CONTEMPORARY
PHOTOGRAPHERS

CONTEMPORARY ARTS SERIES

CONTEMPORARY
PHOTOGRAPHERS

THIRD EDITION

Executive Editor:
Martin Marix Evans

Consultant Editor:
Amanda Hopkinson

Advisers:
Andrey Baskakov, Vladimír Birgus
Ryszard Bobrowski, Becky Cho
Van Deren Coke, Sue Davies
Alastair Fuad-Luke, Helmut Gernsheim
Rune Hassner, Mark Haworth-Booth
Jean-Claude Lemagny, Michael Mack
Pedro Meyer, Radhika Singh
Joyce Tulkens

ST. JAMES PRESS

An International Thomson Publishing Company

I(T)P
Changing the Way the World Learns

NEW YORK • LONDON • BONN • BOSTON • DETROIT • MADRID
MELBOURNE • MEXICO CITY • PARIS • SINGAPORE • TOKYO
TORONTO • WASHINGTON • ALBANY NY • BELMONT CA • CINCINNATI OH

STAFF

Martin Marix Evans, *Executive Editor*
Amanda Hopkinson, *Consultant Editor*

Nigel Cawthorne, Joe da Casa, Angus McGeoch, Daphne A. Williams, *New Entry Editors*
Angela Bambridge, Lynda Maude, *Revision Editors*
Andrew Firth, Susanna Harrison, Gillian Marix Evans, Victoria Mizen, Elizabeth Trundle, *Assistant Editors*
Joann Cerrito, Nicolet V. Elert, Mary K. Ruby, *Contributing Editors*

Suzy Kerr, Barbara Kosińska, Kay Larson, Hildegard Mahoney, Cathy Peck, Valery Stigneev, Susan Yamamoto, *Researchers*

Helenka Fuglewicz, Gabi Griesbach, Amanda Hopkinson, Haruo Itos, Ben Jones, Peter Lewis, Nigel Read, *Translators*

Peter M. Gareffa, *Managing Editor, St. James Press*

Mary Beth Trimper, *Production Director*
Shanna Heilveil, *Production Assistant*
Cynthia Baldwin, *Art Director*
Sherrell Hobbs, *Macintosh Artist*
Pamela A. Hayes, *Photography Coordinator*

⊗™ This book is printed on acid-free paper that meets the minimum requirements of American National Standard for Information Sciences—Permanence Paper for Printed Library Materials, ANSI Z39.48-1984.

The third edition of *Contemporary Photographers* was prepared by Book Packaging and Marketing, 3 Murswell Lane, Silverstone, Towcester, Northants, NN12 8UT, United Kingdom

Cover photo: Luis Poirot, *Portrait of Agustín Centeclas, Spanish Photographer*, 1982. Photograph © Luis Poirot.

ISBN 1-55862-190-3
Printed in the United States of America
Published simultaneously in the United Kingdom

I(T)P™ Gale Research Inc., an International Thomson Publishing Company.
ITP logo is a trademark under license.
10 9 8 7 6 5 4

CONTENTS

INTRODUCTION

Photography is one of the greatest tools of communication to which humanity has ever had access, together with speech, painting and the combination of these two into the refined and sophisticated drawing of signs to represent the written work. However, the timeline for photography is inversely proportionate to the impact it has generated. Given the proliferation of photography, carelessly present in our society, is it really possible to understand just how spectacular an invention it must have appeared to the Victorians?

We currently have an ideal opportunity to re-experience this incredulity thanks to the many complexities that electronic imaging and digital transmission are wreaking on the photographic community. Open virtually any printed publication on photography and it will either contain articles on technological innovation; the wonders of rapid transmission of imagery; or portfolios of new work created with the aid of digital manipulative software. In terms of approach, however, the reaction is polarised, some revelling in the windows of opportunity that electronic imaging has opened, others exhibiting acute anxiety and revealing deep-rooted insecurities with regard to the future of photography. I have to admit to experiencing the same kind of reaction to the continuing avalanche of "digitaphoria" as when faced with the barrage of pre-election political broadcasts. Most "digiphiles" (identified mainly as those preoccupied with the apparatus) proclaiming the wonders of the latest innovations pay little heed to the long term ramifications, whilst the "digiphobes" (identified mainly as those preoccupied with the output) warn of traumatic changes leading to the demise of photography as we now know it.

One can predict that neither of these scenarios will emerge. A careful line between the two will be navigated, although almost certainly the new digital and electronic tools will have less impact on the aesthetics of photography than on its moral and legal implications.

Photographers have manipulated their work since the very beginning of photographic time. Take for example the work of Henry Peach Robinson or Oscar Rejlander, both of whom were in the mid-nineteenth century heavily in pursuit of the classical painterly traditions through the skilful combinations of multiple exposures. The famous *Two Ways of Life* by Rejlander combined no less than thirty-two negatives. Both photographers were in pursuit of fiction, creating tableaux which in true Dickensian tradition worked hard to motivate emotions intended to lead the viewer down the path towards enlightenment and ultimate righteousness. The works could be said to be morally correct even if they are, to our sophisticated tastes, sugar-coated and lacking in emotional subtlety. As yet there is no suggestion that the modern equivalent of combination printing will ever be able to tread a moral path—quite the opposite. The slick ease with which it is now possible to transform photographs *seamlessly* has opened up a well of suspicion and anxiety.

One aspect is the ease with which the subject of the image can be improved. There are comparisons with the twentieth-century amateur pictorialists for whom the stray telegraph pole not removed at printing stage ruins a landscape. A disturbing use of image manipulation is heavily concerned with delivering a level of perfection, creating an image of a plastic world which is as far from reality as the Victorian melodramas. Front cover portraits of models on many recent women's glossies present faces which would not be seen as alien in a cybermovie. Every minute imperfection has been removed and replaced with a plastic skin covering where wrinkles and all manifestations of the elements which make up the characterful and classic beauty are annihilated. (Rembrandt, eat your heart out!) These cybermodels have a more sinister side, as they suggest that this might be the first stage in the rejection of all imperfections. Either the perfecting possibilities of digital manipulation will push us further into believing that anything ugly is unacceptable or it will be used so extensively as to create a dramatic backlash which could result in the worship of ugliness. On a lighter side, Olympus Cameras were quick on the uptake: one of their celebrated April Fool's Day newspaper adverts was to have depicted the fashion photographer John Swannell declaring his discovery of the latest super model, portrayed as being a composite of the best physical features of four real-life super models. Needless to say, the advert disappointingly never made it to the printed page because of extraordinary copyright complexities.

There is also the question of reality, the growing evidence that consumers are increasingly aware that the photographs they view are a constructed reality. The next logical step is the loss of credibility in photography. The credibility factor is a crucial element in some areas of photography, and without it photography will lose its persuasive power. What a disaster this would be for media moguls, art directors and advertising agencies! What an irony that the very techniques they harnessed and exploited to maximise sales of consumer products might well backfire and depress sales. There would then be the perplexing problem of just how a perfected subject could still retain credibility. This is similar to the way in which the sound signals from television satellites are broadcast; although received perfectly, they are often degraded (or squeezed) to ensure that the viewer at home is aware that the broadcast is actually live and coming from a considerable distance. In effect the broadcasters are concerned to ensure the retention of credibility by adding imperfections to a perfect reality.

Aesthetically the results being produced by harnessing computer imaging techniques are at present hugely disappointing. The vast majority of work is reminiscent of acid-induced psychedelia, a nauseating swirl of colour and cacaphony of over-used computer dexterity with little content. With one or two exceptions, the more successful use of computer techniques is found within the advertising sector. There are solid commercial reasons for this. It is cheaper to create the required image by manipulating the resources of an online picture library, and such economies produce improved profit margins and attract forward capital investment in computer "kit." It therefore follows that photographers working in the commercial sector will have greater ease of access to the new imaging technologies.

Increasingly however, the originator of the image is no longer the manipulator. Fred Ritchin[1] suggests that the photographer "may become, like a Third World Country, counted on only as a supplier of raw materials, the photographs to be somehow 'refined' by those who control their publication." William J. Mitchell[2] writes that "images can be received, transformed and recombined like DNA to produce new intellectual structures having their own dynamic and value," a dynamic and value which are not created by the originators of the images. Will photography remain in the hands of photographers, or will digital/electronic wizardry remove the image-making power from photographers and relocate it in the hands of others? The photographic future might well be photographerless. There are now many areas where the traditional rôle of the photographer is being eroded or abandoned altogether.

In the political arena, governments have long been aware of the dichotomous rôle of photography. Take for example war photography, where, particularly since the 1980s, photographers granted access were chosen selectively; in one case, Don McCullin was unable to secure the necessary paperwork to cover the Falklands War. Consider also the dramatic coverage of the destruction of suspected ammunition silos in Iraq, made possible through broadcasts of video excerpts gained directly from cameras mounted alongside (or integral with) the missile range-finder. The camera was there but the photographer was absent. Even aside from government intervention, newspapers (the traditional source of commission funding for photojournalists) are finding their budgets squeezed with the effect that fewer photographers are sent out to war zones. In many cases the problem is "solved" by television/newspaper mergers, thereby reducing costs further as only one television crew is needed at the scene and the still photograph can be grabbed from the video footage produced. Perhaps as a reaction to the ever-decreasing opportunities for individual statements, some photographers have chosen to use ready-made images anonymously taken from a television screen and manipulated to make a fictional interpretation of their perception of the many issues involved. Two such examples would be the work of Jim Adams on Northern Ireland and James Radke on the Gulf. The issues entailed in the work point to a concern over the credibility of the ready-made twenty-four-hour news environment and the implication that tackling this takes precedence over the actual event itself. By using ready-made images there is also a strong point about the dangers inherent in a possibly photographerless society.

That digital manipulation will undoubtedly generate a questioning of the credibility of an image could be the best thing to have happened to photography. To promote scepticism about the "truth" of a photograph is to generate questions. To situate this debate on a wide public platform is to give photography the best opportunity it has ever had to deflect the pervasive myth that photography possesses a unique truth.

Electronic innovations could score the highest creative goal when used by photographers concerned with the creation of a fiction and/or where the resultant image does not need to be anchored in a tangible reality. The single image has its root in a fleeting second of time where the juxtaposition and poetic combination of images can evoke a fluidity of understanding flowing backwards and forwards in a time continuum, as in the work of Mari Mahr or Ania Bien. Electronic creativities remove the need for the photographer to be wedded irrevocably to the raw materials of reality, providing a level of creative freedom ripe for exploration and exciting to consider. In fact, viewers might not only be able to glimpse behind the looking glass, but actually get into virtual reality, a relatively new visual experience which, for commercial reasons, is as yet too expensive for most artists to access. Photographic installations could become a thing of the past and, because of the economical amount of space taken up by virtual technology, installations and walk-round art works could become available at every railway station. The question of course is whether or not virtual reality is photography.

The conclusion I would put forward is that perhaps photographers must mark the millenium by agreeing to let go of the constricting definitions of traditional photography and, for the sake of creative and inspirational imaging, grasp the fact that in spite of the obvious teething problems the new technologies bring with them, they do also provide a burst of energy in which photography can be virtually anything you want it to be. "To the Victorian mind the stereoscope with its three-dimensional views of nature was the visual equivalent of today's virtual reality."[3]

—Amanda Nevill

Director, National Museum of Photography, Film and Television, Bradford, England

[1] Fred Ritchin, "In Our Own Image," *Aperture*, 1990.

[2] William J. Mitchell, *Creative Camera*, 321, 1993.

[3] Roger Taylor, Curator of Photographs, NMPFT, discussion comment, 1994.

EDITOR'S NOTE

This, the third edition of *Contemporary Photographers*, broadly follows the policies laid down by the previous editor, the late Colin Naylor, and an abbreviated version of his editorial note is appended. In the new edition new advisers have joined the ranks of those continuing from the previous edition in order to extend the coverage of African, Indian, Far Eastern and Latin American photographers. Further, it was decided to make a positive effort to secure a better representation of women photographers.

The executive editor has been the beneficiary of exceptional assistance from the advisers and, even more so, from the consultant editor, Amanda Hopkinson. The staff listings acknowledge the contributions of research and editorial workers continuously involved with the undertaking, but without the additional assistance of individuals too numerous to mention this revision, imperfect though it may be, would have been yet the poorer. The special help of Vilnis Auzinš, Jayne Baum, Birgitta Forsell, Professor F. C. Gundlach, Andreas Müller-Pohle, Joke Pronk, Max Scheler and Akiko Yamada cannot go unacknowledged.

The addition of over 140 new entrants has necessitated the omission of many photographers listed in the previous edition. In order to maintain the contemporary relevance of the work, those entrants who died before 1 January 1975, those whom we are advised have not added significantly to their corpus of work since 1987 or whose achievements are not known to us have been excluded; their entries in the second edition of 1988 remain available for study in that volume.

The peripatetic nature of the photographer's work and massive political changes, particularly in Eastern Europe, the former USSR and the former Yugoslavia, since the last revision have combined to make personal contact with entrants difficult, and sometimes impossible. Library research and the assistance of agents, executors and friends has yielded some information, but in certain cases it remains uncertain whether the entrant is alive or dead, working or retired, or now involved in a different field of artistic activity. All information that can assist in the continuing process of revision will be most gratefully received.

Martin F. Marix Evans
Silverstone, England
March 1995

From the Editor's Note to the Second Edition

The choice of entrants is intended to reflect the best and most prominent of contemporary photographers (those who are living and those who have died in the recent past). There are many kinds of photography: the advisers have tried to suggest diversity as well as continuity within the medium.

Entries consist of: biography; individual exhibitions (we list two- and three-person shows in this category); a selection of group exhibitions; a listing of selected public galleries and museums that have the work of the entrant in their collection; and a bibliography of books and articles by and about the entrant. As well, living entrants have been invited to make a statement on their work or on contemporary photography in general and to choose a representative photo. The entry ends with a signed critical essay.

This book has its faults. Most of them probably can be traced to the editors. Others have to do with photography itself. Photography is now more than a century old, but its having been taken seriously as an art form is a recent development, and that very newness creates problems for the compilers of a reference book. Errors introduced in one source—say, an exhibition catalogue—have a way of being perpetuated for years. To correct these errors (and often to find any source of accurate information at all), we had to start at the beginning; we had to rely on the entrants. When the entrants were dead, we had to appeal to the essayists, as well as to families and friends of the entrants—and to curators, scholars, critics and former associates not otherwise connected with this book who were experts on a particular photographer. The response was overwhelmingly co-operative, and one of the disappointments of this book must be that we cannot individually thank the many hundreds of people who helped to create the entries that follow.

Colin Naylor

ADVISERS/CONTRIBUTORS

Hans Christian Adam
James Alinder
Pamela Allara
Marjorie Allthorpe-Guyton
Dana Asbury

Gerry Badger
Roger Baldwin
Lewis Baltz
Nancy Barrett
Thomas F. Barrow
Andrey Baskakov
Derek Bennett
Erika Billeter
Vladimír Birgus
Ulrich Bischoff
M. Teresa Blanch
Lázaro Blanco
Ginette Bléry
Ryszard Bobrowski
Inge Bondi
Robert Booth
Elmer Borklund
John E. Bowlt
Bonnie Boxer
David Brittain
Doris Bry

Alison Carroll
Jean Caslin
Christian Caujolle
Jean-François Chevrier
John Chillingworth
Becky Cho
Monica R. Cipnic
Van Deren Coke
Stu Cohen
A. D. Coleman
Attilio Colombo
Robert W. Cooke
David Corey

Judy Dater
Laura Lee Davies
Sue Davies
A. de Jongh-Vermeulen

Robert J. Doherty
Regis Durand

James L. Enyeart
Eric Eelbode
Lars O. Ericsson
Andrew Eskind
John Esten
Tom Evans

David Featherstone
Vilém Flusser
Joan Fontcuberta
Tina Freeman
Alastair Fuad-Luke
Marianne Fulton
Joseph Fung

Arnold Gassan
Helmut Gernsheim
Norman A. Geske
G.M. Gidley
Marta Gili
Michael Godby
Vicki Goldberg
Arthur Goldsmith
Bradford G. Gorman
Nada Grcevic
Göran Greider
Judith Mara Gutman

Nancy Hall-Duncan
Ellen Handy
Ulf Hård af Segerstad
Margaret Harker
Carole Harmel
David Harris
Martin Harrison
Akira Hasegawa
Yuko Hasegawa
Rune Hassner
Ralph Hattersley
Mark Haworth-Booth
Ted Hedgpeth
Marvin Heiferman
Michael Held

H.K. Henisch
Elena Hill
Francis Hodgson
Mark Holborn
Klaus Honnef

Amanda Hopkinson
Sir Tom Hopkinson
Anne Hoy
F. Jack Hurley

Kohtaro Iizawa

Gavin Jantjes
Ian Jeffrey
Chris Johnson
William Johnson
Rune Jonsson

Takao Kajiwara
Michiko Kasahara
Karen Allen Keenan
Fritz Kempe
Grant Kester
Wolfgang Kil
Hardwicke Knight
Stephen Koch
Michael Koetzle
Barbara Kosińska
Kineo Kuwabara

Martha Langford
Laurence Le Guay
Jean-Claude Lemagny
Lucy Leppard
Jorge Lewinski
Jerome Liebling
Bernd Lohse
Jan-Eric Lundstrom

Aleksandras Macijauskas
Michael Mack
Hildegard Mahoney
Guy Mandery
Katya Mandoki
Jacqueline Markham
Norihiko Matsumoto
Stephen Mayes
Arthur McIntyre
William Messer
Pedro Meyer
Arno Rafael Minkkinen
Francesc Miralles

Marco Misani
Margaretta K. Mitchell
Michael Mitchell
David Moore
Anita V. Mozley
Daniela Mrázková
Andreas Müller-Pohle
Joan Murray

Colin Naylor
Barbara Norfleet
Claude Nori
Michel Nuridsany

Arthur Ollman
Maria Cristina Orive

Daniela Palazzoli
Deba P. Patnaik
Christopher Phillips
Kenneth Poli
Ralph Pomeroy
Elena Poniatowska
Allan Porter
Edo Prando
H. Y. Sharada Prasad
Derrick Price
Uwe Prinz
Sarah Putnam

Shirley Read
Vladimìr Remeš
Jane Richards
Frédéric Ripoll
Grant B. Romer
Naomi Rosenblum
Mike Rowell

Peter Sager
Catharine Sanders
Jean-Michel Sarlet
Aaron Scharf
Jack Schofield
Giuliana Scimé
Julia Scully
Elena Selina
James L. Sheldon
David Sinden
Radhika Singh
Ulf Sjöstedt
Ruprecht Skasa-Weiss
Ján Šmok
Abigail Solomon-Godeau

Ruth Spencer
Heinz Spielmann
Maren Stange
Karl Steinorth
Philip Stokes
Brian Stokoe
William Stott
David Levi Strauss
Maia-Mari Sutnik

Petr Tausk
Liba Taylor
Roger Therond
Ann W. Thomas
Peeter Tooming
Klára Töry
Anne W. Tucker
Joyce Tulkens
Roland Turner

Marina Vaizey
Karel van Deuren
David Vestal
Larry A. Viskochil
Ingeborg von Zitzewitz

Nigel Warburton
Rolf Wedewer
Peter Weirmair
Liz Wells
Leif Wigh
Jürgen Wilde
Jonathan Williams
Sheldon Williams
Ken Winokur
Kelly Wise
Christopher Wordsworth

Italo Zannier

CONTEMPORARY
PHOTOGRAPHERS

LIST OF ENTRANTS

Abbas
Berenice Abbott
Yuri V. Abramochkin
Ansel Adams
Robert Adams
Lucien Aigner
Shotaru Akiyama
James Alinder
Paul Almasy
Max Alpert
Manuel Alvarez Bravo
Heather Angel
Eve Arnold
Vasco Ascolini
Barbara Astman
Ellen Auerbach
Paul Ausloos
Richard Avedon

Gerry Badger
David Bailey
Oscar Bailey
John Baldessari
Walter Ballhause
Richard Baltauss
Dmitri Baltermans
Lewis Baltz
Oladele Bamgboye
Micha Bar-Am
Bruno Barbey
Tina Barney
Thomas F. Barrow
Lillian Bassman
Claude Batho
John Batho
Yngve Baum
Horst H. Baumann
Jean-François Bauret
Herbert Bayer
David P. Bayles
Peter Beard
Cecil Beaton
Bernhard and Hilla Becher
Mitter Bedi
Hans Bellmer
Jim Bengston

Derek Bennett
Roloff Beny
Gianni Berengo-Gardin
Ferenc Berko
Mieczyslaw Berman
Ruth Bernhard
Ian Berry
Zarina Bhimji
Gunar Binde
Ilse Bing
Vladimir Birgus
Michael Bishop
John Blakemore
Lázaro Blanco
Carel Blazer
Donald Blumberg
Anna Bohdziewicz
Dorothy Bohm
Christian Boltanski
Pierre Boogaerts
Walter Bosshard
Enrique Bostelmann
Édouard Boubat
Pierre Boucher
Robert Bourdeau
Guy Bourdin
Dirk Braeckman
Brian Brake
Bill Brandt
Brassaï
Werner Braun
Denis Brihat
Leszek Brogowski
Anton Bruehl
Adam Bujak
Edna Bullock
Wynn Bullock
Jerry Burchard
Victor Burgin
Bill Burke
René Burri
Nancy Burson
Vitaly Butyrin

Debbie Caffery
Romano Cagnoni

Harry Callahan
Jo Ann Callis
Bryn Campbell
Cornell Capa
Paul Caponigro
Lisetta Carmi
Henri Cartier-Bresson
Toni Catany
Agusti Centelles
Chang Chao-Tang
Walter Chappell
Jean-Philippe Charbonnier
Sarah Charlesworth
Peter Chen
John Chillingworth
Václav Chochola
Almond Chu
Arnaud Claass
Larry Clark
Lucien Clergue
William Clift
Lynne Cohen
Mark Cohen
Van Deren Coke
John Collier
Calum Colvin
Linda Connor
Thomas Joshua Cooper
Pierre Cordier
Carlotta M. Corpron
Raúl Corrales
Marie Cosindas
Eileen Cowin
Barbara Crane
Mario Cravo Neto
Donigan Cumming
Robert Cumming
Imogen Cunningham
Douglas Curran

Louise Dahl-Wolfe
Robert D'Allessandro
Stephen Dalton
Alicia D'Amico
Sujoy Das
Judy Dater
Bruce Davidson
Bevan Davies
John Davies
Bob Davis
Dawid
Joe Deal
Roy DeCarava
Liliane DeCock
Carl de Keyzer

Ger Dekkers
Jack Delano
Paul Den Hollander
Paul de Nooijer
Raymond Depardon
Bernard Descamps
Pavel Dias
Jan Dibbets
Ian Dickson
Jean Dieuzaide
Claude Dityvon
Miodrag Djordjević
Zbnigniew Dlubak
Robert Doisneau
John Dominis
Ken Domon
Benedykt Jerzy Dorys
Ed Douglas
Tom Drahos
Antoon Dries
David Douglas Duncan
Max Dupain
Allen A. Dutton

Harold E. Edgerton
Mark Edwards
William Eggleston
Josef Ehm
Gilles Ehrmann
Alfred Eisenstaedt
Sandra Eleta
Rennie Ellis
Paz Errazuriz
Elliott Erwitt
Barbara Ess
Julio Etchart
Walker Evans

Sara Facio
Bernard Faucon
Andreas Feininger
Tamás Féner
Robert W. Fichter
Erwin Fieger
Gabriel Figueroa Flores
Larry Fink
Arno Fischer
Roland Fischer
Steve Fitch
Alain Fleischer
Franco Fontana
Joan Fontcuberta
Anna Fox
Martine Franck
Robert Frank

Leonard Freed
Jill Freedman
Ferran Freixa
Gisèle Freund
Lee Friedlander
Benno Friedman
Toni Frissell
Hideki Fujii
Masahisa Fukase
Hamish Fulton
Joseph Fung

Oliver Gagliani
Charles Gagnon
Avi Ganor
Mario Garcìa Joya
Flor Garduño
William Garnett
Charles Gatewood
Jean-Claude Gautrand
André Gelpke
Helmut Gernsheim
Georg Gerster
Luigi Ghirri
Ashim Ghosh
Mario Giacomelli
Victor Gianella
Ralph Gibson
Tim N. Gidal
Krzysztof Gieraltowski
Bruce Gilden
Sven Gillsäter
Laura Gilpin
Paolo Gioli
Albert Giordan
Burt Glinn
Hervé Gloaguen
Fay Godwin
Frank Gohlke
David Goldblatt
Judith Golden
Luis Gonzalez Palma
Fritz Goro
John R. Gossage
Emmet Gowin
Ken Grant
Mladen Grcević
Joy Gregory
Brian Griffin
Franco Grignani
René Groebli
Jan Groover
Harry Gruyaert
Štěpán Grygar
Sunil Gupta

John Gutmann

Ernst Haas
Betty Hahn
Heinz Hajek-Halke
George Hallett
Philippe Halsman
Hiroshi Hamaya
David Hamilton
Hans Hammarskiöld
Charles Harbutt
Bert Hardy
Erich Hartmann
Edward Hartwig
Sam Haskins
Rune Hassner
Naoya Hatakeyama
Robert Häusser
Milota Havránková
David Heath
Nick Hedges
Eugen Heilig
Robert Heinecken
Adriano Heitmann
Jurgen Heinemann
Keld Helmer-Petersen
Nigel Henderson
Fritz Henle
Florence Henri
Fernando Herraez Gomez
François Hers
Abigail Heyman
Paul Hill
John Hilliard
Hiro
Tana Hoban
Dagmar Hochová
David Hockney
Marta Hoepffner
Volkhard Hofer
Nancy Honey
Thomas Höpker
Thurston Hopkins
William Horeis
Horst
Frank Horvat
Eric Hosking
Eikoh Hosoe
Hsieh Chuen-Te
Hu Wugong
Hanns Hubmann
Miroslav Hucek
Peter Hujar
David Hurn
Roger Hutchings

Walde Huth
Scott Hyde

Tetsuya Ichimura
Boris Ignatovich
Francisco Infante
Irèna Ionesco
Yasuhiro Ishimoto
Miyako Ishiuchi
Yoshihiko Ito
Graciela Iturbide
Izis

Joseph D. Jachna
Lotte Jacobi
Gottfried Jäger
Geoffrey James
Arno Jansen
Pavel Jasanský
Miroslav Jodas
Mimmo Jodice
Tore Johnson
Harold Jones
Pirkle Jones
Philip Jones-Griffiths
Sune Jonsson
Kenneth Josephson
Paul Joyce
Juan I-Jong

Simpson Kalisher
Karol Kalláy
Jonas Kalvelis
Art Kane
Yousuf Karsh
Kikuji Kawada
Peter Keetman
Roshini Kempadoo
Fritz Kempe
Peter Kennard
Gyorgy Kepes
Victor Keppler
Pascal Kern
André Kertész
Dmitri Kessel
Erika Kiffl
Chris Killip
Richard Kirstel
Aart Klein
William Klein
Karen Knorr
Alfred Ko
Viktor Kolář
François Kollar
Michiko Kon

Gennadi Koposov
Péter Korniss
Josef Koudelka
George Krause
Les Krims
Vilem Kříž
Aleksander Krzywoblocki
Kipton Kumler
Seiji Kurata
Kineo Kuwabara
Lyalya Kuznetsova

Syl Labrot
Natalia Lach-Lachowicz
Daniel Laizerowitz
Suzy Lake
Osbert Lam
Michel Lambeth
William Larson
Jacques-Henri Lartigue
Grace Lau
Clarence John Laughlin
Robert Lebeck
Russell Lee
Arthur Leipzig
Saul Leiter
Annette Lemieux
Branko Lenart
Erica Lennard
Joanne Leonard
Cesare Leonardi
Leong Ka Tai
Robert Leverant
Leon Levinstein
David Levinthal
Helen Levitt
Jerzy Lewczyński
Jorge Lewinski
Barry Lewis
Alexander Liberman
Rudolf Lichtsteiner
Jerome Liebling
Tuija Lindström-Caudwell
O. Winston Link
Susan Lipper
Herbert List
Stephen Livick
Giorgio Lotti
Risto Lounema
Markéta Luskacová
Danny Lyon
Joan Lyons
Nathan Lyons

Greg MacGregor

Aleksandras Macijauskas
Ulrich Mack
Michal Macků
Arnaud Maggs
Peter Magubane
Mari Mahr
Frank Majore
Alexandr Makarov
Hans Malmberg
Felix H. Man
Sally Mann
Constantine Manos
Man Ray
Harald Mante
Werner Mantz
Robert Mapplethorpe
Pavel Mara
Jindřich Marco
Richard Margolis
Anna Mariani
Mary Ellen Mark
Knut Maron
Martin Martincek
Max Mathys
Jennifer Matthews
Herbert Matter
Elaine Mayes
Roger Mayne
Angus McBean
Will McBride
Ron McCormick
Donald McCullin
Emila Medková
Ashvin Mehta
Susan Meiselas
Gideon Mendel
Pepi Merisio
Roger Mertin
Ray K. Metzker
Pedro Meyer
Joel Meyerowitz
Duane Michals
Yoichi Midorikawa
Wilhelm Mikhailovsky
Jun Miki
Gjon Mili
Lee Miller
Roger Minick
Arno Rafael Minkkinen
Richard Misrach
Michael Mitchell
Kozo Miyoshi
Lisette Model
Jorge Molder
Paolo Monti

Sarah Moon
David Moore
Raymond Moore
Inge Morath
Barbara Morgan
Jun Morinaga
Daidoh Moriyama

Wright Morris
Stefan Moses
Grant Mudford
Igor Mukhin
Andreas Müller-Pohle
Isabel Muñoz
Carl Mydans

T. S. Nagarajan
Patrick Nagatani
Massatoshi Naitoh
Masaya Nakamura
Hans Namuth
Ikko Narahara
Rafael Navarro
József Németh
Bea Nettles
Floris M. Neusüss
Beaumont Newhall
Arnold Newman
Helmut Newton
Michael Nichols
Pål-Nils Nilsson
Nicholas Nixon
Wim Noordhoek
Sonya Noskowiak
Gabriele and Helmut Nothhelfer
Waclaw Nowak
Ralph Nykvist

Georg Oddner
Lennart Olson
Cas Oorthuys
Ruth Orkin
Detlef Orlopp
José Ortiz-Echagüe
Pablo Ortiz Monasterio
Inge Osswald
Tzachi Ostrovsky
Bill Owens

Hilmar Pabel
Marion Palfi
Prashant Panjiar
Améris M. Paolini
Tod Papageorge
Olivia Parker

Norman Parkinson
Gordon Parks
Martin Parr
Władysław Pawelec
René Peña González
Irving Penn
Gilles Peress
Philip Perkis
Anders Petersen
John Pfahl
Pierre et Gilles
Christopher Pillitz
Ivan Pinkava
Gueorgui Pinkhassov
Wojciech Plewiński
Bernard Plossu
David Plowden
Luis Poirot
Eliot Porter
Marion Post Wolcott
Mark Power
Romualdas Požerskis
Wieslaw Prazuch
Doug Prince
Richard Prince
Josef Prosek
František Provazník
Rosamond Wolff Purcell
Steve Pyke

Edward Quigley

Lucia Radochonska
Enzo Ragazzini
Raghu Rai
Jaroslav Rajzìk
Romualdas Rakauskas
Susan Rankaitis
Robert Rauschenberg
Lilo Raymond
Paul Reas
Vilém Reichmann
Wolfgang Reisewitz
Bruno Requillart
Marcia Resnick
Nancy Rexroth
Marc Riboud
Mirella Ricciardi
Leland Rice
Olivier Richon
Evelyn Richter
Heinrich Riebesehl
Leni Riefenstahl
Herb Ritts
Miguel Rio Branco

Grace Robertson
George Rodger
Fulvio Roiter
Willy Ronis
Walter Rosenblum
Judith Joy Ross
Jaroslav Rössler
Arthur Rothstein
Ernestine Ruben
Meridel Rubenstein
Eva Rubinstein
Edward Ruscha
Marialba Russo
Zofia Rydet

Jan Ságl
Sabastiao Salgado
Lucas Samaras
Karl Sandels
Jan Saudek
Naomi Savage
Boris Savelev
Christian Schad
Jurgen Schadeberg
Max Scheler
Michael Schmidt
Wolfgang G. Schröter
Emil Schulthess
Ferdinando Scianna
Tazio Secchiaroli
Michael Semak
Andres Serrano
Cindy Sherman
Kishin Shinoyama
Yoshikazu Shirakawa
Arkadii Shishkin
Stephen Shore
Jeanloup Sieff
Arthur Siegel
Dayanita Singh
Raghubir Singh
Art Sinsabaugh
Aaron Siskind
Ulf Sjöstedt
Gail Skoff
Sandy Skoglund
Neal Slavin
Henry Holmes Smith
Keith Smith
W. Eugene Smith
Michael Snow
Snowdon
Frederick Sommer
Eve Sonneman
Virgilijus Šonta

Jo Spence
Humphrey Spender
Jan Splìchal
Egons Spuris
Pavel Stecha
Chris Steele-Perkins
Abram Sterenberg
Bert Stern
Joel Sternfeld
Louis Stettner
Jindřich Štreit
Liselotte Strelow
Issei Suda
Josef Sudek
Jean-Pierre Sudre
Wolf Suschitzky
Antanas Sutkus
Risaku Suzuki
Jan Svoboda
Miro Švolík
Manish Swarup
Homer Sykes
Steve Szabo
Karin Székessy
Gabor Szilasi

Maurice Tabard
Keiichi Tahara
Filip Tas
Sam Tata
Petr Tausk
Val Telberg
Joyce Tenneson
Edmund Teske
Lew Thomas
Ernst Thormann
George A. Tice
Tomasz Tomaszewski
Shomei Tomatsu
Peeter Tooming
Michael Torosian
Philip Trager
Mikhail Trakhman
Charles Traub
Arthur Tress
Hiromi Tsuchida
Jakob Tuggener
Lars Tunbjörk
Deborah Turbeville

Shoji Ueda
Jerry N. Uelsmann
Umbo
João Aristeu Urban

Burk Uzzle

John Vachon
Javier Vallhonrat
Ed van der Elsken
James Van Der Zee
Willard Van Dyke
Jean Louis Vanesch
Luigi Veronesi
David Vestal
Roman Vishniac
Christian Vogt
Verena von Gagern

Arne Wahlberg
Robert Walker
Todd Walker
Wang Miao
Nick Waplington
Andy Warhol
Cary Wasserman
Yoshio Watanabe
Alex Webb
Todd Webb
Wolfgang Weber
Carrie Mae Weems
William Wegman
Dan Weiner
Jack Welpott
Henry Wessel, Jr.
Brett Weston
Cole Weston
Minor White
Bob Willoughby
Val Wilmer
Geoff Winningham
Garry Winogrand
Kelly Wise
Joel-Peter Witkin
Stefan Wojnecki
Reinhart Wolf
Don Worth
Wu Jia Lin
Wu Yinxian

Mariana Yampolsky
Max Yavno
Yoshida Tomohiko

Georgij Zelma
Vladimír Židlický
Piet Zwart
Stasys Žvirgždas

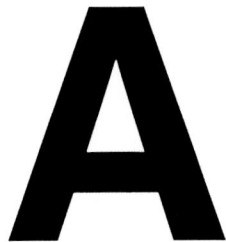

ABBAS.

Nationality: Iranian. **Born:** Iran, in 1944. **Education:** Self-taught in photography, from 1962. **Career:** Reporter and photographer, for *Al Chaab* newspaper, Algiers, 1962-63; photographer for the Olympic Games Committee, Mexico City, 1968-69; freelance photographer, working with *Jeune Afrique* magazine, in Africa, 1970-71; photographer, with Agence SIPA, Paris, working in Biafra, Bangladesh, South Vietnam, Northern Ireland and the Middle East, 1971-73; freelance photographer, working mainly in Ethiopia, 1973-74; photographer, with Agence Gamma, Paris, working in Pakistan, North Vietnam, Sri Lanka, Colombia, Peru, Lebanon, South Africa, Iran and Poland, 1974-80; photographer, with Magnum Photos agency, Paris, working in Gibraltar, Ghana, Algeria, France, the United States, Mexico and Chile, since 1981: has worked on photo assignments for *Time, Life, Newsweek, Sunday Times Magazine, Stern, Geo, Paris-Match, Zeit-Magazin, Actuel* and *Le Monde*, since 1971. From 1987 to 1994 has worked on the resurgence of Islam in 28 countries. **Agent:** Magnum Photos, 5 Passage Piver 75011-Paris, France; and 23 Old Street, London EC1V 9HL, England.

Individual Exhibitions:

1972	*Ganvie People,* Village of Falomo, Nigeria
1977	Galerie Litho, Teheran (retrospective)
	Ce Jour La, FNAC-Montparnasse, Paris
1978	FNAC-Provence, France
1980	Museum of Modern Art, Teheran (retrospective)
	Iran: La Revolution, Galerie Cinefoto, Nice, France
	Darvazeh Ghar Mosque, Teheran
	Iran: La Revolution, Fundacao Cultural, Rio de Janeiro
1982	The Photographers' Gallery, London (retrospective)
	Citizen of the Third World, Open Eye Gallery, Liverpool, England
1983	Consejode Fotografia, Mexico City (retrospective)
1984	GalerieARPA, Bordeaux, France (retrospective)
1986	*Votez pour moi,* Magnum Gallery, Paris
1991	*Imagina,* Almeria (retrospective)
1992	*Retours à Mexico,* Centre Culturel du Mexique, Paris and Maison pour Tous, Calais
1994	*Retornos a Mexico,* Centro Nacional de la Fotografia, Mexico

Selected Group Exhibitions:

1973	*Third World Exhibition of Photography,* Pressehaus Stern, Hamburg (and world tour)
1977	*Gamma Retrospective,* at *Rencontres Internationale de Photographie,* Arles, France
1978	*Ten Years of Gamma,* Nikon Gallery, Paris
1982	*Terrede Guerre,* Magnum Gallery, Paris (travelled to the Ancien Casino, Lausanne, Switzerland)
1983	*Il Reportage Fotografico nelle Guerre Contemporanee,* Palazzo Fortuny, Venice
1985	*South Africa,* FNAC-Montparnasse, Paris
1986	*Magnum Concert,* Musee d'Art et d'Histoire, Fribourg, Switzerland
1989	*In Our Time,* retrospective worldwide travelling exhibition by Magnum (ran until 1994)
1990	*A l'Est de Magnum,* travelling exhibition in Europe
1991	*The Toppan Collection,* I C P, New York
1993	*Mexico Seen through Foreign Eyes,* Tamayo Museum, Mexico and ICP, New York
1994	*Mexico,* Galerie du Chateau d'Eau, Toulouse

Publications:

By ABBAS: Books—*Le Zaire Aujourd'hui,* Paris 1974; *Gamma: Le Secret des Grandes Photos,* with others, Paris 1978; *Iran: La Revolution Confisquée,* Paris 1980; *Retornos a Oapan,* Mexico City 1986; *Return to Mexico, Journeys Beyond the Mask,* New York 1992; *Allah O Akbar, A Journey through Militant Islam,* London 1994.

On ABBAS: Books—The Camera at War by Jorge Lewinski, London 1978; *Gamma 1979,* Paris 1979; *ABBAS: Gamma 1980,* Paris 1980; *A Day in the Life of Australia—March 6, 1981,* with introduction by Thomas Kenneally, Potts Point, New South Wales 1981. **Articles**—"Gamma—One Man's Involvement" in *British Journal of Photography* (London), 18 November 1977; "Iran: les temoins" in *Photo* (Paris), April 1979; "Special Iran" in *American Photographer* (New York), January 1980; "Free" in *American Photographer* (New York), February 1981; "Third World Eyes" by W. Januszcak in *The Guardian* (London), 17 March 1982; "Abbas" by Liba Taylor in *British Journal of Photography* (London), 13/20 August 1982; "Abbas," interview, with Carole Naggar, in *Photo* (Paris), September 1982; "Eye of the Storm" by Liz Nakahara in the *Washington Post,* 6 November 1983; "54 Master Photographers 1960-1979" by Toppan, Japan 1989; "An Eastern Eye" by Amanda Hopkinson in *British Journal of Photography,* July 1991.

*

The photojournalist's gaze is personal to him, of course, but he sees beyond himself, not inside himself, and in doing so he is not a prisoner of reality—he trancends it. . . . The journalist does not refrain the creator—he reveals him.

—Abbas

*　*　*

Abbas taught himself photography while working as a writer and photographer for a newspaper in Algeria, and later for the Olympic Committee covering the Games in Mexico. He began his wider travels as a photojournalist in 1970 when he joined first the Sipa then the Gamma agencies in Paris and travelled widely throughout the world. In 1973 his photographs were the first to bring the world's attention to growing famine in Ethiopia.

Born in Iran, Abbas considers himself a photographer of the "third world." Although there is a school of thought which believes that photojournalism is best served by an entirely objective view, it has become increasingly clear that the most valuable work is done by people who know their subject thoroughly and have had time to study the underlying causes of the dramatic newsworthy incidents, which may catch the attention of the Western world for only a moment. To be born in a country with extremes of riches and poverty gives a fundamental understanding of other such societies not readily available to even the most liberal minded of people brought up in more homogeneous social conditions. Abbas has used this advantage throughout his work.

Before the Shah was overthrown, Abbas returned to Iran to photograph the changes and the potential installation of democracy in his homeland. He stayed for two years documenting the rise of fundamentalism and produced numerous

Diourbel—Senegal, **1988.** Photograph by Abbas.

magazine stories, an exhibition and a book, *Iran: La Révolution Confisquée.* This experience was a personally traumatic one, and although it made him determined to examine Islam more closely, he felt unable to begin this exploration without some time for reflection and research.

Abbas then made eleven trips over a three year period to Mexico, spending a total of twelve months exploring an entirely different world, one in which a social democracy had not eliminanted extremes of wealth and poverty among the people. Here he honed his ability for searching out the root causes of situations and this work also resulted in a book, *Retornos A Oapán,* published by Colección Río de Luz.

In January 1987 Abbas started on his major examination of Islam and this has taken him to 28 countries over the past seven years, culminating in the publication of his latest book, *Allah O Akbar, A Journey through Militant Islam,* published by Phaidon, in 1994. This truly remarkable exploration of one of the world's great religions shows clearly that militancy in this sense does not only apply to actual fighting but to the fervour of prayer and the concentration on the education of the young. Women play a large part in this, both in public rallies and in day-to-day activities and encouragement of their children. The photographs show all forms of Islam from the mystical Dervish and more gentle Sufi through to the seemingly endless fighting in Afghanistan between the Shia and the Shiites. Abbas has also written the text which is a masterly explanation of how the Islamic religion has been interpreted and, in some cases, exploited for political purposes in countries all over the world.

The undertaking of major projects such as these requires both dedication and determination. It is necessary to stand back occasionally, to ensure you are producing photographs that will carry the message clearly and also that your captions cannot be used to twist the meaning of the pictures. Abbas is extremely successful in producing large bodies of work, which, while they remain subjective, are still fair to all concerned. In addition, he produces individual images which are often both beautiful and very moving.

Abbas uses periods of time at home during his long projects both to assess their progress and to undertake shorter assignments, either editorial or, on occasion, for fashion magazines. These help finance the large self-assignments and also give him the opportunity to work with other colleagues in Magnum (which he joined in 1981) on various joint enterprises.

In his future work he plans to continue exploring the great religions of the world, to "stay with God, with whom I now have a cordial relationship—but change the prophet!"

—Sue Davies

ABBOTT, Berenice.

Nationality: American. **Born:** Springfield, Ohio, 17 July 1898. **Education:** Attended public schools in Columbus, until 1916; studied (general studies) at Ohio State University, Columbus, one semester, 1917-18; studied journalism, Columbia University, New York, few weeks, 1918; did independent study of drawing and sculpture, in New York, 1918-21, and in Paris (partially under Antoine Bourdelle), 1921-23; studied at the Kunstschule, Berlin, winter/spring 1923. **Career:** Assistant to Man Ray, Paris, 1923-25; introduced to the work of the photographer Eugène Atget, Paris, 1925: subsequently acquired the Atget archives and promoted his work; independent portrait photographer, establishing own studio, Paris, 1926-29; independent documentary and portrait photographer, New York, 1930-68: worked for *Fortune* and other magazines, and for the W.P.A. Federal Art Project, 1935-39; worked for the Physical Science Study Committee of Educational Services Inc., New York, 1958-61; settled in Abbot Village, Maine, 1968. Instructor in Photography, New School for Social Research, New York, 1935-58. **Recipient:** Honorary doctorate: University of Maine, Orono, 1971; Smith College, Northampton, Massachusetts, 1973; New School for Social Research, 1981; Honorary degree from Ohio State University, 1986; First International Erice Prize for Photography, 1987; International Center for Photography's Infinity Award for Master of Photography, 1989; **Estate:** Commercegraphics, 160E Union Ave., East Rutherford, N.J. 07073, U.S.A. **Died:** (in Monson, Maine) 9 December 1991.

Individual Exhibitions:

1926	*Portraits Photographiques,* Galerie Au Sacre du Printemps, Paris
1930	Contemporary Art Club, Harvard University, Cambridge, Massachusetts
1932	Julien Levy Gallery, New York
	Museum of the City of New York
1934	New School for Social Research, New York
	Photos of New York City, Museum of the City of New York
	Oakland Art Museum, California
	Urban Vernacular of the 40s, 50s and 60s, Yale University, New Haven, Connecticut (toured the United States)
1935	Jerome Stavola Gallery, Hartford, Connecticut
	Springfield Museum of Fine Arts, Massachusetts
	Fine Arts Guild, Cambridge, Massachusetts
1937	*Changing New York,* Museum of the City of New York
1938	Hudson D. Walker Gallery, New York
1939	Federal Art Gallery, New York
1941	Massachusetts Institute of Technology, Cambridge
1947	Galerie de l'Epoque, Paris
1950	Akron Art Institute, Ohio
1951	Art Institute of Chicago
1953	San Francisco Museum of Art
	Caravan Gallery, New York
1955	Currier Gallery of Art, Manchester, New Hampshire
1956	Toronto Art Museum
1957	*Portraits of the 20s,* Limelight Gallery, New York
1959	*Science Photographs,* New School for Social Research, New York
	Science Photographs, Massachusetts Institute of Technology, Cambridge
1960	Carl Siembab Gallery, Boston
	Science Photographs, Currier Gallery of Art, Manchester, New Hampshire
	The Image of Physics, Smithsonian Institution, Washington, D.C. (toured the United States)
	Kalamazoo Art Institute, Michigan
1969	*Women, Cameras and Images III,* Smithsonian Institution, Washington, D.C.
1970	Museum of Modern Art, New York
1973	Witkin Gallery, New York
1975	Focus Gallery, San Francisco
1976	Marlborough Gallery, New York (travelled to Lunn Gallery, Washington, D.C.)
	Allan Frumkin Gallery, Chicago
1977	Vision Gallery, Boston (with Bill Brandt and Brassaï)
	Galerie Zabriskie, Paris (with Eugène Atget)
1979	Gallery for Fine Photography, New Orleans
1980	*Changing New York,* Galerie zur Stockeregg, Zurich
1982	*The 20s and the 30s,* International Center of Photography, New York (toured the United States)
1984	Marlborough Gallery, New York
	Martina Hamilton Gallery, New York (with Ansel Adams and Tod Watts)
1986	*New Portfolio,* Martina Hamilton Gallery, New York
	Retrospective, Ikona Gallery, Venice, Italy
1989	*Retrospective,* New York Public Library
1990	Corcoran Gallery of Art, Washington
	Massachusetts Institute of Technology, Cambridge, MA
1991	Portland Museum of Art

Selected Group Exhibitions:

1929	*Film und Foto/Fifo,* Deutscher Werkbund, Stuttgart (toured Germany)
1932	*New York by New Yorkers,* Julien Levy Gallery, New York
1966	*The Photographer's Eye,* Museum of Modern Art, New York
1967	*Photography in the 20th Century,* National Gallery of Canada, Ottawa (toured Canada and the United States, 1967-73)

City Arabesque, New York, **1938.** Photograph by Berenice Abbott.

1975   *Women of Photography*, San Francisco Museum of Art
1979   *Photography Rediscovered: American Photographs 1900-1930*, Whitney Museum, New York (travelled to the Art Institute of Chicago)
          Recollections: 10 Women of Photography, International Center of Photography, New York (toured the United States, 1979-82)
1980   *The Imaginary Photo Museum*, Kunsthalle, Cologne
1982   *Images of America*, San Francisco Museum of Modern Art (travelled to the St. Louis Art Museum, Missouri; Baltimore Museum of Art, Maryland; Des Moines Art Center, Iowa; Cleveland Museum of Art, Ohio)
1986   *The Animal in Photography 1843-1985*, The Photographers' Gallery, London

Collections:

Museum of Modern Art, New York; Metropolitan Museum of Art, New York; Museum of the City of New York; International Museum of Photography, George Eastman House, Rochester, New York; Museum of Fine Arts, Boston; Smithsonian Institution, Washington, D.C.; Art Institute of Chicago; Museum of Fine Arts, Houston; San Francisco Museum of Art; Bibliothèque Nationale, Paris.

Publications:

By ABBOTT: Books—*Changing New York*, with text by Elizabeth McCausland, New York 1939, as *New York in the Thirties*, New York 1973; *A Guide to Better Photography*, New York 1941, revised edition as *A New Guide to Better Photography*, New York 1953; *The View Camera Made Simple*, Chicago 1948; *Greenwich Village Today and Yesterday*, with text by Henry Wysham Lanier, New York 1949; *Eugène Atget Portfolio: 20 Photographic Prints from His Original Glass Negatives*, portfolio of 20 photos, New York 1956; *Eugène Atget*, Prague 1963; *The World of Atget*, New York 1964; *Magnet*, with text by E.G. Valens, Cleveland, Ohio 1964; *Motion*, with text by E.G. Valens, Cleveland, Ohio 1965; *A Portrait of Maine*, with text by Chenoweth Hall, New York 1968; *The Attractive Universe*, with text by E.G. Valens, Cleveland, Ohio 1969; *Berenice Abbott: Photographs*, with introduction by David Vestal, foreword by Muriel Rukeyser, New York 1970; *Berenice Abbott: 10 Photographs*, portfolio, with an introduction by Hilton Kramer, Roslyn Heights, New York 1976; *Berenice Abbott's New York*, portfolio of 12 photos, New York 1978; *Lisette Model*, editor, New York 1980.
Articles—"Photographer as Artist" in *Art Front* (New York), vol. 16, 1936; "Photography 1839-1937" in *Art Front* (New York), vol. 17, 1937; "Eugène Atget" in *Creative Art* (New York), vol. 5, 1939; "My Ideas on Camera Design" in *Popular Photography* (New York), May 1939; "My Favorite Picture" in *Popular Photography* (New York), February 1940; "Eugène Atget" in *The Complete Photographer* (New York), vol. 6, 1941; "Documenting the City" in *The Complete Photographer* (New York), vol. 22, 1942; "Nadar: Master Portraitist" in *The Complete Photographer* (New York), no. 51, 1943; "View Cameras" in *The Complete Photographer* (New York), no. 53, 1943; "From a Student's Notebook" in *Popular Photography* (New York), vol. 21, no. 6, 1947; "What the Camera and I See" in *Art News* (New York), vol. 50, no. 5, 1951; "It Has to Walk Alone" in *Infinity* (New York), vol. 7, no. 11, 1951; "Photography at the Crossroads" in *Universal Photo Almanac*, New York 1951; "The Image of Science" in *Art in America* (New York), vol. 47, no. 3, 1959.

On ABBOTT: Books—*Photographers on Photography*, edited by Nathan Lyons, New York 1966; *Photography in the 20th Century* by Nathan Lyons, New York 1967; *Masters of Photography* by Beaumont and Nancy Newhall, New York 1969; *Looking at Photographs: 100 Pictures from the Collection of the Museum of Modern Art* by John Szarkowski, New York 1973; *The Woman's Eye*, edited by Anne Tucker, New York 1973; *Women of Photography: An Historical Survey*, edited by Margery Mann and Ann Noggle, San Francisco 1975; *The Magic Image* by Cecil Beaton and Gail Buckland, London and Boston 1975; *Photographs from the Julien Levy Collection, Starting with Atget*, exhibition catalogue, by David Travis, Chicago 1976; *Masters of the Camera: Stieglitz, Steichen and Their Successors* by Gene Thornton, New York 1976; *Photographs: Sheldon Memorial Art Gallery*

Collection, University of Nebraska, with an introduction by Norman A. Geske, Lincoln, Nebraska 1977; *Documenta 6/Band 2*, exhibition catalogue, edited by Klaus Honnef and Evelyn Weiss, Kassel and Cologne 1977; *Helen Gee and the Limelight: A Pioneering Photography Gallery of the Fifties*, exhibition catalogue, by Peter C. Bunnell, New York, 1977; *Fotografie der 30er Jahre: Eine Anthologie*, edited by Hans-Jürgen Syberberg, Munich 1977; *Paris-Berlin 1900-1933*, exhibition catalogue, by Herbert Molderings, Werner Spies, Günter Metken and others, Paris 1978; *Amerika Fotografie 1920-40* by Erika Billeter, Berne 1979; *Photographie als Kunst 1879-1979/Kunst als Photographie 1949-1979*, exhibition catalogue, 2 vols., by Peter Weiermair, Innsbruck 1979; *Photographen der 20er Jahre* by Karl Steinorth, Munich 1979; *Film und Foto der 20er Jahre*, exhibition catalogue, by Ute Eskildsen and Jan Christopher Horak, Stuttgart 1979; *Photography Rediscovered: American Photographs 1900-1930* exhibition catalogue, by David Travis, New York 1979; *Recollections: 10 Women of Photography*, edited by Margaretta Mitchell, New York 1979; *A Ten Year Salute* by Lee D. Witkin, foreword by Carol Brown, Danbury, New Hampshire 1979; *The Photograph Collector's Guide* by Lee D. Witkin and Barbara London, Boston and London 1979; *Life: The First Decade 1936-1945*, with texts by Robert Littmann, Ralph Graves and Doris C. O'Neill, New York 1979, London 1980; *Classic Essays on Photography*, edited by Alan Trachtenberg, New Haven, Connecticut 1980; *Berenice Abbott: the 20s and the 30s*, exhibition catalogue, Washington, D.C. 1982; *Berenice Abbott: Sixty Years of Photography* by Hank O'Neal, New York and London 1982; *Images of America: Precisionist Painting and Modern Photography*, exhibition catalogue, by Karen Tsujimoto, Seattle, Washington 1982.

*   *   *

After almost 60 years in photography, Berenice Abbott claims her rightful place as one of the greatest of American photographers. She has always been an exponent of realism, a tireless and uncompromising advocate for the documentary approach in photography. In 1951 she wrote, "We should take hold of that very quality [realism], make use of it and explore it to the fullest."

Abbott, herself, has achieved excellence in more than one kind of photography. Her earliest work consists of straightforward and penetrating portraits made during the 1920s in Paris. The largest body of work comes from the 1930s when she created an elaborate and systematic documentation of New York City during that dynamic decade of change. Her next vision led her to explore the remote realms of science in order to seek visual explanations for the layman. Her last major project was to follow Route 1 from Maine to Florida, recording the American scene in all its variety.

However, a proper assessment of Berenice Abbott's substantial contribution to the medium was delayed for almost 40 years because of her association with the French photographer, Eugène Atget. The young Berenice Abbott had met Atget while she was photo assistant to Man Ray in Paris where she had gone to study sculpture. She rescued Atget's archives from destruction, preserved and printed it and finally published portions, allowing her own work to languish until she had achieved this remarkable contribution to the history of 19th and 20th century photography.

In Paris during the 1920s Abbott opened a portrait studio on the Left Bank and there photographed writers, artists, aristocrats and collectors such as André Gide, Marcel Duchamp, Max Ernst, Leo Stein, Princesse Marthe Bibesco, Sylvia Beach, James Joyce, Jean Cocteau and Violette Murat as well as an assortment of the now-famous expatriate Americans in Paris such as Edna St. Vincent Millay, Janet Flanner and Peggy Guggenheim. Her portraits have an unusually forthright human dignity based upon her intuitive understanding of the balance of strength in women and gentleness in men; each sitter is treated with individual respect, neither a stereotype nor a sentimental image among them.

On a return visit to New York in 1929 she decided to stay; she set herself the goal of documenting the city, a project which occupied the better part of the next decade. In 1939 her book *Changing New York* was published.

Her later scientific work took years of preparation spent in learning, building apparatus and convincing scientists to collaborate with her work. In 1958, right after the Russian spacecraft Sputnik was launched, Abbott was asked to work for the Physical Science Study Committee at the Massachusetts Institute of Technology in Cambridge. In her scientific "illustrations" Abbott's capacity to clarify complex ideas once again succeeded even though their photographic beauty was originally hidden by the inadequate design of the high school textbook in which they were published.

Living now in Maine, Berenice Abbott makes photographs and prints her work to meet the increased demand for prints. She defines her contribution as one of witnessing the American scene, but to thus summarize her life-work is to give this major photographer only partial praise. The value of her contribution to the medium should be based not only on the enormous concepts she herself developed and photographed but should also include her defense and advancement of the medium itself which can be summed up in her appreciation of Atget's work—which she states has "a relentless fidelity to fact, a deep love of the subject for its own sake, a profound feeling for materials and surfaces and textures, a conscious intent in permitting the subject photographed to live by virtue of its own form and life."

—Margaretta K. Mitchell

ABRAMOCHKIN, Yuri V(asilyevich).

Nationality: Russian. **Born:** Moscow, 11 December 1936. **Education:** Primary and secondary schools, Moscow, 1944-54; studied photography at the Training School of Pictorial Journalism, Novosti Press Agency, Moscow, 1958-60; studied law at the All-Union Juridicial Institute, Moscow, 1963-74, Dip. Legal Science 1974. **Family:** Married Svetlana Viktorovna in 1966; daughter: Tatyana. **Career:** Special Photographer, Novosti Press Agency (APN), Moscow, since 1961. Member, Photo Section, U.S.S.R. Journalists' Union, Moscow, since 1963. **Recipient:** Diploma, Economics Category, *Interphoto*, Prague, 1962; Bronze Medal, *Interpress*, Moscow, 1966; Political Reportage Prize, U.S.S.R. Journalists' Union, 1969; Merited Worker of Culture Award, of the Russian Federation, 1977; Medal, *Interpress*, Havana, 1979; Gold Medal, *Sport as Ambassador of Peace Exhibition*, Moscow, 1980. Lives in Moscow. **Address:** c/o Photo Illustration Department, Novosti Press Agency, 4 Zubovsky Boulevard, Moscow 119021, U.S.S.R.

Individual Exhibitions:

1970   *Photographs from the U.S.S.R.*, City Museum, Sopron, Hungary
1974   *U.S.S.R.: Country and People*, Photo Artists' Salon, Belgrade
1976   *From the Photographer's Album*, House of Culture, Prague
        Photographs from the U.S.S.R., Exhibition Pavilion, West Berlin
1978   *Photographs from the U.S.S.R.*, Soviet Cultural Centre, Damascus
        Sowjetunion: Land und Leute im Foto, Majakowski Galerie, West Berlin
1979   *From the Photographer's Album*, Photo and Cine Club, Belgrade

Selected Group Exhibitions:

1961   *National Photo Exhibition*, Manege Exhibition Hall, Moscow
1962   *International Photo-Agency Exhibition*, Prague
1964   *WorldPress Photo*, Amsterdam (and 1965-69, 1975-76, 1978)
1966   *Interpress Photo '66*, Manege Exhibition Hall, Moscow
1975   *Fotosuit de Sovjet Unie*, Stedelijk Museum, Amsterdam
1976   *Photographs from the U.S.S.R.*, Trade Fair Hall, West Berlin
1979   *Interpress Photo '79*, Havana
1980   *Sportas Ambassador of Peace*, Manege Exhibition Hall, Moscow

Collections:

Novosti Press Agency, Moscow; Photo Section, U.S.S.R. Journalists 'Union, Moscow.

Publications:

By ABRAMOCHKIN: Books—*Soviet Tartaria*, edited by A. Osipenko, Moscow 1975; *Kazan*, edited by N. Tkachenko, Moscow 1976. **Photographs in books**—Soviet Photo Artists, edited by M. Bugayeva, Leipzig 1962; *Photointernational '63*, edited by R. Maahs and H. Bronovski, Leipzig 1963; *Interpress Photo '66*, edited by B. Burkov, Moscow 1966; *Photo '70: Works by Soviet Photographers*, Moscow 1970; *Moments of Happiness*, edited by A. Krasnovsky, Moscow 1972; *Photo Book U.S.S.R.*, Moscow 1975; *Photo Album U.S.S.R.: Country and People*, edited by Vazlav Yiru, Prague 1975; *Photo Album '76: For Life*, edited by D. Ardamatsky, Moscow 1976; *Soviet Photo Artists and Amateurs*, Moscow 1977. **Article**—"APN Photographers" in *Hasselblad Magazine* (Goteborg, Sweden), no. 4, 1977.

On ABRAMOCHKIN: Articles—"Fotos aus der Sowjetunion: Eine Ausstellung des Stedelijk-Museums in Amsterdam" in *Foto Magazine* (Munich), April 1975; "Exportausstellung der USSR 1976" in *Der Abend* (West Berlin), December 1976; "Sowjetunion in Bild" in *DSF Journal* (West Berlin), April 1977; "Creative Biography of Yuri Abramochkin" in *Tishrin* (Damascus), 31 January 1978; "Der Kiosk: Bildende Kunst" in *Die Welt* (Hamburg), 7 April 1978; "Mann, was lauft hier ab" by Ralph Franz and Thomas Krekelius in *Die Wahrheit* (West Berlin), May 1978; "The Soviet State in Photographs" by V. Shatrov in *Sovetskaya Kultura* (Moscow), June 1978; "USSR—Photojournalism: The Art of the State" in *American Photographer* (New York), March 1986.

*

I have been working with a camera for 20 years, trying to be satisfied personally with my shots. I've also been doing my best to draw people's attention to something that might interest them, too. To do this, I release the shutter of my camera at just the right moment for me.

I consider photos from life the most interesting; therefore, an "immediate" moment is preferable. So my task is to "catch" such a moment. Naturally, I admit that a "man with a camera" must have his own secrets of shooting to do his job successfully. And his job is rather complicated, since he should be both in the midst of events and at the same time invisible while shooting.

Here is one of my secrets that I should like to share: a photographer is sometimes too tense during shooting, because he must fix on his subject and always try to keep it. I love to photograph people, and often manage to make each of them my partner. This doesn't mean that the subject tries to play up to me—gradually trust grows between us. Each does his own job in the process of photography. My "hero" doesn't pay any attention to me, but I'm on the alert and can take as many photos as possible, and in a way I like best. I cannot describe exactly how I manage to make contact with so many different people, but usually I succeed.

However, trust alone is not enough. The photographer has another task—for me, a social task, to convey themes of grief and joy, love and hatred, health and disease.

Photography is one of the most truthful means of mass media. It is an expressive and the most convenient language of communication between peoples of different outlooks and taste. No "distance" exists in modern photography.

Because of its emotional impact, photography helps people to understand each other at first glance, to know a lot about each other.

I'm pleased that I can perform such an honorable task.

—Yuri V. Abramochkin

*   *   *

Yuri Abramochkin is well known as one of the leading Soviet agency photographers (he works for APN, the Novosti press agency) and as an important correspondent of outstanding topical events and important political happenings at home and abroad. Because a traditional focus on the most closely covered official events does not offer much scope to journalists, however, Abramochkin, an inventive artist, has taken an individual stand and devised less conventional ways of presenting any given topic. Abramochkin has said of his work that he tries to bring "to contemporary photo reporting, in addition to sensations, emotional and humanistic aspects."

He successfully applied this credo and tested it in practice when, as an amateur, he took snapshots at the *World Festival of Youth and Students* in Moscow in 1957. The various faces and characters that marched past his lens, the noticeable differences in appearance and mentality, the changing situations—all of these aspects of his subjects made him seek out a common denominator in the feelings of short-term yet comradely fellowship of the young people from all parts of the world. He found it in his photo appraisal of friendship.

Abramochkin also took an unusual approach to another task he was to face later, as a professional. He was assigned to photograph the discussions at the 25th Congress of the Communist Party of the U.S.S.R. He did not so much concentrate on the speakers as on the whole atmosphere of the Congress, which always determines the political and economic conditions in the country for years to come. The backstage discussions and the lively reaction of the participants proved to be thematically worthwhile, producing more human effects. These pictures, and his agency photographs of similar events in Soviet political life, have been published, and have made his name known, around the world.

Like most Soviet photojournalists, Yuri Abramochkin has also devoted himself to freelance photography as a kind of compensation for his work at the agency. He has been engaged in long-term projects, cycles on certain themes in Soviet domestic life ("People of My Country," "Siberian Geologists," "Kamchatka," etc.) as well as foreign topics ("Vietnam Diary," "Paris Sketches," "America As It Is," "People of Prague.") Some of these cycles are created after short visits; others, such as the cycle about the inhabitants of Prague, have been created over longer periods and are the result of systematic observation and deepening understanding formed over a number of visits.

But, such versatility, which to a certain extent is essential in work for the press agency, does have its drawbacks. Abramochkin's inventive approach to agency work loses its effect in those instances in which a mere impression is not sufficient, in which the artist cannot make do with just the fascination of first impact. Then the result can be just a pleasing effect or chance vision which, even though professionally inventive and witty, seems too premeditated and facile.

—Vladimìr Remes

ADAMS, Ansel (Easton).

Nationality: American. **Born:** San Francisco, California, 20 February 1902. **Education:** Tutored privately at home; studied piano, San Francisco, 1914-27, and photography with the photofinisher Frank Dittman, San Francisco, 1916-17. **Family:** Married Virginia Best in 1928; children: Michael and Anne. **Career:** Began career as a photographer, 1927, and worked as a commercial photographer, 1930-60; photography correspondent, *Fortnightly Review,* San Francisco, 1931; founder-member, with Willard Van Dyke, Edward Weston, Imogen Cunningham, Sonia Noskowiak and Henry Swift, Group f/64, San Francisco, 1932; director, Ansel Adams Photography and Art Gallery, San Francisco, 1933-34; founder, with Beaumont Newhall and David McAlpin, Photography Department, Museum of Modern Art, New York, 1940; photo-muralist, United States Department of the Interior, in California, 1941-42; photography consultant, Office of War Information, Los Angeles, 1942-44. Consultant to the Polaroid Corporation, Cambridge, Massachusetts, 1949-84. Lived and worked in the Yosemite Valley, California, 1937-62, and in Carmel, California, 1962-84. Instructor, with Edward Weston, *U.S. Camera* photographic forum, Yosemite Valley, 1940; Instructor in Photography, Art Center School, Los Angeles, 1941, and Museum of Modern Art, New York, 1945; Founder-Instructor, Department of Photography, California School of Fine Arts, San Francisco, 1946. Founder/instructor, Ansel Adams Annual Photography Workshops, Yosemite Valley, 1955-84. Member of the board of directors, 1934-71, and honorary vice-president, 1978-84, Sierra Club, San Francisco; founder, 1967, and chairman of the board, Friends of Photography, Carmel. **Recipient:** Guggenheim Fellowship, 1946 (renewed, 1948), 1958; Brehm Memorial Award, Rochester Institute of Technology,

New York, 1958; John Muir Award, Sierra Club, 1963; Conservation Service Award, United States Department of the Interior, 1968; Progress Medal, Photographic Society of America, 1969; Chubb Fellowship, Yale University, New Haven, Connecticut, 1970; Special Citation, American Institute of Architects, 1971; First Ansel Adams Conservation Award, The Wilderness Society, 1980; United States Presidential Medal of Freedom, 1980. D.F.A.: University of California, Berkeley, 1961; Yale University, 1973; University of Massachusetts, Amherst, 1974; University of Arizona, Tucson, 1975; D.H.: Occidental College, Los Angeles, 1967. Fellow, American Academy of Arts and Sciences, 1966, and Society of Photographic Scientists and Engineers, 1975. Honorary Fellow, Royal Photographic Society, London, 1976. **Died:** (in Carmel, California) 23 April 1984.

Individual Exhibitions:

1931	Smithsonian Institution, Washington, D.C.
1932	M.H. de Young Memorial Museum, San Francisco
1933	Delphic Studios, New York
1934	Albright Art Gallery, Buffalo, New York
	Yale University, New Haven, Connecticut
1936	*An American Place,* New York
	Katherine Kuh Gallery, Chicago
	Arts Club, Washington, D.C.
1938	University of California, Berkeley
1939	San Francisco Museum of Art
1944	Museum of Modern Art, New York
1946	Santa Barbara Museum, California
1950	Pasadena Art Institute, California
1951	Art Institute of Chicago
1952	International Museum of Photography, Rochester, New York
	Smithsonian Institution, Washington, D.C. (toured the United States)
1956	Photokina, Cologne
1956	Limelight Gallery, New York
1957	University of Hawaii, Honolulu
1961	American Federation of Arts, Carmel, California
1963	M.H. de Young Memorial Museum, San Francisco (retrospective)
	The Story of a Winery, Smithsonian Institution, Washington, D.C. (with Pirkle Jones; toured the United States)
1967	Boston Museum of Art
1970	Witkin Gallery, New York
1972	Philadelphia Print Club
	Witkin Gallery, New York
	Stanford University, California
	San Francisco Museum of Art
1973	Friends of Photography, Carmel, California
1974	Metropolitan Museum of Art, New York
	University of Arizona, Tucson
1976	Columbia Gallery of Photography, Missouri
	Cronin Gallery, Houston
	Center for Creative Photography, University of Arizona, Tucson
	Victoria and Albert Museum, London
1977	Fotografiska Museet, Stockholm
1979	*Ansel Adams and the West,* Museum of Modern Art, New York
1981	*Ansel Adams, Eliot Porter, William Clift,* Cronin Gallery, Houston, Texas
	Facets of the Permanent Collection: Ansel Adams, San Francisco Museum of Modern Art
	Chrysler Museum, Norfolk, Virginia
	Galerie Lange-Irschl, Munich
1982	*An American Place,* San Francisco Museum of Modern Art (travelled to the Center for Creative Photography, Tucson, Arizona; Seattle Art Museum, Washington; Houston Museum of Fine Arts, Texas; Art Institute of Chicago; Corcoran Gallery, Washington, D.C.)
1984	Martina Hamilton Gallery, New York (with Berenice Abbott and Tod Watts)
1986	Palazzo Fortuny, Venice

Selected Group Exhibitions:

1932   *Group f/64*, M.H. de Young Memorial Museum, San
        Francisco
1937   *Photography 1839-1937*, Museum of Modern Art, New York
1944   *Art in Progress*, Museum of Modern Art, New York
1951   *Contemporary Photography*, Contemporary Arts Museum,
        Houston
1959   *Photography at Mid-Century*, International Museum of
        Photography, Rochester, New York
1963   *The Photographer and the American Landscape*, Museum of
        Modern Art, New York
1978   *Mirrors and Windows: American Photography since 1960*,
        Museum of Modern Art, New York (toured the United
        States, 1978-80)
1980   *The Imaginary Photo Museum*, Kunsthalle, Cologne
1985   *American Images*, Barbican Art Gallery, London (toured
        Britain)
1987   *Photography and Art 1946-86*, Los Angeles County
        Museum of Art

Collections:

Center for Creative Photography, University of Arizona, Tucson (archives); San Francisco Museum of Modern Art; M.H. de Young Memorial Museum, San Francisco; Bancroft Library, University of California, Berkeley; Museum of Modern Art, New York; Victoria and Albert Museum, London; Bibliothèque Nationale, Paris.

Publications:

By ADAMS: Books of photographs—Taos Pueblo, with text by Mary Austin, San Francisco 1930; *Sierra Nevada: The John Muir Trail*, Berkeley, California 1938; *Illustrated Guide to Yosemite Valley*, with Virginia Adams, San Francisco 1940, 8th revised edition 1963; *A Pageant of Photography*, exhibition catalogue, San Francisco 1940; *Michael and Anne in Yosemite Valley*, with text by Virginia Adams, New York and London 1941; *Born Free and Equal: The Story of Loyal Japanese-Americans at Manzanar Relocation Center*, New York 1944; *Yosemite and the High Sierra*, with text by John Muir, edited by Charlotte Mauk, Boston 1948; *My Camera in Yosemite Valley*, Boston 1949; *My Camera in the National Parks*, Boston 1950; *The Land of Little Rain*, with text by Mary Austin and Carl Van Doren, Boston 1950; *Death Valley*, with text by Nancy Newhall, San Francisco 1954, 1963; *Mission San Xavier del Bac*, with text by Nancy Newhall, San Francisco 1954; *The Pageant of History in Northern California*, with text by Nancy Newhall, San Francisco 1954; *The Islands of Hawaii*, with text by Edward Joesting, Honolulu 1958; *Yosemite Valley*, edited by Nancy Newhall, San Francisco 1959; *This Is the American Earth*, with others, with text by Nancy Newhall, San Francisco 1960; *Death Valley and the Creek Called Furnace*, with text by Dewin Corle, Los Angeles 1962; *These We Inherit: The Parklands of America*, San Francisco 1963; *Introduction to Hawaii*, with text by Edward Joesting, Redwood City, California 1964; *Fiat Lux: The University of California*, with text by Nancy Newhall, New York 1967; *The Tetons and The Yellowstone*, with text by Nancy Newhall, Redwood City, California 1970; *Ansel Adams*, edited by Liliane DeCock, New York 1972; *Singular Images*, with text by Edwin Land and David H. McAlpin, Dobbs Ferry, New York 1974; *Ansel Adams: Images 1923-1974*, with text by Wallace Stegner, Boston 1974; *Photographs of the Southwest*, with text by Lawrence Clark Powell, Boston 1976; *The Portfolios of Ansel Adams*, with an introduction by John Szarkowski, Boston and London 1977; *Yosemite and the Range of Light*, Boston 1979; *Ansel Adams: An Autobiography*, with Mary Street Alinder, Boston 1986. **Technical books**—*Making a Photograph*, New York and London 1935; Basic Photo Series: 1) *Camera and Lens*, New York 1948, 1970, 2) *The Negative*, New York 1948, 3) *The Print*, New York 1950, 4) *Natural Light Photography*, New York 1952, and 5) *Artificial Light Photography*, New York 1956; *Polaroid Land Photography Manual*, New York 1963; *Polaroid Land Photography*, Boston 1979; *The Camera*, Boston 1980.

On ADAMS: Books—*The Eloquent Light* by Nancy Newhall, San Francisco 1963; *Photography in America*, edited by Robert Doty, with an introduction

by Minor White, New York and London 1974; *Great Photographers*, by the Time/Life editors, New York 1971; *Looking at Photographs* by John Szarkowski, New York 1973; *Masters of the Camera: Stieglitz, Steichen and Their Successors* by Gene Thornton, New York 1976; *Ansel Adams*, exhibition catalogue, by Ake Sidwall and Wallace Stegner, Stockholm 1977; *Ansel Adams: 50 Years of Portraits* by James Alinder, Carmel, California 1979; *Lichtbildnisse: Das Porträt in der Fotografie*, edited by Klaus Honnef, Cologne 1982; *Master Photographers: The World's Great Photographers on their Art and Technique*, edited by Pat Booth, London 1983; *Ansel Adams: An American Place* by Andrea Gray, Tucson, Arizona 1984. **Films**—*Ansel Adams, Photographer*, directed by David Myers, 1957; *Yosemite, Valley of Light*, directed by Tom Thomas, 1957; *Photography: The Incisive Art*, 5 television films directed by Robert Katz, 1959.

*

Why has photography enjoyed such an extraordinary elevation of interest in recent years? It has always been a popular art and craft, and the appearance of the small "automatic" cameras has excited the interest of millions. We must remember that photography is, in its largest amateur applications, a visual diary system. Passing from the simple recording of interesting facts and events to more selective personal observations and interpretations encourages people to think of photography as something in which they might creatively participate. From there, the steps of appreciation, acquisition and actual production of images are obvious and ever-expanding.

In addition, the photo-journalism explosion has identified the camera image with everyday events, and the proliferation of images in magazines, newspapers and on the television screen competes with the printed word. With the camera image, one feels a strong identity with the world about him. Certainly, only a very small part of photography is "art," but that aspect has been nurtured by the general recognition of photography as a language. This surprises me only because of its vast scale. I think we were all aware of the growth of photography for decades, but the present situation is beyond all expectations. The rate of growth may level off in time, but I am sure photography—in all its forms and manifestations—will remain a permanent and dominant force in our lives.

When I started with photography, about 1916, I certainly had no idea of what photography was or where it was going. My early work was of the "snapshot" diarist character; I was anxious to record and retain recollections of experiences. The expressive potentials (perhaps latent in us all) gradually developed, but when I entered the field professionally around 1931 my knowledge of the techniques and my awareness of creativity were relatively small. Associations with Group f/64 opened new worlds. My experiences with Stieglitz and the Museum of Modern Art in New York confirmed my compelling devotion to the medium. With a few reservations, I feel better now about photography than ever before. I feel the young people of today will carry a brighter torch than any of us of earlier days have ignited and held aloft.

Yet, as a stabilizing comment, I must quote Charles Sheeler after he and I had seen an exhibition of photographs dating from the 1940s through the late 1950s: "Adams, isn't it remarkable how photography has advanced without improving?"

—Ansel Adams (1982)

*   *   *

Everyone at the dinner that evening was noisy, cheerful and a bit intoxicated. Ansel, at 78, presided over his guests at the head of the long table. He entertained us all with an endless round of jokes. His own laughter bellowed and resounded in the large, high-ceilinged room. I was seated to his right, and intermittently, in moments of particular good humor, his gnarled hand would creep along the table and pounce on my arm. My startled reaction sent him into new fits of laughter. Here we all were, enjoying a good dinner at Ansel's, after having come to ask a favor of him. It had all started over 5 o'clock cocktails, a long established tradition, Virginia and Ansel being the most generous and gracious hosts to the endless parade of visitors who came almost daily.

After dinner Ansel continued his joking and with his boundless energy and enthusiasm wanted to show his guests some new "toys," an IBM typewriter and a 4x5 view camera that Virginia had recently given him as a present. We, half his age, were already tired, Virginia had slipped off to bed, but Ansel could have gone on and on. Finally with reluctance, we thanked him, and said good night. We stepped out onto the porch covered with pots of fuschia and white cyclamen, cream colored orchids, and lush ferns. A light mist filtered through Monterey pines standing just outside the windows of the house. Hundreds of feet below the Pacific rolled and broke on the black rocky shore. The night air was cool and moist, aromatic from sea and pines. We left Carmel and drove back to San Francisco, talking of our evening with Ansel: the photographer, the legend, the leprechaun.

As photographer, Adams was an undisputed master of the natural landscape. With clarity and precision he portrayed and heightened the spectacular vistas and rich native details of the western United States. Rivers, mountains, valleys, orchards, deserts and sea—all are chronicled, and fused with his poetic vision and his conservationist instincts. "My approach to photography is based on my belief in the vigor and values of the world of nature—in the aspects of grandeur and of the minutiae all about us."

As technical wizard he was possibly unsurpassed, both in his work and in his writings on the craft of photography. Because of his early training as a concert pianist he often expressed his feelings about the technical aspects of photography in musical terms. "It is futile to visualize the mechanically impossible; we cannot perform something on the violin and expect it to sound like a full orchestra." Or in speaking about the printing quality of a fellow photographer, "Jesus, what a great pianist—but the piano's not very good!" He talked of the negative as being the "score." It was important to him to perform it at the highest possible level.

Though he used the best in equipment he was not "gadget"-oriented. Gadgets in themselves are useless and can ultimately become a distraction. He used only what he needed to achieve superior quality. "I prefer a fine lens because it gives me the best possible optical image, a fine camera because it complements the function of the lens, fine materials because they convey the qualities of the image to the highest degree."

His career is truly legendary. He received every honor and award in the field of photography; he was honored by the United States Medal of Freedom. As photographer, teacher, lecturer, conservationist and writer, he made monumental contributions and has been an important influence. His accomplishments could be overwhelming and intimidating until one had a chance to actually spend some time with the person. It was then that the term leprechaun, while surprising, seems apt. Webster's describes leprechaun this way: "a small fairy, thought of as a sly tricky old man who, if caught, will point out a treasure." Ansel Adams seemed to possess the characteristics of a magical mythical creature. Where he got all of his energy is a mystery. He knew how to delight and to mystify. And indeed, if caught, he could point out a treasure.

—Judy Dater

ADAMS, Robert.

Nationality: American. **Born:** Orange, New Jersey, 8 May 1937. **Education:** Wheat Ridge High School, Colorado, 1952-55; University of Redlands, California, 1955-59, B.A. in English 1959; University of Southern California, Los Angeles, Ph.D. in English 1965. **Family:** Married Kerstin Mornestam in 1960. **Career:** Lecturer and Assistant Professor of English, Colorado College, Colorado Springs, 1962-70. Since 1967, independent photographer and writer. **Recipient:** National Endowment for the Arts Fellowship, 1973, 1978; Guggenheim Fellowship, 1973, 1980; Award of Merit, American Association of State and Local History, 1975; Colorado Governor's Award for the Arts, 1979; Peer Award, Friends of Photography, Carmel, California, 1983. **Agent:** Burden Gallery, 20 East 63rd Street, New York, New York 10010. **Address:** 326 Lincoln Street, Longmont, Colorado 80501, U.S.A.

Individual Exhibitions:

1971	Colorado Springs Fine Arts Center
	Photographs by Robert Adams and Emmet Gowin, Museum of Modern Art, New York
1976	St. John's College, Santa Fe, New Mexico

	Rice University Media Center, Houston
	Salt Lake City Public Library
	Castelli Graphics, New York
1977	Sheldon Memorial Art Gallery, University of Nebraska, Lincoln
	Photographs by Robert Adams and Myron Wood, Colorado Springs Fine Arts Center
1978	Robert Self Gallery, London
	Prairie, Denver Art Museum (travelled to the Museum of Modern Art, New York, and Baltimore Museum of Art, 1979)
1979	Werkstatt für Photographie der VHS Kreuzberg, Berlin
	From the Missouri West, Castelli Graphics, New York
1981	Philadelphia Museum of Art
1983	Milwaukee Art Museum, Wisconsin
1984	*Three Americans,* Museum of Modern Art, New York (with Jim Goldberg and Joel Sternfeld)
1985	Denver Art Museum, Colorado
	Summer Nights, Burden Gallery, New York Fraenkel Gallery, San Francisco
	From the Missouri West, Kunstverein, Munich
	Northlight Gallery, Tucson, Arizona
1990	Dean Jensen Gallery, Milwaukee
1991	Photo Gallery International, Tokyo
1992	Centre d'Art Contemporain, Belgium
1993	*At the End of the Columbia River,* Denver Art Museum
1994	Fraenkel Gallery, San Francisco
	Sprengel Museum, Hannover, Germany

Selected Group Exhibitions:

1973	*Landscape/Cityscape,* Metropolitan Museum of Art, New York
1975	*14 American Photographers,* Baltimore Museum of Art (travelled to Newport Harbor Art Museum, Newport Beach, California; La Jolla Museum of Contemporary Art, California; Walker Art Center, Minneapolis; and Fort Worth Art Museum, Texas)
1976	*Aspects of American Photography 1976,* University of Missouri, St. Louis
1977	*The Target Collection of American Photography,* Museum of Fine Arts, Houston (travelled to the Art Museum of South Texas, Corpus Christi, and Joslyn Art Center, Omaha)
1978	*Mirrors and Windows: American Photography since 1960,* Museum of Modern Art, New York (toured the United States, 1978-80)
1979	*American Images: New Work by 20 Contemporary Photographers,* Corcoran Gallery, Washington, D.C. (toured the United States, 1979-80)
1985	*American Images 1945-80,* Barbican Art Gallery, London (toured Britain)
1986	*Photographs by Artists in Mid-Career,* San Francisco Museum of Modern Art
1987	*Photography and Art 1946-86,* Los Angeles County Museum of Art
1989	*Picturing California,* Oakland Museum
	The 150th Anniversary of the Invention of Photography, Prague
	Photography Now, Victoria and Albert Museum, London
	Decade by Decade, Center for Creative Photography, Tucson
	Photography Until Now, Museum of Modern Art, New York
	On the Art of Fixing a Shadow, National Gallery of Art
1990	*The Indomitable Spirit,* International Center of Photography, New York
	Passages de l'Image, Musée National d'Art Moderne, Paris
	Myth of the West, Henry Art Gallery, Seattle
1991	*Visions/Revisions,* Denver Art Museum
	Timothy O'Sullivan and Robert Adams, Turner/Krull Gallery, Los Angeles
	Changing Visions of the American Landscape, Michener Art Center, Doylestown, Pennsylvania

Pleasures and Terrors of Domestic Comfort, Museum of
Modern Art, New York
The Kiss of Apollo, Fraenkel Gallery, San Francisco
1992   *Photographs of the American West: Robert Adams and Wim
Wenders,* Amerika Haus, Berlin;
Mehr als ein Bild, Sprengel Museum, Hannover, Germany;
A History of Oregon Photography, Portland Art Museum;
Lowinsky Gallery, New York
1993   *Magicians of Light,* National Gallery of Canada, Ottowa
Inherit the Earth, University Corporation for Atmospheric
Research, Boulder
Critical Landscapes, Tokyo Metropolitan Museum of Photogra-
phy; Lowinsky Gallery, New York
A La Recherche du Pere, Esders Gallery, Paris

Collections:

Museum of Modern Art, New York; Metropolitan Museum of Art, New York;
International Museum of Photography, Rochester, New York; Princeton
University Art Museum, New Jersey; Colorado State Museum, Denver;
Colorado Springs Fine Arts Center; Museum of Fine Arts, Houston; Sheldon
Memorial Art Gallery, University of Nebraska, Lincoln; Denver Art Museum;
Australian National Gallery, Canberra.

Publications:

By ADAMS: Books of photographs—*White Churches of the Plains:
Examples from Colorado,* with an introduction by Thomas Hornsby Ferril,
Boulder, Colorado 1970; *The Architecture and Art of Early Hispanic Colo-
rado,* Boulder, Colorado 1974; *The New West: Landscapes Along the Colo-
rado Front Range,* with an introduction by John Szarkowski, Boulder,
Colorado 1974; *Denver: A Photographic Survey of the Metropolitan Area,*
Boulder, Colorado 1977; *Prairie,* Denver 1978; *From the Missouri West,*
Millerton, New York 1980; *Beauty in Photography: Essays in Defense of
Traditional Values,* Millerton, New York 1981; *Our Lives and Our Children:
Pictures Taken Near the Rocky Flats Nuclear Weapons Plant,* Millerton, New
York 1984; *Summer Nights,* Millerton, New York 1985; *Los Angeles Spring,*
Millerton, New York 1986; *Robert Adams: Photographs 1965-1985,* Phila-
delphia and Millerton, New York 1988. **Articles**—''Pictures and the Survival
of Literature'' in *Western Humanities Review* (Salt Lake City), Winter 1971;
review of *Wisconsin Death* by Michael Lesy in *Colorado Magazine* (Denver),
Fall 1974; review of *The West* by David R. Phillips in *Colorado Magazine*
(Denver), Spring 1975; introduction to *A Texas Dozen: 15 Photographs* by
Geoff Winningham, Houston 1976; ''Good News'' in *Untitled* (Carmel,
California), no. 14, 1979; ''Inhabited Nature'' in *Aperture* (Millerton, New
York), no. 81, 1979; ''Robert Adams,'' interview with Thomas Dugan, in
Photography Between Covers: Interviews with Photo Book Makers, Roches-
ter, New York 1979.

On ADAMS: Books—*The Library of World Photography: Landscape,* with
texts by David Plowden and Ian Jeffrey, Tokyo and London 1984; *American
Images: Photography 1945-1980,* edited by Peter Turner, London 1985;
Photography and Art 1946-1986, exhibition catalogue, by Andy Grundberg
and Kathleen Gauss, Los Angeles 1987; *Colorado: Visions of an American
Landscape,* by Kenneth I Helphand and Ellen Manchester, Colorado 1991;
*Magicians of Light: Photographs from the Collection of the National Gallery
of Canada,* exhibition catalogue by James Borcoman, Ottowa 1993. **Arti-
cles**—introduction by John Szarkowski to Adams' *The New West: Land-
scapes Along the Colorado Front Range,* Boulder, Colorado 1974; review of
The New West by Lewis Baltz in *Art in America* (New York), March-April
1975; ''Chronicling Sprawl Across the Plains'' in *Photography Year 1977* by
the Time-Life editors, New York 1977; ''The Sublime and the Anachronistic:
Robert Adams' American Landscape'' by Jan Zita Grover in *Afterimage*
(Rochester, New York), December 1981; ''Landscape as Photograph and
Photograph as Landscape: The New Topographics'' by Shelley Armitage in
Southwest Review, Autumn 1989; ''Robert Adams: l'intuition du paysage'' by
Suzanne Lafont in *Galleries Magazine,* August/September 1989; ''Our Lives
and Our Children'' by Jean-Francois Chevrier in *Passages de l'image,* Paris
1990; ''Ghastly News from Epic Landscapes'' by Max Kozloff in *American

Art, Winter/Spring 1991; ''Faith in the Light: The Photography of Robert
Adams'' by Barry Lopez in *Northwest Review,* Vol 29, No. 2.

*

The subject of most of my pictures is a troubling mixture: buildings and
roads that are often, but not always, unworthy of us; people who are, though
they participate in urban chaos, admirable and deserving of our thought and
care; light that sometimes still works an alchemy; a western scale that, despite
our crowding, persists in long views.

If I hope the pictures show more than this, it is because I share the goal of
most photographers. You may have sensed what that goal is if you have
watched someone with a camera struggle for adequate results; over and over
again he walks a few steps and peers, rather comically, into the camera; to the
exasperation of family and friends, he inventories what seems an endless
number of angles; he explains, if asked, that he is trying for effective
composition, but hesitates to define it. Edward Weston, a photographer who
demonstrated he knew what it was, said simply that good composition was
''the strongest way of seeing.'' What he appears to have meant was that a
photographer wants Form, an unarguably right relationship of shapes, a visual
stability in which all components are equally important. The photographer
hopes, in brief, to discover a tension so exact that it is peace.

Pictures that embody this calm are not synonymous, of course, with what
we might see casually out a car window (they may, however, be more effective
if we can be tricked into thinking so). The form the photographer records,
though discovered in a split second of literal fact, is different because it implies
an order beyond itself, a landscape into which all fragments, no matter how
imperfect, fit perfectly.

—Robert Adams

*   *   *

The work of Robert Adams has, in his three major groups of landscape
photographs to date, balanced two seemingly contradictory concerns: the
inquiry into photography's ability to describe natural beauty and the documentation and acknowledgment of man's wordly presence and intervention in the
landscape.

Adams's first major published series, *The New West: Landscapes Along
the Colorado Front Range,* presents a vision of grandeur tempered with
modesty. The small images present natural land formations, the type generally
presented (in landscape photography) on an operatic, heroic scale. The
pictures in *The New West* document mountains, prairies and foothills but, with
equal gravity and respect, show the tract houses, mobile homes, cities and
suburbs that nestle in them. The images do not encourage judgements but
suggest an uneasy coexistence. Photographed in the harsh light of the
American West, the classical simplicity of the images illustrate Adams's sense
of fairness. The starkness of the confrontation between cultural remembrances
of the ideal landscape and the realities of recent American expansion create
beautiful, troublesome photographs.

The photographs in *Denver: A Photographic Survey of the Metropolitan
Area* continue Adams's earlier interests. The images in this group are more
severe and unrelenting in the attempt to balance the search for form and beauty
with the goal of documenting Denver, a city plagued with urban problems.
Adams's goal is to ''discover a tension so exact that it is peace,'' and these
images of land that undergoes extensive development juggle a wealth of
unpleasant detail, at almost direct odds against the intricate beauty of formal
composition. These are extremely difficult photographs. Disturbing information abounds—motels, shopping malls and highways are carefully described—but Adams's striving for visual order is of equal importance to his
goal in reportage.

From the Missouri West is Adams's most overtly lyrical work to date. The
series documents natural land forms, seen by earlier inhabitants as idyllic or
awesome landscape. Adams allows, in these images, for a lushness that has
come to be expected from landscape imagery, but has tempered these scenes
with carefully selected visual reminders of human presence (bits of litter, tire
tracks, buildings and roads seen in the distance, the opacity of polluted air).
These overtly seductive photographs are no less incisive than Adams's earlier,
more didactic works. But what is communicated, more clearly than ever, is

Adams's quest for beauty, and his affirmation of faith in the possibility of its presence.

John Szarkowski has written eloquently of Adams's work: "Adams's pictures are so civilized, temperate, and exact . . . that some viewers might find them dull. . . . But other viewers, for whom the shrill rodomontade of conventional . . . dialect has lost its persuasive power, may find in these pictures nourishment, surprise, instruction, clarification, challenge and perhaps hope."

—Marvin Heiferman

AIGNER, Lucien (Ladislas).

Nationality: American. **Born:** Ersekujvar, Hungary (now Nove Zamky, Slovakia), 14 September 1901; immigrated to the United States, 1939: naturalized, 1945. **Education:** Studied at Prague University, 1920; theatre and acting at Friedrich Wilhelm University and Reichersche Dram. Hochschule, Berlin, 1921-22; law at the University of Budapest, 1922-24, LL.B. 1924; writing, Columbia University, New York, 1942; and filmmaking, New York University, 1967-68; studied photography at the Winona School of Professional Photography, Winona Lake, Indiana, 1957, 1958 and New England School of Professional Photography, University of New Hampshire, Durham, 1963; also attended photography workshops, under John Freni, Poughkeepsie, New York, 1964. **Family:** Married Anne Lenard in 1932 (divorced, 1953); children: John and Steven, Anne and Kati; married Mildred A. Allen in 1955. **Career:** Worked as assistant film cameraman to Stefan Lorant, Berlin, 1921-22; reporter, then photojournalist, 1924-27, and then assistant to their Paris correspondent, later Paris bureau chief, 1927-39, *Az Est* newspaper group, Budapest; photographic assistant to James Abbe, Paris, 1926-28; editor-in-chief, Aral Press, Paris, 1931-39; Photo-Columnist, *L'Intransigeant* newspaper, Paris, 1932; art director, *Petit Journal* newspaper, Paris, 1933; Paris correspondent, London General Press, 1935-39; contract photographer, *Life* magazine, in Paris, 1936-37; also, freelance photojournalist in Paris, contributing to *Vu, L'illustration, Miroir du Monde,* Paris, *Weekly Illustrated, Lilliput, Picture Post,* London, and *Berliner Illustrierte Zeitung* and *Münchner Illustrierte,* Germany, 1928-39; freelance photojournalist, based in New York, working for the *Christian Science Monitor, New York Times, Look, Click, Coronet, Pageant,* etc., 1939-48; announcer, scriptwriter and producer/director, Voice of America radio broadcasts, New York 1947-53. Owner, the Lucien Aigner Studios, Great Barrington, Massachusetts, also freelance writer-photographer for *Popular Photography, Yankee Magazine, Rotarian, Rangefinder,* etc., since 1954. **Recipient:** Leica Award, 1936; Art Directors Award, New York, 1941; Good Citizens Award, Freedom Inc., 1958; National Endowment for the Arts Grant, 1975, 1977. Master of Photography, 1971, and Life Member, 1973, Professional Photographers of America. Chevalier, Ordre des Arts et des Lettres, Paris, 1986. **Agents:** The Photographers' Gallery, 8 Great Newport Street, London WC2, England; Galerie Viviane Esders, 12 rue Saint Merri, 75004 Paris, France; Anna Obolensky, 29 rue Bressolette, 14110 Arcueil, France; Pacific Press Agency, Tokyo CPO Box 2051, Japan. **Address:** 15 Dresser Avenue, Great Barrington, Massachusetts 01230, U.S.A.

Individual Exhibitions:

1972	*Glimpses of History,* Brandeis University, Waltham, Massachusetts
1973	*Photographs by Lucien Aigner,* International Museum of Photography, George Eastman House, Rochester, New York (travelled to New York University, Focus II Gallery, New York, and Bard College, Annandale-on-Hudson, New York)
	40 Years of Candid Photography, at the *Professional Photographers of America Convention,* Denver
	Einstein and Others, YMHA, Highland Park, New Jersey
1975	*Faces from History,* Amerika Haus, Hamburg (travelled to Amerika Haus, Cologne)

	From Marlene to Churchill, Galerie FNAC-Montparnasse, Paris
	40 Years of Instant History, European Center of Photography, Chalon-sur-Saône, France
	Aigner Laszlo Fotómüvész, Hungarian Cultural Center, Budapest
	Lucien Aigner, Photographer, National Museum of Photography, Helsinki
1976	*Picture Stories of France,* French Institute/Alliance Francaise, New York
	Personal Glimpses of History, Shade Gallery, Lenox, Massachusetts
	Profiles of History, Sindin Gallery, New York
	Glimpses of History, Welles Gallery, Lenox, Massachusetts
1978	*Young Yehudi Menuhin,* The Photographers' Gallery, London
	40 Years of Candid Photography, Temple Emanu-El, Westfield, New Jersey
1979	*Glimpses of History,* International Center of Photography, New York (travelled to Photo-Graphics, New Canaan, Connecticut, and Plymouth College, New Hampshire)
1980	*Around Quatorze Juillet,* French Cultural Center, New York (travelled to the Fine Arts Center, Key West, Florida)
	Lucien Aigner, FNAC-Forum, Paris, and Galleria Il Diaframma, Milan
	Einstein at Work, Waldorf Astoria Hotel, New York, and New York University Medical School
1981	*Lucien Aigner,* FNAC Gallery, Lyons
	Galerie Viviane Esders, Paris
	Paris in the 1930s, The Photographers' Gallery, London Photo Museum, Helsinki (retrospective)
	Paris in the 1930s, FNAC, Toulouse, France (travelled to Marseilles and Clermont-Ferrand)
	New York des Annes 40, Galerie Viviane Esders, Paris
	Paris des Annees 30, Musée Carnavalet, Paris
1982	*Paris in the 1930s,* FNAC, Brussels
	Glimpses of History, Addison Gallery, Andover, Massachusetts Photosalon Nagase, Tokyo (retrospective)

Selected Group Exhibitions:

1979	*Fleeting Gestures: Dance Photographs,* International Center of Photography, New York (travelled to The Photographers' Gallery, London)
1980	*The Statues of Paris,* Musée Bourdelle, Paris
	Albert Einstein, Smithsonian Institution, Washington, D.C.

Collections:

Metropolitan Museum of Art, New York; International Museum of Photography, George Eastman House, Rochester, New York; Library of Congress, Washington, D.C.; Smithsonian Institution, Washington, D.C.; Musée Nicéphore Niepce, Chalonsur-Saône, France; Bibliothèque Nationale, Paris; Staatliche Landesbildstelle, Hamburg; International Center of Photography, New York; Museum of Modern Art, New York; Fotografiska Museet, Stockholm.

Publications:

By AIGNER: Books—*Are We to Disarm,* Geneva 1931; *What Prayer Can Do,* with preface by Norman Vincent Peale, New York 1953; *Windows of Heaven,* with text by Glenn Clark, New York 1954; *As We See Them,* with text by Florence Brumbaugh, New York 1956; *Pictures with Purpose,* Pikesville, Maryland 1956; *Between Two Worlds,* Sarcelles, France 1975; *ICP Library of Photographers: Lucien Aigner,* with an introduction by A.D. Coleman, preface by Cornell Capa, New York 1979; *Aigner's Paris,* Stockholm 1982. **Articles**—approximately 100 articles in the European press, 1927-29; "Sixth Graders on War" in *PM* (New York), 23 June 1940; "Peace and War" in the *Christian Science Monitor* (Boston), 31 July 1940; "Einstein Interview" in the *Christian Science Monitor* (Boston), 14 December 1940; "L'Art d'Etre Grandmere" in *Vu* (Paris), no. 595, 1941; "Einstein Admits" in *Click* (Philadelphia), January 1941; "Famous People Don't Pose" in the *Christian*

Science Monitor (Boston), 24 July 1943; "Celebrity Hunting" in *Popular Photography* (New York), November 1943; "A Movie for Democracy" in *Popular Photography* (New York), May 1944; "Camera at the San Francisco Conference" in *Popular Photography* (New York), August 1945; "Photography in Education" in *Popular Photography* (New York), November 1945; "I Am a Small Town Photographer" in *National Photographer* (Chicago), March 1959; "Children in a Minute" in *Professional Photographer* (Chicago), August 1960; "Stage Photography" in *The Rangefinder* (Santa Monica, California), June 1962; "Steps to Acceptance" in *Professional Photographer* (Chicago), September 1965; "Laubach" in *Boys' Life* (North Brunswick, New Jersey), September 1966; "William Stanley" in *Boys' Life* (North Brunswick, New Jersey), November 1966; "Candid Photo History" in *Professional Photographer* (Chicago), July 1973.

On AIGNER: Articles—"Lucien Aigner in Retrospect" by Warren Fowler in the *Berkshire Eagle* (Pittsfield, Massachusetts), 11 July 1971; "Aigner's 100,000 Photos" by C.R. Wasserman in the *Boston Sunday Globe,* 16 April 1972; "Master of the Picture Story" by A.D. Coleman in the *New York Times,* 25 March 1973; "Who's Been Hiding" in *Yankee* (Dublin, New Hampshire), September 1975; "Lucien Aigner, Pionnier" by Michel Nuridsany in *Le Figaro* (Paris), 22 December 1975; "Stolen Glories" by Atticus in *The Times* (London), 7 March 1976; "Journalism—A Free Pass" by Julie Michaels in *The Sampler* (Pittsfield, Massachusetts), 11 July 1976; "Lucien Aigner, Eyewitness to History" by A.D. Coleman in *35mm Photography* (New York), Winter 1978; "Master of the Picture Story" by P. Lehmbeck in *River Valley Chronicle* (Hudson, New York), January 1979; "Lucien Aigner, un Salomon Francais" by J.J. Naudet in *Photo* (Paris), November 1980; "A Life Behind the Lens" in *The Rotarian* (Chicago), January 1981; "Lucien Aigner" in *Camera Mainichi* (Tokyo), August 1982; "Lucien Aigner" in *Camera Mainichi* (Tokyo), December 1982; "Aigner" in *Historie des Galeries de la FNAC* (Paris), December 1983.

*

For more than fifty years photography has been my profession. The camera—first a discovery, then my obsession, my enemy, my destiny—became my way of life. Early in my professional career as a newspaper correspondent I chose it as my tool to record events and people around me. I tried to capture life as it happened in all its fleeting moments—uninterrupted, spontaneous, unselfconscious.

At first, photography appeared an easy way out of my dilemma of recording my observations about human beings faithfully, but without the burden of recreating them in the laborious process of graphic art. I used photography to illustrate my written stories. As I lacked the skill of a painter or illustrator, I welcomed the magic tool that reproduced without effort what I saw, just by pressing a button. These pictorial notes appeared welcome shortcuts not only to graphic art but also to verbal description. Little did I realize (what I had to find out later, to my chagrin) that my tool, so wonderful when the subject *did* appear before it, was totally worthless when access to the subject was denied or when not all the essential details appeared simultaneously in time. The creative telescoping process of the graphic artist, who can summarize in one picture all the scattered details that appear at different moments, is not available to the photographer. He can take only what appears in that split second in time when he releases his shutter.

I was of the first generation of pioneers of the miniature camera, later called "candid." We enjoyed for a while the privilege of being the few who dared to trust their professional fate to an untried instrument they considered a magic tool.

As a foreign correspondent I was admitted to places from which photographers with their big cameras and obnoxious flashbulbs were barred. This gave me a privileged position at first. But as time progressed and others awakened to the advantages of the miniature camera, it became recognized as a vicious little instrument, dreaded by public figures. Worried about their "image," they tried to avoid it. Authorities and celebrities became sensitized to the danger which the candid camera represented to their pompous self-image. They started their defensive campaign against camera indiscretion. At the same time, competition became keener and keener, and life with the miniature camera became an ordeal.

To make bad things worse, the tolerant attitude of editors toward the poor technical quality of this new kind of photography gradually changed. The

novelty of obtaining pictures with this new technique—using available light mostly—gradually changed. The magic that we could get pictures where usually no pictures were allowed or possible, wore thin. Editors, especially in the United States, wanted technically good pictures—not just unique documents. The need for additional equipment, over and above a miniature camera hidden in one's hip pocket, became imperative. Lights, tripods, lenses (tele and wide-angle) had to be added to the easy-to-carry small camera. The ordeal of being a photographer became more and more gruesome. I began to hate my being a photographer.

There was another reason why I resisted being a photographer—just a photographer: I had been a writer-reporter before I took up camera work. Expressing myself through images alone never satisfied me fully. I realized that while pictures had impact far beyond the written word, they were at times ambiguous. To clarify this ambiguity, words had to be added to the photograph. I have always tried to combine words with pictures in my work. I found this effort a tremendous challenge, not always easy to meet. Expression in words requires entirely different gifts from those required for pictorial expression. To practice both simultaneously is extremely difficult, and consequently practitioners who attempt to combine writing with photography are rare. All my life long I had to face editors who wanted me to be either a photographer OR a writer—but not both. And yet, as hundreds of published illustrated articles and photo-features as well as several books for which I supplied both text and illustrations testify, I have never given up my efforts to combine words with images as a professional.

After a long life spent in photojournalism—and a short period in radio with the Voice of America as a writer-announcer and later as a production director—I settled down during the 1950s in a small New England town, Great Barrington (Massachusetts), to become a "small town photographer." My subjects became my clients instead of my victims, and *they* paid me for the privilege of appearing in front of my camera to be immortalized at their best, instead of my *editors* for capturing them at their off-guard moments—at their worst. This brought about the need for pictures that reveal character, beauty, humanity, without unmasking weaknesses—a much more loving approach than I had practiced in my earlier years. Thus my collection of both kinds of photographs grew when, after the War, my (miraculously preserved) European collection was brought to the U.S., and I became the lucky possessor of a depository of rare historic documents. They eventually earned the reputation of uniqueness, and were sought after by museums, private collectors and publishers.

Today, approaching my 85th birthday, at the end of a photographic career of more than half a century, I have made peace with photography. I enjoy sharing with my contemporaries the episodes of my professional life. They seem to interest young and old. The latter know my subjects: the gloriously famous such as Einstein, Churchill, Sara Delano Roosevelt, Emperor Haile Selassie, Mayor La Guardia—and the infamous such as Hitler, Mussolini and their kind. The former—the young, to whom these names mean little—are eager to know about them. Reviewing the harvest of a lifetime, though obtained at the price of struggles and suffering, gives me joy which compensates for the adversities of the past.

—Lucien Aigner

*   *   *

Lucien Aigner's major contribution to the medium was made in the field of photojournalism between 1925 and 1947. A true photojournalist in the original sense of the word (one who integrates photographs and journalism, words and images), Aigner came to photography as a writer who began photographing because it was easier than collaborating with photographers on assignments.

Aigner's career in the field can be said to have begun in Berlin, where he worked as assistant to Stefan Lorant, whose influence on the emerging genre of photographically illustrated journals was seminal. Aigner's professional photography, however, began after he moved to Paris, working first as manager for James Abbe and as a correspondent for newspapers in his native Hungary. Using the byline "Aral," he perfected his skills at the craft of the small-camera "picture story" or photo-essay, which to him remains the central form of photojournalism.

Aigner's articulacy as a photographer was matched by his adeptness as a writer; his ability to combine the two media effectively was one of his hallmarks. It also resulted in his being able to control the printed presentation of his work to a much greater extent than those photographers who left the contextualizing of their images entirely to their editors.

"While I have great respect for the photographic medium, I feel that pictures are not enough to say what needs saying," he has stated. "I have always been suspicious of the cliché about one picture being worth a thousand words. I think both pictures and words are important: pictures for impact, words for meaning. Pictures are sometimes ambiguous, and words are needed."

Much of Aigner's work from that period addresses the European political scene in the years leading up to World War Two. He covered such events as the 1936 Winter Olympics in Berlin and the 1932 Geneva Conference on Disarmament, photographing Hitler, Mussolini, Churchill, Gandhi, the Roosevelts, Haile Selassie, Anthony Eden and many other major figures of the time.

His approach during this phase of his work exemplifies the now-classic small-camera style which he developed in the company of such other practitioners as Salomon, Eisenstaedt and Kertész. Humanist in its inclinations, with a consistent sense of humor (often sardonically edged), Aigner's imagery—much of it made under low-light conditions—has a distinctive gestural quality which compensates in energy for what is lost in detail.

Upon moving to the United States in 1939, Aigner changed the direction of his work. Prohibited from working on most war-related subjects (due to his technical status as an "enemy alien"), he turned his attention elsewhere: pre-war life in Harlem, the Riker's Island prison, Paderewski in exile, Einstein at Princeton. Adopting the then-prevalent style of American magazine photography, Aigner developed a more formal approach, indicative of a more consciously transactional relationship between the photographer and his subjects and a more directorial attitude.

By 1947 Aigner had virtually ended his career as a full-time photojournalist. In 1954 he opened a professional portrait studio. Not until the late 1960s did he begin to reinvestigate his file of some 100,000 35mm. negatives and re-present this body of work to the public—a process which has included the reassessment of much imagery which he did not publish at the time it was made. The exhibitions, portfolios, monographs and articles he has published over the past decade demonstrate that his is an important visual archive, valuable as both a significant resource for 20th-century history and a fine example of the classic style of European photojournalism.

—A.D. Coleman

AKIYAMA, Shotaro.

Nationality: Japanese. **Born:** Tokyo, 8 June 1920. **Education:** Studied commerce at Waseda University, Tokyo, 1936-43; self-taught in photography, from 1936. **Military Service:** Served in the Japanese Army, in China, 1943-45. **Family:** Married Itsuko in 1943; son: Noriko. **Career:** Amateur student photographer, Tokyo, 1936-43; worked for the Tokyo Fresh Foods Center, Tokyo, 1945-46; established Akiyama Photo Studio, Tokyo, 1946-47; worked in the photography department of Kindai Eiga Sha motion picture company (photographer for *Kindai Eiga* cinema magazine), Tokyo, 1947-51. Since 1951, freelance commercial photographer, for the publishers Bungei Shunju Sha, Kodan Sha, Shogakukan, Shei Sha, etc., Tokyo. Organizer, Nikakai Shashin Bu photography section of the Nika painters' group, Tokyo, since 1953; founder-member from 1959, Chairman 1971-79, and Honorary Chairman since 1979, Japan Advertising Photographers Association (APA), Tokyo. Head of the Nihon Shashin Senmon school, Tokyo, since 1978. Member, Japan Professional Photographers Society (JPS), Tokyo. **Recipient:** Kondansha Publishers Culture Award, Tokyo, 1974. **Address:** 2-25-22 Nishiazabu, Minato-ku, Tokyo 106, Japan.

Individual Exhibitions:

1951	Matsushima Gallery, Ginza, Tokyo (with Tadahiko Hayashi)
1952	Matsushima Gallery, Ginza, Tokyo
1955	Konishiroku Photo Gallery, Ginza, Tokyo

1958	*Josei Hyakutai* (One Hundred Poses of Women), Fuji Photo Salon, Ginza, Tokyo
1960	*Taifutsu Sakuhin Ten* (Photos Taken in France), Fuji Photo Salon, Ginza, Tokyo
1966	Fuji Photo Salon, Ginza, Tokyo
1979	*Watashi no Shigoto* (My Works in Autumn), Fuji Photo Salon, Ginza, Tokyo
1980	Wako Gallery, Ginza, Tokyo (with Ryuichi Yamashiro)
	Coloring in Winter, Olympus Gallery, Tokyo
1981	*One Hundred Beauties*, Fuji Photo Salon, Ginza, Tokyo
1982	*Scenery in Four Seasons*, Contax Salon, Tokyo
1984	*Four Seasons at a Corner*, Takano Gallery, Tokyo
1985	*Coloring in Autumn*, Pentax Forum, Tokyo
	Autumn Flowers, Konishiroku Photo Gallery, Tokyo
1986	Murakoshi Gallery, Ginza, Tokyo (with Tomohide Koizumi)

Selected Group Exhibitions:

1959	*2nd Biennale*, Venice, Italy
1975	*The History of Japanese Contemporary Photography 1945-70*, Seibu Museum of Art, Tokyo

Publications:

By AKIYAMA: Books—*Shadow*, Tokyo 1943; *Beauties and Nudes*, Tokyo 1951; *Women, Men, Europe*, Tokyo 1961; *Flowers, Women*, Tokyo 1970; *Snail Tracks*, Tokyo 1974; *Rose*, Tokyo 1975; *Portraits of Writers*, Tokyo 1978; *The Four Seasons*, Tokyo 1979; *Portraits of One Hundred Beauties*, Tokyo 1981; *Coloring of Perspectives*, Tokyo 1981; *Shotaro Akiyama* (Showa Photographers Series), Tokyo 1982; *Flower Screen of Four Seasons*, Tokyo 1982; *Wonderful Everyday*, Tokyo 1984; *Four Seasons at a Corner*, Tokyo 1985.

On AKIYAMA: Books—*Photography of the World*, edited by Heibonsha Publishers, Tokyo 1956; *Photography of the World '60*, edited by Hiromu Hara, Ihei Kimura and others, Tokyo and New York 1960; *Contemporary Photography and Photographers*, with text by Tsutomu Watanabe, Tokyo 1975; *The History of Japanese Contemporary Photography 1945-1970*, Tokyo 1977; *Nude Photographs of Japan*, with text by Shiroyasu Suzuki, Tokyo 1981; *Showa Photographers Story*, with text by Shozo Kozakai, Tokyo 1983.

*   *   *

Akiyama is currently the most well-known and popular photographer in Japan. It is because his main jobs are fashion photography and taking cover photos for magazines, with many famous actresses and models around him, and he often appears on TV programs. The Japanese love his photographic expression which is both beautiful and lyrical.

The feature of his portraiture lies in the simple, monotone background and simple lightings he uses, but he says that he got the hint of the method from painter Rembrandt he had liked since he was young. He still continues to use the same style. He started shooting flowers and landscapes since around 1960, and these themes are now among his important repertories. Even when shooting these subjects, simplifying images is an important factor for him, and for this reason, he has recently started using a soft-focus lens frequently. His works of flowers and landscapes are close to the expression by Japanese paintings and are also seasoned with European atmosphere. His portrait works have this feeling in common.

When he was a university student (1943), he had a small photography book consisting of about 310 photos and entitled *Shadow* published in a quantity of only 150 copies, at his own expense. He meant it to be an epitaph in his youth, since it was during World War II when he shot those photos and he himself thought he might be killed by the war. The photos in the book are all artless, but it is interesting to note in them part of his current style of photography. He has so far had about 20 photography books published, with so many varied themes such as women's portraits, nudes, novelists' portraits, roses, design-oriented flowers shot in the studio, wild flowers photographed outdoors, landscapes like Japanese paintings, etc., and they are all commercially successful. At present, Akiyama is honorary chairman (since 1979) of the Japan Advertising

Photographers Association (APA) and head of Nihon Shashin Senmon School, and furthermore, as a member of Nika-kai's photography section, he has great influence, especially on amateur photographers.

—Takao Kajiwara

ALINDER, James.

Nationality: American. **Born:** Glendale, California, 31 March 1941. **Education:** Roosevelt High School, Minneapolis, 1956-59; Macalester College, St. Paul, Minnesota, under Jerry Rudquist, 1959-62, B.A. 1962; University of Minnesota, Minneapolis, under Jerome Liebling, 1962-64; University of New Mexico, Albuquerque (graduate fellow; graduate teaching assistant; museum assistant), under Van Deren Coke, Richard Rudisill, and Rod Lazorik, 1966-68, M.F.A. 1968. **Family:** Married Mary Street in 1965. **Career:** Freelance photographer, 1956-64; Peace Corps Volunteer, Somali Republic, East Africa, 1964-66; Professor of Art, University of Nebraska, Lincoln, 1968-77. Since 1977, Director of The Friends of Photography, Carmel, California; also, Editor of *Untitled* (journal of The Friends of Photography). Member, board of directors, 1973-79, editor of *Exposure* (the journal of the Society), 1973-77, and chairman of the board, 1977-79, Society for Photographic Education; trustee, 1983, and chairman of the nominating committee, 1984, International Photography Hall of Fame; president, Photography Arts and Sciences Foundation, 1985; trustee, Monterey Peninsula Museum of Art, 1986. **Recipient:** Photographers' Fellowship, National Endowment for the Arts, 1973, 1980; Woods Foundation Fellowship, 1974. **Agent:** The Weston Gallery, Post Office Box 655, Carmel, California 93921. **Address:** c/o The Friends of Photography, Post Office Box 500, Sunset Center, Carmel, California 93921, U.S.A.

Individual Exhibitions:

1968	*The Somali,* University of Nebraska, Omaha
	Panoramic Pictures, University of Maine, Orono
1969	Sheldon Gallery, University of Nebraska, Lincoln
1970	Focus Gallery, San Francisco
	Blanden Art Museum, Fort Dodge, Iowa
1971	Madison Art Center, Wisconsin
	831 Gallery, Birmingham, Michigan
1972	Center of the Eye, Aspen, Colorado
	Alfred University, Alfred, New York
1973	Sheldon Gallery, University of Nebraska, Lincoln
	East Street Gallery, Grinnell, Iowa
1974	*New Panoramics,* The Once Gallery, New York
	Museum of Art, University of Oregon, Eugene
1975	Gallery f/22, Santa Fe, New Mexico
	Elkhorn Gallery, Sun Valley, Idaho
	University of South Dakota Gallery, Vermillion
1976	University of Colorado, Boulder
1977	St. Michael's College Gallery, Winooski, Vermont
1979	*Instamatic and Diana Pictures,* Camerawork Gallery, San Francisco
1980	*Instamatic America,* Spiva Art Center, Joplin, Missouri
1983	*New Work,* Weston Gallery, Carmel, California
1986	*Images,* Morse Gallery, Pebble Beach, California

Selected Group Exhibitions:

1968	*Light⁷,* Hayden Gallery, Massachusetts Institute of Technology, Cambridge
1969	*Vision and Expression,* International Museum of Photography, George Eastman House, Rochester, New York (toured the United States, 1969-71)
1970	*Be-Ing without Clothes,* Hayden Art Gallery, Massachusetts Institute of Technology, Cambridge

1972	*The Wider View,* International Museum of Photography, George Eastman House, Rochester, New York
1973	*Light and Lens: Methods of Photography,* Hudson River Museum, Yonkers, New York
1977	*The Great West: Real/Ideal,* University of Colorado Art Museum, Boulder (toured the United States)
1980	*The Diana Show,* Wynn Bullock Gallery, Carmel, California
1984	*La Photographie Creative,* Pavillon des Arts, Paris
1985	*American Images 1945-80,* Barbican Art Gallery, London (toured Britain)
1986	*Artist Portraits,* Hudson Gallery, New York

Collections:

Museum of Modern Art, New York; International Museum of Photography, George Eastman House, Rochester, New York; Smithsonian Institution, Washington, D.C.; Art Institute of Chicago; Sheldon Memorial Art Gallery, University of Nebraska, Lincoln; Center for Creative Photography, University of Arizona, Tucson; Museum of Art, Stanford University, California; San Francisco Museum of Modern Art; National Gallery of Canada, Ottawa; Victoria and Albert Museum, London; Bibliothèque Nationale, Paris.

Publications:

By ALINDER: Books of photographs—*Consequences: Panoramic Photographs* by James Alinder, Lincoln, Nebraska 1974; *Kansas Album,* with others, edited by James Enyeart, Lawrence, Kansas 1977; *Picture America,* with text by Wright Morris, Boston 1982. **Other books**—*Wright Morris: Structures and Artifacts,* editor, Lincoln, Nebraska 1975; *Crying for a Vision,* co-editor, Dobbs Ferry, New York 1976; *12 Mid-American Photographers,* Kansas City 1977; *Jerome Liebling: Retrospective,* exhibition catalogue, editor, Carmel, California 1978; *Ansel Adams: 50 Years of Portraits,* Carmel, California 1978; *Self-Portrayal,* editor, Carmel, California 1978; *Photographs of the Columbia River and Oregon,* editor, Carmel, California 1979; *Collecting Light: Photographs of Ruth Bernhard,* Carmel, California 1979; *Robert Cumming: Photographs,* Carmel, California 1979; *9 Critics/9 Photographers,* editor, Carmel, California 1980; *Ansel Adams: Photographs of the American West,* Washington, D.C. 1980; *Discovery and Recognition,* editor, Carmel, California 1981; *Roy DeCarava: Photographs,* editor, Carmel, California 1982; *Wright Morris: Photographs and Words,* Carmel, California 1982; *Ansel Adams: 1902-1984,* editor, Carmel, California 1984.

On ALINDER: Books—*Young Photographers,* exhibition catalogue, with text by Van Deren Coke, Albuquerque, New Mexico 1968; *Light⁷,* edited by Minor White, Millerton, New York and Cambridge, Massachusetts 1968; *Vision and Expression,* edited by Nathan Lyons, Rochester, New York 1969; *Be-Ing Without Clothes,* edited by Minor White, Millerton, New York and Cambridge, Massachusetts 1970; *60s Continuum,* exhibition catalogue, with text by Van Deren Coke, Rochester, New York 1972; *Light and Lens: Methods of Photography* by Donald L. Werner and Dennis Longwell, New York 1973; *The Great West: Real/Ideal,* edited by Sandy Hume and others, Boulder, Colorado 1977; *Photographs: Sheldon Memorial Art Gallery Collection, University of Nebraska,* with an introduction by Norman A. Geske, Lincoln, Nebraska 1977; *70s Wide-View,* exhibition catalogue, by Elaine A. King, Evanston, Illinois 1978; *SX-70 Art,* edited by Ralph Gibson, New York 1979; *The Photograph Collector's Guide* by Lee D. Witkin and Barbara London, Boston and London 1979; *Photography for Collectors: Volume 1: The West,* San Francisco 1979; *The Diana Show,* exhibition catalogue, by David Featherstone, Carmel, California 1980; *La Photographie Creative* by Jean-Claude Lemagny, Paris 1984; *American Images: Photography 1945-1980,* edited by Peter Turner, London 1985. **Articles**—"Spirit Documents" in *Creative Camera* (London), July 1970: review in *Artforum* (New York), March 1975; "Shows We've Seen" by Kirschbrown in *Popular Photography* (New York), May 1975.

* * *

Although the images of James Alinder may seem to fall within the limits of the snapshot tradition, they have nothing in them of the mindless automatism that so frequently characterizes that way of seeing. He is primarily interested in making pictures of people, seen in the setting of their everyday concerns, at home, abroad or, by implication, in their artifacts.

In his early work he gave us a portrait of suburbia: the developer's architecture, the time payment decor, the symbolic culture of the framed reproduction of the Mona Lisa, the comfort, good health and prim perfection of the American dream home. Later there were the panoramic prints which recorded the typical sights of a vacation trip and established him as a distinctive and wryly humorous observer of the American scene in the company of Erwitt, Friedlander and Winogrand but with an accent all his own. Later still, the series entitled "Instamatic America" and a series made with the Diana camera provided the opportunity to expand his exploration of the commonplace with the equipment used by millions. In all this work, so assiduously unexceptional, he has been trying to find, it would seem, an imagery which achieves a kind of quintessential purity but avoids the bland anonymity of the snapshot, the bias of the critic or the dogged factualism of the documentarian. The repeated presence of his wife and children in the well-known prints of the 1970s is some indication of his sense of belonging to the experience he records. The wonders of Mount Rushmore or of a Hinky-Dinky market at Christmas time are, after all, genuine wonders, enveloping us all.

His enthusiasm for his subject, which is his own daily experience, shows. Often enthusiasm shades into amusement. Some of his images are "seriously" funny (witness his family posed between the legs of Michelangelo's David at the Palace of Living Art!). But, with all his sense of humor, Alinder still manages to suggest that these images carry more meaning than is obvious in their subject matter. Possibly popular culture has another side which combines, unaccountably, the real and the surreal.

—Norman A. Geske

ALMASY, Paul.

Nationality: French. **Born:** Budapest, Hungary, 29 May 1906; immigrated to France, 1934: naturalized, 1956. **Education:** Educated in Budapest until 1924; studied political science at the University of Vienna and the University of Heidelberg, 1924-28: trained for a diplomatic career. **Family:** Married Sophie Elina Engelsen in 1953; children: Marietta and Isabelle. **Career:** Free-lance journalist, working for Swiss and German magazines (*Schweizer Illustrierte Zeitung, L'Illustré, Schweizer Allgemeine Volkszeitung, Berliner Illustrierte,* etc.) in Europe and North Africa, 1930-36; photojournalist for Ringier and Company, publishers, Zofingen, Switzerland, 1936-76; also worked as a photographer for Unesco, Paris, 1957-77, World Health Organization, Geneva and Washington, D.C., 1958-73, and the International Labour Office, Geneva, 1960-70. Freelance photographer, Paris, since 1977. Teacher at the Centre de Perfectionnement des Journalistes, Paris, since 1970, International Institute of Journalism, Budapest, since 1975, Ecole de Photographie (ETPA), Toulouse, since 1976, and Université de Paris IV (Sorbonne-Celsa), since 1978. Vice-President, Media Forum, Paris, since 1978; member of the board of directors: Musée Français de Photographie, Bièvres; Europhot, Antwerp; Association des Photojournalistes Français; and Fédération des Associations des Photographes Créateurs, Paris. **Recipient:** Master of Photography Award, Council of Professional Photographers of Europe, 1978. **Address:** 2 Villa des Peupliers, 92200 Neuilly-sur-Seine, France.

Individual Exhibitions:

1964	*La Condition Humaine,* Musée du Havre
	So sehe ich die Welt, Stadttheater, Viersen, Germany
1967	*La Main,* Nouvelles Galeries d'Orléans
1973	*SOS: The Cry of Three Continents,* International Gallery, Budapest
1974	*Appeal for a Better World,* French Chamber of Commerce, London
1975	*Livsvilkaå,* Kunstindustrimuseet, Oslo
1977	*Askpetti humani,* Galleria dell'Immagine, Milan
	Les Humains, Musée de la Photographie, Bièvres, Paris

1978	*La main et son language,* Musée Nicéphore Niepce, Chalon-sur-Saône, France (travelled to the Galleria Libreria-Pan, Rome)
	La Photo: Moyen d'Information, Galerie FNAC, Paris (travelled to Galerie FNAC, Lyons)
	Larmes et sourires du Monde, Galerie Feuillade, Chartres, France
1979	*Souvenirs d'Italie,* Institut Culturel Italien, Paris
	Les Rureaux, Galerie Feuillade, Chartres, France
1980	*La language de la main,* Galerie Canon, Paris
	Le tour du monde en 80 photos, Galerie Neptune, Nantes, France
1982	*Femmes et Sociétés,* Marseille, France
1983	*Le monde a l'école,* Bièvres, France
1984	*Des Dieux et des Hommes,* Paris
1985	*Sauf la Mongolie,* Paris (travelled to Marseille, Toulouse and Brussels)
1986	*Femmes et Sociétés,* Paris

Selected Group Exhibitions:

1952	*Weltausstellung der Photographie,* Lucerne
1955	*Biennale de la Photo,* Paris
1965	*Weltausstellung der Photographie,* Hamburg
1966	*Interpress Foto,* Moscow
	Mostra-Concorso du Fotografie, Ascoli Piceno, Italy
1967	*The Camera as Witness,* Toronto (travelled to New York, Tokyo, and London)
	Vom Gluck des Menschen, Berlin
1968	*Weltausstellung der Photographie,* Hamburg
1971	*Liebe, Freundschaft, Solidaritat,* Berlin
1975	*Golden Eye 75: World Exhibition of Photography,* Novi Sad, Yugoslavia

Collections:

Bibliothèque Nationale, Paris; Musée Francais de la Photographie, Bièvres, France; Musée Nicéphore Niepce, Chalon-sur-Saône, France; Hungarian Photographic Archives, Budapest; Kunstindustrimuseet, Oslo.

Publications:

By ALMASY: Books—*Eves de Paris,* Verviers, Belgium 1964; *Le Mont Saint Michel,* Verviers, Belgium 1965; *Trésors du Val de Loire,* Verviers, Belgium 1967; *La photographie, moyen d'information,* Paris 1975; *Informer par la photo,* Paris 1978; *Képiras—sajtofoto,* Budapest 1979; *La photo à la une,* Paris 1980; *La photographie fonctionelle,* Paris 1981; *Le portrait,* Geneva 1983; *Le paysage,* Geneva 1984; *Sauf la Mongolie,* Paris 1985. **Articles**—"Children of the Americas" in *Photography* (London), March 1962; "La photographie—art anonyme" in *Camera* (Lucerne), March 1965; "La photographie à l'Expo 70" in *Photo Revue* (Paris), September 1970; "La lecture des photos d'information" in *Communication et Langage* (Paris), May 1974; "La visualisation des notions abstraites" in *Communication et Langage* (Paris), October 1976; "Am Anfang war das Bild" in *Filter* (Mainaschaff, Germany), April-October 1979; "L'utilisation des photos de presse" in *Le Photographe* (Paris), October 1979; "Les fonctions magiques de la photo" in *Le Photographe* (Paris), January 1980.

On ALMASY: Book—*Photography Today,* edited by Norman Hall, London 1957. **Articles**—"Almasy" by Norman Hall in *Photography* (London), July 1956; "Almasy" by Yves Lorelle in *Le Photographe* (Paris), October 1966; "Almasy" by Roger Doloy in *Arte Fotografico* (Madrid), January 1972; "Paul Almasy, photojournaliste" by Yves Tessier in *Le Soleil* (Quebec), 24 July 1976; "Almasy, photojournaliste" by André Laude in *Contact* (Paris), August 1976; "Belle ou Bonne Photo" by B.C. in *Le Photographe* (Paris), May 1977; "Visages Humaines d'Almasy" by Edo Prando in *Fotografia Italiana* (Milan), August 1977; "Almasy, photojournaliste" by Olivier Vrooland in *Foto* (Amsterdam), February 1979; "Paul Almasy" by Christian Imbert in

Le Photographe (Paris), October 1979; ''Paul Almasy—Sauf la Mongolie'' in *Contacts* (Paris), 1985.

*

I was simply a journalist and really began taking photographs in order to illustrate some of the problems with which I was dealing in my articles. This led me on to study the functional role of photography as a means of information and communication.

I do not agree with those who define photography as a ''language,'' but think of it as a script. If you look at the etymological derivation of the word, *photos* means light and *graphein* means writing, so that photography, therefore, must be ''writing in light!''

Don't say ''photography *is* a language'' but speak about the ''language *of* photography.'' The biggest nonsense is to say ''photography is a universal language.'' There are billions of photographs in the world, but there is no one of them which would say the same thing to an 18 year old boy in the African bush, to a French girl of 20, to a Chinese farmer, or to an American professor. Of all the media, photography is the one that is most restricted in its efficacy: only persons of the same age, same sex, same culture, same social category, etc. can interpret a photograph *more or less* in the same way.

Similarly, I have decided views on the distinction between the two main branches of photography—the pictorial or artistic and the functional (as used by the press, in advertising, in illustration, etc.) The rules of the one are not at all applicable to the other, and one must never speak of ''photography'' in an overall sense, but must always specify the branch one is alluding to. For myself, I have nothing to do with pictorial photography, and I do not consider myself an artist. My profession is that of photojournalist, and I try to produce photographs that are *good,* not *beautiful.*

I have been studying the rules of photographic writing (in the functional sense) for the past ten years, and I have also considered the ''reading'' of photographs. In fact, my theory concerning the relative importance of the component parts of a picture was the basis of a survey involving 1720 interviewees (50% men, 50% women), a survey that confirmed that the theory was 91% correct. In this theory I distinguish three composition materials, namely: living beings—humans and animals; moving objects—smoke, flames, etc.; and fixed objects—mountains, houses, etc. What happens, in reading, is that the living elements take precedence over both the moving and the still, and the moving elements take precedence over the still. When a photograph contains a living subject, whatever the area or position it occupies within the whole, the ''reading'' of the photograph begins with the living subject, and any moving object comes second in order of priority. We are talking here of a phenomenon which is part optical, part intellectual, and part psychological, and even if the living component is very small, it is still the component that immediately attracts the attention of the ''reader.'' (One must not, of course, confuse ''reading'' with perception. A fixed object, because of its size, shape or light value, can strike the eye within the first tenth of a second. But if one is talking of actual reading, then it will begin with the living object if one exists within the picture.)

If we compare a piece of writing and a photograph (the two media we use to transmit information and messages), the most important difference between them is that the reading of a written text functions on one level only—that of description; whereas the reading of a photograph can always be said to function on two levels—description and suggestion. Over and above that which is actually represented, there is the suggestion of the abstract—ideas, emotions. In reading a text, one's psychological reactions are triggered only indirectly, because the meaning of the words and sentences has to be filtered by the imagination in order to be translated into mental images.

As a photographer my main interest is in people and the ''human condition,'' which I try to portray without any concessions. Whatever happens, I remain firmly committed to reality; I do not sacrifice the truth for the sake of technical quality. If the lighting conditions are inadequate, I do not supplement them with any kind of artificial lighting because this would interfere with the authenticity of the subject. As a photojournalist, I am vehemently against the use of flash: I have taken 325,000 black and white exposures and 115,000 colour transparencies, and not one has involved the use of flash. I prefer to push film sensitivity to the limit; I expose film from 400 ASA to 1600 or 3200 or at times even 6400 ASA, if necessary.

A photojournalist is something of an historian, and an historian must never lie.

—Paul Almasy

*   *   *

A tireless traveller, Paul Almasy, in the course of a long career, has visited every country in the world but two—as he tends to stress with a certain archness. He has always tried to be a careful and exact witness of conditions different from those of his own, and our, everyday life. His archives are enormous, more than 300 thousand shots in black and white and 50 thousand in colour. ''The sum total of my work is a kind of great record of our age,'' he declares. And it is a record, let us add, that reveals a great desire to show that people—black and white, poor and rich—are indissolubly bound by a thread: all belong to the human race. Almasy's attention is always concentrated on man, on the endless adventure in which he is the protagonist, under every sky, under every regime and within every social structure. It is not anthropological research that he aims at, but something different, something wider—a testimony full of optimism even when it records unacceptable facts. A testimony that shows how he has understood many things. His is a classical, composed reportage. He does not fling his truth in people's faces as other reporters do, but presents it with firmness and a great respect for the dignity of man.

Fashions come and go, but the name of Almasy is destined to remain in the histories of photography. A journalist with lens and with pen, he has understood that his profession is to communicate. He has understood that, to be comprehended, it is necessary to communicate in the simplest possible way, so simple as to reveal nothing of the trouble and study that lie behind the pressing of the camera button. The photographic critic of the French daily *Le Monde* has written about Almasy's pictures: ''the more we look at pictures of this quality, the more we want to look at them. This is reportage of great quality. . . . Many of his pictures, it is true, are no more than sketches, with something of the flavour of Bresson. And this is a limitation—if only there were more sketches like Almasy's! In any case, not all his pictures are in this manner. And none of his photographs is an end in itself. . . . 'I am convinced,' he says, 'that photography as an aesthetic art and photography for information must be clearly separated. In the latter there must be more room for the semantic aspect, the points that serve to communicate. But of course I do look for a pleasant aesthetic in my pictures as well as for information. . . . ' ''

Amid this confusion of intentions it is agreeable to converse with Almasy, to listen to him, to learn from his pictures. They are pictures that result from sound preparation, good professionalism, seasoned with a pinch of irony. It may be a commonplace, but it is a question of that quality which the French—and he *is* French—call *esprit.* A quality very hard to find.

—Edo Prando

ALPERT, Max.

Nationality: Russian. **Born:** Simferopol, near Odessa, Ukraine, 18 March 1899. **Education:** Attended the Jewish School, Simferopol, 1906-10; self-taught in photography. **Military Service:** Served in the Red Army, in Odessa, 1919-21. **Family:** Married Glafira Belits-Gaiman in 1947. **Career:** Free-lance photographer, Odessa, 1914-19; agent, Help the Children Commission, Moscow, 1921-24; photo reporter, *Rabochaya Gaseta (Workers' Newspaper),* Moscow, 1924-29; photo correspondent, *Pravda* newspaper, Moscow, 1929-31, and *SSSR na Stroike* magazine, Moscow, 1931-41; war correspondent and photographer, for the TASS Agency, Moscow, at the Russian front, 1941-45; photo correspondent for the Sovinformburo, Moscow, 1945-48, for the *Soviet Union* magazine, Moscow, 1948-51, for Isogis publishing house, Moscow, 1951-58, again for Sovinformburo, 1958-61, and for the APN Press Agency, Moscow, 1961 until his death, 1980. **Recipient:** Silver Medal, *International Photography Exhibition,* Zagreb, 1940; Silver Medal, *International Photography Exhibition,* Boston, 1941; Diploma of the GDR 1958, First Prize, 1959, Gold Medal, 1965, and Grand Prize and Gold Medal, 1974,

The Horse Rider Girl, **1936.** Photograph by Max Alpert.

Bifoto, East Berlin; Silver Medal, *Interpressphoto '66,* Moscow, 1966; First Prize, *Socialist Fotoart Exhibition,* Dresden, 1968; Diploma and Artist Award, Fédération Internationale de l'Art Photographique (FIAP), 1973; Gold Medal for an Individual Exhibition, Czechoslovakia/U.S.S.R. Friendship Association, Prague, 1973; Grand Prix du Président de la République, France, 1976. **Died:** (in Moscow) 1 December 1980.

Individual Exhibitions:

1931   *24 Hours in the Life of the Filippov Family,* Vienna and other European cities (with Shaikhet and Tulesa)
1967   *50 Years with a Camera,* Friendship House, Sofia, Bulgaria (retrospective; toured Eastern Europe, Cuba, Finland, Denmark and France, 1972-80)
1981   Institute of Art History, Moscow

Selected Group Exhibitions:

1929   *Russische Ausstellung,* Kunstgewerbemuseum, Zurich
        Film und Foto/Fifo, Deutscher Werkbund, Stuttgart (toured Germany)
1935   Exhibition of Masters of Soviet Art
1940   *International Photography Exhibition,* Zagreb
1941   *International Photography Exhibition,* Boston
1958   *Bifoto,* East Berlin (and 1959, 1965)
1966   *Interpressphoto '66,* Moscow
1968   *Socialist Fotoart Exhibition,* Dresden
1974   *Bifoto,* East Berlin
        Fotos uit de Sovjet Unie, Stedelijk Museum, Amsterdam
1979   *Film und Foto der 20er Jahre,* Wurttembergischer Kunstverein, Stuttgart (travelled to the Museum Folkwang, Essen; Werkbund Archiv, West Berlin; Kunsthaus, Zurich; Kunstverein, Hamburg; Museum des 20. Jahrhunderts, Vienna)
1989   *150 Years of Photography,* Central Exhibition Hall, Moscow
1992   *The Utopian Dream: Photography in Soviet Russia 1918-1932,* Laurence Miller Gallery, New York
        The Great Utopia: Russian and Soviet Avante-Garde, 1915-1932, Frankfurt; Amsterdam; New York; Moscow; St Petersburg

Collections:

Museum of Photographic Art, Moscow (archives); Shickler/Lafaille Collection, Los Angeles

Publications:

By ALPERT: Books—*Troublesome Profession,* Moscow 1962; *Max Alpert,* edited by Roman Karmen, Moscow 1974.

On ALPERT: Books—*Liberation,* edited by Mikhail Trakhman, Boris Polevoi and Konstantin Simonov, Moscow 1974; *Fotos uit de Sovjet Unie,* exhibition catalogue, Amsterdam 1974; *Photography Yearbook 1975,* edited by John Sanders, London 1974; *Fotografovali Valku,* edited by Daniela Mrázková and Vladimìr Remeš, Prague 1975, as *The Russian War 1941-45,* with an introduction by A.J.P. Taylor, London 1978; *Sowjetische Fotografie 1928-32* by Rosalind Sartori and Henning Rogge, Munich 1975; *Geschichte der Fotografie im 20. Jahrhundert/Photography in the 20th Century* by Petr Tausk, Cologne 1977, London 1980; *Film und Foto der 20er Jahre,* exhibition catalogue, edited by Ute Eskildsen and Jan Christopher Horak, Stuttgart 1979; *Fotografie im Klassen Kampf* by Erich Rinka, Leipzig 1981; *Ciernobiela tvoriva fotografia/Black-and-White Creative Photography* by Petr Tausk, Martin, Czechoslovakia 1981; *Pioneers of Soviet Photography* by Grigory Chudakov, Olga Suslova and Lilya Ukhtomskaya, London and Paris 1983; *Sowjetische Fotografen 1941-1945* by S. Morosov and others, Leipzig 1985; *Anthology of Soviet Photography,* Moscow 1986; *20 Soviet Photographers. 1917-1940,* by Grigory Chudakov, Amsterdam 1990. **Articles**—"Great Joy

Is Work" (80th birthday tribute) by Grigory Chudakov in *Sovetskoye Foto* (Moscow), March 1979.

* * *

Born in 1899, Max Alpert belonged to the young generation of Soviet photojournalists in the 1920s. From the beginning of his career he showed a sensitivity and skill in the depiction of the building of industry. He was interested not only in the significant event—for instance, the celebration of the first car from a new factory—but also in the modest successes that characterized an improved standard of living.

Max Alpert's gift for choosing the representative from within typical situations predestined him to take part in one of the most interesting events in Soviet photography between the two world wars—the picture story, "24 Hours in the Life of the Filippov Family." Together with Shaikhet and Tulesa, Alpert photographed the life of the members of a family of an unknown metalworker in Moscow. From their results, the photographers selected a wonderful collection of 78 photographs which offered unusually complex information about the everyday life of a typical Soviet family in 1931. The whole series was exhibited in Vienna and in other European cities, and a large part of it was published in the journals *USSR in Construction* and *Arbeiter Illustrierte Zeitung.* The creative approach in taking the single images, then combining them in a mutually reflective series, was quite new; it was, in fact, a very important contribution to the evolution of the modern use of photographic information.

In the first half of the 1940s Alpert became a war correspondent for the agency TASS. His extensive experience in live photography in peacetime helped him in his depiction of the dramatic moments in the fight against the Nazi invaders. The eloquence of his images of the period is unique, and they continue to the present day to be examples of great photographic art. Alpert's concern in these works is humanistic, a humanism conveyed by his vision of the particular: for example, the details in the picture of Soviet soldiers, details that, as it were, "speak" of the men's desire to win; the compassion of his pictures of unknown women and children escaping before the onslaught of Fascist troops.

After the war Alpert again returned to his earliest theme, producing magnificent reports on the reconstruction of Soviet industry. Again, in this newest part of his oeuvre, he devoted his attention to people, to their enthusiasm for quick reconstruction after the devastation of wartime.

Later in life Alpert occasionally photographed abroad, and he confirmed in all of these cases his ability to isolate the typical situation, the telling image that would characterize for his audience the style of life in other countries.

Alpert died in 1980, and the great and important work of a modern pioneer of photojournalism came to a close.

—Petr Tausk

ALVAREZ BRAVO, Manuel.

Nationality: Mexican. **Born:** Mexico City, 4 February 1902. **Education:** Attended the Catholic Brothers School, Mexico City, 1908-14; studied painting and music at the Academia Nacional de Bellas Artes, Mexico City, 1918; self-taught in photography. **Family:** Married 3 times, to Dolores Martínez; Doris Heyden; and Colette Urbajtel; children: Manuel, Laurencia, Miguel, Aurelia, and Genoveva. **Career:** Worked as a copy clerk, Mexico City, 1915-16, and for the Mexican Treasury Department, Mexico City, 1916-31. Freelance photographer, Mexico City, since 1931. Instructor in Photography, Escuela Nacional de Bellas Artes San Carlos, Mexico City, 1928-29, 1938-40; proprietor of a commercial photography shop, Mexico City, 1939-42; Photographer/Cameraman and Instructor in Photography, Sindicato de Tecnicos y Manuales de la Industria Cinematografica, Mexico City, 1945-58; Instructor in Photography, Centro Universitario de Estudios Cinematográficos, Mexico City, 1966-68. Since 1959, Founder/Director and Chief Photographer, El Fondo Editorial de la Plástica Mexicana, Mexico City. **Recipient:** Sourasky Art Prize, 1974; National Art Prize, Mexico, 1975. Honorary Member, Academia de Artes, Mexico; Tlacuxlo de Plata awarded by El Salon

El Umbral. Photograph ©Manuel Alvarez Bravo.

de la Plástica Mexicana, 1992; Crêdor Emérito by Fondo Nacional para la Cultura y las Artes, 1993; The Peer Award for Distinguished Career in Photography from Friends of Photography, San Francisco, 1994. **Agent:** Zelda Cheatle Gallery, 8 Cecil Court, London WC2, England. **Address:** Espíritu Santo 83, Coyoacán, 04330 Mexico, D.F., Mexico.

Individual Exhibitions:

1932	Galeria Posada, Mexico City
1934	Palacio de Bellas Artes, Mexico City (with Henri Cartier-Bresson)
1935	*Documentary and Anti-Graphic,* Julien Levy Gallery, New York (with Walker Evans and Henri Cartier-Bresson)
1936	Hull House, Chicago
	Almer Coe Optical Company, Chicago
1939	Universidad Nacional de Mexico, Mexico City
1942	Photo League, New York
1943	Art Institute of Chicago
1945	Sociedad de Arte Moderno, Mexico City
1954	Centro de Relaciones Culturales Anglo-Mexicano, Mexico City
1957	Salon de la Plástica Mexicana, Mexico City
1966	Galeria de Arte Mexicano (Galeria Ines Amor), Mexico City
1968	*Manuel Alvarez Bravo: Fotografias 1928-1968,* Palacio Nacional de Bellas Artes, Mexico City
1971	Pasadena Art Museum, California
	Museum of Modern Art, New York
	International Museum of Photography, Rochester, New York
1972	*Manuel Alvarez Bravo: 400 Photographs,* Palacio Nacional de Bellas Artes, Mexico City
1973	Casa de la Cultura, Hucjitan, Oaxaca, Mexico
1974	Art Institute of Chicago
	Galeria Arvil, Mexico City
	Casa del Lago Universidad, Mexico City
	University of Massachusetts, Boston
1975	Alhondiga de Grananitas, Guanajuato, Mexico
	Witkin Gallery, New York
	Museo de Arte Moderno, Caracas
	Galeria Juan Martìn, Mexico City
1976	Museo de Arte Moderno, Mexico City (opening of permanent exhibit)
	Photogalerie, Paris
	Musée Nicéphore Niepce, Chalon-sur-Saône, France
	Galerie Municipale du Chateau d'Eau, Toulouse
	Alvarez Bravo/Pedro Meyer/Lázaro Blanco, Galleria Il Diaframma, Milan
1978	Photographers Gallery, London
	Corcoran Gallery, Washington, D.C.
1979	*Rencontres Internationale de la Photographie,* Arles, France
1980	Museo de San Carlos, Mexico City
1981	Witkin Gallery, New York
	Photo Art, Basle
1983	Israel Museum, Jerusalem
1984	Quito, Ecuador
	La Habana, Cuba
1985	Madrid Biblioteca Nacional
1986	*Comemora los 50 anos de la exhibicion con Henri Cartier-Bresson,* el INBA
	Rochester Institute of Technology
	Musé d'Art Moderne de la Ville de Paris
1987	International Center of Photography, New York
	Coimbra and Palace of Cascais, Portugal
1988	Alla and Sheinbaum and Russek Gallery, Santa Fe, New Mexico
1989	The Witkin Gallery, New York
	Centro Cultural Arte Contemporaneo, Mexico
	Mucho Sol, Bellas Artes, Mexico
	Museo de Arte Moderno, Buenos Aires
1990	Museum of Photographic Arts, San Diego, California

1992	*90th Birthday Exhibition,* Galería Juan Martin, Mexico; The Witkin Gallery, New York; Musée de l'Elysée, Lausanne. Museo de Arte Moderno, Mexico

Selected Group Exhibitions:

1939	*Souvenir du Mexique,* Galerie Renou et Colle, Paris
1943	*Mexican Art Today,* Philadelphia Museum of Art
1955	*The Family of Man,* Museum of Modern Art, New York (and world tour)
1956	*Alvarez Bravo/Walker Evans/August Sander/Paul Strand,* Museum of Modern Art, New York
1961	*Coloquio Latinoamericano de Fotografia,* Museo de Arte Moderno, Mexico City
1977	*Concerning Photography,* The Photographers' Gallery, London (travelled to the Spectro Workshop, Newcastle upon Tyne)
1978	*Contemporary Photography in Mexico,* University of Arizona, Tucson
1980	*The Imaginary Photo Museum,* Kunsthalle, Cologne
1981	*Photographer as Printmaker,* Ferens Art Gallery, Hull, Yorkshire, (travelled to the Museum and Art Gallery, Leicester; Cooper Gallery, Barnsley; Castle Museum, Nottingham; Photographers Gallery, London)
1982	*Primavera Fotografica a Barcelona,* Fundacion Miro, Barcelona, Spain.

Collections:

Instituto Nacional de Bellas Artes, Mexico City; Museum of Modern Art, New York; Brooklyn Museum, New York; International Museum of Photography, George Eastman House, Rochester, New York; Art Institute of Chicago; Pasadena Art Museum, California; Victoria and Albert Museum, London; Bibliothèque Nationale, Paris; Musée Nicéphore Niepce, Chalon-sur-Saône, France; Museum of Modern Art, Moscow.

Publications:

By ALVAREZ BRAVO: Books—*Manuel Alvarez Bravo,* with text by Luiz Cardoz y Aragon, Mexico City 1935; *Manuel Alvarez Bravo: Fotografias,* Mexico City 1945; *La Pintura Mural de la Revolución Mexicana,* Mexico City 1960; *The Painted Walls of Mexico: From Prehistoric Times until Today,* with texts by Jean Charlot and Emily Edwards, Austin, Texas 1966; *15 Photographs by Manuel Alvarez Bravo,* portfolio, New York 1974; *Manuel Alvarez Bravo,* with text by Denis Roche, Paris 1976; *Photographs by Manuel Alvarez Bravo,* portfolio, Geneva 1977; Exhibition catalogue, Biblioteca Nacional, Madrid, 1985; Exhibition catalogue Musée d'Art Moderne de la Ville de Paris, 1986; *Great Masters of Photography,* New York 1987; *Mucho Sol,* exhibition catalogue, Mexico 1989; *Revelaciones,* San Diego 1990.

On ALVAREZ BRAVO: Books—*Manuel Alvarez Bravo: Fotografias 1928-1968,* exhibition catalogue, by Juan Garcia Ponce, Mexico City 1968; *Manuel Alvarez Bravo,* exhibition catalogue, by Fred Parker, Pasadena, California 1971; *Manuel Alvarez Bravo,* exhibition catalogue, by Jane Livingstone, Boston 1978; *Nude Photographs 1850-1980,* edited by Constance Sullivan, New York 1980; *Photographer as Printmaker,* exhibition catalogue, with texts by Gerry Badger, Peter C. Bunnell and Ansel Adams, London 1981; *World Photography,* edited by Bryn Campbell, London 1981; *The Imaginary Photo Museum* by Helmut Gernsheim, Renate and L. Fritz Gruber, Cologne 1981, London 1982. **Articles**—"Souvenir du Mexique" by André Breton in *Minotaure* (Paris), May 1939; "Manuel Alvarez Bravo" in *Album* (London), October 1970; "Manuel Alvarez Bravo" in *Camera* (Lucerne), January 1972; "Manuel Alvarez Bravo" in *The Magic Image* by Cecil Beaton and Gail Buckland, Boston and London 1975; "The Indigenous Vision of Manuel Alvarez Bravo" by A.D. Coleman in *Artforum* (New York), April 1976, reprinted in Coleman's *Light Readings: A Photography Critic's Writings 1968-1978,* New York 1979; "Manuel Alvarez Bravo" in *Photographs: Sheldon Memorial Art Gallery Collection, University of Nebraska* by Norman A. Geske, Lincoln, Nebraska 1977; "Manuel Alvarez Bravo" in *Concerning Photography,* exhibition catalogue, by Jonathan Bayer, Peter Turner, Ian

Jeffrey, and Ainslie Ellis, London 1977; "Manuel Alvarez Bravo" in *Contemporary Photography in Mexico,* exhibition catalogue, by Rene Verdugo and Terence Pitts, Tucson, Arizona 1978; "Manuel Alvarez Bravo," interview, in *Dialogue with Photography* by Paul Hill and Thomas Cooper, London 1979; "Manuel Alvarez Bravo" by E. C. Garcia in *Photo Vision* (Madrid), April/June 1982.

* * *

When *A Vision of Paris,* recently reissued, was first published in 1963, it demonstrated that the juxtaposition of literature (Proust) and photography (Atget) could create a remarkable synthesis without violating the integrity of either. It is, therefore, equally remarkable that no publisher has thought to combine the words of Malcolm Lowry's *Under the Volcano* with the photographs of Manuel Alvarez Bravo. Alvarez Bravo's pictures provide the perfect counterpoint to Lowry's prose. It was, after all, Mexico which killed Firmin. The terrors and shadows that propelled Malcolm Lowry's protagonist toward his end can be found in Alvarez Bravo's vision of his native land.

Manuel Alvarez Bravo has long been judged "a photographer's photographer," which is a gentle way of saying that, until recently (although he began making photographs in the 1920s), few people, outside of a small group of artists and writers, knew of his achievements. Little wonder; apart from Peter Magubane, how many African photographers, or Brazilian, or Chilean, or—even—Japanese photographers are household names in the West? Precious few. Thus, despite the length of his professional career, and the quality and quantity of his photographs, Manuel Alvarez Bravo's first major U.S. exhibit (at the Pasadena Art Museum) was not mounted until 1971. The catalogue of that exhibit, which was, until 1978, the only collection of his photographs available, has long been out of print.

Despite this long-standing ignorance of his work, Alvarez Bravo was by no means ignorant of what was happening in the world of photography. Yet, there is little outside influence to which one may readily point. "His work," wrote Paul Strand, "is rooted firmly in his love and compassionate understanding of his own country, its people, their problems, and their needs. These he has never ceased to explore and to know intimately."

The typical Alvarez Bravo photograph (as true in the 1920s and 30s as today) is a direct, unmanipulated "straight" print. It succeeds because of his allegiance to and mastery of the formal elements of light, tone, and composition. But one might as easily describe the works of hundreds, thousands, of other photographers in such terms. The salient difference is that Alvarez Bravo's photographs exist on a powerfully symbolic plane as well. In "The Obstacles" (a 1939 image containing four carousel horses), for example, the horses are an obstacle to the viewer, filling the frame so that surrounding buildings are obscured. And that frame is but one of the obstacles preventing the horses' escape. The figures might be waiting impatiently for the Four Horseman of the Apocalypse. In this photographer's world, such conjecture is not far-fetched.

Born in 1902, Alvarez Bravo's world was that of revolutionary Mexico. The street battles of 1910 disturbed his classes; corpses, and a climate of pervasive violence, have remained vivid memories for him. Thus, the tension born of implicit violence recurs in his photographs and is one of the "themes" in his oeuvre. In Alvarez Bravo's world, violence may, as in "The Obstacles," be implied or it may, as with "Striking Worker, Assassinated" (1934), be explicit as death. In this particularly famous example of his work, a corpse is viewed from pelvis to head. The blood-spattered shirt lies partially open and the head lies in a pool of blood. An outstretched arm and the stained sand form a triangle with the lower edge of the frame. That triangle leads directly back to the head; the geometry is as inexorable as death itself.

Death has many symbols for this master: a cemetery wall, animal bones, the grave. But there is lyricism in Alvarez Bravo's world, too. Thus, the reverie of a young woman is caught by the photographer as she is "Day Dreaming" (1931). That particular picture, and a 1974 reprinting, are instructive, too, in revealing changes in the photographer's style.

The older print is, by and large, darker (this is true of others reprinted in the 1974 portfolio). The tonalities which sparkle in the recent print are lost in the style of the older one. "Day Dreaming" (1974) is, therefore, lyrical not only in subject, but in tonality as well. Patches of light on the young woman's shoulder and dress provide points of reference without dominating. In the 1931 print (in which the negative had been cropped considerably), those references become beacons in a dark field—the woman is virtually lost. Thus, the nightmare

qualities implied even in reverie (1931) are softened (1974) and rendered less visceral.

Mystery, in the earlier works, was created, in part, by technical artifice: dark prints, heavy contrasts. In the fine, full-toned recent prints, the mystery inherent in Manuel Alvarez Bravo's vision stands on its own. The comparison is not meant invidiously. Manuel Alvarez Bravo may have selected different methods (including colour) with which to communicate his vision over the past several decades; the power of that vision, however, has never been in question.

—Stu Cohen

ANGEL, Heather (Hazel).

Nationality: British. **Born:** Heather Le Rougetel, in Fulmer, Buckinghamshire, 21 July 1941. **Education:** Attended several schools in Britain and New Zealand, including Gosforth Grammar School, Northumberland, 1956-58, and Wycombe High School, High Wycombe, Buckinghamshire, 1958-59; studied zoology, Bristol University, Gloucestershire, 1959-65, B.Sc. (honours) 1962, M.Sc. 1965; mainly self-taught in photography, from 1966. **Family:** Married the biological oceanographer Martin Angel in 1964; son: Giles, born 1977. **Career:** Assistant Marine Biologist, National Institute of Oceanography, Godalming, Surrey, 1966-67. Since 1967, freelance wildlife and biological photographer working for the magazines *Gardenia, Wildlife, Amateur Photographer* and *Asahi Camera,* and the publishers Fountain Press, Michael Joseph and Ebury Press, in Galapagos, the Seychelles, Sri Lanka, Madagascar, Mauritius, China, Uganda, etc. Founder-Director, Biofotos photo library, Farnham, Surrey, since 1970. Founder-Chairman of the Nature Group, 1965-78, Council Member, 1976-86, and President, 1984-86, Royal Photographic Society, Bath, Avon; Council Member, Royal Society for the Protection of Birds, Sandy, Bedfordshire, 1980-85. **Recipient:** Hood Medal, Royal Photographic Society, 1975; Medaille de Salverté, Société Francaise de Photographie, 1984. D.Sc.: Bath University, Avon, 1986. Fellow: Royal Photographic Society; British Institute of Professional Photography; Linnaean Society. Member: Botanical Society of the British Isles; Hampshire and Isle of Wight Naturalists' Trust; Marine Biological Association; Royal Society for the Protection of Birds; Scottish Marine Biological Association; Surrey Wildlife Trust. **Address:** Highways, 6 Vicarage Hill, Farnham, Surrey GU9 8HJ, England

Individual Exhibitions:

1979   *The Living Shore,* Institute of Biology, London (toured Britain 1979-80)
1981   *The Natural World of Britain and Ireland,* Science Museum, London (toured Britain 1981-84)
1984   *A Camera in the Garden,* Kodak Gallery, London (toured Britain 1984-86)
1986   *Nature in Focus,* Aberystwyth Arts Centre, Wales
        Gardens in Focus, Botanic Garden, Edinburgh
1987   *Nature in Focus,* Natural History Museum, London
1989   *The Art of Wildlife Photography,* Nature in Art, Gloucester.

Selected Group Exhibitions:

1977   *121st RPS Annual Exhibition,* Kodak Gallery, London (travelled to the Grundy Art Gallery, Blackpool; Cathedral Nave, Coventry; Haworth Art Gallery, Accrington)
1982   *Along the Seashore and Under the Sea,* Ellingham Mill Art Society, Suffolk
        Twelve Points of View, Kodak Gallery, London (travelled to Bath, Avon 1983)
1985   *Nikon Exhibition,* Barbican Art Gallery, London
        British Photography, Beijing, China

Cougar or Mountain Lion "Felis Concolor" Kitten, **1992 (original in colour).** Photograph ©Heather Angel.

Collections:

National Maritime Museum, London; National Centre of Photography, Bath, Avon.

Publications:

By ANGEL: Books—*Nature Photography: Its Art and Techniques*, London 1972; *Photographing Nature: Trees*, King's Langley, Hertfordshire 1975; *Photographing Nature: Insects*, King's Langley, Hertfordshire 1975; *Photographing Nature: Flowers*, King's Langley, Hertfordshire 1975; *Photographing Nature: Fungi*, King's Langley, Hertfordshire 1975; *Photographing Nature: Seashore*, King's Langley, Hertfordshire 1975; *Seashore Life on Rocky Shores*, Norwich 1975; *Seashore Life on Sandy Beaches*, Norwich 1975; *The World of a Stream*, London 1976; *Wild Animals in the Garden*, Norwich 1976; *Seashells of the Seashore*, Norwich 1976; *Life in Our Seas*, Norwich 1976; *Life in the Oceans*, London 1976; *Life on the Seashore*, Basingstoke, Hampshire 1976, London 1980; *Seaweeds of the Seashore*, Norwich 1977; *Life in Our Rivers*, Norwich 1977; *Life in Our Estuaries*, Norwich 1977; *Let's Collect Fossils*, with text by Andrew Mathieson, Norwich 1977; *The Jarrold Book of the Countryside of the New Forest*, Norwich 1977; *The Jarrold Book of the Countryside of South Wales*, Norwich 1977; *British Wild Orchids*, Norwich 1977; *Seashells of the Seashore*, 2 vols., Norwich 1978; *Counting Creepie Crawlies*, London 1980; *Ladybirds*, with text by Harold Oldroyd, London 1980; *The Guinness Book of Seashore Life*, Enfield, Middlesex 1981; *The Natural History of Britain and Ireland*, London 1981, 1985; *The Book of Nature Photography*, London 1982; *The Family Water Naturalist*, with Pat Wolseley, London 1982; *The Book of Close-up Photography*, London 1983; *Heather Angel's Countryside*, London 1983; *A Camera in the Garden*, London 1984; *Close-Up*, Goteborg 1986; *A View from a Window*, Sparkford, 1988; *Nature in Focus*, London 1988; *Landscape Photography*, Sparkford 1989; *Animal Photography*, Sparkford 1991; *Kew: A World of Plants*, London 1993; *Photographing the Natural World*, London 1994. **Articles**—"To Sell or Not to Sell" in *Kodak Professional News* (Hemel Hempstead), June 1973; "What Is Nature Photography?" in *British Journal of Photography* (London), December 1973; "Some Aspects of Still Photography" in *Medical and Biological Illustration* (Edinburgh), no. 26, 1976; "Nature in Focus" in *Hasselblad* (Goteborg), no. 2, 1977; "Heather Angel on Nature Sequences" in *Practical Photography Yearbook*, Peterborough, Cambridgeshire 1978; "Guidelines for Tree Photography" in *Arboricultural Journal* (Guildford), October 1980; "Unnatural Selection of Nature Photographs" in *British Journal of Photography* (London), September 1982; "Focus on the Garden" in *Popular Gardening* (London), August 1983; "More Than the Eye Can See" in *Nikon News* (Kusnacht), no. 1, 1985; "The Evolution of Nature Photography" in *The Photographic Journal* (London), September 1986; "The World of Close-Ups" in *Professional Photographer*, September 1986; "Beauty Is in the Eye of the Beholder," in *Modern Eyes*, January 1987; "Down in the Forest," in *Camper*, March 1987; "Selezione Naturale" in *Oasis*, (Italy) March 1988; "A Feast of Fall Foliage" in *World Magazine* (U.K.) September 1988; "A Profusion of Circles" in *World Magazine* (U.K.) October 1988; "Photography as a Tool in Garden Design" in *The Photographic Journal*, September 1989; "Blooming Deserts" in *World Magazine* (U.K.) April 1989; "A History of Nature Photography" in *The BALPA Journal*, Summer 1989; "Garden Photography" in *Telegraph Magazine*, 1989; "How Does Your Garden Grow?" in *The BALPA Journal*, Summer 1989; "Animals in Their Environment" in *The Photographic Journal*, July 1989; "It's a Swan's Life" in *World Magazine* (U.K.) 1989; "Landscapes" in *Hasselblad the System* 1989; "Winter Cameos" in *Regent Magazine*, Hong Kong, December 1989; "Big Eye on the Small World" in *Outdoor Photographer* (U.S.A.), May 1990; "Nature Photographers: Heather Angel" in *The Iris* (RPS Nature Group) No 46, Spring 1990; "A Road of Ancient Traditions" in *World Magazine* (U.K.) September 1990; "Heather Angel's Nature Notebook" in *Amateur Photographer*, monthly Sep-Dec 1990; "Focus on the Natural World" in *Surrey Wildlife Trust*, 1990; "Heather Angel's Nature Notebook" in *Amateur Photographer*, monthly Jan-Dec 1991; "Obituary—Eric Hosking" in *The Times*, February 1991; "Extremes of Exposure" in *BBC Wildlife*, June 1991; "Tribute to Eric Hosking" in *The Photographic Journal*, May 1991; "From the Poles to the Tropics" in *Travel Log* (RPS Travel Group) September 1991; "Heather Angel's Nature Notebook" in *Amateur Photographer*, monthly Jan-Dec 1992; "Picture It" in

Woman's Weekly, 21 April 1992; "Safari Photography" in *Outdoors Illustrated*, May 1992; "Gardens in the Picture" in *Gardeners World*, June 1992; "Photographing Animals" in *Club Rollei*, November 1992; "Douglas Wilson Hon FRPS—An Appreciation" in *The Photographic Journal*, May 1992; "Majestic Cheetahs" in *Cat World*, August 1992; "Horses for Courses" in *The BALPA Journal*, Summer 1992; "Flash Photography," in *Outdoors Illustrated*, 1992; "Heather Angel's Nature Notebook" in *Amateur Photographer*, monthly Jan-Dec 1993; "Natur im Sucher" in *Kosmos* (Germany), January 1993; "Picture in Power" in *The Biologist*, December 1993; "Heather Angel's Nature Notebook" in *Amateur Photographer*, monthly Jan-Dec 1994; "Natural Vision" in *The Photographic Journal*, May 1994; "Close Up," *Hasselblad* brochure 1994.

On ANGEL: Books—*World Photography*, edited by Bryn Campbell, London 1981; *How Famous Photographers Work* by Jack Schofield, John Goldblatt and others, London 1983. **Articles**—"Though the Eye of an Angel" by Jenny Woolf in *Sunday Times Colour Magazine* (London), March 1984; "Heather Angel" in *Asahi Camera* (Tokyo), June 1984; "Natural Selection" by Michelle Hendricks in *The Photographer* (London), October 1984; "Tony Lynch Meets Heather Angel" in *Amateur Photographer* (London), January 1986; "Heather Angel's Nature Course" by Tony Lynch in *Amateur Photographer* (London), March, April, July, October and November 1986; "How Photographers Work—Heather Angel" by Tina Rogers in *You and Your Camera*, No 28, 1979; "Angel Fingers" by Adrian Knowles in *Amateur Photographer*, 5 June 1982; "Focus on Nature" by Dave Curry in *What Camera Weekly*, 19 June 1982; "Portfolio of Heather Angel's Work" in *Asahi Camera* (Tokyo) June 1984; "Heather Angel Talks about Photographing Nature" *Petersen's Photographic Magazine*; "Visit to an Angel" by Victor Blackman in *Amateur Photographer*, 26 May 1984; "So You Want to Be a Nature Photographer" interview in *Practical Photography*, July 1988; "Life through the Lens" by Jackie Bennmett in *The Gardener* October 1988; "A Walk on the Wild Side" by Gillian Thornton in *Home & Freezer Digest*, May 1989; "Heather Angel" by Brian Shuel in *The BALPA Journal*, Winter 1990/91; "Angel of the Morning" by Eamonn Percival in *Photography* July 1991; "Call of the Wild" by Gillian Thornton in *Annabel*, October 1991; "A Question of Wildlife" by Sean Hargrave in *Photo Answers*, February 1992; "In the Bag: Wildlife" by Sean Hargrave in *Buying Cameras*, March 1992; "The World Is Your Lobster" by David Qarr in *Photo Plus*, March 1992; "Recording Angel" by Genevieve Hawks in *Nonesuch*, Spring 1993; "Angel Delights" by Igillian Thornton in *Camping*, September 1993; "Nature's Angel" by Rachel Braverman, *Professional Photographer*, August 1993; Interview with Susan McCartney in the book *Nature Photography: A Complete Guide to Shoot and Sell*, New York 1994; "Pro Choice: Heather Angel" by Jonathan Vince in *Camera Wise*, Issue 117, 1994; "My Gardening World: Heather Angel" in *BBC Gardener's World*, June 1994.

*

To be a successful nature photographer, one must be single-minded yet patient; persistent but not ruthless. Above all, the well-being of the subject must come before achieving the picture. There are two—often conflicting—requirements for a good nature photograph. Firstly, the picture must be truthful; secondly, it needs to arrest the attention of the viewer. My aim is to produce nature photographs which are both visually exciting *and* also make a biological point. I pay great attention to lighting and to detail; for example, if the background distracts and I cannot change the camera viewpoint, I invariably do not expose a frame.

As a dedicated wildlife photographer I have a great love for my subjects and will not photograph a wild animal if it is obviously wary of my presence. Any specimens which are collected for studio photography are returned as soon as possible to their natural habitat.

I now work almost exclusively with colour transparency film for reproduction in magazines, books and calendars. Since colour plays such an important part in communication in the natural world, monochrome pictures simply cannot convey as much information about the biology of a plant or animal as colour ones.

I never had any ambition to be a photographer, and after training as a zoologist and working as a marine biologist, I took up photography to illustrate my lectures and articles on marine life. Entirely self-taught, I have developed my own techniques by trial and error. Writing helps to fuel ideas for pictures, and the observations I make in the field help to trigger off ideas for writing. The two disciplines are now inseparable, and I find one not only complements but is essential to the other.

Unlike many nature photographers who prefer to specialise in one aspect, such as birds, or insects or flowers, I tackle any subject of any size. This involves using a wide range of lenses and equipment and, after the camera itself, I consider a sturdy tripod essential. I use this for 99% of all the pictures I take, the only exception being birds in flight and active insects feeding on flowers. Amongst all the techniques I use, there are probably two which have become my hallmark: birds and mammals shown in context with their natural habitat and critical lighting for close-ups.

Through my nature photographs I aim to make people more aware of the fragility of life on earth. If my photographs make people stop, look, read a caption and thereby learn more about wildlife, then, in a small way I have helped emphasise the need to conserve what is still left in our world of dwindling natural habitats.

Nature photography has taken me to far-flung corners of the globe, including several oceanic islands and, most recently, several times to China. Here, I was able to combine my love for natural scenes with my latest enthusiasm: namely, garden photography. Within gardens, it is textures, colour associations and patterns which attract me. It is particularly interesting to see how plants originating from different corners of the globe are able to grow in combination together in British gardens.

—Heather Angel

*   *   *

Heather Angel has clearly stated the principles on which she works. These, together with photographic skills that have become second nature, her real love and knowledge of her subjects and her astounding energy have made her the leading photographer in her field today. Few other nature photographers will undertake such a wide range of subjects from the smallest of insects to the largest of mammals and equally few will undertake such an enormous amount of travelling to reach them. This is not easy travelling as the equipment needed is extensive and can even include special aquaria to hold tiny water specimens and their background materials when it is necessary to photograph them in laboratory conditions.

Heather Angel makes six or seven trips each year—to a wide variety of locations, often in extremes of heat or cold and usually involving hours or even days of patient waiting for subject and background to come together in a way which satisfies her. No time is wasted during the waiting; every spare minute is used in writing, not only the detailed captions that must accompany any picture, but articles for magazines and text for books, of which she now has over 40 to her credit. She much prefers to arrange her own itinerary and only takes occasional commissions because these might force her to miss the one time in a year when a particular creature or plant can be photographed to the best advantage. While ensuring that the backgrounds are correct and that the lighting shows her subjects clearly, she is not overly precious about the finished prints and has expressed a preference for the Hasselblad format because it enables cropping to suit various layouts more easily than can be done with a 35mil. Her library is now extensive and her work is used in a very wide range of publications, calendars and exhibitions. All possible markets are borne in mind when working, so that a "cute" subject will not be despised any more than the first pictures of a very obscure specimen. She can sometimes be surprised, as in the case of the Pacific Yew tree of which she took six exposures. Because of a special substance found in its bark which has given it news value in the medical and women's press, the picture is now constantly out of the library and she wishes she had taken more!

Heather has immense generosity of spirit. Self-taught in photography, she is keen to help other people in her sphere and has put a great deal of time into starting and chairing the Nature Panel at the Royal Photographic Society as well as undertaking the onerous task of its presidency from 1984 to 1986. She has given lectures across the world and since 1990 has had a regular monthly column in *Amateur Photography* enabling her to share her experiences as widely as possible. She is a member of many learned societies and in 1994 was appointed visiting professor in the Department of Life Science at The University of Nottingham.

Her energy does not diminish and between her forays to foreign parts and writing her books, she has begun the huge undertaking of re-photographing all the British flora and fauna she shot twenty years ago, to take advantage of the vast improvements in film emulsions that are now available.

With the increasing world-wide interest in all aspects of the environment, Heather Angel's photographs will be in constant demand because they do not only give accurate descriptions of hundreds of birds, animals, water creatures and plant life, but also very beautiful ones.

—Sue Davies

ARNOLD, Eve.

Nationality: American. **Born:** Born in Philadelphia to Russian immigrant parents. **Education:** Began photographing and managed photo-finishing plant, in 1946; studied photography with Alexei Brodovitch at New York City's New School for Social Research in 1948. **Career:** First associated with Magnum Photos in 1951; became an associate member in 1955, a full member, 1957; photographed in China and, in 1980, the Brooklyn Museum opened a large travelling exhibition of these photos. **Recipient:** National Book Award for *In China*, 1980; Lifetime Achievement Award from the American Society of Magazine Photographers. **Agent:** Magnum Photos, 23-25 Old Street, London EC1V 7HL, England. **Address:** 26 Mount Street, London W1Y 5RB, England.

Individual Exhibitions:

1980   *In China: Photographs by Eve Arnold,* Brooklyn Museum, New York (toured the United States, 1980-82)
1991   *In Britain,* National Portrait Gallery, London

Selected Group Exhibitions:

1982   *Lichtbildnisse: Das Porträt in der Fotografie,* Rheinisches Landesmuseum, Bonn
1983   *Photography in America 1910-83,* Tampa Museum, Florida
1984   *Sammlung Gruber,* Museum Ludwig, Cologne

Publications:

By ARNOLD: Books—*The Unretouched Woman,* London 1976; *Flashback! The 50s,* New York 1978; *In China,* New York, London, Paris and Tokyo 1980; *In America,* New York and London 1983; *Marilyn Monroe: An Appreciation,* New York, London, Paris, Rome, Madrid, Tokyo 1987; *Private View: Inside Baryshnikov's American Ballet Theatre,* New York and London 1988; *All in a Day's Work,* New York 1989; *In Britain,* London 1991. **Articles**—From 1954 onwards articles have appeared in *Life Magazine* (U.S.A.), *Look Magazine* (U.S.A.), *Geo* (Germany), *Stern* (Germany), *Epoca* (Italy), *Sunday Times* (London), *Paris Match* (France). **Film**—*Behind the Veil,* 1973.

*   *   *

Eve Arnold's life as a working photographer began in the early 1950s. Over the past forty years the world of photojournalism she entered has changed completely and a study of her work reveals a history of the profession from the high point of the photo-based news magazines to the current increasing use of such photographs for books, exhibitions and the sale of individual prints. In one way this can extend our knowledge of the world with far more pictures on one subject available through a book or particular exhibition than could ever have been shown in a magazine. But in another, by selecting an individual picture for sale as a work of art, it may completely change the emphasis that was originally put on it when it was taken. The fact that many of Eve Arnold's early photographs are well able to stand up to such transitions is a measure of her talent.

It was intended that Eve Arnold should be a doctor, but during her studies a boyfriend gave her a Rollei camera, and not content with simply using it for snapshots she enroled at The New School for Social Research where, in 1948, she studied with Alexi Brodovitch. When he assigned a project on fashion Eve

***Marilyn Monroe on the Nevada Desert During the Filming of The Misfits,* 1960.** Photograph by Eve Arnold.

decided to find out if it was possible to cover the subject in Harlem. The resulting pictures of black models and fashion shows so pleased Brodovitch that he encouraged her to continue with the project over the next 18 months. The resulting pictures were sent as a story to *Picture Post* and published in London. In 1952 *Picture Post* asked her to cover her first political story—the Republican Presidential Convention in Chicago—and looking back on the experience she sees that it was the first time that a live news event was widely seen on TV in the States, foreshadowing things to come. For the next ten years she worked all over the United States. As she says, she was learning her trade, and as there was so much going on in New York, she approached all the publicists she could think of until she found herself invited to important events all over the city. Much of this work was done speculatively to begin with, but assignments soon followed. Between engagements she felt she needed to relax on a project of her own and decided to work over a number of years on the recording of her home town which was virtually run by one family who had been given land there in 1706. Here she showed the life of a small town as it grew, and also the terrible conditions in the migrant labour camps that were set up for the southern black potato pickers who came each year to work for the local farmers.

Although magazines were interested in the great and famous there was also a market for "family pictures" in such well paying publications as *The Ladies Home Journal* which used them in a series called "How America Lives," presenting the somewhat idealised lives of people in their striving for "the good and simple life." This was the background against which Senator Joe McCarthy came to power, and Eve was very keen to gain entry to his hearings to photograph them herself. Eventually, by saying she was a freelance who worked for *Fortune*—not untrue but perhaps not the whole truth as it was European magazines who actually wanted these pictures—Eve spent two days

at the hearings, crouching down by the table with the UP and AP photographers and capturing a memorable series of the senator and his cronies at work.

Eve learned one very important lesson from this assignment, that she must be able to control the captions. In Germany when they were published all the captions were pro-McCarthy; not at all what she had given them, and in Italy an additional posed picture of an Italian girl with a big sack of mail was captioned to the effect that this was a tiny part of the post sent protesting against McCarthy—sadly equally untrue!

In 1961 Eve Arnold decided to make her base permanently in London and in her usual thorough way she devised a method of finding out more about her adopted country. The Personal Column of *The Times,* in those days still carried on the front of the paper, contained advertisements from a wide variety of people; a vicar looking for funds for his church roof; a widow looking for companionship; three girls in search of a fourth to share a flat and many more. By contacting them and arranging to photograph the outcomes of their various searches, Arnold was able to both explore the country and produce a series of articles that were published in *Queen* magazine. Several of these stories came to light again when they were included in her book *In Britain,* published in 1991.

Eve Arnold had been associated with the Magnum Agency since 1951 and became a full member in 1957, the second woman to do so (after Gisele Freund). During the early years she covered many stories dealing with "minority" groups—the poor, blacks, the aged and women. Here she succeeded in treating her subjects as individuals, photographing the normal flow of their lives with kindness and candour. During the '60s and '70s she concentrated more on the political movements of both blacks and women, particularly the Black Muslims with Malcolm X. Again her interest lay in showing the individuals rather than striving for instant drama and she was prepared to travel long distances and put up with considerable harassment to fit in with the demands made by Malcolm X. These pictures were shown in 1992 at ICP in New York and still evoke real fear at the possibility of a coalition between the Black Muslims and the American Nazi Party of George Lincoln Rockwell.

Looking back over this work when she was preparing her book *Flash-back—The 50s,* Eve Arnold recognised it as a time of great freedom and adventure for photojournalists. There were many opportunities to travel, to put up ideas and to see them published in the multitude of magazines that then existed. As her friend Charlie Harbutt expressed it, ''photography then was about people, by the end of the seventies it was about photography.'' In the critical self-examination that took place in the late seventies and eighties, photography lost an innocence of purpose which it cannot regain but which truly reflected the straightforward aspirations of the people living in the fifties.

In 1973 Arnold made a film *Behind the Veil* looking at the position of women in Muslim society. In 1976 she expanded on that theme for her second book *The Unretouched Woman,* this time examining the humour, incongruities and pathos of the lives of women around the world. ''I am a woman and I wanted to know about women'' Arnold stated. ''I realise now that through my work. . . .I have been searching for myself, my time, and the world I live in.'' The pictures spanned a period of nearly twenty-five years and ranged from peasants performing backbreaking daily tasks with great dignity to ''behind the scenes'' pictures of Joan Crawford half undressed and Marilyn Monroe on tour. The book was extremely well received and *Newsweek* book critic Walter Clemons found it ''expert photojournalism'' with a text as ''forthright'' as its photos. Eve Arnold had almost always written the texts for her books and although she has had many good writers working with her on magazine stories, her own texts are exemplary in giving clear background information on the subjects and on her feelings about them. They are particularly valuable because Arnold does not load her pictures with her own emotions, leaving us to judge her subjects for ourselves. The texts further satisfy our natural curiosity as to how and why a particular situation came about and conditioned her chosen moment to take the photograph.

In 1979 Arnold made two trips to China—the first to more familiar places; the second to far-flung areas not normally visited by foreigners. ''My goal was to make a photographic book about the lives of the people, to try to get a sense of the sustaining character beneath the surface. . . .I wanted not only to photograph and observe, but to talk to people and to interview them.'' The resulting book, *In China,* contained her text and 179 photographs. While some critics were seduced by the wonderful colour images into finding it too celebratory, Beverly Beyette in the *Los Angeles Times* pointed out that Arnold ''does not take picture post-cards. She photographs laundry drying on the balconies of a modern apartment house, a dormitory for women oil-field workers, a demonstration by the unemployed in Shanghai.'' The pictures were undoubtedly beautiful however, which by the early eighties, was almost considered a crime by some critics. Luckily others had more sense and the exhibition based on the book became a major touring show throughout the United States.

In 1983 Arnold published *In America,* a collection of photographs which showed a composite portrait of the varied races and lifestyles which compose modern America. In 1987 *Marilyn Monroe: An Appreciation* received world-wide publication and reached the bestseller lists, becoming a Book of the Month Club Selection. This was based on several years of photographing Monroe on locations and in relaxed and personal situations. Early in her career Arnold had learned to treat the great and the famous as she treated her less well-known subjects, as people, with respect but not as if they were superhuman. They may be lonely or even suspicious at first, but it is clear that her tact, patience and obvious kindness have given Arnold many of the best pictures ever taken of the great, the good, and sometimes the evil, in the worlds of both politics and the arts. The pictures of Marilyn also brought about the first exhibitions of Arnold's work in commercial galleries in both London and New York and the first sales of her work to collectors. These still continue to grow through both auction houses and galleries.

Over the years between editorial assignments and the occasional commercial one, Eve Arnold has worked as special production photographer on 31 films. During one of these she met Mikail Baryshnikov and from this she went on to produce a book, *Private View: Inside Baryshnikov's American Ballet Theatre* (1988). This had a text by John Fraser and was also a Book of the Month Club Selection and presented as an exhibition at Castelli Graphics in New York.

In 1989 Arnold produced a further collection of photographs, *All in a Day's Work,* published by Bantam in the US and to appear in Britain through Hamish Hamilton. This contained photographs taken over 35 years around the world from Zululand to Afghanistan.

In 1991 a book and an exhibition at The National Portrait Gallery in London continued her series *In Britain,* and showed many of the early black-and-white pictures she had taken when she first arrived as well as many portraits of the famous done when she was working for *Harpers* and *Queen* and then *The Sunday Times.* Photographs of The Queen and Mrs Thatcher are included as well as a housewife, schoolgirls and politicians such as Reginald Maudling and Edward Heath.

Currently Eve Arnold is more in demand than ever, being asked to undertake a wide variety of assignments, and in organising her work for the publication of a major retrospective book which has been contracted to Knopf in New York, who have also asked her to continue her series with *In the USSR.* Plans are currently under discussion for a major retrospective to be shown at the time of the book's publication. It is a long way from the early years when she sometimes felt that no assignments would ever come her way again and was able to relax with the occasional personal projects. She has travelled all over the world and photographed thousands of people. As Mary Blume of the *International Herald Tribune* wrote in 1985: ''In a distinguished career Eve Arnold has photographed Everyone with a capital 'E' and also everyone.''

Throughout her life Eve Arnold has made an enormous number of friends. Most photographers make contacts but with Eve one feels that almost everyone she works with becomes a friend, who both admires her work and her person. This may be part of her secret because friends, like photography, need time and patience as well as natural talent and Eve Arnold has them all in abundance. Her real interest in people, how they think and what they heed, is surely the basis of her life, both in and out of photography. She has taken in her stride the changing markets for photography without ever compromising her style. Now, in the 1990s, when so many photographers seem more concerned with examining themselves than the wider world around them, Eve Arnold is a ''rare bird''—one that we should not only respect but really treasure.

—Sue Davies

ASCOLINI, Vasco.

Nationality: Italian. **Born:** Reggio Emilia, Italy, 10 May 1937. **Education:** Self-taught in photography. **Family:** Married Lidia Paoli in 1963; children: Barbara, Carlotta, Brigida and Claudio. **Career:** Official photographer, Teatro Municipale, Reggio Emilia, 1973-88; freelance architect working on historical monuments and the theatre, since 1988. **Address:** Viale 4 Novembre 2, 42100 Reggio Emilia, Italy.

Individual Exhibitions:

1978   *Cronofotografia di Teatro,* Teatro Muncipale, Reggio Emilia, Italy (travelled to the Oblastni Galerie, Olomouc, Czechoslovakia, 1982)
1980   *The M. Brooks Children's Dance Research Theater,* Corridor Cases and Cullen Library, New York
1981   *L'Imaginaire Collectif,* Université d'Architecture, Grenoble, France
1982   *Fantasmi Fotografici,* Libreria Agora, Turin, Italy (travelled to the Libreria Giocolibri, Pesaro, Italy)
        Pose Teatrali, Teatro Scentifico dei Bibiena, Mantova, Italy (travelled to the Galleria Deposito Figure, Pesaro, Italy, 1984)
1983   *Immagini del Kabuki,* Teatro Poliziano, Milan, Italy
        Le Geste, la Mimique, le Masque, Musée N. Niépce, Chalon-sur-Saône, France (travelled to the FNAC-Istituto Italiano Cultura, Strasburg, France, 1985)
1985   *The Body in its Field,* Lincoln Center Public Library, New York
        Festavanti Regionale, Modena-Reggio Emilia, Italy

***Versailles*, 1990.** Photograph by Vasco Ascolini.

1986   *Teatrarte,* Galleria PHY, Trieste, Italy (and tour)
1987   *Masque, le Visage, le Geste,* Laval, Canada
       Kasvo, Naamio ja Ele, Theatre Museum, Helsinki, Finland
1988   *Un Teatro della Memoria,* Centro Arte Cultura "Il Punto,"
       Bologna, Italy
1989   *Le Corps en Scène,* Bibliothèque Municipale, Laon, France
       Le Fotografie per il Teatro, Casa Cini, Palazzo dei Diamenti,
       Ferrara, Italy
       Aosta Metafisica e altri Luoghi, Torre dei Signori, Aosta, Italy
       Torino Fotografia Biennale Internazionale, Turin, Italy
1990   *Il Corpo in Scena,* Galleria Coppa d'Oro, Parma, Italy
       Danse et Architecture, Centre de la Photographie, Geneva,
       Switzerland (travelled to the Galerie Suzel Berna, Par-
       is, 1992)
1991   *Arles,* at *Rencontres de la Photographie Internationales,* Musée
       Réattu, Arles, France (travelled to the Galerie de la
       Photographie du Hall du Livre, Nancy, France, 1993)
1992   *Mon Italie,* at *1er Printemps des Photographes,* Bastia, France
       Presenze Metafisiche, Galleria "La compagnia dei Fotografi,"
       Milan, Italy
       L'Idea Metafisica, Sala Esposizioni Comunale, Fototeca e
       Biblioteca, Reggio Emilia, Italy
1993   *Villes d'Italie, Parcours de l'art italien à Nice,* Nice, France
       L'Idée Metaphisique, Musée Artur Batut, Labrughière, France
       Paris-Arle, Centro Civico Culturale, Sorbolo, Italy

Selected Group Exhibitions:

1974   *Umijetica Fotografica,* Zara, Yugoslavia
1981   *La Memoria della Città,* Reggio Emilia, Italy
1982   *Una Città, Quattro Fotografia,* Zara, Yugoslavia
1983   *Il Corpo Rappresentato,* Ancona, Italy
       L'Oreille Oubliée, Centre Georges Pompidou, Paris
1985   *La Danza,* Milan, Italy
1989   *Aria, Acqua, Terra, Fuoco,* Castelbolognese, Italy
       Tra le Quinte, Castello di S. Giusto, Trieste, Italy
       Obiettivo Italia, Puebla University, Mexico
1990   *Fixe sur l'Eternité,* Espace Van Gogh, Arles, France
1992   *La Dance Capturé,* Musée de la Photographie, Charleroi,
       Belgium
       Les Trésors du Musée Niépce, Chalon-sur-Saône, France
       La Raccolta Fotografica di Franco Fontana, Galleria Civica,
       Modena
       Mois de la Photographie, Musée Carnevalet, Paris
       Viaggio Fotografico All'Interno Della Vaille D'Aosta,
       Aosta, Italy
1993   *Il Bacio,* Casa di Giulietta, Verona, Italy
1994   *'84-'94, 10 ans au Centre de la Photographie de Genève,*
       Lugano, Switzerland

Collections:

Tokyo College of Photography, Japan; Lincoln Center Public Library, New
York; Metropolitan Museum, New York; Victoria and Albert Museum,
London; Texas University, Austin, U.S.A.; The Solomon R. Guggenheim
Museum, New York; Musée N. Niépce, Chalon-sur-Saône, France; The M.
Brooks Children's Dance Research of Harlem, New York; Museum of
Modern Art, New York; Centre G. Pompidou Musée d'Art Moderne, Paris;
Fototeca Biblioteca Civica, Reggio Emilia, Italy; Gernsheim Collection,
Lugano, Switzerland; Franklin Furnace, New York; Theatre Museum, Helsinki,
Finland; Italian-American Museum, San Francisco; Centre de la Photographie
de Genève, Switzerland; Maison Européenne de la Photographie, Paris;
Musée de la Photographie, Charleroi, Belgium; Musée Réattu, Arles, France;
Musée Carnevalet, Paris; Bibliothèque Nationale, Paris; Visual Studies Work-
shop, Rochester, New York; University of New Mexico Art Museum, Albu-
querque; Galleria Civica, Modena, Italy; Cabinet d'Art Graphique du Domaine
National de Versailles, Paris.

Publications:

By ASCOLINI: Books—Aosta Metafisica e altri luoghi/ Aosta metaphysical and other places, exhibition catalogue, with text by E.H. Gombrich, Aosta,
Italy 1989; *Fotografie per il Teatro/Theatre Photographs,* exhibition catalogue, with text by Aaron Scharf, Bologna, Italy 1989; *Occhi di vetro, Occhi di
legno,* Reggio Emilia 1990; *Arles,* exhibition catalogue, with text by Michèle
Moutashar, Arles, France 1991; *L'Idea Metafisica,* exhibition catalogue, with
text by Aaron Scharf and Laura Gasparini, Reggio Emilia 1992.

On ASCOLINI: Books—La Memoria della Città, exhibition catalogue,
Reggio Emilia 1981; *Il Tempo ritrovato,* A. Ruggero Giorgi, Reggio Emilia
1983; *Reggio Emilia, Una terra la sua storia,* Reggio Emilia 1983; *Il territorio
collinare e montano,* Reggio Emilia 1983; *Montefalcone, contributa alla
Storia di un monumento,* Reggio Emilia 1984; *Trent'anni di balletto a Reggio
Emilia,* Reggio Emilia 1986; *L'occhio si è fermato sui burattini,* Reggio
Emilia 1986; *Milan Sladek Pantominentheater,* Cologne, Germany 1986.
Articles—"Un Mondo Di Rugiada" by Michela Vanon in *Photo Italia*
(Milan), 1986; "Primo Piano" by Romildo Mazzi in *Progresso Fotografico*
(Milan), November 1986; "Defining Space" by Hilda Bijur in *The West Sider*
(New York), 4 July 1985; "Corps de Ballet" by J.M. Lucot in *L'Union* (Laon,
France), 9 February 1989; "Le Fotografie per il Teatro" by Diego Mormorio
in *Photo Italia,* April 1990; "L'Oeuvre au Noir de V. Ascolini" in *Le
Provençal* (Arles, France), 8 July 1991; "Vasco Ascolini" by Marco Bastianelli
and M. Jovine in *Reflex* (Giugno, Italy), 1992; "La foto c'è o non c'è" by
Andrea Ghermandi in *L'Unità* (Rome), 8 January 1992, "Il Segno Metafisico"
by Cristina Righi in *L'Indipendente* (Milan), 9 January 1992; "Plus Noir que
Blanc" by Michel Guerrin in *Le Monde* (Paris), 4 March 1992; "L'Orfèvre du
Vide" by Emmanuelle Bajac in *Le Quotidien de Paris* (Paris), 19 March 1992;
"Sotto l'occhio dell'obiettivo" by Giuliana Scimé in *Il Corriere della Sera*
(Milan), 14 May 1993; "L'Idea Metafisica" by Carlo Rovida in *Photographies
Magazin,* 10 March 1994.

* * *

What I find so immediately striking about many of Vasco Ascolini's
photographs, is the daring way he confronts his subjects head on and close up.
The buildings loom in their frames. All peripheral objects are rendered
extraneous. The concentration on the façade is supreme. Paradoxically, most
of the openings in these buildings, either from the outside looking in, or from
the inside looking out, are blind. Windows, doors and archways for the most
part lead nowhere and present black voids. From the inside looking out, a
white radiance dazzles while it obscures. These flat forms, dark and light,
appear teasingly in a compressed space. Depth, transparency, translucency,
are implied and denied at one and the same time.

Favouring stark contrasts of dark and light, coupled with scrupulously
chosen viewpoints and objects to portray, Ascoloni conveys, with a special
eloquence, an ineffable sense of mystery. He concentrates on the evocative
textures of eroded walls and pavements, on surviving sculpture and fragmented architectural ornaments. Yet he seems wholly unsentimental about the
wounds visited upon these objects: the patina that time endows.

I find little of nostalgia in Ascolini's 'metaphysical' photographs. They
are, to me, essentially austere in spirit; they are by no means bleak or
melancholy. Ascolini dares to enter a treacherous territory, where vestiges of
antiquity and the sculpture and architecture of more recent centuries show
signs of distress: the ravages of the elements, which so easily lure the romantic
into nostalgia and unfettered emotion.

Ascolini doesn't allow himself to succumb to this. His is nevertheless a
strange poetry, a poetry with a steely edge. In his photographs we find no love
of ruins, no Gothic emotionalism. We will not discover here the deadly
embrace of foliage-encrusted artifacts or reverence for the destructive might
of nature. Instead, in these images we are made aware of the photographer's
over-riding curiosity, even sympathy, for the corroded surfaces bestowed on
these objects. Ascolini seems to love these buildings and their decorative
attributes for their own sake.

Despite this absence of romanticism, these pathetic remnants of once
proud structures generate an aura of enigma, invested with quiet dignity by
Ascolini. And who among us has not found himself on a sunlit day, by chance,
alone in some corner or room of a deserted building, where the light
penetrating from outside creates momentarily a self-contained world, where

one experiences quite unexpectedly, new sensations of solids and shadows, of light and atmosphere—a transient but magical experience!

—Aaron Scharf

ASTMAN, Barbara.

Nationality: American. **Born:** Rochester, New York, 12 July 1950; moved to Canada in 1970. **Education:** Irondequoit High School, Rochester, 1964-68; studied design and silversmithing, under Albert Paley, Rochester Institute of Technology, 1968-70; sculpture, under John Chandler, Ontario College of Art, Toronto, 1970-73, Associate 1973; mainly self-taught in photography. **Family:** Married Noel Robert Harding in 1979 (divorced, 1983); Joseph Anthony Baker in 1984; daughter: Amy. **Career:** Independent photographer and mixed media artist, Toronto, since 1973. Photographic Technician, 1973-74, and since 1976 Instructor, Nontechnical Faculty, Ontario College of Art. Faculty, York University, Toronto, 1978-80. Coordinator and Consultant, Color Xerox Artists' Programme, Visual Arts Ontario, Toronto, since 1977. Board Member, Art Gallery at Harbourfront, Toronto, 1983-85. **Recipient:** Ontario Council for the Arts grant, 1974-84; Canada Council Arts Grant, 1976, 1977, 1980, 1981, 1983, 1984, 1986, 1990, 1993. **Address:** 23 Alcina Avenue, Toronto, Ontario M6G 2E7, Canada.

Individual Exhibitions:

1973	Baldwin Street Gallery of Photography, Toronto
1974	Ryerson Photo Gallery, Toronto
1975	National Film Board of Canada, Ottawa
1976	Saw Gallery, Ottawa
	3 Photographers, Deja Vu Gallery, Toronto (with Jerry Uelsmann and Michael Semak)
1977	Sable-Castelli Gallery, Toronto
1979	*Visual Narrative Series,* Sable-Castelli Gallery, Toronto (travelled to the Jean Marie Antone Gallery, Annapolis, Maryland)
	Talking Photos, Artspace, Peterborough, Ontario (with Suzy Lake; travelled to the Whitewater Gallery, North Bay, Ontario, and Brush Art Gallery, Canton, New York, 1980).
1980	*Untitled, I Was Thinking about You,* Sable-Castelli Gallery, Toronto (travelled to the Agnes Etherington Art Centre, Kingston, Ontario; McIntosh Gallery, University of Western Ontario, London; and Galerie Optica, Montreal, 1980; Laurentian University Museum and Art Centre, Sudbury, Ontario, and University of Delaware, Newark, 1981)
1981	*Red,* Sable-Castelli Gallery, Toronto (travelled to the Mendel Art Gallery, Saskatoon, Saskatchewan; University of Alberta, Edmonton; and Southern Alberta Art Gallery, Lethbridge, 1981; and the Centre Culturel Canadien, Paris, 1982)
1982	Art Gallery of Peterborough, Ontario
	Sable-Castelli Gallery, Toronto
1983	*places,* Nickle Arts Museum, Calgary, Alberta
1984	*Settings for Situations,* Sable-Castelli Gallery, Toronto
	Settings for Situations, Concordia University, Montreal
1986	Musée du Quebec, Quebec City
	Sable-Castelli Gallery, Toronto
1988	The Sable-Castelli Gallery, Toronto
1990	The Sable-Castelli Gallery, Toronto
1992	The Laurentian University Museum and Arts Centre, Sudbury, Ontario
	Thunder Bay Art Gallery, Ontario
	St Lawrence College, Saint Laurent Art Gallery, Kingston, Ontario
1993	The Robert McLaughlin gallery, Oshawa, Ontario
1994	McIntosh Gallery, The University of Western Ontario, London, Ontario

Selected Group Exhibitions:

1975	*Chairs,* Art Gallery of Ontario, Toronto
1976	*Woman Photographs Man,* Rockefeller Center, New York
	Xerography, Art Gallery of Ontario, Toronto
1978	*The Canadian Connection,* Neikrug Galleries, New York
1979	*Translations: Photographic Images with New Forms,* Cornell University, Ithaca, New York
	Electroworks, International Museum of Photography, George Eastman House, Rochester, New York
1980	*The Eye of the Beholder,* Harbourfront Art Gallery, Toronto
1983	*Photographic Sequences,* Art Gallery of Peterborough, Ontario
1984	*Responding to Photography,* Art Gallery of Ontario, Toronto
1985	*Generation Polaroid,* Forum des Halles, Paris
1986	*Canada Collects: Contemporary Sculpture from the Art Bank,* Washington, D.C.; Atlanta; San Diego Art Center (travelling)
	Domiciles, Hallwalls Gallery, Buffalo, New York
	The Christmas Stocking, Laurentian University Museum and Art Centre, Sudbury, Ontario
1987	*Olympic Arts Festival,* Billboard Project (travelling)
1988	*Scripta Manent,* La Galerie des Arts Lavalin, Montreal
1988	Persons Award Exhibition (Status of Women, Government of Canada)
	Salon of the National Arts Centre, Ottawa
	Canada-Mexico Photography Exhibition, Mexico City (travelling)
	Porkkana Collection, Pro Museum of Contemporary Art, Finland
1989	The Kamloops Art Gallery, Kamloops, British Columbia
	75 Works for 75 Years: Masterworks from the Permanent Collection of the Art Gallery of Hamilton, The Art Gallery of Hamilton, Ontario
1990	The Koffler Gallery, Toronto, Ontario
1992	*Astman/Dykhuis Exhibition,* Art Gallery of Peterborough, Ontario
1993	*Artists with Their Work,* Art Gallery of Ontario, Toronto, Ontario
	John B Aird Gallery, O.C.A. Faculty Exhibition, Toronto, Ontario
	Group of One, Art Gallery of Hamilton, Ontario
1994	Terminal Art Gallery, Faculty Exhibition, O.C.A., Toronto, Ontario
	Interconnexions Copigraphiques, Montage 93, Visual Studies Workshop, Rochester, New York (touring)
	New Works in the Permanent Collection, Laurentian University Museum and Art Centre, Sudbury, Ontario
	Looking Back II, Southern Alberta Art Gallery, Lethbridge, Alberta
	Hidden Values: Canadian Corporation Collect, The McMichael, Ontario

Collections:

Ontario Arts Council, Toronto; Art Gallery of Ontario, Toronto; Stratford Art Gallery, Ontario; Agnes Etherington Art Centre, Kingston, Ontario; Art Bank, Ottawa, Ontario; Department of External Affairs, Ottawa; National Film Board of Canada, Ottawa; Winnipeg Art Gallery, Manitoba; Victoria and Albert Museum, London; Bibliotheque Nationale, Paris.

Publications:

On ASTMAN: Books—*Exposure: Canadian Contemporary Photographers,* with an introduction by Glenda Milrod, Toronto 1975; *Women Photograph Men,* with an introduction by Molly Haskell, edited by Dannielle B. Hayes, New York 1977; *Alternative Photographic Processes* by Kent Wade, New York 1978; *Copy Art* by Patrick Firpo, Lester Alexander, Claudia Katayanagi and Steve Ditlea, New York 1978; *The Winnipeg Perspective 1979: Photo-Extended Dimensions,* with texts by Roger L. Selby and Karyn Allen, Winnipeg 1979; *Barbara Astman: I Was Thinking about You,* exhibition catalogue, with foreword by Joyan Sanders, London, Ontario, 1980;

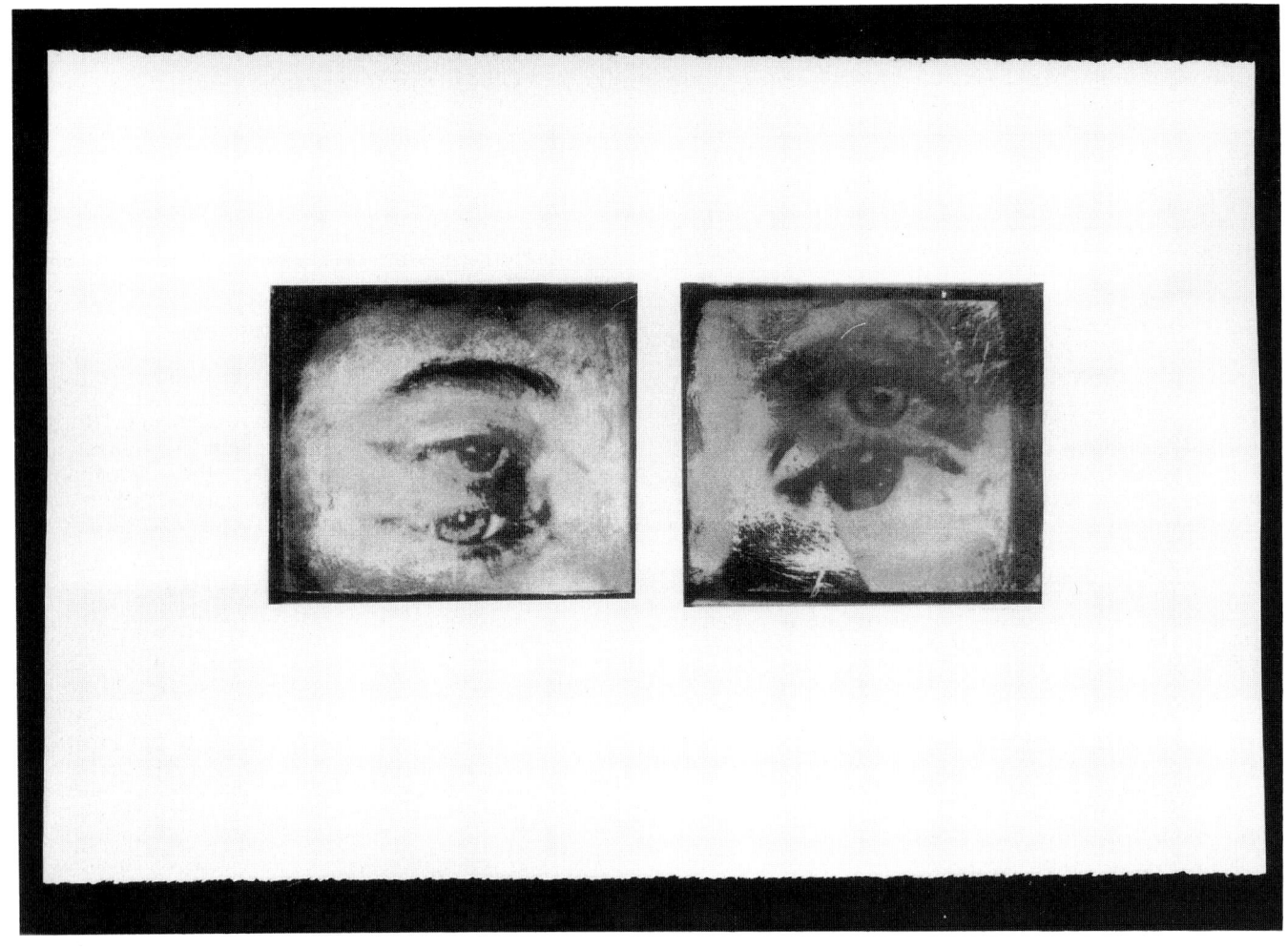

Seeing and Being Seen, **1994.** Photograph by Barbara Astman.

Barbara Astman: Red, exhibition catalogue, with text by Adele Freedman, Toronto 1981; *Contemporary Canadian Photography* by Martha Langford, Edmonton, Alberta 1984; *Visual Facts,* exhibition catalogue with essay by Michael Tooby, Glasgow 1985; *Seventy-Five Years (1914-1989),* exhibition catalogue, Hamilton 1989; *Selections from the John Labatt Limited Collection, 1989,* exhibition catalogue, London (Ontario), 1989; *Rock, is there something you're not telling me?,* exhibition catalogue with essay by Ihor Holubizky, Ontario 1990. **Articles**—"The Impure Narratives of Barbara Astman" by Gary Michael Dault in *Saturday Night Leisure* (Toronto), June 1978; "Gallery Reviews" by Adele Freedman in *Globe and Mail* (Toronto), January 1980; "Barbara's Blow-Up" by Gary Michael Dault in *Toronto Star* (Toronto), 12 January 1980; "Barbara Astman" by Lydia Pawlenko in *Artscanada* (Toronto), April/May 1980; "Art in a Snap" by John Reeves in *Toronto Life* (Toronto), June 1980; "Barbara Astman: I Was Thinking About You" in *Photo Communique* (Toronto), Fall 1980; "Barbara Astman" in *City Woman* (Toronto), Fall 1980; "Barbara Astman: Peut-Etre un 'Body Art' Photographique" in *Parachute* (Montreal), Spring 1981; "Art Is Red, Black and Fine: Photographer Mixed Self Portrait with Kitchen Tools" by Lisa Balfour Bowen in *Sunday Star* (Toronto), 5 April 1981; "Astman Gives Plastic New Meaning" by John Bentley Mays in the *Globe and Mail* (Toronto), 22 March 1984; "Astman's Stepping Out" by Joan Murray in *The Art Post* (Toronto), June/July 1984; "Astman's Travels" by Jane Perdue in *NOW Magazine* (Toronto), 13 March 1986; "Barbara Astman: An Olympian Artist" by Gary Weiner in *Irondequoit* (New York) 9 February 1988; "Astman's Slick Photos Unveil Myths of Romance" by Liz Wylie in *NOW Magazine* (Toronto), 14 April 1988; "Barbara Astman at the Sable Castelli Gallery" by John Bentley Mays in *Globe and Mail* (Toronto), 22 April 1988; "Astman's Fruitful Metaphor Probes the Beauty of Aging" by Dierdre Hanna in *NOW Magazine* (Toronto), 6 September 1990.

*

My work over the past ten years has dealt with the relationship between image and language. Language, through the use of words and symbols, reinforces my explorations of memory. In the *Untitled, I was thinking about you. . . .* series, the words act as a textured barrier or veiling between the viewer and the woman in the photograph. They have a physical presence beyond their narrative presence. In the *RED* series, common objects replace the words. The universality of the objects creates its own language and history unto itself.

In 1983 I began a sculptural exploration, based on memories of different places I had travelled to or lived in. In this *places* series, the patterned tile in conjunction with the printed words creates a narrative based on those memories. In this series I attempted to address the issue of memory based on desire for a location rather than a person. That the desire for either can be as strong. In the *Setting for Situations* series, I explored the psychology of stairs as a metaphor for entering and exiting in a variety of desired locations. In this series, the title of each piece was a crucial key in exploring the work. In the *Travelogue* series, I further explored desire and memory in a more straightforward way through words and images based on actual travel and the varying emotional states induced by observation and participation of "being there." These richly layered images depend on the relationship of the words and images and textures. The textures originated from the actual tiles used in the previous *places* series, which simulate a variety of different surfaces.

In the 1988 *red curtain* series, each piece is composed of three units which construct a vague narrative. The red curtain acts as a framing device evoking a mystery to the memory. It is that special moment we experience in theatre, opera and the movies, that fascination with the relationship between the curtain rising and the event (image) beginning. The series started out being directed by feelings of longing and grew into an exploration of romance, motherhood and power in relationship to longing.

The most recent work deals with the notion of desire. I began exploring ideas that centred on defining beauty, what is considered desirable, through fabricated images. We are all aware as consumers on one level or another of how beauty and desirability, in humans and objects, is portrayed in Western society. I became increasingly fascinated by the reverse of the portrayal, and I began searching out the defects. The resulting photographic images take on an abstraction far more so than any of my previous works and become a metaphor for the beauty of decay.

Although the work has visibly changed over the decade, my concerns build upon one another and create a continuity to the differing bodies of work.

—Barbara Astman

*   *   *

In her art, Barbara Astman strips away and discards elements in pursuit of the most essential aesthetic and psychological statement. It is this de-layering which gives Astman's work its unique power. The artist has referred to the process as "private performance art." Her camera works are an intriguing mixture of various traditional art forms—drawing, painting, photography, sculpture—elements which are redefined by a contemporary sensibility, the impact of which is heightened by the use of experimental technology. This fascination with current technological developments has enabled Astman to realize images of remarkable colour, texture and scale.

Her experimentation with colour xerography led to a series of large-scale murals (1976) organized in the format of a storyboard, composed of 30, 8½ by 11 colour xerox images. The narrative aspect of this series was purely visual; the thematic structure was based on travelogue exotica—postcards and other found images from countries such as Italy, Russia and China—the transformation of photographic images created by new contexts which emerge from the images. Often the images were complemented by a hint of specific time and place, through the use of expanded, handwritten, journalistic notes. The resulting images presented a fictional truth, which becomes even more critical in the later work.

"The Visual Narrative Series" of 1978 represented a honing down of both format and image. This series of photographic, hand-tinted ektacolour murals consisted of 6 SX-70 images in 2 horizontal rows, accompanied by a typewritten narrative. The images are hand-coloured, stark in format and intensely personal. Despite the private/specific connotations of the text, the frontal format and its associations with traditional portraiture, there is a kind of timeless universality, not endemic to a specific point in time or in history.

Astman's work is linked to a classical, painterly tradition. The "I Was Thinking About You" series of 1979 is self-portraiture—the artist, perceived frontally, is posed against a fabric backdrop. These images are a kind of confessional in the format of letter writing. The words and images have become fused, the type literally blending *into* the visual field. This layering results in a consciously ambiguous dissolution of boundaries. Astman has cut the image off beneath the eyes, resulting in a kind of depersonalization. The colour of the backdrop is consistently rich, alluding to sensuous velvet typical of classical portraiture. The mouth is open, the hands poised, at a moment of revelation. It is a rich reduction of elements; the effect of the cut off eyes is to force the issue of abstraction—the result of this compositional strategy is depersonalizing. The blending of the type into the image suggests a kind of marking in time, emotional scarring. The resulting images are poignant yet severe.

The "Red" series of 1980 represents a break-through on several levels—symbology, content, and format. The use of words/text has been eliminated completely from these 4' x 4' ektacolour murals. The artist is posed in a frontal position amidst a carefully balanced composition of objects, which have been spray-painted red. The artist is dressed in black, her face cropped beneath the eyes; there is a tenuous balance in these works. The background objects seem to float in space, assuming something "other" than their typical function. Astman appears as a kind of prophet in this context. She is also something of a magician, using a kind of sensual constructivism, suggestive of El Lissitzky. The words have been replaced as signposts by objects which encourage a conceptual leap on the viewer's part. Recognizable objects assume new connotations related to the various implications of "red," implications that are at once playful and vaguely threatening. Astman has composed a poem-cum-new-wave-lyric to carry these radical (associative) powers of the colour:

> Red feels like a crime
> it relates to that lady
> refers to a diversion
> gets me excited
> tells me I'm new
> red causes me anger
> and can make me a communist.

The hand and the mouth become the agents of prophecy and celebration. These works are indeed a kind of discreet celebration.

It is the immediacy inherent in the implicit properties of the camera which gives the work a power that is almost gothic. There is also an implied relationship with science—objects as tools for discovery and as barometers of change and precision.

Astman is currently exploring the intimacy of private rooms and spaces. This series eliminates altogether the human figure with the result that the objects take on an added symbolic power. It is yet another step in the stripping away of layers, of taking risks, and of exploring the complex realm of memory and dream.

Barbara Astman's work is not only technically and aesthetically exquisite, but it also probes the deepest myteries of the self. The symbolic language is a constant and subtle element in this process of exploration—it offers discreet intimations that hint at voluptuous revelations. It is Astman's own mythological order.

—Karyn Allen Keenan

AUERBACH, Ellen (PIT).

Nationality: American. **Born:** Ellen Rosenberg in Karlsruhe, Germany, 20 May 1906; immigrated to Palestine, 1933, and to the United States, 1937: naturalized, 1942. **Education:** Attended schools in Karlsruhe, 1912-23; studied sculpture at the Karlsruher Kunstakademie under Prof. Speck and Prof. Karl Hubbuch, 1924-27, and at the Kunstschule Stuttgart, 1928; studied photography in Berlin under Prof. Walter Peterhans, 1929; continued studies with Peterhans student Grete Stern; experimented with 16 mm films, 1930-32. **Family:** Married Walter Auerbach in 1937. **Career:** Founded "foto ringl + pit": ringl = Grete Stern; pit = Ellen Rosenberg; specialized in avant-garde advertising, 1932. Official photographer for Women's International Zionist Organization; had "Ishon" studio of photography in Tel Aviv, 1933-35. Began working professionally with Grete Stern in London, 1936. Worked at Lessing Rosenwald Print Collection, Jenkintown, with Walter Auerbach; experimented with infrared, ultraviolet, and Grenz rays; contributor to *Photo Technique, Parents Magazine,* and *Life,* specializing in modern child photography; studied Carbro-colour process, 1937-44. Moved to New York City; freelance projects included portraits in *Time* and record covers for Columbia Masterworks, 1945. Travelled to Argentina, Greece, Mallorca, Germany and Austria, 1946. Photographed children and infants for research conducted by Prof. Sibylle Escalona, Menninger Foundation, Topeka, Kansas, 1946-49. Photographer in San Francisco, Big Sur, Monterey and Los Angeles, 1950-51. Photography teacher, Junior College for Arts and Crafts, Trenton, New Jersey, 1953. Travelled extensively in Mexico with the photographer Eliot Porter to document church interiors, 1955-56. Travelled to New Mexico, Maine, Arizona, Norway and Argentina; increased interests in esoteric, psychological and educational concerns, 1958-65. Educational therapist at the Educational Institute for Learning and Research, New York, under director Dr Edith Schmidt; attended annual Krishnamurti seminars at Saanen, Switzerland,

Lily Woman, Oaxaca, **1956.** Photograph ©Ellen Auerbach.

1965-93. **Agent:** Robert Mann Gallery, 42 East 76th Street, New York 10021, U.S.A. **Address:** 321 East 85th Street, New York 10028-4525, U.S.A.

Individual Exhibitions:

1957   Cosmopolitan Club, Philadelphia, Pennsylvania
           Madonnas and Market Places, Lime Light Gallery, New York
1978   *Mexican Church Interiors,* Sander Gallery, Washington, D.C.
1980   *Images from Mexican Churches,* Cathedral of St John the Divine, New York
1981   *Fotografien ringl + pit, 1930-1933,* Bauhaus Archive, Berlin
1982   *Pictures after 1934, Ellen Auerbach,* The Photographers' Gallery, London
1984   *ringl + pit,* Buenos Aires, Argentina (travelled to the Goethe House, New York, 1985)
1986   *Photography: a Facet of Modernism,* Museum of Modern Art, San Francisco, California
           Photographie & Bauhaus, Kestner Gesellschaft, Hannover, Germany
1988   *Photography Between the Wars,* Metropolitan Museum of Art, New York

           Emigrated, Retrospective 1928-1965, Zentralbibliothek, Wuppertal, Germany
1989   *ringl + pit, Fotografie Werbung,* Museum Folkwang, Essen, Germany
1991   *ringl + pit, Berlin 1928-1933,* Goethe Institute, Vancouver, Canada (travelled to the United States and Germany, 1992-93)
1992   *Ellen Auerbach,* Kunsthaus Fischinger, Stuttgart, Germany
1993-94 *ringl & pit and Walter Peterhans,* Museum Folkwang, Essen; Bauhaus Archive, Berlin; Ulmer Museum, Ulm; Badischer Kunstverein, Karlsruhe; Bauhaus, Dessau
1994   *Ellen Auerbach: From Bauhaus to God's House,* Robert Mann Gallery, New York

Selected Group Exhibitions:

1980   *Avant-garde Photography in Germany, 1919-1939,* travelling exhibition (travelled to San Francisco, Akron, Minneapolis, Baltimore and New York, 1980-82)

1983 *22 Fotografinnen,* Gedok, Hahnentorburg, Cologne (travelled
to the Kunsthaus, Hamburg, and the Schloss Galerie, Bruehl,
Germany, 1983-84)
1984 *Photography of the 1930s,* Sander Gallery, New York
1992 *Mexico Through Foreign Eyes,* Mexico City (and tour,
1992-95)
1993 *Women on the Edge: Twenty Photographers, 1919-1939,* Paul
Getty Museum, California (travelled to the Guggenheim
Museum, New York, 1994)
1994 *Fotografinnen der Weimarer Republik,* Museum Folkwang,
Essen (travelled to the Fundacio "la Caixa," Barcelona and
to the Jewish Museum, New York, 1995)

Collections:

Museum Folkwang, Essen, Germany; John Paul Getty Museum, California;
Cleveland Museum of Art; Bauhaus Archive, Berlin; The Metropolitan
Museum of Art, New York; San Francisco Museum of Art; The St. Louis
Museum of Art

Publications:

By AUERBACH: Books—*Portfolio,* Washington D.C. 1986; *Mexican
Churches,* with Eliot Porter, Albuquerque 1987; *Mexican Celebrations,* with
Eliot Porter, Albuquerque 1989; *ringl + pit,* with Grete Stern, Berlin 1993.
Articles—"Walter Peterhans: Fotografie 1922-82" in *Fotokina,* 1982.

On AUERBACH: Books—*Fotografie 1922-1932,* Cologne 1982; *Geschichte
der Deutschen Film Emigration nach 1933,* Marburg 1989; *Women Photographers,* by Constanze Sullivan, New York 1990; *Fotografie am Bauhaus,*
edited by Jeannine Fiedler, Berlin 1990, and (as *Photography at the Bauhaus*)
Cambridge MA, 1990; *Grete Stern—Ellen Auerback—ringl + pit* by Ute
Eskildsen, Essen 1993; *ringl & pit and Walter Peterhaus* (exhibition catalogue), text by Ute Eskildsen, Essen 1993. **Article**—"ringl + pit: The
representation of women in German advertising, 1929-33" by Maud Lavin in
Print Collector's Newsletter (New York), July 1985, and translated into
German in *Fotogeschichte* (Marburg), No. 29, 1988.

* * *

"One of the most unusual photographers to have had several artistic lives
is Ellen Auerbach." With this sentence Margarett Loke opens her review of
Auerbach's exhibition at the Robert Mann Gallery in New York in the October
1994 issue of *Art News.*

Ellen Auerbach has been a photographer, an educational therapist, and she
has made ends meet by taking jobs as a gardener and a cook. Yet photography
was her destiny, and so was the fact that Walter Peterhans accepted her despite
his reluctance to take on new students because he was about to move from
Berlin to Dessau to become the head of the photographic department at the
Bauhaus. Peterhans introduced his new disciple to modern photography on the
highest level. A good photograph, Auerbach tells her audiences at lectures and
press conferences, requires good taste and good technical skills. A masterpiece, however, has a quality that defies definition; it communicates a meaning
far beyond the subject matter. To illustrate what she means she uses a
metaphor from *Zen and the Art of Archery,* that the archer, his arrow and the
target have to become one, and that the Zen master's arrow would find its
target every time, even in darkness.

Grete Stern, a fellow student, took over the Peterhans studio and asked
Ellen to be her partner. Together they embarked on a new venture, *foto ringl +
pit.* Their original approach to advertising photography was awarded the first
prize at the Deuxième Exposition Internationale de la Photographie et du
Cinéma, 1933 in Brussels.

In 1933, the year Hitler came to power, Pit emigrated to Palestine, then to
London where she married Walter Auerbach. Their odyssey ended in 1937, in
the United States.

An insatiable, inquisitive mind had prompted the child Ellen to ask her
nonplussed mother: "Why is there something and not nothing?" That
curiosity persists to this day. Throughout her professional life, she explored
many aspects of photography, even to conducting experiments with infrared
and ultraviolet rays to detect forgeries in paintings or prints.

Photographs by Ellen Auerbach have appeared in many magazines. In
competition with the photographic élite, her picture of a beaming toddler,
jubilant at a birthday cake with two candles, graced the cover of the second
anniversary issue of *Life,* 28 November 1938.

She rarely used a camera for professional work after her travels through
Mexico with Eliot Porter, to photograph the interiors of churches, mostly in
color and only with available light. This expedition during the winter of 1955/
56 resulted in some 3,000 photographs, 88 of which are reproduced in their
book *Mexican Churches,* published in 1987. Octavio Paz reviewed it in the
New York Times Book Review, "Almost all are excellent, some are magnificent and a few are masterpieces." And the Nobel laureate ended his review as
follows: "There are two families of artists—those like Picasso, who use their
models to serve them, and those who, like Velázquez, serve their models. Mr
Porter and Ms Auerbach belong to this second category."

Success came in the wake of a hiatus from 1965 to 1984, a period
Auerbach, as educational therapist, helped children overcome learning disa-
bilities caused by emotional problems. She brought to this work a rare asset: a
perceptive antenna that reaches into the other person's soul. This asset is
spiced with a magnificent sense of humor. "It is my wish to make one person
laugh every day. Should I make two people laugh on any given day, I get a day
off."

She is very much in demand as a lecturer, and her appointment calendar
has a notation for 1997, the year the Akron Art Institute plans to celebrate the
publication of a new edition of Naomi Rosenblum's reference book *A History
of Women Photographers* and the year Ellen Auerbach expects to celebrate her
91st birthday.

—Ingeborg von Zitzewitz

AUSLOOS, Paul.

Nationality: Belgian. **Born:** Antwerp, 6 January 1927. **Education:** Studied
painting at the Academie voor Schone Kunsten, Antwerp, 1945-50, and
monumental art at the Nationaal Hoger Instituut, Antwerp, 1950-55, Dip.
1955. **Military Service:** Served in the Belgian Army, 1950. **Family:** Married
the ceramic potter Lutgart de Meyer in 1951; sons: Johan and Marc; married
Mia Wuyts in 1973; son: David. **Career:** Painter since 1945; Founder, G58
group, 1958. Photographer, in Antwerp, since 1968. Professor of Publicity
Studies, Academie Sint-Niklaas, Belgium, since 1950; Professor of Photography, Academie of Antwerp, since 1970. **Recipient:** Rome Prize, for painting,
1950. **Agent:** Galerij Paule Pia, Kammenstraat 57, 2000 Antwerp, Belgium.
Address: Kasteelstraat 33, 2000 Antwerp, Belgium.

Individual Exhibitions:

1969 Galerie Venetia, St. Niklaas, Belgium
Foto-Film Academie, Breda, Netherlands
1970 Foto-Kamer Celis, Merksen, Belgium
1971 Academie of Antwerp
Galerie de Zwarte Panter, Antwerp
1976 Bank Brussel-Lambert, St. Niklaas, Belgium
Galerij Paule Pia, Antwerp
1977 Galerie Vecu, Antwerp
1978 Cultureel Centrum, Heusden, Belgium
1983 Galerie Sint-Lucas, Ghent, Belgium
Andre Demedshuis, St. Baafs-Vijve, Belgium
Stadsbibliotheek, St. Niklaas, Belgium

Selected Group Exhibitions:

1975 *G58 Hessenhuis,* Museum voor Schone Kunsten, Antwerp
1976 *15 Photographen aus Flandern,* Kunstlerhaus, Vienna (travelled to the Musée Nicéphore Niepce, Chalon-sur-Saône,
France, 1976, and the Het Sterckshof Museum, Deurne,
Belgium, and the Palais des Beaux-Arts, Brussels, 1977)

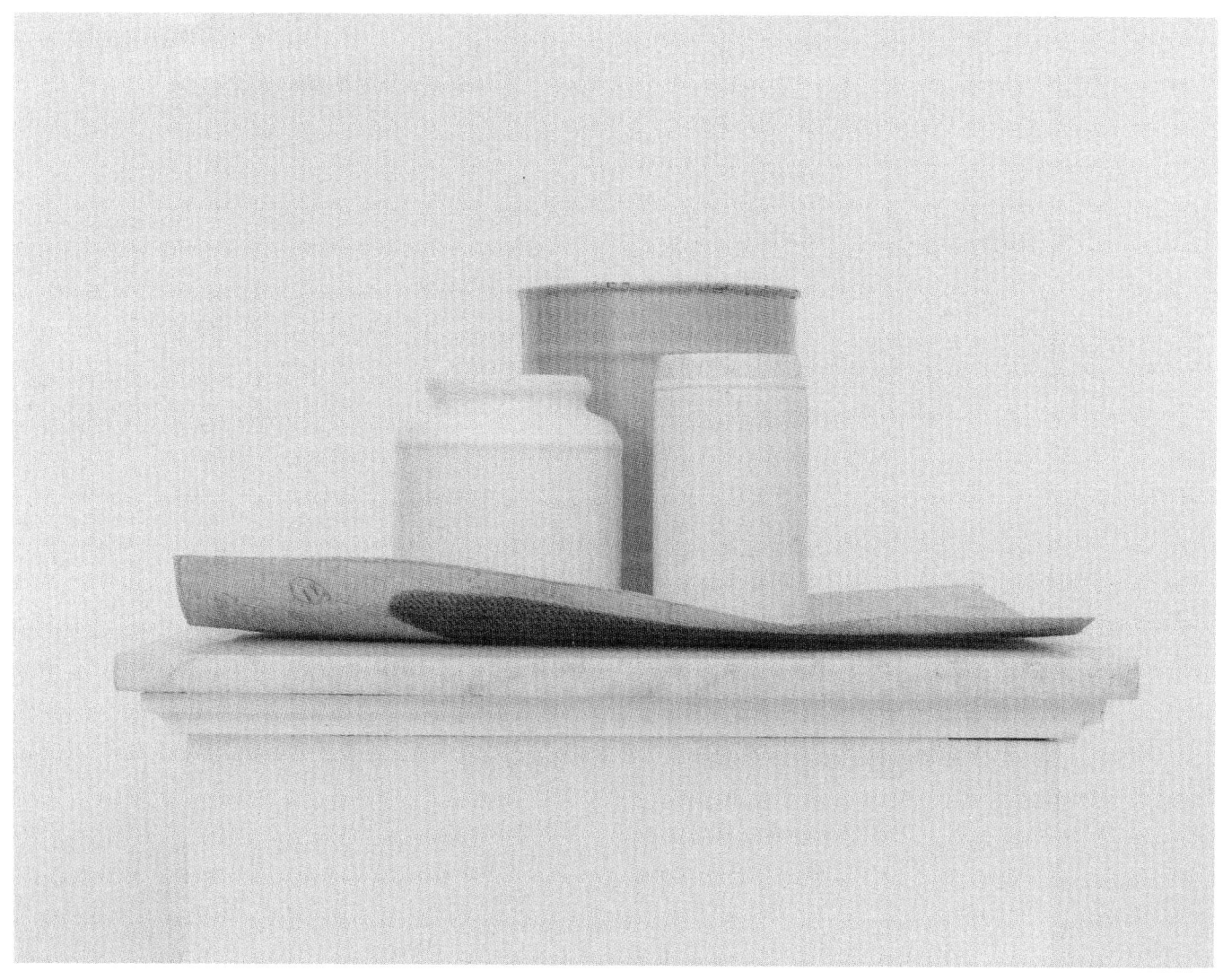

Still Life, **1979 (original in colour). Photograph by Paul Ausloos.**

Fotografen uit Vlaanderen, Galerie de Beierd, Breda, Netherlands (travelled to the Cultureel Centrum, Ghent, 1977)
1978   *Europhot Congress,* Belgrade
        Seconda Triennale della Fotografia, Musée d'Art d'Histoire,
        Fribourg, Switzerland
1980   *Camera Belgica,* Galerie Aslk, Brussels
1985   Galerij Paule Pia, Antwerp
        Het Sterckshof Museum, Deurne, Belgium
        Brakke Grond, Amsterdam
        International Foto-Salon, Tokyo (travelled to Nagoya, Kyoto
        and Sapporo, Japan)
1988   Galerie Bozar, Antwerp

Collections:

Het Sterckshof Museum, Deurne, Belgium; Musée d'Art d'Histoire, Fribourg,
Switzerland; Ministry of Culture, Brussels; Bibliothèque Nationale, Paris.

Publications:

On AUSLOOS: Books—*De Fotografie in Belgie 1940-1980,* exhibition
catalogue, by Roger Coenen and Karel van Deuren, Antwerp 1980; *Foto en*
Film Encyclopedie, (Focus/Elsevier) 1983; *Tekenen des Tijds,* by Jan Smet,
1988; *De Paradox van de Fotografie,* by Joh. M. Swinnen, 1993. **Article—**
''Paul Ausloos'' by Karel van Deuren in *Foto* (Amersfoort), July 1977.
Film—*Puur Cultuur: Fotografen Paul Ausloos,* Belgian television film, 1985.

*

It is rather refreshing for me to come to a certain poetical expression
without any personal handiwork, drawing, painting or photographic manipulation.
Everything has been done *before* I press the button.
There is simply nothing left for handwork.
I work in a room 5 by 5 metres, with a few lamps, a camera and a case full
of objects.

—Paul Ausloos

*   *   *

Paul Ausloos is an artist in photography. Although he has been a
successful painter, his photographs do not have a pictorial character, as was the
case with the pictorialists of the last century or the abstract photographers of
the Bauhaus. His work is purely photographic; it is composed of nothing other
than simple photographic shots.

Except for a limited series of mannered portraits of artists, Ausloos photographs still-lifes of humble objects such as a box with spots of rust, mould at the edges, a loose label—*objets trouvés*. He also uses old photos from his family album and picture postcards. These humble articles, through his strange virtuosity, become redolent of nostalgia and poetry and can be read as the reconstruction of a personal history. Souvenirs of souvenirs.

Then, suddenly, in this series, there is a new subject: fascism. Still-lifes (*nature mortes*) of badges of honour; a portrait of a tomb; postcards of the "Mighty of the Earth" and of "The Beloved" and of "The War Hero." War and patriotism.

This kind of photography continually makes an inventory of what life has to offer through the comforting means of art. *L'Art consolateur.*

After the theme of nostalgia, Paul Ausloos's recent color work is a happy glimpse at newly arranged still-lifes. They are attractive in a strictly intimate and incomparable way.

—Karel van Deuren

AVEDON, Richard.

Nationality: American. **Born:** New York City, 15 May 1923. **Education:** Public School No. 6, New York, 1929-37; DeWitt Clinton High School, New York, 1937-41; studied philosophy at Columbia University, New York, 1941-42; photography, with Alexey Brodovitch, at the New School for Social Research, New York, 1944-50. **Wartime Service:** Served in the photo section of the United States Merchant Marine, 1942-44. **Family:** Married Dorcas Norwell in 1944 (divorced, 1950); married Evelyn Franklin in 1951; son: John. **Career:** Established Richard Avedon Studio, New York, 1946; freelance contributing photographer, *Life, Look, Graphis*, etc., since 1950. Staff Photographer, *Junior Bazaar*, New York, 1945-47, and *Harper's Bazaar*, under Carmel Snow and Alexey Brodovitch, 1945-65; Staff Editor and Photographer, *Theatre Arts*, New York, 1952. Staff Photographer, under Diana Vreeland and Alexander Liberman, *Vogue*, New York, 1966. Visual Consultant on the Stanley Donen film *Funny Face*, 1957; Staff photographer, *New Yorker*, 1994. **Recipient:** Highest Achievement Medal, *Arts Directors' Show*, New York, 1950; World's 10 Greatest Photographers Award, *Popular Photography*, New York, 1958; National Magazine Visual Excellence Award, 1976; Dedication to Fashion Photography Citation, Pratt Institute, New York, 1976; Chancellor's Citation, University of California, Berkeley, 1980; Certificate of Excellence, American Institute for Graphic Arts, 1980; Hall of Fame Award, Art Directors' Club of New York, 1982; Photographer of the Year Award, American Society of Magazine Photographers, 1985. President's Fellow, Rhode Island School of Design, Providence, 1978. **Agent:** Norma Stevens, 1075 Park Avenue, New York, New York 10028. **Address:** 407 East 75th Street, New York, New York 10021, U.S.A.

Individual Exhibitions:

1962	Smithsonian Institution, Washington, D.C.
1970	Minneapolis Institute of Arts (retrospective)
1974	*Jacob Israel Avedon*, Museum of Modern Art, New York
1975	Marlborough Gallery, New York (travelled to the Seibu Museum of Art, Tokyo)
1978	*Photographs 1947-1977*, Metropolitan Museum of Art, New York (travelled to the Dallas Museum of Fine Arts; High Museum of Art, Atlanta; and Isetan, Tokyo)
	Portraits Geants, PPS Galerie, Hamburg
1980	*Retrospective 1946-1980*, University of California, Berkeley
1981	Neikrug Photographica, New York
1985	Light Factory, Charlotte, North Carolina (with Diane Arbus and August Sander)
	Pace Gallery, New York
	In the American West, Amon Carter Museum, Fort Worth, Texas (travelled to the Corcoran Gallery, Washington, D.C.; San Francisco Museum of Modern Art; Art Institute of Chicago; Phoenix Art Museum, Arizona; Institute of

	Contemporary Art, Boston; Pace/MacGill Gallery, New York; and High Museum of Art, Atlanta, Georgia, 1985-87)
1994	Whitney Museum, New York
1995	*Evidence 1944-94*, National Portrait Gallery, London

Selected Group Exhibitions:

1955	*The Family of Man*, Museum of Modern Art, New York (and world tour)
1959	*Photography in the Fine Arts*, Metropolitan Museum of Art, New York (and 1960, 1961, 1963, and 1967)
1964	*The Photographer's Eye*, Museum of Modern Art, New York
1969	*Portrait Photography*, Museum of Modern Art, New York
1974	*The History of Photography in America*, Whitney Museum, New York
1977	*Fashion Photography*, International Museum of Photography, George Eastman House, Rochester, New York (travelled to the Brooklyn Museum, New York; San Francisco Museum of Modern Art; Cincinnati Art Institute, Ohio; and Museum of Fine Arts, St. Petersburg, Florida)
1979	*Photographie als Kunst 1879-1979*, Tiroler Landesmuseum Ferdinandeum, Innsbruck, Austria (travelled to the Neue Galerie am Wolfgang Gurlitt Museum, Linz, Austria; Neue Galerie am Landesmuseum Joanneum, Graz, Austria; and Museum des 20. Jahrhunderts, Vienna)
1980	*The Portrait Extended*, Museum of Contemporary Art, Chicago
1982	*Target III: In Sequence*, Houston Museum of Fine Arts, Texas
1985	*Shots of Style*, Victoria and Albert Museum, London (toured Britain)

Collections:

Museum of Modern Art, New York; Metropolitan Museum of Art, New York; International Museum of Photography, George Eastman House, Rochester, New York; Philadelphia Museum of Art; Museum of Fine Arts, Houston; San Francisco Museum of Modern Art; Haags Gemeentemuseum, The Hague; Amon Carter Museum, Fort Worth, Texas; Victoria and Albert Museum, London.

Publications:

By AVEDON: Books—*Observations*, with text by Truman Capote, New York and London 1959; *Nothing Personal*, with text by James Baldwin, New York 1964; *Diary of a Century: Photographs by Jacques-Henri Lartigue*, editor, New York 1970; *Alice in Wonderland: The Forming of a Company, The Making of a Play*, with text by Doon Arbus, New York 1973; *Richard Avedon: Portraits*, with an introduction by Harold Rosenberg, New York and London 1976; *Avedon: Photographs 1947-1977*, with an essay by Harold Brodkey, New York 1978; *In the American West*, with texts by Laura Wilson, New York and London 1985. **Articles**—"Martin Munkacsi" in *Harper's Bazaar* (New York), June 1964; "Richard Avedon" in *Camera* (Lucerne), November 1974; "The Family" in *Rolling Stone* (San Francisco), 21 October 1976.

On AVEDON: Books—*The Photographer's Eye* by John Szarkowski, New York 1965; *Avedon*, exhibition catalogue, with an introduction by Anthony M. Clark and Carroll T. Hartwell, Minneapolis 1970; *Looking at Photographs: 100 Pictures from the Collection of the Museum of Modern Art* by John Szarkowski, New York 1973; *Avedon*, exhibition catalogue, New York 1975; *The Magic Image* by Cecil Beaton and Gail Buckland, London and Boston 1975; *On Photography* by Susan Sontag, New York 1977; *Geschichte der Photographie im 20. Jahrhundert/Photography in the 20th Century* by Petr Tausk, Cologne 1977, London 1980; *Avedon: Photographs 1947-1977*, exhibition catalogue, with text by Rosamond Bernier, New York 1978; *The History of Fashion Photography* by Nancy Hall-Duncan, New York 1979; *Photographie als Kunst 1879-1979/Kunst als Photographie 1949-1979*, exhibition catalogue, 2 volumes, by Peter Weiermair, Innsbruck, Austria 1979; *Avedon: Retrospective 1946-1980*, exhibition catalogue, with text by David Ross, Berkeley, California 1980; *Camera Lucida: Reflections on*

Red Owens, Oil Field Worker, Velman, Oklahoma, **1980.** Photograph ©Richard Avedon Inc., 1985.

Photography by Roland Barthes, New York 1981; *The Imaginary Photo Museum* by Helmut Gernsheim, Renate and L. Fritz Gruber, Cologne 1981, London 1982; *Shots of Style,* edited by Martin Harrison, London 1985.
Articles—"Richard Avedon, Minneapolis Institute of Arts" in *Arts Magazine* (New York), Summer 1970; "The Mature Portraitist: Richard Avedon" by Dore Ashton in *Studio International* (London), October 1974; "Richard Avedon's Hidden Photographs" by Thomas Hess in *Vogue* (New York), September 1975; "Richard Avedon Will Sell You This Picture" by Owen Edwards in the *Village Voice* (New York), 15 September 1975; "Avedon Rising" by Douglas Davis in *Newsweek* (New York), 22 September 1975; "Avedon's Faces of Power" by Susan Cheever Cowley in *Newsweek* (New York), 11 October 1976; "Avedon" by Roland Barthes in *Photo* (Paris), January 1977; "Looking with Avedon" by Susan Sontag in *Vogue* (New York), September 1978; "The Avedon Look" by Charles Michener in *Newsweek* (New York), 16 October 1978; "Triumph der Modephotographie" by Fritz Neugass in *Du* (Zurich), December 1978; "Photographs by Avedon: A Retrospective, 1947-1980" by Aaron Walden in the *Sentinel* (San Francisco), 21 March 1980; "This Silent Theatre" by Dore Ashton in *Arts Magazine* (New York), September 1985; "Under Western Eyes" by Kay Larson in *Vogue* (New York), September 1985; "In the American West" by Thomas McGuane in *Rolling Stone* (New York), 26 September 1985; "Into the Land of our Dreams" by Richard Lacayo in *Time* (New York), 16 December 1985; "Avedon Goes West" by John Hubner in *West Magazine* (San Jose, California), 23 March 1986.

*

A photographic portrait is a picture of someone who knows he's being photographed, and what he does with this knowledge is as much a part of the photograph as what he's wearing or how he looks. He's implicated in what's happened, and he has a certain real power over the result. We all perform. It's what we do for each other all the time, deliberately or unintentionally. It's a way of telling about ourselves in the hope of being recognized as what we'd like to be. I trust performances. Stripping them away doesn't necessarily get you closer to anything. The way someone who's being photographed presents himself to the camera, and the effect of the photographer's response on that presence, is what the making of a portrait is about.

—Richard Avedon

* * *

Richard Avedon's photography touches the nerve of our identity: who we are, what we are and what we long to be. Through his two types of photography, fashion and portraiture, he has investigated the faces and fashions of our society, its dreams and desires, and told us something of ourselves.

Avedon, only 21 when he did his first work for *Harper's Bazaar* and became a protégé of the legendary art director Alexey Brodovitch, became the boy wonder of fashion photography with an appealing style born of the exuberance and versatility of youth. His stylistic innovation, an improvised and almost accidental quality achieved through blurred motion, was equalled by the fresh new look of his models, who were filled with a carefree joy and love of life. "She laughed, danced . . . ran breathlessly down the Champs-Elysées, smiled and sipped cognac at café tables, and otherwise gave evidence of being human" (Winthrop Sargeant, "Profiles: Richard Avedon," *The New Yorker,* 8 November 1958).

Yet despite their charm, these pictures had a fascinating emotional complexity. Avedon has throughout his career been an unparalled dramatist, able to transform occasions for wearing clothes into moments of high dramatic action. Sargeant again: "It is this power to induce the conviction that one is

witnessing a crucial instant in the emotional life of the subject and to stimulate curiosity as to what brought it about and what will ensue, that give the Avedon photograph its peculiar distinction."

Throughout the 50s Avedon's work changed, maturing, gaining in sophistication and skill and moving progressively away from the straight-forward simplicity he so admired in the work of the Hungarian fashion photographer of the 1930s, Martin Munkacsi. Gradually Avedon gave up not only the outdoor locations in which he had produced his wonderful images of Parisian gambols but also the softly beautiful natural light which had illuminated his early work. He now regarded daylight, which he had loved to use, as a very romantic light. "It's like loving something from long ago that I can't really believe in anymore," he said. "It would be a lie for me to photograph the daylight in a world of Hilton's, airports, supermarkets and television. Daylight is something I rarely see—something I must give up—like childhood" (Cecil Beaton and Gail Buckland, *The Magic Image*).

Avedon moved his fashion into the studio, which he preferred because "it isolates people from their environment . . . they become in a sense symbolic of themselves" (Janet Malcom, "Photography: Men Without Props," *The New Yorker,* 22 September 1975). Though he retained the vitality and movement of the earlier work, he replaced romantic illumination with the harsh, raking light of the strobe. He developed the studio format which became his "signature": the model was seen running, jumping, airborne and giggling across a plain white background. Avedon became the first to combine the static studio tradition of the 20s with the exuberance of Munkacsi's outdoor realism. The Paris jaunt of the early 50s was transformed into a "locationless" shot, a change that reflected Avedon's perception of his own New York environment, which is basically confined to the interior of his studio.

In many ways the development of Avedon's portraiture has paralleled that of his fashion photography. In the *New Yorker* article on Avedon, Janet Malcolm traced the progression of his portraiture from the earliest portraits—"animated by an innovator's spirit of experiment and risk-taking, and by a young man's wish to please and dazzle"—through the fiercely shocking portraits from the period of his book *Nothing Personal* to the current mercurial and analytical work. We find the same progression, if not exactly the same degree of inquiry, informing both portraiture and fashion photography.

The most obvious characteristic of Avedon's portraits is their searing emotional impact, despite—or perhaps, more rightly, because of—their supposed lack of intervention by the photographer. Taken in the studio against white and starkly empty backgrounds, the subjects *confront* the viewer with tight-lipped, vacant expressions and frontal, "informational" poses. When set before this white field Avedon's portrait subjects, who tend to be superstar culturati and political power-dealers, also become "symbolic of themselves" and of the cultural and political values of our society.

The disquiet of Avedon's portraits is heightened by the printing, in which partial borders of the negative become black frames, by the close-up figure-to-frame relationship, and by the size, which ranges from large to vast, encompassing and involving the viewer in their expanse. The 8-foot-high murals shown at the Metropolitan Museum of Art Avedon retrospective—the length of one of them stretched to 35 feet—put the viewer in an entirely new relationship to the photographic image: he was both encompassed by the field and perceived the photographed subject in a one-to-one relationship to his body size. This, in effect, transformed the image from *seen* to *felt.*

Richard Avedon is a stunningly original photographer. He has been able to express the social, material and sexual values of our society in the quick-silver and so-called "ephemeral" medium of fashion photography and to bring new meanings and emotional impact to the field of portraiture. But it is his continued ability to take creative risks, "never to bring the same mental attitude to the same problem twice," which is the key not only to his past work in this medium but also to his future.

—Nancy Hall-Duncan

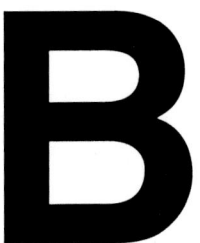

BADGER, Gerry (Gerald David Badger).

Nationality: British. **Born:** Northampton, 13 June 1948. **Education:** Studied architecture at the Duncan of Jordanstone College of Art, Dundee, Scotland, 1964-69, Dip.Arch. 1969; studied photography under Joseph McKenzie, Dundee, 1966-69. **Family:** Married Joyce Masterton in 1964 (divorced, 1986); children: Jane and Emma. **Career:** Architect with the Greater London Council Department of Architecture and Civic Design, 1969-73, and with Peter Wood and Partners, London, 1973-76. Architect in private practice, London, since 1976. Lecturer in Photography, Stanhope Institute, London, since 1976. Member of the Editorial Board, *Creative Camera,* London, 1980-82. **Recipient:** Arts Council Grant for Creative Photography, 1977; Visual Arts Major Award, Greater London Arts Association, 1979. **Address:** 3 Nelson Road, London NW6 9RX, England.

Individual Exhibitions:

1974	Creative Camera Gallery, London
1975	The Photographers' Gallery, London
1978	Brewery Arts Centre, Kendal, Cumbria
1979	Sir John Cass School of Art, London
1980	University of Dundee, Scotland
	Glenrothes Gallery, Scotland
	Open Eye Gallery, Liverpool
1985	Camera Club Gallery, London

Selected Group Exhibitions:

1972	*Young Contemporaries II,* Creative Camera Gallery, London (toured the U.K.)
1973	*Serpentine Photography '73,* Serpentine Gallery, London
1976	*New Photographers,* Boxroom Gallery, London
1978	*Midland Group Photography '78,* Midland Group Gallery, Nottingham (travelled to the Serpentine Gallery, London)
	Stanhope Photographers, Stanhope Gallery, London
1980	*British Art 1940-1980,* Hayward Gallery, London
	Perspectives on Landscape, Arts Council, London (toured the United States)
1981	*Stanhope Photographers,* Stanhope Gallery, London
	Summer Show, B2 Gallery, London
1988	*Towards a Bigger Picture,* Victoria and Albert Museum, London and Tate Gallery, Liverpool
1989	*Through the Looking Glass: Photographic Art in Great Britain 1945-1989,* Barbican Art Gallery, London.

Collections:

Arts Council of Great Britain, London; Department of the Environment, London; London Borough of Hounslow; Royal Photographic Society, Bath, England; Bibliothèque Nationale, Paris; Museum of Modern Art, New York.

Publications:

By BADGER: Books—*New American Still Photography,* exhibition catalogue, Edinburgh 1976; *Singular Realities,* exhibition catalogue, Newcastle upon Tyne 1977; *John Blakemore: British Image III,* London 1977; *Mid-19th Century French Photography,* exhibition catalogue, Edinburgh 1979; *Eugene Atget, Photographer,* London 1985; *American Images: Photography 1945-80,* exhibition catalogue, with Peter Turner and others, London 1985; *Troubled Landscapes* essay in Paul Graham, Troubled Land: The Social Landscape of Northern Ireland (Grey Editions, London, with Cornerhouse Publications, Manchester 1987); *Pages of Experience* text to Joseph McKenxie, Pages of Experience: Photography 1947-1987 (Polygon, Edinburgh and Third Eye Centre, Glasgow 1987); *Phototexts* (Travelling Light, London 1988) anthology of essays with Peter Turner; *Through the Looking Glass: Photographic Art in Britain 1945-1989,* introductory essay (Barbican Art Gallery, London 1989); *The Spider That Spins the Sky,* essay in David Parker *Broken Images* (Cornerhouse Publications, Manchester 1992); *Virtus Pasadas de Moda: El Brick Lane de Marketa Luskacova,* essay in Marketa Luskacova, *Marketa Luskacova: Fotografias de East End De Londres* (Fundacion NatWest and The British Council, Madrid 1992). **Articles**—"Wynn Bullock" in *Photographic Journal* (London), May 1975; "Lee Friedlander" in *British Journal of Photography* (London), March 1976; "Manuel Alvarez Bravo" in *British Journal of Photography* (London), May 1976; "Dr. Thomas Keith" in *British Journal of Photography* (London), May 1977; "Walker Evans" in *Creative Camera* (London), September 1977; "William Klein" in *British Journal of Photography* (London), February 1978; "Garry Winogrand" in *British Journal of Photography* (London), March 1978; "Thomas J. Cooper" in *Artscribe* (London), July 1978; "E.J. Bellocq" in *British Journal of Photography* (London), August 1978; "Mid-19th Century French Photography" in *British Journal of Photography* (London), October 1979; "Early Photography in Egypt" in *Creative Camera* (London), December 1979; "Harry Callahan" in *Creative Camera* (London), August 1981; "Dr. Thomas Keith, Surgeon and Photographer" in *The Photographic Collector* (London), Autumn 1981; "New Californian Colour" in *Creative Camera* (London), October 1981; "Atget and the Garden of Critical Delight" in *The Photographic Collector* (London), Spring 1982; "Beyond Arbus and Bacon—Joel-Peter Witkin" in *The Photographic Collector* (London), Autumn 1982; "Eugene Atget: Peculiarly Non-Conformist" in *The Photographic Collector* (London), Autumn 1983; "Towards a Moral Pornography" in *Creative Camera* (London), May 1986; "Richard Avedon—In the American West" in *The Photographic Collector* (London), Summer 1986; "Bruce Gilden: A Penny to See the Peep Show" in *Creative Camera* (London) August 1986; "The Work of Atget" in *Creative Camera* (London) March 1987;"Light at the Edge of Darkness: Lewis Baltz's San Quentin Point" in *Creative Camera* (London), March 1987; "A Dark Mirror: Thomas Joshua Cooper" in *Creative Camera* November 1987; "Material Witness: Ansekm Kiefer" in *Creative Camera* (London), January 1990; "Voices in the Wilderness: British Photography in the 60s" in *Creative Camera* (London), February 1988; "Serious Photography Matters" in *Creative Camera* (London), May/June 1990; "The Cutting Edge: Danny Lyon at the Photographers' Gallery" in *Arts Review* (London) January 1993; "Nuclear Reactions: Richard Misrach" in *Arts Review* (London) March 1993; "Christmas Crackers: 20 Great Photographic Books" in *The British Journal of Photography* (London) 9 December 1993; "Souther Discomfort: Susan Lipper at the Photographers' Gallery" in *The British Journal* of Photography (London) 17 February 1994.

On BADGER: Books—British Journal of Photography Annual, edited by Geoffrey Crawley, London 1975; *British Journal of Photography Annual,* edited by Geoffrey Crawley, London 1978; *Untitled No. 14,* edited by James Enyeart and James Alinder, Carmel, California 1979; *Perspectives of Land-*

***Whitechapel,* 1982.** Photograph by Gerry Badger.

scape, British Image V, edited by Bill Gaskins, London 1979. **Article**—by William Messer in *U.S. Camera Annual,* New York 1977.

*

Photography, perhaps more than any other graphic art form, is an intensely physical, as well as metaphysical, activity. The relationship between photographer and photographed is a physical one—essentially a purely physical one. The photograph merely transcribes that physical relationship. Photography might be described almost as a performing art. The photographer creates or describes a dance with space and time.

My work is concerned with the photographic art, or the process of photography—on several levels. The physical, the hunting or collecting aspect, is one of the most important. At root—one might say at the first and at the last level—there is the impulse simply to hunt, and capture that which strikes a visual chord, a subjective response. And then to stalk that thing in order to place the camera in an exact physical relationship to it. A relationship whereby the machine may not simply record the subject, but express it, give full expression to the initial chord.

But always this process must begin with the visual. Many things move me in many ways, but not necessarily to make a photograph.

The material in the world that strikes this chord is various, but relates usually to the urban environment. I am concerned not so much with the literal documentation of social fact—a worthy yet near impossible task in terms of the medium anyway—but with a more formal and allusive exploration of the interaction between people and the environment, the interface between natural and built environment. Sometimes this material may seen unprepossessing, the detritus of a profligate society. Sometimes, on the other hand, it might be inspiring, as when one encounters the attempts of individuals to improve their own environments, light years away from the stultifying hands of professional environmentalists. So I am drawn to such things as the spaces between buildings, to cleared sites, modern middens, neglected corners, and particularly to gardens.

Formally, by natural inclination and also as a reaction against the minimalist programmes of so many contemporary photographers, I tend to make texturally and formally dense images. For that purpose, and also because of my great love for early photographic imagery, I use what is basically the same equipment used in the 19th century—a large view camera, complete with black cloth and associated paraphernalia. This is not merely an exercise in nostalgia. I am fascinated by the sheer amount of information that can drop off in a photograph made by such a process. Also, the process slows one down, forcing one to think hard, and making a perhaps protracted yet strangely pleasurable rite out of the whole act of photographing. It tends to produce images that are characterised by a sense of stillness, complexity, and intensity.

For me the delights of photography are its availability as a medium to all and its living continuities with the past, as are evident in the fact that its basic precepts remain as they were at the beginning. They are the same for the ambitious artist as for the most untutored snapshooter. We may experience the same—exactly the same—aesthetic frisson from a Timothy O'Sullivan desert landscape of the 1870's as from a NASA Martian landscape of the 1970's. Both may describe desert, light, space, and a feeling of emptiness to the same degree of perfection.

The root precepts of the medium might be overlaid—as I hope in my own case—with many layers of meaning. But however abstruse these layers of meaning may become, the whole, for me, should be transparent. The simple, mechanical fusion of light, time, space and object.

—Gerry Badger

*   *   *

Gerry Badger's involvement with photography is both practical and theoretical. Trained as an architect, it is perhaps not surprising that his main interest lies in the topographical and his own work is in the formalist tradition.

Badger has written many reviews and critical essays on photography and been involved in the curating of several major photographic exhibitions to which he brings a very personal viewpoint. He has an extensive knowledge of the history of photography and has both written and lectured on the subject although his main area of work has continued to be as a practising architect.

Badger has spent a considerable amount of time in the Middle East and made many photographs while there. One of his early series was based on the minute exploration of a suburban garden in London which resulted in dense and detailed individual photographs which through his use of long exposures and large format camera gave an almost microscopic view of subjects which would be largely ignored by the individual glance. He has followed this approach in a series documenting Luxor, achieving a series of photographs as completely removed from the usual travel documentary as could be imagined. Since the early years of photography Egypt has held a fascination for photographers and Badger has begun to research into these early works and to trace the history of photography in Egypt both by outsiders and by indiginous photographers.

While his personal interest may lie in the formal approach and topographical subject matter his competence as a photographer enables him to take on quite different assignments such as a recent one documenting the youth clubs of Hackney.

—Sue Davies

BAILEY, David (Royston).

Nationality: British. **Born:** London, 2 January 1938. **Education:** Attended schools in London, 1948-53; self-taught in photography. **Military Service:** Served in the Royal Air Force, Malaysia, 1957-58. **Family:** Married Rosemary Bramble in 1960 (divorced); Catherine Deneuve in 1967 (divorced); Marie Helvin in 1975 (divorced); Catherine Dyer in 1986; children: Paloma, Fenton and Sascha. **Career:** Photographic assistant, John French Studio, London, 1959; contract fashion photographer, *Vogue* magazine, London, from 1960; also freelance photographer, working for *Daily Express, Sunday Times, Daily Telegraph, Elle, Glamour,* etc., London, since 1960. Director of television commercials, since 1966, and television documentary films, since 1968. Range of photographic products and accessories, *The David Bailey Collection* with Olympus Cameras in 1994. Fellow, Royal Photographic Society, London, 1972; Fellow, Society of Industrial Artists and Designers, London, 1975. Lives in London. **Address:** Camera Eye Ltd., 24-26 Brownlow Mews, London WC1N 2LA, England.

Individual Exhibitions:

1971   National Portrait Gallery, London
1972   Nikon Galerie, Paris
1973   The Photographers' Gallery, London
1980   *The Boat People,* Olympus Gallery, London
         Trouble and Strife, Olympus Gallery, London
1981   Olympus Gallery, London
1982   *London NW1,* Olympus Gallery, London
1983   *Black and White Memories,* Victoria and Albert Museum, London (travelled to the International Center of Photography, New York, 1984)

1984   *Fotografie 1964-83,* Palazzo Fortuny, Venice
1985   *The Valleys Project,* Fotogallery, Cardiff, Wales
         Photographs from the Sudan, ICA Gallery, London
1989   *Bailey Now!* National Centre of Photography, Bath, England

Selected Group Exhibitions:

1979   *Elements,* Olympus Gallery, London
1982   *Floods of Light,* The Photographers' Gallery, London
1983   *British Photography* 1955-65, The Photographers' Gallery, London
1984   *Sammlung Gruber,* Museum Ludwig, Cologne
1985   *Shots of Style,* Victoria and Albert Museum, London
         Das Aktfoto, Fotomuseum im Stadtmuseum, Munich
1986   *The Animal in Photography 1843-1985,* The Photographers' Gallery, London

Collections:

National Portrait Gallery, London; The Photographers' Gallery, London; Condé Nast Publications, London.

Publications:

By BAILEY: Books—*The Truth About Modelling,* with text by Jean Shrimpton, London 1963; *Box of Pin-Ups,* London 1964; *Goodbye Baby and Amen,* with text by Peter Evans, London 1969; *Andy Warhol,* London 1974; *Beady Minces,* with foreword by Terence Donovan, London 1974; *Another Image: Papua New Guinea,* London 1975; *Mixed Moments,* London 1976; *Masterpieces of Erotic Photography,* with others, London 1977; *David Bailey's Trouble and Strife,* with preface by Jacques-Henri Lartigue, introduction by Brian Clarke, London 1980; *London NW1: Urban Landscapes,* London 1982; *Begin with Bailey,* with text by George Hughes, London 1983; *Black and White Memories: Photographs 1948-1969,* with texts by Martin Harrison and David Mellor, London 1983, New York 1984; *David Bailey: Photographs 1964-1983,* withy text by Martin Harrison, London and Milan 1984; *Nine by Nine,* with others, New York 1984; *Nudes,* London 1984; *Part of the Valleys Project,* Cardiff, Wales 1985; *Shots of Style: Great Fashion Photographs Chosen by David Bailey,* with text by Martin Harrison, London 1985; *Imagine,* London 1985; *If We Shadows,* with preface by George Melly, London 1992. **Article**—"David Bailey," interview, in *Zoom* (Paris), November/December 1972. **Films**—*Beaton by Bailey,* 1971; *Andy Warhol,* television film, 1973.

On BAILEY: Books—*The Magic Image* by Cecil Beaton and Gail Buckland, London 1975; *Geschichte der Fotografie im 20. Jahrhunder/Photography in the 20th Century* by Peter Tausk, Cologne 1977, London 1980; *The Vogue Book of Fashion Photography* by Polly Devlin, with an introduction by Alexander Liberman, London 1979; *World Photography,* edited by Bryn Campbell, London 1981; *Master Photographers: The World's Great Photographers on Their Art and Technique,* edited by Pat Booth, London 1983; *Sammlung Gruber: Photographie des 20. Jahrhunderts,* exhibition catalogue, with foreword by Siegfried Gohr, Cologne 1984. **Articles**—"Goodbye Bailey and Hello!" by Hugh McIlvanney in the *Observer Magazine* (London), 16 November 1969; "Great Photographers of the World: David Bailey" by S. Patterson in *Réalités* (Paris), March 1971; "David Bailey" in *The Image* (London), no. 11, 1973; "Bailey: Not Just a Photographer of Pretty Faces" by G. Hughes in *Amateur Photographer* (London), 3 April 1974; "David Bailey Photographs Faces to Watch" in the *Observer Magazine* (London), 1 March 1981.

*

If I have to explain my pictures in words, it means that my images have not worked.

—David Bailey

*   *   *

David Bailey emerged as a fashion photographer to be reckoned with at the beginning of the 1960's, and he has continued to be one of the most popular and famous figures in that seemingly ephemeral scene. This is because he has both enjoyed his work and taken it seriously, because he is interested in the possibilities of photography in a far wider context than any assigned work he may be given, and probably also because he has always seemed to prefer the women to the clothes, something that his predecessors—with their static and stylised forms of fashion photography—certainly did not.

Keith Waterhouse dubbed them the "Terrible Trio"—Duffy, Donovan and Bailey; but David Bailey is the one who has continued longest in the public eye, partly because his particular style of fashion photography was so revolutionary that his pictures were and are instantly recognisable, and also because his general interest in still photography has continued, and he has published several books of his personal pictures. *Goodbye Baby and Amen,* his hymn to the 1960's, is full of portraits and the dashing spirit of that time, and he has more recently used reportage and other forms to express his ideas.

The freedom that Bailey brought to the previously very stylised forms of fashion photography came from his early realization that it is the girls who wear the clothes that make them work. Both he and Duffy have said that it was the inspiration of the working girls in dance halls, who managed to create style from almost nothing, that led them to the freer expression in their photography, an expression that was so appropriate to the relaxed atmosphere and the breaking down of class barriers that was felt throughout the 60's. This trend has continued and grown, with designers picking up ideas from The Punks and now The Posers, inventing and changing their personna as fast as ever the old designers did.

For me, the best of Bailey is to be found in those portraits made in the intimacy of the studio of his friends or of the models he knew best—the fact that they may have been showing off certain clothes at the same time is immaterial. It has been said of Marilyn Monroe that she had a love affair with the camera. From the other side of the lens, the same could be said of David Bailey. With his camera he can express that freedom from cant and exaggeration that he clearly admires both in photography and in life style, and the best of his pictures will certainly not only show the spirit of their age but also outlive it as portraits in their own right.

In recent years an increasing amount of Bailey's professional work has been on film—and such advertising assignments are uncredited, but this does not mean that his personal work and portraiture does not continue, all over the world. He has also taken up painting, but the camera can never be far from his side as is evidenced by his latest book *If We Shadows* published in 1992 which is laid out in a series of, often surreal, juxtapositions which may well sum up his feelings for the 1980s. For me it is a book about eyes, whether real or imagined and thus makes continual reference to the most important organs in a photographers' body as well as to the camera lens.

—Sue Davies

BAILEY, Oscar.

Nationality: American. **Born:** Barnesville, Ohio, 23 July 1925. **Education:** Wilmington College, Ohio, 1948-51, B.A. 1951; Ohio University, Athens, 1956-58, M.F.A. 1958. **Family:** Married Sara Besco in 1945; children: Susan and Daniel. **Career:** Printer and Designer, Cooperative Recreation Service, Delaware, Ohio, 1951-56. Photographer since 1956. Professor of Photography, State University of New York at Buffalo, 1958-69. Since 1969, Professor of Art, University of South Florida, Tampa. Artist-in-Residence, Artpark, Lewiston, New York, 1977. Founding Member, Society for Photographic Education, 1962. **Recipient:** Faculty Research Fellowship, State University of New York, 1967; Release-Time Grant, University of South Florida, 1974; Photographers Fellowship Grant, National Endowment for the Arts, 1976. **Address:** 2004 Clement Road, Lutz, Florida 33549, U.S.A.

Individual Exhibitions:

1958	Ohio University, Athens
1959	New York State University College at Buffalo
1960	Indiana University, Bloomington
1962	New York State University College at Buffalo
1963	Kalamazoo Institute of Arts, Michigan
1964	Ohio Wesleyan University, Delaware
	International Museum of Photography, George Eastman House, Rochester, New York
1965	University of Tampa
1967	University of New Hampshire, Durham
1969	University of Oregon, Eugene
1970	University of South Florida, Tampa
1971	Penland School of Crafts, North Carolina
1972	Valencia Community College, Orlando, Florida
	University of South Florida, Tampa
1973	Hillsborough Community College, Tampa
1974	University of South Florida, Tampa
1975	Ridge Art Association, Winter Haven, Florida
1976	University of Colorado, Boulder
1977	Southern Illinois University, Carbondale
1978	University of North Florida, Jacksonville

Selected Group Exhibitions:

1960	*The Sense of Abstraction in Contemporary Photography,* Museum of Modern Art, New York
1971	*New Photographics,* Washington State College, Ellensburg
1972	*Wider View,* International Museum of Photography, George Eastman House, Rochester, New York
1973	*Photo-Phantasists,* Florida State University, Tallahassee
	Light and Lens, Hudson River Museum, Yonkers, New York
1974	*New Images in Photography,* University of Miami
1976	*Photo/synthesis,* Cornell University, Ithaca, New York
1977	*The Contemporary American South,* United States Information Agency Exhibition, toured Europe and Southeast Asia
1978	*Extended Frame,* Visual Studies Workshop, Rochester, New York (toured the United States)
1979	*Florida Light,* Loch Haven Art Center, Orlando, Florida

Collections:

Museum of Modern Art, New York; International Museum of Photography, George Eastman House, Rochester, New York; Boston Museum of Fine Arts; Smithsonian Institution, Washington, D.C.; Library of Congress, Washington, D.C.; Ringling Museum of Art, Sarasota, Florida; Florida Center for the Arts, Tampa; Museum of Fine Arts, St. Petersburg, Florida; New Orleans Museum of Art.

Publications:

By BAILEY: Book—*Found Objects,* with Charles Swedlund, Buffalo, New York 1965.

On BAILEY: Books—*Light and Lens,* edited by Donald L. Werner, New York 1973; *Photo/Synthesis,* edited by Jason D. Wong, New York 1976; *Modern Portraits: The Self and Others,* edited by J. Kirk and T. Varnedoe, New York 1976. **Articles**—"Whence Does Wisdom Come?" by Minor White in *Aperture* (Millerton, New York), no. 1, 1959; "Presentation: Oscar Bailey" by Knut Forsund in *Fotografi* (Oslo), September 1978.

*

Whether working with conventional format cameras, 35 mm., 6 x 7 cm., 4 x 5 in., or with my Cirkut 8 (an antique, rotating, panoramic camera, producing negatives 8 by 48 inches in size), I generally deal with the human element. Whether people are in the actual photograph or not, the picture is about mankind—man has done this, has been here.

I enjoy and appreciate all facets of photographic image-making. I do some mixed-media work, constructions, photo-manipulations, but for the most part my work is "straight"—or, in the case of work with the Cirkut camera, "curved."

Statue, Ohio, **1979.** Photograph by Oscar Bailey.

My aim is to present images—images equivalent to my ideas and feelings—with enough vitality to evoke an exchange of understanding. This is, for me, more important than reporting an obvious truth of the external world.

—Oscar Bailey

*   *   *

Oscar Bailey's work is of both a narrative and a compositional nature, but his strongest work is based on the narrative. The juxtaposition of images in a single frame and the relationship of the individual images to each other reveal Bailey's sense of humor, sometimes very subtle and often interjecting very strong opinions by the use of the parts involved. Bailey has made such comments on a range of topics from the vanity of country-western to the unreality of Florida palm trees. His work has transcended the flat plain to the dimensional; the works in gum bicromate fully utilize the visual pun. Bailey has also explored the dot pattern used in the printed image enlarged to the extent of becoming an entity unto itself, thus informing, in these large works, an image of its own structure and abstracting the original reason for its being.

His best known work has been done with his ''cirkut'' camera. In these long horizontals he has explored many of his earlier themes, yet, because of the camera's time lag of 10 to 20 seconds, Bailey has been able to completely throw off reality in his ''backyard happenings,'' creating abstracted forms with a background of undistorted reality, a feat few other mechanically visual media can perform. His backyard experiences also incorporate the narrative by the selection of information in the extreme horizontal format. Because the camera moves from left to right and conceptualization then is from left to right, the natural tendency of ''reading'' the image is strengthened; in ''Old 88 and Friends,'' for instance, there is a very strong sense of narrative. The cirkut images require a great deal of ''pre-visualization'' and precise planning,

including a feeling for movement in a frozen frame. What emerges is Bailey's feeling for his surroundings and his narrative within them.

—Tina Freeman

BALDESSARI, John.

Nationality: American. **Born:** National City, California, 17 June 1931. **Education:** Sweetwater High School, National City, 1945-49; studied painting at San Diego State College, California, 1949-53, 1954-57, B.A. 1953, M.A. 1957. **Family:** Married Carol Wixom in 1962; children: Anna Marie and Antonio. **Career:** Professional artist since 1957. Instructor, Fine Arts Gallery, San Diego, 1953-54, San Diego city schools, 1956-57, San Diego State College, 1956, 1959-61, and Southwestern College, Chula Vista, California, 1962-68; Assistant Professor of Art, University of California at San Diego, 1968-70; also Instructor, La Jolla Museum of Art, California, 1966-70. Professor, California Institute of Arts, Los Angeles, since 1970. Visiting Instructor, Hunter College, New York, 1971. **Recipient:** National Endowment for the Arts Grant, 1973, 1974-75. **Agent:** Sonnabend Gallery, New York. **Address:** c/o Sonnabend Gallery, 420 West Broadway, New York, New York 10012, U.S.A.

Individual Exhibitions:

1960	La Jolla Museum of Art, California
1962	Southwestern College, Chula Vista, California (and 1964)
1966	La Jolla Museum of Art, California
1968	Molly Barnes Gallery, Los Angeles
1970	Richard Feigen Gallery, New York
	Eugenia Butler Gallery, Los Angeles
1971	Galerie Konrad Fischer, Dusseldorf
	Art & Project, Amsterdam
	Nova Scotia College of Art and Design, Halifax
1972	Galerie MTL, Brussels
	Art & Project, Amsterdam
	Galleria Franco Toselli, Milan
	Jack Wendler Gallery, London
1973	Sonnabend Gallery, New York
	Galerie Sonnabend, Paris
	Galleria Schema, Florence
	Galerie Konrad Fischer, Dusseldorf
1974	Galerie Folker Skulima, West Berlin
	Jack Wendler Gallery, London
	Galleria Franco Toselli, Milan
	Art & Project/Galerie MTL, Antwerp
1975	Galerie Felix Handschin, Basle
	Galerie MTL, Brussels
	Saman Gallery, Genoa
	Sonnabend Gallery, New York
	Stedelijk Museum, Amsterdam
	Modern Art Agency, Naples
	Galerie Sonnabend, Paris
	Southwestern College, Chula Vista, California
	The Kitchen, New York
	University of California at Irvine
1976	Ewing Gallery, University of Melbourne, Australia
	Auckland Art Gallery, New Zealand
	University of Akron, Ohio
	Ohio State University, Columbus
	Cirrus Editions Gallery, Los Angeles
	James Corcoran Gallery, Los Angeles
1977	Galleria Massimo Valsecchi, Milan
	Matrix, Hartford Atheneum, Connecticut
	John Baldessari: Films, Fox Venice Theatre, Venice, California
	Robert Self Gallery, London

Baudelaire Meets Poe, **1980, by John Baldessari.** Photograph by Bevan Davies.

1988   *John Baldessari: Recent Work,* Margo Leavin Gallery, Los
        Angeles; Galerie Laage Salomon, Paris; Lisson Gallery,
        London; Galleria Primo Piano, Rome; Kestner-Gesellschaft,
        Hannover.
1989   *John Baldessari: Recent Works,* Galerie Meert Rihoux,
        Brussels
        Ni Por Esas—Not Even So: John Baldessari, Centro de Arte
        Reina Sofia, Madrid
1990   *John Baldessari,* Museum of Contemporary Art, Los Angeles;
        San Francisco Museum of Modern Art; Hirshhorn Museum
        and Sculpture Garden, Washington DC; Walker Arts Center,
        Minneapolis; Whitney Museum of American Art, New York;
        Musee d'Art Contemporain de Montreal.
1991   Galerie Crousel-Robelin Bama, Paris
        Donald Young Gallery, Chicago
1992   Sonnabend Gallery, New York
        John Baldessari, Casa da Parra, Santiago de Compostela, Spain
        Galerie Meert Rihoux, Bruxelles
1993   Galleria Klemens Gasser, Bolzano, Italy
        Galleria Primo Piano, Rome
        Working Materials, Brooke Alexander Editions, New York
        Mai 36 Galerie, Zurich
1994   *John Baldessari at Gemini G.E.L.,* Gemini G.E.L. at Joni
        Moisant Weyl, New York
        John Baldessari: 4 Directional Pieces, The Newark Museum,
        Newark, NJ
        Artist's Choice: John Baldessari, The Museum of Modern Art,
        New York
1995   Cornerhouse, Manchester, England

Selected Group Exhibitions:

1971   *Prospect '71: Projection,* Kunsthalle, Dusseldorf
1974   *Demonstrative Fotografie,* Kunstverein, Heidelberg
1975   *The Extended Document,* International Museum of Photogra-
        phy, George Eastman House, Rochester, New York
1976   *Serial Photography,* Broxton Gallery, Los Angeles
1977   *Contemporary American Photographic Works,* Museum of Fine
        Arts, Houston
1978   *Kirklands International Photographic Exhibition,* Walker Art
        Gallery, Liverpool
1979   *American Photography in the 70's,* Art Institute of Chicago
1980   *Artist and Camera,* Mappin Art Gallery, Sheffield, Yorkshire
        (travelled to the Stoke City Art Gallery; Durham Light
        Infantry Museum and Art Centre; Cartwright Hall, Bradford,
        1980-81)
1983   *Photography in America 1910-83,* Tampa Museum, Florida
1987   *Photography and Art: Interaction since 1946,* Los Angeles
        County Museum of Art, Los Angeles; travelled to Museum
        of Art, Fort Lauderdale; The Queens Museum, Flushing,
        New York; Des Moines Art Center, Des Moines, Iowa
        Coleccion Sonnabend, Centro de Arte Reina Sofia, Ma-
        drid; in 1988 travelled to CAPC, Musee d'Art
        Contemporain, Bordeaux; Hamburger Bahnhof, Berlin;
        Galleria Nazionale d'Arte Moderna, Rome; Museo d'Arte
        Moderna e Contemporanea, Trent, Italy; Musee Rath,
        Geneva; Sezon Museum of Art, Tokyo; The Miyagi Museum
        of Art, Sendai, Japan; The Fukuyama Museum of Art,
        Hiroshima; The National Museum of Modern Art, Kyoto.
1988   *Lost and Found in California: Four Decades of Assemblage
        Art,* James Corcoran Gallery, Santa Monica, CA.
1989   *Magiciens de la Terre,* Centre Georges Pompidou, Paris
        Forty Years of California Assemblage, San Jose Museum of
        Art, Fresno Art Museum, Joslyn, Omaha, Nebraska
        Photography Now, Victoria and Albert Museum, London
1990   *Art Conceptuel: Formes Conceptuelles,* Galerie 1900-
        2000, Paris
        Art That Happens To Be Photography, Texas Gallery, Houston
        The Last Laugh, curated by Collins and Milazzo, Massimo
        Audiello Gallery, New York

1991   *Breakthroughs: Avant-Garde Artists in Europe and America,
        1950-1990,* Wexner Center for the Arts, Ohio State
        University
        *Baldessari, Bernard, Weiss/Fischli, Perlman, Hanne
        Darboven,* Monika Spruth Galerie, Cologne
        Word as Image: American Art 1960-1990, Contemporary Arts
        Museum, Houston (organised by the Milwaukee Art
        Museum)
1992   *Selected Passages,* Galerie Jousse Seguin, Paris
        More Than One Photograph, The Museum of Modern Art,
        New York
        American Art: 1930-1979, Lingotto, Torino, Italy
1993   *Photoplay: Works from The Chase Manhattan Collection,*
        Center for the Fine Arts, Miami; Museo Amparo Puebla,
        Mexico; Museo de Arte Contemporaneo de Monterrey,
        Mexico; Centro Cultural Consolidado, Caracas, Venezuela;
        MASP, Museu de Arte de Sao Paulo, Brazil; Museo
        Nacional de Bellas Artes, Buenos Aires; Museo Nacional de
        Bellas Artes, Santiago, Chile
        Out of Sight, Out of Mind, Lisson Gallery, London
        Art in the Age of Information, Wood Street Galleries, 808 Penn
        Modern, Pittsburgh
1994   *Sixth Biennial Art Auction,* The Museum of Contemporary Art,
        Los Angeles

Collections:

Museum of Modern Art, New York; Los Angeles County Museum of Art; La
Jolla Museum of Art, California; Wallraf-Richartz Museum, Cologne;
Stedelijk Museum, Amsterdam; Kunstmuseum, Basle.

Publications:

By BALDESSARI: Books—*Ingres and Other Parables,* London 1972;
Choosing: Green Beans, Milan 1972; *Throwing Three Balls in the Air to Get a
Straight Line (Best of Thirty-Six Attempts),* Milan 1973; *Throwing a Ball Once
to Get Three Melodies and Fifteen Chords,* Irvine, California 1975; *Four
Events and Reactions,* Amsterdam 1975; *Artists and Photographers,* portfolio,
with others, New York 1975; *Raw Prints,* portfolio, Los Angeles 1976; *Brutus
Killed Caesar,* Akron, Ohio 1976; *A Sentence of Thirteen Parts (with Twelve
Alternate Verbs)Ending in Fable,* Hamburg 1977; ''My Files of Movie Stills''
in *Blasted Allegories: An Anthology of Writings by Contemporary Artists,*
New York and Cambridge, MA 1987. **Articles**—''Photography and Lan-
guage,'' interview, in *John Baldessari,* exhibition catalogue, Los Angeles
1976; ''John Baldessari: Interview,'' with Diane Spodarek, in *Detroit Artists'
Monthly,* June 1976; ''John Baldessari,'' interview with Leo Rubinfein, in *Art
in America* (New York), September/October 1978; untitled statement within
''The State of California'' in *Artcoast* (Los Angeles), May/June 1988.

On BALDESSARI: Books—*Pop Art Redefined* by John Russell and Suzi
Gablik, London and New York 1969; *Conceptual Art* by Ursula Meyers, New
York 1971; *Video Visions: A Medium Discovers Itself* by Jonathan Price, New
York 1972; *Art History of Photography* by Volker Kahmen, New York 1973;
Video Art by Ira Schneider and Beryl Korot, New York 1976; *John Baldessari,*
exhibition catalogue, with texts by Marcia Tucker and Robert Pincus-Witten,
and an interview by Nancy Drew, Dayton, Ohio 1981; *Artist and Camera,*
exhibition catalogue, London 1980; *Photography in America 1910-1983,*
exhibition catalogue by Julie M. Saul, Tampa, Florida 1983; *Photography and
Art 1946-1986,* exhibition catalogue, by Andy Grundberg and Kathleen
Gauss, Los Angeles 1987; *John Baldessari,* by Coosje van Bruggen, New
York 1990. **Articles**—''Baldessari'' by Caroline Tisdall in *The Guardian*
(London), 15 April 1971; ''Pointing, Hybrids and Romanticism: John
Baldessari'' by James Collins in *Artforum* (New York), October 1973;
''Sequential Photographs'' by Mark Power in the *Washington Post,* 7 March
1975; ''What Develops When Painters Pick Up Cameras'' by David Bourdon
in the *Village Voice* (New York), 20 October 1975; ''The Anti-Photogra-
phers'' by Nancy Foote in *Artforum* (New York), September 1976; ''New
Color Photography Is a Blurry Form of Art'' by Gene Thornton in the *New
York Times,* 10 July 1977; ''John Baldessari's 'Blasted Allegories' '' by Hal
Foster in *Artforum* (New York), October 1979; ''Well Hung'' by Ben Lifson

in the *Village Voice* (New York), 5 November 1980; ''John Baldessari's Conceptual Art'' by Hunter Drohojowska in *LA Weekly,* 13-19 July 1984; ''Review: Margo Leavin Gallery'' by Suzanne Muchnic in *Los Angeles Times,* 10 October 1986; ''Review'' by Vince Aletti in *The Village Voice,* 24 November 1987; ''The Artists Who Matter: L.A.'s New Scene Makes History'' by Hunter Drohojowska in *Antiques and Fine Art,* No 4, May/June 1987; ''Review'' by John Roberts in *Artscribe International,* Sept/Oct 1988; ''The Deepest Cut: Montage in the Work of John Balessari'' by John Miller in *Artscribe International,* May 1989; ''Un Planteamiento original y excitante'' by Francisco Calvo Serraller in *El Pais,* 12 January 1989; ''John Baldessari Rises From His Ashes and Finds That He's Hot'' by Michael Small in *People Magazine,* 10 December 1990; ''Subverting Art with Art'' by Peter Plagens in *Newsweek,* 23 April 1990; '''Image World: Art and Media Culture:' Whitney Museum of American Art, New York'' by Liz Markus in *Sculpture,* March/April 1990; ''Sharp Pencils'' by Christopher Knight in *Elle,* March 1990; ''Cerebral Showers'' by Jan Avgikos in *Artscribe,* Nov/Dec 1991; ''Vital Signs: Baldessari, Polke, Sunspots and Truth'' by John Carlin in *Paper Magazine,* November 1991; ''Breaking the Code'' by Kay Larson in *New York Magazine,* 12 August 1991; ''Baldessari Reinvents Himself'' by David Pagel in *The Los Angeles Times,* 28 May 1992; ''From Back Door to Inner Sanctum In the House of Art'' by Vicki Goldberg in *The New York Times,* 24 October 1993; ''Proof'' by Susan Kandel in *Art Issues,* Jan/Feb 1993; ''Art: MOMA Bits'' in *The New Yorker,* 2 May 1994; ''Dear Barbarian'' by Peter Schjeldahl in *The Village Voice,* 12 April 1994.

*

The accompanying piece is a visual equivalent of how I believe Baudelaire must have felt at the moment of reading Poe for the first time.

First the snake, Groveling, Sneaking along the ground, lowly, slow moving, inertia, held down by gravity. A flat point of view, like Flatland. Maybe how one feels having a writer's block? Not much happening until he encounters Poe. But also redolent of indolent voluptuousness, of poetry chained to the earth. Suggestive of the darker regions of the mind, an atmosphere that is infernal. A sign of the demands of the unconscious. I recall that Baudelaire spoke of his mistress as a ''dancing serpent.'' I could have used a snail, I suppose. But a snake just seems better, nearer to the ground, more endless and richer with poetic overtones. Also, this image is in photogravure, but more about that later.

Which gets to the second image. The snake jumps up, curls around, embraces a more specific symbol—a jewel—wraps around it. And a baby snake, a kind of rebirth. Ready to grow. A collision of images, deliberately mixed. High and low. Chosen as Baudelaire says from a ''forest of images.'' Juxtaposing such elements seems very much like Baudelaire. Beauty out of evil Baudelaire would say, though I think my point of view is more indefinite, thus back to Poe. At any rate, it stirs the unconscious and the pre-logical. Repressed ideas and associations begin to awaken.

The frog stands for an explosion made at the moment of impact of the two minds meeting. In color, larger than the other two images, the bursting out of, travelling out of the plane of the wall. A metamorphosis as well, changing from snake to a frog. Repelling but somehow beautiful, standing for magic. Transubstantiation. The idea reified, made flesh but in a sinister non-social fashion.

About the photogravure. It refers to print vs. the color, where the frog is no longer a sign. The frog is the artist freed.

—John Baldessari

*   *   *

One of the most influential of post war generations of American and European artists, John Baldessari's work discloses not only the ubiquity and power of the photographic image, but the usurping of avant garde strategies by mass media. Photomontage and the juxtaposition of text and image play a central role in Baldessari's project where the pictorial is laid bare, its clichés and conventions unpacked with surgical ease and wit. The son of a Danish mother and an Italian father, Baldessari's European background—and not least his unusually tall height—stood him apart from his peers and undoubtedly contributed to his vigorous independence, his polymath intellectual range of mind and his acerbic humour. He studied art, literature and philosophy at

San Diego State College, continued art historical studies at Berkeley and later took a masters degree.

Baldessari's work of the fifties, ranging from painting and teaching to visual effects for a jazz festival which used music and visual images from magazines, newspapers and holiday snapshots, was driven by a compulsion to use everyday experiences as source material and led to the use of photographic notes: backs of lorries on the highway, walls of buildings, advertising posters, film stills. In 1966 Baldessari determined ''that would be the language I was going to use, photographic imagery and words . . . I'm going to give people what they want, and they probably don't want that either!'' Teaching children, he began using an opaque projector enlarging the children's work up to 20 feet high. His play with art conventions of drawing and composition, in theory and practice, persists throughout his work, often acknowledging and appropriating images of modernist masters from Steiglitz to Man Ray and Magritte. A notable series is the set of photographs *Cigar Smoke to Match Clouds That Are Different (By Sight—Side View) and (By Memory—Front View)* 1972-73.

A liking for familiar art historical references, coupled with a sense of the absurdity of the conventions of everyday life, suffuses Baldessari's entire oeuvre which parodies both the illusion of art and the subliminal strategies of media imagery. ''I create my own dictionary of images. . . .I want to feel like a gold miner.'' A rich vein of unrelated words and recycled imagery is exploited through judicious juxtaposition in the disjunctive phototext paintings of 1967, '70s conceptual pieces and '80s composite photoworks. The phototext paintings of 1967-68, on same-size vertical canvasses the proportions of a 35mm slide, use snapshots by the artist and others, as well as images culled from magazines and children's books which are transferred to canvas by the artist using a photo emulsion process and combined with bald texts pained by a sign painter. The matter-of-fact, even banal, immediacy of these images is disrupted by the viewer's awareness of the texts which yield discrepancies of interpretation and reading.

By 1971, when Baldessari had his first one-man show at the Konrad Fischer Gallery in Düsseldorf, he was familiar with the work of both Fluxus and Conceptual artists in New York and Europe, straddling both with the mobility of his own ideas and refusal of dogma. The dominance of photomontage, the collision of anomalous imagery in the violent images of the 80s (such as *Hanging Man with Sunglasses,* 1986) puts the camera to work, as John Miller writes: ''as a kind of stop-action analytical tool'' (*Artscribe* no. 75, 1989).

As well as the stock mentors of contemporary critical theory, from Freud to Levi-Strauss and Wittgenstein, Baldessari's thinking is also steeped in nineteenth century writers, especially Baudelaire and Thoreau. While his work has precedents in Eisenstein, Cage and Warhol, its context lies in that of his peers among Fluxus and Conceptual artists, especially Kaprow, Kosuth and Weiner, and his importance in his happy synthesis of practices. This is revealed with exemplary clarity in the major book by Cooesje van Bruggen, 1990, which is not only the definitive reference but an outstanding tribute to the significance of Baldessari's work. His first major show in Britain in 1995 must exert a shock of recognition for many radical young British artist tyros and their critics whose work and ideas Baldessari anticipated by some decades. His agility and wit overcome the paralysis of modernist traditions, including the rectangular frame in photography, notably *Shape Derived for Subject (Snake), Used as a Framing Device to Produce New Photographs,* 1987 and forces that rare doubletake which poses questions which are as much moral as aesthetic.

—Marjorie Allthorpe-Guyton

BALLHAUSE, Walter.

Nationality: German. **Born:** Hameln an der Weser, 3 April 1911. **Education:** Attended several schools, in Hameln and Hannover, 1917-25; self-taught in photography, from 1928. **Family:** Married Henni Dohrmann in 1936; son: Rolf. **Career:** Worked as a casual labourer and non-professional helper, for Hanomag, Hannover, 1929-31 and 1933-41; independent social documentary photographer, whilst unemployed, Hannover, 1930-33; relinquished photography, from 1934. Apprentice chemical technician, as evening student, Hannover,

***The Unemployed at the Labour Exchange,* 1932.** Photograph by Walter Ballhause.

1939-41; chemical technician and labour-leader, Vomag works, Plauen, 1941-44 (imprisoned by the Gestapo, in Hannover, 1933, and in Zwickau and Plauen, 1944-45); Mayor of Strassburg bei Plauen, 1945-47; Technical Chief and head of the Plamag printing machine works, Plauen, 1947-71. Photographic work of the 1930s rediscovered and exhibited, Hannover, 1971. Member, Sozialist Partei Deutschlands (later, Socialist Workers' Party), 1925; Arbeiterfotogilde, Hannover, 1930-31. **Recipient:** Honour Award for Photography, Kulturbund der DDR, 1976; Johannes R. Becher Silver Medal, Kulturbund der DDR, 1976; Honor Prize for Photography, Kulturbund der DDR, 1984. Executor's **Address:** Henni Ballhause, 08523 Plauen, Strasse der Deutschen, Einheit 4, Germany. **Died:** 8 July 1991

Individual Exhibitions:

1971   Vereinigung Verfolgtendes Naziregimes, Hannover, West
          Germany
1981   Staatliche Galerie Moritzburg, Halle, East Germany
          Kunstmuseum, Hannover, West Germany
1984   Galerie 75, Plauen, East Germany
          Freizeitheim, Hannover-Linden, West Germany
          Sorbisches Institut für Lehrerbildung, Sorbitz, East Germany
          Otto-Nagel-Haus, East Berlin
1986   Kulturbund Galerie, Plauen, East Germany
          Menschen an meiner Seite, at the *Riesaer Fototage 86,* Riesa,
          East Germany
          Maryland University, College Park

1988   Witkin-Galerie, N.Y.
1992   Städt. Galerie, Leipzig

Selected Group Exhibitions:

1931   *Arbeiterfotogilde-Ausstellung,* Kunstlerhaus, Hannover,
          Germany
1973   *Vereinigung Verfolgtendes Naziregimes-Ausstellung,* Hannover
          (toured Germany)
1977   *Medium Fotografie,* Staatliche Galerie Moritzburg, Halle, East
          Germany
1979   *DDR-Fotoausstellung,* Cologne, West Germany
1980   *Fotografie der 20er Jahre,* Informationszentrum, Leipzig, East
          Germany
1981   *Dokumentarfotografien,* Historisches Museum, Hannover, West
          Germany
1983   *Photographien aus zehn Landern in Dresdner Sammlungen,*
          Kupferstichkabinett, Dresden, East Germany
1984   *Arbeiter-Festspiele,* East Germany

Collections:

Kupferstichkabinett, Dresden, Germany; Deutsche Fotothek, Sachsische Landesbibliothek, Dresden, Germany; Fotokinoverlag, Leipzig, Germany; Gesellschaft fur Fotografie—Zentralverband, Berlin; Berliner Verlag, Berlin:

FDGB Bundesvorstand, Berlin; Historisches Museum, Hannover, Germany; Deutsches Historisches Museum, Berlin.

Publications:

By BALLHAUSE: Books—*Uberflussige Menschen,* with text by J. R. Becher and H. Strauss, Leipzig 1981, as *Zwischen Weimar und Hitler: Sozialdokumentarische Fotografie um 1930,* with introduction by Rudolph Fries, Munich 1981; *Licht und Schatten der 30er Jahre,* Munich 1985.

On BALLHAUSE: Books—*Medium Fotografie,* edited by Andreas Huneke, Gerhard Ihrke, Alfred Neumann and Ullrich Wallenburg, Leipzig 1979; *Arbeiterfotografie,* Amsterdam and West Berlin 1979; *Die Arbeiter,* edited by Wolfgang Ruppert, Munich 1979; *Fotografie im Klassenkampf* by Erich Rinka, Leipzig 1981; *Photographien aus zehn Landern in Dresdner Sammlungen,* exhibition catalogue, by Werner Schmidt and Hans-Ulrich Lehmann, Dresden 1983; *Als die Faschisten an die Macht kamen* by Helga Gotschlich, East Berlin 1983; *Bilder aus dunkler Zeit* by Wera and Claus Kuchenmeister, East Berlin 1983; *A World History of Photography,* Abbeville Press, New York 1984; *Unser Jahrhundert in Wort, Bild und Tondie 30er Jahre,* Bertelsmann Lexikothek, 1989; *The Third Reich: Storming to Power* and *The New Order,* Time-Life Books Inc, USA 1989. **Articles**—"Das soziale Foto" in *Volkswillen* (Hannover), August 1930; "Einer von Millionen" in *Kuckdruck* (Vienna), no. 43. 1932; "Zeichen der Krise" in *Fotografie* (Leipzig), no. 10, 1973; "Chronist seiner Zeit" in *Neue Berliner Illustrierte* (East Berlin), May 1981; "Der Arbeiter-Fotograf Walter Ballhause" in *Magazin* (East Berlin), May 1981; "Walter Ballhause—Fotografie 1930-33" in *Galeriespiegel Roter Turm* (Halle), April/May 1981; "Walter Ballhause—1930" in *Sovetskoye Foto* (Moscow), no. 6, 1981; "Ein Arbeiter-Fotograf sah seiner Zeit ins Gesicht" in *Tribuhne* (East Berlin), no. 11, 1981; "Uberflussige Menschen" in *Die Wahrheit* (West Berlin), January 1982; "Der Arbeiter-Fotograf Walter Ballhause" in *Die Horen* (Hannover), no. 126, 1982; "Ein Arbeitsloser registriert die Not seiner Zeit" in *Hannoversche Allgemeine Zeitung* (Hannover), 14/15 November 1983; "Ein Gesprache mit Walter Ballhause" in *Medium* (Frankfurt-am-Main), no. 11/12, 1983; "Klassenauge oder die Macht der Kamera als Waffe" in *Hamburger Rundschau* (Hamburg), 3 April 1986. **Film**—*Einer von Millionen,* Defa-Dokumentarfilm, 1982.

*   *   *

Figures of quite contrasting destinies appear in the development of creative photography: some began early in life and continued through a long career; others have a late start, but are still able to produce a remarkable oeuvre. Walter Ballhause made his unique contribution to social documentary photography as a youth in the space of only a few years. His photographic career was curtailed in 1933 as a result of Germany's political situation in which anyone opposed to the Nazis found his activities considerably limited.

The particular feature of social documentary photography in the Weimar Republic was that its participants were drawn from the working-classes—by contrast with the United States or Britain where photographers were mainly intellectuals or graduates of universities. Ballhause was typical of the German approach. Born in 1911, he belonged to the youngest generation of the *Arbeiter-Fotograf* movement, mainly the sons and daughters of workers who naturally chose as their subject those events most closely connected with working-class life. Despite his youth (he was only twenty years old at the time) he became one of the best documentary photographers of the group. His previous experience as a labourer gave him a sharp insight into the lives of the German poor, and he photographed them with a directness untouched by any aesthetic motives that might have overshadowed the real social message. Ballhause's natural visual sense gave these unsentimental images a documentary and photographic power of their own.

Wounded soldiers, whom Ballhause had seen during his early childhood in the first World War, made a profound impression, and these images of pain were not forgotten when he took up the camera to focus on war invalids begging for alms on Hannover's streets. The streets of the city and its suburbs generally provided him with his subjects: children playing on the pavements, gangs of road-labourers, store assistants, and women returning from a depression-economy shopping trip. More optimistically, Ballhause took part in youth activities, photographing the daily life of Summer camps—the games, sports, as well as kitchen work—all images that signified his trust in the future of the new generation.

Fairly early in his photographic work Ballhause discovered a preference for the Leica—a camera which was remarkably handy for capturing sudden events, and was able to encompass a whole sequence of events thanks to the reserve of 36 shots on its miniature film.

After 1933, Ballhause was forced to change address and identity to avoid Nazi persecution; he was finally captured by the Gestapo in 1944, and only survived due to the destruction of compromising evidence by the air-raids on Dresden. From the end of World War II, he became active in industry, and even in local civic life, and thus his photographic career became a closed chapter. In 1981, a selection of his best photos were gathered in a book which, after half a century, is still impressive for its remarkable vision.

—Petr Tausk

BALTAUSS, Richard.

Nationality: French. **Born:** Chelles-sur-Marne, 18 November 1946. **Education:** Studied at the School of Fine Arts, Marseilles, 1963-65; Ecole de Choreographie, Athens, 1965-67; Ecole d'Art, Marseilles, 1967-69; Ecole des Beaux-Arts, Paris, 1969-71. **Military Service:** Served in the French Army. **Career:** Freelance photographer, working for *Le Monde,* etc., Paris, since 1969. **Recipient:** Prix de la Ville de Paris, 1980; City of Paris Photography Grant, 1985. **Agent:** Galerie Delpire, 13 rue de l'Abbaye, 75006 Paris, France. **Address:** 100 rue d'Amsterdam, 75009 Paris, France.

Individual Exhibitions:

1979	Galerie Delpire, Paris
1982	*Portraits,* Galerie Delpire, Paris (with Frederic Cantor)
1986	*Portrait d'un joueur de tennis,* at *Mois de la Photo,* Musée d'Art Moderne, Paris

Selected Group Exhibitions:

1976	*From the Face to the Mental Model,* Galerie FIAP, Paris
1978	*Portraits,* French Institute, Naples
1980	*Creatis,* Galerie FNAC, Strasbourg, France
	The Month of Photography in Paris, 16th District Hall, Paris
1981	*Faces of Photography: Photography of Faces,* Centre Culturel de Yonnes, Auxerre, France
1983	*Portraits/Visages,* Association Française d'Action Artistique, Paris (toured Europe)
1987	*Un Si Grand Age,* (on tour) Centre National de la Photographie
1989	Expo Centre Culturel de la Communauté Française, Brussels Maison de la Culture d'Amiens
1990	Piazza Beaubourg, Paris

Collections:

Bibliothèque Nationale, Paris; Centre Audiovisuel, Paris; Museum of Modern Art, New York.

Happy Birthday, **1988.** Photograph ©Richard Baltauss.

Publications:

By BALTAUSS: Books—*Hotel d'Amérique,* Paris 1976; *Interior Portraits,* Paris 1979; *Cliches,* with preface by Serge Daney (Brussels) 1988. **Article**—"Photographic Experience" in *Education 2000* (Paris), October 1980.

On BALTAUSS: Books—*La Photographie a la Croisee des Chemins* by Pierre Borhan, 1990. **Articles**—"Portraits by Richard Baltauss" by Christian Caujolle in *Liberation* (Paris), 15 May 1979; "Richard Baltauss: Interiors" by Michel Nuridsany in *Le Figaro* (Paris), May 1979; "Inventory by Richard Baltauss" by Hervé Guibert in *Le Monde* (Paris), June 1979; "Hotel of America by Richard Baltauss" by Sophie Ristelhueber in *Le Matin* (Paris), June 1979; "We Have Seen . . . " in *Le Photographe* (Paris), June 1979; "Hotel of America" by O.H. in *L'Express* (Paris), June 1979; "Photographic Experience" by J.M. Dunoyer in *Le Monde* (Paris), February 1981; "Richard Baltause: Portfolio" in *Cliches* (Brussels), May 1986; Patrick Rogers in *Le Monde,* 1987.

*

The consumer instinct nurtured by our society gives birth to individualism and the cult of personality. This, in its turn, brings about a fresh approach to the environment and a new consciousness of control and yet isolation from which comes the success of the created image: a need to mythicize daily life.

Photography, therefore, becomes a means of immediate expression, a way of reappropriating the environment.

In the depths of the individual we find the universal; that which is the most intimate becomes public; subjectivity is transformed into a product, necessitating an advertising "image" of that which is most private.

It is the creation of another dimension which interests me, the formation of a link between that which is photographed and that which appears in the final result. There is a time lapse between the two that is put into a concrete form by the photograph.

It is to live the present of an experience as the past of a future; for example, I look at a door knob and imagine it at a later time. The act of projecting into the future allows me to grasp that forms have an emotional, sensitive power, resulting from a conjunction of energies and forces which indicate their epoch, and it is this experience, this emotion, which interests me as an image-maker.

—Richard Baltauss

* * *

Perhaps Richard Baltauss' first one-man exhibition should have been entitled *Night and Day.*

It began with wide-angle portraits of the tenants of the Hôtel d'Amérique where for many years Baltauss worked as night watchman. Those people who joined in the game posed one by one in front of a littered table in the lobby. In a hotel where people return only to sleep, everything happens at night: people pass by and meet the photographer loyally at his job. The tenants have no home; they come from an anonymous night, like apparitions. The images are dynamic, worth studying carefully so that their accumulated power can be slowly revealed: Baltauss is heir to the great portraitists of the 19th century who knew how to obtain the collaboration of their models. As if to acknowledge this heritage, he chooses a tinted and faded paper—an image of time past, the ephemeral, the intensity retained in the flow of things.

The solitary faces bring into focus the depth of space and time; the sameness of the decor helps to reveal them. The place begins to move, slowly transformed but always the same. The photograph is transcience at a standstill: a standstill framed in the anonymous movement of a body without fixed identity, without name, without social function. The photographs show without describing.

But this exhibition was also a montage, for it proceeded to a newer series, portraits again, but now with a background. Baltauss had photographed his friends in their daily lives, in their homes. The images lose in intensity, they no longer focus on the figure/face; the people begin to fade; the scene places them, describes them; the images set up a silent sociology. Now everything happens by day. Couples, children—solitude too, but sustained by communal life. In a hotel people live by night, at home by day. There are no couples in the hotel lobby. Above, as it were, in rooms, people form into couples, families, groups, with their furniture, their objects.

Except as they might meet at the exhibition itself, the people from above have probably never met the people from below—but the observer travels through a total space connecting the anonymity of the hotel with the domestic interiors. Private-public, high-low, black-white, full-empty, day-night: Baltauss has found an effective syntax.

Now, Baltauss works differently: models come to pose for the photographer, always within the same framework, with the same lighting, the same setting. It is no longer a question of a stop in a hotel lobby or of a portrait, somewhere, anywhere, "out of this world," everywhere and nowhere, in black-and-white, like an accelerated journey from the other side of the mirror, as if one was both photographer and model, moving in the image.

In the gallery Baltauss told a great story, enigmatic and secret, without literary intent. He strolled through his memory between the hotel and his friends' apartments, night watchman and chronicler of space.

—Jean-François Chevrier

BALTERMANS, Dmitri.

Nationality: Russian. **Born:** Moscow in July 1912. **Education:** Studied mathematics at the University of Moscow, 1928-33; self-taught in photography. **Career:** Worked as a mathematician in Moscow, 1934-38. Photographer from 1936. Photo-Reporter, with the Red Army, for *Izvestia* and *Na Razgrom varaga* newspapers, 1940-45. Chief Press Photographer, *Ogonjok* magazine, Moscow, since 1945. **Recipient:** Second Prize, *World Exhibition of Photography,* Hamburg, 1965. Merited Worker in Culture of the U.S.S.R., 1970. **Address:** Bolshaia Dorogomilovskaia nr. 4, Flat 81, 121059 Moscow, Russia.

Individual Exhibitions:

1972	*Unsteady Reporter,* Foma Gallery, Prague Galerie Profil, Bratislava, Czechoslovakia
1973	House of Art, Brno, Czeckoslovakia
1975	Valokuvamuseon, Helsinki (toured Finland, 1976)
1983	Citizens Exchange Council, New York Soho Photo Gallery, New York
1989	Knopio, Finland
1990	G Ray Hawkins Gallery, Santa Monica, California
	Comptoir de la Photographie, Paris
1992	*War and Peace,* International Center of Photography, New York

Selected Group Exhibitions:

1965	*World Exhibition of Photography: What Is Man?,* Pressehaus Stern, Hamburg (and world tour)
1968	*2nd World Exhibition of Photography: Woman,* Pressehaus Stern, Hamburg (and world tour)
1974	*Sowjetische Kriegsreportage,* Galerie Profile, Bratislava, Czeckoslovakia
1975	*Soviet War Reportage 1941-45,* House of Soviet Science and Culture, Prague
1977	*The Russian War,* International Center of Photography, New York
1978	*The Russian War,* Side Gallery, Newcastle upon Tyne, England
1989	Perpignan, France
1994	G Ray Hawkins Gallery, Santa Monica, California

Collections:

Fotografische Kammergalerie Profil, Bratislava, Czechoslovakia; Tatyana Baltermans, Moscow; G Ray Hawkins Gallery, Santa Monica, California; Paul Harbaugh, Denver, Colorado.

Publications:

By BALTERMANS: Books—*Meeting with Tschikotka,* Moscow 1971; *Dmitri Baltermans: Selected Photographs,* with an introduction by Vasilij Peskov, Moscow 1977.

On BALTERMANS: Books—*World Exhibition of Photography,* exhibition catalogue, edited by Karl Pawek, Hamburg 1965; *Liberation,* edited by Mikhail Trakhman, Boris Polevoi and Konstantin Simonov, Moscow 1974; *Fotografovali Valku,* edited by Daniela Mrázková and Vladimír Remeš, Prague 1975, as *The Russian War,* with introduction by Harrison Salisbury, New York 1977, as *The Russian War 1941-45,* with an introduction by A.J.P. Taylor, London 1978; *Geschichte der Fotografie im 20. Jahrhundert/Photography in the 20th Century* by Petr Tausk, Cologne 1977, London 1980; *The Camera at War* by Jorge Lewinski, London 1979; *Von Moskau nach Berlin* by Danièla Mrázková and Vladimìr Remeš, with an introduction by Heinrich Böll, Munich 1979; *Bilder vom Krieg* by Rainer Fabian and Hans-Christian Adam, Hamburg, 1983, as *Images of War: 130 Years of War Photography,* London 1985. **Articles**—"Dmitry Baltermans: Photographs from World War II" in *Creative Camera* (London), March 1975; "A Cry of Anguish from

Grief, **1942.** Photograph by Dmitri Baltermans.

Wartime Russia'' in *Photography Year 1976,* by the Time-Life editors, New York 1976; ''Il Soldato Fotografo'' in *Fotografia Italiana* (Milan), April 1976; ''The Eye of a Nation,'' *Life,* July 1992; ''Baltermans, Hommage au geant de la photo Sovietique'' in *Photo, 1989.*

*   *   *

For all of the centuries that art has been in existence as the creative impulse of humanity, no artist, medium, or movement—just as no politician, religion, or law—has been Herculean enough to curb the savage impulse of the world for war. One can imagine that many would have anticipated such a task for photography, especially when the medium was first discovered in 1839. Gettysburg, Dachau, or Hiroshima, however, the dumb machine, of course, could only bring back the report. Talbot's ''pencil of nature'' was ultimately no mightier, no more efficacious in such matters than the pen of a poet. It's no wonder that after a century and a half of photographs of mangled bodies, bombed-out churches, and point-blank assassinations, critics have begun to suspect the medium entirely, charging that counteractive influences are far more operative. By inundating our emotional thresholds with repetitive terror, so the accusation goes, the outrage violent images once provoked becomes desensitized and diminished. ''Photographs shock insofar as they show something novel,'' writes Susan Sontag. ''Unfortunately, the ante keeps getting raised—partly through the very proliferation of such images of horror.'' Notwithstanding the legitimacy of such scoldings, one must consider the hypothetical disaster inherent in the opposing argument. What if photography had not been discovered or perfected? What if the grim reality of war—of

clean-sweeping nuclear devastation—lacked the unequivocal confirmation of the photographic record? One shudders at the vision of world-wide destruction civilization might already have inflicted upon itself.

Certainly history must credit those front-line photographers, like the internationally-renowned Russian photojournalist Dmitri Baltermans, for having understood the dilemma before the fact. Balterman's World War II trench reportage on the Russian front restrains the enervating impact of physiological voyeurism by incorporating a psychological involvement for the viewer. His photographs, at their very best, are dramas in human exigency. In the bitter aftermath scene titled *Grief* (1942), one cannot look and expect to leave unaffected. To induce our emotional participation, Baltermans photographs a mud-field full of fresh corpses through the grief and shock of the survivors who have come to measure the loss. The survivors are the people left alive, like us, to deal with the consequences. In another photograph, titled *Tchaikovsky, Germany, 1945,* one half of a living room, perhaps a German household, has been blown to pieces. The massive opening, through which a smoky war-zone landscape can be seen, admits bursts of daylight into what normally might have been a windowless room. Along the one unbroken wall, where a picture-plate still hangs and a vase of flowers sits fresh at attention, a group of war-weary Russian soldiers are gathered about a piano. One of them, having just wiped the plaster dust off the keys, begins to play. No one particularly gives a damn.

Still another persuasive indictment of war was made by Baltermans straight out of the trenches in 1941. Baltermans has focused his camera on several soldiers firing off at an unseen enemy; the soldiers are at the bottom of the picture. Above them, racing at blinding speed, in fragments of coats, boots, and unfurled bayonets, soldiers leap across the ditch. It is an irrevocable "charge" (as the image is titled)—for some of the troops, the final ballet of the battle.

Action or aftermath, it really doesn't matter whose side you're on. For Dmitri Baltermans—a die-hard pacifist before, during and after the war—such an understanding must become an international, world-wide prerequisite. Otherwise, the ultimate—the man-made destruction of mankind—may become the inevitable.

—Arno Rafael Minkkinen

BALTZ, Lewis.

Nationality: American. **Born:** Newport Beach, California, 12 September 1945. **Education:** the San Francisco Art Institute, 1967-69, B.F.A. 1969; Claremont Graduate School, California, 1969-71, M.F.A. 1971. **Family:** Married Mary Ann Rayner in 1974; daughter: Monica. **Career:** Freelance photographer, in California, since 1970. Part-time Instructor, Pomona College, Claremont, 1970-72, and California Institute of the Arts, Valencia, 1972; Visiting Lecturer in Art, University of California, Davis, 1981; Regent's Visitor in Art, University of California, Santa Cruz, 1982; Visiting Artist, Rhode Island School of Design, Providence, 1983; Visiting Associate Professor of Art, University of California, Riverside and Santa Cruz, and University of Victoria, British Columbia, 1984. Member of the Visiting Committee, International Museum of Photography, George Eastman House, Rochester, New York, 1978-81. **Recipient:** National Endowment for the Arts Fellowship in Photography, 1973, 1977; Guggenheim Fellowship, 1977; U.S./U.K. Bicentennial Exchange Fellowship, 1980; Charles Pratt Memorial Award, 1991. **Agents:** Castelli Uptown, 4 East 77th Street, New York, New York 10021; Galerie Michele Chomette, 24 rue Beaubourg, 75003 Paris; and Eaton/Shoen Gallery, 315 Sutter Street, San Francisco, California 94104. **Address:** Post Office Box 42, Sausalito, California 94966, U.S.A.

Individual Exhibitions:

1970	Pomona College, Claremont, California
1971	Castelli Graphics, New York
1972	International Museum of Photography, at George Eastman House, Rochester, New York
1973	Castelli Graphics, New York
1974	Corcoran Gallery of Art, Washington, D.C.
	Jefferson Place Gallery, Washington, D.C.
1975	Leo Castelli Gallery, New York
	Philadelphia College of Art
	Jack Glenn Gallery, Corona del Mar, California
	University of New Mexico, Albuquerque
1976	Galerie December, Dusseldorf
	Corcoran Gallery of Art, Washington, D.C.
	Lunn Gallery/Graphics International, Washington, D.C.
	Baltimore Museum of Art
	La Jolla Museum of Art, California
	Museum of Fine Arts, Houston
1977	Grapestake Gallery, San Francisco
	University of Nebraska, Lincoln
	Ohio University, Athens (with De Lappa and Syl Labrot)
1978	Yarlow-Salzman Gallery, Toronto
	Grapestake Gallery, San Francisco
	University of Nevada, Reno
	Susan Spiritus Gallery, Newport Beach, California
	College of Marin, Kentfield, California
1979	University of Manitoba, Winnipeg
	Nova Scotia College of Art and Design, Halifax
	3 Americans, Moderna Museet, Stockholm (with Mark Cohen and Eve Sonneman; travelled to Alborg Kunstmuseum, Denmark; Kunstpavillionen, Esbjerg, Denmark; Tranegarden,

	Gentofte, Copenhagen; and Henie-Onstad Museum, Oslo, 1980)
1980	MoMing Center for the Arts, Chicago
	Galerie Fiolet, Amsterdam
	Werkstatt für Photographie, Berlin
1981	Castelli Graphics, New York
	San Francisco Museum of Modern Art
	Otis-Parsons Art Institute, Los Angeles
	Light, Los Angeles
1983	Castelli Graphics, New York
	Rhode Island School of Design, Providence
1984	University of California, Berkeley
	University of Victoria, British Columbia
1985	Castelli Uptown, New York
	Victoria and Albert Museum, London
	Fotografiska Museet, Stockholm (with Mikael Levin)
	Dallas Public Library, Texas
	Galerie Michele Chomette, Paris
	Werkstatt für Photographie, West Berlin
	University of New Mexico, Albuquerque
1986	Eaton/Shoen Gallery, San Francisco
	State Historical Society, Reno, Nevada
	University of Arkansas, Little Rock
1987	Galerie Espace l'Orient, France
1988	Galerie Michele Chomette, Paris
	City Museum, Higashikawa-ku, Japan
1989	Castelli Graphics, New York
	Gallery Min, Tokyo
1990	New York Institute for Contemporary Art
1991	Des Moines Art Center
	Galerie DB-S, Antwerp
1992	Cintre Pompidou, Paris
	Stedelijk Museum, Amsterdam
	Los Angeles County Museum of Art
	Kawasaki City Museum, Japan

Selected Group Exhibitions:

1975	*14 American Photographers,* Baltimore Museum of Art (travelled to the Newport Harbor Art Museum, Newport Beach, California, and La Jolla Museum of Contemporary Art, California, 1975; Walker Art Center, Minneapolis, and Fort Worth Art Museum, Texas, 1976)
	New Topographics, International Museum of Photography, at George Eastman House, Rochester, New York (travelled to the Otis Art Institute, Los Angeles, and Princeton University Art Museum, New Jersey, 1976)
1978	*Mirrors and Windows: American Photography since 1960,* Museum of Modern Art, New York (toured the United States, 1978-80)
1979	*American Images,* Corcoran Gallery of Art, Washington, D.C. (travelled to the International Center of Photography, New York; Museum of Fine Arts, Houston; Minneapolis Institute of Arts; and Indianapolis Museum of Art, 1980; American Academy, Rome, 1981)
1980	*The Imaginary Photo Museum,* Kunsthalle, Cologne
1982	*Slices of Time,* Oakland Art Museum, California (travelled to the Security Pacific National Bank, Los Angeles)
1984	*Photography in California 1945-80,* San Francisco Museum of Modern Art (travelled to the Akron Art Museum, Ohio; Corcoran Gallery, Washington, D.C.; Los Angeles Municipal Art Gallery; Cornell University, Ithaca, New York; High Museum of Art, Atlanta, Georgia; Museum Folkwang, Essen; Centre Georges Pompidou, Paris; Museum of Photographic Art, San Diego, California)
1985	*American Images,* Barbican Art Gallery, London (toured Britain)
1986	*The Real Big Picture,* Queens Museum, New York
1987	*Photography and Art 1946-86,* Los Angeles County Museum of Art

Collections:

Museum of Modern Art, New York; International Museum of Photography, George Eastman House, Rochester, New York; Museum of Fine Arts, Boston; Philadelphia Museum of Art; Corcoran Gallery of Art, Washington, D.C.; Art Institute of Chicago; Museum of Fine Arts, Houston; San Francisco Museum of Modern Art; Bibliothèque Nationale, Paris; National Gallery of Australia, Canberra.

Publications:

By BALTZ: Books of photographs—*The New Industrial Parks Near Irvine, California,* New York 1975; *Maryland,* edited by Jane Livingston, Washington, D.C. 1976; *Nevada,* New York 1978; *Park City,* with text by Gus Blaisdell, New York 1980; *San Quentin Point,* with essay by Mark Haworth-Booth, New York and West Berlin 1986; *Candlestick Point,* with essay by Gus Blaisdell, Tokyo 1989; *Lewis Baltz. 5 Projects,* Amsterdam 1992; *Ronde de Nuit* with Olivier Boissiere, Paris 1992. **Other books**—*Contemporary American Photographic Works,* editor, with introduction by John Upton, Houston 1977. **Articles**—"Notes on Recent Industrial Developments in Southern California," with William Jenkins, in *Image* (Rochester, New York), no. 4, 1974; "The New West" in *Art in America* (New York), March/April 1975; "Konsumterror: Notes on Late Industrial Alienation" in *Aperture* (Millerton, New York), Fall 1984; "Robert Adams—Our Lives and Our Children" in *Artspace* (Albuquerque), Fall 1984; "Landscape Problems: Edward Weston—California Landscapes" in *Aperture* (Millerton, New York), Spring 1985.

On BALTZ: Books—*Exposing: Photographic Definitions,* exhibition catalogue, with introduction by Robert Mautner, Los Angeles 1976; *Industry and the Photographic Image,* edited by F. Jack Hurley, New York 1980; *The Imaginary Photo Museum* by Helmut Gernsheim, Renate and L. Fritz Gruber and others, Cologne 1981, London 1982; *Photography in California 1945-1980* by Louise Katzman, San Francisco 1984; *Photography and Art 1946-86,* exhibition catalogue, by Andy Grundberg and Kathleen Gauss, Los Angeles 1987. **Articles**—"Los Angeles" by Peter Plagens in *Artforum* (New York), October 1971; "Latent Image" by A.D. Coleman in the *Village Voice* (New York), 18 January 1972; "Route 66 Revisited: New Landscape Photography" by Carter Ratcliff in *Art in America* (New York), January/February 1976; "The Anti-Photographers" by Nancy Foote in *Artforum* (New York), September 1976; "Contemporary American Photography" by Leo Rubenfein in *Creative Camera* (London), 1976; "Lewis Baltz's Formalism" by Joan Murray in *Artweek* (Oakland, California), 27 August 1977; "San Francisco" by Hal Fischer in *Artforum* (New York), December 1978; "Nevada" by Sally Eauclaire in *Afterimage* (Rochester, New York), April 1980; "Full Photographs of Barren U.S. Scenes" by David Elliott in the *Sun-Times* (Chicago), 25 May 1980; "Lewis Baltz: Irvine, Nevada, Park City Portfolios" by Deborah Bright in *New Art Examiner* (Chicago), June 1980; "Lewis Baltz: Park City oder Landscape as Real-Estate" by Harald Strobl in *Camera Austria* (Graz), December 1981; "The Camera in America" by Marina Vaizey in the *Sunday Times* (London), 12 May 1985; "Lewis Baltz Sceptical Landscapes at the V & A" by William Bishop in *British Journal of Photography* (London), 7 June 1985; "Lewis Baltz" by Michael Schmidt in *Fotoszene* (Frankfurt), September 1985.

* * *

Lewis Baltz came to prominence in the mid 1970s as one of a loose grouping of photographers gathered together in the George Eastman House exhibition *New Topographics*. The rubric 'new topographics' indicates a link with the 'old topographics', those documentary landscape photographers of the old West, such as Timothy O'Sullivan, whose work was marked by its perceived straightforwardness, lack of artifice and apparent objectivity. The New Topographers, who owed at least as much to Walker Evans as to any nineteenth century pioneers, had an oft-quoted maxim—'non-judgemental'—which indicated not that they were without a point of view but that it was subsumed within a desire to let the facts themselves sing, rather than the agent who divined those facts.

Baltz, with his cool, reticent, elevational images of industrial 'sheds' near Irvine, California, was regarded immediately as the purist, or most extreme of the group. It was an impression hardly dispelled by his next major body of work, *Park City,* a record of a tract housing project in Utah that appeared to have all the emotional qualities of an estate agent's display board.

In actuality, there was a lot going on in Baltz's work. It is supported by a broad intellectual framework and a complex web of conceptualisation that places him not only within the mainstream of American photography, but close to various issues in contemporary art. The very luminosity and lucidity of his images, their precise, frontal, mensurative qualities, place him in a line of succession from the Luminist painting school of the nineteenth century and the early limner tradition, both of which were linked with the 'old topographers'. More importantly, such connections place Baltz firmly within the profoundly conceptual strain which characterises much American art. So much American painting has stressed the primacy and integrity of the object, and a mode of intense realism whereby things themselves are seen to radiate a form of impersonal expressionism.

With such an artisitc pedigree, Baltz's links with European conceptual photography seem natural and inevitable. His relation to the Bechers (the only Europeans, interestingly, in *New Topographics*) is obvious, but connections to such more obviously expressive Europeans like Michael Schmidt also become clear when one examines a further tendency of American painting and photography which can be discerned in Baltz and the other New Topographers—Ralph Waldo Emerson's notion of the artist as a vehicle for transcendence, a 'transparent eyeball'.

In recent years many of Baltz's artistic cohorts, including Robert Adas, Frank Gohlke and John Gossage, have been more inclined to allow at least a glimpse of their hearts upon their professional sleeves, and without compromising the integrity of their quietistic style, allow encoded environmental concerns to permeate their work. Although they retain their poise and self-contained air, later projects of Baltz, while venturing further than ever into the rarified realm of fine art, are touched with ever increasing allusions of elemental disquiet. Beginning with *San Quentin Point*—a series shot on a waste ground near San Francisco in the late eighties—Baltz has been in more effusive mood, his metaphors ranging from troubling memories of childhood to portents of the Apocolypse. He continues, as ever, to make exemplary, quietly desperate landscapes. He remains at the vanguard of contempororary art practice.

—Gerry Badger

BAMGBOYE, Oladele Ajiboye.

Nationality: Nigerian and British citizen. **Born:** Odo-Eku, Nigeria, 15 October 1963. Emigrated to Scotland, 1976; lived and worked in Canada, 1989, 1991-92; worked in Germany, 1990 and 1992. **Education:** Attended schools in Nigeria and Glasgow; studied chemical and process engineering, Strathclyde University, Glasgow, 1981-85, B.Sc. (Hons) 1985; self-taught in photography, since 1985. **Career:** Worked in technical photo sales, 1986-88; Committee Member and Joint-Founder, Glasgow Photography Group Ltd, 1987; Joint-Founder, Street Level Gallery, Glasgow, 1988; Co-Founder, with Matthew Dalziel, of the Scottish multi-disciplinary organisation Image and Installation, 1989; Committee Member, Union of Scottish Arts Workers, 1991; Photography Lecturer, Cardonald College, Glasgow, 1991-92; Photography Lecturer, Blake College of Art, London, 1993-95. **Residencies:** Atelier Bomba Colori, Berlin, 1990; Art Studio Summer Residency, Banff Centre for the Arts, Banff, Canada, 1992; Studio Residency, Künstlerhaus Bethanien, Berlin, 1992-93, 1994. **Address:** Top Floor Flat, Holy Trinity Church Hall, 4A Beechwood Road, London E8 3DY, England.

Individual Exhibitions:

1985	Glasgow School of Art, Glasgow
1987	*A Cry for Africa,* Corridor Gallery, Glenrothes, Scotland
	Third Eye Centre, Glasgow
1992-93	*Five Big Images,* Kiek in de Kok Gallery, Tallinn, Estonia, Baltic States
1995	Künstlerhaus Bethanien, Berlin, Germany

Selected Group Exhibitions:

1986   Transmission Gallery, Glasgow
        Nine Photographers at the Glasgow Print Studios, Glasgow
          Print Studios
1987   *New Light in Scottish Photography,* Stills Gallery, Edinburgh
        Images of Glasgow, Third Eye Centre International Touring
          Show (travelled to Dalian, China; Nuremberg, Germany;
          Rostov-on-Don, CIS; and Turin, Italy, 1987-90)
1988   *Fruitmarket Open,* Fruitmarket Gallery, Edinburgh
1989   *Anima Mundi: Still Life in Britain,* Stills Gallery,
        Edinburgh (and Canadian tour, 1989-92)
        Through Photography, Third Eye Centre, Glasgow (travelled to
          the Crawfords Arts Centre, St Andrews, Scotland)
        Smith Biennial, SmithArt Gallery and Museum, Stirling
        Award for Young European Photographers, Frankfurter
          Kunstverein, Frankfurt, Germany
1991   *Culturally (Dis)placed: An Investigation of Ethnology through*
          Contemporary Photography, Burnaby Art Gallery,
          Vancouver, Canada
        De Quelques Troubles d'Identité de la Photographie
          Contemporaine, Dazibao Centre de Photographies Actuelles,
          Montreal, Canada
1992   *Shifting Borders,* Laing Art Gallery, Newcastle-upon-Tyne
        (and international tour)
        Some European Outlooks, Saaremaa Museum, Kuressaare,
          Estonia, Baltic States
1993   *Exposure,* Centre for Contemporary Arts, Glasgow
1994   *Whitechapel Open,* Whitechapel Art Gallery, London
1995   *Das breite Bild,* Frankfurter Kunstverein, Frankfurt, Germany

Collections:

The Scottish Arts Council, Edinburgh

Publications:

By BAMGBOYE: Articles—"Black Male Sexuality" in *Video Out Magazine,* October 1991; artist statement and profile in *Alba Visual Arts Magazine,* No. 4, 1992; "Banff, Benin, Berlin" in *Harbour Magazine* (Montreal), Vol. 2, No. 3.

On BAMGBOYE: Articles—in *Revue de l'Art Actuelle* (Montreal), 1989; in *Photo Selection* (Montreal), 1989; in *Perspektief* (Netherlands), No. 38, 1990; in *Parachute Art Contemporaine* (Montreal), No. 57, 1990; in *Variant Magazine* (Great Britain), No. 8, 1990; in *Artscribe International* (Great Britain), November/December 1990.

*

I emigrated to Scotland with my parents at an early age and continued to live there after they returned to Nigeria five years later. The vast majority of my earlier works were therefore concerned with my immediate environment and self-identity, especially in the total absence of black cultural appreciation.

It would be simplistic to consider my work as addressing only issues of black masculinity or sexuality, but rather as one which has arisen out of the cross-cultural experience that has been directly shaped by my experience and background. I concentrate on self-portraiture in order to give me total control over the image-making process, and ultimately to be directly responsible for the statements that I make in my work.

The sexual objectification of the black male in particular by mass culture is still commonplace, as is the dehumanising of black peoples and their culture as a whole. A significant focus of my work attempts to diffuse and address this unbalanced situation through the process of familiarisation. This is why I deliberately choose to photograph the male body in the most common situation—the domestic home. I choose to photograph the nude as a conscious decision, as this is the most natural state of the human body, stripped of all material wealth and status. I want to make imagery that exudes human warmth and beauty and reflects all levels of human existence and to make work that

focuses on the more sensitive and hidden nature of masculinity that transcends the accepted nature of masculine sexuality.

In London, I have the first opportunity ever to live in a black community since my emigration to Europe, and the effects of this are sure to filter into my new works. Exhibiting my work on African soil is my next ambition. In this way, I feel I will be able to offer the audience there, as I have done in Europe and North America, a unique and alternative perspective of living contemporary black culture.

—Oladele Ajiboye Bamgboye

*   *   *

Oladele Bamgboye, born in Nigeria, left his homeland at a very early age, and now lives in London following periods of study and work in Berlin and Canada. Since 1985 he has been active as an artist, employing photography, arguably the most important medium for self-portraiture, in mainly spatial contexts. Photography is traditionally a medium for self-definition, not only in an artistic but also in an everyday context. Oladele Bamgboye emphasizes the viewer's habitual reactions to the medium. But equally this medium is essentially a reflection of himself as both object and subject, the photographer as well as the photographed. The posed self-portraits involve observer and observed and are informative and enlightening in their expressive quality.

Bamgboye very often employs life-sized images and spatial juxtaposition. The fragmentation of the human body is not fetishistic in a pornographic way, portraying the human body as a sexually available object or as a focus for the myth of sexual superiority. It seeks rather to force the observer to make a judgement. In the documentary photographs of the "body art" movement or in the stills of the performance artists, Bamgboye presents his own body as a teaching aid for cultural and gender comparisons.

All his work deals with his own experience. Other experience that he might simulate is rejected. The authenticity of his work is not the only touchstone of his photography. The laudable aim of this artist is to search for sexual, erotic and cultural identity. All his work strives to achieve a new definition of the body's sexuality and to overcome the conflict between male and female.

"I am trying to understand and discover my own sexuality. I have no fixed standpoint as to what black male sexuality is. I am trying to move into a phase of trisexuality. Trisexuality is the next logical stage that acknowledges the strength, sexuality and spirituality of individual images." His photography serves to invoke an ideal with which we are already familiar from the "body art" movement of the late 1960s. For Oladele Bamgboye this invocation is concerned with questions of cultural identity, with the integration of his original Yoruba aesthetic into the context of western culture, and addresses the topical question of the cultural identity of an African in Europe.

—Peter Weiermair

BAR-AM, Micha.

Nationality: Israeli. **Born:** Berlin, Germany, 26 August 1930; emigrated to Israel, and grew up in Haifa. **Education:** Attended Israeli public schools until age 14. **Family:** Married Orna Zmirin in 1961; children: Barak and Nimrod. **Military Service:** Active in the Haganah, the pre-state underground, 1945-48; served in the Palmach Unit of the Infantry during the Israeli War of Independence, 1948-49. **Career:** Worked as a locksmith, mounted guard and youth instructor, Kibbutz Gesher-Haziv, Western Galilee, 1949-57; Photojournalist, *Bamahane* magazine, Israel, 1957-66; freelance photojournalist, Israeli newspapers, 1966-67. Photo-Correspondent in the Middle East for the *New York Times,* since 1968; Associate Member, Magnum Photos, Paris and New York, since 1968. Advisor on Photography to the Museum of Art, Tel Aviv, since 1977. **Agent:** G. Ray Hawkins Gallery, 9002 Melrose Avenue, Los Angeles, California 90069. **Address:** Post Office Box 923, Ramat Gan 52109, Israel.

Artillery Barrage Near Suez Canal, **October 1973.** Photograph ©Micha Bar-Am/Magnum Photos, Inc.

Individual Exhibitions:

1958   *First Harvest,* Journalists House, Tel Aviv
1960   *West African Diary,* Journalists House, Tel Aviv
1962   *At the Foothills of the Himalayas,* Journalists House, Tel Aviv
1974   Israel Museum, Jerusalem
        The October War, The Little Gallery, Jerusalem
1978   Neikrug Gallery, New York
1979   *Jews in Egypt, Spring '79,* Museum of the Jewish Diaspora,
            Tel Aviv
1981   *La Nacion: Spanish and Portugese Jews in the Caribbean,*
            Museum of the Jewish Diaspora, Tel Aviv
        Safescapes, White Gallery, Tel Aviv
        G. Ray Hawkins Gallery, Los Angeles

Selected Group Exhibitions:

1967   *Photographs from the June War,* Tel Aviv Museum
1968   *Israel: The Reality,* Jewish Museum, New York (toured the
            United States and Canada)
1973   *Jerusalem: City of Mankind,* Israel Museum, Jerusalem
            (travelled to the Jewish Museum, New York, then toured the
            United States)
1978   *Egypt: First Encounter,* Tel Aviv Museum
1981   *10 Photographers at the White Gallery,* White Gallery,
            Tel Aviv

Collections:

Israel Museum, Jerusalem; Tel Aviv Museum; Museum of the Jewish Diaspora, Tel Aviv; Bibliothèque Nationale, Paris; The Photographers' Gallery, London; International Center of Photography, New York.

Publications:

By BAR-AM: Books—*Across Sinai,* Tel Aviv 1957; *Castle of Shells and Sand,* Tel Aviv 1958; *I.D.F. at Eighteen,* as photo editor, Tel Aviv 1966; *Portrait of Israel,* with text by Moshe Brilliant, New York 1970; *The Israel Air Force,* Tel Aviv 1971; *Batchen: The Story of the Women's Corps of the Israeli Army,* Haifa 1971; *When God Judged: A Yom Kippur War Battle Report,* with text by Arnold Sherman, New York 1973; *Jerusalem: City of Mankind,* co-editor with Cornell Capa, New York 1974; *On Beauties, Men, and All the Rest,* with text by Tammar Avidar-Ettinger, Ramat Gan, Israel 1976; *Israel: Face of a People,* Ramat Gan, Israel 1978; *Sinai: The Great and Terrible Wilderness,* with text by Burton Bernstein, New York 1979; *Yoram and the Puppy,* with text by Michal Snunit, Vibatayyim, Israel 1981; *The Jordan,* also author, Giatayyim, Israel 1981.

On BAR-AM: Books—*Israel: The Reality,* edited by Cornell Capa, New York 1969; *Jerusalem: City of Mankind,* edited by Cornell Capa (with Bar-Am as co-editor), New York 1974; *Bilder vom Krieg* by Rainer Fabian and Hans-Christian Adam, Hamburg 1983, as *Images of War: 130 Years of War Photography,* London 1985. **Articles**—"Contact" by Yvette Benedek in *American Photographer* (New York), August 1981; "Images of War and

Peace'' by Suzanne Muchnic in the *Los Angeles Times,* August 1981; ''Micha Bar-Am'' by David Fahey in *Photo Bulletin* (Los Angeles), October 1981.

*   *   *

''Micha Bar-Am has played a very large part in putting Israel on the map in world photography and putting photography on the map in Israel,'' says one of his fellow-photographers. ''His photographs are more than just historical archives, though they are very important as such. They represent the spirit of his generation, the generation that established the State of Israel,'' says one of his co-workers at the Tel Aviv Museum.

Inherent to the spirit of that generation was the mating of an almost anarchic individual freedom to an overriding collective mission. It's a fair definition of the man himself. But it is also an attitude that lends itself well to photography where, as in the most memorable of Bar-Am's photographs, a complex political situation can be distilled into its reflection in one person's concentrated response—the emotions that pour through a woman as she greets a loved one who has returned from a heroic and dangerous mission when it too easily could have been otherwise; one man who looks to see if death is approaching when all others hide their heads from the shelling (all others except the photographer, of course, who keeps his sanity by continuously giving the world order and meaning through his camera. ''The clicking of the shutter becomes a kind of heartbeat,'' he has said).

Bar-Am's professional life is full of contradictions: How to be an objective photojournalist when you are a partisan in the struggle? How to be a museum curator when you are a working photojournalist and a photographer interested in your own aesthetic explorations? How to live with what fate has handed you—a reputation as a war photographer—when you consider that an accident of history that doesn't enter into your self-definition?

Micha Bar-Am is an intensely private person who is intensely committed to the state he has helped build. As it is not in his nature to be a politician, he has used photography to keep himself involved with events in Israel, politically as a photojournalist and culturally as one of the godfathers of photography-as-art.

—Bonnie Boxer

BARBEY, Bruno.

Nationality: French. **Born:** Morocco, 13 February 1941. **Family:** Married Caroline Thienot in 1975; children: Igor and Aurelie. **Agent:** Magnum Photos, 5 Passage Piver, 75011 Paris. **Address:** Square Val d'Osne, Saint Maurice 94410, Paris, France.

Individual Exhibitions:

1967	*Photos d'Italie,* Bibliothèque Nationale, Paris
1972	Galerie Nikon, Paris
1983	*Portrait d'Asie,* Galerie Olympus, Paris (and tour)
	Pologne, FNAC, Paris (and tour)
	Museum of Modern Art, Rome
1991	*Maroc,* Ville du Port, La Reunion
1992	*Maroc,* La Scene National de Bayonne, Bayonne, France

Selected Group Exhibitions:

1973	Photographers' Gallery, London
1976	Musée Réattu, Arles, France
1978	*European Colour Photography,* Photographers' Gallery, London
1979	*This is Magnum,* Tokyo, Japan
1981	*Image pour une page,* Arles, France (and travelling)
1982	*Terre de Guerre,* Galerie Magnum, Paris
1984	*Regard sur l'Art,* Palais de Tokyo, Paris (and travelling)
1985	Galerie Magnum, Paris
1990	*Regards croisés,* Institut du Monde Arabe, Paris

Publications:

By BARBEY: Books—*Naples,* with text by Philippe Dandy, Lausanne 1964; *Bugey,* with text by Suzanne Terrand, Lausanne 1965; *Camargue,* with text by Yuan Audouard, Lausanne 1965; *Kenya,* with text by Claudine La Haye, Lausanne 1966; *Portugal,* with text by Gilbert Ganne, Lausanne 1966; *Koweit,* with text by Meric Dobson, Lausanne 1967; *Ecosse,* with text by Paulette Decraene, Lausanne 1968; *Ceylan: Sri Lanka,* with text by J. Milley, E. Geais and A. Barret, Paris 1974; *L'Iran: Pérennité et Renaissance d'un Empire,* with text by Rene Maheu and Jean Boissel, Paris 1976 (English edition: *Iran: Rebirth of a Timeless Empire*); *Nigeria,* with text by Balogoun, Paris 1978; *Bombay,* with text by Dom Moraes, Amsterdam 1979; *Pologne,* with text by Bernard Guetta, Paris 1982 (English edition: *Poland,* with text by Czeslaw Milosz, London 1982); *Le Gabon,* Paris 1984; *Portugal,* with text by Stefan Reisner, Hamburg 1988. **Articles**—''La Mort à Naples: Essai photographique de Bruno Barbey'' in *Du,* No. 284, October 1964; ''La Galerie de terre d'images: Bruno Barbey: Les italiens'' in *Terre des Images,* No. 28, 17 June 1966; ''Bruno Barbey'' in *Camera,* November 1966; ''Bruno Barbey: Italiener'' in *Du,* No. 340, June 1969; ''Bruno Barbey: Une conception humaine du reportage'' in *Photo* (Paris), No. 31, April 1970; ''Mon Année 1971: Un jeune grand reporter français, Bruno Barbey à travers le monde'' in *Photo* (Paris), No. 52, January 1972; ''Barbey et Shinoyama: Notre carnaval de Rio'' in *Photo* (Paris), No. 80, May 1974; ''Bruno Barbey'' in *Photocinéma Magazine,* November 1975; ''Le Brésil de Barbey'' in *Photo* (Paris), No. 97, October 1975; ''Pushkar'' in *Grands Reportages,* No. 1, May/June 1978; ''Pologne'' in *Photo* (Paris), No. 183, December 1982; ''Bruno Barbey Polonia'' in *Photo* (Milan), No. 93, March 1983; ''Multitudes: Bruno Barbey: Graphisme au carré'' in *Photo* (Paris), No. 190, July 1983; ''Barbey: Photojournalisme: L'Inde de Barbey'' in *Photo-Reporter* (Paris), No. 60, October 1983; ''Multitudini: Bruno Barbey'' in *Photo* (Milan), No. 100, October 1983; ''Art and Style: Feature/Image of Morocco: Bruno Barbey'' in *Styling* (Tokyo), No. 11, January 1988. **Film**—*Mai '68,* 1968.

On BARBEY: Books—*Photography in Switzerland: 1840 to Today,* edited by Hugo Loetscher, Walter Binder, Rosellina Burri-Bischof and Peter Killer, Teufen, Switzerland 1974; *Photography Year 1975,* New York 1975; *Terre de Guerre,* exhibition catalogue, with text by Charles-Henri Favrod, Paris 1982; *Documentary Photography,* Alexandria, Virginia 1983. **Articles**—''Bibliothèque Nationale: Jeune Photo: 21 professionnels, 150 documents, une époque'' in *Photo* (Paris), No. 1, July/August 1967; ''Les Palestiniens vus par Bruno Barbey'' by Jean Genet in *Zoom* (Paris), No. 8, August 1971; ''Barbey Exposé: Au salon, il affirme sa tendance 77: Regarder les hommes vivre'' in *Photo* (Paris), No. 122, November 1977; ''Barbey stellt aus: Festhalten, wie die Menschen leben'' in *Photo* (Munich), No. 63, January 1978; ''Oser la couleur: Barbey, Habans, Dityvon, Piquemal'' in *Photo* (Paris), No. 128, May 1978; ''Le rodeo des taulards'' by Danièle Boone in *Photo-Revue* (Paris), September 1982; ''Barbey en Pologne'' by Petras Gondicas in *Photo-Revue* (Paris), December 1982/January 1983; ''Bruno Barbey: 'L'autre pologne''' by Alain de Penanster in *L'Express,* 8 April 1983; ''Bruno Barbey's Poland'' by Liba Taylor in *British Journal of Photography,* 24 June 1983; ''D'autres regards sur l'Italie'' by Gabriel Bauret in *Camera International,* No. 11, Summer 1987. **Film**—*3 Jours, 3 Photographes,* by F. Moscowitz, 1979.

BARNEY, Tina.

Nationality: American. **Born:** New York, 1945. **Education:** Studied at the Sun Valley Center for Arts and Humanities, 1976-79; workshops with: Frederick Sommer, Roger Mertin, Joyce Niemanas, Duane Michals, Nathan Lyons, John Pfahl, Robert Cumming. Resides in Watch Hill, Rhode Island. **Address:** c/o Janet Borden, Inc., 560 Broadway, New York, New York 10012, U.S.A.

Individual Exhibitions:

1984	Westover School, Middlebury, Connecticut
1985	Tatistcheff & Co., New York

The Trustee and the Curator, 1991 (original in colour). Photograph by Tina Barney. Courtesy Janet Borden, Inc.

1987	Milwaukee Art Center
1988	Tatistcheff Gallery, Los Angeles
	John Good Gallery, New York
1989	The Denver Art Museum
	Janet Borden, Inc.
	Weber College, Ogden, Utah
1990	Museum of Modern Art, New York
	Janet Borden, Inc.
	Cleveland Center for Contemporary Art
1991	International Museum of Photography, George Eastman House, Rochester, New York
1992	Janet Borden, Inc.
1993	Janet Borden, Inc.

Selected Group Exhibitions:

1983	*Big Pictures,* Museum of Modern Art, New York
	The Exhibition Exhibition, University of Arizona, Tucson
1984	*The Lens in the Garden,* Hudson River Museum, Yonkers, New York
	Children through Time & Light, Light Gallery, New York
1985	*Humanistic Visions,* San Jose State University, California

1986	*Relations,* Tatistcheff & Co., New York
	Artists Choose Artists, CDS Gallery, New York
	The Real Big Picture, Queens Museum, New York
1987	*The 1987 Whitney Biennial,* New York
	The Squibb Gallery, Princeton, New Jersey
	Composed for the Photography, Baltimore Art Museum
	American Dreams, Ministry of Culture, Madrid, Spain
1988	*Recent Acquisitions,* Museum of Modern Art, New York
	Cultural Participation, Dia Art Foundation, New York
	Fictitious Truth: Photographs, Real Art Ways, Hartford, Connecticut
	Inaugural Exhibition, Tatistcheff Gallery, Los Angeles
1989	*Recent Acquistions,* Yale University Art Gallery
	Aetna Gallery, Hartford, Connecticut
	Dayton Art Institute, Ohio
	The Photography of Invention, Smithsonian Institution, Washington, D.C.
	San Francisco Cameraworks
1990	*The Art of Photography 1839-1989,* The Seibu Museum of Art, Tokyo
	Identities: Portraiture in Contemporary Photography, Philadelphia Art Alliance
	Thomas Segal Gallery, Boston

Middendorf Gallery, Washington, D.C.
AFR Fine Arts, Washington, D.C.

1991   *This Sporting Life,* High Museum of Art, Atlanta, Georgia
         (and tour)
        Forbidden Games, Jack Tilton Gallery, New York
        Imaging the Family, Brown University, Providence, Rhode
         Island
        The Realm of the Coin, Hofstra University, Hempstead,
         New York
        Blood Relatives, Milwaukee Art Museum
        Houston Center for Photography
        AFR Fine Arts, Washington, D.C.
        Charles N. Moore Gallery, Philadelphia
1992   *Multiple Exposure,* Wesleyan University, Middletown,
         Connecticut
        The Invention of Childhood, Kohler Art Center, Cheboygan,
         Michigan
1993   *In and Out of Place,* Museum of Fine Arts, Boston
        Commodity Image, International Center of Photography,
         New York
        Cleveland Center of Contemporary Art
        Wings of Change, Georgio, Beverly Hills, California
        Fictions of the Self, University of North Carolina (and tour)
        In Camera, Museum of New Mexico, Santa Fe

Collections:

Baltimore Art Museum; Boise Gallery of Art, Idaho; Denver Art Museum; International Museum of Photography, George Eastman House, Rochester, New York; La Jolla Museum of Contemporary Art, California; Los Angeles County Museum of Art; Museum of Fine Arts, Boston; Museum of Fine Arts, Houston; Museum of Modern Art, New York; The National Museum of American Art, Washington, D.C.; The New School, New York; Princeton University Art Museum; San Francisco Museum of Modern Art; Smith College Museum of Art; The Smithsonian Institution, Washington, D.C.; Yale University Art Gallery.

Publications:

By BARNEY: Book—*Swimmers,* with Tina Howe, New York 1991.

On BARNEY: Books—*Mothers & Daughters,* New York 1987; *Women Photographers,* edited by Constance Sullivan, New York 1991; *Friends and Relations,* Washington, D.C. 1992. **Articles**—review in *The New York Times,* 8 May 1984; review in *Modern Photography,* July 1984; review in *Artweek,* 16 February 1985; review in *Arts Magazine,* May 1985; review in *American Photographer,* September 1985; review in *Art in America,* October 1985; review in *The New York Times,* 12 September 1986; in *Modern Photography,* September 1986; in *The Village Voice,* 23 February 1988; review in *Art in America,* July 1988; review in *Los Angeles Times,* 9 December 1988; review by Roberta Smith in *The New York Times,* 26 May 1989; review by Vince Aletti in *The Village Voice,* 30 May 1989; review in *The New Yorker,* 5 June 1989; review in *The New Yorker,* 19 March 1990; profile by Andy Grundberg in *The New York Times,* 1 April 1990; review by Vince Aletti in *The Village Voice,* 10 April 1990; review by Rhonda Lieberman in *Artforum,* November 1991; ''People Like Us'' in *Artforum,* October 1992; review by Charles Hagen in *The New York Times,* 16 April 1993; review by Amy Gamerman in *The Wall Street Journal,* 27 April 1993.

BARROW, Thomas F(rancis).

Nationality: American. **Born:** Kansas City, Missouri, 24 September 1938. **Education:** Studied graphic design at the Kansas City Art Institute, 1959-63, B.F.A. 1963; filmmaking, under Jack Ellis, at Northwestern University, Evanston, Illinois, 1964; and photography, under Aaron Siskind, at the Institute of Design, Illinois Institute of Technology, Chicago, 1965-67, M.S.

Photog. 1967. **Career:** Independent photographer, New York, 1967-73, and New Mexico, since 1973. Assistant Curator of Exhibitions and Associate Curator of the Research Center, 1965-71, Assistant Director, 1971-72, and Editor of *Image,* 1972, George Eastman House, Rochester, New York; Lecturer in the History and Aesthetics of Photography, Rochester Institute of Technology and State University of New York at Buffalo, 1968-71; Lecturer in Photography, Center of the Eye, Aspen, Colorado, 1969-70. Associate Director of the Art Museum, 1973-76, Associate Professor, 1976-85, and Professor since 1985, Department of Art, University of New Mexico, Albuquerque. Director, Summer Photography Workshop, University of California at Riverside, 1976; Visiting Artist, Orange Coast College, Costa Mesa, California, 1985. Editorial Board Member *Artspace* magazine, Albuquerque, New Mexico, 1980-84; Advisory Board Member, Friends of Photography, Carmel, California, 1985-1991. Also works as an exhibition organizer and graphic designer; Elected Full Trustee, Friends of Photography, 1986-91; Visiting Artist, Glasgow School of Art, Scotland 1986-1991; Nominator for the 1987-88 Leopold Godowsky, Jr Color Photography Awards (The Photographic Resource Center, Boston); Reader, The Logan Awards for New Writing in Photography, Photographic Resource Center, Boston 1990; Faculty Member ''Photographic Constructions Workshop,'' The Friends of Photography, August 1990; Juror: Mid-America Arts Alliance and NEA Fellowship Awards CAA Nominating Committee, Spring 1991; CAA Panel member for ''Distinguished Body of Work Exhibition, Presentation or Performance'' 1992-1995; Appointed to Advisory Board Albuquerque Museum 1992. **Recipient:** National Endowment for the Arts Fellowship, 1973, 1978; Honored Photographer, Society for Photographic Education, 1983. **Agent:** Andrew Smith Gallery, Santa Fe, N.M. **Address:** Department of Art, University of New Mexico, Albuquerque, New Mexico 87131, U.S.A.

Individual Exhibitions:

1969   Universityof California at Davis
1972   Light Gallery, New York
1974   Light Gallery, New York
1975   Deja Vu Gallery, Toronto
1976   Light Gallery, New York
1978   *2 from Albuquerque,* Susan Spiritus Gallery, Newport Beach,
         California (with Betty Hahn)
1979   Light Gallery, New York
1980   Susan Spiritus Gallery, Newport Beach, California (with J.
         Thurston)
1981   Film in the Cities, St. Paul, Minnesota (with James Henkel)
1982   *Thomas Barrow/Esther Parada/John Wood,* Northlight
         Gallery, Arizona State University, Tempe
1984   Susan Spiritus Gallery, Newport Beach, California (with Jerry
         Uelsmann)
1985   Light Factory, Charlotte, North Carolina (with Victor Schrager)
1986   *Inventories and Transformations,* San Francisco Museum of
         Modern Art (retrospective; toured the United States)
1990   *Thomas Barrow. The Burning Houses,* Amarillo Art Center
1992   *Notes for the 90's,* Andrew Smith Gallery, Santa Fe
        Studio Notes by Thomas Barrow, Richard Levy Gallery,
         Albuquerque

Selected Group Exhibitions:

1967   *Four Photographers,* Riverside Gallery, Rochester, New York
1969   *Vision and Expression,* International Museum of Photography,
         at George Eastman House, Rochester, New York
1970   *The Photograph as Object,* National Gallery of Canada, Ottawa
1975   *The Extended Document,* International Museum of Photogra-
         phy, at George Eastman House, Rochester, New York
1976   *Aspects of American Photography 1976,* University of
         Missouri, St. Louis
1977   *Contemporary American Photographic Works,* Museum of Fine
         Arts, Houston
1979   *Translations: Photographic Images with New Forms,* Cornell
         University, Ithaca, New York
1981   *Photographer as Printmaker,* Ferens Art Gallery, Hull,
         Yorkshire (travelled to the Museum and Art Gallery,

The World's Eye—Medusa, **1990 (original in colour).** Photograph by Thomas Barrow.

1985   *American Images 1945-80,* Barbican Art Gallery, London
(toured Britain)

Leicester; Cooper Gallery, Barnsley; Castle Museum, Nottingham; Photographers' Gallery, London)

1987   *Photography and Art 1946-86,* Los Angeles County Museum of Art

1988   *Acceptable Entertainment,* ICI travelling exhibition (catalogue)

1989   *Contemporary Landscape Photography from the Permanent Collection,* Los Angeles County Museum of Art, Los Angeles

Decade by Decade, 20th Century American Photography, Center for Creative Photography, Tucson, AZ (catalogue)

The Polaroid 20" x 24" Shoot, Jayne H Baum Gallery, New York City

Nature and Culture, Ansel Adams Center, San Francisco

1990   *Constructed Spaces,* Photographic Resource Center—Boston Architectural Center, Boston, MA

Engaging Transformations: Experiemental Photography of the Sixties, Harnett Gallery, University of Rochester, NY

1991   *Aesthetically Correct—Aesthetically Incorrect,* Jonson Gallery, University of New Mexico, Albuquerque

1992   *Polaroid Selections,* Photokina '92, Cologne, Germany

The Mediated Image: American Photography in the Age of Information, University Art Museum, Albuquerque

1994   *Experimental Vision: The Evolution of the Photogram since 1919,* Denver Art Museum (catalogue)

Artists' Plates, A Celebration, Museum of Fine Arts, Santa Fe

Collections:

International Museum of Photography, George Eastman House, Rochester, New York; Philadelphia Museum of Fine Arts; University of Kansas, Lawrence; Museum of Fine Arts, Houston; University of New Mexico, Albuquerque; San Francisco Museum of Modern Art; Seattle Art Museum; National Gallery of Canada, Ottawa; National Gallery of Australia, Canberra; The Newport Harbor Art Museum; Minneapolis Institute of Art; National Gallery of Australia; Washington Art Consortium (Whatcom Museum of History and Art); The Center for Creative Photography, University of Arizona, Tucson; California State University, Long Beach; DeCordova Museum, Lincoln, MA; University of California, Riverside; The Hallmark Collection; Ohio Wesleyan University; Commodities Corporation Collection; Princeton Art Museum; Los Angeles County Museum of Art; Polaroid International Collection; Tampa Art Museum; The Albuquerque Museum; The Art Institute of Chicago; The Museum of Contemporary Photography, Columbia College, Chicago.

Publications:

By BARROW: Books—designer of numerous books, including *Light and Substance,* Albuquerque, New Mexico 1975; *The New Industrial Parks Near Irvine, California* by Lewis Baltz, New York 1975; *Frederick Hammersley: A Retrospective Exhibition,* catalogue, Albuquerque, New Mexico 1975; *Peculiar to Photography,* exhibition catalogue, Albuquerque, New Mexico 1976; *The Photography of Van Deren Coke,* exhibition catalogue, Albuquerque, New Mexico 1982; *Reading into Photography: Selected Writings, 1959-1981,* editor, with S. Armitage and W. Tydeman, Albuquerque, New Mexico 1982; *Photography and Postmodernism,* editor, with Peter Walch, Albuquerque, New Mexico 1983; *The Beaumont Newhall Lectures,* editor, with Peter Walch, Albuquerque, New Mexico 1984; *Culture and Record,* exhibition catalogue, Madison, Wisconsin 1984; *Inventories and Transformations: The Photographs of Thomas Barrow,* with text by Kathleen M. Gauss, Los Angeles and Albuquerque, New Mexico 1986. **Articles**—"A Letter with Some Thoughts on Photography's Future" in *Album 6* (London), July 1970; "600 Faces by Beaton" in *Aperture* (Millerton, New York), Summer 1970; "The Camera Fiend" in *Image* (Rochester, New York), September 1971; "Talent" in *Image* (Rochester, New York), December 1971; introduction to the *Lewis Hine Portfolio,* Rochester, New York 1971; "Looking Down" in *Image* (Rochester, New York), July 1972; "Notes on the Photoglyphic Process" in *University of New Mexico Bulletin* (Albuquerque, New Mexico), 1973; "Three Photographers and Their Books" in *A Hundred Years of Photographic History,* Albuquerque, New Mexico 1975; "Footnotes," with

Peter Walch, in *New Mexico Studies in the Fine Arts* (Albuquerque), vol. II, 1977; "Some Thoughts on the Criticism of Photography" in *Northlight 8* (Tempe, Arizona), November 1978; "Learning from the Past" in *9 Critics/9 Photographers,* Carmel, California 1980; "Review of Pete Turner Photographs" in *Choice,* June 1990; "Juror's Statement" in *Light Aberrations,* Art Teaching Gallery, University of Texas at San Antonio 1990; Contribution to "Beaumont Newhall: Colleagues and Friends," Museum of Fine Arts, Santa Fe 1993; "Editorial: Beaumont Newhall 1900-1993" in *Views,* Spring/Summer 1993; Reprint of "Some Thoughts on Photography's Future" in *The History of Photography,* Spring 1993; "Moholy-Nagy and the Chicago Bauhaus" *Experimental Vision: The Evolution of the Photogram since 1919,* Denver Art Museum, 1994.

On BARROW: Books—*The Art of Photography,* by the Time-Life editors, New York 1971; *Light and Lens,* edited by Donald L. Werner, New York 1973; *The Extended Document,* exhibition catalogue, Rochester, New York 1975; *The Photographer's Choice,* Danbury, New Hampshire 1976; *Contemporary American Photographic Works,* exhibition catalogue, Houston 1977; *Self-Portrayal,* edited by James Alinder, Carmel, California 1979; *The Photograph Collector's Guide* by Lee D. Witkin and Barbara London, Boston and London 1979; *The Imaginary Photo Museum* by Helmut Gernsheim, Renate and L. Fritz Gruber and others, Cologne 1981, London 1982; *American Images: Photography 1945-1980,* edited by Peter Turner, London 1985; *Photography and Art 1946-1986,* exhibition catalogue, by Andy Grundberg and Kathleen M. Gauss, Los Angeles 1987. **Articles**—"Thomas Barrow" by Henri Man Barendse in *Artspace* (Albuquerque, New Mexico), Summer 1977; "Thomas Barrow's Cancellations" by Henri Man Barendse in *Afterimage* (Rochester, New York), October 1977; "Artists and Their Art: Photographers" by Stephen Sinclair in *The Cultural Post* (Washington, D.C.), July/August 1978; "Currents: American Photography Today" by Andy Grundberg and Julia Scully in *Modern Photography* (New York), April 1980; Cover photograph and internal illustrations in *Aperture,* No 87, 1982; "Dimensions of a Collection: Photographs from the Minneapolis Institute of the Arts" by C T Hartwell in *Aperture Creative Camera,* No 237 September 1984; "Interview with Thomas F Barrow" by John Bloom in *Photo Metro,* March 1986; "Absorbing Inventories, Thomas Barrow's 'Libraries Series'" by Gus Blaisdell in *Artspace,* Autumn 1988; "Thomas Barrow: Material Evidence" by K M Gauss in *Photo Education,* Spring 1989; "Printmaking in New Mexico 1880-1990" by C Adams (UNM Press) 1991.

*

The anomalies of photography have fascinated me for some time now: a physical presence that is ignored while a literal content is described *ad nauseam*; practitioners (especially in the United States) who are determinedly and rather proudly uninformed of the history of art or culture; the almost total absence of a critical literature. The list might be extended to a tedious length. And yet, even at a primitive level of accomplishment, the medium is capable of stimulating questions of significance with regard to truth, virtue, and the areas we label as "serious thoughts." Photography has in common with almost all visual media an inability to provide direct answers to these queries, but the immediacy with which it provokes inquiry is unique. Within these contradictions lay the expressive challenges of the medium. The artist must be able to discern the questions asked by photographs and give form to them; in essence, creating form with the medium's own intrinsic characteristics.

At just this point, one can place the observed questions in opposition to each other creating an argument (dialogue is too passive a word for what occurs at this juncture). Simultaneous with the theoretical are practical aspects, "straight vs. manipulated," "color vs. black and white," that also may be set in opposition for additional clues to evolving ideas and how the images might utilize these ideas. Since the camera and its products are so ubiquitous and seductive, one can easily become the servant of a mindless device. This is, in part, why the preceding "oppositions" are so useful; they allow one to assume an adversary position for the making of art.

Although the preceding has a great deal to do with the way my own work is created, ideas are not always of primary import. I feel a certain sympathy for the following statement by Francis Ponge:

Given such inclinations (distaste for ideas, taste for definitions), it may perhaps be natural that I devote myself first to cataloguing and defining objects in the external world, and among them, the ones that constitute the familiar universe of our culture, our time. (From *The Voice of Things*)

Or even more germane might be John Ashbery's words on Raymond Roussel:

The result in the case of each of his books is a gigantic dose of minutiae: to describe one is like trying to summarize the Manhattan telephone book. Moreover, the force of his writing is felt only gradually; it proceeds from the accumulated weight of this mad wealth of particulars. A page or even a chapter of Roussel, fascinating as it may be, gives no idea of the final effect which is a question of density: the whole is more than the sum of its parts. (From *How I Wrote Certain of My Books*)

It is beyond practicality or hope that all of my pieces might be seen at one time, and yet I have made them as a virtually unbroken series. Certainly not Arthur O. Lovejoy's *Great Chain of Being*, but a definite progression of carefully calculated, occasionally arcane linkages that connect the encyclopedia aspect of photography with the overwhelming materialism of our time.

—Thomas F. Barrow

*   *   *

The photographs of Thomas F. Barrow are intellectual and cerebral; they have often been referred to as conceptual. Yet to connect this artist with the Conceptual Art movement of the last decade is radically to misinterpret him. All of contemporary art photography has, in fact, a peculiar and problematic relationship with Conceptual Art; in a movement that rejected the traditional art product as bourgeois, the photograph often served as the only document of a temporal art event and the only record of the idea. Often with little visual interest of their own, these photographs bear scant philosophical relation to contemporary idea-oriented photography. However conceptual the work of Barrow is, it is also emphatically pictorial. The idea is paramount, but so is the finished print. The work has covered a remarkably varied range of techniques and approaches, yet the underlying thread of continuity is Barrow's investigation of the nature of photography itself, and how, as a system of notation, photographs render information.

"Cancellation" (1975-77) is one of Barrow's most provocative and enigmatic series to date. If it seems at first glance a contemptuous assault on contemporary photography, it yields multiple meanings on closer examination. The "X" suggests the cancellation of printer's plates to limit an edition. If Barrow has thus destroyed his negative to limit the number of prints, he has done so before any edition has been made. These photographs have meaning only if they are cancelled; the casual, deadpan shots of urban debris are enlivened by the compositional tightness lent them by the X; the X itself takes on unique characteristics within the different qualities of the freehand drawing and the variations on how the scratching instrument scraped off emulsion or actually pierced through the acetate film base. As in all of Barrow's work, it is these visual elements that defuse the didacticism that often characterizes Conceptual Art.

The subject matter of this series, the bleak urban landscape, is itself a loaded issue; if Barrow first appears to vandalize his subject by cancelling it, in fact the X can be read as a counteraction against the waste and plunder that mark the landscape and simultaneously as an indication of a photographic trend at mid-decade. An approach to the landscape that has been labelled "New Topographics" incorporated a dispassionate view of the union of nature and city at its most banal. Barrow skillfully raises this issue of a contemporary direction, as if quoting it, and enlarges upon it, paradoxically, by abrogation. This fact, I believe, is the source of the series' dynamism and wit: Barrow is not negating but pointing us toward some of the stickiest questions in contemporary photography—the issue of editions and their limitability, the fashion of recording the defaced urban landscape, and the nature of photographic rendition. The cancellation does not actually affect the facticity of the photograph but draws into question the photographic rendition of information and what we can deduce from it.

Thomas Barrow comes to photography with the background of a painter and a keen interest in design, both of which have served him in his investigation of the properties of the photograph. Yet, it is mostly Barrow's use of the traditional syntax of photographs, their unmatched ability to record and

catalogue information, and his ability to organize it visually that makes his work a skillful transformation of idea into object.

—Dana Asbury

BASSMAN (HIMMEL), Lillian.

Nationality: American. **Born:** New York City, 15 June 1917. **Education:** Painted with Moses Soyez; scholarship in graphic arts (under Alexey Brodovitch) at the New School for Social Research; self-taught in photography. **Family:** Married photographer Paul Himmel in 1938; children: Lizzie and Eric. **Career:** Apprentice, 1941, and later assistant, to Brodovitch at *Harper's Bazaar*; co-art director with Brodovitch at *Junior Bazaar*, 1945-1947. Freelance fashion and advertising photographer since 1947. **Agents:** Howard Greenberg Gallery, 120 Wooster Street, New York 10012; Hamilton's, 13 Carlos Place, London W1Y 5AG. **Address:** 117 East 83rd Street, New York, New York 10028, U.S.A.

Individual Exhibitions:

1978	Staemphli Gallery, New York
1993	Hamilton's, London
	Galeria Sozzani, Milan
	Howard Greenberg Gallery, New York
1994	Jackson Fine Art, Atlanta, Georgia

Selected Group Exhibitions:

1985	*Shots of Style*, Victoria and Albert Museum, London
1991	*Appearances*, Victoria and Albert Museum, London
1993	*Vanites*, Centre National de la Photographie, Paris
1994	*Hommage a Lillian Bassman*, International Festival of Fashion Photography, Carrousel du Louvre

Collections:

Victoria and Albert Museum, London

*   *   *

Working as co-art director of *Junior Bazaar* with Alexey Brodovitch, Lillian Bassman grew intrigued with the potential of photography. She began to experiment in her spare time, teaching herself to print in Hoyningen-Huene's darkroom. Frustrated with creating ideas for others to realise, she gave up art direction and turned full-time photographer in 1947. Many of the characteristics of her early fashion photographs grew directly out of her technical explorations, and an interest in both process and graphic effects continues to distinguish her work today. She evolved a method of producing an evanescent tonal diffusion by enlarging through gauze or tissue, a soft-focus technique tellingly employed in her editorial photographs (principally for *Harper's Bazaar*) of romantic evening wear or lingerie, two categories for which she was especially renowned.

As a woman Bassman was able to establish a close rapport with her favourite models. Studio schedules were more generous when she began and she would spend a whole day on a sitting: conversing, taking lunch with the model, and creating the kind of relaxed environment which facilitated the search for the "intimate gesture" she sought, and which helped lift the photography of lingerie out of its traditional banality and priggishness.

Bassman's oblique but atmospheric photographs placed the expression of mood or emotion above describing detailed fashion information, an impressionistic approach that was increasingly difficult to reconcile with the magazine's need to clearly delineate the merchandise. Even the most extreme of her experiments, however, succeed in conveying the essence of the fashions with considerable dash and fluency, and it is a cause of regret that after about 1950 Bassman's innovatory tendencies were not given freer rein; it is noticeable that

The Wonders of Water, **1959.** Photograph by Lillian Bassman.

her most compelling work was often achieved in response to an open brief (see *The Wonders of Water*, 1959).

Bassman retired from commercial photography in the 1970s, but has continued to experiment with large-scaled colour photographs (male nudes, still lives) and dramatic mixed media monochromes. She also teaches at Parson's School of Design, New York.

—Martin Harrison

BATHO, Claude.

Nationality: French. **Born:** Claude Bodier in Chamalières, 1 June 1935. **Education:** Studied photography at the Ecole des Arts Appliqués, Paris, under Janet le Caisne and Jacques Couturat, 1950-56, Dip. Photog 1956; studied painting at the Ecole des Beaux-Arts, Paris, under Raymond Legueult, 1955-57. **Family:** Married the photographer John Batho, *q.v.,* in 1963; children: Marie Angèle and Delphine. **Career:** Professional photographer, working for the Archives Nationales, Paris, from 1957. Member, Groupe 30 x 40, Paris, from 1972. **Recipient:** First Prize, Images of Women Competition, *F* magazine, Paris, 1980. Chevalier, Ordre des Arts et Lettres, France, 1977. **Agents:** Helene Faggionato, 42 Avenue de Save, 75007 Paris; and Galerie Agathe Gaillard, 3 rue des Pont Louis-Philippe, 75004 Paris. **Died:** (in Paris) in September 1981.

Individual Exhibitions:

1964	*Photographies et Peinture,* Galerie Quai aux Fleurs, Paris
1977	*Le Moment des Choses,* Galerie Agathe Gaillard, Paris (travelled to Galerie 31, Vevey, Switzerland, and Canon Gallery, Amsterdam, 1978; Galerie Contemporaine, Bologna, Galleria Il Diaframma, Milan, Musée d'Angoulème, France, and Fotomania, Barcelona, 1979)
1980	Musée Nicéphore Niepce, Chalon-sur-Saône, France (retrospective; travelled to the Canon Gallery, Geneva)
	Photographies, Galerie du Château d'Eau, Toulouse
1981	Galerie de l'Arpa, Bordeaux
	Photogalerie Portfolio, Lausanne, Switzerland

Selected Group Exhibitions:

1978	*La Photographie Actuelle en France 1978,* Galerie Contrejour, Paris (and world tour, 1978-81)
	20 Photographies, Ecole des Beaux-Arts, Avignon
1980	*Natures Mortes,* Galerie Viviane Esders, Paris
	Transparence, Galerie Viviane Esders, Paris
1984	*La Photographie Créative,* Pavillon des Arts, Paris

Collections:

Bibliothèque Nationale, Paris; Editions des Femmes, Paris; Musée d'Angoulème, France; Musée Nicéphore Niepce, Chalon-sur-Saône, France.

Publications:

By BATHO: Books—*Portraits d'Enfants,* portfolio, with a preface by Jean-Claude Lemagny, Paris 1975; *Le Moment des Choses,* with preface by Irène Schavelzon, Paris 1977, Milan 1978; *Claude Batho, photographe,* with texts by John Batho, Sylviane Heftler and Francoise Marquet, Paris 1982. **Article**—"L'Oeil au bout des doigts" in *Femmes en Mouvements* (Paris), May 1978.

On BATHO: Books—*Photographie Actuelle en France,* exhibition catalogue, Paris 1978; *Des Clefs et des Serrures* by Michel Tournier, Paris 1979; *Transparences: Photographies,* exhibition catalogue, with text by Gilbert Lascault, Paris 1980; *La Photographie Créative* by Jean-Claude Lemagny, Paris 1984. **Articles**—"Le Moment des Choses" by Hervé Guibert in *Le Monde* (Paris), 23 November 1977; "Le Moment des Choses" by Michel Nuridsany in *Le Figaro* (Paris), 28 November 1977; "La Paix de Claude Batho" by Joan Fontcuberta in *Barcelone* (Barcelona), 24 November 1979; "Un Jour, J'aurai une Femme" by Michel Tournier in *Le Monde* (Paris), 5 October 1979; "Esta Mes" in *Nueva Lente* (Madrid), no. 88, 1979.

*

My photographs are too close, too much a part of me, for me to be able to look at them dispassionately. They speak of the way time passes—over people, over children, over the objects that are inanimate; those special moments. . . .

I like to draw attention to the very simplest of fleeting instances. Without breaking the silence.

I find it hard to express in words those things that I am always saying through my photography.

My camera, "the eye at my finger-ends," accompanies me everywhere. Together we search for moments to be singled out. I love the exploring glance; the capturing of the instant; the fight against absence, oblivion, calamity, fate. . . .

But photography also provides another kind of fulfilment. Working in the laboratory is in itself a creative activity, in which there is the fun of developing the film, exposing the negatives, seeing the image spring out of the amber fluid. I love the physical contact of the wet bromide, coming up under my fingertips. The slow materialization of the image on the paper requires a tough and drawn-out struggle to achieve the happy outcome of the successful result.

I photograph in black and white. Perhaps one day I shall turn to colour, but as far as I am concerned black and white already takes so much time and effort—and, besides, it is difficult to do several things well at a time, quite apart from the fact that my life is more than filled by all those feminine domestic duties.

How dearly I should like to have enough time at my disposal to do all the things I want to do; not only photography, but also painting and writing.

But photography—it is for me a necessity of life.

—Claude Batho (1981)

* * *

To write with light. To speak of the self, its inner being and its moods, in gradations of grey, in flashes of white, in deep blacks. To work at nearly the "degree zero" of photography—or at least near the heart of what is most genuine about it.

Like illness, photography was a part of Claude Batho's daily life. We should not be surprised, then, by these quick glances, so full of the experience of living, which characterize her work. Glances at once obvious and yet precise, of completed moments, quiet but charged with energy, with a passion for seeing. The eye of a woman, clearly, for ordinary objects—the light on the wallpaper, the reflection of a window on a family portrait. Austere yet loving glances at children, at little girls playing, at rest, alone.

The work of Claude Batho, full of austerity and tenderness: a perfect demonstration, perhaps, that the eye of the photographer, as it travels around a room, can capture the meaning of a life and recreate the world on a few squares of paper. For here there is no cheating.

—Christian Caujolle

BATHO, John.

Nationality: French. **Born:** Beuzeville, Normandy, 4 March 1939. **Education:** Studied book restoration, Paris, 1961-66. **Family:** Married the photographer Claude Bodier (i.e., Claude Batho, *q.v.*) in 1963; children: Marie Angèle and Delphine. **Career:** Photographer, since 1960. Book Conservationist, Archives Nationales, Paris, since 1961. **Recipient:** Kodak Photography

De Tablier Neuf (The New Blouse), **1967.** Photograph by Claude Batho.

Critics Award, Paris, 1977. **Address:** c/o Galerie Zabriskie, 37 Rue Quincampoix, 75004 Paris, France; Zabriskie Gallery 724 Fifth Avenue, New York, New York 10019, U.S.A.

Individual Exhibitions:

1978	Zabriskie Gallery, New York
	Galerie Zabriskie, Paris
	Madison Art Center, Wisconsin
	University of North Dakota, Grand Forks
1979	Arcade Gallery, Ann Arbor, Michigan
	Photographers Gallery, London
	Galerie Petit Format, Les Baux, France
1980	Camera Obscura, Stockholm
	Couleurs de Fête, Galerie Zabriskie, Paris (travelled to Zabriskie Gallery, New York)
	Galerie Vorlet, Lausanne
	Galerie Municipale du Chateau d'Eau, Toulouse
1981	Zabriskie Gallery, New York
	Galerie Modulo, Lisbon
1982	Maison de Jeune Culture de Saint-Herblain, Nantes, France
	John Batho, at *Printemps Culturel du Valenciennois,* Denain, France
	Coloriages, Galerie Zabriskie, Paris
	Galeria Pro Photo, Nuremberg, West Germany
1983	Galleria Ikona, Venice
	Addison-Ripley Gallery, Washington, D.C.
	Palais des Congres et de la Culture, Le Mans, France

1984	*Burano la couleur et son lieu,* Galerie A.M.C., Mulhouse, France
	Galerie San Sebastian, Dubrovnik, Yugoslavia
	Galerie San Sebastian, Belgrade
	Giverny: comme une peintre deja faite, Musee d'Aurillac, France
	Galerie Zabriskie, Paris
	Centre d'Action culturelle, Le Creuot, France
	Centre d'Action culturelle, Montbeliard, France
1985	*Photocolore,* Centre d'Action culturelle, Privas, France
	Centre d'Action culturelle, Annecy, France
	French Embassy, New York
	Artotheque, La Rochelle, France
	Zabriskie Gallery, New York
	Galerie A.M.C., Mulhouse, France
	Galerie FNAC, Paris (travelled to Lyon, Rouen, Nice and Brussels)
	Galerie Post-Scriptum, Brussels
	Galerie Nei Liitch, Dudelange, Luxembourg
1986	Galerie Ombres Blanches, Toulouse, France

Selected Group Exhibitions:

1977	*Tendances Actuelles,* Musée d'Art Moderne, Paris
1978	*European Colour Photography,* The Photographers' Gallery, London
1980	*L'Amérique aux Indépendants, Petit Palais,* Paris
1982	*Fotografie 1922-82,* at *Photokina 82,* Cologne
1984	*Couleur et la photographie 'Straight',* Art Center, Paris
1985	*Fresson Photographs and Unity of Vision,* Center for Contemporary Art, New Orleans, Louisiana
1986	*Museotrain,* Galerie FNAC, Limousin, France (toured France)

Collections:

Bibliothèque Nationale, Paris; City of Paris; Musée Nicéphore Niepce, Chalon-Sur-Saône, France; Boston Museum of Fine Arts; Galerie FNAC, Limousin, France; FNAC, Champagne-Ardenne, France; FNAC, Alsace, France; Musee d'Aurillac, France.

Publications:

By BATHO: Books—*John Batho,* exhibition catalogue, with text by Jean Dieuzaide, Toulouse, France 1980; *Claude Batho, photographe,* with Sylviane Hefter and Francoise Marquet, Paris 1982; *John Batho: la couleur et son lieu,* exhibition catalogue, with text by Nadhira Lekehal, Mulhouse, France 1984; *John Batho: Giverny comme une peintre deja faite,* with text by Francoise Reynaud, Aurillac, France 1984; *Images-imaginees,* with others, text by Gaston Bachelard and Nadhira Lekehal, Paris 1984; *Photocolore,* with text by Annie Chambonnet, Paris 1985.

On BATHO: Books—*European Colour Photography,* exhibition catalogue, by Sue Davies, Michael Langford and Bryn Campbell, London 1978; *Photographia: La Linea Sottile,* exhibition catalogue, by Giuliana Scimé and Rinaldo Bianda, Locarno 1980; *Fotografie 1922-1982,* exhibition catalogue, with introduction by Manfred Heiting, Rolf-Hasso Ley and Karl Steinorth, Cologne 1982; *La Photographie Creative* by Jean-Claude Lemagny, Paris 1984. **Article**—"7 Maitres du Paysage," in *Photocinema* (Paris), May 1980.

*

I first learnt to photograph in black and white, and continued to do so for ten years or so. At the same time I became interested in ways of capturing colour, and my research in this area ended up by excluding the practice of photographing in black and white.

Black and white concentrate but also reduce the image to a set of related values; I prefer to use colour because the image it obtains seems to me both more alive and more complete. Of course, by its very allure and a certain powdery quality it possesses, colour complicates the image, but it's a delight, an attraction, a meaningful dimension, of which I have no wish to deprive myself. Linked to the action of light on material, colour organizes according to a logic which gives things their relief and their tone. I think of it as more than a language, beyond the laws of physics, like an engaging and active sensation, fascinating both to explore and to transmit.

Through photography, colour, captured and concentrated, becomes pigment. This material translation makes it accessible and malleable, so that it can be modulated, reduced or expanded on its effects and its actions; photographed colour makes concrete and prolongs an attraction, an ability to take hold and to touch.

—John Batho

*   *   *

The work of John Batho was shown publicly in Paris in 1977, although he had been taking photographs for many years before that. He brings to photography a new way of looking at the world by selecting from reality intensely colored pure forms. His studies are similar to those of Rothko in painting, and he has, in a sense, continued one aspect of the work of the Danish photographer Keld Helmer-Petersen, who published in 1949 a work entitled *122 Colored Photographs* in which abstraction and the study of composition with color play a determinant role. Batho took this concept of photography much further by bringing to it other parameters such as time and movement.

Batho is distinguished by his constant evolution: each exhibition marks a new stage in a quest, both true to himself and in constant transformation. A man of contained passion, Batho releases his work only when he believes that he has reached that fragile equilibrium between the idea of the picture and its realization, between the search for expression and its accomplishment in a sensitive form. The dialogue of form with color, together with a concept of the photograph as an object that must be perceived both in its materiality and sensuality, are the pivots around which his creative work evolves. He gives maximum importance to the photographic object: his carbon printings, achieved by entirely manual techniques by Michel Fresson, are produced with extreme care. This manner of completing the photographic object makes Batho very reticent when it comes to showing his photographs in slide form: for him, the picture at this stage is not fully completed; it remains a project which only the materiality of the paper print will perfect.

He believes that photographic space is limited to two dimensions, and he tries to use them in their totality. He has said: "The third dimension can only be hinted at, and, as the photograph itself is only an illusion, I find that even that is too much. . . . In the picture, color reveals, form expresses; it alone will bring out this aspect of evocation, this suggestion which generates the second stage in the reading of the picture."

At the present stage of his work, Batho seems frequently not to regard any picture as a unique object but as part of a sequence of color. A coherence is suddenly discovered in the harmonies of tone; a mysterious connection appears among the most heteroclite worlds: funeral wreaths in cemeteries correspond to fairground dolls, which find an echo in the colored rhythms of oil refinery reservoirs; the movement of children's windmills harmonize with the swirling of merry-go-rounds, which seem to spin round to the rhythm of glittering lights. . . .

—Ginette Bléry

BAUM, Yngve.

Nationality: Swedish. **Born:** Bjärnum, Skåne, 24 October in 1945. **Career:** Freelance photographer since 1965, also working for television and the Swedish Film Institute, in Sweden. **Recipient:** State Art Fellowship, 1967-68 and 1976; City Culture Award, Stockholm 1968; SIDA Grant, 1969; Författarstipendium, 1976-81; Författarfondon Garanterad För fattar-penning, 1982-. **Address:** Kompassgatan 1,413 16 Goteborg, Sweden.

Individual Exhibitions:

1970   *Afro Art,* Tanzania, Stockholm
1974   *Varvsarbetare,* Moderna Museet, Stockholm

Selected Group Exhibitions:

1964   *World Exhibition of Photography: What Is Man?,* Pressehaus
        Stern, Hamburg (and world tour)
1975   *Samlingarna gåvor och köp 1971-75,* Fotografiska Museet,
        Stockholm
1976   *Four Swedish Photographers,* Fotografiska Museet, Stockholm
1978   *Tusen och En Bild: 1001 Pictures,* Moderna Museet,
        Stockholm
1985   *Samlingarna ca 200 fotografer,* Fotografiska Museet,
        Stockholm

Publications:

By BAUM: Books—*Människor vid Hav,* Lofoten 1966; *Kiki-en liten man,* Stockholm 1967; *Berberby,* Algeriet 1967; *Ujama,* Tanzania 1970; *Skeppsvarv,* Göteborg 1974; *Röster från ett varv,* Göteborg 1979; *Två platser på jorden,* Tanzania and Lofoten 1983. **Films**—*Bilder Från ett Skeppsvar,* 1974; *Hamnarbetare,* 1975; *Tiderna skiftar,* 1979; *Fotboll, Herrar och småfolk,* 1980; *På sista varvet,* 1983; *Vi ska tvivla,* 1987; *Människans värde,* 1990; *Husnallen,* 1992.

On BAUM: Books—*Varvsarbetare,* exhibition catalogue, by Åke Sidwall and Leif Wigh, Stockholm 1974; *Four Swedish Photographers,* 1976; *Tusen och En Bild,* exhibition catalogue, by Åke Sidwall, Sune Jonsson and Ulf Hård af Segerstad, Stockholm 1978.

*   *   *

At the end of the 1960's and the beginning of the 70's young photographers in Sweden became increasingly interested in socially committed documentary photography. Many of the students at the schools of photography preferred to turn their cameras towards the reality outside in the community, rather than to practice ingratiating product- and portrait-photography. One of the photographers who became a guiding light to the new generation was Yngve Baum. Not only was he young himself (he was born in 1945), but he had already, in spite of his youth, produced several meticulous documentary reports, which had been reproduced in books and at exhibitions. He had made himself known for sticking obstinately to a self-imposed task until he was himself thoroughly satisfied.

What many of his followers perhaps did not understand was, that his way of exploiting both photographic technique and idiomatic expression gave further weight to content, which was interesting in itself. They photographed work places and they travelled to foreign cultures, but the pictures they brought back often lacked the weight and significance of Baum's. Many of the older photographers were also surprised at the high technical quality of Yngve Baum's reportage. They guessed at large negatives, low sensitivity film and special, home-made developers. But the answer was much simpler. The pictures were taken with a small-format camera (sometimes on a tripod, sometimes in conjunction with a flash). The film was Tri-X and occasionally a medium sensitivity film, which was exposed and developed according to the manufacturer's directions. For—to paraphase Baum—when Kodak has a large specialist staff, who devote all their time to finding a suitable developing-time and a recommended ASA-number, then they ought to know better than the photographer. His simple advice was therefore: "read the instructions!"

But the excellent copies are not simply the result of a chemical/technical process. The prints also reflect a great depth of aesthetic thinking (and a lot of patience). And because of Yngve Baum's great insistence on quality, most of his laboriously produced pictures end up in the waste-paper basket. His aim has been to unite vivid reporting with high technical quality.

After producing various books, Baum went to work for television—in the beginning with still photographs and sound, but fairly soon also with motion pictures. In documentary work the sound-film is often superior to the still picture, as it incorporates the time factor and at the same time integrates picture and sound in a more natural manner. But occasionally he injects a sequence of

Refugee from Kosova, Filipstad, Sweden, **1994.** Photograph by Yngve Baum.

still pictures into his television programmes. They frequently portray the working conditions of various occupations or describe life in small and tucked-away places in Sweden.

For, as time went on, Yngve Baum discovered that you don't have to go to the ends of the world to find what lives on your own doorstep. This is not to denigrate his books from Norway, Algeria or Tanzania. But as a foreigner one always runs the risk of picking out the exotic. At home it is easier to find what is real.

—Rune Jonsson

BAUMANN, Horst H.

Nationality: German. **Born:** Aachen, 19 June 1934. **Education:** Attended the Volksschule, Aachen, 1940-44; Lessing Gymnasium, Dusseldorf, 1946-54; studied metallurgy, Technische Hochschule, Aachen, 1954-57; self-taught in photography. **Family:** Married Ingeborg Geerz in 1971; daughter: Carolin; Regina Neumann in 1973; daughters: Nina, Alice. **Career:** Freelance photojournalist and advertising photographer, working for *Form, Automobile Quar-*

terly, Fiat, Bayer, Aga-Gas, BMW, Sony, Daimler-Benz, McCann Erickson, etc., Dusseldorf, since 1957; also freelance graphic designer, Dusseldorf, since 1960. Founder-Director, Communication Design Baumann studio for communications, planning and design, Dusseldorf, since 1966; Founder with Walther H. Schünemann, Populäre Propaganda Presse (PPP) poster publishing company, Dusseldorf, 1968; has worked with laser displays, since 1968; worked with laser TV production, 1977. Director, City Laser Communications System, Kassel, 1978. Guest Professor of Visual Communications, Hochschule für Gestaltung, Ulm, 1963-64; Lecturer in Communications, Design and Audio Visual Media, Fachhochschule, Dusseldorf, 1974-76. **Recipient:** Young Photographers Prize, *Photokina,* Cologne, 1956, 1958, 1960; Grand Prix for Photography, *Biennale des Jeunes,* Paris, 1967.

Individual Exhibitions:

1966   *Fotografie/Grafik Design,* at *Knauer-Expo,* Stuttgart
1976   Deutsche Gesellschaft für Photographie, Cologne

Selected Group Exhibitions:

1956   *Photokina '56,* Cologne (and 1958, 1960, 1978)

1962	*Das Menschliche Antlitz Europas,* at *Internationaler Münchener Fotosalon,* Munich
1964	*World Exhibition of Photography: What Is Man?,* Pressehaus Stern, Hamburg (and world tour)
1965	*11 International Photographers,* Gallery of Modern Art, New York
1968	*Man in Sport,* Gallery of Modern Art, New York (toured the United States and Europe)
1970	*Architektonische Spekulationen,* Leverkusen, West Germany
1973	*3rd World Exhibition of Photography: On the Way to Paradise,* Pressehaus Stern, Hamburg (and world tour)
1977	*Documenta 6,* Museum Fridericianum, Kassel, West Germany (laser-environment)
1979	*Deutsche Fotografie nach 1945,* Kunstverein, Kassel, West Germany (toured West Germany)
1981	*Farbe im Photo,* Kunsthalle, Cologne

Collections:

Kunstverein, Kassel, Germany; Museum Ludwig, Cologne; Museum of Modern Art, New York.

Publications:

By BAUMANN: Books—*Die Neuen Matadore,* with Ken Purdy, Lucerne 1965; *Fotofutura, Girls, Grand Prix,* Dusseldorf 1966; *Roaring Life: The World of Motorcycling,* West Berlin 1984.

On BAUMANN: Books—*Magie der Farbenfotografie* by W. Boje, Dusseldorf 1961; *Die Welt Der Photographe* by Pollack, Dusseldorf 1962; *Beauty: Variations on the Theme Woman by Masters of the Camera—Past and Present,* edited by L. Fritz Gruber, London and New York 1965; *Uber das Schopferische in der Photographie* by L. Fritz Gruber, Cologne 1966; *Architektonische Spekulationen* by Wedewer and Kempas, Droste, West Germany 1970; *Sportphotographien 1860-1960* by Jean Lattes, Lucerne and Frankfurt 1977; *Fotografie 1919-1979, Made in Germany: Die GDL Fotografen,* edited by Fritz Kempe, Bernd Lohse and others, Frankfurt 1979; *Deutsche Fotografie nach 1945/German Photography after 1945* by Floris Neusüss, Wolfgang Kemp and Petra Benteler, Kassel, West Germany 1979; *Farbe im Photo: Die Geschichte der Farbphotographie von 1861 bis 1981* by Fritz Binder, Gert Koshofer, Rolf Sachasse and others, Cologne 1981. **Article**—"Meister der Leica: Horst Baumann" in *Leica Fotografie* (Wuerzbach, Germany), vo. 11, no. 3, 1962.

* * *

Even in the giddy world of professional photography, it is difficult to think of a professional photographer who has undertaken, and constantly still undertakes, such a variety of work with as much verve and success as Horst Baumann.

When *Photokina*—the photographic *World's Fair*—organized its first "Junior Photography Competition," Baumann, at that time a student of metallurgy in Aachen, was one of the winners—and he went on to win the Young Photographers Prize on two more occasions. His photographs indicated both a positive feeling for form and a social sympathy. It was an irresistible temptation for the creative, perceptive young man: in 1957 he have up his studies, even though they were near to completion, in order to become a press photographer.

It was the time when the popular press in Europe had begun to produce coverage in color. Baumann immediately caused a sensation with essays in color; very quickly he became one of the leading figures of the color avant-garde. Particularly memorable was his coverage of motor racing (he produced a book of these pictures, in collaboration with Ken Purdy, in 1965). Baumann's photos were particularly striking for their audacious blurring effects, and they met with just as much approval in the press as in exhibitions and yearbooks.

Advertising agencies and industrial firms soon offered him commissions, especially when, after 1960, he included graphic design among the services he offered. It is characteristic of Baumann that by 1963-64 he was already a Guest Lecturer in Photography and Film at the Ulm Design Academy, yet he was not afraid to again become a student himself at Aachen in 1972—this time

in pedagogy, sociology and psychology. In 1974-76 he was again lecturing, this time at the Fachhochschule in Dusseldorf, on communication and design.

A reflection of his interests is the firm that he founded in 1966, Communication Design Baumann. Here, since then, he has developed an almost inconceivable versatility—always with photography at the center. It becomes somewhat more understandable when one considers that Baumann is a member not only of eight societies and professional organizations primarily devoted to photography, including design and video, but also of the Society of Futurology. For it is the futuristic phenomenon of the laser which, along with photography and design, determines Baumann's work today. Since *Expo '70* in Montreal, where he took part in the conception of the German Pavilion, he has constantly worked to develop new ideas—always on the basis of photography and visual communication. By this inclusion of inventive futuristic means and methods, Baumann is always one step (or two) ahead of the creative photographic fraternity.

—Bernd Lohse

BAURET, Jean-François.

Nationality: French. **Born:** Paris, 8 September 1932. **Education:** Attended primary and secondary schools in Paris and Villard-de-Lans, until 1950; self-taught in photography, from 1943. Served as Head of the Photo-Services in the Chasseurs Alpins, French Army, Chambéry, 1955-57. **Family:** Married the painter Claude Allard in 1956; children: Frédéric and Isabelle. **Career:** Worked as a photographer, for Sainte La Lys, Paris, 1950-55. Since 1958, freelance magazine, advertising and fashion photographer, working for *Elle, L'Oeil, Figaro, Madame,* Prisunic, Banque Nationale de Paris, Selimaille, Warner, Materna, Parfums Cardin, Renault, Shell, Air France, L'Oreal, Philips, the agencies Havas, Synergie and Publicis, etc.: established studio at Fontenay-Monvoisin, 1958-62, and at rue des Batignolles, Paris, since 1962. Organizer, *Europhot Congress,* Nice, 1970; President, National Association of Publicity and Fashion Photographers, Paris, 1977-82. Instructor in photography workshops in Arles, Avoriaz, Limoges, Paris, Pruniers, Toulouse, etc., since 1978. **Agent:** Bookmakers, 55 Rue de Clignancourt, 75018 Paris, France. **Address:** 34 rue des Batignolles, 75017 Paris, France.

Individual Exhibitions:

1956	Galerie Jean Drevet, Chambéry, France
1957	Librairie de la Cathedrale, Chambéry, France
1966	Galerie 3, Paris
	Galerie de la Baume, Paris
1971	ARC/Musée d'Art Moderne, Paris
	Galerie Tairraz, Paris
1973	Relais de Montmartre, Paris
1975	Galerie Chereau, Caen, France
1977	*Jean-François Bauret,* at *Rencontres Internationales de la Photographie,* Arles, France
1978	Galerie Sylvia Bourdon, Paris
1979	Galerie Polaroid, Paris
1980	Centre des Fontaines, Tours, France
	Galerie Municipale du Chateau d'Eau, Toulouse, France
1981	Photogalerie Portfolio, Lausanne, Switzerland
	Jean-François Bauret, a *2ème Rencontres Internationales de la Photographie,* Montpellier, France
1982	Municipalité de Pruniers, France
	Galerie Contraste, Limoges, France
	Galerie Marion Valentine, Paris
1983	*Jean-François Bauret,* at *3ème Festival de la Photographie,* Avoriaz, France
1984	Fonds National d'Art Contemporain, Marseille, France
1985	Fonds National d'Art Contemporain, Nice, France
	Jean-François Bauret, at *Festival de la Photographie,* Nancy, France

Laurence, 1989. Photograph ©Jean-François Bauret.

	Fonds National d'Art Contemporain, Rouen, France
	Fonds National d'Art Contemporain, Toulouse, France
	Musée de Dunkerque, France
1986	Fonds National d'Art Contemporain, Dijon, France
	Fonds National d'Art Contemporain, Bordeaux, France
	Fonds National d'Art Contemporain, Annecy, France
	Centre des Tanneurs, Nemours, France
1987	EGP Ville de Jarny
	Portraits nus, FNAC, Lyon; Montpellier
	Musée de Bourges
1988	*Autour de la danse,* Lyon
1989	*Chorégraphie silencieuse,* FNAC, Lyon; Paris; Dijon; Rennes
	Isabelle, Darjeeling; Paris
1990	*Chorégraphie silencieuse,* FNAC, Créteil; Lille; Marseille; Grenoble; Bordeaux
	Portraits, Forum des Halles, Paris Audiovisuel, Paris
1991	*Chorégraphie silencieuse,* FNAC, Nice; Strasbourg; Orléans; CNIT (La Défense)
	Isabelle, Salon de Printemps, Clichy
	Grenoble
1992	*Chorégraphie silencieuse,* FNAC, Gand
	Portrait d'Habitants de la ville de Muret, Musée Réattu, Arles; FNAC, Toulouse
1993	*Chorégraphie silencieuse,* FNAC, Parly II
	Portraits d'Habitants de la ville de Muret, Albi
1994	*Chorégraphie nue,* Thomery

Selected Group Exhibitions:

1988	*Splendeur et misére du corps,* Musée d'art et d'histoire, Fribourg; Musée d'art moderne, Paris
	Behold the man nude in photography, Edinburgh
	Picto Bastille, Paris
1989	Salon de la Photographie, Kodak, Paris
	Festival International de la photo de mode, Trouville
1990	Festival International de la photo de mode, Budapest
	Plaisir du Photographe, Cargése, Club Méditerranée; Galerie Maeght, Paris
	Behold the man nude in photography, London
	Fondation Agfa, Chateau d'Eau, Toulouse; Fondation Charles Cante, Mérignac; Cathédrale d'Images, Baux de Provence; Arsenal de Metz, Metz
1991	*Danser: Corps et Ame,* Blois; Douai; Annecy; Vandoeuvre
	Plaisir du photographe, New York
1993	*A la recherche du père,* Espace Photographique de Paris

Collections:

Musée d'Art Moderne, Paris; Ville de Paris Collection, Paris; Bibliothèque Nationale, Paris; Fonds National d'Art Contemporain, Paris; Musée de Toulon, France; Musée du Chateau d'Eau, Toulouse, France; Musée de Dunkerque, France.

Publications:

By BAURET: Books—*Charchoune,* Paris 1958; *Asse,* Paris 1959; *Boulez,* Paris 1959; *Bram van Velde,* Paris 1959; *Hadju,* Paris 1959; *Pallut,* Paris 1959; *Penalba,* Paris 1959; *Szenes,* Paris 1959; *Vieira da Silva,* Paris 1959; *Villon,* Paris 1959; *Morandi,* Paris 1961; *Portraits d'Hommes nus, Connus et Inconnus,* Paris 1975; *Jean-François Bauret,* with introduction by Jean Dieuzaide, Toulouse, France 1980; *Portraits Nus,* with text by Gabriel Bauret, Paris 1984; *Passeport Paris Audiovisuel,* exhibition catalogue, Paris 1990; *Portraits d'habitants de la ville de Muret,* Parchemins du Midi 1992. **Article**—"Bauret au Musée d'Art Moderne," interview, in *Zoom* (Paris), November/December 1971.

On BAURET: Books—*Jean-François Bauret,* exhibition catalogue, by Jerome Hinstin, Paris 1971; *Die Geschichte der Photographie im 20. Jahrhundert/Photography in the 20th Century* by Petr Tausk, Cologne 1977, London 1980; *French Photography From Its Origins to the Present* by Claude Nori, Paris 1978, London 1979; *Glanzlichter der Photographie: 30 Jahre Photokina Bilderschauen,* exhibition catalogue, edited by L. Fritz Gruber, Cologne 1980; *The Imaginary Photo Museum* by Helmut Gernsheim, Renate and L. Fritz Gruber and others, Cologne 1981, London 1982; *Histoire Mondiale de la Photographie en Couleurs* by Roger Bellone, Paris 1981; *La Photographie Créative* by Jean-Claude Lemagny, Paris 1984; *Photo Poche: Le Nu,* Paris 1986. **Articles**—"Artistes et modeles: Jean-François Bauret" in *Photo* (Paris), September 1969; "Jean-François Bauret" in *Zoom* (Paris), no. 3, 1970; "Le point sur le sexisme" in la *Zoom* (Paris), February//March 1971; "Huit photographies autour d'une modele de 18 ans" in *Photo* (Paris), June 1971; "Bauret et Cramer, ARC" in *Opus International* (Paris), May 1975; "L'Homme nu a encore frappé" in *Contrejour* (Paris), June 1975; "The Autoportrait" in *Camera* (Lucerne), September 1978; "Jean-François Bauret" in *Camera International* (Paris), November 1984; *Das Aktfoto* (München and Luzern) 1985; *Photographie,* April 1987; *Nude,* Japan 1988; *Vis à Vis,* No 5, 1989; *Photographies Magazine,* October 1990; *France Photographie,* No 119, 1990; *Obscéne?* Pamphlet sur 2 enfants nus, California 1990; *Photographis Magazine,* July 1992; *Réponses Photo,* December 1992; *A la recherche du père,* Paris Audiovisuel, May 1993; *Portraits de Mots,* 1994.

*

I like photography to exalt without words, to transmit emotion rather than information, and to go beyond the mere sign. The existential is not enough; it has to merge with the essential.

—Jean-François Bauret

*   *   *

Jean-François Bauret is a French photographer from the middle generation who specializes in portraits, nudes, fashion and advertising photography. He had photographed since boyhood as an amateur, but the first sight of Mary Ray's unusual portrait of the artist Meret Oppenheim made him determined to become a professional photographer. In this, he was supported by his wife, a painter, and at the beginning of their careers they exhibited portraits and landscapes together.

The major part of Bauret's assignment work is in fashion and publicity. Gifted with a powerful imagination, he executes this work with a unique freshness and eye-catching individuality. A number of posters based on his photos aroused both admiration and controversy when first seen in France—a barometer of the newness and nonconformity of his conceptions. Probably no photographer influences the visual taste of a society so much as one whose work is featured on billboards. The satisfaction felt at one's contribution to contemporary culture, however, is tempered by the constraints placed on creativity by the client, and the fact that the poster itself is ephemeral. The photograph made as an independent work and finished as an original print, on the other hand, may enjoy a longer life in the collection of museums or galleries, and offers greater freedom as a creative act. Bauret's own personal independent work is centered on the portrait and nude study, subjects for which he is well-equipped through his other studio assignment work.

His series of portraits of well-known people, including artists and scientists, got a warm public reception. Bauret's nudes, however, caused some

commotion. His unconventional approach did not focus on the familiar glamour pin-up, but was closer to an objective portrait of the body without any erotic context. This conception allowed Bauret a very wide choice of models—children, men, pregnant women, old people. No sensational presentation was intended, since the series appeared as a fair cross-section of human society without anything signified by garment or decoration. The majority of his audience may still be convinced that for public presentation only "nice nudes" are suitable (despite their apparent power to evoke erotic imaginings), but Bauret is surely entitled to show a fair picture of the real world in "straight" photos of individuals in chaste and calm poses.

—Petr Tausk

BAYER, Herbert.

Nationality: American. **Born:** Haag, Austria, 5 April 1900; emigrated to the United States, 1938: naturalized, 1944. **Education:** Attended gymnasium, Linz, Austria, 1911-17; apprentice in architecture and decorative arts, under architect George Schmidthammer, Linz, 1919; graphic design and typography assistant to architect Emanuel Margold, Darmstadt, Germany, 1920; studied mural painting and design, with Vasily Kandinsky, at the Staatliche Bauhaus, in Weimar, 1921-23, and in Dessau, 1925-28. **Military Service:** Served in Infantry Regiment 14, Austrian Army, 1917-19. **Family:** Married Irene Hecht in 1925 (divorced): daughter: Julia; married Joella Haweis Levy in 1944. **Career:** First photographs, with Irene Hecht, Dessau, 1924; independent photographer, from 1928. Young Master of Typography and Graphic Design, Staatliche Bauhaus, Dessau, 1925-28; Director, Dorland Studio of Design, Berlin, 1928-38; Art Director, *Vogue* magazine, Berlin 1928-30; freelance photographer, contributing to *Die Neue Linie,* etc., Berlin, 1930-36; painter, photographer, graphic designer, and exhibition architect, New York, 1938-45; Director, Dorland International design company, New York, 1945; Consultant Designer, 1945-56, and Chairman of Department of Design, 1956-65, Container Corporation of America, Chicago. Consultant and Architect, Aspen Institute of Humanistic Studies, Colorado, 1964-85; Art and Design Consultant, Atlantic Richfield Company, Los Angeles, 1966-85. **Recipient:** First Prize, *Foreign Advertising Photography* exhibition, New York, 1931; Medal, City of Salzburg, Austria, 1936; Gold Medal, Art Directors Club of Denver, Colorado, 1957; Gold Medal, Art Directors Club of Philadelphia, 1961; Trustees Award, Aspen Institute for Humanistic Studies, Colorado, 1965; Ambassador's Award for Excellence, London, 1968; Kulturpreis for Photography, Cologne, 1969; Gold Medal, American Institute of Graphic Arts, 1970; Adalbert Stifter Preis für Bildende Kunst Verliehen, Linz, Austria, 1971; Austrian Cross of Honor for Art and Science, 1978. Honorary Doctorate: Technische Hochschule, Graz, Austria, 1973; D.F.A.: Philadelphia College of Art, 1974. Honorary Member, Alliance Graphique Internationale, 1975; Honorary Fellow, Royal Academy of Fine Art, The Hague, Netherlands, 1975. Fellow, American Academy of Arts and Sciences, 1979. **Agent:** Marlborough Gallery, 40 West 57th Street, New York, New York 10019. **Died:** (in Montecito, California) 30 September 1985.

Individual Exhibitions:

1953	Hans Schaeffer Galleries, New York
1954	Kunstkabinett Klihm, Munich
	Galleria del Milione, Milan
1955	Aspen Institute for Humanistic Studies, Colorado
1956	*33 Years of Herbert Bayer's Work,* Germanisches Nationalmuseum, Nuremberg, West Germany (retrospective; travelled to Munich, Zurich, Berlin, Braunschweig and Vienna, 1956-57)
1957	Kunstkabinett Klihm, Munich
1958	*Recent Works,* Fort Worth Art Center, Texas (travelled to Minneapolis, Minnesota and Norman, Oklahoma)
1959	Kunstkabinett Klihm, Munich
1960	Stadtische Kunsthalle, Dusseldorf
	Museum am Ostwall, Dortmund, West Germany
1961	Bauhaus Archiv, Darmstadt, West Germany
1962	Stadtisches Kunstmuseum, Duisberg, West Germany (retrospective; toured the United States, Germany and Italy)
1963	Andrew Morris Gallery, New York
	Neue Galerie, Linz, Austria
1964	Aspen Institute for Humanistic Studies, Colorado
	5207 Galleries, Oklahoma City
1965	Byron Gallery, New York
	Esther Robles Gallery, Los Angeles
	Boise Art Association, Idaho
1966	University of New Hampshire, Durham
1967	Galerie Klihm, Munich
	Galerie Conzen, Dusseldorf
	Philadelphia Art Alliance
1968	Marlborough New London Gallery
1969	University of California at Santa Barbara
	Two Visions of Space: Herbert Bayer and Ingeborg ten Haeff, Hudson River Museum, Yonkers, New York
1970	Dunkelman Gallery, Toronto
	Germanisches Nationalmuseum, Nuremberg
	Galerie Conzen, Dusseldorf
1971	Marlborough Gallery, New York
	Centre Culturel Allemand, Paris
	Goethe-Institut, Paris
	Die Neue Sammlung, Munich
	Österreichisches Museum für Angewandte Kunst, Vienna
1972	Marlborough Gallery, Montreal
	Mer-Kup Galerias, Mexico City
1973	Landesbildstelle, Hamburg (travelled to Krefeld and Leverkusen)
	Saarland Museum, Saarbrücken
	Herbert Bayer: A Total Concept, Denver Art Museum (retrospective)
1974	Marlborough Galerie, Zurich
	Galerie Klihm, Munich
	Galerie Nächst St. Stephan, Vienna (travelled to Innsbruck and Graz)
	Marlborough Graphics, New York (toured the United States, 1974-75)
	Das Druckgrafische Werk bis 1971, Haus Deutscher Ring, Hamburg (retrospective; toured Germany, Switzerland, Portugal and Spain)
1975	Marlborough Gallery, Toronto
	Arte Contacto Galeria, Caracas
1976	*Beispiele aus dem Gesamtwerk 1919-1974,* Neue Galerie, Linz, Austria
	Graphics and Small Sculptures, Marlborough Gallery, New York
	Photomontages, Marlborough Gallery, New York
1977	Marian Locks Gallery, Philadelphia
	From Type to Landscape, Hopkins Center, Darmouth College, Hanover, New Hampshire (American Federation of Art show: toured the United States)
	Photographic Works, Arco Center for visual Art, Los Angeles (toured the United States)
1978	*Tapestries and Environmental Designs,* Galerie Klihm, Munich

	Museum Bochum, West Germany
1979	Marlborough Gallery, New York
	Photographic Exhibition, Galerie Breiting, West Berlin
1980	*Inaugural Exhibition of the Herbert Bayer Archive,* Denver Art Museum
	Neue Gallery, Linz, Austria
	Galerias Mer-Kup, Mexico City
1981	*A Selected Survey,* Grapestake Gallery, San Francisco
	Centre Georges Pompidou, Paris (with Umbo)
1982	*Das kunstlerische Werk 1918-38,* Bauhaus-Archiv, West Berlin (travelled to the Gewerbemuseum, Basle, Switzerland)
1983	*Bilder, Aquarelle, Zeichnungen,* Galerie Thomas, Munich
1984	*Works on Paper 1969-84,* Galerie Lopes, Zurich
	Saidenberg Gallery, New York

Selected Group Exhibitions:

1923	*Kunst and Technik: Eine neue Einheit,* Bauhaus und Staatliches Landesmuseum, Weimar
1929	*Film und Foto,* Stuttgart
1936	*Entartete Kunst,* Haus der Deutschen Kunst, Munich
1967	*50 Jahre Bauhaus,* Württembergische Kunstverein, Stuttgart (toured Europe, the United States, Canada, Argentina and Japan)
1973	*Die Zwanziger Jahre: Kontraste eines Jahrzehnts,* Zurich
1980	*Avant-Garde Photography in Germany 1919-1939,* San Francisco Museum of Modern Art (toured the United States)
1981	*Photographer as Printmaker,* Ferens Art Gallery, Hull, Yorkshire (travelled to the Museum and Art Gallery, Leicester; Cooper Gallery, Barnsley; Castle Museum, Nottingham; Photographers' Gallery, London)
1983	*Bauhausfotografie,* Institut for Auslandbeziehung, Stuttgart (and world tour)
1984	*Subjektive Fotografie: Images of the 50s,* San Francisco Museum of Modern Art (toured the United States and Europe)
1985	*Das Aktfoto,* Fotomuseum im Stadtmuseum, Munich

Collections:

Museum of Modern Art, New York; Denver Art Museum, Colorado (Archives); Santa Barbara Museum of Art, California; Neue Galerie der Stadt Linz, Austria; San Francisco Museum of Modern Art; Museum Folkwang, Essen, Germany; Bauhaus-Archiv, Berlin.

Publications:

By BAYER: Books—*Fotomontagen,* portfolio of 11 photomontages, Berlin 1932; *Fotoplastiken,* portfolio of 10 photos, Berlin 1937; *Bauhaus 1919-1928,* with Ise and Walter Gropius, New York 1938, 1959, 1975; *Seven Convolutions,* portfolio of lithographs, Colorado Springs 1948; *World Geo-Graphic Atlas,* Aspen, Colorado 1953; *Book of Drawings,* Chicago 1961; *Eight Monochrome Suite,* portfolio of lithographs, Los Angeles 1965; *Herbert Bayer: Paintings,* portfolio of reproductions, Chicago 1965; *Herbert Bayer: Painter/Designer/Architect,* New York, Ravensburg, London and Tokyo 1967; *Herbert Bayer,* portfolio of 6 silkscreens, with introduction by Dieter Honisch, Stuttgart 1968. **Articles**—"Reflections from One of the Sculptors Who Contributed to the 'Route of Friendship'" in *Architecture Formes et Fonctions* (Lausanne), 1969; "Typography and Design" in *Concepts of the Bauhaus: Busch-Reisinger Museum Collection,* exhibition catalogue, Cambridge, Massachusetts 1971; "Herbert Bayer," interview, in *Dialogue with Photography,* edited by Paul Hill and Thomas Cooper, London 1979; "Many Paths from the Bauhaus," interview, in *Darkroom Photography* (San Francisco), January/February 1981.

On BAYER: Books—*Foto-Auge/Oeil et photo/Photo-Eye: 76 Fotos der Zeit,* edited by Franz Roh and Jan Tschichold, Stuttgart 1929, London 1974; *The Way Beyond Art: The Work of Herbert Bayer* by Alexander Dorner, New York 1947; *Fotoauge Herbert Bayer,* exhibition catalogue, edited by Jan

Tschichold, Munich 1967; *Herbert Bayer,* exhibition catalogue, with text by Ludwig Grote, London 1968; *50 Jahre Bauhaus,* exhibition catalogue, by Wulf Herzongenrath, Stuttgart and London 1968; *Two Visions of Space: Herbert Bayer and Ingeborg ten Haeff,* exhibition catalogue, with introduction by Carl Black, Jr., New York 1969; *The Bauhaus* by Hans M. Wingler, Cambridge, Massachusetts 1969; *Herbert Bayer: A Total Concept,* exhibition catalogue, with introduction by Karl Otto Bach, Denver 1973; *Herbert Bayer: Das Druckgrafische Werk bis 1971,* with text by Hans M. Wingler and Peter Hahn, Berlin 1974; *Herbert Bayer,* exhibition catalogue, with introduction by Ida Rodriguez Prampolini, Zurich 1974; *Photographie als Kunstlerisches Experiment* by Willi Rotzler, Lucerne and Frankfurt 1974; *Herbert Bayer: Un Concepto Total* by Ida Rodriguez Prampolini, Mexico City 1975; *The Magic Image* by Cecil Beaton and Gail Buckland, London and Boston 1975; *Beispiele aus dem Gesamtwerk 1919-1974,* exhibition catalogue, with introduction by Peter Baum, Linz 1976; *Photomontage* by Dawn Ades, London and New York 1976; *Herbert Bayer: From Type to Landscape,* exhibition catalogue, with text by Jan van der Marck, New York 1977; *Herbert Bayer: Photographic Works,* exhibition catalogue, with text by Leland Rice and Beaumont Newhall, Los Angeles 1977; *Geschichte der Fotografie im 20. Jahrhundert/Photography in the 20th Century* by Petr Tausk, Cologne 1977, London 1980; *Fotographische Kunstlerbildnisse,* exhibition catalogue, by Dieter Ronte, Evelyn Weiss and Jeane von Oppenheim, Cologne 1977; *Kunstler-photographie im XX. Jahrhundert,* exhibition catalogue, edited by Carl-Albrecht Haenlein, Hannover 1977; *Neue Sachlichkeit and German Realism of the Twenties,* exhibition catalogue, by Wieland Schmied and Ute Eskildsen, London 1978; *Das Experimentelle Photo in Deutschland 1918-1940* by Emilio Bertonati, Munich 1978; *Germany: The New Photography 1927-33,* edited by David Mellor, London 1978; *Paris-Berlin 1900-1933,* exhibition catalogue, by Herbert Molderings, Werner Spies, Günter Metken and others, Paris 1978; *Photographie als Kunst 1879-1979/Kunst als Photographie 1949-1979,* exhibition catalogue, 2 vols., by Peter Weiermair, Innsbruck 1979; *Photographen der 20er Jahre* by Karl Steinorth, Munich 1979; *Film und Foto der 20er Jahre,* exhibition catalogue, by Ute Eskildsen and Jan Christopher Horak, Stuttgart 1979; *Internationale Ausstellung des Deutschen Werkbundes "Film und Foto" 1929,* facsimile reprint, edited by Karl Steinorth, Stuttgart 1979; *Bauhaus Fotografie,* edited by Roswitha Fricke, Dusseldorf 1982; *Herbert Bayer: Das kunstlerische Werk 1918-1938,* exhibition catalogue, West Berlin 1982; *The Artist as Photographer* by Marina Vaizey, London 1982; *Bauhausfotografie,* exhibition catalogue, by Wulf Herzogenrath, Stuttgart 1983; *Subjektive Fotografie: Images of the 50s,* exhibition catalogue by Dorothy Martinson and Ute Eskildsen, San Francisco 1984; *Herbert Bayer: The Complete Work* by Arthur A. Cohen, Cambridge, Massachusetts 1984. **Articles**—"Herbert Bayer: Photograph und Maler" by Paul Westheim in *Das Kunstblatt* (Berlin), May 1929; "Foreign Commercial Photographs Make Brilliant Showing" by Margaret Breuning in *New York Evening Post,* 7 March 1931; "Photographie" by Eberhard Holscher in *Gebrauchsgraphik* (Berlin), 1935; "From a Portfolio of Photomontages by Herbert Bayer" by Julien Levy in *Coronet* (New York), January 1940; "Die Zwischenposition von Herbert Bayer" by Franz Roh in *Die Kunst* (Munich), May 1956; "Herbert Bayer's Photographic Experiments" by Eckhard Neumann in *Typographica* (London), no. 2, 1965; "Herbert Bayer und seine Fotographischen Experimente" by Eckhard Neumann in *Foto Prisma* (Stuttgart), November 1969; "The Bayer Blitz: Two Views of a Bauhaus Veteran" by Henry J. Seldis, Jr. in the *Los Angeles Times,* 8 May 1977; "Herbert Bayer and Photography" by Leland Rice in *Exposure* (New York), May 1977; "Masters of Photography: Herbert Bayer" by Janis Bultman in *Darkroom Photography* (San Francisco), January/ February 1981; "Herbert Bayer: Typography at the Bauhaus" in *The Times* (London), 4 October 1985. **Film**—*Bayer: The Man and His Work* by Max Ewings, 1975.

*

Photography as well as photomontage has become one medium among many other mediums for the contemporary artist. It was in the depressed years after the First World War that a new optimism became evident to the artist who began to look for the liberating forces of a new technological and scientific age. Great interest was concentrated on the newly created technologies among which was photography.

The invention of the small format camera developed in the wake of this attitude. The miniature camera became a flexible instrument on the way to new imagery. The small camera is a handy tool of creativity, and it led to the discovery of new points of view. We suddenly saw a great possibility in hitherto unexplored perspectives such as the "bird's-eye view" or the "frog's-eye view." Furthermore, new photography was inspired by photography being used for scientific aims, making it possible to look through the human body, to photograph the microcosmos as well as the macrocosmos of the universe.

From the mid-1920's, it became a preferred pictorial medium in the exploration of a new visual language. The combined use of typography and photography (typo-photo) unified these previously isolated mediums. It was seen as imparting information clearly, precisely, and when used well, aesthetically and forcefully. The discoveries of the possibilities inherent in photography made it a tool to record realism, to freeze motion and speed, to convey the invisible.

The invention of photomontage added further richness. Photomontage, collage, montage and assemblage, as used early in posters, announcements and graphics became an artistic technique at the Bauhaus and by the Dadaists of a more intimate and playful nature.

We believed that any technique is permissible when it serves the problem better than another one. Choice of a medium is therefore often suggested by the nature of the problem. Consequently, several different techniques were mixed and used simultaneously.

The one static viewpoint from which to look upon a given subject gave way to a dynamic "multipoint of view" concept to which montage lends itself naturally. Furthermore, montage not only makes images of an unreal character possible, but can also be a powerful tool to convey the invisible as well as that of a succession of complex events. It is particularly compatible with advertising psychology and the imagery of ideas.

Photography explored in many different ways is today an esteemed medium of art. Future technologies will give to the artist yet unknown concepts of exploration.

—Herbert Bayer (1982)

*   *   *

While considering himself primarily a painter, Herbert Bayer has distinguished himself in a variety of fields, including sculpture, typography, graphic design—and photography. His initial encounter with photography came in the 1920's, when he was a student and later teacher at the Bauhaus. Established in the aftermath of World War I, the Bauhaus urged artists to come to terms with industrial society and the machine age. Its embrace of technology and machine aesthetics furnished a particularly receptive atmosphere for experiments with the image-producing machine, the camera.

Bayer, who came to the Bauhaus in 1921 as a student and remained to teach typography and graphic design, was stimulated to take up photography by the example of László Moholy-Nagy. It was Moholy's provocative opinion (expressed in his 1925 book *Painting Photography Film*) that photographic technology had dramatically extended and intensified the visual sense, opening up a "new wealth of optical expression" available for artistic exploration.

Bayer's first investigations of what Moholy called the "new vision" shared many of Moholy's visual concerns, and the photographs that Bayer made with a small hand-held camera in the mid-1920's are strongly reminiscent of Moholy's own. In these photographs, conventional picture relations were systematically disrupted by means of a variety of then-novel devices. Everyday scenes or objects were presented from unusually high or low vantage points—the so-called "bird's-eye" and "frog's-eye" views. Extreme close-ups revealed unexpected textures and forms. Shadows were called into play as an important graphic element. The resulting images were unprecedented for their combination of graphic clarity and spatial ambiguity, and went far toward establishing the camera's potential as an instrument of abstract vision. A large group of Bayer's photographs was exhibited at the 1929 *Film und Foto* exhibition in Stuttgart, which brought together some of the most advanced work being done in Europe and America.

Bayer's very different and highly personal approach to photomontage dates from the period after 1928 when he left the Bauhaus and moved to Berlin. In "Lonely Metropolitan" (1932), a pair of eyes unexpectedly stare out of the palms of two imploring hands set before a desolate cityscape. The mingling of photographic realism and dreamlike fantasy is characteristic of the surrealist art of the time, but Bayer's emphatic design and technical polish far surpass the typical surrealist production.

A related and somewhat later group of photographic images, which Bayer called *fotoplastiken,* dates from around 1936. These originated as groups of everyday objects and geometric solids which were arranged expressly to be photographed. The objects might be held in place by strings, which would later be removed by retouching. Backgrounds might be airbrushed in, serving to situate Bayer's strangely evocative collections of objects in a receding, illusionistic space.

These relatively private researches into fresh uses of photographic methods and imagery have received renewed attention in recent years. As a highly influential graphic designer, Bayer adapted many of the visual principles which inform his photomontages and *fotoplastiken* to use in posters and advertisements. By insisting on the importance of visual images in modern mass communication, he played a leading role in introducing the visual language of modern art to the public at large.

—Christopher Phillips

BAYLES, David P.

Nationality: American. **Born:** The Dalles, Oregon, 10 July 1952. **Education:** Studied at Moorpark Community College, California, 1970-72; Brooks Institute of Photography, Santa Barbara, California, 1978-80, BA (honours) 1980. **Career:** Independent photographer, from 1981. Worked as a color printer, Richard Armstrong Color Printing, Santa Barbara, California, 1981-82; Laboratory Manager, Maine Photographic Workshops, Rockport, 1984; Sound Editor, Bonnie Durrance Productions, Washington, D.C., 1984; commercial and portrait photographer, Jeffrey Alan's Photography Studio, Canoga Park, California, since 1985. Instructor at weekend photography workshops, The Learning Tree University, Chatsworth, California, since 1985. **Address:** P.O. Box 90238, Santa Barbara, California 93190, U.S.A.

Individual Exhibitions:

1982   Carnegie Cultural Arts Center, Oxnard, California
1983   Hooker Gallery, Carpinteria, California
1984   Maine Photographic Workshops, Rockport
        Cycle of Visions, Western States Museum of Photography, Santa Barbara, California
1986   Ventura College, California

Selected Group Exhibitions:

1982   *Erotic Art Show,* Artist Response, Isla Vista, California
        The Way We See It, Gallery Lens, Santa Barbara, California
1984   *Four Photographers,* Studio 10, Santa Barbara, California
        National Print Exhibition, Ledel Gallery, New York
        Association of Photographic Art Dealers, Roosevelt Hotel, New York
1986   *Landscape as Metaphor,* San Diego Museum of Art, California (travelled to Santa Barbara Museum of Art, California)
        Images of Excellence, Santa Barbara Arts Council, California
        The Golden Light, San Diego Museum of Art, California

Collections:

Bibliothèque Nationale, Paris; Los Angeles County Museum of Art, California; University of Texas, Austin; Santa Barbara Museum of Art, California; Gernsheim Collection, Lugano, Switzerland.

Publications:

By BAYLES: Articles—"Santa Barbara Vignettes" in *The News and Review* (Santa Barbara), May 1979; "It Takes a Lot to Laugh, It Takes a Train to Cry" in *The News and Review* (Santa Barbara), December 1979.

On BAYLES: Articles—"Cycle of Visions" by Pat Fish in *The Weekly* (Santa Barbara), January 1984.

*

I work in color as well as in black and white. My color work is of found objects, both man made and natural. It tends toward the abstract and is a simple expression of purity in color, texture and form. My black and white images originate from an inner perspective. Through it I explore various relationships between humanity and the natural environment. The two processes are complementary. My color work begins as a recognition by the eye and moves inward, while the black and white originates from within and reaches outward for expression through the eye.

—David P. Bayles

*   *   *

When on a visit to Brooks Institute of Photography in Santa Barbara a few years ago I came across an exhibition of very original and highly competent colour abstractions of a former student. Always on the look-out for new talent, it was not long before Bayles came to see me bringing with him additional work.

Abstract forms in nature and man-made creations have long fascinated me, and Bayles' close-ups might be called concentrated nature. Compared with the hieroglyphics of Gianella or Siskind they are easily dicipherable. A few descriptions may clarify my meaning: Peeling paint, window-reflections, rock patterns, drain stained by minerals, seed-stems of a flower. In all these images form is accentuated by concentration and becomes striking by isolation from the surroundings. Our gain is an aesthetic pleasure in the new forms and patterns that are revealed, as Blossfeldt discovered in the magnifications of plants sixty years ago.

However, despite obvious success David Bayles enjoyed with these colour abstractions he abandoned this field as "too easy" about a year ago. "They became second nature to me requiring no mental effort." A creative mind, he rightly argues, requires constant confrontation with new problems. Once he knows the solution to one he must move on to the next or he will lose himself in repetition. Bayles now specializes in b/w landscapes with figures-landscapes in which he sees qualities analogous with or complementary to the figures, nude or clothed. A symbolism which I admit is not easy to comprehend by an outsider not familiar with the personality of the "portrayed," or rather involved. Whatever the difficulties which any exploration of new ideas will throw up, eventually, we hope, they may be mastered. We must leave Bayles to it, for this problem is a psychological and not a photographic one.

—Helmut Gernsheim

BEARD, Peter (Hill).

Nationality: American. **Born:** New York City, 22 January 1938. **Education:** Attended Buckley School, New York, 1945-52; Pomfret School, Vermont, 1950-54; Felsted College, Essex, England, 1956-57; studied art, under Josef Albers, at Yale University, New Haven, Connecticut, 1958-61, B.A. 1961. **Family:** Married Mary O. Cushing in 1967 (divorced, 1971); married the model Cheryl Tiegs in 1981. **Career:** Photographer/diarist since 1950. First visited Africa, 1955; settled in Kenya, on "Hog Ranch," below the Ngong

Untitled, **1986.** Photograph by David P. Bayles.

Hills near Nairobi, 1961; met and worked with Karen Blixen (Isak Dinesen), Denmark, 1961-62; worked in Tsavo Park, Kenya, documenting the elephant habitat crisis, 1964-65; worked with the Nuffield Unit and Wildlife Services, Dick Laws and Ian Parker in documenting elephant and hippo populations, 1966, and with Alistair Graham on a Lake Rudolf crocodile survey for Kenya Game Department, 1966-68; established second residence in Montauk, Long Island, New York, 1973. **Agent:** Blum-Helman Gallery, 20 West 57th Street, New York, New York 10019. **Address:** Post Office Box 603, Montauk, Long Island, New York 11954, U.S.A.

Individual Exhibitions:

1975   Blum-Helman Gallery, New York
1977   *The End of the Game,* International Center of Photography,
            New York
1979   *Last Word from Paradise,* Seibu Museum, Tokyo
            The Diary of Peter Beard, Watari Gallery, Shibuya-ku, Tokyo

Selected Group Exhibitions:

1979   *NASA: Voyager Time Capsule Exhibition,* The Photographers'
            Gallery, London

Collections:

Museum of Modern Art, New York; International Center of Photography, New York; Musée Réattu, Arles, France.

Publications:

By BEARD: Books—*The End of the Game,* New York 1965, revised edition as *The End of the Game: Last Word from Paradise,* with an introduction by Joseph Murumbi, epilogue by Richard M. Laws, New York and London 1977; *Eyelids of Morning,* New York 1974; *Longing for Darkness: Kamante's Tales from Out of Africa,* New York and London 1975. **Articles**—interview in *Interview* (New York), December 1973; "Last of the Nuba" in *Natural History Magazine* (New York), December 1975; "Introduction" to *Francis Bacon,* Metropolitan Museum exhibition catalogue, New York 1976; *Interview* (New York), January 1978; interview in *Photo* (New York), January/ February 1978; "Another Last Word from Paradise," interview, with Esmond Martin, in *Africana Magazine* (Nairobi), August 1978; "Introduction" to *Leni Riefenstahl,* exhibition catalogue, Tokyo 1980. **Films**—*Hallelujah the Hills,* as actor, directed by Jonas Mekas, 1963; *Longing for Darkness,* 1975; *The Bicentennial Diary,* 1976; *Africa: The End of the Game,* ABC television film, 1979.

Hog Ranch, 1976. Photograph by Peter Beard.

On BEARD: Articles—"Peter Beard: The Death of a World" by Owen Edwards in the *Village Voice* (New York), 29 December 1975; "Endpaper: Four Days in the Life" by Glenn Collins in the *New York Times Magazine,* 15 February 1976; "This Is the End of the Game" by Boyce Rensberger in the *New York Times Magazine,* 6 November 1977; "Notes on the Lost Books of Peter Beard" by Jonas Mekas in *Soho Weekly News* (New York), 10 November 1977; "Epitaph on Film: Images of Ruin in Africa" by Robert Hughes in *Time* (New York), 12 December 1977; "The Collector: Photographer Peter Beard's Life and Times" by Doon Arbus in *Rolling Stone* (San Francisco), 16 November 1978; "The Last Great Herds" by Jeffery A. Davis in *Ecology* (San Diego, California), June 1979; "Peter Beard's Diary" by Carol DiGrappa in *Upper and Lower Case* (New York), June 1979.

*

Not to take pictures in this century is crazy. If people only knew how easy it was, everyone would be "a photographer." Photography is a great field for phony artists and frustrated technicians. All you need is enough brain to recognize good subject matter and enough money to buy a reflex camera.

I'm not much of a message bearer, but I like the idea of documentation, particularly photographic, in a sort of collage over a period of time. The thing that occurs to me, now that speeds are so accelerated, is how much we're losing in terms of values in daily life; how much quality of life we're losing, and how willingly we accept this, adapt ourselves to it, and make excuses for ourselves. Particularly in East Africa—the Paradise slum.

I mean, the capacity of human beings to fool themselves—to behave more destructively than any other animal and call it love. The human behaviorist Ronald Laing describes it perfectly in *The Politics of Experience:* "Human beings seem to have an almost unlimited capacity to deceive themselves into taking their own lies for truth. . . . The double action of destroying ourselves with one hand and calling this love with the other, is a sleight of hand we can marvel at. . . . By such mystification, we achieve and sustain our adjustment, our adaptation."

The first *End of the Game* was an amateur swan through areas I'd always read about and became interested in through Karen Blixen, and it seemed almost acceptable to carry out as a sort of corny homework assignment—I was still in school. The idea of redoing it came from a new publisher, and I was relieved to be able to fix up a half-assed project that was unmistakeably thrown together between classes. The new version encompasses 23 years of fresh observations, collections, researches, photos, documentation. It is completely rewritten, completely redone.

I keep thinking of what Faulkner said: "The ruined wood we used to know won't cry for retribution—the men who have destroyed it will accomplish its revenge." What amazes me most is that we are so willing to lose things that we can never get back—even further, we appear hell-bent on our own destruction. It's rivetting.

The End of the Game says that we have deprived the elephants of the habitat they require. It won't be long before this can be said of our own species—*they were deprived of the habitat they required.* To require means to need, to depend on. We are losing many things on earth, irreplaceable things, and we will soon find out the degree of our dependency, the extent of our need and the thoughtlessness of our expanding populations.

The End of the Game is a sort of photo album based on field studies by internationally qualified scientists who had integrity and were therefore replaced. It shows the road to hell paved with benevolence and short-term politics. Hopefully, this will give confidence and direction to the nervously emerging African citizens who do not want to denude, domesticate and ruin everything as we have—who are tired of being sucked up to and manipulated with lies: it will forever record for them a wilderness they lived in for many hundreds of years and saw mangled and over-run by our well-meaning missionaries and high-velocity heroes. As Karen Blixen says in the introduction: "The wilderness of only half a century ago, then so completely itself, has been reduced tree by tree, animal by animal, shadow by shadow, rock by rock, to its last rutted corners. The few remaining spaces have been infiltrated, divided up, domesticated, deprived of natural systems, denuded of natural processes, systematized, similarized, artificialized, sterilized, commercialized. . . . "

The play period is over. We no longer have the luxury of living in a world where there is the time or the space for playing games in the wild-deerness. The speeds are too great. By tracing fossil series we know that evolution has favored size and numbers—but trends in evolution have their own limiting factors, their own built-in demise. Sheer size may do us in. We are poised at the lily pond like dinosaurs.

—Peter Beard

*　　*　　*

Peter Beard's photographs deal with only one subject and place—the natural life of the African bush—but they give such a complex and sensitive view that their meaning is universal. As a boy of seventeen Beard began to make the beautiful and melancholy photographs that appear in his three books, *Eyelids of Morning, Longing for Darkness,* and the classic *End of the Game.* The latter book in particular is a moving memorial to Kenya as it was in the days of its first generation of European explorers, hunters and settlers. Hoping to create "a memory of the past, a record of the present, and an image of the future," Beard photographed the extraordinary wildlife, and its human counterparts, that surrounded him on safari.

The special experience of Beard's photographs is their personal immediacy: in a sequence of shots he captures the charge of a lion—directly toward the camera. He presents the spectacular sight of an elephant herd observed from an airplane's height, but he can also find beauty in a close shot of an elephant's gigantic, decaying carcass. He shows the splendor of the impala's flight and also the moment of its death. Color photography is used for both the intricate beadwork of the African tribespeople and the bloody flesh of a flayed zebra.

Courage and humor rescue Beard's photographs from sentimentality. Certainly their beauty is melancholy; at least half of the images in *End of the Game* show death rather than life. Yet, when we see the lined and tired face of one of Africa's great old hunters sharing a spread with a tough bull rhino, mortally wounded, the humorous visual comparison helps drive home Beard's point. It is "the end of the game" in more senses than one.

Perhaps because he has arranged them in collage-like diaries that he has kept for many years, Beard's photographs work well with text and other documentary materials. His characteristically soft-focus, low contrast images convey both the urgency of his actual safari experience and the underlying preservationist concern that is the impetus of his entire project. Beard has grasped the special documentary power that is photography's. He possesses the rare ability to use the documentary aspect of the camera's power for his creative personal expression. Photographer, writer, film-maker, sportsman, this protean artist has succeeded not only in expressing his deep and complex feelings about his beloved Africa, but also in putting the photographic medium to a use for which it is uniquely suited.

—Maren Stange

BEATON, Cecil (Walter Hardy).

Nationality: British. **Born:** London, 14 January 1904. **Education:** Attended Heath Mount School, London; Harrow School, Middlesex; and St. Cyprian's School, Eastbourne, until 1921; studied history and architecture, St. John's College, Cambridge, 1922-25; self-taught in photography. **Career:** Served as photographer with the Ministry of Information, London, 1939-45. Worked as a clerk, Schmiegelow and Company cement company, London, 1925-26. Freelance portrait and fashion photographer, 1926-30; contract fashion photographer, Condé Nast Publications, mainly for *Vogue* magazine, New York and London, 1930 until the mid-1950's, thereafter freelance photographer, until his death, 1980; also stage designer, 1925-70, and film designer, 1941-70, London and Hollywood. **Recipient:** Neiman Marcus Award, 1956; Antoinette Perry Award for costume, 1957; Academy Award for film sets and costumes, 1957, 1965; Honor Award, American Society of Magazine Photographer, 1963. Honorary Fellow, Royal Photographic Society, London, 1964. Chevalier, Légion d'Honneur, 1960. C.B.E. (Commander, Order of the British Empire), 1957; knighted, 1972. **Agent:** Sotheby's Belgravia, 19 Motcomb Street, London SW1X 8LB, England. **Died:** (in Broadchalke, near Salisbury, Wiltshire) *18 January 1980.*

Individual Exhibitions:

1929	Everglades Club, Palm Beach, Florida
	Elsie de Wolfe Galleries, New York
1930	Cooling Galleries, London
1931	Delphic Galleries, New York
1936	Redfern Gallery, London
1937	Carroll Carstairs Gallery, New York
1942	Estudio do Spu, Lisbon
1951	Sagittarius Gallery, New York
1956	Sagittarius Gallery, New York
1958	Redfern Gallery, London
1960	Sagittarius Gallery, New York
1964	Redfern Gallery, London
1966	Lefevre Gallery, London
1968	Palm Beach Gallery, Miami
	Wright Hepburn Gallery, London
	Portraits 1928-1968, National Portrait Gallery, London
1969	*600 Faces by Beaton 1928-69,* Museum of the City of New York
1970	Palm Beach Gallery, Miami
1971	*Fashion: An Anthology,* Victoria and Albert Museum, London (with costumes and designs by others)
1972	Palm Beach Gallery, Miami
1973	Impressions Gallery, York
	The First 10 Years, Sonnabend Gallery, New York
	Record of a Period, Draytons Gallery 12, Minneapolis
1974	Kodak Gallery, London (retrospective)
1980	Galerie Zabriskie, Paris (with Joseph Cornell)
1981	*War Photographs 1939-45,* Imperial War Museum, London
	Fotogalleriet, Oslo
1982	*Fotografie 1922-71,* Palazzo Fortuny, Venice
1983	*Studied Beauty,* Smithsonian Institution, Washington, D.C. (toured the United States and Canada)
1985	Barbican Art Gallery, London (retrospective)
	Brooks Museum of Art, Memphis, Tennessee

Selected Group Exhibitions:

1929	*Film und Foto/Fifo,* Deutscher Werkbund, Stuttgart (toured Germany)
1959	*Hundert Jahre Photographie 1839-1939,* Museum Folkwang, Essen (travelled to Cologne and Frankfurt)
1964	*The Painter and the Photograph: From Delacroix to Warhol,* University of New Mexico, Albuquerque
1972	*Personal Views 1850-1970,* British Council, London (toured Europe)
1977	*Fashion Photography,* International Museum of Photography, George Eastman House, Rochester, New York (travelled to Brooklyn Museum, New York; San Francisco Museum of Modern Art; Cincinnati Art Institute, Ohio; and Museum of Fine Arts, St. Petersburg, Florida)
1979	*Photographie als Kunst 1879-1979,* Tiroler Landesmuseum Ferdinandeum, Innsbruck, Austria (travelled to Neue Galerie am Wolfgang Gurlitt Museum, Linz, Austria; Neue Galerie am Landesmuseum Joanneum, Graz, Austria; and the Museum des 20. Jahrhunderts, Vienna)
1980	*The Queen Mother: A Celebration,* National Portrait Gallery, London
1983	*British Photography 1955-65,* The Photographer's Gallery, London
1985	*Das Aktfoto,* Fotomuseum im Stadtmuseum, Munich
1987	*Hollywood Photographers,* Los Angeles County Museum of Art

Collections:

National Portrait Gallery, London; Imperial War Museum, London; Sotheby's Belgravia, London; Life Picture Collection, New York; Boston Public Library; Yale University, New Haven, Connecticut; Rhode Island School of Design, Providence; New Orleans Museum of Art; University of Nebraska, Lincoln; Gernsheim Collection, University of Texas at Austin.

Publications:

By BEATON: Books—*The Book of Beauty,* London 1930; *Cecil Beaton's Scrapbook,* London 1937; *Cecil Beaton's New York,* London 1938, 1948, as *Portrait of New York,* New York 1938; *My Royal Past, by Baroness von Bulop, as Told to Cecil Beaton (or Rather Written by Him),* London 1939, revised edition, London and New York 1960; *Time Exposure,* with text by Peter Quennell, London 1941, 1946; *History under Fire,* with text by James Pope-Hennessy, London 1941; *Winged Squadrons,* London 1942; *Near East,* London 1943; *British Photographers,* editor, London 1944; *Face to Face with China,* with text by H.B. Rattenburg, London 1945; *Far East,* London 1945; *Air of Glory,* with text by Ministry of Information editors, London 1946; *Indian Album,* London 1946; *Chinese Album,* London 1946; *Designs for the Theatre by Rex Whistler,* editor, London 1947; *Ashcombe: The Story of a 15 Year Lease,* London 1947; *The School for Scandal,* with text by R.B. Sheridan, London 1949; *Ballet,* London and New York 1951; *Photobiography,* London 1951; *Persona Grata,* with Kenneth Tynan, London 1953; *The Glass of Fashion,* London 1954; *It Gives Me Great Pleasure,* London 1955, as *I Take Great Pleasure,* New York 1955; *The Face of the World,* London and New York 1957; *Images,* with an introduction by Christopher Isherwood, London 1959; *The Importance of Being Earnest,* with text by Oscar Wilde, London 1960; *The Wandering Years: Diaries 1922-39,* London and Boston 1961; *Quail in Aspic: The Life Story of Count Charles Korsetz,* London 1962; *Royal Portraits,* with an introduction by Peter Quennell, London 1963; *Cecil Beaton's My Fair Lady,* London, as *Cecil Beaton's "Fair Lady,"* New York 1964; *The Years Between: Diaries 1939-44,* London 1965; *The Best of Beaton,* with an introduction by Truman Capote, London 1968; *Fashion: An Anthology Compiled by Cecil Beaton,* exhibition catalogue, edited by Madeleine Ginsburg, London 1971; *My Bolivian Aunt: A Memoir,* London 1971; *The Happy Years: Diaries 1944-48,* London 1972; *Memoires of the Forties,* New York 1972; *Salisbury: A New Approach to the City and Its Neighbourhood,* with text by Hugh de Shortt, London 1972; *The Strenuous Years: Diaries 1948-55,* London 1973; *The Magic Image: The Genius of Photography from*

A Ghurka Soldier Transporting a Wounded Man on His Back Through the Jungle, c 1945. Photograph by Cecil Beaton.

1839 to the Present Day, with Gail Buckland, London and Boston 1975; *The Restless Years: Diaries 1955-63,* London 1976; *The Parting Years: Diaries 1963-74,* London 1978; *Self-Portrait with Friends: The Selected Diaries of Cecil Beaton 1922-1974,* edited by Richard Buckle, London and New York 1979; *Cecil Beaton: War Photographs 1939-45,* with forward by Peter Quennell, introduction by Gail Buckland, London 1981; *Oliver Messel,* exhibition catalogue, with others, London 1983.

On BEATON: Books—*A Hundred Years of Photography 1839-1939* by Lucia Moholy, London 1939; *The Man Behind the Camera* by Helmut Gernsheim, London 1948; *Some Designs for Stage and Screen* by Orville K. Larson, East Lansing, Michigan 1961; *Beaton Portraits,* exhibition catalogue, London 1968; *The Painter and the Photograph: From Delacroix to Warhol* by Van Deren Coke, Albuquerque, New Mexico 1972; *Photography into Art,* exhibition catalogue, by Colin Osman, Ainslie Ellis and Margaret Harker, London 1973; *The Photographs of Sir Cecil Beaton,* exhibition catalogue, by Andrew Sproxton, York 1973; *American Fashion,* edited by Sarah Tomerlin Lee, New York 1975, London 1976; *Cecil Beaton: Stage and Film Designs* by Charles Spencer, London 1976; *Geschichte der Fotografie im 20. Jahrhundert/ Photography in the 20th Century* by Petr Tausk, Cologne 1977, London 1980;

Happy and Glorious: 130 Years of Royal Photographs, exhibition catalogue, edited by Colin Ford, London 1977; *Photographen der 20er Jahre* by Karl Steinorth, Munich 1979; *Film und Foto der 20er Jahre,* exhibition catalogue, by Ute Eskildsen and Jan Christopher Horak, Stuttgart 1979; *The History of Fashion Photography* by Nancy Hall-Duncan, New York and Paris 1979; *The Vogue Book of Fashion Photography* by Polly Devlin, with an introduction by Alexander Liberman, New York and London 1979; *30's: British Art and Design Before the War,* exhibition catalogue, by Ian Jeffrey, William Feaver and others, London 1979; *Dialogue with Photography,* edited by Paul Hill and Thomas Cooper, London 1979; *Life: The First Decade 1936-1945* by Robert Littman, Ralph Graves and Doris C. O'Neill, New York 1979, London 1980; *Beaton,* edited with text by James Danziger, London 1980; *Cecil Beaton* by Philippe Garner, London 1982; *Bilder vom Krieg* by Rainer Fabian and Hans-Christian Adam, Hamburg 1983, as *Images of War: 130 Years of War Photography,* London 1985; *Hollywood Photographers: Interpreting American Culture Through Photographs,* exhibition catalogue, by Linda Rich, David Fahey and Kathleen M. Gauss, Los Angeles 1987. **Articles**—"600 Faces by Cecil Beaton 1928-1969" by T. Barrow in *Aperture* (New York), Summer 1970; "Beaton at His Own Game" by P. Glynn in *The Times* (London), 12 October 1971; "Sir Cecil Beaton at the RPS" by Gail Buckland in *Photographic Journal* (London), July 1973; "Knight in White Satin: Cecil Beaton Talks to Penelope Tree" in *Inter/View* (New York), April 1973; "Cecil Beaton" by G. Hughes in *Amateur Photographer* (London), 10 April 1974; "Living Masters of Photography: Cecil Beaton" by Allan Porter in *Camera* (Lucerne), June 1974; "Obituary: Sir Cecil Beaton, Photographer, Writer and Stage Designer" in *The Times* (London), 19 January 1980; "Cecil Beaton: Arbiter of Elegance" by Richard Buckle in *The Observer* (London), 20 January 1980; "Cecil Beaton: Garbo Inconnue" in *Photo* (Paris), February 1980; "A Dramatic Achievement: The Life and Works of Cecil Beaton" by Ainslie Ellis in *British Journal of Photography* (London), 15 February 1980; "Sir Cecil Beaton C.B.E., 1904-1980" by Colin Osman in *Creative Camera* (London), March 1980; "Beaton: The Final Selection" by James Danziger in the *Sunday Times Magazine* (London), 5 October 1980.

*   *   *

Born in 1904, Cecil Beaton was educated at Harrow and Cambridge. A member of the British social elite, Beaton was and is best known as a photographer of high fashion, a portraitist of the rich and the royal, and as a designer of theatrical sets and costumes.

"I had two careers—photography and set designing. They overflowed constantly." As a young boy, Beaton was introduced to photography by his sisters' nanny, and with a Kodak 3a folding camera, began photographing his sisters, his mother, and any family friends who were willing to sit and model. Inspired by the romantic portraits by Baron de Meyer, the lavish fashion photographs by Steichen, and allegorical photographs of the Edwardian age, young Beaton's imagination and energy were unbounded.

He would go to great lengths to construct elaborate sets, using materials ranging from mirrors to cellophane, frequently painting large backdrops in strong abstract designs. He photographed his sitters posed statue-like, dressed in fanciful costumes or wrapped in silver cloth. Human subjects became elements of an entire decorative tableau. His camera did the work of a painter or a designer: the sitter became part of a preconceived schema in which the focus was not the figure or the clothes, but the creation of an entire "ambience."

In the late 1920's and 1930's, the introduction and availability of small hand-held cameras opened new possibilities in journalistic and documentary photography, leading to an interest in naturalism and depiction of "truth." Beaton did not participate in these developments. His work did not involve itself with the general social concerns of the times, but, rather, reflected Beaton's own private social interests. He continued to explore the artifice and constructed environments within the constraints of a studio. He worked as a freelance portrait photographer, patronized by members of the British upper class and old family friends like the Sitwells.

A trip to New York in 1930 began a long relationship with Condé Nast; he worked during the 30's under exclusive contract for *Vogue.* It was Condé Nast that insisted that Beaton finally abandon his beloved old Kodak 3a, and acquire an 8 x 10 view camera. Although he initially hated its cumbersome-

ness, the quality of his photographs improved dramatically, and Beaton was soon won over to this new camera. Throughout his photographic career he worked in large format, using a smaller Rolleiflex only on his travels and during his years as a war photographer.

From New York, Beaton went to Hollywood in 1931. This was the heyday of a new movie industry, and Beaton loved it. Here, his love of the theatrical could integrate unrestrainedly with his love of photographing. He spent days photographing movie stars in back lots and unused sets. The photographs were new, and exciting, and many had a surrealist quality to them as Beaton placed human forms amid the enormous scale and chaotic aura of back lots. On his return to London, Beaton became the official photographer for the royal family.

During World War II, the Ministry of Information hired Beaton to take pictures of war-torn London and of Allied operations in North Africa and the Far East. The pictures were for propaganda purposes, to document the destruction of London, and to enlist American support. One image from this period, of a young victim of the bombings sitting in a hospital bed with a bandaged head, clutching a rag doll, was widely circulated and is said to be largely responsible for gaining American sympathy.

This wartime assignment presented a new challenge to Beaton, and the results are radically different from his previous work. The photographs of London are stark, simple, and straightforward, and imbued with the tense alienation of a vulnerable population. His photographs of North Africa and China do not have the drama of Capa's or Smith's, but their strength is in their grace and subtle, poetic spirit.

Following the war, Beaton returned to fashion photography, still under contract to *Vogue.* The pictures were different though, adopting the style of "new realism," in which women dressed in high fashion were photographed in everyday situations. In the 1950's, new stars in fashion photography began to emerge. The energy of Avedon and the clean grace of Penn began to make Beaton's pictures seem outdated, and his contract with *Vogue* was terminated. It had been a long and fruitful relationship.

The late 1950's and early 1960's led to his increased involvement with theater and cinema. Beaton designed the sets and costumes for both *Gigi* and *My Fair Lady,* and won Oscars for both. In 1956 he began working for *Harper's Bazaar,* photographing such personalities as Marilyn Monroe, Evelyn Waugh, Carson McCullers, and Mick Jagger. The photographs of this period are looser, more personal and engaging.

Sir Cecil Beaton was knighted in 1972. In 1974 he suffered a stroke, and was not able to photograph for several years. Sotheby's purchased his entire photographic output in 1977 (150,000 photographs, one million negatives, countless color transparencies, more than a dozen scrapbooks). In 1979 he began photographing again, and continued to do so right up until the time of his death.

—Sarah Putnam

BECHER, Bernhard and Hilla.

Nationality: German. **Born:** Bernhard Becher in Siegen in 1931; Hilla Becher born Hilla Wobeser in Potsdam in 1934 **Education:** Bernhard Becher studied painting and lithography at the Staatlichen Kunstakademie, Stuttgart, 1953-56, and typography at the Staatlichen Kunstakademie, Dusseldorf, 1957-61; self-taught in photography; Hilla Becher studied photography in Potsdam, and painting at the Staatlichen Kunstakademie, Dusseldorf. **Career:** Bernhard and Hilla Becher married in 1961; they have worked together as freelance photographic artists, concentrating on industrial photography, Dusseldorf, since 1959. Both are instructors in photography at the Staatlichen Kunstakademie, Dusseldorf. **Recipient:** British Council Photo Study Grant, 1966; Fritz-Thyssen-Stiftung grant, West Germany, 1967-68. **Agents:** Galerie Konrad Fischer, Platanenstrasse 7, Dusseldorf, Sonnabend Gallery, 420 West Broadway, New York, New York 10012, and Nigel Greenwood Inc., 41 Sloane Gardens, London SW1, England. **Address:** Wittlauer 4, Am Muhlenkamp 16, Dusseldorf, Germany.

Individual Exhibitions:

1963	Galerie Ruth Nohl, Siegen, West Germany
1965	Galerie Pro, Bad Godesburg, West Germany
1966	Staatliche Kunstakademie, Dusseldorf
1967	Staatliches Museum, Munich
	Technische Hochschule, Karlsruhe
	Bergbau-Museum, Bochum, West Germany
	Kunstakademie, Copenhagen
1968	Wachsman Institute, Los Angeles
	Goethe Center, San Francisco
	Stedelijk Van Abbemuseum, Eindhoven, Netherlands
	Galerie Ruth Nohl, Siegen, West Germany
	Städtisches Museum, Monchengladbach, West Germany
1969	Städtische Kunsthalle, Dusseldorf
1970	Städtisches Museum, Ulm, West Germany
	Moderna Museet, Stockholm
	Galerie Konrad Fischer, Dusseldorf
1971	Kabinett für Aktuelle Kunst, Bremerhaven, West Germany
	Gegenverkehr, Aachen, West Germany
1972	Sonnabend Gallery, New York
	Bennington College, Vermont
1973	Galleria Forma, Genoa
	Nigel Greenwood Inc., London
	Sonnabend Gallery, New York
1974	Institute of Contemporary Arts, London (toured the U.K.)
	Sonnabend Gallery, New York
1975	*Fotografien 1957-1975,* Rheinisches Landesmuseum, Bonn
	Galleria Castelli, Milan
	Museum of Modern Art, New York
	Sonnabend Gallery, New York
1976	Kunsthalle, Tubingen, West Germany
1977	Sonnabend Gallery, New York
1981	Stedelijk Van Abbemuseum, Eindhoven, Netherlands
	Kunstverein, Siegen, West Germany
	Sonnabend Gallery, New York
	Carl Taylor Gallery, Dallas, Texas
1982	Sonnabend Gallery, New York
1986	Architekturmuseum, Basle, Switzerland

Selected Group Exhibitions:

1969	*Prospekt '69,* Städtische Kunsthalle, Dusseldorf
1970	*Information,* Museum of Modern Art, New York
1975	*New Topographics: Photographs of a Man-Altered Landscape,* International Museum of Photography, George Eastman House, Rochester, New York (travelled to the Otis Art Institute, Los Angeles, and Princeton University Art Museum, New Jersey)
1977	*Documenta 6,* Museum Fridericianum, Kassel, West Germany
1979	*Photographie als Kunst 1879-1979/Kunst als Photographie 1949-1979,* Tiroler Landesmuseum Ferdinandeum, Innsbruck, Austria (travelled to the Neue Galerie am Wolfgang Gurlitt Museum, Linz, Austria; Neue Galerie am Landesmuseum Joanneum, Graz, Austria; and Museum des 20. Jahrhunderts, Vienna)
1980	*Artist and Camera,* Mappin Art Gallery, Sheffield, Yorkshire (travelled to the Stoke City Art Gallery; Durham Light Infantry Museum; Cartwright Hall, Bradford)
1982	*Counterprarts: Form and Emotion in Photographs,* Metropolitan Museum of Art, New York (travelled to the Contemporary Arts Center, Cincinnati; Dallas Museum of Fine Arts; San Francisco Museum of Modern Art; Corcoran Gallery, Washington, D.C.)
1983	*The Medium is Photography,* San Francisco Museum of Modern Art
1984	*La Photographie Créative,* Pavillion des Arts, Paris
1987	*Photography and Art 1946-86,* Los Angeles County Museum of Art

Collections:

Wallraf-Richartz Museum, Cologne; Moderna Museet, Stockholm; Museum of Modern Art, New York; Allen Memorial Art Museum, Oberlin College, Ohio; Metropolitan Museum of Art, New York; Art Gallery of Ontario, Toronto; Tate Gallery, London; International Museum of Photography at George Eastman House, Rochester, New York.

Publications:

By the BECHERS: Books—*Anonyme Skulpturen: Eine Typologie Technische Bauten,* Dusseldorf 1970; *Die Architektur der Förder- und Wasser-Türme,* with text by W. Schoenberg, J. Werth and T. Aachen, Munich 1971; *Industrial Buildings,* portfolio of 14 photos, Munich 1975; *Framework Houses of the Siegen Industrial Region,* Munich 1977. **Article**—"Photographing Industrial Architecture," interview, with Angela Graverholz and Anne Ramsden, in *Parachute* (Montreal), Spring 1981.

On the BECHERS: Books—*Visuelle Kommunikation,* edited by Hermann K. Ehmer, Cologne 1971; *Bernhard and Hilla Becher,* exhibition catalogue, edited by Lynda Morris, London 1974; *Bernhard and Hilla Becher: Fotografien 1957-1975,* exhibition catalogue, with text by Klaus Honnef, Bonn 1975; *New Topographics: Photographs of a Man-Altered Landscape,* exhibition catalogue, with text by William Jenkins, Rochester, New York 1975; *Documenta 6/Band 2,* exhibition catalogue, edited by Klauf Honnef and Evelyn Weiss, Kassel and Cologne 1977; *Geschichte der Fotografie im 20. Jahrhundert/ Photography in the 20th Century* by Petr Tausk, Cologne 1977, London 1980; *Typologien Industrieller Bau 1963-1975,* exhibition catalogue, Sao Paulo 1977; *Photographie als Kunst 1879-1979/Kunst als Photographie 1949-1979,* exhibition catalogue, 2 vols., by Peter Weiermair, Innsbruck, Austria 1979; *The Imaginary Photo Museum* by Helmut Gernsheim, Renate and L. Fritz Gruber and others, Cologne 1981, London 1982; *The Artist as Photographer* by Marina Vaizey, London 1982; *La Photographie Créative* by Jean Claude Lemagny, Paris 1984; *Photography and Art 1946-1986,* exhibition catalogue, by Andy Grundberg and Kathleen M. Gauss, Los Angeles 1987. **Articles**—"Bernhard and Hilla Becher," special monograph issue of *Kunst-Zeitung,* January 1969; "Two Books of Ultra-Topography" by Robert Sobieszek in *Image* (Rochester, New York), September 1971; "A Note on Bernhard and Hilla Becher" by Carl Andre in *Artforum* (New York), December 1972; "Bernd and Hiller Becher" by Lynda Morris in *Art Press* (Paris), May 1973; "Bernhard and Hilla Becher: Nigel Greenwood Gallery" by Georgina Oliver in *Connoisseur* (London), February 1973.

* * *

That which Hilla and Bernhard Becher depict in their photographs is exclusively an architectonic record of industrial culture. They once called their work "anonymous sculptures." Hilla, a trained photographer, and Bernhard, originally a painter, invariably represent their subjects as a composite interlocking system. They either create a formal comparison between their subjects in which socalled typologies are formed—i.e., they place mining pithead gears, gas tanks, water towers, blast furnaces, cooling towers, locomotive engine houses, grain silos, cement mixers, even standardized residences, in contrast to one another—or they execute a certain development as if it were a course of action, with the camera moving around the object so that it fixes upon a different view after each 45 degrees.

The pithead as such, in fact, is irrelevant to them, just as irrelevant as the normal residence, but the serial character of their photographic practice corresponds to the character—pre-stamped mass-manufacture—of their chosen subjects. Photographic subject and method remain in direct reciprocal relation to one another—they provide comment on and heighten each other mutually. Like the photographs of August Sander, whose photographic/artistic concepts the Bechers seized upon and consequently followed (the only German photographers to do so), their images are also documents in the truest sense of the word: visually clear proofs of the historical process of development. It is not all of social development that is portrayed, but rather only one of its aspects, that of the process of industrialization. The Ruhr District, once Germany's most important industrial area, now exists as a landscape of coal mines and steel mills only in the Bechers' photographs.

When the Bechers depict these industrial structures—which for the most part remind one of tools, of overly-enlarged objects from the realm of everyday use—they are essentially uninterested in any picturesque view of the surrounding region. They reveal their subject by means of a comparison of all available structures of a particular type and by means of a successive unfolding of different points of view—directly head on, at an angle, from the side: in this way they reveal the inner framework as well as means of production and function. Sander proceeded similarly in this presentation of the social types of the Weimar Republic. In the Bechers' photographs, the subjects continue to exist—on the strength of the methods used—with such a sense of the present that one can grasp them literally and consequently comprehend them visually. The sense of the present in the subjects results as much from a kind of plastic accuracy—the subjects in front of a neutral sky setting the language of the picture—as from the penetrating analysis of their structures.

For a long time the Bechers' work was misunderstood in photographic circles. Only with the emergence of Conceptual Art—the shift from artistic concept to reliance on pictorial result as based on artistic process—did their kind of comparative photographic interpretation begin to be understood. In it Alfred Döblin saw, with some accuracy, as he wrote in the preface to Sander's *Das Antlitz der neuen Zeit,* a scientific point of view.

—Klaus Honnef

BEDI, Mitter.

Nationality: Indian. **Born:** Lahore, 26 January 1926. **Education:** Attended D.A.V. School, Lahore, 1930-40; Vidyasagar College, Calcutta, 1942-43. **Family:** Married Sarla Goenka in 1956; children: Preeti, Jyoti, and Gayatri. **Career:** Photographer from 1954; established studio, Bombay, 1956; industrial photographer, Bombay, 1958 until his death in 1985. Visiting Professor, K.C. College of Journalism, Bombay, 1974-75, National Institute of Design, Ahmedabad, 1976, Rajendra Prasad Institute of Communication, Bombay, 1978, and SNDT Women's University, Bombay, 1978. Chairman, Leica Club of India, 1969-72. **Recipient:** First Prize for Applied Photography, Commercial Artists Guild, Bombay, 1968, 1969, 1970, 1974; Silver and Bronze Trophy, CAG India, 1977; Photographer of the Year Award, Commercial Artists Guild of India, 1984. **Died:** (in Bombay) 10 March 1985.

Individual Exhibitions:

1969   *Industrial Photography,* Jehangir Art Gallery, Bombay
1986   *Man and Legend,* Bedi Studio, Bombay (retrospective)

Selected Group Exhibitions:

1970   *Commercial Artists Guild Annual Exhibition,* Jehangir Art
             Gallery, Bombay (and subsequent exhibitions through 1980)
1982   *Photography in India 1858-1980,* The Photographers' Gallery,
             London
             The Other India, Museum of Modern Art, Oxford, England

Publications:

By BEDI: Book—*Mitter Bedi: Man and Legend,* edited by Sarla Bedi, Bombay 1986. **Articles**—"Those Good Old Days of Photography" in *First All-India Photographic Products Exhibition,* catalogue, Bombay 1978; "A Commitment to Industrial Photography" in *Kodak News* (Bombay), September 1978; "Photokina: The World of Photography" in *Dharamyug* (Bombay), 23 September 1979; "A Homage to Photography" in *Advertising Directory,* Bombay 1979; "High Adventure in Photography" in *Agfa Photo Gallery* (Bombay), January 1980.

On BEDI: Books—*Photography in India 1858-1980: A Survey,* exhibition catalogue, by Partha Mitter, London 1982; *The Other India: Seven Contemporary Photographers,* exhibition catalogue, with introduction by David Elliott, Oxford 1982. **Articles**—"Leading Photographers of India" by Dr. Chinwala

in *Illustrated Weekly of India* (Bombay), 2 January 1959; "Mitter Bedi, Indian Photographer" by Ulf Sjöstedt in *Hasselblad Magazine* (Gothenburg, Sweden), January 1973; "Art in Industry" by Gayatri Sondhi in *Fortnight Weekly* (New Delhi), 25 July 1979; "Photographers on Models" by Mohan Deep in *Caravan* (New Delhi), August 1979; "Future Shock" in *Bombay Magazine,* 7 April 1980; "A Pioneer in Industrial Photography" in *Business India* (Bombay), 23 June 1980.

*

A few years ago, after Independence, India was moving towards industrialization. I started in the profession around 1954, and noticed the change that was coming in.

In 1958 I quit being a general photographer and became, exclusively, an industrial photographer. My own inexperience and the very low demand for this little-known branch of photography made the first few years very tough. It took a lot of hard work and patience to create an awareness of proper industrial photography among the business community. I did feel a bit discouraged—having given up a lucrative business. But, thank God, I did not give up. At that time the shortages of manufactured goods in India kept industrial and advertising photography next to nil, which meant very little work for me. But, with the gradual increase in production, my work caught on. I literally grew with industry, sharing its growth and prosperity. I contributed a lot of useful work towards our export promotion abroad, and I felt myself really doing a service to my country through the medium of photography. The promotion of tourism created many new challenges, and I am proud that I met them creditably.

I did a few important jobs for advertising agencies, as they too were growing rapidly, but I preferred industrial photography, which gave me much more satisfaction. I am glad that I pioneered this branch of photography in my country, and pleased that a good number of promising young people are now entering this field. Photography has still a long way to go in India, but I am sure we will "make it" sooner than is generally expected. We are already the 8th largest industrial nation in the world.

My generation of photographers in India had to meet the demand of changing times with numerous handicaps and very low fees, and I do not think we were able to evolve a philosophy of our own contemporary photography. I have, however, I hope, set standards that younger people can follow. I really did not have the kind of time available to indulge in the luxury of "Art Photography" or "Photography-for-Art's Sake."

A few of us now have international acceptance, and I have been extensively rewarded both by private institutions and by the government. I have been a teacher of photography for over five years, and I have now started my own academy, teaching both Basic and Advanced photography.

Photography in India is slowly discovering its place in society and its role as a communicator. The efforts of photographers are helping to bridge the gap created by many languages and many more dialects throughout the country, besides promoting business and industry, and aiding the growing field of education.

—Mitter Bedi (1982)

*   *   *

As a boy he played with a Kodak box camera, worked in his family printing press in his teens, then he moved into the movie world of India as a public relations assistant. Photography was a suppressed passion in Mitter Bedi until, at the age of 27, he finally decided to devote his life to the art. His career in photography has passed through stages—a short stint in photojournalism, a period of unusual theatre-photography, and advertising. His huge enlarged pictures in the 1956 *International Industry Fair* in New Delhi immediately attracted national and international attention. And it was industrial photography that Bedi took up in 1958 as his life's vocation. Twenty-five years later, he was India's finest industrial photographer with a worldwide reputation. With his Hasselblads, he has not only recorded the industrial growth of a new nation, but also has made industrial photography an art-form.

For Bedi, this kind of photography did not mean just taking publicity pictures of machines and machine-hands. His firm belief was that "the subject must come alive, communicate . . . in the most creative manner possible." This is the unique feature of his photography—the power of communication.

Lathes, pipes, cranes, bottles, and structures convey the sense of their particular materiality as well as suggest a story. This is evident even in the photographs of interiors like those of the Taj Hotel in Bombay and the Royal Palace in Muscat. The pictures of pharmaceutical bottles of all shapes and sizes carefully arranged, in the simplicity of composition and subtle manipulation of light and colour, are remarkable examples of aesthetic and communicational effectiveness. Long pipes zooming out from the bottom to the top of the picture, slightly out of focus at the bottom and becoming more and more clear and shimmering in the middle of the frame, then becoming all lighted and shining at the top, while from the two sides the pipes get smaller in size, creating the illusion of convergence, is a masterful manipulation of photographic elements. His ''Piston'' images are a brilliant series.

Another strong feature in his industrial photography is the dimension of human value, even though no human figure is in the image. The pictures of small or giant machines, ordinary bottles, unglamourous pipes or cranes become a tribute to human ingenuity, craft and knowledge. Bedi's sense of colour, texture, and tone, and his manipulation of light and space in his better photographs are always so precise and subtle. It is this sense which gives a peculiar sensuous reality to his pictures of arrangements of forks and spoons, dead lobsters, and party-tables, or those remarkable pictures of a steel tube factory in operation with all sorts of firecrackerish designs.

Mitter Bedi was also an outstanding teacher; his Academy in Bombay is a major photography institution with national and international students and teachers. Despite many difficulties, Mitter Bedi continually displayed his talents both as a photographer and teacher in a matchless manner.

—Deba P. Patnaik

BELLMER, Hans.

Nationality: German. **Born:** Katowice, Silesia, Germany/Poland border (now in Poland), 13 March 1902. **Education:** Studied engineering, Technische Hochschule, Berlin, 1923-24; drawing and perspective studies with artist George Grosz, Berlin, 1924; mainly self-taught in photography. **Family:** Married Margarete Bellmer in 1927 (died, 1937); 2 daughters; married again in 1942 (separated, 1946); twin daughters: Doraine and Beatrice; lived with poetess Nora Mitrani, 1946, and with writer Unica Zurn, 1953-70 (died, 1970). **Career:** Worked as coal-miner, Katowice, 1920-23; designer, typographer and illustrator, for Malik Publishing Company, Berlin, 1924-25; independent painter and designer, Berlin, 1926-36, in Paris, 1936-39; interned in prison camp, Aix-en-Provence, France, 1940; independent painter and designer, Toulouse, France, 1941-45, and Paris, 1946 until his death, 1975. Worked on photographs of puppet doll (Die Puppe), Berlin, 1934-36, and in Paris, 1936-39, 1946-75. **Recipient:** William and Noma Copley Foundation Prize, Chicago, 1958. **Died:** (in Paris) *23 February 1975.*

Individual Exhibitions:

1943	Galerie Trentin, Toulouse
1945	Galerie du Luxembourg, Paris
1963	Galerie Daniel Cordier, Paris
1966	Robert Fraser Gallery, London
	Galerie Sydow, Frankfurt
	Robert Self Gallery, London
	Ulmer Museum, Ulm, West Germany
	Galerie Benador, Geneva
	Galerie Gmurzynska, Cologne
1967	Galerie A.F. Petit, Paris
	Kestner Gesellschaft, Hannover (retrospective)
	Galerie Wolfgang Ketterer, Munich
	Galleria d'Arte Moderna, Turin
	Galerie Thomas, Munich and Cologne
1969	Galerie A.F. Petit, Paris
1970	Stedelijk Museum, Amsterdam
	Galerie La Pochade, Paris
1971	Centre National d'Art Contemporain, Paris (retrospective)

	Von der Heydt Museum, Wuppertal, West Germany
1971	Lerner-Misrachi Gallery, New York
	Sidney Janis Gallery, New York
	Editions Graphiques, London
1974	Sidney Janis Gallery, New York
	Galerie Schindler, Berne
1975	Museum of Contemporary Art, Chicago
	Galerie A.F. Petit, Paris
1980	*Les Jeux de la Poupée,* Vision Gallery, Boston
1983	Centre Georges Pompidou, Paris
1985	Barbara Gladstone Gallery, New York

Selected Group Exhibitions:

1935	*Exposicion Surealista,* Galeria Ateneo, Tenerife, Canary Islands
1936	*International Surrealist Exhibition,* Museum of Modern Art, New York
1947	*Exposition Internationale du Surrealisme,* Galerie Maeght, Paris
1960	*Exposition Internationale du Surrealisme,* Galerie Daniel Cordier, Paris
1977	*Künstlerphotographien im 20. Jahrhundert,* Kestner Gesellschaft, Hannover
1979	*Photographic Surrealism,* New Gallery of Contemporary Art, Cleveland, Ohio (travelled to Dayton Art Institute, Ohio; and Brooklyn Museum, New York)
1980	*Masks, Mannequins and Dolls,* Prakapas Gallery, New York *Avant-Garde Photography in Germany 1919-39,* San Francisco Museum of Modern Art (toured the United States)
1981	*Germany: The New Vision,* Fraenkel Gallery, San Francisco
1985	*L'Amour Four: Photography and Surrealism,* Corcoran Gallery of Art, Washington, D.C. (travelled to San Francisco Museum of Modern Art; Centre Georges Pompidou, Paris; Hayward Gallery, London)

Collections:

Musée d'Art Moderne, Paris; Ulmer Museum, Ulm, Germany; Galerie Brusberg, Hannover; Museum of Modern Art, New York; Institute for Sex Research, University of Indiana, Bloomington; Art Institute of Chicago; International Museum of Photography at George Eastman House, Rochester, New York.

Publications:

By BELLMER: Books—*Die Puppe,* Karlsruhe 1934, Paris 1936, revised edition, Berlin 1962; *The Story of Eve,* with text by Georges Bataille, Paris 1944; *Les Jeux de la Poupée,* with text by Paul Eluard, Paris 1949; *L'Anatomie de l'Image,* Paris 1957; *A Sade,* Paris 1967; *Madame Edwarda,* with text by Georges Bataille, Paris 1965; *Mode d'Emploi,* Paris 1967; *Bilder fran den aren 1934-1950,* with text by Ragnar von Holten, Stockholm 1978.

On BELLMER: Books—*Hans Bellmer* by Christian d'Orgeix, Paris 1950; *Hans Bellmer* by Alain Jouffroy, Chicago and London 1959; *Les Dessins de Hans Bellmer,* edited by Constantin Jelenski, Paris 1966; *Hans Bellmer: Oeuvre Gravé* by André Pieyre de Mandiargues, Paris 1969; *CNAC Archives I: Hans Bellmer,* exhibition catalogue, by Paul Eluard and others, Paris 1971; *The Drawings of Hans Bellmer,* edited by Alex Grall, London 1972, New York 1973; *Hans Bellmer* by Sarane Alexandrian, Paris 1972, New York 1973; *Photography as Art* by Volker Kahmen, London 1974; *Künstlerphotographien im XX. Jahrhundert,* exhibition catalogue, by Carl-Albrecht Haenlein, Hannover 1977; *Geschichte der Fotografie im 20. Jahrhundert/Photography in the 20th Century* by Petr Tausk, Cologne 1977, London 1980; *Dada and Surrealism Reviewed,* exhibition catalogue, by Dawn Ades, London 1978; *Le Trésor*

Cruel de Hans Bellmer by André Pieyre de Mandiargues, Paris 1979; *Photographic Surrealism,* exhibition catalogue, by Nancy Hall-Duncan, Cleveland 1979; *Avant-Garde Photography in Germany 1919-39,* exhibition catalogue, by Van Deren Coke, Ute Eskildsen and Bernd Lohse, San Francisco 1980; *Nude Photographs 1850-1980,* edited by Constance Sullivan, New York 1980; *L'Amour Fou: Photography and Surrealism* by Rosalind Krauss and Jane Livingston, Washington, D.C., and New York 1985; *Hans Bellmer* by Peter Webb, London 1985. **Articles**—"Hans Bellmer: The Machine-Gun in a State of Grace" by John Lyle in *Art and Artists* (London), August 1970; "Balthus, Klossowski, Bellmer: Three Approaches to the Flesh" by Michael Peppiatt in *Art International* (Lugano, Switzerland), October 1973; "Le Rêve et le Désir: Au Regard de la Poupée" by J.C. Bailly in *XX Siècle* (Paris), June 1974; "Hans Bellmer: Obituary" in *Connaissance des Arts* (Paris), May 1975.

* * *

Hans Bellmer received acclaim on many levels and was internationally accorded the highest praise for the amazing delicacy of his draughtsmanship paralleled by an extraordinary facility to top pornography with a lacing of humour. As a brilliant and totally original sculptor, he turned lay-figures into doll-fetiches—in a sense, almost sophisticated toys—whose limbs, head, hands and feet could be disjointed and then reassembled differently, yet so harmoniously that somehow this new pattern of conjunctions was visually acceptable. The roundedness in Bellmer's sculpture of every ancillary part of the female human form offered a peculiarly photo-attractive opportunity to the camera, so it was not surprising that Bellmer should expand his artistic range to include photography.

However, what is more to the point in this book of modern photographers is that Bellmer proved to be much more than merely adept in this medium. Sometimes the "photographs" would be an assemblage of several photos pieced together. At other times the original photo or parts of photo would be enlarged to twice or more times the size of the original object; the largest of these might enjoy dimensions of 6 ft. x 31 ft. and were usually laid on hard card. Working in black-and-white, he would sometimes "invent" tints to colour the finished work, drenching the image in an all-over transparency of pink or blue.

But apart from experimental subject matter and the application of personal techniques, what else had this one-time friend of and co-exhibitor with Man Ray and the other proto-surrealists to add to the history of modern creative photography?

The question is at once easy and difficult to answer. Easy, because Bellmer enjoyed his personal relationship with cameracraft. In this medium, not only could he experiment and record plans—both projected and achieved—as an aid to his work as draughtsman and sculptor, but he was also able to bring positive intentions to fruition before their official naissance. Furthermore, he could imbue the *quality* of photography (by no means lacking in the hands of others, even those favouring similar visual investigations) with a special ingredient: that of an over-powering point-of-contact with absolute carnal femininity, both shameless and shameful at the same time. Because of his obsession with puppetry (through his incredible dismemberable female lay-figures whose every segment was rich in rotundity), he could endow these dolls with an anonymity insofar as character was concerned, and yet could express through them an archetypical femininity.

Of course, there are many who would say: "What about the drawings? What about the actual sculptures? Don't they achieve ends just as 'identical?' " A summation of his work with the camera is difficult because in a sense, photography was for him almost a private activity. He created his photographic oeuvres partly for his own pleasure, partly to aid and abet the working requirements of his other artistic talents. Therefore, his photographic works were likely to languish in his studio—unless they fell by sheer chance into the hands of friends and acquaintances. If they appeared at all in exhibitions, it was to add emphasis to works in quite different media. Only later, when his world reputation as a creative genius was confirmed, were the photographs put on view to the public in their own right.

On this evidence, does Bellmer qualify as one of modern photography's giants? As in the case of the multi-faceted Picasso, he was able to disprove the traditional view, "Jack-of-all-trades; master of none!"

—Sheldon Williams

BENGSTON, Jim.

Nationality: American. **Born:** Evanston, Illinois, 31 March 1942. **Education:** B.A. from Lake Forest College (literature), 1964. Mainly self-taught in photography from 1964. Originally influenced by work of Robert Frank, Cartier Bresson and FSA photographers. Later influences: Timothy O'Sullivan, Carleton Watkins and Atget. **Military Service:** Served as Photo Assistant, US Army in Germany, 1965-68. **Family:** Married Trine Thorkelsen (Norwegian), 1968; children: Espen (b.1969) and Marius (b. 1971). **Career:** Photo Editor Associated Press, New York, 1969 and 1970; Copywriter/ photographer, Young and Rubicam, Oslo, 1971-75; Freelance Photographer in advertising, architecture and design since 1975. Photographed the official sports posters for the 1994 Winter Olympics at Lillehammer. **Recipient:** First Prize, Nikon International Photo Contest, 1970. Member, Forbundet Freie Fotografer, Oslo, 1978. **Agent:** Fotogalleri, Oscarsgate 50b, Oslo 2, Norway. **Address:** Grakamveien 7c, 0389 Oslo 3, Norway.

Individual Exhibitions:

1979	Fotogalleri, Oslo
1980	Camera Obscura, Stockholm
1981	Henie-Onstad Kunstsenter, Oslo
1982	Trondheims Kunstforening, Norway
	Galleri Anders Tornberg, Lund, Sweden
	Galerie Renner, Munich
1983	Galerie Lindemann, Stuttgart
1984	Galeria Image, Madrid
	Henie-Onstad Kunstsenter, Oslo
	Alcatraz, Carnegie Recital Hall, New York (with composer Ingram Marshall; toured Europe and the United States)
1986	*Eberbach,* Newport Harbor Art Museum, Newport Beach, California (with composer Ingram Marshall)
1987	*Construction Site,* Galleri Melhuus, Oslo
1990	*Empty Landscape,* Preus Foto Museum, Horten; Galleri Cafe Opera, Bergen
1991	*Empty Landscape,* Henie Onstad Kunstsenter, Oslo
1992	*Empty Landscape,* Kunstnersenteret i Oppland, Lillehammer; Naturhus, Jeløy
1993	*Construction Site,* Gallery AHO, Norwegian School of Architecture, Oslo
	Empty Landscape, Jernigan/Wicker Fine Arts, San Francisco
1994	*Utah,* Galleri Wang, Oslo

Selected Group Exhibitions:

1978	*Mirrors and Windows,* Museum of Modern Art, New York (toured the United States)
1979	*Photography Here and Now,* Henie-Onstad Kunstsenter, Oslo
1981	*Extended Photography,* at the *Biennale,* Vienna
1982	*The Frozen Image,* Walker Art Center, Minneapolis (travelled to the International Center of Photography, New York; University of California at Los Angeles; Portland Art Museum, Maine; Museum of Contemporary Art, Chicago; Tacoma Art Museum, Washington; Kjavalsstadir, Reykjavik; Louisiana Museum, Humlebaek, Denmark; Fotografiska Museet, Stockholm; Henie-Onstad Kunstsenter, Oslo)
	Floods of Light, The Photographers' Gallery, London
1983	*Nordic Landscape,* Sveaborg, Helsinki
1984	*La Photographie Créative,* Bibliotheque Nationale, Paris
1985	*Scandinavian Photography,* Brandts Klaedefabrik, Odense, Denmark
1986	*The Animal in Photography 1843-1985,* The Photographers' Gallery, London
	Crosscurrents, San Francisco Museum of Modern Art
1987	*Legacy of Light,* International Center for Photography, New York

From the series *Empty Landscape,* **Portør, Norway, 1992 (original in colour).** Photograph by Jim Bengston.

1988	*Swimmers,* Burden Gallery (Aperture), New York
	Norwegian Prospects, Fotogalleri, Oslo
	Different Family Pictures, Museum of Photographic Art (Brandts Klædefabrikk), Odense
1990	*You Wish to See, Listen,* Aterforum Festival, Ferrara, Italy
1991	*The Fourth Wall,* (Photography as Theater), Amsterdam
1992	*Photo of My Father* (Month of the Photo), Paris
	Sprung in Die Zeit, Berlinische Galerie, Berlin
1993	Museum of Modern Art, New York, photohistorical installations
	Position 1, Fotogalleri, Oslo
	Landscape Archetypes, Seafirst Gallery, Seattle
	Photographs from the Real World, Lillehammer Art Museum in conjunction with the Winter Olympics

Collections:

Art Institute of Chicago; Bibliothèque Nationale, Paris; Henie-Onstad Kunstsenter, Oslo; Museum Ludwig, Cologne; Museum of Modern Art, New York; National Museum of American Art/Smithsonian Institution, Washington, D.C.; Trondheims Kunstforening, Norway; Walker Art Center, Minneapolis; Polaroid Collection, Cambridge, Massachusetts.

Publications:

By BENGSTON: Books—*Afterwords,* New York 1978; *Fiber,* Ahus, Sweden 1981; *Slow Motion,* with introduction by Robert Meyer, Gottingen, West Germany 1986.

On BENGSTON: Books—*The Frozen Image: Scandinavian Photography,* edited by Martin Freeman, Minneapolis and New York 1982; *Floods of Light: Flash Photography 1851-1981,* exhibition catalogue, by Rupert Martin, London 1982; *La Photographie Créative* by Jean-Claude Lemagny, Paris 1984. **Articles**—''Bengston's recipe for light and motion'' by Don Leavitt in *Popular Photography* (New York), June 1980; ''Jim Bengston'' by Allan Porter in *Camera* (Lucerne), November 1980; ''Jim Bengston'' in *Fotoforum* (Oslo), November 1980; ''Jim Bengston'' in *Album* (Malmo), no. 1, 1984; ''Bengston—Troubles Biographiques'' by Pierre Borhan in *Cliches* (Brussels), no. 17, 1985.

*

I started making photographs in 1964 because Robert Frank's pictures, which I saw by chance in a photo magazine, moved me.

After our children were born in 1969 and 1971 and until about 1982, most of my work was related to family and friends. My main concern, however, was not simply to present a family album. The photos dealt perhaps just as much with their own reality—or the reality of photographs per se—as with any other theme. Interpretation of movement was of prime importance. This work culminated with the 1986 publication of *Slow Motion* by European Photography in Gottingen, Germany.

More recently, I've been doing landscape photographs, including the series *Norway, Illinois, Empty Landscape* and *Utah, a Four-Letter Word.* I've also collaborated with American composer Ingram Marshall (*Alcatraz,* 1984, and *Eberbach,* 1986). *Alcatraz* and *Eberbach* can be seen either as photographic series experienced temporally with musical accompaniment, or as musical compositions with pictorial "texts." From either vantage point, the equal parts add up to a whole which is an artistic statement on a specific subject—in these cases a former Californian prison and a 12th-century German monastery. The pieces are presented as slide shows using dissolves with live and electronic musical accompaniment, performed by the composer. Another series in a similar mode is *Construction Site* (1987). These color photos build upon each other (often in groups of two to four prints which function together) to present a "landscape" of the structure being photographed. Since 1986 I have photographed exclusively in color.

Whereas most of my earlier work showed people and their activities, most of the present pictures are of empty rooms, empty buildings and depopulated landscapes. Despite this development, I hope the human element hasn't disappeared.

—Jim Bengston

*   *   *

Although Jim Bengston was born in America, his father was of Scandinavian origin (his grandfather being Swedish and his grandmother Danish), and his mother was half-French and half-English. He studied German literature at Lake Forest College and later at Princeton University, and it is perhaps this early orientation towards verbal communications that prompted his particular interest in a kind of documentary photography, at times reaching out to the narrative. Some of his observations are directed toward episodic events from everyday life. In his choice of the "decisive moment" for clicking the camera's shutter, Bengston stands closer to Robert Frank than to Cartier-Bresson, although, having absorbed the influences of both, Bengston produces a highly individual kind of work.

During a long sojourn in Germany, he met and married the Norwegian Katrine Thorkelsen, and they lived for some years in New York; gradually, the recognition that they were not "big city people" led to a move to a lovely house on a hill in the suburbs of Oslo. The beauty of Bengston's current environment influences his work not only by providing handy nearby motifs suited to his particular vision, but also in the atmosphere generated by the lifestyle of the region. Many of his pictures of children playing, dogs jumping, and so on, have an optimistic mood—with the implication that Bengston himself is a real participant, not merely an observer. His personal engagement is again evident in photographs of his family, where he often appears as a subject.

Bengston's feeling for play develops with his use of new cameras and technical systems, especially so in the case of Polaroid instant photographs. He uses the facility of seeing results within a minute or so of exposure to make series of trial-and-error images, frequently in combinations of daylight, flash and instant photography. The results suggest something close to an organized happening.

Although much of this work revolves around Bengston's interest in live-photography and visual jokes, he also likes to work with landscapes, especially the Norwegian mountain regions. His first book, *Afterwords,* features all sorts of work from his varied repertoire in the one volume. Very little text is evident; frequently only the name of the location for a landscape or even a live event. Clearly, Bengston feels that a photograph should be able to speak for itself.

—Petr Tausk

BENNETT, Derek.

Nationality: American. **Born:** Buffalo, New York, 13 October 1944. **Education:** Sir George Williams University, Montreal, 1964-69, B.A. in English 1969. **Family:** Married Ruth Huber in 1973; children: Leif and Jennifer. **Career:** Freelance photographer, in Switzerland, since 1971. Contributor to the magazines *Fotografie* and *European Photography,* Gottingen, West Germany, since 1979. **Address:** Finsterwaldstrasse 23, CH-8200 Schaffhausen, Switzerland.

Individual Exhibitions:

1974	*Fathers and Sons,* Silver Image Gallery, Tacoma, Washington
	Schaffhausen Kunstverein, Switzerland
1976	Arnolfini Arts Centre, Bristol
	The Swiss Photographs, Silver Image Gallery, Seattle (travelled to Gallery 38, Zurich)
	Paul Caponigro/Edward Weston/Derek Bennett, Silver Image Gallery, Seattle
	Gallery Tolgge, Zurich
1978	*Spaces,* Gallery Paule Pia, Antwerp (travelled to Il Diaframma, Milan, Photo Art, Basel, and Canon Gallery, Geneva, 1979)
1981	Galerie Novum, Hannover
1983	Museum Ludwig, Cologne
	Sprengel Museum, Hannover
	Kunstverein, Kassel, West Germany
	Josef Haubrich Museum, Bottrop, West Germany
	Salzburg College, Austria
1984	Saarland Museum, Saarbrücken, West Germany
	Fotomuseum im Stadtmuseum, Munich
	Stadtische Galerie, Erlangen West Germany
	Kunstverein, Ingolstadt, West Germany
	Wessenberg Galerie, Konstanz, West Germany
	Rathaus, Bielefeld, West Germany
	Kunstverein, Dortmund, West Germany
	Museum zu Allerheiligen, Schaffhausen, Switzerland
1985	Salzburg College, Austria

Selected Group Exhibitions:

1976	*The Human Image in 20th Century Photography,* University of Washington Art Museum, Seattle
1981	*10 Schaffhausen Künstler,* Kunstverein, St. Gall, Switzerland
1983	*Zeitgenössische europäische Fotografie,* Museum zu Allerheiligen, Schaffhausen, Switzerland
1985	*Il Jornades Fotografique,* Valencia, Spain

Collections:

Bibliothèque Nationale, Paris; Polaroid Collection, Amsterdam; Museum zu Allerheiligen, Schaffhausen, Switzerland; Museum Ludwig, Cologne; Hartkamp Collection, University of Leiden, Netherlands; Generalitat Valencia, Spain; Goethe-Institut, Munich; San Francisco Museum of Modern Art; Center for Creative Photography, University of Arizona, Tucson.

Publications:

By BENNETT: Books—*A Silent Dialogue: Images of Germans,* Cologne 1983; *In Schaffhausen,* Schaffhausen Switzerland 1984; *In Zürich,* Feuerthalen, Switzerland 1986. **Articles**—"Arles Meeting in Critical Phase," with Marco Misani, in *Print Letter* (Zurich), September 1976; "The Arles Book Workshop: Stalemate" in *Print Letter* (Zurich), September 1977; "Evolution and Revolution in Book Publishing" in *Print Letter* (Zurich), November 1977; "Moving Past the Mind, Past the Heart. . . . ," interview with Paul Caponigro, in *Print Letter* (Zurich), November 1977; "Jan Saudek: 'I'm Led by Instinct' " in *Print Letter* (Zurich), March 1978; "The Limited Edition Portfolio: A Special Report" in *Print Letter* (Zurich), May 1978; "European

Zurich, 1978. Photograph ©Derek Bennett.

Photography and the American Sensibility" in *European Photography* (Göttingen), January 1980; "Image and Reality: Seven Aspects of Subjective Photography" in *European Photography* (Göttingen), April 1980; "Photography Criticism" in *European Photography* (Gottingen), October 1980; "European Photography and the American Dream" in *European Photography* (Gottingen), July 1981; "The Outsider in Photography," in *European Photography* (Gottingen), October 1981; "From Object to Vision" in *European Photography* (Gottingen), April 1983; "Essays on Documentary Photography" in *European Photography* (Gottingen), April 1985; "Fotografie und der nachindustrielle Verkehrsstau" in *Fotokritik* (West Berlin), March 1985; "(A) e (s) the (et) ics" in *European Photography* (Gottingen), January 1986.

On BENNETT: Books—*10 Schaffhausen Künstler,* exhibition catalogue, St. Gall, Switzerland 1981; *Zeitgenössische europäische Fotografie,* exhibition catalogue, Schaffhausen, Switzerland 1983; *Dumont Foto 4,* Cologne 1983. **Articles**—"Derek Bennett," interview, with Marco Misani, in *Print Letter* (Zurich), July 1978; "Portfolio: Derek Bennett" in *Fotografie* (Göttingen), January 1979; "Porträts" in *Schweizerische Photorundschau* (Zurich), March 1980; "Porträts" in *Zoom* (Munich), June 1983; "In Schaffhausen/Stille Zwiesprache: Bildnisse von Deutschen" in *Perspektief* (Rotterdam), June 1985.

*

My work keeps changing, in some cases very drastically, because my personal and photographic concerns keep changing. Even so, in specific images I can see the single thread running through all the various series I have worked on. It's this thread which interests me the most. In a sense, the various series simply form a context within which I can follow the thread wherever it leads me. The first photographs I took more or less consciously were street portraits of Castro's Cuban revolutionary soldiers when I was 14 years old. About 20 years later, I suddenly found myself doing approximately the same thing, but in Germany. The "coincidence" shocked me at first, but it soon took on another kind of significance.

All art is largely a process of distillation, and photography itself has always seemed almost alchemical to me. I think probably most photographers expect to discover a kind of personal philosopher's stone within the medium, or at least within their own work. The darkroom is obviously alchemical in nature—especially when exactly that photograph you wanted begins slowly to appear in the developer. There is an urge to jump up and shout "Eureka!" Something in the nature of the world or in the nature of simply being is clarified at that moment, and the seemingly endless process of distillation you have gone through suddenly makes itself manifest.

Photography is an eminently visual medium, more so than painting because a photograph is less tactile than a painting. Some photographs may ultimately speak to the intellect, but if they don't first attach themselves directly to the eye of the viewer, I think they ultimately fail. Personally, I have never seen a "logical" photograph, although I have seen many which attempt to express the visual world logically. But the best photographs always contain something that we cannot quite explain. I suspect that the world functions a lot differently than we think it does, and, often enough, I find that photographs bear out my suspicions.

I also suspect that photography serves an historical function having little to do with the relatively simple process of making photographs. Possibly, like the wheel, the abacus, or moveable type, photography will be seen in the future to have been the result of a kind of spontaneous combustion within the process of human "progress" or a *deusex-machina*. I doubt that we have even begun to understand what the camera has "done" to us, and probably it will take the death of the medium for us to find out. In the meantime, Man-the-imagemaker continues to take pictures, trying to find something in his experience of the world which has the nature of a revelation.

—Derek Bennett

* * *

As Derek Bennett himself once noted, apparently the highest goal of the photographic critic is to place the photographer's work in one or another "school." Such would in any case be difficult to do with Bennett's own work: one would be hard put to recognize if his work is of "mirrors" or of "windows" (in the Szarkowskian sense).

Bennett's early work—from the late 1960's to the mid-1970's—took its cues from what has come to be known as street photography—windows, definitely. But then his work took a sudden turn, as if photography were now a two-way mirror, to reflect and to be looked through simultaneously. His "Spaces" series of 1976-78 consisted of easily identified, subjectively perceived and realized details of his personal environment. The "subjectivity" of these photographs arose primarily from an intellectual process influenced by personal experience, valuations, reflexes and recognitions. With time, all of these mental attitudes were transformed, and thus Bennett's approach to photography was also transformed, sometimes less, sometimes more. In the "Spaces" photographs, it is not the objects themselves—say, a nearly framefilling white shirt on a man in a crowd—which visually please, but their suggestive aesthetic qualities, the transformation of objects, the abstractions, the intellections.

Bennett's next large series was seemingly informed solely by the tenets of straight documentary photography. It dealt with portraits of Germans—"in the footsteps of August Sander." Bennett says. That would admit of an attempt to choose subjects according to a typology, which of course invariably reflects the photographer himself. The apparent documentary nature of the attempt resulted in the subjectivity of Bennett's eye belying anything more than a superficial difference—resting, so to speak, on the surface of the photographic paper—between "Spaces" and the German portraits.

Bennet has continued his series on personal, subjective documentation with an exhibition project and a book on his chosen hometown of Schaffhausen, Switzerland, and is now aiming for a similar—though in its results probably quite different—project on the city of Zurich. However, he has never restricted himself to working on a single self-chosen assignment only, and has produced many images of experimental character when he found himself at a certain place, at a certain time, in a certain mood. For example, a small series on trees, taken at night with multiple exposure or multiple flashes resulted from a ten-day invitation by the local Spanish government of the Province of Valencia in 1985. In Bennett's work as a whole, if it is not always windows or always mirrors, it is conceivably both at once.

Bennett also has won a reputation as a teacher of photography in many workshops throughout Europe, and is, with his critical and theoretical essays, comments and book reviews, a permanent contributor to magazines like *Photographie* and *European Photography*.

—Hans Christian Adam

BENY, Roloff.

Nationality: Canadian. **Born:** Wilfred Roy Beny in Medicine Hat, Alberta, 7 January 1924. **Education:** Attended elementary and high schools in Medicine Hat, 1931-39; Banff School of Fine Arts, Alberta, 1939-41; Trinity College, University of Toronto, 1941-45, B.F.A. 1945; Ohio State University, Columbus, 1946-47, M.F.A. 1947; Columbia University, New York, 1947; Institute of Fine Arts, New York University, 1947-48; American School of Classical Studies, Athens, 1948-49. Freelance photographer, mainly of photographic books, and working for *Vogue, Harper's Bazaar, Bunte, Sunday Times, Connaissance des Arts, Time*, etc., in Lethbridge, Alberta, and Rome, 1949

until his death in 1984; also, a painter (had more than 25 individual exhibitions in Canada, Europe and the United States). **Recipient:** Guggenheim Fellowship, 1953, 1954; Centennial Medal, Canada, 1967; Visual Arts Award, Canada Council, 1968; Gold Medal, *Leipzig International Book Fair,* 1968; Silver Eagle Award, *Nice International Book Fair,* 1969. LL.D.: University of Lethbridge, 1972. Knight of Mark Twain, 1967; Life Member, Royal Canadian Academy of Arts, 1973. Member, Order of Canada, 1972. **Died:** (in Rome) *15 March 1984.*

Individual Exhibitions:

1955	Institute of Contemporary Arts, London
1956	Galleria Sagittarius, Rome
1962	*A Time of Gods,* Royal Ontario Museum, Toronto
1967	*Image Canada* at Expo '67, Montreal
1968	*A Visual Odyssey,* Gallery of Modern Art, New York (travelled to Huntington Hartford Museum, New York, and Toronto Dominion Bank, Ontario)
1974	*In the Closter of San Francisco,* Sorrento, Italy
1980	Palazzo dell'Esposizioni, Rome
1981	*The Churches of Rome,* Royal Institute of British Architects, Rome

Selected Group Exhibitions:

1967	*Photography in Canada 67,* National Film Board of Canada, Montreal
1968	*Internationale Buchkunstausstellung,* Leipzig, East Germany

Publications:

By BENY: Books—*An Aegean Notebook,* Lethbridge, Alberta 1950; *The Thrones of Earth and Heaven,* with texts by Herbert Read, Freya Stark, Jean Cocteau, Bernard Berenson, Rose Macaulay and Stephen Spender, London and New York 1958; *A Time of Gods,* London and New York 1962; *Pleasure of Ruins,* with text by Rose Macaulay, London and New York 1964, 1977; *To Everything There Is a Season,* London 1967; *Japan in Colour,* with text by Anthony Thwaite, London and New York 1967; *India,* with text by Aubrey Menen, Toronto and London 1969; *Island: Ceylon,* with text by John Lindsay Opie, Toronto and London 1971; *Roloff Beny in Italy,* with texts by Anthony Thwaite, Peter Porter and Gore Vidal, London and Toronto 1974; *Persia: Bridge of Turquoise,* with text by S.H. Nasr, Toronto, London and Boston 1975; *The Churches of Rome,* with text by Peter Gunn, London 1981; *Odyssey: Mirror of the Mediterranean,* with text by Anthony Thwaite, London 1981; *The Gods of Greece,* with text by Arianna Stassinopoulos, London 1983; *Rajasthan: Land of Kings,* with text by Sylvia A. Matheson, London 1984.

On BENY: Books—*Image 2: Photography in Canada 1967,* edited by Lorraine Monk, Montreal 1967; *Image 6: A Review of Contemporary Photography in Canada,* edited by Lorraine Monk, Toronto 1970; *The Magic Image* by Cecil Beaton and Gail Buckland, London and Boston 1975.

* * *

Roloff Beny was a seeker after grandeur. He searched for it in such places as India, Persia, Japan and the shores of the Mediterranean and Aegean seas. It is the shadow of gods and kings he tracks. He was in sympathy with the splendid, and he records splendid architecture, splendid landscapes, splendid animals, splendid ruins.

Beny was, in fact, a little in love with ruins, even seeing "majestic ruins" in the sky. Because of his special response to certain situations of beauty we have another knowledge of temples and palaces, mosques and villas, the deserted, the dissolving, the magnificent, the awesome.

The gods still inhabit the world he visited—perhaps just off-stage, but *there.* Royal ghosts invisibly tread his terraces and gardens. His choice of color

John Butler in Saint Nicholas Church, Spoleto, **1969.** Photograph by
Roloff Beny.

is as complex and beautiful as some Persian carpet; his choice of light, that
certain clarity born of brightness.

—Ralph Pomeroy

BERENGO-GARDIN, Gianni.

Nationality: Italian. **Born:** Santa Margherita Ligure, 10 October 1930.
Education: Attended the Liceo Scientifico, Venice, until 1950. **Family:**
Married Caterina Stiffoni in 1957 (separated, 1979); children: Alberto and
Susanna. **Career:** Did various jobs connected with the tourist industry, in
Paris and Venice, 1950-60. First concentrated on photography, associating
with La Gondola group of photographers, Venice, 1954; freelance photojournalist,
working for *Domus, Epoca, Il Mondo, L'Espresso, Time, Stern, Harper's,
Réalités, Vogue,* etc., Venice, 1960-64, and Milan, since 1964. Founder-
Member, Il Ponte group of photographers, Venice, 1958. **Recipient:** Artist
Award, International Federation of Photographic Art (FIAP), 1957. **Agent:**
Galleria Il Diaframma, Via Brera 10, Milan. **Address:** Via San Michele del
Carso 21, I-20144 Milan, Italy.

Individual Exhibitions:

1968   Galleria Il Diaframma, Milan
1972   Galleria Il Diaframma, Milan (retrospective)
1978   *Great Britain,* Galleria Il Diaframma, Milan
1981   *Gianni Berengo-Gardin,* at *Napoli 81,* Naples
1983   Fotografi Centrum, Stockholm
        Il Mondo, Palazzo Stelline, Milan
        Gianni Berengo-Gardin, at *Incontro Rimini,* Rimini, Italy
1984   FNAC-Galerie, Paris
        Bund Freischaffender Fotodesigner, Dusseldorf
1985   Palazzo Dugnani, Milan

Selected Group Exhibitions:

1965   *Contemporary Photographic Expression,* International Museum
        of Photography, Rochester, New York
1967   *Expo '67,* Montreal
1968   *New York, a City,* Galleria Il Diaframma, Milan
1973   *3rd World Exhibition of Photography,* Pressehaus Stern,
        Hamburg (and world tour)
1975   *The Land: 20th Century Landscape Photographs Selected by
        Bill Brandt,* Victoria and Albert Museum, London (travelled
        to the National Gallery, Edinburgh; Ulster Museum, Belfast;
        and National Museum of Wales, Cardiff, 1976)
1979   *Venezia '79*
1980   *30 Anni di Fotografia a Venezia,* Palazzo Fortuny, Venice
        Fotografia e Immagine dell'Architettura, Galleria d'Arte
        Moderna, Bologna, Italy
1981   *L'Informazione Negata: Fotogiornalismo,* Pinacoteca
        Provinciale, Bari, Italy
1985   *Il Dopoguerra dei Fotografi,* Galleria d'Arte Moderna,
        Bologna, Italy

Collections:

Università di Pisa; Bibliothèque Nationale, Paris; Museum of Modern Art,
New York; International Museum of Photography, George Eastman House,
Rochester, New York; Museum of Aesthetic Art, Beijing, China.

Publications:

By BERENGO-GARDIN: Books—*Venise des Saisons,* with text by
Giorgio Bassani and Mario Soldati, Paris 1965; *Toscana,* 2 volumes, Milan
1966; *Viaggio in Toscana,* with an introduction by Giorgio Soavi, Venice
1967; *Morire di Classe,* edited by Franco Basaglia, Turin 1969; *L'Occhio
come Mestiere,* with an introduction by Cesare Colombo, Milan 1970;
Francia, Milan 1975; *Grecia,* Milan 1976; *Un Paese, Venti' Anni Dopo,* with
Cesare Zavattini, Turin 1976; *England, Wales and Scotland,* Milan 1977;
Dentro le Case, Milan 1977; *Dentro il Lavoro,* Milan 1978; *Case Contadine,*
Milan 1979; *India,* Como 1980; *Spazi dell'Uomo,* Ivrea, Italy 1980; *Cagliari,
Marina,* with Antonio Romagnino and Magda Arduino, Milan 1981; *Venezia,*
with text by Giorgio Soavi, Milan 1981; *Germania,* Milan 1982; *Scandinavia,*
Milan 1983; *Archeologia Industriale,* Milan 1983; *I Navigli,* Milan 1984; *Il
Mondo,* Milan 1985; *Veneto,* Milan 1985; *Roma,* Milan 1986; *Toscana,*
Milan 1986.

On BERENGO-GARDIN: Books—*Nuova Fotografia Italiana* by Giuseppe
Turroni, Milan 1959; *Photography Year Book,* edited by Norman Hall,
London 1961-65, 1967, 1970, 1972; *The Land,* exhibition catalogue, edited by
Mark Haworth-Booth, London 1975; *The Magic Image* by Cecil Beaton and
Gail Buckland, London and Boston 1975; *Geschichte der Fotografie im 20.
Jahrhundert/History of Photography in the 20th Century* by Petr Tausk,
Cologne 1977, London 1980; *70 Anni di Fotografia in Italia* by Italo Zannier,
Modena, Italy 1978; *30 Anni di Fotografia a Venezia,* exhibition catalogue, by
Italo Zannier, Venice 1980; *L'Informazione Negata: Il Fotogiornalismo in
Italia 1945/80,* edited by Uliano Lucas and Maurizio Bizziccari, Bari, Italy
1981; *Photography Year 1982* by Time-Life editors, Amsterdam 1982; *The
Image and the Eye* by E. H. Gombrich, London 1982. **Articles**—"Young
Italian Photographers" by Romeo Martinez in *Camera* (Lucerne), January
1963; "Gianni Berengo-Gardin" by P. Racanicchi in *Popular Photography*
(New York), October 1964; "Gianni Berengo-Gardin" by Bill Jay in *Album*
(London), no. 12, 1970; "Gianni Berengo-Gardin" in *Modern Photogra-
phy*(New York), December 1972; "Gianni Berengo-Gardin" by A. Natali in
Zoom (Paris), May 1973; "Gianni Berengo-Gardin" by Gilardi in *Photo*
(Milan), March 1977; "Gianni Berengo-Gardin" by Piovani in *Progresso
Fotografico* (Milan), May 1979; "Gianni Berengo-Gardin" in *Zoom* (Mu-
nich), August 1980.

*   *   *

Gianni Berengo-Gardin has always been a freelance reporter, and he has
been producing pictures for decades, investigating and revealing the weak-

nesses and the conventions of human life in an insistent, ironic way. Cesare Zavattini, a great Italian script-writer, has written of him: "This man, with a sort of absent-mindedness, has always heard the trumpets of a universal justice, a little painful perhaps in a vague sort of way but always insistently moral, hidden in the wings." Berengo-Gardin's photography takes a view that is sometimes indiscreet but is never aggressive, a view that is assimilated from reality and becomes his own, inescapably his, thanks to the effect of the acute cultural penetration and precise moral judgment that are evident in his work.

With his great skill in composing his pictures (nearly always in black and white, since color strikes him as superfluous to the true needs of "fundamental" investigation), in fitting the figure to the background, in styling the picture within the frame, Berengo-Gardin often achieves highly original results. Indeed, in Italy, and not only in Italy, he has built a reputation as an excessively "cultured" photographer—a reputation which, if it in practical terms means that he cannot work for certain magazines and periodicals, still makes him much sought after for book after book of photographs.

His photographs are, in fact, always the fruit of careful production, a period of unhurried interpretation as if to urge the beholder to look beyond that which the picture itself seems to pass over in silence. Not that Berengo-Gardin ever fails to give his subjects all the attention they require; and he will deal with a subject all the more closely the more nearly it is in line with his own convictions. The most eloquent examples of his work come from his "love affair" with Venice, from the splendid series of pictures of villages in India, or from his pictures of Luzzara, the village visited 20 years after Strand went there. Then there are his great social reportages ("High-Class Death" is the most affecting example), which he regards as his most important project—a project that is half precise, detailed documentation and half personal, literary interpretation.

Berengo-Gardin likes best to work without a set plan, so that he can move around in the most creative way. All the same, he certainly does not look upon himself as an artist; he describes himself as "an honest photographic craftsman" who learned long ago how to use his tools and employs them to tell others about the world.

—Attilio Colombo

BERKO, Ferenc.

Nationality: American. **Born:** Nagyvárad, Hungary, 28 January 1916; emigrated to Germany, 1921, and England, 1932: naturalized, 1947; and to the United States, 1947: naturalized, 1969. **Education:** Primary school in Weisser Hirsch Spa, near Dresden, 1921-26; gymnasia in Dresden, 1926-27, Berlin, 1928, and Frankfurt, 1929-31, and grammar school in London, 1932; mainly self-taught in photography. **Family:** Married Mirte Hahn-Beretta in 1937; daughters: Nora and Gina. **Career:** Began photographing, in Dresden, 1927; freelance documentary photographer and cinematographer, Paris and London, 1936-38; Director of Photography, Bhavnani Film Productions, Bombay, 1938-39; also produced photo stories for Michael Powell and Emeric Pressburger, London Film Productions, 1938-49; established own commercial and portrait studio, in conjunction with British Advertising Agency, Bombay, 1939-44; worked as a director (Staff Captain) with the British Directorate of Kinematography, Bombay, 1944-47; Instructor in Photography and Film, Institute of Design, Chicago, 1947-48; settled in Aspen, Colorado, 1948; worked as a photographer/filmmaker for the Container Corporation of America, Chicago, 1948-51. Independent photographer and filmmaker, Aspen, since 1952. Photographed for the Music Associates of Aspen and the Aspen Institute for Humanistic Studies since 1949, and documented Aspen from that date on. Organizer, Photo Conference, Aspen Institute for Humanistic Studies, 1951. **Agent:** Rudolf Kicken, Vintage Prints, Köln, Germany; USA representative: Yancey Richardson, Lumina, 251 W 19th Street, New York, NY 10011.

Individual Exhibitions:

1947   *Bronzes of Southern India,* Victoria and Albert Museum,
        London

1967   *Berko: 75 Color Prints,* Cincinnati Museum of Art, Ohio
        (toured the United States)
1968   *Beauty Perceived,* Pat Moore Gallery, Aspen, Colorado
1970   *3 Color Photographers,* Neikrug Gallery, New York
1971   *Berko: Retrospective,* Institute for Humanistic Studies, Aspen,
        Colorado
1972   *Color Photography by Berko,* Amon Carter Museum, Fort
        Worth, Texas
1976   *Images of Nature,* Amon Carter Museum, Fort Worth, Texas
        (toured the United States)
1979   *50 Color Photographs,* Institute for Humanistic Studies, Aspen,
        Colorado
        Berko/Fontana/Gianella, University of Texas at Austin
1980   *Berko/Bruehl,* Center for Creative Photography, University of
        Arizona, Tucson
1981   *Ferenc Berko,* New Gallery for Contemporary Photography,
        Cleveland
        Ferenc Berko, 5th Avenue Gallery of Photography, Scottsdale,
        Arizona
        Selected Photographs 1937-79, Aspen Art Museum, Colorado
1983   Unicorn Gallery, Aspen Colorado (retrospective)
1984   *Aspen Portraits,* Aspen Institute for Humanistic Studies,
        Colorado (travelled to the Modernage Gallery, New
        York 1985)
1991   *Ferenc Berko: 60 Years of Photography—The Discovering
        Eye,* Arles, France (travelled to Museum of Photography,
        Bradford, 1992; toured Germany, Prague, Milan, Budapest,
        1992-1993)
1994   *Ferenc Berko: 60 Years of Photography—The Discovering
        Eye,* ICP, USA
        New Retrospective, Musée de L'Elysée, Lausanne

Selected Group Exhibitions:

1959   *Photography at Mid-Century,* International Museum of
        Photography, George Eastman House, Rochester, New York
1964   *Santos of New Mexico,* Amon Carter Museum, Fort
        Worth, Texas
1968   *Photography U.S.A.,* De Cordova Museum, Lincoln,
        Massachusetts
1978   *Color Photography 30 Years Ago,* at *Photokina '78,* Cologne
1980   *American Portraits of the 60's and 70's,* Center for Visual
        Arts, Aspen, Colorado
        The Carter Cabinet Portraits, National Portrait Gallery,
        Washington, D.C.
1984   *Subjektive Fotografie: Images of the 50s,* San Francisco
        Museum of Modern Art (travelled to the University of
        Houston, Texas; Museum Folkwang, Essen; Vasterbottens
        Museum, Umea; Kulsturhuset, Stockholm; Saarland Museum, Saarbrucken; Palais des Beaux-Arts, Brussels)
1985   *Das Aktfoto,* Fotomuseum im Stadtmuseum, Munich
1986   *Fifty Years of Modern Colour Photos,* at *Photokina 86,*
        Cologne

Collections:

Museum of Modern Art, New York; Metropolitan Museum of Art, New York; Gernsheim Collection, University of Texas at Austin; San Francisco Museum of Modern Art; Center for Creative Photography, University of Arizona, Tucson; Museum Folkwang, Essen, Germany.

Publications:

By BERKO: Books—*Nudes by Berko, Basch and Bullock,* portfolio, with text by Lou Parella, New York 1960; *The Aspen Idea,* with text by Sidney Hyman, Norman, Oklahoma 1975; *Ferenc Berko: 12 Color Dye Transfers,* portfolio, edited by ARCO, Los Angeles 1978; *Berko: Color Photographs,* limited edition, with an introduction by Helmut Gernsheim, Los Angeles 1979; *Ferenc Berko—Early Images,* portfolio of 12 black-and-white photos, edited by the Unicorn Gallery, Aspen, Colorado 1983. **Films**—3 documentary

Satin Nude. Photograph ©Ferec Berko.

films for the Epidaurus Trust, London, 1935-36; government documentaries on aspects of Indian Army life, Bombay 1942-43; documentary recruiting films, for the Directorate of Kinematography, Bombay, 1944-46; experimental color shorts, at the Institute of Design, Chicago, 1947-52; 2 documentary/publicity films for Container Corporation of America, Chicago, 1949-51; *Time Capsule, World's Fair,* for Westinghouse Corporation, 1950; Anne Morrow Lindbergh's "Gift from the Sea" section of the Charles Eames' film *The Sea,* for CBS-TV, 1950; film for Samsonite, Denver, 1962.

On BERKO: Books—*Akt International/International Nudes,* with introduction by Otto Steinert, Munich and London 1954; *Photography Today,* edited by Norman Hall, London 1957; *Beauty: Variations on the Theme Woman by Masters of the Camera—Past and Present,* edited by L. Fritz Gruber, London and New York 1965; *Subjektive Fotografie: Images of the 50s,* exhibition catalogue, by Ute Eskildsen, Manfred Schmalriede and Dorothy Martinson, Essen, West Germany 1984; *A Concise History of Photography,* 3rd edition, by Helmut Gernsheim, New York 1986. **Articles**—in *Modern Photography* (New York), December 1952; in *Grossbild-Technik* (Munich), December 1955; "The Abstract Work of Ferenc Berko" by Giuseppe Turroni in *Ferrania* (Milan), April 1958; "Ferenc Berko: A Many-Sided Talent" by Jacquelyn Balish in *Modern Photography* (New York), November 1958; "3 Photo-Journalists" by Bernd Lohse in *Camera* (Lucerne), October 1976; "Ferenc Berko: Ein Meister der Stillen Farbe" by Carl Steinorth in *Format* (Karlsruhe), September 1978; "Ferenc Berko" in *Creative Camera* (London), October 1978; "Ferenc Berko" by James Enyeart in *American Photographer* (New York), July 1980; "Ferenc Berko" by Helmut Gernsheim in *Fotomagazin* (Munich), July 1983; "Ferenc Berko—Portfolio" in *Photo Technik International* (Munich), March 1986.

*

I believe photography that endures, like any other form of art, does not need explanations.

I have no quarrel with so-called "experimental" photography, inside or outside the studio or darkroom. However, I do not feel that something is better simply because it is new, or that there is nothing left to photograph any more. The world is rich and beautiful and unendingly full of subject matter to take, be it small or large, "abstract" or "real," "documentary" or "scenic"—however we tend to compartmentalize it.

—Ferenc Berko

*   *   *

Shape, form and colour are Ferenc Berko's *forte,* though he is an extremely versatile photographer who it is impossible to pigeonhole. His superb colour reportages of Morocco, Mexico, Japan, India and many other countries and his striking close-ups of nature and man-made objects have strong graphic design, geometric composition and often unusual perspective in common. Long before anyone else, Berko discovered gorgeous colour designs in water reflections, sand dunes, bird feathers, lichen-covered stones, patterns of petrified wood, torn billboards. Photographs taken 30 years ago have now earned him a reputation as one of the great masters of colour photography.

Many of these fragments of nature were taken for Berko's own pleasure, others for the Container Corporation of America, which drew him in 1949 from the Chicago Institute of Design to Aspen, Colorado.

Yet not all of Berko's work is in colour. It includes many monochrome portraits of men and women famous in music, literature, painting and architecture taken in his capacity as official photographer to international music festivals and design conferences arranged by the Institute for Humanistic Studies at Aspen. They are fine character studies or photojournalistic documents of subjects taken unawares while speaking or performing.

Berko is an extremely sensitive artist, a careful observer, and an acute interpreter of nature. I have watched the overpowering impact of his striking colour shots not only on myself but also on most visitors during exhibitions.

—Helmut Gernsheim

BERMAN, Mieczyslaw.

Nationality: Polish. **Born:** Warsaw, 7 July 1903. **Education:** Studied at the School of Decorative Art, Warsaw, 1921-26; mainly self-taught in photography, from 1927. **Military Service:** Served in the Polish division of the Soviet Army, U.S.S.R., 1943-44. **Family:** Married Irena Chojnacka in 1930. **Career:** Independent photographer and photomontagist, for the magazines, *Kuznia, Ze Swiata, Trybuna Wolnosci, Zolnierz Polski,* etc., Warsaw 1927-39, 1947-75. Assistant Editor, *Przekroj* magazine, Warsaw, 1930-31; founder-member, with Bartoszek, Bobowski, Gede, Hanft, etc., Phrygian Cap artists' group, Warsaw, 1934-37; member, KAGR artists' group, Warsaw, 1934-39; lived in the U.S.S.R., making anti-nazi photomontages for the Polish emigre magazines *Wolna Polska* and *Nowe Widnokreg,* 1939-46. **Recipient:** Gold Medal, *Exposition des Arts et Technique dans la Vie Moderne,* Paris 1937; National Prize for Political Caricature, Warsaw, 1950. Honorary Corresponding Member, Deutsche Akademie der Kunst zu Berlin, East Germany, 1971. **Died:** (in Warsaw) *6 May 1975.*

Individual Exhibitions:

1947	Galerie Purkyne, Prague
1948	Club of Young Artists, Warsaw
1969	Galeria Zacheta, Warsaw (retrospective)
1966	*Satyra Mieczsława Bermana,* Galeria Zacheta, Warsaw
	Arsenal, Poznan, Poland
	Internationale Ausstellungszentrum, East Berlin (travelled to Dresden)
1967	Galerie Daniel Keel, Zurich
1968	Galerie im Taxispalais, Innsbruck, Austria Karther Landesgalerie, Klagenfurt, Austria
1973	Galleria Schwarz, Milan
	Galleria Milano, Milan
1990	*Mieczysław Berman,* retrospective, National Museum, Wrocław

Selected Group Exhibitions:

1934	*KAGR,* Institute of Propaganda Art, Warsaw
1937	*Phrygian Cap Artists,* Railwaymen's Trade Union Building, Krakow, Poland
1950	*Affiches Polnaises,* Palais des Beaux-Arts, Brussels
1961	*Im Kampf vereint,* Pavillion der Kunst, East Berlin (travelled to Weimar, East Germany)
1965	*Arte e Resistenza in Europa,* Bolonia and Torino, Italy
1966	*Engagierte Kunst,* Linz
1967	*Polski plakat polityczny 1944-1967,* Museum Historii Polskiego Ruchu Rewolucyjnego, Warsaw
1968	*Collagen,* Kunstgewerbemuseum, Zurich
1969	*Die Fotomontage,* Stadttheater, Ingolstadt, West Germany
1970	*Fotomontaze 1924-34,* Galeria Wspolczesna, Warsaw
	Mahnung—Kunst des Widerstandes gegen den Faschismus, Weimar Kunsthalle, Weimar
1973	*Medium—Fotografie, Stadtisches Museum,* Leverkusen, West Germany (toured Germany and Italy)
1974	*Ars 74—International Modern Art Exhibition,* The Art Museum of the Ateneum, Helsinki and Tampereen Taidemuseo, Tampere
1980	*Experimental Photography,* Stills Gallery, Edinburgh, Scotland (toured Britain)
1981	*Photographie Polonaise 1900-81,* Centre Georges Pompidou, Paris
1983	*Presences Polonaises,* Centre Georges Pompidou, Paris
1989	*Co je fotografie (What is Photography),* Galerie Manes, Prague
1994	*Europa, Europa—Das Jahrhundert der Avantgarde in Mittelund Osteuropa,* Kust und Ausstellungshalle der BRD, Bonn

Collections:

Mieczyslaw Berman Archive, Galleria Schwarz, Milan; National Museum, Warsaw; Historical Museum of the Polish Revolutionary Movement, Warsaw; Museum Sztuki/Museum of Art, Łódz, Poland; Kupferstichkabinett, Dresden, East Germany; National Museum, Wrocław

Publications:

By BERMAN: Books—*Mieczyslaw Szczuka,* with Anatol Stern, Warsaw 1965; *Fotomontaze 1924-1934,* exhibition catalogue, Galeria Wspòłczesna, Warsaw 1970. **Articles**—"John Heartfield—moj przyjaciel i mistrz" in *Fotografia* (Warsaw), no. 7, 1968; "My Meeting with John Heartfield" in *Sonntag* (East Berlin), 11 May 1969; "The Photomontage" in *Berliner Zeitung* (East Berlin), August 1972.

On BERMAN: Books—*Fotomantaze Mieczyslawa Bermana* by Tadeusz Borowski, Warsaw 1948; *Fotomontaze artystyczne Mieczyslawa Bermana* by Ignacy Witz, Warsaw 1964; *Fotomontagen Mieczyslaw Berman* by John Heartfield, East Berlin 1966; *Fifty Years of History in Berman's Photomontages,* edited by Arturo Schwarz, Milan 1973; *Photomontage* by Dawn Ades, London 1976; *Polska fotografia artystyczna do roku 1939,* exhibition catalogue by Adam Sobota, Wroclaw, Poland 1977; *Dada Photomontagen,* exhibition catalogue by Carl-Albrecht Haenlein and others, Hannover 1979; *Fotografia Polska 1839-1979,* exhibition catalogue by Julius Garztecki, Adam Sobota, Urszula Czartoryska and others, New York 1979; *Experimental Photography,* exhibition catalogue by Dawn Ades, London 1980; *Photographie d'Avante-Garde en Pologne,* exhibition catalogue by Urszula Czartoryska, Paris 1981; *Sztuka Polski Ludowej,* by Janusz Bogucki, Warsaw 1983; *Fotografia Polska 1945-1985* by Ryszard Bobrowski and others, Gorzów Wielkopolski, Poland 1985; *Europa, Europa—Das Jahrhundert der Avantgarde in Mittelund Osteuropa,* exhibition catalogue, Bonn 1994. **Articles**—"Ag Visit to Mieczyslaw Berman" by Marian Bielicki in *Zwierciadlo* Warsaw), March 1964; "The Photomontages of Mieczyslaw Berman" by Ewa Garztecka in *Trybuna Ludu* (Warsaw), May 1966; "Politically Committed Art from Poland" by Grete Misar in *Kliene Zeitung* (Klagenfurt, Austria), March 1968; "A Challenge to Indifference" by Sybille Pawel in *Berliner Zeitung* (East Berlin), August 1972; "Poland Through the Camera Eye" by Gene Thornton in the *New York Times,* 13 August 1979; "The Eye of Poland" by Douglas Davis in *Newsweek* (New York), 13 August 1979; "Photos Through Polish Shutters" by David Elliot in *Sun-Times* (Chicago), 14 October 1979; "Fotografia Polska" by John Russell Taylor in *The Times* (London), 28 September 1980; "Wystawa-Fotografia polska 1839-1979" by Ryszard Bobrowski in *Fotografia* (Warsaw), no. 3, 1980; "140 lat fotografii polskiej" by Marcin Gizycki in *Projekt* (Warsaw), no. 4, 1980; "La Photographie Polonaise 1900-1981" by Chris Miller in *European Photography* (Gottingen), no. 7, 1981.

* * *

Mieczyslaw Berman was a political artist par excellence. Interested in communist ideology and political writings from an early age, Berman dedicated his whole life to art and politics—two passions that he attempted to join into one. Aware of the distinctive characteristics of the new era and of its consequent problems, he demanded both realism and idealism from his work and, regardless of its context, saw it as a vehicle for exposure and propaganda, demystification and controversy. He made frequent use of photographic material taken from periodicals and super-imposed on original photographs—a technique of photomontage or, more accurately, photo-collage that enabled him to respond quickly to events and that substantiated his ideas and facilitated their understanding.

Berman began his artistic career in advertising. Here, in the 1920s, he became familiar with Russian constructivism and the works of Bauhaus. His first attempts at photomontage incorporate pure geometric forms and criss-crossing vertical and horizontal lines representative of new towns and their construction. In this period, he strove towards commemoration and unification and also to a simplicity of expression. Berman's constructivist themes took on the aspect of universal signs and symbols.

This stage of his work ended around 1930 when, thanks to Kurt Tucholski's *Deutschland, Deutschland über Alles,* Berman discovered John Heartfield's

graphic works. The initial contact between these artists, which rapidly grew into an enduring friendship, made a great impression on Berman's art. He rejected strict constructivism in favour of socio-political satire which, it seems, better suited his personality and general disposition. This satire arose not from honour or a sense of the grotesque, however, but from anger and a passion for disclosure. Using anecdotes and making no attempt to mute their force, Berman created a truly grotesque theatre of people, objects and events through which he portrayed current affairs—for the most part—accurately and justly. Through his art, he attacked both the political Right in Poland and the expanding Hitler movement, middle-class conventions and the small-mindedness of man. Berman's photocollages reveal his sense of caricature and his satirical talent albeit through violent and uncompromising accusations levelled at the prevailing socio-political conditions and the sense of threat felt in the

After the war, Berman, now a recognised artist, continued his commitment to his art. This time, he made his stand against imperialism and neocolonialism, against the Vietnam war and nuclear threat. His photocollages, supplemented from 1943 onwards by watercolours and tempera, show the same emotional and intellectual commitment—a commitment that attempts to compel an immediate response. His work reflects Berman's unalterable conviction as to the functional nature of art and its subservience to universal ideas and values.

—Ryszard Bobrowski

BERNHARD, Ruth.

Nationality: American. **Born:** Berlin, Germany, 14 October 1905; emigrated to the United States, 1927: naturalized, 1935. **Education:** the Akademie der Künste, Berlin, 1926-27. **Wartime Service:** Served in the Women's Land Army during World War II. **Career:** Freelance photographer in New York, 1927-36, in Los Angeles, 1936-53, and San Francisco, since 1953. Since 1965, Instructor at Utah State University, Logan. Instructor, University of California Extension, Berkeley and San Francisco, 1967-75; Instructor, Photography Master Class, Columbia University, New York, 1971. Honorary Member, Board of Directors, Photographic Center of Monterey Peninsula, Carmel, California, 1993. **Recipient:** National Urban League Award, 1961; Dorothea Lange Award, Oakland Museum, California, 1976; City and County of San Francisco Award, 1978. Award of Honor for Outstanding Achievement in Photography, San Francisco Art Commission, 1984; The Professional Photographers of California, Los Angeles; Honored by the Society of Photographic Education Midwest Regional Conference for a Distinguished Career in Photography, in Chicago,1987; Presidential citation for outstanding service to Utah State University, 1990; Cyril Magnin Award bestowed by the San Francisco Chamber of Commerce for Distinguished Achievement in Photography, 1994. **Address:** 2982 Clay Street, San Francisco, California 94115, U.S.A.

Individual Exhibitions:

1936	Pacific Institute for Music and Art, Los Angeles
	Jake Zeitlin Gallery, Los Angeles
1938	P.M. Gallery, New York
1941	Little Gallery, San Francisco
1956	Gump's Gallery, San Francisco
1958	Institute for Cultural Relations, Mexico City
1959	City College of San Francisco
1962	San Francisco Public Library
	Carl Siembab Gallery, Boston
1963	Portland State College, Oregon
1965	Toren Gallery, San Francisco
1966	Jacksonville Art Museum, Florida
	Aardvark Gallery, San Francisco
1971	Neikrug Gallery, New York
1973	Chicago Center for Contemporary Photography
1975	Mills College, Oakland, California

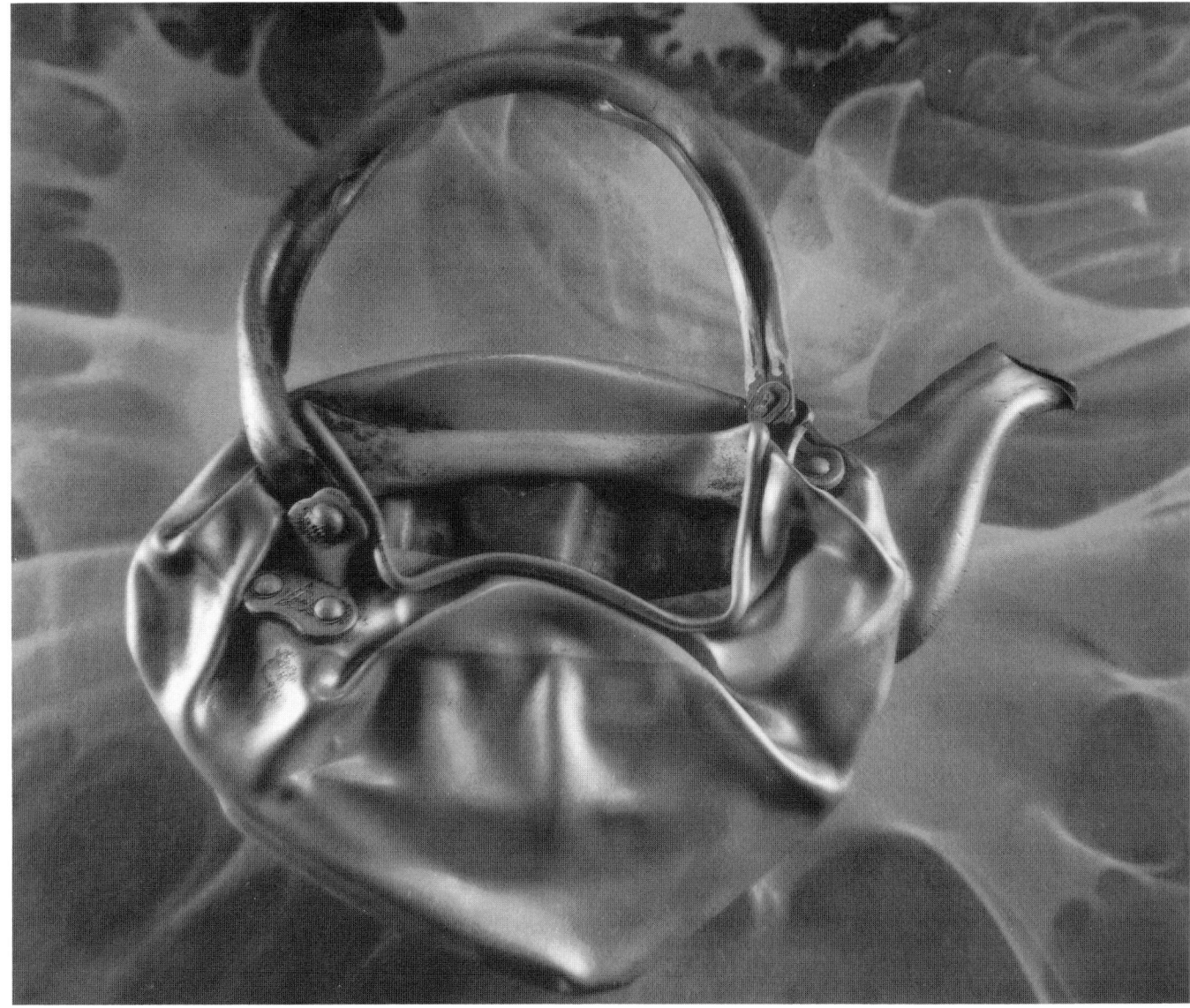

Teapot, **1976.** Photograph ©Ruth Bernhard. Courtesy Collected Visions, Berkeley, California.

1976	Halsted Gallery, Birmingham, Michigan	
	Creative Eye Gallery, Sonoma, California	
	Secret City Gallery, San Francisco	
	Edison Steet Gallery, Salt Lake City, Utah	
	Fullerton State College, California	
1977	Stephen White Gallery, Los Angeles	
	J. Hunt Gallery, Minneapolis	

1976   Halsted Gallery, Birmingham, Michigan
         Creative Eye Gallery, Sonoma, California
         Secret City Gallery, San Francisco
         Edison Steet Gallery, Salt Lake City, Utah
         Fullerton State College, California
1977   Stephen White Gallery, Los Angeles
         J. Hunt Gallery, Minneapolis
1978   Halsted Gallery, Birmingham, Michigan
         Canon Gallery, Amsterdam
1979   Image Gallery, Sarasota, Florida
         Friends of Photography, Carmel; California (restrospective)
1980   5th Avenue Gallery, Scottsdale, Arizona
         Stephen White Gallery, Los Angeles
         Photogenesis, Albuquerque, New Mexico Equivalents, Seattle
1981   Photography West, Carmel, California
         Edwynn Houk Gallery, Chicago (with Marsha Burns)
         Images Gallery, Cincinnati, Ohio
         Halsted Gallery, Birmingham, Michigan
         Pierce Street Gallery, Birmingham, Michigan
1982   Douglas Elliott Gallery, San Francisco

         University of Santa Clara, California
         Jeb Gallery, Providence, Rhode Island
         Portland Art Museum, Oregon
1983   Photographer's Gallery, Palo Alto, California
         P.G.I. Gallery, Tokyo
         Galerie Athanor 538, Marseille, France
         Grand Palais, Paris
1984   Utah State University, Logan
         Maryland Institute, Baltimore
         University of Utah, Salt Lake City
1985   Edwynn Houk Gallery, Chicago
         Milwaukee Center for Photography, Wisconsin
1986   *The Eternal Body: Photographs by Ruth Bernhard,* San
              Francisco Museum of Modern Art
         The Best of Ruth Bernhard, Tokyo Institute of Polytechnics
              College (Japan). Retrospective
1987   *The Eternal Body: Photographs by Ruth Bernhard,* Internation-
              al Center of Photography, New York
         Vision Gallery, San Francisco. Retrospective. Vintage and
              modern prints

1988	*The Eternal Body: Photographs by Ruth Bernhard,* The Museum of Contemporary Photography, Columbia College, Chicago; Galerie Zur Stockeregg, Zurich; Amerika Haus, US Cultural Center, Berlin; IF Immagine Fotografica, Milan; Lichtbild Gallery, Ingolstadt, Germany; Forum Bottcherstrasse, Bremen
1989	*The Eternal Body: Photographs by Ruth Bernhard,* Fotografie Forum Frankfurt, Germany
	Palm Beach Photographic Workshops Gallery. Retrospective
	The Eternal Body: Photographs by Ruth Bernhard, Preus Fotomuseum, Horten, Norway
	Photo Forum Gallery, Pittsburgh, PA
1990	Gallery Min, Tokyo, Japan
	Vision Gallery, San Francisco. Retrospective
1991	Photographic Image Gallery, Portland, Oregon
	Form and Light, Alinder Gallery, Gualala, CA
	The Human Figure, University Art Gallery, California State University, Chico
1992	*Ruth Bernhard: Photographs,* G Gibson Gallery, Seattle, WA
	Gift of the Commonplace, Vision Gallery, San Francisco. Retrospective
1993	Arvada Center for the Arts and Humanities, Denver. Retrospective
	Peter Fetterman Gallery, Santa Monica, CA
1994	*Ruth Bernhard: Classic Images,* G Gibson Gallery, Seattle, WA

Selected Group Exhibitions:

1965	*Contemporary Photography,* University of Illinois, Urbana
1967	*Photography in the Fine Arts,* Metropolitan Museum of Art, New York
1968	*Light 7,* Massachusetts Institute of Technology, Cambridge
1970	*Be-Ing Without Clothes,* Massachusetts Institute of Technology, Cambridge
1972	*Photography West,* Alliance for the Visual Arts, Logan, Utah
1973	*Through One's Eyes,* Muckenthaler Cultural Center, Fullerton, CA
1975	*Women of Photography,* San Francisco Museum of Modern Art
1979	*Recollections: 10 Women of Photography,* International Center of Photography, New York (toured the United States)
1981	*A Show of Hands,* San Francisco Museum of Modern Art
1984	*Photography in California 1945-80,* San Francisco Museum of Modern Art (travelling exhibition)
1987	*Women See Men,* Frankfurter Kunstverein, Frankfurt, Germany
1990	*Ninety Photographs: Fifteen Master Photographers,* Community Gallery of Lancaster, Pensylvannia
1991	*Classic Nudes: 1920-1970,* Redding Museum and Art Center, Redding, CA
	Alinder Gallery, Gualala, CA
	West Coast Photographers, Gail Severn Gallery, Ketchum, Idaho

Collections:

Museum of Modern Art, New York; Metropolitan Museum of Art, New York; International Museum of Photography, George Eastman House, Rochester, New York; Massachusetts Institute of Technology, Cambridge; Museum of Fine Arts, St. Petersburg, Florida; University of Illinois, Urbana; Utah State Institute of Fine Arts, Logan; Oakland Museum, California; San Francisco Museum of Modern Art; Norton Simon Museum, Pasadena, California; Bibliothèque Nationale, Paris.

Publications:

By BERNHARD: Books—*The Big Heart,* with text by Melvin Van Peebles, New York 1957; *Ruth Bernhard: The Eternal Body,* edited by Margaretta Mitchell, published by Photography West Graphics, Carmel, California 1986; second edition published by Chronicle Books, San Francisco, 1994. **Article**—

"Ruth Bernhard," interview, with Morrie Camhi, in *Photoshow* (Los Angeles), no. 2, 1979.

On BERNHARD: Books—*Recollections: 10 Women of Photography,* edited by Margaretta Mitchell, New York 1979; *Collecting Light* by James Alinder, Carmel, California 1979; *The Library of World Photography: Photography as Fine Art,* with introduction by Douglas Davis, Tokyo 1982, 1983, London 1983; *Photography in California 1945-1980* by Louise Katzman, San Francisco 1984; *Ruth Bernhard: The Collection of Ginny Williams,* Denver 1993. **Articles**—"Photographs by Ruth Bernhard" in *Creative Camera* (London), October 1971; "Ruth Bernhard" by Ben Helprin in *Photo Image* (Fullerton, California), vol. I, no. 1, 1976.

*

For me, photographing is a heightened experience perhaps most akin to poetry and music. The image is an attempt to express my sense of wonder at the miraculous visible world and the mysteries that lie beyond our limited human perceptions. Intensified observations lead to exciting discoveries. Looking at everything as if for the first time reveals the commonplace to be utterly incredible, if only we can be alive to the newness of it. I see a tiny seed and a mountain range as equally significant in the order of the universe, as are life and death. These are some of the concepts that have challenged me in my work.

—Ruth Bernhard

* * *

Ruth Bernhard's enthusiasm not only for photography but also for life itself is infectious. The depth of her involvement is persuasive. For the past fifty years she has been doing what she has had to do as an artist. Now well into her 70's, she welcomes the growing chorus of accolades. Perhaps she wonders why it has taken us so long to discover her.

Ruth became the assistant to Ralph Steiner's assistant photographer at *The Delineator,* a popular woman's magazine. Ruth remembers the job as primarily one of darkroom scullery maid, but she did learn the basics of photography. She was fired six months later because of erratic attendance and general lack of interest; a love affair had taken priority in her life. With the $90 she received as severance pay Ruth purchased an 8 x 10 view camera along with an assortment of darkroom equipment. Her first serious photograph was of candy *Lifesavers* made in 1930. It is more than remarkable that all of the elements which remain important to her are present in this image—the use of light, found objects, formal perfection, symbolism.

Ruth's first important commission came in 1934. The Museum of Modern Art asked her to make photographs for an exhibition and publication called *Machine Art.* It was while photographing an oversized stainless steel bowl for this assignment that the idea of her first nude emerged:

I had a friend who loved to take off her clothes and loved to dance. I said, "Get in the bowl." She did, and I made two exposures with the 8 x 10. I wasn't aware that it was unusual to photograph nudes. I didn't even know it was unusual to be a woman photographer. I just tried very hard to be a good one.

During this period Ruth continued photographing for personal satisfaction. Despite her commercial success a fortuitous meeting in 1935 was to change the course of her life. Ruth was visiting in California. While walking along the beach at Santa Monica her companion introduced her to two of his friends, Edward and Brett Weston. Ruth accepted Edward's invitation to see his work and was profoundly affected by it.

"Although I had been a practicing photographer for more than five years, the personal power of his photographic statements made me respect my own craft for the first time. I was 30 years old and ready to make a long-term commitment to my chosen work.

I saw Edward as often as I could over the years. I much admired his frugal lifestyle. Beans never tasted better!"

Ruth's move to the West Coast was responsible for the great change in the kind of assignments she was to do. In New York she had been involved primarily with advertising, architecture and industrial design. In California, however, she began to photograph children and movie starlets. There was still ample time for personal photography, however, and she began to exhibit her work. In 1936 she exhibited at both the Zeitlin Gallery and the Pacific Institute in Los Angeles. She moved into a new studio across from the Hollywood Bowl, and after concerts there she opened her house to photographers, artist, musicians and other friends. She had become integrated into the Los Angeles art community.

During World War II, Ruth felt the need to be a part of the war effort. She became a farm hand in the Women's Land Army, taking her basic training at the Agriculture College in Farmingdale, Long Island. After this she was assigned to a large farm in Mendham, New Jersey, where she was able to become completely involved in the growing of crops and care of the animals. She remembers this period in her life with a sense of deep satisfaction. In 1947, soon after she returned to Southern California, Ruth became gravely ill. From that time until 1958 her creative efforts came to a virtual standstill while she underwent, and slowly recovered from, two major operations.

In 1952 she gave up her 8 x 10 view camera in favor of the smaller 4 x 5 Graphic View and, later, a 2¼-square negative format. A 1953 trip to Northern California excited Ruth and provided the stimulus for her move to San Francisco in April of that year. She found an ideal studio and flat on Clay Street that continues to be her home.

Ruth's studio is large enough to double as a classroom for photography students. They began arriving in the mid-1950's for informal sessions, and by 1967 she was also teaching at the University of California Extension in San Francisco. Over the past two decades she has lectured across the country and has taught many workshops and master classes.

Photography for Ruth is a mystical experience. She explains:

"My own creative work comes to me like a gift, pushing itself into my consciousness. A powerful feeling comes over me. It is a timeless experience, almost like being in a trance. Often I have struggled for days to get the image of the photograph to overlap the spirit I seek. It is an awesome responsibility and a lonely one."

The relatively small volume of Ruth's work can be attributed, in part, to her unproductivity during almost two decades of illness, coupled with her discarding of hundreds of negatives at a time when she felt her work was not important to others. An even greater reason lies in her uncompromising belief in the need for exquisite perfection for each exposure. Ruth truly feels a oneness with the universe which she attempts to communicate in her photographs. When all is right, there is no question in her mind as to which objects in what arrangement will complete that communication. While Ruth insists on harmony, beauty and perfection, her overriding concern is with light itself.

—James Alinder

BERRY, Ian.

Nationality: British. **Born:** Preston, Lancashire, 4 April 1934. **Education:** Ramillies Hall, Cheadle Hulme, Cheshire, and Rossall School, Fleetwood, Lancashire, until 1951. **Career:** Worked as a general photographic assistant, 1952-56, then press photographer, 1956-58, *Rand Daily Mail,* Johannesburg; photographer, *Drum* magazine, Johannesburg, 1959-60; freelance photographer, in Johannesburg, 1960-62, in Paris, 1962-67, and in London, since 1967: has worked for *Paris-Match, Stern, Life, Observer Colour Magazine, Encyclopedia Brittanica, Geo, Sunday Times, Der Spiegel, Fortune,* etc. Member, Magnum Photos co-operative agency, Paris and New York, from 1963. **Recipient:** First and Third Prizes, Nikon World Photo Contest, 1959; Features Photographer of the Year Award, British Press Pictures Association, 1959, 1960; Photo Award, Art Directors Club of New York, 1969; Arts Council Photo Bursary, London, 1974; Nikon Photographer of the Year Award, 1977; Pix of the Year Award, Missouri School of Journalism/National Press Photographers of America 1981. Honorary Fellow, University of Lancashire, 1990. **Address:** c/o Magnum Photos, 5 Passage Piver, 75001 Paris, France.

Individual Exhibitions:

1972   The Photographers' Gallery, London
        This Is Whitechapel, Whitechapel Art Gallery, London
1973   *2 Views,* travelling exhibition (toured the U.K.)

1976   *The English,* The Photographers' Gallery, London
        Colour Photos, Photo Fair, Paris
1977   House of Culture, Hamburg
1986   *The English,* XYZ Gallery, Brussels
        South Africa, Fonds Nationale d'Art Contemporain, Paris

Selected Group Exhibitions:

1972   *Personal Views 1850-1970,* British Council, London
1977   *Concerning Photography,* The Photographers' Gallery, London
            (travelled to the Spectro Workshop, Newcastle upon Tyne)
1976   *British Photographers,* Photo Fair, Paris
1978   *Magnum Photographers,* at *Rencontres Internationale de
            Photographie,* Arles, France
1979   *This is Magnum,* Takashimaya Department Store, Tokyo
1981   *Berry/McCullin/Snowdon/Lichfield,* Kodak Gallery, London
1983   *Geographis,* Olympus Gallery, Paris (travelled to Hamburg)
1984   *Britain in 1984,* National Museum of Photography, in
            Bradford, Yorkshire
1985   *Contemporary British Photography,* Musée d'Art
            Moderne, Paris
1991   *A L'Est de Magnum,* Paris

Collections:

Arts Council of Great Britain, London; British Council, London; Museum Ludwig, Cologne.

Publications:

By BERRY: Books—*King Kong,* with text by Mona Glassner, London 1960; *The English,* London 1978; photos for *The Sporting Horse,* Paris 1984; *Women in Wine,* Paris 1985; *Great Italian Restaurants,* Paris 1985; *L'Afrique du Sud,* with foreword by President Mitterand, Paris 1989; *Nature's Wonderlands—Natural Parks of the World,* Washington 1989; *Les Grands Travaux,* Paris 1989.

On BERRY: Books—*Personal Views 1850-1970,* exhibition catalogue, with an introduction by Bill Jay, London 1972; *British Image 2,* London 1976; *Concerning Photography,* exhibition catalogue, by Jonathan Bayer and others, London 1977; *World Photography,* edited by Bryn Campbell, London 1981; *Eye Witness: 25 Years Through World Press Photos* by Harold Evans, London 1981; *Sammlung Gruber: Photographie des 20. Jahrhunderts,* exhibition catalogue, with foreword by Siegfried Gohr, Cologne 1984. **Articles**—"Ian Berry" in *Photo* (Paris), March 1972; "Personal Views 1895-1970" in *Creative Camera* (London) May 1972; "Portfolio: Ian Berry" in the *British Journal of Photography* (London), 23 June 1972; "This Is Whitechapel" by Peter Fuller in *Connoisseur* (London), October 1972; "What They Leave Behind Them: Photographs by Ian Berry," with text by Nicholas Tomalin, in the *Sunday Times Magazine* (London),21 January 1973; "Bursary for Berry" in *Photographic Journal* (London), November 1974.

*   *   *

He arrived on the photographic scene to the sound of gunfire, which he would hear much more of over the next decade. It was March 21, 1960, and the place Sharpeville, a dusty settlement in the veldt outside Johannesburg.

"Get down, you bloody fool!" shouted his companion from the South African magazine *Drum,* as Ian Berry stood up to photograph the African crowd rushing towards him from the police firing at them from the tops of their vehicles.

"Yes, I did hear things whizzing past me," he explained in the office afterwards, "But if I hadn't been standing up, how could I have got the pictures?"

In each of the next two years the young unknown would win the top British photographic award—first with a set of a witch-doctor at work, then with his coverage of the Congo uprising. Slightly-built, diffident and bearded, Berry

Refugee Camp, Natal, S. Africa, **1994.** Photograph ©Ian Berry/Magnum.

looked more like an artist than a trouble-shooter, but he came to life with danger, like a racing man when he catches sight of the horses in the paddock. So for the next few years he ranged the troubled continent of Africa, shooting story after story for the big picture magazines of America and Europe, and for the Magnum agency he had been invited to join.

But by the time he came to settle in Britain, Ian Berry, then in his 30's, had expanded his range of interest and vision, and could find all the stimulus he needed in the life of everyday humanity. At first on his own, and later on the first bursary ever awarded by the Arts Council, he ranged over the British scene, making pictures in Whitechapel and clubland, at Ascot and Southend; the North of England particularly seemed to give him what he was looking for. In his work a new sympathy and tenderness developed, so that he seemed to be taking pictures *with* people and not of them, he and his camera having become part of the surroundings.

Berry works out of a direct response, going to a place or occasion intuitively and shooting with little conciously-formed plan:"You're there waiting for the moment that makes the whole thing work, moving around so the shapes relate to each other and fall together.'' And he operates almost entirely with black-and-white: ''If you're concerned with form and content, colour can be an intrusion and distraction. Also it has technical limitations— so that it becomes less easy just to walk around all day, moving in and out of situations, simply shooting.''

In his early trouble-shooting days, Ian Berry let the world know what went on in places few would ever visit, recording with his camera mainly what was frightening and extraordinary. Today he photographs those scenes and events we all can see, but few of us ever notice. Drifting almost imperceptibly around

to record the weakness and oddity, the callousnes, humor and affection of everyday life, he tells us about ourselves and one another.

—Tom Hopkinson

BHIMJI, Zarina.

Nationality: British. **Born:** Mbarara, Uganda, 30 August 1963; emigrated to Great Britain in 1974. **Education:** Studied art foundation at Leicester Poly-technic, 1982-83, fine art at Goldsmiths' College, University of London, 1983-86, and mixed media postgraduate studies at Slade School of Fine Art, University College London, 1988-89, B.A. 1986. **Career:** Artist in residence at the Victoria and Albert Museum (India Department), Plymouth Art Gallery, Whitechapel Art Gallery, Highbury Islington Secondary School, 1992; artist in residence at Kettle's Yard, Cambridge and visiting fellow of Darwin College, Cambridge, 1993. **Recipient:** Julian Sullivan award, Slade School of Art, 1989, Coopers & Lybrand award for the most outstanding work in any medium by artists under the age of 35 in the Whitechapel 1989 Open. **Address:** 50 Heron House, Pelican Estate, London, SE15 5NJ, England.

Individual Exhibitions:

1989   Tom Allen Community Art Centre, London
1992   *I will always be here*, Ikon Gallery, Birmingham
1995   Kettle's Yard, Cambridge

Selected Group Exhibitions:

1985   *Mirror Reflecting Darkly*, Brixton Gallery, London
        Struggle & Success, Jubilee Gardens, London
        Artists Against Apartheid, South Bank, London
        F Stops, Chelsea School of Art, London
1986   *Darshan*, Camerawork, London (and tour)
        From Two Worlds, Whitechapel Art Gallery, London (and tour)
        Jagrati, Greenwich Peoples Gallery, London
1987   *Dislocation*, Kettles Yard, Cambridge
        The Devil's Feast, Chelsea School of Art, London
        The Image Employed The Use of Narrative in Black Art,
            Cornerhouse Gallery, Manchester
        The South London Open Exhibition, South London Art Gallery
        Black Women Photographers, Camden Arts Centre, London
1988   *The Essential BLACK ART*, Chisenhale Gallery, London
        (and tour)
        Insights, Battersea District Library, London
1989   *Whitechapel Open*, Whitechapel Art Gallery, London
        Towards a Bigger Picture, Victoria & Albert Museum
            (and tour)
1990   *Selections 5, Photokina '90*, Cologne, Germany (and
            world tour)
        Intimate Distance, Photographers' Gallery, London (and tour)
        Fabled Territories (New Asian Photography in Britain), Leeds
            City Galleries, Viewpoint and tour
        The Women in My Life, Acton Community Workshop, London
            and tour
        In Focus, Horizon Art Gallery, London
        From Object to Image, Watershed Media Centre, Bristol
        Black Markets, Cornerhouse Gallery, Manchester (and tour)
        Shocks to the System '90s Political Art, Arts Council
            Collection
1992   *Whitechapel Open*, Whitechapel Art Gallery, London
        Critical Decade, Museum of Modern Art, Oxford
1993   *Antwerp '93*, MUHKA Museum, Antwerp, Belgium

Collections:

New Hall, Cambridge; Victoria and Albert Museum, London; Polaroid International Collection, Germany; Leicester Museum and Art Gallery; Arts Council Collection, London.

Publications:

On BHIMJI: Articles—*Artrage*, No. 18, Autumn 1987; *Third Text*, Nos. 3 and 4, 1988; *Art Monthly*, March 1988; *Aperture*, No. 113, Winter 1988; *The Independent*, 15 August 1989; *Artscribe the International Magazine of New Art*, November 1989; *Art Forum International*, November 1990; *Creative Camera*, April-May 1991; *The Guardian*, 6 May 1992; *Womens Art*, No. 51, March/April 1993; *Creative Camera*, No. 321, 1993; *Third Text*, No. 22, 1993.

*   *   *

I went to Chisenhale Studios, an old whitewashed factory in Hackney, east London, to see *The Essential Black Art* in 1988. In the last part of the exhibition I found four images sandwiched in plexi-glass hanging from the ceiling above a wild pattern on the floor—a Jackson Pollock of red and orange spices. The images were photographs—an embroidered slipper, a bird jewellery—lightly tinted photographs placed on linen. There were words in blue and red printed on the fabric. You had to get up close to read them: "*Slowly she raised her arm, thin dark brown in the sun-haze circled by two*

heavy gold bangles. This had come from home—every Ismaili girl wore from birth." The words followed the weave and stretch of the threads, like the undulation of something being spoken. Perhaps the images swayed in the space, and the eye scanned them as if they were on a film screen: as part of a surface rather than the contents of a frame. In one panel the muslin was twisted and there was no picture—but there was an image. There was a pair of rubber surgical gloves. Negotiating round the spices, I turned to look at the back of the panels and saw another image—a Home Office visa stamp, enlarged and silk-screened in blue on the cloth. 'The time limit', I read, 'on the holder's leave to enter the United Kingdom is hereby removed'. There was the date and a signature. Whose fate hung on that signature? One of the women from the Indian sub-continent whose virginity was examined by Home Office Immigration Department officials in the 1970's—wearing surgical gloves?

That installation by Zarina Bhimji was titled *She Loved to Breathe—Pure Silence, 1987*. A new artist had emerged from silence: an artist working with language, film-like pictures, raw and manufactured materials (some stating an Indian origin), with mixed-media, performance, memory, anecdote, telling tales of immigration and humiliation, of mothers and daughters, of private and public, of anger and loss. The artist wrote in 1989: "I am drawn towards the challenge of my own people. I fight them and I fight for them." And in 1988: "I want to create, communicate new meanings by bringing Indian languages, objects, memory, dreams, conversations from East African and Indian backgrounds, as well as my experience of Western culture, to play in between two realities."

She works from her own identity, history and sense of community, framing questions which history in general and her own personal history have forced upon her. She was eight when civil war erupted in Uganda and her family spent two years behind closed curtains. Old shoe-boxes were her playthings. Her contribution to the exhibition *Intimate Distance* (1989) has been described by Gilan Tawadros as picturing "the traumas of premature sexual knowledge . . . reenacted in the process of discovering a specific cultural history of disenfranchisement, colonialism and migration, where this awakening is fraught with tensions and conflicts." Zarina Bhimji's work relies on intuition—hers and ours—and speaks with courage, vulnerability and pride.

—Mark Haworth-Booth

BINDE, Gunar.

Nationality: Latvian. **Born:** Aluksnes district of Latvia, 27 December 1933. **Education:** Bejas Elementary School, Aluksnes, 1940-47; studied agriculture, Priekuli Technical and Mechanical College, Cesis, 1950-57; photography, under Povilas Karpjavicius and Genady Koposov, Moscow House of Journalists (correspondence-lecture course), 1961-63. **Family:** Married Sarmite Kviesite in 1969; children: Ieva, Mara, and Elina. **Career:** Worked as a theatre lighting technician, Palace of Culture, Aluksne, 1957-61, Municipal Theatre, Valmiera, 1961-62, and Youth Theatre, Riga, 1962-64; Lecturer in Photography, School of Art, Riga, 1964-75. Photographer of the Historical Museum, Dole, since 1975. Lecturer since 1978, and Head of the Youth Master Studio since 1979, Photo Club of Riga. **Recipient:** Artist Award, Federation Internationale de l'Art Photographique (FIAP), 1975. Member of the Photo Club of Riga, since 1964, and the Union of Journalists of the U.S.S.R., since 1967. Honorary Member, Association of Finnish Camera Clubs, 1967; Cegledi Foto Club, Hungary, 1968; Danish Camera Society, 1969; Anpas Photo Society, Sri Lanka, 1970; Osterreichische Gesellschaft der Photografie, (OGPh), Austria, 1979; Honorary Fellow, A-74 Photo Society, Poland, 1975; Honorable Worker of Art of the Latvian S.S.R., 1981. **Address:** Post Office Box 82, Riga 226011, Latvia.

Individual Exhibitions:

1965   Tallinn Photo Club, Estonia
1968   Photo Club, Kaunas, Lithuania
1970   School of Art, Bechin, Czechoslovakia
1971   Galerie PP, Linz, Austria
        Staatliche Landesbildstelle, Hamburg

1972	Gdansk Photo Club, Poland
1973	Society of Friendship, Sofia, Bulgaria
	Tbilisi Photo Club, Georgia
1975	Photo Gallery of Poland, Warsaw
	Krakow Photo Society, Poland
1979	Photo Society of Lithuania, Vilnius
	Photo Club of Tshelyabinsk, Russia
	Gunar Binde/Egons Spuris/Peeter Tooming, Dum Panu ź
	Kunstatu, Brno, Czechoslovakia (travelled to the Museum of
	Czeske-Budejovica, Czechoslovakia, 1979, and Kiek in de
	Kök, Tallinn, Estonia, 1980)
	City Academy of Science, Dubna, Russia
	Church of St. Peter, Riga, Latvia (retrospective)
1980	Riga Photo Club, Latvia

Selected Group Exhibitions:

1968	*Second World Exhibition of Photography: Woman,* Pressehaus
	Stern, Hamburg (and world tour)
1970	*10 Top European Photographers: East and West,* Galerie PP,
	Linz, Austria (toured the United States, 1971-72)
1972	*Prezentacje,* Galerie ZPAF, Warsaw
1978	*10 Weltspitzen Fotografen,* Krakow Photographic Society,
	Poland (travelled to the *Innsbrucker Fotoschau,* Innsbruck,
	Austria)

Collections:

Photo Club, Riga, Latvia.

Publications:

By BINDE: Films—*Hello, Moscow,* 1966; *A Moment of the Epoch,* 1967; *With Own Hands,* 1967; *The Salute,* 1975.

On BINDE: Books—*Foto 71 USSR* by the Sovetskoye Foto editors, Moscow 1971; *Pobaltska sovetska fotografie* by Vaclav Jiru, Prague 1974; *Latvijas Fotomaksla* by Peteris Zeile and others, Riga, Latvia 1985. **Articles**—"Binde" by Pavel Bojar in *Revue Fotografie'64,* Prague 1964; "Gunar Binde Ja Hanen Mallinsa" by P.K. Jaskari in *Kamera Lehti* (Helsinki), no. 6, 1967; "Zu Unseren Bilder" by J. Drausinger in *Osterreichisches Photo-Zeitung* (Vienna), no. 10, 1971; "Gunar Binde" by V. Robert in *Photo-Cine Revue* (Paris), no. 3, 1971; "Thinking Over the Subjects We Had Sighted" in *Sovetskoye Foto* (Moscow), no. 3, 1978; "Camera Artist Gunar Binde" in *Soviet Life* (Moscow), no. 7, 1978; "Latviesu fotografijas 'enfant terrible," by Vilnis Folkmanis in *Maksla* (Riga, Latvia), no. 4, 1979.

*

Purely documentary photography is, to me, too primitive, and the subjective portrayal of one's world is incomprehensible; the real values in photoart are somewhere between the two.

I don't pursue sensationalism, striking events or characters, nature photography, documentarism or portraiture. I am looking for a resonance between the visible world and my soul. If I perceive such a harmony, I take a picture.

When taking pictures, I influence the people who are my subject. If they submit to this influence, the result is a positive one. However, very few people actually submit to it. This influence occurs in a mysterious way; the photographer, with his sophisticated and strange apparatus, communicates his intention and feelings without words, or any sign at all. . . .

Concerning contemporary trends in photography, I'll mention those aspects that seem to me to be negative: conceptualism, now developed to a highly personalized and individualist degree, has replaced genuine feeling in current photography; contemporary photography is short of great ideas, glutted with insignificant subjects; photographers are lazy concerning significant world events, social as well as humane.

Perhaps, however, I am not correct about this: I am coming to an age when a person must be careful about the conclusion he draws, which can prove too conservative.

—Gunar Binde

*   *   *

Ten or fifteen years are nothing in the cultural history of a nation, but that is exactly the time which Latvian photography needed to develop by the end of the 1960's into a quite specific expression of national culture, based on the age-old tradition of folk art. Up until that time Gunar Binde was a synonym for Latvian photography. By his own example, as well as in his teaching, he trained literally scores of contemporary photographers.

Although he is not yet old, Gunar Binde is an historical figure, inseparably linked with the post-war development of Latvin photography—not just Latvian photography but also Soviet photography in general. At a time when a superficial, optimistic recording of outward reality prevailed, Binde presented pictures of an inward reality—psychological portraits that delved deep into the heart, mind and character of the persons depicted. And he also depicted the nude, which in Soviet photography had been taboo for a long time as something unsuitable for publication. From the outset, however, Binde's nudes were not only gentle, charming and erotically effective but also dignified. His nude women are not just attractive beings; as well, they personify the noble charm of womanhood, of motherhood, the philosophy of life of those who give life. They are filled with a strong internal tension, a promise of something that remains forever unspoken, which, for that very reason, continually attracts one's attention.

Gunar Binde was first introduced abroad in 1964 in the pages of the Czech quarterly *Revue Fotografie.* At that time he was still an amateur, working in the theatre as a lighting technician, but he was soon to become a professional photographer. There was a growing interest in his work, especially abroad. He was included in international year-books, he gained recognition at exhibitions, and he began to win awards. One of the first foreign awards for this work—a Gold Medal for a portrait of the director Eduard Smilgis, which he won at an exhibition in Argentina in 1965—had a tremendous impact on many of his followers, the amateurs who followed in his footsteps: they turned their hobby into a profession, now finding in photography a suitable form for creative self-realization. This evolutionary leap, which was suddenly and almost immediately valid with regard to quality, was quite logical in a nation that for centuries had withstood the vagaries of fate and managed to preserve its own national culture. Modern photographic expression was generally fully accepted, and Gunar Binde had the lion's share in that accomplishment. It was he who in the 1960's helped to free Soviet photography in general from its pathos, who helped it to gain a direct and lively approach, full of semantic depth.

In the 1970's Binde also devoted himself to landscape photography. To a certain extent he had, in the past, already dealt with landscape: he was, for example, a pioneer in the formal placement of the female nude in landscape, which is still much imitated. But just as in those photos he made use of the symbiosis of the beauty of various shapes found in nature, in his purely landscape photos he was also above all concerned with the relationship between man and nature. This he usually expresses by a symbolic sign, which, by joining mutually incongruous elements, produces something of a surreal dramatic arrangement.

—Daniela Mrázková

BING, Ilse.

Nationality: American. **Born:** Frankfurt am Main, Germany, 23 March 1899; emigrated to the United States, 1941: naturalized 1946. **Education:** Primary school, and the Schiller Gymnasium, Frankfurt, until 1920; studied mathematics and art history, University of Frankfurt, and University of Vienna, 1920-29; mainly self-taught in photography, from 1928. **Family:** Married the pianist Konrad Wolff in 1937. **Career:** Freelance photographer, working for

Eiffel Tower with Thermometer, **1934 (solarized negative).** Photograph by Ilse Bing.

Das Illustrierte Blatt, Bader Blatt, Frankfurter Zeitung and *Das Neue Frank-furt,* Frankfurt, 1929-30; freelance press, fashion, portrait and documentary photographer, working for *Algemeen Handelsblad, Frankfurter Illustrierte, Vogue, Le Monde Illustre, Harper's Bazaar,* etc., in Paris, 1930-39 (interned in a concentration camp, Gurs, France, 1940-41); freelance portrait, press and still-life photographer, for *Baby Talk, Two to Six, Pageant, Town and Country,* New York, 1941-59; relinquished photography to concentrate on poetry, painting and collage, New York, 1959. **Agent:** Houk Friedman, 851 Madison Avenue, New York, NY 10021, U.S.A.

Individual Exhibitions:

1932	Galerie Trittler, Frankfurt am Main
1933	American Library, Paris
	Maison Tiranty, Paris (with Studio Shall and Jacques Azema)
1936	June Rhodes Gallery, New York
1939	Galerie Chasseurs d'Images, Paris
1947	*Visages et enfants des Etats-Unis,* Galerie de l'Arc-en-Ciel, Paris
1948	Brooklyn Museum, New York
1949	Carroll-Knight Gallery, St. Louis, Missouri
1950	*New York 1947-50,* Galerie-Librairie Palmes, Paris

	Galerie Pares, Paris
1951	*Photographs 1931-51,* New York Public Library
1953	American Institute of Architects, Washington, D.C.
1954	Junior League Gallery, St. Louis, Missouri
1955	New York Public Library
1958	Bennett College, Millbrook, New York
1959	*Color Photographs,* Designer's Gallery, San Francisco
1976	Witkin Gallery, New York (retrospective)
1978	Council of the Arts, Las Vegas, Nevada
1979	*Vintage Photographs of the 1930s,* Allan Frumkin Gallery, Chicago
	Vintage Photos from the 1920s and 1930s, Simon Lowinsky Gallery, San Francisco
	Heusenstamm Stiftung, Frankfurt am Main
1981	Galerie Zabriskie, Paris (with Ella Bergmann-Michel)
1982	*Fashion Photographs from the 1930s,* Simon Lowinsky Gallery, San Francisco
	Femmes de l'enfance a la vieillese 1929-55, Galerie des Femmes, Paris
1983	Columbia Museum of Art, South Carolina
1984	*Work from Three Decades,* Light Factory, Charlotte, North Carolina
	Mains, Galerie des Femmes, Paris

1985	*Three Decades of Photography,* New Orleans Museum of Art, Louisiana (retrospective; travelled to the International Center of Photography, New York; Frankfurter Kunstverein; Baltimore Museum of Art, Maryland)
1986	*Photos of the '50s,* Branstein Gallery, San Francisco
1990	*Ilse Bing Collages, 1979-1990,* Lowinsky Gallery, New York
1992	*Ilse Bing: Frankfurt, Paris, New York,* Houk Friedman, New York
1994	*Ilse Bing,* Goethe House, New York
1995	*Ilse Bing—Vintage Photographs,* Galerie für Kunstphotographie zur Stockeregg, Zürich

Selected Group Exhibitions:

1930	*Groupe Annuel des Photographes,* Galerie de la Pleiade, Paris (and 1931-33, 1938)
1931	*Das Lichtbild,* Museum Folkwang, Essen, Germany
1932	*Modern European Photography,* Julien Levy Gallery, New York
1937	*Photography 1839-1937,* Museum of Modern Art, New York
1943	*Art in Exile,* New York Public Library
1976	*Photographs from the Julien Levy Collection,* Art Institute of Chicago (toured the United States)
1978	*French Photography: the new spirit 1925-40,* Galerie Zabriskie, Paris
1981	*Autoportraits photographiques 1898-1981,* Centre Georges Pompidou, Paris
1985	*Das Aktfoto,* Fotomuseum im Stadtmuseum, Munich
1986	*La nouvelle photographie en France 1919-39,* Museum of Poitiers, France
1988	*Vintage Photographs by Women of the 20's and 30's,* Houk Gallery, Chicago
1991	*Summer Exhibition,* Houk Friedman, New York
1992	*de l'Ancien Regime aux Temps Modernes: Paris et ses Environs,* Houk Friedman, New York
	Flora Photographica: La Fleur dans la Photographie, de 1835 à nos jours, Vancouver Art Gallery, Vancouver
1993	*Urban Visions,* Houk Friedman, New York
	Flora Photographica: La Fleur dans la Photographie, de 1835 à nos jours, The New York Public Library, New York; The Royal Ontario Museum, Toronto
1994	*Flora Photographica: La Fleur dans la Photographie, de 1835 à nos jours,* Musée des beaux-arts de Montréal, Montréal, Quebec
	Non-Objective Photography between the Wars, Houk Friedman, New York
	Vintage Photographs by Women of the 20's and 30's, Houk Friedman, New York
	Women Photographers of the Weimar Republic, Museum Folkwang, Essen; Fundacio 'la caixa', Centre Cultural, Barcelona
1995	*Women Photographers of the Weimar Republic,* The Jewish Museum, New York

Collections:

Art Institute of Chicago; Brooklyn Museum, New York; Center for Creative Photography, University of Arizona, Tucson; Museum of Modern Art, New York; International Center of Photography, New York; New Orleans Museum of Art, Louisiana; San Francisco Museum of Modern Art; National Gallery of Canada, Ottawa; Bibliotheque Nationale, Paris; Museum Folkwang, Essen, Germany.

Publications:

By BING: Books—*Words as Visions,* poems, drawings and collages, New York 1974; *Numbers in Images,* poems, drawings and collages, New York 1976; *Women from the Cradle to Old Age,* Paris 1982.

On BING: Books—*Photography 1839-1937* by Beaumont Newhall, New York 1937; *L'Art de photographier* by Robert Andreani, Paris 1952; *Photographs from the Julien Levy Collection, starting with Atget,* exhibition catalogue, by David Travis, Chicago 1976; *The Julien Levy Collection* by Lee D. Witkin, New York 1977; *The Photograph Collector's Guide* by Lee D. Witkin and Barbara London, Boston and London 1979; *Zur Geschichte der Pressefotografie 1930-1936* by Annemarie Troger, West Berlin 1938; *The Dog Observed: Photographs 1844-1983,* edited by Ruth Silverman, New York 1984; *Ilse Bing: Three Decades of Photography,* exhibition catalogue, by Nancy Barrett, New Orleans, Louisiana 1985; *Vintage Photographs by Women of the 20's and 30's,* exhibition catalogue by Edwyn Houk Gallery, Chicago 1988. **Articles**—"Photo-Ausstellung Ilse Bing" in *Frankfurter Zeitung,* 18 September 1932; "Les photographies de Mlle. Ilse Bing" by H.F. Pottechel in *Comedia* (Paris), 22 August 1934; "Ilse Bing" by Emmanuel Sougez in *L'Art Vivant* (Paris), December 1934/January 1935; "Ilse Bing, Photographer, To Display Her Works" in *New York Herald Tribune* (Paris), 21 March 1939; "Freed from French Camp, Ilse Bing Carries on Here" by Helen Stephenson in *New York World-Telegram,* 13 August 1941; "Ilse Bing, 35mm Specialist" by Mildred Stagg in *U.S. Camera* (New York), August 1949; "Ilse Bing" by Robert Andreani in *Photo-revue* (Paris), February 1953; "Ilse Bing" by Hilton Kramer in the *New York Times,* 7 January 1977; "Ilse Bing" in *Creative Camera* (London), November 1978; "At 80, still in focus: A long reign for the 'Queen of the Leica'" by Alan G. Artner in *Chicago Tribune,* 1 April 1979; "Ilse Bing, une vie" by Herve Guibert in *Le Monde* (Paris), 4 June 1981; "Ilse Bing, une pionniere de la photographie des annees 30" by Alain Beaufils and Dominique Gaessler in *Photographiques* (Paris), April 1983; "Camera Pioneer Saluted at ICP" by Roberta Hershenson in the *New York Times,* 23 February 1986; "Two Pioneers Rediscovered" by Douglas Davis in *Newsweek* (New York), 31 March 1986. **Film**—*Frankfurt, Paris, New York: Die 3 Leben der Ilse Bing,* Z.D.F. German television film, Wiesbaden 1986.

*

(1) A good photographer is the one who knows when NOT to take a picture.

(2) It may be difficult for a photographer with high skills and high reputation to give up as soon as new works do not represent new ideas. But the task of any artist may be defined as the revelation of something new or as the showing of something old under a new light. Repetition, even at the highest level of craftsmanship, is empty. Therefore: SAY IT ONCE!

(3) Photography is a means of expression like language. Language can be used for trivial sayings, for scientific work, in literature; etc. Photography, too, covers vastly different fields. In all of these—document, journalism, portrait, pictorial, etc.—, if the photographer is an artist, his work will automatically be a work of art. One cannot *become* an artist. As artist you have a gift and you have a responsibility; and if you are honest, this is often painful.

(4) The abstract in life has always fascinated me. The abstract painting or drawing does not come to grips with this phenomenon, for here it is the painter himself who decides on each line and on each dot. But in a photograph, if I show something abstract, I must make it clear in which way real-life incidents have created this particular abstract shape.

—Ilse Bing

*   *   *

Ilse Bing was born in Frankfurt in 1899, in her youth studying mathematics and art, and eventually pursuing a doctoral degree in art history at the University of Frankfurt. In 1928, she began using a camera to make illustrations for her dissertation; shortly, however, she was given commissions for photostories by the Frankfurt newspaper. The following year, in a flash of self-knowledge, Bing gave up art history to pursue a career as an artist, an artist using photography as her creative medium, with the newly-marketed Leica camera as her artistic tool. Through the Constructivist architect Mart Stam for whom she photographed architectural projects in Frankfurt, she began associating with Ella Bergmann-Michel, developing close personal and artistic ties. In 1930, Bing moved to Paris, and soon built a successful and varied career which included photojournalism, magazine illustration, and fashion, portrait, and architectural photography. Her photographs were seen in the most important Parisian publications of the period, such as *Vu, Arts et Métiers graphiques,* and *Photographie*; she was commissioned with all fashion accessory work for *Harper's Bazaar,* and she was included in all major Parisian exhibitions of photography, as well as the landmark Museum of Modern Art "Photography 1839-1937" organized by Beaumont Newhall.

In the 1920s and 1930s, photography, particularly in Europe, underwent a sudden burst of creativity which expanded its frontiers and largely determined its development over the next half century. Modern photojournalism, and photography's use in advertising and illustration, science and industry evolved, and photography matured as a creative medium. Bing was among the vanguard contributing to this florescence. She was a pioneer of the new technology, cropping minute fragments from 35-mm negatives and enlarging them many times their original size, improvising lenses, experimenting with highly sensitive night film, and gleaning such darkroom secrets as solarization. She was the only professional photographer in Paris to use the 35-mm camera exclusively, mastering it with such authority that the respected French photographer and critic Emmanuel Sougez was moved to call her the "Queen of the Leica."

However, we are drawn to Bing's photographs less from the inquisitiveness of the historian, than from the beauty of their craftsmanship and artistic vision. Hers was a very personal style combining unposed Leica imagery with a rigorous pictorial organization and strongly felt emotion. Bing used the techniques of photojournalism, not to produce objective documents of reality, but to transform reality through artistic emotion, capturing what Sougez described in them as the "enchantment surrounding reality." While they verge on abstraction, the reality before the camera lens is not stilled; the life and movement of the subject is never stilled. Rather, the strong composition imposed upon it intensifies its life and hints at the universal laws giving shape to nature. Her photographs are spontaneous and intuitive, yet equally measured and controlled fusing the precision of science with the poetry of art.

In 1940, Bing and her husband, the pianist and musicologist Konrad Wolff, were interned by the Vichy government as enemy aliens, and immigrated to the United States in 1941. She continued her work, but in a style radically different from that of the 1930s. She began using electronic flash and the larger format Rolleiflex camera; her printing became harsher and cooler, and she began working on a larger scale, dry-mounting photographs to thick boards and trimming to their edges. "As I got older," she explains, "I was at a greater remove which manifested itself at a greater optical remove."

By 1957, Bing was working exclusively in color, doing all lab work herself with masterful results. Two years later, she gave up photography altogether. "Photographic work is possessive," she says, "I didn't want to hold the moment anymore. A hand holds water. The moment flows through and you are part of it. I needed another medium." Instead, she writes poetry in three languages and makes drawings and collages, newer pieces incorporating fragments of photographs. Life is a continuing stream from which she continues to drink deep. Of her life today, she says, "I had the luck to have found out that when one gets old, one may let essential matters join up; the parallels meet."

—Nancy Barrett

BIRGUS, Vladimír.

Nationality: Czechoslovakian. **Born:** Frýdek-Místek, Czechoslovakia, 5 May 1954. **Education:** Attended Gymnasium in Olomouc, Czechoslavakia, 1969-73. Studied literature, theatre and cinema in the Faculty of Philosophy, Palacký University, Olomouc, 1973-78 and photography as an external student in the Faculty of Film and Television, Academy of the Performing Arts (FAMU), Prague, 1974-78. **Family:** Married Darina Tauskova; children Daniel and Helena. **Career:** Assistant Lecturer, Department of Photography, Faculty of Film and Television, Academy of the Performing Arts (FAMU), Prague, 1978-94; Associate Professor since 1994. Director of the Institute of Creative Photography, Silesian University, Opava, since 1990. Member of the Board of the Prague House of Photography since 1990. **Agent:** Prague House of Photography, Husova 23, 110 00 Prague 1, Czech Republic. **Address:** Na poříčním prá-128 00 Prague 2, Czech Republic.

Individual Exhibitions:

1971	Galerie pod podloubím, Olomouc, Czechoslovakia
1972	Theatre Rokoko, Prague
	Gallery Fotochema, Ostrava, Czechoslovakia
1976	Galerie mladých, Brno, Czechoslavakia
1978	Kormoná galéria fotographie, Žilina, Czechoslovakia
	Národní dům, Prostějov, Czechoslovakia
1979	Gallery BWA, 9th Photographic Confrontation, Gorzów, Poland
1980	Malá galerie Československého spisovatele, Prague
1981	Fotografijos galeria, Kaunas, Lithuania
	Fotografijos salon, Vilnius, Lithuania
	Fotografijos museos, Šjauljaj, Lithuania
1983	Galerie F, Banská Bystrica, Czechoslovakia
1984	Galeria ZPAF, Gorzów, Poland
1985	Canon Photo Gallery, Amsterdam
	Galeria SČF, Česká Lípa, Czechoslovakia
1986	Kellergalerie, Munich, Germany
1988	Stara galeria ZPAF, Warsaw
	Museum für Photographie, Braunschweig, Germany
1989	Funkův kabinet, House of Lords of Kunštát, Brno
	Galerie 4, Cheb, Czechoslovakia
1990	Salzburg College, Salzburg, Austria
	Galerie Mathurin, Tours, France
	Galerie Foma, Prague
1991	Fotogalerie im Haus Bohl, Eisenbach, Germany
	Gallery FM, Siegen, Germany

Selected Group Exhibitions:

1970	*Young Photographers Show Europe,* Munich, Germany; and from 1971 to 1976.
1974	*Fotographia academica,* Pardubice, Czechoslovakia; and from 1975 to 1978.
1976	*Portrait in Contemporary Moravian Photography,* Regional Gallery of Fine Art, Hodonín, Czechoslovakia
1979	*Young Photographers,* Galerie Aréne, Recentres International de la Photographie, Arles, France
1982	*Actual Photography,* Moravian Gallery, Brno
1984	*Czech Creative Photography,* Gallery D, Prague
	Aspects of Czechoslovakian Photography, Gallery Thackeray and Robertson, San Francisco, CA
	Salon of the Invited, Gallery BWA, Lódź, Poland
1985	*27 Czechoslovakian Photographers,* The Photographers Gallery, London
	Nude Photography in Eastern Europe, Torino Fotographia 85, Turin, Italy (travelled to Amsterdam)
1986	*Young Czechoslovakian Photographers,* Galerie Aréne, Arles, France
1988	*Photographs of Teachers and Students of FAMU Prague,* Helsinki
1989	*Contemporary Czechoslovakian Photography,* Foto 89, Nieuwe Kerk, Amsterdam
1992	*What's New: Prague,* Art Institute of Chicago, Chicago, IL
1993	*Czech and Slovak Photography from between the Wars to the Present,* Fitchburg Art Museum, Fitchburg, MA

Collections:

Moravian Gallery, Brno, Czech Republic; Collection of the Union of Czech Photographers, Prague; Silesian Museum, Opava, Czech Republic; Regional Gallery of Fine Art, Hodonín, Czech Republic; Museum Ludwig, Cologne, Germany; Museet for Fotokunst, Odense, Denmark; The Photographers' Gallery, London; Maison Européenne de la Photographie—Paris Audiovisuel, Paris; Bibliothéque National, Paris; Lithuanian Museum of Photography, Šjuljai, Lithuania; Lituanian Union of Photographers, Vilnius, Lithuania; Internation Center of Photography, New York.

From the cycle *Something Unspoken*, Scheveningen, 1984. Photograph by Vladimír Birgus.

Publications:

By BIRGUS: Books—*Miroslav Bílek,* Ostrava, 1982; *Město (Town),* (with Miroslav Hucek and Pavel Jasanský) Prague, 1984; *Milan Borovička,* Ostrava, 1984; *Informatorium 2—Photography,* Prague, 1984; *František Drtikol,* (with Antonín Braný) Prague 1988; *Československo 1989,* Prague, 1990; *Tschechoslowakische Fotografie der Gegenwart,* Heidelberg, 1990; *Vývoj československé fotografie v datech 1945-1989 (History of Czechoslovakian Photography 1945-1989),* Prague, 1990; *Fotograf František Drtikol,* Prague, 1994. **Articles:**—more than 300 articles in *Československ fotografie* (Prague), *Revue Fotographie* (Prague), *Fotographie Magazín* (Prague), *Ateliér* (Prague), *Výtvarníctvo-fotografia-film* (Bratislava), *Reflex* (Prague), *Mladý svět* (Prague), *European Photography* (Göttingen), *Focus* (Amsterdam), *PF* (Amsterdam), *Fotografia* (Moscow), *Fotografi* (Helsingborg).

On BIRGUS: Books—*Encyclopédie internationale des photographes* by Michéle & Michel Auer, Hermance/Geneva, 1985; *27 Contemporary Czechoslovak Photographers,* exhibition catalogue, by Antonín Dufek and Sue Davies, London, 1985; *Černobílá fotografie (Black and White Photography)* by Antonín Dufek, Prague, 1987; *What is Photography?—150 Years of Photography,* Prague, 1989; *Who's Who in the Czech Republic,* Prague, 1994. **Articles**—"Vladimir Birgus" by Petr Klimpl in *Československá fotografie* (Prague), no.4, 1977; "Vladimir Birgus" by Gerhard Ihrke in *Fotografie* (Leipzig), no.4, 1978; "Cosi nevysloveného na fotografiích Vladimíra Birguse" by Alena Nádvorníková in *Revue Fotografie* (Prague), no.2, 1980; "Vladimir Birgus" by Václav Zykmund in *Fotoforum* (Oslo), no.3, 1982; "Im Bild: lauter Gerechte" by Georg Soller in *Fotomagazin* (Munich), no.7, 1983; "Člověk na fotografiích Vladimíra Birguse" by Martin Hruška in *Československá fotografie* (Prague), no.2, 1985; "Birgus, Maršálrek, Friedlander" by Barbara Kosińska in *Fotografia* (Warsaw), no.1, 1985; "Vladimir Birgus" by Dirk van der Spek in *Focus* (Amsterdam), no.9, 1985; "Irgend etwas Unausgesprochenes—Fotografien van Vladimír Birgus" in *Fotografie* (Leipzig), no.12, 1988; "Rozmowa z Vladimirem Birgusem" by Barbara Kosińska in *Foto* (Warsaw), no.1, 1989; "Fotografie Vladimíra Birguse" by Ladislav Šolc in *Revue Fotografie* (Prague), no.1, 1989; "Subjektivnyj fotodokument" by Valery Stigneev in *Sovetskoe foto* (Moscow), no.11, 1989; "Vladimir Birgus" by Petr Balajka in *Professional News* (Chemnitz), no.1, 1991; "Vladimir Birgus" by Manfred Zollner in *Fotomagazin* (Munich), no.4, 1992.

*

In my photographs I try above all to express some aspects of present-day life and its effect on human relations and psychic conditions. I am particularly attracted by the unusual and often absurd confrontations of people and environment, or by a number of parallel actions whose emotive photographic depiction can help the viewer to reassess the conventional significance of the external and internal world and see it anew and in greater depth. I am interested in a subjective document; I do not try to put forward my own view as being the only correct one but rather to stimulate viewers with my photographs to make their own interpretations of the problems I outline. I realize that this is a very ambitious aim in which success is the exception.

—Vladimír Birgus

*   *   *

The early days of Vladimír Birgus's photographic career were marked by a measure of hesitation or even vacillation between art and documentary photography. Recollecting that period, his configurations of black and white human bodies are what most spring to mind. Constrained by the confines of the decisive and non-decisive moment, Birgus succeeded in treading his own path, pregnant with thought and profoundly rich in human qualities. The name "Something Unspoken" has been rightly associated with his most extensive cycle of photographs, pointing out just how difficult it is to define the core of the photographer's work.

In his photographs Vladimír Birgus himself presents man as just having detached himself from the context of the surrounding universe and turned into himself, into his innermost world. Whether walking or moving in any other way, man seems to be just about the same as if standing, sitting or sun-bathing. The actual outward appearance of his existence is irrelevant at such moments, since during those split seconds man is deaf to the outside world, oblivious to it. The world's physical environment has been exchanged for an inner world of his own, whether he is awake or dreaming. This constitutes a specific form of contemplation, through which Western man escapes to the realm of Eastern mental techniques out of a desire to be on his own with his fate for a time, rather than outside any chosen programme.

This could easily give the impression that Vladimír Birgus is actually bent on glorifying a passive kind of man. But that would be a dangerous over-simplification. It is necessary to come back to firm ground every now and then for man to be able to rebel against heaven; it is vital to return to the sources of rivers in order to appreciate the vastness of the ocean.

On several occasions Birgus's photographs have given rise to the criticism that he has been guilty of violating or, indeed, negating valid laws of art. But the truth lies elsewhere: he has applied these laws very consistently, but to creative materials where we are simply unaccustomed to encounter them. All the signs are that these artistic tendencies of his early years have found their expression there. The outcome is a rare symbiosis of life photography with the sophistication and refinement of an artist. Just observe how Birgus restricts the number of pictorial elements applied; how he handles tonality; how ingeniously he often uses colours; how he avoids emotional and optical perfection of any kind and how carefully he distributes his elements in order to focus attention on the main figure, to highlight to the viewer the pausing of man in time, his immersion in his own inward world.

True, there is "Something Unspoken" involved, but still it is expressed sufficiently clearly for us to understand the imagery, however hard it is to spell it out in words.

—Ján Šmok

BISHOP, Michael.

Nationality: American. **Born:** Palo Alto, California in 1946. **Education:** Studied at Foothill College, Los Altos Hills, California, and at the San Francisco Art Institute; studied photography, under Henry Holmes Smith, San Francisco State College, B.A. 1970, M.A. 1971. **Career:** Independent photographer. Instructor, San Francisco Art Institute, 1971-74; University of California at Los Angeles, 1974-75; Visual Studies Workshop, Rochester, New York, and State University of New York, Buffalo, 1975. Founder-Member, Visual Dialogue Foundation, San Francisco. **Recipient:** National Endowment for the Arts Grant, 1975. **Agent:** Light Gallery, 724 Fifth Avenue, New York, New York 10019. **Address:** 43 Surrey Street, San Francisco, California 94103, U.S.A.

Individual Exhibitions:

1970	Loomis Institute, Windsor, Connecticut
	Silver Image Gallery, Ohio State University, Columbus
1971	School of the Art Institute of Chicago
	Light Gallery, New York
1973	University of Rhode Island, Kingston (with Linda Connor)
1974	Imageworks, Boston
1975	Light Gallery, New York
1976	Light Gallery, New York
1979	Center for Contemporary Photography, Chicago
	Center for Creative Photography, University of Arizona, Tucson
1981	*Michael Bishop/Mark McFadden: Sleight of Eye,* Creative Photography Gallery, Cambridge, Massachusetts

Selected Group Exhibitions:

1967	*Photography for the Arts in Embassies,* Focus Gallery, San Francisco (and Oakland Museum, California)
1969	*Vision and Expression,* International Museum of Photography, George Eastman House, Rochester, New York (toured the United States, 1969-71)
1972	*60's Continuum,* International Museum of Photography, George Eastman House, Rochester, New York
1973	*Light and Lens: Methods of Photography,* Hudson River Museum, Yonkers, New York
1975	*The Extended Document: An Investigation of Information and Evidence in Photographs,* International Museum of Photography, George Eastman House, Rochester, New York
1978	*One of a Kind: Polaroid Color,* Corcoran Gallery, Washington, D.C. (toured the United States)
1979	*Photographic Surrealism,* New Gallery of Contemporary Art, Cleveland (travelled to Dayton Art Institute, Ohio; and the Brooklyn Museum, New York, 1980)
1984	*Photography in California 1945-80,* San Francisco Museum of Modern Art (travelled to the Akron Art Museum, Ohio; Corcoran Gallery, Washington, D.C.; Los Angeles Municipal Art Gallery; Cornell University, Ithaca, New York; High Museum of Art, Atlanta, Georgia; Museum Folkwang, Essen; Centre Georges Pompidou, Paris; Museum of Photographic Arts, San Diego, California)
1985	*American Images 1945-80,* Barbican Art Gallery, London (toured Britain)
1987	*Photography and Art 1946-86,* Los Angeles County Museum of Art

Collections:

Museum of Modern Art, New York; International Museum of Photography, George Eastman House, Rochester, New York; Fogg Art Museum, Harvard University, Cambridge, Massachusetts; Museum of Fine Arts, St. Petersburg, Florida; University of Tennessee, Knoxville; University of New Mexico, Albuquerque; San Francisco State University; National Gallery of Canada, Ottawa; Ryerson Polytechnical Institute, Toronto; Musée Réattu, Arles, France.

Publications:

On BISHOP: Books—*Vision and Expression* by Nathan Lyons, New York 1969; *California Photographers 1970,* exhibition catalogue, by Fred R. Parker, Davis, California 1970; *Photo Media: Elements and Technics of Photography Experienced as an Artistic Medium,* exhibition catalogue, New York 1971; *60's Continuum,* exhibition catalogue, with text by Van Deren Coke, Rochester, New York 1972; *Light and Lens: Methods of Photography* by Donald L. Werner and Dennis Longwell, Dobbs Ferry, New York 1973; *The Extended Document: An Investigation of Information and Evidence in Photographs,* with text by William Jenkins, Rochester, New York 1975; *Peculiar to Photography,* exhibition catalogue, by Van Deren Coke, Thomas

F. Barrow and others, Albuquerque, New Mexico 1976; *One of a Kind: Recent Polaroid Color Photography,* with a preface by Belinda Rathbone, and an introduction by Eugenia Parry Janis, Boston 1979; *Michael Bishop,* exhibition catalogue, with text by Charles Desmarais and Charles Hagen, Chicago 1979; *Color as Form: A History of Color Photography,* exhibition catalogue, with introduction by Robert A. Sobieszek, Rochester, New York 1982; *Photography in California 1945-1980* by Louise Katzman, San Francisco 1984; *American Images: Photography 1945-1980,* edited by Peter Turner, London 1985; *Photography and Art 1946-1986,* exhibition catalogue, by Andy Grundberg and Kathleen M. Gauss, Los Angeles 1987. **Articles**—in *Esquire* (New York), February 1976; in *Modern Photography* (New York), July 1976.

* * *

Since Michael Bishop's banal photographic subjects present no immediately evident esthetic or other kind of value, they require special resources on the viewer's part. "Familiar, non-obtrusive objects and forms," Bishop calls his sepia-toned, overturned lawnchair in a deserted late-winter yard, his metal stepladder flashlighted in front of an open closet, his isolated traffic signs. Yet, having once agreed to yield to the photographer the extra effort that his subject matter insists upon, we become free to savor his peculiar formalism.

Bishop's universe is boxed and hedged by the junctures of such hard, nonporous, man-made surfaces as concrete, steel, and other more mysterious materials. Rarely does a fleshly being intrude, and it is these dreary intersections that seem to define and limit the world. Confining himself to the apparently trivial and mundane, eschewing, if not truth, at least beauty, the artist presents an idea of photography that has little to do with the our usual thoughts about the medium.

Bishop does not pursue the illusionistic, nor engage the topical, social or narrative concerns that preoccupy many photographers. Rather, the ever more spare and elemental subject matter that he has developed over the years actively prevents any appreciation of his work on such levels. Bishop's interest is in photographic composition—that is, in the stripped down elements of the artistic vision—and in the tonal possibilities of photography. Having found the black-and-white tonal range "visually unrewarding," he has experimented with tints and now works in color. If we are to be interested by Bishop's work, it is his ideas about, and mastery of, the formal elements of his medium that will provoke us.

Bishop's vision is, of course, surreal, trading on the unexpected, momentary juxtapositions that it is photography's special power and irony to make permanent. What gives humanity to his apparently inhuman images is his invocation of a fundamental surrealist notion. The photographs need no human subjects because, he implies, their subjects are all of us, as we endure each day of forced yet haphazard encounters with the familiar, inhuman surfaces of our own making that have increasingly become our world.

—Maren Stange

BLAKEMORE, John.

Nationality: British. **Born:** Coventry, 15 July 1936. **Education:** John Gulson School, Coventry, 1947-52; self-taught in photography. **Career:** Worked as a farmhand in Warwickshire and Shropshire, 1952-54. Served as a nurse in the Royal Air Force in England and Libya, 1954-56. Freelance photographer with the Black Star agency, London and the Midlands, 1956-58; Photographic Studio Manager, Taylor Brothers Studio, Coventry, 1958-61; Photographer, Beryl Houghton Studio, Coventry, 1961-62, Richard Sadler Studio, Coventry, 1962-63, Courtaulds Company, Coventry, 1963-68, and Hilton Studios, London, 1968-69. Freelance photographer, in Derby, since 1970. Lecturer in Photography, Derby Lonsdale College, 1970-91. **Recipient:** Arts Council of Great Britain bursary, 1974, 1976, 1979. Appointed Reader in Photography, University of Derby, 1991. Awarded Fellowship of Royal Photographic Society; **Agent:** Zelda Cheatle, Zelda Cheatle Gallery, 8 Cecil Court, London WC2N 4HE. **Address:** 39 Gerard Street, Derby DE1 1PA, England.

Individual Exhibitions:

1964	*Area in Transition,* Coventry College of Art
1965	*Girls School,* City Architects Gallery, Coventry
1966	*West Side Story,* City Architects Gallery, Coventry
1967	*Two Photographers,* Belgrade Theatre, Coventry (with Richard Sadler)
1972	Midland Group Gallery, Nottingham
	Photographs and Paintings, Morgan Gallery, Coventry (with David Eddington)
1975	*A Vision of Landscape,* Impressions Gallery, York
	3 Photographers, Galleria Il Diaframma, Milan (with Paul Hill and Thomas Cooper)
1976	*Stand Before the World,* Arnolfini Gallery, Bristol (travelled to The Photographers' Gallery, London, then toured the U.K.)
1978	*Michael House, A Rudolph Steiner School,* Michael House School, Ilkeston, Derbyshire
1979	*Spirit of Place: Photographs in Wales 1971-78,* Photographic Gallery, Cardiff (toured the U.K.)
1980	*Lila,* The Photographers' Gallery, London (toured the U.K.)
1981	Contrasts Gallery, London
	Camera Obscura Gallery, Stockholm
	Impressions Gallery, York
1985	*Still Life: 1981-1984,* Untitled Gallery, Sheffield
	Axiom Arts Centre, Cheltenham
1987	*The Killing Fields,* Metro Gallery, Derby (East Midlands touring exhibition)
1989	*Year of the Tree,* Crompton Gallery, Derby
1990	*Still Life,* Photographers' Gallery, London
1991	*Inscape,* Zelda Cheatle Gallery, London
	Beyond Landscape, Retrospective 1971-1991, Derby Photography Festival, Derby City Museum and Art Gallery
1992	*Inscape,* Portfolio Gallery, Edinburgh, Scotland
	Poseurs Gallery, Birmingham
	Intimate Rituals, Mai de la Photo, Reims, France
	Beyond Landscape, Oldham Museum and Art Gallery, Oldham
	Cambridge Darkroom, Cambridge
	Recent Photographs, Laurence Miller Gallery, New York
	Still Life, Contratype Gallery, Brussels, Belgium
1993	*Tulipa,* Pendle Art Gallery, Nelson, Lancashire
	Los Angeles International Invitational, Paul Kopeikin Gallery, Los Angeles, USA
	Beyond Landscape, Royal Photographic Society, Bath; Focal Point Gallery, Southend on Sea; Photography Gallery, Dublin; City Gallery, Limerick; Brewery Arts Centre, Kendal
	Recent Works, Bergen Museum of Art and Science, Paramus, New Jersey, USA
	Inscape, Gronigen Festival of Photography, Netherlands
	The Photographs of John Blakemore (British Council Touring Exhibition) Fotogaleria del Tertro General San Maretin, Buenos Aires, Centro Cultural Victoria Ocampo Mardel Plata, Argentina, Centro Cultural Bernardino Rivadaria, Rosario, Salón Cultural Calle, Mendoza
1994	*Beyond Landscape,* Howarth Gallery, Accrington

Selected Group Exhibitions:

1968	*International Photography,* Midland Arts Centre, Cannon Hill, Birmingham
1971	*Those Who Can Do,* Derby College of Art and Technology
1973	*Serpentine Photography 73,* Serpentine Gallery, London
1974	*New Photography,* Midland Group Gallery, Nottingham
1975	*The Romantic Landscape,* Kodak House, London
1977	*Singular Realities,* Side Gallery, Newcastle upon Tyne
1978	*Tusen och en bild/1001 Pictures,* Fotografiska Museet, Moderna Museet, Stockholm
1979	*The Native Land,* Mostyn Gallery, Llandudno, Wales
1980	*British Art 1940-1980,* Hayward Gallery, London

Tulipa—Mutations No. 6, **1992.** Photograph by John Blakemore.

1981   *Photographer as Printmaker,* Ferens Art Gallery, Hull,
        Yorkshire (travelled to the Museum and Art Gallery,
        Leicester; Cooper Gallery, Barnsley; Castle Museum,
        Nottingham; Photographers' Gallery, London)
        Contemporary British Photography, Massachusetts Institute of
        Technology, Boston, USA
1984   *Second Nature,* London
1986   *Tomorrow,* Council for the Protection of Rural England, Royal
        Festival Hall, London Royal Photographic Society, (commission) Bath
1987   *Realities Revisited,* Saidye Bronfwyan Centre, Montreal,
        Canada
1988   *Images of British Landscape,* Meyerhof Gallery, Baltimore, USA
1989   *Through the Looking Glass,* British Photography 1948-89, The
        Barbican, London
1990   *The Garden,* Newcastle Arts Centre (and touring)
        Landscape, The Zelda Cheatle Gallery, London
1991   *Road and Sky,* Japan (touring)
1992   *Fox Talbot Photographic Awards Exhibition,* National Portrait
        Gallery, London; National Museum of Photography, Film &
        Television, Bradford, England
        Flora Photographica, Serpentine Gallery, London, Royal
        Botanical Gardens, Edinburgh, Scotland, City Museum and
        Art Gallery, Manchester (and touring)
        Shared Light, Oriel Mostyn Gallery, Llandudno, Wales
        British Photography, Rencontres Internationale de la
        Photographie, Arles, France
        Works on Paper, The Armoury, New York, USA, Chicago Arts
        Fair, Chicago, USA
1993   *Aspects of Land,* Zelda Cheatle Gallery, London
        Flora Photographica, Vancouver Art Gallery, Canada; The
        New York Public Library, New York, USA; The Royal
        Ontario Museum, Toronto, Canada; The Meade Gallery,
        University of Warwick, Coventry

Collections:

Arts Council of Great Britain, London; Department of the Environment,
London; Victoria and Albert Museum, London; Royal Photographic Society,
Bath, England; West Midlands Arts Association, Birmingham; National
Library of Wales, Cardiff; Derby Lonsdale College, Derby; Fotografiska
Museet, Moderna Museet, Stockholm; Los Angeles County Museum of Art;
National Museum of Photography, Film & TV, Bradford; The British Council:
Los Angeles County Museum, Los Angeles, USA; Bibliotheque Nationale,
Paris; The Vernon Collection, Los Angeles, USA; University of Parma, Italy.

Publications:

By BLAKEMORE: Books—*British Image 3: John Blakemore,* with an
introduction by Gerry Badger, London 1977; *Thistles,* portfolio, London 1981;
Inscape, Zelda Cheatle Press, London 1991, *Tulipomania,* Zelda Cheatle Press
1994. **Article**—"John Blakemore: Interview," with Helen Shield and Jan
Segieda, in *Ten 8* (Birmingham), August 1979.

On BLAKEMORE: Books—*British Journal of Photography Annual,*
London 1976; *Creative Camera International Yearbook,* edited by Colin
Osman and Peter Turner, London 1976; *Geschichte der Fotografie im 20.
Jahrhundert/Photography in the 20th Century* by Petr Tausk, Cologne 1977,
London 1980; *Exploring Photography* by Bryn Campbell, London 1978;
Tusen och en Bild, exhibition catalogue, by Ake Sidwall, Sune Jonsson and Ulf
Hard af Segerstad, Stockholm 1978; *British Image 5: Perspective on Landscape,* edited by Bill Gaskins, London 1978; *John Blakemore: Spirit of Place:
Photographs in Wales 1971-78,* exhibition catalogue, Cardiff 1979; *World
Photography,* edited by Bryn Campbell, London 1981; *Photographer as
Printmaker,* exhibition catalogue, with texts by Gerry Badger, Peter C.
Bunnell and Ansel Adams, London 1981; *England's Glory,* Council for the
Protection of Rural England, London 1987; *Mai de la Photo,* exhibition
catalogue, Reims 1992; *The Photographs of John Blakemore,* exhibition
catalogue, The British Council, London 1993. **Articles**—"Reflections on

John Blakemore" by Edward Martin in the *British Journal of Photography*
(London), January 1976; "John Blakemore" in *Camera* (Lucerne), August
1976; "John Blakemore" in *Nye Foto* (Oslo), December 1976; "Blakemore's
Moving Spirit" in *Amateur Photographer* (London), February 1980; "John
Blakemore" in *Print Letter* (Zurich), January 1981; "John Blakemore: Path to
Perfection" in *Amateur Photographer* (London), February 1981; *British
Journal of Photography* (London), issues 6840 and 6851, 1991; *Creative
Camera,* issue 311, 1991; *Vis à Vie* (Paris), 1992; *Portfolio Magazine,*
(Edinburgh), issue 14, 1992; *Zoom* (Italy), issue 122, 1993.

*

For me, photography revolves around the relationship of the photographer
to his subject, upon an acceptance of the descriptive base of the medium. The
photographer must express himself, his feelings, his ideas, through a discovery
of the world external to himself. The work process is a refinement of one's
ability to see, to respond; it is a process of recognition, the recognition of the
significance of an object, an event.

Intensity of relationship, of understanding, is, to me, the core of photography. Formal and craft decisions are the means of translating experience to
image, not ends in themselves.

Our civilization has lost its sense of dependence upon, connection with,
nature; our relationship has become one of reckless exploitation. In a sense, I
see my work in the landscape as an attempt to re-establish relationship; to
become aware of, to acknowledge, myself as part of nature, not merely an
observer of a process from which I am separated by consciousness.

To be alone in the landscape, to experience that aloneness with intensity, is
to feel awe. It is to be made aware of one's insignificance, one's isolation—
occasionally, to experience a sense of oneness, to be made aware of oneself as
part of a continuum. My photography is both a response to such experience
and a means of renewing it. My work is generally confined to limited areas, a
stretch of river, a wooded hillside, a length of beach: places which I visit again
and again, which become intensely familiar to me, allowing the possibility of
understanding, of communion. What I hope to suggest through my photographs is the continuity, the spiritual and physical dynamic, the essential
mystery of nature. I try to work as simply as possible—for the last five years
all my photographs have been made with a 5 x 4 camera and one lens. I want
my prints to suggest the qualities that fascinate me in the landscape. To have a
richness of texture, of tonality, a sense of light that can evoke the richness, the
fecundity of nature. I seek to make images that function both as a celebration
of the landscape and as a metaphor of my response to and my connection with
it. The camera provides a link, a means, both of communion and communication.

Since 1981 the main focus of my practice has shifted from the 'natural'
landscape to the studio, the constructed image. My underlying concerns
remain unchanged, a fascination with an activity of picture making, a
celebration of nature and an exploration of the complex relationship of nature
and culture.

—John Blakemore

*   *   *

Steichen's exhibition *The Family of Man* (1956) inspired John Blakemore
to become a photographer. When his national service finished he put together a
portfolio and spent two years doing freelance assignments. In his spare time he
photographed what concerned him, showing the pictures anywhere and
everywhere he could. His dislike of the hassle involved in the freelance world
resulted in his setting up a studio and funding his personal work through
commercial commissions. Over the next ten years his own interests changed
from people to landscape, partly because of a growing disbelief in the ability of
photography to bring about social change but also because he felt a growing
concern with self-development and with the use of photography as a medium
of artistic expression.

It is Blakemore's work in the landscape that has given him international
recognition. It is intensely personal and avoids documenting a romantic and
nostalgic evocation of the past or seeking to illustrate its degradation under the
heavy hand of man.

He has said that it was while spending the winter of 1968 in Wales that his
decision to concentrate on this work was crystalised. He walked daily in the
hills and along the shore and became increasingly aware of the minute activity

within any small piece of the land, streams or seashore without taking photographs. Returning to Derbyshire he began working with a 4 x 5 camera and tripod, going out early in the morning, spending time listening to the sounds, tuning in to a specific area where he wanted to work. He was dissatisfied with this early work, but through continual experiment and hours of undoubted physical discomfort he began to make the pictures that we know and appreciate so much. Water seems always to have fascinated him, how it can reflect light, be still, or allowed to sparkle and how it can hold rocks and stones which in turn serve as symbols and metaphors.

Blakemore has always enjoyed darkroom processes and how he prints his negatives can reflect his feelings as surely as the way in which the negatives were made.

In 1970 he became a full time teacher of photography at Derby Lonsdale College and since 1991 has been a Reader in Photography at the University of Derby. His teaching has been of enormous importance to his students as he has not forced them to follow his way, but encouraged them always to find their own, giving them the necessary skills to realise their ideas clearly.

In 1985, facing something of a crisis in his own work and beginning to work through this with a period of writing for his doctorate, John Blakemore began to photograph indoors. What began as a practical exploration of the theory he was working on has become a major body of work published in 1994 as *The Stilled Gaze* by Zelda Cheatle Press. Over the years in various series of work, Blakemore has shown us the power, strength and on occasion even the menace within nature, but also the lightness and sweetness of the air as it moves through a grove of young trees. If some of the early work owed a little to American influences it has become increasingly European and in the latest series on tulips there are certain homages to Sudek with which the old master would surely be delighted. There are many levels to this work, the use of light reflected in the water or on the surface of the tables and the walls; the almost scientific collection and arrangement of specimens; and the history from birth to death of the flower which must feed its bulb to ensure its future regeneration.

Blakemore's work grows out of a process of self exploration but it carries understandable messages for those prepared to spend time reading the images. In the process they will enjoy an uplifting of the spirit through the sheer beauty of the pictures.

—Sue Davies

BLANCO, Lázaro.

Nationality: Mexican. **Born:** Ciudad Juárez, Chihuahua, 1 April 1938. **Education:** Attended primary and secondary schools in Ciudad Juárez, and in El Paso, Texas, 1944-56; studied architecture, 1957, and experimental physics, 1958-63, Universidad Nacional Autónoma, Mexico City; science, Eastern Michigan University, Ypsilanti, and Instituto Politecnico Nacional, Mexico City, 1967; physics, New York State University at Geneseo, 1971; self-taught in photography. **Career:** Worked as an actor and technician, Teátro Universitario, Mexico City, 1961; instructor in mathematics and physics at various schools, Mexico City, 1963. Photographer since 1966. Physics Instructor and I.P.S. Instructor, American School, Mexico City, since 1964; Instructor, Photography Workshop, Casa del Lago, Universidad Nacional Autonoma, Mexico City, since 1969. Contributor, *Fotozoom* magazine, Mexico City, since 1977. Founder Member, Ciné Club Ciencias, Universidad Nacional Autónoma, 1959, 35-6 x 6 Photographers Group, Mexico City, 1968, and V.O.D. Photographers Group, Mexico City, 1973; Founder Member, Head of the Exhibition Commission, Museographer, and Vice-President, Consejo Mexicano de Fotografia, since 1976; Museographer and Photography Adviser, Museo Carrillo Gil, Mexico City, since 1979. **Recipient:** First Prize, *National Cattle and Agriculture Exposition,* Mexico City, 1973; Acquisition Prize, *Plastic Arts National Salon,* Mexico City, 1979. **Agent:** Prakapas Gallery, 19 East 71st Street, New York, New York 10021, U.S.A. **Address:** Rep. Argentina 17-402, Mexico 1, D.F., Mexico.

Individual Exhibitions:

1967   Eastern Michigan University, Ypsilanti

	Club Fotografico, Mexico City
1971	*Fiesta del Dolor,* Galería del Bosque, Casa del Lago, Mexico City
	Little Gallery, Hudson Park Branch, New York Public Library
1975	*Las Moradas del Tiempo,* Fine Arts Institute, Guadalajara
	Modernage Gallery, New York
	Galeria de Fotografia, Casa del Lago, Mexico City
1976	Instituto Nacional de Bellas Artes, Mexico City
	Modernage Gallery, New York
	Alvarez Bravo/Pedro Meyer/Lázaro Blanco, Galleria Il Diaframma, Milan
1977	Galleria Il Diaframma/Canon, Milan
	Azienda Autonoma Soggiorno e Turismo, Salerno, Italy
	Galería Pro-Arte, Mexico City
1980	Museo Carrillo Gil, Mexico City

Selected Group Exhibitions:

1968	*National Newspaper Snapshot Exhibition,* National Geographic Society, Washington, D.C.
1969	*Grupo 35-6 x 6: Fotografías,* Little Gallery, Hudson Park Branch, New York Public Library
1974	*La Muerte: Expresion Mexicana de un Enigma,* Universidad Nacional Autónoma, Mexico City
1977	*Bienal de Grafica,* Palacio de Bellas Artes, Mexico City
1978	*Contemporary Photography in Mexico,* Northlight Gallery, Arizona State University, Tempe (travelled to the Center for Creative Photography, University of Arizona, Tucson)
	Mexico Today, Nexus Gallery, Atlanta (travelled to Meridian House, Washington, D.C.)
1980	*7 Portfolios Mexicanos,* Casa de Mexico, Paris (travelled to the Picasso Museum, Antibes)
	El desnudo Fotográfico, Casa del Lago, Universidad Nacional Autónoma, Mexico City
1981	*Hecho en Latino America 2,* Palacio de Bellas Artes, Mexico City
1982	*La Photographie Contemporaine en Amerique Latine,* Centre Georges Pompidou, Paris

Collections:

Instituto Nacional de Bellas Artes, Mexico City; Consejo Mexicano de Fotografia, Mexico City; Fototeca de la Casa del Lago, Mexico City; Museo de Artes y Ciencias, Universidad Nacional Autónoma, Mexico City; Museo Carrillo Gil, Mexico City; Casa de las Américas, Havana, Cuba; National Geographic Society, Washington, D.C.; United Nations Archives, Geneva; Hartkamp Collection, Amsterdam.

Publications:

By BLANCO: Books—*Science Experiments That Really Work,* with others, Chicago 1970, Mexico City 1973; *El Paisaje del Espectáculo en México,* with others, Mexico City 1974; *El Paisaje Religioso de México,* with others, Mexico City 1975; *Obras en Parques Naturales,* with others, Mexico City 1975; *Caminos y Desarrollo,* with others, Mexico City 1975; *Hecho en Latinoamérica,* with others, Mexico City 1978; *America en la Mira,* with others, Mexico City 1978; *7 Portafolios Mexicanos,* exhibition catalogue, with others, Mexico City 1980; *El desnudo Fotográfico,* exhibition catalogue, with others, Mexico City 1980; *Mexican Women in Statistics,* Mexico City 1981; *Percepcion y Analisis,* Mexico City 1981; *Fiesta del Dolor,* Mexico City 1981; *El Auto,* Mexico City 1981; *Hecho en Latino America 2,* exhibition catalogue, with others, Mexico City 1981. **Articles**—"Niños in the Camera Eye" in the *Christian Science Monitor* (Boston), 22 August 1967; "La Fotografía, imagen de la realidad o una manera de ver" in *Arte Sociedad e Ideología*(Mexico City), July 1977; "La difícil facilidad de la fotografia" in *Artes Visuales* (Mexico City), Spring 1977.

On BLANCO: Book—*La Photographie Contemporaine en Amerique Latine*, exhibition catalogue, by Alain Sayag, Paris 1982. Articles—in *Revista de Bellas Artes* (Mexico City), September/October 1975; "Lázaro Blanco" in *Camera* (Lucerne), October 1978; "Lázaro Blanco" in *Zoom* (Paris), April 1979; in *Printletter* (Zurich), May/June 1980.

*

Those pieces of transformed reality we call photographs may awaken in the viewer latent or hidden feelings about his world by allowing him to see, observe, interpret, redefine, notice and become aware of all that he has lost due to his immersion in a deafening, numbing society. Photographs may very well represent the outcries of those struggling to emerge from the marsh to see the light.

The self-exploration brought about when sights are consolidated into more or less permanent reminders or records may help a man better understand his past and look at himself with a clearer eye. This self-exploration that photography allows is undoubtedly due to its strong and powerful link with reality.

People are beginning to realize that photographs are not only tangible fragments of their own existence, but also of their illusions and dreams of events which may never come to pass, as well as materialized flares of imagination and of a nonexisting world.

The ambiguity of photographs plays tricks on even the most clever minds in an interplay established between the photographic image and its observer. Some observers are satisfied with immediate recognition of that which is depicted while other non-conformists search for meanings in all they see.

The photographer must give nurtured and nutritious responses to everyone. His images must contain something of importance even though he may fail to recognize it as readily as someone studying them more closely.

He must lean on the common ordinary tactics of the use of form and content enhanced by the interaction with lines, shapes, textures, etc., to direct the observer's attention to a certain point. But then, each photographer must be able to release the viewer so that he uses this frozen semi-reality to fly away on his own, to reach his own heights, and from that viewpoint see the world, see himself.

Since the beginning of awareness, the artist, generally a painter or draftsman, has had the receptive ability to give new meanings to that which surrounds him and communicate his feelings to others. Scientists did as well. In this sense, scientists and artists are no different from the photographer, but unlike the draftsman's or painter's tools, the extra flexibility lent to the photographer by the use of sophisticated equipment and processes enables him to concentrate on the most difficult part of it all: discovery and capture.

The photographer's widespread use of odd and strange techniques as well as bizarre environments and subjects to depict his own creations sometimes causes the world to wonder at his audacity or even depravity and his ability to repel and disgust yet inform and communicate. Still, he has not forgotten to look at the simple things around him and to discover the magic within an ordinary subject without sensationalism or unusual treatment to capture attention.

I like simplicity—even more when I recognize the kind that results from careful elaboration. Real simplicity may jump out at you from a street corner, or make its presence known when you stand staring at a point without really knowing why and from the blurred, out-of-focus vision, a relationship of lights and shadows emerges that makes your heart skip a beat with your urgency to capture it, to materialize it.

I also enjoy seeing something that another photographer has put together, whether I discover it in a book, a gallery, or a magazine. I always have the same pleasurable reaction when I feel cleverness, originality and ability blended together to produce a photographic image that makes my heart and head turn. I have also great respect for this type of experience.

Conversely, I feel offended when I discover a poorly-executed trick. I have nothing against tricks but their purpose should always be unequivocally defined. I, as the observer, should always recognize the meaning and justification. I feel betrayed when a trick is used for the sole purpose of attracting attention which otherwise would be quickly lost.

I never lean on the importance of content in my own work, nor the emotions resulting from witnessing a dramatic, grotesque, comical or other kind of attention-arresting event. I would rather use the content as a pretext to make myself seen.

—Lázaro Blanco

* * *

A sensitive and acute interpreter of his people and his country, Lázaro Blanco has transformed documentary photography into a poetic narration of facts, realities and opinions. Inheriting the concepts of the great Mexican school of photography, which has decisively influenced more than one famous photographer—Cartier-Bresson, Weston, Modotti, Strand—Blanco has created a new and personal style in which tradition goes through a profound process of innovation.

Certain themes that form part of the Mexican visual heritage—sociopolitical declarations, religious ritual, the influences of the cultures that preceded Columbus, the mass of habits and customs—are all tackled by Blanco, but allusively. This cultural network, always an integral and essential part of Mexican society, is actually revealed in his pictures through minute, apparently insignificant details, almost confused and hidden by other elements of contemporary life.

There is also in his work a subtle contrast between surviving symbols of the past and symbols of the present, a truthful and faithful representation of a society in evolution. The two ways of life and thought in a society that lives in daily contradiction with itself, unable to abandon the ancient myths yet already living in a futuristic age, are depicted by Blanco with delicate sensitivity. And he succeeds in harmonizing within himself two approaches to reality that are normally in conflict: intellectual acuteness in recognizing the significant subject and a warm-hearted human sympathy. As a result, certain asperities that come from too clear a vision of the world and a facile tendency to sentimentalism are resolved by Blanco in pictures of a composed and expressive harmony.

Blanco examines the little lives, the less obvious realities, the humdrum events, things from which significant elements can be extracted as a means to an overview, avoiding anything easy, obvious, exceptional or extraordinary. He is accustomed to reason and self-discipline and never allows himself to be distracted by a passing emotion; with meticulous care he controls every detail of a picture constructed from a few essential, irreplaceable elements. His graphic composition seems to be the result of complex mathematical and geometrical calculations, which create a perfect balance of lines, forms, and tone. Every one of his pictures is the result of slow deliberation; he purges anything superfluous or redundant until he arrives more at the suggestion than at the crude statement of an idea.

There is nothing flashy about his work, nor does he look for the "decisive moment." His approach is patient and restrained. First, he assimilates the fragments of actuality before his eyes; once his emotional response to his subject has subsided, he looks for essence in his everyday event; then, when he has reached harmony between emotional impulse and exterior image, he takes his picture. This slow intellectual and psychological process creates photographs that also take a long time to observe: the picture makes no instant, profound impact on the viewer. The totality of the message, with its myriad of minute details, is comprehended only gradually.

Lázaro Blanco "writes" with light, creating visual poems with the tempo and rhythms of an old traditional dance. And just as the dance is a metaphorical representation of life and fantasy, so we discover in his pictures how much magic is within reality.

—Giuliana Scimé

BLAZER, Carel.

Nationality: Dutch. **Born:** Amsterdam, 16 June 1911. **Education:** Attended schools in Amsterdam, 1919-27; trained in electronics; studied photography, under Hans Finsler, at the Kunstgewerbeschule, Zurich, 1934. **Career:** Worked in photographic studio of Eva Besnyö, Amsterdam, 1934; freelance photojournalist and industrial photographer, working for *De Lach, Het Leven,*

Wereldkroniek, and Metz and Company, Bruijnzeel, Matex-Rotterdam, etc., Amsterdam, 1934-75: did photo-reportage in Netherlands and abroad, including the Spanish Civil War, 1937, and Anschluss in Czechoslovakia, 1938; also produced monumental photo-murals for Economische Voorlichtingsdienst, etc., Amsterdam, from 1938; Persoons Bewijs Centrale, 1942-45; retired, living in Altforst, Netherlands, 1975 until his death. Instructor in Photography, under Paul Citroen, Nieuwe Kunstschool, Amsterdam, 1939-42. **Recipient:** Gebonden Kunstenfederatie Prize, Amsterdam, 1968. **Died:** (in Altforst) 16 January 1980.

Individual Exhibitions:

1958   Steendrukkerij De Jong, Hilversum, Netherlands
1968   *May Peace Be,* Stedelijk Museum, Amsterdam
        Raadhuis, Heerlen, Netherlands
1979   Gemeentemuseum, The Hague
1992   *Carel Blazer. Zeeland droog,* Zeeuwse Bibliotheek, Middelburg

Selected Group Exhibitions:

1937   *Foto '37,* Stedelijk Museum, Amsterdam
        World's Fair, Paris
1945   *Ondergedoken Camera,* Atelier Meijboom, Amsterdam
1948   *Foto '48,* Stedelijk Museum, Amsterdam
1957   *Fotografie als Uitdrukkingsmiddel,* Van Abbemuseum,
        Eindhoven, Netherlands
1958   *Gebonden Kunstenfederatie,* Rijksuniversiteit, Leiden
1964   *Mensen op Weg,* Stedelijk Museum, Amsterdam
1978   *Fotografie in Nederland 1940-1975,* Stedelijk Museum,
        Amsterdam
1979   *Fotografie in Nederland 1920-1940,* Haags Gemeentemuseum,
        The Hague
1980   *De ondergedonken camera,* Paleis op de Dam, Amsterdam
1985   *Amsterdam 1950-1959 20 fotografen,* Gemeentearchief,
        Amsterdam
1986   *50 Jahre moderne Farbfotografie 1936-1986* (Photokina),
        Keulen
1989   *Foto in omslag. Het Nederlandse documentaire fotoboek na
        1945.* De Zonnehof, Amersfoort
1991   *Confrontaties. Nederlands fotografen en hun betrokkenheid bij
        (inter)nationale conflicten,* Grote Kerk, Den Haag

Collections:

Stedelijk Museum, Amsterdam; Gemeente Archief, Amsterdam; Haags Gemeentemuseum, The Hague, Prentenkabinet, Rijksuniversiteit, Leiden; Maria Austria Instituut, Amsterdam; Rijksmuseum, Amsterdam; Rijksdienst Beeldende Kunst, Den Haag; Museum voor Volkenkunde, Rotterdam.

Publications:

By BLAZER: Books—*Rome/Amsterdam,* Antwerpen 1950; *Leve de Vrede,* exhibition catalogue, Stedelijk Museum, Amsterdam 1968; *Anderland. Carel Blazer fotograaf,* with text by Willem Frederik Hermans, Amsterdam 1979.

On BLAZER: Books—*Waar Nederland Trotsch op Is* by Paul Schuitema, Leiden 1940; *Holland and the Canadians* by Norman Phillips and J. Nikerk, Amsterdam 1946; *50 Jaar Bruijnzeel, 1897-1947,* Amsterdam 1947; *Verwoesting en Wederopbouw* by Ir. Th. P. Tromp, Amsterdam 1948; *Fotogoek over Rome,* Amsterdam 1951; *De Dijken* by Max Dendermonde, Amsterdam 1956; *Wegen naar morgen* by Max Dendermonde and others, Wormerveer, Netherlands 1962; *Carel Blazer,* exhibition catalogue, Amsterdam 1968; *Fotografie in Nederland 1940-1975,* exhibition catalogue, by Els Barents, Amsterdam 1978; *Fotografie in Nederland 1920-1940,* exhibition catalogue, by Flip Bool and Kees Broos, The Hague 1979; *Anderland: Carel Blazer Fotograaf,* with an introduction by Willem Frederik Hermans, Amsterdam 1979; *De Arbeidersfotografen: Camera in Crisis in de Jaren '30* by Flip Bool and Jeroen de Vries, Amsterdam 1982; *Foto in omslag. Het Nederlandse documentaire fotoboek na 1945,* by Mattie Boom, Amsterdam 1989. **Arti**-cles—in *Haagse Post* (The Hague), 27 September 1958; "Carel Blazer" by Wim Alings Jr. in *De Groene Amsterdammer* (Amsterdam), 4 April 1968; "Fotograaf Blazer" by Taco Swart in *Algemeen Dagblad* (Amsterdam), 9 April 1968; *Algemeen Handelsblad* (Amsterdam) 13 April 1968; "De tweede generatie" by Ursula den Tex in *Vrij Nederland-bijlage* (Amsterdam), 15 May 1976; "Carel Blazer was 'nieuwe fotograaf'" by Bas Roodnat in *NRC Handelsblad* (Amsterdam), 21 January 1980; "Bij de dood van Carel Blazer, een virtuoos fotograaf" by Ursula den Tex in *Vrij Nederland* (Amsterdam), 26 January 1980; "Leve de vrede. Carel Blazer 1911-1980" by Willem K. Coumans in *Foto* (Amersfoort), March 1980; "Carel Blazer" by Tineke de Ruiter and Ingeborg Th. Leijerzapf in *Alphen aan den Rijn/Amsterdam,* 15 April 1991.

*   *   *

In 1932 Carel Blazer, while still an amateur photographer, made a photograph of a performance by an anti-fascist labour ballet group. This photograph was a surprisingly and highly successful version of the avant-garde trends of the 1930's, complete with the very characteristic dynamic diagonal accent. The reasons for so precocious a performance are these: his contacts with the Association of Worker Photographers created an incentive to choose photography as a profession; because he had trained as an electro-technician, he was already technically oriented; and, most important, he had, even at that very early age, already obtained a perfect command of the techniques of photography. That this was so soon became apparent in his photographic reports for newspapers and industry. Later on, he invested in special equipment, which allowed him to improve on his color photography—and his enlargements, for example the one he produced for the Dutch Pavilion at the *World's Fair* in Brussels in 1958. He enlarged a miniature photo into one of 100 square meters, and every photographer in Holland wanted to know how he had done it.

Blazer always went out into the world to "report." He enjoyed participating in and conveying what was happening in other people's lives. Because he was religious, he longed for a peaceful world. *May Peace Be* was the title of his exhibition at the Stedelijk Museum in Amsterdam in 1968. This title was inspired by the title of one of his photographs in the exhibition, "Viva la Pace," which both before and during the war had been the slogan in the fight against fascism. Blazer made some very moving photographs of 14 July 1936 in Paris; of the Spanish Civil War in 1937; of the "Anschluss" in Czechoslovakia in 1938; and of Amsterdam just before and after the capitulation of the Germans in 1945; but he sometimes felt frustrated that he could not do more to help fight fascism except via his photographs. He wanted at least to capture what he saw. This "capturing," which always involved ordinary people, he did continuously throughout his life, travelling all over the world. He did it with modesty and sincerity. "When I take pictures, I take them to show to others, not so much to show the sorrow, but more to show the positive things."

For his many industrial reports Blazer still found time to improve techniques and to experiment. His reports on the Delta works in Zeeland are both dynamic and technically excellent; his series on various firms in Rotterdam are of an equally high standard. Even in these industrial pictures, he managed to achieve something special.

Another Dutch photographer once said of Blazer: "I do not think there exists any Dutch photographer who has not learned something from his work."

—A. de Jonge-Vermeulen

BLUMBERG, Donald.

Nationality: American. **Born:** Brooklyn, New York, 4 April 1935. **Education:** Attended Cornell University, Ithaca, New York, 1957-59, B.S. in biology 1959; University of Colorado, Boulder, 1959-61, M.S. in biology 1961. **Military Service:** Served in the United States Army, in the U.S. and Germany, 1955-57: Corporal. **Family:** Married Grace Ganz in 1959; daughter: Rachel. **Career:** Photographer since 1962. Instructor, Brooklyn College, New York, 1962-63, City College of New York, 1963-64, and Mobilization for Youth (Federal anti-poverty program), Lower East Side, New York, 1962-65. Assistant Professor of Art, 1965-69, Associate Professor of Art, 1969-72, and since 1972 Professor of Art and Director of the Photography Program, State University of New York at Buffalo. Visiting Professor in Creative Photography, Massachusetts Institute of Technology, Cambridge, 1972-74; Distinguished Visiting Professor of Art (Photography), California State University at San Jose, 1979-80. **Recipient:** SUNY at Buffalo Research Fellowship, 1966, 1967, 1969, 1972, 1973; SUNY at Buffalo Institutional Funds Research Grant, 1967-71, 1975; Creative Artist Public Service Grant, New York State Council of the Arts, 1971, 1975. **Agents:** Visual Studies Workshop, 31 Prince Street, Rochester, New York 14607; and Light Gallery, 800 North La Cienega Boulevard, Los Angeles, California 90069. **Address:** 16918 Donna Ynex Lane, Pacific Palisades, California 90272, U.S.A.

Individual Exhibitions:

1963	Camera Infinity Gallery, New York
1966	International Museum of Photography, George Eastman House, Rochester, New York
1969	University/Community Living Arts Center (Domus), Buffalo, New York
1970	State University of New York at Buffalo
1971	*Daily Photographs,* Visual Studies Workshop, Rochester, New York
	Portraits of Students, State University of New York at Buffalo
1972	International Museum of Photography, George Eastman House, Rochester, New York
1973	Harvard University, Cambridge, Massachusetts
	Massachusetts Institute of Technology, Cambridge
	Cranbrook Academy of Art, Bloomfield Hills, Michigan
	Worcester Art Museum, Massachusetts
1974	International Cultureel Centrum, Antwerp (toured Europe)
	Memorial Gallery, Rochester, New York
1976	Visual Studies Workshop, Rochester, New York
1979	*Photographs 1965-1978 by Donald Blumberg,* Cranbrook Academy of Art, Bloomfield Hills, Michigan (retrospective)
	Donald Blumberg: Recent Photographs in Series, Albright-Knox Art Gallery, Buffalo, New York
	Recent Photographs, Addison Gallery of American Art, Andover, Massachusetts
	Recent Photographs, California State University at San Jose
1980	*Photographs 1965-1980 by Donald Blumberg,* DeSaisset Museum, University of California at Santa Clara
	Photographs 1965-1980 by Donald Blumberg, Glenbow Museum, Calgary, Alberta
	Donald Blumberg: Cityscapes/Landscapes, Markham Gallery, San Jose, California
1981	*Photographs 1965-1981 by Donald Blumberg,* Los Angeles Municipal Museum at Barnsdall Park
	Glenbow Museum, Calgary, Alberta
1983	Light Factory, Charlotte, North Carolina

Selected Group Exhibitions:

1966	*Current Report II,* Museum of Modern Art, New York (toured the United States, 1966-75)
1967	*The Persistence of Vision,* International Museum of Photography, George Eastman House, Rochester, New York (toured the United States, 1967-70)
	Photography in the 20th Century, National Gallery of Canada, Ottawa (toured Canada and the United States, 1967-73)
1968	*Contemporary Photographer III,* International Museum of Photography, George Eastman House, Rochester, New York (toured the United States, 1968-71)

1969	*Vision and Expression,* International Museum of Photography, George Eastman House, Rochester, New York (toured the United States, 1969-71)
1970	*New Acquisitions,* Museum of Modern Art, New York
1971	*Edward Steichen Permanent Collection,* Museum of Modern Art, New York
	The Permanent Collection, Visual Studies Workshop, Rochester, New York
1977	*Eye of the West: Camera Vision and Cultural Consensus,* Hayden Gallery, Massachusetts Institute of Technology, Cambridge
1980	*The Painterly Photograph,* Washington Project for the Arts, Washington, D.C.

Collections:

Museum of Modern Art, New York; International Museum of Photography, George Eastman House, Rochester, New York; Carpenter Center for the Visual Arts, Harvard University, Cambridge, Massachusetts; Library of Congress, Washington, D.C.; Art Institute of Chicago; Minneapolis Institute of Arts; Norton Simon Museum, Pasadena, California; Oakland Museum, California; National Gallery of Canada, Ottawa.

Publications:

By BLUMBERG: Books—*Daily Photographs,* portfolio, New York 1971; *Portraits of Students,* New York 1972; *In Front of St. Patrick's Cathedral: Photographs by Donald Blumberg,* with an introduction by Nathan Lyons, preface by Minor White, Cambridge, Massachusetts 1973; *Photographs 1965-1978 by Donald Blumberg: Recent Photographs in Series,* Buffalo, New York 1979. **Films**—*The Art Department, State University of New York at Buffalo,* with Charles Gill, 1967; *The American Seduction,* with SUNY-Buffalo Film Club, 1967; *P.S. 32, Class 4A, 1907,* with Grace Blumberg, 1967; *Buffalo to New York, New York to Buffalo,* with Grace Blumberg, 1968; *Exorcise,* with Grace Blumberg, 1968.

On BLUMBERG: Books—*Photography in the Twentieth Century* by Nathan Lyons, New York 1967; *The Persistence of Vision* by Nathan Lyons, New York 1967; *Vision and Expression* by Nathan Lyons, New York 1969; *The City: American Experience* by Alan Trachtenberg, Peter Neill, and Peter Bunnell, New York 1971. **Articles**—"Daily Photographs" by A.D. Coleman in the *Village Voice* (New York), 28 October 1971; "In Front of St. Patrick's Cathedral" by Peter Galassi in *Afterimage* (Rochester, New York), December 1973; "From Formal to Family" by Anthony Bannon in *Afterimage* (Rochester, New York), December 1979.

*

My work over the past fifteen years represents a series of transitions that generally parallel my picture-making, socio-political, and family concerns. At first, my photography was dominantly concerned with expanding the photographic vernacular. *In Front of St. Patrick's Cathedral* (1965-67) dealt with extending the concepts of the photographic frame and collage concepts. The collaborative work with the painter Charles Gill (1966), involving large-format photo-linen and smaller cliché-verre, was a continuation of this phase.

In the late 1960's, during the war in Vietnam, I found egocentric production repugnant. I turned to *Daily Photographs* (transient newspaper war and domestic atrocity images transposed to large scale photographs) as a photographic political act. This was also my intention in *Portraits of Students,* which frontally records students subjected to the abuse of war-time politics.

Since 1972 and the birth of my daughter Rachel, I have been involved with images that relate to the family. They are intended (as defined by John Berger) to be "private," rather than "public" photographs. Although they are regularly shown in museums, they are made as a family document—primarily for my daughter, so that she can look back in future time and say, "This is how I was in time past and place. This is how my father chose to make the record."

—Donald Blumberg

* * *

Donald Blumberg is one of the leading practitioners of the experimental photograph. This tradition, drawn from the work of the surrealist and Dada photographers (Man Ray, Lázló Moholy-Nagy and Herbert Bayer), was long neglected until Blumberg and a few others (e.g., John Wood, Keith Smith) began to experiment in the 1960's. Their inspiration and rationales for working came not just from these earlier photographers, but from works in many media. The making of Art was undergoing many radical approaches during the decade and these new attitudes infected and influenced the photographic community. One could do anything.

For the last 20 years, Blumberg has created an incredible amount of differing kinds of work. His images are exploratory, often irrelevant and at times political; he is one of the few photographers to have made anti-Vietnam war images. The photographs surprise, confuse, contradict. Formal concerns chiefly inform Blumberg's aesthetics. He has used collage extensively; there are photographs within photographs, gridded in various patterns, and pasted or sewn on additions of other elements such as buttons and drawings. The portrait and various approaches to it has been a continuing concern as has the relationship of color to black and white. His use of cliché verre and stain photographs were revolutionary when done in 1966. However, the work always transports the viewer through the structure to discover a profound emotional and personal content. By creating a world of his own in his photographs of this world, Blumberg can reveal the issues he is concerned about. The series, "Collaboration with Rachel" (his daughter), which he has pursued for the past five years, is a powerful and evocative document of both the growth of a child and of the evolution of a father-daughter relationship in 20th century America.

Blumberg belongs to no easily described school of image-making. His work is unique because the technique of photography is not his cage; it's only one of the many tools for touching his experience to ours.

—James L. Sheldon

BOHDZIEWICZ, Anna Beata.

Nationality: Polish. **Born:** Lódz, 15 April 1950. **Education:** Attended Warsaw University, 1967-74; self-taught in photography. **Family:** Married Janusz Lipinski in 1983; children: Agnieszka, Edyta, Andrzej and Adam. **Career:** Worked as a director's assistant and second unit director for Polish Feature Films Enterprise. In 1981, became a freelance photographer for Solidarity. Worked for the underground press and *L'Express* and *The Independent*. Photo Editor for *Gazeta Wyborcza* 1991-92. **Address:** ul. Profesorska 4 m 2, 00-433 Warsaw, Poland.

Individiual Exhibitions:

1974   *First Exhibition,* studio of Professor Zofia Demkowska, Warsaw
1978   *Chorasan,* Art Critics' Gallery, Warsaw

1980   *Afghanistan,* Lódz Photo Society Gallery, Lódz
1983   *Almost a Year,* Polish Photographers' Union Gallery, Cracow
1984   *Afghanistan—memories from a journey,* Foto-Video Gallery, Cracow
        More Than a Year—Photodiary—A Song on the End of the World, OD NOWA Gallery, Poznan
        Warsaw Courtyard Chapels, FORMA Gallery, Warsaw
        The Way of the Cross, Maxymilian Kolbe's Church, Cracow
1985   *Ein Fototagebuch aus Polen,* Galerie Zyndikat, Berlin
        Photodiary, Bielsko Photo Gallery, Bielsko-Biala, Poland
1986   *Rome—Photodiary,* Visual Scene Gallery, Lublin
1987   *Photodiary,* FF-Gallery, Lódz (travelled to Natalie Klebenow Gallery, Boston; Grey Gallery, New York University)
        Photodiary—The Fifth Year, Polish Photographers' Union Gallery, Cracow
1988   *Photodiary,* Salzburg College Gallery, Salzburg
1989   *Photodiary,* Red Eye Gallery, Rhode Island School of Design
        Fototagebuch, Bartolomäuskirche, Berlin
1990   *Ten Years of Solidarity in Poland* (shown in sixty countries throughout the world)
1991   *The Way of the Cross,* Wolów
        Warsaw Courtyard Chapels, Radom Regional Museum, Poland
        Pope John Paul II in Poland—Photodiary, BWA Gallery, Koszalin
1994   *Fototagebuch,* Humbold Bibliothek and Rathaus-Galerie, Berlin

Selected Group Exhibitions:

1986   *The Second International Portfolio of Artists' Photography,* Liget Gallery, Budapest
1987   *Out of Eastern Europe—Private Photography,* List Visual Arts Center, MIT, Boston (travelled to Rosa Esmon Gallery, New York; Art Space, San Francisco; The Baxter Gallery, Portland; Randolph Street Gallery, Chicago)
1988   *Polish Experimental Photography,* Liget Gallery, Budapest, Hungary
        Zwischen Wolga und Elbe, Lenbachhaus, Munich
        Polish perceptions, Collins Gallery, Glasgow
1989   *Zwischen Wolga und Elbe,* Neue Gesellschaft für Bildende Kunst, Berlin
        XXth Biennale of Arts, Sao Paulo
1990   *Fotoberichte aus Polen,* Gasteig Gallery, Munich

Collections:

Art Museum, Lódz; National Museum, Wroclaw; National Library, Warsaw; Musée de L'Elysée, Lausanne; Check-Point-Charlie Museum, Berlin.

Publications:

By BOHDZIEWICZ: Books—*The Way of the Cross,* n.p. 1984; *Droga Nadziei,* Wydawnictwo 1988; *Der Friedens-Nobelpreis von 1983 bis 1988. Lech Walesa.* **Articles**—"A Window on Poland" (under pseudonym Victoria) in *TriQuarterly,* Spring-Summer 1983; "Z Magicznej Szkatulki" in *Fotografia,* number one, 1984; "Afgánská Setkánf" in *Ceskoslovenska Fotografie,* December 1984; *L'Autrement* (numero sur la Pologne), (Paris) 1990; "Fotodziennik, Piosenka o Koncu Swiata" in *Konteksty,* 3 April 1992; "Fotodeník—Dokument Nebo Kreace?" in *Revue Fotografie,* April 1993; also criticism in *Gazeta Wyborcza, Fototapeta* and *Exlibris.*

On BOHDZIEWICZ: Articles—"Fotodziennik, czyli notatki o koncu swiata" by Tadeusz Szyma, *Tygodnik Powszechny,* 26 February 1984; "Rzeby

The Pope Has Not Come Yet, But Is Already with Us, 1991. Photograph ©Anna Bohdziewicz.

na podwórzu'' by Andrzej Oseka, *Przeglad Powszechny,* December 1984; ''Mala apokalipsa—o fotografiach Anny Beaty Bohdziewicz'' by Krystyna Czerni, *Res Publica* April 1988; ''Time intensified'' by Urszula Czartoryska, 1988; ''Public projections and private images—Krzysztof Wodiczko and Eastern European Photography at MIT,'' *Afterimage,* May 1987.

*

I think that the real world is far more interesting than anything we can make up. Using photography, I am making notes on the odds-and-ends that make up our lives. They speak of its quality. I think photography is a very powerful medium but it needs words to fix it precisely in time and space. That is why all my photos have captions. I believe that a simple documentary photograph becomes, in time, a metaphor. I hope that my photos—that show everyday life in Poland in 1980s and 1990s—will become one day a big metaphor of the times in which I have lived. They were so painfully real—though they now seemed unreal, even surreal. The surrealistic aspect of reality is also very important in my photographic work.

—A. Bohdziewicz

* * *

The art of Anna Bohdziewicz belongs to that current in Polish photography in which the photographic image is primarily a register of emotional experi-

ence and of events—past or present—seen from a very individual point of view.

Within this current Anna Bohdziewicz occupies a special position thanks to the freshness and authenticity of her work, the relevance of its intellectual message and the purely artistic values of her photographs.

Her debut as an independent photographer came in 1978 with the *Afghanistan* series, which she lent the status of a metaphor and nostalgic meditation on human existence. In it she revealed her sensitivity to the social aspect of life, derived from her academic background in ethnography.

It was in 1980-81, the period of political change in Poland brought about by strikes on the coast and the subsequent formation of ''Solidarity'' that Anna Bohdziewicz defined herself as a photographer. ''We live in a political world'' she says, ''There is no point pretending that politics does not concern us, that it is best left to 'statesmen'. For the artist, too, there is no escaping politics.''

Her photography is strongly involved in public and political events: it is marked by a journalist's inquisitiveness and professionalism, while her way of photographing people and situations is indebted to André Kertesz as well as Robert Frank and Henri Cartier-Bresson.

In Anna Bohdziewicz's photographs politics is usually combined with privacy. Important events co-exist with fleeting moments, famous people are portrayed on a par with the artist's friends and relatives.

Alongside this Bohdziewicz's art displays a fascination with the sacred and the various forms in which it appears in our lives and contrasts with the banality of the everyday. This is the subject of the *Corpus Christi* series dating from 1980-81 and the particularly interesting *Warsaw Chapels* series from 1980-84, an unassuming, almost scientific record of folk chapels preserved in urban courtyards. Bohdziewicz is also the author of *The Way of the Cross* (1984) and a tireless and consistent observer of successive Papal visits to

Poland, which she has turned into a separate series constituting a remarkable testimony to the emotional attachment of Poles to the present pontiff.

In one of her catalogues the artist quotes the art critic Urszula Czartoryska: "Photography is a specific way of intensifying man's existence in the world . . . it is waiting for the world to reveal and express itself. Revelation of the world in thousands of photographs is meant to lend it sense, coherence and permanence in time and space that would be visible on the photographs." This, too, is the way Bohdziewicz perceives photography.

Her most extensive and important project, which she has been working on since 1982 when Poland was under martial law, is the *Photo-diary—A Song on the End of the World*. These "notes" photographed almost at random from day to day compare her "private history of mankind" governed by a specific logic of narrative determined by the logic of absurdity of surrounding events.

The *Photo-diary* consists of white square sheets of paper on which the photographs are placed together with hand-written captions that complement the whole.

"My captions," the author says "are very diverse. Often their function is restricted to providing information, sometimes they form my personal commentary, sometimes they are puns or jokes, sometimes a poetic counterpoint. Often my captions are intended to draw the viewer into a kind of game between the image and the word, between what is visible and the way in which—I feel—others see it."

—Barbara Kosinska

BOHM, Dorothy.

Nationality: British. **Born:** Königsberg, Germany (then East Prussia), 22 June 1924; emigrated to England, 1939: naturalized, 1946. **Education:** Attended schools in Germany and England; studied photography, Manchester College of Technology, obtained City and Guilds Final Certificate in Photography. **Family:** Married Dr Louis Bohm in 1945; daughters: Monica and Yvonne. **Career:** Worked in Manchester portrait studio; taught photography at the Manchester College of Technology, 1945; established and operated own photographic studio in Manchester, specializing in portraiture, graduation portraits, fashion pictures and some advertising and publicity work, 1945-60; since 1971, active at The Photographers' Gallery in London, and Associate Director, 1973-86; former trustee at the Camden Arts Centre, London; Patron of The Photographers' Gallery. **Address:** 15 Church Row, London NW3 6UP, England.

Individual Exhibitions:

1961   *People at Peace,* Institute of Contemporary Arts, London
1975   Il Diaframma Gallery, Milan, Italy
1976   *Impressions of South Africa,* The Photographers' Gallery, London
1981   Contrast Gallery, Dover Street, London
        Camden Arts Centre, London (major retrospective)
1984   The Photographers' Gallery, London
1986   *Dorothy Bohm—Photographs,* Israel Museum, Jerusalem
1994   *Dorothy Bohm: Retrospective,* The Photographers' Gallery, London

Selected Group Exhibitions:

1977   *Women Photographers,* Marjorie Neikrug Gallery, New York (and US tour)
1978   *Paris Seen,* Graves Art Gallery, Sheffield, England
1988   *City Lights,* Goldsmiths College, University of London (and tour)
1989   *Through the Looking Glass—Photographic Art in Britain 1945-1989,* Barbican Art Gallery, London

Collections:

Victoria and Albert Museum, London; Arts Council Collection, London; Israel Museum, Jerusalem; Exelrod Collection, Los Angeles, and many other US collections.

Publications:

By BOHM: Books—*A World Observed,* with foreword by Sir Roland Penrose, 1970; *Hampstead—London Hill Town,* with text by Ian Norrie, 1981; *A Celebration of London,* with text by Ian Norrie, 1984; *A Celebration of London,* published in paperback and in USA 1986; *Dorothy Bohm—Photographs,* exhibition catalogue, with text by Nissan Perez, Jerusalem 1986; *Egypt,* with foreword by Lawrence Durrell and essay by Ian Jeffrey, London and New York 1989; *Venice,* with text by Ian Jeffrey, London and New York 1992; *Dorothy Bohm Colour Photography 1984-94,* foreword by Sue Grayson-Ford, introduction by Ian Jeffrey, 1994. **Articles**—in *Creative Camera,* April 1969; in *British Journal of Photography,* April 1969; in *Creative Camera,* December 1970; in *Amateur Photographer,* 17 February 1971 and 7 June 1972; in *Photographic Journal,* May 1975; in *British Journal of Photography,* June 1980.

On BOHM: Film—*Dorothy Bohm—Photographer,* BBC television film, 1980.

*

I have spent a lifetime taking photographs. It has given me the opportunity to express myself, to search and to look at the world with great interest and intense observation, and to try and show in my pictures a world which is both private and universal. It has been said of my pictures "that they compensate for a sense of loss." There is some truth in this.

The photograph stops things from disappearing. It makes transience less painful, retains some of the special beauty and magic which I have found in the most unlikely places.

I have tried to create order out of chaos, to find stability in flux. I am conscious of the universality of human longing and have tried to express this in my photographs.

—Dorothy Bohm

*   *   *

In 1945 Dorothy Bohm opened a photographic studio in the centre of Manchester and for the next twelve years worked as a portraitist. She is known, though, primarily as a colourist. She began to concentrate on colour photography in 1971, and this important phase in her work has been summed up in her exhibition in the Photographers' Gallery, London, in 1994. Her first major book in colour was *Egypt,* published by Thames & Hudson, London, who also published her *Venice,* in 1992. Good selections of her work in black and white appear in *A World Observed,* published by Cape, London, in 1970 and in *Dorothy Bohm—Photographs,* published by the Israel Museum in 1986, with a foreword by Nissan Pérez.

One of the determining factors in her works was her marriage in 1945 to Louis Bohm, a research chemist whose work took him all over the world. During the late 1940s they lived in Paris and went on prolonged journeys to the United States, Mexico and Spain. She managed, throughout this period, to maintain her photographic studio in Manchester on a part-time basis. Life in Paris introduced her particularly to the work of such Italian film-makers as Fellini, whose *La Strada* she lists as a principal influence. She and her husband also spent prolonged periods during the 1940s and 1950s in Ascona, in the Italian speaking area of Switzerland, where they were in touch with a flourishing community of German and Swiss artists. Like many of her contemporaries she was also impressed by the work of Henri Cartier-Bresson as it was published during the 1950s.

Her dependence on portraiture, however, meant that she could develop her own photographic poetics relatively undisturbed. She was not working to order, nor in any very anxious relationship to the contemporary scene. Thus she was able to develop, quite unselfconsciously, a distinctly personal poetics. It is a bitter-sweet aesthetic of festival shot through with melancholia. On the

Children in Sussex, **1986.** Photograph ©Dorothy Bohm.

one side stand the beauties of the world, comestible and charming, and on the other those, including herself, who have knowledge of more bracing realities.

She works, like anyone conscious of the neo-realist art of the 1940s, with respect for metaphor. Her particular psycho-drama, which is at the core of her art, is displaced, enacted by found figures, by imposing, tender and abraded statuary, for instance. She is interested in ceremonials, because of their splendours—but also because many of them involve rites of passage and the loss of innocence. She has been engrossed, above all, by the staging of women in complex custodial roles. She is, to a degree, a theatrical photographer conscious of the make-up of appearances, of cosmetics in the broadest sense. Vitrines and advertising always catch her eye, as do painted landscapes—or the real thing responding excessively to art's challenge. She can be thought of as continuing the inventive studio photography of the 1920s practised by, for example, ringle & pit, by Germaine Krull and by Florence Henri. She has, of course, worked usually in the mode of reportage, taking things as they come, but fundamentally has addressed the world out there as if it were a studio, contrived to elicit that qualified delight of which she was always capable.

Through her work with and support for The Photographers' Gallery, London, which she helped found in 1971, she came into contact with such established photographers as André Kertész and Manuel Alvarez Bravo, but her direction had been settled long before. Her circumstances, which include a childhood in Lithuania, the traumas of the war, and a consciousness of Europe lost and found again, have made her one of the most rewarding of auteur-photographers.

—Ian Jeffrey

BOLTANSKI, Christian.

Nationality: French. **Born:** Paris, 6 September 1944. **Education:** Self-taught in photography. **Career:** Professional photographer and artist, Paris, since 1969. **Agent:** Sonnabend Gallery, 420 West Broadway, New York, New York 10012, U.S.A. **Address:** 746 Boulevard Camelinat, 92240 Malakoff, France.

Individual Exhibitions:

1970 Galerie Templon, Paris (with Jean Le Gac)
   Musée d'Art Moderne, Paris

1971	Galerie Sonnabend, Paris
1972	Galerie Folker Skulima, Berlin
1973	Galleria Lucio Amelio, Naples
	Kunsthalle, Baden-Baden, West Germany
	Museum of Modern Art, Oxford
	Israel Museum, Jerusalem
1974	Westfalischer Kunstverein, Münster, West Germany
	Louisiana Museum, Humlebaek, Denmark
	Centre National d'Art Contemporain, Paris
1975	Sonnabend Gallery, New York
	Kunsthalle, Kiel, West Germany
	Centre d'Art Contemporain, Geneva
	Württembergische Kunstverein, Stuttgart
	Galerie Seriaal, Amsterdam
1976	Musée d'Art Moderne, Paris
	Rheinisches Landesmuseum, Bonn
1977	Museum of Contemporary Art, La Jolla, California
	Galleria Bruno Soletti, Milan
	Galerie Sonnabend, Paris
1978	Badischer Kunstverein, Karlsruhe, West Germany
	Galerie Jollenbeck, Cologne
	Galerie Malacorda, Geneva
	Galerie Foksal, Warsaw
1979	The Kitchen, New York
	Maison de la Culture, Chalon-sur-Saône, France
	Sonnabend Gallery, New York
1980	Musée de Peinture, Calais
	Galerie Sonnabend, Paris
	Carpenter Art Center, Harvard University, Cambridge, Massachusetts
1981	Musée d'Art Moderne, Paris (retrospective)
1982	Sonnabend Gallery, New York
	Le Nouveau Musée, Lyon, France
1983	Aldrich Museum, Ridgefield, Connecticut
1984	Centre Georges Pompidou, Paris
	Kunsthaus, Zurich
	Kunsthalle, Baden-Baden, West Germany
	Galerie 't Venster, Rotterdam
1985	Galerie Crousel-Hussenot, Paris
1986	Kunstverein, Munich

Selected Group Exhibitions:

1969	*Biennale de Paris,* Musée d'Art Moderne, Paris
1971	*Prospekt '71,* Kunsthalle, Dusseldorf
1972	*Documenta 5,* Museum Fridericianum, Kassel, West Germany
1975	*Biennale,* Venice
1977	*Documenta 6,* Museum Fridericianum, Kassel, West Germany
1979	*Biennale,* Museum of Modern Art, Sydney
	Aspectes de l'Art en France, Musée d'Art Moderne, Paris
1980	*Art in Europe,* Museum van Hedendaagse, Ghent
	Artist and Camera, Mappin Art Gallery, Sheffield, Yorkshire (travelled to the Stoke City Art Gallery; Durham Light Infantry Museum; Cartwright Hall, Bradford)
1986	*Photography as Performance,* Photographers' Gallery, London

Collections:

Musée d'Art Moderne, Paris; Kunsthalle, Hamburg; Kunsthalle, Kiel, West Germany; Neue Galerie, Aachen, West Germany; Louisiana Museum, Humlebaek, Denmark; Boymans-van Beuningen Museum, Rotterdam; Museum of Fine Arts, Lodz, Poland; Israel Museum, Jerusalem; Art Institute of Chicago.

Publications:

By BOLTANSKI: Books—*Reconstitutions des Gestes,* Paris 1971; *10 Portraits Photographiques,* Paris 1972; *Album Photographique,* Hamburg 1972; *Inventaire,* Munster, West Germany 1973; *Quelques Interpretations,* Paris 1974; *20 Regles et Technique,* Copenhagen 1975; *Les Morts pour Rire,*

Antibes, France 1975; *Modellbilder,* with others, Bonn 1976. **Film**—*La Vie Impossible de Christian Boltanski,* 1968.

On BOLTANSKI: Books—*Photography as Art* by Volker Kahmen, Tubingen, West Germany 1973, London 1974; *150 Jahre Fotografie* by Klaus Honnef, Mainz, West Germany 1977; *Reconstitution* by Andreas Franke, Paris 1978; *Les Modeles* by Paul-Hervé Würz, Paris 1979; *Spurensicherung* by Günter Metken, Cologne 1979; *Artist and Camera,* exhibition catalogue, by M.S.C., London 1980.

*

If I wanted to describe the images I make up, I would say that they are photographs—but that, at the same time, they are all about painting; that they show, and yet have nothing to do with, reality; that some of them are based on Japanese design, but they are all concerned with our (Western) culture only; that they are both the expression of my pessimistic viewpoint and motives for hope; that I would like them to be collective, but that they are intensely personal.

All that would be true, as would be dozens of other statements or restrictions. Words are too clear-cut to describe an image; they enclose it within limits, and I hope my photographs will be vague or fuzzy enough for each person, depending on his own background and his present mood, to "see" them each time in a different way.

—Christian Boltanski

* * *

Christian Boltanski is a painter, a painter who uses the photograph to the exclusion of every other medium. As an artist belonging to the post-1968 generation, he has rejected "great art." He uses the photograph, he says, "because it is popularized, reduced art, the art of quotation. . . . " At the end of the Roman Empire there were poets who wrote brief plays that consisted entirely of quotations from ancient authors; collages, fragments of poetry. There is an equivalent phenomenon among the painters of today. It is as if they can create only portraits of culture, cultural quotations. As if nature can no longer be copied, only culture.

This is the impetus that makes Boltanski focus on stereotypes in his work: whether it be *Reconstitutions* of his past life or catalogues of the Western myths of today or photo albums from 1971 or Japanese gardens from 1978, Boltanski does not give us pictures but clichés. "For me," he has said, "the photograph is the equivalent of what the frame was for Lichtenstein—something that limits, which precludes, which indicates that this is not the thing itself. When Lichtenstein paints a landscape, he doesn't really paint a landscape; he paints a picture of a landscape. And this is what I want to do: these are pictures of pictures."

Pictures that have already been seen—Boltanski worked with notions of memory for a long time. The viewer, in fact, does not see nature, but recognizes a picture of this reality seen through a photograph, a scene, a movie. We know it in this way: the vision that we have of nature is a photographic vision. The green of the prairie appears beautiful only if it is Kodak green. The stereotype is a detonator of common memories.

The year 1976, with his "Composition fleuries," marked Boltanski's rupture with the "ugly" photograph in black and white, the deliberately "amateur" photograph of his early career: according to him, during this period the more ugly and "rotten" a work was, the more it was art. Boltanski now does beautiful pictures in the style of Vilmorin advertisements, "because what is 'nice' is meaningless."

Since 1976 the format of Boltanski's composition has become increasingly comprehensive. Using a background that makes everything unreal, he presented, in 1981, at the Musée d'Art Moderne, Paris, in a superb retrospective, his "Compositions heroiques," considerably enlarged photographs of little plastic soldiers placed in the dark and lighted in a very theatrical fashion: the effect was magical. Even though this work is divorced from that of the traditional artist approaching the traditional painting, and though the photographed objects are always inventories of pictures, these real objects yet possess the illusory aspect of art.

Born in 1944 and in the full effervescence of his resources, he is an artist who has always refused what could lead him to stagnate. He has always been concerned with remaining in an uncomfortable position, refusing to adhere to anything established, escaping all enclosures, all ossifications. His concern to always leave form open, malleable, to pattern himself, as it were, on matter in perpetual motion, assures for the rest of us innumerably more upheavals and surprises. Boltanski clearly exceeds the simple scope of the photograph and even of painters who use the photograph: he is, with Buren, one of the greatest French artists of today.

—Michel Nuridsany

BOOGAERTS, Pierre.

Nationality: Belgian. **Born:** Brussels, 30 October 1964; moved to Canada, 1973. **Education:** Studied at the Institut Supérieur Saint Luc, Brussels, 1963-66; Académie Royale, Brussels, 1966-67. **Family:** Married Nicole Renson in 1971. **Career:** Independent painter until 1972; began working with photography in 1971; based in Montreal, since 1973. **Recipient:** Canada Council Arts Grant, 1977, 1978, 1980. **Agent:** Galerie Gilles Gheerbrant, 307 Ste. Catherine West, Montreal, Quebec H2Y 2A3. **Address:** 500 rue de Gaspé, Apt. 309, Ile des Soeurs, Montreal, Quebec H3E 1E8, Canada.

Individual Exhibitions:

1973	*3 Plantations à Véhicle,* Véhicule Art Gallery, Montreal
1975	*Références: Plantation, Jaune-Bananier,* Galerie Optica, Montreal
	"Synthetization" of the Sky, Galerie Gilles Gheerbrant, Montreal
1977	*Arte Fiera '77,* Galerie Gilles Gheerbrant, Bologna, Italy
	New York, N.Y., Galerie Gilles Gheerbrant, and Galerie Optica, Montreal
	Palais des Beaux-Arts, Brussels
1978	International Center of Photography, New York
1979	*Une Après-Midi sur mon Balcon,* Galerie Marielle Mailhot, Montreal
	Screen Series: Street Skies, N.Y. 1978-79, Galerie Gilles Gheerbrant, Montreal (travelled to Ydessa Gallery, Toronto, 1980)
1980	*Street Corners (Pyramids) N.Y. 1978-79,* Musée d'Art Contemporain, and Galerie Gilles Gheerbrant, Montreal (travelled to the Vancouver Art Gallery, 1981)
1981	*Une Après-Midi sur mon Balcon* (second montage), Galerie Photo Vu, Quebec
	Screen Series: Street Skies, N.Y. 1978-79 (second series), National Gallery of Canada, Ottawa
	Camera Series, N.Y. 1979, Galerie Sans Nom, Moncton, New Brunswick
	Pierre Boogaerts, N.Y. 1976-79, 49th Parallel: Centre for Contemporary Canadian Art, New York

Selected Group Exhibitions:

1972	*Pour une Replantation,* Palais des Beaux-Arts Hall, Brussels
1974	*Camerart,* Galerie Optica, Montreal (travelled to Paris and London)
1975	*Conceptual,* Burpee Art Museum, Chicago
1976	*Photography as Art,* Galerija Grada Zagreba, Zagreb
	7 Photographers: Destination Europe, Galerie Optica, Montreal (travelled to Toronto, and toured Europe)
1978	*The Winnipeg Perspective,* Winnipeg Art Gallery
1979	*Black/White and Color,* Bertha Urdang Gallery, New York
1980	*Pluralities,* National Gallery of Canada, Ottawa
	Nuages, Bibliothèque Nationale, Paris
	Art et Photographie, Caisse Génerale d'Epargne et de Retraite, Brussels
1981	*Suite, Serie, Sequence,* Musée des Beaux-Arts, Nantes, France

Collections:

Collection de l'Etat, Brussels; Caisse Générale d'Epargne et de Retraite, Brussels; Bibliothèque Nationale, Paris; Art Bank, Ottawa; National Film Board of Canada, Ottawa; National Gallery of Canada, Ottawa; Musée d'Art Contemporain, Montreal.

Publications:

By BOOGAERTS: Books—*3 Plantations à Véhicule,* Montreal 1974; *Bic Banana,* Montreal 1974; *New York, N.Y.,* Montreal 1977; *Pierre Boogaerts: Série Ecran—Screen Series—Scherm Serie,* Brussels 1977; *Coins de Rues (Pyramides)/N.Y. 1978-79/Street Corners (Pyramids),* c. 1980. **Articles**—"Pierre Boogaerts: The 'Banana-Tree Yellow' Reference" in *Flash Art* (Milan), December 1974/January 1975; "Référence: Plantation, Jaune-Bananier" in *Parachute* (Montreal), November 1975; "Conversation entre Pierre Boogaerts et Michel Denée" in *Parachute* (Montreal), Summer 1980.

On BOOGAERTS: Books—*Camerart,* exhibition catalogue, with texts by Les Levine, Chantal Pontbriand and others, Montreal 1974; *Photography as Art,* exhibition catalogue, Zagreb 1976; *The Winnipeg Perspective,* exhibition catalogue, Winnipeg 1978; *Pluralities,* exhibition catalogue, with text by Chantal Pontbriand, Ottawa 1980; *Art et Photographie,* exhibition catalogue, Brussels 1980; *Nuages,* exhibition catalogue, Paris 1980; *Contemporary Canadian Photography* by Martha Langford, Edmonton, Alberta 1984. **Articles**—"From Object to Image" by Georges Bogardi in the *Montreal Star,* 10 May 1978; "Pierre Boogaerts" by Walter Klepac in *Artscanada* (Toronto), July-August 1976; "Référence Faite: New York; N.Y. de Pierre Boogaerts" by Thierry de Duve in *Parachute* (Montreal), Winter 1977-78; "Canada's Artists with Cameras" by William E. Ewing in *Art News* (New York), April 1978; "'Synthétisation' du Ciel" in *Le Nouvel Observateur Special Photo* (Paris), June 1978; "Erasing the Line Between Art and Photography" by Georges Bogardi in the *Montreal Star,* 28 July 1979; "Boogaerts: Les Ciels de New York" by Gilles Toupin *La Presse* (Montreal), 27 October 1979; "Pierre Boogaerts, N.Y., La Pyramide et La Photo" by René Viau in *Le Devoir* (Montreal), 20 December 1980; "Shows We've Seen" by N. Canavor in *Popular Photography* (New York), June 1981.

*

A few rough notes about my work, 1978-80:

What interests me most in photography are its aberrations. It seems to me that its faults, its neglects (what is eliminated) and its obstructions (that which eliminates) are strangely similar to those of the society we live in.

I know that my photographs are not durable. I like to think of their fragility as an echo of the fragility of our industrial society. I work with photography's immediacy—we don't function along the same rhythm or the same "slowness" as preceding societies. I like its democratic nature—doesn't everyone own a camera?—its waste: isn't the same landscape often photographed by thousands of people?

In a way science cannot do without it; current events, the arts and their teachings are linked to it.

Our society was born of machines and the photomachine can only (re)produce its image.

Consumer society: a society of waste, one of form more than content (are these not the very problems of the image today?).

This is why I both love and hate photography. This may also be why my work in photography consists essentially of "shifting" or "distorting" the givens of properties of the medium. By thwarting and contradicting those properties, I emphasize them on one hand, and on the other hand, by using simple images of our environment, I draw a parallel with our society, with us, with me.

Surface:

A photograph is a surface (like a painting). It can only show us the appearance, the surface of things. When working with photography, one must therefore begin with the externals of things; one must use "photographic evidence." We are condemned to start from the superficial aspect of things, the common, the banal, what everyone sees, from democratic reality. The photographic image, with its accessibility, its waste and its reproducibility is a democratization of the world, a popularization (simplification, superficiality).

But a surface is also, by definition, the borderline between two areas. When working with photography, therefore, one must take into account, besides the external aspect of things, things outside the photograph.

Framing (Screen):

On our face, along a horizontal line, two eyes; the angle of perception is about 180°; our sight frames reality. Moreover, when we look at something, the rest fades away, becomes blurred: to regard is to re-frame.

To photograph is to frame (like a window). In a photograph, the hidden reality is greater than the visible reality; framing is an eclipse.

To photograph is to frame (like blinkers). It is, therefore, to select. Like all specializations, this specialized view demarcates a territory: photography raises walls as easily as a dog raises a leg.

Framing is the border line between what is visible and what is not and consequently between reality and imagination, culture and myth. Framing is the border line between what we see and what we are.

To the *subtractive process* (taking a photograph, a fragment of a whole) I add an *additive process:* the group of photographs and the series.

To change the viewing angle is to modify the frontiers of looking. Chance (or aberration) and the exclusiveness of framing (or the fragility of a prejudice) modify the frontiers of vision (or the parochiality of our territory).

The logic of working with photography is the logic of framing. If one photograph refers to its borders, several photographs, as well as enlarging their respective frames of view, refer to their respective borders. The sum total of these borders will determine the shape of a piece. The sum total of these pieces will determine the shape of the work.

This multiplication of images, each of them limited but at the same time working in a larger context, reminds me of the division of cells.

A photograph is a fragment, photographs are fragments; a piece is the passage from one to several, from the individual to the group. Working with photography is therefore working at the level of connections, joints (. . . in any event, it's a world in pieces . . .).

The group of photographs—a succession of screens—opens, in the end, on the physical presence of the wall and the importance of that wall depends on whether it points out screens that are beyond photography: the screen of the wall on the landscape, of the gallery on art; of art on life; the screens of education, ideas, personality. . . . The piece is a knot which intertwines two visions: in one, the purpose is to see as well as we can (as much), to broaden our field of vision; in the second, the purpose is to hide, to insist on the partial aspect of vision.

The Series:

The series is the group of photographs included in a piece; it is the group of pieces included in one work.

A photograph is like a readymade, and all framings are possible. As far as I am concerned, the difference between two photographs is the difference between two stones found on a road. Anyone can find one that is more or less beautiful or one can be more or less lucky (or patient) or some may even have found a "beautiful quarry." (apparently, what makes a good photographer is 90% subject matter.) What is important to me is that these stones—these possible framings—be found on one road, that they fit into a perspective, that they indicate an *itinerary* (to photograph is also to organize, to arrange time and space). This itinerary can only be decoded through a succession of such readymades. (Repetition: endless reflection.)

By using series, I use one of the characteristics of the medium: reproducibility, *quantity*—consequently, its characteristics of being non-unique and fragmented. This is what I mean by a series.

Weightlessness:

Like light, photography has no weight. It is a "pure" image. For this reason, it cannot be "ugly." To achieve ugliness, one would have to paint it, scratch it, etc., add elements to weight it down, make it "impure." This is why, for example, there is the aberration of war photographs or photographs of disasters which are serenely "beautiful" ("what a beautiful black, what beautiful framing, what a beautiful glossy, satin finish . . . ").

Even if photographs stem from a certain type of perspective, they do not belong to the world of gravity. They have the lightness (and the fragility) of the image, of the simplified surface (and its thinness). The objects represented belong to the world of the sea or to the world of space (at NASA, simulated exercises in weightlessness are conducted in a liquid environment): they owe nothing to the gravity of real life but are situated in the weightlessness of the psyche.

The positioning of a photograph on the wall stems either from the logic of sight, which puts the image black right side-up (this is its figurative logic), or, from the logic of form: a photograph is a rectangle which we can position horizontally or vertically. The two types of logic usually go together. Therefore, if you follow only one type of logic at a time, what results is either a photograph which shows, for example, an upside-down New York architecture, an inversion of right and left, or else a situation in which the rectangle of the photograph will have to be placed askew on the wall, thus re-situating the image in relation to gravity.

One More Note to Avoid Conclusion:

Through individuality (framing) we rejoin a globality: man in the universe. Rediscovering space and the universe through certain aerial/aqueous qualities of the vision and of time; thus regaining along with the viewer the freedom which is also my dependency, and this at every level of my work.

—Pierre Boogaerts

*   *   *

Pierre Boogaerts' monumental panoramas of the Manhattan skyline are the ultimate expressions of his longstanding fascination with the edge of things, particularly the resonant edge where the urban landscape confronts and blends with nature. From the time of his first exclusively photographic works (Boogaerts was trained as a painter in his native Belgium and the earliest works he exhibited were in mixed media), Boogaerts has reached for images which would fuse and reconcile the nature-culture duality into a single entity which he has called a "synthetic image."

The New York scenes were shot from a stationary position, with Boogaerts standing on a street corner and panning his camera first upward, toward the sky, and then downward, toward the horizon. The shape of the sequence corresponds to that of the view: X-shaped sequences, for instance, resulted from a given location affording four divergent views; T-shaped and vertical columns are similarly logical configurations. In some earlier works the "synthetic image" was a fictitious one, entirely invented by the artist, but the New York shots are documentary views, faithful to the eccentricities of the urban scene even in the shape of the over-all assemblage.

With each photograph measuring 16 X 24, the sequence's scale becomes monumental, forcing the spectator to re-enact in his "reading" the panning motion of the camera: a kinesthetic experience that is almost without precedent in photography.

Boogaerts' New York photographs are slightly under-exposed so that the sky becomes a dark, unmodulated shape whose visual density is equal to that of the buildings' shapes. Through this manipulation, the usual figure-ground relationship is dispensed with: foreground and background—culture and nature—are both strained through the camera lens and made to align along a single plane. This is Boogaerts' strategy for conquering the traditional dichotomy, his way of noting that the eternal figure-ground "relationship" has always been, in effect, a schism. The "synthetic image" is thus an agent of healing, of mediation and reconciliation.

But behind this apparent fusion there is still a struggle going on. Beyond the luminous calm of the photographic surface and the seamless perfection of the sequence, two forces oppose each other: the panning movement of the camera can be taken to represent culture in all its greed for distance and information, while the converging perspective which brings each sequence to a close is an eloquent reminder of the limits nature imposes on perception.

—Georges Bogardi

BOSSHARD, Walter.

Nationality: Swiss. **Born:** Richterswil, Lake Zurich, 8 November 1892. **Education:** Educated in Kusnacht, Maennedorf and Zurich, 1899-1910; studied pedagogy and art history, University of Zurich, 1910-14; photography, privately, with advice from Photohaus Ruedi, Lugano, Switzerland, 1927. **Military Service:** Served in the Swiss Army, Fort Brunnen (in the Alps), Switzerland, 1914-18. **Career:** Worked on plantation, and as gemcutter's agent, travelling in Sumatra, Siam and India, 1920-27; documentary photographer and researcher, with Dr. Trinkler and Dr. H. de Terra, German Central Asia Expedition to Tibet and Turkestan, 1927-28; photographer, with agency Dephot (Deutsche Photodienst), Berlin, 1930; correspondent (writer and photographer) for Ullstein publishing house (Berlin), in East Asia, 1930-35; photographer, expedition to Arctic on *Graf Zeppelin* airship, 1931; with Black Star agency, New York, 1935-39; staff correspondent, *Neue Zurcher Zeitung*, Washington, D.C., 1942-45. Also freelance travel and documentary photographer, and journalist, 1926-56: in East Asia (especially Peking), 1936-39, in Balkans, Middle East, Greece, Turkey, and India, 1940, in Chunking, China 1940-41, in San Francisco (United Nations Assembly), 1947, in East Asia (Jenan and Peking), 1948, in Middle East (especially Cairo) and East Asia, 1952, in Korea (suffered accident and ceased photographic activity), 1953, in Geneva and East Asia, 1954: worked for *Berliner Illustrierte, Atlantis, Schweizer Illustrierte Zeitung, Münchner Illustrierte Presse, London Illustrated News, Daily Sketch, Neue Zurcher Zeitung*, etc. Retired, living in Torremolinos and Ronda, Spain, 1960 until his death. **Died:** (in Ronda) 18 November 1975.

Individual Exhibitions:

1977	Kunsthaus, Zurich (retrospective)
1978	International Center of Photography, New York

Selected Group Exhibitions:

1974	*Photographes Suisses depuis 1840 à nos Jours,* Kunsthaus, Zurich
1980	*Arbeitsgemeinschaft Öffentlicher Fotosammlungen* (AÖFS), Zurich (travelled to Essen and Vienna)
1981	*Aus der Sammlung der Stiftung für die Photographie,* Kunsthaus, Zurich
1984	*Swiss Photography from 1840 until Today,* Pro Helvetia Foundation, Zurich (and world tour)

Collections:

Stiftung für die Photographie, Kunsthaus, Zurich.

Publications:

By BOSSHARD: Books—*Durch Tibet und Turkistan,* Stuttgart 1930; *Indien Kämpft,* Stuttgart 1931; *Results of the Botanical Findings, German Centralasian Expedition,* Zurich 1932; *Kühles Grasland Mongolei,* Berlin 1938, Zurich 1949, 1950; *Erlebte Weltgeschichte,* Zurich 1947; *Gefahrenherd der Welt: Generale-Könige-Rebellen,* Zurich 1954; *Thut,* Zurich 1960; *Im Goldenen Sand von Asswan,* Zurich 1962. **Film**—*Mao Tse-Tung and Chou-en-Lai,* 1948.

On BOSSHARD: Books—*Deutschland: Beginn des Modernen Photojournalismus/Photojournalism: Origin and Evolution 1910-1933* by Tim N. Gidal, Lucerne and Frankfurt 1972, New York 1973; *Photographes Suisses depuis 1840 à nos Jours,* exhibition catalogue, by Manuel Gasser, Hugo Loetscher, Walter Binder and Rosellina Burri-Bischof, Zurich 1974; *Walter Bosshard, ein schweizer Pionier des Photojournalismus: Photographien 1927-1939,* exhibition catalogue, with text by Guido Magnaguagno, Zurich 1977; *Neue Sachlichkeit und Surrealismus in der Schweiz 1915-1940,* edited by Rudolf Koella, Berne 1979; *Swiss Photography from 1840 until Today,* exhibition catalogue, with introduction by Hugo Loetscher, Zurich 1984. **Articles**—"Walter Bosshard Siebzigjährig" in *Neue Zürcher Zeitung,* 8 November 1962; "Walter Bosshard Achtzigjährig" in *Neue Zürcher Zeitung,* 8 November 1972; "Walter Bosshard Gestorben" in *Neue Zürcher Zeitung,* 20 November 1975.

*   *   *

Walter Bosshard is still a fragmented, not yet fully explored, fascinating figure. From the start, he accompanied his photographs with articles. He worked in long stretches on one subject, consolidating it into an illustrated book, before going on to the next one. What we do not know is whether he regarded himself as a photographer or as a journalist. Nor have we had the opportunity to see what is on those 15,000 captioned negatives that passed into the hands of the Stiftung für die Photographie, Zurich, after his death. What is certain is that as he became a brilliant political analyst, he disparaged and diminished his photographic efforts. Insight became more important than evidence.

The quality of the work I have seen is uneven, but from the start his best pictures turn out to be portraits of the powerful, spiritual or temporal, perhaps because he realized how power can stabilize or destroy lives. Ultimately his subject was "human rights." He was fearless: remained behind when the Japanese arrived in a Chinese village; flew on the first Japanese flight on their new Charbin-Mukden line, and when they claimed to be dropping only leaflets, showed in a moving photograph two Chinese emerging from a hole in the ground, looking up at departing aircraft.

If he was a pioneer in everything he did, he was also a person who believed in making use of every development modernity offered. Already in India in 1930 he worked with three Leicas, rarely using his little tripod, with flash only for occasional outdoor nightshots.

Whatever the final judgment, Bosshard's photographic coverages of Gandhi and Mao on the threshold of power guarantee him a place in the pantheon of history. Gandhi had vowed not to pose for photographers, but allowed Bosshard to snap him asleep, eating his soup, reading reports on the troubles he had just begun to provoke with his passive resistance efforts.

Bosshard was the first European to interview Mao at Yenan in 1938. His photographs were more mature than before, but he judged rightly that his information was more far reaching. Accordingly, he published this series as articles, illustrated with a few pictures, in the important *Neue Zürcher Zeitung,* which carried them in prime space on their front page.

—Inge Bondi

BOSTELMANN, Enrique.

Nationality: Mexican. **Born:** Guadalajara, 22 March 1939. **Education:** Schools in Mexico; studied photography, under Heinz Schlicht, Alexander Von Humboldt German College, Mexico City, 1956-57; under Franz Bartel, Bayerische Staatslehranstalt der Fotografie, Munich, 1958-60, Dip. Photog. 1960. **Family:** Married the photographer Yevette Noetzel del Castillo in 1966; children: Saskia and Alexis. **Career:** Founder-Director, Fotografia Creativa, S.A., photography studios, Mexico City, since 1960. Secretary, Club Fotografico, Mexico City, 1961-62. Secretary, Foro de Arte Contemporaneo, Mexico City, since 1977. Treasurer, Consejo Mexicano de Fotografia, Mexico City, since 1980. Instructor in Photography, Instituto Paul Coremans, Mexico City, 1964-67. **Address:** (studio) Fotografia Creativa S.A., Nautla 23, Mexico 7, D.F., Mexico.

Individual Exhibitions:

1967	JWT Gallery, New York
1969	Galleria Due Mondi, Rome
1970	Casa de la Cultura, Quito, Ecuador
1971	Galleria de Arte Moderna, Perugia, Italy
1973	*Paisaje del Hombre,* Museo de Arte Moderno, Mexico City
	Universidad de Panama, Panama City (toured Mexico)
1974	*La Piel de las Aguas,* Galería José María Velasco, Mexico City (also at Unidad Xochimilco, Universidad Metropolitana, Mexico City; and travelled to Museo Guayasamin, Quito, Ecuador, and Biblioteca Municipal, Guayaquil, Ecuador, 1975)
1975	Galería Geller, Cali, Colombia
1976	*Fotomorfosis I,* Galería Jose Clemente Orozco, Instituto Nacional de Bellas Artes, Mexico City
	La Piel de las Aguas, Museo de Maracaibo, Barquisimeto, Venezuela (travelled to Valencia, Venezuela)
1977	*Proposiciones Fotográficas,* Galería Arvil 2, Mexico City

Secretaría de Relaciones Exteriores, Mexico City
Mexican Ceramics and Photos, World Trade Center, New York
1978 *Estructura y Biografía de un Objeto,* Galeria Juan Martin,
Mexico City
Fotomorfosis II, Museo de Bellas Artes, Caracas, Venezuela
(travelled to Museo de Artes Graficas, Maracaibo, Venezue-
la; Biblioteca Luis Angel A., Bogota, Colombia; Museo de
Arte Moderno, Buenos Aires)
1979 *Suicidio y Muerte Natural,* Colegio de México, Mexico City
Estructura y Biografía de un Objeto, Universidad Ibero
Americana, Mexico City

Selected Group Exhibitions:

1958 *Photokina '58,* Cologne
1976 *10 Fotografos Mexicanos,* Salon de la Plastica Mexicana,
Mexico City
1977 *Homenaje a Posada,* Academia de Artes Plasticas, San Carlos,
Mexico City
1978 *La Primavera,* Galería Arvil, Mexico City
Exposición Inaugural, Foro de Arte Contemporaneo, Mexico City
Coloquio Latinoamericano de Fotografía, Museo de Arte
Moderno, Mexico City
1980 *Retrato Contemporaneo,* Museo Carrillo Gil, Mexico City
1981 *Hecho en Latino America 2,* Palacio de Bellas Artes,
Mexico City
1982 *La Photographie Contemporaine en Amerique Latine,* Centre
Georges Pompidou, Paris

Collections:

Secretaria de Relaciones Exteriores, Mexico City; Universidad Nacional
Autónoma, Mexico City; Museo Guayasamin, Quito, Ecuador; Museo de
Bellas Artes, Caracas, Venezuela.

Publications:

By BOSTELMANN: Books—*American: Un Viaje a Traves de la Injusticia,*
Mexico City 1970; *El Paisaje de Mexico,* Mexico City 1972; *Estructura y
Biografía de un Objeto,* Mexico City 1979.

On BOSTELMANN: Books—*Photokina '58,* exhibition catalogue, by L.
Fritz Gruber and others, Cologne 1958; *Primer Coloquio Latinoamericano de
Fotografía,* exhibition catalogue, Mexico City 1978; *Hecho en Latino Ameri-
ca 2,* exhibition catalogue, with texts by Pedro Meyer, Lázaro Blanco and
others, Mexico City 1981; *La Photographie Contemporaine en Amerique
Latine,* exhibition catalogue, by Alain Sayag, Paris 1982.

*

Light surrounds the world. The world has so many facets that it is
impossible to capture them all. That is why I feel that the responsibility of the
photographer is to select those which are closest to his way of thinking, feeling
and acting. To achieve this is an arduous process but one which gives great
satisfaction. The quest for achievement as an end in itself should never stop
because, with the help of new impulses and situations, it will regenerate itself.
Ideally it will only end with the end of life itself.

—Enrique Bostelmann

*   *   *

The work of Enrique Bostelmann is quite unusual in the context of
Mexican photography. He is one of those rare photographers who uses color
for works of personal expression; moreover, many of his photographs are a
kind of objectual art: they are made up in real space of three-dimensional
geometric structures. His work involves a somewhat paradoxical investigation. On the one hand he works with virtual space, the legacy of Renaissance

notions of volume and perspective, as is common in photography; on the other
hand, he plays with format in real space, following the experiments of the new-
concretists and of the Argentinian group Madi. Both trends are found in a
single work. Whereas most of his colleagues are mainly concerned with the
relevance of implicit meaning in a photograph, Bostelmann places the
emphasis of his search on formal innovation.

The originality of the endeavors and the photographic solutions of
Bostelmann's work do not emerge without reason. The objectual and elegant
geometrism with which he builds his forms is presently the dominating style in
the spaces of private enterprise and of government institutions. It may be said
as well that Bostelmann's color photography probably emerges from the
chromatic vigor that throbs in all those places that haven't been completely
soiled by smog or made drab by industrial and financial centers. A particular
sense of color is found in the handicrafts, the clothing and the walls of the
houses in Mexico. Bostelmann uses it to convey a harmony of man and his
environment.

To search for anger, criticism, sarcasm or malice in his photographs is to
view them from the wrong perspective. For him the camera is not an
instrument of protest; it is a means for the magic dignification of man. In this
search for the beauty that may appear in the grandiose and in the insignificant,
even in poverty, there is a genuine playfulness. One could say he even has a
certain childlike candor. Another characteristic of his work is his curiosity. In a
search that reminds us of the experiments made by the cubists, he represents an
object from different perspectives. His recent portraits and his formal exploration of a coffee pot are examples of this trend.

Unrelenting in his search for originality and innovation of language,
Enrique Bostelmann astonishes by his unaccustomed combinations and by his
technical virtuosity. He is a classicist in pursuit of balance and beauty, a
photographer who has inherited the western artistic tradition and who expresses himself with reticence, subtlety and joy.

—Katya Mandoki

BOUBAT, Édouard.

Nationality: French. **Born:** Paris, 13 September 1923. **Education:** Studied
printing, design, and typography at the Ecole Estienne, Paris, 1938-42.
Family: Married Bernadette Boubat in 1957; son: Bernard. **Career:** Worked
as a photogravure printer, Paris, 1942-45; first photos, Paris, 1946; free-lance
photographer, Paris, 1946-50; Staff Photographer, *Réalités* magazine, Paris,
1951-68; freelance photojournalist and portrait photographer, Paris, since
1968. **Recipient:** Kodak Prize, 1947; Grand Prix National de Photographie,
Paris, 1984. **Agent:** Agence Rapho, 8 rue d'Alger, 75001 Paris. **Address:** 12
rue Bouchut, 75015 Paris, France.

Individual Exhibitions:

1955 Limelight Gallery, New York
1967 *Edouard Boubat: Ogonblick av Lycka,* Moderna Museet,
Stockholm
1971 Galerie Rencontre, Paris
1973 Bibliothèque Nationale, Paris
1976 Witkin Gallery, New York
Art Institute of Chicago
1978 Museo d'Arte Moderna, Mexico City
Photographers Gallery, London
Musée Nicéphore Niepce, Chalon-sur-Saône, France
1979 Fondation Nationale de la Photographie, Lyons
1980 Musée d'Art Moderne, Paris
1981 Camera Obscura, Stockholm
1982 Witkin Gallery, New York
1985 Galerie Agathe Gaillard, Paris

Selected Group Exhibitions:

1951   *Izis/Brassaï/Doisneau/Facchetti/Boubat,* Galerie La
Hune, Paris
1954   *Great Photographs,* Limelight Gallery, New York
1959   *Salon National de la Photographie,* Bibliothèque
Nationale, Paris
1964   *World Exhibition of Photography: What Is Man?,* Pressehaus
Stern, Hamburg (and world tour)
1977   *Helen Gee & the Limelight,* Carlton Gallery, New York
1978   *Tusen och en bild,* Moderna Museet, Stockholm
1979   *Photographie als Kunst 1879-1979,* Tiroler Landesmuseum
Ferdinandeum, Innsbruck, Austria (travelled to Neue Galerie
am Wolfgang Gurlitt Museum, Linz, Austria; Neue Galerie
am Landesmuseum Joanneum, Graz, Austria; and Museum
des 20. Jahrhunderts, Vienna)
1980   *10 Photographes pour le Patrimoine,* Centre Pompidou, Paris
1982   *Counterparts: Form and Emotion in Photographs,* Metropolitan
Museum of Art, New York (travelled to the Contemporary
Arts Center, Cincinnati; Dallas Museum of Fine Arts, Texas;
San Francisco Museum of Modern Art; Corcoran Gallery,
Washington, D.C.)
1984   *Subjektive Fotografie: Images of the 50s,* San Francisco
Museum of Modern Art (travelled to the University of
Houston, Texas; Museum Folkwang, Essen; Vasterbottens
Museum, Umea; Kulturhuset, Stockholm; Saarland Museum,
Saarbrucken; Palais des Beaux-Arts, Brussels)

Collections:

Bibliothèque Nationale, Paris; Musée Nicéphore Niepce, Chalon-sur-Saône,
France; Museum of Modern Art, New York; Metropolitan Museum of Art,
New York; Art Institute of Chicago; Fondation Cartier, Paris; Museum
Folkwang, Essen, Germany; University of Kansas, Lawrence; Virginia Com-
monwealth University, Richmond.

Publications:

By BOUBAT: Books—*Ode Maritime,* with an introduction by Bernard
George, Tokyo 1957; *Les Nouvelles Messageries de la Presse Parisienne,*
with a preface by Antoine Blondin, Paris 1960; *Edouard Boubat: Collection
Terre d'Images,* with an introduction by Bernard George, Paris 1966; *Femmes/
Woman,* Paris and London 1972, New York 1973; *Miroirs: Autoportraits,*
Paris 1973; *Anges,* with text by Antoine Blondin, Paris 1974; *La Photographie,*
Paris 1974; *La Survivance,* Paris 1976; *L'Ombre de l'Autre,* with text by
Dominique Preschez, Paris 1979; *Preferées,* Paris 1980; *Au Pays du Cheval
d'Orgueil,* with text by Pierre Helias, Paris 1980; *Edouard Boubat,* portfolio,
with an introduction by Robert Doisneau, Paris 1981; *Vues de dos,* with text by
Michel Tournier, Paris 1981; *Jardins et Squares,* with text by Bernard Noel,
Paris 1982; *Les Grandes Photographes: Edouard Boubat,* with text by Jean
Luc Mercie, Paris 1982; *Pauses,* Paris 1983; *I Grandi Fotografi: Edouard
Boubat,* Milan 1983; *Journal de Voyage au Canada,* with text by Michel
Tournier, Paris 1984. **Films**—*Chambre Noire,* television film, 1966; *Photos
by Boubat,* television film, with Rune Hassner, 1967.

On BOUBAT: Books—*Edouard Boubat: Ogonblick av Lycka,* exhibition
catalogue, by Rune Hassner, Stockholm 1967; *Edouard Boubat* by Bernard
George, Lucerne and Frankfurt 1972, New York 1973; *Edouard Boubat,*
edited by Daniel Mauprey, Paris 1973; *La Photographie Français des
Origines à nos Jours* by Claude Nori, Paris 1978; *10 Photographes pour le
Patrimoine,* exhibition catalogue, edited by Jean-Claude Gautrand, Paris
1980; *The Imaginary Photo Museum* by Helmut Gernsheim, Renate and L.
Fritz Gruber and others, Cologne 1981, London 1982; *Counterparts: Form
and Emotion in Photographs* by Weston J. Naef, New York 1982; *Subjektive
Fotografie: Images of the 50s,* exhibition catalogue, by Ute Eskildsen,
Manfred Schmalriede and Dorothy Martinson, Essen, West Germany 1984.
Articles—"Edouard Boubat" by Louis Stettner in *Camera* (Lucerne), May
1950; "Edouard Boubat" in *Photography of the World,* Tokyo 1956; "Boubat,
un des plus poetiques parmi les photographes contemporains" by Romeo
Martinez in *Camera* (Lucerne), June 1956; "Edouard Boubat, Star Photogra-

pher" in *Photography Year Book,* London 1958; "Edouard Boubat" by
Tetsuo Abe in *Molders of Modern Forms,* Tokyo 1959; "Un Temoignage sur
les Vraies Dimensions de l'Art Photographique: l'Univers d'Edouard Boubat"
by Jean Danielou in *Réalités* (Paris), November 1962; "Edouard Boubat,
photographe des instants privileges" by Bernard George in *Terre d'Images*
(Paris), November/December 1964; "Edouard Boubat" by Rune Hassner in
Popular Fotografi (Stockholm), May 1967; "Objectif sur l'Agence Vu" in
Reporter Objectif (Paris), September/October 1971; "Edouard Boubat:
Photographs of Women" in *Creative Camera* (London), June 1972; "Edouard
Boubat" in *Modern Photography Annual,* New York 1974; "Les Cinq Sens
en Eveil: Photos Boubat" by E. Renaudin in *Elle* (Paris), 16 December 1974;
"The Humanistic Eye: Edouard Boubat" by Walter Rosenblum in *35mm
Photography* (New York), Summer 1975; "Edouard Boubat" by Dominique
Dubois in *Photo Cine Review (Paris),* November 1979; "Edouard Boubat" by
Danielle Boune in *Beaux Arts* (Paris), February 1985.

*

I am not ashamed of being a photographer! I love music, painting, and,
above all, life. Life gives me my photos. I need other people. Photography is a
profession for encounters! It is in praise of life, an attempt to come close to
nature and my fellow creatures.

—Édouard Boubat

*   *   *

It was only in the years following World War II that French photographers,
after the years of restrictions and horrors, were able fully to express their
originality through press and magazine photography. Whatever their mode or
method, photographers participated in the moral and economic reconstruction
of the country and attempted a clarification of the social and political milieu.
Two kinds of photographers emerged. Photojournalists analyzed the facts,
informed the public, and tried to provide a witness of the flagrant upheavals of
this world: their pictures were, above all, examples of actuality, fragments of
reality, and often redundant of the texts they accompanied. Another kind of
photographer, difficult to categorize but which one might call humanist,
expressed the poetry of daily life by conveying its simple joys and emotions—
lovers, public balls, children, etc. The images of these photographers took the
form of "Storytelling Pictures" in magazines, and slowly they began to be
exhibited in galleries—for instance, in La Hune in 1951.

Édouard Boubat, who has much in common with the humanists, still
occupies a completely unique place in French photography, a place where
graphic traditions and photographic modernity meet. Always counter-current,
often cut off from "actuality," creating with the passage of time his own
individual space, Boubat remains a kind of living point of reference for young
photographers.

His first photo, in 1946, at the age of 23, "Little Girl in the Dead Leaves,"
is a symbol of all of his work. (It is interesting to remember that at the same
time Capa, Cartier-Bresson and Seymour had begun to lay the foundations of
the Magnum Agency: Boubat's little girl seems to turn her back on them.) In
this slightly blurred photo of not very impressive technique (Boubat was, after
all, a beginner), a little girl drags a train of dead leaves which seem to be poised
as if by magic. We cannot tell where the action takes place or at what point in
time: we are confronted by a photograph which is not only a reflection of
reality but which is also, above all, a photograph by Édouard Boubat. It is a
photograph that refers us to other photographs—"Lella en Bretagne," 1947;
"Le Jardin du Luxembourg," 1955; "Le Masque au Mexique," 1978—as a
word in a sentence or a verse in a poem might suggest the whole—or as one
might say of a Rembrandt—"Ah, this is a Boubat!"

Since 1952, the date of his first reportage for *Réalités,* Boubat has travelled
around the world, from Spain to Africa, from India to China, going through the
United States and capturing there, under the folklore and the brilliance, that
which is true and unchanging. Whereas Robert Frank, like the writers of the
beat generation who let themselves be carried away by their typewriters, threw
in our faces a reality of chaotic emotions and spatterings, Boubat seems to
organize apparent disorder to create a harmonious ensemble within which a
thousand years of human history are interwoven. Consider his depiction of
woman. She is strangely eternal and contemporary, not only an object for
contemplation that fuses architecture and the environment, but also, and more

so, the light that crystallizes vital forces and spiritual energy. She is at once Eve, Beatrice, Juliet and Angela Davis.

Today, Édouard Boubat continues to photograph with the joy and delight of a college boy on vacation. The world may have shrunk around him, but that seems only to have enlarged his creative freedom. More than ever Boubat does Boubat. The subject, the anecdote, may be passé, dissipated. What interests is the meeting of the man with forms and with light, the meeting of the photographer with the images that he carries within himself.

The photographs of Édouard Boubat are the traces of our collective past, the imprints of a paradise invented by our own social subconscious. We truly need them to lighten, to enhance, our daily lives.

—Claude Nori

BOUCHER, Pierre.

Nationality: French. **Born:** Paris, 29 February 1908. **Education:** Studied at the Ecole des Arts Appliqués a l'Industrie, Paris, 1921-25; apprentice at Draeger Frères printing firm, Paris, 1926. **Military Service:** Served as a photographer in the French Air Force, Morocco, 1928-30, 1939-40. **Family:** Married Yvonne Prieur in 1931 (divorced, 1941); son: Jean-Louis; married Suzanne Laroche in 1950. **Career:** Worked as a designer for Printemps and Tolmer publishers, Paris, 1926-28. Since 1930, freelance designer, advertising photographer and photo-muralist, mainly in Paris: worked for Arts et Métiers Graphiques, Printel, Moroccan Railways, Tweedales and Smalley, the British Northern Gas Board, etc. Founder-Member, with Robert Capa, Chim, P. Verger and others, Agence Alliance-Photo photographers agency, Paris, 1933-40, and Agence de Documentation et d'Edition Photographique, Paris, 1945-72; Director of Graphic Services, Marshall Plan, Paris, 1948-52; Artistic Director, Multiphoto agency, Paris, 1952-72.

Individual Exhibitions:

1941	*L'Esprit et la Matière* mural, Convent of the Carmelites, Lyons (permanent exhibition)
1951	*Textile Industry* mural, Tweedales and Smalley, Manchester (permanent exhibition)
1961	*Petrol* mural, Northern Gas Board, New-castle-upon-Tyne (permanent installation)
1974	*Polarisations Photo,* Galerie Camille Renault, Paris
1975	Maison de la Culture, Biot, France
1980	*Projection sur la Vie et l'Humour,* Musée Reattu, Arles, France
1984	*Pierre Boucher temoin de son epoque,* Salle du Consortium, Dijon, France
1986	Musée du Brou, Bourg en Bresse, France

Selected Group Exhibitions:

1937	*Affiche Photo Typo,* Maison de la Culture, Paris
1972	*Salon des Decorateurs,* Grand Palais, Paris
1974	*Art Contemporain,* Hotel de Ville, Pernes les Fontaines, France
1975	*Ecole de Paris de la Photo,* Porte de Versailles, Paris
1976	*Exposition Nationale de la Photo,* Maison de la Culture, Biot, France
1979	*La Photographie Francaise 1925-1940,* Galerie Zabriskie, Paris (and Zabriskie Gallery, New York)
	Photographic Surrealism, New Gallery of Contemporary Art, Cleveland, Ohio (travelled to the Brooklyn Museum, New York)
1983	*Le Corps et Son Image,* Centre Culturel de Bretigny, France
1984	*Groupe d'Animation de la Photographie,* Hotel de Ville, Cholet, France
1985	*Bauhaus-Photographie,* Musée d'Art Moderne de la Ville, Paris

Collections:

Bibliothèque Nationale, Paris; Ministry of Culture, Paris; Musée National d'Art Moderne, Paris; Musée d'Art Moderne de la Ville de Paris; Musée Nicephore Niepce, Chalon sur Saone, France; San Francisco Museum of Modern Art; Museum of Fine Arts, Houston, Texas.

Publications:

By BOUCHER: Books—*Truquages en Photographie,* Paris 1938; *Methode Francaise de Ski,* Paris 1947. **Articles**—"La Photographie Sous-Marine" in *Photo France* (Paris), August 1950; "Photographie Sous Marine" in *Camera* (Lucerne), May 1953.

On BOUCHER: Books—*Formes Nues,* Paris 1935; *Nu en Photographie* by Marcel Natkin, Paris 1935; *Photography of the World,* Tokyo 1956; *Exempla Graphica,* Zurich 1969; *Idea 93* by Noboru Sakamoto, Tokyo 1969; *Idea 150* by Noboru Sakamoto, Tokyo 1978; *La Photographie Francaise* by Claude Nori, Paris 1979; *Le Surrealisme en Photographie,* Paris 1982; *Bauhaus-Photographie,* Paris 1983. **Articles**—"Pierre Boucher" by Remy Duval in *Arts et Metiers Graphiques* (Paris), June 1935; "Photos et Montages de Pierre Boucher" by Walter Herdeg in *Graphis* (Zurich), November 1945; "Pierre Boucher" in *Camera* (Lucerne), January 1947; "The Frieze of Pierre Boucher" in *Photography* (London), July 1950; "La Publication Instructive" in *Camera-Europhot* (Lucerne), May 1960; "La renaissance 1930" in *Photo* (Paris), no. 138, 1979; "La Photographie en Laboratoire: Pierre Boucher" in *Cliches* (Brussels), no. 10, 1984; "Pierre Boucher" in *Camera International* (Paris), no. 3, 1985.

*

From very early on, man felt the need to fix the representation of his environment, to capture the fleeting moment and hold on to the present, to make concrete the intangible. The means have been numerous and each age has produced new methods of realizing this aim.

The inevitable discovery of photography (the brainwave of the painters Leonardo da Vinci, Porta and Daguerre) has opened up a new way of representing the image by using photons of light like a paintbrush and allowing us to go beyond the limitations of our senses, to see the invisible—infra-red, ultra-violet, x-rays—to cut time up into intervals more or less long according to the lengths of obturation which, for example, represent running water as ice or mist.

An area which has interested me for some time is that of polarized light. Although the process, which I call "Optical Painting," is solely concerned with light, it allows me to represent things in new ways which are closest to the methods of painters. Painters too, in their work, use more or less automatic methods in which chance intervenes to reveal new materials and renew their inspiration.

I think that in the not very distant future we will be able, with the aid of electromagnetic waves, to create directly out of our own minds the images of our dream visions and I would not be surprised if such a thing were not already happening via synthesizers and computers.

—Pierre Boucher

*   *   *

The earth and the sky. Between the two the domain of light. There is where the nudes evolve, where the parts of the mural are linked together. Let water flow, and you have the elements of the work of Pierre Boucher.

This play of elements both determine and characterize his work. And Boucher is a unique case, perhaps; he did not learn photography on the ground, but in the air, on airplanes. Similarly, he learned photographic montage by working with military aerial maps, over a table, with a razor blade.

He said of himself in 1935: "I am a wanderer, a nomad. I like nature, sports, cycling, Munkacsi, simplicity and travel. Canoeing and sunbathing are a religion with me."

A religion which led him naturally to the nude. Naturist and unaffected at first, they became increasingly more elaborate, with double exposures, phantasmagorical landscapes. He also liked to photograph his friends in leaps that the shot itself makes aerial.

During the war, for the Pierre Schaeffer group, Boucher worked on a 17-meter long mural on the theme *L'Esprit et la Matière*. By virtue of his training, his experience in photography and in photomontage, he managed to create a veritable visual symphony. The mural form suited him well, and he went on to create three others. Each includes hundreds of negatives and represents several months of work. For the *Methode Francaise de Ski*, he was responsible for all aspects of production, and this book, with its very elaborate structure, can perhaps be considered his manifesto on photography.

With color, too, his creativity never diminishes. His centerfolds and publicity brochures from the 1960's combine invention with graphic expertise. And today his work has to do with large prints on which his virtuoso use of the chromatic scale make geometric subjects vibrant.

Recent publications and exhibitions try to limit Boucher to his surrealist nudes. His domain is much wider. From the first nudes to the iridescent color, from the leaping friends to the cosmic murals, from advertising montages to geometric polychromatics—his work is very rich. It is also consistent in its pursuit of plastic means to enhance images of the aerial, the immaterial, and the dream.

Pierre Boucher is nothing less than one of the outstanding creators in photography of the 20th century.

—Guy Mandery

BOURDEAU, Robert.

Nationality: Canadian. **Born:** Kingston, Ontario, 14 November 1931. **Education:** Self-taught in photography, from 1959. **Family:** Married Mary Eardley in 1961; sons: Robbie and Sean. **Career:** Since 1969, freelance photographer, Ottawa. Master Class Instructor, Banff School of Fine Arts, Alberta, 1979; Part-time Professor, University of Ottawa, 1980-81. **Recipient:** Canada Council Grant, 1971, 1974, 1978; Ontario Arts Council Grant, 1976, 1980. **Agent:** Jane Corkin Gallery, 144 Front Street West, Toronto, Ontario. **Address:** 1462 Chomley Crescent, Ottawa, Ontario K1G OV1, Canada.

Individual Exhibitions:

1966	National Film Board of Canada, Ottawa (toured Canada)
1969	Bibliothèque Centrale, Lucerne, Quebec
1971	Toronto Gallery of Photography
	Université de Sherbrooke, Quebec
	Federation des Centres Culturels de Quebec, Montreal (toured Quebec)
1973	The Photographers Gallery, Saskatoon, Saskatchewan
	The Photography Gallery, Bowmanville, Ontario
1974	Photo Image 33 Limited, Kingston, Ontario
1975	Deja Vu Gallery, Toronto
1976	Owens Art Gallery, Sackville, New Brunswick
	National Film Board of Canada, Moncton, New Brunswick
	The Banff Centre, Alberta
	Yajima Gallery, Montreal
	The Gallery of Photography, North Vancouver, Ontario
	Sunbury Shores Arts Centre, St. Andrews, New Brunswick
	Village Olympique, Montreal
	Southern Alberta Art Gallery, Lethbridge
	Vanier College, St. Laurent, Quebec
1977	Carleton University, Ottawa

	Secession Gallery of Photography, Victoria, British Columbia
	Artspace, Peterborough, Ontario
1978	Moulinette Gallery, Cornwall, Ontario
	Musée Regional des Mines et des Arts, Malartic, Quebec
	Memorial University Art Galley, St. John's, Newfoundland
1979	New Brunswick Craft School, Fredericton
	Mt. Allison University, Sackville, New Brunswick
	Agnes Etherington Art Center, Queen's University, Kingston, Ontario
	Edward's Art and Books, Toronto
1981	Art Gallery of Ontario, Toronto (with Philip Pocock)
1983	Jane Corkin Gallery, Toronto
	Afterimage Gallery, Dallas, Texas

Selected Group Exhibitions:

1967	*Photography '67*, National Film Board of Canada, Ottawa
1968	*Light⁷*, Hayden Gallery, Massachusetts Institute of Technology, Cambridge
1970	*The Photograph as Object*, Art Gallery of Ontario, Toronto
1972	*Canada, C'Est Quoi*, National Film Board of Canada, Ottawa
1973	*Commonwealth Conference Exhibition*, Canadian Government Conference Centre, Ottawa
	7 Photographers, National Film Board of Canada, Ottawa
1979	*The Banff Purchase*, Banff Centre, Alberta
1984	*Canadian Contemporary Photography*, National Film Board of Canada, Ottawa

Collections:

National Gallery of Canada, Ottawa; Canadian Centre for Contemporary Photography, Ottawa; Canada Council Arts Bank, Ottawa; Ontario Institute of Studies in Education, Toronto; Agnes Etherington Arts Centre, Queen's University, Kingston, Ontario; Musée d'Art Contemporain, Montreal; The Banff Centre, Alberta; Smithsonian Institution, Washington, D.C.

Publications:

By BOURDEAU: Book—*Robert Bourdeau*, edited by Lorraine Monk, Toronto 1979. **Articles**—"The Meditated Image" in *Photo Age* (Montreal), March 1965; "A Portfolio of Photographs" in *Habitat* (Ottawa), September 1972.

On BOURDEAU: Books—*Canada: A Year of the Land*, edited by Lorraine Monk, Ottawa 1967; *Image 2: Canada*, edited by Lorraine Monk, Ottawa 1967; *Light⁷*, edited and with text by Minor White, Millerton, New York 1968; *Image 3: Other Places*, edited by Lorraine Monk, Ottawa 1968; *Image 5: Seeds of the Spacefields*, edited by Lorraine Monk, Ottawa 1969; *The Photographers' Choice*, edited by Kelly Wise, Danbury, New Hampshire 1976; *12 Canadians*, edited by Jane Corkin, Toronto 1980; *Canadian Contemporary Photography* by Martha Langford, Edmonton, Alberta 1984. **Articles**—"Robert Bourdeau" in *Camera* (Lucerne), August 1969; "An Inquiry into the Aesthetics of Photography," edited by Anne Brodzky, special issue of *Artscanada* (Toronto), December 1974; "Robert Bourdeau's Landforms" in *Artscanada* (Toronto), May/June 1977; "Robert Bourdeau, Ultimate Amateur" in *Photo Life* (Toronto), July 1978; "More Than the Eye Can See" in *Maclean's* (Toronto), December 1979; "La Mise Entre Parentheses du Sublime par la Photographie et Quelques Examples Chez Robert Bourdeau" in *Parachute* (Montreal), Spring 1981.

*

I work in the landscape and, through its forces and rhythms, have sought its inner strength and mystery.

Many things are significant and must come together before an image is realized on the ground glass and ultimately in the fine print. Areas of activity must function individually within the whole context of the picture and have a life of their own. All things in the image must have substance and be revealed. Working with amorphous subjects, the organization of the structural complexities within the format becomes extremely important. The logic of photographic space must be well served.

A sensitivity to nuances and an interaction between myself and the landscape are paramount. A lucid craftsman is central to all of these things. The beauty, subtlety and presence of the contact print is also central to my camerawork.

I have discovered that one of the most significant functions of "camerawork" may be based on the developed ability to stand aside and watch oneself be lost in one's own photograph or object to be photographed, or one understood, and thereby find oneself. Others may also find rapport with their own inner feelings while in a state of receptivity with an intense image.

So many pictures today cry out shrilly, Stop and look at me. And the "me" they ask you to look at is not the photographer's gifts of vision, but the photographer himself. The forced drama of tone and line, the stunts, the visual shocks force the onlooker to feel not the object or person photographed, but the author's obsessive demand for attention and recognition. The quantity of work today that asks instead of gives is tragic. It speaks of the waste of human beings and their creativity. It says that we are not strong enough to make what contributions we can without the applause of an audience.

It is the responsibility of the photographer who employs "camerawork" as his medium to produce pictures which are as free of the author's personal contingencies as possible. His images must have a "transparency."

Only an image born, not made, is free. And freedom of the eye and heart will come to him who loves things not for his egotistical self to exploit for personal gain or satisfaction, but who loves things and other persons as they are—for their own unique being.

—Robert Bourdeau

*   *   *

Robert Bourdeau is the most paradoxical photographer in Canada. The gelatin silver contact prints from his view camera (11 x 14 or 8 x 10) contain immense vistas, crackling with energy in all four corners. When he chooses the bare landscape of the southwestern United States like Utah and Arizona (1973 and 1976), the images are sparse and austere. Places like Canada's Muskoka, which he visited in the late 1960's and early 70's, Gatineau Park (1965 onwards) or the Wordsworthian England (1975 and 1980) are rich and lush. But it's not the imagery which matters as much as his perception, especially of the structure of the land and its complexity. Bourdeau met Minor White in 1958, and it meant something to him, not so much because White's photographs were the "equivalent of a frame of mind" but because White told him about photography's way of seeing.

Bourdeau wants to reveal everything, he says—as much depth as possible (the perspective is almost hallucinatory), the immensity of distance. But he stresses an exquisitely subtle and continous tonal range in black and white. Nothing is out of focus, but the space is ambiguous. The landscape tilts into two-dimensions. Scale is hard to determine. There's an underlying sense of tension. In seeing everything, the viewer notices, most of all, the passage of time. Tombstones, though fused to and absorbed by the landscape, are time made visible—and Bourdeau uses the space which surrounds them positively; he plays with almost tactile views of astonishing clarity, stressing the interacting forces on the surface to create a complex, overall tapestry. "I like things to flow," he says.

There are other paradoxes. These "things as they are" are filled with an inner luminosity and radiance, a sense of mystery and quiet power. At first glance cool, they have a compelling emotional and hypnotic life. They are riveting evidence of Bourdeau's "new-found land."

—Joan Murray

BOURDIN, Guy.

Nationality: French. **Born:** Paris, in 1933. **Education:** Studied art and design, Paris; self-taught in photography, from 1950. **Military Service:** Served in the French Army, in Africa, 1950-51. **Career:** Independent painter and photographer, Paris, 1952-55. Since 1955, freelance professional fashion and advertising photographer, Paris: worked for *Vogue* magazine, in New York, 1957-58, and in Paris, from 1960; for Charles Jourdan shoes, Paris, from 1966; for *Harper's Bazaar* magazine, in Paris, 1969; for Grès and Bloomingdale's fashions, 1976. Worked with M.A.F.I.A. (Maime Arnodin Fayolle International Associés) agency, Paris, 1973.

Selected Group Exhibitions:

1961	*Salon International du Portrait Photographique,* Bibliothèque Nationale, Paris
1977	*Documenta 6,* Museum Fridericianum, Kassel, West Germany
	The History of Fashion Photography, International Museum of Photography at George Eastman House, Rochester, New York, (travelled to Brooklyn Museum of Art, New York; San Francisco Museum of Modern Art; Cincinnati Art Institute, Ohio; Museum of Fine Arts, St. Petersburg, Florida)
1978	*Photokina 78,* Cologne
1982	*Color as Form,* International Museum of Photography at George Eastman House, Rochester, New York

Publications:

On BOURDIN: Books—*Women by 10,* edited by the Playboy Press, Chicago 1973; *Photography as Art* by Volker Kahmen, Tubingen, West Germany 1973, London 1974; *Documenta 6: Band 2,* exhibition catalogue, edited by Klaus Honnef and Evelyn Weiss, Kassel, West Germany 1977; *French Photography from its Origins to the Present* by Claude Nori, Paris 1978, London 1979; *The History of Fashion Photography* by Nancy Hall-Duncan, New York 1979; *The Vogue Book of Fashion Photography* by Polly Devlin, with introduction by Alexander Liberman, New York and London 1979; *World Photography,* edited by Bryn Campbell, London 1981. **Articles**— "Pussy Galore: The Cat Drawings of Guy Bourdin" in *Avant-Garde* (New York), March 1969; "Huite photographes aoutour d'une modele de 18 ans" in *Photo* (Paris), June 1971; "Guy Bourdin" in *Photo* (Paris), September 1972; "Vogue Paris" by Claude Nori in *Progresso Fotografico* (Milan), December 1972; "MAFIA: A successful Advertising Agency in Paris" by A. Alexandre in *Novum* (Munich), September 1974; "Guy Bourdin for Charles Jourdan" in *Art Direction* (New York), December 1975; "French Fashion's Kinky Look" by M. Orth and others in *Newsweek* (New York), 4 October 1976; "The Fanciful Catalogue" in *Art Direction* (New York), November 1976; "Guy Bourdin" in *Photo* (Paris), August 1977.

*   *   *

While the birth of fashion photography—and, indeed, commercial photography generally—can be traced back to the mid 19th century, in the sense in which it is regarded today, it can only be properly discussed with reference to the period immediately preceding the First World War and the 1920s and '30s. The convergence of diverse factors such as developments in photography, innovations in photographic techniques of printing and developing, and a general relaxation of the rules governing fashion, gave rise to conditions in which magazines such as *Harper's Bazaar, Art et Décoration* or *Vogue* could set a trend that, with changes and modifications, has continued to the present day.

Although the aims of commercial and fashion photography vary, they converge, in reality, in a single ambition—to draw attention and to convey select information. It was soon apparent that women could be of great use here and that the allure of the female body as well as that of femininity and beauty could be turned to advantage. As time passed, woman-as-tool became not only a useful but also a perfected technique and successive generations of photographers extended the degree and range of uses to which it could be applied. On the whole, and like their models, these photographers were anonymous and simply addressed themselves to fulfilling the tasks they were set. In this sense, this photography is predominantly utilitarian rather than artistic. However, there is a small group of photographers who, thanks to their talent, imagination and ability to impose their vision on others, were able to break away from this pattern. One of the most interesting of these was definitely Guy Bourdin.

Bourdin, who studied drawing and art in his youth and, as a painter, hoped to become Man Ray's assistant, attributes his success to his rejection of rules that had prevailed for decades—he did not attach ultimate importance to the advertised product but, instead, concentrated on the ways in which he could use it to draw attention. Putting his artistic education to good use and remaining, as he himself admits, under the early influence of Edward Weston's abstract ideas, he created photographs that were startling in their composition, colour combinations, make-up techniques, etc. Rejecting all the photographic conventions used in advertising up to that time, he presented astonishing pictures in which it was not immediately apparent just what was being advertised and in which models appeared without heads or torsos—photographs with no clear content that appeared simply fortuitous if not indifferent. Despite appearances, however, the composition of these photographs was not fortuitous but explicitly calculated with a great deal of attention to detail, particulars, etc. While there is no action or narrative in these photographs, their strangeness or drama makes itself felt immediately. For, through photography, Bourdin masterfully creates a diversity of moods—from melodrama, through surrealism and expressionist visions, even to sexual desire. "Whether or not I create art is not of importance to me," Bourdin replies to critics. "For me, photography is a means of expressing my wonderment at objects or certain people, a way of celebrating the poetry of nature or the melancholy of passing time. . . . "

This photography, as novel as it was absurd when it first appeared, has, with the passage of time, become an accepted vehicle for modern advertising. Given its visual attraction and photographic interest, it has found imitators. It was Bourdin, however, who formed the style.

Now, not only Charles Jourdan's shoes but also perfumes, jewelery, underwear and many other products are advertised in this way. While, in the accumulation of this photography, Bourdin's originality and power is sometimes lost, the awareness that yet another standard has been overthrown and that photography has moved forward, even in as commonplace and commercial a field as advertising, remains.

—Ryszard Bobrowski

BRAECKMAN, Dirk (Raymond Angèle).

Nationality: Belgian. **Born:** Eeklo, Belgium, 15 June 1958. **Education:** Studied film and photography at the Royal Academy of Fine Arts, Ghent, 1977-81. **Career:** Co-founder of Gallery XYZ, Ghent, 1982-89; co-founder of photography magazine *XYZ*, 1983-85. **Recipient:** 1st prize "Provinciale Prijs Oost-Vlaanderen," Belgium, 1985; 1st prize "Photographie Experimentale," Jette, Belgium, 1985; 1st prize "Provinciale Prijs Antwerpen," Antwerp, 1987; 1st prize "Kodak Award," Brussels, 1989; 1st prize "Preis für Junge Europäische Fotografen," Germany, 1990. **Address:** Leest 29, 9950 Waarschoot, Belgium.

Individual Exhibitions:

1985-89	Gallery Perspektief, Rotterdam, Netherlands
	Gallery Ken Damy, Milan, Italy
	Gallery Vrais Rêves, Lyon, France
	Espace Contretype, Brussels
	Maison de la Culture Côte-des-Neiges, Montreal, Canada
	Studio 666, Paris
	Gallery Moment, Hamburg, Germany
1990	Gallerie Forum, Tarragona, Spain
	Gallery DBS, Antwerp, Belgium
	Contretype, Hôtel Hannon, Brussels
1991	Gallery Détour, Namur, Belgium
	Gallery S. and H. De Buck, Ghent, Belgium
1992	Gallery L.A., Frankfurt, Germany
	Gallery Réverbère 2, Lyon, France
1993	Contretype, Hôtel Hannon, Brussels
	Gallery S. and H. De Buck, Ghent, Belgium

Selected Group Exhibitions:

1985-89	*Junge Europäische Fotografen,* Frankfurt, Germany
	Iniatief '86, Gallery XYZ, Ghent, Belgium
	Jeune Peinture, Museum for Fine Arts, Brussels
	Troisième Triennale Internationale de la Photographie, Museum for Fine Arts, Charleroi, Belgium
	Autorretrato, Narcissismo or Provocación? Foco, Circulo de Bellas Artes, Madrid, Spain
	Journées Internationales de la Photographie, Hôtel de Ville, Montpelier, France
	Festival Photo, Museum for Modern Art, Liège, Belgium
	Bruce Vellick Gallery, San Francisco
	Mise-en-scène, Museum for Photography, Antwerp, Belgium (travelled to Brakke Grond, Amsterdam, Netherlands)
	Belgian Contemporary Photography, Marcus Pfeifer Gallery, New York
	Het Portret, Canon Gallery, Amsterdam, Netherlands
	Biennal Barcelona, Centre de la Cultura Contemporania, Barcelona, Spain
	Kodak Award, Arles, France
1990	*Mai de la Photo,* Reims, France
	Junge Europäische Fotografen, Martin Grophius Bau, Berlin
1991	*D'oeil et Mémoires,* Centre Culturel Namur, Namur, Belgium
	La Photographie Belge, Palais de Tokyo, Paris
1992	*Portret,* ICC, Antwerp, Belgium
	Mai de la Photo/A l'image de rien, Epernay, Reims, France
	L'Echappée Européenne, Leverkusen, Germany (travelled to Pavillon des Arts, Paris)
1993	*A la recherche du Père,* l'Espace Photographique, Paris
	L'Histoire de la Photographie Belge, Museum for Photography, Charleroi, Belgium
	Jonge Helden, Museum for Photography, Antwerp, Belgium
	Europese Oefeningen, Galerie DBS, Antwerp, Belgium
	Contemporary Belgian Photography, Gallery Philippe Staib/ Art Wall + B, New York
	La Matière L'Ombre, La Fiction, Bibliothèque National de France

Collections:

Bibliothèque Nationale, Paris; Provinciaal Museum voor Fotografie, Antwerp, Belgium; Musée de la Photographie, Charleroi, Belgium; Ministerie van Vlaamse Gemeenschap, Belgium; Musée de l'Elysée, Lausanne, Switzerland; Museum of Modern Art, San Fransico; Paris Audiovisuel; Fondation Nationale d'Art Contemporain, Paris; Museum of Modern Art, Houston, Texas.

From the ''E'' Series, **1993.** Photograph by Dirk Braeckman.

Publications:

By BRAECKMAN: Book—*Dirk Braeckman,* 1992.

On BRAECKMAN: Articles—*European Photography* (Germany), No. 25, 1985; *Magazine Perspektief* (Rotterdam), No. 22, 1985; *Progresso Fotografico* (Milan), No. 12, 1986; *Photovision 18,* (Madrid), 1987; *Café Crème,* No. 6, 1987; *Photographias* (Greece), May/June 1988; *Clichés* (Brussels), No. 43, 1988; *Foto* (Netherlands), No. 4, 1988; *European Photography,* No. 40, 1989; *Photojournal 9, Asahicamera* (Japan), 1990; *Openbaar Kunstbezit* (Belgium),

No. 2, 1990; *Photographies,* No. 33, 1991; *European Photography,* No. 45, 1991; *European Photography,* No. 53, 1993.

*   *   *

Much has already been written about Dirk Braeckman: that he created tormented icons of wretchedness or that he was the photographic counterpart of Francis Bacon; that he involved himself only with the dark side of life, with the ''black holes'' of being; or that the demons of his obsessions urged him into an extravagant form of photographic expressionism.

I doubt whether these statements say anything significant about Braeckman's photographs. They simply place his work in a very isolated corner. Dirk Braeckman is neither a pessimist flirting with personal perversions, nor an eccentric clairvoyant or a "photographer maudit." His motivation is as simple as it is clear. He takes photos and continues to take photos because he has to. His work is thus in a constant process of evolution.

If it is true that you never get a second chance at a first impression, then my first, indelible glimpse of Dirk Braeckman's work is forever encapsulated in words such as overwhelming, feverish, disturbing, passionate, intangible, by the grace of darkness.

Together with Marc Trivier, Dirk Braeckman (born in Eeklo, 1958) is, in my opinion, one of the most important exponents of contemporary Belgian photography. Whereas the former, with his portraits of world famous artists, of maniacs and slaughtered animals, works in a somewhat academic but rebellious manner—the essence of Trivier's oeuvre lies in the erudite connections which can be made between the photographs—Dirk Braeckman actually defines his images in the darkroom. In the past the figures portrayed were almost violated by his techniques of rubbing and brushing with developer. More recently the processing has been more subtle, more concerned with the final image. Partial solarisation and purposive manipulation by rubbing the developer creates one-off images of what took place in front of the camera.

The story remains in the first instance autobiographical (photo-biographical). Every portrait is a self-portrait. Together they form fragments of an extremely selective diary of images; the life, loves and encounters of Dirk Braeckman. He selects and preserves. In the end he is the only person who saw his friends, colleagues and acquaintances. . . .as they were, there at that very moment. He was the only person who spoke with them, gave some indications or said absolutely nothing. . . .They gave him exactly what we see and they more or less bared themselves to him. What is intriguing is this dramatic tension between what people want to reveal about themselves and what they actually reveal.

Braeckman's language in images formulates itself further in frontal portraits, often almost life-sized with a claustrophobic frame and veiled in a dark matt silver grey haze. Reality is enhanced and at the same time his models do not become exposed. He seems to assure them that they can show everything and still remain safe. No-one can touch their deepest self.

Dirk Braeckman is concerned, above all, with his existence as an event. His conflicting emotions which give rise to an intuitive unveiling of a strictly personal reality, transforms the voyeur into a visionary. Braeckman does not make photos with malice aforethought; the staging seems to occur spontaneously, without being staged. "Whatever happens near the frame also wants to be inside it." A photograph by Dirk Braeckman is not a mirror; at the moment it is a momentary reflection.

"So what was life? It was warmth, the heated product of a restlessness taking form, a fever of matter. . . .It was the existence of that which could not actually exist, of that which balanced on the edge of existence as on a knife-edge in this enclosed and frenzied process of decay and renewal." (Thomas Mann, *The Magic Mountain,* 1924)

—Erik Eelbode

BRAKE, (John) Brian.

Nationality: New Zealander. **Born:** Wellington, 27 June 1927. **Education:** Attended Papanui primary school in Christchurch, and at Christchurch Boys' High School, 1941-44. **Career:** Photographer since 1945: Assistant, Spencer Digby Portraiture Studio, Wellington, 1945-49; Cameraman/Director, New Zealand National Film Unit, Wellington, 1949-53; Member of Magnum Photos, Paris and New York, 1955-66; freelance photographer, as member of Rapho agency, working for *Life, Paris-Match, National Geographic, Epoca, Horizon,* etc., since 1966, now based in Auckland. Founder-Director, Zodiac Films documentary film unit, Hong Kong, 1970. **Recipient:** British Council Bursary, 1949; Award of Merit, American Society of Magazine Photographers, 1961; Merit Award, Art Directors Club of New York, 1965, 1967, 1984; Award of Excellence, 9th Exhibition of Communication Arts, 1968; Award of Excellence, *Communication Graphics,* 1970; Order of Merit, Government of

Egypt, 1970; Art Directors and Artists Club of San Francisco Merit Awards, 1978; Pata Film Festival Award, 1984. Associate, Royal Photographic Society, London, 1947; Honorary Fellow, New Zealand Professional Photographers Association, 1978, and Photographic Society of New Zealand, 1984; Fellow, New Zealand Academy of Fine Arts, 1986. M.Sc.: Brooks Institute of Photography Art and Science, Santa Barbara, California, 1983. Officer, Order of the British Empire(O.B.E.), 1981. **Agents:** Photo Researchers Inc., 60 East 56th Street, New York, New York 10022, U.S.A.; Agence Rapho, 8 rue d'Alger, 75001 Paris, France; and John Hillelson Agency, 145 Fleet Street, London EC4, England.

Individual Exhibitions:

1956	*We the People,* Auckland Art Gallery (toured New Zealand)
1976	*Brian Brake: 40 Photographs,* Dowse Art Gallery, Lower Hutt, Wellington (toured New Zealand, 1976-78)
1978	*Tangata: The Maori Vision of Man,* Musée de l'Homme, Paris (and world tour, 1978-80)
1983	*China of the Chinese,* Galerie Legard, Wellington (travelled to Canterbury Arts Centre, Christchurch; Art Gallery of Omarau; Otago Museum, Dunedin)
1984	*Kahurangi,* Pacific Asia Museum, Pasadena, California

Selected Group Exhibitions:

1963	*Photo Essays,* Museum of Modern Art, New York
1964	*World Exhibition of Photography: What Is Man?,* Pressehaus Stern, Hamburg (and world tour)
1975	*The Land: 20th Century Landscape Photographs Selected by Bill Brandt,* Victoria and Albert Museum, London (travelled to the National Gallery, Edinburgh; Ulster Museum, Belfast; and National Museum of Wales, Cardiff, 1976)
1976	*Eye of the Beholder,* Squibb and Sons, Princeton, New Jersey
1980	*Body Electric,* Squibb and Sons, Princeton, New Jersey
1983	*British Photography 1955-65,* The Photographers' Gallery, London
1984	*Sammlung Gruber,* Museum Ludwig, Cologne

Collections:

Victoria and Albert Museum, London; National Gallery of New Zealand, Wellington.

Publications:

By BRAKE: Books—*The Chinese Smile,* with text by Nigel Cameron, London 1958; *New Zealand: Gift of the Sea,* with text by Maurice Shadbolt, Christchurch, New Zealand 1963, 1964, 1974; *Peking: A Tale of Three Cities,* New York 1965, 1977; *The House on the Klong,* Bangkok 1968; *The Sculpture of Thailand,* New York 1972; *Form und Farbe,* Cologne 1972; *New Zealand Potters: Their Work and Words,* with text by Doreen Blumhardt, Wellington 1976; *Hong Kong,* with text by R.S. Elegant, London 1977; *Legend and Reality: Early Ceramics from South East Asia,* with text by Roxanna M. Brown and others, Kuala Lumpur 1977; *Rome and Her Empire,* with text by Barry Cunliffe, New York and London 1978; *The Sacred Image,* Cologne 1979; *The Art of the Pacific,* with text by James McNeish and David Simmons, London and New York 1980; *Sydney,* with Time-Life editors, London 1980; *Craft New Zealand,* with text by Doreen Blumhardt, Wellington 1981; *Batik— Fabled Cloth of Java,* with text by Inge McCabe-Elliott, New York 1984. **Films**—*Ancient Egypt,* with Time-Life, 1969; documentaries on Indonesia, including *Borobudur: The Cosmic Mountain, Batik: The Magic Cloth, Ramayana, The Eternal Cycle: Festivals of Life and Death,* and *Indonesian Safari,* 1970-75.

On BRAKE: Books—*Histoire d'Aujourd'hui,* with texts by G. Bonheur, M. Clerc, J. Farran and M. Bisiaux, Paris 1957; *The Picture History of Photography* by Peter Pollack, New York 1958; *Photojournalism,* by Time-Life editors, New York 1971; *Brian Brake: 40 Photographs,* exhibition catalogue, Wellington 1976; *British Photography 1955-1965: The Master Craftsmen in*

Print, exhibition catalogue, by Sue Davies, Michael Rand, Mark Boxer and others, London 1983; *Sammlung Gruber: Photographie des 20. Jahrhunderts,* exhibition catalogue, with foreword by Siegfried Gohr, Cologne 1984.

*

Photography is my life and language.

—Brian Brake

*   *   *

Looking at some of Brian Brake's photographs, one feels that there was a series of shots leading up to the one chosen. Brake intuitively anticipates: he takes what might be called a past, present and future record of the subject or event; he then selects a frame that represents the present, which is in fact the psychological moment at which a photograph epitomises the build-up and hints at the denouement. The student with a 35mm camera would find it instructive to see the entire film strip, for the selection of the frame is part of Brake's art.

Though he has gained international fame, Brake is a born New Zealander, and it is in his home photography that he is most individual and shows the fullest interpretation of nature into photography. The work he exhibits—such as his *40 Photographs*—reveals more of his ambition than of his style. It is when he has to provide photographs for his books, such as *New Zealand: Gift of the Sea,* where he portrays subjects as varied as sheep mustering, the Rugby scrum, placid lakes, and boiling springs, that it becomes evident that he is consciously documenting. This has given him a recognizable style, a character similar to that of Cartier-Bresson. The New Zealand scene, neither human nor landscape, is not patently tense; there are no scenes of poverty, there is no majesty like the Grand Canyon. It is necessary to create a photographic tenseness to arrest and interest. Brake uses black-and-white and colour. His tendency is to show human activity in terms of the tonal scale, and to use the spectral scale for portraying moods, atmosphere, and superlatives.

Brake's creativity in photography is in presenting highly informative illustrations. He is not always so successful when he is commissioned to photograph given subjects, such as the large number of ethnographic artefacts in museum collections used in *The Art of the Pacific,* where a desire to create pictures with dramatic lighting detracts from the information inherent in the items.

But the failures are few. Brake takes his place in the tradition of intensive documentary photography which New Zealand has nurtured. Though early New Zealand photographers such as J.W. Allen and D.L. Mundy are known only to photohistorians, Alfred Burton was awarded the Fellowship of the Royal Geographical Society for his ethnographic photography of the Maori people, and his work has been valued by museums throughout the world. Others followed this documentary approach. Brake's *Monsoon,* which was exhibited at the Museum of Modern Art in New York, is a most sensitive documentary in this tradition, and it has received international recognition.

Brian Brake concentrates on the more intrinsic aspects of life and avoids the trivialities of the passing scene. But though he is objective and serious in showing life as it is, he is also thrilled by his subjects and excited about his photography—and his attitude is infectious.

—Hardwicke Knight

BRANDT, Bill.

Nationality: British. **Born:** Hamburg, Germany in May 1904; raised mainly in Germany and Switzerland. **Education:** Largely self-taught in photography, from 1925; student-assistant to the photographer Man Ray, Paris, 1929-30. **Family:** Married to Noya Brandt. **Career:** Freelance social documentary photographer, working for *Weekly Illustrated, Picture Post, Verve,* etc., London, 1931-39; photographer for *Lilliput* magazine, London, 1939-45; worked on photographic survey of bomb shelters for the Home Office, London, also as a documentary photographer for the National Buildings

Record, London, 1940-45. Freelance photographer, London, 1945 until his death in 1983; spent part of each year in Provence, from 1959. Honorary doctorate: Royal College of Art, London, 1977. Member of the Faculty, Royal Designers for Industry. Honorary Fellow, Royal Photographic Society of Great Britain, 1980. **Agent:** Marlborough Fine Art, 6 Albemarle Street, London W1X 3HF, and Marlborough Gallery, 40 West 57th Street, New York, New York 10019. **Died:** (in London) 20 December 1983.

Individual Exhibitions:

1938   *Londres de Nuit,* Galerie du Chasseur d'Images, Paris
1948   Museum of Modern Art, New York
1969   Museum of Modern Art, New York (retrospective; travelled to the Hayward Gallery, London, 1970, then toured the U.K.)
1972   British Council Travelling Exhibition (toured European cities)
1973   Witkin Gallery, New York
1974   The Photographers' Gallery, London
          Collages, Kinsman Morrison Gallery, London
1975   *Early Photographs 1930-1942,* Hayward Gallery, London
          Musée Nicéphore Niepce, Chalon-sur-Saône
          Photogalerie, Paris
1976   Marlborough Fine Art, London
          Marlborough Gallery, New York
          Cronin Gallery, Houston
          Galerie du Chateau d'Eau, Toulouse
          Palais des Beaux-Arts, Charleroi, Belgium
1977   Vision Gallery, Boston (with Brassaï and Berenice Abbott)
          Brandt/Gibson/Klein, Vrije Universiteit, Amsterdam (with Ralph Gibson and Aart Klein)
1978   Moderna Museet, Stockholm
1979   *Perspective of Nudes,* Zeit-Foto Salon, Tokyo Galerij Paule Pia, Antwerp
1980   *Nudes,* Petit Trianon de Bagatelle, Paris
          Early Nudes, Galerie zur Stockerreg, Zurich
          Galerie et Fils, Brussels (with Mario Giacomelli and Aleksandras Macijauskas)
1981   Worcester Art Museum, Massachusetts
          National Centre of Photography, Bath, England
          Marlborough Gallery, London
          Edwynn Houk Gallery, Chicago
          Early Photographs 1930-1942, University of Kent Library, Canterbury (toured the U.K.)
          Zeit Foto Salon, Tokyo
1982   *Photographs by Bill Brandt: 1929-1975,* Art Gallery of Ontario, Toronto
          Selected Works 1930-76, Perimeter Press, Chicago
1983   International Center of Photography, New York
          London by Night, The Photographers' Gallery, London
1984   De Beyerd Centrum, Breda, Netherlands Impressions Gallery, York
          Literary Britain, Victoria and Albert Museum, London
1986   *Behind the Camera,* Burden Gallery, New York
1993   *Bill Brandt Photographs 1928-1983,* Barbican Art Gallery, London
          Bill Brandt: Assemblages, Reed's Wharf Gallery, London
1994   *Bill Brandt Photographs 1928-1983,* Centre National de la Photographie, Paris

Selected Group Exhibitions:

1955   *The Family of Man,* Museum of Modern Art, New York (and world tour)
1967   *Photography in the 20th Century,* National Gallery of Canada, Ottawa (toured Canada and the United States, 1967-73)
1975   *The Land: 20th Century Landscape Photographs Selected by Bill Brandt,* Victoria and Albert Museum, London (travelled to the National Gallery, Edinburgh; Ulster Museum, Belfast; and National Museum of Wales, Cardiff, 1976)

Francis Bacon Walking on Primrose Hill, London, **1963.** Photograph by Bill Brandt.

1977   *Concerning Photography,* The Photographers' Gallery, London (travelled to the Spectro Workshop, Newcastle upon Tyne)
1979   *Photographie als Kunst 1879-1979,* Tiroler Landesmuseum, Innsbruck (travelled to the Neue Galerie am Wolfgang Gurlitt Museum, Linz, Austria; Neue Galerie am Landesmuseum Joanneum, Graz, Austria; and Museum des 20. Jahrhunderts, Vienna)
1980   *Modern British Photography 1919-39,* Museum of Modern Art, Oxford
1982   *Lichtbildnisse: Das Porträt in der Fotografie,* Rheinisches Landesmuseum, Bonn
1983   *British Photography 1955-65,* The Photographers' Gallery, London
1984   *Subjektive Fotografie: Images of the 50s,* San Francisco Museum of Modern Art (travelled to the University of Houston, Texas; Museum Folkwang, Essen; Vasterbottens Museum, Umea; Kulturhuset, Stockholm; Saarland Museum, Saarbrucken; Palais des Beaux-Arts, Brussels)
1986   *The Animal in Photography 1843-1985,* The Photographers' Gallery, London

Collections:

Victoria and Albert Museum, London; Bibliothèque Nationale, Paris; Museum of Modern Art, New York; International Museum of Photography, George Eastman House, Rochester, New York; Art Institute of Chicago; National Gallery of Victoria, Melbourne; Museum Ludwig, Cologne; Museum Folkwang, Essen, Germany.

Publications:

By BRANDT: Books—*The English at Home,* with an introduction by Raymond Mortimer, London 1936; *A Night in London,* with an introduction by

James Bone, London and New York 1938, as *Londres de Nuit,* Paris 1938; *Bill Brandt: Camera in London,* edited by Andor Kraszna-Krausz, commentary by Norah Wildon, London and New York 1948; *Literary Britain,* with an introduction by John Hayward, London 1951; *Perspective of Nudes,* with texts by Lawrence Durrell and Chapman Mortimer, London and New York 1961, as *Perspectives sur le Nu,* Paris 1961; *Shadow of Light,* with an introduction by Cyril Connolly, notes by Marjorie Beckett, London and New York 1966, as *Ombre d'une Ile,* with an introduction by Michel Butor, notes by Marjorie Beckett, Paris 1967, revised edition, with introductions by Cyril Connolly and Mark Haworth-Booth, London and New York, 1977, Tokyo 1979, as *Ombre de Lumiere,* Paris 1977; *Bill Brandt: Nudes 1945-1980,* with an introduction by Michael Hiley, London and Boston 1980; *Portraits,* with introduction by Alan Ross, London 1982; *London in the Thirties,* London 1983, New York 1984. **Articles**—"Bill Brandt," interview, in *Album* (London), February and March 1970; "Bill Brandt," interview, with Ruth Spencer, in *British Journal of Photography* (London), 9 November 1973.

On BRANDT: Books—*Photography in the 20th Century* by Nathan Lyons, New York 1967; *Bill Brandt: Photographs,* exhibition catalogue, by Aaron Scharf, London 1970; *The Land: 20th Century Landscape Photographs Selected by Bill Brandt,* exhibition catalogue, edited by Mark Haworth-Booth, London 1975; *Bill Brandt: Early Photographs 1930-1942,* exhibition catalogue, by Peter Turner, London 1975; *The Magic Image* by Cecil Beaton and Gail Buckland, London and Boston 1975; *Bill Brandt,* exhibition catalogue, with an essay by Norman Hall, London 1976; *Geschichte der Photographie im 20. Jahrhundert/Photography in the 20th Century* by Petr Tausk, Cologne 1977, London 1980; *The 30's: British Art and Design Before the War,* exhibition catalogue, by Ian Jeffrey, William Feaver, Brian Lacey and others, London 1979; *Photographie als Kunst 1879-1979,* exhibition catalogue, 2 vols., by Peter Weiermair, Innsbruck 1979; *Old and Modern Masters of Photography,* exhibition catalogue, by Mark Haworth-Booth, London 1980; *World Photography,* edited by Bryn Campbell, London 1981; *Of This Our Time: A Journalist's Story 1905-50* by Tom Hopkinson, London 1982; *Master Photographers: The World's Great Photographers on their Art and Technique,* edited by Pat Booth, London 1983; *Literary Britain—Photographed by Bill Brandt,* exhibition catalogue, edited by Mark Haworth-Booth, London 1984; *Bill Brandt Behind the Camera* by David Mellor and Mark Haworth-Booth, London 1985; *Bill Brandt Photographs 1928-1983,* exhibition catalogue with introduction by Ian Jeffrey, London 1993; *Bill Brandt: Selected Texts and Bibliography,* edited by Nigel Warburton, Oxford 1993. **Articles**—"Bill Brandt" by Ainslie Ellis in *British Journal of Photography* (London), 15 May 1970; "Bill Brandt: How Significant Is His Photography?" by John Bardsley and R. Dunkley in *Photographic Journal* (London), July 1970; "The Brandt Collection" by C. Faraldi in *The Observer* (London), 9 June 1974; "Bill Brandt: Not Resting on His Laurels" by Dave Saunders in *Hot Shoe* (London), no. 15, 1981; "Obituary: Bill Brandt—Contribution to British Photography" in *The Times* (London), 21 December 1983; "Bill Brandt, 79, Photographer of Foreboding Images, Dead" in the *New York Times,* 22 December 1983; "Bill Brandt: Behind the Camera" by David Mellor, special issue of *Aperture* (Millerton, New York), no. 99, 1985; "Bill Brandt's Balancing Act" by Tom Goodman in *Afterimage* (Rochester, New York), February 1986.

*

The photographer must possess and preserve the receptive faculties of a child who looks at the world for the first time. . . . As a rule, we are all too busy, too preoccupied, too eager to be right, too obsessed by certain ideas, to find the time to stand and stare. We look at something and think that we have seen it. And yet what we see is often only what our preconceived ideas prepare us to see, or else what our past experience compels us to see, or else what our desires want us to see. Only rarely are we able to free ourselves from the burden of our thoughts and emotions and to see for the simple pleasure of seeing. And as long as we cannot do this, the essence of things remains hidden from us.

It is essential for a photographer to know his lens. The lens is his eye and is responsible for the success or failure of the work.

Composition is an important element and mainly, in my opinion, a matter of instinct. It can be developed, but I doubt that it can be learned.

To achieve the best possible work, the young photographer has to discover what moves him visually. It is up to him to discover his own personal world.

—Bill Brandt (1982)

*   *   *

Bill Brandt's late prints, with their harsh black/white contrasts and strong formal elements are instantly recognisable. By the time of the publication of the second edition of his retrospective *Shadow of Light* (1977), which included reportage, landscapes, portraits and nudes, he had evolved a printing style which rendered flesh and stone as pure white and shadow jet black. This device, emphasising composition and form, gave a coherence and unity to the photographic output of half a century. Images which had originally been commissioned as photojournalistic documents were transformed by the removal of extraneous detail. The results were stark, mysterious and beautiful.

Following a period as Man Ray's assistant in Paris in 1929, and travels in Europe, he settled in London, working on assignment for various magazines including *Weekly Illustrated, Picture Post* and *Lilliput*. In his first three books, *The English at Home* (1936), *A Night in London* (1938) and *Camera in London* (1948) he gave an outsider's view of the British class system with its exaggerated social contrasts: images of rich and poor were juxtaposed in a manner which many contemporary reviewers thought highly critical of the status quo. However, Brandt later repudiated the idea that he'd ever intended his photography as political propaganda, and his images of this period are now often used as neutral records of a vanished age of parlourmaids, toffs and street urchins. Yet Brandt's attitude to the medium even in this phase was never purely documentary: for him the effect was always more important than how it was achieved, or as he put it "I am not interested in rules and conventions. . . .Photography is not a sport." He staged seemingly candid shots when it suited him: some of the photographs of the thirties, for instance, feature Brandt's brother and sister-in-law cast as working class Londoners.

His wartime work included commissions from the Ministry of Defence to photograph London Underground tunnels which were being used as air-raid shelters, and from the newly-formed National Buildings Record to document cathedral monuments under threat from the Blitz. After the war Brandt was drawn to what he called the poetic trend in photography. He worked in three genres: landscape, portraiture and the nude, making distinctive contributions to each.

In his photographs of the British landscape, many of which were collected in *Literary Britain* (1951), his aim was to recreate the atmosphere of particular locations, "the spirit that charged the commonplace with beauty" rather than simply to reproduce the visible. He achieved this by scrupulous and patient attention to form and to weather conditions and by the selection and intensification of detail in the printing process, sometimes, as in a famous picture of Top Withens, resorting to combination printing. His portraits of artists and writers, many of them commissioned for the American *Harper's Bazaar*, capture the inwardness and self-reflection of his subjects, rather than fleeting expressions. In the best of them, such as the portrait of Francis Bacon on Primrose Hill at dusk, setting, printing style and subject combine to produce an intensity of vision seldom seen in photographic portraiture. Brandt's late nudes are perhaps the most obviously surreal of his photographs. In these distorted and dreamlike images a woman's limbs on a beach are scarcely separable from the stone on which she lies, bodies have become integrated with landscape, rendered as abstract patterns of line and texture, or else lie, stand or sit in half-empty rooms, perspective and proportions transformed by the unpredictable distortions of the wide angle lens of an old Kodak police camera: "The lens produced anatomical images and shapes which my eyes had never observed. . . .It taught me how to use acute distortion to convey the weight of a body or the lightness of movement."

In the sixties it looked as if the next phase of Brandt's career would be non-naturalistic colour photography: he included eight colour photographs of rock formations in the first edition of *Shadow of Light* (1966). But, dissatisfied with the results, he abandoned these experiments, devoting much of his energy in later years to constructing 3-dimensional assemblages of beach debris which he glued to a painted background and encased in perspex boxes.

The New York Museum of Modern Art's retrospective exhibition organised by John Szarkowski in 1969, which later moved to the Hayward Gallery in London, confirmed Brandt's place in the pantheon of great photographers of the twentieth century. He has been an acknowledged influence and inspiration for most photographers working in Britain in the post-war period.

—Nigel Warburton

BRASSAÏ.

Nationality: French. **Born:** Gyula Halász in Brasso, Transylvania, Hungary, now Rumania, 9 September 1899; emigrated to France, 1924: naturalized, 1948; adopted the name "Brassaï" (literally, "from Brasso"), Paris, 1925. **Education:** Attended schools in Brasov and Budapest, 1917; studied at the Academy of Fine Arts, Budapest, 1918-19; Akademische Hochschule, Berlin-Charlottenburg, 1921-22, B.A. 1922. **Military Service:** Served in the Austro-Hungarian Army, 1917-18. **Family:** Married Gilberte-Mercedes Boyer in 1947. **Career:** Worked as a painter, sculptor and journalist, associating with Picasso, Dali, Braque, etc., Paris, 1924-30; took up photography, Paris, 1930; freelance magazine photographer, Paris, working for *Minotaure, Verve, Harper's Bazaar*, etc., 1930-40; lived in the South of France, 1940, then returned to Paris, refused to photograph during the German occupation, but worked in Picasso's studio photographing his sculptures and designing and writing *Conversations avec Picasso*; resumed career as photographer, 1945, working for *Picture Post, Lilliput, Coronet, Labyrinthe, Réalités, Plaisirs de Franc*, and *Harper's Bazaar* (1936-63); also designed for ballets (creating first stage decors in photographs), Paris, 1945-50. **Recipient:** Emerson Medal, London, 1934; Gold Medal, *Daguerre Centennial Exhibition*, Budapest, 1937; Gold Medal, *Biennale de Fotografia*, Venice, 1957; Prize, *Cannes Film Festival*, 1956; Obelisk of Honor, *Photokina*, Cologne, 1963; American Society of Magazine Photographers Award, with Ansel Adams, 1966; Medal, City of Arles, France, 1974; Premier Grand Prix National de la Photographie, 1978. Chevalier des Arts et Lettres, 1974; Chevalier de la Légion d'Honneur, 1976. **Died:** (in Nice, France) 8 July 1984.

Individual Exhibitions:

1933	*Paris de Nuit,* Arts et Métiers Graphiques, Paris (travelled to the Batsford Gallery, London)
1946	Palais des Beaux-Arts, Brussels
1952	*Cent Photographies de Brassaï,* Musée des Beaux-Arts, Nancy, France
1954	Interclub, Toulouse
	Art Institute of Chicago
1955	Walker Art Center, Minneapolis
	International Museum of Photography, George Eastman House, Rochester, New York
	Delgado Museum, New Orleans
1956	Hansa Gallery, New York
1957	*Graffiti,* Museum of Modern Art, New York
1958	*The Language of the Wall: Parisian Graffiti Photographed by Brassaï,* Institute of Contemporary Arts, London
1959	*Eye of Paris,* Limelight Gallery, New York
1960	*Graffiti,* at the *Triennale di Milano*
1962	*Graffiti,* Galerie Daniel Cordier, Paris
	Galleria dell'Obelisco, Rome
1963	Maison de la Culture, Caen, France
	Worcester Art Museum, Massachusetts
	Brassaï: Exhibition Retrospective, Bibliothèque Nationale, Paris
	Residence du Louvre, Menton, France
1964	Staatliche Kunsthalle, Baden-Baden, West Germany
	Picasso/Brassaï, Galerie Madura, Cannes (with Pablo Picasso sculptures)
1965	Musée du Vieux-Chateau, Dieppe, France
1966	Kölnischer Kunstverein, Cologne (retrospective)
1968	Staatliche Landesbildstelle, Hamburg
	Museum of Modern Art, New York (retrospective; travelled to the City Art Museum, St. Louis, 1969; toured Australia, New Zealand, and South America, 1971-74)

Two Apaches in Paris. Photograph by Brassaï. Courtesy of the Art Institute of Chicago.

1970	*L'Art Mural par Brassaï,* Galerie Rencontres, Paris
1971	Robert Schoelkopf Gallery, New York
1972	Lunn Gallery, Washington, D.C.
1973	Corcoran Gallery, Washington, D.C.
	Friends of Photography, Carmel, California
	Witkin Gallery, New York
1974	Santa Barbara Museum of Art, California
	University of Iowa Museum of Art, Iowa City
	University of California, Berkeley
	Brassaï: Hommage, Musée Réattu, Arles, France
1975	Museum of Art, Utica, New York
	Brassaï: The Eye of Paris, Baltimore Museum of Art
1976	Cornblatt Gallery, Baltimore
	David Mirvish Gallery, Toronto
	The Secret Paris of the 30's, Marlborough Gallery, New York
1977	*Paris Secret des Années 30,* Marlborough Gallery, Zurich
	Neue Galerie der Stadt Linz, Austria
	Das Geheime Paris, Galerie Levy, Hamburg
	Halsted 831 Gallery, Birmingham, Michigan
	Vision Gallery, Boston (with Berenice Abbott and Bill Brandt)
1978	*Paris Secret,* Banque Lambert, Brussels
	Le Paris Secret, Musée des Beaux-Arts, Arnhem, Netherlands
	Galerij Paule Pia, Antwerp
	Paris Secret, Camera Obscura, Stockholm
1979	*Artists and Studios,* Marlborough Gallery, New York
	The Photographers' Gallery, London
	Zeit-Foto Salon, Tokyo
1982	*Artists and Studios,* Marlborough Gallery, New York
	Artists and Studios, Marlborough Fine Art, London
1984	Marlborough Gallery, New York
	Celebrations, Zabriskie Gallery, New York
1986	*Brassaï: Les Artistes de ma vie,* Galerie municipale du Château d'eau, Toulouse
1987	*Picasso vu par Brassaï,* Musée Picasso Reunion des Musées nationaux, Paris
1988	*Brassaï: Paris le jour, Paris la nuit,* Musée Carnavalet, Paris
1990	*Brassaï,* Printemps Ginza, Tokyo
1993	*Brassaï: The Eye of Paris,* Hourk Friedman Gallery, New York; Fundacio Antoni Tapies, Barcelona

Also, exhibitions of designs, sculpture and tapestry, including: Galerie Renou et Colle, Paris, 1945; Galerie du Pont-Royal, Paris, 1960; Galerie Daniel Cordier, Paris, 1962; Galerie Les Contards, Lacoste, 1966; Galerie des Ponts des Arts, Paris, 1968; Gallery La Boétie, New York, 1968; Galerie Verrière, Paris, 1972; and Galerie Verrière, Lyons, 1973.

Selected Group Exhibitions:

1932	*Modern European Photographers,* Julien Levy Gallery, New York (as Halász)
1937	*Photography 1839-1937,* Museum of Modern Art, New York
1948	*Exposition des Photographes Hongrois de France,* Union Democratique des Hongrois de France, Paris
1953	*Post-War European Photography,* Museum of Modern Art, New York
1955	*The Family of Man,* Museum of Modern Art, New York (and world tour)
1963	*Great Photographers,* at *Photokina,* Cologne
1976	*Photographs from the Julien Levy Collection, Starting with Atget,* Art Institute of Chicago
1981	*Les Réalismes,* Centre Georges Pompidou, Paris
1982	*Counterparts: Form and Emotion in Photographs,* Metropolitan Museum of Art, New York (travelled to the Contemporary Arts Centre, Cincinnati; Dallas Museum of Fine Arts, Texas; San Francisco Museum of Modern Art; Corcoran Gallery, Washington, D.C.)
1985	*L'Amour Fou: Photography and Surrealism,* Corcoran Gallery, Washington, D.C. (travelled to San Francisco Museum of Modern Art; Centre Georges Pompidou, Paris; Hayward Gallery, London)

Collections:

Bibliothèque Nationale, Paris; Musée Réattu, Arles, France; Victoria and Albert Museum, London; Museum of Modern Art, New York; Metropolitan Museum of Art, New York; International Museum of Photography, George Eastman House, Rochester, New York; Smithsonian Institution, Washington, D.C.; Art Institute of Chicago; Walker Art Center, Minneapolis; National Gallery of Victoria, Melbourne.

Publications:

By BRASSAÏ: Books—*Paris de Nuit,* with text by Paul Morand, Paris and London 1933, republished Paris, New York, London and Tokyo, 1987; *Trente Dessins,* with poems by Jacques Prévert, Paris 1946; *Les Sculptures de Picasso,* with text by Daniel-Henry Kahnweiler, Paris 1948, London 1949; *Brassaï: Camera in Paris,* London and New York 1949; *Histoire de Marie,* novel (unillustrated), with an introduction by Henry Miller, Paris 1949; *Formes,* Paris 1951; *Brassaï,* with an introduction by Henry Miller, Paris 1952; *Seville en Fête,* with an introduction by Henri de Montherlant, Paris 1954, Munich 1955, as *Fiesta in Spain,* New York 1956; *Graffiti de Brassaï,* with text by Pablo Picasso, Stuttgart and Paris 1961, republished Paris 1993; *Brassaï,* with text by Ludvic Soucek, Prague 1962; *Conversations avec Picasso,* Paris 1964 and 1987, as *Picasso and Company,* New York 1966; *Transmutations,* portfolio, Vaucluse, France 1966; *Portfolio Brassaï,* with text by A.D. Coleman, New York 1973; *Henry Miller: Grandeur Nature,* Paris 1975; *Le Paris Secret des Années 30,* Paris, London, New York and Frankfurt 1976, republished Paris 1988; *Paroles en L'Air,* Paris 1978; *Henry Miller Rocher Heureux,* Paris 1978; *Revelation: Letters from Brassaï to His Parents 1920-1940,* Bucharest 1980; *The Artists of my Life,* London 1982; *Paris tendresse,* with text by Patrick Modiano, Paris 1990. **Articles**—"Du Mur des Cavernes au Mur d'Usine" in *Minotaure* (Paris), nos. 3/4, 1933; "Le Paris Insolite" in *Réalités* (Paris), December 1960; "Mon Ami André Kertész" in *Camera* (Lucerne), April 1963; introduction to *Images de Camera,* Paris, London and Lucerne 1964; "My Memories of Eugène Atget, P.H. Emerson and Alfred Stieglitz" in *Camera* (Lucerne), January 1969; "Brassaï par Brassaï: Propos Recueillis par Viviane Berger" in *Jardin des Arts* (Paris), March 1972; "Lewis Carroll: Photographe" in *Zoom* (Paris), no. 11, 1972; "Le Regard de Picasso" and "Picasso et Goethe" in *Gazette des Beaux-Arts* (Paris), October 1973; "Texte sur Man Ray (a sa Mort)" in *Nouvelles Lettres* (Paris), 23 November 1975; "Brassaï," interview, in *Dialogue with Photography,* edited by Paul Hill and Thomas Cooper, London 1979. **Film**—*Tant qu'il y Aura des Betes,* 1955.

On BRASSAÏ: Books—*Art de Voir en Photographie* by Marcel Natkin, Paris 1935; *Photography 1839-1937,* exhibition catalogue, by Beaumont Newhall, New York 1937; *Histoire de la Photographie* by Raymond Lecuyer, Paris 1945; *Masters of Modern Art* by Alfred H. Barr, Jr., New York 1954; *Photography of the World,* Tokyo 1956; *The Language of the Wall: Parisian Graffiti Photographed by Brassaï,* exhibition catalogue, with an introduction by Roland Penrose, London 1958; *The Picture History of Photography* by Peter Pollack, New York 1958, 1969; *Brassaï: Exposition Retrospective,* exhibition catalogue, with a preface by Julien Cain, text by Jean Adhémar, Paris 1963; *Great Photographers of Our Century* by Fritz Gruber, Dusseldorf and Vienna 1964; *The Painter and the Photograph: From Delacroix to Warhol* by Van Deren Coke, Albuquerque, New Mexico 1965, 1972; *Photography in the 20th Century* by Nathan Lyons, New York 1967; *Brassaï,* exhibition catalogue, with a preface by John Szarkowski, and an introduction by Lawrence Durrell, New York 1968; *Looking at Photographs* by John Szarkowski, New York 1973; *The Magic Image* by Cecil Beaton and Gail Buckland, London and Boston 1975; *Photographs from the Julien Levy Collection, Starting with Atget,* exhibition catalogue, by David Travis, Chicago 1976; *The Grotesque in Photography* by A.D. Coleman, New York 1977; *Faces,* edited by Ben Maddow, Boston 1977; *Geschichte der Fotografie im 20. Jahrhundert/Photography in the 20th Century* by Petr Tausk, Cologne 1977, London 1980; *Histoire de la Photographie Francaise* by Claude Nori, Paris 1978; *Nudes,* edited by Constance Sullivan and Ben Maddow, New York 1980; *World Photography,* edited by Bryn Campbell, London 1981; *L'Amour Fou: Photography and Surrealism,* edited by Jane Livingston and Rosalind Krauss, New York 1985. **Articles**—"Brassaï," special monograph issue of *La Revue Neuf* (Paris), no. 5, 1951; "Brassaï" by André Kertész, special monograph issue of *Infinity* (New York), vol. 15, no. 7, 1966; "Brassaï, Photographer of Paris Night Life, Dies" in the *New York Times,* 12 July 1984; "Obituary: Brassaï—Recorder of the Paris demi-monde" in *The Times* (London), 12 July 1984; "Brassaï Explored More than the Seedy Life of Paris" by Andy Grundberg in the *New York Times,* 23 September 1984.

*

"I invent nothing, I imagine everything." I have never looked for subjects that are exotic or sensational in themselves. Most of the time I have drawn my images from the daily life around me. I think that it is the most sincere and humble appreciation of reality, the most everyday event that leads to the extraordinary. Or, as Jean Giono said: "Reality pushed to the extreme leads to unreality/the visionary."

My subject matter, field of research: Paris by day; Paris by night; portraits of artists, writers, etc.; nudes; graffiti; abstract colors; walls; Greece, Italy, Spain, Turkey, Morocco, Sweden, Sicily, Brazil, the United States, Ireland, England, etc.; engravings; glass negatives.

—Brassaï (1982)

* * *

He was born in Transylvania at Brasso (hence his pseudonym, Brassaï) on 9-9-1899 at 9 p.m. "Nothing but 9 or multiples of 9," Brassaï remarked, and laughed. He laughed a lot. Everything amused him. Humor was not, however, a determining factor in his work; it is, rather, a counterpoint that accompanies it, a detour, a diversion, or, more exactly, one of those glissandi by which violinists start from a low note then go up the string until they achieve perfection in the note they seek.

Curiosity—it was Brassaï's driving force. Perhaps it is what drove him to abandon drawing, in which he excelled, for the photograph—to the great dismay of Picasso. Curiosity is certainly what drove him to follow Léon Paul Fargue, the famous Paris pedestrian, on his nocturnal wanderings, far from the Dôme, far from the cosmopolitan quarter of Montparnasse which he so loved. About these peregrinations and the illicit universe that he knew so well Brassaï had a thousand anecdotes: he adored the world of the night; he studied, judged, sized up, marvelled at, criticized, all his being on alert—yet laughter was always ready to burst out. He often said, "I nearly created sociological studies of certain milieux of this period."

Even though he belatedly discovered photography, and in Paris, Brassaï was influenced by the New Objectivity movement in Germany. If he transcends the limits of the "applied" photo where others of his era stop, it is because his reflection proceeds less from the diktats of the theorists limited by an objective combination of art and industry and much more from an in-depth analysis which finds its source in the scientific and literary thought of Goethe. The work of Goethe nourished Brassaï; he was, in fact, a disciple. It was Henry Miller who best explained Brassaï's particular philosophy: "This desire that Brassaï displays with so much force, this desire that seeks not to alter the object but to take it in its essence, *as it is,* is it not provoked by a deep humility, respect and veneration for the object itself? The more this man puts aside his vision of life and the objects and beings which compose it, plus all the interference of individual volition and of the ego, the easier it is for him to quickly assume multiple identities that usually remain foreign and closed to us. Because he was able to become depersonalized, he was able to discover his personality in everything and everywhere." And this is why, it seems to me, that his art is characterized by a kind of definitive "seizure" of things.

"I like living beings; I like life," said Brassaï, "but I like to capture it in such a way that the photo does not move. I don't really like the snapshot, the Leica with its 36 views, all of which distract attention." For Brassaï the photograph was something static. And, indeed, all of his great pictures appear immobile in their density of sculpture—yes, sculpture: his prostitutes, his low-life figures, they are *volumes* brought into light, revealed by light.

The snapshot more or less reveals nuance, psychology, detail. Brassaï sought rather to restrict, to assemble, to contain. A mysterious power, opaque, disengages itself from these incredibly concentrated forms: it is not so much

involved with the complexities of the mind or irregularities of the heart as, always, with more essential truths.

Brassaï himself did not stand still: he simply photographed the motionless. He did not capture a face when the muscles are stretching, tensed or contorted, when the mouth opens onto an interior countryside of mucous membranes and tooth decay. He waited—until the being collected itself, was contained, had ceased to disperse, to reach out from itself—when, ceasing to be an anecdote, it became its own story. And that is why Brassaï restricts the authority of the eye of the beholder, challenges its authority: he does not distract with detail, and he allows no escape from his own vision.

—Michel Nuridsany

BRAUN, Werner.

Nationality: Israeli. **Born:** Nuremberg, Germany, 12 June 1918; emigrated to Israel (then Palestine), 1946; naturalized Israeli citizen, 1948. **Education:** Attended the Reform Gymnasium, Nuremberg, 1925-34; self-taught in photography. **Military Service:** Served in the Israeli Army, 1948, 1967, and as a photo-correspondent during the Yom Kippur War, 1973. **Family:** Married Yael Fleischmann in 1941 (divorced, 1976); children: Dani and Ruth; married Anat Rotem in 1977. **Career:** Worked as a farmer in Sweden, 1937-39, Denmark, 1939-43, and again in Sweden, 1943-46. Owner of the Braun Photo Laboratory, Jerusalem, since 1949; freelance news, magazine and documentary photographer, Jerusalem, specializing in aerial and underwater photography, since 1950. **Recipient:** Third Prize, Nikon International Contest, 1979; First Prize, Jerusalem Post International Photo Contest, 1992. **Agent:** Camera Press, Russell Court, Coram Street, London WC1, England. **Address:** Post Office Box 8024, 91080 Jerusalem, Israel.

Individual Exhibition:

1983   *Thirty Years of Photography,* Brown Gallery, Jerusalem
            (retrospective)

Selected Group Exhibitions:

1975   *Jerusalem,* Israel Museum, Jerusalem
1976   *Jerusalem,* Stadt der Menschheit, Charlottenburg, West Berlin

Collections:

Jewish Museum, New York.

Publications:

By BRAUN: Books—*Olive Trees,* Teufen, Switzerland 1958; *Tel Aviv/Jaffa,* Tel Aviv 1958; *The Red Sea Is Blue,* Tel Aviv 1966; *Akko,* Tel Aviv 1967; *Israel and the Holy Land,* New York 1967; *Haifa,* Haifa 1968; *Jerusalem,* with text by G. Rosenthal, Munich 1968; *Israel, Land of Faith,* with text by Rinna Samuel, Tel Aviv 1970; *Night of the Wadi,* with text by Dvora Ben-Shaul, New York 1970; *Shalom Israel,* Tel Aviv 1972; *Sinai and the Negev,* with text by Rinna Samuel, London 1972; *Jerusalem, The Holy,* Tel Aviv 1972; *Jerusalem,* portfolio, with others, New York 1973; *Levanon,* with text by

Aerial Fisheye Shot of Jerusalem—"Center of the World," **1992.** Photograph ©Werner Braun.

Giladi, Tel Aviv 1974; *Israel,* with text by Gisela Bischof-Elten, Lucerne, Switzerland 1986. **Article**—"Seeing the U.S.A.—the Israeli Way" in the *Chicago Tribune,* August 1965.

On BRAUN: Articles—"Production Specialists: Photo Werner Braun" in *Israel Book World* (Tel Aviv), December 1973; "Leading Israeli Photographers" by Helen Davis in *Israel Scene* (Jerusalem), November 1980.

*

To be a photographer is more than a profession; it's a challenge that never, never ends. Since absolutely everybody can shoot pictures, you always have people glancing over your shoulder, even if they are not near you physically. This is the tension in our lives, the Darwinian survival of the fittest: every shot taken is a competition against thousands of unseen opponents. And that challenge really *does* keep you functional in body and soul. You never want to stop; you remain young. Many photographers, if they do not expose themselves to too much danger, live to a very ripe old age. Doctors look at my x-rays and tell me ominously, you are 68 and your bone-structure has changed. Yes, it has; the joints do ache sometimes; so does my back. I have difficulty in carrying around 2 Hasselblads with 5 lenses, and often I switch to the easier Nikon. But would I give up flying, diving, skiing or roaming through half the world in a camper—all these activities closely and intimately related to my profession? No, I would not. Not yet; not ever, if I can help it.

It is good to specialize, because only then can you reach real perfection. I have seen the truth of that advice in the careers of many of my colleagues. But what can you do if EVERYTHING interests you, be it fashion, advertising, public relations, micro, macro, tele, animals, sports, aerials, underwater, book illustration, photo essays, calendars, posters, and the struggle of a young state called Israel? So much for *my* specialization.

Yet I do believe that photographers can be artists. The bulk of our work might not be art. But there are rare moments (you feel them in your blood) when you know that you have hit it. It can happen any time, anywhere. You can sit in an airplane and be doing routine work and suddenly you see it, and you coax the pilot to put the plane in precise position, and you get the shot in a million, the ultimate. Sometimes you have to think a lot and search and walk and wait in order to find the moment that means the difference between a shot and a photograph. When it comes, it is the most rewarding moment of your life.

—Werner Braun

*   *   *

Werner Braun has had a life of struggle ending in adventurous delight.

Like many other Israelis, he arrived in the country at a time of great upheaval. He had spent ten years in Scandinavia after fleeing Nazi Germany, waiting to be allowed to enter Palestine. Once there, he had the world before him, and yet nothing before him. What occupation should he follow? Upholstery?—the family business he had been trained for? Agriculture?—he had worked as a farmer in Sweden and Denmark. But he already had hypo in his blood. In those days, however, the profession of photographer was unheard of, so he went to work as a darkroom technician in Jerusalem's only professional lab. Soon he was running it. And then, during the War of Independence (mind you, *during* the war), while he was still a soldier, he bought the place. After the war—a pioneering effort in itself—he became a photographer.

With incredible energy and stamina, Braun has helped to create the profession of photographer in Israel. Starting with the usual studio shots, he moved on to recording his country's growth, as a press photographer, as an aerial photographer, and as the creator of a series of outstanding books about his country. Many of his photos have become classics, known around the world.

Perhaps the spirit of the man is best captured by allowing him to speak for himself—his description of the photo that accompanies this entry:

"This is my favorite aerial shot. I was flying over Jerusalem, and it was getting late as I had planned. The lower the sun, the better the color transparencies. But suddenly clouds were covering the sky, completely shutting out the sun. Only the far-off desert and Dead Sea to the East remained bright. I gave up; the pilot turned back in the direction of the airfield. But just then a window opened in the sky. The shaft of light fell on the Old City, but its position was changing rapidly; the luminous patch moved toward the Temple Mount. I prayed that this precious window should not close. Now, I'm not religious and I don't normally pray, but maybe because I was so near to God, He heard me. The Temple Mount and the Jewish Quarter of the Old City were bathed by the eerie sunlight. I took the shot in black-and-white because color would never stand up to this tremendous contrast. And I shouted for joy as I pressed the shutter release. It was what we call in German *eine Sternstunde.*"

—Bonnie Boxer

BRIHAT, Denis.

Nationality: French. **Born:** Paris, 16 September 1928. **Education:** Brief studies at the Vaugirard School, Paris, 1947; self-taught in photography. **Military Service:** Served as a Photographer in the French Army Press Service, in Germany, 1949-50. **Family:** Married Solange Robert in 1967: children: Anne and Pierre. **Career:** Professional photographer, in Paris, 1947-52, Biot, 1952-56, and in Provence, since 1958: studio established, 1970. Co-Founder and Instructor, Department of Photography, Marseille-Provence University, 1975-77. Former Director, Brihat Annual Photography Workshops, Provence. **Recipient:** Prix Niepce, 1957; Prix Nadar, Paris, 1963; Vermeil Medal, City of Paris, 1982; Grand Prix de la Ville de Paris 1987. **Agent:** Martine Portelette d'Arc, 11 rue Daniel Stern, F.75015, Paris; Anne Berthoud, 4A Stanley Crescent, London W11 2NB. **Address:** 84480 Bonnieux, Vaucluse, France.

Individual Exhibitions:

1952	Brihat Studio, Biot, France
1957	*Prix Niepce,* Société Française de Photographie, Paris
1962	*Aventure de Matière,* Galerie Montaigne, Paris (with Jean-Pierre Sudre)
	Réalité Poètique, Galerie Pierre Coren, Aixen-Provence
	Réalité Poètique, Galerie Michel, Carpentras, France
1963	*Réalité Poètique,* Galerie La Proue, Lyons
1965	Musée des Arts Decoratifs, Paris
	Galerie Les Contards, Lacoste, Vaucluse, France
1967	*Denis Brihat/Pierre Cordier/Jean-Pierre Sudre,* Galleri Artek, Helsinki (with Jean-Pierre Sudre and Pierre Cordier)
	Museum of Modern Art, New York
	Wooster School, Danbury, Connecticut
1968	Orly Airport Gallery, Paris
1971	Galerie La Lampe à Huile, Marseilles
1972	Galerie La Demeure, Paris
	Witkin Gallery, New York
	Art Center, Washington, Connecticut
1973	Fondation Grand Cachot de Vent, Neuchâtel, Switzerland
1974	Galleria 291, Milan
1975	Palais des Congrès, Antibes
1976	Photo-Galerie Fiolet, Amsterdam
	Galerie Paule Pia, Antwerp, Belgium
	Musée d'Angoulème, France
1977	Galerie Agathe Gaillard, Paris
	Galerie Jean Dieuzaide, Toulouse
	Musée Nicéphore Niepce, Chalon-sur-Saône, France
1978	Galerie Photo-Art, Basle (with Jean Dieuzaide)
	Musée des Beaux-Arts, Besançon, France
1979	Galerie Portfolio, Lausanne
1980	*Denis Brihat: Photographies 1947-80,* Galerie Municipale à Chateau d'Eau, Toulouse (partial retrospective)
1981	Musée de Grignan, Drome, France
	Brihat Studio, Bonnieux, France
	Musée des Beaux-Art, Neuchâtel, Switzerland
1982	Musée d'Orange, Vaucluse, France
	Photogralerie Portfolio, Lausanne, Switzerland
	Galerie Alexandre de La Salle, St. Paul de Vence, France
	Galerie Photogramme, Montreal
	Galerie Espace Canon, Paris
	Galerie Agathe Gaillard, Paris
1983	Galleria Luisella d'Alessandro, Turin
	Santa Fe Center for Photography, New Mexico
	Camera Obscura Gallery, Denver, Colorado
	Galerie Suzanne Kuepfer, Bienne, Switzerland
1984	Galerie Le Tournesol, Bonnieux, France
1985	Wooster Art Center, Danbury, Connecticut
	Galerie Alexandre de La Salle, St. Paul de Vence, France
	Galerie Le Mas de l'Enfant, Barbentane, France
1986	Musée Henri Fabre, Montpellier, France
	Galerie Suisse, Paris
1987	Gal. "L'imagerie," Lanion, France.
1988	Societé française de photographie, Paris
	Photographers' Gallery, Palo-Alto, California
	Centre de la photographie du Nord, Douchy, France
1989	Galerie Hall du Livre, Nancy, France
	Galerie de la gare, Bonnieux, France
	Anne Barthoud Gallery, London
1990	Photo-Forum Pasquart, Biehl, Switzerland
1991	Anne Barthoud Gallery, London
	Maison française, New York University, New York.
1992	Galerie de la Gare, Bonnieux, France
1993	Palais de Tokyo, Paris
1994	Musee de Salon de Provence, France
	Galerie clairefontaine, Luxembourg
	Musée de l'Elysée, Lausanne, Switzerland

Selected Group Exhibitions:

1951	*Salon National de Photographie,* Bibliothèque Nationale, Paris (and 1952, 1953, 1954)
1963	*Salon Comparaisons,* Musée d'Art Moderne, Paris (and 1964)
1968	*L'Oeil Objectif,* Musée Cantini, Marseilles (with Lucien Clergue, Robert Doisneau, and Jean-Pierre Sudre)
1972	*La Photographie Française,* Moscow
1978	*European Colour Photography,* The Photographers' Gallery, London
1980	*Photographia: La Linea Sottile,* Galleria Flaviana, Locarno, Switzerland
	Jeune Photographie, Château Lumiere, Lyon, France
1984	*La Photographie Créative,* Pavillon des Arts, Paris
1985	*SIF 85: Semana Internacional de la Fotografía,* Palacio del Infantado, Guadalajara, Spain
1990	*High-Tech Plants Photo-Exhibition,* Osaka, Japan.
1993	*Flora Photographica,* USA, Canada, England

***Larch,* 1991.** Photograph ©Denis Brihat.

Collections:

Bibliothèque Nationale, Paris; Musée Réattu, Arles, France; Musée Nicéphore Niepce, Chalon-sur-Saône, France; Musée d'Angoulème, France; Het Sterckshof Museum, Antwerp; Museum of Modern Art, New York; Center for Creative Photography, University of Arizona, Tucson; Musée d'Orange, Vaucluse, France; Musée des Beaux-Arts, Toulon, France; Musée des Béaux-Arts, Neuchatel, Switzerland.

Publications:

By BRIHAT: Books—Edition *le nez dans l'herbe,* portfolio of 12 originals printed at 16 (ed. Ottezec, 1988).

On BRIHAT: Books—*Denis Brihat: Photographies* by Charles Estienne, Paris 1965; *European Colour Photography* by Sue Davies, Michael Langford, and Bryn Campbell, London 1978; *Denis Brihat: Photographies 1947-80* by Jean Dieuzaide, Toulouse 1980; *Photographia: La Linea Sottile* by Rinaldo Bianda and Giuliana Scimé, Locarno, Switzerland, 1980; *Jeune Photographie,* exhibition catalogue, with introduction by Bernard Chardere, Paris 1980; *I Grandi Fotografi: Denis Brihat,* Milan 1983; *La Photographie Créative* by Jean-Claude Lemagny, Paris 1984. **Articles**—in *Point de Vue* (Paris), December 1959; *Camera* (Lucerne), May 1964; *Techniques Graphiques* (Paris), June 1965; *Popular Fotografi* (Stockholm), April 1966; *Arte Fotografico* (Madrid), October 1971; *Photo Revue* (Paris), April 1972; *Progresso Fotografico* (Milan), October 1972.

*

Photography is a sum of techniques—mechanical, chemical, optical—allowing about 50 different crafts.

For fifteen years I practised many of these crafts. Through the opportunities they gave me, I learned a lot. I finally understood what must be my way in life. That is why since 1958 I have lived in Provence, growing my garden, looking after my rabbits and chickens, and making what is now called "creative photography." I work on small pieces of nature, flowers or vegetables, more a kind of portrait than still life.

Since 1968, my pictures have been mostly in colour, but from black-and-white material, using toning processes. Their purpose is to be a "poetical decoration" for the wall: the same goal as in painting, engraving, etc.

I sell my work through galleries or at home.

—Denis Brihat

* * *

Since 1958 when he left the world of commercial photography to live in Bonnieux, Denis Brihat has sought to combine both truth and beauty in his photographs and to make works of art with the sole intention that they should grace our walls. His subjects have been the flowers, vegetables and plant life that grows in his garden and he has photographed them truthfully in black and white.

Dissatisfied with the colour available through commercial films he has worked his magic in his studio and darkroom, giving his images the colours that he feels brings out their essential truth and beauty through the use of various chemical toners and metallic combinations. Occasionally he will also use a tool on the emulsion to clarify a subject and make it more readable. These manipulations do not result in any garish exaggerations but rather bring out the subtle underlying value of the plant. His work is based on a thorough love and understanding of the way plants grow and, in the past, he has insisted that his students also work in the garden so that they too can reach an empathy with their subjects.

Denis Brihat is an artist who combines his emotional response to his subjects together with his scientific knowledge, and experiments with techniques to express his feelings in just the same way as a painter uses his tools and knowledge of materials. It is a long and often painstaking process and each negative may only be used 3 or 4 times, with each picture being both different and absolutely stable.

Each of his pictures is a poem—almost a haiku—which celebrates the spirit of the subject and the beauty that Brihat finds in all the natural world.

—Sue Davies

BROGOWSKI, Leszek.

Nationality: Polish. **Born:** Gdańsk, 15 March 1955. **Education:** Studied at the Building Machine Faculty, Polytechnic of Gdańsk, 1973-78, M.S. 1978; philosophy, University of the Sorbonne, Paris, from 1985; self-taught in photography, from 1970. **Family:** Married Hanna Sidorowicz in 1985. **Career:** Photoreporter, *Kronika Studencka* student journal, Gdańsk, 1973-75; independent painter and artist-photographer, concentrating on intellectual expression in photography, in Gdańsk since 1975, and in Paris since 1983. Vice-President, Gdańsk branch of the Union of Polish Art Photographers, 1975-85; Director, Gallery GN, Gdańsk, 1978-81. Professor, High School of Fine Arts, Gdańsk, 1978-81. Member, Union of Polish Visual Artists, 1983. **Agent:** Galerie Alain Oudin, Paris. **Addresses:** Danusi ul.11, 80 434 Gdańsk, Poland; c/o Galerie Alain Oudin, 28 bis, Boulevard de Sebastopol, 75005 Paris, France.

Individual Exhibitions:

1975	Zak Students' Club, Gdańsk, Poland
1978	*Idioms,* Gallery GN, Gdańsk, Poland
	Stara Galerie, Warsaw (with P. Borkowski)
1979	*Fotografia Kolorowa,* Gallery GN, Gdańsk, Poland
1980	Gallery Foto-Medium-Art, Wroclaw, Poland (with P. Borkowski)
	Iconology, Mala Galeria, Warsaw
1981	*Drawing Considerations,* Gallery Studio, Warsaw
	Drawing Considerations, Znak Gallery, Bialystok, Poland
	Labirynth Gallery, Lublin, Poland
	Idioms V, Gallery GN, Gdańsk, Poland
	Drawing Considerations, Kunoldstrasse 34, Kassel, West Germany
1982	Galerie L'Ollave, Lyon, France
	Galerie St. Agnes, Roskilde, Denmark
1983	*Consideration sur le dessin,* Galerie Alain Oudin, Paris
1984	*Passe-Partout/Painting Action,* Dluzniewscy residence, Warsaw
1985	*Photos and Drawings on the 'One',* Mala Galeria, Warsaw
	Painting Book and Beyond, Galeria Akumulatory 2, Poznań, Poland
	BWA Gallery, Lublin, Poland (retrospective)
	The Cross, On Gallery, Poznań, Poland
	Museum of Chelm Lubelski, Poland (retrospective)
	Idioms VII, Dluzniewscy residence, Warsaw
	Dessins et photos sur 'Un', Galerie Alain Oudin, Paris
1986	Aspex Gallery, Portsmouth, Hampshire (with David Connearn)
	Gallery Krzysztofory, Krakow, Poland (with David Connearn)

Selected Group Exhibitions:

1979	*Fotografia Polska,* International Center of Photography, New York (travelled to Art Institute of Chicago; Centre Georges Pompidou, Paris; Whitechapel Art Gallery, London)
1980	*Fotografia Polska 1900-80,* Zacheta Galeria, Warsaw (travelled to the Museum of Art, Lodz, Poland)
1981	*Neue Kunst aus Polen,* Kunstlerhaus, Stuttgart
1984	*Conceptions of Space in Contemporary Art,* National Museum, Warsaw
	To Get Close Human Contact, Galerie Makkom, Amsterdam
	International Art Exposition, Chicago
	Forum 84, Zurich

1985   *Berdyszak/Brogowski/Dlubak* . . . , Galerie L'Ollave, Lyon,
         France

Collections:

Bibliothèque Nationale, Paris; National Museum, Warsaw; National Museum, Poznań, Poland; Museum of Art, Lodz, Poland; Studio Gallery, Warsaw; Museo Vostell, Malpartida de Caceres, Spain; Polaroid Corporation, Cambridge, Massachusetts.

Publications:

By BROGOWSKI: Books—*Kazimierz Malewicz,* editor, Gdańsk, Poland 1983; *Ad Reinhardt,* Gdańsk, Poland 1984; *Sztuka i Czlowiek* (Art and the Human Being), Warsaw 1987; *Sztuka Wobec Przemian* (Art and Question of Change), Warsaw 1988. Articles—"Myth of Credible Photography" in *Revue Fotografie* (Prague), no. 3, 1980; "Ad Reinhardt: Discoverer of Ideas and Paintings Maker" in *Miesiecznik Literacki* (Warsaw), May 1982; "Participation as Personal Authorship" in *Makkom Press* (Amsterdam), November 1984; "Idioms IV and V" in *European Photography* (Göttingen, West Germany), nos. 4-6, 1984; "Idioms V" in *Fotografia* (Warsaw), no. 1, 1985.

On BROGOWSKI: Books—*Granice Fotografii* by Jerzy Busza, Warsaw 1983; *Wszystko Fotografii,* with text by Ryszard Bobrowski and others, 1984; *Fotografia Polska 1945-1985* by Ryszard Bobrowski, Jerzy Busza and others, Gorzow Wielkopolski, Poland 1985; *Generative Photography* by Gottfried Jäger, Ravensburg, West Germany 1986. Articles—"Golden Umber 77" by K. T. Toeplitz in *Fotografia* (Warsaw), no. 7, 1977; "Polish Photography in the Years 1939-1979" by Ryszard Bobrowski in *Fotografia* (Warsaw), special issue, 1979; "Bioracy Zojecia" by M. Bacciarelli in *Fakty* (Bydgoszcz, Poland), no. 8, 1980; "Drawing Considerations" by J. Busza in *Studio News* (Warsaw), no. 1, 1981; "Leszek Brogowski" by I. Sadowska-Guillon in *Art Press* (Paris), no. 6, 1983; "Polnische Praesenz in Paris" by M. L. Syring in *Du* (Zurich), no. 8, 1983; "Voyage en Pologne" by J. de Breyne in *La Voix du Lyonnais* (Lyon, France), no. 9, 1984; "Brogowski" by J. Baron in *La Croix* (Paris), no. 11, 1985; "Photoset Dessin de Leszek Brogowski" in *Le Quotidien du Medecin* (Paris), no. 11, 1985.

*

IDIOMS IV, 1978: The popular belief regularly functioning with respect to photography tends to ignore the ontological difference between the world and its photographic presentation. This attitude appears to be fixedly coded in the spoken language. We can see a photo and ask who it is, instead of enquiring whose picture it is, whom does it represent. We also reply: this is Marilyn Monroe, this is Ali Bhutto or Pele . . . However, almost always there is a boundary line between the situation and its photographic reproduction. This "almost" leaves space for one unique instance when the photograph and the reality being photographed are precisely reality and the same, when for a moment the ontological difference between reality and its photographic presentation ceases to exist. This moment takes place in *Idioms IV.*

In *Idioms IV,* I take a photo of two and later three white sheets of paper, first arranged on one another, then subsequently detached from each other in various ways. The first and the last photo in each piece in this series is a white sheet of paper. It is the photo of a white sheet of paper too. A white sheet of paper exists both as a picture and as a white sheet of paper. A white sheet of paper is what is it—both the photo and the object.

> IDIOMS V, 1981: The photo of a white sheet of
> paper is the white sheet of paper.
> The photo of the photo of a white sheet of paper is
> the white sheet of paper.
> The photo of the photo of a white sheet of paper is
> not the white sheet of paper.
> The photo of a dirty sheet of paper is not a dirty
> sheet of paper.
> The photo of a lined sheet of paper is a lined sheet
> of paper.
> The photo of a white object is a white object.
> The photo of a white object is another white object.

> The photo of a white object is the white sheet of
> paper.
> The photo of a white object is not the white sheet of
> paper.
> The photo of a monotone white surface is a
> monotone white surface.
> The photo of a monotone white space is a monotone
> white surface.
> The photo of a white space is the white sheet of
> paper.
> The photo of the back side of a white sheet of paper
> is the white sheet of paper.
> The photo of the back side of a white sheet of paper
> is not the back side.
> The photo has not the back side.
> The photo that would represent its own back side
> would probably be the white sheet of paper.
> The photo of a white flatness is flat.
> The photo is always flat.
> The photo of nothingness is white.

—Leszek Brogowski

*   *   *

It is generally accepted that photography is illimitably authentic, faithful, real, etc., as it originates by mechanical-chemical means. While even the most realistic painting is, of necessity, merely an interpretation or individual expression of nature, photography, by virtue of its impartiality and objectivity, is a complete and certain rendition. The camera's objective is neither to select nor to choose. Photography, eliminating chance and emotion, does not imitate the world but simply presents it, becoming no more than a transparent pane of glass through which knowledge and understanding of reality are achieved. Leszek Brogowski has been concerned with the theory and practice of photography since the mid-1970s yet still appears to question this general verdict on the fidelity of photography.

For all its realism and authenticity, photography can perform various functions—it can, for example, be a maker of myths. As Brogowski points out, this is not merely a reference to the old magical dependence between man and his likeness that can be found in the magical rites of numerous cultures and is based on the belief that the person himself can be affected by manipulations of his image. In those cases, images representing the hated figure were pierced or stabbed, destroyed, etc. Photography, supplying likenesses of objects and people as it does, became included here in the practice of pure magic. There are also various known instances of lost people being found, and of others having their state of health diagnosed, on the sole basis of their photographs. Regardless of these general applications, however, photography can and does perform a myth-creating role simply in the context of art itself.

Man Ray toyed with the idea of photography as an excellent tool in the creation of myths with Duchamp, as did Witkacy and his friends as well as many other artists. Many more or less successful examples of the use of photography in exactly this way could be quoted. However, there is also an opposite side to this coin—that of the demythification of myths according to new cultural values. A significant part of the art, and photography, of the last few decades exemplifies this. In all of these examples, the verity or objectivity of photography is problematic to say the least.

Brogowski himself sees reality and fidelity in photography in a still different way. What interests him most is the question of the philosophical, or more accurately, the ontological difference between reality and its photographic image. "The current trend," he comments, "links accurate and faithful making of images with photography. The most naive cases of this come close to losing any sense of ontological boundary between the thing that is photographed and its photograph. Nevertheless, this boundary almost always exists. The word 'almost' allows for a single exception to this—the case when the photograph and the reality being photographed are exactly one and the same, when for a moment the ontological difference between reality and its photographic representation ceases to exist. A moment such as this occurs in 'Idioms IV.' In 'Idioms IV,' I take photographs of two, and later three, sheets of white paper, first lying on top of each other and then separated in various ways. The first and last photograph in each piece of this series is of a sheet of white paper. At the same time, it *is* a sheet of white paper. The object of the photograph and the photograph of this object become identified. A sheet of white paper is what *is*—both as a photograph and as an object."

A careful theoretical approach, great parsimony and the effectiveness of his means of visual expression, distinguish Brogowski from other Polish photographers concerned with similar issues. It should also be stressed that this photography is not an addendum to his verbal theories but that, in fact, through photography, he attempts to unravel the problems and questions that interest him. This is what makes it so interesting.

—Ryszard Bobrowski

BRUEHL, Anton.

Nationality: American. **Born:** Hawker, South Australia, 11 March 1900; emigrated to the United States, 1919: naturalized, 1940. **Education:** Studied electrical engineering at Christian Brothers School, Melbourne; studied photography at the Clarence White School, New York City and New Canaan, Connecticut, 1924-25. **Family:** Married Sara Barnes in 1940; children: Stevan, David and Tony. **Career:** Worked as an engineer for the Western Electric Company, New York City, 1922-24; Teacher, Clarence White School of Photography, New York, 1924-26; also worked as part-time assistant to the photographer Jessie Tarbox Beals, New York, 1924. Freelance fashion and advertising photographer, working for *Vogue, Vanity Fair, House and Garden,* etc., New York, from 1926: maintained Anton Bruehl Studio, New York, 1927-66; Chief of Color Photography for Condé Nast Publications, New York, in the 1930's. Member of the Executive Committee, Pictorial Photographers of America. **Recipient:** Harvard Award, 1929, 1931; Illustrated Book Award, American Institute of Graphic Arts, 1933; 8 Gold Medals, Art Directors Club of New York, 1934-58. **Died:** (in San Francisco) 10 August 1982.

Individual Exhibitions:

1931	Delphic Galleries, New York
	Annual Exhibition of Advertising Art, New York (with Margaret Bourke-White; art works by others)
1932	Julien Levy Gallery, New York
	Museum of Modern Art, New York
1933	*Mexican Photos,* Delphic Galleries, New York
1978	Witkin Gallery, New York
	Center for the Arts, Boca Raton, Florida
1979	G. Ray Hawkins Gallery, Los Angeles
1980	Center for Creative Photography, University of Arizona, Tucson

Selected Group Exhibitions:

1929	*Pictorial Photographers of America Annual Exhibition,* Art Center, New York
	Film und Foto, Deutscher Werkbund, Stuttgart
1932	*Murals by American Painters and Photographers,* Museum of Modern Art, New York
	New York by New Yorkers, Julien Levy Gallery, New York
1937	*Photography 1839-1937,* Museum of Modern Art, New York
1975	*Fashion 1900-1939,* Victoria and Albert Museum, London
1976	*Photographs from the Julien Levy Collection, Starting with Atget,* Art Institute of Chicago
1979	*Fleeting Gestures: Dance Photographs,* International Center of Photography, New York (travelled to The Photographers' Gallery, London)
1982	*Color as Form,* International Museum of Photography at George Eastman House, Rochester, New York
1985	*Signs of the Times,* San Francisco Museum of Modern Art

Collections:

Museum of Modern Art, New York; Whitney Museum of American Art, New York; International Museum of Photography, George Eastman House, Rochester, New York; Art Institute of Chicago; New Orleans Museum of Art; University of New Mexico, Albuquerque; Center for Creative Photography, University of Arizona, Tucson; San Francisco Museum of Modern Art.

Publications:

By BRUEHL: Books—*Mexico,* New York 1933, with text by Sally Lee Woodall, New York 1945; *Color Sells,* with text by Fernand Bourges, New York 1935; *Magic Dials: The Story of Radio and Television,* with text by Lowell Thomas, New York 1939; *Tropic Patterns,* Hollywood, Florida 1970. **Article**—"Why I Don't Like the Photographic Press" in *Popular Photography* (New York), January 1938.

On BRUEHL: Books—*Pictorial Photography in America,* annual, with a foreword by Frank Crowninshield, New York 1929; *Form and Re-Form: A Practical Handbook of Modern Interiors* by Paul T. Frankl, New York 1930; *Fashion 1900-1939,* exhibition catalogue, by Valerie Lloyd and others, London 1975; *Photographs from the Julien Levy Collection, Starting with Atget,* exhibition catalogue, by David Travis, Chicago 1976; *The Julien Levy Collection,* edited by Lee D. Witkin, New York 1977; *The Vogue Book of Fashion Photography* by Polly Devlin, with an introduction by Alexander Liberman, London 1979; *The Photograph Collector's Guide* by Lee D. Witkin and Barbara London, Boston and London 1979; *Lichtbildnisse: Das Porträt in der Fotografie,* edited by Klaus Honnef, Cologne 1982; *Color as Form: A History of Color Photography,* exhibition catalogue, by Robert A. Sobieszek, Rochester, New York 1982; *The Library of World Photography: Portraits,* with introduction by Colin Ford, Tokyo 1982, 1983, London 1983; *Masterpieces of Photography from George Eastman House,* edited by Robert A. Sobieszek, New York 1985. **Articles**—"Anton Bruehl, Master of Color" by Etna M. Kelly in *Photography* (New York), November 1936; "The Brothers Bruehl" in *U.S. Camera* (New York), March/April 1939; "Anton Bruehl" in the "Camera" issue of *Vogue* (New York), June 1941; "The First of the Beautiful People" by Helen Lawrenson in *Esquire* (New York), March 1973; "Anton Bruehl" by Joe Deal in *Image* (Rochester, New York), June 1976; "Anton Bruehl" by Howard Batchelor in *The Annual Obituary 1982,* London and New York 1983.

*   *   *

Trained in electrical engineering, Anton Bruehl turned to photography in 1924; after studying under Clarence White, he took up portraiture and advertising illustration. In the 1920's, improvements in reproduction technology produced a revolution in photography for the printed page. Along with his better-known contemporaries, Edward Steichen, Paul Outerbridge, Jr., and Ralph Steiner, Bruehl emerged as a leader of photography's successful challenge to the older methods of commercial illustration.

In 1927 Bruehl and his brother Martin opened what proved to be one of New York's most durable and highly acclaimed commercial studios. However, Bruehl's reputation as a photographer of great originality extended well beyond the commercial world. His work was included in the 1929 *Film und Foto* exhibition in Stuttgart, selected for the Museum of Modern Art's 1937 survey of photography's first hundred years, and shown at the Julien Levy Gallery in New York.

Bruehl wrote, "The technical side of photography can be learned in three hours. After that, it's up to one's imagination." Working primarily in the studio, he produced images remarkable for their unusual lighting effects and angles of view; their strong, simple graphic organization; their meticulous craftsmanship; and their understated humor. Although he was best known for his stylish still life and table-top arrangements for advertising illustration, Bruehl was equally adept at the celebrity portraiture and fashion photography he contributed to *Vogue.*

In 1932 *Vogue* published the first of the color photographs Bruehl produced in collaboration with the color technician Fernand Bourges. Bourges, drawing upon his knowledge of color dyes, had devised a method of making near-perfect color transparencies to guide the Condé Nast engravers in reproduction. The Bruehl-Bourges process set the standard for color repro-

Mexico, **1932.** Photograph by Anton Bruehl.

duction in the 1930's, and Bruehl became chief of color photography for Condé Nast Publications. His own work represents some of the most effective color photography used in advertising and editorial illustration in that decade.

Mexico, a book of twenty-five black and white photographs published in 1933, contains Bruehl's major body of work done outside the studio. His keenly-observed portraits of Mexican villagers mirror the gravity and unaffected grace of his subjects.

—Christopher Phillips

BUJAK, Adam.

Nationality: Polish. **Born:** Kraków, 12 May 1942. **Education:** Attended primary and secondary schools in Kraków; self-taught in photography from 1958. **Family:** Married Ewa Chmielnicka in 1980; children: Maria and Marcin. **Career:** Since 1960, freelance photographer, working with *Tygodnik Powzechny* magazine, Kraków; photographer of Karol Wojtyla, bishop, archbishop and cardinal of Kraków, now Pope John Paul II, since 1963; worked for *Sweden Now* magazine, Stockholm, 1975. **Recipient:** more than 50 medals and diploma awards in Kraków; Ministry of Art and Culture Prize, Warsaw, 1965; Art Photographer Diploma, Warsaw 1967; National Museum Prize, Oswiecim, Poland 1967; National Foto-Expo Prize, Warsaw, 1969; National Award, Kraków, 1973; Solidarity Award, Warsaw, 1985; Ehrendiplom der Internationalen Buchkunst—Ausstellung, Leipzig, 1989; "Most Beautiful Book of the Year" for *Nekropolie Krolow i Ksiazat Polskich,* Warsaw, 1989; Medal of Goreujskitisk City for *Nekropolie Krolow i Ksiazat Polskich,* 1989; Grand Prix of II National Triennale for Landscape and Tourist Books, 1990; Honour Prize for Outstanding Achievements in Art Photography, Warsaw, 1991; Prize of the Year for *Echo Krakowa,* Cracow, 1992; Decoration of St Mary Magdalene for *Tysiac Lat Chrzescijanstwa na Rusi,* 1992; Prize of the year, awarded by Civitas Crystiana, 1993. Member, Royal Photographic Society, London, 1970; Artiste, Fédération Internationale d'Art Photographique (FIAP), 1973. **Agent:** Union of Polish Art Photographers, ul. Sw. Anny 3, Kraków, Poland. **Address:** ul. Praska 5, 30-328 Kraków, Poland.

Individual Exhibitions:

1960   Galerie Jazz Club, Kraków, Poland (and 1961)
1963   *Pamieć meczeństwa,* Galeria WSP, Kraków, Poland
1965   *Wizja lokalna Trybunalu we Frankfurcio w O'swiecimiu,* Galeria Krzysztofory, Kraków, Poland
1966   *Synagogi i cmentarze Polski poludniowej,* Muzeum Historyczne, Kraków, Poland (with S. Gostynski; travelled to Muzeum Historii Zydow, Warsaw)
1970   *Misteria,* Galeria Prezentacje, Torun, Poland (travelled to Galeria Krzysztofory, Kraków; Galeria Wspolczesna, Warsaw; Museum of Fine Arts, Lodz; Galeria Fotografii, Wroclaw; Galeria BWA, Tarnow; Galeria ZPAR, Warsaw)
1971   *Polish Synagogues and Cemeteries and their Destruction,* Museum of Ethnography and Folklore, Tel Aviv, Israel (with S. Gostynski)
1980   *Polski papiez,* Galeria Kamieniolomy, Kraków, Poland
        Watykan, Ziema Swieta, Góra Athos, Galeria ZPAF, Kraków, Poland
1983   *Weit Stos,* St. Klara Kirche, Nuremberg, West Germany
1990   National Academic Science Library, Leningrad

Adam Bujak's photo-series *Jan Pawel II, Ziemia Swieta* and *Jan Pawel II i misteria z Kalwarii* are on permanent exhibit at Bernardine and Franciscan convent, Kalwaria Zebrzydowska, Poland.

Selected Group Exhibitions:

1969   *Starptautiska 100 Fotomeisteru i Zstade,* Riga, Latvian U.S.S.R.
        World Press Photo, The Hague

1971   *Deuxième Salon International d'Art Photographique,* Monte Carlo
1973   *Weltausstellung der Photographie,* Pressehaus Stern Hamburg, West Germany (and world tour)
1977   *Artists 77,* Union Carbide Building, New York
1978   *APA International Photography Exhibition,* Tokyo
1980   *Sztuka reportazu,* National Museum, Wroclaw, Poland
1981   *Photographie Polonaise,* Centre Georges Pompidou, Paris
1984   *Pogrzeb ks. Jerzego Popieluszki,* Kraków, Poland (travelled to Warsaw)
1985   *Apokalipsa-Swiatlo 2 ciemności,* Kościól Sw. Krzyza, Warsaw

Collections:

International Museum of Photography at George Eastman House, Rochester, New York; National Museum, Wroclaw, Poland; Museum of Fine Arts, Lodz, Poland; Ethnography Museum, Kraków, Poland; Ethnography and Folklore Museum, Tel Aviv, Israel; Museum Auschwitz, Birkenau.

Publications:

By BUJAK: Books and portfolios—*O'swiecim/Auschwitz,* with others, text by Kazimierz Smolén, O'swiecim, Poland 1965; *O'swiecim-Brzezinka,* with text by Adolf Gawlewicz, Warsaw 1973; *Misteria kalwaryjskie,* with text by Wieslaw Murawiec, Kalwaria Zebrzydowska, Poland 1973; *Des Pierres Racontent . . .* , Paris 1973; *Journeys to Glory,* with text by Marjorie B. Yong, New York 1976; *Solange noch Zeit ist Kavalaer,* Kavalaer, West Germany 1977; *Katedra Krakowska na Wawelu,* with text by Michal Rozek, Kraków, Poland 1978; *Un Papa sull' orizonte del duemilia,* with others, text by Grigiel-Citterich, Rome 1979; *The Polish Pope and North,* with others, text by Stan Obodiac, Toronto 1979; *Orle gniazda,* with text by Tomasz Jurasz, Warsaw 1979; *Johannes Paul II,* with text by Mieczyslaw Maliński, Graz, Austria 1979; *Krakowskie pejzaze,* with text by Zbigniew Swiech, Kraków, Poland 1980; *Myslac Ojczyzna,* with text by John Paul II, Rome 1980; *Jan Pawal II,* with text by Tomasz Turowski, Rimini, Italy 1980; *Pieśń Wawelu,* with text by Stanislaw Wyspanski, Kraków, Poland 1980; *Ojciec Swiety, Pielgrzym kalwaryski,* with text by John Paul II and Mikolaj Rudyk, Kalwaria Zebrzydowska, Poland 1981; *Santuarium Maryjne w Rzeszowie,* with text by Mieczyslaw Maliński, Kalwaria Zebrzydowska, Poland 1982; *Ojczyzna,* with text by John Paul II, Kraków, Poland 1982; *Mutter der Versohnung,* with text by Teo Mechtenberg, West Germany 1982; *Zycie Jezusa Chrystusa,* Kalwaria Zebrzydowska, Poland 1983; *Kraków nieznany,* with text by Tadeusz Zychiewicz, Kraków, Poland 1983; *Wege des Lebens mit Jezus und Maria,* with text by Mieczyslaw Maliński, Graz, Austria 1983; *Masters of Polish Photography,* with others, Geneva 1986; *Kwiaty Zalipia,* text by Dereta Gromezakiewiez, Krakow 1987; *Miejsee Pietrewe,* text by Marek Skwarnicki, Kalwaria Zebrzyaswska, 1987; *Misteria,* Warzaw 1989; *Auschwitz Birkenau,* text by Wlacyslaw Barteszewski and others, Freiburg, Basel and Wien 1989; *Jan Pawel II,* Krakow 1990; *In the gardens of the Vatican and castel Gandolfe,* text by Wlcesimierz Redziech, Warsaw 1990; *Bazylika Sw Pietra,* text by Wladzimierz Redziech, Terni 1991; *John Paul II,* with Anerzej Wajaa, Paris and San Francisco 1992; *Polskie Krajabrazy,* text by Anna Szezucka, Warsaw 1993; *Auschwitz,* text by Teresa i Henryk Swiebeezki, Krakow-Oswieim 1993; *Ziemua Jezusa,* text by Jan Pawel II i Miwezyslaw Malinski, Warsaw 1994.

On BUJAK: Books—*Wszystko o fotografii,* Warsaw 1984; *Fotografia polska 1945-1985* by Ryszard Bobrowski, Jerzy Busza and others, Gorzów Wielkopolski, Poland 1985; *Masters of Polish Photography,* with text by Ryszard Bobrowski, Geneva 1986. **Articles**—in *Foto Magazin* (Munich), September 1969; *Tygodnik Polski* (Warsaw), April 1972; *Aktuelt* (Copenhagen), September 1974; *Tygodnik Powszechny* (Kraków, Poland), March 1974; *Sweden Now* (Stockholm), May 1975; *Aktuell Fotografi* (Helsingborg, Sweden), 1976; *Outcry* (Toronto), no. 25, 1975; *Przekroj* (Kraków, Poland), January 1976; *Kultura* (Warsaw), November 1976; *The Drama Review* (New

Untitled. Photograph ©Adam Bujak.

York), September 1977; *Daily News* (Chicago), May 1977; *Fotografia* (Warsaw), special issue, 1979; *Projekt* (Warsaw), January 1983; "Fotograficzne oratoria" by Jerzy Busza in *Fotografia* (Warsaw), no. 4, 1984; interview with Mata Janos in *Képes* (Budapest), 7 December 1989; review by Czeslaw Czaplinski in *Kariera* (New York), no. 6, June 1990; "Hunting for Men's Faces" by Andrzej Lisowski in *Tygodnik Wybrzeze*, no. 3-4, 27 January 1991; book review by Jerzy Piekarczyk in *Przekroj* (Krakow), no. 14, 3 April 1994; "Wandering to Holy Places" by Krzysztof Maslon in *Rzeczpospolita* (Warsaw), no. 112, 16 May 1994.

*   *   *

Press photography is one of the main branches of Polish contemporary photography. Despite the fact that the most important postwar journal for this type of work, the weekly publication *Swiat*, no longer appears and that a further weekly, *Polska*, has lost its primary purpose, there are still many illustrated periodicals on the market—such as *ITD*, *Perspektywy* or *Razem*— that afford it a great deal of space. While the outlet for aspiring journalistic photography exists, there is a lack of individuality capable of breaking through current editorial views and imposing its own themes, interests and passions on the papers. An exception to this, not linked to any particular publication, is Adam Bujak.

Bujak expressed no particular interests in his youth and, forever attempting different careers did not really know whether he would become a businessman, a dancer or a priest. He became a photographer. "The arrival of photography in my life," Bujak remembers, "was not accidental but conditional on my coming across things that fascinated me. My photography was born from the need to fix events that I witnessed by chance and that I hadn't been able to predict. When I first came across mementos of past epochs, I felt the need to inform society of things that the average 20th century man is ignorant about. I am convinced that the things I witnessed should not remain merely between myself and the other people concerned, that the information in my photographs is a necessary supplement to our knowledge of contemporary man."

The first of the events mentioned by Bujak was the Passion Play enacted at Kalwaria Zebrzydowska not far from Kraków. Here, for over 280 years, in the last week of Lent, local actors, mostly workers and peasants, put on a Passion Play that traces the events from Christ's journey to Jerusalem to Pilate's judgement and the Crucifixion. The religious character of this play and its pageantry, folklore and mysticism prompted Bujak to pilgrimages with members of other religious groups in Poland. Over the next few years, he travelled with members of the Orthodox, Protestant and Islamic churches, with Adventists and other religious sects. "Religion," Bujak admits, "is the subject closest to me. Without it, I would not be the person I am. I have not only photographic links with this subject but spiritual ones as well. In fact, in all of this I'm rarely a photographer. I live with people, share experiences and sometimes, without thinking about it, take photographs by some reflex action. Even then I feel an abominable intruder."

It must be emphasised that this attitude distinguishes Bujak from other photographers who are interested in similar issues. The thing which most clearly separates Bujak from other reporters of his time is not only his rare inner conviction, his fascination with his subject and the piety with which he approaches disappearing and often unrepeatable human phenomena—it is also, and maybe above all, his personal religious quest. "I hold fast with the Catholic faith," the photographer stresses, "but I have experience of Orthodox, Jewish and even Islamic religions. I believe these are enormously powerful subjects .... I have behind me twenty years of searching but that's not enough. I think that's only the beginning of a lengthy affair.

Perhaps, in my declining years, I will put together an extensive album, a publication of religions of the world .... "

At the heart of Bujak's photography lies the need to reveal and describe hopes and dreams that are never fully realised and aspirations to something beyond that which is offered by man's daily life and work. There is also—and, for Bujak, this is probably the most important thing of all—the conviction that, despite their separateness and even their hostility to one another, all the great religions of the world are part of a larger whole. Like branches growing from the tree of human fate, despite different directions and obstacles, they all reach towards one end—to light.

—Ryszard Bobrowski

BULLOCK, Edna.

Nationality: American. **Born:** Edna Jeanette Earle in Hollister, California, 20 May 1915. **Education:** Studied at Modesto Junior College, A.A. 1936; University of California at Los Angeles, B.E. in Physical Education 1938; University of California at Berkeley, Certificate of Completion for General Secondary Teaching Credential 1940; studied photography under Henry Gilpin, Ron James, Tom Millea and David Fuess, Monterey Peninsula College, 1976-78; archival processing, mounting and 32 years of life experiences with Wynn Bullock; workshops with Ansel Adams, Morley Baer, Judy Dater, Eihoh Hosoe, Eva Rubenstein, Jerry Uelsmann, Al Weber and others. **Family:** Married the photographer Wynn Bullock in 1943 (died, 1975); step-daughter: Mary Wynne; daughters: Barbara Ann and Lynne Marie. **Career:** Taught physical education and dance, Fresno High School, 1940-43; settled in Monterey, California, 1946; full-time mother, homemaker and helpmate until late 1950s when teaching career was resumed, first as a substitute, then as full-time teacher; taught physical education, dance and home economics at high school and junior high levels; retired in 1974 to care for Wynn who was ill with cancer; began own photographic career, 1976; lecturer, teacher and workshop leader, since 1976. **Address:** 155 Mar Vista Drive, Monterey, California 93940, USA.

Individual Exhibitions:

1977	Country Club Camera Store, Pacific Grove, California
	Shado Gallery, Portland, Oregon
1979	Governors State University, University Park, Illinois
	Pacific Grove Art Center, California
	Photo-Synthesis Gallery, Clovis, California
1980	Cafe Balthazar Gallery, Pacific Grove, California
	Collectors Gallery, Pacific Grove, California (with Wynn Bullock)
1981	Focus Gallery, San Francisco (with Wynn Bullock)
	San Jose City College, California (with Wynn Bullock)
1982	Exposures Gallery, Libertyville, Illinois (with Wynn Bullock)
	Jeb Gallery, Providence, Rhode Island (with Wynn Bullock)
1983	Ledel Gallery, New York (with Wynn Bullock)
	Neikrug Gallery, New York (with Wynn Bullock)
	Santa Fe Center for Photography, New Mexico (with Wynn Bullock)
1985	Cape Cod Museum of Natural History, Brewster, Massachusetts
	Spectrum Gallery, Fresno, California (with Martha Duff)
	Vision Gallery, San Francisco (with Wynn Bullock)
1986	Photography at Oregon Gallery, Eugene, Oregon (with Wynn Bullock)
	University of Santa Clara, California
	Yellowstone Art Center, Billings, Montana (with Wynn Bullock)
1987	Betty Garland Gallery, San Francisco (with Morrie Camhi and Martha Casanave)
	Exposure Gallery, Orleans, Massachusetts
	Olive Hyde Art Gallery, Fremont, California (with Wynn Bullock)
1989	Axis/291, Richmond, Virginia
	Michigan State University, East Lansing, Michigan
	Pacific Grove Art Center, California
1990	Foto Galerie, Chincoteague, Virginia (with Wynn Bullock)
	South Suburban College, South Holland, Illinois
1991	Carl Cherry Foundation, Carmel, California (with sculptor Ken Wiese)
	Monterey Peninsula Unitarian Church, Carmel, California
	California State University, Chico, California (with Ruth Bernhard)
1993	G. Ray Hawkins Gallery, Santa Monica, California (with Wynn Bullock)
	Halsted Gallery, Birmingham, Michigan (with Wynn Bullock)
	Photo Forum, Pittsburgh, Pennsylvania (with Wynn Bullock)

Peggy and Round Rocks, **1991.** Photograph ©Edna Bullock.

PhotoZone Gallery, Eugene, Oregon (with Wynn Bullock)
Fotofeis--the Scottish International Festival of Photography,
  Edinburgh (with Wynn Bullock)

1995   *Edna's Nudes,* Marjorie Evans Gallery, Carmel, California; F.
          Stops Here Gallery, Santa Barbara, California; Halsted
          Gallery, Birmingham, Michigan; S.K. Josefberg Studio,

Portland, Oregon

Selected Group Exhibitions:

1977　*Portrait of the Earth,* Southwest Center of Photography,
　　　　Austin, Texas
　　　　Women, Southwest Center of Photography, Austin, Texas
1978　*Fifty Outstanding Photographers,* Silver Image Gallery, Seattle
　　　　Friends of the Door, The Print Gallery, Carmel, California
　　　　Twenty Western Photographic Artists, Reflections Gallery of
　　　　Photography, Sedona, Arizona
1981　*Master Photographers of the 20th Century,* Edwynn Hauk
　　　　Gallery, Chicago
　　　　Western Images, William K. Lyons Gallery, Coral Gables,
　　　　Florida
　　　　Women Photographers, Palo Alto Cultural Center, California
1983　*Photographs from the Collection of Jane Reese Williams:
　　　　Photographs by Female Photographers,* Santa Fe Center for
　　　　Photography, New Mexico
1984　*The Nude: Classic Beauty,* Silver Image Gallery, Seattle
　　　　(and 1992)
　　　　The Unseen Photographs, The Photography Gallery, La Jolla,
　　　　California
1985　*The Nude Show,* Photographic Image Gallery, Portland, Oregon
1986　*Commitment to Vision,* University of Oregon, Eugene
　　　　(and tour)
1988　*Behold the Man,* Stills Gallery, Edinburgh, Scotland
　　　　The Human Vessel, Museum of Photography, Antwerp,
　　　　Belgium
1989　*Women in Photography International,* Pacific Grove Art
　　　　Center, California (and tour)
1990　*A Celebration—150 Years of Photography,* David Adler
　　　　Cultural Center, Libertyville, Illinois
　　　　Educational Steps, Santa Fe Center for Photography, New
　　　　Mexico
1991　*International Exhibit of Women Photographers,* sponsored by
　　　　the Union of Photographers of the USSR (opened in Ryazan
　　　　and travelled throughout the Soviet Union)
1993　*Figures, Portraits, Persona—Photographic Works by Female
　　　　Artists,* Clarion University, Pennsylvania
1994　*Dreaming Art—Visual Aids,* Carl Cherry Center for the Arts,
　　　　Carmel, California
　　　　The Male Nude, Scott Nichols Gallery, San Francisco

Selected Collections:

Bibliothèque Nationale, Paris; Center for Creative Photography, University of
Arizona, Tucson; Michigan State University, East Lansing; Monterey Penin-
sula Museum of Art; National Museum of Modern Art, Kyoto, Japan;
University of California, Santa Cruz.

Selected Publications:

By BULLOCK: Book—*Edna's Nudes,* text written and edited by Barbara
Bullock-Wilson with afterword by Karen Sinsheimer, Santa Barbara, California 1995.

On BULLOCK: Books—*Happy, Happy, Happy* by Lois Earle, Mesa,
Arizona 1977; *Cows, Poets & Other Loves* by Caryl Hill and Deborah Weston,
Carmel, California 1978; *A Taste of Honey* by Lois Earle, Mesa, Arizona
1981; *Combing the Coast I* by Ruth A. Jackson, San Francisco 1981; *Combing
the Coast II* by Ruth A. Jackson, San Francisco 1982; *Combing the Coast,
Highway One from San Francisco to San Luis Obispo* by Ruth A. Jackson, San
Francisco 1985; *En Marcha—Spanish Reading Series,* New York 1985;
Photographers' Encyclopaedia International, 1839 to the Present, Switzer-
land 1985; *The Naked and the Nude: A History of Nude Photography* by Jorge
Lewinski, London 1987; *Erotic by Nature,* edited by David Steinburg, North
San Juan, California 1988. **Articles**—"Edna Bullock" by Patricia Gardner in
The Creative Woman (Illinois), Vol. 9, No. 4, Summer 1989; "A Gathering of

Friends—An Interview with Edna Bullock" by Donna Conrad in *Camera &
Darkroom* (Los Angeles), February 1993; "A Nude Awakening" by Ruth
Wishart in *The Scotsman* (Edinburgh), 5 June 1993; "Through a Lens
Magically" by Richard Pitnick in *Coast Weekly* (Carmel, California), 19
August 1993; "A Conversation with Edna Bullock and Barbara Bullock-
Wilson" by Brooks Jensen in *LensWork Quarterly* (Portland, Oregon), No. 7,
Fall 1994.

* * *

Edna Bullock was sixty in 1975 when her husband, Wynn Bullock, the
noted Northern California photographer, died. Trained as a dancer, then a
school teacher of dance, physical education and home economics, she had
spent 32 years as a wife, mother and assistant to the artist. He was best known
for his mysterious and mystical *Child in the Forest* (their daughter Barbara
along the Redwood Highway), the most popular photograph in the *Family of
Man* exhibition and book of 1955. Edna inherited Wynn's darkroom and fine
view cameras. She decided to learn to use them.

Bullock enrolled at Monterey Peninsula College and took workshops with
such photographers as Ansel Adams (an old family friend), Judy Dater, Jerry
Uelsmann, Eikoh Hose and Morley Baer. She chose her first subjects—
gnarled wood in closeup, objects in flea markets—because Wynn had *not*
photographed them. She found her own voice in relation to those of his friends:
Edward Weston and his son, Brett; Ansel Adams; Ruth Bernhard; and others.
She began exhibiting in 1977, and regularly lectured and ran workshops from
then on.

Bullock's work blossomed when she turned to the subject of the nude: in
the studio and outdoors, on the coast and in the desert, and she soon added male
models and couples to a genre most identified, especially in Northern
California, with woman and nature. Her conception of the union of nude and
landscape reflects the idealization of both in the vitalist philosophies of the f/
64 group and their disciples in the Bay Area before World War II. But unlike
such photographers as Edward Weston, she often puts her models in balletic
motion, or shows them in quiet interaction, adding energy and emotion to an
otherwise distanced style of careful composition and rich texture, generally in
black and white.

Bullock also makes portraits with a keen eye for characteristic expression
and gesture; takes amusing street photographs; and experiments with soft
focus, double exposure, sandwiched negatives and negative printing.

Her first book, *Edna's Nudes,* was published in 1995 for the 80th
anniversary of her birth, and a travelling exhibition of that title is planned.

—Anne Hoy

BULLOCK, Wynn.

Nationality: American. **Born:** Percy Wingfield Bullock in Chicago, Illinois,
18 April 1902. **Education:** Attended elementary and secondary schools,
South Pasadena, California, 1907-21; attended Columbia College, New York,
1925-27; University of West Virginia, Morgantown, 1931-32; studied voice
and music in New York 1921-28, in Paris 1928 and in Milan and Berlin 1930;
studied photography, under Edward Kaminski, Art Center School, Los Angeles, 1938-40; influenced by the work of semanticist Alfred Korzybski, Los
Angeles, 1940-41. **Military Service:** Served in the United States Army, in
California, 1942-44. **Family:** Married Mary Elizabeth McCarty in 1925
(divorced, 1941); children: Mary Wynne (Mimi) and George (died, 1942);
married Edna Jeanette Earle in 1943; daughters: Barbara Ann and Lynne
Marie. **Career:** Worked as singer in music revues, New York, 1921-28; gave
concerts in Europe 1928-30; managed wife's real estate business, Clarksburg,
West Virginia, 1931-37; commercial and portrait photographer, producing
and selling tourist postcards, Los Angeles and Santa Monica, California, 1940-
42, 1944-46; commercial photographer, 1946-68, working mainly for Fort
Ord military base, Monterey, California, 1946-59. Taught at the Institute of
Design, Illinois Institute of Technology, Chicago, University of California at
Santa Clara, and San Francisco State College. Trustee and Chairman of

Tree Trunk, **1971.** Photograph ©Wynn Bullock. Courtesy of the Wynn and Edna Bullock Trust.

Exhibition Committee, Friends of Photography, Carmel, California, 1968-70.
Died: (in Monterey, California), 16 November 1975.

Individual Exhibitions:

1941	Los Angeles County Museum of Art
1947	Santa Barbara Museum of Art, California
1954	University of California at Los Angeles
1955	Limelight Gallery, New York
1956	Cherry Foundation, Carmel, California
	M.H. de Young Memorial Museum, San Francisco
	International Museum of Photography, George Eastman House, Rochester, New York
1957	Photographic and Cine Society, Johannesburg, South Africa
	Photographia de Assoução dos Velhos, Pietermaritzburg, Portuguese East Africa
	Photographia de Assoução dos Velhos, Lourenco Marques, Portuguese East Africa
1958	Federation of Arts, Prague
1959	Gull Pacific Arts Gallery, Richmond, California
1960	Princeton University, New Jersey
	Monterey Peninsula College, California

1961	Fine Art Galerie Pierre Venderburght, Brussels
	Icon Gallery, Venice, California
	3 Photographers, Kalamazoo Institute of Arts, Michigan (with Aaron Siskind and David Vestal)
1962	Carl Siembab Gallery, Boston
	Cheney Cowles Memorial Art Gallery, Spokane, Washington
1963	Toren Gallery, San Francisco
1964	University of Florida, Gainesville
	Heliography Gallery, New York (with Jerry Uelsmann)
1966	Foothill College, Los Altos, California
	International Museum of Photography, George Eastman House, Rochester, New York
1967	Jacksonville Museum of Art, Florida
1968	Camera Work Gallery, Newport Beach, California
	Rhode Island School of Design, Providence
	University of St. Thomas Media Center, Houston
1969	Institute of Design, Illinois Institute of Technology, Chicago
	Phoenix College, Arizona
	Reed College, Portland, Oregon
	San Francisco Museum of Art
	Skidmore College, Saratoga Springs, New York
	University of Iowa, Iowa City

University of North Carolina, Greensboro
University of the South, Sewanee, Tennessee
University of Washington, Seattle
Witkin Gallery, New York (with Les Krims)
1970   Amon Carter Museum, Fort Worth, Texas
Colorado Springs Fine Art Center, Colorado
Minneapolis Institute of Arts, Minnesota
Rice University, Houston
Santa Barbara Museum of Art, California
Temple University, Philadelphia
1971   Bathhouse Gallery, Milwaukee, Wisconsin
Columbia College, Chicago
The 831 Gallery, Birmingham, Michigan
Friends of Photography, Carmel, California
Maryland Institute of the Arts, Baltimore
University of Georgia, Athens
1972   Limited Edition Gallery, Chicago
Shado Gallery, Oregon City, Oregon
United States Information Agency, Washington, D.C. (toured Europe and North Africa)
University of Santa Clara, CA
1973   Light Gallery, New York
Pasadena Museum of Art, California
Ohio University, Athens
Bibliothéque Nationale, Paris
3 Photographers, University of Colorado, Boulder (with Aaron Siskind and Edmund Teske)
1974   Madison Art Center, Wisconsin
1976   Metropolitan Museum of Art, New York
Art Institute of Chicago
San Francisco Museum of Art
1981   Focus Gallery, San Francisco (with Edna Bullock)
1982   Photography West Gallery, Carmel, California
1983   Santa Fe Center for Photography, New Mexico (with Edna Bullock)
1985   Vision Gallery, San Francisco (with Edna Bullock)
1986   Photo Gallery International, Tokyo (with Edna Bullock)
Photography at Oregon Gallery, Eugene, Oregon (with Edna Bullock)
Yellowstone Art Center, Billings, Montana (with Edna Bullock)
1987   Olive Hyde Art Gallery, Fremont, California (with Edna Bullock)
1988   La Reverbere Galerie Photographique, Lyon, France
1989   The Photographic Center of the Monterey Peninsula, Carmel, California
1990   Foto Galerie, Chincoteague, Virginia (with Edna Bullock)
1992   Center for Photographic Art, Carmel, California
1993   G. Ray Hawkins Gallery, Santa Monica (with Edna Bullock)
Photo Forum, Pittsburgh, Pennsylvania (with Edna Bullock)
PhotoZone Gallery, Eugene, Oregon (with Edna Bullock)
The Halsted Gallery, Birmingham, Michigan (with Edna Bullock)
University of Edinburgh, Edinburgh, Scotland (with Edna Bullock)
1994   Ansel Adams Gallery at the Inn at Spanish Bay, Pebble Beach, California
Photo Gallery International, Tokyo

Selected Group Exhibitions:

1955   *The Family of Man,* Museum of Modern Art, New York (and world tour)
1960   *The Sense of Abstraction,* Museum of Modern Art, New York
1974   *Photography in America,* Whitney Museum of American Art, New York
1975   *The Land: 20th Century Landscape Photographs Selected by Bill Brandt,* Victoria and Albert Museum, London (travelled to the National Gallery, Edinburgh; Ulster Museum, Belfast; and National Museum of Wales, Cardiff, 1976)
1977   *Corroborations & Constructions,* Chicago Center for Contemporary Photography, Chicago
1978   *From the Collection of Mr and Mrs Arnold Gilbert,* University of Wisconsin, Milwaukee
1979   *Message from the West Coast,* Photo Gallery International, Tokyo
1980   *Photography of the 50's,* International Center of Photography, New York (travelled to the Center for Contemporary Photography, University of Arizona, Tucson; Minneapolis Institute of Arts, Minnesota; California State University at Long Beach; and Delaware Art Museum, Wilmington)
1981   *Master Portraits of the 20th Century,* Edwynn Hauk Gallery, Chicago
1982   *Color as Form,* International Museum of Photography at George Eastman House, Rochester, New York
1984   *Photography in California 1945-80,* San Francisco Museum of Modern Art (travelled to the Akron Art Museum, Ohio; Corcoran Gallery, Washington, D.C.; Los Angeles Municipal Art Gallery; Cornell University, Ithaca, New York; High Museum of Art, Atlanta, Georgia; Museum Folkwang, Essen; Centre Georges Pompidou, Paris; Museum of Photographic Arts, San Diego, California)
1985   *American Images 1945-80,* Barbican Art Gallery, London (toured Britain)
1986   *In Love with the Universe,* Dartmouth College, Hanover, New Hampshire
1987   *Photography and Art 1946-86,* Los Angeles County Museum of Art, Los Angeles (travelled throughout US)
1988   *The Influence of Chinese Art on the Recent Art of the American West Coast,* Taiwan Museum of Art, Taichung, Taiwan
Master Photographs from the ''Photography in the Fine Arts'' Exhibitions 1959-1967, International Center for Photography, New York
1989   *Earthscape,* Expo 90 Photo Museum, Tokyo
1990   *Picturing California: A Century of Photographic Genius,* Oakland Museum, Oakland (and then travelling)
1992   *The Nude—Classic Beauty,* Silver Image Gallery, Seattle, Washington
1994   *Hidden Faces,* Paul Kopeikin Gallery, Los Angeles, California

Selected Collections:

Center for Creative Photography, University of Arizona, Tucson (prints, negatives and private papers); Museum of Modern Art, New York; Metropolitan Museum of Art, New York; International Museum of Photography, George Eastman House, Rochester, New York; Museum of Fine Arts, Boston; Smithsonian Institution, Washington, D.C.; Museum of Fine Arts, St. Petersburg, Florida; University of Nebraska, Lincoln; Oakland Museum, California; San Francisco Museum of Art; Australian National Gallery, Canberra, Australia; National Gallery, Ottawa, Canada; Princeton University, Princeton, NJ;Royal Photographic Society, Bath, England; Stanford University Museum of Art, Stanford, Ca; Tokyo College of Photography, Tokyo, Japan; University of Texas, Austin, Texas; Victoria and Albert Museum, London, England; Yale University, New Haven, Connecticut.

Publications:

By BULLOCK: Books—*Monterey's Adobe Heritage,* Monterey 1965; *The Widening Stream,* with text by Richard Mack, Carmel, California 1965; *Wynn Bullock,* with text by Barbara Bullock, San Francisco 1971; *Wynn Bullock: Photography, A Way of Life,* with text by Barbara Bullock-Wilson, edited by Liliane DeCock, Dobbs Ferry, New York 1973; *Photographs, 1951-1973,* portfolio of 12 photos, with an introduction by Ansel Adams, Monterey, California 1973; *The Photograph As Symbol,* Capitola, California 1976; *Wynn Bullock,* with text by David Feuss, 4th in the *Aperture History of Photography* series, New York 1976; *Wynn Bullock: Photographing the Nude,* with introduction by Barbara Bullock-Wilson, Utah 1984; *Wynn Bullock: The Enchanted Landscape—Photographs 1940-1975,* with poem by Ursula LeGuin and essay by Raphael Shevelev, New York and London 1993.

Articles—"Portfolio" in *Aperture* (Rochester, New York), October 1953; "A Lyrical Journey to Big Sur" with poetry by Eric Barker in *Carmel Pacific Spectator Journal* (Carmel), September-October 1954; "Partial Reversal Line" in *The Photographic Journal* (London), April 1955; "Virtues of Large and Small Cameras Are Evaluated" in *Monterey Peninsula Herald* (California), 3 November 1956; "Line Photography" in *Medical and Biological Illustration* (London), April 1957; "The Fourth Dimension" in *Photography* (London), September 1962; "Nature Photography: A Boy Fishing" in *Pacific Discovery* (San Francisco), May-June 1963; "Space and Time" in *Photographers on Photography*, edited by Nathan Lyons, New York, 1966; "Wynn Bullock Nudes," with George F. Pollack, in *Creative Camera* (London), June 1969; "Introduction to the Work of Edward Weston" in *Edward Weston Portfolio* (New York) 1971; "Photographer's Statement" in *Wynn Bullock: Twenty Color Photographs,* (Santa Clara, California) 1972; "Wynn Bullock," interview, in *Dialogue with Photography*, edited by Paul Hill and Thomas Cooper, London 1979.

On BULLOCK: Books—*The Family of Man,* edited by Edward Steichen, New York 1955; *American Photography: The Sixties,* exhibition catalogue, Lincoln, Nebraska 1966; *Photography in the Twentieth Century* by Nathan Lyons, New York 1967; *Photography, USA,* exhibition catalogue, Lincoln, Massachusetts 1967; *Not Man Apart* by David Brower, San Francisco 1969; *The Land: 20th Century Landscape Photographs Selected by Bill Brandt,* exhibition catalogue, edited by Mark Haworth-Booth, London 1975; *The Photographers' Choice,* edited by Kelly Wise, Danbury, New Hampshire 1975; *Helen Gee and the Limelight: A Pioneering Photography Gallery of The Fifties,* exhibition catalogue, by Peter C. Bunnell, New York 1977; *Geschichte der Fotografie im 20. Jahrhundert/Photography in the 20th Century* by Petr Tausk, Cologne 1977, London 1980; *Darkroom 1,* edited by Eleanor Lewis, New York 1977; *Amerikanische Landschaftsphotographie 1860-1978,* exhibition catalogue, with an introduction by Klaus-Jürgen Sembach, Munich 1978; *The Photograph Collector's Guide* by Lee D. Witkin and Barbara London, Boston and London 1979; *Photography of the Fifties: An American Perspective* by Helen Gee, Tucson, Arizona 1980; *American Landscapes* by John Szarkowski, New York 1981; *The Imaginary Photo Museum* by Helmut Gernsheim, Renate and L. Fritz Gruber and others, Cologne 1981, London 1982; *Wynn Bullock Archive—Guide Series #6,* edited by Charles Lamb and Cynthia Ludlow, Tucson 1982; *Color as Form: A History of Color Photography,* exhibition catalogue, with introduction by Robert A. Sobieszek, Rochester, New York 1982; *Photography in California 1945-1980* by Louise Katzman, San Francisco 1984; *A World History of Photography* by Naomi Rosenblum, New York 1984; *American Images: Photographs 1945-1980,* edited by Peter Turner, London 1985; *Decade by Decade: 20th Century American Photography,* edited by James Enyeart, Boston 1989. Articles—"Photographic Horizon" by C. Weston Booth in *U.S. Camera* (New York), August 1946; "Creative Photography 1956" by Van Deren Coke in *Aperture* (Rochester, New York), January 1956; "Wynn Bullock" by Lew Parella in *U.S. Camera Annual,* New York 1956; "Thoughts on Wynn Bullock: The Landscape—An Object of Philosophy" by George Bush in *International Photo Technik* (Munich), no. 1, 1961; "The Eyes of Three Phantasists: Laughlin, Sommer, Bullock" by Jonathan Williams in *Aperture* (Rochester, New York), October 1961; "Wynn Bullock: A Critical Appreciation" by Nat Herz in *Infinity* (New York), November 1961; "Wynn Bullock: Tracing Man's Roots in Nature" by Barbara Bullock and Jerry Uelsmann in *Modern Photography* (New York), May 1970; "Wynn Bullock, a Retrospective View" by Colin Osman in *Creative Camera* (London), June 1971; "Wynn Bullock" by Gerry Badger in *The Photographic Journal* (London), May 1975; "Wynn Bullock" by Jean-Claude Gautrand in *Le Nouveau Cinema* (Paris), February 1976; "Wynn Bullock 1902-1975" in *Popular Photography* (New York), March 1976; "Wynn Bullock: Visionary and Philosopher" in *Artweek* (Oakland, California), 3 October 1981; "The Magic Eye of Wynn Bullock" by Ruth Jackson in *American West* (Tucson) October 1989; "Wynn Bullock and the Magic of Point Lobos" by Barbara Bullock-Wilson in *The Herald's Alta Vista Magazine* (Monterey), 18 November 1990; "Wynn Bullock and Point Lobos: A Loving Tribute to Man and Place" by Barbara Bullock-Wilson in *The Photographic Journal* (Bath), October 1992; "A Gathering of Friends—An Interview with Edna Bullock" by Donna Conrad in *Camera and Darkroom* (Los Angeles), February 1993. Films—*Two Photographers: Wynn Bullock and Imogen Cunningham* by Fred Padula, 1966; *Wynn Bullock: Reflections* by Tom Tyson, 1975.

*   *   *

Wynn Bullock was one of the most widely respected photo-artists of our time. And yet, in many ways, he was also one of the least understood. Wynn became well known for his evocative and striking photographs of trees, nudes in nature, and moving water; but in order to appreciate the scope of his creative life and work, it is important to know that in addition to being a gifted image maker, Wynn was also a deeply inspired and intellectually curious man.

Wynn Bullock's photographs have a penetrating, enigmatic and almost mystical quality that sets his work apart from that of other photographers who work with similar subjects. The best of his photography tends to catch you off guard with its combination of formal beauty and disturbingly provocative imagery. We see rocks shrouded in a luminous atmosphere that defies simple comprehension and haunting interiors with undertones of loneliness, alienation, and death. There are intimations of dynamic forces and intriguing implied narratives in many of his images, but somehow the mysteries are never explained; we are simply left to wonder in awe.

Many great works of art raise questions in the mind of the viewer without offering any obvious or immediate answers. The enigma of Mona Lisa's smile is a good example. It is this quality of mystery held in suspension that gives many of Wynn's photographs their power and depth. And yet, because Wynn's images are so visually satisfying, this is as far as most of us go in appreciating his work. To go further one needs to ask, What provided the motivating force for his creative life? Where do images like his come from?

The question is a relevant one because as well as being a skilled photographer, Wynn Bullock was also a teacher. Through his lectures and writing he wanted us to understand that our presumptions about the nature of the visual world are superficial and overly simple. Every serious artist knows this intuitively, but Wynn made the effort to formulate his ideas into a philosophical system that he demonstrated through his work and interactions with students and followers. Wynn's interest in spreading his ideas made him controversial—not everyone is comfortable with the idea of an artist lecturing on abstract philosophy. Yet he firmly believed that we can and should advance to profound conclusions about nature by asking apparently simple and impertinent questions. In a lecture he might ask for example, "What color is this red apple?" Our first reaction might be to consider the question ridiculous. A red apple is obviously red! He would then invite us to consider the intriguing fact that the apple only appears red to our eyes because its skin is reflecting the red wavelengths of light while invisibly absorbing the others. With this idea firmly in our minds we are left with the confounding question: "What color is the apple *unto itself?*" Of course a question like this one is inherently impossible for us to answer. But then, Wynn's objective was not for us to solve the problem, but rather to begin questioning our stubborn convictions that our senses are giving us an accurate view of the world. The point that he was trying to make with exercises like this was that our proper responses to nature should be closer to wide-eyed awe than to comfortable familiarity. It was Wynn's desire to record this feeling of awe on film that motivated him to photograph the way that he did.

Wynn took this process a step further by rationalizing his awareness of nature's mystery into a number of philosophical principles that provided him with a systematic way of communicating his insights. The list of these principles includes such statements as "time is the fourth dimension," "opposites are one," and, "ordering is not the thing ordered." There were times when an experience that Wynn encountered in nature would inspire these concepts; at other times the concepts themselves would give him ideas for how to photograph more creatively. For Wynn, philosophical exploration became the natural counterpoint to this instinctive impulse to create. Consciousness and feeling merged to complete the creative process.

Wynn would happily discuss these and other subjects for hours, but of course he did more than simply think and write about these ideas; his response was to begin photographing natural subjects in a way that challenged the inherent conservatism of our senses. To this end, any photographic technique that worked was fair. Wynn loved to experiment with photography's ability to create the appearance of an altered reality, and it is for this reason that we see such a wide variety of departures from straight-forward printmaking techniques in his work. Pieces of wood appear as negative images that glow where a positive print would show a shadow. Photographs of tide-pools are printed upside down so that what we know to be depressions seem to rise out of the ground. If one technique didn't satisfy or interest him he would simply try another. It was Wynn's ability to so consistently translate his ideas into persuasive images that confirms his place among the masters of creative photography. The concept "Time is the fourth dimension" became his famous study of sea palms and waves. "Opposites are one" appears as the haunting image of the naked child in the woods. We could easily dismiss these statements as being relatively unimportant when compared with the photographs themselves, but to do so would limit our understanding of Wynn's approach to life and art.

To an artist, an individual work of art is more than an isolated statement; it is also a benchmark that records his progress along the path of personal growth. When we consider the greater body of Wynn's work in this light, his progressive development as an artist/philosopher becomes easier to see. His earliest photographs show the influence of Edward Weston, but even then he experimented with the process of solarization as a way of taking his images beyond the familiar idiom. Later his work becomes strongly romantic, psychological and enigmatically sensual. He photographed nudes and children, but often in lonely and dilapidated settings that give the images a somber quality that suggests vulnerability and pathos.

Later still, Wynn formulated what was to become the central theme of his aesthetic/philosophical system. He came to believe that there is an inherent and profound difference between Reality, which he defined as the limited impression of the world that we derive from our senses—the redness of the apple; and Existence, those intangible and underlying qualities of the universe that are beyond the reach of our perceptions—the apple's true color. The more sensitive Wynn became to the presence of Existence in the world around him, the less content he became with strictly representational images. At this point in his career he began producing a large body of dramatically abstracted close-up studies of wood and other common objects. In these images Wynn left the world of appearances behind; the essential nature of things was all that mattered. There's a soberness that pervades this work, a dense encompassing quiet that suggests the presence of the unknown. One can feel that the attention of the artist is focussed through these photographs to sensations beyond the reach of ordinary life. In many ways these images are less accessible than his earlier descriptive work, but to many they represent the height of Wynn's accomplishment as an image maker, iconographer, and sensitive human being.

—Chris Johnson

BURCHARD, Jerry.

Nationality: American. **Born:** Rochester, New York, 1 December 1931. **Education:** Studied at the California School of Fine Arts, now the San Francisco Art Institute, 1956-60, B.F.A. 1960. **Military Service:** Served as a photography mate, in the United States Navy, in Italy, 1952-56. **Career:** Worked for the Kodak Photographic Products Company, Rochester, New York, 1950-52. Freelance photographer, now based in San Francisco, since 1960. Instructor in Photography, San Francisco Art Institute, since 1966 (Head of the Photography Department, 1968-71, 1978-79). **Recipient:** Photography Fellowship, 1976, 1978, and Survey Grant, 1979, National Endowment for the Arts. **Agent:** Jehu-Wong Galleries, 2719 Bush Street, San Francisco, California 94115. **Address:** 1014 Greenwich Street, San Francisco, California 94133, U.S.A.

Individual Exhibitions:

1968   *Italian Circus,* San Francisco Art Institute
1975   Texas Gallery, Houston
        A Selection of Photographs, American Gallery, San Francisco
1976   Center of the Eye, Sun Valley, Idaho
1978   Corcoran Gallery, Washington, D.C.
        Addison Gallery, Phillips Academy, Andover, Massachusetts
1979   *Color Photographs,* Jehu Gallery, San Francisco

        *3 San Francisco Photographers: Jerry Burchard, Jyo Kushida,
        Joel Sackett,* Nickle Arts Museum, University of Calgary,
        Alberta
        *Jerry Burchard/Ingeborg Gerdes/John Spence Weir: Photo-
        graphic Viewpoints,* San Francisco Museum of Modern Art
1981   *New Color Landscapes,* Jehu Gallery, San Francisco

Selected Group Exhibitions:

1966   *Experience,* San Francisco Art Institute
1969   *Recent Acquisitions,* Pasadena Art Museum, California
1970   *California Photographers 1970,* University of California at
        Davis (travelled to the Oakland Art Museum, California, and
        Pasadena Art Museum, California)
        8 Photographers, Pratt Institute, Brooklyn, New York
1975   *Dimensional Light,* California State University at Fullerton
        San Francisco Renaissance: Photographs of the 50's and 60's,
        Gotham Book Mart Gallery, New York
1976   *Camera in Common,* Wheelock Gallery, Boston
        Contemporary Photographs, Fogg Art Museum, Harvard
        University, Cambridge, Massachusetts
1979   *Burchard/Cohen/Hallman/Mertin,* Southwest Missouri State
        University, Springfield
1984   *Photography in California 1945-80,* San Francisco Museum of
        Modern Art (travelled to the Akron Art Museum, Ohio;
        Corcoran Gallery, Washington, D.C.; Los Angeles Municipal
        Art Gallery; Cornell University, Ithaca, New York; High
        Museum of Art, Atlanta, Georgia; Museum Folkwang,
        Essen; Centre Georges Pompidou, Paris; Museum of
        Photographic Arts, San Diego, California)

Collections:

International Museum of Photography, George Eastman House, Rochester, New York; Visual Studies Workshop, Rochester, New York; Fogg Art Museum, Harvard University, Cambridge, Massachusetts; Addison Gallery, Phillips Academy, Andover, Massachusetts; Library of Congress, Washington, D.C.; Target Collection, Museum of Fine Arts, Houston; Pasadena Museum of Art, California; San Francisco Museum of Modern Art; Seattle Art Museum, Washington; Australian National Gallery, Canberra.

Publications:

On BURCHARD: Books—*Recent Acquisitions,* exhibition catalogue, Pasadena, California 1969; *San Francisco Renaissance: Photographs of the 50's and 60's,* exhibition catalogue, New York 1975; *Dimensional Light,* exhibition catalogue, Fullerton, California 1975; *A Kind of Beatness,* exhibition catalogue, San Francisco 1975; *Jerry Burchard,* exhibition catalogue, Washington, D.C. 1978; *Jerry Burchard/Ingeborg Gerdes/John Spence Weir: Photographic Viewpoints,* exhibition catalogue, San Francisco 1979; *Photography for Collectors,* vol. I, *The West,* Carmel, California 1980; *Photography in California 1945-1980* by Louise Katzman, San Francisco 1984. **Articles**—review by A.D. Coleman in the *Boston Phoenix,* 28 November 1978; "Star Streaks" by Thomas Albright in *Art News* (New York), 4 April 1979; "Photographs Are Larger Than Life" by Thomas Albright in the *San Francisco Chronicle,* 3 December 1979; "Jerry Burchard's Sensuous Color" by Ted Hedgpeth in *Artweek* (Oakland, California), 15 December 1979; "Jerry Burchard: Recent Photographs" by Robert Atkins in the *San Francisco Bay Guardian,* 15 December 1979.

*

There's a certain thickness in time, a reacquaintance of a dream, an exciting match of doppelgangers from an imagined, or even quite valid, past or future sequence. I can smell the film roll through the camera. Each satisfactory depressing of the shutter leads to greater confidence. A black rainbow shimmers in the darkness. Love and lust whirl with the fingertips and sharp pain wells deep in my lungs, tiny flecks of light float across my eyes. The shutter is released and I breathe deeply, reality impinges and I am mortal again. I stand alone as sounds of the night return, a distant bicycle or buzzing of a streetlight announcing the world of others once more. Looking again at the tree, the house, the beach, I continue walking, hoping for more. Every few months, I scrape through thousands of such illusions to see if any came true. My real partner in these adventures is my camera. It sees where I am blind. My landscapes don't actually exist except on film. They certainly are not conceptual. They come from the other of the creative spectrum, the unconscious rendering of light as an advent.

Paradoxically, my work on nude still-lifes is always in brilliant sunlight, taking five and ten hours at a stretch, covering three to five hundred frames, but often hardly more deliberate, the eye more important than thought, the folds of flesh and silk and flowers flowing like a spring wine in a vision. In the end, the frequency of satisfactory images is on a par with the nightwork: sparse.

I also photograph my breakfasts, my orchids, my fish and my friends. As any artist, I record my life. My fantasies record themselves.

—Jerry Burchard

* * *

Extended night exposures have, in the last five years, become a popular and widely used technique, especially among San Francisco Bay area photographers. Long before night photography reached its current popularity, Jerry Burchard was exploring its possibilities and continues to do so now while the faddists dwindle. As John Szarkowski noted in his exhibition *Mirrors and Windows* in 1978, photography for the last two decades has become increasingly personal and private in its imagery. In its introspection, the work of Jerry Burchard substantiates this thesis; it belongs to contemporary trends in the medium.

Burchard's best photographs seem to confound what the camera does best; rather than the sharply focused, clean, informative images one once associated with photographic vision, Burchard presents us with vague, misty, romantic compositions that depend on their titles for facts about their subjects. His technique is studiedly casual, although his results, despite skewed angles and distorted shapes, never are or even seem accidental. The approach is intuitive, but the intuition is both informal and much less naive than Burchard's statements such as ''the camera sees more than I can'' would indicate. Burchard's work recalls the pictorialist genre, where light and form take on a greater symbolic importance than the actual objects they represent, but there is a uniquely mystical cast to these pictures to which Burchard's own words testify:

If you allow the camera to overexpose long enough, it starts discovering new levels of gray and new planes. Some things get so overexposed that they turn into new objects.

Despite the luxuriant drama of the places Burchard visits—Casablanca, Thailand, Chiang Rai—his photographs of the landscape are not so much pictures of a place as they are Burchard's personal reveries. The work is personal to such an extent that even the ineluctable specificity of the photograph is transcended and ''Rochester at Christmastime'' has the same emotional ring as ''Washington Square.''

What is ultimately most provocative about Jerry Burchard's works, besides the way they toy with and offer new variations on the way we expect a photograph to look, is their use of metaphor. Because of the privacy of his imagery, the meaning of these pictures remains open-ended. With the romantic associations that the lush, dense rain forest evokes, one may be assured that Burchard's photograph ''Monsoon, Thailand'' is not a meteorological document but a subjective response to the jungle lushness. The circumstances of these photographs may be vague, an effect heightened by the odd, nocturnal light, yet their existence is clearly, if ineffably, a personal pipe dream in which the viewer is invited to participate.

Burchard has been experimenting with color for the past several years and exploring more literally his attraction to the sensual and seductive. While he continues to make landscapes, his imagery now includes close, fragmented views of the human body which are often specifically sexual and juxtaposed against brightly patterned fabrics. In the color work, there is less use of the distortion of motion and long exposures, but the pictures retain their private and mysterious overtones.

—Dana Asbury

BURGIN, Victor.

Nationality: British. **Born:** Sheffield, Yorkshire, 24 July 1941. **Education:** Studied at the Royal College of Art, London, 1962-65, A.R.C.A. (1st class) 1965; Yale University, New Haven, Connecticut, 1965-67, M.F.A. 1967. **Career:** Photographer, based in London, since 1967. Lecturer, Trent Polytechnic, Nottingham, 1967-73. Senior Lecturer in the History and Theory of the Visual Arts, School of Communication, Polytechnic of Central London, 1973. Picker Professor of Fine Arts, Colgate University, Hamilton, New York, 1980. Professor of Art History, University of California, Santa Cruz, 1989. **Recipient:** U.S./U.K. Bicentennial Arts Exchange Fellowship, 1976-77; Deutscher Akademischer Austauschdienst (DAAD) Fellowship, Berlin, 1978-79. **Agents:** John Weber Gallery, 420 West Broadway, New York, New York 10012, U.S.A.; Liliane and Michel Durand-Dessert, 43 rue de Montmorency, 75003 Paris, France.

Individual Exhibitions:

1976	Institute of Contemporary Arts, London
	Robert Self Gallery, London
1977	*Victor Burgin: Work,* Stedelijk van Abbemuseum, Eindhoven, Netherlands (travelled to the John Weber Gallery, New York)
1978	Museum of Modern Art, Oxford
1979	Deutscher Akademischer Austauschdienst, Berlin (travelled to the John Weber Gallery, New York; Liliane and Michel Durand-Dessert Gallery, Paris; and Max Hetzler Gallery, Stuttgart)
1980	*Victor Burgin: US 77/Zoo 78,* Picker Art Gallery, Colgate University, Hamilton, New York
1981	Zwigzek Polskich Artystow Fotografikow, Warsaw
	Musée de la Ville, Calais, France
1982	John Weber Gallery, New York
1984	Galerie Durand-Dessert, Paris

Selected Group Exhibitions:

1969	*When Attitudes Become Form,* Institute of Contemporary Arts, London
1970	*Idea Structures,* Camden Arts Centre, London
1971	*6th Guggenheim International,* Guggenheim Museum, New York
	The British Avant-Garde, New York Cultural Center
1972	*Documenta,* Kassel, West Germany
	The New Art, Hayward Gallery, London
1976	*Arte Inglese Oggi,* Palazzo Reale, Milan
1977	*Europe in the 70's,* Art Institute of Chicago
1978	*23 Photographers—23 Directions,* The Walker Art Gallery, Liverpool
1979	*3 Perspectives on Photography,* Hayward Gallery, London
1980	*Artist and Camera,* Mappin Art Gallery, Sheffield, Yorkshire (travelled to the Stoke City Art Gallery; Durham Light Infantry Museum; Cartwright Hall, Bradford)
1987	*State of the Art: Ideas and Images in the 1980s,* London
1989	*On the Art of Fixing a Shadow: 150 Years of Photography,* National Gallery of Art, Washington D.C.; The Art Institute of Chicago, Chicago, IL
	The Art of Photography: 1839-1989, The Royal Academy of Arts, London
	Through the Looking Glass: Photographic Art in Britain 1945-1989, Barbican Art Gallery, London
1991	*Shocks to the System,* South Bank Centre, London

Collections:

Tate Gallery, London; Victoria and Albert Museum, London; Arts Council of Great Britain, London; British Council, London; Walker Art Gallery, Liverpool; Graves Art Gallery, Sheffield; Museum of Modern Art, Oxford; Musée d'Art Moderne, Paris; Bibliothèque Nationale, Paris; Van Abbemuseum, Eindhoven, Netherlands.

Publications:

By BURGIN: Books—*Work and Commentary*, London 1973; *Two Essays on Art, Photography, and Semiotics*, London 1976; *Family*, New York 1977; *Victor Burgin: Work*, exhibition catalogue, Eindhoven, Netherlands 1977; *Thinking Photography: Essays in the Theory of Photographic Representation*, editor, London 1981; *Between*, London 1986; *The End of Art Theory: Criticism and Modernity*, New York 1986; contribution to *Other than Itself* edited by John X Berger and Olivier Richon, Manchester 1989. **Articles**—"Art Society Systems" in *Control* (London), no. 4, 1968; "Situational Aesthetics" in *Studio International* (London), October 1969; "Thanks for the Memory" in *Architectural Design* (London), August 1970; "Rules of Thumb" in *Studio International* (London), May 1971; "Interview with Varsity" in *Varsity* (Cambridge), October 1971; "Margin Note" and "Interview" in *The New Art*, exhibition catalogue, edited by Anne Seymour, London 1972; "In Reply" in *Art-Language* (Leamington Spa, Warwickshire), Summer 1972; "Photographic Practice and Art Theory" in *Studio International* (London), July/August 1975; "Socialist Formalism" in *Studio International* (London), March/April 1976; "Art, Common-Sense and Photography" in *Camerawork* (London), no. 3, 1976; "Modernism in the Work of Art" in *20th Century Studies* (Canterbury, Kent), no. 15/16, 1976; "Looking at Photographs" in *Screen Education* (London), Autumn 1977; "Images of People" in *Studio International* (London), no. 2, 1978; "Seeing Sense" in *Artforum* (New York), February 1980; "Photography, Fantasy, Function" in *Screen* (London), Spring 1980.

On BURGIN: Books—*Artist and Camera*, exhibition catalogue, by M.S.C., London 1980; *State of the Art: Ideas and Images in the 1980s* by Sandy Nairne with Geoff Dunlop and John Wyver, London 1987; *The Art of Photography 1839-1989* by Mike Weaver, London 1989. **Articles**—"Victor Burgin: La Representation par le Text" by A. Pacquement in *Art Press* (Paris), no. 5, 1973; "Victor Burgin" by E. Tynan in *Studio International* (London), September/October 1976; "Victor Burgin in Oxford" by D. Reed in *British Journal of Photography* (London), March 1978; "Chasing Dreams" by Jean Fisher in *Artforum* (New York), May 1984; *Camera Austria*, No. 25, 1988.

*

How would you describe US 77?

I'll take the question literally: there are 12 photographs, each 40 x 60 inches, with a text superimposed on each; these sections are ordered in no particular sequence—there's no linear narrative—and they're designed so that they can be viewed either together, or individually, or in groups smaller than twelve; the graphic conventions governing their appearance derive from illustrated magazines and advertising. In terms of content, the work is built around the themes of power, identity, sexuality.

It's easy to see the reference to mass-media in the way the words are put directly over the photograph, but it's not always quite so obvious what, precisely, the relationship of the text to the image is. Could you say something about this? Take, for instance, the one called "Framed."

We usually see words used to *comment* on the image in some way; for example, to give some extra information about what is shown in the image. Alternatively, we see an image used to illustrate a text—to show pictorially what has already been mentioned verbally. I tend not to do either of these things. To take the example you mention: the key word "framed" is used to relate together a number of pictured and "written" frames: the frame of the panel itself; the frame of the Marlboro poster; the frame of the photograph described in the text; and the frame of the mirror in which the woman watches herself. Secondly, the word "framed"—in the language of cowboy and gangster films—has the meaning of the misrepresentation of an individual: the good guy is "framed" by the bad guys. The cowboy in the poster helps this sort of reading. Now this idea of being framed, of having a certain "picture" of yourself imposed on you by others, against your will, can then be attached to the stereotypes which are arranged as oppositions: young girl/middle-aged woman; male hairdresser/cowboy—these are clearly distinguished cliché representations of people used in the media, and in culture in general. We can go even further with this sort of reading, although you'll probably find this a bit

extreme: the cowboy in the poster is smoking a cigarette; a slang term for a cigarette, in England, is "fag," and "fag" is also a term of insult used against homosexual men. And again, under the poster there's a bag: the term "bag" is a similar sexist insult used to describe a woman "past her prime." These sorts of "literarizations" of elements in an image aren't often picked up consciously, but I think that they contribute to what we might call the "unconscious" of an image—contribute to that certain "taste" that an image has and which we find so difficult to account for.

You've always used black-and-white photos, never colour, yet your work has got an overt relationship with advertising which now predominantly appears in colour, presumably to give more pleasure. Apart from reasons of cost, why do you not use colour photographs yourself?

Colour photography *is* pleasurable, but in terms of pleasure it can also be the "cheap shot," the easy way of giving an image a rather meretricious appeal—there are very few photographers who use colour intelligently. Colour photography is also more on the side of illusion than is black-and-white; additionally, so long as black-and-white photography exists—and there may be commercial threats to its continuing existence—colour photography will tend to look anecdotal by comparison. I want to stress the image not as illusion but as *text*, to be read. Black-and-white is, of course, the combination we associate with the printed word, so again this helps my intention more than colour would. The words in my work are formed from the same substance, the same grain-structure, as the image—they aren't added later by some other process: another way of emphasizing the indivisibility of word and image, a sort of crude analogue of the way in which the mind forms both words and images from the same "substance," on the same "surface."

Could you say something more about the more practical aspects of your work? What equipment do you use? What procedures?

Strictly standard equipment for the sort of pictures I take: HP5 in D-76; Leica M-4 with 35mm lens although I used to use the 50mm more often. But these are almost embarrassing questions for me to answer—they're the sort of questions you ask a photographer.

You don't consider yourself a photographer?

Not in the sense of the word where "photographer" means someone totally involved with the *image*. What I'm involved with is the way images and words mesh together into what we might call a "scripto-visual" discourse. The reason I'm so interested in this form of discourse is quite simply because it's the one we are most exposed to—advertising, magazines, newspapers, and so on. You see, once you're interested in photography as a discursive form, as a practice of representation, as a social *fact*, then you're bound to accept the use of writing—it's not a matter of personal choice, it just happens to *be a fact*.

It's a fact you can choose to ignore.

You can choose to ignore a fact, but if you think that makes the fact any less factual then you're in a state of delusion.

So are you saying that "art photographers" ought to take the social use of photography, this use of words, into account?

Not at all; I'm merely pointing out that my own concerns are very different from theirs.

What about the moment when you are actually taking the photograph—aren't you, at least for that moment, dealing with their concerns? Or do you only think about the text you're going to use?

I'd say that even though I may have a text in mind, and even though I may have selected the thing to photograph on the basis of that text, I'm nevertheless making an *image*, and I try to make that image as well as I can—which means dealing with "purely visual" things, but also with the *medium* as a *craft*.

So, for that moment, you're a photographer in the sense you've just objected to.

It's a very brief moment! It's what comes afterwards that's most important to the final result. Let me give you an example. You asked about technical procedures. I begin with a 35mm negative. Then I make a print on 12 x 16 paper. This print is then photographed on a 10 x 8 negative film. Another 10 x 8 negative is made of the typesetting. The two 10 x 8 negatives—one for tone, one for line—are then taped together, one superimposed on the other. Finally, a print is made from this "neg-sandwich" which, in the case of US 77 for example, is 40 x 60 inches. Now every stage of this process is accompanied by a degree of image degradation, and it's this that gives that harsh, gritty quality to the work. Now the current taste in "fine photography" is for a very low contrast, pearly effect—with very fine grain and fine detail—on a relatively small scale. They're totally different ends.

What are these ends?

They have to be very broadly defined, because, obviously, different people have different ideas about what they're trying to do. But I think there are two very broad areas of practice: the ''fine photography'' camp are, at base, concerned with the image as a source of *fascination,* a form of *captivation,* a sort of trap for the eye in which one's sense of being is somehow condensed into the exercise of the visual faculty—what we might call the ''mesmeric'' school of photography. Against this tendency there's the attempt to involve the viewer's sense of *social* existence, in addition to the more narcissistic pleasures of ''just looking''—this involves much more of an attempt to organize more particular sorts of meanings: we could call this the ''discursive'' tendency. There's a spectrum of concerns ranged across these two broad areas, which moves from the contemplation of one's navel, at one extreme, to the crudest sort of propaganda at the other.

—Victor Burgin (from an interview with Tony Godfrey)

* * *

In an essay written in 1975, Victor Burgin wrote: ''One thing conceptual art has done, apart from underlining the central importance of theory, is to make the photograph an important tool of practice. The consequence of such moves has been to further render the categorical distinction between art and photography ill-founded and irrelevant.'' Burgin's own photographic practice is itself grounded in the conceptual art pioneered in the 1960's and involves the creation of photographs with texts that demand the active participation of the viewer, as opposed to passive consumption, in order to elicit meaning.

Few contemporary photographers have been as critically preoccupied as Burgin with the ideological, social, and cultural implications of photographic practice, and Burgin's articles and essays collectively constitute one of the most thoughful and provocative bodies of photographic criticism to be produced in the past ten years. Burgin's theoretical understanding of photography and his own practice have roots in the thinking of the Frankfurt School philosophers—principally Walter Benjamin—and among contemporary theoreticians he has been most influenced by Roland Barthes. From these various sources he has distilled certain crucial insights regarding the uses of photography in mass culture, its reiteration, transmission and reinforcement of dominant bourgeois values, its simultaneous activation and frustration of the mechanisms of desire, and its functioning as a comprehensive sign system of hidden but nonetheless persuasive meaning. By thus utilizing a system of analysis derived from Marxism and semiology, Burgin attempts in his own work to subvert and deconstruct the normative ploys and strategies of the photographic image. And because the overwhelming majority of images we are exposed to are those of advertising, it is the format of the advertising image that Burgin chooses to re-present. This is a less obvious strategy than might at first appear, for Burgin perceives clearly that although ''photos *appear* gratuitously provided, they are not so much objects as environment.'' Burgin's awareness that the proliferation of photography is not so much a plurality of discrete images as a global environment of images which are absorbed unconsciously and effortlessly dictates that the form of his own radical practice must be to compel the viewer to *conscious* apprehension of the image and to knowledge of the photograph's textuality. It is, preeminently, in order to effect this recognition that Burgin's photographs are constructed.

Burgin's photographs consist typically of rather straightforward images of mass culture, or banal and quotidian scenes of urban life often including advertising images and messages (billboards, posters, etc.). On these images Burgin superimposes texts—the form in which we see most photographs, be they in newspapers, magazines, or in advertising. The text may itself be derived from advertising or magazine copy. Sometimes it will be scrambled, as in a photograph of a Pakistani woman factory worker: superimposed is a text which begins ''St. Laurent demands a whole new life style . . .'' and ends disconcertingly with ''three months ago/are a ramble through/Eastern Europe.'' In other cases, the text will be unambiguous and didactic. A photo of workers whose upper bodies are engulfed in the autos of their assembly line is captioned STILL IN THE DARK; this is followed by government exhortations that workers privilege the ''national interest'' over class, ''moderate'' trade unionism over more radical demands, etc., and Burgin's own analysis of the political manipulation involved. Another photograph showing a space-suited astronaut, a smiling woman with a camera, and two children—each figure unrelated to the others—is entitled ''Nuclear Power.'' The text concerns the fact that only 6% of American families consist of a husband, wife,

and two children. A photograph of a banal surburban street scene, bisected by electrical wires, contains a flowery travel brochure text describing the California coast and is captioned TODAY IS THE TOMORROW YOU WERE PROMISED YESTERDAY.

Burgin's consistent strategy is to use the very instruments of ideological and cultural control against themselves. By juxtaposing images of the kind one sees all the time, with texts that initiate a dialectic between photograph and viewer, Burgin subverts and deconstructs the cultural myths that are so ubiquitous and internalized they have become almost invisible.

—Abigail Solomon-Godeau

BURKE, Bill.

Nationality: American. **Born:** Derby, Connecticut, 8 April 1943. **Education:** Studied art history, Middlebury College, BA 1966; studied photography, Rhode Island School of Design, BFA 1968 and MFA 1970. **Career:** Instructor at the School of the Museum of Fine Arts, Boston, since 1971. Contributor to *Christian Science Monitor,* since 1984. Magazine work for *Fortune* and *Esquire.* Gordon Graham Lecturer, Harvard University, 1991. **Recipient:** National Endowment for the Arts Grant to a Visual Artist, 1976, 1982, 1988, 1994; Ford Foundation grant for faculty enrichment, 1980; John Simon Guggenheim Fellowship, 1979; Placem em Homenagem Au Presidente da Associacao Dos Fotografos do Rio de Janeiro, 1980; Artists Foundation Award, 1985; Englehard Award, 1987; Mellon Foundation Faculty Enrichment Grant, 1990; Gahan Lectureship, Harvard University, 1991; Graham Foundation for Advanced Studies in the Fine Arts, 1994. **Agent:** Etherton Gallery, 135 South 6th Avenue, Tuscon, Arizona 85701. **Address:** 6 Melville Avenue, Dorchester, Massachusetts 02124, USA.

Individual Exhibitions:

1970	Johnson Gallery, Middlebury College, Middlebury, Vermont
1974	Porch Gallery, Wesleyan University, Middleton, Connecticut
1981	Nexus Gallery, Atlanta, Georgia
1982	Clarence Kennedy Gallery, Cambridge, Massachusetts
1983-87	*Encounters,* travelling exhibition
1984	San Francisco Camera Work Gallery
1987	*I Want to Take Picture,* International Center of Photography, New York
1988	Stanford University Museum of Art, Stanford, California
1990	North Kentucky University
1994	*Mine Fields,* Photographic Resource Center, Boston University Etherton Gallery, Tucson

Selected Group Exhibitions:

1973	*The Dog Show,* George Eastman House, Rochester, New York
1976	*Kentucky Bicentennial Photo Project,* J.B. Speed Museum, Louisville, Kentucky
1978	*Private Parts,* Electron Movers Gallery, Providence, Rhode Island
1979	*Kentucky Seen,* George Eastman House, Rochester, New York
1980	*Three American Photographers,* Conjunto Universitario Candido Mendez, Rio de Janeiro, Brazil
1983	*A Reasonable Likeness,* University of Louisville Photo Archives, Kentucky
1984	*Boston '84,* Federal Reserve Bank, Boston, Massachusetts
1985	*Travelling,* The Addison Gallery, Andover, Massachusetts
	Boston Now, Institute of Contemporary Art, Boston, Massachusetts
	Stanley Wise Gallery, New York (with Mike Disfarmer)
1986	*Conflict and Caring,* Catskill Center for Photography, Woodstock, New York (with Susan Meiselas, Mary Ellen Mark and Gilles Peres)
1987	*Spirit in the Land,* San Francisco Camera Work Gallery

Untitled. Photograph by Bill Burke.

1988   *Southeast Asia Experience,* Lowell, Massachusetts
        Real Faces, Whitney Museum, Midtown, New York
        City Limits, North Gallery, Massachusetts College of Art,
            Boston, Massachusetts
        Return of the Hero, Burden Gallery, New York
1989   *Photo Journals,* Center for Book Arts, New York (with Peter
            Beard, Ed Grazda and Rosalind Solomon)
        Poetic Document, Drexel University, Philadelphia, Pennsylva-
            nia (with Phyllis Galembo and Larry Fink)
1990   *Forced Out,* P.S.1, Brooklyn, New York
        *The Indomitable Spirit, Photographers and Friends United
            Against AIDS,* International Center of Photography, New
            York (travelled to Sotheby's Auction House, New York)
1991   *People of Southeast Asia,* Addison Gallery, Philips Andover
            Academy, Andover, MA
        Some of the Consequences, with Bill Short, Keene State
            College, Keene, NH

Collections:

Addison Gallery, Andover, Massachusetts; International Center of Photography, New York; Stanford University Museum of Art; Museum of Modern Art, New York; George Eastman House, Rochester, New York; Getty Museum, Los Angeles; Museum of Fine Arts, Boston; Smithsonian Institution Museum of American Art, Washington, D.C.; Museum of Art, Rhode Island School of Design, Providence; Polaroid Collection, USA; Polaroid Collection, Europe; Dansen Art Center, Wesleyan University, Middleton; Kentucky Historical Society, Frankfort; University of Louisville Photo Archives; Los Angeles County Museum of Art.

Publications:

By BURKE: Books—*They Shall Cast Out Demons,* with text by Richard Selzer, 1983; *Bill Burke Portraits,* monograph, with texts by Raymond Carver and Andy Grundberg, 1987; *I Want To Take Picture,* Atlanta, 1987; *Mine Fields,* Atlanta, 1994.

On BURKE: Books—*Harry Callahan and His Students,* Atlanta 1983; *Visible Light* by Michael Lesy, New York 1985; *American Dreams,* Madrid 1987; *Legacy of Light,* edited by Constance Sullivan, 1987; *Real Faces,* exhibition catalogue, essay by Max Kozloff, 1988; *Poetic Document,* exhibition catalogue with essay by J Hugenin, 1989; *Forced Out,* exhibition catalogue, edited by Carle Kismaric, 1989; *The Indomitable Spirit,* exhibition catalogue, edited by Marvin Heiferman, 1990.

*

For me, pictures are part poetry and part fact. They hover between metaphors for internal states and proofs of experience.

—Bill Burke

*   *   *

"Like all American boys in the '50s, I was raised to be in a war in Asia," Bill Burke recalls. "I looked at *LIFE's Picture History of World War II.* I watched 'Victory at Sea' on TV . . . When I was of military age, we had the war in Vietnam, but I was in college taking courses in Far Eastern Art and Far Eastern Religion, taking psychedelics. Then I was in art school learning to be a photographer, learning about space (studying under Harry Callahan) . . . I was immensely relieved when, with some effort, I failed my draft physical.

"In the '70s I learned to use photography as an excuse to go where I had no business and to make pictures in places where I was uncomfortable (the rural South, Central America, Brazil). I saw and was greatly moved by (the films) *Apocalypse Now* and *The Deer Hunter.* I began to feel in some way sorry to have missed the Southeast Asia experience my government had set up for my generation.

"I wanted to make pictures where I didn't know the rules, where I'd be off-balance. Friends who had been there recommended Thailand: nice people,

easy transportation, good food." Burke's first trip was in 1982. "Without even trying, I bumped into the Cambodian border and people running away from the Khmer Rouge (the régime responsible for the deaths of up to 2 million Cambodians between 1975 and 1979). The 'heart of darkness' was right on the other side of the border."

Burke plunged into it. And he has returned yearly to Cambodia till today. In the black-and-white photographs he presented in the books he designed, *I Want to Take Picture,* (1987) and *Mine Fields,* (1995), he chronicled his encounters with Khmer Rouge soldiers, their leaders, and the victims of their genocide, and of US bombings during the Vietnam war and later internal conflicts. At ease in their environments, his subjects pose for his camera, reflecting a nonjudgmental curiosity on both sides of the lens and letting us note their "otherness," from bristling weapons to multiple amputations.

Burke's Polaroid prints are reproduced full-frame, including their unevenly developed dark edges. This technique signifies veracity (no cropping), yet also heightens the imagery's uneasy recollections of 19th century photographs of exotic exploration and ethnography. Is this another chapter of Western imperialism? Such associations are countered by Burke's integration of autobiography into his publications and exhibitions. *I Want to Take Picture* is organized as a dramatic private travelogue, compressing three trips into one, and it moves from Burke's arrival in Bangkok to a last negative, scratched in the highway accident that broke his neck. *Mine Fields* also reproduces mementoes of his trips; pages from his journals; news clips and the like in collage form; and in addition weaves between Southeast Asia and his highly charged life at home in Boston. "What was an adventure in the first book—trying to find the Khmer Rouge—has now become this endless crusade," he says, "but what happens to me in the process is still an adventure . . . still exciting."

His previous books, including *They Shall Cast Out Demons* (1983), which involved his design, and *Bill Burke Portraits* (1987) are not overtly self-revealing, but they can similarly be placed in the tradition of personal journalism emergent since the 1960s.

A talisman for Burke and others was Robert Frank's odyssey across the United States and the resultant photography in *The Americans* (1959): Frank and later photographers shifted photojournalism from a detached public voice to an engaged private communication; from a predictable narrative form to an open-ended poetry; from idealistic, quasi-socialist concern for the underdog to a more ambivalent fascination with human oddities and extremes. The older photojournalism had flourished in *LIFE* which ceased publication as a weekly in 1972, outdated by television with its speed in delivering news and its power in selling ads. The camerawork pursued by Burke and the photographers he admires, such as Gilles Peress, Peter Beard, Ed Grazda, and Gaylord Oscar Herron, is conceived instead for exhibitions and books, venues with more sympathetic editors and quieter communication between photographer and viewer. Indicative of this situation, Burke calls his work "docu-art."

Currently (1995) he is photographing French colonial architecture in Indochina before the new Western capitalist influences sweep it away. "I'm methodical, like Atget, going out every morning with a view camera," Burke says. "I like being productive without worrying about being blown up."

—Anne Hoy

BURRI, René.

Nationality: Swiss. **Born:** Zurich, 9 April 1933. **Education:** Attended primary and secondary schools in Zurich, 1940-49; studied photography, under Hans Finsler, 1949-53, and filmmaking, 1953-54, at the Kunstgewerbeschule, Zurich; mainly self-taught as a photojournalist, but influenced by Werner Bischof. **Military Service:** Served in the Swiss Army, 1954. **Family:** Married Rosellina Bischof in 1963; children: Yasmine and Oliver. **Career:** Freelance photojournalist, working for *Life, Look, Paris-Match, Stern, Fortune, Epoca, Sunday Times, Geo, Du, Twen,* etc., also a filmmaker, Zurich, since 1955. Member, Magnum Photos co-operative agency, Paris and New York, since 1959. **Recipient:** *International Film and Television Festival* Award, New York, 1967. **Agent:** Magnum Photos, 20 rue des Grands-Augustins, 75006 Paris; and Magnum Photos Inc., 251 Park Avenue South, New York, New York 10010. **Address:** Wegackerstrasse 7, 8041 Zurich, Switzerland.

Individual Exhibitions:

1965	*China,* Galerie Form, Zurich
1967	*Selected Works,* Art Institute of Chicago
1971	*Selected Works,* Galerie Rencontre, Paris
1972	*Selected Works,* Raffi Photo Gallery, New York
	Selected Works, Galleria Diaframma, Milan
1980	*Die Deutschen,* Museum Folkwang, Essen
1981	*Die Deutschen,* Galerie Kicken, Cologne

Selected Group Exhibitions:

1960	*The World as Seen by Magnum,* Takashimaya Department Store, Tokyo (and world tour)
1967	*Photography in the 20th Century,* National Gallery of Canada, Ottawa (toured Canada and the United States, 1967-73)
1972	*Behind the Great Wall of China,* Metropolitan Museum of Art, New York (toured the United States)
1974	*Photographie Suisse depuis 1840 à nos jours,* Kunsthaus, Zurich (and world tour)
1977	*Concerning Photography,* The Photographers' Gallery, London (travelled to the Spectro Workshop, Newcastle upon Tyne)
1979	*Fleeting Gestures: Dance Photographs,* International Center of Photography, New York (travelled to *Venezia '79* and The Photographers' Gallery, London)
1980	*The Imaginary Photo Museum,* Kunsthalle, Cologne
1982	*Lichtbildnisse: Das Porträt in der Fotografie,* Rheinisches Landesmuseum, Bonn
1984	*Sammlung Gruber,* Museum Ludwig, Cologne
	Swiss Photography from 1840 until Today, Pro Helvetia Foundation, Zurich (and world tour)

Collections:

Stiftung für die Photographie, Kunsthaus, Zurich; Museum Folkwang, Essen; Musée Réattu, Arles, France; Bibliothèque Nationale, Paris; Palais des Beaux-Arts, Charleroi, Belgium; Museum of Modern Art, New York; Art Institute of Chicago; Museum Ludwig, Cologne.

Publications:

By BURRI: Books—*Die Deutschen/Les Allemands,* Zurich and Paris 1962; *The Gaucho,* with text by J.L. Borges, Buenos Aires and London 1968; *In Search of the Holy Land/Im Heiligen Land,* with text by H.V. Morton, London, New York and Lucerne 1979. **Films**—*The Two Faces of China,* BBC and German television film, 1965; *After the Six-Day War,* German television film, 1967; *Braccia si, uomini no!,* Swiss television film, 1968, also several industrial films, 1967-68.

On BURRI: Books—*Photography of the World '60,* edited by Hiromu Hara, Ihei Kimura and others, Tokyo and New York 1960; *Photography in the 20th Century* by Nathan Lyons, New York 1967; *Behind the Great Wall of China,* edited by Cornell Capa, with an introduction by Weston J. Naef, New York 1972; *Concerning Photography,* exhibition catalogue, edited by Jonathan Bayer and others, London 1977; *World Photography,* edited by Bryn Campbell, London 1981; *Die Deutschen: René Burri,* exhibition catalogue, edited by Galerie Kicken, Cologne 1981; *A Day in the Life of Australia—March 6, 1981,* with introduction by Thomas Kenneally, Potts Point, New South Wales 1981; *The Imaginary Photo Museum* by Helmut Gernsheim, Renate and L. Fritz Gruber and others, Cologne 1981, London 1982; *Lichtbildnisse: Das Porträt in der Fotografie,* edited by Klaus Honnef, Cologne 1982; *Bilder vom Krieg* by Rainer Fabian and Hans Christian Adam, Hamburg 1983, as *Images of War: 130 Years of War Photography,* London 1985; *Swiss Photography from 1840 until Today,* exhibition catalogue, with introduction by Hugo Loetscher, Zurich 1984; *After the War Was Over,* with introduction by Mary Blume, London 1985; *Cuba y Cuba* by Marco Melere and Miguel Barnet, Milan 1994. **Articles**—by Romeo E. Martinez in *Camera* (Lucerne), no. 2, 1959; in *Leica Magazin* (Frankfurt), no. 5, 1962; in *Leica Magazin* (Frankfurt), no. 1, 1967; by Allan Porter in *Camera* (Lucerne), no. 1, 1970; in *Photo* (Paris), no. 46, 1971; in *British Journal of Photography* (London), no. 32, 1971; in *Popular Photography* (New York), no. 6, 1972; in *Fotografia Italiana* (Milan), no. 168, 1972; in *Nikon News* (Zurich), no. 4, 1976; in *Creative Camera* (London), no. 162, 1977; "René Burri" in *Glasherz* (Munich), no. 6, 1981.

*   *   *

René Burri's photographic career began with his interest in motion pictures. After studying filmmaking, he worked on several pictures, and was assistant cameraman on Walt Disney's *Switzerland.* He studied photography under Hans Finsler at the Kunstgewerbeschule in Zurich, and through Finsler met the photojournalist Werner Bischof. Recognizing Burri's outstanding abilities as a photographer, Bischof recommended him to the important co-operative agency Magnum. Burri became an associate photographer with Magnum in 1956, and a full member in 1959.

From the inception of his career with Magnum, Burri's progress as a photojournalist has been a full and superbly successful one. His reportages include a sensitive story on hearing-impaired children at Zurich's Institute of Musical and Rhythmic Education (1955), in-depth coverage of the Suez crisis from Cairo (1956), and a series of hectic magazine and industrial assignments which took him to Italy, Spain, Greece and Turkey in 1957. In 1958, he followed Nasser throughout Egypt during the country's union with Syria, trailed across Brazil and Iran (a story on the birth of an heir to the Shah) in 1960, went to Korea and Japan in 1961, then interviewed Cuba's Che Guevara for *Look,* did a colour essay on the Holy Land for *Paris-Match,* and reported on the escalation of the Vietnam war in 1963.

His best-known reportages—"Argentine Gaucho," "Japan at Work," and "Island in the Gulf of Siam"—were done for the Swiss magazine *Du,* for which he also produced the widely-seen photo-essay on the architect Le Corbusier. At the same time he created his now out-of-print book *The Germans* for publication in Switzerland and France—a little-known classic in the spirit of Robert Frank's *The Americans.*

Simultaneous with his busy career as a photojournalist, however, Burri has continued to make films; he spent much of the year 1964-65 making test photos and shooting a feature movie in the Far East. His Xerox film *What's It All About?* won the New York *International Film and Television Festival* Award in 1967.

Today, René Burri's Zurich studio buzzes with film acitivity: he has concentrated on movie work almost exclusively in recent years, producing industrial films as well as programmes for the British Broadcasting Corporation and for German television.

—Colin Naylor

BURSON, Nancy.

Nationality: American. **Born:** St. Louis, Missouri, 1948. **Education:** Attended Colorado Women's College, Denver. **Recipient:** CAST, in conjunction with the New York State Council on the Arts and Syracuse University, 1977; National Science Foundation Grant for "Composite" Machine exhibit, 1987; National Endowment for the Arts, Photography, 1990. **Address:** c/o Jayne H. Baum Gallery, 588 Broadway, New York, NY 10012, USA.

Individual Exhibitions:

1974	Bertha Urdang Gallery, New York
1977	Hal Bromm Gallery, New York
1978	C.W. Post College, Installation, Long Island University, Brookville, New York
1984	Holly Solomon Gallery, New York
	Bruce Velick Gallery, San Francisco
1985	International Center of Photography, New York
	Institute of Contemporary Art, Boston
	Baker Gallery, Kansas City
1986	Greathouse Gallery, New York
	Chrysler Museum, Norfolk, Virginia
1987	Holly Solomon Gallery, New York
	Torino Fotographia, Turin, Italy
	New Britain Museum of American Art, New Britain, Connecticut
	Baker Gallery, Kansas City
1989	Jan Kesner Gallery, Los Angeles
1990	Museum of Contemporary Photography, Columbia College, Chicago
	Massachusetts Institute of Technology, List Visual Arts Center, Cambridge, Massachusetts
	Jayne H. Baum Gallery, New York
1991	Galerie Michèle Chomette, Paris
	Jan Kesner Gallery, Los Angeles
1992	Jayne H. Baum Gallery, New York
	Faces, Contemporary Arts Museum, Houston, Texas (and tour)
	The New Museum, New York
1993	Jayne H. Baum Gallery, New York
	University of Rhode Island, Fine Arts Center Galleries, Kingston, Rhode Island

Selected Group Exhibitions:

1976	Susan Caldwell Gallery, New York
	Bertha Urdang Gallery, New York
1977	*Arte Fierra,* Hal Bromm Gallery, Bologna, Italy
1978	*Atypical Works,* Julian Pretto Gallery, New York
1979	*Big Drawing Show,* P.S.1, Long Island City, New York
1980	*Pool Show,* Artists Space, New York
1981	Julian Pretto Gallery, New York
	New Acquisitions, Stadt Galerie in Lembachhaus, Munich, Germany
1982	*Androgyny,* Emily Lowe Gallery, Hofstra University, Hempstead, New York
	Nuclear Disarmament, Ronald Feldman Gallery, New York
1983	London Regional Art Gallery, Ontario, Canada
	Invitational, Bertha Urdang Gallery, New York

1984	*1984,* Ronald Feldman Gallery, New York
	Seven Women Artists, Zurich Art Fair, Switzerland
1985	*Signs of the Times, Some Recurring Motifs in 20th Century Photography,* San Francisco Museum of Modern Art
	Identity, Palais de Tokyo, Paris
	Biennale, Sao Paulo, Brazil
1986	*Stills: Cinema and Video Transformed,* Seattle Art Museum
	Television's Impact on Contemporary Art, Queens Museum, Flushing, New York
1987	*Fake,* The New Museum, New York
	Portraits, Virginia Museum, Richmond, Virginia
	Extending the Boundaries of Contemporary Photography, Museum of Contemporary Photography, Chicago
1988	*Two to Tango: Collaboration in Recent American Photography,* International Center of Photography, New York (travelled to the Center for the Fine Arts, Miami)
	Fabrication: Staged, Altered and Appropriated Photographs, Carpenter Center, Harvard University, Cambridge, Massachusetts
	Education and Democracy and Cultural Participation, Dia Art Foundation, New York
1989	*Photography Now,* Victoria and Albert Museum, London
	Fotografie, Wissenschaft und Neuetechnologien, Kunstmuseum, Dusseldorf, Germany
	AIDS and Democracy, Dia Art Foundation, New York
1990	*"Rien Que La Chose Exhorbitée . . . ,"* Galerie Michèle Chomette, Paris
	Critical Realism, Perspektief, Rotterdam, Netherlands
	Selections Five, at *Fifth Cologne Biennale,* Cologne, Germany
1991	*L'oeuvre photographique considérée comme un état de sculpture,* Galerie Michèle Chomette, Paris
	Sculpter Photographier, Centre national de la photographie, Palais de Toyko, Paris
	JFK in Memorium: Myth and Denial, Renee Fotouhi Fine Art East, East Hampton, New York
	Practicing Beauty, Art Gallery of Hamilton, Hamilton, Canada
1992	*Numerical Proof,* Centre national de la photographie, Palais de Tokyo, Paris
	The Evolution of the Portrait in Photography, The Photography Museum, The International Cultural Centre, Antwerp, Belgium
	Americas, at *Expo '92,* Mar Villaepesa, Tarifa, Spain
	In Vitro: De Les Mitologies de la Fertilitat als Limits de la Ciencia, Foundation Joan Miro, Barcelona, Spain
1993	*Konstruktion Zitat: Kollektive Bilder in der Fotografie,* Sprengel Museum, Hannover, Germany
	Breda Fotografica '93, Breda, Netherlands
	Danse Macabre: Portraits Photographiques, Abbaye aux Dames, Caen, le FRAC, Basse-Normandie, France
1993-94	*Beyond Recognition: Contemporary International Photography,* Australian National Gallery, Canberra
1994	*Body and Soul: Contemporary Art and Healing,* DeCordova Museum, Lincoln, Massachusetts
	Photography Now: Facts and Fantasies, Rye Arts Center, Rye, New York
	Stealth, Seafirst Gallery, Columbia Seafirst Center, Seattle

Collections:

Allentown Art Museum, Oberlin, Ohio; Australian National Gallery, Canberra; Bayly Museum of Art, University of Virginia, Charlottesville, Virginia; Chrysler Museum, Norfolk, Virginia; Emily Lowe Gallery, Hofstra University, Hempstead, New York; Fonds National d'Art Contemporain, Paris; Fonds Regional d'Art Contemporain de Basse-Normandie, France; International Museum of Photography, George Eastman House, Rochester, New York; Library of Congress, Washington, D.C.; Los Angeles County Museum; The Metropolitan Museum of Art, New York; Musée National d'Art Moderne, Centre Georges Pompidou, Paris; Museum of Fine Arts, Houston, Texas;

Untitled, **1993.** Photograph ©Nancy Burson. Courtesy of Jayne H. Baum Gallery, New York.

National Museum of American Art, Smithsonian Institution, Washington, D.C.; San Francisco Museum of Modern Art; Stadt Galerie in Lembachhaus, Munich, Germany; The Tampa Museum of Art; Victoria and Albert Museum, London.

Publications:

By BURSON: Books—*COMPOSITES Computer Generated Portraits,* with an introduction by William A. Ewing and Jeanne A. McDermott, New York 1986; *Nancy Burson: The Age Machine and Composite Portraits,* with an

essay by Dana Friis-Hansen, Cambridge, Massachusetts 1990; *Faces—Nancy Burson,* with an essay by Jeanne A. McDermott, Santa Fe, New Mexico 1993.

On BURSON: Books—*Photography Now* by Mark Haworth-Booth, England 1989; *The Photography of Invention, American Pictures of the 1980s* by Joshua P. Smith, Cambridge, Massachusetts 1989; *About Faces* by Terry Landau, New York 1989; *Artspeak* by Robert Atkins, New York 1990; *Artificial Nature* by Jeffrey Dietch, Athens, Greece 1990; *Crisis of the Real: Writings on Photography 1974-1989* by Andy Grundberg, New York 1990; *The History of Photography, an Overview* by Alma Davenport, Stoneham,

Massachusetts 1991; *The Reconfigured Eye: Visual Truth in the Post-Photographic Era* by William J. Mitchell, Cambridge, Massachusetts 1992. **Articles**—"Patents: A Method That Pictures a Person at Any Age" by Stacy Jones in *The New York Times,* 14 July 1981; "Her Computer Art Maps the Faces of the Future" by Richard Story in *USA Today,* 24 January 1984; "Images in the Computer Age" by Andy Grundberg in *The New York Times,* 14 April 1985; "Face to Face, it's the Expression that Bears the Message" by Jeanne A. McDermott in *Smithsonian Magazine,* March 1986; "The Serious Implications of Digital Image Processing" by Michael O'Connor in *Print Magazine,* March/April 1986; "Books: Prodigies & Identities" by Vicki Goldberg in *American Photographer,* Vol. XVII, July 1986; "New Faces" by Art Kleiner in *Aperture,* Issue No. 106, 1987; "Nancy Burson: Chimaeras" in *European Photography,* January/February/March 1988; "Photographing AIDS; Difficult Subject" by Robert Atkins in *The Village Voice* (New York), 28 June 1988; "Portraits with Bursonality" by Owen Edwards in *American Photographer,* Vol. XXII, No. 5, May 1989; "Images Abundant: Anything's Possible" by Andy Grundberg in *The New York Times,* 12 January 1990; "Choices" by Vince Aletti in *The Village Voice* (New York), 24 January 1990; "Ask No Questions the Camera Can Lie" by Andy Grundberg in *The New York Times,* 12 August 1990; "Nancy Burson Making Faces" by Robert Atkins in *Contemporanea,* Vol. 24, January 1991; "Figure de l'au-dela" by Patrick Roegiers in *Le Monde* (Paris), 5 June 1991; "VISION USA" by Gianni Romano in *Zoom* (Italy), No. 116, March/April 1992; "Composites of Reality" by Sue Heinemann in *New Environment* (Tokyo), No. 2, 1992; "About Face, Redefining Normality With Nancy Burson" by Vince Aletti in *The Village Voice* (New York), 21 April 1992; "Fast Forward, Art Goes High Tech" by Mark Dery in *ARTnews* (New York), February 1993; "Visions of the Future" by Sue Alexander in *American Photo,* May/June 1994.

*   *   *

Nancy Burson is one of the photographers who has most closely embraced new technologies of photographic manipulation and the alteration of photographic images by means of computers. Her computer-altered photographs are deliberate uses of this technology as a complement, dialectical opposite or reproach to the fabled accuracy and truth of the camera. All are self-conscious applications of the computer's ability to combine or alter images, rather than merely imaginative or expressive explorations. Burson's computer-altered photographic images tell truths by representing and altering reality, much as conventional photographs, written reportage and scientific predictions do.

Burson's composite portraits use computers to integrate and blend disparate images, arriving at a final product at once unreal and hyper-real. It is the enduring value of her work that she never reduces this technique to the mere gimmick it might so easily be. Rather, her photographs address the largest of social questions through the often witty understatement of her technique. Gender, race, world politics and the nature of evil are among the topics addressed by her composite portraits. For instance, *Big Brother,* of 1983 combines the visages of Stalin, Mussolini, Mao, Hitler and Khomeini, while *Businessman* (1982) is comprised of ten unnamed investment bankers from Goldman Sachs and Company.

Burson has put her artistic methods at the service of the police in her updatings of the snapshots of missing children, presumed abducted. She is able to simulate the changing appearance of a growing child at any age, based on existing photographs of that child and its family. A project related to this endeavor is Burson's *The Age Machine,* a computer controlled video display of one's own face which can be instructed to perform simulated agings by various increments of years. More recent projects have included images of healthy and damaged tissue from AIDS patients (1989) and a series of portraits of children with craniofacial deformations (1992). This last series, made with a Diana camera and without computer manipulation, is a startling change from her previous work, and a challenge to the viewer. The rather ethereal blurry images question the distinctions between normal and exceptional.

—Ellen Handy

BUTYRIN, Vitaly.

Nationality: Russian. **Born:** Kaunas, Lithuania, 30 May 1947. **Education:** Attended schools in Kaunas; mainly self-taught in photography, from 1963. **Family:** Married Dana Kucinskaite in 1977; daughter: Lina. **Career:** Photographer, Vilnius, Lithuania, and Member of the Lithuanian Photography Art Society, Vilnius, since 1965 (Board Member and Art Council Member, since 1970). Liaison Officer of FIAP in Lithuania. Honorary Member, Ploen Photography Society, East Germany, 1972; Honorary Member, Kaunas Photography Club, 1973; Honorary Member, NATRON Photography Club, Maglay, Yugoslavia, 1974; Honorary Salon Member, First International Salon of Photography, Landernau, France, 1976; Artist, Federation Internationale d'Art Photographique, Berne, 1976; Honorary Member, A-74 Photography Club, Warsaw, 1977; Honorary Member, Virton Photography Society, Belgium, 1980. **Recipient:** Gold Medal, Yugoslav Union of Photographers, Maglaj, 1974; Gold Medal, Federation of Photography Art, Brussels, 1974; Trophy of Corato City, Italy 1974; Trophy of Lanciano City, Italy, 1974; Gold Medal, Federation Internationale d'Art Photographique, 1974, 1975, 1977; Niepce Medal, France, 1974, 1977, 1979; Grand Prix, Golden Eye Exhibition, Novi Sad, Yugoslavia, 1975, 1977; Grand Prix, *Auteurop 76,* Paris, 1976; Gold Medal, *Man and Sea* exhibition, Zadar, Yugoslavia, 1976; Grand Prix, *Fotomontaz 77,* Grudziaz, Poland, 1977; Belgian Royal Medal, Antwerp, 1977; Gold Medal, *Delta 81,* Brussels, 1981; Gold Medal, *Uzvara 85,* Bauska, U.S.S.R., 1985; Gold Medal, *Koper 85,* Yugoslavia 1985; Owner of the Supreme Title of the International Art Photography Federation (FIAP)—MFIAP (Master). **Address:** National Association of Lithuania Photographers, Universiteto str. 4, Vilnius 2600, Lithuania.

Individual Exhibitions:

1965   Azuolynas Movie Theatre, Kaunas, Lithuania
1969   International Friendship House, Moscow
1971   U.S.S.R. People's Ethnographical Museum, Leningrad
1972   Central Library, Kaunas, Lithuania
1973   U.S.S.R. People's Ethnographical Museum, Leningrad
1975   International Friendship House, Moscow
1977   Graphic Art Society, Moscow
1979   Galeria Fotografiki, Torun, Poland
1980   *Meines Fotografijos Parados,* Vilnius, Lithuania (retrospective; toured Kaunas, Siauliai, Riga, Tallinn, Murmansk, Minsk, Lvov, Ryazan, Moscow, Alma-Ata, Chelyabinsk, Novosibirsk, and Vladivostok—all U.S.S.R.)
        Salzburg Kunstlerhaus, Austria
1982   Exhibition Hall, Mogilyov, U.S.S.R.
1983   Palace of Culture, Neringa, U.S.S.R.
1984   Klub Johannes R. Becher, Neubranderburg, East Germany
1985   Galerie im Keller, East Berlin
        Kezys Gallery, Chicago
        Tautas Fotostudija, Riga, Latvia
        Plovdiv Fotoklub Gallery, Bulgaria
        Galerie Brennpunkt, West Berlin
        Vilnius Photography Gallery, Lithuania
1986   State Youth Theatre, Vilnius, Lithuania
        Klaipeda Photography Salon, U.S.S.R.
        Kaunas Photo Gallery, Lithuania
        Photo Museum, Siauliai, U.S.S.R.
1987   Preus Fotomuseum, Horten, Norway

Selected Group Exhibitions:

1969   *Nine Lithuanian Photographers,* USSR Journalists Union, Moscow
1975   *First International Triennale of Photography,* Musee d'Art et d'Histoire, Fribourg, Switzerland
1976   *Fantastic Photography in Europe,* Caon Gallery, Amsterdam
1977   *Photographers' Eyes,* Helsinki (travelled to Tampere and Turku, Finland)

From *Childhood Reminiscences* **series.** Photograph by Vitaly Butyrin.

Collections:

Lithuanian State Photography Museum, Siauliai; Musée Francais de la Photographie, Bièvres, France; Bibliotheque Nationale, Paris; Federation Internationale de l'Art Photographique Historical Collection, Paris; Moderna Galerija, Liubliana, Yugoslavia; Preus Fotomuseum, Horten, Norway; Canon Gallery, Amsterdam; Prakapas Gallery, New York.

Publications:

By BUTYRIN: Book—*Vitaly Butyrin,* Vilnius, Lithuania 1980. **Article**—"Technology Is Our ABC" in *Fotografie* (Leipzig), 1978.

On BUTYRIN: Books—*Photography Yearbook* edited by Norman Hall, London 1968, 1971; *Fotojahrbuch International,* Leipzig 1972, 1973, 1975; *Im Blickpunkt unsere Epoche,* Leipzig 1975; *Lietuvos Fotografija,* with an introduction by Romualdas Pacésa, Vilnius, Lithuania 1978; *Vitaly Butyrin: Meines Fotografijos Parados,* exhibition catalogue, Vilnius, Lithuania 1980; *Great Soviet Encyclopedia,* volume 27, Moscow 1979; *La Photographie Fantastique* by Lorenzo Merlo, Paris 1979; *Fotografen aus den USSR,* Baden-Baden, West Germany 1982; *Essays on Lithuanian Photography* by L. Anninsky, Vilnius, Lithuania 1984; *Vitaly Butyrin,* Neubranderburg, East Germany 1984; *Creative Photography* by S. Morosov, Moscow 1985; *Vitaly Butyrin: Fotografik—Fotomontage* by Ursula Petsch and Viktor Dyomin, Leipzig 1987. **Articles**—in *Revue Fotografia* (Prague), no. 4, 1968; "The Sharp and Inimitable Handwriting" by Valery Kichin in *Sovetskoye Foto* (Moscow), no. 8, 1978, reprinted in *Bulgarsko Foto* (Sofia), 1979; "Photographer of Allegory and Fantasy" by Valery Kichin and M. Leontyev in *Sputnik* (Moscow), 1979.

*

Photography is my entire life. What scares me most is when I start talking about photography. It is not because I would deprive the numerous critics and photography experts of their bite, or that I would be included in the immeasurable crowd of photo-impotents with their incessant photo-gossip. It is because I would deprive myself of my greatest source of happiness—creating my own world, seen, experienced and interpreted by myself, and given to other people. That is why I am happy that my arsenal of ideas is far richer than my arsenal of words, and I can make photographs without talking about it, in spite of the perceived truth that photography at present seems to have exhausted all, or nearly all, its possibilities.

I imagine photographic art as an immense and impenetrable fence. Once I am lucky enough to find a gap in the fence, I feel I must force myself through headfirst or feetfirst. However, this must be done without making other people's noses bleed by forcing the boards aside. It must help them to find their path to . . . the following fence.

—Vitaly Butyrin

*   *   *

Vitaly Butyrin, the grand master of photo arrangement, did not begin his career with the photomontage. When he began shooting at the Kaunas Photo Club in the 1960's he was fascinated by real life, by the world around him. But even then he worked towards a laconic style. To be more exact is to put stress where perhaps it doesn't belong, but in general he began to leave out every superfluous detail (using cropping, etc.); still later, in order to stress generality, independence in existence, and to a certain extent symbolism, Butyrin completely disposed of background and replaced it with a screen. From then on, it was no great step for Butyrin to become the artist we know today, the creator of his own world.

Among the photo-montages that have been created by various artists, one can distinguish different styles and perceive different degrees of conventionality, and perhaps the artists themselves can be said to divide into two groups. The first group creates a new environment or situation on the basis of real and familiar elements, and the new reality so created is perceived as a real one. The other group creates a new world that exists only in the artist's imagination. Butyrin is of the latter group, artists whose worlds have been created by themselves and are unique.

Many observers perceive Butyrin's style as excessively aggressive and individual in a world where everything seems to reduce to the same level; whatever one's response, there is no denying that Butyrin has forged his own individuality. He doesn't hide his arrangements; he offers his world as the only possibility; we have to accept him as he is. Yet, Butyrin's photos are still conventional to the extent that there is no incentive to reduce them to some recognizable reality. Not that they immediately suggest their equivalents in reality; rather, they represent universal human feelings and everyday problems to which one can respond. Love and dreams, respect for the dead, pollution of the environment, youth and age—these are some of the subjects that Butyrin likes to present, with great suggestiveness and eloquence.

Is it necessary to know the nature of the elements of Butyrin's world? One has to give in to the artist's fantasy as well as his thoughts, and doing so results in a new experience: visual effectiveness is combined with philosophical import. The series "Terra Incognita" and "Sea Tales" are something more than either thrilling or bizarre. The attentive observer notes that the sand drifts or the sea have become the sky, the clouds and stones have become the sea— and these photos allow our thoughts and fantasies their freedom; one can imagine a fairytale, good and beautiful world. Butyrin's photos may be mysterious, symbolic, and enigmatic, but they are never cruel. He is like the good teller of fairytales, whose story may be mystically dark but the end of which is necessarily happy.

—Peeter Tooming

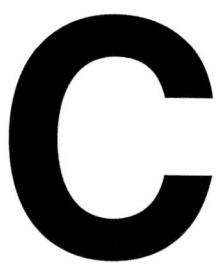

CAFFERY, Debbie (Deborah Ruth) Fleming.

Nationality: American. **Born:** New Iberia, Louisiana, 6 March 1948. **Education:** Graduated from the San Francisco Art Institute, Bachelor of Fine Arts. **Family:** Children: Joshua, Ruth Martin and Brennan. **Recipient:** Outstanding Achievement in the Arts, Acadiana Arts Council, Lafayette, Louisiana, 1988; Governor's Art Award, Professional Artist of the Year, Louisiana, 1989. **Agent:** Howard Greenberg, 120 Wochester Street, New York, New York 10012. **Address:** P.O. Box 298, Franklin, Louisiana 70538, U.S.A.

Individual Exhibitions:

1980	Contemporary Arts Center, New Orleans
1981	Arthur Roger Gallery, New Orleans
	Duke University, Durham, North Carolina
1984	Arthur Roger Gallery, New Orleans
1988	Martin Gallery, Washington, D.C.
	Museum of Southeast Texas, Beaumont, Texas
1989	Jane Corkin Gallery, Toronto
	Museum of Photographic Arts, San Diego, California
	Galerie Jean Pierre Lambert, Paris
	Galerie Junod, Lausanne, Switzerland
	Arthur Roger Gallery, New Orleans
1990	*Quatrième Triennale Internationale de la Photographie,* Palais des Beaux-Arts, Charleroi, Belgium
	Opsis Foundation, New York
	National Museum of American History, Smithsonian Institution, Washington, D.C.
1991	University Art Museum, Lafayette, Louisiana
	Arthur Roger Gallery, New Orleans
	Benteler Morgan Gallery, Houston
1992	Jackson Fine Arts, Atlanta, Georgia
	Robert Koch Gallery, San Francisco
	Photo Gallery International, Tokyo
1993	Museum of Contemporary Photography, Chicago
	Galveston Arts Center, Galveston, Texas

Selected Group Exhibitions:

1973	*Louisiana Photographs,* New Orleans Museum of Art
1980	*Louisiana Photography 1900-1980,* New Orleans Museum of Art
1982	*A Louisiana Focus,* Louisiana State Museum
1984	*A Century of Vision—Louisiana Photography, 1884-1984,* Louisiana State Museum
1985	*The Fertile Crescent,* Florida State University Fine Arts Gallery, Tallahasse, Florida
1986	Jane Corkin Gallery, Toronto
1988	Light Factory, Charlotte, North Carolina
	Twining Gallery, New York
1989	*The Deep South,* at *Recontres Internationales de la Photographie,* Arles, France
	New Southern Photographers, Burden Gallery, New York
1990	*Touched by Man: Landscape Photographs from Around the World,* Weil Gallery, Corpus Christi State University, Corpus Christi, Texas
	The Lloyds Bank Photographs of Children: 150 Years, Canadian Museum of Civilization, Ottawa
1991	*O Coracao Da Ciencia,* Centros Estudos Photographia, Coimbra, Portugal
	Découvertes, Grand Palais, Paris
1992	*Visages, Paysages et Autres Rivages,* Centre d'Art Contemporain, Brussels
1993	*Vale do Mondego,* Encontros De Photographie, Montemor-o-Vélho, Portugal
	Home, at *Fotomanifestatie, Noorderlicht,* Groningen, Holland
	Contemporary American Photography, Jingshan Jushnguan, Juangzhon, China
1994	*Devotion, Faith and Fervor,* Howard Greenberg Gallery, New York

Collections:

Museum of Modern Art, New York; Metropolitan Museum of Art, New York; George Eastman House, Rochester, New York; Smithsonian Institution, National Museum of American History, Washington, D.C.; New Orleans Museum of Art; Louisiana State Museum, New Orleans; Harvard University, Carpenter Center for Visual Studies, Cambridge, Massachusetts; St Louis Museum, Missouri; New York Public Library; Houston Museum of Fine Arts, Houston, Texas; Louisiana State University, Baton Rouge, Louisiana; Museum of Photographic Arts, San Diego, California; National Museum of American Art, Washington, D.C.; Museum für Kunst und Bewerbe, Hamburg, Germany; Bibliothèque Nationale, Paris; Maison Européenne de la Photographie, Paris; New Orleans Aquarium; Spencer Museum of Art, University of Kansas, Lawrence, Kansas; Arts Council of New Orleans; Fonds National d'Art Contemporain, Paris; Birmingham Museum of Art, Birmingham, Alabama; Harry Ransom Humanities Research Center, University of Texas, Austin; Los Angeles County Museum of Art; Center for Creative Photography, Tuscon, Arizona; High Museum of Art, Atlanta, Georgia.

Publications:

By CAFFERY: Book—*Carry Me Home,* with text by Pete Daniels and Anne Wilkes Tucker, Washington 1990.

On CAFFERY: Book—*Women Photographers* by Connie Sullivan, 1990. **Articles**—in *Popular Photography* (New York); in *Photoblätter* (Frankfurt); in *Photographies Magazine* (Paris); in *Cliches* (Brussels); in *Art Press* (Paris).

*

My search in photography has been a continuously refined response to what is beautiful, energetic, curious and mysterious. Many of my images portray fog, fire-smoke, steam and long exposures, with blurred or out-of-focus elements that help suggest the unexplainable.

My preference for black and white allows me to work with darkness, light and shadow to impart a mood into my work which reflects the sense of mystery that I feel. Certain conditions of weather and appearances of light and shadow and expressions or gestures of my subjects arrest me and the resonation begins.

Papa and Kojack, **1987.** Photograph ©Debbie Fleming Caffery. Courtesy Howard Greenberg Gallery.

I am trying to distill in my photographs a visual sense of mystery and grace, creating order in each frame from the clarity and chaos of what I see and feel. An emotional organization of feelings, textures and light.

—Debbie Fleming Caffery

*   *   *

You can feel the heat, the intense penetration of the heat working on your back. And the heaviness of the air, the blanket of sweaty, steaming air too thick and salty to breathe. No breeze to freshen or cool the back of the neck. And the endless row of green cane ahead to be stroked to promote a crop of sugar. Your back is wet, heavy and throbbing, afraid to straighten up, afraid of the pain; you might just snap from stretching against the constant curve of the planting-picking posture. Hands, raw and dry. Strange how everything else is wet but the hands are dry and split and stinging.

Later, the fields are picked over, stubble like a three-day growth on the chin of a drunken giant in the gutter; the husk of a field resting after working too hard, trying to forget the commerce that was just yanked out of it; an unwilling birth. It will take the full fury of the Louisiana July sun and plenty of chemicals to coax another crop out of this tired dirt. A cold dry wind blows dust against a steel drum filled with flames and scrap wood sending bad smoke and cinders into the air. Dark, huddled figures crowd the drum. This smoke is choking but smelling it means you can finally straighten your back. Shoulders hunched, hands still dry and cracked, deep in the pockets.

The images flow like smoke out of Debbie Caffery's portfolio. Reminders of Dorothea Lange, Doris Ulmann, and Walker Evans—a gesture, a back-against-the-wall full-faced portrait, a detail of soft texture in a calloused life. It is impossible for an urban audience to approach this work without these reminders because we scarcely see it as contemporary. Is life, somewhere, still like this? It's 1989 and the stock market has gone over the 2300 mark, star wars is on the agenda, one can go to a Skin Gym in Los Angeles, and the mailman is being retired by the fax machine. Who is still living in the sharecropper's cabin? Whose hands are these, whose profile? Whose milky brown eyes on a lizard sleeping on the screen?

There is an intimacy in these sweet revelations, mixed with monumental regard for the personalities. Caffery's respect is showing. She has developed access to a world we haven't seen in-depth since the FSA. These are not, however, documentary passages. They are poetry to their core. Tough and tender, sweet and bitter slices of a reality we seem to remember, though we've never seen it before. They are as current as this morning's news. These fields, these shacks, these tools may be very old, but it's a new crew—new faces, hands and backs putting the sugar in your 1989 coffee.

Ms Caffery makes a ''leit motif'' of the elderly Polly. In a series of intimate images Polly is seen in various contexts. She exudes tender strength, wisdom and simplicity. She seems so at ease with our intrusion that we feel we may be violating a trust by looking. Polly is an earth mother archetype, round, solid, monumental. She is passive and inscrutable, bearing the deep dignity of rural royalty. A closer view yields only more mystery. It is the mystery of life in the rural South. It is the riddle of Faulkner and Zora Neale Hurston, a glimpse of the melodic, impenetrable core of southern agrarian life.

The enervating soggy heat, the dry crackling cold wind, the smoke filled with cinders and creosote, lizards sleeping on broken window screens, and Polly's heavy round shoulder up against gray weathered wood are all seen through a veil of memory, a veil woven of literature and photographs. Debbie Fleming Caffery is the magician revealing what is under the veil while only deepening the puzzle. By referring to romantic memory, literary imagination, the sensuousness of a very physical existence and the history of rural American photography she has illustrated a lineage, through time, of the cracked hands and bent backs that have been feeding us for generations from off-camera. Debbie Fleming Caffery gives us a sweet and bitter ballad of Bayou Memoirs.

—Arthur Ollman

CAGNONI, Romano.

Nationality: Italian. **Born:** Pietrasanta, 9 November 1935. **Education:** Attended schools in Italy; self-taught in photography. **Career:** Freelance photographer and photojournalist, working for *The Observer, Paris-Match, Life, Bunte, The Times, Stern, L'Espresso, Newsweek, France Soir,* etc., in London, since 1958. **Recipient:** Overseas Press Club Award, New York, 1970; Gold Medal, International Academy of Photographic Art, Salsomaggiore, Italy, 1983; Bronze Medal, Art Directors Club of Germany, 1992. **Agent:** The Photographers' Gallery, 8 Great Newport Street, London WC2. **Address:** via Osterietta 38, Pietrasanta 55045 (Lucca), Italy.

Individual Exhibitions:

1966   *Florence Floods,* Swiss Cottage Library, London
1969   *Biafra,* Trafalgar Square Marquee, London

1975   *Romano Cagnoni, Presented by Olivetti,* Galleria II Diaframma, Milan
1976   University Museum, Mexico City
1977   Italian Institute of Culture, London (retrospective)
1978   Museo Civico, Bologna
1984   Palazzo Braschi, Rome
1985   Galleria d'Arte, Pietrasanta, Italy
1986   Galleria d'Arte, Carrara, Italy
        Arts Council Gallery, Desenzano, Italy
1988   *Caro Marmo,* IF Gallery, Milan; Versiliana, Lucca
1989   *Caro Marmo,* I.I.F.T., Los Angeles
1990   *Caro Marmo,* Palazzo Lanfranchi, Pisa
1991   *Caro Marmo,* Foto Expo, Gorizia
1993   *War in Yugoslavia,* Italian Institute of Culture, New York, Chicago, Los Angeles and Washington, D.C.
1994   *15 Best Photographs,* Acta International Gallery, Rome

Selected Group Exhibitions:

1971   *Witness,* The Photographers' Gallery, London
        Color Supplement Photojournalists, Royal Photographic Society, London
1975   *Romano Cagnoni and the U.S.A. Avantgarde,* Museo Correr, Venice
1978   *Italian Photographers,* at *Rencontres Internationales de la Photographie,* Arles, France
1979   *Italian Eye,* ACIA Gallery, New York
1980   *African Photos,* Palazzo Isimbardi, Milan
        Politics and Photography, P.S.1., New York
1981   *L'Informazione Negata,* Biblioteca Provinciale, Bari, Italy
1983   *Kindness,* Keflex Collection, London
1984   *Trees,* The Photographers' Gallery, London

Collections:

Bibliothèque Nationale, Paris; Arts Council of Carrara, Italy: Arts Council of Bologna, Italy; Keflex Collection, London; John C. De Prez Jr., Indianapolis, USA; Paul Arden, London.

Publications:

By CAGNONI: Books—*Bury Me in My Boots,* with text by Sally Trench, London 1968; *The Brother's War,* with text by John de St. Jorre, Boston 1972; *Middle East War,* with text by the *Sunday Times* editors, London 1974; *Southern Italy: History and Technology,* Turin 1978; *Bologna,* Bologna 1979; *The South of Italy,* Turin 1980; *Trees,* exhibition catalogue, with others, London 1984; *Geometry of Pain,* Rome 1984; *Pietrasanta and Figli,* Milan 1985; *Italy,* with Time-Life editors, New York and Amsterdam 1986; *Caro Marmo,* edited by Iveco-Fiat, Italy 1987; *Sculptors in Pietrasanta,* edited by La Subbia, Italy 1991; *Kan Yasuda Sculptor,* with Kozo Watabiki, edited by Leonardo, De Luca, Italy 1991.

On CAGNONI: Books—*English Painting* by R.H. Wilenski, London 1964; *The Art of Photography,* by the Time-Life editors, New York 1971; *Romano Cagnoni, Presented by Olivetti,* exhibition catalogue, with text by Bruno Segre, introduction by Renzo Zorzi, Milan 1975; *70 Anni di Fotografia in Italia* by Italo Zannier, Modena, Italy 1978; *Pictures on a Page* by Harold Evans, London 1978; *The Camera at War* by Jorge Lewinski, London 1979; *L'Informazione Negata: il fotogiornalismo in Italia 1945/1980,* edited by Uliano Lucas and Maurizio Bizziccari, Bari, Italy 1981; *European Photography 1981* by Edward Booth Clibborn, London 1981; *I Grandi Fotografi: Romano Cagnoni,* Milan 1983; *How Famous Photographers Work* by Jack Schofield, John Goldblatt and others, London 1983; *Bilder vom Kreig* by Rainer Fabian and Hans Christian Adam, Hamburg 1983, as *Images of War: 130 Years of War Photography,* London 1985; *Achieving Photographic Style,* Macdonald, London 1984; *The Magic of Black and White* by Kodak editors, London 1985, New York 1986; *Life 50 Years,* Time Life Books, New York 1986. **Articles**—''Romano Cagnoni'' in *Life* (New York), August 1968; ''Best Photographic Reporting'' in *Dateline* (New York), April 1969; ''Romano

The Painter, My Late Wife, Berenice Sydney. Photograph ©Romano Cagnoni.

Cagnoni: Total Photography'' by J.J. de Lucio-Meyer in the *Penrose Annual,* London 1970; ''Photographic Documents by Romano Cagnoni, London'' by J.J. de Lucio-Meyer in *Gebrauchsgraphik* (Munich), March 1971; ''Romano Cagnoni: Biafra'' in *Schweizerische Photorundschau* (Visp, Switzerland), August 1971; ''Romano Cagnoni'' in *Fotografia Italiana* (Milan), October 1974; ''10 Years of Photographing Historical Events'' in *Domenica del Corriere* (Milan), April 1975; ''Sight-Insight-Foresight'' by J.J. de Lucio-Meyer in *Novum* (Munich), December 1975; ''Romano Cagnoni,'' special issue of *Progresso Fotografico* (Milan), November 1976; ''Romano Cagnoni'' in *You and Your Camera* (London), May/June 1980; ''Das War 1989'' *Stern,* Hamburg 1989.

*

A human pictorial document: that is the description of the best photograph. A fashion photographer, advertising, ''creative'' wouldn't perhaps agree with me, nor would many others. Yet, the camera, this technological tool, has no limit to document human beings' feelings, but has boundaries to record forms if one is to compare photographs to painting. I am not talking of bad painting. I have yet to see a photograph so rich in construction as Picasso's or Berenice Sydney's; to compare visual medias is an old argument and I will stop here.

I rather enjoy comparing photography to literature, many books of prose of plays, in which very sensitive writers describe their characters' feelings by their expressions: the light in their eyes, the curve the mouth might take, the lines of their faces changing according to what they feel, etc. Also I enjoy, like writers, sharing the relationship that my ''characters'' have with their environment, with other people and most of all the relationship they have with themselves.

In moments of doubt I wonder that perhaps a photograph is beautiful only because of its pictorial impact; then I remember that psychological research is an incredible event of this century and feel again confident to go along on my itinerary. Certainly the communication is visual, the challenge is at times how to break rules of compositional equilibrium to further a research towards more dramatic photographs.

For me though, the most lively aspects of this work of photographer remains the search and discovery of human beings' contradictions and I, first to be mutable, still manage sometimes to remain surprised by the results.

—Romano Cagnoni

*　　*　　*

Many of Romano Cagnoni's photographs are beyond criticism. When a man risks his life for a picture, or gets them in almost impossible circumstances, it reduces any complaints about technical quality or composition to churlishness. Cagnoni does take risks. He was one of the first photographers into the war in Biafra (and one of the last to leave). He was the first independent photographer into North Vietnam, travelling with the writer James Cameron. He penetrated into Afghanistan shortly after the Soviet invasion, and secretly took pictures through his partly unbuttoned coat. . . . As well as all this, Cagnoni's black-and-white pictures show a rare gift for capturing powerful emotions. Stark, contrasty lighting and/or printing suffuse his pictures with a sense of drama, or even danger, though the source of the danger may not be shown in the frame. For example, one shot taken in Biafra and published in *Life* in 1970 seems to sum up the whole agony of that wretched war, yet all it shows is a negro's head. In theory it could have been taken anywhere, but the man's haunted expression, the fear implied by the whites of his eyes, speak volumes about that particular conflict.

Another sequence taken in Biafra the year before was so powerful it was given a whole page display in *The Times* (12 March 1969). That newspaper had so long been renowned for its failure to use pictures well, it was astonishing for them to publish a dramatic set in the *Life* manner.

Cagnoni's pictures rarely show the fighting, or tell you which side is winning. What they tell you is that people are losing. People are suffering. Often the pictures show people trying, as best they can, to help one another. A nurse, crouching, beckons an emaciated child; doctors operate on the wounded; a man kneels before a missionary; a mother clutches at her children: the raw emotions of these pictures give them a continuing appeal long after the battles have been forgotten. In these and in more everyday newspaper pictures, Cagnoni tends to crop tightly round his figures to emphasize the points of contact between them. Unimportant parts of the picture might well be out of focus, or so grainy (due to the greatness of the enlargement) that they do not hold the eye. Everything is subordinated to the central emotion which is the point of the picture. Cagnoni's colour work is less dramatic. Colour film does not lend itself to reducing scenes to extreme contrasts of light and shade. Also, it is not built to withstand the kind of rough treatment Cagnoni gives it, and his cameras, and himself, in the pursuit of impossible pictures.

I believe that Romano Cagnoni has always had the respect of his peers in photography both in England and the rest of the world. Because he chose not to join any of the agencies and largely decided his own stories, he has not had the back-up that allows a photographer to pursue personal work over a long period. However in Italy, to which he has now returned, this is sometimes possible with the sponsorship of large companies. Such was the case with his book *Caro marmo* on the marble mines of Carrara which was underwritten by Iveco, which chose some of the pictures for its calendar. This book, entirely in colour, shows a different side of his work as it contains not only extremely beautiful pictures but also documents the difficulties and dangers of the work which seems hardly changed over the centuries.

Cagnoni remains primarily interested in the human condition and while a good selection of his photographs, both from war and in peace, can be found in *Geometry of Pain* and in his contribution to the *I Grand Fotografi* series edited by Fabbri, he is now turning more to the creative side. His two latest books explore his interest in sculpture and its creation. While, like McCullin, he may feel he has seen enough of war and disaster, his own talent is undiminished and continues to flower in more positive environments.

—Jack Schofield

CALLAHAN, Harry.

Nationality: American. **Born:** Detroit, Michigan, 22 October 1912. **Education:** Attended public school in Royal Oak, Michigan; studied engineering at Michigan State College, East Lansing, 1931-33; self-taught in photography. **Family:** Married Eleanor Knapp in 1936; daughter: Barbara. **Careeer:** Photographer since 1938. Worked for Chrysler Motor Parts Corporation, Detroit, 1934-44; Processing Assistant, General Motors Photographic Laboratories, Detroit, 1944-45. Instructor in Photography, 1946-49, and Head of the Department of Photography, 1949-61, Institute of Design, Illnois Institute of Technology, Chicago; Associate Professor, 1961-64, Professor, 1964-77, and Chairman of the Department of Photography, 1961-73, Rhode Island School of Design, Providence. Visiting Instructor, Black Mountain College, North Carolina, 1951, University of California Extension, Berkeley, 1966, and University of Massachusetts, Boston, 1974. **Recipient:** Diploma and Plaque, *Photokina* exhibition, Cologne, 1951; Graham Foundation Grant, 1956; Photography Award, *Rhode Island Arts Festival,* 1963; Rhode Island Governor's Award for Excellence in the Arts, 1969; Distinguished Contribution Award, National Association of Schools, 1972; Guggenheim Fellowship, 1972; Photographer and Educator Award, Society for Photographic Education, 1976; Brandeis Award, Brandeis University, Waltham, Massachusetts, 1985. Honored Photographer, *Rencontres Internationale de la Photographie,* Arles, France, 1977. D.F.A.: Rhode Island School of Design, 1978. **Agent:** Pace/MacGill, 32 East 57th Street, New York, New York 10022, U.S.A.

Individual Exhibitions:

1946	750 Studio Gallery, Chicago
1951	Art Institute of Chicago
	Black Mountain College, North Carolina
	Museum of Modern Art, New York (toured the United States)
1956	Kansas City Art Institute
1957	*Harry Callahan/Aaron Siskind: Photographes Americains,* Centre Culturel Americain, Paris (travelled to Algiers and London)
	Abstract Photography, American Federation of Arts, New York (with Aaron Siskind and Arthur Siegel; toured the United States)
	3 Photographers: Harry Callahan/Walter Rosenblum/Minor White, White Museum of Art, Cornell University, Ithaca, New York
1958	International Museum of Photography, George Eastman House, Rochester, New York (retrospective)
1960	*Aaron Siskind/Harry Callahan,* The Cliff Dwellers, Chicago
1962	Museum of Modern Art, New York (with Robert Frank)
	University of Warsaw
1963	Galeria Krzysztofory, Krakow, Poland
	Galeria Towarzystwo, Warsaw
1964	Heliography Gallery, New York
	Hallmark Gallery, New York (toured the United States)
	El Mochuelo Gallery, Santa Barbara, California
1966	Kiosk Galleries, Reed College, Portland, Oregon
1968	Massachusetts Institute of Technology, Cambridge
	Museum of Modern Art, New York (toured the United States)
1969	International Museum of Photography, George Eastman House, Rochester, New York (toured the United States)
1970	Friends of Photography, Carmel, California
	Witkin Gallery, New York
	Siembab Gallery, Boston
1971	831 Gallery, Birmingham, Michigan
	International Museum of Photography, George Eastman House, Rochester, New York
1972	Light Gallery, New York
1974	Light Gallery, New York
1975	Massachusetts Institute of Technology, Cambridge
	Cronin Gallery, Houston
1976	Museum of Modern Art, New York (retrospective)
	Minneapolis Institute of Arts

Picture Gallery, Zurich
Galerie Lichttropfen, Aachen, West Germany
Light Gallery, New York
Photographs by Aaron Siskind and Harry Callahan, Washington Gallery of Photography, Washington, D.C.
Aaron Siskind/Harry Callahan/Stephen Shore, Silver Image Gallery, Tacoma, Washington
1977   Galerie Zabriskie, Paris
Enjay Gallery, Boston
David Mirvish Gallery, Toronto
Rencontres Internationales de la Photographie, Arles, France
Susan Spiritus Gallery, Newport Beach, California
Grapestake Gallery, San Francisco
1978   Galerie Fiolet, Amsterdam
Light Gallery, New York
Biennale, Venice (with Richard Diebenkorn)
1980   Light Gallery, New York
Light Gallery, Los Angeles
1981   *Color Photographs 1940-1980,* Colorado Mountain College, Breckenridge
1983   *Posed and Unposed Portraits,* Zabriskie Gallery, New York (with Lee Friedlander)
1984   *Pictures of Eleanor,* Center for Creative Photography, University of Arizona, Tucson (toured the United States 1985-87)
Chicago Photos, Edwynn Houk Gallery, Chicago
1985   Ffotogallery, Cardiff, Wales (retrospective)
1987   Pace/MacGill Gallery, New York City
1991   Pace/MacGill Gallery, New York City
1992   *Harry Callahan: City Pictures 1950,* Pace/MacGill Gallery, New York City

Selected Group Exhibitions:

1948   *In and Out of Focus,* Museum of Modern Art, New York
1950   *Photography at Mid-Century,* Los Angeles County Museum of Art
1954   *Subjecktive Fotografie 2,* State School of Arts, Saarbrucken
1955   *The Family of Man,* Museum of Modern Art, New York (and world tour)
1967   *Photography in the 20th Century,* National Gallery of Canada, Ottawa (toured Canada and the United States, 1967-73)
1977   *The Photographer and the City,* Museum of Contemporary Art, Chicago
1980   *The Magical Eye,* National Gallery of Canada, Ottawa
1982   *Counterparts: Form and Emotion in Photographs,* Metropolitan Museum of Art, New York (travelled to the Contemporary Arts Center, Cincinnati, Ohio; Dallas Museum of Fine Arts, Texas; San Francisco Museum of Modern Art; Corcoran Gallery, Washington, D.C.)
1985   *American Images 1945-80,* Barbican Art Gallery, London (toured Britain)
1987   *Photography and Art 1946-86,* Los Angeles County Museum of Art
1990   Pace/MacGill Gallery, New York City
1992   Pace/MacGill Gallery, New York City

Collections:

Center for Creative Photography, University of Arizona, Tucson (archives); Museum of Modern Art, New York; International Museum of Photography, George Eastman House, Rochester, New York; Art Institute of Chicago; Hallmark Collection, Kansas City; National Gallery of Canada, Ottawa; Bibliothèque Nationale, Paris.

Publications:

By CALLAHAN: Books of photographs—*On My Eyes,* with text by Larry Eigner, Highlands, North Carolina 1960; *The Multiple Image: Photographs by Harry Callahan,* edited by Gordon Martin and Aaron Siskind, text by Jonathan Williams, Chicago 1961; *Photographs: Harry Callahan,* with text by Hugo

Weber, Santa Barbara, California 1964; *Photographs by Harry Callahan,* Hallmark calendar, with text by Edward Steichen, New York 1966; *Harry Callahan,* with preface by John Szarkowski, text by Paul Sherman, New York 1967; *Callahan,* edited by John Szarkowski, Millerton, New York 1976; *Harry Callahan,* text by Peter C. Bunnell, New York 1978; *Harry Callahan: Color,* New York 1980; *Water's Edge: Photographs by Harry Callahan,* with an introductory poem by A.R. Ammons, afterword by Callahan, Lyme, Connecticut 1980; *Eleanor,* New York and Carmel, California 1984. **Articles**—"Learning Photography at the Institute of Design," with Aaron Siskind, in *Aperture* (Millerton, New York), no. 4, 1956; "Pattern" in *American Society of Magazine Photographers Annual,* New York 1957; "Harry Callahan: Conventional Subjects Become Extraordinary Photographs," with David Ebin, in *Modern Photography* (New York), February 1957; "Harry Callahan: An Interview," with A.D. Coleman in the *New York Photographer,* January 1972; "Quotes from Callahan," edited by Harvey Lloyd, in *Infinity* (New York), March 1973; "An Interview with Harry Callahan," with James Alinder, in *Exposure* (New York), May 1976; "Harry Callahan: Questions," with Jacqueline Brody, in *Print Collector's Newsletter* (New York), January/February 1977; "Callahan," edited by Melissa Shook, in *Photograph* (New York), Summer 1977.

On CALLAHAN: Books—*Photography as Art* by Volker Kahmen, Tubingen, West Germany 1973, London 1974; *Faces: A Narrative History of the Portrait in Photography* by Ben Maddow, Boston 1977; *Nude Photographs 1850-1980,* edited by Constance Sullivan, New York 1980; *Visions and Images; American Photographers on Photography,* edited by Barbaralee Diamonstein, New York 1981; *The Imaginary Photo Museum* by Helmut Gernsheim, Renate and L. Fritz Gruber, Cologne 1981, London 1982; *Counterparts: Form and Emotion in Photographs* by Weston J. Naef, New York 1982; *The Library of World Photography: Landscape,* with texts by David Plowden and Ian Jeffrey, Tokyo and London 1984; *Photography and Art 1946-1986,* exhibition catalogue, by Andy Grundberg and Kathleen M Gauss, Los Angeles 1987. **Articles**—"An Exhibition: Creative Photography" by Van Deren Coke in *Aperture* (Millerton, New York), no. 1, 1956; "The Photographs of Harry Callahan" by Minor White in *Aperture* (Millerton, New York), no. 2, 1958; "Harry Callahan in Polske" by Ursula Czartoyska in *Fotografia* (Warsaw), March 1963; "Photographs: Harry Callahan" by Margery Mann in *Artforum* (New York), September 1964; "Harry Callahan: The Multiple Image" in *Creative Camera* (London), August 1968; "Callahan Teaching Method" by Jacob Deschin in the *New York Times,* 12 January 1969; "Who Is Callahan?" by David Vestal in *Travel and Camera* (New York), May 1969; "Is His Genius Underrated?" by A.D. Coleman in the *New York Times,* 27 September 1970; "Harry Callahan" by A.D. Coleman in the *New York Times,* 31 December 1972; "Harry Callahan" by Thomas Barrow in the *Britannica Encyclopaedia of American Art,* Chicago 1975; "Harry Callahan's Detente with Experience" by Leo Rubinfen in the *Village Voice* (New York), 10 April 1978; "Romance without Pain or Anxiety: Harry Callahan's Photos of Eleanor" by Alan G. Artner in the *Chicago Tribune,* 22 January 1984; "When Woman Is Idealized Without Resorting to Cliche" by Andy Grundberg in the *New York Times,* 1 July 1984.

*   *   *

The person who one day writes Harry Callahan's definitive biography may not have to make a very fat book of it, unless, of course, photographs are included. Then the volume could easily bulge at the seams.

True, much is known and has been recorded about the biographical events in Callahan's life—that his parents were farmers, that he received no formal photographic education, that he's been head over heels about Eleanor ever since the two met on a blind date in '33, or that he once worked as a clerk in the accounting department at Chrysler Motors. And Callahan himself has informed us that it was Ansel Adams who first put the bug in him, cleared away "the monkey business," and made tone and texture *a priori* conditions that liberated him for pure camera work thereafter. We know, too, of Callahan's reputation as a teacher, enduring and indisputable even after his own candid claims to the contrary—admissions that teaching for him could be murder at times. While it will never be said that Callahan made a better teacher than he is a photographer, few artist-teachers have been as influential: his great passion for photography as a way of life was eagerly adopted by generation after generation of students at both Chicago's Institute of Design and later the

Rhode Island School of Design. Incontrovertible as well is Callahan's reputation as an American photographer turned international artist, his work the subject of numerous exhibitions and publications, including major retrospectives at the Museum of Modern Art and the Venice *Biennale.* Yet these events, while assuredly significant and nourishing to Callahan himself, to his biographer may ultimately be nonevents.

Personal attributes and accomplishments have never been easy to embellish, not without some trail of gossip or legend. Callahan's chronology contains no tales of fervent pursuit by government agents, no confiscated or destroyed negatives, no model/mistress mix-ups, no abject solitude or gross impecunity. Marked by grace and peace, the story of Harry Callahan is a triumph of self-motivation and inner volition. The details progress like inches along a yardstick—a logical and predictable chain of achievements, a checklist growing ever more prestigious with every new exhibition, publication, honor, and award. In short, Harry Callahan epitomizes the new American photographer approaching a 21st century art world, a world where artistic success with financial stability for a photographer within his or her lifetime is no longer an impossible dream.

For Alfred Stieglitz and his contemporaries, things were never that certain. For Callahan, in his seventies, there is now the blessed knowledge, and the confidence and satisfaction it must bring, that one's daily exercises of eye and heart are already in safe keeping, not just in the history of photography but the history of art. Callahan, along with Ansel Adams and a handful of others, is among the first living masters of the medium to witness the future Stieglitz had in mind, to benefit from the concepts he sought to reify.

"Photography is an adventure just as life is an adventure," Callahan has stated. "If man wishes to express himself photographically he must understand, surely to a certain extent, his relationship to life." Looking then at this adventure, this remarkably clear and straightforward life, the pictures, every one of them, tell the story. Harry Callahan is his work. And therein lies his legend.

The titles of Callahan's photographs—limited to place and year snapped—inform where and when, rarely what, never why, and only who if Eleanor, his wife, or Barbara, his daughter, are the subjects before his camera. While his images have been grouped into a variety of categories—geographic, chronologic, camera format used and the like—most appropriate would be to survey his life's work as he organized it himself, by some half-dozen thematic concerns. These themes—landscapes, seascapes, cityscapes, anonymous strangers, intimate loved ones, camera-confined multiple exposures (mostly combinations of his single-image subject matter), and, as it now turns out, a full-fledged career in color photography too—were all initiated in his very first years as a photographer and have preoccupied him ever since. Callahan himself was quick to recognize these first "good ones" as images he could build on, but rarely surpass. Some of them were indeed as good as any he has ever made.

As theoretician, Callahan was an ardent disciple of the Bauhaus tradition, a staunch supporter of a discipline that treated an art form like photography as machine-made as much as it was manmade. His photographs can be viewed as a lifelong challenge to the camera's eye, a series of neverending questions on the nature of the medium itself. What do varying shutter speeds accomplish with sunlight on water? At what camera distance does the human eye stop searching for detail in a print? How contiguously can tones be rendered and still stand apart? Can a silhouette also be three-dimensional? How will the same scene overlapped upside down against itself appear on film? Or how black-and-white can a color photograph be? Callahan's answers, contained in his photographs, have never ceased to surprise with their uncanny blend of directness and subtlety.

Aesthetically, Callahan was often compelled by images that pitted perfection against imperfection, that countered visual chaos with visual order. A classic example is the 1950ish photograph of starkly bared trees set against a gray paste of Chicago sky and harbor. The branches are a mish-mash of polywebbed obfuscation, yet the trunks are distinctively poised like impeccably mannered guests in black tuxedos. A more recent illustration of Callahan's penchant for balance with imbalance occurs in his Cape Cod series. In one of these, an imperfect horizon line, bowed slightly at center like an Ellsworth Kelly curve painting, perfectly divides a landscape into equal parts of cloudless gray sky and wind-mogulled, glittering sand. That a tiny speck of black in the distance is, in fact, the mighty Atlantic further underscores Callahan's fondness for dualities. In another photograph, a volleyball net levitates near the shoreline of a listless beach. The top cord of the net hangs in a

perfect arch from pole to pole. The bottom cord, lighter in weight, catches the slight breeze and visually breaks apart.

From image to image, dichotomies reverberate in Callahan's work. When he is inside, it is the intimacy of his home life that he embraces. Sunlight filters through venetian blinds into a womb-like room where Madonna and child, Eleanor and Barbara, rest in the nude. It is a scene of tenderness only a father and husband, tip-toeing with a tripod, would catch. When Callahan is outside, it is often the anonymity of the street—two strangers and one dead lamplight—that he utilizes to symbolize the broken circuitry of human interaction.

In almost any Callahan photograph it is possible to see every Callahan photograph. There is the 1952 image of his friend Bob Fine standing in a shaft of city sunlight at the far end of an alleyway. Fine is so tiny, he at first appears as if seen on stage from the very last row of the top balcony. A similar scale illusion takes hold in a 1972 photograph on Cape Cod. A wind-tussled surf is about to pound a beach like a bedsheet slapped flat for a tight fit. At first, the rushing breaker threatens our toes—we think it so near—then, spying a jogger skirting the surf edge, we grasp where Callahan must be: high on the peak of a sand dune overlooking the whole ocean.

Recently, Callahan has claimed to have abandoned black-and-white photography altogether. If that turns out to be the case (and it will be verified only after many more years have passed), the switch to color signals the first true dividing line in a career notable for a paucity of turning points. With the color work fresh out of the drum—even though most of it was photographed decades ago—there is a natural inclination, almost temptation, to compare both modes of expression, especially among concurrent images. In the work with Eleanor and Barbara particularly, Callahan's choice of film seems to have made little difference. There is the black-and-white photograph of the two of them, taken in 1953, thigh and neck deep in Lake Huron. Callahan isolates and incubates his family in tranquillity and softness, out of the reach of strangers scurrying near the edges of the frame. By comparison, there is no loss of intimacy—no compromise in compassion or beauty—in the color photograph of Eleanor leading Barbara by the hand, elephant trunklike, into a windowsill of sunlight. Here, as in the color work with Providence houses, with their spanking paint jobs and Kodachrome blue skies vs. their black-and-white brethen, the choice is a toss up. Like two sides of a coin, the value is the same.

As any major artist in his 70s must come to know, you rarely get any better than you already are. Callahan's great achievements may have been predicated on having accepted this knowledge right from the start. There are photographers whose life-span outstretches their vision. Then there are photograpers like Harry Callahan who, after 40 years, still show no sign of let-up. Callahan's genius as an artist may ultimately rest as much with the purity of his vision as with this remarkable, rejuvenating continuum.

—Arno Rafael Minkkinen

CALLIS, Jo Ann.

Nationality: American. **Born:** Jo Ann Levin in Cincinnati, Ohio, 25 November 1940. **Education:** Attended Ohio State University, Columbus, 1958-60; California State University at Long Beach, 1962-65; University of California at Los Angeles (studied under Robert Heinecken), 1971-77, B.A. 1974, M.F.A. 1977. **Family:** Married Gilbert Callis in 1960 (divorced, 1975); children: Stephen and Michael; married David Pann in 1980. **Career:** Teaching Assistant, University of California at Los Angeles, 1976-77. Since 1976, Instructor, California Institute of the Arts, Valencia. **Recipient:** Ferguson Award, Friends of Photography, Carmel, California, 1978; Photography Fellowship, National Endowment for the Arts, 1980, 1985 and 1991; Awards in the Visual Arts, 1989; Guggenheim Fellowship, 1990. **Agents:** Laurence Miller Gallery, 138 Spring Street, New York 10012; Craig Krull Gallery, 2525 Michigan Avenue B3, Santa Monica, California 90404, U.S.A.

Individual Exhibitions:

1975   Orange Coast College, Costa Mesa, California
1977   *Callis, Kasten and Zimmerman,* University of Southern
        California, Los Angeles

Performance, **1985.** Photograph by Joanne Callis.

1978	Gallery of Fine Photography, New Orleans
1979	*Callis/Cumming,* Blue Sky Gallery, Portland, Oregon (with Robert Cumming)
	Color Transformations, University of California, Berkeley (with John Divola)
1980	G. Ray Hawkins Gallery, Los Angeles
1985	H. F. Manes Gallery, New York
	The Temporary Contemporary, Museum of Contemporary Art, Los Angeles
1986	Gallery Min, Tokyo
1988	Richard Green Gallery, New York
1989	*Objects of Reverie, Selected Photographs,* Des Moines Art Center, Des Moines, Iowa
1992	Dorothy Goldeen Gallery, Santa Monica, California
1993	*New Work in Color,* Laurence Miller Gallery, New York
1994	*Color Mysteries,* Cleveland Museum of Art, Cleveland, Ohio

Selected Group Exhibitions:

1976	*Emerging L.A. Photographers,* Friends of Photography, Carmel, California
1978	*The Photograph as Artifice,* California State University at Long Beach
1979	*Southern California Invitational Exhibition,* University of Southern California
1980	*The Imaginary Photo Museum,* Kunsthalle, Cologne
1982	*Color as Form,* International Museum of Photography at George Eastman House, Rochester, New York
1984	*Photography in California 1945-80,* San Francisco Museum of Modern Art (toured)
1986	*Photography as Performance,* The Photographers' Gallery, London
1987	*Photography and Art 1946-86,* Los Angeles County Museum of Art
1989	*California Photography: Remaking Make-Believe,* Museum of Modern Art, New York
	The Photography of Invention: American Pictures of the 80's, National Museum of American Art, Smithsonian Institution, Washington, D.C.
1991	*Pleasures and Terrors of Domestic Comfort,* Museum of Modern Art, New York
1992	*Patterns of Influence,* Center of Creative Photography, University of Arizona, Tuscon, Arizona
1993	*American Made—The New Still Life,* Isetan Museum of Art, Tokyo

Collections:

Museum of Modern Art, New York; Center for Creative Photography, University of Arizona, Tucson; Museum of Modern Art, San Francisco; International Museum of Photography, George Eastman House, Rochester, New York; Denver Museum of Art; Minneapolis Institute of Art; New Orleans Museum of Art; Bibliothèque Nationale, Paris; Tasmanian Museum of Art, Hobart; Corcoran Gallery of Art, Washington, D.C.; Mito Museum, Japan.

Publications:

By CALLIS: Portfolio—*Dye Transfer Portfolio,* 8 prints, Los Angeles 1984.

On CALLIS: Books—*Glass Eye* by Kikuo Mori, Los Angeles 1975, 1977; *Creative Camera Annual,* edited by Colin Osman, London 1976; *Photography Annual,* New York 1978, 1979; *Ten Year Salute* by Lee Witkin, Danbury, New Hampshire 1979; *The Imaginary Photo Museum* by Helmut Gernsheim, Renate and L. Fritz Gruber and others, Cologne 1981, London 1982; *Color as Form: A History of Color Photography,* exhibition catalogue, with introduction by Robert A. Sobieszek, Rochester, New York 1982; *Photography in California 1945-1980* by Louise Katzman, San Francisco 1984; *Photography and Art 1946-1986,* exhibition catalogue, by Andy Grundberg and Kathleen M. Gauss, Los Angeles 1987; *Anti Olympus, Catalogue for 10 Photographers,*

by Peter Schjeldahl, 1985. **Articles**—"A New York Welcome" by Guy Trebay in the *Village Voice* (New York), 28 February 1977; "Jo Ann Callis" in *Popular Photography* (New York), no. 4, 1977; "Jo Ann Callis" in *Picture Magazine* (Los Angeles), no. 6, 1978; "Le Vertige des Sens" in *Photo* (Paris), no. 131, 1978; "Jo Ann Callis" by Cathy Coleman in *Artweek* (Oakland, California), 11 February 1978; "Collector's Eye" by Peter Plagens in *New West Magazine* (Los Angeles), 8 November 1978; "Between Eroticism and Morbidity" in *LAICA Journal* (Los Angeles), no. 24, 1979; "Jo Ann Callis" in *Creative Camera* (London), October 1979; "Memorable Visions" by Joan Murray in *Artweek* (Oakland, California), 8 September 1979; "Jo Ann Callis" by Don Owens in *Photo Show Magazine* (Los Angeles), May 1980; "Callis' Photographs—Telling it Like it May Be" by Suzanne Muchnic in *Los Angeles Times,* 18 July 1985; "A Strangeness in the Ordinary" by Mark Johnstone in *Artweek,* 24 August 1985; "Re-Presenting Presentation" by Amelia Jones in *Artweek,* 26 December 1987; "JoAnne Callis: Conjured Visions" by Peter Clothier in *Angeles Magazine,* January 1989; "Jo Ann Callis" by Susan Kandel in *Arts Magazine,* September 1991; "Jo Ann Callis" by Amelia Jones in *Art Issues,* September/October 1991; "Jo Ann Callis at Dorothy Goldeen" by Janet Koplos in *Art in America,* December 1991; "Enigmatic Fabrications" by Susan Kandel in *Los Angeles Times,* 11 June 1992; "JoAnn Callis: A Fascination with Transformation" in *Cal Arts Current,* Vol 5 No 3, May 1993.

*

I have always made photographs that are fabricated and have a psychological edge to them. I find that my pictures communicate sensations and evoke feelings that leave the viewer with a sense of uneasiness as well as pleasure. The dualities of attraction and repulsion, and reality and fantasy are often present in my work, whether the images are color or black and white. My artwork reflects my ongoing interest in performance and presentation or display, using familiar interior spaces as my chosen arena.

—Jo Ann Callis

*   *   *

The color photographs of Jo Ann Callis are resonant with familiarity, yet one would find it difficult to describe exactly what is happening in them. Using a medium noted for its literal specificity, Callis makes photographs that slip by, like dreams, with only a trace of resemblance to the occurrences of the everyday world. She describes them as originating from pictures she sees in her mind; translated onto film, they retain a dislocated sense of unreality that defies their existence as photographs.

Callis is aware of the tensions she creates in setting up these scenes, and, like the Surrealists drawn to an Atget photograph of a headless mannequin, she understands how disturbing pristine but dislocated photographic detail can be. In order to maintain the sense that these scenes are visions, tapped from the archive of memory, Callis uses models more as objects than as recognizable persons. They are anonymous, seen either from the back or with their faces turned away, covered in shadow or masked by gesture. They are the nameless characters of dreams; their unnamed presence carries also the undertones of coercion and reluctance. Two people sit before a table, an empty red bowl in front of the woman, a bowl of strawberries and cream off to the side. Although nothing is pointedly amiss in the scene, there is a general uneasiness that is almost sinister, and a tight-lipped determination not to reveal more. In fact, in many of Callis's pictures, one has the unpleasant feeling of having walked into the scene unwelcome. A woman sits with her back to us, facing an empty chair and an illuminated lamp. Questions hover about these pictures with a foreboding that both attracts and repels us. Other of Callis's photographs, however, seem to have been arranged and performed expressly for the viewer. A nude female torso is bathed in light and surrounded with organza netting and a spray of flowers; the initial response to the loveliness is undercut by the slightly sour and acidic color that Callis has achieved with subtle effect.

Reproduction does not do justice to Callis's large-format prints. The elegance of their physical presence and their reliance on the sensual tactility of flesh and fabric are important to their ability to entice the viewer.

The set-up or directed photography has been a vital approach to the medium ever since O.J. Rejlander's and H.P. Robinson's Victorian efforts; Jo Ann Callis distinguishes herself with a confrontation of the ritualistic nature of this act. She does not cover her tracks, and yet, as studied and dramatic as these works are, they do not ring false because they trigger the viewer's recognition. Callis has discovered in the extreme economy of a simple gesture or a certain color or form a wealth of innuendo. The photograph is, by its nature, already the record of a past confrontation; Callis amplifies this fact until we are seeing recollections of memories many times removed, and the response they evoke is as loaded, compelling, and individual as the images are simple.

—Dana Asbury

CAMPBELL, Bryn.

Nationality: British. **Born:** Mountain Ash, Glamorgan, Wales, 20 May 1933. **Education:** Attended Mountain Ash Grammar School, 1943-51; University of Manchester, 1953-55. **Career:** Served as a photographer in the Royal Air Force, 1951-53. Assistant Editor, *Practical Photography* and *Photo News Weekly,* London, 1959-60; Editor, *Cameras and Equipment,* London, 1960-61; Associate Editor, *British Journal of Photography,* London (and Picture Editor of the *British Journal of Photography Annual*), 1962-63; Picture Editor, *The Observer* newspaper, London, 1964-66. Freelance photographer, London, since 1966. Picture Editor, *Sunday Express Magazine,* 1984-85, *The Illustrated London News,* 1985-87 and 1989-93; Consultant Picture Editor, *Daily Telegraph Magazine,* 1987-88. Honorary Associate Lecturer in Photographic Arts, Polytechnic of Central London, 1974-77. Member of the Photography Board, Council for National Academic Awards, 1977, 1978; Member of the Photography Committee, Arts Council of Great Britain, 1978-80. Trustee, The Photographers' Gallery, London, 1974-84; Member of the Art Panel, Arts Council of Great Britain, 1980-82; Chairman "Sports Picture of the Year" judging panel 1984-88; British judge "World Press Photo Competition" 1985. **Recipient:** First Prize for News Pictures, British Press Picture Awards, 1969; Kodak Bursary, 1973; Photography Award, Arts Council of Great Britain, 1974. Fellow, Institute of Incorporated Photographers, 1969, and Royal Photographic Society, 1971. **Address:** 11 Belsize Park Mews, London NW3 5BL, England.

Individual Exhibitions:

1973 *Reports and Rumours,* The Photographers' Gallery, London (retrospective; toured the U.K.)
1975 *Village School,* at the *Chichester 900 Festival,* Sussex
   Village School, Photographic Gallery, Southampton (and regional tour)
1976 *Caring and Concern,* Kodak Gallery, London (toured the U.K.)
1977 *Sports View,* Watford Sports Centre, Hertfordshire (toured eastern England)
1978 Salzburg College, Austria (retrospective)
1979 *Experimental Colour Work,* Salzburg College, Austria
1980 *Antarctic Expedition,* Olympus Gallery, London
1981 *Colour Photographs,* The Photographers' Gallery, London

Selected Group Exhibitions:

1973 *Up the Blues,* The Photographers' Gallery, London
   The English by the English, Salon de Paris
1975 *The Camera and the Craftsman,* Crafts Centre, London
1976 *Photography Helps,* Kodak Gallery, London
1977 *Personal View,* British Council, London (and world tour)
1978 *European Colour Photography,* The Photographers' Gallery, London
1982 *Kindness: the Keflex Collection,* Hamiltons Gallery, London
1983 *British Photography 1955-65,* The Photographers' Gallery, London

1983 *The Other Britain,* National Theatre, London

Collections:

Arts Council of Great Britain, London; Victoria and Albert Museum, London; Keflex Collection, London.

Publications:

By CAMPBELL: Books—*British Journal of Photography Annual,* picture editor, London 1963, 1964; *Loneliness,* with text by Jeremy Seabrook, London 1973, Stockholm 1975; *The Headless Valley,* with others, with text by Ranulph Fiennes, London 1973; *The Experience of Sport,* with text by John L. Foster, London 1975; *British Image I,* with others, London 1975; *The Camera and the Craftsman,* exhibition catalogue, with others, London 1975; *Children and Language,* London 1976; *The Facts about a Football Club,* with text by Alan Road, London 1976; *Goalkeepers Are Crazy,* with text by Brian Glanville, London 1977; *Newspaper Dragon,* with text by Alan Road, Swansea 1977; *Exploring Photography,* London 1978, New York 1979; *European Colour Photography,* exhibition catalogue, with others, London 1978; *World Photography,* editor, London and New York 1981, 1983; *Great Action Photography,* editor, London 1983; *I Grandi Fotografi* (series of monographs), co-editor, Italy 1982; *The Great Photographers,* (selected translations of Italian series), consultant editor, London 1983. **Film**—*Exploring Photography,* television series, 1978.

On CAMPBELL: Books—*British Journal of Photography Annual,* London 1968, 1969, 1971, 1972, 1973, 1974; *Popular Photography Annual,* New York 1972; *The History of Photography in the 20th Century* by Petr Tausk, London 1980; *British Photography 1955-1965: The Master Craftsmen in Print,* exhibition catalogue, by Sue Davies, Michael Rand, Mark Boxer and others, London 1983; *British Journal of Photography Annual,* London 1984. **Articles**—"Bryn Campbell: Picture Portfolio" in *Camera* (Lucerne), June 1963; "Professional Photography '71" by Ainslie Ellis in *British Journal of Photography* (London), 9 April 1971; "Death of a President" by Philippe Barraud in *Schweizerische Photorundschau* (Visp, Switzerland), October 1971; "Bryn Campbell: Portfolio" in *Photo* (Paris), July 1972; "Exploring Photography" by Ainslie Ellis in *British Journal of Photography* (London), 27 October 1978; "Bryn Campbell: Portfolio" in *You and Your Camera* (London), 1 November 1979; Portfolio, *Photographers International,* Taiwan, June 1994.

*

I seem to have run two parallel careers, as a photographer and as an editor/critic of photography.

In my work as a photo-journalist, I have always tried to be as alert to shape as to incident and I always look for a simple, direct image. I add to the satisfaction I get from my professional activities by being constantly involved in long-term personal projects.

Most of my work has a strong documentary bias, but for the last 29 years I have also been fascinated by images that convey impressions rather than information. This curiosity has taken up much of my time in the last 16 years, and I have concentrated my experiments in the field of colour. Purely abstract compositions did not appeal to me, but I did enjoy exploring the borderline between the abstract and the representational. I wanted to see how far one could take an image before it became too vague and lost the tension of its basic shape. Then I realized that colour held the form together long after other detail had disappeared.

That is at the heart of my present preoccupation, pushing the colour image to that point beyond which its sense and structure disintegrates.

My tastes in photography are very catholic, and I am in debt to so many people for the pleasure their pictures have brought me. As an editor, I enjoy sharing this work and this enthusiasm for photography with others.

—Bryn Campbell

* * *

Hampstead Heath, London, **1972.** Photograph ©Bryn Campbell.

Bryn Campbell's lifelong involvement with photography has been both as a photographer and as a picture editor. To both he has brought a love and understanding of the medium and a commitment to make clear and compassionate photographs and to show work by others that is the best of its kind.

His main photographic work has been in black and white beginning with many photographs both in Wales and in many other parts of the world, but he has also explored the medium in a personal series of experimental colour photographs which are concerned with how far a colour image can be pushed in time and still remain comprehensible and graphically coherent.

As a photographer he has worked for many newspapers and magazines and undertaken both news and long term assignments. He went with Sir Ranulf Fiennes on two of his explorations, The Headless Valley and Transglobe Expeditions, and has worked for international publications such as *Geo,* as well as the British colour magazines. His personal work has explored the worlds of sport and of children and he has an on-going project on the school life of children. His work has been seen in many group and several one man exhibitions and combines a strong graphic line with a respect for the integrity of his human subjects, whatever their situation.

His editorial work has been extremely successful because he understands how photographs are made and has a real interest in other people's work and showing it to its best advantage. He also has considerable talent as a writer and interviewer and this was shown particularly in a series he made for television and for book publication, *Exploring Photography.* Here he was able to ask all the questions of leading photographers that we would like to ask and to get

intelligent and clear responses. This was followed by an excellent book of interviews and portfolios of many of the world's leading photographers, *World Photography.*

While fully appreciating that a certain ambiguity in an image can produce work of lasting interest and value he is impatient with slickly produced work that seeks to hide the paucity of ideas under a gloss of over production. His own work continues to show the honesty and integrity which is the mark of a photographer who fully realises the true value of his medium.

—Sue Davies

CAPA, Cornell.

Nationality: American. **Born:** Kornel Friedmann in Budapest, Hungary, 10 April 1918; immigrated to the United States, 1937: naturalized, 1943. **Education:** Attended the Imre Madacs Gymnasium, Budapest, 1928-36; studied French, Alliance Francaise, Paris, 1936-37. **Military Service:** Served in a Photo-Intelligence unit in the United States Air Force, 1941-45: Sergeant. **Family:** Married Edith Schwartz in 1940. **Career:** Worked as a photo-printer, with his brother Robert Capa, Paris, 1936; photographer, adopting the name

Image from *Margin of Life,* Honduras 1973. Photograph by Cornell Capa. ©Magnum Photos, Inc.

"Capa," with PIX Inc. photo agency, New York, 1936-37; photo-printer with *Life* magazine, New York, 1937-41; Staff Photographer, 1946-54, and Contributing Photographer, 1955-67, *Life* magazine. Photographer with Magnum Photos co-operative agency, Paris and New York, since 1955; Executive Director, International Center of Photography, New York, since 1974. Founder, Robert Capa/David Seymour Photographic Foundation, Israel, 1958-66; Founder-Director, Bischof/Capa/Seymour Memorial Fund, New York, 1966-74. **Recipient:** American Newspaper Guild Citation, 1956; Overseas Press Club Citation, 1956; Photo-Journalism Award, 1968, and Honor Award, 1975, American Society of Magazine Photographers; Mayor's Award of Honor, City of New York, 1978. **Agent:** Magnum Photos, 2 rue des Grands Augustins, 75006 Paris, France, and 251 Park Avenue South, New York, New York 10010. **Address:** 275 Fifth Avenue, New York, New York 10016, U.S.A.

Individual Exhibitions:

1974   *Margin of Life,* Center for Inter-American Relations, New York (travelled to the Johnson Museum, Ithaca, New York, and Amarillo Art Center Association, Amarillo, Texas)

Selected Group Exhibitions:

1951   *Memorable Life Photographs,* Museum of Modern Art, New York
1960   *The World as Seen by Magnum,* Lever House, New York (toured Japan, the United States, and Europe)
1963   *John F. Kennedy: In Memoriam,* Library of Congress, Washington, D.C. (toured under the auspices of the United States Information Agency)
1966   *Adlai E. Stevenson,* Hallmark Gallery, New York (toured the United States)
1973   *Jerusalem: City of Mankind,* Israel Museum, Jerusalem (toured the United States and Europe)
1977   *Fotografische Kunstlerbildnisse,* Museum Ludwig, Cologne
1980   *Photography of the 50's,* Center for Creative Photography, University of Arizona, Tucson (toured the United States and Europe)
1983   *Figure della danza,* Teatro R. Valli, Reggio Emilia, Italy
1984   *Sammlung Gruber,* Museum Ludwig, Cologne

Collections:

Museum of Modern Art, New York; International Center of Photography, New York; Israel Museum, Jerusalem; Museum Ludwig, Cologne.

Publications:

By CAPA: Books—*Retarded Children Can Be Helped,* with text by Maya Pines, New York 1957; *Through the Gates of Splendor,* with text by Elisabeth Elliot, New York 1957; *Savage My Kinsman,* with text by Elisabeth Elliot, New York 1959; *Let Us Begin,* photographic editor, New York 1961; *Farewell to Eden,* with text by Matthew Huxley, New York 1964; *The Emergent Decade of South American Painting,* with text by Thomas Messer, New York 1966; *The Andean Republics,* with Time-Life editors, New York 1966; *Adlai E. Stevenson's Public Years,* with text by Adlai E. Stevenson, New York 1966; *Swift Sword,* with others, New York 1967; *The Concerned Photographer,* editor, 2 volumes, New York 1969, 1972; *New Breed on Wall Street,* with text by Martin Mayer, New York 1969; *Israel: The Reality,* editor, New York 1959; *Behind the Great Wall of China,* editor, New York 1972; *Language and Faith,* New York 1972; *Margin of Life,* with text by J. Mayone Stycos, New York 1974; *Jerusalem: City of Mankind,* editor, New York 1974; *ICP Library of Photographers,* editor, 6 volumes, New York 1974; *Cornell Capa: Photographs,* joint editor with Richard Whelan, New York 1992. **Articles**—"Cornell Capa: An Interview," with Ruth Spencer, in *British Journal of Photography* (London), 29 October 1976; "Cornell Capa" in *Interviews with Master Photographers* by James Danziger and Barnaby Conrad III, New York and London 1977.

On CAPA: Books—*Memorable Life Photographs,* with text by Edward Steichen, New York 1951; *Life Photographers: Their Careers and Favorite Pictures,* edited by Stanley Rayfield, New York 1957; *America in Crisis: Photographs for Magnum,* edited by Charles Harbutt and Lee Jones, with an essay by Michael Levitas, New York 1969; *Fotografische Kunstlerbildnisse,* exhibition catalogue, by Dieter Ronte, Evelyn Weiss and Jeane von Oppenheim, Cologne 1977; *Geschichte der Fotografie im 20. Jahrhundert/Photography in the 20th Century* by Petr Tausk, Cologne 1977, London 1980; *Great Photo Essays from Life,* edited by Maitland Edey, Boston 1978; *Visions and Images: American Photographers on Photography,* edited by Barbaralee Diamonstein, New York 1981; *Figure della danza/Visions of the Dance 1859-1982,* exhibition catalogue, by C. Traub, R. Silverman and G. Ackerman, Reggio Emilia, Italy 1983; *Sammlung Gruber: Photographie des 20. Jahrhunderts,* exhibition catalogue, with foreword by Siegfried Gohr, Cologne 1984; *After the War Was Over,* with introduction by Mary Blume, London 1985. **Articles**—"Cornell Capa l'Universal" in *Photo* (Paris), June 1968; "ICP: Photography's Fabulous New Center" by Harvey Fondiller in *Popular Photography* (New York), April 1975; "International Center of Photography" in *Minolta Mirror* (Tokyo), 1976; "Ten Year Odyssey of Cornell Capa" by Michael Edelson in *Camera 35* (New York), March 1978; "Lighthouse of Photography" by Richard Whelan in *Art News* (New York), April 1979; "Photo Visite Venise 1979" in *Photo* (Paris), August 1979; "The Concerns of Cornell Capa" by Norman Schreiber in *Camera Arts* (New York), November/December 1980.

*

Single photographs are not representative of what I do best. My most effective work is groups of photographs which hang together and tell stories. My pictures are the "words" which make up "sentences" which, in turn, form the story. Just as words by themselves, removed from context, are seldom at their most meaningful, so it is with many of my photographs—singly, they do very little. I am not a maker of images which are to be enjoyed by the viewer for their purely aesthetic value. I hope that as often as possible my pictures have feeling, composition, and sometimes beauty—but my preoccupation is with the story and not with attaining a fine art level in the individual pictures. If I work well, my pictures mean something when they are connected in story from. And the images, by being connected, seem to gain in editorial impact and visually as well.

It took me some time to realize that the camera is a mere tool, capable of many uses, and at last I understood that—for me—its role, its power and its duty are to comment, describe, provoke discussion, awaken conscience, evoke sympathy, spotlight human misery and joy which otherwise would pass unseen, un-understood and unnoticed. I have been interested in photographing the everyday life of my fellow humans and the commonplace spectacle of the world around me, and in trying to distill out of these their beauty and whatever is of permanent interest.

The greatest joy that the camera has given me is my gained capacity to see. The next gain is that I can "be there" where things are going on and have the opportunity to partake. It also gives me a central seat in front (and, more importantly, a backstage vantage point as well) of the Greatest Spectaculars that man has created to impress others. It has given me rich opportunities to be one with fellow human beings of all varieties in their hours of trial and triumph. Thus I can live a thousand lives during my lifetime. Finally, there is the satisfaction of showing others what experiences I have gone through.

Today, so many pictures are being taken that no one is really interested in what has gone on before. Man's witness of his own times dies with him. Added to that, the technological advances in camera design have made photography seem easy. It has become so popular—so used and abused—that, because of its popularity, it is in danger of losing its own self-respect as well as the trust and confidence of viewers in its veracity and artistry.

The Fund (for Concerned Photography and *The Concerned Photographer* exhibit and book) is dedicated to the recognition of photography as a very personal means of communication, to the recognition of the photographer as an individual with his very own recognizable graphic style and human content, who translates what he sees into frozen reality. The resulting images bear the photographer's own respect for the truth. They also reveal his appreciation of the aesthetic values for light and form, and his artistic concepts of composition.

The Fund has dedicated itself to encouraging and assisting photographers of all ages and nationalities who are vitally concerned with their times. It aims not only at finding and helping new talent, but also at uncovering and preserving valuable and forgotten archives and presenting them to the public.

There are many concerned photographers all over the world whose work will provide the visual history of our century—the first century of which such a documentation will exist. In carrying out a program of documentation of "Man in His World," recovering the perishable past documents, and in capturing our rapidly changing present, the concerned photographer finds much in the present unacceptable, which he tries to alter.

—Cornell Capa

* * *

Cornell Capa photographs people. He photographs them when their empty bellies are filled with promises, with expectant wishes. He shows us leaders who parade, crowds that flood barricades, schoolrooms, demonstrators, priests, police. Usually photographing in bold black-and-white, he often uses crashing angles to emphasize a grainy black, while sections in these photographs rebound with glaring lights. Capa grabs viewers. Sometimes he enlarges the image of a foreground figure, making that figure devour a picture's frontal plane to encroach on a picture's total space—especially if the space is filled with people narrowing into a sharply angular, perspectively reached vanishing point. He did this when photographing Adlai Stevenson waving to a crowd from the rear of a train during the 1952 presidential campaign, the camera in back of Stevenson as Stevenson faced the crowd, his head and shoulders pre-empting the frontal space as viewers looked beyond him into the crowd converging on the horizon line with the train tracks. Twenty years later when Capa photographed a crowd marching through a Bolivian street, foreground figures cried out as they marched towards the viewers, their cries emphasized by the camera's light, all as torchlights simmered in the surrounding dark and angles faded in back of them to punctuate the figures' anguish. These 1970s figures no longer encroached on the picture's space. They took it over, their grainy black movements emphasized by light. Capa's photographs glow with the power that the living produce. Don't try to find the beauty of the human condition in Capa's photographs. Don't look for intimate personal touches. Capa's photographs are of the power the living can produce.

Sometimes that power spills with laughter, as it did in a toast that a mixed religious group of four offered in Jersalem, the ceiling's whitened pattern swirling behind the four, they in their blackened robes as the camera, from its deep perch below them, enhanced their image against the ceiling's swirls. Sometimes that power marches across the picture's space as it does in a Jerusalem iron sculpture which mastered the picture's frontal plane with grid-like strength and revealed a lightened building set in the distance behind the sculpture's spaces. Bold blacks, set against whites, dominate so many of Capa's pictures, while foregrounds and backgrounds—each fully employed— work to focus on the living. It's not a generalized "life" Capa is after. It's the dynamic, explosive force of the living that snares him . . . and that he, in turn, brings to his viewers.

When he portrays people—and I am thinking of a beautiful portrait of a woman in San Salvador—he works from the same ideas and extends the same principles. A deepened silky black profile becomes the foreground. But more, it is framed by a halo of light, that delicate band outlining the profile against a darkened background, while her hand—held to her head—and the clothing which falls diagonally across her body—and the picture plane—use a slightly richer light to reveal a human texture in a grim world. That light is marginal. So is the human texture. This is just as Capa would have it. Bold visual statements need to be made about the living.

Capa's photographs contain very few grays. Gray is much too indiscriminate. Capa is looking for clear statements. Even when he took color photographs—as he did for much of his professional career as a photographer with *Life*—he reached for heightened color and stark emotional impact. Reds, especially on a rich woman's dress, dazzle his viewers, while glittering black velvets worn by cigar-smoking politicos, sharpen his viewer's perception. Avoiding middling tonalities, Capa avoids the world of middling thoughts. For not only do Capa's photographs tell us about the living, and the power the living can produce, but they also tell us about the drive the living possess once

they strip indecisiveness away. Capa's photographs are clarion calls to the living as they are clear direct statements about the living.

—Judith Mara Gutman

CAPONIGRO, Paul.

Nationality: American. **Born:** Boston, 7 December 1932. **Education:** Attended high school in Boston, 1946-50; studied piano, College of Music, Boston University, 1950-51; studied photography, with Benjamin Chin and Alfred W. Richter, at California School of Fine Arts, San Francisco, 1956, and with Minor White, at Rochester Institute of Technology, New York, 1957-58. **Military Service:** Served as photographer in the United States Army, 1953-55. **Family:** Married Eleanor Morris in 1964; son: John Paul. **Career:** Worked as apprentice in commercial photographic studio, Boston, 1952; freelance photographer since 1955, resident in Santa Fe, New Mexico, since 1973. Photo-Research Consultant, Polaroid Corporation, Cambridge, Massachusetts, from 1960. Teaching Assistant, with Minor White, Summer Photographic Workshops, San Francisco and Portland, Oregon, 1959; Visiting Instructor in Photography, at numerous colleges and workshops throughout the United States, including Boston University, 1960, St. Lawrence University, Canton, New York, 1966-71, New York University, 1967-70, Yale University, New Haven, Connecticut, 1970-73, and Maine Photographic Workshop, 1972, 1979-81 and 1984-85. Founder-Member, Association of Heliographers, New York, 1963. **Recipient:** First Prize for Photography, *10th Boston Arts Festival*, 1961; Guggenheim Fellowship, 1966, 1975; National Endowment for the Arts Photography Fellowship, 1971, 1974; Art Directors Club of New York Award, 1974; National Endowment for the Arts Grant, 1975 and 1982; Arts Council of Great Britain Grant, 1978; Peer Award, Friends of Photography, Carmel, California, 1983; Annual Governor's Award, New Mexico, 1984. **Address:** Route 3, Box 96D, Santa Fe, New Mexico 87501, U.S.A.

Individual Exhibitions:

1958	*In the Presence Of*, International Museum of Photography, George Eastman House, Rochester, New York
1960	Carl Siembab Gallery, Boston
	Image Study, Boston University
	Limelight Gallery, New York (with Minor White)
1962	Wellesley Free Library, Massachusetts
	Creative Arts Center, University of New Hampshire, Durham
1963	A Photographer's Place, Philadelphia
	Carl Siembab Gallery, Boston
1965	Gallery 216, New York
1968	Garik Gallery, Philadelphia
	Museum of Modern Art, New York (toured the United States)
	Creative Arts Center, University of New Hampshire, Durham
	Phoenix College, Arizona
	Carl Siembab Gallery, Boston
	University of Louisville, Kentucky
1969	Focus Gallery, San Francisco
	Friends of Photography, Carmel, California
	Pine Manor Junior College, Chestnut Hill, Connecticut
	Smith College, Northampton, Massachusetts
	State College, Fitchburg, Massachusetts
1970	Princeton University, New Jersey
	San Francisco Museum of Art
	Bathhouse Gallery, Milwaukee
1971	Baldwin Street Gallery, Toronto
	Image Gallery, Stockbridge, Massachusetts
	Perspective Gallery, Poughkeepsie, New York
	State University of New York at New Paltz
	Wooster School, Danbury, Connecticut
1973	Art Institute of Chicago
	University of Maryland, Baltimore
1974	Springfield Museum of Fine Art, Massachusetts

Lakeview Center for the Arts and Sciences, Peoria, Illinois
1975   Victoria and Albert Museum, London
Friends of Photography, Carmel, California (with Abigail Heyman)
Robbins Library Gallery, Arlington, Massachusetts
1976   Cronin Gallery, Houston
G. Ray Hawkins Gallery, Los Angeles
Albright-Knox Art Gallery, Buffalo, New York
Columbia College, Chicago
Paul Caponigro/Edward Weston/Derek Bennett, Silver Image Gallery, Tacoma, Washington
Carl Siembab Gallery, Boston
Museum of Fine Arts, Santa Fe, New Mexico
Douglas Kenyon Gallery, San Francisco
1977   David Mirvish Gallery, Toronto
Robert Schoelkopf Gallery, New York
1978   Delaware Art Museum, Wilmington
Susan Spiritus Gallery, Newport Beach, California
1979   High Museum of Art, Atlanta, Georgia
Photo Gallery International, Tokyo
Photographers Gallery, South Yarra, Australia
1980   Simon Lowinsky Gallery, San Francisco
University of Wisconsin, Lacross
1981   *Stonehenge,* Galerij Paule Pia, Antwerp, Belgium
Photography Gallery, La Jolla, California
Images Gallery, Cincinnati, Ohio
Marlborough Gallery, New York
PhotoGraphics Workshop, New Canaan, Connecticut
Photography Gallery, Philadelphia
Worcester Art Museum, Massachusetts
Werkstatt für Photographie, West Berlin
Photogalerie II, Bienne, Switzerland
1982   Plymouth Arts Centre, Hampshire
South Woodford Library, London
Rozelle House Museum, Ayr, Scotland
Uppermill Library, Manchester, Lancashire
Scheinbaum and Russek Gallery, Santa Fe, New Mexico (with Eliot Porter)
1983   Miami-Dade Community College, Miami, Florida
Stevenage Museum, Hertfordshire
Prema Project, Bethesda Chapel, Gloucester, England
The Old Goal Arts Centre, Oxford, England
Lairthwaite Centre, Keswick, Cumbria
Stanwix Gallery, Carlisle, Cumbria
1984   Detroit Institute of Art, Michigan
Huntsville Museum of Art, Alabama
Clarence Kennedy Gallery, Boston, Massachusetts
St. John's College, Santa Fe, New Mexico
Photo West Gallery, Carmel, California
Utah State University, Logan
Arizona Bank Galleria, Phoenix
1985   Photographer's Gallery, Palo Alto, California
Oklahoma Arts Institute, Oklahoma City
Scottish National Gallery, Edinburgh
Gallery of Photography, Dublin
Brentford Watermans Art Center, London
International Center of Photography, New York
Cincinnati Art Museum, Ohio
Art Gallery of Hamilton, Ontario
Tel Aviv Museum, Israel
Sammlung Fotografis Landerbank, Vienna
National Museum of Photography, Bradford, Yorkshire
United States Ambassador's Residence, Moscow
National Museum, Bucharest
1986   Center for Creative Photography, University of Arizona, Tucson
Rachel Davis Gallery, Houston, Texas
Athens Cultural Centre, Greece
Municipal Gallery, Thessaloniki, Greece

Selected Group Exhibitions:

1960   *The Sense of Abstraction in Contemporary Photography,* Museum of Modern Art, New York
1963   *The Photographer and the American Landscape,* Museum of Modern Art, New York
1967   *Photography in the 20th Century,* National Gallery of Canada, Ottawa (toured Canada and the United States, 1967-73)
1972   *4 Directions in Modern Photography: Paul Caponigro, John T. Hill, Jerry N. Uelsmann, Bruce Davidson,* Yale University Art Gallery, New Haven, Connecticut
Photography in America, Whitney Museum, New York
1975   *14 American Photographers,* Baltimore Museum of Art (travelled to the Newport Harbor Art Museum, California, and La Jolla Museum of Contemporary Art, California, 1975; and Walker Art Center, Minneapolis, and Fort Worth Art Museum, Texas, 1976)
1978   *Mirrors and Windows,* Museum of Modern Art, New York (toured the United States, 1978-80)
1979   *Discovering America 1959-70,* Art Institute of Chicago
1982   *Color as Form,* International Museum of Photography at George Eastman House, Rochester, New York
1985   *American Images 1945-80,* Barbican Art Gallery, London (toured Britain)

Collections:

Metropolitan Museum of Art, New York; Museum of Modern Art, New York; International Museum of Photography, George Eastman House, Rochester, New York; Fogg Art Museum, Harvard University, Cambridge, Massachusetts; Art Institute of Chicago; Target Collection of American Photography, Museum of Fine Arts, Houston; Center for Creative Photography, University of Arizona, Tucson; National Gallery of Canada, Ottawa; Victoria and Albert Museum, London; Bibliothèque Nationale, Paris.

Publications:

By CAPONIGRO: Books—*Portfolio One,* portfolio of 12 photos, Redding, Connecticut 1960; *The Music of Willem Nyland,* New York 1963, 1964; *Paul Caponigro,* Millerton, New York 1967, revised edition 1972; *Portfolio Two,* portfolio of 8 photos, Redding, Connecticut 1973; *Sunflower,* New York 1974; *Landscape: Photographs by Paul Caponigro,* New York 1975; *Portfolio Three: Stonehenge,* portfolio of 12 photos, Santa Fe, New Mexico 1977.

On CAPONIGRO: Books—*American Photography: The 60's,* Lincoln, Nebraska 1966; *The Photographer and the American Landscape,* exhibition catalogue, by John Szarkowski, New York 1963; *The Photographer's Eye* by John Szarkowski, New York 1966; *Photography in the 20th Century* by Nathan Lyons, New York 1967; *Photographie Nouvelle des Etats-Unis* by John Szarkowski, Paris 1969; *Photography in America,* edited by Robert Doty, with an introduction by Minor White, New York and London 1974; *The Magic Image* by Cecil Beaton and Gail Buckland, London and New York 1975; *Photographs: Sheldon Memorial Art Gallery Collection, University of Nebraska,* with an introduction by Norman A. Geske, Lincoln 1977; *Mirrors and Windows: American Photography since 1960* by John Szarkowski, New York 1978; *The Photograph Collector's Guide* by Lee D. Witkin and Barbara London, Boston and London 1979; *Dialogue with Photography,* edited by Paul Hill and Thomas Cooper, London and New York 1979; *Fourteen Photographers from Santa Fe,* exhibition catalogue, with introduction by Beaumont Newhall, Palm Beach, Florida 1981; *Paul Caponigro Photography: 25 Years,* exhibition catalogue, edited by D. W. Mellor, with introduction by Peter C. Bunnell, Philadelphia 1981; *Color as Form: A History of Color Photography,* exhibition catalogue with introduction by Robert A. Sobieszek, Rochester, New York 1982; *The Library of World Photography: Landscape,* with texts by David Plowden and Ian Jeffrey, Tokyo and London 1984; *American Images; Photography 1945-1980,* edited by Peter Turner, London 1985. **Articles**—"Discovery No. 44: Paul Caponigro" by Patricia Caulfield in *Modern Photography* (New York), August 1959; "Paul Caponigro" by Herb Snitzer in *Contemporary Photographer* (Culpeper, Virginia), Spring 1963; "Paul Caponigro" by Matt Herron in *Contemporary Photographer*

(Culpeper, Virginia), Summer 1963; ''Camera Notes: Caponigro and Heath at Heliography'' in the *New York Times,* 12 April 1964; ''New York: Paul Caponigro, Museum of Modern Art'' by Emily Wasserman in *Artforum* (New York), January 1969; ''Paul Caponigro'' in *Camera* (Lucerne), January 1973; ''Paul Caponigro: Portrait of Nature'' by Peter C. Bunnell in *Modern Photography* (New York), December 1973; ''Caponigro and Heyman'' by Joan Murray in *Artweek* (Oakland, California), 23 August 1975; ''Caponigro's Sense of Site'' by Margaret R. Weiss in *Saturday Review* (New York), 15 May 1976; ''Caponigro: A Respect for the Activities of Existence'' by Rolf Koppel in *Santa Fe Reporter* (New Mexico), 28 October 1976; ''An Interview with Paul Caponigro'' by Kurt Markus in *Creative Camera* (London), November 1978; ''Paul Caponigro'' by Nicholas Dean in *Close-Up* (Milwaukee), no. 2, 1981; ''The Gravity of Stone'' by Owen Edwards in *American Photographer* (New York), August 1981.

* * *

''My concern'' as a photographer, writes Paul Caponigro, is ''to maintain, within the inevitable limitations of the medium, a freedom which alone could permit contact with the greater dimension—the landscape behind the landscape.'' He has relentlessly pursued his passion to capture in silver ''the elusive image of nature's subtle realms.'' Caponigro's mastery and subtlety in the area of nature photography are distinctive and remarkable. There is a kind of lyrical profundity that sustains his imagery which in tone and composition display his very own style and attitude. Not so much the grandeur and majesty of nature, but the subtle harmonies and mysterious nuances are evoked in his photographs; these simultaneously being corresponded with the inner dimensions of human beinghood.

The striking element in these photographs of nature is the unromantic, unidealized, undramatic evocation and realization that Caponigro so masterfully conveys. His images are not statements, not messages—only hints, evocations, visual notations of states of being. As one is drawn to see the specific objects in a particular image, one is instantly stirred to see into and beyond them—be they sunflower, cabbage leaf, a stone-house, running white deer, snowflakes on windowpanes, rocks, or trees. A sense of waiting—time destroyed—pervades. No foreground or background, each image presents itself with a kind of austerity and starkness nuanced by subtle rhythms.

Caponigro's photographs are not metaphors or symbols attempting to propound metaphysical concepts or ideas. They are more like epiphanic revelations of the inherent nature of things and being. The pictures of the monuments of Stonehenge as well as of the Japanese shrines among his recent work demonstrate this quality.

Caponigro is a fastidious artist. His distinctive strength lies in the tonal quality of his images. Not given to contrast or light-and-shadow play, he uses the material and medium essentially through an amazing control and subtlety of tonal values. Here again, his method and the meaning of his imagery are in perfect balance, harmony. Normally, one would get somewhat bored with such tonality. But this does not happen with Caponigro, primarily because of the element of surprise combined with the subtle evocativeness in his images. In this sense, he is innovative in the use of the photographic material and medium and in inspiring viewers in *seeing.*

—Deba P. Patnaik

CARMI, Lisetta.

Nationality: Italian. **Born:** Annalisa Carmi in Genoa, 15 February 1924. **Education:** Attended Gymnasium School, Genoa, until 1938, when, as a Jew, she was disallowed from attending public school; thereafter studied privately; studied piano at the Conservatorio di Milan, and awarded a high school diploma there, 1951; mainly self-taught in photography. **Career:** Professional pianist and piano teacher, 1952-60; Music Teacher, Italsider workers' music courses, Genoa, 1961-62. Photographer since 1960. **Recipient:** Niepce Prize, 1966; Cultura nella Fotografia Prize, Milan, 1966; World Book Prize, Leipzig, 1978. **Address:** Casella 56, 72014 Cisternino (Brindisi), Italy.

Individual Exhibitions:

1964   *Genova Porto,* Societa di Cultura, Genoa (travelled to the
        Circolo Gobetti, Turin, and Societa di Cultura, Milan)
1969   *I Travestiti,* at the *Festival dei Popoli,* Florence
1970   *I Travestiti,* at the *Congress of Cultural Anthropology,*
        Perugia, Italy
1974   *I Travestiti,* Galleria Il Diagramma, Milan
1978   *I Travestiti,* Canon Photo Gallery, Amsterdam (travelled to
        the Contrejour Gallery, Paris, and to Voir Photogalerie,
        Toulouse)

Selected Group Exhibitions:

1967   *World Press Photo,* Amsterdam
1968   *Welt Austellung der Photographie: Die Frau,* Hamburg (and
        world tour)
1974   *Anagrafe di Genova,* at *SICOF,* Milan
1978   *Biennale,* Venice

Publications:

By CARMI: Books—*Israele,* with text by Giovanni Russo, Milan 1965; *Ezra Pound,* with text by David Heymann, New York 1968, with text by Eve Hesse, Munich 1978; *I Travestiti,* with text by Elvio Facchinelli, Naples 1972, 2nd edition Milan 1980; *Il Teatro in Italia,* edited by E. Fadini, Turin 1977; *Acque di Sicilia,* with text by Leonardo Sciascia, Bergamo, Italy 1977.

On CARMI: Books—*Primo Almanacco Fotografico Italiano,* edited by Lanfranco Colombo and Roberta Clerici, Milan 1969; *70 Anni di Fotografia in Italia* by Italo Zannier, Modena, Italy 1978. **Articles—**''I Travestiti'' by Marcantonio Muzi Falconi in *Photo 13* (Milan), 1971; ''I Travestiti'' by Ando Gilardi in *Fototredici* (Milan), 1973; ''I Travestiti'' by Ferdinando Scianna in *L'Europeo* (Milan), 1973; ''I Travestiti'' by Sergio Daho in *Zoom* (Milan), 1973; ''I Travestiti'' by Elvio Fachinelli in *L'Erba Voglio* (Milan), 1974; ''Acque di Sicilia'' by Ando Gilardi in *Fototredici* (Milan), September 1978; ''Acque di Sicilia'' by M.C. in *Il Fotografo* (Milan), no. 17, 1978.

*

Work for me has always been a means of understanding myself as well as being instrumental in my search for truth.

Until the age of 35 I was a pianist. Music was then at the center of my life as an inner guide towards the attainment of a total equilibrium of man and universe.

For the following twenty years, from the age of 35 to 55, I worked as a photographer. From being totally concentrated on the inner life I plunged into the world outside: man in all his expressions and modes of being was my constant interest, taking me to all parts of the world. In this way I discovered the human soul and with it the problems that make our society so rich, fascinating and contradictory.

Today, after several travels to India, where in 1976 I encountered my spiritual master, Babaji, the avatar of the Himalayas, my search for truth continues without intermediaries, so that for the moment I have even abandoned photography. Yet I know that it has been a great help to me, a means to acquire greater knowledge and a new consciousness of life.

—Lisetta Carmi

* * *

In the years just after the Second World War Italian photographers declared their intention of using the photograph chiefly to analyze the social realities of their country, the realities that the Fascist regime had preferred to keep hidden during their ''20 years,'' when a mediocre pictorialism was the only alternative to photographs celebrating the Mussolinian myths—apart, that is, from the experiments of artists like Pagano, Mollino, Veronesi and a few others within the sphere of the European avant-garde movements, whose work had been reviewed and compared in the pages of the *Fotografia* yearbook published by Domus in 1943.

The photography of the time involved what in the cinema and in literature has been called neorealism, an ideology characterized by a kind of political imperative to practice a sociological analysis of every sector of society but most of all in the world of the peasant and the laborer, the weakest and most vulnerable. This theme of the "under-privileged" dominated Italian photography between 1948 and the 1960's, a period of excitement and revival; it affected photojournalism and the picture publishing industry, able at last to face up to international competition.

There were a few photographers who opposed this trend (one might say demand) for the sociological documentary (Cavalli, Veronesi, Vender), but they were mostly people who were involved in art photography—though even amongst these photographers there were discussions of the premise that the function of a photographer is as a cultural agent who cannot stand aloof from everyday realities, who must sometimes put considerations of form to one side, even to the point of creating a new aesthetic nourished by the photographic qualities inherent in the "ugly," the "poor," the "under-privileged."

Lisetta Carmi was not a member of the nucleus of neo-realistic photographers; she did not enter photography until the beginning of the 1960's, when the arguments between the supporters of "form" and those of "content" were coming to an end and many of the naive and pretentious ideas and aspirations were being abandoned in favor of a professionalism which, from Patellani to Roiter, Monti to Mulas, has led to a more comprehensive, profitable and functional theory and practice. Lisetta Carmi also fortunately remained outside the realm of "art" photography, even though such photography has been the fundamental—almost the only—"school" in Italy for the training of young photographers. Her visual education had external origins, not only territorially but also culturally; it was the result, too, of an eclectic reading, generally "underground," and of an apprehension that encompassed both the "pop" experiments of a William Klein or a Robert Frank and the rediscovery of the European masters, who for Carmi are Brassaï or Kertész rather than Cartier-Bresson.

Carmi's most important book, the one that made her famous, was *I Travestiti (The Transvestites)*. The subject of transvestites (taken up later by Warhol) was, at that time (and still is), a particularly controversial one in Italy; Carmi's photography, with its communicative aggressiveness, opens up a world of "outsiders" unknown to many people; her pictures reveal, unveil, that world with great expressiveness but wholly without malice or suggestiveness. "It was all the fruit of inside investigation," she has said, "of a sincere wish to understand and to communicate." And, indeed, for Carmi social research means above all participation and adherence to a reality of which we all, in some way and to some extent, form a part.

Carmi has produced a deeply poetic, deeply affecting account, in pictures of delicacy and understanding, of a world that is normally kept out of sight, a world that many people refuse to see. Basically, and not only from the point of view of postwar European photography, *I Travestiti* is evidence of a lucid capacity to read and transcribe society visually, a capacity confirmed in Carmi's other never uninteresting works.

—Italo Zannier

CARTIER-BRESSON, Henri.

Nationality: French. **Born:** Chanteloup, Seine et Marne, France, 22 August 1908. **Education:** Attended the École Fénelon and Lycée Condorcet, and also studied painting with Cotenet, Paris, 1922-23; studied painting with André Lhote, Paris, 1927-28, and painting and literature at Cambridge University, 1928-29. **Military Service:** Served in the French Army, 1930. **Family:** Married the photographer Martine Franck, *q.v.,* in 1970. **Career:** Began as a photographer, 1931; photographer on an ethnographic expedition to Mexico, 1934; studied filmmaking with Paul Strand, New York, 1935; Assistant Director, with Jacques Becker and André Zvoboda, to filmmaker Jean Renoir, France, 1936, 1939; worked on documentary films in Spain, 1937; prisoner-of-war, Württemberg, Germany, 1940, until he escaped, 1943; active in the MNPGD (French underground for helping escaped war prisoners, etc), 1943-

45. Since 1945, freelance photographer in Paris; worked in the United States, 1946; Founder, with Robert Capa, David Seymour ("Chim"), and George Rodger, Magnum Photos co-operative agency, New York and Paris, 1947-66 (Magnum continues to act as his agent); worked in India, Burma, Pakistan, China and Indonesia, 1948-50, in the U.S.S.R., 1954, in China, 1958-59, in Cuba, Mexico, and Canada, 1960, and in India and Japan, 1965; has concentrated on drawing since 1974 (drawings exhibited: Carlton Gallery, New York, 1975; Bischofberger Gallery, Zurich, 1976; Forcalquier Galerie, Paris, 1976; Musée d'Art Moderne, Paris, 1981; Museo Nacional de Belas Artes, Mexico City, 1982; French Institute, Stockholm, 1983; Padiglione d'Arte Contemporanea, Milan, 1983; Museum of Modern Art, Oxford, 1984; Palais Liechtenstein, Vienna, and Salzburg, 1985; French Institute, Athens, 1985; Manheim, 1986; Herstand Gallery, New York, 1987; Ecole des Beaux Arts, Paris, 1989; Printemps Ginza, Tokyo, 1989; Musée d'Art Moderne, Taiwan, 1991; Parma, Italy, 1992; Saragosse, Logrono, 1993; La Caridad, Barcelona, 1994). **Recipient:** Overseas Press Club of America Award, 1948, 1954, 1960, 1964; American Society of Magazine Photographers Award, 1953; Prix de la Société Français de Photographie, 1959; Culture Prize, Deutsche Gesellschaft für Photographie, 1979; Hasselblad Award, 1983; Novecento Award, 1986. D.Litt.: Oxford University, 1975. Member, American Academy of Arts and Sciences, 1974. **Address:** c/o Magnum Photos, 5 Passage Piver, 75011 Paris, France and c/o Helen Wright, 135 East 74th Street, New York NY10021, USA.

Individual Exhibitions:

1932	Gallery Julien Levy, New York; Club Atheneo, Madrid
1934	Palacio de Bellas Artes, Mexico City (with Manuel Alvarez Bravo)
1935	*Documentry and Anti-Graphic,* Gallery Julien Levy, New York (with Walker Evans and Manuel Alvarez Bravo)
1946	Museum of Modern Art, New York (retrospective)
1952	Institute of Contemporary Arts, London
1954	Art Institute of Chicago
1955	Musée des Arts Décoratifs, Paris (retrospective; toured Europe, Japan, and the United States)
1964	Phillips Collection, Washington, D.C.
1965	Asahi Gallery, Tokyo (retrospective; toured Europe and the United States)
1968	Museum of Modern Art, New York
1970	*En France,* Grand Palais, Paris (and world tour)
1974	International Center of Photography, New York
1978	Fruit Market Gallery, Edinburgh (and Side Gallery, Newcastle-upon-Tyne)
1979	International Center of Photography, New York (retrospective; toured the United States, 1979-82)
	Galerie Delpire, Paris
	Zeit-Foto Salon, Tokyo
1980	*Paysage et Hommes,* Zeit-Foto Salon, Tokyo
1981	Kunsthaus, Zurich
	Colorado Photographic Arts Center, Denver (with Jacques-Henri Lartique)
1991	Art University, Osaka
1992	Palazzo Sanvitale
	L'Amerique, FNAC, Paris
	Zaragoza, Museo Camon Aznar
1994	A Propos de Paris, Hamburg
	I.C.P., New York
	Early Work, Caridad, Barcelona

Selected Group Exhibitions:

1951	*Memorable Life Photographs,* Museum of Modern Art, New York
	5 French Photographers: Brassai/Cartier-Bresson/Doisneau/Izis/Ronis, Museum of Modern Art, New York
1959	*Hundert Jahre Photographie 1839-1939,* Folkwang Museum, Essen (travelled to Cologne and Frankfurt)
1964	*The Painter and the Photograph: From Delacroix to Warhol,* University of New Mexico, Albuquerque

A Family of News Vendors: Two Women Resting on Ground, **Mexico City 1934.** Photograph by Henri Cartier-Bresson. Courtesy of The Art
Institute of Chicago.

1972   *Behind the Great Wall of China*, Metropolitan Museum of Art, New York

1977   *Concerning Photography*, The Photographers' Gallery, London (travelled to the Spectro Workshop, Newcastle upon Tyne)

1979   *La Photographie Francaise 1925-1940*, Galerie Zabriskie, Paris (travelled to the Zabriskie Gallery, New York)

1980   *Looking for Picasso*, International Center of Photography, New York

1981   *Photographer as Printmaker*, Ferens Art Gallery, Hull, Yorkshire (travelled to the Museum and Art Gallery, Leicester; Cooper Gallery, Barnsley; Castle Museum, Nottingham; Photographers' Gallery, London)

1984   *Subjektive Fotografie: Images of the 50s*, San Francisco Museum of Modern Art (travelled to the University of Houston, Texas; Museum Folkwang, Essen; Vasterbottens Museum, Umea; Kulturhuset, Stockholm; Saarland Museum, Saarbrucken; Palais des Beaux-Arts, Brussels)

Collections:

Bibliothèque Nationale, Paris; Magnum Photos, Paris; Victoria and Albert Museum, London; University of Fine Arts, Osaka, Japan; Museum of Modern Art, New York; International Museum of Photography, George Eastman House, Rochester, New York; Art Institute of Chicago; DeMenil Foundation, Houston (390 photographs).

Publications:

By CARTIER-BRESSON: Books--*Photos of Henri Cartier-Bresson*, text by Lincoln Kurstein and Beaumont Newhall, New York 1947; *Images à la Sauvette/The Decisive Moment*, Paris and New York 1952; *Les Danses à Bali*, with text by Antonin Artaud, Paris 1954; *D'Une Chine à l'Autre*, with a preface by Jean-Paul Sartre, Paris 1954, as *China in Transition*, with text by Han Suyin, New York 1956; *Les Européens/The Europeans*, Paris and New York 1955; *Moscow/The People of Moscow*, Paris, London and New York 1955; *China as Photographed by Henri Cartier-Bresson*, with text by Cartier-Bresson and Barbara Brakeley-Miller, New York 1964, 1966; *The Galveston That Was*, with Ezra Stoler and Howard Barstone, New York and Houston 1966; *Photographs by Henri Cartier-Bresson*, with text by Claude Roy and Ryoichi Kojima, Paris 1963, Tokyo 1966; *Flagrants Délits/The World of Henri Cartier-Bresson*, Paris, Lucerne, Frankfurt and London 1968; *Impressions de Turquie*, booklet, with text by Alain Robbe-Grillet, Paris and Istanbul 1968; *L'Homme et la Machine/Man and Machine*, Paris and New York 1968, London 1972; *The Mandate of Heaven: Photos by Henri Cartier-Bresson*, edited by John F. Melby, London 1969; *Vive la France/Cartier-Bresson's France*, with text by Francois Nourissier, Paris, London, New York, Lucerne and Frankfurt 1970; *The Face of Asia*, with text by Robert Shapley, London and New York 1972, as *Visage d'Asie*, Paris 1972; *A Propos de l'U.R.S.S.*, Paris 1973, as *About Russia*, New York and London 1974; *Henri Cartier-Bresson, Photographer*, with a foreword by Yves Bonnefoy, Paris and Boston 1979, London 1980, new edition 1992; *Henri Cartier-Bresson: Portraits*, with text by André Pieyre de Mandiargues and Ferdinando Scianna, Paris, London and New York 1984; *Early Work*, text by Peter Galassi, Paris 1987; *India*, London 1987; *The Drawings of Henri Cartier-Bresson: Line by Line*, text by John Russell and Jean Clair, English, French and German editions, 1988; *America in Passing*, German and American editions 1989; *Paris a vue d'oeil*, French, English and German editions, 1994. **Articles**—"The Moment of Truth" in *Camera* (Lucerne), no. 4, 1954; "La Seine: das Leben eines Stromes" with texts by Robert Delpire and René Haury, in *Du*, 18:6 (Zurich), June 1958; "The Deciding Eye" in *Lilliput* (London), no. 3, 1959; "One-Man Shows Are Best" in *Infinity* (New York), no. 10, 1959; "Henri Cartier-Bresson on the Art of Photography," interview with Yvonne Baby, in *Harper's* (New York), November 1961; "Porträtaufnahmen" in *Du* 21:4 (Zurich) April 1961; "Le flâneur des deux rives" in *Asahi Camera* No.1, 1966; "La Basilicata" in *Du* 34:7 (Zurich) July 1974; interview in *Le Monde* (Paris), 5 September, and subsequent correspondence 17 October, 1974; "Henri Cartier-Bresson," interview, in *Dialogue with Photography* by Paul Hill and Thomas Cooper, London 1979. **Films**—*Victorie de la vie*, 1937; *Le Retour*, with J. Lemare (for the United States Office of War Information), 1945; *Flagrants Délits*, directed by Robert Delpire, 1967; *Impressions of California*, with J. Boffety, CBS-TV film, 1970; *Southern Exposures*, with W. Dombrow, CBS-TV film, 1970. **Compact disc recording**—*"Le Bon Plaisir d'Henri Cartier-Bresson"* interviews by Vera Feyder 1991 (for France Culture).

On CARTIER-BRESSON: Books—*Photographs by Henri Cartier-Bresson and an Exhibition of Anti-Graphic Photography*, exhibition catalogue, by Julien Levy, New York 1932; *The Photographs of Henri Cartier-Bresson* by Lincoln Kirstein and Beaumont Newhall, New York 1947, new edition as *Photographs of Cartier-Bresson*, New York 1963, as *Henri Cartier-Bresson: Photographs*, London 1964; *Masters of Photography* by Beaumont and Nancy Newhall, New York 1958; *Henri Cartier-Bresson* by Anna Farova, Prague 1958; *Photographers on Photography*, edited by Nathan Lyons, New York 1966; *The Magic Image* by Cecil Beaton and Gail Buckland, London and Boston 1975; *Henri Cartier-Bresson* by Claude Roy, Paris 1976; *Henri Cartier-Bresson* (Aperture monograph), Millerton, New York 1976; *Concerning Photography*, exhibition catalogue, by Jonathan Bayer, Peter Turner, Ian Jeffrey and Ainslie Ellis, London 1977; *Documenta 6*, exhibition catalogue, edited by Klaus Honnef and Evelyn Weiss, Kassel 1977; *Henri Cartier-Bresson* by Daniela Palazzoli, Milan 1978; *Henri Cartier-Bresson*, exhibition catalogue, by E.H. Gombrich, Edinburgh 1978; *Bilder vom Krieg* by Rainer Fabian and Hans Christian Adam, Hamburg 1983, as *Images of War: 130 Years of War Photography*, London 1985; *Henri Cartier-Bresson: Drawings and Paintings*, exhibition catalogue, by David Elliott and Carol Brown, Oxford 1984; *Henri Cartier-Bresson: dessins et tempéras (exhibition catalogue)* with texts by Michael Brenson, André Berne Joffroy and James Lord, Athens 1985; *Henri Cartier-Bresson: Zeichnung and Fotografie*, exhibition catalogue, introductions by Roland Scotti, Thomas Schirmböck and Friedrich W Kasten, Mannheim 1986; *Henri Cartier-Bresson: Drawings and Paintings*, exhibition catalogue, introduction by Arnold Herstand, New York 1987; *Henri Cartier-Bresson*, exhibition catalogue, Tokyo 1989; *Henri Cartier-Bresson/Martine Franck*, exhibition catalogue, Taipei 1991; "Henri Cartier-Bresson" in *Peinture et Regard: Ecrits sur l'art*, Paris 1991; *Henri Cartier-Bresson*, exhibition catalogue, text by Jean Leymarie, Noyers-sur-Serein, Parma and Noceto 1992. **Articles**—"Henri Cartier-Bresson" by Ben Shahn in *Magazine of Art*, May 1947; "The Instant Vision of Henri Cartier-Bresson" by Beaumont Newhall in *Camera* (Lucerne), October 1955; "Stieglitz and Cartier-Bresson" by Dorothy Norman in *Saturday Review* (New York), no. 38, 1962; "Henri Cartier-Bresson" by P. Donzelli and P. Racanicchi in *Quaderni di Critica e Storia della Fotografia*, Milan 1963; "Henri Cartier-Bresson Today" by Bob Schwahlberg in *Popular Photography* (New York), May 1967; "Henri Cartier-Bresson: Schweiz" by Manuel Gasser in *Du* (Zurich), 27:8, 1967; "Henri Cartier-Bresson: l'Immagine Riferita" by Italo Zannier in *Fotografia Italiana*, (Milan), April/May 1971; "Henri Cartier-Bresson: A Lyrical View of Life" by Ernst Haas in *Modern Photography* (New York), November 1971; "Ce Cher Henri" by Claude Roy in *Photo* (Paris), November 1974; entire issue of *Camera* (Lucerne), July 1976; "50 Years of Decisive Moments" in *Photography Year 1980*, by the Time-Life editors, New York 1980; "The Sad Fate of Henri Cartier-Bresson" by Roger Clark in the *British Journal of Photography* (London), 30 May 1980; "HCB: 255 ritratti" by Ferdinando Scianna in *Photo* (Milan) no.125, 1985; "Profiles: Stealing a March on the World" by Dan Hofstader in *The New Yorker* (New York) 23 and 30 October 1989; "La jouissance de l'oeil" by Michel Guerrin in *Le Monde* (Paris) 21 November 1991; "From Photography to Painting" by Jean Leymarie in *Bostonia Magazine*, Spring 1993; Doctorial thesis: Jean-Pierre Montier "Esthetique Photographique à propos d'Henri Cartier-Bresson" (Université d'Aix en Provence) 1993; "A propos de Paris," 1994 editions in French, German, English and Japanese. **Films**—*Henri Cartier-Bresson, Photographer* by Gjon Mili, 1958; *Henri Cartier-Bresson* by Sarah Moon, 1994.

*   *   *

An affable and unassuming man presented himself, at the time of the 1974 presidential elections, at the headquarters of the Ecologist candidate on a barge beside the Pont de l'Alma in Paris. He had given his support, and he was ready, he said, if it were necessary, to take some pictures. It was 48 hours later that the Ecologist militants noticed for the first time that the name written in the membership book was that of Henri Cartier-Bresson.

This is, of course, only an anecdote, but it is significant, for it reveals the two constants of Cartier-Bresson's personality: his deep-seated horror of all notoreity and his fidelity to an almost anarchistic/surrealistic distrust of all political ideologies.

And, how else does one speak about Cartier-Bresson except through anecdotes? He is the master theorist; he is God the father, the son and Holy Ghost; he is the *eminence grise* (or *noire*), Talleyrand or Machiavelli; he is the Caesar that no Brutus (and Brutus is legion) has succeeded in deposing. He is a guru, a high priest, a living legend.

When in Toulon in 1930 he pressed a shutter release for the first time, no one, least of all himself, realized what was to come. He was a very young man; he had been a student of André Lhote, and he dreamed only of drawing and painting; he had just returned sick from a trip to the Ivory Coast with Marc Allégret. But, little by little, he discovered the virtues of the fixed image. What followed is inscribed in the Pantheon of Photography: New York, and the friendship of Julien Levy, who gave him his first exhibition, and Helen Snow of *Harper's Bazaar* who gave him his first assignments. Paris, and it is *Vogel pour Vu* which gives him his first assignments—then the Spanish Civil War, then Germany, as a prisoner of war, where he tried to escape three times before succeeding in 1943. After the war, in 1947, the foundation of Magnum with Robert Capa, Chim and George Rodger. The discovery of China and of the U.S.S.R. Then the books—*Images à la Sauvette/The Decisive Moment,* with a cover by Matisse, *Les Européens,* with one by Miro, *Vive la France,* with a text by Nourissier, *Flagrants Délits,* and finally the book published by Delpire in 1980, a superb and definitive photographic testimonial.

Everything becomes outrageous, extreme, when one speaks of Cartier-Bresson, from the hatred he provokes to the admiration and devotion that his spiritual sons accord him. Then there are his statements, his theories. The least of them, as for example his casual comments in an interview in *Le Monde* in 1974—about chance and objectives and fleeting, privileged moments—change the milieu of photography, become axioms that the rest of us continue to debate in the schools of photography. Yet the durability of Henri Cartier-Bresson in photography comes from nothing so much as from his incredible vision, his perfect sense of composition, his genius for being there at the precise moment that allows the significant image, the timelessness of his pictures.

As for everything else, his own words are best:

1) "I want to prove nothing, demonstrate nothing. Things and beings speak sufficiently."

2) "I never 'cook.' I loathe work in a laboratory or a studio."

3) "I feel a sense of solidarity with every photographer who works on the street and in the city, but absolutely none with 'aestheticians' who pose 'belle jeunes filles en fleur.' "

4) "One does not learn how to become a photographer."

5) "Finally, the photograph itself does not interest me. I want only to capture a minute part of reality."

6) "The photo that succeeds is the photo that is looked at for more than a second."

7) "I really want to be a taxi driver, but I don't want to become a chauffeur."

8) "It's like having a fish on a line. You have to approach your prey carefully and strike at the right time."

9) "I love principles. I detest rules."

Growing older, Henri Cartier-Bresson has slowly turned away from photography to rediscover his first love: drawing. It seems unpardonable, even though it was he himself who warned, ''Not only am I an amateur; even worse, I am a dilettante.'' But, of course, finally our disapproval of the way he chooses to spend his last days is unimportant. For the work of Cartier-Bresson in photography is as jealousy in *Othello*: other things will die—it, never.

—Roger Therond

CATANY, Toni.

Nationality: Spanish. **Born:** Llucmajor, Majorca, 15 August 1942. **Education:** Attended Instituto Ramon Llull, Palma, Majorca, 1954; self-taught in photography. **Career:** Freelance photographer, in Barcelona, since 1967.

Address: Carrer Nou de la Rambla 34, Principal, Barcelona 08001, Spain.

Individual Exhibitions:

1972   *Cantants,* Galeria Aixela, Barcelona
1975   *Ballet,* Galeria 4 Gats, Palma, Majorca (travelled to Galeria Spectrum, Barcelona, Centre Culturel, Toulouse, and Museo del Teatro, Barcelona, 1975-76)
1978   *Statues,* Fotomania, Barcelona (travelled to Galerie Voir, Toulouse, 1979)
1980   *Calotypes/Still Life,* Fotomania, Barcelona (travelled to Ca'n Duai, Majorca)
        Las Fiestas de San Juan, Bank Union, Menorca
1981   Canon Photo Gallery, Amsterdam
        Galeria Cop D'Ull, Lleida, Spain
1982   Galerie Suzanne Kuepfer, Nidau, Switzerland
        Sala Municipal de Cultura, Seville, Spain
        Galeria Forum, Tarragona, Spain
        Photographic Center, Athens, Greece
        Studio 666, Paris
1983   Sala Aixela, Barcelona
        Sala d'Art Els Setze, Martorell, Spain
        Galerie Ton Peek, Utrecht, Netherlands
        Galeria Spectrum Canon, Saragossa, Spain
        Galleria Il Diaframma, Milan
        Galerie Pro Photo, Nuremberg, West Germany
        Berner Photogalerie, Berne, Switzerland
        Galeria Image, Madrid
1984   Photographic Center, Athens, Greece
        Fotoforum, Bremen, West Germany
        Galeria Visor, Valencia, Spain
        Galeria I.D.E.P., Barcelona
        Jornadas Universitarias de Fotografia, Madrid
        The Photographers Gallery, Auckland, New Zealand
        Galerie Viviane Esders, Paris
        Galerie Junod, Lausanne, Switzerland
1985   Galerie XYZ, Ghent, Belgium
        Canon Photo Gallery, Amsterdam
        Nikon Fotogalerie, Zurich
        Galerie Pro Photo, Nuremberg, West Germany
        Galerie Les Somnambules, Toulouse, France
        Galerie Post-Scriptum, Brussels
1986   Galerie La Reverbere, Lyon, France
        Fotogalerie 68, Hoensbroek, Netherlands
        ARCO 86 Festival, Madrid
        Benteler Galleries, Houston, Texas (with Reinhart Wolf and Cay Lang)

Selected Group Exhibitions:

1975   *Foto-Arte 75,* Galeria Fontana d'Or, Gerona, Spain
1979   *4 Punts de Vista,* Galeria Lleonart, Barcelona
1980   *Metaphysical Presence,* at *Grupa Junij '80,* Ljubljana, Yugoslavia
        Spanish Photography, Night Gallery, London (travelled to the Photographic Gallery, Cardiff, and the Open Eye Gallery, Liverpool)
1981   *Cinco Fotografos Espanoles,* Canon Photogallery/Le Trepied, Geneva
1982   *Fotografs de Barcelona,* FNAC-Montparnasse, Paris (travelled to Toulouse, Brussels and Metz)
1983   *European Photography,* Northeastern University, Boston, Massachusetts (toured the United States)
1984   *Triennale Internationale de Photographie,* Palais des Beaux-Arts, Charleroi, Belgium
1985   *Fotografia Espanola Contemporanea,* Museo de Bellas Artes, Madrid
1986   *La Fotografia en el Museo,* Museo Espanola de Arte Contemporanea, Madrid

Collections:

Bibliothèque Nationale, Paris; Musée d'Art Moderne de la Ville de Paris; Musée Nicephore Niepce, Châlon sur Saone, France; Università di Parma, Italy; Polaroid Collection, Cambridge, Massachusetts.

Publications:

By CATANY: Books—*Les Illes,* edited by Abadia de Monserrat, with an introduction by Maria Antonio Oliver, Barcelona 1975; *Jorge Donn Danse Béjart,* with text by France Ferran, Paris 1977; *Tomas Monserrat,* editor, Palma, Spain 1983; *Natures Mortes,* portfolio, Brussels 1984. **Articles**—"Ballet" in *Imagen y Sonido* (Barcelona), February 1974; "Les Velles" in *Imagen y Sonido* (Barcelona), January 1975; "Els Viatjes" in *Eikonos* (Barcelona), September 1976; "Superman" in *Reflections* (Amsterdam), June 1978.

On CATANY: Books—*4 Punts de Vista,* exhibition catalogue, by Francesc Miralles, Barcelona 1979; *La Novetat de la Tradició,* exhibition catalogue, by Francesc Miralles, Barcelona 1980; *Primavera Fotografica a Barcelona 1982,* exhibition catalogue, with introduction by J. Corredon-Matheos, Barcelona 1982; *SIF 85: Semana Internacional de la Fotografia,* exhibition catalogue, by Marie Genevieve and others, Guadalajara, Spain 1985. **Articles**—"La Calidad de la Luz" by Joan Fontcuberta in *El Correo Catalan* (Barcelona), October 1980; "Catany, tradicion y novedad" by Luis Revenga in *El Pais* (Madrid), 7 January 1984; "Toni Catany" by E. Peral in *Arte Fotografico* (Madrid), no. 388, 1984; "Un art photographique" by P. Borhan in *Cliches* (Brussels), October 1984; "Toni Catany" by P. Borhan in *Camera Mainichi* (Tokyo), April 1985.

*

Since 1976, I've been using for my personal work old cameras (13 x 8 cm; 18 x 24 cm) and using the technique of Talbot—the calotype. I try to combine this old technique with modern photographic aesthetics.

But sometimes I have new ideas that I'm not able to accomplish with these cameras and this old technique. Consequently, there is another side to my work: still-lifes done with a 6 x 6 cm camera in which I'm interested in emphasizing the composition inside a square, the light, the shadows, the reflections, transparencies, and the quality of objects (plastic, glass, flowers, etc.)

—Toni Catany

* * *

Toni Catany occupies a singular position among the younger generation of Spanish photographers. While the majority have become progressively more specialized, both conceptually and aesthetically, Toni Catany strikes one with his versatility and constant experimentation. Even more impressive is the very high level of accomplishment he attains. Outstanding in his work, to my mind, are: the reports from the Middle East and Africa; the ethnographic pictures made in Majorca; his documentation of dance; the "metaphysical" series of statues; the experiments with collage and hand-coloring; his work with "procedures" such as calotypes; and his most recent still-lifes—first in black-and-white and later in colour.

Certain observations that apply to the whole of his work can be derived from an analysis of the calotypes and still-lifes.

The series of calotypes was started in 1976 when Catany had the idea of conducting a series of experiments with an old, bulky wooden camera. His next idea was to use the camera with a photographic process equally as archaic, the calotype, a system devised by Fox Talbot for obtaining prints from negatives made of paper. The project obviously presented a certain challenge—how to merge a contemporary vision with a method whose antiquity and characteristics confer an aura of primitivism or aesthetic anachronism to the resulting image. Conditions effectively enforced this appearance: a lack of clarity due to the smooth focal lens; the lack of contrast due to the irregular transparency of the paper negative; the static quality of the composition due to the slow movement of the camera.

The results demonstrate the give and take of the creative challenge, between methods that imposed certain limitations of presentation and the perseverance of the photographer, who tried to hold those limitations in check and himself direct the result. If we arrange the calotypes in chronological order, we can see a transition from a classic concept of nature as passive to one full of force and energy. Fairly unorthodox contexts and perspectives reveal themselves to an imaginative and ironic eye, which controls the situation: one is aware that a combination is being formed of contradictory methods and propositions.

This eagerness to take on a challenge, to extract the best that a particular method or style has to offer, to take it as far as it is able to go, is characteristic of Catany's creative attitude. And that is the difference between his still-lifes and those of Baron de Meyer or Josef Sudek, with whom he certainly shares similarities—in the feeling of tranquility, for example. He maintains the same kind of creative tension in his still-lifes as in his calotypes, though here the creative energy, the vitality, is conveyed in a more subtle form, given the greater control of his medium. Here, he sacrifices the irregular texture of the calotypes for precision and detail and, in turn, for the natural textures of the subjects photographed. The images acquire tactile qualities—along with a warmth and sensuality—that the calotypes lack.

It is a sensitivity to light that helps to create the vitality of these works. Much as the evocative atmosphere Sudek infuses into his images comes in great measure from the soft light of his Prague studio, so Toni Catany has a predilection for "indigenous" light, the warmer, more vigorous Mediterranean light, for a delicate but pronounced play of light and shade that is his work's principal source of inspiration. His collection of still-lifes from the mid-1980s is also filled with the delicate colouring of the Mediterranean. Here, colour plays a substantial part. He is not only striving to create a personal world through the nature of objects—sometimes using an approach similar to the *objet trouve* technique—but one finds that the harmony of tones prevails over the object itself, which is thus converted into a mere support for the colour. Hence the fact that the arbitrary choice of object goes on to intensify this nostalgic and sometimes surrealist dimension. This preponderance of colour has grown so strong that it has become an exploration of pure colour, an approach which has probably meant that his work may no longer be thought of as still-life but as constructed or staged photography. Objects in his photos are shot through sheets of glass or transparent plastic spattered with coloured paint. This technique approaches that of abstract art, but, as Jean-Francois Chevrier has pointed out, it also offers an ironic parody of the pyrotechnics we find in some types of mass-culture such as science fiction films. The nature of the objects photographed also contributes—at times in the style of the *objet trouvé,* but they are always the objects of his own personal world. A visit to his studio-home would reveal most of the elements which have been the protagonists of his images.

—Joan Fontcuberta

CENTELLES, Agustì.

Nationality: Spanish. **Born:** Grau, Valencia, 21 May 1909. **Education:** Attended the Escola Santa Maria, Grau, until 1923; self-taught in photography, from 1923. **Family:** Married Eugenia Martin Montserrat in 1936; children: Sergi and Octavi. **Career:** Press photographer, principally for *Diario Grafico* newsapaper, Barcelona, 1934-39; war photographer, with the Republican forces, Spain, 1936-37; assigned to photographic services with the Catalonian Army, Barcelona, 1937-39; worked as a photographer in the Studio Porte, Carcassonne, France, 1939-44; industrial and publicity photographer, working for Siemens, Maquinista Terrestre y Marìtima, Cordoniu, Juvé i Camps, Flamminer, Coca-Cola, etc., in Barcelona, 1945-83. Pre-1939 photo files recovered from Carcassonne, France, 1976. **Recipient:** Premio Nacional de Artes Plasticas, Ministry of Culture, Madrid, 1984. Estate: Sergi and Octavi Centelles, calle Ciutat de Balaguer 31, 08021 Barcelona, Spain. **Died:** (in Barcelona) 1 December 1985.

Individual Exhibitions:

1977   Centre de Convergencia Democratica de Catalunya, Gracia,
        Barcelona, Spain
1978   Centro Internacional de la Fotografia, Barcelona, Spain
1984   Galeria Primer Plano, Barcelona, Spain
        Galeria Visor, Valencia, Spain
1986   Institut d'Estudis Fotografics de Catalunya, Barcelona, Spain
        La Guerra Civil Espanola, Ayuntamiento de Barcelona, Spain
        Spanish Civil War Photographs, Queens College, City
        University of New York

Selected Group Exhibitions:

1984   *Idas and Chaos: Trends in Spanish Photography 1920-45,*
        Biblioteca Nacional, Madrid (travelled to the Fundacion Joan
        Miro, Barcelona; Museo de Bellas Artes, Bilbao; Sala de
        Exposiciones del Ayuntamiento, Valencia; International
        Center of Photography, New York; Museum Folkwang,
        Essen, West Germany)
1986   *Visio fotografica d'una epoca,* Sala Arcs, Barcelona, Spain
        No Pasaran, Arnolfini Gallery, Bristol, England

Collections:

Biblioteca Nacional, Madrid.

Publications:

By CENTELLES: Books—*Visiones de guerra y retaguardia,* with text by
Josep Fontana, Barcelona/Palma de Mallorca 1977; *Anos de muerte y
esperanza,* with Eduard Pons Prades, Barcelona 1979.

On CENTELLES: Books—*Idas and Chaos: Trends in Spanish Photography 1920-1945,* exhibition catalogue, with texts by Joan Fontcuberta, Marta
Gili and others, Madrid 1985; *Primavera Fotografica a Catalunya 1986;
Homenatje a Agustì Centelles,* exhibition catalogue, with texts by Marie-Loup
Sougez, Josep Benet and Xavier Miserachs, Barcelona 1986. **Articles**—"Un
imago de la imagen" by Eduardo Chamorro in *Cambio-16* (Madrid), no. 333,
1978; "Agustì Centelles: la identidad de un reportero" by Maria Jesus Perez
in *Flash-Foto* (Madrid), no. 62, 1979; "Agustì Centelles: el gran reportero de
nuestra guerra" by Juan Ramon Anguera in *Flash-Foto* (Madrid), no. 78,
1980; "Una Leica y un hombre: Agustì Centelles" by Martias Antolin in
Nueva Lente (Madrid), no. 107/108, 1981; "Mi 18 de julio disparando fotos"
in *Interviu* (Madrid), no. 7, 1982; "Agustì Centelles" in *Westermann's*
(Munich), no. 7, 1986.

*   *   *

Even today, very little is known about Spanish photography during the
Civil War, 1936-39. Scholars have been more involved in analysing the use
for propaganda purposes—rather than purely for information—of the photojournalism which appeared for the first time in the mass media, than in
rescuing from oblivion the many nameless photojournalists. To make matters
worse, Franco's troops seized many photographic files and shut them away in
the Army archives in Salamanca. With the information now available, there
emerges the figure of Agustì Centelles, considered to be the most accomplished Spanish photographer to work during the conflict and whose output
from this period may be compared both in quality and technique to that of the
best known in the field such as Capa, Seymour, Namuth, etc.

Centelles was trained in photo-journalism during the Second Republic
when the prevailing liberalism encouraged freedom and competition among
the Press (somewhat like what had happened some years previously under the
Weimar Republic). Newspapers and magazines were eager to obtain spectacular and powerful images, and the emergence of small format cameras made
possible more lively and skilful reporting. At the end of the twenties and the
beginning of the thirties, the prototype press photographer in Barcelona was
embodied in Alejandro Merletti, who would turn up at every event bearing his
heavy plate camera, his tripod and his primitive magnesium flash. With this

equipment that today seems so crude, Merletti has left us with a visual record
that is both static and picturesque. In contrast to this conception of photojournalism, Centelles was the first Spanish cameraman to go on to the streets
with just a Leica and attempt to capture the news as it happened, and to freeze
climactic moments for posterity. With his strong intuitive sense and great
powers of anticipation, Centelles was to create a whole new school in his effort
to harmonise the camera's newsgathering possibilities with the demands of the
times he sought to record.

What most characterises Centelles' work is the desire to capture a fleeting
expression, a meaningful gesture or the unrepeatable coincidence of several
images in the viewfinder; however, he cannot be considered a master of
composition, which is always sacrificed in favour of immediacy in his
pictures. Even so, the frames should be seen as ingenuous or accidental, since
they obey a certain rhetorical strategy, sometimes providing an aseptic
description of an event in a balanced configuration and sometimes producing
tension with disproportion in the foreground and a diagonal horizon. Thus
Centelles' work embodies a mature understanding and practice of the photojournalist's craft using all the expressive resources that the medium can
provide—a kind of photo-journalism which not only informs but expresses
opinions and emotions. This is why Centelles' vision of the Civil War,
compared with that of foreign cameramen, is all the more passionate and
intense, since a greater feeling of conflict and involvement can be sensed in his
pictures.

—Joan Fontcuberta

CHANG, Chao-Tang.

Nationality: Taiwanese. **Born:** Pan-Chiao, Taipei, Taiwan, 17 November
1943. **Education:** Studied civil engineering, National Taiwan University,
1961-64; self-taught in photography, since 1960. **Family:** Married Liao Shu-
Cheng in 1965; sons: Shih-Ho and Shih-Lun. **Career:** Worked as a news
cameraman, film and video maker, 1968-81; freelance photographer, editor
and director for television documentary series; also consultant in visual design
for stage and print, 1982-89; cinematographer, 1986; senior producer,
Chinese Public Television Organizing Committee, since 1991; part-time
teacher of photography and television news production, Graduate School of
Journalism, National Taiwan University, since 1992. **Agent:** Ruth Silverman,
Photos Gallery, 403 Francisco Street, San Francisco, California 94133, U.S.A.
Address: 5th Floor 9, Lane 3, Tung-Shan Street, Taipei, Taiwan.

Individual Exhibitions:

1974   *Farewell to Photography,* Artist Gallery, Taipei
1983   *Human Grace and Forgiveness,* Spring Gallery, Taipei
        (travelled to the Eye Gallery, San Francisco; Zuni
        Icosahedron, Hong Kong; and Chinese Cultural Center, New
        York, 1983-85)
1986   *Images from the East,* Soho Photo Gallery, New York
        Trip Reverse, Lion Art Gallery, Taipei (travelled to the
        Olympus Photo Gallery, Tokyo)
1994   *Voyage à rebours,* La Laverie, Paris

Selected Group Exhibitions:

1965   *Contemporary Photography Show,* toured in Taiwan Island
1967   *Womanolozy,* Lin-Yun Gallery, Taipei
1972   *Livingolozy,* China Gallery, Taipei
1976   *'76 Exhibition,* American Culture Center, Taipei
1983   *'83 Taipei,* Hong Kong
1986   *The Free Roaming,* Jazz Photo Gallery, Taipei
1991   *Seeing—Nine Taiwanese Photographers' Perspective,* Eslite
        Art Gallery, Taipei (travelled to the Eye Gallery, San
        Francisco)
1993   *View on the River Tamsui in 50 Years,* toured in Taipei County

Wu-Fong Village, Hsin Chu, Taiwan, 1986. Photograph by Chang Chao-Tang.

Cloud Gate Dance Theatre in 20 Years, toured in Taiwan
    Island
1994   *Contemporary Photography from Mainland China, Hong Kong*
    and Taiwan, Hong Kong Arts Centre

Collections:

Taipei Modern Art Museum.

Publications:

By CHANG: Books—*In Search of Photos Past,* Taipei 1988; *Chang Chao-Tang,* Taipei 1989; *Aspects and Visions,* editor, Taipei 1989 and 1994; *View on the River Tamsui in 50 Years,* exhibition catalogue, editor, Taipei 1993. **Articles**—"Journey Image" in *Artist Magazine* (Taipei), Nos. 79-92, 1981-82; "Silent Island—Peng-Hu" in *Taiwan Geography Magazine* (Taipei), July 1985; "Young Photographer from Mainland China," commentator, in *Echo Magazine* (Taipei), Nos. 19-25, 1988-89; "Vision of Chinese Photography: 1935-1990," commentator, in *The Independence Morning Post* (Taipei), 1991-92; "Alternative Image," commentator, in *Echo Folk Art Magazine* (Taipei), Nos. 28-67, 1991-94; "Shadows and Footprints—Tracing the Development of Taiwan Photo-Journalism," commentator, in *Three Photographic Perspectives—Hong Kong, Mainland China, Taiwan* (Hong Kong), February 1994.

On CHANG: Articles—"Seeing and Reading" by Chien Yung-Bin in *Hsiung Shih Art Monthly* (Taipei), May 1986; "A Circle of Life" by Lin Hwai-Min in *The United News* (Taipei), May 1986; "Facing Life Straight" by Hou Wu-Kong in *PHOTOGRAPHY* (China), October 1989.

*

For me, photography is a process of freezing instants of the mundane . . . of melancholy, of directionless despair . . . into silently emotional expressions of time and space. Life, however, does not change because of this. The oppression and tedium remain.

I am merely trying to find a little consolation in these frozen moments.

—Chang Chao-Tang

*   *   *

Chang Chao-Tang's importance in the history of photography in Taiwan, where he remained at the forefront of Chinese contemporary photography, cannot be overstated. Although trained as a civil engineer, Chang Chao-Tang's interest in the arts made it inevitable that he would pursue a photographic career since the late 1950s. Once an amateur salon pictorial photographer, Chang found himself obsessed with emerging artistic trends when ideas such as surrealism and the Theatre of the Absurd were introduced in his college days.

"Recording an emotion is easy but expressing a spirit is not," said Chang, who is among probably the first generation of truly indigenous Taiwanese photographers. His realisation that one is free to express oneself, resulting in a muting of artistic political criticism of the results of the disintegration of society and the environment in Taiwan, are reflected throughout Chang's documentary works since the 1970s. Chang believes that one should ''photograph because of a hunger, a passion, not in order to exhibit or to prove anything.'' And it is exactly this principle of not having a ''mission'' which freed him from the burden and allowed him to see more clearly. Chang's black and white images drawn from Taiwanese history, aboriginal culture and contemporary society are often used to criticise or satirise Taiwan society. Symbols such as Chinese mythology, animals' parts and urban landscapes are also used as metaphors to interpret current phenomena. Chang's almost surreal photographs exhibit an anxiety which is conveyed by the destruction of urban and country life demonstrated in his works. His social landscapes and human portraits, hiding the misery and depression of people who are marginal and have fallen by the wayside, remain his finest works.

Chang Chao-Tang's concentration on his reminiscences of things, places, family and cultures is not only reflected in his photographs but also in the documentary films to which he has devoted most of his time in recent years. As one of the most influential figures in, and a witness of Taiwanese photographic development, Chang has also been donating his time and efforts to preserving its history through organising publications and exhibitions of past and contemporary photographers. Unlike other countries where such activities are financed and encouraged by the governments, Chang's projects helping to preserve and promote Taiwanese photography are mostly initiated, researched and produced by him, with the occasional support from different organisations. These occupations have been a major contribution to the industry of photography but at the same time limited our chance to appreciate Chang's photography in the 1990s.

—Becky Cho

CHAPPELL, Walter.

Nationality: American. **Born:** Portland, Oregon, 8 June 1925. **Education:** Attended the Ellison-White Conservatory of Music, Portland, majoring in piano, 1932-43, and the Benson Polytechnical School, Portland, majoring in architectural drawing, 1939-43; studied architecture at Frank Lloyd Wright's Taliesin West, Paradise Valley, near Scottsdale, Arizona, 1953-54; apprentice photographic student with Nile Root and Winter Prather, Denver, 1954-57; studied photographic printmaking with Minor White, Rochester, New York, 1957-58. **Military Service:** Served as a private in the 13th Airborne Division, United States Army, stationed in the eastern United States, 1943-47. **Family:** Lived with Leslie Spears from 1948 (separated, 1952); married Patricia Schmid in 1956 (died, 1959); lived with Nancy Dickinson from 1960 (separated, 1974); married Suzanne Lichau in 1977; children: Dharma, Theo, Aryan, Piki, Robin, Riversong, and Anja. **Career:** Painter, poet, musician and craftsman, in Portland, San Francisco, Los Angeles, New Orleans, New York and Big Sur, California, 1942 until the early 1950s; turned to serious work in photography while hospitalized for tuberculosis in Denver, 1954-56; Curator of Exhibitions and Prints, International Museum of Photography, George Eastman House, Rochester, New York, 1957-61; Director, Association of Heliographers, New York, 1962-65; lived in Big Sur, 1965, Taos, New Mexico, 1965-70, San Francisco, 1970-74, and New Mexico, since 1974: settled on land in the Rio Grande Gorge, near Taos, 1981, and in Santa Fe, 1982. Artist-in-Residence, Volcanoes National Park, Hawaii, 1977-79. **Recipient:** National Endowment for the Arts Photography Fellowship, 1977, 1980, 1984. **Address:** P.O. Box 8736, Santa Fe, New Mexico 87504, U.S.A.

Individual Exhibitions:

1956	Photography Workshop, Denver
	Alegro Music FM Station, Denver
	National Jewish Hospital, Denver
1957	George Wittenborn Gallery, New York
	International Museum of Photography, George Eastman House, Rochester, New York
1959	Smithsonian Institution, Washington, D.C.
	Boston University
1960	Carl Siembab Gallery, Boston
	Under the Sun, Poindexter Gallery, New York (with Syl Labrot and Nathan Lyons)
1961	Polaroid Corporation, Cambridge, Massachusetts
1963	Gallery Archive of Heliography, New York
	VII Photographers Gallery, Provincetown, Massachusetts
1964	Coast Gallery, Big Sur, California
	San Francisco State College
	El Mochuelo Gallery, Santa Barbara, California
1965	Hip Pocket Book Gallery, Santa Cruz, California
1966	Craft House, Arroyo Saco, New Mexico
	Quivira Gallery, Corrales, New Mexico
	Demasiado, Santa Fe, New Mexico
	Levin Gallery, Santa Fe, New Mexico
1967	Atlantis Gallery, Santa Fe, New Mexico
	Museum of New Mexico, Santa Fe
	Antalope Press, Santa Fe, New Mexico
1968	Nirvana, Santa Fe, New Mexico
1970	Coast Gallery, Big Sur, California
	Dennis Hopper Residence, Hollywood, California
1971	Sun Gallery, San Francisco
1972	Phos-Graphos Gallery, San Francisco
	New Prints, Caryl Hill Residence, Carmel, California
	San Francisco Art Institute (presentation)
	San Francisco State College
1973	Visual Studies Workshop, Rochester, New York
	Rochester Institute of Technology, New York (presentation)
	Massachusetts Institute of Technology, Cambridge (presentation)
	80 Prints, Light Gallery, New York
	Musée d'Art Moderne de la Ville, Paris
1974	*Image Without Credential,* Camerawork Gallery, San Anselmo, California
	Metaflora, Annex Gallery, Santa Rosa, California
1975	University of Iowa, Iowa City
	Enjay Gallery, Boston
	Creative Eye Gallery, Sonoma, California
	Everett Community College, Washington
	Wells College, Aurora, New York
1976	Vanderbilt University, Nashville, Tennessee
	Visual Studies Workshop, Rochester, New York
	Volcano Art Gallery, Volcanoes National Park, Hawaii
1977	Millersville State College, Pennsylvania
	Volcano Art Center, Volcanoes National Park, Hawaii
	Bank of Hawaii, Hilo
	The Foundry, Honolulu
1978	Vision Gallery, Boston
	Oakton Community College, Morton Grove, Illinois
	Light Factory, Charlotte, North Cardina
	Silver Image Gallery, Seattle
	Susan Spiritus Gallery, Newport Beach, California
	Philadelphia Museum of Art
	Volcano Art Center, Volcanoes National Park, Hawaii
1979	Silver Image Gallery, Ohio State University, Columbus
	Catskill Center for Photography, Woodstock, New York
	Neuberger Museum, Purchase, New York
	Santa Fe Gallery of Photography, New Mexico
1980	Nicholas Potter Gallery, Santa Fe
	Colorado Photographic Art Center, Denver (retrospective)
1981	Center for Media Art, American Center, Paris
	Grapestake Gallery, San Francisco
1982	The New Gallery, Taos, New Mexico
	Photography Gallery, La Jolla, California
1983	Scheinbaum and Russek Gallery, Santa Fe, New Mexico
	The American Center, Cairo, Egypt
1984	DVS Gallery, Taos, New Mexico (with Bob Saltzman)

Selected Group Exhibitions:

1958	*5 Masters of Photography,* I.F.A. Galleries, Washington, D.C.

1959	*Photography at Mid-Century,* International Museum of Photography, George Eastman House, Rochester, New York
1960	*The Sense of Abstraction,* Museum of Modern Art, New York
1963	*Heliography 1963,* Lever House, New York (and 1964)
1967	*Photography in the 20th Century,* National Gallery of Canada, Ottawa (toured Canada and the United States, 1967-73)
1968	*Light⁷,* Hayden Gallery, Massachusetts Institute of Technology, Cambridge
1974	*Photography in America,* Whitney Museum, New York
1978	*Mirrors and Windows: American Photography since 1960,* Museum of Modern Art, New York (toured the United States, 1978-80)
1981	*Onze Photographes de Santa Fe,* at *Rencontres Internationales de Photographie,* Arles, France (travelled in France, Iceland, Spain, Russia, Turkey and Israel, 1981-84)
1982	*Twentieth Century Photographs from MOMA,* Seibu Museum of Art, Tokyo

Collections:

Museum of Modern Art, New York; Metropolitan Museum of Art, New York; International Museum of Photography, George Eastman House, Rochester, New York; Massachusetts Institute of Technology, Cambridge; Polaroid Corporation, Cambridge, Massachusetts; Fogg Art Museum, Harvard University, Cambridge, Massachusetts; Alfred Stieglitz Center, Philadelphia Museum of Art; Smithsonian Institution, Washington, D.C.; Exchange National Bank, Chicago.

Publications:

By CHAPPELL: Books—*Gestures of Infinity,* New York 1957; *Logue and Glyphs,* New Orleans 1950; *Under the Sun: The Abstract Art of Camera Vision,* with Syl Labrot and Nathan Lyons, New York 1960, 1970; *Edmond Kara Portfolio One,* 10 prints, Big Sur, California 1963; *Sharon Tate Portfolio,* 12 prints, Big Sur, California 1964; *Edmond Kara Portfolio: Elizabeth Taylor Sculpture,* 12 prints, Big Sur, California 1964; *Metaflora,* portfolio, Santa Fe, New Mexico 1980; *Solar Incarnate,* portfolio of 12 prints, Taos, New Mexico 1981. **Films**—*Legend at Big Sur,* 1967; *The Doll,* 1968; *Fleshstones,* 1968; *Bambu,* 1968; *Yeas, 1968; Hammock,* 1970; *Yet-Ta-Hey-Alcatraz,* 1971; *Veterans' Day,* 1972.

On CHAPPELL: Books—*Photography in the 20th Century* by Nathan Lyons, New York 1967; *Photography in America,* edited by Robert Doty, with an introduction by Minor White, New York and London 1974; *The Photographer's Choice,* edited by Kelly Wise, Danbury, New Hampshire 1975; *Photographs: Sheldon Memorial Art Gallery Collection, University of Nebraska,* edited by Norman A. Geske, Lincoln, Nebraska 1977; *Mirrors and Windows: American Photography since 1960* by John Szarkowski, New York 1978; *The Nude,* edited by Constance Sullivan, New York 1981; *Onze Photographes de Santa Fe,* exhibition catalogue, Arles, France 1981; *20th Century Photographs from the Museum of Modern Art,* exhibition catalogue, by John Szarkowski, Tokyo and New York 1982.

*

Camera vision operates as an intelligent function between the human eyes and the totality of understanding in a moment of active awareness. No camera is needed for this experience, only the keen sensibility of the human mind.

To arrest and refine this flow of impressions, creating an independent image in space, I use my camera with the same care and immediacy as I have become accustomed to practice with my eyes. The camera allows me to arrest my vision as a realization in outer space, precisely at that moment when my understanding and conscience intuitively experience a reality most important for my awareness of Life's essential presence.

This image of my "camera vision," when fully expressed in the perfected print, stands independently as a fusion, or a blending of two otherwise opposing worlds within a unified whole. By Nature invested with countless impressions, such imagery functions for me as a richly compressed emotional language, liberating ideas and gestures from the vast possibilities hidden beyond the common experience of Life.

The art of creative work in any medium is, for me personally, the struggle to unify my discovery of Nature with the growing discovery of my inner being; to find every opportunity to create a new image of understanding for my senses—these senses which can aid as well as hinder my growth of understanding. It is an extra experience in mutual communication when others experience understanding in the material results of my work.

Photography originally attracted me as a medium akin to music, both being an instantaneous vehicle for the experience of perceiving, decision, and expression; both relating precisely to the spontaneous functioning potential within our human life. All at once.

—Walter Chappell

*   *   *

Walter Chappell began working seriously with photography in Denver, Colorado in 1955 when he was a patient at the National Jewish Hospital, where the medical triumph of creating an effective cure for tuberculosis was celebrated. The Hospital program required each patient to be vocationally rehabilitated as part of the psychological program preceding release. Chappell had been a painter and during previous years in San Francisco had produced enormous, elegant batiks—but the fumes of the wax and of the solvents were now forbidden to him. Photography seemed a logical and productive replacement. The Hospital funded equipment and lessons with a local professional photographer who was also concerned with creative work. When Chappell left Denver, he went to Rochester, New York and continued growing as a photographic printmaker under the tutelage of Minor White, with whom he had been friends in San Francisco in the late 1940's. White introduced Chappell to Beaumont Newhall at George Eastman House and encouraged Newhall to hire Chappell as an assistant curator when White moved on from the House to R.I.T. At the same time, Chappell introduced Minor White to the ideas of G.I. Gurdjieff and P.D. Ouspensky, and together they explored the concept that the photographer ought to be responsible for the content of his work—knowledgeable about the associations and evocations implicit in the image and accepting responsibility for the general thrust and purpose of those tacit meanings—and the way to achieve knowledge of this hidden content was through careful analysis of the obvious and subtle sign language of the photograph seen as gestalt. The result of their investigation was published in a series of articles in *Aperture* in the late 1950's dealing with "reading" photographs.

Chappell's photographs were, from the first negatives, rediscoveries of images already present in his paintings. Reality is seen on more than one level, both as a transcription of what is obvious and as a revelation of what is imminent. The photograph was perceived as a "medium for the realization of inner realities." As Chappell says in his statement above, the camera is a tool which permits the artist to "arrest . . . vision as a realization in outer space, precisely at that moment when . . . understanding and conscience intuitively experience a reality. . . ." The unfamiliar use of the word conscience in an aesthetic argument indicates the fundamentally religious structure of Chappell's relationship to photographic art.

Chappell worked with White for little more than a year before moving to downstate New York where he built a house (later destroyed by a fire which also destroyed most of his prints and negatives). In 1962, he was a moving force in the creation of the Association of Heliographers, a cooperative photographic gallery on Madison Avenue, which sponsored a series of large exhibits in Lever House and other public spaces as well as providing exhibits for the members: Paul Caponigro, Jerry N. Uelsmann, Scott Hyde, etc. Although he initially defined the Heliographers as being "a magnetic center for Gurdjieffism," this definition was discarded by the general membership when Chappell moved West to New Mexico.

In the first days in Rochester, he became aware of the work done on resonance dowsing and adapted some of the concepts to his own photography, ideas which found parallel voicing in the writings of Castenada in the late 1960s; he also became interested in the Kirlian aura photography and since 1975 has produced a portfolio of images combining aesthetic and psycho-religious responses. The *Metaflora* portfolio invites meditation on the radiance of living forms, suggesting a spiritual documentary. Chappell's formal and spiritual needs find simultaneous statement in this work.

—Arnold Gassan

CHARBONNIER, Jean-Philippe.

Nationality: French. **Born:** Paris, 28 August 1921. **Education:** Attended Lycée Condorcet, Paris, 1930-39, B.Phil. 1939; self-taught in photography and as assistant to movie portraitist Sam Levin. **Family:** Married Gisèle Gonfreville in 1951 (divorced, 1965); married the gallery owner Agathe Gaillard in 1968 (divorced, 1982); children: Marie-Christine, Prune, and Eglantine. **Career:** Layout Artist, *Liberation* newspaper, Paris, 1944-49; Staff Photographer, *Réalités* magazine, Paris, 1950-74; freelance photographer, Paris, since 1974. Instructor in Photography, Ecole Superieur des Arts Graphiques, Paris, and Annual Photography Workshop, Derby Lonsdale College, England, since 1976. **Recipient:** Vermeil Medal, City of Paris, 1983. **Agents:** Top Agency, 15 Rue de Verneuil, 75007 Paris, and Galerie Agathe Gaillard, 3 rue du Pont Louis-Philippe, 75004 Paris. **Address:** 1 rue du Pont Louis-Philippe, 75004 Paris, France.

Individual Exhibitions:

1972	*Jean-Philippe Charbonnier: Un Photographe Français,* Maison de la Culture, Le Havre (travelled to the Centre Culturel, Brussels, and The Photographers' Gallery, London)
1974	*Jean-Philippe Charbonnier/Marc Riboud: Reporters-Photographes,* French Institute, Stockholm
1976	*I Think We Met Before,* Galerie Agathe Gaillard, Paris (travelled to Galerie Nagel, Berlin)
	Portraits and Situations, Berlin Cultural Centre
1978	*50 Photographies Nouvelles,* Galerie Agathe Gaillard, Paris (travelled to Galerie Nagel, Berlin)
1983	Musée d'Art Moderne de la Ville, Paris (retrospective) Cultural Center, Chicago
1984	Fotografi Centrum, Stockholm
1985	Maison de la Culture, St. Etienne, France
1986	Cultural Center, Angoulême
1987	Town Hall, Cholet
1990	Nicephore Niepce Musem, Chalon-sur-Saône Zelda Gallery, London Portfolio Gallery, Edinburgh
1991	Mountains House, Chamonix Andre Malraux Mediatheque, Tourcoing Arabic World Institute, Paris
1992	Argentière (Hte Savoie) Le Mans
1993	Agathe Gaillard Gallery, Paris

Selected Group Exhibitions:

1964	*World Exhibition of Photography: What Is Man?* Pressehaus Stern, Hamburg (and world tour)
1968	*2nd World Exhibition of Photography: Woman,* Pressehaus Stern, Hamburg (and world tour)
1973	*3rd World Exhibition of Photography: On the Way to Paradise,* Pressehaus Stern, Hamburg (and world tour)
1974	*Six Great French Photographers,* touring exhibition (toured Moscow, South America, Algiers, etc., 1974-78)
1979	*Fleeting Gestures: Dance Photographs,* International Center of Photography, New York (travelled to The Photographers' Gallery, London, and *Venezia '79*)

Collections:

Bibliothèque Nationale, Paris; Musée Réattu, Arles, France; Musée d'Art Moderne de la Ville de Paris.

Publications:

By CHARBONNIER: Books—*Les Chemins de la Vie,* with introduction by Philippe Soupault, Paris 1957; *Un Photographe vous Parle,* Paris 1961; *107*

Photographies en Noir et Blanc 1945-1971, with an introduction by Michel Tournier, Paris 1972; *Jean-Philippe Charbonnier,* exhibition catalogue, Paris 1983; *Chamonix: Forty Years in the Valley,* (Glenat edition); *Banalités,* in preparation. **Other**—"France," 1954, "Around the World," 1955, and "Red China," 1956, all special issues of *Réalités* (Paris); 6 photo albums on Morocco for Royal Air Maroc, 1968-73.

On CHARBONNIER: Book—*Jean-Philippe Charbonnier/Marc Riboud: Reporters-Photographes,* exhibition catalogue, Stockholm 1974. **Articles**—"Les Tribulations de Jean-Philippe Charbonnier" by Francoise Riss in *Photo-Reporter* (Paris), March 1979; "Ile de Sein" by Hervé Le Gall in *Photo-Journal* (Paris), June 1980.

*

Ansel Adams said (more or less): "It's strange how photography advanced without improving." Man Ray said: "Don't ask with what camera and exposure a picture is done." Robert Capa said: "If a picture is not good, it's because you were not close enough." Henri Cartier-Bresson said: "To me, photography is the simultaneous recognition, in a fraction of a second, of the significance of an event as well as of a precise organization of forms which give that event its proper expression." (*The Decisive Moment,* 1952). Mies van der Rohe said: "Less is more, and more is too much." Also, one should read what the Bauhaus people said, and Moholy-Nagy, and Oscar Niemeyer. And Picasso said: "On ne cherche pas, on trouve."

Norman Hall was a very fine person, a marvellous friend, and he knew photography much better than anyone ever did. And he published pictures in *The Times* just for the beauty of the gesture—and said nothing, but did much. Nobody ever did it before or after.

I say: Exoticism is around the corner, but if *Geo* is out, *National Geographic Magazine* is in. One should make movies of the lives of Edward Weston, Edwin Land and Howard Hughes. I love Halsman; Karsh is out forever. *Jamming the Blues* (Gjon Mili) and *Citizen Kane* and the Kubrick movie *Barry Lyndon* are a must for every photographer. As for *Citizen Kane,* I am sure that charming Bill Brandt agrees (he told me so). Larry Burrows was much greater than W. Eugene Smith (for Smith was also 100% concerned and 100% honest, but more a sculptor-artist than a candid-shooter). Irving Penn and Hoyningen-Huene are aristocrats; Avedon is a good salesman; André Kertész is the ever-marching statue of modern photography.

It took me thirty years and a lot of pain to discover the truth of what H. C.-B. always said. One should use only ONE camera with one lens that coincides with your angle of vision, with the same film at its normal speed. The rest is gimmick and hardware.

—Jean-Philippe Charbonnier

*   *   *

A way of seeing and a commanding presence—vigor, passion, and an unfailing way of catching his contemporaries, placing them among his other discoveries and desires in order to give some coherence to the life of contradictions he finds around him: this is the same man who travels all over the world for *Réalités* and submits his strong and astonishing reports, discovering the unusual in the heart of Africa and in the sumptuous nudes in a corridor of the Folies Bergères.

The great unrecognized photographer of the "French" school of reporting in the 1950's, Jean-Philippe Charbonnier is, of his generation, the man who has understood best that one does not make photographs in the same way as one works for the press or for exhibitions; he is the true professional who has made a coherent, analytic statement of his way of seeing things. To be convinced of this we need only look at his shifts in lighting, the sudden breaks in his severe style and the emergence of new intentions.

Teacher, reporter, graphic artist, typography fanatic, a colorful character, sincere, sensitive, passionate—Jean-Philippe Charbonnier is an exemplary photographer. This would be true if only because of the continuous series of photographs in which he uses the "fixed image" to question the meaning of an entire era.

—Christian Caujolle

CHARLESWORTH, Sarah E.

Nationality: American. **Born:** East Orange, New Jersey, 29 March 1947. **Education:** Graduated from Barnard College with a BA in 1969. Largely self-taught in photography, though studied with Lisette Modell in 1970. **Family:** Married Amos Poe in 1984; children: Nicholas and Lucy. **Career:** Graduate instructor at New York University 1983-85 and at the School of Visual Arts, New York, 1992 to the present. **Recipient:** National Endowment for the Arts grants, 1976, 1980, and 1983; and New York State Creative Artists Public Service grant, 1977. **Agent:** Jay Gorney Modern Art, 100 Greene Street, New York, New York 10012. **Address:** 31 Great Jones Street, New York, New York U.S.A.

Individual Exhibitions:

1977	MTL Gallery, Brussels
1978	Galerie Eric Fabre, Paris
	Centre d'Art Contemporain, Geneva
	Zona, Florence
	Pio Monte Gallery, Rome
	C Space, New York
1979	New 57 Gallery, Edinburgh
1980	Tony Shafrazi Gallery, New York
1981	Galerie Micheline Scwajcer, Antwerp
1982	CEPA Gallery, Buffalo
	Larry Gagosian, New York
1984	The Clocktower, New York
	Light Work, Syracuse
1985	International with Monument, New York
	California Museum of Photography, Riverside, California
1986	S.L. Simpson Gallery, Toronto
	International with Monument, New York
1987	Tyler Gallery, Temple University, Philadelphia
	International with Monument, New York
	Margo Leavin Gallery, Los Angeles (with Joel Otterson)
1988	Galerie Xavier Hufkens Noirhomme, Brussels
1989	Interim Art, London
	Jay Gorney Modern Art, New York
1990	S.L. Simpson Gallery, Toronto
1991	Paley Wright Gallery, London (with Graham Gussin)
1992	*Herald Tribune: November, 1997/Herald Tribune: January 18-February 28, 1991,* The Queens Museum of Art, New York.
	Galerie Carola Mosch, Berlin
	Rena Bransten Gallery, San Francisco
1993	Jay Gorney Modern Art, New York
	Galerie Rizzo, Paris (with Laurie Simmons)
	Natural Magic, S.L. Simpson Gallery, Toronto

Selected Group Exhibitions:

1980	*The Times Square Show,* New York
1984	*Sex Specific: Photographic Investigations of Contemporary Sexuality,* School of Art Institute of Chicago
1985	*Biennial Exhibition,* Whitney Museum of American Art, New York
1987	*Aperto,* Venice Biennale
1988	*The Biennale of Sydney,* Sydney
1988	*Fabrications,* Carpenter Center for the Visuals Arts, Harvard University
1989	*The Photography of Invention: American Pictures of the 1980s,* National Museum of American Art, Smithsonian Institution, Washington, D.C. (travelled to the Museum of Contemporary Art, Chicago and the Walker Art Center, Minneapolis)
1990	*Figuring the Body,* Museum of Fine Arts, Boston
1991	*Post-modern Printmaking,* Victoria and Albert Museum, London

	Beyond the Frame: American Art 1960-1990, Setagaya Art Museum, Tokyo (travelled to the National Museum of Art, Osaka, and the Fukuoka Art Museum, Fukuoka)
1992	*Special Collections: The Photographic Order from Pop to Now,* International Center of Photography Midtown, New York
1993	*Commodity Image,* International Center of Photography, New York (travelled to the Institute of Contemporary Art, Boston)

Collections:

Allen Memorial Art Museum, Oberlin, Ohio; Birmingham Museum of Art, Atlanta; International Center of Photography, New York; Museum of Contemporary Art, Los Angeles; Los Angeles County Museum of Art, California; Museum of Fine Arts, Boston; Museum of Modern Art, New York; New York Public Library, New York; Museum of Art, Princeton; National Museum of American Art, Smithsonian Institution, Washington, D.C.; Stedelijk Van Abbemuseum, Eindehoven; Victoria and Albert Museum, London; Whitney Museum of American Art, New York.

Publications:

By CHARLESWORTH: Articles—"Interview with Sarah Charlesworth" by Betsey Sussler, *Cover* magazine, Spring-summer 1980; "Photo pieces by Sarah Charlesworth" in *Aperture,* Autumn 1985; "Interview with Sarah Charlesworth" by David Clarkson, in *Parachute* (Canada), December 1987; "Sarah Charlesworth: L'Immaculee Conception," interview by Pierre Stiwer and Paul Di Felic, *Cafe Creme* (Luxembourg), Summer 1991.

On CHARLESWORTH: Books—*Art After Modernism: Rethinking Representation,* edited by Brian Wallis, New York 1984; *Beyond Boundaries: New York's New Art* by Jerry Saltz, New York, 1986. **Articles**—"Questioning Authority" by David Dietcher in *After-Image,* Summer 1984; "Imagining the Other" by Dena Shotenkirk in *C* magazine, Spring 1987; "Where Do Pictures Come From? Sarah Charlesworth and the Development of the Sign" by Jeremy Gilbert-Rolfe in *Arts* magazine, December 1987; "The Implacable Distance: Sarah Charlesworth's 'Unidentified Woman, Hotel Corona, Madrid (1979-1985)'" by Jerry Slatz in *Arts* magazine, March 1988; "Born Again: Seeing the End of Photography" by Bill Jones in *Arts* magazine, October 1989; "Profile on Sarah Charlesworth" by Betsey Sussler in *Bomb* magazine, Winter 1989; "What's in a Word" by G. Roger Denson in *Contemporanea,* July-October 1990; "Fragments d'un Paysage d'images" by Regis Durand in *Arts Press,* December 1990; "Sarah Charlesworth's Abracadabra" by Susan Weiley in *Arts News,* March 1991; "Shifted Images of the Renaissance" by Michael Brenson in *The New York Times,* 22 March 1991; "Traces of Femininity: Sarah Charlesworth, Jan Groover & Ida Applebroog" (reprint of "What's in a Word") by G. Roger Denson in *Bijutsu-Techno* (Japan), Summer 1991; "Sarah Charlesworth" by Maria Campitelli, in *Juliet* (Italy), February-March 1992; "Materialized Girls" by Elizabeth Hess in *The Village Voice,* 20 April 1993; "Sarah Charlesworth" by Gianni Romano in *Zoom* (Italy), November-December 1993.

*   *   *

Among the artists who emerged in the 1980s and who appropriate photographs, Sarah Charlesworth may be the most conceptual and learned. In her career from 1983 to 1993 her iconic arrangements of her found images have remained consistently simple and declarative: in diptychs or triptychs she centers a single, easily identified motif or a line of them on a field of saturated, symbolic color. Yet her choice and comparison of the motifs—drawn from world religions and cultures high and low, as well as animal, vegetable, and mineral kingdoms—trigger readings from philosophy, histories of art and spirituality, linguistics, psychoanalysis, gender studies and other disciplines as well as, recently, her own life. Immensely articulate, a lecturer and visiting artist at many colleges since 1983, Charlesworth invites viewers to complete the interpretation of her works.

Like contemporary appropriators such as Richard Prince, Sherrie Levine and Barbara Kruger, Charlesworth emphasizes that she is not a photographer but an artist who uses photographs. She glues her photo-reproductions to colored boards and sends them to a commercial lab where 4 x 5-inch transparencies are made and then printed on Cibachrome materials. She does not need a camera.

Though Charlesworth briefly trained with photographer Lisette Model, she was most affected by her study with conceptualists Douglas Huebler and Joseph Kosuth (she lived with Kosuth for most of the 1970s), and like them she asserts that "art is made of ideas." She continues: "I am not so much concerned with the expression of a 'personal' vision as I am with uncovering the deeply rooted and complex structure of [photography's] primary visual language, the values it implicitly asserts, the expectations it describes, the common ground of our vision as a culture. My work involves the endless unmaking and remaking of meaning."

In her first series, *Objects of Desire,* begun in 1983, Charlesworth deconstructed pop culture's portrayals of the sexes by juxtaposing object-metaphors that she selected from her photo files. In *Figures* she paired a satin gown with a body shrouded in fabric, thus suggesting the bondage of notions of glamour. Like all her motifs, the clothed form functions linguistically, as a sign that changes meaning according to context.

By 1989 Charlesworth's focus turned inward, and in the series *Academy of Secrets,* she executed such works as *Of Myself,* in which a round cauldron circled by body parts alluded to her pregnancy of that year. In this series she sought the "recreation of a new metaphor" and found herself in "a kind of *lange* and *parole* situation where I am speaking of the world through things of the world but via my own particular arrangement."

In 1991 Charlesworth's treatment of her chosen photographs, this time reproductions of Renaissance paintings, was more invasive. By cutting embracing angels apart, for instance, or removing Christ's dead body from Raphael's *Entombment,* she imposed her contemporary commentary on the content of these "master" pieces of Christianity and Western culture. Meaning is not immutable and reducible, but time-bound and individual, she seemed to say.

In 1993 Charlesworth overturned expectations again: she photographed herself doing magic tricks, in a kind of self-portrait series that smiled at both art's artifice and photography's assumed veracity. This was the first work to contain her own photographs. It signalled no break, however, but an extension of her interests in psychic phenomena. It reminded viewers that her earlier Cibachromes, for all their heraldic formality and ideological freight, were still personal investigations, and that here as always she is the art director, whether in charge of scissors or film.

—Anne Hoy

CHEN, Peter Ke Yong.

Nationality: Singaporean. **Born:** Singapore, 8 September 1954. **Education:** Self-taught in photography. **Family:** Married Patsy Ng Chweekim in 1980; son: Gerald Chen Wei Shan. **Career:** Freelance photographer, specializing in advertising and commercial projects, since 1974. **Address:** Blk. 110, Bukit Purmei Road, #03-174 Singapore 0409.

Individual Exhibitions:

1990   Studio Tang, Singapore

Selected Group Exhibitions:

1991   Notices Gallery, Singapore

Publications:

On CHEN: Books—*City, Island, State Book of Singapore* by Didier Millet; *Abode of Peace* by Didier Millet, 1993.

*   *   *

In Singapore, artistic photographers need a strong determination to stand by their ideas. This clean, regulated city state is an antidote for creative energy.

It is therefore all the more surprising that a self-taught photographer like Peter Chen, born and raised in Singapore, managed quietly to realise his vision of the spirit of this city without compromising his integrity.

In that light however it is not surprising that Chen's photographs are clean, pure and uncluttered. They could well have been taken in the Californian sun but for the typical Singaporean identification marks. He uses large areas of bold, primary colours which turn almost, but not quite, into abstract forms. Or he plays with the linear patterns of buildings, often in monochrome or sepia tones. He says "I like distortions, but it is important to be able to identify the object." That seems a valid point, considering that one of his objectives is to preserve or evoke memories.

When he is not at his advertising jobs, Chen can be found in Chinatown where he has been roaming about for twenty years. He says "The different times of day throw different shadows. I'm always fascinated by that."

Chen is concerned with the phenomenon that a person's familiar environment can be wiped out rigorously within a mere decade. But instead of creating moody, nostalgic pictures, he chooses to bring out the essentials, loud and clear in generous compositions. He blows up a detail with the aim of evoking a recognition of the total object: a part of a wall, the canvas of an awning, the vault of a car. At the same time he seeks to satisfy the eye's need to "feel" an object; the textures of plastic, chrome or paper have an almost tangible quality, brought about by clever lighting, reflection and a keen eye for technical detail.

An introvert by nature, Chen expresses his thoughts exclusively in his work, which seems extrovert by contrast.

Like a child who is invariably attracted to tiny insects, Peter Chen has always been intrigued with things others overlook. But while enlarging mundane objects is in itself nothing new, the choice of the objects and the luminosity of the colours give the prints a refreshing originality.

—Joyce van Fenema-Tulkens

CHILLINGWORTH, John (Henry).

Nationality: British. **Born:** London, 18 January 1928. **Education:** Darkroom and photographic training at the Hulton Press Ltd (*Picture Post*). **Family:** Married to Roslyn; children: Mark, Paul, Jonathan, Lisa, and Nicola. **Career:** Staff photographer at *Picture Post,* 1949-56; freelance photographer, assignments for national newspapers and magazines, 1956-68; documentary/magazine photography for industry—steel, rail, chemicals, 1959-75. Visual communication consultancy, copywriting and graphic design, since 1975. Consultant to the Hulton-Deutsch Collection, 1989-91. **Address:** 5 Thames Close, Warminster, Wiltshire, BA12 9QB, England.

Selected Group Exhibitions:

1960   *Save the Children Fund,* Albert Hall, London
1972   *Colour in Industry,* Kodak House, London
1989   *Picture Post,* National Theatre, London
1994   *All Human Life,* Barbican Art Gallery, London

Collections:

The Hulton-Deutsch Collection; *The Steel Industry,* National Museum of Photography, Film and Television, Bradford; *Oral History of British Photography,* The British Library.

Publications:

By CHILLINGWORTH: Books—*Policeman,* picture career book, Lutterworth; *Nursing,* picture career book, Lutterworth; *Fashion,* picture career book, Lutterworth; editor, *BIPP Directory of Professional Photography,* 1986. **Articles**—numerous articles over a period of 30 years, including photographer profile series in *The Photographer,* "What Is photo-journalism?"; "Photographic Journalism—The Moving Finger Writes"; "Spot the Press!";

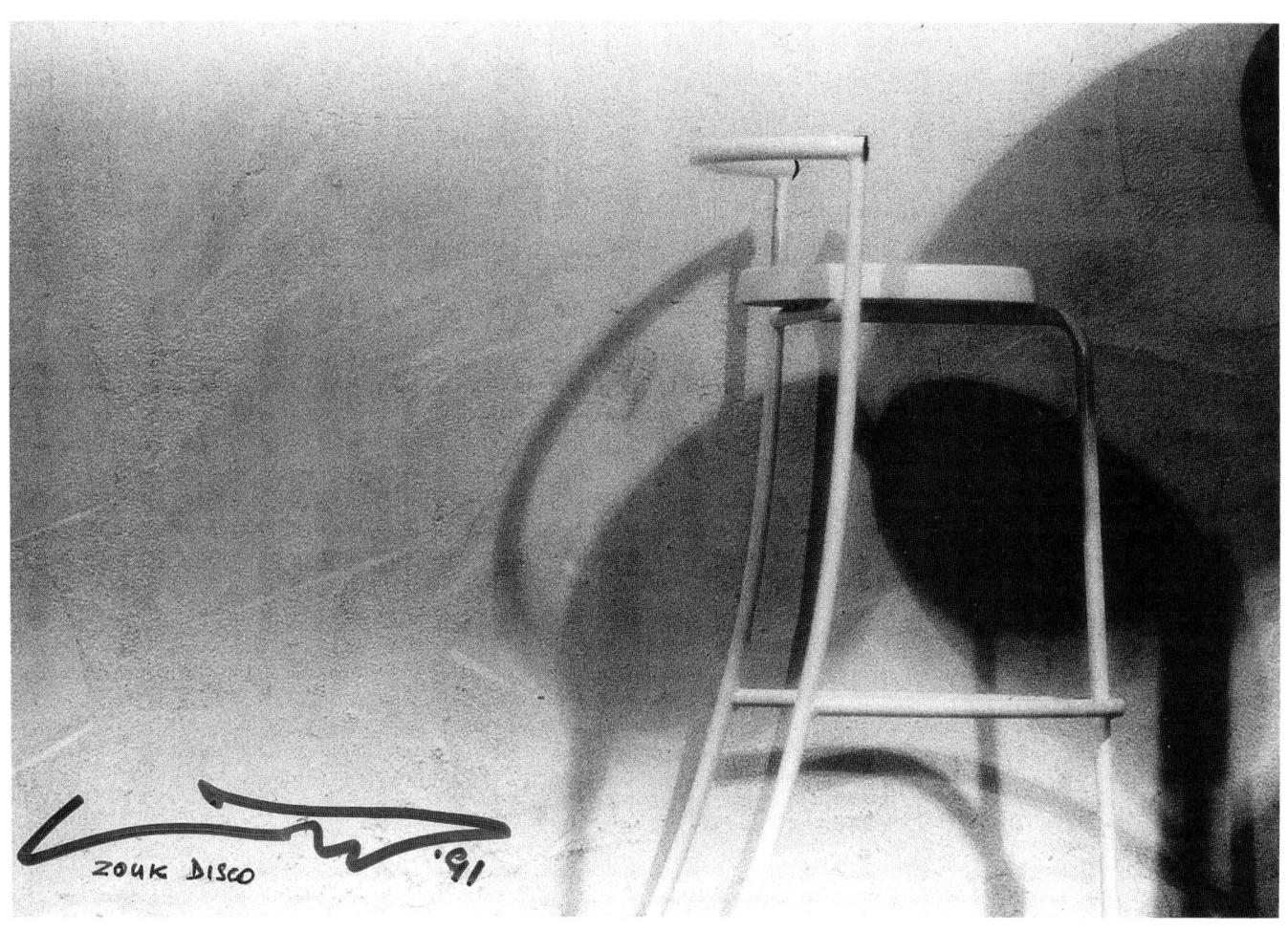

Zouk Disco, **1991.** Photograph by Peter Ke Yong Chen.

"Star Photographer" in *BAPLA Journal.* **Film**—*How to Take Pictures* (presenter), BBC TV series, 1965.

*

At the National Museum of Photography, Film and Television in 1989, I was described, with some of my former colleagues from *Picture Post,* as a "Maker of Photographic History."

As a professional photographer, taught by personal contact with the original "masters" of photographic journalism, Kurt Hutten and Hans Baumann, and encouraged by Tom Hopkinson, the legendary magazine editor, I had a head start! However, in the style demanded by the medium in its "classic" period, I have remained largely unrecognised by the wider public, except through picture credits, through the years. Yet to my peers I have always been a net contributor to the progress of the profession, receiving a Presidential Award for long and distinguished service to the British Institute of Professional Photography in 1989.

I joined Hulton Press, publishers of *Picture Post,* with the ambition to earn more than thirty shillings a week, but from the age of twenty-two, I travelled the world practising my craft. In disgust at the appalling things that had been done to the greatest picture magazine of its time, I resigned from the photographic team in 1956.

My experience made me fiercely independent in my professional approach to magazine, advertising and industrial photography. However there came a time when it was important to adjust my sights and work using all my communication skills. Today, I write on a wide range of subjects, including photography. My images continue to be used in the media, via the archives of the Hulton-Deutsch Collection. Also, with world-wide print sales through the publication *Photo-Art for Sale,* I am persuaded that I have a positive place in the contemporary history of photography.

—John Chillingworth

* * *

What does it mean to have been a staff photographer during the golden years of *Picture Post* magazine? For John Chillingworth, who joined in 1943 "to make the tea" for the darkroom staff, it was clearly the formative experience of his career. After National Service, he rejoined the magazine as a photographer in 1950.

Over the next six years he was to create a greater number of memorable, sensitive images than most photographers manage in a lifetime. For a keen young photographer, it was a fantastic opportunity. Even though the staff included many talented writers, *Picture Post* was always picture-led: "The photographer was always the team leader," he remembers, "we were writing stories with pictures."

Every Monday morning there was an editorial meeting to decide who would be doing what. It seems to have been quite a democratic affair, with many of the stories self-generated. In fact, Chillingworth recalls, you would be in trouble if you *didn't* bring along several good ideas.

Looking at Chillingworth's pictures from that period, one is struck by their vitality and their intimacy. Nothing was stage-managed. In an age that was perhaps less media-aware, the *Picture Post* photographers, always supremely confident, quickly won the trust of their subjects and shot stunningly believ-

Innocence—Kyoto, Japan, **1955.** Photograph by John Chillingworth. ©The Hulton-Deutsch Collection.

able pictures. How was it done? "It's not something you can learn," says Chillingworth. "You just look for something that will read. Often the picture comes alive when something unexpected happens. We didn't believe in setting things up."

Even though they were clearly an elite, the *Picture Post* photographers were expected to be all-rounders. After harrowing experiences in war-torn Korea, photographing children dying of starvation and disease, Chillingworth's next assignment was the Paris fashion shows.

Perhaps it is significant that some of Chillingworth's best images from this period are of children. Because a good journalist probably requires that strange mixture of wonder and sharpness which is peculiar to childhood. Clearly Chillingworth relates to children in a direct, unpatronising manner, and finds no difficulty in entering and sharing their world. How does he gain their trust? He smiles. "By making a fool of myself."

—Chris Wordsworth

CHOCHOLA, Václav.

Nationality: Czechoslovakian. **Born:** Prague, 30 January 1923. **Education:** Attended secondary school in Prague, 1935-41; apprentice photographer to Otto Erban, Prague, 1941-45. **Family:** Married Božena Stopkova in 1953; daughter: Blanka. **Career:** Part-time photographer for the Větrník avant-garde theatre, Prague, 1943-45; freelance photojournalist working for the newspapers and periodicals *Ruch, Stadion, Svět v obrazech*, etc., in Prague, 1945-54. Since 1954, freelance photographer, working with the Ministry of Forestry, the S.K. Neuman theatre, and various journals, in Prague. In 1970, arrested photographing grave of Jan Poloch and given two-year suspended sentence. Archive confiscated. Member, Union of Czechoslovak Fine Artists, 1949. **Recipient:** Charter 77 stipend, 1990. **Address:** (studio) Za Mlýnem 1566/33, CS-14700 Prague 4, Czech Republic.

Individual Exhibitions:

1945	Větrník Theatre, Prague
1961	Fotokabinett Jaromir Funke, Brno, Czechoslovakia
1963	S.K. Neuman Theatre, Prague
1965	Czechoslovak Writers Gallery, Prague
1966	Czechoslovak Cultural Center, Warsaw
	Czechoslovak Cultural Center, East Berlin
	Czechoslovak Cultural Center, Budapest
1967	Czechoslovak Cultural Center, Bucharest
	Czechoslovak Cultural Center, Cairo
1968	Czechoslovak Writers Club, Prague
1969	Czechoslovak Writers Club, Prague
1974	Fotokabinett Jaromir Funke, Brno, Czechoslovakia
1980	Music Theatre, Olomouc, Czechoslovakia
1982	Exhibition Hall, Hradec Králové, Czechoslovakia Town Hall, Prague
1983	Cultural Centre, Liberec, Czechoslovakia
1984	Exhibition Hall, Bánská Bystrice, Czechoslovakia
1985	Photogalerie, East Berlin (travelled to Budapest, Havana and Sofia)
1988	Malá galerie Melantrich, Prague
1989	Fotochema, Prague
1989/90	Jacques Baruch Gallery, Chicago, USA
1993	Galerie Václava Špály, Prague

Selected Group Exhibitions:

1946	*The End of the War in Prague*, Gallery ULAV, Prague
1959	*Members of the Artists Union*, Czechoslovak Writers Gallery, Prague
1963	*Vietnam Today*, Gallery Ars, Prague
1966	*Surrealism and Photography*, Folkwang Museum, Essen
1967	*Exhibition 7 x 7*, Gallery Spála, Prague

1970	*Cien Grabados i Cien Fotografías*, University Gallery, Mexico City
1971	*Czechoslovak Photography*, Moravian Gallery, Brno, Czechoslovakia
1979	*Czechoslovak Photography 1918-78*, Fotoforum, Kassel, West Germany
1980	*Chochola/ Ludwig/ Straka/ Tmej*, Umeleckoprumyslovem Muzeu, Prague
1985	*Czech Creative Photography*, Gallery of Czech Writers, Prague
1987	Okamžik, Brno
1988	*Autoportrét II*, Malá galerie Sporiteiny, Kladno
1990	*Review and Preview*, Jacques Baruch Gallery, Chicago
1991	*Salvador Dali*, Odeon, Prague
1992	*Self Portraits*, Galerie Les Lieux, Lorient
1993	*Max Ernst*, Odeon, Prague

Collections:

Museum of Decorative Arts, Prague; Moravian Gallery, Brno, Czechoslovakia; District Gallery, Olomouc, Czechoslovakia; Museo Universitario de Ciencas y Arte, Mexico City; Jacques Baruch Gallery, Chicago; Thackrey and Robertson Gallery, San Francisco; New Orleans Museum of Art; Houston Museum of Art, Texas; Victoria and Albert Museum, London; Kicken Gallery, Cologne.

Publications:

By CHOCHOLA: Books of photographs—*Pferde/ Horse*, with an introduction by Matyášová, Prague 1958, 1960; *Artists' Studios in Prague*, with others, edited by J. Prošek, 1960; *Light and Shadow*, with others, Prague 1960; *Painter Frantisek Tichý*, with text by F. Dvořák, Prague 1961; *Václav Chochola 1940-1960*, edited by Jiři Kolář, Prague 1961; *Václav Chochola: Meisterfotografien*, edited by Jiři Kolář, Prague 1961; *Memory in Black and White*, edited by J. Prošek and J. Rezáč, Prague 1961; *Nudes*, with others, edited by Z. Pilar and J. Rezáč, Bratislava 1968; *Spring in Prague*, with text by Anna Fárová and Václav Holzknect, Prague 1970; *The Paintings of František Tichý*, with text by Jan Tomeš, Prague 1976; *Václav Talich—Orchestra Conductor*, with text by Milan Kuna, Prague 1980; *Karel Ludwig, Pressfoto*, Prague 1980; *Vaclav Chochola—Fotografie 1940-1982*, with text by A. Dufek, Prague 1982. **Articles**—"A Musical Play for Josef Sudek on His 70th Birthday" in *Ceskoslovenská Fotografie* (Prague), March 1966; "Fotografický Přehled 1967" in *Kulturní Tvorba* (Prague), no. 12, 1968; "Fotografie podobné patentkám Ko-hi-noor" in *Tvorba* (Prague), no. 51, 1982; "Jak jsem fotografoval Salvadora Daliho" in *Magazin dramatického uměni*, 1989.

On CHOCHOLA: Books—*Licht und Schatten/Light and Shadow*, edited by Milos Hrbas, Prague 1959; *The Life and Work of Václav Chochola* by Blanka Chocholová, Prague 1980; *The Evolution of Czechoslovak Photography from 1918 to Today* by Petr Tausk, Prague 1986; *Cernobilá fotografie*, by A. Dufek, Prague 1987; *Ceskoslovensky biograficky slovník*, Akademia, Prague 1992; *Cabinets of Vaclav Chochola*, edited by Blanka Chocholova, Prague 1993. **Articles**—"Roláže V. Chocholy a Jiriho Kolaře" by Adolf Hoffmeister in *Svět. Literatura* (Prague), no. 5, 1962; "Spiknutí Krásy" by Bohumil Hrabal in *Rudé Právo* (Prague), October 1965; "Czech Points on Surrealism" by Petr Tausk in *Modern Photography* (New York), no. 9, 1969; "Jak se co dělá" by A. Sourkové in *Ceskoslovenská Fotografie* (Prague), no. 10, 1969; "Photographie Tschécoslovaque" by V. Fiala in *Photo Ciné Revue* (Paris), no. 12, 1971; "Tvar Ceskoslovenska Fotografie" by Karel Dvořák in *Ceskoslovenská Fotografie* (Prague), no. 12, 1972; "Painting and Photography" by Petr Tausk in *British Journal of Photography Annual*, London 1973; "Jubilee of Václav Chochola" in *Výtvarná kultura* (Prague), no. 3, 1983; "Chapters from the History of Czech Sport-photography" by J. Kolis in *Stadion* (Prague), no. 8, 1986.

*

A good photograph is a witness of the time when it was taken. The more simple the image, the better the interpretation of the spirit of the time.

My archive of negatives comprises a harvest of more than forty-five years. The older photographs capture my own attitudes and impressions of past years, and I now see a record of the sort of person I was—thanks to the photos resulting from my creative efforts.

The strength of photography comes from the vision of the photographer, from his ability to discover the hidden poetry in everyday life.

—Václav Chochola

*   *   *

Václav Chochola once collaborated with an avant garde theatre, and in that work he became better acquainted with Dada and the surrealistic trends of the first half of the 1940s. The dreamlike situations on stage that he had to photograph helped him to find his own way to the realm of poetry of subconscious forces. Once his creative vision and skill developed in capturing the chance meeting of subjects, he began to discover his *objets trouvés* in all parts of the world. Chochola never hunted his subjects at any price; he found them naturally, without intruding on the reality of their environments. For this reason his photographs are free from artifice, the artificiality that always conveys a certain coldness. His work is simple, direct and honest; it demonstrates the hidden richness of everyday life.

In fact, Chochola's work is more eclectic than this description suggests; he has always worked within a broad spectrum. Besides his predilection for the *objet trouvé*, he has also a sincere interest in the "live" photograph at that moment when the happening is in its most eloquent arrangement, so that he may express most clearly visual information about the event. Chochola also responds to the beauty of disciplined movement: he has been a photographer of sports, particularly in the early part of his career.

Chochola has always had close contacts with modern painters, sculptors, poets and actors, and these friendly connections have created the necessary and fertile basis for a series of psychological portraits of outstanding personalities. This theme has attracted him since practically the beginning of his creative career, and in several of his one-man shows of the 1980s he exhibited a unique collection of famous faces from both Czechoslovakia and abroad.

His interest in modern art was accompanied by an enthusiasm for technical progress. The admiration, however, is of a platonic nature, since Chochola himself is a clean-cut antitechnical character, and despite his fascination with new camera systems, for his own work always uses an old Leica. On advertising assignments using colour slides in medium and large formats, he works with his daughter Blanka, a graduate of the Prague Film and Television Faculty well acquainted with the latest techniques and creative practices.

Chochola's work has principally been in black-and-white. After reaching the age of sixty, he began returning to those topics with which he had initiated his career. His first ever published photograph was a snapshot of the annual walking race in Prague-Podebrady; he now returns to photograph it every year. A similar fidelity may be observed in his continuing interest in the annual "Prague Spring" concerts and music festivals. The recurrent photography of periodic events feeds his well-preserved archive, a practice which allows him to make fascinating series of chronologically connected images.

—Petr Tausk

CHU, Almond (Tak Wah).

Nationality: British/Hong Kong. **Born:** Hong Kong, 8 September 1962. **Education:** Attended Cognitio College, Hong Kong, 1974-79; studied advertising and graphic design, Caritas Bianchi College of Careers, Hong Kong, 1979-80; studied commercial art and design, First Institute of Art and Design, Hong Kong, 1980-82; studied Japanese, Asian-African Language Institute, Japan, 1982-83; studied fine art photography, Tokyo College of Photography, Japan, 1983-86. **Career:** Worked under the supervision of Yoshida Taiho, Tamura Akihide and various reputable photographers in Japan, 1985-86. Established own studio, Hong Kong. Interviewed by *Asahi Camera, Asian Art News, Nippon Camera, Déja-vu, Photo Asia, Photo Camera Review, Photoart, Photopictorial, Photography Magazine, Vogue,* etc. **Recipient:** Agfa Fellowship Young Photographer Award, 1993; HKIPP

Awards, Certificates of Merits, 1993. **Address:** Ground Floor, 33 Mosque Junction, Mid-level, Hong Kong.

Individual Exhibitions:

1987   *Isolated Object,* City Contemporary Gallery, Hong Kong
            (travelled to Fringe Club, Hong Kong)
1990   *Portraits,* Le Cadre Gallery, Hong Kong
1994   *Asian Artists in New York,* Agfa Gallery, Goethe-Institut,
            Hong Kong

Selected Group Exhibitions:

1986   Fuji Salon Gallery, Tokyo
1992   *Vision,* Lan Kwai Fong, Hong Kong
            Arts in June, Hong Kong Cultural Centre
1993   *Portraits of Life,* Hong Kong Arts Centre
1994   *Contemporary Photography from Mainland China, Hong Kong
            and Taiwan,* Hong Kong Arts Centre
            Aktuell, Agfa Gallery, Goethe-Institut, Hong Kong
            City Colors, The 10th Anniversary Art Exhibition, City
            Polytechnic of Hong Kong

Publications:

By CHU: Books—*Portraits of Life,* exhibition catalogue, with an introduction by Iizawa Kohtaro, Hong Kong 1993; *Asian Artists in New York,* exhibition catalogue with introduction by Hans Lodders, Hong Kong 1994.

*   *   *

Almond Chu's work distinguishes itself by deep blacks. His models are mostly dressed in black and his objects are set against a black background. Traditionally, Chinese artists are most comfortable with the graphic elements of black and white, as can be seen in their calligraphy in which words are turned into an artform.

The abundance of black allows Chu to express his heavy handed nature while at the same time enveloping his slightly over-exposed closeups, sharp and monumental in a deep, saturated background. He says "Black represents what I feel. Its function is space. Space to think."

Chu finds the psychological complexity of his chosen subjects so overwhelming that he prefers a direct, simple approach, no distracting niceties, but only urgent features. Instead of adding illustrative elements to a single image, Chu prefers a series of individual shots which together amount to a total story line. For example, he may express a turn of the head in two separate photographs: a three-quarter profile and the back of the head. Or the character of his model may be such that he chooses to turn two mirrored profile shots sideways resulting in a sexually insinuating form.

His models never smile: they reflect Almond Chu's own outlook on life. He comments: "I use my models to translate my experience and feelings. They are my 'alter ego.'"

However, there is a lighter side to his nature that is at least as intriguing, for example in the series "Patrick and the Egg" in which he associates his model's bald head with an ostrich egg. Or in the "Violet" series which includes a print of the colour violet.

Life, death and sex are recurring themes in his work. It is not in his Oriental nature to display common realities explicitly. Instead he subtly introduces design elements and symbolic shapes to express his ideas, leftovers from studying graphic design.

After leaving the First Institute of Art and Design he started painting; first he made realistic oil paintings, later he ventured into distortionist surrealism, but eventually he found he didn't get satisfaction from it. It was during an art course in Tokyo that he started to seriously take up photography, which he discovered as a technique ideally suited to his needs.

—Joyce van Fenema-Tulkens

Body of Mr. A, **1993.** Photograph by Almond Chu.

CLAASS, Arnaud.

Nationality: French. **Born:** Paris, 16 June 1949. **Education:** Studied music with the composer Janine Charbonnier, Paris, 1959-67; attended Cours Hattemer, Paris, 1963-67; self-taught in photography, but influenced by work of André Kertész, Henri Cartier-Bresson and Bill Brandt. **Career:** Assistant fashion photographer, Studio Camera, Montreal, 1968-69; freelance photojournalist, working for *Le Nouvel Observateur, L'Express, Elle,* etc., United States and France, 1970-72. Independent photographer, Paris, since 1973. Photography critic, working for *La Nouvelle Critique, Zoom,* etc., Paris, 1974-79. Cofounder, *Contrejour* photo magazine and publishing company, Paris, 1975; visiting instructor in photography, Contrejour workshops, École Nationale des Arts Décoratifs, etc., Paris, since 1975; Professor, École Nationale de la Photographie, Arles, France, since 1983. **Agent:** Michelle Chomette, 240 bis Boulevard St. Germain, 75007 Paris, France.

Individual Exhibitions:

1972	F.I.A.P. Galerie, Paris
1973	Underground Gallery, New York
1974	Galerie Le Signe, Paris
	Galerie L'Oeil 2000, Chateauroux, France
1976	Galerie Contrejour, Paris
1978	Centre Georges Pompidou, Paris
1979	Galleria Civica, Modena, Italy
1981	The Photographic Gallery, Cardiff, Wales
	Kathleen Ewing Gallery, Washington, D.C.
	Collectors' Gallery, Milwaukee
	Galerie Montesquieu, Agen, France
1982	Bibliothèque Nationale, Paris
1986	Galerie Michelle Chomette, Paris

Selected Group Exhibitions:

1977	*Architecture,* Vinci 1840, Paris
1978	*Histoire de la Photographie Francaise,* Galerie Contrejour, Paris (toured France)
	Junge franzosische Photographen, Werkstatt für Photographie, West Berlin
1979	*La Photographie Contemporaine en France,* at the *Festival d'Avignon*
1980	*21 Photographes Contemporains,* Vinci 1840, Paris
	Acquisitions Photographiques, Musée Cantini, Marseilles
1981	*Portraits d'Arbres,* Centre Culturel de Boulogne-Billancourt, Paris
1984	*Construire les Paysages de la Photographie,* Metz, France
	La Photographie Créative, Pavillon des Arts, Paris

Collections:

Centre Georges Pompidou, Paris; Bibliotheque Nationale, Paris; City of Paris Collection; Musée Cantini, Marseilles; Polaroid Collection, Amsterdam.

Publications:

By CLAASS: Books—*Ellipses,* Paris 1976; *Contretemps,* Paris 1978. **Articles**—''Vues sur la Photographie Créative'' in *Photographie Nouvelle* (Paris), April 1973; ''Conversacion con Arnaud Claass,'' with Roger Doloy, in *Arte Fotografico* (Madrid), May 1973; ''Eva Rubinstein'' in *La Nouvelle Critique* (Paris), September 1975; ''Raoul Hausmann'' in *La Nouvelle Critique* (Paris), April 1976; ''Lewis Carroll: Maître de la Chasteté'' in *Contrejour* (Paris), September 1976; ''Bruno'' in *Zoom* (Paris), December 1976; ''J.P. Charbonnier'' in *Contrejour* (Paris), March 1977; ''La Photographie à Beaubourg: Perspectives'' in *La Nouvelle Critique* (Paris), May 1977; ''Robert Frank'' in *Contrejour* (Paris), October 1977; ''André Kertész'' in *Zoom* (Paris), January 1978; ''D. Seylan'' in *Zoom* (Paris), May 1978; ''William

Klein'' in *Zoom* (Paris), April 1979; ''Peter Klasen'' in *Zoom* (Paris), March 1980.

On CLAASS: Books—*Junge franzosische Photographen,* exhibition catalogue, with introduction by Jean-Claude Lemagny, West Berlin 1978; *Histoire de la Photograpie Francaise des Origine à nos Jours* by Claude Nori, Paris 1978; *Arnaud Claass,* exhibition catalogue, Paris 1982; *La Photographie Créative* by Jean Claude Lemagny, Paris 1984; *Construire les Paysages de la Photographie,* exhibition catalogue, by Jean-Francois Chevrier, Jean-Marc Poinsot and Michelle Chomette; Metz, France 1984. **Article**—in *Fotografia* (Warsaw), May 1977.

*

Photography is incapable of ''representing reality.'' Reality is fluid, sonorous and without boundaries; photography is fixed, silent, and centered. Photography is, for me, essentially an art of evocation. It allows us to fix the sensations provoked in us by that which we believe to be real. Human sight involves deciphering, a re-creation that follows physical and emotional laws. Photography is proof of the fragility of sight. It is in the recognition of this fragility that its strength, its drama, and its beauty reside.

The best way to display this strength and this beauty is by having faith in the camera. It is not necessary to seek to ''express oneself'' or ''to be an artist.'' If the sight of grass in a field evokes for me the image of fur, then this evocation is already an expression of myself. The camera and the suitably used emulsion can visually fix it. That is their true objectivity.

For a series of miniature landscapes, I chose a very small printing format for the sake of aesthetic economy (that is, the most possible with the least possible) and to compel the viewer's concentration. This choice is the result of my sustained interest in the delicacy and severity of Chinese painting.

—Arnaud Claass

* * *

In one of Claass's recent landscape photos, the familiarity of the natural shapes and ''feel'' of the foliage escorts the viewer comfortably into the picture, as the trees themselves are easily taken for small bushes or even lichen-covered rocks, as though in scale to one standing before and just above them. Just as these assumptions begin to be cast into doubt, the figures are discovered—human and dwarfed. For an instant, in realisation, as though an Alice approaching Wonderland, the viewer feels like a rapidly shrinking giant, until coming to harmonious rest somewhere on the park grounds in identifiably proper scale once again, and at peace. That is until, in exhibition, it is time to move on to the next Claass miniature.

This is a big jump from the earlier work of Arnaud Claass as seen in his self-published book *Contretemps.* There the photographing is more pensive and less contemplative, more critical, less classical. Made in the USA from 1970 to 1973 and in Paris between 1976 and 1977, they are images of alienated romance and masochistic abandon, disturbing beauty and condemnative precision, a darker fascination in the revolving Doors of Perception, more like an Alice Cooper in Wonderland. Only two years elapsed between the two bodies of work, but the change is dramatic; yet equally compelling is the thread of connection as aerial perspective appeared effectively and gardens too were visited, perceptively. *Contretemps* means literally ''against time.'' I am provoked to imagine photographs, frozen in their quadrangular packages of the past, struggling like salmon, forward, against ''the current,'' against the flowing moments, occasionally leaping into the air, showing themselves— glistening, future-moving fragments of time. Some succeed, reaching the spawning grounds, producing new photographs to repeat the process over again; these are the fertile and potent ones, the strong swimmers and high-jumpers, the good pictures. Only the good photographer will make them repeatedly, and Arnaud Claass is proving he can do this.

In an introductory note to *Contretemps* (a quote by Claude Simon), Arnaud Claass points us toward a way he correlates his pictures, ''. . . as in the lush and rigourous disorder of the memory.'' The description also fits gardens (although perhaps more English than French, and perhaps more American than either). Is this the metaphor behind the work which followed the miniatures, the Garden as Memory? It seems likely and it seems to work. The fascination with the imaging of memory continued in Claass's work of the mid-1980s. Each time I encounter new work from Claass, another jump has occurred, another evolution of organic growth, carefully nurtured and tended, though not directed or controlled; and each time I discover new respect for the gardener.

—William Messer

CLARK, Larry.

Nationality: American. **Born:** Tulsa, Oklahoma, 19 January 1943. **Education:** Attended schools in Tulsa, 1956-61; studied photography, under Walter Sheffer, Layton School of Art, Milwaukee, Wisconsin, 1961-63. **Military Service:** Served in the United States Army, in Vietnam, 1964-66. **Career:** Worked in family commercial portrait photo business, Tulsa, 1956-61. Freelance photographer, New York, 1964, 1966-70, and in Tulsa and New York, since 1970. **Recipient:** National Endowment for the Arts Photographers' Fellowship, 1973; Creative Arts Public Service Photographers' Grant, 1980. **Agent:** Luhring Augustine, 130 Prince Street, New York 10012. **Address:** 225 Hudson Street, Apartment 6, New York, New York 10013, U.S.A.

Individual Exhibitions:

1971	San Francisco Art Institute
1973	University of North Dakota, Grand Folks
1973	State University of New York at Buffalo
1974	Oakton College, Morton Grove, Illinois
1975	International Museum of Photography, George Eastman House, Rochester, New York (toured the United States, 1975-78)
1976	New England School of Photography, Boston
1977	Photography Gallery Society, Saskatoon, Saskatchewan
1979	Robert Freidus Gallery, New York
	Vision Gallery, Boston
1980	The Photographers' Gallery, South Yarra, Victoria, Australia
	James Madison University, Harrisonburg, Virginia
	Glyph Gallery, Amherst, Massachusetts
1981	G. Ray Hawkins Gallery, Los Angeles
	Simon Lowinsky Gallery, San Francisco
	Zenith Gallery, Pittsburgh
	Galerie Agathe Gaillard, Paris
1982	Rhode Island School of Design, Providence
	3 New Yorker Fotografen: Peter Hujar/Larry Clark/Robert Mapplethorpe, Kunsthalle, Basel
1984	Madison Art Center, Wisconsin
1986	Fotografiska Museet, Stockholm
1987	Finphoto, Helsinki
1990	Anderson Ranch Public Gallery, Aspen
	Luhring Augustine Gallery, New York
1991	Grazer Kunstverein, Graz
1992	L'Espace Photographique de Paris, Paris
	Kunsthalle, Lucerne
	Galerie Urbi et Orbi, Paris
	Galerie Gisela Capitain, Koln
	Luhring Augustine Gallery, New York
	Galerie Barbara Weiss, Berlin
1993	Galerie Christian Nagel, Koln
	Fraenkel Gallery, San Francisco
	Zwemmer Fine Photographs, London
1994	Taka Ishii Gallery, Tokyo
	Picture Photo Space, Osaka
	Karsten Schubert, London

Selected Group Exhibitions:

1978	*Photos from the Sam Wagstaff Collection,* Corcoran Gallery of Art, Washington, D.C. (toured the United States and Canada)
1981	*Whitney Biennial,* Whitney Museum, New York
1982	*International Photography 1920-80,* Australian National Gallery, Canberra
	Lichtbildnisse: Das Porträt in der Fotografie, Rheinisches Landesmuseum, Bonn
1984	*La Photographie Créative,* Pavillon des Arts, Paris
1985	*SIF 85: Semana Internacional de la Fotografia,* Palacio del Infantado, Guadalajara, Spain
	American Images 1945-80, Barbican Art Gallery, London (toured Britain)
1986	The Museum of Contemporary Art, Los Angeles
1989	*Constructing a History: A Focus on MoCA's Permanent Collection,* Museum of Contemporary Art, Los Angeles
1990	*Le Mois de la Photo,* Galerie du Jour, Paris
	Strip-tease de l'Intime, Galerie Urbi et Orbi, Paris
1991	*Erotic Desire,* Perspektief, Rotterdam
	Letters, Christine Burgin Gallery, New York
	Louder, Gallery 400, The University of Illinois at Chicago
	1969, Daniel Newburg Gallery, New York
1992	*JFK in Memoriam: Myth and Denial,* Renee Fotouhi Fine Art East, East Hampton; B4A Gallery, New York
	American Documents in the Fringe, Tokyo Metropolitan Museum of Photography, Tokyo
	Addressing the Forbidden, The Art Gallery of Brighton Polytechnic, Brighton; Stills Gallery, Edinburgh
	Spielholle, Akadamie der Kunste und Wissenschaften, Frankfurt am Main
1993	*Spielholle,* Grazer Kunstverein, Graz; Galerie Sylvana Lorenz, Paris
	Changing I Dense Cities, Shedhalle, Zurich
	Repression, Enkehuset Foundation, Stockholm
	Several Exceptionally Good Recently Acquired Pictures VII, Fraenkel Gallery, San Francisco
	Slipping Through My Fingers, Galerie Snoei, Rotterdam
1994	*New Acquisitions 2,* Art Metropole, Toronto
	The Use of Pleasure, curated by Bob Nickas, Terrain, San Francisco
	Larry Clark and Robert Frank, Galerie Rudiger Schottle, Munich
	Under Development: Dreaming in the MCA's Collection, MCA, Chicago
	Nobuyoshi Araki and Larry Clark, Sala Parpallo, Valencia
	Puber-Alles (Why am i who i am?), Stedelijk Museum, Amsterdam
1995	University of Massachusetts, Amherst

Collections:

Metropolitan Museum of Art, New York; Museum of Modern Art, New York; International Center of Photography, New York; International Museum of Photography, George Eastman House, Rochester, New York; Philadelphia Museum of Art; Princeton Art Museum, New Jersey; Chrysler Museum, Norfolk, Virginia; St. Louis Museum; Washington Arts Consortium, Seattle; Australian National Gallery, Canberra.

Publications:

By CLARK: Books—*Tulsa,* New York 1971; *Teen Lust,* portfolio of 7 photos, Tulsa, Oklahoma 1974; *Tulsa,* portfolio of 10 photos, New York 1975; *Teenage Lust,* Millerton, New York 1982; *Larry Clark 1992,* New York and Koln 1992; *The Perfect Childhood,* Zurich 1993. **Article**—interview in *Photography Between Covers* by Thomas Dugan, Rochester, New York 1979.

On CLARK: Books—*Darkroom,* edited by Eleanor Lewis, New York 1977; *A Book of Photographs from the Collection fo Sam Wagstaff,* designed by Arne Lewis, New York 1978; *SX-70 Art,* edited by Ralph Gibson, New York 1979; *The Photograph Collector's Guide* by Lee D. Witkin and Barbara London, Boston and London 1979; *Light Readings: A Photography Critic's Writings 1968-1978* by A.D. Coleman, New York 1979; *3 New Yorker Fotografen,* exhibition catalogue, with texts by Dieter Hall, Jean-Christophe Ammann, and Sam Wagstaff, Basel 1982; *Lichtbildnisse: Das Porträt in der*

Fotografie, edited by Klaus Honnef, Cologne 1982; *International Photography 1920-1980,* edited by Ian North, Canberra 1982; *La Photographie Créative* by Jean-Claude Lemagny, Paris 1984; *American Images: Photography 1945-1980,* edited by Peter Turner, London 1985. **Articles**—"Larry Clark: Tulsa" by Italo Zannier in *Fotografia Italiana* (Milan), April 1973; "Larry Clark" in *Camera* (Lucerne), May 1980; "Larry Clark: Adieu Junkies" in *Photo* (Paris), September 1980; "New York: Larry Clark, Robert Freidus Gallery" by Lynn Zelevansky in *Flash Art* (Milan), January/February 1981; "Dillon Plays a Hyped-Up Dude" by Ron Wolfe in *The Tulsa Tribune,* 15 January 1990; "Protest Forces Photo Show to Move" by Mark Huffman in *Aspen Times Daily,* 14 June 1990; "So, What Else Do You Want to Know About Me?" by Andy Grundberg in *The New York Times,* 21 September 1990; "Photo Choices: Larry Clark" by Vince Aletti in *The Village Voice,* 2 October 1990; "Larry Clark 1962/1990, Photographs" by Francesco Bonami in *Flash Art,* November/December 1990; "Larry Clark at Luhring Augustine" by Catherine Liu in *Artforum,* December 1990; "The Bad and the Beautiful" by Richard Merkin in *GQ,* February 1991; "I Am a Camera: Larry Clark walks in the teenage world" by Ralph Rugoff in *LA Weekly,* 11-17 October 1991; "Larry Clark, Adolescence et Drogue: La poudre aux yeux" by Michel Guerrin in *Le Monde,* 20 February 1992; "Larry Clark, les gosses dans la peau" by Beatrice Bocard in *Liberation,* 19 February 1992; "L'Amerique de Larry Clark: Le reve brise" by Pierre Bastin in *La Wallonie,* 28 February 1992; "Larry Clark" by Jutta Koether in *Journal of Contemporary Art,* Vol. 5, No. 1, Spring 1992; "The Young Rebel in American Photography, 1950-1970" by Edward Robinson in *MOMA Members' Quarterly,* Summer 1992; "Nihilistic Narcissists" by Malcolm Jones Jr in *Newsweek,* 21 September 1992; "Berlin-Kultur: Larry Clark at Galerie Barbara Weiss" in *Die Tageszeitung,* 9 November 1992; "Larry Clark" by Jean-Christophe Ammann in *Metropolis M,* No. 6, December 1992; "Teenage Wasteland" by Roberto Friedman in *Bay Area Reporter,* 25 February 1993; "Obsession with seeing truth" by David Bonetti in *San Francisco Examiner,* 5 March 1993; "Coming to Terms with Difficult Art" by Marcia Tanner in *San Francisco Chronicle,* 17 March 1993; "Kaputtheit, Retuschen" by Brita Sachs in *Frankfurter Allegmeine,* 26 February 1994; "Under the Influence" by Charles Gandee in *Vogue,* April 1994; "Foco no lado escuro da America" by Edney Silvestre in *O Globo* (Rio de Janeiro) 5 February 1994; "Bookforum: The Perfect Childhood by Larry Clark" by Dennis Cooper in *Artforum,* Summer 1994.

* * *

Like that of Robert Frank, who must certainly be counted as a spiritual forebear, Larry Clark's reputation was both immediately established and largely based on the publication of a single book. The now legendary *Tulsa,* long out of print and, because of a lawsuit, never re-issued, is a gritty and wholly unsentimentalized chronicle of the violent and blasted lives of the friends of his youth, for several of whom *Tulsa* came to serve as epitaph. During the 1960's, in a double role as witness and participant, Clark assiduously recorded a Middle American netherworld bounded and defined by amphetamine addiction; a closed world of speed freaks whose emblem and device are respectively the needle and the gun. *Tulsa* traces their dark passage throughout the Vietnam war years as they evolve in the photographs from shorthaired rednecks to longhaired addicts, a passage punctuated by anomic sex, by beatings (of girlfriends, of informers), gunshot wounds, the ubiquitous needle, and death (of a baby, of Clark's two close friends). *Tulsa* concludes with photographs of the younger brothers and sisters of Clark's friends, hanging out and shooting up, initiating (it would appear) a reprise of all that came before, an apt coda to Clark's quintessentially American heart of darkness.

Although Clark has cited Dorothea Lange and Eugene Smith as important influences, the socially committed ethos of the former and the sentimental humanism of the latter have played little part in his work. It is in fact the very absence of such liberal and distancing sentiments that contributes to the particular power of his photographs and separates them so emphatically from the comparable (in terms of subject matter) work of Bruce Davidson or Danny Lyon. Pathos and compassion, those staples of much photographic documentation of American subculture, be it of the poor, the marginal, or the criminal, are utterly abolished in Clark's abrasive and non-rhetorical images. Insisting on his status as participant rather than detached observer, Clark accepts the milieux he photographs on its own terms, neither moralizing nor anecdotalizing his subjects.

Following the internal logic of the later photographs in *Tulsa,* Clark's next body of work evolved into the series entitled *Teenage Lust,* published in 1982 by Aperture. But these photographs done in the 70's, although probably destined to be as shocking to many sensibilities as were the *Tulsa* pictures by virtue of their casual acceptance and graphic depiction of adolescent sexuality, are in fact less sensational and disturbing than their subject matter would lead one to expect. In part this is due to the greater degree of formal mediation—of artfulness—that Clark brought to bear in making the photographs. Between *Tulsa* and *Teenage Lust,* Clark had inevitably lost the raw charge of the primitive in the process of becoming a more self-conscious and sophisticated photographer. But perhaps even more significantly, the very nature of the subject matter compelled Clark to assume the role of voyeur and thus to forfeit the absolute intimacy, and hence, identification, that gave *Tulsa* its special authority and power.

Clark's most recent work is an ongoing documentation of what has been termed the "feral youth" of New York City, the adolescent and preadolescent boys who survive as hustlers, thieves, and small-time dope dealers on 42nd Street. As with his previous projects, the point of departure is the privileged knowledge of the insider in a subculture, here derived from the preliminary months of gaining the confidence of the youths, insinuating the camera to the degree that it ceases to be an intrusive and unnatural presence.

Clark quite correctly recognizes that his projects have nothing to do with the values and imperatives of conventional photojournalism. Speaking of his 42nd Street work he has said "If this project looked like photojournalism, even if it told the truth, I would probably burn it." Clark's fascination with and attraction to the outlaw, the fringe, the forbidden, the dangerous, is more than tinged by romanticism, linking him more to the *poéte maudit* than the documentarian. As Clark gets older, and his subjects younger (and more "other," as are the largely Hispanic boys he is now photographing), it remains to be seen whether he will again find the perfect congruence of subject and sensibility that made *Tulsa* such a unique and powerful achievement.

—Abigail Solomon-Godeau

CLERGUE, Lucien (Georges).

Nationality: French. **Born:** Arles, 14 August 1934. **Education:** Attended the Lycée Frederic-Mistral, Arles, 1948-52; self-taught in photography. **Family:** Married Yolande Wartel in 1963; children: Anne and Olivia. **Career:** Freelance photographer and teacher, Arles, since 1960. Founder, *Rencontres Internationales de la Photographie,* Arles, 1970; Artistic Consultant,*Festival of Arles,* 1970-75, and since 1983. Instructor in Photography, University of Provence, Marseilles, since 1976, New School for Social Research, New York, since 1979 and École Nationale de la Photographie, Arles, since 1982. Member of the Administrative Council, Fondation Nationale de la Photographie, Lyons, since 1979. **Recipient:** Prix Louis Lumière, for film, 1966; Photographer of the Year Award, Photo Festival of Japan, Tokyo, 1986. LL.D.: University of Provence, 1979. Member, Academie d'Arles, 1974; Chevalier, Ordre National du Merité, 1980. **Address:** 17 Rue A. Briand, B.P. 84, 13632 Arles, France.

Individual Exhibitions:

1958	Kunstgewerbemuseum, Zurich
1960	Musée Réattu, Arles, France
1961	Museum of Modern Art, New York
1962	Musée des Arts Décoratifs, Paris
	Folkwang Museum, Essen
1963	Kunstgewerbemuseum, Zurich (retrospective)
1964	Gewerbemuseum, Basle
	München Stadtmuseum, Munich
1965	Worcester Museum of Art, Massachusetts
1969	Moderna Museet, Stockholm
1970	Art Institute of Chicago
	Galerie de France, Paris
	Kunsthalle, Dusseldorf

Kunstsenter Sonja Henie, Oslo
1971   Chateau-Musée, Lunéville, France
        Maison de la Culture, Amiens, France
1972   Witkin Gallery, New York
1973   Jacques Baruch Gallery, Chicago
        Hommage à Picasso, at the *Festival d'Avignon,* France
        University of Reading, Berkshire
        Institute of Contemporary Arts, London
1974   Leopold-Hoesch Museum, Duren, West Germany
        Musée des Beaux-Arts, Ixelles, Brussels
        Israel Museum, Jerusalem
1975   French Institute/Alliance Francaise, New York
        French Institute, Copenhagen
        Bibliothèque Nationale, Abidjan, Ivory Coast
1976   Jacques Baruch Gallery, Chicago
        Galerie Municipale du Chateau d'Eau, Toulouse
1977   French Institute, West Berlin
        Galleria II Diaframma, Milan
1978   Musée Réattu, Arles, France
        Galerie Le Balcon des Arts, Paris
        Shadai Gallery, Tokyo
1979   Witkin Gallery, New York
        Jacques Baruch Gallery, Chicago
        G. Ray Hawkins Gallery, Los Angeles
        Musée Nicéphore Niepce, Chalon-sur-Saône, France
        Gallery Portfolio, Lausanne
1980   Editions Gallery, Houston
        Centre Georges Pompidou, Paris
        Gallery Portfolio, Lausanne
        Galleria II Diaframma, Milan
1981   Equivalents Gallery, Seattle, Washington
        Picasso, Hall du Livre, Nancy, France
1982   University of Maryland, Baltimore
        Serra Galleria de Arte, Caracas, Venezuela
        Equivalents Gallery, Seattle, Washington
        Brentano's Gallery, New York
        Hommage a Ansel Adams, Musée Reattu, Arles, France
        Château-Musée, Luneville, France
1983   French Institute, Athens, Greece
        Maison de Malte, Rhodos, Greece
        Galerie FNAC, Paris (toured France and Belgium)
        Milwaukee Center for Photography, Wisconsin
        Galleria Lotti, Bologna, Italy
        Maison des 4 Vents, Garches, France
        Galerie Arena, Arles, France
1984   Maison de la Culture, Aubagne, France
        Musée d'Art Moderne de la Ville, Paris
        Allison Center, Washington, D.C.
        Centure Culturel des Penitents Montbrison, France
        Galleria Pleiadi, La Spezia, Italy
        Gallery Grafika 3, Haifa, Israel
        French Cultural Center, Tel Aviv, Israel
1985   Canon Photo Gallery, Amsterdam
        Biennale de l'Image, Nancy, France
        Musée Municipale, Ornage, France
        International Museum of Photography at George Eastman
            House, Rochester, New York
1986   International Center of Photography, New York (retrospective)
        De Rempich Gallery, New York
        Grand Angle, Voiron, France
        Centre Regional d'Art Contemporain, Beziers, France
        Musée du Volvic, France
        The Photographer's Gallery, Palo Alto, California

Selected Group Exhibitions:

1964   *The Painter and the Photograph,* University of New Mexico,
            Albuquerque
1968   *L'Oeil Objectif,* Musée Cantini, Marseilles (with Denis Brihat,
            Robert Doisneau and Jean-Pierre Sudre)

1975   *The Nude,* at *Reconctres Internationales de la Photographie,*
            Arles, France
1978   *The Nude,* Musée Fabre, Montpellier, France
1979   *Les Photographes Imaginaires,* Palais de la Découverte, Paris
1981   *Four Generations of French Photographers,* Friends of
            Photography, Carmel, California
1983   *Il Corpo Rivelato,* Chiostro Brunelleschiano, Florence (trav-
            elled to Viareggio, Italy)
1984   *La Photographie Créative,* Pavillon des Arts, Paris
1985   *SIF 85; Semana Internacional de la Fotografie,* Palacio del
            Infantado, Guadalajara, Spain
1986   *La Femme et la Plage,* Musée de Menton, France

Collections:

Bibliothèque Nationale, Paris; Centre Georges Pompidou, Paris; Israel Muse-
um, Jerusalem; Shadai College, Tokyo; Museum of Modern Art, New York;
Metropolitan Museum of Art, New York; Art Institute of Chicago; Center for
Creative Photography, University of Arizona, Tucson; Gernsheim Collection,
University of Texas at Austin; International Center of Photography, New York.

Publications:

By CLERGUE: Books—*Corps Memorable,* with poems by Paul Eluard and
Jean Cocteau, Paris 1957, 1969; *Poesie der Photographie,* with texts by Jean
Cocteau and Jean-Marie Magnan, Cologne 1960; *Birth of Aphrodite,* with
poems by Federico Garcia Lorca, Brussels, New York, Stuttgart and Paris
1963; *Toros Muertos,* with texts by Jean Cocteau and Jean-Marie Magnan,
Brussels, New York, Stuttgart and Paris 1963; *Lucien Clergue: A Retrospec-
tive Monograph,* with texts by Jean Cocteau and others, Zurich 1963; *Numero
Uno: A Portrait of Antonio Ordonez in 24 Photographs,* with text by Jean
Cocteau, Paris 1963; *Le Taureau au Corps,* with text by Daniel Schmitt, Paris
1963; *Le Testament d'Orphée,* with text by Jean Cocteau, Monaco 1963; *El
Cordobes,* with texts by Jean-Marie Magnan and others, Paris 1965; *Le
Temple Tauromacique,* with text by Jean-Marie Magnan, Paris 1968; *Née de
la Vague,* Paris 1968, 1978, as *Nude of the Sea,* New York 1980; *Genese,* with
poems by St. John Perse, Paris 1973; *Lucien Clergue,* with text by Michel
Tournier, Paris 1974; *Le Quart d'Heure du Taureau,* with text by Jean-Marie
Magnan, Paris 1976; *Camargue Secrete,* with text by Mario Prassinos, Paris
1976; *Musique aux Doigts,* with text by Manitas de Plata, Paris 1976; *La
Camargue est au Bout des Chemins,* Marseilles 1978, 1981; *Belle des Sables,*
Marseilles 1979; *The Best Nudes,* designed by Eikoh Hosoe, Tokyo 1979;
Langage des Sables, with a foreword by Roland Barthes, Marseilles 1980; *Les
Saltimbanques,* Marseilles 1980; *Practical Nude in Photography,* New York
and London 1982; *Eve est noire,* Monza, Italy 1982; *Nude Workshop,* New
York 1982; *Lucien Clergue,* Kristianstad, Sweden 1982; *Lucien Clergue:
Photographs 1953-1981,* exhibition catalogue, Baltimore 1982; *Lucien
Clergue,* Tokyo 1983; *Vivre la Provence et la Camargue,* Paris 1983; *I Grandi
Fotgrafi: Lucien Clergue,* edited by Gianni Rizzoni, Milan 1983, Barcelona
1984; *Variations sur la Croix,* with Jean Dieuzaide, Colmar, West Germany
1983; *Passion de Femmes,* Paris 1985. **Portfolios**—*Caco au Grand Herbier,*
20 photos, with a foreword by the model, Arles, France 1978; *Jeux de l'Eté,* 12
photos, Arles, France 1980; *Chicago Suite,* 5 photos, Arles, France 1980;
Pablo Picasso, 15 photos, Arles, France 1981; *Urban Nude,* 12 photos, with a
foreword by Jain Kelly, New York 1981; *Nude of the Sea,* 11 photos, New
York 1981. **Films**—*Drame du Taureau,* 1965; *Delta del Sel,* 1966; *Sables,*
1968; *Manitas de Plata,* television film 1968; *Picasso: Guerre, Amour et Paix,*
television film, 1971.

On CLERGUE: Books—*The History of the Nude in Photography* by Peter
Lacey and Anthony La Rotonda, New York 1964; *The Painter and the
Photograph: From Delacroix to Warhol* by Van Deren Coke, Albuquerque,
New Mexico 1964, 1972; *A Picture History of Photography* by Peter Pollack,
revised edition, New York 1969; *The Photograph Collector's Guide* by Lee D.
Witkin and Barbara London, Boston and London 1979; *Nude: Theory,* edited
by Jain Kelly, New York 1979; *Le Nu Français by Jacques Laurent,* Paris
1982; *Classic Glamour Photography* by Ian Banks, New York and London
1983; *La Photographie Créative* by Jean-Claude Lemagny, Paris 1984.
Articles—"Artistes et Modeles: Lucien Clergue" in *Photo* (Paris), May
1969; "Ni Limites, ni Frontieres" in *La Galerie* (Paris), November 1971;

"Lucien Clergue" in *Modern Photography Annual,* New York 1972; "Lucien Clergue: She/Sea" in *Zoom* (Paris), no. 21, 1973; "Lucien Clergue" by Ruth Spencer in *British Journal of Photography* (London), 20 December 1974; "Urban Nudes: Lucien Clergue" by J. Brody in *Camera 35* (New York), April 1978; "Lucien Clergue: Photographies en couleurs" in *Zoom* (Paris), March 1982; "Lucien Clergue—a master class on the nude" by David Marcus in *American Photographer* (New York), January 1983.

*

Freedom in photography is my major interest. It is why I worked in a factory until 1959, so that I could continue to do the kind of photography I wanted to do. Since 1960 I have been free to do what I like—and no boss, no director of any agency, can order me to do anything.

Three subjects are my main interest: death, life, and a kind of no-man's-land in between. The death of the bull at the bullfight, the nude female in true nature, landscape, seascape, sandscape, are the essentials of my permanent research—to find the beginning of our world and of ourselves.

I try to build a story, like I did with *Camargue Secrete* or with *Langage des Sables.* The difficulty for a photographer is the fact that he is producing "fine" photographs, and he forgets sometimes to remember to what they belong. It's one thing to know how to read and write; it's another to know how to put together all those words.

My master was Edward Weston: the way he looks at the woman as she is, or at a vegetable as it is—this influenced me very much. The technical expertise of such a man is not mine. I try, in using a 35mm camera, to be as fresh as possible. But I'm not saying that I will never use a larger camera. I am prepared to learn how to work with a large camera (I already have a 4 x 5 camera and three lenses). I still remember what my friend Picasso used to say: "It takes time to become young." I do hope that I have years enough ahead of me to discover my childhood.

Since 1981 I have experimented with Polaroid SX 70, and made a group of composites, which opened up new territories for me and pushed me to work more in color—with Ciba Print, Fresson, and also Polaroid 20 x 24 inch formats.

—Lucien Clergue

*   *   *

"My mother had very Puritanical ideas about sex and women. However they might appear, they were Evil. . . . " So Lucien Clergue once said in an interview. It is only a very short mental step to endow him with a guilt complex that he tried to exorcise by photographing nude women. But that is too simple an explanation, too superficial; it does nothing to account either for his success or for his skill as a photographer. Undoubtedly, there is something else behind his photographs—his shyness, for example, which still dogs him even now that he is famous. "To tell the truth, the first nudes I did, which I've still never exhibited, were just a good excuse to have a naked girl in front of me. Since then I've been unveiling a whole world, extolling woman. Hence the symbols: woman and water. I wanted to be a ballet-dancer and a bullfighter, but I didn't have the capacity or the courage; I've taken possession of the world thanks to photography." So Clergue tells us. But are a poet's explanations the best guide to his poetry? Surely not. He is too deeply involved. Clergue has also and most certainly been influenced in his development by the environment in which he has worked—Provence, which has always attracted artists and poets.

Clergue photographs female nudes, but he also photographs dead animals, abandoned cemeteries; an entire book of his photographs is dedicated to the death of the bull in the bullring. Eros *and* thanatos, then? Maybe so. But beyond this simple classification there is something else, a pagan vein, a joy in living justified and made possible by its antithesis, death. It is the essential vision of life of the Latin world. "First they will publish your nudes, then the rest," his friend Picasso prophesied when he was still an unknown provincial amateur photographer. And the prophecy came true.

Today Clergue is better known for his nudes than for his other pictures, nudes that bear his special stamp. His models are not the ambiguous adoles-

cents of Hamilton, still less the mysterious figures of Newton. His models are women of flesh and blood, with opulent figures and glowing skin. Woman as portrayed by Clergue is never idealized, romantic, ambiguous, mysterious; she is a woman who enjoys being alive and does not hide it. A passion for life shines out of these pictures; there is no sense or suggestion or intellectualist intervention.

"I brought my models down to the beach and made them go into the water. The sea is a destroyer, even in photography, and it can sometimes happen that it is stronger than oneself. Its waves do not readily allow a slender girl's body to stand quite still. . . . " That is how Clergue explains his first series of nudes. Since then he has looked for other backgrounds, other landscapes in which to set his statuesque bodies. There are the nudes of the woods, the "urban nudes" of New York. At the window, on the balconies of skyscrapers, his models with their majestic forms contrast strangely with the city below with its chaotic traffic. Clergue, it seems, wants to demonstrate again the eternal contrast between nature and culture, between culture and civilization.

—Edo Prando

CLIFT, William.

Nationality: American. **Born:** Boston, Massachusetts, 5 January 1944. **Education:** Attended Browne and Nichols High School, Cambridge, Massachusetts, 1957-61; mainly self-taught in photography, but attended workshop under Paul Caponigro, Boston, 1959; studied humanities at Columbia University, New York, 1962. **Family:** Married Vida Chesnulis in 1971; children: Charis, Carola and William. **Career:** Charter Member, Association of Heliographers, New York, 1962; commercial architectural photographer, with Stephen Gersh, as Helios Photography, Cambridge, Massachusetts, 1963-71. Freelance photographer, Santa Fe, New Mexico, since 1971. Commissioned by Readers' Digest Assocation to photograph New York State Capitol (1984) and Hudson River Highlands (1985). **Recipient:** Massachusetts Council on the Arts and Humanities Commission, 1970; National Endowment for the Arts Photography Fellowship, 1972, 1979; Guggenheim Photography Fellowship, 1974, 1980; A.T. & T. Photography Project Participant, 1978; Governor's Award for Excellence and Achievement in the Arts, New Mexico 1987. **Address:** Post Office Box 6035, Santa Fe, New Mexico 87502, U.S.A.

Individual Exhibitions:

1963	Cafe Florian, Boston
1964	Gallery Archives of Heliography, New York (with Scott Hyde)
1969	Carl Siembab Gallery, Boston
	University of Oregon, Eugene
1970	*Old City Hall, Boston,* New City Hall, Boston (travelled to the University of Massachusetts, Amherst; Berkshire Museum, Pittsfield, Massachusetts; Williams College, Williamstown, Massachusetts; Addison Gallery, Andover, Massachusetts; Wheaton College, Norton, Massachusetts; and Worcester Art Museum, Massachusetts, 1971; and Creative Photography Gallery, Massachusetts Institute of Technology, Cambridge, 1972)
1972	Carl Siembab Gallery, Boston
1973	*New Mexico Landscapes,* St. John's College, Santa Fe, New Mexico
1974	Boston Public Library
1975	Fine Arts Museum, Santa Fe, New Mexico (with Arthur Lazar)
1977	Photographers Gallery and Workshop, Melbourne

Landscape #2, New Mexico. Photograph by William Clift.

Eliot Porter/Laura Gilpin/William Clift, Horwitch Gallery, Santa Fe, New Mexico
1978   Australian Centre for Photography, Sydney
1979   Susan Spiritus Gallery, Newport Beach, California
        Focus Gallery, San Francisco
        Fine Arts Museum, Santa Fe, New Mexico
1980   Creative Photography Gallery, Massachusetts Institute of Technology, Cambridge
        William Lyons Gallery, Coconut Grove, Miami
        Atlanta Gallery of Photography
1981   Phoenix Art Museum, Arizona
        Jeb Gallery, Providence, Rhode Island
        Ansel Adams/Eliot Porter/William Clift, Cronin Gallery, Houston
        Sheldon Art Gallery, University of Nebraska, Lincoln
        Portfolio Gallery, Oklahoma City
1982   Images Gallery, Cincinnati, Ohio
1983   Atheneum, Boston, Massachusetts
        Eclipse Gallery, Boulder, Colorado
1984   Bank of Sante Fe, New Mexico
        Susan Harder Gallery, New York
1985   The Cleveland Art Museum, Ohio
1987   *Certain Places,* Chicago Art Institute; Amon Carter Museum, Fort Worth, Texas
1988   *Family Pictures* (with Judith Black), Clarence Kennedy Gallery, Cambridge, Massachusetts

1993   *Major Retrospective,* The Equitable Gallery, New York
1994   *A Hudson Landscape,* The Frances Lehman Loeb Art Center, Vassar College, Poughkeepsie, New York

Selected Group Exhibitions:

1963   *Association of Heliographers,* Lever House, New York
1973   *6 New Mexico Photographers,* Museum of Fine Arts, Santa Fe, New Mexico
1976   *12 Artists Working in New Mexico,* University of New Mexico, Albuquerque
1977   *The Great West: Real/Ideal,* University of Colorado, Boulder (toured the United States)
1978   *Court House: A Photographic Document,* Art Institute of Chicago (toured the United States, 1978-79)
1979   *American Images: New Work by 20 Contemporary Photographers,* Corcoran Gallery, Washington, D.C. (toured the United States, 1979-80; travelled to the American Academy, Rome, 1981)
1981   *Photography in the National Parks,* Oakland Art Museum, California
1982   *Counterparts: Form and Emotion in Photographs,* Metropolitan Museum of Art, New York (travelled to the Contemporary Arts Center, Cincinnati, Ohio; Dallas Museum of Fine Arts, Texas; San Francisco Museum of Modern Art; Corcoran Gallery, Washington, D.C.)

1984   *Exposed and Developed*, National Museum of American Art, Washington, D.C.
1985   *Western Spaces*, Burden Gallery, New York
1986   *The Capitol at Albany*, New York State Capital Building, Albany
1987   *Legacy of Light*, The International Center for Photography, New York City
        American Dreams, The Centro Reina Sofia, Madrid, Spain
1988   *Shades of Light, Photography and Australia 1839-1988*, Australian National Gallery, Canberra
1989   *Landscape Photographs from the Permanent Collection*, The Corcoran Gallery of Art, Washington, D.C.
1990   *Site Work: Architecture in Photography Since Early Modernism*, The Photographers' Gallery, London
1991   *The Intuitive Eye—Photographs from The David C. and Sarajean Ruttenberg Collection*, The Art Institute of Chicago
1994   *Allan Chasanoff Photographic Collection: Tradition and the Unpredictable*, The Museum of Fine Arts, Houston

Collections:

Museum of Modern Art, New York; Metropolitan Museum of Art, New York; Museum of Fine Arts, Boston; Boston Public Library; Library of Congress, Washington, D.C.; Art Institute of Chicago; Denver Art Museum; University of New Mexico, Albuquerque; Center for Creative Photography, University of Arizona, Tucson; Bibliothèque Nationale, Paris; The Houston Art Museum; Fogg Art Museum, Harvard University; Roswell Museum and Art Center, Roswell, New Mexico; The National Gallery of Australia at Canberra; The National Gallery of Ausralia at Adelaide; New Orleans Art Museum; Amon Carter Museum, Fort Worth, Texas; National Gallery of Canada; George Eastman House, Rochester, New York; University of New Mexico at Santa Cruz; National Museum of American Art, Washington, D.C.; The Corcoran Gallery of Art, Washington, D.C.

Publications:

By CLIFT: Books—*Old Boston City Hall*, Portfolio of 108 photos, Boston 1971; *New Mexico*, portfolio of 8 photos, Santa Fe, New Mexico 1975; *Beacon Hill: A Walking Tour*, with text by A. McVoy McIntyre, Boston 1975; *Court House*, portfolio of 6 photos, Santa Fe, New Mexico 1979; *Certain Places, Photographs by William Clift*, Santa Fe 1987; *A Hudson Landscape, Photographs by William Clift*, Santa Fe 1994. **Articles**—"Introduction" to *The Darkness and the Light: Photos by Doris Ulmann*, New York 1974; "Court House" in *Vision Magazine* (Melbourne), November/December 1977.

On CLIFT: Books—*The Great West: Real/Ideal*, exhibition catalogue, edited by Gary Metz, Boulder, Colorado 1977; *Mirrors and Windows: American Photography since 1960* by John Szarkowski, New York 1978; *Court House*, edited by Richard Pare, New York 1978; *American Images: New Work by Twenty Contemporary Photographers*, edited by Renato Danese, New York 1979; *Photography in New Mexico*, edited by Van Deren Coke, Albuquerque, New Mexico 1979; *Photography in the National Parks*, edited by Robert Ketchum, New York 1981; *Counterparts: Form and Emotion in Photographs* by Weston J. Naef, New York 1982; *International Photography 1920-1980*, edited by Ian North, Canberra 1982; *The Library of World Photography: Landscape*, with texts by David Plowden and Ian Jeffrey, Tokyo and London 1984; *Photographic Viewpoints* by Clifford Ackley, Boston 1985; *The Capitol at Albany*, exhibition catalogue with text by William Kennedy, New York 1986; *Legacy of Light—Anthology of Polaroid Instant Photography*, edited by Constance Sullivan, New York 1987; *Site Work—Architecture in Photography Since Early Modernism*, edited by Martin Caiger-Smith, London 1990. **Article**—"Romancing the Stones" by Erla Zwingle in *American Photographer*, June 1987.

*   *   *

At a time when the spontaneous gesture in the form of snapshots has been glorified by installation on the walls of our art museums, William Clift has worked with a sense of the seriousness of his medium. His photographs are significant not only for what they document, but also as wonderful prints.

Clarity of thought and vision characterizes Clift's photographs—in his choice of subject; in their composition and structure; and in his use of light. All of these elements are integrated in the completed prints. These works have centered, over the years, on two principal themes: architectural subjects, such as his earlier work in Boston and his more recent photographs of courthouses of the United States; and landscapes, especially of the American Southwest where he now lives. The seeming simplicity of these subjects, however, covers many possible levels of meaning, so that an appreciation of the full complexity of his photographs may depend on other levels of analysis.

First and foremost, there is the sheer beauty of his prints. Clift is a superb craftsman; his intense vision is best expressed through the physical presence of his prints, which are suffused with an understanding of light, of tonalities, and balance that is rare indeed in photography today. At the dark end of the photographic scale, noticeable in many of the courthouse series, he achieves these qualities by his ability to give life to the shadowed areas in the print, while at the opposite end of the scale, especially in the high-key desert landscapes, he has created some of his most masterly work. His prints in the highest keys—whites on white—are often his finest, with their extraordinary brilliance and subtlety, the brilliance of the print a perfect echo of the light and color of a dream landscape. Indeed, so rich is his use of the black-white scale that color would seem garish and untrue to what is before his camera.

If Clift's print quality and structure impose an order on his photographs which makes them works of art, there is also a more abstract level from which other meanings emerge. For Clift's photographs may also be taken as quiet expressions of two forms of human ritual which impose order on chaos: law and religion. They seem to be a subtle thread which runs through many of the photographs—knowingly or not, one cannot tell. In the architectural forms, indoors and out, as well as in the trappings of justice shown within the courthouse walls, we feel the somber weight of the law. Similarly, while observing some of nature's most anti-human landscapes, we feel that Clift has tamed wildness, material few can cope with. At times, in certain other of his Southwest landscapes, we find Clift's respectful choice of places sacred to the Indians of the region—sometimes a group of found sacred objects, a sign, a stone, a magic mountain—ways which cultures other than ours evolved to deal with the powers of the natural world long before we came on the scene with cameras and modern means for the making of works of art. Throughout this work, the absence of the human figure gives Clift's prints an additional symbolic weight.

None of this could be done without intelligence—a trait not always present in artists, and mistakenly all too often taken for granted. But William Clift is intelligent, and that is probably one reason his photographs are so satisfying. He has been, and remains, his own man. In photography, as well in today's art world, that is extraordinary.

—Doris Bry

COHEN, Lynne.

Nationality: Canadian. **Born:** Racine, Wisconsin, U.S.A., 3 July 1944; immigrated to Canada, 1973. **Education:** Attended Horlick High School, Racine, 1959-62; studied at University College, London, England, 1964-65; University of Wisconsin, Madison, 1965-67, B.S. 1967; University of Michigan, Ann Arbor, 1968; Eastern Michigan University, Ypsilanti, 1968-69, M.A. 1969. **Family:** Married Andrew Lugg in 1968. **Career:** Artist and photographer, based in Ottawa since 1973. Teaching Fellow, 1968, Lecturer, 1969-70, and Instructor, 1970-73, Eastern Michigan University; Instructor, Algonquin College, Ottawa, 1973-75; Instructor, 1974-81, and Assistant Professor, from 1981, University of Ottawa. **Recipient:** Canada Council Award, 1975, 1978, 1979-80; Ontario Arts Council Special Project Grant, 1978; Canada Council Victor Martyn Lynch-Staunton Award, 1991; Canada Council Short-Term Grant, 1992. **Agents:** PPOW, 532 Broadway, New York, New York 10012; Galerie Rodolphe Janssen, Brussels; Ehlers/Caudill, Chicago; Printworks, Chicago and Louise Spence, Canada. **Address:** 216 Metcalfe, Apartment 3, Ottawa, Ontario K2P 1R1, Canada.

Laboratory. Photograph by Lynne Cohen.

Individual Exhibitions:

1973	A-Space Gallery, Toronto
1975	University of New Mexico, Albuquerque
	Yajima Gallery, Montreal
1978	*Futuric Scientific,* International Center of Photography, New York
	Galerie Delphire/Nouvel Observateur, Paris
	Carpenter Center, Harvard University, Cambridge, Massachusetts
1979	Yarlow-Salzman Gallery, Toronto
	Lightwork Gallery, Syracuse, New York
1981	The Floating Gallery, Winnipeg
1986	49th Parallel Gallery, New York (with Donegan Cumming)
1987	Printworks, Chicago
1988	Art Gallery of Windsor
	PPOW, New York
	Interim Art, London
	Samia Saouma, Paris
1989	Museum fur gestaltung, Zurich
1990	Gokelaere & Janssen, Brussels
1991	Mackenzie Art Gallery, Regina
1992	Robert Klein Gallery, Boston

	FRAC, Limousin, Limoges
1993	Hôtel des Arts, Paris
	Robert Koch, San Francisco
1994	M Louise Spence 20th Century Art and Design

Selected Group Exhibitions:

1973	*Photography: Midwest Invitational,* Walker Art Center, Minneapolis
1976	*5 Photographers,* Owens Art Gallery, Sackville, New Brunswick
	The Photographers' Choice, Witkin Gallery, New York
	New Acquisitions, University of New Mexico, Albuquerque
	Destination Europe: 6 Canadian Photographers, Optica Galerie, Montreal
1977	*Rooms* (Winter Penthouse Exhibition), Museum of Modern Art, New York
1979	*The Banff Purchase,* Walter Phillips Gallery, Banff, Alberta (toured Canada)
1980	*Environments,* National Film Board of Canada, Ottawa
1981	*Suite, Serie, Sequence,* Cultural Centre, Nantes, France
1984	*La Photographie Créative,* Pavillon des Arts, Paris

1986	PPOW, New York
1987	Jeffrey Linden Gallery, Hollywood
1988	DIA Art Foundation, Aperture, New York
1989	Stills Gallery, Edinburgh
	Galerie Samia Saouma, Paris
	Victoria and Albert Museum, London
	Serpentine Gallery, London
	Manes Gallery, Prague
1990	Ehlers Caudill, Chicago
	Biennale Internationale de Marseilles
	Lineart Gand Belgique
1991	Newport Harbor Art Museum
	Barbican Art Gallery, London
	Barbara Gross Galerie, Münich
	Corcoran Gallery of Art, Washington
1992	Maryland Institute
	Galerie Rodolphe Janssen, Brussels
	Dazibao, Montreal
	Canadian Museum of Contemporary Photography
	Center for Creative Photography, Tucson
1994	Galerie Nationale du Jeu de Paume

Collections:

Art Bank, Canada; Art Gallery of Ontario; Art Gallery of Windsor; Art Institute of Chicago; Australian National Gallery; Bibliotheque Nationale, Paris; Canadian Centre for Architecture; Canadian Museum of Contemporary Photography; Center for Creative Photography, Tucson; Department of External Affairs, Canada; Edmonton Art Gallery; Fonds National d'Art Contemporain, Paris; Fonds Regional d'Art Contemporain, Basse-Normandie, Limousin, Lorraine, Bretagne; International Center of Photography, New York; International Museum of Photography, George Eastman House, Rochester; Light Work, Syracuse; Metropolitan Museum of Art, New York; Musée d'Art Contemporain, Montreal; Musée d'Art Moderne de la Ville de Paris; Musée de Nîmes; Museum voor Fotografie, Antwerp; National Film Board of Canada; National Gallery of Canada; National Public Archives of Canada; New Orleans Art Museum; Owens Art Gallery, Mount Allison University; Photographers' Gallery, Saskatoon; Prudential Insurance Company, New York; University of New Mexico Art Museum; Walter Phillips Gallery, Banff; Winnipeg Art Museum.

Publications:

By COHEN: Book—*Occupied Territory,* foreword by David Byrne, text by David Mellor, edited by William Ewing, New York 1988.

On COHEN: Books—*The Photographers' Choice,* edited by Kelly Wise, Danbury, New Hampshire 1975; *The Female Eye,* Ottawa 1975; *Exposure,* Toronto 1975; *The Banff Purchase,* with text by Penny Cousineau, Toronto 1979; *La Photographie Créative* by Jean-Claude Lemagny, Paris 1984; *Contemporary Canadian Photography* by Martha Langford, Edmonton, Alberta 1984; *Seeing People, Seeing Space,* exhibition catalogue, London 1984; *Art and the Law,* exhibition catalogue, Minnesota 1988; *Shifting Focus,* exhibition catalogue, London 1989; *Public Exposures,* exhibition catalogue, Toronto 1990; *No Laughing Matter,* exhibition catalogue, New York 1991; *Living Evidence,* exhibition catalogue, Vancouver 1991; *Thirteen Essays on Photography,* by Carol Corey Phillips, Canadian Museum of Contemporary Photography, 1991; *De la curiosité: Petite Anatomie d'un Regard,* exhibition catalogue, Montreal 1992. **Articles**—"Photos Reflect Our Culture" by Henri Man Barendse in the *New Mexico Daily Lobo* (Albuquerque), 12 February 1974; "Lynn Cohen: Interiors—Portfolio" by William Jenkins in *Image* (Rochester, New York), September 1974; "Gallery Roundup" by Henry Lehmann in *The Montreal Star,* 17 September 1975; article by Penny Cousineau in *Parachute* (Montreal), Autumn 1976; "The Emptiness of Our Empty Rooms" by Owen Edwards in the *Saturday Review* (New York), 8 July 1978; "Photography: The Banff Purchase" by Gail Fisher-Taylor in *Artmagazine* (Toronto), May/June 1979; "Walter Phillips Gallery" by Nancy Tousley in *Vanguard* (Vancouver), October 1979; "Photography: The Banff Purchase" by Gail Fisher-Taylor in *Artmagazine* (Toronto), February/March 1980; "The Banff Purchase: Tentative Beginnings" by Derek Bennett in

Printletter (Zurich), March/April 1980; Sally Eauclaire in *Chicago Tribune,* 23 January 1987; *Printcollectors Newsletter,* Spring 1988; Elizabeth Hess in *Village Voice,* 24 May 1988; Patrick Roegiers in *Le Monde,* 14 September 1988; William Zimmer in *New York Times,* 26 February 1989; Marina Warner in *New Statesman and Society,* 17 March 1989; Abigail Foerstner in *Chicago Tribune,* 12 January 1990; Jacques Meuris in *La Libre Belgique,* 16 February 1990; Jean-Louis Poitevin in *Clichés,* #61, 1990; Kelly Wise in *Boston Globe,* 21 May 1992; Michel Guerrin in *Le Monde,* 7 October 1992.

*   *   *

Formica is everywhere in Lynne Cohen's visions of an unpeopled land of filing cabinets and potted plants. Her subjects are empty rooms, often classrooms (like her stark "Classroom in a Mortuary Science School," Pittsburgh, 1980), lobbies in apartment buildings, community centre halls, and Shriners' boardrooms. Her spaces resonate with loneliness, like stage sets for a play by Samuel Beckett. There's an element of gentle irony and sad, quirky humour in the precision of her imagery too—its extreme frontality, the way the scene in so many of her works is exactly parallel to the picture plane (lately she's become more interested in oblique space). The scenes are bare and stark, with little abstract elements and absurd details—a small plaster statue of the Venus de Milo is plugged into a pool in front of a mobile home, an office has bizarre wallpaper. Often a just visible ceiling adds to the general claustrophobia. "The rooms pose for me," Cohen says—and they seem to be talking back.

Cohen has been working with her 8 x 10 inch view camera since 1972: her prints are immaculately black and white. Her way of looking at culture as revealed by objects and the spaces between them has been carefully tutored, a product of her training as a sculptor and painter. Her anonymous places in strange cities suggest her own feelings about herself—that she is alien, a visitor. For Cohen, there's clearly something ironic about the world. Her work is a testament to photography's folk culture.

—Joan Murray

COHEN, Mark.

Nationality: American. **Born:** Wilkes-Barre, Pennsylvania, 24 August 1943. **Education:** Attended Forty Fort High School, Pennsylvania, 1957-61; Pennsylvania State University, University Park, 1961-63. **Career:** Photographer since 1956; established Mark Cohen Studio, Wilkes-Barre, 1966. Instructor, Kings College, Wilkes-Barre, 1967-71; Princeton University, New Jersey, 1977; Rhode Island School of Design, Providence, 1979; Cooper Union School of Art, New York, 1980; Corcoran School of Art, Washington, D.C., 1981; and New School for Social Research, New York, 1982. **Recipient:** Guggenheim Fellowship, 1971, 1976; National Endowment for the Arts Award, 1975. **Address:** Mark Cohen Studio, 32 West South Street, Wilkes-Barre, Pennsylvania 18702, U.S.A.

Individual Exhibitions:

1962	Pennsylvania State University, University Park
1965	Wilkes College, Wilkes-Barre, Pennsylvania
1973	Museum of Modern Art, New York
1974	International Museum of Photography, George Eastman House, Rochester, New York
	Light Gallery, New York
1975	Art Institute of Chicago
	Light Gallery, New York
1976	Iowa University Art Gallery, Iowa City
	English Photographs, Visual Studies, Workshop, Rochester, New York
1977	Castelli Graphics, New York
1978	Castelli Graphics, New York

Scranton, 1992. Photograph by Mark Cohen.

Robert Self Gallery, London
1979   *3 Americans,* Moderna Museet, Stockholm (with Lewis Baltz
        and Eve Sonneman; travelled to the Alborg Kunstmuseum,
        Denmark; Kunstpavillionen, Esbjerg, Denmark; Tranegarden,
        Gentofte, Copenhagen; and Henie-Onstad Museum, Os-
        lo, 1980)
1981   *Recent Photographs,* Pennsylvania Academy of Fine Arts,
        Philadelphia
        Corcoran Gallery, Washington, D.C.
        Marlborough Gallery, New York
1984   Jones Troyer Gallery, Washington, D.C.
1986   Zabriskie Gallery, New York
1988   Galerie Zabriskie, Paris
1990   Zabriskie Gallery, New York
1993   Muhlenberg College, Frank Martin Gallery, Allentown, PA

Selected Group Exhibitions:

1968   *Vision and Expression,* International Museum of Photography,
        George Eastman House, Rochester, New York (toured the
        United States, 1969-71)
1970   *New Photographers,* Museum of Modern Art, New York
1973   *Documentary Photography,* Tyler School of Art, Philadelphia
1975   *Photography in America,* Whitney Museum, New York
1976   *Other Eyes,* Hayward Gallery, London (toured the U.K.)
1977   *10 Photographes Contemporains,* Galerie Zabriskie, Paris

1978   *Mirrors and Windows: American Photography since 1960,*
        Museum of Modern Art, New York (toured the United
        States, 1978-80)
1979   *Burchard/Cohen/Hallman/Mertin,* South-west Missouri State
        University, Springfield
1982   *Counterparts: Form and Emotion in Photographs,* Metropolitan
        Museum of Art, New York (travelled to the Contemporary
        Arts Center, Cincinnati, Ohio; Dallas Museum of Fine Arts,
        Texas; San Francisco Museum of Modern Art; Corcoran
        Gallery, Washington, D.C.)
1985   *American Images 1945-80,* Barbican Art Gallery, London
        (toured Britain)
1991   *Mexico Through Foreign Eyes,* Museo Rufino Tamayo,
        Mexico City

Collections:

Art Institute of Chicago; University of New Mexico Art Museum, Albuquer-
que; Carnegie Institute, Pittsburgh; Emily Lowe Gallery, Hofstra University,
Hempstead, New York; Fogg Art Museum, Harvard University, Cambridge,
Massachusetts; International Museum of Photography at George Eastman
House, Rochester, New York.

Publications:

By COHEN: Article—"Mark Cohen," interview, with Michael Sigrin, in
Camera (Lucerne), March 1980.

On COHEN: Books—*Vision and Expression,* edited by Nathan Lyons, New
York 1968; *Photography in America,* edited by Robert Doty, with an introduction by Minor White, New York 1974; *Faces: A Narrative History of the
Portrait in Photography* by Ben Maddow, Boston 1977; *The Imaginary Photo
Museum* by Helmut Gernsheim, Renate and L. Fritz Gruber and others,
Cologne 1981, London 1982; *Counterparts: Form and Emotion in Photo-
graphs* by Weston J. Naef, New York 1982; *American Images: Photography
1945-1980,* edited by Peter Turner, London 1985; *Masterpieces of Photogra-
phy from George Eastman House,* edited by Robert A. Sobieszek, New York
1985. **Articles**—"Mark Cohen" in *Creative Camera Yearbook,* edited by
Peter Turner, London 1976; "Persistence of Vision" by Kenneth Poli in
Popular Photography (New York), April 1977; "New York: Mark Cohen,
Castelli Graphics" by Leo Rubinfein in *Artforum* (New York), April 1977;
"Mark Cohen" by Allan Porter in *Camera* (Lucerne), November 1977;
"Mark Cohen" by Carol Squiers in *Artforum* (New York), March 1978;
review by Sally Eauclaire in *Art in America* (New York), June 1979; "Mark
Cohen's Other Realities" by Julia Scully and Andy Grundberg in *Modern
Photography* (New York), November 1979.

*   *   *

Photography may be the most difficult art in which to develop a truly
original style. Dealing in images based on the real world, a photographer needs
both extraordinary craftsmanship and a restless imagination to add a distinguishing *cachet* to his work. So, it is refreshing to find a still-young
photographer who is a complete original with a style so distinct that his prints
can often be attributed to him at sight, even without the signature "Mark
Cohen."

For many observers, Cohen's images are an acquired taste. Fragmented,
often harshly lit and visually disheveled, chaotic and surreal, they at first tend
to baffle, even repel the viewer. But if he continues to look and search, a viewer
soon begins to find rewards. Mark Cohen's best images are visually powerful
and communicate in a strikingly direct and non-verbal way. Although they are
not obviously "about" anything, Cohen pictures often set the viewer to
musing, following his thoughts through the labyrinth of his own mind. This
can be anything from a pleasant to an extremely unpleasant experience. But it
is a proof of aliveness—both in the photographer and his audience—that is
doubly welcome at a time when so much photography leaves one either bored
or repelled.

Despite its uniqueness, a Cohen photograph is "straight"—made with
purely photographic equipment and materials. There are no artful scratches,
water-colors, sequins, burns or wool stitching added to the print to point out

the photographer's originality. The individuality comes from Cohen's mind, vision—and a certain amount of chance.

Most of Mark Cohen's images are totally spontaneous. His working methods, as described by someone who accompanied him on one of his picture-hunting strolls, can be as fantastic as his photographs. Approaching his subject, he holds a 35mm camera with 28mm superwide angle lens attached, in one hand. The lens, prefocused for close work, takes in much of the subject. As he engages his subject in conversation, Cohen snaps pictures, seemingly at random as he talks, moving the camera up, down, out to the side, shooting without looking through the finder, trusting to experience, skill and the reactions of his subject to the encounter with the photographer to provide him with starting images.

Like other artists in other media before him, Mark Cohen has continued to experiment, to change approaches and techniques to expand his growth in photography. For a while, he was fascinated with flash illuminations and combined flash and low daylight. More recently he has been doing large color prints.

Cohen admits to being under urgent, internally generated pressure to produce new work constantly. Yet when he leaves his home or studio to go out to make pictures, he has no clear concept of what he is looking for. It is life, people, the photographer, chance, impulse, emotion and intuition interacting that produce Mark Cohen images.

—Kenneth Poli

COKE, (Frank) Van Deren.

Nationality: American. **Born:** Lexington, Kentucky, 4 July 1921. **Education:** Attended Woodberry Forest Preparatory School, Orange, Virginia, 1935-39; University of Kentucky, Lexington, 1939-42, A.B. in history and art history; Indiana University, Bloomington, 1957-58, M.F.A. in art history and sculpture; Harvard University, Cambridge, Massachusetts, summers 1959, 1960, 1961; studied photography with Nicholas Haz, 1939, at the Clarence White School of Photography, New York, 1940, and with Ansel Adams, 1952, 1955. **Military Service:** Served in the United States Navy, 1942-45. **Family:** Married Eleanor Barton in 1943 (divorced, 1980); children: Sterling and Eleanor; married Joan Gillberry Morgan in 1983. **Career:** Photographer since 1936. Assistant Professor, University of Florida, Gainesville, 1958-61; Associate Professor, Arizona State University, Tempe, 1961-62; Director of the Art Museum and Professor of Art, 1962-68, 1972-79, and Chairman of the Department of Art, 1962-70, University of New Mexico, Albuquerque; Deputy Director and Director, International Museum of Photography at George Eastman House, Rochester, New York, 1970-72. Director, Department of Photography, San Francisco Museum of Modern Art, 1979-87. Visiting Lecturer, St. Martin's School of Art, London, 1968; Distinguished Visiting Professor, University of California at Davis, 1974; Distinguished Professor, Arizona State University, Tempe, 1988-91; Senior Fulbright Scholar, Elam School of Fine Arts, University of Auckland, New Zealand 1989. Curated and wrote catalogue for *Twenty-one Photographers from New Mexico*, Vision Gallery, San Francisco 1991; *Cerámica de Arte Popular,* Pewabic Pottery Museum, Detroit 1991; *Three Generations of Hispanic Photographers Working in New Mexico,* The Harwood Foundation Museum of the University of New Mexico, Taos 1993; *Forecast: Shifts in Direction* (modern photography from six European countries, Canada and the United States), Museum of Fine Arts, Santa Fe, New Mexico 1994. **Recipient:** Photography International Award, 1955, 1956, 1957; International Prize, *Modern Photography,* 1956; International Prize, *U.S. Camera,* 1957, 1958, 1960; New Talent USA Award, *Art in America,* at the University of New Mexico Art Museum, Albuquerque, 1986; D.H.L.: San Francisco Academy, 1986; Annual Governor's Awards for Art History, Photography by Governor Tony Anaya, Governor of New Mexico, 1986; The E. Leitz, Inc. Medal of Excellence "Educator of the Year Award," 1988; The Joseph Sudek Medal for "Recognition of the Highest Contributions to the Sphere of Photography" awarded by the Ministry of Culture of the Czech Socialist Republic, 1989; Friends of Photography, San Francisco, "Distinguished Career in Photography," 1992; "Premio Internazionale della Fotographia Award Medal,"

Republica di San Marino, at II International Photo Meeting, 1992. **Address:** 1053 Governor Dempsey Dr., Santa Fe, New Mexico 87501, U.S.A.

Individual Exhibitions:

1940	University of Kentucky, Lexington
1955	Caravan Galleries, New York
	University of Texas at Austin
1956	International Museum of Photography, George Eastman House, Rochester, New York
1957	A Photographer's Gallery, New York (with Ralph Eugene Meatyard)
1958	University of Florida, Gainesville
1959	Davison Art Center, Wesleyan University, Middletown, Connecticut
	Tulane University, New Orleans
	University of Kentucky, Lexington
1960	University of Florida, Gainesville
1961	International Museum of Photography at George Eastman House, Rochester, New York
1962	Arizona State University, Tempe
	Carl Siembab Gallery, Boston
1963	Phoenix Art Museum, Arizona
1965	Florida State University, Tallahasee
1967	University of Oregon, Eugene
	University of New Hampshire, Durham
1968	Quivira Gallery, Corrales, New Mexico
	Quivira Gallery, Corrales, New Mexico (with Ralph Eugene Meatyard)
1972	Focus Gallery, San Francisco
	Madison Art Center, Wisconsin
1973	Witkin Gallery, New York
1974	Oakland Art Museum, California
1975	Galerie Die Brucke, Vienna
	Galerie Nagel, West Berlin
1976	Schoelkopf Gallery, New York
	La Photogalerie, Paris
	Susan Spiritus Gallery, Newport Beach, California
1978	Kansas State University, Wichita
1980	University of Wisconsin at Menominie
1981	University of New Mexico, Albuquerque (retrospective)
1985	Instituto Nacional de Bellas Artes, San Miguel de Allende, Mexico
1986	Phoenix Art Museum, Arizona
	Albuquerque Museum, New Mexico
1988	*Van Deren Coke: Black and White Into Color, 1937-1987,* Northlight Gallery, School of Art, Arizona State University, Tempe, Arizona
	Van Deren Coke, Vision Gallery, San Francisco
1989	Exposure Gallery, Wellington, New Zealand
	Van Deren Coke: Recent Photographs of Mexico and Morocco, Andrew Smith Gallery, Santa Fe, New Mexico
1990	*Van Deren Coke,* A Gallery of Fine Photography, New Orleans, Louisiana
1991	*Streets of Mexico: Photographs by Van Deren Coke,* University of New Mexico Art Museum, Albuquerque
	Van Deren Coke: Recent Photographs, Heike Pickett Gallery, Lexington, Kentucky
1992	Roswell Museum, New Mexico
	Linda Durham Gallery, Santa Fe, New Mexico

Selected Group Exhibitions:

1960	*Fotografi della Nuova Generazione,* Milan
1962	*Les Grands Photographes de Notres Temps,* Versailles
1967	*Photography U.S.A. '67,* De Cordova Museum, Lincoln, Massachusetts
1969	*13 Photographers,* Pratt Institute, Brooklyn, New York
1973	*Light and Lens,* Hudson River Museum, Yonkers, New York

Portrait of my Great Grandfather, **1973.** Photogravure by F. Van Deren Coke.

1974   *National Invitational,* Virginia Commonwealth University,
          Richmond
1977   *Painting in the Age of Photography,* Kunsthaus, Zurich
1978   *Photographie New Mexico,* Centre Culturel Americain, Paris
1981   *Photographer as Printmaker,* Ferens Art Gallery, Hull,
          Yorkshire (travelled to the Museum and Art Gallery,
          Leicester; Cooper Gallery, Barnsley; Castle Museum,
          Nottingham; Photographers' Gallery, London)
1983   *Fotogramme—die lichtreichen Schatten,* Fotomuseum im
          Stadtmuseum, Munich
1989   *The Monterey Photographic Tradition: The Weston Years,*
          Monterey Peninsula Museum of Art, Monterey, California
          *Das Foto als Autonomes Bild. Experimentelle Gestaltung 1839-
          1989,* Bielefeld, Germany
          Contemporary Photography after 'The Americans', The Muse-
          um of Contemporary Photography, Chicago
1991   *Pictures from the Fifties,* San Francisco Museum of Mod-
          ern Art
1992   *Patterns of Influence,* Center for Creative Photography,
          University of Arizona, Tucson
          Van Deren Coke, Friends of Photography Gallery, San
          Francisco
1993   *10th Anniversary Exhibition,* Heike Pickett Gallery, Lexington,
          Kentucky

Collections:

Museum of Modern Art, New York; International Museum of Photography at George Eastman House, Rochester, New York; Addison Gallery of American Art, Andover, Massachusetts; Smithsonian Institution, Washington, D.C.; University of Kentucky, Lexington; Sheldon Memorial Art Gallery, Bibliotheque Nationale, Paris.

Publications:

By COKE: Books—*Young Photographers,* exhibition catalogue, Albuquerque, New Mexico 1968; *The Painter and the Photograph: From Delacroix to Warhol,* Albuquerque, New Mexico 1974; *One Hundred Years of Photographic History,* editor, Albuquerque, New Mexico 1975; *Ralph Eugene Meatyard: A Retrospective,* exhibition catalogue, Illinois State University, 1976; *La Gente de Luz: Portraits from Near Mexico,* by Meridel Rubenstein, exhibition catalogue, Santa Fe 1977; *Photography in New Mexico,* Albuquerque, New Mexico 1979; *Fabricated to Be Photographed,* exhibition catalogue, San Francisco 1979; *Photography's Response to Constructivism,* exhibition catalogue, San Francisco 1980; *Avant-Garde Photography in Germany 1919-1939,* exhibition catalogue, San Francisco 1981; *Avantgarde Fotografie in Deutschland,* Munich 1982; *Pedro Meyer: Photographs of Latin America,* San Francisco 1988; *Secular and Sacred: Photographs of Mexico,* Albuquerque 1992. **Articles**—"The Photographs of Eugene Meatyard" in *Aperture* (Rochester, New York), no. 4, 1959; "60's Continuum" in *Image* (Rochester, New York), March 1972; "Notes on Walker Evan and W. Eugene Smith" in *Art International* (Lugano), June 1972; "Wider View I" in *Image* (Rochester, New York), July 1972; "Dorothea Lange" in *Modern Photography* (New York), no. 5, 1973; "Giorgio Sommer" in *UNM Art Museum Bulletin* (Albuquerque), no. 9, 1975: "An Interview with Van Deren Coke," with James Hajicek, in *Northlight 8* (Tempe, Arizona), November 1978; "No Party Line: A Conversation with Van Deren Coke," in *Exposure* (New York), vol. 20, no. 2, 1982; "Joel Peter Witkin: Forty Photographs." exhibition catalogue, San Francisco, 1985; "A New Vision in Europe and America: 1920-1930" in *Decade by Decade* (Tucson), 1989; "Earthscape," in exhibition catalogue (Osaka), 1990; "Proto-Modern Photography" in *Art News* (Santa Fe), October 1992.

On COKE: Books—*Van Deren Coke: Photographs 1956-1973* by Henry Holmes Smith and Gerald Nordland, Albuquerque, New Mexico 1973; *History of Photography Instruction: A Report of Present Trends and Future Directions* by Donald Lokuta, Union, New Jersey 1975; *Die Geschichte der Fotografie im 20. Jahrhundert/History of Photography in the 20th Century* by Petr Tausk, Cologne 1977, London 1980: *Photographer as Printmaker,* exhibition catalogue, with texts by Gerry Badger, Peter C. Bunnell and Ansel

Adams, London 1981; *Fotogramme—die lichtreichen Schatten,* exhibition catalogue, by Floris M. Neususs, Kassel, West Germany 1983. **Articles**—"Cycles into Darkness" by Joan Murray in *Artweek* (Oakland, California), March 1974; "Is the Photography Class an Anachronism" by Robert Routh in *Petersen's Photographic Magazine* (Los Angeles), no. 11, 1976; "Taccuino Americano," edited by G.R. Namias in *Progresso Fotografico* (Milan), March 1978; "Van Deren Coke: Pied Piper of the Avant-Garde" by Liz Lufkin in *American Photographer* (New York), June 1985; "Interview with Van Deren Coke" by John Bloom in *Photo Metro* (San Francisco), December 1986/January 1987; "Van Deren Coke: Unanswered Questions" by Sally Euclaire in *Pasatiempo Magazine* (Santa Fe), 21 April 1989; "Conversation with Van Deren Coke" by Henry Brimmer in *Photo Metro* (San Francisco), March 1990; "Art in the Realm of Ideas" by Rebecca Clay in *Southwest Profile,* March 1990.

*

It is very difficult to make art with a camera.

—Van Deren Coke

*   *   *

Although he is known primarily as an educator, a scholar, and, more recently, as the innovative Director of Photography at the San Francisco Museum of Modern Art, Van Deren Coke originally came to the medium as a practicing photographer. He was inspired by traditional masters of West Coast view camera photography such as Ansel Adams and Edward Weston, and he made photographs that reflected their straight, purist heritage. Documentary scenes (a statue of Christ in a crate, the front of a Museum of the Old West), figure studies (his wife sleeping, a young girl on a bed), a found imagery (the word GOD sprayed on a wall in expressionistic style, a gruesome dessicated rodent lying on a wooden floor), though they carried ideas to which he was committed, gave way to photo montages in which the processes and techniques more directly articulated his visual concerns.

Directly inspired by the Rayographs of Man Ray and the Schadographs of Christian Schad, Coke's manipulated photographic prints embody the mystery he aspired to attain. They combine pictures from newspapers, images from old ambrotype plates, and straight and double exposed photographs of real scenes together on photographic paper that has been selectively solarized and often includes, in photogram fashion, a shadow of the hand that has put them all together. An oppressive sense of melancholy weighs heavily on the autobiographical subjects which come from art history as well as personal history, intuition, and dream. The combination of elements comes not from rational choice but from subjective, emotional attraction to the subjects and intuitive, visual attraction to the arrangements. Even his most recent color works—which are straight cibachrome prints) contain a strong element of ambiguity mixed with a slight dose of surrealism.

All of his photographs deny easy reading, making the viewer absorb the totality of the image in order to experience the full impact of Coke's inescapable fascination with the passage of time, and the eventuality of death.

—Ted Hedgpeth

COLLIER, John (Jr.).

Nationality: American. **Born:** Sparkhill, New York, 22 May 1913. **Education:** Studied painting, under Maynard Dixon, California School of Fine Arts, now San Francisco Art Institute, 1931-35; mainly self-taught in photography, but assisted initially by Dorothea Lange, from 1935. **Military Service:** Served in the United States Merchant Marine, 1943-45. **Family:** Married Mary Trumbull. **Career:** First photographic project, University of California Bancroft Library, Berkeley, 1938; Assistant to commercial photographer Gabriel Moulin, San Francisco, 1939-40; photographer, under Roy E. Stryker, Farm Security Administration, throughout the United States, 1941-42, Office of War Information, Rhode Island and New Mexico, 1942-43, and Standard Oil

Company of New Jersey, 1945-49; also worked with anthropologist Anibal Buitrón, Otavalo study project, Ecuador, 1946; with anthropologists Alexander H. Leighton and Allan R. Holmberg, in Canada, Navajo Indian Reservation, and Peru, 1951-54. Freelance photographer, working for *Fortune, Ladies Home Journal,* etc., since 1949; has concentrated on anthropological photo studies, since 1955. Professor of Education and Anthropology, California State University, San Francisco; Instructor in Photography, San Francisco Art Institute. **Recipient:** Wennergen Fellowship, 1950; Guggenheim Fellowship, 1957. **Address:** Muir Beach, Sausalito, California 94965; and General Delivery, Ranchos de Taos, New Mexico 87557, U.S.A.

Selected Group Exhibitions:

1955   *FSA Anniversary Show,* Brooklyn Museum, New York
1962   *The Bitter Years: FSA Photographs 1935-41,* Museum of
           Modern Art, New York (toured the United States)
1968   *Just Before the War,* Newport Harbor Art Museum, Newport
           Beach, California
1976   *FSA Photographers,* Witkin Gallery, New York
1978   *Roy Stryker: Humane Propagandist,* International Museum of
           Photography, George Eastman House, Rochester, New York
1979   *Images de l'Amérique en Crise: Photos de la FSA,* Centre
           Georges Pompidou, Paris
           Amerika Fotografie 1920-1940, Kunsthaus, Zurich
1980   *Les Années Ameres de l'Amérique en Crise 1935-42,* Galerie
           Municipale du Chateau d'Eau, Toulouse, France
           Images of America: Photography from the FSA, Sonoma State
           University, California
           Amerika: Traum und Depression 1920-40, Kunstverein,
           Hamburg (toured West Germany)

Collections:

Museum of Modern Art, New York; Library of Congress, Washington, D.C.; University of New Mexico, Albuquerque; San Francisco Art Institute.

Publications:

By COLLIER: Books—*The Awakening Valley,* with Anibal Buitrón, Chicago 1949; *Visual Anthropology: Photography as a Research Method,* New York 1967, revised and expanded edition, with Malcolm Collier, Albuquerque 1986; *Alaskan Eskimo Education: A Film Analysis of Cultural Confrontation in the Classroom,* New York 1973. **Article**—"Navajo Housing in Transition," with M.A. Tremblay and T.T. Sasakai in *America Indigena* (Mexico City), vol. 14, no. 3, 1954.

On COLLIER: Books—*Poverty and Politics: The Rise and Fall of the FSA* by Sidney Baldwin, Chapel Hill, North Carolina 1968; *The Years of Bitterness and Pride: FSA Photographs 1934-1943,* edited by Haig Akamakjian, compiled by Jerry Kearns and Leroy Bellamy, New York 1975; *Portrait of a Decade: Roy Stryker and the Development of Documentary Photography in the Thirties* by F. Jack Hurley, Baton Rouge, Louisiana 1972, New York 1977; *A Vision Shared: A Classic Portrait of America and Its People 1935-43,* edited by Hank O'Neal, New York and London 1976; *Dorothea Lange: A Photographer's Life* by Milton Meltzer, New York 1978; *Amerika Fotografie 1920-1940* by Erika Billeter, Berne 1979; *Maryland: Time Exposures 1840-1940* by Mame Warren and Marion E. Warren, Baltimore and London 1984; *Official Images: New Deal Photography,* by Pete Daniel et al, Washington DC 1987; *Documentary America, 1935-1943,* edited by Carl Fleishhauser and Beverley W Brannan, Berkeley, Los Angeles, Oxford, 1988.

*   *   *

John Collier's ideas on the status of his photography are suggestive: he has said, for instance, that he would not be interested in a compilation of his pictures "as art"; "being there" was more important than "the print"; the photograph, rather, is a "testament" to being there, a record. While such views might seem to place the emphasis fundamentally on the phenomena of the material universe—and he has also said that the photographer, unlike the painter, cannot photograph "what is in his head"—I suspect that this degree of reverence for materiality is actually more akin to transcendentalism.

He has always been attracted to sequential stories, to film-making and, especially, to the photo-essay. An accomplished writer, from his fine descriptive letters to Roy Stryker, his first employer at the Farm Security Administration in the 1940's, to the present, it is as if words emphasize the movement through time which the photograph simultaneously denies and affirms. From this perspective, perhaps his most exciting work is *The Awakening Valley,* on Otavalo, Ecuador, with its stunning views of the Andes, journeys to and from market, the processes of crafts, and people in all their variety.

His father, John Collier Sr., was President F.D. Roosevelt's radical Commissioner for Indian Affairs. As he was brought up to be aware of and respectful towards other cultures, it is not surprising that the bulk of Collier's photography has been devoted to anthropological subjects, whether pictures of munitions factory life for the FSA, Native American tribal activities, or Canadian Maritime communities. And in both his conversation and writing—especially his classic *Visual Anthropology*—he views photographs as a means to materialize people themselves through such things as their worn doorsteps, the fabric of their houses, etc. His famous portrait of "Grandfather Romero, Trampas, New Mexico," 1943, depicts an old man oddly situated in the bottom left of the frame with part of his bed in the bottom right and a large expanse of wall behind him—at least he seems oddly situated until we realize that that is precisely the point: behind him, like a religious tryptich, is a picture of Jesus, a genre print and, between them, a group of family snapshots and the elaborately framed portrait of a young man in military uniform. These objects visually balance Romero in the picture and literally indicate the rounds of his life: religion, family, traditional community activities and the place he lays his head.

—G.M. Gidley

COLVIN, Calum.

Nationality: British. **Born:** Glasgow, Scotland, 26 October 1961. **Education:** Studied sculpture, Duncan of Jordanstone College of Art, Dundee, 1979-83, Dip. 1983; studied photography, Royal College of Art, London, 1983-85, M.A. 1985. **Family:** Married Shirley Moore in 1988; children: Heather and Robbie. **Career:** Part-time Lecturer in Fine Art and Printmaking, Duncan of Jordanstone College of Art, Dundee, since 1993. **Agent:** Zelda Cheatle Gallery, 8 Cecil Court, London WC2N 4HE. **Address:** 7 East Brighton Crescent, Edinburgh EH15 1LR, Scotland.

Individual Exhibitions:

1987   Riverside Studios, London
           Seagate Gallery, Dundee
1988   Friedman-Guinness Gallery, Heidelberg, Germany
           Galeria 57, Madrid, Spain
           DC Art, New South Wales, Australia
1989   California State University, Long Beach
           Salama Caro Gallery, London
           Friedman-Guinness Gallery, Frankfurt, Germany
1990   Haggerty Museum, Wisconsin, U.S.A.
           Torch Gallery, Amsterdam, Netherlands
           Fruitmarket Gallery, Edinburgh
1991   Salama Caro Gallery, London
           The Two Ways of Life, Art Institute of Chicago, U.S.A.
           Willy d'Huysser Gallery, Knokke Zout, Belgium
1992   *The Two Ways of Life,* San Francisco Museum of Modern Art,
           U.S.A.; Nickle Arts Museum, Calgary, Canada; Winnipeg
           Art Gallery, Canada
1993   *The Seven Deadly Sins and the Four Last Things,* Portfolio
           Gallery, Edinburgh; The Photographers' Gallery, London
           Badischer Kunstverein, Karlsruhe, Germany

The Deaf Man's Villa (detail), **1990 (original in colour).** Photograph by Calum Colvin.

1994   *The Seven Deadly Sins and the Four Last Things,* Photography
        Centre of Athens, Greece; Royal Photographic Society, Bath,
        England

Selected Group Exhibitions:

1985   *The 85 Degree Show,* Serpentine Gallery, London
1986   *Constructed Narratives,* (with Ron O'Donnel) Photographers'
        Gallery, London; Stills Gallery, Edinburgh; Watershed,
        Bristol; Arts Centre, Glasgow; Primavera Photographie,
        Bracelona; Recontres Internationales de la Photographie,
        Arles, France
1987   *Towards a Bigger Picture,* Victoria and Albert Museum,
        London
        The Vigorous Imagination, Scottish National Gallery of
        Modern Art
1988   *Two Scottish Photographers,* Richard Pomoroy Gallery,
        London
1989   *Machine Dreams,* Photographers' Gallery, London
        Through the Looking Glass, Photographic Art in Britain 1945-
        89, Barbican Art Gallery, London (travelled to the
        Manchester City Art Gallery)
        Das Konstruierte Bild, Kunstverein Munich; Kunsthalle,
        Nurnberg; Forum, Bremen; Kunstverein, Karlsruhe; Ansel
        Adams Center, San Francisco
1990   *Photography on Site,* California State University
        New Scottish Photography, at *Fotofest,* Houston, (travelled to
        the Scottish National Portrait Gallery)

Collections:

Victoria and Albert Museum, London; Metropolitan Museum of Modern Art,
New York; Scottish National Portrait Gallery, Edinburgh; Scottish Arts
Council; The British Council; Contemporary Art Society, London; Museum of
Fine Art, Houston, Texas; Museum of Modern Art, Edinburgh; Museum
Ludwig, Cologne, Germany.

Publications:

On COLVIN: Books—*Constructed Narratives,* exhibition catalogue, with
text by David Brittain, London 1986; *The Vigorous Imagination,* exhibition
catalogue, with text by Keith Hartley, Edinburgh 1987; *New Scottish Photography,* exhibition catalogue, with text by David Brittain and Sara Stevenson,
Edinburgh 1990; *British Photography towards a Bigger Picture,* New York
1988; *Through the Looking Glass, Photographic Art in Britain 1945-1989,*
exhibition catalogue, with text by Gerry Badger and John Benton-Harris,
London 1989; *The Two Ways of Life,* exhibition catalogue, with text by Colin
Westerbeck and David Mellor, London 1991; *Calum Colvin,* exhibition
catalogue, Edinburgh 1990; *The Seven Deadly Sins and the Four Last Things,*
exhibition catalogue, with text by Tom Normand, Edinburgh 1993. **Articles**—
"Calum Colvin" by Natasha Edwards in *Artforum,* September 1990; "Calum
Colvin" by Robert MacDonald in *Contemporanea,* February 1990; "Calum
Colvin and the Seven Deadly Sins" by James Lawson in *Portfolio Magazine,*
1993. **Films**—*Arena—New Scottish Art,* BBC television, 1988; *Gallery,*
Channel 4 television, 1989; *Prudential Awards for the Arts,* London Weekend
television, 1993.

*

My work consists of constructed photographic images, utilising painted
scenery, montage and trompe l'oeil techniques to construct sculptural tableaux, predominantly dealing with issues of culture and society.

The most recent body of work I have produced, *The Seven Deadly Sins and
the Four Last Things,* utilises computer manipulation to produce meditations
on Bosch's *Tondo* and references to history, politics and literature.

—Calum Colvin

*   *   *

Training in Scotland at a time when Scottish painters were once again
making a worldwide name for themselves with fresh figurative work, Calum
Colvin decided to change direction from sculpture to photography. Although
he was accepted at the Royal College of Art on the basis of a portfolio of black
and white street pictures, he had already begun to work on his made images.
By the time he left college, he had a fine body of work which was new, exciting
and obviously Scottish. This was shown very quickly by the Photographers'
Gallery and subsequently toured extensively in Britain and abroad under the
auspices of the British Council. He has continued to work extremely hard and
successfully, showing extensively and selling well.

Calum's work came as a breath of fresh air because while it has some self-
referential iconography within it, it also makes references to art history, myths
and legends, which are part of our common heritage, and contains a humourous
element which has been missing from contemporary photography for some
time. Much was made of his method of working, building his sets from various
items of junk collected from car boot sales, painting over them to make an
image which could only be seen to make sense through the camera lens and
usually introducing his kilt-clad "Action-man" figure to represent himself or
one of the protagonists in the dramas his pictures portrayed. He is now
exploring the possibilities of computer technology combined with his photographs and chosen texts, and although the first experiments resulted in rather
flat images, the latest ones are, to an increasing extent, restoring the original
depth.

Method alone would not hold our attention for long and the real interest in
this work lies in the ideas behind it. Calum is political in a humanist sense, and
combines his knowledge of history and legend with the way in which we treat
our planet and ourselves to point out the repetitive nature of our mistakes. His
research is very thorough and both old writings and painting from the past can
inspire him as in his series *The Seven Deadly Sins and the Four Last Things*
based on the Hieronymous Bosch tondo. His use of colour adds to the drama of
these story pictures and his wry sense of humour encourages us to explore the
messages they contain.

—Sue Davies

CONNOR, Linda (Stevens).

Nationality: American. **Born:** New York City, 18 November 1944. **Educa-
tion:** Studied photography, under Harry Callahan, at the Rhode Island School
of Design, Providence, 1962-66, B.F.A. 1967; and under Aaron Siskind at the
Institute of Design, Illinois Institute of Technology, Chicago, 1966-69, M.S.
1969. **Career:** Freelance photographer, based in San Francisco, since 1966.
Instructor, San Francisco Art Institute, since 1969 (held Graduate Chair, 1975;
Co-Chairperson, Photography Department, 1973-75). Has also taught at San
Francisco State University, 1972; California College of Arts and Crafts,
Summer 1970, Spring 1973; University of California Extension at Berkeley,
1973; and School of the Museum of Fine Arts, Boston, Fall 1978. **Recipient:**
National Endowment for the Arts Individual Grant, 1976 and 1988; Photo
Survey Grant, 1981; AT&T. Photography Project Grant, 1978; Guggenheim
Fellowship, 1979; Individual Artist Grants, Marin Arts Council, 1986; "Pho-
tographer of the Year Award," Peer Awards, Friends of Photography, 1986;
The Charles Pratt Memorial Award, 1988. **Agents:** Haines Gallery, 49 Geary
Street, San Francisco, California 94108; Howard Greenburg Gallery, 120
Wooster, New York, New York 10012; Scheinbaum and Russet Gallery, 328
Guadalupe, Santa Fe, New Mexico 87501. **Address:** 87 Rutherford Avenue,
San Anselmo, California 94960, and c/o Department of Photography, San
Francisco Art Institute, 800 Chestnut Street, San Francisco, California 94133,
U.S.A.

Individual Exhibitions:

1969   School of the Dayton Art Institute, Ohio
1970   San Francisco Art Institute
1971   Focus Gallery, San Francisco

Lotus, Kashmir, India, **1985.** Photograph by Linda Connor.

Corcoran Photographic Workshop, Washington, D.C.
Lomis School, Connecticut
School of the Art Institute of Chicago
1972 Let A Dark, San Rafael, California
1973 Hallway Gallery, San Francisco Art Institute Light Gallery,
      New York
1974 Tyler School of Art, Philadelphia
      Portland School of Art, Oregon
      Merramec Community College, St. Louis
1975 University of Colorado, Boulder
      218 Gallery, Memphis, Tennessee
      Center Gallery, University of California Extension at Berkeley
      Slightly Sloping Gallery, Visual Studies Workshop, Rochester,
      New York
1976 Spectrum Gallery, Tucson, Arizona
      Susan Spiritus Gallery, Newport Beach, California
      Center Gallery, Sun Valley, Idaho
      Center for Photographic Studies, Louisville, Kentucky
1977 Bard College, Annandale-on-Hudson, New York
      De Young Memorial Museum, San Francisco
1978 Light Gallery, New York
      Linda Connor and Nicholas Nixon, Massachusetts College of
      Art, Boston

1979 Los Angeles Institute of Contemporary Art
1980 Light Factory, Charlotte, North Carolina
      Eclipse Gallery, Boulder, Colorado
      Light Gallery, Los Angeles
      *Landscape Images: Recent Photographs by Linda Connor,
      Judy Fiskin, Ruth Thorne-Thomsen,* La Jolla Museum of
      Contemporary Art, California
1981 *Images of Asia,* Light Gallery, New York
      North Light Gallery, Arizona State University, Tempe
      Linda Connor: Images Past and Present, Vision Gallery,
      Boston
      Ancient Currents Gallery, San Francisco
      Silver Image Gallery, Ohio State University, Columbus
1983 California Museum of Photography, Riverside (with Francois
      Descamps)
1984 *Foreign Views,* Friends of Photography, Carmel, California
1985 *Linda Connor,* Metropolitan Museum and Art Center, Coral
      Gables, Florida
1986 Kalamazoo Institute of Art, Kalamazoo, Michigan
1987 Colorado Gallery of the Arts, Arapahoe Community College,
      Little Colorado
1988 *Linda Connor,* Art Institute of Chicago, Chicago
      Gallery Min, Tokyo

1990   *Spiral Journey,* Museum of Contemporary Photography,
        Chicago (travelling tour for two years)
1992   *Earthly Constellations,* San Francisco Museum of Modern Art,
        San Fancisco (travelling)
1993   *Sacred Places from Around the World,* Cuesta College Art
        Gallery, San Luis Obispo, California
        Tibet, A Land of Light and Shadow, Haines Gallery, San
        Francisco

Selected Group Exhibitions:

1969   *Vision and Expression,* International Museum of Photography,
        George Eastman House, Rochester, New York (toured the
        United States, 1969-71)
1973   *Light and Lens,* Hudson River Museum, Yonkers, New York
1974   *14 American Photographers,* Baltimore Museum of Art
        (travelled to the Newport Harbor Art Museum, California;
        La Jolla Museum of Contemporary Art, California; Walker
        Art Center, Minneapolis; and Fort Worth Art Museum,
        Texas)
1977   *The Great West: Real/Ideal,* University of Colorado, Boulder
        (subsequently Smithsonian Institution travelling exhibition:
        toured the United States)
1978   *Mirrors and Windows: American Photography since 1960,*
        Museum of Modern Art, New York (toured the United
        States, 1978-80)
1980   *New Landscapes, Part II,* Friends of Photography, Carmel,
        California
1981   *American Photographers and the National Parks,* Corcoran
        Gallery, Washington, D.C. (toured the United States)
1984   *Photography in California 1945-80,* San Francisco Museum of
        Modern Art (travelling)
1985   *American Images 1945-80,* Barbican Art Gallery, London
        (toured Britain)
1986   *Artists in Mid-Career,* San Francisco Museum of Modern Art,
        San Francisco
1987   *Photography and Art 1946-86,* Los Angeles County
        Museum of Art
        Reclaiming Paradise—American Women Photograph the Land,
        Tweed Museum of Art, University of Minnesota, Duluth
        (catalogue)
1988   *Landscapes from the Permanent Collection,* Corcoran Gallery
        of Art, Washington D.C.
1989   *Photography's Sesquicentennial—Masterpieces from the Col-
        lections,* Stanford Museum, California
        Selected Photographs, 17 American Embassies in Europe
        through USIA
1990   *The Indomitable Spirit—Photographers and Artists Respond in
        the Time of AIDS,* International Center of Photography,
        Midtown, New York City
1991   *To Collect the Art of Women: The Jane Reese Williams
        Collection of Photography,* Museum of New Mexico, Santa
        Fe, New Mexico
1992   *Between Home and Heaven: Contemporary American Land-
        scape Photography,* National Museum of American Art,
        Washington D.C. (travelling)
        *The Country Between Us: Contemporary American Landscape
        Photographs,* Huntington Gallery, Massachusetts College of
        Art, Boston
        Charles Pratt Memorial Award Exhibition, Center for Creative
        Photography, The University of Arizona, Tucson, Arizona
        Harry Callahan and Linda Connor, Light Factory, Charlotte,
        North Carolina
        Mexico Thrugh Foreign Eyes, Museo de Arte Contemporaneo,
        Rufino Tamayo, Mexico City
1993   *Women in Photography,* Scheinbaum & Russek Ltd, Santa Fe,
        New Mexico
        Recent Acquisitions in the Siskind Center, Museum of Art,
        Rhode Island School of Design, Providence, Rhode Island

1994   *Beauty in the Beast,* National Wildlife Art Museum, Jackson
        Hole, Wyoming

Collections:

Museum of Modern Art, New York; International Museum of Photography,
George Eastman House, Rochester, New York; Visual Studies Workshop,
Rochester, New York; Museum of Fine Arts, Boston; Polaroid Corporation
Collection, Cambridge, Massachusetts; Art Institute of Chicago; High Muse-
um, Atlanta; Center for Creative Photography, University of Arizona, Tucson;
San Francisco Museum of Modern Art; Australian National Gallery, Canberra;
Center for Creative Photography, University of Arizona; J. Paul Getty
Museum; Stanford Art Museum; National Museum of American Art, Wash-
ington D.C.

Publications:

By CONNOR: Book—*Solos,* Millerton, New York 1979.

On CONNOR: Books—*Be-Ing Without Clothes* by Minor White, Millerton,
New York 1970; *Private Realities,* exhibition catalogue, Boston 1974; *14
American Photographers,* exhibition catalogue, Baltimore 1974; *The Less
Than Sharp Show,* exhibition catalogue, Chicago 1977; *Darkroom,* New York
1977; *Mirrors and Windows: American Photography since 1960* by John
Szarkowski, New York 1978; *American Images: New Work by 20 Contempo-
rary Photographers,* edited by Renato Danese, New York 1979; *American
Photographers and the National Parks,* New York 1981; *International
Photography 1920-1980,* edited by Ian North, Canberra 1982; *Photography in
California 1945-1980* by Louise Katzman, San Francisco 1984; *American
Images: Photographs 1945-1980,* edited by Peter Turner, London 1985;
Photography and Art 1946-86, exhibition catalogue, by Andy Grundberg and
Kathleen M. Gauss, Los Angeles 1987; *Marks in Place,* New Mexico 1987;
Spiral Journey, with introduction by Denise Miller-Clark and essay by
Rebecca Solnit, Chicago 1990; *Women in Photography,* edited by Constance
Sullivan, New York 1990; *Between Home and Heaven: Contemporary
American Landscape Photography,* National Museum of American Art,
Smithsonian Institution and the University of New Mexico Press, 1992.
Articles—''Singular Developments: Polaroid's Paean to Color'' by Allen
Robertson in *TWA/Ambassador* (St. Paul, Minnesota), December 1979;
''Linda Connor, Light Gallery'' by Lynn Zelevansky in *Flash Art* (Milan),
Summer 1981; ''Currents: American Photography Today'' in *Modern Pho-
tography* (New York), August 1981.

*

I can clearly recall watching the clouds moving past my window and
perceiving, for the first time, their passage around the earth; my breathless
investigations of snowflakes on my sleeve before they would melt; the
intricate patterns of an Oriental rug which, decades later, I would recognize
again instantly.

As a child I was alone amidst the substance and power of the world, an
awed and fascinated witness. Photography re-establishes that state of absorption and wonderment, of unfiltered experience. It both grounds and nurtures
my imagination.

Discipline and an attitude of openness provide the proper medium for the
flow of creative energy. It is a privilege to serve and transform this elusive
force; it enriches my life, surpasses my knowledge, and remains far more
profound than I.

—Linda Connor

*   *   *

For Linda Connor, more than for most photographers, the act of photographing is a conscious probing of her subconscious, rather than an expression
of an emotion toward the subject—an act of discovery rather than a
confirmation of self-recognition. This has led, as the work of years has been
gathered, to a disparate group of images, bound together by the strong thread
of a formal structure, initiated, she believes, by her admiration for the work of
Walker Evans. In the late 1960's Connor photographed collage-like arrange-

ments of photographs, some distinctly biographical, such as portraits from her mother's high-school yearbook; the production involved negative and print manipulation and some hand-coloring. From this she moved to still-life arrangements; the material she collected for them continued to suggest the appeal to her of subjects with a personally sentimental history. It reflected as well her exploration of the relationship between art and nature—a reproduction of Botticelli's *Venus* combined with shells, for instance. She also recycled earlier photographs of her own, combining them with found objects or reproductions of fine and folk art in unlikely juxtapositions that produced, for her, revelatory images.

This search for revelation has continued in Connor's view photographs. The earliest of these were taken with a camera her great-aunt had used when she studied with Clarence White, an 8 x 10 Century with a lens as soft as an astigmatic eye. The prints were produced by contact and toned with goldchloride, a procedure used more for its somewhat antique effect than for notions of purity. Because of the soft focus and the blossom of ambient light that appeared around the center of the image, these photographs of landscapes and objects in them have a mysterious, tantalizing effect. The subject, though recognizable, can not be fully grasped, and the failure of definition often suggests something other than what is actually portrayed.

After publishing these soft-focus photographs in her book *Solos*, Connor started using a view camera with a hard lens. Her object then became to find subjects that even when fully revealed would appear surreal. Her search for personally meaningful subject matter—which she most often has found in non-Western cultures, in ancient architecture and in wilderness—has taken her to Central America, to the Far East and Europe, as well as to the Southwest of the United States. While her photographs in these various locations may include people, more often she places a ritual site, an ancient tree or an inscription in stone at the center of them. She makes these photographs of objects as animated as those with people in them through her attention to tone and continuous line, which provides a sort of gesture.

The visual jolt of an image that transcends reality is felt in Linda Connor's best photographs. That is what she is really after. "When my pictures stop telling me things," she says, "I will stop making them."

—Anita V. Mozley

COOPER, Thomas Joshua.

Nationality: American. **Born:** San Francisco, California, 19 December 1946. **Education:** Attended Arcata High School, California, 1960-64; studied art, philosophy and literature, Humboldt State University, Arcata, California, 1965-69, B.A. 1969; photography, under Van Deren Coke, Jim Kraft, Richard Rudisill and Beaumont Newhall, University of New Mexico, Albuquerque, 1970-72, M.A. **Career:** Independent photographer, in England, 1976-79, in the United States, 1979-83, and in Scotland, since 1983. Teacher of Photography, Arcata High School, California, 1969; Instructor of Photography, College of the Redwoods Community College, Eureka, California, 1970; Teacher, Dana Elementary School, Nipoma, California, 1971; Visiting Lecturer in Photography, Institute of American Indian Art, Sante Fe, New Mexico, 1973; Senior Lecturer in Photography and History of Photography, and Course Director, Trent Polytechnic, Nottingham, England, 1973-76. Visiting Assistant Professor of Art, Humboldt State University, Arcata, California, 1979-82; Head of the Photography Department, Glasgow School of Art, Scotland, since 1983. **Recipient:** James D. Phalen Award in Art, Oakland Museum of Art, California, 1971; New Mexico Biennial Fine Art Award, New Mexico Museum of Fine Art, 1973; National Endowment for the Arts Grant, 1978. Photography Bursar for Arts Council of Great Britain, with Joseph Koudelka, 1976-77. **Address:** c/o Glasgow School of Art, 167 Renfrew Street, Glasgow G3 6RQ, Scotland.

Individual Exhibitions:

1971   *I See the God in You,* The Art Center, San Luis Obispo, California

1972   *The Fields We Know: A Myth of Recollection,* University of New Mexico Fine Art Museum, Albuquerque
1973   *Sweet Play,* Quivera Gallery, Albuquerque, New Mexico
        The Shado Gallery, Portland, Oregon
1974   *She Rain,* The Midland Group Gallery, Nottingham, England
        Indications, The Photographers' Gallery, London
1975   *Remnants and Prenotations,* The Arnolfini Gallery, Bristol, England (with Paul Hill)
        The Warwick Gallery, England (with Paul Hill)
        The Spectrum Art Photographic Gallery, Barcelona
1977   *Images of Our Mortality,* The Robert Self Gallery, London
1979   *Paysages,* Bibliothèque Nationale, Paris
        A Place In Between, College of the Redwoods Art Gallery, Eureka, California (with watercolorist Robert Benson; toured the United States)
1981   *Intimations,* Northcoast Art Gallery, Arcata, California (with fiber sculptor Beckie Evans)
1985   Third Eye Centre, Glasgow
        Orchard Gallery, Londonderry, Northern Ireland

Selected Group Exhibitions:

1971   *James D. Phalen Awards Exhibition,* Oakland Museum of Art, California
1972   *New Mexico Biennial Fine Art Exhibition,* New Mexico Museum of Fine Art, Santa Fe
1974   *New Photography: British Arts Council Juried Travelling Exhibition,* Midland Group Gallery, Nottingham, England (toured the U.K.)
1976   *Open Photography: British Arts Council Juried Travelling Exhibition,* Midland Group Gallery, Nottingham, England (toured the U.K.)
1978   *Critic's Choice,* Institute of Contemporary Arts, London
1979   *3 Perspectives on Photography,* Hayward Gallery, London
1980   *A Survey of British Photography 1935-1979,* Arts Council of Great Britain, London
1981   *Photographer as Printmaker,* Ferens Art Gallery, Hull, Yorkshire (travelled to the Museum and Art Gallery, Leicester; Cooper Gallery, Barnsley; Castle Museum, Nottingham; Photographers' Gallery, London)
1984   *La Photographie Créative,* Pavillon des Arts, Paris
1985   *American Images 1945-80,* Barbican Art Gallery, London (toured Britain)

Collections:

Center for Creative Photography, University of Arizona, Tucson; University of New Mexico, Albuquerque; Oakland Museum, California; Humboldt State University, Arcata, California; National Gallery of Canada, Ottawa; Arts Council of Great Britain, London; Open University, London; Victoria and Albert Museum, London; Trent Polytechnic, Nottingham, England; Bibliothèque Nationale, Paris.

Publications:

By COOPER: Books—*The Reflecting Pool,* Arcata, California 1969; *Remnants and Prenotations,* exhibition catalogue, with Paul Hill, London 1975; *Dialogue with Photography,* with Paul Hill, New York, London and Madrid 1979; *Between Dark and Dark,* Edinburgh 1985. **Articles**—"The Carlotta House" in *Hilltopper Review* (Arcata, California), 1967; "Such Were the Joys . . . " in *Hilltopper Review* (Arcata, California), 1968; "Can British Photography Emerge from the Dark Ages?" with Paul Hill, in *Creative Camera* (London), September 1974; "Paul Strand: An Appreciation," with Paul Hill, in *British Journal of Photography,* (London), 13 February 1976; "Imogen: A Celebration," with Gerry Badger, in *The British Journal of Photography Annual,* London 1978.

On COOPER: Books—*New Photography,* exhibition catalogue, by Jean-Claude Lemagny and Aaron Scharf, Nottingham, England 1974; *Open Photography,* exhibition catalogue, by Allan Porter and Keith Arnatt, Nottingham, England 1976; *Other Eyes,* exhibition catalogue, by Peter Turner, London 1976; *Photomiscellany: 120 Years of International Photographic History,* exhibition catalogue, by Angus Stokes, Bakewell, Derbyshire 1978; *Critics Choice,* exhibition catalogue, by John McEwen, London 1978; *Perspectives on Landscape: British Image 5,* selected and edited by Bill Gaskins, London 1978; *Photography in New Mexico* by Van Deren Coke, Albuquerque, New Mexico 1979; *Three Perspectives on Photography: Recent Photography in Britain,* exhibition catalogue, by Paul Hill, London 1979; *The History of Photography in the 20th Century* by Petr Tausk, Cologne 1977, London 1980; *New Works of Contemporary Art and Music,* edited by Graeme Murray, Edinburgh 1981; *La Photographie Créative* by Jean-Claude Lemagny, Paris 1984; *American Images: Photographs 1945-1980,* edited by Peter Turner, London 1985. **Article**—"The British Obsession—About to Pay Off" by William Messer in *U.S. Camera Annual,* New York 1977.

*

My photographs are meditations; it is as simple as that. They are concerned with myths and rituals of the land, and with a yearning to more fully comprehend them. For over a decade I have been involved in concentrated research into the attitudes of the mythic and the meditative in photography. My photographs generally suggest these researches by containing three primary areas of inquiry: Ritual Indications, Ritual Guardians, and Ritual Grounds. It is around such ritual "sightings" that both the conceptual and formal basis for my work occurs.

The works are often autobiographical in reference, always sequentially structured, and invariably reliquarily involved. Early "primitive" myths and legends from North America and the British Isles seem to inspire the work and to infuse its making. The works are, however, constructions, illusions, inventions—*discoveries.*

Photography is the form of my art. Myth is the essence. For me, photography must always be a function and a process of Heart. My photographs, then, are more the products of revelation than that of actual direct documentation of place.

—Thomas Joshua Cooper

*   *   *

Although the hard work associated with heading the department of photography at Glasgow Art School might be expected to lessen one's time and energy for the creation of new work, for Thomas Joshua Cooper it has the opposite effect. He has always been an inspirational teacher and clearly there is a reciprocal process with his students. His work is increasingly recognised throughout Europe and he has been chosen on more than one occasion to represent Great Britain abroad.

The major retrospective of his work chosen by the Gulbenkian Foundation to mark the end of Lisbon's year as European City of Culture and the beginning of Portugal's Presidency of the EEC took place during the winter of 1994/95 and includes many of his large photographs of the sea. This departure from landscape to seascape has taken place over the past four or five years and at the same time the pictures themselves are made in a much larger format, sometimes reaching almost a metre square. Although he does still make contact prints on occasion, like all artists he is continually searching for the right means to express his intentions and ideas. This may take the form of small books such as *Handful of Stones,* currently in production, or taking part in group or one man exhibitions. He also enjoys the workshops he gives each year in Salzburg, Invernaid and for Paul Hill in Derbyshire. Art, however made, has to be received, appreciated and understood. As he matures Cooper feels as excited by the possibilities of photography as ever and continues to give pleasure and inspiration to those who appreciate his energy and commitment.

—Sue Davies

CORDIER, Pierre.

Nationality: Belgian. **Born:** Brussels, 28 January 1933. **Education:** Studied political and administrative sciences at the Université Libre, Brussels, 1952-55, and photography with Otto Steinert, in Saarbrucken, 1958. **Military Service:** Served in the Belgian Army, in Longerich, Germany, 1955-57. **Career:** Has worked with "Chimigrams" (chemically produced images on photosensitive materials), Brussels, since 1956; also, freelance photographer, Brussels, 1957-67. Lecturer, Ecole Nationale Supérieure d'Arts Visuels, Brussels, since 1965. Corresponding Member, Deutsche Gesellschaft für Photographie (DGPh), since 1971. Member, European Society for the History of Photography; AMINA World Association for Inventors and Researchers. **Address:** Pié Le Breou, Hameau Les Cordiers, F-84490 Saint-Saturnin-lès-Apt.

Individual Exhibitions:

1962	*Pierre Cordier,* Studio 28, Paris
1964	*Chimigrammes de Pierre Cordier,* Galerie Vanderborght, Brussels
1967	*Denis Brihat/Pierre Cordier/Jean-Pierre Sudre: A European Experiment,* Museum of Modern Art, New York
1970	*Chimigrammi di Pierre Cordier,* Galleria Il Diaframma, Milan
1974	*Chimigrammes de Pierre Cordier,* Galerie Michel Vokaer, Brussels
1975	*Pierre Cordier: Chimigrammes,* Galerie du Disque Rouge, Brussels (travelled to Gesbanque, Amis du Musée, Verviers, Belgium)
1976	*Pierre Cordier: Chimigrammi,* Galeria Spectrum, Barcelona
	Pierre Cordier: Chimigramme, Galerie Die Brücke, Vienna
	20 Ans de Chimigrammes, Palais des Beaux-Arts, Brussels (retrospective; travelled to the Maison de la Culture, Namur, Belgium, 1977)
1977	*Chimigrammes de Pierre Cordier,* Galerie du Château d'Eau, Toulouse (retrospective)
	20 Years of Chimigrams, Neikrug Galleries, New York
	Chimigrammen van Pierre Cordier, Galerie Paule Pia, Antwerp
1979	*Pierre Cordier: Chimigrammes,* Bibliothéque Nationale, Paris
1980	*Pierre Cordier,* Galerie Anne Van Horenbeeck, Brussels
	Pierre Cordier, Atelier Charles de Trooz, Louvain-la-Neuve, Belgium
	Pierre Cordier: Chimigrammes, Musée Réattu, Arles, France (retrospective; travelled to the Musée Nicéphore Niepce, Chalon-sur-Saône, France)
1981	*Photography and Chemigram,* Galerie FNAC, Paris
1982	*Le Désespoir du Peintre,* Galerie l'Autre Musée, Brussels
	Chimigrammen, Akademie, Antwerp, Belgium
1983	Benteler Galleries, Houston, Texas
	Imprimatur Gallery, Minneapolis, Minnesota
	Université Catholique de Louvain-la-Neuve, Belgium
	Galleria Il Diaframma, Milan (with T. Wroblewski and A. Grippo)
1984	Laurence Miller Gallery, New York
1985	Shadai Gallery, Tokyo
1986	Galerie Photo Art, Basle, Switzerland (with Gérald Minkoff)
	Hergrammes, Hommage à Hergé, Libreria Agorà, Turin, Italy
1987	Galerie d'Art Actuel Georgette Ballegeer, Liège
1988	Musées Royaux des Beaux-Arts de Belgique, Art Moderne, Brussels
	Notre-Dame de Beauregard, Orgon, Provence
1991	Galerie Le Miroir d'Encre, Brussels

Selected Group Exhibitions:

1958	*Subjektive Fotografie III,* at *Photokina,* Cologne
1967	*A European Experiment,* Museum of Modern Art, New York
1968	*Generative Fotografie,* Kunsthaus, Bielefeld, West Germany

Chemigram Detail **from** ***La Suma*** **by Jorge Luis Borges, 1991.** Photograph by Pierre Cordier.

1969   *Vision and Expression,* International Museum of Photography,
        George Eastman House, Rochester, New York (toured the
        United States, 1969-71)
1972   *Octave of Prayer,* Massachusetts Institute of Technology,
        Cambridge
1976   *Generative Fotografie,* Galerie Spectrum, Hannover
1981   *Auto-Portraits Photographiques,* Centre Georges
        Pompidou, Paris
1983   *Lensless Photography,* Franklin Institute Science Museum,
        Philadelphia (travelled to IBM Gallery, New York)
1984   *Subjektive Fotografie: Images of the 50s,* San Francisco
        Museum of Modern Art (toured the United States and
        Europe)
1985   *Signes et Ecritures,* Centre d'Art Contemporain, Brussels
1986   *Subjektive Fotografie,* Palais des Beaux-Arts, Brussels
1987   *Photographs beget photographs,* The Minneapolis Institute of
        Arts, Minneapolis
        Photogrammes, 1918 jusqu'à nos jours, Goethe-Institute,
        München
1988   *Naissance d'une collection,* Fondation Vincent Van
        Gogh, Arles
1989   *Materia Prima,* Fonds Régional d'Art Contemporain, Marseille
1990   *Tire la langue ou les irrégulliers du langage,* Beaunord, Centre
        Wallonie-Bruxelles, Paris
1991   *Otto Steinert und Schüler. Fotografie und Ausbildung 1948 bis
        1978,* Museum Folkwang, Essen
1992   *Denis Brihat et ses amis: Jean-Pierre Sudre, Jerry Uelsman et
        Pierre Cordier,* Galerie de la Gare, Bonnieux
1993   *Jorge Luis Borges,* Centre Georges Pompidou, Paris
1994   *La Ville,* Centre Georges Pompidou, Paris
        Les mots dans la peinture, l'Autre Musée-Martyrs, Brussels
        Visiones Urbanas-Europa 1870-1993, Centro de Cultura
        Contemporanea, Barcelona

Collections:

Folkwang Museum, Essen; Ministry of Culture, Brussels; Musées Royaux des Beaux-Arts, Brussels; Musée d'Ixelles, Brussels; Crédit Communal, Brussels; Provinciaal Museum voof Fotografie, Antwerp; Musée des Beaux-Arts, Liège; Musée de Verviers; Musée de la Photographie, Charleroi; Musée d'Art Moderne, Brussels; Museum of Modern Art, New York; International Museum of Photography, George Eastman House, Rochester, New York; Fogg Art Museum, Harvard University, Cambridge, Massachusetts; Gernsheim Collection, University of Texas at Austin; Center for Creative Photography, University of Arizona, Tucson; Institute of Art, Minneapolis; Bibliothèque Nationale, Paris; Musée Nicéphore Niépce, Chalon-sur-Saône; Musée de Toulon; FRAC, Metz; Musée Réattu, Arles; Fondation Vincent Van Gogh, Arles; Maison Européenne de la Photographie, Paris; Institute of Polytechnics, Tokyo; Centro Cultural, Arte Contemporaneo, Mexico.

Publications:

By CORDIER: Books—*Chimigrammes,* with an introduction by Jean-Michel Folon, Brussels 1974; *20 Years of Chemigrams,* with an interview by Pierre Baudson, Brussels 1976. **Articles**—"Billet de Saarbrücken" in *Contact* (Brussels), May/June 1958; "Dialogue avec les faiseurs d'Images" in *L'Arc* (Aix-en-Provence, France), April 1963; "11 apunti sui chimigrammi" in *Centro Culturale Fiat* (Turin), January 1972; "Denis Brihat" in *Lens en Mens* (Antwerp), February 1976; "John Vink" in *Zoom* (Paris), December 1979; "I Fotografins Gränsområde" in *Album* (Helsinborg, Sweden), January/March 1980; "The Secrets of Chemigrams and Photo-Chemigrams" in *Print Letter* (Zurich), March/April 1980; "Chemigram—A New Approach to Lensless Photography" in *Leonardo* (Oxford), no. 4, 1982; "Edited By" in *European Photography* (Gottingen), no. 18, 1984; "Aux confins de la photographie et de la peinture: le chimigramme" with Jean-Loup Wastrat in *La Recherche Photographique* (Paris), May 1988. **Films**—*Chimigramme,* with Philippe Dasnoy, 1963; *Start,* with Marc Lobet, 1976; *Pierre Cordier, autogramme,* 1991; television—*Puur Cultuur,* interview with Luddo Bekkers, BRT 1, 1984; *Six Nez en l'Air,* magazine of Sélim Sasson, RTBF 1, 1992;

Entretien avec Pierre Cordier, Maison Européenne de la Photographie, Paris, 1994.

On CORDIER: Books—*Selbstportraits* by Otto Steinert, Gütersloh, Germany 1961; *L'Arte Moderna 121: La Fotografia* by Grytzko Mascioni, Milan 1967; *Il Linguaggio Fotografico* by Renzo Chini, Turin 1968; *The Picture History of Photography* by Peter Pollack, New York 1969; *Photography Without a Camera* by Patra Holter, London 1972; *Photographis,* edited by Walter Herdeg, Zurich 1973; *Apparative Kunst* by Herbert W. Franke and Gottfried Jäger, Cologne 1973; *Generative Fotografie* by Gottfried Jäger and K. Holzhäuser, Ravensburg, Germany 1975; *Die Geschichte der Fotografie im 20. Jahrhundert* by Petr Tausk, Cologne 1977, London 1980; *Lexikon der Fotografie,* edited by Hugo Schöttle, Cologne 1978; *Time-Life Photography Yearbook,* edited by Ed Brash, New York 1979; *World Photography,* edited by Bryn Campbell, London 1981; *Fotogramme—die lichtreichen Schatten* by Floris M. Kassel, West Germany 1983; *Subjektive Fotografie: Images of the 50s,* exhibition catalogue, by Ute Eskildsen, Manfred Schmalriede and Dorothy Martinson, Essen, West Germany 1984; *La Photographie Créative* by Jean-Claude Lemagny, Paris 1984; *Pierre Cordier dans le cadre des rappots peinture-photographie,* Université Libre de Bruxelles 1991; *Pour une histoire de la photgraphies en Belgique,* Charleroi 1993; *Right Brain, Left Brain Photography* by Kathryn Marx, New York 1994. **Articles**—"Pierre Cordier" by Allan Porter in *Camera* (Lucerne), May 1971; "Pierre Cordier, uitvinder van de chemigraphie" by Else M. Hooykaas in *Foto* (Amersfoort, Netherlands), September 1970; "Pierre Cordier and His Chemigrams" by Charles Rohonyi in *Novum-Gebrauchsgraphik* (Munich), August 1972; "Chemigrams-Chimigrammes" by Gottfried Jäger in *Graphis* (Zurich), no. 164, 1972; "Chimigrammes, oeuvre ouverte" by Carole Naggar in *Zoom* (Paris), March 1975; "Chemigraphy" by Ed Scully in *Modern Photography* (New York), September 1976; "Technique Alternative" by Roberto Salbitani in *Progresso Fotografico* (Milan), November 1978; "Pierre Cordier" by Jean-Claude Lemagny in *Connaissance des Arts* (Paris), March 1980; "Images Aléatoires de l'Inconnu" by Yves Aubry in *Zoom* (Paris), June 1980; "Art and Alchemy" in *Camera Arts* (New York), December 1982; "Chance and Design" in *Omni* (New York), September 1984; "La Ligne Obscure" in *Clichés* (Brussels), March 1986; "Pierre Cordier: le Coït alchimique" by Michel Baudson in *Clichés* (Brussels), March 1988; *Design Journal* (Seoul, Korea), no. 15, May 1989; *Journal of Contemporary Art* (New York), spring/summer 1990.

*

Painters nowadays ask themselves many questions: what is a painting? What is it to paint? I ask the same questions about photography.

Photography is the "bisociation" (Arthur Koestler) of two sciences: chemistry and optics. And yet, photographers and painters almost always use only optics, pictures made with cameras, and they ignore the creative possibilities of chemistry. The first pioneers (Niépce, Daguerre, Talbot, Bayard) mostly invented photographic chemistry, because the Camera Obscura—and its optics—had already existed for several centuries and were readily used by painters. One can therefore deduce that the chemigram, being the systematic use of photographic chemistry, is more related to the research of the photographic pioneers than to that of the modern photographers.

The CHEMIGRAM (1956) owes its existence to the localized action of chemical substances on a photosensitive surface, without the use of the camera, enlarger or darkroom. From "chemistry" and the Greek "gramma," a written sign, the word "chemigram" conveys both the technique and the resulting image. The chemigram results from the encounter of two chemistries: one is solid, that of the photosensitive surface; the other is liquid, that of the developer and fixer. The developer is the equivalent of the pencil: it produces the blacks and the colors. The fixer, used before the developer, neutralizes its effect and thus produces the white; its role is similar to that of an eraser which, in this case, precedes the pencil. Like a camera, the localizing substances determine the forms and structures of the chemigram. These substances are numberless: they can be hard, soft, oily, dry, sticky, or brittle. By varying these three elements separately or together (photosensitive surfaces, localizing substances, and developer-fixer), the possibilities available to the chemigram process are infinite.

Chemigram = Photography? In conventional photography, the effects of light are localized by the camera, and the developer and fixer act upon the whole photosensitized surface. Inversely, in the chemigram process, light plays only a passive role on the whole photosensitive surface, and the developer and fixer are localized, either successively or simultaneously.

Chemigram = Painting? In painting, matter is applied, accumulated, preserved. It is thus used in an additive manner, by sedimentation. A chemigram, however, is produced by erosion. It is the result of a subtractive action. Indeed, matter is first applied, then gradually eroded until it reaches the absence of matter particular to photography. Thus, lines or shapes are never applied as they are in painting; they are produced by negative action, resulting not from the accumulation of matter but rather by the retraction and elimination of that same matter which creates it.

Chemigram = Photography *and* Painting? The chemigram has no place of its own: it is a painting for a photographer, and a photograph for a painter. This proves that there are at least two possible readings: one by inclusion, the other by exclusion. One interpretation would consist of saying that it combines painting and photography in various ways that are all conveyed by the conjunction "and." Examples: 1) Painting has always been a manual process, in opposition to photography which is a direct physico-chemical process. A chemigram is both one and the other at the same time. 2) The surface in a painting is progressively annexed, again in opposition to photography where the whole surface is treated at once. The chemigram does both at the same time. 3) A painting is unique (and cannot be multiplied); a photograph is multiple (it is directly linked to reproduction). A chemigram, once again, is both at the same time.

One could go on, to describe what a chemigram really is: doing so would define its essential characteristic as being not the conjunction of two elements (photography and painting) but rather the realization of their disparity.

—Pierre Cordier

* * *

Pierre Cordier calls his technique "chemigram." He consistently exploits the nuances of photo-chemicals and coloured dyes acting on photographic emulsions (developers, fixatives and toning materials as examples) without recourse to the camera and other conventional photographic means. Conventional procedures are reversed in order to extend the range of form, tone and colour. Often the fixing solution is used before the developer. Sometimes the solutions are employed simultaneously. Moreover, calculated alterations in the dilution or saturation of these baths, in temperature and immersion time, will produce effects which, carefully noted by Cordier, can, with a degree of precision, be repeated. To concentrate these general effects of colour and tone (in a sense to "draw" the shapes and contours making up the image) Cordier uses what he calls "localizing substances," which in fact replace the camera.

Even the darkroom is superfluous, for chemigrams can be made in full light. Though indispensable in the process, light itself plays a minimal role. The versatility of chemigram techniques is great. Accidental and often striking aberrations occur as an inevitable consequence of operating by such methods. "Chance is my best collaborator," says Cordier, "but it only favours a receptive medium."

Unique images are produced when the base employed directly is photographic paper. If, however, a photographic film or plate is used initially, as in ordinary photographic processes, this negative can be the source of multiple prints virtually identical in appearance.

Cordier has employed his cameraless methods since 1956. The soft, muted colours of his earlier chemigrams for which fixatives and developers were used are permanent; those requiring the application of dyes for heightening the colours less so. Chemigrams do not simply augment a tradition stretching from Fox Talbot to Man Ray and Moholy-Nagy, but bring "light painting" to a colouristic fulfilment in the context of contemporary imagery. Pierre Cordier *invented* the chemigram technique in the true sense of the word. In essence, he produces works which visually combine characteristics attributable both to photography and painting. By a diversity of highly refined techniques Cordier, in his choice of images, is able to marry the impersonal tonal fluency of photography with the painter's "touch." In an important sense his explorations echo the perennial Surrealist concern with the violation of materials and its concomitants in bringing to light new pictorial mechanisms. These means for giving expression to inspiration make tangible the Surrealist idea of a "photography of the mind." In this way Cordier is able to explore an inner and very personal imagery, yet present it in an impersonal and concrete way.

However recondite chemigrams may appear, they are, in a photographic way, believable—as are, for example, crystalline fragments viewed through an electron microscope.

Cordier's synthesis of art and science is entirely in keeping with contemporary preoccupations reflected in cinema, television, video-recording, holography and computer-generated images. As in those media, the artist guides the machine. The means, though vital, play a passive role.

Colour is essential in Cordier's chemigrams. In his commanding hands, it has become immensely efficacious, and so versatile that it can even be chosen (in Cordier's words) "according to a programme similar to Goethe's theory of colours." The hues achieved in his later work, their rich metallic tones mostly derived from photo-emulsion dyes, are wholly compatible with his synthetic light-chemical means. With dyes, Cordier's range of colour is greatly enlarged: cyan, magenta, cobalt blues, chrome greens, alizarin crimson, cadmium yellows and orange make it possible, with the earlier earth colours, to embrace the whole chromatic spectrum.

Though hazard must play its part in Cordier's procedures, it is only within the parameters set by the artist himself. As in painting, the construction of a chemigram is mutable and extensive in time. It is not, as in most conventional photography, instantaneous. Moreover, far from being mass-produced, it sometimes takes Cordier several days to complete one or two chemigrams.

Cordier's subjects, for all their impersonality and uniformity in tonal rendering, appear as organic entities made by the machine, evocative and inviting interpretation. This is so partly by virtue of the medium's intrinsic properties, but mainly I suspect at Cordier's bidding. A subliminal sense of growth is often conveyed: objects or forms appear in genesis or in transition. They materialize or dissolve in improbable ways. This implied movement—indeed, life force—is enhanced by Cordier's predilection for sequential imagery. The source is occasionally in the early consecutive series photographs of Muybridge or in the chronophotography of Marey. Cordier pays homage to both these pioneers in several enigmatic series of photo-chemigrams based on their photographs.

—Aaron Scharf

CORPRON, Carlotta M(ae).

Nationality: American. **Born:** Blue Earth, Minnesota, 9 December 1901. **Education:** Attended English boarding schools, Himalayan Mountains, India, 1905-20; University of Omaha, Nebraska, 1920; studied art, Michigan State Normal College, now Eastern Michigan University, Ypsilanti, 1920-25, B.S. 1925; Teachers College, Columbia University, New York, 1926, M.A. 1926; University of Chicago, 1933; photographic technique, Art Center School, Los Angeles, 1936; private photographic studies, under Gyorgy Kepes, Texas Women's University, Denton, 1944. **Career:** Independent photographer, since 1933. Instructor in Design, Michigan State Normal College, Ypsilanti, 1926; Instructor in Design and Art Education, Women's College of Alabama, now Huntington College, Montgomery, 1926-28; Instructor in Design, Art History and Creative Photography, Texas Women's University, Denton, 1935 until her retirement, 1968. **Agent:** Marcuse Pfeifer Gallery, 568 Broadway, Suite 102, New York, New York 10012. **Address:** 206 Forest, Denton, Texas 76201, U.S.A.

Individual Exhibitions:

1948	Dallas Museum of Fine Arts
1952	Louisiana Art Commission, Baton Rouge
1953	Art Institute of Chicago
	University of Georgia, Athens
1954	Women's University of North Carolina, Chapel Hill
1955	Ohio University, Athens
1977	*Carlotta Corpron: Form and Light: 1942-1949,* Marcuse Pfeifer Gallery, New York
1978	Galleria del Milione, Milan
1980	Texas Women's University, Denton

Carlotta Corpron: Designer with Light, Amon Carter Museum,
Fort Worth, Texas
1985   Avrom Gallery, Dallas, Texas

Selected Group Exhibitions:

1944   *Captured Light,* Norlyst Gallery, New York
1945   *Design with Light,* Art Alliance, Philadelphia
1951   *Contemporary Photography,* Contemporary Arts Association,
Houston
1952   *Abstraction in Photography,* Museum of Modern Art,
New York
1975   *Women of Photography: An Historial Survey,* San Francisco
Museum of Art
1978   *Works on Paper: Southwest 1978,* Dallas Museum of Fine Arts
1979   *Recollections: 10 Women of Photography,* International Center
of Photography, New York (toured the United States)
1980   *Photography's Response to Constructivism,* San Francisco
Museum of Art
        Light Abstractions, University of Missouri, St. Louis
1985   *Light: From Illumination to Pure Radiance,* San Francisco
Museum of Modern Art

Collections:

Museum of Modern Art, New York; Art Institute of Chicago; University of
Indiana, Bloomington; New Orleans Museum of Art, Louisiana; Amon Carter
Museum of Western Art, Fort Worth, Texas; Dallas Museum of Fine Arts;
Center for Creative Photography, University of Arizona, Tucson.

Publications:

By CORPRON: Articles—"Designing with Light" in *Design* (New York),
October 1949; "Light as a Creative Medium" in *Art Education* (New York),
May 1962.

On CORPRON: Books—*The Language of Vision* by Gyorgy Kepes,
Chicago 1944; *Vision in Motion* by László Moholy-Nagy, Chicago 1947; *The
New Landscape in Art and Science* by Gyorgy Kepes, Chicago 1956; *Women
of Photography: An Historical Survey,* edited by Margery Mann and Anne
Noggle, San Francisco 1975; *Works on Paper: Southwest 1978,* exhibition
catalogue, by Robert M. Murdoch, Dallas, Texas 1978; *Recollections: Ten
Women of Photography,* edited by Margaretta K. Mitchell, New York 1979;
Light and Abstraction, exhibition catalogue, by Jean S. Tucker, St. Louis,
Missouri 1980; *Carlotta Corpron: Designer with Light,* exhibition catalogue,
with text by Martha A. Sandweiss, foreword by Gyorgy Kepes, Austin, Texas
and London 1980. **Articles**—"A Creative Approach to Photography" by
Mabel E. Maxey in *Texas Trends in Art Education* (Dallas, Texas), Autumn
1960; "Carlotta Corpron" by Paula E. Bennett in *Photographic Portfolio*
(Dallas, Texas), June 1979; "The Language of Light" by Ken Barrow in
Texas Artist (Dallas), September 1981.

*

Light can literally illumine a commonplace object; model and outline
form; bend and follow curves or straight lines; pass through openings and
transparent objects to create wonderful patterns; create new and exciting
shapes when reflected from surfaces which distort familiar objects; and
dramatically emphasize textures. With all of these fascinating possibilities, the
creative photographer never lacks inspiration or subjects for photographs with
inner vitality and interest.

I photographed for the great joy and satisfaction I experienced. I was
particularly interested in working with glass, plastics, and all surfaces and
materials that reflect and refract light. When an idea for a new series evolved, I
spent hours exploring the subject with LIGHT. I was fascinated by the
geometric purity of a glass cube, and the wonderful patterns that were formed
as the lights played over and through it. Suddenly, I saw a picture in the ground
glass of the camera that I wanted to capture.

My designs with Light were the natural result of having been both a Design
and Creative Photography teacher for many years. I considered myself
fortunate because my vocation and avocation merged.

My photographs represent ten years of exciting, intensive experimentation. After 1955, due to serious health problems, I had to discontinue spending
long hours in the darkrooms. My teaching schedule was very heavy, including
History of Art courses, Advertising Design, Sophomore and Freshman Design—as well as Creative Photography.

My problem through the years is that I have been neither "fish nor fowl,"
that is, photographers could not understand what I was doing, and very few
artists were willing to accept photography as art. I really had photographed to
please myself, not anyone else. If my work has any value it is due to its
originality and my design background. Light always determined the character
of the photograph, and I never approached any subject matter with preconceived ideas.

The subject matter of my work can be classified as follows: nature—
flowers, leaves, shells, etc.; light drawings—moving lights in amusement
parks; light follows form studies; light through glass cubes and glass bricks—
forming designs; space compositions with eggs distorted in reflecting surfaces; fluid light designs reflected from plastic; solarization of flowers and
portraits.

—Carlotta M. Corpron

*   *   *

Carlotta M. Corpron speaks of herself as a "designer with light," a title
that accurately describes her creative expression in photography. As a full-
time teacher of design, art history and photography, she managed to spend a
decade of spare time, nights and weekends, to create a remarkable collection of
elegant black and white light abstractions.

She first started photographing during the 1930's when she tried to interest
students in her class of textile design to study patterns in nature through the use
of a close-up lens. Later in the early 1940's at Texas Women's University in
Denton, Texas, she was asked to develop a course in creative photography. She
began working with light the way a painter works with color. She encouraged
students to make photograms (designs of light and shadow made without a
camera on sensitized paper). In 1942 Moholy-Nagy, the director of the
Institute of Design in Chicago, led a light workshop in Denton; Carlotta
assisted, teaching the students to work with a "light modulator," made by
folding and bending white paper against the light source so as to create patterns
from the interplay of light and form.

Carlotta Corpron, however, credits the visit of another member of the
Institute of Design in Chicago, Gyorgy Kepes, with the true guidance of her
vision. Kepes spent part of 1944 at North Texas State University working on
his seminal book *Language of Vision.* Kepes advised Corpron to work in the
controlled setting of a light box in order to completely control the light source.
She made such a 2 x 3-foot portable studio where subtle amounts of light from
long exposures could be allowed to dwell on the subject, perhaps something as
simple as cut paper. In order to create even more abstract shapes through
repetition of form the photographer often reversed or overlapped the negative.
Her experiments often produced a new kind of metaphorical imagery inspiring
the photographer to use fanciful titles such as "Wind Between the Worlds." In
some compositions, she shone light through and reflected it from paper
weights and glass bricks, cubes and sheets of plastic; in others she used the
pattern of light and shadow created with venetian blinds.

The light abstractions by Carlotta Corpron can be grouped according to
different technical uses of light. They include a series she calls "Nature
Studies" that show her personal delight in lighting natural forms in new ways;
another called "Light Drawings" in which she has tracked moving lights at
night to create lively abstract rhythms; "Light Patterns," a series which
explores the light and shadow of light reflected by and through cut and folded
and different translucent materials; "Light Follows Form," which are experiments with light changing on sculpture and space compositions which work
with illusions of depth and reflection; "Fluid Light Designs" in which the
photographer has transcended the material and captured light as a subject in
itself. There seemed to be no end to her capacity to imagine new light designs
until illness during the 1950's compelled her to cease experimentation. She
continued to teach until her retirement in 1968 and now prints her work for a
new generation of admirers.

The light abstractions of Carlotta Corpron are proof of the strength of her own teaching methods which encouraged students to experiment, to create something new out of material and the imagination. Her own experiments with reflections and refractions of light combine a clear understanding of optical phenomena with a poetic vision of nature to produce visual metaphors for that visible energy we call light.

—Margaretta K. Mitchell

CORRALES, Raúl.

Nationality: Cuban. **Born:** Raúl Corral Varela in Ciego de Avila, Cuba, 29 January 1925. **Education:** Attended C. Arenal High School, Havana; studied graphics technology, Manuel Marquez Sterling School of Press (newspaper) Production, Havana, 1957-59. **Family:** Married Norma Lopez Martinez in 1953; children: Raúl, Norma and Saul. **Career:** Photographer, *Noticias de Hoy* newspaper, Havana, 1945-53; *Revista Carteles* magazine, Havana, 1953-59; and *Periodico Revolución* newspaper, Havana, 1959-62; advertising photographer, Publicitaria Siboney company, Havana, 1957-59; Graphics Editor, *INRA Cuba* magazine, Havana, 1959-62; Director, Central Photo Department, Academia de Ciencias, Havana, 1962-73; Section Director, Consejo de Estado, Havana, 1964-80. **Recipient:** First Prize, *Salon Nacional de Artes Plasticas,* UNEAC, 1979; First Prize, *Salon E. Hart Davalos,* Havana, 1979; Grand Prize, *Salon Nacional,* Havana, 1980; Ministry of Culture Prize, *Salon Nacional,* 1980; Premio de Fotografia Contemporanea y Latinoamericana, Havana, 1981; Premio de Fotografia, Salon de Artes Plasticas, Havana, 1982; Premio Enrique Hart Davalos, Havana, 1982; Special Prize, Ministro de la F.A.R., Havana, 1986. **Address:** 26 Nro. 9015, Cojimar, Havana, Cuba.

Individual Exhibitions:

1980	Galeria de La Habana (retrospective)
	35 con la 35, Casa de la Cultura, Ciego de Avila, Cuba (retrospective; travelled to Union Nacional de Escritores y Artistas de Cuba, Santiago de Cuba)
	Salon de Premiados, Galeria L, University of Havana
1981	Museo Nacional de Bellas Artes, Havana
1982	Museo del Pueblo Combatiente, Havana
1984	Galeria Alejo Carpentier, Camagúey, Cuba
	Ministry of Culture, Moa Holguìn, Cuba
1985	*Homenaje a Raúl Corrales,* Museo Nacional de Bellas Artes, Havana

Selected Group Exhibitions:

1960	*10 Años de Revolución,* Museo de Bellas Artes, Havana (toured Europe and Asia)
1967	*Muestra de la Cultura Cubana,* Pabellon Cuba, Havana
1978	*Historia de la Fotografìa Cubana,* Palacio de Bellas Artes, Mexico City
	Hecho en Latinoamerica, Museo de Arte Moderno, Mexico City (travelled to *Venezia '79*)
1979	*Salon Nacional de Artes Plasticas,* Union Nacional de Escritores y Artistas de Cuba, Havana
1980	*Dos Momentos Revolucionarios,* Consejo Mexicano de Fotografia, Mexico City
1982	*La Photographie Contemporaine en Amerique Latine,* Centre Georges Pompidou, Paris
1984	*Portrait of a Distant Land,* Photography, Paddington, New South Wales

1985	*Cuba: A View from Inside,* Ledel Gallery, New York
1986	*Girón,* Centro de Arte, Havana

Collections:

Union de Escritores y Artistas de Cuba, Havana; Instituto Nacional de Bellas Artes, Museo de Bellas Artes, Mexico City; Consejo Mexicano de Fotografia, Mexico City; House of Culture, Prague; Casa de las Americas; Havana; Biblioteca Nacional, Havana; Ministry of Culture, Managua, Nicaragua; Ryerson College, Toronto; University of Parma, Italy.

Publications:

By CORRALES: Books—*Geografia de Cuba,* with text by A.N. Jiménez, Havana 1959; *Cuba Z.D.A.,* with text by Lisandro Otero, Havana 1959; *Asì es mi Patria,* with text by A.N. Jiménez, Havana 1960; *Un Año de Liberación Agraria,* with text by the Ministerio de Relaciones Exteriores, Havana 1960; *La Liberación de las Islas,* with text by A.N. Jiménez, Havana 1961; *Patria o Muerte,* with text by A.N. Jiménez, Havana 1961; *Cuba,* Moscow 1961; *Nazim Hikmet,* with poems by Hikmet, Milan 1961; *Nicolás Guillén,* with poems by Guillén, Milan 1964; *Jorn-Cuba,* with texts by G. Limbour, A. Saura, W. Lam and C. Franqui, Turin 1970; *Obra Gráfica Casa de las Americas,* Mexico City 1979; *Cuevas y Pictografias,* with text by A.N. Jiménez, Havana 1980; *Playa Giron,* Havana 1981, 1985; *En Marcha con Fidel,* with text by A. N. Jiminez, Havana 1984; *Un Pueblo Entero,* Havana 1984.

On CORRALES: Books—*Hecho en Latinoamerica,* exhibition catalogue, Mexico City 1978; *Venezia '79: La Fotografia,* edited by Daniela Palazzoli, Vittorio Sgarbi and Italo Zannier, Milan and New York 1979; *Historia de la Fotografia Cubana* by Maria Eugenia Haya, Mexico City 1979; *Raul Corrales: 35 con la 35* by Gerardo Mosquera, Havana 1980; *Hecho en Latino America 2,* exhibition catalogue, with texts by Pedro Meyer, Lazaro Blanco and others, Mexico City 1981; *La Photographie Contemporaine en Amerique Latine,* exhibition catalogue, by Alain Sayag, Paris 1982; *La Fotografie en Cuba* by A. J. Navarrete, Havana 1983; *Cuba: A View from Inside,* exhibition catalogue, by Max Kozloff, New York 1985. **Articles**—"Premios del Salon de la UNEAC" by A. Alonso in *Juventud Rebelde* (Havana), December 1979; "La Imagen en Dos Tiempos" by Angel Tomas in *El Caiman Barbudo* (Havana), December 1979; "Arte y Testimonio" by M. Sanchez Alfonso in *Revolución y Cultura* (Havana), January 1980; "35 con la 35" by Ele Nussa in *Bohemia* (Havana), July 1980; "De Reportero a Reportero" by A. Fleitas in *Juventud Rebelde* (Havana), August 1980; "Sobre la Fotografia Cubana" by Maria E. Haya in *Revolución y Cultura* (Havana), no. 93, 1980; "Un Fotografo en la Revolucion" by Gerardo Mosquera in *Granma Internacional* (Havana), 25 December 1983; "El Testimonio de Raúl Corrales" by Sergio Lopez in *Fotografia* (Medellin, Colombia), no. 5, 1984; "Fotos aus Kuba" by Stefan Wendel in *Fotografie* (Leipzig), no. 7, 1984; "La Pasión del Fotógrafo" by Jaime Sarusky in *Revolución y Cultura* (Havana), no. 7, 1985; "Colgar las Fotos" by J. A. Navarrete in *Bohemia* (Havana), 26 July 1985; "Un Testimonio de su Paso por la Tierra" by Toni Pinera in *Granma* (Havana), July 1985; "El Todo por la Parte" by A. G. Alonso in *Juventud Rebelde* (Havana), 7 December 1985; "Sul Filo della Memoria" by Lanfranco Colombo in *Infinito* (Milan), February 1986.

*

Man makes and records history. Somebody in this world must photograph that history in order that future generations may have the chance of seeing those images which we create today. I've had the experience of living through a time of profound and radical socio-economic change in my country.

As a photographer closely concerned with my own time, I have not remained indifferent to events. In order not to be so, it has been sufficient to follow what the Consejo Mexicano de Fotografia has laid down as its objectives: "that the photographer concerned with the spirit of his own time must face the responsibility of interpreting, with the help of his images, the beauty and the conflict, the triumphs and the defeats and the aspirations of his own people." Class division and conflict was what hit me most in my first years as a photographer and upon that I based my work. I feel one can find the best of my work in the products of that period. My work, independent of any aesthetic considerations, is, in effect, a visual testimony.

—Raúl Corrales

*　　*　　*

It could be said that Raúl Corrales developed his skills as a photographer in pre-revolutionary Cuba and that, after the Revolution, he was able to exploit that skill as a particularly appropriate means of documenting the attempts of his society to break away from the vices born of the decadent institutions of the previous regime. Prior to the revolution his photographs often had to consist of propaganda images, enforced indoctrination; despite this limitation, he succeeded in transcending such tendentious material to subtly register the facts, documenting social reality in various newspapers and magazines.

His development reveals both his honesty and a passion for his work—particularly in his capacity as the editor of the work of other photographers. Of humble origin, Corrales has retained a spirit of humility, which is always the principal attribute of those who, like himself, are disposed to help and make themselves accessible to beginners. He is a very important historical figure in Cuban photography, for his contribution was made during the most significant and turbulent period of that country's history, a time of transition from a government imposed to one freely accepted by the people. His heroic figures are the people themselves, and his themes are their contributions to the creation of a new era. Recently, after a long period spent in organizing and documenting his country's historic photographic archives, Corrales (along with Cuban artists in other disciplines) has been able to rejoin the artistic mainstream in Latin America.

In the variety of his work one recognizes rigor and spontaneity, in well-balanced proportions, which inform and simultaneously reveal his own sentiments concerning his subjects. The rigor is present not so much in the purely visual and formal aspects of his work as in the content and in the range of information offered. The spontaneity is of a kind derived from experience: it is one that allows him to sensitively emphasize the important and transcendental aspects of the witnessed fact.

—Lázaro Blanco

COSINDAS, Marie.

Nationality: American. **Born:** Boston, Massachusetts, in 1925. **Education:** Attended schools in Boston; studied at Modern School of Fashion Design, Boston; studied painting at the Boston Museum School; attended photography workshops, under Ansel Adams, 1961, and Minor White, 1963, 1964. **Career:** Worked as illustrator and designer, 1945-60. Freelance photographer, Boston, since 1960. Instructor, Colorado College Summer Photo Workshops, Colorado Springs, 1972-78; Artist-in-Residence, Dartmouth College, Hanover, New Hampshire, 1976; Visiting Lecturer in Visual and Environmental Studies, Harvard University, Cambridge, Massachusetts, 1977-78. **Recipient:** Artist-in-Television Award, WGBH/Rockefeller Foundation, Boston, 1967; Guggenheim Fellowship, 1967; National Academy of Television Arts and Sciences Award, 1976. D.F.A. Moore College of Art, Philadelphia, 1967. **Address:** 770 Boylston Street, Boston, Massachusetts, U.S.A.

Individual Exhibitions:

1962	University of New Hampshire, Durham
1963	Arlington Street Church, Boston
	Harvard University, Cambridge, Massachusetts
1964	National Shawmut Bank, Boston
	3 Women Photographers, International Museum of Photography, George Eastman House, Rochester, New York
1966	*Polaroid Color Photographs,* Museum of Fine Arts, Boston
	Polaroid Color Photographs, Museum of Modern Art, New York

	Philadelphia College of Art
	2 Photographers, Gropper Galleries, Cambridge, Massachusetts
1967	*Polacolor Photographs,* University of North Carolina, Chapel Hill
	Polaroid Color Photographs, Art Institute of Chicago
	40 Polaroid Color Photographs, at *10th Festival of Two Worlds,* Spoleto, Italy
1968	*Polaroid Color Photographs,* Currier Gallery of Art, Manchester, New Hampshire
	3 Women Photographers, Moore College of Art, Philadelphia (with Barbara Crane and Naomi Savage)
	Portraits in Beauty, Kenyon and Eckhardt, New York
	4 x 5 Polaroid Color Photos, at *Photokina '68,* Cologne
1969	Louisburg College, North Carolina
	Bi-National Cultural Institute, Mexico City (and Monterrey, Mexico)
	University of Wisconsin, Madison
	Marie Cosindas: A Color Retrospective, Brockton Art Center, Massachusetts
1971	*Polaroid Color Photographs,* University of Connecticut, Storrs
1976	*Artsist-in-Residence Exhibition,* Dartmouth College, Hanover, New Hampshire
	Polaroid Photos 1960-76, Institute of Contemporary Art, Boston
1977	Amsterdam Art Center
	New Faculty Show, Carpenter Center, Harvard University, Cambridge, Massachusetts
	Künstlerhaus, Vienna
1980	Art Institute of Chicago

Selected Group Exhibitions:

1966	*American Photography: The 60's,* Sheldon Memorial Art Gallery, University of Nebraska, Lincoln
1967	*Photography in the 20th Century,* National Gallery of Canada, Ottawa (toured Canada and the United States, 1967-73)
1975	*In Just Seconds,* International Center of Photography, New York
1977	*A Century of Fashion Photography,* Boston Atheneum
1978	*Mirrors and Windows: American Photography since 1960,* Museum of Modern Art, New York (toured the United States, 1978-80)
1979	*One of a Kind: Polaroid Color,* Corcoran Gallery, Washington, D.C. (toured the United States)
1980	*The Imaginary Photo Museum,* Kunsthalle, Cologne
1982	*Color as Form,* International Museum of Photography at George Eastman House, Rochester, New York
1984	*Sammlung Gruber,* Museum Ludwig, Cologne
1987	*Hollywood Photographers,* Los Angeles County Museum of Art

Collections:

Museum of Modern Art, New York; Metropolitan Museum of Art, New York; Visual Studies Workshop, Rochester, New York; International Museum of Photography, George Eastman House, Rochester, New York; Addison Gallery of American Art, Andover, Massachusetts; Polaroid Corporation, Cambridge, Massachusetts; Art Institute of Chicago; Exchange National Bank, Chicago; University of Nebraska, Lincoln; National Gallery of Canada, Ottawa.

Publications:

By COSINDAS: Book—*Marie Cosindas: Color Photographs,* with text by Tom Wolfe, Boston 1978 (includes bibliography).

On COSINDAS: Books—*Marie Cosindas: Polaroid Color Photographs,* exhibition catalogue, with text by John Szarkowski, New York 1966; *Photography in the 20th Century* by Nathan Lyons, New York 1967; *This Fabulous Century,* by the Time-Life editors, New York 1969; *A Picture History of*

Photography by Peter Pollack, New York 1969; *Discovery: Inner and Outer Worlds Portfolio II*, by Friends of Photography, Carmel, California 1970; *Photography Year 1973*, by the Time-Life editors, New York 1973; *Faces and Facades*, with texts by L. Fritz Gruber and Peter C. Bunnell, edited by the Polaroid Corporation, Cambridge, Massachusetts, 1977; *Polaroid Land Photography* by Ansel Adams, revised edition, Boston 1978; *Mirrors and Windows: American Photography since 1960* by John Szarkowski, New York 1978; *The Photography Collector's Guide* by Lee D. Witkin and Barbara London, Boston and London 1979; *One of a Kind: Recent Polaroid Color Photography,* with a preface by Belinda Rathbone, introduction by Eugenia Parry Janis, Boston 1979; *The Imaginary Photo Museum* by Helmut Gernsheim, Renate and L. Fritz Gruber and others, Cologne 1981, London 1982; *Color as Form: A History of Color Photography,* exhibition catalogue, with introduction by Robert A. Sobieszek, Rochester, New York 1982; *Hollywood Photographers: Interpreting American Culture Through Photographs,* exhibition catalogue, by Linda Rich, David Fahey and Kathleen M. Gauss, Los Angeles 1987. **Articles**—"A Show of Color" by Margaret R. Weiss in *Saturday Review* (New York), 24 September 1966; "Beyond Realism" in *Life* (New York), 3 May 1968; "Marie Cosindas" in *Photographs: Sheldon Memorial Art Gallery Collection, University of Nebraska,* with an introduction by Norman A. Geske, Lincoln 1977; "Singular Developments: Polaroid's Paean to Color" by Allen Robertson in *TWA/Ambassador* (St. Paul, Minnesota), December 1979.

*   *   *

It has been the fate of color photographs to remind us either of advertising, of illustrations, or of paintings. The photographic museum world does not recognize advertising or illustrations as art, and when a photograph does remind us of a painting, the painting is almost always better.

The photographs of Marie Cosindas also remind us of paintings. The difference is that her photographs are better. Perhaps this is why Cosindas is the only successful art photographer I know of who readily accepts the idea that her photographs do indeed look like paintings. It may also be relevant that she began as a painter.

Cosindas was the first serious photographer to explore successfully the possibilities of Polaroid color film. Important photographers had rejected the 60 second process as trifling, color as inconsequential, and the 4 by 5-inch print size as impossibly small. Cosindas took advantage of the quick prints to make endless experiments for each picture, she turned the inconsequential color into the lushest and most sensual photographs ever seen, and she contrived her shots so well that smallness transformed paper into precious gems. The likes of her pictures had never been seen before in the photographic world. Many tried to imitate her, but no one seemed to be able to make Polaroid do what she could make it do. Even when it became known that she used her own view camera rather than the Polaroid camera; that she used natural light rather than artificial; and that she experimented by varying color filters, development time, and temperature for every picture, no one could achieve the heat and lushness of her pictures.

Everything is calculated in a Cosindas still-life—whether it is a portrait of a person or an object. Her use of sensual materials, flowers, exotic clothes, and evocative objects make her pictures look old fashioned, timeless, and slightly overripe. They hover on the line between the decadent and the superbly gorgeous. Sittings proceed with long periods of trial and error. The subject sooner or later relaxes, wipes off his public face, and portrays the expression and posture which makes for a serious portrait rather than a superficial one. They are simply the person revealed—not the person transformed into strangeness by being caught off guard.

It took courage for Cosindas to go against the fashion of art photography. Photography of the 1960's emphasized black and white unstaged street pictures of unimportant people and places. This aesthetic is still with us. Cosindas is a strong woman with an independent mind and was not to be influenced by such fashion. She made it in the art world by producing exactly the kind of picture she wanted.

Cosindas has also been successful in the world of commercial photography. Not as others by doing one kind of work for commerce and another for art, but by producing the same kind of work for both. Her portraits are for people as well as of people; the still lifes for corporate advertising hang on museum walls. Cosindas does not need to teach at a university or have another job to support her photography. She earns a comfortable living through her work and

she never compromises. She is in many ways the purest example of what a photographer should be.

—Barbara Norfleet

COWIN, Eileen.

Nationality: American. **Born:** Brooklyn, New York, 17 August 1947. **Education:** Studied education, State University of New York at New Paltz, B.S. 1968; studied photography, Illinois Institute of Technology, Chicago, M.S. 1970. **Recipient:** National Endowment for the Arts Grants, Photography, 1979, 1982, 1990-91. **Address:** c/o Jayne H. Baum Gallery, 588 Broadway, New York, New York 10012, U.S.A.

Individual Exhibitions:

1970	Cooper Union, New York
1971	Witkin Gallery, New York
1972	School of the Dayton Art Institute, Dayton, Ohio
1973	School of the Dayton Art Institute, Dayton, Ohio
1975	Portland School of Art, Portland, Minnesota
1976	Light Gallery, New York
1977	O.K. Harris Gallery, New York
1978	Metropolitan State College, Denver, Colorado
1979	The Light Factory, Charlotte, North Carolina
	San Francisco Camerawork, San Francisco
1980	Orange Coast Gallery, Costa Mesa, California
1983	Orange Coast College, Costa Mesa, California
	Blue Sky Gallery, Portland, Oregon
1984	H.F. Manes' Gallery, New York
	The Light Factory, Charlotte, North Carolina
	Lightsong Gallery, University of Arizona, Tucson
1985	Los Angeles County Museum of Art
	Viviane Esders Gallery, Paris
1987	Min Gallery and Studio, Tokyo, Japan
	Centre for Photography, Osaka, Japan
1988	Jayne H. Baum Gallery, New York
	Cleveland Museum of Art, Cleveland, Ohio
1989	Roy Boyd Gallery, Santa Monica, California
1991	Museum of Contemporary Photography, Columbia College, Chicago
	Roy Boyd Gallery, Santa Monica, California
	Jayne H. Baum Gallery, New York
1993	Jayne H. Baum Gallery, New York

Selected Group Exhibitions:

1970	*Photographic Celebration,* University of Florida, Gainesville, Florida
1972	*The Multiple Image,* University of Rhode Island, Kingston, Rhode Island
1973	*Photo Phantasists,* Florida State University, Tallahassee, Florida
	Light and Substance, The University of New Mexico Art Museum, Albuquerque, New Mexico
1974	*Photography Unlimited,* Fogg Museum, Harvard University, Cambridge, Massachusetts
1975	*The Human Image: Sociology and Photography,* New York State University, Fredonia, New York
	Colors, Florida State University, Tallahassee, Florida
	New American Graphics, Madison Art Center, Madison, Wisconsin
1976	*Exposing: Photographic Definitions,* The Los Angeles Institute of Contemporary Art

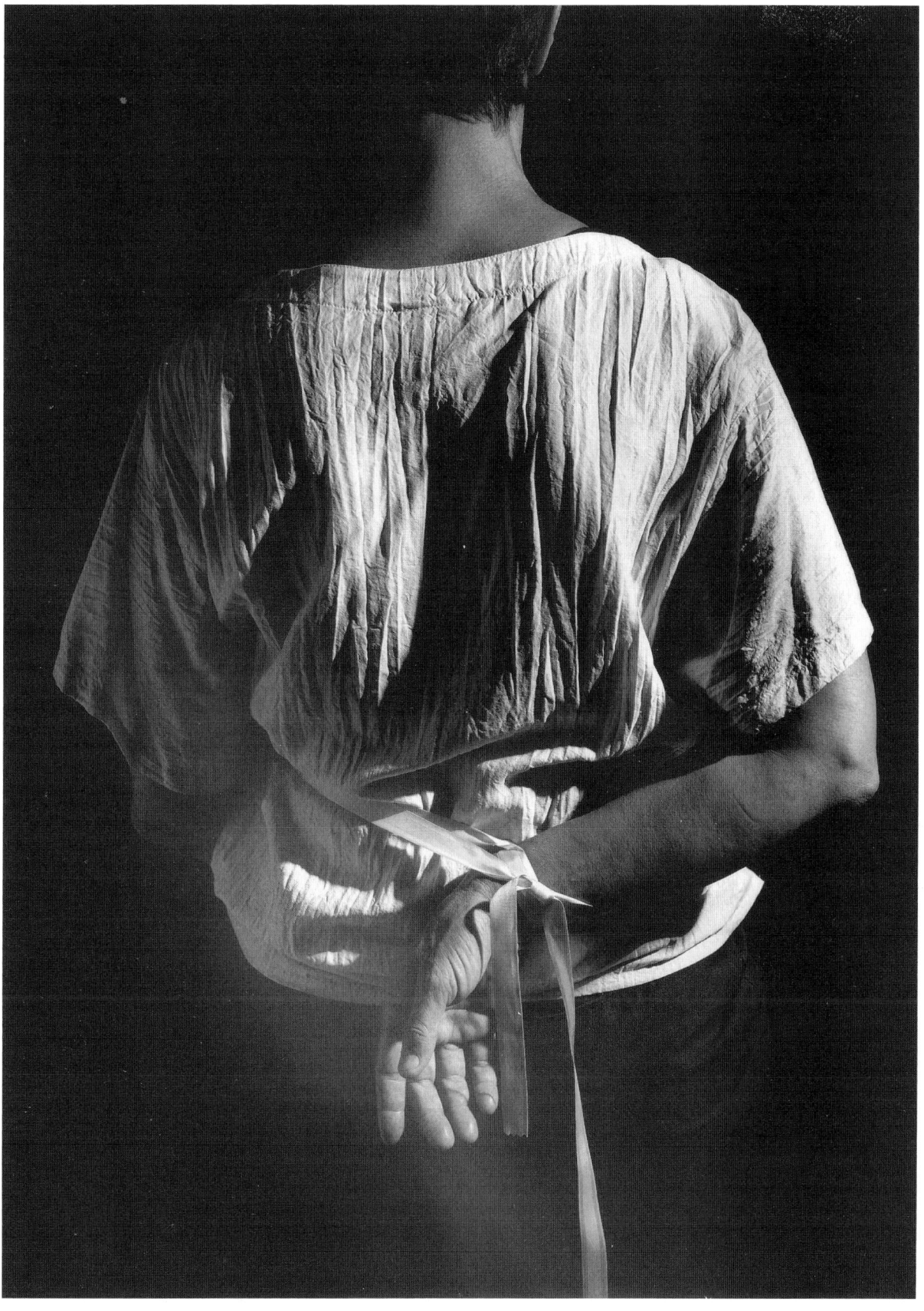

***Untitled*, 1993.** Photograph ©Eileen Cowin. Courtesy of Jayne H. Baum Gallery, New York.

1977   *Language and Image: Photo Linguistics,* Contemporary Graph-
        ics Gallery, Santa Barbara Museum of Art, Santa Barbara,
        California
        Silver See, The Los Angeles Institute of Contemporary Art
        (travelled to the Los Angeles County Museum of Art, 1978)
1979   *Soirée Americaine,* Arles, France
        Polaroid Art in the White Gallery, Tel-Aviv, Israel
1980   *Vis à Vis,* Art Institute of Boston, Boston, Massachusetts
        The New Vision, Light Gallery, New York
1981   *Perceptions on Paper: A Visual Dialogue,* Long Beach Gallery,
        Long Beach, California
1982   *Contemporary Photography as Phantasy,* Santa Barbara
        Museum of Art, Santa Barbara, California (and tour,
        1982-83)
        The Photographer as Printmaker, Ferens Art Gallery, Hull,
        England (and UK tour)
1983   *Biennial Exhibition,* Whitney Museum of American Art,
        New York
        Group Exhibition, Musée Réattu, Arles, France
1984   *Photography in California, 1945-1980,* San Francisco Museum
        of Modern Art (and tour, 1984-86)
        Anxious Interiors, Laguna Beach Museum of Art, Laguna
        Beach, California (and tour, 1984-85)
1985   *Extending the Perimeters of 20th Century Photography,* San
        Francisco Museum of Modern Art
        *Eileen Cowin and John Divola: Recent Work, No Fancy
        Titles,* California/International Arts Foundation (and tour,
        1985-87)
1986   *Spectrum 3: Selections from the Poloroid Collection,* Cologne,
        Germany
        Théatre des Réalités, Metz, France
1987   *Fabrications: Staged, Altered and Appropriated Photographs,*
        International Center for Photography, New York
        Photography and Art: Interactions Since 1946, Des Moines Art
        Center, Des Moines, Iowa (and tour, 1987-88)
1988   *Towards the Photograph as Vulgar Document,* Optica, Center
        for Contemporary Art, Montreal, Canada
1989   *The Photography of Invention: American Pictures of the 1980s,*
        National Museum of American Art, Smithsonian Institution,
        Washington, D.C. (and tour, 1989-90)
        *Fantasies, Fables and Fabrications: Photoworks from the
        1980s,* Herter Art Gallery, University of Massachusetts,
        Amherst (and tour)
1990   *Seductive Deceptions: The Theatrical Image,* University
        Gallery, University of Florida, Gainesville, Florida
        The Big Picture: Selections from the Permanent Collection,
        San Francisco Museum of Modern Art
1991   *Individual Realities,* Sezon Museum, Tokyo, Japan (travelled to
        Tsukashin Hall, Osaka, Japan)
        De Oude Kerk, Amsterdam (travelled to de Beijerd, Breda,
        Netherlands)
        U.S. Photographers, Vooruit Kunstencentrum, Ghent, Belgium
        Erotic Desire, Perspektief, Rotterdam, Netherlands
1992   *Instant-Imaging-Stories,* Museum Moderner Kunst, Vienna,
        Austria
        *SOMETHING'S OUT THERE, Danger in Contemporary
        Photography,* The National Arts Club, New York
1994   *Love in the Ruins,* Long Beach Museum of Art, Long Beach,
        California

Collections:

Aaron Spelling Productions, West Hollywood; Brooklyn Museum of Art;
Baltimore Museum of Art; Bayly Art Museum, University of Virginia,
Charlottesville; Boise Gallery of Art; Shirley Burden Collection; The Chicago
Art Institute; The Colorado College, Colorado Springs; Fogg Museum,
Harvard University, Cambridge, Massachusetts; First National Bank of Chica-
go, Chicago; Grunwald Center for the Graphic Arts, University of California,
Los Angeles; Institute of Design, Illinois Institute of Technology, Chicago;
International Museum of Photography, George Eastman House, Rochester,

New York; Los Angeles County Museum of Art; The Minneapolis Institute of
Arts; The Museum of Contemporary Photography, Columbia College, Chica-
go; The Museum of Modern Art, New York; The Museum of Photographic
Arts, San Diego; Museum of Art, Rhode Island School of Design, Providence;
National Gallery of Canada, Ottawa; National Museum of American Art,
Smithsonian Institution, Washington, D.C.; Newport Harbor Art Museum,
Newport Beach, California; Northlight Gallery, University of Arizona, Tempe;
Polarid Collection, Cambridge, Massachusetts; The Princeton Art Museum;
San Francisco Museum of Modern Art; Santa Barbara Museum of Art; Seattle
Art Museum; Security Pacific National Bank Corporation, Los Angeles; State
University College of New York, New Paltz, New York; Tampa Museum of
Art; University Art Museum, California State University, Long Beach;
University of Kansas Museum of Art, Lawrence; University of Maryland,
Catonsville; Weatherspoon Art Gallery, Charlotte, North Carolina.

Publications:

By COWIN: Article—"On Robert Fichter" in *Working Papers,* 3 May
1982. **Films—***Seeing With the Camera,* with Grant Mudford, part of *The
Photographic Vision,* telecourse production for PBS, KOCE-TV, California,
1984; *The Search for the Mind: Thinking,* PBS program produced by WNET-
TV, New York, 1988.

On COWIN: Books—*The Art of Photography,* New York 1971; *Who's Who
in American Art,* 1984; *New American Photography* by Kathleen Gauss, Los
Angeles 1985; *Masters and Masterpieces: Photographs from The George
Eastman House* by Robert Sobieszek, New York 1986; *Photographs: The
1987 International Yearbook of Photography,* Zurich 1987; *The Privileged
Eye* by Max Kozloff, Albuquerque 1987. **Articles—**"Archetypes, Talis-
mans" by A.D. Coleman in *The Village Voice* (New York), 25 November
1971; "Studio Work: Color it Large" by Chuck Nicholson in *Artweek,* 4
September 1982; "Photography: Biennial Show" by Andy Grundberg in *The
New York Times,* 1 April 1983; "Family Fables" by Andy Grundberg in
Modern Photography, June 1983; "A Postmodern Look at the World" by
Melissa Taylor in *Artweek,* 7 April 1984; "Reappraising Photography's
Status" by Andy Grundberg in *The New York Times,* 7 June 1984; "Cowin's
Facts on Display" by Colin Gardner in *Los Angeles Times,* 30 August 1985;
"Altered Images" by Claire Accomando in *Artweek,* 7 September 1985;
"Voice Choice" by Vince Aletti in *The Village Voice* (New York), 22
November 1988; "Urbane Images of Alienation and Voyeurism," review by
Andy Grundberg in *The New York Times,* 2 December 1988; "Amid Train
Data, Images of Danger and Intrigue," review by Andy Grundberg in *The New
York Times,* 17 August 1990; "Représentation publique de l'image privée
dans l'autoportrait mis en scène" by Patrick Roegiers in *Art Press Special
Photo* (Paris), November 1990; "A Group With Night on Its Mind," review
by Charles Hagen in *The New York Times,* 23 August 1991; "Home Snapshots
of America's Arty White Middle Class" by A.D. Coleman in *The New York
Observer,* 14 October 1991; "Photography and the Sin of Voyeurism" by
Vicki Goldberg in *The New York Times,* 8 March 1992; "The New Season on
Photography" by Vicki Goldberg in *The New York Times,* 11 September 1993;
"Voice Choice" by Vince Aletti in *The Village Voice* (New York), 30
November 1993.

*   *   *

The term "directorial photography" seems tailor-made for Eileen Cowin's
work. Since she turned from painting to photography in 1976, the year critic
A.D. Coleman coined the phrase, she has sketched the tableaux she envisions;
chosen lighting, sets, actors and their dress; staged their interaction; and,
finally, photographed them. She doesn't take photographs; she makes them,
and with conventions openly borrowed from TV soap operas, melodramas of
stage and screen, and recently short stories. Her scenes are "set up to look set
up," she says. "The believable picture has no basis in my work."

Like the fabrications of Cindy Sherman and Laurie Simmons, which also
came to attention in the early '80s, Cowin's photographs are obvious fictions
that exaggerate and thereby offer a critique of how media from art history to
Hollywood have dramatized gender roles, especially women's, and engaged
the viewer's emotions and imagination. But Cowin's work seems more poetic
than political, more open-ended in meaning. Like theater-goers, her audiences can be moved yet be simultaneously aware of her mechanisms.

In her "Family Docu-Drama Series," begun in 1980 and named for TV's merger of fact and fiction, Cowin directed her husband, two stepchildren, and her identical twin sister in scenes fraught with domestic "Sturm und Drang." Sexual and generational conflicts were obvious but unresolved. Indecisive moments were played out in . . . rooms (Cowin's home), suggesting the tumult beneath contemporary family relations.

In the mid 1980s Cowin added elderly figures to her cast and without clichés suggested loneliness, pathos, boredom, and other nuances of feeling. In diptychs and triptychs of larger prints (up to four by five feet), she encouraged temporal readings, and she used black-and-white as often as color and homed in on faces and gestures for increased expressiveness. Stressing the archetypal in her stories, she soon substituted models for her family members, eliminated their middle-class settings in favor of backgrounds of inky darkness, and focused on one or two figures.

If these pictures seemed relatively personal, Cowin's next work appeared media-conscious again, but with a broader take on American culture's image bank. Old Master references alternate with film stylizations. A woman reclining like a Velásquez Venus watches television; a female with hooded head poses before a reproduction of Magritte's similarly draped lovers (both 1988). In 1990 Cowin had eleven light boxes with her black-and-white transparencies displayed in New York's Grand Central Station. Recalling director Alfred Hitchcock's use of such settings, her images of men in trench-coats, women glimpsed at windows, an open envelope, a telephone receiver, etc, hinted at intrigue and danger and implicated viewers as voyeurs. Irrational shifts in space and focus and looming shadows that formed independent shapes heightened the sinister savor. Cowin had found some of the Surrealist and Expressionist roots of *film noir* and grafted them onto her own hybrid of the familiar and the mysterious.

In her pictures from the early 1990s, Cowin continued this cinematic exploration (just as current television and films directed by David Lynch et al were rediscovering the '30s and '40s genre).

And in her New York exhibition of 1993 she tightened her work's allusions to the movies: she displayed her black-and-white images in bands on the gallery walls, suggesting film strips. In each group of six pictures she inserted a TV monitor showing a closeup of a single, enigmatic, but evocative event: water pouring through a pair of cupped hands; blood oozing from a man's mouth. The movement was so slow it was barely perceptible, and both the videos and photographs shared the same family of resonant images and portentous feelings, so the media were at first glance almost indistinguishable. The latent action in her photographs and their resemblance to film stills was underlined by the videos. Their minimalism emphasized the Zen-like ellipsis of her photographs. As before, Cowin used the realism of photography to insist on the reality of stereotypes in expressing her viewers' experience. But like a number of other artists in the 1990s, she heightened the emotive impact of her work in theatrical installations and shifted their subjects from the mediated to the more mythic.

—Anne Hoy

CRANE, Barbara.

Nationality: American. **Born:** Barbara Bachmann in Chicago, Illinois, 19 March 1928. **Education:** Studied art history, under Alfred Neumeyer, Mills College, Oakland, California, 1945-48; New York University, 1948-50, B.A. 1950; photography, under Aaron Siskind, Institute of Design, Illinois Institute of Technology, Chicago, 1964-66, M.S. 1966. Freelance professional photographer, 1948-64; Professor, School of the Art Institute of Chicago, 1967-94; Professor Emeritus, School of the Art Institute of Chicago, 1995—. **Family:** Married Alan Crane in 1948; children: Elizabeth, Jennifer and Bruce. **Career:** Independent photographer from 1948, and freelance professional photographer since 1960. Professor, School of the Art Institute of Chicago, since 1967; Lecturer in the History of Photography, Illinois Institute of Technology, Chicago, 1969; Visiting Professor of Photography, Philadelphia College of Art, 1977; Visiting Artist in Photography, School of the Museum of Fine Art, Boston, 1979; Visiting Professor, Cornell University, Ithaca, New York, 1983. Board Member, Society for Photographic Education, 1972-76; Trustee,

Friends of Photography, Carmel, California, from 1975. **Recipient:** National Endowment for the Arts Grant, 1974; Guggenheim Fellowship, 1979; Polaroid Corporation Grant, 1979; Illinois Art Council Grant, 1985. **Agent:** Jones Troyer Gallery, Washington, D.C. **Address:** 1230 W. Washington, Chicago, Illinois 60607, U.S.A.

Individual Exhibitions:

1969	Friends of Photography, Carmel, California
1971	Limited Image Gallery, Chicago
1972	Museum of Science and Industry, Chicago
1973	University of Iowa, Iowa City
1975	Friends of Photography, Carmel, California
	University of Iowa, Iowa City
1980	Vision Gallery, Boston
1981	Center for Creative Photography, University of Arizona, Tucson (retrospective; toured the United States)
1983	Douglas Elliot Gallery, San Francisco
1986	Tweed Museum of Art, University of Minnesota, Duluth
1987	Museum of Contemporary Photography, Columbia College, Chicago
	Bezalel Academy of Art and Design, Mt Scopus, Jerusalem
1989	Hanmadang Gallery, Seoul, Korea
	Barbara Crane: New Work, Jones Troyer Fitzpatrick Gallery, Washington D.C.
	Catherine Edelman Gallery, Chicago
1991	*A Decade of Photography 1980-1990*, Sarah Spurgeon Gallery, Central Washington University, Ellensburg
1992	*Israeli Suite*, Spertus Museum of Judaica, Chicago
1993	*Harmonic Distortions*, Prague House of Photography, Prague, Czech Republic
	Transformations and Aberrations, Gallery 954, Chicago
	Barbara Crane: Photographie, Galerie Suzel Berna, Paris, France

Selected Group Exhibitions:

1968	*Young Photographers '68*, Purdue University, Lafayette, Indiana
1970	*Be-ing Without Clothes*, Massachusetts Institute of Technology, Cambridge
1976	*One Hundred Years of Chicago Architecture*, Museum of Contemporary Art, Chicago
1977	*The Photographer and the City*, Museum of Contemporary Art, Chicago
1980	*The New Vision*, Light Gallery, New York and Chicago Public Library, Chicago
1983	*Big Pictures by Contemporary Photographers*, Museum of Modern Art, New York
1987	*Modern Photography and Beyond*, National Museum of Modern Art, Kyoto, Japan
1989	*L'Oeil de la Lettre*, Palais de Tokyo, Paris
1991	*American Photography Since 1920*, Barcelona and Madrid
1993	*Essential Art: 140 Years of American Photography*, Center for Creative Photography, Tucson, Arizona
	Flora Photographica, Montreal Museum of Fine Arts, Montreal, Quebec

Collections:

Museum of Modern Art, New York; International Center of Photography, New York; International Museum of Photography at George Eastman House, Rochester, New York; Art Institute of Chicago; Museum of Contemporary Photography at Columbia College, Chicago; Center for Creative Photography,

University of Arizona, Tucson; Library of Congress, Washington, D.C.; Bibliothèque Nationale, Paris; Getty Museum, Malibu, California; National Museum of Modern Art, Kyoto, Japan; Musée de L'Elysée, Lausanne, Switzerland; National Museum of American Art, Smithsonian Institution, Washington, D.C.; Paris Audiovisual, Paris.

Publications:

By CRANE: Books—*Barbara Crane: Photographs 1948-1980,* with texts by Estelle Jussim and Paul Vanderbilt, Tucson, Arizona 1981; *Barbara Crane: The Evolution of a Vision,* exhibition catalogue, Baltimore 1983.

On CRANE: Books—*Be-ing Without Clothes,* exhibition catalogue, by Minor White, New York and Cambridge, Massachusetts 1970; *Object and Image: An Introduction to Photography* by George M. Craven, New York 1975; *The Photographer and the City,* exhibition catalogue, with text by Gail Buckland, Chicago 1977; *American Photography, A Critical History 1945 to the Present,* by Jonathan Green and Harry N Abrams, New York 1984; *Landscape as Photograph,* Estelle Jussim and Elizabeth Lindquist-Cock, New Haven 1985; *Instant Projects,* Robert Baker and Barbara London, edited by Henry Horenstein, Polaroid Corp 1986; *Mothers and Daughters,* Aperture Books 1987; *Swimmers,* Aperture Books 1988; *Decade by Decade: Twentieth Century American Photography,* edited by James Enyeart, Bullfinch Press 1989; *The Eternal Moment: Essays on the Photographic Image,* Estelle Jussim, Aperture 1989; *A Kiss Is Just a Kiss* by Bruce Velick, New York 1990. Articles:—''Barbara Crane'' in *Photography Annual* (New York), 1970; ''Barbara Crane'' in *Creative Camera* (London), August 1974; ''Photos by Barbara Crane'' in *Camera 35* (New York), December 1979.

*

I like to get specific. More and more that seems to be the point of my work as a photographer and as a teacher.

The camera is indiscriminate, but the photographer uses it to discriminate. I want to get rid of everything but the one thing I want to show. I find myself inching closer, physically, to my subject. I used to be ten feet or ten yards from a body or building. Now it's ten inches.

This physical closeness relates to an emotional inching closer. And it interests me that getting specific often means accepting and exploring emotional paradoxes—tenderness and pain existing, not just side by side, but as parts of each other. Form and design have always come easily to me. Translating emotional content into visual form has come by a slow, indirect route, through and around obstacles and experience.

When I'm photographing, I try to put my weight on the balls of my feet, like a runner. Otherwise, I lose. I have to be poised to catch the accident that must be harnessed, the chance juxtaposition that will reveal what I'm searching for. By getting specific, I am trying to transcend that which is merely eccentric. I am trying for what I suppose I would call the sublime. I would love to make a sublime photograph.

As a teacher, the same needs and excitements are involved in the intense one-to-one communication with individual students, the attempt to help each student discover the special thing that he or she can do. I bring my new work and discuss my doubts about it, letting them learn from my experience with my work as well as from my specific knowledge.

—Barbara Crane

*   *   *

Among the dichotemies relied upon by critics for purposes of categorizing their subjects can be found the distinction between those whose primary motive is fame/fortune and those who have an inner compulsion to DO or to create. Although she has achieved a measure of the type of recognition that counts after forty prolific years of photography, Barbara Crane clearly is a member of the latter class (and the medium might be more lively today if she had more company).

There are no contradictions between Crane's life and her photography. Born and raised in Chicago, studying photography with Aaron Siskind at the Institute of Design, teaching photography at the School of the Art Institute of Chicago, much of her photography done at Chicago beaches, parks, museums, architecture, corporate offices—it should come as no surprise that Crane's work fits into the Chicago/Bauhaus tradition of Moholy-Nagy, Harry Callahan, Ray Metzker, Ken Josephson, et al. In fact, Crane's work contributes substantially to the definition of ''Chicago School.'' Yet Crane acknowledges some West Coast affinities dating from her undergraduate study at Mills College in Oakland and personified through friendships with both Imogen Cunningham and Ansel Adams.

Critical to an understanding of Barbara Crane is her experience teaching photography. First at highly regarded New Trier High School (her own alma mater) in the mid-1960s, and since 1967 at the School of the Art Institute of Chicago, Crane has poured the same energies into teaching as she has, simultaneously, into series after series of photographic projects. As befits a good teacher, Crane generates a steady stream of visual ideas. She is open to the exploration of all techniques and materials both for herself and for student work. In her own work she has employed every format from 35mm to press camera to 8 x 10 view camera. Her subjects range from commuters to figure study to architecture to found objects. Color, collage, murals, repetition, sequence have all been explored in successive series of images from ''Human Forms'' in the mid-1960s through ''Chicago Beaches and Parks'' in the mid-1970s to the ''Monster Series,'' ''Chicago Dry Docks'' and ''Objects Trouvés'' of the 1980s.

Crane has successfully intermixed commissions and commercial projects with her own creative work. The murals done in 1975 for Baxter/Travenol Labs brilliantly bridge the interests of a corporate client with her own aesthetic concerns without compromise to either. Scaled at 8 x 8 feet and 7 x 9 feet, they were well ahead of the 1980s trend toward photographs having the presence of paintings.

Crane's work can be viewed as a long-running alternation between primarily humanistic concerns and more strictly formal concerns. Beginning with simple portraiture, formal concerns soon assert their presence in the figure studies. The ''Neon'' series literally double exposes human faces and lighted forms—a most straightforward way to achieve this balance. ''People of the North Portal'' followed by strictly formal architectural work followed again by the ''Community Discourse'' series represent rather extreme swings between two extremes. The elements are mixed in the most complex ways by the 1980s in Crane's Polacolor work and the more recent ''Object Trouvé'' series. It is said of the fugue that when all the voices have ''arrived,'' then there are no rules.

If Barbara Crane's work today has shed itself of the rules to which she has up until how adhered, it is because her oeuvre is a grand intellectual fugue.

—Andrew Eskind

CRAVO NETO, Mario.

Nationality: Brazilian. **Born:** Salvador, Bahia, Brazil, 20 April 1947. **Education:** Initiated in sculpture and photography, 1964. Moved to Berlin with his father, the sculptor Mario Cravo Junior, 1964; moved to New York City as a student of the Art Students League, 1969. **Family:** Married Eva Christensen in 1979 (divorced); children: Lua Diana and Christian; married Angela Cunha in 1987; children: Lukas and Akira. **Career:** Set up his studio in Soho, New York

Lord of the Head, **1988.** Photograph ©Mario Cravo Neto.

City, 1969; returned to Brazil, 1971. **Agents:** Witkin Gallery, 415 West Broadway, New York, New York 10012, U.S.A.; Fahey/Klein Gallery, 148 North La Brea Avenue, Los Angeles, California 90036, U.S.A. **Address:** Av. Genaro de Carvalho 11, 41.320-100 Salvador, Bahia, Brazil.

Individual Exhibitions:

1965	Galeria Convivium, Salvador
1971	Galeria Documenta, São Paulo
	Museu de Arte Moderna da Bahia, Salvador

	XI Bienal Internacional de São Paulo, São Paulo
1972	Galeria Grupo B, Rio de Janeiro
	Galeria Documenta, São Paulo
1973	Galeria Documenta, São Paulo
	XII Bienal Internacional de São Paulo, São Paulo
1974	A Galeria, São Paulo
1975	*XIII Bienal Internacional de São Paulo,* São Paulo
1976	Modern Art Gallery, Munich
1977	Galeria Multipla, São Paulo
	XIV Bienal Internacional de São Paulo, São Paulo

1979	Museu de Arte da Bahia, Salvador (with Pierre Verger)
	Museu de Arte de São Paulo, São Paulo (with Pierre Verger)
1980	Foto Galeria, São Paulo
	Galleria Il Diaframma, Milan
1981	Galleria La Parisina, Turin
	Galeria Monica Filgueiras, São Paulo
1982	Brazilian American Cultural Institute, Washington, D.C.
1983	Galleria Il Diaframma, Milan
	Museu de Arte de São Paulo, São Paulo
	Arco Arte Contemporanea, São Paulo
	XVII Bienal Internacional de São Paulo, São Paulo
1984	Museu de Arte Moderna, Rio de Janeiro
	Fotografia Oltre, Chiasso, Switzerland
1985	Yuen Lui Gallery, Seattle
	IF—Immagine Fotografica, Milan
1986	Arco Arte Contemporanea, São Paulo
1987	Vision Gallery, San Francisco
	Billedhusets Gallery, Copenhagen
1988	Suomen Valokuvataiteen Museo, Helsinki
	Palazzo Fortuny, Venice
1989	La Galeria Kahlo, Coronel, Mexico
	Galeria O Cavalete, Salvador
	Arco Arte Contemporanea, São Paulo
1990	Galerie Springer, Berlin
	Canon Image Centre, Amsterdam
1991	Galería del Teatro General San Martín, Buenos Aires
	Ada Galeria, Salvador
1992	*Houston FotoFest*, Houston, Texas
	Galeria Modulo, Lisbon
	Fahey/Klein Gallery, Los Angeles
	Witkin Gallery, New York
1993	Vision Gallery, San Francisco
	Kathleen Ewing Gallery, Washington, D.C.
	Fisher Gallery, University of Southern California, Los Angeles
1994	Museum of Photographic Art, San Diego, California
	Frankfurter Kunstverein, Frankfurt
	Susan Spiritus Gallery, Los Angeles
	Witkin Gallery, New York
1995	Catherine Edelman Gallery, Chicago

Selected Group Exhibitions:

1965	*I Bienal de Artes Plasticas da Bahia*, Salvador
1971	*V Exposicão Jovem Arte Contemporanea*, Museu de Arte Contemporanea de São Paulo
1972	*Panorama da Arte Brasileira Atual*, Museu de Arte Moderna de São Paulo
1975	*Art Systems in Latin America*, Institute of Contemporary Arts, London (travelled to l'Espace Pierre Cardin, Paris; Galleria Civica d'Arte Moderna, Ferrara)
1976	*Arte Agora I*, Museu de Arte Moderna do Rio de Janeiro
1978	*Subterranean Art*, Architecture and Objects, Galería Huan Martin and Museo Carrillo Gil, Mexico D.F.
1980	*SICOF—Salone Internazionale della Cinematografia, Ottica e Fotografia*, Milan
1981	*Fotografia Lateinamerika*, Kunsthaus Zürich (travelled to Akademie der Künste, Berlin)
	Panorama 81, Museu de Arte Moderna, São Paulo
1982	*Biennale Internazionale di Fotografia*, Caserta, Italy
1983	*Brazilian Photography, Six Contemporaries*, The Photographers' Gallery, London
	Brésil des brésiliens, Centre Georges Pompidou, Paris
1984	*Photoamerica/84, Objettivi sull'America Latina*, Geneva
	Corpo e Alma, at *Mois de la Photo*, Espace Latino Américain, Paris
1985	*I Quadrienal de Fotografia*, Museu de Arte Moderna, São Paulo
	A Arte e seus Materiais—Atitudes Contemporaneas, Galeria Sergio Millet, Funarte, Rio de Janeiro

	Panorama da Arte Atual Brasileira, Museu de Arte Moderna de São Paulo
	50 Years of Color, Circulo de Bellas Artes, Madrid
1988	*Het Portret*, Canon Image Centre, Amsterdam
	Brazil Projects, P.S. ONE, Institute for Art and Urban Resources, New York
	Splendeurs et misère du corps, Musée d'art et d'histoire de Fribourg (travelled to the Musée d'Art Moderne de la Ville de Paris)
1989	*Réalités Magiques, Photografie Latino Américaine Contemporaine*, Museet for Fotokunst, Odense, Denmark (travelled to the Museum voor Fotografie, Antwerp)
1990	*Von der Natur in der Kunst*, Messepalast Wien, Vienna
	Op Position, 2ème Fotografie Biennale Rotterdam
1991	*13 Photographers*, Witkin Gallery, New York
	Incursão pelo Imaginario na Fotografia Brasileira Contemporanea, at *Rencontres Internationales de la Photographie*, Arles, France
1992	*Arte Amazonas*, Museu de Arte Moderna, Rio de Janeiro (travelled to the Staatliche Kunsthalle, Berlin)
	Encuentro de los Mundos, Museu de Arte de la Tertulia, Cali, Colombia
	Ante América, Biblioteca Luis Angel, Bogota, Colombia
	América Latina, at *V FotoBienal de Vigo*, Vigo, Spain
1993	*Cartographies*, Winnipeg Art Gallery, Winnipeg, Canada (travelled to the National Gallery of Canada, Ottawa, 1994)
1994	*Canto a Realidad*, Casa de América, Madrid
	Romper los Márgenes, at *Encuentro de Fotografía Latino Americano*, Museo de Artes Visuales Alexandro Otero, Caracas, Venezuela
	A Hidden View, Images of Bahia, Barbican Centre Concourse Gallery, London
	Bienal Brasil Seculo XX, São Paulo

Collections:

Museet for Fotokunst, Odense; Museum of Fine Arts, Houston, Texas; Museum of Photographic Arts, San Diego, California; Princeton Art Museum; Museu de Arte de São Paulo; Stedelijk Museum, Amsterdam; Volukvataiteen Museum, Helsinki; Museu de Arte Contemporanea de São Paulo; Museu de Arte Moderna, Rio de Janeiro; Museu de Arte Moderna de São Paulo; Museu de Arte Moderna da Bahia, Salvador; Museum voor Fotografie, Antwerp.

Publications:

By CRAVO NETO: Books—*Bahia*, São Paulo 1980; *Cravo*, Salvador, Bahia 1983; *A Cidade da Bahia*, Salvador, Bahia 1984; *Os Estranhos Filhos da Casa*, Salvador, Bahia 1985; *Exvoto*, Salvador, Bahia 1986; *Mario Cravo Neto*, exhibition catalogue, Milan 1988; *Mario Cravo Neto*, exhibition catalogue, Salvador, Bahia 1991. **Article**—"Scars of Our Inheritance" in *View Camera* (Sacramento, California), September/October 1993. **Films**—*Ubirajara*, feature film, directed by André Luis Oliveira, 1975; *Smetak*, documentary film, directed by Walter Lima, 1978; *Nos*, directed by Walter Lima, 1978; *Iya-Mi-Agba*, documentary film, directed by Juana Elbain, 1979; *GW-43, Gulf War*, video film, 1990; *Nash, U 19, Amazonia*, video film, 1991; *Exu Dos Ventos*, video film, 1992.

On CRAVO NETO: Books—*Mario Cravo Neto* by Carole Naggar in *Encyclopedie Internationale des Photographes*, Paris 1982; *Encyclopedie Internationale des Photographes, 1939-1984* by Michel Auer, Berne; *A Hidden View, Images of Bahia*, exhibition catalogue, with text by Amanda Hopkinson, London 1994; *The Witkin Gallery 25th*, with portfolio selected by Evelyne Daitz and text by Peter C. Bunnell, Toronto and New York 1994. **Articles**—"Woman" in *Popular Photography* (New York), Spring 1971; "Phill Marco, Lucien Clerque, Cravo Neto" by Luigi Carluccio in *Panorama* (Milan), 1981; "Mario Cravo Neto" by Attilio Colombo in *Progresso Fotografico* (Milan), March 1981; "Portraits Sculpturaux" in *Zoom Magazine* (Paris), 1986; "The Sculptural Nude" by Joan Murray in *Artweek* (Piedmont), June 1987; "Mario Cravo Neto" by Casimiro Mendonça in *Atlante* (São Paulo), 1989; "Bestiaire" in *Camera International* (Paris),

Winter 1991; "A New Lens or Two on the Mythologizing of Latin America" by A.D. Coleman in *The New York Observer* (New York), 12 October 1992; "Mario Cravo Neto" by Charles Hagen in *The New York Times* (New York), 16 October 1992; "Mario Cravo Neto" by Margareth Loke in *Art News* (New York), December 1992; "Three Artists From Brazil" by Suzanne Muchnic in *Art News* (New York), April 1993; "Miracles of Fishes and Flesh" by Lee Fleming in *The Washington Post,* 10 April 1993; "Mario Cravo Neto" by Edward Leffingwell in *Poliester,* Spring 1993.

*

It is my intention to charge these photographs with the mystical and religious energy which expresses itself in the temperament, sentiment and humanity of religious and cultural syncretism in Bahia. These photographs are a psychological portrait of our people through facial expressions and gestures characteristic of the indigenous, Portuguese, and African population and the racial mixture of these three ethnic groups—generators of a new temperament and passion that characterizes us.

The colonial city of Bahia is the richest repository of Portuguese architecture and African culture in South America and as such the central radiating source of these contributions from both races.

The cultural and religious roots can be eloquently seen in the emotional presence of the photographed subjects. The contemplative and dramatic visages presented are the scars of our inheritance.

To speak about my photography is to speak about my experience with art and artists, my inner feelings and dreams. Now in my forties, my photography is the result of my activity as an artist in several different media. Sculpture, drawing and conceptual art gave me the knowledge and the basis of my future works on photography.

—Mario Cravo Neto

* * *

Mario Cravo Neto's images are among the most strikingly powerful to have emerged on the contemporary art scene. One says "art" because Cravo Neto started as a fine artist and retains many of the preoccupations appropriate to that field of work, right down to being a gallery-based worker. Although, increasingly, his giant black-and-white portraits are receiving magazine exposure, it's important to see the originals in order to gain the full impact of their dramatic size, their artistic and technical quality.

My entry into the new acquisitions gallery of the Stedelijk Museum was arrested just as surely as if someone had barred the door. Across the hall a man was holding a turtle up to conceal his face. Neither the oddity of his action nor the incongruousness—in that setting—of a naked black man against a stark background were what stopped me. It was the strength, almost the stridency, of the image itself that halted me in my tracks. The first image I'd ever seen by Mario Cravo Neto.

Since then I've had pleasurable reason to become familiar with Cravo Neto's vocabulary of predominantly "voodoo" portraits of humans and animals. For the northeastern region of Brazil where he comes from has miraculously conserved the culture and religion of the Yoruba peoples once transported there as slaves. Called *candomblé* (or, in its bowdlerised, Western version, *voodoo*), it connects with ancestor worship through an intricately sophisticated cycle of celebrations involving dance and music, elaborate costumes and foods, offertories and sacrifices. Cravo Neto is steeped in that culture and strips it down to the most intimate and immediate of relationships between the natural worlds. This admits of humans, no more clothed than the birds and animals who also have their parts to play, of plants and inanimate objets trouvés. Some of these have ritual aspects, as with certain stones and obsidian knives; others are more purely artistic, selected for their aesthetic qualities.

Beyond these immensely striking portraits, taken usually in Cravo Neto's own studio at home into which parrots fly and monkeys scamper (for there, on the fringes of Salvador da Bahia, it is hard to be certain where the house ends and the jungle enters: perhaps "home" is both), Cravo Neto has a substantial body of other work more identifiably within photographic and video traditions. He has done a considerable amount of colour reportage, most recently using Salvador's street carnival as something of a pretext for pursuing his fascination with the street carts used both by local traders and then as carnival

floats. He has made video films on subjects as diverse as the Gulf War, the perilous—and endangered—region of Amazonas, and ExO (messenger of the candomblé gods).

Despite visits to Lusiphone Africa and periods of study ad production in the United States, Cravo Neto is very much a son of Bahia. Indeed, his name intimates as much—meaning as it does, Mario Cravo Grandson, that his father and grandfather were also artists before him. Passionate about his work to the point of constant insomnia, Mario Cravo Neto avoids the tropical heat and works at night, moving between his various chosen disciplines with consummate ease and expertise. But his portraits of children clasping geese or playing with dogs; the man covering his eyes with two baby birds or his back with two slithering fish; the woman (his wife, and fellow artist, Angela Cunha) holding a stone to her ear or a branch aloft; the interplay of black-and-white photography and black or white models with natural lights and shades—these, to me, are the quintessential Mario Cravo Neto.

—Amanda Hopkinson

CUMMING, Donigan.

Nationality: American. **Born:** Danville, Virginia, 5 July 1947. Resident in Canada since 1970. **Education:** Attended Florida High School, Tallahassee, Florida; studied at Florida State University, Tallahassee, Florida, B.Sc. 1978; studied at Concordia University, Montreal, Canada, M.F.A. 1985; mainly self-taught in photography; studied with Evon Streatman and Tom Gibson. **Family:** Married Martha Langford in 1994. **Recipient:** Photographers' Fellowship, National Endowment for the Arts, Washington, D.C., 1980; John Simon Guggenheim Memorial Foundation Fellowship, New York, 1984; Ministère des Affaires culturelles, Quebec, Grant "A," 1988, 1993; Canada Council Arts Grant "A," 1990, 1991, 1993. **Agents:** Bravin Post Lee, NYC, 80 Mercer St, New York, New York, 10012, USA; Galerie Pons, 38 rue Sainte Croix de la Bretonnerie, 75004 Paris, France. **Address:** 2191 Souvenir Street, Montreal, Quebec, H3H 1R9, Canada.

Individual Exhibitions:

1974	*Hommage to John Marlowe (as John Marlow),* Photo Progression, Montreal
1978	*Gardens (as Georgia Freeman),* Photo Progression, Montreal
	Boxing, Photo Progression, Montreal
	Portraits of Men (as C.D. Battey), Photo Progression, Montreal
1983	*Selections from Reality and Motive 1,* The Photography Gallery, Toronto
	Bourget Gallery, Montreal, Quebec
1984	University of Ottawa, Ottawa
1985	Glengarry Historical Society, Cornwall, Ontario
	Coburg Gallery, Vancouver, British Columbia
1986	*La Réalité et le Dessein dans la photographie documentaire,* Centre National de la Photographie, Paris
	Reality and Motive in Documentary Photography 1 & 2, O.K. Harris, New York; 49th Parallel, New York
	Selections from Reality and Motive 1 & 2, Grünwald Gallery, Toronto
	Blue Sky Gallery, Portland, Oregan
1987	Université Laval, Quebec
	Photographers Gallery, Saskatoon, Saskatchewan
1988	Musée de la Photographie, Charleroi, Belgium
	Gallery Connexion & New Brunswick Craft School Gallery, Fredericton, New Brunswick
	Selections from work in progress for The Mirror, The Hammer and The Stage, Grünwald & Watterson Gallery, Toronto
	Richard F. Brush Gallery, Canton, New York
1989	XYZ Fotografie vzw, Ghent, Belgium
1990	*The Mirror, The Hammer and The Stage,* The Museum of Contemporary Photography, Chicago, Illinois, USA (trav-

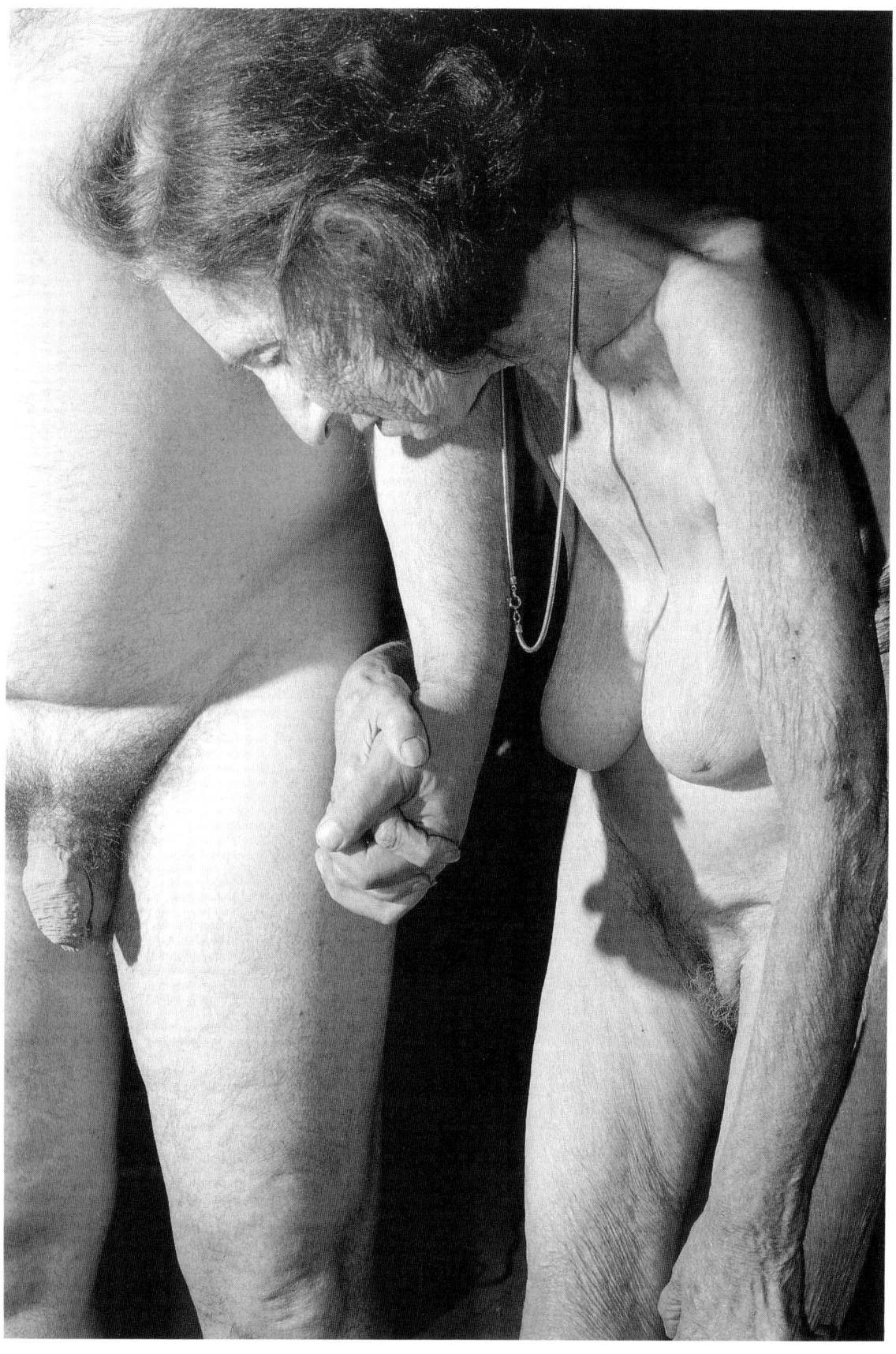

Harry's Diary: Extract from Pretty Ribbons, **1992.** Photograph ©Donigan Cumming.

elled to the Photographic Resource Center, Boston, Massachusetts, 1992)

The Floating Gallery & Main/Access Gallery, Winnipeg, Manitoba

1991 Glendon Gallery, York University, Toronto

1993 *Donigan Cumming: Diverting the Image/Détournements de l'image,* Les cents jours d'art contemporain, Montreal; Art Gallery of Windsor, Windsor, Ontario

1994 *Pretty Ribbons,* Les Rencontres d'Arles, Arles, France

Harry's Diary: Extracts from Pretty Ribbons, Bravin Post Lee Gallery, New York (travelled to the Genereux Grunwald Gallery, Toronto)

Selected Group Exhibitions:

1983 Photo Union Gallery, Hamilton, Ontario

Fait, Galerie Articule, Montreal

Document: Aspects of Canadian Life, The Photo Gallery, National Film Board, Ottawa (toured in Canada and the United States, 1985-87)

1984 *Contemporary Canadian Photography from the National Film Board,* Edmonton Art Gallery, Edmonton, Alberta

Photographers Gallery, Saskatoon, Saskatchewan

1985 *Contemporary Canadian Photograpy,* National Gallery of Canada, Ottawa

Portraits, Galerie Articule, Montreal

1986 *Photography: Suggestions and Facts,* Mandeville Gallery, La Jolla, California

Art Support, Galerie John Schweitzer, Montreal

1987 *Foto(con)tekst,* Perspektief Gallery, Rotterdam, Netherlands

The Working Artist, A Space, Toronto (and tour)

Un si grand âge . . . , Centre National de la Photographie, Paris (and tour)

Photographs from the Permanent Collection, Concordia Art Gallery, Montreal

1988 *Vivre Longtemps,* Musée de la Civilisation, Quebec (toured in Quebec, 1988-91)

Art Gallery of Ontario, Toronto

Bányászati Museum, Sopron, Hungary

Photographic Truth, The Bruce Museum, Greenwich, Connecticut

1989 *Culture Medium,* International Center of Photography, New York

What Is Photography? Manes Centre, Union of Czechoslovak Creative Artists, Prague, Czechoslovakia

Krakow Gallery, Polish Art Photographers Association, Krakow, Poland

Power Plays: Contemporary Photography from Canada, Stills Gallery, Edinburgh, Scotland (and UK tour)

Artunion, Budapest, Hungary

1990 *Strip-Tease de l'intime,* at *Mois de la Photo à Paris,* Galerie Urbi et Orbi, Paris

Op-Positions: commitment and cultural identity in contemporary photography from Japan, Canada, Brazil, The Soviet Union and The Netherlands, Rotterdam, Netherlands

Public Exposures: One Decade, Toronto Photographers Workshop, Toronto

Grünwald Gallery, Toronto

1991 *Découvertes,* Grand Palais, Paris

Portraits, autoportrait et représentation(s), Galerie Photogramme, Montreal

1992 *Women Photographed 1849-1988,* National Gallery of Canada, Ottawa

Genereux Grunwald Gallery, Toronto

Real Stories: Revisions in Documentary and Narrative Photography, Museet for Fotokunst, Odense, Denmark (toured Scandinavia and Europe)

Beau: a reflection on the nature of beauty in photography, Canadian Museum of Contemporary Photography, Ottawa

(travelled to the *Mois de la photo à Paris,* Centre culturel canadien, Paris)

1993 *Site Survey,* Canadian Museum of Contemporary Photography, Ottawa

Observing Traditions: Contemporary Photography 1975-1993, National Gallery of Canada, Ottawa

1994 *Harry's Diary: Extracts from Pretty Ribbons,* Kunsthalle Bielefeld, Germany (travelled to the Kunstverein, Frankfurt and Haus am Waldsee, Berlin)

Auction of Fine Art Photographs, Photographic Resource Center, Boston, Massachusetts

Collections:

Art Gallery of Windsor, Windsor, Ontario; Asolo Theater Festival Archives, Sarasota, Florida; Bibliothèque Nationale, Paris; Canada Council Art Bank, Ottawa; Canadian Museum of Contemporary Photography, Ottawa; Leonard and Bina Ellen Art Gallery, Concordia University, Montreal; Maison Européenne de la Photographie, Paris; Musée de la Photographie, Charleroi, Belgium; Museet for Fotokunst, Odense, Denmark; National Gallery of Canada, Ottawa; National Museum of American Art, Washington, D.C.; The Museum of Fine Arts, Houston, Texas; Winnipeg Art Gallery, Winnipeg, Manitoba; FNAC, Paris, France.

Publications:

By CUMMING: Book—*The Stage,* Montreal 1991.

On CUMMING: Books—*In Camera: The Photography of Donigan Cumming* by Georges Bogardi in *Thirteen Essays on Photography,* Ottawa 1990; *Autobiographie au Québec* by Patrick Roegiers in *L'il multiple,* Paris 1992. **Articles**—"Document: Aspects of Canadian Life" by Peter Wollheim in *Vanguard,* Vol. 12, No. 7, September 1983; "Brian Collins, Donigan Cumming, Robert Ouellet" by Thérèse St-Gelais in *Vanguard,* Vol. 12, No. 9, November 1983; "Open Parody, Hidden Agenda: Donigan Cumming" by Clara Gutsche in *Vanguard,* Vol. 13, No. 4, May 1984; "Donigan Cumming: Undoing Documentary" by Robert Graham in *Parachute* (Montreal), No. 34, March/April/May 1984; "Donigan Cumming Photographs" by Keith Wallace in *Issue* (Vancouver), Vol. 2, No. 4, March/April 1985; "The Dark Visions of Donigan Cumming" by Georges Bogardi in *Canadian Art,* Vol. 3, No. 1, Spring 1986; "Exploring art's potential to refuse its viewers the privilege of control" by Carole Corbeil in *The Globe and Mail* (Toronto), 29 May 1986; "Photographer of gloss fascinated by ordinary" by Nick Auf Der Maur in *The Gazette* (Montreal), 4 June 1986; "Donigan Cumming" by O'Reilly in *The Village Voice* (New York), 17 June 1986; "A New Breed Puts Its Own Stamp on the Medium" by Andy Grundberg in *The New York Times,* 28 December 1986; "Donigan Cumming: Centre National de la Photographie, Palais de Tokyo" by Françoise Orsini in *Des Arts* (Rennes), No. 5, Winter 1986/1987; "Donigan Cumming au Palais de Tokyo: l'insolite quotidien" by Patrick Roegiers in *Le Monde* (Paris), 7 January 1987; "Photosocio" by Danielle Boone in *Révolution* (Paris), No. 364, 20-26 February 1987; "Donigan Cumming: Palais de Tokyo (C.N.P.)" by Noël Bourcier in *Art Press,* No. 112, March 1987; "Le regard limitrophe de Donigan Cumming" by Richard Baillargeon in *Photo Sélection,* July/August 1987; "Cumming/Golberg/Woodman: Beyond Semiotics" by Peter Wollheim in *Photo Communique,* Vol. 9, No. 2, Summer 1987; "Documentary in a New Context" by Michael Gibbs in *Perspektief* (Rotterdam), No. 31/32, April 1988; "Donigan Cumming, photographe: le procès du 'naturel'" by Daniele Gillemon in *Le Soir* (Brussels), 24 November 1988; "Disturbing challenges to documentary photography" by Murdo Macdonald in *The Scotsman* (Edinburgh), 17 January 1989; "Power Plays: Contemporary photography from Canada" by Claire Henry in *The Glasgow Herald* (Scotland), 3 February 1989; "Show at International Center Turns the News into a Snooze" by A.D. Coleman in *The New York Observer,* August 1989; "A Montréal: La Photographie Canadienne Contemporaine" by Annie Walther in *Photographies Magazine,* No. 17, November 1989; "Espaces révélateurs: là, au travers, hors de là et retour" by Sylvain Campeau in *Parachute* (Montreal), No. 57, January/February/March 1990; "Taking Photography to Pieces" by Terry Byrnes in *Photo Life,* Vol. 15, No. 2, March 1990; "Public Exposures: One Decade Mapping the Photo Ghetto" by David Hlynsky in *Views,* Vol. 7, No. 2, May 1990; "Impasse et modernité du reportage—À Rotterdam, la 2e Biennale repose sur une exposition au concept original et provocant'' by Patrick Roegiers in *Le Monde* (Paris), 7 September 1990; ''Lines of Photographic History'' by Scott Ellis in *Border Crossings* (Winnipeg), Vol. 10, No. 1, January 1991; ''Pretty Ribbons: Photographs by Donigan Cumming'' by Robert Enright in *Border Crossings* (Winnipeg), Vol. 10, No. 1, January 1991; ''Stage Fright'' by Terry Byrnes in *Photo Life*, Vol. 16, No. 9, November 1991; ''Pumping up the drama'' by Kelly Wise in *The Boston Globe*, 22 September 1992; ''Up Canada Way: Mois de la Photo à Montreal'' by A.D. Coleman in *European Photography*, Vol. 13, No. 49, Winter 1992; ''Un monde sans pitié'' by Stéphane Aquin in *Voir* (Montreal), Vol. 7, No. 38, 19-25 August 1993; ''Cumming le provocateur'' by Julie Vaillancourt in *MTL* (Montreal), Summer 1993; ''Donigan Cumming: Centre international d'art contemporain de Montréal'' by Guy Bellavance in *Parachute* (Montreal), No. 73, January/February/ March 1994; ''La fonction sociale du photographe'' by Marie-Michèle Cron in *ETC Montréal*, No. 25, 15 February–15 May 1994; ''Reflexions sur l'irregardable'' by Dominique Baqué in *Le Monde* (Paris), 30 June 1994; ''Donigan Cumming: Le Journal de Harry = Donigan Cumming: Harry's Diary'' by Nicole Gingras in *CV Photo* (Montréal), Summer 1994.

*

In 1982 I was expanding my cast of characters for Part 1 of *Reality and Motive in Documentary Photography,* when I was reintroduced to a woman named Nettie Harris. I had known of Nettie for a decade through Montreal's network of bars and cafés. She was a widow in her sixties who had once worked as a journalist, raised a family and was embarking on a third career as an actress. When I met her again, she was an elderly woman, not without means, but living in the kind of disarray that dominates popular perceptions of the ageing poor.

My initial interest in Nettie was largely circumstantial, based on her age, her sex and her environment. As we worked, I discovered in her a powerful and affecting model whose qualities were concentrated by the still photograph. She took direction and drew from the répertoire of her experience, real and imagined. In directing her for the camera, I never tried to curb Nettie's urge to improvise. I discovered the compelling images in the spaces between her gestures and moods.

More to the point, though, is what Nettie came to represent in my work. One of the most troubling aspects of my imagery—the harsh theatre that I've mounted as a form of thick description—is that it is in fact fed from a specific reality, as provisional as my intervention. As she aged, Nettie's eccentricity was inflected by her physical decline. Her body decayed; the mess around her became more severe. She began to face the real difficulties that people encounter in old age.

When I began *Reality and Motive in Documentary Photography,* I was absorbed with the history and applications of the social documentary tradition. I pursued them by quoting, repeating and loading my photographs with a mannered vocabulary, emotional hooks and multiple versions of decisive moments. Like many critics at that time, I was appalled by the arrested development of documentary photography and wanted to offer some correction—not polemical, but visual. Instead, almost in spite of myself, I began to generate an alternative that manifested itself in the climax of the work.

The alternative was based on a theatrical model that I carried into *The Mirror, The Hammer and The Stage,* and later, into *Pretty Ribbons.* I stopped imitating objectivity and made a broader spectacle of my emotional entanglement with the people that I photographed. These projects involved a chorus of voices that rose and fell in the visual density of their physical and social surroundings. Working with Nettie Harris, I wanted to isolate one of those voices, to entwine my own in the biography of her imagination.

I worked with Nettie Harris until her death in 1993.

—Donigan Cumming

*   *   *

Donigan Cumming, although born and raised in the American South, is now considered a Canadian photographer. He is an ideal example of North America's ''free trade'' agreement between the United States and Canada. Since the early 1980s support for his work has alternated between Canada Arts Council sponsorship and The National Endowment for the Arts, Washington

D.C. His most provocative photographs were taken in and around his adoptive city of the last 24 years, Montreal. Although principally self-taught in photography, he holds an M.F.A. from Concordia University, Montreal, Canada. His curriculum vitae is extensive, with over 35 national group exhibitions, more than 65 selected articles in periodicals, 25+ publications and thirteen solo exhibitions.

Robin Laurence, in *Border Crossings* (vol. 12, no. 1, Winter 1993) said ''By exaggerating the contrived and theatrical aspects of photo-journalism and photo documentation, and declaring his own presence in the process, Donigan Cumming asserted the impossibility of extricating the photographer's taste and vision from the vaunted notion of objectivity.''

Questioning the authenticity and realism of the documentarian's image is an integral part of Donigan Cumming's photography. It is an ambitious objective and there is much controversy surrounding whether he has been successful at this. Cumming explains that his work involves devising a new postulate for the documentary genre. ''The documentary photographic tradition is a process of loading the pictures ... with mannered vocabulary, emotional hooks, and multiple versions of deceive moments.''

He has spent the best part of the last decade demonstrating the pitfalls of reportage photo-journalism by bolstering its sensationalism. In his 1986 exhibition/catalogue, *Reality and Motive in Documentary Photography,* Cumming along with a ''cast of thousands'' (over 250 individuals participated in this project) trailblazes towards this ''new frontier'' of documentary deconstruction. In *Reality and Motive* the viewer is challenged by contentious imagery. His subjects collaborate with him, allowing him to manipulate and pose them like plasticine. He is also permitted to expose them at their most banal. It is obvious that the subjects are under his direction. His images are awash in post-modern fetishised symbolism and icons: lingerie, television, kitsch and ''Elvis'' memorabilia. The exhibition is intended to shock and elicit emotional dander, drawing on the imagery of the more controversial sector, pornography. At its best Cumming's work is the embodiment of the fundamental problems which underlie photography. The medium can never be objective, everything hinges on the effect produced in the viewer, and is therefore subjective.

Cumming's work suggests that both the photographer and the viewer of documentary photography are voyeurs. This notion is best tested in his 1994 catalogue *Pretty Ribbons,* possibly the most problematic selection of his work. In this catalogue the spectators are invited to trespass and look at a woman's introspective space. The viewer is challenged by the photographer's brutal mise-en-scène. In one of the pictures Nettie, an elderly woman who Cumming uses in over 50 photographs, poses sprawled out in a seductive lamé slip dress with the hemline just skirting the ''os pubis.'' With this body of work the viewer is forced to confront his own voyeurism and this comes perilously close to exploitation. Cumming's work has been repeatedly described as demeaning and repellent, but to whom? The subjects collaborate under paid contract. The photographer confidently defends this work. ''Nettie and I are old friends and we have a wonderful rapport. All the photographs taken of her were a collaborative effort,'' justifies Cumming.

—Elena Hill

CUMMING, Robert.

Nationality: American. **Born:** Worcester, Massachusetts, 7 October 1943. **Education:** Studied painting at the Massachusetts College of Art, Boston, 1961-65, B.F.A. 1965, and at the University of Illinois, Urbana, 1965-67, M.F.A. 1967. **Family:** Married Sandra Staples in 1969; daughter: Avonell. **Career:** Professional artist since 1967, photographer since 1972. Instructor, University of Wisconsin at Milwaukee, 1967-70; Assistant Professor, California State College at Fullerton, 1970-72, California State University at Long Beach, 1972-74, University of California at Riverside, 1973, University of California at Los Angeles Extension, 1974-77, Otis Art Institute, Los Angeles, 1975-76, Orange Coast College, Costa Mesa, California, 1976,

California Institute of the Arts, Valencia, 1976-77, and University of California at Irvine, 1977-78; Associate Professor, Hartford Art School, West Hartford, Connecticut, 1978-86. **Recipient:** Elmer Winter Sculpture Award, Milwaukee Art Center, 1968; Frank Logan Sculpture Award, Art Institute of Chicago, 1969; Sculpture Purchase Prize, San Diego State College, California, 1972; National Endowment for the Arts Fellowship, 1972, 1976, 1983; Guggenheim Fellowship, 1980-81; Exchange Artist Fellowship, Japan/U.S. Friendship Commission, The Bunkacho, Japan, 1981; Visual Arts Award, Southeast Center for Contemporary Art, Winston-Salem, North Carolina, 1984; Creative Arts Award, Brandeis University, Waltham, Massachusetts, 1985. **Agent:** Castelli Uptown, 4 East 77th Street, New York, New York 10021, U.S.A. **Address:** 1604 North Grand, West Suffield, Connecticut 06093, U.S.A.

Individual Exhibitions:

1973	Phoenix College, Arizona
	California Institute of the Arts, Valencia
	John Gibson Gallery, New York
	University of California at Irvine
	The Photograph as Object, Metaphor and Document of Concept: Robert Heinecken, Minor White and Robert Cumming, California State University at Long Beach
1975	Verelst-Poirer Galerie, Brussels
	John Gibson Gallery, New York
	A Space Gallery, Toronto
1976	University of Iowa, Iowa City
	Newspace Gallery, Los Angeles
	Los Angeles Institute of Contemporary Art
1977	Artons, Calgary, Alberta
	John Gibson Gallery, New York
1978	University of Rhode Island, Kingston
	Grossmont College, El Cajon, California
	Thomas-Lewallen Gallery, Los Angeles
	Real Artways, Hartford, Connecticut
	Gilbert Gallery, Chicago
1979	Friends of Photography, Carmel, California (retrospective)
	Institute of Modern Art, Brisbane, Queensland (retrospective; travelled to the Ewing-Paton Gallery, University of Melbourne; Burnie Art Gallery, Tasmania; Experimental Art Foundation, Adelaide, South Australia; and Australian Centre for Photography, Sydney, 1979-81)
	Callis/Cumming, Blue Sky Gallery, Portland, Oregon (with Jo Ann Callis)
	Evergreen State College, Olympia, Washington
	Nova Gallery, Vancouver
	Gilbert Gallery, Chicago
1980	Bard College, Annandale-on-Hudson, New York
	Film in the Cities Gallery, Minneapolis
	Gilbert Gallery, Chicago
1981	Art Institute of Chicago
1982	Castelli Graphics, New York
	Real Artways, Hartford, Connecticut
	Monmouth College, West Long Branch, New Jersey
	Hampshire College, Amherst, Massachusetts
	Werkstatt für Photographie, West Berlin
1983	Northlight Gallery, Arizona State University, Tempe
	Central Michigan Gallery, Mount Pleasant
	Blue Sky Gallery, Portland, Oregon
1984	Castelli Graphics, New York
	Gallery Watari, Tokyo
	Van Straaten Gallery, New York (with Sandro Chia)
1985	Castelli Graphics, New York
	Cirrus Gallery, Los Angeles
	Wadsworth Atheneum, Hartford, Connecticut
	University of California, Berkeley
	Carpenter-Hochman Gallery, Dallas, Texas
1986	Reynolds-Minor Gallery, Richmond, Virginia
	San Francisco Museum of Modern Art
	Castelli Uptown, New York

Whitney Museum, New York

Selected Group Exhibitions:

1976	*The Artist and the Photograph,* Israel Museum, Jerusalem
1977	*Biennale de Paris,* Musée d'Art Moderne, Paris
1978	*23 Photographers: 23 Directions,* Walker Art Gallery, Liverpool
	Mirrors and Windows: American Photography since 1960, Museum of Modern Art, New York (toured the United States)
1979	*Fabricated to Be Photographed,* San Francisco Museum of Modern Art
1980	*Aspects of the 70's,* De Cordova Museum, Lincoln, Massachusetts
1982	*Target III: In Sequence,* Houston Museum of Fine Arts, Texas
1984	*Photography in California 1945-80,* San Francisco Museum of Modern Art (travelled to the Akron Art Museum, Ohio; Corcoran Gallery, Washington, D.C.; Los Angeles Municipal Art Gallery; Cornell University, Ithaca, New York; High Museum of Art, Atlanta, Georgia; Museum Folkwang, Essen; Centre Georges Pompidou, Paris; Museum of Photographic Arts, San Diego, California)
1985	*American Images 1945-80,* Barbican Art Gallery, London (toured Britain)
1987	*Photography and Art 1946-86,* Los Angeles County Museum of Art

Collections:

Museum of Modern Art, New York; Johnson Library, Cornell University, Ithaca, New York; Hopkins Center, Dartmouth College, Hanover, New Hampshire; Corcoran Gallery of Art, Washington, D.C.; Art Institute of Chicago; Museum of Fine Arts, Houston; University of New Mexico, Albuquerque; Academy of Motion Picture Arts and Sciences, Los Angeles.

Publications:

By CUMMING: Books—*Picture Fictions,* Los Angeles 1971, 1973; *The Weight of Franchise Meat,* Los Angeles 1971; *A Training in the Arts,* Toronto 1973; *Discourse on Domestic Disorder,* Los Angeles 1975; *Interruptions in Landscape and Logic,* Los Angeles 1977; *Equilibrium and the Rotary Disc,* Providence, Rhode Island 1980; *Robert Cumming: Drawings for Props and Photographs,* Adelaide 1980. Articles—''Through Western Eyes,'' interview, with Leo Rubinfein, in *Art in America* (New York), September 1978; ''Robert Cumming,'' interview, with Ted Hedgepeth in *San Francisco Camerawork,* Fall 1983.

On CUMMING: Books—*Robert Cumming: Nation's Capitol in Photographs* by Jane Livingston, Washington, D.C. 1976; *Robert Cumming: Photographs* by James Alinder, Carmel, California 1979; *American Photography, 1946 to the Present* by J. Green, New York 1984; *Photography in California 1945-1980* by Louise Katzman, San Francisco and New York 1984; *American Images: Photography 1945-1980,* edited by Peter Turner and John Benton-Harris, London and New York 1985; *Photography and Art 1946-1986,* exhibition catalogue, by Andy Grundberg and Kathleen M. Gauss, Los Angeles 1987. Articles—''Robert Cumming'' by P. Kraniak in *Tempest* (Milwaukee), Fall 1970; ''Robert Cumming's Eccentric Illusions'' by Patricia Foschi in *Artforum* (New York), June 1975; ''The Directorial Mode'' by A.D. Coleman in *Artforum* (New York), September 1976; ''The Photographer and the Drawing: Fitch, Misrach, Cumming'' by L. Fishman in *Creative Camera* (London), August 1977; ''Robert Cumming'' by I. Applebaum in *Impressions* (Toronto), June 1978; ''Robert Cumming: Trucage; Falsehoods'' by J. Hugunin in *Afterimage* (Rochester, New York), December 1978; ''Robert Cumming: Objects and Their Photographs'' by R. Keziere in *Vanguard* (Vancouver), December 1978; ''Robert Cumming's Recent Work'' by J. Hugunin in *LAICA Journal* (Los Angeles), March 1979; ''Currents: American Photography Today'' by Andy Grundberg and Julia Scully in *Modern Photography* (New York), November 1982; ''Robert Cumming's Subject-Object'' by C. Hagen in *Artforum* (New York), Summer 1983.

*

My work progresses seriously—despite the doubt and despite the suspicions of folly—much the same as it did 20 years ago. The works of the 1960's (when I defined myself primarily as a sculptor) represented an approach to art making as a means to understanding the world through its objects and phenomena. Once one understood, I thought, a very broad (but finite) set of systems—engineering, psychology, philosophy, etc.—much of the inexplicable would clear aside and one would come to see the rough shape of a ''truth'' or ''reality.'' One only had to apply oneself diligently to the details of currently accepted ''universals,'' principles and theorems governing cause and effect throughout the cosmos.

Instead of an emergent clarity of overview, the whole became a detail-laden morass with no specific shape. Voices of intellectual and creative brilliance lead the way and provide frequent short-cuts. But, indiscriminately listened to, the more the answers of their own accord expand the central paradox. Logic and rationale begin to rebound in hazy conceptual spaces . . . contradictions abound . . . dualistic dilemmas go unchecked . . . and the whole swells accordingly.

Now my work still looks to satisfactory answers to questions I have about the world. The work, like the world, incorporates the false echoes and detours as part of its natural by-product. Pragmatically, it looks earnestly for nuts and bolts solutions, but accepts now too the permanent presence of mystery. The compulsion of the earlier work to ''make sense'' is simply seen as the common inner need to assert order over chaos. That each of us through life draws up a satisfactory, orderly shape, its simple proportions the result of a lifetimes' alterations, is an intriguing proposition. Suspiciously, the emergent profile resembles that of its owner, despite claims of objectivity. I think, from birth, we're given the onerous task of filling in details; I think the work of any successful artist must transmit, in covert visual terms, the results of that personal fabrication.

—Robert Cumming

* * *

An undercurrent for decades, conceptual art emerged as a formal movement in the 1960's as an extreme response of the dictum ''less is more.'' Its philosophical roots lie in the belief that ideas are the most important human product; presentation through an actual art object is secondary. Taken to its logical extreme, this theory implies that art ultimately has no physical object. While a few visual artists found the idea of art without objects appealing in its pure form, most felt the need for a vehicle to share their ideas with an audience. Photography was often the medium selected for that sharing because of its utility in the documentation of ideas. It thus entered at the core of the conceptual movement. Of the several artists who refined their use of photography while maintaining a distinctly conceptual approach, Robert Cumming is one of the most important.

As a child, Cumming was a self-taught and compulsive artist. His formal art education, which included both bachelor's and master's degrees, initially focused on drawing and painting, but later on sculpture and, finally, photography. While his primary statement over the past few years has been in photography, he continues to work actively in other media. In fact, he calls on his skills as a sculptor to construct the basic ''subject matter'' for many of his photographs. For most photographers the object to be photographed is raw material. For Cumming, the objects which he constructs to be used in his photographs are an inherent part of the creative process as well as subjects.

The evolution of Cumming's photography over the past decade, on close inspection, shows both continuity and change. The change is not always clear, however, because Cumming often returns to earlier themes. His themes include interruptions in landscape and logic, reappraisal of everyday objects, debunking of the polished presentation of art photographs, ironic and absurd reversals of the expected, distorted time relationships, reconsideration of form and function, out-and-out illusionism and magic tricks, satires on the misreading of natural phenomena, and sardonic commentaries on the history

of art and photography. To present these ideas as photographs, Cumming has purposefully directed the objects placed in front of the camera; he has carefully constructed and arranged them to provide the visual expression of his concept.

A central theme in Cumming's work is his desire to remind us that we are looking at a photograph; he wants his ''hand'' to show. He often includes the floodlights, the source of illumination of the photograph, within the frame. Cumming usually leaves more around the edges of the subject than we expect; he does not fill the frame with the central subject, but allows us to see its context.

The relationship between the amount of time spent conceptualizing, constructing and photographing in Cumming's work is radically different from what we commonly expect in photography. Of course the percentages vary with each piece, but Cummings spends perhaps an average of 45% of his time thinking, 45% building the subject—100 mosquitos, for example—and 10% actually making the picture.

Despite a long-standing public notion that photographs tell the truth, that they can and should be believed, there is abundant evidence that *all* photographs are replete with lies and fabrications. At the very most they give us a modest monocular appearance of one aspect of a subject. Amazingly, we still routinely expect approximate truth from still photographs, and we are nonplussed when confronted with sleight of hand. For Cumming, illusionism and artifice are fundamental, and as with the magician, we are advised not to pose technical questions, but simply to enjoy.

The captions which accompany Cumming's photographs are sometimes merely labels, yet often they are vital links to understanding. While drawing on the narrative abilities of the photograph, Cumming uses the captions to spark out interpretation. He points out connections which the viewer may not have been able to determine from the photographs alone. However, Cumming has also been known to add a caption that leads nowhere.

While most conceptual artists use photography merely as a tool to document their ideas, Cumming is concerned with the medium of photography itself. His photographs, with their environmental backgrounds, are considerably more interesting as pictures than are typical conceptual documents. Cumming has also chosen the 8 x 10 view camera as the instrument for his picture making. He selected the format for its ability to resolve detail, but he does not place emphasis on other potential advantages of the large negative. It would seem too fussy for him to be concerned with elegant fine prints; after all, craft must not dominate concept. It is clear, however, when viewing Cumming's original prints, that there has been an overall refinement in his craft during the past decade.

One of the most consistently appealing aspects of his photographs is that they are metaphors which can be appreciated on many levels. Robert Cumming is a magician who seems to be explaining the secret of his magic, but is one step ahead of us.

—James Alinder

CUNNINGHAM, Imogen.

Nationality: American. **Born:** Portland, Oregon, 12 April 1883. **Education:** Attended Seattle public schools; studied chemistry at the University of Washington, Seattle, and photographic chemistry at the Technische Hochschule, Dresden, 1909-10. **Family:** Married the printmaker Roi Partridge in 1915 (divorced, 1934); son: Rondal. **Career:** Began photographing in 1901; worked in the studio of the photographer Edward S. Curtis, Seattle, 1907-09; maintained own studio, Seattle, 1910-16; moved to San Francisco and established studio, 1917, and worked there until her death, 1976: created series of ''plant studies,'' 1922-29; did free-lance work for *Vanity Fair* magazine, 1931-36; Founding Member, with Willard Van Dyke, Ansel Adams, Edward Weston, Sonya Noskowiak, John Paul Edwards and Henry Swift, Group f/64, San Francisco, 1932-35. Visiting Instructor in Photography, California College of Arts and Crafts, Oakland: Ansel Adams Workshop, Yosemite Park, California; and at the San Francisco Art Institute. Founded the Imogen Cunningham Trust, San Francisco, 1974. **Recipient:** Guggenheim Fellowship, 1970; Artist of the Year Award, San Francisco Art Commission, 1973; Summa Laude

Dignatus Award, University of Washington, 1974. D.F.A.: California College of Arts and Crafts, 1969. **Died:** (in San Francisco) 24 June 1976.

Individual Exhibitions:

1912	Brooklyn Institute of Arts and Sciences, New York
1932	Los Angeles County Museum of Art
	M.H. de Young Memorial Museum, San Francisco
1935	Dallas Art Museum
1936	E.B. Crocker Art Gallery, Sacramento, California
1951	San Francisco Museum of Art
1953	Mills College, Oakland, California
1956	Cincinnati Museum of Art, Ohio
	Limelight Gallery, New York
1957	Oakland Art Museum, California
1959	Oakland Public Museum, California
1961	International Museum of Photography, George Eastman House, Rochester, New York
1964	San Francisco Museum of Art
	Art Institute of Chicago
1965	Henry Gallery, University of Washington, Seattle
1967	*Imogen Cunningham: Photographs 1921-1967,* Stanford University Art Gallery, California
1968	California College of Arts and Crafts, Oakland
	North Beach and Haight-Ashbury, Focus Gallery, San Francisco
1969	Siembab Gallery, Boston
	Women, Cameras and Images I, Smithsonian Institution, Washington, D.C.
	Phoenix College Library, Arizona
1970	M.H. de Young Memorial Museum, San Francisco
1971	Seattle Art Museum
	Friends of Photography, Carmel, California
	Bathhouse Gallery, Milwaukee
	Atholl McBean Gallery, San Francisco Art Institute
1972	Mt. Angel Abbey, Oregon
	Ohio Silver Gallery, Los Angeles
1973	Witkin Gallery, New York
	Metropolitan Museum of Art, New York
	Artist of the Year, Capricorn Asunder Gallery, San Francisco
1974	*Imogen! . . . Imogen Cunningham Photographs 1910-1973,* Henry Art Gallery, University of Washington, Seattle
1977	*Imogen Cunningham: 75 Years as a Photographer,* Union Gallery, University of Michigan, Ann Arbor
1979	*Imogen Cunningham: 75 Anni di Fotografia,* Galleria-Libreria Pan, Rome
1981	*Imogen Cunningham: Vintage and Modern Photographs,* David Mancini Gallery, Philadelphia
	Photographs of People over 90 Years of Age, Milwaukee Art Center
	Camera Obcura Gallery, Stockholm
	Photogallery International, Tokyo
1983	*A Centennial Selection,* California Academy of Arts and Sciences, San Francisco (toured the United States 1983-86)
	Dolls and Doubles, Camerawork Gallery, San Francisco
	Vanity Fair Photos, Focus Gallery, San Francisco
	Portraits of Artists, San Francisco Art Institute

Selected Group Exhibitions:

1929	*Film und Foto,* Deutscher Werkbund, Stuttgart
1932	*Group f/64,* M.H. de Young Memorial Museum, San Francisco
1937	*Photography 1839-1937,* Museum of Modern Art, New York
1940	*A Pageant of Photography,* at the *Golden Gate International Exposition,* San Francisco
1959	*Photography at Mid-Century,* International Museum of Photography, George Eastman House, Rochester, New York (toured the United States)
1970	*Platinum Prints,* Friends of Photography, Carmel, California

1973	*Images of Imogen 1903-73,* Focus Gallery, San Francisco (travelled to the Henry Art Gallery, University of Washington, Seattle, where it appeared with the one-woman show *Imogen Cunningham Photographs 1910-1973,* 1974)
1974	*Photography in America,* Whitney Museum, New York
1982	*Images of America,* San Francisco Museum of Modern Art (travelled to the St. Louis Art Museum, Missouri; Baltimore Museum of Art, Maryland; Des Moines Art Center, Iowa; Cleveland Museum of Art, Ohio)
1985	*Das Aktfoto,* Fotomuseum im Stadtmuseum, Munich (toured West Germany)

Collections:

Imogen Cunningham Trust, Berkeley, California; Henry Swift Collection, San Francisco Museum of Modern Art; Oakland Museum, California; Center for Creative Photography, University of Arizona, Tucson; Art Institute of Chicago; International Museum of Photography, George Eastman House, Rochester, New York; Museum of Modern Art, New York; Metropolitan Museum of Art, New York; Library of Congress, Washington, D.C.; Smithsonian Institution, Washington, D.C.

Publications:

By CUNNINGHAM: Books of photographs—*Imogen Cunningham: Photographs,* with an introduction by Margery Mann, Seattle and London 1970 (includes bibliography); *After Ninety,* with an introduction by Margaretta Mitchell, Seattle and London 1977; other books—*Imogen Cunningham: Portraits, Ideas and Design,* interviews, with Edna Tartual Daniel, Berkeley, California 1961. **Articles**—"Imogen Cunningham," interview, in *Interviews with Master Photographers* by James Danziger and Barnaby Conrad III, New York and London 1977; "Imogen Cunningham," interview, in *Dialogue with Photography* by Paul Hill and Thomas Cooper, London 1979.

On CUNNINGHAM: Books—*Imogen Cunningham* (Aperture monograph), Millerton, New York 1964; *Imogen Cunningham: Photographs 1921-1967,* exhibition catalogue, by Beaumont Newhall, Stanford, California 1967; *Imogen! . . . Imogen Cunningham Photographs 1910-1973,* exhibition catalogue, by Margery Mann, Seattle and London 1974; *Imogen Cunningham: A Portrait* by Judy Dater, Boston and London 1979; *Images of America: Precisionist Painting and Modern Photography,* exhibition catalogue, by Karen Tsujimoto, Seattle, Washington 1982; *American Images: Photography 1945-1980,* edited by Peter Turner and John Benton-Harris, London and New York 1985. **Articles**—"Imogen Cunningham" by Norman Hall in *Photography* (London), May 1960; "Imogen Cunningham" by George M. Craven in *Aperture* (Millerton, New York), November 1964; "Imogen Cunningham" by Margery Mann in *Infinity* (New York), November 1966; "Imogen Cunningham" by Bill Jay in *Album* (London), June 1970; "Photographs by Imogen Cunningham" by Colin Osman in *Creative Camera* (London), July 1971; "Group f/64" by Allan Porter in *Camera* (Lucerne), February 1973; "Abigail Heyman and Imogen Cunningham" by A.D. Coleman in the *New York Times,* 30 June 1974, reprinted in his book *Light Readings: A Photography Critic's Writings 1968-1978,* New York 1979; "Homage to Imogen," special issue of *Camera* (Lucerne), October 1975.

* * *

Her career spanned the first three-quarters of the 20th century, paralleling and at times advancing the major directions of the period's art photography. Imogen Cunningham began in 1901, when she was 19, as an amateur correspondent of a photography school. In 1907, after a lapse in her interest in the medium, she saw the work of Gertrude Käsebier and was moved to give again to photography the energy she had been devoting to painting and drawing. On her return to Seattle in 1910 from a year at the Dresden Polytechnic, where she studied photo-chemistry, she opened a portrait studio; the light, settings and poses were natural, in the Käsebier manner. Outside of the studio, she took her view camera to Seattle's misty woods, where she draped friends in exotic cloths and posed them in tableaux representing scenes from William Morris's prose romance *The Wood Beyond the World,* the poetry of Swinburne, and moral themes such as "Conscience" and "Eve Repentant.'' She hired a family of models and posed them naked over reflecting pools, affording revelations that shocked Seattle when the photographs were exhibited in 1915. After marriage and the birth of three sons, she moved with her family to Northern California. There, in the 1920's, she joined in the general rejection of pictorialism that Stieglitz had evidenced by at least 1915. She was then in touch with Edward Weston and Margrethe Mather; the double portraits that she made of the pair just before Weston went to Mexico in 1923 mark the beginning of her break with the earlier style. She quickly moved to a mode that put her at the forefront of the international style of the 1920's: in 1925, she produced ''Magnolia Blossom,'' the first of a series of closeups of plant forms that were exhibited in 1929 at the Stuttgart *Film und Foto* exhibition. The group, which included ''Glacial Lily,'' ''Callas,'' ''Rubber Plant,'' ''Agave,'' ''Aloe Bud'' and others, were seen as among the most powerful demonstrations of the impulse toward the abstract in photography that typified the decade.

Edward Weston's essay for the *Film und Foto* catalogue looked forward to another development, strictly American, that she and Weston shared. In it, he equated impressionism with skepticism, and declared that photography is ''a way of extreme exactitude . . . honest, straightforward and free of compromise when it is used purely.'' Within three years a group of seven West Coast photographers sympathetic with Weston's example exhibited together in San Francisco. They called themselves Group f/64, signifying the shutter stop that would produce the greatest detail in depth on their preferred view cameras. Besides Cunningham and Weston, the members of f/64 were Ansel Adams, John Paul Edwards, Sonya Noskowiak, Henry Swift and Willard Van Dyke. Ansel Adams recognized the variety of individual approaches that the fact of organization tended to obscure: ''the variety of approach, emotional and intellectual—of subject material, of tonal values, of style—which we evidence in our respective fields is proof sufficient that pure photography is not a *metier* of rigid and restricted rule. It can interpret with beauty and power the wide spectrum of emotional experience.'' Cunningham's subject matter became increasingly portraits, especially after she opened a professional portrait studio in San Francisco in the mid-1930s. During these years she thought of herself as a portraitist of individuals; the portrayal of American society that occupied the photographers of the Farm Security Administration was not, she stated, for her. A commission from *Vanity Fair* to photograph Herbert Hoover led her to introduce herself thus: ''I am not a snapshot candid camera worker—but try to the best of my ability to establish a feeling of confidence between my sitter and myself and what I call an honest portrait, not a caricature.''

Until 1939, when she first used a Rolleiflex, she made portraits with an 8 x 10 view camera or a 4 x 5 Graflex. After that she used the Rollei for portraits, but preferred a larger camera on a tripod for still subjects. By 1965 she had photographed so many artists and craftsmen of the West Coast that a publisher proposed that they be gathered into a volume called *West Coast Creators*. But her field was not limited to local artists, and among her finest portraits are those of José Limon, Merce Cunningham, Darius Milhaud, Amadee Ozenfant, Lionel Feininger, Gertrude Stein, John Masefield, Marianne Moore, Stephen Spender, Alfred Stieglitz, Morris Graves, Minor White, and Theodore Roethke. A list of these portraits constitutes a selective *Who's Who* in the arts during the years of her greatest portrait activity, c. 1935-1965. Many of the portraits remain the most convincing representation we have of their subjects. They share her absolute respect for the sitter as an individual whose identity is regarded at a distance; the sitter's mood and style dominates, not the photographer's. She does not introduce props, but takes them as she finds them: who can forget that Stieglitz stands in front of a painting by O'Keeffe, that the bemused Feininger has a passion flower in his buttonhole, that Roethke sits by a concrete wall inscribed with a ragged ''R''?

At the same time that she practiced a straight use of her medium, she also investigated unstraight ways and printing processes to produce intense statements of private meanings. She acknowledged that ''unreality is interesting to me but difficult, in such an exact medium, to achieve.'' Her way out of this difficulty was a way she practiced early: a negative print, 1929; a double exposure, 1931. In later portraits (''Dream Walking,'' 1968; ''Warning,'' 1970; ''Pentimento,'' 1973), she combined negatives to produce images that continued the dreamlike scenarios of her 1912-1914 illustrations.

The body of work by which she is widely known is but a small part of that produced throughout the years of her career. It has been skimmed from the top, the ''artistic'' cream of her whole production. The rest includes, to name typical examples, color covers for *Sunset* magazine, a Southern Pacific

Railroad poster, 103 shots of a wedding that she covered with her photographer son Rondal, documentary photographs of the weavings and ceramics of craftsmen, bound booklets of photographs of children: all of the bread-and-butter part of her working life that we disregard in the gallery and museum world of today.

In the last years of her life she was overwhelmed by interviews, students seeking advice, and preparations for important exhibitions that were finally offered to her. She also had a major photographic project in mind. She was consciously pursuing it in 1974, when she went to Fidaglio Island, near Seattle, to photograph the 93-year-old father of a friend. While she prepared herself for death in an orderly, practical way, she explored the worlds of her peers, people over 90, for the experience of its approach that could be derived, both for her own and others' use, from her photographs. Making these portraits of her contemporaries occupied her until June 1976, when she was still planning a trip up the California coast to Elk, where a friend had found an ancient Indian basketmaker for her to photograph. But she died that month, and the book that resulted from her project is without the photograph of the basketmaker.

Throughout her life Imogen Cunningham had thought of herself as a self-employed photographer. She had believed that work was essential to life; it was through work, she had said in 1914, that ''the human mind finds a form in which to express itself.'' Near the end of her life, after over half a century of hard and often unrewarded work, she could still say, ''To have real work is the only way to live.''

—Anita V. Mozley

CURRAN, Douglas.

Nationality: Canadian. **Born:** Seaforth, Ontario, 7 August 1952. **Education:** Studied at Loyalist College of Applied Arts, Belleville, Ontario, 1971; Photographic Arts Department, Ryerson Polytechnic Institute, Toronto, 1972-76; The Banff Centre, Alberta, 1979 (studio scholarship). **Family:** Married Kate Davis in 1981. **Career:** Independent photographer, from 1968; freelance photographer and stillsman, for various motion picture companies, in Canada and internationally, since 1983. Instructor in photography and guest speaker: University of New Mexico, Albuquerque, 1980; American Culture Convention, Detroit, Michigan, 1980; City of Edmonton Parks and Recreation, Alberta, 1981; Daziboa Gallery, Montreal, Quebec, 1982; Alberta Culture, Edmonton, 1983; University of Alberta, Edmonton, 1983-84; Grant McEwan College, Edmonton, Alberta, 1984; Toronto Photographers Workshop, Ontario, 1986. **Recipient:** Canada Council Grants, 1977, 1978, 1981, 1984; Alberta Writers' Guild Non-Fiction Award, 1985. **Address:** 6002 Bow Crescent N.W., Calgary, Alberta, Canada.

Individual Exhibitions:

1977	*Picton*, Ryerson Polytechnical Institute, Toronto, Ontario
1978	*Tangent Series*, Between Spaces, Ottawa, Ontario
	Folk Concepts of Outer Space, Prairie Light Gallery, Saskatoon, Saskatchewan
	Folk Concepts of Outer Space, University of Ottawa, Ontario
1981	*In Advance of the Landing*, Edmonton Art Gallery, Alberta (toured Canada)
1983	*Doug Curran's Other Photographs*, Latitude 53 Gallery, Edmonton, Alberta
1984	*In Advance of the Landing*, Coburg Gallery, Vancouver, British Columbia
	Gallery-In-Transit, travelled to Winnipeg, Manitoba; Edmonton, Alberta; Vancouver, British Columbia
1985	*The Metis Settlements of Alberta*, Edmonton Art Gallery, Alberta (toured Canada)

Selected Group Exhibitions:

1978	*Alberta-Saskatchewan-Manitoba*, National Film Board of Canada, Ottawa, Ontario (toured Canada)

1980	*Seven: Weegee/Szilasi/Arbus/Kertesz/Levinson/Curran/ Max,* Banff Centre, Alberta
1981	*New Acquisitions,* National Film Board of Canada, Ottawa, Ontario
1982	*Primary Colour,* Art Gallery at Harbourfront, Toronto, Ontario
1983	*Document,* National Film Board of Canada, Ottawa, Ontario (toured Canada)
	Ten-83, Alberta Art Foundation, Edmonton
1984	*Canadian Contemporary Photography,* National Film Board of Canada, Ottawa, Ontario (toured Canada)
	Enigma, Nickle Arts Museum, Calgary, Alberta
1985	*Structured Paradise,* Banff Centre, Alberta
1986	*1985 Acquisitions,* Edmonton Art Gallery, Alberta

Collections:

Canadian Museum of Contemporary Photography, Ottawa, Ontario; Banff Centre, Alberta; Edmonton Art Gallery, Alberta; Winnipeg Art Gallery, Manitoba; Alberta Vocational Centre, Lac LaBiche; Alberta 75th Commission, Edmonton; Alberta Art Foundation, Edmonton.

Publications:

By CURRAN: Books—*Keepsake: Photographs from the Alberta 75th Photo Project,* with introduction by Doug Clark and Lyn Wedman, Calgary, Alberta 1982; *Metisism: A Cultural Identity,* Edmonton, Alberta 1983; *The Metis Settlements of Alberta,* calendar, Calgary, Alberta 1984; *In Advance of the Landing: Folk Concepts of Outer Space,* with foreword by Tom Wolfe, New York 1985. **Articles**—"Chronicler of Flying Saucer Lore," interview, in *People Magazine* (New York), 8 September 1986; "In Advance of the Landing" in *Whole Earth Review* (Sausalito, California), Fall 1986.

On CURRAN: Book—*Canadian Contemporary Photography* by Martha Langford, Edmonton, Alberta 1984. **Articles**—"Close Encounters with the Saucer Sects" by Salem Alaton in the *Globe and Mail* (Toronto), 22 February 1986; "The Flying Saucer Set" by Brian D. Johnson in *Maclean's Magazine* (Toronto), 17 March 1986.

*   *   *

For nearly a decade Douglas Curran has been turning himself into a witness for the culturally marginal peoples of North America. He makes periodic sorties from his northwestern outpost in Edmonton into the rest of the continent, gumshoeing his way through the gas stations and cafes strung along secondary highways until he finds his subjects. For more than half a dozen years he tracked UFO cultists, people who believed in a high technology Second Coming. His recent book of this material, *In Advance of the Landing: Folk Concepts of Outer Space,* documents the awkward sythesis of traditional religion and modern science that inspires both those who believe that Jesus will return in a flying saucer as well as those individuals building their own

space ships in order to rise up and meet him. Curran's photographs are those of a born storyteller. Although he pays homage to Walker Evans and August Sander, the real paradigms are the Weegee of *Naked City* and Bill Owens' *Suburbia.* His pictures have little of the austere and classical formal qualities of Evans'; rather, they are those of a reporter—one who gets everything we need to know within the frame and relies on content to carry the image.

If, at times, one wishes that the photographs in *Folk Concepts* were less casual in construction, one is rewarded by his more recent work with the Metis people of Alberta. His collaboration with these descendants of French fur trappers and native indian women has produced a series of handsome photographs with a clear pictorial structure that perfectly supports the information they contain. The organization of elements within each picture goes beyond simple reporting—it interprets what we are seeing. Although Curran, like Owens, always photographs with the consent and complicity of his subjects, his Metis people, unlike the UFO cultists, no longer consistently stand near the centre of the frame staring at the camera. Instead we witness a people hard at their work and play or lost in their own private thoughts. When they do stand and face the camera the photographs really do approach the elegant simplicity of Sander's most memorable portraits. In this work we know what Curran feels for this largely disenfranchised people. Despite the greater physical distance and wider views in this work, the cumulative effect is one of greater intimacy. The photographs reflect a partnership with a people rather than simply the encounter of photographer and cultist. As a result, we no longer glance and smile, we look hard and care.

Curran's ambition is not so much to make art as to record information and make photographs that are useful. Unlike Owens or Weegee who photographed people of their own class, Curran follows documentary tradition and points his camera down the social scale. However he is not yet another photographer out slumming for exotica; there is always a much larger issue at stake. His current project, a documentary on itinerant evangelists, seems, along with *Folk Concepts,* to be a reflection on the belief crisis in our secular culture. Both projects remind us that the ideas and established learning that inform everyday life are often quite incompatible with late-twentieth-century science and technology. However much we may smile at the homespun attempts of the flying saucer millenialists to integrate old fashioned Bible thumping with modern science, we all, in truth, share their confusion and anxiety. Fear of atomic annihilation is the leitmotiv in believers' statements in Curran's book. Like the rest of us they are scared; their belief system helps them manage that fear.

In the course of working on *Folk Concepts* Curran occasionally revisited some of his subjects after several years had intervened. Some had abandoned their saucers and embraced new beliefs. Their withdrawal demonstrated what they perhaps only unconsciously understood—that a patchwork of Christian fundamentalism, patriotism, and popularized science refuses to stay stuck together. These searchers are not charlatans but people trying to find value and meaning in the modern world. By photographing these seemingly marginal people Curran is documenting a contemporary crisis of the spirit.

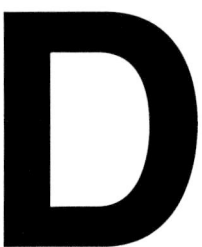

DAHL-WOLFE, Louise (Emma Augusta).

Nationality: American. **Born:** Louise Dahl in Alameda, California, 19 November 1895. **Education:** Studied design and color under Rudolph Schaeffer, and painting under Frank Van Sloan, at the San Francisco Institute of Art, day classes 1914-17, night classes 1921-22; studied design and decoration in New York, 1923, and architecture at Columbia University, New York, Summer 1923; mainly self-taught in photography, but influenced initially, in the early 1920s, by the work of photographer Anne Brigman. **Family:** Married the painter and sculptor Meyer (Mike) Wolfe in 1928. **Career:** Electric sign designer for the Federal Electric Company, San Francisco, 1920-22; assistant to an interior decorator, New York, 1923; assistant to the decorator Beth Armstrong, at Armstrong, Carter and Kenyon, San Francisco, 1924; worked for Stroheim and Roman wholesale fabrics company, San Francisco, 1925-1927; travelled with the photographer/journalist Consuela Kanaga in Europe, 1927-28; worked for the interior decorating firm Hofstatten and Company, New York, 1929; concentrated on photography, San Francisco, 1930-32 and Gatlinburg, Great Smoky Mountains, Tennessee, 1932-33; maintained own photographic studio in New York, 1933-60: freelance advertising and fashion photographer, working for *Woman's Home Companion,* and for the stores Saks Fifth Avenue and Bonwit Teller, New York, 1933-36; Staff Fashion Photographer, under editor Carmel Snow, *Harper's Bazaar,* New York, 1936-58; freelance magazine photographer, working for *Vogue,* New York, 1958-59, and *Sports Illustrated,* New York, 1958-60; now retired. **Recipient:** Art Directors Club of New York Medal, 1939, and Award, 1941. **Agent:** Staley-Wise Gallery, 560 Broadway, New York, New York 10012, U.S.A. **Died:** 11 December 1989.

Individual Exhibitions:

1955	Southern Vermont Art Center, Manchester (with Meyer Wolfe)
1965	*Louise Dahl-Wolfe: Photographs/Meyer Wolfe: Sculpture and Drawings,* Country Art Gallery, Westbury, Long Island, New York
1983	Staley-Wise Gallery, New York Grey Art Gallery, New York University (retrospective)
1984	Staley-Wise Gallery, New York
1986	Center for Creative Photography, University of Arizona, Tucson
1992	Staley-Wise Gallery, New York

Selected Group Exhibitions:

1937	*Photography 1839-1937,* Museum of Modern Art, New York
1961	*Fashion: 7 Decades,* Hofstra University, Hempstead, New York
1975	*Women of Photography: An Historical Survey,* San Francisco Museum of Modern Art (travelled to the Sidney Janis Gallery, New York, 1976)
1977	*The History of Fashion Photography,* International Museum of Photography, George Eastman House, Rochester, New York (travelled to the San Francisco Museum of Modern Art; Cincinnati Art Institute; and the Museum of Fine Arts, St. Petersburg, Florida)
1979	*Recollections: 10 Women of Photography,* International Center of Photography, New York (toured the United States)
1980	*Fashion Photographs,* Tennessee Fine Arts Museum at Cheekwood, Nashville
1982	*Color as Form,* International Museum of Photography at George Eastman House, Rochester, New York
1986	*The Animal in Photography 1843-1985,* The Photographers' Gallery, London
1987	*Hollywood Photographers,* Los Angeles County Museum of Art

Collections:

Fashion Institute of Technology, New York; Museum of Modern Art, New York; International Museum of Photography, George Eastman House, Rochester, New York; San Francisco Museum of Modern Art.

Publications:

By DAHL-WOLFE: Book—*A Photographer's Scrapbook,* New York 1984. **Articles**—"America's Outstanding Woman Photographers," interview, with Kary H. Lasch, in *Foto* (Stockholm), no. 9, 1950; "Louise Dahl-Wolfe" in *Inter/View* (New York), February 1981.

On DAHL-WOLFE: Books—*The Wheels of Fashion* by Phyllis Lee Levin, New York 1965; *Harper's Bazaar: 100 Years of the American Female* by Jane Trahey, New York 1967; *American Fashion* by Sarah Tomerlin Lee, New York 1975, London 1976; *Women of Photography: An Historical Survey,* exhibition catalogue, by Margery Mann and Ann Noggle, San Francisco 1975; *The Magic Image* by Cecil Beaton and Gail Buckland, London and Boston 1975; *The Photograph Collector's Guide* by Lee D. Witkin and Barbara London, Boston and London 1979; *The History of Fashion Photography* by Nancy Hall-Duncan, New York 1979; *Recollections: Ten Women of Photography* by Margaretta Mitchell, New York 1979; *Color as Form: A History of Color Photography,* exhibition catalogue, with introduction by Robert A. Sobieszek, Rochester, New York 1982; *Hollywood Photographers: Interpreting American Culture Through Photographs,* exhibition catalogue, by Linda Rich, David Fahey and Kathleen M. Gauss, Los Angeles 1987. **Articles**—"World History of Photography on Exhibition at the Museum of Modern Art" in the *New York Times,* 17 March 1937; "Look Behind Success" by Helen Morgan in *You* (New York), Summer 1940; "Good Housekeeping Finds Out What a Woman Photographer Does" in *Good Housekeeping* (New York), August 1941; "La Photos de Louise Dahl-Wolfe" in *Norte* (Mexico City), October 1942; "Great American Photographers 1: Louise Dahl-Wolfe" in *Pageant* (New York), September 1947; "The Individualist" by Sarah Tomerlin Lee in *House Beautiful* (New York), March 1965; "Louise Dahl-Wolfe: Quiet at Home" in the *New York Times,* 16 December 1973; "Louise Dahl-Wolfe: A Discerning Eye, A Cordial Heart" in the *Nashville Tennessean,* 1 June 1980; "Profile: Louise Dahl-Wolfe" by Vicki Goldberg in *American Photographer* (New York), June 1981; "When Illustration Becomes Artistic Expression" by Gene Thornton in the *New York Times,* 2 October 1983; "A Chronicler of Fashion, at 88, Reflects on Change" by John Duka in the *New York Times,* 28 September 1984.

*

Upon thinking over my long career in photography, particularly the years spent on *Harper's Bazaar,* I've arrived at the following conclusion: that if there were any successes, they were due to the knowledge I gained from the 5 years I spent at the San Francisco Institute of Art and also from the opportunity of working under an outstanding editor, Carmel Snow.

It is easy to learn the technique of the camera by oneself, but by working in design I learned the principles of good design and composition. Drawing from the nudes in life class made me aware of the grace and flow of line, body movements, and the differences in the way a male poses from that of a female. This was helpful in photographing fashion.

I was exceedingly fortunate in studying color with a great teacher, Rudolph Schaeffer, who at the age of 90 is still teaching the art and science of color in San Francisco.

—Louise Dahl-Wolfe

*   *   *

Although Louise Dahl-Wolfe is known primarily as a fashion photographer whose achievement equals or surpasses that of her contemporaries, such as Horst, Cecil Beaton and Richard Avedon, she has also created a significant body of portrait and landscape work. Dahl-Wolfe credits her study at the San Francisco Institute of Art with training her eye for composition and color. In particular, she cites the influence of her instructor, Rudolph Schaeffer, who was one of the few teachers in the U.S. at the time to encourage the use of intense "Fauve" color. In 1916, the Diaghilev Ballet's visit to San Francisco provided further inspiration for the imaginative settings and unusual color harmonies for which she became known. Indeed, the exquisite interiors which she created for her own home, a renovated farmhouse in Frenchtown, New Jersey, served as the backdrop for some of the most memorable of the fashion photographs which she made during her 22-year career with *Harper's Bazaar*.

Dahl-Wolfe became interested in photography in 1921 when she was shown the Pictorialist photographer Anne Brigman's studies of nudes posed against the cypress trees on Point Lobos. The dramatic poses and averted faces of Brigman's nudes may have influenced Dahl-Wolfe's approach to the model, just as her Tennessee-born artist-husband Meyer Wolfe may have expanded her innate interest in people of all nationalities and social levels to include blacks and rural poor. Dahl-Wolfe was also impressed with the work of another San Francisco based photographer, Francis Bruguièr, but it is unlikely that his abstractions had any direct influence on her resolutely representational style.

Dahl-Wolfe met and later married Meyer Wolfe on a trip to Europe and North Africa in 1928, and her first published photograph was a portrait of a Mrs. Ramsey, which was made in her husband's home state of Tennessee. "Tennessee Mountain Woman" (*Vanity Fair*, November 1933) presages the Farm Security Administration photography of the Depression, but Dahl-Wolfe was less concerned with documenting poverty than with reflecting the personality of the sitter. Framing an intricately lined face, Mrs. Ramsey's 25-year-old straw hat has a poignant elegance which constitutes a naive counterpart to the sophisticated young models in Paulette hats which Dahl-Wolfe sat against the Louvre in May 1950. The same direct address of the camera marks Dahl-Wolfe's portraits of the bedridden Colette (1951) and the starkly lit, androgynous face of Cecil Beaton (1950).

Color fashion photography was in its infancy when Dahl-Wolfe began experimenting with the Kodak "one-shot" camera. She gained experience by photographing shoes and accessories before receiving her first fashion assignments in 1937. With the advent of 8 x 10-inch Kodachrome transparencies several years later, Dahl-Wolfe's instinct for elegance was unleashed, and her control of color ranges was extraordinary from the beginning. In her justifiably famous "discovery" photograph of Lauren Bacall for the cover of the March 1943 *Harper's*, for instance, Dahl-Wolfe accentuates a nearly monochrome composition with three touches of red, each of a different intensity and hue, yet not appearing applied as do most strong colors in photographs from this period. Again, in a picture of a Dior gown made by a window inside Richelieu's Palace in Paris, Dahl-Wolfe highlights the champagne colors of the dress and decor with a multicolored shawl.

Dahl-Wolfe was able to maintain such virtuosity by color-correcting all of her plates for the engraver. As a result, her more than 600 pages for *Harper's* are comparable in quality to the gravures in *Camera Work*, which served as her standard, and in subtlety to the prints of Paul Outerbridge, whose "Music" (c.1924), clipped from a magazine reproduction, hangs by Dahl-Wolfe's bed even today.

Dahl-Wolfe feels that publishing standards are too lax and the photographer's role too compromised by editorial control for great fashion photography to exist today. Her perfectionism—her insistence that her work can only be reproduced under the most exacting criteria—has in part contributed to the lack of publications on this important artist and gracious woman. An exhibition of her portrait and landscape work, organized by International Exhibitions (Smithsonian Institution) and circulated throughout the United States in 1982, should help redress the imbalanced historical view of the photography of the 1940s and 50s.

—Pamela Allara

D'ALESSANDRO, Robert (Philip).

Nationality: American. **Born:** New York City, 29 November 1942. **Education:** Attended Islip High School, Islip, New York, 1956-60; studied graphic design at the Pratt Institute, New York, 1960-65, B.F.A. 1965; Peace Corps Volunteer in Brazil, 1965; studied photography and drawing at Brooklyn College, New York, 1969-71, M.F.A. 1971. **Family:** Married Sara Hankinson in 1965. **Career:** Freelance photographer, working for *American Journal, National Lampoon, Readers Digest, Pageant Magazine, New York Magazine,* etc., New York since 1968; also Director of Photography and cameraman, for On Television Ltd., and Yural Productions Inc., New York, since 1983. Instructor in Advanced and Basic Photography, New School for Social Research, New York, and Adjunct Instructor in Basic Photography and Art, Brooklyn College, New York, 1970-72; Associate Adjunct Professor of Graduate Photography, New York University, 1972; Photographer-in-Residence, University of New Mexico, Albuquerque, 1973. Associate Professor of Art, Brooklyn College, New York, since 1974; also Visiting Lecturer, School of Visual Arts, New York, 1985-86, and Cooper Union, New York, 1986. **Recipient:** Judges' Prize, *City of Man* exhibition, University of Chicago, 1970; Creative Artists Public Service Grant, New York, 1971; First Prize, Mount Holyoke College Art Museum Exhibition, Massachusetts, 1971; National Endowment for the Arts Grant, 1975; New York State Council on the Arts Grant, 1980; City University of New York Grant, 1984-85. **Agents:** Marcuse Pfeifer Gallery, 568 Broadway, Suite 102, New York, New York 10012; and Andrew Smith Gallery, 76 East San Francisco, Santa Fe, New Mexico 87501. **Address:** 388 Broadway, Studio 4, New York, New York 10013, U.S.A.

Individual Exhibitions:

1972	*The Life Fantastic,* Floating Foundation of Photography, New York
1973	*Letters to My Congressman,* Washington Gallery of Photography, Washington, D.C.
1977	*Glory,* International Museum of Photography, George Eastman House, Rochester, New York (travelled to Galerie Nagel, West Berlin)
1980	Nicholas Potter Gallery, Santa Fe, New Mexico
1981	East End Arts and Humanities Council, Riverhead, New York
1982	Marcuse Pfeifer Gallery, New York
1990	*Robert D'Allessandro,* Picture Photo Space, Osaka, Japan

Selected Group Exhibitions:

1968	*Photography '68,* International Museum of Photography, George Eastman House, Rochester, New York
1970	*City of Man,* University of Chicago
1972	*60s Continuum,* International Museum of Photography, George Eastman House, Rochester, New York
	3 Young American Photographers: Fredrich Cantor, Paul Diamond, Robert D'Alessandro, The Photographers' Gallery, London
1973	*Threads and No Threads,* Floating Foundation of Photography, New York

IBM and Fuller Building, **1990.** Robert D'Alessandro.

1974   *C.A.P.S. Photographers,* Soho Photo Gallery, New York
1977   *Brooklyn College Art Department 1942-77,* Schoelkopf
        Gallery, New York
1978   *How Photography Clicked,* Floating Foundation of Photogra-
        phy, New York
1979   *Attitudes: Photography in the 1970s,* Santa Barbara Museum of
        Art, California
1984   *Exposed and Developed,* American Museum of American Art,
        Washington, D.C. (toured the United States)
1986   *Sky Writing,* Kunstverein, Kassel, West Germany
1987   *Permanent Collection/Recent Acquisitions,* Center for Creative
        Photography, North Light Gallery, Arizona State Universi-
        ty, Tempe
1988   *Swimmers,* Burden Gallery, New York (touring until 1992)
1989   *Long Island Artists,* Nassau County Museum of Fine Arts,
        Roslyn Harbor
        Contemporary Photography in New Mexico, Taos Art Associa-
        tion, Stables Art Center
        Attitudes Revisited, Santa Barbara Museum of Art, California
1991   *On the Edge—Contemporary Photographs of the Perimeter of
        Manhattan,* Henry Street Settlement Louis Abrons Center,
        New York

Collections:

New School for Social Research, New York; James Van Der Zee Institute, New York; International Museum of Photography, George Eastman House, Rochester, New York; Lincoln First Bank, Rochester, New York; University of New Mexico, Albuquerque; Ryerson Polytechnical Institute, Toronto; National Gallery of Canada, Ottawa; Bibliothèque Nationale, Paris.

Publications:

By D'ALESSANDRO: Book—*Glory,* New York 1973. **Articles**—"Teaching Photography," interview with Marian Stanley, in *Grain* (Brooklyn, New York), 1974; "Robert D'Alessandro: Portfolio from Glory," interview with Jacob Deschin, in *Popular Photography Annual,* New York 1976; "Teaching in Individualism," interview with Scott Hornstein, in *Photograph Magazine* (New York), September 1976.

On D'ALESSANDRO: Books—*Vision and Expression,* edited by Nathan Lyons, New York 1968; *Light Readings* by A.D. Coleman, New York 1979; *The Photographers' Cookbook,* edited by Deborah Barsel, Rochester, New York 1979; *Photography in New Mexico from Daguerrotype to the Present,* edited by Van Deren Coke, Albuquerque, New Mexico 1979; *Signs of Life* by Alfred Appel, Jr., New York 1983; *Exposed and Developed,* exhibition catalogue, Washington, D.C. 1984; *Swimmers,* text by Stephen Dobyns and Hans Christian Adam, New York 1988; *Photographic Possibilities,* by Robert Hirsch, Boston/London 1990. **Articles**—picture features in *The Age* (Australia) 1987 and 1988; *Sfera Magazine* (Rome), No. 35, 1993.

*

I photograph what is interesting to me at the time. This changes as my life moves along.

For me, my work is about change—change in my awareness of what life is and can be. I move from one theme to the next, trying to see more clearly.

What fascinates me is when what I see transforms into an image. The photograph as an image does not supply an answer; it stands alone and complete as a statement of vision. I wonder at this point whether I have photographed it or it has photographed me.

Through photography, I feel I can open a dialogue between the picture and the viewer by creating a space in the viewer's imagination which he can ultimately fill with his own responses.

In my recent work in video, I am investigating the nature of the moving image, in a series of public television documentaries examining the social functions and impacts of television. How this will affect my future work in still photography remains to be seen.

—Robert D'Alessandro

*   *   *

The photographic work of Robert D'Alessandro is varied and complex. Few have viewed its entirety, and those who have, without knowing the man, might be hard-pressed to account for its logic. He is perhaps best known for his satirical depiction of the American myth. These images are clever, lively, and sustained descriptions of the character and acts of Americans. In the grand traditions of satire, his images falsify characters and transgress proper limits in the service of exposing what is defective, blameworthy or vicious in public administration and conduct, or in personal morals. However, it would be a mistake to think of his work as being solely concerned with condemning political statements about what is wrong with America.

D'Alessandro's vision and his use of the camera to express it are very much a product of the world he depicts. He is of the post-war generation of Americans who grew up being visually informed by the early days of television. Uncountable hours by this generation were spent studying intensely a framed image of not only the culture of the 1950s but also the popular visual culture of the 1920s, 30s, and 40s. So much of early television fare was comprised of movies and cartoons produced for other generations. Without a doubt, whether consciously or unconsciously absorbed, this visual and cultural education lies at the foundation of D'Alessandro's vision, as it does for many other American visual artists.

Of further influence is American urban life. A child growing up in an urban environment must keep its eyes wide open and must be informed of harsh realities in order to survive. One must be "street-wise" and all that that implies. One of the basic tools of survival in the city is a sense of humor, which given the above influences and daily stimulae, becomes quite complex and highly developed. Surely, D'Alessandro was called a "wise-guy" more than once, and, indeed, he is just that.

Fate has allowed D'Alessandro to further develop his visual tastes and appetites. He definitely is among the best informed of today's American photographers about the traditions of photography and painting. He fully realizes the peculiar tool which is the camera. He knows how to use the frame to capture and reveal information. He knows the powerful time-magic that is uniquely available to him with the photographic imaging medium.

Central to his personality and survival is that he is aware. Awareness belongs to the knowledge which is needful for one's own sake in the regulation of interests. It refers to matters of ordinary, common or practical information, or to any facts or truths as bearing upon ourselves. Such knowledge is the result of observation and experience. When we are aware of a thing, we bear in mind its relative nature and consequences. Thus, whether of the ruins of Brooklyn or the skies of New Mexico, each of D'Alessandro's images are evidence of what he is aware of. He is aware of much that is threatening, false and unpleasant. But also, he is aware of much that is humorous, ironic and magical. He has a particular eye out for evidence of the metaphysical. Any of his images can give proof of one, some, or all of the above. For this reason, his images often transcend the limits of the subject and have tremendous appeal to others aware of the same.

D'Alessandro's work is proof that he is aware, and when it is offered to the public, it is an invitation and inducement to beware.

—Grant B. Romer

DALTON, Stephen (Neal).

Nationality: British. **Born:** Kingswood, Surrey, 2 October 1937. **Education:** Attended Wrekin College, Shropshire; studied photography under Margaret Harker, Regent Street Polytechnic, London, 1961-63. **Family:** Married Elizabeth Anne MacAndrew in 1977; children: Joanna, Philip, Lee and Lucy. **Career:** Freelance photographer, specializing in wildlife and high-speed photography, London and Sussex, since 1963: established studio in Ardingly,

Sussex, 1976. **Recipient:** Kodak Scholarship in Advanced Photography, London, 1962; Associate, 1963, and Honorary Fellow, 1978, Royal Photographic Society; Kodak Award, London, 1970; Hood Medal, 1971, and Silver Progress Medal, 1978, Royal Photographic Society, London; Nikon Award, London 1977. **Address:** Holly Farm-house, Cob Lane, Ardingly, Sussex RH17 6ST, England.

Individual Exhibitions:

1963	*Six Sixty Three,* Aldeburgh Festival, Suffolk
1973	*Borne on the Wind,* Photographers' Gallery, London
1977	*The Miracle of Flight,* Pentax Gallery, London
1986	*The Secret Life of an Oakwood,* London Ecology Centre; Leeds Museum; York Museum
1989	*At the Water's Edge,* Barbican Centre, London
1990	*Vanishing Paradise,* Ecology Centre, London
1991	*Vanishing Paradise,* Royal Botanical Gardens, Edinburgh
1993	*The Secret Life of a Garden,* Royal Photographic Society, Bath

Selected Group Exhibitions:

1963	*Six Sixty-Three,* Aldeburgh Festival, Suffolk
1982	*Floods of Light,* Photographers' Gallery, London

Collections:

Science Museum, London; Royal Photographic Society, Bath, Avon.

Publications:

By DALTON: Books—*Ants from Close-up,* New York 1967; *Bees from Close-up,* New York 1968; *Looking at Nature,* Norwich, Norfolk 1971; *Borne on the Wind,* New York and London 1975; *The Miracle of Flight,* London and New York 1977; *Caught in Motion: High Speed Nature Photography,* London, New York, France, Germany and Japan 1982; *Split Second,* with others, London and New York 1983; *The Secret Life of an Oakwood,* edited by Jill Bailey, London and New York 1986; *Secret Lives,* London, New York, France, Germany and Holland 1988; *At the Water's Edge,* London 1989; *Vanishing Paradise,* London, USA, France, Germany, Holland, Italy and Japan 1990; *The Secret Life of a Garden,* London, USA, France, Germany 1992. **Articles**—"First on the Wind," with Howard Ensign, in *Audubon Magazine* (New York), September 1975; "The Fantastic World of Insects" in *Popular Photography* (New York), 1976.

On DALTON: Books—*World Photography,* edited by Bryn Campbell, London 1981; *Floods of Light: Flash Photography 1851-1981,* exhibition catalogue by Rupert Martin, London 1982. **Articles**—"Stephen Dalton" by Robert Booth in *Industrial and Commercial Photographer* (Croydon, Surrey), November 1975; "Photographers at Work: Stephen Dalton" by James Clement in *British Journal of Photography* (London), 5 November 1976; "Stephen Dalton" by Gordon Barn in *Radio Times* (London), May 1978; "Flight Fantastic" by Richard Hopkins in *Practical Photography* (Peterborough, England), May 1978; "Stephen Dalton in Person" by John Hall in *New Scientist* (London), September 1978; "Nature Spectacular" by Richard Hopkins in *Camera* (Lucerne), April 1980; "Miracle of Flight" in *SLR Camera* (London), May 1980; "Macrobatics" in *Practical Photography* (Peterborough, England), March 1983.

*

In 1970, after some five years of professional wildlife photography, I cut short my normal work and set out to do something totally new—to photograph insects in free flight.

Until then, there was no means of observing the way an insect used its wings to make the incredible manoeuvres we take for granted. No technique was capable of stopping an insect with absolute clarity in free flight. It was the solution of this problem which became my overriding obsession. I was determined to achieve two things. First, I wanted to record flight behaviour and wing movements which had never been seen before—to show every twist of the wing, every scale and hair in critical focus. Second, and just as important, I wanted to create real pictures—the insect had to be flying in a setting evoking the beauty of its natural habitat. It was also vital to show the animal behaving naturally.

Over the next decade or so all this was achieved, and I was lucky enough to specialise in the type of photography which I enjoy most—recording animal movements which are too fast to be seen by the human eye, working not only with insects but also with birds, bats, frogs and even snakes. More recently my work has become far more general in scope, with my later books containing photography of a more conventional style.

Finding natural beauty far more emotive than anything man contrives, I sometimes find it disturbing to work in a profession where there are constant reminders of the accelerating destruction of earth's wild places and the creatures which live in it. Thus an increasingly important driving force behind my work is the wish to convey to others some of the excitement and exquisite perfection of the natural world.

—Stephen Dalton

* * *

Unlike most photographers, Stephen Dalton did not move into the medium because of a fascination with its machinery, an attraction to its glamour or through aspiring to its cultural pretensions. His intense motivation came from outside the world of photography, and has led ironically to innovative high technology being used in a most intimate rapport with nature. This same motivation has also led to creative ambitions, some of which could not have been realised with ready-made equipment purchasable at any price.

Dalton has gone further than any other wildlife photographer in understanding high-speed movement in nature, particularly flight and insect activity, and the devising and developing suitable equipment for the project in hand. This inventiveness arises from his need to serve nature with truthful and sympathetic images, which time and again have revealed a beauty of detail previously unseen by the human eye. It has, for example, often required a very brief but powerful electronic flash and fast-response triggering of the shutter—and all this in a flexible system that could be adapted to a wide range of field and studio conditions.

His work in the 1970s achieved a quite remarkable level of technical perfection. Looking at one of his photographs from this period, one cannot help speculating about the hundreds of exposures he must have rejected as "failures." Dalton was the first to capture the beauty of insects and birds in free, uncontrolled flight with such exquisite clarity. We can now see how the most minute anatomical feature behaves during uninhibited movement.

Much of his photography has been seen in the many books devoted to his work which were published during the first twenty years of his professional life. The earliest work of the 1960s showed an overriding concern with technical craftsmanship and zoological factors. However, from this base he has developed an ever-widening range of techniques together with a deep knowledge of, and sensitivity to, creatures in the wild. This is best seen in his 1985 book *The Secret Life of an Oakwood,* in which both the photographic and emotive quality of the 150 colour plates is so consistently high that it totally misleads the viewer about the difficulties, persistence and patience involved in capturing such images. A versatile range of techniques was necessary to cover such subjects as weather, life-death and rebirth, trees, insects, reptiles, light, fungi, ferns and flowers, bats, birds and badgers. This book established his maturity, not as a photographer (which, by any standards, he reached long ago) but as a man who has a close and caring empathy with nature, and the humility to bypass self in telling us about it. Whilst the ecological information and detail could even make this a definitive textbook, the words together with the pictures are so evocative that the total effect is profoundly moving.

Dalton has been commissioned to travel widely abroad and his picture library has most things from Venezuelan moths to British mammals. His work has been the subject of a BBC TV *World About Us* programme, most United Kingdom colour magazines and many natural history, photographic and technical journals around the world. Nevertheless, Dalton's work is more familiar than his name. He lives amongst his work. Both in location and spirit he is closer to the world of wildlife than the world of business and institutional and media recognition.

All his work throughout the 1970s and into the 1980s has been characterised by an unsurpassed level of photographic craftsmanship. He has made thousands of pictures using every last micron of quality allowed by the slower films and finest lenses available at the time. His photographs always have a directness and lack of ambiguity. There is never any doubt about the precise and explicit purpose of any image. Nor is there hidden meaning or deference to current style. Dalton's latest work comes from a man not only enthralled by the living world but, fortunately for us, with such an understanding of both it and photography that he can move its wonders right into our vision.

—Robert Booth

D'AMICO, Alicia.

Nationality: Argentinian. **Born:** Buenos Aires, 6 October 1933. **Education:** Studied art at the Escuela Nacional de Bellas Artes, Buenos Aires, 1947-53, Dip. 1953; art history in Paris (French Government Scholarship), 1955; photography in the studio of her father, Luis D'Amico, Buenos Aires, 1957, and color photography at Kodak, Rochester, New York, 1960; student-assistant, studio of Annemarie Heinrich, Buenos Aires, 1960. **Career:** Freelance photographer, with joint studio with Sara Facio, q.v., as Alicia D'Amico/Sara Facio, Fotograffas, Buenos Aires, since 1960. Editor of the Photographic Section, *La Nación* newspaper, Buenos Aires, 1966-74, and *La Azotea* magazine, Buenos Aires, 1973-86. Founder-member and organizer, Consejo Argentino de Fotografia, Buenos Aires, since 1979. **Recipient:** Artist Award, Fédération International de l'Art Photographique, 1965; Olivetti-Comunidad Award, Buenos Aires, 1968; Book Prize, Congress of Books, Vienna, 1969; Premio Konex, Buenos Aires, 1982. **Address:** Santa Fe 2088-piso 13A, Buenos Aires 1123, Argentina.

Individual Exhibitions with Sara Facio:

1963   *Escritores Argentinos*, Galería Riobbo, Buenos Aires (travelled to the Biblioteca Nacional, Mexico City)
1964   *Mutaciones*, Galería Lirolay, Buenos Aires
1965   *Escritores Argentinos*, Consejo Deliberante, Buenos Aires
        50 Fotografías, Agfa-Gevaert Gallery, Buenos Aires (travelled to Image 65, Cordoba, Argentina)
1966   *"Luv" in Fotografía*, Casa del Teatro, Buenos Aires (travelled to the Rosario Gallery, Argentina)
1967   *Fotografías Premiadas*, Image 67, Cordoba, Argentina
1968   *Buenos Aires, Buenos Aires*, Peña Fotográfica, Rosario, Argentina (toured Argentina, 1968-70)
1969   Biblioteca Popular de San Pedro, Buenos Aires
1971   *Escritores y Actores Argentinos*, Ateneo Foto-Cine, Rosario, Argentina
1974   *Retratos y Autorretratos*, Casa del Fotografo, Buenos Aires
1981   *Buenos Aires*, Gallery Tsukada, Tokyo
        Humanrio, Gallery Tsukada, Tokyo
        Buenos Aires y su Gente, Museo de Arte Moderno, Sao Paulo
1982   *Geografia de Pablo Neruda*, Palazzo Reale, Caserta, Italy (travelled to Galleria San Fedele, Milan)
1984   *Buenos Aires, Buenos Aires*, Universita de Genova, Italy
        Encuentros con Julio Cortazar, Museo J. C. Castagnino, Mar del Plata, Argentina
        Buenos Aires, Galerie Municipale du Chateau d'Eau, Toulouse, France
1985   *Julio Cortazar*, Centro Cultural San Martin, Buenos Aires
        25 Anos de Fotografia, Centro Cultural, Mar del Plata, Argentina
1986   *25 Anos de Fotografia*, Casa Argentina, Rome

Individual Exhibitions

1983   *Mujeres*, United Nations Information Centre, Buenos Aires (travelled to the Consejo de Ciencias Sociales, Buenos Aires; Foto Galeria Omega, La Plata; and to *II Encuentro Feminista*, Lima, Peru)

1984   *Creacion de la Propia Imagen*, Villa Victoria Ocampo, Mar del Plata, Argentina (travelled to Museo de Arte Moderno, Bogota, Colombia; Museo Angel maria de Rosa, Junin, Argentina)
        Autorretratos, Lugar de Mujer, Buenos Aires
        Portafolio, at *Rencontres Internationales de la Photographie*, Arles, France
1985   *Creacion de la Propia Imagen*, Biblioteca Rivadavia, Bahia Blanca, Argentina
        Imagen y Cambio, El Barberillo, Madrid
1986   *Creacion de la Propia Imagen*, at *Encuentro de Mujeres del cono sur*, Mendoza, Argentina

Selected Group Exhibitions:

1977   *Maestros de la Fotografía Argentina*, YMCA Salon, Buenos Aires
1978   *Hecho in Latinoamérica*, Museo de Arte Moderno, Mexico City (travelled to *Venezia 79*)
1979   *Fotografia Argentina*, House of Friendship, Moscow (toured the U.S.S.R.)
1980   *Miembros Fundadores del Consejo Argentino de Fotografia*, Galería Praxis, Buenos Aires
1981   *Fotografie Lateinamerika*, Kunsthaus, Zurich
1982   *Fotografia Contemporanea Argentina*, Palazzo Reale, Caserta, Italy
1983   *Los Fotografos-Autorretratos*, Foto Galería Omega, La Plata, Argentina
1984   *El Retrato en Buenos Aires*, Museo Isaac Fernandez Blanco, Buenos Aires
1985   *Photographies Argentines*, Espace Culturel Graslin, Nantes, France

Collections:

Bibliothèque Nationale, Paris.

Publications:

By D'AMICO: Books—*Buenos Aires, Buenos Aires*, with Sara Facio, Buenos Aires 1968; *Argentina*, with text by H.S. Ferns, London 1969; *Geografía de Pablo Neruda*, with Sara Facio, Barcelona 1973; *Retratos y Autorretratos*, with Sara Facio, Buenos Aires 1974; *Humanario*, with Sara Facio, Buenos Aires 1976; *Como tomar Fotografías*, with Sara Facio, Buenos Aires 1977; *Rostros de Buenos Aires*, Buenos Aires 1978; *Argentine Turistique*, Paris 1978; *Fotografia Argentina Actual*, Buenos Aires 1981; *Sara Facio/ Alicia D'Amico, 1960-1985*, with Sara Facio, Buenos Aires 1985. **Articles**— "Todas la realidades, la realidad" in *La Nación* (Buenos Aires), 31 January 1967; "Historia de una pasion . . . " in *La Nación* (Buenos Aires), 25 July 1967; "Stieglitz: el antes y el despues" in *La Nación* (Buenos Aires) 6 January 1970; "Oh, aquellos fotógrafos" in *La Nación* (Buenos Aires), 21 July 1970; "El legado de la Bauhaus" in *La Nación* (Buenos Aires), 8 September 1970; "El Muchacho de la cámara" in *La Nación* (Buenos Aires), 22 September 1970; "Henri Cartier-Bresson" in *Fotografia Universal* (Buenos Aires), August 1971; "El rol fotográfico" in *La Nación* (Buenos Aires), 16 November 1971; "El impacto visual" in *La Nación* (Buenos Aires), 18 July 1972; "La opinión de cada uno" in *La Nación* (Buenos Aires), 26 September 1972; "La fotografía social" in *Hecho en Latinoamerica*, exhibition catalogue, Mexico City 1978; "Mexico—May 1978" in *Camera* (Lucerne), no. 10, 1978; "Salud, identidad y socializacion" in *El Espectador de Bogotá* (Colombia), 3 June 1984; "Ralph Gibson o la sensación visual" in *La Prensa* (Buenos Aires), 15 September 1985; "Como se fotografían los animales" in *La Nación* (Buenos Aires), 2 February 1986.

On D'AMICO: Books—*Territorios* by Julio Cortázar, Mexico City 1978; *Pintores Argentinos del siglo XX, no. 98: D'Amico*, with text by Sara Facio, Buenos Aires 1982. **Articles**—"3 Photographes . . . " by Ives Lorelle in *Le Photographe* (Paris), October 1968; "Pablo Neruda . . . " by Michel Nuridsany in *Le Figaro* (Paris), 14 January 1974; "Geografia Doméstica" in *El Correo*

Catalan (Barcelona), 24 January 1974; "El escritor y su espejo" in *La Nación* (Buenos Aires), 24 February 1974; "La Azotea presentó Humanario" in *Fotografia Universal* (Buenos Aires), April 1976; "Fotografia en A" by M.C. Orive in *Artes Visuales* (Mexico City), May 1976; "Vision de un mundo . . ." by O.H. Villordo in *La Nación* (Buenos Aires), 23 May 1976; "Humanity in Camera" by Robert Cox in the *Buenos Aires Herald,* 23 October 1976; "La Argentina presente" in *Foco* (Buenos Aires), no. 22, 1979; "Buenos Aires e sua gente, nas fotos de Alicia y Sara" in *Estado de Sao Paulo* (Brazil), 28 April 1981; "Humanario" in *Nippon Camera* (Tokyo), 9 September 1981; "Alicia D'Amico dice todo lo que sabe" by Orlando Barone in *Mercado* (Buenos Aires), 7 October 1982; "Alicia D'Amico: luz natural a las mujeres" in *Tiempo Argentino* (Buenos Aires), 15 March 1983; "La camara como espejo" in *Clarin* (Buenos Aires), 18 February 1984; "Sara Facio, Alicia D'Amico: 25 anos de fotografia" by Maria Elena Walsh in *La Prensa* (Buenos Aires), 30 June 1985.

*

Nowadays anyone can use a camera with accuracy. In the midst of so many records, documents, and conventional illustrations, photographers who choose photography as a means of expression have to be much more aware of the world and of their surroundings. In the "civilization of the image" a certain kind of photography becomes a marginal activity within the vortex of meaningless graphics that surround us.

I do not believe in the objectivity of a photographer. It is perhaps for this reason that the medium which most resembles reality seems to me more and more difficult. The compromise which most attracts me, and which I most appreciate in other photographers, is to achieve a successful image through one's own subjectivity.

I feel that I am a humanist photographer; photography is for me a means of knowledge. We photographers are laid bare in our photos, which eventually become a long drawn out self-portrait.

—Alicia D'Amico

*   *   *

Contemporary society has been described as a "civilization of consumer goods and pictures." And even the pictures are consumed—worn out, rather—at a dizzying rate, in bombardments from the mass media. The public's voracious appetite for photographic documentation has caused the photographer, engaged in an endless search for some freshly shocking event, to forget the feeling of *pietas*. Press photography is becoming more and more a pretext for the exhibition of dreadful horrors than a search for the true essence of man. Yet a true, a humane, photo-journalism ought to engage the photographer in constant reflection on the significance of events and a consciousness of essential values. Reflection and consciousness are the moral bases of the work of Alicia D'Amico.

D'Amico's approach to external realities is based on a profound respect for the feelings of other people, the people depicted and the people who look at her photographs. She reveals the true man—his joy, hopelessness, meanness, greatness, pity and ferocity—through descriptive details in an harmonious photography that aims not to evoke morbid curiosity but to penetrate. In practice, the picture that makes a violent impact leaves only a superficial impression: the instant reaction disappears almost as soon as it is aroused. Since the photo is not the fruit of reflection, it cannot stimulate reflection. D'Amico's photography—and that of all those who practice humane photo-journalism—combines awareness of solid reality with what lies within it, and her vision does penetrate our consciousness. The photo is no longer purely representational, a visual depiction of events, but involves implication, an expression of values and universal concepts.

Perhaps it is no longer even important that certain events, captured at a certain place and time, should be printed on a piece of photographic paper. Such subjects have been transformed into symbols of the human condition, of feelings, of emotions, and transformed into historical proclamations, social declarations—but are they? The very limitations of time and space in objective photography preclude any kind of real outline of the essence of man; they might just as well be replaced by a general caption: "Earth, any year." It is in this context that we can understand how Alicia D'Amico's documentary photographs perform the function appropriate to creative photography: the

communication not so much of information about the visible world as about the intangible world of the individual.

Even the composition of her pictures transmits her message. The choice of point-of-view, the color contrasts, the highlights and black areas, the geometrical balance of the figures that form a background to the action of the subject—all are symbolic elements. Every symbol embodies some etymological meaning. Comprehension of the message comes with perceptive coordination of the totality of the symbols.

—Giuliana Scimé

DAS, Sujoy.

Nationality: Indian. **Born:** Calcutta, 6 January 1961. **Education:** Attended St Xaviers School, 1968-78, and St Xaviers College, 1979-82, Bachelor of Commerce (Hons), 1982; Fellow Member of the Institute of Chartered Accountants of India, 1980-84; self-taught in photography. **Career:** Since 1978, freelance photojournalist, working mainly on editorial photography and photo essays, specializing in the Himalayas. **Agents:** Ms. Radhika Singh, Director, R Fotomedia (P) Ltd., E 540 Greater Kailash II, New Delhi 110 048, India; Ms. Alice Caroll, Stock Boston Inc., 36 Gloucester Street, Boston, Massachusetts 02115, USA. **Address:** 8 Short Street, Calcutta 700 017, India.

Individual Exhibitions:

1992　　*Land of the Lotus Born—Photographs from Sikkim,* India
　　　　International Centre, New Delhi
　　　　The Sikkim Years—A Retrospective, Academy of Fine Arts,
　　　　Calcutta

Selected Group Exhibitions:

1987-88　*Festival of India Photo Exhibition Pratibimba,* toured the
　　　　major cities of the U.S.S.R. as part of the Festival of India
　　　　in Russia
1991　　*Mountaineering in the Indian Himalayas,* Indian Mountaineer-
　　　　ing Foundation Museum, New Delhi
1993　　*2nd Indian Biennale of Creative Photography,* Lalit Kala
　　　　Akademi, New Delhi

Publications:

By DAS: Books—*Calcutta,* edited by Michel Vatin, Singapore 1991; *Sikkim, Darjeeling and Kalimpong,* with text by Wendy Brewer Lama, Singapore 1992; *South India,* with text by Manjulika Dubey and Bikram Grewal, Singapore 1992; *Flowers of the Western Himalayas,* with text by Rupin Dang, Dehli 1993; *The Himalayas,* with text by Shankar Barua, New Dehli 1994. **Articles**—"Rediscovering Darjeeling" in *Frontline,* 10-23 August 1985; "Darjeeling—Perspectives in the 150th Anniversary Year" in *Destination In1985;* "The Abode of the Dorji—Darjeeling" in *Swagat,* January 1986; "The Serampore Press and Library" in *The India Magazine,* June 1986; "Feat of Clay—The Clay Modellers of Krishnagar" in *Frontline,* 9-22 August 1986; "P.N. Bose—From the Travel Journals of a Geologist" in *The India Magazine,* July 1989; "Sikkim Himalaya" in *Sawasdee,* December 1989; "Beauty at it's Peak—North Sikkim" in *The Telegraph Sunday Magazine,* 11 March 1990; "Great Escapes" in *The Telegraph Sunday Magazine,* 29 April 1990; "The Dance of Death—Lama Dances in Sikkim" in *The Telegraph Sunday Magazine,* 16 December 1990; "Kalimpong" in *The Economic Times,* 19 May 1991; "Anglo Indians—Pioneers and Prodigies" in *Discover India,* June 1991; "The Yak Herdsmen of Lhonak Valley" in *The India Magazine,* September 1992; "Journey down the Hoogly" in *The India Magazine,* June 1993.

On DAS: Articles—"Focusing on a Vanishing Culture" in *Evening News,* 22 May 1992; "Framing the Soul of Sikkim" by Amit Prakash in *The Pioneer,* 27 May 1992; "Land of the Lotus Born" by Anjali Abhayankar in *India*

A Lama Looks out onto a Monastery Courtyard at Enchey, Gangtok, Sikkim, **1989 (original in colour).** Photograph by Sujoy Das.

Today, 15 June 1992; "Striking Images" in *Business World,* 17-30 June 1992; "In Camera" by Sara Adhikari in *The Times of India,* 27 June 1992; "Land of Mystery, of Myth" by Soumitra Das in *The Statesman,* 1 December 1992; "Sikkim Visited" by Ella Datta in *Business Standard,* 6 December 1992.

*

I have trekked and climbed extensively in the Himalayas, often scaling heights of 5000 metres in my quest for the "magic moment."

—Sujoy Das

DATER, Judy.

Nationality: American. **Born:** Judy Rose Lichtenfeld in Hollywood, California, 21 June 1941. **Education:** Attended Fairfax High School, Los Angeles, 1956-59; University of California at Los Angeles, 1959-62; studied photography, under Jack Welpott, San Francisco State University, 1962-66, B.A. 1963, M.A. 1966. **Family:** Married Dennis Dater in 1962 (divorced, 1964); Jack Welpott in 1970 (divorced, 1978). **Career:** Freelance photographer, in California, since 1967. Instructor in Photography, University of California Extension, San Francisco, 1966-74, and San Francisco Art Institute, 1974-78; Guest Lecturer, Kansas City Art Institute, Missouri, 1985. **Recipient:** Dorothea

Lange Award, Oakland Art Museum, California, 1974; National Endowment for the Arts Photography Fellowship, 1976; Guggenheim Photography Fellowship, 1978. **Address:** Box 709, San Anselmo, California 94960, U.S.A.

Individual Exhibitions:

1965	Aardvark Gallery, San Francisco
1972	School of the Art Institute of Chicago
	Witkin Gallery, New York
1973	University of Maryland, Baltimore
	Center for Photographic Studies, University of Louisville, Kentucky
	University of Colorado, Boulder
	Musée Réattu, Arles, France (with Imogen Cunningham and Linda Connor)
	Women, International Museum of Photography, George Eastman House, Rochester, New York (with Jack Welpott)
1974	Oakland Museum, California
1975	Silver Image Gallery, Tacoma, Washington
	Spectrum Gallery, Tucson, Arizona
1976	Evergreen State College, Olympia, Washington
1977	Susan Spiritus Gallery, Newport Beach, California
	Grapestake Gallery, San Francisco
1978	Witkin Gallery, New York
1979	Contemporary Arts Center, New Orleans
	Kimball Art Center, Park City, Utah
	Yuen Lui Gallery, Seattle, Washington
	G. Ray Hawkins Gallery, Los Angeles

1980	Delaware Technical College, Wilmington
	Photography Southwest, Scottsdale, Arizona
	Jeb Gallery, Providence, Rhode Island
1981	Orange Coast College, Costa Mesa, California
	University of North Dakota, Grand Forks
	Atlanta Gallery, Georgia
	Catskill Center of Photography, Woodstock, New York
	Camera Obscura Gallery, Denver, Colorado
	Spectrum Gallery, Fresno, California
1982	*New Work,* Yuen Lui Gallery, Seattle
	Burton Gallery, Toronto
	Baker Gallery, Kansas City, Missouri
	Kathleen Ewing Gallery, Washington, D.C.
	Lightworks/Film in the cities, St. Paul, Minnesota
	Girls of the Golden West, Santa Fe Center for Photography, New Mexico (with Gail Skoff)
1983	Lone Star Photographic Workshop, Austin, Texas
	The Photographic Center, Dallas, Texas
	University of Oregon, Eugene
	Hasselblad Galleri, Goteborg, Sweden
	Idaho State University, Pocatello
	North Carolina State University, Raleigh
1984	Yuen Lui Gallery, Seattle, Washington
	Portraits of Disabled Artists, San Francsico Museum of Modern Art
	Kathleen Ewing Gallery, Washington, D.C.
	Grapestake Gallery, San Francisco
1985	Northern Arizona University, Flagstaff
1986	*Judy Dater: 20 Years,* University of Santa Clara, California
	Webster University, St. Louis, Missouri

Selected Group Exhibitions:

1967	*Light⁷,* Massachusetts Institute of Technology, Cambridge
1968	*Vision and Expression,* International Museum of Photography, George Eastman House, Rochester, New York
1973	*60s Continuum,* International Museum of Photography, George Eastman House, Rochester, New York
1974	*Photography in America,* Whitney Museum, New York
1977	*The Great West: Real/Ideal,* University of Colorado, Boulder
1978	*Mirrors and Windows,* Museum of Modern Art, New York (toured the United States, 1978-80)
1979	*Photographie als Kunst 1879-1979/Kunst als Photographie 1949-1979,* Tiroler Landesmuseum Ferdinandeum, Innsbruck, Austria (travelled to Neue Galerie am Wolfgang Gurlitt Museum, Linz; Neue Galerie am Landesmuseum Johanneum, Graz; Museum des 20. Jahrhunderts, Vienna)
1981	*Photo Facts and Opinions,* Addison Gallery of American Art, Andover, Massachusetts
1984	*Photography in California 1945-80,* San Francisco Museum of Modern Art (travelled to the Akron Art Museum, Ohio; Corcoran Gallery, Washington, D.C.; Los Angeles Municipal Art Gallery; Cornell University, Ithaca, New York; High Museum of Art, Atlanta, Georgia; Museum Folkwang, Essen; Centre Georges Pompidou, Paris; Museum of Photographic Arts, San Diego, California)
1986	*Self-Portrait Photography 1840-1945,* Plymouth Arts Centre, Devon (toured Britain)

Collections:

Museum of Modern Art, New York; International Museum of Photography, George Eastman House, Rochester, New York; Museum of Fine Arts, Boston; Fogg Art Museum, Harvard University, Cambridge, Massachusetts; Center for Creative Photography, University of Arizona, Tucson; San Francisco Museum of Modern Art, California; Oakland Museum, California; Bibliothèque Nationale, Paris; Moderna Museet, Stockholm.

Publications:

By DATER: Books—*Women and Other Visions,* with Jack Welpott, introduction by Henry Holmes Smith, New York 1975; *Imogen Cunningham: A Portrait,* editor, Boston and London 1979; *Judy Dater: 20 Years,* with text by James Enyeart, Tucson, Arizona 1986.

On DATER: Books—*Photography Year 1973,* by Time-Life editors, New York 1973; *The Woman's Eye* by Anne Tucker, New York 1974; *Faces* by Ben Maddow, Boston 1978; *Darkroom II,* edited by Jain Kelly, New York 1978; *A Ten Year Salute,* edited by Lee D. Witkin, New York 1979; *The Photograph Collector's Guide* by Lee D. Witkin and Barbara London, Boston and London 1979; *Light Readings: A Photography Critic's Writings 1968-1978* by A.D. Coleman, New York 1979; *Contact* by Ralph Gibson, New York 1980; *The Library of World Photography: Portraits,* with introduction by Colin Ford, Tokyo 1982, 1983, London 1983; *Subjective Vision,* exhibition catalogue, with introduction by A. D. Coleman, Atlanta, Georgia 1983; *La Photographie Créative by Jean-Claude Lemagny,* Paris 1984; *Photography in California 1945-1980* by Louise Katzman, San Francisco and New York 1984; *A World History of Photography* by Naomi Rosenblum, New York 1984. **Articles**—"Judy Dater" by Shelley Rice in *Ms.* (New York), June 1978; "Bay Area Photography" by Hal Fisher in *Picture Magazine* (Los Angeles), June 1979; "Judy Dater and Jack Welpott," interview with Gilles Walinski, in *Zoom* (Paris), November/December 1979; "Judy Dater" by Richard S. Street in *Pacific Sun* (San Rafael, California), 1-7 February 1980. **Film**—*The Woman Behind the Image: Photographer Judy Dater* by John Stewart, 1981.

*

From the beginning people have been my favorite subject. The human face and body attracted me in all its infinite variety. I built my photographs around the person I had chosen. An evolution began, starting with self-portraits, then with friends, and ultimately with strangers.

I find my themes ebb and flow. The earliest portraits were done in the landscape. Occasionally an uninhabited landscape would materialize, but generally a person dominated. I moved closer with my camera and eventually concentrated on interior environmental portraits.

From 1980 to 1985, I have dealt with the self-portrait in a variety of ways; by incorporating the landscape, use of costumes and props, and diaristic writings. I have employed both color and black-and-white, video stills, painting, photo-lithography and hand cast paper in the most recent work. I am currently producing a series of images of women, in black-and-white, on a large scale, minimum of 30 by 40 inches.

—Judy Dater

* * *

When Judy Dater says that her work is rooted in 19th century portraiture, she pays homage to a tradition which goes back to the beginning of photography. The desire to see oneself rendered with such amazing clarity and naturalistic detail (which the most meticulous painting could not begin to match) made portraiture incredibly popular in those early years of photography. Even today, after the novelty has worn off, photographic renderings of the human face carry an intense appeal. Dater has updated the tradition by using available natural light instead of artificial, studio illumination, and by employing a classical, straightforward approach to undercut the romanticism of the past. Using a 4 x 5 inch view camera, which reflects the influence of California's f64 school, she makes fine black-and-white prints that in themselves have a sensuous appeal.

She selects her subjects intuitively, first through her attraction to them, and then through their willingness to be photographed. Working with Jack Welpott on her well-known book *Women and Other Visions,* she chose somewhat bohemian, urban women and photographed them clothed and unclothed in their home environments. These photographs examine female identity through costume and role playing, and they question both personal and societal attitudes toward sexuality.

In Dater's pictures the naked body is often less revealing than the face. Her knack is to allow people's experience to appear in their posture and facial expression, then click the shutter. The total expression her subjects adopt exposes elements of both their conscious and their unconscious persona, making the viewer confront some essential quality of personality which often remains hidden in the movement of everyday life.

While she is careful about imposing her point of view on the subject, Dater often allows suggestive symbols to appear. When she photographs Cheri, whose expression and exposed body belie years of experience, standing naked holding a long, horizontal picture of an army regiment, Dater is not making a literal statement about Cheri's sex life; she is simply indicating what a woman's experience can sometimes seem like. Similarly, when she photographs Joyce Goldstein in her kitchen with utensils hanging over her head, Dater emphasizes Goldstein's individual strength of character; yet she subtly manages to raise some questions about the roles contemporary women choose to adopt.

The dynamic quality of Dater's work comes from her understanding of the inherent mystery of the photographic portrait, which conceals as much as it reveals. The feeling that you know something special about the person in the picture is always undercut by your inability to say what it is; the descriptive truth of the photograph is always balanced by its theatrical and fictional nature. Judy Dater takes full advantage of this duality: her photographs offer the rich tonalities and the engaging detail of traditional black-and-white photographs, but they focus on ephemeral, elusive qualities which no camera can really record.

—Ted Hedgpeth

DAVIDSON, Bruce.

Nationality: American. **Born:** Chicago, Illinois, in 1933. **Education:** Attended Oak Park High School, 1948-51; studied photography, Rochester Institute of Technology, New York, 1951-54, and painting, philosophy and photography, under Herbert Matter, Alexey Brodovitch, and Josef Albers, Yale University, New Haven, Connecticut, 1955. Served in the United States Army, in Georgia, Arizona and France, 1955-57. **Family:** Married Emily Haas in 1967; children: Jenny and Anna. **Career:** Worked as an apprentice to photographer Al Cox, Oak Park, 1947; Dark-room Technician, Eastman Kodak, Rochester, 1954-55; freelance photographer, working for *Life, Réalités, Du, Esquire, Queen, Look, Vogue,* etc., in New York, Paris and Los Angeles, since 1958; Member, Magnum Photos co-operative agency, New York and Paris, since 1958. Photographer, *Life* magazine program for young photographers, New York, 1958; Instructor in Photography, School of Visual Arts, New York, 1964; also conducts private photography workshops. **Recipient:** Guggenheim Fellowship, 1962; National Endowment for the Arts grant, 1967, 1970; American Film Institute grant, 1970, 1972, and A.F.I. Critics Prize, 1971. **Address:** c/o Magnum Photos, 251 Park Avenue South, New York, New York 10010, U.S.A.

Individual Exhibitions:

1965	Art Institute of Chicago
	International Museum of Photography, George Eastman House, Rochester, New York
	San Francisco Museum of Art
1966	Museum of Modern Art, New York
	Moderna Museet, Stockholm
1970	Museum of Modern Art, New York
1971	San Francisco Museum of Art
1976	Addison Gallery, Andover, Massachusetts
1979	FNAC Gallery, Paris
	Galerie Delpire, Paris
	Galerie Fiolet, Amsterdam
1982	Douglas Kenyon Gallery, Chicago
1983	*New York Subway Color,* International Center of Photography, New York

Selected Group Exhibitions:

1959	*Photography at Mid-Century,* International Museum of Photography, George Eastman House, Rochester, New York
1960	*The World as Seen by Magnum,* Takashimaya Department Store, Tokyo (and world tour)
1962	*Ideas in Images,* American Federation of Arts, New York (and world tour)
1966	*Contemporary Photography since 1950,* International Museum of Photography, George Eastman House, Rochester, New York (toured the United States)
1973	*The Concerned Photographer 2,* Israel Museum, Jerusalem (toured Europe)
1974	*Photography in America,* Whitney Museum, New York
1977	*Concerning Photography,* The Photographers' Gallery, London (travelled to the Spectro Workshop, Newcastle upon Tyne)
1980	*The Imaginary Photo Museum,* Kunsthalle, Cologne
1982	*Color as Form,* International Museum of Photography, George Eastman House, Rochester, New York
1985	*American Images 1945-80,* Barbican Art Gallery, London (toured Britain)

Collections:

Museum of Modern Art, New York; International Museum of Photography, George Eastman House, Rochester, New York; Visual Studies Workshop, Rochester, New York; Yale University, New Haven, Connecticut; Addison Gallery of American Art, Andover, Massachusetts; Carpenter Center and Fogg Art Museum, Harvard University, Cambridge, Massachusetts; Art Institute of Chicago; University of Nebraska, Lincoln; Norton Simon Museum, Pasadena, California.

Publications:

By DAVIDSON: Books—*The Negro American,* edited by T. Parsons and K. Clark, New York 1966; *East 100th Street,* with an introduction by John Szarkowski, Cambridge, Massachusetts 1970; *Subsistence U.S.A.,* with Carol Hill, New York 1973; *Photographing Children,* with others, edited by Time-Life, New York 1973; *Bruce Davidson: Photographs,* with an introduction by Henry Geldzahler, New York and London 1979; *New York Subway,* Millerton, New York, 1986. **Article**—"What Photography Means to Me" in *Popular Photography* (New York), May 1962. **Films**—*On Your Way Up,* 1966; *Living Off the Land,* 1970; *Zoo Doctor,* series, 1971; *Isaac Singer's Nightmare and Mrs. Pupko's Beard,* 1972; *Enemies: A Love Story,* screenplay, 1979.

On DAVIDSON: Books—*Photography of the World '60,* edited by Hiromu Hara, Ihei Kimura and others, Tokyo and New York 1960; *Towards a Social Landscape: Contemporary Photographers,* edited by Nathan Lyons, New York 1966; *American Photography in the 20th Century* by Nathan Lyons, New York 1967; *America in Crisis: Photographs for Magnum,* edited by Charles Harbutt and Lee Jones, with an essay by Mitchel Levitas, New York 1969; *New Photography USA,* exhibition catalogue, by John Szarkowski, Arturo Carlo Quintavalle and Massimo Mussini, Parma, Italy 1971; *The Concerned Photographer 2,* edited by Cornell Capa, New York and London 1972; *Photography in America,* edited by Robert Doty, with an introduction by Minor White, New York and London 1974; *The Magic Image* by Cecil Beaton and Gail Buckland, London and Boston 1975; *Other Eyes,* exhibition catalogue, by Peter Turner, London 1976; *Concerning Photography,* exhibition catalogue, by Jonathan Bayer and others, London 1977; *Photographs: Sheldon Memorial Art Gallery Collection, University of Nebraska,* with an introduction by Norman A. Geske, Lincoln, Nebraska 1977; *Geschichte der Fotografie im 20. Jahrhundert/Photography in the 20th Century* by Petr Tausk, Cologne 1977, London 1980; *Mirrors and Windows: American Photography since 1960* by John Szarkowski, New York 1978; *Light Readings: A Photography Critic's Writings 1968-1978* by A.D. Coleman, New York 1979; *The Vogue Book of Fashion Photography* by Polly Devlin, with an introduction by Alexander Liberman, London 1979; *The Photograph Collector's Guide* by Lee D. Witkin and Barbara London, Boston and London 1979; *The Imaginary Photo Museum* by Helmut Gernsheim, Renate and L. Fritz Gruber and others, Cologne 1981, London 1982; *The Library of World*

Photography: Portraits, with introduction by Colin Ford, Tokyo 1982, 1983, London 1983; *After the War Was Over,* with introduction by Mary Blume, London 1985; *American Images: Photography 1945-1980,* edited by Peter Turner and John Benton-Harris, London and New York 1985; *Masterpieces of Photography from George Eastman House,* edited by Robert A. Sobieszek, New York 1985. **Articles**—"The Bruce Davidson Show" by David Vestal, in *Infinity* (New York), August 1966; "Bruce Davidson: New York, East 100th Street," in *Du* (Zurich), March 1969; "Bruce Davidson: Photographe en Liberté," in *Photo* (Paris), October 1969; "Bruce Davidson," in *Infinity* (New York), September 1970; "East 100th Street: A Review by Jonathan Green," in *Aperture* (Rochester, New York), no. 16, 1971; "Concerned Photographers" by Cornell Capa, in *Zoom* (Paris), no. 16, 1973; "Bruce Davidson," in *Progresso Fotografico* (Milan), December 1973; "Bruce Davidson: A Guided Tour," in *Exposure* (New York), Spring 1979; "Bruce Davidson" by C.G. Cupic, in the *International Herald Tribune* (Paris), 3 July 1979.

* * *

At 24, some 28 years ago, and less than two years out of the United States Army, Bruce Davidson was the youngest member of Magnum, then and now the definitive photographers' cooperative agency. Like many (perhaps most) outstanding photographers, he had been using a camera since his early teens, moving single-mindedly toward becoming a professional with obvious success.

But it takes more than energy and purposefulness to join the foremost group of one's peers at such an early age. It also takes talent so impressive that it cannot be ignored, even in a profession that has long been glutted with it.

Bruce Davidson's talent is for the poetry of everyday life. It combines a vision that sees beauty in the meanest of surroundings with a sensibility that prevents sentiment from dissolving into sentimentality. His is a partisan way of seeing that speaks out on behalf of the poor, the old, the ill—a sympathetic voice that will not let us ignore those whom it is more comfortable to overlook in a sometimes conscienceless world. Perhaps because so many of his subjects tend to be the overlooked members of our society, Davidson's photographs are often suffused with both sympathy and a gentle sadness. Not the shocked outrage of a W. Eugene Smith or a Don McCullin, but a strong concern that these people must be given attention, seen and appreciated for their humanity.

Thus, much of his work is in low key, shadowy, subdued, but telling in its observation and choice of moment and detail. The latter two aspects are always strong in a Davidson photograph. In a single photo in an early essay on a widow whose late husband was a friend of many French impressionist painters, for example, four simple picture elements sum up the old woman's past and present. Featured are her hands, arranging flowers in a vase; hinted at in the shadows, we see a suggestion of her face; and looming large, next to the flowers, the fragment of a painting, perhaps by one of the friends of her late husband. So much of her story is conjured up by these simple details.

Another memorable Davidson image shows a dwarf circus clown standing in the rain, smoking a cigarette, circus tents visible behind him, a sad expression on his face. Again, a few simple elements tell a life story with the speed and impact of an uppercut.

Even in sports photography, Davidson eschews the frantic action and emotion to express instead the stresses of the players. The tension of a sidelined footballer is shown not by his face (only the chin of which is visible), but by a closeup of his hands tightly twisting a towel as he watches the action on the field.

Unlike many of his contemporary photojournalists, Bruce Davidson is not completely self-taught. He graduated from Rochester Institute of Technology and worked as a photographic illustrator before becoming a full-time photojournalist—the Leica.

But in doing his classic project *East 100th Street,* Davidson turned to the 4 x 5 view camera as his recording tool. It provided a sharp break with the style that had built his reputation. To begin with, the 4 x 5 camera had to be tripod-mounted. There could not be grabbing of the precise split-second during continuing action. Nor could there be a quick retreat should the subject object with violence to the taking of his picture. So, *East 100th Street* was not a two-day picture essay. Rather it was a two-year project that involved visiting, and getting to know and be known by the people who populate that block in New York City's East Harlem. It involved trust, friendship and cooperation among

the photographer and his new friends as he documented their faces and their lives.

His choice of a larger-format camera and a deliberate approach to the subject has seemingly made his sympathies and eye for detail even more piercing. Areas that were once shadowed and coarse-grained in earlier pictures are opened up so that we may see clearly into every crumbling, littered inch of his subjects' home territory. But if it is less shadowy than before, Davidson's lighting is no less dolorous. And, although many of his subjects are children and lovers, virtually no smiles are to be seen on Bruce Davidson's East 100th Street.

In mid-career, Bruce Davidson's vision remains sharp, sympathetic and full of poetry; his picture-making style adapts gracefully to either small or large-format camera, and his images remain timeless because they spring from the basic emotions, troubles and triumphs that will always be understood by viewers related to one another by common humanity.

—Kenneth Poli

DAVIES, Bevan.

Nationality: American. **Born:** Chicago, Illinois, 8 October 1941. **Education:** Attended Waller High School, Chicago; University of Chicago, for 2 years. **Family:** Married Michele Vallery in 1970; daughter: Stephanie. **Career:** Worked as a drummer in jazz and dance bands, and taught percussion players, Chicago, 1957-64. Photographer since 1965. Guest Lecturer, New York University, New York, 1978, and Napier College, Edinburgh, 1979. **Recipient:** National Endowment for the Arts grant, 1977, 1979. **Agent:** Sonnabend Gallery, 420 West Broadway, New York, New York 10012. **Address:** 431 West Broadway, New York, New York 10012, U.S.A.

Individual Exhibitions:

1969	Gotham Book Mart, New York
1976	Sonnabend Gallery, New York
	Broxton Gallery, Westwood, California
1977	International Museum of Photography, Rochester, New York
	Palais des Beaux-Arts, Brussels
1978	Sonnabend Gallery, New York
	Galleriaforma, Genoa
1979	Galerie Wilde, Cologne

Selected Group Exhibitions:

1964	*Photography '64,* International Museum of Photography, Rochester, New York
1976	*New York—Downtown Manhattan—Soho,* Akademie der Künste, Berlin
1977	*Photography as an Art Form,* Ringling Museum of Art, Sarasota, Florida
	Contemporary American Photographic Works, Museum of Fine Arts, Houston (travelled to the Museum of Contemporary Art, Chicago, and the La Jolla Museum of Contemporary Art, California)
1978	*Summer Group Exhibition,* Sonnabend Gallery, New York
1979	*Space in Two Dimensions,* Museum of Fine Arts, Houston
	American Images: New Work by 20 Contemporary Photographers, Corcoran Gallery, Washington, D.C. (travelled to the International Center of Photography, New York, and the Museum of Fine Arts, Houston)

Collections:

Art Institute of Chicago; International Museum of Photography, Rochester, New York; Museum of Fine Arts, Houston.

Publications:

On DAVIES: Books—*Contemporary American Photographic Works,* exhibition catalogue, edited by Lewis Baltz, Houston 1977; *American Images,* edited by Renato Danese, New York 1979; *Photographie als Kunst, Kunst als Photographie* by Peter Weiermair, Vienna 1979; *Presences* by Marilyn A. Zeitlin, Reading, Pennsylvania 1980. **Articles**—"Document: The American Point of View" by Allan Porter in *Camera* (Lucerne), May 1978; "Deepening the Definition of the Art" by Gene Thornton in the *New York Times,* 31 December 1978; "Post-Modern Photography: It Doesn't Look 'Modern' At All" by Gene Thornton in *Art News* (New York), April 1979; "Photo Works Laid Back with Sobriety" by David Elliott in the *Chicago Sun-Times,* 20 May 1979.

*

The motivations for being an artist are simply too complex to allow me to make an intelligent statement. Contemporary cynicism and old-fashioned Protestant ethics are uncomfortable bedfellows, and I don't feel capable of evaluating how and to what degree they affect me and my work.

—Bevan Davies

*   *   *

Bevan Davies' observation that the camera should be allowed to "see by itself" articulated one of the major ambitions of American photography in the 1970s. The bankruptcy of the dominant photographic styles of the 1960s contributed to the distrust that Davies and others of his generation felt toward "style" as the distinguishing element of serious photography. From this basis Davies proceeded to investigate the fundamental conditions in which a photograph might function as a work of art. The result of this investigation has been a body of photographs based upon the principles of economy, clarity, and disinterested intelligence.

If Davies' esthetic has been reductive and self-critical, his results have not been, in any sense, diminished. In Davies' work the world appears to present itself, and it is for precisely this reason that Davies' photographs provide a rewarding experience for the viewer.

Davies' work is conspicuously public in content and rigorous in execution. He has taken as his subjects prominent buildings, some of inherent architectural or historic interest, others whose chief claim on our attention is that they occupy and define substantial areas of the urban environment. In both cases Davies' mode is presentational. He does not confer distinction upon his subjects nor does he deny their essential dignity; his photographs neither condescend nor do they aggrandize. In this respect his work has been likened to that of the Bechers, although for obvious reasons of methodological difference it would be inaccurate to extend this comparison too far.

Davies' photographs acknowledge no interest in the transient, the aleatory, the anecdotal, or the gratuitous. Consequently, they have proved to be a maddening, if uncalculated, affront to viewers whose grasp of photographic esthetics is confined to the simplistic formulas of candid street photography.

Davies works with an 8 x 10-inch camera, a point worth mentioning only to illustrate his commitment to a deliberate work method and his insistence that the camera define equally and precisely each object within its field of vision.

Davies' prints are 16 x 20 inches, and the visual power of these expansive and richly detailed surfaces is difficult to deny. Nevertheless, it is obvious that Davies' concern is not with the production of handsome objects *per se*; rather, they are the logical outcome of his vision and method. The properties of Davies' prints are the result of necessity, rather than style. The size and resolution of his prints is required to convey the density of information that is the cornerstone of his vision. The harsh, glossy surfaces, with their unavoidable commercial associations, act to subvert any sense of preciousness. The final effect of these astringent and carefully made images is curiously anti-decorative, in keeping with Davies' seriousness of purpose.

Bevan Davies has made a significant and fundamental contribution to contemporary American photography; his work is a testament to the intrinsic strength of the photographic image and suggests its significance in the context of contemporary art.

—Lewis Baltz

DAVIES, John (A.).

Nationality: British. **Born:** Sedgefield, County Durham, 11 December 1949. **Education:** Graduated from Trent Polytechnic (now Nottingham Trent University), 1974. **Family:** Daughter: Alix. **Career:** Worked as a photographer/printer for Sotheby's, London, 1976; Visiting Lecturer in Photography, Blackpool College of Art, 1978-81; Photography Fellowship, Sheffield Polytechnic, 1981; Visiting Lecturer in Photography, West Surrey College of Art, 1985-89; Chair of Counter Image, Manchester's film and photography workshop, 1986-90; Visiting Lecturer in Photography, Nottingham Polytechnic, 1989-91. **Recipient:** Fellow of Royal Photographic Society, 1992. **Agents:** Zelda Cheatle Gallery, 8 Cecil Court, London, WC2N 4HE; Galerie Claire Burrus, 16 Rue de Lappe, Paris 75011; Galerie Rodolphe Janssen, Rue de Livourne 35, Brussels, B1050, Belgium. **Address:** 88 Kings Road, Cardiff, CF1 9DD, England.

Individual Exhibitions:

1976	The Photographers' Gallery, London
1977	Institute of Contemporary Arts, London
1979	*West Coast of Ireland,* The Photographic Gallery, Southampton (and tour)
1981	*Landscapes,* Side Gallery, Newcastle-upon-Tyne (and tour)
1982	*Above and Beyond,* Sheffield (and tour)
1983	*Durham Coalfield,* Side Gallery, Newcastle-upon-Tyne (and tour)
1984	*The Valleys Project,* Ffotogallery, Cardiff (and tour)
1985	*On the Edge of White Peak,* Buxton Art Gallery and Museum (and tour)
1986	*In the Wake of King Cotton,* Rochdale Art Gallery (and tour)
1987	*Skylines,* Viewpoint, Salford (toured the United Kingdom; travelled to Valencia and Salamanca Universities, Spain, 1993)
	A Green and Pleasant Land, The Photographers' Gallery, London (and tour)
1988	XYZ Gallery, Ghent, Belgium
	Taking Stock, Stockport Art Gallery (and tour)
1990	Centro de Estudos Fotograficos, Vigo, Spain
1991	*Phase 11,* The Photographers' Gallery, London (and tour)
	Jacques Gordat Gallery, Paris
1992	*Cross Currents,* Ffotogallery, Cardiff (and tour)
	Vigovisions, at *IV Fotobienal,* Vigo, Spain
1993	*British and Italian Landscapes,* Galleria Dell'Immagine, Rimini, Italy
	The Rhondda Valleys, Galerie Claire Burrus, Paris
1994	*Fos-sur-Mer,* Fos-sur-Mer, France
	Saint-Benoit-du-Sault, France (retrospective)
1995	Galerie Claire Burrus, Paris

Selected Group Exhibitions:

1983	*For Druridge,* Side Gallery, Newcastle-upon-Tyne (and tour)
1984	*Britain in 1984,* National Museum of Photography, Film and Television, Bradford (travelled to The Photographers' Gallery, London)
1985	*Nuova fotografia Inglese,* British Council, Italian touring exhibition
	Centre Nationale du Photographie, Paris
1986	*Coming of Age,* Wilhiem Gallery, Houston, Texas (travelled to the Columbia College Gallery, Chicago)

Goats and Sheep, Barcelona, **1990.** Photograph by John Davies.

Urban Landscapes, Perspektief Gallery, Rotterdam, Netherlands (and tour)

1987   *Poignant Sources,* Artspace, San Francisco

1989   *Autoroute A26,* Douchy, France (and tour)

Towards a Bigger Picture, Victoria and Albert Museum, London (travelled to the Tate Gallery, Liverpool)

Ausbeute (Mining), Ruhrlandmuseum, Essen, Germany

Through the Looking Glass, Barbican Art Gallery, London

The Art of Photography, Royal Academy of Arts, London

1990   Lia Rumma Gallery, Naples, Italy

Association of Catalan Architects, Barcelona, Spain

1991   *British Photography from the Thatcher Years,* Museum of Modern Art, New York (and tour)

Western Styria, Haus der Architektur, Graz, Austria

1992   *Level but not Plain,* Houston Center for Photography, Houston, Texas

Shared Light, Oriel Mostyn, Llandudno, Wales

Wasteland, Perspektief Gallery, Rotterdam, Netherlands

1993   *Coal Mining Landscape,* Angela Flowers Gallery, London

Antwerp 93—A City in Photographs, Museum voor Fotografie, Antwerp, Belgium (and tour)

Gardens of Eden, at *Encontros de Fotografia,* Coimbra, Portugal

Iron River, Bilbao Metropolitan Museum, Spain

1994   *La Ville,* Centre Georges Pompidou, Paris (and tour)

Galerie Rodolphe Janssen, Brussels

The Loire, Art Contemporain Guerigny, France

Neapolis Metropolis, G7 Economic Summit, Naples, Italy

L'Observatoire Photographique du Paysage, Cite des Sciences at de l'Industrie, Paris

Collections:

Arts Council of Great Britain; Association of Catalan Architects, Barcelona, Spain; Bibliothèque Nationale, Paris; BBC Wales; British Council, Leipzig, Germany; British Council, London; Buxton Art Gallery and Museum; Centro de Estudos Fotograficos, Vigo, Spain; Centrum voor Architectuur en Stedebouw, Groningen, Holland; Ffotogallery, Cardiff; Haus der Architektur, Graz, Austria; Maison Européenne de la Photographie, Paris; Manchester City Art Gallery; Musée de la Photographie, Charleroi, Belgium; Museum of Modern Art, New York; National Library of Wales; National Museum of Photography, Film and Television, Bradford; Perspektief Gallery, Rotterdam, Netherlands; Photographers' Gallery, London; Rochdale Art Gallery; Ruhrlandmuseum, Essen, Germany; Side Gallery, Newcastle-upon-Tyne; Stockport Art Gallery; Victoria and Albert Museum, London.

Publications:

By DAVIES: Books—*The Rhymney Valley,* exhibition catalogue, Cardiff 1984; *On the Edge of White Peak,* exhibition catalogue, Buxton 1985; *In the Wake of King Cotton,* exhibition catalogue, Rochdale 1986; *Mist Mountain Water Wind,* monograph, 1986; *A Green and Pleasant Land,* monograph, Manchester 1987; *Taking Stock,* exhibition catalogue, Stockport 1988; *Broadgate—Visitors' Guide,* monograph, London 1989; *Autoroute A26,*

Calais-Reims, monograph, with Michel Kempf, Douchy, France 1989; *Phase 11*, monograph, London 1991; *Broadgate—Photographs by Brian Griffin and John Davies*, London 1991; *Cross Currents*, monograph, Cardiff and Manchester 1992; *Skylines*, monograph, Valencia, Spain 1993.

On DAVIES: Book—*History of Photography* by Peter Turner, 1987. **Articles**—in *Creative Camera* (London), November 1985; in *Amateur Photographer* (London), 22 November 1986; in *The Guardian* (London), 12 November 1987; in *British Journal of Photography* (London), 19 November 1987; in *Aperture* (New York), No. 113, 1988; in *Camera Austria* (Graz), No. 26, 1988; in *The Sunday Times* (London), 8 May 1988; in *Foto* (Holland), July/August 1989; in *The Evening Standard Magazine* (London), 7 March 1991; in *Creative Camera* (London), February/March 1991; in *The Guardian* (London), 3 April 1991; in *British Journal of Photography* (London), 4 July 1991; in *Le Monde* (Paris), 30 December 1993.

*

A fundamental aspect of the landscape is the sense of power which it can symbolise and evoke. Images of land, water and sky can become metaphors which reflect our emotional and spiritual states. But the landscape can also represent power in terms of land ownership and material wealth. It is this dual representation of the metaphysical and the material in the landscape that underlies my photographic work.

I began to document the urban landscape of Britain in 1981 by photographing the city of Sheffield from high vantage points to make ''map-like'' images. I wanted to see how social environments have emerged and how they function—to try to untangle the complex web of urban development.

Industrial developments have been a major influence in shaping our landscape since the Industrial Revolution. I am fascinated by the role industry plays in altering the landscape and the way industrial and living environments co-exist.

We live in a landscape that has a multi-layered history. This history and our relationship to it can be revealed and symbolised by the various building developments that have survived. I am impressed by the structures that have remained throughout the changes in our social history and the way they have continued to be functional.

The impact of our surroundings affects the quality of our lives. My work is about observing the changes in our landscape and I want to make visually stimulating images that celebrate as well as question the forces of change on our environment.

—John Davies

* * *

Working for himself, John Davies would always choose black and white. As a successful architectural photographer, he has often used colour which he does with great success. His reputation has grown steadily in the field of landscape and urban photography and he has made excellent use of his commissions and grants to explore both the United Kingdom and other countries in Europe. His particular interest lies in the cross-over spaces between town and country and the effect that man has had even in the seeming depths of the countryside. His point of view is often from a slightly high vantage point, giving him a wide sky and enabling him to show a range of man-made structures, or the detritus that has been left behind by mining or manufacture. The sky may be overcast and grey or contain clouds which give an added drama to the scene but it is always as carefully considered as the main subject of the picture.

The photographs give one an impression of an explorer. Someone sympathetic but possibly slightly bemused by what we do to our spaces. In *Green and Pleasant Land* there was compassion rather than criticism in the way in which we let decay seemingly take us unaware until it becomes unnoticeable to those who pass it everyday. In *Cross Currents*, John Davies had the opportunity to visit countries throughout the European Community and although there is diversity, the work shows a commonality which is then the photographic viewpoint and which should encourage us to see and appreciate similarities with our European neighbours rather than our differences.

Although the majority of his work is taken from a distance that makes any human or animal figure minimal in size, when he undertook the complete

record of the building of Phase 11 of the Broadgate Development in London, he took many photographs of construction workers, in close-up or as the subjects of the pictures, and spent many hours high on the scaffolding as the building grew. These are not photographs of ''hero workers'' as have been made in the past, but very real pictures of men at work in difficult and dangerous surroundings which give a true feel of their involvement in the construction—as true a picture as of the building itself; which becomes organic rather than monumental because we have seen it growing and know how it happened. It also illustrates how much care and attention is given by human beings to their constructions which may well become the detritus of the future.

—Sue Davies

DAVIS, Bob (Robert James Davis).

Nationality: Australian. **Born:** Melbourne, Victoria, 8 August 1944. **Education:** Attended various schools in Australia; self-taught in photography. **Career:** Cinematographer and photographer, Department of Film Production, Hobart, Tasmania, 1963-65; freelance photographer, in Sydney, 1965-70, in London and Japan, 1970-78, in Hong Kong, since 1978. Owner-Director, The Stock House photo library/agency, Hong Kong, since 1980. **Recipient:** Honor Award, Pacific Area Travel Association, San Francisco, 1986. **Agents:** Aspect Picture Library, 40 Rostrevor Road, London SW6 5AD, England; Woodfin Camp and Associates, 415 Madison Avenue, New York, New York. **Address:** The Stock House, 310 Yu Yuet Lai Building, 43-55 Wyndham Street, Hong Kong.

Individual Exhibitions:

1974	*Light and Shade of Europe: Color Photographs*, Pentax Gallery, Tokyo
1979	*Faces of Japan*, Australian Centre of Photography, Sydney (travelled to Church Street Photographic Centre, Melbourne, 1980)
1980	*China*, at the *Hong Kong Arts Festival*
1991	*Mont Blanc*, Hong Kong

Publications:

By DAVIS: Books—*Faces of Japan*, paperback, Tokyo 1974, as hard cover with an introduction by Murray Sayle, Tokyo 1978; *A Day in the Life of Australia*, Tokyo 1981; *A Day in the Life of Japan—June 7, 1985*, with others, edited by Rick Smolan and David Cohen, New York and London 1985; *Historic Postcards of Hong Kong*, Hong Kong 1991; *Hong Kong Today*, Tokyo 1992. **Article**—''Winnie the Pooh'' in *Observer Colour Magazine* (London), December 1973.

On DAVIS: Articles—''Bob Davis'' in *British Journal of Photography Annual*, London 1971; ''Portfolio: Bob Davis'' in *British Journal of Photography* (London), April 1971; ''Bob Davis'' in *British Journal of Photography* (London), July 1971; ''Bob Davis'' in *The Image* (London), February 1973; ''Bob Davis'' in *British Journal of Photography* (London), June 1973; ''Bob Davis'' in *Photo Technic* (London), February 1974; ''Bob Davis'' in *British Journal of Photography Annual*, London 1975; ''Faces of Japan'' in *The Australian* (Sydney), March 1979; ''Bob Davis'' in *British Journal of Photography* (London), March 1979; ''Bob Davis: Portfolio'' in *Zoom* (Paris), May 1979; ''Travel Photography'' by Jim Bell in *You and Your Camera* (London), June 1980; ''A Day in the Life of Australia'' in *Life* (New York), October 1981; ''Bob Davis'' in *Photo District News* (New York), April 1986.

*

Photography to me has become my life-style—a combination of commercial work (advertising, editorial and corporate), editing and running a photoagency (as owner of the Stock House, Asia's largest agency outside of Japan), and personal work mainly evolving around books (working on three books at present).

—Bob Davis

* * *

Bob Davis is essentially a travel photographer who works in colour with 35mm SLR cameras; but at the same time he also shoots black-and-white reportage using Leicas.

The colour work is eminently suitable for uses such as travel advertising, airline calendars and posters, magazines and brochures. It presents a picturesque world of invitingly exotic subjects in lush colours. But Davis manages to be romantic without cloying the palette. The pictures are toughened by an acute sense of perception and by their strong graphic design. The "design" is the careful arrangement of the main lines of the subject in the composition, such as strong patterns of shadows in flat plains or the receding lines of a road or pathway in a landscape. The "sense of perception" comes from the reportage feel of the work. Davis does not shoot "picture postcards"; he takes the kind of pictures *you* would want to take on holiday to preserve, in idealized form, pleasant memories. It is very satisfying.

The black-and-white work is after the style of Cartier-Bresson, to judge by the 88 plates in *Faces of Japan*. This contains a few pictures where the subject is reacting to the camera, but in most of them the photographer is making a point of not being noticed.

Many of the reportage pictures show the same type of strong graphic arrangement as the colour work, though often an unacceptable subject is included in the frame. In travel photography terms, an "unacceptable subject" is the overflowing wastepaper bin at the edge of the lake (plate 83) or the wrecked car which despoils the beautiful beach (plate 60). Davis places these unsightly objects smack in the front of his black and white pictures as if in protest against the colour shots where he would go to even greater pains to exclude them.

Now based permanently in Hong Kong, Bob Davis continues to build up his Stock House agency, working with other photographers, and travels all over the world for both magazines and corporate clients. He works chiefly in colour, both in his books and on assignment, and intends to stay on after 1997.

—Jack Schofield

DAWID (Björn Dawidsson).

Nationality: Swedish. **Born:** Örebro, Sweden, 7 June 1949. **Family:** Married to Åsa; daughter: Fabian. **Address:** Pilgatan 19A, 11223 Stockholm, Sweden.

Individual Exhibitions:

1972	Liljevalchs Konsthall, Stockholm
1973	Västerbottens Museum, Umeå, Sweden
1978	Fotograficentrum, Stockholm (with Håkan Lind)
1980	Galleri Camera Obscura, Stockholm
1982	Malmö Konsthall, Malmö, Sweden
	Galleri Camera Obscura, Stockholm
1983	Fotografiska Museet, Stockholm
1984	Galleri BarBar, Stockholm
1985	Upplands Konstmuseum, Uppsala, Sweden
1986	Galleri Nordenhake, Malmö, Sweden
	Galleri Olsson, Stockholm
	Centre Culturel Suédois, Paris
1987	Galerie Nemo, Eckernförde, Germany
	Galleri Finnfoto, Helsinki, Finland
1989	Galleri Wallner, Malmö, Sweden
	Malmö Konsthall, Malmö, Sweden
	Galerie Le Lieu, Lorient, France
	Thielska Galleriet, Stockholm
1990	Galleri Riis, Oslo, Norway
1991	Lido, Stockholm
	Galleri Nordanstad-Skarstedt, Stockholm
	Fotografiska Museet, Stockholm
1992	Pieni Agora, Helsinki, Finland
	Galleri Wallner, Malmö, Sweden
	Bildmuseet, Umeå, Sweden
	Mölndals Konsthall, Mölndal, Sweden
1993	Museum Folkwang, Essen, Germany
	Galerie Nemo, Eckernförde, Germany
1994	Upplandsmuseet, Uppsala, Sweden
	Encontros da Imagem, Braga, Portugal

Selected Group Exhibitions:

1975	*Vargen,* Moderna Museet, Stockholm
1981	*Sju svenska fotografer,* Konsthallen, Pori, Finland
	Le Moderna museet de Stockholm à Bruxelles, Palais des Beaux-Arts, Brussels
	Swedish Photographers, Photographers Gallery, Wales
1982	*The Frozen Image,* Walker Art Center, Minneapolis, USA (travelling exhibition)
1984	*Het stilleven in de fotografie,* Rotterdamse Kunststichting, Netherlands
	Valokuva Taiteena, Sveaborg, Helsinki, Finland
1985	*Nordic Art Photography,* Brandts Klaedefabrik Museum, Odense, Denmark
1986	*Conversions,* Germans van Eck Gallery, New York
1987	*Nordic Artistic Photography—a viewpoint,* Brandts Klaedefabrik Museum, Odense, Denmark (travelling exhibition)
	Fred, Louisiana Museum, Humlebaek, Denmark
1990	*Spegling,* Moderna Museet, Stockholm (travelling exhibition)
	Nordic, Charlottenborg, Copenhagen, Denmark
1991	*Zehn Jahre junger Kunst in Malmö,* Kampnagelfabrik, Hamburg, Germany
	Yttre, Södertälje Konsthall, Sweden
	Konst-Fotografi, Hasselblad Centre, Gothenburg, Sweden (travelling exhibition)
	Lika med, Moderna Museet, Stockholm (travelling exhibition)
1992	*Från Skåne,* Malmö Konsthall, Malmö, Sweden
	Konkret, Museet for samtidskunst, Oslo, Norway
	Ostsee-Biennale 1992, Kunsthalle Rostock, Germany
	Elkida, D'Arte Galleria, Helsinki, Finland (travelled to the Forum, Stockholm, 1994)
1993	*Prospekt,* Fotografiska Museet in the Moderna Museet, Stockholm
	Spelets Regler, Stockholm
	Pod ostona nieba, Centrum Szuki Wspótczesnej Patac Ujazdowski, Warsaw, Poland
	De Refuserade, Liljevalchs Konsthall, Stockholm
1994	*Stranger Than Paradise,* ICP, New York

Collections:

Camera Obscura, Stockholm; Centro Cultural Arte Contemporaneo, Mexico City; Fotografiska Museet in the Moderna Museet, Stockholm; Malmö Museum, Malmö, Sweden; Nykytaiteen museo, Helsinki, Finland; Statens Konstrad, Stockholm; Upplands Konstmuseum, Uppsala, Sweden.

Publications:

By DAWID: Book—*Verkligen?!,* with Håkan Lind, Stockholm 1978.

On DAWID: Books—*Dawid* by Jan-Gunnar Sjölin, Stockholm 1980; *ROST* by Leif Wigh, Stockholm 1983; *Dawid* by Johan Ehrenberg, Stockholm 1988;

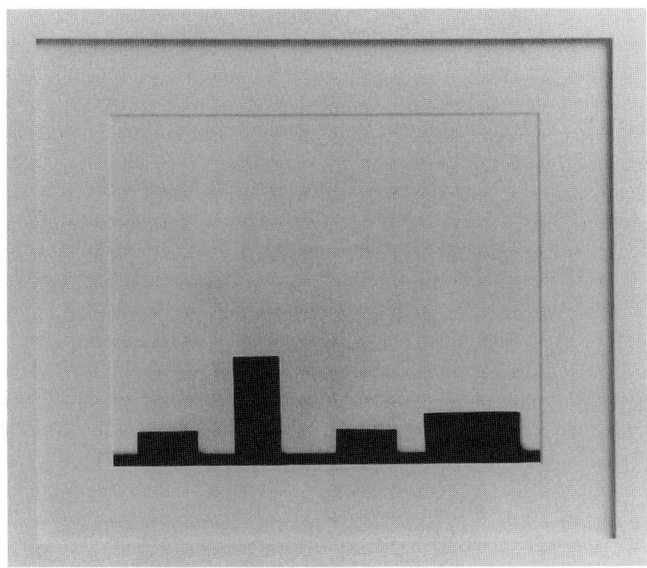

3206, from the series *Arbetsnamn Skulptur,* **1988.** Photograph by Dawid
(Bjorn Dawidsson).

Dagram by Stig Larsson and Björn Springfeldt, Malmö, Sweden 1989; *Mot fotografiet/Arbetsnamn Skulptur* by Ulf Linde, Stockholm 1989; *Etthundra Fotografier/1968-1991* by Peder Alton and Björn Springfeldt, Stockholm 1991.

*   *   *

"I make each place my own" says Dawid. And where there is no place, he creates one for himself. For Dawid, photography is such a place; a place that he uses and integrates into his works. Thus it hardly needs mentioning that Dawid does not like to travel. He has no need to. He always finds something, however small and insignificant it may be, to make into a picture: a rusty nail, for example, or a piece of wire. Not even the camera is always necessary. "If the camera had never been invented, I would have found some other way to create pictures," he said in an interview.

The state of being oblivious is, according to Dawid, the supreme moment of artistic creation, and also a form of annihilation or death. "In schematic work a pleasant obliviousness arises." Dawid does everything himself: he develops film, designs and paints frames, cuts matboard. He delegates nothing. Dawid seeks complication in simple, uncovered things. His pictures are so "simple" that trying to understand them becomes a real challenge. When representation is uncovered, only the image remains, the photographic image, the image that is reduced to photography.

—Lars O Ericsson

DEAL, Joe.

Nationality: American. **Born:** Topeka, Kansas, 12 August 1947. **Education:** Studied at Kansas City Art Institute, 1967-70, B.F.A. 1970; University of New Mexico, Albuquerque, 1973-74, M.A. 1974, M.F.A. 1978. **Career:** Photographer since 1969. Director of Exhibitions, International Museum of Photography, George Eastman House, Rochester, New York, 1975-76. Since 1976, Assistant Professor of Art, University of California at Riverside. **Recipient:** National Endowment for the Arts Photography Fellowship, 1977, 1980; Guggenheim Fellowship, 1984. **Agent:** Light Gallery, 724 Fifth Ave-

nue, New York, New York 10019. **Address:** 3540 Watkins Drive, Riverside, California 92507, U.S.A.

Individual Exhibitions:

1973	Light Gallery, New York
1975	Light Gallery, New York
1976	Orange Coast College, Costa Mesa, California
1977	University of California at Riverside
1978	Light Gallery, New York
	Los Angeles Institute of Contemporary Art
	University of New Mexico, Albuquerque
	University of Arkansas, Little Rock
1980	Colorado Mountain College, Breckenridge
1981	Light Gallery, Los Angeles
	Joe Deal: The Fault Zone/William Larson: Recent Color Work from Arizona, Light Gallery, New York
	New Topographics, Arnolfini Gallery, Bristol, Avon (with Robert Adams and Lewis Baltz; travelled to the Open Eye Gallery, Liverpool; B2 Gallery, London; Ikon Gallery, Birmingham)
1983	Center for Creative Photography, University of Arizona, Tucson
	Real and Potential Disasters, Film in the Cities, Minneapolis, Minnesota (with Frank Gohlke)
1986	Nagase Photo Gallery, Tokyo

Selected Group Exhibitions:

1972	*Summer Light,* Light Gallery, New York
1973	*Sharp-Focus Realism: A New Perspective,* Pace Editions, New York
1975	*New Topographics: Photographs of a Man-Altered Landscape,* International Museum of Photography, George Eastman House, Rochester, New York (travelled to the Otis Art Institute, Los Angeles, and Princeton University, New Jersey)
1977	*Contemporary American Photographic Works,* Museum of Fine Arts, Houston (travelled to the La Jolla Art Museum, California)
	The Great West: Real/Ideal, University of Colorado, Boulder (toured the United States)
1978	*Baltz/Deal/Gohlke/Shore/Toth,* Werkstatt für Photographie der VHS Kreuzberg, Berlin
1979	*New California Views,* International Center of Photography, New York (travelled to the Minneapolis Institute of Art, and Mills College, Oakland, California)
1981	*Slices of Time: California Landscapes,* Oakland Museum, California (travelled to the Security Pacific National Bank Plaza, Los Angeles)
1984	*Photography in California 1945-80,* San Francisco Museum of Modern Art (travelled to the Akron Art Museum, Ohio; Corcoran Gallery, Washington, D.C.; Los Angeles Municipal Art Gallery; Cornell University, Ithaca, New York; High Museum of Art, Atlanta, Georgia; Museum Folkwang, Essen; Centre Georges Pompidou, Paris; Museum of Photographic Arts, San Diego, California)
1985	*American Images 1945-80,* Barbican Art Gallery, London (toured Britain)

Collections:

Museum of Modern Art, New York; International Museum of Photography, George Eastman House, Rochester, New York; Minneapolis Institute of Art; University of Louisville, Kentucky; University of Colorado, Boulder; University of New Mexico, Albuquerque; Center for Creative Photography, University of Arizona, Tucson; Museum of Fine Arts, Houston; Neue Sammlung, Munich.

Publications:

By DEAL: portfolio—*The Fault Zone,* with Anita Mozley, Los Angeles 1981.

On DEAL: Books—*New Topographics: Photographs of a Man-Altered Landscape,* exhibition catalogue, by William Jenkins, Rochester, New York 1975; *Photographer's Choice,* edited by Kelly Wise, Danbury, New Hampshire 1975; *The Light Gallery Catalogue of Contemporary Photography,* New York 1976; *Contemporary American Photographic Works,* exhibition catalogue, by Lewis Baltz and John Upton, Houston 1977; *The Great West: Real/ Ideal,* exhibition catalogue, edited by Sandy Hume, Ellen Manchester, and Gary Metz, Boulder, Colorado 1977; *New California Views,* portfolio, edited by Victor Landweber and Arthur Ollman, Los Angeles 1979; *Long Beach: A Photographic Survey,* exhibition catalogue, edited by Constance W. Glenn and Jane Bledsoe, Long Beach California 1980; *New Topographics: Photographs by Robert Adams, Lewis Baltz and Joe Deal,* exhibition catalogue, by Paul Highnam, Bristol 1981; *Photography in California 1945-1980* by Louise Katzman, San Francisco and New York 1984; *American Images: Photography 1945-1980,* edited by Peter Turner and John Benton-Harris, London and New York 1985; *Landscape as Photograph* by Estelle Jussim and Elizabeth Lindquist-Cock, London and New Haven, Connecticut 1985. **Articles**— "Route 66 Revisited: New Landscape Photography" by Carter Ratcliff in *Art in America* (New York), January/February 1976; "Joe Deal: New Topographics" by James Hajicek and Bill Jay in *Northlight 4* (Tempe, Arizona), 1977; "Aspekte der Amerikanischen Fotografie der Gegenwart" by Janet Borden in *Dumont Foto 1: Fotokunst und Fotodesign International,* edited by Hugo Schöttle, Cologne 1978; "Joe Deal's Optical Democracy" by James Hugunin in *Afterimage* (Rochester, New York), February 1979.

*   *   *

Early in his career, Joe Deal photographed decisively shaped natural objects and strictly rectangular architecture: pines clipped to cones, bulbous cacti, square white plaster, linear dark metal. All these textures and the shapes that were made of them were conjoined in coherent, deliberately designed photographs. Increasingly, the area of the photograph given over to expansive nature, or what was left of it as it was prepared for man's invasion, was extended. An ecological concern became evident as he focused, for instance, on land cut through with barbaric swathes, the preparations for what we call, without a trace of irony, its development. In his photographs, the land was seen as impotent, while the houses bred. Along with this messier subject came an increasing complication of the image; strictness of design gave way to a sense for existing disorder, the disorder of change. He moved from close focus on discrete objects to as wide a view as his square format camera would admit, from exclusiveness to inclusiveness. This interest in the man-altered landscape, shared by a number of American photographers in the 1970s, was exhibited at the International Museum of Photography in 1975 under the title *New Topographics.* Deal, however, differed from others in the exhibition in his advancing freedom from self-conscious stylization.

When he became a resident of Southern California in 1976, Deal was well-prepared for one subject that he found in that population-explosive area. In "Beach Cities," a series made in 1978-79, he presented powerful arguments for the incompatability of those two terms; read rightly, his images of urbanized sea shores were photographic object lessons. In his most recent series, "The Fault Zone," 1978-80, he goes beyond depiction or analysis. The physical incidents in his view are given in a pictorially tense structure that is analogous to the tension between subterranean and superficial events. Man's artifacts depend from the sides of the square frames of these recent photographs; porches and roadways, concrete beginnings (or remains?) seem perched and tentative on the inscrutable earth. His nominal subject is the landscape of earthquake country, but his essential subject is time—man's time and the earth's time. As an artist, Deal has thus moved from well-designed description to philosophic comment. Throughout his career, his mode has been coolly dispassionate, reminiscent of that of the 19th-century survey photographer Tomothy O'Sullivan. His straight technique is consistently impeccable.

—Anita V. Mozley

DeCARAVA, Roy (Rudolph).

Nationality: American. **Born:** New York City, 9 December 1919. **Education:** Attended New York public schools, 1924-38, including Textile High School, 1934-38; studied architecture and sculpture, and painting with Byron Thomas and Morris Kantor, at Cooper Union Institute, New York, 1938-40; painting with Elton Fax and printmaking, Harlem Art Center, New York, 1940-42; and drawing and painting with Charles White, at George Washington Carver Art School, New York, 1944-45. **Military Service:** Served as a topographical draftsman in the United States Army, 1943. **Family:** Married Sherry Turner in 1970; children: Susan, Wendy and Laura. **Career:** Worked in New York as a sign painter and display artist, 1936-37, technical draftsman, 1939-42, and commercial artist and illustrator, 1944-58. Freelance photographer, in New York, working for various advertising agencies, recording and television companies, and such magazines as *Scientific American, Fortune, McCall's, Look, Newsweek, Time, Life,* 1959-68 and since 1975; Contract Photographer, *Sports Illustrated* magazine, New York, 1968-75. Founder-Director, A Photographers Gallery, New York, 1954-56; Founder-Director, Kamoinge Workshop for black photographers, New York, 1963-66; Member, Curatorial Council, Studio Museum, Harlem, New York, 1976. Adjunct Professor of Photography, Cooper Union Institute, New York, 1969-72. Associate Professor, 1975-78, Professor of Art, 1978-88 and since 1988 Distinguished Professor of Art, Hunter College, New York. Chairman, Committee to End Discrimination Against Black Photographers, American Society of Magazine Photographers, 1963-66. **Recipient:** Guggenheim Photography Fellowship, 1952; Art Service Award, Mt. Morris United Presbyterian Church, New York, 1969; Benin Creative Photography Award, 1972; Artistic and Cultural Achievement Award, Community Museum of Brooklyn, New York, 1979. Honorary Citizen of Houston, Texas, 1975. Honorary Doctorates from Rhode Island School of Design, 1985, and The Maryland Institute, 1986. **Agent:** Witkin Gallery, 415 West Broadway, New York 10012. **Address:** 81 Halsey Street, Brooklyn, New York 11216, U.S.A.

Individual Exhibitions:

1950	Forty-Fourth Street Gallery, New York
1951	Countee Cullen Branch, New York Public Library
1954	*Guggenheim Photographs,* Little Gallery, New York Public Library
1955	A Photographers Gallery, New York
1956	Camera Club of New York
1967	*US,* Countee Cullen Branch, New York Public Library
1969	*Thru Black Eyes,* Studio Museum, Harlem, New York
1970	Sheldon Memorial Art Center, University of Nebraska, Lincoln
1974	*Photographic Perspectives,* University of Massachusetts, Amherst
1975	Museum of Fine Arts, Houston
1976	*The Nation's Capitol in Photographs,* Corcoran Gallery, Washington, D.C.
	Benin Gallery, New York
1977	Witkin Gallery, New York
	Light Work Gallery, Syracuse, New York
1978	Port Washington Public Library, New York
1980	Friends of Photography, Carmel, California
	Akron Art Institute, Ohio
1983	*Jazz Photographs,* Studio Museum, Harlem, New York
1988	Museum of Modern Art, Stockholm (toured to Paris and London)
1990	*Recent Photographs,* The Witkin Gallery, New York

Selected Group Exhibitions:

1953	*Always the Young Strangers,* Museum of Modern Art, New York
1955	*The Family of Man,* Museum of Modern Art, New York (and world tour)
1964	*Photography in the Fine Arts,* Metropolitan Museum of Art, New York

1967   *Photography in the 20th Century,* National Gallery of Canada,
        Ottawa (toured Canada and the United States, 1967-73)
1978   *Mirrors and Windows: American Photography since 1960,*
        Museum of Modern Art, New York (toured the United
        States, 1978-80)
1980   *Photography of the 50s,* Center for Creative Photography,
        University of Arizona, Tucson
1983   *Photography in America 1910-83,* Tampa Museum, Florida
1985   *American Images 1945-80,* Barbican Art Gallery, London
        (toured Britain)
1986   *Jazz pa Fotografiska,* Fotografiska Museet, Stockholm

Collections:

Museum of Modern Art, New York; Metropolitan Museum of Art, New York;
Harlem Art Collection, New York State Office Building, New York; Andover
Art Gallery, Phillips Academy, Andover, Massachusetts; Corcoran Gallery,
Washington, D.C.; Atlanta University; Sheldon Memorial Art Gallery, Uni-
versity of Nebraska, Lincoln; Museum of Fine Arts, Houston; Center for
Creative Photography, University of Arizona, Tucson.

Publications:

By DeCARAVA: Book—*The Sweet Flypaper of Life,* with text by Langston
Hughes, New York 1955, 1967 and Washington D.C. 1984.

On DeCARAVA: Books—*Photography in the 20th Century* by Nathan
Lyons, New York 1967; *Roy DeCarava, Photographer,* exhibition catalogue,
with text by James Alinder, Lincoln, Nebraska 1970; *Black Photographers
Annual,* New York 1975; *Roy DeCarava: Photographs,* exhibition catalogue,
with text by Alvia Wardlaw Short, Houston 1975; *Roy DeCarava: The
Nation's Capitol in Photographs,* with text by Jane Livingston and Frances
Fralin, Washington, D.C. 1976; *Mirrors and Windows: American Photogra-
phy since 1960* by John Szarkowski, New York 1978; *Light Readings: A
Photography Critic's Writings 1968-1978* by A.D. Coleman, New York 1979;
American Images: New Work by 20 Contemporary Photographers, edited by
Renato Danese, New York 1979; *The Photograph Collector's Guide* by Lee
D. Witkin and Barbara London, Boston and London 1979; *Photography of the
50s,* exhibition catalogue, by Helen Gee, Tucson, Arizona 1980; *Roy DeCarava:
Photographs,* Carmel, California, 1981; *Photography in America 1910-1983,*
exhibition catalogue, by Julie M. Saul, Tampa, Florida 1983; *American
Images: Photography 1945-1980,* edited by Peter Turner and John Benton-
Harris, London and New York 1985.

*

    Photography allows me to be of use by enabling me to share my concerns
and my priorities with others, known and unknown.

—Roy DeCarava

*   *   *

    Roy DeCarava could be described as an exponent of a black point of view,
the creator of a black aesthetic, an interpreter of black experience. All of these
claims are demonstrable, and certainly their validity is nowhere better demonstrated than in his remarkable collaboration with Langston Hughes in his first
book, *The Sweet Flypaper of Life.* There is in these images the warmth of total
identification and their truth is unmistakable, and yet if his work is compared
with that of another black artist, James Van Der Zee, a significant difference
makes itself felt. DeCarava is seen to have broken out of the ghetto of color and
exercises his vision and sensibility in a world much less enclosed and
exclusive. It is apparent that he is able to look at and see human beings, black
and white, with a straight-forward sympathy and insight.
    DeCarava has said: "Most photographers are motivated by form. I'm
motivated by content." Form in his work is by no means a negligible quality.
His images are structured with a rightness that reveals the completely unselfconscious craftsman. The moment seized by the click of the camera or, if as
may be, by the choice made in the darkroom, is the only one, the one that
contains the insight that defines the picture. In this, his sense of form is

instinctive, utterly simple and, in effect, invisible. No structures of climate or
emotion or process stand between the eye of the photographer and his
witnessing of the subject. His images are as a whole tonally dark, sometimes
suggesting a mood of thoughtful melancholy, but it is clear in the rapport that
links every image with the sensibility of the photographer, that his sense of the
content of his subject is one of recognition.
    And in the very act of recognition, DeCarava is set apart from the
multitude of photographers who specialize in an uncritical record of the
commonplace of everyday experience. His images have nothing of the look of
the accidental or the irrelevant, nothing of the bland monotony of thousands of
shots taken, from which one is selected as somehow more significant than the
rest. He sees and catches, with inevitable rightness, the entire ambience of
living, the wash of light along a street, the abstractions of walls and windows,
of surfaces and voids, and invests them with a richness of tone and texture that
makes these places and events palpable to the senses and evidence to the mind
of the human experience which has shaped them.

—Norman A. Geske

DeCOCK, Liliane.

Nationality: American. **Born:** Antwerp, Belgium, 11 September 1939; immi-
grated to the United States, 1960, subsequently naturalized. **Family:** Married
the publisher Douglas Morgan in 1972. **Career:** Freelance photographer.
Worked as photographic assistant to Ansel Adams, Carmel, California, 1963-
72; graphics editor, Morgan and Morgan publishers, from 1972. Trustee,
Friends of Photography, Carmel. **Recipient:** Guggenheim Fellowship, 1972.
Address: c/o Morgan and Morgan, 145 Palisades Street, Dobbs Ferry, New
York 10522, U.S.A.

Individual Exhibitions:

1968   Jacksonville Museum of Art, Florida
        Friends of Photography, Carmel, California
1969   University of California at Berkeley
        Harnell College, Salinas, California
1970   Bathhouse Gallery, Milwaukee
        International Museum of Photography, George Eastman House,
            Rochester, New York
1971   Massachusetts Institute of Technology, Cambridge
1972   Limited Image Gallery, Chicago
        Film-Com Gallery, Berwyn, Pennsylvania
        Witkin Gallery, New York
        University of Rhode Island, Kingston
1980   Milwaukee Center of Photography

Selected Group Exhibitions:

1980   *De Fotografie in Belgie 1940-1980,* Het Sterckshof Museum,
            Deurne-Antwerp

Collections:

Princeton University, New Jersey; Exchange National Bank, Chicago; Amon
Carter Museum of Western Art, Fort Worth, Texas; Phoenix College, Arizona;
Glendale College, California; Norton Simon Art Museum, Pasadena, California

Publications:

By DeCOCK: Book—*Liliane DeCock: Photographs,* with a foreword by
Ansel Adams, New York 1973.

On DeCOCK: Book—*De Fotografie in Belgie 1940-1980,* exhibition catalogue, by Roger Coenen and Karel van Deuren, Antwerp 1980.

* * *

The photographic landscape is always a fragment. A person can be glanced from head to toe; the earth's skin just stretches too far. Even from as far back as the moon, only half the earth is visible. Landscapes are landscapes within landscapes, atomized chunks of earth cut loose by the camera, intimating the character of the greater surround. Oddly enough, to fragment, to tease with the frame, to swerve attention from the picture to its edges or outside it has not been a traditional imperative of strength of the landscape photographer. Rather, the chosen views of masters such as Ansel Adams and Wynn Bullock impart wholeness and completeness, such that we come to experience the scene firsthand, as if we too had been there, standing beside the photographer at the moment of recording, sensing peripherally, seeing it all.

Such is the essence of the land in the landscapes of the Belgian-born photographer Liliane DeCock. In one striking example, a cloud mass swathes the face of Yosemite's *El Capitan* with steamy softness, never subduing the majesty of the precipice over which the translucent, enveloping wisps roll. We see the fragment, yet feel the totality.

Frame evaporates in other DeCock landscapes. In one of these, a spinning windmill generator on a prairie near Santa Fe, New Mexico spits and scatters thunder clouds every which way, becoming itself the eye of the gathering storm, the center of our undivided attention.

As it appears, DeCock's photographs are as much about the weather as they are about the land. Her camera often points upward. With a kind of ascensional gesture of the tripod head heavenward, DeCock embraces the elements as equal collaborators with the earth in formulating the picture. Sky becomes background transfigured. A storm front in Nevada sweeps our eyes up with the billowing clouds, like a balloon released from underwater, or as in many of her architectural images of pinnacled barnroofs, like a congregation standing in unison. It is indeed uncanny that these photographs of uplift and optimism should begin their creative life upside down on the ground glass of DeCock's view camera. Earth above, sky below. Perhaps her intention in making images that exhilarate, subconscious though that driving force may be, is a matter of compensation for the ground glass, or could it be more likely that these magnificent celebrations of the American West are instead an eloquent compensation for Belgian flatness.

—Arno Rafael Minkkinen

DE KEYZER, Carl.

Nationality: Belgian. **Born:** Kortrijk, Belgium, 27 December 1958. **Education:** Studied Latin and science, St Amand College, Kortrijk, 1971-77; studied photography and film-making, Kask Royal Academy of Fine Arts, Ghent, 1977-81. **Career:** Photography teacher, Royal Academy of Fine Arts, Ghent, 1982-89. Co-founder and co-director of the photo gallery "XYZ Photography," 1982-89. Freelance photographer, since 1982. Member of the MAGNUM Agency. **Recipient:** 1st prize, experimental film festival for young Belgian filmmakers, Brussels, 1982; Hasselblad Award Belgium, Brussels, 1986; Grand Prix de la Triennale de la Photographie—Photographie Ouverte, Charleroi, Belgium, 1986; Grand Prix Triennale de la Ville de Fribourg, Fribourg, Switzerland, 1988; Louis-Paul Boon Award, Ghent, 1990; Book Award—Prix du Livre, Festival International de la Photo, Arles, France, 1990; Eugene Smith Award, International Center for Photography, New York, 1990; The Kodak Award Prix de la Critique—Kodak, Paris, 1992. **Agent:** Magnum, 5 Passage Piver, 75011 Paris. **Address:** Brabantdam 110, 9000 Gent, Belgium.

Individual Exhibitions:

1984   CCH Hasselt, Belgium
1987   XYZ-Fotografie, Ghent
        Canon Gallery, Amsterdam

Galerie Contretype, Brussels
Galerie Nueva Imagen, Pamplona, Spain
Gallery Focus, Amsterdam
1988   Fotografie Museum, Antwerp
        Centre Culturel d'Art Contemporain, Amiens, France
        Museum of Modern Art, Ghent
        Centre for Photography as an art form, Bombay, India
        Canon Rotown, Rotterdam, Netherlands
        Fotogalerije Novo Mesto, Novo Mesto, Yugoslavia
        Congress Center, Lubljana, Yugoslavia
        Galerie Frederic Basille, Montpellier, France
1989   CCH, Hasselt, Belgium
        Canon Image Centre, Amsterdam
1990   Musée de la Photo, Charleroi, Belgium
        Museum of Modern Art, Ghent
        Galerie DBS, Antwerp
        Musée de l'Elysée, Lausanne, Switzerland
        Photokina, Belgisch Huis, Cologne, Germany
        Centre Culturel d'Art Contemporain, Amiens, France
1991   Galerie du Chateau d'Eau, Toulouse, France
1992   Canon Image Centre, Amsterdam
        Museum of Modern Art, Ghent
        The Photographers' Gallery, London
        FNAC FORUM, Paris
        California Museum of Photography, Riverside, California
1993   Frankfurt Forum Galerie—Frankfurter Buchmesse, Frankfurt
        Nikon Galerie, Zurich, Switzerland
1994   Galerie Polaris, Brussels

Selected Group Exhibitions:

1982   Galerie Siegfried De Buck, Ghent
        Galerie Pennings, Eindhoven, Netherlands
        Galerie J. Walter Thompson, Amsterdam
        Galerie XYZ, Ghent
1983   *Paysages Urbains,* at *Festival International de la Photo,* Huy, Belgium
        Galerie Images, Brussels
1984   *15 Vlaamse Fotografen,* De Brakke Grond, Amsterdam (travelled to the Fotografie Museum, Antwerp, 1985; Rathaus, Essen, Germany, 1986)
        CCH, Hasselt, Belgium
1986   *Initiatief '86,* Galerie XYZ, Ghent
        Galerie Portfolio, Antwerp
        Photographie Ouverte, Charleroi, Belgium
1987   *Festival International de la Photo,* Liège, Belgium
        View '87—La Photo en Belgique, Brussels
        Prospect 6, Gele Zaal, Ghent
        Young European Photography, Frankfurt, Germany
1988   Musée d'Art Moderne, Fribourg, Switzerland
        Forum Photo, Club Méditerrannée, Gregolimano, Greece
        Forum Gregolimano, FNAC, France
        Festival International de la Photographie Actuelle, Montreal
        Young European Photography, Galerie Faber, Vienna
1989   *Foto Festival,* Athens, Greece
        5 Ans Clichés, Le Botanique, Brussels (travelled to the Centre Culturel de la Wallonnie, Paris; Centre Culturel d'Art Contemporain, Amiens)
        European Prizewinners 1988, Bielefeld, Germany
1990   *Zomer van de Fotografie,* Fotografie Museum, Antwerp
1991   *Panorama des Panoramas,* Centre National de la Photo, Palais de Tokyo, Paris
        La Photographie Belge, Centre National de la Photo, Palais de Tokyo, Paris
        The Eugene Smith Legacy, Centre Georges Pompidou, Paris (and tour, 1991-93)
        MAGNUM à l'Est—East of MAGNUM, world tour
1992   *La Danse,* Musée de la Photo, Charleroi, Belgium
        Carl De Keyzer & Miguel Rio Branco, Zeno-X Gallery, Antwerp

Photofollies, Centre National de la Photo, Palais de Tokyo, Paris

Portretten van Papier, Paleis voor Schone Kunsten, Brussels

1993 *Metro Pictures,* Passage 44, Brussels

Photographie Belge, Musée de la Photo, Charleroi, Belgium

Three Magnum Photographers, University of Santiago de
Compostella, Spain (with Miguel Rio Branco and Martin Parr)

Première Photo, Paris

Photos de Pères, Paris

1994 *Rural Europe,* FNAC, Paris

Collections:

Museum of Modern Art, Ghent; Photography Museum, Charleroi; Photography Museum, Antwerp; FNAC Collection, Paris; Ministry of Culture, Brussels; ICP, New York.

Publications:

By DE KEYZER: Books—*Oogspanning—Fotografie Carl De Keyzer
1981-1984,* with an introduction by Johan Anthierens, 1984; *India,* with an
introduction by Dirk Van Der Spek, Amsterdam 1987 and 1990; *U.S.S.R.—
1989—C.C.C.P.,* Amsterdam/The Hague 1989 (English edition: *Homo
Sovieticus*); *God, Inc.,* Amsterdam 1992.

On DE KEYZER: Articles—in *The Independent Magazine* (Great Britain);
Rolling Stone (USA); *Life Magazine* (USA); *The Daily Telegraph Magazine*
(Great Britain); *Frankfurter Allegmeine* (Germany); *GEO* (Germany); *Mos-
cow* (USSR); *Sette* (Italy); *Los Angeles Times Magazine* (USA); *The Guardian*
(Great Britain); *Globe* (France); *Nieuwe Revue* (Netherlands); *Elsevier* (Neth-
erlands); *Knack* (Belgium); *De Volkskrant* (Netherlands); *Libération* (France); *Le
Figaro Magazine* (France); *De Morgen* (Belgium); *NRC Handelsblad* (Neth-
erlands); *De Standaard Magazine* (Belgium); *Clichés, Foto, PHOTO, Photo
Reporter, Fotomagazine, Focale, Focus, European Photography, Neuva
Imagen, Kamera, Fotografie, Photographie, Photomagazine, Camera Inter-
national, Fotografisk Magazine,* etc., films, television interviews—*Eiland,*
BRT Belgium, 1987; *Kunstzaken,* BRT Belgium, 1987; *Zeker Weten,* BRT
Belgium, 1992; *Karel,* AVRO Holland, 1992; *Roerend Goed,* VPRO Hol-
land, 1994.

*   *   *

Carl de Keyzer is one of that younger generation of talented photographers
who are picking up the baton at the Magnum agency. He made a considerable
name with his first major project on India, published in 1987, and has been a
successful working photojournalist ever since. But this simple description
leaves a great deal unsaid: the world is full of photojournalists who are only as
good as their last story. De Keyzer has fused his interests and his manner of
photographing into something that is identifiably a style of his own. He prefers
to work on large, ambitious projects which come to their full realisation in
books put together some time after the events he has described. The magazine
pieces that pepper his career are works-in-progress. He leaves news and
newsworthiness to others or to video crews, choosing instead to make long
reports in which the way things are photographed is at least as important as the
fact that they are. The impression he gives is of somebody photographing the
world for his own understanding, allowing viewers to share some of the sense
of the search that he has made to bring us the pictures. In an era when the
picture magazines are alleged to be in a permanent decline he has found a way
of using photographs that does not depend on their immediacy, but where each
one quite plainly conveys the outcome of serious thought. The picture story in
de Keyzer's hands becomes a way of tying together all those news reports that
busy or lazy readers of today, with their dwindling attention spans and
mountains of information to digest, haven't quite got around to understanding.

De Keyzer has shown impeccable timing when glasnost and perestroika
were exciting new words and the West began seriously to wonder what life
might be like in the newly thawed Russian states, producing his *Homo
Sovieticus.* When we in western Europe first began to hear words like
televangelist and wonder why our neighbours went to Morris Cerullo's or
Billy Graham's meetings, he was ready with *God Inc.* They are very different

books, but both had sharp aptness and a quality of slightly startled honesty that
won him prizes. In some ways de Keyzer functions less like his illustrious
predecessors at Magnum (although his pictures are full of references to theirs)
than like a new-improved nineteenth-century travel photographer. They were
able to bring back pictures confident that the vast majority of their viewers had
seen nothing like them; de Keyzer knows that everything has been photographed and still manages to come back from his travels with a collector's
enthusiasm: "You won't believe this, but . . ." He can be acid, even a little
spiteful in his pictures, but the general tone remains one of enormous
enjoyment of the vagaries that a journalist's life can involve. His characters
teeter on the edge of caricature but remain, just, ordinary folks. De Keyzer
seems to refuse to make people ridiculous. But of course, if they already are,
then what can a good journalist do but show it? It is a fine line to tread, and one
that de Keyzer managed with great surefootedness.

—Francis Hodgson

DEKKERS, Ger(rit Hendrik).

Nationality: Dutch. **Born:** 21 August 1929. **Education:** Attended secondary
school in Hengelo, 1942-46; studied graphics at the Academy of Art,
Enschede, 1950-54. **Military Service:** Served in the Dutch Army, in
Indonesia, 1948-50. **Family:** Married Hilda Hartsuiker in 1954; children:
Henriette and Jose. **Career:** Freelance artist and photographer, Enschede,
1954-76, and in Giethoorn, since 1976. Member, Photo Section, Gebonden
Kunstenfederatie (GKf), since 1969. **Recipient:** Dutch Ministry of Culture
Grant, 1970, 1971, 1975, 1976; City of Amsterdam Stipendium 1976. **Agents:**
Galerie M, Haus Weitmar, 463 Bochum-Weitmar, Germany; and Galerie
Nouvelles Images, Westeinde 22, The Hague, Netherlands. **Address:**
Dwarsgracht 31, 8355 CV Giethoorn, Netherlands.

Individual Exhibitions:

1972 *Ger Dekkers: Landscape Perceptions,* Rijksmuseum Kröller-
Müller, Otterlo, Netherlands

1973 *Ger Dekkers: Landscape Perceptions,* Museum Bochum-
Kunstsammlung, Bochum, West Germany

Ger Dekkers: Landscape Perceptions, Neue Galerie-
Kunstsammlung Ludwig, Aachen, West Germany

1974 *Ger Dekkers: Landscape Perceptions,* Stedelijk Museum,
Amsterdam

Ger Dekkers: Landscape Perceptions, Haagse
Gemeentemuseum, The Hague

1975 *Ger Dekkers: Landscape Perceptions,* Palais des Beaux-Arts,
Brussels

Ger Dekkers: Landscape Perceptions, Galleria del Cavallino,
Venice

1976 *Ger Dekkers: Landscape Perceptions,* Kunstmuseum, Aarhus,
Denmark

Ger Dekkers: Landscape Perceptions, Print Gallery Pieter
Brattinga, Amsterdam

Ger Dekkers: Landscape Perceptions, Galerie M, Bochum,
West Germany

1977 *Planned Landscapes,* Rijksmuseum Kröller-Müller, Otterlo,
Netherlands

Plastic, Museum Boymans-van Beuningen, Rotterdam

1978 *Plastic,* Gemeentemuseum, Arnhem, Netherlands

Planned Landscapes, De Vishal, Haarlem, Netherlands

1979 *New Dutch Landscapes,* Hayden Gallery, Massachusetts
Institute of Technology, Cambridge

Planned Landscapes, Print Gallery Pieter Brattinga, Amsterdam

Planned Landscapes, Provincaal Begijnhof, Hasselt, Belgium

1980 *Planned Landscapes,* Kunstcentrum Markt 17, Enschede,
Netherlands

Planned Landscapes, Rijksplanologische Dienst, The Hague
1981   *Planned Landscapes,* Studium Generale, Wageningen,
            Netherlands
        Planned Landscapes, Städtische Galerie, Nordhorn, West
            Germany

Selected Group Exhibitions:

1969   *Atelier 6,* Stedelijk Museum, Amsterdam
1971   *Sonsbeek '71,* Central Station, Amsterdam
1974   *Projekt '74,* Kunsthalle, Cologne
1977   *Sequenzen,* Kunstverein, Hamburg
        Documenta 6, Museum Fridericianum, Kassel, West Germany
        Museum of Drawers, Kunsthaus, Zurich (now permanent
            installation)
1978   *Fotografie in Nederland 1940-75,* Stedelijk Museum,
            Amsterdam
        Photography as Art/Art as Photography, Fotoforum, Kassel,
            West Germany (and world tour)
1979   *To Do with Nature,* travelling exhibition, (toured the
            Netherlands, Sweden, Belgium, Germany, Denmark, and
            Portugal, 1979-81)
        Photographie als Kunst 1879-1979, Tiroler Landesmuseum
            Ferdinandeum, Innsbruck, Austria (travelled to the Neue
            Galerie am Wolfgang Gurlitt Museum, Linz, Austria; Neue
            Galerie am Landesmuseum Joanneum, Graz, Austria; and
            Museum des 20. Jahrhunderts, Vienna)

Collections:

Rijksmuseum Kröller-Müller, Otterlo, Netherlands; Stedelijk Museum, Amsterdam; Museum Boymans-van Beuningen, Rotterdam; Haagse Gemeentemuseum, The Hague; Gemeentemuseum, Arnhem, Netherlands; Ministry of Culture, The Hague; Posts-Telegraph-Telephone (P.T.T.), The Hague; Museum Ludwig, Cologne; Kunsthalle, Hamburg; Museum Bochum-Kunstsammlung, Bochum, Germany.

Publications:

By DEKKERS: Book—*Planned Landscapes: 25 Horizons,* with an introduction by R.W.D. Oxenaar, Amsterdam 1977; *Graven en begrave in Overijssel,* editor, with H. Schelhaas and B. Molenaar, Zwolle, Netherlands 1980.

On DEKKERS: Books—*Ger Dekkers: Landscape Perceptions,* exhibition catalogue, with text by R.W.D. Oxenaar, Otterlo, Netherlands 1972; *Ger Dekkers: Landscape Perceptions,* exhibition catalogue, with text by P. Spielmann, Bochum, West Germany 1973; *Ger Dekkers: Landscape Perceptions 1968-1975,* exhibition catalogue, with text by J.L. Locher and M. Schneckenburger, The Hague 1974; *Fotografie in Nederland 1940-1975,* exhibition catalogue, with text by Els Barents, Ingeborg Leyerzapf and others, The Hague 1978; *New Dutch Landscape,* exhibition catalogue, by Marc S. Gerstein, Cambridge, Massachusetts 1979; *The Artist as Photographer* by Marina Vaizey, London 1982. **Articles**—"Demonstrative Fotografie" by Hans Gercke in *Das Kunstwerk* (Baden-Baden), March 1974; "Ger Dekkers" in *Flash Art* (Milan), December 1974/January 1975; "Ger Dekkers" by A. Von Berswordt-Wallrabe in *M-Bochum* (Bochum, West Germany), no. 3, 1976; "Ger Dekkers" by Betty van Garrel in *Volker Post* (Rotterdam), no. 4, 1978; "Ger Dekkers" by Dolf Welling in *Holland Herald* (Amsterdam), July 1979; "Ger Dekkers" by H.P. Platz in *Basler Magazin* (Basle), January 1980; "Ger Dekkers" by Fred Hazelhoff in *Foto* (Hilversum, Netherlands), September 1980; "Ger Dekkers" by Herman v. Buuren in *Bijvoorbeeld* (Amsterdam), no. 2, 1981.

*

My actual subject is the effect that our culture has on landscape. The Dutch landscape with its polders provides an excellent example.

I am aware that my work is a personal expression, in which my personality is one factor. My principal action—to record a situation that I encounter—I experience myself as an intruder.

My concern with the subject and its surroundings does not go further than emotionally choosing the angle of the camera and focussing it, and later on making a selection and carefully completing the process.

The horizon acts as a middle line in the square pictures: this gives a continuous line that runs throughout the series and thus the whole project.

The medium I use is another factor.

I find only a limited number of phototechnical possibilities important. It is not the gimmicks of photography that mean the most to me, but its very irrevocability, its inevitability. From these factors, but mainly, I hope, from its essence, my work derives its validity.

—Ger Dekkers

*   *   *

Until recently comparatively unknown, Ger Dekkers was first recognized for his photographs on calendars while he was working as a photographic collaborator with a graphic designer in a small commerical firm in Enschede. Then, at the *Atelier 6* exhibition at Amsterdam's Stedelijk Museum in 1969, Dekkers received attention from the art world as well. At that time, his work consisted of single photographs of landscape subjects. Simple, clear situations in which space, pattern and order were presented in a calm, precise and austere manner. What attracted the subsequent widespread critical attention was that Dekkers' photos were not commonplace: they have an unmistakable concept and shape of their own, and the undeniable presence of works of art.

The point of departure for his colour photographs is the desire to record situations in the landscape arising from man-made alterations, vegetation, weather conditions, or fauna. He never manipulates or interferes with his subject matter. The moment of choice and insight are important. He neither works with special exposures or exposure-times nor with extreme optical angles. For him developing and printing are first and foremost technical, not creative, processes. Only the position of the camera, the framing of the photograph, angle of light and time of day are allowed to determine the final picture. His aim is always a matter-of-fact realistic reproduction of some part of reality. The photos show a preference for great shapes, or a few simple shapes are grouped well-balanced round the centre or along one of the diagonals of the picture surface. The viewer is made more aware of spatiality, and hence the "ordinary" may be experienced as novel once more.

Dekkers began to make series of photos in 1971, the visible principles of ordering being a uniform size of 100 x 100cm and a limitation to a series of 4 related photographs. The total absence of human beings is typical. That is: the personal presence of human beings. Numerous traces of human existence are evident, even strongly emphasized—coloured tubes of synthetic material on a lawn, goalposts, electric cables, road surfaces, ensilaged grass, etc. Dekkers does not observe landscape as a piece of unspoilt scenery. Visible tension between culture and nature is the central theme. He has recently occupied himself with the way culture literally penetrates into nature and transforms it: a straightened ditch, purposeful plantings of a row of trees, a ploughed-up plot of land, etc. The series are arranged into analogous shots of allied objects, but also into series of various photos of the same subject with only a slight but continuous shift of viewpoint. Occasionally, a similar series is added, but taken at a different season. The different locations, distances and details fall into sequence with a continuous horizon. One's eye follows the camera, takes up position and joins it in its directional swings. This imbues the motif with spatial rhythms to produce landscapes of triptych-like unity.

Since 1973, Dekkers has been concerned with the coastal areas of Holland, and with the polders in particular. The polder is a paradigm of human intervention in nature, as it is land that has been reclaimed from the sea. Every feature of the landscape, every bit of woods and farmland has been planned and created by man in these programmed new spaces of Holland which are laid out as on a drawing-board in a mass of straight lines. In Dekkers' photos, the horizon line remains a major visual component—a flat horizon which bisects the square image as nearly as possible: it remains in a fixed position through parts of the series and through a set of *Planned Landscapes* as a whole. Dekkers imposes order on the already highly ordered landscape.

He divides his work into *Landscape Situations,* akin to art areas like "land art" or "earth works," and *Objects in a Landscape,* similar to "ready-mades" or "objets trouvés," with a certain surreal or superreal flavour. These art terms indicate that Dekkers looks at his themes in the context of his time, and his insights are related to the vision of many contemporary artists.

Dekkers is often compared to his compatriot photo-artist Jan Dibbets. But whereas Dibbets visualizes a concept of perception criticism, Dekkers remains in the sphere of immediate cognition. For Dibbets, who corrects perspective and rectifies both the camera lens and the eye, photography is a means of posing theoretical problems which have more to do with determinations of time than of place. Dekkers never tries to change the landscape, but sums up its angles and verses the eye in differentiated perception.

More importantly, however, in Dekkers' photographic groups, the work of art does not exist without the photographs. They are not mere clues to a process of mental and visual deduction, nor is their process the primary thing. The series are complete and self-sufficient. For Dekkers, the series is ultimately an account of a continuous and psychological response to the landscape.

—Colin Naylor

DELANO, Jack.

Nationality: American. **Born:** Jack Ovcharov in Kiev, Russia, 1 August 1914; immigrated to the United States in 1923: naturalized, 1928; adopted the name Delano, 1940. **Education:** Attended the Settlement Music School, Philadelphia, 1925-33 (scholarship student: studied violin, viola, and composition); Central High School, Philadelphia, 1928-32; Pennsylvania Academy of Fine Arts, Philadelphia, 1932-37 (Cresson Travelling Scholar, 1936-37), Dip. 1937. **Military Service:** Served in the Air Transport Command, United States Army Corps of Engineers, 1943-46: Captain. **Family:** Married Irene Esser in 1940; children: Pablo and Laura. **Career:** Took first photographs while travelling in Europe, 1936-37; photographer with the Works Progress Administration (WPA) Project, New York, 1937-39; freelance photographer, working mainly for the United Fund, New York, 1939-40; Staff Photographer, under Roy Stryker, Farm Security Administration, Washington, D.C., and throughout the United States and Puerto Rico, 1940-43; Photographer, Government of Puerto Rico, 1946-47; Director of Motion Picture Services, Government of Puerto Rico, 1947-53; independent film-maker, San Juan, Puerto Rico, 1953-57; Director of Programming, Puerto Rican Educational Television, 1957-64; General Manager, Puerto Rican Government Radio and Television Service, 1969; independent photographer, film-maker, book illustrator, and graphics consultant, and music teacher at the Puerto Rico Conservatory, 1969-79; teacher of film animation techniques at Sacred Heart University; designer of San Juan Children's Museum and Pablo Casals Museum. Since 1979, working as a photographer on grant from the National Endowment for the Humanities. **Recipient:** Guggenheim Fellowship in Photography, 1945; Unesco Travelling Fellowship, Europe and Asia, 1960; Children's Art Books Award, with Irene Delano, Brooklyn Museum, New York, 1973; National Endowment for the Arts Grant, 1979; Certificate of Merit, Casa Aboy, San Juan, 1983; Composers Award, Institute of Puerto Rican Culture, 1984; ASCAP Award for Musical Composition, 1987. **Agent:** Sonnabend Gallery, 420 West Broadway, New York, New York 10012, U.S.A. **Address:** R.F.D. 2, Box 10, Rio Piedras, Puerto Rico 00928.

Individual Exhibitions:

1938   *Anthracite Coal Miners,* Pennsylvania Railroad Station Gallery, Philadelphia

1977   Sonnabend Gallery, New York
1978   Art Students League, San Juan, Puerto Rico
1979   *Our Humility, Our Pride,* Springfield Museum of Fine Arts, Massachusetts
1982   University of Puerto Rico Museum, San Juan
1983   Hostos Community College, New York
1984   University of Michigan, Ann Arbor
1985   Daytona Beach Community College, Florida
          Casa Aboy, San Juan, Puerto Ridao
1986   *Before and After: The FSA,* Daytona Beach Community College, Florida (with Arthur Rothstein and Marion Post Wolcott)
1992   Retrospective, Vigo, Spain
          Contrasts, toured USA and to Buenos Aires, Argentina and Caracas, Venezuela

Selected Group Exhibitions:

1955   *The Family of Man,* Museum of Modern Art, New York (and world tour)
1962   *The Bitter Years,* Museum of Modern Art, New York
1976   *FSA Photographers,* Witkin Gallery, New York
1977   *Documenta 6,* Kassel, West Germany
1978   *Work,* Fine Arts Museum, San Francisco
1979   *Images de l'Amerique en Crise,* Centre Georges Pompidou, Paris
1980   *Les Années Ameres de l'Amerique en Crise,* Galerie Municipale du Chateau d'Eau, Toulouse, France
1981   *Farbe im Photo,* Josef-Haubrich-Kunsthalle, Cologne
1982   *Floods of Light,* The Photographers' Gallery, London
          Lichtbildnisse: Das Porträt in der Fotografie, Rheinisches Landesmuseum, Bonn
1994   *Fotofest,* Houston, Texas

Collections:

Library of Congress, Washington, D.C.; New York Public Library; International Museum of Photography, George Eastman House, Rochester, New York; University of Louisville, Kentucky; Institute of Puerto Rican Culture, San Juan.

Publications:

By DELANO: Book—*The Iron Horse at War,* with text by James Valle, Berkeley, California 1977; *From San to Ponce on the Train,* Puerto Rico 1992; *In Search of Maestro Rafael Cordero,* with Irene Delano, Puerto Rico 1994. **Articles**—"Educational TV in Puerto Rico" in the *San Juan Star,* 1964; "Documentary Photography" in *Southern Exposure* (Chapel Hill, North Carolina), 1977.

On DELANO: Books—*Portrait of a Decade* by Jack Hurley, Baton Rouge, Louisiana 1972; *In This Proud Land* by Roy E. Stryker and Nancy Wood, Greenwich, Connecticut 1973; *A Vision Shared: A Classic Portrait of America and Its People 1935-43,* edited by Hank O'Neal, New York and London 1976; *Les Années Ameres de l'Amerique en Crise 1935-1942,* exhibition catalogue, by Jean Dieuzaide, Toulouse 1980; *Farbe im Photo: Die Geschichte der Farbphotographie von 1861 bis 1981* by Fritz Binder, Gert Koshofer, Rolf Sachsse and others, Cologne 1981; *Floods of Light: Flash Photography 1851-1981,* exhibition catalogue, by Rupert Martin, London 1982; *Jack Delano—Humanista,* thesis, by Maria del Rosario Fraticelli, University of Puerto Rico, San Juan, 1982; *Puerto Rico Mio,* Washington 1990. **Articles**—"Jack Delano: Clicking in Puerto Rico for 30 Years" by Erin Hart in the *Sunday San Juan Star,* June 1975; "FSA Color" by Sally Stein in *Modern Photography*

(New York), January 1979; "Jack Delano: Interview" by Ed Miller in *Combinations: A Journal of Photography* (Green-field Center, New York), July 1979; "The Serious Pleasures of Commitment: Jack and Irene Delano" by Marshall Morris in *San Juan Star* (Puerto Rico), 11 January 1981; "La Permanencia del Pasado en las Foto de Jack Delano" by Edgardo Rodriguez Julia in *San Juan Star* (Puerto Rico), 6 December 1982.

*

I don't like to pontificate about my ideas on photography. But if I must say something, here it is: the lens of a camera is, to me, one of the most powerful instruments ever invented for showing us as we really are. It can focus with equal sharpness on our stupidity and our brilliance, on our brutality and on our gentleness, on our arrogance, and on our humility, on our destructiveness and on our creative genius. It can show us at our best and at our worst, to shake us up and make us ponder. And that is precisely what it *should* do.

—Jack Delano

* * *

During the course of his career Jack Delano has worked, often simultaneously, as photographer, director of a national television service, book designer and composer. His interest in photography began in 1936 when, an art student in Pennsylvania, he travelled to Europe and took along a camera in order to record his trip visually. Four years later he was to join the Historical Section of the Farm Security Administration on the recommendation of Paul Strand.

At that time the FSA was very successful, with a record of important work behind it, and was preparing for its transition to the new kinds of work which would be necessary in time of war. Delano contributed greatly to the work of the Section, travelling first to Virginia and then on an extended journey around the Southern states. He also managed to work in some unique locations, so far as the Section was concerned. Alone of all FSA photographers he was sent overseas in order to document life in the Virgin Islands and in Puerto Rico—which was later to become his permanent home. Even within America itself he managed to gain access to locations formerly considered closed to the photographer. For example, he penetrated a defense plant and also was allowed to work inside Greensboro County Jail. The powerful photographs he took within that institution exemplify two major aims of documentary photography: they are moving representations of people living under extreme conditions and a straight record of the nature of life in a Southern jail at the time.

Jack Delano's work has been influenced by the work produced by other FSA photographers, notably by that of Walker Evans. In common with Evans he belongs to that group of photographers whose aim is to reveal, to demonstrate, the nature of things at a stroke, within the frame of a single, definitive photograph. This imposes on the photographer an exceptional concern for technique and consideration for compositional detail. In simple technical terms it meant, for example, that Delano often used an 8 x 10 camera rather than a 35 mm. But the use of a large format camera and a highly developed concern with composition must not be seen as an obsession with form. Delano has always been primarily concerned with recording and interpreting the ways of life and condition of human beings around the world. His work has a unity and an integrity which transcends any formal considerations and made him into a fine and important documentary photographer.

—Derrick Price

den HOLLANDER, Paul.

Nationality: Dutch. **Born:** Breda, 5 July 1950. **Education:** Studied at St. Joost Academy of Fine Arts, Breda, 1968-73. **Family:** Married Annemarie Aardewerk in 1980, divorced 1991. Now living with Pascale Mons and daughter Claire. **Career:** Freelance photographer, working for the Naples Tourist Board, Yugoslav Tourism Authority, Studio Trisorio of Naples, Société des Autoroutes du Sud de la France, etc., in Breda, since 1976. **Recipient:** City of Breda Prize, 1973; Black-and-White Prize, Triennale of Photography, Fribourg, Switzerland, 1981; Grand Prix International de la Recherche Photographique, Arles, 1981. **Address:** Haagweg 386, 4813, XG Breda, The Netherlands.

Individual Exhibitions:

1976	Canon Photo Gallery, Amsterdam
1978	Galerij Paule Pia, Antwerp
	A.B.N. Gallery, Amsterdam
	Centro Culturale, Modena, Italy
1979	Fotomania, Barcelona
	Internationaal Cultureel Centrum, Antwerp
	Galerie Phot'Oeil, Paris
	Canon Photo Gallery, Amsterdam
1980	Kruithuis Cultural Centre, Den Bosch, Netherlands
	Galerie Voir, Toulouse
	Photographic Centre, Athens
	Photogallery, Thessaloniki
	Cultural Centre, Hasselt, Belgium
1981	Canon Photo Gallery, Geneva
	Galleria Il Diaframma, Milan
	Galerie Suzanne Kupfer, Nidau-Biel, Switzerland
	Institut Neerlandais, Paris
	The Photographic Gallery, Cardiff, Wales
	Night Gallery, London
	Galerie Beeld en Aambeeld, Enschede, Netherlands
	Galerie Novum, Hannover, West Germany
1982	Fotogalerie Hugo Minnen, Dessel, Belgium
	Galerie Renner, Munich
	Cultureel Centrum, Hoensbroek, Netherlands
	Galerie 't Pepertje, Diepenbeek, Belgium
	FNAC-Forum, Les Halles, Paris
	Centrum De Beyerd, Breda, Netherlands
	Galerie Perspectief, Rotterdam
1983	Photographers Gallery, Christchurch, New Zealand
	Galleria Figura, Biella, Italy
1984	Canon Photo Gallery, Amsterdam
	Galeria Modulo, Lisbon
1985	Galerie Musée de la Photographie, Charleroi, Belgium
	Canon Photo Gallery, Amsterdam
	Galerie XYZ, Ghent, Belgium
1986	Galeria Forum, Tarragona, Spain
	Galerie FNAC, Paris
1987	FNAC Forum, des Halles, Paris
	Galeria Polleria Immaginaria, Genoa, Italy
	Galerie Fotomania, Leiden, The Netherlands
	Galeria Nueva Imagen, Pamplona, Spain
	Galeria Spazio Immagine, Bari, Italy
	De Beyerd, Centre for Contemporar Arts, Breda
	Museo Civico G. Fiorelli, Lucera
	Galleria Rondini, Osimo
1988	Galerie Parvis-2, Centre de Developpment Culturel, Tarbes, France
1989	*Paul den Hollander,* Volkshochschule Haneburg, Leer, Germany
1990	Galerie S & H: de Buck, Ghent, Belgium
	Centre Regional de la Photographie, Douchy, France
1991	Noordbrabants Museum, Den Bosch, The Netherlands
1992	*Les Pyramids du Nord,* De Beyerd, Centre for Contemporary Arts, Breda; Galerie Pons, Paris; Galeria Graca Fonseca, Lisbon, Portugal

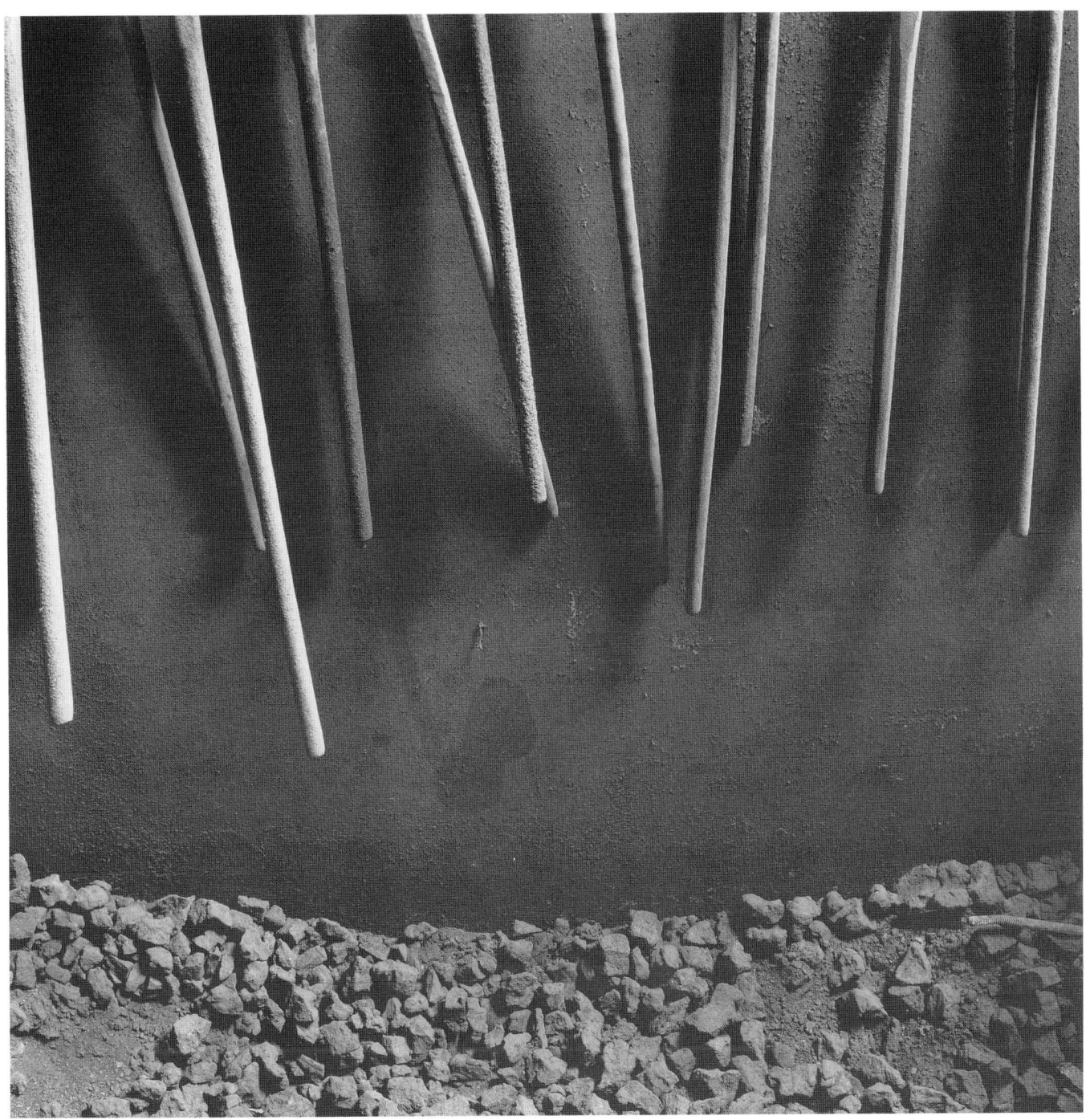

Untitled, **from the series** *Les Pyramides du nord,* **1988.** Photograph by Paul den Hollander.

1993	Musée Municipal, Orange, France
	Musée d'Histoire Naturelle, Grenoble, France
1994	*Les Pyramids du Nord,* Contretype, Brussels
	Paul den Hollander. Fotowerken, Wetering Galerie, Amsterdam

Selected Group Exhibitions:

| 1972 | *Ooggetuige,* Ministry of Cultural Affairs, Amsterdam (toured The Netherlands) |

1978	*Photography since 1955,* at *Arte Fiera,* Bologna
1979	*Fotofacetten,* Kruithuis Cultural Centre, Den Bosch, Netherlands
	Foto 78, Ministry of Cultural Affairs, Amsterdam (toured The Netherlands)
1980	*Triennale Internationale de Photographie,* Palais des Beaux-Arts, Charleroi, Belgium
1982	*In My View: 30 Dutch Photographers,* KLM Plaza, New York
1983	*Contemporary European Photography,* Museum zu Allerheiligen, Schaffhausen, Switzerland

1984	*Entgegnung mit den Niederlanden*, Galerie Pro-Photo, Nuremberg, West Germany
1985	*Rives et Rivages*, Société des Autoroutes du Sud de la France, Paris
1986	*Foto '86*, Koopmansbeurs, Amsterdam
	50 Years of Colour Photography, Photokina, Cologne, Germany
	Vigo: View of the Town of Vigo by Six Photographers, Vigo, Spain
	50 Jahre moderne Farbfotografie 1936-1986, (Photokina), Keulen
	Nature morte, nature vive. 7es Journeés Internationales de la Photographie et de l'Audiovisuel, Montpellier
1987	*Quatro Fotografia Olandesi*, Sesto Fiorentino
	Kunst over de vloer, Entrepôtdok, Amsterdam
1988	*Roots and Turns: 20th Century Photography in the Netherlands*, Houston, Texas
	9os Encontros e Fotografia, Coimbra
	Events, Gulbenkian Modern Art Centre, Lisbon, Portugal
1989	*What is Photography?150 Years of Photography*, Mánes Gallery, Prague
	Grotesque, Rijksmuseum voor Geologie en Mineralogie, Leiden
	12 Villages en Europe, Ministry of Agriculture, Paris
1990	*Grotesque: Natural Historical and Formaldehyde Photography*, Musée Zoölogique, Strasbourg, France
1991	*O Coracáo da Ciência, 700 Anos da Universidade de Coimbra*, Portugal
1992	*De la Curiosité—Petite Anatomie d'un Regard*, with Lynne Cohen, Joel-Peter Witkin, John Coplans, Joan Fontcuberta and Roberto Pellegrinuzzi, Centre de Photographies Actuelles 'Dazibao,' Montreal, Canada
	Muse Museum: Contemporary Photographers at Barcelona Museums, Palau de Virreina, Barcelona, Spain
	L'Echappée Européenne: Collection de la Maison Européenne de la Photographie à Paris, Pavillon des Arts, Paris
	Minimal Relics, Zoölogisch Museum, Amsterdam
1993	*Minimal Relics*, Natuurmuseum, Rotterdam, The Netherlands
1994	*Eindhoven, aspekten van een stad*, Museum Kempenland, Eindhoven, The Netherlands

Collections:

University of Leiden; Musée Royale des Beaux-Arts, Brussels; Musée Nicéphore Niepce, Chalon-sur-Saône, France; Bibliothèque Nationale, Paris; National Museum of Modern Art, Tokyo; Musée d'Art et d'Histoire, Fribourg, Switzerland; Università di Parma, Italy; Victoria and Albert Museum, London; Gulbenkian Modern Art Centre, Lisbon; National Museum of Photography, Bradford; Het Nederlands Fotomuseum, Sittard, The Netherlands; Polaroid Collection, Amsterdam; Provinciaal Museum voor Fotografie, Antwerpen; Artotheek, Breda; Rijksdienst Beeldende Kunst, Den Haag; Museum De Lakenhal, Leiden; Gulbenkian Modern Art Centre, Lisbon; Fond National d'Art Contemporain, Paris.

Publications:

By den HOLLANDER: Books—*Moments in Time*, with introduction by Lorenzo Merlo, Amsterdam 1982; *Paul den Hollander, een keuze uit zijn foto's*, edited by Het Noordbrabants Genootschap, 1991; *Les Pyramides du Nord*, exhibition catalogue 1992.

On den HOLLANDER: Books—*Kunst als Fotografie/Fotografie als Kunst*, exhibition catalogue, by Peter Weiermair, Innsbruck 1979; *Nederlands Landschap/Dutch Landscape*, exhibition catalogue, by Lorenzo Merlo, Amsterdam 1979; *New Dutch Photography* by Lorenzo Merlo, Amsterdam 1980; *Dumont Foto 4: Fotografie in Europa Heute* by Andreas Muller-Pohle, Cologne 1982; *Zeitgenossische Europaische Fotografie*, exhibition catalogue, by Derek Bennett, Schaffhausen, Switzerland 1983; *Roots and Turns: 20th Century Photography in the Netherlands*, exhibition catalogue (The Hague)

1988; *Fribourg, vu par 5 Photographes* (Fribourg) 1991; *L'Echappée Européenne*, by Gilles Mora (Paris) 1992; *Vrij Spel*, by Willemijn Stokvis and Kitty Zijlmans, Amsterdam 1993. **Articles**—"European Portfolio One" in *Printletter* (Zurich), August 1980; "Visualism" in *European Photography* (Gottingen), no. 3, 1980; "Works in Progress" in *European Photography* (Gottingen), no. 16, 1983; "Paul den Hollander" in *Camera International* (Paris), November 1984; *Clichés*, No. 17, 1985; *Photovision*, (Madrid) no 16, December 1986; "Paul den Hollander" by Ingeborg Th. Leijerzapf in *Geschiedenis van de Nederlandse fotografie in monografieën en thema-artikelen* (Amsterdam), 11 April 1989; "Paul den Hollander" by Steffen Thomas in *Clichés*, No. 54, March 1989; "Ordering the Chaos" in *Photovision* (Madrid), No 24, 1993.

* * *

Paul den Hollander once said: "I take photographs to allow other people to share my experiences. My photography is an image-reflection of what goes on in myself." With that statement, he almost places himself in the tradition of the New Objectivity—photography as a means to realize your place in the world and as a medium to convey it to others.

Den Hollander's photographs are compositionally balanced and reveal a quiet world in which people create things then leave them behind, almost as if they are no longer important—cultural/social landscapes, parks, roads, farmland, towns and buildings. Often his works are almost graphic illustrations of abstract structures: sides of houses, a row of garden chairs, line reflections near a stair-shaft, the architecture of Versailles.

The human being plays only a passive, impersonal role in his work. He is shown as a blurred passer-by or as a shadow in his own landscape. No need to distinguish him. Sometimes he is suggested only in the form of a departing car, a piece of paper thrown away, or footprints in the sand.

Den Hollander tries to record with his technically and compositionally fine photographs the continuously changing process of the world. "In my photographs everything is equally important," he says. "The landscape is not a background nor is the passer-by most important. I aim to create so that space and the human being merge together. I do not analyze situations in which reality collapses. It is of more importance to keep the experience of totality—and is it not true that in reality things happen by accident and none of the elements has our exclusive attention?"

—A. de Jonge-Vermeulen

de NOOIJER, Paul (us).

Nationality: Dutch. **Born:** Eindhoven, 15 June 1943. **Education:** Studied industrial design at the Akademie voor Industriele Vormgeving, Eindhoven, 1960-65. **Family:** Married Francoise Neeteson in 1965; son: Menno. **Career:** Freelance advertising/illustration photographer, Eindhoven, 1968-73. Freelance photographer and filmmaker, Eindhovern, since 1974. Guest Instructor, Vrije Akademie, The Hague, 1974; Instructor in Photography, G.I.K.O., Helmond, 1975-76; Guest Lecturer, Academie St. Joost, Breda, 1978, and Academy of Arnhem, 1978; Guest Instructor, Gerrit Rietveld Akademie, Amsterdam, 1979. Since 1978, Instructor, Akademie voor Beeldende Vorming, Tilburg. **Recipient:** Municipal Prize, Eindhoven, 1968; Grand Prix Internationale de la Photographie, Royan, France, 1974; Bronze Medal, *International Triennale of Photography*, Fribourg, 1975; Dutch Ministry of Cultural Affairs Fellowship, 1975, 1976, 1977; First Prize, *West Deutscher Kurz Film Tage*, Oberhausen, 1979.

Individual Exhibitions:

1974	Canon Photo Gallery, Amsterdam
	Galleria Il Diaframma, Milan
	Art Center, Venlo, Netherlands
1975	Galleria Broletto, Varese, Italy
	Galerie 5.6, Ghent
	Galeria Spectrum, Barcelona
	Photographers Gallery, Melbourne

't Meyhuis, Helmond, Netherlands
1976   Galerie 2.8, Mechelen, Belgium
        Cultureel Centrum, Tilburg, Netherlands
1977   Galerie Fiolet, Amsterdam
        Stedelijk Van Abbemuseum, Eindhoven, Netherlands
1978   Photographers Gallery, Saskatoon, Saskatchewan
        Photo/Graphic Gallery, Seattle
        Nikon Gallery, Zurich
        Galerie Jesus Moreno, Geneva
        Galerij Paule Pia, Antwerp
        Trockenpresse Galerie für Fotografie, Berlin
        Photo Art Gallery, Basle

Selected Group Exhibitions:

1974   *Salon Internationale de la Recherche Photographique,* Royan,
            France
        4 Dutch Photographers, Fotogalerie Die Brücke, Vienna
            (travelled to the Internationaal Cultureel Centrum, Antwerp)
        Op-th-iek, University of Eindhoven, Netherlands
1975   *6 Dutch Photographers,* The Photographers' Gallery, London
        Sequences, Stedelijk Museum, Amsterdam
        Fantastic Photography in Europe, at Rencontres
            Internationales de la Photographie, Arles, France (toured
            Europe and the United States, 1976-79)
1978   *Tusen och En Bild/1000 Pictures,* Moderna Museet,
            Stockholm
1979   *Beelden van de Eigen Werkelijkheid,* Van Reekum Museum,
            Apeldoorn, Netherlands
1984   *La Photographie Créative,* Pavillon des Arts Paris

Collections:

Stedelijk Museum, Amsterdam; Ministry of Cultural Affairs, Amsterdam;
Prentenkabinet, Rijksuniversiteit Leiden, Netherlands; Stedelijk Van Abbemuseum,
Eindhoven, Netherlands; Bibliothèque Nationale, Paris; Moderna Museet,
Stockholm.

Publications:

By de NOOIJER: Books—*Losing One's Head,* with an introduction by
Ingeborg Th. Leijerzapf, Eindhoven, Netherlands 1978; *Losing One's Photos,*
Eindhoven, Netherlands 1981. **Articles**—"Pierrot" in *Avenue* (Amsterdam),
no. 2, 1977; "De Jaguar Club" in *Avenue* (Amsterdam), no. 7, 1977;
"Moderne Architectuur" in *Avenue* (Amsterdam), no. 10, 1977. **Films**—*The
Pie,* 1975; *Say Goodbye,* 1975; *Extra Ball,* 1976; *Transformation,* 1976;
Review, 1976; *Tarzan and Jane,* 1977.

On de NOOIJER: Books—*Geschichte der Fotografie im 20. Jahrhunderts/
Photography in the 20th Century* by Petr Tausk, Cologne 1977, London 1980;
Dumont Foto 1, edited by Hugo Schöttle, Cologne 1978; *La Photographie
Fantastique* by Attilio Colombo, Paris 1979; *Beelden van de Eigen Werkelnkeid*
by Jerven Ober, Apeldoorn, Netherlands 1979; *La Photographie Créative* by
Jean-Claude Lemagny, Paris 1984. **Articles**—"Royan: Le Festival '74" by
Jean-Claude Gautrand in *Photo Review* (Paris), June 1974; "Paul de Nooijer"
by Jean Gohelle in *Le Nouveau Photocinema* (Paris), no. 11, 1974; "Imagenes-
Imaginadas" by Jean-Claude Gautrand in *Nueva Lente* (Barcelona), April
1975; "Paul de Nooijer: Between Concept and Intuition" by Marco Misani in
Print Letter (Zurich), 9/10, 1978; "Paul de Nooijer: Tussen Retro en Veto"
by Filip Tas in *De Standaard* (Antwerp), 13 October 1978; "Paul de Nooijer"
by Aloys Ginjaar in *Foto* (Amsterdam), no. 9, 1978; "Paul de Nooijer" by
Frits Oppenoorth in *Avenue* (Amsterdam), no. 3, 1979; "Boterhammen op de
vloer: over het werk van Paul de Nooijer" by R. Dirven and R. Hendrikx in
Skrien (Amsterdam), Summer 1983.

*   *   *

If I had to choose the two contemporary photographers who have most
known how to construct a more intense personal world by means of the absurd,
I would choose Les Krims in the United States and Paul de Nooijer in Europe.
Both possess a particular morbidity—the former is caustic, the latter sarcas-
tic—and for both of them the image is a provocation, but the photos of de
Nooijer are more fantastic, more humorous.

If we accept Umberto Eco's thesis that artistic reaction distinguishes
different levels of codification, then without a doubt the psychological and
aesthetic would be the most preponderant in de Nooijer's work. In effect, if we
carefully examine his photographic world, we discover a series of constants: a
delight in certain fetishes; oppressive surroundings; dramatic landscapes;
similar but always surprising incongruities. Is an image by de Nooijer a replay of a nightmare or is the world really like that, at least for those who have
been endowed with perspicacity?

This same question is still incessantly asked about the work of Hieronymus
Bosch, and the uncertainty that he provoked is still his major attraction. This
comparison should not seem completely inappropriate, since both artists share
in good measure the same "ironic space." What distinguishes them, naturally,
is the ontology of the different languages they employ. Bosch moved his
brushes according to the dictates of his lucid imagination. De Nooijer implies
that all we see in the cliché comes from the truth. The very creator oversteps
the mere photographer in order to enter into the scenography, into the *mise-en-
scène* or into the art of the "happening." The model actors represent their roles
in a wild theatrical representation that has a finality, an end established in a
photosensitized format. Why does de Nooijer choose the photographic medium as the vehicle of his conceptions? Evidently for the (apparent) fidelity of
reproduction. The scenes are elaborated with such detail, the facial expressions are so apt, that it is best to reproduce them as they are, very precisely.

But, fortunately, Paul de Nooijer is not a purist; he does employ the
creative resources of photography to reinforce the general effect of his work.
And they are so well realized that his aesthetic code is one of the most
identifiable among contemporary photographers of the actual. Two elements
are most typical: a bold texture, which adds a certain turbulence while it
compresses the planes and creates a more pictorial resolution; and the use of
the wide-angle lens to amend reality, distorting the human body and creating
impossible spaces. His nonpurist attitude sometimes carries him away—for
example, when he paints prints by hand, producing a coloration of "short-
circuit hallucination."

No one is ever going to know whether de Nooijer is a genius who
experiences revelations or a lunatic who experiences fantasies—but it does
not much matter, just so long as he continues using his expressive facilities and
his dominion over his medium in the ways he has done so far. For we need
revolutionaries of the collective conscience, who keep alive a vision of the
"great theatre of the absurd"—that is to say, life.

—Joan Fontcuberta

DEPARDON, Raymond.

Nationality: French. **Born:** Villefranche-sur-Saône, 6 July 1942. **Education:** Studied at an agricultural school in Lyons. **Military Service:** Served in
the French Army, as a war reporter in Algeria, 1962-63. **Career:** Worked as
an assistant to the commercial photographer Louis Foucherand, Paris, 1958-
60; photographer with Agence Dalmas, Paris, working for *Life, Paris-Match,*
etc. 1960-62, 1963-66. Freelance photojournalist, Paris, since 1967. Founder
Member, with Gilles Caron, Hugues Vassal and Hubert Henrotte, Agence
Gamma photographers agency, Paris, 1967-70. Member, Magnum Photos,
Paris, since 1978. **Recipient:** Prix Georges Sadoul, for film, 1980. **Address:**
c/o Magnum Photos, 20 rue des Grand-Augustins, 75006 Paris, France.

Individual Exhibitions:

1974   *Chili,* Galerie FNAC, Paris (with David Burnett and Charles
            Geretsen)

Selected Group Exhibitions:

1981   *Paris Magnum,* Palais du Luxembourg, Paris

1985   *Paysages Photographies,* Galerie DATAR, Paris (toured
          France)

Publications:

By DEPARDON: Books—*Chili,* with David Burnett and Charles Geretsen,
Paris 1973; *Tchad: Images de Guerre,* Paris 1978; *Notes Arfuyen X,* Paris
1979; *Correspondance Newyorkaise,* with Alain Bergala, Paris 1981; *Le
Desert Américain,* Paris 1983; *San Clemente,* Paris 1984; *Les Fiancés de
Saigon,* Paris 1986. **Articles**—"Raymond Depardon: Le Profil du Photographe
Journaliste de 1980," interview, with Robert Y. Pledge, in *Zoom* (Paris),
December 1970; Interview in *Cahiers du Cinema* (Paris), December 1979;
"Reportages: Un Film de Raymond Depardon," interview, with Michael
Maingois, in *Zoom* (Paris), July/August 1981. **Films**—*Ian Pallach,* 1969;
Yemen, 1972; *Tibesti Two,* 1976; *Numeros Zeros,* 1977; *Reportages,* 1981;
San Clemente, 1981.

On DEPARDON: Books—*Eye Witness: 25 Years Through World Press
Photos* by Harold Evans, London 1981; *Paysages Photographies: La Mission
Photographique de la DATAR—Travaux en cours 1984/1985,* with texts by
Francois Hers, Jean-Francois Chevrier and others, Paris 1985. **Articles**—
"Raymond Depardon: Auschwitz: La Memoire" in *Photo* (Paris), May 1979;
"Photojournalism's Fearless Point Man" in *American Photographer* (New
York), September 1980.

                    *   *   *

What is it, then, that makes Raymond Depardon run?

A certain intellectual discomfort and internal contradictions. That, at least,
is his own analysis. One is tempted to believe that this analysis is erroneous
because the individual and the photographs are harmonious and express
generous bursts of humanism. But the facts and the intentions of his life and
work demonstrate his lucidity.

Depardon has belonged to several agencies—he even founded one of
them: Gamma—but he seems always to have felt an uneasiness in such
groupings, both morally and materially, and he is never able to decide whether
to remain independent; put another way, he feels at ease neither in an agency
nor outside of one. He avoids like the plague that which he calls the "pseudo-
artistic ghetto of the photograph" and the tendency to create "beautiful"
pictures. But his own pictures are beautiful, even when they bear witness to
tragedy, which comes from another kind of restlessness ("I am torn," he says,
"between aestheticism and content"). Above all, he dreads the picture that
bears the conventional mark of the photojournalist ("a kind of cowboy
romantic"), but he well realizes—another complication—that his own
notoriety came to him from his perilous campaigns in those regions where
blood was flowing—and where he was forced, against his own nature and a
nauseating fear, to play the hero of reportage. He works alone, but he devoutly
asks for the judgment of his peers. He yearns for authenticity, but he suffers in
his professional relations with those "in high places" from having to behave
as a character of convention ("the photographer, this puppet, this buffoon") in
charge of trying to validate the "show business" game of politicians. He is a
photographer, but he says (it is not necessary to believe him) that "this is by
accident," brought about by the cinema. And when he places himself behind
the camera to shoot films that he knows are commercially unviable, do we see
that in his vision? His brothers, the photojournalists—that is to say, himself—
are detached from that primary function which fascinates and consumes him.
Voilà, it is tied together; the introspection is recorded on film.

Far from sterilizing him, his uncertainties stimulate Depardon. So high
does he tower—even if he is not alone—over French photojournalism. That
agencies now treat reporters better than they did—to a great extent, his
colleagues owe that change to him. That photographs are used that are faithful
to the spirit of the photographer, without an alteration of meaning—for this,
they are also indebted. That the exploitation of bloody scenes has been
denounced—for this too, credit is due him. That the spirit of Capa lives, that it
is possible for a photographer to adhere to a cause, that there has been a
restoration of an attitude of militancy in photography—for all of these things,
we are indebted to Depardon. Beyond the work, in which the strength and
quality are beyond dispute, there is a great leader in the man himself.

                                        —Roger Therond

DESCAMPS, Bernard.

Nationality: French. **Born:** Paris, 16 January 1947. **Education:** Doctorate in
biology. **Career:** Freelance photographer, since 1975. Member of the Métis
agency. **Recipient:** Villa Medicis Hor les Murs Award, 1992. **Agent:** Galerie
Le Réverbère 2, Lyon, France. **Address:** c/o METIS IMAGES, 4 Impasse du
Mont Tonnene, 75015 Paris, France.

Individual Exhibitions:

1974   Galerie-Librarie de Seine, Paris
1975   Bibliothèque Nationale, Paris (with Plossu, Requillart and
          Duligowski)
          Galerie M, Bochum, Germany (with Florence Henri)
1976   Museum Leverkusen, Germany (with André Kemesz)
1977   Musée National d'Art Moderne, Centre Georges
          Pompidou, Paris
1979   Museée Réattu, Arles, France
          Galerie Pennings, Eindhoven, Netherlands
1981   Galerie Agathe Gaillard, Paris
1983   *Sahara,* Galerie Agathe Gaillard, Paris (travelled to Galerie Le
          Réverbère 2, Lyon, 1985)
1987   Galerie du Château d'Eau, Toulouse, France
1988   Musée N. Niépce, Chalon-sur-Saône, France
1991   *Photographies 1975-1990,* Galerie Le Réverbère 2, Lyon,
          France
          Et si demain, nous allions au zoo, Picto-Bastille, Paris
1992   *Paris couleur nuit,* Galerie FNAC Etoile, Paris (travelled to
          Berlin and Tokyo)
1994   *Le Japon de Bernard Descamps,* at *Mois de la Photo,* Paris
          Galerie Le Réverbère 2, Lyon, France
          Galerie du Théatre, Gap, France
          Les gens de Tana, Centre Culturel Albert Camus, Tananarive,
          Madagascar (with Perrot Men)

Selected Group Exhibitions:

1975   *4 Photographes,* Bibliothèque Nationale, Paris (with Plossu,
          Bruno and Kuligowski)
1977   *La Photographie Créatrice aux XX Siècle,* Centre Georges
          Pompidou, Paris
1978   *La Photographie Actuelle en France 1978,* Galerie Contreiour,
          Paris (and world tour, 1978-81)
          Concerning Photography, The Photographers' Gallery, London
          (travelled to the Spectro Workshop, Newcastle-upon-Tyne)
1979   *6 Photographes en Quête de Banlieues,* Centre Georges
          Pompidou, Paris (with Doisneau, Le Querrec, Raimond-
          Dityvon, Lattés and Freire)
          Bruxelles Photographique, L'Association Intercommunale
          Culturelle, Brussels (toured Belgium and travelled to the
          Centre Culturel Belge, Paris)
1980   *10 Photographes pour le Patrimoine,* Musée d'Art Moderne,
          Centre Georges Pompidou, Paris
1984   *La Photographie Créative,* Pavillon des Arts, Paris
          Objectif: Monuments, Chappelle St. Louis-de-la-
          Salpetrière, Paris
1988   *Regards sur le Palais Garnier,* at *Mois de la Photo,* Paris
1994   *L'esprit Métis,* Galerie Le Réverbère 2, Lyon (travelled to
          Galerie du Château d'Eau, Toulouse)
          Paris, la nuit, at *Mois de la Photo,* Paris

Collections:

Bibliothèque Nationale, Paris; Fondation Nationale de la Photographie, Lyon;
Musée National d'Art Moderne, Centre Georges Pompidou, Paris; Musée
Cantini, Marseille; Musée Réattu, Arles; Musée N. Niépce, Chalon-sur-
Saône; Galerie du Château d'Eau, Toulouse; FRAC (Aquitaine, Centre,

Limousin, Côte d'Azur); FNAC, Paris; Musée européenne de la Photographie, Paris.

Publications:

By DESCAMPS: Books—*Rencontres,* Paris 1976; *Balméaires,* Amiens 1984; *Sahara,* with text by Tahar Ben Jelloun, Mulhouse 1986. **Article**—text in *10 Photographes pour le Patrimonie,* exhibition catalogue, Paris 1980.

On DESCAMPS: Books—*Bernard Descamps: Photographies,* exhibition catalogue, with introduction by Jean-Claude Gautrand, Chateauxroux, France 1978; *Histoire de la Photographie Française* by Claude Nori, Paris 1978; *Jeune Photographie,* Lyons 1980; *Objectif: Monuments,* exhibition catalogue, with texts by Francoise Berce and Elvira Perego, Paris 1984; *La Photographie Créative* by Jean-Claude Lemagny, Paris 1984. **Articles**—in *Caméra* (Lucerne), text by Allan Porter, 1974; in *Photographies Magazine* (Paris), text by Brigitte Ollie, 1991; in *Photographers International* (Taiwan), December 1993.

*

Photography to me nowadays is something simple—I mean, in the way I go about it.

The camera is the extension, both natural and indispensable, of my visual sensibility, a recorder of feelings and visions.

My photographs are an encounter, a profound but instantaneous interchange between a moment of myself and a "subject," whether it be an object, place, situation or individual.

My technique is minimal, neutral, so that I may remain faithful and close to this encounter which is so fragile and difficult to capture.

Every day I capture in flight a flood of fleeting images: they make up a "different reality," whether it is "*the* reality" or "*my* reality," my image of the world, myself through my encounters.

I walk alone, recording my emotions in everyday space, where I travel according to chance desires.

Among the multitude of captured images, there are sometimes those that go beyond self, which are ahead of me, which are a result of my dreams and hidden desires, of my subconscious. It is usually these images that I select, which through interpretative printing, become photographs.

—Bernard Descamps

* * *

There is an age-old antagonism between "image" and "word" in which, in general, extreme positions have prevailed. Yet the Gutenburg world has not disappeared with the world of Niepce, nor will it disappear with the world of Marconi. They merely influence and compliment one another.

The image is a poly-semantic statement or message—i.e., subject to various possible interpretations. For this reason, many photos carry a legend which clearly defines the meaning. What might seem a limitation to effective communication is actually a great advantage to effective expression, or so, at least, some photographers believe.

Observing the works of Bernard Descamps, for example, one asks himself: why are they so ambiguous? Why does Descamps make ambiguity his banner? An initial response might be that from the ambiguous nature of the image stems its evocative power. Another response, no less valid, is that the photographer might assume reality itself to be ambiguous. From this metaphysical revelation, the photographer would wish to demonstrate that things are as we wish to see them—that their arrangement in a given context and their more or less paradoxical relationship to that context depends on the consciousness of the observer. Reality does not exist in and of itself but as a function of our experience. Perhaps from here one can go a step further to the theoretical contribution of Minor White when he affirms that creation stems from the "mystical state of seeing." Descamps seems to suggest, in addition, that reality itself is affirmed and even shaped by our vision.

Without a doubt, external reality, like its representation, allows many readings—from the literal interpretation defined by cultural conventions to the intuitive interpretation found in the work of Descamps. Here commonplace objects come to reveal occult dimensions, at times mystical, at times absurd,

but always in conflict with the familiarity of the objects. In his own words, Descamps deals with "subversion of the glance." And this subversion is supported by an unusual and turbulent aesthetic. The work of Descamps is sufficiently agile so as not to require a set of stylistic tables. Empty spaces and imbalances predominate. The graphic constitution of the image appears at times baroque owing to the great density of elements which introduce new information.

There is no gratituous formalism, but rather the opposite, the maximum economy of means, a naked vision, a piece of reality captured through the rectangular window of the camera. Disproving the effects of all concession to gratuitous aesthetics, Descamps shapes a final image with precision, despite the risk of its being interpreted contrarily. He reaches a reality-image interaction without artificiality despite the danger that the spectator might view it as creative barrenness. These seem to be the norms that Descamps has imposed upon himself in his strange, rigorous and enduring "ambiguous vision."

—Joan Fontcuberta

DIAS, Pavel.

Nationality: Czechoslovakian. **Born:** Brno, 9 December 1938. **Education:** Studied drawing and photography, under K.O. Hrubý, at the Middle Art School, Brno, 1954-58, and photography and filmmaking, at the Academy of Musical Arts, Prague, 1958-63. **Family:** Married Hilda Misurova in 1961; son: Marek. **Career:** Assistant Cameraman, Czechoslovak Film Studio, Gottwaldov; subsequently Photographer, Barrandov Film Studio, Prague, 1959-61, and Central Institute of Folk Arts, Prague, 1963-65. Freelance photographer, working for *Mladý svet, Svet v obrazech,* etc., Prague, since 1965. Member, Czech Art Photography Society, and Union of Czech Journalists. Teacher and Chief of Photography Department at Middle Art School, Brno, 1983-1988. Teacher of Documentary Photography at Academy of Performing Arts, Film and TV Faculty, Department of Photography in Prague since 1989. **Address:** Studio—Jana Masaryka 51, 120 00 Prague 2, Czech Republic.

Individual Exhibitions:

1961	*Bartušek/Dias/Hucek,* Lucerna Ciné, Prague
1963	Jaromir Funke Fotokabinett, Brno, Czechoslovakia
1964	Malostranksá beseda, Prague
1965	Gallery, Luhacovice, Czechoslovakia
	Klutzr House, Gottwaldov, Czechoslovakia
1966	Foto-Gallery, Děčin, Czechoslovakia
1979	*Without Blinkers,* Gallery D, Prague
	Torso, Osvětim Museum, Osvětim, Poland (travelled to Sachsenhausen Museum, Oranienburg, East Germany, 1980)
1980	*Turf,* Gallery Pardubce, Pradubice, Czechoslovakia
1981	*Without Blinkers,* Jaromir Funke Fotokabinett, Brno, Czechoslovakia
1984	*Turf Photography,* Napajedla, Czechoslovakia
1988	*Retrospective: 1957-1987,* Uhersky brod, Czechoslovakia
	Arts Gallery, Hodonin, Czechoslovakia
1989	*Reminiscence/Paris,* Boskovice, Czechoslovakia
	Velvet Revolution, Mahen's Theatre, Brno, Czechoslovakia
1990	*Sacral Motives,* Theatre Uherské Hradiště, Czechoslovakia
	Without Blinkers, Dům Uměni, Brno, Czechoslovakia
1992	Museum of Modern Arts, Tehran, Iran

Selected Group Exhibitions:

1958	*Fotokina,* Köln am Rhein
1959	Students Photography exhibition, Hong Kong
1963	*Photographers of Mladý svet,* Prague
1977	*Contemporary Creative Photography,* Fragner's Gallery, Prague

1979   *Tschechoslowakische Fotografie 1918-78,* Fotoforum, Kassel,
        West Germany
1985   *Czech Creative Photography,* Gallery of Czechoslovak Writers,
        Prague
1987   *Photography of FAMU,* Holland
1989   *150 Anniversary of Photography,* Prague Gallery, Zvon
        Velvet Revolution, Prague, Vienna, Loisane, Strasbourg,
        Norimberg

Publications:

By DIAS: Books—*Kone formule 1/1* (Horses Formula 1/1), Prague 1985;
Svet lidi a svet koni (The World of People and the World of Horses), Prague
1986. **Films and television**—*Jazz,* Czech Television 1977; *Torso,* Czech
Television 1981; *Turf,* Czech Television 1981; *Photographers in Moravia,*
Czech Television 1992.

On DIAS: Book—*The Evolution of Czechoslovak Photography 1918 to
Today* by Petr Tausk, Prague 1986. **Articles**—"Chceme vidět zivot ve vsem"
by J. Spousta in *Ceskoslovenská Fotografie* (Prague), no. 3, 1961; "Medailon-
foto" in *Mladý svet* (Prague), no. 2, 1962; "Pavel Dias fotograf" by I.
Soeldner in *MY 64* (Prague), no. 4, 1964; "Medailon Pavel Dias" in
Ceskoslovenská televize (Prague), no. 5, 1964; "Paris by Pavel Dias" in *Svět v
obrazech* (Prague), no. 2, 1969; "Pavel Dias" by K. Dvořák in *Ceskoslovenská
Fotografie* (Prague), no. 4, 1969; "Mongolsko by Pavel Dias" in *Mladý svět*
(Prague), no. 7, 1969; "Concentration Camps" in *Mladý svet* (Prague), no. 2,
1974; "Torso" by O. in *Ceskoslovenská Fotografie* (Prague), no. 5, 1979;
"Pavel Dias" by Karel Dvořák in *Fotografie* (Prague), no. 12, 1979; "Pavel
Dias" in *Ceskoslovenská televize,* (Prague), no. 1, 1981.

*

I was interested at first in drawing, and for that reason I enrolled at the
Střední uměleckoprmyslová škola (Middle Art School) in Brno. But Professor
K.O. Hrubý at the school influenced me in the direction of photography. I
discovered that photography, far from being only a technically strict reproduction of reality, is a formally technical art. And Steichen's book *The Family of
Man* had a strong impact on me. My interest in drawing gradually lessened,
and I began working at the film studio in Gottwaldov and at the Barrandov
Film Studio in Prague. These meetings, and meetings with film directors,
cameramen and actors, my contributions to daily newspapers and magazines,
meetings with newsmen, and, most importantly, the events of my daily life,
were all very important for the formation of my views. After completing my
studies at the film faculty in Prague, I began to concentrate on documentary
photography. I studied the works of Cartier-Bresson, Robert Capa, Werner
Bischof, David Seymour, Dorothea Lange, etc. Among Czech photographers
the great influence was the Photo-Film Group of the Left Front, mainly R.
Kohn. My photos were published in some cultural magazines. After a couple
of years of freelance photojournalism, I discovered something about myself: I
prefer to work with thematic series or cycles.

My first important series was of Nazi concentration camps, photos taken
20 or 30 years after the Second World War. These photos document impressions created by the places and their local details—thirty years after the events.
I also took photos of more recent human horror, and the resultant series got the
name *Torso.* It is meant as a warning.

Another theme is horses, the people around them, and their world. The
horse has always been man's best helper; nevertheless, the number of horses in
the world today is less than it used to be, and some breeds are nearly extinct. I
believe, however, that the horse—a long-time friend and natural partner of
man—will, in this "over-civilized" world, again become important as an aid
to man's psychological balance. The horse will, in future, serve more than just
its historical roles of transport and war-machine.

One of the main and inevitable parts of this series is racing and its milieu.
This series is called *The Face of the Horserace,* and the book I am preparing is
called *Without Blinkers.* While shooting "on location," I meet men of a very
large family, people of different nations and different skin color, who have one
common interest—horses. It is just one of the possible ways of understanding
the world by means of a universal language, by photography.

Photography as a specific means of expression, speaking with a common
understandable language all over the world, and by its ability to express the
truth, must help to uphold mankind's highest ideals. In my work, that's what I
strive to do. At the same time, I am fully aware that to do it well is by far the
most difficult part of photography.

—Pavel Dias

*   *   *

Pavel Dias was one of the first artists to receive a complete photographic
education at university level in Czechoslovakia. After his studies at the Film
and TV Faculty of the Academy of Musical Arts in Prague he came to regard
the "live" image as the most interesting and most appropriate to his own
notions regarding the nature of photography. Although he frequently works on
assignment for various journals, Dias does not believe that his kind of work
ought to be reproduced exclusively on the printed page of weeklies or books;
rather, he is one of those photographers who prefers to present his oeuvre in the
form of original prints. Naturally, it follows that Dias is convinced that in using
an image as an autonomous work of art it is necessary to select those
photographs that are informed by personal emotion in the act of observation.
For this reason—the final goal, as it were—he prefers always to choose those
subjects that attract him, regardless of whether he will be able to publish the
results. He confirms the theory that the decision "what to photograph" may be
the ultimate creative act in photography.

One of his most extraordinary conceptions has been a cycle on former Nazi
concentration camps. His subject was actually the reaction of contemporary
visitors to these camps—the faces of visitors revealing that uncomprehending
sorrow that it was possible for humans to inflict such atrocities on their fellow
men. Dias does not show the horror—nor the vision of the photographers who
accompanied the Allied troops into the camps in 1945—but bases the rather
complex expression of this cycle purely on the emotions of contemporaries
who were highly moved by these places redolent of memory.

The most recent of his cycles concerns horses. When looking at these
photographs it is impossible not to feel the ways in which the photographer
meditated on the changing status of these animals in an era when the tractor
took over their role in agriculture in most countries. For this series Dias has
visited Mongolia, in order to photograph big herds of horses, and has also
visited important breeding farms in Europe. He has photographed numerous
horse-races and steeple-chases, again in various parts of the world, and he has
tried to convey the relationship of jockeys and other people of the turf world to
the thoroughbred animals. He does so in a very personal way. Dias possesses a
sensitivity for both very dynamic and for nearly static situations which enables
him to express different messages from image to image.

In the 1980s Dias began teaching photography at a school of arts and crafts
in Brno. The new employment allowed him some independence from photo-
assignments, so that he was able to find time to arrange his cycles of
photographs taken over the years for his personal expression. As a result, two
fine picture volumes were published. The first, *Horses Formula 1/1,* was
dedicated to the Czechoslovak turf. Dias had selected images showing
dramatic moments from the races as well as the tension mirrored on the faces
of enthusiastic spectators. The major part of the book is composed of black-
and-white photos to better depict this dynamic tension, whilst the additional
colour supplement presents the atmosphere of brightly-hued silks of the
jockeys against the green grass of the track itself, along with shots of the race's
rapid blur.

The second volume, *The World of People and the World of Horses,* is
conceived more philosophically. Employing only black-and-white images,
the book is a creative compendium of the life of the horse and its relationship to
people in various countries. It examines a variety of horse breeds and the role
of the horse in human history. Apart from revealing Dias' skill as a photographer, the book provides an insight into his ideas on social development. Thus
we are given an important instance of the Photographer's art making full use of
the medium's semantic strengths.

—Petr Tausk

DIBBETS, Jan.

Nationality: Dutch. **Born:** Gerardus Johannes Maria Dibbets in Weert, Netherlands, 9 May 1941. **Education:** Attended Bisschoppelijk College, Weert, 1953-59; studied art, Academie voor Beeldende an Bouwedde Kunsten, Tilburg, 1959-63; private painting studies, with Jan Gregor, Eindhoven, 1961-63; St. Martin's School of Art, London, 1967; self-taught in photography. **Family:** Married Bianka Francisca de Poorter in 1967; daughter: Hiske Karool. Independent photographic artist, Amsterdam, since 1963. Co-founder, with Reiner Lucassen and Ger van Elk, International Institute for the Reeducation of Artists, Amsterdam, 1968. Art Instructor, Enschede, 1964-67, and Atelier 63, Haarlem, 1968-71; Visiting Artist, Nova Scotia College of Art and Design, Halifax, 1971. **Recipient:** British Council Scholarship, London 1967; Heineken Prize, The Hague, 1969; Cassandra Foundation Award, New York, 1971. **Agent:** Waddington Galleries, 11 Cork Street, London W1X 1PD, England. **Address:** Boerhaaveplein 6, 1091 Amsterdam, Netherlands.

Individual Exhibitions:

1965	Galerie 845, Amsterdam
	Galerie Swart, Amsterdam (and 1966, 1967)
1968	Galerie Konrad Fischer, Dusseldorf
1969	Seth Siegelaub Gallery, New York
	Videogalerie Gerry Schum, Dusseldorf
	Art and Project, Amsterdam
	Museum Haus Lange, Krefeld, West Germany
1970	Galerie Yvon Lambert, Paris
	Galleria Françoise Lambert, Milan
	Zentrum für Aktuelle Kunst, Aachen, West Germany
	Aktionsraum 1, Munich
	Videogalerie Gerry Schum, Dusseldorf
1971	Galleria Gian Enzo Sperone, Turin
	Galerie Konrad Fischer, Dusseldorf
	Art and Project, Amsterdam
	Stedelijk Van Abbemuseum, Eindhoven, Netherlands
	Bykert Gallery, New York
1972	Galerie MTL, Brussels
	Galerie Yvon Lambert, Paris
	Jack Wendler Gallery, London
	Galleria Toselli, Milan
	Israel Museum, Jerusalem
	Stedelijk Museum, Amsterdam
	Dutch Pavilion, *XXXVI Biennale,* Venice
1973	Leo Castelli Gallery, New York
	Galleria Sperone-Fischer, Rome
	Galerie Konrad Fischer, Dusseldorf
	Art and Project, Amsterdam
	Kabinett für Aktuelle Kunst, Bremerhaven, West Germany
	Jack Wendler Gallery, London
1974	Galleria Gian Enzo Sperone, Turin
	Galerie Rolf Preisig, Basle
	Galerie Yvon Lambert, Paris
	Galerie Konrad Fischer, Dusseldorf
1975	Galerie MTL, Brussels
	Art and Project, Amsterdam
	Cusack Gallery, Houston
	Claire Copley Gallery, Los Angeles
	Leo Castelli Gallery, New York
	Jan Dibbets: Autumn Melody, Kunstmuseum, Lucerne
1976	Galleria Gian Enzo Sperone, Rome
	Galleria Marilena Bonomo, Bari, Italy
	Scottish Arts Council Gallery, Edinburgh (travelled to Arnolfini Gallery, Bristol; Chapter Arts Centre, Cardiff; Museum of Modern Art, Oxford)
1977	Galerie Konrad Fischer, Dusseldorf
	Gálerie Yvon Lambert, Paris
1978	Leo Castelli Gallery, New York
1980	Van Abbemuseum, Eindhoven, Netherlands

	Galerie Yvon Lambert, Paris
	Kunsthalle, Berne, Switzerland
	Musée d'Art Moderne de la Ville, Paris
1981	Galleria Christian Stein, Turin
	Galleria Locus Solus, Genoa, Italy
1982	Anthony D'Offay Gallery, London
	Centre International de Création Artistique, Paris
1983	Galerie Karen and Jean Bernier, Athens, Greece
	Leo Castelli Gallery, New York
1984	Galerie Dam 43, Middelburg, Netherlands
	Waddington Galleries, London
1985	Galerie Maeght Lelong, Paris
	Van Abbemuseum, Eindhoven, Netherlands
	Musej Savremene Umetnosti, Belgrade (travelled to Galerija Suvremene Umjetnosti, Zagreb, Yugoslavia)
1987	Walker Art Center, Minneapolis, Minnesota (toured the United States)

Selected Group Exhibitions:

1970	*Information,* Museum of Modern Art, New York
1971	*Guggenheim International,* Guggenheim Museum, New York
1972	*Konzept-Kunst,* Kunstmuseum, Basle
1976	*The Artist and the Photograph,* Israel Museum, Jerusalem
1978	*23 Photographers/23 Directions,* Walker Art Gallery, Liverpool
1979	*Photographie als Kunst 1879-1979/Kunst als Photographie 1949-1979,* Tiroler Landesmuseum Ferdinandeum, Innsbruck, Austria (travelled to Neue Galerie am Wolfgang Gurlitt Museum, Linz, Austria; Neue Galerie am Landesmuseum Joanneum, Graz, Austria; and Museum des 20. Jahrhunderts, Vienna)
1980	*Artist and Camera,* Mappin Art Gallery, Sheffield, Yorkshire (travelled to the Stoke City Art Gallery; Durham Light Infantry Museum; Cartwright Hall, Bradford)
1982	*International Photography 1920-80,* Australian National Gallery, Canberra
1984	*Construire les Paysages de la Photographie,* Musée de Metz, France
1987	*Photography and Art 1946-86,* Los Angeles County Museum of Art

Collections:

Stedelijk Museum, Amsterdam; Haagse Gemeentemuseum, The Hague; Kaiser Wilhelm Museum, Krefeld, West Germany; Von der Heydt Museum, Wuppertal, West Germany; Stedelijk Van Abbemuseum, Eindhoven, Netherlands; Rijksmuseum Kroller-Muller, Otterloo, Netherlands; Australian National Gallery, Canberra; Weisman Foundation, Los Angeles.

Publications:

By DIBBETS: Book—*Robin Redbreast's Territory: Sculpture 1969, April-June,* Cologne and New York 1970. **Articles**—"Voor Beeldende Kunst Moet Je Kunnen Kijken" in *Museumjournaal* (Amsterdam), no. 13, 1968; "Jan Dibbets: TV as Fireplace" in *Interfunktionen* (Cologne), no. 4, 1970; "Jan Dibbets: Interview" in *Avalanche* (New York), Fall 1970; "Jan Dibbets in Conversation with Charlotte Townsend" in *Artscanda* (Toronto), August/September 1971; "Jan Dibbets" in *Art and Project Bulletin* (Amsterdam), no. 56, 1972. **Films and videotapes**—*Land Art,* 1968; *Fire/Feuer/Feu/Vuur,* 1968; *12 Hours Ride Objects with Correction of Perspective,* 1969; *Painting 1,* 1970; *Painting 2,* 1970; *Vertical-Horizontal-Diagonal-Square,* 1970; *Horizon I: Sea,* 1970; *Horizon II: Sea,* 1971; *Horizon III: Sea,* 1971; *Vibrating Horizon,* 1971; *Venetian Blinds,* 1971; *Video: 2 Diagonals,* 1971; *Video: 3 Diagonals,* 1971.

On DIBBETS: Books—*Jan Dibbets: Autumn Melody,* exhibition catalogue, with text by Jean-Christophe Amman, Lucerne 1975; *Jan Dibbets,* exhibition catalogue, with text by Barbara Reise and M.M.M. Vos, Edinburgh 1976; *23*

Photographers/23 Directions, exhibition catalogue, by Valerie Lloyd, Liverpool 1978; *Photographie als Kunst 1879-1979/Kunst als Photographie 1949-1979,* exhibition catalogue, 2 vols., by Peter Weiermair, Innsbruck, Austria 1979; *Jan Dibbets: Photographic Works from 1967 to 1980,* exhibition catalogue, with introduction by Rudi Fuchs, Eindhoven, Netherlands 1980; *Jan Dibbets,* exhibition catalogue, with introduction by Suzanne Page, M.M.M. Voos and Carole Naggar, Paris 1980; *International Photography 1920-1980,* edited by Ian North, Canberra 1982; *Jan Dibbets,* exhibition catalogue, with texts by Jesa Denegri and M. M. M. Vos, Belgrade 1985; *Photography and Art 1946-1986,* exhibition catalogue, by Andy Grundberg and Kathleen M. Gauss, Los Angeles 1987. **Articles**—"Notities over het Werk van Jan Dibbets" by Carel Blotkamp in *Musemjournaal* (Amsterdam), July 1971; "Notes on Jan Dibbets: Contemporary Nature to Realistic Classicism in the Dutch Tradition" by Barbara Reise in *Studio International* (London), June 1972; "Jan Dibbets: Biennale de Venise" by Irmeline Lebeer in *L'Art Vivant* (Paris), June/July 1972; "Jan Dibbets: A Perspective Correction" by Barbara Reise in *Art News* (New York), Summer 1972; "Modes of Visual Experience: New Works by Jan Dibbets" by Rudi H. Fuchs in *Studio International* (London), January 1973; "Some Work by Jan Dibbets" by M. Vos in *Flash Art* (Milan), January 1973; "Jan Dibbets: The Photograph and the Photographed" by Bruce Boice in *Artforum* (New York), April 1973; "The Art of Discovering Conflicts in Perception" by A. von Graevenitz in *Data* (Milan), Summer 1973; "Jan Dibbets" in *Art Annual* (New York), 1973/74; "Jan Dibbets at Jack Wendler Gallery" by Lynda Morris in *Studio International* (London), no. 187, 1974.

* * *

Many established prejudices encourage an elitist distinction between artists and photographers—who are also artists. It is often thought, at least in some quarters of the art world, that *artists'* photographs are inherently "high art" and somehow superior to "mere" photography. Jan Dibbets is one of those who use photographs, but identify themselves primarily with the art world and its concerns.

Dibbets' move to photography in 1968, after a period of making abstract paintings, grew out of his reflection on the fundamental relationship between art and reality. In fact, his approach to photography was initially related to concept art. For a show in 1970 at the Galerie Yvon Lambert in Paris, for instance, he photographed the walls of the gallery, which he had divided up into numbered sections. The 14 resultant photos were subsequently exhibited over the corresponding numbers. He also reconstructed the pattern of the walls in several series of photographs on a separate sheet. A ground plan of the gallery was added. The emphasis of this work—as in most "concept" art—still lay fairly strongly on the idea, but soon Dibbets developed a more delicate balance between concept and realization through his rich and meticulous application of sequential photography.

Dibbets' preference for sequential photography springs from an intuitive understanding of the phenomenological characteristics of photography. Because the characteristics of "art photography" do not interest him, the singular relationship between photography and reality offers him—as far as the individual photo is concerned—little scope for his creativity as an artist. But the possibilities afforded by the photographic sequence are totally different. The structure of the sequence spans the fragmentary and descriptive nature of the individual photographs.

Dibbets uses photographs within the framework of abstraction: not as a means of producing aesthetic images, but of developing a way of seeing.

He shifts our attention from the object that is photographed to the camera taking the photograph. In "Comets" (1973) the structure of the work is based on a meticulous combination of the choice of motif on the one hand and the manipulation of the camera on the other. In "Perspective Corrections" the position of the camera is the result of careful calculation. In the series "Panoramas," "Dutch Mountains" and "Comets," the camera is rotated around different axes, taking photos at regular intervals; in another group of works, the structure is obtained by using increasing shutter speeds, or by registering natural and artificial changes of light. Slight changes in light and shade are also recorded every 10 minutes in "The Shortest Day" (1970); the camera rotates on a perpendicular axis taking a photo every 15 degrees.

The rise of photography was accompanied last century by a deterioration of descriptive painting—"from today, painting is dead." But Dibbets' interest in light and colour, in abstract structure, in the expressive qualities of

visually perceptible reality, are a painter's concerns, even though he uses photographs instead of paint and brushes. He has discovered in photography a possibility for grafting visual art onto nature once more. The photograph is not used as a means of documentation; his concern is with the final image shown by the photographs.

Leaving an exhibition of Dibbets' photo-works, a critic exclaimed in surprise: "But that man Dibbets is a real painter." And Dibbets, standing nearby, answered: "So I am."

—Colin Naylor

DICKSON, Ian (Andrew).

Nationality: British. **Born:** Glasgow, Scotland, 20 September 1945. **Education:** Attended Clydebank Secondary High School and Newcastle College of Art; self-taught in photography. **Career:** Worked as a graphic designer. In-house photographer, University Theatre, Newcastle-upon-Tyne, 1970-72; freelance rock music photographer, working for *Disc, NME, Sounds, Vox,* etc., since 1973. **Address:** 36 New Road, Shenley, Herts WD7 9EA, England.

Individual Exhibitions:

1992   *It Was Twenty Years Ago Today,* Gallery on the Lane, Acton, London
1993   *Hit the Road Jack,* Madrid, Spain (travelled to the FNAC Brussels, Belgium)

*

One day in 1970, with a little extra cash in my pocket, I paused outside the window of my local camera shop and looked in. Purely on impulse, I bought a second-hand Zenith B, a Russian basic 35 mm camera, and photography became my life's passion. At work, I sat at my desk and daydreamed about being a professional photographer—so much so, in fact, that my employers helped me realise my dream by sacking me. They said, quite understandably, that if my mind was elsewhere, the rest of my body should be with it!

Under the circumstances, they were generous with the amount which they paid me off with, and so I bought my first Nikon and set about becoming a freelance photographer. After six months of photographing babies and junior marching bands, I was appointed as house photographer to the Tyneside Theatre Company, based at the University Theatre in Newcastle. It was there that I met Bob Brown, the manager of the City Hall, Newcastle's major concert venue. He invited me along whenever I wished and soon I was making frequent visits to the Hall where I began photographing rock musicians.

When I discovered how much I could earn photographing rock bands, I hitched a lift to London on Roxy Music's tour coach, and I've been here ever since.

In November 1992, I had my first London exhibition and, encouraged by the reaction to the photographs, I decided to put the show itself "on the road." *Hit the Road Jack* has already been seen in Madrid and Brussels, and there are plans to visit further European cities, not to mention the North American continent!

—Ian Dickson

* * *

Ian Andrew Dickson was born in Glasgow in 1945. Originally working as a graphic designer, he first took up photography over 20 years ago, when his previous boss finally decided he had been caught daydreaming about Nikons once too often. Having stayed on in Newcastle Upon Tyne after completing his studies at Newcastle College of Art, he began to make use of the secondhand Zenith B which had been the cause of his newfound obsession, picking up work by hanging out at the University Theatre. It was here that he first met Bob Brown, manager of the town's biggest rock venue, the City Hall. With an open invitation to hang out there, Dickson spent all his time snapping pictures of

The Power of Love (Frankie Goes to Hollywood), **1984, from his series** ***Hit the Road Jack.*** Photograph by Ian Dickson.

artists in performance and backstage, drawn to the sudden realisation that he could make money taking photos of pop stars. In the early '70s, access to pop groups was a lot easier than the "three songs and then you're out" system of today, and from this time Dickson made valuable contacts with the likes of Rod Steward and Roxy Music.

In fact, Dickson jumped ship, returning to London on the coach with Bryan Ferry's pre-glam pop gods and spending the next two years working closely with them. In those pre-promo video days, few bands could promise such image-aware access to a photographer, and from this invaluable time Dickson has gone on to be one of the most respected music photographers we have.

Although Dickson's portfolio features a whole collection of stunning portraits and on-the-road, backstage snaps of everyone from stadium-filling pop stars to American blues legends, it's his live, onstage footage which he personally prefers. With dimly lit venues, a spaghetti of wires and a crammed space up against the amps to deal with, most photographers rely on those moments when the lead singer is perhaps doing something a little unusual with the microphone, or pulling some rock and roll pose. Dickson, however, often captures the moments of rare intimacy between artist and audience, as can be seen in this classic picture of Frankie Goes to Hollywood's Holly Johnson.

With published work in *Disk, NME, Vox* and *Sounds,* Dickson has worked through hippy rock and even survived the '80s pop music merry-go-round. He is currently putting together a collection of shots from the punk era for a special box set to be published in the near future, and continues to freelance for music journals and record companies. In the past couple of years he has also begun to exhibit his work (his two shows so far are *Hit The Road Jack* and *It was 20 Years Ago Today*) both in London and abroad.

—Laura Lee Davies

DIEUZAIDE, Jean.

Pseudonym: Yan. **Nationality:** French. **Born:** Grenade-sur-Garonne, 20 June 1921. **Education:** Attended secondary school in Nice, 1938-40; did preparatory year for Saint-Cyr Military School, but left because of the war. **Family:** Married Jacqueline Manuquet in 1950; children: Michel and Marie-Francoise. **Career:** Freelance photographer, in Toulouse, since 1944: Founder and Art Director, Galerie du Château d'Eau, Toulouse, since 1974; established Jean Dieuzaide Gallery, Toulouse, 1976. Instructor in Photography Workshops, *Rencontres Internationales de Photographie,* Arles, France, since 1969. Instructor, Ecole Audiovisuelle de Saint-Cloud, Paris, 1978. Chairman, Artistic Committee, Fédération Internationale d'Art Photographique (FIAP), since 1970. **Recipient:** French Cup for Portraits, Fédération Internationale de d'Art Photographique, 1951; Niepce Prize, 1955; International Prize, Colour Tourist Poster Competition, New Delhi, 1956; French Cup for Industrial Research and Edouard Belin Medal, Fédération Internationale de l'Art Photographique, 1957; French National Prize for Posters, 1959; Nadar Book Prize, 1961; French Cup for Landscape Photography, Fédération Internationale d'Art Photographique, 1967; Lucien Lorell Cup, Bordeaux, 1969; Clemence Isaure Prize, Languedoc Academy, 1979; Grand Prix de la Ville de Paris, 1985. Honorary Member, French Committee of Photographic Art, 1969. Chevalier, Order of Merit, France, 1966; Officer, Ordre des Arts et Lettres, France, 1981. **Address:** 7 rue Erasme, 31400 Toulouse, France.

Individual Exhibitions:

1948	Publicity Club, Paris
1952	Inter-Club, Toulouse
1955	Galerie d'Orsay, Paris
	Knights of St. Joan, Toulouse
1960	Augustin Museum, Toulouse
1961	Municipal Museum, Sete, France
1962	Galeria Imagen y Sonido, Barcelona
	Pavillon de Marsan, Paris
1963	Municipal Museum, Tel Aviv
1964	Cloister Gallery, Moissac, France
1965	Cultural Center, Toulouse

1966	Rangueil University, Toulouse
1967	Association of Culture and Photographic Art, Avignon
1968	Maison des Quatres Vents, Paris
1969	Fiat Cultural Center, Turin
1970	Musée Réattu, Arles, France
	Toussaint Gallery, Angers, France
1971	Galerie de l'Oeuvre, Toulouse
	Cultural Center, Toulouse
	Galerie La Demeure, Paris
1976	Ecole des Beaux-Arts, Tourcoing, France
1977	Musée Nicéphore Niepce, Chalon-sur-Saône, France
1978	Galerij Paule Pia, Antwerp
1979	*Dialogue avec la Lumière,* Credit Commercial de France, Toulouse
1981	Galerie Le Trepied, Geneva
1983	*Un photographe de la réalité,* Fondation nationale de la Photographie, Lyon, France
1984	*Variation sur Croix,* Musée du Colmar, France (with Lucien Clergue)
1986	*Quarante Ans de Vie Professionelle,* Réfectoire des Jacobins, Toulouse, France

Selected Group Exhibitions:

1952	*Photokina '52,* Cologne
1961	*Salon International du Portrait Photographique,* Bibliothèque Nationale, Paris
1968	*2nd World Exhibition of Photography: Woman,* Pressehaus Stern, Hamburg (and world tour)
1972	*15 French Photographers,* National Museum, Moscow
1980	*7 Photographers,* University of Oklahoma, Norman
1981	*Farbe im Photo,* Josef-Haubrich-Kunsthalle, Cologne
1982	*Fotografie 1922-82,* at *Photokina 82,* Cologne
1984	*La Photographie Créative,* Pavillon des Arts, Paris
	Sammlung Gruber, Museum Ludwig, Cologne
1985	*SIF 85: Semana Internacional de la Fotografia,* Palacio del Infantado, Guadalajara, Spain

Collections:

Bibliothèque Nationale, Paris; City of Paris Collection: Musée Réattu, Arles, France; Musée Nicéphore Niepce, Chalon-sur-Saône, France; Musée Cantini, Marseilles; Het Sterckshof Museum, Antwerp; Metropolitan Museum of Art, New York; Virginia Museum, Norfolk; Museum Ludwig, Cologne.

Publications:

By DIEUZAIDE: Books—*The South of Spain,* with text by Jean Sermet, Paris 1953; *St. Sernin de Toulouse,* with text by Jean Peyrade, Toulouse 1955; *Spain,* with text by Yves Bottineau, Paris 1955; *Portugal,* with text by Yves Bottineau, Paris 1956; *Pictures of Alsace,* with text by Victor Beyer, Paris 1956; *Sardinia,* with text by Antonio Borio, Paris 1957; *Treasures of Turkey,* with text by Ml de St-Pierre, Paris 1957; *Roussillon Roman,* with text by Marcel Durliat, La Pierre que Vire, France 1958; *Basque Country,* with text by Rd Ritter, Paris 1958; *Béarn-Bigorre,* with text by Rd Ritter, Paris 1958; *History of Toulouse,* with text by Ph. Wolff, Toulouse 1958; *Blue Guide of the Pyrenees,* with text by P. de Gorsse, Paris 1959; *Romanesque Quercy,* with text by M. Vidal, La Pierre qui Vire, France 1959; *Catalogne Romane,* with text by Edouardo Junyent, La Pierre qui Vire, France 1960; *The Ways to Santiago,* with text by Yves Bottineau, Paris 1961; *Toulouse and Haut-Languedoc,* with text by Robert Mesuret, Toulouse 1961; *Voix et Images de Toulouse,* with text by Ph. Wolff, Toulouse 1962; *L'Art Roman en Espagne,* with text by Marcel Durliat, Paris 1962; *My Pyrenees,* with text by Raymond Escholier, Paris 1962; *Rouergue Roman,* with text by G. Gaillard, La Pierre qui Vire, France 1963; *Toulouse,* with text by Pierre Cabanne, Toulouse 1963; *Splendours of Spain,* with text by Yves Bottineau, Paris 1964; *St. Foy de Conques,* with text by Mère E. de Solms, La Pierre qui Vire, France 1965; *Romanesque Art,* with text by A. Fernandes Arenas, Barcelona 1965; *Los Caminos de Santiago,* with text by Yves Bottineau, Barcelona, 1965; *Rutas del Romanico,* with text by Subias Galter, Barcelona 1965; *Périgord,* with text by

Paul Fènelon, Paris 1966; *History of Languedoc,* with text by Nougier/ Gallet, Toulouse 1967; *El movimento romanico en Espagna,* with text by Blai Bonnet, Barcelona 1967; *Toulouse, City of Fate,* with text by René Mauriès, Toulouse 1974; *My Adventure with Pitch,* with text by Jean Claude Lemagny, Toulouse 1975; *Albi,* with text by Pierre de Gorsse, Toulouse 1977; *Toulouse as It Was in the Nineties,* with text by M. St. Saens, Toulouse 1978; *Dialogues avec la lumière,* Paris 1979; *Cataluna,* with text by Eduard Junyent, Madrid 1980; *Voyages en Ibérie,* Paris 1983; *Toulouse d'Hier et d'Aujourd'hui,* Toulouse 1984.

On DIEUZAIDE: Books—*Photography Today,* edited by Norman Hall, London 1957; *Transparences: photographies,* exhibition catalogue, with text by Gilbert Lascault, Paris 1980; *10 Photographes pour le Patrimoine,* exhibition catalogue, by Jean-Claude Gautrand, Paris 1980; *Farbe im Photo: Die Geschichte der Farbphotographie von 1861 bis 1981* by Fritz Binder, Gert Koshofer, Rolf Sachsse and others, Cologne 1981; *Fotografie 1922-1982,* exhibition catalogue, with introduction by Manfred Heiting, Rolf-Hasso Ley and Karl Steinorth, Cologne 1982; *Sammlung Gruber: Photographie des 20. Jahrhunderts,* exhibition catalogue, with foreword by Siegfried Gohr, Cologne 1984; *La Photographie Créative* by Jean-Claude Lemagny, Paris 1984.

*

People often think it is necessary to go to the far ends of the world to act as a photographer. But photography is not synonymous with being removed from one's usual surroundings; it also has to do with rediscovering the common things of everyday life that we can no longer see, things we do not take the time to see. The thousands of objects that share our intimacy have something to tell us, but our eye does not listen to them: they play with light to draw our attention, and they are surely sorry for our indifference, as they feel they are a part of ourselves.

I really don't care much whether I create "Art" with my pictures or not.

For always my inward joy, that which I can't be deprived of without being shut in a dark closet, is to look at the *interplays of light* and photograph them: light gives richness to the swaying of a solid, a form, a body, a tool, a trifle. It makes all my being vibrate intensely, and sometimes it brings a small tear of joy to the corner of my eye, escaping as a visual expression of my gratitude.

Without light nothing exists, and there is no more liberty. With it everything is present, simple, precise, and matter to think about, be it a grain of flesh or flesh of stone: it is a marvellous present offered us to gather the pictures and sensations which help us to understand better others and ourselves.

It is a sin not to acknowledge it; it is our duty to make it understood—and photography is here to help us do it. I would even say that it is here to make us rediscover the "spiritual" way to which so many young people aspire and from which our stupid world separates them as well as ourselves. Since I saw the "cabbage leaf" as photographed by Weston, I have had a much greater respect for the cabbage. . . .

Photography helped me to rediscover the leaf of a tree, then the tree itself, then the landscape of which it is a part and the man who comes to speak with it or to rest in its shadow.

The look of that man made me understand that he had many things to teach me—about himself, his life, his problems which are also mine: rich with the lessons received since antiquity, passing through the Middle Ages, he made me understand that his experience could be of some use to me; he called my attention to this rapport between surfaces and proportions arising from nature and pure science and ruled by a simple mechanism which is the very means of communication of all time.

Finally, this man made me understand that the same rapport must also exist spontaneously in any work, artistic or not, so that man may perceive it; otherwise, he rejects it as he rejects physically a bitter perfume, a sour fruit, a harsh noise or contact with lifeless flesh.

There is no doubt that the game of proportions in any work created by the hand of a man known as an artist is nothing less than the transposition of certain laws of equilibrium and relationship in which we find a permanent example in all living organisms put on earth by the "prodigious clock-maker" of whom Voltaire spoke. Fatuity makes us blind to everything that is obvious and to that which is offered daily and *freely* to each of us.

To me, photography is now one of the rare means by which we can make man understand the stupidity of his megalomania and *wash* humanity clean of this sin of pride, but to come to it we must learn again how to look at things humbly and without hate, respecting man and everything that surrounds him, even far beyond our unreliable eyes.

Science, art, light, mysticism—they will doubtless be the essential components of our next civilization: photography comes in its time to help us to this desirable evolution. Light, essential to photography, reveals the truth. Plato wrote, more than two thousand years ago, "Beauty is the splendor of truth."

—Jean Dieuzaide

*   *   *

If anyone can be said to be at one with photography, it is surely Jean Dieuzaide. Not only, like many others, has he devoted his entire life to photography, but he has also made himself its apostle. Where others strive for their own interest and for personal success, Dieuzaide struggles for photography—so that it may be better understood, so that it may be better defended, so that, at last, it may enjoy an appropriate status among the arts.

Dieuzaide is, however, first of all a photographer, and one of the characteristics of his career is the great variety of photographic styles in which he has practiced. He began to establish a reputation as a recorder of events with his portrait of General de Gaulle in Toulouse in 1944. As an illustrator he has excelled in descriptive regional photography; he has collaborated for many years with a variety of writers on books about the regions of France and other countries. He has been an industrial photographer and an advertising photographer. Artistically eclectic, he has also been technically ingenious. In 1949, for example, he had a water-tight box constructed to his own specifications so that he might shoot under water. His taste for action has also led him to aerial photography. And he must be one of the few photographers (maybe the only photographer) to have taken photos from astride the shoulders of a tightrope walker: "The Marriage of the Tightrope Walkers" (1954), published in *Life.* Given this range of activity, it is not surprising that his archives contain nearly 300,000 pictures, 6 x 6, 24 x 36, color and black-and-white, all appropriately catalogued.

Yet if Dieuzaide has excelled in all genres, and has been recognized by an impressive series of awards, there are still high points in his work—his architectural photographs, for example. They bear witness—whether they are of industrial architecture, the architecture of landscape or the architecture of objects—to his vast culture and to the perfection of his vision in relation to the composition of masses. Also noteworthy are the products of his passion for the region of his birth, the southwest. Long before it was fashionable to do so, he felt all the strength and sincerity of regional life; he was an early ecologist and never lost contact with nature, the most humble manifestations of which are celebrated in his photographs.

Emotion plays a great part in his work, emotion continually contained, expressed in the very great sensuality of the photographs. Dieuzaide belongs to that generation of photographers who brought great love to photography: expression, essentially in black-and-white, passes through, as it were, a complete mastery of technique, from the taking of a shot to the work in the laboratory, in the service of sensitivity. To the formal perfection of the composition is added a restitution of the subject in all its graininess or smoothness. Dieuzaide's photographs are very tactile; they invite touch, a caress. The sensuality which seeps from the sensitive surface is present in all his photography, but it finds its most complete achievement in the work entitled *My Adventure with Pitch.* From 1956 to 1960 he concentrated on this work, creating a series of photographs of rare sensual abstraction and strength, which he did not show publicly until 1968. This work reveals one of his most particular characteristics, his vision of a nature of symbolic significance beyond form, beyond literal content. His pictures bear witness to that mysterious exchange produced in nature: the lowliest vegetable, the dankest marsh, speak to us of totality, of beauty within which Dieuzaide sees the manifestation of God.

The year 1971 marked a turning point in his career. Since then he has more and more deserted his own work to devote himself to the social activity of exhibitions and the publication of texts and manifestos. A sad choice, because an artist who has not completed his own creation remains continually torn by his need to produce new images. The time he has devoted to the popularization of photography—notably at the Galerie du Château d'Eau in Toulouse, opened in 1974, where so far there have been more than 100 exhibitions—has taken away the freedom necessary for artistic work. It remains to be seen whether the need to invent obstacles is a process peculiar to Jean Dieuzaide's creative methods, whether those obstacles are the difficulty against which he must now struggle to reach his own emotional resources.

—Ginette Bléry

DITYVON, Claude.

Nationality: French. **Born:** La Rochelle, 12 March 1937. **Education:** Attended technical school in La Rochelle; self-taught in photography. **Family:** Married Christiane Le Rumeur in 1966; son: Thomas. **Career:** Photographer since 1968. Founder Member, Viva Photo agency, Paris, 1972-85; Co-Director of Viva, 1981-82. Since 1986, freelance photographer, Paris. **Recipient:** Prix Niepce, 1970; Fondation Nationale de la Photographie Award, 1976; City of Paris Award, 1978. **Address:** 24 Avenue Edison, 75013 Paris, France.

Individual Exhibitions:

1970	Maison de Jeunes du 5ème, Paris (retrospective)
	Visage de la Ville, Maison de la Culture, Chalon-sur-Saône, France
1972	Musée d'Art Moderne (ARC), Paris (retrospective)
1974	Photogalerie, Paris (retrospective)
1975	*Regard sur un Exil,* Maison de la Culture, Bobigny, St. Denis, France
1977	*L'Homme et le Travail,* Maison de la Culture, La Rochelle, France
	Presence, Maison de la Culture, La Rochelle, France
1978	*Territoire d'Enfance,* Maison de la Culture, La Rochelle, France
	La Marée Noire, Maison de la Culture, Rennes, France
	Un Jour comme les Autres, Hôpital Universitaire, Limoges, France
	Dityvon, Bibliothèque Nationale, Paris (retrospective)
1979	*Presence,* Musée du Mans, Le Mans, France Maison des Jeunes, Angers, France (retrospective)
	Musée du Châtellerault, France (retrospective)
1980	*Portrait d'une Ville,* Maison des Jeunes, Châtellerault, France
	Centre Culturel, Rabat, Morocco (retrospective)
	Maison des Jeunes, Nanterre, France (retrospective)
1981	Centre Formation Technologique, Gobelin, Paris
	Les Heros du Moment, Espace Canon, Paris (toured France)
	Fotografiska Museet, Stockholm (retrospective)
	Portraits, Galerie Canon, Paris
1982	*L'Homme et le Travail,* toured France
	Recherches Personnelles, Centre d'Art Contemporain, Montbéliard, France
1985	*Album de Tournage,* Galerie Canon, Paris (toured France)
1986	*Humeurs de la Ville,* Douchy-les-Mines, CRP-Nord Pas de Calais, France
	A Propos de Cannes, Centre d'Art et de Culture de Marne la Vallée; Maison du temps de libre, Torcy; Librairie Actes Sud, Arles, France
	Album de Tournage, Maison des Arts, Montbéliard; Centre culturel de Sain-Nazaire, France
1987	*Monographie,* Centre de la photographie, Geneva
	Mes Préférées de 1986, Galerie Sillages, Paris
1988	*Mai 1968,* La Chambre Claire, Paris; Musée de Charleroi, Belgium
	Les immigrés, Bibliothèque Agagon, Fontenay-sous-Bois, France
	Album de Tournage, Espace des Arts, Châlon-sur-Saône, France
1989	*Monographie,* Centre Social Europe, St Quentin, France
1990	*Au-delà des apparences,* Culture commune, Béthune, France
1991	*Canal du Nord. Béthune,* Centre régional Nord-Pas-de-Calais, France
1992	*Canal du Nord,* Onyx, L'éspace culturel de Saint-Herblain, France
1993	*Balade en Red Star,* Conseil Général de la Seine-St-Denis, Bobigny, France
1993-94	*Monographie 1967-1993,* L'Espace photographique de Paris, Paris audio-visuel, Paris; Fondation Charles Comte, Mérignac, France
1994	*Hommes au travail,* Espace Louise Michel, Lille, France
	Portrait de Châlon-sur-Saône, Photographie de 1970, Espace des Arts, Châlon-sur-Saône, France
	Album de Tournage, Douchy-les-Mines, France

Selected Group Exhibitions:

1973	*Viva: Familles en France,* Galleria Il Diaframma, Milan (travelled to the French Consulate, New York; The Photographers' Gallery, London; International Cultureel Centrum, Antwerp; and Optica Gallery, Montreal)
1976	*Les Français en Vacances,* Musée du Lyon
1977	*Six Photographes en Quête de Banlieu,* Centre Georges Pompidou, Paris
	Photos from Viva, Side Gallery, Newcastle upon Tyne
1978	*Beaubourg vu par six photographes,* Centre Beaubourg, Paris (and world tour)
1979	*Paris 1979: Les Parisiens,* Salon de la Photo, Paris
1980	*Jeune Photographie,* Château Lumière, Lyon, France
1981	*Viva,* Centre Culturel, Tunis
1982	*Les Français en Vacances,* Centre Georges Pompidou, Paris
1983	*Immigrés,* Centre Georges Pompidou, Paris
1987	*Mois du sport,* Conseil général Seine-St-Denis, Bobigny, France
	Marne-la-Valée. Les images, Ecole Essie, Centre d'action culturelle, Torcy, France
1988	*Regards sur les musées,* Centre régional Nord-Pas-de-Calais, France
1989	*La Navale,* Musée d'Art moderne, Dunkerque, France
1990	*Jazz comme une image,* Banlieues Bleues, conseil général de la Seine-St-Denis, France
	25 ans Prix Niepce 1955-1990, Musée d'Art contemporain, Dunkerque, France
	Sept Regards, Sept Villes—Fete de l'Humanite, France
	Quatre Saisons de la ruralité dans le Tarn, Centre Culturel, Albi, France
1991	*Portrait de la création photographique. Région Nord-Pas-de-Calais,* Centre culturel de Vitré, France
1992	*La Mission photograpique transmarche,* Galerie du Forum, rez-de-chaussée, Centre Pompidou, Paris
	Photos de classes et autres enfances, Maison de la photo, Maison du Geste et de l'Image, Paris
1993	*Le chantier et les hommes,* Centre d'information, Bibliothèque de France, Paris

Collections:

Bibliothèque Nationale, Paris; Fond National d'Art Contemporain, Paris; Musée Nièpce, Châlon sur Saône, France; Bibliothèque Municipale, La Rochelle, France; Arthothèque Agora, Evry, France; Centre Culturel Régional Nord Pas de Calais, Douchy-les Mines, France; Rencontres internationales de la Photographie, Arles, France; Musée de la photographie de Charleroi, Belgium; Paris audiovisuel, Maison Européenne de la Photographie, Paris.

Publications:

By DITYVON: Books—*Visages de la Cité,* edited by H. Calba, Paris 1972; *Etrepilly-Glasherz,* with text by Hans J. Scheurer, Cologne 1975; *La Marée Noire,* Paris 1978; *Un Jour Comme les Autres,* Limoges, France 1978; *Gens de La Rochelle,* Paris 1979; *59 Auteurs de Bande Dessinee,* with Christiane Raimond-Dityvon, Paris 1981; *Basket,* Limoges, France 1983; *Album de*

Cherbourg, France, **1990.** Photograph ©Claude Dityvon.

Tournages, Paris 1985; *Douchy-les-Mines*, text by Denis Roche, 1986; *la Navale*, Dunkerque 1988; *Mai 68*, text by Renaud, Paris, 1988; *Dityvon*, St Quentin 1989; *Au-delà des apparences*, text by Alain Demouzon, Calais, 1990; *Dityvon. Monographie 1967-1993*, Paris, 1993. **Films**—*Est-ce ainsi que les Hommes Vivent*, 1976; *Un Jour comme les Autres*, 1977; *Basket*, 1983; *Le couloir, Patrick*, with Catherine Deneuve, 1994.

On DITYVON: Books—*Dityvon*, exhibition catalogue, Paris 1978; *Un Jour comme les Autres*, exhibition catalogue, Limoges, France 1978; *Paris 1979*, exhibition catalogue, by Christian Caujolle, Paris 1979; *Jeune Photographie*, exhibition catalogue, with introduction by Bernard Chardere, Paris 1980. **Articles**—"Claude Raimond-Dityvon" by Robert Salbitani in *Progresso Fotografico* (Milan), February 1974; "Le Régard Politique de Dityvon" by André Laude in *Quotidien de Paris*, October 1974; "Photographe du Non-Evenement" by Yves Bourde in *Le Monde* (Paris), 16 October 1974; "Etrepilly" by Christian de Bartillat in *Nouveau Photo-Cinema* (Paris), October 1974; "Régard sur un Exil" by Jean-Marie Dunoyer in *Le Monde* (Paris), 22 June 1975; "Raimond-Dityvon" in *Zoom* (Paris), March 1976; "Claude Raimond-Dityvon" in *Creative Camera* (London), July 1977; "Un Photographe en Limousin" by Liliane Boyer in *Nouveau Photo-Cinema* (Paris), February 1978; "Le Monteur d'Ours" by Christian de Bartillat in *Zoom* (Paris), March 1978; "May 1968" in *Photo* (Paris), May 1978; "Une Emotion Minimale" by Hervé Guibert in *Le Monde* (Paris), 18 October 1978; "Dityvon" by André Laude in *Nouvelles Litteraires* (Paris), October 1978; "Hommes au Travail" in *Grand Angle* (Lyons), October 1978; "Dityvon" by Ghislaine de la Villeguerin in *Photo-Reporter* (Paris), July/August 1979; "Dix tournaged de Dityvon" by Louis Skorecki, Serge Daney in *Libération*, December,1985; in *L'Express* by Nadine Descendre, January 1986; "Douchy n'est pas Venise" in *Le Monde*, 25 December 1986; "Les enfants secrets de Dityvon" by Louis Skorecki in *Libération*, February 1990; "Une ville, deux regards. Cherbourg." by Michel Besnier in *L'Humanité Dimanche*, September 1990; "Le mystère Dityvon" in *Libération*, 9 April 1991; "Canal du Nord. La Nonchalante" by Alain Demouzon in *L'Humanité Dimanche*, June 1991; "Voyage sur terrain de foot" in *L'Humanité Dimanche*, 18 February 1993; "Dityvon" by Dominique Graessler in *Photographie Magazine*, December 1993; "L'échappée belle" in *Le Photographe*, December/January 1994; "Un nostalgieque inclassable" by Michel Guerrin in *Le Monde*, 8 Janaury 1994.

*

I want to assume entirely my function as a professional photographer, yet at the same time I wish to be someone who walks around, a man among men.

To go beyond the created photo that is an end in itself, I want, with the help of photographic art, to convey the ideology of an economic and political system.

Initially, at the beginning of my career, I wished to do what one could call social reporting. Now, I want to express the inexpressible, to convey that incommunicability that restrains the individual, to go beyond the anecdotal for a deeper truth—the importance of the unsaid, of atmosphere, of the impalpable.

—Dityvon

*   *   *

Claude Dityvon did not come to photography until 1967 when he was already 30. One of the paradoxes of the man (and not the least of them) is that he is a reporter who does not like photo-journalism; he thinks that the press photographer has a tendency to produce stereotype or shock photos of superficially treated subjects. Yet Dityvon was one of the instigators of the revival of the profession of the photo-reporter: he was one of the founders of the now famous Viva agency in Paris.

The paradox is explainable. The goal of his work is a new kind of photojournalism, and that goal is two-fold. The photograph must involve a "responsible" look at reality; it should not be the means to a "scoop," but rather, an effort to go to the depths of everyday existence, to show the ways in which the ordinary contains the marvellous. He attempts, therefore, a sociological approach to reality without forfeiting its poetry. Also, he does not forget that photography is itself a creator, that it brings about a certain point of view, that, as a consequence, one must not forget the formal exigencies of craft. And, in the manner of Goya, he believes that the horror, whatever it may

be, cannot be disassociated from the beauty. His work is rather like the performance of a tightrope walker: it involves rapt attention to a particular activity, yet that activity is also the means of expression of being.

Dityvon's work comprises a variety of in-depth reportages: miners; fishermen; May 1968; families in France; a chronicle of a village in the Paris region; the black tide of 1978; La Rochelle. . . . This poet of the banal and the ordinary has also produced films, audiovisual montage and animation—to all of which he brings the same deep commitment. To help others to see, to teach them to discover their surroundings with new eyes, to teach them to discover their own personal sensibility—these are all parts of the task of the photographer as Dityvon conceives it.

Space and time meet in his photos to create slices of everyday life of rare density. There are always many things happening in his photos; they succeed in being a concentrate. The scenes unfold on several planes, and space achieves a depth rarely attained in photography. The photo ceases to be a flat surface of two dimensions and includes a third dimension—an essential dimension, but one that it is very difficult to create—call it the complexity of life. Each picture encloses confrontations, a game of glances. Lines of force are therefore created which translate themselves as broken lines that intersect at the interior of the field, creating there a mysterious but compelling dynamic. The exchanges, the fleeting glances, create a passage to the interior of the picture, evoking the space of non-communication. This space is not particularly dramatic, and it is not agonizing; simply, each person is about his own business. A part of life has been photographed, the most banal, that of the everyday, made up of affections and oversights, desires and unexpressed dreams: it is life at the limits of consciousness that this master of photographic art succeeds in rendering perceptible to us.

—Ginette Bléry

DJORDJEVIĆ, Miodrag (Borislav).

Nationality: Yugoslavian. **Born:** Valjevo, 7 December 1919. **Education:** Attended high school in Negotin, 1935-39; studied medicine at the University of Belgrade, 1939-49, M.D. 1968; self-taught in photography. **Military Service:** Served in the Yugoslav National Liberation Movement, 1941-45. **Family:** Married Branka Petrovic in 1956 (divorced, 1968); married Dusanka Miljkovic in 1978; son: Nenad. **Career:** Freelance artist and photographer, Belgrade, since 1947. Professor of Photography, School of Design, Belgrade, 1968-78. Since 1978, Head of the Photography and Film Department, Medical Center, University of Belgrade. **Recipient:** Janez Puhar Award, *Yugoslav Photography Exhibition*, 1953; First Prize, *International Exhibition of Photography*, FIAP, Cologne, 1956; First Prize, *Exposicion Internacional Universitaria de Fotografia de Montant*, Madrid, 1957; Golden Plate Award, *Yugoslav Photography Exhibition*, Osjek, 1958; Artist of Photography Award, 1961, and Award of Excellence, 1972, Federation Internationale de l'Art Photographique (FIAP); ULUPUS Award, Belgrade, 1963; Master of Photography Award, Association of Photographers of Yugoslavia, 1969; *October Salon* Award, Belgrade, 1975; City of Belgrade Award, 1986. **Agents:** Singidunum, Knez Mihajlova 40, 11000 Belgrade; and B. Moravec's Gallery, rua Augusta, Sao Paulo, Brazil. **Address:** Studio—Stanka Vraza 6, 11000 Belgrade, Yugoslavia.

Individual Exhibitions:

1951	*Mountains*, Dom žljeznicara, Belgrade
1952	*Landscapes*, Stanko Vraz, Belgrade
1957	Grafički kolektiv, Belgrade
1961	*Wystawa fotografi*, Cultural House, Nova Huta, Poland
1963	*Nature-Man*, Museum of Applied Arts, Belgrade
	Abstract-Concrete, City Museum, Subotica, Yugoslavia (travelled to the City Museum, Rovinj, Yugoslavia, 1964)
1966	*Retrospective 1944-1966*, Nadezda Petrović, Cačak, Yugoslavia
	10 Nudes and a Portrait, Grafički kolektiv, Belgrade
	Somatic Metaphors, City Museum, Rovinj, Yugoslavia

1967	*Vystava 80 fotografi,* Dum Panu z Kunštatu, Brno, Czechoslovakia
1968	*A Woman and Stone,* Kamen mali, Cavtat, Yugoslavia
1970	*Photo-Design,* Applied Arts Gallery, Belgrade
	Artists' Portraits, GUF Gallery, Zagreb
1971	*Portraits of Artists of Belgrade,* Museum of Applied Arts, Belgrade (travelled to the Cultural House, Cačak, Yugoslavia, 1972)
1972	*Kunst-fotos,* Stadtmuseum, Erlangen, West Germany
	Students' Centre, Novi Sad, Yugoslavia
1976	*Nascimento de Megalopole,* Avenida das Nacoes Gallery, Brasilia (travelled to the Tower Gallery, Nis, Yugoslavia, 1977)
1977	*100 Photographics and Photopictures,* Museu de Arte Moderna, Sao Paulo
1978	*Luminokinets,* Museum of Modern Arts, Belgrade (travelled to the Museum of Modern Arts, Skopje, Yugoslavia, 1979, and Gallery of Modern Arts, Zagreb, 1980)
1979	Gallery of Arts, Shanghai
1985	Cvijeta Zuzorić Gallery, Belgrade (retrospective; travelled to the Collegium Artisticum Gallery, Sarajevo, Yugoslavia)

Selected Group Exhibitions:

1952	*1st Exhibition of Yugoslav Photographers,* Dom Sindikata, Belgrade
1958	*Photos by ULUPUS Members,* Museum of Applied Arts, Belgrade
1965	*October Salon of Arts and Applied Arts,* Museum of Applied Arts and Cvijeta Gallery, Belgrade (and annually until 1979)
	ULUPUS Exhibition, Museum of Applied Arts and Cvijeta Gallery, Belgrade (and annually until 1979)
1969	*Contemporary Yugoslav Photography,* Nadežda Petrović, Cačak, Yugoslavia
1970	*Serbian Photography,* Museum of Applied Arts, Belgrade
1974	*5th International Biennale of Posters,* National Museum, Warsaw
1975	*BIO 6,* Gospodarsko rastavišče, Ljubljana, Yugoslavia
	ZGRAF '75, Gallery of Arts, Zagreb
1978	*1st Triennial of Plastic Arts,* Collegium Artisticum, Sarajevo, Yugoslavia
1979	*Photographic Media,* Museum of Modern Arts, Belgrade

Collections:

Museum of Applied Arts, Belgrade; Museum of Modern Arts, Belgrade; Serbian Academy of Science and Arts, Belgrade; Museum of Modern Arts, Skopje, Yugoslavia; Gallery of Contemporary Arts, Zagreb; Monastery Chilander, Athos, Greece; Museu de Arte Contemporante, Sao Paulo; Museu de Arte Moderna, Sao Paulo.

Publications:

By DJORDJEVIĆ: Books—*Studenica,* with an introduction by Mandić Sveta, Belgrade 1963; *Rovinj,* with an introduction by Anton Paulentić, Belgrade 1963; *Art on the Soil of Yugoslavia: From Prehistoric Times to the Present,* with others, edited by France Stele, Belgrade and Sarajevo 1971; *Istorija Beograda,* 3 volumes, edited by Vasa Cubrilović, Belgrade 1974; *Icônes Byzantines,* edited by Paul Johannes Müller, Paris 1977; *Hilander,* with an introduction by Pavle Savić, Belgrade 1978; *Tisnikar,* with an introduction by Nebojša Tomasevic, Belgrade 1979; *China,* with others, with an introduction by No Myth, Belgrade and New York 1980; *Traditional Arts and Crafts in Yugoslavia,* with text by N. Pantelic, Belgrade 1985; *Famous Byzantine Frescos,* with text by Paul Muller, Munich 1986. Articles—"Fotograf mora da napravisliku" in *Fotokino revija* (Belgrade), May 1971; "Fotografija Anastasa Jovanovića" in *Sveska 32 Galerije SANU* (Belgrade), August 1977; "Jusuf Karč" in *Katalog izlozbe FSJ* (Belgrade), November 1979; "Anastas Jovanović, the First Serbian Photographer" in *History of Photography* (University Park, Pennsylvania), April 1980.

On DJORDJEVIĆ: Books—*42 Photographs: Nature-Man* by Mića Popović, Belgrade 1963; *Portret: beogradskih umetnika* by Lazar Trifunović, Belgrade 1971; *Portreti umetnika* by Zvonimir Golob, Zagreb 1972; *Foto-grafica e foto quadros de Miodrag Djordjević* by Oto Bihalji Merin, Sao Paulo 1977; *Razgovor sa Miodragom Djordjićem* by Irina Subotić, Belgrade 1978. Articles—"Prirodačovek" by Dragoslav Djordjević in *Borba* (Belgrade), April 1963; "Pogled ptice" by Mića Popović in *Umetnost* (Belgrade), April 1968; "Miodrag Djordjević" by Masaru Katzumie in *Graphic Design* (Tokyo), December 1975; "Izložba Dr. Miodraga Djordjevića u Brazilu" by Grozdana Sarčević in *Industrijsko Oblikovanje* (Belgrade), April 1976; "Miodrag Djordjević" by Ernestina Karman in *Folha de Tarde* (Sao Paulo), April 1977; "Miodrag Djordjević" by Alberto Beuttenmüller in *Visao* (Rio de Janeiro), April 1977; "Fotoslikarstvo Miodraga Djordjevića" by Gordana Harašić in *Covjek i prostor* (Zagreb), June 1977; "Povodom izložbe u Muzeju moderne umetnosti u Sao Paulu" by Oto Bihalji Merin in *Umetnost* (Belgrade), October 1977; "Miodrag Djordjević" by Josip Depolo in *Oko* (Zagreb), August 1980; "Retrospectiva Miodraga Djordjevica" by Balsa Raicevic in *Odjek* (Sarajevo), May 1985; "Nadrealna vizija sveta" by Gordana Vidakovic in *Foto-kino revija* (Belgrade), June 1985; "Miodrag Djordjevic" by Goran Malic in *Oko* (Zagreb), June 1985.

*

If you ask me why I take photographs, that is like asking me why I breathe. It is through photography that I have for many years studied life and the dynamics of existence; I react to the signs, symbols and sounds that surround me. My initial impulse is to photograph everything that I see and also that which I do not see but which I feel is hidden within a second layer of the visible, everything that moves and yet does not move at all, everything that I love or hate, that inspires or irritates me. To me it is still a game, and only a game, my game of life.

From my earliest days I have felt the need to express myself through the fine arts: I learned to draw, I studied sculpture, so that I would finally have an eye capable of seeing, of knowing.

All my sense impressions become images; music, touch, taste convert spontaneously into lively pictures.

I create by playing, but that does not exclude my accumulated experience and knowledge; I experiment consciously, I search, I test, I make mistakes, I reject, I adopt.

I sort out my negatives into related groups and come back to them when I am free from the business and social activities; in peace and with complete concentration, I select and bring together the results of similar experiments and in this way my various cycles of photographs are born. They are never definitive, and afterwards, in my work, they intersect, cross fertilize and generate new ones. . . . Cycles: *Somatic Metamorphoses, Abstraction Equal to the Concrete, Poetic Fantasy, Luminokinetic,* and others.

Once the photo-negative process is completed, I work on the photograph with different techniques and technologies. I think that everything in art is allowed that contributes to the artist's expression. Personally I use anything that can ennoble and humanize the photograph.

I pay attention to size because I think that it is an important part of the composition. I look very carefully for the true dimension of each image destined for exhibition, also taking into account its relationship in space.

Dealing with photography in general—I think that it must finally break away from the dogmatic and academic norms that have imposed limitations on it for years and prevented its development. It is essential that photography should quite freely start permeating through the great family of the fine arts, while still retaining the original characteristics of the photographic medium.

—Miodrag Djordjević

*   *   *

The search for a photography that will be not only an extension of the eye but also an extension of the mind could be said to be the constant preoccupation of Miodrag Djordjević, an explorer in the field of imaginative photography.

Djordjevic's early fascination with photography was caused by mountains, by the grandeur of the Alpine landscape, to which he devoted his first complete photographic cycle nearly 30 years ago. That first step was within the tradition of pictorial photography, but he soon turned his attention to the depiction of people in a realistic manner. At the same time, he began a new cycle of photographs of macro-structures, which led him to the thesis that "abstract equals concrete." From then on, the combination of the two visions, the realistic and the abstract, became the principal concern of his work. Balancing the two extremes, and juxtaposing objective with imaginative, constructive with destructive, static with dynamic, humanistic with spiritual, he came very close to the limits of graphic art. In his Laser cycle, he drew patterns and lines by means of various light sources, then subsequently dyed his photographic canvasses by hand.

From time to time Djordjević has exhibited the results of his experiments, arranging several thematic cycles for viewing at once. Because of his continuous searching, the cycles are not necessarily sharply delimited; they permeate each other, some cycles originate others. Yet, within this continuous change, there is a single constant, his joy in experimentation. Djordjević's favorite cycle is fantastic, a kind of poetic fiction. In it he combines two or more different and unexpected contents by means of multiple overprinting, and in this way creates a strange, surrealistic atmosphere. A small but very interesting part of this cycle consists of portraits obtained by reverse double printing of a single negative. With this method he creates non-existing physiognomies of a peculiar and striking expression.

Djordjević's efforts in photographic exploration were crowned by a very successful one-man show at the Museu de Arte Moderna in Sao Paulo in 1977. Since then he has been involved with new cycles and, simultaneously, with new means of visual communication, as well as with illustrating books about modern and ancient art, especially Byzantine painting and, most recently, Chinese art and architecture.

—Nada Grcević

DLUBAK, Zbigniew.

Nationality: Polish. **Born:** Radomsko, 26 April 1921. **Education:** Self-taught in photography. **Career:** Independent painter since 1946, and freelance photographer since 1948. Chief Editor, *Fotografia* magazine, Warsaw, 1953-72; Member, Editorial Committee, *Polish Art Review,* 1971-72. Founder Member, Grupa 55 artists group, 1955-56; Co-Founder, Galeria Permafo, Wroclaw, 1970-74, President, Union of Polish Art Photographers (ZPAP), 1979-81. Currently living in Paris. **Recipient:** Kosciuszko Foundation Scholarship, U.S.A., 1972. **Address:** 43 Av. du General Gallieni, F-92, 190 Meudon, France and Pulawska 24a. M. 26, 02-512 Warsaw, Poland.

Individual Exhibitions:

1948   Club of Young Artists and Scientists, Warsaw
1967   *Ikonosfera 1,* Contemporary Gallery, Warsaw
        Malarstwo/Painting, Galeria Krzysztofory, Cracow
1970   International Press and Book Club Ruch, Warsaw
        Ikonosfera 2, Galeria Od Nowa, Poznan, Poland
1971   *Mutanty* and *Relop,* Galeria Bod Mona Liza, Wroclaw (with
            Natalia Lach-Lachowicz and Andrzej Lachowicz; travelled
            to the Contemporary Gallery, Warsaw)
        Tautologie, Galeria Permafo, Wroclaw
        Contemporary Gallery, Warsaw
1973   *Ocean,* Galeria Permafo, Wroclaw
1974   *Gestykulacje,* Gallery "Znak," Bialystok, Poland
        Galeria 72, Chelm, Poland
1975   *Fotografia,* Galeria Labirynt, Lublin, Poland
        Systemy, Galeria Remont, Warsaw
1976   *Systemy efemeryczne,* Salon of Contemporary Art, Lodz
1978   *Desymbolizacje,* Museum of Fine Arts, Lodz; Mala Galeria,
            Warsaw; Muzeum Sztuki, Lodz
        Systemy, Galeria Znak, Bialystok
        Pokaz prac/Works, Galeria Permafo, Wroclaw
1981   *Zbigniew Dlubak: Fotografia,* Institute Polonais, Paris
        National Museum, Warsaw (retrospective)
        Photographie Artistique, Polish Institute, Paris

1988   *Asymetria,* Mala Galeria, Warsaw
1989   *Assymetry,* Gallery PAAS, New York
1990   *Metamorphoses,* Librarie Galerie, Paris
1992   *Zbigniew Dlubak—prace z lat 1965-1991/Works from 1965-
            1991,* Centrum Sztuki Wspolczesnej Zamek Ujazowski,
            Warsaw
        Asymetria, Galeria Foto-Medium-Art, Wroclaw
1993   *Przeciw stereotypom/Against Stereotypes,* International Cultur-
            al Centre Gallery, Cracow

Selected Group Exhibitions:

1948   *Modern Polish Photography: Polish Association of Photogra-
            phy,* Club of Young Artists and Scientists, Warsaw
1957   *Exhibition of Modern Art,* Zacheta Galeria, Warsaw
1964   *Polnische Kunst heute,* Bochum, Kassel
1965   *All-Poland Exhibition of Applied Photography,* Galeria
            Zacheta, Warsaw
1966   *All-Polish Exhibition of Utilitarian Photography,* Zacheta
            Galeria, Warsaw
1968   *Fotografia Subiektywna/Subjective Photography,* Krakow;
            Warsaw; Szczecin
1969   *Moderne Polnische Malerei und Grafik 1959-1969,* Berlin
1971   *Fotografowie poszukujacy/Searching Photographs,* Galeria
            Wspolczesna, Warsaw
1972   *NS New Situation,* Galeria Permafo, Wroclaw; Galeria
            Wspolczesna, Warsaw; Museum Sztuki, Lodz
        Modern Polish Photography, Patio Foundation, Geneva;
            Kunsthalle, Nuremberg
1973   *Permafo Group,* Galeria Remont, Warsaw
        Modern Polish Photography, New York; Chalon-sur-Saône;
            Kassel; Tokyo
1974   *Permafo Group,* Galerie Paramedia, West Berlin; CAYC, Club
            Universitario, La Plata
        Polish Art, The Hall Galleries, London
1975   *Modern Polish Photography,* Jose Clement Orosco Gallery,
            Mexico City
1976   *17 Contemporary Artists from Poland,* Albright-Knox Art
            Gallery, Buffalo, New York; Polish Contextual Artists,
            CEAC Gallery, Toronto
        Contextual Art, Gallerie St Petri, Lund, Sweden
1979   *Fotografia Polska 1839-1979,* International Center of
            Photography, New York (travelled to the Museum of
            Contemporary Art, Chicago, Zacheta Galeria, Warsaw,
            Museum of Fine Arts, Lodz, and the Whitechapel Art
            Gallery, London, 1979-80)
1980   *Contact—From Agitation to Contemplation,* Palac Sztuki,
            Cracow; galeria Foto-Medium-Art, Wroclaw
        Medium and Recognition, Art Gallery, Tokyo
        Polish Painting, Finland
1981   *Photographie Polonaise 1900-1981,* Centre Georges
            Pompidou, Paris
1982   *Banque d'image pour la Pologne,* La Maison des
            Artistes, Paris
1984   *Wystawa Fotografii Wspolczesnej,* Galeria Zacheta, Warsaw
1985   *Modern Polish Art Photography,* Galeria Zacheta, Warsaw
1986   *Hommage à 1956,* Musée de Neuilly-sur-Seine
        Die Ecke, Galerie Hoffmann, Friedberg
        Polish Photography 1955-1984, Umeleckoprumyslove Muse-
            um, Prague
1988   *Die Ecke,* Museum in Sion, Switzerland
1989   *Frele Raum It,* Villa Toscana, Gmunden, Austria
        *150 Years of Photography in the Collection of the National
            Museum,* Wroclaw
        What is Photography? Galerie Manes, Prague
1990   *Hommage Stazewskiemu,* Galeria Studio, Warsaw
1992   *International Triennial of Drawing,* Wroclaw
        Permafo 1970-1981, Centrum Sztuki Wspolczesnej Zamek
            Ujazowski, Warsaw

Collections:

National Museum of Art, Warsaw; National Museum of Art, Poznan; National Museum of Art, Wroclaw; Museum of Contemporary Art, Lodz; Museum of Architecture, Wroclaw; Lublin Museum; Koszalin Museum; Chelm Museum; Mala Galeria, Warsaw; Stadtische Kunsthalle, Bochum, Germany; Museum of Modern Art, New York; Bibliothéque Nationale, Paris.

Publications:

By DLUBAK: Books—*Wybrane Teksty o Sztuce 1948-1977/Selected Text on Art 1948-1977,* Warsaw 1977; *Fotografia Permafo,* exhibition catalogue, Wroclaw 1977; *Desymbolizacje,* exhibition catalogue, Lodz, Poland 1978; *Asymetria,* exhibition catalogue, Warsaw 1988; *Rozmowa z Barbara Askanas o Galerii Kryzywe Kolo,* exhibition catalogue. Warsaw 1990; *Autoportrety,* text by Wieslawa Wierzchowska, Warsaw 1991; *150 Years of Polish Photography,* Warasaw 1991. **Articles**—"Zrozmyslan o fotografice" in *Swiat Fotografii* (Warsaw), nos. 9/10, 1948, no. 11, 1949; "Uwagi o sytuacji w fotografice polskiej" in *Fotografia* (Warsaw), no. 2, 1953; "Na marginesie IV Ogolnopolskiej Wystawy Fotografiki" in *Fotografia* (Warsaw), no. 7, 1954; "O Specyficznych Cechach Fotografiki" in *Fotografia* (Warsaw), no. 6, 1955; "O Fotografii Nowoczesney Avangardowosci" in *Fotografia* (Warsaw), no. 10, 1956; "O Metaforze Fotograficznej" in *Fotografia* (Warsaw), no. 1, 1957; "Patrzac na Fotografie," series of essays, in *Ty i Ja* (Warsaw), nos. 4-12, 1963, nos. 1-7, 1964; "Problemy Pogranicza Fotografii i Plastyki" in *Fotografia* (Warsaw), no. 12, 1966; "Podawac w Watpliwosc" in *Fotografia* (Warsaw), no. 8, 1969; statement in *Tautologie,* exhibition catalogue, Wroclaw 1971; "Sztuka Poza Swiaten Znaczen" in *Biuletyn ZPAP* (Warsaw), no. 3/4, 1976; "Uwagi o Sztuce i Fotografii" in *Odra* (Wroclaw), no. 6, 1977; "Nie martwi mnie, ze nie bede znany. . . . " in *Kontact,* Paris 1987.

On DLUBAK: Books—*Wsrod Polskich Mistrzow Kamery* by L. Grabowski, Warsaw 1964; *Przygody Plastyczne Fotografii* by U. Czartoryska, Warsaw 1965; *Od Pop-Artu do Sztuki Konceptualnej* by U. Czartoryska, Warsaw 1974; *Historia Fotografii Warszawskiej* by W. Zdzarski, Warsaw 1974; *Nowa Sztuka Polska 1945-1978* by A. Kepinska, Warsaw 1981; *Photographie d'avant-garde en Pologne,* exhibition catalogue, by Urszula Czartoryska, Paris 1981; *Fotografie in Europa Heute,* with text by Petr Tausk, Cologne 1982; *Dictionnaire des photographes,* by Carole Naggar, Paris 1982; *Who is Who in Poland,* Warsaw 1984; *Who is Who in the World,* 7th edition, Chicago 1984; *Encyclopédue Internationale des Photographes de 1849 a nos jours,* Geneva 1985; *Fotografia polska 1945-85,* with texts by Ryszard Bobrowski, Lech Lechowicz and Jerzy Busza, Gorzow Wielkopolski, Poland 1985; *Polska wspolczesna fotografia artystyczna,* exhibition catalogue, text by Adam Sobota, Warsaw 1985; *What is Photography,* exhibition catalogue, Prague 1989; *Galeria Krzywe Kolo,* exhibition catalogue, Warsaw 1990. **Articles**—"Spotkania Fotografii z Plastyka" by U. Czartoryska in *Fotografia* (Warsaw), no. 11, 1960; "Dlubak, Zbrozyna i Epizod G55" by J. Bogucki in *Kultura* (Warsaw), no. 6, 1966; "Gzlowiek z Kamera: Zbigniew Dlubak" by J. Garztecki in *Fotografia* (Warsaw), no. 12, 1976; "Tworzyno i Wyobraznia" by U. Czartoryska in *Projekt* (Warsaw), no. 1, 1969; "Tautologia Zbigniewa Dlubaka" by A. Dzieduszycki in *Fotografia* (Warsaw), no. 10, 1971; "Pseudoavangarda" by W. Borowski in *Kultura* (Warsaw), no. 12, 1975; "Systemy i Gestykulaoje" by J. Ladnowska in *Sztuka* (Warsaw), no. 5, 1976; "Zbigniew Dlubak" by J. Olek in *Nuri* (Wroclaw), no. 10, 1977; "Desymbolizaoja" by E.M. Malkowska in *Literatura* (Warsaw), no. 14, 1979; "The Eye of Poland" by Douglas Davis in *Newsweek* (New York), 13 August 1979; "Polish Photography" by Owen Edwards in *American Photographer* (New York), November 1979; "Fotografia Polska 1839-1979" by Ryszard Bobrowski in *Fotografia* (Warsaw), no. 3, 1980; "La Photographie Polonaise" by Chris Miller in *European Photography* (Gottingen), no. 7, 1981; "Tworcze Watpienie" by Jan Kowalski in *Kontakt* (Paris), XI 1987; "Seminarium Warszawskie" by Jerzy Olek in *Kontakt* (Paris), no. 4, 1989; "Living Through the Ages of Zbigniew Dlubak—Polish Photography" by Takuya Tsukahara in *Portfolio* (Tokyo), no. II-III, 1991; "Widzenie znaczace czyli o Dlubaku" by Jerzy Olek in *Exit* (Warsaw), no. 9, 1992; "Permafo" by Adam Sobota in *Format* (Wroclaw), no. 6-7, 1992; "Beyond the formal order. Remarks on the Art of Zbigniew Dlubak" by Andrzej Turowski, introduction by Marek Grygiel in exhibition catalogue *Zbigniew Dlubak—Works from 1965-1991* (Warsaw) 1992; "Against Stereotypes" by Adam Sobota and

"From Constructivism to Deconstruction" by Leszek Brogowski in exhibition catalogue *Against Stereotypes* (Cracow) 1993. **Film**—*Zywa Galeria* (An Alive Gallery), by Jozef Robakowski, 1975;

*   *   *

In 1948 an exhibition on *Modern Polish Photography* opened in Warsaw. In an introduction to the catalogue Zbigniew Dlubak wrote: "The convention of naturalism has exerted such strong pressure on our artistic consciousness that we are not courageous enough to eschew from art this unnecessary ballast, and reach for other more fruitful and not yet fully exploited means—the suggestiveness of forms and their associational value. Instead of treating these aspects marginally we should give them full expression and in them look for new potential in photography—to enrich its scope and raise it to a high standard of artistic expression."

Dlubak's artistic manifesto was based on a formal link between photography and its practical technique (with photographic paper as the basic creative element), yet he also linked it ideologically with the fine arts and even with more general cultural trends. Also the use of the intellect ("associational value") was emphasized as an essential element of creativity and of perception in photography. Dlubak followed this programme with few modifications throughout the post-war years.

His early photographs showed close-ups of small objects, strong enlargements of plant fibre, embryonic forms—in other words, the structure of the micro-world. These photographs, moving beyond the boundaries of legibility and at the same time full of a strange surrealistic atmosphere, consciously used poetic metaphor, exemplified by the titles of the photographs, such as "Children Dream about Birds," and by a series of illustrations to Pablo Neruda's poem "Magellan's Heart." Later Dlubak moved away from this surrealistic photography, presenting simple and banal, uninteresting, even ugly subjects. This series of photographs, conceived in opposition to current artistic fashion, bore the title "Existences."

The next significant trend in Dlubak's photography can be seen in the series "Ikonosfera" (Iconosphere; 1967). The most expressive work is "Ikonosfera 1," which consists of a labyrinth of chaotically suspended, "drying out" photographs representing nudes and other subjects of everyday life. This theme was an interesting attempt to use photography not only for recording single shots but also for recording a consciously treated, prearranged space, forcing the viewer into physical and intellectual contact with the elements of an artist's environment.

In Dlubak's photography of the 1970s, there is a domination of tendencies which urge a revision of the traditional image of photography (the photograph as a work of art) and the need to redefine its essence: this work is influenced by the conceptual art of Joseph Kosuth and his polemics. It started in 1970 with a series "Gestykulacje" (Gesticulations), followed by "Tautologie" and "Systemy" (Systems) in the next years. Dlubak concentrated increasingly on descriptions of the way art functions in particular cultural contexts, and this brought him to a revision of contemporary definitions and to a neutralization or even the outright destruction of traditionally established meanings in art. A significant role was played in these reductionist actions by the theory of unism painting created back in 1927 by Wladyslaw Strzeminski. Strzeminski contrasted rich baroque composition with unist composition based on the extreme simplicity and purity of elements making up a visual picture. Following this destructive direction, Dlubak created a series under the title "Desymbolizacje" (Desymbolization) where with the use of repetitions, distortions and deformations of highly meaningful and symbolic themes (taken, for example, from the history of painting or from the mythology of religion) he achieved works wherein the separate fragments of this theme interrelate, mutually eclipsing one another.

"In this way," he claims, "the general structure of art reveals itself. The new avant-garde should therefore be involved in experiments desymbolizing existing and new artworks, in all elements of their meaning. New works should create situations in which the desymbolization results from their structure and becomes the only sensible form of perception."

All of these works suggest that photography is a way of seeing the world in which artistic values are not inherently contained in a work of art, nor should they impose themselves on the subjective valuation of the viewer. Art is the process of forming an artistic idea, an idea which discloses itself with empty visual signs. Its value is defined through changing meanings which exist in a particular cultural context.

—Ryszard Bobrowski

DOISNEAU, Robert.

Nationality: French. **Born:** Gentilly, Seine, 14 April 1912. **Education:** Attended schools in Gentilly; studied lithography at the Ecole Estienne, Paris, 1926-29. **Military Service:** Served in the French Army Infantry, 1939-40, and with the French Resistance, 1940-45. **Family:** Married Pierrette Chaumaison in 1934; daughters: Annette and Francine. **Career:** Worked as an engraver and lithographer, Paris, 1929-31; photographer, beginning 1930: photographic assistant to André Vigneau, Paris, 1931-33; Industrial Photographer, Renault Car Company, Billancourt, Paris, 1934-39. Photojournalist and magazine photographer, working for *Excelsior, Point de Vue, Life, Fortune, Noir et Blanc, Paris-Match, Vogue* (1949-52), etc., Paris, beginning 1945: Member, Alliance Photo Agency, later known as Adep, Paris, 1945; Member, Rapho Agency, Paris, beginning 1946. **Recipient:** Kodak Prize, 1947; Niépce Prize, 1956; Grand Prix National de la Photographie, Paris, 1983. Chevalier, Légion d'Honneur, France, 1984. **Agent:** Rapho, 8 rue d'Alger, 75038 Paris, France. **Died:** 1 April 1994.

Individual Exhibitions:

1951   *Le Monde des Spectacles,* La Fontaine des Quatre Saisons, Paris
1959   Limelight Gallery, New York
1960   Art Institute of Chicago
1968   Bibliothèque Nationale, Paris
1972   International Museum of Photography, George Eastman House, Rochester, New York
1974   Galerie Municipale du Château d'Eau, Toulouse
           Vieille Charité, Marseilles
           Witkin Gallery, New York
1975   Galerie Bardawil, Paris
           La Galerie et Fils, Brussels
           Musée des Arts Décoratifs, Nantes, France Musée Réattu, Arles, France
1976   Photo Art, Basle
           Town Hall, Dieppe, France
1978   *Ne Bougeons Plus!,* Galerie Agathe Gaillard, Paris
           Witkin Gallery, New York
           Musée Nicéphore Niepce, Chalon-sur-Saône, France
1979   Musée Eugène Boudin, Honfleur, France
           Paris: Les Passants que Passent, Musée d'Art Moderne, Paris
           Quelques Secondes d'Éternité, Galerie Municipale du Château d'Eau, Toulouse
1981   Grapestake Gallery, San Francisco
           Gallery for Fine Photography, New Orleans
1983   Palace of Fine Arts, Beijing
           Portrait Exhibition, Tokyo
1987   *Saint Denis,* Musée Saint Denis, Paris
           Kyoto Museum, Japan
1988   Villa Médicis, Rome
1989   *Doisneau-Renault,* Grande Halle de la Villette, Paris
1990   *La Science de Doisneau,* Jardin des Plantes, Paris
1992   Retrospective, MOMA, Oxford
1994   Galerie du Château d'Eau, Toulouse
           Doisneau 40/44, Centre d'Histoire de la Résistance et de la Déportation, Lyon
1995   Musée Carnavalet, Paris

Selected Group Exhibitions:

1951   *5 French Photographers: Brassaï/Cartier-Bresson/Doisneau/ Izis/Ronis,* Museum of Modern Art, New York
1954   *Great Photographs,* Limelight Gallery, New York
1965   *6 Photographes de Paris,* Musée des Arts Décoratifs, Paris
1968   *L'Oeil Objectif,* Musée Cantini, Marselles (with Denis Brihat, Lucien Clergue, and Jean-Pierre Sudre)
1972   *Boubat/Brassaï/Cartier-Bresson/Doisneau/Izis/Ronis,* French Embassy, Moscow
1977   *6 Photographes en Quête de Banlieue,* Centre Georges Pompidou, Paris
1980   *The Imaginary Photo Museum,* Kunsthalle, Cologne
1982   *Counterparts: Form and Emotion in Photographs,* Metropolitan Museum of Art, New York (travelled to the Contemporary Arts Center, Cincinnati, Ohio; Dallas Museum of Fine Arts, Texas; San Francisco Museum of Modern Art; Corcoran Gallery, Washington, D.C.)
1984   *Subjektive Fotografie: Images of the 50s,* San Francisco Museum of Modern Art (travelled to the University of Houston, Texas; Museum Folkwang, Essen; Vasterbottens Museum, Umea; Kulturhuset, Stockholm; Saarland Museum, Saarbrucken; Palais des Beaux-Arts, Brussels)
1986   *The Animal in Photography 1843-1985,* The Photographers' Gallery, London

Collections:

Musée d'Art Moderne, Paris; Bibliothèque Nationale, Paris; Musée Nicéphore Niepce, Chalon-sur-Saône, France; Victoria and Albert Museum, London; Museum of Modern Art, New York; International Museum of Photography, George Eastman House, Rochester, New York; New Orleans Museum of Art; Center for Creative Photography, University of Arizona, Tucson; Metropolitan Museum of Art, New York.

Publications:

By DOISNEAU: Books—*Le Banlieue de Paris,* with text by Blaise Cendrars, Paris 1949, 1983; *Sortilèges de Paris,* with text by François Cali, Paris 1952; *Les Parisiens Tels Qu'ils Sont,* with text by Robert Giraud and Michel Ragon, Paris 1954; *Instantanées de Paris,* Paris 1955; *1,2,3,4,5—Compter en s'Amusant,* Lausanne 1955; *Paris Parade,* London 1956; *Pour que Paris Soit,* with text by Elsa Triolet, Paris 1956; *Gosses de Paris,* with text by Jean Donques, Paris 1956; *Nicolas Schöfer,* Neuchâtel, Switzerland 1963; *Marius le Forestier,* with text by Dominique Halévy, Paris 1964; *Le royaume d'argot,* with text by Robert Giraud, Paris 1965; *Epouvantables Épouvantails,* Paris 1965; *Catherine la danseuse,* with text by Michèle Manceaux, Paris 1966; *Témoins de la vie quotidienne,* with text by Roger Lecotte and Jacques Dubois, Paris 1971; *My Paris,* with text by Maurice Chevalier, New York 1972; *Le Paris de Robert Doisneau et Max-Pol Fouchet,* Paris 1974; *Manuel de St.-Germain des Prés,* with text by Boris Vian, Paris 1974; *La Loire,* Paris 1978; *Trois Secondes d'Éternité,* Paris 1979, as *Robert Doisneau, Photographs,* London 1980; *Doisneau,* portfolio, New York 1979; *L'Enfant et la Colombe,* with text by James Sage, Paris 1979; *Robert Doisneau,* Paris 1980; *Le Mal de Paris,* with text by Clement Lepidis, Paris 1980; *Passages et galeries du 19e Siecle,* with text by Bernard Delvaille, Paris 1981; *Ballade pour violoncello et chambre noir,* with text by Maurice Baquet, Paris 1981; *Robert Doisneau,* edited by Jean-Francois Chevrier, Paris 1983; *Pour saluer Cendrars,* with text by Jérome Camilly, 1987; *Les Grandes Vacances,* with text by Daniel Pennac, Paris 1990; *Portrait de Saint-Denis,* Paris 1992; *Rue Jacques Prévert,* 1992; *Les Enfants de Germinal,* (with Charbonnier and Ronis) with text by Cavanna, Paris 1993; *La Vie de Famille,* with text by Daniel Pennac, Paris 1993; *Doisneau 40/44,* with text by Pascal Ory, Paris 1994; *La Vie d'un Photographe, Robert Doisneau,* Paris 1995; interviews—with Aloys Ginjaar in *Foto* (Amersfoort, Netherlands), September 1976; with Walter Rosenblum in *Popular Photography* (New York), January 1977; in *Dialogue with Photography* by Paul Hill and Thomas Cooper, London 1979; in *Voyons Voir: 8 Photographes,* edited by Pierre Borhan, Paris 1980.

L'Enfer, **1952.** Photograph by Robert Doisneau.

On DOISNEAU: Books—*The Picture History of Photography* by Peter Pollack, New York 1958; *The Magic Image* by Cecil Beaton and Gail Buckland, London and Boston 1975; *La Photographie Française des Origines à nos Jours* by Claude Nori, Paris 1978; *World Photography,* edited by Bryn Campbell, London 1981; *Counterparts: Form and Emotion in Photographs* by Weston J. Naef, New York, 1982; *Subjektive Fotografie: Images of the 50s,* exhibition catalogue, by Ute Eskildsen, Manfred Schmalriede and Dorothy Martinson, Essen, West Germany 1984; *Paysages Photographies: La Mission Photographique de la DATAR—travaux en cours 1984/1985,* with texts by Francois Hers, Bernard Latarjet, Jean-Francois Chevrier and others, Paris 1985; *Robert Doisneau* by Sylvain Roumette, London and New York 1991. Articles—"Robert Doisneau" by Peter Pollack in *Infinity* (New York), February 1959; "Le Secret du Succès pour l'Agence Rapho" by Yves Lorelle in *Le Photographe* (Paris), October 1965; "Robert Doisneau et la Recherche des Moments Perdus" by Jean-Claude Gautrand in *Phototribune* (Paris), no. 1, 1969; "Le Paris de Robert Doisneau" by Jean-Jacques Deutsch in *Photo-Cinéma* (Paris), January 1973; "Doisneau le Photographe fait Tourner Thuiland le Pottier" by Eveline Schlumberger in *Connaissance des Arts* (Paris), February 1973; "Robert Doisneau" by Michel Nuridsany in *Le Figaro* (Paris), 5 August 1974; "Harbutt et Doisneau" by Jean-Jacques Naudet in *Photo* (Paris), August 1974; "Robert Doisneau" by Jean Leroy in *Photo Revue* (Paris), February 1975. Films—*Trois Jours, Trois Photographes* (Doisneau, Sieff and Barbey), Paris 1979; *Bonjour, Monsieur Doisneau,* by Sabine Azéma, 1992; *Doisneau des Villes et Doisneau des Champs,* by Patrick Cazals, 1993.

*

My photographs are completely subjective. In particular, they grasp that "unevenness" that goes against the order of things. They show the world as I would like it to be at all times. And, for me, this world exists . . . because I create photographic proof of it. I don't wish to pretend to be the wretched photographer who goes (comfortably) to photograph the poor. And I don't want to make photographs that say to people: "look at what wretches you are, look at how ugly your life is."

On the contrary, I try to slip in softly, "Look at that which I have seen. You passed near to it today, but look for yourselves, and tomorrow you will find things around you that will make you laugh or move you."

—Robert Doisneau

*   *   *

For more than thirty years, Robert Doisneau has been photographing ordinary people engaged in unexceptional activities. However, his concern is not with the boredom or the banalities of everyday life. He has evolved a personal variant of "decisive instant" street photography in order to reveal fragile moments of urban existence that are bouyant with warmth, feeling and wit.

Soon after graduating from Ecole Estienne, where he studied printing arts, Doisneau began a career in commercial photography, first in the studio of André Vigneau and later as an industrial photographer for Renault Motor Company. At the end of World War II, following a period in the French Army and the Resistance, he decided to seek economic security as a fashion photographer for *Vogue* magazine, an interlude he later characterized as " . . . an absolute mistake, a kind of prostitution." Eventually his free-lance photography was handled by an agency headed by Charles Rado, an arrangement that allowed Doisneau to devote more time to street photography in Paris and its environs.

In the early 1930s Doisneau became interested in the possibilities of the 35 mm camera through his admiration of the work of Brassaï and Kertesz, which he saw in Paris. His own images of street life often contrast nature and machinery, youth and age, laughter and sorrow, giving plastic form to his conviction that in a culture dominated by technology, one must cherish the most basic human responses. In seeking out unexpected moments of frailty, humor or even ridiculousness, Doisneau proclaims the uniqueness of the individual. Above all, by making the fortuitous permanent, he has upset the proscribed routine of existence and substituted a world of enhanced sensibility.

As is evident in a number of images, including the well known one of the married couple regarding the objects in an art dealer's display window,

Doisneau employs satire as a corrective for the presumptuousness he feels is endemic in bureaucratized societies. In this, he continues a visual tradition exemplified by Daumier and other 19th century graphic artists. But he also is convinced that of itself ridicule is too simplistic a reaction, and prefers to portray situations in which the complex interplay between individuals and their surroundings is only slowly revealed, and then on several levels of meaning.

As is true of a number of photographers who address the passing scene with a small camera, Doisneau's aesthetic approach is intuitive. Less ingenious than Bresson's, it nevertheless reveals the sophistication of an eye that can create a seamless harmony between reality and pictorial necessity. Furthermore, the exceptional visual variety in Doisneau's images, including close-ups, long shots, distortion, sharply focused and blurry forms, indicates that the photographer does not approach his subject with a preconceived aesthetic formula but lets the moment create the form.

Like Atget, whose work he admires, Doisneau is a romantic who has sought to arrest time. As economic relationships have changed and neighborhoods have been destroyed, he has used the camera to rescue architecture, artifact gesture and expression from the technological dust-bin. His document of Les Halles, the Paris produce market that was dismantled to modernize the area around the Centre Pompidou, is concerned with an irrecoverable physical environment that encompassed a disorderly but creative humanity. As such, it was a consummate subject for Doisneau's lens. His recent work for the Mission Photographique de la DATAR, a government-sponsored effort to document the natural and built landscape of France today, is notable not only for being part of a group project with a social perspective, but because Doisneau has chosen to work in colour.

Doisneau claims that his interest is in "survival"—in leaving on earth a record of his own brief visit. In his case, he has given vivid life to the ephemeral. Through his special sensitivity to the feelings and textures of his own time and place, he has made the anonymous passing moment poignant and redemptive.

—Naomi Rosenblum

In the decade before his death in 1994 Doisneau's work achieved an enormous popularity, especially with young people, and largely through the reproduction of many of his images of Paris as posters and postcards.

His affectionate humorous portrait of French life in the years before, and immediately after, the Second World War caught the nostalgic mood of the 1980s. At a time when, with economic union, Europe itself was changing rapidly, his quintessentially romantic view of France had an enormous charm and widespread appeal. Doisneau's France was a country of the popular imagination and many a television sitcom showed his posters on the wall, while brandy advertisements used his photographs to demonstrate the Frenchness of their product.

This had its negative aspect for Doisneau. In French law an individual owns the right to his or her image and he was sued for damages more than once. In 1992 two separate couples in their sixties claimed to be the young couple made immortal in the 1950 photograph *Kiss at the Hôtel de Ville*. This image, originally commissioned as part of a series for *Life* magazine, became the classic icon of the French romantic temperament. By then Doisneau was a widely known figure in France and his income from this image alone constituted a considerable sum.

Despite operations for cataracts Doisneau was still photographing in the streets of Paris in his eighties, although he lamented the passing of the old street life of the city. It remains to be seen whether these photographs will have the same nostalgic appeal in years to come as his wonderfully affectionate portrait of a disappeared city does for us now.

—Shirley Read

DOMINIS, John.

Nationality: American. **Born:** Los Angeles, California, 27 June 1921. **Education:** Studied photography, under C.A. Bach, Fremont High School, Los

Angeles, 1936-40; and filmmaking, at the University of Southern California, Los Angeles, 1940-44. **Military Service:** Served as a Photographer in the United States Air Force, in Japan, 1944-46: 2nd Lieutenant. **Family:** Married Frances Clausen in 1948 (died, 1974); children: Paul, Dori and Greg. **Career:** Freelance photographer in Japan, working for *Saturday Evening Post, Colliers, Life,* etc., 1946-48; freelance photographer for Three Lions picture agency, New York, 1948-50. Associated with Time-Life since 1950: Staff Photographer, *Life* magazine, New York, 1950-74 (covered the Korean War; worked in *Life* bureaus in Atlanta, San Francisco, Dallas, and Chicago, also in Singapore and Hong Kong, as Southeast Asian Photographer, 1956-62; based in New York from 1964); Picture Editor, *People* magazine, New York, 1975-78, and *Sports Illustrated* magazine, New York, since 1978. **Recipient:** Photographer of the Year Award, University of Missouri, Columbia, 1966; White House Photographer of the Year, 1967. **Address:** c/o *Sports Illustrated,* Time and Life Building, Rockefeller Center, New York, New York 10020, U.S.A.

Individual Exhibitions:

1970   Nikon Gallery, New York

Selected Group Exhibitions:

1951   *Memorable Life Photographs,* Museum of Modern Art, New York

Collections:

Time-Life Inc., New York; Museum of Modern Art, New York.

Publications:

By DOMINIS: Books—*The Forbidden Forest,* with text by Darrell Berrigan, Tokyo 1947; *The Cats of Africa,* with text by Maitland Edey, New York 1968; *Life Great Dinners,* with text by Eleanor Graves, New York 1970; *Caribbean Wilderness,* with text by Peter Wood, New York 1975; *Adirondack Wilderness,* with text by Li Barnett, New York 1976.

On DOMINIS: Books—*Memorable Life Photographs,* with text by Edward Steichen, New York 1951; *Life Photographers: Their Careers and Favorite Pictures,* edited by Stanley Rayfield, New York 1957; *Bilder vom Krieg* by Rainer Fabian and Hans Christian Adam, Hamburg 1983, as *Images of War: 30 Years of War Photography,* London 1985.

*

I love photojournalism, with all of the opportunities to witness great events and to pursue the most variety in assignments.

At this time, I also admire the work of young photographers and gallery photographers who are very creative and imaginative. I like the manipulations of the black-and-white and color prints that they employ; it is stimulating to me, and has advanced the breadth of photography immeasurably since my days at *Life* magazine.

—John Dominis

*   *   *

One of Time Inc.'s most versatile photographers, John Dominis joined the staff of *Life* in 1950. Like several other *Life* staffers, Dominis began his apprenticeship to photography in C.A. Bach's class in practical photojournalism at Fremont High School in Los Angeles, where he practiced shooting high school sports and eventually succeeded in selling occasional prints to a local sports editor.

Also, like many *Life* contemporaries, Dominis served in World War II as a combat photographer. Stationed with the Air Force in Japan, he began an affectionate association with the Orient that has continued throughout his career. He remained in Japan after the war, freelancing for American magazines, and produced a book of photographs of Japanese children, *The Forbidden Forest.*

As a *Life* staffer, Dominis covered the Korean War before returning to America for several years to work in various *Life* bureaus. In 1956 he went east again and spent six years in Singapore and Hong Kong as the magazine's Southeast Asian photographer, sending back poignant coverage from that wartorn part of the world. Using his sharply honed reportorial skills to the utmost, Dominis covered Indonesia's movement toward independence, reported on the beginning of the Laotian conflict in 1958, and was one of the few American photographers present to record the civil strife in Vietnam that was the prelude to American involvement.

After being transferred permanently to New York in 1964, Dominis developed his talents in a new direction, covering Broadway shows and such entertainers as Frank Sinatra, Steve McQueen, Dustin Hoffman, and Robert Redford. His coverage of President Kennedy in the early 1960s earned him the White House Photographer's Award in 1967.

In addition to his coverage of sports and personalities, and his vivid reportage, Dominis has contributed to many Time-Life books on a wide variety of subjects. He showed his editorial abilities in 1975 when he assumed duties as picture editor of Time Inc.'s newly launched *People* magazine, where he was responsible for staff and freelance photographers. Since 1978, following in the footsteps of Mark Kauffman, another Bach alumnus, Dominis has been picture editor at *Sports Illustrated.*

—Maren Stange

DOMON, Ken.

Nationality: Japanese. **Born:** Sakata City, Yamagata Prefecture in 1909. **Education:** Studied at University, Tokyo, 1932; apprentice at Kotaro Miyauchi Photo Studio, Tokyo, 1933-35. **Career:** Staff photographer, Nihon Kobo Studio, Tokyo, from 1935. Freelance photographer, since 1945. Member, Society for Promotion of International Cultural Relations, 1939; Founder, Shudan Photo group, 1950; Vice President, Japan Photographers Society, 1959. **Recipient:** Photographic Culture Prize, 1942; Photographer of the Year Award, Japan Photo Critics Association, 1958; Mainichi Photo Prize, 1958; Minister of Education Award of Arts, 1959; Photographic Society of Japan Award, 1960; Japan Journalists Congress Award, 1960; Grand Prix, *International Exhibition of News Photographs,* The Hague, 1960; Mainichi Art Award, Tokyo, 1961; The Kan Kikuchi Award, 1971. **Address:** 903 Kojimachi Sky Mansion, 4-8 Kojimachi, Chiyoda-ku, Tokyo 102, Japan.

Individual Exhibitions:

1955   *Children of Downtown Tokyo,* Takashimaya Department Store, Tokyo
1960   *Children of Chikuho Coal Mines,* Fuji Photo Salon, Tokyo
1968   *Days of Hatred and Disappointment: Hiroshima,* Ginza Nikon Salon, Tokyo
1972   *Pilgrimages to Ancient Temples,* Odakyu Department Store, Tokyo
1973   *Bunraku,* Waho Gallery, Tokyo
1981   Shadai Gallery, Tokyo

Selected Group Exhibitions:

1974   *New Japanese Photography,* Museum of Modern Art, New York (toured the United States)
1979   *Japanese Photography Today and Its Origin,* Galleria d'Arte Moderna, Bologna (travelled to the Palazzo Reale, Milan; Palais des Beaux-Arts, Brussels; Institute of Contemporary Arts, London; Museum für Kunst und Gewerbe, Hamburg; Gemeente Museum, Arnhem; Pulchri Studio, The Hague)
1980   *The Imaginary Photo Museum,* Kunsthalle, Cologne

Publications:

By DOMON: Books—*Fubo,* Tokyo 1953; *Hiroshima,* Tokyo 1958; *Children of Chikuho Coal Mines,* Tokyo 1960; *Rumie's Daddy Is Dead,* Tokyo 1960; *Pilgrimage to Ancient Temples,* 4 vols., Tokyo 1963-71; *Taishi-no-Midera: The Taji,* Tokyo 1965; *Bunraku,* Osaka 1972; *The Todai-ji,* Tokyo 1973; *Living Hiroshima,* Tokyo 1978.

On DOMON: Books—*Photography of the World,* edited by Heibonsha Publishers, Tokyo 1956; *Photography of the World '60,* edited by Hiromu Hara, Ihei Kimura and others, Tokyo and New York 1960; *Nihon Shashin Shi, 1840-1945,* edited by the Japanese Photographers Association, Tokyo 1971, as *A Century of Japanese Photography,* with introduction by John W. Dower, New York and London 1980; *New Japanese Photography,* exhibition catalogue, by John Szarkowski and Shoji Yamagishi, New York 1974; *Japanese Photography Today and Its Origin* by Attilio Colombo and Isabella Doniselli, Bologna 1979; *Nude Photographs of Japan,* with text by Shiroyasu Suzuki, Tokyo 1981; *The Imaginary Photo Museum* by Helmut Gernsheim, Renate and L. Fritz Gruber and others, Cologne 1981, London 1982; *The Library of World Photography: Landscape,* with texts by David Plowden and Ian Jeffrey, Tokyo and London 1984.

*   *   *

Ken Domon became a photographer in the late 1930s, a decade in which Japan moved towards an economic domination of South East Asia, the occupation of Manchuria and finally towards world war. Domon was still a young man when war was declared. The dramatic and terrible events of the decade were to shape his photography for the span of his working life. As a result of radical student activities he was expelled from university in 1932 and then started an apprenticeship at the Kotaro Miyauchi Photo Studio, after which he joined the Nihon Kobo agency. During this period of rapid industrialisation, there was great social unrest and the rise of the authoritarian power of the state. Though a Marxist photo-collective had been established by Kimura, much of Japanese photography was an imitative, shallow pictorialism. The war, surrender and Occupation made such photographic material irrelevant. Domon faced the aftermath with a cold objectivity; it may well have been the only way to accommodate such a disaster. Domon's new realism replaced the abundant, obsolete trivia of glamour and nude photography from the war years. Hiroshima was the turning point.

In October 1950 he established the Shudan Photo group to spearhead his new realism in the midst of the Occupation and the first stirrings of national recovery. The Shudan group held eight annual exhibitions in conjunction with Western photographers including Bourke-White, Eugene Smith, Irving Pen, Cartier-Bresson and Bill Brandt. Japan was emerging from the isolation prevalent for nearly two decades.

As well as establishing a new realist school, Domon was recording classical Japanese art. Between 1940 and 1954 he photographed Muroji, the temple close to the Muro river near Nara. On the banks of the river he photographed the giant figure of Miroku carved in the rock. Within the temple he photographed the sculpture, which includes the finest examples of carving from the Heian period of Esoteric Buddhism. He isolated the details of the limbs and the expressive hand gestures. With the skill he applied to sculpture, he also recorded the horrifying scars of Hiroshima. The photographs were published as a book in 1958. It contained formal and explicit portraits of the victims, their scar tissue and skin grafts and detailed photographs of surgery. The nearest modern parallel to this book is Eugene Smith's Minamata document. However appalling the scars, there is also the hint of survival. Twenty years after that publication Domon returned to publish another stage in the recovery in *Living Hiroshima.*

He continued to reaffirm his interest in traditional Japan with the publication and exhibition of his works *Bunraku, The Pilgrimages to Ancient Temples,* and *Todai-ji.* This assertion of his native tradition has been paralleled by his uncompromising documentary work, including his work with Tomatsu in the "Hiroshima-Nagasaki Document" (1961).

By the early 1960s, Japanese economic recovery was accelerating rapidly. The Shudan group was replaced by the new wave of the Junin-no-me and Vivo groups. Modern Japanese photography was established. Ken Domon had been the pioneer.

—Mark Holborn

DORYS, Benedykt Jerzy.

Nationality: Polish. **Born:** Kalisz, 25 May 1901. **Education:** Attended the Humanistic Grammar School, Kalisz, 1910-19; studied violin at Music School, Kalisz, 1918-22; self-taught in photography. **Military Service:** Served in the Polish Army, 1920, and in the defence of Warsaw, 1939. **Family:** Married Halina Preger in 1928. **Career:** Photographer since 1914: maintained a studio in Warsaw, Photo-Dorys, 1929-39, 1947-49. Founder Member, 1946, Member of the Qualifying Commission, 1946-47, Member of the General Council, 1947-50, Secretary, 1950-52, and Vice-President of the General Council, 1952-56, Chairman and Member of the Bar of Conscience, 1956-81, also Member and Chairman of the Artistic Commission, 1953-58, and Chairman of the Qualifying Commission of the Warsaw section, 1969-72, of the Union of Polish Art Photographers (UPAP); Founder Member, Warsaw Photographic Society, 1947; Founder Member of the Photo-Section, 1947, Secretary of the Council, 1956-59, and Member of the Board of Conscience, 1959-78. Zaiks authors society, Warsaw. **Recipient:** 10th Anniversary of the Polish People's Republic Medal, 1955; Gold Cross of Merit, Poland, 1955; Award of Excellence, 1957, and Honorary Excellence Award, 1968, Federation Internationale de l'Art Photographique (FIAP); Ministry of Culture and Art Award, 1960, 1973, 1975; Honorary Member, 1961, Silver Medal, 1960, and Gold Medal, 1974, Union of Polish Art Photographers (UPAP); Cavalier Cross, 1964, and Commandery Cross, 1980, Order of Polonia Restituta; Golden Badge of Merit, 1968, and Commemorative Medal, 1978, Zaiks authors society, Warsaw; 30th Anniversary of the Polish People's Republic Medal, 1974; Jan Bulhak Medal, Warsaw, 1976, 1985; Culture Activist's Badge, Poland, 1978; 40th Anniversary of the Polish People's Republic Medal, 1985. Honorary Member, Warsaw Photographic Society, 1981. **Died:** (in Warsaw) 19 September 1990.

Individual Exhibitions:

1929   Polish Photographic Society, Warsaw
1960   Ministry of Culture and Art Kordegarda Gallery, Warsaw
            (retrospective; toured Poland)
1974   *Actors and Fashions of the 1930s,* ZPAF (Zwiazek Polskich
            Artystow Fotografikow) Gallery, Warsaw (toured Poland)
        Men of Polish Arts and Culture, ZPAF Gallery, Warsaw
1977   *Kazimierz on the Vistula 1931-32,* ZPAF Gallery, Warsaw
1983   *Kazimierz nad Wista 1931-1932,* Museum in Kazimierz
            Dolny, Poland
1994   *Benedykt Jerzy Dorys,* Stara Galeria, ZPAF/Old Gallery UPAP

Selected Group Exhibitions:

1977   *Polish Creative Photography until 1939,* National Museum,
            Wroclaw, Poland
1978   *Polish Portraiture 1840-1939,* UPAP Gallery, Warsaw
1979   *Fotografia Polska 1839-1979,* International Center of
            Photography, New York (travelled to the Museum of
            Contemporary Art, Chicago, and the Whitechapel Art
            Gallery, London)
        The Art of Reportage, National Museum, Wroclaw, Poland
            (travelled to the Museum of Arts, Lodz, Poland)
1980   *Fotografia Polska 1840-1939,* Galeria Zacheta, Warsaw
            (travelled to the Museum of Arts, Lodz, Poland)
1981   *Photographie Polonaise 1900-81,* Centre Georges
            Pompidou, Paris
1984   *Exhibition of Contemporary Photography,* Zacheta Gallery,
            Warsaw
1990   *L'annee de l'Est,* Musee d'Elysee, Lausanne, Switzerland

1992   *Les chefs d'oeuvre de la photographie polonaise 1912-1948,*
         Institut Polonais, Paris (travelled to the Muzeum Sztuki/
         Museum of Art in Lodz)

Collections:

National Museum, Wroclaw, Poland; Museum of Arts, Lodz, Poland; Navigator Foundation, Boston, Massachusetts; Instytut Sztuki PAN/Art Institute of Polish Academy of Science, Warsaw; National Library, Warsaw.

Publications:

By DORYS: Books—*Kazimierz on the Vistula, 1931,* with an introduction by Romuald Klosiewicz, Warsaw 1979; *Benedykt Jerzy Dorys,* with an introduction by Tomasz Moscicki, Warsaw 1994.

On DORYS: Books—*Das polnische Lichtbild,* with introduction by Zbigniew Pekoslawski, Halle, East Germany 1961; *Among the Polish Masters of the Camera* by Lech Grabowski, Warsaw 1964; *History of Warsaw Photography* by Waclaw Zdzarski, Warsaw 1974; *Polska fotografia artystyczna do roku 1939,* exhibition catalogue, by Adam Sobota, Wroclaw, Poland 1977; *La Photographie d'Art en Pologne,* exhibition catalogue, by Adam Sobota, Urszula Czartoryska and others, Paris 1981; *Wobec fotografow,* by Jerzy Busza, Warsaw 1983; *Fotografia polska 1945-1985* by Jerzy Busza, Ryszard Bobrowski and others, Gorzow Wielkopolski, Poland 1985; *Sztuka reportazu,* exhibition catalogue, Wroclaw 1979; *Kazimierz nad Wisla 1931-1932,* exhibition catalogue with text by Adam Johann, Kazimierz Dolny 1983; *Wobec fotografow,* by Jerzy Busza, Warsaw 1983; *Czy istnieje fotografia socjologiczna? (Does sociological photography exist?),* Krakòw 1987; *Wobec odbiorcòw fotografii,* by Jerzy Busza, Warsaw 1990; *150 lat fotografil polskiej (150 years of Polish Photography),* Warsaw 1991; *Les chefs d'oeuvre de la photographie polonaise 1912-1948,* exhibition catalogue, Paris 1992. **Articles**—"An Exhibition of B.J. Dorys' Photographs" by Jerzy Ficowski in *New Culture* (Warsaw), 20 November 1960; "Blue Sheets" by A. Rudnicki in *Swiat* (Warsaw), 20 November 1960; "Photographer and Musician" by W. Kicinski in *Trybuna Ludu* (Warsaw), 23 November 1960; "The Work of B.J. Dorys" by M. Sadzewicz in *Stolica* (Warsaw), 4 December 1960; "Afterthoughts on Authenticity" by U. Czartoryska in *Fotografia* (Warsaw), January 1961; "The Versatile Dorys" by O. Galdynski in *Pomorze* (Bydgoszcz, Gdansk and Szczecin, Poland), 1-15 March 1961; "The First Photographic Reportage" by Jerzy Busza in *Culture* (Warsaw), 19 June 1977; "The Leica Folly in Kazimierz" by R. Klosiewicz in *Photography* (Warsaw), No. 2, 1977; "Polish Photography" by Owen Edwards in *American Photographer* (New York), November 1979; "Wystawa-Fotografia polska 1839-1979" by Ryszard Bobrowski in *Fotografia* (Warsaw), no. 3, 1980; "Benedykt Jerzy Dorys" by Kathryn Livingston in *American Photographer* (New York), January 1981; "Portret niepozowany Benedykta Jerzego Dorysa" ("Unposed Portrait of Benedykt Jerzy Dorys") by Barbara Kosinska in *Fotografia* (Warsaw) no. 2/1983; "Mistrz fotografii" ("Master of Photography") by Krzysztof Lipka in *Express Wieczorny,* (Warsaw) no. 42/1994. **Films**—*By the Vistula,* directed by M. Kwiatkowska, commentary by Maria Kuncewicz, 1961; *Photo-Dorys,* TV film, directed by Urszula Litynska, 1980.

*

Some personal details: I started to photograph in 1914, whilst studying music, the violin. Since 1926 I have been active in the Polish Society of Amateur Photographers, later known as the Polish Photographic Society, in Warsaw. I concentrated on landscape, architectural, nude and portrait photography. I have mastered such techniques as the duplicate, the gum, the bromoil, the transfer, mono- and polychromatic, and others. Since 1927, I have contributed to many exhibitions of artistic photography in Poland and abroad, receiving many medals, awards and honorable mentions. All evidence of this activity was destroyed during the war, the occupation and the Warsaw Insurrection.

Portraiture interests me most. I opened a photo studio in Warsaw in 1929. I have made a tremendous number of portraits of men of culture, the arts, science and politics. I also do fashion, commercial photography, etc. In 1931-32 I made a large series of photographs entitled *Kazimierz on the Vistula,* which is regarded as the first photographic reportage to be made in Poland. A

part of that work was exhibited for the first time in my retrospective show in 1960.

I don't feel entitled to cast a critical eye on my photography or to state my views on photography in general. I am tolerant enough not to make evaluations of a photograph dependent on when it was made or upon the problems in which it indulges. The abuse of photography marks the limits of my tolerance. I think that there simply happen to be good and bad photographs. I think that in my own work I have managed to remain true to myself. As far as the future is concerned, I hope that, in its evolution, photography doesn't lose what I consider to be its most essential, almost innate, aspect—namely, its ability to penetrate and interpret the phenomena of the world that surrounds us, and its ability to make visible that which is invisible.

—Benedykt Jerzy Dorys

*   *   *

Benedykt Jerzy Dorys was to have been a musician. In his early years he studied violin, and he intended to devote himself to music as a form of expression. But, instead, he became a photographer, though no ordinary one. Right at the beginning of his long and varied career Dorys became a portrait photographer of people who were well-known and famous—actresses, politicians, artists, the elegant people. His photography was elegant to match—carefully designed, well-mannered, pretty. There was no place in it for ugliness, for protest, or for destruction. Now and then one can find in these portraits wisdom or sometimes a reflective mood, but it is a buoyant and cheerful reflectiveness. There is no question that throughout this early period Dorys was a happy man; so also was his photography.

Yet, in the history of Polish photography Dorys is known not only as an elegant contributor to the portrait tradition but also as the founder of modern camera reportage. In the years 1931-32 Dorys went twice to Kazimierz on the Vistula, a small, picturesque and neglected town populated mainly by Jews. It was not the picturesque which interested Dorys. As always, he was fascinated by people. Not his usual subjects—but people met by chance, often dirty, dishevelled, people of the street and gutter.

And this work from Kazimierz is something quite startling in his career. Wrestling with his subject, Dorys is now inelegant in capturing the dynamics of the street, impulsively captured in snapshots with a 35 millimetre camera. This large series contains much that has now gone forever, things that were then the center of the world for this small provincial town. It is a world of trade and of bitter, anguished destitution, a world of circus attractions, of the music of gypsies, of slums and barefooted children in the street; a world of calm, people as if arrested in time, a world of hopeless waiting and helplessness. It is remarkable that Dorys saw in Kazimierz not those things for which the town was famous but what few people would at that time have perceived: a world stopped in time as though waiting for its own catastrophe. In these photographs, often hurriedly and secretly taken, accidentally composed, there is silence and anxiety; one feels a poignant drama, as if misfortune waits just around the corner.

"Kazimierz on the Vistula" constitutes a sociological study of a town's life. It is also, and perhaps primarily, a study of man. For if there is a common denominator in his radically varied output, it is man. Man is the theme to which Dorys has always remained faithful, whether he was photographing the elegant world of urban Warsaw or taking the group portrait of a dying community.

—Ryszard Bobrowski

DOUGLAS, Ed.

Nationality: American. **Born:** San Rafael, California, 6 May 1943; immigrated to Australia, 1973. **Education:** Attended Wade Thomas Primary School, San Anselmo, California, 1949-57; Sir Francis Drake High School, San Anselmo, 1957-61; studied fine arts and photography, under Lou Callait, College of Marin, California, 1961-63, A.A. 1963; San Francisco Art Institute, under Joe Humphrey, Geraldine Sharpe, and Blair Stapp, 1964; San

Untitled, **from the series** *Lore of Unrealised Desire,* **1993 (original in colour). Photograph by Ed Douglas.**

Francisco State University, under Don Worth, John Gutmann, Jack Welpott, and Imogen Cunningham, 1965-69, B.A. 1967, M.A. 1969. **Family:** Married Nancy Wehrheim in 1964 (divorced, 1969). **Career:** Photographer since 1963. Worked as a boat-builder near San Francisco, 1964-65; teaching assistant to Imogen Cunningham, San Francisco State University, 1968-69; Instructor in Photography, College of Marin, 1969-73; farmed in Nimbin, New South Wales, 1973-76; Lecturer, Sydney College of the Arts, 1976-77. Since 1977, Head of the Photography Section, South Australian School of Art, Adelaide. Founder-Member, with Jack Welpott, Judy Dater, Linda Connor, Don Worth and others, Visual Dialogue Foundation, San Francisco, 1969. **Recipient:** XV Grand Prix, 'Le Provencal' du Festival d'Avignon, France 1971; Special Equipment Grant: Australia Visual Arts Board, 1976; Project Grant: Australia Council, Visual Arts Board, 1981; C.S.R. Artist's Project Commission: CSR gypsum mine, Kangaroo Island, South Australia 1982-83; Project Grant: Sydney, 1983; Parliament House Project, Canberra: Australian Capital Territory 1984-86; Canon Australia: Artist Sponsorship Program, 1993. **Address:** 85 Aldgate Valley Road, Aldgate, South Australia 5154.

Individual Exhibitions:

1971	Anima Mundi Gallery, Mill Valley, California
1972	Diablo Valley Junior College, Concord, California
	Hartnell College, Salinas, California
	Studio Gallery, Bolinas, California
1974	Hogarth Gallery, Paddington, New South Wales
1975	Australian Centre for Photography, Sydney
1976	Sydney College of the Arts, Balmain, New South Wales
1978	Contemporary Art Society, Parkside, South Australia
1982	Australian Centre for Photography, Sydney

	Developed Image Gallery, Adelaide, South Australia
1983	Christine Abrahams Gallery, Melbourne, Victoria
1993	Perth Institute of Contemporary Art, Perth, Western Australia
1994	University of South Australia Art Museum, Adelaide, South Australia

Selected Group Exhibitions:

1970	*California Photographers,* University of California at Davis
1971	*XV Le Provencal,* at the Festival of Avignon
1975	*California Photographers,* National Gallery, Melbourne
1980	*8 South Australian Photographers,* Australian Centre for Photography, Sydney
1981	*Visions After Light,* Art Gallery of South Australia, Adelaide
1982	*Contemporary Colour Photography,* Newcastle Regional Art Gallery, New South Wales
1983	*C.S.R. Photographic Project,* Art Gallery of New South Wales, Sydney
1984	*Time Present and Time Past,* Australian Centre for Photography, Sydney
1985	*New Landscapes,* Tasmanian School of Art, Hobart
1986	*New Views: Landscape Photographs from Two Continents,* Gallery 210, University of Missouri, St. Louis, USA.
1987	*Constructed Images: Photographs of the New Parliament House,* Pod Gallery, Drill Hall Annexe Gallery, A.C.T.
1992	*Con-Temporary,* Curated by Alan Cruickshank, Capital Building, Adelaide, South Australia.
1993	*Australia Exposed,* Art Gallery of South Australia, Adelaide.
	Carte Blanche, Anima Gallery, Adelaide, South Australia

Collections:

Australian Centre for Photography, Sydney; Phillip Morris Collection, Melbourne; Gallery of South Australia, Adelaide; Museum of Modern Art, New York; International Museum of Photography, George Eastman House, Rochester, New York; San Francisco Museum of Modern Art; Bibliothèque Nationale, Paris; Open University, England; Australian National Gallery, Canberra; Parliament House Collection, Canberra.

Publications:

By DOUGLAS: Articles—"The Gypsy Truck" (photographic series) in *Earth Garden* (Sydney), March 1974; "Search and Discovery" in *Light Vision* (Melbourne), November/December 1977; "Artist's Proof" in *Artlink* (Adelaide), nos. 2/3, 1984.

On DOUGLAS: Books—*California Photographers,* exhibition catalogue, Davis, California 1970; *New Photography Australia: A Selective Survey,* edited by Graham Howe, Sydney 1974; *Australian Photography 1976,* edited by Laurence LeGuay, Sydney 1976; *Australian Photography: A Contemporary View* by Laurence LeGuay, Sydney 1978; *Australian Photographers: The Phillip Morris Collection,* Melbourne 1979; *Australian Photography Yearbook 1983,* edited by Jean-Marc Le Pechoux, Melbourne 1983; *The Centre: Works on Paper by Contemporary Australian Artists* by Alison Carroll, Adelaide 1984; *New Landscapes: Photographs from Two Continents* by David Stephenson, Hobart, Tasmania 1985; *Common Ground: Personal I* by Alan Cruickshank, Adelaide, South Australia 1985; *New Landscapes: Photographs from Two Continents,* by David Stephenson, University of Tasmania, Hobart 1985; *New Views: Landscape Photographs from Two Continents* by Tom Patton, University of Missouri, St. Louis 1986; *CSR Photography Project Collection* by Robert McFarlane, Art Gallery of NSW 1988; *Expressing Australia: Art in Parliament,* Parliament House Construction Authority, Canberra, ACT 1988; *Ed Douglas: The Lure of Unrealised Desire* by John Neylon, University of South Australia Art Museum, Adelaide 1994. **Articles**—"Visual Dialogue Photographers: Portfolio" in *Album* (London), October 1970; "An Extraordinary Backyard" by Peter Ward in *The Australian/Weekend Magazine* (Sydney), 30 October 1982; "Photography in South Australia" by Alison Carroll in *Bulletin of the Art Gallery of South Australia* (Adelaide), vol. 39, 1983; "The Geographic Tradition" by Alison Carroll in *Studio International* (London), March/April 1984; "Australian Photography Now" by Andreas Muller-Pohle and Alan Cruikshank in *European Photography* (Gottingen), no. 3, 1985.

*

From the late 1970s my work has involved an exploration of a subjective inner landscape, always with the intention of referencing the archetypal and the mythic.

Since 1990 I have been working with found photographic fragments—usually quite small in scale. Using a Canon laser copier I enlarge and extend the colour and contrast of these image fragments. The final laser copy is then transferred to a Canon 'Bubblejet' A1 copier to produce a larger scale work. The 'Bubblejet' process sprays fine dots of ink onto paper. To complete the image I use coloured pencils and ink.

"The Lure of Unrealised Desire," my latest exhibition, is based on Jungian conepts of 'individuation' which extol an honouring of the psychological opposites: masculine/feminine, self/shadow, consciousness/unconsciousness, lust/love. A narrative reference, in this particular exhibition, is Dante's journey as portrayed in his "The Divine Comedy."

—Ed Douglas

* * *

Ed Douglas is a sharp professional with a soft focus—aware of all the angles but never letting go of his belief in the natural gentle side of man.

He explores this dichotomy in his photographs, where there is the hard reality of the picture but always an enigma or, better, an illusion of something else. Art and illusion; illusion and reality. Douglas works with the age-old duality of art as a central premise of his work.

Douglas usually explores it in self-images, following a very conscious duality in himself: art school lecturer and alter ego, the primitive man called Glenson Tealeaf—the one aggressive, assertive, sharp, harsh, conforming to the demands of professional life; the other accepting, receptive, sensitive to the nuances of nature. Neither can live easily in the other's environment, and it is, of course, the tensions between the two which give Douglas's photographs their edge.

Douglas started using self-portraits against an environment in California in the late 1960s, an important image being *Self Portrait with Taurus-Ego Figure,* a slow exposure resulting in a shadowy, illusory figure—of Douglas the artist—against a fresco of dubious merit shown in full clarity. A further image, in Arles, made of layers of pale tones, shows the disappearing artist stiffly standing near an almost tactile advertisement for the "reality" of beauty "aid." The human being is ephemeral compared with his material products.

For his first years in Australia, living on a farm in northern New South Wales, Douglas continued his exploration of dual roles, with objects literally superimposed over alien environments, as for example, his images of man on the moon collaged over the Australian desert. Later, the harshness and threats of returning to city life, in Sydney in 1976, were translated in a series on plants struggling to live amidst the concrete of the metropolis. In these works (reproduced in the short-lived Australian photographic magazine *Light Vision*), the ideas of the earlier self-images are repeated in the metaphor of these other natural creatures trying to maintain some sense of self-worth: other soft focuses amidst the harsh, bright shapes of the material city. And again, ironically (like the man who is essential to the production of the fresco and the beauty advertisement), these plants are essential to physical and mental and spiritual health of their seeming "sponsors."

The Glenson Tealeaf series, made in South Australia, again leads from this concern. Now the previous illusive, threatened, natural man takes on a substantial persona. In his own quiet way, Glenson Tealeaf asserts the values of his being: the softness of focus, the delicacy of colour, the seeming low-key but subtly, sweetly all-pervasive wholeness of the chosen subjects; the absence of hard, sharp aggression. This is indeed a positive statement, even a triumph, only attained after difficult and on-going personal struggle. For still, over all Glenson's work watches—and judges—the other side, the professional man, Ed Douglas himself.

—Alison Carroll

DRAHOS, Tom.

Nationality: French. **Born:** Jablon, Czech Republic, 17 November 1947; immigrated to France, 1968; naturalized, 1978. **Education:** Studied at the Cinema Academy, Prague, 1967-68; Institut des Hautes Etudes du Cinéma, Paris, 1969-72. **Family:** Married Christine Gennetier in 1977; sons: Alexis and Jean Baptiste. **Career:** Photographer, in Paris, since 1968. Instructor, Institut des Hautes Etudes du Cinéma, Paris, 1983, Ecole Nationale de la Photographie, Arles, France, 1985 and Ecole des Beaux Arts, Rennes. **Recipient:** Kodak Photo Book Prize, Paris, 1980. **Address:** 52 rue Montmartre, 75002 Paris, France.

Individual Exhibitions:

1972	Galerie Rencontre, Paris
1980	Ufficio dell'Arte, Paris
1981	Galerie Voir, Toulouse, France
1982	Ikon Gallery, Birmingham, England
	Espace AGF, Paris
	Galerie 666, Paris
1983	Ufficio dell'Arte, Paris
1984	Galerie ARPA, Bordeaux, France
	Galleria Canon, Milan
	Galerie Gabrielle Maubrie, Paris
	Galerie Samia Saouma, Paris
1985	Palais des Congrès, Le Mans, France

1986	Galerie Montenay Delsol, Paris
1987	*Retrospective 1967-1987*, Aurillac, France
1989	Galerie Montenay, Paris
	Centre Georges Pompidou, Paris
1991	*Continuité Discontinuité*, Galerie Joseph Dutertre, Rennes; Charlotenborg, Copenhagen; Kampnagelfabrik, Hamburg; Kunstverein, Friburg
1992	Kunstverein, Bonn
	Université de Strasbourg, Strasbourg
1993	Galeries Manes, Prague
1994	*Apparences*, Maison de l'Art et de la communication, Sallaumines

Selected Group Exhibitions:

1973	*Séquences*, Musée d'Art Moderne, Paris
1974	*Révisions*, Institut de l'Environnement, Paris
1980	*Ils Se Disent Peintres; Ils Se Disent Photographers*, Musée d'Art Moderne, Paris
1983	*Images Fabriquées*, Centre Georges Pompidou, Paris
	Photographie France Aujourd'hui, Musée d'Art Moderne de la Ville, Paris
1984	*Contemporary European Photography*, Benteler Galleries, Houston, Texas
	Construire les Paysages de la Photographie, Musée de Metz, France
1985	*Sol et Mur*, Musée du Havre, Le Havre, France

Collections:

Bibliothèque Nationale, Paris; Musée d'Art Moderne, Paris; Musée Rodin, Paris; Musée d'Art Moderne de la Ville de Paris; Fondation Nationale de la Photographie, Paris; Musée Nicéphore Niepce, Chalon sur Saône, France; Museum of Modern Art, New York.

Publications:

By DRAHOS: Books—*Metamorphoses*, Paris 1981; *Le vieux mystère*, with René Thom, Strasbourg 1987; *Le corps, la galère*, exhibition catalogue with text by François Soulages, Toulon 1988. **Films**—*Metroshima*, 35mm NB, 80 min; *Le Mangeur de Bonbons*, 35mm NB, 80 min; *India*, 16mm/Betacam Coul, 25 min; *Prague*, 16mm/BVU Coul, 25 min; *Reims*, 16mm/BVU/Coul, 24 min; *Frankfurt*, 16mm/BVU Coul, 25 min; *Barcelone*, 16mm/BVU Coul, 25 min; *Antony*, 16mm/BVU Coul, 22 min; *Singen*, 16mm/BVU Coul, 22 min; *Sallaumines*, 16mm/BVU Coul, 21 min; *Arras*,16mm/BVU Coul, 21 min; *Coppenhague*, 16mm/BVU Coul, 22 min; *Paris*, 16mm/BVU Coul, 22 min; *Périphérie*, 16mm/BVU Coul, 22 min; *Mystères*, 16mm/BVU Coul, 22 min; *Odradek*, 16mm/Betacam, 30 min; *Une Sentinelle*, 16mm/Betacam, 30 min; *Chevauchée*, 16mm/Betacam 30 min; *Une Grosse Motte*, 16mm/Betacam, 30 min; *Le Pont*, 16mm/Betacam, 30 min; *Une Petite Femme*, 16mm/Betacam, 30 min; *Carrefour*, 16mm/Betacam, 30 min; *Le Terrier*, 16mm/Betacam, 30 min; *L'Esprit Malin*, 16mm/Betacam, 30 min; *K'Oua Fou ou Wou*, 16mm/Betacam, 20 min.

On DRAHOS: Books—*Album Photographique* by Pierre de Fenoyl, Paris 1979; *Construire les Paysages de la Photographie*, exhibition catalogue, by Jean-Francois Chevrier, Jean-Marc Poinsot and Michele Chomette, Metz, France 1984; *La Photographie Créative* by Jean-Claude Lemagny, Paris 1984; *Paysages Photographies: La Mission Photographique de la DATAR—travaux en cours 1984/1985*, with texts by Bernard Latarjet, Jean-Francois Chevrier, Francois Hers and others, Paris 1985; *Le regard pensif*, by Régis Durand, Paris 1988. **Articles**—"Humains" by Allan Porter in *Camera* (Lucerne), January 1970; articles by F. Petri in *Nuova Fotografia* (Naples), August 1971; by J. Deutsch in *Le Nouveau Photo* (Paris), July 1972; by A. Pozner in *Zoom* (Paris), November 1973; by J. Rueda in *Nueva Lente* (Madrid), January 1977; by Carole Naggar in *Zoom* (Paris), May/June 1977;

"Tom Drahos: mises en scene" in *Canal* (Paris), May 1980; "Tom Drahos, l'insatiable" by Patrick Roegiers in *Revolution* (Paris), no. 239, 1984; "Tom Drahos" in *Beaux Arts* (Paris), October 1984.

      *

Photography, like all art, passes by three essential axes: sensation, ability, and knowledge. All art has to be a path without compromise, a determination of the predominant essentials of contemporary life. Whoever makes a true analysis of our surrounding reality will never refuse to accept the fine line between beauty and ugliness and will reject all mediocrity in whatever form. In his eyes a perfect work is achieved only by rejecting all ambiguity and false artifice. He knows that each work demands an ethic and a rigor without which it will be banal and dull; he attacks all conventional ideas and the conscience of the age to reach his true creative dimensions. It is in his affirmation or—on the contrary—in his questioning that he depicts his environment without bothering about its reactions. In this respect he is in a privileged position; at the same time, he is also a prime target. Attached to the phenomena peculiar to Man, he is not embarrassed by any of their manifestations and uses all his strength to find a new definition of life.

After its beginning, when it borrowed much from painting, photography has gradually, over the years, detached itself from pictorial imitations to find its own nature. While contemporary painting now is being influenced by photography, the image of the surface sensitive to the action of light enters a new phase. Although photographic film was devised to record visible reality, nowadays we witness numerous experiments in which the photographer tries to record an "invisible" materiality; the photographer is no longer content to record the evidence; he wants to interpret or even create it.

Without doubt, it is in this direction, in which the photographer insists on his own intervention and participation in the creation of the image in all its complexity, that photography will find its own freedom and its true development. The photographer's eye will cease to be passive and impotent; it will, on the contrary, suggest new dimensions of sensitivity, extend creativity, and push forward towards new and unknown spheres. To be sure, the vocation of photography will remain the same, but its future development will make us reconsider its true significance.

            —Tom Drahos

     *   *   *

For many young, questing photographers, the "real" is no longer a genuine subject matter. They prefer to invent and then fix a world which bears witness to their visions, to play with representation, to recount their explorations. Optical illusions, ladders, graphic work form the stage settings of Tom Drahos' work.

Drahos' photographs make conceptual worlds concrete and bring together our various fears—of mutants, of the atomic age, the pressure of daily life, the element of the absurd: threatening forces, but always fixed and frozen. We are reminded of the clarity of certain parts of his Czechoslavakian heritage and his determination to define his role as an artist.

In his quest, in his slow progress towards perfection of subject matter, lighting, and the evocation of moods, Drahos has not been taken in, either by the world around him or by photography itself. He practices the art of clear-sightedness.

            —Christian Caujolle

DRIES, Antoon.

Nationality: Belgian. **Born:** Antwerp, 14 October 1910. **Education:** Attended the School for Dentistry, Antwerp, 1931-35; self-taught in photography.

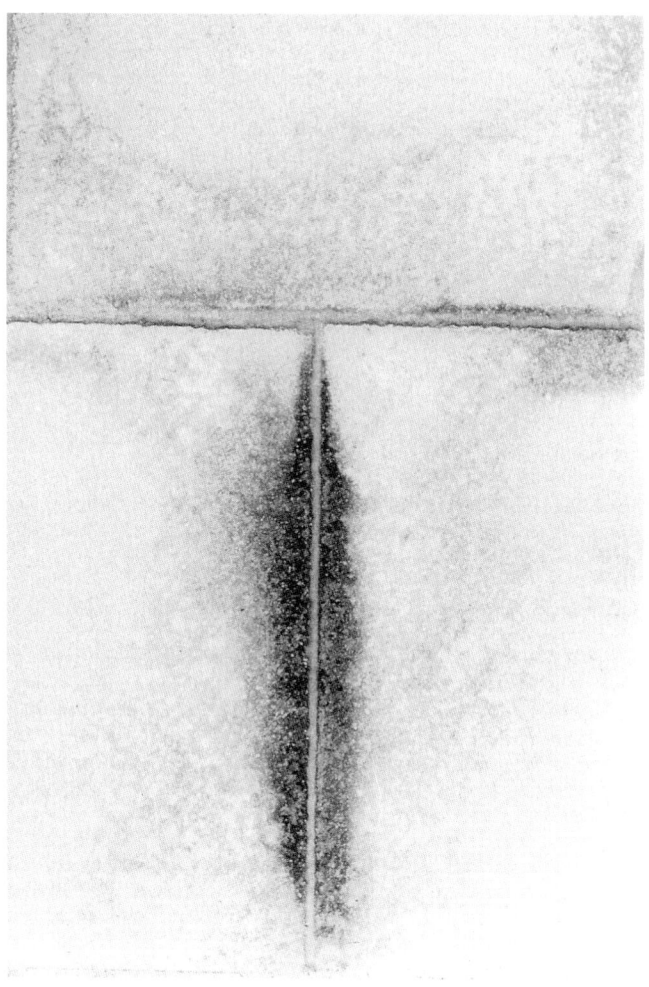

***Untitled,* 1990.** Photograph by Anton Dries.

Family: Married Dora Verbert in 1937; children: Luc and Ilse. **Career:** Dental surgeon, Antwerp, since 1935. Freelance photographer, Antwerp. Member since 1938, and Vice-President since 1939, Photoclub "Iris," Antwerp. **Recipient:** Flemish Ministry of Culture Prize, Brussels, 1984. **Address:** Raymond Delbekestr. 39, 2080 Zoessel, Belgium.

Individual Exhibitions:

1961	*Tensions,* Galerie du Studio 8, Paris
1962	*Tensions,* Studio De Braeckeleer, Antwerp
	Tensions, Studio Rik Wouters, Brussels
1965	*Photos 1940-1965,* Looszaal Koninklijke Maatschappy voor Dierkunde, Antwerp
1968	*Natuur-Vorm-Magie,* Huidevettershuis, Brugge, Belgium
1971	*Jan Dries: Sculptures,* Galerie Jeanne Buytaert, Antwerp
1974	*Sequences,* Internationaal Cultureel Centrum, Antwerp
1976	*Sequences II,* Galerie Jeanne Buytaert, Antwerp
1977	*Beneath the Oaks,* Provinciaal Centrum Arenberg, Antwerp
1979	*House, Garden and Kitchen,* Galerie Jeanne Buytaert, Antwerp (travelled to Gallery 68, Hoensbroek, Netherlands)
1981	*House, Garden and Kitchen,* Galerie Drieghe, Wetteren, Belgium
1982	*Een spel met drie wertolkers,* Galerie Jeanne Buytaert, Antwerp (toured Belgium)
1984	*Fotosequenties,* Galerie Neu, Saint-Niklaas, Belgium
1985	Provinciaal Museum voor Fotografie, Antwerp (retrospective)

1986	*Beschouwende Fotografie,* Galerie Jeanne Buytaert, Antwerp
1988	Galerie Jeanne Buytaert, Antwerp
1990	*Drempel 80,* Galerie Jeanne Buytaert, Antwerp
1992	*Fotos 1935-1990,* Museum voor Fotografie, Antwerp (with illustrated cataglogue)
	Gebonden-Geschonden-Gespleten-Gekliefd-Gevild-Genoogd zot Rust, Galerie Jeanne Buytaert, Antwerp
	Koesteel Hoensbrock, Fotogalerie 68, The Netherlands
1993	Kopelgalerie St Maria, Antwerp (retrospective)
1994	*Parcours,* Galerie Jeanne Buytaert, Antwerp

Selected Group Exhibitions:

1956	*Contemporary Photography,* Galerie St. Laurent, Brussels
1960	*5 Belgian Photographers,* Värmlands Museum, Karlstad, Sweden
1969	*Photomundi,* Philips Showroom, Eindhoven, Netherlands
1976	*15 Photographers from Flanders,* Künstlerhaus, Vienna (travelled to Cologne, West Germany, and Chalon-sur-Saône, France)
1978	*3/4 Century Fotokring "Iris,"* Het Sterckshof Museum, Deurne-Antwerp
1980	*De Fotografie in Belgie 1940-1980,* Het Sterckshof Museum, Deurne-Antwerp
1982	*Fotografie Vroeger en Nu,* Passage 44, Brussels
1983	*Fotografie 16 + 1,* Saint-Lucasinstitut, Ghent, Belgium
1984	*Vier Fotografen,* Cultureel Centrum Jesus-Eik, Overijse, Belgium
1985	*Vyftien Vlaamse Fotografen,* Stedelijk Museum, Amsterdam (toured the Netherlands and Belgium)
1993	*Pour une histoire de la photographie en Belgique,* Musée de la Photographie, Charleroi (with publication of the illustrated book)

Collections:

Provinciaal Museum voor Kunstambachten Het Sterckshof, Deurne-Antwerp; Galerie Jeanne Buytaert, Antwerp; Belgian State Archives, Brussels; Bibliothèque Nationale, Paris; Museum Folkwang, Essen, West Germany; The Photographers Gallery, Saskatoon, Saskatchewan, Canada; Musée de la Photographie, Charleroi, Belgium.

Publications:

By DRIES: Articles—"Fotosalon in Het Stadhuis van Brussel" in *Fotografie* (Eindhoven, Netherlands), no. 1, 1956; "Fotografi del B.A.G." in *Fotografia* (Milan), May 1956; "Fotografie d'Oggi" in *Fotografia* (Milan), February 1957; "Photographie d'Aujourd'hui" in *Aujourd'hui Art et Architecture* (Paris), June 1957; "Photographie Moderne" in *Flash* (Brussels), December 1957; "Antoine Dries" in *Les Beaux-Arts,* (Brussels), March 1959; "Blick nach Draussen" in *Fotopost* (Mannheim, West Germany), February 1960; "Belgisk Fotografi i Dag" in *Nordisk Tidskrift för Fotografi* (Gothenburg, Sweden), May 1960; "Old and New Photography in Brussels" in *Foto-Tribune* (Antwerp), August 1962; "Photographie" in *L'Arc* (Aix-en-Provence, France), Spring 1962; "Antoon Dries: Poète de l'Image" in *Asahi Pentax Family* (Brussels), September 1966.

On DRIES: Books—*De Fotografie in Belgie 1940-1980,* exhibition catalogue, by Roger Coenen and Karel van Deuren, Antwerp 1980; *De Paradox van de Fotographie* by Johan M. Swinner, 1992. **Articles**—"Antoine Dries" by Julien Coulommier in *Foto* (Doetichem, Netherlands), April 1955; "Spanningen in de Fotograaf Antoine Dries" by Julien Coulommier in *Focus* (Haarlem, Netherlands), April 1961; "Antoon Dries fotografeert Kunstgalery" by Filip Tas in *De Standaard* (Antwerp), March 1976; "Antoon Dries: De Fotograaf en de Objectiviteit" by Ludo Bekkers in *Kunstbeeld* (Alphen aan de Rijn, Netherlands), January 1980; "Antoon Dries: Objectieve Fotografie" by Karel van Deuren in *Foto* (Doetichem, Netherlands), January 1981; "Quatre Regards de Chez Nous" by Guy Vaes in *Le Nouvel Impact* (Brussels), June 1981; "Der Verwondering" by Karel van Deuren in *Vorm-Info* (Brussels),

281

January/February 1983; "Antoon Dries ou l'experience photographique" in *La Libre Belgique* (Brussels), 1984. **Film**—*Over Fotografen*, Belgian television series, by Ludo Bekkers, 1984; broadcast—*De pioniers van den Fotografie*, 1994.

*

To put it briefly, what I am doing now is a sort of beholding of the simple reality around me, registering it, without transposition or dramatization, in photo-series which are in parallel with abstract thought.

—Antoon Dries

*   *   *

What is noteworthy in the enormous oeuvre of Antoon Dries, apart from its continuously high artistic quality, is that it alters and evolves just as life itself changes. In the late 1930s Dries began to take photographs as exercises in photographic techniques and classical composition. After World War II, he identified with the subjective photography propagated by Steinert, but then moved on. In an unbroken process of both condensation and invention, he has moved to a style that says more with less visual information. His most recent work is endowed with a touch of Japanese asceticism.

Since 1970 he has worked mainly, as he says, in "series and sequences or at least joined or confronted photos." Yet each individual photo is important; each is of excellent quality. The accent is more on the print than on the conveying of "concept." It is perhaps correct to say that each series of prints is an attempt to integrate time, to visualize an organic process, to establish relativities. In their subtle variations on a theme, the series might be said to show a musical structure. It is extraordinarily enthralling and original work which requires the observer's close attention.

Above all, Antoon Dries looks at the wondrous phenomena that occur all around us with a strong personal response—the melting of a snow-flake, the drying up of a puddle, and slow rotting and shrivelling of fruit.

—Karel van Deuren

DUNCAN, David Douglas.

Nationality: American. **Born:** Kansas City, Missouri, 23 January 1916. **Education:** Studied archaeology at the University of Arizona, Tucson, 1935, and marine zoology and deep-sea diving at the University of Miami, 1935-38, B.A. 1938. **Military Service:** Served as a combat photographer in the United States Marine Corps, in the South Pacific, 1943-46: Lieutenant-Colonel; Legion of Merit, Distinguished Flying Cross, Air Medal, and Purple Heart. **Family:** Married Leila Khanki in 1947 (divorced, 1962); married Sheila Macauley in 1962. **Career:** Has worked as a boxer, deep-sea diver, airline publicity photographer, etc.; photographer, foreign press correspondent and art historian, since 1938: Official Cameraman, Michael Lerner Chile/Peru Expedition, for the American Museum of Natural History, New York, 1940-41; Photographer and Chile/Peru Coordinator, Office of Inter-American Affairs, Washington, D.C., 1941-42; Staff Photographer, *Life* Magazine, in Palestine, Greece, Korea and Indo-China, 1946-56; freelance photographer, working for *Collier's, Life,* ABC-TV, NBC-TV, etc., in the U.S.S.R., Vietnam, the United States and Europe, since 1966. **Recipient:** Gold Medal, *U.S. Camera,* 1950; Overseas Press Club Award, 1951; Robert Capa Gold Medal, 1968; Photographer of the Year Award, American Society of Magazine Photographers, 1968. Honorary Khan of the Qashqui Tribe, Iran. **Address:** Castellaras 53, Mouans-Sartoux, Alps Maritime 06, France.

Individual Exhibitions:

1971 William Rockhill Nelson Gallery, Kansas City, Missouri (retrospective)
1972 Whitney Museum, New York
1981 *250 Photographs of Picasso,* Sidney Janis Gallery, New York

Selected Group Exhibitions:

1951 *Memorable Life Photographs,* Museum of Modern Art, New York
1964 *The Painter and the Photograph: From Delacroix to Warhol,* University of New Mexico, Albuquerque
1967 *Photography in the 20th Century,* National Gallery of Canada, Ottawa (toured Canada and the United States, 1967-73)
1977 *Documenta 6,* Kassel, West Germany
1980 *Photography of the 50s,* International Center of Photography, New York (travelled to the Center for Creative Photography, University of Arizona, Tucson; Minneapolis Institute of Arts; California State University at Long Beach; and Delaware Art Museum, Wilmington)
1983 *Il Reportage Fotografico nelle Guerre Contemporanee,* Palazzo Fortuny, Venice

Collections:

Time-Life Library, New York; International Museum of Photography, George Eastman House, Rochester, New York; Nelson-Atkins Museum of Art, Kansas City, Missouri.

Publications:

By DUNCAN: Books—*This is War!,* New York and London 1951; *The Private World of Pablo Picasso,* New York 1958; *The Kremlin,* London 1960; *Picasso's Picassos,* London 1961, 1968; *Yankee Nomad,* London 1966; *War Without Heroes,* New York 1970; London 1971; *Portfolio,* Lausanne 1972; *Prismatics: Exploring a New World,* Paris 1972, London and Dusseldorf 1973; *Goodbye Picasso,* New York and London 1974; *The Silent Studio,* London 1976.

On DUNCAN: Books—*Memorable Life Photographs,* with text by Edward Steichen, New York 1951; *Words and Pictures: An Introduction to Photojournalism* by Wilson Hicks, New York 1952; *How Life Gets the Story: Behind the Scenes in Photo-Journalism,* edited by Stanley Rayfield, New York 1955; *The Picture History of Photography* by Peter Pollack, New York 1958; *The Painter and the Photograph: From Delacroix to Warhol* by Van Deren Coke, Albuquerque, New Mexico 1964, 1972; *Photography in the 20th Century* by Nathan Lyons, New York 1967; *The Magic Image* by Cecil Beaton and Gail Buckland, London and Boston 1975; *Documenta 6,* exhibition catalogue, by Klaus Honnef and Evelyn Weiss, Kassel and Cologne 1977; *Geschichte der Fotografie im 20. Jahrhundert/Photography in the 20th Century* by Petr Tausk, Cologne 1977, London 1980; *Photography of the 50s: An American Perspective* by Helen Gee, Tucson, Arizona 1980; *Bilder vom Krieg* by Rainer Fabian and Hans Christian Adam, Hamburg 1983, as *Images of War: 130 Years of War Photography,* London 1985. **Articles**—"Korea: David Douglas Duncan" in *U.S. Camera Annual 1951,* edited by Tom Maloney, New York 1950; "Seized Moment" in *Time* (New York), 20 September 1971; "David Douglas Duncan" in *Modern Photography Annual,* New York 1972; "Duncan Photo Show Is First at Whitney" by G. Fraser in the *New York Times,* 15 June 1972; "Les Prismatiques de David Douglas Duncan" in *Zoom* (Paris), no. 20, 1973; "Living Masters of Photography" by Allan Porter in *Camera* (Lucerne), June 1974.

*   *   *

Yankee Nomad is the title of one of David Douglas Duncan's books and an apt title it is. Duncan has been all over the place—a photo-journalist with Everywhere as his location. He has caught fishermen in Mexico; shrines in Japan; Christmas in Kansas City; bullfights in Spain; flying in small planes; golf amid the oil pipelines of the Middle East; sheep, painted for easier spotting by their shepherds, in Ireland. He has done portraits of Eisenhower and Farouk, recorded Lord Mountbatten during the last days of British rule in India. Out of all his observations of historic places, persons and events has come a deep insight into history with overtones of the ironic along with something of the resignation of a seasoned fighting man.

Duncan has been an active Marine and "gone to war" gung ho. He has covered the French in Vietnam, bomber missions, Palestinian terrorism, warriors in south Iran, the Korean war. A number of his images of exhausted G.I.'s have become contemporary icons, immediately recognized as true pictures of the awfulness of war. He has managed to convey such things as fear, death, destruction, the terrain, the weather of combat along with the trivia of cigarettes, coffee, idiosyncrasies of clothing, beards. But above all he has got on paper the haunted and haunting expression in soldiers' eyes.

This response to eyes may be one of the reasons for Duncan's other great subject: Pablo Picasso. Duncan took countless photographs of Picasso over many years, thereby superbly documenting one of this century's great artists. One of the outstanding features of Picasso's face were his big dark eyes with their humor and sadness and relentless scrutiny. Duncan ''snuck'' into the artist's life, capturing not only the famous eyes but also his work and play, ''fair weather and foul,'' night and day. His camera has recorded how Picasso went about making his art, what he worked on, where he worked. And, by way of compliment, he documented Picasso's world of loved ones, associates, friends, homes, landscapes, games—not to mention such things as Picasso in his underpants, Picasso in an Indian war bonnet, and, of course, Picasso's eyes peering through the cut-out eyes of one of his playful drawings.

—Ralph Pomeroy

DUPAIN, Max.

Nationality: Australian. **Born:** Sydney, New South Wales, 22 April 1911. **Education:** Attended Sydney Grammar School, under F.G. Phillips, 1925-30; studied drawing and painting, East Sydney Technical College and Julian Ashton School, Sydney, 1933-35; photographic apprentice to Cecil Bostock, Sydney, 1930-34. **Military Service:** Served as a camouflage officer, Royal Australian Air Force, in Australia, New Guinea, and the Admiralty Islands, 1939-45; Photographer, Department of Information, Canberra, 1945-47. **Family:** Married Diana Illingworth in 1944; children: Danina and Rex. **Career:** Freelance industrial, architectural, fashion, portrait and advertising photographer, Sydney, 1934-39, 1947-92: joined Hartland and Hyde, process engravers, and established Max Dupain and Associates Pty. Ltd., Sydney, 1961. Photography Critic, *Sydney Morning Herald*, 1980-81. **Recipient:** Silver Jubilee Medal, 1977. Honorary Fellow, Royal Australian Institute of Architects, 1980. O.B.E. (Order of the British Empire) for services to Photography, 1982; President's Medal, Royal Australian Institute of Architects, Sydney Chapter, for services to architectural photography, 1989; A.C. for services to photography, 1992. **Agent:** Diana Dupain, 23 The Scarp, Castlecrag, NSW, 2068, Australia. **Died:** 1992.

Individual Exhibitions:

1938	University of Sydney
1960	University of New England, Armidale, New South Wales
1962	*No Time to Spare*, David Jones Gallery, Sydney
1967	*Australian Colonial Architecture*, Art Gallery of New South Wales, Sydney
	Old and New Buildings, Manly Art Gallery, Sydney
1969	*Burley Griffin's Architiecture*, Castlecrag, Sydney
	From Amateur to Top Professional, Photographic Society of New South Wales, Sydney
1973	*Sydney Opera House*, at the *Triennale*, Milan
1975	Australian Centre for Photography, Sydney (retrospective)
	National Gallery of Victoria, Melbourne (retrospective)
1978	Church Street Photographic Centre, Melbourne (retrospective)
	Max Dupain: New Work, Powell Street Gallery, Melbourne
1980	*Max Dupain: Retrospective 1930-1980*, Art Gallery of New South Wales, Sydney
	Max Dupain: Architectural Photographs, Australian Centre for Photography, Sydney
1981	The Photographers' Gallery, London
	Ray Hughes Gallery, Brisbane
	Church Street Gallery, Melbourne
1983	City of Horsham Regional Gallery

	Castlemaine Art Gallery
	Max Dupain: New Work, Old Work and Very Old Work, A.C.P.
1987	*Max Dupain's Australia*, Staley Wise Gallery, New York
	All Passion Spent—Bar Love, Christine Abrahams Gallery, Melbourne
1988	*To Orange with Love*
1990	*Max Dupain's Dancers*, Blaxland Gallery, Sydney
	Christine Abrahams Gallery, Melbourne
1991	*A Celebration*, David Jones Gallery
	80th Birthday, Christine Abrahams Gallery, Melbourne
1992	BMG Fine Art, Adelaide

Selected Group Exhibitions:

1932	*Salon Internationale de Photographie*, Paris
1934	*London Salon of Photography*
	Victorian Salon of Photography, Melbourne
1955	*Six Photographers*, David Jones Gallery, Sydney
1960	*Third Sydney International Exhibition of Photography*
1979	*Australian Pictorial Photography*, Art Gallery of New South Wales, Sydney
1980	*The 30s*, Erwin Museum and Art Gallery, Sydney
	International Photography: The Last 10 Years, Australian National Gallery, Canberra
1983	*Australian Photography 1930-60*, Art Gallery of New South Wales, Sydney

Collections:

Australian National Gallery, Canberra; National Gallery of Victoria, Melbourne; Adelaide Art Gallery; Hobart Art Gallery.

Publications:

By DUPAIN: Books—*Soul of a City*, text by John Thompson, edited by Oswald Ziegler, Sydney 1940; *Flower Pieces*, text by Helen Blaxland, Sydney 1946; *Max Dupain: Photographs*, with an introduction by Hal Missingham, Sydney 1948; *Georgian Architecture in Australia*, with texts by Morton Herman, Marjorie Barnard and Daniel Thomas, Sydney 1963; *Australia Square, Sydney*, Sydney 1967; *Sydney Builds an Opera House*, edited by Oswald Ziegler, Sydney 1973; *Architecture for the New World, the work of Harry Seidler*, text by Peter Blake, Sydney 1973; *The Golden Decade of Australian Architecture*, with text by James Broadbent, Sydney 1978; *Harry Seidler, Australian Embassy*, text by Peter Blake, Sydney 1979; *Francis Greenway: A Celebration*, with an introduction by J.M. Freeland, Sydney 1980; *Old Colonial Buildings of Australia*, with an introduction by J.M. Freeland, Sydney 1980; *Fine Houses of Sydney*, text by Robert Irving and John Kinstler, Sydney 1982; *Leslis Wilkinson, A Practial Idealist*, compiled and edited by Suzanne Falkiner, Woollahra, NSW 1982; *Leaves of Iron: Glen Murcutt, Pioneer of an Australian Architectural Form*, text by Philip Drew, Sydney 1985, *Max Dupain's Australia*, 1986; *Max Dupain's Australian Landscapes*, 1988; *To Orange with Love, Orange NSW*, Orange City Council 1988; *Max Dupain*, 1991. **Articles**—''Man Ray'' in *The Home Magazine* (Sydney), October 1935; ''The Photography of Henri Mallard'' in *Building the Sydney Harbour Bridge*, Sydney 1976.

On DUPAIN: Books—*Australian Photography*, annual, edited by Oswald Ziegler, Sydney 1947; *Creative Camera Collection 5*, edited by Colin Osman and Peter Turner, London 1978; *Max Dupain: 50 Years Work*, with text by Gael Newton, Sydney 1980; *Silver and Grey: Fifty Years of Australian Photography 1900-1950*, edited by Gael Newton, Sydney 1980. **Articles**—''Australian Camera Personalities'' by Laurence Le Guay in *Contemporary Photography* (Sydney), January/February 1947; ''Max Dupain'' by Gael Newton and others, in special monograph issue of *Light Vision* (Melbourne), May/June 1978.

*

The Sunbaker, **1937.** Photograph by Max Dupain.

The technique of etching and that of oil and watercolour painting and sculpture has not changed basically for hundreds of years. They are established mediums. What remains to be done with them is forever an eternity of exploration and adventure.

Not so with photography. Every month in the picture magazines there are pages devoted to new gadgets, new flash units, new automatic devices with which to do something differently and more quickly than before; in short, to gratify the whims of mechanically minded amateur photographers and create a profitable industry out of profitless indulgence.

Those who practice this gadget-ridden "folk art of 20th century people" have substituted "nostalgia" for "opium." Because in the long run this element, this photo soporific, is the sum total of their efforts.

After nearly half a century of pretty close involvement in photography I'm convinced that we have to assess the product of this art of ours by its significance. So much of it is banal and trivial and meaningless. There is

currently a rash of urban landscapes appearing in every magazine you pick up, and the majority of these pictures are boring and proletarian.

On the other hand, there are photographers with a great sense of discipline, who work with unsophisticated equipment and who possess an acute sense of selection and spontaneous composition. They are able to extract every ounce of pictorial sensibility from their subject, and I support their doctrine to the last. Sensitivity, piercing awareness, emotional and intellectual involvement, self-discipline are some of the elements which create that rapport with the subject, be it a rock or a woman or a woman on a rock!

Once this is established—and it takes only fractions of seconds—the camera takes over. But without that subjective liaison as the first flash upon the inward eye, the result is almost always sterile and useless.

Subject matter comes to you, you don't go to it (as in Russian television—it watches you!). Like a theme which comes to a composer; straight from heaven; three or four notes and you've got it to work on, to elaborate, improvise, exercise counterpoint until you have a symphony or concerto based on that original theme of several notes.

Likewise you may be on a walk through the bush, a street, a park, or driving to work, and spontaneously an inner voice will call out to you and, behold, there it is. Although I shoot extemporaneously a lot of the time, I prefer to have half a dozen shots in my mind. Probably I have seen them many times under different conditions and have been thinking about them. The moment will come when I shall go to them and make the photographs (in black and white)! I find the contemplation of the subject brings it closer to you, and when you are there face to face and under the stress of knowing this is it and there's no turning back, something just goes bang inside and it's all over. I'm sorry I cannot give you a formula for this one; but I stress two things, simplicity and directness. This means reduction of the subject to elementary or even symbolic terms, by devious selection of viewpoint, by lighting, by after-treatment. I do not always print the total negative. This practice has become a bit of a fetish. What the hell. The result is all that matters. Also I work mostly in black and white—it suits my will to interpret and dramatize. I have more control with black and white, without which the personal element is lost forever.

Working as a professional photographer in insular Australia has been my self-chosen lot. In such a "cultural backwater," as Norman Lindsay expressed it, mental stimulation is anything but over-plus, especially the further one moves into the rural regions. So one is thrown up against one's inner resources, and visual excitement comes from over there by proxy in picture books and printed text; music, poetry, painting and sculpture provide the vital ingredients for soul fodder in the local scene. Direct influential impact is at half-strength capacity. I think this is a good thing if one has the courage and endurance to sustain and promote his individuality by sheer brute assertion of belief in himself. God help those who can't muster this will unless they migrate, absorb and return to us, temporarily stimulated and refreshed, but possibly as other human beings lost to their real selves in the wilderness of the world's pictorial paradise.

After reading over what I have written, I am reminded of an article by Beatrice Faust in an issue of *Light Vision*. She declares, "There is an incredible amount of bullshit being written and spoken about photography," simultaneously adding her share to the heap! At the same time, she issues an alert against the seduction of words. No doubt her findings are correct, but they do not pertain only to photography; the whole subjective world is full of it. The prime endeavour of art critics and writers about aesthetic matters is to enlarge the chimera which is emitted by their subject and recreate the dictum that "all is illusion." Let's not talk too much; there is a great deal of material out there to be taken hold of, grappled with and hammered down into beautiful photographic prints. Let's get on with it.

By the way, this credo establishes a very personal attitude to the art I practice. Great art is *not* persona; it's impersonal. Shakespeare is not personal, he embraces all men. Beethoven is not personal, he reaches heights beyond this earth. How about Rembrandt? That light is divine. Listen to the Gods entering Valhalla in Wagner's *Rhinegold,* and think of photography. I dare you!

—Max Dupain

*   *   *

Max Dupain was possibly *the* photographer extraordinary of contemporary Australia. His formative years in the late 1920s and early 1930s were beset by visual clichés emanating from the pictorial, salon school of photography which boasted a vast following. Bromoil prints, misty landscapes and the ubiquitous S curve of "the line of grace" were everywhere to be seen on exhibition walls. Dupain too produced some of these sentimental works—and did them very well. But quite suddenly—and perhaps by accident—he discovered a new world that dealt with reality and the power of industrial form. From this modernism stance he never retreated.

An early picture dated 1932 of a stone quarry with demanding diagonal shadows was followed closely by a superb image of grain silos towering into a clear Australian sky. The concrete forms vibrated within the frame edge of the picture to unleash a new visual strength. This was Dupain's radical turning point; it set him apart from his contemporaries in Australia and related his work directly to the international understanding of the documentary approach. When later (1947) he read *Grierson on Documentary* it served to reinforce his attitudes. He was particularly impressed by the great film-maker's definition of Documentary as "the creative treatment of actuality," and he used this quotation to support his philosophy on many future occasions.

Should it be surprising that Dupain became a leader in modern Australian photography, it is even more surprising that his personal images continued to be produced alongside a varied output of commercial work which included architecture, industry, fashion, portraits and product advertising. For many successful Australian photographers there is no time or inclination for personal production after commercial activities, but for Dupain the two always went hand in hand.

Dupain found photography as his means of expression during his years at Sydney Grammar School. It was here that he won his first award for "the productive use of spare time" with an exhibition of landscape photographs. This was in 1928 at the age of seventeen. He later received many prizes and awards, including an honorary fellowship of the Royal Australian Institute of Architects for his services to the photography of architecture. His first retrospective was mounted by The Australian Centre for Photography in 1975, and 1980 saw a further retrospective at The Art Gallery of New South Wales. Both these exhibitions paid long overdue tribute to a major Australian artist.

Writing in the monograph *Max Dupain,* Gael Newton states: "Max Dupain has created a body of work unmatched by his contemporaries. . . . His best images simultaneously belong to Australian culture and to the expression of the modern era which first inspired his work in 1931."

—David Moore

DUTTON, Allen A(yers).

Nationality: American. **Born:** Kingman, Arizona, 13 April 1922. **Education:** Attended Mohave County Union High School, Kingman, 1936-40; Los Angeles Art Center, 1940-41; Arizona State University, Tempe, 1941-42, 1945-47, M.A. in education 1947; Bennington College, Vermont, 1961 (John Hay Fellow); San Francisco Art Institute, 1964. **Military Service:** Served as a staff-sergeant in the United States Army, in the U.S.A. and North Africa, 1942-46. **Family:** Married Harriet E. Freeberg in 1946 (divorced, 1962); married Mary Ann Enloe in 1963; children: Nels, Elizabeth and Wendy. **Career:** Worked as an entomologist, Arizona Agro Chemicals, Phoenix, 1948-54; Instructor, North Phoenix High School, 1954-61. Freelance photographer, Arizona, since 1964. Instructor in Photography, Phoenix College, 1961-68 and since 1969. Film Producer, Encyclopaedia Brittanica Films, Chicago, 1968-69. **Agents:** Vision Gallery, 216 Newbury Street, Boston, Massachusetts 02116; and Photography Southwest Gallery, 4223 North Marshall Way, Scottsdale, Arizona. **Address:** 15235 North 11th Street, Phoenix, Arizona 85022, U.S.A.

Individual Exhibitions:

1964	Union Gallery, Phoenix, Arizona
1965	Arizona State University, Tempe
1967	Phoenix College, Arizona
1970	Instituto Mexicano-Norteamericano, Mexico City
1973	Nikon Salon, Tokyo
1974	Galeria Garcia, Carefree, Arizona
1976	Shinju Gallery, Tokyo
	Galleria Il Diframma, Milan (and Galleria Il Diframma, Florence and Rome)
	Focus Gallery, San Francisco
1977	Galerie Bardiwill, Paris
	Massachusetts Institute of Technology, Cambridge
1978	Photography Southwest Gallery, Scottsdale, Arizona
1979	Northlight, Tempe, Arizona
1980	Photography Southwest Gallery, Scottsdale, Arizona
	Phoenix College, Phoenix, Arizona
1985	Vision Gallery, San Francisco (with Jack Foss)
1987	*Retrospective,* Arizona State University, Tempe, Arizona
1991	Hal Martin Fogle Gallery, Scottsdale, Arizona
1993	Hal Martin Fogle Gallery, Scottsdale, Arizona

1995   Phoenix College, Phoenix, Arizona

Selected Group Exhibitions:

1968   *Light,* Hayden Gallery, Massachusetts Institute of Technology, Cambridge
1972   *Multiple Image,* University of Rhode Island, Kingston
         Octave of Prayer, Hayden Gallery, Massachusetts Institute of Technology, Cambridge
1978   *The Great West: Real/Ideal,* University of Colorado, Boulder (toured the United States)
         Self-Portrayal, Friends of Photography, Carmel, California
1980   *Silver Sensibilities,* Newhouse Gallery, Staten Island, New York

Collections:

Museum of Modern Art, New York; University of Kentucky, Lexington; University of New Mexico, Albuquerque; Arizona State University, Tempe; Phoenix College, Arizona; Bibliothèque Nationale, Paris; Tokyo College of Photography.

Publications:

By DUTTON: Books—*Mental Retardation: An Image,* Phoenix, Arizona 1968; *The Great Stone Tit,* Tempe, Arizona 1974; *A.A. Dutton's Compendium of Relevant But Unreported 20th Century Phenomena,* Phoenix, Arizona 1977; *Hide and Seek,* portfolio, Phoenix, Arizona 1979; *Fantastic Photographs Folio 1,* portfolio, Phoenix, Arizona 1980; *Mythology for the Twenty First Century,* Tempe, Arizona 1992.

On DUTTON: Book—*Photography for Collectors: The West,* edited by James Alinder, Carmel, California 1980. **Article**—"Allen A. Dutton," special monograph issue of *Northlight* (Tempe, Arizona), May 1977.

             *

The advent of photography caused a revolution in the graphic arts. This medium made it possible to accurately record aspects of the world which, until then, had only been hinted at. The photograph's ability to give us as realistic a record of the visual world in two dimensions is unsurpassed and yet seldom used today with the sharpest intent. The documentary photograph has alternately been venerated and left to languish.

I feel that I am in a small degree unique in that I have used the photographic image not only to record my libido but also the physical environment in which I live. For more than a decade I have been an exponent and practitioner of the photomontage. I feel that this mode of using the photographic image is most valid when my business has been that of documenting my own psyche. I also contend that when I turn my attention to the physical world, the documentary camera style, which so vivified the photography of the last half of the 19th century, is most appropriate. This is why I generally utilize an 8 x 10-inch view camera at such times. It lends itself to making as accurate a record of the physical characteristics of this world as any photographic tool ever has.

I enjoy recording every minute detail of the desert where I live. I discover in my photographs more than I ever can when I contemplate the Arizona landscape directly. Unfortunately, many contemporary photographers attempt to use a 35mm camera to do what the large-view camera does so well. When they are seduced by the ease of use of the small hand camera for this purpose, I am sure that everyone is the loser.

—Allen A. Dutton

       *   *   *

Claiming that his paintings could never look like his dreams, Allen Dutton turned to photography to create his own private world of surrealistic imagery. In his exploration of both personal and societal fetishes and in his re-creation of dreams, he has produced many strange but engaging images.

The Great Stone Tit is an irreverant look at "titenvy," which in Dutton's vernacular is a counterpart to penis envy. Sometimes attacked by feminists as chauvinist, sexist, and exploitive, this book is actually meant as a humorous tribute to womankind. The pages and pages of women's breasts are aimed more at the obsessions of men than those of women. As he says in the introduction, "He [man], therefore, has developed an overpowering titenvy which far surpasses any envy displayed by women."

The title of Dutton's later book, *A.A. Dutton's Compendium of Relevant But Unreported 20th Century Phenomena,* is a good indication of the somewhat farcical nature of his concerns. In this work a rambling text, made up of fables, parables, and pseudo-critical essays, accompanies his surrealist inspired photo montages. Here he creates an entire universe of fictional characters, events, heroes, religious rites, truths (which he numbers 1 through 57), legends and myths. Dr. Amy Abletung, world-renowned symbologist from the Center for Creative Symbology located at Mount Grundy, Iowa, adds to the volume a half dozen mock-serious psychological profiles of Dutton's individual pictures; Tungger Rasmussen, "a connoisseur of various sundry and arcane pastimes," is purported to be author of a number of verses accompanying the photos; and Shibo Lethum, an artist working around the time 2,351,012 B.C., is supposed to have contributed a master print showing 29 buttocks. The rest of the compendium is filled with truths (such as "Diligence should be exercised in the care and maintenance of vegetable gardens and external sex organs, for when either is neglected they can easily become overgrown and unproductive") and many other indescribable myths and fables surrounding photographs of parts of bodies and nude women in totally fabricated dreamscapes.

More than anything, Dutton's work seems designed to challenge a viewer's sense of believability, and to push him into the nether realms of imagination.

—Ted Hedgpeth

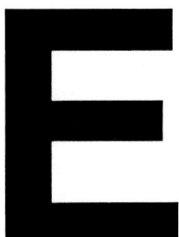

EDGERTON, Harold E(ugene).

Nationality: American. **Born:** Fremont, Nebraska, 6 April 1903. **Education:** Educated in Aurora, Nebraska, 1914-21; studied at the University of Nebraska, Lincoln, 1921-25, B.S. 1925; Massachusetts Institute of Technology, Cambridge, 1926-27, M.S. 1927, D.Sc. 1931. **Military Service:** Served as a consultant to the United States Army, in Italy, France and England, 1942-43. **Family:** Married Esther May Garrett in 1928; children: Mary, William, and Robert. **Career:** Worked as an electrical engineer, Nebraska Power and Light Company, Aurora, 1919-21, and General Electric Company, Schenectady, New York, 1926. Teacher of electrical engineering, Massachusetts Institute of Technology, Cambridge, since 1928 (now Emeritus). Independent photographer, developer of stroboscopic high-speed motion and still photography equipment, Cambridge, since 1930. Founder-Partner, 1947, and Honorary Chairman of the Board until retirement, 1972, Edgerton, Germeshausen and Grier (now EG&G Inc.); purveyor of technical and scientific products and services, Cambridge. **Recipient:** Potts Medal, Franklin Institute, Philadelphia, 1941; Royal Photographic Society Medal, London, 1944; Gold Medal, National Geographic Society, Washington, D.C., 1968; Albert A. Michelson Medal, American Optical Society, 1969; Culture Award, Deutsche Gesellschaft für Photographie (DGPh), West Germany, 1981. Member, National Academy of Sciences, 1964, and National Academy of Engineering, 1966. **Agent:** Palm Press Inc., 23 Bradford Street, Concord, Massachusetts 01742, U.S.A. **Died:** (in Cambridge, Massachusetts) 4 January 1990.

Individual Exhibitions:

1976	*Seeing the Unseen,* Ikon Gallery, Birmingham, England (travelled to the Photographers' Gallery, London; Hatton Gallery, Newcastle upon Tyne; Midland Group Gallery, Nottingham; Museum of Modern Art, Oxford; and Arnolfini Gallery, Bristol)
1977	Margaret Compton Gallery, Massachusetts Institute of Technology, Cambridge
	Vision Gallery, Boston
	Stephen Wirtz Gallery, San Francisco
	G. Ray Hawkins Gallery, Los Angeles
1978	Galerie Agathe Gaillard, Paris
1980	Museum of Science, Boston
1981	Gallery of Photographs, New Haven, Connecticut
	Haverford College, Pennsylvania
	Daniel Wolf Inc., New York
1982	University of Nebraska, Lincoln
1986	*The Split Second,* Silver Image Gallery, Columbus, Ohio
1994	*Seeing the Unseen: Dr Harold E. Edgerton and the Wonders of Strobe Alley,* George Eastman House, Rochester, New York

Selected Group Exhibitions:

1959	*Hundert Jahre Photographie 1839-1939,* Museum Folkwang, Essen (travelled to Cologne and Frankfurt)
1960	*The Sense of Abstraction,* Museum of Modern Art, New York
1964	*The Painter and the Photograph: From Delacroix to Warhol,* University of New Mexico, Albuquerque

1978	*Photos from the Sam Wagstaff Collection,* Corcoran Gallery, Washington, D.C. (toured the United States and Canada)
1979	*Fleeting Gestures: Dance Photographs,* International Center of Photography, New York (travelled to *Venezia '79* and to The Photographers' Gallery, London)
	Life: The First Decade 1936-45, Grey Art Gallery, New York University
1982	*Floods of Light,* The Photographers' Gallery, London
1983	*Invention and Allegory,* Daniel Wolf Inc., New York
1984	*Sammlung Gruber,* Museum Ludwig, Cologne

Collections:

Massachusetts Institute of Technology, Cambridge; International Museum of Photography, George Eastman House, Rochester, New York; Plainsman Museum, Aurora, Nebraska; Gernsheim Collection, University of Texas at Austin; Science Museum, London; Bibliothèque Nationale, Paris; Centre Georges Pompidou, Paris; Moderna Museet, Stockholm; Museum Ludwig, Cologne.

Publications:

By EDGERTON: Books—*Flash! Seeing the Unseen by Ultra-High-Speed Photography,* with J.R. Killian, Boston 1939, 1954; *Electronic Flash, Strobe,* New York 1970, as paperback, Cambridge, Massachusetts 1979; *Seeing the Unseen,* portfolio, with an introduction by Geoffrey W. Holt, Cambridge, Massachusetts 1977; *Moments of Vision: The Stroboscopic Revolution in Photography,* with James R. Killian Jr., Cambridge, Massachusetts 1979.

On EDGERTON: Books—*A Hundred Years of Photography 1839-1939* by Lucia Moholy, London 1939; *Histoire de la Photographie* by Raymond Lecuyer, Paris 1945; *Hundert Jahre Photographie 1839-1939 aus der Sammlung Gernsheim,* exhibition catalogue, by Helmut and Alison Gernsheim, Essen 1959; *Polaroid Portfolio No. 1,* edited by John Wolbarst, New York 1959; *The Painter and the Photograph: From Delacroix to Warhol* by Van Deren Coke, Albuquerque, New Mexico 1964, 1972; *Looking at Photographs: 100 Pictures from the Collection of the Museum of Modern Art* by John Szarkowski, New York 1973; *The Magic Image* by Cecil Beaton and Gail Buckland, London and Boston 1975; *Geschichte der Fotografie im 20. Jahrhundert/Photography in the 20th Century* by Petr Tausk, Cologne 1977, London 1980; *Tusen och en Bild,* exhibition catalogue, by Ake Sidwall, Sune Jonsson and Ulf Hard af Segerstad, Stockholm 1978; *A Book of Photographs from the Collection of Sam Wagstaff,* designed by Arne Lewis, New York 1978; *Amerika Fotografie 1920-1940* by Erika Billeter, Berne 1979; *Life: The First Decade 1936-1945* by Robert Littman, Ralph Graves and Doris C. O'Neill, New York 1979, London 1980; *The Photograph Collector's Guide* by Lee D. Witkin and Barbara London, Boston and London 1979; *La Chambre Claire* by Roland Barthes, Paris 1980; *Floods of Light: Flash Photography 1851-1981,* exhibition catalogue, by Rupert Martin, London 1982; *Sammlung Gruber: Photographie des 20. Jahrhunderts,* exhibition catalogue, with foreword by Siegfried Gohr, Cologne 1984; *Stopping Time,* by Jussim, Kayafas, Dagata and Mooney, New York 1987. **Articles**—"Edgerton

Densmore Shute Bends the Shaft, **1938.** Photograph by Dr. Harold E. Edgerton. ©The Harold E. Edgerton 1992 Trust.

Magique'' in *Photo* (Paris), March 1979; ''Papa Flash's Magic Strobes'' in *Photography Year 1980,* by the Time-Life editors, New York 1980; ''Stroboscopic Lighting in the Realm of Art'' by Gene Thornton in the *New York Times,* 10 January 1982.

*

As I see it, photography is entirely dependent upon light energy. Perhaps I am biased, but electronic flash is the best known method today of producing high-intensity flashes that can be controlled. Once strobe sources became available, multiple applications have immediately followed, not only in conventional photography, but in a myriad collection of ever developing scientific projects.

An old article in the *British Journal of Photography* (September, 1864), when referring to Fox-Talbot's relatively weak spark experiments, stated, '' . . . further progress in this direction would not be difficult.'' So correct, but it has taken over 100 years for electronic flash to become a commonly used source of light for all types of photography.

The modern xenon-filled flash lamp, in contrast to the open spark of early days, as a photographic source, has three important qualifications: (1) the lamp can be made to operate at relatively low voltages: (2) the lamp is an efficient converter of electrical to radiant energy; and (3) the spectral distribution of energy is such that daylight color emulsions can be used.

A commercial market analysis made a few years ago predicted that flash photography was ''out'' since the improved films and lenses made photography possible with available light. Just the opposite has happened. The electronic flash, especially for portable photography, has blossomed since now a very *small* unit can serve because of fast lenses and films. However, the use of chemical flash bulbs has decreased, because they were too powerful and also they needed to be changed after each use.

Speciality electronic flash units for bullet photography (1 millionth of a second flash duration), golf ball close ups (1/100,000 of a second), birds (1/10,000 of a second) are now in demand since the conventional flash units in the market place have exposure times of greater than 1/1000 of a second. Photographs without blur are desired. The future of electronic flash is very bright!

—Harold E. Edgerton

*   *   *

Dr. Harold Edgerton was a photographer of extended vision. More exactly, he was a scientist who used photography to extend the capabilities of the human eye to micro-second vision. How radical this accomplishment is—for Edgerton has virtually changed the way we see in the 20th century—is the measure of his contribution to photography.

Dr. Edgerton's idea was simple but revolutionary. In 1931 he combined the camera with the stroboscope, a device invented in 1832, in which a moving object was viewed either through a slotted disk or by flashes of light. Edgerton utilized blinding-bright flashes of light, electrical discharges from neon-filled tubes, which could be very accurately controlled. The exposure was made in the infinitesimally small periods of time—as fast as one fifty-thousandth to one-millionth of a second—that the light flashed, thus overcoming the restrictions of a normal camera's mechanical shutter which could only open to top speeds of 1/1500th of a second. Since the camera and flash were synchronized and the speed of the flash could be made to equal that of a moving object, the object appeared to be standing still. This literally allowed objects to be photographed in mid-flight: water hung in mid-air, a speeding bullet was stopped before our very eyes, and a hummingbird's wings were transfixed in flight. The motion could be photographed as a single image, or superimposed in multiples of up to 600 per second, or linked to a motion picture camera to produce moving high-speed images.

One of the most important reasons that high-speed stroboscopic photography can not be ignored is that it has virtually changed our notion of time. Edgerton said of his photographs that they embody the possibility for ''time itself to be chopped up into small bits and frozen so that it suits our needs and wishes.'' Timing on a micro-scale nearly impossible to imagine is essential to this work. Thus, through photography we are able to see bodies moving through units of time so small they could not have been imagined by previous generations.

There are many implications to Edgerton's work. Not only has his stroboscopic photography been the foundation for the development of modern electronic flash, but he also took strobe to the depths of the ocean to reveal another unseen realm. This oceanographic work included designing watertight cameras and strobes, working aboard the *Calypso* with Jacques-Yves Cousteau, and developing sonar devices for geological research and underwater archaeological exploration.

All of Edgerton's photographs exploit potentials of the medium overlooked by an art-dominated view of photography. Edgerton considered himself primarily an electrical engineer; these photographs are primarily scientific documents. They were taken and are put to the use of photographic evidence of phenomena and are, as Geoffrey Holt stated, ''as neatly conclusive as the lengthiest equations.'' They have allowed scientists to chart the unknown, to see the previously unseen, and to analyze principles such as those governing impact, flight and velocity.

Yet these photographs, though they embody rational principles, exist also in the realm of wonder. They bring the marvel of our existence to us simply and directly, translating the aspects of science into a universal language which can be appreciated by the layman. They are accessible and many are familiar, but their wonder and significance can not be forgotten.

—Nancy Hall-Duncan

EDWARDS, Mark.

Nationality: British. **Born:** London, 12 June 1947. **Education:** Sibford School, Banbury, 1958-63; studied at the Guildford School of Art, Surrey, 1965-68, Dip.A.A. 1968. **Career:** Freelance photojournalist, London and Copenhagen, since 1968. **Recipient:** Publication Grant, Arts Council of Great Britain, 1974; Danish Government Book Grant, 1977; Silver Award, Design and Art Directors Association, London, 1981; United Nations *Global 500* Award for Outstanding Services to the Environment, 1990; Cherry Kearton Medal for Environmental Photography, awarded by Royal Geographic Society, 1992; **Addresses:** c/o Earthscan, 3 Endsleigh Street, London WCI, England; and 199A Shooters Hill Road, Blackheath, London SE3, England.

Individual Exhibitions:

1971	*The Face of Bengal,* Half Moon Gallery, London (with Chris Steele-Perkins; toured Britain)
1974	Serpentine Gallery, London
1977	*Film Ends,* Photographers Gallery, Southampton, Hampshire (with Chris Steele-Perkins; travelled to Spectro Workshop, Newcastle-upon-Tyne; Photographers' Gallery, London; Centre Culturel du Marais, Paris; International Center of Photography, New York)
1979	*Christiania,* The Photographers' Gallery, London (travelled to Galleri Loppen, Copenhagen, 1980)
1982	*Indians Here and Now,* The Photographers' Gallery, London (toured Britain)
	English Reportage, Moderna Museet, Stockholm
1984	*Two Folios,* The Photographers' Gallery, London (with George Rodger)

Selected Group Exhibitions:

1971	*8 Young Photographers,* The Photographers' Gallery, London
1972	*The Inquisitive Eye,* Institute of Contemporary Arts, London
1973	*One Hundred Photographs,* Chelsea School of Art, London
1975	*Young British Photographers,* The Photographers' Gallery, London (toured Europe, the United States and Canada)
1982	*Floods of Light,* The Photographers' Gallery, London
1984	*Trees,* The Photographers' Gallery, London
1987	*Realities Revisited,* Saidye Bronfman Centre, Montreal

Collections:

Victoria and Albert Museum, London; Arts Council of Great Britain, London; Danish Royal Library, Copenhagen.

Publications:

By EDWARDS: Books—*The Awakening of Intelligence,* with text by J. Krishnamurti, London 1973; *Young British Photographers,* editor, with Chris Steele-Perkins, London 1975; *Photography,* London 1977; *Christiania,* Copenhagen 1979; *Christiania Versuche, anders zu Leben,* Reinbek, West Germany 1980; *Karneval i Kobenhavn,* Copenhagen 1982; *Mark Edwards' Tivoli,* Copenhagen 1983; *To Landsbyer,* Copenhagen 1985; *Last Talks at Saanen,* with text by J. Krishnamurti, London 1986, USA 1987; *Two Cities,* WWF, UK 1988; *Changing Consciousness,* with Professor David Bohm, USA 1991; Photographs for *Defending the Future* and *Facing the Future,* London 1991.

On EDWARDS: Exhibition catalogues—*8 Young Photographers,* London 1971; *Film Ends,* London 1979; *Floods of Light: Flash Photography 1851-*

Topsoil Blowing Away in a Dust Storm, Ethiopia. Photograph ©Mark Edwards/Still Pictures.

1981 by Rupert Martin, London 1982. **Articles**—"Portfolio: Mark Edwards" in *British Journal of Photography* (London), 11 June 1971; "Mark Edwards: Pictures from India" in *Creative Camera* (London), July 1971.

*

Most of the photographs I have taken since I left Art School in 1968 are of people living in Third World countries. These pictures do not emphasise the extremes of poverty or political unrest—I have never quite come to terms with the enthusiasm the picture media has for dramatic suffering. Instead, I try to show what ordinary life is like in the villages and cities in a way that gives some insight into the causes of environmental problems which lead to the well-documented disasters reported throughout the world.

—Mark Edwards

*   *   *

Shortly after he left college Mark Edwards spent nearly two years travelling in India. This was not simply a hippy-trail experience but it did give him a direction for his life and for his work. The contrast between poverty and riches was so marked that he has spent the major part of his working career trying to illustrate the reasons for and responses to it throughout the third world. At the same time, an interest and growing understanding of the teachings of Krishnamurti has helped him retain a sane and balanced outlook in the face of the sometimes inexplicable behaviour of human beings towards one another.

During the seventies and early eighties Edwards exhibited widely and published books. Between long excursions to Africa and India he spent periods of time in Christiania, the commune on the outskirts of Copenhagen which acted as a kind of "rest and recreation" space in his life. He did not stop photographing however and made his first experiments with colour there, which resulted in one book on Christiania itself and two others on Tivoli and Carnivals in Copenhagen, commissioned in Denmark.

In all his work Mark Edwards has tried to show the whole picture. He works for long periods in particular places and is more interested in giving complete and correct information rather than going for a simple dramatic shot. In the early years much of this work was done for organisations such as Oxfam and Christian Aid, but as more of the world became interested in environmental issues the market expanded, and by the mid-1980s it was necessary to organise the growing library so that a wider public could be reached. Initially this was done through Panos, attached to Earthscan. Not long afterwards Mark established Still Pictures—now called Still Pictures-Moving Words.

During the past seven years Mark Edwards has continued to travel all over the world on assignments for a wide range of publications and environmental and development organisations. His work has been shown at many conferences on the earth's problems, and the library has continued to expand to include work by other well-known reportage and environmental photographers. The library also acts as an agency for like-minded organisations from both Eastern and Western Europe.

This is really the success story of a photographer who discovered early what he wanted to do and stuck to it through lean years until the wider world found that it too needed to look for reasons and methods of dealing with the world's growing problems of human and environmental resources.

—Sue Davies

EGGLESTON, William.

Nationality: American. **Born:** Memphis, Tennessee, in July 1937. **Education:** Attended public school in Sumner, Mississippi; Webb School, Bell Buckle, Tennessee; Vanderbilt University, Nashville, Tennessee; Delta State College, Cleveland, Mississippi; and University of Mississippi, Oxford. **Family:** Married, wife's name Rosa; children: William, Andrea, and Winston. **Career:** Freelance photographer, Memphis and Washington, D.C., since 1962. Lecturer in Visual and Environmental Studies, Carpenter Center, Harvard University, Cambridge, Massachusetts, 1974; Researcher in Color Video, Massachusetts Institute of Technology, Cambridge, 1978-79. **Recipient:** Guggenheim Fellowship, 1974; National Endowment for the Arts Photographer's Fellowship, 1975, and Arts Survey Grant, 1978. **Address:** 4382 Walnut Grove Road, Memphis, Tennessee 38117, U.S.A.

Individual Exhibitions:

1974   Jefferson Place Gallery, Washington, D.C.
1975   Carpenter Center, Harvard University, Cambridge, Massachusetts
1976   *William Eggleston's Guide,* Museum of Modern Art, New York (travelled to the Seattle Art Museum; Santa Barbara Museum of Art, California; Wight Galleries, University of California at Los Angeles; Reed College Art Gallery, Portland, Oregon; and University of Maryland Art Galleries, College Park)
1977   Brooks Memorial Art Gallery, Memphis, Tennessee
         Castelli Graphics, New York
         Allan Frumkin Gallery, Chicago
         Lunn Gallery, Washington, D.C.
         Grapestake Gallery, San Francisco
         William Eggleston/William Christenberry, Morgan Gallery, Shawnee Mission, Kansas
1978   *Color Photographs,* Cronin Gallery, Houston (with Nicholas Nixon)
1980   *Troubled Waters,* Charles Cowles Gallery, New York
1983   *Colour Photos from the American South,* Victoria and Albert Museum, London
         Recent Work, Fraenkel Gallery, San Francisco
1984   *Graceland and the South,* Art Institute of Chicago
1985   Middendorf Gallery, Washington, D.C.
         Recent Color Photos, Friends of Photography, Carmel, California
1986   *William Eggleston's Early Black and White Photography,* Memphis Brooks Museum, Memphis
1987   Southern Texas Museum, Austin
1988   Middendorf Gallery, Washington, D.C.
1989   Laurence Miller Gallery, New York
         New Orleans Museum of Art
         University Museum, Oxford, Mississippi
1990   *Democratic Forest,* Corcoran Gallery, Washington, D.C.
1992   *Ancient and Modern,* Barbican Gallery, London (travelled to Louisiana Museum, Copenhagen; Faulkwang Museum, Essen; Fotomuseum Winterthur, Zurich)
1993   Robert Miller Gallery, New York
1994   *From Graceland to Wasteland,* Laurence Miller Gallery, New York

Selected Group Exhibitions:

1974   *Straight Color,* Rochester Institute of Technology, New York
1975   *14 American Photographers,* Baltimore Museum of Art (travelled to Newport Harbor Art Museum, California; La Jolla Museum of Contemporary Art, California; Walker Art Center, Minneapolis; and Fort Worth Art Museum, Texas)
1976   *Spectrum,* Rochester Institute of Technology, New York
1977   *Contemporary American Photographic Works,* Museum of Fine Arts, Houston (travelled to the Museum of Contemporary Art, Chicago; La Jolla Museum of Contemporary Art, California; and Newport Harbor Art Museum, California)
1978   *Mirrors and Windows: American Photography since 1960,* Museum of Modern Art, New York (toured the United States, 1978-80)
1979   *American Images: New Work by 20 Contemporary Photographers,* Corcoran Gallery, Washington, D.C. (travelled to the International Center of Photography, New York; Museum of Fine Arts, Houston; Minneapolis Institute of Arts; and Indianapolis Institute of Arts, 1980; and American Academy, Rome, 1981)
1980   *The Imaginary Photo Museum,* Kunsthalle, Cologne
1982   *Slices of Time: California Landscapes,* Oakland Museum, California (travelled to Security Pacific National Bank, Los Angeles)
1983   *Subjective Vision,* High Museum of Art, Atlanta, Georgia
1985   *American Images 1945-80,* Barbican Art Gallery, London (toured Britain)
1989   Seibu Gallery, Tokyo
1993   *In Camera,* Museum of New Mexico, Santa Fe, New Mexico
         Daydream Nation, Luhring Augustine Gallery, New York
1994   *A Sense of Place,* Elizabeth Leach Gallery, Portland, Oregan

Collections:

Museum of Modern Art, New York; Corcoran Gallery of Art, Washington, D.C.; National Collection of Fine Arts, Washington, D.C.; Brooks Memorial Art Gallery, Memphis, Tennessee; New Orleans Museum of Art; Museum of Fine Arts, Houston; Birmingham Museum of Art, Alabama; Madison Art Center, Wisconsin.

Publications:

By EGGLESTON: Books—*14 Pictures,* portfolio, Washington, D.C. 1974; *William Eggleston's Guide,* edited by and with text by John Szarkowski, New York 1976; *Election Eve,* with a preface by Lloyd Fonvielle, New York 1977; *Troubled Waters,* portfolio, New York 1978.

On EGGLESTON: Books—*14 American Photographers,* exhibition catalogue, edited by Renato Danese, Baltimore 1975; *Amerikanische Landschaftsphotographie 1869-1978,* exhibition catalogue, Munich 1978; *Mirrors and Windows: American Photography since 1960* by John Szarkowski, New York 1978; *American Images: New Work by 20 Contemporary Photographers,* edited by Renato Danese, New York 1979; *The Imaginary Photo Museum* by Helmut Gernsheim, Renate and L. Fritz Gruber and others, Cologne 1981, London 1982; *William Eggleston: Colour Photographs from the American South,* exhibition catalogue, with text by Mark Haworth-Booth, London 1983; *New Color/New York* by Sally Eauclaire, New York 1984; *American Images: Photography 1945-1980,* edited by Peter Turner and John Benton-Harris, London 1985. **Articles**—"Photography: A Different Kind of Art" by John Szarkowski in the *New York Times Sunday Magazine,* 13 April 1975; "The Commonplace in Living Color" in *Photography Year 1976,* by the Time-Life editors, New York 1976; "New Frontiers in Color" by Douglas Davis in *Newsweek* (New York), 19 April 1976; "Art: Focus on Photo Shows" by Hilton Kramer in the *New York Times,* 28 May 1976; "Photographed Silence" by Malcolm Preston in *Newsday* (Long Island, New York), 10 June 1976; "MOMA Lowers the Color Bar" by Sean Callahan in *New York,* 28 June 1976; "Seeing Pictures" by Julia Scully in *Modern Photography* (New York), August 1976; "The Colors of William Eggleston" by Joan Murray in *Artweek* (Oakland, California), 18 September 1976; "How to Mystify Color Photography" by Max Kozloff in *Artforum* (New York), November 1976; "The Second Generation of Color Photographers" by Allan Porter in *Camera* (Lucerne), July 1977; "William Eggleston, Charles Cowles

Gallery" by Lynn Zelevansky in *Flash Art* (Milan), January/February 1981; "Graceland: Images of a Fallen King" by Richard Harrington in *Washington Post,* 10 December 1983; "Color Codes" by Mark Holborn in *Aperture 96,* 1984; "William Eggleston's Early Black and White Photography" by J Richard Gruber, Memphis 1986; "William Eggleston: Democracy and Chaos" by Mark Holborn in *Artforum,* Summer 1988; "An Interview with William Eggleston" by Charles Hagan in *Aperture 115,* Summer 1989; "The Democratic Forest" by Andy Grundberg in *New York Times,* 3 December 1989; "Translating Ideas into Color" by Malcolm Jones in *Newsweek,* 1 January 1990; "Los Alamos-A Fragment" by Walter Hopps in *Grand Street 36,* New York 1990; "William Eggleston: Seen and Unseen" by Carol Thompson in *The Print Collector's Newsletter,* vol xxi-5, November-December 1990; "Memphis Beau" by Richard Woodward in *Vanity Fair,* October 1991; "William Eggleston: An Interview" by Mark Haworth-Booth in *History of Photography,* v.17, no 1, Spring 1993.

*   *   *

If William Eggleston's photographs had been in black and white they would not have been noticed. They do not make us laugh, they do not shock or titillate us, they do not make us marvel at how he managed to stage the world so perfectly. But Eggleston's photographs are in color; he was one of the first serious photographers to take advantage of new color technologies. His first color work was shown at the Museum of Modern Art in 1976. The prints were made from color slides. The hues in color slides are intense and contrasty—superreal. Eggleston had large dye transfer prints made from his slides and was able to reduce contrast, increase saturation, and to reproduce on paper this superreal quality of color slides. The result was incredible. A worn out farm truck abandoned in a field glows with an inner heat—it is transformed into a gorgeous object. In the same way, road signs caught by the setting sun are transformed into incandescent jewels. The colors glow the way out-of-tune TV colors glow. Those who know Eggleston's work now see the beauty in the commonplace, in the fantasy world of objects shining in a setting sun. He has freed our senses. Eggleston likes to stay up late and sleep into the afternoon. His is a good fit between lifestyle, technology, and choice of subject matter.

Eggleston makes no fetish of discovery. His pictures are straightforward; they neither strive for the accidental, the sensational, the shocking, nor for the clever juxtaposition of unlikely objects and precise organization of diverse forms. They do share, however, a few of the other characteristics of the candid snapshot. Eggleston chooses the same kind of unimportant places and people, and his pictures have the seemingly unsophisticated casualness of snapshots. The difference is that Eggleston's are totally lacking in either the intrusiveness or the cuteness of much snapshot art photography. If there is irony in his pictures it is in the subject matter, not in the condescending attitude of the photographer. His goal seems to be to capture the normal moment which is always quietly present. He takes his pictures in the places he knows best—Memphis and northern Mississippi. It might be said that his pictures are more like the snapshots that amateurs take of friends and places than they are like the snapshots taken by other art photographers for museum walls.

Eggleston's banal and slightly decadent subject matter combines with his honorable attitude toward reality to save his pictures from any touch of sentimentality. He is, nonetheless, a romantic. His more recent works of sky and nature, using a larger camera and exchanging color negatives for slides, insures his position as a romantic. These may be the photographs he wanted to take all along, but only after shocking the art world into accepting color photography as serious and important could he indulge himself and make the pictures which earlier might have been foolishly rejected as the work of a talented camera club enthusiast.

—Barbara Norfleet

EHM, Josef.

Nationality: Czechoslovakian. **Born:** Habartov, 1 August 1909. **Education:** Attended public school in Poděbrady, Czechoslovakia, 1923-27; apprentice in the portrait studio of K. Podlipný, Poděbrady, Czechoslovakia, 1923-27.

Family: Married Marie Nesměrákova in 1956. **Career:** Worked as a photographer in various studios, Prague, 1927-34; Instructor, State Graphic School, Prague, 1934-46, 1960-67; freelance photographer, Prague, 1946-60, and from 1967. Contributing Editor, *Fotograficky Obzor* magazine, Prague, 1939-42. **Recipient:** Silver Medal, *Professional Photographers Exhibition,* Prague, 1938; Silver Medal, *International Photography Exhibition,* Poland, 1956; Silver Medal, *Bifota Exhibition,* Berlin, 1958; Silver Medal, *International Exhibition of Photography,* Budapest, 1958; Memorial Award, Panorama Publishers, Prague, 1979. **Died:** (in Prague) 8 November 1989.

Individual Exhibitions:

1947	SVU Purkyně Gallery, Prague (retrospective)
1948	Photographic Society, Plzeň, Czechoslovakia (retrospective)
1957	Photographic Society, Pardubice, Czechoslovakia (retrospective)
1959	Funke's Gallery, Brno, Czechoslovakia
1984	Gallery of Czechoslovak Writers, Prague House of Art, Brno, Czechoslovakia
1989	Robert Koch Gallery, San Francisco
1990	Jacques Baruch Gallery, Chicago

Selected Group Exhibitions:

1936	*International Exhibition of Photography,* Mánes Gallery, Prague
1939	*100 Years of Photography,* Museum of Decorative Arts, Prague
1948	*Czechoslovak Photography* (toured Switzerland)
1950	*Members' Exhibition,* Mánes Gallery, Prague
1959	*Union of Fine Artists Exhibition,* Mánes Gallery, Prague
1968	*2nd World Exhibition of Photography: Woman,* Pressehaus Stern, Hamburg (and world tour)
1970	*Cien Grabados y Cien Fotografias,* Museo Universitario, Mexico City
1975	*The Lyricism of Czech Photography,* Municipal Museum, Freiburg, West Germany
1979	*Man and Time,* Town Hall, Prague
1984	*Tschechische Fotografie 1918-48,* Museum Folkwang, Essen, West Germany (travelled to the Kunstverein, Frankfurt; Museum Moderner Kunst, Vienna)
	Body in Czechoslovak Photography, Musuem Kromerizska, Kromeriz, Czechoslovakia
1988	*Line, Color, Form,* Municipal Gallery, Prague
1989	*What is Photography—150 Years of Photography,* Gallery Mánes, Prague
1989	*Czechoslovakia Photography 1945-1989,* Gallery Valdstejnska jizdarna, Prague
1993	*Czech and Slovak Photography from Between the Wars to the Present,* Fitchburg Art Museum, Massachusetts (travelled to Boston and Middlebury)

Collections:

Museum of Decorative Arts, Prague; Moravian Gallery, Brno, Czechoslovakia; San Francisco Museum of Modern Art; Robert Koch Gallery, San Francisco; Howard Greenberg Gallery, New York; The Anne & Jacques Baruch Collection Ltd., Chicago; The Navigator Foundation Collection, Boston; Galerie Rudolf Kicken, Cologne; Institute for Theory and History of Art of the Czech Academy of Sciences, Prague.

Publications:

By EHM: Books—*St. George Church,* with text by Cibulka, Prague 1936; *The Sculptor Myslbek,* with text by V.V. Stech, Prague 1939; *The Sculptor Myslbek,* with text by V. Volavka, Prague 1942; *Prague,* with text by V.V. Stech, Prague 1948; *Glass Dream,* with text by N. Papoušková, Prague 1949; *Italian Majolics,* with text by J. Vydrová, Prague 1955; *Bohemian Porcelain,* with text by E. Poche, Prague 1956; *Prague of Yesterday and Today,* with text by E. Poche, Prague 1958, 1965; *Czech Gothic Sculpture,* with text by A.

Kutal, Prague 1962; *Czech Castles and Chateaux,* with text by J. Wagner, Prague 1971; *Prague,* with text by Frantisek Kožík, Prague 1973; *Prague's Interiors,* with text by E. Poche, Prague 1973; *Prague in Colour,* with text by J. Janáček, Prague 1979; *Das alte Prag,* with text by J. Janacek, Leipzig 1980, 1983; *Cechy—umelecke pamatky,* with text by Emanuel Poche, Prague, 1983. **Article**—"Interview with Josef Ehm," with Jiří Macku, in *Revue Fotografie* (Prague), no. 3, 1972.

On EHM: Books—*Modern Czech Photography* by Karel Teige, Prague 1943; *Licht und Schatten/Light and Shadow,* edited by Milos Hrbas, Prague 1959; *Josef Ehm* by Jiří Masìn, Prague 1961; *Josef Ehm—Profile* by Jiří Masìn, Prague 1963; *The Ways of Modern Photography* by Ludvìk Souček, Prague 1964; *History of Photography* by Rudolph Skopec, Prague 1964; *Art Which Can Be Done by Everybody?* by V. Zykmund, Prague 1964; *The Portrait in Photography* by Ludvik Baran, Prague 1965; *Encyclopedia of Practical Photography* by Petr Tausk and others, Prague 1972; *Fotografie im 20. Jahrhundert* by Petr Tausk, Cologne 1977, London 1979; *Josef Ehm: Portfolio* by Petr Tausk, Prague 1980; *Praha Objectiven Mistru/Prague Through the Lens of Masters,* with introduction by Ludvik Baran, Prague 1981; *Tschechische Fotografie 1918-1948,* exhibition catalogue, by Ute Eskildsen, Essen, West Germany 1984; *Encyclopédie internationale des photographes* by Michel and Michele Auer, Geneva 1985; *The Evolution of Czechoslovak Photography from 1918 to Today* by Petr Tausk, Prague 1986; *Cernobila fotografie,* by Antonin Dufek, Prague 1987; *Cesty ceskoslovenské fotografie* by Daniela Mrazkova and Vladimir Remes, Prague 1989; *Josef Ehm,* exhibition catalogue by Zdenek Kirschner, Chicago 1990. **Articles**—"Czechoslovak Photography" by Karel Teige in *Blok* (Brno, Czechoslovakia), 1948; "The 60th Birthday of Josef Ehm" by Petr Tausk in *Kvety* (Prague), no. 30, 1969; "Dear Josef Ehm" by Jiří Macku in *Ceskoslovensko Fotografie* (Prague), August 1969; "Josef Ehm" by Petr Tausk in *Revue Fotografie* (Prague), no. 3, 1979; "Roots of Modern Photography in Czechoslovakia" by Petr Tausk in *History of Photography* (University Park, Pennsylvania), no. 3, 1979; "Fotografie der tschechoslowakichen Avantgarde: Das Prinzip des 'object trouve'" by Petr Tausk in *Form und Zweck* (Munich), no. 1, 1982; "Josef Ehm jubilantem" by Vladimir Birgus in *Ceskoslovenska fotografie* (Prague), no. 8, 1984; "Za profesorem Ehmem" by Vladimir Birgus in *Ceskoslovenska fotografie* (Prague), no. 5, 1990.

*

I think that depicting by means of photography is of a documentary nature. I have always enjoyed taking photographs for my own pleasure, but at the same time I have never been ashamed to take photos purely for purposes of information. All of the art of the Gothic, Renaissance, and the Baroque was done on commission, and we admire still the greatness of these works. I believe that no photographer should be offended if he is forced to do a large part of his work on public or official commission—so long as he can make it good and approach it creatively.

—Josef Ehm

*   *   *

Josef Ehm became a photographer in Czechoslovakia in the second half of the 1920s. According to the custom of the time, he started his career as an apprentice in a portrait studio, and there he acquired the brilliantly precise craftsmanship and respect for the qualities of the image that were to characterize his work in all the years that have followed.

Throughout his apprenticeship and his first jobs in various Prague studios, Ehm was concerned not merely with mastering the fundamentals, but even more with finding his own way, his means to self-expression. This search is particularly obvious in those photographs he made outside the studio, in his images from nature and the landscape—though, in fact, throughout this period of experimentation, he never neglected his own further development in portraiture.

Because of the great quality of his often unconventional results, Ehm was appointed to the faculty of the Photographic Department of the State Graphic School in Prague in 1934. As a teacher he felt it was his responsibility to create all kinds of images as examples for his students. His oeuvre was thus enriched by photographs of architectural and artistic monuments, as well as by reportage, advertising photographs, and still-lifes. And, during these years, he also missed no opportunity to continue to experiment, to define the limits to which creative photography might be extended. He created Photograms; he developed unusual laboratory techniques.

Enthusiasm for anything new and his spontaneous joy in daring creative experiments led him quite legitimately into the ranks of the artistic avantgarde of the 1930s. In this community he came under the influence of surrealism, which in his case meant the poetry of the everyday world as revealed through the *objet trouvé.* And, as was not unusual in Czechoslovakia at the time, in Ehm's attempts to emphasize the modest poetry of reality, surrealistic influences were colored by the precepts of the "New Objectivity."

As well as using *object trouvé* methods, surrealist influences also became evident with his pictures of artificially-arranged subjects, and it was the photography of nude models which exemplified this trend. In the mid-1930s Ehm created his now-famous photograph *Imaginary Space,* where the image of hands in gloves contrasts with thigh and leg to completely hide the rest of the body. His best-known nude photos, however, were made some ten years later, the finished works employing a modicum of solarization. At the same time, up to the end of the 1950s, Ehm also made portraits of Czech celebrities, most of them known to him personally. In these, he always managed to attain a high degree of technical perfection to complement the precisely desired psychological mood and expression.

Shortly after World War II, Ehm left his post at the State Graphics School to devote himself to creating photos for numerous books on Prague, Czech castles and the works of sculptors. His esteem for technical perfection made him one of the best photographers of architecture and cultural monuments.

During the 1960s, after working for a long time in black-and-white, Ehm began to take a greater interest in colour work—mainly in response to the demand from publishers. He quickly acquainted himself with the language of this "new medium," as evidenced by his 1979 picture book on Prague, composed entirely of colour images.

Having more or less retired from professional photography in 1982, Ehm donated the major part of his archive of negatives relating to cultural monuments to the Institute of Theory and History of Arts at the Czech Academy of Sciences in Prague. His personal work, spanning the experiments of the 1930s up to his recent colour work of the 1980s, he collected for a big 75th birthday retrospective exhibition in 1984. Despite the wide variety of subjects from different periods, the whole oeuvre could be seen immediately as the "creative manuscript" of one man.

—Petr Tausk

EHRMANN, Gilles.

Nationality: French. **Born:** Metz, 3 September 1928. **Education:** Attended primary school in Metz, 1934-40, and secondary school in Avignon, 1940-45; studied at the Ecole des Arts Decoratifs, Paris, 1946-55; self-taught in photography, from 1950. **Career:** Freelance photographer from 1955, and with Agence Rapho/Top, Paris, since 1984: has worked with the architects André Bloc, Claude Parent and André Jacqmain, and the magazines *Aujourd'hui* and *Architecture d'aujourd'hui,* from 1956, with Electricité de France (EDF) and *Realites* magazine, from 1958, with *Vogue Pelle* magazine, 1981, and *Casa Vogue* magazine, 1984. **Recipient:** Prix Nadar, Paris, 1963. **Agent:** Agence Rapho/Top, 1 rue St. Georges, 75009 Paris, France. **Address:** 48 rue Pigalle, 75009 Paris, France.

Individual Exhibitions:

1965   Maison de la Culture, Caen, France
1970   Maison de la Culture, Suresnes, France (projection)
1971   Maison de la Culture, Rennes, France (projection; with
            Gherasim Luca)
         Galerie Albertus Magnus, Paris (projection; with
            Gherasim Luca)
1974   Festival de Fylkingen, Stockholm (projection; with
            Gherasim Luca)

Maison de la Culture, Rennes, France (projection; with
Gherasim Luca)
1975   Bibliothéque Nationale, Paris
Maison de la Culture, Firminy, France (projection; with
Gherasim Luca)
Musée d'Art Moderne de la Ville, Paris (projection; with
Gherasim Luca)
Comédie, Caen, France (projection; with Gherasim Luca)
1976   Maison de la Culture, Bourges, France
Nörrköpings Museum, Sweden
Franska Institutet, Sockholm
1977   Centre Culturel Les Gemeaux, Sceaux, France
Maison de la Culture, Rennes, France
1978   Musée d'Art Moderne de la Ville, Paris
1979   Maison des Arts et de la Culture, Creteil, France
1980   Galerie Agathe Gaillard, Paris
1981   Maison des Jeunes et de la Culture, La Souterraine, France
Musée des Sables d'Olonne, France
Palais de Chaillot, Paris
Maison de la Culture, Amiens, France
Musée de Chartres, France
1982   Centre St. Martial, Angouleme, France
1983   Hotel d'Escoville, Caen, France
Musée des Beaux Arts, Caen, France (projection; with
Gherasim Luca)
Centre Georges Pompidou, Paris (projection; with
Gherasim Luca)
1985   *Architecture contemporaine en Bretagne,* travelled to Brest,
Rennes and Nantes, France
1986   Galerie Agathe Gaillard, Paris
Galerie de la Salle, Saint Paul de Vence, France

Selected Group Exhibitions:

1964   *World Exhibition of Photography: What Is Man?,* Pressehaus
Stern, Hamburg (and world tour)
1966   *Exploration du Futur,* Salines Royales, Arc et Senans, France
1973   *3rd World Exhibition of Photography,* Pressehaus Stern,
Hamburg (and world tour)
1979   *La Famille des Portraits,* Musée des Arts Décoratifs, Paris
1980   *Dix Photographes pour le Patrimoine,* Centre Georges
Pompidou, Paris
1981   *French Photography,* Zabriskie Gallery, New York
Jacques Prevert et ses Amis Photographes, Centre National de
la Photographie, Lyons France (travelled to the Musée d'Art
Moderne de la Ville, Paris)
1982   *Les Prevert de Prevert,* Bibliothèque Nationale, Paris
1984   *Six Photographes chez Le Corbusier,* Centre Georges
Pompidou, Paris
1985   *Les Stations Thermales,* École des Beaux Arts, Paris

Collections:

Bibliothèque Nationale, Paris; Musée d'Art Moderne de la Ville, Paris; Fonds
National d'Art Contemporain, Paris; Musée des Sables d'Olonne, France;
Musée de Toulon, France; Photothèque de Pret, Arles, France; Nörrköpings
Museum, Sweden.

Publications:

By EHRMANN: Books—*Provence Noire,* with text by André Verdet, Paris
1955; *. . . De Saint Paul de Vence,* with text by Andre Verdet, Geneva 1956;
Les Inspirés et leurs Demeures, with preface by André Breton, poems by
Gherasim Luca and Benjamin Peret, Paris 1962; *Salines Royales d'Arc et
Senans,* with text by M. Parent, Arc et Senans, France 1973; *Oedipe Sphinx,*
with poems by Gherasim Luca, Paris 1987. **Articles**—"Gilles Ehrmann,"
interview, with Catherine Jajolet, in *La Vie Electrique* (Paris), no. 151, 1981;
"Un Nuit Lumineuse," interview, with Herve Guibert, in *Le Monde* (Paris), 9
January 1981.

On EHRMANN: Books—*Gilles Ehrmann,* exhibition catalogue, with text
by André Breton and Gherasim Luca, Nörrköping, Sweden 1976; *Bilder for
Miljoner* by Rune Hassner, Stockholm 1977; *La Famille des Portraits,*
exhibition catalogue, with text by Jean-Claude Lemagny, Paris 1979; *Dix
Photographes pour le Patrimoine,* exhibition catalogue, edited by Jean-
Claude Gautrand, Paris 1980; *Gilles Ehrmann,* exhibition catalogue, with texts
by Henri-Claude Cousseau, André Breton and Gherasim Luca, Les Sables
d'Olonne, France 1982; *Les Mystères de la Chambre Noire,* edited by Edouard
Jaguer, Paris 1982.

                          *   *   *

Poetry is shy of noise and commotion, which is why Gilles Ehrmann is
never represented at photographic exhibitions or in specialist journals. And yet
Ehrmann is one of the very foremost French photographers to have produced
their most important work since the war.

His career began with a flourish in the mid-1950s when he published one
after another, at the age of twenty-seven and twenty-eight, two books,
Provence Noire and *. . . De Saint Paul de Vence,* which he both conceived and
executed himself. In retrospect, we can only marvel at the young man's artistic
daring. To have produced at such a time a book of photographic poems lacking
either picturesque element or any kind of narrative was a stroke of absolute
genius that could very easily have backfired. Shadow effects, ruined walls,
bare stone are the dominant themes. Here and there, sparsely scattered, a
young girl or a group of youths figure as landmarks among the stones. Round
the edge of one page we see, close together, the faces of Braque, Léger and
Picasso—faces that fix the level of these photos. These two books already
exhibit distinctive Ehrmann features: an irresistible attraction to the mineral
world and a method of photographing which, rather than faithfully reproducing, or dissecting, things and people, evokes them poetically through a kind of
prolonged resonance.

The publication of *Provence Noire* and *. . . De Saint Paul de Vence* gained
Ehrmann entry into the world of magazines and in the fifties and sixties he
collaborated with Boubat, Charbonnier and others on the great French
illustrated magazine of those years, *Réalités.* But Ehrmann was principally
concerned with producing books and he caused a second sensation with *Les
Inspirés et leurs Demeures* (The inspired ones and their dwellings). Created at
a time (1962) when naive art was only appreciated by a few specialists,
Ehrmann's book was inspired by those who realize their dreams in stone or
cement, spangled with porcelain. Imaginary landscapes, a reconstituted animal world, anthropomorphic gardens, and all manner of dream elements, are
recorded and photographed with affection and understanding. The harmony
between the photographer and his subject matter is complete, the method
transparent and the emotion conveyed pure and intact. André Breton wrote a
brief text to *Les Inspirés* and the book had a profound impact on the artistic
sensibilities of the sixties.

Gilles Ehrmann's photography continues to create a sensation today. He is
still producing books, though not all of them have been published. In his
collection he has a number that have been ready for publication for years,
others are in the process of coming together. Two of these books are
particularly impressive and may in turn become works of primary importance.
Faire un pas (Take a step) centres on the region of Nepal and unrolls with
careful precision, but without contrivance of any sort, a touching fresco of
human beings surrounded by their landscape of stone. In *Oedipe Sphinx* the
mineral world now relates to whatever remains after death, whether it be the
image of the dead person fashioned in marble, or the dust, bones and blood
vessels strangely petrified into a bewildering human tree. In this book, which
Gilles Ehrmann spent sixteen years producing, the partnership between man
and stone has become a terrifying marriage of extraordinary beauty.

It should be clear by now that Ehrmann's subject matter is not light. He
goes straight to the primordial: matter, life, and death. This is Ehrmann's
manner of being and of photographing, which he succeeds in sharing with us
by means of his style. It is a style of great simplicity and transparency. There is
no artifice here which might enable us to identify the artist at first glance but
which would falsify reality. Nor is there any attempt to create a significant
geometrical effect or a significant moment. The power of Ehrmann's photography lies elsewhere. "Ehrmann rejects anything that displaces, anything that
clings or adds to the simple and authentic presence of things and people" (J.C.
Lemagny). What counts in his work is indeed this ability to go straight to the
heart of his subject and to stay with it; a careful attention towards human

beings and things; an intense, almost obsessive gaze which forces us in our turn to look hard. By maintaining for thirty years this constant attitude of "discreet intransigence" (H.H. Cousseau), Gilles Ehrmann has carved for himself a place of primary importance in French photography.

—Guy Mandery

EISENSTAEDT, Alfred.

Nationality: American. **Born:** Dierschau, West Prussia, now Poland, 6 December 1898; emigrated to the United States, 1935: naturalized, 1943. **Education:** Attended the Hohenzollern Gymnasium, Berlin, 1906-12; University of Berlin, 1913-16; self-taught in photography. **Military Service:** Served in the German Army, 1916-18. **Career:** Worked as a belt and button salesman, Berlin, 1919-29; also active as a freelance photographer and photojournalist, mainly for *Weltspiegel* magazine, Berlin, 1927-29; photojournalist, with Pacific and Atlantic Picture Agency, later part of Associated Press, and working for *Berliner Illustrierte Zeitung*, etc., Berlin and Paris, 1929-35; freelance photographer, New York, working for *Harper's Bazaar, Vogue, Town and Country*, etc., 1935-36; Staff Photographer, *Life* magazine, New York, from 1936. **Recipient:** Photographer of the Year Award, Britannica Books, 1951; Clifton C. Edom Award, 1953; Culture Prize, Deutsche Gesellschaft für Photographie (DGPh), 1962; International Understanding Award, 1967; *Popular Photography* Award, 1968; Joseph A. Sprague Award, National Press Photographers Association, 1971. **Address:** Time-Life Building, Room 2850, Rockefeller Center, New York, New York 10020, U.S.A.

Individual Exhibitions:

1955 *2 Photographers: Alfred Eisenstaedt and Walter Rosenblum,* Philadelphia College of Art
1966 *Witness to Our Time,* Time-Life Building, New York (travelled to the Smithsonian Institution, Washington, D.C.)
1980 *Eisenstaedt: Germany,* Smithsonian Institution, Washington, D.C. (and world tour)
1981 International Center of Photography, New York (retrospective)
1986 *Eisenstaedt and Company,* National Theatre, London (travelled to Hamburg and New York)

Selected Group Exhibitions:

1951 *Memorable Life Photographs,* Museum of Modern Art, New York
1959 *Hundert Jahre Photographie 1839-1939,* Museum Folkwang, Essen (travelled to Cologne and Frankfurt)
1967 *Photography in the 20th Century,* National Gallery of Canada, Ottawa (toured Canada and the United States, 1967-73)
1973 *Die Zwanziger Jahre,* Kunstgewerbemuseum, Zurich
1974 *Photography in America,* Whitney Museum, New York
1979 *Life: The First Decade 1936-45,* Grey Art Gallery, New York University
1980 *The Imaginary Photo Museum,* Kunsthalle, Cologne
1982 *Lichtbildnisse: Das Porträt in der Fotografie,* Rheinisches Landesmuseum, Bonn
1984 *Sammlung Gruber,* Museum Ludwig, Cologne

Collections:

Time-Life Library, New York; International Center of Photography, New York; International Museum of Photography, George Eastman House, Rochester, New York; National Gallery of Canada, Ottawa; Royal Photographic Society, London; Museum Ludwig, Cologne.

Publications:

By EISENSTAEDT: Books—*Witness to Our Time,* New York 1966; *The Eye of Eisenstaedt,* as told to Arthur Goldsmith, New York 1969; *Martha's Vineyard,* with text by Henry Beetle Hough, New York 1970; *Witness to Nature,* New York 1971; *Wimbledon: A Celebration,* with text by John McPhee, New York and London 1972; *People,* New York 1973; *Panoptikum,* Lucerne and Frankfurt 1973; *Eisenstaedt's Album: 50 Years of Friends and Acquaintances,* New York and London 1976; *Eisenstaedt's Guide to Photography,* New York 1978; *Eisenstaedt: Germany,* Washington, D.C. 1981; *Eisenstaedt: Aberdeen,* New York and London 1984; *Eisenstaedt on Eisenstaedt: A Self Portrait,* New York and London 1985.

On EISENSTAEDT: Books—*Memorable Life Photographs,* with text by Edward Steichen, New York 1951; *Words and Pictures: An Introduction to Photojournalism* by Wilson Hicks, New York 1952; *How Life Gets the Story: Behind the Scenes in Photo-Journalism,* edited by Stanley Rayfield, New York 1955; *Life Photographers: Their Careers and Favorite Pictures,* edited by Stanley Rayfield, New York 1957; *Hundert Jahre Photographie aus der Sammlung Gernsheim,* exhibition catalogue, by Helmut and Alison Gernsheim, Essen 1959; *Fame: Famous Portraits of Famous People by Famous Photographers,* edited by L. Fritz Gruber, London and New York 1960; *Great News Photos and the Stories Behind Them* by John Faber, New York 1960, 1978; *Photography in the 20th Century* by Nathan Lyons, New York 1967; *Deutschland: Beginn des Modernen Photojournalismus* by Tim N. Gidal, Frankfurt 1972; *Photography in America,* edited by Robert Doty, with an introduction by Minor White, New York and London 1974; *The Magic Image* by Cecil Beaton and Gail Buckland, London and Boston 1975; *Geschichte der Fotografie im 20. Jahrhundert/Photography in the 20th Century* by Petr Tausk, Cologne 1977, London 1980; *Great Photographic Essays from Life* by Maitland Edey, Boston 1978; *Amerika Fotografie 1920-1940* by Erika Billeter, Berne 1979; *Life: The First Decade 1936-1945* by Robert Littman, Ralph Graves and Doris C. O'Neill, New York 1979, London 1980; *The Photograph Collector's Guide* by Lee D. Witkin and Barbara London, Boston and London 1979; *The Imaginary Photo Museum* by Helmut Gernsheim, Renate and L. Fritz Gruber and others, Cologne 1981, London 1982; *Lichtbildnisse: Das Porträt in der Fotografie,* edited by Klaus Honnef, Cologne 1982; *Bilder vom Krieg* by Rainer Fabian and Hans Christian Adam, Hamburg 1983, as *Images of War: 130 Years of War Photography,* London 1985. **Articles**—"Legend in Our Times: Alfred Eisenstaedt" by Arthur Goldsmith in *Infinity* (New York), September 1971; "Alfred Eisenstaedt" in *Modern Photography Annual,* New York 1972; "Why I Use an SLR: Alfred Eisenstaedt, Peter Turner, Neal Boenzi" by R. Busch in *Popular Photography* (New York), May 1973; "Eisenstaedt's People" by Arthur Goldsmith in *Popular Photography* (New York), December 1973; "Allemagne Année 30" in *Photo* (Paris), April 1981.

* * *

No man stands taller in the ranks of photojournalists than does Alfred Eisenstaedt at 5'4''. Eisenstaedt continued working into his late 80s, filled with the enthusiasm for photography that started him on his career in Germany between the first and second world wars.

Like many of his colleagues on *Life* magazine in the 1930s, Eisenstaedt was a generalist, with no particular area of specialty for his photographs—although he's at his best working with people. For more than five decades "Eisie" has photographed the important, the unimportant, the famous and the infamous people whose doings change or inform the world they inhabit. In the late 1920s in Berlin he photographed, among other theater personalities, the young Marlene Dietrich, just become a star for her work in *The Blue Angel.*

His portrait of a glowering Joseph Goebbels, Nazi propaganda minister, made in 1933, is almost a definitive picture of the sinister spirit of the Hitler regime. Another Eisenstaedt classic shows merely the cracked, bare soles of the feet of an Ethiopian soldier during his country's war with Italy. This simple, powerful image evokes many overtones of the miseries of war.

Great physical energy is packed into Alfred Eisenstaedt's small frame. He is a disciplined sit-up and push-up devotee, walks a great deal, carrying a pedometer to keep track of his daily mileage.

On the job, too, he is all action, moving from spot to spot, looking for the proper perspective and viewpoint, checking the light, leaving, if necessary, to return hours later when the light is right. As he works with people, Eisenstaedt maintains a stream of commentary—questions, commands, observations—designed to distract the subject, to put him or her at ease, to make the all-seeing lens of his camera invisible.

When Eisenstaedt learned his craft, lenses were slow and/or less than needle sharp, films were unresponsive and coarse-grained in most cases. Nevertheless, he helped to pioneer the small, maneuverable camera that has today become the hallmark of the photojournalist. First with a little Ernemann taking glass plates, later with the Leica using 35-mm roll film, Eisenstaedt made his photo essays, whenever possible, by light that existed on the scene. This led often to slow exposures of a quarter- or a half-second with the camera mounted on a tripod. The process removed a certain amount of spontaneity (what subject could stay unaware of a tripod-mounted camera?) but gave a natural ''here's-how-it-was'' atmosphere to the scene by preserving the actual lighting rather than substituting bright lamps or flash. He was a pioneer of ''existing-light'' photography.

Colorful as a personality, Eisenstaedt was otherwise conservative as photojournalists go. He was an unflamboyant dresser, has no recorded vices other than (as some colleagues would have it) regular exercise. His manner was mild and friendly. On the job, he showed intense concentration, yet shot minimally—enough to provide his editor with variety, yet not with the motor-winder abandon exhibited by some of his peers.

The balanced Eisenstaedt personality is evident in many of his photographs. Seldom are they passionately partisan, angry, shocking, derogatory. Humor is often there—visual, human, perhaps the hardest kind to bring off successfully. Affection, symbolism and the revealing side glance that gives character to a photo essay are there. An Eisenstaedt photograph is cleanly composed, perhaps through disciplines learned when 35-mm photographers had to make every square millimeter of negative space count to preserve technical quality in the print.

His pictures have rarely been labeled as great art. And yet their consistent excellence over a half-century gives them a staying power that many of the images by lately-acclaimed artist-photographers sadly lack. There was nothing trendy or temporary in Eisenstaedt's approach. His images are products of dispassionate observation tempered with the reactions, likes and dislikes of an urban personality—visually refined and distilled by the eye of the definitive photojournalist.

—Kenneth Poli

ELETA, Sandra.

Nationality: Panamanian. **Born:** Panama, 4 September 1942. **Education:** Elizabeth Seton High School, New York, 1959-60; studied art history at Finch College, New York, 1961-64, and literature at the New School for Social Research, New York, 1970-71. **Career:** Painter, in Spain, 1964-67; worked in the Art Department of Campagnani and Quelquejeu, Panama, 1968-69; Art Guide/Lecturer, Metropolitan Museum of Art, New York, 1970-71; Instructor of Photography, Universidad de San Jose, Costa Rica, 1972-73. Freelance photographer, Panama, since 1974, working for Latin American periodicals, 1974-76, and on the Portobelo study project, since 1976. International Juror in Photography, Latin American Art Meeting, 1990. **Recipient:** Crystal Apple Award, New York Film Festival, 1985. **Agent:** Galerie Agathe Gaillard, Paris. **Address:** Post Office Box 157, Panama, Zone 1, Republic of Panama.

Individual Exhibitions:

1975   *Solentiname,* Center for Inter-American Relations, New York
1979   *3 American Women,* Canon Photo Gallery, Amsterdam
1980   *Portobelo,* Consejo Venezolano de Fotografia, Caracas
1983   *Portobelo,* Galerie Agathe Gaillard, Paris
1984   *Portobelo,* Nikon Photo Gallery, Zurich
        Portobelo (Audio-Visual), Consejo Argentino de Fotografia,
           Centro Cultural Ciudad de Buenos Aires; Museo del
           Hombre Panameño, Panama City

1985   *Portobelo* (Audio-Visual), Alcaldia del Municipio de
           Portobelo, Panama
        Sirenata en B (Audio-Visual), Teatro Nacional, Ciudad de
           Panama; New York Film Festival, Joseph Papp Theater;
           Casa de las Américas, La Habana, Cuba
1986   *Taller Portobelo,* Centro de Convenciones, La Habana, Cuba
1991   *Portobelo,* Recontres Internationales de la Photographie, Arles

Selected Group Exhibitions:

1976   *The Latin Woman,* McGraw-Hill Exhibition Center, New York
1978   *Ritos y Minorias,* La Photogaleria, Madrid
        Muestra de Fotografia Latinoamericana Contemporanea,
           Museo de Arte Moderno, Mexico City
1979   *Venezia '79*
        Rencontres Internationales de la Photographie, Arles, France
1981   *Hecho en Latino America 2,* Palacio de Bellas Artes,
           Mexico City
1982   *La Photographie Contemporaine en Amerique Latine,* Centre
           Georges Pompidou, Paris
1987   *Contemporary Latin American Photographers,* Burden Gallery,
           New York
1989   *Festival des Trois Continents,* Nantes

Collections:

Museo de Arte Moderno, Mexico City; Bibliothèque Nationale, Paris.

Publications:

By ELETA: Books—*Portobelo,* Buenos Aires 1981; *Solentiname,* with text by Ernesto Cardenal, Wuppertal, Germany 1981; *Nostalgia del Futuro,* with text by Ernesto Cardenal, Nicaragua 1982. **Film:** *The Empire Visits us Again,* Panama 1990.

On ELETA: Book—*Hecho en Latinoamerica,* edited by the Consejo Mexicano de Fotografia, Mexico City 1978; *Hecho en Latino America 2,* exhibition catalogue, with texts by Pedro Meyer, Lazaro Blanco and others, Mexico City 1981; *La Photographie Contemporaine en Amerique Latine,* exhibition catalogue, by Alain Sayag, Paris 1982. **Articles**—''Portobelo o la Magia del Espacio'' by Edison Simons in *Zoom* (Madrid), 31 January 1978; ''Three American Women'' in *Reflexions* (Amsterdam), March 1979; article by Michel Nuridsany in *Le Figaro* (Paris), 17 July 1979; article in *Camera* (Lucerne), January 1980; ''Las Tribolaciones del Señor Vatifafotti'' by Paolo Gasparini in *Bulletin of Consejo Venezolano de Fotografia* (Caracas), May 1980.

*

My development as a photographer is parallel to my personal development. As a former painter, I found it to be a lonely mental world and, having the need for a more physical way of expressing myself, turned to photography. At the beginning my pictures were closed in: I used to photograph cryptic symbols, worlds in the shadows, in a perpetual alienation. In my first workshop I was forced to become more real, to participate with my work in the daily task of living.

To participate—that was the word that opened the world for me. Since then I have been involved in the process of navigating to the vital center of being, where establishing contact and participating in the flow of life are open possibilities. Being and seeing merge as in the moments of poetic epiphanies; vision becomes an extension of the totality of being.

The eye doesn't respond solely to the mechanical, conditioned vision. The visionary poets have been able to travel, sometimes, around the eye; some photographers too (and as filmmaker Jean-Luc Godard once said, ''To look around oneself—that is to be free''). Part of the new dimension that contemporary photography has offered is the great range of feeling and subjectivity to explore reality. Visionaries like Gene Smith, Bill Brandt, Diane Arbus, and Robert Frank mastered the documentary style by adding a strong

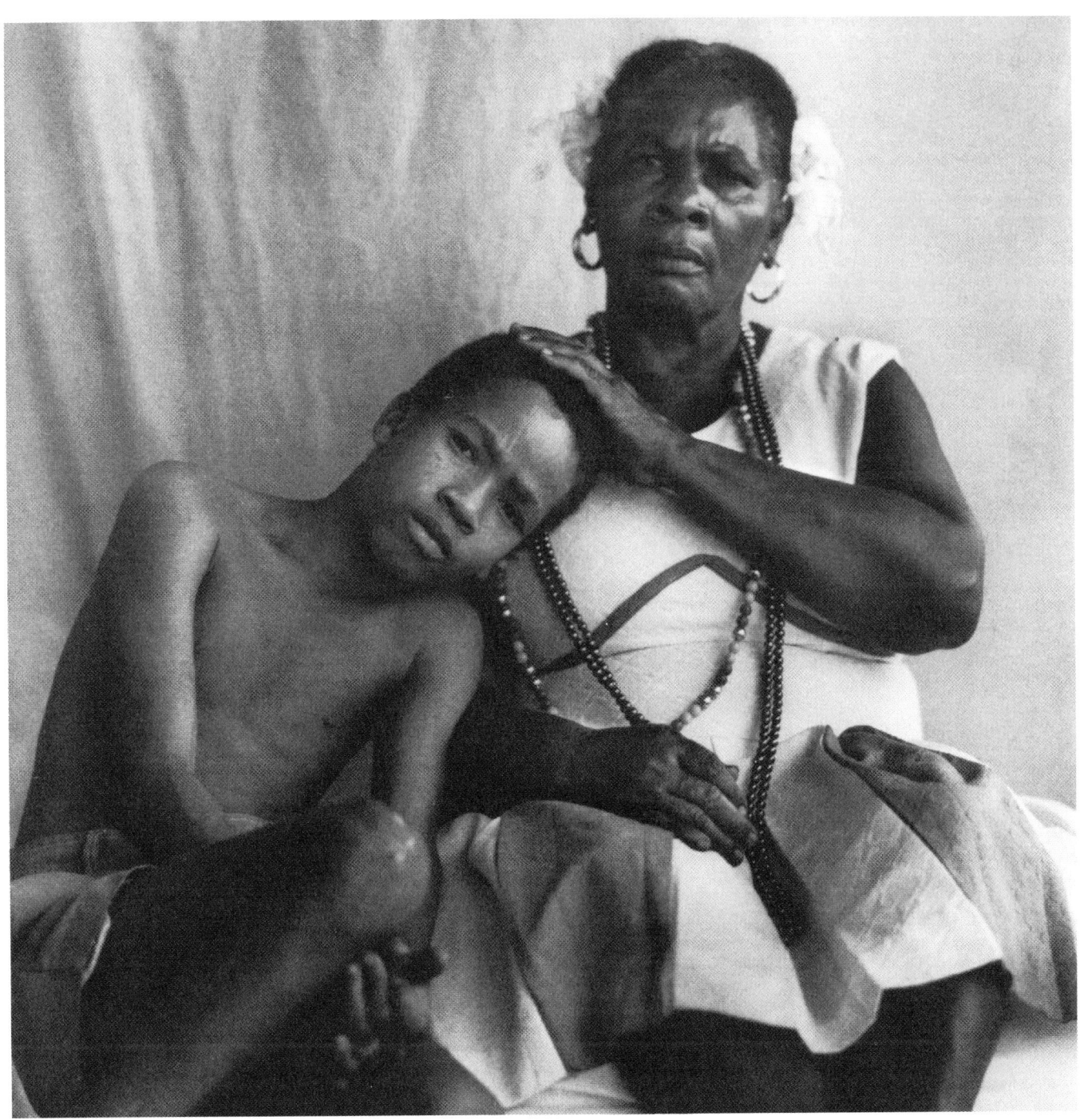

Image from *Portobelo.* Photograph by Sandra Eleta.

personal dimension, deep psychological insight—and sometimes by using reality as a symbol to convey another reality, rendering visible the invisible. Reality as such was perceived on many different levels, contemporary styles of photography being enriched with different ideas generated by various branches of photography, which now converge as part of a natural process of assimilation.

—Sandra Eleta

*   *   *

"I try to reach, as deeply as possible, within the theme, searching for a dialogue, rather than chasing after separate moments." And for Sandra Eleta the theme is always the same: people, human beings. It is difficult to think of her photographing buildings or stones or landscapes. All of her photographs are portraits. Portraits with or without a background. Human beings clothed in all their dignity, their strength, even their invisible reality—but never naked, vulnerable, or weak.

Sandra Eleta feels herself incapable of photojournalism or of catching decisive moments. When she does work in that way, she suffers; it is simply not her style. Nor do we find any evidence of a search for particular composition or particular illumination. The contrary is true: everything is simple. The emphasis is on detail, anything that can reveal the subjective commentary, the theme.

She worked from the beginning with a Hasselblad with a normal lens (80 mm). Later she added a Leica and Nikon, each of them having only one lens. Changing lenses seems to her as inconceivable as changing eyes. Each camera has its own way of seeing things. When she starts with a theme, she experiments with different film and its various sensitivities and with her cameras; once she has decided which medium is the most appropriate to her purposes, she forgets the technicalities to concentrate on theme.

Apart from her first essay on the Nicaraguan poet Ernesto Cardenal and his work in Solentiname, the most important and successful of her work is the series on Portobelo and its inhabitants, a people full of dignity, independence, and magic. Her work on three peasant women from the Valley of Tonosi is especially fine. She describes them: "work becomes rite, dance, celebration of the cycles of sowing and reaping; they are priestesses of eternal laboring." She captures with great success the incredible inner beauty of these three women.

There is a further series of photographs taken in the house of relatives in Madrid. All the servants, cooks, helpers, drivers, butlers are included, portrayed while at their individual tasks, in their own places within that world—with their pride, their ambitions, their fleeting jealousies, and perhaps their unconscious emulation of their masters' attitudes. In this series of photographs, as in the others, Sandra Eleta does not denounce or condemn. She has searched for the profound truth of her theme. She portrays her subjects with wit and with joy and as human beings rather than clichés. Every one of the characters portrayed reveals himself or herself totally, even the aunt—surprisingly, because the portrait of the aunt seems to be of somebody already not of this world, someone who has left only a ghostly form behind. The aunt was delighted with the photo: she said it looked exactly as she felt. But the series remains unfinished.

Sandra Eleta has been working with color, always in Portobelo and the Atlantic coast of her country. She says: "I feel less prejudice against using color now. I think I have found some new depth, and I have tried hard to escape the commonplace. I have very substantial material and will continue to polish my work."

The photography of Sandra Eleta seems not merely very Latin American but also important because it blends a humanistic concern with a contemporary language.

—Maria Cristina Orive

ELLIS, Rennie.

Nationality: Australian. **Born:** Melbourne, 11 November 1940. **Education:** Brighton Grammar School, Melbourne, 1951-58; University of Melbourne, 1959; studied advertising at Royal Melbourne Institute of Technology, 1960-62, 1966, Dip.Adv. 1966; self-taught in photography. **Family:** Married Carol Silk in 1966 (divorced, 1978); son: Joshua. **Career:** Television Producer, Orr, Skate and Associates, Melbourne, 1960-62; Copy Chief, Jackson Wain Advertising, Melbourne, 1966-67; Creative Director, Monahan Dayman Advertising, Melbourne, 1967-69. Freelance photographer, filmmaker, and writer, working for *The Age, The Australian, Pol, Mode, Pacific, Playboy, Australian Geographic, Panorama, Women's Weekly,* etc., in Melbourne, since 1969: established studio, Rennie Ellis and Associates, 1975. Founder-Director, Brummel's Gallery of Photography, Melbourne, 1972-80, and Scoopix Photo Library, Melbourne, 1975. Part-time Lecturer in Creative Writing, Preston Institute of Technology, Melbourne, 1973. **Recipient:** Silver Medallion, Art Directors Club of Melbourne, 1972; United Nations "Habitat" Award for Australia, 1976; Visual Arts Board Grant, Australia Council, 1976, 1979; Melbourne Art Directors Club Awards, 1984, 1985. **Address:** Rennie Ellis and Associates, 154 Greville Street, Prahran, Victoria 3181, Australia.

Individual Exhibitions:

1971   *Kings Cross, Sydney,* Yellow House, Sydney (travelled to Gallery A, Melbourne)

1975   *Aussies All,* 500 Collins Street, Melbourne
1976   *Heroes and Anti-Heroes,* The Photographers' Gallery, Melbourne
1978   *The Way of Flesh,* Australian Centre for Photography, Sydney

Selected Group Exhibitions:

1973   *Children,* Brummels Gallery of Photography, Melbourne
1975   *Snapshots,* Australian Centre for Photography, Sydney
       Recent Australian Photography, touring exhibition (toured the Far East)
1977   *Five Photographers,* Benalla Art Gallery, Benalla, Victoria
1978   *5th Philip Morris Arts Grant Exhibition,* at the *Adelaide Festival of Arts*
1979   *Australian Photographers,* Hyde Park, Sydney
1980   *Through the Looking Glass,* Ray Hughes Gallery, Brisbane
       Australian Photographers: The Philip Morris Collection, Alexander Gardens, Melbourne
1983   *Australian Street Photography—1970s,* Australian National Gallery, Canberra
1984   *Tenth Anniversary,* Australian Centre for Photography, Sydney

Collections:

Australian National Gallery, Canberra; National Gallery of Victoria, Melbourne; Australian Centre for Photography, Sydney; Tasmanian Museum and Art Gallery, Hobart; Bibliothèque Nationale, Paris.

Publications:

By ELLIS: Books—*Kings Cross, Sydney,* with Wes Stacey, Melbourne 1971; *Australian Graffiti,* Melbourne 1975; *Ketut Lives in Bali,* with Stan Marks, London 1977; *L'Australie,* with Ursula Marcus, Zurich 1978; *Australian Graffiti Revisited,* Melbourne 1979; *Railway Stations of Australia,* with text by Andrew Wards, Melbourne 1982; *We Live in Australia,* Hove, Sussex 1982; *Life's a Beach,* Melbourne 1983; *Life's a Beer,* Melbourne 1984; *Life's a Ball,* Melbourne 1985; *The All New Australian Graffiti,* Melbourne 1985; *Life's a Parade,* Melbourne 1986. **Articles**—"Follow the Fence, Follow Your Nose" in *Walkabout* (Melbourne), October 1970; "Once a Jolly Oddball" in *Pol* (Sydney), vol. 5, no. 7, 1973; "Recognizing Snaps as Art" in *Nation Review* (Melbourne), 5 October 1973; "A Taste of Honeys" in *Man* (Sydney), November 1973; "Ikons of the Dreaming" in *BHP Journal* (Melbourne), March 1975; "Mykonos" in *Vogue Men* (Sydney), July 1977; "The Pool Where Parisians Meet" in *The Age* (Melbourne), 30 July 1977; "Rennie Ellis on Looking at Photographs" in *Light Vision* (Melbourne), September 1977; "The Driving Force Behind LRB" in *Australian Playboy* (Sydney), February 1980; "The Legend Lives On" in *Detours* (Sydney), Winter 1980; "Local Heroes" in *Mode* (Sydney), March 1985; "Ron Barassi Interview" in *Australian Playboy* (Sydney), September 1985; "The Flames of Passion" in *Mode* (Sydney), January 1986; "The World's Sexiest Carnival" in *Australian Playboy* (Sydney), December 1986.

On ELLIS: Books—*Australian Photography—A Contemporary View,* edited by Laurence Le Guay, Sydney 1979; *A Day in the Life of Australia—March 6, 1981,* with introduction by Thomas Kenneally, Potts Point, New South Wales 1981. **Articles**—"Rennie Ellis: Brummels Gallery" in *Professional Photography in Australia* (Melbourne), July 1973; "Rennie Ellis, Photographer" in *Australian Photography* (Sydney), June 1976; "Youthful Celebration of Fleshly Pleasures" by Sandra McGrath in *The Australian* (Sydney), 31 January 1978; "Camera on the Threshold" by Nancy Borlace in *Sydney Morning Herald,* 4 February 1978.

*

While I make a living as a commercial photographer, the medium is also my vehicle for self-expression—my art form, if you like. I take photographs for fun, for the people it brings me into contact with, for the doors it unlocks, for the thresholds it allows me to cross. I like to put myself in "a state of grace with chance." My presence with a camera often triggers off the image I capture. I like to document things that happen around me, the situations I find myself in, my friends. I like to photograph interesting ladies I find in the street. I like to embrace the moment. I like adventures and I collect images. I respond to things erotic and things bizarre. Perhaps my photographs give visual form to vague feelings and fantasies that I have. Maybe.

—Rennie Ellis

*   *   *

The most significant aspect of Rennie Ellis's photography is his overriding concern with images and ideas, as opposed to virtuoso displays of technical facility. This does not mean that he pays no attention to technique. For Ellis, technique is merely a means to an end. The first image should reach out, engage the interest of the viewer, and perhaps change his way of seeing a specific aspect of the world around him.

Ellis is an enthusiastic supporter of education in the Aesthetics of Photography. He believes that the way one looks at photographs is as important as learning how to use a camera and puddle around in the dark room. While bemoaning the lack of tradition in Australian photography, Ellis believes that the last five years have seen great advances in terms of critical sensitivity to the underlying subtleties and inner motivations of the photographic artist.

He explains his personal attitude to his art as follows: "Taking photographs is very important to me; it somehow helps me to define my place in the universe."

At times he has expressed doubts about the significance of the photographer's art, compared to that of a painter, printmaker or filmmaker, but is reassured by public response to the photographic image in the gallery context.

At a symposium at Prahran C.A.E. on April 30th, 1977, Ellis commented: "I think photography is full of contradiction, full of mysteries, and I hope its potential for innovation is as great as any of the art forms, because the way I see it, the boundaries of our visual experience are limitless—the horizons keep on receding!"

He summed up his ideas about his own work and what he feels should be the attitude of other practitioners by quoting Alfred Steiglitz: "Art or not art, that's immaterial. I continue on my own way, seeking my own truth ever affirming today."

Ellis, founder of the Pentax-Brummels Gallery of Photography in Melbourne, has exhibited regularly since 1971, presenting one-man shows with telling insights into aspects of the human condition as he sees it.

In his Sydney exhibition *The Way of Flesh* Ellis incorporated lively written commentaries to embellish his photographic images of the human body in all its glory and ugliness. Goddesses sunbaking on rooftops in Hydra stimulated an erotic viewer response, while overweight Australian males swilling beer from tins invoked laughter and repulsion. In a sense these works provided viewers with an almost voyeuristic pleasure, akin to peeking into someone's private diary. Ellis revealed much about himself and his subjects with a refreshing honesty.

After *The Way of Flesh* exhibition he set about documenting interesting aspects of Australian railway stations, no doubt spurred on by the knowledge that the original architectural delights which heralded the coming of the steam train in Australia were doomed to extinction by the rapid onslaught of progress.

—Arthur McIntyre

ERRÁZURIZ, Paz.

Nationality: Chilean. **Born:** Santiago, Chile, 2 January 1944. **Education:** Studied education at the Catholic University, Santiago, Licenciada (B.A.) 1972; self-taught in photography. **Family:** Married Thomas Daskam in 1972; children: Daniela and Thomas. **Career:** Worked as a primary school teacher; illustrated children's books. **Recipient:** John Simon Guggenheim Fellowship, 1986 and 1987; Fundación Andes, 1990; Fulbright Fellowship, 1992. **Address:** Av. R. Lyon 2509, Santiago, Chile.

Individual Exhibitions:

1981   *Personas,* Instituto Norteam de Cultura, Santiago
1982   *Fotografías 1982,* Galería Sur, Santiago
1986   *Fotografías,* Galería Carmen Waugh, La Casa Larga, Santiago
1987   *Combate contra el Angel,* Galería la Plaza, Santiago
1988   *De A Dos,* Galeria Carmen Waugh, La Casa Larga, Santiago
1989   *Adam's Apple,* Galería Ojo de Buey, Santiago (travelled to the Centre for Photography, Sydney, Australia)
1991   *A Certain Time,* Museo Nacional de Bellas Artes, Santiago
1992   *Photographs by Paz Errázuriz,* The Photography Gallery, Harbourfront York Quay Centre, Toronto, Canada
        Paz Errázuriz: Photographs 1981-1991, Chile, Museo Carrillo Gil, Mexico City

Selected Group Exhibitions:

1990   *Museo Abierto,* Museo Nacional de Bellas Artes, Santiago
1991   *Old World New World,* Seattle Art Museum, Washington
1992   *Desires and Disguises,* The Photographers' Gallery, London
1993   *Recovering Histories,* Zimmerli Art Museum, New Jersey
1994   *States of Loss,* Jersey City Museum
        Bienal, Havana, Cuba

Collections:

Museo de Bellas Artes, Santiago.

Publications:

By ERRÁZURIZ: Books—*Amalia,* Santiago 1973; *Adam's Apple,* with text by Claudia Donoso, Santiago 1990; *Una Mirada en los Intersticios,* with text by Diamela Eltit, Santiago 1992; *Infarto del Alma,* with text by Diamela Eltit, Santiago 1994; *Fotografías de Paz Errázuriz,* with text by Waldemar Sommer, Santiago 1994.

On ERRÁZURIZ: Book—*Desires and Disguises,* exhibition catalogue, edited by Amanda Hopkinson, London 1992.

*

A search for identity is always present in my photography, and I think it deals primarily with a look at "the other," i.e. elements of the society outside the mainstream. My work is neither removed nor distant. I prefer to think of it as a look through the back door into my own life, my own world. To make the invisible visible is like carefully following an endless line of footprints, prying into and recording a world that is unspeakably mine.

—Paz Errázuriz

*   *   *

Paz Errázuriz is an example of how women's working lives still frequently have a trajectory different from men's. While her children were young, she worked as a primary school teacher in her native Santiago. Her way into photography occurred with taking class photographs and illustrating children's books. (Her first publication, about a pet hen called *Amalia* and with her own text, was commissioned by Isabel Allende and published in 1973.) As her own children grew up, her work grew beyond the bounds of childhood, the photography taking over from the teaching and compiling of projects in which images might emerge as important but remained incidental to her career. She is

***Couple of Lovers in Mental Institution, Chile,* 1992.** Photograph ©Paz Errázuriz.

self-taught in photography, borrowing a friend's darkroom to work in at night, until she gained the experience and confidence to describe herself as "a photographer."

By 1980 she was moving on from "taking another—a different—look" at childhood to looking at other groups she regarded as outsiders within society. Her camera roved over the age spectrum, visiting state-run old people's homes, where to be elderly means to be impoverished financially but allows for the richness of perpetuated illusions. Errázuriz works frequently on the ambivalent edge between dreams and disasters, performance and parody. Her images of the old ladies' contest to be "beauty queen" both accepts their premise that beauty is more than skin-deep and questions a traditional equation of prettiness with purity, dressing up the frilled white of the *quinceannera* (the fifteen-year-old at her white-clad Confirmation service) topped with the regal tiara and satin sash of the fashion show winner.

Errázuriz' fascination with the marginalised and anachronistic extended to other groups with political overtones. Under the military dictatorship of General Pinochet (1973-90)), the armed forces both exploited and attacked the easily identifiable community of transvestite prostitutes. Having lived and worked for a while in a house used by women prostitutes, Errázuriz became friends with some of the transvestites. She uncovered their story of persecution, being locked up on a notorious "torture ship," the Esmeralda, off the Valparaiso coast. On their eventual release, the survivors relocated to Talco in the south, where for five years (1983-88) Errázuriz and the sociologist Claudia Donoso visited and documented their stories. The outcome was *Adam's Apple,* a homage to the vitality of their profoundly ambiguous but extraordinarily candid lifestyle, and a reference to both a denied Garden of Eden and to the velvet ribbon the performers wear around their throat, to conceal a protuberant voicebox.

The next group of "people outside society" (their self-description) that Errázuriz turned to was the boxers. Mainly born and raised in the shanty towns, unable to make more than bantam-weight, they fascinated Errázuriz with the demonstration of "how far poverty can push you. Into brutality." She came to know boxers who died and others, like the former champion Martin Vargas, who ended up permanently punch-drunk. Her portraits, like Diane Arbus before her, showed the bravado and pathos of those who don't quite belong in the world they aspire to. Unlike Arbus, however, Errázuriz works with compassion, often reaching her subjects through their mothers who may also appear in the frame with the transvestites, the boxers, the gypsy children. "I find the unconditional nature of mother-love, the utter acceptance of their children whoever they become, an attractive phenomenon in itself."

This, presumably, partly explains Errázuriz' affinity with her subjects, however unlikely. Rarely working on the street—the only exception being when, under Pinochet's dictatorship, she joined the Association of Independent Photographers to maintain a photojournalistic presence even in the face of totalitarian censorship, documenting strikes and demonstrations—she prefers to slowly come to know her subjects, sharing with them a rare degree of dignity and intimacy. From a black-and-white project with patients in a psychiatric hospital she has moved into colour for a series on the *animitas,* the wayside shrines that have been adapted from pre-Columbian tombs to become chapels for the victims of road accidents. "I am always looking for a different viewpoint, yet always remembering that every portrait is a self-portrait. We all spend our lives attempting to fathom who we really are, the photographer no less than the transvestite. So far I can only say that, not having found myself, I'll keep on looking."

—Amanda Hopkinson

ERWITT, Elliott.

Nationality: American. **Born:** Born, of American parents, in Paris, France, in 1928. **Education:** Educated in Milan, 1935-38, in Paris, 1938-39, in New York, 1940, and in Hollywood, 1942-44; studied at Los Angeles City College, 1945-47; studied film at the New School for Social Research, New York, 1948-50. **Military Service:** Served as a photographic assistant in the United States Army Signal Corps, in Germany and France, 1951-53. **Family:** Twice married; children: Jennifer, George, David, Misha and Ellen. **Career:** Worked as a drugstore sales and photographic darkroom assistant, Los Angeles, 1947-48; film cameraman in France, 1949-50; photographic assistant, Valentino Sarra Studio, New York, 1950; staff photographer, under Roy E. Stryker, for Standard Oil Company of New Jersey and Pittsburgh Photo Library, 1950-52; freelance photographer, working for *Collier's, Look, Life, Holiday,* etc., New York, since 1953. Member of Magnum Photos co-operative agency, New York and Paris, since 1953 (President, Magnum, New York, 1966). **Address:** c/o Magnum Photos, 72 Spring Street, New York, New York 10012, U.S.A.

Individual Exhibitions:

1947	Artists Club, New Orleans
1957	Limelight Gallery, New York
1963	Smithsonian Institution, Washington, D.C.
1965	Museum of Modern Art, New York
1971	The Photographers' Gallery, London
1972	Art Institute of Chicago
1974	*Son of a Bitch,* Witkin Gallery, New York
1978	*Elliott Erwitt at 50,* Witkin Gallery, New York
1979	Jeb Gallery, Providence, Rhode Island Kunsthaus, Zurich
1981	Canon Photo Gallery, Geneva (with Marius Hermanovicz)
	Douglas Kenyon Gallery, Chicago (with Arthur Bell)
1989	*Retrospective* based on *Personal Exposures,* New York; Palais, Tokyo
	Chateau d'Eau, Toulouse
	Canal de Isabel Museum, Madrid
	Retrospective, Fiesole, Italy
	Retrospective, Matsuya, Tokyo; Osaka and touring
	Personal Exposure, touring USA, Europe and Japan
1990	Hamilton Gallery, London
	Danziger Gallery, New York
	Photo Fair, Houston
	Retrospective, Milan
	A Moment in Time Gallery, Toronto
	Michael Shapiro Gallery, San Francisco
1991	Galerie Photogramme, Montreal; Vancouver
	On the Beach, touring FNAC Galleries, France
1992	Knoxville Museum of Art, Tennessee
	Mitsukoshi, Yokohama
	G Ray Hawkins Gallery, Los Angeles
	Travelli Williams Gallery, Aspen
	Janet Jackson Gallery, Atlanta
	Danziger Gallery, New York
	Friends of Photography, Ansel Adams Center, San Francisco
	To The Dogs, touring USA and Europe
1993	Agenzia Contrasto, Milan
	Royal Photographic Society, Bath, England

Selected Group Exhibitions:

1966	*The Photographer's Eye,* Museum of Modern Art, New York
1967	*Photography in the 20th Century,* National Gallery of Canada, Ottawa (toured Canada and the United States, 1967-73)
1977	*Concerning Photography,* The Photographers' Gallery, London (travelled to the Spectro Workshop, Newcastle upon Tyne)
1978	*Mirrors and Windows: American Photography since 1960,* Museum of Modern Art, New York (toured the United States, 1978-80)
1979	*American Images: New Work by 20 Contemporary Photographers,* Corcoran Gallery, Washington, D.C. (travelled to the International Center of Photography, New York; Museum of Fine Arts, Houston; Minneapolis Institute of Arts; and Indianapolis Institute of Arts, 1980; and American Academy, Rome, 1981)
1980	*Photography of the 50s,* International Center of Photography, New York (travelled to the Center for Creative Photography, University of Arizona, Tucson; Minneapolis Institute of Arts; California State University at Long Beach; Delaware Art Museum, Wilmington)
1983	*Photography in America 1910-83,* Tampa Museum, Florida
1984	*Sammlung Gruber,* Museum Ludwig, Cologne
1985	*American Images 1945-80,* Barbican Art Gallery, London (toured Britain)
1986	*The Animal in Photography 1843-1985,* The Photographers Gallery, London
1993	*The Photographers Who Opened the Age: 1960-70s,* Metropolitan Museum of Art, Tokyo

Collections:

Museum of Modern Art, New York; Smithsonian Institution, Washington, D.C.; Art Institute of Chicago; New Orleans Museum of Art; Bibliothèque Nationale, Paris; Museum Ludwig, Cologne, California Museum of Photography, University of California at Riverside; J. B. Speed Art Museum, Louisville, Kentucky; Cincinnati Art Museum, Ohio; Museum of Fine Arts, Houston, Texas.

Publications:

By ERWITT: Books—*Observations on American Architecture,* with text by Ivan Chermayeff, New York and London 1972; *Photographs and Anti-Photographs,* with text by Sam Holmes and John Szarkowski, Greenwich, Connecticut and London 1972; *The Private Experience: Elliott Erwitt,* with text by Sean Callahan, Los Angeles and London 1974; *Untitled,* portfolio of 10 photos, with an introduction by Peter C. Bunnell, New York 1974; *Son of a Bitch,* with text by P.G. Wodehouse, New York 1974; *15 Photographs,* portfolio, Geneva 1977; *Recent Developments,* with an introduction by Wilfred Sheed, New York 1978; *The Angel Tree,* with text by Howard Linn and Mary Jane Pool, New York 1984; *Personal Exposures,* New York 1988; *Elliott Erwitt: On The Beach,* New York 1991 (English, French, Italian, German and Japanese editions); *To The Dogs,* New York and Tokyo, 1992 (English, French, German, Italian, Japanese editions); *Between the Sexes,* New York 1994 (English, German and Japanese editions). **Films**—*Dustin Hoffman; Arthur Penn; Beauty Knows No Pain,* 1971; *Red, White and Bluegrass,* 1973; *Glass Makers of Herat,* 1977.

On ERWITT: Books—*American Photography: The 60s,* exhibition catalogue, Lincoln, Nebraska 1966; *Photography in the 20th Century* by Nathan Lyons, New York 1967; *America in Crisis: Photographs for Magnum,* edited by Charles Harbutt and Lee Jones, with an essay by Michael Levitas, New York 1969; *Looking at Photographs* by John Szarkowski, New York 1973; *Interviews with Master Photographers,* edited by James Danziger and Barnaby Conrad III, New York and London 1977; *Geschichte der Fotografie im 20. Jahrhundert/Photography in the 20th Century* by Petr Tausk, Cologne 1977, London 1980; *Concerning Photography,* exhibition catalogue, by Jonathan Bayer and others, London 1977; *Mirrors and Windows: American Photography since 1960* by John Szarkowski, New York 1978; *A Ten Year Salute* by Lee D. Witkin, with a foreword by Carol Brown, Danbury, New Hampshire 1979; *American Images: New Work by 20 Contemporary Photographers,* edited by Renato Danese, New York 1979; *Contact: Theory,* edited by Ralph Gibson, New York 1980; *Photography of the 50s: An American Perspective* by Helen Gee, Tucson, Arizona 1980; *World Photography,* edited by Bryn Campbell, London 1981; *Visions and Images: American Photographers on Photography,* edited by Barbaralee Diamonstein, New York 1981; *Sammlung Gruber: Photographie des 20, Jahrhunderts,* exhibition catalogue, with foreword by Siegfried Gohr, Cologne 1984; *American Images: Photography 1945-1980,* edited by Peter Turner and John Benton-Harris, London 1985. **Articles**—"Elliott Erwitt: Improbable Photographs" by Arthur Goldsmith in

California 1955. Photograph ©Elliott Erwitt.

Infinity (New York), August 1965; "Travelling Photographer" in *Infinity* (New York), October 1967; "Elliott Erwitt," with an introduction by P.G. Wodehouse, in *Album* (London), no. 12, 1970; "A Superbly Printed Sense of Fun: Elliott Erwitt, The Photographers' Gallery" by Ainslie Ellis in the *British Journal of Photography* (London), 9 July 1971; "Elliott Erwitt ou le Sourire à Fleur d'Objectif" in *Photo* (Paris), September 1971; "The Man Who Kept Something for Himself" by Sam Holmes in *Infinity* (New York), May 1972; "Elliott Erwitt" in *The Image* (London), no. 8, 1972; "Les Animaux Tristes d'Elliott Erwitt" in *Photo* (Paris), November 1972; "Elliott Erwitt, Photographs and Anti-Photographs" in *Photography Year 1973,* New York 1973; "Elliott Erwitt" in *Creative Camera* (London), March 1973; "Elliott Erwitt" in *Camera* (Lucerne), April 1973; "Elliott Erwitt" in *Zoom* (Paris), November/ December 1974; "Elliott Erwitt" in *News Reporter* (Paris), January 1976; "Les collections dans 'l'atmosphere Carne'" in *Vogue* (Paris) September 1978; "What's So Funny About Elliott Erwitt" by Wilfred Sheed in *American Photographer,* October 1978; "Klassiska bilder" by Rune Jonsson in *Aktuell Fotografi,* May 1979; "Short Takes: Recycling a Great Notion" by Kathryn Livingston in *American Photographer,* November 1981; "Enter Elliott Erwitt" in *Artforum,* January 1988; "Slices of Life" by Susan Piperato in *Popular Photography,* February 1988.

*   *   *

Humor has never been as highly regarded in the visual arts as it has in literature, perhaps because no one can hold a laugh too long, and literature has sufficient social grace to move along. The hybrid forms, like theater and film, fare better than the visual arts alone, but recently painting, sculpture, and especially still photography have been making some headway. It may be that the rise of absurdist and black humor in the postwar era has made more acceptable a photographic view that the world is a comic stage where men and animals accidentally fall into an unrehearsed ballet set up by a subversive set designer. Cartier-Bresson gave a boost to the notion that humor in photography might be valuable by proving that a serious photographer could also be funny. Doisneau carried the cause forward with pictures that proved a photographer with a funny bone, or at least one with his delicate understanding of the poignancy of life, could maintain an amazingly high standard. Elliott Erwitt, who clearly learned from both, polishes up the idea that a humorous photographer can be a serious man as well.

Erwitt's work swerves between journalism and formalism. He can build on a spare, eccentric, but highly controlled sense of design, holding his formal strategies as reserve weapons, always at the ready, not always at the front. One minute he catches the psychological tremor in a news event (see his 1959 pictures of Nixon and Kruschev's "kitchen debate" in Moscow); the next minute he compares the zigzag outline of a gull's body to the zigzag balconies that modern architects and poured concrete have foisted on Florida. Sometimes he has a quirky view of space, where objects shift slightly out of proportion or out of place, much as normal patterns of behavior do when he regards them closely. In his pictures, one small staccato mark—a walking man, a kite, a bird—gathers an odd force in a great empty field. Then, too, feet, paws, and socks assume a new importance when viewed at ankle height. Whether the aim is humor or graphic design, Erwitt can achieve an absolute poise of unrelated elements.

The main thrust of his work lies in his comic awareness of the gap between nobility and reality or between subject and setting, which blunder unpredictably into rhyme or battle with each other. He has forged a happy alliance with incongruity. A stolid matron in Las Vegas plies the metal arm of a ferocious cowboy slot machine. A couple wages intense and oblivious conversation between screaming mummies in Guanajuato. Erwitt's humor also depends heavily on visual puns, like that of the woman seen through a set of open shelves on which are two round pieces of fruit which stand for her breasts. He capitalizes on visual obstacles: a woman in a middle eastern *chador* walks past a flag that takes the place of her head. Mostly he concentrates on the disparity between the orderly world we imagined was out there and the actual place they sneaked in on us for daily use.

Dogs inhabit this real world. Sometimes they have their humans with them on the other end of a leash. Erwitt has a lot of sympathy for dogs (he is said to have had a growling contest with a strange dog once, and won). Dogs are rather like humans with a few mistakes in the engineering. They know shame, grow fat, assume ungainly postures, and lead the life of misfits among other bewildered creatures. Dogs comment succinctly on human activities. In 1962, Erwitt took three pictures of Nelson Rockefeller politicking on a street corner. In the first, a mutt watched closely, in the second he turned aside, and in the third he moved away to lift his leg.

That dogs, as Auden said, go on with their doggy life no matter what happens around them, is a reminder that there are no accidents in Erwitt's pictures. He uses the kind of accident and chance coincidence that "serious" photographers like William Klein and Robert Frank gave status in the 1950s, but he uses them as proofs that the world is a silly predicament we have agreed to inhabit. It does have its ideals. The Parthenon was one, Brasilia another, but a small dog can show up either one for an empty bastion. Anyway, human beings are always shaping trees and carving stones, and somehow the shapers and carvers never end up looking as neat as their endeavors. Erwitt apparently doesn't think this place that people and dogs have been plunked into is particularly welcoming. It does have its enjoyments, but a good many of these would suggest to a reasonable person that we are in a pickle. Three of Erwitt's movies trace the gargantuan effort and emotional tension involved in reaching such goals as marching in a brief costume between the halves of a football game. No one in Erwitt's viewfinder has any large measure of control. The camera alone proves the rebellious nature of the environment, where statues make faces behind the innocent, and cannons take aim at bus stops. Sometimes a person does retain authority over, say, a broom, or perhaps the model, if only the model, or an area to be bombed.

But limited or not, furred or otherwise, the inhabitants of Erwitt's terrain cock an eye, stick out a tongue, and keep on moving. They do not move through a wide range of emotions—at times they are touching, more often wry. But they provoke a smile the first, the second and third times around. That can only mean that we are amused with us. How grand of Mr. Erwitt to introduce us to our inconsequential selves.

—Vicki Goldberg

ESS, BARBARA

Nationality: American. **Born:** Brooklyn, New York, 4 April 1948. **Education:** Graduated from University of Michigan, Ann Arbor, in 1969 and attended the London School of Film Technique in 1971; self-taught in photography. **Recipient:** Mid Atlantic Arts Foundation Regional Fellowship Photography, 1990-91; National Endowment for the Arts Fellowship in Photography, 1994. **Agent:** Curt Marcus Gallery, 578 Broadway, New York, New York 10012, U.S.A. **Address:** 8 Spring Street, No. 4EF, New York, New York 10012, U.S.A.

Individual Exhibitions:

1978	*Census,* Franklin Furnace, New York
1981	*Shameless Longing,* J.N. Herlin Bookstore, New York
	Have You Ever Experienced Ecstasy?, Printed Matter, New York
1985	*The Doppler Effect,* New Museum of Contemporary Art, New York Cable Gallery, New York
1986	Curt Marcus Gallery, New York
	Middendorf Gallery, Washington, D.C.

	CEPA Gallery, Buffalo
1987	*Food for the Moon & Other Photos,* Johnen & Schottle Galerie, Cologne
	Michael Kohn Gallery, Los Angeles
	Interim Art, London (with James Casebere)
	Honolulu Academy of Arts, Honolulu
1988	Galerie Micheline Szwajcer, Antwerp
	Curt Marcus Gallery, New York
1989	Galerie Ghislaine Hussenot, Paris
1990	Curt Marcus Gallery, New York
	Galeria La Maquina Espanola, Madrid
1991	Michael Kohn Gallery, Los Angeles
1993	Curt Marcus Gallery, New York
	High Museum of Art, Atlanta
	Galeria La Maquina Espanola, Madrid
	Barbara Ess: Photography, Installation and Books 1978-1991, The Queens Museum, New York (travelled to Miami Center for The Arts, Florida; Anderson Gallery, Virginia Commonwealth University, Richmond Virginia)
1994	Fundacio, "La Caixa," Barcelona
	Faggionato Fine Arts, London
	Curt Marcus Gallery, New York

Selected Group Exhibitions:

1979	*Library,* 5 Bleecker Street, New York
1980	*Speaking Volumes* AIR Gallery, New York
1981	*Pictures and Promises,* The Kitchen, New York
1982	*Audio Arts at the Tate Gallery,* The Tate Gallery, London
1984	*Sextet,* Coburg Gallery, Vancouver
1985	Rudiger Schottle Gallery, Munich
	Currents, Institute of Contemporary Art, Boston
1986	*Ultrasurd,* S.L. Simpson Gallery, Toronto
	New New York, Cleveland Center for Contemporary Art, Cleveland
1987	*The New Romantic Landscape,* Whitney Museum of Art, Stamford, Connecticut
	In Black and White, The Carnegie Museum of Art, Pittsburgh
	Non in Codice, Gallerie Pieroni & American Academy, Rome
1988	*Twelve from New York,* Grey Art Gallery, New York University
	Made in Camera, Galleri Sten Erikson, Stockholm
1989	*Arrangements I,* Mai 36 Gallerie, Lucerne
	Galeria La Maquina Espanola, Madrid
	The Photography of Invention, National Museum of American Art, Washington, D.C.
1990	*Romance and Irony,* Art Gallery of Western Australia, Perth (travelled to National Gallery of New Zealand)
	The Indomitable Spirit, International Center of Photography Midtown, New York
	Figures et Lectures, Galerie Samia Saouma, Paris
	Images in Transition: Photographic Representation in the Eighties, The National Museum of Modern Art, Tokyo and Kyoto
1991	*Contemporary Abstract Photography,* CompassRose, Chicago
	Postmodern Prints, Victoria and Albert Museum, London
1992	*Aspects de la Collection Photographique Contemporaine,* Musee de La Roche-Sur-Yon, France
	Group Exhibition, Curt Marcus Gallery, New York
1993	*VIVID: Intense Images by American Photographers,* Raab Galerie, Berlin (travelled to London and Milan)
1994	*World of Tomorrow,* Thomas Solomon's Garage, Los Angeles
	Digressions, Caren Golden Fine Art, New York

Collections:

Art Gallery of Western Australia, Perth; The Art Institute of Chicago, Illinois; The Carnegie Museum of Art, Pittsburgh; The Chase Manhattan Bank; First National Bank of Minneapolis; FRAC Loire, France; FRAC Limousin, Limoges; Kunsthaus, Zurich; La Jolla Museum of Contemporary Art, Califor-

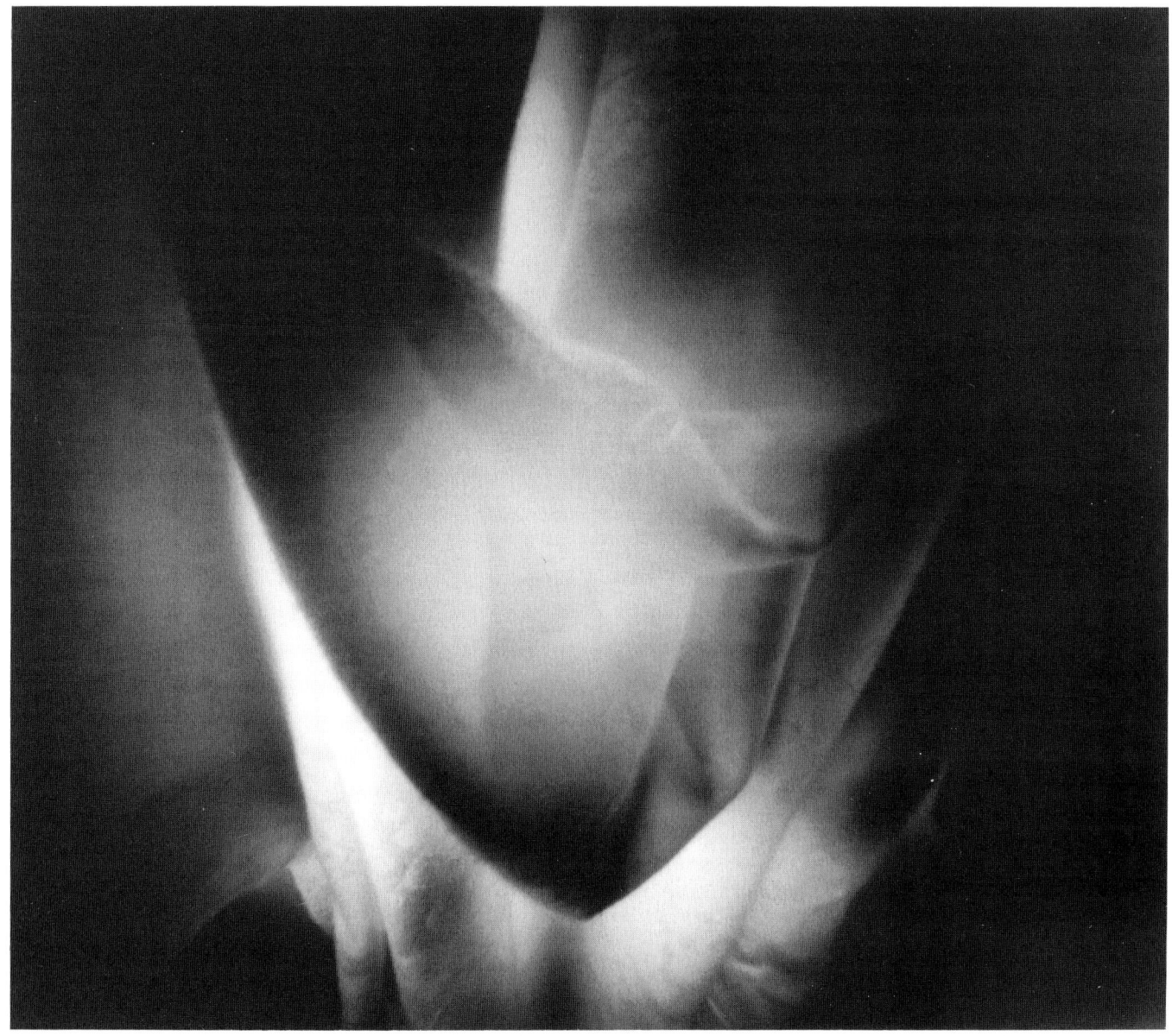

Untitled, **1994.** Photograph by Barbara Ess. Courtesy Curt Marcus Gallery, New York.

nia; List Art Center/David Winton Bell Gallery, Brown University, Providence, Rhode Island; Museum of Contemporary Art, Los Angeles; The Museum of Fine Arts, Houston; National Museum of American Art, Smithsonian Institution, Washington, D.C.; Musee National d'Art Moderne, Centre Pompidou, Paris; New School for Social Research, New York; The New Orleans Museum of Art; Princeton University of Art Museum, New Jersey; The Tampa Museum of Art, Florida; Toledo Museum of Art, Ohio; The Whitney Museum of American Art, New York.

Publications:

By BARBARA ESS: Books—*JAA #1* and *JAA #2,* 1978; *JAA #6,* 1983; *Thought Objects,* 1987; *Barbara Ess: Photography, Installation and Books 1978-1991,* The Queens Museum of Art (New York), 1993. **Articles**—*JAA #3,* 1979; *JAA #4,* 1980; *Camera Austria,* October 1988.

On BARBARA ESS: Books—*Beyond Boundaries: New York's New Art* by Jerry Saltz, Alfred Van der Mark Editions, 1986; *The Photography of*

Invention, American Pictures of the 1980s by Joshua P. Smith. The National Museum of American Art, Smithsonian Institute and MIT Press, 1989; *Woman Photographers* by Constance Sullivan (New York), 1990; *Barbara Ess* by Juan Vicente Aliaga, Fundació "la Caixa" (Barcelona), 1994. **Articles**—"Amerikanen en Het Medium Foto III: Barbara Ess" by Rob Perree in *Kunst Beel* (Amsterdam), 1985; Cookie Mueller in *Details,* June 1985; Andy Grundberg in *The New York Times,* June 1985; Kristine Mckenna in *Los Angeles Times,* July 1985; "Minimal Representation: Another View of New York" by Peter Clothier in *L.A. Weekly,* August 1985; *Suddendeutsche Zeitung* (Munich), August 1985; Jean Fisher in *Artforum,* September 1985; "Springtime on the Fringe" by Dan Cameron in *Arts Magazine,* September 1985; Jamey Gambrell in *Art in America,* October 1985; Richard Huntington in *The Buffalo News,* February 1986; Mark Power in *The Washington Post,* May 1986; "Ess's Essence" by Gerald Marzorati in *Vanity Fair,* September 1986; Valentin Tatransky in *Arts Magazine,* October 1986; *Bomb* magazine, number XVII, Fall 1986; "Pick of the Week" by A. Zelchner in *L.A. Weekly,* 19-26 December 1986; Holland Cotter in *Flash Art,* December 1986; *Redtape* magazine, #6, 1986; "Future Perfect" by Gary Indiana in *The Village Voice,*

10 March 1988; *The Los Angeles Times,* 19 June 1988; "Mental Theater: The Art of Barbara Ess" by Dan Cameron in *Arts Magazine,* Summer 1988; Shaun Caley in *Flash Art,* Summer 1988; "The Mind's Eye" by Mary Haus in *Art News,* November 1988; "Shooting from the Hip" by Vince Aletti in *The Village Voice,* 1988; "Les Territoires de Barbara Ess" by Mary Haus in *ArtPress,* January 1989; Barry Schwabsky in *Flash Art,* January/February 1989; Isabella Graw in *Wolkenkratzer Art Journal,* March 1989; "A Photographic Observatory" by Christopher Knight in the *Los Angeles Herald Times,* 16 June 1989; "Fuzz Box" by Vince Aletti in *The Village Voice,* 22 May 1990; "XY Ess" by Carlo McCormick in *Artforum,* Summer 1990; Roger G. Denson in *Artscribe,* October 1990; Dina Sorenson in *Arts Magazine,* October 1990; "Barbara Ess: Machine Dreams" by Nancy Princenthal in *The Print Collector's Newsletter,* Vol XXI Number 5, November/December 1990; Mary Haus in *Tema Celesta,* N. 27-28, November/December 1990; "Sibyllinisches Auge" in *FAZ,* 26 January 1991; "Sibyllinisches Auge der Frauen" by Peter Bode in *AZ feuilleton,* January 1991; "The Rush of Light" by Barbara Barg in *Cover Magazine,* January 1991; "Geschichten im Betrachter-Kopf" by Carin Steinlechner in *Kultur,* January 1991; "Jenseits Des Reinen Bildes" by Harion Mahren in *Munchner,* January 1991; "The Library" by Roberta Smith in *The New York Times,* 14 June 1991; "The Library at Josh Baer Gallery" in *The New Yorker,* 17 June 1991; "Barbara Ess: Visioni Strettamente Personali" by Gianni Romano in *Temporale,* Edizioni Dabbeni, N. 25; "Frauen und Foto" by Maribel Koniger in *Applaus,* 1991; "Dysfunction in the Family Album" by Charles Hagen in *The New York Times,* 31 January 1992; "Fogmeister" by Peter Schjeldahl in *The Village Voice,* 28 April 1992; "Through A Pinhole Darkly" by Ken Day in *NYQ,* April 1992; "Interview: Barbara Ess" by Patti Belle Hastings in *Art Papers,* May/June 1992; "Barbara Ess: Aquello que nos rodea" by Jose Ramon Danvila in *El Punto,* 5-11 June 1992; "Barbara Ess, Fotografo Inteligente" by Adolfo Castano in *ABC de las Artes,* 12 June 1992; "Barbara Ess, Curt Marcus Gallery" by Keith Seward in *Artforum,* September 1992; "Barbara Ess, Curt Marcus" by Mary Haus in *Artnews,* September 1992; "Art at the Edge, High Museum of Art" in *Journal of the Print World,* Winter 1992; Barbara Barg in *Flash Art,* Vol. XXV, No. 167, 1992; "Prasent und wahrnehmbar, ohne als Korper sichtbar zu sein" by Gabriela Hiltmann in *Basler Zeitung Ausgabe Fricktal,* 1 March 1993; "Odysseen mit der Kamera" by Ursula Eggennberger in *Zuri-tip,* 5 March 1993; "Complex Vision" by P.C. Smith in *Art in America,* March 1993; "Ausstellung, Korper im Ubergang" by Sabine Weder Arlitt in *Annabelle,* 8 April 1993; "Barbara Ess: Photography, Installation and Books 1978-1991" by Alan Schwartzman in *The New Yorker,* 17 May 1993; "Camera Obscura" by Katherine Dieckmann in *The Village Voice,* 2-8 June 1993; "Barbara Ess" by Vince Aletti in *The Village Voice,* 29 June 1993; "Gallery Go 'Round" by Victoria Pedersen, June 1993; "Memories, Facts and Lies" by Holland Cotter in *The New York Times,* 16 July 1993; "Summer Compendia: Memories, Facts and Lies" in *The Art Newspaper,* July-September 1993; "Photographs' Truth Are In the Eyes of The Beholder" by Helen Kohen in *The Miami Herald,* 15 August 1993; "The Gorgeous Distortions of Barbara Ess" by Sandra Schulman in *XS* Fun & Frolic, 1 September 1993; "Voice Choice" by Vince Aletti in *The Village Voice,* 19 April 1994; "The Ess Word" by David Lillington in *Time Out,* 4-11 May 1994; Sacha Craddock in *The Times* (London), 17 May 1994; "The World of Tomorrow" by David Pagel in *Art Issues,* May-June 1994; "Barbara Ess at Faggionato Fine Art" in *Art Monthly,* June 1994; "Barbara Ess: Curt Marcus Gallery" by David Levi-Strauss in *Artform,* Summer 1994; "Barbara Ess: Curt Marcus" by Dike Blair in *Flash Art,* Summer 1994; "Barbara Ess, Curt Marcus" by Gregory Volk in *ARTnews,* September 1994.

* * *

Though she came to notice in the ironic 1980s, Barbara Ess ignores the media-conscious content and forms of that decade's most visible camera art as well as the conventions of familiar photography—the hyper-real detail of advertising and portraiture, the snapshot veracity of photojournalism. In her antique technique and the hallucinatory scenes she often stages, she denies notions of the medium as literal, public, and modernist, and gives the soft-focus introspection associated with Pictorialism and some Surrealism a contemporary psychic edge. Using a camera yet subverting photography as fact, she underlines, in her words, "how emotion and thought interact with the phenomenal world."

Evolving since the mid-1980s, Ess's emblematic motifs—a baby on a bed, domestic animals, a rose-covered fence, a snake in a living room—mix feminine and Freudian overtones and evoke interpenetrating states of longing, memory, fear and fantasy. Like a number of 1990s artists in her interest in internalized perceptions of the body, she explores what she calls "ambiguous perceptual boundaries: between people, between the self and the not self, between in here and out there."

"I use primal imagery," says Ess, "so maybe it's fitting that I use the most primitive of cameras." She refers to her pinhole equipment, a lens-less box holding a 4 by 5 inch negative that she built for herself in 1983. In the long exposure demanded by the process, focus is relatively sharp at the center but moving figures blur into wraiths while shadows gather and perspectives dive at the margins of the picture. These traits enhance the subjectivity of Ess's images, which she shoots on black-and-white film, enlarges up to seven feet wide—with dust, scratches and all—and prints in a single, symbolic hue.

Making the private public, Ess has mounted her photographs like wallpaper (1988) and on a billboard (1994), and she also integrates them with the handmade books, audio-cassettes, videos and sculptures she produces. Coming out of the process and conceptual art of the 1970s, she uses the camera like any other device: indeed, her education was not in photography but philosophy (at the University of Michigan, Ann Arbor) and filmmaking (in London in 1971) and her first works were artist's books, which culminated in the seven numbers of the anthology of projects (by Ess and others) that she called *Just Another Asshole* (1973-87).

Ess's first exhibition exploring extreme states was "Have You Ever Experienced Ecstasy?"—an audio/photo/text installation of 1981 that gave some of her public's answers to this question, all linked by the theme of transcending the body. In 1994 her technical means and themes of eroticism, spirituality, and near-death were similar but more resonantly employed in the exhibition she called "Duvetyn." From the root of this word for down quilt cover (or "duvet"), she explained, come such meanings as "breath," "spirit," "to rise in a cloud" like dust or vapor and such derivatives as "deer," "dove," "deaf," "dusk," and "down." With her photographs of a deer, a dove in flight, and billowing duvets, she presented an altered video loop of the climax of the dance film *The Red Shoes* and pillows printed with excerpts from Freud's famous case study of Dora's dreams.

Beyond the literal connections among these sources, Ess suggested analogies between the dreamer, the ballerina and the visual artist and the need for all their languages—words, movements, images, objects—to conjure up the internal and external forces of nature, eros and thanatos working upon the psyche. Ess's photographs were the most memorable component of the display, but given her poetic ambitions, "Duvetyn" foretold that they will never be her only medium. As she "re-mystifies the world," in curator Susan Krane's phrase, Ess can be expected to use every magic tool.

—Anne Hoy

ETCHART, Julio (Alejandro Pedro).

Nationality: Uruguayan and British. **Born:** Montevideo, Uruguay, 20 May 1950; emigrated to Paris, 1974, and to London, 1975: naturalized, 1992, but retained Uruguayan citizenship. **Education:** Attended several schools in Montevideo; studied applied sciences, University of Montevideo, 1969-72; attended evening classes in photography and 16 mm film-making, Montevideo, 1966-68; studied documentary photography, Newport, Gwent, Wales, 1979-80. **Family:** Married Karen Greenhill in 1975 (divorced, 1979); married Linda Briggs in 1990; children: Alexander and Camille Etchart Briggs. **Career:** Worked as an interpreter/researcher, 1976-79; community media worker, St Paul's, Bristol, 1981-83; freelance photojournalist, working for *The Guardian, The Sunday Times, The Observer, Sunday Telegraph, The Independent, BBC Worldwide, New York Times, Newsweek, Der Spiegel,*

Fishermen and Empty Baskets, Guayaquil, Ecuador, **1984.** Photograph ©Julio Etchart.

Stern, Tiempo, Cambio 16, War on Want, OXFAM, Christian Aid, CAFOD, Amnesty International, Survival International, UNAIS, etc., since 1980. Co-founder and co-director of REPORTAGE Photos, London, since 1992. **Recipient:** First Prize, Environment category, World Press Photo Foundation, 1993. **Agent:** REPORTAGE Photos, 28 Norcott Road, London N16 7EL, England. **Address:** 50 Patshull Road, London NW5 2LD, England.

Individual Exhibitions:

1981   *Tales of Two Cities,* Bristol Arts Centre, Bristol
1985   *After the Dictators,* Watershed, Bristol (and UK tour, 1985-88)
1989   *Cuba Now,* ICA, London (and UK tour, 1989-92)
1990   *Songs, Faces and Winds: Photographs from Three Continents,* Bolivar Hall, London (travelled to the Galería del Notariado, Montevideo, Uruguay, 1991)
1991   *From a Common Past to a Better Future,* international touring display
1992   *The Forbidden Rainbow,* The Photographers' Gallery, London

Selected Group Exhibitions:

1986   *New Perspectives,* Crocodile Gallery, London
1991   *Our World in Photographs,* Museum of Modern Art, Oxford (and tour)
1993   *The Peopling of London,* Museum of London (and UK tour)
          Votes for Freedom, The Photographers' Gallery, London
          Parenthood, Whiteleys Gallery, London (and tour)

Collections:

The Photographers' Gallery, London; World Press Photo Foundation, Amsterdam.

Publications:

By ETCHART: Book—*Forbidden Rainbow,* with text edited by Amanda Hopkinson, London 1992.

On ETCHART: Book—*Latin Americans* by Hugh O'Shaughnessy, London 1988. **Articles**—"Etchart Mirrors Cuba" in *British Journal of Photography,* January 1989. **Films**—interview by Jo Shinner on BSB TV, 28 October 1990; interview by Sonia Brescia on Channel 5 SODRE (Uruguayan State TV), 20 December 1990.

*

    Although I started practising my experimenting with photography when I was a teenager, I did not become a professional photographer until I had completed the documentary photography course at Newport in 1980, which enabled me to focus my energies and abilities. I thus became a relatively "late" starter at the tender age of 30. However, I found that to be to my advantage, since I was able to apply my experience and my social and political awareness to my work. Although I undertake a fair amount of "straight" editorial work for newspapers and magazines, and have published a conventional photo book and exhibited in galleries, my main body of work has taken the shape of touring educational/campaigning displays produced by British and European non-governmental organisations and aid agencies that has allowed me to focus on important social issues and make photography an instrument of cultural awareness and discussion. I am now beginning to experiment with computer designed CD-ROM projects for educational markets.

—Julio Etchart

* * *

Julio Etchart has long been at the cutting edge of contemporary photojournalism. Apparently at home wherever in the world he happens to be working, nowhere is taken as exotic or "other"; the focus is always on the story, never its trappings. Whether photographing the fetishist religious practices of *santeria* in Cuba, the North African community in Paris or Indian women making *beadies* to smoke, the viewer is always aware of the larger picture, of the wider story beyond the frame and behind the image.

Etchart's formation in the work of reportage—incidentally also the name of the agency he founded, with fellow-photographer Carlos Guarita, in 1992—was consolidated by the course he took at Newport, Gwent from 1979-80. Famous for its training of documentary photographers, Newport was an important catalyst for a generation of photojournalists—nowhere more than in this instance, with the work that hitherto had only existed as a counterpart to Etchart's concerned involvement in a number of community and political enterprises. Born (to parents of Basque origin) in Montevideo in 1950, Etchart grew up during a period of maximum political upheaval in Latin America. While he was studying for school matriculation, taking evening classes in photography and film-making, Uruguay was in the throes of military dictatorship and the tupamaros guerrilla movement. Etchart's capacity to see beyond the immediate and persist against the odds was forged at this time.

By the mid-1970s Etchart was joining the ranks of Latin American exiles in Europe, first in Paris, then in Bristol and London. Community politics and media studies combined in a considerable body of work for consciousness-raising publicity of various kinds from the fightback against racism in St Paul's to exhibitions for Amnesty International (AI). To demonstrate how constant a preoccupation this remains requires one to look no further than the still-current row over a picture used by AI in June 1994, part of a press campaign by AI about street children in Colombia. Reproduced in the London *Guardian, Independent, Sunday Telegraph, Times, Financial Times* and *Observer* newspapers, it shows a boy with an open bullet wound to his stomach, sprawled on the street, his glue-bottle still in one hand. The row involved members of both the British and Colombian governments, regarded (in the words of Tristan Garel-Jones, Minister of State at the Foreign Office) as "a friendly democratic state whose aims and objects are ours."

The politics surrounding issues of national representation and international diplomacy have never given Etchart much cause for pause. On the one hand, his good relations with the Uruguayan Embassy in London have caused him to become their unofficial photographer of visiting dignitaries. On the other, his work—particularly on pollution and contamination—has proved conflictive in many regions, despite winning him awards with the World Press Photo Association including first prize (1993) in the ecological topics category. His ability to exercise the common touch and locate the people affected by and affecting those who make the news render his editorial work tailored to the kind of weekend magazines that, alas, few newspapers still produce. Nonetheless, Etchart remains a regular contributor, in particular to Saturday newspapers in Britain and to major continental magazines (*Stern, Der Spiegel, Tiempo* and *Cambio 16* among them). To expose this kind of work beyond the international aid agencies to a mass readership such as this is itself a signal achievement.

—Amanda Hopkinson

EVANS, Walker.

Nationality: American. **Born:** St. Louis, Missouri, 3 November 1903. **Education:** Loomis School, Windsor, Connecticut, until 1922; Phillips Academy,

Andover, Massachusetts, 1922; Williams College, Williams-town, Massachusetts, 1922-23; Sorbonne, Paris, 1926-27; mainly self-taught in photography. **Family:** Married and divorced twice. **Career:** Worked in the Public Library, New York City, 1923-25; freelance photographer, New York, from 1928; Staff Photographer, under Roy Stryker, Farm Security Administration (FSA), mainly in the southern United States, 1935-37; Associate Editor and Photographer, *Fortune* magazine, New York, 1945-65; retired from professional photography, 1965. Professor of Graphic Arts, 1964-74, and Emeritus Professor, 1974-75, Yale University, New Haven, Connecticut; Artist-in-Residence, Dartmouth College, Hanover, New Hampshire, 1972. **Recipient:** Guggenheim Fellowship, 1940, 1941, 1959; Carnegie Corporation Award, New York, 1962; Mark Rothko Foundation Grant, New York, 1973. D.Litt.: Williams College, 1968. Fellow, American Academy of Arts and Sciences, 1968; Member, National Institute of Arts and Letters, Washington, D.C., 1973. **Died:** (in New Haven, Connecticut) 10 April 1975.

Individual Exhibitions:

1931	*Photographs by 3 Americans,* John Becker Gallery, New York (with Ralph Steiner and Margaret Bourke-White)
1932	*Walker Evans and George Platt Lynes,* Julien Levy Gallery, New York
1933	*Walker Evans: Photographs of 19th Century Houses,* Museum of Modern Art, New York
1935	*Documentary and Anti-Graphic,* Julien Levy Gallery, New York (with Henri Cartier-Bresson and Manuel Alvarez Bravo)
1938	*Walker Evans: American Photographs,* Museum of Modern Art, New York (toured the United States)
1948	Art Institute of Chicago
1962	*Walker Evans: American Photographs,* Museum of Modern Art, New York (toured the United States and Canada)
1964	Art Institute of Chicago
1966	*Walker Evans' Subway,* Museum of Modern Art, New York
	Robert Schoelkopf Gallery, New York
	National Gallery of Canada, Ottawa (toured Canada)
1970	*Walker Evans: Paintings and Photographs,* Century Association, New York
1971	Robert Schoelkopf Gallery, New York
	Museum of Modern Art, New York (retrospective)
1972	Yale University, New Haven, Connecticut
1973	Robert Schoelkopf Gallery, New York
1974	Robert Schoelkopf Gallery, New York
1975	Kluuvin Galleria, Helsinki
1976	Bibliothéque Royale, Brussels
	Museum of Modern Art, New York (toured the United States and Europe)
	America Observed: Etchings by Edward Hopper, Photographs by Walker Evans, California Palace of the Legion of Honor, San Francisco (also shown at Acherbach Foundation for Fine Art, San Francisco)
1977	Cronin Gallery, Houston
	Robert Schoelkopf Gallery, New York
1978	Sidney Janis Gallery, New York
	Walker Evans at Fortune 1945-1965, Wellesley College, Massachusetts
1981	Milwaukee Art Center (with Ralph Steiner)
	Walker Evans:250 Photographies, Galerie Baudoin Lebon, Paris
	Walker Evans and Robert Frank:An Essay on Influence, Fraenkel Gallery, San Francisco
	Photographs of Chicago by Walker Evans, Kelmscott Gallery, Chicago
1984	Krannert Art Museum, University of Illinois, Champaign

Selected Group Exhibitions:

1936	*Fantastic Art, Dada and Surrealism,* Museum of Modern Art, New York
1937	*Photography 1839-1937,* Museum of Modern Art, New York

1938	*First International Photographic Exposition,* Grand Central Palace, New York
1939	*Art in Our Time:7 American Photographers,* Museum of Modern Art, New York
1962	*The Bitter Years:FSA Photographs 1935-41,* Museum of Modern Art, New York (toured the United States and Canada)
1976	*Photographs from the Julien Levy Collection, Starting with Atget,* Art Institute of Chicago
1979	*Images de l'Amerique en Crise,* Centre Georges Pompidou, Paris
1980	*The Magical Eye,* National Gallery of Canada, Ottawa (toured Canada)
1981	*Photographer as Printmaker,* Ferens Art Gallery, Hull, Yorkshire (travelled to the Museum and Art Gallery, Leicester; Cooper Gallery, Barnsley; Castle Museum, Nottingham; Photographers' Gallery, London)
1984	*Sammlung Gruber,* Museum Ludwig, Cologne

Collections:

Museum of Modern Art, New York; Metropolitan Museum of Art, New York; Yale University, New Haven, Connecticut; Wadsworth Atheneum, Hartford, Connecticut; Fogg Art Museum, Harvard University, Cambridge, Massachusetts; Library of Congress, Washington, D.C.; New Orleans Museum of Art; University of New Mexico, Albuquerque; San Francisco Museum of Modern Art; National Gallery of Canada, Ottawa.

Publications:

By EVANS: Books—*The Bridge,* with text by Hart Crane, Paris and New York 1930; *The Crime of Cuba,* with text by Carleton Beals, Philadelphia 1933, New York 1970; *African Negro Art,* with text by J.J. Sweeney, New York 1935; *American Photographs,* with text by Lincoln Kirstein, New York 1938, 1962, 1975; *Let Us Now Praise Famous Men,* with text by James Agee, New York 1941, Boston 1960, New York 1966; *Wheaton College Photographs,* with text by J. Edgar Park, Norton, Massachusetts 1941; *The Mangrove Coast,* with text by Karl Bickel, New York 1942; *African Folk Tales and Sculpture,* with text by Paul Radin and James Johnson Sweeney, New York 1952, 1964, revised edition, as 2 vols., *African Folktales,* with text by Paul Radin, and *African Sculpture,* with text by James Johnson Sweeney, Princeton, New Jersey 1970; *Many Are Called,* with an introduction by James Agee, Boston 1966; *Message from the Interior,* with an afterword by John Szarkowski, New York 1966; *Walker Evans,* portfolio of 14 photos, with an introduction by Robert Penn Warren, New Haven, Connecticut 1971; *Selected Photographs,* portfolio of 15 photos, with an introduction by Lionel Trilling, New York 1974; *I,* portfolio of 15 photos, New Haven, Connecticut and Washington, D.C. 1977; *Walker Evans: First and Last,* New York and London 1978. **Articles**—"The Reappearance of Photography" in *Hound and Horn* (Concord, New Hampshire), October-December 1931; "Labor Anonymous" in *Fortune* (New York), November 1946; "Chicago" in *Fortune* (New York), February 1947; "In the Heart of the Black Belt" in *Fortune* (New York), August 1948; "The Wreckers" in *Fortune* (New York), May 1951; "The U.S. Depot" in *Fortune* (New York), February 1953; "Over California" in *Fortune* (New York), March 1954; "The Congressional" in *Fortune* (New York), November 1955; "These Dark Satanic Mills" in *Fortune* (New York), April 1956; "Robert Frank" in *U.S. Camera Annual 1958,* New York 1957; "The Last of Railroad Steam" in *Fortune* (New York), September 1958; "James Agee in 1936" in *Atlantic* (Boston), July 1960; "When 'Downtown' Was a Beautiful Mess" in *Fortune* (New York), January 1962; "Those Little Screens" in *Harper's Bazaar* (New York), February 1963; "Walker Evans on Himself" in *Exposure* (New York), February 1977.

On EVANS: Books—*Fantastic Art, Dada And Surrealism,* edited by Alfred H. Barr Jr., New York 1936, 1937; *Walker Evans:Photographs,* with an introduction by John Szarkowski, New York 1971, London 1972; *Walker Evans: Photographs for the Farm Security Administration 1935-38,* with an introduction by Jerald C. Maddox, New York 1973; *Documentary Expression in Thirties America* by William Stott, New York 1973, London 1976; *Walker Evans: Photographs from the "Let Us Now Praise Famous Men" Project,* edited by William Stott and David Farmer, Austin, Texas 1974; *Photography in America,* edited by Robert Doty, with an introduction by Minor White, New York and London 1974; *The Years of Bitterness and Pride: FSA Photographs 1935-1943,* compiled by Jerry Kearns and Leroy Bellamy, edited by Hiak Akmakjian, New York 1975; *A Vision Shared: A Classic Portrait of America and Its People 1935-43,* edited by Hank O'Neal, New York and London 1976; *America Observed: Etchings by Edward Hopper, Photographs by Walker Evans,* exhibition catalogue, San Francisco 1976; *Photographs from the Julien Levy Collection, Starting with Atget,* exhibition catalogue, by David Travis, Chicago 1976; *Walker Evans: Photographs,* exhibition catalogue, by Valerie Lloyd, London 1976; *Concerning Photography,* exhibition catalogue, edited by Jonathan Bayer, London 1977; *Photographs: Sheldon Memorial Art Gallery Collection, University of Nebraska,* with an introduction by Norman A. Geske, Lincoln 1977; *Images of the South: Visits with Eudora Welty and Walker Evans,* edited by Carol Lynn Yellin, Memphis, Tennessee 1977; *A Book of Photographs from the Collection of Sam Wagstaff,* designed by Arne Lewis, New York 1978; *Walker Evans at Fortune 1945-1965,* exhibition catalogue, by Leslie K. Baier, Wellesley, Massachusetts 1978; *The Presence of Walker Evans* by Alan Trachtenberg, Boston 1978; *Life: The First Decade 1936-1945* by Robert Littman, Ralph Graves and Doris C. O'Neill, New York 1979, London 1980; *SX-70 Art,* edited by Ralph Gibson, New York 1979; *A Ten Year Salute* by Lee D. Witkin, with a foreword by Carol Brown, Danbury, New Hampshire 1979; *The Photograph Collector's Guide* by Lee D. Witkin and Barbara London, Boston and London 1979; *Les Années Ameres de l'Amerique en Crise 1935-1942,* exhibition catalogue, by Jean Dieuzaide, Toulouse, France 1980; *Instantanées* exhibition catalogue, by Michel Nuridsany, Paris 1980; *The Artist as Photographer* by Marina Vaizey, London 1982; *Walker Evans at Work* by Jerry L. Thompson, New York 1982, London 1983; *The Library of World Photography: Landscape,* with texts by David Plowden and Ian Jeffrey, Tokyo and London 1984;*The Hungry Eye,* by Giles Mora and John T Hill, London 1993. **Articles**—"Evans' Brilliant Camera Records Modern America" by Martha Davidson in *Art News* (New York), 8 October 1938; "Walker Evans' Photographs of America" by Thomas Dabney Mabry in *Harper's Bazaar* (New York), 1 November 1938; "Photographs by Walker Evans" by Lincoln Kirstein in *Print* (New York), February 1957; "Walker Evans: American Photographs" by Josephine Herbst in *Arts Magazine* (New York), November 1962; "Walker Evans: Photography as Representation" by Sidney Tillim in *Artforum* (New York), March 1967; "Notes on Walker Evans and W. Eugene Smith" by Van Deren Coke in *Art International* (Lugano, Switzerland), June 1971; "Walker Evans: A Crusty Colossus" in *Photography Year 1976* by Time-Life editors, New York 1976; "An Introduction to Evans' Work and His Recollections" by Peter C. Bunnell in *Exposure* (New York), February 1977; "Walker Evans" by M. Maingois in *Zoom* (Paris), April 1981. **Film**—*Walker Evans: His Time, His Presence, His Silence* by Sedat Pakay, 1969.

*   *   *

Since his 1971 retrospective at the Museum of Modern Art, Walker Evans has been generally acknowledged America's finest documentary photographer of this century and the artist who more than any other created the image Americans have of the Great Depression of the 1930s.

The special character of his work—his style and tone—is recognized to have influenced photographers, filmmakers, graphic artists, and indeed artists in other fields. His style has been described as straight, direct, unhurried, unobtrusive, transparent; his tone, as calm, timeless, staring, silent, sad, nostalgic. All these words are true but in a sense misleading. They point attention to the mystery of Evans' art, which can't be satisfactorily defined, and away from his pictures themselves and what matters most in each of them: the subject.

Consider one of Evans' photographs from *Let Us Now Praise Famous Men,* the classic documentary book on Southern tenant farming he did with the writer James Agee. The photo is a full-length portrait of the sharecropper farmwife the book calls Sadie Ricketts. Mrs. Ricketts is wearing a dress she made of an undyed canvaslike material. She is looking at the camera with her arms at her side, her right hand gently holding back her skirt so that the dress hangs better. There is a piece of paper and bits of trash—leaves? food?—at her feet. Her feet are bare.

This is the sort of picture Evans always took. Its subject is human (Mrs. Ricketts) or of human contrivance (Mrs. Ricketts' way of standing, her very special dress). "I am for man's work and the civilization he's built," Evans said. "Nature bores me as an art form." The subject, though "lower class," is decent. Mrs. Ricketts' dress is dirty but the dirt is the rubbed-in residue of many washings; Mrs. Ricketts wears the dress as though it were clean. The three safety pins holding its bodice closed are carefully set parallel, making them an ornament. Mrs. Ricketts is not taken off guard in a piteous or dramatic candid. On the contrary, she presents herself as she is willing to be seen, directly, consciously, to us, the viewers. In Evans' world, the critic Lincoln Kirstein noted, "even the inanimate things, bureau drawers, pots, tires, bricks, signs, seem waiting in their own patient dignity, posing for their pictures."

For Evans, it is the subject that counts—here, Sadie Ricketts and what she visibly and actually is. Behind her, left and right, are awkward clusters of hands, arms, pieces of her children. This awkwardness does not matter. The point of the photo is not silky composition, as it would be in, say, an Edward Weston picture. The point is Mrs. Ricketts, her face and dress, the way she presents her body, her worried regal diffidence. Evans might have agreed that the background was awkward, cluttered. "I find a howling error in composition, because something is in the wrong place, and I leave it there," he once said. "God arranged that; I wouldn't touch it."

Evans didn't change his subjects physically, and he did what he could not to change them *spiritually*. He tried to add nothing to them: no ideology, no polemic, no extrinsic excitement, no razzmatazz technique. His reluctance to polemicize helped lose him the best job he ever had, photographing rural America for the New Deal's Farm Security Administration. His hatred of sham excitements kept him from usual photojournalism and made him impatient with the technical extravagances of "concerned" photographers who pep up their photos with faux-casual framing, vignetting, bleach-enhanced chiaroscuro. Such techniques are spectacular but wrong, Evans thought, because they draw attention from the picture's subject. Of two virtuoso photographers he once remarked, "They do the perfect thing with the camera, and you say ohh and ahh, how perfect. Then you don't get their content clearly enough, however. As in typography and printing, technique shouldn't arrest you."

Content was what counted, the subject itself. The chief reason the subjects in Evans' photos matter is of course that they are, like Mrs. Ricketts, beautiful.

As I have argued elsewhere, Evans showed the lives and appurtenances of the poor to be works of art. This was a magnificent achievement, the central imaginative act of the Depression. He put the life of the poor in a frame, the photograph itself, wherein sensitive onlookers could see its aesthetic respectability.

In ways difficult to pin down Evans' vision of beauty was influenced by the Purist aesthetic of the 1920s. Though his work is scrupulously "straight," the effect he achieves in his best-known pictures of the 1930s, like the portrait of Mrs. Ricketts, has some of the neatness and bright permanence of streamlining. Part of his greatness, in fact, may be to bring together the two major 1930s aesthetics: documentary and Art Deco.

Since there is a purism in his work, though, is he not liable to the same criticism that the Marxist critic Walter Benjamin leveled at the German Neue Sachlichkeit (New Objectivist) photographers? Is Evans not guilty of beautifying hardship and thus "mystifying," camouflaging, social wrongs? Evans himself was deeply aware of this question—which is much discussed in *Let Us Now Praise Famous Men*—and knew it couldn't be settled to his own or others' satisfaction. He wanted to insist on both the beauty of his subjects *and* the obscenity of the social conditions in which their beauty grew. The beauty he documented, then, is not a gentle thing; "it's not beauty in the conventional sense," he said. It is beauty with blood on it, beauty tragic twice over: because of the abominable conditions that fed it and because it could not be recognized or appreciated by those who created it.

Of those of us who can appreciate it, this beauty asks a lot. It asks us, for example, to see that Mrs. Ricketts didn't want to be dressed as she was and yet still was proud of the dress she had made. Evans didn't mind asking a lot; he once said, "If an audience can only be moved by a picture of someone with his guts pouring out, they're not a very interesting audience." He wanted to bring his audience subjects whose beauty would not only amaze them but appall them—move them, as he was moved, to wonder, compassion, anger, self-hatred. For most of his career Evans didn't have the audience he needed; he has us now.

—William Stott

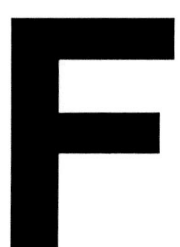

FACIO, Sara.

Nationality: Argentinian. **Born:** Buenos Aires, 18 April 1932. **Education:** Studied drawing and painting at the Escuela Nacional de Bellas Artes, Buenos Aires, 1947-53; studied color photography at Kodak, Rochester, New York, 1960; studied photography in the studio of Annemarie Heinrich, Buenos Aires, 1960; studied color photography at Agfa, Buenos Aires, 1965. **Career:** Freelance photographer, with joint studio with Alicia D'Amico, q.v., as Alicia D'Amico/Sara Facio, Fotografias, Buenos Aires, since 1960. Editor of the Photographic Section, *La Nación* newspaper, Buenos Aires, 1966-74, and *Autoclub* magazine, Buenos Aires, 1970-74. Editor, La Azotea photographic book publishers, Buenos Aires, since 1973. "Camara clara" columnist, *Vigencia* magazine, Buenos Aires, since 1980. Founder-Member, Consejo Argentino de Fotografia, Buenos Aires, since 1979; Director, Foto Galeria Permanente, Teatro San Martin, Buenos Aires, since 1985. **Recipient:** National Salon of Argentina Prize, 1964; Bifota Medal, Berlin, 1965; Artist Award, Fédération International de l'Art Photographique, 1967; Olivetti-Communidad Award, Buenos Aires, 1968; Book Prize, Congress of Books, Vienna, 1969; SAS Prize, Copenhagen, 1969; Special Prize, Federacion Argentino de Fotografia, 1970; First Prize, *Fotografia Argentina* exhibition, Moscow, 1977; Ten Major Figures of Argentine Visual Arts Award, 1982; Ten Women of Argentine Life Award, 1985; Premio Feria del Libro Leipzig-Alemania, 1986; Premio Cámara Argentina de Publicaciones, 1990, 1991 and 1993; Medalla de los XXII Encuentros de Arles-Francia, 1991; Konex de Platino (Mayor Figure Photographic 1982/92), 1992. **Agent:** Galerie Agathe Gaillard, 3 rue du Pont Louis-Philippe, 75004 Paris, France. **Address:** Paraguay 1480, (1061) Buenos Aires, Argentina.

Individual Exhibitions (with Alicia D'Amico):

1963	*Escritores Argentinos,* Galería Rioboo, Buenos Aires (travelled to the Biblioteca Nacional, Mexico City)
1964	*Mutaciones,* Galería Lirolay, Buenos Aires
1965	*Escritores Argentinos,* Consejo Deliberante, Buenos Aires
	50 Fotografias, Agfa-Gevaert Gallery, Buenos Aires (travelled to Image 65, Cordoba, Argentina)
1966	*"Luv" en Fotografia,* Casa del Teatro, Buenos Aires (travelled to the Rosario Gallery, Argentina)
1967	*Fotografias Premiadas,* Image 67, Cordoba, Argentina
1968	*Buenos Aires, Buenos Aires,* Peña Fotográfica, Rosario, Argentina (toured Argentina, 1968-70)
1971	*Escritores argentinos,* Ateneo Foto Cine, Rosario, Argentina
1974	*Retratos y Autorretratos,* Casa del Fotografo, Buenos Aires (toured Argentina)
1981	*Buenos Aires, Buenos Aires,* Gallery Tsukada, Tokyo
	Humanario, Gallery Tsukada, Tokyo
	Buenos Aires, Buenos Aires, Museo de Arte Moderno, Sao Paulo, Brazil
1982	*Geografia de Pablo Neruda,* Palazzo Reale, Caserta, Italy (travelled to the Galleria San Fedele, Milan)
1984	*Encuentros con Julio Cortazar,* Museo de la Ciudad, Mar del Plata, Argentina (travelled to Centro Cultural San Martin, Buenos Aires)
1985	*25 Anos de Fotografia,* Centro Cultural de Buenos Aires (travelled to the Auditorium of Mar del Plata; Casa Argentina, Rome)
1992	*Humanario,* Fotofest, Houston, Texas

Figures et caracteres, (Retratos y Autorretratos), Centre Pompidou, Paris

Individual Exhibitions:

1981	*Actos de Fe en Guatemala,* Galerie Agathe Gaillard, Paris; The Photographers' Gallery, London
1988	*La mujer y el Cine,* Mar del Plata, Argentina
1989	*Gente de Cine,* Mar del Plata, Argentina
	Retratos, Universidad de Lima, Peru
1990	*Las Hechiceras,* Fundación Goldstein, BS.As.
1991	*Bestias en New York,* Harrod's en el Arte, BS.As.
	Retratos de Escritores, Encuentros Inter nacionales de Fotografia, Arles, France
	Retratos, Amsterdam
1992	*Retratos,* Santa Fe, Mar del Plata, Argentina
1993	*Escritores de America Latina,* Buenos Aires

Selected Group Exhibitions:

1963	*La Selección Argentina,* Federación Argentina de Fotografia, Buenos Aires (toured Germany, Belgium, Greece, and Colombia)
1977	*Maestros de la Fotografia Argentina,* YMCA Salon, Buenos Aires
1978	*Hecho en Latinoamérica,* Museo de Arte Moderno, Mexico City (travelled to *Venezia '79*)
	Argentine Exhibition, House of Friendship, Moscow
1980	*Miembros Fundadores del Consejo Argentino de Fotografia,* Buenos Aires (toured Argentina)
1981	*Hecho en Latino America 2,* Palacio de Bellas Artes, Mexico City
1982	*La Photographie Contemporaine en Amerique Latine,* Centre Georges Pompidou, Paris
1984	*Fotografia Argentina,* Kasteel Hoensbroek, Netherlands
1985	*Photographie Argentine,* Espace Graslin, Nantes, France
1986/87	*La mujer en la creación,* toured Argentina
1991	*Fotografia para coleccionar,* Buenos Aires
1992	*Desires and Desguises,* The Photographers' Gallery, London (travelled)
1993	*El niño y la Imagen,* La Plata, Buenos Aires
	La otra Cara, Kassel, Germany
	Canto a la Realidad, Madrid, Spain

Collections:

Bibliothèque Nationale, Paris; Art Institute of Chicago; Library of Congress, Washington, D.C.; Museum of Modern Art, New York; Musée Municipale du Chateau d'Eau, Toulouse, France.

Publications:

By FACIO: Books—*Buenos Aires, Buenos Aires,* with Alicia D'Amico, Buenos Aires 1968; *Geografía de Pablo Neruda,* with Alicia D'Amico, Buenos Aires 1973; *Seven Voices,* with Rita Guibert, New York 1973; *Retratos y Autorretratos,* with Alicia D'Amico, Buenos Aires 1974; *Hasta aqui,* with Mario Benedetti, Buenos Aires 1974; *Humanario,* with Alicia D'Amico, Buenos Aires 1976; *Cancionero Contra . . . ,* with Maria Elena

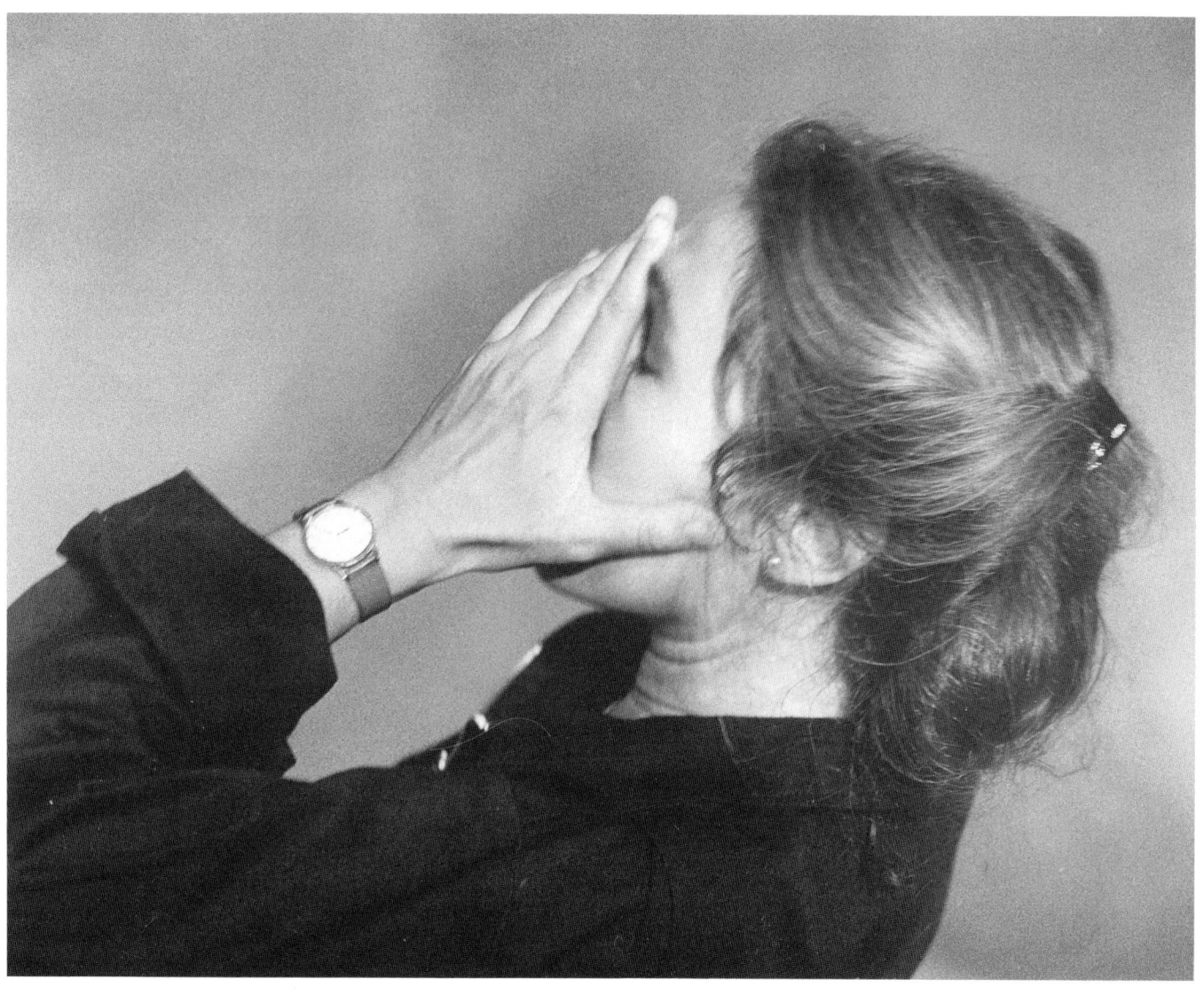

Jeanine Meeratfel, **from series** *Las Hechiceras,* **1990.** Photograph ©Sara Facio.

Walsh, Buenos Aires 1976; *Cómo tomar Fotografías,* with Alicia D'Amico, Buenos Aires 1977; *Rostros de Buenos Aires,* Buenos Aires 1978; *Fotografía Argentina Actual,* editor, Buenos Aires 1981; *Sara Facio/Alicia D'Amico: 25 anos de fotografía,* with text by Maria Elena Walsh, Buenos Aires 1985; *Actos de Fe en Guatemala,* with text by Miguel Angel Asturias, Buenos Aires 1980; *Pablo Neruda,* with text by Neruda, Buenos Aires 1988; *Sara Facio, Retratos,* with introduction by Maria Elena Walsh, Buenos Aires 1992; *Fotografía Argentina Actual,* Buenos Aires 1981; *Alicia D'Amico,* Buenos Aires 1982; *Martin Chambi,* Buenos Aires 1986; *Annemare Heinrich,* Buenos Aires 1987; *Grete Stern,* Buenos Aires 1988; *La fotografía en la Argentina 1840/1920,* Buenos Aires 1988; *La Fotogaleria del Teatro San Martin,* Buenos Aires 1990; *Witcomb, nuestro ayer,* Buenos Aires 1991; *Marcos López,* Buenos Aires 1993. **Articles**—"Juegos de J. Cortázar" in *La Nación (Buenos Aires),* 4 May 1967; "San Pablo 67; no fué" in *La Nación* (Buenos Aires), 12 September 1967; "Edward Weston" in *La Nación* (Buenos Aires), 26 November 1968; "Denis Gabor: Holograma" in *La Nación* (Buenos Aires), 12 February 1972; "Tambien la mujeres" and "Tikal, encuentro . . ." in *La Nación* (Buenos Aires), 10 August 1972; "Francoise Giroud" in *La Nación* (Buenos Aires), 10 December 1972; "Steichen siempre foto" in *La Nación* (Buenos Aires), 2 April 1973; "Tim, humor para vivir" in *La Nación* (Buenos Aires), 30 December 1973; "Jeanine Niepce" in *Crisis Magazine* (Buenos Aires), 3 April 1974; "Fotografia es Cultura" in *Diario Clarin* (Buenos

Aires), 20 March 1980; "Cuando la fotografia es una excusa" in *La Nación* (Buenos Aires), 8 November 1981; "La fotografia creativa" in *Diario Clarin* (Buenos Aires), 7 May 1982; "Confesiones" in *Diario La Voz* (Buenos Aires), 5 November 1982; "Fotos, trompadas y privelegios" in *Diario Clarin* (Buenos Aires), 26 October 1983; "Andre Kertesz" in *Diario Clarin* (Buenos Aires), 7 September 1985; Special section in *La Revista,* ACAFO 1986/87; "Sander: un maestro en la ciudad" in *Diario Clarin* (Buenos Aires) 4 September 1987; Special section in *La Revista Cultura* 1989/93; "El desnudo de ayer y de hoy" in *Revista Actualidad,* N.66; "Hace 150 años" in *Diario Ambito Financiero,* 8 August 1989; "Sebastiano Salgado" in *Diario Clarin,* 22 September 1989; Special section in *La Revista Fotomundo,* 1992/93.

On FACIO: Books—*Territorios* by Julio Cortázar, Mexico City 1978; *Photography Yearbook,* by Time-Life editors, New York 1979; *Hecho en Latino America 2,* exhibition catalogue, with texts by Pedro Meyer, Lazaro Blanco and others, Mexico City 1981; *Sara Facio* by J. Potenze, Buenos Aires 1982; *La Photographie Contemporaine en Amerique Latine,* exhibition catalogue, by Alain Sayag, Paris 1982; *The Library of World Photography: Portraits,* with introduction by Colin Ford, Tokyo 1982, 1983, London 1983. **Articles**—"Approche a la Vie" by Ives Lorelle in *Photo-Cinema* (Paris), February 1968; "Tercera Fundación" by Tomás E. Marinex in *Primera Plana* (Buenos Aires), 13 August 1968; "Pablo Neruda . . ." by Michel Nuridsany in *Le Figaro* (Paris), 14 January 1974; "Itinerario por . . . " by Robert Saladrigas in *Destino* (Barcelona), 16 February 1974; "Dos Fotografas" by Nestor Barreiro in *Vandidades* (Santiago), May 1976; "Fotografía en A" by M.C. Orive in *Artes Visuales* (Mexico City), May 1976; "Humanity in Camera" by Robert Cox in the *Buenos Aires Herald,* 23 October 1976; "Sara Facio, caza . . . " by Vilma Colina in *Convicción* (Buenos Aires), 11 May 1980; "Argentina" in *Printletter* (Zurich), no. 36, 1981; "Sara Facio" in *Fotomundo* (Buenos Aires), no. 178, 1983; "Sara Facio" in *Revista Cultura* (Buenos Aires), no. 10, 1985; "25 años" by A. Bécque Casaballe in *Revista Fotomundo*, 1985; "Argentina Hoy" by Diana Mines-Diario in *Jake* (Uruguay), 1985; "Hay que educar la mirada" by Cristina Civale in *Revista el Periodista*, 1986; "Sara Facio: Testimonio visual" by Fermin Fevre in *Diario Clarin*, 1988; "Actos de Fe" by Pablo Avelluto in *Revista Babel*, 1989; "Sara Facio" by Nora L. Jabif in *Diario Sur*, 1990; "La Fotogaleria" by A. Bacquer Casaballe in *Revista Fotomundo*, 1990; "Un hito en la fotografia argentina" by Lilina Fariña in *Diario La Prensa*, 1991; "Argentinos en el Pompidou" by Mabel Itzcovich in *Diario Clarin,* 1992.

*

I came to photography by way of a long apprenticeship in classical art. Painting, with its decorative aestheticism somehow implying—even in a physical sense—an evasion of reality, proved a disappointment; and I discovered instead that photography was the perfect medium for representing the reality that I saw around me. I noticed that each individual photographer, according to his level of intensity, could demonstrate his own particular brand of reality subjectively, with credibility, giving it a personal touch that was different.

It was a late discovery, but in the 1960s, from the age of about 30, I began to dedicate myself entirely to photography. It is my profession, at which I make my living; it is my means of self-expression. For the past twenty years I have been reading, writing, and taking pictures without interruption. I have remained faithful to realism and naturalism, without using artificial aids for lighting, taking the pictures, or laboratory work; and, in general, I base my work on the human figure. Those photographers whose work affects me most are those who take the same direction. I am not dazzled by sheer technique or enormous scale.

Another reason for my commitment to realism is the awareness that I cannot dissociate myself from my own context—my country, my city, my people. I have travelled widely, learned to know other cultures and races, and have, indeed, photographed them and written about them. But it is only in Argentina that I somehow feel authentic and secure—photographing my own people, whether well-known or anonymous. I feel the urge to record them with my camera and to show them to the world—writers, artists, dancers, townsfolk, and peasants. Argentina has no colorful folklore, "picturesque" natives, or gaudy and exotic costumes. There is no special architecture or handicrafts, nor are there any quaint established customs. Everything is "antiphotogenic." It is a constant challenge to take good pictures that are natural and lively, when faced with subjects that have so little visual attraction.

A few months ago, during a journey to the almost unpopulated north of my enormous country, while taking photographs of the desolate landscapes, I felt the overwhelming need to incorporate *myself* into that landscape, so strong was the anxiety I felt at the absence of any living soul. Thus came about my latest series, *Autopaisajes* ("Self-Landscape"). Perhaps, quite apart from the way in which my photographs need people, there was also a need in me to be included quite literally and physically. Probably that is the ultimate way of linking myself indissolubly with this abiding passion I feel for photography.

—Sara Facio

* * *

A year or so before he died, Steichen said: "The mission of photography is to explain man to man and every man to himself." This is indeed the very essence of every kind of photographic picture, and is still more true in photography that has a social commitment. Photography, in fact, which never has been the faithful mirror of objective reality, is none the less an interpretation of reality that enables us to know both the single individual and the whole community. In the final analysis the task of social photography is really to translate into pictures the events, situations and personalities that form part of

our daily life, which, added together, express man and his nature. That is the method that Sara Facio follows in her work; every one of her pictures seeks to describe some detail, however minute, of the historic period in which we live.

Her photographs seldom depict the sensational or unusual; Sara Facio is far from being one of those legendary, fascinating press photographers who are always on the spot whenever and wherever there is hot news. Paradoxically, our historical narrative is unfolded through unhistorical photographs. A great event is of course the tip of a submerged iceberg, the visible part, but by no means the whole, though it gives us facts that are basic to our understanding of the entire phenomenon. Facio records moments in life for what they are worth, claiming no special significance for them, but despite their modesty, they are representative of contemporary society.

For Sara Facio photography is the most suitable medium to fix the moment which can never be repeated. And that is the true key to the creativity of the photographer who, faced by a world in continuous evolution, chooses a picture, a tiny piece of life, in order to transmit a personal concept of it. Every picture thus represents a purely subjective reaction and may be interpreted by the viewer equally subjectively. But there does exist a common linguistic code between photographer and viewer that makes an intelligible communication possible. The code consists of the commonplaceness of the event represented; it is in fact that which every one of us knows very well by instinct but cannot isolate from the whole visual panorama. This then is a photography that does not remain circumscribed by the limits of mere reproduction of the concrete world. The picture chosen is transformed into evidence, indelible and immutable, of a fugitive reality obliterated as soon as it comes into being. Like an enormous jigsaw puzzle, the sum of all this evidence makes up an authentic portrait, but certainly an incomplete, partial one, since Sara Facio is not so absurdly presumptuous as to claim that her photography is a full record of objectivity.

Rather, her sensibility, her feelings and emotions are the psychological instruments that enable her to penetrate the world around her. And it is with those same instruments that the public can start on its voyage of exploration through her pictures. Thanks to the balance in them between concrete information and emotive expressivity, Sara Facio's photographs stimulate the mechanism of intellectual perception and the processes of psychological intuition in the beholder.

The mission of photography is thereby realized: the photographer describes a part of external reality with the visual story, helping to enhance our consciousness of the world; at the same time she conveys an emotional response, giving us the means to look deeper into ourselves.

—Giuliana Scimé

FAUCON, Bernard.

Nationality: French. **Born:** Apt-en-Provence, 12 September 1950. **Education:** Attended the Lycée d'Apt, 1962-69; studied at the Sorbonne, Paris, 1969-73, M.Ph. 1973. **Career:** Freelance photographer, in Paris and Apt, since 1976. **Recipient:** Prix du Premier Livre de Photo de la Ville de Paris, 1979; Grand Prix National, 1989; Prix Léonard de Vinci 1991. **Agents:** Galerie Yvon Lambert, 108 rue Vieille du Temple, 75003, Paris and Agathe Gaillard, 3 rue du Pont Louis Philippe, 75004 Paris **Address:** 6 rue Barbanègre, 75019 Paris, France.

Individual Exhibitions:

1977	Galerie Lop-Lop, Paris
	Galerie-librairie la Quotidienne, Aix-en-Provence, France
1978	Galeria Fotomania, Barcelona, Spain
1979	Galerie Agathe Gaillard, Paris
	Galeria Castelli Graphics, New York
1980	Galerie 't Venster, Rotterdam
	Canon Photogallery, Geneva
1981	Galerie Napalm, Saint-Etienne, France
	Castelli Photographs, New York
	Galerie Junod, Lausanne, Switzerland

La tempetêde neige, la quatorzième chambre d'amour, **1985 (original in colour).** Photograph by Bernard Faucon.

1982	Galerij Paule Pia, Antwerp, Belgium
	Syracuse University, New York
	Zeit-Foto Salon, Tokyo
	Musée de Toulon, Toulon, France
1983	Castelli Graphics, New York
	Galerie Fiolet, Amsterdam
	Galerie Imagique, Saint-Saturnin d'Apt, France
	Galerie Junod, Lausanne, Switzerland
1984	Galerie Agathe Gaillard, Paris
1985	Axe Actuel, Toulouse, France
	Van Reekum Museum, Apeldoorn, Netherlands
	Galerie Images Nouvelles, Bordeaux, France
	Galerie de Pret, Angers, France
	Musée Nicephore Niepce, Chalon sur Saône, France
	Galerie Artem, Quimper, France
	Galeria Modulo, Lisbon
	Galerie Alexandre de la Salle, Saint-Paul-de-Vence, France
1986	Houston Center for Photography, Texas
	Galerie Jade, Colmar, France
	Musée d'Auriac, France
	Galerie Agathe Gaillard, Paris
	Castelli Graphics, New York
	Centre d'Art Contemporain, Forcalquier, France
	Galerie Images Nouvelles, Bordeaux, France
	Galerie Fiolet, Amsterdam
	Galerie Agathe Gaillard, Paris
	10 ans de photographie, Musée de la Vieille Charité, Marseille, France
1987	L'Hypodrome, Douai
	Galerie Fiolet, Amsterdam
	Maison de la culture, Amiens
	Watershed, Bristol
	Centre culturel, Montbeliard
	Parco, Tokyo
	Slills Gallery, Edinburgh
	Institute of Contemporary Art, London
	Darkroom, Cambridge
	Torino Fotografia, Turin

	Centre Culturel Français, Berlin Est
	Galerie Carré d'art, Larmor, Bretagne
	Galerie Junod, Lausanne
	Cross References, Sculpture into Photography, Walker Art Center, Minneapolis; Museum of Contemporary Art, Chicago
1988	Centre culturel français, Prague
	Arthothèque, La Rochelle
	Centre culturel Français, Berlin, RDA
	Galerie Junod, Lausanne
	Journées de la photo, Galerie Bazille, Montpellier
	Galerie Agathe Gaillard, Paris
	Espace photo de la ville de Paris: Rétrospective, Paris
	Parco Gallery, Sapero, Japon
	Interform gallery, Osaka
	Hotel Hannon, Galerie Contretype, Bruxelles
	Artifices, Chapelle des recollets, Apt, France
	Espace Gérad Philippe, Jarny
	Rebecca Hossack Gallery, London
	Centre culturel André Malraux, Vandoeuvre les Nancy
	Galerie Fiolet, Amsterdam
	Maison Descartes: Rétrospective, Amsterdam
	Galerie Jean-François Dumont, Bordeaux
	Galerie Joachim Becker, Cannes
1989	Arthothèque du centre ville, Grenoble
	Arthothèque de la grande place, Grenoble
	Alliance française, Manilla, Philippines
	Hotel Oriental, Bangkok
	Alliance française, Hong Kong
	Cadran solaire, Troyes, France
	Galeria Spectrum, Saragossa, Spain
	Zeit Foto Salon, Tokyo
	Festival Photographique, Taragona, Spain
	Centre fotografic Visor, Valencia
	Modulo, Lisbon
	Nueva imagen fotogaleria, Pamplona, Espagne
	Léo Castelli, New York
	Centre national de l'audiovisuel, Luxembourg
1990	Duta Fine Arts Foundation, Jakarta, Indonesia
	la peur du voyage, Impressions d'Edimbourg, Institut Français d'Ecosse: Edinburgh
	Nikon live galerie, Zurich
	Institut Français, Freiburg, Germany
	Galerie Agathe Gaillard, Paris
1991	Picture Photo space, Osaka, Japan
	Rebecca Hossack, London
1992	Centre culturel Français de Casablanca
	Centre culturel Français de Marrakech
	Centre culturel d'Albi
	Moments contemporains, Galerie L., Saint Etienne, France
1993	Picture Photo Space, Osaka
	Il Tempo, Tokyo
	Château d'Eau, Toulouse
	Aberdeen Art Gallery, Aberdeen Museum
	Institut Français de Turin
	Institut Français de Budapest
1994	Rebecca Hossack Gallery, London
	Galerie Delacroix, CCF, Tangier
	Centre culturel Français, Marrakech
	Selected Group Exhibitions:
1980	*Invented Images,* University of California, Santa Barbara
1981	*French Photographers,* Friends of Photography, Carmel, California
1982	*Color as Form,* International Museum of Photography at George Eastman House, Rochester, New York
	Staged photo events, Lijnbaancentrum/Rotterdam kunstichting
1983	*Peindre et Photographier,* Espace Niçois d'Art et de Culture, Nice, France
	Images fabriquées, Musée Georges Pompidou, Paris
1984	*French Spirit Today,* La Jolla Museum of Contemporary Art, California

La Puissance de la Photographie, Forum Stadtpark, Graz, Austria

1985   *Paris, New York, Tokyo,* Tsukuba Museum of Photography, Japan

Semana International del fotografia, Guadalajara, Spain

1986   *Photography as Performance,* The Photographers' Gallery, London

La Magie de l'image, Musée d'art contemporain de Montréal

1987   *Arrangements for the Camera, a view of contemporary Photography,* Baltimore Museum of Art, Maryland.

1988   *Art or Nature, 20th century French Photography,* Barbican Art Gallery, London

1989   *L'invention d'un art, 150éme anniversaire de la photographie* Musée Beaubourg, Paris

20 ans de photographie créative en France, Ludwig Museum, Koln

Prospect fotografie, Frankfurter Kunstverein, Frankfurt

Das konstruierte Bild, Kunstverein München, Munich

1990   *Fotografia actual em França* Fundacao Gulbenkian, Lisbonne

The International garden and greenery exhibition, Photo Museum, Osaka

1991   *Photographie Française en Liberté,* International Center for Photography, New York

1992   *Photographie Française: La décennie créative 1980-1990,* Tokyo Metropolitan Museum of Photography

1993   *Images fabriquées* Musée Sarret de Grozon, Arbois

Sie nennen es Liebe, Künstlerhaus Bethanien, Berlin

De Brancusi à Boltanski, Castelo di Rivoli, Turin

1994   *Sans domicile fixe* Théâtre de l'Agora, Evry

Pour les chapelles de Vence, Chateua de Villeneuve, Fondation Emile Hugues, France

Collections:

Fond national d'art contemporain/Ministère de la culture, Paris; Albert Museum, London; The Contemporary Arts Society, London; San Francisco Museum of Modern Art; Musée d'art moderne de la ville de Paris; Bibliothèque nationale, Paris; Musée de Toulon; Musée de Nice; Musée Nicéphore Niepce, Chalon sur Saône, Musée de la photografie, Mexico; The Chase Manhattan Art Program, New York; Museum of Art, Oklahoma University, Norman; Fine Art Advisory Service, Denver; Nouveau Musée, Lyon; CAPC, Bordeaux; Tsukuba Museum of Photography, Japan; International Museum of Photography at George Eastman House, Rochester; Musée de Guadalajara, Spain; Musée Georges Pompidou, Paris; Musée d'art moderne de Montréal; Van Rekum Museum, Apeldoorn, Holland; Fondation Lucien Henry, Forcalquier, France; Museum of Fine Arts and Museum of Photography, Houston; Musée Guggenheim, New York; Walker Art Center, Minneapolis; Musée de Strasbourg; Musée d'Auriac; Musée de Dunkerque; Maison Européenne de la photographie, Paris; Musées de Marseille; Centre d'art contemporain, Mito, Japan; Tampa Museum of Art; Fine Art Museum, Osaka; Australian National Gallery, Canberra, Australia; Fondation Vincent Van Gogh, Arles; Musée d'art moderne de Lisbonne; Readers Digest Corporate Collection, New York; Fondation Select, Lausanne; Artothèques. France; Evry-Dunkerque-Anger-Toulouse-Lyon-Grenoble; Fonds régionaux d'art contemporain, France; Limousin-Pays de Loire-Champagne Ardenne-Rhône/Alpes-Lorraine-Alsace-Aquitaine-Poitou charentes-Franche Comté.

Publications:

By FAUCON: Books—*Les Grandes Vacances,* Paris 1980, as *Summer Camp,* New York 1981; *La part du calcul dans la grâce,* William Blake and Co, Bordeaux 1985; *Les papiers qui volent,* Hazan, Paris 1986, as *Parco,* Tokyo; *Les chambres d'amour* as *Love Chambers,* William Blake and Co, Bordeaux 1987; *Chambres d'amour, Chambres d'or,* William Blake and Co, Bordeaux 1989; *Tables d'amis* William Blake and Co, Bordeaux 1991; *Les Idoles et les Sacrifices,* Parco, Tokyo 1991; *Dernier Portrait,* Nanasaï, Kyoto, 1991; *Les Ecritures,* William Blake and Co. Bordeaux and Yvon Lambert, Paris, 1993.

On FAUCON: Books—*Invented Images,* exhibition catalogue, by Phyllis Pons, Santa Barbara, California 1980; *Quinze Critiques/Quinze Photographes,*

Paris 1981; *Lichtbildnisse: Das Porträt in der Fotografie,* edited by Klaus Honnef, Cologne 1982; *Images imaginées,* exhibition catalogue, with text by John Batho, Champagne-Ardenne, France 1984; *La Part du Calcul dans la Grace* by Jean-Michel Michelena, Bordeaux, France 1988; *Les Grands Photographs* by Pierre Borhan, Paris 1988. **Articles**—"Bernard Faucon" by Roland Barthes in *Zoom* (Paris), November 1978; "Les Plaisirs d'Enfance" by Hervé Guibert in *Le Monde* (Paris), 5 April 1979; "L'Enfance Rêvée" by Michel Nuridsany in *Le Figaro* (Paris), 10 April 1979; "Bernard Faucon" by André Laude in *Les Nouvelles Litteraires* (Paris), 26 April 1979; "Entretein avec Bernard Faucon" by Hervé Guibert in *Le Monde* (Paris), 14 January 1981; "Bernard Faucon" by Christian Caujolle in *Photo* (Paris), February 1983; "Faucon l'inspire" by Hervé Guibert in *Le Monde* (Paris), 13 November 1984; "Bernard Faucon" by Christian Caujolle in *Beaux-Arts* (Paris), no. 18, 1984; Regis Durand in *Art Press,* May 1988; Michel Guerrin in *Le Monde* (Paris), 29 March 1991, 19 March 1993.

*

It is the setting that controls the entire frame. I do not cut the landscape but try to incorporate as vast an area as possible—to create a world without limits. Sometimes it takes me two whole days to decide on how to do it. The setting must act as a background; it must be precisely delineated; but, nevertheless, it must retain a certain fragility in rather the same way as does the square shape of the film I use, which emphasizes the sky and so gives rise to unexpected resonances.

Next, it is time to people the landscape—a laborious task. I move things from one place to another; I excavate, pull things around, put them into the ground, join them together—great feats of ingenuity! and a constant struggle against the wind and weather, not to mention the perversity of inanimate objects.

Finally, I add the lighting. I recreate the entire illumination, even out of doors. I take no notice of photography in achieving the right effect. I draw my own lines onto the countryside, and when they do not suffice I deploy great panels of aluminium, or mirrors, or white sheets. I will even use gunpowder, controlled quantitites of herbicide, yellow ochre—even sugar!

When the whole thing has worked out, the scene comes alive. Not with "theatrical" life, but with the life of an image whose apotheosis is in the moment of its happening, in the "click."

Then, immediately afterwards, I pull it all apart; tidy up; remove all traces. I allow myself no way of return.

—Bernard Faucon

*   *   *

We must never stop at the apparent "subject matter" of a photograph. Only the treatment counts; the affirmation, by means of a style, of a specific point of view, organized around several fundamental elements of photographic expression. For a long time regarded merely as a "photographer of models, childhood and stage productions," Bernard Faucon surprised those who would restrict him to that simple world and produced new works without characters—indoor scenes and scenes of the countryside. In fact, this young French photographer, one of the most passionate of his generation, has worked steadily and scrupulously on particular expressive elements, which he successfully combines, and announced to the world that he is to be recognized as a poet and metaphysician.

Using square formats, organizing a world in which he never settles for the mere reconstruction of reality, he has gradually produced compositions of rare precision and played unexpected games with "ordinary pictures" (advertisements, religious images and so on). He is one of those who has chosen to work in color, but integrates it into his own view of things and wisely never makes the play of colors his primary aim. Because he tries to produce only those pictures which could not be done in black and white and because he is in control of the whole color process, he belongs to that new generation of photographers who are perfectly aware of the possibilities and limitations of the medium—the photographers who have finally come of age.

—Christian Caujolle

FEININGER, Andreas (Bernhard Lyonel).

Nationality: American. **Born:** Paris, 27 December 1906. **Education:** Attended public schools in Germany; studied cabinet-making, under Walter Gropius, at the Bauhaus, Weimar, 1922-25, and architecture at the Bauschule, Weimar, 1925-26, and at the Staatliche Bauschule, Zerbst, Germany, 1926-28; self-taught in photography. **Family:** Married Gertrud Wysse Hägg in 1933; son: Toma. **Career:** Practising architect, Dessau and Hamburg, 1928-31; Assistant Architect, Office of Le Corbusier, Paris, 1932-33; architectural and industrial photographer, Stockholm, 1933-39; freelance photojournalist, with Black Star Photo Agency, New York, 1940-41; War Correspondent/Photographer, United States Office of War Information, 1941-42; Staff Photographer, *Life* magazine, New York, 1943-62. Freelance photographer, New York and Connecticut, since 1962. Instructor in Creative Photocommunications, New York University, 1972. **Recipient:** Bronze Medal, Fotografiska Föreningen, Stockholm, 1938, 1939; Gold Medal, Art Directors Club of Metropolitan Washington, 1965; Robert Leavitt Award, American Society of Magazine Photographers, 1966. **Agent:** Daniel Wolf Inc., 30 West 57th Street, New York, New York 10019. **Addresses:** (studio) 5 East 22nd Street, New York, New York 10010; (home) 18 Elizabeth Lane, New Milford, Connecticut 06776, U.S.A.

Individual Exhibitions:

1957	*The Anatomy of Nature,* American Museum of Natural History, New York (travelled to the Smithsonian Institution, Washington, D.C.)
	Pratt Institute, Brooklyn, New York
1961	Carl Siembab Gallery, Boston
	Heinz Held Gallery, Cologne
1963	*The World through My Eyes,* Smithsonian Institution, Washington, D.C. (retrospective)
	Landesbildstelle, Hamburg
1965	Cambridge Art Association, Massachusetts
	New York in Farbe, Deutsche Gesellschaft für Photographie, Cologne
1967	Trinity College, Hartford, Connecticut
	New Haven Festival of Arts, Connecticut
1968	Heckscher Museum, Huntington, Long Island, New York
1970	Oakland Museum, California
1972	Neikrug Galleries, New York
	Shells, American Museum of Natural History, New York
1976	International Center of Photography, New York (retrospective)
1978	*New York in the 40s,* New York Historical Society
1980	Southwest Texas State University, San Marcos
1981	Center for Creative Photography, University of Arizona, Tucson
1982	Daniel Wolf Gallery, New York
1985	Daniel Wolf Gallery, New York

Selected Group Exhibitions:

1929	*Film und Foto/Fifo,* Deutscher Werkbund, Stuttgart (toured Germany)
1948	*50 Photographs by 50 Photographers,* Museum of Modern Art, New York
1955	*The Family of Man,* Museum of Modern Art, New York (and world tour)
1958	*70 Photographers Look at New York,* Museum of Modern Art, New York
1959	*Photography at Mid-Century,* International Museum of Photography, George Eastman House, Rochester, New York
1962	*Ideas in Images,* American Federation of Arts, New York (toured the United States)
1967	*Once Visible,* Museum of Modern Art, New York
1971	*Photo-Eye of the 20s,* International Museum of Photography, George Eastman House, Rochester, New York (travelled to the Museum of Modern Art, New York)
1980	*Avant-Garde Photography in Germany 1918-1939,* San Francisco Museum of Modern Art
1983	*Bauhausfotografie,* Institut fur Auslandsbeziehung, Stuttgart (and world tour)

Collections:

Center for Creative Photography, University of Arizona, Tucson (archives); Metropolitan Museum of Art, New York; Museum of Modern Art, New York; International Center of Photography, New York; International Museum of Photography, George Eastman House, Rochester, New York; Carpenter Center for the Visual Arts, Harvard University, Cambridge, Massachusetts; Smithsonian Institution, Washington, D.C., New Orleans Museum of Art; Victoria and Albert Museum, London; Bibliothèque Nationale, Paris.

Publications:

By FEININGER: Books—*Stockholm,* Stockholm 1936; *New Paths in Photography,* Boston 1939; *New York,* with text by John Erskine and Jacqueline Judge, New York and Chicago 1945; *The Face of New York,* with text by Susan Lyman, New York 1954; *Changing America,* with text by Patrica Dyett, New York 1955; *The Anatomy of Nature,* New York 1956, Munich 1957, Barcelona 1962; *Man and Stone,* Dusseldorf 1960, New York 1961, Amsterdam 1962; *Maids, Madonnas and Witches,* with text by Henry Miller and J. Bon, Cologne 1960, New York and London 1961; *The World through My Eyes,* New York, Dusseldorf, Milan and Amsterdam 1963; *New York,* with text by Kate Simon, New York and Dusseldorf 1964; *Lyonel Feininger: City at the Edge of the World,* New York and Munich 1965; *Forms of Nature and Life,* New York, London and Dusseldorf 1966; *Trees,* New York, London and Dusseldorf 1968; *Shells,* with text by William K. Emerson, New York, London, Dusseldorf and Milan 1972; *Roots of Art,* New York, London, Dusseldorf and Milan 1975; *The Mountains of the Mind,* New York and Dusseldorf 1977, as *Nature Close Up,* 1981; *New York in the Forties,* with text by John von Hartz, New York 1978; *Feininger's Hamburg,* Dusseldorf 1980; *Feininger's Chicago, 1941,* New York 1980; *Industrial America,* New York 1982; *Leaves,* New York 1984; photographic textbooks—*Menschen vor der Kamera,* Halle, Germany 1934; *Selbst Entwickeln und Kopieren,* Harzburg, Germany 1935; *Vergrössern, Leicht Gemacht,* Harzburg, Germany 1935; *Entwicken Kopieren Vergrössern,* Harzburg, Germany 1936; *Aufnahmetechnik,* Harzburg, Germany 1936; *Fotografische Gestaltung,* Harzburg, Germany 1937; *Motive in Gegenlicht,* Harzburg, Germany 1939; *Feininger on Photography,* Chicago and New York 1949, 2nd edition, New York 1953; *Advanced Photography,* New York 1952; *Successful Photography,* New York 1954, Stockholm 1956, Helsinki 1957, Dusseldorf 1959, Milan 1961, 2nd edition, New York 1975; *Successful Color Photography,* New York 1954, Stockholm 1957, Helsinki 1958, Dusseldorf 1959, Milan 1962, 4th edition, New York 1966; *The Creative Photographer,* New York 1955, Dusseldorf and Stockholm 1958, Bucarest 1967, 2nd edition, New York 1975; *Total Picture Control,* New York and Dusseldorf 1961, London and Copenhagen 1962, Prague 1968, Barcelona 1969, Amsterdam 1973, 2nd edition, New York 1970; *The Complete Photographer,* New York, Dusseldorf and Amsterdam 1965, London and Milan 1966, Tokyo 1969, Prague 1971, Barcelona 1972; *The Color Photo Book,* New York, Dusseldorf, London and Amsterdam 1969; *Basic Color Photography,* New York, Dusseldorf and London 1972, Milan and Helsinki 1974; *Photographic Seeing,* New York 1973; *Principles of Composition in Photography,* New York and London 1973, Dusseldorf 1974; *Darkroom Techniques,* 2 volumes, New York 1974; *The Perfect Photograph,* New York 1974; *Light and Lighting in Photography,* New York 1976, Dusseldorf 1980; *Experimental Work,* New York 1978; *Total Photography,* New York 1982.

On FEININGER: Books—*Foto-Auge/Oeil et photo/Photo-Eye: 76 Fotos der Zeit,* edited by Franz Roh and Jan Tschichold, Stuttgart 1929, London 1974; *How Life Gets the Story: Behind the Scenes in Photo-Journalism,* edited by Stanley Rayfield, New York 1955; *Grosse Photographen unseres Jahrhunderts* by Fritz Gruber, Dusseldorf 1964; *The Picture History of Photography* by Peter Pollack, second edition, New York 1969; *Andreas Feininger* by Ralph Hattersley, New York 1973; *Farbe in Photo,* edited by Fritz Binder, Gert Koshofer and others, Cologne 1981; *Bauhaus Fotografie,* edited by Roswitha Fricke, Dusseldorf 1982. **Articles**—in *Modern Photogra-*

phy (New York), December 1949; *Popular Photography* (New York), February 1964; *Infinity* (New York), November 1968; and *Modern Photography* (New York), August 1973.

*

Photography, as I see it, is a picture-language, a form of communication. This, of course, implies that a photograph, at least as far as I am concerned, must have something to communicate that is of interest to the viewer. A photograph that fails in this respect, is, in my opinion, worthless.

I believe that the key to good photography is interest on the part of the photographer, *not* in photography but in his subject. Unless a potential subject "speaks to me," I wouldn't consider photographing it. Only if I feel "turned on" by a subject can I hope to make pictures capable of evoking a response in other people.

As in speech or in writing, in photography, too, a statement can be presented well or badly. A well-presented statement is, of course, more effective and enjoyable than a badly-presented one. In photography, this makes it important to pay attention to the technical execution of the picture—the form of presentation. But while phototechnique is important, it should never be more than a means to an end. Excessive preoccupation with the technical aspects of photography shifts the emphasis from the end to the means. Basically, in my opinion, an interesting visual statement badly presented is still preferable to the technically most accomplished picture that has nothing to say. The first, at least, is meaningful, whereas the second is a total waste of the viewer's time.

To me, good presentation means three things: clarity, simplicity, organization. I found this most easy to accomplish by keeping my means and equipment simple.

I always strive to produce images which show the viewer *more* than he would (and often could) have seen had he been confronted with my subject in reality. A photograph which shows only what anybody can see in reality is visually less valuable and informative than one that shows the viewer something which he wouldn't or couldn't have seen, something he didn't know or something he hadn't thought of before. The first is merely a record, while the second can enrich and stimulate the mind.

Despite a superficial similarity in regard to construction, important functional differences exist between the human eye and the camera. As a result, eye and camera "see" the same subject differently. Unless a photographer takes these differences into account, is able to "see in terms of photography," and acts accordingly, his pictures are bound to be inferior to the experience that triggered them.

On the other hand, the camera can also show us *more* than we were able to see at the moment the picture was taken. Examples are certain types of tele- and wide-angle photographs, extreme close-ups, pictures in cylindrical and spherical perspectives, high-speed photographs, stroboscopic motion studies, time exposures involving blur as a means of symbolizing subject motion, selectively focussed images, double exposures and superimpositions, pictures taken on infra-red film, X-ray photographs, and so on. However, to make the most of such opportunities, it is essential that the photographer is able to think and see in terms of photography.

—Andreas Feininger

*   *   *

Andreas Feininger is one of the great pioneers who made photography into what it is today. He and his peers found a medium that was struggling to express itself and turned it into a great visual language capable of communicating literally millions of things. Photography has grown so influential that life in a modern culture would hardly make sense without it. Everywhere you turn are photographs, and they all have something to say. But it was men like Feininger who first made them speak clearly.

Photography has never been easy to understand, for it works on the non-verbal level. Many have tried to explain it and have failed. Equipped with a piercing intellect, Feininger has provided successful explanations for many years and shows no sign of stopping. He is justly famous for his books on photography, though he has also written on other subjects. Thirty-two of his books have been published in America, and he has been translated into thirteen

foreign languages. He is a great favorite of librarians, for he writes clearly and logically about a very abstruse subject. His explanations are the best available.

Trained as an architect, Feininger is still very interested in structures and constructions, photographing them with both power and sensitivity. He finds them in man-made things and in nature and is primarily a photographer of objects. He is fascinated by the myriad forms of organization that he finds and in the relationship between form and function. You can almost always tell how the objects in his photographs will function, for that is his intent. If he photographs a bone, for example, you can see how its structure makes it function well as a support.

Feininger looks at the camera as an instrument of discovery related to the telescope and the microscope. His pictures help viewers to discover things that they wouldn't ordinarily see. His typical photograph is a veritable feast of things waiting to be seen. He firmly believes that the photographer's vision is his most important asset and that he should use it to show the wonders of the world to those less well endowed. He is especially good at making people see what he wants them to see. In this sense his pictures have great power, though he is also a master of subtleties.

Feininger's hero is the person who can really see. Such a person must have a hyper-acute awareness of the surrounding world, must have eyes as sensitive as a child's, must be fully conscious of the things he is looking at. The person who really sees is always fascinated with the idea, finding his vision an endless source of amazement. Thus it is with Feininger himself—he is constantly discovering new things to marvel at. Fortunately he is able to communicate this feeling to others with his photographs.

A part of good seeing is to know what light can do, because vision depends on it entirely. Thus photographers concentrate their attention both on ambient lightings and on lightings fully under their control, striving to make themselves fully aware of what they are looking at. In both areas Feininger is the expert's expert. The ambient lightings that he chooses to use usually emphasize power, while his controlled lightings put the accent on great subtlety. Though his controlled lightings are masterful they are never tricky. Very often they are as simple as can be, for simplicity may fill the bill.

Through his definitive books Feininger is probably the world's foremost teacher of photography. Many thousands of people have been led to a sound understanding of this difficult medium, led firmly and with authority by this master teacher. His work as a writer-teacher may lead some to overlook his other accomplishments, however. For example, he was one of the select few who developed magazine photojournalism into its present form. For twenty years he was a staff photographer on *Life* magazine, then as now the acknowledged leader in photojournalism. While there he participated in hundreds of decisions that helped shape the art. Though inclined to be shy, he always stood up for his own opinions, which were always well-reasoned and logical. So he left a definite mark on the magazine. He did 346 assignments for *Life*—in magazine photojournalism this is a great many. He left *Life* in 1962 to devote himself to his own work, which has kept him very busy ever since.

Feininger's favorite tools are the telephoto lens and the close-up camera. He has personally built four telephoto cameras and three close-up cameras, highly specialized instruments of a kind not available commercially. The telephoto lens gives him the perspectives that he likes and helps him maintain certain size relationships in his subjects. The close-up camera enables him to photograph very small objects—seashells, rocks, insects, structures created by insects, and so on. He is especially interested in small things, often making them appear very large in his pictures.

Feininger works almost exclusively in black-and-white, for it gives him much greater control over the ultimate appearance of his pictures than color. It is also much simpler and helps keep down the cost of book production. On the other hand, he did a lot of color work for *Life* and earned a considerable reputation as a color photographer.

Feininger's entire photographic archive will go to the Center for Creative Photography in Tucson, Arizona, where it will be available to scholars and for study. The transfer has largely taken place already. The archive will include thousands of negatives and prints, scrapbooks, reviews of exhibitions and books, personal papers and documents, and a complete set of Feininger's books. Since he is a very careful and methodical person, the archive is in splendid shape.

In sum, Andreas Feininger is a great historical figure in photography whom everyone should know about.

—Ralph Hattersley

FÉNER, Tamás.

Nationality: Hungarian. **Born:** Budapest, 17 November 1938. **Education:** Attended secondary school in Budapest, 1953-57; studied at the school of Journalism, Budapest, 1960-61. **Family:** Married Judit Rónaszéki in 1967 (divorced in 1973); lives with the writer Zsuzsa Tóth since 1973; children: Viktor and Sára. **Career:** Photographer, then art editor, *Film, Szinház, Muzsika* weekly paper, Budapest, 1957-86; editor-in-chief, *Fotómüveszet* quarterly bulletin, Budapest, since 1968; assistant editor-in-chief, *Képes 7* weekly paper, Budapest, since 1986. Freelance since 1994. Secretary-General, Hungarian Artist Photographers' Union, Budapest, 1978-86. Professor, School of Journalism, Budapest, 1980-83; Teaches the profession of press photography on the faculty of Media and Visual Anthropolgy at Eötvös Lóránd University. **Recipient:** World Press Photo Awards, Amsterdam, 1963, 1965; Socialist Civilization Award, Budapest, 1965; Béla Balász Prize, Budapest, 1973; Artist Emeritus Award, Budapest, 1984; Grand Prize Beth Hatsefutsoth, Tel Aviv, 1993. **Address:** Roskovics utca 6, 1122 Budapest XII, Hungary.

Individual Exhibitions:

1969	*Portraits of Artists,* Fészek Artists' Club, Budapest
1971	*Portraits and Situations,* Mücsarnok Art Gallery, Budapest
1972	Hungarian Cultural Institute, Warsaw
1974	*Cserhalmi Miners Brigade/Gipsy Colony,* Picture-Gallery, Miskolc, Hungary
1976	*Four Sociographic Series,* Hungarian Workers Movement Museum, Budapest
1978	*1400° C,* Hungarian Workers Movement Museum, Budapest
1979	*1400° C,* Hungarian Cultural Institute, East Berlin
1981	*Stunt-Flying,* Mücsarnok Art Gallery, Budapest
1983	*And You Shall Tell Your Son,* Ethnographical Museum, Budapest
	Stunt-Flying, Havana, Cuba
	1400° C, Belgrade, Yugoslavia
1984	*And You Shall Tell Your Son,* Canon Gallery, Amsterdam
	Four Series, Bibliothèque Forney, Paris
1985	*And You Shall Tell Your Son,* Centro San Fedele, Milan
	And You Shall Tell Your Son, Gorizia, Italy
1986	*Stunt-Flying,* Vilnius, U.S.S.R.
	And You Shall Tell Your Son, Rathaus, Heidenheim, West Germany
	That was the factory. . . . , Hungarian Workers Movement Museum, Budapest
1988	*And You Shall Tell Your Son,* Hungarian Cultural Institute, East Berlin
	And You Shall Tell Your Son, Jewish Community, West Berlin
	Hortobágy, Photo Gallery, Budapest
	S.P.Q.R., Hungarian National Gallery, Budapest
1990	*Berlin mal anders,* Hungarian Cultural Institute, East Berlin
	And You Shall Tell Your Son, The House of Hungarian Culture, Sofia
1991	*And You Shall Tell Your Son,* Hungarian Embassy, Washington
1992	*pepsifeeling,* Vigadó Gallery, Budapest
1993	*And You Shall Tell Your Son,* Ortodox synagogue, Budapest
1994	*Landscapes and Polsters,* National Museum

Selected Group Exhibitions:

1966	*125 Years of Hungarian Photographic Art,* Hungarian National Gallery, Budapest
1981	*Facts and Pictures: Hungarian Photography 1840-1981,* Art Gallery, Budapest
1986	*Studio Nadar,* Ernst Museum, Budapest

Collections:

Federation of Hungarian Photographers, Budapest; *Film, Szinhá, Muzsika* Archives, Budapest.

Publications:

By FÉNER: Books—*Ballet in Budapest,* with others, Budapest 1972; *Koszeg,* with introduction by Dezso Dercsényi, Budapest 1976 *Theatre in Hungary,* with others, Budapest 1978; *Weekday,* with introduction by Iván Vitányi, Budapest 1979; *And You Shall Tell Your Son . . . ,* with introduction by Sándor Schreiber, Budapest 1984; *Obscure by Lights—A Life's Work Volume* with introduction by Miklós Almasi, Budapest 1993.

On FÉNER: Books—*Dictionnaire des Photographes* by Carole Naggar, Paris 1982; *Photographers' Encyclopedia International* by Michel Auer, Hermance, Switzerland 1985. **Articles**—"Masks Squared" by Iván Rozgonyi in *Fotómüveszet* (Budapest), no. 2, 1969; "The Portrait of Th. Fener" by Mihály Gera in *Fotómüveszet* (Budapest), no. 3, 1973; "On the Photo-Series" in *Fotómüveszet* (Budapest), no. 1, 1977; "About Béla Bartók" by Zsolt Molnár in *Napjaink* (Budapest), March 1981; "Interview with Th. Fener" by Hugó Salamon in *Uj Forrás* (Tatabanya, Hungary), December 1982; " . . . What a Story!" in *Liberation* (Paris), 9 December 1984.

*

Photography from the beginning until today has been an alternation of realistic and non-realistic tendencies. Better if you believe me—I don't want to interfere in vulgar aesthetics. The composita and the realism of the "explorers," the pictorialism with the rhyming Neue Sachlichkeit, the Group f64 in America, etc., etc. And then the period from pop-art to concept-art was followed dramatically and suddenly by the alternation of the realistic, romantic-eclectic, the postmodern . . .

I can draw a lesson from all this: in the rapid flow of events, it is better to remain true to your *own* style. Now the world and its fashions passes you by, and perhaps this is the time for really absorbing work; then the full glare of publicity comes close. From the point of view of form, my own work was first influenced by the German illustrated press, especially the press of the Weimar Republic, and by the American magazines of the 1940s and 1950s. Under these influences, I have exhibited since the 1970s only series, and—considering the whole exhibition as a scripto-visual system—I have set a high value not only on the individual pictures, but on their placing and measurement as well. Perhaps it's a press-mentality (or a book-mentality), but I am forced to consider the exhibition in terms of the pressure on space in Hungarian magazines and the similar difficulties encountered in publishing books. In my exhibitions, I assign a prominent role to the formation of an evocative milieu, and for this purpose use all kinds of objects referring to the places where the photographs were taken. Sometimes I create exhibitions of colour photos, sometimes only of black-and-white, depending on the subject. Essentially, my works are of sociographic origin, relating to certain specific social problems or phenomena of today. I have made a series on miners, the steelworkers' brigade, and on gipsies. A recent work was devoted to the life of Jews in Budapest; I was particularly interested in preserving a memory of a disappearing lifestyle, the relation between individual and community, its orthodoxy, and the specifies of a closed milieu. Later my interest has moved from the people to the environment, created by the people, because I had felt that the modern society does not need the presence of the artist. So I allowed myself that luxury, to chase out the people from my pictures and just to photograph the world which was created by the people. I prepared a series on a ruined factory on the Hungarian plain, one on the bleak East Berlin, Budapest, and during my grant in Rome I prepared one about it. Recently I deal with giant posters, or with their damaging influence on the land and on the city.

—Tamás Féner

*   *   *

Tamás Féner is a major figure in contemporary Hungarian photography. In addition to working for three decades as a press photographer, he has been remarkably prolific in his own independent work. A wide range of topics,

Hortobagy—Gray Cattle, Hungary. Photograph by Tamás Féner.

including pictures of ballet and drama productions to portraits of artists has resulted in a number of fascinating portfolios.

Within this varied range of subject, Féner has essentially one major theme: the human being in specific social and historical situations—an exploration he has pursued in a series of albums and exhibitions. Going beyond the mere documentary study, he has attempted to communicate an essential truth beneath the external phenomena of his subjects.

In Hungary during the 1950s, human labour was customarily depicted with a kind of false optimism and idealised gloss—the theme becoming so devalued that many photographers abandoned it altogether. By the mid-1960s, however, the drive for a more authentic realism in literature, film and the fine arts began to arise, and Féner was among the first photographers to react to this new mood. A prime motive of this movement was to revive the once internationally-famed Hungarian social documentary tradition of the 1930s and 1940s with its direct and honest imagery and commitment to essential features of the theme.

Starting from a contemporary but well-researched viewpoint, Féner began by examining transformations in social and employment circumstances. His results were starkly objective, without a trace of heroic overtones. The pictures not only confronted the viewer, but exposed social phenomena in a way that posed difficult questions about society's self-image. What was revealed in this series of photos was no embellished hymn to the beauty of labour; we see a reality in which the harshness and immense effort of labour, the low status accorded the workforce, the out-of-date factory conditions, dismal bunkhouses, and meagre—sometimes non-existent—recreational facilities are plainly

evident. Nor is Féner's preoccupation a view of those on the fringes of society, but one that deals with the mainstream of working life.

Whilst uncovering such unpalatable visions, however, Féner does not consider them as absolutes, for he frequently shows a wider picture in which the negative is countered by the sheer human strength of the community and its satisfaction with the fulfilment of a good day's work. The message, perhaps idealist, is that we need to think and act for a better life.

Feńer's recent project on traditional Hungarian Jewish life has both sociological and lyric qualities. Through the course of individual lives and deaths, festivals and daily routines, and the orthodoxy of an enclosed world, he uncovers the whole life of a community. By exhibiting these photographs as a newspaper photo-essay with narrative elements lined up horizontally and associated images on a vertical axis, Féner makes evident every detail of his many-sided study, the entire series forming a rational and cohesive whole.

—Klára Töry

FICHTER, Robert W(hitten).

Nationality: American. **Born:** Fort Meyers, Florida, 30 December 1939. **Education:** Attended P.K. Yonge High School, Gainesville, Florida, 1954-

58; studied printmaking and painting, University of Florida, Gainesville, under Jerry N. Uelsmann, 1959-63, B.F.A. 1963; photography and printmaking, under Henry Holmes Smith, Indiana University, Bloomington, 1963-66, M.F.A. 1966. **Career:** Independent photographer, since 1966. Assistant Curator of Exhibitions, George Eastman House, Rochester, New York, 1966-68. Visiting Instructor in Photography, University of Florida, Gainesville, 1967; Instructor, Penland Craft School, North Carolina, Summers, 1968, 1970, 1971; Assistant Professor, 1968-70, Lecturer, 1971, Visiting Associate Professor, 1976, University of California at Los Angeles; Visiting Artist, Art Institute of Chicago, 1977. Associate Professor, 1972-82, and Professor since 1982, Florida State University, Tallahassee. **Recipient:** National Endowment for the Arts Grant, 1980, 1984; Florida Fine Arts Fellowship, 1981. **Agent:** Robert Freidus Gallery Inc., 158 Lafayette Street, New York, New York 10013. **Addresses:** 612 West 8th Avenue, Tallahasee, Florida 32303; and c/o Department of Art, Florida State University, Tallahassee, Florida 32306, U.S.A.

Individual Exhibitions:

1968   *Robert Fichter's Trips,* International Museum of Photography, George Eastman House, Rochester, New York
1970   *Recent Photo-Drawings,* University of California at Davis
1972   Infinite Gallery, Seattle
        Center of the Eye, Aspen, Colorado
        Visual Studies Workshop, Rochester, New York (toured the United States)
1974   Light Gallery, New York
        School of the Art Institute of Chicago
1975   University of New Mexico, Albuquerque
1976   Light Gallery, New York
1978   Cameraworks Gallery, San Francisco
1980   Robert Freidus Gallery, New York
        Northlight Gallery, Tempe, Arizona
        Gulf Coast Gallery, Tampa, Florida
1981   Robert Freidus Gallery, New York
        Los Angeles Center for Photographic Studies
        Drawings, University of Florida, Gainesville
1982   *New Paintings and Cibachromes,* Robert Freidus Gallery, New York
        Photography and Other Questions, International Museum of Photography at George Eastman House, Rochester, New York (toured the United States)
1983   Center for Creative Photography, University of Arizona, Tucson
        Mattingly Baker Gallery, Dallas, Texas
        James Madison University, Madison, Virginia
        Paintings and Cibachromes, Freidus/Ordover, New York
        Constructions and Photographs, Fay Gold Gallery, Atlanta, Georgia
1984   University of Central Florida, Orlando
        After Eden, University of South Florida, Tampa (travelled to Pensacola Junior College, Florida)
1986   CEPA Gallery, Buffalo, New York

Selected Group Exhibitions:

1967   *4 Photographers,* Riverside Gallery, Rochester, New York
1968   *Contemporary Photographers,* University of California at Los Angeles
1969   *Serial/Modular Imagery,* Purdue University, Lafayette, Indiana (toured the United States)
1970   *The Photograph as Object 1843-1969,* National Gallery of Canada, Ottawa (toured Canada)
1972   *60s Continuum,* International Museum of Photography, George Eastman House, Rochester, New York
1973   *Photography into Art,* Scottish Arts Council Gallery, Edinburgh
1977   *Painting in the Age of Photography,* Kunsthaus, Zurich
1980   *Invented Images,* University of California at Santa Barbara
1984   *Photography in California 1945-80,* San Francisco Museum of Modern Art (travelled to the Akron Art Museum, Ohio;

Corcoran Gallery, Washington, D.C.; Los Angeles Municipal Art Gallery; Cornell University, Ithaca, New York; High Museum of Art, Atlanta, Georgia; Museum Folkwang, Essen; Centre Georges Pompidou, Paris, Museum of Photographic Arts, San Diego, California
1987   *Photography and Art 1946-86,* Los Angeles County Museum of Art

Collections:

International Museum of Photography, George Eastman House, Rochester, New York; Visual Studies Workshop, Rochester, New York; Museum of Fine Arts, Boston; Princeton University, New Jersey; Museum of Fine Arts, St. Petersburg, Florida; Minneapolis Institute of Art, Minnesota; Los Angeles County Museum of Art; Pasadena Art Museum, California; National Gallery of Canada, Ottawa; Australian National Gallery, Canberra, A.C.T.

Publications:

By FICHTER: Books—*Robert Fichter: Photography and Other Questions,* edited by Robert A. Sobieszek, Albuquerque, New Mexico 1982; *After Eden,* Tampa, Florida 1984.

On FICHTER: Books—*California Photographers 1970,* exhibition catalogue, by Fred R. Parker, Davis, California 1970; *Into the 70s: Photographic Images by 16 Artists/Photographers,* exhibition catalogue, by Tom Muir Wilson, Orrel E. Thompson and Robert M. Doty, Akron, Ohio 1970; *Photography into Art,* exhibition catalogue, by Pat Gilmour, Edinburgh 1973; *Light and Lens: Methods of Photography,* exhibition catalogue, by Donald L. Werner and Dennis Longwell, New York 1973; *The Great West: Real/Ideal,* edited by Sandy Hume and others, Boulder, Colorado 1977; *The Photograph Collector's Guide* by Lee D. Witkin and Barbara London, Boston and London 1979; *International Photography 1920-1980,* edited by Ian North, Canberra 1982; *Photography in California 1945-1980* by Louise Katzman, San Francisco and New York, 1984; *Masterpieces of Photography from George Eastman House,* edited by Robert A. Sobieszek, New York 1985; *Photography and Art 1946-1986,* exhibition catalogue, by Andy Grundberg and Kathleen M. Gauss, Los Angeles 1987. **Articles**—"Photography: Charles Traub and Robert Fichter" by Hal Fischer in *Artweek* (Oakland, California), 16 September 1978; "Apocalyptic Images" in *Flash Art* (Milan), March 1983; "Robert Fichter: Photography and other questions" in *Choice* (Chicago), February 1984.

*

I am a student of photography—not a photographer.

Photography is an ad hoc device for me; I use it to record, to amplify, to distort, to simplify, to complicate the images that I receive from this poor, glad, sad, radiant universe.

My work lies at the fringe of what most people would call photography. I work from "straight" to "funny" and back. I am currently trying to make my work much more direct, less diagrammatic, and in general richer and more intense. I use my hand as often as my lens.

The theory of photography as a creative means of self-expression is one I derived from studying with Jerry Uelsmann and Henry Holmes Smith—both marvellous poet-photographers and photo-intellects.

I hope someday to make a "photo-icon" that will float through time and that will be used to transfigure man's existence, should biology survive the nuclear age.

—Robert W. Fichter

*   *   *

One notable aspect of contemporary photography is the softening, perhaps actual breakdown, of its erstwhile clearly defined borders. A great many photographers, no longer satisfied with their lack of hands-on participation in the final product, have incorporated painting, drawing, and printmaking techniques into their photographic imagery. Yet few photographers have managed to dismantle and shuffle off the confines of the medium as easily as

Robert Fichter. The body of his work is more diverse in both approach and technique than an essay of this length could acknowledge with justice; his recent 20 X 24 color Polaroids, however, do represent an adequate and distinctive summary of his work to date and an extraordinary example of what can be achieved within that format.

In the now substantial body of work from the 20 X 24 camera sponsored by the Polaroid Corporation, a specific mode emerges from and characterizes the various photographers' results. The camera, by its enormous size and non-mobility, seems to demand the kind of careful, often laborious, compilations of things, patterns, textures and colors that most artists bring to it. Were it not for the work of Fichter, we might also think the procedure demanded a certain mordant seriousness as well. Fichter seems enough at ease with the technique to be able to relinquish the diamond-hard focus, the meticulous rendering of photographic detail and the sense of a space densely stuffed. He uses a loose, raw drawing style which unleashes a primitive, intense energy that belies the hours required to set up these compositions. Fichter also uses the tear-off, negative material, the residue of other prints, in some images, which lends them a ghostly, mysterious backdrop, a kind of mirage of past images. Many of his scenes are primarily painted or drawn; Fichter thus imbues the well-chosen photographic elements with heightened significance.

Eugenia Parry Janis noted in her introduction to *One of a Kind* (Boston, 1980), that this camera encourages photographers into a peculiar kind of hermeticism. They fill the frame with quantities of quirky objects primarily to revel in their shape, color and texture, in their objectness. It is a lavish indulgence in materialism. Fichter, by contrast with most, constructs pictures to be deciphered, personal observations on contemporary affairs. Against the background of a gaudy, gold-fringed Lackland Air Force Base souvenir scarf are toy Indians, cowboys, soldiers and space monsters and a picture of forest animals, perhaps reminiscent of earlier, more bucolic times. Fichter is comfortable and experienced in working with the additive mode; unlike many photographers, he is used to beginning with a blank space or page.

In seeing a number of Fichter's Polaroids, one recognizes recurrent symbols and a personal iconology. A toy dinosaur skeleton frequents the scenes as a reminder, one suspects, of great beasts, once powerful and now extinct. The military references are profuse with emphasis on the underlying violence of conquering the frontier, whether that frontier is the American West or outer space. Animals of all kinds abound: a stuffed bird, drawn dogs, pinned butterflies, a plastic crab, and the imaginary "born again art ass." This world is whimsical and sometimes cartoonlike, but the apparent playfulness underscores the ultimate irony of his messages.

In an idiosyncratic language, Fichter comments upon a world that exists beyond the narrow confines of art photography. His 20 X 24 color Polaroids have all of the bejewelled brilliance that characterizes the format without the epicurean weightlessness. In disregarding the limits of the medium and format alike, and with a healthy dose of irreverence, Fichter has infused his constructed toy world with topical and personal significance. A compelling mixture of drollery and irony gives this work its tautness and its unexpected bite.

—Dana Asbury

FIEGER, Erwin.

Nationality: German. **Born:** Toplei, Czechoslovakia, 10 December 1928; emigrated to West Germany, and subsequently naturalized. **Education:** Studied commercial art and graphics, under Eugen Funk, Staatliche Akademie der Bildenden Kunste, Stuttgart, 1951-55; self-taught in photography. **Career:** Freelance photographer, Germany and Italy, since 1956; has concentrated on color photography since 1962. Member, Gesellschaft Deutscher Lichtbildner (GDL), 1960-62. **Recipient:** Nadar Prize, France, 1969; Gold Medal, Art Directors Club of Germany, 1972; Cultural Prize, Deutsche Gesellschaft für Photographie (DGPh), 1974; Honorary Award of the German Foundation for the Promotion of Culture, 1989; Kodak Photo-Book Award for *Ganges*, 1990; Award of Merit, Art Directors' Club, New York. Scheufelin's advertising campaign *The Papermakers*, using photographs from *Ganges*, won the Grand Prix of the International Advertising Association of New York, 1993; Bronze Medal of the Econ Verlag, Düsseldorf, 1993; Kodak EPICA Prize, Paris, 1993; Silver Award from *Business to Business,* Stuttgart, 1993. **Address:** La Lama Casa le Mura, Castelfranco di Sopra, Italy.

Selected Group Exhibitions:

1974   *Photokina '74,* Cologne
1979   *Deutsch Fotografie nach 1945,* Kunstverein, Kassel, West
            Germany (toured West Germany)
1981   *Farbe im Photo,* Josef-Haubrich-Kunsthalle, Cologne
1989   *Light and Shade,* Landesgirokasse, Stuttgart; Bayrische
            Landesbank, Munich

Collections:

Deutsche Gesellschaft für Photographie, Cologne; Gesellschaft Deutscher Lichtbildner, Stuttgart.

Publications:

By FIEGER: Books—*Farbiges London,* Dusseldorf 1962; *Grand Prix,* Stuttgart 1963; *13 Photo Essays,* with an introduction by Helmut Gernsheim, Dusseldorf 1969; *Japan: Sunrise Island,* Dusseldorf 1971; *Olympia: Sapporo,* Munich 1972; *Olympia: Munich,* 1972; *Mexico,* Dusseldorf 1973; *Live—Foto: Eine Epoche in Farbe,* Dusseldorf 1973; *Ski WM St. Moritz,* Munich 1974; *Fussball WM Germany,* Munich 1974; *Winterolympiade Innsbruck,* Munich 1976; *Sommerolympiade Montreal,* Munich 1976; *Was die Menscheit bewegt,* Munich 1977; *Ski WM Garmisch-Lathi,* Munich 1978; *Fussball WM Argentinien,* Munich 1978; *Die Zukunft unserer Kinder,* Munich 1979; *Sommerolympiade Moskau,* Munich 1980; *Sommerolympiade Los Angeles,* Munich 1984; *Ganges,* preface by Helmut Gernsheim, Munich 1990; *Emotions,* Munich 1993; *Yin and Yang,* Munich 1994.

On FIEGER: Books—*A Concise History of Photography* by Helmut Gernsheim, London and New York 1965, 1971, 1986; *Uber das Schopferische in der Photographie* by L. Fritz Gruber, Cologne 1966; *Geschichte der Fotografie im 20. Jahrhundert/Photography in the 20th Century* by Petr Tausk, Cologne 1977, London 1980; *Deutsche Fotografie nach 1945/German Photography after 1945* by Floris Neususs, Wolfgang Kemp and Petra Benteler, Kassel, West Germany 1979; *Fotografie 1919-1979, Made in Germany: Die GDL-Fotografen,* edited by Fritz Kempe, Bernd Lohse and others, Frankfurt 1979; *Farbe im Photo: Die Geschichte der Farbphotographie von 1861 bis 1981* by Fritz Binder, Gert Koshofer, Rolf Sachsse and others, Cologne 1981; *Light and Shade,* exhibition catalogue, Stuttgart 1989. **Articles**—"Erwin Fieger: Photo-Essays" in *German Photography Annual,* Stuttgart 1970; "Magnet Japan" in *German Photographic Annual,* Stuttgart 1972; "Erwin Fieger" in *Zoom* (Paris), September/October 1972.

*

My photographic work has always had one goal—to praise creation. Not only do I take care with still-life subjects, but search for humanity in all corners of the world. For a number of years, I have been working on the theme "Life and Death on the Ganges."

—Erwin Fieger

*   *   *

In our photographic age the concerned photographer is in danger of being drowned by a flood of illustrators. Our senses are being blunted by seeing too much and understanding too little. Aware of this danger, Erwin Fieger discovered a new conception and interpretation. The impact of his telephoto-lens close-ups are breathtaking, marking a personal style that proved to be a landmark influence on reportage photography. Fieger's colour photo-essays on cities and countries raised the power of photographic expression to hitherto unknown heights. From his first book, *Farbiges London* (1962), to his fabulous album on Japan ten years later, and others following it, we are confronted with the work of an outstanding photographer, gifted with the vision of an artist. A great sensitivity for poetical situations and an ability to

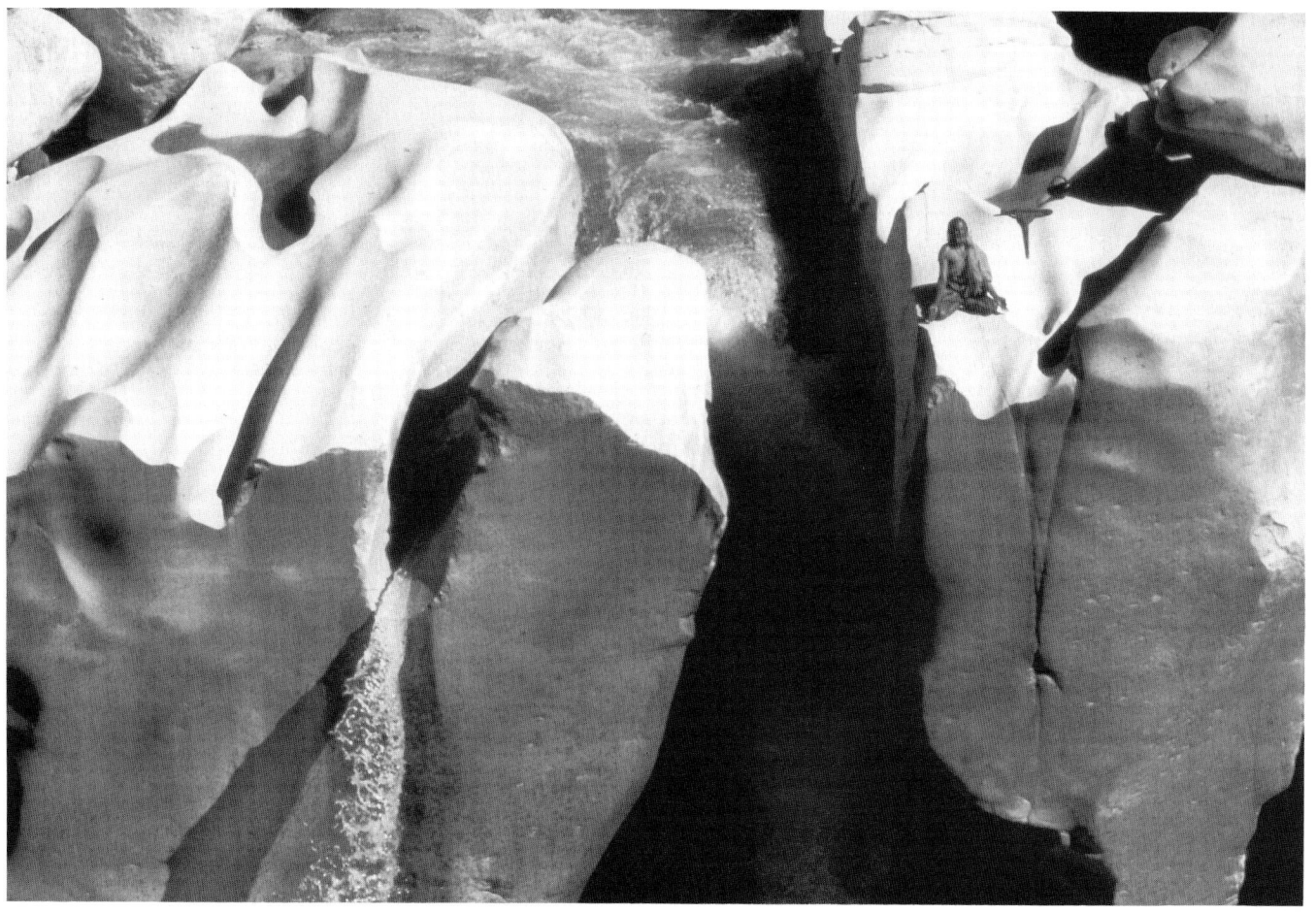

Image from *Life and Death on the Ganges,* 1985. Photograph by Erwin Fieger.

transform a fleeting impression into a permanent design of high aesthetic value led the former graphic designer to the creation of unusual images. He directs our attention to things we have seen, and yet not noticed. The isolation of the subject from its surroundings, the "freezing" of a fleeting impression, the closing-in on a detail—they all contribute to the novel way of interpretation and unexpected grandeur.

The lenses of our eyes are of short focal length and have consequently great depth of focus. This makes it possible for us to view near and far objects in quick alternation. The zoom lens which Fieger chiefly employs has only a small depth of focus. The desired picture plane is sharp, everything in front or behind it appears unsharp, throwing the subject in focus into greater relief. The, to us, unaccustomed tele-vision, the blurring of colour outlines due to comparatively long exposure times, the snatching of a detail out of the immense mosaic of reality, allow a very personal interpretation which fascinates on account of its revelation of entirely new visual effects.

Fieger's photo-essays are optical voyages of discovery into uncharted territories. He is on the whole not concerned with documentation in the established sense, with the representation of facts or events. Our discovery lies in his "shorthand" impressions of what he saw, and the magic of colour. The importance of his essays lies in the originality of his vision and the purely aesthetic pleasure of his interpretation. Landscape motifs are rendered symbolically; their geographical region is only of secondary importance to satisfy our curiosity. His people are types: Indians, Japanese, Africans, Mexicans—not representatives of a social class; they are solely human beings whose faces, gestures, joy or grief express everything without words. Describing his work for someone who does not know it is difficult. Seeing it opens new worlds. Fieger works for a small, discriminating public, appreciative and willing to pay for the highest printing quality achievable. The reproductions in his folio

volumes are as good as original prints, which, surprisingly, Fieger neither makes nor sells from his 35mm diapositives. Respect for his medium and individual expression oblige him to continue on his chosen path rather than dancing to the dictates of picture editors.

—Helmut Gernsheim

FIGUEROA FLORES, Gabriel.

Nationality: Mexican. **Born:** Mexico City, 16 October 1952. **Education:** Attended the German School, Mexico City, 1956-65; Universidad Iberoamericana, Mexico City, 1971-74; attended Ansel Adams Photography Workshop, Yosemite Park, California, 1973; studied mass media communications at the Polytechnic of Central London, 1974-77, B.A. Photog. 1977. **Military Service:** Served in the Mexican Army, 1967-68. **Career:** Freelance photographer, Mexico City, since 1978. **Agent:** Galeria Juan Martin, Calle de Amberes 17, Mexico 6, D.F. **Address:** Alberto Zamora 39, Mexico 21, D.F., Mexico.

Individual Exhibitions:

1978   *3 Jovenes Fotografos,* Galeria Juan Martin, Mexico City (with
        Pablo Ortiz Monasterio and Julieta Gimenez Cacho)
1980   Galeria Juan Martin, Mexico City

Selected Group Exhibitions:

1978   *Los Fotografos Eligen,* Galeria Arvil, Mexico City
1979   *Fotografia Urbana,* Galeria B. Franklin, Mexico City
1981   *Astrazione e Realta,* Galleria Flaviana, Locarno, Switzerland

Publications:

By FIGUEROA FLORES: Book—*Caminos y Mano de Obra,* Mexico City 1976. **Articles—**"La Fotografia in Messico" in *Fotografia Italiana* (Milan), February 1979; "Los Fotografos Crtesanos" in *Siempre* (Mexico City), August 1979; "Mulege" in *New West Magazine* (Los Angeles), August 1979; "Gabriel Figueroa Flores: Fotografias" in *Arquitecto* (Mexico City), August 1980.

*

One always tries to find a commitment in life. Some people are completely dedicated for many years, to a specific activity. I have spent my life trying to find out if I have a commitment, and what it might be.

What I do most—and perhaps this is my commitment—is to make objective my subjective feelings through a mental process and via a language. I respond to visual stimuli because of my early training and education. I realize that this could be compared to a digestive process: one sees, learns, retains, blends, distorts and so on, until one day something from all those inputs becomes a coherent part (or parts) of another process which transforms those previous experiences.

What I photograph is a condensation of my previous thought processes. These images tell about other lines of process in a specific place and time: a man's trace or gesture, even the most insignificant or trivial accident, becomes very important to me, because it is part of our unconscious made manifest, leaving a temporary—sometimes even permanent—wound in our world.

Objects—worn out, faded, torn, scratched, beaten, repainted, demolished, oxidized, left behind: all these are evidence of a particular moment, representing visually my idea of what is significant. The colour of these impressions acts as a form in itself, not merely as a factor serving to delimit the forms of the objects.

I seek harmony with the outer visual world, and, when I find it, I make a picture or several images until they are integrated to my system; then, I begin again.

—Gabriel Figueroa Flores

*   *   *

Gabriel Figueroa Flores is an unconventional photographer who has annihilated the graphic traditions of his country. Mexican representative art—painting, sculpture, film and photography—performs an essentially didactic and narrative role. To avoid the visual temptations that lead inevitably to folklore, and the ideological influences that lead to the imitation of hallowed models, Flores has had to engage in a profound analysis of his historic inheritance, from which has come a visual representation that is essential and severe, purged of symbols and free of preconceived plans.

His pictures are pictures of real life, of things that exist but of which we are often unaware, tangled up as they are with so many other things that make their presence felt much more conspicuously.

Flores uses the photographic medium as a selector of aesthetic banality. His is a refined intellectual operation to recover a microcosm and, at the same time, to scale down the actual meaning of artistic expression. In effect, through his work he reaffirms that creative photography is wholly subjective and makes no claim to be an all-embracing, exhaustive representation of "truth." Absolute truth does not exist. What does exist is a number of probable, individual truths, no less valid for that reason, and it is only through the assembling of such individual truths that we can approach a real truth.

With Flores, photography, too often interpreted as a faithful representation, once more finds its true dimensions as a recorder of minute realities. The camera is not an extension of the eye, which in every microsecond takes in an infinite series of objects that are then lost to our consciousness. Its function is

to isolate different elements, to restore to each one its predominance over the others. The grating over a manhole cover, the body of a truck, the walls of a room, the structure of an individual wall—all take on again their true meaning in our visual world.

While it is easy enough for all of us to perceive beauty where centuries of tradition and culture have taught us to see it—in a flower, a face, a landscape, a sunset—it is far from easy to discover it where we never knew it existed. The photo thus becomes a sensitive interpretation, the communication of an emotional message.

The use of color has a basic function in that emotional message and is fully justified by the balanced relationships between form and structure of spaces. It is also the element that reveals the subtle tension between the rational and emotional. In fact, the graphic structure of Flores's pictures is based on simple linear geometry, and violent color contrasts fill them with pathos and give them vivid life. Black and yellow, red and deep blue, grey and orange define the spatial rhythms and smooth the outlines. The severity of the form loses its hardness, and a whole world of visual emotions breaks out from the rectangle of photographic paper that momentarily contained them.

Another characterisitic of Flores's photographs is the absence of people. People are suggested by the details of the objects photographed. Every detail carries unmistakable traces of the human race, as the organizer of harmonic forms and violator of nature, as the creator of order and of passion. These poles have been set up by Flores in his pictures, creating works that are both exciting and mysterious. The excitement and mystery of the photographic process become metaphors of human nature.

—Giuliana Scimé

FINK, Larry.

Nationality: American. **Born:** Brooklyn, New York, 3 November 1941. **Education:** Attended Stockbridge High School, Massachusetts; Coe College, Cedar Rapids, Iowa; and New School for Social Research, New York; studied photography, privately, with Lisette Model, New York. **Career:** Freelance photographer. Instructor, Parsons School of Design, New York, 1967-72, and New School for Social Research, New York, 1968-72; Assistant Professor, Kingsborough Community College, New York, 1969-73; Instructor, Lehigh University, Bethlehem, Pennsylvania, 1976; Walker Evans Professor of Photography, 1977-78, and Professor, 1978, Yale University, New Haven, Connecticut; Instructor, International Center of Photography, New York, 1977, and Cooper Union, New York, 1979; Instructor, Yale School of Fine Arts, MFA Program, New Haven, CT, since 1987; Instructor, School of Visual Arts, MFA Program, New York, since 1987; Professor of Photography, Bard College, Annandale on the Hudson, New York, since 1987. **Recipient:** Creative Artists Public Service Grant, New York State Council on the Arts, 1971, 1974; Guggenheim Fellowship, 1976, 1979; National Endowment for the Arts Photography Fellowship, 1978. **Agent:** Light Gallery, 724 Fifth Avenue, New York, New York 10019. **Address:** Post Office Box 295, Martins Creek, Pennsylvania 18063, U.S.A.

Individual Exhibitions:

1960   *Cannes Film Festival*
1971   Paley and Lowe Gallery, New York
1972   Harcus-Krakow Gallery, Boston
1973   Light Works, Syracuse, New York
        Ohio Wesleyan University, Delaware
        Diana Gallery, New York
        Yale Summer School, New Haven, Connecticut
1975   Muhlenberg College, Allentown, Pennsylvania
        Cedar Crest College, Allentown, Pennsylvania

Sarte and Kara's Wedding, **1991.** Photograph by Larry Fink.

	Kirkland College, Clinton, New York	1979	Museum of Modern Art, New York
	Midtown Y Gallery, New York	1980	Light Gallery, New York
1976	Bucks County Community College, Newtown, Pennsylvania	1981	San Francisco Museum of Modern Art (with Joel Sternfeld)
	St. Lawrence University, Canton, New York		*Larry Fink/Andreas Müller-Pohle/Michael Schmidt,*
	Light Works, Syracuse, New York		Kunstmuseum, Dusseldorf
	Broxton Gallery, Los Angeles	1985	Burden Gallery, New York (with Anthony Hernandez)
	Carl Solway Gallery, Cincinnati, Ohio	1989	Gallery Foto, Oslo
1977	Yale University, New Haven, Connecticut	1992	Vigo, Spain
	University of Arizona, Tucson		Catherine Edelman Gallery, Chicago
1978	Sander Gallery, Washington, D.C.	1993	Newberger Museum, Purchase, New York
	Lehigh University, Bethlehem, Pennsylvania		Gallery Forum, Tarragona, Spain
	Hayden Gallery, Massachusetts Institute of Technology,		*Les Recontres de Photographie,* (major retrospective) Arles,
	Cambridge		France

Silver Eye Gallery, Pittsburgh
1994   Photo Forum, Frankfurt
Musée de la Photographie, Brussels, Belgium
Musée de l'Elysee, Lausanne, Switzerland

Selected Group Exhibitions:

1968   *Great Photographs,* American Society of Magazine Photographers, New York
1970   *Metropolitan Middle Class,* Massachusetts Institute of Technology, Cambridge
1973   *The Jew in New York,* Midtown Y Gallery, New York
1976   *Celebration,* Floating Foundation of Photography, New York
1978   *Mirrors and Windows: American Photography since 1960,* Museum of Modern Art, New York (toured the United States, 1978-80)
1979   *American Images: New Work by 20 Contemporary Photographers,* Corcoran Gallery, Washington, D.C. (travelled to the International Center of Photography, New York; Museum of Fine Arts, Houston; Minneapolis Institute of Arts; and Indianapolis Institute of Arts, 1980; and American Academy, Rome, 1981)
1980   *The Imaginary Photo Museum,* Kunsthalle, Cologne
1982   *Floods of Light,* The Photographers' Gallery, London
1983   *Photography in America 1910-83,* Tampa Museum, Florida
1985   *American images 1945-80,* Barbican Art Gallery, London (toured Britain)
1991   *Pleasures and Terrors of Domestic Comfort,* Museum of Modern Art, New York
1992   *The Young Rebel in American Photography,* Museum of Modern Art, New York
1994   National Institute of Photography in the Netherlands

Collections:

Museum of Modern Art, New York; Museum of Fine Arts, Boston; Corcoran Gallery, Washington, D.C.

Publications:

By FINK: Books—*Un Printemps à New York,* with Marc Albert Levin, Paris 1969; *Tour de Force,* with Marc Albert Levin, Paris 1969; *Social Graces,* Millerton, New York 1984. **Articles**—editorial portfolios published in *Leica Magazine,* Germany 1993; *Schwarzweiss,* Germany 1994; *Zoom,* Italy, NYC 1994.

On FINK: Books—*Mirrors and Windows: American Photography since 1960* by John Szarkowski, New York 1978; *American Images: New Work by 20 Contemporary Photographers,* edited by Renato Danese, New York 1979; *Photographie als Kunst 1879-1979/Kunst als Photographie 1949-1979,* exhibition catalogue, 2 vols., by Peter Weiermair, Innsbruck, Austria 1979; *Larry Fink/Joel Sternfeld,* exhibition catalogue, by Dorothy Martinson, San Francisco 1981; *The Imaginary Photo Museum* by Helmut Gernsheim, Renate and L. Fritz Gruber and others, Cologne 1981, London 1982; *Floods of Light: Flash Photography 1851-1981,* exhibition catalogue, edited by Rupert Martin, London 1982; *Lichtbildnisse: Das Porträt in der Fotografie,* edited by Klaus Honnef, Cologne 1982; *Photography in America 1910-1983,* exhibition catalogue, by Julie M. Saul, Tampa, Florida 1983; *American Images: Photography 1945-1980,* edited by Peter Turner and John Benton-Harris, London 1985. **Articles**—"Larry Fink: San Gennaro Festival" in *Print* (New York), January/February 1973; "New Work: Larry Fink, Light Gallery" by Lynn Zelevansky in *Flash Art* (Milan), Summer 1980; *Le Fotografia* (Paris), July 1993; *Le Monde* (Paris), July 1993; *Le Figaro* (Paris), July 1993; *La Creation, Revolution* (Paris), July 1993; *International Herald Tribune,* July 1993; *Globe* (Paris), July 1993.

* * *

Perhaps Larry Fink's photographs are best described under the rubric "new social photography." Like other "new" types of photography—documentary, landscape, topography—Fink's social documents have become "new" because they are made with an added detachment and self-consciousness unavailable to those who originally dealt with the then-fresh subject matter.

Clearly reliant on the styles of Robert Frank, Garry Winogrand, Diane Arbus and his teacher Lisette Model, Fink's work reflects not only the mood of the period in American life that he photographs, but also the currency of the social and artistic forces and institutions that have developed and formed him as an artist. Travelling in both the urban and the quasi-rural social landscapes, Fink specializes in the types and activities found in lower middle class locales and gatherings. Having studied the lessons in romance offered by America's tradition of photographer-travellers who have explored the country through photography since the Western expeditions, Fink has learned how to heroicize the capture of "quintessential" American scenes and moments. His forte is the carefully framed 21/4 image in black and white, highlighted by flash or other harsh lighting, and printed in high contrast to bring out all the details.

Equally transparent as his lower middle class subjects are opaque, however, is the story to be read in Fink's photographs of his own development as photographer-artist-teacher. In their detachment from the lives and habits of the people they show, Fink's photographs are highly expressive of his own social point of view; they suggest that he photographs a social milieu from which he himself has narrowly escaped. Fink seems at once closer to and less comfortable with his subjects than are Frank, Winogrand or Arbus.

Fink is a highly successful teacher, capable of not only stylistic proficiency and grace but also the ability to convey the fundamentals of these accomplishments to younger photographers. Nor is this success surprising, for the work itself pays unabashed homage to art school training, trends in collecting, and curatorial tastes—the agents, certainly, of his rescue from that very lower middle class which he photographs. In the unself-conscious grins and the television-inspired, banal gesture of his subjects, all too lovingly caught, one senses the artist's faint sigh of relief—"there but for the grace of God go I"—and realizes anew the power of photography in American life today.

—Maren Stange

FISCHER, Arno.

Nationality: German. **Born:** Berlin, 14 April 1927. **Education:** Studied sculpture at the Kunsthochschule, Berlin, 1947-48; under Heinrich Drake, Hochschule für Angewandte Kunst, East Berlin, 1948-52; Hochschule für Bildende Künste, West Berlin, 1952-54. **Family:** Married Sibylle Bergemann in 1986; children: Kathleen, Jenny, Oliver and Robert. **Career:** Senior Assistant in Photography, Kunstchochschule, Berlin-Weissensee, 1956-71. Since 1971, freelance portrait, reportage, fashion and advertising photographer, working for *Sibylle, Magazin, Freie Welt,* Verlag Volk und Welt, etc., in East Berlin. Instructor, 1984, and Professor of Photography since 1985, Hochschule für Graphik und Buchkunst, Leipzig. **Recipient:** Bronze Medal, Fédération Internationale d'Art Photographique (FIAP), 1974. **Address:** Schiffbauerdamm 12, Berlin 1040, Germany.

Individual Exhibitions:

1977   *Am Wege,* Fotogalerie, Bratislava, Czechoslovakia
1978   Kunstmuseum, Vienna
1979   Galerie Berlin, East Berlin
1983   *Indien,* Club der Kulturschaffenden der DDR, East Berlin
        Alt Delhi—Neu Delhi, Galerie Sophienstrasse 8, East Berlin
1986   *Fotografien aus vier Jahrzehnten,* Fotogalerie Helsinforser Platz, East Berlin

Selected Group Exhibitions:

1977   *Medium Fotografie,* Staatliche Galerie Moritzburg, Halle, East Germany

1979   *DDR Fotografie,* Galerie Gurzenich, Cologne, West Germany
1981   *II. Porträtfotoausstellung,* Fucik Hallen, Dresden, East
        Germany
1982   *9. Kunstausstellung DDR,* Fucik Hallen, Dresden, East
        Germany
1985   *Photographes Contemporains en R.D.A.,* Cherbourg, France
        (travelled to Brest and Rheims, France)
        10 Fotografen aus der DDR, Graz, Austria (travelled to
        Vienna)
        Begegnungen, Altes Museum, East Berlin
        Frühe Bilder: Photographie in DDR 1945-65, Leipzig, East
        Germany (travelled to East Berlin)

Collections:

Gesellschaft für Photographie, Berlin.

Publications:

By FISCHER: Books—*Polens Hauptstädte,* with Rolf Schneider, East
Berlin 1974; *Leningrad—Erinnerungen und Entdeckungen,* with Daniil
Granin, East Berlin 1981; *Alt Delhi—Neu Delhi: Zwischen Affenstadt und
Rotem Fort,* with Richard Christ, East Berlin 1983. **Article**—"Mit Kleinbild
und Schwarzweiss in Afrika" in *Fotografie* (Leipzig), no. 8, 1974.

On FISCHER: Books—*U.S. Camera Annual 1958,* New York 1958;
Erlebnis, Bild, Personlichkeit—fünf Fotografen, fünf Sichten, edited by B.
Beiler and H. Föppel, Leipzig 1973; *Gebrauchsgrafik in der DDR,* Dresden
1975; *Die Geschichte der Fotografie im 20. Jahrhundert/Photography in the
Twentieth Century* by Petr Tausk, Cologne 1977, London 1980; *Medium
Fotografie,* edited by Andreas Hüneke, Gerhard Ihrke, Alfred Neumann and
Ullrich Wallenburg, Leipzig 1979. **Articles**—"Arno Fischer" by Jutta Voigt
in *Sonntag* (East Berlin), no. 16, 1973; "Arno Fischer" by Colin Osman in
Creative Camera (London), no. 5, 1979; "Das geht eben nur in Farbe" by P.
Voigt in *Fotografie* (Leipzig), no. 1, 1983; "Gruppe Direkt" by Wolfgang Kil
in *Bildende Kunst* (East Berlin), no. 4, 1984; "Arno Fischer" by Wolfgang Kil
in *Sonntag* (East Berlin), no. 1, 1986.

*   *   *

Two important names are connected with photographic innovation in East
Germany in the mid-1950s: those of Evelyn Richter and Arno Fischer. After
studying sculpture for several years, in 1954 Arno Fischer began capturing
photographic impressions of his home town, Berlin. This first important cycle
of his photographic output, on which Fischer continued to work up until 1960,
completely broke from the start with every photographic convention and
tradition current in East Germany at the time. Fischer's way of seeing, as these
photos demonstrated, was most closely related to that of the American Robert
Frank, whose book *The Americans* continues to epitomize for Fischer the kind
of photography to which he aspires: a photography that transforms everyday
situations into symbols for the general, existential questions of human life.

Although all his photographs relate to real-life incidents, Fischer has
never thought of himself as a photo-journalist. In order to make a living from
photographic work and at the same time to follow his own inclinations, in 1956
he took up a teaching post in photography at the Berlin Academy of Art. For
the next decade he exerted a marked influence on photographic fashion in East
Germany and began to collect around himself an increasing number of pupils
and colleagues, whose search for original and intensive pictorial expression he
furthered. One of the temporary photographic groups that formed around him
was that of "Direkt," to which such important East German photographers as
Sibylle Bergemann and Roger Melis belonged.

Since 1971 Arno Fischer has been working as a freelance photographer,
producing, among other things, an important series of travel pictures from
various continents, principally as commissions for publishing firms. His
method of capturing everyday situations in vivid, symbolic moments has
barely altered over the course of time: his 1984 New York photos exert the
same, almost magical fascination as his Berlin pictures of 1958. The photograph always deals with the same thing: the same unavoidable confrontation
with anonymous individuals, with a segment of life unfamiliar to us.

Arno Fischer is a teacher *par excellence,* possessing a sure eye for his
pupils' talent and an open mind towards other ways of looking at things. Since
1981 he has been teaching photography at the Academy of Graphics and Book
Production in Leipzig, where he was granted a Professorship in 1985. This
regular contact with students ensures the continuation in the next generation of
young East German photographers of that humanist tradition which, since the
beginning of his career, Fischer has sought to advance by his remarkable
photographic achievements.

—Wolfgang Kil

FISCHER, Roland.

Nationality: German. **Born:** Saarbrücken, Germany, 21 December 1958.
Resident in Los Angeles, USA and Munich, Germany. **Education:** Studied
mathematics at University of Munich. **Family:** Married Dr Barbara Fisher.
Recipient: Photography Prize, Arteder '82, Bilbao, Spain, 1982. **Agent:**
Galerie Six, Friedrich Cuvilliesstrasse 15, D 81679 Munich, Germany.

Individual Exhibitions:

1980   Amerikahaus, Munich
1981   Goethe-Institut, New York
1983   Galerie Loft, Munich
1987   Galerie Mosel und Tschechow, Munich
1989   Musée d'art Moderne de la Ville de Paris, Paris
        Galerie Mosel und Tschechow, Munich
1990   Akademie Weingarten
        Galerie Schneider, Frankfurt
        Saarland Museum, Saarbrücken, Germany
1991   Gallery Carine Campo, Antwerp
        Landesmuseum, Linz, Austria
        Städtische Galerie, Marstall Rastatt
        Galerie Mathias Kampl, Passau
1992   Kunsthalle, Bielefeld
        Kunstverein, Ludwigsburg
        Städtische Galerie, Cordonhaus, Cham
        Galerie Christine et Isy Brachot, Paris
1993   Gallery Carine Campo, Antwerp
        Gallery Storm, Amsterdam
1994   Galérie Sollertis, Toulouse, France
        Museum Nijmegen, Nijmegen, Holland
        Galerie Six Friedrich, Munich
        Gallery Carine Campo, Antwerp
        Galérie Le monde de l'art, Paris
1995   Galerie Raab, Berlin/London
        Galerie Beatrice Wassermann, Köln

Selected Group Exhibitions:

1983   *6 Münchner Kunstler,* Centre d'Art Belgrad, Belgrade
1985   *Alles und noch viel mehr,* Kunstmuseum, Munich;
        Kunsthalle, Bern
1990   *To be and not to be,* Centre d'Art Contemporain, Barcelona
1992   *Einsamkeit, fünf deitsche Fotokünstler,* (travelled to Tarragona,
        Madrid, Barcelona and Palma)
        Iemand, Niemand En Honderdduizend, Internationales
        Kulturelles Zentrum, Antwerp
1993   *Danse Macabre,* Portraits Photographie Contemporaine,
        Rennes, France
        Le Printemps de la Photo, Cahors, France
        Presences, The Photographers' Gallery, London

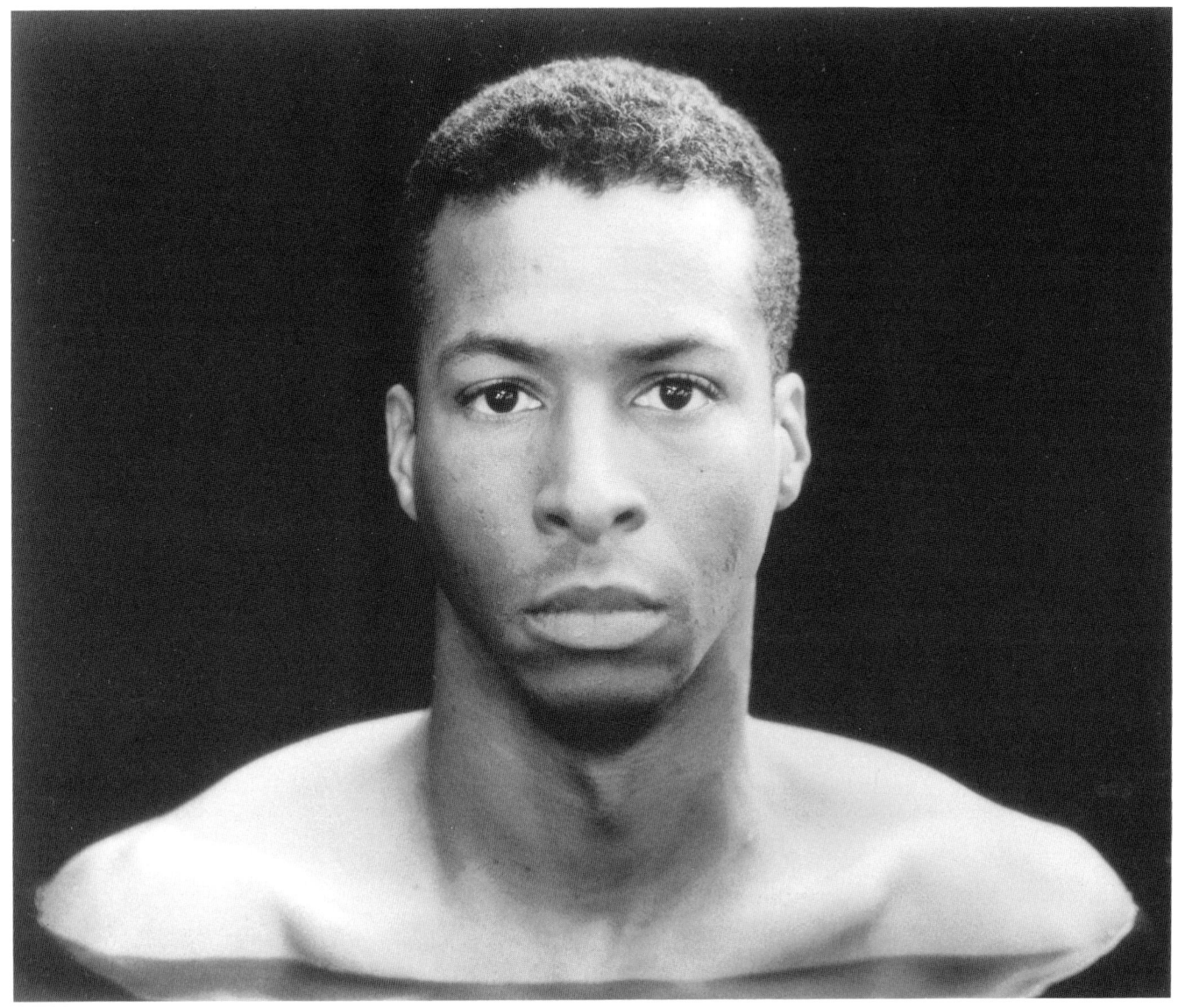

Untitled, **1993 (original in colour).** Photograph ©Roland Fischer.

Collections:

Musée d'art Moderne de la ville de Paris; Städtische Galerie im Lenbachhaus, Munich; Saarland Museum, Saarbrücken; Museum für Moderne Kunst, Antwerp; FRAC, Normandie; Städtische Galerie Rastatt; FNAC, Paris.

Publications:

By FISCHER: Article—"Portraits" in *Humanitas* (Rastatt), 1989.

On FISCHER: Articles—"Portraits of Roland Fischer" by Christoph Wiedemann in *Süddeutsche Zeitung,* December 1983; "Portraits besonderer Art" by Hans Michael Herzog in *Süddeutsche Zeitung,* No. 285, December 1987; "La transparence passionée de Roland Fischer" by Régis Durand in *Art Press* (Paris), No 132, January 1989; "Visages de Silence" by Oliver Clément in *Artics 2* (Barcelona), 1989; "Les Visions de l'esprit de Roland Fischer" in *Le Monde,* February 1989; "Stille Macht des Augenblicks" by Gabi Czöppan in *Pan,* January 1990; "A l'abbaye du Val d'Antheit, boulversante recontre avec l'invisible" by Jacques Henrard in *Vers l'Avenir,* August 1990; "La Part de l'ombre," a series of essays by Régis Durand in *Edition La Difference*

(Paris), 1990; "Das alte Element im neuen Medium, zur Wasserthematik in der Kunstfotografie" by Christoph Blase in *Artis,* January 1990; "L'oeil à l'oeuvre: images fixes et visions sans objet" by Sylvie Couderc in *La Photographie,* 1990; "Grösser als das Leben" by Freddy Langer in *Frankfurter Allgemeine Zeitung,* January 1991; "Suche nach Ruhe, aus der Spannung kommt" by Wolfgang Koch in *Saarbrücker Zeitung,* January 1991; "Spannung zwischen Nähe und Distanz" by Freddy Langer in *Frankfurter Allegmeine Zeitung,* January 1991; "In Kloster und Swimmingpool" by Wolfgang Koch in *Saarbrücker Zeitung,* December 1991; "Die glatte Asthetik von Runzeln und Falten" by M. Schmitt-Rilling in *Die Rheinpfalz,* January 1991; "Frau im Wasser" by Kai Hoffmann in *Frankfurter Rundschau,* December 1991; "Roland Fisher" by Anne Wauters in *Art Press* (Paris), July/August 1991; "Zwischen Freiheit und Bestimmung" by Kirsten Voigt in *Badisches Tagblatt,* September 1991; "Kühle Blicke aus den Schwimmbädern Kaliforniens" by Freddy Langer in *Faz-Magazin,* February 1992; "Photographie: Thomas Struth und Roland Fischer" by Sabine Scheltwort in *Die Zeit,* March 1992; "Amerikanischer Traum und Kunstwirklichkeit" by Konstanze Crüwell in *Frankfurter Allgemeine Zeitung,* September 1992; "Mais l'arbre ne doit pas. . . ." by Anne Wauters in *Art et Culture,* March 1993; "Esto no es fotografia" by Santiago B. Olmo in *Diario de Mallorca,* March 1993; "Le

Printemps de la photo'' by Anne Dagbert in *Art Press*, No. 183, September 1993; ''Los Angeles Portraits'' by M. Koetzle in *Photo* (Munich), March/April 1994.

*

One common theme in my projects *Nuns and Monks,* the *Los Angeles Portraits* and *Tertullian* is the concept of human consciousness and perception, form and freedom. On the visual side I was always interested in the simultaneous presence of two conflicting principles, like the face surrounded by black and white masses (*Nuns and Monks*) or the human bust in the monochrome blue or black of the water (*Los Angeles Portraits*).

—Roland Fischer

* * *

At the turn of the century the search for the ''valid'' portrait was a search for character, essence, individuality. The innermost depths were to be brought out with the help of the camera. At the end of the twentieth century Roland Fischer questions in a fundamental way the mimetic qualities of photography. ''I only believe in the reality of the picture itself'' he says. And: ''Only if one looks at a picture in a state of detachment from reality, do its true qualities bear fruit.''

Roland Fischer is a painter with a camera: not in the sense of a traditional aesthetic of artistic photography, but rather in the sense of portraying a vision, for whose interpretation the artist simply relays via a technical medium. Long before Fischer presses the shutter release, he is developing an idea, a concept. In this process he seems to be more interested in mathematically comprehensible laws of composition or the formulation of philosophical questions than in professional standards of photographic practice.

After taking the Abitur test Fischer did in fact first study mathematics, but then increasingly found his real vocation in photography, which he had already been practising in his school days. In 1983 he showed his work in Munich, large-format black-and-white portraits which at first glance appear traditionally structured and whose formal unity (close detail, full-face shot, collected expression) refer of course to his predilection for the abstract. The breakthrough, or if you prefer, the international recognition occurred at the end of the eighties with—again large-format—colour portraits of monks and nuns, mostly close up, more rarely full-figure. Here too he is not concerned with psychology or even the sociology of monastic life. The reason for approaching this particular theme was rather the rigorous geometry of a way of life that is meagre in all its facets.

Fischer's most recent colour work could be described as ''Nude Studies.'' But just as the ''Los Angeles Portraits'' (1989-1994) were in no way portraits in the classical sense, so the ''Tertullian'' series is not simply an interpretation of the body. Once more what concerns Fischer is the visualisation of diverse conflicts of opposites; space and time; body and spirit; materiality and transparency. The combinations of traditional photographic techniques and digital reworking (which seems to interest the artist more and more) is technically interesting and offers an explanation of the strange appearance of pictures.

When, to prevent misunderstandings, he himself comments on his photographs, Roland Fischer likes to speak of ''tense relationships,'' which he wishes to bring out through his pictorial discoveries. Also of the contrast of organically free and solid forms, of ''masses,'' which he pushes around until he has composed his picture. In Fischer's work logic and the power of suggestion, mathematical calculation and the old theme of humanity combine in a fascinating way.

—Michael Koetzle

FITCH, Steve.

Nationality: American. **Born:** Tucson, Arizona, 16 August 1949. **Education:** Attended the University of California at Davis, 1967-68, and University of California, Berkeley, 1968-71, B.A. in anthropology 1971; San Francisco Art Institute, 1977; University of New Mexico, Albuquerque, 1978, M.A. in photography 1978. **Family:** Married A. Lynn Grimes in 1980; son: Daniel Luke. **Career:** Photographer since 1965. Instructor, A.S.U.C. Studio, University of California, Berkeley, 1971-77; Teaching Assistant, University of New Mexico, 1978; Visiting Lecturer, 1979-80, and Assistant Professor of Art, 1980-85, University of Colorado, Boulder; Visiting Associate Professor, University of Texas at San Antonio, 1985. **Recipient:** National Endowment for the Arts Photography Grant, 1973, 1975, 1981; Purchase Awards in exhibitions in California, 1973, New York, 1975, Colorado, 1984, Missouri, 1984, and New Mexico, 1985. **Agents:** Ursula Gropper and Associates, 10 Laurel Lane, Sausalito, California 94965; and Etherton Gallery, 424 East 6th Street, Tucson, Arizona 85705. **Addresses:** 801 LaFarge, Louisville, Colorado 80027; or Post Office Box 4626, Berkeley, California 94704; permanent address—870 Helen Avenue, Ukiah, California 95482, U.S.A.

Individual Exhibitions:

1975	Darkroom Workshop Gallery, Berkeley, California
	University Art Museum, Berkeley, California
	Shado Gallery, Oregon City, Oregon
	Sacramento State University, California
1976	Orange Coast College, Costa Mesa, California
	College of Marin, Kentfield, California
1977	Santa Fe Gallery of Photography, New Mexico
1979	Foto Gallery, New York
	Blue Sky Gallery, Portland, Oregon
1980	Simon Lowinsky Gallery, San Francisco
1981	Colorado Mountain College, Breckinridge
1982	Hills Gallery, Denver, Colorado
	University of Colorado, Boulder
1983	Texas Technical University, Lubbock
	Arizona State University, Tempe
1984	Southern Exposure Gallery, Amarillo College, Texas
1985	University of Colorado, Boulder
	Auraria Higher Education Center, Denver, Colorado

Selected Group Exhibitions:

1973	*Places,* San Francisco Art Institute
1974	*Light and Substance,* University of New Mexico, Albuquerque
1975	*Young American Photographers,* Kalamazoo Institute of Arts, Michigan
1977	*Radical Photography and Bay Area Innovators,* Sacred Heart School, Menlo Park, California
1978	*The Aesthetics of Graffiti,* San Francisco Museum of Modern Art
1979	*Attitudes: Photography in the 70s,* Santa Barbara Museum of Art, California
1980	*Beyond Color,* San Francisco Museum of Modern Art
1982	*Color as Form,* International Museum of Photography at George Eastman House, Rochester, New York
1984	*Exposed and Developed,* National Museum of American Art, Washington, D.C. (toured the United States)
1985	*New Landscapes,* Tasmanian School of Art, Hobart (travelled to The Developed Image Gallery, Adelaide; Australian Centre for Photography, Sydney)

Collections:

Museum of Modern Art, New York; Museum of Fine Arts, Boston; Fogg Art Museum, Harvard University, Cambridge, Massachusetts; Rhode Island School of Design, Providence; Minneapolis Institute of the Arts; Houston Museum of Fine Arts; University of New Mexico, Albuquerque; Center for Creative Photography, University of Arizona, Tucson; Oakland Art Museum, California; Grunwald Center for the Graphic Arts, University of California at Los Angeles.

Publications:

By FITCH: Book—*Diesels and Dinosaurs,* Berkeley, California 1976. **Articles**—"The Recording of Maya Sculpture" in *Berkeley Archaeological Research Facility Reports* (Berkeley, California), no. 16, 1972; "Personal Notes on Teaching the History of Photography" in *Exposure* (Chicago), Spring 1981.

On FITCH: Books—*Light and Substance,* exhibition catalogue, by Ralph Bogardus, Albuquerque, New Mexico 1973; *Beyond Color,* exhibition catalogue, by Louise Katzman, San Francisco 1980; *Color as Form: A History of Color Photography,* exhibition catalogue, with introduction by Robert A. Sobieszek, Rochester, New York 1982; *American Photography: A Critical History* by Jonathan Greene, New York 1984. **Articles**—"Roadwork" by Lois Fishman in *Afterimage* (Rochester, New York), May/June 1975; "Transformation of the Ordinary" by Dana Asbury in *Artweek* (Oakland, California), 26 November 1977; "Interactive Visions" by Ted Hedgpeth in *Artweek* (Oakland, California), 9 February 1980; "Review" by Hal Fischer in *Artforum* (New York), May 1980; "Shows We've Seen" by Natalie Canavor in *Popular Photography* (New York), June 1980.

*

The photographs I make are primarily observations about the American vernacular, in particular the highway and strip developments of the West. Details of this vernacular include drive-in movie theatres, motels, neon and neon signs, billboards, styles of landscaping, even the road itself. Recent photographs have also included images of Native American rock art sites located in the Southwest.

Why I am interested in photographing this sort of evidence is difficult to explain. A simple reason is that I wish to document it—for my own purposes as well as in an archival sense: for the society. Another, more complicated and perhaps mystical reason is that I feel an attachment and profound respect for both the experience of the road and the physical facts of it.

How I formally approach this experience and these facts as an artist varies. Much of my work has been—and continues to be—done at night. As a result I use an assortment of light sources (singly and in combination): ambient sky light, strobe, artificial street and neon lighting, the headlights of my truck. I have always been interested in the nuances of the photographic process: how can I affect or alter the image by using a particular process or photographing with a certain attitude about time and place in mind. Originally, I began to work at night because I was curious about what photographs made then would look like, and I felt it was necessary for the subject matter that I was photographing (for example, neon signs).

I consider photography to be an important means for collecting, transmitting and storing information as well as a curious set of possibilities for altering and commenting on that information. Also, it is an important source of ideas for drawings, constructions, expeditions. Not only does the medium allow me a chance to exercise my obsessions; it also gives me an opportunity to understand and perhaps explain their importance.

—Steve Fitch

*   *   *

Steve Fitch's first book, *Diesels and Dinosaurs,* has its source in family vacations he took as a child, but it was realized when he later wandered the western highways alone and with his friends. It is a personal documentary revealing his romantic attraction to this uniquely American phenomenon. The photographs concentrate on single iconic aspects of the experience; billboards, neon and handpainted signs, building facades, drive-in movies, a truckstop waitress, and anonymous motels are preserved within the borders of these black and white photos. What makes this more than a routine documentary study, though, is the recurring motif of semi-trucks that dominate the highways and wooden prehistoric creatures that populate roadside attractions. His focus on these elements carries the metaphorical implication that these diesels are like modern day dinosaurs moving slowly toward extinction.

After this project Fitch's concerns shifted away from the documentary image toward an interest in the picture as an entity in itself, separate from its subject. His series of bushes illuminated by strong flash at night were technically and stylistically innovative studies which not only signalled a new direction in his work, but opened up new avenues for many other photographers as well. Their sophisticated use of space, perspective, color, and movement was meant to create new forms of content in the image.

The large, color prints which followed (for which he mastered the dye-transfer process) were a natural outgrowth of his technical experimentation and his fascination with road signs. Vibrant, saturated color and captivating movement in the photograph itself recreate the visual intensity of neon seen in the darkness of the desert highways. The signature piece of this series contains a pulsating orange neon arrow mounted on a shimmering steel pole. Set against a deep purple sky, it illuminates an unreal scene as it points diagonally down to unrecognizable squiggles of light. The thematic implication of this and many other works in this group is that all photographs act like signs because they direct viewers back to the world they have captured. The irony, of course, is that, like the arrow-sign in his picture, Fitch's photographs always point to an unreal, imaginative world.

—Ted Hedgpeth

FLEISCHER, Alain.

Nationality: French. **Born:** Paris, 10 January 1944. **Education:** Attended the Sorbonne, Paris, and l'Ecole des Hautes Etudes en Sciences Sociales, Paris. **Agents:** Galerie Michèle Chomette, 24 rue Beaubourg, 75003, Paris, France; and Jayne H. Baum Gallery, 588 Broadway, New York 10012, U.S.A.

Individual Exhibitions:

1975	Musée National d'Art Moderne, Centre Georges Pompidou, Paris
1980	Studio 666, Paris
1981	Multi-Media Gallery and French Institute, Zagreb, Yugoslavia
	Students Gallery, Belgrade, Yugoslavia
	French Institute, Ljubljana, Yugoslavia
	French Institute, Split, Yugoslavia
1982	Musée National d'Art Moderne, Centre Georges Pompidou, Paris
1983	Studio 666, Paris
1984	*A Month of Photography in Paris,* Studio 666, Paris
1985	Musée de l'Abbaye Sainte Croix, Les Sables d'Olonne, France
1986	Centre of Photography, Patino Foundation, Geneva
1987	French Institute, Prague, Czechoslovakia
	Villa Medicis, Rome
	Galerie Michèle Chomette, Paris
1988	Galleria M.R., Rome
	Galerie des Beaux-Arts, Nantes, France
	Photography Gallery, Kladno, Czechoslovakia
1989	Jayne H. Baum Gallery, New York
	Musée Ancien Eveché, Evreux, France
	Past Rays Gallery, Yokohma, Japan
	French Institute, Budapest, Hungary
	French Institute, Naples, Italy
	French Institute, Cologne, Germany
1990	Sala Joseph M. Gugol, Catalonia, Spain
	Le Match, Le Fresnoy, Tourcoing, France
	Galerie Michèle Chomette, Paris
1991	Galerie Optica, Montreal, Canada
	Museo de Bilbao, Spain
	Ateneum Museum, Helsinki, Finland
1992	*Les Lions de Rome et autres papiers d'argent,* Galerie Michèle Chomette, Paris
1993	Museo d'Arte Moderna, Rio de Janeiro, Brazil (retrospective; and worldwide tour, 1993-95)
1995	*Names and Numbers,* Jayne H. Baum Gallery, New York

Selected Group Exhibitions:

1981   Studios 81-82, ARC/Musée d'Art Moderne, Paris
        Suites, Series, Sequences, Musée National d'Art Moderne,
          Centre Georges Pompidou, Paris
1982   *Photography in France Today,* ARC/Musée d'Art Moderne,
          Paris (travelled to New York and Tokyo)
        International Biennial, Paris
1983   *Rencontres Internationales de la Photographie,* Paris
1984   *Attention to Painting,* at *Rencontres Internationales de la
          Photographie,* Arles, France
1985   *Das Aktphoto,* Fotomuseum im Stadtmuseum, Munich (trav-
          elled to Hamburg, Vienna and Tokyo)
        5 x 5, French Institute, Berlin (travelled to Bonn, Dusseldorf
          and Munich)
1986   *Machines Affected/Affected Machines,* Nexus Contemporary
          Art Center, Atlanta, Georgia (travelled to Chicago and New
          York, 1987)
1987   *Vice Versa, Artistes Français aux Pays-Bas,* Vleeshalle de
          Middelburg, Netherlands
1988   *Festival des Arts Electroniques,* Rennes, France
        L'image dans l'image, travelling exhibition (toured Finland)
        Art or Nature, Barbican Art Centre, London
        Tendances actuelles de la photographie en France, Centre
          National de la Photographie, Paris (and international tour)
        Homages and Remakes, Perspektief Gallery, Rotterdam,
          Netherlands
1989   Tolarno Gallery, Melbourne, Victoria, Australia
        Bad Women, Elefanten Press Galerie, Berlin
        20 Years of French Photography, Bayer Foundation,
          Leverkusen, Germany (and tour, 1990-91)
        L'Absence, Musée Réattu, Arles, France
        Internationale Foto Triennale, Esslingen, Germany
        L'Invention d'un Art, Musée National d'Art Moderne, Centre
          Georges Pompidou, Paris
1990   *Odalisque,* Jayne H. Baum Gallery, New York
        Sydney Biennial, Sydney, Australia
        *L'oeuvre photographique considerée comme un état de
          sculpture,* Galerie Michèle Chomette, Paris
1991   *La Photographie Française en Liberté,* Gulbenkian Foundation,
          Lisbon, Portugal (travelled to the United States, Mexico and
          Japan, 1991-92)
        Macchine de Luce, Galleria Il Millennio, Rome
1992   *Voyeurism,* Jayne H. Baum Gallery, New York
        Internationale Foto Triennale, Esslingen, Germany
        Metropolitan Museum, Tokyo, Japan

Collections:

Musée d'Art Moderne de la Ville de Paris; Musée National d'Art Moderne,
Centre Georges Pompidou, Paris; Musées de Marseille, France; Musées
d'Aurillac, France; Musée de l'Abbaye Sainte Croix, Les Sables d'Olonne,
France; Musée Réattu, Arles, France; Fonds National d'Art Contemporain,
Paris; Fonds Régional d'Art Contemporain des Pays de Loire, Clisson, France;
Fonds Régional d'Art Contemporain d'Aquitaine, Bordeaux, France; Fonds
Régional d'Art Contemporain de Languedoc Roussillon, Montpelier, France;
Fonds Régional d'Art Contemporain Champagne Ardennes, Reims, France;
Fonds Régional d'Art Contemporain de Franche Conté, Dole, France; Fonds
Régional d'Art Contemporain de Bourgogne, Dijon, France; Fonds Régional
d'Art Contemporain de Basse Normandie, Caen, France; Fonds Régional
d'Art Contemporain Provence Alpes Cote d'Azur, Marseille, France; Muse-
um of Modern Art, Jerusalem, Israel; The Art Institute, Chicago.

Publications:

By FLEISCHER: Books—*Kafka,* with text by Regis Durand, Paris 1990;
Quelques Obscurcissiments, Paris 1991; *Pris au mot,* Paris 1992. **Films**—*Le
jeune cinema français à Cannes,* 1977; *Zoo Zero,* 1978; *La pour Ca,* Bourges
1982; *Pierre Klossowski, portrait de l'artiste en souffleur,* Paris 1982; *Ombres
d'Asie,* 1982; *Riverrun,* 1983; *L'embarquement pour Cythère,* 1983; *Le

voyage du brise-glace ou pays des miroirs, 1983; *L'Aventure Générale,* 1984;
L'Art d'exposer, Paris 1984; *Boltanski par Fleischer,* 1984; *Cinéma et
Photographie,* 1984; *L'Art d'exposer II,* Paris 1985; *Daniel Buren,* 1985;
Demi-frères, 1985; *Le dernier voyage en Italie,* 1987; *Romeo Romeo,* 1990;
Daniel Cordier: le Regard d'un Amateur, 1990; *Grands Artistes observés par
un veilleur de nuit,* 1992; *Bukitrok,* 1992.

On FLEISCHER: Articles—"Photography: A New Era" by Bonnie Barrett
Stretch in *ARTnews,* Vol. 91, No. 3, March 1992; "Paris: The Ghost of
Hippolyte Bayard is Still Among Us" by Valerie Morlot in *Center Quarterly*
(New York), Vol. 51, No. 3, 1992; "ALAIN FLEISCHER: son film *Romeo
Romeo* sort le 15 avril à Paris" by Vincent Ostria in *Jardin des Modes* (Paris),
No. 158, April 1992; "Voyeurism" by Mary Haus, review, in *ARTnews,* Vol.
91, No. 5, May 1992.

*   *   *

As Alain Fleischer has frequently said of himself: he was born at the
crossroads of several cultures and raised with the knowledge of several
languages and countries. Clearly gifted in several fields of activity, he would
have wished—he wished—not to surrender any part of it. In fact he is
endowed with something of the appetite of a Renaissance man, at the stage
where an individual could still hope to embrace the near-totality of human
knowledge. This is clearly no longer the case, and such an ambition is today no
more than nostalgia, *hubris,* neurosis according to some.

Where Alain Fleischer is concerned, this immoderation takes the form of a
practice at once blazed across numerous fields and yet remarkably homogeneous. Film-maker, writer, photographer, artist, teacher—Alain Fleischer, in his
own words, "elaborates work projects as though endowed with a lie expectation of 200-300 years" (interview with Hervé Gauville, November 1994). As
a film-maker, he alternates fiction films with theses of the art and artists of his
time. Most recently he has produced a montage of previously unedited rushes
from Jean Renoir's *Une Partie de Campagne (A Day in the Country).* The
cinema is perhaps, without him really recognising it, his first choice, the one
where every other melds and regenerates itself—without him experiencing the
least desire of becoming the "professionals' professional" berated by Jean-
Luc Godard. As a writer, he has published works of fiction (a novel, four
volumes of narrative), sometimes overtly autobiographical in nature, in which
the writing resembles the mechanism of memory and desire, at the same time
implacable and elegant.

One rediscovers the taste for the mechanisms of sight in his photographic
works and installation, which represent an important part of his work in their
own right. His slides are both highly sophisticated and very simple; Alain
Fleischer makes great play with mechanical toys, with reflective surfaces,
mirrors, metals, water etc., along with whatever introduces a sense of
displacement or a ripple within a fixed image: ventilators, mobile toys,
anamorphoses, superimpositions, etc. All is in keeping with that great seventeenth century tradition of catoptrics. Alain Fleischer ceaselessly employs it in
a game of historical references to painting, which turns his work into a
museum without walls—"a museum-like anti-space which is my imaginary
space"—as he has accounted it with precision. A partitioned and intermittent
space, in which however nothing mixes, as each project is always quite
specifically designated for a particular medium. A *nomadic* space, in which all
the forms work with and or each other, photography with cinema, cinema with
painting, text for the images, etc., etc. and in which the construction is rendered
impressive by dint of its breadth and mastery.

—Régis Durand

FONTANA, Franco.

Nationality: Italian. **Born:** Modena, 9 December 1933. **Education:** Attended
Modena schools; self-taught in photography, from 1959. **Family:** Divorced;
daughters: Laura and Andrea. **Career:** Freelance industrial, advertising and
magazine photographer, working for Fiat, Alitalia, Kodak, Ferrari, Sony,
Volkswagen, Time/Life, Mondadori Editore, Lustrum Press, Conde-Nast,

Amphoto, Gruppo Editoriale Fabbri, Abbeville Press, *Photovision, Frankfurter Allgemeine Zeitung, Photo, Nippon Camera, Glamour,* etc., Modena, since 1961. **Recipient:** Photographic Society of Japan "The 150 Years of Photography Award," Tokyo 1992; Premier Guitarra 199, Cordoba 1993; **Agents:** Peter Riva, 116 East 95th Street, New York, New York 10128, U.S.A.; Goro Kuramochi, 1103, 2-33-8 Jingumae, Shibuya-ku, Tokyo 151, Japan. **Address:** Via R. Benzi 40, 41010 Cognento, Modena, Italy.

Individual Exhibitions:

1965	Subalpina Società Fotografica, Turin
1968	Sala di Cultura, Commune di Modena
1970	Centro Culturale Pirelli, Milan
	Centro Attività Visive, Palazzo dei Diamanti, Ferrara, Italy
	Sala Esposizioni, Isolato San Rocco, Reggio Emilia, Italy
	Saletta 70, Modena
	Galleria dell'Immagine/Il Diaframma, Milan
1971	Scuola di Belle Arti, Somma Lombardo, Italy
	Associazione Fotografica Napoletana, Naples
	Galleria Tempo, Bologna
	Palazzo del Turismo, Rovereto, Italy
1972	Palazzo dei Musei, Modena
	Fotogalerie Die Brücke, Vienna
	Galleria Il Camauro, Venice
	Neue Galerie, Klagenfurt, Austria
	Artemide Showroom, Milan
	Artemide Showroom, Naples
1973	Sala della Rocca, Vignola, Italy
	The Photographers' Gallery, London
1974	Galleria Documenta, Turin
	Canon Photo Gallery, Amsterdam
	Galleria dell'Immagine/Il Diaframma, Milan
	Galleria Il Broletto, Varese, Italy
	Galleria Il Gelso, Lodi, Italy
	Palazzo d'Accursio, Bologna
	Palazzo Strozzi, Florence
1975	Fotogalerie 5.6, Ghent
	Galeria Spectrum, Barcelona
	Galerie Nagel, Berlin
	Internationaal Cultureel Centrum, Antwerp
	Galerie Spectrum, Brussels
	Fotogalerie in Forum Stadtpark, Graz, Austria
1976	Sala delle Scuderie in Pilotta, Parma
	The Darkroom, Chicago
	Canon Photo Gallery, Geneva
	La Photogaleria, Madrid
	Mariani Showroom, Lucca, Italy
	Galerie Optica, Montreal
	Deja Vu Gallery, Toronto
	St. Gallen Photogalerie, St. Gallen, Switzerland
	Museu de Arte de Sao Paulo, Brazil
	Galleria del Cavallino, Venice
1977	Galleria Il Diaframma, Brescia, Italy
	Chiesa di Sn. Caterina, Treviso, Italy
	Salon de Actos, Alicante, Spain
	Palazzo Broletto, Novara, Italy
	Galleria Ghelfi, Vicenza, Italy
	Galleria La Città, Verona
	Arte Centrum, Bilbao, Spain
	Image Gallery, New Orleans
	Photo Art Gallery, Basle
	Galerie Dieuzaide, Toulouse
	The Photographers' Gallery, London
	Galerie Lange Irschl, Munich
	Galeria Spectrum Canon, Barcelona
1978	Nikon Gallery, Zurich
	The Photographic Gallery, Southampton, England
	Escuela Tecnica Superior de Arquitectura, La Coruna, Spain
	Galleria Il Diaframma, Milan
	Galleria d'Arte Moderna Emilio Mazzoli, Modena

	Galleria Spectrum Canon, Zaragoza, Spain
	Galeria Yem, Alcoy, Spain
1979	Galleria Il Vicola, Genoa
	The Photographic Gallery, Dublin
	Galleria Fonte d'Abisso, Modena
	Foto Cine Club San Paolo, Turin
	Cine Foto Club, Portomaggiore, Italy
	Palazzo Pallavicino, Busseto, Italy
	Fiaf 1979, Pescara, Italy
	The Photographic Gallery, South Yarra, Victoria, Australia
	Canon Photo Gallery, Amsterdam
	Gruppo Artistico Leonardo, Cremona, Italy
	Fotogalerij Paule Pia, Antwerp
	White Gallery, Tel Aviv
	Jane Corkin Gallery, Toronto
	Nuova Galleria, Treviso, Italy
	Galleria d'Arte Moderna Rondanini, Rome
	The Space Gallery, New York
	The Photographic Gallery, Melbourne
1980	Galleria Ideogramma, Turin
	Focus Gallery, San Francisco
	FNAC Forum, Paris
	Galerie Koffiehuisje, Hasselt, Belgium
	Centro Internacional de Fotografia, Barcelona
	Galleria Ikona, Venice
	G. Ray Hawkins Gallery, Los Angeles
	Galleria Diaframma, Brescia, Italy
	Galleria Fotografis, Bologna
	Galerie Fiolet, Amsterdam
	The Photographic Gallery, Dublin
	Galleria Grandangola, Padua
	Photographic Center, Athens
	Galleria d'Arte Moderna Rondanini, Rome
	Galleria Agora, Turin
1981	Forum Gallery, Nice
	Rizzoli Gallery, New York
	Jane Corkin Gallery, Toronto
	Silver Image Gallery, Seattle
	Galeria Photo Copy, La Coruna, Spain
	FNAC Centre Jaude, Clermont-Ferrand, France
	Nagase Salon, Tokyo
	Shadai Gallery, Tokyo
	Chiostro di San Nicolo, Spoleto, Italy
	Galerie Vogt, Zurich
	Galerie Viviane Esders, Paris
	Galleria Ikona, Venice
	Galleria Il Diaframma, Milan
	Photo Art Gallery, Frankfurt
1982	Forum Stadtpark, Graz, Austria
	Galerie Photo Art Basel, Basle, Switzerland
	Galleri Camera Obscura, Stockholm
	Galleria Rondanini, Rome
	Galerie Aspect, Brussels
1983	Galerie Le Reverbere, Lyon, France
	Canon Salon, Tokyo
	The Photographers' Gallery, London
	Galerie Viviane Esders, Paris
1984	Fondation Nationale de la Photographie, Lyon, France
	Museo de Bellas Artes, Caracas, Venezuela
	Musee Nicephore Niepce, Chalon sur Saone, France
	Galerie Municipale du Chateau d'Eau, Toulouse, France
	Akashiya Gallery, Hiroshima, Japan
	Syracuse University, Florence, Italy
1985	Circulo de Bellas Artes, Madrid
	Ken Damy Gallery, Milan
	White Gallery, Ghent, Belgium
	Musée Réattu, Arles, France
	Porin Taidemuseo, Finland
1986	Galerie Pro Photo, Nuremberg, West Germany
	Fuji Foto Salon, Tokyo

1987	Galleria Rondanini, Rome
	Galleria Fotochema, Prague
	Greg Foto gallery, Catania
1988	Hilton and Towers, Chicago
	Palazzo Sonvila, San Daniele, Italy
	Desireé, Washington, D.C.
1989	Instituto Culturale Italiano, Nairobi, Kenya
	Palazzo San Giorgio, Genoa, Italy
1990	Palazzo del Comune, Modena, Italy
	Ken Damy Foto Gallery, Milan
	Galleria Venice Design, Venice
	Kodak Photo Salon, Tokyo
	Museum of Photography, Helsinki
1991	Castello di San Giusto, Trieste
	Espace Photographique, Paris
	Biblioteca Comunale, Palermo
1992	Palazzo di Re Enzo, Bologna
	Instituta San Gabriele, Rome
	Milano Design, Milan
	Premio Sorrento, Sorrento, Italy
1993	Posada del Potro, Cordoba, Spain
	Palazzo della Ragione, Padua, Italy
	Galleria Railowsky, Valencia, Spain
1994	Museo Ken Damy, Brescia, Italy
	Federacio Andorrana de Fotografia, Andorra
	Acquario Romano, Rome
	Teatro San Martino, Buenos Aires

Selected Group Exhibitions:

1973	*Modern Experimental Color Photography,* The Photographers' Gallery, London
1974	*Aspects of Photography,* at *Photokina '74,* Cologne
1975	*Aspetti della Natura,* at *SICOF,* Milan
1978	*Tusen och En Bild,* Moderna Museet, Stockholm
1980	*19 Fotografos Italianos,* Museo de Arte Carrillo Gil, Mexico City
1981	*Astrazione e Realtà,* Galleria Flaviana, Locarno, Switzerland
1982	*Color as Form,* International Museum of Photography at George Eastman House, Rochester, New York
1984	*La Photographie Créative,* Pavillon des Arts, Paris
1985	*L'Autoportrait a l'epoque de la photographie,* Musée Cantonal des Beaux Arts, Lausanne, Switzerland (toured Europe)
1986	*Houston and the Rodeo,* Texas Commerce Tower, Houston, Texas
1987	*Pasion Et Jardins De Photographes,* Trianon de Bagatelle, Paris
	Jane Corkin Gallery, Toronto
	Fondation Vasarely, Aix en Provence, France
1988	*Collezione FNAC,* Hotel de la ville, Grenoble, France
	Studio Marconi, Milan
1989	*L'insistenza dello sguardo,* Museo Fortuny, Venice
	Manes, Prague
	Terra, acqua, aria, fuoco, Castelbolognese, Italy
	Immagini famose, Fiera del Mare, Genoa
	Light and Shadow, Printemps, Tokyo
1990	*Photographie Italienne Contemp,* Galerie Traing, Brussels
	International Viewpoints, Muesum of Fine Art, Houston
	OP Reportage, Canon Image Center, Amsterdam
1991	*Fotografia Italiana 1900-1990,* Museo Ken Dami, Brescia
	Toppan Collection, I.C.P., New York
	Campidoglio—Valentino—30 anni di Magia, Rome
	Galerie Faber, Vienna
1992	*Un'America, 4 Americhe,* Nuova Galleria del teatro, Parma
	Einladung, Galleria Prisma, Bolzano
	La Photographie dans le monde, Musée Nicéphore Niépce, Chalon-sur-Saône
	Dentro la citta altre le mura, Galleria di Palazzo Patrizi, Siena
	La collection photo de la FNAC, Epace Drouet d'Erlon, Reims
1993	*A la recherche du pere,* Espace des Halles, Paris

	7x7 Vizi Capitali, Archivio di Stato, Milan
	Palazzo del Turismo, Riccione
	Collection Van Gogh, Musée de la photographie, Mougins
	1960-1970: Photographers who Created a New Age, Metropolitan Museum, Tokyo
1994	*Provini d'Autore,* Galleria del centro Cult Francese, Rome
	Cappello nel Mondo, Palazzo Ghilini, Alessandria
	Chasanoff collection, Museum of Fine Art, Houston

Collections:

Museo della Fotografia, University of Parma; Galleria d'Arte Moderna, Ferrara, Italy; Bibliothèque Nationale, Paris; Musée Réattu, Arles, France; Musée Cantini, Marseilles; Musée d'Art et d'Histoire, Fribourg, Switzerland; Photographic Museum, Helsinki; Museum of Modern Art, New York; International Museum of Photography, George Eastman House, Rochester, New York; Art Museum, University of New Mexico, Albuquerque; The Israel Art Book Musem, Jerusalem; University of Texas, Austin, USA; National Gallery of Pechino, China; Collection Manuel Alvarez Bravo, Mexico City; Collection FNAC, Paris; Canadian Center of Photography, Toronto; Art Institute of Chicago; Piskin State Museum of Fine Arts, Moscow; Musée d'Art Modern, Paris; American Expresso Collection, Frankfurt; Collectio Unio Bank of Finland, Helsinki; Kyushu Industrial University, Tokyo.

Publications:

By FONTANA: Books—*Modena una Città,* with text by Pier Paolo Preti, Modena 1971; *Terra da Leggere,* with text by Pier Paolo Preti, Modena 1975; *Bologna: Il Volto della Città,* with text by Pier Luigi Cervellati, Modena 1975; *Franco Fontana,* with text by Giuliana Ferrari, Parma, Italy 1976; *Laggiù gli uomini,* with text by Enzo Biagi, Modena 1977; *Presenze Veneziane,* with text by Achille Bonito Oliva, Modena 1978; *Franco Fontana: Skyline,* with an introduction by Helmut Gernsheim, Milan and Paris 1978; *Paesaggio Urbano: Selezione d'Immagini,* with text by Angelo Schwarz, Monza, Italy 1980; *Photoedition 3: Franco Fontana,* Schaffhausen, Switzerland 1982; *I grandi fotografi: Franco Fontana,* with text by Achille Bonito Oliva and Giuliana Scime, Milan 1983; *Presenzassenza,* with text by Giuliana Scime, Monza 1983; *Meisterfotos Gestalten,* Munich 1983; *Fullcolor,* with text by Guy Mandery, Paris 1983; *Iprimi dieci ristoranti e alberghi d'Italia,* with introduction by Giovanni Agnelli and Giovanni Nuvoletti, Milan 1983; *Piscina,* Milan 1984; *Franco Fontana,* Tokyo 1984; *Landscape Photography,* with text by Gene Thornton, New York 1984; *EU 42,* with introduction by Paolo Portoghesi and G. Bilancioni, Rome 1984; *Emilia Romagna,* with text by C. Bonvicini, Milan 1986; *Università oggi,* with text by Paolo Portoghesi and others, Rome 1986; *Il Nudi di Franco Fontana,* Turin 1989; *Viaggio in Sicilia,* Bologna 1992; *Landscape Moments,* Modena 1994; *Landscape,* Franco Fontana and Mario Giacomelli, Bologna 1994.

On FONTANA: Books—*Immagini del Colore,* exhibition catalogue, by C. Bonvicini, P. Racanicchi, F. Vaccari and others, Modena, Italy 1968; *Subject: Landscape,* exhibition catalogue, by Pier Paolo Preti, Amsterdam and London 1974; *Photography Year,* by the Time-Life editors, New York 1975; *Bolaffi Arte,* Turin 1976; *British Journal of Photography Annual,* London 1979; *Contact Theory,* New York 1980; *Das Imaginare Photo Museum,* Cologne 1981; *Histoire Mondiale de la Photographie en Couleurs,* Paris 1981; *Farbe im Photo: Die Geschichte der Farbphotographie von 1861 bis 1981* by Fritz Binder, Gert Koshofer, Rolf Sachsse and others, Cologne 1981; *Color as Form: A History of Color Photography,* exhibition catalogue, with introduction by Robert A. Sobieszek, Rochester, New York 1982; *La Photographie Créative* by Jean-Claude Lemagny, Paris 1984; *Sammlung Gruber: Photographie des 20. Jahrhunderts,* exhibition catalogue, with foreword by Siegfried Gohr, Cologne 1984; *Franco Fontana,* exhibition catalogue, by Jean Dieuzaide, Toulouse, France 1984; *Franco Fontana,* Turin 1987; *Franco Fontana* by Flaminio Gualdoni, Milan 1994. **Articles**—"La Materia che non Vediamo" by Pier Paolo Preti in *Ottagono* (Milan), September 1972; "Si Puo Fare Ancora del Paesaggio? Franco Fontana" by Pier Paolo Preti in *Fotografia Italiana* (Milan), July 1974; "Paesaggio come Franco Fontana" by Giuseppe Turroni in *Nuova Fotografia* (Milan), June 1975; "Significato come Valore di Scambio" by A.C. Quintavalle in *Il Mulino* (Bologna), December 1975; "Nuove Realtà" by Antonio Pitta in *Ottagono* (Milan), September 1976;

"Franco Fontana" by Sean Callahan in *American Photographer* (New York), October 1978; "The Landscape as Nude" by David Steigman in *Popular Photography* (New York), December 1978; "Franco Fontana" by A.C. Quintavalle in *Zoom* (Paris), August 1979; "Ein Meister aus Modena" by Rolf Paltzer in *Art* (Hamburg), November 1979; "Landscapist" by Michael Edelson in *Newsweek* (New York), 15 September 1980; "A Lens to Serve a Vision" by David Livingston in *Maclean's* (Toronto), 6 April 1981; "Leçon de Couleurs" in *Photo Reporter* (Paris), July 1981.

*

My story as a photographer began in 1961, and my work then was connected to amateur circles.

At the beginning I was not following any specific line of research; I just photographed any subject around me that was beautiful in itself: sunsets, reflected light, etc. Anyone can recognize the beauty of nature, and I was nothing but a re-producer of images, a re-presenter of facts—things that were not mine. But behind the camera there was still no man, no discoverer of hidden realities.

Very slowly and with much humility I started to feel conscious of my own inner requirements, and my attention was concentrated on rustic dwellings, on windows, facades, walls corroded by time—investigating their materiality. This first conscious experiment marks the beginning of my personal research, aiming for a progressive essentiality, which I believe has been consistent in its development during all the years since then.

My best known work is on the natural landscape. I try to isolate, in space and time, that which is normally dispersed and mixed up with an infinity of details. This work of cleansing, of extracting a few essential elements from the entirety that presents itself to the human eye, has to do with one of my inner requirements: to achieve an harmonic unity through the elimination of all disturbing natural elements. In this way, a landscape is born which is made up by subtle relations of space, form, drawing and color.

The fascination of the image lies in the play between reality—the lens has registered what was actually in front of my camera—and seeming unreality. This is a clear example of how the camera should be at the service of man, and not vice versa.

As compared to other artistic forms, photography is the most castrating: between intention and realization the camera imposes its limits. The photographer is kept tied by a strong umbilical cord to a variety of alien situations: subject, light, time, color, etc. A photographer could hardly express his own creativeness if he had to live in a single room—unlike an author, a painter or a musician. The photographer has to do violence to reality, or at least to what is believed to be reality. In fact, reality, in its absolute signification, does not exist and escapes from our daily experience.

Accustomed as we are to rational analysis, we mortify imagination by preventing it from endowing the surrounding world with original and unconsuetudinary significance. Imagination is the great force that provokes, stimulates and puts images into action—and gives life to them by penetrating beneath the surface. The subjects and situations we photograph are a pretext for communicating our interior experiences. Our personal story appears through the images: a lamp is not merely a lamp, it loses its concrete connotations; in the moment we see it, the lamp becomes a projection of a part of ourselves.

The fascination of an image lies in the violence that created it, a violence which is necessary to shake off the mental attitudes that make our looking blind.

We are the bearers and witnesses of the only possible significance.

Objectivity is always and in any case destined to escape our grasp.

—Franco Fontana

*　　*　　*

With his investigations of the world of concrete forms, Franco Fontana overturns the erroneous and superficial conceptions we have of reality. That reality that surrounds us—that which we believe to be "truth"—is built on spatial relationships according to the rules of perspective: every object exists within the function of every other, and we perceive its position on the basis of successive planes. Amid all the visual information that the eye takes in at any

given time, Fontana emphasizes only certain details which are concealed in the whole so that we never "see" them.

He was attracted in the 1960s by the capacity of light to create new plastic forms which do not really exist, and he went on in the following years to refine his vision until he had removed from his work everything that was redundant. His picture is simple, but certainly not simplistic, pure in form and strictly balanced in color, showing us a representation of a reality existent but unknown. Fontana enables us to penetrate a new spatial dimension, freeing us from the physical and intellectual constrictions to which we are slaves.

And even if his pictures are often completely abstract—we lose the connotation of the subject represented and can no longer recognize it as something known and familiar—they are still a "record of reality." The old debate between those who argue for a pure photography and those who support freedom in the employment of the medium—that argument is settled, paradoxically, in Fontana's work: it is a representation of the real with no technical elaboration or manipulation during the photo-chemical-mechanical process. There is just his capacity to see, to select, that enables him to extract certain elements from the immense panorama of the concrete world. But he carries out a rigorous analysis of that world and provides us, in the photographic medium, with a tool for the free interpretation of it unprejudiced by cultural conditioning or social and environmental situations.

It is equally clear that his photographs, albeit a documentary record, do not conform to the commonly accepted meaning of that term, either in the kind of information they give us or in the unusual design of their composition. But Fontana extends the meaning of documentary photography, recording the vitality of a universe parallel to and intermixed with the universe more evident to our ordinary perception; and, at the same time, he also extends the use of the photographic medium, which in his hands reveals that other universe.

He may be regarded as an innovator of contemporary creative photography and as the author of a new visual language. His landscapes, assembled with the refinement of an extremely sensitive eye, represent a moment of intimate reflection on the tangible world; they have the quality of a biographical confession. His refusal to reproduce scenes of life as we know it—either contaminated nature or urban sprawl—and his preference for the unveiling of the secrets of the harmonious relationships contained in them, reveal a special way of thinking. Fontana uses photography to lay bare the emotions, sensations, anxieties and disturbances of an artist never content with the surface of things.

The "information" that he gives us is completely subjective; it awakens the mechanism of emotional intuition in us, enabling us to know ourselves, and especially the world we live in, more deeply.

Fontana's inimitable language nullifies the rules of ordinary perception and overturns conceptions of space and form, the bases of our visual culture. His forms exist in a new relation with space in which the perspective planes are abolished—and, in that, Fontana's picture is perfectly in line with the reality of the photographic object, which is of necessity bi-dimensional.

Even Fontana's partiality for using color underlines the function of analytical realism in his photography. It is always a natural color. Indeed, he never uses either filters or any other technical refinements, because "everything is there already in the infinite scenery of nature."

—Giuliana Scimé

FONTCUBERTA, Joan.

Nationality: Spanish. **Born:** Barcelona, 24 February 1955. **Education:** Studied journalism and advertising at the University of Barcelona, Faculty of Communications, 1971-77; self-taught in photography. **Career:** Photographer since 1972. Instructor, Grup Taller d'Art Fotogràfic, Barcelona, 1975-76, and Faculty of Communications, University of Barcelona, 1977-78. Since 1977, Instructor, CEI (Center for Image Studies), Barcelona; since 1980, Professor of Photography, Faculty of Fine Arts, University of Barcelona. Freelance exhibition curator, for the Spanish Ministry of Culture, the Catalan Autonomous Government and other institutions, since 1982. Columnist, *Nueva Lente* magazine, Madrid, 1975-78. Columnist, *El Correo Catalán* newspaper, Barcelona, since 1977, and *La Vanguardia* newspaper, Barcelona,

Iris Puffs **(iron-toned photogram on a family-size tissue paper), 1991 (original in colour).** Photograph by Joan Fontcuberta.

since 1979; Barcelona Correspondent, *American Photographer,* since 1980; Co-Founder and Co-Editor of *Photovision,* Madrid, since 1981. Co-Founder, Foto FAD, and editor of its publication *La Titafolla,* Barcelona, 1975; Co-Founder, Grup Alabern, Barcelona, 1976; Co-Founder, 1977, Vice-President, 1977-79, and editor of its publication *Fotodossier,* Anfa FAD, Barcelona. **Address:** Avda. Infanta Carlota 113, Barcelona 29, Spain.

Selected Individual Exhibitions:

1974	Sala Aixela, Barcelona
	Galería Spectrum, Barcelona
1975	La Photogalería, Madrid
1976	Galería Spectrum, Barcelona
1977	Canon Photo Gallery, Amsterdam
	Galerie Upsilon, Nantes, France
	Galería Tretze, Valencia
	Galería A, Vilafranca, Spain
1978	Canon Photo Gallery, Geneva
	Galerie 31, Vevey, Switzerland
	Galería Fotomanía, Barcelona
	Galerie Voir, Toulouse
	Galerie de l'Image, Liège
1979	Galerie Agathe Gaillard, Paris
	Il Laboratorio d'If, Palermo
	Galerie Trockenpresse, Berlin
	Galería Tretze, Valencia
	Fotogalerie Pennings, Eindhoven, Netherlands
	Work Gallery, Zurich
1980	Paule Pia Fotogalerij, Antwerp
	Canon Photo Gallery, Amsterdam
	The White Gallery, Tel Aviv
	Galerie 11, Nidau, Switzerland
	Photographic Center of Athens
1981	FNAC Gallery, Les Halles, Paris
	FNAC Gallery, Strasbourg
	Rudi Renner Fotogalerie, Munich
	Novum Fotogalerie, Hannover
	The Photographic Gallery, Cardiff
	ARPA Gallery, Bordeaux
	Centro Civico Irnerio, Bologna
	Galería 491, Barcelona
1982	Galleria II Diaframma-Canon, Milan
	Galleria Rondanini, Rome
	Galería Redor, Madrid
	Image Center for Photography, Aarhus, Denmark
	Galerie S.I.R.P., Royan, France
	Forum Stadtpark, Graz, Austria
1983	Galerie Pro Photo, Munich
	Galerie Municipale du Chateau d'Eau, Toulouse, France
	Galerie Zabriskie, Paris
	Galerie Junod, Lausanne, Switzerland
	Galería Visor, Valencia, Spain
	Atelier Yves Humbert, Nyon, Switzerland
	The Photographers' Gallery, Christchurch, New Zealand
	Fotogalleri, Lund, Sweden
	Galerie Jutta Rössner, Stuttgart
1984	Fotoforum, Bremen, West Germany
	Museo Comunale, Rimini, Italy
	Galerie Contretype, Brussels
	Museu d'Art, Sabadell, Spain
	Galería Guadalquivir, Seville, Spain
	Sala Arcs, Barcelona, Spain (toured Spain)
	Salzburg College, Austria
1985	Galerie XYZ, Ghent, Belgium
	Galería Redor, Madrid
	Galería Eude, Barcelona, Spain
	Galería Forum, Tarragona, Spain
	Galerie 52, Luxembourg
	Galería Alfos, Lleida, Spain
	La Polleria Immaginaria, Genoa, Italy

	Spazio Immagine, Bari, Italy
	Galleria Frank Paludetto, Turin, Italy
	Shadai Gallery, Tokyo
	Hochschule der Künste, West Berlin
	Sala dos Peiraos, Vigo, Spain
	Salzburg College, Austria
	Sala de Arte Granvia, Bilbao, Spain
	Centro de Estudios Fotograficos, Coimbra, Portugal
	International Museum of Photography at George Eastman House, Rochester, New York
1986	Zabriskie Gallery, New York
	Hadler/Rodriguez Gallery, Houston, Texas
	Presentation House Gallery, Vancouver, British Columbia
	Théâtre Municipal, Montpellier, France
	Galería Maeght, Barcelona, Spain
1987	Folkwang Museum, Essen
	Galerie Zabriskie, Paris
	Centro de Arte-Palacio Almudi (Murcia)
1988	Galerie Jütta RoBner, Stuttgart
	Zabriskie Gallery, New York
	The Photographers' Gallery, London
	The Museum of Modern Art, New York
1989	Perspektief, Rotterdam
	Galería Juana Mordó, Madrid
1990	Museet for Fotokunst, Odense
	Zeit Foto Co, Tokyo
	Museum of Natural History, Aarhus
	The Art Institute of Chicago, Chicago
1991	Galerie Zabriskie, Paris
	Lothar Albrecht Galerie, Frankfurt
	Gallery of Art, University of Missouri, Kansas City
	Lieberman & Saul, New York
	Zabriskie Gallery, New York
1992	Galería Angels de la Mota, Barcelona
	The Ansel Adams Center, San Francisco
	Parco Gallery, Tokyo
	Old Pueblo Museum, Tucson
	Midtown Plaza, Saskatoon, Canada
1993	Galeria Pedro Oliveira, Oporto
	Galerie Zabrinskie, Paris
	Lothar Albrecht Galerie, Frankfurt
	Galerie Beeld & Aambeeld, Enschede, Holland
	Cultureel Centrum Alden Biesen, Bilzen, Belgium
	Zabriskie Gallery, New York
1994	Palacio de Revillagigedo—Centro Internacional de Arte, Gijon

Selected Group Exhibitions:

1974	*Spanish Photographers,* Spectrum Gallery, Brussels
1976	*European Photography,* Allen Street Gallery, Dallas
1977	*Grup Alabern,* Galerie de l'Instant, Paris (travelled to Galleria Altre Immagini Politecnico, Rome)
1978	*New Spanish Photography,* at *Rencontres Internationales de la Photographie,* Arles, France
1979	*Die Zweite Avantgarde der Fotografia,* Fotogalerie 68, Hoensbroek, Netherlands
1980	*Photographia: La Linea Sottile,* Galleria Flaviana, Locarno, Switzerland
1981	*Photographer as Printmaker,* Ferens Art Gallery, Hull, Yorkshire (travelled to the Museum and Art Gallery, Leicester; Cooper Gallery, Barnsley; Castle Museum, Nottingham; Photographers' Gallery, London)
1982	*Four Spanish Photographers,* Santa Fe Center for Photography, New Mexico
1984	*Images Imaginées,* Musée Rimbaud, Cherleville-Mezières, France (travelled to the Centre Culturel, Cherbourg; University of Niigata, Japan)
1985	*The European Edge,* Museum for Photographic Arts, San Diego, California

1986	*Contemporary Spanish Photography,* University of New Mexico, Albuquerque
	4 Fotografia Catalani, Limonaia di Villa Corsi Salviati, Florence
1987	*Künstlichkeit und Wirklichkeit,* Appendix Galerie, Wuppertal
	After Franco, Marcuse Pfeiffer Gallery, New York
	Haute Sensibilité, Galerie d'Art du Centre Saint Vicent, Herblay, Paris
1988	*Fotovision, Projekt Fotografie nach 150 Jahren,* Spengel Museum, Hannover (travelled to Kunstraum im Messepalast, Vienna and Museum für Gestaltung, Zurich, 1989)
	Four Spanish Photographers, Tucson Art Museum, Tucson
1989	*On the Art of Fixing a Shadow,* The Art Institute of Chicago; National Gallery of Art, Washington; and Los Angeles County Museum of Art
	Photography Until Now, The Museum of Modern Art, New York; Cleveland Museum of Art
1990	*Natural History Recreated,* Woodstock Center for Photography, New York
	Corps de l'Image, Palais du Tau, Reims
1991	*La Photographie en miettes,* Musée National d'Art Moderne, Centre George Pompidou, Paris
1992	*More Than One Photography: Works Since 1980 from the Collection,* Museum of Modern Art, New York
	De la curiosité. Petite anatomie d'un regrad, Dazibao, Montreal
	Musa Museus, Palau de la Virreina, Barcelona
	La Ménagerie du Palais, Centre National de la Photographie, Paris
1993	*Curios et Mirabilia,* Château d'Oiron, France
	Flora Photographica, New York Public Library; Musée des Beaux Arts, Montreal
1994	*Barcelona a vol d'artista,* Centre de Cultura Contemporània, Casa de la Caritat, Barcelona
	Lessons in Life, The Art Institute, Chicago

Collections:

Fundació Joan Miró, Barcelona; Bibliothèque Nationale, Paris; Musée Réattu, Arles, France; Galerie Municipale à Chateau d'Eau, Toulouse; Musée d'Art Moderne, Brussels; Polaroid Collection, Amsterdam; Metropolitan Museum of Art, New York; Centro Cultural Hidalgo, Michuca, Mexico; Museum Folkwang, Essen, West Germany; San Francisco Museum of Modern Art; Museum of Modern Art, New York; Danish National Library, Copenhagen; ShadaiGallery, Tokyo Polytechnic, Tokyo; Museum für Kunst und Gewerge, Hamburg; Centre National de la Photographie, Paris; Center for Creative photography, Tucson; Museo Español de Arte Contemporáneo, Madrid; Zeit-Foto/Green Museum, Tokyo; Fons d'Art de la Generalitat de Catalunya, Barcelona; Museet for Fotokunst, Odense; Museum of Fine Arts, Houston; The Art Institute, Chicago; Musée d'Art Moderne—Centre Georges Pompidou, Paris.

Publications:

By FONTCUBERTA: Books—*Joan Fontcuberta: Fotograflas,* Zaragoza, Spain 1976; *Derrière l'Arbre (Duchamp no ha comprendido Rembrandt),* Barcelona 1976; *Platja 30.9.75,* Barcelona 1976; *Pintades,* Barcelona 1977; *Joan Brossa: Poems Objecte,* with Brossa, Barcelona 1978; *Photographie Catalane des années 30,* Paris 1982; *Wolfgang Weber,* Barcelona 1984; *Fotografia Mediterranea,* Barcelona 1984; *Idas y Chaos: Aspectos de las vanguardias fotograficas en España,* Madrid 1984, as *Idas and Chaos: Trends in Spanish Photography 1920-1945,* New York 1986; *Estetica Fotografica,* Barcelona 1984; *Josep Renau, fotomontador,* Mexico City 1985; *Creation Photographique en Espagne: 1968-88,* Marseille 1988; *Creació Fotogràfica a Espanya 1968-88,* Barcelona 1989; *La Fotografia: Conceptos y Procedimientos,* Barcelona 1990. **Articles**—"La Photo Catalane et ses Fantômes" in *Contrejour* (Paris), March/April 1977; "La Subversion Photographique de la Réalité" in *The Village Cry* (Basle), September 1977; "La Fotografia Revisa els seus Origens" in *Avui* (Barcelona), 11 June 1978; "Contravisiones: la subversión fotografica de la realidad" in *Nueva Lente* (Madrid), no. 75, 1978, reprinted in

Fotografie (Göttingen), August 1978; "Apologìa de la 5a Generación" in *Nueva Lente* (Madrid), no. 76/77, 1978; "La Fotografia contra la Realtà" in *Il Diaframma: Fotografia Italiana* (Milan), August 1978; "Participación Española en Arles" in *Estudios pro Arte* (Barcelona), October 1978; "Fotograflas al Cuadrado" in *Batik* (Barcelona), April 1979; "Fotografía Española y la Búsqueda del Tiempo Perdido" in *Batik* (Barcelona), June 1979; "Arte y Fotografia: El Intelecto Contra la Sensibilidad" in *El Correo Catalan* (Barcelona), 3 November 1979; "Percepción y Vanguardia Fotografica" in *Zoom* (Madrid), November 1979; "Photography in Spain: An Effort of Private Initiative" in *Print Letter* (Zurich), March 1980; "Spanish Photography in the 80s: Normalization or Loss of Identity" in *European Photography* (Göttingen), April 1980; "1965-1976: La Consolidacion de la Fotografia Creativa" in *Enciclopedia Espasa: Supplement,* Barcelona 1980; "Pla Janini: Axis of Catalan Photography" in *Camera* (Lucerne), December 1980; "Introduccio a la fotografia catalana dels anys 30" in *Anals* (Barcelona), no. 1, 1983; "Mediterranean Photography" in *European Photography* (Göttingen), October/December 1984; "Fotografia estenopeica" in *Photovision* (Madrid), no. 15, 1986; "Countervision: Zeus's eye against Zeiss' eye" in *European Photography* (Göttingen), October/December 1986; "Opera Prima. Spain's New Photography" in *European Photography* (Göttingen), no. 35, July/August/September 1988; "Cuando el arte engulle a la fotografia" in *Lapiz* (Madrid), no. 60, 1989; "Arte, ciencia y naturalezas" in *Lapiz* (Madrid) no. 63, 1989; "Fauna: Conception and Genesis" in *ArtLetter* (Los Angeles), no. 1, 1990; "Fauna: de la impostura a la fe" in *Nexus* (Barcelona), Fall 1990; "Verdad, tiempo, memoria" in *Lapiz* (Madrid) no. 72, 1990; "Del pigmento a la luz" in *III Biennal Europea/Facultats i Escoles Superiors d'Art* (Barcelona), 1991 ; "La generación espejismo, la Barcelona fantasma" in *Lapiz* (Madrid), no. 88, 1992; "Imágenes para un epitafio" in *Sobre Santiago: Tres de Magnum* (Santiago de Compostela), 1993; "Fotografia como pecado" in *El teléfono en la fotografia* (Madrid), 1993; "Col.lecionar per a la història" in *Imatges Escollides. La Col.lecció Cualladó* (Valencia), 1993; "Reconfigurar la experiència" in *Papers* (Barcelona) no. 5, 1994; "Videncia y evidencia" in *Luna Córnea* (Mexico DF), no. 5, 1994.

On FONTCUBERTA: Books—*Photographer as Printmaker,* exhibition catalogue, with texts by Gerry Badger, Peter C. Bunnell and Ansel Adams, London 1981; *Joan Fontcuberta,* exhibition catalogue, by Jean Dieuzaide, Toulouse, France 1983; *Joan Fontcuberta, fotografies,* Barcelona 1984; *Herbarium,* text by Vilém Flusser, Barcelona 1984, Göttingen 1985; *Dr Ameisenhaunfen's Fauna,* text by Pere Formiguera and Joan Fontcuberta, Göttingen 1987; *Animal Trouvé,* Bilbao, Spain 1985; *Herbarium,* portfolio, with texts by Jean-Francois Chevrier and Pere Formiguera, Barcelona 1986; *Contemporary Spanish Photography* by Betty Hahn, Albuquerque 1987; *Botanica: L'Essence des Formes* by Pierre Gascar, Paris 1987; *Joan Fontcuberta: Science and Fiction,* Flushing (New York) 1989; *Artists who Love Nature: from Barbizon School to Contemporary Photography,* by Yoshio Abe, Osaka 1990; *Signs of Life,* by Melissa E Feldman, Philadelphia 1990; *Fauna Secreta,* with text by Hiroshi Aramata, Pere Alberch and Pere Formiguera-Joan Fontcuberta, Tokyo 1991; *Costel lacions,* text by Joan Durán and Anatxu Zabalbeascoa, Lleida 1994. **Articles**—"Joan Fontcuberta, en quête du point sublime" by José Vigo in *Contrejour* (Paris), no. 2, 1976; "Joan Fontcuberta" by Roberto Salbitani in *Progresso Fotografico* (Milan), June 1977; "Joan Fontcuberta" by Daniel Giralt-Miracle in *Avui* (Barcelona), 15 January 1978; "Joan Fontcuberta" by Josep Rigol in *Zoom* (Madrid), no. 20, 1978; "Joan Fontcuberta en Fotomania" by Matias Antolin in *Ozono* (Madrid), June 1978; "Fantástico Fontcuberta" by Jorid Socias in *La Calle* (Madrid), 2-8 January 1979; "Fontcuberta chez Agathe Gaillard" by Hervé Guibert in *Le Monde* (Paris), 24 January 1979; "La Fotografia Miente" by A. Torralva and J. Valenzuela in *Valencia Semanal,* 18-25 March 1979; "Fontcuberta Fotografa anche la Solitude" by Gian Mauro Costa in *Il Diario* (Palermo), 23 March 1979; "Raffinate Techniche di Manipolazione" by Eduardo Rebulla in *L'Ora* (Palermo), 30 March 1979; "Erwachen aus Einerlangen Agonie" by Rolf Paltzer in *Art* (Hamburg), no. 1, 1979; "Fontcuberta" by Francesc Miralles in *Zoom* (Paris), no. 67, 1979; "Joan Fontcuberta: Animalesche Visionen" by Jörg Kirchbaum in *Zoom* (Munich), March 1980; "Fontcuberta" in *Camera* (Lucerne), November 1980; "Le Bestiare de Joan Fontcuberta" by Christian Caujolle in *Contact* (Paris), May 1981; "A propos de Joan Fontcuberta, quelques remarques sur le réalisme et le surréalisme en photographie" by Claude Pitot in *ARPA* (Burdeus), 7 May 1981; "Arriba, Joan Fontcuberta" by Christian Caujolle in *Liberation* (Paris),

30 November 1983; "La otra cara del progreso, vista por Joan Fontcuberta" by Marina Pino in *El Correo Catalan* (Barcelona), 11 November 1984; "Darwin, los Zoos y la Fotografia" by Derek Bennett in *Ikuspen. Comunicación visual* (Bilbao), September 1985; "Joan Fontcuberta: la fotografia como ensayo intelectual" by Pilar Comesana in *Faro de Vigo* (Vigo), 10 November 1985; "Joan Fontcuberta: la ficcion de la fotografia" by Manuel Clemente in *Trama Art* (Barcelona), no. 6, 1986; "Joan Fontcuberta: L'Herbier Imaginaire" by Jean-Louis Godefroid in *Clichés*, Brussels, May 1984; "Der magische Augenblick. Interview mit Joan Fontcuberta" by Helmut Brandt in *Die Tageszeitung*, Frankfurt 18 April 1984; "Joan Fontcuberta" by Andreas Müller-Pohle in *XYZ Fotografie*, Gant, January 1985; "El ojo mecánico: Paradoja y Fotografia en el Herbarium de Joan Fontuberta" by Luis Rodriguez Baena in *Actas Noesis* (Terol), April 1987; "Un Bestaire en Peau de Lapin" by Louis Mesplé in *Liberation* (Paris), 27 November 1987; "O Monstruario de Joan Fontcuberta" by Bernardo Pinto in *Journal da Lisboa* (Lisboa), 14 December 1987; "Sales Bêtes! Le Bestiare Fantastique de Joan Fontcuberta" by Jerôme Saglio in *Le Monde* (Paris), December 1987; "Entdeckt. Ameisenhaufens Fauna" by Volker Rapsch in *Landshuter Zeitung* (Frankfurt), 22 April 1988; "El Bestiario Fantástico de Fontcuberta y Formiguera o el fotógrafo como fingidor" by Elena Hevia in *ABC* (Barcelona), 7 June 1988; "A Furry-footed Fish and Other Gallery Rogues" by Roberta Smith in *The New York Times* (New York), 29 July 1988; "Frottograms" by Roberta Smith in *The New York Times* (New York) 29 July 1988; "Genetik und generative Fotografie" by Vilém Flusser in *Fotografische Akademie Bulletin* (Bielefeld), September 1988; "Entretien avec Joan Fontcuberta" by Chantal Grande in *Frottogrammes*, Paris November 1988; "Frottogrammes de Joan Fontcuberta" by Pilar Parcerisas in *Avui* (Barcelona), 11 December 1988; "Herbarium" by Agnés Clerc in *Nueva Imagen* (Pamplona), January 1989; "Dr Ameisenhaufen's Fauna" by Giuliana Scimé in *Progresso Fotografico* (Mila), February 1989; "Hier Is Iets Grondig Mis" by Mariette Havemann in *Telegraaf* (Rotterdam), May 1989; "Weird Science: Animal Quackers" by David Cary Tuck in *Taxi* (New York), May 1989; "Arti et Scientiae" by Midas Dekkers in *Perspektief* (Rotterdam), June 1989; "El Bestiario como parodia" by Julià Guillamon in *La Vanguardia* (Barcelona), 4 September 1989; "Fauna Secreta, una exposició insólita" in *Revista de Catalunya* (Barcelona), September 1989; "Joan Fontcuberta y Pere Formiguera" by Jeffrey Swartz in *Arena* (Madrid), December 1989;"Joan Fontcuberta" by Manuel Santos in *Lápiz* (Madrid), 1989; "Von den kunstlerischen Strategien der Falsifikation zur allmaehlichen Verfertigung der Kunst in den Etagen der Bank" by Peter Dimke in *Künstlich* (Barterode), 1989; "Clichés Rigolades, Mise en Scène de Vertige et les Mondes Extrapoles de Fontcuberta" by Edouard Waintrop in *Liberation* (Paris), 17 March 1990; "Una visió plurisensorial de la Fotografia" by Pilar Parcerisas in *Avui* (Barcelona), 22 August 1990; "Joan Fontcuberta. Les Voies de l'Image" by Pierre Stiwer in *Café Crème*, Luxembury, December 1990; "A Vast Dialogue Between Nature and Culture" by A.D. Coleman in *Journal of Contemporary Art,* New York April 1991; "Seeking the Reality that Lurks in the Shadows" by Charles Hagen in *The New York Times* (New York), 2 June 1991; "En Bildernas Ateruppfinnare" by Cecilia Anderson in *Svenska dagbladet* (Estocolm) 3 August 1991; "Joan Fontcuberta" by Alisa Tager in *Arts Magazine* (New York), September 1991; "La naturaleza simulada o la naturaleza del simulacro" by Anatxu Zabalbeascoa in *La Fotografia* (Barcelona), December 1991; "Estem en condicions de revisar la Fotografia" by Isidre Estévez in *Diari de Barcelona* (Barcelona) 22 January 1992; "En la huyella está el unico valor testimonial de la Fotografia" by Oscar Fontrodona in *ABC* (Barcelona), 31 January 1992; "Madonna Inn Majestic, de Joan Fontcuberta" by Angels Vilana in *Diari de Barcelona* (Barcelona), 8 January 1992; "Joan Fontcuberta: Foto-Ficción" by Pepa Bueno in *Elle* (Madrid), February 1992; "Joan Fontcuberta" by Anatxu Zabalbeascoa in *Art Forum* (New York), March 1992; "Joan Fontcuberta" by Task Wanatabe in *Gulliver* (Tokyo), April 1992; "Joan Fontcuberta" by Celia Montolio in *Lápiz* (Madrid), April 1992; "Joan Fontcuberta Interview" by Masa Sai in *Asahi Camera,* Tokyo November 1992; "Fauna Secreta" by Akiko Miyeda in *Moe* (Tokyo), December 1992; interviews:—"Der Magische Augenblick" by Helmut Brandt in *Die Tageszeitung* (Frankfurt), 18 April 1984; "A Fotografia nao e Servil em Relaçao a Realidade" by Bernardo Pinto in *Jornal da Lisboa* (Lisboa), November 1987; "Joan Fontcuberta: El tema de la subversión de la Realidad" by Vitor Vaquero in *No Artes e Ideas* (Vigo), December 1987; "Entrevista: Joan Fontcuberta" by Josep Rigol in *Camera International* (Madrid), May 1988; "A Vast Dialogue Between Nature and Culture" by A D Coleman in *Journal of Contemporary Art* (New York), April 1991; "Reviving the Exquisite Corpse" by Diane Neumaier in *Afterimage* (Rochester), April 1991; "Más allá de la Fotografia" by Jorge Ribalta in *ADGráfica* (Barcelona), February 1992; "La Veritat a través de la Falsedat" by Anatxu Zabalbeascoa in *Diari de Barcelona* (Barcelona), 9 February 1992.

*

The photographer is, in my opinion, a specialist in looking. His mission is to filter his own vision of the world and to offer a personal view in which he firstly says something about himself and then something of his times and their social forces.

In my own work I am interested in transmitting, above all, an atmosphere of mystery. I believe that all means to this end are valid, from the distortions required to express an oneiric world, including the distillation of enigma itself, to the incongruities produced by chance in representing the same reality.

Recently, this concern has been prevalent in my work. I think it is ascribable to a certain development—or, at least, to a certain maturity—in photographic language. Previously, my images were more direct and shocking; later, they possibly reached a more subtle level, which demanded the definite, personal, and poetic interpretation of the spectator. To me, participation by the spectator is important: the creative cycle in the visual arts is completed through the artist-audience symbiosis; it adds new significance to the work; it helps to make it even richer. In this sense I see photography as a stimulation of the imagination of the spectator. This is a part of the philosophy of "open photography," which is evocative, as opposed to "closed" or descriptive photography—for instance, photojournalism or the photography of advertisements.

Formally I pursue two basic interests: composition (that is, the design and placement of elements in space) and texture. Composition is the vital element in the translation of sensations into silver images. I use texture afterwards to increase the sensual charge of the image. It is vital for me to furnish my work with this "sensual tension." That is what drives me to take a photograph of determined subjects in a determined manner.

—Joan Fontcuberta

*　　*　　*

Until a few years ago Spain was considered to be one of the last bastions of that original, classic surrealism found chiefly under authoritarian political regimes and in isolation from international evolution in the arts—a surrealism whose obsolete weapons seem to us still appropriate only where they are directed against an even more obsolete kind of society. Since the death of Franco there has been a change in Spain's socio-cultural conditions towards a progressive opening up and liberalization. And so opportunities have developed for artists and photographers to broaden their range of themes and to refine their repertoire of expression. Joan Fontcuberta has not only analysed and systematically expressed the changed conditions of Spanish photography; he also visibly reflects them in his own photographic work.

Fontcuberta's early works in surrealistic style between 1973 and 1976 are simple, direct and, at times, based on an unequivocal idea: a bird leaving behind it the vapour trails of a jet fighter; a hand rising from a flower pot being cut off by hedge shears; a man stabbing himself in the forehead with a fork—shock montages that provoke and challenge the spectator unawares, which also soon yield their "mystery."

Fontcuberta himself describes as an important development in perception and maturity his ability to give up by degrees such artificial, staged and manipulated subjects and to express his ideas in a more subtle manner. He discovered that the surreal, the mysterious, the enigmatic do not need to be constructed but are present in visible reality itself. After 1976 his works show first of all gloomy arrangements in which snakes and fishes, ivy and moss occur as elements of a complex symbolism; the gentle hint replaces the loud accusation, the poetic cypher takes the place of the direct provocation. And in his portfolio "Animals," completed in 1977, and in his work after 1978 he has finally given up artificial arrangement; direct vision now determines his pictures. The visual estrangement changes to ever more frequent experimental methods to win from his subjects—found in museums, parks and zoos—a sometimes magical, sometimes fantastic, but always disturbing, enigmatic and provocative vision. The photographer's eye takes over the task previously performed by the process of thought.

In his book *Herbarium,* published in 1985, Fontcuberta has finally applied what might be called a "post-modern" stratagem. What at first appears to be a collection of Blossfeldt's botanical photographs, at a closer look turns out to be the result of photographically created mutations: it is not Blossfeldt being revived here, it is a recycled Blossfeldt.

From the first shock pictures of the '70s to the ironic understatements in his most recent works, Fontcuberta has developed a repertoire of subversionary tools, whose theoretical basis and maxims have been formulated in his theory of *countervision.* According to this, everything amounts to one point: to present things as a contradiction to prevailing concepts of reality and to interpret the world contrary to its established ideologies.

—Andreas Müller-Pohle

FOX, Anna.

Nationality: British. **Born:** Alton, Hampshire, 9 September 1961. **Education:** Attended Bedales School, Hampshire, 1972-77; Peter Symmonds 6th Form, Hampshire, 1977-79; West Surrey College of Art and Design, Foundation Course, 1977-80; studied photography, West Surrey College of Art and Design, 1983-86, B.A. (Hons) 1986. **Family:** Partner: Kitt Parsons, since 1986; children: Felix and Louis Fox. **Career:** Worked as an insurance agent and catering assistant, 1980-83; freelance documentary photographer, since 1986; part-time lecturer in photography, since 1989. Member of Format Agency, 1993. **Recipient:** Second Prize, Deutsche Leasing Award for European Photography, 1993. **Address:** 41 Hewitt Road, Haringay, London N8 OBS, England.

Individual Exhibitions:

1988	Camerawork, London
1989	Espace St Cyprien, Toulouse, France
	Eigen + Art, Leipzig, Germany
	Photography Festival, Vigo, Spain
	Festival of Photography, Helsinki, Finland
1990	The Photographers' Gallery, London
1991	*Les Rencontres Photographiques en Bretagne,* France
	Portfolio Gallery, Edinburgh
1992	*Primavera,* Barcelona, Spain
	Tarazona Festival of Photography, Spain
	ARAP, Bordeaux, France
1993	Galeria Spectrum, Zaragoza, Spain
	Worthing Museum and Art Gallery
1994	The Edge Gallery, London
	Braga Festival of Photography, Portugal
	Vigo Festival of Photography, Spain

Selected Group Exhibitions:

1987	The Museum of London
1989	*Through the Looking Glass,* Barbican Art Gallery, London
	Sun Life Awards, National Museum of Photography, Film and Television, Bradford
1990	*Triennale de la Photographie,* Charleroi, Belgium
1991	*San Francisco Photoscape*
	The Fourth Wall, Amsterdam
	The Mappin Gallery, Sheffield
	The Untitled Gallery, Sheffield
1992	*Festival of Photography,* Estonia and Lithuania
	Mai de la Photo, Rheims, France
	ICI Fox Talbot Awards, The National Portrait Gallery, London
1993	*Documentary Dilemmas,* Sao Paulo, Brazil (travelled to the Dublin Gallery of Photography, 1994)
	Academy of Arts, Berlin
	Royal Photographic Society, Bath
	Deutsche Leasing Awards, Frankfurt

1994	*Positive View,* The Saatchi Gallery, London
	Viewfindings, Newlyn Art Gallery, Penzance; The Watershed, Bristol
	Warworks, Rotterdam Biennale
1995	*Warworks,* Victoria and Albert Museum, London

Collections:

The National Museum of Photography, Film and Television, Bradford; The Royal Photographic Society, Bath; The Museum of London; The British Council; Photographie Forum, Frankfurt; Department of Cultural Affairs, Toulouse; Musée de la Photographie, Charleroi; Galerie le Lieu, Lorient; The Michael Wilson Collection; ARAP, Bordeaux; Victoria and Albert Museum, London.

Publications:

By FOX: Book—*Workstations,* London 1988. **Film**—*Moving Stills,* Channel 4 television film, 1989.

On FOX: Books—*Warworks* by Val Williams, exhibition catalogue, London 1994; *Viewfindings,* by Liz Wells, exhibition catalogue, Bristol 1994. **Article**—"Village People" by Val Williams in *The Guardian* (London), 13 November 1993.

*

In 1986 I photographed the town of Basingstoke. I wanted to convey what it was like to live in a new town which became successful in the consumerist eighties and occupied the no-man's-land between the city and the countryside.

In the late 1980s I began documenting office life in London, aiming to explore the hierarchies of the workplace, and became fascinated by the aggression which fuelled success.

My series of photographs of the small village of Compton in West Sussex looked at the reality which lies behind the rural idyll, and explored the lives of wealthy retirees.

Since 1990 I have been photographing weekend wargames in the south of England for the project "Friendly Fire." My primary concern is to photograph ordinary people in ordinary places.

—Anna Fox

*   *   *

In 1986, as a second year student of photography, Anna Fox undertook a work placement with me at *Camerawork* magazine (based in the East End of London). The magazine subsequently folded but Anna's link with *Camerawork* resurfaced in the form of her first major project, *Workstations,* which was commissioned and exhibited there.

Her work falls within the new colour documentary tradition now established as, internationally, perhaps the best-known strand of contemporary British photography. As such, the influence of Martin Parr in supporting and promoting her work should be acknowledged. Anna Fox is the most prominent woman photographer within the younger group who could loosely be defined as the new generation of documentarians, those who grew up associating colour with documentary practices. Her work always stands out in exhibitions. She shoots with confidence, very close-up, and is never afraid to experiment with use of words, or shifts in scale, in order to further fuel the rhetoric of her imagery.

Given her energy and commitment, and her willingness to take risks, it should come as no surprise that some of her more recent work is in black and white. *The Village,* shot in 1992, was shown as a series of black and white framed photographs accompanying a slide-tape installation. Her concern, as always, is with people and everyday occurrences whether in the office, in the village, or enjoying leisure pursuits such as *Wargames* (in which participants dress up as soldiers and engage in pretend military pursuits). Her eye is always upon the details and paradoxes of social behaviour. Broader political ramifications are not entirely lost. (*Wargames* includes an image of Margaret Thatcher

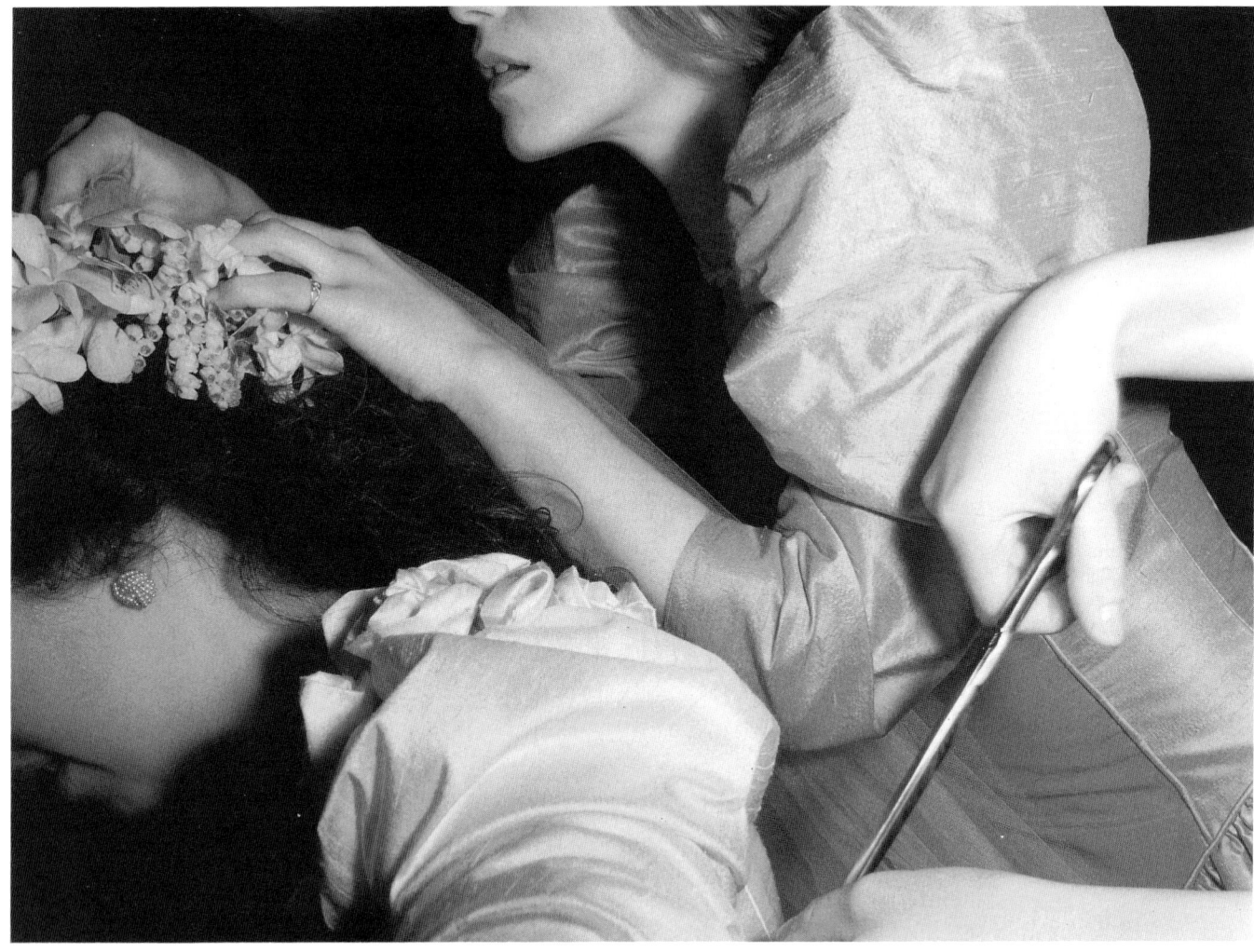

From the series *The Village*, 1992 (original in colour). Photograph ©Anna Fox.

as target.) But her work is never strident, and always focuses primarily upon the human as individual.

—Liz Wells

FRANCK, Martine.

Nationality: Belgian. **Born:** Antwerp, 2 April 1938. **Education:** Attended primary schools in New York and Arizona, 1942-44, and Heathfield School, Ascot, England, 1947-54; studied at the University of Madrid, 1956-57, and the Ecole du Louvre, Paris, 1958-63. **Family:** Married the photographer Henri Cartier-Bresson, *q.v.,* in 1970. **Career:** First photographs, in China, Japan, and India, 1963; photographic assistant to Eliot Elisofon and Gjon Mili, Time-Life Photo Laboratories, Paris, 1964; freelance photographer, working for *Life, Fortune, Sports Illustrated, New York Times, Vogue,* etc., Paris, since 1965; also, photographer for the Théâtre du Soleil co-operative, Paris, since 1965. Member, Vu photographers agency, Paris, 1970-71. Founder Member, Viva photographers Agency, Paris, 1972-79; Associate Member, 1980, and Member since 1983, Magnum Photos co-operative agency, Paris. **Address:** c/o Magnum Photos, 5 Passage Piver, 75011, Paris, France.

Individual Exhibitions:

1971	*Le Theatre du Soleil,* Galerie Rencontre, Paris
1974	*La Paroisse St.-Pierre de Chaillot,* Chaillot-Galliera, Paris
	Le Quartier Beaubourg, Centre Georges Pompidou, Paris
1978	Carlton Gallery, New York
1979	Pentax Gallery, Tokyo
	Northern Images, Side Gallery, Newcastle upon Tyne
	Photogalerie Portfolio, Lausanne
1980	Galerie A.M.C., Mulhouse, France
	Galerie Agathe Gaillard, Paris
1981	Musée Nicéphore Niepce, Chalon-sur-Saône, France
1982	Galerie Municipale du Château d'Eau, Toulouse, France
1983	*Des Femmes et la Creation,* Maison de la Culture, Le Havre, France
1984	Maison Descartes, Amsterdam
1985	*Portraits,* Centre Georges Pompidou, Paris
1986	Galerie A.R.P.A., Bordeaux, France
1987	Centro Culturale Pier Paolo Pasolini, Agrigento, Sicily
1988	*65 Portraits,* Maison de la Culture, Amiens
	Le Théâtre du Soleil, Centre Culturel Français, Berlin
	Portraits, Galerie Nikon, Zurich
1989	*De Temps en Temps,* Centre National de la Photographie, Paris
1990	*De Temps en Temps,* Almeria, Spain
1991	*Des métiers et des femmes,* FNAC, Paris

Kyabje Kalou Rimpoche, During His Enthronement Celebration, Sonada Monastery, India, **1993.** Photograph ©Martine Franck/Magnum.

Retrospective, 150 Photographs, Taipei Fine Arts Museum,
Taiwan
Mannheim Kunstverein, Germany
1992   *Retrospective, 150 Photographs,* Museo d'Arte
Contempeoraneo, Santiago, Chile; Institut Français, Buenos
Aires, Argentina
1993   *Le Théâtre du Soleil,* Bradford, England

Selected Group Exhibitions:

1973   *Viva: Familles en France,* Galleria Il Diaframma, Milan
(travelled to the French Consulate, New York; The
Photographers' Gallery, London; Internationaal Cultureel
Centrum, Antwerp; and Optica Gallery, Montreal)
1974   *There Is No Female Eye,* Neikrug Galleries, New York (toured
the United States)
1976   *French Photography,* French Consulate, New York (toured the
United States)
1977   *Le Photojournalisme,* Musée Galliera, Paris
1979   *Paris 1979: Les Parisiens,* Salon de la Photo, Paris
1980   *Jeune Photographie,* Foundation Nationale de la
Photographie, Lyons
1981   *Four French Photographers,* Friends of Photography, Carmel,
California
1982   *Photographier le Theatre,* Maison Jean Vilar, Avignon, France
1984   *Six photographes chez Le Corbusier,* Centre Georges
Pompidou, Paris
1985   *Magnum Concert,* Musée d'Art et d'Histoire, Fribourg,
Switzerland
1987   *Magnum 40th Anniversary*
1994   *Couvent des Cordeliers,* Magnum Cinema, Paris

Collections:

Bibliothèque Nationale, Paris; Ministère de la Culture, Paris; Ministère des
Affaires Etrangères, Paris; Musée Cantini, Marseilles; Musée Nicéphore
Niepce, Chalon-sur-Saône, France; Museum of Modern Art, New York;
Metropolitan Museum of Art, New York; Musée d'Art Moderne de la Ville de
Paris.

Publications:

By FRANCK: Books—*Etienne Martin, Sculpteur,* with text by Michel
Ragon, Brussels 1970; *La Sculpture de Cardenas,* with text by Jose Pierre,
Brussels 1971; *Le Théâtre du Soleil: 1789,* Paris 1971; *Le Théâtre du Soleil:
1793,* Paris 1972; *Martine Franck,* with preface by Ariane Mnouchkine, Paris
1976; *Quartier Beaubourg,* exhibition catalogue, Paris 1977; *Les Luberons,*
with text by Yves Berger, Paris 1978; *Le Temps de Vieillir,* with text by Robert
Doisneau and Dr. L. Kaprio, Paris 1980; *I grandi fotografi: Martine Franck,*
with text by Vera Feyder, Milan 1983; *Martine Franck: des Femmes et la
Creation,* Le Havre, France 1983; *De temps en temps,* preface by Claude Roy,
Paris 1988; *Portraits,* text by Yves Bonnefoy, Amiens 1988; *Le College de
France,* Paris 1995. **Articles—**"Le Theatre du Soleil: Shakespeare" in
Double Page (Paris), no. 21, 1982; "Le Theatre du Soleil: Shakespeare" in
Double Page (Paris), no. 32, 1984; "L'Indiade," text by Hélène Cixous, in
Double Page (Paris), no. 49, 1987; "La Famille," text by Jacques Rivette, in
Du, No. 5, (Switzerland), 1994.

On FRANCK: Books—*Jeune Photographie,* exhibition catalogue, with
introduction by Bernard Chardère, Paris 1980; *Martine Franck,* by Vera
Feyder and Attilio Colombo, Milan 1982; *Madrid Visto par. . . . ,* Madrid
1994; *Portraits de Mots,* Paris 1994. **Articles—**"Martine Franck" in *Leica
Photography* (New York), vol. 27, no. 1, 1974; "Martine Franck" in *Creative
Camera* (London), November 1974; "Martine Franck" by Anna Farova in
Revue Fotografie (Prague), no. 2, 1976; "Martine Franck" by Shoji Yamagishi
in *Mainichi Camera* (Tokyo), June 1976; "Martine Franck" in *Camera*
(Lucerne), June 1976; "Martine Franck" in *Zoom* (Paris), November 1977;
"Portrait: Martine Franck" in *Le Nouveau Photo Cinema* (Paris), April 1979;
"Martine Franck" in *Asahi Pentax Annual,* Tokyo 1979; "Le Temps de

Vieillir" in *Photo* (Paris), October 1980; "Martine Franck" in *Photography
Annual,* New York 1982; "Martine Franck: Tory Island," in *Photographers
International* (Taipei), February 1995.

*

If we look at the history of photography we discover the continual presence
of women. Perhaps they directed their attention more towards the portrait
which was a kind of work more in keeping with the constraints of their lives;
nevertheless, since the beginnings of photo-reportage, women such as
Margaret Bourke-White and Dorothea Lange have made their impression as
remarkable witnesses of their time. Nowadays they are much more numerous,
and I see in that the sign of an evolution in our society which gradually allows
women greater freedom. For a certain time, for reasons usually associated with
their family life, many choose not to roam the world. If because of this they are
more limited in their choice of themes, it is not because of their feminine nature
but because of the conditions of their lives. A good photographer is not always
a globetrotter. Photographers do not have to model themselves on a certain
kind of reporter. They have to try to be themselves. If women do not have any
more difficulty than men in selling their photographs through an agency, they
can have difficulty when it comes to photographic commissions, even
assuming that they have already overcome resistance to their work and its
"seriousness"—a difficulty that women encounter in all professions.

I really do not think that there is a specifically feminine as opposed to a
masculine view. Our view depends on our sensitivity, on our being, on our
personality. I do not think either that one can tell whether a photograph has
been taken by a man or a woman. On the other hand, one can recognize the
style of this man or that woman. Certain women have taken extraordinary war
photographs: I am thinking particularly of those of Cathy Leroy in Vietnam
and of those of Susan Meiselas in Nicaragua. All their pictures are as powerful
and over-whelming as those of their male colleagues.

We all have latent elements, attributed traditionally to the other sex, which
photography can in fact reveal. It is not because a photograph has been taken
by a woman that I necessarily acclaim it.

As for myself, I feel concerned by what goes on in the world and involved
in my surroundings. I don't want merely to "document," I want to know why
a certain thing disturbs or attracts me and how a situation can affect the person
involved. I do not try to create a situation, and I never work in a studio; I try
rather to understand and grasp reality. In photography I have found a language
that suits me.

My studies of the history of art would have led me to follow a profession
involving writing, but I do not like writing—nor do I particularly like talking
about photography! If I do have something to say, I hope that it shows in my
pictures. I think that everything can be painted because painting can transform
reality, but not everything can be photographed and the photographer often
comes home empty-handed with pictures that often have a documentary
interest but that rarely go beyond that. One has to remain available and
extremely tenacious, admit that many subjects produce nothing . . . and then,
sometimes, the miracle happens, without warning.

—Martine Franck

*   *   *

In Paris in 1972 Martine Franck, together with six other young photographers, founded the Viva agency and remained one of its moving spirits until
1979 when the agency collapsed due to the departure of its best personnel.
Now she is associated with the Magnum agency, which draws increasingly
from the crucible of the May 1968 generation.

If the social and progressive preoccupations of Viva were obvious, it is
extremely difficult to perceive a common style or particular aesthetic method,
although Cartier-Bresson's influence was apparent, at least in the vision of
what could be photographed. At the heart of the agency, Martine Franck
developed an original approach based on aesthetic rigour, and gradually she
affirmed her own personality. Her photograph of a provincial swimming pool,
taken in 1976 and published with success, marks an important step in the
development of her style and, as a point of reference, allows a detailed study of
her particular characteristics.

Background and form are perfectly united in this picture and provoke
cultural, social, existential and poetic reflection. Spontaneity has no place

here, for everything down to the smallest detail is perceived, imagined, revealed and planned with remarkable intelligence. The composition draws together four important elements, four actions, four subjects, which act in keeping with an unequal tension. This work makes one think of the paintings of Piero della Francesca or of Indian mural paintings and of the miniatures of the Mogul school and of Rajastan where people move in groups of three or four. The difference in contemporary photography—and with Martine Franck, in particular—is that the God Krishna has been replaced by the common man, by an anonymous being in an urban environment that makes of him both hero and victim.

In her book, *Le Temps de Vieillir,* Martine Franck deals with a typically photographic theme which functions on three levels—as it were, on three superimposed epidermic layers—so that the portrait of old age is fixed as ferociously present, as a testimony of the past and of childhood, and finally as an inexorable reflection of death. Within this mask of old age, and in the functioning of the common man articulated by threads that often imprison him (sometimes provoking a grating humor)—in this slice of life freshly cut from reality, everything acts as enigma rather than as testimony.

One of the great lessons of contemporary photography, in which Martine Franck finds her place, is to teach us to react, to investigate a problem, to interpret reality for what it is—a photographic framework, a matter of choice, a political action where we, as spectators and actors, have something to say.

—Claude Nori

FRANK, Robert.

Nationality: Swiss. **Born:** Zurich, 1924; moved to the United States, 1947, and to Canada, 1969. **Education:** Attended schools in Zurich; apprenticed to the photographer Herman Eidenbenz, Basle, 1940-41, and to Michael Wolgesinger, Zurich 1942; also influenced by the photographer Gotthard Schuh. **Family:** Married Mary Lockspeiser, 1950; children: Pablo and Andrea (d.1974); separated 1969. Married June Leaf, 1975. **Career:** Still Photographer, Gloria Films, Zurich, 1943-44; freelance photographer, Zurich, 1945-47; freelance photographer, under Alexey Brodovitch, for *Harper's Bazaar,* and for *Fortune, Life, Look,* etc., New York, 1948, in Europe, 1949-51, and New York, 1951-55; independent photographer and filmmaker, New York, 1956-69, in Cape Breton, Nova Scotia, since 1969. Concentrated on filmmaking, with Allen Ginsberg, Larry Rivers, Peter Orlovsky and Jack Kerouac, New York, 1958; Founder Member, with Shirley Clarke, Jonas Mekas, Peter Bogdanovich, Gregory Markopoulos and others, New American Cinema Group, New York, 1960, and Film-Makers Co-operative, New York 1962. Visiting Instructor in Filmmaking, University of California at Davis, 1977. **Recipient:** Guggenheim Fellowhip, 1955; First Prize, *San Francisco Film Festival,* 1959. **Agent:** Pace/MacGill Gallery, 32 East 57th Street, New York, 10022, U.S.A.

Individual Exhibitions:

1948	Museum of Modern Art, New York
1955	Helmhaus, Zurich
1960	*Spring,* Art Institute of Chicago, Chicago
1962	Museum of Modern Art, New York (with Harry Callahan)
1976	Kunsthaus, Zurich
1979	Galerie Zabriskie, Paris
1980	Scottish Photography Group, Edinburgh (travelled to the Institute of Contemporary Arts, London)
	Art Gallery of Ontario, Toronto (retrospective)
1981	*Walker Evans and Robert Frank: An Essay on Influence,* Fraenkel Gallery, San Francisco
1987	*New York to Nova Scotia,* Museum of Fine Arts, Houston, Texas (travelled to Cleveland Museum of Art, Ohio; Minneapolis Institute of Arts, Minnesota; Los Angeles County Museum of Art; University of California, Berkeley)
	Fotografie Forum, Frankfurt (with Diane Arbus)
1992	Pace/MacGill Gallery, New York

1994	*Robert Frank: 27 Photographs,* Pace/MacGill Gallery, New York
	Robert Frank: Moving Out, (retrospective), National Gallery of Art, Washington, D.C. (travelling to (1995) Yokohama, Zurich, and Amsterdam)
1995	Whitney Musem of American Art, New York
1996	Lannan Foundation, Los Angeles (projected)

Selected Group Exhibitions:

1954	*Great Photographs,* Limelight Gallery, New York
1955	*The Family of Man,* Museum of Modern Art, New York (and world tour)
1967	*Photography in the 20th Century,* National Gallery of Canada, Ottawa (toured Canada and the United States, 1967-73)
1974	*Photography in America,* Whitney Museum, New York
1979	*Photographie als Kunst 1879-1979/Kunst als Photographie 1949-1979,* Tiroler Landesmuseum Ferdinandeum, Innsbruck, Austria (travelled to the Neue Galerie am Wolfgang Gurlitt Museum, Linz, Austria; Neue Galerie am Landesmuseum Joaneum, Graz, Austria; and the Museum des 20. Jahrhunderts, Vienna)
1980	*Photography of the 50s,* International Center of Photography, New York (travelled to the Center for Creative Photography, University of Arizona, Tucson; Minneapolis Institute of Arts; California State University at Long Beach; Delaware Art Museum, Wilmington)
1982	*Counterparts: Form and Emotion in Photographs,* Metropolitan Museum of Art, New York (travelled to the Contemporary Arts Center, Cincinnati, Ohio; Dallas Museum of Fine Art, Texas; San Francisco Museum of Modern Art; Corcoran Gallery, Washington, D.C.)
1984	*Exposed and Developed,* National Museum of American Art, Washington, D.C. (toured the United States)
1985	*American Images 1945-80,* Barbican Art Gallery, London (toured Britain)
1987	*Photography and Art 1946-86,* Los Angeles County Museum of Art
1990	Pace/MacGill Gallery, New York

Collections:

Museum of Modern Art, New York; International Museum of Photography, George Eastman House, Rochester, New York; Philadelphia Museum of Art; Smithsonian Institution, Washington, D.C.; Art Institute of Chicago; National Gallery of Canada, Ottawa; San Francisco Museum of Modern Art; Houston Museum of Fine Arts, Texas; University of New Mexico, Albuquerque.

Publications:

By FRANK: Books—*New York Is,* New York 1955; *Indiens pas morts,* with Werner Bischof and Pierre Berger, with text by Georges Arnaud, Paris 1956, as *From Incas to Indians,* with an introduction by Manuel Tuñian de Lara, New York 1956; *Les Américains,* edited by Alain Bosquet, Paris 1958, Milan 1959, as *The Americans,* with an introduction by Jack Kerouac, New York 1959, revised editions Millerton, New York 1969, 1978; *Pull My Daisy,* with Jack Kerouac and Alfred Leslie, New York 1961; *Zero Mostel Reads a Book,* New York 1963; *The Lines of My Hand,* Tokyo 1971, Los Angeles 1972; *Robert Frank,* with an introduction by Rudi Wurlitzer, Millerton, New York 1976 (includes bibliography). **Articles**—"Bus Ride Through New York: The Bridge from Photography to Cinematography" in *Camera* (Lucerne), no. 45, 1966; "Films: Entertainment Shacked Up with Art" in *Arts* (New York), no. 41, 1967; "The Lines of My Hand" and "Uneasy Words While Waiting: Robert Frank Interviewed by Sean Kernan" in *U.S. Camera/Camera 35 Annual,* New York 1972; "Dialogue Between Robert Frank and Walker Evans" in *Still* (New Haven, Connecticut), no. 3, 1973. **Films**—*Pull My Daisy,* 1959; *The Sin of Jesus,* 1961; *O.K. End Here,* 1963; *Me and My Brother,* 1968; *Conversation in Vermont,* 1969; *Life Raft—Earth,* 1969; *About Me: A Musical,* 1971; *Cock-sucker Blues,* 1972; *Keep Busy,* with Rudi Wurlitzer, 1975; *Life Dances On,* 1980.

On FRANK: Books—*Photographers on Photography,* edited by Nathan Lyons, New York 1966; *Photography in the 20th Century* by Nathan Lyons, New York 1967; *New Documents,* exhibition catalogue, with text by John Szarkowski, New York 1967; *11 American Photographers,* exhibition catalogue, by Robert Doty and Robert Littman, Hempstead, New York 1972; *Looking at Photographs* by John Szarkowski, New York 1973; *Une Histoire du Cinema,* exhibition catalogue, by Peter Kubelka and others, Paris 1976; *Concerning Photography,* exhibition catalogue, by Jonathan Bayer and others, London 1977; *Photography Within the Humanities,* edited by Eugenia Parry Janis and Wendy MacNeil, Danbury, New Hampshire 1977; *A Book of Photographs from the Collection of Sam Wagstaff,* designed by Arne Lewis, New York 1978; *Photographie als Kunst 1879-1979/Kunst als Photographie 1949-1979,* exhibition catalogue, 2 volumes, by Peter Weiermair, Innsbruck, Austria 1979; *Light Readings: A Photography Critic's Writings 1968-1978* by A.D. Coleman, New York 1979; *The Photograph Collector's Guide* by Lee D. Witkin and Barbara London, Boston and London 1979; *Photography of the 50s,* exhibition catalogue, by Helen Gee, Tucson, Arizona 1980; *Walker Evans and Robert Frank: An Essay on Influence* by Tod Papageorge, New Haven, Connecticut 1981; *The Robert Frank Coloring Book* by Jno Cook, Chicago 1983; *Contemporary Canadian Photography* by Martha Langford, Edmonton, Alberta 1984; *Robert Frank: Fotografias/Films 1948-1984,* edited by Artur Heras and Vicente Todoli, Valencia, Spain 1985; *American Images: Photography 1945-1980,* edited by Peter Turner and John Benton-Harris, London 1985; *Robert Frank: New York to Nova Scotia,* exhibition catalogue with text by Allen Ginsberg, Houston, Texas 1987; *Photography and Art 1946-1986,* exhibition catalogue, by Andy Grundberg and Kathleen M. Gauss, Los Angeles 1987; *Robert Frank: Moving Out,* exhibition catalogue, National Gallery of Art, Washington 1994. **Articles**—"Robert Frank" in *Camera* (Lucerne), no. 12, 1949; "A Letter Addressed to Robert Frank" by Gotthard Schuh in *Camera* (Lucerne), no. 8, 1957; "Robert Frank" by Walker Evans in *U.S. Camera Annual,* New York 1958; "Black and White Are the Colors of Robert Frank" by Edna Bennett in *Aperture* (Rochester, New York), no. 1, 1961; "Der Photograph Robert Frank" by Willy Rotzler and Hugo Loetscher, special issue of *Du* (Zurich), January 1962; "Robert Frank: The Americans" in *Creative Camera* (London), January 1969; "Robert Frank" in *Camera* (Lucerne), March 1969; "Robert Frank's Dilemma" by Gene Thornton in the *New York Times,* 20 August 1972; "Robert Frank: Seeing Through the Rain" by Charles Hagen in *Afterimage* (Rochester, New York), February 1973; "Robert Frank: An Appreciation" by Ian Jeffrey in *Photographic Journal* (London), July 1973; "Walker Evans, Robert Frank and the Landscape of Dissociation" by William Stott in *Artscanada* (Toronto), December 1974; "Robert Frank's Most Recent Work Part of His Exhibition" by Maia-Mari Sutnik in *The Gallery* (Toronto), February 1980; "Robert Frank: Dissecting the American Image" by Jno Cook in *Exposure* (New York), Spring 1986.

*

I wished my photographs (the old ones) would move—or talk—to be a little more alive. But I can't talk for them. That's why there's so much written about photography today—by "experts." Contemporary photography is competent, often exquisite. It's easy to look at, and I prefer it if it's not in colour and not about whores in India or South America. The few photographs I'm trying to make show my interior against the landscape I'm in. At times I put in words—Soup—Strength—Fate—Blind.

—Robert Frank

*   *   *

During the first half of the history of photography—a short and comparatively sweet seventy years—cameras were basically heavy, cumbersome, and unyielding as the mules and camels that hauled the machinery across the continents. Added to this intractability of mechanical means, light sensitive materials, by 1980s standards, were semi-conscious at best. Not surprisingly, most photographers focused their cameras on easy targets—people forsworn not to bat an eyelash or occasional immobile knick-knacks and the like. Even in photographs taken worlds away by daring itinerants, the impression left was that life stood still, that nothing happened. Whether the photograph depicted a battle-scarred Sioux warrior or a white picket fence, the emphasis rested on the noun and the adjectives used to embellish it. While Stieglitz caught the

breath of horses as early as 1893 and little Lartigue the spill and splash of family friends some dozen years later, the verb, the controlling factor on the noun, had little influence or business in photography's early development. It wasn't until after the First World War, in fact, with the advent of small, hand-held cameras and faster films that the fluidity of real events finally opened to unmitigated scrutiny. Photography became, to carry the metaphor to its logical conclusion, a completed sentence.

Some photographers, like Henri Cartier-Bresson, made the moment, the verb, decisive. Others, like André Kertész and Bill Brandt, ultimately placed their sympathies alongside the noun. In the middle was Robert Frank, who, influenced in part by these masters from Europe as well as in part by the astringent, verbless images of Walker Evans in America, blended both the subject and the action, the noun and the verb, with exquisite clarity, compassion, and grace.

It was in 1947 that Robert Frank left Switzerland on a steamer bound for New York, one of several auspicious journeys he would make in his life. Once he got to America, his break with traditional modes of photography, perhaps precipitated by the sudden withdrawal from Swiss serenity, was immediate, clear-cut and self-propelled. It was, for Frank, an irrevocable shift in life style as much as life vision.

From the first photographs on, taken in the streets of New York and later in Paris and London, Spain and Peru, one discovers performers and performances inextricably woven in what can best be described as the real feel of life. Indeed, as sentences, the photographs of Robert Frank are among the most complex and intelligent ever made in photography.

Moments are caught as they reflect the ironies and agonies of life, not for the joys of abstraction or symmetry. The moment itself never engulfs the person, yet the person is never without the moment. No matter what the mood or circumstance, people preserve their identities as human beings, maintain their physical and emotional integrity. Whether expressions are resilient or forbearing, despondent or gleeful, there is always a countenance that must be confronted and reckoned with. Even when their faces are concealed—covered by a hand in the midst of a shoe shine or by an unruly flag when watching a parade, Frank's protagonists never appear exploited, mere faceless pawns in some clever graphic scheme.

Frank's things—the jukeboxes, the cars, the barbershop chairs, the stars and the stripes—radiate the human presence of the people that surround them, inhabit them, accelerate them, adore them, swear by them. They bring in the sound effects, like the glowing jukebox in New York that visually blares away.

There are those who regard Frank's achievement primarily on visual grounds, pointing out how he roughed up the medium with a blurry, blinding vision that left whole sections of the picture out-of-focus, horizon lines helter-skelter, and edges messy with the residue of careless cropping. Yet considering the messages of Frank's pictures, as dreary as they sometimes could be, it is difficult to tolerate such claims. More convincing would be to say that by forcing photography to conform to and obey the beat of life, Frank was able to seize upon some of life's most haunting, poignant, tragicomic, sad, bizarre, and crazy phenomena. Ultimately, feeling overshadows appearance.

There is the picture of two passers-by in Paris, one reaching for a coin, the other holding a tulip behind his back, neither aware of the actions of the other. The picture counters life's random absurdity with the dignity of human courtesy and kindness. Then, in drizzling London, in what may be his most famous early photograph, Frank captures a little girl racing down the street, a bundle of energy dissolving fast. Looming in the picture's foreground sits a hearse, the back door of death swung wide open. The child's foot race against the inevitable is simply out of a dream.

In 1955, and it is legend now, Robert Frank, riding on a Guggenheim fellowship, rented a used car, packed in the family, and criss-crossed America. Sweeping through big cities and backroads, stopping in poolhalls, parks, barrooms, bus depots, assembly lines and lunch counters, Frank photographed what he saw. His ground rules were clear: "With these photographs, I have attempted to show a cross-section of the American population. My effort was to express it simply and without confusion. The view is personal and, therefore, various facets of American life and society have been ignored," he wrote later of his experience. The book based on these photographs with the simple title, *The Americans,* was first published in France, then a year later in America. Why it wasn't published first in the United States is self-evident from the pictures. Frank's personal view was not the view of America Americans wished to see or acknowledge, especially when coming from an outsider.

Affluent, free, and deep in the middle of an American dream that blanketed the memories of Hiroshima and the Holocaust, Americans didn't want to be caught dimeless in front of the jukebox, have their cocktail parties ruined by a funeral procession, or be reminded that blacks on a bus actually rode in the back. No one much appreciated seeing the stars and stripes so translucent, hanging across a fourth of July picnic like prison bars, or church and state—St. Francis and City Hall—separated by a greasy garage.

It was the great symbol of the American dream—the car—the perfect get-away machine, the king of the road, that Robert Frank celebrated in what is perhaps his best known photograph. Parked on a street in Long Beach, California, a car is draped by a shimmering, silvery sheet, covering it all, right to the tip of the radio antenna. Flanked by two majestic palm tree pillars, the automobile-in-absentia becomes a veritable curbside altarpiece, a holy vessel.

On U.S. Highway 66, between Winslow and Flagstaff, Arizona (next plate in the book), automobile worship turns suddenly sour. Instead of a liturgical vestment, a beaten bedspread covers a corpse or two at the scene of an accident. Our sorrow lies not with the victims, but with the witnesses huddled but alone in the lightly falling snow—the snow James Joyce describes in the final story of *Dubliners* as "falling faintly through the universe and faintly falling like the descent of their last end, upon all the living and the dead."

Americans have little appetite for despair, remorse, or depressive bore-dom. Like miserable diseases, such feelings in life are best to avoid if you can. To Europeans, like Frank, the grim, darker aspects are part and parcel of life's ups and downs, its give and take. In *The Americans,* Robert Frank, who would later in his life know despair and pain at its highest pitches with the loss of his daughter in a plane crash over Guatemala, dared to raise such existential questions. Perhaps because photography couldn't answer them fully, Robert Frank put aside the still camera in 1958 and moved on to the ultimate visual verb, the making of films.

Living in Nova Scotia, Canada since 1969 and with a dozen or more films, like *Pull My Daisy, Keep Busy,* and *Cocksucker Blues* to his credit, Robert Frank has returned to a kind of photography that resembles the game of solitaire. Snapshots of gelid landscapes replete with mailboxes, telephone lines, clotheslines, and horizon lines are combined with postcards and assem-bled into collages, then painted, often the blues and oranges of gas stove flames. Some are hand scrawled with words that couldn't be more perspicu-ous: "The wind will blow the fire of pain across everyone in time"; or in dripping paint across a mirror reflecting a doll-sized skeleton held in a hand: "Sick of goodbyes"; or of his lost daughter: "She was 21 years and she lived in this house and I think of Andrea every day."

Frank also continues to film, dedicating his most recent film, *Life Dances On,* also to his daughter's memory. In the harrowing final scene, Andrea's face appears for the first time, super-imposed over the jagged Canadian coastline. While it is impossible for anyone to interpret someone else's private inten-tions, could it be that in this film, steered by its title, Frank encompasses and conquers the grief of eternal separation. The existential predicament of those left behind to continue their lives can be resolved, he seems to faintly voice, not by forgetting, but rather by embracing the beautiful ghosts that will haunt us. Only then can we move on with life and become again its governor.

Ultimately, words written about the films and photographs of Robert Frank will always sit on the dull edge of the knife. Frank himself has written, "The best would be no writing at all."

—Arno Rafael Minkkinen

FREED, Leonard.

Nationality: American. **Born:** Brooklyn, New York, 23 October 1929. **Education:** Attended Tilden High School, Brooklyn, 1944-48; studied painting; self-taught in photography. **Family:** Married Brigitte Kluck; daugh-ter: Elke. **Career:** Freelance photographer, New York, since 1958, working most recently for the London *Sunday Times Magazine, New York Times Magazine, Der Speigel, Der Stern, GEO, l'Express, Liberation* and *Fortune.*

Member, Magnum Photos co-operative agency, New York, since 1970. Taught at the New School for Social Research, New York. **Recipient:** National Endowment for the Arts Grant, 1980. **Address:** c/o Magnum, 72 Spring Street, New York, New York 10012, U.S.A.

Individual Exhibitions:

1959	Steendrukkerij De Jong, Hilversum, Netherlands
1960	Kunstkring, Rotterdam
1967	*What is Man,* Roman Catholic Benedictine Nuns of Cockfosters, London
1969	Smithsonian Institution, Washington, D.C.
1973	*The Spectre of Violence,* The Photographers' Gallery, London
1980	*Made in Germany 1970,* Museum Folk-wang, Essen
1984	F.N.A.C., Paris
1987	Galerie Municipale du Chateau d'Eau, Toulouse, France
1989	San Daniele del Fruili, Friuli, Italy
1991	Alinari, Florence, Italy
1992	F.N.A.C., Berlin, Germany
1993	Palazzo delle Esposizioni, Rome, Italy
1994	*Leonard Freed: Vintage Photographs,* 292 Gallery, New York

Selected Group Exhibitions:

1961	*Dag Amsterdam,* Stedelijk Museum, Amsterdam
1964	*World Exhibition of Photography: What Is Man?,* Pressehaus Stern, Hamburg (and world tour)
1967	*The Concerned Photographer,* Riverside Museum, New York (and world tour)
1968	*2nd World Exhibition of Photography,* Pressehaus Stern, Hamburg (and world tour)
1970	*Fotoportret,* Gemeentemuseum, The Hague
1973	*Inside Whitechapel,* Whitechapel Art Gallery, London
1974	*Celebrations,* Hayden Gallery, Massachusetts Institute of Technology, Cambridge
1978	*Fotografie in Nederland 1940-75,* Stedelijk Museum, Amsterdam
1983	*Die fotografische Sammlung,* Museum Folkwang, Essen, West Germany
1985	*American Images 1945-80,* Barbican Art Gallery, London (toured Britain)
1986	*Native Americans,* State Capital Building, Albany, New York
1991	*Magnum 50th Anniversary,* Palais du Luxembourg, Paris (and worldwide)
1993	*Focus,* Ljubljana, Slovenia

Collections:

Riverside Museum, New York; International Center of Photography, New York; Museum Folkwang, Essen; Stedelijk Museum, Amsterdam; Bibliothèque Nationale, Paris; Prenten Kabinet Der Rijksuniversiteit Te Leiden, Nether-lands; Metropolitan Museum, New York City; Israel Museum, Jerusalem; Alinari, Florence, Italy; Swiss Foundation, Zurich, Switzerland; Fundacion Cultural Banesto, Madrid, Spain; Galerie Municipale du Chateau d'Eau, Toulouse, France; Smithsonian Institution, Washington, D.C.

Publications:

By FREED: Books—*Joden van Amsterdam,* Amsterdam 1959; *Deutsche Juden Heute,* Munich 1965; *Black in White America,* New York 1968;

Seltsame Spiele, with Shinkichi Tajiri, Frankfurt 1970; *Made in Germany 1970,* Munich 1970, as *Leonard Freed's Germany,* New York and London 1971; *Police Work,* New York 1980; *La Danse des Fideles,* Paris 1984; *New York Police,* Paris 1990; *Libertate Roumanie,* Paris 1990; *Leonard Freed: Photographies 1954-1990,* Paris 1991; *Miradas Fin de Siglo,* Madrid 1992. **Films**—*Dansende Vromen,* 1962; *The Negro in America,* 1968; *Joey Goes to Wigstock,* 1992.

On FREED: Books—*2nd World Exhibition of Photography,* exhibition catalogue, edited by Karl Pawek, Hamburg 1968; *The Concerned Photographer,* edited by Cornell Capa, New York 1969; *Inside Whitechapel,* exhibition catalogue, by John Furse, London 1973; *The Spectre of Violence,* exhibition catalogue, by Sue Davies, London 1973; *Geschichte der Fotografie im 20. Jahrhundert/Photography in the 20th Century* by Petr Tausk, Cologne 1977, London 1980; *Museum Folkwang: die fotografische Sammlung,* exhibition catalogue, with introduction by Ute Eskildsen, Essen, West Germany 1983; *American Images: Photography 1945-1980,* edited by Peter Turner and John Benton-Harris, London 1985. **Articles**—"Leonard Freed: Portfolio for the Concerned Photographer" in *Infinity* (New York), October 1967; "The Concerned Photographer," special issue of *Contemporary Photographer* (Culpeper, Virginia), vol. 6, no. 2, 1968; "Leonard Freed" in *Camera* (Lucerne), May 1969; "Deauville: Photographs by Leonard Freed" in *Du* (Zurich), August 1969; "Way Out Westbeth: A Photographic Essay by Leonard Freed" in *Avantgarde* (New York), Summer 1971; "Leonard Freed" in *Modern Photography Annual,* New York 1972; "Leonard Freed's Germany" in *Creative Camera* (London), January 1972; "Leonard Freed à New York: Une Nuit commes les Autres" in *Photo* (Paris), May 1973; "Leonard Freed" in *The Image* (London), vol. 2, no. 6, 1974; "Leonard Freed: Vive les Flics New-Yorkais" in *Photo* (Paris), October 1980; "La Police, C'Est Nous" in *Photo* (Paris), April 1981.

                              *   *   *

To get the eye, the head and the heart together on the same sight-line—that was the goal of the founding fathers of the Magnum agency. Leonard Freed is a member of Magnum and has conformed absolutely to their precepts. His interest in social affairs is not a mere fashion, born perhaps from the pressure of the roaring 60s: Freed is not of an age to have grown up culturally in that period, and he shows it in his pictures. He is not a man disenchanted with the lens, one of those photographers who, using as an excuse the dullness of everyday life, the absence of any kind of decisive moment, make convenient alibis for themselves to produce pictures expressing intimate experiences. He does not take refuge in contemplation of the misfortunes of the photographer rather than those of the photographed. At the same time Freed's interest in the dramatic situations in life was not born in dangerous times when it was fashionable to play at revolution, fighting it with a camera round one's neck. Freed was born at the time of the great American slump of 1929, and when he began to take photographs it was to document the life of the Jewish community in New York, their problems and their hopes. After the Second World War a journey to Europe reinforced his interest in the Jewish problem. Cineaste and photographer, he produces pictures of denunciation, cruel pictures, as it were a warning to the guilty conscience. The problem of the blacks, the Six Days war, the Germany of the period of reconstruction: he is not one who sings of optimism, even if, paradoxically, his denunciation has implicit in it the hope for a better tomorrow—a tomorrow to which, perhaps, his pictures too can contribute.

A dream, an optimistic presumption about the powers of photography? "Suddenly," Freed said at the opening in 1967 of the New York exhibition *The Concerned Photographer,* in which he took part with five colleagues, "suddenly I feel that I belong to a tradition. . . ." It is the same tradition that informs Luce's famous program for the newborn *Life:* ". . . to see life, see the world, be witness to great events, peer into the faces of the poor, the mad, to understand the shadows of the jungle, hidden things, to see, to rejoice in

seeing, to be spiritually enriched. . . ." For his spiritual enrichment Freed does not hesitate to throw reality in your face, the reality he has picked as his objective. It is the reality of the people, of the man. He does not like to photograph objects or backgrounds. There in the foreground are the people, the faces of the people, the bodies of the people. He does not go looking for the man's reflection in objects; he does not look for the tracks of his passing. He looks the man directly in the face, frankly and loyally.

There is great humanism in this placing of the human figure at the centre of interest, with no deceit or false pity. Even when his pictures seem rough and cruel, there is never less in the photographer of what the Romans called *pietas.* A humble approach to the subject, but with a capacity to grow angry, to cry out against injustices. Freed does not go in for "beautiful photography," photography in the Cartier-Bresson manner, unless it is to catch our eye. For him the age-old argument about the relative importance of content and form has clearly been settled in favour of the former.

                                                              —Edo Prando

FREEDMAN, Jill.

Nationality: American. **Born:** Pittsburgh, Pennsylvania, in October 1939. **Education:** Studied sociology and anthropology at the University of Pittsburgh; self-taught in photography. **Career:** Formerly worked as a musician. Photographer, based in New York. **Address:** 181 Sullivan Street, Brooklyn, New York 11231, U.S.A.

Individual Exhibitions:

1968	*From Points of View on Resurrection City,* Brooklyn Children's Museum, New York
1972	Soho Photo Gallery, New York
1974	The Photographers' Gallery, London
1976	Nikon Gallery, Zurich
1978	Galerie Trockenpresse, Berlin
1979	Hippolyte Gallery, Helsinki
1981	Photograph Gallery, New York
1984	Museum of Contemporary Photography, Columbia College, Chicago

Selected Group Exhibitions:

1969	*Vision and Expression,* International Museum of Photography, George Eastman House, Rochester, New York
1986	*Jazz pa Fotografiska,* Fotografiska Museet, Stockholm
	The Animal in Photography 1843-1985, The Photographers' Gallery, London

Publications:

By FREEDMAN: Books—*Old News: Resurrection City,* New York 1970; *Circus Days,* New York 1975; *Firehouse,* with text by Dennis Smith, New York 1977; *Street Cops,* New York 1981. **Article**—"Circus" in *U.S. Camera/Camera 35 Annual,* New York 1975.

On FREEDMAN: Books—*Photography Annual,* New York 1969; *World Photography* by Bryn Campbell, London 1981; *Dictionnaire des Photographes* by Carole Naggar, Paris 1982. **Articles**—"Jill Freedman: Welfare Hotel" in *Print* (New York), January/February 1973; "Jill Freedman's Street Gallery" by Y. Kalmus in *Camera 35* (New York), November 1973; "Jill Freedman Stalks America for Unflinching Portraits" by Abigail Foerstner in the *Chicago Tribune,* 14 December 1984.

* * *

Jill Freedman is a most unusual and independent photographer. Her involvement with her subjects becomes total, whether that involvement is for a period of months or even years. Her first book *Old News: Resurrection City,* told of the poor people's march on Washington, and from it to *Circus Days* (a three-month period spent with circus people, moving on every night after the show) to her latest book, *Street Cops,* about the New York police, she has lived and breathed the subjects, from taking the pictures right through to the final design and writing of the texts.

At a time when it is more fashionable to provide a cool look at the world, Freedman is totally committed to everything she does. Her uncompromising attitude means that she has little time for the "photo-scene," and apart from some occasional one-off assignments, she prefers to live from one book to the next without allegiances to any particular newspaper, magazine or agency. Such independence makes it necessary for her to be particularly hard on herself—self-discipline demands more over a long period than working with any kind of group with whom one can share responsibilities. And this discipline extends to her ruthless sorting and sifting of her work, to make sure that only the best is seen.

Luckily, through all this intensity, there shines a rare sense of humour. Compassion there certainly is, a fine sense of composition, and an eye that seeks and finds the secret and quiet moments as well as the dramatic ones without ever giving the impression of being that of an outsider. If the world belongs to Jill Freedman, she also belongs to it—the Irish pub musicians, the brave fireman or the old beaten down-and-out are all part of the same world. She is not showing us things in the hope that we will change them, just that we will admit them to our minds, and agree that the human condition, however imperfect, is the one that we share: by coming to terms with it we may get some hard knocks, but we certainly get the best highs too—and with her help, some truly great pictures.

—Sue Davies

FREIXA, Ferran.

Nationality: Spanish. **Born:** Barcelona, 11 November 1950. **Education:** Attended Escola Laietana, Barcelona, 1964-66; studied drawing and painting, Escola Massana and Cercle Artistic St. Lluc, Barcelona, 1965-68; mainly self-taught in photography. **Military Service:** Served in the Spanish Army, Barcelona, 1968-69. **Career:** Freelance photographer and graphic designer, establishing own studio, Barcelona, since 1969. **Recipient:** Laus 85 Trophy, Art Directors Club of Barcelona, 1985; Award of Honor, Catalan Government, Barcelona, 1986. **Address:** Provenca 285 entlo., Barcelona 08037, Spain.

Individual Exhibitions:

1976	La Photogaleria, Madrid
	FAD (Foment de les Arts Decoratives), Barcelona
1977	Galeria Rosa Bisbe, Barcelona
	Galeria Lletra Menuda, Ciutadella-Menorca, Spain
	Galeria Fotoarte, Bilbao, Spain
	Galeria Spectrum-Canon, Barcelona
	Galeria Il Diaframma-Canon, Milan
1978	Atelier-Galerie de Photographie, Aix-en-Provence, France
1979	Galerie Demi-Teinte, Paris
	Galeria Fotomania, Barcelona
	La Photogaleria, Madrid
	Sala de Imagen (Caja de Ahorros), Castellón, Spain
	Galeria Desalt, Girona, Spain
1980	Galeria Spectrum-Canon, Girona, Spain
1982	Galeria El Setze, Martorell, Spain
	Galeria Cop d'Ull, Lleida, Spain
1983	Berner Photo-Galerie, Berne, Switzerland
	Galerie Agathe Gaillard, Paris
	Forum Fotogaleria, Tarragona, Spain
	Galerie Spectrum, Zaragoza, Spain
1985	Club de la Imatge, Barcelona
1986	Contraluz, Barcelona, Spain
	Sala Dos Peiraos, Vigo, Spain
1991	*VII Mes de la Fotografia Iberoamericana,* Museo Provincial de Huelva, Spain
1992	*Cocktails,* Gimlet series, Barcelona, Spain
1993	Museu Tèxtil i de l'Indumentaria, Barcelona, Spain

Selected Group Exhibitions:

1973	*La Bella y la Bestia,* Galeria Da Barra, Barcelona
1976	*El Fotògraf Fotografiat,* Casal de La Floresta, Barcelona
1977	*Photographies d'Architecture,* Chez Rove/Vinci 1840, Paris
1978	*Fotografia Española Contemporánea,* Centro Cultural Juana Mordó, Madrid
1979	*Expo Lìmite, Oficina de Turismo Español,* New York
1980	*Autorretratos,* Galeria Fotomania, Barcelona
1982	*Fotografos Españoles,* Galleri Camera Obscura, Stockholm
1984	*Fotografia Mediterrania,* Centre Cultural de la Caixa de Pensions, Barcelona
1985	*Natures Mortes,* Galerie ARPA, Bordeaux, France
1986	*Contemporary Spanish Photography,* University of New Mexico, Albuquerque
1987	*Tarraco: Objecte i Imatge,* Museu Nacional Arqueològic, Tarragona, Spain
	Escenarios de la guerra, Canal de Isabel II, Madrid
	Contemporary Spanish Photography, Center for Creative Photography, University of Arizona, Tuscon, USA
1989	*Porta d'aigua (Ten Photographers in the Port of Barcelona),* Sala Arcs de la Caixa de Barcelona
1991	*Fotògrafs Catalans Contemporanis,* biennial "Taula de fotografia," Club Universitari, Tarragona, Spain
	Cuatro Direcciones, Fotografia Contemporánea Española 1970-1990, Museo Nacional Centro de Arte Reina Sofia
1992	*Musa Museu: 15 Contemporary Photographers in the Museums of Barcelona,* Palau de la Virreina, Barcelona
	Objectiu: MD'A, El museu vist per 7 fotògrafs, Museu d'Art de Girona, Spain
	Imatges textuals, Laie, Barcelona
1992	*Cuatro Direcciones,* Travelling exhibition in Spain and elsewhere
1994	*Spanish Photography,* The Special Photographers Company, London
	Cuatro Direcciones, Photographers' Gallery, London
	Barcelona-Berlin moments de canvi, Catalonia Institute of Architects, Barcelona

Archeologic National Museum of Tarragona, Spain, **1987.** Photograph ©Ferran Freixa.

Collections:

Musée d'Art et d'Histoire, Fribourg, Switzerland; Bibliothèque Nationale, Paris; Fundacion Cultural Televisa, Mexico City; Fundacion Joan Miro, Barcelona; Museo Español de Arte Contemporaneo, Madrid.

Publications:

By FREIXA: **Books**—*Polen d'Entrecuix,* with text by Joan Brossa, Barcelona 1978; *Immagini della Fotografia Europea Contemporanea,* Milan 1985; *Carmen, Ballet Antonio Gades,* Barcelona 1986; *Porta d'aigua (Ten Photog-*

raphers in the Port of Barcelona), Barcelona 1989; *Le grand livre de l'eau,* Paris 1990; *El Gran Teatre del Liceu,* Barcelona 1990; *El Prado Vivo,* Madrid 1992; *Bien de salud y otros cuentos de autobuses en Barcelona,* text by María José Furió, Barcelona 1993. **Articles**—''Portafolio Holanda'' in *Zoom* (Madrid), October 1976; ''Sotto il sole di Minorca'' in *Il Fotografo* (Milan), September 1977; ''Exposición Lìmite'' in *Nueva Lente* (Madrid), March 1979; ''Spanish Photography'' in *European Photography* (Göttingen), April/ June 1980.

On FREIXA: **Books**—*Dictionnaire des Photographes* by Carole Naggar, Paris 1982; *Primavera Fotogràfica a Barcelona 1982,* exhibition catalogue, with introduction by J. Corredor-Mateos, Barcelona 1982. **Articles**—"Conversaciones en el Laboratorio" by Jordi Palarea Fonts in *Flash-Foto* (Barcelona), November 1980; several publications in the most important international magazines of architecture and interiors.

* * *

The series "Escaparates" of 1978-79 suggests a change in the work of Ferran Freixa. The same elements as in his previous two series ("Holanda" in 1976 and "Menorca" in 1976-77) are still present, and these elements demonstrate a continuity in his work. But there are also differences, much more subtle than they at first appear to be.

As far as composition is concerned, Freixa constantly maintains the principle of not presenting us with an object in its totality but with merely a fragment. In terms of technique, he presents us with a negative which is free from any previous or subsequent manipulation. Thematically, he analyzes those elements that evoke lost worlds or worlds nearing their ends. In "Holanda" the Dutch houses evoke the bourgeoisie of the 17th and 18th centuries. The sculptured walls and aristocratic houses in "Menorca" are reminders of the presence of the English on the island during the 18th century. And in "Escaparates" the shop windows of Barcelona are a kind of final evidence of the world of the artisans' guilds, a world that is vanishing before our eyes. The work of Ferran Freixa, in other words, always obliges the viewer to make some effort of the imagination. His work is highly suggestive and intellectual.

So much the series have in common. Yet, in the current work, there is a difference—because of its concrete theme; because of his use of a different focal distance. The objects he now depicts are invariably of a smaller dimension than the subjects of "Holanda" and "Menorca": they are seen more closely and they are personal—some gloves, a hat. The theme is bold and to be "read," but the photos of "Escaparates" distance us from an atmosphere of analysis; they evoke an immediate emotional response, bringing us nearer to humanity.

—Francesc Miralles

FREUND, Gisèle.

Nationality: French. **Born:** Berlin, Germany, 19 December 1912; emigrated to France, 1933: naturalized, 1936. **Education:** Studied sociology and art history at the University of Freiburg im Breisgau, 1931; under Karl Mannheim and Norbert Elias, Institute for Social Sciences, University of Frankfurt, 1932-33; and at the Sorbonne, Paris, 1933-36, Ph.D. in sociology and art 1936. **Career:** Freelance journalist and writer, working for *Life, Weekly Illustrated, Vu, Picture Post, Paris-Match, Du,* etc., in Paris, 1935-40, 1946-50, and since 1953. **Recipient:** Kulturpreis, Deutsche Gesellschaft für Photographie (DGPh), 1978; Grand Prix National des Arts, France, 1980. Officer de la Legion d'Honneur. **Agent:** Galerie de France, 52 rue de la Verrerie, 75004 Paris. **Address:** B.P. 509, 75666 Paris, Cedex 14, France.

Individual Exhibitions:

1939	*Ecrivains célèbres,* Galerie Adrienne Monnier, Paris
	Peggy Guggenheim Jeune Gallery, London
1942	Amigos del Arte, Buenos Aires
1945	Palacio de Bellas Artes, Valparaiso, Chile
1946	*Amerique Latine,* Maison de l'Amerique Latine, Paris
1963	Bibliothèque Nationale, Paris
1964	French Institute, London
1965	Princeton Art Museum, New Jersey
1968	*Au Pays des Visages 1938-68,* Musée d'Art Moderne de la Ville, Paris
	Fondation Royaumont, Asnières, France
	Maison de la Culture, Grenoble, France
1971	Musée de la Cataye, Mont-de-Marsan, France
	Musée de la Cataye, Pau, France

	Musée Municipale, Angoulème, France
1972	Association Mulhousienne pour la Culture, Mulhouse, France
	Maison de la Culture, Dôle, France
	Centre Culturel des Premontres, Pont-à-Mousson, France
1973	Musée Sandelin, Saint-Omer, France
	Theatre Gerard Philippe, Saint-Denis, France
	La Mairie, Amboise, France
	Centre Culturel, St. Savin-sur-Cartempe, France
	Descartes Huis, Amsterdam
	Comite d'Enterprise E.D.F., Chatou, France
	Musée d'Art et d'Histoire, Nimes, France
1974	Maison de la Culture, Cannes
	Maison de la Culture, Brive-la-Gaillarde, France
	Maison de la Culture, St.-Ouen-L'Aumone, France
	Maison de la Culture, Aquitaine, France
	Association Bourguignonne, Dijon, France
1975	Maison de la Culture, Rennes, France
	Maison de la Culture, Fougeres, France
	Maison de la Culture, Laval, France
	Robert Schoelkopf Gallery, New York
1976	Focus Gallery, San Francisco
1977	*Fotografien 1932-1977,* Rheinisches Landesmuseum, Bonn (retrospective)
	Fotoforum der Gesamthochschule, Kassel, West Germany (retrospective)
1978	Galerie Dreiseitel, Cologne
	Galerie Lange-Irschl, Munich
	Musée Réattu, Arles, France
	Galerie La Hune, Paris
	Watari Gallery, Tokyo
	Shadai Gallery, Tokyo
	Mirvish Gallery, Toronto
	Harcus Krakow Gallery, Boston
1979	Sidney Janis Gallery, New York
1980	Galerie Agathe Gaillard, Paris
	Photo Art Gallery, Basle
	Canon Gallery, Geneva
1981	Axiom Gallery, Melbourne
	Galerie Rudolf Kicken, Cologne
	Galerie Municipale du Château d'Eau, Toulouse
1983	Photographers' Gallery, London
1985	Musée d'Art Moderne de la Ville, Paris
	Kunstraum München, Munich
1991/92	Musée d'Art Moderne, Centre Georges Pompidou, Paris
1993/94	Berlin; Hamburg

Selected Group Exhibitions:

1951	*Memorable Life Photographs,* Museum of Modern Art, New York
1961	*Salon International de la Photographie,* Bibliothéque Nationale, Paris
1963	*Das Französische Porträt im 20. Jahrhundert,* Akademie der Künste, Berlin (travelled to the Kunsthalle, Dusseldorf)
1965	*Femmes Photographes,* Les 30/40, Paris
1966	*Commemoration Joyce,* Centre Culturel Americain, Paris
1972	*Photographes Français,* Moscow Museum, U.S.S.R.
1975	*Women of Photography,* San Francisco Museum of Art (toured the United States, 1975-77)
1977	*Photographes Français,* Centre Beaubourg, Paris
1981	*Les Réalismes,* Centre Beaubourg, Paris
1982	*Color as Form,* International Museum of Photography at George Eastman House, Rochester, New York

Collections:

Bibliothèque Nationale, Paris; Musée Réattu, Arles, France; Stedelijk Museum, Amsterdam; Moderna Museet, Stockholm; Shadai Gallery, Tokyo; International Museum of Photography, George Eastman House, Rochester, New York; Princeton University, New Jersey; Center for Creative Photography,

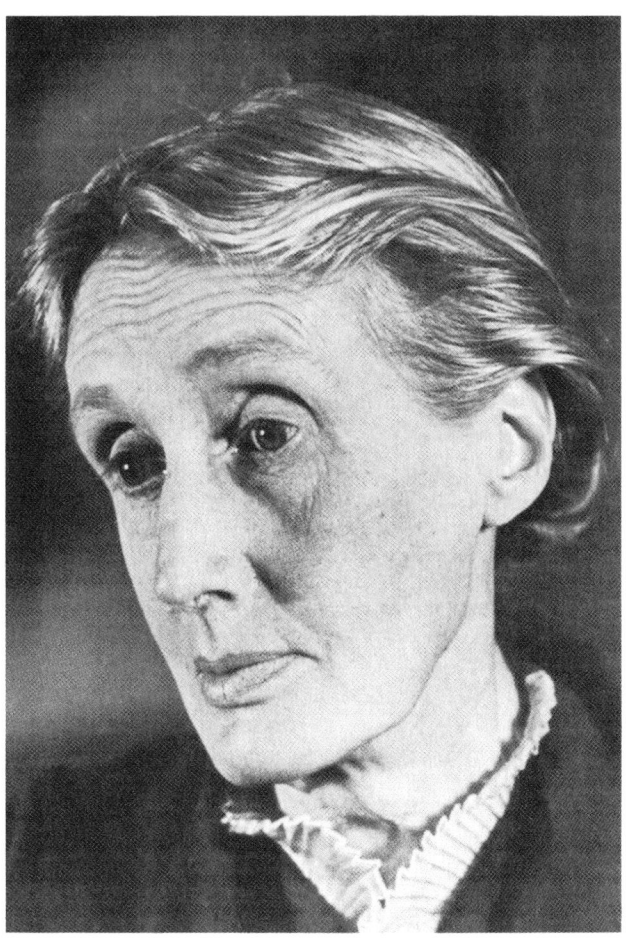

Virginia Woolf, **1939.** Photograph by Gisèle Freund.

University of Arizona, Tucson; Musée d'Art Moderne/Centre Georges Pompidou, Paris; Musée d'Art Moderne de la Ville de Paris.

Publications:

By FREUND: Books—*La Photographie en France au 19me Siècle,* Paris 1936, Buenos Aires 1947, Munich 1968; *Mexique Précolombien,* Neuchâtel, France 1954, Munich 1955; *James Joyce in Paris: His Final Years,* New York 1965, London 1966; *Le Monde et Ma Camera,* Paris 1970, New York 1974; *Photographie et Société,* Paris 1974, 1975, Turin, Barcelona, Munich, Boston, Stockholm and London 1980; *Memoires de l'Oeil,* Paris and Frankfurt 1977; *Gisèle Freund,* Portfolio, Washington, D.C. 1978; *Trois Jours avec Joyce,* Paris 1982, New York 1985; *Itineraires,* Paris 1985; *Gisèle Freund, Photographer,* New York and Munich 1985; *Portrait,* conversation with Rauda Jamis, Paris 1992. Articles—"A French Woman Visits the North and Asks: Is This Your England?" in *Weekly Illustrated* (London), 5 October 1935; "Northern England," under pseudonym "Girix," in *Life* (New York), 14 December 1936; article in *Arts et Metiers Graphiques* (Paris), no. 65, 1937; "David Octavius Hill" in *Verve* (Paris), October 1939; "Some Scenes from the Economic War Front of Parisian Fashions" in *Life* (New York), 15 April 1940; "Kein Schnappschuss, Kein Pose: Langzeitaufnahmen einer Epoche," interview with Georg Puttnies, in *Frankfurter Allgemeine Zeitung,* 3 April 1975.

On FREUND: Books—*Memorable Life Photographs* with text by Edward Steichen, New York 1951; *Au Pays des Visages 1938-1968,* exhibition catalogue, by Pierre Gaudibert, Paris 1968; *Women of Photography,* exhibition catalogue, by Margery Mann, San Francisco 1975; *Gisèle Freund: Fotografien 1932-1977,* exhibition catalogue, by Klaus Honnef, Bonn 1977;

Farbe im Photo: Die Geschichte der Farbphotographie von 1861 bis 1981 by Fritz Binder, Gert Koshofer, Rolf Sachsse and others, Cologne 1981; *International Photography 1920-1980,* edited by Ian North, Canberra 1982; *Lichtbildnisse: Das Porträt in der Fotografie,* edited by Klaus Honnef, Cologne 1982; *The Library of World Photography: Portraits,* with introduction by Colin Ford, Tokyo 1982, 1983, London 1983. Articles—"Au Pays des Figures" by Adrienne Monnier in *Verve* (Paris), no. 5/6, 1939; "Miroirs Francs" by Annette Vaillant in *Les Nouvelles Litteraires* (Paris), 28 March 1963; "Oh Young Men, Oh Young Comrades" by Cyril Connolly in the *Sunday Times Magazine* (London), 22 December 1963; "The Key to Inner Character" by Geraldine Fabrikant in *Ms* (New York), March 1975; "Gisèle Freund" in *Kunstforum International* (Mainz), vol. 16, 1976; "Gisèle Freund" by Fritz J. Oberli in *Camera* (Lucerne), November 1978; "Gisèle Freund" by Rosellina Burri-Bischof in *Du* (Zurich), January 1981; "Gisèle Freund, la femme aux portraits" in *Le Matin* (Paris), 26 September 1985; "L'oeil du Maitre" in *Paris-Match* (Paris), 4 October 1985; "Gisèle Freund: Philosopher of Photography" in *Photo District News* (New York), January 1986; "Exploring the Origins of Glamour" in *American Photographer* (New York), May 1986; "Erzahlte Augenblicke" in *Suddeutsche Zeitung* (Munich), 3/4 May 1986; "L'amicizia e y pudore nell' obiettivo de Gisèle Freund" in *Corriere della Sera* (Milan), 16, May 1986.

*

To create a photograph which possesses originality, an emotion that nobody before has expressed, is as difficult as it is for a painter to realize a painting which expresses new ideas. Newspapers, magazines and books publish every day millions of photographs, but it is extremely seldom that one discovers a great work among this multitude, one that touches the heart and enchants the spirit.

Yet it seems so easy to take a photograph! One forgets that, apart from the technical aspects, photography can be a mental creation and the affirmation of a personality. What is marvellous about photography is that its possibilities are infinite; there aren't any subjects "done to death," for, as Brassaï says: "A fresh eye can still disclose anew unknown aspects."

To reveal man to man, to be a universal language accessible to all—that, for me, is the prime task of photography.

—Gisèle Freund

*   *   *

In her touching memoirs and reflections on the art of photography, *Le Monde et Ma Camera* (1970), Gisèle Freund makes the surprising confession that originally she had wanted to be a sociologist "because the diversity of social problems fascinated me." She became a photographer out of necessity, she continues, "and I never regretted it, for I soon understood that my most vital concerns were directed toward the individual, with his sorrows and hopes and anguishes. My camera led me to pay special heed to that which I took most to heart: a gesture, an isolated expression. Gradually, I came to believe that everything was summed up in the human face." And although she also describes herself as a "photoreporter" and has taken memorable pictures of her visits to Argentina and Mexico, she is primarily a portraitist. Her photographs of Joyce, Virginia Woolf, Colette and André Malraux (many of them done in color as early as 1938) are probably the best-known "literary" portraits of our time, but the impressive list of artists and intellectuals who sat for her should not suggest that she is a kind of court photographer. There is nothing idealized about most of these portraits: she does not disguise the muted terror in Virginia Woolf's eyes, for example, or Malraux's fierce arrogance. What she looks for is the "symbolic essence of an individual."

About the art of photography in general she remarks that while an observer takes in countless details when he glances at a scene, the camera remains fixed. It must select, it must choose, and thereby gains its special power: "it captures an isolated reality in a fraction of a second. The immediate present thus takes on a symbolic value." But at the same time "*I* am the one who decides at exactly what moment the button must be pressed. . . . And in the end, the intrinsic value of a photograph depends on the photographer's ability to select, among a mass of impressive and jumbled details, those that reveal the most meaning." Thus the expressive value of a photograph depends ultimately on the character of the photographer and the point of view he chooses. With

Gisèle Freund that point of view is poised, objective, even classical in its assumption that there are essences to be revealed, and at the same time alert to the intensity of the particular moment. "My goal," she writes, "has always been to make my camera the witness of the time in which I live."

—Elmer Borklund

FRIEDLANDER, Lee (Norman).

Nationality: American. **Born:** Aberdeen, Washington, 14 July 1934. **Education:** Studied photography, under Edward Kaminski, Art Center School, Los Angeles, 1953-55. **Career:** Began photographing, 1948; freelance photographer, working for *Esquire, McCall's, Collier's, Art in America,* etc., since 1955. Artist-in-Residence, University of Minnesota, Minneapolis, 1966; Guest Lecturer, University of California at Los Angeles, 1970; Mellon Professor of Fine Arts, Rice University, Houston, 1977. **Recipient:** Guggenheim Fellowship, 1960, 1962, 1977; National Endowment for the Arts Fellowship, 1972, 1977, 1978, 1979, 1980; Friends of Photography Peer Award, 1980; Medal of the City of Paris, 1981; Edward MacDowell Medal, 1986; John D. and Catherine T. MacArthur Foundation Award, 1990. **Address:** 44 South Mountain Road, New City, New York, U.S.A.

Individual Exhibitions:

1963	International Museum of Photography, George Eastman House, Rochester, New York
1967	*New Documents,* Museum of Modern Art, New York (with Diane Arbus and Garry Winogrand; toured the United States, 1967-75)
1968	University of California at Los Angeles
1970	Garrick Fine Arts Gallery, Philadelphia
1971	*Gatherings I Got Myself Invited To,* Focus Gallery, San Francisco
1972	Focus Gallery, San Francisco
	Gatherings, Museum of Modern Art, New York
	Witkin Gallery, New York
1973	Jefferson Place Gallery, Washington, D.C.
	Galerie Wilde, Cologne
	East Street Gallery, Grinnell, Iowa
1974	Museum of Modern Art, New York
1975	Broxton Gallery, Los Angeles
	Museum of Modern Art, New York
1976	*Portfolios,* Minneapolis Institute of Arts
	Kunsthaus, Zurich
	Texas Center for Photographic Studies, Dallas
	The Nation's Capital in Photographs, Corcoran Gallery, Washington, D.C.
	Yajima Galerie, Montreal
1977	*The American Monument,* Institute of Contemporary Art, Boston (toured the United States)
	Light Gallery, New York
	Cronin Gallery, Houston
	Center for Contemporary Photography, Chicago
1978	Hudson River Museum, Yonkers, New York
	Galerie Zabriskie, Paris
	Light Gallery, New York
1979	Fraenkel Gallery, New York (retrospective)
1980	Work Gallery, Zurich
1981	Jeb Gallery, Providence, Rhode Island
	California Museum of Photography, University of California at Riverside
	Arbres et Fleurs, Galerie Zabriskie, Paris
1983	*Portraits 1958-83,* Zabriskie Gallery, New York
	Shiloh, International Museum of Photography at George Eastman House, Rochester, New York
	Portraits 1958-80, Fraenkel Gallery, San Francisco

	Industrial Valleys, San Francisco Museum of Modern Art
	Posed and Unposed Portraits, Zabriskie Gallery, New York (with Harry Callahan)
1986	*Shiloh,* Fraenkel Gallery, San Francisco
1987	Zabriskie Gallery, Paris
	Seibu Museum of Art, Tokyo
1988	Fraenkel Gallery, San Francisco
1989	Seattle Art Museum, travelling and catalogue
1990	Fraenkel Gallery, San Francisco
1991	San Francisco Museum of Modern Art
	Museum of Modern Art, New York
1993	Institute for Contemporary Art, Boston
	Walker Art Center, Minneapolis
	Canadian Centre for Architecture, Montreal
1994	Museum of Modern Art, New York
	Fraenkel Gallery, San Francisco

Selected Group Exhibitions:

1966	*Contemporary Photography since 1950,* International Museum of Photography, George Eastman House, Rochester, New York (toured the United States)
1967	*Photography in the 20th Century,* National Gallery of Canada, Ottawa (toured Canada and the United States, 1967-73)
1975	*4 Amerikanische Photographen: Friedlander/Gibson/Krims/ Michals,* Stadtisches Museum, Leverkusen, West Germany
1976	*Peculiar to Photography,* University of New Mexico, Albuquerque
1977	*Contemporary American Photographic Works,* Museum of Fine Arts, Houston (travelled to the Museum of Contemporary Art, Chicago; La Jolla Museum of Contemporary Art, California; and Newport Harbor Art Museum, California)
1978	*23 Photographers/23 Directions,* Walker Art Gallery, Liverpool
1979	*Photographie als Kunst 1879-1979/Kunst als Photographie 1949-1979,* Tiroler Landesmuseum Ferdinandeum, Innsbruck, Austria (travelled to the Neue Galerie am Wolfgang Gurlitt Museum, Linz, Austria; Neue Galerie am Landes-museum Joanneum, Graz, Austria; and Museum des 20. Jahrhunderts, Vienna)
1981	*Robert Frank Forward,* Fraenkel Gallery, San Francisco
1985	*American Images 1945-80,* Barbican Art Gallery, London, (toured Britain)
1987	*Photography and Art 1946-86,* Los Angeles County Museum of Art
1988	*Three on Technology,* Massachusetts Institute of Technology, Cambridge, catalogue
1993	*In Camera,* Museum of Fine Arts, Museum of New Mexico, Santa Fe
1994	*One Hundred Years of Street Photography,* Wright State University, Dayton, Ohio

Collections:

Museum of Modern Art, New York; Museum of Fine Arts, Boston; Fogg Art Museum, Harvard University, Cambridge, Massachusetts; Smithsonian Institution, Washington, D.C.; New Orleans Museum of Art; University of Kansas, Lawrence; University of New Mexico, Albuquerque; San Francisco Museum of Modern Art; University of California at Los Angeles; National Gallery of Canada, Ottawa; Victoria and Albert Museum, London.

Publications:

By FRIEDLANDER: Books—*Work from the Same House,* with Jim Dine, London and New York, 1969; *Photographs by Lee Friedlander and Etchings by Jim Dine,* portfolio of 16 photos and etchings, London 1969; *Self-Portrait,* New City, New York 1970; *E.J. Bellocq: Storyville Portraits,* editor, New York 1970; *15 Photographs by Lee Friedlander,* portfolio, with an introduction by Walker Evans, New York 1973; *Photographs of Flowers,* portfolio of 15 photos, New York 1975; *The American Monument,* with text by Leslie

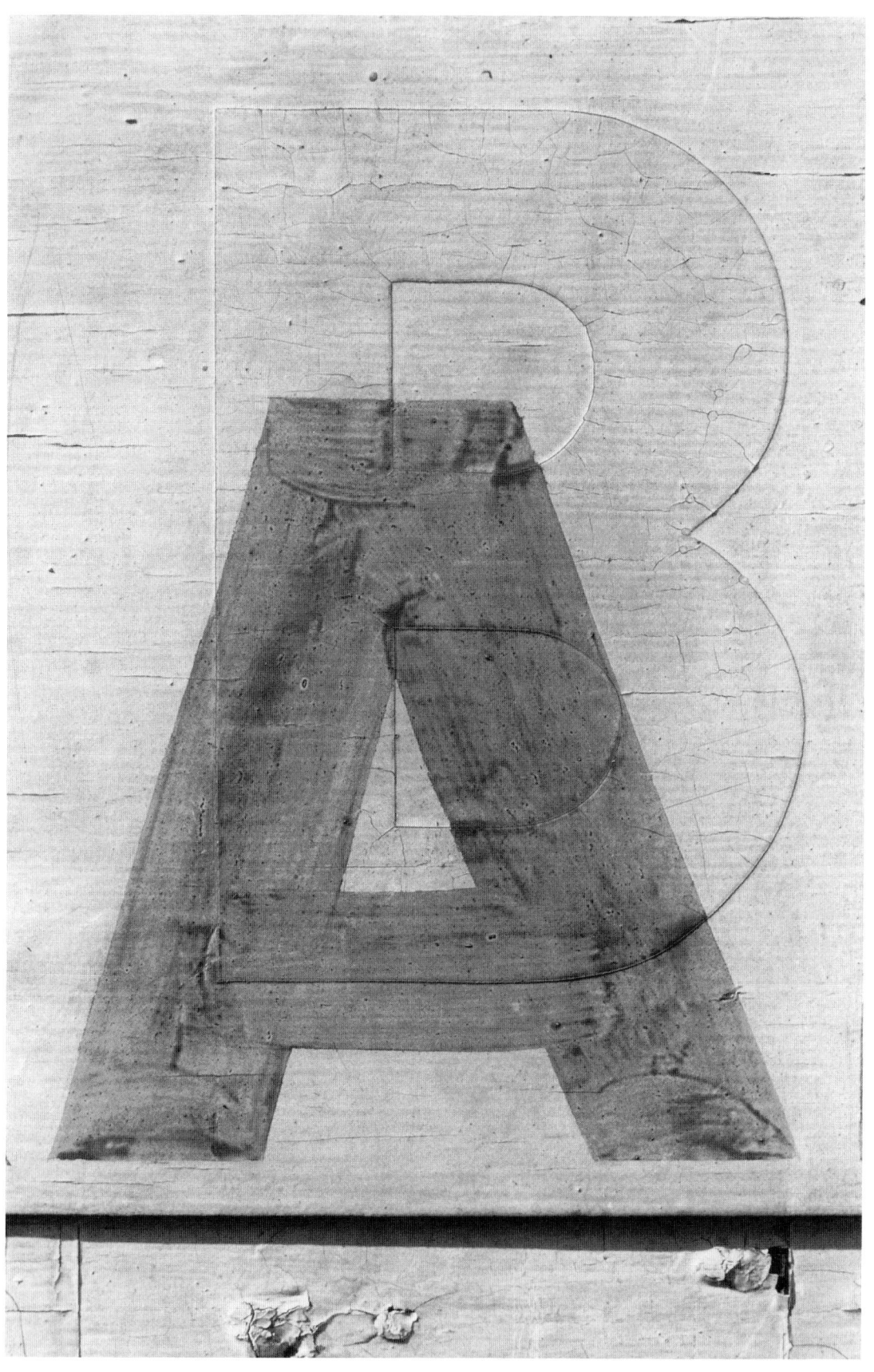

New Orleans, **1979.** Photograph by Lee Friedlander. Courtesy Fraenkel Gallery, San Francisco.

George Katz, New York 1976; *The Nation's Capital in Photographs 1976,* exhibition catalogue, with an introduction by Jane Livingston, Washington, D.C. 1976; *Lee Friedlander: Photographs,* New City, New York 1978; *Flowers and Trees,* portfolio of 40 photos, New York 1981; *Factory Valleys,* New York 1982; *Lee Friedlander: Portraits,* New York 1986; *Cherry Blossom Time in Japan,* New York 1986; *Cray at Chippewa Falls,* Cray Research MN 1987; *Lee Friedlander: Nudes,* New York 1991; *Maria,* Massachusetts, 1992; *The Jazz People of New Orleans,* New York 1992; *Letters from the People,* New York 1993. **Articles**—"Looking at Television" in *Current* (New York), April 1963; "The Little Screens" in *Harper's Bazaar* (New York), February 1963; "E.J. Bellocq: Storyville Portraits" in *Camera* (Lucerne), December 1971.

On FRIEDLANDER: Books—*Photography in the 20th Century* by Nathan Lyons, New York 1967; *New Photography USA,* exhibition catalogue, by John Szarkowski, Arturo Quintavalle and Massimo Mussini, Parma, Italy 1971; *Peculiar to Photography,* exhibition catalogue, by Van Deren Coke, Thomas F. Barrow and others, Albuquerque, New Mexico 1976; *Geschichte der Fotografie im 20. Jahrhundert/Photography in the 20th Century* by Petr Tausk, Cologne 1977, London 1980; *Contemporary American Photographic Works,* edited by Lewis Baltz, Houston 1977; *The Magic Image* by Cecil Beaton and Gail Buckland, London and Boston 1975; *Concerning Photography,* exhibition catalogue, by Jonathan Bayer, Peter Turner, Ian Jeffrey and Ainslie Ellis, London 1977; *Photographs: Sheldon Memorial Art Gallery Collection, University of Nebraska,* with an introduction by Norman A. Geske, Lincoln, Nebraska 1977; *Tusen och En Bild,* exhibition catalogue, by Ake Sidwall, Rune Jonsson and Ulf Hard af Segerstad, Stockholm 1978; *Mirrors and Windows: American Photography since 1960* by John Szarkowski, New York 1978; *23 Photographers/23 Directions,* exhibition catalogue, by Valerie Lloyd, Liverpool 1978; *Photographie als Kunst 1879-1979/Kunst als Photographie 1949-1979,* exhibition catalogue, 2 vols., by Peter Weiermair, Innsbruck, Austria 1979; *Old and Modern Masters of Photography,* exhibition catalogue, by Mark Haworth-Booth, London 1980; *Lichtbildnisse: Das Porträt in der Fotografie,* edited by Klaus Honnef, Cologne 1982; *American Images: Photography 1945-1980,* edited by Peter Turner and John Benton-Harris, London 1985. **Articles**—"Lee Friedlander" by James Thrall Soby in *Art in America* (New York), June 1960; "The Little Screens" by Walker Evans in *Harper's Bazaar* (New York), February 1963; "Lee Friedlander: 5 Portraits" in *Creative Camera* (London), April 1969; "Lee Friedlander" in *Camera* (Lucerne), January 1969; "E.J. Bellocq: Storyville Portraits, from Prints by Lee Friedlander" in *Creative Camera* (London), August 1971; "Lee Friedlander: Self-Portraits" in *Creative Camera* (London), September 1971; "Le Foto di Friedlander" by Ugo Mulas in *NAC* (Milan), January 1972; "Lee Friedlander: Self Portrait" by J. Kelly in *Art in America* (New York), May/June 1972; "Lee Friedlander" in *Documentary Photography,* by the Time-Life editors, New York 1973; "Lee Friedlander" in *Photo* (Paris), February 1974; "All of a Sudden Friedlander Seems Passé" by Gene Thornton in the *New York Times,* 15 December 1974; "Lee Friedlander" by Gerry Badger in the *British Journal of Photography* (London), 5 March 1976; "Constancy Marks an Artistic Vision" by Andy Grundberg in the *New York Times,* 6 November 1983.

*   *   *

One of the most significant American photographers of the past four decades, Lee Friedlander photographs the social landscape as an unobserved observer. His photographs are resolutely visual, but they deny themselves the customary assertions and annunciatory associations of vernacular photography. Quite often an enigma to the viewer, they seek their own inherence of form. Why, may be asked, photograph a dog with his tongue lolling out waiting at a street corner in Albuquerque, New Mexico? Why, too, a monument of a rifleman with a klatch of pigeons fluttering at its base? Friedlander's work is deceiving with its understatement, its carefree manner, as if he just happened to be somewhere in urban America one day and also just happened to snap a picture. Of course, his photographs escape the innocence of a snapshot. Their meaning cannot be reduced to a phrase of facile interpretation.

Friedlander has created a formidable body of work: reflections in store front windows; urban landscapes with and without people; a series of American monuments; closeups of people frolicking at social gatherings and lounging within the privacies of their homes; and a study of trees and flowers, the ways their forms inhabit urban spaces.

Friedlander is the master of store front reflections in which clouds, a plane, a drugstore menu, a saleswoman or customer, and a glittering movie marquee across the street all gracefully mix as on a brilliant groundglass. What lies behind a window and what is reflected in its shiny surface unite in a two dimensional format that, accordion-style, expands and contracts in gradations of space. In these photographs his presence is often inserted as a shadow or partially concealed form, his face opaqued by the camera or a telltale part of his body merging into the flux of detail. By shooting from within a store or a phone booth, sometimes he will reverse the accustomed perspective, achieving a similar result.

The urban landscapes are broad reaches of space where parts of buildings, curbing, parked cars, telephone lines, unaware pedestrians, streetlamps, and awnings oddly relate and intersect. Flat and unassuming, the photographs interest one by their precision of detail and stubborn refusal to make interpretative comment. Perhaps because they are so fresh and originally conceived, they are not immediately winsome. But indeed they are unalloyed, real. They observe what most Americans pass by unblinkingly each day, doubtless some of the artifacts of contemporary urban culture. Neither self-consciousness nor self-congratulation taints these images. Many are shot in bright sunlight, and when printed the contrast of shadows and highlights is downplayed. Their impact is dry with a lingering assertion; what they behold is subtle, witty, as unique as the taste of hotdogs or roasted chestnuts served by a street vendor.

An extended portrait of monuments in America and their unintentionally amusing and banal placements has taken Friedlander throughout the country. With deadpan alertness, his photographs tout bronze figures and stone sculptures, their backs turned to a clutter of drab school buildings and brassy Thom McAn and Coca-Cola signs and towering flagpoles which intrude like jealous cousins at a picnic.

The tree for Friedlander has become another kind of monument. Reminiscent of his work with store front reflections, his photographs in the mid-70s began to cast trees as though they were unappreciated yet dominant objects of the American landscape. With such raw and unpromising subjects, Friedlander has fashioned some enduring photographs; his trees, their branches tangled and bare, offer an almost transparent surface through which other objects of the social landscape emerge.

A trademark of his work is a hand or an object like a plaster urn or a fire hydrant placed somewhere in the foreground of the photograph, a device allowing him to heighten the illusion of space. Another trademark is the unobtrusive manner in which he photographs. The human figures that snare his attention are rarely aware of his presence, as if before they can truly lock him into their thoughts he has already turned away.

Friedlander is not a causer, nor a satirist who pleads for change. His is the visual scholarship of an historian. He makes no towering social indictments or judgments. He has created a rich and diverse lexicon of urban America. People are certainly part of that lexicon, but his abiding fascination with them seems rooted in the ways they move in and inhabit their familiar spaces.

The apparent eclecticism of his subject matter is an index of his assurance and versatility. With a small, hand held camera and a hawk's eye for the unnoticed, he has forged an unmistakable style. Though easeful on the viewer's eyes, Friedlander's photographs are difficult and original conceptions. Their cohesions are intangible and secure, as if bound by invisible thread. What others would pass by as unphotographic, he gently tucks into his lexicon: an unpeopled street with a deep shadow splayed across it like a languorous whale; or a woman asleep, arms upthrust over her eyes, her head sunk softly between two pillows. His vision, his style, his wordless visual assertions have unequivocally affected the ways many contemporary American photographers envisage the urban environment.

—Kelly Wise

FRIEDMAN, Benno.

Nationality: American. **Born:** New York City, 28 March 1945. **Education:** Attended Brandeis University, Waltham, Massachusetts, 1962-66, B.A.

(honors) in fine arts 1966. **Career:** Photographer since 1966; established studio in New York City. Artist-in-Residence, Massachusetts College of Art, Boston, 1972-73. **Recipient:** *Photovision '72* Award, Boston; Massachusetts Council on the Arts and Humanities Fellowship, 1975; New York State Creative Arts Program Services Grant, 1978. **Agent:** Marcuse Pfeifer Gallery, 568 Broadway, New York, New York 10012. **Address:** 26 West 20th Street, New York, New York 10011, U.S.A.

Individual Exhibitions:

1969	Underground Gallery, New York
1972	Andover Museum of Art, Massachusetts
	Massachusetts College of Art, Boston
1973	Light Gallery, New York
	Tucson Art Center, Arizona
1975	Light Gallery, New York
1976	Center for Creative Photography, University of Arizona, Tucson
	Light Gallery, New York
1977	Light Gallery, New York
	Port Washington Library, Port Washington, New York
	Yajima Gallery, Montreal
1978	Arco Center for the Arts, Los Angeles
	Light Gallery, New York
1980	Asher-Faure Gallery, Los Angeles
	Honey Shop Gallery, Lenox, Massachusetts
	Susan Spiritus Gallery, Newport Beach, California
1981	Yajima Gallery, Montreal
	Photograph Gallery, New York
1982	Susan Spiritus Gallery, Newport Beach, California
	Film in the Cities, St. Paul, Minnesota
	David Mancini Gallery, Boston
	Charles Cowles Gallery, New York
1983	Elizabeth Leach Gallery, Portland, Oregon
1984	Yajima Gallery, Montreal
	Chiaroscuro Gallery, Lenox, Massachusetts
	Southwest Craft Center, San Antonio, Texas
1985	Berkshire Museum, Pittsfield, Massachusetts
	Vision Gallery, San Francisco (with David Holland and Chris Bastien)
1986	Marcuse Pfeifer Gallery, New York

Selected Group Exhibitions:

1970	*Recent Acquisitions,* Museum of Modern Art, New York
1972	*60s Continuum,* International Museum of Photography, George Eastman House, Rochester, New York
1973	*Light and Lens: Methods of Photography,* Hudson River Museum, Yonkers, New York
1974	*Private Realities,* Museum of Fine Arts, Boston
1976	*Photo/Synthesis,* Herbert F. Johnson Museum, Cornell University, Ithaca, New York
1979	*One of a Kind: Polaroid Color,* Corcoran Gallery, Washington, D.C. (toured the United States)
1981	*The Markers,* San Francisco Museum of Modern Art
1982	*International Photography 1920-80,* Australian National Gallery, Canberra
1984	*Altered Photos,* Jane Baum Gallery, New York
1985	*American Photography Today,* University of Denver, Colorado

Collections:

Museum of Modern Art, New York; Wertheim and Company, New York; International Museum of Photography, George Eastman House, Rochester, New York; Vassar College, Poughkeepsie, New York; Museum of Fine Arts, Boston; Fogg Art Museum, Harvard University, Cambridge, Massachusetts; Massachusetts Institute of Technology, Cambridge; Virginia Museum of Fine Arts, Richmond; Australian National Gallery, Canberra.

Publications:

On FRIEDMAN: Books—*Darkroom Dynamics,* edited by Jim Stone, New York 1979; *International Photography 1920-1980,* edited by Ian North, Canberra 1982. **Articles—**in *Art in America* (New York) February/March 1970; in *Esquire* (New York), March 1976.

*

I do not believe in the distinction between "pure" and altered photography. Black and white. It is all shades of grey. All photographs are both manipulated and manipulating. Webster: ". . . to control or change especially by artful or unfair means so as to achieve a desired end. . . . " The pure photographic moment (if the beast lives at all) is that fraction of an instant during which the image is perceived and desired, but prior to the moment of acquisition (the click of the shutter). All that follows is less than pure.

The realization/actualization of the photograph is manipulated by the photographer, and the image content of the photograph manipulates the viewer/audience. Process and narration. There is no 100% anything in our universe. No photograph is the exclusive product of either narration or process, yet so many photographers love their images without loving their photographs.

All photographs are manipulated, in that each step, each photographic process from image-collecting to print drying, is a variable (choice of camera, lens, developer, temperature, paper, etc., etc.). Each decision in this familiar family of activities is a specific alteration/manipulation, affected by and affecting each other. Using Spot-Tone is a manipulation . . . it is a choice to spot out a dust mark or scratch; it is no less a photograph if everything but the scratch is blackened.

Photography is manipulating in the illusions it has created and successfully perpetuated. The illusion of truth. The illusion of honesty. The illusion of substance. The illusion of a mirror. The illusion of reality. The only reality a photograph conforms to is that of being a photograph. All photographs could have been conceived and actualized on a film-lot in Hollywood. Today that is well within our illusionary abilities. All photographs are in substance no more than the outcome of a restricted reaction of silver salts to light and chemical bathing. All photographs at best only resemble things with which we are familiar. Our imaginations supply the missing details.

Today's photographic technology makes it available to man, chimpanzee, and computer. It is the faculties of critical choice that distinguish the deliberate from the random. Both chimp and man can make art; only man can be an artist. Computers have eliminated the necessity for the chimp's hand: a camera mounted and programmed to fire automatically, attended by blind technicians, the film processed and printed by machine. . . .

Commitment, evolution, exploration and intent. It is not enough to make well-printed, well-composed photographs. They are the cheapest form of visual currency, filling our publications, overflowing from the libraries; the silver has become more precious than the imagery.

Uneven edges, not-squared corner angles, erasures, alternate and superimposed rectangles, corrections, broken lines, reaffirmed demarcations, fingerprints, smudges, possibilities of mistakes, errors in the initial ordering process, statements replaced by questions: my attempt to define a series of visual interrelationships between the shaky, imperfect hand of man and the frozen exactitude of machine.

A wondrous and exciting time in the photographic experience is the transitional, alchemical time between neutral, undefined white paper and the finality of a fully developed print; the process of becoming, rather than the definiteness of having become. The Cubists struggled to reveal a multiplicity of facets and angles of the same object within a single frame . . . both this and that, frontal and profile, seen from above and at eye level. I wrestle with the quality of the absolute in photography—breaking it open, leaving room for additional information from other sources . . . a tree, photographically cut in half; what of its other half? I help reunite the two . . . reaffirming significant patterns, combinations of shapes, spatial relationships . . . an end, the edge is here, no—there, no—further over . . . this image is a segment ripped from a larger unphotographed place, an incomplete fraction which, like a single bone to an anthropologist, excites and reveals by its presence even that much more that is still yet unknown.

—Benno Friedman

* * *

The nature of Benno Friedman's work is such that some controversy exists as to whether it should be considered as photography at all. To photography purists, the extent of his manipulation of the print—bleaching, coloring, painting, and now, in his most recent work, re-drawing the image in pencil—raises questions about how far a photograph can be transformed and reworked and still remain a photograph. However, Friedman's insistence that the photograph is by definition an image made with a camera, and not a transcription of reality, is fully in keeping with the modernist dictum that a photograph is a photograph, be it a seemingly unmediated documentary image or an extensively manipulated abstraction. Whether the latter constitutes a *good* photograph is of course another question.

As Friedman's work has evolved, his real subject matter, *proprement dit,* can be said to be the very properties of photographic imagery. In calling attention to the arbitrary conventions and technical determinants of the photograph (the crop, the frame, the shape, and the properties of abstraction and flattening which derive from the camera registering the world in two-dimensional monochrome) he is above all asserting the fictional quality of photography. Much of his recent work, for example, involves either an extension of the image beyond its borders, a partial vignetting of the photographic image within the frame, or a pencilled continuation and elaboration of the image. Such devices emphasize that the most fundamental of photographic properties—the crop—is itself a convention, a fiction, a formal construction. Further, the presentation of two types of image making (the hand drawn and the photographed) within a single pictorial field asserts the primacy of image making as such and undercuts the tendency to privilege the photographic as more real or optically truthful. In Friedman's photographs, both elements have equal weight and neither element is more or less true than the other.

In much the same way that Friedman expands the image beyond the frame to allude to the physical world which continues and extends outside of the photographic crop, so too does his use of color refer to the reality excluded by the photograph. The imposition of arbitrary or unnatural hand coloring implies both the true colors of the natural world and the monochrome conversion that occurs in a black and white photograph (color photography imposes its own fictions).

Because the 140 year old battle to legitimize photography as art has been waged on painting's terms, it is not surprising that even now art photographers such as Friedman emphasize the "made" rather than the "taken" aspects of photography. The modernist insistence on the autonomous and self-referential nature of art informs a good deal of contemporary photography and Friedman's work is very much within this tradition. But inasmuch as the formalist criteria employed in modernist criticism involve such concepts as truth to materials, it is an open question as to whether photography can renounce its indexical relation to the world and still succeed as photography. Friedman takes as his aesthetic foundation and modus operandi these notions of autonomy and self-referentiality. By consistently producing images that challenge conventional assumptions of what constitutes the photographic, and which often approach total abstraction, he can be seen to have carried the position to its logical extreme.

—Abigail Solomon-Godeau

FRISSELL, Toni.

Nationality: American. **Born:** New York City, 10 March 1907. **Education:** Attended Lincoln School, New York, 1914-20; Miss Porter's School, Farmington, Connecticut, 1920-25; mainly self-taught in photography, but influenced by brother Varick, a documentary filmmaker. **Family:** Married Francis McNeill Bacon III in 1932; children: Varick and Sidney. **Career:**

Caption writer, 1930-31, and Fashion Photographer, 1931-42, *Vogue* magazine, New York; Official Photographer, American Red Cross, also working for the Women's Army Corps, United States Air Force and Office of War Information, in England and Scotland, 1941, 1944-45; freelance photographer, New York, working for *Harper's Bazaar, Life, Look, Vogue,* and *Sports Illustrated,* from 1942; retired, 1967. **Address:** Toni Frissell Collection, Prints and Photographs Division, Library of Congress, Washington DC 20540-5230, U.S.A. **Died:** 1988.

Individual Exhibitions:

1961   *A Number of Things,* IBM Gallery, New York (retrospective; toured the United States)
1967   *View from My Camera,* Philadelphia Museum of Art (toured the United States)
1975   *The King Ranch,* Amon Carter Museum, Fort Worth, Texas (toured the United States)

Selected Group Exhibitions:

1955   *The Family of Man,* Museum of Modern Art, New York (and world tour)
1964   *World Exhibition of Photography: What Is Man?,* Pressehaus Stern, Hamburg (and world tour)
1968   *Man in Sport,* Baltimore Museum of Art (toured the United States)
1975   *Fashion Photography: 6 Decades,* Hofstra University, Hempstead, New York (toured the United States)
1976   *Women Look at Women,* Library of Congress, Washington, D.C. (toured the United States)
1977   *The History of Fashion Photography,* International Museum of Photography, George Eastman House, Rochester, New York (travelled to the Brooklyn Museum, New York; San Francisco Museum of Modern Art; Cincinnati Art Institute; and Museum of Fine Arts, St. Petersburg, Florida)
1979   *The Fashionable World,* Stephen White Gallery, Los Angeles
       Recollections: 10 Women of Photography, International Center of Photography, New York (toured the United States)
1985   *Shots of Style,* Victoria and Albert Museum, London

Collections:

Library of Congress, Washington, D.C. (main collection); Metropolitan Museum of Art, New York; Fashion Institute of Technology, New York; International Museum of Photography, George Eastman House, Rochester, New York.

Publications:

By FRISSELL: Books—*A Child's Garden of Verses,* with poems by Robert Louis Stevenson, New York 1944; *The Happy Island,* New York 1946; *Toni Frissell's Mother Goose,* New York 1948; *The King Ranch,* with others, with an introduction by Holland McCombs, Fort Worth, Texas and New York 1975. **Article**—"I Went to England for the American Red Cross" in *Vogue* (New York), 1 February 1943.

On FRISSELL: Books—*U.S. Camera 1936,* annual, edited by Tom J. Maloney, New York 1936; *The Studio,* by Time-Life editors, New York 1972; *The Vogue Book of Fashion Photography* by Polly Devlin, with an introduction by Alexander Liberman, London 1979; *The History of Fashion Photography* by Nancy Hall-Duncan, New York 1979; *Recollections: 10 Women of Photography,* edited by Margaretta K. Mitchell, New York 1979; *The Library of World Photography: Portraits,* with introduction by Colin Ford, Tokyo 1982, 1983, London 1983; *Shots of Style: Great Fashion Photographs Chosen by David Bailey,* with text by Martin Harrison, London 1985; *Toni Frissell: Photographs 1933-1967,* introduction by George Plimpton, foreword by Sidney Frissell Stafford, New York and London 1994. **Articles**—"American Aces: Toni Frissell" by Frank Crowninshield in *U.S. Camera* (New York), December 1939; "Toni Frissell: A Number of Things" in *Photography*

Annual 1962, New York 1961; ''When the Cameraman Is a Woman'' in the *Chicago Sunday American Magazine,* 25 October 1964; ''Toni Frissell: Portfolio'' in *Infinity* (New York), December 1967; ''Toni Frissell Bacon: 'I'm Sixty-Six and I Love It' '' in *Vogue* (New York), June 1973.

*   *   *

For the photographer Toni Frissell the camera was an extension of her eye, leading her to adventures in every part of the world. Her career was initiated by a series of summer pictures of her young friends called ''Beauties at Newport,'' published by *Town and Country* in 1931. From there she began an eleven-year career as a staff photographer for *Vogue.* In the 1940s she turned free lance, working over the years for many journals including *Harper's Bazaar, Sports Illustrated,* and *Life.*

Best known for her work in fashion, Toni Frissell was the first to work out-of-doors and on location with models, promoting the casual, unselfconscious, scrubbed, sporty look which she herself exemplified. As a sports photographer she was one of the few women photographers included in an exhibition called *Man in Sport* in 1968 at the Baltimore Museum of Art. She and her husband loved travel and sports, and assignments took them over the years to ski in remote areas of the Alps, and to visit unusual, privately held places such as Medway Plantation and the King Ranch. Her most proud moment came when she traveled to Europe with both the Red Cross and the Air Corps during World War II, bringing back photo documents of their work.

After the war, her interests turned from fashion to people and events. She was drawn particularly to the British for much of her photojournalism during this period. One of the great treasures in the Frissell Collection is a series of photographs of Winston Churchill and his family, and over the next decade Toni Frissell recorded the way of life of the upper class in Britain—nannies and their prams in Hyde Park, royalty at garden parties and fox hunts, dukes and duchesses behind the scenes at the coronation of Queen Elizabeth II in 1953 and a series of fine portraits of families and children.

If her camera was a passport to a wide world of action, sports and glamour, she also created her own storybook at home, using family and friends to pose much as the Andrew Wyeth family and neighbors posed for the painter. Some of her most personal work portrays children dressed up in old costumes. In her mind the camera has the innocence of a child's vision. When her own two children were young, Toni made many photographs of them, some illustrating Robert Louis Stevenson's *A Child's Garden of Verses,* published in book form in 1944, and others illustrating *Mother Goose* published in 1948.

A Frissell photograph is a straightforward record of the photographer's response to the moment or the person. She photographed the worlds in which she lived and traveled as she let her subjects speak for themselves.

Both Hallmark and IBM have sponsored solo shows of a broad cross-section of her work. And her complete collection, now in the Library of Congress, stands as a remarkable record of a stratum of society. Most of the time she herself was as much a participant as a spectator, a fact that gives to her photographs the comfortable inside view: a midcentury album. As Toni Frissell commented in *Recollections: 10 Women of Photography,* ''I've been lucky to observe a segment of society as it was lived and I think that my work will have greater value in the next century as a record of a vanished way of life.''

—Margaretta K. Mitchell

FUJII, Hideki.

Nationality: Japanese. **Born:** Tokyo in 1934. **Education:** Attended Tokyo schools; studied photography at Nihon University, Tokyo. **Career:** Worked as an assistant to the photographer Shotaro Akiyama, Tokyo, 1953-56; fashion and magazine photographer with the Fujin Seikatsusha publishing company, working for *Fukuso* (Costume) magazine, Tokyo, 1957-60; advertising photographer with the Nihon Design Center, Tokyo, 1960-63. Since 1963, freelance advertising and fashion photographer, working for Max Factor, Jal Japan Airlines, *Vogue, Elle,* etc., in Tokyo. **Recipient:** Film Prize, 20th Festival International de Film Publicitaire, Cannes, France, 1973; Silver Lion

Award, Art Directors Club of New York, 1985; Annual Award, Photographic Society of Japan, Tokyo, 1985. **Address:** 4396-2 Iiyama, Atsugi-shi, Kanagawa Prefecture 243-02, Japan.

Individual Exhibitions:

1970	*Past,* Nikon Salon, Ginza Tokyo
1974	Spectrum Gallery, Hannover
1975	Canon Gallery, Amsterdam
	Musée d'Art Moderne, Paris
1977	Trent Polytechnic, Nottingham, England
	Galleria Il Diagramma, Milan
	Fuji Foto Salon, Tokyo
1978	Contax Salon, Tokyo
1981	*The Makeup,* Olympus Gallery, Tokyo
	Kompositionen, Olympus Gallery, Hamburg
1983	*The Best of Hideki Fujii,* Nikon House, New York
1985	*L'Image de Pastel,* Nagase Photo Salon, Tokyo
1986	*Woman in Oriental Mood,* Pentax Forum, Tokyo

Selected Group Exhibitions:

1979	*Japanese Photography from 1848 to Today,* Galleria d'Arte Moderna, Bologna, Italy (travelled to the Palazzo Reale, Milan; Palais des Beaux-Arts, Brussels; Institute of Contemporary Arts, London; Museum für Kunst und Gewerbe, Hamburg; Gemeente Museum, Arnhem; Pulchri Studio, The Hague)
1984	*Sammlung Gruber,* Museum Ludwig, Cologne

Collections:

Museum Ludwig, Cologne.

Publications:

By FUJII: Books—*Hideki Fujii, Fotografo,* Milan 1981; *The Makeup,* Tokyo 1984.

On FUJII: Books—*De Japanse Fotografie van 1848 tot Heden,* exhibition catalogue, by Attilio Colombo and Isabella Doniseli, Amsterdam 1980; *Hideki Fujii: Kompositionen,* exhibition catalogue, Hamburg 1981; *How Famous Photographers Work* by Jack Schofield and others, London 1983; *Sammlung Gruber: Photographie des 20. Jahrhunderts,* exhibition catalogue, with foreword by Siegfried Gohr, Cologne 1984.

*   *   *

Hideki Fujii is a fashion photographer in modern Japan. He was born in Tokyo in 1934, and became interested in photography while still in high school. He joined an amateur photographic society, and eventually his interest became more serious. At that time, quite by chance, he happened to photograph a cinema on fire: that snapshot was published in a newspaper, a decisive factor in Fujii's electing to enter photography professionally. He studied at the Department of Photography, Nihon University, and while there, he was employed as an assistant to the professional photographer Shotaro Akiyama. Having spent three years as Akiyama's assistant, he joined the publishing house Fujin Seikatsusha. There, he took fashion photographs for the magazine *Fukuso (Costume).* He quit after three years, and joined the Nihon Design Center, an advertising agency, where he was in the commercial photography department. After another three years, he left to freelance.

Fujii says that he had gradually acquired the basic techniques during these formative years: in the first three years with Akiyama, he mastered the rudiments of photographic art; in the second term of three years with Fujin Seikatsusha he added the techniques of fashion photography to his repertoire; in the final three years with Nihon Design Center he began to appreciate the commercial aspects of photography. His experiences in these years must have been invaluable in the making of his mature photographic sensibility.

The first major commission Fujii received as a freelance came from Max Factor. Prior to this, he had met a model, Hiromi Oka, with whom he had done a series of sessions; it was mainly on the strength of these photographs that Max Factor were persuaded to hire him. The first poster he produced for them employed a photo from one of those sessions with Oka. The collaboration between Oka and Fujii rocketed them to preeminence in the fashion world.

Fujii is a perfectionist, trying every technical experiment to fix his image in print. He is exceptional in his explorations, devoting much time and effort to his work: it is almost abnormal the effort he puts into a single image. Someone unfamiliar with his work as whole, on seeing him at work, might think him simply a technician. Yet his techniques of fixing, with their artisan-like overtones, are most intriguing and must be very difficult for others to emulate. As for the almost-stylized, noble and beautiful images Fujii creates—these are beyond technique.

Lately, he has taken another direction, towards the aesthetic of the oriental, using female portraiture to investigate the exotic East. These photographs have been particularly appreciated in Europe and in the United States.

—Takao Kajiwara

FUKASE, Masahisa.

Nationality: Japanese. **Born:** Bifuka, Hokkaido, 25 February 1934. **Education:** Studied photography at the Nihon University, Tokyo, Dip.Photog. 1956. **Family:** Married Yohko Fukase (now divorced). **Career:** Worked as a photographer for the Daiichi Advertising Company, Tokyo, 1956-65, and for the Nihon Design Center and Kawada Shobo, Tokyo, 1965-68. Freelance photographer, Tokyo, since 1968. **Recipient:** Nobuo Ina Prize, Tokyo, 1977. **Address:** Room 501, 2-33-16 Jingumae, Shibuya-ku, Tokyo, Japan.

Individual Exhibitions:

1960	*Sky over an Oil Refinery,* Konishiroku Gallery, Tokyo
1961	*A Slaughterhouse,* Ginza Gallery, Tokyo
1973	*Big Fight,* Waren House, Seibu, Tokyo
1976	*Aha!/Crows,* Ginza Nikon Salon, Tokyo (also shown at Shinjuku Nikon Salon, Tokyo, and Nikon Salon, Osaka)
1978	*Yohko,* Nikon Salon, Tokyo (also shown at Shinjuku Nikon Salon, Tokyo)
1979	*Blackbirds,* Ginza Nikon Salon, Tokyo (also shown at Shinjuku Nikon Salon, and Nikon Salon, Osaka)
1981	*Blackbirds—Tokyo,* Ginza Nikon Salon, Tokyo (also shown at Nikon Salon, Osaka)
1988	*Crows* Israel, Photo Biennale
1990	*Personal Landscapes—travel correspondence,* Nikon Salon, Tokyo
1992	*Personal Landscapes '92,* Nikon Salon, Tokyo

Selected Group Exhibitions:

1974	*New Japanese Photography,* Museum of Modern Art, New York (toured the United States)
1977	*Neue Fotografie aus Japan,* Kulturhaus, Graz, Austria (travelled to Vienna)
1979	*Japanese Photography Today and Its Origins,* Galleria d'Arte Moderna, Bologna (travelled to the Palazzo Reale, Milan; Palais des Beux-Arts, Brussels; Institute of Contemporary Arts, London; Museum für Kunst und Gewerbe, Hamburg; Gemeente Museum, Arnhem; Pulchri Studio, The Hague)
	Japan: A Self-Portrait, International Center of Photography, New York
1985	*A Day in the Life of Japan,* Tokyo (toured Japan)
	Black Sun, Museum of Modern Art, Oxford, England (travelled to the Serpentine Gallery, London; Philadelphia Museum of Art)
1988	*Memory's revenge,* Form Stadtpark, Graz
1989	*Japanese Photographers,* Europaria Japan, Belgium
1989	*11 People over 1965-75,* Yamaguchi Prefectural Art Museum
1989	*Photography Now,* Victoria and Albert Museum, London
1990	*New documents '90,* Toyama Prefectural Museum of Modern Art

Collections:

Nihon University, Tokyo; Museum of Modern Art, Tokyo.

Publications:

By FUKASE: Books—*Homo Ludens,* Tokyo 1971; *Yohko,* Tokyo 1978; *The Straw Hat Cat,* Tokyo 1978.

On FUKASE: Books—*New Japanese Photography,* exhibition catalogue, by John Szarkowski and Shoji Yamagishi, New York 1974; *Neue Fotografie aus Japan,* exhibition catalogue, by Otto Breicha, Ben Watanabe and John Szarkowski, Graz and Vienna 1977; *Japanese Photography Today and Its Origin,* exhibition catalogue, by Attilio Colombo and Isabella Doniselli, Bologna 1979; *Japan: A Self-Portrait,* exhibition catalogue, by Shoji Yamagishi, Cornell Capa and Taeko Tomioka, New York 1979; *Nude Photographs of Japan,* with text by Shiroyasu Suzuki, Tokyo 1981; *A Day in the Life of Japan—June 7, 1985,* edited by Rick Smolan and David Cohen, New York and London 1985. **Article**—"Black Sun: The Eyes of Four," special issue of *Aperture* (Millerton, New York), no. 102, 1986.

*   *   *

The exhibition *New Japanese Photography* at the Museum of Modern Art in New York in 1974 included work by Masahisa Fukase, who had used his wife Yohko as a model. There have been several examples of the intimacy between photographer and model emanating throughout their mutual work, notably Weston's pictures of Charis and Callahan's pictures of Eleanor. Fukase was attempting to explore neither Weston's sensuality nor Callahan's plastic, sculptural sense. His intimacy with Yohko surfaced in a long, narrative drama with Yohko at the centre of the stage and himself as both voyeur/spectator and leading protagonist. He continued to photograph Yohko until 1976. In the wake of their divorce he returned to his native Hokkaido. The chance picture of a flock of crows crystallised images of solitude and death appropriate to his sombre mood, and he began a series on the birds. He photographed the crow in the snow and in the night, the bird as symbol and the bird in death. The silver eye and black silhouette were photographed in a similar convention to sumi-e ink painting, like brush strokes in the sky. The crows became a running image punctuating the Yohko series to which he returned and exhibited and published in 1978.

The complete series opens with the black silhouette of the crow in flight followed by a macabre image of dead flesh—two pigs on hooks hang against the blood-splattered walls of the slaughter-house. Yohko appears in white on her wedding day; the optimism is soon destroyed on masked walks across the wastelands of Tokyo housing. The intimate domesticity is broken by Yohko in rehearsal then in performance on the Noh stage. The drama continues in the fields, by the coast and in a northern town, until Yohko is transported to the back streets of New York, a stranger hurrying on the sidewalk or lost among the winos of some Bowery slum. The personal relationship is charted to the final separation with Yohko resolute again on the Noh stage and Fukase himself left with a final image of a sky swarming with crows.

Fukase's series sustains an intimate but deeply melancholic narrative. In his recent work, exhibited in Europe in 1979, he has moved from such personal exposure to a much more formal use of an old, large format Anbako camera in a reaction back to the meticulous detail of early photography.

—Mark Holborn

FULTON, Hamish.

Nationality: British. **Born:** London, 1946. **Education:** Attended Hammersmith School of Art, London, 1964-65; St. Martin's School of Art, London, 1966-68; Royal College of Art, London, 1968-69. **Career:** Professional artist since 1970. Lives in Canterbury, Kent. **Address:** c/o Annely Juda Fine Art, 23 Dering Street, London W7R 9AA, England.

Individual Exhibitions:

1969	Galerie Konrad Fischer, Dusseldorf
1970	Galleria Sperone, Turin
1971	Galerie Konrad Fischer, Dusseldorf
	Situation, London
	Richard Demarco Gallery, Edinburgh
1972	Galleria Sperone, Turin
	Art and Project, Amsterdam
	Galleria Toselli, Milan
	Galerie Konrad Fischer, Dusseldorf
	Museum of Modern Art, Oxford
	Galerie Yvon Lambert, Paris
1973	Kabinett für Aktuelle Kunst, Bremerhaven
	Stedelijk Museum, Amsterdam
	Galleria Sperone-Fischer, Rome
	Situation, London
	Galerie Yvon Lambert, Paris
	Art and Project-M.T.L., Antwerp
1974	Galleria Marilena Bonomo, Bari, Italy
	Museum of Modern Art, Oxford
	Galleria Sperone, Turin
	Galerie Konrad Fischer, Dusseldorf
1975	Art and Project, Amsterdam
	Galerie Rolf Preisig Basle
	P.M.J. Self Gallery, London
	Kunstmuseum, Basle
1976	Sperone-Westwater-Fischer Gallery, New York
	Cusack Gallery, Houston
	Institute of Contemporary Arts, London
	Hester van Royen Gallery, London
	Robert Self Gallery, London
	Claire Copley Gallery, Los Angeles
1977	Galerie Rolf Preisig, Basle
	City Museum, Canterbury, Kent
	Stedelijk Van Abbemuseum, Eindhoven, Netherlands
	Robert Self Gallery, London
	Sonnabend Gallery, New York
1978	Galerie Konrad Fischer, Dusseldorf
	Galerie Nancy Gillespie/Elisabeth de Laage, Paris
	Museum of Modern Art, New York (project exhibition)
	Centre d'Art Contemporain, Geneva
	Galerie Tanit, Munich
1979	Whitechapel Art Gallery, London
	Galerie Rolf Preisig, Basle
	Art and Project, Amsterdam
1980	Galerie Gillespie de Laage, Paris
	Thackrey and Robertson Gallery, San Francisco
	Sperone-Westwater-Fischer Gallery, New York
	Graeme Murray Gallery, Edinburgh
	Kanransha Gallery, Tokyo
	Waddington Galleries, London
1981	Galleria Massimo Valsecchi, Milan
	Centre Georges Pompidou, Paris
1982	Waddington Galleries, London
	Orchard Gallery, Londonderry, Northern Ireland
1983	Galerie Salomon Gillespie Laage, Paris
	Kanrancha Gallery, Tokyo
	Galleria Massimo Valsecchi, Milan
	John Weber Gallery, New York
1984	Waddington Galleries, London
	Centre d'Art Contemporain, Geneva
1985	Van Abbemuseum, Eindhoven, Netherlands (travelled to Le Nouveau Musée, Lyon; Fruit Market Gallery, Edinburgh; Mendel Art Gallery, Saskatoon; Castello di Rivoli, Turin)
1986	Galerie Tanit, Munich
	Moderne Kunst Dietmar Werle, Cologne
1988	Kanransha, Tokyo
	Painted Wall Texts, Delfryd Celf, Wales
	Galerie Tanit, Munich
	Temple University, Philadelphia
	Gallery Senda, Hiroshima
1989	*Here and There Travels,* The Clocktower Gallery, New York
	East South West North, Graeme Murray Gallery, Edinburgh
	Kanransha, Tokyo
1990	*Selected Walks 1969-1989,* Albright-Knox Art Gallery, Buffalo, New York (toured to National Gallery of Canada, Ottawa; La Fundacion Cultura Televisa, A.C. and El Centro Cultural/Arte Contemporaneo, Mexico City
	Musée de Grenoble, France
	John Weber Gallery, New York
	Galerie Laage-Salomon, Paris
1991	Galerie Tanit, Koln
	Serpentine Gallery, London
	Haags Gemeentemuseum (Project Space), Netherlands
1992	John Weber Gallery, New York
	Statliche Kunsthalle, Baden-Baden, Germany
	Galleri Riis, Oslo
1993	Annely Juda Fine Art, London
	Massimo Minini, Brescia, Italy
1994	John Weber Gallery, New York
	Galerie Lydie Rekow, Crest, France

Selected Group Exhibitions:

1969	*Konzeption/Conception,* Städtisches Museum, Leverkusen, West Germany
1970	*Information,* Museum of Modern Art, New York
1972	*Documenta 5,* Kassel, West Germany
1973	*Medium Fotografie,* Städtisches Museum, Leverkusen, West Germany

1975   *Artists over Land,* Arnolfini Gallery, Bristol
1978   *Art as Photography, Photography as Art,* Institute of
            Contemporary Arts, London
1979   *Altered Photographs,* Project Studio One, New York
1980   *Artist and Camera,* Mappin Art Gallery, Sheffield, Yorkshire
            (travelled to the Stoke City Art Gallery; Durham Light
            Infantry Museum; Cartwright Hall, Bradford)
1982   *Slices of Time: California Landscapes,* Oakland Museum,
            California (travelled to the Security Pacific National Bank,
            Los Angeles)
1984   *Construire les Paysages de la Photographie,* Caves Sainte-
            Croix, Metz, France
            A Contemporary Focus 74-84, Hirshorn Museum, Washington
1985   *Second Nature,* Common Ground, London
1986   *The Real Big Picture,* The Queens Museum, New York
1988   *Raw Materials,* Althea Viafora Gallery, New York
            Images of British Landscapes, Maryland Institute College of
            Art, Baltimore
            In Praise of Walking, Cairn Gallery, Nailsworth, England
1989   *Line Art '89,* Galerie Ronny van de Velde, Brussels
            Maskunow: A Trail, A Path, Memorial University Gallery, St
            John's, Newfoundland
            Topography, Fuller Gross Gallery, San Francisco
1990   *Signs of Life: Process and Materials, 1960-1990,* Institute of
            Contemporary Art, University of Pennsylvania, Philadelphia
            Savour-Faire, Savoir-Faire, Savoir-Etre, Centre International
            Contemporain, Montreal, Quebec
1991   *Telekinesis,* Mincher/Wilcox Gallery, San Francisco
            About Collecting, Ronny Van de Velde, Antwerp

Collections:

Tate Gallery, London; Museum of Modern Art, New York; The Brooklyn Museum, New York; Princeton Art Gallery, Princeton; Philadephia Museum of Art, USA; Los Angeles County Museum, USA; Eastman House, Rochester, New York; National Gallery of Canada; Metropolitan Museum, Tokyo; National Museum, Osaka, Japan; Victoria and Albert Museum, London; Biblioteque National, Paris; Australian National Gallery, Canberra; Stedelijk Museum, Amsterdam; Stedelijk Van Abbemuseum, Eindhoven, Holland; Art Gallery of Ontario, Toronto; National Gallery of Scotland, Edinburgh; British Council, London; Kunstmuseum, Basel, Switzerland; Centro Cultural Arte Contemporaneo, Mexico City; Centre d'Art Contemporain, Geneva; Musée de Grenoble, France; Musée St Pierre, Lyon, France; FRAC, Rennes, France.

Publications:

By FULTON: Books of photographs—*Hollow Lane,* London 1971; *The Sweet Grass Hills of Montana,* Turin 1971; *10 Views of Brockman's Mount,* Amsterdam 1973; *Hamish Fulton,* Milan 1974; *Skyline Ridge,* London 1977; *Nepal 1975,* Eindhoven, Netherlands 1977; *Nine Works, 1969-1973,* London 1977; *Roads and Paths,* Munich 1978; *Wild Flowers,* Paris 1981; *Song of the Skylark,* London 1982; *Horizon to Horizon,* Londonderry 1983; *Twilight Horizons,* Bordeaux, France 1983; *Camp Fire,* Eindhoven, Netherlands 1985; *Coast to Coast Walks,* London 1985; *Cloud River,* London 1985; *Jet Car Owl Mud,* Neuss 1987; *Ajawaan,* Toronto 1987; *The Snow Mountain,* New York 1987; *No talking for Seven days,* Munchen 1988; *Straight Smoke,* Philadelphia 1988; *Hamish Fulton, Selected Walks, 1969-1989,* Buffalo 1990; *Alps Horizon,* Grenoble 1990; *A Twelve Day Walk and 84 Paces,* London 1991; *Bird Song,* London 1991; *Touching By Hand One Hundred Rocks,* Tokyo 1991; *One Hundred Walks,* Den Haag 1991; *Hamish Fulton 1992,* Baden-Baden 1992; *Walking Passed Standing Stones Cairns Milestones Rocks and Boulders,* Valencia 1992.

On FULTON: Books—*Photography as Art* by Volker Kahmen, Tubingen, West Germany 1973, London 1974; *Artist and Camera,* exhibition catalogue,

London 1980; *The Artist as Photographer* by Marina Vaizey, London 1982; *International Photograph 1920-1980,* edited by Ian North, Canberra 1982; *Construire les Paysages de la Photographie,* exhibition catalogue, by Jean-Francois Chevrier, Jean-Marc Poinsot and Michele Chomette, Metz, France 1984. **Articles**—"Photography as Sculpture" by Rudi Fuchs in *Studio International,* October 1973; "Artist over Land" by William Packer in *Studio International,* November 1975; "Hamish Fulton" by Peter Fuller in *Studio International,* May/June 1976; "Hamish Fulton" by Hal Foster in *Artforum,* February 1978; "Richard Long and Hamish Fulton" by Allan Davies in *Art Monthly,* 25 April 1979; "Hamish Fulton: The Residue of Vision/The Opening of Mind" by Robert Morgan in *Arts Magazine,* March 1986; "A Journey into the Realm of Meditative Art" by John Bentley Mays in *The Globe and Mail* (Toronto), 4 March 1990; "Mexico City, Hamish Fulton" by Roger Bevan in *Burlington Magazine,* June 1990.

*

My work is about the experience of walking. The framed artwork is about a state of mind—it cannot convey the experience of the walk. A walk has a life of its own; it does not need to be made into art. I am an artist and choose to make my artworks from real life experiences. All the walks I make are easy. I prefer to go out into the world and be influenced and changed by events rather than work from my imagination in one fixed place. (1979)

My artform is the short journey—made by walking in the landscape. (1986)

—Hamish Fulton

*   *   *

Hamish Fulton is a sculptor who takes photographs, and the photographs become the exhibited art. His concern is not documentary reportage, but the photograph as a kind of souvenir, memento, allusive metaphor, for his work. Definition, print quality, brilliance of composition, accuracy of description of the observed scene are thus not necessarily part of the work, which is not in any event professional photography in the usual sense.

The action of his work—walking through landscape—takes place throughout the world; sometimes he works alone, sometimes he walks with friends. His photographs, very often strongly horizontal in bias so that the spectator has a sense of walking as a passage through time which crosses space, are grainy, and typically unpeopled. Photographs are usually taken with the forward thrust of the walk, not looking backwards. A number of books of his photographs have been published, and photographs as exhibited and as published are captioned. But the captions may not be directly descriptive of the photograph, rather an amplification of mood, feeling or even observation that has taken place beyond the picture frame. A few, or hundreds of photographs may be taken on each walk. Invariably only a very few are used.

It may well be argued that what Fulton has done is to join in with his own distinctive way of working and looking in a tradition that is specifically British, even, perhaps, English: the romantic attitude towards the meaning of landscape, the desire to be part of it as well as to show it. Thus Fulton's photographs are paradigms of effort. While normally a half hidden reaction to a photograph is a belief in its authenticity—no matter how much our conscious mind may grasp the fact, in fact, of a photograph's having been manipulated, handled, treated—the reaction to captioned framed photographs by Fulton (which are sometimes isolated, sometimes in series) is a variation: the photograph is a proof not of itself, the authenticity of the depicted scene, but of Fulton's activity in the landscape, of his presence.

Some of his work has indeed extracted segments of landscape, or landscape seen through time, as in Brockman's Mount, a hill in Kent near his home, which he photographed over a period of nearly a year, to produce *10 Views,* under varying conditions of light, time, weather, atmosphere. *Hollow Lane* shows in photographs part of the Pilgrims Way between Canterbury and Winchester. After 1973 Fulton decided that work did not exist without the relationship of his walking in landscape: much of the walked landscape has been over well-worn tracks, paths, old ways, particularly poignant in remote landscapes. At some point in the activity, Fulton, who hardly ever acts in the landscape, other than walking through it (that is, unlike other land sculptors, he does not rearrange landscape elements such as stones or pieces of wood to form manipulated sculptures in the natural environment), decides that a certain view, or segment, coinciding with his feelings, distills the work: this distillation is confirmed in a photograph, or photographs. Thus the photograph is an analogue for the experience of the walk. "Views are chosen because they symbolize the walk." This is borne out by the titles for exhibitions and publications: for example, *Skyline Ridge,* "16 Selected Walks," or *Roads and Paths.*

Interestingly, Fulton claims not to be interested in Western landscape painting, but rather in the Oriental landscape tradition. Certainly in terms of certain Eastern attitudes towards the importance simply of being and feeling, this is understandable.

The photographs exist as an expression of that being and feeling: for instance, the size of the photograph reflects his attitude and feeling toward the walk in landscape it commemorates. Fulton does not develop or print his photographs, and he uses a hand-held camera, working exclusively in black-and-white.

By his use of photography in this way Fulton implicitly questions traditional views of art and photography. Certainly his photographs are not professional in the commonly held view of the term. Yet fundamentally images convey experience, and with its combination of caption and image, in art work exhibited on gallery walls, in the pages of magazines and periodicals, and in books, Fulton's work is amongst that which has expanded the public response to the individual experience of landscape—remote, exotic, near and intimate. Again, it is the "examination of life" which is the impetus behind Fulton's work.

—Marina Vaizey

FUNG, Joseph (Hon-kee).

Nationality: Chinese. **Born:** Guangzhou, China, 10 October 1938. **Education:** Studied at the College of Medicine, National Taiwan University, Taipei, Taiwan, 1956-60; studied photography, The School of the Art Institute of Chicago, Illinois, USA, 1985-87, MFA 1987. **Family:** Married Sok Mai Leung in 1971; children: Michelle and Joey. **Career:** Freelance photographer, specializing in fashion, advertising and editorial work, since 1967. Instructor of Photography, Applied Design Certificate Course, Extramural Studies, Chinese University, 1968; co-ordinated and taught the Certificate Course of Commercial Photography, Extramural Studies, Chinese University, 1979-81. Founder of Fotocine School of Photography, 1979-81. Founder of Photo Centre, co-ordinated and taught photography courses, 1981-88. Supervisor, AEB-GCE "A" Level Photography Examination, since 1981. Teaching Assistant to Ken Josephson, Large Format Photography, The School of the Art Institute of Chicago, 1986, and to Karen Savage, Color Photography, The School of the Art Institute of Chicago, 1987. Tutor, 2D and 3D Studies, Diploma Course; Architecture and Industrial Photography, HAP2, Part-time Evening Course; Major Projects, HAP2, Part-time Evening Course; and Fashion Photography, BA Fashion Design, 1987-88; BA Graphic Course Committee Member and China Contacts Forum Member, 1987-88; Tutor, Photography, BA Graphic Design, 1988-89; Course Leader, Higher Certificate Applied Photography Evening Course, since 1990; Senior Tutor and Course Committee Member, BA (Honours) Photographic Design Course,

since 1990; Tutor and Course Committee Member, BA (Honours) Art and Design in Education Course, 1992; Lecturer (College of Degree Studies), Swire School of Design, Hong Kong Polytechnic, 1992. Editorial Consultant and column writer, *InPhoto* magazine, Shenzhen, China, since 1988; Member of Editorial Board and column writer, Jejiang Photographic Press, Hangzhou, China, since 1988; Member, Hong Kong Artists' Guild, 1988; Chairman, Photo Art League, Hong Kong, since 1989; Member of the Executive Committee, Hong Kong Artists' Guild, since 1990; Member of the Executive Committee, Hong Kong Federation of Writers & Artists, 1991; Member of Selection Panel, *1991 Photographer of the Year Award,* 1992; Member and Endorser, Hong Kong Cultural Sector Joint Conference Ad-hoc Committee, March 1992; Member, Steering Committee, Hong Kong Cultural Sector Joint Conference, April 1992; Editorial Associate, *Photographer International,* Taipei, Taiwan, 1992; Contributing Artist to Spring 1993 issue of *Aperture,* New York, 1992-93; Selection Panel, *Artists of the Year Awards, 92,* Hong Kong Artists' Guild & Urban Council, 1992-93; Board of Directors, Hong Kong Cultural Sector Joint Conference, 1993-94; Judging Panel Member, *Miss Photogenic of the Miss Asia Pageant 1993,* Asia Television, Hong Kong, August 1993; Official Photographer, *Miss Asia Pageant 1993,* Asia Television, Hong Kong, August 1993. Invited to join as member of the "Circle of 24 Photographers," a group of international established photographers with workshop and gallery in the Hague, Netherlands, March 1994. Formally invited to join the Editorial Advisory Board by Aperture Publications, New York, March 1994. **Recipient:** Associateship, Royal Photographic Society of Great Britain, 1965; Bronze Award for *National Minority Costume in China,* Hong Kong Designer Show, 1986. **Address:** 75B, Block 47, Savanna Garden, Tai Po Kau, N.T., Hong Kong

Individual Exhibitions:

1975   *Recent Work,* Hong Kong Arts Centre
1976   *Image & Reality,* Quorum Galleries, Hong Kong
1981   *Glimpses of China,* Hong Kong Arts Centre
1983   *Glimpses of Mainland China,* Taipei, Taiwan
1985   *Tales of Two Cities—Taipei & Shenzhen,* Photo Centre
          Gallery, Hong Kong
1993   *New Perspectives,* F-Stop Gallery Bar/Restaurant, Hong Kong

Selected Group Exhibitions:

1983   *Self Portraits,* Hong Kong
          Hong Kong—Faces & Places, Hong Kong
1990   *Visits to the Homeland: Photographs of China,* Hampshire
          College Photography Gallery, Amherst, Massachusetts, USA
          (travelled to the Visual Studies Workshop, Rochester, New
          York, 1991)
1992   *City Vibrance—Recent Works in Western Media by Hong
          Kong Artists,* Hong Kong
          Contemporary Chinese Photographers, travelling exhibition
          (toured the United States)
1994   *Contemporary Photography of Hong Kong, Mainland China &
          Taiwan,* Hong Kong Arts Centre
          Jurors' Photographic Exhibition, Exposition Hall, Hong Kong
          University of Science & Technology
          Aktuell, Hong Kong Arts Centre

Publications:

By FUNG: Books—*A Han Tomb—Li Cheng UK Estate,* Hong Kong 1970; *Beijing XXXI,* monograph, Hong Kong 1983; *National Minority Costume in*

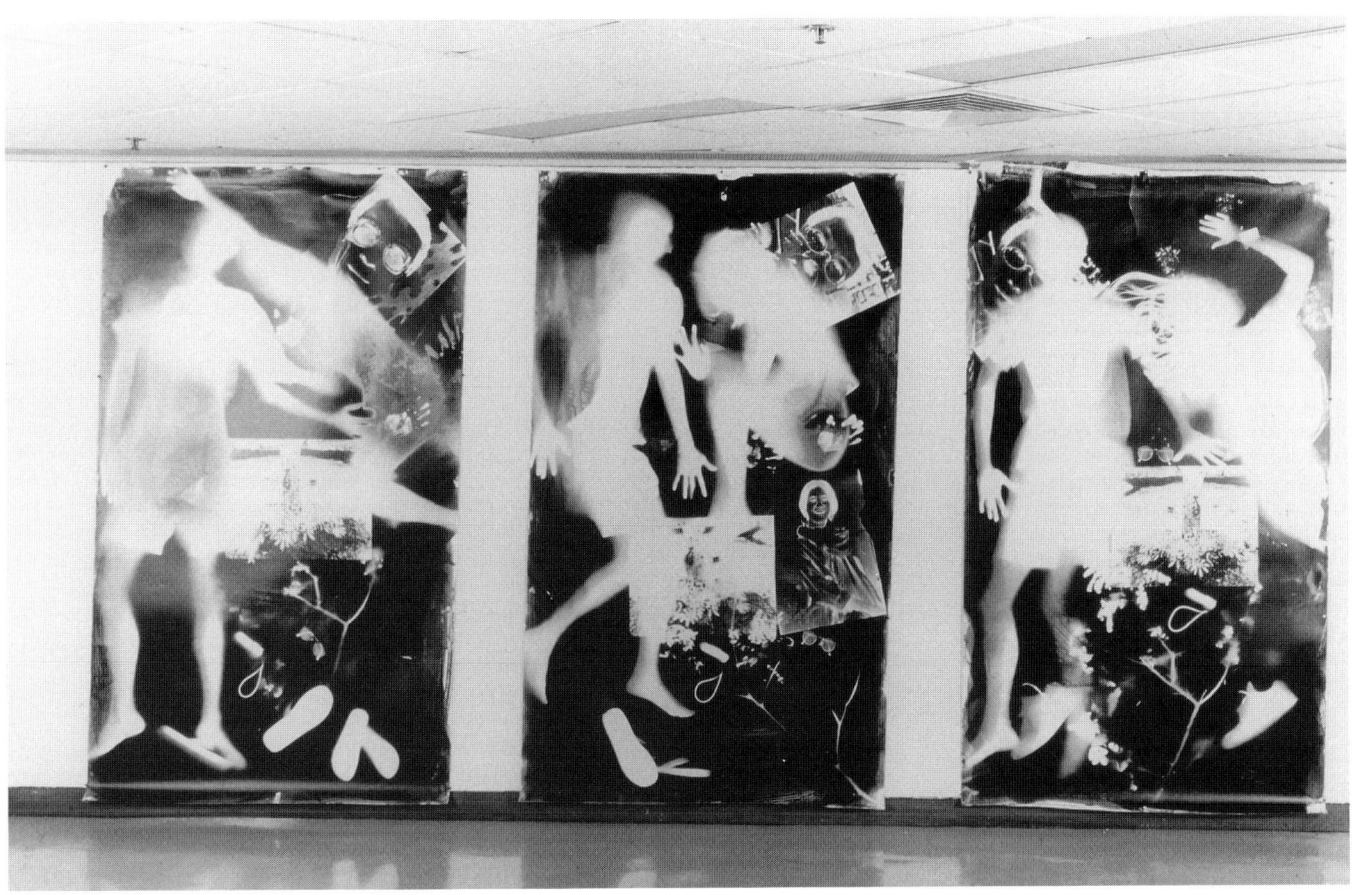

Fantasy Nos. 2, 1, 3, **1992.** Photograph by Joseph Fung.

China, Hong Kong 1985; *Yuen Ming Yuen—Imperial Garden,* co-photographer, Hong Kong and Beijing, China 1985.

*   *   *

It is not always easy to put contemporary Chinese culture into perspective. Radical changes in modern Chinese history divided "China" into three main parts, namely, the mainland, Taiwan and Hong Kong. The lifestyles and behaviour between these places differ in many ways and yet they share the same cultural roots. It is exactly this combination of differences as well as their similarities that formulated the foundation for Joseph Fung's photographic development. Born in Guangzhou, raised in Hong Kong and educated in Taiwan: Fung's photographic practice only began after returning from his medical training in Taiwan. Photography was first a hobby for Fung and later turned into a profession in the late 1960s, thus making him one of the pioneers in the industry as a Chinese photographer.

Always working from a position of discontent, Joseph Fung has made certain dramatic changes in his photographic journey. A rebel by nature, Fung questioned the "salon" and pictorial photography which was the only school of creativity at the time of his early years. His academic background and enthusiasm for exploring new schools of thought drove Fung's career in the direction of education. Founder of "The Fotocine School of Photography," "PhotoCenter" and photography instructor at the Hong Kong Polytechnic, Fung combined careers in teaching with free and experimental picture-making of his own. However, it was not until the conclusion of *Beijing XXXI*—an honest black-and-white portrayal of a real China which has just opened her

door to the West and, more importantly, to the son who left home—that Fung realised he was no longer fascinated by social documentary. This marked the beginning of Fung's two years of fine art training in Chicago, during which he questioned the identity and culture of overseas Chinese immigrants in the colour series *Chinatown.* Behind the mythical symbol of dragon, buddha and red lantern these photographs show a surrealistic influence on the artist's interpretation of these phenomena.

Openness and receptiveness in Fung's character once again drove Fung's attention to other means of expression. In the years following his return from the States Fung experimented, exhibited and taught the use of photogram and Polaroid manipulation in Hong Kong. Whether the subject is a Coca-Cola can, a rose or a human body, an emotional emphasis is expressed through the manipulation of material and the texture of the subjects used. But for Fung, photography is also as much an occult science as an art. The recent development of digital imaging has triggered Fung's curiosity to explore a new approach. His latest works, using a computer as the tool of composition, alter our normal perception of scale, tone and colour. It is also about manipulating symbols, only this time they have become more cynical. For an artist who cannot be restrained by a single medium of expression, digital photography seems to be the immediate attraction to Joseph Fung. Before the next stage, that is.

—Becky Cho

GAGLIANI, Oliver (Lewis).

Nationality: American. **Born:** Placerville, California, 11 February 1917. **Education:** Attended San Francisco schools, 1928-37; studied music at San Francisco State College, now California State University at San Francisco, 1940-42; studied at the California School of Fine Arts, now San Francisco Art Institute, 1946, and studied engineering at the Heald College of Engineering, San Francisco, 1951-53; mainly self-taught in photography from 1940, but attended workshops under Ansel Adams, Minor White, and Ruth Bernhard. **Military Service:** Served as an aircraft mechanic in the United States Army, in the Pacific, 1942-45. **Family:** Married Laura Frugoli in 1948; Gayle Anderson in 1981; children: Laurence and Olivia. **Career:** Independent photographer, San Francisco, since 1948. Instructor in Photography, South San Francisco High School, 1967-69, University of California Extension at San Francisco, 1969-74, Image Circle, Berkeley, California, 1970-71, and Zone System Workshop, Ansel Adams Gallery, Yosemite, California, 1974-75; Graduate Instructor in Photography, California State University at San Francisco, 1973-74; also, instructor in private photography workshops, San Francisco, since 1965. Founder Member, Visual Dialogue Foundation, San Francisco, 1969; Advisory Trustee, Friends of Photography, Carmel, California, 1974-76. **Recipient:** National Endowment for the Arts Grant, 1976; Fisher Grant, University of Arizona, Tucson. **Address:** 605 Rocca Avenue, South San Francisco, California 94080, U.S.A.

Individual Exhibitions:

1953	Peninsula Art Association, San Mateo, California
1954	California Palace of the Legion of Honor, San Francisco
1955	International Museum of Photography, George Eastman House, Rochester, New York
1958	*California State Park Series,* Oakland Public Museum, California (travelled to the Santa Barbara Museum of Art, California)
1961	*Color in the Photographic Print,* San Francisco Museum of Art (travelled to Indiana University, Bloomington, 1962, and Fresno State University, California, 1963)
1964	Underground Gallery, New York
1968	*The Magic of the Image,* Focus Gallery, San Francisco (travelled to Arizona State University, Tempe)
1969	*The Visual Dialogue of Oliver Gagliani,* Camera Work Gallery, Costa Mesa, California
	University of Iowa, Iowa City
	International Museum of Photography, George Eastman House, Rochester, New York (with Todd Walker)
1970	Ohio State University, Columbus
	Bakersfield College, California
	Middle Tennessee State University, Murfreesboro
1971	St. Mary's Art Center, Virginia City, Nevada
1974	Witkin Gallery, New York
1975	Diablo Valley College Art Gallery, Pleasant Hill, California
1976	Printworks Gallery, Seattle
	Chapman College, Orange, California
1977	*Festival of Tasmania,* Hobart
	Photographer's Gallery, Melbourne
1978	Neary Gallery, Santa Cruz, California
	Photosynthesis, Fresno, California
	Glanville Gallery, Perth, Western Australia

1979	Galleria Il Diaframma, Milan (toured Europe)
	Photogallery International, Tokyo
1980	Yuen Lui Gallery, Seattle
	Afterimage, Dallas
1981	Daniels Gallery, Carmel, California
	Susan Spiritus Gallery, Newport Beach, California
	Jeb Gallery, Providence, Rhode Island
1984	*Retrospective 1937-84,* Fresno Arts Center, California
	Josephus Daniels Gallery, Carmel, California
1985	Monterey Peninsula Museum of Art, California
	Selections from the Retrospective, Silver Image Gallery, Seattle, Washington
1989	*Past and Present,* Witkin Gallery, New York

Selected Group Exhibitions:

1954	*9 Bay Area Photographers,* Photographers Gallery, San Francisco
1959	*9 Photographers from the West Coast,* Indiana University, Bloomington
1967	*Oliver Gagliani's 1966 Workshop,* San Francisco State College
1968	*Light7,* Massachusetts Institute of Technology, Cambridge
1969	*Vision and Expression,* International Museum of Photography, George Eastman House, Rochester, New York (toured the United States, 1969-71)
1973	*Polaroid Photography,* Focus Gallery, San Francisco (travelled to the Neikrug Gallery, New York)
1976	*American Photography of the 20th Century,* Mt. St. Mary's College, Los Angeles
1977	*The Great West: Real/Ideal,* University of Colorado, Boulder (subsequently Smithsonian Institution travelling exhibition: toured the United States)
1983	*Arboretum,* University of Denver, Colorado
1986	*The Other Image,* Josephus Daniels Gallery, Carmel, California

Collections:

Museum of Modern Art, New York; International. Museum of Photography, George Eastman House, Rochester, New York; Visual Studies Workshop, Rochester, New York; Massachusetts Institute of Technology, Cambridge; Art Institute of Chicago; Center of the Eye, Sun Valley, Idaho; Phoenix College, Arizona; Pasadena Art Museum, California; San Francisco Museum of Modern Art; Bibliothèque Nationale, Paris.

Publications:

By GAGLIANI: Books—*Color Portfolio Number One,* San Francisco 1960; *Oliver Gagliani,* with introductions by Van Deren Coke and Leland Rice, and an afterword by Jack Welpott, Menlo Park, California 1975; *Oliver Gagliani,* portfolio of 4 photos, Sunnyvale, California 1978; *Meniscus,* portfolio, with others, San Francisco 1983; *Oliver Gagliani: A Retrospective 1937-1984,* exhibition catalogue, Fresno, California 1984. **Film**—*One Final Expression,* 1974.

On GAGLIANI: Books—*Light7,* edited by Minor White, Rochester, New York 1968; *Vision and Expression* by Nathan Lyons, New York 1969; *The Great West: Real/Ideal* edited by Sandy Hume and others, Boulder, Colorado 1977; *The Photograph Collector's Guide* by Lee D. Witkin and Barbara

London, Boston and London 1979. **Articles**—"Gallery: Oliver Gagliani" in *American Photographer* (New York), February 1980.

*

Everything that exists in this world, whether it be a tree or a rock, a building or a chair, every object has a life of its own. It is a living thing to me, a being that exists within a given span of time. At some point it was put together, it had its birth as a unit, then it fills its life span of so many years, and eventually reaches decay and death. The problems it faces are the same problems that face human beings. And from the experience of these problems, these objects have gained a special wisdom.

I believe that the only thing we are after as human beings, the only real goal of this life, is to acquire wisdom, the knowledge of something outside of ourselves which in turn gives a further knowledge of ourselves. Everything else is secondary. And from these objects of the world, from their own lives which often far outlast our own, we can acquire a wisdom which would otherwise be inaccessible to us. It is the photographer, through the medium of light, who must confront these objects directly, not as he would like them to be, but as they are in themselves. It is the measure of his success as to how deeply he is able to perceive the life which they have experienced, and penetrate the surface to tap the wisdom which they have to offer.

—Oliver Gagliani

*   *   *

Oliver Gagliani is one of those poets of the lens who focus their attention on the smallest things around us. A broken-down wall, a broken window, a corner of the landscape—these are for him, and through his pictures also for us, a whole universe. He takes objects and images that look ordinary and humdrum and draws from them a visual symphony that helps us to understand the world better.

The word symphony is not used by chance. Gagliani began by studying music. Only later, at a mature age, did he take up photography. As he himself tells us, two exhibitions that he saw in San Francisco just after the war made a great impression on him. One was by Paul Strand, the other by Weston. "The contrast that Strand could make between light and shade, between object and space, was marvellous," says Gagliani. "It made me think of music, which I had been studying for a long time." We can find abundant traces in his photographs of this passion of his for grey tones and the arrangement of masses and planes in the composition of the picture. It is no coincidence that, at the beginning of his career as a photographer, he attended a workshop run by Ansel Adams. The whole of Gagliani's work is shot through with this master's vision, his love of nature. Gagliani opens up to us a secret world of lights and shadows, of spaces, of textures. His representations are never pointless, but reveal the inward essence of things. Heir to the great American photographic tradition known as the West Coast School, in photography he leads, and to some extent has actually outrun, the path of hyperrealism. The object depicted has reference to something else, something that goes beyond the mere object itself. Gagliani's reality is reinvented, transfigured. We can also find distant echoes of the school of Subjective Photography, and this has preserved him from empty exercises in form without content. His photographs are not imitations of abstractism but are always recognizable as pictures of something, of perfectly definite objects, even if the significance of them transcends the pure and simple descriptive datum. The photographic medium is adapted to the need to extend our perception; a process of search that magnifies and makes memorable the signals received by the human eye.

Gagliani does not simply look; he succeeds in seeing, and in making us see. His technique is highly refined, very precise; like every good workman, he attributes great importance to it without becoming subject to it. A complete tonal scale of greys, a strict and subtle framing, cannot be improvised. They are the result of long study, many trials, many failures, many experiments. Gagliani does not take his photographs on the spur of the moment; he holds them within himself for a long time until they emerge, almost by magic, and easily. "You have to establish a kind of understanding with your subject," he says. "You have to go all around it, you have to observe it for a long time, until this mutual exchange, the atmosphere that is created, enables you to take the right picture, the picture that, more than any others, is full of meaning."

Mindful of his musical studies, Gagliani has not forgotten that, in photography too, accurate execution lies behind the success of a work. The greatest composer's sonata will make a poor effect if it is played by a bad musician. In the same way, in the pictures that Gagliani wants to produce, and does indeed produce, form and content must go strictly arm in arm. Each serves the other in a reciprocal exchange, resulting in a work inseparable into two parts. Hence the fascination of his pictures and of the poetry that shines out from them.

—Edo Prando

GAGNON, Charles.

Nationality: Canadian. **Born:** Montreal, Quebec, 23 May 1934. **Education:** Studied at College Stanislas, Montreal, 1942-48; Loyola College, Montreal, 1948-50; Parsons School of Design, New York, 1956-57; New York University, 1956-57; New York School of Design, 1958-59. **Family:** Married Michiko Yajima in 1960; children: Monika, Erika and Eames. **Career:** Designer, Harvey Probber Inc., New York, 1959-60; Founder-Director and Designer, Charles F. Gagnon Inc., and Gagnon/ Valkus Inc., Montreal, 1961-68. Independent photographer, Montreal, since 1968. Also a painter. Associate Professor, Department of Communication Arts, Concordia University, Montreal, 1967-75. Professor, Department of Visual Communication Arts, University of Ottawa, since 1975. **Recipient:** Design Award, New York School of Design, 1959; Canada Council Award, 1961, 1969, 1978; National Award, and Donald Cameron Medal, Banff Centre School of Fine Arts, Alberta, 1981. **Agent:** Yajima/Galerie, 307 Ste. Catherine West, Montreal, Quebec H2X 2A3, Canada. **Address:** 3510 Addington Avenue, Montreal, Quebec H4A 3G6, Canada.

Individual Exhibitions:

1971	Art Gallery of Vancouver
	Art Gallery of Edmonton, Alberta
1972	Mendel Art Gallery, Saskatoon, Saskatchewan
	Sir George Williams University, Montreal
	Yellowknife Library and Art Centre, Yukon
1973	Moose Jaw Art Gallery, Saskatchewan
	Mount St. Vincent University, Halifax, Nova Scotia
	Université de Sherbrooke, Quebec
	York University, Toronto
	Owens Art Gallery, Mount Allison University, Sackville, New Brunswick
1974	Memorial University, St. John, Newfoundland
1975	Yajima/Galerie, Montreal
1978	*Paintings-Drawings-Photographs,* Musée des Beaux-Arts, Montreal (travelled to the National Gallery of Canada, Ottawa, Vancouver Art Gallery, and Art Gallery of Ontario, Toronto, 1979; and Winnipeg Art Gallery, 1980)

Selected Group Exhibitions:

1972	*5 Montreal Photographers,* Optica Gallery, Montreal
1975	*5 Canadian Photographers,* Mount Allison University, Sackville, New Brunswick
1976	*Destination Europe,* Art Gallery of Ontario, Toronto (travelled to The Photographers' Gallery London, and Galleria Il Diaframma, Milan)
1979	*The Banff Purchase,* Walter Phillips Gallery, Banff, Alberta
	An Exhibition of Photography in Canada, Edmonton Art Gallery, Alberta (travelled to Glenbow Institute, Calgary, Alberta, and Mendel Art Gallery, Saskatoon, Saskatchewan)
1984	*Contemporary Canadian Photography,* National Film Board of Canada, Ottawa (toured Canada)

Collections:

National Gallery of Canada, Ottawa; Canada Council Art Bank, Ottawa; Department of External Affairs, Ottawa; Musée d'Art Contemporain, Quebec; Montreal Museum of Fine Arts; Walter Phillips Gallery, Banff Centre, Alberta; Owens Art Gallery, Mount Allison University, Sackville, New Brunswick.

Publications:

On GAGNON: Books—*Charles Gagnon,* exhibition catalogue, with text by Philip Fry, Montreal 1978; *The Banff Purchase: A Survey of Photography in Canada* by Penny Cousineau, Banff and Toronto 1980; *Contemporary Canadian Photography* by Martha Langford, Edmonton, Alberta 1984. **Articles**—"Charles Gagnon" by N. Theriault in *Vie des Arts* (Montreal), December 1968; "Charles Gagnon" by D. Corbeil in *Artscanada* (Toronto), April 1970; "Charles Gagnon" by G. Guerra in *Ovo/Photo* (Montreal), June 1974; "A Canadian Portfolio" by Geoffrey James in *Artscanada* (Toronto), December 1974; "Two Exhibitions" by Penny Cousineau in *Parachute* (Montreal), Fall 1976; "Charles Gagnon—Making and Trying" by Philip Fry in *Parachute* (Montreal), Fall 1977; "Charles Gagnon: Das Fenêtre sur l'Ambigu" by Gilles Toupin in *La Presse* (Montreal), 21 October 1978; "Charles Gagnon: Le Culte de l'Ambiguité" by L. Lamy in *Vie des Arts* (Montreal), Spring 1979; "Charles Gagnon: The Ambiguous Object" by David Burnett in *Vanguard* (Vancouver), June 1979; "Charles Gagnon's Point of View" by Dore Ashton in *Artscanada* (Toronto), August 1979; "Focusing on Urban and Inner Landscapes" by Georges Bogardi in *Chimo* (Montreal), May 1981.

*

Among some thoughts/Works of art raise questions rather than answer them/Talking about my own work too specifically is contradictory to its aim/I am not interested in raising such questions directly about anything in particular but possibly to record a catalytic non-event which rang true at the time (for me)/Art is but a distillation concocted at a particular time and place (not about a particular time and place) thru unknown filters permitting us to clarify for ourselves what "being" is about/Someone wrote: "Art is the mirror conscience of the soul"/In my work I am concerned with communion rather than communication/The material stuff of the arts which is normally labeled "the formal issues" is but a part of the vocabulary not the content itself/The content hinted by the work really comes from the interaction between it (the work) and the spectator, and the quality of this interaction is to a great extent the responsibility of the viewer, although it is not as much a question of effort as it is a matter of compatibility/When I photograph I don't "make" anything; I don't have to. It's all around me for the seeing and taking. The seeing amazes me. The taking confirms that I am.

—Charles Gagnon

*   *   *

"It's the photographer's mind that clicks—not the camera's shutter," says Charles Gagnon. His subtle photographs investigate the fascination of the ordinary. They concern non-events, "nothing," Gagnon says—"irreverent irrelevance." He's not only seeing (and using) his environment as a work of art but choosing things stopped and still, or out of context (they're supposed to serve a function but don't). The effect in his photographs is of suspense: something is going to happen, but the viewer is not sure what it is. In a way, the results recall early de Chirico or Magritte. But Gagnon has a serious intent: it is society which is out of order, malfunctioning. In "Exit—Montreal" (1973), his most stripped down formal presentation, the light over the closed door is on—and there's an alarm system visible. The potential of danger from a mysterious source exists.

Gagnon's photographs are charged with spiritual and mental truths. They imply the tensions, ambiguities, and contradictions of life. For him, the camera is a tool which forces him to look at the "unbelievable" world which surrounds him. It's in the dark room, his "altar," where everything comes together. Gagnon prints dark to capture the richness and intensity of what he sees, and bring the viewer closer to the print. "The situation creates a conflict

of territory between the photograph's pregnant moment and the viewer's private world."

—Joan Murray

GANOR, Avi.

Nationality: Israeli. **Born:** Kfar-Saba, 8 October 1950. **Education:** Hasharon High School, Neve-Magen, 1964-68; studied aeronautics at the Technion Institute of Technology, Haifa, 1969-73; studied at the San Francisco Art Institute, 1975, Pratt Institute, New York, 1976, and Parsons School of Design, New York, 1977. **Family:** Married Ofra Steinman in 1977. **Career:** Instructor at Bezalel Academy of Art and Design, Jerusalem, and Beit Zvi, Ramat Gan since 1977. Head of Department of Computerized Images, Camera-Obscura School of Art, Tel Aviv since 1991. Freelance photographer, with own studio at 2 Chlenov Street, Tel Aviv 66181, since 1977. **Address:** 6 Shalom-Aleichem Street, Ramat-Hasharon 47265, Israel.

Individual Exhibitions:

1980   White Gallery, Tel Aviv
1985   Tel Aviv Museum, Israel

Selected Group Exhibitions:

1978   *Hard Sale/Soft Sale,* White Gallery, Tel Aviv
1979   *Polaroid Photos,* White Gallery, Tel Aviv
1980   *Photographers' Exhibition,* Artist's House Gallery, Tel Aviv
1981   *10 Israeli Photographers,* White Gallery, Tel Aviv
1982   *Here and Now,* Israel Museum, Jerusalem
1983   *A Pear and an Apple,* Tel Aviv Museum, Israel
        Personal View, Israel Museum, Jerusalem
1985   *The Enrique Kavlin Photography Grant,* Israel Museum, Jerusalem
1986   *First Israeli Biennale*
1987   *Still Life,* Artist's House, Tel Aviv
1990   Jerusalem Museum Photography Collection
1991   *Image and Text,* Kalisher Gallery, Tel Aviv
        Intimate Art, Kalisher Gallery, Tel Aviv
        New Acquisitions, Tel Aviv Museum

Collections:

Tel Aviv Museum; White Gallery, Tel Aviv; Bezalel Art Academy, Jerusalem; Israel Museum, Jerusalem; The Photographers' Gallery, London.

Publications:

By GANOR: Books—*The First Israeli Biennale* (Editor), Israel 1986; *Taste of Israel,* (co-author), New York 1990; *The Garden of Childhood* (co-author), Israel 1991; *The Grill* (co-author), USA 1991. **Article**—"About Photography" in *Zilum* (Tel Aviv), August/September 1985.

On GANOR: Books—*Here and Now,* exhibition catalogue, Jerusalem 1982; *Personal View: Works by Contemporary Israeli Photographers,* exhibition catalogue, with foreword by Eyal Onne, Jerusalem 1983; *Avi Ganor,* exhibition catalogue, Tel Aviv 1985. **Articles**—"Suddenly I See a Photograph" by Ronit Shanie in *Yedioth-Ahronoth* (Tel Aviv), 28 March 1980; "A Matter of Time" by Adam Baruch in *Yedioth-Ahronoth* (Tel Aviv), 11 April 1980; "Avi Ganor: interview" by Eyal Onne in *Zilum* (Tel Aviv), June/July 1985; "Ganorama" by Meir Agasi in *Monitin* (Tel Aviv), June 1985; "Ganor at Home" by Tzvika Reich in *Tel Aviv,* 24 May 1985.

*   *   *

Avi Ganor is one of a handful of people in Israel who are feeding fresh photographic ideas to the public through the wide dissemination of commercial images. He is, however, operating in a market that he describes as "small and poor": "It's good there is what there is, but there isn't much. Israel is not a society with a high level of consumption. Therefore advertising is not a top developmental priority, nor should it be."

What does this mean in practice? At the most obvious level, it means a lot more organizational work for the photographer: an elaborate back-up industry simply does not exist. There are, for example, no agents to represent him to clients, no bureaux through which to book models, no stylists, no color retouchers. In fact, he can't even use Kodachrome, because there is no place in all of the Middle East to get it processed. Also, a small, restrained economy can only allot small budgets. Ganor sees himself as one of a group of photographers who've recently returned to Israel after studying abroad. "We've brought new blood to what was a pretty ossified, conventional scene. We have as much imagination or technical competence as our peers in New York or Paris, but we don't have as much money to explore our ideas." Because Israel is a very small country—there are, after all, fewer than four million of us—Ganor cannot afford that discipline which is also a luxury, style. "Style is a positive word elsewhere, something you're constantly urged to develop, to make yourself recognizable. That just doesn't go in a small market that is quickly saturated. Here I am under constant, anxiety-producing pressure to change all the time, to come up with new ideas all the time. Nor is there such a thing as specialization; it might be surreal fashion today and a complicated technical shot tomorrow."

Nevertheless, Ganor, who has the round, curlframed face of a mischievous cherub, is very happy about his profession. He is convinced that photography's future lies with commercial photographers because, like pianists, they practice their craft every day. They work primarily in color, and Ganor has no doubt that color will soon dominate photography. Also, as commercial photography mirrors the values of the society that commissions it, the photographs increase in value over time, becoming eloquent historical records.

Ganor looks to his commercial colleagues as much for their personal work as for their professional work. His own deepest commitment, for example, is to the development of his self-assignment—street photography: "People are photography's true subject and, for me, the only interesting reality." He believes that photography as a medium has barely begun to express its potential. He feels much the same about himself: "My photographs are temporary achievements in a process of constant research. I'm creating raw material. I need to live more life before I start making conclusions."

—Bonnie Boxer

GARCÍA JOYA, Mario (also known as Mayito).

Nationality: Cuban. **Born:** Santa María del Rosario, 28 July 1938. **Education:** Studied musical theory and harmonics, Guanabacoa Conservatory, Havana, 1953-54; fine arts, San Alejandro Academy, Havana, 1955-57; graphic design, under the painter Raúl Martínez, Havana, 1957-58; history of photography, under Mario Rodriguez Alemán, Cuban Institute of Film Art and Industry, Havana, 1963-64; photographic evaluation, under Adelaide de Juan, Jose Marti National Library, Havana, 1965-66; and philology, specializing in Cuban studies, Havana University, 1972-78. **Family:** Married Leonor Fayat in 1960 (divorced, 1963); children: Kattia and Abigail; married the photographer María Eugenia Haya in 1964; children: Mario and María. **Career:** Photographer, for Otpla and Mestre y Conill advertising agencies, Havana, 1957-58; photographer, *Revolución* newspaper, Havana, 1959-65; Member of the Creative Group, Channel 4, Cuban Television, 1961-62; Director of Photography, Cuban Institute of Film Art and Industry, Havana, 1961-68; photographer, *Cuba* magazine, Havana, 1963-65. Lecturer in Photography, Vedado House of Culture, Havana, 1977. Advisory Group Member, Fine Arts Department, Cuban Ministry of Culture, 1977-80; Founder-member, Latin American Photography Council, Mexico City, 1978; President of the Photographic Section, Unión Nacional de Escritores y Artistas de Cuba (UNEAC), 1978-80; Evalutation Committee Member, Creativity Group, Cuban Institute of Film Art and Industry, Havana, 1980. **Recipient:** Cifsa Silver Cup, Cuba

One and Only Contest, Havana, 1959; Komsomolkaya Pravda Prize, Prague, 1961; Photojournalism Prize, Union Nacional de Escritores y Artistas de Cuba, 1964; First Prize, *Havana Carnival*, 1966; Photo graphic Award, *Internationale Buchausstellung*, Leipzig, 1977; Minfar Prize for Photomontage, Havana, 1979; First International Prize, Socialist Ministries of Culture, Budapest, 1979. **Address:** c/o Unión Nacional de Escritores y Artistas de Cuba (UNEAC), 17 no. 351, Vedado, Havana, Cuba.

Individual Exhibitions:

1963   *Expresionismo Abstracto,* Havana Gallery, Cuba

Nuez y Mayito, Ercidez Perez Gallery, Camaguey, Cuba (with the caricaturist Nuez)

1964   *Dos Momentos,* Havana Gallery, Cuba

1965   *Foto-Mentira,* Havana Gallery, Cuba

1967   *Audiovisual Scenography,* Maisonneuve Theatre, Montreal

1968   *El tren blindado,* open-air exhibition, Santa Clara City, Cuba

1969   *Campaña de Alfabetización,* open-air exhibition, Grenoble, France

1970   *Cuba Va!,* at *Salón 70,* Museo Nacional, Havana

1980   *Influencia Africana en la Cultura Cubana,* Museo Carillo Gil, Mexico City (with María E. Haya; travelled to the Museo Nacional, Havana)

Selected Group Exhibitions:

1962   *10 Años de Revolución,* Museo Nacional, Cuba (toured Europe and Asia)

1966   *Primera Muestra de la Culture Cubana,* Pabellón Cuba, Havana

1967   *Cuban Pavilion Exhibition,* at *Expo '67,* Montreal (photomontage and script)

1968   *Del Tercer Mundo,* Pabellón Cuba, Havana (photomontage and script; travelled to Grenoble, France, 1969)

1978   *Hecho en Latinoamerica,* Museum of Modern Art, Mexico City (travelled to the *Biennale,* Venice, 1979)

1979   *Historia de la Fotografía en Cuba,* Museo Carillo Gil, Mexico City

Soirée Latinamericaine, at *Rencontres Internationales de la Photographie,* Arles, France

1980   *Culture in the Socialist Countries,* Museum of Contemporary Art, Budapest

Dos Momentos Revolucionarios, Consejo Mexicano de Fotografia, Mexico City

1981   *Hecho en Latinoamerica II,* Palacio de Bellas Artes, Mexico City

Collections:

Museo Nacional, Havana; Biblioteca Nacional José Martí, Havana; Casa de las Americás, Havana; Unión Nacional de Excritores y Artistas de Cuba (UNEAC), Havana; Escuela de Filología, University of Havana; Havana Musical Theatre (murals; permanent installation); Museo de Santiago de Cuba, Oriente (murals; permanent installation); Consejo Mexicano de Fotografia, Mexico City; House of Culture, Prague.

Publications:

By GARCÍA JOYA: Photographs in books—*Páginas de Memorias,* Havana 1964; *La Historia, la Provincia, la Revolución,* Havana 1965; *A la Plaza con Fidel,* Havana 1970; *Diana Habanera o la Rumba se llama Chano,* Havana 1971; *Un Mundo Amasado por los Trabadores,* Havana 1975; *Fotos de Cuba,* Havana 1975; *XX Aniversario Casa de las Americás: Obra Gráfica,* Mexico City 1979. **Articles**—"La Otra Historia de la Fotografía" in *Revolución y Cultura* (Havana), no. 56, 1977; "Delante y detrás de la cámera" in *El Caimán Barbudo* (Havana), no. 113, 1977; "La Ultima Cena" in *El Caimá Barbudo* (Havana), no. 112, 1978; "Relación entre Realidad y Estilos de la Fotografía en Latinoamerica" in *Hecho en Latinoamerica,* exhibition catalogue, Mexico City 1978; "Notas para la Historia de la Fotografía" in

Fototéchnica (Havana), vol. 9, no. 1, 1978; "Sobre el Coloquio Latinoamerica de Fotografía" in *La Gaceta de Cuba* (Havana), no. 170, 1978; "Disparos de una Cámara" in *Constantinos Arias,* exhibition catalogue, Havana 1980; also, numerous feature films and documentaries, 1964-79.

On GARCÍA JOYA: Books—*Diez Años de Arquitectura Revolucionaria* by Roberto Segre, Havana 1968; *Las Artes Plásticas* by Adelaide de Juan, Havana 1968; *Pintura Cubana: Temas y Variaciones* by Adelaide de Juan, Havana 1978; *Breve Historia de la Fotografía Cubana* by María E. Haya, Havana 1980; *Hecho en Latinoamerica 2,* exhibition catalogue, with texts by Pedro Meyer, Lazaro Blanco and others, Mexico City 1981. **Articles**—"Dos Momentos de Mayito" by David Fernández in *Pueblo y Cultura* (Havana), January 1964; "En el Mundo de la Alucinación" by Graziella Pogolotti in *Cuba* (Havana), February 1964; "La Imagen Fotográfica del Subdesarrollo" by Edmundo Desnoes in *Casa* (Havana), no. 34, 1966; "Foto-Mentira" by Edmundo Desnoes in *Bohemia* (Havana), July 1966; "Expo '67—Pabellón Cuba: Una Revolución es asi" by Norberto Fuentes in *Cuba* (Havana), August 1967; "Cuba en la Expo '67" by Jorge Timosi in *Granma* (Havana), 9 August 1967; "Una Pelea Cubana contra los Demonios" by Mario Rodriguez Alemán in *Granma* Havana), March 1972; "Historia de la Fotografía Cubana" by María E. Haya in *XX Aniversario Casa de la Americas: Obra Grafica,* Mexico City 1979; "Influencias Africanas en la Cultura Cubana" by Katya Mandoki in *Uno más Uno* (Mexico City), May 1980.

* * *

Mario García Joya is perhaps the best-known mid-generation Cuban photographer alive today. To assess such a personality, one must take into account the relatively small number of professional photographers in Cuba, compared with Europe or North America. Nevertheless, the public appetite for visual images is as great there as in any part of the world.

The prime focus of attention for Cuban photographers is contemporary life, the immediate environment and the Cuban people. Such subject matter is, of course, also the concern of the photojournalists, who in Cuba are either editorial staff members on periodicals and newspapers or attached to the national press agency. In addition, there are around thirty photographers registered with the Union of Writers and Fine Artists of Cuba, some of them freelancers. At the head of this last group is the photographer Mario García Joya, called Mayito, who is also vice-president of the whole Union. García Joya's erudition in the arts extends beyond photography, having studied at the Escuela Superior de Arte San Alejandro and completed his graphics studies with the painter Raul Martinez. He became attracted to photography for its ability to depict life's events so directly. As a founder-member of the photographers' team at the newspaper *Revolucion* in 1959, he was able to expand his photographic experience, and went on to formal photography training at Havana's National Library. Later still, after producing a number of films, he completed a course of literary studies at Havana University in 1978.

These extensive studies in several branches of the arts gave him a broader understanding of the specific properties of photography. García Joya prefers to make enlarged prints of his favourite photographs, giving them the concrete presence of autonomous works of art, and in this format his pictures have represented Cuban photography at numerous exhibitions abroad. Seeing his work alongside that of foreign contemporary photographers is an important stimulus in clarifying his own role as a photographer.

García Joya is no exception to the Cuban tradition of the "human interest" photographer. He has made numerous portraits of the typical inhabitants of both city and countryside, and likes to reinforce narrative qualities by including symbolic props in the pictures. One of his most characteristic series is of Cuban house interiors in which the furnished rooms offer as much information about their inhabitants as the direct portrait shot of the person. His intimate understanding of many areas of fine art invests his images of quite ordinary daily life with an aesthetic quality which justifies their status as works of art.

—Petr Tausk

GARDUÑO, Flor.

Nationality: Mexican. **Born:** Mexico City, 21 March 1957; emigrated to Switzerland, 1989. **Education:** Studied visual art, Escuela Nacional de Artes Plasticas San Carlos UNAM, Mexico City, 1976-78; studied under Kati Horna, 1978. **Family:** Married the photographer Adriano Heitmann in 1989; daughter: Azul. **Career:** Worked as assistant to Manuel Alvarez Bravo, 1978-80; freelance photographer, working on art reproductions for books, 1980-86. **Recipient:** Kodak Prize (Germany) for the Best Book of the Year, for *Witnesses of Time,* 1992. **Agent:** Argento Immagine, PO Box 59, CH-6855 Stabio, Switzerland. **Address:** Via Ufentina 17B, CH-6855 Stabio, Switzerland.

Individual Exhibitions:

1980	*Fotografías de Flor Garduño,* Gallery of the National Art College, San Carlos UNAM, Mexico City
1985	*Magia del Juego eterno,* Galería de Arte Contemporaneo, Mexico (travelled to Galerie La Chambre Claire, Paris; and Museo de América Latina, Monte Carlo, 1987)
1988	*Bestiarium,* Galería de Arte Contemporaneo, Mexico City (toured in Europe, the United States and Canada, 1989-93)
1992	*Witnesses of Time,* Musée de l'Elysée, Lausanne, Switzerland (toured in Europe, the United States and Mexico, 1992-94)
1993	*Indios,* Nikon Gallery, Zurich, Switzerland

Selected Group Exhibitions:

1983	*Four from Mexico,* The Mexican Museum, San Francisco
	La Fotografía por la Fotografía/Photography for Photography, Museo de Arte Moderno, Mexico City
1984	*Primera Bienal de Grafica de la Habana,* Casa de Las Américas, La Habana, Cuba
1987	*Exposicion Imagen de Mexico/Exhibition Images from Mexico,* Museum Schirn, Frankfurt, Germany
1988	*Friburgo Tip 88,* Fribourg, Switzerland (travelled to the Teatro San Martin, Buenos Aires, Argentina)
1989	*La Memoria del Tiempo/Memory of Time,* Museo de Arte Moderno, Mexico City
1990	*Other Images, Other Realities: Mexican Photography since 1930,* Sewall Art Gallery, Rice University, Houston, Texas
	Between Worlds, Impressions Gallery, York, England (toured in England, Ireland and the United States, 1990-92)
1991	*The Fourth Wall,* De Oude Kerk, Amsterdam
	The First Ten Years, Galleria Gottardo, Lugano, Switzerland
	Selection, at *Rencontres d'Arles,* France
1992	*5 FotoBienal,* Vigo, Spain
1993	*Canto a la Realidad. Fotografía Latinoamericano, 1860-1993,* Casa de América, Madrid, Spain
	Photographs from the Real World, Lillehammer Art Museum, Lillehammer, Norway (travelled to Bergen Kunstforening, Bergen, Norway; Hasselblad Centre, Göteborg, Sweden; and Museet for Fotokunst, Odense, Denmark, 1994)
	European Photography Award 1993, Bad Homburg, Germany

Collections:

Museum of Modern Art, New York; Museum Ludwig, Cologne; Museum of Fine Arts, Houston, Texas; Museo de Arte Moderno, Mexico City; Casa de la Cultura de Juchitán, Oaxaca, Mexico; Museo Nacional de Historia, INAH, Mexico; Swiss Foundation for Photography, Zurich; Bibliothèque Nationale, Paris.

Publications:

By GARDUÑO: Books—*Magia del Juego eterno,* with introduction by Eraclio Yepeda, Oaxaca, Mexico 1985; *Bestiarium,* edited by Allan Porter,

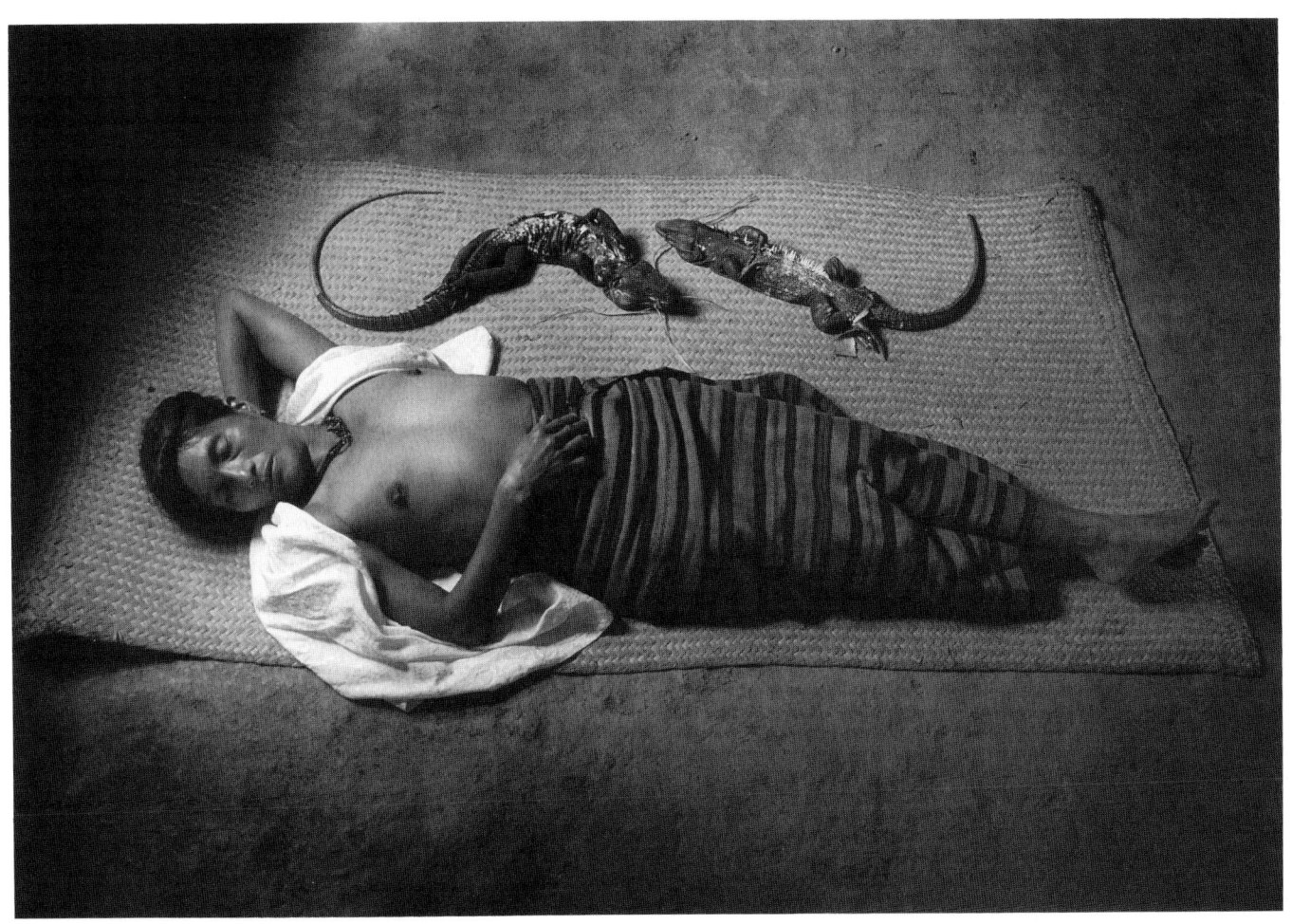

La mujer que sueña (Dreaming Woman), **1991.** Photograph ©Flor Garduño.

Zurich and Stabio, Switzerland 1987; *Witnesses of Time,* Paris, London, New York, Milan, Mexico City, Zurich and Heidelberg, 1992.

On GARDUÑO: Book—*Other Images, Other Realities: Mexican Photography since 1930,* exhibition catalogue, Houston, Texas 1990. **Articles**—in *Camera International* (Paris), 1991; special monographic issue of *Du* (Zurich), January 1992; in *Airone* (Milan), 1992.

*   *   *

Few photographers have been catapulted to world renown almost overnight through a book, an exhibition or both. Names that spring to mind in the last thirty years are Jacques-Henri Lartigue (exhibition of his boyhood photographs at Museum of Modern Art, 1963); Lennart Nilsson ("A Child Is Born," 1965); Mirella Ricciardi ("Vanishing Africa," 1971); Sebastião Salgardo (exhibition of the gold miners of Serra Pelada, 1986); Cristina García Rodero ("España Oculta," 1989), and lastly Flor Garduño ("Witnesses of Time," 1992).

There is a certain kinship in theme between the last two publications: Rodero's occult, religious celebrations in Spain today and Garduño's esoteric, mystic Indian customs and festivals of Hispanic America. Mexican-born Flor Garduño is of mixed Indian and Spanish extraction. She worked for 2-3 years with Manual Alvarez Bravo, as did her compatriot Graciela Iturbide. Flor had an inborn fascination for the rituals of peasant culture, and by approaching the shy Indians with understanding and sympathy was able to interpret Indian culture and traditions. Aesthetically her mentor is the Hungarian-born photographer Kati Horna who had fled to Mexico City from Berlin in 1933. Flor admired this ardent follower of surrealism who enlivened the artistic scene for her intelligence and progressive spirit. As an example of different interpretation compare Iturbide's Indian woman carrying a head-dress of Iguanas and Garduño's sleeping peasant, naked at the top, lying on a mat, watched by two bound iguanas decoratively spaced.

Or let us consider the cemetery pictures from Guatemala with animal-masked figures guarding cave-like tombs and upturned stone-blocks. Such scenes seem closer to a Dalí concept than to holy ground. Yet the native writer Eduardo found the cemetery pictures "a perfect reflection of the complex religious, political, cultural and magic reality of Latin America—death, happiness, play, religion and magic." If you want to know what has been left to the Indios of their original culture after 500 years of supremacy of the catholic church and European political influence Flor's understanding eye and gift for dramatization and chiaroscuro may help to find an answer.

Flor Garduño started work on this theme in Mexico in 1987. Three years later she received a grant from the Mexican National Council for Culture and from other institutions enabling her to continue and extend the series travelling hundreds of miles in Ecuador, Guatemala, Columbia, Peru and Bolivia. The well known Swiss cultural magazine *DU* devoted its entire January 1992 issue to her work.

Her book "Witnesses of Time" produced by her husband Adriano Heitmann and published in 1992 in several languages has made her work known in many countries and has led to numerous exhibitions. She is presently engaged on a new book on indigenous peoples, this time commissioned by a publisher. Flor and Adriano, a well known reportage photographer and her manager, got married in 1989 to celebrate the 150th anniversary of photography. They live close to the Swiss border with Italy in Canton Ticino.

—Helmut Gernsheim

GARNETT, William A(shford).

Nationality: American. **Born:** Chicago, Illinois, 26 December 1916. **Education:** John Muir High School, Pasadena, California, until 1937; Art Center School, Los Angeles, 1939. **Military Service:** Served as a cameraman in the United States Army Signal Corps during World War II. **Family:** Married Eula Beal in 1942; children: William, Jay and Don. **Career:** Freelance photographer, in California, since 1947: noted for aerial photography. Photographer for *Life* magazine, New York, and for *Fortune* magazine, New York, since 1954. Fellow in Advanced Visual Studies, Massachusetts Institute of Technology, Cambridge, 1967. Professor of Design, University of California, Berkeley, 1968-84. **Recipient:** Guggenheim Fellowship, 1953, 1956, 1975; Outstanding Achievement Award, American Society of Magazine Photographers, 1983. **Agents:** Photography West Gallery, Dolores at Ocean Avenue, P.O. Box 4829, Carmel, California 93921; Vision Gallery, 1151 Mission Street, San Francisco, California 94103. **Address:** 1286 Congress Valley Road, Napa, California 94558, U.S.A.

Individual Exhibitions:

1955	International Museum of Photography, George Eastman House, Rochester, New York
1979	Robert Mondavi Winery, Oakville, California
1980	University of Oregon, Eugene
	William Lyons Gallery, Coconut Grove, Florida
	Douglas Elliott Gallery, San Francisco
	Friends of Photography, Carmel, California
	Silver Image Gallery, Seattle, Washington
	Daniel Wolf Gallery, New York
1981	The Halsted Gallery, Birmingham, Michigan
1983	Douglas Elliott Gallery, San Francisco
	Sterling Vineyards, Napa, California
	Susan Spiritus Gallery, Newport Beach, California
	Stephen White Gallery, Los Angeles

Selected Group Exhibitions:

1955	*The Family of Man,* Museum of Modern Art, New York (and world tour)
1956	*Diogenes IV,* Museum of Modern Art, New York
1967	*Photography in the 20th Century,* National Gallery of Canada, Ottawa (toured Canada and the United States, 1967-73)
1976	*100 Master Photographers,* Museum of Modern Art, New York
1978	*Landscapes in Photography 1859-1978,* Vision Gallery, Boston
1979	*The Photographer and the National Parks,* The White House, Washington, D.C.
1980	*A Survey of Western Landscape Photography 1950-1980,* Crocker Art Institute, Sacramento, California
1981	*Our Beautiful Earth: The View from Air and Space,* National Air and Space Museum, Washington, D.C.
1982	*Counterparts: Form and Emotion in Photographs,* Metropolitan Museum of Art, New York (travelled to the Contemporary Arts Center, Cincinnati, Ohio; Dallas Museum of Fine Arts, Texas; San Francisco Museum of Modern Art; Corcoran Gallery, Washington, D.C.)
1983	*The View From Above,* The Photographers' Gallery, London
1991	Vision Gallery, San Francisco, California

Collections:

Museum of Modern Art, New York; Metropolitan Museum, New York; Gilman Paper Company, New York; Polaroid Corporation, Cambridge, Massachusetts; Smithsonian Institution, Washington, D.C.; John Deere Corporation, Moline, Illinois; Pentax Corporation, Japan.

Publications:

By GARNETT: Books—*The American Aesthetic,* with text by Nathaniel Alexander Owings, New York 1969; *The Leica Manual,* Dobbs Ferry, New York 1973; *The Extraordinary Landscape,* Boston 1982; *William Garnett Aerial Photographs,* Berkeley 1994.

On GARNETT: Books—*The World from Above* by Hanns Reich, New York 1966; *Photography in the 20th Century* by Nathan Lyons, New York 1967; *Airborne Camera* by Beaumont Newhall, New York 1969; *Landscape: Theory* by Ralph Gibson, New York 1980; *World Photography,* edited by Bryn Campbell, London 1981; *Counterparts: Form and Emotion in Photographs* by Weston J. Naef, New York 1982; *The View From Above: 125 Years of Aerial Photography,* exhibition catalogue, edited by Rupert Martin, London 1983; *The Library of World Photography: Landscape,* with texts by David Plowden and Ian Jeffrey, Tokyo and London 1984. **Articles**—"Over California" by Walker Evans in *Fortune* (New York), March 1954; "The Eye of Bill Garnett Looks Down on the Commonplace and Sees Art" by Edward Parks in *Smithsonian* (Washington, D.C.), May 1977; "William Garnett" by Eric Lax in *American Photographer* (New York), February 1980; "A Lofty View" in *Natural History* (New York), October 1982; "America How Beautiful" in *Life* (New York), October 1982; "William Garnett: Flying a 37-year Mission" in *Popular Photography* (New York), December 1982; "William Garnett" in *Reader's Digest* (Pleasantville, New York), February 1983.

*   *   *

William Garnett has been making aerial photographs for more than three decades; his infatuation with the view from above began as a child when he took an airplane sightseeing tour. He began his career in commercial photography in the 1930s, but it was not until after World War II that he was able to combine flying with photography. His early aerial photographs were made for commercial clients, but the reputation for his personal, creative work spread rapidly.

Garnett pioneered the use of oblique light in aerial photography, and prefers to photograph the dramatic forms of the landscape when they are illuminated by the early morning or evening sun. He uses his hand-polished silver 1955 Cessna 170-B not only as transportation to reach his subjects, but also as an active tool in the creation of his images. Working at an altitude ranging from a few hundred to several thousand feet, and at a speed of up to 100 miles per hour, he keeps his light meters in a holster in the plane's window and his cameras—each equipped with a lens of a different focal length, permanently set at infinity—tucked away behind him in the cockpit.

Once he has located a potential subject he circles the area to study the changing patterns of light and land below, framing the picture both by selection of altitude and lens-length. By moving laterally he is able to place the reflection of the sun in an exact relationship to land forms, or to select certain tones or colors in ground-water reflecting the sky. Once his subject has been determined he circles again, opens the cockpit window, aims the camera behind the wing-strut and makes the exposure at the exact point where the photograph had been visualized.

In the air Garnett faces the same problems of pollution and natural haze—in magnified form—that ground photographers must confront. Added to these problems are the effects of plane vibration, ground speed and the resolution by the lens of objects photographed at great distances, plus the demands of the concentration required to fly his plane and to watch for other air traffic.

The details of Garnett's photographic technique in the air become all the more fascinating when they are seen in the context of the exquisite photographs he produces. Aerial photographs are always intriguing because of their unusual point of view. The popularity of pictures sent to earth from satellites or from the planetary space-probes have demonstrated this. Garnett is not satisfied, however, simply to depict the land below him. He abstracts sections from the landscape and often has a greater interest in the forms and textures within his camera's view than in the geographical or geological descriptions of those forms.

The diversity he is able to achieve in images of similar subject matter is clearly seen in the series of photographs he made during the 1950s in a few square miles of Death Valley. Through the combination of the ever-changing landscape and his active manipulation of the camera's position in relation to the light transforming the land, Garnett made a remarkably varied group of photographs.

Other clearly defined groups of work exist in his oeuvre, including a continuing series of reflections of the sun in the landscape made in many different parts of the country, and an on-going investigation of patterns in cultivated farm land. Garnett has also actively worked in color, and has made a series of large, 24'' x 36'' prints. Many of these have unexpected colors that result from the response of the film to the oblique light on his subjects and to the unusual coloring he finds in many of the land forms he photographs.

—David Featherstone

GATEWOOD, Charles.

Nationality: American. **Born:** Chicago, Illinois, 8 November 1942. **Education:** Parkview High School, Springfield, Missouri, 1956-60; University of Missouri, Columbia, 1960-64, B.A. in anthropology 1963; University of Stockholm, 1964-66; self-taught in photography, from 1965. **Career:** Staff Photographer, *Manhattan Tribune* newspaper, 1969-73, and *Rolling Stone* magazine, 1973-74, in New York. Freelance photographer, New York, since 1974. Publisher, *The Flash* tabloid magazine, New York, 1977-82. Lecturer in Photography, New York University, 1972, Educational Alliance, New York, 1974-77, International Center of Photography, New York, 1975-77, San Francisco Art Institute, 1977, and Rutgers University, New Brunswick, New Jersey, 1977, 1979; Artist-in-Residence, Light Work, Syracuse University, Syracuse, New York, 1976; also visiting lecturer at numerous universities and photography workshops in the United States and Europe, since 1976. **Recipient:** Creative Artists Public Service Photography Fellowship, New York, 1974, 1977; American Institute of Graphic Arts Award, 1975; Catskill Center for Photography Grant, Woodstock, New York, 1980; Artist-Sponsored Fellowship, New York State Council on the Arts, 1983; Leica Medal of Excellence, New York 1985; Merit Award, Art Directors Club of New York, 1985. **Address:** P.O. Box 745, Woodstock, New York 12498, U.S.A.

Individual Exhibitions:

1968	Lewison Gallery, City College of New York
1972	Light Gallery, New York
1975	Neikrug Gallery, New York
	Brummels Gallery, Melbourne
1976	Australian Centre for Photography, Sydney
1977	University of West Virginia, Morgantown
	X-1000, Levitan Gallery, New York
1978	*Wall Stret,* Stieglitz Gallery, New York
	Forbidden Photographs, Light Work, Syracuse University, Syracuse, New York (travelled to the Project Arts Center, Cambridge, Massachusetts)
	Contemporary Arts Center, New Orleans
	Galerie Contrejour, Paris
	Catskill Center for Photography, Woodstock, New York
	Metropolitan State College, Denver
	University of Colorado, Boulder
	Fat Tuesday, Midtown YMHA, New York (with George W. Gardner)
1979	Galerie Voir, Toulouse
	Pushing Ink, Neikrug Gallery, New York (with Spider Webb)
1981	*Forbidden Photographs,* Robert Samuel Gallery, New York
	Hamilton College, Amherst, Massachusetts (with Bruce Gilden)
1984	Rhode Island School of Design, Providence

Selected Group Exhibitions:

1967	*Photography U.S.A. '67,* De Cordova Museum, Lincoln, Massachusetts
1971	*Images of Concern,* Neikrug Gallery, New York (travelled to the Focus Gallery, San Francisco
1972	*Octave of Prayer,* Hayden Gallery, Massachusetts Institute of Technology, Cambridge
1974	*Celebrations,* Hayden Gallery, Massachusetts Institute of Technology, Cambridge
1976	*Exposition Phot-Univers,* Musée Francais de la Photographie, Bièvres, France
1977	*Rated X,* Neikrug Gallery, New York (and 1978, 1979, 1980)
1978	*The Grotesque in Photography,* Art Resources of Connecticut, New Haven
1980	*Art in a World Gone Mad,* Art Awareness Gallery, Lexington, New York
1983	*Past Tensions/Present Tense,* Philadelphia College of Art, Pennsylvania
1985	*Das Aktfoto,* Fotomuseum im Stadtmuseum, Munich (toured Germany)

Collections:

International Center of Photography, New York; Light Work, Syracuse University, Syracuse, New York; Portland Museum of Art, Maine; Kalamazoo Institute of Art, Michigan; Musée Francais de la Photographie, Bièvres, France; Museum of Modern Art, New York; Metropolitan Museum of Art, New York.

Publications:

By GATEWOOD: Books—*Sidetripping,* with text by William S. Burroughs, New York 1975; *People in Focus,* New York 1977; *X-1000,* with Spider Webb and Marco Vassi, New York 1977; *Pushing Ink,* with Spider Webb and Marco Vassi, New York 1979. *Forbidden Photographs,* Woodstock, New York 1981; *How to Take Great Pictures with Your Simple Camera,* New York 1982; *Wall Street,* New York 1984.

On GATEWOOD: Books—*Octave of Prayer,* edited by Minor White, Millerton, New York and Cambridge, Massachusetts, 1972; *Celebrations,* with texts by Minor White and Jonathan Green, Millerton, New York and Cambridge, Massachusetts 1974. **Articles**—"Thomas Barrow and Charles Gatewood" in *Light Readings: A Photography Critic's Writings 1968-1978* by A.D. Coleman, New York 1979; "Why Does Charlie Do Those Things?" by Casey Allen in *Camera 35* (New York), March 1980.

*

I quote A.D. Coleman: "Once the idea of any work enters the bloodstream of a culture, its vehicle becomes a corpse—exquisite, perhaps, but a corpse nonetheless. The calling of the artist is not simply to be a manufacturer of objects, a craftsman, but to be a progenitor of new myths, new truths, new definitions."

My book, *Forbidden Photographs,* is a new experiment in defining and developing such a visionary expressionism. Please publish my address: I welcome correspondence.

—Charles Gatewood

*   *   *

One of the earliest photographs in *Sidetripping* contains, in capital letters, the words "See life as it really is! 24hrs. Pay up front!" That just about sums up the book, which is photographed in capital letters too. Charles Gatewood shoots life not only "in the raw" but also flat on its back, masturbating in front of a mixed audience. He must have the sort of instinct for sex that Weegee had for crime and death. It draws him, as a moth is drawn to a naked candle flame.

Sidetripping: like the moth, Gatewood will never master the art of flying straight. But like the moth, he shows no fear of situations that are, to say the least, threatening and could be highly dangerous. There is nothing sneaky about his approach: he stares his subjects right in the face, or in the nipple or the crotch. He clearly does not hide the camera, or his own presence, and some of his subjects are reacting to, or acting for, the camera. He emphasizes the nature of his approach by placing his subjects near the centre of the frame, and by using direct flash in poor lighting—again, like Weegee and the newspapers' other crime photographers.

But this is not to say his compositions are artless: far from it. Though they are made to appear casual, to persuade you they are simply a "slice of life," they are tightly cropped for impact, and usually only essential information is retained in the frame.

More important than framing, however, is timing. A lot of pictures have been captured because of the photographer's sharp eye and quick reactions. For example, he has caught a policeman in the act of expectorating into a waste-basket labelled "our city," which could illustrate any low-life version of Cartier-Bresson's account of the "Decisive Moment." More often the timing shows in the capturing of precise expressions: the twisted ones that convince us that normal people are actually quite bizarre, and the human ones which persuade us that those bizarre-looking people are actually quite normal. For example, there's a woman standing on a bar with her knickers partly down to show off her backside (and a reversed sign, Hot Sausages, in the mirror): from the smile on her face she could easily be someone you'd that to on the bus. The two girls, shirts lifted, comparing their breasts on the subway, could easily be from the local library.... Most of Gatewood's subjects are not down-and-outs, like those in Anders Petersen's pictures taken in the Lehmitz café in Hamburg; nor is there the undercurrent of violence which runs through Seiji Kurata's *Flash Up* book. Gatewood's subjects probably enjoyed their normal, middle-class upbringing before they decided that being weird might be more fun. Gatewood's pictures are quite fun too, with the added spice of being slightly threatening.

—Jack Schofield

GAUTRAND, Jean-Claude.

Nationality: French. **Born:** Sains-en-Gohelle, Pas de Calais, 19 December 1932. **Education:** the Lycée Colbert, Paris, baccalauréat 1951; mainly self-taught in photography. **Family:** Married Gisèle Omar in 1955 (died, 1965); daughter: Brigitte; married Dominique Buré in 1968 (divorced, 1973); son: Philippe. **Career:** Has worked for the French Postal Service (PTT), in Paris, since 1952: currently, Superintendent. Joined the PTT Photo Club, 1956; professional photographer, since 1958. Also, contributor as journalist/ critic/ historian to *Jeune Photographie, Photo Tribune, Point de Vue, Photo Revue, Le Nouveau Photo-Cinéma, Le Photographe, Nueva Lente, Fotografia Italiana, Photo Journal,* etc. Founder Member, with Jean Louis Moré and Gérard Contant, Gamma Photo Group, Paris, 1963, and, with Jean Dieuzaide and others, Libre-Expression Photo Group, Paris, 1964; Vice-President, 1968, and President, 1976-79, 30 x 40 Photo Club, Paris. Founder, and Cultural and Artistic Counsellor for the Photography Section, *Festival d'Art Contemporain,* Royan, France, since 1972; Member of the Council, *Rencontres Internationales de la Photographie,* Arles, France, 1976-1993; Secretary-General, Prix Nadar, Paris, from 1983; Member of the Consultative Committe for Artistic Creation, Paris, 1985. **Recipient:** Grand Prix, Fédération Internationale de Photographie (FIAP), 1965; Grand Prix de la Photo d'Avant Garde, Spain, 1967; Grand Prix des Arts, City of Marseilles, 1969, 1968; Prix Vasari, Paris, 1986. Chevalier, Ordre des Arts et des Lettres, France, 1984. **Address:** 45 rue d'Avron, 75020 Paris, France.

Individual Exhibitions:

1967   Société Francaise de Photographie, Paris
1968   FNAC, Paris
        Grand Prix Musée Cantini, Galerie des Quartre Vents, Marseilles

1970   Galerie Toussaint, Angers, France
1972   *L'Assassinat de Baltard,* Centre International de Séjour, Paris (travelled to the Centre Culturel, Limoges, France, and the Centre Culturel, Gueret, France)
1974   Neikrug Gallery, New York (retrospective)
1977   Artcurial, Paris
        La Photogalerie, Paris
        Rencontres Internationales de la Photographie, Arles, France
        Galerie du Chateau d'Eau, Toulouse
        Galerie des Philosophes, Geneva
        Galerie 74, Vienna
        The Photographers' Gallery, London
1978   Musée Nicéphore Niepce, Chalon-sur-Saône, France
        Galerie FNAC, Strasbourg
        Galerie FNAC, Metz, France
        Galerie FNAC, Grenoble, France
        Galerie FNAC, Lyons
1979   Galerie Paule Pia, Antwerp
1980   Galerie ARPA, Bordeaux
        Work Gallery, Zurich
        Mai de Flandres, Bergues, France
        Musée de Grignan, France
1983   Berner Photo Gallery, Berne, Switzerland
1989   *Photofolies,* Rodez
1992   Jarny

Selected Group Exhibitions:

1963   *Photography '63,* International Museum of Photography, George Eastman House, Rochester, New York
1965   *Groupe Libre-Expression,* Société Française de Photographie, Paris (and 1966, 1971)
1972   *Biennale de Paris*
1975   *Triennale de la Photographie,* Musée d'Art et d'Histoire, Fribourg
1977   *Collection Bibliothèque Nationale,* Centre Georges Pompidou, Paris
1979   *The Concrete Eye,* French Cultural Center, New York (toured American universities)
1980   *5 French Photographers,* Australian Center for Photography, Sydney
        Des Clés et des Serrures, Canon Photo Gallery, Geneva
1981   *Ten Contemporary French Photographers,* Santa Barbara Museum of Art, California (travelled to Fifth Avenue Gallery, Scottsdale, Arizona; Lincoln Arts Center, Santa Rosa, California; Southwestern College, Chula Vista, California)
1984   *La Photographie Créative,* Pavillon des Arts, Paris
1989   *Vingt ans de photographie créative en France,* Leverküssen, Cologne, Paris Audiovisuel
1990   *Acquisitions récentes du Cabinet de la Photographie,* Musée d'Art Moderne, Centre Georges Pompidou
        En Train, Mission du Patrimoine, Palais de Tokyo, Paris
1991   *Matières et actes photographiques,* Espace Photo de Paris
1994   *Du Mur de l'Atlantique au Mur de Berlin,* FRAC, Caen; Musée de St. Lô
        Bercy la dernière balade, with Philippe Gautrand, Fondation Willums, Pourrières.

Collections:

Bibliothèque Nationale, Paris; Collection des Affaires Culturels, City of Paris; Musée Réattu, Arles, France; Musée Cantini, Marseilles; Musée Nicéphore Niepce, Chalon-sur-Saône, France; Musée des Arts Décoratifs, Nantes, France; Musée du Chateau d'Eau, Toulouse, France; Musée du Toulon,

***Bercy—La Dernière Balade, Paris,* 1989.** Photograph by Jean-Claude Gautrand.

France; International Museum of Photography, George Eastman House, Rochester, New York; Fond National d'Art Contemporain; Centre Pompidou, Paris; Paris Audio Visuel; Bibliothèque Historique de la Ville de Paris; Museum of Fine Arts, Houston, Texas.

Publications:

By GAUTRAND: Books—*Libre-Expression I,* exhibition catalogue, editor, Paris 1965; *Murs de Mai 1968,* Brussels 1967; *Libre-Expression V,* exhibition catalogue, editor, Paris 1971; *L'Assassinat de Baltard,* Paris 1972; *Forteresses du Dérisoire,* with text by Jean-Pierre Raynaud and Georg Ramseger, Paris 1977; *Paris des Photographes,* Paris 1985; *Hippolyte Bayard, Naissance de la Photographie,* editions des Trois Cailloux, 1986; *Le Temps des Pionniers,* Collection Photopoche Editions C.N.P., 1987; *Visions du Sport,* Editions Admira, 1989; text of *En Train,* edition Mission du Patrimoine/La Manufacture, 1990; *Rene-Jacques—Chroniques d'époques,* collection Les Grands Photographes, editions Belfond/Paris Audiovisuel, 1992; *Les Seeberger, l'aventure de trois frères photographes au début du siècle,* Collections Les Poches du Patrimoine, Edition la Manufacture, 1992; *Jean Dieuzaide—Yan. L'authenticité d'un regard,* Editions Marval, Paris 1994; *Bercy, la dernière balade,* with Philippe Gautrand, text by Alphonse Boudard, Paris 1994. **Articles**—numerous articles on photographers in *Photo-Ciné Revue* (Paris), April 1966-July 1975; "Les Grandes Maitres de la Photographie," series (Paris), 1973-76; "La Place de la Photographie dans l'Art Contemporain" in *Photo-Ciné-Guide,* Paris 1974; numerous articles on photographers in *Nouveau Photo-Cinéma* (Paris), June 1975-July 1979; "Photographie Aujourd'hui" in *Photo-Ciné-Guide,* Paris 1978; "Une Histoire de la Photographie" in *Photo-Journal* (Paris), November 1979-July 1980; "Les Plus Belles Photos de Paris," series, in *Point de Vue* (Paris), 1980-81; "L'Appareil et ses Applications Créatives" in *Almanach de la Photographie '81,* Paris 1981; "Cent Cinquante Ans de Portraits" in *Photo-Ciné-Guide,* Paris 1981; "Histoire du Surréalisme en Photographie" in *Images* (Paris), no. 1, 1981; "Histoire des Rencontres Internationales de la Photogaphie—Arles 1970-1994" in *Caméra International spécial,* 1994; videos—Producer, video interviews for Paris Audiovisuel: *Bernard Plosu—Sabine Weiss,* 1992; *Denis Brihat—Willy Ronis,* 1993; *Pierre Cordier—Jean Pierre Sudre,* 1994.

On GAUTRAND: Books—*Jean-Claude Gautrand,* exhibition catalogue, with text by Jean Dieuzaide, Toulouse 1977; *Jean-Claude Gautrand,* exhibition catalogue, with text by Paul Jay, Chalon-sur-Saône, France 1978; *La Photographie Créative* by Jean-Claude Lemagny, Paris 1984. **Articles**—"Jean-Claude Gautrand" by Maurice Bernard in *Photo-Ciné Revue* (Paris), June 1967; "Jean-Claude Gautrand" by Robert Doloy in *Arte Fotografico* (Madrid), November 1969; "Jean-Claude Gautrand" by Roberto Salbitani in *Progresso Fotografico* (Milan), August 1972; "Jean-Claude Guatrand" in *Photo* (Paris), September 1972; "Jean-Claude Gautrand" by Pablo Perez Minguez in *Nueva Lente* (Madrid), February 1973; "Jean-Claude Gautrand" by Michel Nuridsany in *Arts et Techniques Graphiques* (Paris), May 1974; "Jean-Claude Gautrand" in *Camera* (Lucerne), April 1977; "Jean-Claude Gautrand: l'Illusioniste" by Michel Cournot in *Nouveau Photo-Cinema* (Paris), May 1977; "Jean-Claude Gautrand: An Interview and Series Portfolio," with an interview by Bernard Plossu, in *Minolta Mirror* (Tokyo), 1977.

*

My photography is based on two essential elements: form and light. These two elements interact with each other to create images that go beyond simple reality to a personal and passionate subjectivism. It is a photographic style that asks more for imagination than for observation: the viewer cannot remain passive. For me, photography that does not include magic and mystery reveals itself immediately and is only, at best, anecdotal.

I have been strongly influenced by the rigor and poetry of Straight Photography, but also, and especially, by the wealth of possibilities in Otto Steinert's Subjective Photography.

I work with themes in time and space, to form long series of photographs which I call "poems of imagery." Each photograph should be considered as a word in a sentence; each sentence offers its meaning within the total context of the "poem." A subject unveils itself only little by little; it must revolve to invest itself and thus restore its body, its mystery, its relationship to the environment and especially to the photographer.

My principal series are: La Galet (1967), which illustrates one of the myths about the world's origin; Les Boues Rouge (1970), on industrial pollution; Les Murs de Mai (1968), on revolutionary graffiti; L'Assassinat de Baltard (1972), an indictment of the destruction of a cultural patrimony; Forteresses du Dérisoire (1977), a testimony on human pride, a passionate discourse, and a genuine archaeological work. Within the framework of preparing the book *Paris des Photographes,* of which the first volume appeared in 1985, my subject for some years has essentially been the city of Paris. *Bercy, la dernière balade,* (1993) is, for instance, an extensive study of the last Parisian village, where the 19th century warehouses of the wine merchants are being destroyed.

Focussing on the life and death of things, these series are often cries of revolt; they are commitments against injustice, effacement, and oblivion. Oblivion and death are everywhere, like an obsessive idea that pierces the mystery of deep shadows, immersing these lyrical images.

—Jean-Claude Gautrand

* * *

French photography is above all strongly characterized by documentary and photojournalism. Photographers such as Eugéne Atget, Henri Le Secq, Charles Négre, Victor Regnault, Cartier-Bresson and Robert Doisneau have created the framework for our national photography, traditionally dedicated to rendering social testimony in a sincerely socialist spirit. Man is always at the center; it is towards him that in the end the photographer's attention is directed. When one thinks of misery, of exploitation, of work, it is always to a face or to a body in action that our visual memory responds. So-called "committed" photography therefore has more to do with the subject photographed (a worker leaving a factory, for example) than with the progressive vision of the photographer himself, and sometimes photos of this kind, with this kind of social pretension, do not ultimately serve the good cause because of the banality of their internal functioning.

Jean-Claude Gautrand belongs half-way between this documentary tradition and a naturalistic trend that developed in the French Midi during the 1960s in the work of such photographers as Denis Brihat, Jean-Pierre Sudre, Jean Dieuzaide and Lucien Clergue, all of whom were definitely influenced by the School of Weston. These artists select as subjects, whatever they may be, that which will allow them to create maximumly effective metaphors of their interior lives.

Gautrand was one of the founders of the group Libre-Expression, the manifesto of which attempted to create the basis of a new kind of subjectivity. From his first book, *Murs de Mai,* through *L'Assassinat de Baltard,* to *Forteresses du Dérisoire,* Gautrand has followed a path that has put him in the midst of social tensions and political occurrences, the result of his willingness to record the presence of man in architectural constructions and structures. His photographs immortalize human activity; at the same time, they are creative spaces—because of their great technical quality and because of Gautrand's consummate craftmanship in printing. One feels that Gautrand (and the other "naturalists") wants to re-establish the concept of the artisan, to "work" the material, in hand-to-hand combat, as it were, with the gelatin. For, if it is important to show all the gestural and subversive beauty of the graffiti, it is also necessary to understand the wall, that which permitted the graffiti's existence.

Sometimes using a wide-angle lens and a red filter, Jean-Claude Gautrand creates grandiose and dramatic images. Their lyricism excites the senses. It can also deaden the political message—if one does not wish to *read* his photographs as within a global perspective. Gautrand occupies a special place in French photography, a position in which it is difficult to exist, between the "decisive moment" of Cartier-Bresson and the "charming" aestheticism of the pictorial tradition.

—Claude Nori

GELPKE, André.

Nationality: German. **Born:** Beienrode, Gifhorn, 15 March 1947. **Education:** Attended volksschule in Beienrode and Rheydt, 1953-59, and gymnasium in Rheydt and Krefeld, 1959-62; studied photography, under Otto Steinert, Folkwangschule, Essen, 1969-74. **Military Service:** Served as an infantryman in the German Army, in Bremen, 1967-68. **Career:** Bricklayer, cement worker, and truck driver, 1962-67. Photographer since 1974: Founder-Member, Visum Photo Agency, Essen, now Hamburg, 1975-78; freelance photographer, Essen, 1978-83, and in Dusseldorf, 1983-1990; Visiting Lecturer, Fachhocschule, Dortmund 1989-90. Moved to Zürich, Switzerland 1990. Lecturer Höhern Schule für Gestaltung, Zürich. Member, Gesellschaft Deutsche Lichtbildner (GDL), 1975-78. **Address:** Bächerstrasse 37, 8004, Zürich, Switzerland.

Individual Exhibitions:

1974	Galerie Schürmann und Kicken, Aachen, West Germany
1975	Galerie Spectrum im Kunstmuseum, Hannover
1979	Galerie Krebaum, Weinheim, West Germany
	Galerij Paule Pia Antwerp
	University of Salzburg
1980	*Ein Monolog: Ein Dialog,* Sander Gallery, Washington, D.C. (travelled to Work Gallery, Zurich)
	Vernissagen, Museum Folkwang, Essen
1981	Fotomuseum im Stadtmuseum, Munich Galerie Foto Art, Frankfurt
1982	Galerie Forum Stadtpark, Graz, Austria
	Benteler Galleries, Houston, Texas
	Werkstatt für Photographie, Berlin-Kreuzberg
	Galerie Foto Art, Frankfurt
1983	Universität Essen, West Germany
	Galerie Rudi Renner, Munich
1984	Galerie Rudolf Kicken, Cologne
	Benteler Galleries, Houston, Texas
	Centre Georges Pompidou, Paris
1986	Museum für Photographie, Braunschweig, West Germany
	Forum Galeria, Tarragona, Spain
	Goethe Institut, Coimbra, Portugal
	Goethe Institut, Porto, Portugal
1987	Fotogalleriet, Oslo, Norway
	Goethe Institut, Turin, Italy
1988	*Fotofest,* Houston, Texas
	Fotoforum, Hamburg, Germany
1989	Fotomuseum, Braunschweig, Germany
1990	Sprengelmuseum, Hannover, Germany

Selected Group Exhibitions:

1977	*German Photography,* Arles, France
1978	*Bildjournalismus,* Museum Folkwang, Essen
1979	*Deutsche Fotografie nach 1945,* Kunstverein, Kassel, West Germany (toured West Germany)
1980	*Vorstellungen und Wirklichkeit: 7 Aspekte Subjektiver Fotografie,* Städtisches Museum, Leverkusen, West Germany (travelled to the Künstlerhaus, Vienna, and Fundució Joan Miró, Barcelona, 1980; Palais des Beaux-Arts, Brussels, 1981)
1981	*Absage an das Einzelbild,* Museum Folkwang, Essen, West Germany
1982	*Floods of Light,* The Photographers' Gallery, London
1983	*Fotografie in Deutschland—Heute,* Cultureel Centrum Hasselt, Belgium
1984	*Six Contemporary German Photographers,* Santa Fe Center for Photography, New Mexico
1985	*Europa-America/Hello-Goodbye,* Forum Stadtpark, Graz, Austria
1986	*7 Tendencias en la Fotografia Contemporanea Europea,* Museo De Bellas Artes, Caracas, Venezuela
1987	*Endlich so wie überall,* Ruhrlandmuseum, Essen, Germany
1988	*Twentieth Century Photographs,* Museum of Fine Arts, Houston, Texas
1989	Circulo Bellas Artes, Madrid, Spain
	Landscape, Alden Biesen, Belgium
	Stipendien für Zeitgenössische Deutsche Fotografie, Folkwangmuseum, Essen, Germany
1990	*Otto Steinert und Schüler,* Museum Folkwang, Essen, Germany
1992	*Zustandsberichte: Deutsche Fotografie der fünfziger bis achziger Jahre,* IfA Galerie, Berlin, Germany
1993	*Antwerpen 93,* Museum foor Fotografie, Antwerp, Belgium
1994	*8 Fotografen zum gleichen Thema,* Siemens Fotoprojekt Städtische Galerie Nordhorn, Germany

Collections:

Museum Folkwang, Essen; Neue Sammlung, Munich; Münchner Stadtmuseum, Munich; Stedelijk Museum, Amsterdam; Bibliothèque Nationale, Paris; Centre Georges Pompidou/Musée d'Art Moderne, Paris; Museum für Kunst und Gewerbe, Hamburg; Polaroid Collection, Amsterdam; Museum of Fine Art, Houston, Texas.

Publications:

By GELPKE: Books—*Sex-Theater,* Munich 1981; *Fluchtgedanken,* Munich 1983; *Der Schiefe Turm von Pisa,* Braunschweig, West Germany 1986; *Siemens Fotoprojekt,* Munich 1991. **Articles**—texts in *André Gelpke,* exhibition catalogue, Hannover 1975; "Die Autorität Steinerts" in *Print Letter* (Zurich), no. 9, 1977; "Sextheater" in *Fotografie*(Göttingen), no. 8, 1978; text in *Neue Wege in der Fotografie,* exhibition catalogue, Munich 1980.

On GELPKE: Books—*Deutsche Fotografie nach 1945,* exhibition catalogue, by Floris Neusüss, Petra Benteler, and Wolfgang Kemp, Kassel, West Germany 1979; *Fotografie 1919-1979, Made in Germany: Die GDL-Fotografen,* edited by Fritz Kempe, Bernd Lohse and others, Frankfurt 1979; *Vorstellungen und Wirklichkeit,* exhibition catalogue, by Dieter Wellershof, Vienna and Cologne 1980; *The Imaginary Photo Museum* by Helmut Gernsheim, Renate and L. Fritz Gruber and others, Cologne 1981, London 1982; *Floods of Light: Flash Photography 1851-1981,* exhibition catalogue, by Rupert Martin, London 1982; *Museum Folkwang: Die fotografische Sammlung,* exhibition catalogue, with introduction by Ute Eskildsen, Essen, West Germany 1983. **Articles**—"André Gelpke: Auswahl" by Allan Porter in *Camera* (Lucerne), no. 11, 1970; "André Gelpke" in *Creative Camera* (London), July 1972; "Foto-Galerie" by Peter Sager in *Zeitmagazin* (Hamburg), no. 49, 1977; "Neue Experimente" by Allan Porter in *Camera* (Lucerne), no. 4, 1977; "André Gelpke" by Jög Kirchbaum in *Fotografie* (Göttingen), no. 5, 1978; "Die Verweigerte Ansicht" by Peter Sager in *Zeitmagazin* (Hamburg), no. 43, 1979; "Vernissagen" by Rolf Paltzer in *Art* (Hamburg), no. 6, 1980.

*

In this visual age, when our consciousness of reality is increasingly permeated by the actualities of television, photography and advertising, my aim is to present the photographic-bureaucratic fact collector with a selection of my reality clippings from an only apparent "pseudo reality" and thereby to bring about a new questioning of reality.

Even though I have worked for many years as a photojournalist, the medium has continued to bewilder me deeply. While I have the feeling on the one hand that photography has altered or expanded my consciousness, I am certain that it has, on the other hand, and to the same extent, led to a contraction of my awareness. For example, the indirect reality of a printed image of war which lies open in an illustrated magazine on the dining table next to the soup

Chiffre 389506

Series *Inkognito,* **1993.** Photograph by Andre Gelpke.

tureen doesn't prevent us from going on eating. The information that this image carries no longer reaches our manipulated consciousness. Reality, conditioned by the remoteness of such happenings, by the torrent of such images of cruelty, becomes fiction.

I am not interested in supplying such ''real fiction.'' I am interested in tracking down just this encounter of ''war report and soup tureen'' so that I can demonstrate it with photographic means and thereby make visible a ''counter-reality.''

The answer to the question, can photography be art, is, for me, to be found in the fact that artistic creation consists as much in the rejection of what is false as in the selection of the right solution to a self-imposed problem.

Photography is primarily a school of seeing. And there is the question of the head behind the camera, the "what" and "how" it sees, the way it reproduces this "what" with the necessary "photo apparatus." Since the discovery of photography, this "reproduction" has always been the starting point of all art criticism.

And since, with most of them, we are dealing with a particularly work-shy and failed form of human existence, art critics have naturally very quickly recognized the use for their own purposes of this "reproducibility." One critic, for example, visits exhibitions only fleetingly and simply uses photographs as a means to review painting. Shall we now say that that which was always only an aid to easier work is now suddenly an art in itself? Seeing is only a part of reality, and this lofty stance can have nothing to do with reality. The inspiration, the divinely gifted hand that creates, is missing.

Another kind of critic considers that photography's only claim to art (with the emphasis on "only") lies precisely in its capacity to "reproduce." But isn't this opinion only a wish to clarify the relationship between painting and photography?—caused by the discovery of photography and the consequences for naturalistic painting? If it has to do with "you can do this" and "I can do that," then art comes down to "being able to."

And on the so-called "photography art scene" there are now many photographers who resign themselves to this "fixing of boundaries" and see everything as everyone else sees it. The photographer sees a car and reproduces it; the viewer says, "Look, a car," and thinks that instead of a picture he sees a car in front of him. The picture is, therefore, anonymous; it is defined according to "classification."

A third kind of critic is a fetishist of the unique. He is not very interested in the creation of the picture; he is interested in the fact that it can be reproduced, that one print from the original negative cannot be distinguished from another: the prints are not "original." This kind of critic understands art only in terms of its "rarity value."

In fact, most critics of photography are not at all interested in what is to be seen in the photograph. They do not judge the image but the conditions of its manufacture and whether or not it can be traded. Any more serious analysis is feared.

Photography, with its multiple print (and I consider this the most important form of diffusion for photography), is accessible to a wide public. For this reason, I think photography can be compared to literature—I think literature most closely resembles photography's true nature . . . the literature of images, from the cheap novel for sale on every corner to the poetry that is little understood and not much sold. In the same way that literature is classified— essay, poetry, novel, journalism, etc.—so photography and its current practitioners can also be classified, so that the public, the reader, can choose between, say, the cheap photographic novel and good photographic prose. Criticism, and appraisal, of these genres does not need to involve comparisons: one would not compare a textbook with a volume of verse. We must, instead, establish criteria against which any one of the photographic genres can be judged according to its "quality."

—André Gelpke

*   *   *

André Gelpke tends to speak of two categories when referring to his work: the monologues (introspection) and the dialogues (relationships with the external). There is no opposition between them—they are complementary because they basically try to exercise two distinct types of vision upon the same reality: sensual vision and intellectual vision.

Sensual vision would be that which involves the senses, which, for example, relate to an atmosphere or the sensation of temperature. The camera acts spontaneously as an extension of sensibility—it functions more to the rhythm of the heart than of the mind. The photographs included in the touring show *Vorstellungen und Wirklichkeit* (most of which belong to the series entitled "Sea Pieces") constitute good examples of this sensual vision. In them Gelpke uses a precise visual rhetoric: violence of light, tension of space, a predilection for compact masses and for geometric forms, fragmented frames, etc. It is not a question, as Dieter Wellershof states, of "pure exercises of vision," or, at least, it is not only a question of this. Beyond the appearance

of simply visual gymnastics there is an underlying energy of greater expressive potential. Although these images also have a metaphysical dimension— as do those of Herbert List with which there are certain formal similarities— there is not so much a search for the enigma of the *objet trouvé* as for the banality of the situation, for the congelation of its static and immobile qualities, and for the "decisive moment of light." The first two of these are essentially painterly characteristics, as in the work of Magritte, but the third is essentially photographic.

The intellectual vision, on the one hand, would be that which withdraws from the aesthetic and favors content. We can clearly see this aspect if we compare the aforementioned works with the series titled "Plastic People" and "Sankt Pauli." In these the photographer shows evidence of greater reflection, and his ethical attitude becomes clear. The camera appears much more controlled because the goal is more precise. Again, Gelpke knows how to use visual rhetoric intelligently: direct shots in the best documentary tradition, which dignify the faces of the transvestites and strippers of the red-light district of Hamburg, thereby permitting the spectator to take part in an intimate one-to-one encounter. In contrast, he uses a fine and disturbing irony in the series "Plastic People," using a "decapitated" frame which emphasizes the extravagant details of certain social rituals such as receptions and *vernissages*. As in the images of Larry Fink, the use of flash emphasizes the character of the scene.

The history of photography has advanced through successive dialects, doctrines, and binary methods which negate one another. At the moment, we think the medium has reached its maturity, and there is no need to demand radical or dogmatic positions. He who understands photography in this way and knows how to creatively combine attitudes which appear antagonistic— sensuality and intellect in this case—is in a position to bequeath us a body of work as fruitful as that of Gelpke.

—Joan Fontcuberta

GERNSHEIM, Helmut (Erich Robert).

Nationality: British. **Born:** Munich, Germany, 1 March 1913; emigrated to England, 1937: naturalized, 1946; settled in Switzerland, 1965. **Education:** St. Anna College, Augsburg, Germany, 1931-33; studied art history at the University of Munich, 1933-34; photography at the Bayerische Staats-Lehr- und Versuchsanstalt für Lichtbildwesen, Munich, 1934-36, and colour photography at Uvachrome, Munich, 1936-37. **Family:** Married Alison Eames in 1942 (died, 1969); married Irene Guenin in 1971. **Career:** Professional photographer, 1936-45 (Photographer for the Warburg Institute, London, 1942-45); photo-historian and collector since 1945: established Gernsheim Collection of Historic Photographs, 1945 (at University of Texas at Austin, since 1964). Coeditor, *Yearbook of Photography,* London, 1953-55; Adviser, Granada Television, Manchester, 1958-62. Since 1968, Editorial Adviser to *Encyclopaedia Britannica,* Chicago. Lecturer in the History of Photography and African Art, Franklin College, Lugano, Switzerland, 1971-72; Lecturer in the History of Photography, Unesco, Venice, 1979; Distinguished Visiting Professor, University of Texas at Austin, Spring 1979, Arizona State University, Tempe, Spring 1982, University of California at Riverside, 1984; Regents Professor, University of California at Santa Barbara, 1985 and 1989. British Representative, *World Exhibition of Photography,* Lucerne, 1952, and Unesco Conference on Photography, Paris, 1955; Chairman, History of Photography, *Rencontres Internationales de Photographie,* Arles, France, 1978. Trustee, Stiftung für Photographie, Zurich, 1975-82. Curator/organizer of numerous photographic exhibitions, including: *Masterpieces of Victorian Photography,* Victoria and Albert Museum, London, 1951; Historical Section, *World Exhibition of Photography,* Lucerne, 1952; *A Century of Photography from the Gernsheim Collection,* Art Museum, Gothenburg, 1956, Nordisk Museum, Stockholm, and *Triennale,* Milan, 1957; *Portraits of 19th Century Authors from the Gernsheim Collection,* Folio Society, London, 1958; *Hundert Jahre Photographie 1839-1939,* Folkwang Museum, Essen, and Wallraf-Richartz Museum, Cologne, 1959, City Art Gallery, Frankfurt, 1960; *The History of Photography from the Gernsheim Collection,* Art Museum, Newcastle upon Tyne, 1960; *120 Jahre Photographie aus der Gernsheim Sammlung,*

Martinique, **1977 (original in colour).** Photograph by Helmut Gernsheim.

Stadtmuseum, Munich, 1961; *Creative Photography 1826 to the Present from the Gernsheim Collection,* in 4 parts, at Wayne State University, Institute of Arts, Historical Museum, and the Public Library, all Detroit, 1963; *200 Color Photographs by Berko, Fontana, Henle, Dal Gal, Sudre, Gianella Recently Acquired for the Gernsheim Collection,* Michener Gallery, University of Texas at Austin, 1979; *Photographic Abstractions,* University of California at Riverside, 1984; etc. **Recipient:** American Photographers Association Award, 1955; Kulturpreis, Deutsche Gesellschaft für Photographie, 1959; Cross of Merit, First Class, German Federal Republic, 1970; Gold Medal, Accademia Italia, Parma, 1980; David Octavius Hill Medal, Deutsche Fotografische Akademie, Leinfelden, West Germany, 1983; International Association of Photographic Art Dealers Award, New York, 1984; Master of Science degree, Brooks Institute, Santa Barbara, California, 1984; Honorary Doctorate, University of Bradford, England, 1989; Sudek Gold Medal awarded by the Czecho-Slovak State, 1989; Daguerre Medal, Societé Français Daguerre, Paris 1989; Photography Prize, San Merino Republic, 1991; Leitz Silver Medal "In Recognition of a Lifetime Achievement in Photography," 1994. Honorary Fellow Photographic Historical Society of America, 1978; Honorary Fellow of the European Society for the History of Photography, Antwerp, 1985; Honorary Member, Swedish Photographic Society, Stockholm, 1972; Honorary Member Club Daguerre, Frankfurt am Main, 1980; Honorary Member German Photographic Academy, Leinfelden, 1983; Honorary Member Spanish Photohistorical Society, Seville, 1990. Trustee Alinari Museum, Storia della Fotografia, Florence, 1985; Adjunct Professor of Art History, Arizona State University, Tempe 1990. **Address:** Residenza Tamporiva, Via Tamporiva 28, CH-6976 Castagnola, Switzerland.

Individual Exhibitions:

1937   *Photographs of the Munich Marionette Theatre,* at the *World Exhibition,* Paris
     Old Master Drawings Gallery, Stratford Place, London
1938   Old Master Drawings Gallery, Stratford Place, London
1945   *Westminster Abbey,* Courtauld Institute of Art, London
     Churchill Club, London (6 exhibitions of work for the National Buildings Record, 1945-46)
1946   *St. Paul's Cathedral,* Courtauld Institute of Art, London
1948   Royal Photographic Society, London
1983   *Helmut Gernsheim 1935-82,* Galerie Gundlach, Hamburg (retrospective; travelled to Spectrum Gallery, Hannover; Stadtmuseum, Munich; and Augustiner Museum, Freiburg im Breisgau, 1984-86)

Selected Group Exhibitions:

1944   *National Building Record,* National Gallery, London
1959   *Hundert Jahre Photographie 1839-1939,* Museum Folkwang, Essen, West Germany (travelled to Wallraf-Richartz Museum, Cologne; City Art Gallery, Frankfurt)
1961   *120 Jahre Photographie,* Stadtmuseum, Munich
1963   *Creative Photography 1826 to the Present,* Detroit Art Institute, Michigan; Wayne State University, Detroit

1964   *The Painter & the Photograph: From Delacroix to Warhol,*
        University of New Mexico, Albuquerque
1984   *Subjektive Fotografie: Images of the 50s,* San Francisco
        Museum of Modern Art (travelled to the University of
        Houston, Texas; Museum Folkwang, Essen; Vasterbottens
        Museum, Umea; Kulturhuset, Stockholm; Saarland Museum,
        Saarbrucken; Palais des Beaux-Arts, Brussels)
1986   *Art in Exile in Great Britain 1933-45,* Schloss Charlottenburg,
        West Berlin (travelled to Oberhausen, Graz and London)

Collections:

Bibliotheque Nationale, Paris; The Museum of Fine Arts, Houston; Folkwang
Museum, Essen; Fotografiska Museet, Stockholm; International Museum of
Photography, George Eastman House, Rochester, New York; Gernsheim
Collection, University of Texas, Austin.

Publications:

By GERNSHEIM: Books—*New Photo Vision,* London 1942; *Julia Marga-
ret Cameron,* London 1948, Millerton, New York 1975; *Focus on Architec-
ture and Sculpture,* London 1949; *Lewis Carroll, Photographer,* London
1949, 1968; *Beautiful London,* London 1950, 1960; *Masterpieces of Victorian
Photography,* London 1951; *The Man Behind the Camera,* London 1948, New
York 1979; *Those Impossible English,* with Quentin Bell, London 1952;
Roger Fenton, Photographer of the Crimean War, with Alison Gernsheim,
London and New York 1954, 1973; *The History of Photography,* London and
New York 1955, 1969, Berlin 1983; *Churchill: His Life in Photographs,*
London and New York 1955; *L.J.M. Photographer,* with Alison Gernsheim,
London and New York 1956, 1969; *Queen Victoria: A Biography in Word and
Picture,* with Alison Gernsheim, London and New York 1959; *Historic Events
1839-1939,* with Alison Gernsheim, London and New York 1960; *Edward VII
and Queen Alexandra: A Biography in Word and Picture,* with Alison
Gernsheim, London 1962; *Creative Photography: Aesthetic Trends,* London
and Boston 1962, New York 1975, 1986; *A Concise History of Photography,*
with Alison Gernsheim, London and New York 1965, 1971, 1986; *Alvin
Langdon Coburn, Photographer,* with Alison Gernsheim, London and New
York 1966, 1978; *The Origins of Photography,* Milan, London and New York
1982; *Incunabula of British Photographic Literature 1839-1875,* London and
Berkeley, California 1984; *The Rise of Photography,* Milan, London and New
York 1987. **Articles**—more than 300 articles in European and American
publications, interview—in *Dialogue with Photography,* edited by Paul Hill
and Thomas Cooper, London and New York 1979; "Gernsheim on Gernsheim:
A Lecture given by H.G. at George Eastman House in October 1983" in
Image, (New York) Vol 27, April 1984.

On GERNSHEIM: Books—*The Man Behind the Camera,* London and New
York 1948, New York 1979; *The Picture History of Photography* by Peter
Pollack, New York 1958; *Fotografica '67* by Bo Lagercrantz, Stockholm
1966; *The Painter and the Photograph: From Delacroix to Warhol* by Van
Deren Coke, Albuquerque, New Mexico 1972; *Faces: A Narrative History of
the Portrait in Photography* by Ben Maddow, Boston 1977; *Helmut Gernsheim
1935-1982,* exhibition catalogue, by Fritz Kempe, Hamburg 1983; *Subjektive
Fotografie: Images of the 50s,* exhibition catalogue, by Ute Eskildsen,
Manfred Schmalriede and Dorothy Martinson, Essen, West Germany 1984.
Articles—in *Photography* (London), February 1939; by Sir Kenneth Clark in
Architectural Review (London), July 1943; in *Statesman and Nation* (Lon-
don), June 1944; by Fritz Gruber in *Foto Magazin* (Munich), May 1952; by
Otto Zoff in *Das Kunstwerk* (Baden-Baden), October 1958; by Beaumont
Newhall in *Image* (Rochester, New York), September 1959; by Rudolf Skopec
in *Ceskoslovenska Fotografie* (Prague), December 1961; by Ulla Bergstrand-
Wilhsson in *Foto* (Stockholm), January 1962; by Allan Porter in *Camera*
(Lucerne), October 1968; by Angelo Schwartz in *Fotografia Italiana* (Milan),
December 1977; "Helmet Gernsheim" an interview by James Hajicek, *Visual
Arts Vol L,* (Arizona) 1981/82; "Der Architektur Photograph, Sammler und
Fotohistoriker Helmet Gernsheim" by Prof Friedrich Herneck in *Fotografie*
(Leipzig) 1983; "Helmut Gernsheim" by Lanfranco Colombo in *Infinito,*
(Milan) 1986; "Helmut Gernsheim" by Steffan Wolff in *The Photograph
Collector, Vol V* (London) 1986; "Gernsheim" by Urs Tillmann in *Photographie*
(Düsseldorf) May 1989; "Helmut Gernsheim der Sammler" by Peter Sager in
Die Zeit (Hamburg) July 1989; "Helmut Gernsheim zum 80 Geburtstag" by
Claudia Gabriele Philipp in *Bulletin of the Deutsche Fotografische Akademie*
(Leinfelden) April 1993. **Film**—*Helmut Gernsheim: Portrait,* Norddeutscher
Rundfunk Television film, by Manfred Eichel, 1985.

*

I have been brought up in the spirit of "Neue Sachlichkeit," which
established itself in the early 1920s as a reaction against the manipulated, arty
Salon pictures of the previous generation. They were an expression of late
Victorian grandeur, fake photographs simulating High Art. The new realism
was a return to the origins of photography—a truthful image of the world
around us. Paul Strand and Albert Renger-Patzsch, the founders of modern
photography, even believed they had attained objectivity, yet this was an
illusion. All creative photography is bound to be subjective, a personal
viewpoint and expression of the man behind the camera.

Though my eight years' activity as a professional photographer (1936-45)
has been completely over-shadowed by my work as an historian and collector,
I still take hundreds of colour shots every year on my extensive travels, which
have taken me to every continent. They are my impressions of distant
countries, their beauty and squalor, the people and customs, flora, fauna, and
architecture. No one, apart from my wife and a few friends, had seen them—
yet a recent retrospective has given the public an opportunity to get acquainted
with my work.

Meanwhile, I am content to admire, advise, and sometimes criticize the
pictures others produce. Only a small percentage of the annual output can
satisfy a critical eye, and mine has been sharpened by a lifetime's study of art,
ancient and modern, classical and primitive, good, mediocre and bad. I have
acquired an instinctive response to it, and, to judge by the reputation enjoyed
by the art I have collected, my perception has been sound. A photograph has to
speak to me. If it fails to strike a chord, if it is meaningless, tasteless, contrived,
badly composed, or in some other way assails my eyes, my susceptibility
shrinks to zero. Some noise pretending to be modern music has the same effect
on my ears.

Great reputations are usually justified, but nowadays they can also be
acquired by manipulation. I use solely my eyes. Quality speaks for itself and
requires no publicity hand-out and no recommendations. I delight in supporting photographers whose work fails to gain official recognition—if it
impresses me. I fought too many battles with the blind and ignorant myself, not
as a photographer but in my efforts to get photography officially recognized
and appreciated by museums. Many 19th century photographers—and quite a
few contemporary ones—owe their present renown to a happy crossing of our
paths. Reputations rise and fall, and none of the entrants in the present volume
has any control over the vagaries of time. Whether your name or mine will
survive and be resurrected in fifty years' time in a *Who Was Who* is fascinating
speculation but not important. The Romans said: *Carpe Diem*—take your
chance.

It is easy to fake photographs, but difficult to master photography. Hence
the disproportionately high percentage of meaningless or boring images that
find their way into print via editors lacking in critical discernment. A
frightening mental emptiness, visual illiteracy and sensationalism are debas-
ing the contemporary photo-scene. Let us beware of accepting every novelty
as instant success or as a trend-setter. There is no substitute for hard work,
talent, intelligence, sound judgement, and experience—and without these
there will be no creative photography.

—Helmut Gernsheim

*   *   *

Gernsheim discovered for himself the characteristic properties of the
photograph very early in his career. He came to appreciate the particular ability
of the camera to depict the real world with the greatest possible exactness, and
he meditated on the appropriate ways to use the medium for creative self-
expression. Probably this intellectual approach was what led him, before the
Second World War, to embrace the "New Objectivity." Perhaps, too, his
profound knowledge of German photography as it had evolved during the
1920s, and his special training in color photography by means of the
Uvachrome technique, brought him to a belief in straightforward contact to
achieve a truthful depicting of reality. Whatever the reasons, Gernsheim

devoted himself to images of details in which he discovered interesting forms. This approach served him well whether he was depicting the works of man (piano hammers, for instance) or the works of nature. Often he experimented with strongly magnified images, which allowed him to present (for instance) the surprising construction of plants. He liked also to explore perspective as a means toward creative interpretation—for instance, his downward view of a spiral staircase at St. Paul's Cathedral in London. Though his career as a professional photographer was a comparatively short one, he created photographs, whatever his subject or his method, that were always accomplished with perfect technique, a reflection of his belief in precise work.

That belief is as clearly reflected in his later work as a photo historian, for which he is now best known, internationally known, to the general public. Before Gernsheim, in collaboration with his wife Alison, published his fundamental book on the history of photography, there existed only a few publications, of which probably the most important were the works by Josef Maria Eder and Beaumont Newhall. Eder was concerned mainly with the evolution of technique; Newhall chose the approach of following creative trends. The accomplishment of Gernsheim in *The History of Photography*, first published in 1955, was to have combined these subjects, to have added the crucial subject of the use of photographs by human society, and to have offered this amalgam with a scholarship, precision and control that remain unique. Gernsheim, with Eder and Newhall, must be counted as among the very few gifted and important historians of photography.

—Petr Tausk

GERSTER, Georg (Anton).

Nationality: Swiss. **Born:** Winterthur, 30 April 1928. **Education:** Attended gymnasium in Winterthur, 1941-47; studied German literature and philology, University of Zurich, 1947-53, Ph.D. 1953; self-taught in photography. **Family:** Married Isabel Hummel in 1954; children: Franziska and Thomas. **Career:** Science Editor, *Die Weltwoche* weekly newspaper, Zurich, 1952-56. Freelance scientific and aerial writer-photographer, working for *Neue Zürcher Zeitung, National Geographic Magazine, Sunday Times Magazine, Geo, Paris-Match, Graphis, Epoca, Omni,* etc., Zurich, since 1956; also, Contract Advertising Photographer, Swissair national airline, Zurich, since 1960. **Recipient:** Die Goldene Blende, Germany, 1973; Ehrengabe des Kantons Zurich, 1974; Prix Nadar, Paris, 1976; Picture of the Year Award, University of Missouri, Columbia, 1976 and 1980; Anerkennungsgabe der Stadt Winterthur, 1977; Zurcher Journalistenpreis, Zurich, 1984. **Agents:** Comstock, New York and London; Agence Rapho, 8 rue d'Alger, 75038 Paris, France; Pacific Press Service, Tokyo; Anne Hamann, Munich; Grazia Neri, Milan; A.G.E. FotoStock, Barcelona. **Address:** Tobelhusstrasse 24, 8126 Zumikon-Zurich, Switzerland.

Individual Exhibitions:

1965   *Swissair: North America,* at the *Basle Trade Fair*
1966   *Swissair: Africa,* at the *Basle Trade Fair*
1967   *Swissair: South America,* at the *Basle Trade Fair*
1968   *Swissair: North America,* at the *Basle Trade Fair*
        Kirchen im Fels, Zürich (toured Switzerland)
1969   *Swissair: Japan,* at the *Basle Trade Fair*
1970   *Swissair Worldwide,* at the *Basle Trade Fair*
1971   *Swissair: USA,* at the *Basle Trade Fair*
1975   *Der Mensch auf Seiner Erde* (toured Switzerland and Austria)
1979   *Le Pain et le Sel: Vues Aériennes,* Centre Kodak, Paris (toured France, 1979-81)
        US Farmlands, Swiss Center, New York
1989   *Salz in Afrika,* Deutsches Salzmuseum, Lüneburg
1990   *Grand Design drawn by the Earth and Man,* Museum for Salt and Tobacco, Tokyo
1992   *Le Pain et le Sel: Vues Aériennes,* Bordeaux
        Life between Artifact and Nature: Design and the Environmental Challenge, 18th Triennale, Milan

Selected Group Exhibitions:

1980   *Our Beautiful Earth: The View from Air and Space,* National Air and Space Museum, Washington, D.C. (toured the United States)
1983   *The View From Above: 125 Years of Aerial Photography,* The Photographers' Gallery, London
1984   *Swiss Photography from 1840 until Today,* Pro Helvetia Foundation, Zurich (and world tour)
1991   *Premier Festival International du Ciel et de l'Espace,* F-32500, Fleurance, France

Collections:

Swissair National Airlines, Zurich; Smithsonian Institution, Washington, D.C.; Zürich Versicherungen, Zurich; Third National Bank of Ohio, Dayton; Bank Leu, Zurich; Museum for Salt and Tobacco, Tokyo; Schweizer Rück, Zürich; Schweizerische Stiftung für die Photographie. Kunsthaus, Zürich; Duriron, Dayton, Ohio; Zürcher Kantonalbank, Zürich.

Publications:

By GERSTER: Books—*Die Leidigen Dichter,* thesis, Zurich 1954; *Eine Stunde mit . . . ,* Frankfurt and Berlin 1956, as *Aus der Werkstatt des Wissens 1,* Frankfurt and Berlin 1962; *Aus der Werkstatt des Wissens 2,* Frankfurt and Berlin 1958; *Sahara: Reiche Fruchtbare Wüste,* Berlin, Frankfurt and Vienna 1959, as *Sahara: Desert of Destiny,* London 1960, New York 1961; *Sinai: Land der Offenbarung,* Berlin, Frankfurt and Vienna 1961, as *Sinai,* Paris 1962, new edition, Zurich 1970; *Augenschein in Alaska,* Berne 1961; *Nubien: Goldland am Nil,* Zurich 1964; *Faras: Die Kathedrale aus dem Wüstensand,* with text by K. Michalowski, Zurich and Cologne 1966; *The World Saves Abu Simbel,* Berlin and Vienna 1968; *Kirchen im Fels,* Stuttgart 1968, as *L'Art Ethiopien,* Paris 1968, as *Churches in Rock,* London and New York 1970, new edition, Zurich 1972; *Frozen Frontier,* brochure, Washington, D.C. 1968; *Countdown fur die Monlandung,* brochure, Zurich 1969; *The Nubians: Peaceful People in Egypt,* with text by Robert A. Fernea, Austin, Texas 1973; *Aethiopien: Das Dach Afrikas/L'Ethiopie: Toit de l'Afrique,* Zurich 1974; *Der Mensch auf seiner Erde: Eine Befragung in Flugbildern/La Terre de l'Homme: Vues Aériennes,* Zurich 1975, as *Grand Design: The Earth from Above,* London and New York 1976, paperback edition (one half of original) as *Flights of Discovery,* The London and New York 1978; *Brot und Salz: Flugbilder/Le Pain et le Sel,* Zurich and Paris 1980; *Flugbilder: 133 aus der Luft gegriffene Fundsachen,* Basel, Stuttgart and Boston 1985, as *Below from Above,* New York 1986; *The Most Beautiful Place in the World,* New York 1986; *China. The Long March,* Hong Kong 1986; *Die Welt im Sucher,* Zürich 1988; *Over China,* Hong Kong 1988; *Face of the Earth,* Tokyo 1990; *The Art of the Maze,* London 1990, as *Labyrinth. Solving the Riddle of the Maze,* New York 1990; *Amber Waves of Grain. America's Farmlands from Above,* New York 1990; *Over Europe,* Sydney 1992.

On GERSTER: Books—*The Next Whole Earth Catalog,* New York 1982; *The View from Above: 125 Years of Aerial Photography,* exhibition catalogue, edited by Rupert Martin, London 1983. **Article**—"Sky High Portraits of the Earth" in *Photography Year 1980,* by the Time-Life editors, New York 1980.

*

When my plans for an aerial view of the earth were beginning to crystallize, I still uninhibitedly indulged, as I flew, in a hedonism of the eyes. I was sometimes completely overpowered by the beauty—it was always there, lying in wait for me, and I had nothing but an arsenal of cameras with which to confront it. The calligraphy of roads, the graphics of plantations, the unwitting art of salt recovery ponds and the mosaics of small cultivated fields still delight me and tempt me to board planes. But in addition to this beauty "out of the blue," and of equal importance, I am now aware of the information gained from the air. The aerial view by far exceeds the ground-level view in informational content; occasionally it even achieves something like the quadrature of the circle: the volume of information grows with abstraction. Admittedly, first doubts are stirred by the realization that even Man's worst offenses are aesthetically upgraded by sufficient distance. The automobile scrapyard in a natural setting is an eyesore on the ground, but even from kite-flying heights it is transformed into an attractive multicolored design. And as for the profuse, untidy settlement growth that eats into field, forest and meadow: at jet altitudes, if not lower, the eye begins to recognize a gratifying order in the chaos. Contemplation from a spacecraft redeems the earth from Man completely: to a lunar astronaut it appears as a habitable, though perhaps uninhabited, blue planet. This phenomenon of redemption through distance is the one drawback of an approach that otherwise has only advantages. Distance creates clarity and transforms the single image into a symbol: into an accusation here, a hymn of praise there, a manifesto everywhere. Coincidence turns to fact. On the ground we worry about an inventory of what is, but the lofty contemplation of the aerial photograph shows us also what might be—it is a stocktaking of our chances. Aerial photography x-rays the environments created by Man and reveals the intensity of the ecological give-and-take. It follows Man on his precarious way between foolishness and efficiency, conquest and coercion; manifests Man's conflict between the biblical order to subdue the earth and the necessity, only recently recognized, to submit himself to it. The currently popular condemnation of Man, which sees him as an incurable disease of his own planet, passes judgment without trial. I regard my aerial photographs as the interrogation of the accused; but if they plead at all, it is for one who has built up rather than against one who has destroyed.

—Georg Gerster

*   *   *

If aerial photography were simple, the work of Georg Gerster would not be so highly prized. But just as a cart-load of monkeys will not type Shakespeare, so a dozen orbiting satellites will not produce the kind of picture that Gerster has become almost uniquely famous for.

His pictures have something in common with modern art in offering colourful patterns, full of repeated motifs, of a flat "canvas." Then—unlike modern art—the eye finds and identifies objects, and the picture suddenly acquires scale and depth. Gerster varies the height and angle of his shots, so they are not all equally easy to "read." However, the joy of this recognition is a potent force in his photography.

With the joy of recognition comes the pleasure of seeing something from a new and therefore refreshing angle. Even rail yards and quarries take on a certain charm when seen from above, with massive tipper-trucks seeming like toys in a sandpit. In some cases the distance lends an unwarranted enchantment to the view, and Gerster appreciates that the aerial view is not an unalloyed benefit.

In some shots an extra favor is the discovery of order in what has previously seemed to be chaos. A town or a patchwork of fields or an irrigated landscape which seems, from ground level, to be a jumble can, from the air, be seen to have an organized or even an organic appearance. The result is that order is brought out of chaos, which is a satisfying experience.

Gerster rarely produces the complete abstract or "puzzle picture" with an interesting form but no informational content. Nor does he produce the sort of record shot which is so common in an aerial view, but which is only of real interest to people whose houses are in the picture. It is his combination of the factors of strong design with revelation that makes his pictures so enjoyable. It makes them effective both in books like the magnificent *Grand Design* and as eye-stopping posters stuck on the wall advertising Swissair, who have used so many of the pictures.

—Jack Schofield

GHIRRI, Luigi.

Nationality: Italian. **Born:** Scandiano, Reggio Emilia, 5 January 1943. **Family:** Divorced; daughter; Ilaria. **Career:** Freelance Photographer, in Modena, since 1971. **Agent:** Galleria Rondanini, Piazza Rondanini 48, Rome.

Individual Exhibitions:

1973   Sette Arti Club, Modena
1974   *Paesaggi di Cartone,* Galleria Il Diaframma, Milan (travelled to Galleria Il Gelso, Lodi, Italy)
         Colazione sull'Erba, Galleria Il Diaframma Sud, Naples (travelled to Galleria Nadar, Pisa, and Galleria Comunale, Modena, 1975)
1975   *Atlante,* Galleria Documenta, Turin (travelled to the Canon Gallery, Geneva, 1976)
         Canon Gallery, Amsterdam
         Centro Divulgazione, Castano Primoli, Italy (travelled to the Galleria Comunale, Fusignano, Italy)
1976   Forum Stadtpark, Graz, Austria
         Galleria Rondanini, Rome
         Photographic Gallery, University of Southampton
1978   *Kodachrome* Galerie Contrejour, Paris (travelled to the Studio Fossati, Alessandria, Italy, Laboratorio d'If, Palermo, and the Fotostudio, Treviso, Italy, 1979; and Galleria Photo 13, Cagliari, Italy, 1980)
1979   Galleria CSAC, University of Parma *Still Life,* FNAC, Paris (travelled to FNAC, Metz, France, Galerie Stenope, Nice, and the Light Gallery, New York, 1980)
1980   Palazzo dei Diamanti, Ferrara, Italy (travelled to the Galleria Rondanini, Rome)
1983   Galerie Junod, Lausanne, Switzerland
1992   *200 Fotografie in Emilia Romagna,* Galleria d'Arte Moderna, Bologna

Selected Group Exhibitions:

1976   *Photography as Art/Art as Photography,* Maison Européenne de la Photographie, Chalon-sur Saône, France (and world tour)
1977   *Personali,* at *SICOF,* Milan
1978   *Fotografie Italiana,* at *Rencontres Internationales de la Photographie,* Arles, France *Arte e Natura,* at the *Biennale,* Venice
1979   *Iconicittà,* Padiglione Arte Contemporanea, Ferrara, Italy
         Symposium über Fotografie, Forum Stadtpark, Graz, Austria
1980   *Das Imaginare Photo-Museum,* at *Photokina '80,* Cologne
1982   *Lichtbildnisse: Das Porträt in der Fotografie,* Rheinisches Landesmuseum, Bonn
1984   *Construire les Paysages de la Photographie,* Caves Sainte-Croix, Metz, France
         La Photographie Créative, Pavillon des Arts, Paris

Collections:

Centro Studi e Archivio della Communicazione, Parma, Italy; Bibliothèque Nationale, Paris; Musée Réattu, Arles, France; Museum of Modern Art, New York; Stedelijk Museum, Amsterdam; Polaroid Collection, Amsterdam.

Publications:

By GHIRRI: Books—*Kodachrome,* Modena and Paris 1978; *Luigi Ghirri,* with introduction by Massimo Mussini, Parma and Milan 1979; *Luigi Ghirri,* with text by Franco Vaccari Ennery Taramelli, Milan 1982; *Il Palazzo del Arte,* with text by Arturo Carlo Quintavalle, Milan 1988; *Paesaggio Italiano,* Milan 1989; *Il Profilo delle nuvole,* with text by Gianni Celati, Milan 1989; *Atelier Morandi,* with text by Giorgio Messori, Paris and Bari 1992. **Articles—**"Mondi senza fine" in *Camera Austria* (Graz), no. 13, 1983/84; "Cahiers de photographie" in *Contrejour* (Paris), no. 15, 1984; "L'Italia by night" in *La Repubblica* (Rome), 4 September 1986; "Da Contarina a Prince" in *Racconti di fotografi* (Rome), 21/22 May 1989.

On GHIRRI: Books—*Photography Yearbook,* by the Time-Life editors, New York 1975; *70 Anni di Fotografia Italiana* by Italo Zannier, Modena 1979; *Venezia '79: La Fotografia,* edited by Daniela Palazzoli, Vittorio Sgarbi and Italo Zannier, Milan and New York 1979; *Photokina 1980: Glanzichter der Photographie,* edited by L. Fritz Gruber, Cologne 1980; *Fotografie 1922-1982,* exhibition catalogue, with introduction by Manfred Heiting, Rolf-Hasso and Karl Steinorth, Cologne 1982; *Lichtbildnisse: Das Porträt in der Fotografie,* edited by Klaus Honnef, Cologne 1982; *Construire les Paysages de la Photographie,* exhibition catalogue, by Jean-Francois Chevrier and others, Metz, France 1984; *La Photographie Créative* by Jean-Claude Lemagny, Paris 1984; *Vista con Camera Luigi Ghirri* by Paola Ghirri and Ennery Taramelli, Milan 1994. **Articles**—"Luigi Ghirri: Cardboard Cityscapes" in *TIME-LIFE Photography Year* (New York), 1975; "Kodachrome de Luigi Ghirri" by Michele Nuridsany in *Figaro Magazine* (Paris), 9 October 1978; "I riti simbolici della camera oscura" by Ennery Taramelli in *Paese Sera* (Rome), 11 March 1979; "Ghirri: inventer le reél" by Michelle Nuridsany in *Figaro* (Paris) 7 November 1979; "Un art trompeur" by Jean Claude Lemagny in *Connaissance des Arts* (Paris), no. 337, November 1980; "Italy Rome, Ghirri, Rondanini Gallery" by George Targe in *Artforum* (New York), no. 12, December 1980; "Arles: 15eme Recontres Internationales de la Photographie" by Regis Durand in *Argus de la Presse* (Paris), September 1984;"Limmersion dans la couleur" by Jeanne Baumberger in *Soir* (Paris), August 1987; "Le foto di Ghirri, una tappa d'obbligo" by Adriano Bertolini in *Il Resto del Carlino* (Bologna), 1 August 1989; "Luigi Ghirri e le sue foto: anche le emozioni hanno un profilo" by Angela Pancrazio in *L'Arena* (Verona) 6 February 1990; "Paisagista italiano" in *Journal do Brasil* (Brasilia), 8 March 1990; "Tre fotografie e l'immagine della città" by Roberto Muti in *La Repubblica* (Rome), 24 March 1991.

*

In 1969 the photo taken from the space shuttle on its way to the Moon was published in all newspapers: this was the first photograph of the world.

The picture pursued for centuries by man was presented to our eyes, containing contemporarily all the preceding images, incomplete, all books written, all signs deciphered and not.

It was not only a picture of the world, but the picture which contained all pictures of the world: graffiti, frescoes, prints, paintings, writings, photographs, books, films. Simultaneously the representation of the world and all the representations of the world in one time only.

On the other hand, this total view, this *redescription* of everything, destroyed one more possibility of translating the hieroglyphic whole. The power of containing everything vanished in front of the impossibility of seeing everything at the same time.

The event and its representation, to see and to be contained, reappeared to man as not sufficient to solve eternal questions. This possibility of *total duplication,* however, allowed us to glimpse the possibility of deciphering the hieroglyph; we had the two poles of doubt and of the secular mystery: the picture of the atom and the picture of the world, finally one in front of the other. The space between the infinitely small and the infinitely big was filled by the infinitely complex problem: man and his life, nature. The need for information and consciousness thus arises between two extreme points, oscillating from the microscope to the telescope in order to be able to translate and interpret reality or the hieroglyph.

My work rises from the necessity and the desire to interpret and translate the sign and meaning of this sum of hieroglyphs. So, not only a reality that is easily identifiable or highly loaded with symbols, but also thought, imagination, the fantastic, and strange meanings.

The photograph is extremely important for the goal that I have set myself because of certain characteristic features of its language, which I shall try to explain:

The cancellation of the space surrounding the framed part is for me as important as the represented part; it is because of this cancellation that the picture assumes a meaning and becomes measurable.

At the same time, the picture continues in the *visible part* of the cancellation, and it invites us to *see* the rest of the not-represented reality.

This double aspect of representation and cancellation not only evokes the absence of limits (excluding any idea of completeness, of a finished thing), but also it indicates something that cannot be delimited—the real.

The possibility of seeing and penetrating the universe of reality involves passing through all the known cultural representations and models, which have been given to us as definite and decisive, and our relationship with reality and life is the same as that of the picture from the satellite with the earth itself.

So the photograph, with its indeterminates, is privileged: it is able to go beyond the symbolism of definite representations to which a certain value of *truth* has been given. The possibility of analysis in time, in the space of signs that form the reality whose completeness has always slipped our minds, thus permits the photograph, because of its *fragmentary character,* to be closer to things that cannot be delimited, that is, physical existence.

That is why I am not interested in "pictures" or "decisive moments," or the study or analysis of their language as an end in itself, aesthetics, the concept or totalizing idea, the emotions of the photographer, the well-bred quotation, the search for a new aesthetic creed, the use of a style.

I am occupied with *seeing* clearly. That is why I am interested in all possible functions, without separating any one from the whole; I wish to assume them totally in order to show and render recognizable, at one time or another, the hieroglyphs I have met.

The daily encounter with reality, with the fictions and the surrogates, the ambiguities, poetical or alienating, seems to deny any way out of the labyrinth, the walls of which are always increasingly illusive, even to the point of our confusing ourselves with them. The meaning that I try to give to my work is that of verification, of how it is still possible to wish to face the way of knowledge, possible at last to tell the real identity of man, of things, from the image of man, of life.

—Luigi Ghirri

*   *   *

The discussion between those who are partisans of conceptual art and those who are partisans of an expression more emotive and formally rich will find a point of equilibrium in the work of Luigi Ghirri. His photos, usually created in series, represent a moderation between intellect and sensibility, which is to say that they are images clearly realized within the function of a concept—paradoxically, they are reflections upon the same image, each time more pointed, in a progressive process that the creator himself has classified as "intellectual strip-tease"—but without falling into excessive seriousness, boredom or lack of imagination which plagues many conceptual photographers. Ghirri, instead, boasts an irony that alone would justify his creative labor.

It is difficult to talk in general terms of photographic activity as prolific—at times even dangerously excessive—but it is the aspect of irony which seems fundamental to me. The paradox and *trompe de l'oeil* are rhetorical devices which time and again, and with a peculiar visual intelligence, appear to be the leitmotif of Ghirri's creations. With our civilization remaining as a backdrop, he creates a sort of critical X-ray photograph of this image-oriented civilization—that is to say, of the multiplicity of images which it produces and consumes, of its mass production, of its depersonalization, of its decontextualization, and, above all, of its "thingification" (an image is today an object-thing more than a representation of some-thing).

To a certain extent, this is reminiscent of "pop": the taste for the industrial image, for its "parasitic" elements such as the photomechanical fraud—the *decollages,* the reflection which the paper itself produces, etc.—for the "*objet trouvé*" (which in this case would be called the "*image trouvé*") or for "*kitsch*" imagery.

Without doubt, it is for these reasons which Jean-Claude Lemagny—one of those who best knows Ghirri's work—affirms that in him "we find ourselves in contact with two artifices: that of the modern world and that of color photography." It is a modern world evidently filtered through a lens which is both cunning and implacably critical. The question of color deserves special attention. The color in Ghirri's photography turns out to be a means that is consubstantial with the very nature of both the medium and the world (a world which we view in color). Color photography appears more neutral, more transparent, renouncing the artificiality and the artiness to which a priori black-and-white lends itself by pure cultural convention. Nevertheless, it is obviously not a question of an innocent or naive use of color, but one full of intention. Approaching the inoffensive aesthetic of the amateur, with its mass-produced, fully automated snapshots, Ghirri uses the same weapons of the ambient contemporary sensibility suitable to the capitalistic world, but purely in order to disqualify it. In this way the factor of color—as well as many other factors—constitutes a profound subversion of the sensibility of the system.

—Joan Fontcuberta

GHOSH, Ashim.

Nationality: Indian. **Born:** Griffithstown, Wales, 12 December 1962. **Education:** St. Columba's High School, New Delhi, 1966-81; B.A. (Hons) Economics, Hans Raj College, Delhi University 1981-84; self-taught in photography. **Career:** Worked as a corporate/industrial/travel photographer, 1984-90. Also freelance bass player/vocalist, songwriter since 1983. **Agent:** FOTOMEDIA, Flat No. 301, E-540 Greater Kailash II, New Delhi 110048, India. **Address:** A-M/164, Shalimar Bagh, New Delhi 110052, India.

Individual Exhibitions:

1991	*PROJECT L.O.N.D.O.N.#1,* New Delhi (travelled to Calcutta, Bombay and Madras, 1992)
1992	*METROPOLIS,* Shridharani Gallery, New Delhi (travelled to the Centre for Photography as an Art, N.C.P.A., Bombay)
1994	*Masses of Opiate,* Max Mueller Bhavan, New Delhi (travelled to the Centre for Photography as an Art, N.C.P.A., Bombay, 1995)

Selected Group Exhibitions:

1990	*An Economy of Signs,* The Photographers' Gallery, London (and toured the UK, 1990-92)
1993	*2nd Creative Photography Biennale,* Lalit Kala Akademi, New Delhi
1994	*Project Punjab,* National Gallery of Modern Art, New Delhi

Publications:

By GHOSH: Book—*Schoolhours, Days, Years, Centuries . . . ,* with Shankar Barua and Ravi Pasricha, New Delhi, 1994.

*

I started off as a corporate/industrial/travel photographer in 1984. Fulfilling corporate requirements, I travelled extensively around India, quenching an inherent wanderlust, while capturing in fascination the diverse variegations of my country. I also regularly wrote for most mainstream travel publications.

By 1990, the images I had shot during my travels around India became my prime source of income. Stocked with FOTOMEDIA, India's prime image bank, they continue to be widely published. The same year, I stopped corporate capers, concentrating on my growing interest in human documentation. From classic portraiture, my style swung to photographing human interaction, innocent of its capture on celluloid. This took my work to an intuitive/spiritual front, striving to be aware of my self, while explaining the use of photography as an instrument heralding sound social change. Since then I have moved on to constructed imagery and other methods to fully express my creative energies as they emerge from the cultural synthesis I represent. A synthesis of both global influences and my root identity as an Indian.

—Ashim Ghosh

GIACOMELLI, Mario.

Nationality: Italian. **Born:** Senigallia, Ancona, 1 August 1925. **Education:** Attended schools in Senigallia, 1935-40; studied typography; self-taught in photography, from 1945. **Military Service:** Served in the Italian Army, 1944. **Family:** Married Anna Giacomelli in 1954; children: Rita, Neris and Simone. **Career:** Worked as a shop assistant, later becoming the proprietor, of a typography workshop, Senigallia, from 1938. Professional typographer, and independent photographer, Senigallia, since 1953. Member, La Bussola group of photographers, 1956. **Recipient:** Numerous medals and prizes in national photography competitions, Italy, since 1955. **Agent:** Davide Faccioli, Galleria Photology, Via della Moscova 25, Milan, Italy. **Address:** Via Mastai 24, 60019 Senigallia, Ancona, Italy.

Individual Exhibitions:

1966	*Breve Omaggio,* Novara, Italy
	Circolo d'arte Falconarese, Falconara, Italy
1975	*100 volte Giacomelli,* Circolo Fotografico Potenza, Italy
1976	Museo di Ascoli Piceno, Italy
	Museo San Adrian de Besos, Spain
1979	Visual Studies Workshop, Rochester, New York (with Joseph Jachna)
1980	*Brandt/Giacomelli/Macijauskas,* Galerie et Fils, Brussels (with Bill Brandt and Alexandras Macijauskas)
	Università di Parma, Italy
1981	Contrasts/Visions Gallery, London
	Paesaggi 1955-81, Galleria Rondanini, Rome
1982	Photography Gallery, Philadelphia
1983	*A Retrospective 1955-83,* Ffotogallery, Cardiff, Wales
	Fotografie 1953-83, Palazzo degli Anziani, Ancona, Italy
1984	Honolulu Academy of Arts, Hawaii (with Stefano Brigidi)
1986	The Photographers' Gallery, London
1987	*Mario Giacomelli Retrospective,* Galeries Pablo Picasso, Denain; Centre National de la Photographie, Palais de Tokyo, Paris
1988	Shadai Gallery, Tokyo
	Mario Giacomelli 50 photos pour le Musée de l'Elysée, Galerie Chalet Muri, Bern, Switzerland
	Mostra di fotografie di Mario Giacomelli, Galleria Fotochema, Prague
1990	Photofind Gallery, New York
	Catherine Eldman Gallery, Chicago
1992	Galerie Agathe Gaillard, Paris
	Galleria Castello di Rivoli, Torino
1993	Metropolitan Museum of Tokyo
	Galleria Riflessi, Fermo, Italy
	Le Musée de l'Elysée, Lausanne, Switzerland
	Photology Galleria, Milan
1994	*The Photography Show,* Hilton Hotel, New York
	Palazzo di Beiteddine, Ostelio Remi, Beirut
	Galleria Matasci-Tenero, Switzerland
	Galleria Diego Chiesa, Chiasso, Switzerland
	Galleria Photology, Milan
	Film su Giacomelli, Regista Claudio Adorni, Chiasso, Switzerland
	Museo d'Art Moderno, Bologna, Italy

Selected Group Exhibitions:

1955	*Personale,* Castelfranco, Italy
1956	*Mostra Internazionale di Fotografia Artistica,* Palazzo Pomponi, Pescara, Italy
1960	*Fotografi italiane oggi,* Cine Club Udinese, Udine, Italy
1964	*World Exhibition of Photography: What Is Man?,* Pressehaus Stern, Hamburg (and world tour)
1967	*Photography in the 20th Century,* National Gallery of Canada, Ottawa (toured Canada and the United States, 1967-73)
1975	*The Land: 20th Century Landscape Photographs Selected by Bill Brandt,* Victoria and Albert Museum, London (travelled to the National Gallery, Edinburgh; Ulster Museum, Belfast; and National Museum of Wales, Cardiff, 1976)
1978	*The Spirit of New Landscape,* Bowdoin College, Brunswick, Maine
1983	*The View From Above,* The Photographers' Gallery, London
1984	*La Photographie Créative,* Pavillon des Arts, Paris
1985	*Il dopoguerra dei fotografi,* Galeria d'Arte Moderna, Bologna, Italy

From the book *Schoolhours, Days, Years, Centuries ...,* **1993.** Photograph ©Ashim Ghosh.

Le mire Marche, **1980.** Photograph by Mario Giacomelli.

Collections:

Galleria Photology, Milan; Università di Parma, Italy; Bibliothèque Nationale, Paris; Victoria and Albert Museum, London; Museum of Modern Art, New York; International Museum of Photography, George Eastman House, Rochester, New York; Visual Studies Workshop, Rochester, New York; Virginia Museum of Fine Arts, Richmond; Rhode Island School of Design, Providence; James Danziger Gallery, New York.

Publications:

By GIACOMELLI: Book—*Mario Giacomelli, fotografie,* edited by Angelo Schwarz, Ivrea, Italy 1980.

On GIACOMELLI: Books—*Nuova Fotografia Italiana* by Giuseppe Turroni, Milan 1959; *Breve Omaggio,* exhibition catalogue, by Paolo Monti, Novara, Italy 1966; *Photography in the 20th Century* by Nathan Lyons, New York 1967; *Primo Almanacco Fotografico Italiano,* edited by Lanfranco Colombo and Roberta Clerici, Milan 1969; *The Print,* by Time-Life editors, New York 1972; *Looking at Photographs* by John Szarkowski, New York 1973; *The Magic Image* by Cecil Beaton and Gail Buckland, London and Boston 1975; *The Land: 20th Century Landscape Photographs Selected by Bill Brandt,* exhibition catalogue, edited by Mark Haworth-Booth, London 1975; *Geschichte der Fotografie im 20. Jahrhundert/Photography in the 20th Century* by Petr Tausk, Cologne 1977, London 1980; *Mario Giacomelli* by Arturo C. Quintavalle, and others, Parma, Italy 1980; *Mario Giacomelli: a retrospective 1955-1983,* exhibition catalogue, by Alistair Crawford, Cardiff

1983; *La Photographie Créative* by Jean-Claude Lemagny, Paris 1984; *Photo Poche: Mario Giacomelli,* Paris 1986; *Mario Giacomelli risponde a Emilio de Tullio,* by E de Tullio, Milan 1987; *Il reale e l'immaginario di Mario Giacomelli,* by E. Carli, Bologna 1988; *Mario Giacomelli: Spazi interiori* by E. Carli, Nova Jesi 1990; *Viaggio in Puglia. Fotografie di Mario Giacomelli* by R. Nigro, Bari 1991; *Foto di Mario Giacomelli* by E. Taramelli, Paris 1992; *Mario Giacomelli: Universita Camerino* by A. Pellegrino, 1993; *Mario Giacomelli,* exhibition catalogue, Museo d'Arte Contemporaneo, Turin 1993; *Mario Giacomelli,* exhibition catalogue, Riflessi 1993; *Prime Odere,* exhibition catalogue, Milan 1993; *Ninna Nanna,* by Alberto Pellegrino, S Severino Marche 1994; *Mario Giacomelli 1954-1994,* Tenero 1994; *Ritrottie e Film Mario Giacomelli,* by Claudio Adorni, Chiasso 1994; *Omaggio a Spoon River* by Roberto Sanesi, Milan 1994; *La Fotografie di Mario Giacomelli,* editore Ostelio Remi, Beirut 1994. **Articles**—"Giacomelli, Prima e Secunda Maniera" by Giuseppe Turroni in *Fotografia* (Milan), May 1959; "Grande Artista" by S. Genovali in *Regione Marche* (Ancona), July 1960; "Io Non Ho Mani" by P. Racanicchi in *Popular Photography* (Milan), February 1964; "Giacomelli" by Nathan Lyons in *Popular Photography* (New York), September 1965; "Giacomelli" by Attilio Colombo in *Progresso Fotografico* (Milan), October 1974; "Giacomelli" by Arturo Schwartz in *Fotografia Italiana* (Milan), May 1978; "Giacomelli" by Hervé Guibert in *Le Monde* (Paris), January 1980.

* * *

Mario Giacomelli lives in a small town, Senigallia, on the shores of the Adriatic Sea, where the original spirit of the Italian mentality remained virtually untouched by foreign influences for a long time. Because he is very shy by nature, Giacomelli never felt himself entirely at home in the big cities of the North: the traffic, the newly acquired customs, seemed to him completely at odds with national traditions. The environment in which he was born and in which he has lived his entire life has formed his mental background and attitudes. Giacomelli likes everything, intuitively, that has been typical of the old Italy. In the arts in general he has preferred works that represent the purest domestic approach. Thus among his favorite poets he reserves a place of honor for Giacomo Leopardi, traditionally beloved by the whole nation, whose work is considered to be among the most pessimistic in the world's literature. And on the wall of Giacomelli's darkroom there is a small photograph showing the face of the painter Giorgio Morandi whose still-lifes have profoundly penetrated his subconscious.

This close connection to his native ground is significant in Giacomelli's interpretation of the inner truth of the Italian reality. His optical communications have always been based on his belief that he had something important to say about the world, and he never takes the camera into his hands before he feels that he has found the right relation to his subject. He is the kind of photographer whose activity is based more on intuition than on theoretical reasoning, and the means by which he determines themes for future photographs could be described as purely emotional. The time needed for this "ripening of ideas" often lasts a few months, but once he is sure of his orientation he takes his images without hesitation and quite quickly.

Giacomelli has never worked according to the trial-and-error method of many photojournalists. Although a great part of his work belongs to the realm of "live" photography, he is able to enlarge about 80% of his negatives into definitive prints. Using a little-known camera, Kobell Press, he takes on one strip of film only 10 photographs: he saves his spare shots, prepared to take more pictures if still better situations occur.

In Italy the sun shines from the bright blue sky, and the white walls of the houses reflect the sun. At night the towns and cities are full of light, and the atmosphere is gay. However, under the apparent jollity of the surface there is sorrow, mourning and a fear of death, deep within the Italian soul. Giacomelli discovered very early on his own way to resonate this melancholic sense in his photographs—not only through the choice of motif but also in his use of dark tones. The scenes from Italian country life in Abruzzi, where the village women wear black clothes, is a good and logical rendering of some of his favorite motifs.

Giacomelli likes the high contrast between the pictures of persons and the white walls of houses in the background, because within such contrasts forms become most evident. For this reason he also uses high contrast paper. Sometimes, the profound contrast of black-clad people and white backgrounds creates an almost graphic effect—as, for instance, in the cycle showing young seminarians playing in the snow. The "solution" of these photos suggests that his sense for interesting forms was combined closely with an art in choosing the right moment for both an eloquent and poetic depiction.

Although Giacomelli has shown himself a master of form, one cannot speak of him merely as a formalist, since much of his oeuvre has displayed a warm human interest in life. In this context, it is necessary to consider those images made in old people's rest-homes, his even more evident compassion in photographs of the sick at Lourdes, and among the starving of Ethiopia.

All periods of Giacomelli's work, however, are imprinted with the key preoccupation with the landscape—photographed in its myriad of forms over the past thirty years. The early photos showed a realist observation, concentrating on planes of light across the land; this was followed by a fascination for the abstract shapes of the Italian flatlands punctured by the verticality of trees. More recent work has focussed on textural patterns found in wood-surfaces, and even on birds-eye-view images.

Just as one needs time to become acquainted with a subject, so Giacomelli takes time in meditating on his images of the land. Frequently, he will make at first only a small contact print—leaving the production of a definitive enlargement until several weeks later. Giacomelli's patience parallels the fact that his photos often ripen to their full emotional impact quite outside the geographical or time sphere in which they were originally made.

—Petr Tausk

GIANELLA, Victor.

Nationality: Swiss. **Born:** Paris, France, 5 January 1918; settled in Switzerland, 1949. **Education:** Studied typography and book production under Georges Lecomte at the Ecole Estienne, Paris, 1934-37; self-taught in photography, from 1934. **Military Service:** Served in the 18th Regiment of Engineers, French Army, Nancy, 1938-40; deported, as prisoner-of-war, to work-camp, Vienna, 1942-45. **Family:** Married Clara Darani in 1947; children: Francois and Daniel. **Career:** Worked as a typographer, Paris 1945-49, and in his own business, Brusino-Arsizio, Switzerland, from 1949. Freelance photographer since 1969. **Agent:** Galleria d'Arte Ca dal Portic, Via della Motta 13, 6600 Locarno, Switzerland. **Address:** CH-6923 Brusino-Arsizio, Ticino, Switzerland.

Individual Exhibitions:

1978	*Victor Gianella,* at the *Rencontres Internationales de Photographie,* Arles, France
1979	*Fotografie di Victor Gianella,* Serfontana, Chiasso, Switzerland
	Victor Gianella: Retrospettiva, Galleria d'Arte, Mendrisio, Switzerland
1981	Galleria Diaframma/Canon, Milan
1982	Galleria Pretorio, Faido, Switzerland
1984	*La Fotografia e Poesia,* Galleria Fotografia Oltre, Chiasso, Switzerland
1985	*Il fantastico nel paesaggio,* Galleria Ca dal Portic, Locarno, Switzerland
	Abstractions, Galerie zur Stockeregg, Zurich
1986	*Fotografi ticinesi,* Finter Bank, Chiasso, Switzerland
1987	*Il Fantastico del paysage,* Galleria del Postic, Locarno, Switzerland
1993	*Fotografie di Victor Gianella,* Biblioteca comunale, Brusino-Arsizio, Switzerland

Selected Group Exhibitions:

1974	*Swiss Photography from 1840 until Today,* Kunsthaus, Zurich (travelled to the Villa Malpensata, Lugano, and Musée Rath, Geneva)
1975	*Triennale de la Photographie,* Musée d'Art et d'Histoire, Fribourg
1979	*Modern European Color Photography,* Michener Gallery, University of Texas

1981	*Astrazione e Realtà,* Galleria Flaviana, Locarno, Switzerland
1982	*400th Anniversary of Saint Francis,* Convento del Bigorio, Lugano, Switzerland
1984	*La Photographie Créative,* Pavillon des Arts, Paris
1985	*Art 16/85,* Basle, Switzerland
1987	*Fotografie d'Autore,* Comune di Como, Varese, Lugano; Palazzo Broletto, Como
	Il Ticino e i suoi fotografi, Museo Cantonale d'Arte, Lugano, Switzerland; Kunsthaus, Zürich
1991	*Das Tessin und seine Photographen,* Freiburg; Kassel; Nürnberg; Köln

Collections:

Bibliothèque Nationale, Paris; Fotoforum der Gesamthochschule, Kassel, West Germany; Gernsheim Collection, University of Texas at Austin; University of Parma, Italy; Hartkamp Collection, Amsterdam; Kunsthaus, Zurich.

Publications:

By GIANELLA: Book—*Abstractions,* preface by Helmut Gernsheim, Zurich 1988.

On GIANELLA: Books—*Triennale de la Photographie,* exhibition catalogue, Fribourg 1975; *La fotografia di Victor Gianella,* exhibition catalogue, Chiasso, Switzerland 1984; *La Photographie Créative* by Jean-Claude Lemagny, Paris 1984. **Articles**—*Photographie,* leaflet, by Helmut Gernsheim, Mendrisio, Switzerland, 1979; "Victor Gianella" by Giuliana Scimé in *Cenobio* (Lugano), January/February 1979; "Collection Shows Photos and Art" by Laura Fatal in *The Daily Texan* (Austin), April 1979; "Encyclopédie internationale des photographes 1839/1983," *Camera Obscura,* 1985; "Das Tessin und seine Photographen," *Pro Helvethia,* 1991.

*

I have taken photographs since my youth. My development, however, dates from 1968-69. How can I explain the reasons for this development? A choice, an abstraction? I might even dare to say: "the heart has reasons that reason does not understand." Or then I might also say that "poetry is loved rather than understood."

For me, taking photographs is neither work nor a profession; it is, on the contrary, a necessity, a duty. It is like travel unlimited by time or space, towards distant shores, towards a kind of infinite. . . .

It is true that I enjoy taking photographs of simple insignificant everyday objects, trying to give them form and soul. I would even like to make them worthy of admiration—like the "great things" of this world.

Contemporary photography is very rich in interesting subjects. Today, perhaps reason eclipses everything else. But, tomorrow, might it not be the heart?

—Victor Gianella

*   *   *

Photography is a form of abstraction, a selection from nature, a segment. Complete abstraction—the reduction to a minimum of lines—is the most difficult form of composition, and probably no one is so much the master of this Mondrian-like way of seeing in photography as Victor Gianella.

His work is not achieved, as some people assume, by cropping in the enlarger but by careful selection before shooting. In the apparent simplicity of composition lies long practice in reducing the image to its fundamental elements. The more a detail is isolated from its context and seen in juxtaposition to another fragment normally not associated with it in our minds, the stranger is the visual effect. We fail to recognize the subject altogether, and the fragment assumes a life of its own.

Gianella is fascinated by this fragmentation of the visible world into facets that remain hidden to most of us. His magic images, transcending the reality of the object, are painterly in conception yet achieved by purely photographic means. They are all of everyday subjects, such as close-ups of children's balloons, a gas ring, a rent in a tent, brush strokes, bore-holes in metal.

These and other superb colour compositions make him the most original abstract expressionist in photography.

—Helmut Gernsheim

GIBSON, Ralph.

Nationality: American. **Born:** Los Angeles, California, 16 January 1939. **Education:** Notre Dame High School, North Hollywood, 1952-56; studied photography at the San Francisco Art Institute, 1960-61. **Military Service:** United States Navy, Mediterranean Fleet, 1956-60. **Career:** Photographer since 1961: worked as an assistant to Dorothea Lange, San Francisco, 1961-62; worked for Robert Frank on the film *Me and My Brother,* New York, 1967-69; cameraman on *Conversations in Vermont,* 1969; moved to New York, and established a studio there, 1969. Founder-Director, Lustrum Press, New York, since 1969. Founder Member, with Frosty Meyers, Larry Clark, Rich Ferrar, and Larry Bennett, Sex 'n' Drugs Band, New York, 1975. Honorary Doctor of Fine Arts, University of Maryland, 1991. **Recipient:** National Endowment for the Arts Photography Fellowship, 1973, 1975, 1986; Creative Artists Public Service Grant, New York, 1977; DAAD Exchange Fellowship, Berlin, 1979; Welsh Arts Council Grant, Cardiff, 1980; Guggenheim Fellowship, New York, 1985; Leica Medal of Excellence Award, 1988; Grand Medal of the City of Arles, France, 1994. **Agent:** Castelli Gallery, 420 W. Broadway, New York, New York 10021. **Address:** 331 West Broadway, New York, New York 10013, U.S.A.

Individual Exhibitions:

1970	San Francisco Art Institute
1971	Focus Gallery, San Francisco
1972	Pasadena Art Museum, California
1973	Centre Culturel Americain, Paris
	International Museum of Photography, George Eastman House, Rochester, New York
	Galerie Wilde, Cologne
1974	Miami-Dade Community College
	Wilkes College, Wilkes-Barre, Pennsylvania
	Palais des Beaux-Arts, Brussels
1975	Hoesch Museum, Düren, West Germany
	Galerie Agathe Gaillard, Paris
	Photopia Gallery, Philadelphia (with Mary Ellen Mark)
	Madison Art Center, Wisconsin
	Broxton Gallery, Los Angeles
1976	University of Guelph, Ontario
	Castelli Graphics, New York
	Baltimore Museum of Art
	Moderna Museet, Stockholm
	Focus Gallery, San Francisco
	Light Impressions, Rochester, New York
	Galerie Fiolet, Amsterdam
	Silver Image, Tacoma, Washington
	Texas Center for Photographic Studies, Dallas
	Center for Contemporary Photography, Chicago
	Photogenesis, Columbus, Ohio
	Galerie Jean Dieuzaide, Toulouse
1977	*Brandt/Gibson/Klein,* Vrije Universiteit, Amsterdam (with Bill Brandt and Aart Klein)
	Van Reekum Galerij, Apeldoorn, Netherlands
	Galerie Agathe Gaillard, Paris
	Moderna Museet, Stockholm
	CEPA Gallery, Buffalo, New York
	Silver Image Gallery, Seattle

	Museum of Modern Art, Oxford
	Side Gallery, Newcastle upon Tyne, England
	Photographers' Gallery, Melbourne
	Galerie Breiting, Berlin
1978	Robert Self Gallery, London
	Castelli Graphics, New York
	Center for Creative Photography, University of Arizona, Tucson
	Camera Obscura, Stockholm
	Photographers' Gallery, Melbourne
	Galerie Daniel Templon, Paris
	Galerie Fiolet, Amsterdam
	Van Reekum Galerij, Apeldoorn, Netherlands
	Museum of Modern Art, Brisbane
	Galerie Givaudan, Geneva
	Atlanta Gallery of Photography
1979	Werkstatt für Photographie, Berlin
	Canon Photo Galerie, Geneva
	Grapestake Gallery, San Francisco
	I.C.A. Museum of Art, Richmond, Virginia
	Galerie Pennings, Eindhoven, Netherlands
	Nouvelle Image, The Hague
1980	Castelli Graphics, New York
	Kunstmuseum, Dusseldorf
	Galleria Arco d'Alibert, Rome
	The Black Series, The Photography Gallery, Cardiff
	Olympus Showroom, Hamburg
	Open Eye Gallery, Liverpool
	Night Gallery, London
1981	P.P.S. Gallery, Hamburg
	Galleria La Giudecca, Venice
	Sprenger Museum, Hannover
	Silver Image Gallery, Seattle
	Mattingly Baker Gallery, Dallas, Texas
	Museum Folkwang, Essen, West Germany
	Spectro Arts Workshop, Newcastle-on-Tyne, England
1982	Centre Georges Pompidou, Paris
	Galerie Agathe Gaillard, Paris
	Castelli Graphics, New York
	Shadai Gallery, Tokyo
	Olympus Gallery, London
	Ralph Gibson, at *FIAC 82,* Paris
1983	Seattle Art Museum, Washington
	Sun Valley Center for the Arts, Idaho
1984	Weston Gallery, Carmel, California
1985	Leo Castelli Gallery, New York
	Galerie Agathe Gaillard, Paris
	Castelli Uptown, New York
	Bouwfonds Hovelaken, Netherlands
	Consejo Argentino de Fotografia, Buenos Aires
1986	United States Information Agency, Washington, D.C. (toured Africa)
	Galerie-FNAC, Paris
	Benteler Galleries, Houston, Texas
1987	International Center of Photography, New York
	Circulo de Bellas Artes, Madrid
	Museo Archivi Alinari, Florence
	Museum of Fine Arts, Alexandria, Egypt
	Hellenic Center of Photography, Athens
	Fotografie Forum, Frankfurt
	Olympus Gallery, Amsterdam
	Alliance Francaise, New York
	Photo Art Basel, Basel
	FNAC, Nice
1987	Villa Medici, Rome
	Leo Castelli Gallery, New York
1988	The Photographers' Gallery, London
	Bibliotheque Nationale, Paris

Galerie Agathe Gaillard, Paris
7'eme Recontres Photographique in Bretagne, Villa Margaret,
Lorient
Encontros de Fotografia, Coimbra, Portugal
1990   *Quatrieme Triennale Internationale de la Photographie,* Musee
de la Photographie, Charleroi, Belgium
Voyage en Riberac, Espace Culturel de l'Ancienne Eglise,
Notre Dame, Riberac
Drew University Art Gallery, Madison, New Jersey
Musée Nicephore Niepce, Chalon sur Saone, France
Albin O Kuhn Library and Gallery, University of Maryland,
Baltimore
Colegio Oficial de Arquitectos de Canarias (COAC), Tenerife
1991   Castelli Graphics, New York
Espace Photo, Paris Audiovisuel, Paris
ICAC/Weston Gallery, Tokyo
Vision Gallery, San Francisco
Leica USA, Northvale, New Jersey
1992   Photography House, Prague
Pictures of Peace, Louise Jones Brown Gallery, Duke
University
1993   *L'Aire de Bourgogne,* Espace des Arts, Chalon sur Saone
Women, Boca Museum of Art, Boca Raton, Florida
Landscapes, Light Impressions, Rochester, New York
1994   Butler Institute of American Art, Youngstown, Ohio
25 éme Anniversaire, Les Recontres, D'Arles, France
French Cultural Services, New York
Leo Castelli, Art Jonction Canne

Selected Group Exhibitions:

1967   *12 Photographers of the American Social Landscape,* Brandeis
University, Waltham, Massachusetts
1970   *U.S.A. in Your Heart,* San Francisco Art Institute
1975   *4 Amerikanische Photographen: Friedlander/Gibson/Krims/
Michals,* Städtischer Museum, Leverkusen, West Germany
1977   *Concerning Photography,* The Photographers' Gallery, London
(travelled to the Spectro Workshop, Newcastle upon Tyne)
1978   *23 Photographers/23 Directions,* Walker Art Gallery,
Liverpool
Mirrors and Windows: American Photography since 1960,
Museum of Modern Art, New York (toured the United
States, 1978-80)
1979   *Photographie als Kunst 1879-1979/Kunst als Photographie
1949-1979,* Tiroler Landesmuseum Ferdinandeum,
Innsbruck, Austria (travelled to the Neue Galerie am
Wolfgang Gurlitt Museum, Linz, Austria; Neue Galerie am
Landesmuseum Joanneum, Graz, Austria; and the Museum
des 20. Jahrhunderts, Vienna)
1982   *Counterparts: Form and Emotion in Photographs,* Metropolitan
Museum of Art, New York (travelled to the Contemporary
Arts Center, Cincinnati, Ohio; Dallas Museum of Fine Arts,
Texas; San Francisco Museum of Modern Art; Corcoran
Gallery, Washington, D.C.)
1985   *American Images 1945-80,* Barbican Art Gallery, London
(toured Britain)
1987   *Photography and Art 1946-86,* Los Angeles County Museum
of Art;
Three Decades of Exploration, Homage to Leo Casteli,
Museum of Art, Fort Lauderdale, Florida
Contemporary American Figurative Photography, Center for
the Fine Arts, Miami, Florida
1988   *Photography and Art,* The Queens Museum, Queens, New
York City
Castelli Graphics, 1969-1988, Leo Castelli Gallery, New York
Legacy of Light, National Portrait Gallery, Washington

Instant Likeness: Polaroid Portraits, National Portrait Gallery,
Washington
1989   *Landscape Photographs from the Permanent Collection,*
Corcoran Gallery of Art, Washington, D.C.
*Decade by Decade: Twentieth Century American Photography
from the Center for Creative Photography,* Tucson, Arizona
Fotografi 159 AR, Moderna Museet, Stockholm
At The Waters Edge, Tampa Museum of Art, Tampa, Florida
What is Photography?, Manes Gallery, Prague
54 Master Photographers of 1960-1979, Toppan Collection,
Photographic Society of Japan, Tokyo
1990   *The Year of Tibet,* Haines Gallery, San Francisco
Expo '90, Osaka Museum, Osaka, Japan
Masterpieces of American Photography 1899-1982, Cornell
Fine Arts Museum, Rollins College, Winter Park, Florida
1991   *Pictures of Peace* (travelling exhibition)
Museum of Modern Art, Rio de Janiero
War and Peace, Alinder Gallery, Gualia, California
1992   *At Home And On The Beach,* Art Finds Marsha Fogel Gallery,
East Hampton, New York
About Face: Portraits from the Permanent Collection, ICP
Midtown, New York
Decouvertes 1992, Grand Palais, Paris
Works from the Permanent Collection, Seattle Art Museum,
Washington
1993   *Four Friends,* Murray and Isabella Rayburn Foundation
LaForet Museum, Harajuku, Tokyo
An Image of Class, Park Avenue Showroom, New York City
Photographers Who Created a New Age, Tokyo Metropolitan
Museum of Photography, Tokyo
Selections from the Permanent Collection; Image and Text,
Center for Creative Photography, Tucson
1994   *Selections from the Permanent Collection,* Mexico
*New Acquisitions/New Work/New Directions 2, Photography
from the Collection,* Los Angeles County Museum of Art,
Los Angeles
Four Friends, Oklahoma City Art Museum

Collections:

Fondation Select, Switzerland; Museum of Modern Art, New York; Bibliotheque
National, Paris; National Gallery of Ottawa, Canada; Pasadena Art Museum,
California; International Museum of Photography at George Eastman House,
Rochester, New York; University of New Mexico, Albuquerque, New Mexi-
co; Whitney Museum of American Art, New York; University of California,
Los Angeles; Visual Studies Workshop, Rochester, New York; Seattle Art
Museum, Volunteer Park, Seattle; Fogg Art Museum, Boston, Massachusetts;
Metropolitan Museum of Art, New York; Center for Creative Photography,
Tucson, Arizona; Australian National Gallery, Canberra; National Gallery of
Victoria, Australia; Allen Art Museum, Oberlin College, Oberlin, Ohio; Dalls
Museum of Art, Texas; John Simon Guggenheim Memorial Foundation;
Museum of Fine Arts, Saint Petersburg, Florida; Musee Reattu, Arles; High
Museum of Art, Atlanta, Georgia; San Francisco Musem of Modern Art;
Musee Contini, Marseilles; Virginia Museum of Fine Art, Richmond, Virgin-
ia; Whatcom Museum of History and Art, Bellingham, Washington; Museum
fur Kunst und Gwerbe, Hamburg; Stedelijk Museum, Amsterdam; Museum
Ludwig, Cologne; New Orleans Museum of Art; Dallas Museum of Art;
Fotografiska Museet, Stockholm; Atkins Museum of Fine Art, Kansas City;
Israel Museum, Tel Aviv; Jerusalem Museum, Israel; Museo Fratelli Alinari,
Florence; Smithsonian Institution, Washington, D.C.; Library of Congress,
Washington, D.C.; Galleria Civica de Modena, Italy; The Museum of Modern
Art, Mexico City.

Publications:

By GIBSON: Books—*The Strip,* Los Angeles 1966; *The Hawk,* Indianapolis
1968; *The American Civil Liberties Union Calendar,* New York 1969; *The*

Somnambulist, New York 1970; *Deja-Vu,* New York 1973; *Days at Sea,* New York 1974; *Mit Konkreten Bildern die Welt Ordnen,* portfolio, with text by Rolf Paltzer, Hamburg 1980; *Syntax,* New York 1983; *Nine by Nine,* with others, New York 1984; *L'Anonyme,* New York and London 1986; *Tropism,* New York, Florence, London 1987; *Archive 24,* Tucson 1988; *In Situ,* Paris 1988; *Les Cahiers de la Photographie #22,* Paris 1988; *Chiaroscuro,* Paris 1990; *Apropos de Mary Jane,* Paris 1990; *L'Histoire de France,* Paris 1991; *Bookworks: Four Projects,* Paris 1992; *Women,* Boca Raton 1993; *Tropical Drift,* New York 1994; *L'Aire de Bourgogne,* Paris 1994; *The Spirit of Burgundy,* New York 1994. **Articles**—"A Statement on the Photographic Print Market" in *Print Letter* (Zurich), September/October 1979; interview in *Photography Between Covers* by Thomas Dugan, Rochester, New York 1979.

On GIBSON: Books—*Ralph Gibson,* exhibition catalogue, by Ake Sidwall and Leif Wigh, Stockholm 1976; *Nude: Theory* by Jain Kelly, New York 1979; *The Black Series,* exhibition catalogue, by Ian Walker, Cardiff 1980; *Counterparts: Form and Emotion in Photographs* by Weston J. Naef, New York 1982; *Master Photographers: The World's Great Photographers on their Art and Technique,* edited by Pat Booth, London 1983; *American Images: Photography 1945-1980,* edited by Peter Turner and John Benton-Harris, London 1985; *Photography and Art 1946-1986,* exhibition catalogue, by Andy Grundberg and Kathleen M. Gauss, Los Angeles 1987. **Articles**—"Ralph Gibson: The Somnambulist" in *Creative Camera* (London), November 1971; "Ralph Gibson" in *Photography Annual 1972,* New York 1972; "Ralph Gibson: Deja-Vu" by A.D. Coleman in the *New York Times,* 25 February 1973, reprinted in Coleman's *Light Readings: A Photography Critic's Writings 1968-1978,* New York 1979; "Ralph Gibson: Pictures from Deja Vu" by H.M. Kinzer in *35mm Photography* (New York), Spring 1973; "Ralph Gibson" in *Photo* (Paris), September 1973; "Ralph Gibson" in *Modern Photography Annual,* New York 1973; "Ralph Gibson: The Future Returns" in *US Camera/Camera 35 Annual,* New York 1973; "Ralph Gibson" by Douglas Davis in *Newsweek* (New York), 18 November 1974; "Ralph Gibson" in the *British Journal of Photography* (London), 20 December 1974; "Ralph Gibson" by William Wilson in the *Los Angeles Times,* 13 June 1975; "Ralph Gibson: How He Creates His Fractional Images" in *Popular Photography* (New York), April 1977; "An Imaginary Interview with Ralph Gibson" in *Camera* (Lucerne), April 1979; "Ralph Gibson's Early Work" by Cynthia Gano Lewis in *Center for Creative Photography No. 10* (Tucson, Arizona), October 1979; "Formalism Stretched to Vacuity" by Hal Fischer in *Artweek* (Oakland, California), 12 January 1980; "Interview with Ralph Gibson" in *Camera International* (Paris), November 1984.

*

I have been involved with this image since it was made, in 1975. It satisfies my need for structure, content, surrealism, religion, society, etc. I can still vividly recall the moment I made this photograph. It was a moment of clarity.

—Ralph Gibson

*   *   *

Ralph Gibson's art is one of structure, analogy, and sequence. Individually, his pictures have a broad and compelling organization and consequent force such that they can stand as autonomous works, yet it is in the progressive building of image upon image that their full meaning is realized. Characteristically working in series, Gibson endeavors to amplify each image by all those around it, so that the subtleties of each emerge in the context of the others.

This process permits—or more to the point, demands—the effort of his audience, who must become partners with him in discovery. Since sequence is vital to the logic of this process, the photographer needs an absolute control over it—thus the photographic book, unburdened with verbal accounts and functioning to physically preserve the sequence, has become the ideal medium

for Gibson's work. Implicit in this is a revised concept of just what constitutes a finished work. The silver image, emerging from the darkroom to live on as artifact, is less to the point than the series of which it is a part; "a work," as an artistic totality encompassing thought, plan and intention, means the whole series. And the book, rather than suggesting a secondary status as once-removed from the original, becomes in effect the original in that it is the final product of the artist's insight and exercise of control.

The trilogy of books from the early 1970s *(The Somnambulist; Deja-Vu; Days at Sea)* have in common the editorial acumen which associates itself directly with the creative process rather than with a secondary act of sorting and piecing together. The enchantment with the potential of the carefully planned book has resulted in a considerable contribution to the field through Gibson's Lustrum Press.

By and large, the content of Gibson's images is elusive and even mysterious. The human form is generalized beyond the associative specificity of portraiture; by way of this, individuals in the pictures, denied as they are those props and signs of distinct locale, are elevated to a plateau of human-kind-ness. The result is an invitation to metaphysical speculation based on the images, yet (much to their advantage) the pictures utterly lack the rhetorical grandiosity that so often emerges from pictures alluding to the state of mankind in the world and the universe.

Frequently figures appear as but fragments. This draws attention to the framing of the shot, one of the photographer's most powerful tools. Edge is critical, as are the proportions of the rectangle and the tensions established by forcing the compositional thrust of the image to the periphery. Such pictures, though, ring with an organic completeness of structure, so that this device connotes nothing fortuitous in the process of picture-making or the encounter with a subject. While capitalizing on the properties of the small hand-held camera, the photographer virtually discards the stylistic tradition associated with 35mm work.

The technical conditions of Gibson's work are at odds with the current ideal of the richly tonal print. He aims for a maximum saturation of the blacks at the expense of (irrelevant) detail, and maximizes the harshness of grain with contrasty printing that abbreviates the tonal scale. Every technical decision has a reverberation in the aesthetic quality of the image: in Gibson's photographs the local textures of objects sacrifice a degree of their identity to the quality of the surface of the picture; space contracts as spatial clues are submerged; the sheer graphic punch of the two-dimensional image compels attention.

The structural distinctiveness of the pictures often depends as well on the isolation of parts, to the degree that the authority Gibson can invest in parts forestalls one's speculations about the whole. His "The Priest" typifies the taut severity of design that one finds again and again. The painstaking calculation of the relative visual weights of sky and black frock yields a variation of shape and tension of positive and negative space which results in a solemn austerity of conception, a monumentality defiant in the face of a visual world of flux and ephemeral appearance.

Gibson's sophisticated analogical thinking—or analogical intuition of eye—is another persistent trait. It is best exemplified in *Deja-Vu,* wherein pairs of images of different size confront one another in each spread. In some pairs, the comparison back and forth is based on a formal similarity of objects one would not generally associate. This is a testimony not just to one person's capacity of recognition, but to an innate syntactical feature of the medium itself. Gibson is attuned not just to the potentials of the visible world, but to the unique capacity of photography to rebuild that world. In one instance, the collar of a sailor reacts with the curve of a newspaper in the adjacent frame; in another, a figure cut by the edge is completed by the arm of a different figure in a different setting—the arm outstretched and holding a gun. The shock value of this (a recurrent symbol) is less effective (and more overtly contrived) than the purely photographic aspect of the pair.

Other analogies are less explicit. The windblown hair of a woman is compared to a cloud. The remarkable quality of this pairing and others of the same sort is a capacity to evoke sensation beyond the visual. The tactile conjuring of Gibson's work is often downright synaesthetic: a limited vocabulary of repeated but differently inflected motifs excites the broadest range of responses.

Finally, while many photographers seem to consciously establish a gulf between themselves and their work, Gibson's seems intensely personal. In a sense, the pictures are autobiographic, but so obliquely that their public accessibility is not diminished. Their meaning is in a realm of suggestion rather than fact; they are equally capable of rewarding eye, mind, and whatever it is that some dare to call soul.

—Roger Baldwin

GIDAL, Tim N(achum).

Nationality: Israeli and American. **Born:** Nachum Ignaz Gidalewitsch, of Jewish/Russian parents, in Munich, Germany, 18 May 1909; emigrated to Israel, 1936: naturalized, 1975. **Education:** the Neues Real-Gymnasium, Munich, 1928; studied art history, history and economics at the University of Munich, 1928-29, University of Berlin, 1929-31, and University of Basle, 1933-35, Ph.D. 1935. **Military Service:** Served as Chief Staff Reporter, *Parade* magazine, British 8th Army, North Africa and Mediterranean, 1942-43, and with the British 14th Army in China, Burma, India, and the Middle East, 1943-44: Captain. **Family:** Married Sonia Epstein in 1944 (divorced, 1970); son: Peter; married Pia Karp, 1975; married Pia Lis in 1980. **Career:** Photo-reporter and journalist, working for the *Münchner Illustrierte Zeitung, Woche,* etc., Berlin, 1929-33, and for British and American magazines in Palestine, 1936-38; Photo-Reporter, under Stefan Lorant, *Picture Post,* London, 1938-40; freelance photographer, Jerusalem, 1940-42, 1945-48; Editorial Consultant, *Life* magazine, New York, 1950-53; Lecturer in Visual Communications, New School for Social Research, New York, 1955-58; writer/photographer, 1955-70. Senior Lecturer, 1971-86, and Associate Professor of Visual Communications, since 1976, Hebrew University, Jerusalem. Editorial Board Member, *History of Photography* magazine, State College, Pennsylvania. **Recipient:** Kalvin Prize, Israel Museum, Jerusalem, 1980; Dr. Erich Salomon Prize, Deutsche Gesellschaft fur Photographie, 1983. Honorary Fellow, Royal Photographic Society, 1992; Corresponding Member, Deutsche Gesellschaft für Photographie, 1972. **Address:** 16 Nili Street, Jerusalem, Israel.

Individual Exhibitions:

1937	Steimatzky Gallery, Jerusalem
1974	Galerie Schürmann and Kicken, Aachen, West Germany
1975	*Tim Gidal: In the 30s,* Israel Museum, Jerusalem (travelled to The Photographers' Gallery, London, 1976; Witkin Gallery, New York, 1978; Galerie Nagel, Berlin, and Galerie Photo Art, Basle
1981	*Tim Gidal: In the 40s,* The Photographers' Gallery, London
1984	*Memories of Jewish Poland, 1932,* Museum of the Diaspora, Tel Aviv (travelled to the Wolffsohn Museum, Jerusalem; Mane Katz Museum, Haifa; and toured the United States, 1986-87, Germany, Switzerland, Poland, 1988-1993)
	Bilder der 30er Jahre, Museum Folkwang, Essen, West Germany (travelled to the Staatliche Lichtbildstelle, West Berlin, Cologne, Vienna)
1985	Spectrum Gallery, Hannover
1986	Sammlung Fotografis Landerbank, Vienna
	Vision Gallery, Los Angeles (retrospective)
	Kuwait: A Visual Documentation, 1942, Lempertz Art Gallery, Cologne
	Color Photos, Jerusalem, Fisher House
1992	Retrospective, Open Museum, Tefen, Israel
1993	*Life of a Photoreporter,* Göteborg, Sweden
1995	*The World in my Camera,* Israel Museum, Jerusalem

Selected Group Exhibitions:

1978	*Photokina '78,* Cologne
1980	*Avant-Garde Photography in Germany 1919-39,* San Francisco Museum of Modern Art (toured the United States, 1981-82)
1982	*Floods of Light,* The Photographers' Gallery, London

1984	*Sammlung Gruber,* Museum Ludwig, Cologne
	Color, Israel Museum, Jerusalem
1985	*Place-Scape,* Paley Center, Jerusalem
1986	*Art in Exile in Great Britain 1933-45,* Schloss Charlottenburg, West Berlin (travelled to Oberhausen, Graz and London)
1993	*The Freudeans,* Jeudisches Museum der Stadt, Wien
1995	*My Way,* Israel Museum, Jerusalem

Collections:

Victoria and Albert Museum London; Berlinische Galerie, Berlin; Photo Museum, Munich; Israel Museum, Jerusalem; International Museum of Photography, George Eastman House, Rochester, New York; Gernsheim Collection, University of Texas at Austin; City Art Museum, Melbourne; Bibliothèque Nationale, Paris; Sammlung Fotografis Länderbank, Vienna; Los Angeles Museum of Art; Museum of Modern Art, New York; Folkwang Museum, Essen.

Publications:

By GIDAL: Books—*Bildberichterstattung und Presse/Picture Reporting and the Press,* Tübingen, Germany 1935, 1952; *Kinder in Eretz Israel,* Berlin 1936; *Israel Year,* Berlin 1936; *Meir Shfea,* New York 1947; *This Is Israel,* with Robert Capa and Jerry Cooke, New York 1948; *My Village,* series (23 books), co-author and photographer, New York 1956-70; *Modern Photojournalism: Origin and Evolution 1910-1933,* Frankfurt and Lucerne 1972, New York 1973; *Everybody Lives in Communities,* Boston 1972; *100 Years and 30: Photography in Palestine/Israel 1840-1978,* Jerusalem 1979; *Ewiges Jerusalem/Eternal Jerusalem,* Lucerne 1980; *Land of Promise,* New York, Munich and Tel Aviv 1982; *The Jews in Germany from Roman Times to the Republic Weimar,* Munich 1988; *The Freudeans—1934,* Munich 1990; *Nachum Tim Gidal: Photographs 1929-1992,* Tefen 1992; *Chronicles of Life—The Modern Photoreportage,* Berlin 1993; *Begegnung mit Karl Valentin,* Munich 1995; *Jerusalem in 3000 Years,* Cologne 1995. **Articles**—"Eye Witness"in *Der Bildjournalist* (Leverkusen, West Germany), no. 1-2, 1967 and no. 1-2, 1968; "Photojournalism's First Two Decades" in *35mm Photography* (New York), Summer 1974; "Letter to Young Photographers" in *Creative Camera International Yearbook,* London 1978; "Working for *Picture Post*" in *Creative Camera* (London), Winter 1980-81; "Modern Photojournalism: The First Years" in *Creative Camera* (London), January 1981; "The Beginning of Modern Photojournalism: a reply to Felix H. Man's false claims" in *Intern* (Cologne), 1981; "My Life as a Photoreporter in Israel" in *Ariel*(Jerusalem), no. 57, 1984; "Jews in Photography" in *Leo Baeck Yearbook,* London 1987; "Discovering S. Narinsky, A Great Photographer" in *History of Photography,* Oxford 1989; "The Photographer E.M. Lilien" in *Ariel,* Jerusalem 1990; "The Freudians" in *Judisches Museum,* Vienna, 1993; "A Robert Capa Hoax" in *Intern,* Cologne 1993/94.

On GIDAL: Books—*Words and Pictures: An Introduction to Photojournalism* by Wilson Hicks, New York 1952; *The Magic Image* by Cecil Beaton and Gail Buckland, London and Boston 1975; *Tim Gidal: In the 30s,* exhibition catalogue, Jerusalem 1975; *Geschichte der Photographie im 20. Jahrhundert/ History of Photography in the 20th Century* by Petr Tausk, Cologne 1977, London 1980; *The Photograph Collector's Guide* by Lee D. Witkin and Barbara London, Boston and London 1979; *Tim Gidal: In the Forties,* exhibition catalogue, with introduction by Nigel Trow, London 1981; *Floods of Light: Flash Photography 1851-1981,* exhibition catalogue, by Rupert Martin, London 1982; *Tim Gidal: Bilder der 30er Jahre,* exhibition catalogue, with texts by Ute Eskildsen, Carl Frankenstein and others, Essen, West Germany 1984; *Tim Gidal: Memoirs of Jewish Poland, 1932,* exhibition catalogue, Tel Aviv 1984; *Sammlung Gruber: Photographie des 20. Jahrhunderts,* exhibition catalogue, with foreword by Siegfried Gohr, Cologne 1984. **Articles**—"Tim Gidal" by Colin Osman in *Creative Camera* (London), September 1974; "Tim Gidal" by Bernd Lohse in *Camera* (Lucerne), January 1975; "Tim Gidal: Before the Storm" in *London Magazine,* December 1976; "The Revolution in Reportage" by Gene Thornton in the *New York Times,* 23 April 1978; "Tim Gidal" by Colin Osman in *Creative Camera* (London), May 1979; "Tim Gidal, a photographic ethic" by Nigel Trow in *British Journal of Photography Yearbook,* London 1982; "Photoreporter Tim Gidal" in *Zeit Magazin* (Hamburg), 12 September 1983; "Nachum Tim Gidal" in *Encyclo-*

The Last Judgement (Sistine Chapel), **Rome, 1973.** Photograph ©Dr. Tim Gidal.

pedia Judaica, Jerusalem 1989; "Nachum T. Gidal at 80" *History of Photography,* July 1989; "Tim Gidal, Photographed Cultural History" in *Süddeutsche Zeitung,* Munich, September 1990; "A Tourist Through History" in *The Jerusalem Report,* July 1992; "The Man who Photographed the Twentieth Century" by Avi Katzmann in *Ha'Aretz,* Tel Aviv, September 1992; "Photographer of the Freudeans" by Anna Auer in *Falter,* No. 47, 1993; "A Private Passion" by Michael Hallett in *British Journal of Photography,* 3 March 1994; "Tim Gidal, Grandmaster of Photography" by Renate Schönhagen-Gericke in *Panorama,* October 1994.

*

Photography was always an essential part of my adult life. As a photographer, I published in many magazines, from the early German illustrated magazines (since 1929) to *Life* and *Look* and, with great pleasure, in *Picture Post,* where I had the chance to create visual novellas or essays.

But the greater part of my photographs I did, a private passion, for myself, as a great experience of life itself. This explains the fact that for more than 40 years I never contributed to a photographic magazine, never sent photos to exhibitions. These photographs were, as a rule, seen only by my friends.

In 1974 I decided to exhibit my photos of the 30s. I had one-man shows (about 120 photos) at the Israel Museum in Jerusalem (1975), The Photographers' Gallery, London (1976), Witkin Gallery, New York (1978), and the Nagel Gallery in Berlin (1979). I had much fun when I showed people my photos (most of them had not known my name) and watched the startled expressions on their faces.

Cecil Beaton and Gail Buckland, Colin Osman of *Creative Camera,* and Allan Porter of *Camera* were the first to publish my photos in their books and magazines. The *taking* of the photos, not the showing, was, and is, for me, of the essence.

My photos, I like to think, are variations on the everlasting theme of the tragi-comedy of human life, facets of life itself. In contrast to, say, Henri Cartier-Bresson, I do not wait until the formal quality of the selected rectangle in my viewfinder satisfies a constructivist formal urge. I am directed, I believe, more by intuition and participation, which leads on occasion to a sort of participation mystique.

My photos should show what I saw and experienced. I can't explain them; I have no mission. The viewer can take what attracts him (or leave it). But it gives me much satisfaction when some, especially younger, people "are sent" by some of my pictures—as the saying went in the 1960s.

As a rule, I do not crop my photos. As a rule, cropping destroys their meaning (at least for me). Some editors cursed me, because they found it almost impossible to crop my pictures; which amused me.

I admire the late André Kertesz, friend since 1930 in Paris, New York and other places. I admire some of my opposites: Aaron Siskind, Erwin Blumenfeld, some of Penn's work.

Good Art is good Art, bad Art is horrible art. Good paintings are good paintings, bad paintings are bad. Good photography is good photography, bad photography is bad, and much of the new pictorialism and imitation of third-class literature is bad photography. So is most of what is called "conceptual photography," because it tries to imitate literature and shows mostly first drafts of second-class minds.

But, as I say, there is much good photography around, especially amongst the younger photographers who go their own way and don't try to imitate.

—Tim N. Gidal

* * *

Tim Gidal's engaging summary of his career in photography suggests an initially puzzling distinction between his public and private work. He tells us that he enjoyed providing "visual novellas and essays" for German and British illustrated magazines during the 30s and 40s; and yet he also speaks of photographs made during that same period which had their origin in a purely "private passion," which were rarely exhibited or reproduced and are not to be explained—at least by their creator—in terms of any conscious goal or mission.

Gidal's public career is closely associated with the rise of photojournalism in Germany between 1929 and 1933. In his own lively account of this influential movement, *Modern Photojournalism: Origin and Evolution 1910-1933,* he asserts that unlike "aesthetic" photography, photojournalism "took its cues not from art or literature, but from the many and varied aspects of the *condition humaine* itself." Photojournalism should provide "a visual historical documentation of the events, social conditions, culture, and civilization—as well as the barbarism and lack of culture—of a given time. Didactically defined, it is the instigator of political agitation. The motto of the photojournalist—in our time—is the phrase "Yo lo vi" which Goya scribbled under one of his battle scenes." Walter Bosshard, Felix Man, Martin Munkacsi, Erich Salomon and some of his other colleagues might not have agreed wholeheartedly with this rousing definition of photojournalism, but Gidal's own political sensitivity and commitment are obvious. And for all their diversity, he goes on, each of the major photojournalists had a central motif. In his own case, he explains, it was simply "Gesture and Expression: Man in the Community."

As for the private work, at least some of which appeared in two of his major exhibitions, *In the 30s* and *In the 40s,* Gidal remarks that he was motivated by innate sympathy: his theme remains "the tragi-comedy of human life." In one of the quieter moments of *Photojournalism* he observes that the photographer must have "a talent for observation and the ability to experience and participate intensely and . . . sensitivity, empathy and intuition for capturing the essential quality of the whole in the single picture." Moreover, to be "worthy of his camera," the photographer "must identify himself with the human problems which, tangibly or intangibly, have to form the basic core of his work." Shortly after making this last statement, he alludes briefly to Martin Buber, and it is tempting to speculate that his respect for Buber may help explain an essential connection between Gidal's public and private work. Although Gidal does not refer to it explicitly, Buber's conception of the "I-It" as opposed to the "I-Thou" relationship is probably crucial here. Very briefly, the I-It attitude refers to our visual treatment of objects and other persons simply as objects, to be used as need or desire dictates. The I-Thou attitude, however, refers to our sense of others as existences in themselves: it involves a moral, reciprocal relationship, a true encounter with the other in himself. Authentic existence for Buber is a "meeting," although we are unable to sustain the encounter for very long. "Without *It* man cannot live. But he who lives with *It* alone is not a man."

Gidal's photojournalism is frankly rhetorical and deals with such "meetings" in the realm of large, public concerns. But his private work is concerned with the same problems as they appear in the details of daily living, in what Professor Carl Frankenstein calls ordinary events in ordinary lives and "the absurd in the performances of life"—in the embarrassing encounter, for example, between a faded Bright Young Thing and Hamlet. Gidal's technique remains constant: sympathetic penetration and an attempt to discover—and to share with the viewer—what it must have felt like to be alive and vulnerable at a particular moment. Gidal himself says modestly that these private reflections

have no "mission." But this is surely too self-effacing: trust the tale, D.H. Lawrence once advised, not the teller.

—Elmer Borklund

GIERALTOWSKI, Krzysztof.

Nationality: Polish. **Born:** Warsaw, 10 August 1938. **Education:** Studied at the BD-Gimnazjum Ogolnoksztalcace, Slupsk, 1956; Akademia Medyczna, Gdansk, 1956-58; Akademia Medyczna, Warsaw, 1958-59; Panstwowa Wyzsza Szkola Filmowa (PWSTiF), Lodz, 1961-64. **Family:** Married Maria Gerô in 1964 (divorced, 1969); married Elzbieta Skulska in 1977. **Career:** Photographer, Publicity Enterprise AGPOL, Warsaw, 1966; senior photographer, Warsaw, 1967; permanent collaborator, *TY IJA* magazine, Warsaw, 1967-72; chief adviser, Zjednoczenie Przemyslu Odziezowego, Lodz, 1968-69; freelance advertising photographer, working for *Elle,* Zurich, 1969-70; photographer, *Perspektywy* weekly, Warsaw, 1971-72; permanent collaborator, *Razem* weekly, Warsaw, 1977-78; deputy chief photographer, *ITD* weekly, Warsaw, 1978-81; freelance portrait photographer, Europe, 1982-91; adviser to the Polish Press Agency Chairman for the reorganisation of the former Central Photo Agency, 1992; established Gieraltowski Studio, Warsaw, 1993; photography for Leo Burnet Agency, campaign for the Ministry of Finance, and for Lintas Agency, campaign for the Polish Airlines LOT, 1994. Member of the Polish Authors' Association (ZAIKS) and of the Polish Journalists' Association (SDP). Corresponding Member of the Deutsche Gesellschaft für Photographie (DGPh). **Address:** 01-577 Warszawa, ul. Wyspianskiego 2 m 25, Poland.

Individual Exhibitions:

1963   *Przeglad,* Galeria Wspolczesnosci, Warsaw
1980   *Drukowane Twarze,* Foto-Medium-Art, Wroclaw, Poland (and tour, 1980-81)
1983   *Ritratti Polacchi,* Sezione Culturale SICOF, Milan
        Polen Porträts, Rheinisches Landesmuseum, Bonn
1984   *Krzysztof Gieraltowski,* Galerie PPS, Hamburg
        Porträts, Fotomuseum, Stadtmuseum, Munich
        Polen in Portretten, Gemeentemuseum, Arnhem (travelled to the Frans Halsmuseum, Haarlem)
        Menschen aus Polen, Staatliche Kunsthalle, Baden-Baden, Germany
        Krzysztof Gieraltowski, Sonia Henie Artcenter, Oslo
1985   *Puolalaisia Muotokuvia,* Alvar Aalto Museo, Jyväskylä, Finland
1986   *Portrety,* Galeria Fotografiki BWA, Kielce, Poland
1987   *Nowe Portrety,* Brama Krolewska, Szczecin, Poland
1988   *Portrety Subiektywne,* Royal Castle, Warsaw
        Fotoportrety, Dom Esterki-Dom Gaski BWA, Radom, Poland
        Portrety, Maly Salon BWA, Wroclaw, Poland
1990   *Portrety,* Dum Panu z Kunstatu-Jaromira Funke, Brno, Czechoslovakia
        Neue Porträts, Evangelisches Bildungswerk, Berlin
        Passage Oost-Europa, Gemeentemuseum, Arnhem
1992   *Porträtfotografie,* IFA-Galerie, Berlin (travelled to the Staatliche Galerie Moritzburg, Halle)
1993   *Scientists,* at Expo 93, Taejon, Korea

Selected Group Exhibitions:

1979   *Fotografia Polska 1889-1979,* International Center of Photography, New York (travelled to the Museum of Modern Art, Chicago; Galeria Zacheta, Warsaw; Muzeum Sztuki, Lodz; and Whitechapel Art Gallery, London, 1980)
1980   *Wizerunek Miasta,* Galeria Warexpo, Warsaw
        Pejzaz Spoleczny, Galeria Krytykow, Warsaw

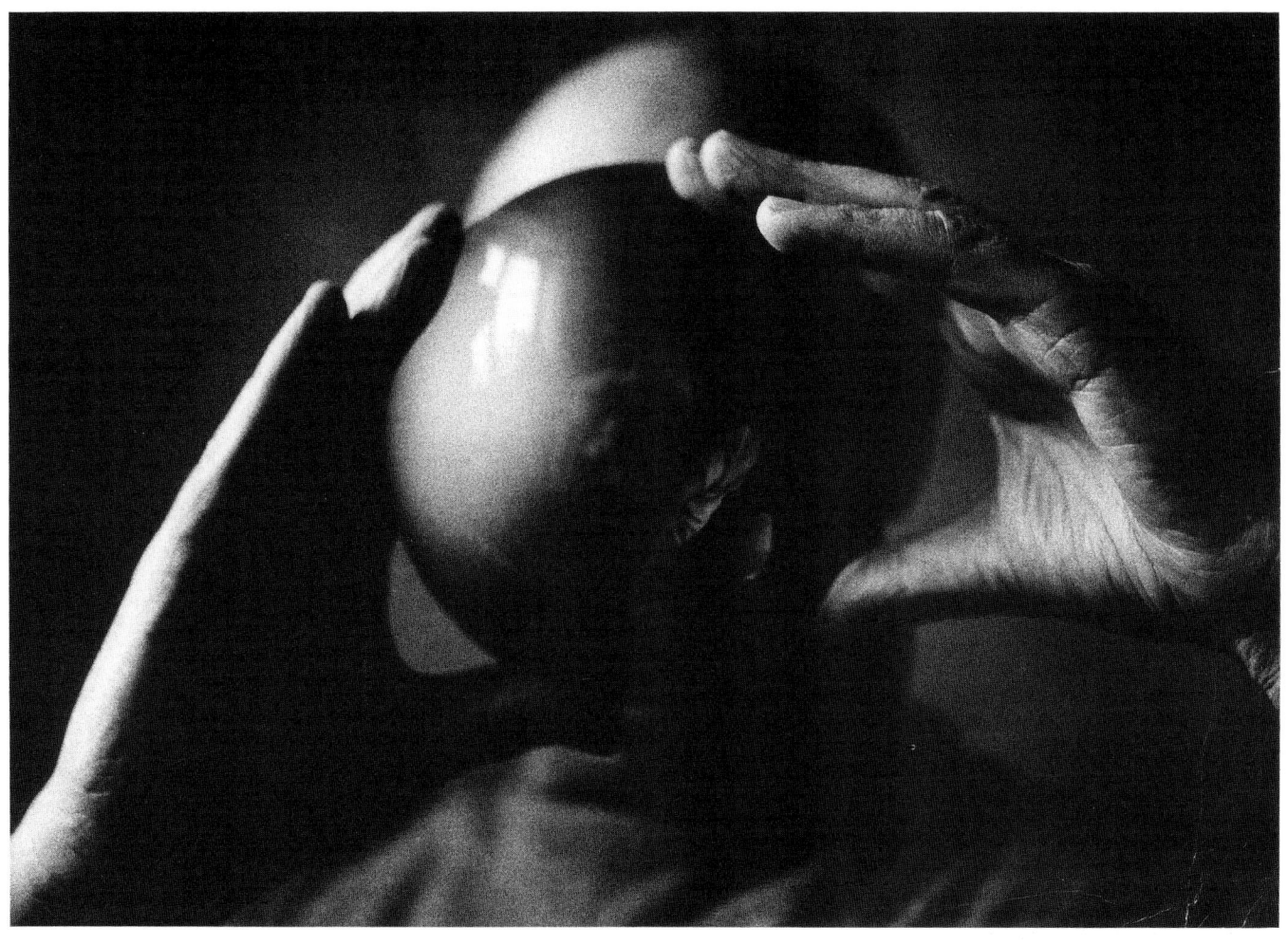

Erwin Axer, Theater Director. Photograph ©Krzysztof Gieraltowski.

1984	*Polska Wspolczesna-Fotografia Artystyczna,* Galeria Zacheta, Warsaw (travelled to the Muzeum Narodowe, Wroclaw)
1986	*Fotografier,* Charlottenbourg, Copenhagen
	Mastiera Polskoj Fotografii Pressy, Wsiesojuznyj Muzej Fotografii, Moscow (travelled to the Etnograficzeskij Muzej, Leningrad)
1987	*Realismus-Metaphor-Geometrie,* Palais Palffy, Vienna
1988	*Het Portret,* Canon Image Centre/Pulitzer Art Gallery, Amsterdam
1989	*Wols, Janssen, Gieraltowski,* Kupferstitch-Kabinett, Staatliche Kunstsammlungen, Dresden
	Spojrzenia/Wrazenia, Muzeum Sztuki, Lodz, Poland
	Co Je Fotografie, Dum Umieni, Manes, Prague
	Wystawa Z Okazji 150 Lat Fotografii, Muzeum Narodowe, Wroclaw, Poland
1991	*Vor der Wende,* Museum Ludwig, Cologne

Collections:

Library of Congress, Washington, D.C.; Museum of Modern Art, San Francisco; Henie-Onstat Artcenter, Oslo; Preus Fotomuseum, Horten, Norway; Det Kongelige Bibliotek, Copenhagen; Prentenkabinet, Rijksuniversiteit, Leiden; Bibliothèque Nationale, Paris; Musée d'Art Moderne de la Ville de Paris; Museum für Kunst und Gewerbe, Hamburg; Museum Ludwig, Cologne; Rheinisches Landesmuseum, Bonn; Fotomuseum im Stadtmuseum, Munich; Il Diaframma/Canon, Milan; Kupferstitch-Kabinett, Staatliche Kunstsammlungen, Dresden; Staatliche Galerie Moritzburg, Halle; Staatliche Museen zu Berlin, Kunstbibliothek, Berlin; Muzej Isobrazitelnich Iskusstv, Moscow; Moravska Galerie, Brno, Czechoslovakia; Muzeum Narodowe, Warsaw; Muzeum Narodowe, Wroclaw; Muzeum Sztuki, Lodz; Biblioteka Narodowa, Warsaw; Muzeum Plakatu, Warsaw; Muzeum Essen, Warsaw; Muzeum Lahti, Warsaw.

Publications:

On GIERALTOWSKI: Articles—in *Fotografia* (Warsaw), No. 3, 1979; in *Revue Fotografie* (Prague), No. 3, 1980; in *European Photography* (Göttingen), No. 1, 1984; in *Clichés* (Brussels), No. 12, 1988; in *Camera International* (Paris) No. 2, 1988; in *Ceskoslovenska Fotografie* (Prague), No. 3, 1989; in *Fotografie* (Dresden), No. 1, 1991; in *6x9 Fotografia* (Warsaw), No. 2, 1991.

*   *   *

Krzysztof Gieraltowski's photography is an interesting Polish phenomenon. He began in the 1960s with press photography and this is the forum in which he expressed himself best. In those days he worked for a number of publications, but most notably for the student magazine *ITD*. At that time the magazine had a clear policy of inviting contributors who held widely differing views; most frequently these would be famous people with very strong personalities. The magazine's journalists would then conduct highly unconventional exchanges with these celebrities, debates which resembled rounds in a boxing match rather than dignified salon discussions with professors, artists, politicians and the like. The upshot of this editorial stance was both that the magazine was very popular and that the debates in its columns carried a certain weight. The combative and even aggressive nature of the interviews in *ITD* suited Gieraltowski's own character. It gave him an excellent opportunity to develop an equally unconventional style of photography. What interested him most was not taking elegant photographs of successful people, which they were, in the main. Rather, he went much further, bypassing the image these individuals aspired to convey, and showing them as he saw them during the numerous rounds of these metaphorical boxing matches—anxiously calculating by turns incisive then brutal, resolute then indecisive, with their weaknesses mercilessly exposed. Indeed, Gieraltowski not only photographed them as they appeared to him, he further dramatised these images with a natural talent for capturing an expression, and the creating or even caricaturing of a subject. Interestingly, each of these photographs was reproduced on a full page in the magazine, and their impact was immediate. They provoked admiration or criticism, and were accorded praise or denigration, but could not be ignored. By developing and perfecting this type of portrait photography, Gieraltowski eventually created his own inimitable form of portraiture. He had created a new style.

Alongside and somewhat in the shadow of this expressive and biting style of photography are to be found his other portrait photographs. Now and again Gieraltowski would photograph his subjects much as the medieval painters depicted saints, showing the symbols of their sanctity or the instruments of their martyrdom. This device is echoed in a series of Gieraltowski's photographs in which the sitters are pictured with the tools of their trade, or with objects reflecting their particular interests or emphasising the nature of their work. Compared to his other work, these photographs lack Gieraltowski's characteristic dynamism and vigour.

Viewed together, Gieraltowski's photographs occupy a unique place in Polish photography. They transcend their origins in press photography, which was so crucial to his style, but they cannot be described as analytical, conceptual or avant-garde. Indeed, they do not aspire to these forms. Their defining characteristic is a combination of expressiveness and visual impact, such that they occupy a hitherto empty middle ground which had separated these two major photographic trends. Along with a handful of other Polish photographers, Gieraltowski can be credited with introducing a set of new and important values into this unclaimed no-man's land, thus contributing to the emergence of a completely new direction for Polish contemporary photography.

—Ryszard Bobrowski

GILDEN, Bruce.

Nationality: American. **Born:** 16 October 1946. **Education:** Self-taught photographer. **Recipient:** Won the Grand Prize at the International Triennial Exhibition of Photography, Fribourg, in 1985 and the Special Jury Prize in 1988. Commissioned by the ARCO Festival, Madrid, in 1991; Medecins Sans Frontieres's Twentieth Anniversary, in 1991; Mission Photographique Transmanche, Centre Regional de la Photographie, Nord Pas de Calais, in 1993, and the Metropoli 30, Bilbao, in 1993. Received the Artist's Fellowship Award from the New York Foundation for the Arts in 1979 and 1992 and the National Endowment for the Art Photographer's Fellowship in 1980, 1984 and 1992. **Address:** 25 Mercer Street, New York, New York 10013, U.S.A.

Individual Exhibitions:

1977	O.K. Harris Gallery, New York City
1979	O.K. Harris Gallery, New York City
1984	O.K. Harris Gallery, New York City
1986	Les Rencontres D'Arles
	Focus Gallery, Amsterdam
	Fotograficentrum, Stockholm
1987	Nikon Salon, Tokyo
	Fotografisk Galeri, Copenhagen
1988	Ffoto Gallery, Cardiff

	Houston Center for Photography, Texas
	Blue Sky Gallery, Portland, Oregon
1989	Galeria d'Arte Moderne, Bologna
	Bibliotheque Nationale, Paris
1990	Agatha Gaillard Gallery, Paris
1991	Blatent Image/Silver Eye, Pittsburgh
	Canon Image Centre, Amsterdam
	Fotograficentrum, Stockholm
	Photographic Museum of Finland, Helsinki
1992	Schlossmuseum, Kleve Fotogalerie in der Schwanenberg, Germany
	Fotographie Forum, Frankfurt
	Galerie FNAC, Paris (also travelled)
	The Chrysler Museum, Norfolk, Virginia
	German-American Institute, Tubingen
1993	German-American Institute, Heidelberg
	Galeria Forum, Tarragona
	The Special Photographers Company, London
	Centre Regional de la Photographie, Nord Pas de Calais
	Musee de l'Elysee, Lausanne, Switzerland
	Galerie Bodo Niemann, Berlin
	Musee de la Photographie, Charleroi, Belgium
	Fotogaleria San Martin, Buenos Aires
1994	Centre Regional de la Photographie, Nord Pas de Calais
	Leica Gallery, Solms, Germany
	Galerie Sephiha, Brussels, Belgium
	Agatha Gaillard Gallery, Paris

Selected Group Exhibitions:

1985	International Triennial Exhibition of Photography, Fribourg, Switzerland
	American Images 1945-1980, Barbican Art Gallery, London
1987	International Triennial Exhibition of Photography, Musee de la Photographie, Charleroi, Belgium
	From Time to Time, Centre National de la Photographie, Paris
	Movement, Centre National de la Photographie, Paris
	Twelve Photographers Look At Us, Philadelphia Museum of Art
	57th & 5th, Pace/MacGill Gallery, New York
	Galerie Municipale du Chateau d'Eau, Toulouse
1988	*NYC—Same Streets—3 Views,* Houston FotoFest
	Victoria and Albert Museum, London
	Splendeurs et Miseres du Corps, Mois de la Photo, Musee d'Art, Moderne de la Ville de Paris
1989	Cliche Magazine Anniversary Exhibition (also travelled)
	Mois de la Photo, Montreal
	Stated As Fact: Photographic Documents of New Jersey, New Jersey State Museum, Trenton, New Jersey
1991	P.P.S. Gallerie, Hamburg
	Mean Streets: American Photographs from the Collection, Museum of Modern Art, New York
	Regards sur Medecins Sans Frontieres, MSF Twentieth Anniversay (three simultaneous travelling exhibitions in America, France and the rest of Europe)
1992	Casa des Artes, Vigo, Spain
1993	*Uber dir Grossen Stadte,* Marstall, Berlin
	Recent Acquisitions, Museum of Modern Art, New York
1994	*Who's Looking at the Family?,* Barbican Gallery, London
	Magic Moments: 40 Years of Leica M, Hasselblad Centre, Goteborg, Sweden

Collections:

Museum of Modern Art, New York; Galerie Municipale du Chateau d'Eau, Toulouse; Bibliotheque Nationale, Paris; Schomburg Center, New York Public Library; Museum of Art and History, Fribourg, Switzerland; Paris Audiovisuel, France; Union Bank of Finland; Moderna Museet, Stockholm; Helmut Gernsheim Collection, Switzerland; Bert Hartkamp Collection, The Netherlands; ARCO Collection, Madrid; Galeries Photo FNAC, Paris; The

Untitled, Haiti, **1990.** Photograph ©Bruce Gilden.

Dreyfus Corporation, New York; Center for Creative Photography, Tucson, Arizona; National Gallery of Canada, Ottawa; Centre Regional de la Photographie, Nord Pas de Calais; Victoria and Albert Museum, London; Philadelphia Museum of Art, Pennsylvania; Library of Congress, Washington, D.C.; Museum of Fine Arts, Houston; Toledo Museum of Art, Ohio; Musee de la Photographie, Belgium; Museet for Fotokunst, Odense, Denmark; Photographic Museum of Finland; F.C. Gundlach Collection, Germany; Manfred Heiting Collection, Belgium; Musee de l'Elysee, Lausanne; The Chrysler Museum, Norfolk, VA; Fonds National d'Art Contemporain, Paris; Hasselblad Center, Goteberg, Sweden; Brooklyn Museum, New York.

Publications:

By GILDEN: Books—*Bruce Gilden: The Small Haiti Portfolio,* Helsinki 1990; *Facing New York: Photographs by Bruce Gilden,* Cornerhouse Publications (England), Fall 1992; *Bleus,* Cahier number 13, Mission Photographique Transmanche, (Nord Pas de Calais) 1994.

On GILDEN: Books—*Camera Lucida* by Roland Barthes, Hill & Wang (New York), 1981; *Photographic Artists and Innovators,* Brown & Partnow (New York), 1983. **Articles**—"Young Contempories" in the *Creative Camera International Yearbook,* London 1978; *Amateur Photographer* (England), 1981; *Aperture Magazine* (New York), number 101, 1986; *Bild Magazine* (Sweden), number 33, 1986; *Cliches Magazine* (Belgium), number 28, 1986; *Valokuva Magazine* (Finland), 1986; *PF Magazine* (The Netherland), 1986; *Creative Camera Magazine* (England), 1986; *Focus Magazine* (The Netherlands), number 10, October 1986; *Asahi Camera* (Japan), 1987; "Un Si

Grand Age . . ." in *Photo Copies,* (Paris) number 7, (Paris) 1987; "Le Temps d'un Movement" in *Photo Copies,* (Paris) number 8, 1987; *Camera International* (France), number 22, 1989; *Vis-a-Vis* (France), number 6, 1990; *Photo Metro* (San Francisco), June/July 1990; *The Independent* (England), number 94, Summer 1990; *Prat* (Stockholm), Spring 1991; *Musta Taide* (Helsinki), number 1, 1990; "Street Life" in the *Observer Magazine,* 17 March 1991; "Cannes Film Festival" in *Liberation,* (Paris) May 1991; *Photographers International* (Taiwan), number 5, December 1992; *Aperture* (New York), issue 126, Spring 1992; "Haiti; Hope in Hell" in the *Observer Magazine,* 3 February 1993; *Globe Hebdo* (Paris), number 3, 1993; *British Vogue,* February 1993; *La Fotografia,* number 5 (Spain), 1993; *Aktuel Photographie* (Helsingborg) 1994.

* * *

In many ways Bruce Gilden is the archetypal New York street photographer, the natural heir to Strand, Frank, Klein, Levinstein and Winogrand. Like his mentor, William Klein, Gilden has even moved to Paris in recent years, his frequent trips between the two great cities adding a cosmopolitan edge to his previously localised vision. However, Gilden is very much a photographer of the late twentieth century, and we must not suppose that his concerns match those of his predecessors who brought a determinedly humanist, even overtly political stance to their street photography—the members of the Photo League for example. Bruce Gilden is a self-confessed formalist, a fact which has not pleased those for whom any formalist tendencies are anathema. Yet we must not suppose that the humanists were uninterested in formal matters, or subjective psychology, nor assume too readily that social or psychological concerns do not lurk somewhere in Gilden's imagery.

Essentially, Bruce Gilden, like any photographer, reflects the *zeitgeist*, and if his pictures seem more nervy and psychotic than those of former decades, then one might point to the mood of our times. If his frame seems more sharply energised by his favoured combination of quick, close confrontation and flash lighting, such a vision seems perfectly in accord with the asocial, amoral angst of inner city life in contemporary America.

Gilden's stated credo is "to energise the frame"—not only in a formal sense, but in a way that captures the nervous and psychological energies of city life. In every Gilden image there is a psychodrama taking place. He tends not to show much of the *mis en scène* of city life around his subjects, frequently isolating in a miasma of flash blur and removing them from any clearly identifiable activity or setting, thus pouring our concentration upon them and their inner selves. Their psychological profiles and personal stories seem to have been sucked out of them, almost miraculously, in a mere fraction of a second, by Gilden's probing flash light. Of course, these "stories" are fictions, elicited by Gilden and his camera. They are not the whole truth, but neither are they lies. For all his formalist bent, Gilden is saying something about his view of modern society and it is not entirely a joyful vision. "Manic-depressive" might be an apt term for the way it swings violently between aggressive energies and slow motion smash-ups.

So many of Gilden's subjects seem to be alienated, wandering and rootless, and this may relate to his Jewishness, which is an important factor to him. In his essay, *First Diasporist Manifesto*, the painter R B Kitaj wrote about the terrible fate of his people in this century and went on to consider whether rootlessness and wandering have not become more than just a Jewish preoccupation—whether indeed they are the modern human condition. Gilden's vibrant echoes of existential life on the streets of New York City would seem to confirm Kitaj's views.

—Gerry Badger

GILLSÄTER, Sven.

Nationality: Swedish. **Born:** Njutaanger, Hälsingland, 28 February 1921. **Education:** Studied at Hudiksvalls Laeroverk College, Hudiksvall, 1935-39; School of Journalism, Stockholm, 1947-48. **Military Service:** Served as a mountain soldier with the Kiruna Ski Battalion, Swedish Army, in northern Sweden, 1942-45. **Family:** Married the actress and singer Harriet Forssell in 1964; children: Pia and Björn. **Career:** Worked with the photographer Sven Hoernell, in Riksgraensen, Sweden, 1944. Since 1947, freelance press and sports photographer, and photojournalist, Stockholm, working for the daily and weekly publications *Paris-Match, Natural History Magazine, Epoca, Stern, Quick, Das Tier, La Vie de Bafes,* etc., with the agencies Black Star (New York), Fot (Copenhagen) and Bildnytt (Stockholm); has worked mainly on nature and animal photography, from 1957. Founder-member, with Hans Malmberg, Hans Hammarskiold, Rune Hassner and others, Tio Fotografer group, Stockholm, 1958. Swedish Board Member, World Wildlife Fund, Stockholm, since 1980. **Recipient:** Animal Friend of the Year Award, Swedish Society for the Protection of Animals, 1976. **Address:** Steninge 375, 310 42 Haverdal, Sweden.

Individual Exhibitions:

1985   *Animals,* Hasselblad Gallery, Goteborg, Sweden
        Animals, Flamingo Gallery, Falkenberg, Sweden
        Animals, Persasen Gallery, Ostersund, Sweden
1986   *Five Continents,* Museum of Natural History, Stockholm

Selected Group Exhibitions:

1949   *Young Photographers,* Rotohallen, Stockholm
1958   *Tio Fotografer,* Lunds Konsthall, Sweden
1960   *Tio på Svensk Form,* Svensk Form Gallery, Stockholm
1971   *Contemporary Photographs from Sweden,* Library of Congress, Washington, D.C.

1975   *Samlingarna gavor och kop 1971-75,* Fotografiska Museet, Stockholm
1977   *Ten Photographers,* Aronowitsch Gallery, Stockholm
1982   *Fotograferna och det Svenska Landskappet,* Fotografiska Museet, Stockholm

Collections:

Fotografiska Museet, Stockholm; Museum of Photography, Oslo; Museum of Photography, Helsinki; Bibliothèque Nationale, Paris; Library of Congress, Washington, D.C.

Publications:

By GILLSÄTER: Books—*A Turn in the Snow,* with text by Curt Paulson, Stockholm 1955; *Eye to Eye,* Stockholm 1958; *We Ended in Bali,* Stockholm 1958, London 1961; *Susan in the Holy Land,* with Pia Gillsäter, Stockholm 1960, London 1961; *Strange Animals in Tropical Nature,* Stockholm 1962; *Wave After Wave,* Stockholm 1962, London 1964; *See You at Liseberg,* with text by Axel Miltander, Stockholm 1963; *Pia's Safari,* Stockholm 1964; *Island After Island,* Stockholm 1966, London 1968; *Pia in Alaska,* Stockholm 1968; *Penguins in the Wind,* Stockholm 1969; *Kolmården: The Environment for the Wild,* with text by Nils Linnman, Hoganas, Sweden 1972; *More Wild Than Tame,* Hoganas, Sweden 1974; *Wings Over Kattegatt,* Halmstad, Sweden 1977; *Gillsäter's Ark,* Stockholm 1979; *Oland: Nightingale and Orchids,* edited by Sigvard Malmberg, Stockholm 1983; *What An Animal Life—Kolmården,* Hoganas, Sweden 1983; *Galapagos,* Hoganas, Sweden 1986. **Article**—"Antarktis" in *Hasselblad* (Goteborg), March 1985.

On GILLSÄTER: Books—*Contemporary Photographs from Sweden: An Exhibition of the Work of the Tio Photographers,* catalogue, Washington, D.C. 1971; *Photographic Communication,* edited by R. Smith Schuneman, London and Toronto 1972; *Tio Fotografer,* Stockholm 1976; *Bilder for Miljoner* by Rune Hassner, Stockholm 1977; *Writers of Nature Close Up* by Rune Bollvik, Stockholm 1980; *Fotograferna och det Svenska Landskappet,* exhibition catalogue, with text by Leif Wigh, Stockholm 1982; *Tio Fotografer Bildbyra,* Stockholm 1983; *Nature Photographers* by Arne Schmitz, Hoganas, Sweden 1985. **Articles**—"Sven Gillsäter—reporterfotograf" in *Fotografisk Arsbok 1962,* Stockholm 1962; "Sven Gillsäter" in *Hasselblad* (Goteborg), March 1970; "Sven Gillsäter" by Evald Karlsten in *Hasselblad* (Goteborg), September 1982; "Antarktis" by Bertil Hagerhäll in *Swedish Nature* (Stockholm), October 1985; "The Most Well-Known Nature Photographer" by Bertil K. Johansson in *Foto* (Stockholm), no. 7/8, 1985.

*

I was born in a crofter's cottage at Njutånger in a district called Hälsingland, up 300 miles north of Stockholm. The real countryside was my camera hunting grounds already at school. My father was a keen nature lover and his forest was an oasis for the animals. When chopping wood for the usually rough winter, we should always have a double set of sandwiches for the mice, the weasel, for the fox. The moose was often standing watching us from close range. No shooting ever had frightened the "park"'s inhabitants. I also think I got a very useful experience of life under harder conditions during military service above the Arctic Circle with the skiing battalion of Kiruna. I was so lost in the mountains that I asked for a job as a photographer in Riksgränsen near the Norwegian border—only an hotel and three houses, the rest was tundra. There I got to know the animal life of the treeline and how important it was to try to conserve the life able to survive in such a strange climate. After a year of pretty isolated life among the Lapps and the mountains I went down to Stockholm and attended a school of journalism. I thought I had to know how to write a caption for my pictures. The pictures became picture stories and the articles became books.

This is in brief how the globetrotter life started: reportage travels all over the world, sometimes for such a long time that the Foreign Office had to make inquiries for me. They sometimes got a cable from an Embassy that I probably had a good time with the dragons of Komodo.

Through the years I have learned that human beings could be much more dangerous than the animals. If one behaves like a polite guest in their environment and respects them as inhabitants you do not have to fear the animals at all.

I think I have tried to work as a conservationist—with World Wildlife Fund rules and thoughts—long before the word was known to the general public. Now I dedicate most of my time to WWF as a member of the Swedish board. In my picture stories, articles, books, television- and radio-programs I have always tried to inform how important it is to be careful with the environment and its inhabitants. All sorts. In my pictures I have also tried to make them as artistic as possible and have tried to avoid the "museum-picture" impression. My ambition is to avoid pictures of threatened animals— or threatening animals. I think I am a little bit on the right way: many of my TV-films have been shown in different countries all over the world and many of my books have been translated into English, German, Italian, Russian, Spanish, Hungarian, Bulgarian, Jugoslavian and other languages. Picture reports for Swedish and foreign press from all continents—the latest picture stories from three travels to the Antarctic. That way I hope and believe that I have spread out the information to those who can assist in helping to "Save the World."

—Sven Gillsäter

*   *   *

Sven Gillsäter is one of the most serious and ambitious photographers I know in his particular field of animal, nature and environmental photography. It is a fascinating experience to have followed his photography from when he was a young and angry photographer in the late 1940s and the early 1950s.

When he worked as a newspaper reporter and sports photographer I know he was interested in nature and animals, being born deep in the Swedish forests, and when he began full-time work in the 1950s, it was as a nature and animal photographer. I am sure his first ambition was to tell beautiful stories about animal life. But soon, he discovered that many species were already extinct and many others on their way to extermination. Despite his wish to tell of nature's beauty, his pictures became more and more critical.

Since the beginning of the World Wildlife Fund (WWF), Gillsäter has been its most important propagandist and contributor. He has used his camera as a weapon in defence of those species still remaining on our earth. Few have collected so much in funds for the WWF in Sweden as Gillsäter, who has constantly lectured and exhibited all over Sweden on WWF's behalf.

Why has nature, animal and landscape photography been so important in Sweden? Because we live so close to nature or within it. Long ago, some photographers used as models stuffed animals, or half-dead ones (for instance, a trampled mouse would enable an owl to make its kill within range of the photographer's viewfinder). To get away from this sort of photography, a number of Swedish photographers started the group "Naturfotograferna," Gillsäter being one of the first and still one of its most important members.

Many young Swedes have learned much from this, and today can pass on their valuable heritage. The late Victor Hasselblad, a good nature photographer himself, often worked with Gillsäter, and their influence was mutual. The Hasselblad camera and system that Victor Hasselblad invented have been very important to Gillsäter's photography. Since he acquired his first Hasselblad camera in the early 1950s he has remained faithful to it, unlike so many others in his field who turned to the 35mm system.

For me, most nature and animal pictures are no manifestations of art. They are seldom what Otto Steinert called "subjective photography," or what Andreas Feininger has called "creative photography"; they are more like, to borrow Feininger's term, "an artistic controlled documentation." At any rate, there are pictures by Gillsäter that I would call manifestations of art—i.e., pictures which have more of a symbolic language than documentary.

Robert Capa said that words are more important than pictures. I don't think he was right; I think the most useful way to communicate is to use *both* words and pictures. Gillsäter is brilliant at doing just that. He writes the text for most of his books, and the message is all the stronger for that. Nor would his words alone have been enough, nor his pictures. Text and pictures need each other. In much the same way as he combines word and image in his television films. Some of them are unforgettable—not least because of his brilliant commentary. He is one of the best story-tellers in Sweden.

Gillsäter has travelled the world to save and preserve animal life, and he looks set to continue for as long as he can use the camera for this purpose. His strong feeling for both animal and human life (despite his fame as an animal photographer, he never stopped photographing people), is something for which we owe a debt of thanks.

—Ulf Sjöstedt

GILPIN, Laura.

Nationality: American. **Born:** Colorado Springs, Colorado, 22 April 1891. **Education:** Baldwin School, Bryn Mawr, Pennsylvania, and Rosemary Hall School, Greenwich, Connecticut, 1904-08; studied photography, under Max Weber and Paul Anderson, Clarence White School, New York, 1916-18; did graduate studies in photogravure, under Anton Bruehl, Bernard Horn and Clarence White, New York, 1918. **Career:** Independent professional photographer, from 1915: staff photographer, Central City Opera House Association (University of Denver), Colorado, 1932-36; chief photographer, Boeing Aircraft Company, Wichita, Kansas, 1942-45; concentrated on Navaho Indian photography project, Santa Fe, New Mexico, 1946-68; Canyon de Chelly project, Santa Fe, 1968-79. Instructor in Photography, Chappell School of Art, Denver, 1926-30; Colorado Springs Fine Arts Center, 1930, 1940-41. Regional Vice-President, Pictorial Photographers of America, 1930; Chairman, Indian Arts Fund, Santa Fe, New Mexico, 1958. **Recipient:** Medal, International Salon, Madrid 1935; Award of Merit, Photographic Society of America 1947; Honored Photographer, St. John's College, Santa Fe, New Mexico, 1966; Appreciation Award, Indian Arts and Crafts Board, United States Department of the Interior, 1967; Southwest Library Association Award, 1969; Western Heritage Award, 1969; Headline Award, Theta Sigma Phi Society of Women in Journalism and Communications, Albuquerque, New Mexico, 1970; Hidalgo de Calificada Nobleza Award, State of New Mexico, 1970; Research Grant, School of American Research, Santa Fe, New Mexico, 1971; Fine Arts Award, Industrial Photographers of the Southwest, 1971; Brotherhood Award, National Conference of Christians and Jews, 1972; Governor's Award, State of New Mexico, 1974; Guggenheim Fellowship, 1975. D.H.L.: University of New Mexico, Albuquerque, 1970. Honorary Life Member of the Board, School of American Research, Santa Fe, New Mexico, 1967; Honorary Colonel, Aide-de-Camp, to Governor of New Mexico, 1970. Associate, Royal Photographic Society, London, 1930. **Estate:** Mr. Gerald Richardson, 703 Don Felix Street, Santa Fe, New Mexico 87501. **Died:** (in Santa Fe) 30 November 1979.

Individual Exhibitions:

1918	Clarence H. White School, New York
	Camera Club Galleries, New York
1924	Pictorial Photographers of America, New York
	Baltimore Photographic Club
1933	Denver Art Museum
1934	Library of Congress, Washington, D.C.
	Taylor Museum for Southwestern Studies, Colorado Springs
	American Museum of Natural History, New York
1935	Beacon School, Wellesley, Massachusetts
1936	J.B. Speed Museum, Louisville, Kentucky
	Taylor Museum for Southwestern Studies, Colorado Springs
1946	Museo Arqueologico e Historico de Yucatan, Merida, Mexico
1948	*Follow the Rio Grande,* Colorado Springs Fine Arts Center
1949	Santa Barbara Museum of Art, California
	Galeria Mexico, Santa Fe, New Mexico
	The Town Hall Club, New York
	Portal Gallery, First National Bank, Santa Fe, New Mexico
	Dallas Museum of Fine Arts
1951	Roswell Art Center, New Mexico
	The Arts Club, Washington, D.C.
	Wichita Art Association, Kansas
1953	*The Architecture of John Gaw Meem,* Fine Arts Museum of New Mexico, Santa Fe
1955	Tucson Art Center, Arizona
	The Arts Club, Washington, D.C.

1956	American Museum of Natural History, New York
1957	Laboratory of Anthropology, Santa Fe, New Mexico
	International Museum of Photography, George Eastman House, Rochester, New York
1958	Colorado Springs Fine Art Center
	Fine Arts Museum of New Mexico, Santa Fe (with Eliot Porter)
1960	Nelson Gallery of Art, Kansas City
1962	Fine Arts Museum of New Mexico, Santa Fe (with Eliot Porter and Todd Webb)
1965	Tucson Fine Arts Association, Arizona
1966	*50th Anniversary Exhibition,* St. John's College, Santa Fe, New Mexico
1968	*Rio Grande: River of the Arid Land,* Museum of Albuquerque, New Mexico
	Museum of the Southwest, Midland, Texas
	The Enduring Navaho, Amon Carter Museum, Fort Worth, Texas
1969	West Texas Museum, Texas Technological University, Lubbock
	Communication from the Reservation, Riverside Museum, New York (photos by Gilpin; with Southwestern Indian artefacts)
1970	*Retrospective 1923-1968,* Institute of American Indian Arts, Santa Fe, New Mexico
	Oklahoma City Art Museum
	Colorado Springs Fine Arts Center
1971	St. John's College, Santa Fe, New Mexico
1972	*Churches and Public Buildings by Architect John Gaw Meem,* St. John's College, Santa Fe, New Mexico
1973	Witkin Gallery, New York
1974	Farmington Museum, New Mexico
	Laura Gilpin: Retrospective, Museum of New Mexico, Santa Fe (toured the United States)
1977	*Laura Gilpin/William Clift/Eliot Porter,* Horwitch Gallery, Santa Fe, New Mexico
1978	*Laura Gilpin: Photographer,* National Cowboy Hall of Fame and Western Heritage Center, Oklahoma City
	Amon Carter Museum, Fort Worth, Texas (retrospective)
1979	*Laura Gilpin: Ranch School Photographs,* The Los Alamos Historical Society, New Mexico
1980	Witkin Gallery, New York
1986	*An Enduring Grace,* IBM Gallery, New York

Selected Group Exhibitions:

1975	*Women of Photography,* San Francisco Museum of Art (toured the United States, 1975-77)
1977	*5 Santa Fe Photographers,* Horwitch Gallery, Santa Fe, New Mexico
	Photographs: Sheldon Memorial Art Gallery Collection, University of Nebraska, Lincoln
1979	*Photography Rediscovered: American Photographs 1900-1930,* Whitney Museum, New York (travelled to Art Institute of Chicago)
	The History of Photography in New Mexico, University of New Mexico, Albuquerque (travelled to Tyler Museum of Art, Texas; and Roswell Museum, New Mexico)
	Recollections: 10 Women of Photography, International Center of Photography, New York (toured the United States)
1981	*11 Photographers of Santa Fe,* at *Rencontres Internationales de la Photographie,* Arles, France
	Masterworks from the Photography Collection, Amon Carter Museum, Fort Worth, Texas
	American Photographers and the National Parks, Corcoran Gallery, Washington, D.C. (toured the United States, 1981-83)
1983	*Subjective Vision,* High Museum of Art, Atlanta, Georgia

Collections:

Amon Carter Museum, Fort Worth, Texas (26,000 negatives, 20,000 photos, library and personal papers); Museum of Modern Art, New York; International Museum of Photography, George Eastman House, Rochester, New York; Library of Congress, Washington, D.C.; Smithsonian Institution, Washington, D.C.; Princeton University, New Jersey; Colorado Springs Fine Arts Center; Center for Creative Photography, University of Arizona, Tucson; University of New Mexico, Albuquerque; Museum of New Mexico, Santa Fe.

Publications:

By GILPIN: Books—*The Pikes Peak Regions: Reproductions from a Series of Photographs by Laura Gilpin,* Colorado Springs 1926; *The Mesa Verde National Park: Reproductions from a Series of Photographs,* Colorado Springs 1927; *The Pueblos: A Camera Chronicle,* New York 1941; *Temples in Yucatan: A Camera Chronicle of Chichen Itza,* New York 1948; *The Rio Grande: River of Destiny,* New York 1949; *The Enduring Navaho,* Austin, Texas and London 1968. **Articles**—interview and comment in *Gazette* (Colorado Springs), 4 July 1920; "Some Thoughts on Portraiture" in *Portraiture by Photography,* brochure, Colorado Springs, 1920; "Historic Architecture Photography: The Southwest" in *The Complete Photographer: Volume 6,* New York 1942; "Portraiture" in *Graphic Graflex Photography,* New York 1945; "Rio Grande Country" in *U.S. Camera* (New York), February 1950; pictures and commentary in *Photography: The Selected Image* by Gerald Lang and James Baker, University Park, Pennsylvania 1978.

On GILPIN: Books—*Laura Gilpin: Retrospective 1910-1974,* exhibition catalogue, with texts by Anne Noggle and others, Sante Fe, New Mexico 1974; *Women of Photography: An Historical Survey* by Margey Mann and Anne Noggle, San Francisco 1975; *Color Photography: Inventors and Innovators 1850-1975* exhibition catalogue, by Laura Geringer, New Haven, Connecticut 1975; *Aspects of American Photography 1976,* exhibition catalogue, by Jean S. Tucker, St. Louis, Missouri 1976; *The Great West: Real/Ideal,* edited by Sandy Hume and others, Boulder, Colorado 1977; *Photographs: The Sheldon Memorial Art Gallery Collection, University of Nebraska,* with an introduction by Norman A. Geske, Lincoln, Nebraska 1977; *Dialogue with Photography,* edited by Paul Hill and Thomas Cooper, London 1979; *Recollections: 10 Women of Photography,* edited by Margaretta K. Mitchell, New York 1979; *Photography Rediscovered: American Photographs 1900-1930* by David Travis, New York 1979; *A Ten Year Salute* by Lee D. Witkin, with a foreword by Carol Brown, Danbury, New Hampshire 1979; *The Photograph Collector's Guide* by Lee D. Witkin and Barbara London, Boston and London 1979; *American Photographers and the National Parks,* exhibition catalogue, by Robert Glenn Ketchum, Los Angeles 1983; *Subjective Vision,* exhibition catalogue, with introduction by A. D. Coleman, Atlanta, Georgia 1983; *The Library of World Photography: Landscape,* with text by David Plowden and Ian Jeffrey, Tokyo and London 1984. **Articles**—"Laura Gilpin, Photographer of the Southwest" by David Vestal in *Popular Photography* (New York), February 1977; "The Photography of Laura Gilpin" by Marni Sandweiss in *Four Winds* (Austin, Texas), vol. 1, no. 4, 1980.

*   *   *

Laura Gilpin was an artist whose affinity for her chosen subject, the landscape and native cultures of the American Southwest, was such that her life's work has become a part of the primary documentation of these places and people. For almost 60 years she devoted her energies and consummate skill to the depiction of the society and environment of the Pueblo and Navajo people. Unlike her predecessors in the field she was not limited in her procedures and point of view to the creation of an exclusively anthropological record of disappearing patterns of life. While commanding her attention and respect, the "old ways" were seen in the context of the many changes affecting Indian life in the 20th century and the resulting archive of many thousands of prints is imbued with the remarkable rapport that operated between the artist and her subjects.

It is interesting to note that Laura Gilpin, like so many of her contemporaries, began as a pictorialist, producing autochrome and platinum prints of notably artistic character. In her maturity the character of her work changed, moving away from the soft focus ideal which she had learned in the Clarence

White School and ultimately achieving the objective clarity and warmth of tone which was the special quality of her style.

In her several books, the landscape, architecture and people of her chosen world achieved a kind of classic definition in the public mind which in recent years, with the proliferation of photographic exhibitions, has been enhanced by the recognition of her impeccable craftsmanship in printing. In these books, particularly in *The Enduring Navaho*, she demonstrated her very considerable skill as a writer and proponent of social and environmental integrity.

Taken as a whole Laura Gilpin's work represents the function of photography as a social art at its highest level, embodying history in the terms of visual experience.

—Norman A. Geske

GIOLI, Paolo.

Nationality: Italian. **Born:** Sarzano di Rovigo, 12 October 1942. **Education:** Schools in Rovigo and Venice. **Family:** Married Carla Schiesari in 1969. **Career:** Freelance photographer and filmmaker, Rovigo and Milan, since 1968; has worked with Polaroid color photography since 1977, with Cibachrome since the end of the seventies. **Recipient:** Premio Italia, for photography, Verona, 1976; Premio Friuli Venezia Giulia Fotografia, Spilimbergo, 1989. **Address:** via Pradespin, 29, 45026 Lendinara (Rovigo) Italy.

Individual Exhibitions:

1977	*Il Tempo della Ricera Ritrovata*, Galleria Il Diaframma, Milan (travelled to Libreria e Galleria Pan, Rome, 1978)
1978	*Terra di Land*, Galleria Il Diaframma, Milan (travelled to Libreria e Galleria Pan, Rome)
1979	*Antropolaroid*, Galleria Il Diaframma, Milan
1981	*A Hippolyte Bayard Gran Positivo*, at *SICOF 1981*, Milan
	Ritratto Gran Positivo, Galleria Agora, Turin
1982	*Il Punto Trasparente*, Istituto Nazionale per la Grafica-Calcografia, Rome
	Cameron Obscura, Galerie des Arènes, Arles, France (travelled to Contrasts Gallery, London)
1983	*Hommage à Niepce*, Musée Nicéphore Niepce, Chalon sur Sâone, France
	Marey/Eakins: L'Uomo Scomposto, at *SICOF 83*, Milan
	Corps et Torax, Centre Georges Pompidou, Paris (travelled to the Castello Sforzesco, Milan)
	Il Punto Trasparente/Grafie, Palazzo dei Priori, Volterra, Italy
	Niepce et Poitevin, Parc des Expositions, Paris
1984	*Paolo Gioli à Ornans*, Maison Natale Courbet, Ornans, France
	Il Volto Inciso, Palazzo dei Priori, Volterra, Italy
1985	*I Volti Riflessi*, Palazzo dei Priori, Volterra, Italy
1986	*Obscura la natura riflessa*, Museo del Paesaggio, Verbania
	Planches naturelles, empreintes anatomiques, Galerie Michèle Chomette, Paris
	Autoanatomie, Galerie Michèle Chomette, Paris
1987	*Autoanatomie*, Musée Reattu, Arles
1990	*Nature volti e maschere dormienti*, Galerie Michèle Chomette, Paris
1991	*Paolo Gioli, Polaroids*, L.A. Galerie, Frankfurt
	Gran positivo nel crudele spazio stenopeico, Palazzo Fortuny, Venice; Museo Alinari, Florence
1993	*Paolo Gioli*, L.A. Galerie, Frankfurt; Galleria Federica Inghilleri, Milan; Galleria Comunale d'Arte Moderna, Bologna

Selected Group Exhibitions:

1978	*Fotografia Italiana*, at *Rencontres Internationales de la Photographie*, Arles, France
1979	*Il Ritratto*, at *SICOF 1979*, Milan

	The Italian Eye, Alternative Center for International Arts, New York
	Fotografia italiana contemporanea, Magazzini del Sale, Venice
1980	*Fotografia e Immagine dell'Architettura*, Galleria d'Arte Moderna, Bologna
	La Linea Sottile, Galleria Flaviana, Locarno, Switzerland
	Lo spazio audiovisivo—spazio eale/spazio virtuale, XVI Triennale, Milan
	Camera incantate—espansione dell'immagine, Palozzo Reale, Milan
1981	*Linee della Ricerca Artistica in Italia 1960-80*, Palazzo delle Esposizioni, Rome
1982	*Foire des Photographies*, at *FIAC 82*, Grand Palais, Paris
	Paesaggio, Immagine e realtà, Galleria Comunale d'Arte Moderna, Bologna
	Photo Art 1, PhotoKina, Köln
1983	*Five Contemporary Italian Photographers*, Pushkin Museum, Moscow
1984	*II. Triennale de la Photographie*, Palais des Beaux Arts, Charleroi, Belgium
1985	*Das Aktfoto*, Fotomuseum im Stadtmuseum, Munich
	Generation Polaroid, Pavillon des Arts, Paris
	Photo Couleur Critique, Palais de Congres, Royan
1986	*50 Jahre Moderne Farbphotographie: Selections 3 Polaroid*, Photokina, Koln
1987	*Photographs Beget Photographs*, Minneapolis Institute of Art
	Memoires de l'origine, Centre de la Vielle Charité, Marseille
	Le temps du mouvement, Palais de Tokyo, Paris
	Les miroirs qui se souviennent, Cormeilles-en-Parisis
	Il nudo maschile nella fotografia del XIX e del XX secolo, Pinacoteca Comunale, Ravenna
1988	*Through a Pinhole Darkly*, Fine Art Museum of Long Island, Hampstead, New York
	Splendeurs et miseres du corps, Musèe d'Art et d'Histoire de Fribourg, Triennale International de Photographie; Musée d'Art Moderne de la Ville de Paris, Paris
	Hommages and Remakes, Perspektief Gallery, Biennale of Photography, Rotterdam
1989	*L'insistenza dello sguardo*. Fotografie italiane 1839-1989, Palazzo Fortuny, Venice; Museo di Storia della Fotografia Fratelli Alinari, Florence
	On the Art of Fixing a Shadow. 150 Years of Photography, National Gallery of Art, Washington DC; The Art Institute of Chicago, Chicago
	La nouvelle photographie ancienne, Saint Malo and Quimper, France
1990	*On the Art of Fixing a Shadow. 150 Years of Photography*, Los Angeles County Museum of Art
	The International Pinhole Photography Exhibition, Contemporary Arts Museum, Houston
	150 anni di fotografia in Italia. Un itinerario, Palazzo Rondanini alla Rotonda, Rome
	L'invention d'un art, Centre Georges Pompidou, Paris
1992	*Le mouvement décomposé*, Musèe Marey, Beaune
	Il Internationale Foto-Triennale, Esslingen
1993	*Segni di luce*, Castello di Spilimbergo
	Immagini italiane, Peggy Guggenheim Foundation, Venice; Museo Villa Pignatelli, Naples
1994	*Segni di luce*, Biblioteca Civica, Ravenna
	Il ruolo della critica, Palazzo Comunale, Modena
	Immagini italiane, Smithsonian Foundation, New York

Collections:

Museum of Modern Art, New York; Art Institute of Chicago; Musée National d'Art Moderne, Centre George Pompidou, Paris; Cabinet des Estampes, Bibliothèque Nationale, Paris; Musée Nicéphore Niépce, Chalon-sur-Saone; International Polaroid Collection, Cambridge, Massachusetts; FRAC, Champagne Ardennes, Haute Normandie, Aquitaine, Languedoc-Roussillon; Bert Hartcamp, Amsterdam; C. Galitzine, Paris; J. von Hoppenheim, Cologne;

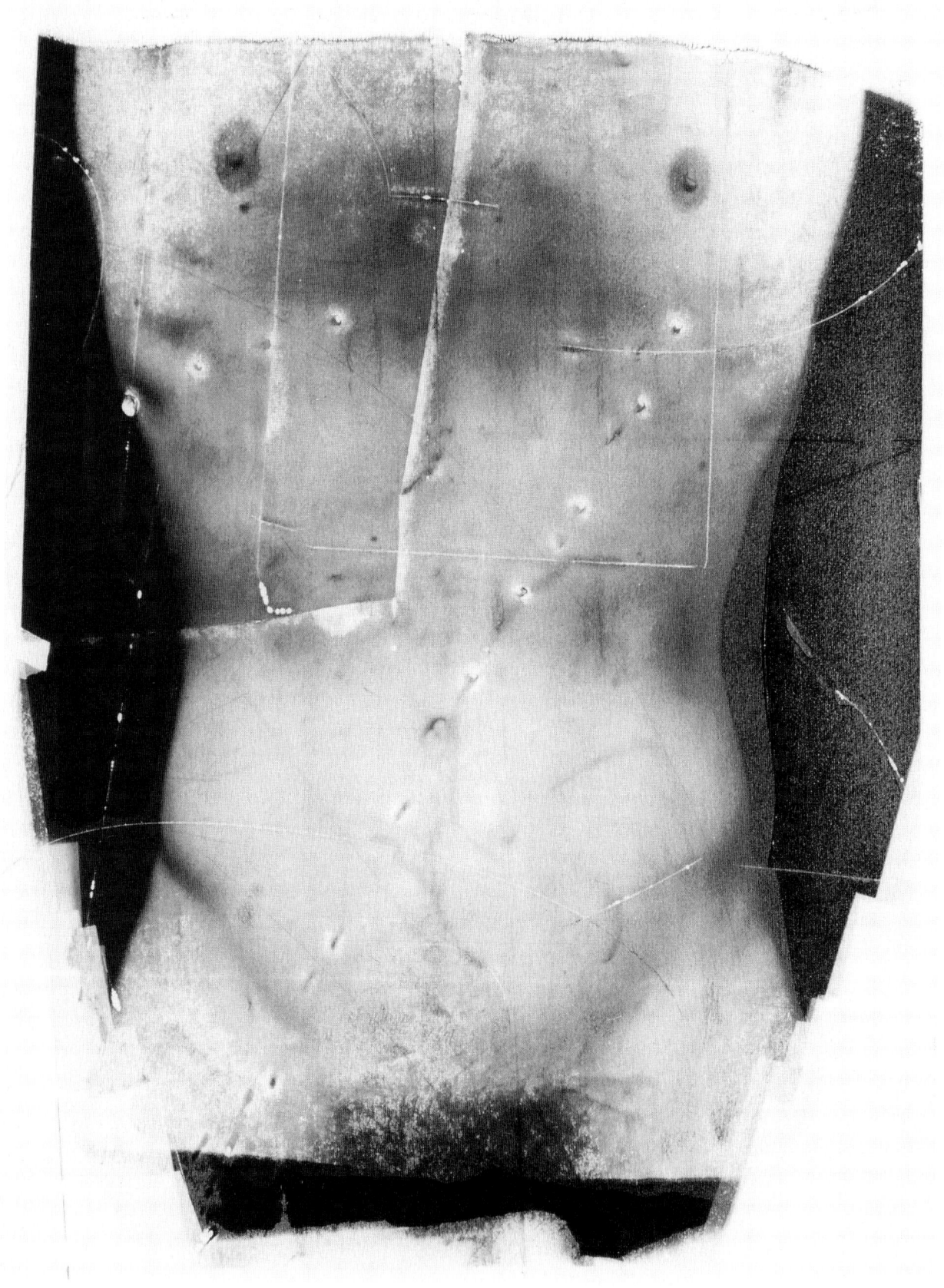

Corpo di Sebastiano (The Body of Sebastian), **1993 (original in colour).** Photograph by Paoli Gioli.

Museo del Paesaggio, Verbania;Museo di Fotografia Fratelli Alinari, Florence; Musei Civici, Modena, Centro Studi e Archivio della Comunicazione, Parma; Accademia Carrara, Bergamo.

Publications:

By GIOLI: Books—*Immagini Disturbata da un Intenso Parassita*, lithographic portfolio, Rome 1974; *Ispezione e Tracciamento sul Rettangolo*, lithographic portfolio, Rome 1975; *Dadathustra*, lithographic portfolio, Rome 1976; *Paolo Gioli: Monografia Fotografica*, Milan 1977; *Paolo Gioli: Spiracolografie*, with a preface by Ando Gilardi, Milan 1980; *Il Punto Trasparente*, Rome 1981; *Hommage a Niépce 1833-1983*, text by P Jay, M. Chomette, J F Chevrier, Chalon-sur-Saone 1983; *Il volto inciso*, text by V. Fagone, Comune di Volterra, Volterra 1984; *Obscura la natura riflessa*, text by R Valtorta, Milano 1986; *Autoanatomie*, text by M Moutashar, I Zannier, C Gattinoni, Firenze/Arles 1987; *Alidades*, text by P Aigrain (one hundred copies, numbered and signed, with reproductions of original works) Rémanences Editions 1988; *La conchiglia dissoluta* (fifty copies numbered and signed, with original Polaroids SX-70), realizzata in proprio 1990; *Gran positivo nel crudele spazio stenopeico*, text by P Costantini and I Zannier, Firenze 1991 films—*Passando da una Situazione ad un'Altra*, 1968; *Tracce di Tracce*, 1969; *Commutazioni con Mutazione*, 1969; *Immagini Disturbate da un Intenso Parassita*, 1970; *Secondo il Mio Occhio di Vetro*, 1971; *Immagini Reali/Immagini Virtuali*, 1972; *Del Tuffarsi e dell'Annegarsi*, 1972; *Cineforon*, 1972; *Anonimatografo*, 1972 *Ispezione e Tracciamento sul Rettangolo*, 1973; *Geometrico Continuo*, 1973; *Hillarisdoppio*, 1973; *Traumatografo*, 1973; *Film per Flauto da Presa*, 1973; *Figure Instabili nella Vegetazione*, 1974; *Quando la Pellicola è Calda*, 1974; *Schermo Inciso*, 1978; *Schermo-Schermo*, 1978; *L'Operatore Perforato*, 1979; *L'Assassino Nudo*, 1984; *Il Volto Inciso*, 1984; *Piccolo Film Decomposto*, 1985; *Geneation Polaroid*, with essay by M. Nuridsany, Paris 1985;*Memoires de l'origine*, exhibition catalogue with text by M. Deregibus and O. Menanteay, Marseilles 1987; *Les miroirs qui se souviennent*, text by Lobjoy, Paris 1987; *Quando l'occhio trema*, 1988; *Splendeurs et miseres du corps*, text by P. Borhan, Paris 1988; *Hommages et Remakes*, text by B. Vroege, ROtterdam 1988; *Colore caldo*, 1988; *Finestra davanti a un albero*, 1984-89; *Film stenopeico*, 1973-81-89; *Sfarfallio*, 1992; *Immagini travolte dalla ruota di Duchamp*, 1992, *Metamorphoso*, 1992; *Vita circolare*, 1992; *Il quadrato generale delle ore*, 1992. Articles—"Architettura nello Spazio Stenopeico" in *Fotografia e Immagine dell'Architettura*, exhibition catalogue, Bologna 1980; "A Hippolyte Bayard Gran Positivo" in *SICOF '81*, exhibition catalogue, (Milan) 1981; "Nota sul lavoro" in *Il punto trasparente*—'grafie (Rome), 1981; "Quest'anno tocca a lui" in *Zoom* (Milan), July-August 1982; "La ligne transparente" in *Exin* (Paris), no. 2, 1982; "Niépce di Land, La prova stenopeica, Poitevin, Corps et thorax, Eakins/Marey: l'uomo scomposto, Cameron Obscura" in *Fotologia* (Florence), no. 2, 1985; "Appunto per cassa stenopeica su Antonio Canal" in *Fotologia* (Florence), no. 2, 1985; "La conchiglia dissoluta" in *La conchiglia dissoluta* (Lendinara), 1990; "Figura esausta da accoppiamento, Natura alterata da una finestra, Movimento con eccessive venature sui corpi" in *Gran positivo nel crudele spazio stenopeico* (Florence) 1991.

On GIOLI: Books—*Catalogo Bolaffi per la Fotografia No. 2*, 1977-78, Turin 1977; *70 Anni di Fotografia Italiana* by Italo Zannier, Milan 1978; *Venezia '79. La fotografia*, exhibition catalogue, with texts by I. Zannier and D. Palozzoli, Milan 1979; *Lo spazio audiovisivo, spazio reale/spazio virtuale*, with essays by U Bettetini and U. la Pietre, Milan 1980; *Fotografie a immagine dell'architettura*, VV.A.A., Bologna 1980; *La Linea sottile*, with essay by G. Scine, Locarno, 1980; *Camere incantate, espansione dell'immagine*, with essay by V. Fagone, Milano 1980; *Linee della ricerca artistica in Italie*, with essay by A C Quintavalle, Rome 1981; *Guida alla Critica Fotografica* by G. Turroni, Milan 1980; *Fotomedia 2*, exhibition catalogue, with an essay by Daniela Palazzoli, Ravenna 1980; *Storie e tecnica della fotografie*, by I. Zammier, Bari 1982; *Paolo Gioli à Ornans*, exhibition catalogue, by D. Leguay, Ornans, France 1984; *Photo Couleur Critique*, by C Gattinoni, Paris 1985; *Das Aktfoto*, by M. Köhler, Munchen 1985; *Generation Polaroid*, essay by M. Nuridsany, Paris 1985; *Storia della fotografia italiana*, by I. Zannier, Bari 1986; *Photographs Beget Photographs*, Exhibition catalogue with text by A Peterson, Minneapolis 1987; *Il nudo maschile nella fotografie del XIX e del XX secolo*, by P Weilsman, Ravenna 1987; *Le temps du movement*, by M Frizot, Paris 1987; *Memoires de l'origine*, exhibition catalogue with text by M. Deregibus and O. Menanteau, Marseille 1987; *Les miroirs qui se souviennent*, text by Lobjoy, Paris 1987; *Through a Pinhole Darkly*, exhibition catalogue with text by L Tortora, New York 1988; *Splendeurs et miseres du corps*, text by P. Borhan, Paris 1988; *Hommages et Remakes*, text by B. Vroge, Rotterdam 1988; *On the Art of Fixing a Shadow*, exhibition catalogue, Washington 1989; *L'invention d'un art*, by A. Sayag, Paris 1989; *De la photographie comme un des beaux arts*, by A. Sayag, Paris 1989; *The International Pinhole Photography Exhibition*, exhibition catalogue with text by B Besold and E Renner, Houston 1990; *Segri di luce*, by I. Zannier, Ravenna 1993; *Il ruolo della critica*, by R Valtorta, Udine 1994. Articles—"Paolo Gioli e il Magnifico Bottone" by Ando Gilardi in *Il Diaframma/Fotografia Italiana* (Milan), June 1977; "Paolo Gioli: La Fotografia Vergine" by Ando Gilardi in *Photo Italiana* (Milan), February 1979; "Venise-Venezia 79 la fotografia" by George Tatge in *Artforum* (New York) November 1979; "Zeitgenössische Fotografie in Italien" by Italo Zannier in *Zoom* (Munich), August 1980; "Dentro al Labirinto: Meandri Pubblici Ecc." by G. Bonini in *Progresso Fotografico* (Milan), February 1981; "Paolo Gioli: Le Strane Fotocamere" by Eduardo Prando in *Fotografare* (Milan), March 1981; "Paolo Gioli: Antropolaroid" in *Zoom* (Milan), April 1981; "Les Polaroids de Paolo Gioli" by R. Loaec in *Le Photographe* (Paris), July/August 1982; "Paolo Gioli" by R. Valtorta in *Zoom* (Milan), February 1983; "Paolo Gioli—Hommage à Poitevin" in *Zoom* (Milan), March 1984; "Paolo Gioli" by Italo Zannier in *Fotologia* (Milan), no. 2, 1985; "Objeto: Hombre" by Giuliana Scimè, Giuseppe Turroni in *Fotologia* (Firenze) no 2 inverno 1985; "Paolo Gioli: Publication" by Vilem Flusser in *European Photography* (Gottingen), no 35 estate 1988; "Paolo Gioli, Appunto per cassa stenopeica su Antonio Canal" in *Fotologia* (Firenze) no 10 1989; "Paolo Gioli" by Roberta Valtorta in *Photographers International* (Taipei/Parigi) no 9 August 1993; "Paolo Gioli—Atelier" in *European Photography* (Gottingen) no 54, autunno-inverno 1993.

*

My prevalent tendency to blend creative techniques with techniques from the history of art is the result of my conviction that it is an extremely complicated matter to understand the contamination, the spectacular invasions, that follow one after another in the disciplines of science and expression. For myself, I believe that I have reached such complexity within research that I no longer really know which lines are going to lead to which changes.

I should like to re-examine photographic history, and if that quest involves sensitive material, my own working materials, that is pure chance. Perhaps what I mean *is* primarily material, dusted and treated with technological sediment, starting from the countless anthropological bifurcations that such a combination has to offer.

What interests me enormously is the formidable capacity of photosensitive material to distort and fantasticate, nearly always dramatically, everything it touches. Thus, my interest must involve a thorough examination of all that has happened in the history of photography, by way of that which has manipulated it even as it fed it—chemistry.

The Polaroid, that most delicate membrane, iconophotography, is a liquid incunabulum of modern history.

I have take the pinhole as a "viewpoint," both plastic and ideological. I discovered the pinhole picture because I had no camera. Later this picture provoked a fascination with the scene portrayed: I was fascinated by the purity of this "poor" method of filming, by the equally pure reproduction—not poor at all but absolutely marvellous.

I am not aiming at an academic thesis but at a definite way of comprehending space through a point in space. Thus the fade-in effect; the magnificent figures all around us conveyed by the purest ways; with no shutters, no stopping down, no focussing.

Cibachrome, that voluptuous technological page printed from subtle marks traced in secret, is a page of enchanted iridescence.

—Paolo Gioli

* * *

One of the first people in Italy (1970) to draw attention to the urgent need for some kind of check on photography's capacity for documentary visualization was Ugo Mulas, who upset the traditional conviction that photography should be a medium for the objective representation of reality. Mulas's ideas, his experiments with the language of photography (*La Fotografia,* 1973), were something of a revelation and aroused interest in many cultural circles. Above all, his work was a stimulus to interest in the uses of the photographic image, so challenging in the immediacy of its communication, an interest that many artists then working in the field of "conceptualism" pursued following the vogue of "pop art"—which, in its turn, had suggested a whole new range of expressive possibilities inherent in the very "mechanicalness" of photography, a concern previously regarded as of secondary importance, as non-creative.

Paoli Gioli took up photography while the polemics provoked by Mulas's investigations were still going on and while a mannerism imported from America and France was spreading, one that was to characterize modern Italian photography after the general crisis of photographic journalism in the 1970s had revived "art photography" as an interesting solution.

Gioli's interest in photography (as well as his interest in film and video-tape) was chiefly one of experimentation, an effort to locate and specify the creative possibilities offered by modern technology, which now determines not only photography but also every other kind of communicative function in the modern world. And it was via this very technology—so sophisticated, so amazingly complex—that Gioli moved to his meditation on the media, a meditation that has involved almost a physiological rejection as an antidote to their pervasive penetration of the unconscious. With a jesting, playing, quixotic provocativeness, Gioli has become a ruthless debunker of the photographic medium, waxing especially ironic about its "technique," or rather its technicality, which must now, in his view, become an end in itself if one wants to avoid the risk of the stereotype, the repetitive banalities of daily picture output, which leads to collective hypnosis and an inevitable vulgarization of the image.

"Technical investigations, based on the revival and reconsideration of 'primordial' methods and equipment for photography," writes Piergiorgio Dragone, are for Gioli the starting-point of an argument that inevitably comes up against the basic problem of the nature of the photographic image, its essential ambiguity. Gioli, always a Jack-of-all-trades, has actually himself created various devices and methods the brilliant simplicity of which have enabled him to achieve unexpected explorations of the "real"—often far distant not only from convention but also from any ordinary documentation. Photo-finishes obtained by making the film move during the shot by means of a lever fitted to a simple camera; manipulations of the "sandwich" of Polaroid film whereby the photo is directly transferred to pieces of paper or silk; *spiracolografie* ("aperturegraphs") obtained with a wooden camera obscura as ingenious as it is precarious; stenopeic (pin-hole) aperture, which he uses for a reinterpretation of urban space according to archaic principles of "perspective"—Gioli has in fact examined countless new possibilities with an instinctive freshness and often with brilliant skill.

Gioli's photography is manageable, accessible, because of the unexpected, brilliant visual inventions; it is often also a game by which he aspires to "return to the technical immediacy of the origins of photography" (Daniela Palazzoli, *Fotomedia Due,* 1980). Gioli's journey, then, is one backwards into the development of photographic language, starting from the most advanced technology, particularly that of photo-sensitive materials, in search of the primordial, elementary imprints of light, to rediscover the origin of vision and at the same time create exciting illusions of reality.

—Italo Zannier

GIORDAN, Albert.

Nationality: French. **Born:** Nice, 24 June 1949. **Education:** Attended the Lycée d'État, Nice, 1960-65; studied architecture, École Nationale des Arts Décoratifs, Nice, 1965-66; apprenticed in a photo laboratory, Nice, 1967; self-taught in photography, from 1968. **Career:** Freelance sports reporter and photographer, Nice, 1968-69; fashion photographer, working for ready-to-wear design houses, and the magazines *20 Ans* and *Le Guide d'Achat du Prêt-a-Porter Français,* Paris, 1969-72; audiovisual technician, Ministry of Works, Nice, 1972-75. Since 1976, independent architectural and still-life

photographer, Villefranche: worked with the Mission Photographique de la DATAR (Délégation a l'Aménagement du Territoire et a l'Action Régionale), Paris, 1984-85. Head of the Montreal Mission, Ministry of External Relations, 1983; Artistic Director, Centre National d'Art Contemporain, Nice, 1985. Professor, École Nationale de la Photographie, Arles, France, since 1985. **Recipient:** Laureate, Fondation Nationale de la Photographie, Lyon, 1982. **Agents:** Gerry Fiolet, Art Photography Agency, Herengracht 86, Amsterdam, Netherlands; Alexandre De La Salle, Galerie De La Salle, Saint Paul de Vence, France. **Address:** Villa "Les Yuccas," 44 Boulevard Settimelli-Lazare, 06230 Villefranche-sur-Mer, France.

Individual Exhibitions:

Selected Group Exhibitions:

Collections:

Musée d'Art et d'Histoire, Fribourg, Switzerland; Galerie du Château d'Eau, Toulouse, France; Musée Cantini, Marseille, France; Fonds National d'Art Contemporain, Paris; Photothéque, Arles, France; Fonds Régional d'Art Contemporain, Marseille, France; Bibliothéque Nationale, Paris; Fondation Nationale de la Photographie, Lyon, France; Musée Nicéphore Niepce, Chalon-sur-Sâone, France.

Publications:

By GIORDAN: Book—*Un Anniversaire,* Paris 1983.

On GIORDAN: Books—*Cartes Postales et Posters,* Paris 1982, 1985, 1986; *La Photographie Créative* by Jean-Claude Lemagny, Paris 1984; *Paysages Photographies,* with texts by Francois Hers, Bernard Latarjet, Roger Brunet and others, Paris 1985. **Article**—"Albert Giordan" by G. Bauret in *Camera International* (Paris), April 1985.

*

My thoughts essentially concern the means proper to "photographic writing" and its chances of portraying a three-dimensional universe by means of propositions that are logical, but nevertheless two-dimensional.

The image is emptied of anecdote. I wish to avoid the extraordinary and the spectacular, since that will permit me to experience the play of tones and shades whereby the object photographed appears ambiguously hovering between its own reality and that of a pure graphism.

Among other things, I have taken up again the tradition of the Still Life, for this allows me to reflect exclusively on problems of a plastic nature, more particularly on the relationship between the object and the space in which it is confined, and on the reciprocal transformations taking place between these two elements. When I photograph an object I use it as an indication of spatiality. What I am looking for in my compositions is for the play between the various grey expanses to subvert our habits of visual perception.

—Albert Giordan

* * *

In the 1920s, 1930s and 1940s, France made a great contribution to the development of contemporary art, photography included. Paris was then the great centre of world art and familiarity with what went on there was more or less compulsory. Less is known, however, about the achievements of contemporary French photography and especially about photographers whose work is connected to the art of, for example, Maurice Tabard or Man Ray, or the work of the Bauhaus. Albert Giordan is one such photographer.

Giordan was an architect by training and, presumably, this background is, in part at least, responsible for his predilection for form and structure. In fact, his photographs truly look as if they had been constructed or built up, part by part. Their affiliation with architecture, however, can only be partial. The two-dimensional element of the photography differentiates it from architecture. Architecture is clearly spatial whereas Giordan's photography is flat. In essence, therefore, it is more closely aligned with painting—for example, with geometric abstracts—than with architecture.

Giordan is exceptionally meticulous in his choice of subjects and affords them a great deal of concentration and attention. The objects he photographs are usually commonplace—books and other things that are found in any home—and stripped of decoration or detail or other distracting features. Hence, they have a sterile purity—there is only the object itself, nothing more. The inevitable frontal aspect and the intensity of the photographs suggest that, in trying to represent these objects in their purest form, Giordan wishes to grasp their very substance and to convey it through photography.

Of course, the thing that interests Giordan most is not the object itself but its image. The object is only an intermediary, raw material stripped of all possible meaning or significance. Only when it is used discerningly, when thoughts or artistic ideas are expressed through it, is it endowed with any artistic value. Giordan's merit lies in the way in which he tries to create images that are not commonplace from trivial objects of everyday use and, in this way, to forward the development of photography in the 1980s.

—Ryszard Bobrowski

GLINN, Burt.

Nationality: American. **Born:** Pittsburgh, Pennsylvania, 23 July 1925. **Education:** Schenley High School, Pittsburgh, 1939-43; Harvard College, Cambridge, Massachusetts, 1943, 1946-49, B.A. 1949 (Dana Reed Award, 1949); mainly self-taught in photography. **Military Service:** Served as an artilleryman, United States Army, in the United States and Germany, 1943-46: Lieutenant. **Family:** Married Elena Prohaska in 1981. **Career:** Assistant Photographer, 1949-50, and Photographer, under editor Wilson Hicks, 1950, *Life* magazine,

New York. Freelance photographer, New York, since 1950: commissions include industrial photography for Pepsico, General Motors, Richardson-Merrill, Xerox, Revlon, Bristol-Myers, AMF, Seagrams, Inland Steel, Goldman Sachs, Warner Communications, etc.; advertising photography for IBM, TWA, British Airways, Chase Manhattan Bank, Seagrams, ITT, etc.; magazine photography for *Holiday, Esquire, Fortune, Travel and Leisure, Life, Paris-Match, Newsweek,* etc.; also, Contributing Editor, *New York Magazine,* 1974-77. Member since 1952, and President, 1972-74, Magnum Photos Inc., New York. President, American Society of Magazine Photographers, 1980-81. **Recipient:** Matthew Brady Magazine Photographer of the Year Award, University of Missouri and *Encyclopaedia Britannica,* 1960; Overseas Press Club Award, 1967; Gold Medal, Art Directors Club of New York, 1972; Gold Medal, *Financial World,* New York, 1979. **Agents:** Magnum Photos Inc., 251 Park Avenue South, New York, New York 10010; and Elena Prohaska Fine Arts, 61 East 77th Street, New York, New York 10021, U.S.A. **Address:** 41 Central Park West, New York, New York 10023, U.S.A.

Individual Exhibitions:

1976   Nikon House Gallery, New York (with George Haling)
1978   The Photographers' Gallery, London

Selected Group Exhibitions:

1955   *The Family of Man,* Museum of Modern Art, New York (and world tour)
1979   *This Is Magnum,* Takashimaya Department store, Tokyo
1980   *This Is Magnum,* Galerie Le Clôitre, St. Ursanne Switzerland

Collections:

International Center of Photography, New York; Museum of Modern Art, New York; Harvard College, Cambridge, Massachusetts; Kimberley-Clark Corporation, Neenah, Wisconsin.

Publications:

By GLINN: Books—*A Portrait of All the Russias,* with text by Laurens van der Post, New York and London 1967; *A Portrait of Japan,* with text by Laurens van der Post, New York and London 1968. **Articles**—"Otto Preminger" in *Esquire* (New York), March 1961; "Burt Glinn" in *Camera* (Lucerne), August 1962; "The Art of Discovering Pictures" in *Professional Photographer,* February 1978; interview in *Photographers on Photography,* edited by Jerry C. LaPlante, New York 1979; "The Avalanche since Ice on the Roof" in *American Showcase 1980,* New York 1980; "Photography Now and Then" in *The American Society of Magazine Photographers at 35,* New York 1980.

On GLINN: Books—*The Family of Man,* with text by Edward Steichen, New York 1955; *America in Crisis: Photographs for Magnum,* edited by Charles Harbutt and Lee Jones, with an essay by Michael Levitas, New York 1969; *World Photography,* edited by Bryn Campbell, London 1981; *Eye Witness: 25 Years Through World Press Photos* by Harold Evans, London 1981; *The Library of World Photography: Portraits,* with introduction by Colin Ford, Tokyo 1982, 1983, London 1983; *The Library of World Photography: Landscape,* with texts by David Plowden and Ian Jeffrey, Tokyo and London 1984; *After the War Was Over,* with introduction by Mary Blume, London 1985. **Articles**—"Burt Glinn's Japan" in *Photography Annual 1963,* New York 1962; "Burt Glinn: A Portrait of All the Russias" in *Creative Camera* (London) July 1968; "Photographers' Photographer: Burt Glinn, The Epitome of Professionalism in That Complicated Art of Picture Taking" by Michael Edelson in *Flight Time,* June 1976; "Burt Glinn: The Right Lens for the Right Look" by Mary O'Grady in *Modern Photography* (New York), August 1977; "The Costly New Look" by Arlene Hershman and G. Bruce Knecht in *Dun's Review,* June 1981.

*

I have been taking pictures for a living for more than 30 years. A lot of people think of me as an old professional. I like to think of myself merely as experienced. At least I am experienced enough to view this literary exercise with some doubt. The problem with writing about photography is that taking pictures seems so simple. Of course, it is not, but explanations why it is not have led to some very defensive, somber, arcane, and pretentious prose.

Some of this has slopped back onto the taking of pictures. This is not the most encouraging thing to come out of the growing interest in photography. Pretentiousness has done more harm to good photography than automated exposure.

I became a photographer almost by accident, and I stayed a photographer over all these years because I like taking pictures. It is a wonderful way to make a living. It does get me around and keeps me out in the air.

However, it is not a life without complications. I make my living completely from photography, and, mostly as a result of my photographic exercises working on an essentially acquisitive nature, my appetites are hardly monastic. As a result, I spend a lot of my photographic time working for large corporations, either for advertising or for corporate reports. It is serious work, and I take it very seriously. Even though I do it very well—humility is neither a common nor useful trait in our work—the selection of my work for this book is not industrial. Even the most sophisticated commercial assignments have very specific goals, and, handsome and striking as some of the pictures may be, this specificity deprives them of what I hope is the depth and complexity of the other part of my work.

That other part has evolved into a kind of cultural journalism-cum-anthropology. It started with assignments from *Holiday* magazine in the fifties and sixties when *Holiday* magazine was really a magazine. These assignments, at least for me, were a kind of unrestricted grant. Frank Zachary, the art director and dominant figure on the magazine, once sent me on their most expensive assignment—four months to photograph an entire issue on the then not too open Soviet Union. His only instructions were, "Hey kid, I want you to take some snaps of Russia."

Over the years, shooting wherever assignments took me, I began to discover a pattern in the pictures I liked best. I have come to believe that all societies, from the most primitive to the most sophisticated, are driven by similar fears, myths, and superstitions. As a result, all their rituals, no matter how different their appearance, have a certain basic similarity. Most of my personal favourites, among all the pictures I have taken, document these varieties of religious experience. At the simplest level, the New Guinea woman with her collection of Bird of Paradise feathers and seashells is satisfying the same urge as the top-hatted, frock-coated gentleman in the Royal Enclosure at Ascot. There are more icons of Lenin in Moscow than there are images of Christ in Rome. In getting to this place I have discovered a basic attitude that works for me. It is not writ in stone and it may not be true for everyone else, or even for anyone else. But for my photography I have come to believe in the superiority of discovery to invention. What is important is not what I make happen, but what happens to me. I can work in a studio, but I would rather work in the world. Even in my industrial work when I have created a situation, I try to keep it as loose and unconstructed as possible so that there is the maximum chance for fortuitous accident to happen and be recognized and photographed.

I am not fond of technique for its own sake, and I do not use lenses for effects: I use them to take pictures. Even in the most restrictive assignments I try to avoid preconception. Our world is so flooded with photographic images that when we preconceive, we end up, probably unwittingly, taking pictures of pictures we have already seen.

I work most of the time in color because I see in color. It is a fact, it is there. I react to minimal color, and my feeling is that color alone is not enough. Color photographs must have the same discipline of content and structure that good black-and-white photographs have. If I made black-and-white prints of the color pictures I like best, they would not be the same and they probably would not be as good, but they would still have real photographic value.

I am glad I am a photographer. I am afraid I am a bit promiscuous because I enjoy it all, even when I know better. It forces me to start each day with fresh eyes. I have even been lucky in my timing. Photography is young enough and I am old enough so that even in my middle years I have been able to sit with, eat with, drink with, and exchange truthful exaggerations with most of the people whose work I have admired. I look forward to a lot more years of all of this and

a lot more photographs. Our world in photography is changing at an almost unimaginable pace—and who knows—it may even be for the better.

—Burt Glinn

*   *   *

Burt Glinn can justly lay claim to the title of New York's freelance photographer *par excellence*. Not only a long-time member but also a three-term president of Magnum, the international photographers' cooperative agency, Glinn has excelled at skillful and stylish photography of subject matter ranging from Fidel Castro's revolution in Cuba to Revlon's annual report.

At Harvard in the late 1940s Glinn was photographer and photography editor for the *Crimson*, where he attracted the attention of talent scouts for *Life* and other picture magazines. Beginning as a photographer's assistant at *Life*, he quickly parlayed that position into part-time freelance work for the magazine as well as developing a clientele at other publications. He began a career that included both reportage and the kind of spectacular travel coverage that earned him complete issues of *Holiday* magazine devoted throughout to his color photographs of the South Seas (October/November 1960), Japan (October 1961), Mexico (October 1962), Russia (October 1963), and California (October 1965). His reportorial range, developed in the 1950s and 60s, now seems almost limitless: Glinn has covered the Sinai War, the U.S. Marines' invasion of Lebanon, Khrushchev's tour of the United States, and several American political conventions, and he has produced sensitive profiles of such personalities as Sammy Davis Jr. and Robert Kennedy. Throughout, he has remained resolutely freelance.

Glinn is known as something of an "editor's photographer," both for his ability to turn in consistently solid high quality pictures and for his wide intellectual interests, his knowledge of politics and current affairs. Perhaps his early *Crimson* experience encouraged his abilities to develop editorial ideas and to bring a fresh approach to material that others might find stale.

Glinn was one of the original contributing editors to *New York Magazine* and continued in the capacity until 1977. He has also served as President of the American Society of Magazine Photographers. In recent years, Glenn has developed numerous corporate and advertising clients. And, in addition to the prizes for his magazine work, Glinn has also been awarded the Gold Medal from the Art Directors Club of New York for the best print ad of the year (his Foster-Grant sun glasses ads) and *Financial World's* Gold Medal for the best annual report of 1979 (Warner Communications).

—Maren Stange

GLOAGUEN, Hervé.

Nationality: French. **Born:** Rennes, 11 May 1937. **Career:** Assistant to the photographer Gilles Ehrmann, Paris, 1963; freelance photographer, mainly for *Réalités* magazine, Paris, 1964-71. Founder-Member, Viva photographers agency, Paris, 1972-82. Since 1982, freelance photographer, working mainly with *Geo* magazine, in Africa, India, Japan, Thailand, Senegal, Uruguay, Madagascar, Niger, Mali, Brazil and the United States. **Agent:** Agence Rapho, Paris. **Address:** c/o Rapho, 8 rue d'Alger, 75001 Paris, France.

Individual Exhibitions:

1974	*Photographs of Contemporary Artists,* Musée d'Art Moderne (A.R.C.), Paris
1977	Galerie Gloux, Concarneau, France
1980	*30 Photographs,* at *Albi Festival of Photography,* France
1985	*Biennele de l'Image,* Nancy, France
1989	*Le miel et le bronze,* Arles, France
1990	*Afriques,* FNAC, Montparnasse, Paris

Selected Group Exhibitions:

1973   *Viva: Familles en France,* Galleria Il Diaframma, Milan
          (toured Europe, the United States and Canada, 1973-76)
1977   *Photojournalisme,* Musée Galliera, Paris
1978   *European Colour Photography,* The Photographers' Gallery,
          London
1980   *Jeune Photographie,* Château Lumière, Lyon, France
1981   *A Day in the Life of Australia,* Sydney, New South Wales
          (toured Australia)

Collections:

Bibliothèque Nationale, Paris; Musée Nicéphore Niepce, Chalon-sur-Saône, France.

Publications:

By GLOAGUEN: Books—*L'Art Actuel en France,* with text by Anne Tronche, Paris 1973; *La Loire Angevine,* with text by Gaston Humeau, Paris 1979; *Lyon,* Paris 1981; *Hervé Gloaguen: Photographies,* Paris 1981; *Lyon: photographies Hervé Gloaguen,* with text by Jean-Francois Chevrier, Paris 1982; *Droit d'Asile,* Paris 1986. **Article**—"Vétérinairs sans frontiéres" in *Geo,* 1988.

On GLOAGUEN: Books—*Photographie Actuelle en France,* Paris 1976; *A Certain Image of French Photography,* Paris 1977; *La Photographie Francaise des Origines à nos Jours* by Claude Nori, Paris 1978; *European Colour Photography,* exhibition catalogue, by Sue Davies, Bryn Campbell and Michael Langford, London 1978; *Jeune Photographie,* exhibition catalogue, with introduction by Bernard Chardere, Paris 1980; *A Day in the Life of Australia—March 6, 1981,* with introduction by Thomas Kenneally, Potts Point, New South Wales 1981. **Articles**—"Gloaguen: 2 Ans de Travail dans l'Intimité de 8 Artistes Contemporains" in *Photo* (Paris), July 1972; "Gloaguen" in *Progresso Fotografico* (Milan), April 1974; "Gloaguen" in *Zoom* (Paris), November 1974; "Hervé Gloaguen Fotografier Förändrar inte Menökar Medvetenheten" in *Aktuell Fotografi* (Helsingborg, Sweden), September 1978.

*

I started as a photojournalist because I wanted to see the world, because I wanted to show the good and bad sides of life and people, and because I was feeling guilty. Also because, in those days, galleries, museums and books were not presenting photography as they do today.

Like many photographers of my generation, I find the photojournalist-witness kind of situation stimulating but frustrating. We have been influenced by Robert Frank and have developed a more contradictory and ambiguous sense of information. I think that my own photographs are the result of a constant struggle between information and self-portrait.

My attitude can be irritating to many people, and painful for the photographer, and that is how I have been able to produce, perhaps, some good photographs.

—Hervé Gloaguen

*   *   *

Hervé Gloaguen likes the jazz of New Orleans. He likes to work with others, and thinks that in the Viva group he has found a slightly similar ensemble. At the same time, he believes that photography is a solitary pursuit: his pictures are obsessed with solitude, the coldness of the modern town, the clinical atmosphere of a laboratory. He looks for a gesture of sympathy, a hint of warmth, a suggestion of co-operation to challenge a stiff and congealed universe.

His pictures are discreet. They are very graphic, but do not play with the effects of depth, do not create volume by contrasts of light—and their human presences are ambiguous. For example, a factory girl, in her working clothes, taken from a distance, looks sideways. The photo is simple, but the delicacy of the face, the thin lips, the high forehead under slightly tilted headgear, the

elegance of the high collar under the chin, assert, in the abstraction of the context, a resistance to the environment that is both fragile and monumental. And, as with this portrait, Gloaguen's photos are never overloaded. He does not look for complexity in the composition. Like Robert Doisneau, he seems to have created his oeuvre inadvertently, by playing the bad pupil, by accepting rules only the better to get around them.

This art is sentimental; it is an art of the game and therefore of ambiguity. It belongs to a French tradition, but it has found its own theme. Although Gloaguen is very professional (he respects the rules because he loves the game), he does not look for great themes; he keeps to a minor register and jumps from one subject to another.

His own impression is that he chose photography for its inconsequence and frivolity—so that he could continue to play and run away in even the most tragic circumstances. He has too much humor to take himself seriously, but he also recognizes himself in the man whom he saw one time in Poland, in an industrial landscape, running away from a nightmare.

—Jean-François Chevrier

GODWIN, Fay.

Nationality: British. **Born:** Fay Simmonds in Berlin, Germany, 17 February 1931. **Education:** Attended various schools all over the world (father a diplomat); self-taught in photography, from 1966. **Family:** Married; sons: Nicholas and Jeremy. **Career:** Freelance photographer, London, since 1970. **Recipient:** Arts Council Bursary in Photography, 1978; Fellow at the National Museum of Photography, Bradford, 1986/87; Received Honorary Fellowship from the Royal Photographic Society, 1990; President of the Rambler's Association 1987-1990. **Agent:** The Photographers' Gallery, London. **Address:** c/o The Photographers' Gallery, 8 Great Newport Street, London WC2, England.

Individual Exhibitions:

1974   *Writers Portraits/Young Music Makers,* Swiss Cottage Library,
          London
1975   *Ridgeway,* Anthony Stokes Ltd., London (and simultaneously
          at the Photographic Gallery, University of Southampton;
          subsequently toured the U.K.)
1977   *Drovers' Roads, Wales,* Anthony Stokes Ltd., London (and
          simultaneously at the Oriel Bookshop, Welsh Arts Council,
          Cardiff; subsequently toured Britian)
        The Oil Rush, Aberdeen Art Gallery, Scotland (travelled to the
          National Theatre, London)
1978   *Drovers' Roads, Wales and Ridgeway,* Chester Arts Centre
1979   *Calder Valley,* Anthony Stokes Ltd., London (and simultane-
          ously at the Impressions Gallery, York, and Open Eye,
          Liverpool; travelled to the Ulster Museum, Belfast, and
          Photographic Gallery, Dublin, 1980)
1980   *Selected Landscapes,* Aarhus Photographic Museum, Denmark
        East Neuk, Crawford Arts Centre, St. Andrews, Scotland (with
          local photographers)
1981   *Romney Marsh,* Anthony Stokes Ltd., London (and simultane-
          ously at the Rye Art Gallery, Sussex; subsequently toured
          Britain)
1983   *The Saxon Shore Way,* Photogallery, St. Leonards on Sea,
          Sussex (toured Britain)
        The Whisky Roads of Scotland, Crawford Arts Centre, St.
          Andrews, Scotland (toured Britain)
        Portraits of Writers, Midland Arts Centre, Birmingham,
          Warwickshire
1984   *Landscape Photographs,* British Council, London (toured
          Europe)

Private Land, Brassington, Derbyshire, from *Our Forbidden Land,* **1990.** Photograph ©Fay Godwin.

1985	*Land,* Serpentine Gallery, London (toured Britain and the United States, 1986)
	Wessex, The Photographers' Gallery, London
1986	*Literary Portraits,* Poetry Society, London
1990	*Our Forbidden Land,* Royal Photographic Society, Bath
1994	*Glassworks, Recent Colour Work* at The Print Room, The Photographers' Gallery, London

Selected Group Exhibitions:

1976	*The Land: 20th Century Landscape Photographs Selected by Bill Brandt,* Victoria and Albert Museum, London
1978	*Sussex Photographers,* Rye Art Gallery, Sussex
1979	*Wales,* Mostyn Art Gallery, Llandudno, Wales
1980	*British Art 1940-1980,* Hayward Gallery, London
	Fairies, Brighton Museum, Sussex
1981	*Acquisitions 1973-80,* International Museum of Photography at George Eastman House, Rochester, New York
1982	*Presences of Nature,* Carlisle Museum, Cumbria (toured Britain)
1986	*The Secret Forest of Dean,* Arnolfini Gallery, Bristol, Avon (toured Britain)

Collections:

Victoria and Albert Museum, London; Department of the Environment, London; Arts Council of Great Britain, London; National Portrait Gallery, London; Aberdeen Art Gallery, Scotland; Royal Library, Copenhagen; Bibliothèque Nationale, Paris; International Museum of Photography at George Eastman House, Rochester, New York; Scottish National Portrait Gallery, Edinburgh; Halifax Museum, Yorkshire; The National Museum of Film, Photography and Television, Bradford.

Publications:

By GODWIN: Books—*The Oldest Road: An Exploration of the Ridgeway,* with text by J.R.L. Anderson, London 1975; *The Oil Rush,* with text by Mervyn Jones, London 1976; *The Drovers' Roads of Wales,* with text by Shirley Toulson, London 1977; *Islands,* with text by John Fowles, London and Boston 1978; *Remains of Elmet,* with poems by Ted Hughes, London and New York 1979; *Romney Marsh and the Royal Military Canal,* with text by Richard Ingrams, London 1980; *The Whisky Roads of Scotland,* with text by Derek Cooper, London 1981; *Tess: The Story of a Guide Dog,* with text by Peter Purves, London 1981; *Bison at Chalk Farm and Other Snaps,* with foreword by Frank Muir, London 1982; *The Saxon Shore Way from Gravesend to Rye,* with text by Allan Sillitoe, London 1983; *Land,* with text by John Fowles, London and Boston 1985; *Wessex,* with text by Patricia Beer, London 1985; *The Secret Forest of Dean,* Bristol 1986; *Our Forbidden Land,* London 1990.

On GODWIN: Books—*Acquisitions 1973-1980, George Eastman House,* exhibition catalogue, by Robert A. Sobieszek, Marianne Fulton and Philip Condax, Rochester, New York 1981; *The Library of World Photography: Landscape,* with texts by David Plowden and Ian Jeffrey, Tokyo and London 1984. **Articles**—by Lesley Adamson in *The Guardian* (London), 28 July 1976; by William Packer in the *Financial Times* (London), 11 October 1977 and 15 May 1979; by Mark Haworth-Booth in *Art Monthly* (London), no. 27, 1979; by John Taylor in *Ten-8* (Birmingham), Autumn 1979.

*

I have worked mainly in the landscape in the UK, from walkers' handbooks to *Land* in 1985. In 1990 I published *Our Forbidden Land* which is an examination of access to land on foot in the UK, and an investigation of the degradation of our environment. Since then I have been working in colour, close up, still originating from the landscape, purely creative.

—Fay Godwin

* * *

The British landscape's intimacy of scale, diversity in kind, and the infinite subtleness of its textural variations are altogether matched by the qualities of the light. In the nature of things, then, only rarely can the experience of an encounter with this landscape be adequately recapitulated in a photographic image. All too often photographers' accounts range in gist from the vapidly charming, through the tedious, to falsely theatrical. Few photographers have either the sensitivity to place or the mastery of material necessary to produce a body of work consistently true to the spirit of this subject.

Fay Godwin is one of the small number whose photographic studies of landscape have a felicity which flows from their rightness, rather than from any gentling of her view of the places photographed. Indeed, some convey a sense of formidable, cold hardness. Many are located in the old, used lands formed by the activities of predecessor tribes, ranging from bronze age agriculturists to early industrial man. The marks of each upon the earth are recorded by Fay Godwin with such impartial completeness that the limitations on information lie with the perceiver, rather than in the image.

Her photographs have had wide currency whether as the visual strand in some of the more original and imaginative guidebooks, or in company with the poems of Ted Hughes. Fay Godwin's images survive remarkably well the cheap reproductive processes inevitable to some of them. Higher printing standards, as seen for example in *Remains of Elmet,* remind the viewer of her interest in the photograph as fine print.

Indeed, it is that interest which was the dominant factor in the reception of Fay Godwin's work over a significant phase of her photographic career. However closely the images were contextualised, or even let us say, bound to an author's intention by layout and association with text, however inadequately they may have been reproduced, they always retained the character of autonomous art objects. Sometimes the consequence of this was admiration for the strength and consistency of Fay Godwin's aesthetic principles; sometimes that very strength was regarded with suspicion as a sign of romantic idealisation.

Only with the publication of *Our Forbidden Land* did Fay Godwin unequivocally show that her aesthetic could be the perfect vehicle for an impassioned, political message. *Our Forbidden Land* was a cry, or to be accurate, a diatribe against the closing off of vast areas of Britain by commercial and government interests. Only images so powerfully conceived and executed as hers could adequately represent the pain and outrage perpetrated upon ordinary citizens as they have been deprived of the access to the countryside that they thought had been re-won permanently through the struggles of the thirties and the subsequent post-war legislation.

Comparison may in many ways be invidious, but it is hard to resist the temptation to draw attention to similarities between Fay Godwin's work and the output of those illustrious protesters against the first Industrial Revolution, William Blake and his friends in the Brotherhood of Ancients. Neither in her

case nor in theirs may beauty be seen as a ruse to avoid painful issues; on the contrary, it is in aesthetic perfection that the consequence of loss is most powerfully expressed by Fay Godwin, as it was by her predecessors.

—Philip Stokes

GOHLKE, Frank.

Nationality: American. **Born:** Wichita Falls, Texas, 3 April 1942. **Education:** Attended Wichita Falls High School, Wichita Falls, Texas, 1957-60; Davidson College, North Carolina, 1960-63; University of Texas at Austin, 1960-64 B.A. in English literature 1964; Yale University, New Haven, Connecticut, 1964-67, M.A. in English literature 1967; studied photography with Paul Caponigro, Bethel, Connecticut, 1967-68. **Family:** Married Madelon Sprengnether in 1966 (divorced, 1981); daughter: Jessica Lee; married Lucy Flint in 1985; daughters Emma Flint and Grace Clayton. **Career:** Freelance photographer since 1967. Adjunct Instructor, Middlebury College, Vermont, 1968-71; Teacher, Blake Schools, Minneapolis, 1973-75; Assistant Professor, University of Minnesota Extension, Minneapolis, 1975-79; Visiting Instructor in Art, Colorado College, Colorado Springs, 1977-81; Visiting Professor, Carleton College, Northfield, Minnesota, 1980, and Yale University Graduate School, 1981. **Recipient:** Guggenheim Fellowship, 1975; Minnesota State Arts Council Fellowship, 1973; Seagram Bicentennial Courthouse Project Award, 1975; National Endowment for the Arts Fellowship, 1977 and 1986-87; Bush Foundation Artists Fellowship, 1979; McKnight Foundation Film in the Cities Photographic Fellowship, 1983. **Agent:** Light Gallery, 724 Fifth Avenue, New York, New York 10019, U.S.A. **Address:** 65 Cross Street, Ashland, Massachusetts 01721, U.S.A.

Individual Exhibitions:

1969	Middlebury College, Vermont
1971	Underground Gallery, New York
1974	International Museum of Photography, George Eastman House, Rochester, New York
	Art Institute of Chicago
1975	Light Gallery, New York
	Amon Carter Museum, Fort Worth, Texas
1977	Viterbo College, La Crosse, Wisconsin Boston Museum School
1978	University of Nebraska, Lincoln
	Museum of Modern Art, New York
	Light Gallery, New York
1980	University of Massachusetts, Amherst
	Carleton College, Northfield, Minnesota
1981	Kalamazoo Institute of Arts, Michigan
	Light Gallery, New York
1983	University of Minnesota, Minneapolis
1986	Daniel Wolf Gallery, New York
1988	*Landscapes from the Middle of the World,* Museum of Contemporary Photography, Columbia College, Chicago (travelled)
1992	Franklin Parrasch Gallery, New York
1993	*Living Water: Photographs of the Sudbury River by Frank Gohlke,* DeCordova Museum and Sculpture Park, Lincoln, Massachusetts

Selected Group Exhibitions:

1972	*60s Continuum,* International Museum of Photography, George Eastman House, Rochester, New York
1973	*Photographers: Midwest Invitational,* Walker Art Center, Minneapolis
1975	*New Topographics: Photographs of a Man-Altered Landscape,* International Museum of Photography, George Eastman

Spring Floods, the Sudbury River, Sudbury, Massachusetts, **April 1993 (original in colour), from** *Living Water:* **Photographs of the Sudbury River.**
Photograph by Frank Gohlke.

House, Rochester, New York (travelled to the Otis Art
Institute, Los Angeles, and Princeton University Art
Museum, New Jersey)

1976   *Recent American Still Photography,* Fruit Market Gallery,
Edinburgh

1978   *Mirrors and Windows: American Photography since 1960,*
Museum of Modern Art, New York (toured the United
States, 1978-80)

1979   *American Images: New Work by 20 Contemporary Photogra-*
phers, Corcoran Gallery, Washington, D.C. (travelled to the
International Center of Photography, New York; Museum of
Fine Arts, Houston; Minneapolis Institute of Arts; and
Indianapolis Institute of Arts, 1980; American Academy,
Rome, 1981)

1980   *New Landscapes, Part II,* Friends of Photography, Carmel,
California

1982   *20th Century Photographs from MOMA,* Seibu Museum of
Art, Tokyo

1983   *New Work by Eight Photographers,* Daniel Wolf Gallery,
New York

        An Open Land: Photographs of the Midwest 1852-1982, Art
Institute of Chicago (travelled)

1985   *Paris-New York-Tokyo,* Tsukuba Museum of Photography,
Tsukuba, Japan; Miyagi Museum of Art, Japan

1986   *Variance,* MoMA, New York

1987   *American Dreams,* Centro de Arte Reina Sofia, Madrid, Spain

1988   *The Second Israeli Photography Biennial,* Mishkan Le'Omanut,
Museum of Art, Ein Harod, Israel

        Tradition and Change: Contemporary American Landscape
Photography, Houston Center for Photography, Houston, Texas

1989   *Photography Now,* Victoria and Albert Museum, London
        Photography Until Now, MoMA, New York

1992   *More Than One Photography,* MoMA, New York

Collections:

Museum of Modern Art, New York; International Museum of Photography,
George Eastman House Rochester, New York; Art Institute of Chicago;
Minneapolis Institute of Arts; Museum of Fine Arts, Houston; Amon Carter
Museum of Western Art, Fort Worth, Texas; Santa Barbara Museum of Art,
California; Die Neue Sammlung, Munich; National Gallery of Australia,
Canberra; Bibliothèque Nationale, Paris; Victoria and Albert Museum, Lon-
don; National Gallery of Canada, Ottawa, Ontario; Walker Art Center,

Minneapolis, Minnesota; Cleveland Museum of Art; Metropolitan Museum of Art, New York.

Publications:

By GOHLKE: Book—*Measure of Emptiness: Grain elevators in the American Landscape,* with essay by John C. Hudson (Baltimore) 1992. **Articles**—"Frank Gohlke" in *Camera* (Lucerne), May 1976; introductory essay in *Photographs,* edited by Ben Lifson, El Cajon, California 1977; in *Darkroom 2,* edited by Jain Kelly, New York 1978; "Silos of Life" in the *New York Times,* 18 January 1979; "A Photographer's View of Grain Elevators" in *GTA Digest* (Minneapolis), March/April 1979; "Frank Gohlke: An Interview," special issue of *Northlight* (Tempe, Arizona), vol. 10, 1979. **Videotape**—*Prairie Castles,* co-director, St. Paul, Minnesota 1979.

On GOHLKE: Books—*New Topographics: Photographs of a Man-Altered Landscape,* edited by William Jenkins, Rochester, New York 1975; *Court House,* edited by Richard Pare, New York 1978; *Mirrors and Windows: American Photography since 1960* by John Szarkowski, New York 1978; *American Images: New Work by 20 Contemporary Photographers,* edited by Renato Danese, New York 1979; *Photography and Beauty* by Robert Adams and others, Millerton, New York 1981; *20th Century Photography from the Museum of Modern Art,* exhibition catalogue, by John Szarkowski, Tokyo and New York 1982; *The Sudbury River: A Celebration,* exhibition catalogue, Lincoln 1983; *Masterpieces of Photography from George Eastman House,* edited by Robert A. Sobieszek, New York 1985; *Landscapes from the Middle of the World,* exhibition catalogue, introduction by Ben Lifson, Chicago 1988; *Photography Until Now,* exhibition catalogue, by John Szarkowski, New York 1989; *Photography Now,* exhibition catalogue, by Mark Haworth-Booth, London 1989. **Articles**—"Route 66 Revisited: The New Landscape Photography" by Carter Ratcliff in *Art in America* (New York), January/February 1976; "Frank Gohlke's Entrance into the Provinces" by Ben Lifson in the *Village Voice* (New York), 8 May 1978; "Showing an America of Wheat and Wheaties" by Sami Klein in *Minneapolis Star,* 16 June 1979; "Midwest Icons" by Peter Picard in *Minnesota Daily* (Minneapolis), 26 October 1979; "Our Town: Gohlke's Tulsa Murals" by Robert Silberman in *Art in America,* July 1985; "Frank Gohlke at Daniel Wolf" by Charles Hagen in *Artforum,* XX, 7 March 1987; "What Landscapes Really Mean" by Vicki Goldberg in *American Photographer,* December 1988; "Frank Gohlke" by Ingrid Sischy in *The New Yorker,* 17 May 1992; "High and Mighty" by Nonya Grenader in *Cite: The Architecture and Design Review of Houston,* No 31, Winter-Spring 1994.

*

A sense of taking and being taken by the world (and I want to insist on the erotic edge of that word) is central to my understanding of photography. My perceptions depend, tautologically, on what there is to see. The world forms my ideas and imaginings; but I'm also aware that I give form to the world in the act of seeing and photographing it; and if I manage to do it right, it's a form which is peculiar to me. The paradox is that you only do that which is uniquely yours by forgetting yourself, by losing yourself in the world you photograph.

The photograph I want to make (which I never will, because it is unmakable) would replicate that experience of self-loss and recovery in all its complexity, intensity, temporal depth and conviction of utter completeness, as if for that moment the whole universe is concentrated there. That's quite a bit to expect from a flat piece of paper with some grey smudges on it, but thanks to metaphor we can give a persuasive illusion that such is the case. The things described in a photograph are akin to the words of a poem, and the form of the photograph is analogous to the poem's structure. Word and structure, thing and form, act upon one another. The form mirrors the movement of the mind and feelings, as the possibility of the photograph is first sensed, then pursued, and finally given a shape. The photograph is itself a gesture, a compound of the gesture of the world and the gesture of the photographer in response to it.

If I were forced to come up with one word to characterize my photography, the word would be "lyrical." Lyricism as a mode strives to give each impulse, each curve of emotion, the form that is unique to it and unrepeatable. It is concerned to describe with fidelity and clarity that interaction between inner and outer realities that is the occasion for the photograph. For me, that implies that the appearances, the physical things and the spaces they inhabit must be rendered with the same fidelity and clarity. Whatever system there is in my work grows out of a body of encounters which have things in common, and so will have resolutions in common.

What I'm looking for is a way of photographing that is internally consistent, but that will also allow me to photograph *anything* I want without a sense of strain, dislocation or anomaly. My ideal style involves the disappearance of an obvious "style" altogether. Pure transparency is the goal, but of course it's unattainable. It is the effort toward the goal that feeds the imagination.

—Frank Gohlke

* * *

The groundglass of a camera has always been dead set against the idea of a landscape. Aiming essentially down at the land with a viewfinder that is positioned essentially upright is a kind of delight in a dilemma that all landscape photographers in some fashion or other have faced. Frank Gohlke, who has been photographing the flat world of the American Midwest from Texas to Minnesota for the last decade, regards the levelness of the land—the prone prairie that must somehow be lifted vertically on its feet—as "an active force in the landscape [and not simply] a passive container of objects." Describing the sensation of driving through the plains of Kansas and the Texas Panhandle, Gohlke writes, "I felt the presence of space rather than the absence of things."

In such vastness as Gohlke has photographed, we welcome interruptions that would secure focus and bearing, "things" that would calm our distended, often disoriented, optic nerves. For Frank Gohlke, as well as for most temporally minded true believers on the plains, that blessed intermission, that resting point of focus, has been the grain elevator. Out there in all that recumbency, these sky-scraping, perpendicular refreshments not only mark where road and rail intersect, they are the beacon for a mini-city of workers who gravitate from hundreds of miles out to toil in their shadows. "Grain elevators," Gohlke writes, "exist in the present, testaments to the timeless but immediately crucial powers of soil and sun, water and wind. The future they anticipate is next year's harvest, not eternity."

The excitement of discovery often draws an artist within surface sight of the subject. Such, it appears, was the nature of Frank Gohlke's quest on the prairie. The earliest photographs are frame-filled with the gleaming sheet metal or chipped clapboards of the granaries. The images are replete with razor-sharp creases between abutting columns and walls, creases so impeccable they resemble paper folded in half and pressed tightly between two fingers.

In subsequent years, Gohlke pulled away from the elevators, sometimes so far back that telephone lines clearly visible at the edges of his frame vanished in the center of his prints. While the elevators were still in sight, sky and land flooded the scene.

In a three-dimensional world, heaven and earth never touch. In a photograph, there's no way to keep them apart. The horizon line where the contact is made—that endless line of obfuscating conclusions that Gohlke characterizes as being "unreachable except by sight"—behaves as catalyst and kingpin in a number of these mid-1970s pushedback landscapes. The horizon line causes us to consider at which distances Gohlke's landmarkers actually lie as well as what particular relationships among them are formed. In a photograph taken in Perryton, Texas in 1973, for example, Gohlke establishes an engaging equivalence in scale and function between the dividing line (normally tiny) on a highway and the white columns of a grain elevator (normally colossal) in the distance. Seen (and photographed) from one specific spot, and one specific spot only, the road dashes and the elevator columns are in perfect line, the one over the other. What's more—and it is indeed astounding to witness this in the photograph—both are rendered in exactly the same size. The dashes mark the path ahead, the towers indicate how far there is to go.

Gohlke addresses not only formal equivalencies, but also mechanical laws interacting with human aspirations. In "Near Kinsley, Kansas," 1973, the elevators are reduced to the size of trees, the manmade and the natural standing neck and neck on the horizon reaching for the firmament. "Physical orientation," Gohlke states in his writings, "is never far distant from spiritual orientation." A woman from Texas once told him, "Our churches don't need steeples; we have grain elevators."

Gohlke's handling of "decisive distance and decisive place" gains momentum as the hallmark of his vision in much of his recent work, not just of grain elevators and their surroundings, but of prairie-sized parking lots, amusement parks, sports complexes, marsh fires, power stations, and highway construction sites. There is the image taken in Albuquerque, New Mexico in 1977 of what appears to be, at first sight, one half of a freshly paved highway (seen parallel to the film plane). The other lane (tiny and far away in the flatness of the landscape) easily consolidates the moderately light traffic of the day. Upon closer inspection, however, we realize—and it works like a charm every time—that Gohlke has, in fact, positioned the traffic, the road lights and power line poles precisely on top of a smoothly cemented wall. Certainly it is an uplifting landscape, if not a classic.

—Arno Rafael Minkkinen

GOLDBLATT, (Lewis) David.

Nationality: South African. **Born:** Randfontein, 29 November 1930. **Education:** Attended Krugersdorp High School, near Johannesburg, until 1948; studied commerce, University of the Witwatersrand, Johannesburg, 1952-57, B.S. 1956; self-taught in photography, from 1947. **Family:** Married Lily Psek in 1955; children: Steven, Brenda and Ron. **Career:** Since 1963, freelance photographer, Johannesburg. Director of Photography, *Leadership* magazine, Cape Town. **Address:** 35 Forbes Street, Fellside, Box 1464, Johannesburg 2000, South Africa.

Individual Exhibitions:

1974	Photographers' Gallery, London
1975	National Gallery of Victoria, Melbourne
	Photography Place, Sydney, New South Wales
1977	Durban Art Gallery, Natal, South Africa
1983	South African National Gallery, Cape Town
1984	Johannesburg Art Gallery, South Africa
	Durban Art Gallery, Natal, South Africa
1986	Photographers' Gallery, London
	Market Photo Gallery, Johannesburg

Selected Group Exhibitions:

1978	*Some South African Photographers,* Durban Art Gallery, Natal, South Africa
1986	*The Cordoned Heart* (until 1993) USA
1990	*Zabalaza,* London
1991	*Die Vierde Wand,* Amdsterdam
	amaNdebele, Huas der Kulturen der Welt, Berlin
1993	*Fotomanifestatie Noorderlicht 1993,* Groningen, Holland

Collections:

South African National Gallery, Cape Town; National Gallery of Victoria, Melbourne; Museum of Modern Art, New York; Durban Art Gallery, Natal, South Africa; Johannesburg Art Gallery, South Africa; Bibliothèque Nationale, Paris; Victoria & Albert Museum, London.

Publications:

By GOLDBLATT: Books—*On the Mines,* with text by Nadine Gordimer, Cape Town 1973; *Some Afrikaners Photographed,* Johannesburg 1975; *Cape Dutch Homesteads,* with Margaret Courtney-Clarke, text by John Kench, Cape Town 1981; *In Boksburg,* Cape Town 1982; *Lifetimes: Under Apartheid,* with Nadine Gordimer, New York 1986; *The Transported of KwaNdebele,* New York 1989. **Articles**—"The Afrikaners" in *Camera* (Lucerne), June 1969; "The Structure of Things Here" in *Camera Austria,* No 46, 1994.

Widow in Her House Near Flagstaff, **1975.** Photograph by David Goldblatt. Courtesy of The Photographers' Gallery, London.

On GOLDBLATT: Books—*Some South African Photographers,* exhibition catalogue, Durban, South Africa 1978; *Nichts Wird Uns Trennen,* Berne 1983; *South Africa—The Cordoned Heart,* Cape Town 1986. **Articles**—"David Goldblatt" in *Camera* (Lucerne), April 1973; interview in *ADA Magazine,* (Cape Town) No. 8, 1990.

*   *   *

David Goldblatt is a photographer of sensitivity and passion. Perhaps because of his Jewish background—his grandfather left Lithuania at the time of the pogroms—he has been more than usually aware of the racial tensions within his country since he was a child. He began to photograph professionally in the early sixties combining his personal work with that of professional assignments for many magazines and several books.

Some of his photographs echo memories of his childhood as he recognises something within a subject that brings back earlier experiences. All of them search for the essential—what he would call the 'isness' of the person or situation being photographed. This search is carried out across all levels of society and all races in South Africa. He has become the most influential of all the photographers in that country and inspired many of his younger countrymen and women.

Goldblatt did not photograph the increasing violence that took place in South Africa after the Sharpeville Massacre. His photographs showed the reasons for that violence, the situations and expectations of a wide range of people, both the fearful and the fearsome, living under a system that in legalising prejudice gave it a force that made everyone concerned frightened of somebody or something.

David Goldblatt is unique among the photographers of his generation in that his personal work has concentrated for thirty years on one, albeit enormous, subject—the people of South Africa, the effect they have on each other and on their countryside and cities. With the joyful ending of apartheid and the beginning of reconstruction it is certain that his work will continue to give us a clear and true document of immense historical importance and photographic integrity.

—Sue Davies

GOLDEN, Judith.

Nationality: American. **Born:** Judith Greene in Chicago, Illinois, 29 November 1934. **Education:** Studied at the School of the Art Institute of Chicago, 1968-73, B.F.A. 1973; University of California at Davis, 1973-75 (Chancellor's Fellowship, 1974; Regents' Fellowship, 1975), M.F.A. 1975. **Family:** Married David Golden in 1955 (divorced, 1968); children: David and Lucinda. **Career:** Freelance photographer, in California, since 1973. Visiting Lecturer, University of California at Los Angeles, 1975-79, University of California at Davis, 1980, and California College of Arts and Crafts, Oakland, 1980; Associate Professor, University of Arizona, Tucson, 1981-1989; Full Professor, University of Arizona, Tucson, since 1989. **Recipient:** National Endowment for the Arts Photography Fellowship, 1979; Artists Fellowship, Arizona Commission on the Arts, 1984; Arizona Foundation Grant, 1984; Honorary Ph.D., Moore College of Art, 1990. **Agent:** Etherton Gallery, 424 East 6th Street, Tucson, Arizona 85705, U.S.A. **Address:** 135 South 6th Avenue, Tucson, Arizona 85701, U.S.A.

Individual Exhibitions:

1977	University of Colorado, Boulder
	University of California at San Francisco
	The Women's Building, Los Angeles
1978	G. Ray Hawkins Gallery, Los Angeles
1979	Quay Gallery, San Francisco
1980	Galerie Nagel, West Berlin
1981	*Photo/Trans/Forms,* San Francisco Museum of Modern Art (with Joanne Leonard)
	Quay Gallery, San Francisco
1982	Colorado Mountain College, Breckenridge
	Catskill Center for Photography, Woodstock, New York
1983	Center for Creative Photography, University of Arizona, Tucson
1984	University of Oregon, Eugene
1985	Andover Gallery, Massachusetts
	Coburg Gallery, Vancouver, British Columbia
	Union Gallery, University of Arizona, Tucson
	Etherton Gallery, Tucson, Arizona
1986	Museum of Photographic Arts, San Diego, California (retrospective)
1987	Friends of Photography, Carmel, California
	Tucson Museum of Art, Arizona (retrospective)
1988	Museum of Contemporary Photography, Chicago
1990	Visual Arts Center, Anchorage
1991	Etherton/Stern Gallery, Tucson
1993	Scottsdale Center for the Arts, Scottsdale, Arizona
	Gallery 954, Chicago

Selected Group Exhibitions:

1977	*Contemporary Photography,* Fogg Art Museum, Harvard University, Cambridge, Massachusetts
1978	*Silver and Ink,* Oakland Museum, California
	20th Century Photography: 1959 to the Present, University of New Mexico, Albuquerque
1979	*Translations: Photographic Images with New Forms,* Cornell University, Ithaca, New York
1980	*Rated X,* Photographica Gallery, New York
1981	*Contemporary Hand-Colored Photographs,* de Saisset Museum, University of Santa Clara, California
	A Look at the Boundaries, Memorial Union Gallery, University of California at Davis
1983	*The Self as Subject,* University of New Mexico, Albuquerque
1984	*Photography in California 1945-80,* San Francisco Museum of Modern Art (travelled to the Akron Art Museum, Ohio; Corcoran Gallery, Washington, D.C.; Los Angeles Municipal Art Gallery; Cornell University, Ithaca, New York; High Museum of Art, Atlanta, Georgia; Museum Folkwang,

Essen; Centre Georges Pompidou, Paris; Museum of Photographic Arts, San Diego, California)

1986	*Self Portrait Photography 1840-1985,* National Portrait Gallery, London (travelled to Plymouth Arts Centre, Hampshire; John Hansard Gallery, Southampton; Ikon Gallery, Birmingham)
1987	*Photography and Art: Interactions since 1946,* Los Angeles County Museum of Art
1989	*Nature and Culture,* Inaugural exhibition, Ansel Adams Center, San Francisco
	Self and Shadow, Burden Gallery at Aperture, New York
1990	*Selection 5 from the Polaroid Corporation Collection,* Photokina 90, Cologne (touring until 1993)
1991	*American Photography Since 1920: From the Collection of the Center for Creative Photography,* Fundacion La Caixa, Barcelona; De Beyerd Center for Contemporary Art, Breda, Netherlands
	A Portrait Is Not a Likeness, Center for Creative Photography, University of Arizona, Tucson
	Self-Portraits of Contemporary Women: Exploring the Unknown Self, Tokyo Metropolitan Museum of Photography
1992	*Proof: Los Angeles Art and the Photograph, 1960-1980,* Laguna Art Museum, Laguna Beach (travelled until 1994)
	On Death/La Muerte, Bridge Center for Contemporary Art, El Paso
1993	*The Mediated Image: American Photography in the Age of Information,* University Art Museum, Albuquerque
1994	*The Irmas Collection of Photographic Self-Portraits,* Los Angeles County Museum of Art

Collections:

Art Institute of Chicago; Center for Creative Photography, University of Arizona, Tucson; Fogg Museum of Art, Harvard University, Cambridge, Massachusetts; Grunwald Center for the Graphic Arts, University of California, Los Angeles; International Musuem of Photography at George Eastman House, Rochester, New York; Los Angeles County Museum of Art; Minneapolis Institute of the Arts, Minnesota; Muesum of Contemporary Photography, Columbia College, Chicago; Museum of Photographic Arts, San Diego; Newport Harbor Museum of Art, Newport Beach, California; Oakland Museum of Art, Oakland; Osaka Museum of Photography, Japan; Polaroid Corporation, Cambridge, Massachusetts; San Francisco Museum of Modern Art; Tokyo Metropolitan Museum of Photography, Japan.

Publications:

On GOLDEN: Books—*In/Sights: Self-Portraits by Women,* edited by Joyce Tenneson Cohen, Boston 1978, London 1979; *Self-Portrayal: The Photographer's Image,* Carmel, California 1979; *Autoportraits Photographiques 1898-1981,* exhibition catalogue, by Alain Sayag and Dennis Roche, Paris 1981; *Photo/Trans/Form,* exhibition catalogue, by Louise Katzman, San Francisco 1981; *Photography in California 1945-1980* by Louise Katzman, San Francisco and New York 1984; *Cycles: A Decade of Photographs by Judith Golden,* by Claire Peeps, San Francisco 1988; *Self-Portraits of Contemporary Women: Exploring the Unknown Self,* by Michiko Kasahara, Japan 1991. **Articles**—"Judith Golden's Explorations of Self" by Joan Murray in *Artweek* (Oakland, California), 26 March 1977; "Discoveries: Judith Golden" in *Time-Life Photography Annual,* New York 1978; "Judith Golden and Sherrie Sheen" by Barbara Noah in *Art in America* (New York), March 1978; "Judith Golden" by David Fahey in *G. Ray Hawkins Photo-Bulletin* (Los Angeles), September 1978; "Judith Golden's Self-Portrait Fantasies" by Diana Portner in *Artweek* (Oakland, California), 16 September 1978; "Dialogue with Judith Golden" by Diana Portner in *Bulletin of the Los Angeles Center for Photographic Studies,* October 1978; "Forbidden Fantasies" by Ted Hedgpeth in *Artweek* (Oakland, California), 27 September 1979; "Selbstporträt und Narzissus" by Bernd Linhart in *Tip* (West Berlin), 17 July 1980; "Judith Golden" by Hal Fischer in *Artforum* (New York), January 1982; "Judith Golden Exhibit a Knockout" by Kelly Wise in the *Boston Globe,* 12 May 1985; "Myths unveil many faces of Judith Golden" by Mark Elliott Lugo in the *San Diego Tribune,* 7 March 1986; "Judith Golden: The

***Water Boy,* 1989.** Photograph by Judith Golden.

Chameleons, The Personas, The Cycles" by Sheldon Reich in *Artspace* (Albuquerque), Winter 1986-87; "Photographer Through the Looking Glass" by Robert Cauthorn in *Arizona Daily Star* (Tucson) 19 July 1987; "Emotional, Cerebral Transformations of the Traditional Print" by Larry Thall in *Chicago Tribune* (Chicago) 9 September 1988; "Judith Golden at MCP" by Joanna Freuh in *Art in America* (New York), February 1989; "Lively Visions at Ansel Adams Center" by Liz Lupkin in *San Francisco Chronicle* (San Francisco) 8 October 1989; "Shuffling the Deck" by Charlotte Rowe in *Tucson Citizen* (Tucson), 2 April 1991; "Infinite Twists" by Margaret Regan in *Tucson Weekly* (Tucson), 21 October 1992; "Realidad Virtual: Retratos de America" by Joseph R Wolin in *Luna Cornea* (Mexico City), No. 3, 1993.

*

Beauty. Innocence. Joy. Pain. Life. Death. Dreams. Light. Shadow. My work leads me on a visual journey through the labyrinth of life's many contradictions and challenges. My intent is to keep in touch with the magical timeless realm that is not always visible.

—Judith Golden

*   *   *

Trained as a painter and printmaker, Judith Golden was not interested in straight photography's somewhat passive role of recording the world. Instead, she looked on photography as a tool to generate images containing a high degree of believability. Thus she began to integrate photography with printing techniques to create imaginative works based on popular myths and fantasies.

Her meticulously crafted, one-of-a-kind pieces which grew out of this combination are accomplished with a series of color toners, hand-applied paints, and various other devices including stitching cloth borders around the pictures and attaching hair, ribbon, and other items to their surfaces. Although some prints rely on purely photographic illusionism—her most recent works, in fact, are straight color prints—they all exploit the convincing realism inherent in the photographic process.

When discussing her work, Golden expresses a longstanding interest in the ways we are made to conform to mass media images. Using herself as model—which makes these essentially self-portraits—she tries on different costumes, takes on different roles, or substitutes her face for that of some famous person. In the "People Magazine" series, her face appears through a hole cut out of the magazine's cover which contains recognizable features of such stars as Louise Lasser and Woody Allen; in the series entitled "Ode to Hollywood" her face appears in place of the heroine in madeover movie posters; and in the portrait series "Chameleon," she assumes other identities so totally she herself becomes unrecognizable. The thoroughly illusionistic quality of the images—which makes the fantasy seem very real—underscores Golden's message about the seductive nature of roles fabricated by the media.

"Forbidden Fantasies," her series of explicit sexual fantasies made from retouched reproductions of a 16th century Chinese marriage manual, illustrates Golden's sense of humor as well as her daring honesty. Expressions of delight on the pasted-on faces and lavishly colored genitals make her private desires (she is shown in the body of a Chinese maiden having sex with famous artists like Henry Miller, Picasso, Edward Weston, and Robert Heinecken) embarrassingly public. With these images, as with her others, Golden seems to be saying that it is OK to have such fantasies. Using herself as example, she is encouraging her viewers to develop their imaginations in order to create and to live out their own personal fantasies.

—Ted Hedgpeth

GONZÁLEZ PALMA, Luis.

Nationality: Guatemalan. **Born:** Guatemala, 3 August 1957. **Education:** Studied architecture and cinematography at the Universidad de San Carlos, Guatemala; self-taught in photography. **Family:** Married to Delia Vigil. **Recipient:** Fellowship at Cité des Artes, Paris, 1992-93; fellowship at Château Beychevalle, France to work on the theme of "Valour," 1993. **Agent:** Martha Schneider, 230 West Superior, Chicago, Illinois 60610, U.S.A. **Address:** 444 Brickell Avenue, Suite 51-187, Miami, Florida 33131, U.S.A.

Individual Exhibitions:

1989	Museum of Contemporary Hispanic Art, New York
1990	Fotogalería Teatro San Martín, Buenos Aires, Argentina
1991	Galería Arte Contemporaneo, Mexico D.F., Mexico
	Galería El Cadejo, Antigua Guatemala, Guatemala
1992	Art Institute of Chicago
	V Fotobienal de Vigo, Spain
	Simon Lowinsky Gallery, New York
	Galleri Image, Arhus, Denmark
	Schneider-Bluhm-Loeb Gallery, Chicago
	FOTOFEST, International Month of Photography, Houston, Texas
	Galería Sol del Río, Guatemala
1993	Moderna Museet, Fotografiska Museet, Stockholm, Sweden
	Musée de la Photographie, Charleroi, Belgium
	Simon Lowinsky Gallery, New York
	A.B. Galeries, Paris
	FOTOFEIS, Scottish International Festival of Photography, Scotland
	Schneider-Bluhm-Loeb Gallery, Chicago
	XX Century Photography, Stephen Cohen Gallery, Los Angeles
	Jane Jackson Gallery, Atlanta, Georgia
1994	Royal Festival Hall, London (and tour)
	Museo de Bellas Artes de Caracas, Venezuela
	25 Rencontres Internationales de la Photographie, Arles, France
	Cleveland Center for Contemporary Art, Cleveland, Ohio
	Month of Photography, Bratislava, Czechoslovakia

Selected Group Exhibitions:

1988	*Angelogia,* Galería Imaginaria, Antigua Guatemala, Guatemala
	Refigura, Arte Moderno Gallery, San Antonio, Texas
1989	*Presencia Imaginaria,* Museo de Arte Moderno de Mexico (travelled to the Museo de Arte Moderno de Guatemala)
1990	*Cent Ans de Photographie au Guatemala,* Maison de l'Amérique Latine, Paris
1991	*Rencontres Internationales de la Photographie,* Arles, France
	Fotografía Contemporanea de Latinoamerica, Museo de Huelva, Spain
1992	*Salón Latinoamericano de desnudo, Bienal de São Paulo,* Brazil
	Alianza Francesa, Lima, Peru
1993	*Encuentro Latinoamericano de Fotografía,* Caracas, Venezuela
	Canto de la Realidad, Fotografía Latinoamericana 1860-1990, Casa de América, Madrid, Spain
1994	*V Bienal de la Habana,* Cuba
	Image & Memory: Latin American Photography 1880-1992, Akron Art Museum; (travelled to the Meadows Museum of Art, Southern Methodist University, Dallas, Texas)
	Schneider Gallery, Chicago
	Courage, Château Beychevelle, Bordeaux, France

Collections:

Art Institute of Chicago; Museum of Fine Arts, Houston; Museum of Art, New Orleans; The Minneapolis Institute of Art; Los Angeles County Museum of Art; Centro Cultural de Arte Contemporaneo, Mexico D.F.; The Bronx Museum of Art, New York; Musée de la Photographie, Charleroi, Belgium; Museo de Bellas Artes de Caracas, Venezuela; Centro de Estudios Fotograficos, Vigo, Spain; Maison de l'Amérique Latine, Paris.

Cherub, **1991.** Photograph by Luis González Palma.

Publications:

On GONZALEZ PALMA: Book—*Luis González Palma,* Buenos Aires 1993. **Articles**—"Foto Instalacíon" by Nilda Durante in *Diario Clarín,* (Buenos Aires), 26 May 1990; "Fotografía de devociones" by Graciela Kartofel in *Vogue-México,* August 1991; "Past and Present, Far and Near" by Patricia C. Johnson in *Houston Chronicle,* 15 March 1992; "Two Artists' Works Provide a Visual Counterpoint" by Larry Thall in *Chicago Tribune,* 24 April 1992; "A New Lens, or Two, on the Mythologizing of Latin America" by A.D. Coleman in *The New York Observer,* 12 October 1992; "Luis González Palma/A Thoroughly Modern Artist with the Soul of a Baroque Painter" by Peter H. Halpert in *Arts & Antiques,* December 1992; "Los iluminados" by Fernando Castro in *Art Nexus* (Colombia), January-March 1993; "Luis González Palma" by Alisa Tager in *Art News* (USA), February 1993; "Luis González Palma" by Tage Poulsen in *Katalog, Quarterly Magazine for Photography* (Denmark), March 1993; "Magic Touch from Guatemala" by Clare Henry in *The Glasgow Herald,* 4 June 1993. **Film**— *Randam no 99,* FRANCE 3TV, directed by Caroline Jauffrer, Paris 1993.

* * *

I first encountered Luis González Palma's work in 1990 at a mixed Guatemalan exhibition at the Maison de l'Amérique Latine in Paris. At once strikingly different to anything I had ever seen before, it was also entirely in place alongside the nineteenth century Guatemalan photography portraits by Yas and Noriega—of "native indians," dead babies and local dignitaries. My response was clearly commonplace: in the last three years, González Palma's work has been shown at every major photographic festival in the Americas and Europe, including Fotofeis, the Scottish photographic festival held in June 1993. Although first exhibited only six years ago, the work was impressively mature almost from its inception.

Perhaps this connects to the fact that photography is González Palma's self-taught second career, commencing in his late twenties. Certainly his architectural training remains evident in his meticulous planning, the use of interlinked spaces in assembled panels and triptychs, and his recent move towards creating installations. There is evidence, too, of a frustrated painter in him. Possibly most important of all, however, is his powerful sense of belonging to a dislocated culture.

González Palma's work depends exclusively on Maya models, people who Columbus' errant sense of geography indiscriminately labelled as "indians," although the Maya people alone belong to twenty-three distinct language groups.

González Palma's photography takes as its starting point the period of ecclesiastical High Baroque that became known as the churriguerresco style. Reaching its bizarre apex in the eighteenth century, it combined a decadent European Rococo with fantastical designs worthy of the great Maya city states of 700 years earlier. His themes frequently belong to the Church and its cycles: crowns of thorns and haloes of roses; the depiction of Saints, Virgins and Christs; ceremonies, rites and sacraments based on the Mysteries of the Rosary.

Luis González Palma describes a privileged education remote from many of his models. "While I wouldn't now call myself a religious person, I was educated by the Marist fathers . . . I admit I am imbued with its images. Mariolatry, the cult of sanctity, the Stations of the Cross are all things that were inculcated in us at a very early age." His models enjoy acting their way into the rôles of saints and angels: "I always offer them examples of my work and they never choose the 'passport photos,' always the more imaginative portraits that a part of them clearly identifies with."

Picking up a camera, recognising that he wanted to make portraits that had nothing to do with standard portraiture, came partly with the rejection of religion and the summary end of formal education. "Throughout the time I was at San Carlos (the national university in Guatemala City), there were bombs going off, students and teachers were abducted and any protest sparked a shooting. Eventually I left."

Institutionalised violence finds its way into González Palma's work in its torn borders, scratched negatives and fragmented images. Although shot in black and white, many are then sepia-coated, frequently leaving only the staring white of an eye or a flower or the brilliant scarlet of a trailing ribbon to break disturbingly with the gentle mulatto tones.

Since being invited to work at the Château de Beychevelle, near Bordeaux, González Palma has had further opportunity to investigate artistically the relativism of human values. The Château is a peculiarly Galic institution inviting individual artists working in a variety of media to come together around a particular theme. 1993 was the second year of developing the "Four Cardinal Virtues": after *Justice* came *Valour*. "I learnt that to the orientals, Valour was not described as a virtue—other values, such as obedience, might be more important. Within my own culture there is also a clash: the conquistadores introduced the whole medieval panoply of the lottery cards, showing weapons and armour, using the helmet as an emblem. Whereas to the Maya the quetzal bird is the symbol of courage."

There is a difference in attitude that haunts González Palma's work and his country's history. The quetzal is on Guatemala's national flag and its currency, yet was long believed to have become extinct. Its recent rediscovery in the tropical forests of the altiplano is regarded as a symbol of hope. When the Spaniards arrived, the Maya were horrified that their priceless feather capes and head-dresses were subjected either to wholesale destruction or to occasional looting as "curiosities"—dusty specimens are still displayed at Vienna'a Ethnological Museum—in the rampage to unearth gold. The feathers were worked into shields and standards, entering battle against the Europeans' plated armour.

The mythic dimensions of confronting metal with quetzal feathers is one that González Palma is now exploring, alongside the historical theme of Maya resistance, promising that something radical will appear in *Valour*.

—Amanda Hopkinson

GORO, Fritz.

Nationality: American. **Born:** Bremen, Germany, 20 April 1901; emigrated to France, 1933, to the United States, 1936: naturalized, 1944. **Education:** Attended the Lessing Gymnasium, Berlin, until 1919; studied at the State School of Applied Arts, Berlin, 1919-21, and at the Bauhaus School, Weimar, 1921-23. **Family:** Married the sculptress Grete Goro; has one son. **Career:** Worked in the Magazine Division of Ullstein Publishing House, Berlin, as art director, designer, writer and editor, 1924-28; Assistant to the Managing Director, and editor, designer and art director, *Münchner Illustrierte,* Munich, 1928-33; freelance photographer, Paris, 1933-36, and New York, working mainly for *Life* magazine, 1936-44; Science Staff Photographer, *Life* magazine, New York, 1944-66, and for *Life* on contract, 1966-71; freelance science photographer, working mainly for *Scientific American* and for the Research Division of the Polaroid Corporation, since 1971. Regents Professor, University of California at San Diego, 1969; Visiting Fellow, Yale University, New Haven, Connecticut, 1969-70. **Recipient:** American Medical Association Award, 1948; National Society for Medical Research Award, 1949; 4 Art Directors Club of New York/ American Institute of Graphic Arts Awards, 1974-75; New York Microscopical Society Award, 1977; Society of Photographic Scientists and Engineers Award, 1977; Life Achievement Award, American Society of Magazine Photographers, 1978; Louis Schmidt Award, Biological Photographic Association, 1980. Fellow, Biological Photographic Association, 1969, and New York Microscopical Society, 1976. **Address:** 324 North Bedford Road, Chappaqua, New York 10514, U.S.A.

Individual Exhibitions:

1969   Lowe Art Gallery, University of Miami
1981   *Microcosmos,* Polaroid Corporation, Cambridge, Massachusetts (travelled to the Chappaqua, New York Library, 1982)

Selected Group Exhibitions:

1951   *Memorable Life Photographs,* Museum of Modern Art, New York
1955   *The Family of Man,* Museum of Modern Art, New York (and world tour)
1979   *Life: The First Decade 1936-1945,* Grey Art Gallery, New York University

Publications:

By GORO: Article—"Footnotes from a Member of the Jubilee," with Kay Reese, in *Infinity* (New York), January 1971.

On GORO: Books—*Memorable Life Photographs,* with text by Edward Steichen, New York 1951; *How Life Gets the Story: Behind the Scenes in Photo-Journalism,* edited by Stanley Rayfield, New York 1955; *Life Photographers: Their Careers and Favorite Pictures,* edited by Stanley Rayfield, New York 1957; *Photographic Communication,* edited by R. Smith Schuneman, London and Toronto 1972; *Life: The First Decade 1936-1945* by Robert Littman, Ralph Graves and Doris C. O'Neill, New York 1979, London 1980.

*   *   *

It all happened by chance in 1937. Fritz Goro was photographing the beaches of Cape Cod for *Life* when the editors of the magazine assigned him to check out the Wood's Hole Marine Biological Laboratory along the coast of Massachusetts. It was Goro's first acquaintance with science and oceanography and was to influence the rest of his life. Today his name is not only closely associated with photography of science, but also Fritz Goro is one of the very few recognized microscopists in the world.

Born in Germany, Goro was trained as a designer and sculptor at the State School of Applied Arts in Berlin as well as at the Bauhaus. He became the youngest designer/writer on the staff of the *Berliner Illustrierte* (Ullstein Verlag) and somewhat later an executive at the *Münchner Illustrierte.* In 1933, Goro and his sculptress wife Grete fled from Nazi Germany to Paris, literally leaving all their belongings behind them. They both became freelance photographers, and some of their work was published in magazines such as *Vogue* and *Vue.* In 1936 they moved to New York, where Fritz Goro has worked for *Life* ever since.

Life was very supportive and interested in scientific experiments and, after the Wood's Hole episode, assigned Goro as scientific photographer for marine sciences and marine biology without strings attached to his time. Thus Goro was able to develop his own very precise approach to scientific photography, his own optical equipment and his own highly personal style. In 1938 he photographed the pioneering work of Enrico Fermi with the fission of uranium, and he has ever since worked on nuclear physics and nuclear chemistry. In 1942 he made his first essay for Polaroid on quinine; he has continued to experiment with Polaroid technologies to this day. In 1945 he made the first photographs in color of blood circulation in living animals. In the 60s he worked intensely on the structure of DNA and RNA.

Widely travelled, including various expeditions to the Arctic, Fritz Goro works now mostly out of his own darkroom-laboratory set up in his home.

Many of his present assignments come from well-known scientific companies and magazines such as *Scientific American.*

Goro's pictures, taken with microscopes and specially designed lenses and lighting, reach far beyond the recording of items invisible to the naked eye. His continuous search to make understandable images out of abstract concepts has resulted in the most sophisticated and beautiful photographs in which science blends intimately with art.

—Ruth Spencer

GOSSAGE, John R.

Nationality: American. **Born:** New York City, 15 March 1946. **Education:** Studied photography privately with Lisette Model, Alexey Brodovitch, and Bruce Davidson, New York, 1962-64. **Family:** Married Terri Weifenbach in 1992. **Career:** Freelance photographer, New York, 1963-65, and Washington, D.C., since 1965. **Recipient:** Washington Gallery of Modern Art Fund Award, 1969, 1970; National Endowment for the Arts Short Term Project Grant, 1973, and Photography Grant, 1974, 1978; Stern Family Foundation Grant, 1974. **Agent:** Castelli Graphics, 4 East 77th Street, New York, New York 10021, U.S.A. **Address:** 2070 Belmont Road N.W., Washington D.C., 20009, U.S.A.

Individual Exhibitions:

1963	Camera Infinity Gallery, New York
1968	Hinkley Brohel Gallery, Washington, D.C.
1971	Ohio University, Athens
1972	*John Gossage: Photographs/Anne Truitt: Color Fields,* Pyramid Gallery, Washington, D.C.
1974	*Cultivation and Neglect,* Jefferson Place Gallery, Washington, D.C.
1976	Castelli Graphics, New York
	Max Protetch Gallery, Washington, D.C.
	Better Neighborhoods of Greater Washington, Corcoran Gallery of Art, Washington, D.C.
1978	*Gardens,* Castelli Graphics, New York (travelled to Wekstatt für Photographie der VHS Kreuzberg, Berlin)
1980	Castelli Graphics, New York
	Lunn Gallery, Washington, D.C.
1982	Wekstatt für Photographie der VHS Kreuzberg, West Berlin
	Forum Stadtpark, Graz, Austria
	Galerie Lang-Irschl, Munich
	Kunstmuseum, Hannover
1983	*LA to Berlin,* Castelli Graphics, New York
1984	University of Maryland, Baltimore
1987	*Stadt Des Schwarz,* Castelli Graphics, New York; Jones Troyer Gallery, Washington, D.C.
1989	*Secret Life of Goethe,* Jones Troyer Gallery, Washington, D.C.
1990	*Berlin,* Hilman Holland Gallery, Atlanta, Georgia
1991	Mueusm of Contemporary Photography, Chicago
1992	Ehler Cavdill Gallery, Chicago
1993	*The Photograph and its Double,* Grimaldis Gallery, Baltimore

Selected Group Exhibitions:

1975	*14 American Photographers,* Baltimore Museum of Art (travelled to Newport Harbor Museum, Newport Beach, California; La Jolla Museum, California; Walker Art Center, Minneapolis; Fort Worth Art Museum, Texas)
1976	*Peculiar to Photography,* University of New Mexico, Albuquerque
1977	*Contemporary American Photographic Works,* Museum of Fine Arts, Houston (travelled to the Museum of Contemporary Art, Chicago; La Jolla Museum, California; Newport Harbor Art Museum, Newport Beach, California)
1978	*23 Photographers/23 Directions,* Walker Art Gallery, Liverpool
1979	*American Images: New Work by Twenty Contemporary Photographers,* Corcoran Gallery, Washington, D.C. (travelled to the International Center of Photography, New York, Museum of Fine Arts, Houston, Minneapolis Institute of Arts, and Indianapolis Institute of Arts, 1980; and American Academy, Rome, 1981)
1981	*Slices of Time: California Landscapes,* Oakland Museum, California (travelled to the Security Pacific National Bank, Los Angeles, 1982)
1982	*Lichtbildnisse: Das Porträt in der Fotografie,* Rheinisches Landesmuseum, Bonn
1983	*New York, New York,* Seibu Museum of Art, Tokyo
1985	*American Images 1945-80,* Barbican Art Gallery, London (toured Britain)
1987	*Dialectical Landscapes,* Palazzo Fortuny, Venice
1988	*California Photography,* Oakland Museum of Art, Oakland, California
	Photography Now, Victoria and Albert Museum, London
1989	*Photography at Night,* Hallmark Collection, Kansas City
1990	*Recent Acquisitions,* National Museum of American Art, Washington, D.C.
1992	*Summer '92,* C Grimaldis Gallery, Baltimore, Maryland
1993	*Recent Acquisitions,* Los Angeles County Museum, Los Angeles

Collections:

Museum of Modern Art, New York; International Museum of Photography, George Eastman House, Rochester, New York; Princeton University, New Jersey; Pan American Union, Washington, D.C.; Corcoran Gallery of Art, Washington, D.C.; Philadelphia Museum of Art; Museum of Fine Arts, St. Petersburg, Florida; Museum of Fine Arts, Houston; Bibliothèque Nationale, Paris; Australian National Gallery, Canberra.

Publications:

By GOSSAGE: Books—*Gardens,* with text by Walter Hopps, New York and Washington, D.C. 1978; *American Images,* New York 1979; *The Pond,* Millerton, New York 1986; *Stadt des Schwarz* Washington DC and Berlin, 1987; *Three Days in Berlin,* Berlin 1988. **Article**—"Blow Up: The Story of Photography in Today's Art Market" in the *New York Times,* 12 October 1975.

On GOSSAGE: Books—*14 American Photographers,* exhibition catalogue, by Renato Danese, Baltimore 1975; *Time-Life Textbook of Photography,* edited by John and Barbara Upton, Boston 1976; *Better Neighborhoods of Greater Washington,* exhibition catalogue, by Jane Livingston, Washington, D.C. 1976; *Slices of Time: California Landscapes 1860-1880, 1960-1980,* exhibition catalogue, by Therese Thau Heyman and Ted Hedgpeth, Oakland, California 1981; *La Photographie Créative* by Jean-Claude Lemagny, Paris 1984; *American Images: Photography 1945-1980,* edited by Peter Turner and John Benton-Harris, London 1985. **Articles**—"As They See Themselves" in *Esquire* (New York), July 1965; "John R. Gossage" in *Camera* (Lucerne), August 1970; "Photos by John R. Gossage" in *Camera* (Lucerne), September 1973; "Four Photographs of John Gossage" in *The Georgia Review* (Durham, North Carolina), Winter 1975; "New York: John R. Gossage, Leo Castelli Gallery Uptown" by Phil Patton in *Artforum* (New York), April 1976; "Galleries" by Paul Richard in the *Washington Post,* 12 April 1976; "John R. Gossage" by Jane Livingston and Allan Porter in *Camera* (Lucerne), March 1977; "Gardens" by Noel Frackman in *Artsmagazine* (New York), May 1978; "Art in Washington" in *Art in America* (New York), July/August 1978.

*   *   *

John Gossage's photographs stand in the mainstream tradition of Atget, Evans, Frank, and Friedlander. Like them his concerns are with the world, and, like them, he has a keen appreciation of the world's ironies. What distinguishes Gossage's work is his ability to extend and enrich his traditional base

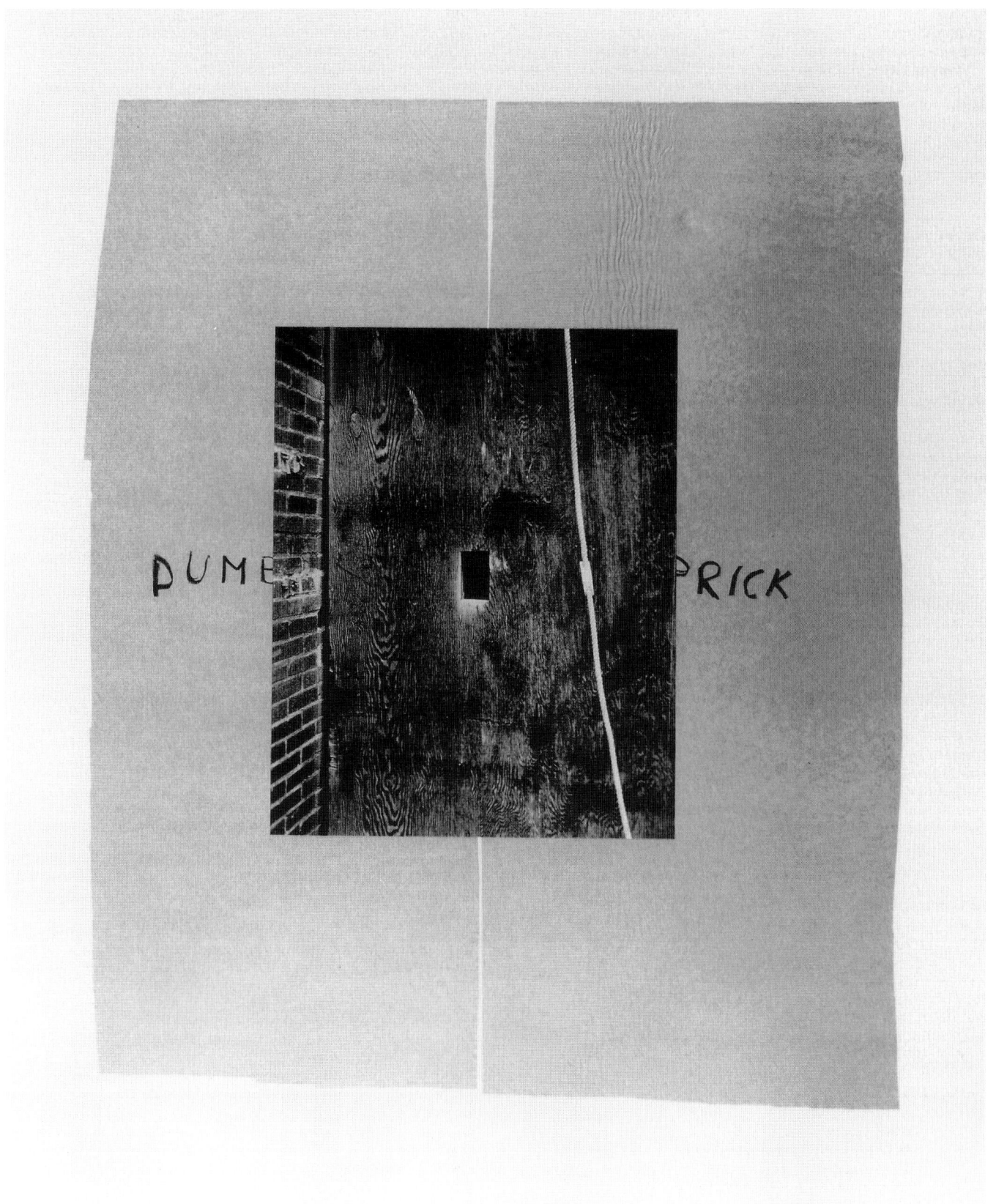

From the series *Plains of Hell*, Solvay, New York, 1984-90 (original in colour). Photograph ©John Gossage.

while, often in the same image, using his vision to remark upon the procedures, accomplishments, and occasional pretensions of the documentary point of view. All photographs are subversive; Gossage's a bit more so than most.

The complexity and subtlety of Gossage's images have made him the center of much critical controversy. To accept Gossage's work one must also accept, or at least acknowledge his assertions about the possibilities of photographic seeing. On this point Gossage is uncompromising. While Gossage's work has never been sufficiently anecdotal to a broad public, it is difficult to think of another photographer of his generation who has enjoyed a more profound influence within the field, or whose work has been more widely imitated.

Gossage's work from the 1970s (*Cultivation and Neglect,* 1974; the book, *Gardens,* with Walter Hopps, 1978) established the formal vocabulary and philosophic intentions that characterize his particular vision. Much of this work derives its authority from the apparent contradictions that Gossage introduces between the superficial confusion of elements within the photographic frame and the sophisticated, often nearly hidden, structure of the image. His subjects are often mean and trivial and are presented in such a way as to subvert the viewer's hierarchies of significance, yet the photographs themselves are intelligent, witty, and often perversely beautiful.

In his portfolios (*Seattle,* 1979; *Chevy Chase,* 1979-80) Gossage has shown himself unwilling to repeat the strategies of his earlier work. These newer works employ a tighter formal structure and make more explicit use of deep pictorial space. This, along with an increased concern for detail, has allowed Gossage to further objectify and externalize his interests and to turn his attention to subjects of broader documentary possibilities while retaining his characteristic fascination with the ambiguities of photographic vision.

—Lewis Baltz

GOWIN, Emmet.

Nationality: American. **Born:** Danville, Virginia, 22 December 1941. **Education:** Studied at the Richmond Professional Institute, Virginia, 1961-65, B.F.A. 1965; studied photography, under Harry Callahan, at the Rhode Island School of Design, Providence, 1965-67, M.F.A. 1967. **Family:** Married Edith Morris in 1964; children: Elijah and Isaac. **Career:** Independent photographer, since 1967. Graduate Assistant Instructor in Photography, Rhode Island School of Design, 1966-67; Instructor in Photography, Dayton Art Institute, 1967-71, and Bucks County Community College, Newtown, Pennsylvania, 1971. **Recipient:** Guggenheim Fellowship, 1974; National Endowment for the Arts grant, 1977. **Agent:** Pace/MacGill Gallery, 32 East 57th Street, New York, New York 10022, U.S.A.

Individual Exhibitions:

1968	University of Richmond, Virginia
	Dayton Art Institute, Ohio
	Illinois Institute of Technology, Chicago
1969	International Museum of Photography, George Eastman House, Rochester, New York
1971	Massachusetts Institute of Technology, Cambridge
	Photographs by Robert Adams and Emmet Gowin, Museum of Modern Art, New York
	The Photographers' Gallery, London
1972	Light Gallery, New York
	Art Institute of Chicago
1973	Friends of Photography, Carmel, California Light Gallery, New York
1974	Galerie Lichttropfen, Aachen, West Germany
	La Photogalerie, Paris
	Light Gallery, New York
1976	Light Gallery, New York
1977	Susan Spiritus Gallery, Newport Beach, California
1981	Photography Gallery, Philadelphia
1983	Northlight Gallery, Arizona State University, Tempe

1985	Chrysler Museum, Norfolk, Virginia (with David Levinson)
1986	*Emmet Gowin: Petra and Mount St. Helen's,* Pace/MacGill Gallery, New York
1988	Pace/MacGill Gallery, New York
1994	*Emmet Gowin: A Review 1990-1993,* Pace/MacGill Gallery, New York

Selected Group Exhibitions:

1969	*Vision and Expression,* International Museum of Photography, George Eastman House, Rochester, New York (toured the United States, 1969-71)
1970	*Be-Ing Without Clothes,* Hayden Gallery, Massachusetts Institute of Technology, Cambridge (toured the United States)
1973	*Light and Lens: Methods of Photography,* Hudson River Museum, Yonkers, New York
1975	*Celebrations,* Massachusetts Institute of Technology, Cambridge
1978	*Mirrors and Windows: American Photography since 1960,* Museum of Modern Art, New York (toured the United States, 1978-80)
1979	*Photographie als Kunst 1879-1979/Kunst als Photographie 1949-1979,* Tiroler Landesmuseum Ferdinandeum, Innsbruck, Austria (travelled to the Neue Galerie am Wolfgang Gurlitt Museum, Linz, Austria; Neue Galerie am Landesmuseum Joanneum, Graz, Austria; and the Museum des 20. Jahrhunderts, Vienna)
1980	*The Portrait Extended,* Museum of Contemporary Art, Chicago
1982	*Color as Form,* International Museum of Photography at George Eastman House, Rochester; New York
1983	*Subjective Vision,* High Museum of Art, Atlanta, George
1985	*American Images 1945-80,* Barbican Art Gallery, London (toured Britain)
	The Nude in Photography, Munchner Stadtmuseum, Munich, Germany
	History of Photography Survey, International Museum of Photography, George Eastman House, Rochester
1990	Pace/MacGill Gallery, New York
1992	Pace/MacGill Gallery, New York

Collections:

Museum of Modern Art, New York; Rhode Island School of Design, Providence; Fogg Art Museum, Harvard University, Cambridge, Massachusetts; Dayton Art Institute, Ohio; Cincinnati Art Museum, Ohio; Art Institute of Chicago; Minneapolis Institute of Arts; University of Kansas, Lawrence; University of New Mexico, Albuquerque; National Gallery of Canada, Ottawa.

Publications:

By GOWIN: Book—*Emmet Gowin: Photographs,* New York 1976.

On GOWIN: Books—*Vision and Expression* by Nathan Lyons, New York 1969; *Be-Ing Without Clothes,* exhibition catalogue, by Minor White, Cambridge, Massachusetts and Millerton, New York 1970; *11 American Photographers,* exhibition catalogue, by Robert Doty and Robert Littman, Hempstead, New York 1972; *Light and Lens: Methods of Photography,* edited by Donald L. Werner and Dennis Longwell, New York 1973; *Celebrations,* edited by Minor White and Jonathan Green, Cambridge, Massachusetts, and Millerton, New York 1974; *Photography in America,* edited by Robert Doty, with an introduction by Minor White, New York and London 1974; *The Snapshot,* edited by Jonathan Green, Millerton, New York 1974; *Private Realities: Recent American Photography,* exhibition catalogue, by Clifford S. Ackley, Boston 1974; *The Land: 20th Century Landscape Photographs Selected by Bill Brandt,* exhibition catalogue, edited by Mark Haworth-Booth, London 1975; *Photographs: Sheldon Memorial Art Gallery Collection,* University of Nebraska, with an introduction by Norman A. Geske, Lincoln, Nebraska 1977; *Geschichte der Fotografie im 20. Jahrhundert/Photography* *in the 20th Century* by Petr Tausk, Cologne 1977, London 1980; *Mirrors and Windows: American Photography since 1960* by John Szarkowski, New York 1978; *Darkroom 2,* edited by Jain Kelly, New York 1978; *Light Readings: A Photography Critic's Writings 1968-1978* by A.D. Coleman, New York 1979; *Photographie als Kunst 1879-1979/Kunst als Photographie 1949-1979,* exhibition catalogue, 2 volumes, by Peter Weiermair, Innsbruck, Austria 1979; *Nude Photographs 1850-1980,* edited by Constance Sullivan, New York 1980; *International Photography 1920-1980,* edited by Ian North, Canberra 1982; *Masterpieces of Photography from George Eastman House,* edited by Robert A. Sobieszek, New York 1985; *American Images: Photography 1945-1980,* edited by Peter Turner and John Benton-Harris, London 1985. **Articles**—"Emmet Gowin" in *Album* (London), nos. 5 and 6, 1970; "Photographs: Emmet Gowin" in *Aperture* (Rochester, New York), no. 2, 1971; "Emmet Gowin" in *Camera Mainichi* (Tokyo), October 1972.

*   *   *

Emmet Gowin's photographs are deceptively simple; many appear to be straightforward pictures of family life in a small town and others look casual—they are not. In them an intensely personal iconography is presented as a manifestation of universal experience. The mixture of life's basic elements, pregnancy, death, children, slaughter, unite into a finely tempered moral energy that cuts through the common scene.

Gowin's pictures of people and places in Danville, Virginia, are a head-on collision of the forthright with the mysterious which seems to say that this place, this person is both unique and universal. The cycles of life appear with ritualistic intensity heightened in many pictures by the use of vignetting.

Photographs of Edith, Gowin's wife, recur throughout his work. She seems at times to be the soul of his work, a symbolic center that ties all together. Her image fluctuates between a very real mother/housewife to an eternal feminine force. In these shifting roles she represents a paradox of the metaphysical in the physical and the timeless within constant change. In one of his best known pictures, "Edith, Danville, Virginia, 1971," she sits at the foot of their bed, one hand placed behind her head, one hand on her knee; a wooden horse sits in the window. The undulant, sculptural pose breaks into the severely horizontal lines of the bed, rugs and windows. The paradoxical suggestion of a typical artificial, showgirl pose is completely arrested by the stillness of the contemplative female presence in the simple room.

By comparison the European landscapes are lighter and more open. The textural complexity of the detail disperses the heavier ambiguous symbolism of the Danville pictures. Less autobiographical, the images still extol the riches of the earth. The subject matter, composition and the exquisite printing recall the work of Gowin's mentor, Frederick Sommer. Gowin's view has become more expansive and the tonal variations and print detail have become more delicate, marking a major stylistic change from his early moodier prints.

—Marianne Fulton

GRANT, Ken.

Nationality: British. **Born:** Liverpool, 5 June 1967. **Education:** Calday Grammar School, 1978-83. Studied photography, Wirral Metropolitan College, Wallasey, Merseyside, 1985-87, B.T.E.C. 1987; studied photography, West Surrey College of Art and Design, Farnham, Surrey, 1987-90, B.A. (Honours) 1990. **Career:** Part-time Lecturer in Photography, Wirral Metropolitan College, 1991-92, and since 1993; Lecturer in Photography, Dublin, 1993. **Recipient:** Arts Foundation Fellow in Photography, 1993-94; *Creative Review* magazine "Editorial Photography" nomination, 1994. **Address:** c/o 7 Speedwell Drive, Heswall, Merseyside L60 2SY, England.

Individual Exhibitions:

1991	The Open Eye Gallery, Liverpool
1992	*The Great Georges Project,* Liverpool
	Irish Gallery of Photography, Dublin
	Irish Life Centre, Dublin

St. Domingo Vale, Everton, **1989.** Photograph by Ken Grant.

Tallaght Arts Centre, Dublin
Limerick City Art Gallery

Selected Group Exhibitions:

1990	The Mall Galleries, London
1992	*Mai de la Photo,* Rheims, France
	Royal Liver Buildings, Liverpool
1993	Royal Photographic Society, Bath
1994	Open Eye Gallery, Liverpool

Collections:

The Victoria and Albert Museum, London.

Publications:

On GRANT: Articles—"The Mersey Beat" by Amanda Hopkinson in *The British Journal of Photography,* 2 December 1993; "Unguided Tours" by Graham Coster in *Reportage,* May 1994; "Editorial Photography, Creative Futures" in *Creative Review,* June 1994.

*

I worked through my early teens with my cabinet-maker father and our ever-changing colleagues. Through the eighties, work undertaken shifted from precision craft to general labour; Saturday mornings were for repairing shops after Friday night break-ins, with floor safes, wrenched from basements, away across roofs. I photographed the parts of the workshops we used and personalised—cupboards decorated with newsprint, playing cards around tables. I had seen few photographs of the labours we were involved in. Only the exceptions drew merit: E Chambre Hardman's Ark Royal on the Mersey; Lewis Hines workmen were elevated to a dignity remote from the weight of experience.

With such experience, and with regular work uncertain, I trained as a photographic technician, alongside redundant welders, electricians and taxi drivers—all of us new to a craft of chemistry and interpretation. I was encouraged in finding work relative to my own situation; Friedlanders factory valley convinced me of the impersonal nature of factory work; Raymond

Moores reminded me of temperamental caravan holidays on the Welsh seafront. My own experience was important, more than the generality of Spender's mass observation and less uncomfortable than Orwell's Wigan tea parties. I supported the work with small jobs and commissions, and constantly returning to manual work fuelled my concerns. In studying for a degree at Farnham, I found it natural to continue the work I had begun in Merseyside, and through family interest photographed the web of terraces and parkland that houses the Liverpool football ground.

Liverpool, as an illustration of post-industrial decline, is widely photographed. A history of casual labour has left generations naturally suspicious of a stranger's attention, so it has been to my advantage to work locally, producing work over months rather than hours. I enjoy the comfort of involvement and considering my position through photography. Nan Goldin, in her *Ballad of Sexual Dependency* argued, "this is our party—I'm involved and have every right to be here." My approach has involved using medium and large format cameras, imploring patience and commitment, allowing me to photograph with, rather than at people.

—Ken Grant

*   *   *

Ken Grant comes above all else from a sense of place and tradition. His grandfather was a cooper, his father is a joiner, and he enjoys helping in the building trade in his native Liverpool. Born little more than a mile from the city centre, Grant concentrates on working in the neighbourhood he knows best. After all, he says, "if you're unknown, you stick out like a sore thumb. To do the work I do, you have to be known and know the people there. I'm not out of context. I don't flash at them all the time." He doesn't ask questions either, not even of the guy with the impressive bruise on his neck, whom he never manages to snap twice with the same woman.

He remembers with discomfort when he started out, around 1987 and with a borrowed camera, only discovering too late when he'd taken a picture out of turn. "It is when everything just stops, and there's no way you're not made aware of it." He recalls with something akin to awe that Chris Killip, also working in Everton, ended up rolling entangled in the street with a passerby who took exception to the scene he was shooting. Given that at times Grant can end up photographing beachcombing cocklers alongside DSS workers keen on collecting the evidence to cut dole payments, or showing guys taking dope and strong ale as they mind their babies, doesn't this ever give him cause to pause even to consider whether to intervene. . . .? "You're asking me, and obviously I ask myself how much am I involved? Do I really care about these people? I think I am concerned, and there are certainly jobs I wouldn't take on." The example of documenting city housing for a Conservative corporation, whose commitment of the work he couldn't corroborate, is offered, before he added "At the same time I've got a hell of a frigging job with my own life and I'm not sure I'm doing so well at that."

There's a considerable amount of drinking and football that shows in Grant's documentation. Of Scottish Protestant extraction himself, he grew up with the jargon of the last remnants of the Orange Halls and Lodges, of references to Fenian estates and Paddies' pubs. Even *Songs of Praise* got switched off if it happened to be one of the Papist variety. While many of his images show the cultural relics of either side, the graffiti—like the lives—tells another story. It is really of far greater interest to learn who is using who—and what—than to worry overmuch about race and religion.

Gossip is a useful antidote to the boredom that results from endemic unemployment and poverty and much of that revolves around pubs and football. These have a gender division of their own at variance with the increased sharing of childcare. While the men play away, the women stay put in the pub of a Sunday afternoon with the booze and the kids. To judge from the photographic evidence there can be few more merry all-female gatherings than the latter and competing for the local club beats trying for the England team, if the expressions on the faces of the agonised contenders are any indicator.

While already expert at capturing a range of human emotion in his subjects, Grant regards himself as an emotionally committed participant. He uses the term "subjective documentary" to describe his work, taking it as axiomatic that every image reflects as much of his inner feelings as of the outside world. Combining sensitivity towards his subjects with familiarity with regard to location, he still admits "I have a problem getting the places I live in to look how I feel. In some instances, the streets are really bland, so it is harder to get my feelings across."

One way of overcoming such problems is through technique. Whether the initial gift of a Polaroid camera for his 12th birthday was decisive or not, Grant favours square images, often taken at a diamond angle. He also holds his square-format camera down, getting an almost child's-eye view, looking up at his subject from below. These are frequently set middle-distance with what Grant calls his "references" foregrounded rather than kept in the background. On one, this is the fellow's "inky," a tattoo on a jutting wrist; in another a woman's sprawled legs fronts an image of cigarette-filled boredom; in a third a hairy fist getting in the way of two pubbers beginning to converse with their hands.

Increasingly, however, Grant says "I'm starting to do stuff that's a lot more topographical, a lot more meditative." Given his working background, it is small wonder that he sees his photography as something highly crafted especially in the processing. Working with a 1960s Koni Omega Rapid, he plays with getting new angles, photographing into sunlight with maximum flare to achieve images worthy of the surreal film director David Lynch.

Having so far only travelled to Wales and Ireland, Grant still has a whole world beyond to discover, if he wants it. In the meantime the 1993 National Arts Foundation Award brought him a deserved £12,500 nearer towards subjectively documenting what he knows best: his own surroundings and how he feels about them.

—Amanda Hopkinson

GRČEVIĆ, Mladen.

Nationality: Croatian. **Born:** Zagreb, 8 October 1918. **Education:** Attended the University of Zagreb, 1937-42, B.L. in law 1942, and 1956-60, B.A. in art history 1960, M.A. in art history 1965. **Family:** Married Nada Suljak in 1943. **Career:** Instructor, School of Graphic Arts, Zagreb, 1946-52; also photographer, working with the magazine, *Yugoslavia*, Belgrade, 1949-64; Professor, Academy of Applied Arts, Zagreb, 1952-54. Freelance photographer and art historian, Zagreb, since 1954: worked for *Stern, Vogue* and *Graphis* magazines, 1968-71. Researcher in photographic history, for the University of Zagreb, 1960-65; Editorial Board Member for Photography, *Yugoslav Art Encyclopedia,* Zagreb, since 1984. **Recipient:** First Prize, Yugoslav Photo Competition, Liubliana, 1950; International Photo-Competition Award, Lucerne, 1951; Rollei Award, Vienna, 1953; First Prize, Yugoslav Photo Competition, Sarajevo, 1953; First Prize, I Salao Internacional de Arte Fotografica, Lisbon, 1956; First Prize, *The Sea* exhibition, Rijeka, 1958; Life Achievement Award, Yugoslav Federation of Photography, 1971; First Prize, International Book Fair, Moscow, 1975; Toso Dabac Award, Zagreb, 1975; First Prize, International Tourist Poster Competition, Manila, 1980. Master of Art Photography, Yugoslav Federation of Photography, 1954. Honorary Member, National Federation of Photographic Societies of France (FNSPF), 1955, and International Federation of Photographic Art (FIAP), 1967 (Member of the Art Commission, FIAP, since 1972). **Address:** Dvorničićeva 19, 41000 Zagreb, Croatia.

Individual Exhibitions:

1944   Salon Ulrich, Zagreb
1945   *Naša Istra,* Salon Ulrich, Zagreb
1948   *Dabac/Grčević/Szabo,* Salon Ulrich, Zagreb
1954   Galerie Yougoslave, Paris (travelled to the Yugoslav Tourist Office, London)
1956   Cairo Art Gallery (travelled to the Public Relations Department, Rangoon)
        From London to Hong Kong, Salon LIKUM, Zagreb (travelled to the Photo Club Gallery, Osijek, Croatia, 1957)
1970   *Quest for Man,* Art Gallery, Sisak, Croatia.

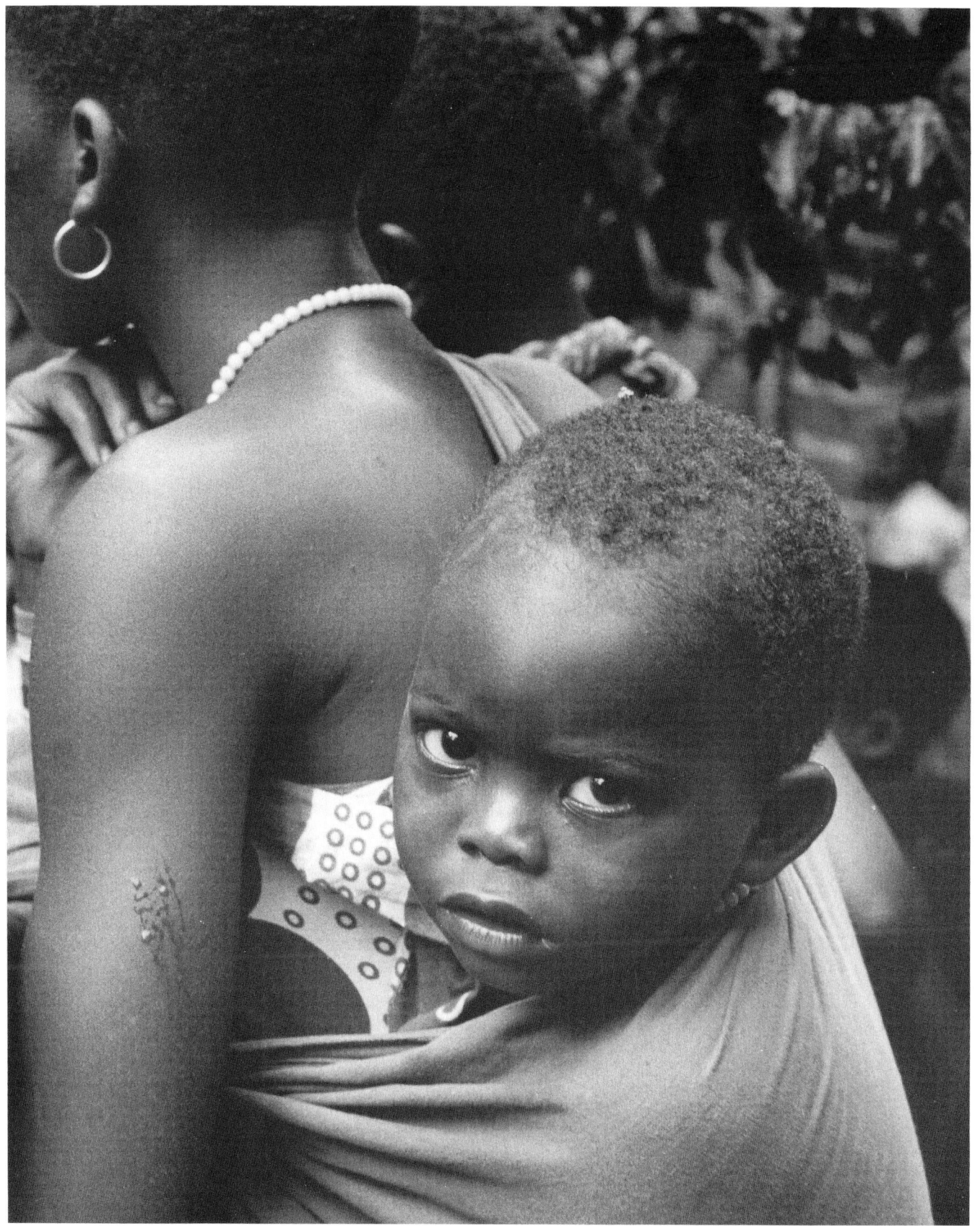

Kenya, **1977.** Photograph by Mladen Grčević.

Selected Group Exhibitions:

1951	*World Exhibition of Photography,* Lucerne
1952	*Photokina,* Cologne
	Swedish Master Competition, Stockholm
1953	*Marine Photography,* Mariners' Museum, Newport News, Virginia (travelled to the Smithsonian Institution, Washington, D.C.)
1954	*PSA International Exhibition,* Chicago
1964	*Was ist der Mensch, Stern* magazine travelling exhibition
1968	*Die Frau, Stern* magazine travelling exhibition
1970	*Asia,* at *Photokina,* Cologne
1973	*Unterwegs zum Paradies, Stern* magazine travelling exhibition
1977	*Die Kinder Dieser Welt, Stern* magazine travelling exhibition
1980	*The Nude in Art Photography,* Museum of Art, Zagreb
1993	*Croatian Photography Since 1950,* Museum of Modern Art, Zagreb
1993	*Picture Freedom,* Photographers' Gallery, London

Collections:

Arts and Crafts Museum, Zagreb; Permanent Collection of Photography, Havdrup, Denmark; Photographic Association of Bengal, Calcutta; The Mariners' Museum, Newport News, Virginia; Smithsonian Institution, Washington, D.C; Bibliothèque Nationale, Paris; New York Public Library, New York; Museum Ludwig, Köln; Photographers' Gallery, London; Museum of Modern Art, Zagreb.

Publications:

By GRČEVIĆ: Books—*Yougoslavie,* with text by L. Peillard, Paris 1955; *Dalmatien,* with text by K. Edschmid, Munich 1961; *Situla Art,* with text by J. Kastelic, Belgrade and New York 1965; *Icons from Macedonia,* with text by K. Balabanov, Belgrade 1969; *Gold and Silver of Zadar,* with text by M. Krleža, Zagreb 1971; *Sibenik,* with text by S. Grubišić, Zagreb 1971; *Poreč,* with text by Z. Crnja, Pazin, Yugoslavia 1975; *Early Croatian Heritage,* with text by S. Gunjača, Zagreb 1976; *Zadar,* with text by V. Cestarić, Zadar, Yugoslavia 1978; *The Shrine of Saint Simeon in Zadar,* with text by I. Petricioli, Zagreb 1983; *Optical Memories,* Zagreb 1988. **Articles**—"Grand Succès de la Photographie Francaise à Zagreb" in *Photo-Cinéma* (Paris), July 1955; "Za jednu univerzalnu povijest fotografije" in *Zivot umjetnosti* (Zagreb), no. 6, 1968; "Mladen Grčević," interview, in *Fotografie* (Leipzig), December 1975; "The Beginnings of Art Photography in Zagreb" in *Zagrebačka fotografija Almanac,* Zagreb 1978; "Die Anfänge der künstlerischen Amateurfotografie in Zagreb" in *Fotografie* (Leipzig), no. 7, 1980; "Soziale Tendenzen in der Zagreber Fotografie der dreissiger Jahre" in *Fotografie* (Leipzig), no. 11, 1981.

On GRČEVIĆ: Book—*Mladen Grčević* by Oto Bihalji-Merin, Belgrade 1973. **Articles**—"Photos de Mladen Grčević" by R. Andreani in *Photo-Ciné Revue* (Paris), November 1954; "Mladen Grčević" by G. Paterne in *Photo-Cinéma* (Paris), April 1955; "Un Maitre Photographe Expose au Caire" by R. Mosseri in *Progrès Egyptien* (Cairo), May 1956; "Mladen Grčević" by Z. Jeremić in *Foto-Kino Revija* (Belgrade), January 1972; "In Search of Man" by B. Aleksić in *Review* (Belgrade), October 1974; "Nagrada jugoslavenskom turističkom plakatu" by F. Marinković in *Čovjek i prostor* (Zagreb), December 1980; "Optička sjećanja Mladen Grčevića" by R. Ivančević in *Zivot Umjetnosti* (Zagreb) No 45-46, 1989; "Optični Spomini" by I Maroević in *Sinteza* (Ljubljana), October 1990; "Die optischen Erinnerungen eines Livefotografen" by A. Seferović in *Fotografie* (Leipzig), January 1991.

*

The first period of my photographic activity belonged to the sphere of pictorial photography. It was a time of learning, of gaining the security and discipline of the camera, of mastering the composition and searching for order in the chaotic picture of the world. It culminated in one-man shows in London and Paris in 1954.

A considerable change occurred during my journey to Africa, South Asia, and the Far East in 1955-56. Fascinated, and at the same time shocked, by the drama and dynamics of life among a tumult of races and religions, I spontaneously arrived at a particular variant of *Life* photography, with an accent on humanity and social criticism. In my quest for man in this immense and unknown vastness, I found love and hatred, self-contentment and wisdom, fatalism and loneliness. Taking photographs, I was no longer attracted by the exotic but by the truth behind the visible.

I am still a passionate traveller. My camera does not cease to capture the contrasts of life equally in Mexico or in Brazil as in Kenya and Japan. I still inquisitively penetrate the human and social dimensions, as well as the dimension of time—especially in contact with ancient cultures, where the time-distance becomes more impressive than the terrestrial one. These trips into time brought me into contact with the historical course of art. Being both a photographer and an art historian, I started to illustrate and design books dealing with the art of several epochs. I tried to create a synthesis of a strictly scientific approach with the personal view of a photographer.

There is one sphere more, one that I have repeatedly entered during the 40 years of my work as a photographer: that of experimental photography. In 1965 I finally published some interesting results of photographic multiplication. For a *Life* photographer it would have been an unexpected digression, but in my case I believe it was the result of an unconscious necessity to transcend the boundaries of the natural world and to penetrate the trans-human world of form, an expanded and still unknown multi-dimensional space.

Nevertheless, I did not change my views on "creative" photography. Out of the complex and broad spectrum of contemporary photography, I still have the deepest appreciation for that work that is directed towards the human being and the complicated problems of his existence. That attitude makes for a deeply engaged photography that is still primarily searching for the truth behind the visible.

—Mladen Grčević

*   *   *

If it is true that contemporary photography has its roots in life and is fed by life, then that might just be the right starting point for viewing and understanding the photographic work of Mladen Grčević. For years Grčević recorded with his camera the story of human life—from its most primitive manifestations to its most civilized—in different parts of the globe.

The first phase of his work however, was within the traditions of the so-called "Zagreb School of Photography," which was, at that time, internationally known for its specific style and typical national content. With his photographs in this manner—photographs of the land, its life and people— Grčević gained a considerable reputation in his native country.

In the early 1950s Grčević was the first and only photographer among the group of outstanding Yugoslav modern artists who began to exhibit in Paris. His one-man show there in 1954 brought him invitations for other exhibitions in London, Cairo and Rangoon, as well as offers from well-known publishing houses and photographic magazines. His intense photographic activity in Paris also involved a resolute break with tradition.

In 1955 Grčević undertook a long journey to remote parts of the Middle and Far East. That journey was the beginning of a new—and, in my opinion, the most significant—phase in his photographic career. Confronted with life in uncommon and unexpected manifestations in the very cradle of mankind, he tried to find adequate means of photographic expression, and spontaneously came to what might be called a "meditative verism." There is some social criticism in these striking pictures, but there is still more of humanity and profound sympathy. When he focused on common people while at work, in the street, or contemplating in temples, he was successful in capturing expressions not only of bitterness and fatality, but also of serenity, dignity, and nobility. In these pictures the inner psychological reality is more important than any visual or social one: they make one think. It is obvious now that Grčević's 1955 photographs signalled a modern concept of documentary, the "truth" of which was confirmed by public response when these pictures appeared in contemporary publications or were shown in the travelling exhibitions organized by *Stern* magazine.

Thereafter Grčević developed a more public career, presenting his photographs in numerous magazines and illustrating more than 100 books in nine different countries. As well, he has become a complete maker of books—as creator of the concept, author, photographer, and graphic designer. If one had to select the most successful work of this kind, it would have to be his photographic interpretation of prehistoric *Situla Art,* published in Belgrade and New York in 1965, which was nominated by the *New York Times* as one of the year's best art books.

—Nada Grčević

GREGORY, Joy.

Nationality: British. **Born:** Bicester, Oxfordshire, 7 November 1959. **Education:** Studied foundation art, Buckinghamshire College of Higher Education, 1980-81; studied communication art and design, Manchester Polytechnic, 1981-84, B.A. (Honours) 1984; studied photography, Royal College of Art, 1984-86, M.A. (RCA) 1986. Member of the *Spectrum Women's Photo Festival* Steering Group, 1987-89; Administrator/Co-ordinator, North Paddington Community Darkroom, 1987-90; Visiting Lecturer, Staffordshire Polytechnic, 1987-93, and Senior Lecturer, 1989-91; *Photofusion* Education Co-ordinator, 1991-93; *Creating the Subject* Exhibition Group Co-ordinator, 1992; *Autograph Open Show* Selection Panel Member, 1992; ACGB Photography Advisor, since 1993. **Recipient:** Princess of Wales Scholarship, 1984-86; RCA Minor Travel Award, 1985; Chestertons Award, 1986; 3M Award, 1986. **Agent:** Zelda Cheatle Gallery, Cecil Court, London WC2, England. **Address:** 34 Brocket House, Union Road, London SW8 2RE, England.

Individual Exhibition:

1988   *Silent Life,* Great Smith Street Library, London

Selected Group Exhibitions:

1983   *Young Northern Contemporaries,* Whitworth Gallery,
                 Manchester
1988   *Women and Space,* The Tabernacle, London
1989   *The Nude,* The Pride Gallery, London
                 Secret Spaces: Interiors and Still Life, The Pride Gallery,
                 London
                 Compelling Eye, Henry Moore Gallery, London
1990   *Autoportraits,* Camerawork, London
                 Ecstatic Antibodies, Impressions Gallery, York (and tour,
                 1990-93)
1991   *The Bottom Drawer,* The Small Mansion Gallery, London (and
                 tour, 1991-93)
                 Treading a Fine Line, Zelda Cheatle Gallery, London (travelled
                 to The Focal Point, Southend)
                 The 6th International Art Fair, London Olympia, Earls Court
                 The Honeymoon Project, Ikon Gallery, Birmingham (travelled
                 to Barcelona, Spain, 1992)
                 Who Do You Take Me For, Institute of Modern Art, Brisbane,
                 Australia (and tour, 1992-93)
1993   *Rencontres au Noir,* at *Rencontres Internationales de la
                 Photographie,* Arles, France

Collections:

Queensland Art Gallery, Brisbane, Australia.

Publications:

On GREGORY: Articles—in *Critical Decade,* 1992; in *Creative Review,* 1993. **Film**—*The Other Observers,* video, 1987.

*

I use photography to depict my life, my perceptions and experiences. Each piece is a window to a phase of my life. Over the last five years, my work has been in the area of self-identity, which has inevitably involved a lot of work around self-portraiture. For me, self-portraiture is looking for your back which is always hidden in the variety of fronts that the human face offers. It is the most delicate and compromising confrontation. A genre inexhaustible in its variations. It may be shaped from psychological symbols, the tradition of the cathartic performance, a study of different concepts of the nude and naked, the list is endless. It also illustrates phases of great personal development, understanding, acceptance and appreciation of the self and others.

Since 1994 I have been researching and reflecting on notions of beauty and wish to take my work into the domain of body image. I plan to look at body size and shape, ageing while challenging commonly held concepts of beauty. My interest in ideologies of beauty stem from my past interest in fashion photography and women's magazines. Fashion photography is absent in its call for women to cultivate their independence. It is presented as a contradiction, as freedom is laced with notions of beauty resulting in self-hatred, physical obsession, terror of ageing and dread of loss of control. It appears that women are increasingly willing to regard their bodies as photographic images which are unpublishable, invisible and shameful until retouched at the hands of a surgeon.

—Joy Gregory

*   *   *

Joy Gregory is an immensely thoughtful photographer. Her photographs, in turn, afford considerable food for thought. Her fine art training imbues her work with an immense sensitivity to the subtleties of colour, particularly in the blues and yellows of her flower prints made according to early techniques. Her careful consideration of what she does, the application of the most appropriate materials and processes across a spectrum of innovative series of images, makes her a serious but not a solemn artist. In her words: "I enjoy *all* the photography I do. It doesn't matter if it's food, fashion, interiors or portraits. I even created a group called *Love* for the magazine *I-D.* Not that they paid. Ever noticed how the more glamorous the outlet the less they pay you?."

Joy Gregory's commitment to her work is such that not only does she ride out the financial vicissitudes, she at times appears to court them. Alongside the work for which she receives commissions, awards, accolades and sales, she dedicates a part of her time to scantily-funded community projects and teaching posts. She also serves in an advisory capacity for such organisations as the Arts Council of England and on the management committees of both the British festivals of women photographers (*Spectrum* in 1988 and *Signals* in 1994) at a time when all cultural funds are under constant attack and cutback. Her political consciousness as a black woman in a racist society is explicit, there as a continuum integrated in both her choice of subject and as platforms for her work. She is both a member of *Autograph* (the association of black photographers, for whom she has served as a selection panel member and whose magazine has profiled her work) and has shown at the *Rencontres au Noir* at the 1993 Arles photo-festival.

Otherwise, the main outlets for her own work are principally in galleries, where sequences on subjects as divergent as *Ecstatic Antibodies* (on HIV and AIDs, 1990-93, which travelled England and France). This has subsequently given rise to a peer education project among fifteen and sixteen-year-olds on the same theme, which employs posters and videos to pass warning messages in images and five languages between the youth of Europe. Similarly, her series on the theme of beauty, showing dress and fashion uninhabited by any human body, has been the springboard for another called *Real Life,* an uncynical examination of the myths we tell ourselves to justify our prejudices and vindicate our apportioning of blame.

By contrast, there is the genuine innocence with which Joy Gregory dismantles traditional notions of the pose and the portrait in her documentation of the nude. Often working through self-portraiture, she asserts: "I realise I'm now looking for my own identity. I used to hate catching sight of myself in mirrors, convinced of my ugliness. I was always the last person chosen as a dancing partner so of course I thought I was the most hideous girl in the

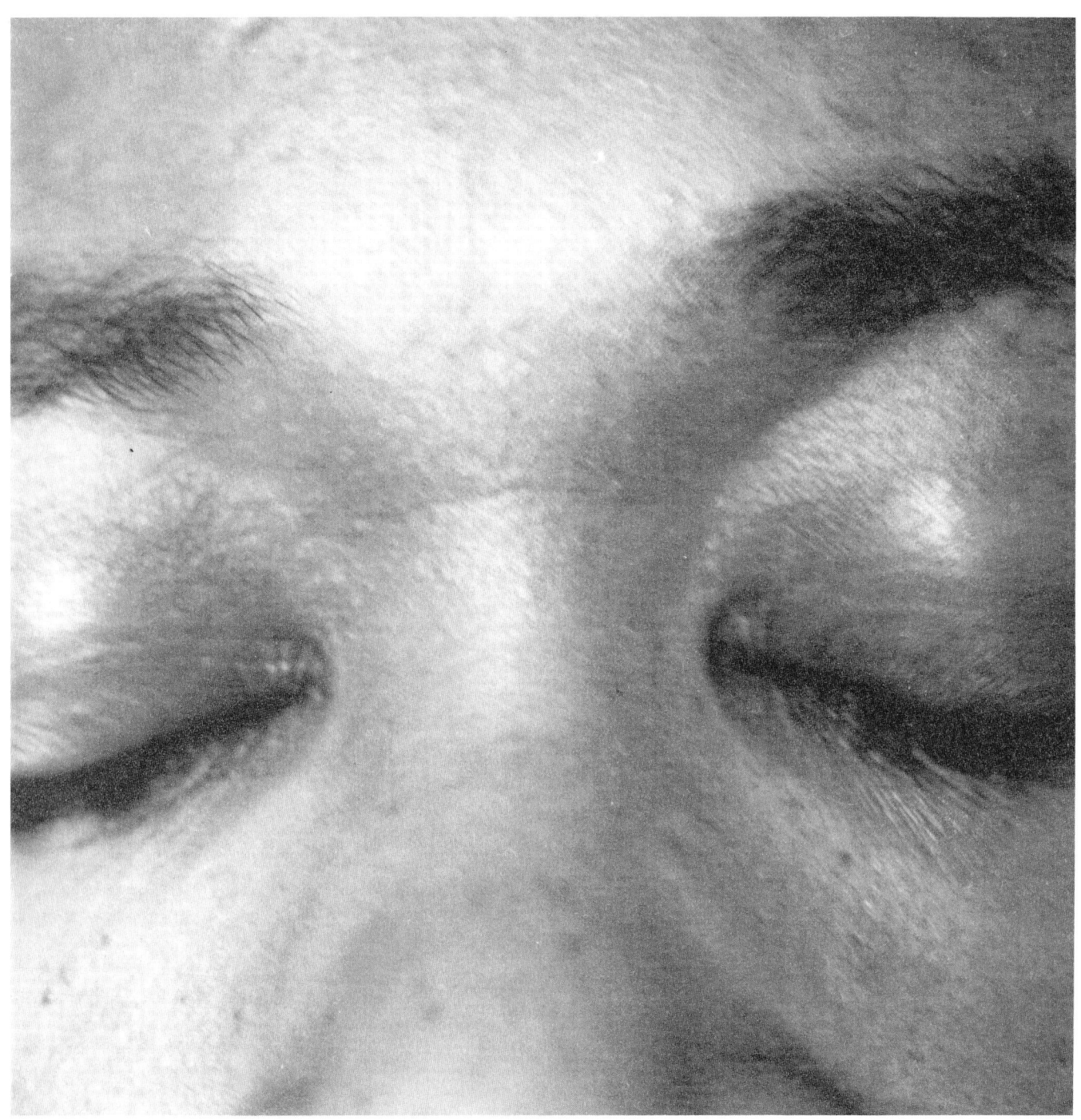

Autoportrait II, **1990.** Photograph by Joy Gregory.

school.'' Now she's less concerned with formal concepts of beauty and ''more concerned with seeing all around myself.'' This desire to get beyond and behind is part of her overall practice of stripping away preconceptions and consensus definitions. If beauty is in the eye of the beholder so, palpably, is photography and the photographer is free to break with standard practice in investigating the body's form of changing and ageing. So far Joy Gregory's autoportraiture has been backview and backlit—so often it is difficult for a photographer to face the other side of the camera!

—Amanda Hopkinson

GRIFFIN, Brian.

Nationality: British. **Born:** Birmingham, 13 April 1948. **Education:** Attended Halesowen Technical School, Worcestershire, 1959-64, O.N.C. in mechanical engineering 1968; Dudley College of Further Education, Worcestershire, 1964-69; studied photography at the Manchester Polytechnic, 1969-72, Dip.Photog. 1972. **Family:** Married Frances Newman in 1980. Worked as estimating engineer for British Steel Corporation, Birmingham, 1966-69.

Career: Freelance photographer, working for British Airways, Rolls Royce, Lloyds Bank, British Rail, Barclays Bank, British Leyland, Olivetti, Smirnoff Vodka, Hewlett Packard, *Vogue, Harpers and Queen, Tatler, Rolling Stone, Life, Sunday Times Magazine,* and the pop musicians Kate Bush, Elvis Costello, Frankie Goes to Hollywood, etc., London, since 1972: established Brian Griffin Studio, Rotherhithe, 1980. Granted Freedom of the City of Arles, 1987. **Address:** (studio) 121/123 Rotherhithe Street, Rotherhithe, London SE16 4NF, England.

Individual Exhibitions:

1978	*Portrait of Our Time,* The Photographers' Gallery, London
1980	*1979,* Photogallery, St. Leonard's-on-Sea, Sussex
1981	*Rock n' Roll and The Office,* Contrasts Gallery, London
1982	Galerie Viviane Esders, Paris
1983	Savile Club, London
	Auras, Olympus Gallery, London
	Manchester Polytechnic, Lancashire
1984	Olympus Gallery, Tokyo
1986	The Photographers' Gallery, London
1989	*Work,* National Portrait Gallery, London
1992	*Beyond The Portrait,* City Museum and Art Gallery, Derby

Selected Group Exhibitions:

1975	*Young British Photographers,* Museum of Modern Art, Oxford
1979	*Three Perspectives on Photography,* Hayward Gallery, London
1981	*Half a Dozen Photographers,* Stafford Art Gallery, England
1982	*Lichtbildnisse: Das Porträt in der Fotografie,* Rheinisches Landesmuseum, Bonn
1983	*London at Night,* The Photographers' Gallery, London (toured Britain)
1984	*Razzle Dazzle Pop,* Institute of Contemporary Arts, London
1985	*Human Interest,* Cornerhouse Gallery, Manchester, Lancashire
1986	*British Contemporary Photography,* at the *Foto Fest,* Houston, Texas
1987	*Cite Des Photographes,* Arles
1988	*Towards a Bigger Picture,* Victoria and Albert Muesum, London
1989	*150 Years of Photography,* Prague
1991	*Beyond Japan,* Barbican, London

Collections:

Victoria and Albert Museum, London; Arts Council of Great Britain, London; British Council, London; Stills Gallery, Edinburgh; City Museum, Braga, Portugal; Museum Fokwang, Essen, Germany; National Portrait Gallery, London.

Publications:

By GRIFFIN: Books—*Brian Griffin: Copyright 1978,* London 1978; *Power,* London 1981, 1984; *''Y,''* London 1983; *Auras,* London 1983; *Open: Twenty-one Photographs by Brian Griffin,* London 1986; *Portraits,* London 1987; *Work,* London 1988.

On GRIFFIN: Books—*Exploring Photography* by Bryn Campbell, London 1979; *Three Perspectives on Photography,* exhibition catalogue, by Paul Hill, Angela Kelly and John Tagg, London 1979; *Lichtbildnisse: Das Porträt in der Fotografie,* edited by Klaus Honnef, Cologne 1982; *Nuova Fotografia Inglese,* edited by Giovanni Chiaramonte, Milan 1984. **Article**—by Clive Lancaster in *British Journal of Photography Annual 1980,* London 1979.

*

My concerns in photography at present lie in the symbolic photographic realization of the emotional and political tensions that have arisen in my world and country today.

—Brian Griffin

*   *   *

Photographers draw their inspiration from a variety of sources—some from nature, others from the beauty of men and women, still others from chunks of rocks or wood. Brian Griffin will have none of these. His life was always firmly rooted in the city and its inhabitants.

Born into an industrial community near Birmingham, Griffin started his adult life as a minor executive in an engineering firm. Not long after he had started in that career he suddenly decided to switch to photography. Three years' course at the Manchester Polytechnic gave him a start, but not much else. He did there, he says, some uninteresting fashion and polished a number of still-life tables. In 1972, as a mature 25 year old, he found himself pounding the streets of London in search of work. It took him four months to find. His industrial background paid off, for his first assignment—and the beginning of his distinctive style—was a commission to photograph a business tycoon for the magazine *Management Today.* His strongly designed, simple but original image caught the eye of his editors, and a new career was born.

During the eighties Griffin was known mainly for these politically biased, cold, stilted, disrespectful portraits of a number of industrialists, directors and politicians. These photos were always very graphic, with large areas of black and white, and most of them based on an unusual, often startling idea. A little later he consolidated his style with a series of rock 'n' roll personalities, mainly for *The Rolling Stone.* With both groups his portrayal, he insists, came only from his own strong opinions and tendencies. He feels that his photographs are never superficial, but always committed and involved, springing from personal beliefs and also from intuition. In fact, he acts, in his characterization of the sitters, from instantaneous impression. This—the on-the-spot impression rather than a pre-sitting study—gives him his idea for the image, which he proceeds to create by careful arrangement of props and lights. Although he considers himself a ''straight'' photographer, Griffin does not hesitate to prearrange and fabricate his pictures almost entirely.

After his involvement with portraiture, which lasted several years, he has allowed his portrait sessions to become far less frequent; in fact, he does not want to do any more portraits of tycoons. He feels that this phase of his work is now thoroughly exhausted. Now, the majority of his work comes from advertising, which, like his portraiture, has come initially from his industrial beginnings. Most of his early advertising was based on industry and on the use of ''high finance'' figureheads. During the late eighties and early nineties Brian Griffin found his interests expanding into film, music, poetry and performance art. This crystalised into an ambition to make his own films utilising the experience he had gained in the making of TV commercials and combining his experiments with other art forms. Although he had exhibitions of photographs at The National Portrait Gallery and in Arles in 1987, film became his major preoccupation and his first short film, *Claustrophomia,* was submitted at the Berlin Film Festival in the winter of 1994/95.

—Jorge Lewinski

GRIGNANI, Franco.

Nationality: Italian. **Born:** Pieve Porto Morone, Pavia, 4 February 1908. **Education:** the Istituto Tecnico and Liceo Scientifico, Pavia; studied at the Polytechnic of Architecture, Turin, 1933, but never practised as an architect; mainly self-taught in photography. **Military Service:** Served as a Lieutenant in the Italian Army Artillery, 1939-43. **Family:** Married Jeanne Michot in 1942; daughters: Daniela and Manuela. **Career:** Freelance painter, designer, graphic artist and photographer, Milan, since 1932: Art Director for Alfieri and Lacroix, printers, and *Bellezza d'Italia* magazine, Milan, 1948-64. Art Director, *Pubblicità in Italia* editions, Milan, since 1954. Participated in the second Futurist movement, Milan, in the 1930s; Founder Member, Gruppo

Exhibition Design, Milan, 1969. **Recipient:** Grand Prize, *9th Triennale,* Milan, 1951; Gold Medal for Publicity/Advertising, Milan, 1954; Gold Medal, *Triennale,* Milan, 1957; Silver Lion Award, Il Ponte photographic group, Venice, 1962; Gold Medal, Centro Culturale G. Puecher, Milan, 1974. Member, Alliance Graphique Internationale, 1951; Honorary Member, Society of Typographic Arts, Chicago, 1967. **Address:** Via Bianca di Savoia 7, 20122 Milan, Italy.

Individual Exhibitions:

1958	*Experiments in Abstract Photography,* Liberia Salto, Milan
	Photographs for Graphic Design, Libreria Comunale, Milan
	Experiments in Dissolving View, Libreria Salto, Milan
1960	*Experiments in Visual Tension,* Libreria Salto, Milan
	Experimental Photographics, Normandy House STA Gallery, Chicago
1967	*18 Years of Creative Research,* Centro Culturale Pirelli, Milan
1970	500 D Gallery, Chicago
1975	*Methodology of Vision,* Museo Rotonda Besana, Milan (retrospective)
1977	*Experimental Paintings and Photographs,* Museo de Bellas Artes, Caracas (retrospective)
1979	*Experimental Paintings and Photographs,* Salone Comunale, Reggio Emilia, Italy (retrospective)
1980	*Projection of 79 Slides,* at the *Congress of the Alliance Graphique Internationale,* Munich
1981	*Experimental and Graphic Photography,* Galleria Flaviana, Locarno, Switzerland
	Lorenzelli Arte, Milan
1983	*151 Photo-graphies,* Palestra Civica di Pieve Porto Morone, Paiva, Italy
1984	*Type nel filtro ottico,* Galleria Quanta, Milan
1985	*In Valori del segno,* Galleria Municipale di La Salle, Aosta, Italy
	Dai moires alle strutture iperboliche, Galleria Il Salotto, Como, Italy

Selected Group Exhibitions:

1962	*Gruppo Il Ponte,* at the *1st National Gold Lion Exhibition,* Venice
1963	*2nd Competition for Black and White Photography,* Bollate, Milan
1970	*Creative Photography,* Centro Gamma, Trieste
1972	*Technology Versus Man,* Salone Arengario, Milan
1977	*Between Painting and Photography,* Acireale, Sicily
1978	*Italian Photographers,* Musée Réattu, Arles, France
1980	*Cine-Graphia: La Linea in Movimento,* Galleria Flaviana, Locarno, Switzerland
1983	*La Sperimentazione Fotografico in Italia 1930-70,* Galleria d'Arte Moderna, Bologna, Italy
1985	*Experimental Italian Photography,* Montclair State College, New Jersey
1986	*L'Ideogramma universale,* Galleria Il Segno, Turin

Collections:

Museum of Modern Art, New York; Stedelijk Museum, Amsterdam; Museum of Modern Art, Warsaw; Victoria and Albert Museum, London.

Publications:

By GRIGNANI: Book—*Franco Grignani: Art and Graphic,* edited by Willy Rotzler, Zurich 1983. **Articles**—"Photographie et Graphique" in *Camera* (Lucerne), June 1957; "Concerto in MI b1" in *Linea Grafica* (Milan), May/June 1963; "La Fotografia Grafica" in special issue of *Pubblirama Italiano* (Milan), 1963; "Franco Grignani" in *Graphis* (Zurich), no. 108, 1963.

On GRIGNANI: Books—*Fotografia* by Ermanno Scopinich, Milan 1943; *Fotografi Italiana,* Milan 1953; *Nuova Fotografia Italiana* by Giuseppe Turroni, Milan 1959; *Photo-Graphism International* by Tobias M. Bartel, Munich 1965; *Optical Illusions and the Visual Arts* by Ronald G. Carraher, New York and London 1966; *Franco Grignani: Graphic Designer in Europe,* Tokyo 1971; *Franco Grignani: Arte come Sperimentazione e Metodo,* Rome 1974; *Una Metodologia della Visione* by Giulio Carlo Argan and Guido Montana, Milan 1975; *Franco Grignani: El Sentido de una Larga Busqueda* by Giulio Carlo Argan, Caracas 1977; *70 Anni di Fotografia in Italia* by Italo Zannier, Modena, Italy 1978; *Franco Grignani: Il Segno come Matrice, Il Fenomeno come Variabilita Analitica* by Giuseppe Turroni, Milan 1978; *Mostra Antologica di Franco Grignani,* exhibition catalogue, by Bruno D'Amore and Giuseppe Berti, Reggio Emilia, Italy 1979; *Venezia '79: La Fotografia,* Milan and New York 1979; *Cine-Graphia: La Linea in Movimento,* exhibition catalogue, by Giuliana Scimé, Locarno, Switzerland 1980; *La Sperimentazione Fotografica in Italia 1930/1970,* exhibition catalogue, with text by Carlo Gentili, Bologna, Italy 1983. **Articles**—"Franco Grignani" in *Idea* (Tokyo), June 1961; "Franco Grignani, ricerca pura" by Giovanni Brunazzi in *Graphicus* (Turin), July/August 1967; "Franco Grignani and His Experimental Graphics" by Katzumie Masaru in *Graphic Design* (Tokyo), no. 28, 1967; "Franco Grignani and His Characteristic Graphic Style" by Raimund Hrabak in *Novum Gebrauchsgraphik* (Munich), February 1972; "Franco Grignani: A Methodology of Vision" by Stanley Mason in *Graphis* (Zurich), vol. 180, 1976; "Il Movimento" by Giuliana Scimé in *Il Diaframma* (Milan), October/November 1980; "Subpercezioni 1949-52 di Franco Grignani" by Arturo Carlo Quintavalle in *Enciclopedia Practica per Fotografare,* Milan 1981.

*

I have long thought that graphic design, though maintaining its essential character as a "service" to visual communication, must be supported by a wide range of experimental experiences from which one can attain the desired freedom from the routine of daily activities. Urgency conditioning quality; thematic limitations dwarfing creativity; certain style coherences—all combine to fetter the graphic designer's individual character.

I have done my best to oppose such external conditioning, and tried to widen the range of my own activities, concentrating on major experimental work that often overlaps into scientific fields such as psychology and physics. With the influence and adaptation of these scientific resources, graphic design can find its own evolution in new ways of expression. My tendency to experiment—and more especially to borrow from various scientific disciplines—probably comes from my having studied architecture. My experimental work isn't restricted merely to a mathematical framework; I have, for instance, worked with optical distortion and structural tension.

The human eye "sees" through emotion and suggestion; therefore, simple geometry and balanced composition don't provide the necessary stress for triggering off a reaction in the human eye. Advertisements are seen mostly side-by-side with other advertisements, and this proximity calls for an expression of physical autonomy (by "autonomy" I mean a traumatic value that instantly catches the viewer's eye, making him feel uneasy, perceiving the irregularity caused by tension).

Graphic design is nowadays the chief means by which cultural change is disseminated, because it can be mechanically reproduced. Every day we browse through a newspaper; our eyes receive a sequence of images from posters; we are constantly and unconsciously absorbing messages. It is evident that the graphic designer is a fundamental power in the modern world: he pours culture out onto the streets; he distributes culture to ordinary people via our mass communications.

My experimental research is of different kinds:

The flou period: My research was devoted to creating indefinite images or signs, intended to stimulate observation and creativity. This study, afterwards, included incomplete images (by means of photographic cuts) whose informational content was a stimulant to thought.

Research on distortions: The reality of an image is optically altered in order to compete with the logic imposed by the human eye. An attentive eye will absorb new visual discoveries beyond the rules of logic, when shapes are anthropomorphous, free from geometric limitations, free from any man-made structure. The result is one of visual trauma, due to the dynamics and individuality imposed on what is frequently an otherwise orderly geometric space. After distortions I turned—as a natural development of these studies—to a period of *tension in shapes and space.*

The breaking-up of the "even-ness" of a space brings about tensions that are more vividly experienced because of the physical uneasiness they create and the consequent process of re-orientation they call for, while—ultimately—creating a stimulus towards the completion of the proposed image. All these are fundamental phenomena of visual communication.

Nevertheless, we can say that even a human expression, bodily posture or gesture can create tension. Their power to create tension is equal to the effects caused by a certain space, or imbalance in tonal or color quantities, or by spoken or non-vocalized words.

Visual induction: by which I mean stimulus, concentration and absorption. Good examples are: any circular shape; shapes based on a radical-stressed balance; shapes having a focalizing, compelling core.

Recently I began to concentrate on art: that is, painting. The borderline, however, between graphic design and painting is rather blurred. But, because of the absence of any restraint, painting gives me the illusion of a wide-ranging freedom.

I have always been interested in photography, especially as an element of graphic design (so-called "vanguard photography"). Photography must not be simply good documentation, even poetic documentation. It must intrigue through the use of light, chemistry, etc. In my work there is little drawing. What drawing exists has always been modified through photography or optical equipment to make it express a different sort of sign.

Currently, I am involved in research on periodical images (that is, the creation of an organized structure by repeating a basic shape or sign, mostly a very simple one). The result is an altered geometry, usually computer-programmed to create a multi-directional spreading of the image. The observer is thus unconsciously compelled to re-coordinate the perspective distortions and finally to become involved in visual communication.

During the last few years much has been said about visual communication: human nature tends to seek solutions, discover the unknown, ask why things are as they are. Communication is not simply "seeing." Appearances in the visual world that are already filed in one's experience are uninteresting. The task of the graphic designer is not merely to stick printed texts on cardboard; he must attempt new and individual graphic experiments, since these are the "vital humus" from which he can draw those elements that will make his message a valid and lasting one.

—Franco Grignani

*   *   *

Italian photography, especially in the first decades of the century, was led astray by the attractions of "pictorialism" with all of its attendant *kitsch,* and only began to break free in the 1940s with the decline in power of the Fascist regime, a regime that had forced many people into a photography of evasion, which had, in effect, stifled any opportunity for a genuine photo-journalism. There were, however, some who even during that period had begun to make valuable contacts with European cultural movements, with countries where photography had long since assumed a specific role of its own as an autonomous medium of expression, particularly among the *avant-garde.* In fact, it was a group of architects, designers, illustrators, painters—artists quite outside the world of professional, or even of amateur, photography—who recognized that photography could allow them a new visual analysis of reality and space and who created a movement which has had a profound influence on the work of many creative artists in architecture and design. By the 1930s the rhetorical message of Second Futurism, though it had stimulated photographers such as Tato, Bertieri and Wulz for almost 20 years after the explosive "photo-dynamic" phenomenon of the Bragaglia brothers, was becoming exhausted—yet, at the same time, this group of architects and designers (from Pagano to Steiner, from Peressuti to Comencini) was organizing itself around the editorial offices of Gio Ponti's journal *Domus,* which from then on became an important reference point for photography as well. Working in the group at that time were Luigi Veronesi, who had already experimented with abstract photography in 1928, and Antonio Boggeri, whose exciting photographic experiments were mirrored in the advertisements he was then producing. It was in this context that Franco Grignani took up photography in 1930.

Grignani came to photography with a compelling curiosity about everything that this medium of expression would allow him to reveal about that mysterious reality that he envisaged as beyond visible appearances and the conventions of the traditional picture. And, ever since his first experiments, Grignani has been exploring this unknown "landscape," which exists in a dimension into which photography allows him to penetrate, to visualize, with a "mechanical" precision that has become the hallmark of his style—just as it was of the severe experiments of the Bauhaus, at the beginning a cultural reference point for Grignani as were the theories of the *Gestalt.*

"I knew all about photography," Grignani has written, "but the lens gave me only the ordinary picture; what I was looking for then was more disparate media—moving lenses, sheets of glass, condensers, prisms, water, oil"—any medium, in other words, that would lead him to a "transfiguration" of ordinary, objective reality. But his photographic creativity was also controlled by a remarkable scientific strictness, something almost compulsive.

It has characterized all of his work. "His research," writes G.C. Argan, "aims essentially at pinpointing the thought processes that develop not beyond perception but within it. . . . ''

The imaginary, the invisible, the fantastic are expressed in photographic rectangles that Grignani constructs with a geometrical precision by means of rhythms that are suggested to him primarily on the philosophical, conceptual level by those "existential problems of our technological civilization which are beyond the physical limits of the human eye."

Through a progression of optical-visual experiments, Grignani has discovered the "importance of reality changed through the internal tensions of the *distortion, the flux,* of pictures"; it is a graphic art ("multiple writing," as D'Amore puts it) of what is outside our immediate capacity to perceive but the cryptic language of which is revealed by photography, a language in which the *symbol* emerges and is freed from the physical object that gives rise to it, becoming itself the sole subject of the picture.

His optical research of the 1960s bears a certain resemblance to that of Vasarely and Bridget Riley, but it originates from studies in 1949-52 of *subperception* ("analysis of total space through the analysis of lateral space") and of *distortion,* obtained from an interpretation of the "specular surfaces of buildings, of metals, of the paintwork of car bodies"—but also against "the mechanicity of typography." He followed this work with research in 1959 on "permutation," derived from experiments on moire, whose reticular systems he is now studying, and he also spent some time, in 1967-68, on the analysis of structures described as "fluctuating," "diachronic," "radial" and "periodic," these last being almost identifiable with the work of others on the cinematographic photogram. After his studies in 1969 of "psychoplastic" and "isoplastic," which are "volumetries to be read mentally, experienced in a time too swift for the human eye," and his studies in 1975 on "concealed diagonals," Franco Grignani is at present carrying out increasingly significant research on the concept of "space," which he says "is eternally in equilibrium between the abstract and the concrete"—as indeed his own photographs regularly tend to demonstrate.

—Italo Zannier

GROEBLI, René.

Nationality: Swiss. **Born:** Zurich, 9 October 1927. **Education:** Attended elementary and high schools in Zurich, until 1942; studied photography, under Hans Finsler, Kunstgewerbeschule, Zurich, 1945. **Family:** Married Rita Dürmüller in 1951. **Career:** Apprenticed to documentary filmmakers Central Film and Gloria Film, Zurich, 1945-48. Freelance photographer, since 1949; stringer for *Life* magazine, Zurich, 1949-51; with Black Star Agency, London, 1951-53, also worked for *Picture Post, Time, Life, Photography,* etc., 1951-54; concentrated on color, working as freelance advertising and industrial photographer, Zurich, since 1953; established Studio Groebli and Partner AG, Zurich, 1955. **Agent:** Michèle Auer, 10 Rue du Couchant, CH. 1248, Hermance, GE.

Individual Exhibitions:

| 1949 | Anliker keller, Berne |
| 1954 | Galerie 16, Zurich |

From the series *Magie du Rail*, 1949. Photograph ©René Groebli.

1966	Galerie 58, Rapperswil, Switzerland
1978	*New York,* Portfolio Gallery, Lausanne, Switzerland
	Fantasies, Images Gallery, New York
	New York, at *Rencontres Internationales de la Photographie,* Arles France
1979	*Fantasies,* Neufeld Galerie, St. Gall, Switzerland
	Fantasies, Galerie Jean Dieuzaide, Toulouse
	Reverie sur New York, FNAC, Centre St. Jacques, Mulhouse, France (toured France)
1980	*Fantasies,* Galerie Contact, Bordeaux
	Babylon, Babylon, Galerie Limbach, Cologne
1983	Galerie Yves Humert, Nyon, Switzerland
1984	Galerie Poseidon, Zurich
1985	*Hommage au féminin,* Galerie Djélal, Isle-sur-Sorgue; Galerie Yves Humbert, Nyon
1989	*Babylon, Babylon,* Galerie Ideereal, Zurich
	Hommage au féminin, Galerie Yves Humbert, Nyon
1991	*Retrospective,* Tarazona 91
1992	*Retrospective,* Centre de la photogrpahie, Genève

Selected Group Exhibitions:

1953	*Kollegium Schweizer Photographen,* Helmhaus, Zurich
1955	*Family of Man,* Museum of Modern Art, New York (and world tour)
1974	*Photographes Suisses Depuis 1840 à Nos Jours,* Kunsthaus, Zurich (toured the United States)
1976	*Fantastic Photography in Europe,* at *Rencontres Internationales de la Photographie,* Arles, France (toured Europe and the United States, 1976-79)
1978	*Triennale della Fotografia,* Musée d'Art et d'Histoire, Fribourg, Switzerland
1981	*European Museums Collect,* Kunsthaus, Zurich (toured Europe)

1983	*Die fotografische Sammlung,* Museum Folkwang, Essen, West Germany
1984	*Swiss Photography from 1840 until Today,* Pro Helvetia Foundation, Zurich (and world tour)
	Subjektive Fotografie: Images of the 50s, San Francisco Museum of Modern Art (travelled to the University of Houston, Texas; Museum Folkwang, Essen; Vasterbottens Museum, Umea; Kulturhuset, Stockholm; Saarland Museum, Saarbrucken; Palais des Beaux-Arts, Brussels)
1986	Neuerwerbungen und Geschenke, Kunsthaus, Zurich
1989	Erotiques, Ateliers Fontana, Geneva
1990	Le Train, C.N.P. Paris, Collezione Fontana Centro Maestri Stranieri

Collections:

Kunsthaus, Zurich; Museum Folkwang, Essen.

Publications:

By GROEBLI: Books—*Magie der Schiene/Rail Magic,* Zurich and London 1949; *Das Auge der Liebe/The Eye of Love,* with text by Basil Burton, Zurich and London 1954; *Variation,* Teufen, Switzerland and New York 1965; *Variation 2,* Teufen, Switzerland and New York 1971; *Fantasies,* with an introduction by J. Hennessey, London 1978; *Dia Muschel,* Switzerland 1984; *R.G. Visionen/Visions, Photographies 1946-1991,* Switzerland 1992. **Article**—"How I Work in Color" in *Popular Photography* (New York), April 1962.

On GROEBLI: Books—*Schweizer Künstler,* Zurich 1964; *Museum Folkwang: die fotografische Sammlung,* exhibition catalogue, with introduction by Ute Eskildsen, Essen, West Germany 1983; *Swiss Photography from 1840 until Today,* exhibition catalogue, with introduction by Hugo Loetscher, Zurich 1984; *Subjektive Fotografie: Images of the 50s,* exhibition catalogue, by Ute Eskildsen, Manfred Schmalriede and Dorothy Martinson, Essen, West Germany 1984; *Encyclopédie internationale des photographes de 1839 à nos Jours,* Switzerland 1985; *The Naked and the Nude,* by Jorge Lewinski, London 1987; *Le Train,* Paris 1990; *Vache d'utopie,* ed. Slatkine, Genève 1991. **Articles**—"Vision of Love" in *U.S. Camera Annual,* New York 1957; "René Groebli Photo: Variation 2" by M. Nakamura in *Idea* (Tokyo), September 1971; "New Portraits by René Groebli" in *Camera 35* (New York), June 1973.

* * *

René Groebli has never been afraid to break a taboo. For him the documentary is but a dull relation to the world of imagination. Dominant in his work is a sense of what is prevailing, a Zeitgeist of what pleases and of what disturbs now.

A few years ago, Groebli decided to concentrate on his own work and on commissions he can execute freely in his own style. Formerly he worked much in the studio, pioneered in lighting, manipulated dye transfers into montage. His color dazzled, his techniques puzzled. Now, in more muted tones, he expresses surreal contemporary verities, as in "Babylon-Babylon." In this work Groebli invested his feelings for New York in 1976: attraction for its dynamic, but also repulsion, fear of it. In "Going Down to Hell" a blurred, blue spaceman, with horns reminiscent of the devil, descends, all alone on his side of the moving staircase, while its upward-moving counterpart is filled with people. All but his figure is in porous black and white. The picture gives off an eerie premonition. Will today's technological gain—the man on the moon, the shuttle in space—will they deteriorate as the subway, yesterday's gain, has deteriorated into a threatening conveyance, where murder takes place?

Feelings of power and terror and isolation, because of the fast moving tempo of our time, of alienation by technological pollution—that is what we are experiencing now. Groebli enlarged on his vision by making a mural 2m. x 2.50 of this picture. Composed of a grid of 12 sections, "Going Down to Hell" has inserted into it a neon tube, bent into a dart of lightning, so that when you confront the larger than life apparition you can imagine him hurling it.

René Groebli's satisfaction continues to come, as it always has, in completing every stage of the imagery he makes. His medium now is a combination of black and white and cibachrome. Past techniques are specified in his books *Variation* and *Variation 2*, a treasure trove of recipes for craft magic. He has always been a wanderer, searching out new techniques, to meet his inner needs. His first publication, then in black and white, was a visualization of what it feels like to "get away." It was 1949; the medium was the train. His blurred pictures were then defamed as mistakes. Five years later, he published his *The Eye of Love*, a sensitive tale of what he felt then—in Paris. That lyrical world is now a memory, not only for Groebli. Anticipation has been displaced by knowledge.

—Inge Bondi

GROOVER, Jan.

Nationality: American. **Born:** Plainfield, New Jersey, in 1943. **Education:** Studied painting at the Pratt Institute, New York, 1961-65, B.F.A. 1965; Ohio State University, Columbus, 1966-70, M.F.A. 1970. **Career:** Freelance photographer, New York, since 1971. Instructor, University of Hartford, Connecticut, 1970-73. **Recipient:** Creative Artists Public Service Grant, 1974, 1977; National Endowment for the Arts Grant, 1978 and 1990; Guggenheim Fellowship, 1979. **Agent:** Robert Miller Gallery, 41 East 57th Street, New York, New York 10022, U.S.A.

Individual Exhibitions:

1974   Light Gallery, New York
1976   Max Protetch Gallery, New York
        The Nation's Capital in Photographs, Corcoran Gallery, Washington, D.C.
        Max Protetch Gallery, Washington, D.C.
        International Museum of Photography, George Eastman House, Rochester, New York
1977   Sonnabend Gallery, New York
        Galerie Sonnabend, Paris
        Baltimore Museum of Art
        Galleria Bruna Soletti, Milan
1978   Sonnabend Gallery, New York
        Whitney Museum, New York (with David Haxton)
        Viewpoints, Walker Art Center, Minneapolis (with Michael Manzavrakos)
1979   Thomas Segal Gallery, Boston
        Waddington Galleries II, London
        Akron Art Institute, Ohio
        Wright State University, Dayton, Ohio
        Galerie Sonnabend, Paris
        Galerie Wilde, Cologne
1980   Rutgers University Art Gallery, New Brunswick, New Jersey
        Sonnabend Gallery, New York
        Bard College, Annandale-on-Hudson, New York
        Hansen Fuller Gallery, San Francisco
        Milwaukee Art Museum
        Galerie Fiolet, Amsterdam
1981   Light Gallery, New York
1983   Neuberger Museum, State University of New York at Purchase
1985   Laguna Gloria Art Museum, Austin, Texas
1986   Cleveland Museum of Art, Cleveland
1987   *Jan Groover: Retrospective 1973-1985*, Museum of Modern Art, New York (travelled)
1988   Michael H Lord Gallery, Milwaukee, Wisconsin
        Robert Miller Gallery, New York
1989   Richard Green Gallery, Los Angeles
        Demeure Bossuet, Metz, France
1990   *Jan Groover: Vintage Color Triptychs*, Janet Borden, New York
        Recent Photographs, Robert Miller Gallery, New York
1991   *Jan Groover, 1981-1990*, Betsy Rosenfield Gallery, Chicago

1992   *Recent Photographs*, Robert Miller Gallery, New York
1993   *Jan Groover*, Nancy Drysdale Gallery, Washington
        Hamiltons Gallery, London
        Jan Groover Photographs, Fahey/Klein Gallery, Los Angeles
        Jan Groover: Recent Photographs, Jacksonville Art Museum, Jacksonville, Florida
1994   Photo Gallery International, Sata Corporation, Tokyo

Selected Group Exhibitions:

1975   *(Photo) (Photo)2...(Photo)n: Sequenced Photographs*, University of Maryland, College Park (travelled to San Francisco Museum of Art, and University of Texas at Austin)
1976   *Photographers' Choice*, Mount St. Mary's Art Gallery, Los Angeles (travelled to Enjay Gallery, Boston and Witkin Gallery, New York)
1977   *Contemporary American Photographic Works*, Museum of Fine Arts, Houston
1978   *Mirrors and Windows: American Photography since 1960*, Museum of Modern Art, New York (toured the United States, 1978-80)
1979   *American Photography in the 1970s*, Art Institute of Chicago
        Photographie als Kunst 1879-1979/Kunst als Photographie 1949-1979, Tiroler Landesmuseum Ferdinandeum, Innsbruck, Austria (travelled to Neue Galerie am Wolfgang Gurlitt Museum, Linz, Austria; Neue Galerie am Landesmuseum Joanneum, Graz, Austria; and Museum des 20. Jahrhunderts, Vienna)
1980   *Polacolor: A Survey of Color and Scale in Recent Polaroid Photographs*, Philadelphia College of Art
1981   *Color Photography: New Images*, University of California at San Diego
1982   *Counterparts: Form and Emotion in Photographs*, Metropolitan Museum of Art, New York (travelled to the Contemporary Arts Center, Cincinnati, Ohio; Dallas Museum of Fine Arts, Texas; San Francisco Museum of Modern Art; Corcoran Gallery, Washington, D.C.)
1985   *American Images 1945-80*, Barbican Art Gallery, London (toured Britain)
        Messages from 1985, Light Gallery, New York
        Aquenous Chamber, Gallery Hirondelle, New York
1986   *The Animal in Photography*, The Photographers' Gallery, London
        Women View New York, Ledel Gallery, New York
        Platinum Portraits, Lieberman & Saul Gallery, New York
1987   *Still Life*, Tibor de Nagy Gallery, New York
        A Visible Order, Lieberman & Saul Gallery, New York
1988   *Lifelike*, Lorence Monk Gallery, New York
        Columnar, Hudson River Museum, Yonkers, New York
        Three on Technology, M.I.T., Cambridge, Massachusetts
1989   Group Show, Betsy Rosenfield Gallery, Chicago
1990   *The Indomitable Spirit*, The International Center of Photography, Midtown, New York (travelled)
        Constructed Realty, New Jersey Center for Visual Arts, Summit, New Jersey
        The Technological Muse, The Katonah Gallery, Katonah, New York
        The Knife in the Picture, Galerie du Jour, Paris
1991   *The Kiss of Apollo, Photography and Sculpture 1845 to the Present*, Fraenkel Gallery, San Francisco
        National Gallery of Victoria, Melbourne, Australia
        Photography from 1980 to 1990, Ginny Williams Gallery, Denver, Colorado
        Portraits on Paper, Robert Miller Gallery, New York
        Colour, Hamiltons Gallery, London
1992   *The Modernist Still Life-Photographed*, University of Missouri, St. Louis (travelled to Greece, Algeria, Morocco, Saudi Arabia, Jordan, Egypt and South America)
        Flora Photographica, Royal Botanical Garden, Edinburgh; Manchester City Art Gallery; Mead Gallery, Coventry

1993   *American Made: The New Still-Life,* Japan Art and Culture
        Association, Isetan Museum, Tokyo, Japan
        Photographs from the Real World, Lillehammer Art Museum,
        Lillehammer, Norway
1994   *A Sense of Place,* Elizabeth Leach, Portland, Oregon
        Pictures of the Real World, New York (travelled to Le
        Consortium, Dijon, France; Stadtische Galerie, Goppingen,
        Germany; Galleria Massimo De Carlo, Milan, Italy)

Collections:

Museum of Modern Art, New York; Metropolitan Museum of Art, New York; Whitney Museum of American Art, New York; International Museum of Photography, George Eastman House, Rochester, New York; Museum of Fine Arts, Houston; Centre Georges Pompidou, Paris.

Publications:

By GROOVER: Books—*Jan Groover,* with an introduction by Jane Livingston, Washington, D.C. 1976; *Jan Groover: Photographs,* Boston 1993. Article—"The Medium Is the Use" in *Artforum* (New York), November 1973.

On GROOVER: Books—*The Photographers' Choice,* edited by Kelly Wise, Danbury, New Hampshire 1975; *The Nation's Capital in Photographs,* exhibition catalogue, Washington, D.C. 1976; *Mirrors and Windows: American Photography since 1960* by John Szarkowski, New York 1978; *American Images: New Work by 20 Contemporary Photographers,* edited by Renato Danese, New York 1979; *Photographie als Kunst 1879-1979/Kunst als Photographie 1949-1979,* exhibition catalogue, 2 vols., by Peter Weiermair, Innsbruck 1979; *Lichtbildnisse: Das Porträt in der Fotografie,* edited by Klaus Honnef, Cologne 1982; *Counterparts: Form and Emotion in Photographs* by Weston J. Naef, New York 1982; *International Photography 1920-1980,* edited by Ian North, Canberra 1982; *Masterpieces of Photography from George Eastman House,* edited by Robert A. Sobieszek, New York 1985; *American Images: Photography 1945-1980,* edited by Peter Turner and John Benton-Harris, London 1985. Articles—"Photographs in Sequence" by Joan Murray in *Artweek* (Oakland, California), 4 October 1975; "Jan Groover" by Phil Patton in *Artforum* (New York), April 1976; "Jan Groover's Abstractions Embrace the World" by Ben Lifson in *Village Voice* (New York), November 1978; "Jan Groover: Degrees of Transparencies Illustrated" by Jeff Perrone in *Artforum* (New York), January 1979; "Jan Groover at Sonnabend" by Pepe Karmel in *Art in America* (New York), May 1980; "Susan Rankaitis' Materiality, Jan Groover's Structuralism" by Mark Johnstone in *Artweek* (Oakland, California), 14 February 1981; "A Knife is a Knife" by Linda André in *Afterimage,* October 1983; "Jan Groover at Robert Miller" by Stephen Ellis in *Art in America,* July 1986; "Jan Groover: Melancholy Modernist" by Max Kozloff in *Art in America,* June 1987; "Jan Groover: The Still Life seen in an Enigmatic New Light" by Carol Squiers in *American Photographer,* March 1989; "Jan Groover" in *Art Forum,* March 1991; "Jan Groover: The Afternoon of the Sensual Objects" by Hiroko Tanaka in *Hi Fashion Magazine,* March 1991.

*   *   *

Jan Groover began photographing in 1971, producing color diptychs and triptychs which are still perhaps her best-known works. Her artistic choices were clearly taken: she rejected sociologically-oriented "street" photography and embraced formal aesthetics, conceptual art, and systemic imagery. Groover's double and triple images, whose subjects were vehicles passing a significant landmark, illustrated changes which happened in a short span of time, playing in a sophisticated way with the stop-action imagery of Eadweard Muybridge which she so admired. Rather than Muybridge's analysis of movement, however, Groover's interest was in formal and coloristic changes and the manipulation of space within and between the images. Groover's training as a painter (at Pratt and Ohio State University) thus informed but did not determine her artistic position.

Groover next experimented with different kinds of space changes. During a trip to Washington D.C. in 1975 she changed her shooting procedure so that

the camera rather than the subject moved. The basic concerns remained the same, but the results and formal discoveries differed.

As Groover became less interested in the systemic nature of images and increasingly concerned with photographic form, she began producing "single image" photographs. Her photographic variables changed as well: artificial replaced natural light, found images were replaced with constructed compositions, and inherent color gave way to reflected hue. Most significant, however, was the increasingly baroque use of form and space.

The still-lifes of plant forms and kitchen objects, to which Groover turned next, constitute her most accomplished and intelligent use of the medium to date. The real subject is the content of color photography, which is both accepted (for these *are* very beautiful color images) and questioned. Silver foil and flatware, mirrors and variegated plants are used to create disjunctures and distortions that raise the question of spatial integrity in photographs. The surface of objects, their space and the effects of reflected colored light change constantly with the reflected objects, severely threatening the integrity of the objects photographed and our preconceptions about photographic replication. In addition, the images are printed slightly larger than lifesize, which tampers with our sense of bodily scale and plays subtly with traditions of photographic seeing by altering our normal compensation for scale in looking at photographs.

Most recently, Jan Groover has signalled a new direction in her photography by beginning to shoot portraits in black and white. Though still in the experimental stage, this departure will undoubtedly open new formal directions in which Groover can continue her intelligent questioning of photographic form.

—Nancy Hall-Duncan

GRUYAERT, Harry.

Nationality: Belgian. **Born:** Antwerp, 25 August 1941. **Education:** Studied photography and cinema, Brussels, 1959-62. **Family:** Children: Saskia and Marieke. **Career:** Worked as director of photography on films for Flemish television and began working in Paris as a fashion and advertising photographer, 1963-67; first visited the United States, 1968, and Morocco, 1969; photographed the Munich Olympic Games and the first Apollo space flights on a television screen, using colour manipulation, 1972; began work on Belgium, 1975; first visited India, 1976; Egypt, 1987; the Soviet Union, 1989; Santo Domingo and Haiti, 1990. Member of the Magnum Agency since 1981 (Associate), 1986 (Full). **Recipient:** 1st Prize, Kodak Photography Critics Award, Paris, 1976. **Agent:** Magnum Photos, 5 Passage Piver, Paris 75011, France. **Address:** 60 Rue Traversière, Paris 75012, France.

Individual Exhibitions:

1974   *TV Shots,* Galerie Delpire, Paris (travelled to the Palais des
        Beaux-Arts, Brussels; International Center of Photography,
        New York; and FNAC, Paris, 1975-84)
1978   *Maroc,* Galerie Delpire, Paris (and tour, 1978-80)
1980   *Belgique,* Palais des Beaux-Arts, Brussels (travelled to the
        Galerie Delpire, Paris, 1981)
        Couleur 1980, Centre Saint Gervais, Geneva
1985   Photographers' Gallery, London (with Alex Webb)
1986   *Lumières blanches,* Palais de Tokyo, Paris (and tour)
1990   *Morocco,* FNAC, Paris

Selected Group Exhibitions:

1986   *The New Colour Photojournalism,* Walker Art Center,
        Minneapolis (and tour)
1988   *Regards d'Acier,* Sollac, Dunkirk (travelled to the Palais de
        Tokyo, Paris)
        Alors, c'est comment?, Bourse, Paris (toured the USSR)
1989   *Magnum, 50 ans de photographies,* Palais de Tokyo, Paris
        (and tour)
1990   *Regards croisés,* Institut du Monde Arabe, Paris

1993 *La photographie belge,* Musée de Charleroi, Belgium
1994 *Cinéma,* Magnum, Paris

Publications:

By GRUYAERT: Books—*Morocco,* Munich 1990; *La Somme,* Amiens 1992.

On GRUYAERT: Books—*Lumières blanches,* exhibition catalogue, Paris 1986, Madrid 1990; *Regards d'Acier,* exhibition catalogue, Dunkirk 1988. **Articles**—"TV Shots" in *Zoom* (Paris), No. 27, 1974; "Maroc" in *Zoom* (Paris), No. 53, 1978; "Inde" in *Photo* (Paris), No. 127, 1978; "Belgique" in *Photographique,* March/April 1983; "Las Vegas" in *Clichés* (Brussels), No. 17, June 1985; "Maroc" in *Stern* (Hamburg), April 1986.

GRYGAR, Štěpán.

Nationality: Czechoslovakian. **Born:** Prague, 10 July 1955. **Education:** secondary school in Prague, 1970-74; studied photography, FAMU Film Academy, Prague 1975-79. **Military Service:** Served in the Czech Army, 1980. **Career:** Worked in the photo documentation department, National Technical Museum, Prague, 1974-75. Since 1980, freelance photographer in Prague; Lecturer at FAMU Film Academy, Prague since 1993. **Address:** Nikoly Tesly 4, 160 00 Prague 6, Czech Republic.

Individual Exhibitions:

1983 Fotochema Gallery, Prague
1984 Funke Fotokabinett, House of Arts, Brno, Czechoslovakia
1985 Foto-Medium-Art Gallery, Wroclaw, Poland
1986 House of Music, Olomouc, Czechoslovakia
 Culture Centrum Gallery, Liberec, Czechoslovakia
 Gallery of Arts, Karlovy Vary, Czechoslovakia
1988 The International House, Munich
 The International House, Madrid
1989 Akademia Lacunza, San Sebastian
1989 Liget Galeria, Budapest
1989 Cankarjev Dom, Ljubljana
1990 Galerie Foto-Medium-Art, Wroclaw
 Galerie Mathieu, Besançon
1991 Vystavni Sin, FOMA, Praha
1992 Malá galerie spořitelny Kladně
1993 *Planeta,* Galerie Staradnice, Brno; Galerie 4, Cheb
 Galerie Zamec, Pribram (with Milan Grygar)
1994 *Planeta,* Galerie FOMA, Liberec

Selected Group Exhibitions:

1982 *Aktuálni Fotografie,* Moravian Gallery, Brno, Czechoslovakia
1983 *Rencontres Internationale de Photographie,* Arles, France
1984 *Czech Photography,* Galerie Antrazit, Essen, West Germany
 Photography in Czechoslovakia, Galleria San Fedele, Milan
 Aspects of Czech Photography, Thackrey and Robertson Gallery, San Francisco
 XI Biennale of Applied Graphic Art, Moravian Gallery, Brno, Czechoslovakia
1985 *Origin and Presence of Czech Photography,* Fotoforum, Frankfurt, West Germany
 27 Contemporary Czech Photographers, The Photographer's Gallery, London
 Zeitgenössische Fotografie Ost-und Südosteuropas, Kunstmuseum, Düsseldorf, West Germany
1986 *Elementary Photography,* Gallery of Contemporary Art, Szczecin, Poland
1987 *Award for Young European Photographers,* Frankfurt
1988 *De Prague et de Boheme,* Paris-Ville de Bretigny
1989 *Prix Air France/Ville de Paris,* Espace Photo, Paris

1990 *Choice,* Fotofest, Houston
1990 *Photographie Progressive en Tcheccslovaque,* Galerie R. Doisneau, Nancy
1991 *The Wall/The Fall,* Shayder Art Gallery, Denver, Colorado
 Contemporary Czechoslovak Photographers, Jacques Baruch Gallery, Chicago
 New Spaces of Photography, Wroclaw
 Zeitgenössische Tschechoslowakische Fotografie und Glas Kunst, Kunsthaus, Hamburg
1992 *Autoportraits,* Galerie le Lieu, Lorient
 Aarhus Festival Week, Galleri Image
1993 *What's New: Prague,* The Art Institute of Chicago
 In and Out Czechoslovakia, The Zelda Cheatle Gallery, London
1994 *Sélénographie (Collection de photographies contemporines),* Espace, Nantes.
 Czech and Slovak Photographers, The Photographers' Gallery, Perth, Australia

Collections:

Museum of Industrial Arts, Prague; Moravian Gallery, Brno, Czechoslovakia; Muzeum Sztuki, Lodz, Poland; Bibliothèque Nationale, Paris; National Museum, Wroclaw, Poland; Centre Georges Pompidou, Paris; The University of Texas at Austin; The Museum of Fine Arts, Houston, Texas; Museum Ludwig, Köln, The Art Institute of Chicago.

Publications:

By GRYGAR: Books—*An Accident,* with text by Jiří Švejda, n.p. 1981; *Bet on Love,* with text by Jan Suchl, n.p. 1983; *Naked in the Thorns,* with text by Milena Lukešova, Prague 1985; *A Planet,* with text by Zdenek Primus, Edition Umbrella, Prague 1993.

On GRYGAR: Books—*Aktuálni Fotografie,* exhibition catalogue, by Antonìn Dufek, Brno, Czechoslovakia 1982; *Štěpán Grygar,* exhibition catalogue, with text by Antonìn Dufek, Prague 1983; *27 Contemporary Czechoslovakian Photographers,* exhibition catalogue, with texts by Jiří Hlušička, Sue Davies and Antonìn Dufek, London 1985. **Article**—"The New Sensitiveness of Štěpán Grygar" by Antonìn Dufek in *Revue Fotografie* (Prague), no. 3, 1984; *Photonews* No 8/1989; *Revue Fotographie* No. 3/93 with text by Zdeneck Primus.

*

Photography does not represent reality, but it creates a new reality. The more is the conception of photographic series clean, the more exact is its process.

—Štěpán Grygar

*   *   *

He is sometimes ranked among the so-called visualists, i.e. those who concentrate on the visual experience and in the name of the latter negate the usual perception of the visible world, trying to make each image of the latter unique and unexpected, wanting to transform the visible reality into a mystery and a revelation. This, after all, is nothing new because Moholy-Nagy, Rodchenko or Funke did the same during the 1920s and 30s and so did later the Surrealists. Only the aesthetics differ, as does the psychological and social experience from which it stems.

"When I photograph, I try to work without a preconceived idea which I would pursue, nor do I want to project myself into the photographed objects. On the contrary, I give reins to the new reality, although the freedom may be somewhat determined by my own visual experience," says Grygar, yet his fragments of reality which seem as if captured by chance undoubtedly constitute a very personal message. It is a message of a child who grew in the city streets and was affected as much by the *genius loci* of medieval Prague as by the rapid advancement of the technical civilization, as much by the unique charm of the city that has been a living history as by phenomena of a new

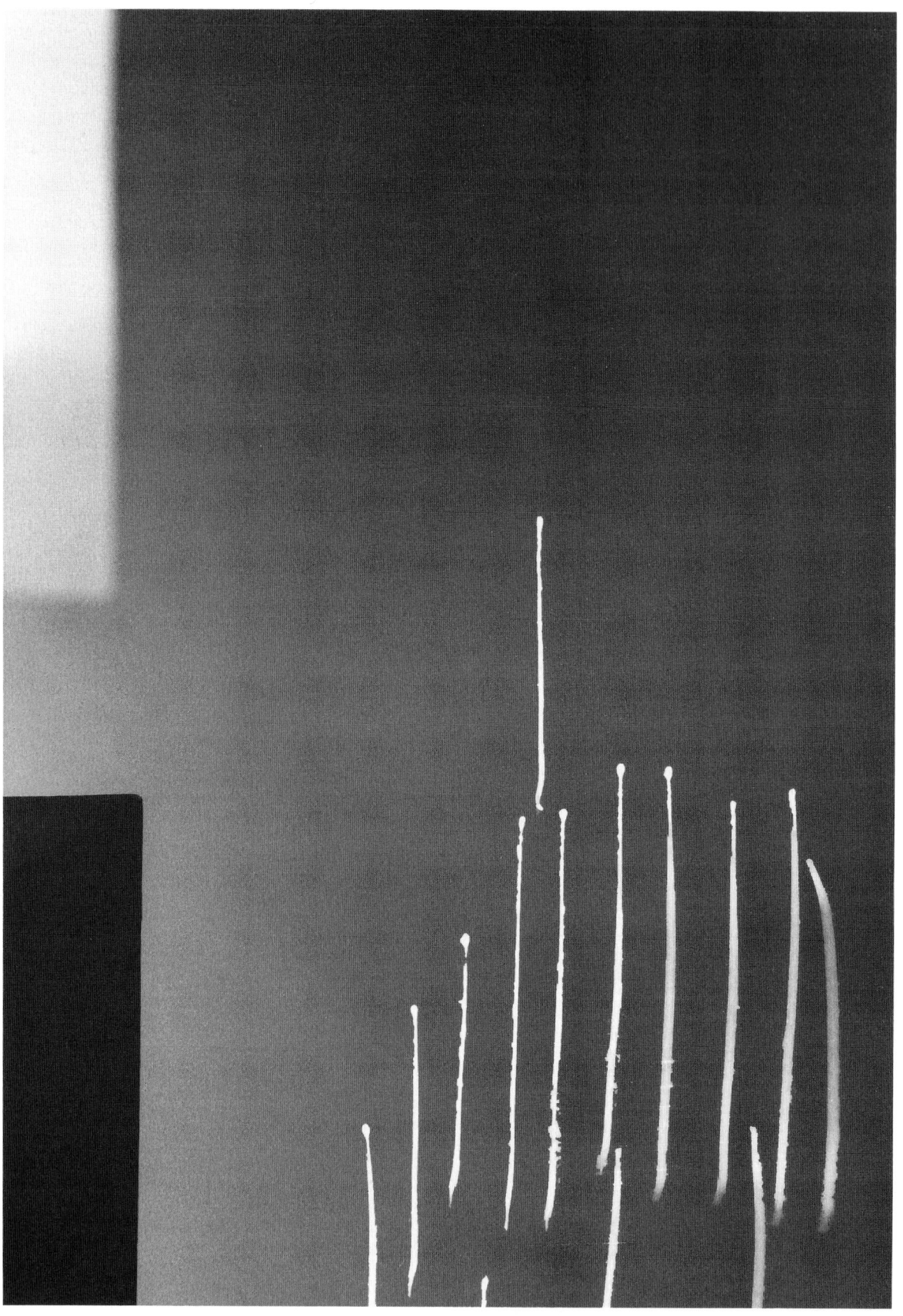

Untitled, **1989.** Photograph ©Štěpán Grygar.

lifestyle marked by gadgetry and absurd consumerism. Perhaps Grygar's "new free reality" is but a result of an inner, maybe even subconscious need to come to terms emotionally with the world in which he lives.

Although he does not depend on a preconceived idea of what he is going to photograph, he still works with it: it is his essential philosophy of life and his undeniable visual sensitivity which make him select his objects, associate them visually and semantically, select his camera angles or tonal presentation. Grygar photographs nothing but reality, and even a reality unarranged, unexpected—in fact a reality discovered, or more precisely, a reality glimpsed. And yet his pictures feel like surreal mysteries which inspire and excite us as anything ambiguous does. This is not only due to the fact that Grygar is so fond of mere fragments of reality torn out of context, but also because we strongly feel the irresistible appeal of a moment frozen still. A moment in which we glimpse a house, a figure, a quay or a poster wall. Comes the next moment and we see a totally different view. And in the next moment a car, human legs, a lamppost sneak as if inadvertently into a corner of the picture, yet a second later everything is empty and void again. The aesthetics of snap photography, that is the essence of Grygar's work, as if the photographer had to verify constantly his vision of the world, as if he had to subject it to a torrent of new impulses and reevaluate it through new experience.

The eeriness of his objects is even enhanced by shifts of tonality used in the positive process. The result is a cool chiaroscuro, oppressive and even mesmerizing. Then suddenly the captured reality, which objectively existed in front of the lens when the shutter was released, is almost gone, for gone is the natural context of objects, their static character and even their original dynamism; gone is also the original light. The new reality starts living a life of its own, independent of the previous one. The phenomenon of the city has acquired new qualities.

However, the popular presentation of Grygar in his native country as something essentially new in the Czech photographic tradition, a phenomenon stemming from nobody and nothing, is not true. Grygar's pictures indeed are a continuation of a tradition, for they integrate the experience of modern poetry, and if not consciously, then at least subconsciously resonate with the imagination of the Czech inter-war and post-war generations—Functionalism of J. Funke, Civilism of J. Sever, Surrealism of J. Štyrský or E. Medková . . . . Besides, Grygar's work also reveals an intimate knowledge of the world's contemporary creative photography, and even the artistic traditions of his own family. In fact, his photographs concern always the same problem: the relation of man and encroaching technocratic civilization. But whereas photographers of the inter-war period were much impressed and even intoxicated by technology, in more recent authors such civilization provokes conflicting thought and even anxiety since man becomes more and more fettered by his own creation.

—Daniela Mrázková

GUPTA, Sunil.

Nationality: Canadian. **Born:** New Delhi, India, 8 September 1953; emigrated to Canada 1969; naturalized, 1972. **Education:** Attended Dawson College, Montreal, 1970-72; studied accountancy at Concordia University, Montreal, 1972-77; attended the Philip Halsman and Lisette Model Workshop, The New School, New York, 1976; studied for Dip. Photography at West Surrey College of Art and Design, Farnham, Surrey, 1978-81 and for M.A. (Photography) at Royal College of Art, London 1981-83. **Career:** Worked as an auditor in Canada 1974 and 1977; worked as a part-time teacher in basic photographic skills to design students at East Ham College of Technology, 1985-86; founded Autograph—The Association of Black Photographers—London, 1986-88; tutor to fine art students, Chelsea College of Art, London, 1988; worked as co-administrator of Autograph, London 1988-89; half-time lecturer in Photography at Humberside Polytechnic, Hull, 1991-92; curator at INIVA (the Institute of New International Visual Arts), London since 1992. **Recipient:** RCA-3M Portfolio Award, 1983. **Agent:** Network Photographers, London. **Address:** 4 Bellefields Road, Brixton, London SW9 9UQ, England.

Individual Exhibitions:

1980	India International Centre, New Delhi, India
1983	Commonwealth Institute, London
1984	International Maritime Organisation, London
	Museum and Art Galleries, Nottingham, England
	Museum and Art Galleries, Leicester, England
1986	South Hill Park, Bracknell, England
	Leica Gallery, Wetzlar, Germany
1988	*Social Security,* The Showroom, London
1991	Edinburgh Festival Theatre Workshop, Edinburgh
	Film in the Cities, St. Paul, Minnesota
1994	Contemporary Art Gallery, Vancouver, British Columbia, Canada

Selected Group Exhibitions:

1980	*Salford '80,* Salford, England
1982	*The Living Arts,* Serpentine Gallery, London
1983	*New Contemporaries,* ICA, London
	Snap, Oval House, London
1984	*Brilliance Books,* People's Gallery, London
	Five Dials Gallery, London
1985	*Staying On,* The Photographers' Gallery, London
	Riverside Open, Riverside Studios, London
1986	*The Black Experience,* Brixton Art Gallery, London
	Darshan, GLC/Camerawork, London
	Same Difference, Camerawork, London
1987	*The Body Politic,* The Photographers' Gallery, London
1988	*Monologue/Dialogue,* Randolph Street Gallery, Chicago
1989	*Through the Looking Glass,* Barbican Gallery, London
	Partners in Crime, Camerawork, London
	Fabled Territories, Leeds City Art Gallery, Leeds, England
1990	*Ecstatic Antibodies,* Impressions Gallery of Photography, York
	Autoportraits, Camerawork. London
	Post Mortality, Kettle's Yard, Cambridge
1991	*Shocks to the System,* The South Bank Centre, London
1992	*Dis/Orient,* UIC Gallery 400, Chicago
	Queer Landscape, Evergreen State College, Olympia, Washington State
	How Do I Look?, Institute of Modern Art, Brisbane, Australia (and touring)
	Fine Materials for a Dream, Harris Museum, Preston (toured to Hull and Oldham, England)
	Trophies of Empire, Amolfini, Bristol
1993	*Trophies of Empire,* Ferens Art Gallery, Hull, England
	They Call it Love, NGBK, Berlin
1994	*Havana Biennale,* Cuba

Collections:

Arts Council of Great Britain, London; National Museum of Film, TV and Photography, Bradford, England; Queensland Art Gallery, Brisbane, Australia.

Publications:

By GUPTA: Books—*Ecstatic Antibodies: Resisting the AIDS Mythology,* with Tessa Boffin, London 1990; *An Economy of Signs,* London and Boston 1990; *Disrupted Borders,* London and Boston 1993. **Television/video**—photographs used in *This is not an AIDS Advertisement* by Isaac Julien/Sankofa, 1987; *Indian Postcard,* 1988/89; *de Souza,* 1989/90; *Cock Crazy or Scared Stiff,* co-directed with Laura MacGregor, 1991/92.

*   *   *

Sunil Gupta is both photographer and curator and his work is at the forefront of developments in contemporary documentary photography. This work emerges very directly from his own politics around race and sexuality and his experience of cultural difference. His photographs have an eclecticism

From *Trespass* series, 1992. Photograph ©Sunil Gupta.

and a range of sources of imagery which reflect the many and diverse influences of Sunil's early life. Born in Delhi, of an Indian father and a Tibetan mother, he grew up in an environment which included Hinduism, Christianity, Indian and American film, music and literature. At home a mixture of English, Urdu and Hindi was spoken, while at school he worked to the English curriculum and learned English history and culture. At the age of thirteen his family moved to Canada, which he says was like "entering the movies," later he moved to New York and then to Britain.

Sunil came to photography relatively late, having trained in business studies. It was the experience of living in New York where "everyone is an artist" that started his photographic training. He took classes with Lisette Model at the New School and learned and enjoyed the craft aspects of print making. When he came to Britain he initially trained in documentary photography and worked for a number of years as a freelance photojournalist for magazines and newspapers, often working with Network photo agency.

His work, however, operates on a fine line between truth and fiction; it might perhaps be called post-documentary. Frequently he deals with an issue or situation in an apparently documentary mode but has in fact constructed the image and left a clue somewhere that he has done so. He describes this practice as the result of working for magazines and newspapers and "realising that the opportunity for innovation or presenting a point of view was non-existent because magazine people want you to produce work which fits their house style." He became increasingly bored with journalism, realising that "once you've got one decisive moment you can produce hundreds—it's problem solving with either technical or time pressure."

However, it was working as a photojournalist in the 1980s which gave Sunil the opportunity to return to India for the first time since he had left as a teenager. At the same time as carrying out a commission he was able to pursue more personal work, looking at the hidden face of homosexuality in India. The need to protect the identity of the men he was photographing and current theory in British photographic circles dovetailed and confirmed his emerging practice of setting pictures up rather than documenting events as they occur.

Much of his work is collaborative and has come about through joint projects developed to address issues of concern in the gay and lesbian or the Black community. He became actively involved in public sector arts and in making work and issues of race though the GLC in the mid-1980s when he was invited to contribute to a show of the work of Black photographers by the GLC and to be on the GLC Anti-Racist Design Committee. His administrative and business skills were crucial to his involvement in setting up Autograph, the Association of Black Photographers, and managing it with Monika Baker.

Subsequently he set up OVA, the Organisation for Visual Arts, and has received an INIVA franchise to curate a number of touring exhibitions. The first of these *Disrupted Borders,* he describes as an intervention in definition of boundaries. In his curatorial work he continues to construct a view where, working always from a position as the "other," he places the "other" very clearly at the centre of his vision.

—Shirley Read

GUTMANN, John.

Nationality: American. **Born:** Breslau, Germany (now Wroclaw, Poland), 28 May 1905; emigrated to the United States, 1933: naturalized, 1940. **Education:** Attended the Johannes Gymnasium, Breslau, 1914-23; studied art, under Otto Mueller, Staatliche Akademie für Kunst und Kunstgewerbe, Breslau, 1923-27, B.A. 1927; history of art and philosophy, Schlesische Friedrich Wilhelms Universität, Breslau, 1926-27; Preussisches Schulkollegium für Höhere Erziehung, Berlin, 1927-28, M.A. 1928; post-graduate studies at the Humboldt Universität, and the Berliner Akademie der Bildenden Künste, Berlin, 1929-30; self-taught in photography, from 1933. **Military Service:** Served as a still and motion picture cameraman, United States Army Signal Corps, and with the Psychological Warfare Team, United States Office of War Information, in China, Burma and India, 1943-45. **Family:** Married the artist Gerrie von Pribosic in 1949. **Career:** Independent painter, in Berlin, 1929-33, and in San Francisco, from 1934; freelance photographer, in Berlin 1933, and in San Francisco, 1934-63 and since 1974; also independent filmmaker, San Francisco, from 1949; worked with the Presse-Foto agency, Berlin, 1933-36, and with Pix Inc., agency, New York 1939-63, photographing for *Berliner Illustrierte Zeitung, Die Woche, Beatrys, Das Illustrierte Blatt, Sirene, Hamburger Woche, Saturday Evening Post, Time, Life, Look, Picture Post, National Geographic, Pictorial Press, Coronet, Asia,* etc.; Staff Photographer, *The Dispatch* army newspaper, Camp Roberts, California, 1942-43. Member, California Camera Club, San Francisco, 1934-40. Instructor in art at several schools in Berlin, 1929-32; part-time instructor in art, 1936-38, Assistant Professor, 1938-42 and 1946-49, Associate Professor, 1949-55, Professor, 1955-73, and Emeritus Professor, 1973, San Francisco State College (now

San Francisco State University). **Recipient:** Distinguished Teaching Award, California State Colleges, 1968; Guggenheim Fellowship, New York, 1977. Member, American Association of University Professors; College Art Association of America. **Agents:** Fraenkel Gallery, 49 Geary Street, San Francisco, California 94108-5730, U.S.A.; Castelli Graphics, 4 East 77th Street, New York, New York 10021, U.S.A. **Address:** 1543 Cole Street, San Francisco, California 94117, U.S.A.

Individual Exhibitions:

1938	*Colorful America,* M. H. de Young Memorial Museum, San Francisco
1941	*Wondrous World,* M. H. de Young Memorial Museum, San Francisco
1947	*The Face of the Orient,* M. H. de Young Memorial Museum, San Francisco
1974	Light Gallery, New York
1976	*As I Saw It,* San Francisco Museum of Modern Art
	Vintage Photographs of the 1930s, Phoenix Gallery, San Francisco (with Walker Evans)
1979	*The Fourth Decade,* Castelli Graphics, New York
1980	*San Francisco 1934-39,* Fraenkel Gallery, San Francisco
	Halsted Gallery, Birmingham, Michigan
1981	*Photographs of San Francisco and New Orleans ca.1937,* Gallery for Fine Photography, New Orleans, Louisiana
	Women, Castelli Graphics, New York
1983	*Ten Photographs,* Fraenkel Gallery, San Francisco
	A Portfolio of Photographs, Robert Freidus Gallery, New York
	Women, Fraenkel Gallery, San Francisco
	American Images 1930s-40s, Giannini Gallery, Bank of America, San Francisco
1984	Museum of Photographic Arts, San Diego, California (with Berenice Abbott)
	The Restless Decade, Books & Co., New York
1985	*By My Choice,* Castelli Uptown Gallery, New York
	Art Gallery of Ontario, Toronto
	Vintage Photographs, Fraenkel Gallery, San Francisco
	Fotografias 1934-39, Il Jornades Fotografiques, Valencia, Spain
1986	*Photographs of the South 1937,* Houston Center for Photography, Texas
1988	Fraenkel Gallery, San Francisco
1989	*Beyond the Document,* San Francisco Museum of Modern Art (travelled to Museum of Modern Art, New York; Los Angeles County Museum of Art)
	99 Photographs Museo Casa Natal de Jovellanos, Spain
1990	Fahey/Klein Gallery, Los Angeles
	Castelli Graphics, New York
1991	Fraenkel Gallery, San Francisco
1993	Ehlers Caudill Gallery, Chicago
1994	*Talking Pictures,* Centre National de la Photographie, Paris

Selected Group Exhibitions:

1941	*Image of Freedom,* Museum of Modern Art, New York
1976	*Photography and Language,* La Mamelle, San Francisco (and Camerawork, San Francisco)
1978	*Aesthetics of Graffiti,* San Francisco Museum of Modern Art
1979	*Amerika Fotografie 1920-40,* Kunsthaus, Zurich (toured Europe)
1980	*Avant-Garde Photography in Germany 1919-39,* San Francisco Museum of Modern Art (travelled to Akron Art Institute, Ohio; Walker Art Center, Minneapolis; Baltimore Museum of Art, Maryland; Chicago Center for Contemporary Photography, Columbia College; International Center of Photography, New York; Portland Art Museum, Oregon)
1982	*Cityscapes,* Fine Arts Museum of San Francisco
1983	*American Bathing Styles 1900-40,* Wadsworth Atheneum, Hartford, Connecticut
1984	*Automobile and Culture,* Museum of Contemporary Art, Los Angeles
1985	*L'Autoportrait à l'Age de la Photographie,* Musée Cantonal des Beaux-Arts, Lausanne, Switzerland (toured Europe)
	American Photography 1945-80, Barbican Centre, London
1986	*The Artist and the Machine 1910-40,* De Saisset Museum, Santa Clara, California
	The Machine Age, Brooklyn Museum, New York
1989	*Photography from California Collections,* San Francisco Museum of Modern Art
	L'Oeil de la Lettre, Centre National de la Photographie, Paris
	The Blues Aesthetic, Washington Project for the Arts, Washington, D.C.
1991	*En Bateau,* Mission du Patrimoine Photographique, Paris
	The Kiss of Apollo, Fraenkel Gallery, San Francisco
1992	*This Sporting Life, 1878-1991,* High Museum of Art, Atlanta
	101 Years of California Photography, Santa Barbara Museum of Art
1994	*Graffiti,* Zabriskie Gallery, New York
	Hidden Faces, Paul Kopeikien Gallery, Los Angeles

Collections:

San Francisco Museum of Modern Art; Boston Museum of Fine Art, Massachusetts; New Orleans Museum of Art, Louisiana; Metropolitan Museum of Art, New York; Museum of Photographic Arts, San Diego, California; Los Angeles County Museum of Art; Center for Creative Photography, University of Arizona, Tucson; Australian National Gallery, Canberra; Museum of Modern Art, New York; Amon Carter Museum, Dallas; Art Institute of Chicago; Corcoran Gallery of Art, Washington, DC; Indiana University Art Museum, Bloomington; Lehigh University, Bethlehem, Pennsylvania; Museum of Fine Arts, Houston; National Gallery of Canada, Ottawa; Saint Louis Museum of Modern Art; Solomon Guggenheim Foundation Collection.

Publications:

By GUTMANN: Books—*Out of State,* portfolio, with others, text by Henry Holmes Smith, San Francisco 1978; *John Gutmann: 10 Photographs,* portfolio, San Francisco and New York 1982. **Article**—"Interview with John Gutmann," with Paul Raedeke, in *Photo Metro* (San Francisco), September 1985. **Films**—*The Chinese Peasant Goes to Market,* 1949; *Journey to Kunming,* 1949; *Le Palais Idéal,* 1983.

On GUTMANN: Books—*Land of the Free* by Archibald McLeish, New York 1938; *As I Saw It: Photographs by John Gutmann,* exhibition catalogue, by John Humphrey, San Francisco 1976; *Photography and Language,* edited by Lew Thomas, San Francisco; *Photography in Germany 1919-1939,* exhibition catalogue, by Van Deren Coke, Ute Eskildsen and Bernd Lohse, San Francisco 1980; *Still Photography: The Problematic Model,* edited by Lew Thomas and Peter D'Agostino, San Francisco 1981; *Photography in California 1945-1980* by Louise Katzman, New York and San Francisco 1984; *The Restless Decade: John Gutmann's Photographs of the Thirties* by Max Kozloff, edited by Lew Thomas, New York 1984; *John Guttman: 99 Photographs,* exhibition catalogue, Spain 1984; *Gutmann,* exhibition catalogue, by Maia-Mari Sutnik, Toronto 1985; *John Gutmann: 1934-1939* by Alain Dupuy, Valencia, Spain 1985; *The Artist and the Machine 1910-1940,* exhibition catalogue, by Georgianna M. Lagoria, Santa Clara, California 1986. **Articles**—"Wondrous World Exhibition" by Alfred Frankenstein in the *San Francisco Chronicle,* 14 May 1941; "Profile: John Gutmann, American Icons" by Margaretta K. Mitchell in *35mm Photography* (New York), Winter 1977; "John Gutmann: A Transported Vision" by Carol Squiers in *Artforum* (New York), January 1980; "John Gutmann: San Francisco 1934-1939" by Robert Atkins in the *San Francisco Guardian,* 24 April 1980; "The Extravagant Depression: John Gutmann's Photographs of the Thirties" by Max Kozloff in *Artforum* (New York), November 1982; "The Restless Decade: John Gutmann" by Alan Trachtenberg in *Exposure* (New York), Fall 1985; "A Photographic Maverick" by Joan Murray in *Artweek* (Oakland, California), 9 November 1985; *Zyzzyva* (San Francisco), Volume III, no. 4, Winter 1987; *Zyzzyva* (San Francisco), Volume IX, no. 3, Fall 1993.

*

Most important to me is the meaning of my photographs, the finding of subject matter significant for myself and, hopefully, for the viewer. Pictorial effectiveness and formal inventiveness are self-understood but secondary. I am not addicted to aesthetic perfection and technical fetishism. I want my pictures to be read for the expression of my feelings and for the information in my visual discoveries.

—John Gutmann

*   *   *

John Gutmann's photography is a synthesis of both social and aesthetic concerns; it springs from his impulse to respond clearly, to capture an immediate impression, and to define its visual possibilities. His remarkable vision is offset by a spontaneous expression of imagery that fuses reality with the illusory and the allusive. The importance of this dualism, and Gutmann's methodology of organizing and cross-referencing the content of his photographs, serve to create a system of resonance between the images and the designated categories. His categorical spectrum originates to meet the requirements of photojournalism, and more significantly, to personal choices of themes suited to the tenor of his experience and as a reflection of the general times.

Born in 1905 and raised in Breslau, Germany, Gutmann—a former master student of Die Brücke Expressionist Otto Mueller—took up photography in 1933 when Hitler's regime proscribed an end to his artistic career. Gutmann bought an expensive camera, faked the role of a photojournalist and armed with a contract from the Berlin agency of Presse-Foto, promptly departed for San Francisco to record America for European magazines. As Gutmann learned the rudiments of his new profession, he discovered in America a country with a "marvellous extravagance of life," where he found a kind of surrealist experience—everything bizarre, exotic and marvellous. Gutmann would seek out the kind of subject matter that would record an aspect of life and reveal the momentum of an event that was most American for the illustrated magazines in Europe. He felt he knew how to get a good picture, relying on what he describes as "his painter's consciousness."

Gutmann's stylistic development demonstrated variance in resolution. Notwithstanding the demands of making a living and the press's demands for pictures that were graphically suited for layout or cropped to fit editorial formats, Gutmann established his visual vocabulary with distinguishing marks and attributes that decoded a new culture. Certain subjects necessitated certain methods of production, as both spontaneity and pre-judgement played a role in the creative process. He would exploit the characteristics of the medium to purvey the unanticipated and give ascendancy to multiple possibilities. Gutmann easily accepted the potentials of the camera: its disposition towards fragmentary framing and its relative tension, description of seductive surface, vantage point, and segmentation of time. The out-of-focus foreground subjects are often blunt and snappish. Framing in bold spatial crops and in angular configurations already apparent in his first experimental images, and patterning of light and dark all convey visual uniqueness and spontaneity in the treatment of his subject matter. At his most brilliant, Gutmann's quick wit and the camera's slow shutter speed merge in *The Jump* (1939). In this enigmatic moment, there is a hand pointing to a painted white spot on the ground, a full-length curving shadow of a man, and a blurred amorphous form springing from some concealed force, expelled over the spot. The jumping frog suggests free association with some previously experienced moment more than a transcription of current fact.

In such approaches to his subject matter, Gutmann forecast tendencies and visual motifs that were to be explored by subsequent photographers. The images of Robert Frank, Diane Arbus, Lee Friedlander, Bruce Davidson, Garry Winogrand have become so familiar now that Gutmann's precursory photographs do not seem startling until one is alerted to their date. In his 1948 series of *Hunter's Point*, he predicted the cool topographical work seen almost thirty years later in the urban landscape work of Lewis Baltz, Robert Adams, and Joe Deal.

Although Gutmann joined the Pix agency in New York and supplied photographs for their use over two decades, it is not surprising that many of Gutmann's photographs were not part of magazine assignments at all. The ambiguous, the ambivalent, the tentative, and the personally expressive did not always meet the taste of editors. Gutmann retained many of his pictures and organized them into a personal archive. His methodology depended on a wide spectrum of themes: Documents of the Street, Automobile Culture, The Depression, Ethnic Minorities, Women, Death, Graffiti, Structured Vision, and an enigmatic category Beyond Reality, among several other themes that would cross-reference and overlap. Throughout these categories, form and content transpose and fuse. Often the visually straightforward information in one image would contrast with an expressionistic, gestural approach to the same subject matter in another.

For Gutmann, no subject proved as limitless as the celebrated automobile, and America's obsession with it was fertile territory. Gutmann saw it as the quintessential American icon; it symbolized power, glamour, prosperity and a wondrous inventiveness. Gutmann observed its every facet: fenders, headlights, adornments, decals, its relationship to life and its surrounding, the homage it paid to itself, its own aggrandizement in advertising—as a transport for ideological proclamations and a billboard for commerce. From the beginning Gutmann has sustained an incomparable breadth and bite in this subject.

In the mid-thirties, concurrent with his photography, Gutmann established himself as professor of art at San Francisco State College (now University) and continued his teaching affiliation until 1973. In 1943 Gutmann volunteered for overseas duty and worked on film and photography assignments in Southwest China, Burma, and India. There he remained stimulated by the challenge of finding subject matter that would reveal the new and reflect the themes he had developed in America. He focused on his established categories, and yet his overall approach was more classical, more proportioned, and for him more appropriate for the subjects. They detail vignettes: what people do, how they live, their environment of land, canals, and the streets; the pictures are also supported by lengthy captions that transcribe direct information about the content. While much of this work disappeared into government files, there remained enough images in his possession to be later published internationally into many photo-essays.

Gutmann's fertile vision has existed in distinct spheres: in the sphere of expressive documentary observation drawing from reality, in the formal, and in the sensual and the poetic. Within each sphere, the complexity of expression, be it gestural or subtle, has expanded his artistic invention to suit subject matter and content. Inspired both by pre-existing European resources and by his own profound originality, through his extraordinary diversity he has used varied pictorial means to serve his medium, and to project different realms of his experience. To stress his belief in the importance of subject matter in recurring human themes and events, it was feeling for the irrational and the rational that polarized his vision. Photographic history has no name-tag for Gutmann; he himself prefers to be linked with the "unclassifiables." At the heart of his photographic genius is a surefootedness and a positive vision of the multiplicity that life offers.

—Maia-Mari Sutnik

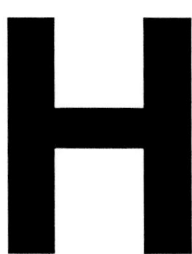

HAAS, Ernst.

Nationality: Austrian. **Born:** Vienna, 2 March 1921; moved to the United States, 1950. **Education:** Studied medicine in Vienna; subsequently studied photography at the Graphische Lehr- und Versuchsanstalt, Vienna. **Family:** Married; children: Alexander and Victoria. **Career:** Freelance photographer, in Paris, 1948-50, and in New York, working for *Life, Paris-Match, Esquire, Holiday, Queen, Look,* etc., 1950 until his death in 1986. Member, Magnum Photos co-operative agency, Paris and New York, from 1949. Stills Photographer on films *The Bible, Little Big Man, Hello Dolly,* etc. Lecturer (one week a year), Maine Photographic Workshop, Rockport, and Anderson Ranch Foundation, Aspen, Colorado, 1975-85. **Recipient:** Newhouse Award, Syracuse University, New York, 1958; Der Kulturpreis, Deutsche Gesellschaft für Photographie (DGPh), 1972; Honor Roll Award, American Society of Magazine Photographers, 1952; Wilson Hicks Award, University of Miami, 1978; State of New York Executive Chamber Citation, 1979; Merit Award, Art Directors Club of New York, 1980. **Died:** (in New York City) *15 September 1986.*

Individual Exhibitions:

1947	*Homecoming of Austrian Prisoners of War,* Red Cross Headquarters, Vienna
1962	*Ernst Haas: Color Photography,* Museum of Modern Art, New York
1964	*Poetry in Color,* IBM Gallery, New York
1968	*Angkor and Bali: Two Worlds of Ernst Haas,* Asia House, New York
1971	*The Creation,* Rizzoli Gallery, New York (travelled to *Photokina,* Cologne, 1972)
1978	*In Germany,* at *Photokina,* Cologne
1980	*Ernst Haas: Retrospective: 1960-1980,* Museum of Art, Sao Paulo, Brazil
1983	Jeb Gallery, Providence, Rhode Island

Selected Group Exhibitions:

1951	*Memorable Life Photographs,* Museum of Modern Art, New York
1960	*The World as Seen by Magnum Photographers,* Takashimaya Department Store, Tokyo
1967	*Photography in the 20th Century,* National Gallery of Canada, Ottawa (toured Canada and the United States, 1967-73)
1970	*The Concerned Photographer 2,* Israel Museum, Jerusalem (toured Europe)
1973	*Photography into Art,* Camden Arts Centre, London
1978	*Mirrors and Windows: American Photography since 1960,* Museum of Modern Art, New York (toured the United States, 1978-80)
1979	*Photographie als Kunst 1879-1979,* Tiroler Landesmuseum Ferdinandeum, Innsbruck, Austria (travelled to the Neue Galerie am Wolfgang Gurlitt Museum, Linz, Austria; Neue Galerie am Landesmuseum Joanneum, Graz, Austria; and Museum des 20. Jahrhunderts, Vienna)
1980	*Photography of the 50s,* International Center of Photography, New York (travelled to the Center for Creative Photography, University of Arizona, Tucson; Minneapolis Institute of Arts;

California State University at Long Beach; and the Delaware Art Museum, Wilmington)

1982	*Color as Form,* International Museum of Photography at George Eastman House, Rochester, New York
1984	*La Photographie Créative,* Pavillon des Arts, Paris

Collections:

Museum of Modern Art, New York; International Center of Photography, New York; International Museum of Photography, George Eastman House, Rochester, New York; Exchange National Bank, Chicago; Royal Society of Photography Collection, Bath, England; Museum des 20. Jahrhunderts, Vienna; Museum Ludwig, Cologne.

Publications:

By HAAS: Books—￼*The Creation,* New York, Paris and London 1971; *In America,* New York and London 1975; *Ende und Anfang,* with text by Hellmut Andics, Dusseldorf and Vienna 1975; *In Germany,* with text by Thilo Koch, Dusseldorf, Vienna and New York 1976; *Himalayan Pilgrimage,* with text by Gisela Minke, New York and London 1978; *Realm of Light,* edited by Samuel Walker, New York 1979; *The Joy of Photography,* Rochester, New York 1979; *The Joy of Photography II,* Rochester, New York 1981; also, contributor to many books in the Time-Life book series—color portfolio for the "Photography" series; *The Grand Canyon* and *Cactus Country* for the "Wilderness" series; and *Venice* for the "Great Cities" series. **Articles—**"Man and Nature: The Wilderness Debate" in *GEO* (New York), July 1979; "Cloudland of the Spirits: Himalaya" in *Life* (New York), November 1979.

On HAAS: Books—*Memorable Life Photographs,* with text by Edward Steichen, New York 1951; *Photography of the World '60,* edited by Hiromu Hara, Ihei Kimura and others, Tokyo and New York 1960; *Photography in the 20th Century* by Nathan Lyons, New York 1967; *The Concerned Photographer 2,* edited by Cornell Capa, New York and London 1972; *Photography into Art,* exhibition catalogue, by Colin Osman, Ainslie Ellis and Margaret Harker, London 1973; *The Magic Image* by Cecil Beaton and Gail Buckland, London and Boston 1975; *Geschichte der Fotografie im 20. Jahrhundert/ Photography in the 20th Century* by Petr Tausk, Cologne 1977, London 1980; *Mirrors and Windows: American Photography since 1960* by John Szarkowski, New York 1978; *Photographie als Kunst 1879-1979/Kunst als Photographie 1949-1979,* exhibition catalogue, 2 volumes, by Peter Weiermair, Innsbruck, Austria 1979; *Photography of the 50s,* exhibition catalogue, by Helen Gee, Tucson, Arizona 1980; *The Great Photographers: Ernst Haas,* edited by Bryn Campbell, London 1983; *Bilder vom Krieg* by Rainer Fabian and Hans Christian Adam, Hamburg 1983, as *Images of War: 130 Years of War Photography,* London 1985; *The Library of World Photography: Landscape,* with texts by David Plowden and Ian Jeffrey, Tokyo and London 1984; *La Photographie Créative* by Jean-Claude Lemagny, Paris 1984; *After the War Was Over,* with introduction by Mary Blume, London 1985. **Articles—**"Classics of Photography: Ernst Haas" by Inge Bondi in *Modern Photography* (New York), July 1970; "Ernst Haas Poem" in *Camera* (Lucerne), October 1970; "Ernst Haas" in *Modern Photography Annual,* New York 1972; "Ernst Haas" in *Color,* by the Time-Life editors, New York 1972; "Ernst Haas" in *Camera Mainchi* (Tokyo), July 1973; "Close-Up on Nature" in *Amateur Photographer* (London), 19 September 1973; "Ernst Haas" by Andre Laude in *Zoom* (Paris), June/July 1974; "Ernst Haas" by Inge Bondi in *Die Weltwoche* (Zurich), 13 October 1976; "New York" in

Zoom (Paris), November/December 1979; "7 Maitres du Paysage" in *Photocinema* (Paris), May 1980.

*

At my age the scales of what I did and what I still have to do is in constant movement and competition. For me, photography became a language with which I have learned to write both prose and poetry.

Whatever I did and do, it always became the extension of my interests. The interrelationship of all senses and arts is very important to me. I wanted to connect photography with words through books and articles, with music through audio-visuals. In exhibits, single pictures have to speak their pure visual language. I want to be open to everything in this world, and I am even willing to unlearn.

Important is the end result of your works, the opus; therefore, I want to be remembered much more by a total vision than a few perfect single pictures.

—Ernst Haas (1982)

* * *

The visual inspired Ernst Haas to give us successive innovations in photography. Their purpose: to communicate reality on all its planes, from the seen to the sensed, to the metaphysical. Expression and impression, the subjective and the objective mirror in his oeuvre the multiplicity of perception that enriches our lives. Though Haas is generally identified with color, he himself referred to differentiate between it and black and white, as "racism." In his work in both, form and content coincide at their peak, accentuating each other. In both, his vision has been radical, his solutions original. Edward Steichen described him as a free spirit, untrammeled by tradition.

Even as a child in Vienna, Haas looked at life as he saw fit. The changing shapes, movement of hues of clouds were more rewarding to him than the stereotyped information of the classroom. He was sent home from photography school. His work was too individual; he would not conform. In hungry, post-war Vienna, he traded with his mother's help a pound of butter for a camera and photographed: among the ruins, serene, two little girls with bare bottoms were taking a sunbath; a young soldier stuffed his artificial foot into his rucksack, adjusting to reality—one leg and a crutch; like a wish or premonition, birds flew over the ruins.

It was a time for hope and new beginnings. He had made a magazine connection. On a fashion assignment to be photographed at the railway station, Haas' models were late. A train brought prisoners of war, returning home from Russia. Ernst's photographs of the waiting, tense relatives, of their searching in the crowd, of reunions, of resignation to more waiting, were published. Bob Capa saw them and invited Haas to join the then small band of Magnum photographers. Now Haas flew, like the birds he had photographed over the ruins of Europe on assignment, and when *Life* offered him a job he preferred winging his photographic life, which soon took him to the United States.

Fascinated and frustrated, he could not get New York into his lens. In the changing light of the New Mexico desert, again on the fringe of an assignment, he encountered another milestone in his life: color. In his "Magic Images of New York," a story which *Life* published on 24 pages, at a time when color was used little and then to make subject matter more real, color transformed reality. Brooklyn Bridge in a haze of gold at dusk became every immigrant's symbol of hope; orange reflections in which a peacock struts on 42nd Street remind us that, in this city, the impossible can be beautiful. A swing in Central Park speaks of the exhilaration of riding high; a pile of junked cars, a skyscraper in the background, tells us that extravagant waste is part of it all. A smudge of oil on the road turns into an angel with an aureole. In Haas' New York, color accentuates mood, induces sensations, activates the viewer to participate. To do the same for Venice, a city whose presence is shrouded in associations of the past, Haas photographed it in November mists. The muted glow of lamps on cafe tables in the Piazza San Marco seems to come from long ago; calm greys echo the low vibrations of a guitar, gondolas loom out of the blue.

As the brilliant reflections of traffic moving in New York's glass facades turned into shimmering images of buildings reflected in canals, so the slow motion of gliding gondolas was electrified in his next essay, "Bullfight." With delicate colors, with indeterminate outlines, Haas accentuated the fast

changing beauty and unity of toreador and bull, hypnotised in their ritual, a minuet of death. This was the prelude to Haas' exploration of speed in sport, called "Motion," which matched, with its blurred effect, the exuberance of the 50s in the United States far better than any story concentrating on the specific could.

All these essays can now be seen only in the pages of old copies of *Life* magazine, yet their impact revised the vernacular of color, which, up to the publication of this work, had been only colored photography.

The Museum of Modern Art commemorated ten years of Ernst Haas' color by devoting to his work its first exhibition in that medium. Five years after it had appeared, Haas' concept of motion was still so new that a statement on it by him was included. He, however, was already far into his next project, which was published almost a decade later as his first book, *The Creation*.

It is a visualization of the story of Genesis, but also a code to Haas' way of seeing and photographing, going far beyond his previous work. His *In America, Ende und Anfang,* (End and Beginning, his b/w Vienna photographs), *In Germany* and *Himalayan Pilgrimage* followed, but much remains unseen and unpublished.

Though in his approach to the visual, Ernst Haas regarded himself as an impatient painter, his day to day work consisted of commercial assignments. While solving his client's problems, he had moments of quietude when the good accident provides for images which evoke the most frequent response from his viewers.

Ernst Haas' last color photographs speak more plainly than ever their message in that language he invented that does not follow the logic of words, but radiates the quintessence of those polar forces that make up the wheel of life. Awareness, endurance and discipline led Ernst Haas to beauty, dignity and tolerance. With gentle humour, he pursued the absolute in truth. To achieve it in photography, he said, you have to give of yourself, while taking your picture. Then the circle is closed. If not, there is no contact.

—Inge Bondi

HAHN, Betty.

Nationality: American. Born: Chicago, Illinois, 11 October 1940. Education: Studied under Henry Holmes Smith at Indiana University, Bloomington, A.B. in art 1963, M.F.A. in photography 1966. Family: Married Daniel Andrews in 1970. Career: Freelance photographer. Assistant Professor of Photography, Rochester Institute of Technology, 1969-75. Since 1976, Professor of Photography, University of New Mexico, Albuquerque. Recipient: Pratt Graphics Center Award, New York, 1971; Purchase Award, Sheldon Memorial Art Gallery, University of Nebraska, Lincoln, 1972; National Endowment for the Arts Fellowship, 1974, 1979; New York State Council on the Arts Grant, 1975; Research Grant, University of New Mexico, 1977; Polaroid Artists on "20x24" camera, 1988; Fellowship, Visual Arts Research Institute, Arizona State University. Agent: Andrew Smith, 76 East San Francisco Street, Santa Fe, New Mexico 87501; Witkin Gallery, 415 West Broadway, New York, New York 10012. Address: c/o Art Department, University of New Mexico, Albuquerque, New Mexico 87131, U.S.A.

Individual Exhibitions:

1966	Fine Arts Museum, Indiana University, Bloomington
1969	Smithsonian Institution, Washington, D.C. (with Gayle Smalley)
1971	Center for Photographic Studies, Louisville, Kentucky
1973	*Betty Hahn: Photo Images,* Riverside Studio, Rochester, New York
	Witkin Gallery, New York
1974	*Betty Hahn: Stitched Gum Bichromate Prints,* Focus Gallery, San Francisco
1976	*Betty Hahn and Steve Hale,* Nexus Gallery, Atlanta
	Betty Hahn: Passing Shots, New England School of Photography, Boston
1977	Archetype Gallery, New Haven, Connecticut

Carnation, **1988.** Photograph by Betty Hahn.

Sheldon Art Gallery, University of Nebraska, Lincoln
Southern Illinois University, Carbondale
Blue Sky Gallery, Portland, Oregon
Sandstone Gallery, Rochester, New York
1979   Witkin Gallery, New York
Miami-Dade Junior College
1980   Washington Project of the Arts, Washington, D.C.
Wildine Galleries, Albuquerque, New Mexico
1981   *Betty Hahn*, Colorado Mountain College, Breckenridge
Crime, Center for Creative Photography, University of Arizona,
Tucson
1982   *20 x 24 Color Polaroids*, Looking Glass Photography Gallery,
Royal Oak, Michigan
Columbia College, Chicago
1983   University of Alabama, Tuscaloosa
1984   University of New Mexico, Albuquerque
University of Arkansas, Fayetteville
Louisiana Technical University, Ruston
1985   Ruth Ramburg Gallery, Albuquerque, New Mexico
1986   Santa Fe Museum of Fine Arts, New Mexico
Passing Shots, Georgia State University, Atlanta
1988   *Crime and Intrigue*, Fort Wayne Museum of Art, Indiana
Non-Silver Prints, Baker Gallery, Kansas City
Lehigh University Art Galleries, Bethlehem, Pennsylvania
1989   *Shinjuku*, University Gallery, Fine Arts Center, University of
Massachusetts at Amherst
1991   *Berlin Time Frames*, Andrew Smith Gallery, Santa Fe, New
Mexico
1994   *Passing Shots: A Travel Series*, University of New Mexico Art
Museum, Albuquerque

Selected Group Exhibitions:

1967   *Photography in the 20th Century*, National Gallery of Canada,
Ottawa (toured Canada and the United States, 1967-73)
1969   *Vision and Expression*, International Museum of Photography,
George Eastman House, Rochester, New York (toured the
United States and Canada, 1969-71)
1972   *Photography into Art*, Camden Arts Centre, London
1973   *New Images 1939-1973*, Smithsonian Institution, Washington, D.C.
1975   *Women of Photography*, Sidney Janis Gallery, New York
1977   *The Great West: Real/Ideal*, University of Colorado, Boulder
(subsequently Smithsonian Institution travelling exhibition;
toured the United States)
1978   *Photography: New Mexico*, Centre Culturel American, Paris
1979   *20 x 24 Light*, Light Gallery, New York
1981   *Acquisitions 1973-80*, International Museum of Photography at
George Eastman House, Rochester, New York
1986   *Photographs by Artists in Mid-Career*, San Francisco Museum
of Modern Art
1990   *Artists Who Love Nature: From Barbizon School to Contemporary Photographers*, The Green Museum, Osaka, Japan
Fantasies, Fables and Fabrications, Phillips Exeter Academy
Gallery, Andover, MA
1991   *Photography from New Mexico*, Mosfilm Studio Gallery,
Moscow
1992   *The Modernist Still Life Photographed*, Touring exhibition
arranged by the USIA travelled to Karachi, Dehli, Riyadh,
Amman, Cairo, Algiers, Rabat, Athens, Thessaloniki
1993   Denver Art Museum, Denver Colorado
Intentions and Techniques, Lehigh University Art Gallery,
Bethlehem, Pennsylvania
1994   *Flora Photographica: The Flower in Photography from 1835
to the Present*, Musée des beaux-arts de Montreal, Montreal

Collections:

Museum of Modern Art, New York; International Museum of Photography,
George Eastman House, Rochester, New York; Smithsonian Institution,

Washington, D.C.; Virginia Museum of Fine Art, Richmond; Art Institute of
Chicago; Pasadena Art Museum, California; San Francisco Museum of
Modern Art; Crocker Art Museum, Sacramento, California; National Gallery
of Canada, Ottawa; Bibliothèque Nationale, Paris.

Publications:

By HAHN: Books—*Contemporary Spanish Photography*, editor, Albuquer-
que 1987. **Articles**—"Henry Holmes Smith: Speaking with a Genuine
Voice" in *Image* (Rochester, New York), December 1973; "Betty Hahn: On
Gum Bichromate Printing" in *Darkroom*, edited by Eleanor Lewis, New York
1977; "Photo Artist Betty Hahn," interview, with Brad Hill, in *Black and
White* (Albuquerque, New Mexico), July 1980.

On HAHN: Books—*Die Geschichte der Photographie im 20. Jahrhundert-
Photography in the 20th Century* by Petr Tausk, Cologne 1977, London 1980;
The Color Print Book by Arnold Gassan, Rochester, New York 1981; *Printed
by Women* by Judith Brodsky and Ofelia Garcia, Philadelphia 1983; *The
Modernist Still Life—Photographed*, by Jean S Tucker, St Louis 1989;
Photography at Bay: Interviews, Essays and Reviews by John Bloom, Albu-
querque 1993. **Articles**—"Woman Photographer Betty Hahn" by Robert
Sobieszek in *Ceskoslovenska Fotografie* (Prague), no. 2, 1973; "Anne Noggle/
Betty Hahn" by Lois Fishman in *Artweek* (Oakland, California), 24 Novem-
ber 1974; "Mums and Kitsch" by Dana Asbury in *Afterimage* (Rochester,
New York), Summer 1979; "Large Scale Exuberance" by Dana Asbury in
Artweek (Oakland, California), 17 May 1980;

*

The picture was no longer synonymous with the subject because I could
manipulate the process and exercise some intellectual control over those
details recorded by the camera while incorporating other ideas. Photographic
information could be provided where details were included, or it could remain
hidden where details were obscured.

—Betty Hahn

*   *   *

The work of Betty Hahn displays a wide range of process, techniques, and
imagery, but despite its variance, her work retains a coherence because of the
recurrent themes that weave throughout her many innovations. Hahn's career
now spans nearly 20 years; during this time she has constantly investigated
new ways to make pictures, from stitched photo-canvases to toy cameras.

Photography in the western world may be a nearly universal folk art, and
one interest evident in Hahn's work is in the naive, snapshot roots of the
medium. Her earliest works use family album imagery in casual shots of
children, friends and groups, underscoring the informality with bright colors
and bold brushstrokes of the hand-applied emulsions. Just as this early work
predates the renewed interest in the snapshot, evidenced by Jonathan Green's
book *The Snapshot* (1974), so her Mick-a-matic series (c. 1976) prefigures
the popularity among art photographers of the Diana and other toy cameras. In
this series, Hahn uses the softness and distortion of the plastic lens to
romanticize her vernacular and nostalgic imagery; pink flamingos and carnival horses, closely viewed and unsituated, take on a dreamlike presence. In
some of her most recent 20 x 24 color Polaroids, still-lifes comprised of
clippings and memorabilia recall a family member in a sentimental but elegant
composition. Using the simplest and most naive techniques or state-of-the-art
technology, Hahn explores photography's ability to preserve the past and the
almost fetishistic appeal that photographs as surrogates have maintained since
the first elaborately encased daguerreotypes.

Akin to this examination of the folk roots and vernacular symbols of
photography is Betty Hahn's attraction to the American hero; she explored at
great length the figure of the Lone Ranger in an extended series using, with one
image, numerous combinations of techniques and variations. The symbol was
well-chosen; not only did it represent a tongue-in-cheek statement about
media heroism but also a protracted look at the persistence of the photograph.
Despite Hahn's drawing on and extreme manipulation of the image, throughout the series it clings to that unmistakable quality—"photographicness."

If the cowboy on his horse occupies a solid place in American mythology as the virile loner, it is a place he shares in the popular imagination with the detective. Hahn's series of set-up color photographs posing as documents of the scene of the crime amplifies the mystique of crime detection, as do her recent color Polaroid arrangements of clues to fictional crimes. Hahn plays with her role, the artist as detective, and understands that it is the persistence of the photograph that makes crime photography so compelling. As in Antonioni's movie *Blow-Up* (1966), there is a superstitious and sometimes obsessive belief in the photograph's ability to yield clues or answers if examined minutely enough. There has been a curious popular reluctance to admit the limitations of photography; Hahn focuses upon those limitations and the myths and draws them out in these series that are both visually exciting and culturally abundant.

Another recurrent theme in Betty Hahn's work is her attraction to flowers. From the Mick-a-matic pictures of gardens bathed in warm afternoon light to her groups of mums in large blue and brown prints with extensive use of paint and handwork to her most recent 20 x 24 color Polaroids, "Botanical Layouts," the flower remains both a fragile and feminine symbol of beauty and an element which evokes a wealth of art historical tradition. Hahn uses the conventions of 18th century botanical prints, Japanese prints, and some of Piet Mondrian's devices from his chrysanthemum series, yet her mastery of the characteristics of hand-applied emulsions or the jewel-like renditions of large format contact prints make this body of work both evocative and fresh.

Botanical layouts, publicity stills, family album snapshots or wherever Hahn finds inspiration for her imagery, it all unites around an investigation of a popular use of the photograph. She amplifies the inherent charm of her subject matter with her sophistication as a designer and colorist.

—Dana Asbury

HAJEK-HALKE, Heinz.

Nationality: German. **Born:** Berlin, 1 December 1898. **Education:** Educated in Argentina, until 1910, in Berlin, 1910-15; studied painting, Königlichen Kunstschule, Berlin, under Emil Orlik and Baluschek, 1915-16, 1919-23; mainly self-taught in photography, but influenced by photojournalist Willi Ruge, Berlin, from 1925. **Military Service:** Served in the German Army, 1917-19; served as aerial photographer, Dornier Company, Friedrichshafen/Bodensee, 1939-44: prisoner-of-war, France, escaped 1945. **Career:** Worked as copperplate printer, poster designer, and press illustrator, for Presseverlag Dr. Dammart, Berlin, 1919-23; worked on a fishing boat, Hamburg, 1923-25; photojournalist and advertising photographer, working for Presse-Photo agency, Berlin, 1925-33; scientific and biological photographer, as Heinz Halke, Bodensee (Lake Constance), 1933-37; filmmaker on snake farm, Brazil, 1937-38; after escape from prisoner-of-war camp, founder-proprietor, snake venom farm, West Berlin, 1945-47. Independent photographer and photomontagist, West Berlin, 1947, until his death in 1983. Member, via Toni Schneiders, Fotoform group of photographers, Saarbrücken, 1949-54. Instructor in Photography and Photomontage, Kunstgewerbeschule, Berlin-Charlottenburg, 1925; Lecturer in Photo-Graphics, Hochschule für Bildende Künste, West Berlin, from 1955. Member, Deutsche Gesellschaft für Photographie (DGPh), 1955; Gesellschaft für Deutsche Lichtbildner, (GDL), 1957. **Recipient:** Culture Award, Deutsche Gesellschaft für Photographie, 1965; David Octavius Hill Medal, Gesellschaft Deutsche Lichtbildner (GDL), 1978. Guest of Honor, *Rencontres Internationales de la Photographie*, Arles, France, 1977; Honorary Professor, Bürgermeister of Berlin, 1978. **Died:** (in West Berlin) *in 1983.*

Individual Exhibitions:

1954   *Foto-Grafik,* Suermondt-Museum, Aachen, West Germany

1956   *Lichtgrafik,* Franklin-Institut, Lindau, West Germany
        Foto-Grafik, Museum für Angewandte Kunst, Vienna
1957   *Herbert Bayer—Hajek-Halke,* Kunstgewer-bemuseum, Zurich
        Lichtgrafik, Deutsche Gesellschaft für Photographie, Cologne
1958   *Lichtgrafik,* Landesbildstelle, Hamburg
        Lichtgrafik, Virchow-Krankenhaus, Berlin (with Paul Dierke's *Plastik*)
1959   *Fotografia Sperimentale di H-H,* Biblioteca Communale, Milan
        Angenendt, Coppens, Hajek-Halke, Palazzo Azienda di Soggiorno, Pescara, Italy
1960   *Deutsche Lichtgrafik Werke von Hajek-Halke,* National Museum of Modern Art, Tokyo (travelled to the Fuji-Photo Salon, Osaka, Japan)
1965   *Lichtgrafik,* Werkkunstschule, Bielefeld, West Germany
        Deutsche Gesellschaft für Photographie, Cologne
1966   Modus Department Store, Berlin
        Lichtgrafik, Galerie am Dom, Frankfurt
1967   *Lichtgrafik,* Galerie Clarissa, Hannover
1968   *Lichtgrafik,* Galerie Seestrasse 67, Ludwigsburg, West Germany
        Lichtgrafik, Carleton University, Ottawa
        Lichtgrafik, University of Montreal
1969   *Lichtgrafik,* Galleria dell'Immagine di Popular Photography Italiana, Milan
        Lichtgrafik, Museum Het Sterckshof, Deurne/Antwerp
1970   *Fotografie—Fotografik—Lichtgrafik,* Landesbildstelle, Berlin
1978   *Die Freiheit des Fotografen: Montagen/Collagen/Lichtgrafiken,* Fotomuseum in Stadtmuseum, Munich
        Heinz Hajek-Halke: Fotografie, Foto-Grafik, Licht-Grafik, Galerie Werner Kunze, West Berlin
1979   *Fotografie—Fotografik—Lichtgrafik,* Gallerie Lewi, Hamburg
        Lichtgrafik, Galerie Duc et Camroux, Paris
1980   *Lichtgrafik,* Foto-Art-Galerie, Basle

Selected Group Exhibitions:

1968   *Light7,* Massachusetts Institute of Technology, Cambridge
1979   *Deutsche Fotografie nach 1945,* Kunstverein, Kassel, West Germany (toured West Germany)
1980   *Photographia: La Linea Sottile,* Galleria Flaviana, Locarno, Switzerland
        Avant-Garde Photography in Germany 1919-1939, San Francisco Museum of Modern Art (toured the United States, 1981-82)
1981   *Farbe im Photo,* Josef-Haubrich-Kunsthalle, Cologne
1983   *Fotogramme—Die lichtreichen Schatten,* Fotomuseum im Stadtmuseum, Munich
1984   *Subjektive Fotografie: Images of the 50s,* San Francisco Museum of Modern Art (travelled to the University of Houston, Texas; Museum Folkwang, Essen; Vasterbottens Museum, Umea; Kulturhuset, Stockholm; Saarland Museum, Saarbrucken; Palais des Beaux-Arts, Brussels)
1985   *Das Aktfoto,* Fotomuseum im Stadtmuseum, Munich

Collections:

Kunstbibliothek, Berlin; Kupferstich-Kabinett, Berlin; Landesgalerie, Hannover; Kestner Museum, Hannover; Museum für Kunst und Gewerbe, Hamburg; Museum Folkwang, Essen; Foto-Historama der Agfa-Gevaert AG, Leverkusen, Germany; Stadtmuseum, Munich; Museum Het Sterckshof, Deurne/Antwerp; Museum of Modern Art, New York.

Publications:

By HAJEK-HALKE: Books—*Experimentelle Fotografie,* Bonn 1955; *Magie der Farbenfotografie,* with text by W. Boje, Dusseldorf 1961; *Lichtgrafik,* Dusseldorf and Vienna 1964, as *Abstract Pictures on Film,* London 1965.

On HAJEK-HALKE: Books—*Europa-Camera* by Kurt Zentner and Bernd Lohse, Frankfurt 1951; *Subjektive Fotografie I* by Otto Steinert, Munich 1952; *Akt International* by Otto Steinert, Munich 1954; *Das Aktfoto* by Herbert Rittlinger, Dusseldorf 1954; *Subjektive Fotografie II* by Otto Steinert, Munich 1955; *Photography of the World,* Tokyo 1957; *Photographie Heute* by G. Basner, Bernd Lohse and Niels Reuter, Frankfurt 1958; *Parteilichkeit im Foto* by Berthold Beiler, Halle, East Germany 1959; *Deutsche Lichtgrafik Werke von Heinz Hajek-Halke,* exhibition catalogue, with an introduction by Arryo Orsi, Tokyo 1960; *Fotografisk Arsbok '60,* Stockholm 1960; *Selbstportraits* by Otto Steinert, Berlin 1961; *Fetisch des Jahrhunderts* by Fritz Kempe, Dusseldorf 1964; *Die Welt der Camera,* Lucerne 1964; *Esthètique du Nu dans le Monde* by Lucien Lorelle, Paris 1964; *Werbarium der Zwanziger Jahre,* Hamburg 1965; *Light7,* edited by Minor White, Rochester, New York 1968; *Generative Fotografie* by Gottfried Jäger and Karl Martin Holzhäuser, Ravensburg, West Germany 1975; *Geschichte der Fotografie im 20. Jahrhundert/Photography in the 20th Century* by Petr Tausk, Cologne 1977, London 1980; *Heinz Hajek-Halke,* exhibition catalogue, Göttingen, West Germany 1978; *Heinz Hajek-Halke: Fotografie, Foto-Grafik, Lichtgrafik,* exhibit introduction by Eberhard Roters, West Berlin 1978; *Deutsche Fotografie nach 1945/German Photography after 1945* by Floris Neusüss, Wolfgang Kemp and Petra Benteler, Kassel, West Germany 1979; *Fotografie 1919-1979, Made in Germany: Die GDL-Fotografen,* edited by Fritz Kempe, Bernard Lohse, and others, Frankfurt 1979; *Photographia: La Linea Sottile,* exhibition catalogue, by Rinaldo Bianda and Giuliana Scimé, Locarno, Switzerland 1980; *Avant-Garde Photography in Germany 1919-1939,* exhibition catalogue, by Van Deren Coke, Ute Eskildsen and Bernd Lohse, San Francisco 1980; *The Imaginary Photo Museum* by Helmut Gernsheim, Renate and L. Fritz Gruber and others, Cologne 1981, London 1982; *Fotogramme—die lichtreichen Schatten,* exhibition catalogue, by Floris M. Neusüss, Kassel, West Germany 1983; *Subjektive Fotografie: Images of the 50s,* exhibition catalogue, by Ute Eskildsen, Manfred Schmalriede and Dorothy Martinson, Essen, West Germany 1984.

*   *   *

Heinz Hajek-Halke, who really wanted to be a painter, became a master of experimental photography in Germany with his *Lichtgrafiken.*

He was born in Berlin in 1898, the son of a painter, and he studied in that city at the arts academy under Emil Orlik. After the First World War he designed film posters, became a press illustrator, then a photojournalist and an advertising photographer. Even during this early period, at the end of the 1920s, his first photo-montages had begun to appear, among them the exemplary work, "Evil Gossip": three gentlemen in frock coats and top hats talk together in a street which, at the same time, is the torso of a recumbent female nude—body and asphalt, nude and street, two levels of image and sensation, superimposed to produce a double entendre, a doubly sensual new image. In works such as this Hajek-Halke reflected the photomontages of the Dadaists and Surrealists, particularly the pictures of the Berlin Dadaists, Hanna Höch, John Heartfield, and Raoul Hausmann.

How suggestively—with cross exposure, cross copying and mounting—reality could be photographically altered, and with what virtuosity Hajek-Halke could carry it out, was also recognized by the Nazis. In 1933 they asked him to falsify documentary photographs for the Ministry of Propaganda. Hajek-Halke avoided their grasp by moving to Lake Constance where he specialized in macro-photographs in the field of small animal biology. In 1939, however, he was obliged to serve as works and flight photographer at the Dornier factories in Friedrichshafen.

After the war Hajek-Halke founded a snake farm in order to finance a new set of photographic equipment from the sale of snake venom to the pharmaceutical industry. And during this period he began to make photogrammes and *lichtgrafiken,* without a camera, in the tradition of the photogrammes of Man Ray, Christian Schad and Moholy-Nagy. Hajek-Halke's work became abstract yet at the same time, in the sense of the photographic medium, highly concrete. His artistic, object-less photography extended from the luminogramme, the recording of tracks of light, to the graphic and chemical treatment of the film negative. It is a poetic photography in parallel with nature, with art, just as much related to the informal painting of the 1950s as to the structures and organic processes of nature.

In 1955 the Berlin Hochschule für Bildende Künste appointed him Dozent für Foto-Grafik—the first professorship of this kind in a German arts academy. An alchemist among photographers of the 20th century, Heinz Hajek-Halke also became known to a wide public with his books *Experimentelle Fotografie* and *Lichtgrafik.*

—Peter Sager

HALLETT, George.

Nationality: South African. **Born:** in Cape Town, 31 December 1942. **Education:** High School, Cape Town, Senior Certificate 1960; self-taught in photography. **Family:** Married to Marie-Madeleine Olong; children: Mymoena and Natasha. **Career:** Worked freelance for *The Times Educational Supplement,* London, and designed book covers for *Heinemann Educational Books,* 1970-82. Lecturer, Central London Polytechnic, 1972-73. Worked as freelance photographer and farmer, France, 1974-80. Lecturer, Zimbabwe Institute of Mass Communications (ZIMCO), Harare, Zimbabwe, 1981-82. Lecture tour of universities in the United States, 1982. Worked for *South Magazine,* London, 1983. Artist in Residence, University of Illinois, 1983. Freelance work in Holland and England, 1986. Lecturer, St Martins School of Art, The London Institute, London, 1987; and Centre for Photographic Studies, Cape Town, 1993. Since 1992, lives in Paris and Cape Town. **Address:** 1 Avenue Victor Hugo, 91860 Epinay sous Senart, France.

Individual Exhibitions:

1970	The Artists Gallery, Cape Town
1971	Westekerk, Amsterdam
1972	Anne Frank Huis, Amsterdam
	Presence Africaine, Paris
	University of Brussels, Belgium
1973	Susan Loppert Graphics, London
	Central London Polytechnic
	John Hansard Gallery, Southampton University, England
1975	Midi Libre Journal, Perpignan, France
1976	Sonja Henie Kunstzentrum, Oslo
	University of Lund, Sweden
	Gothenburg Museum, Sweden
1977	Provinciehuis Groningen, Netherlands
1979	Künstlerhaus Bethanien, Berlin
1980	Atelier Six, Ceret, France
1982	Women of Southern Africa Conference Centre, Harare, Zimbabwe
	University of Illinois
1983	Howard University Gallery, Washington, D.C.
	Michigan State University, Lansing
	Emory University, Atlanta, Georgia
	Tuskegee Institute, Atlanta, Georgia
	Carbondale Southern Illinois University
1984	Stadhuis Leiden, Netherlands
	Schomburg Center, New York
1985	University of Illinois
1988	Aschenbach Gallery, Amsterdam
1989	Afrika Centrum Cadier en Keer, Maastricht, Netherlands

Selected Group Exhibitions:

1969	*New Photography,* University of Cape Town, Architecture Faculty Gallery, South Africa
1973	Serpentine Gallery, London
1982	*Culture and Resistance Festival,* The National Museum of Botswana, Gaborone, Botswana
1983	*Nothing Will Separate Us,* toured Germany
1984	*14 Black Photographers,* Schomburg Center, New York (and toured the United States)
	Black Photography from South Africa to South Carolina, Castillo Gallery, New York

Untitled. Photograph by George Hallett.

1986   *Allemal Amsterdamers,* Stadhuis Amsterdam, Netherlands

Collections:

Sonja Henie-Nils Onstad Collection, Oslo; Künstlerhaus Bethanien, Berlin.

Publications:

By HALLETT: Books—*Present Lives Future Becoming,* with Wilfred Paulse and Clarence Coulson, and text by Cosmo Pieterse, London 1973;

Images, with text by James Matthews, South Africa 1979. **Films**—*District Six,* television documentary, 1975; *Morokaners uit Amsterdam,* information video, 1984.

On HALLETT: Books—*Nichts wird uns trennen/Nothing will separate us,* Berne 1983; *An Illustrated Bio-Bibliography of Black Photographers 1940-1988* by Deborah Willis-Thomas, New York 1989.

*   *   *

George Hallett's photographs narrate the significance of people by establishing humanity as an emotive subject for contemplation. Fact, fiction and speculation are part of the spectrum of light captured in his work and ultimately one's engagement with his images are a kinetic en-coding and re-coding of the world.

Hallett's vision offers a counter balance, a thankful release in fact, from the threat of indifference posed by the swamp of photographic images that abound in the post-modern metropolis. By seeking the re-location of feeling and the evocation of an emotional response, it quietly chants a rebellious anthem for a different kind of life. His response to the cool remoteness of contemporary looking is to place before us the pulse and texture of the people and things that once moved him.

His photographs aim to permeate one's subconscious, giving insights beyond appearances. He evokes the spirit of one's humanity in so many ways. By choosing to serve his subjects rather than a contemporary style or theory, his work displays great care and respect for what is transformed into image. Hallett has engineered a complex world filled with cultural differences, an imagined world that unfolds at two levels. Firstly, in the spectacle of each individual photographic moment, when coincidences tessellate to construct a particular image whose character is distinct and succeeds in unlocking the magic of the reality from which it came. Secondly, in the manner one's imagined sense of humanity is objectified. Nothing in the picture frame is inadvertent. Encoding and translating his work serves not to construct a description, but rather to investigate and prove that the spirit of an image is not absent or dead. One is engaged in unwrapping the word *humanity* from the layers of meaning our tongues have placed around it, each unwrapping disclosing humanity's presence and vitality. Moreover, the work's success is its quiet insistence that what is seen is somehow contextualized socially and/or historically, that one must appraise with an open mind cultures and people one may just have encountered but cannot yet fully comprehend.

Hallett is a black South African, who had no access to any academic training in photography when he started. He recalls that in desperation he sought inspiration in black visual artists, writers and musicians. He found in this fraternity not only an understanding for his photographic aspirations but located dissonant voices who like himself believed that South African visual expression needed strategies to take it beyond the assertion that art should strictly serve the anti-apartheid struggle. Those early alliances brought him to the realisation that South African art had to be more than complaint about the inane and monstrous acts of racists or narrations of the revolutionary struggle of black people. It had also to show its ability to visualise a culture, and avoid parochialism.

His work challenges viewers to use the re-generative power of their imagination. To rethink the world, and avoid the dichotomy that moulds all African photography into ethnographic or anthropological fact. In doing this he has assumed the role of an empathetic and knowledgeable seer, rather than that of ethnographer.

—Gavin Jantjes

HALSMAN, Phillippe.

Nationality: American. **Born:** Riga, Latvia, 2 May 1906; emigrated to the United States, 1940: naturalized, 1949. **Education:** Vidus Skola, Riga, 1922-24, B.A. 1924; studied electrical engineering, Technische Hochschule, Dresden, Germany, 1924-28; studied at the Sorbonne, Paris, 1931; self-taught in photography. **Family:** Married Yvonne Moser in 1937; children: Irene Alene and Jane Ellen. **Career:** Worked as part-time freelance photographer, mainly for Ullstein publishing house in Berlin, while still a student, 1924-28; then moved to Paris; freelance portrait and fashion photographer with own studio in

Paris working for *Vogue, Vu, Voila,* etc., 1931-40; freelance photographer, New York, working for *Life, Saturday Evening Post, Look,* etc., 1941-79. Instructor, Famous Photographers School, Westport, Connecticut, 1969-79. President, American Society of Magazine Photographers, New York, 1944, 1954. **Recipient:** 10 Greatest Photographers Award, *Popular Photography,* New York, 1958; Newhouse Award, 1963; Golden Plate Award, American Academy of Achievement, 1967; Life Achievement Award, American Society of Magazine Photographers, 1975. **Died:** (in New York) *25 June 1979.*

Individual Exhibitions

1979	International Center of Photography, New York (retrospective)
1981	Foto Galerij Paule Pia, Antwerp, Belgium
1985	Galerie zur Stockeregg, Zurich

Selected Group Exhibitions:

1936	*Exposition Internationale de la Photographie Contemporaine,* Musée des Arts Decoratifs, Paris
1951	*Memorable Life Photographs,* Museum of Modern Art, New York
1965	*12 International Photographers,* Gallery of Modern Art, New York
1978	*Photos from the Sam Wagstaff Collection,* Corcoran Gallery of Art, Washington, D.C. (toured the United States and Canada)
1979	*Fleeting Gestures: Dance Photographs,* International Center of Photography, New York (travelled to The Photographers' Gallery, London; and *Venezia '79*)
	Life: The First Decade 1936-1945, Grey Art Gallery, New York University (toured the United States)
1980	*Photography of the 50s,* International Center of Photography, New York (travelled to Center for Creative Photography, University of Arizona, Tucson; Minneapolis Institute of Arts; California State University at Long Beach; and Delaware Art Museum, Wilmington)
1982	*Lichtbildnisse: Das Porträt in der Fotografie,* Rheinisches Landesmuseum, Bonn
1983	*Photography in America 1910-83,* Tampa Museum, Florida
1984	*Sammlung Gruber,* Museum Ludwig, Cologne

Collections:

Metropolitan Museum of Art, New York; Museum of Modern Art, New York; Life Picture Collection, New York; International Center of Photography, New York; Smithsonian Institution, Washington, D.C.; Library of Congress, Washington, D.C.; New Orleans Museum of Art; Royal Photographic Society, London; Museum Ludwig, Cologne.

Publications:

By HALSMAN: Books—*The Frenchman: A Photographic Interview with Fernandel,* New York 1949, London 1950; *The Candidate,* New York 1952; *Piccoli,* New York 1953; *Dali's Mustache: A Photographic Interview with Salvador Dali,* New York 1954; *Polaroid Portfolio no. 1,* with others, edited by John Wolbarst, New York 1959; *Philippe Halsman's Jump Book,* New York and London 1959; *Halsman on the Creation of Photographic Ideas,* New York and London 1961; *Halsman: Sight and Insight,* New York 1972; *Halsman,* with an introduction by Owen Edwards, New York 1979; *Photographers on Photography,* edited by Jerry C. LaPlante, New York 1979; *Halsman Portraits,* edited by Yvonne Halsman, New York 1983. **Articles**—"Artificial Light" in *Popular Photography Annual,* New York 1957; "Philippe Halsman Interview," with Casey Allen, in *Camera 35* (New York), July 1978; "Marilyn Jumps" in *American Photographer* (New York), March 1979. **Film**—*For a Livable America.*

On HALSMAN: Books—*Memorable Life Photographs,* with text by Edward Steichen, New York 1951; *Fame: Famous Portraits of Famous People by Famous Photographers,* edited by L. Fritz Gruber, London and New York 1960; *The Magic Image* by Cecil Beaton and Gail Buckland, London and

Boston 1975; *Geschichte der Fotografie im 20. Jahrhundert/Photography in the 20th Century* by Petr Tausk, Cologne 1977, London 1980; *A Book of Photographs from the Collection of Sam Wagstaff,* designed by Arne Lewis, New York 1978; *Life: The First Decade 1936-1945* by Ralph Littman, Ralph Graves and Doris C. O'Neill, New York 1979, London 1980; *Photographie als Kunst 1879-1979/Kunst als Photographie 1949-1979,* exhibition catalogue, 2 vols., by Peter Weiermair, Innsbruck, Austria 1979; *Photographic Surrealism,* exhibition catalogue, edited by Nancy Hall-Duncan, Cleveland 1979; *Halsman,* exhibition catalogue, New York 1979; *The Photograph Collector's Guide* by Lee D. Witkin and Barbara London, Boston and London 1979; *Photography of the 50s,* exhibition catalogue, by Helen Gee, Tucson, Arizona 1980; *Lichtbildnisse: Das Porträt in der Fotografie,* edited by Klaus Honnef, Cologne 1982; *The Library of World Photography: Portraits,* with introduction by Colin Ford, Tokyo 1982, 1983, London 1983; *After the War Was Over,* with introduction by Mary Blume, London 1985. **Articles—** "Philippe Halsman" in *U.S. Camera Annual 1952,* edited by Tom Maloney, New York 1951; "Halsman: Sight and Insight" in *Popular Photography* (New York), August 1973; "Philippe Halsman's Mini Course in Portrait Lighting" by Renee Bruns in *Popular Photography* (New York), November 1973; "Philippe Halsman" by Ruth Spencer in the *British Journal of Photography* (London), 10 October 1975; "Halsman on Portraits" by Janet Nelson in the *New York Times,* 9 April 1978; "Fantasies of Philippe" by Charles Reynolds in *Popular Photography* (New York), July 1979; "Philippe Halsman 1906-1979" by Arthur Goldsmith in *Popular Photography* (New York), September 1979; "Halsman: A Tribute" by Owen Edwards in *Portfolio* (New York), October/November 1979.

* * *

Latvian-born Philippe Halsman achieved his greatest photographic reputation in the United States as a master of graphically powerful, psychologically penetrating, and technically superb portraiture. During the heyday of the old (weekly) *Life* magazine, Halsman's photographs frequently appeared on its pages, and he is the only photographer ever to make the cover 100 times; in fact, he added one more for good measure. In addition to his portraiture, Halsman also found time to express a rich, delightful sense of fantasy in the vein of surrealism, concocting outrageous visual puns and startling juxtapositions of images. In the latter work he often collaborated with his long-time acquaintance, Salvador Dali.

The son of a dentist, Halsman left his native Riga during his teens to study electrical engineering in Dresden for three years. He then moved to Paris where the stimulating intellectual climate of the 20s was more to his liking. He decided to abandon engineering for the world of arts and letters, first as a poet (writing in French) and then increasingly as a photographer. An interest in psychology led him to photographic portraiture. He believed that through an understanding of psychology it was possible for a photographer "to capture the essence of a human being." In later developing his theory of "psychological portraiture," he wrote: "Very often it is not the good photographer who makes the good portrait but the good psychologist. In many sittings I have felt that what I said to the client was more important than what I did with my camera and my lights."

Rebelling against the soft-focus pictorial style then in vogue, he believed that making sharply-focused images was the only proper way to use a camera, and he remained passionately dedicated to image sharpness thereafter. He sought clarity and precision in his images as he did in his thinking and writing. Although emphasizing that technique was only a means to an end, he became a master technician. "Each technical step must contribute.... This is the meaning of the interrelation of technique and emotion," he said. "An uncut diamond has only a potential value. Only after it is cut and polished does it shine in the dark."

By the time World War II broke out, Halsman had established himself as a successful portrait photographer in Paris; his clients included leading personalities in the avant garde cultural scene there such as André Malraux and Jean Cocteau. As the German army approached Paris in 1940, Halsman, his French wife, Yvonne, and their baby daughter left for New York on an emergency visa obtained with the help of Albert Einstein.

Before long, Halsman began to earn a new reputation and receive even greater success in the United States than he had in Paris. Although never on the staff of *Life,* he achieved his greatest fame through assignments for that publication. During many years of active relationship with *Life* and other

leading picture magazines, Halsman photographed many of the most celebrated personalities of the times: Winston Churchill, Albert Einstein, The Duke and Duchess of Windsor, John F. Kennedy, Marilyn Monroe, Bertrand Russell, Matisse, Chagall, Joan Baez, and many others. Some of these Halsman portraits, especially the 1947 Einstein portrait, have become the definitive image of the person photographed, indelibly burned into the retina and brains of millions of people. Three have been issued as U.S. postage stamps.

In addition to his more serious work, Halsman pursued the whimsical, fantastic aspect of his personality. Among the most striking of his studio-created surrealism is "Dali Atomicus" in which the painter is caught in mid-air amidst levitating furniture, flying cats, and a stream of water. Halsman's books include *The Frenchman, Piccoli,* a non-photographic fairy tale which has since been translated into three languages, *Dali's Mustache, Philippe Halsman's Jump Book,* which reveals famous people jumping, and *Halsman on the Creation of Photographic Ideas,* an exposition of his psychological and visual theories.

During the last years of his life Halsman was plagued by ill-health and fits of depression, although he continued to carry out magazine assignments and continue his portrait practice on a limited scale. Shortly before his death in 1979 he completed work on a major retrospective exhibition at Manhattan's International Center of Photography, which reflected both his achievements as a portrait photographer and his imaginative play with the absurdity of vision.

The heritage of his portraits includes images in which emotion and technique merge in sharp focus, capturing the "quintessential" aspects of a human personality that always was his goal. However, the originality and imagination of his created photographs, made for his own amusement, are not submerged by his more serious work, revealing as they do a vision both whimsical and disturbing. He belongs to both the tradition of portraiture and that of surrealism.

—Arthur Goldsmith

HAMAYA, Hiroshi.

Nationality: Japanese. **Born:** Tokyo, 28 March 1915. **Education:** Kanto Daiichi High School, Tokyo, 1929-33; mainly self-taught in photography. **Family:** Married Asa Nanbu in 1948. **Career:** Freelance photographer, Tokyo, 1937-45, Takada City, Niigata Prefecture, 1945-52, and in Oiso, Kanagawa Prefecture, since 1952; Contributing Photographer, Magnum Photos co-operative agency, New York and Paris, since 1960. Has photographed in Manchuria, 1940, 1942, in China, 1956, in Thailand, 1960, Western Europe, 1963, the United States, Mexico and Canada, 1967, 1969, 1973, Nepal, 1974, Australia and the South Pacific, 1975, Greenland, 1976, Nepal, 1978, Algeria and Turkey, 1979, China, 1980, and Australia, 1981. **Recipient:** Master of Photography Award, International Center of Photography, New York, 1986. **Agents:** Magnum Photos, 251 Park Avenue South, New York, New York 10010, and 20 rue des Grands-Augustins, 75006 Paris; Pacific Press Service (PPS Tsushinsha), 3-4-4 Iidabashi, Chiyoda-ku, Tokyo 102. **Address:** 534 Higashikoiso, Oiso-machi, Kanagawa-ken 255, Japan.

Individual Exhibitions:

1946	*Heavy Snowfall in 1945 in Takada,* Izumoya Gallery, Takada, Niigata Prefecture
1947	*7 Artists in Echigo,* Daishi Bank Hall, Takada, Niigata Prefecture, Japan
1957	*The Red China I Saw,* Takashimaya Department Store, Tokyo
1959	*Ook Dit is Japan,* Leiden Museum, Holland
1960	*The Document of Grief and Anger,* Matsuya Gallery, Tokyo
1969	*Hamaya's Japan,* Asia House, New York
1970	*Nature of Japan,* at Photokina '70, Cologne
1981	*Hiroshi Hamaya: 50 Years of Photography,* Takashimaya Department Store, Wako Hall and Fuji Photo Salon, Tokyo
1982	*Form of the Earth,* Takashimaya Department Store, Tokyo
1983	*Fifty Years of Photography,* Beijing Museum, China

1986   *Fifty Years of Photography*, International Center of Photography, New York, (travelled to the Matsuya Department Store, Tokyo)

Selected Group Exhibitions:

1959   *Biennale Internazionale di Fotografia*, Venice
1960   *The World as Seen by Magnum*, Takashimaya Department Store, Tokyo (and world tour)
1965   *12 Photographers*, Gallery of Modern Art, New York
1972   *The Concerned Photographer*, Smithsonian Institution, Washington, D.C.
1979   *Japan: A Self-Portrait*, International Center of Photography, New York
        Venezia '79
        Japanese Photography Today and Its Origin, Galleria d'Arte Moderna, Bologna (travelled to the Palazzo Reale, Milan; Palais des Beaux-Arts, Brussels; the Institute of Contemporary Arts, London; Museum für Kunst und Gewerbe, Hamburg; Gemeente Museum, Arnhem; Pulchri Studio, The Hague)
1980   *The Imaginary Photo Museum*, Kunsthalle, Cologne
1984   *Sammlung Gruber*, Museum Ludwig, Cologne
1985   *A Day in the Life of Japan*, Tokyo (toured Japan)

Collections:

National Museum of Modern Art, Tokyo; Bibliothèque Nationale, Paris; Museum of Modern Art, New York; International Museum of Photography, George Eastman House, Rochester, New York; International Center of Photography, New York; Museum Ludwig, Cologne; Art Museum of Kawasaki, Japan.

Publications:

By HAMAYA: Books—*Yuki Guni(The Snow Country)*, Tokyo 1956; *Ura Nihon (Back Regions of Japan)*, Tokyo 1957; *Umruch-Hsinchiang, China/Urumchi, The Remote City*, Tokyo 1957; *The Red China I Saw*, Tokyo 1958; *Contemporary Japanese Photography: A Volume of Selected Works by Hiroshi Hamaya*, Tokyo 1958; *Children in Japan*, Tokyo 1959; *Det Gomda Japan*, Stockholm 1960; *A Record of Anger and Sorrow*, Tokyo 1960; *Landscapes of Japan*, with an introduction by Taro Tsujimura, Tokyo 1964; *Latentimage Afterimage: Hiroshi Hamaya's Memoirs*, Tokyo 1971; *American America*, Tokyo 1971; *Nature*, portfolio, Tokyo 1971; *A Treasury of Japanese Poetry*, Tokyo 1972; *Yaichi Aizu: Portfolio of a Master Calligrapher*, Tokyo 1972; *Tokyo 1936*, with Katsuya Nakamura, Tokyo 1974; *Landscape of Japan National Park*, Tokyo 1975; *Mount Fuji: A Lone Peak*, Tokyo 1978; *Summer Shots: Antarctic Peninsula*, Tokyo 1979; *Hiroshi Hamaya: 50 Years of Photography*, in 2 volumes: *Aspects of Nature* and *Aspects of Life*, Tokyo 1981; *The Collected Works of Hiroshi Hamaya*, Tokyo 1981; *Landscapes*, New York 1982; *Travel*, Tokyo 1982; *Japanese Scholars and Artists*, Tokyo 1983; *Women in the Showa Era*, Tokyo 1985; *Calendar Days of Asa Hamaya*, Tokyo 1986.

On HAMAYA: Books—*Photography of the World*, edited by Heibonsha Publishers, Tokyo 1956; *Nihon Shashin Shi, 1840-1945* by the Japan Photographers Association, Tokyo 1971, as *A Century of Japanese Photography*, with introduction by John W. Dower, New York and London 1980; *The Concerned Photographer 2*, edited by Cornell Capa, New York and London 1972; *Japan: A Self-Portrait*, edited by Shoji Yamagishi and Cornell Capa, New York 1979; *Japanese Photography Today and Its Origins* by Attilio Colombo and Isabella Doniselli, Bologna, Italy 1979; *A Day in the Life of Australia—March 6, 1981*, with introduction by Thomas Kenneally, Potts Point, New South Wales 1981; *The Imaginary Photo Museum* by Helmut Gernsheim, Renate and L. Fritz Gruber and others, Cologne 1981, London 1982; *The Library of World Photography: Landscape*, with texts by David Plowden and Ian Jeffrey, Tokyo and London 1984; *A Day in the Life of Japan—June 7, 1985*, edited by Rick Smolan and David Cohen, New York and London 1985. Articles—''River, Swamp, Sea and Fire Mountains:

Pictures of Japan by Hiroshi Hamaya'' in *Du* (Zurich), February 1970; ''Hiroshi Hamaya'' in *Modern Photography Annual*, New York 1972; ''The Concerned Photographers'' by Cornell Capa in *Zoom* (Paris), no. 16, 1973; ''Hiroshi Hamaya and the Art of No Art'' by Owen Edwards in *American Photographer* (New York), July 1986.

*

From the preface to *Landscapes of Japan*, 1964:
It has been 33 years since I began photography, and 31 years since the time that I decided to take up photography as my life's work. During all this period what captured and held my interest was people and their problems. I, who was born in down-town Tokyo, first began taking pictures of urban man. My thoughts at that time about photography were, of course, shallow, and, because I was young, my interest was limited to manners and customs—but, anyway, my work began with pictures of human beings.

In the winter of my 25th year, I visited the ''snow country'' for the first time and saw the ways of people living in those regions. What I saw there was completely different from anything I had ever seen of people in Tokyo, and my interest was aroused. My first photo series, *The Snow Country*, was a collection of photographs about the lives of peasants living in a deep, snow-filled valley, and centered on their six-day New Year festival.

In order to know people, from those living in a limited world of their own to others living in a wider world, for 4 years, from 1954 to 1957, I walked the districts of western Japan, ''Ura Nihon.'' There, I thought about man, his environment, his life styles.

The peculiar features of a region—''Fudo,'' pronounced foodo—generally means the topography of a certain district, the nature of its soil, scenery, climate, etc. Whether we are consciously aware of it or not, we are all living in our own particular kind of Fudo. This Fudo envelopes us, it encircles us; man comes to acquire a deep-rooted relation to his Fudo. And this relationship is never one-sided; it is a mutual influence, with the result that there is created the nature of a particular Fudo with the particular nature of man.

Fudo therefore changes with the nature of a particular region and with the character of the people living there. According to climatology, there are 3 main kinds of Fudo: the monsoon, the desert, the pastoral. And, there are accompanying human characters.

Japan is of the monsoon type. The Japanese Fudo has complicated features related to the extensively long longitudinal position of Japan from north to south, with its intensive climatic changes. Within this Fudo, our ancestors cultivated not only the tropical rice plant but also wheat, oats and barley. This was accomplished through active co-operation and intermingling of Man and Fudo. And I felt, with my study of people, that I had to study the Fudo in close relation with people. This was at the time I began taking pictures of Ura Nihon. The result was another series, *Ura Nihon* (Back Regions of Japan), which recorded my travels in these parts. In that book I wrote that my purpose was for ''man to understand man, so that the Japanese may understand the Japanese.'' And I thought that I had come to understand the Japanese rather well as a result of my wanderings all over Japan; however, I also began to realize more and more the difficulty of really knowing my own people.

In 1960 Japan was plunged into a sort of political crisis that reminded one of the night before a revolution. Never before had the Japanese people evinced so much concern for political issues as at that time. And I, who never took pictures of political happenings, felt that I had to make a record of this historical period. During that year—from May 20 to June 22—I took pictures of every aspect of the times to the limit of my ability and energy, and completed a full and precise record. This resulted in another documentary series, *A Record of Anger and Sorrow*.

The Japanese, who had lived through a long history as though they had no relation to politics, had shown, at this particular point, an unexpected awareness of politics. But it was only a momentary phenomenon. The heightening of awareness was transitory. A superficial economic prosperity supplanted it. I do not speak in an abstract way. I have walked through all parts of Japan, experiencing things by myself, seeing and feeling things through my own experience, and, through having seen the actual ways of living of the people, I have come to understand the unscientific thinking habits of the Japanese. Their tendency is to limit their thinking only to their own feelings, to build their lives upon it. This unscientific and strictly private habit of thinking has darkened the history of my people.

I wondered why I was always so obsessed with people, particularly about common people, the masses of the lowest social stratum. During history class in school, I often wondered why history should always stress royalty, the aristocrats, and the warriors. I would have learned history better, as my own personal problem, through studying the lives of common people and how they had lived through the ages. Those facts are connected to our present problems, and they can show us future direction.

Later, in 1960, I was led to think again about the problem of historical necessity and the influence of Fudo on the people. If one goes deep into the subject, one comes finally to People and Nature: the problem of the Japanese and Japanese soil. Since we have lost sight of the Japanese people, the kind of people they are, I decided to look instead and deeply at the land. I felt the urgency to find out and see for myself what kind of land Japan is.

To look intently at nature—that was something I had never even thought about. For me, it was a completely new subject.

Although I have travelled through all the regions of Japan, I have never been particularly conscious of nature in itself. Always, for me, there were people in nature. I became conscious of nature itself for the first time in 1956 in China. When I flew over the desert between Kwantung province and Sinkiang, I was overwhelmed by the vastness of nature. The desert that spread out in that most interior part of earth made me imagine the earth's skin in primordial times; it made me think of the earth as becoming fossilized in the blowing cosmic wind. This was an extreme world that shut out the lives of plants and animals.

From that time on an unexpected, fantastic thing called Nature loomed before me. And I thought, I will have to look more closely and deeply into nature some day.

During the course of time the relation between man and nature has gone on changing. Today there are many individual ways of thinking about nature. Civil engineers think about opening the land for their work; sponsors of tourist enterprises think only about how to use it to make a profit; hunters think about the whereabouts of game animals; poets and painters look for beauty; and geologists approach nature on the basis of their scientific obsession. But what attitude should a photographer take towards nature?

When nature is the subject matter of photography, it is called landscape. And landscape, along with portraiture, was one of the mainstays in the early days of photography. And one could say of the landscape photography of that early period that nature was "taken" because it was there to be taken. Along with the rapid development of photographic technique, the photographing of landscapes underwent many changes, corresponding to a variety of attitudes: as record, as document, as a trophy of tourism, and finally as a motif for art photography. The taking of pictures of landscapes for an artistic end has persisted to this day.

Landscape prevailed from quite an early time in Japanese photography. Its purpose was not the taking of landscapes as such; it was, rather, a way to reveal the beauty of lighting and its harmonies. It was the means to a photography that suited the temperament of the Japanese, and this trend continued for a long time. Since then, landscape photography has continued, but it has not involved any new dialectic or any fresh vision.

In my series *Ura Nihon* I used the word Fudo instead of the usual Fukei (landscape) because I was in search of a new way. How, as a photographer, I was going to look at the Japanese archipelago now became my theme. To look at the scenery of the archipelago as "fukei" was what I wanted most of all to avoid. Also, to reveal the landscape as an artistic expression goes against my way of thinking. My method was to look at the land in an objective, scientific way, as much as it was possible for me to do. I thought of taking my photographs as with the support of physical science, so that, on this solid basis, I could explore fresh camera angles and focus. I value science, to explore and clarify my own path. And I use it as my resistance to unscientific thinking, so as not to fall into that narrow, self-enclosed way of thinking I mentioned earlier.

But the road was rugged. Despite the fact that great progress has been made by science, there are still too many things that are not known, that remain mysteries.

Now, to look at nature, to mingle with nature, or to conquer nature is not my purpose. I don't want to drown, and I don't want to conquer. I want to look intently at nature, as objectively as possible.

To understand nature, I soon discovered, was far more difficult than to understand people. I became so enthusiastic that my wife began to worry that, maybe, I was neurotically shunning people. Actually, I had a feeling of distrust towards men, a gap did exist; and this feeling was, for me, a new experience.

What remained of pure nature on the Japanese Islands was unexpectedly little. People had been everywhere; I tried to avoid any place that "smelled" of people. I deliberately separated everything that was not nature from nature; and it could be said that this process began with my turning away from people.

Now, having finished my compilation of the *Landscapes of Japan,* what I am now thinking about is Man. This may be only my way of feeling, but in each of these pictures I sense and feel Man. Thus, I have gained some new insights into Man through having looked deeply at Nature.

—Hiroshi Hamaya

* * *

Hiroshi Hamaya is the most eminent documentary photographer in Japan today. His preferred subjects are people and nature. In the context of the romantic expressionism of many contemporary Japanese photographers, he is an exception in that he approaches his subjects scientifically and objectively.

In his first book of photographs, *Yuki Guni* (The Snow Country), there is a series of images of the New Year customs in a remote village: the photographer dramatically records the harmony between nature and the villagers' lives. This could be said to mark the beginning of his interest in the delicate balance of man and nature. A second book, *Ura Nihon* (Back Regions of Japan), saw his original interest more strongly represented and his theory of documentary photography more highly developed. A third series, *Nihon Retto* (Japan's Archipelago), includes a good many aerial views, and the imagery is more stark: Hamaya seems to be intent on arriving at the relation between man and nature through Japan's geomorphology.

His interest in nature is not, however, limited to the Japanese countryside but to unspoiled nature around the world. While recording nature globally, Hamaya has also documented human life in its many variations. In 1981 his travels culminated in two books, *Aspects of Nature* and *Aspects of Life.* The photographs are not so "dry" as this description suggests. Although Hamaya intended the photos to be scientific records, he has also, with his usual skill, given them an aesthetic rendering: he has made an art form of documentary.

At the same time a complementary exhibition of his work, *Hiroshi Hamaya: 50 Years of Photography,* was mounted in Tokyo. It included a group of portraits of artists and scholars not included in the books: they reveal the successful amalgamation of simple composition techniques with his usual objective distancing.

From these two books and the exhibition it is now obvious that Hamaya's accomplishment has been to combine Japanese poetry with Western theory, and that his fastidious, perfectionist character is the motivating force behind his creativity.

—Takao Kajiwara

HAMILTON, David.

Nationality: British. **Born:** London, 15 April 1933. **Career:** Worked as Graphic Designer and Art Director, *Queen* magazine, London, and *Printemps* magazine, Paris. Professional Photographer, Paris, working for *Twen, Réalités, Vogue,* etc., since 1966. **Address:** 41 Boulevard du Montparnasse, 75006 Paris, France.

Individual Exhibitions:

1981   Photogalerie Portfolio, Lausanne, Switzerland

Selected Group Exhibitions:

1975   *Foto-Arte 75,* Galeria Fontana d'Or, Gerona, Spain

Publications:

By HAMILTON: Books—*Dreams of Young Girls,* with Alain Robbe-Grillet, London 1971; *Sisters,* with text by Alain Robbe-Grillet, Zug, Switzerland 1972, 1973, London 1976, New York 1977; *Souvenirs,* with text by Denise Couttes, Zug, Switzerland 1974, London 1978; *The Best of David Hamilton,* with text by Denise Couttes, Zug, Switzerland 1976, London 1977; *La Danse,* Zug, Switzerland 1976; *David Hamilton's Private Collection,* Zug, Switzerland 1976; *Erinnerungen an Bilitis,* Kehl, West Germany 1977, as *Hamilton's Movie Bilitis: a photographic scrapbook from the movie,* New York 1977, London 1982; *A Summer in Saint Tropez,* London 1982; *Tender Cousins,* New York and London 1982. **Article**—"David Hamilton par Lui-Même," interview, with Edith Cottrell, photos by Claude Raimond-Dityvon, in *Zoom* (Paris), December 1970. **Film**—*Bilitis,* 1976.

On HAMILTON: Books—*Geschichte der Fotografie im 20. Jahrhundert/ Photography in the 20th Century* by Petr Tausk, Cologne 1977, London 1980; *French Photography from its Origins to the Present* by Claude Nori, Paris 1978, London 1979; *Classic Glamour Photography* by Iain Banks, New York and London 1983. **Articles**—"La Demeure Immobile de David Hamilton" by Alain Robbe-Grillet in *Zoom* (Paris), December 1970; "David Hamilton" in *Penthouse Photo World* (New York), February/March 1977; "Hamilton en Quinze Secondes" in *Photo* (Paris), February 1981.

*   *   *

In photographic circles it would be a mistake to show any interest in David Hamilton. His critics prefer to excommunicate him, to emphasize the incessant repetition of the same diaphanous nymphs, the same gestures, the exploitation of a shameful aesthetic eroticism, the "commercial" aspects of his work. Still, to shrug our shoulders in disapproval is to deny a captivating and disturbing force.

Hamilton is not a bad photographer, as we can see clearly enough by looking at some of his early nudes and some of his recent still-lifes. He is not a photographer of genius, however, as his color albums and post cards more than prove. Yet he is a kind of sociological phenomenon, and one of the few photographers accessible to a mass audience, largely because he works with only two fixed devices: a clear pictorial intention and a latent eroticism, ostensibly romantic but asking for trouble.

The last fashionable pictorial photographer of this century, Hamilton seduces us by artistic means and manages to avoid bad taste and vulgarity (pictures of adolescents, for example, which merely arouse the usual erotic fantasies). His work is pretty-pretty and decorative, and he knows how to market it successfully. The individual photos of the last century became collector's items; now Hamilton turns out millions of copies of his conventional pictures. But it would be pointless to admire the prettiness or cultivate the paradox that because the public lacks visual sophistication he will leave his mark on the history of photography.

—Christian Caujolle

HAMMARSKIÖLD, Hans (Arvid).

Nationality: Swedish. **Born:** Stockholm, 17 May 1925. **Education:** The Östra Real, Stockholm, 1936-44; self-taught in photography. **Family:** Married Caroline Hebbe in 1951 (divorced, 1976); children: Suzanne, Viveca, and Richard; married Magdalena Ander in 1978 (divorced 1993). **Career:** Photographer, Bellander Studio, Stockholm, 1950, and *Vogue* Studios, Condé Nast Publications, London, 1955-56. Freelance photographer, Stockholm, since 1957. Member, Tio Fotografer group, Stockholm, since 1958. **Address:** 5 Slåntunet, 181 48 Lidingö, Sweden.

Individual Exhibitions:

1951   Rotohallen, Stockholm

1956   *London,* Institute of Contemporary Arts, London (travelled to Artek, Stockholm, 1958)
1962   *Swedish Design,* Svensk Form, Stockholm
1979   Camera Obscura, Stockholm (retrospective)
         Douglas Elliott Gallery, San Francisco (retrospective)
1981   Stephen White Gallery, Los Angeles
1993   Fotografiska Museet, Stokholm

Selected Group Exhibitions:

1949   *Unga Fotografer,* Rotohallen, Stockholm
1951   *Subjektive Fotografie,* State Art and Crafts School, Saarbrucken (and 1954)
1953   *Postwar European Photography,* Museum of Modern Art, New York (toured the United States, 1953-56)
1955   *The Family of Man,* Museum of Modern Art, New York (and world tour)
1962   *Svenskarna sedda av 11 fotografer,* Moderna Museet, Stockholm
1970   *Tio Fotografer,* Bibliothèque Nationale, Paris
1971   *Contemporary Photographs from Sweden,* Library of Congress, Washington, D.C.
1978   *Tusen och En Bild/1001 Pictures,* Moderna Museet, Stockholm
1982   *The Frozen Image: Scandinavian Photography,* Walker Art Center, Minneapolis, Minnesota
1984   *Subjektive Fotografie: Images of the 50s,* Museum Folkwang, Essen

Collections:

Fotografiska Museet, Stockholm; Bibliothèque Nationale, Paris; Museum of Modern Art, New York; Library of Congress, Washington, D.C; Museum Folkwang, Essen, Germany; Museum Ludwig, Cologne.

Publications:

By HAMMARSKIÖLD: Books—*Objektivt sett,* Stockholm 1955; *Billa och jag,* Stockholm 1959; *Lillasyster och jag,* Stockholm 1960; *Forna dagars Sverige III,* 1962; *Storsudret-kring vast och täun,* 1987; *Nära Linné,* 1993; *Stockholms Fasader,* 1993.

On HAMMARSKIÖLD: Books—*Photography Today,* edited by Norman Hall, London 1957; *Tio Fotografer,* Stockholm 1976; *Tusen och en bild/1001 Pictures* exhibition catalogue, by Ake Sidwall, Sune Jonsson and Ulf Hard af Segerstad, Stockholm 1978; *Hans Hammarskiöld* by Rune Jonsson, Helsingborg, Sweden 1979; *The Frozen Image: Scandinavian Photography,* edited by Martin Freeman, Minneapolis and New York 1982; *Subjektive Fotografie: Images of the 50s,* exhibition catalogue, by Ute Eskildsen, Manfred Schmalriede and Dorothy Martinson, Essen, West Germany 1984.

*

I started off as a freelance photographer in 1950 working mainly with fashion and picture stories for Swedish magazines. During 1955-56 I was a staff photographer at British *Vogue* and *House and Garden* doing fashion, portraits, advertising, food and interiors. I came back to Sweden in 1957, where I have been a freelance photographer since then. I became a member of the group Tio when it started in 1958, and during the period 1958-68 I continued to do picture stories, food photography, still lifes, portraits and also industrial photography.

In 1968 I was asked to make a multi-screen show for a Swedish company, and I have since then worked mainly with multi-screen shows and industrial photography. Besides that type of work, I have done a lot of nature photography, which has been my special interest since I got my camera. My old nature pictures were in black-and-white. Today they are mainly in colour. I use a lot of them in my multi-screen shows, but I also print some on Cibachrome for my gallery shows. I have by now made about twenty multi-screen shows, and the two biggest have been with 36 projectors each for permanent showing at the

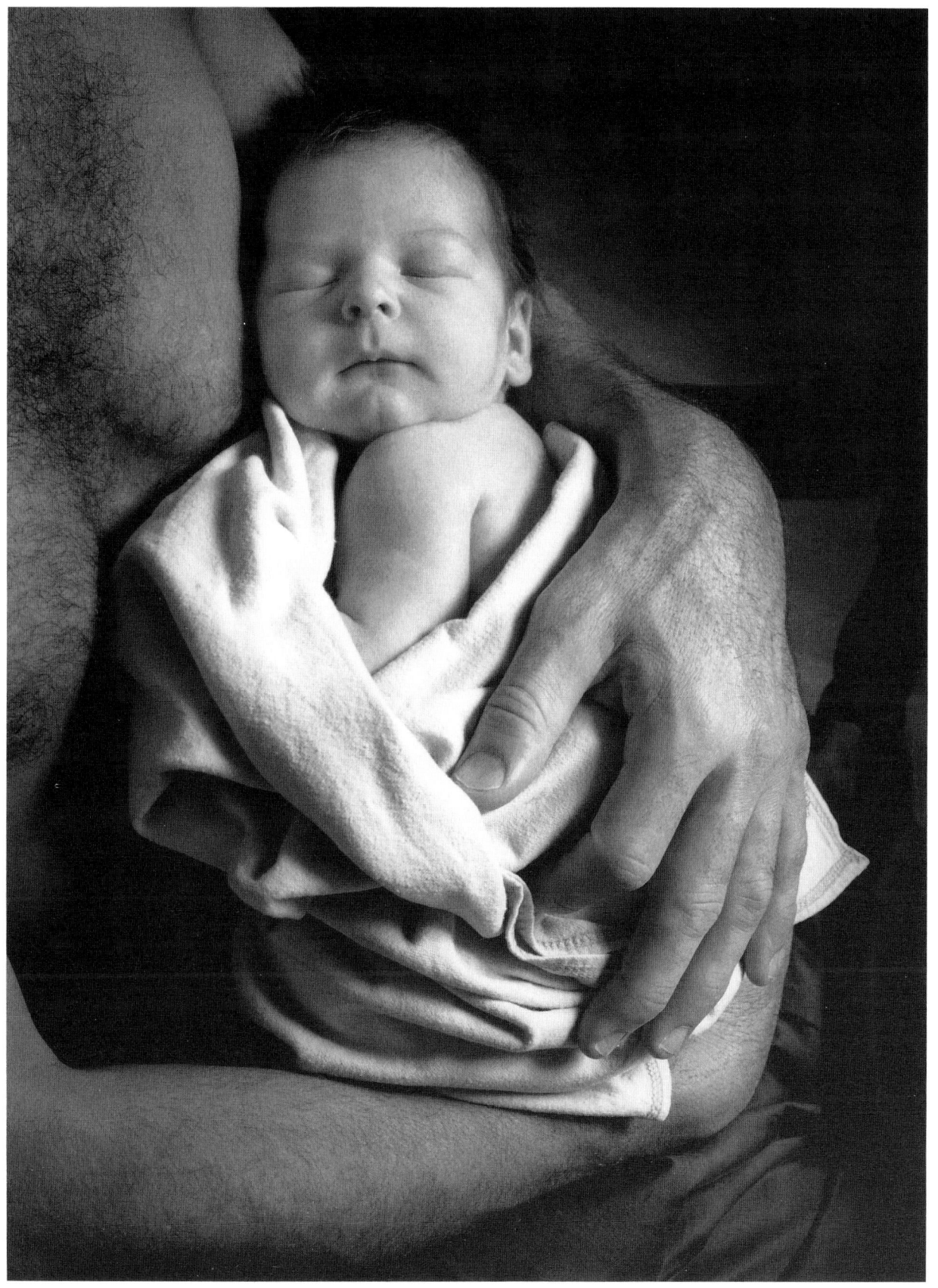

Newborn, **1989.** Photograph ©Hans Hammarskiöld.

Swedish company Asea, in Vasteras. They have been running since 1972, and will soon be replaced by two new programs of the same size.

—Hans Hammarskiöld

* * *

At the end of the 1940s a kind of change of generations took place in Swedish photography. Hans Hammarskiöld was one of "The Young" (*De Unga*), and, along with his contemporaries, he used provocative exaggeration to underline his dissociation from the pre-war generation. The old rules about grey scale and fine grain were casually slung on the dungheap—which itself often became a favorite motif. For in their subject matter, too, the new generation tried to distance itself from the conventional photographers and their ingratiating motifworld.

After their isolation during the Second World War, many of the younger Swedish photographers turned their sights towards Paris; a number of them even moved there for short or extended periods of time. But Hammarskiöld's interests were directed west of Paris. He visited the United States early in his career and made contact with its leading photographers—W. Eugene Smith, Irving Penn and Edward Steichen. So it is not surprising that Hammarskiöld's pictures from the 1950s show American influences, notably those of Weston and Callahan—razor-sharp representations of surface structures and details of nature, in which form is more important than the matter-of-fact pictures of species. The pictures are often characterized by a deep solemnity and a decorative line-play, in which the accentuated silhouettes have a constructive function.

But in these works there are also traces of the national romanticism that dominated Swedish photography during the 1930s and 1940s. And it may be worth noting, too, that Hammarskiöld made his competition debut with a romantic picture of a backlighted ploughman.

Hammarskiöld's engagement as a photographer on *Vogue* and *House and Garden* in London in 1955 and 1956 resulted in a renewal in his pictorial expression. Besides doing his commercial work, he wandered around London and took reportage photos with a small-picture camera in the spirit of Cartier-Bresson. He exhibited the pictures in Stockholm and other cities, and the critics wrote ecstatically that he had succeeded in capturing the London of Sherlock Holmes and Dickens. Mood and light were accentuated. The confident idiomatic expression was still there but was now combined with a more descriptive content.

In the course of time Hammarskiöld had come to be regarded as a typical black-and-white photographer. Few were as expert as he at mastering the graphic construction of a picture in clearly defined grey tones. No doubt many people thought he had betrayed his ideals, therefore, when in the late 1960s he began increasingly to work in color. These pictures were primarily used for multi-screen shows or were examples of the Cibachrome method.

In choosing his subjects Hammarskiöld often returns to his work from the 1950s—severely cut details of nature, with distinctly decorative value. He has at times been criticized for this work, for in it little is seen of the violation of nature by the industrial world. Challenged on this point in an interview Hammarskiöld responded that many other photographers already specialize in this aspect of nature in the modern world. "But I prefer doing it the opposite way. To show the beauty and magic in nature. To try to make people see and feel what's really at stake."

—Rune Jonsson

HARBUTT, Charles (Henry).

Nationality: American. **Born:** Camden, New Jersey, 29 July 1935. **Education:** Marquette University, Milwaukee, 1952-56, B.S. in journalism 1956. **Family:** Married Alberta Steves in 1958 (divorced, 1978); children: Sarah, Charles, and Damian; married Joan Liftin in 1978. **Career:** Associate Editor, *Jubilee* magazine, New York, 1956-59; freelance magazine photographer, New York, 1959-63. Since 1963, Photographer with Magnum Photos Inc., co-operative photo agency, New York and Paris (President, Magnum, New York, 1970-72, 1976-78). Photographic Consultant, New York City Planning Commission, 1968-70. Lecturer, Cooper Union and Pratt Institute, New York, 1970-72; Visiting Artist, Art Institute of Chicago, 1975, Rhode Island School of Design, Providence, 1976, and Massachusetts Institute of Technology, Cambridge, 1978. Vice-President, American Society of Magazine Photographers, 1970-71. **Recipient:** Magazine Photography Award, University of Missouri, Columbia, 1969; Gold Medal, *Atlanta Film Festival,* 1970; Creative Artists Public Service Award, New York, 1972; Photo Book of the Year Award, *Rencontres Internationales de Photographie,* Arles, France, 1974. Lives in New York. **Address:** c/o Magnum Photos Inc., 251 Park Avenue South, New York, New York 10010, U.S.A.; or Magnum Photos, 20 rue des Grands-Augustins, 75006 Paris, France.

Individual Exhibitions:

Selected Group Exhibitions:

Collections:

Museum of Modern Art, New York; Metropolitan Museum of Art, New York; International Museum of Photography, George Eastman House, Rochester,

New York; Smithsonian Institution, Washington, D.C.; Art Institute of Chicago; New Orleans Museum of Art; University of Nebraska, Lincoln; University of Manchester, England; Bibliothèque Nationale, Paris; Moderna Museet, Stockholm.

Publications:

By HARBUTT: Books—*America in Crisis,* with others (also editor), New York 1969; *The Plan for the City of New York,* 6 volumes, with the New York City Planning Commission, Cambridge, Massachusetts 1970; *Travelog,* Cambridge, Massachusetts 1973; *New York Street Kids,* with others, text by Victor Remer and John von Hartz, New York 1978. **Articles**—"The Multi-Level Picture Story" in *Contemporary Photographer* (Boston) 1965; "The Concerned Photographer" in *Album* (London), no. 9, 1970; "The Harbutt Workshop" in *Modern Photography* (New York), January-April 1976.

On HARBUTT: Exhibition catalogues—*Sympathetic Explorations: Kertész/ Harbutt* by Andy Grundberg, Moorhead, Minnesota 1978; *Tusen och En Bild* exhibition catalogue by Ake Sidwall, Sune Jonsson and Ulf Hard af Segerstad, Stockholm 1978; *La Photographie Créative* by Jean-Claude Lemagny, Paris 1984; *American Images: Photography 1945-1980,* edited by Peter Turner and John Benton-Harris, London 1985. **Article**—"In Search of the Honest Photograph" by Julia Scully and Andy Grundberg in *Modern Photography* (New York), July 1979.

*

I take pictures because it gives me pleasure. Having taught for ten years, I feel to say more is idiocy.

—Charles Harbutt

*   *   *

In her book *Flashback! The 50s,* Eve Arnold recalls that she was trying to understand the difference between the photography of the 50s and the 70s, so she called her friend and fellow Magnum photographer Charles Harbutt and asked him. "Oh that's easy," he said. "Photography in the 50s was about people. Now it's about photography." Harbutt's own photography seems to have followed this line of development (Arnold's hasn't), and not just because of the trumpeted death of the established markets for photojournalistic work.

Originally Harbutt stopped being a writer and started being a photographer because photographers had to *be* there. It required more contact with reality. His photography developed in the great reportage style of the Magnum agency. He photographed the 6-Day War for *Paris-Match* and *Newsweek,* Spiro Agnew for *Life,* ghettos for *Look* and so on. The culmination of this "concerned" style came with the book he edited, *America in Crisis,* which was photographed by Magnum members and included many of his own pictures.

But by this time Harbutt was trying to find a new way of taking pictures: one that more truly represented his own experience of the world. Now that he saw this as alien and fragmentary, it no longer fitted the journalistic tradition in which he had been working. Part of the stimulus for this reconsideration was provided by reality in the form of a speeding bullet. In May 1967, he recalls, "I turned casually around a high-noon street in Aden to see the hammer drawing back on a pistol aimed at me."

His reconsideration resulted in a new style and an award-winning book, *Travelog.* For a while he called the new style "Superbanalisme," perhaps because he was focusing on the trivialities of everyday life instead of the "Great Themes." The implied mockery hid the fact that he was involved in a radical reassessment of the relationships between photography and reality and photography and art.

Thus many of the pictures in *Travelog* are concerned with identifying areas of reality that the camera records in a way that is different from our everyday experience of them. For example: reflections in windows and puddles, lighted windows, clouds, shadows, and pictures with pictures. To the camera's eye these phantoms are just as real as solid objects. Also Harbutt experimented with breaking the rules of composition that had fundamentally been derived from painting, in the search for a specifically photographic aesthetic. He used wide-angle distortion, tilting the camera, cut people's heads off *etc.* The resulting book is by no means consistent. Some pictures are *avant garde* while others are reportage, but the effects are always interesting.

Underneath the philosophical overlay, Harbutt's photography tells another story—of depersonalisation and the search for human contact. In most of the pictures in the book, people are cut off—you see only their legs or shoulders or whatever—or they are behind glass, or safely sealed inside their cars, or distant, or in their own little groups which exclude the photographer. The few people who relate to the photographer directly include a beaming man on an advertising poster, a distant beauty queen on a passing carnival float, and a small child with a gun. It is the geometrical lines of the city buildings, the patterns of walls, windows and pavements, that dominate the pictures, while the figures are isolated in the space. In a sense this is as cold and alienating a vision as it sounds. In another sense, the photographs themselves are a warm act of communication and a way of sharing the beauty of their formal conception. In *Travelog* Harbutt is making the simplest and most basic statement, "I am here." I photograph, therefore I am.

—Jack Schofield

HARDY, Bert.

Nationality: British. **Born:** Albert Hardy in London, 19 May 1913. **Education:** Friar Street Elementary School, London, 1918-27; self-taught in photography. **Military Service:** Served as a photographer in the British Army, in France and Germany, 1942-46. **Family:** Married Sheila Marshall in 1965; children (from first marriage): Michael and Terence. **Career:** Worked as a messenger and laboratory assistant, Central Photo Services, London, 1927-36; Photographer, for William Davis, General Photographic Agency, London, contributing to *Illustrated London News, Tatler, Sphere,* etc., 1936-39; Founder-Director, with Bertram Collins, Criterion Press photo agency, London, 1939-40; Staff Photographer, *Picture Post,* London, 1941-57; freelance advertising photographer, London, 1958-63. Founder-Director, with the late Gerry Grove, Grove Hardy Ltd. photo processing company, London, since 1960; has also farmed in Limpsfield Chart, Surrey, since 1964. President, Photogallery, St. Leonard's on Sea, Sussex. **Recipient:** *Encyclopaedia Britannica* Award, 1948, 1950, 1951, 1952; Gold Medal, *Unifoto,* 1951; National Outdoor Advertising Award, 1960. Honorary Fellow, Royal Photographic Society, London, 1986. **Address:** Chartlands Farm, Limpsfield Chart, Surrey, England.

Individual Exhibitions:

1974	Maidenhead Public Library, Berkshire (toured the U.K.)
1975	*3 from Picture Post,* The Photographers' Gallery, London (with Thurston Hopkins and Kurt Hutton; toured the U.K. 1976-77)
1978	Photo Gallery, St. Leonards on Sea, Sussex
1983	Side Gallery, Newcastle-on-Tyne, Northumberland
1984	Buddle Arts Centre, Newcastle-on-Tyne, Northumberland
1985	National Museum of Photography, Bradford, Yorkshire
	Royal Photographic Society, Bath, Avon
	The Photographers' Gallery, London
	Open Eye Gallery, Liverpool, Merseyside
	Arts Centre, University of Wales, Cardiff
	New Metropole Arts Centre, Folkestone, Kent
	Manchester Polytechnic, Lancashire
	Bourne Hall, Ewell, Surrey
1986	MacLaurin Art Gallery, Ayr, Scotland
	Graves Art Gallery, Sheffield, Yorkshire

Selected Group Exhibitions:

1955	*The Family of Man,* Museum of Modern Art, New York (and world tour)
1972	*Personal Views 1850-1970,* British Council, London (toured Europe)

1975	*The Real Thing: An Anthology of British Photographs 1840-1950,* Hayward Gallery, London (toured the U.K.)
1978	*Images des Hommes,* Palais des Beaux-Arts, Brussels (travelled to Ghent, Hasselt and Charleroi, Belgium)
1982	*Floods of Light,* The Photographers' Gallery, London
1983	*British Photography 1955-65,* The Photographers' Gallery, London
1984	*Subjektive Fotografie: Images of the 50s,* San Francisco Museum of Modern Art (travelled to the University of Houston, Texas; Museum Folkwang, Essen; Vasterbottens Museum, Umea; Kulturhuset, Stockholm; Saarland Museum, Saarbrucken; Palais des Beaux-Arts, Brussels)
1986	*British Character,* The Photographers' Gallery, London

Collections:

Radio Times Hulton Picture Library, London; Arts Council of Great Britain, London; Imperial War Museum, London (war pictures, 1942-46); Victoria and Albert Museum, London; Science Museum, London; National Museum of Photography, Film and Television, Bradford, Yorkshire; Museum Folkwang, Essen, Germany.

Publications:

By HARDY: Books—*A Horse Grows Up,* New York 1972; *Bert Hardy, Photojournalist,* with an introduction by Tom Hopkinson, London 1975; *My Life,* (autobiography), London 1985. **Articles**—"How I Photograph People" in *Photography* (London), June 1949; "Bert Hardy: Comment Je Photographe les Gens" in *Photo-Monde* (Paris), November 1952; "Bert Hardy: Comment Je Photographe le Mouvement" in *Photo-Monde* (Paris), March 1953; "Covering the Berlin Conference" in *Photography* (London), March 1954; "On Using a Miniature" in *Photography* (London), April 1956; "Anything for a Story" in *Creative Camera* (London), December 1971.

On HARDY: Books—*Picture Post 1938-50* by Tom Hopkinson, London 1970; *Personal Views 1850-1970,* exhibition catalogue, with an introduction by Bill Jay, London 1972; *The Magic Image* by Cecil Beaton and Gail Buckland, London and Boston 1975; *The Camera at War* by Jorge Lewinski, London and New York 1978; *Pictures on a Page* by Harold Evans, London 1978; *Cameramen at War* by Ian Grant, Cambridge 1980; *Of This Our Time: A Journalist's Story* by Tom Hopkinson, London 1982; *British Photography 1955-1965: The Master Craftsmen in Print,* exhibition catalogue, by Sue Davies, Michael Rand, Mark Boxer and others, London 1983; *Bilder vom Krieg* by Rainer Fabian and Hans Christian Adam, Hamburg 1983, as *Images of War: 130 Years of War Photography,* London 1985. **Articles**—"Bert Hardy's Piccadilly Story" in *Photography* (London), August 1953; "Bert Hardy" in *Camera* (Lucerne), August 1954; "Bert Hardy" by Harry Deverson in *Camera World* (London), November 1956; "What Photography Means to Bert Hardy" in *Popular Photography* (New York), October 1957; "A Day in the Life of a Ghost That Won't Lie Down" by Lionel Birch in *Creative Camera* (London), April 1973; "Giants of Fleet Street: Bert Hardy" by Leslie S. Shaw in the *British Journal of Photography* (London), 25 July and 1 August 1980; "The Compassionate Camera of Bert Hardy" in *The Observer* (London), 10 March 1985; "Hardy Perennial" in *British Journal of Photography* (London), 12 April 1985; "Bert Hardy—Fleet Street Legend" in *Photo District News* (New York), July 1985. **Films**—*Life and Death of Picture Post,* BBC television film, 1977; *Bert Hardy,* Tyne Tees Television film, 1983.

*

By sheer luck I became a photographer. It was the first job I got when I left school at the age of 14. I had no choice, as I needed the job to help my parents support our large family. I think I was very lucky, because I took to photography naturally; also, the period of the 35mm was just, but only just, starting. In the early days I learned only photo-processing, which it is essential to know about if you are going to be a successful photographer. As a

photographer I was completely self-taught, chiefly by trial and error on old plate cameras. It was when I got my first 35mm camera—a Leica—that my photographic talent emerged, but from the beginning I did photographic sequences, now known as photo-journalism. I also made use of the 35mm camera's large aperture lenses fl.4 and used natural light no matter how poor. I never used flash, which in those early days was flashbulbs; there were no electronics.

When *Picture Post* was launched in October 1938, I started to get stories published in it almost immediately through the firm I then worked for, General Photographic Agency. Later, in 1941, I joined the staff of the magazine and worked for it until it closed in 1957, except for my service as an Army Photographer from June 1942 until September 1946. After *Picture Post* folded I went into advertising. I retired gradually from serious photography from about 1967 and now happily farm, still taking a few photographs and retaining an interest in photography through my processing business, Grove Hardy Ltd. Since the publication of my autobiography, I have been very busy doing television programmes and lecturing on my photography to young students at universities, colleges and camera clubs.

—Bert Hardy

*   *   *

During his working life Bert Hardy was looked on as a photojournalist devoted to his craft, with a gift for being in the right place at the crucial moment and for making memorable pictures out of what he saw. Today he is coming to be considered one of the great recorders of social conditions in the tradition of John Thomson, Jacob Riis and Lewis Hine. "He belongs," one critic wrote, "to a British tradition which favours anecdote and human incident. He pictures people as characters, and his work is a rich source for any study of the folk-life of Britain, a modern continuation of the graphic tradition of Hogarth and Rowlandson."

From birth Hardy's life was cast in the classic mould of the poor boy who makes good by his own efforts: "We lived in a tenement. My father was a splint maker, a right old drunk. My mother went out charring. There were seven kids. I left school on a Friday afternoon, aged 14. On Saturday morning I answered a 'Boy Wanted' notice in a film developing and printing works. My job was to cycle round chemists, collect films and process them, and deliver the films back. Pay was ten bob a week. . . . "

When he joined *Picture Post* early in the war Hardy's talent began to flower. He was ready to tackle anything, and his pictures of the Blitz were among the finest—and the closest to the action—taken by any cameraman. Later as an Army Photographer he roamed the world, photographing terrible sights, without ever losing his capacity to feel intensely the suffering he recorded. On entering the concentration camp at Luneberg, he says, "I was so sick with rage I could hardly take pictures."

Back in Britain after the war he moved, imperceptibly and almost unconsciously, into photographing the social scene, particularly life from the underside. His pictures in the Gorbals, and the Elephant and Castle before its demolition, have become classics, but what today are regarded as exposures were for him a recording of the flow of life as it goes on—not a denunciation but a tribute to the way humans cope with what life brings them, made with admiration and affection, not, like the Luneberg pictures, out of rage. In making them, however, Hardy learned something new about himself. As a man and a photographer he had long since found his strength, but he now began to realise that he was also—though he never used the word—an artist: "When I left the Gorbals I had a rare feeling, and then when I saw my pictures, I realized for the first time what I could do."

Though in his work he has ranged over a vast field, making pictures over half the world and of many of the great men of our day, in the end Hardy always comes back to the individual, the ordinary man or woman and—with a special perception but no sentimentality—the child. He has to feel and to make contact; it is impossible for him to be just a lens. Now retired to the country, he still misses taking pictures, "although it used to kill me with nerves. I've never used a light meter or a range-finder in my life. It's not my style. What would I like to photograph now? People. Faces. That man over there talking with his hands. Ordinary things. Life happening. I've always got on with ordinary people."

—Tom Hopkinson

HARTMANN, Erich.

Nationality: American. **Born:** Munich, Germany, 29 July 1922; emigrated to the United States in 1938; naturalized, 1943. **Education:** Attended primary school, Munich, 1928-38; and at night school in the United States; self-taught in photography, but influenced by Alexei Brodovitch, E.H. Cassidy and Werner Bischof. **Military Service:** Served in the United States Army, in Europe, 1943-45. **Family:** Married Ruth E. Bains in 1946; children: Nicholas and Celia. **Career:** Freelance photographer, New York and Maine, since 1946: industrial and advertising photography for IBM, Mead Paper, Bristol Myers, Boeing, Litton Industries, RCA, Merck, Ford Motor Company, Citroen, etc.; magazine and newspaper photography for *Fortune, The Daily Telegraph, The Sunday Times,* and *The Sun,* London, *Johns Hopkins Magazine, Venture, US, Geo, Stern, Travel and Leisure, Americana,* etc.; Member, Magnum Photos, New York and Paris, since 1952. Lecturer, School of Journalism of Syracuse University, New York, 1969-70; Lecturer, New York University, since 1971. **Recipient:** Art Directors Award, New York, 1968, 1977; *Photokina* Award, 1972; **Address:** c/o Magnum Photos Inc., 251 Park Avenue South, New York, New York 10010, U.S.A.

Individual Exhibitions:

1956	*Sunday under the Bridge,* Museum of the City of New York
1962	*Our Daily Bread,* New York Coliseum (travelled to the Department of Agriculture Gallery, Washington, D.C., 1963)
1971	*Mannequin Factory,* The Underground Gallery, New York
1973	*Europe in Space,* The Photographers' Gallery, London
1976	*Carnet de Voyage,* Photogalerie, Paris
1977	*Photographs with a Laser,* AIGA Gallery, New York
1978	*Play of Light,* Neikrug Gallery, New York
1979	*Mannequins and Lasers,* Galerie Fiolet, Amsterdam
1981	*Vu du Train,* Galerie Olympus, Paris

Selected Group Exhibitions:

1972	*Photokina,* Cologne
1979	*This Is Magnum,* Takashimaya Department Store, Tokyo
1980	*Magnum,* Galerie Le Cloître Hotel de Ville, St. Ursanne, Switzerland

Collections:

Museum of Modern Art, New York; Museum of the City of New York.

Publications:

By HARTMANN: Book—*Au Clair de la Terre,* with text by Georges Bardawil, Brussels 1972.

On HARTMANN: Books—*This Is Magnum,* exhibition catalogue, Tokyo 1979; *Magnum Photos,* exhibition catalogue, St. Ursanne, Switzerland, and Paris 1980; *Dictionnaire des Photographes* by Carole Naggar, Paris 1982.

*

Photographing combines the disciplines of craft with the ambiguities of language. It is a way of speaking which (I discovered by accident) suits my temperament.

I have a long-standing preoccupation with "commonplace" subject matter, especially with the world in which we are inescapably imbedded. Thus a good deal of my work is autobiographical.

I suspect that photography will continue to waver between the counterpoints of technique and meaning and that, as now, most photographs will have form without content or vice versa. But, as now, among the millions of photographers there will always be some (it takes only a few) who will be able to make form and content into a clear and personal record of what they saw and felt in their time.

Those photographs will endure and that, in the end, is the purpose of the exercise.

—Erich Hartmann

*   *   *

Erich Hartmann claims a preoccupation with the commonplace; however, his idea of the "commonplace," hardly common, is based on an interest in industry and high technology, out of which he has developed an expertise in laser photography. To date he has exhibited several collections of his laser work in Europe and America.

Hartmann's photography is distinguished by an unstinting concern for documentary authenticity combined with great precision of composition. Whether his subject is the fluorescent-lit plastic circuitry of an analog computer or the sunny greensward of an English garden, Hartmann renders its mood, its colors, its very presence with an image that seems to represent precisely the essence of the object.

It is no doubt Hartmann's ability to bring out the fascinating and even the poetic in the technological world that has attracted his numerous corporate and advertising clients. A master of technique, he does not hesitate to use the surprising angle or the unusual lens; however, his effect is always authenticity rather than manipulation. Since the 1950s Hartmann has published regular portfolios on industry and the industrial landscape in *Fortune* in the U.S. and the *Daily Telegraph Magazine* in London.

A measure of his versatility is Hartmann's contribution to *Au Clair de la Terre,* a book on the development of European space satellites. Hartmann's hundreds of photographs cover the full range of satellite production and use from the physics seminar to the testing lab to, as Hartmann puts it, the "ideas, speculations and intentions" that inevitably accompany man's penetration of space. In his sensitive visual realizations of such intangibles, Hartmann has made use of techniques that refract and filter light in fascinating ways—how well he understands that the root-meaning of the word "photography" is "light-writing!" As Hartmann knows, the images so achieved are symbolic rather than descriptive, and they help to express the optimistic mood that accompanies scientific and technological achievement. Yet, like all Hartmann's photographs, they express as well his precise vision and his pride in superior craftsmanship.

—Maren Stange

HARTWIG, Edward.

Nationality: Polish. **Born:** Moscow, of Polish parents, 6 September 1909. **Education:** Attended a gymnasium in Lublin, Poland; studied under Professor Rudolph Kopitz and Professor Hans Daimler at the Graphische Institut, Vienna, 1932-34. **Family:** Married Helena Jagiello in 1931; daughters: Danuta and Eva. **Career:** Instructor in Art, College of Engineering, Lublin, 1937-38. Freelance photographer in Warsaw, since 1938. Member of the Editorial Board, *Almanach of Polish Art Photography,* Warsaw, 1969-74. Co-Founder, 1953, Vice-President (and President of the Art Council), 1953-63, and Member of the Art Council, 1963-80, Polish Art Photographers Union; International Committee Member, Fédération Internationale de l'Art Photographique (FIAP), 1969-74. **Recipient:** Gold Cross of Merit, 1954; Knight's Cross of the Polish Resurgence, 1959; Award for Achievements in Art Photography, City of Warsaw, 1961; Annual Cultural Award, Polish Ministry of Culture, 1965; Medal of the City of Bordeaux, France, 1968; Medal of the City of Paris, 1986; Meritorious for the City of Lublin, 1986; Meritorious for National Culture Awards, 1988. Honorary Member, Union of Polish Art Photographers (ZPAF), Warsaw, Fédération Internationale de l'Art Photographique (FIAP), Union of Czechoslovak Photographers, Union of Rumanian Photographers, Union of Danish Photographers, Photo Club, Linz, Austria, and the Photo Club, Bordeaux. **Agent:** Gallery of the Polish Art Photographers Union (ZPAF), Plac Zamkowy 8, Warsaw, Poland. **Address:** Al. Jerozolimskie 31/10,00-508 Warsaw, Poland.

Individual Exhibitions:

1937	City Museum, Lublin, Poland
1944	City Museum, Lublin, Poland
1954	National Museum Wroclaw, Poland
1957	Zacheta Gallery, Warsaw
1959	Société Francaise de Photographie, Paris
1963	*Behind the Theatrical Scenes,* Palace of Culture, Warsaw (toured Europe and the United States)
	Gallery of the Central Bureau of Artistic Exhibitions/Union of Polish Art Photographers, Toruń, Poland (travelled to Gdansk)
1965	Art Foto Gallery, Prague
1971	Société Francaise de Photographie, Paris
1972	Zacheta Gallery, Warsaw
1975	*Behind the Theatrical Scenes,* travelling exhibition (toured Poland and the United States)
	Art Gallery, Athens, Greece
	Berlin DDR, City Gallery, Wroclaw, Poland
	Foto Gallery, Bratislava, Czechoslovakia
1979	Budapesti-Fotoclub, Budapest
	My World 1930-78, Zacheta Gallery, Warsaw (retrospective)
	A Master from Poland, Stadtische Galerie, Hamburg
1980	Bureau of Artistic Exhibitions Gallery, Toruń, Poland
	Union of Polish Art Photographers Gallery, Warsaw (retrospective)
1983	*Vintage Photography,* UPAP Gallery, Kielce, Poland
	Warsaw Impressions, Kordegarda Gallery, Warsaw
	Old Lublin: Town of My Youth, Press House, Lublin, Poland
1984	Biblioteca ZVIS, Bogota, Colombia (travelled to the Pruna Sala de Esposiciones, Bogota)
	Thackrey and Robertson Gallery, San Francisco
1986	*Polskie wierzby (Polish Willows),* Gallery of Bielsko-Biala, Poland
1987	*Works from 1923-1987,* BWA Salon Sztuki, Wspolczesnej, Bydgoszcz
1988	*Zaproszenie do szatni (Inviting to the cloakroom),* Foto-Medium-Art Gallery, Wroclaw
1989	*Edward Hartwig,* BWA Gallery, Sopot, Poland
	Moja galeria (My Gallery), Retrospective, Zacheta Gallery, Warsaw
1990	*Edward Hartwig,* PTF Gallery, Poznan
1991	*Edward Hartwig,* Zamek Wojnowice, Wroclaw, Poland
1992	*Najnowsze. . . . .,* Mala Galeria, Warsaw
1993	*Ludzie teatru: Impresje fotograficzne (People of the Theatre: Photographic Impressions,* Teatr Boguslawskiego, Kalisz, Poland
1994	*Edward Hartwig,* Gallery of the Union of Latvian Photographers, Riga, Latvia

Selected Group Exhibitions:

1938	*Wystawa Fotografii Polskiej,* Lublin, Poland
1948	*Nowoczesna Fotografika Polska (Modern Polish Photography),* Club of Young Artists and Scientists, Warsaw
1955	*International Photography Exhibition,* Richmond Art Gallery, Surrey
1965	*Photokina,* Cologne
1969	*10 Photographers of the World,* Neustadt Galerie, Vienna
1975	*10 Great Art Photographers of FIAP,* at the *FIAP International Congress,* Padua
1976	*10 European Photographers,* Gallery of the Cracow Photographic Society
1979	*Fotografia Polska 1839-1979,* International Center of Photography, New York (travelled to the Museum of Contemporary Art, Chicago; Galeria Zacheta, Warsaw; Museum of Fine Arts, Lodz; Whitechapel Art Gallery, London)
1981	*La Photographie Polonaise 1900-81,* Centre Georges Pompidou, Paris

1984	*Contemporary Photography,* Galeria Zacheta, Warsaw
1987	*Kolekcja,* Mala Galeria, Warsaw
1988	*Fotofest Houston,* Houston, USA
1989	*!50 lat fotografii ze zbioròw,* National Museum, Wroclaw, Poland
1990	*L'annee de l'Est,* Musee d'Elysee, Lausanne, Switzerland
	Foto's uit Oost Europa, De Beurs van Berlage, Amsterdam
1992	*Les chefs d'oeuvre de la photographie polonaise 1912-1948,* Institute Polonais, Paris

Collections:

Museum of Contemporary Art, Lodz, Poland; National Museum, Wroclaw, Poland; Murray Forbes Collection, Cambridge, Massachusetts; Biblioteka Narodowa (National Library), Warsaw; Museum in Kazimierz Dolny, Poland; Castle Museum and BWA Gallery, Lublin, Poland; Portrait Collection Museum of Fine Arts, Houston; Navigator Foundation, Boston, Massachusetts; Israel Museum, Tel Aviv.

Publications:

By HARTWIG: Books—*Photo-Graphics,* Warsaw, 1958, 1960; *My Country,* Warsaw 1960; *Acropolis,* Warsaw 1962; *Pieniny,* Warsaw 1963, 1966; *Cracow,* Warsaw 1965, 1969; *Behind the Theatrical Scenes,* Warsaw 1969; *Warsaw,* Warsaw 1974, 1978; portfolios—*Edward Hartwig,* Prague 1966; *Edward Hartwig: Photographic Subjects,* Warsaw 1978; *Edward Hartwig: Photographic Impressions,* Warsaw 1979. **Articles**—"Kilka uwag o fotografice dzisiejszej" in *Swiat Fotografii* (Poznan), no. 6, 1947; "Dlaczego Lublin?" in *Fotografia* (Warsaw), no. 8, 1955; "Spotkanie z Cartier-Bressonem" in *Fotografia* (Warsaw), no. 2, 1957.

On HARTWIG: Books—*Das Polnische Lichtbild,* with introduction by Zbigniew Pekoslawski, Halle, East Germany 1961; *Wsrod polskich mistrzow kamery* by Lech Grabowski, Warsaw 1964; *Przygody plastyczne fotograffi* by Urszula Czartoryska, Warsaw 1965; *Historia fotografii warszawskiej* by Waclaw Zdzarski, Warsaw 1974; *Portret polski 1840-1939,* exhibition catalogue, by Ryszard Bobrowski, Warsaw 1978; *La Photographie d'Art en Pologne,* exhibition catalogue, by Adam Sobota, Paris 1981; *Fotografia polska 1945-1985* by Ryszard Bobrowski, Pawel Pierscinski and others, Gorzow Wielkopolski, Poland 1985; *Masters of Polish Photography* by Ryszard Bobrowski, Geneva 1986; *Edward Hartwig—moga galeria,* exhibition catalogue by Paweł Pierści'ski, Warsaw 1989; *Wobect odbiorcow fotografii,* by Jerzy Busza, Warsaw 1990; *150 lat fotografii polskiej (150 years of Polish Photography,* Warsaw 1991; *Les chefs d'oeuvre de la photographie polonaise 1912-1948,* exhibition catalogue, Paris 1992; *Edward Hartwig,* exhibition catalogue with text (in Polish, English and Latvian) by Marek Grygiel, Riga 1994. **Articles**—"Wystawa E. Hartwig" by Jan Klosowski in *Swiat Fotografii* (Poznan), no. 2, 1949; "Opowiesc o starym Lublinie" by Lech Grabowski in *Fotografia* (Warsaw), no. 11, 1956; "Edward Hartwig" by Bogdan Lopienski in *Fotografia* (Warsaw), no. 10, 1965; "Edward Hartwig" by Fritz Kempe in *Foto Magazin* (Munich), no. 1, 1971; "Wystawa-Fotografia polska 1839-1979" by Ryszard Bobrowski in *Fotografia* (Warsaw), no. 3, 1980; "140 lat fotografii polskiej" by Marcin Gizycki in *Projekt* (Warsaw), no. 4, 1980; "Nazwisko z encyklopedii" by Aldona Grabarczyk in *Panorama Polska,* no. 4, 1986; "Dojrzewanie spokoju—rozmowa z Edwardem Hartwigiem" by Zdzislaw Toczynski in *Kamena,* (Lublin) no. 10, 1987; "Zajalem sie wierzba" by Wojciech Kicinski in *Trybuna Ludu,* (Warsaw), no. 66, 1988; "Edward Hartwig" by Kazimierz Sobolewski in *Kurier Polski,* (Warsaw), no. 142, 1989; "Wierzby i fotografia" by Piotr Bialek in *Stolica,* no. 33, 1989; "Czas pozyskany—rozmowa z Edwardem Hartigiem" by Barbara Osterloff in *Teatr,* no. 12, 1991; "Hartwiga pejzaz katastrofy" by Zbigniew Taranienko in *Nowa Europa,* no. 14, 1992; "Kompozycja powyborcza" by Anna B Bohdziewicz in *Gazeta Wyborcza* (Warsaw) no. 41, 1992.

*

During my youth I had a nonchalant attitude to life, and my time spent with writers, painters, actors and musicians resulted in long-lasting friendships.

The impressionist paintings of the pre-war period had a strong influence on my own work—especially the works of 1925 to 1939. Later on, I became fascinated by the creations of Polish photodesigners, scenographers and graphic artists. Those phases of my creative development are now over, and I tend to work in areas to which I have become well accustomed. My portfolios and exhibitions reflect my strong interest in graphics and black and white studies, with little photography in colour.

Intuition plays a great role in the creation of any work of art—including the photograph—and I therefore have involved myself in an examination of my own artistic development. Despite this search for a personal expression, I find that my favourite subject from the very beginning of my career up to the present has been nature itself.

Experience has taught me that photography (as with other arts) brings us closer to a universal truth—without allowing us to reveal it completely. Every new style and artistic novelty eventually shows itself as a new aesthetic form. Photography, as with other arts, creates a world of artificial forms and feelings.

It now seems that photography is trying to live through an era of philosophical form. It is therefore important that photographers preserve their own integrity, and make photographs true to their maker.

—Edward Hartwig

*   *   *

Edward Hartwig has created a large and diverse output of photographs. In the beginning he was a photographer of nature, and landscape is a theme to which he has repeatedly returned throughout his career. This interest developed very early in his life: in his teens he wished to become a painter and took classes in drawing and painting and, although he never did become a painter, his work has always shown a fascination with nature, the soil and the landscape—traditional subjects in the fine arts. Hartwig's landscapes are not empty or depersonalized; quite frequently (especially in his work of the inter-war years) there are people in them, people within their own landscapes. He is not only a photographer of landscape but also an ethnographer.

Hartwig was educated in fine arts at the Graphische Institut in Vienna, where he attended life classes and studied portraiture in the studio of Rudolph Kopitz and Hans Daimler. Among the courses he took there were photography and graphics, which involved a wide range of technical experiments at the "boundaries" of those subjects. This experience was to play a significant part in his work, for, later, he was to apply various formal experiments to his photographs. Frequently they were technical experiments in his darkroom, involving processes such as over-exposure, superimposition, numerous optical effects with light, mirrors, etc. These treatments so radically transformed the character of his work that, in a sense, it ceased to be photography and became a sort of photo-graphics. It is relevant that Hartwig was involved with this kind of photography in the 1950s and 60s, a period in which expressive abstraction and the continuous questioning of traditional art-forms predominated.

Applied to Hartwig's usual landscape themes, these experiments produced various results. On the one hand, the move from bland pictorialism to powerful and decisive lines and strongly drawn contrasts did give this photography a contemporary look. On the other hand, however, the fascination with the possibilities raised by these new techniques marked a shift from purely visual values to artistic pictures created in accordance with novel avantgarde proposals.

As in his youth, apart from landscape photography, Hartwig is also involved with urban photography, portrait, stage and experimental photography. His work in all these areas is characterized by an unconstrained use of the darkroom and a constant search for new means of expression. It is very clear that he would like to continue to discover and attempt new forms of artistic expression. It is probable that he is also preoccupied with photography of a totally different kind—one that would be able to distance itself totally from all that has gone before in the field.

Edward Hartwig occupies a quite significant position in the history of Polish photography. He is noted for his interest in traditional landscape and portrait photography; at the same time, he is known for his continuous search for new forms and methods, a search in which his photographic ideas run parallel with various trends in painting and graphic arts.

—Ryszard Bobrowski

HASKINS, Sam(uel Joseph).

Nationality: British. **Born:** Kroonstad, South Africa, 11 November 1926. **Education:** Attended Helpmekaar High School, Johannesburg; studied graphics at the Witwatersrand Technical College, Johannesburg, and photography at Bolt Court (London College of Printing) School, 1948-50. **Family:** Married Alida Elzabe van Heerden in 1952; sons: Ludwig and Konrad. **Career:** Freelance photographer/designer, Johannesburg, 1952-1968, London, since 1968: established Haskins Studio and Haskins Press in London. Engaged in an international lecture programme since 1970. **Recipient:** Prix Nadar (for *Cowboy Kate*), France, 1964; Silver Medal, *International Art Book Competition* (for *African Image*), 1969; Gold Medal, Art Directors Club of New York (for *Haskins Posters*), 1974; Book of the Year Award, Kodak, (for *Photo Graphics*) 1980. **Address:** 9A Calonne Road, London SW19 5HH, England.

Individual Exhibitions:

1953	*Haskins Photographs,* Castle Mansions, Johannesburg
1960	*Photographic Illustration,* Orrco Theatre, Johannesburg
1970	*Sam Haskins,* Pentax Gallery, Tokyo
	Sam Haskins '70, Isetan Gallery, Tokyo
1972	*Haskins Posters,* The Photographers' Gallery, London (travelled to the FNAC Gallery, Paris, 1973, and the Canon Gallery, Amsterdam, 1974)
1973	*The Girls—Haskins Posters in Tokyo,* Isetan Gallery, Tokyo
	Haskins Posters, FNAC Gallery, Paris
1974	*The Pentax Calendar '75,* Pentax Gallery, London
1976	*Scandinavian Landscape,* Isetan Gallery, Tokyo
	Calendar '77, Pentax Gallery, London
1979	*New Work,* Pentax Gallery, London
1980	*Photo Graphics,* National Theatre, London (travelled to the Kodak Gallery, London, Sainsbury Centre, Norwich, and Royal Photographic Society Gallery, Bath, 1980; and Hillhead Gallery, Glasgow, Pentax Gallery, Rotterdam, Pentax Gallery, Zurich, Pentax Forum Gallery, Tokyo, and Marjorie Neikrug Gallery, New York, 1981)
1984	*Sam Haskins a Bologna,* Galleria d'Accursio, Bologna
1985	*The Best of Sam Haskins,* Pentax Forum Gallery, Tokyo (travelled to Printemps Gallery, Osaka)
1987	*Graphic Work,* Saatchi and Saatchi, London
	Pentax '88 Calendar, Pentax Forum Gallery, Tokyo
1990	*The Image Factor,* Pentax Forum Gallery, Tokyo (travelled to Pentax Forum, Osaka 1990; and Auckland, Sydney, Hong Kong, Taipei, Singapore in 1991)
1992	*Remember Barcelona,* Pentax Forum Gallery (travelled to Pentax Forum Osaka and the Industrial Palace, Prague in 1993)
	Graphic Work, San Paolo Palace Hotel, Palermo
1993	*Hearts,* Pentax Forum Gallery, Tokyo (travelled to Pentax Forym Osaka and the San Paolo Palace Hotel, Palermo)

Selected Group Exhibitions:

1970	*4 Masters of Erotic Photography,* at *Photokina '70,* Cologne (toured Europe)
1972	*Who Are You,* Gimpel Fils Gallery, London
1973	*The Top 10 Photographers,* McMaster University, Hamilton, Ontario
1985	*Das Akt Foto,* Fotomuseum im Stadtmuseum, Munich (toured Germany)
1986	*Fifty Years of Modern Colour Photography 1936-1986,* Photokina, Cologne
1989	*150 Years of Photography,* Narodni Galerie, Prague

Publications:

By HASKINS: Books—*5 Girls,* New York 1962 and 1963, London and Bonn 1964, paperback editions New York 1968, London 1969, Bonn 1969;

***Dancer,* 1978.** Photograph by Sam Haskins.

Cowboy Kate and Other Stories, with an introduction by Norman Hall and text by Desmond Skirrow, London 1964, 1966 and 1976, New York, Paris, Bonn, Amsterdam 1965, paperback editions London 1967, 1968, New York, Paris, Bonn 1968; *November Girl,* with text by Desmond Skirrow, London 1966, paperback editions New York 1968, 1973, London, Paris, Bonn 1968; *African Image,* with a foreword by L. Fritz Gruber, London 1967; *Haskins Posters,* London and Zurich 1972; *Photo Graphics,* Geneva 1980; *Sam Haskins a Bologna,* text by Prof Carlo Gentili and Prof Renzo Renzi, Bologna 1984.

On HASKINS: **Books**—*Photography of the World,* Heibonsha Ltd, Tokyo 1964 and 1969; *Silver Images,* History of photography in Africa by Dr A D Bensusan, Cape Town 1966; *The British Journal of Photography,* Annuals 1966 and 1968, London 1965 and 1967; *Photographis,* edited by Walter Herdeg, Zurich 1966, 1968, 1971-75, 1977-82, 1984; *Art Directors Index to Photographers,* Geneve 1970, 1971, 1973, 1975, 1977; *4 Meister der Erotischen Fotografie: Dokumentation einer Fotoausstellung,* with texts by Robbe-Grillet, Mishima, Naumann and Cau, Munich 1970; *Graphis Posters 1974,* edited by Walter Herdeg, Zurich 1974; *Glamour Calendar Art,* by Michael Colmer, London 1976; *The One Show,* NY Art Directors Club exhibition documentation; New York 1974; *Photography—Using a 35mm camera,* by R H Mason, London 1977; *Asahi Pentax Annual,* Tokyo 1977; *Geschichte der Fotografie im 20. Jahrhundert/Photography in the 20th Century* by Petr Tausk, Cologne 1977, London 1980; *Brno Biennale '78,* Catalogue of the 8th Biennale of graphic art, Brno 1978; *Dumont Foto 1—Fotokunst + Fotodesign International,* Cologne 1978; *Snoeck's Almanacs '78, '81,* Gent 1977, 1980; *The Visual Dictionary of Sex,* London 1978; *Modern Publicity,* London 1979; *The Language of Graphics,* by Edward Booth-Cliborn, London 1980; *Black-and-White Creative Photography* by Petr Tausk, Czechoslovakia 1981; *Women in the Magic Mirror,* Milan 1981; *How Famous Photographers Work* by Jack Schofield, London 1983; *The Autograph Book,* Cambridge 1983; *Stern Bibliothek der Fotografie,* Hamburg 1984; *Colour Creative Photography* by Petr Tausk, Czechoslovakia 1985; *Das Aktfoto,* Munich 1985; *50 Years Modern Colour Photography 1936-1986,* Frankfurt 1986; *Ansichten vom Korper Das Aktfoto 1840-1986,* by Michael Kohler, Frankfurt 1986; *Masters of Photography—A thematic history,* by Daniela Mrazkova, London 1987; *The Naked and the Nude,* by Jorge Lewinsky, London 1987; *Pentax Photo Annual,* Tokyo 1987-88, 1988-89, 1990-91, 1991-92, 1992-93; *Professional Photographic Illustration,* Rochester 1989; *Twelve Instant Images—The S-70 Experience,* Polaroid 1975. **Articles**—"Glamor by Sam Haskins" in *Photography Annual 1963,* New York 1962; "Five Girls" by Andreas Feininger in *Infinity* (New York), March 1963; "Sam Haskins" in *Camera* (Lucerne), April 1969; "Sam Haskins by Ulf Sjostedt" in *Hasselblad* (Gothenburg, Sweden), no. 4, 1969; "Four Masters of Erotic Photography, Photographers' Gallery" by G.S. Whittet in *Art and Artists* (London), July 1971; "Haskins: The Man, The Photographer, The Technician" by J. Shire in *Photo Technique* (London), November 1972; "The Apple in Sam's Eye" by J. Sandilands in the *Daily Telegraph Magazine* (London), 13 October 1972; "Sam Haskins: The Apple" by Shoji Yamagishi in *Camera Mainichi* (Tokyo), June 1973; "Sam Haskins" by J. Boivin in *Zoom* (Paris), no. 16, 1973; "Sam Haskins: Fashion Photographs" in the *Daily Telegraph Magazine* (London), 8 November 1974; "Sam Haskins, Photographer" in *Idea* (Tokyo), May 1974; "Art: Fun and Eros" by L. A. Mannheim in *Modern Photography* (New York), August 1975; "Sam Haskins' Photo-Graphics" by Walter Nurnberg in *British Journal of Photography* (London), 22 August 1980; "Sam Haskins: Paper Chaste" in *American Photographer* (New York), April 1981; "Sam Haskins' Schone Frauen" in *Photo* (Munich) 4 April 1981; "Photo Graphics" in *Fotografi* (Oslo), June 1981; "Arizona Shoot" in *SLR Camera,* London October 1981, May 1985; "Sam Haskins—The man, the pictures, the driving force" by Dave Saunders in *Hot Shoe No. 10* (London) 1982; "Aspects of Sam Haskins—Zanders calendar" in *Print,* (New York) September 1982; "Haskins shoots Pentax" by B Hunter in *Practical Photography,* (London) December 1982; "Sam Haskins a Bologna" in *Bolognaincontri No 3,* (Bologna) March 1984; "So fotografiert Sam Haskins" by Rene Uhlman in *Fotoheft* (Dusseldorf) September 1985; "Haskins—The Italian Job" by Nigel Skelsey in *Photography* (London) March 1987; "The JPS International Calendar" in *Kodal Professional,* (London), Winter 1989; "Sam Haskins, The Image Factor" in *Photo Asia* (Hong Kong) May 1991; "Playing it again Sam" by K Y Kiew in *Mondial Collections* (Singapore), No 3 1991; "Remember Barcelona" in *Nippon Camera,* (Tokyo) August 1992; "9 Convegno Internazionale della Fotografia" in *La Gazzetta della Fotografie*

(Palermo) November 1993. **Film**—*Sam Haskins,* directed by W. Webb, London 1973; *Grandi Fotografi—Sam Haskins,* produced by Polyvideo SA-Locarno, 1987; *Sam Haskins—Pentax 67,* directed by Luke Jeans, London 1990.

*

My approach to image making is deeply rooted in the graphic ethos of the artists who were working at the time when I first became aware of the world around me.

Eclecticism being my most pronounced character trait, my heroes were chosen from a pretty wide spectrum of endeavour. All the way from so called "fine artists" to "commercial" giants of the Ben Shahn, Cassandre ilk and including many splendid "craftspeople," children and naive artists who express themselves so directly and honestly.

After the Arcadian life at art school, when the time came to enter the real world and earn a living I decided to become a graphic designer using photography as my medium.

Over the years Multiple Image Montage has become a very important field of research for me. With the advent of computer manipulated imagery where anything is possible, and therefore in a sense meaningless, the old basic "in camera" techniques have been challenged but not conquered—they remain rich and rewarding. From within my own personal niche I love, respect and enjoy every other genre of photography and art.

—Sam Haskins

*   *   *

Born in South Africa, Sam Haskins was fascinated by tribal art ever since he could remember. From early on, one observes a certain dreamlike quality in his work that ripens into a predilection for Surrealism and unexpected juxtapositions. His studio in London is filled with a great collection of objects, either discovered on his many travels or made in his workshop. Haskins enjoys creative games. He might, for example, reassemble familiar elements in such a way that a new object emerges, the tangible result of some lateral visual thoughts. Some of these creations have become familiar through their use as subjects in his photographs where they function as supplements to the final image.

The fame of Sam Haskins is closely connected with his figure photography. His wonderful sense of whimsy was already apparent in his second book *Cowboy Kate* in which he created charming visions of an unclothed girl acting as a sheriff hunting a felon. It is marvellous persiflage, a meeting of the worlds of glamour and the Western.

The creative fantasies are, however, combined with an unerring sense of composition; surprising subjects are shown to have an epic content, expressed in a perfect form. Perhaps that may be the reason why so many of his images have been used on large format calendars and posters; they are dominating photographs, yet they repay continual contemplation.

Haskins' images are perhaps most dramatic when they depict the worlds of his own construction; however, this is not the only approach that he has used in his work. He has produced extensive reportage documentation of the indigenous, rural African cultures—ritual dances, the hunt that still involves simple weapons—and discovered in these motifs some almost magical features. In his magnificent book *African Image* he juxtaposed these photographs with, on opposite pages, images of old artefacts—and the comparison serves to emphasise the poetry of his subconscious.

Thus the same mental and emotional impetus informs such apparently quite diverse subjects as figure work and tribal life.

—Petr Tausk

HASSNER, Rune.

Nationality: Swedish. **Born:** Östersund, 13 August 1928. **Education:** Studied photography with Rolf Winquist, Stockholm, 1947-49. **Family:** Married

Yangtse Kiang at the "Three Gorges," between Chungking and Hankow, China, **1956.** Photograph ©Rune Hassner/Tio.

Eva Polasek in 1958 (divorced, 1984). **Career:** Freelance photographer, Paris, 1949-57, and Stockholm, since 1957; also documentary filmmaker, from 1965, and photo-historian and teacher, from 1968. Founder-Member, Tio Fotografer group, Stockholm, since 1958; Founder-Member and Board Member, European Society for the History of Photography, 1977. Head of Photography Department, Göteborg University, 1982-83. Director of Hasselblad Center, Göteborg, 1988-94 **Recipient:** *Svenska Dagbladet* Photo Prize, Stockholm, 1957. **Agent:** Tiofoto, Box 3252, 103 65 Stockholm, Sweden. **Address:** Bastugatan 12B, 118 20 Stockholm, Sweden.

Individual Exhibitions:

1951   Rotohallen, Stockholm
        Teaterhuset, Östersund, Sweden
1962   *Indian Village,* Pub Gallery, Stockholm
        Nimba, Museum of Art, Eskilstuna, Sweden
        Indian Village, Domus, Visby, Sweden
        Indian Village, Domus, Sundsvall, Sweden
        Indian Village, Casselska, Grängesberg, Sweden
1964   *Nimba,* Norrköpings Museum, Sweden
1982   Fotohuset, Göteborg, Sweden (retrospective)
        Nikon Gallery, Stockholm (retrospective) Camden Arts Centre,
            London (retrospective)
1985   Dalarnas Museum, Falun, Sweden (retrospective)
        Länsmuseet, Gävle, Sweden (retrospective)
        Upplands Konstmuseum, Uppsala, Sweden (retrospective)
        Jämtlands läns museum, Östersund, Sweden (retrospective)
1986   Norrbottens Museum, Luleå, Sweden (retrospective)
1990   Konstmuseet, Trollhättan, Sweden
1995   Hasselblad Center, Göteborg, Sweden

Selected Group Exhibitions:

1949   *Unga Fotografer,* Rotohallen, Stockholm
1951   *Jeunes Photographes Suédoises,* Galerie Kodak, Paris
        Subjektive Fotografie 1, Staatliche Schule für Kunst und
            Handwerk, Saarbrucken (and 2, 1954)
1959   *Young European Photography,* Van Abbemuseum, Eindhoven,
            Netherlands
1963   *Photography '63,* International Museum of Photography,
            George Eastman House, Rochester, New York
1971   *Contemporary Photographs from Sweden,* Library of Congress,
            Washington, D.C. (toured the United States)
1976   *Tio Fotografer,* Galerie Aronowitsch, Stockholm
1977   *Tio Fotografer,* at *Rencontres Internationales de Photographie,*
            Arles, France (travelled to La Photogalerie, Paris)
1982   *11 fotografos suecos,* Palacio de Bellas Artes, Mexico City
1984   *Subjektive Fotografie: Images of the 50s,* San Francisco
            Museum of Modern Art (travelled to the University of
            Houston, Texas; Museum Folkwang, Essen; Vasterbottens
            Museum, Umea; Kulturhuset, Stockholm; Saarland Museum,
            Saarbrucken; Palais des Beaux-Arts, Brussels)

Collections:

Moderna Museet, Stockholm; Norsk Fotohistorisk Forening, Oslo; Museum of Photography (Valokuvamuseon), Helsinki; Bibliothèque Nationale, Paris; Library of Congress, Washington, D.C; Provinciaal Museum voor Fotografie, Antwerp; Museum Folkwang, Essen, Germany; Hasselblad, Center, Göteborg, Sweden.

Publications:

By HASSNER: Books—*Parispromenad,* with text by Sven Aurén, Stockholm 1951; *Sköna Frankrike,* with text by Sven Stolpe, Stockholm 1953; *Jambo,* with text by O. Strandberg, Stockholm 1954; *Lättjans Öar,* with text by O. Strandberg and Hassner, Stockholm 1956; *Det Nya Kina,* Stockholm 1957; *Vår Indiska By,* with text by S.O. Andersson, Stockholm 1962; *Hassner Foto,* Stockholm 1993; *Edouard Boubat,* exhibition catalogue, Stockholm

1967; *Jacob A. Riis: Reporter med Kamera i New Yorks Slum,* Stockholm 1970; *Rolf Winquist,* exhibition catalogue, Stockholm 1970; *De Bittra Aren,* exhibition catalogue, Stockholm 1970; *André Kertész,* exhibition catalogue, Stockholm 1971; *Jacob A. Riis,* exhibition catalogue, Essen 1971; *Hur den Andra Hälften Levde,* exhibition catalogue, Stockholm 1972; *Erich Salomon,* exhibition catalogue, Stockholm 1974; *Felix H. Man,* exhibition catalogue, Stockholm 1975; *Bilder för Miljoner,* Stockholm 1977; *Mexikansk fotografi,* exhibition catalogue, Stockholm 1982; *Rune Hassner,* exhibition catalogue, Stockholm 1985; *Nine Masters of Photography,* exhibition catalogue, Göteborg 1989; *Rolf Winquist—Porträttör,* exhibition catalogue, Göteborg 1989; *Arbete pågår,* exhibition catalogue, Göteborg 1990; *Eric G Matson & the American Colony Photographers, Jerusalem,* exhibition catalogue, Göteborg 1990; *William Klein,* exhibition catalogue, Göteborg 1990; *Lennart Nilsson—fotografier 1945-90,* exhibition catalogue, Göteborg 1990; *Richard Avedon—Portraits, Fashion and Reportage,* exhibition catalogue, Göteborg 1991; *Josef Koudelka—Gypsies,* exhibition catalogue, Göteborg 1992; *Sune Jonsson—Focus on people and landscapes in Northern Sweden,* exhibition catalogue, Göteborg 1993. **Articles**—"Sir Jake och Survey-Fotograferna" in *Populär Fotografi* (Helsingborg, Sweden), September 1970; "David Douglas Duncan och Krig Utan Hjältar" in *Fotonyheterna* (Stockholm), no. 5, 1972; "När kulturrevolutionen kom till USA" in *Paletten* (Gothenburg), January 1976; "Rol & Meurisse" in *Aktuell Fotografi* (Helsingborg, Sweden), December 1978; "Mass Observation, Picture Post och Humphrey Spender" in *Aktuell Fotografi* (Helsingborg, Sweden), November 1980; "SSSR na stroike—USSR in Construction" in *Album* (Halsingborg, Sweden), no. 2, 1981; "Fotografins historia—fakta och myter" in *Svenska Dagbladet* (Stockholm), 19 May 1984; "Fransk fotografi—mot en ny realism" in *Svenska Dagbladet* (Stockholm), 9 June 1984; "Modefotografins historia" in *Svensk Fotografisk Tidskrift* (Stockholm), no. 3, 1986.

On HASSNER: Books—*Photography Today,* edited by Norman Hall, London 1957; *Photographic Communication,* edited by R. Smith Schuneman, London and Toronto 1972; *Museum Folkwang: die fotografische Sammlung,* with introduction by Ute Eskildsen, Essen, West Germany 1983. **Articles**—"Rune Hassner: From Morocco to Cape Town" by B. Dobell in *U.S. Camera* (New York), January 1955; "Entretien avec Rune Hassner" by Romeo Martinez in *Camera* (Lucerne), September 1956; "Rune Hassner: Världsreporter" by B. Gustafsson in *Foto* (Stockholm), March 1962; "Rune Hassner, Star Photographer" by Norman Hall in *Photography Yearbook,* London 1963; "Rune Hassner: Forskande Fotograf" by Kurt Bergengren in *Fotonyheterna* (Stockholm), no. 10, 1970; "Rune Hassners pionjärinsats" by Guy Jamais in *Foto* (Stockholm), no. 11, 1977; "Rune Hassner—Bilder for miljoner" by Bernd Lohse in *Fotomagazin* (Munich), no. 5, 1979; "Hassner—Bildskapare" by Gun Kessle in *Folket i bild* (Stockholm), no. 21, 1981; "Rune Hassner—var förste bildlektor" by Kurt Bergengren in *Aftonbladet* (Stockholm), 11 September 1982; "Världen i svart och vitt" by Peder Alton in *Dagens Nyheter* (Stockholm), 24 September 1993; "Bildkännare av mått" by Margartea Artsman in *Svenska Dagbladet* (Stockholm), 12 August 1993.

*   *   *

During the Second World War neutral Sweden experienced an increase in national pride. In photography this found expression in romantic-patriotic imagery. The idyllic dominated the photoclub competitions and exhibitions—far removed from the tragic reality outside the country's borders. When the war was over, there was, not surprisingly, a counter-reaction among the country's young photographers. They reacted not only against charmingly seductive images of reality, as reflected in these photographs, but also against an idiom which had become a stereotype. In 1949 a group of young photographers organized an exhibition in Stockholm: it amounted to open provocation. These 11 photographers were dubbed "De Unga" (The Young). But they had no long-term objectives, and after their attack on the photographic establishment, each one returned to his own speciality: fashion, journalism, nature photography, etc. Rune Hassner was the one who came to represent the young radicals. He readily entered into polemics in the trade journals with his older and shocked colleagues. His literary style was just as hard-hitting as his pictorial.

Having attempted to demolish the photographic idyll with both words and pictures, Hassner left for Paris, along with a number of other young Swedish photographers. In France he quickly established himself as a creator of reportage, and he supplied the Swedish newspapers with photos from the worlds of culture, politics and fashion. But for preference he would saunter around and photograph daily life, and these photos were the basis of two books. At the same time he provided Swedish photographic periodicals with reports on the new European photography.

Hassner's photographic ideals were similar to those of the more personally and poetically engaged photojournalists. Experimental photography—as for example in the exhibition *Subjektive Fotografie*—he found largely meaningless and superficially picturesque. His attacks on the experimental as well as the romantically idyllic may seem inconsistent, but, as he asserted, he felt that photographs should communicate something essential about our surroundings, not function as playgrounds for aesthetic games.

During the 1950s Hassner produced another three books—on Africa, the West Indies and China, the last with his own text. After this period he gradually became involved with motion pictures. He has made more than fifty documentary films for Swedish television, many of them about photographers and photographic history. His interest in the latter is also evidenced by books and by the number of his articles in journals.

During recent years, therefore, Rune Hassner has appeared mostly in the roles of filmmaker, photographic historian and teacher—but at the same time he has continued collecting his visual impressions in still photography, a medium that is still obviously very close to his heart, which he also showed in a large retrospective exhibition that circulated in 1985/86 and a large retrospective at the Hasselblad Center in January 1995.

His previous teaching experience made him the obvious choice to start the development of the new photographic department at Göteborg University in 1982-83 and to start the Hasselblad Center in 1989. The one-time Paris bohemian proved to be a capable organiser and administrator.

—Rune Jonsson

HATAKEYAMA, Naoya.

Nationality: Japanese. **Born:** 19 March 1958. **Education:** Graduated from the University of Tsukuba's School of Art and Design in 1980 and completed post-graduate studies at the University of Tsukuba, 1984. **Address:** 6-3-12, Nagasaki, Toshima-ku, Tokyo 171.

Individual Exhibitions:

1983	Zeit-Foto Salon, Tokyo
1986	Tokyo University of Art and Design, Tokyo
1987	Photo Interform, Osaka
1988	Zeit-Foto Salon, Tokyo
1989	Théâtre d'Hérouville, Caen
1990	Artothèque de Nantes, France
	Bibliothèque de Falaise, France
	Institute du Monde Arabe, Paris
1991	Photo Interform, Osaka
1994	Gallery NW House, Tokyo
	Fox Talbot Museum, Lacock, UK

Selected Group Exhibitions:

1981	*Camera Works Exhibition,* University of Tsukuba, Ibaraki
1985	*Paris, New York, Tokyo,* Tsukuba Museum of Photography 85, Ibaraki
1986	*Fotographia Japonesa Contemporanea,* Barcelona (travelled throughout Spain)
1988	*Contemporary Photographs from Japan,* Columbia College, Chicago
	Tama Vivant 88, Seed Hall, Tokyo
1989	*The 9th Hara Annual,* Hara Museum of Contemporary Art, Tokyo
	Orientalism, White Museum, International Design Exposition, Nagoya
1990	*A Selection of Photographs on the Sea,* Shimonoseki City Museum, Yamaguchi
	Japanese Contemporary Photography—Twelve Viewpoints, Tokyo Metropolitan Museum of Photography (travelled to the Pavillion des Arts, Paris)
1991	*Vach' image,* Saint Gervais Genèva mjc, Switzerland
	Make-believe, The Photographers' Gallery, London (toured throughout UK)
1992	*Matrix of Photography 3,* Kawasaki City Museum, Kanagawa
1993	*Contemporary Japanese Photography,* Kunsthaus, Zürich
1994	*Liquid Crystal Futures,* The Fruitmarket Gallery, Edinburgh (travelled throughout Europe and America)
	Desert of Desires, Spiral Garden, Tokyo
	Kawasaki Monuments, Kawasaki City Museum, Kanagawa

Collections:

Artothèque de Nantes, France; Kawasaki City Museum, Japan; Tokyo Metropolitan Museum of Photography, Japan; The Swiss Foundation for Photography; Conoco plc, UK; Baring Securities (Japan) Ltd.

Publications:

By HATAKEYAMA: Book—*Contour Line,* Camera Works Tokyo, No. 9, 1982.

On HATAKEYAMA: Books—*Camera Works Exhibition at Tsukuba University,* 1981; *Paris-New York-Tokyo,* 1985; *Fotographia Japonesa Contemporanea,* 1986; *New Wave,* Complete Collection of Japanese Photography, Vol. 12, Shogakukan, 1988; *Tama-Vivant 88,* exhibition catalogue, 1988; *The 9th Hara Annual,* 1989; *Orientalism,* 1989; *A Selection of Photographs on the Sea,* 1990; *Japanese Contemporary Photography—Twelve Viewpoints,* 1990; *14 Japanese Photographers,* Mitsukoshi, 1991; *Make Believe,* 1991; *Matrix of Photography 3,* 1992; *In die Felsen bohren sich Zikadenstimmen/Contemporary Japanese Photography,* 1993; *Desert of Desires,* 1994; *Kawasaki Monuments,* 1994. **Articles**—"Contour Line" in *Art View,* No. 2, 1982; "Contour Line" in *Camera-Mainichi,* July 1983; "Contour Line" by Chizuru Miyasako in *Commercial Photo,* August 1983; "Standard-Bearers of New Wave" in *Bijutsu-Techo,* January 1984; "Academic City" in *Sho,* 1984; "New Photography" in *Bijutsu-Techo,* January 1985; "Return and Revival—Academic City" in *Zoom Japon,* January 1986; "Photography of Today" in *Asahi Camera,* extra issue 1986; "Factory Survey" in *Graphication,* No. 28, 1986; essay on the artist by Osamu Hiraki in *Nihon-Camera,* September 1987; "Lime Hills" in *Nihon-Camera,* February 1987; "Best Artists of Serious Photography" in *Photo-Technique,* May-June 1988; "Lime Hills" in *WAVE,* No. 25, 1990; "Series of River" in *Tokyo-jin,* February 1994; "Lime Works" by Arturo Silva in *déjà-vu,* No. 16, 1994.

HÄUSSER, Robert.

Nationality: German. **Born:** Stuttgart, 8 November 1924. **Education:** Attended gymnasium in Stuttgart, until 1941; Graphische Fachschule, Stuttgart, 1941-42; Meisterschule für Handwerk und Kunst, Weimar, 1950, Meisterdiplom, 1950. **Military Service:** Served in the German Army, 1944-45. **Family:** Married Elfriede Meyer in 1946; daughter: Regine. **Career:** Photographer since 1950: established studio, Mannheim, 1952. Member since 1950, Jury Chairman, 1965-68, Executive Director, 1976-80, Acting Chairman, 1980-83, and Vice-President of the Photographic Academy since 1986, Gesellschaft Deutscher Lichtbildner (GDL); Member, Deutsche Gesellschaft für Photographie, since 1960, Deutschen Werkbundes, since 1960 and Akademie der Künste, Mannheim, since 1985; Founder-Member, Bund Freischaffender Fotodesigner (BFF), since 1969; Member, Deutschen Künstlerbundes, since 1979, and Neuen Darmstädter Sezession, since 1980. **Recipient:** Silver Medal, Swedish Master Competition, 1950; *Photokina*-Plaque, Cologne, 1960; Gold Medal, *Biennale,* Venice, 1961; Special Prize, City of San Remo, Italy, 1963; German City Prize, 1965; Schiller Plaque, City of Mannheim, 1977; Kunstpreis

From the series *Lime Hills*, 1990 (original in colour). Photograph by Naoya Hatakeyama.

Nordhorn, 1984; David Octavius Hill Medal, Gesellschaft Deutscher Lichtbildner, 1984; Cross of Honour, First Class, Federal Republic of Germany, 1984. Professor honoris causa for the work, 1989. **Agents:** Benteler Galleries, 2409 Rice Boulevard, Houston, Texas 77005, U.S.A.; Galerie Jutta Rössner, Vogelsangstrasse 13, 7000 Stuttgart; and Galerie Rudolf Kicken, Albertusstrasse 1, D-5000 Cologne 1, Germany. **Address:** Ladenburgerstrasse 23, D-68309 Mannheim, Germany.

Individual Exhibitions:

1959	Galerie Probst, Mannheim
1960	Landesbildstelle, Hamburg
	Swansea-Toulon-Mannheim, Reiss-Museum, Mannheim
1961	*Toulon-Mannheim,* Toulon Opera
1970	Galeria Van der Voort, Ibiza, Spain
1971	Kunstverein, Augsburg, West Germany
1972	Kunsthalle, Mannheim
	Leopold-Hoesch-Museum, Düren, West Germany
	Konfrontatie, Van Abbemuseum, Eindhoven, Netherlands
	Magischer Realismus, Institut für Moderne Kunst, Nuremberg
	Kunsthalle, Cologne
	Die Neue Sammlung, Munich

1973	Kunsthalle, Bielefeld, West Germany
	Kunstmuseum, Bonn
	Paula-Modersohn-Becker-Haus, Bremen
	Kulturhaus, Soest, West Germany
1974	Museum am Dom, Lubeck
1975	*Magischer Realismus,* Galerie der Deutsche Gesellschaft für Photographie, Cologne
1977	Galerie Spectrum, Hannover
1978	Galerie Lauter, Mannheim (partial retrospective)
	Industriefotografie and *Magischer Realismus,* Kulturhaus der BASF, Ludwigshafen, West Germany
1979	Kunstverein, Pforzheim, West Germany
1982	Karl-Ernst-Osthaus-Museum, Hagen, West Germany
1983	Nationalgalerie, West Berlin
1984	Benteler Galleries, Houston, Texas
	Städtische Galerie, Nordhorn, West Germany
	Studio für moderne Kunst, Otterndorf, West Germany
	Kunsthalle, Mannheim
1985	Saarland Museum, Saarbrücken, West Germany
	Kunsthalle, Nuremberg, West Germany
1987	Galerie spectrum, Sprengel-Museum, Hannover
1988	Galerie für Fotografie Rössner-Kropp, Stuttgart
	Württembergischer Kunstverein, Stuttgart

J.R., 5.9.70, **1970.** Photograph by Robert Häusser.

Allunionzentrum für Fotografie, Moscow
Nationalgalerie, Berlin
Museum für Kunst und Gewerbe, Hamburg
Augustinermuseum, Marienbad Freiburg
1989   Cankarjev Dom, Lubljana
Galerie Rothe, Frankfurt
1992   Galerie Holzwarth, Stuttgart
Galerie Städt Schwäbisch Hall
1993   Kunstverein Eislingen
1994   *foto forum nord,* Worpswede

Selected Group Exhibitions:

1951   *Mostra fotografica europea,* Milan
1961   *3 Biennale internazionale della fotografica,* Venedig
1963   *Angewandte Kunst in Europa nach 1945,* Museum für Kunst und Gewerbe, Hamburg
1969   *Vision and Expression,* International Museum of Photography, George Eastman House, Rochester, New York; Media Center University, Houston; Museum of Westerm Art, Houston; Museum of Art, El Paso
1971   *Eros en el arte actual en Espana,* Galerie Vandrés, Madrid
1973   *Das kleinste Museum der Welt - Tabu Format,* Kunstverein, Wolfsburg, West Germany (travelled to the Kunsthalle, Baden-Baden, West Germany)
1974   *The First Communications X 0001,* New York
1975   *Fotoauge-gestern und heute, Fotografie 1929-1975,* Württembergischer, Kunstverein, Stuttgart

1976   *Obras Graficas 1966-1976,* Museo de Arte Vontemporaneo de Ibiza, Spain
1977   *Recontres International de la Photographie,* Arles, France
1979   *Deutsche Fotografie nach 1945,* Kunstverein, Kassel, West Germany (toured West Germany)
70 Meisterwerke der Fotografie, Staatl. Museum für Kunst und Gewerbe, Hamburg
Fotografie 1919-1979 made in Germany, Photomuesm i, Stadtmuseum, München
1980   *Deutsche Fotografie nach 1945,* PPS-Galerie, Hamburg; Kunstmuseum, Hannover; Overbeck-Gesellschaft, Lübeck; Kunstverein, Wolfsburg
1981   *Photography Europe 1,* Benteler Galleries Inc, Houston
Die Sammlung Otto Steinert, Museum Folkwang, Essen
Deutsche Fotografie nach 1945, Goethe Institut, Italy
1982   *Lichtbildnisse: Das Porträt in der Fotografie,* Rheinisches Landesmuseum, Bonn
1983   *Kunstpreis Villa Romana Florenz,* Märkisches Museum, Witten
Die 50er Jahre in der Fotografie, Staatl. Museum für Kunst und Gewerbe, Hamburg
1984   *4 Aspekte Deutscher Fotografie,* Goethe-House, New York
1985   *Das Aktfoto,* Fotomuseum im Stadtmuseum, Munich (toured Germany)
Das Selbstporträt im Zeitalter der Photographie, Württbg. Kunstv. Stuttgart; Akademie der Künste, Berlin
1986   *Sammlung Otto Steinert,* Wilhelm-Hack-Museum, Ludwigshafen
Das Automobil in der Kunst, Haus der Kunst, München

1987 *Deutsche Lichtbildner—Wegbereiter zeitgenössischer Fotografie*, Museum Ludwig, Köln; Helsinki; Erlangen
1988 *Deutsche Lichtbildner—Wegbereiter zeitgenössischer Fotografie*, Galerie Ingolstadt
Das Auge des Zyklopen-Das Bild der Photographie, Fotomuesum im Münchner Stadtmuseum
Kunst der 80 er Jahre, III, Akademie der Künste Mannheim mit Künstlerbund Rhein-Neckar
Moderne Kunst in Deutschland, Taiwan Kulturzentrum
1989 *Dokument und Erfindung, Fotografien aus der Bundesrepublik Deutschland 1945 bis heute, Berlin*, Haus am Lützowplatz
Augustiner Museum, Freiburg
Das Foto als autonomes Bild-Experimentelle Gestaltung, Kunsthalle Bielefeld, Akademie d. schönen Künste, München
1990 *Document and Invention*, Goldie Paley Gallery, Moore College of Art and Design, Philadelphia; Department of Art, Morehead State University, Kentucky
Subjektive Fotografie—Der deutsche Beitrag 1984-1963, Galerie Agora, Turin; Kulturstiftung Grossbank, Palermo; Kulturzentum Ausoni, Rome; Accademia delle Belle Arti, Cantania
1991 *Subjektive Fotografie—Der deutsche Beitrag 1984-1963*, Palazzo Sera Gerace, Genoa; Galeria Idea Books, Mailand Instituto Europeo di Design, Mailand; Gal. Freidrichstrasse, Berlin
Dokument und Erfindung-Fotografische Akademie, C.E.P.A. Center, Buffalo
1992 *Sprung in die Zeit—Bewegung und Zeit als Gestaltungsprinzip in der Photographie von den Anfängen bis zur Gegenwart*, Berlinische Galerie, Museum für monderne Kunst, Photographie und Architektur, Gropis-Bau, Berlin
1993 *Kunst im 20 Jahrhundert*, Neuerwerbungen 1982-1993, Städt. Galerie Wolfsburg

Collections:

Museum of Modern Art, New York; International Museum of Photography, Rochester, New York; George Eastmann House, USA; Kunsthalle, Mannheim; Leopold-Hoesch-Museum, Düren; Wilhelm-Hack-Museum, Ludwigshafen; Städt. Kunstsammlungen, Erlangen; Die Neue Sammlung, München; Kunstmuseum, Bonn; Kunsthalle, Bielefeld; Van Abbe Museum, Eindhoven; Museum Folkwang, Essen; Sammlung Gernsheim, Lugano, Switzerland; Museum für Kunst und Gewerbe, Hamburg; Sammlung Steinert, Museum Folkwang, Essen; Städt. Kunstsammlung, Wolfsburg; Kunstsammlung IBM Deutschland; Städt Sammlung Stadt Sindelfingen (Lütze II); Karl-Ernst-Osthaus-Museum, Hagen; Museum of Fine Art, Houston; Photomuesm des Münchner Stadtmuseums; Kunstsammlung der Stadt Nordhorn; Kunstsammlung Cuxhaven/Otterndorf; Foto-Museum, Burghausen; Moderne Galerie des Saalandmuseums, Saarbrücken; Museum Ludwig, Köln; Staatsgalerie, Stuttgart; Sprengel-Museum, Hannover; Schleswig-Holsteinisches Landesmuseum, Schleswig; Fränkisch-Hällisches Museum, Schwäb. Hall; Städt. Kunstsammlung Rastatt; Sammlung der Bundesrepublik Deutschland; Sammlung Preussischer Kulturbesitz, Berlin.

Publications:

By HÄUSSER: Books—*Ein Fotograf sieht Mannheim*, Mannheim 1957; *Heidelberg*, Konstanz 1961; *Welt am Oberrhein*, Karlsruhe 1961, 1962, 1963; *Aus unseren Fenstem*, Mannheim 1962; *Das Elsass*, Karlsruhe 1962; *Weinland Baden*, Mannheim 1969; *Ladenburg*, Mannheim 1970; *Gelsenkirchen*, Dusseldorf 1970; *Der Bildhauer Hans Nagel*, Nuremberg 1971; *Der Maler K.F. Dahmen*, Munich 1972; *Mannheim*, Mannheim 1975; *Die Welt der Oper*, Karlsruhe 1977; *Weinland Pfalz*, Mannheim 1979; *Das Geschenk der Erde*, Dusseldorf 1980; *Kunst-Landschaft-Architektur in der Bundesrepublik Deutschland*, Berlin 1983; *II. Internationale Bildhauersymposion*, Bentheim, West Germany 1984; *Die Wirklichkeit ist subjektiv*, Deutscher Werkbund 1986; *Land an der Vechte*, Nordhorn 1990; *Da Elsass*, Kazlsruhe 1993. Articles—"Zur Fotografie in der Kunstszene" in *Kunstreport* (Berlin), no. 2/3, 1975; "Fragen an einen Fotografen" in *Werk und Zeit* (Darmstadt), no. 6, 1976; "Spuren und Zeichen im Um-Raun" in *Leica Fotografie* (Frankfurt),

no. 7, 1978; "Schwarzweiss oder Farbe?" in *Leica Fotografie* (Frankfurt), no. 5, 1980; "Uber die Kunst, Kunst zu fotografieren" in *Leica Fotografie* (Frankfurt), no. 6, 1980; "Anmerkungen zur Fotografie von Kunstwerken" in *Kunstreport* (Berlin), no. 3, 1981; "Aus meinem Moor-Tagebuch" in *Leica Fotografie* (Frankfurt), no. 1, 1985.

On HÄUSSER: Books—*Ein Meister der neuen Ding-Magie*, exhibition catalogue, by Juliana Roh, Augsburg, West Germany 1970; *Robert Häusser* by Heinz Fuchs, Mannheim 1972; *Robert Häusser: Fotografische Bilder*, exhibition catalogue, by Horst Keller, Cologne 1972; *Robert Häusser: Konfrontatie*, exhibition catalogue, by Jan Leering, Eindhoven, Netherlands 1972; *Robert Häusser*, exhibition catalogue, by J.W. von Moltke, Bielefeld, West Germany 1973; *Die Fremdheit des Vertrauten* by Ulrich Weisner, Lubeck 1974; *Geschichte der Fotografie im 20. Jahrhunder/History of Photography in the 20th Century* by Petr Tausk, Cologne 1977, London 1980; *Robert Häusser*, exhibition catalogue, with text by J. H. Muller, Hagen, West Germany 1982; *Robert Häusser: Ausstellung und Kunstpreis*, exhibition catalogue, with text by Klaus Honnef, Nordhorn, West Germany 1984; *Retrospektive Robert Häusser*, exhibition catalogue, by J. A. Schmoll, M. Fath and others, Mannheim 1984. Articles—"Robert Häusser" by Robert d'Hooghe in *Foto Prisma* (Dusseldorf), October 1958; "Robert Häusser" in *Das Deutsche Lichtbild*, portfolio, Stuttgart 1959; "Robert Häusser: Meister der Leica" by Fritz Kempe in *Leica Fotografie* (Frankfurt), no. 6, 1971; "Kamera-Magie" by E. Pfeiffer-Belli in *Süddeutsche Zeitung* (Munich), 29 July 1971; "Robert Häusser: Poetischer Naturalismus" by Rainer Fabian in *Die Welt* (Hamburg), 17 August 1971; "Robert Häusser: Fotografischer Realismus" by Juliana Roh in *Gebrauchsgraphik* (Munich), no. 10, 1972; "Robert Häusser: Erfüllung durch Fotografie und Lebenskunst" by Gunther Lensch in *Foto-Magazin* (Munich), December 1974; "Zwei Weisen sich ein Bild zu machen" by R. Skasa-Weiss in *Stuttgarter Zeitung*, 2 October 1975; "Magie der Banalität" by Hugo Schöttle in *Leica Fotografie* (Frankfurt), no. 1, 1976; "Robert Häusser" by Hans Christian Adam in *Fotografie* (Riesweiler, West Germany), no. 4, 1977; "Robert Häusser: Die Wahrheit hinter der Schonheit" by F. Adler in *Photo Revue* (Munich), no. 12, 1983; "Kunstfiguren eines Fotografen" by R. G. Dienst in *Frankfurter Allgemeine Zeitung* (Frankfurt), 5 February 1985; "Robert Häusser—Fruhe Bilder 1941-1950" by F. Adler in *Photo Revue* (Munich), no. 1, 1986; "Robert Häusser—Eine Welt aus Traum und Magie" by Klaus Reitz in *Mannheimer Morgen*, 1988; Robert Häusser—Wiederbesichtigter Klassiker" by Sigrid Feeser in *Rhienpfalz*, 31 March 1988; "Robert Häusser—Wirklichkeit-Wahrheit" by Heiner Stachelhaus, exhibition catalogue, Württbg. Kunstverein, Stuttgart 1988; "Robert Häusser—Den Zufall in die Schranken weisen" by Rainer Vogt in *Stuttgarter Nachrichten*, 14 March 1988. Films—*Sprache aus Licht und Zeit*, ARD German television documentary, 1972; *Das Unsichtbare sichtbar machen—Der Fotograf Robert Häusser*, ARD German television documentary, 1986.

*

I use photography not to try to produce an autonomous picture of reality; what interests me is an interpretation of reality. I find it more important to evoke the creative quality of reality than to compose a picture of the world.

Photography ensures that I stay within the bounds of reality and that along the way I may perhaps make visible a further reality. Such pictures are records not as reproductions but as the making visible of an inner state by visual and optical articulation. If this is successful, the picture is conclusive. It means analysis, recognition and an adequate formal proficiency. The discovery of form is accounted for by the content because form serves content, illuminates it, and is determined by it. But the discovery of form presupposes the discovery of content: an analysis of the visible and invisible. This spiritual process requires us to question and learn by listening to the inner reality which hides behind the visible. It is the other dimension which constitutes existence: the essential. But I will have nothing to do with formal tricks, however great their aesthetic appeal. They are, and remain, only decorative.

I take that which is, I ask what is, and I try to show that which is.

—Robert Häusser

* * *

459

Robert Häusser is something of a classic in modern post-war German photography. It is difficult to think of any other contemporary photographer who has, over a period of 30 years, followed so straight a course in the shaping, development and consistent pursuit of his own creative handwriting. For Häusser photography is a medium with not only strict graphic principles but also its own laws, with which the photographer can interpret both his environment and his own personal world.

Häusser's black-and-white landscapes of the 1950s and 60s are rich in contrast and are distinguished by their perfect stillness. They are nearly always devoid of people. If a human figure is included, it is frozen to a black silhouette or signifies by its transitoriness, by the blurring of an isolated movement within otherwise rigid elements of the picture, that complete stillness will return immediately.

Even the subjects of Häusser's pictures are not important; they serve only to construct the whole. Häusser takes up the principles of "land art": he finds impressive lines in the man-made environment. He reduces everything (by selective cutting, black-and-white contrast and other creative possibilities of photography) that could trigger an idea other than that which he wishes for his composition; he "subtracts" objects until there remains only what is important to the picture in the way of strong shapes and lines.

In recent years Häusser's realism has become increasingly subjective and now contains mysterious, magical elements: he adds to his pictures (as always void of all superfluity) objects, forms, veiled bodies; he leaves a human figure to perform in a room otherwise reduced to abstraction (the series "Wing," 1976). The veiling: the enigma under the white cloth, the desire for a resolution—this stimulus to fantasy is increasingly evident in his photographs.

One of Häusser's best-known photographs shows a racing car, wrapped in awnings like a Christo, with severe black/white contrast on a concrete road—a picture that symbolizes bridled energy. Häusser's photographs, however coldly and graphically rationalized, have an unbridled strength.

He spends part of his time on the Spanish island of Ibiza, where some years ago he acquired an ancient whitewashed farmhouse of *finca*, a constant inspiration for many of his later images. Häusser has received much recognition for his life's work through the 1984/85 retrospective exhibition travelling in Germany, which was accompanied by an excellent major catalogue.

—Hans Christian Adam

HAVRÁNKOVÁ, Milota.

Nationality: Czechoslovakian. **Born:** Košice, 7 August 1945. **Education:** Attended primary school in Košice, 1951-59; studied photography, High School of Art and Design, Bratislava, 1959-63; School of Photography, FAMU Academy of Art, Prague, 1963-67. **Family:** Married Peter Breza in 1977; children: Igor and Milota. **Career:** Independent photographer and film animator, Bratislava, since 1970. Lecturer in Artistic Photography, High School of Art and Design, Bratislava, 1972-78. Member, Union of Slovak Artists, 1969. **Agents:** Dielo-SFVU: Slovak Institution for Fine Arts, Štúrova Street 3, 800 00 Bratislava, Czechoslovakia; Slovart, Gottwaldovo námestie 48, 800 00 Bratislava, Czechoslovakia. **Address:** Benediktiho Street 1, 811 05 Bratislava, Czechoslovakia.

Individual Exhibitions:

1969	Student Gallery, Tübingen, West Germany
1970	Student Gallery, Krakow, Poland
1972	Gallery of Fine Art, Nové Zámky, Czechoslovakia
1973	Galerie Profil, Bratislava, Czechoslovakia
1974	Regional Gallery, Vysoké Mýto, Czechoslovakia
1975	Theatre Gallery, Martin, Czechoslovakia
1978	Cyprian Majernik Gallery, Bratislava, Czechoslovakia
1980	Gallery of Photography, Wroclaw, Poland

1981	ZPAF Old Gallery, Warsaw
1982	Gallery of Fine Art, Bratislava, Czechoslovakia

Selected Group Exhibitions:

1971	*Czechoslovak Photography,* Moravian Gallery, Brno, Czechoslovakia
1972	*Women with Camera I,* Gallery of the Capital, Prague
1973	*Slovak Land,* Gallery of Fine Art, Bratislava, Czechoslovakia
1976	*Rencontres Internationale de la Photographie,* Galerie Municipale, Arles, France
1979	*Photography 1918-1978,* Galerie Fotoforum, Kassel, West Germany
1980	*Generation 45,* Gallery of Young Artists, Bratislava, Czechoslovakia
1983	*Contemporary Photography in Bratislava,* Community Centre, Bratislava, Czechoslovakia
1984	Czechoslovak Photography, Gallery Show, San Francisco, California
1985	*FAMU Academy Photography Graduates,* Gallery of Fine Arts, Brno, Czechoslovakia
1986	*Tenth Exhibition of Design in Slovakia,* Gallery of Fine Art, Bratislava, Czechoslovakia

Collections:

Moravian Gallery, Brno, Czechoslovakia; Slovak National Gallery, Bratislava, Czechoslovakia; Matica Slovenská Museum of Literature, Martin, Czechoslovakia; Museum of Design, Prague.

Publications:

By HAVRÁNKOVÁ: Books—*Skamenely,* with text by J. Král, Martin, Czechoslovakia 1972; *Milena,* with text by V. Filipová, Bratislava, Czechoslovakia 1983; *Spain,* with P. Breza, Bratislava, Czechoslovakia 1985. **Films**—*Fotografie Milota Havránková,* 1978; *Plný čas,* 1980.

On HAVRÁNKOVÁ: Books—*Ceskoslovenska Fotografie 1971/72,* exhibition catalogue, by Antonin Dufek and Ludovit Hlavac, Brno, Czechoslovakia 1973; *Absolventi FAMU a ich vplyv na Slovenskú fotografiu,* thesis, by Peter Breza, Prague 1980; *Milota Havránková,* thesis, by Anton Sladek, Prague 1982; *Slovenská fotografia* by Rudolf Ciliak, Bratislava, Czechoslovakia 1987. **Articles**—in *Revue Fotografie* (Prague), no. 2, 1969, no. 4, 1971, and no. 1, 1977; *Výtvarný život* (Bratislava), no. 4, 1973, and no. 7, 1978; *Šeskoslovenská Fotografie* (Prague), no. 4, 1976; *Film a doba* (Prague), no. 3, 1979; *Life-Czechoslovakia* (Prague), no. 10, 1979; *Fotografia* (Warsaw), no. 10, 1980; *Život* (Bratislava), no. 7, 1983; *Vlasta* (Prague), no. 30, 1983.

*

Photography is one of the most exciting inventions in man's history. It provides an infinite number of experiments, expressive ideas and ideals of our times. Photography is a creative tool documenting the atmosphere of our rapidly changing world.

Today photography is a real part of our life. We meet it everywhere. You cannot miss it. And thus, photography met me.

I love photography. It has become my profession—a real part of my life, a creative tool I can handle immediately. The philosophy of my work has been crystallizing slowly in the light of new experiences and knowledge. In my work there is a phenomenon, the presence of which has been evident from the very beginning of my career. It is an attempt to impress onto every photograph my own personal expression. I was never satisfied merely by perfect technique or documentary values alone. I have always tried to change my surroundings through photography, to express the essence, simplicity and sincerity of an immediate idea. Colour and the multiple use of elements play an important role in my work, but the concept itself remains the predominant feature. In the course of my career, I have made many experiments whilst looking for something to link photography more closely with the fine arts. Sound and motion are elements which are able to open new horizons in photography. I made the films *Fotografie Milota Havránková* and *Plný čas* (Full Time) using special-effects and animated photos. I wrote the film-script myself, which, together with the rich colours and music, expresses my personal ideas. The film is a springboard for my next career.

I firmly believe in a future for a photography incorporated in the fine arts and in the mainstream culture of our society.

—Milota Havránková

*   *   *

Slovakia, the land under the rugged Tatra Mountains north of the Danube, the "nation of sheep" as it used to be derisively called by its Hungarian rulers, continues to be a great font of inspiration to art because of its vital heritage of folk art. Besides painting on glass, embroidery, dress design, utility objects and decorative bric-à-brac, the inspiration of folk art finds its outlet even in less traditional fields, as proved by the work of Milota Havránková, daughter of a folk embroidery artist. The author of numerous book illustrations and monumental interior decoration projects, she is one of the exponents of the application of the photographic process to visual art. She can be said to have made applied photography an integral part of architectural design in Czechoslovakia.

As early as 1969 when she graduated from the photography department of Prague's Film Academy, she tried to liberate photography from its traditional framework of a wall-mounted picture and lend it a wider application. She set out to prove that photography, essentially a product of optics and chemistry, could play a novel role in a number of new modes of expression and that it was possible to obliterate the division between photographic documentarism and artistic stylization. She tried out novel creative projects in which photography was but a part of the technique employed (toners, solarization, montage, photographic printing, etc.) which she used to make her "photographic paintings." In time her post-Surrealist visions began using diverse materials selected for their specific properties, i.e. not only photographic paper but also canvas, plastics, glass, wood, nonferrous metals and ultimately also movie film with sound and musical accompaniment, resulting in audiovisual mobiles of sorts. Only a dependence on conventional means of reproduction makes it impossible for her to create effects produced by holography and laser technology, i.e. an effect of total spatial experience.

Havránková's main interest lies in innovative interior decoration. Her original idea of blending photography and graphics has found practical use in two-dimensional frescoes of monumental dimensions. Collaborating with architects, she has made projects that are an integral part of interior decoration of various public places, coffee shops, restaurants, shopping marts and even industrial plants, as in the complex of a gas company near Bratislava where her monumental frescoes are a prominent feature of the architectural design of an entrance hall, several conference rooms and a clubroom, lending the architecture a markedly technicist character.

The atmosphere of these interiors is largely dominated by Havránková's contribution to the overall architectural design. Her creations envelop the visitor, hinting subtly at the complex sensibility of contemporary humanity, but it is a sensibility which is firmly rooted in national cultural heritage, in a need to put an inbred artistic talent to a practical use, to decorate objects of everyday use as well as one's whole environment, albeit in accordance with the contemporary lifestyle. And thus Havránková, prodded by her mother's example, manages in her creations to reflect truthfully the emotional and intellectual position of her own generation whose environment is no longer rural, but industrial and urban.

The great economic and social changes that have taken place in her native Slovakia during the past few decades have thus found an adequate counterbalance in artistic expression while maintaining a continuity of national cultural heritage. In her efforts, Havránková does not remain isolated; her programme has been adopted by a whole generation of young Slovak photographers she has helped shape while teaching for several years at the School of Applied Arts in Bratislava.

—Vladimìr Remeš

HEATH, David (Martin).

Nationality: American. **Born:** Philadelphia, Pennsylvania, 27 June 1931; landed immigrant in Canada since 1970. **Education:** Germantown High School, Philadelphia, 1945-47; studied art at the Philadelphia College of Art, 1954-55, and photography, under Richard Nickel, at the Institute of Design, Illinois Institute of Technology, Chicago, 1955-56; studied photography, under W. Eugene Smith, at the New School for Social Research, New York, 1959, and in Smith's Photo Workshop, New York, 1961. **Military Service:** Served in the 3rd Infantry Division of the United States Army, in Korea, 1952-54. **Family:** Married Angelika Karin de Kornfeld in 1970 (divorced, 1975). **Career:** Photographer since 1947. Darkroom assistant in a commercial photo-finishing firm, Philadelphia, 1948-62; Photographic Assistant, Shigeta-Wright Studio, Chicago, 1955-56; Photographic Assistant to Wingate Paine, Carl Fischer and Bert Stern, New York, 1957-65. Instructor in Photography, School of the Dayton Art Institute, Ohio, 1965-67; Assistant Professor, Moore College of Art, Philadelphia, 1967-70. Since 1970, Professor of Photography, Ryerson Polytechnical Institute, Toronto. Artist-in-Residence, University of Minnesota, Minneapolis, 1965; Visual Studies Workshop, Rochester, New York, 1976-77; and International Center of Photography, New York, 1978. **Recipient:** Guggenheim Fellowship in Photography, 1963, 1964; Canada Council Grant, 1981; Ontario Arts Council Grant, 1984. **Agent:** The Collected Image, 806 Monroe Street, Evanston, Illinois 60202, U.S.A. **Address:** 120 Wolfrey Avenue, Toronto, Ontario M4K 1L3, Canada.

Individual Exhibitions:

1958	*Neither Peace Nor War,* 7 Arts Gallery, New York
1961	Image Gallery, New York
1963	*A Dialogue with Solitude,* Art Institute of Chicago (travelled to the International Museum of Photography, George Eastman House, Rochester, New York, 1964)
1964	*David Heath/Paul Caponigro,* Heliography Gallery, New York
1965	*Work in Progress,* Westbank Gallery, Minneapolis
1968	Phoenix College, Arizona
	David Heath/Richard Garrod, Focus Gallery, San Francisco
1969	*Beyond the Gates of Eden* (audio-visual show), University of Connecticut, Storrs
1971	*An Epiphany* (audio-visual show), Society for Photographic Education, Chicago
1973	*Le Grand Album Ordinaire* (audio-visual show), Ryerson Polytechnical Institute, Toronto
1979	*Songs of Innocence,* Walter Phillips Gallery, Banff, Alberta
1980	*Ars Moriendi: A Masque* (audio-visual show), Rochester Institute of Technology, Rochester, New York
1981	*A Dialogue with Solitude and SX-70 Polaroid Works,* National Gallery of Canada, Ottawa
1982	*Omnia Vanitas,* International Center of Photography, New York
1985	*Dew-World or, dancing with frenzy before God,* Ryerson Polytechnical Institute, Toronto
1988	*Dave Heath: Work from the 50s and 60s,* Photofind Gallery, New York
	Le Plasir de Voir; La Passion du Regard, Light Impressions Spectrum Gallery, Rochester, New York
1993	*Photographs by Dave Heath,* Stephen Cohen Gallery, Los Angeles
1994	*A Dialogue with Solitude,* Minneapolis Art Institute

Selected Group Exhibitions:

1963	*Photos from the Permanent Collection,* Museum of Modern Art, New York
1964	*Association of Heliographers,* Lever House, New York
1965	*Recent Acquisitions,* Museum of Modern Art, New York
1966	*Guggenheim Fellows in Photography,* Philadelphia College of Art

Sheila and Arnie at 7 Arts Cafe, **1957 from** *A Dialogue with Solitude.* Photograph by David Heath.

1968	*Contemporary Photographs,* University of California at Los Angeles
1970	*Contemporary Photography,* Peale House, Philadelphia
1974	*Photography in America,* Whitney Museum, New York
1978	*Mirrors and Windows: American Photography since 1960,* Museum of Modern Art, New York (toured the United States, 1978-80)
1980	*The Magical Eye,* National Gallery of Canada, Ottawa (toured Canada)
1986	*The Polaroid Project,* Visual Studies Workshop, Rochester, New York
1988	*Robert Frank: The Americans/Dave Heath: A Dialogue with Solitude,* The Museum of Contemporary Photography, Columbia College, Chicago
1989	*Lesley Walker: A Collaborative Portrayal,* Artscourt, Ottawa; Ryerson Bond Street Gallery, Toronto, Ontario
1990	*Street Engagements, Social Landscape. Photography of the 60s,* International Museum of Photography, George Eastman House, Rochester
1993	*Magicians of Light, Photographs from the Collection,* National Gallery of Canada, Ottawa
1994	*The Family,* Canadian Museum of Photography, Ottawa

Collections:

National Gallery of Canada, Ottawa; National Film Board of Canada, Ottawa; Museum of Modern Art, New York; Yeshiva University, New York; International Museum of Photography, George Eastman House, Rochester, New York; University of Rochester, New York; Philadelphia Museum of Art; Art Institute of Chicago; Minneapolis Art Gallery; University of California at Los Angeles; Minneapolis Art Institute.

Publications:

By HEATH: Book—*A Dialogue with Solitude,* with a foreword by Hugh Edwards, New York 1965. **Article**—"Portfolio '64" in *Contemporary Photographer* (Culpeper, Virginia), Fall 1964.

On HEATH: Books—*Photography of the World '60,* edited by Hiromu Hara, Ihei Kimura and others, Tokyo and New York 1960; *The City and the Camera,* symposium proceedings, edited by Nelson Wiseman, Toronto 1979; *The Polaroid Project* by William Johnson and Susie Cohen, with introduction by Carl Chiarenza, Rochester, New York 1986. **Articles**—"A Dialogue with Solitude" by Linda Knox in *Aperture* (Millerton, New York), no. 4, 1966;

"Le Grand Album Ordinaire" by Charles Hagen in *Afterimage* (Rochester, New York), February 1974; "David Heath: A Dialogue with Solitude" by James Borcoman in *National Gallery of Canada Journal* (Ottawa), October 1979; "David Heath: from 'A Dialogue with Solitude' to 'Songs of Innocence'" by Katherine Tweedie in *Photo Communique* (Toronto), January/ February 1980; "Art in a Snap: SX70 expression" by John Reeves in *Toronto Life,* June 1980; "A Window on Wistfulness" by David Livingstone in *Maclean's* (Toronto), 14 December 1981; "Killed by Roses," essay by Ann Thomas in *Journal 45* (Ottawa), January 1984.

*

Introduction: Dave Heath's Folly, David Heath's Doubt: small drolleries from a life in progress:

Ah! you, this glorious crowd so hell-bent on celebration, and you scholars, you most of all who best love a festival . . . come! one and all, and as clowns of God, share my bread of bitterness, my salt and vinegar of contrition. Then together might we hear His laughter at the shattering of the world.

Envoi: Valediction Forbidding Mourning, with Apologies to John Donne:

> Maintaining myself in a state of doubt
> I sit among the crazy shapes both time and
>   objects take,
> having wanted to give to this age its emblematic
>   beast.
> Having sought after new knowledge through means
>   of experience
> and declaimed old truths through the crafting of
>   my art,
> I find I have lost the wit for such inspired madness,
> seeing the imposture in it all.
> Now in the autumn twilight
> of my 49th turn through the gravity of time's grief,
> I languor before Hell's gates
> Listening to the Pleiades wail that I am none,
> nor can my sun renew.
> For I am a dead thing
> in whom no love has wrought its true alchemy,
> no quintessence transmuted
> from dull privations and lean emptiness.
> Study me then, you
> who out of the demiurge of communion shall
>   lovers be
> at the next world (that is, the next spring),
> and make of me what you will,
> and from this long journey out of self
> take small mappings
> of a heart's brute solitude.
> Sweet lovers, for whose sake the greater sun
> at wintertime to the goat is run
> to fetch new lust and give it you—
> Enjoy our summer all!

—David Heath

*   *   *

Moved by the emotional power of a story in *Life* magazine, Dave Heath began to photograph seriously in the late 1940s. By the middle 1950s he was successfully attempting to expand the expressive potential of the extended photo-essay. His book, *A Dialogue with Solitude,* created in 1961 and finally published in 1965, pushed that form into a personal and poetic dimension which was almost unique at that time and which has rarely been matched to this day.

In the late 1960s Heath found the largely unexplored and technically uncertain medium of the slide-tape program singularly suited to his needs. During the next decade he produced a number of slide-tapes ("Beyond the Gates of Eden" (1969); "An Epiphany" (1971); "Le Grand Album Ordinaire" (1974); and "Ars Moriendi" (1980) which have exponentially enlarged the creative potential of the medium.

Heath has always been particularly aware of the powerful forces of isolation and community on the human condition, and he has addressed his art to comment upon those events and actions of humanity that display these basic influences most clearly at work. In his own search for community, Heath has drawn sustenance (as well as specific materials for his art) from his wide ranging through the arts and their histories. He uses the music and literature, the poetry, painting and photography of both the past and the present in his own work. And his own work is informed with the despair and passion of his search for a meaning in life and with the compassion and hope of his answers, which he finds in the large community of human creativity.

—William Johnson

HEDGES, Nick.

Nationality: British. **Born:** Bromsgrove, Worcestershire, 31 December 1943. **Education:** Kings School, Worcester, 1955-62; studied photography, under Ted Martin, at the Birmingham College of Art and Design, 1964-68. **Family:** Married Diana Roberts in 1977 (separated 1991); children: Ruth and Annie. **Career:** Photographer and researcher, Shelter National Campaign for the Homeless, London, 1968-72. Freelance photographer since 1972. Part-time Lecturer, Polytechnic of Central London, 1972-76, and Derby College of Art and Technology, 1976-77; West Midlands Arts Association Fellow in Photography, Wolverhampton Polytechnic, 1976-78; Senior Lecturer in Photography, West Midlands College of Higher Education, Walsall, 1980-86. Since 1988, Course Leader B.A. Hons Photography, University of Wolverhampton. **Address:** 57 Canon Street, Cherry Orchard, Shrewsbury, Shropshire, England, SY2 5HH.

Individual Exhibitions:

1971	*Shelter Photographs,* Impressions Gallery, York
	Shelter Photographs, Half Moon Gallery, London
	Shelter Photographs, Royal Photographic Society Gallery, London
1972	*Shelter Photographs,* Kodak Gallery, London
1973	*3 Photographers,* Victoria and Albert Museum, London (with Cristabel Melian and Sylvester Jacobs)
1976	*Worship in Wolverhampton,* Wolverhampton Art Gallery
1977	*Factory Photographs,* Birmingham Arts Laboratory
1978	*Factory Photographs,* Half Moon Gallery, London (toured the U.K.)
1979	*Mental Handicap,* Pentax Gallery, London (travelled to the Midland Arts Centre, Birmingham)
1980	*Factory Photographs,* Side Gallery, Newcastle upon Tyne
1981	*The Fishing Industry,* Side Gallery, Newcastle upon Tyne
1989	*Black Country Working Women,* Wolverhampton Art Gallery
1990	*Double Visions,* The Gateway Arts Centre, Shrewsbury
1991	*From the Centre: Living Through Change in an Industrial Society,* Lighthouse Media Centre (subsequently toured UK)

Selected Group Exhibitions:

1976	*Problem in the City,* Institute of Contemporary Arts, London
1978	*Art for Society,* Whitechapel Art Gallery, London
	Photokina '78, Cologne
1979	*Un Certain Art Anglais,* ARC Galerie, Paris
	Contemporary Portraits, Half Moon Gallery, London
1981	*Hecho en Latino America 2,* Palacio de Bellas Artes, Mexico City
1982	*Lichtbildnisse: Das Porträt in der Fotografie,* Rheinisches Landesmuseum, Bonn
1983	*A Woman's Place,* Royal Festival Hall, London
1984	*William Morris Today,* ICA, London
1985	*Human Interest,* Cornerhouse Gallery, Manchester

Assembly Line Worker, Lock Factory, Willenhall, 1976. Photograph by Nick Hedges.

1988   *Arbetets Varld,* Norrkoping, Sweden

Collections:

Victoria and Albert Museum, London; West Midlands Arts Associations, Stafford; National Museum of Film, Photography and TV, Bradford.

Publications:

By HEDGES: Books—*Shelter Reports*(5), London 1968-72; *Born to Work: Images of Factory Life,* with text by Huw Beynon, London 1981; *Believers,* London 1982; *Milestones,* London 1984; *From the Centre: Living Through Change in an Industrial Society,* text by Paul Lewis, London 1991. **Articles**—interview, with Ainslie Ellis, in *British Journal of Photography* (London), 23 December 1969; "Problem in the City" in *Camera Work* (London), no. 1, 1976; "Factory Fantasies" in *Camera Work* (London), no. 6, 1977; "Factory Photographs" in *Camera Work* (London), no. 10, 1978; "Charity Begins at Home" in *Photography/Politics* (London), no. 1, 1979; "Documentary Photography" in *Ten-8* (Birmingham), 1981.

On HEDGES: Books—*Hecho en Latino America 2,* exhibition catalogue, with texts by Pedro Meyer, Lazaro Blanco and others, Mexico City 1981; *Lichtbildnisse: Das Porträt in der Fotografie,* edited by Klaus Honnef, Cologne 1982. **Article**—"The Meanings of the Environment" by Jeremy Seabrook in *Ten-8,* no. 36, 1990.

*

I am a documentary photographer, and I have always worked within the convention that accepts and uses photography as a substitute for reality. Most of my work has, from choice, been for agencies of social reform. More recently I have chosen to photograph aspects of contemporary society which have been largely uncelebrated by the conventional mass media: working life in factories and aspects of life amongst ethnic minority communities.

Whilst I am interested in the current debate which questions the "reading" of photographs as substitutes for reality, I prefer to work within the documentary tradition. I want to try to find new ways to create a fuller context for documentary photographs.

I do not like the trend towards a purely gallery existence for fine art photographs, nor the trend towards introspection in photography. I like photographs to be published and used, rather than strung along the walls in a gallery.

—Nick Hedges

*   *   *

Nick Hedges produces photographs which document aspects of working people's lives. The images achieve public circulation through being exhibited and through their use as illustrations to printed material, generally intended to record or influence social conditions. By acknowledging the different demands of his photographs' functions, Nick Hedges not only assures their maximum effectiveness, but also, inevitably, builds into them the clearest demonstration of the paradoxes inherent in the documentary mode.

For even if it should be that his central intention in making a set of images is towards establishing self-knowledge and a group consciousness among his subjects, one might reasonably suspect that the numerically largest and most influential audience will be the regular gallery goers and readers of serious publications. The vehemence of the exchanges amongst certain commentators from these groups, as they attempt the Procrustean task of imposing Nick Hedges' images upon their contradictory stereotypes, has tended to obscure the actual record, that his exhibitions attract the widest popular interest in venues far removed from the fashionable circuit. That in truth the audience is probably made up to a relatively minor extent of the traditional "us" with "our" traditions of seemly composure or ritual rage in the face of "their" sufferings and hard times. And if commentators' perceptiveness withers as their vehemence burgeons, his unschooled audience can exercise its advantage, and experience the photographs in a way which does justice to their informational richness.

Questions as to how information from the world shall be selected and converted into the photographic record may be answered in purely technical terms, but every choice of technique is shadowed by an aesthetic counterpart. His concern for efficacy in communication leads Nick Hedges into making his final prints with a sharp and distinctive consonance between the qualities of his images, which has from time to time exposed him to accusations of aestheticising for its own sake.

Whether these charges are justified, or important, or even represent an inevitable concomitant of successful communication are problems for each maker or viewer to deal with. To someone so involved in the world and his craft as Nick Hedges is, the relationships between informational and aesthetic factors must be of major influence upon the evolution of his photography; and the way in which they are reconciled and balanced will be fascinating to watch.

—Philip Stokes

HEILIG, Eugen.

Nationality: German. **Born:** Neckargröningen, Württemberg, 13 May 1892. **Education:** the Volksschule, Stuttgart, 1899-1906; studied electro- and stereotype printing, Deutsche Verlagsanstalt, Stuttgart, 1906-10; under Professor Wiesenmüller, Kunstge-werbeschule für Kriegsversehrte, in Bedburg-Hau, near Gelsenkirchen, 1915-17; self-taught in photography, from 1912. **Military Service:** Served in the German Army, 1914-17. **Family:** Married Hermine Hess in 1919; son: Walter. **Career:** Worked as an electrotype printer for several companies in Germany and Italy, 1910-14, and for the Deutsche Verlagsanstalt, Stuttgart, 1917-27; editor and photoreporter, *Arbeiter-Illustrierte-Zeitung (AIZ)* magazine, Berlin, 1927-30; also acting editor, *Der Arbeiterfotograf* magazine, Berlin, 1927-33; editor and archivist, Union-Bild picture agency, Moscow and Berlin, 1930-33; worked as an electrotype printer, Schütte-Behling printing company, Berlin, 1933-42; keeper of the negatives archives (compulsory war work), in Glogau-Berlin, 1942-45; Press Spokesman, Foreign Trade Department, Potsdam/Berlin, 1945 until he retired in 1964. Photo-section Director, Naturfreunde Group, Stuttgart, 1917-26; Founder-President of the Stuttgart section, 1926-27, and Württemberg Regional Director, Erfurt, 1927-29, Vereinigung der Arbeiter Fotografen Deutschlands; Regional Photography Commission Member, Kulturbund der DDR, Berlin, 1960-75. Member Social Democratic Party of Germany, 1911; Spartakusbund, Germany, 1917; German Communist Party, 1917. **Recipient:** Title of Excellence, Fédération Internationale d'Art Photographique (FIAP), 1961; Gold Honour Award for Photography, Kulturbund der DDR, Berlin, 1964; National Order of Honour, German Democratic Republic, 1972. Honorary Member, Photography Association of the Estonian SSR, 1974. **Estate:** Gesellschaft für Fotografie, Wallstrasse 68, 1020 Berlin, German Democratic Republic; and Walter Heilig, Germanenstrasse 125, 1185 Berlin, German Democratic Republic. **Died:** (in East Berlin) *28 January 1975.*

Individual Exhibitions:

1928   *Reise eines Arbeiterfotografen in die Sowjetunion,* Radesfo,
          Stuttgart
1980   Kunsthandel der DDR, East Berlin
1984   Kongress der Arbeiterfotografen, Stuttgart

Selected Group Exhibitions:

1965   *Arbeiterfotografie,* Zentrale Kommission Fotografie, Erfurt,
          East Germany
1966   *Bilder deutscher Arbeiterfotografen,* Museum für Deutsche
          Geschichte, East Berlin
1977   *Medium Fotografie,* Staatliche Galerie Moritzburg, Halle, East
          Germany
1980   *Fotografie der 20er Jahre,* Zentrale Kommission Fotografie,
          Leipzig, East Germany
1981   *Der Arbeiterfotograf,* Creative Camera, London
1983   *Auferstanden aus Ruinen,* Magistrat Building, East Berlin
1984   *Bruder Eichmann,* foyer of the Deutsches Theater, East Berlin

Collections:

Museum für Deutsche Geschichte, Berlin; ADN-Zentralbild, Berlin; Institut für Marxismus-Leninismus, Berlin; Sovetskoye Foto Archives, Moscow; Technisches Museum, Dresden, Germany; Staatlicher Kunsthandel der DDR, Berlin.

Publications:

By HEILIG: Books—*Jugend Fotografieret,* Berlin 1947; *Ich lerne fotografieren,* Berlin 1948; *Berichte, Erinnerungen, Gedanken zur Geschichte der deutschen Arbeiterfotografie,* co-editor, East Berlin 1967. **Articles**—in *Arbeiter-Illustrierte-Zeitung* (Berlin), and *Der Arbeiterfotograf* (Berlin), 1927-33, and in *Sovetskoye Foto* (Moscow), 1928-33 and 1945-64; "Arbeiterfotografie—ein Kapitel deutscher Arbeitergeschichte" in *Neue Deutsche Presse* (East Berlin), April 1966; "Wiedersehen nach 40 Jahren" in *Neue Deutsche Presse* (East Berlin), October 1966; also numerous book jackets and posters for John Heartfield's photomontages, Berlin 1927-33.

On HEILIG: Books—*Die Anfange der Arbeiter-fotografenbewegung,* thesis, by Gunther Danner, Karl-Marx-Universität, Leipzig 1966; *Medium Fotografie,* edited by Andreas Hüneke, Gerhard Ihrke, Alfred Neumann and Ullrich Wallenburg, Leipzig 1979; *Fotografie im Klassen Kampf* by Erich Rinka, Leipzig 1981. **Articles**—"Erinnerungen an einen Arbeiterfotografen" by Walter Heilig in *Fotografie* (Leipzig), no. 2, 1980, reprinted in *Creative Camera* (London), May/June 1981.

*   *   *

An amateur photographer, Eugen Heilig was one of those German Communists who recognized very early on the documentary potential of photography and enlisted it in the service of agit-prop.

As a youth he first joined a photography group called "Naturfreunde" (Friends of Nature), a widespread social democratic section of the Workers' Movement in Germany in the 1920s. The representative works of this group differed little in essentials from those of the bourgeois amateur clubs of the time; dream-like idylls and so-called "noble printing techniques" in imitation of painting were valued highly by both types of amateur club. Eugen Heilig broke with salon photography entirely after a few years and devoted himself whole-heartedly to propagandist photography. Nevertheless, it was to his association with "Friends of Nature" that Heilig owed his first attempts at successful formal solutions and his overall photographic style.

His first political photographs appeared when Heilig worked as a travelling journeyman, and photographed with a 9 x 12 inch camera Italian workers in Milan engaged in strike action. A few years later, in 1917, Heilig became a member of the Spartakusbund and in 1918 he joined the German Communist Party. These facts are important for his development as a photographer since Heilig may be regarded as one of the spiritual fathers of German Worker-Photography. He was one of the founder members of the "Vereinigung der Arbeiter-Fotografen Deutschlands" (Association of Worker-Photographers of Germany), whose 1931 programme stated that one of its aims was: "to influence and enlighten the broad masses of the people through pictorial propaganda in all areas of political, educational and cultural conflict."

Heilig was one of the leading representative photographers of the group, which regarded social and political documentation as the single worthwhile goal of photography, rejecting any other functions as the expression of bourgeois ideology. One ought not to overlook here the fact that the Worker-Photographers had little access to information regarding contemporary tendencies in bourgeois photography abroad. Heilig's impressions of a trip he made to the Soviet Union in 1927 (as a delegate of the Association of Worker-Photographers of Germany) must have been all the more powerful as a result. In Russia he met famous representatives of early Soviet photojournalism and familiarized himself with working methods of the mass application of photography. As a consequence of Heilig's visit, photo-reportage, till then regularly discussed by the publication *Arbeiter Illustrierte Zeitung,* but rarely actually appearing among its pages, became the dominant working method of the Worker-Photographers in Germany.

Eugen Heilig's contributions were not merely theoretical in this area. He is also the author of a series of powerful agitational reportages on social and political themes that appeared in *AIZ:* poor housing, the increased exploitation of working women, demonstrations and agitational marches by the German Communist Party, etc. A typical example is the piece "Hunger im Frankenwald" (1931), with its characteristically objective documentary, almost lapidary style, and the strongly emotive quality of its simple, balanced composition.

Heilig's main creative period as a photographer ended with the break-up of the Association of Worker-Photographers by the Fascists in 1933. But Heilig was one of those who, though hourly in danger of their lives, continued to work illegally against the Fascists, producing important photographic documents even in those difficult years. Heilig's documentary photo "Faschistische Rassenhetze" (Racial persecution by the Fascists, 1935) is world famous.

—Uwe Prinz

HEINECKEN, Robert (Friedli).

Nationality: American. **Born:** Denver, Colorado, 29 December 1931. **Education:** the Polytechnic High School, Riverside, California, 1945-49; University of California at Los Angeles, 1951-53, 1958-60, B.A. 1959, M.A. 1960. Military **Service:** Served as a Jet Fighter Pilot in the United States Marine Corps, 1953-57: Captain. **Family:** Married Janet Marion Storey in 1955 (divorced, 1980); children: Kathe, Geoffrey, and Karol. **Career:** Photographer/artist since 1960. Professor, Department of Art, University of California at Los Angeles, since 1960. Instructor, Advanced Studies Workshop, George Eastman House, Rochester, New York, 1967, State University of New York at Buffalo, 1969, San Francisco Art Institute, 1970, School of the Art Institute of Chicago, 1970, and Harvard University, Cambridge, Massachusetts, 1971. Chairman of the Board of Directors, Society for Photographic Education, 1970-72; Trustee, Friends of Photography, Carmel, California, 1974-75; Professor Emeritus, UCLA 1990. **Recipient:** Guggenheim Fellowship, 1976; National Endowment for the Arts grant, 1977, 1981 and 1986; Peer Award, Friends of Photography, Carmel, California, 1985; First Annual Members Award, California Museum of Photography, Riverside, 1985. **Agent:** Pace/MacGill Gallery, 32 East 57th Street, New York, New York 10022, U.S.A. **Address:** 1501 West Wadansia Avenue, Chicago, Illinois, 60622, U.S.A.

Individual Exhibitions:

1964	Mount St. Mary College of Fine Arts, Los Angeles
1965	Long Beach Museum of Art, California (with Coar and Rink)
1966	California State University at Los Angeles
	Mills College Art Gallery, Oakland, California
1968	Focus Gallery, San Francisco
1969	Occidental College, Los Angeles
1970	Phoenix College Art Gallery, Arizona
	Witkin Gallery, New York
	California State University at Northridge (with Daryl Curran and Bart Parker)
1971	University of Oregon Art Gallery, Eugene
	University of Colorado Art Gallery, Boulder
1972	Pasadena City College Gallery, California
	University of Rhode Island, Kingston

	Pasadena Art Museum, California
1973	California State College at San Bernardino
	The Photograph as Object, Metaphor and Document of Concept: Robert Heinecken, Minor White and Robert Cumming, California State University at Long Beach
	Friends of Photography, Carmel, California
	Light Gallery, New York
1974	Madison Art Center, Wisconsin
1976	Light Gallery, New York
	Texas Center for Photographic Studies, Dallas
	International Museum of Photography, George Eastman House, Rochester, New York
1978	Old Dominion University Gallery, Norfolk, Virginia
	Center for Contemporary Photography, Chicago
	San Francisco Museum of Modern Art
	Frederick Wight Art Gallery, University of California at Los Angeles
	Susan Spiritus Gallery, Newport Beach, California
1979	Light Gallery, New York
	Sesnon Gallery, University of California at Santa Cruz
	University of Northern Illinois Art Gallery, DeKalb
	Forum Stadtpark, Graz, Austria
1980	University of Nevada Art Gallery, Las Vegas
	Nova Gallery, Vancouver, British Columbia
	Werkstaff für Fotografie, West Berlin
1981	Light Gallery, Los Angeles
	Light Gallery, New York
	University of Oregon, Eugene
1982	Northlight Gallery, Arizona State University, Tempe (with Joyce Neimanas)
	Rhode Island School of Design, Providence
1983	Film in the Cities, St. Paul, Minnesota
	Fotoforum der Gesamthochschule, Kassel, West Germany
	Los Angeles Center for Photographic Studies (with John Wood)
	Rio Hondo College Art Gallery, Whittier, California (with JoAnn Callis and Eileen Cowin)
1986	*Heinechen: Selected Works 1966-1986,* Gallery Min, Tokyo
	Center for Creative Photography, University of Arizona, Tucson
1987	*Television/Source/Subject,* The Art Institute of Chicago
	Robert Heinecken/New Works, Printworks Ltd, Chicago; Fahey/Klein Gallery, Los Angeles
1988	*The Nuclear Family,* Vision Gallery, Boston
1989	*Retrospective 1962-1989,* Pace MacGill Gallery, New York
	A Case Study in Finding an Appropriate TV Newswoman, (A CBS docudrama in words and pictures) University of St Louis (circulating exhibition)
	Roert Heinecken 1966-1989, Sunnygate Gallery, Taipei, Taiwan
1990	*I/You: Dorit Cypis/Robert Heinecken,* Walter McBean Gallery, San Francisco Art Institute
1992	*Robert Heinecken: Recent Photograms,* Printwork Gallery, Chicago
	Robert Heinecken: Recent Work, Pace/McGill Gallery, New York
	Robert Heinecken: New Work, Fahey/Klein Gallery, Los Angeles
1994	*Robert Heinecken: Altered Magazines,* Linda Cathcart Gallery, Santa Monica

Selected Group Exhibitions:

1967	*Photography in the 20th Century,* National Gallery of Canada, Ottawa (toured Canada and the United States, 1967-73)
1969	*Vision and Expression,* International Museum of Photography, George Eastman House, Rochester, New York (toured the United States, 1969-71)
1970	*Photography into Sculpture,* Museum of Modern Art, New York

Barbara Campaign Fund Raising in Middle America, **1992. 72'' x 48'' color photograph of collaged life-size free-standing, advertising display figures.** Photograph by Robert Heinecken.

1974   *Photography in America*, Whitney Museum, New York
1978   *23 Photographers/23 Directions*, Walker Art Gallery,
        Liverpool
1980   *The Magical Eye*, National Gallery of Canada, Ottawa (toured
        Canada)
1983   *Fotogramme—die lichtreichen Schatten*, Fotomuseum im
        Stadtmuseum, Munich (toured Germany)
1984   *Photography in California 1945-80*, San Francisco Museum of
        Modern Art (travelled to the Akron Art Museum, Ohio;
        Corcoran Gallery, Washington, D.C.; Los Angeles Municipal
        Art Gallery; Cornell University, Ithaca, New York; High
        Museum of Art, Atlanta, Georgia; Museum Folkwang,
        Essen; Centre Georges Pompidou, Paris; Museum of
        Photographic Arts, San Diego, California)
1985   *American Images 1945-80*, Barbican Art Gallery, London
        (toured Britain)
1987   *Photography and Art 1946-86*, Los Angeles County Museum
        of Art (and circulating)
        *Photographs in the Collection of The National Museum of
        Modern Art*, Kyoto, Japan
        Fotogramme: 1918 bis heute, Goethe Institute, Germany
        Faces, Metropolitan Museum of Art, New York
        Fabrications: Staged, Altered and Appropriated Photographs,
        International Center of Photography Museum Shop,
        New York
1988   *Under Construction: New Photomontage*, Cranbrook Academy
        of Art Museum, Bloomfield Hills, MI
        *Evocative Presence: 20th Century Photographs in the Perma-
        nent Collection*, Museum of Fine Arts, Houston
        John Baldessari/Robert Heinecken/Ed Rusha, Pace/MacGill
        Gallery, New York
        Fabrications: Staged, Altered and Appropriate Photographs,
        Harvard University, Cambridge, MA
        *Active Process: Artists' Books, Photographic and Contempo-
        rary*, Gallery TPW, Toronto
1989   *California Photography Remaking Make-Believe*, Museum of
        Modern Art, New York
        On the Art of Fixing a Shadow: 150 Years of Photography,
        The National Gallery of Art, Washington DC; Art Institute
        of Chicago; Los Angeles County Museum of Art
        That Was Then—This Is Now, Museum of Photographic Arts,
        San Diego, CA
        Lies and More Lies: The Photography of Representation,
        Contemporary Arts Center, New Orleans, LA
        One Hundred Years of Photography: What Is Photography,
        Manes Gallery, Svac Ceskych, Prague
1990   *Photography Until Now*, Museum of Modern Art, New York
        *Anwesenheit bei Abwesenheit: Das Fotogram in die kunst im
        20. Jahrhundert*, Kunsthaus Zurich
        Street Engagements: Social Landscape Photography of the 60s,
        International Museum of Photography, Rochester
        Amb Els Media Contra Els Media, Sala Arcs Fundacio Caixa
        de Barcelona
        *Engaging Transformations: Experimental Photography of the
        60s*, University of Rochester Harnet Gallery
1991   *Toppan Collection*, International Center for Photograph,
        New York
        *American Photography Since 1920: From the Collection of the
        Center for Creative Photography* University of Arizona;
        Fundacion Caja de Pensiones, Madrid
        *Past/Present: Photographs from the Collection of the Museum
        of Fine Arts*, Houston
        *Spheres of Influence: Teacher/Student Relations in American
        Photography Since 1945*, Center for Creative Photography,
        University of Arizona
1992   *Proof: Los Angeles Art and the Photograph 1960-1980*,
        Laguna Art Museum, California
        *Special Collections: The Photographic Order from Pop
        to Now*, International Center of Photography, Midtown,
        New York

Fotographica '92, Brada, Netherlands
Permanent Collection Gallery, Muesum of Modern Art,
        New York
Notes from the Material World: Contemporary Photo Montage,
        John Michael Kohler Arts Center, Sheboygan, WI
1993   *Multiple Images: Photographs Since 1965 from the Collection*,
        Museum of Modern Art
        The Photographers Who Opened the Age: 1960s-70s, Tokyo
        Metropolitan Museum of Photography
        *The Mediated Image: American Photography in the Age of
        Information*, University Art Museum, University of New
        Mexico, Albuquerque
        Selections from the Permanent Collection: Image and Text,
        Center for Creative Photography, University of Arizona
        Recent Acquisitions, Museum of Modern Art, New York
1994   *Lessons in Life: Photographic Works from the Boardroom
        Collection*, Art Institute of Chicago
        *Experimental Vision: The Evolution of the Photogram since
        1919*, Denver Art Museum, Denver Colorado
        Dialogues with Photography: The Monson Collection, Henry
        Art Gallery, University of Washington, Seattle
        *New Acquisitions/New Works/New Directions: Photography
        from the Collection*, Los Angeles Country Museum of Art
        Selections from the Permanent Collection: Fictions, Center for
        Creative Photography, University of Arizona
        Recent Acquisitions, University Art Museum, University of
        New Mexico

Collections:

Museum of Modern Art, New York; University of Nebraska, Lincoln;
Museum of Fine Arts, Houston; University of New Mexico, Albuquerque;
Center for Creative Photography, University of Arizona, Tucson; Norton
Simon Art Museum, Pasadena, California; Pomona College, Claremont,
California; San Francisco Museum of Modern Art; Oakland Art Museum,
California; University of Washington, Seattle; Art Institute of Chicago;
Australian National Gallery; Commodities Corporation, New York; Fogg
Museum, Harvard University, Cambridge, Massachusetts; Frito Lay Collec-
tion, Los Angeles; Fundacion CTVC, Mexico City; Grunwald Center for the
Graphic Arts, UCLA, Los Angeles; Library of Congress, Washington, D.C.;
Mills College, Oakland, California; Museum of Fine Arts, St. Petersburg,
Florida; Museum of Photographic Arts, San Diego California; National
Gallery of Canada, Ottawa; Newport Harbor Museum, Newport Beach,
California; Princeton University, Princeton, NJ; Santa Monica College, Santa
Monica, California; University of Louisville Archive, Louisville, Missouri;
University of Massachussets, Boston; Sheldon Gallery, University of Kansas,
Laurence; Washington Consortium, Bellingham, Washington.

Publications:

By HEINECKEN: Books—*Are You Rea*, portfolio, Los Angeles 1968;
Mansmag, portfolio, Los Angeles 1969; *Just Good Eats for U Diner*, portfolio,
Los Angeles 1971; *He/She*, Chicago 1980; *Naked*, Portfolio, Boulder,
Colorado 1985; *Selected Works from 1966-1986*, exhibiton catalogue, Tokyo
1986. **Articles**—"The Photograph: Not a Picture of, but an Object about" in
ADLA (Los Angeles), October 1965; "Manipulative Photography" in *Con-
temporary Photographer* (Boston), August 1969; statement in *Continum*,
exhibition catalogue, Los Angeles 1970; "Teaching Interview" in *Photogra-
phy: Source and Resource*, University Park, Pennsylvania 1973; "Eulogy" in
William Doherty, exhibition catalogue, Los Angeles 1973; "On Change and
Exchange" in *Untitled 7/8* (Carmel, California), April 1974; introduction to
UCLA Collection of Contemporary Photographs, exhibition catalogue, Los
Angeles 1976; "Robert Heinecken: An Interview" in *Afterimage* (Rochester,
New York), April 1976; "Introduction: Emerging Los Angeles Photogra-
phers" in *Untitled 11* (Carmel, California), October 1977; "An Interview with
Robert Heinecken" in *LAICA Journal* (Los Angeles), September/October
1981; "Photographic Installation/West Coast Revision" in *San Francisco
Camerawork Quarterly*, no. 2, 1985.

On HEINECKEN: Books—*Heinecken,* edited by James Enyeart, Carmel, California 1980; *Nude Photographs 1850-1980,* edited by Constance Sullivan, New York 1980; *Robert Heinecken: Food, Sex and TV,* exhibition catalogue, by Suzanne E. Pastor and Susan E. Cohen, Kassel, West Germany 1983; *Photography in California 1945-1980* by Louise Katzman, San Francisco and New York 1984; *American Photography: A Critical History 1945 to the Present* by Jonathan Greem, New York, 1984; *American Images: Photography 1945-1980,* edited by Peter Turner and John Benton-Harris, London 1985; *Ansicheten Von Korper: Das Aktfoto 1840-1985,* by Michael Kohler, 1986; *Photography and Art 1946-1986,* exhibition catalogue, by Andy Grundberg and Kathleen M. Gauss, Los Angeles 1987; *Stills: Cinema and Video Transformed,* by Rod Slemons, Seattle 1986; *Photography and Art: Interactions since 1946,* by Andy Grundberg and Kathleen Gauss, Los Angeles 1987; *Fotogramme: 1918 bis heute,* exhibition catalogue, Munich 1987; *Modern Photography and Beyond,* exhibition catalogue, Kyoto 1987; *On the Art of Fixing A Shadow,* exhibition catalogue, text by Colin Westerbeck, Chicago 1989; *New Acquisitions, New Work, New Directions,* exhibition catalogue with text by Robeert Sobieszek, New York 1989; *Lies and More Lies,* exhibition catalogue, text by Lew Thomas, New Orleans 1989; *Das Fotogram in der Kunst des 20 Jahrhunderts,* exhibition catalogue, text by Floris M Neususs, Koln 1990; *The History of Photography: An Overview,* by Alma Davenport, London 1991; *Proof: Los Angeles Art and the Photograph 1960-1980,* exhibition catalogue (Laguna Beach) 1992. Articles—''The Photography of Robert Heinecken'' by Carl Belz in *Camera* (Lucerne), January 1968; ''Heinecken: A Man for All Dimensions'' by A.D. Coleman in the *New York Times,* 2 August 1970, reprinted in Coleman's *Light Readings: A Photography Critic's Writings 1968-1978,* New York 1979; ''Heinecken: Photograph as Object'' by John Upton in *The Photograph as Object, Metaphor and Document of Concept: Robert Heinecken, Minor White, and Robert Cumming,* exhibition catalogue, Long Beach, California 1973; ''Phenomenology of Sex'' by James Hugunin in *Dumb Ox* (Los Angeles), Fall 1977; ''The Medium as Subject'' by Charles Desmarais and ''Space-Time and the Syzygy'' by Candida Finkel in *Exposure* (Lincoln, Nebraska), December 1977; ''Two Decades of Work'' by Hal Fischer in *Artweek* (Oakland, California), September 1978; ''Robert Heinecken'' by William Jenkins in *Image* (Rochester, New York), September 1978; ''He/She: Heinecken's SX-70 Conversations'' by Carl Toth in *Afterimage* (Rochester, New York), May 1979; ''Relations: Some Work by Robert Heinecken'' by Irene Borger in *Exposure* (Lincoln, Nebraska), Summer 1979; ''Provoking Without Judging'' by Mark Johnstone in *Artweek* (Oakland, California), 5 December 1981; ''The Neurotic Erotic'' by Martha Gever in *Afterimage* (Rochester, New York), Summer 1982; ''Don't Call Him an Artist'' by Joan Murray in *Artweek* (Oakland, California), 27 August 1983; ''California by Strobe Light'' by Douglas Davis in *Newsweek* (New York), 5 March 1984; ''Is There Life After California Photography?'' by Donna Stein in *Catskill Center Quarterly* (Woodstock, New York), Spring 1985; ''Paraphotographer Robert Heinecken'' by Claire Peeps in *Insight* (Bristol, RI) Winter-Spring 1988; ''Case Study picks up perfect TV anchor'' by Christine Craft in *Sacramento Bee,* 2 February 1990; ''Letter from New York'' by A.D. Coleman in *Photo Metro* (San Francisco), February 1990; ''A Conversation with Robert Heinecken'' by Philip Bergen in *Art Week* (San Jose), 23 July 1992.

*

I am involved in using subjective artifice to produce photographic evidence and in using photographic evidence to create subjective artifice, and am interested in the confusion which results.

—Robert Heinecken

*   *   *

Robert Heinecken was university trained in printmaking, and then adapted the photograph to his interests in problems of content and form. In the 1960s he assembled similarly shaped photographs of water, wood, clouds and a nude onto slices from a large prismatic solid, arranged so that the nine slices could be turned to make different combinations of original subjects yet retain the general gestalt. He fragmented a nude over a cube, which was shown mounted on one corner, an orientation that forces the viewer to see three parts of the body at any one time, in a visual/verbal interplay reminiscent of some of the

problems of Duchamp and of cubist art. During the late 1960s he published a portfolio of 25 prints entitled *Are You Rea,* which combined investigation of the medium, formal relationships, and social-emotional implications drawn from the images. By examining hundreds of fashion magazines and other popular magazines of the time, Heinecken found enough pages which, when examined on a light-table, revealed pictures and words on opposite sides that interacted in useful ways. By using the page as a negative and exposing an offset printing plate directly, he was able to print a tonally reversed image that provided information from the change-operation montages he had discovered. The total content is a bitter comment on the values of American society in the 1960s.

He examined the common sexual concerns of the times in a series of large assembled images which were then reproduced in photolithographed versions, sometimes with color added. The ''Cliche Vary'' set was composed of three large assembled pieces of photographs on sensitized canvas: ''Cliche Vary/ Autoeroticism, -Fetishism, -Lesbianism,'' all done in the mid-1970s. The photographs were printed from negatives supplied in undeveloped rolls from the soft-pornographic sales houses that flourish in southern California. The straight image was then drawn and painted on, as well as being montaged, repeated, and overprinted to achieve the final complex relationship he desired.

Heineken writes of his own work: ''Because I was never in a school situation where someone said 'This is the way a photograph is supposed to look,' I was completely free to cut them up, combine them, or do anything. . . . Some of my enthusiam for the photograph was based on the fact that there was some residual illusion of reality in it always, no matter what I did to it. . . . '' Heinecken is concerned both with what the art materials will do and with the social implications that are covertly dealt with in his art. In the ''Cliche Vary'' series he is using the word cliché to deal with the social meaning of the word and ''cliche vary'' as a pun on the term for the hand-made negative of photographic art history, plus of course the variations on the themes of this central cliché of our culture, the search for sexual expression without emotional content.

By the end of the 1970s, his art work had carried him further from the act of photographing in a traditional sense. He produced a series of SX70 prints showing himself, women, cluttered rooms, and other bits and pieces of a life, accompanied by short dialogues written in a blunt, schoolbook style beneath the mounted prints. These pungent dialogues between He and She are sometimes painful, often evocative, and in conjunction with the photographs remind a viewer of the Italian cartoon books that are so popular on the Continent. The immensely personal and specifically erotic SX70 prints were replaced, in a published small book of these dialogues, with deliberately bland and depersonalized drygoods advertising photographs masked so as to appear to be SX70 prints, creating an artistic abstraction from the deeply personal and often painful initial image/word structure. Heinecken, like most of the photographers who manipulate, or who permit the word to interact with the photograph, appears to be within a continuation of an essentially romantic tradition, finding new forms with which to express himself in an era that is very strongly classical in spirit.

—Arnold Gassan

HEINEMANN, Jürgen.

Nationality: German. Born: Osnabrück, Germany, 13 September 1934. Education: Studied photography under Otto Steinert, in Saarbrücken, 1957-59, and in Essen, 1959-62. Career: Photojournalist, working for *Ruhrwort,* since 1962; has made numerous trips to South America, mainly for the Catholic Church organization Adveniat, since 1962. Part-time Instructor in Photojournalism, Fachhochschule, Dortmund, and Fachhochscule, Würzburg. Professor of photojournalism at Fachhochschule Bielefeld since 1981. Member, (GDL) now Deutsche fotografische Akademie, since 1962. Recipient: Artistic Photography Prize, *World Press Photo,* Amsterdam, 1963; first Prize at Concorso Internationale di Fotografia, Francesco di Assisi, 1965; David Octavius Hill Medal of Deutschen Fotografischen Akademie, 1994. Address: Dammstr. 36, D 33824 Werther, Germany.

Individual Exhibitions:

1992   *Jürgen Heinemann-Amèrika,* travelled throughout Germany

Selected Group Exhibitions:

1956   *Photokina '56,* Cologne
1960   *Photokina,* Cologne
1962   *Otto Steinert und Schüler,* Frankfurt
         World Press Photo, Amsterdam
1964   *World Exhibition of Photography: What Is Man?,* Pressehaus
         Stern, Hamburg (and world tour)
1967   *GDL,* Frankfurt
1968   *2nd World Exhibition of Photography,* Pressehaus Stern,
         Hamburg (and world tour)
1979   *Deutsche Fotografie nach 1945,* Kasseler Kunstverein, Kassel,
         West Germany (toured West Germany)
         Fotografie 1919-1975, Frankfurt
1983   *Die fotografische Sammlung,* Museum Folkwang, Essen, West
         Germany
1985   *Unterwegs,* Leinfelden-Echterdingen
1989   *Dokument und Erfindung,* Berlin
1991   *Steinert Schüler,* Folkwangmuseum, Essen

Collections:

Museum Folkwang, Essen, Germany; Fachhochschule, Bielefeld; Bibliotheque
National, Paris.

Publications:

By HEINEMANN: Books—*Ich habe dein Gesicht gesehen,* Kevelaer 1975;
Amèrica, Berlin 1992.

On HEINEMANN: Books—*2nd World Exhibition of Photography,* exhibi-
tion catalogue, edited by Karl Pawek, Hamburg 1968; *Fotografie 1919-1979,
Made in Germany: Die GDL-Fotografen,* edited by Fritz Kempe, Bernd
Lohse and others, Frankfurt 1979; *Deutsche Fotografie nach 1945/German
Photography after 1945* by Floris Neusüss, Wolfgang Kemp and Petra
Benteler, Kassel, West Germany 1979; *Museum Folkwang: die fotografische
Sammlung,* exhibition catalogue, with introduction by Ute Eskildsen, Essen,
West Germany 1983.

* * *

Can one pursue humanitarian photography as a profession? That the
answer to this question is yes can be proved by many examples from history:
one thinks, for example, of Jacob Riis and Lewis Hine who, with the aid of the
camera, fought against the slum conditions of New York and the exploitation
of child labour in the United States—or of Chim, founder member in 1947 of
Magnum, whose main concern was the fate of children in post-war Europe. It
would not occur to Jürgen Heinemann, a quiet, reserved, reflective man, to
compare his own work with such renowned historic figures. Nevertheless, he
follows in their tradition—in a contemporary manner.

Heinemann was born in 1934 in the Ruhr area of Germany into the family
of a salesman; both his parents and his brother took pictures as a hobby, and he
soon learned to handle a camera. As he was only 14 years old at the time, it
was, of course, a completely automatic box camera. But as time went on his
secret interest in the world of art went so far that, though he too seemed
destined to become a salesman, he privately dreamed of being allowed to take
photographs for the rest of his life. Then a handshake with Theodor Heuss, the
first president of the Federal Republic of Germany, led to a definite decision,
for in a junior photography competition in 1956 Heinemann was among the
prize winners. The direct consequence was that he went to Saarbrucken to see a
certain Professor Otto Steinert, and as Steinert was prepared to take him into
his class, Heinemann said goodbye to the life of a salesman. The study of the
first volume of Steinert's *Subjective Photography* had already made his future
path clear to him. In 1959 Heinemann followed his teacher to the Folkwang

School in Essen. In vacations he toured Europe, almost as a tramp, taking
photographs.

Even before he completed his studies in photography in 1962, Heinemann
had begun working for the newspaper *Ruhrwort* (The Ruhr Word). It was a
Catholic Church publication for the industrial area of the Ruhr, and it
attempted to reach its public with modern publicity methods, particularly with
lively press photography. The paper's connection with the Catholic humanitarian organizations Misereor and Adveniat, which in the undeveloped countries help in the fight against hunger with practical development aid, also
became an interest for Heinemann: he made his first journeys to South
America in 1962 and 1963, and thereafter made a lengthy journey each
summer, mainly for Adveniat.

What does the photographic work from such journeys look like? It is as
many-sided and diverse as the human problems—according to the country—
encountered by the ecclesiastical aid organizations and missionary societies. It
is part of Heinemann's individuality that he does not concentrate on "official"
photographs—as, for example, the mechanics of food distribution. The
depiction of such problems is, of course, also part of his commission, but
Heinemann's particular and splendid forte is in conveying everyday human
interest scenes. He photographs with a feeling for the "decisive moment"
with an instinctive sense of pictorial composition, in the pattern of Cartier-
Bresson. Perhaps he will photograph the radiant happiness on the face of a
peasant in El Salvador, who has merely been able to find work in a distant town
and can return only on Sundays to his family in their wretched hut in the
remote village. Or the moving scenes that occur when—in the destitute
drought areas of North Eastern Brazil—a child dies and only the small
playmates accompany the tiny coffin, adorned with their gifts of flowers, to the
cemetery where it will be buried in a hastily dug hole in the ground.

—Bernd Lohse

HEITMANN, Adriano.

Nationality: Swiss. **Born:** in Zurich, 17 August 1951. **Education:** Attended
elementary and secondary schools in Ticino, Switzerland; self-taught in
photography. **Family:** Married the photographer Flor Garduño in 1989;
daughter: Azul. **Career:** Sports photographer, 1972-80. Contributor to
magazines and newspapers, including *Neue Zürcher Zeitung, Du, Tages-
Anzeiger Magazin, Berlitz-guides, Bilanz, Airone, Epoca, Foto, Zeit-Magazin,
GEO, Merian,* since 1974. Photoreporter at the Olympic Games, Lake Placid,
USA, 1980. Special correspondent at the World Cup Football Championship,
Mexico, 1986. Photographer for the architect Mario Botta, since 1986.
Address: Via Ufentina 17B, CH-6855 Stabio, Switzerland.

Individual Exhibition:

1986   Photoforum Pasquart, Biel, Switzerland

Selected Group Exhibitions:

1990   *24 Swiss Photographers,* toured Switzerland

Publications:

By HEITMANN: Book—*Mexico Today,* Vevey, Switzerland 1983. **Articles**—"Brazil" in *Geo* (Hamburg), March 1991; "Senegal" in *Du* (Zurich),
April 1991.

* * *

Adriano Heitmann and his Mexican wife Flor Garduño are both reportage
photographers, yet the different aspects of their work makes them often seem a
world apart.

Born in Zürich in 1951 Adriano started as a photo reporter of sports events
for *Swiss Illustrated* after finishing school with a Federal matric. He was 20
and an autodidact in photography. He soon tired of sport preferring to travel

and meeting with different cultures in distant lands. By 1974 his goal was achieved. His reportages appeared in the leading newspapers and cultural magazines of Switzerland, Italy and Germany, such as *Du, Airone, Zeit Magazine, GEO* and *Merian.* The rapid progress continued and at the age of 30 the Swiss Federal government acknowledged his achievement with a Federal grant for culture, an honour which was bestowed on him for a second time a few years later.

In 1982 the Swiss publisher Mondo sent Heitmann to Mexico for several months to produce a comprehensive series of pictures which were published a few years later in their book *Mexico Today.* During his stay in Mexico Adriano met his future wife, the photographer Flor Garduño. They were married in Mexico in 1989 and live since then partly in Mexico and partly in their house in Tessin close to the Italian border. The famous architect Mario Botta lives in the neighbourhood and for many years Adriano has been Botta's photographer. When Botta was invited for a bit retrospective show at the Museum of Modern Art in 1989 Heitmann had the pleasure of collaborating with him both on the layout of the catalogue and on the design of the exhibition in New York with a large number of his photographs.

During the last ten years he has travelled extensively for many leading cultural magazines in which his reportages appear, *GEO* in particular. He was also the designer and producer of his wife's much admired book on the rites, myths and customs of the South American Indians, *Witness of Time,* 1992. He also managed the travelling exhibition of the same title. This work occupied him for several years during which his own photography had of necessity to be neglected.

—Helmut Gernsheim

HELMER-PETERSEN, Keld.

Nationality: Danish. **Born:** in Copenhagen, 23 August 1920. **Education:** Attended the Metropolitan Gymnasium, Copenhagen, 1931-37; studied English at Trinity College, Cambridge, 1938-39; studied photography, under Harry Callahan, at the Institute of Design, Illinois Institute of Technology, Chicago, 1950-51. **Wartime Service:** Served in the Civil Defense Corps, Copenhagen, 1943. **Family:** Married Birthe Dalsgaard in 1945; children: Jan and Finn. **Career:** Photographer since 1939; established studio, Copenhagen, 1955. Camera Assistant, Minerva Film, Copenhagen, 1948; Film and Video Cameraman, Danish State Radio and Television, Copenhagen, 1951-54. Instructor in Photography, School of Interior Design, Copenhagen, 1951, and School of Graphic Arts, Copenhagen, 1960-63. Lecturer and Instructor, Department of Visual Communication, School of Architecture, Royal Academy of Arts, Copenhagen, 1964-1990. **Recipient:** Arts and Crafts Award, Royal Danish Academy of Arts, 1981; Danish Crafts Council Annual Award, 1981. Chairman of Board, Museum for Fotokunst, Odense, Denmark, 1986-1994. **Address:** Kristianiagade 14, 2100 Copenhagen, Denmark.

Individual Exhibitions:

1954	*Experiment and Documentation,* Charlottenborg, Copenhagen (travelled to the Röhsska Museet, Gothenburg, Sweden, 1955)
1962	Stiftsmuseum, Viborg, Denmark
	Helmer-Petersen and Renger-Patzsch, Dansk Centralbibliotek, Flensburg, Germany
1965	Galleri Exi, Odense, Denmark
	Queedens Gård, Ribe, Denmark
1970	Centralbiblioteket, Nakskov, Denmark
	Hjørring Museum, Denmark
1980	*Color Photographs by Keld Helmer-Petersen,* American-Scandinavian Foundation, New York
1982	Image Gallery, Århus, Denmark
1984	Rådhus, Albertslund, Denmark
1989	Museum of Decorative Art, Copenhagen
1990	Keld Helmer-Petersen retrospective, Museum for Fotokunst, Odense, Denmark

Selected Group Exhibitions:

1954	*Post-War European Photography,* Museum of Modern Art, New York
1955	*Subjektive Fotografie,* Saarbrücken
1958	*12 International Photographers,* Värmlands Museum, Karlstad, Sweden
1965	*Strukturer,* Ole Palsby, Copenhagen
1966	*5 Danish Designers,* Museum of Decorative Art, Copenhagen
1975	*Gråtoner,* Museum of Decorative Art, Copenhagen
1976	*Charlottenborgs Forårsudstilling,* Charlottenborg, Copenhagen
1979	*7th Biennale of Photography of the Baltic Countries,* National Museum, Gdansk, Poland
1985	*Nordic Photographic Art,* Museum for Fotokunst, Odense, Denmark
1986	*Fifty Years of Modern Color Photography 1935-86,* at *Photokina 86,* Cologne
1992	*13 Critics, 26 Fotografs,* Primavera Fotogràfica, Barcelona
1994	Fotografisk Galleri, Copenhagen

Collections:

Royal Library, Copenhagen; Stiftung für die Fotografie, Zurich; Museum of Modern Art, New York; Museum Folkwang, Essen, Germany; Museum for Fotokunst, Odense, Denmark.

Publications:

By HELMER-PETERSEN: Books—*122 Colour Photographs,* Copenhagen 1949; *Colour Before the Camera,* London 1952; *Fragments of a City,* Copenhagen 1960; *Romansk Billedhuggerkunst i Viborg Amts Kirker,* Viborg, Denmark 1963; *København,* Copenhagen 1965; *Frameworks, Photographs 1950-1990,* Copenhagen 1993. **Articles**—"On Photographic Experimentation" in *Fra A til Z* (Copenhagen), no. 3, 1952; "Den Fotografiske Udtryksform" in *Vindrosen* (Copenhagen), March 1954; "A New Personality: Jørn Utzon" in *Zodiac* (Milan), no. 5, 1959; "Fotografen og billedet" in *Flensborg Avis* (Flensborg, West Germany), 8 May 1962; "Fjaes" in *Vindrosen* (Copenhagen), no. 2, 1963; "2 Svenske Grafikere" in *Dansk Kunsthåndvaerk* (Copenhagen), no. 8, 1963.

On HELMER-PETERSEN: Books—*Die Geschichte der Fotografie im 20. Jahrhundert/History of Photography in the 20th Century* by Petr Tausk, Cologne 1977, London 1980; *Museum Folkwang: die fotografische Sammlung,* exhibition catalogue, with introduction by Ute Eskildsen, Essen, West Germany 1983. **Articles**—"Camera Abstractions" by Wilson Hicks in *Life* (New York), 28 November 1949; "Helmer-Petersen, Kopenhagen" by Ludwig Ebenhoh in *Gebrauchsgraphik* (Munich), no. 4, 1954; "Von der Phantasie des Auges" by Robert d'Hooghe in *Leica-Fotografie* (Frankfurt), May/June 1954; "Black on White" by Willa Percival in *Infinity* (New York), November 1954; "Patterns in Line" in *U.S. Camera* (New York), January 1957; "Fra et besog i bygningen" by Palle Nielsen in *Perspektiv* (Copenhagen), no. 5, 1960; "Der Experimentator" by Bruno Schleifer in *Foto Prisma* (Dusseldorf), September 1962; "Crop as You See" by Jacqueline Balish in *Modern Photography* (New York), June 1963; "Keld Helmer-Petersen" by Vance Jonson in *CA Magazine* (Palo Alto, California), no. 9/10, 1963; "Strukturer" by Henrik Bramsen in *Dansk Kunsthåndvaerk* (Copenhagen), no. 3, 1966; "Retrospective Look at the Formative Years" by Finn Thrane in *Katalog* (Odense), vol. 3, no. 1, 1990; "Postmodernisme: Albans i despréo" by Finn Thrane in *13 Critics, 26 Fotogras,* Primavera Fotografica, Barcelona, 1992.

*

I am inspired by the look of things that man has put his mark on, their strangeness, their visual power, even their magic, and—not least—the way they often take on the appearance of works of art. I would like my photographs to become as powerful as the work of the artists I admire most, be they composers, sculptors, architects, engineers, graphic artists, painters or photographers.

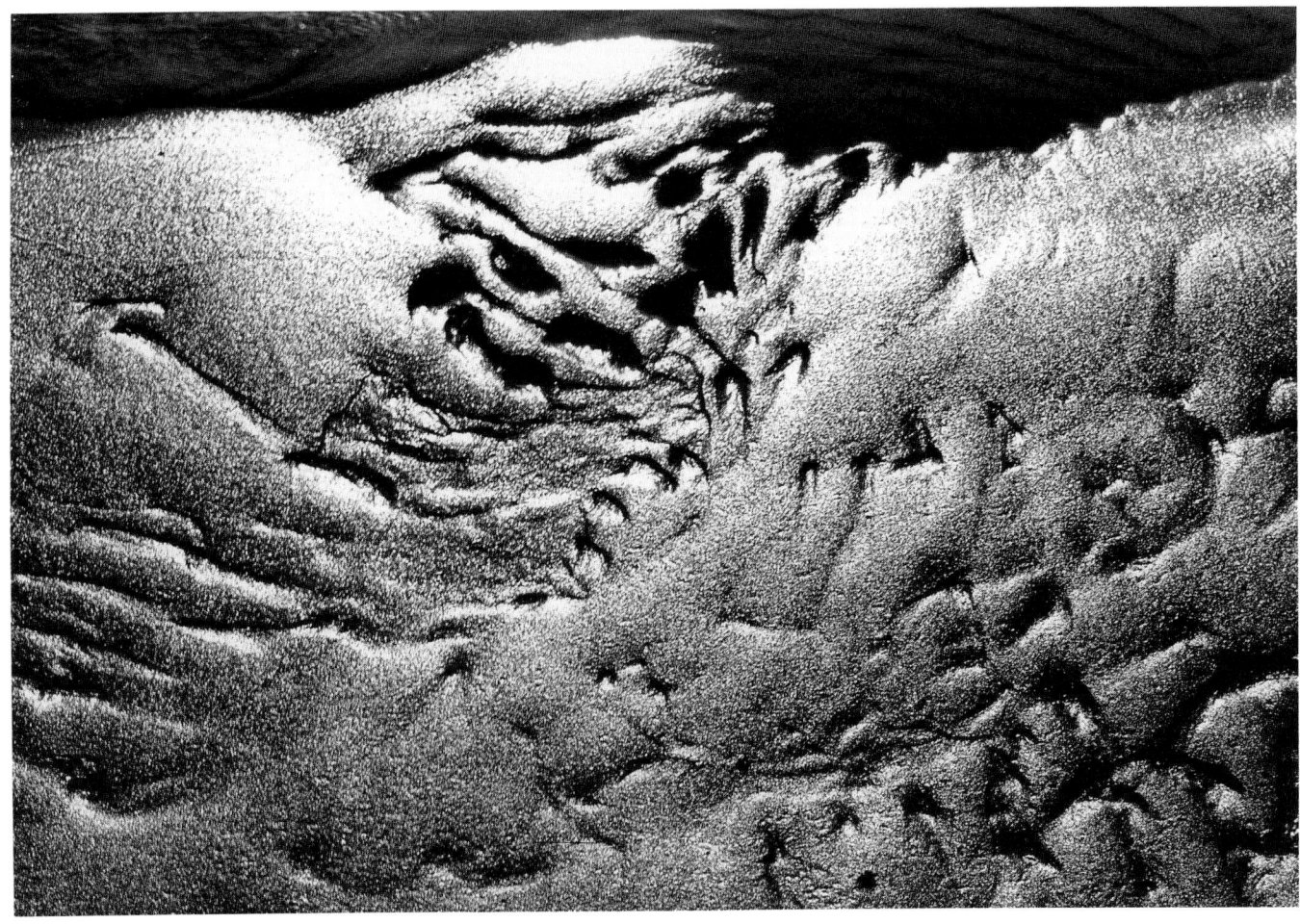

Sand Relief, **1961.** Photograph ©K. Helmer-Petersen.

I suppose I should be labelled a purist and a formalist in that I strive for simplicity and clarity of expression. The viewer should be struck by carefully balanced compositions, bold graphic patterns, and impeccable craftsmanship.

In later years I have, however, also become increasingly attracted to what I imagine should be called surrealism, in that I would also like there to be in my pictures something more and beyond what meets the eye. Something like a subconscious appeal to the imagination, when the eye has been satisfied. This extra layer of meaning is what to me makes a picture really interesting and of lasting value.

Man himself or the portrayal of the human condition in a direct sense is not my concern, much as I admire the artists who can turn this kind of subject matter into forceful imagery.

I would like my statements to excite the mind and eye no matter how humble or apparently ordinary the subject, and to be able to stand the test of time and of being hung on the wall. To achieve this, we enter the realm of the photographer's creative means and methods, such as lighting, rendering of texture, grey tones, minute definition, size and format. I would strive to enrich the vocabulary of photography through constant experimentation and refinement, thus keeping photography abreast with the best achievements of the related arts. I see no reason for photography's not rising to the level of, and achieving the status of, a respected graphic medium, and finding its way into more and more museum collections all over the world—besides playing its inferior role as a slave of the mass picture industry.

—Keld Helmer-Petersen

*   *   *

The primary characteristic of the work of Keld Helmer-Petersen has to do with his sensitive vision, a vision that exists within a respectful concern for the proper function of photography. All of his images reveal an honest approach to that part of the world that he has chosen as his subject. He does not manipulate reality; his photographs are always truthful.

Perhaps the clue to his work is that he attempts to choose the right way, given their nature, to photograph his various subjects. In the case of his photos of modern iron constructions, he often reduces the tonal composition to black-and-white because in this way, through contrast, he can better show the beauty and spirit of the engineers' work. On the other hand, in his depiction of traces left by trucks on sand, he uses the ability of photography to show great richness of detail, interpreting his subject as a landscape of marvellous hills and mountains. Towards the end of the 1970s and in the early 1980s, Helmer-Petersen made a brilliant cycle of "Winter Graphics" focussing on the patterns made by the white patches of snow on the dark earth. His metaphoric interpretation of these phenomena reaffirmed his sense of the everyday world's modest poetry.

Helmer-Petersen also responds to the times in which we live (whether that reaction is conscious or not is irrelevant). Besides photographing the constructions of contemporary engineers, he has shown actual changes in our environment. The problem of waste is growing considerably in every industrially developed country. The reaction to this problem need not be the same in every photographer—and the reaction need not be specifically critical. Poetic and striking forms can be found in that which human society changes by its use into waste, and it is surely a measure of Helmer-Petersen's art the extent to which he is able to present his "found objects" by means of well-chosen perspective and lighting in such a way that everyone understands his interpretation at first glance. He possesses the sensitivity that is necessary for both the discovering and the depicting of the fascinating by-products of contemporary everyday life.

Helmer-Petersen presents his subjects in both black-and-white and colour, but perhaps his colour work is better known. For it is probably true to say that his book *122 Colour Photographs,* published in 1949, was the first really modern publication to be composed of unusual colour-images of the surprising objects of a modest reality.

His researches in the realm of colour still continue today. Following his pictures based on abstract patterns discovered in the outside world, Helmer-Petersen began work on a series of close-up images of distorted found objects. The cycle, simply entitled "Distortions," is composed of both monochrome and colour images—a magnificent use of both media.

—Petr Tausk

HENDERSON, Nigel.

Nationality: British. **Born:** St. John's Wood, London, 1 April 1917. **Education:** Stowe School, Buckingham, 1931-33; studied biology, Chelsea Polytechnic, London, 1935-36; drawing and painting, Slade School of Fine Art, London 1945-49 (ex-serviceman's study grant); mainly self-taught in photography. **Military Service:** Served as a pilot in the Coastal Command, Royal Air Force, with 608 Squadron, Thornaby, Yorkshire, 1939-45; Flight Lieutenant. **Family:** Married anthropologist Karin Judith Stephen in 1943 (died, 1972); children: Jo, Justin, Edward and Stephen. **Career:** Worked as an assistant to the picture-restorer Dr. Helmut Ruhemann, National Gallery, London, 1936-39. Freelance documentary photographer, working occasionally for *Vogue, Flair, Architectural Review* and *Melody Maker,* in London, 1948-52, and in Essex, 1952 until his death in 1985. Founder-Member, with Eduardo Paolozzi, Lawrence Alloway, Richard Hamilton and others, Independent Group, Institute of Contemporary Arts, London, 1952-54, Founder-Director, with Eduardo Paolozzi, Hammer Prints Ltd., wallpaper, textile and ceramic design company, Landermere Quay, Essex, 1955-61. Part-Time Instructor in Creative Photography, Central School of Arts and Crafts, London, 1951-53, and Colchester School of Art, Essex, 1957-65. Lecturer in Charge of Photography Department, Norwich School of Art, Norfolk, 1965-68, and 1972-85. **Recipient:** Edwin Austin Abbey Senior Scholarship, London, 1969. **Died:** (in Thorpe-le-Soken, Clacton-on-Sea, Essex) *15 May 1985.*

Individual Exhibitions:

1953	*Photo-Images,* Institute of Contemporary Arts, London
1957	Arts Council Gallery, Cambridge, England (with Eduardo Paolozzi)
1960	School of Architecture, Cambridge University, England
1961	*Photo-Images, Collages, Paintings,* Institute of Contemporary Arts, London
1977	*Photographs, Collages, Paintings,* Kettle's Yard, Cambridge, England (retrospective)
	Paintings, Collages, Photos, Anthony D'Offay Gallery, London
1978	*Photographs of Bethnal Green 1949-52,* Midland Group Gallery, Nottingham
1983	*Headlands: photos 1960-83,* Serpentine Gallery, London

Selected Group Exhibitions:

1953	*Parallel of Life and Art,* Institute of Contemporary Arts, London
1954	*Collages and Objects,* Institute of Contemporary Arts, London
1956	*This Is Tomorrow,* Whitechapel Art Gallery, London
1981	*Photographer as Printmaker,* Ferens Art Gallery, Hull, Yorkshire (travelled to the Museum and Art Gallery, Leicester; Cooper Gallery, Barnsley; Castle Museum, Nottingham; Photographers' Gallery, London)

Collections:

Tate Gallery, London; Victoria and Albert Museum, London; Arts Council of Great Britain, London; Eastern Arts Association, Cambridge; Welsh National Gallery, Cardiff; Museum of Modern Art, New York.

Publications:

On HENDERSON: Books—*Nigel Henderson: Photographs, Collages, Paintings,* exhibition catalogue, with text by Frank Whitford, Cambridge 1977; *Nigel Henderson: Photographs of Bethnal Green 1949-52,* exhibition catalogue, Nottingham, England 1978; *Photographer as Printmaker,* exhibition catalogue, with texts by Gerry Badger, Peter C. Bunnell and Ansel Adams, London 1981. **Articles**—"Notes Towards a Chronology Based on Conversations with the Artist" (by Anne Seymour) in *Nigel Henderson: Paintings, Collages and Photographs,* exhibition catalogue, London 1977; "Nigel Henderson" by David Mellor, interview by Dave Hoffman and Shirley Read, in *Camerawork* (London), September 1978; "Four Years in the Life of Nigel Henderson" in *British Journal of Photography,* (London) January 1979; "Obituary: Mr. Nigel Henderson" in *The Times* (London), 24 May 1985.

*

When I got involved in photography after the War, I worked, as it were, on two fronts, each reflecting important aspects of my life at that time, which were:

1. I had been given an ex-serviceman's grant to study at the Slade School of Fine Art.

2. My wife, who had studied anthropology in America under Margaret Mead, had been offered a job running a newly-conceived course on sociology in Bethnal Green in the East End of London. It was a condition of her appointment that she should live in the borough.

1. My work at the Slade School was drawing exclusively in the Life Room. I was not very gifted at drawing. I had no facility. It was an uphill struggle to try to delineate, as accurately as I could, what I saw before me. No more than that—an attempt to gain some skill—some small command of what I was about.

2. My wife (née Judith Stephen) and I both had public school backgrounds. We knew we must experience alienation living in a completely working-class environment. Always a rather withdrawn person, this alienation intensified the feeling that I had that I was watching live theatre. My neighbors seemed to be living out their lives in response to some pre-determined script, as if under post-hypnotic suggestion. The social rites were very strongly moulded, coercive, and seemed to me (because of their unfamiliarity) exotic—however absurd this may sound.

"Limitation of means creates style," said the French painter Georges Braque of painting. I thought this was true of the life around me, as I recognized a sort of poetic homogeneity linking the tired faces of people, of houses, of pavements, of prams and utensils. I soon wanted to get some of this down, and decided to try my hand with a camera.

By the time I had acquired an enlarger, I was in my third year of study at the Slade. Photography was taboo there; I worked at home, buying large quantities of Government Surplus papers cheaply, so that I could print down anything I had a mind to. I was really excited by the simple change of scale of things, and by the possibilities of the photogram. I drew on glass and I floated liquids on it as well. I was involved in a kind of drawing. I would cut out ravelled pieces of cloth and mesh and that war-time glass substitute, and shove them into the enlarger to investigate their projections. The bomb sites were, of course, goldmines of semi-transmuted things, fused, torn, twisted, corroded, eroded. Gradually, this aspect of my work began to predominate, and I began to think of myself as an image-maker working in the medium of photography. This is how I would describe myself now.

—Nigel Henderson (1982)

*   *   *

In subject matter, in the way he combines photographic with other elements, and in his attitude towards his work, Nigel Henderson is highly unusual. Brought up in a world of art and artists, he started work as a picture restorer, helped with the hanging of exhibitions, began himself to draw, paint and make collages. After the war, in which he saw the world largely from the air, he and his wife settled in the East End where he started to make photograms, using debris from bomb sites. Later, excited by the "very strong, coherent and highly exotic image of Bethnal Green," he turned to a special kind of documentary photography.

Regarding the detritus of city streets as though he had just arrived from Saturn or a coral beach, he photographed broken hoardings, pieces of sacking, torn posters, roofless dwellings. One of his best-known pictures shows a small tobacconist-cum-sweetshop almost entirely obscured by placards and advertisements. "I want to release an energy of image from trivial data. I feel happiest among discarded things, vituperative fragments cast casually from life, with the fizz of vitality still about them."

To handle such "vituperative fragments" he made use of double exposure, overprints, distortion, crumpling of negatives, drawing on the unexposed film—indeed of every kind of darkroom manipulation—to produce prints, collages or photographic murals. He has created designs for wallpapers and textiles, and made experiments with ceramics. His productions have links with those of surrealist painters, many of whom as a young man he knew and talked to, through a similiar exploitation of casual effects to stimulate memory and imagination.

His own attitude towards his work is completely unpretentious. He never received any formal photographic training, but picked up what knowledge he needed "largely on the linoleum floor of the bathroom." Nor did he ever, he says, "decide that I wanted to be a photographer. I felt I'd like to try taking a camera around with me," and his aim in shooting a picture is "just to get the image in, not to kill it at a blow."

During his last years Henderson made his living mainly through teaching, while operating as an artist in a No-Man's-Land between a variety of forms, using a medley of techniques on the basis of a wide experience. The results are regarded with respect, not only by galleries, critics and sociologists, but also by many conventional photographers.

—Tom Hopkinson

HENLE, Fritz.

Nationality: American. **Born:** Dortmund, Germany, 9 June 1909; emigrated to the United States, 1936; naturalized, 1942. **Education:** Attended gymnasium in Dortmund, 1920-29; University of Heidelberg, 1930, and University of Munich, 1930; studied photography, under Hanna Seewald, at the Bayrische Staatslehranstalt für Lichtbildwesen, Munich, 1930-31, Dip. Photog. 1931. **Family:** Married Atti van den Berg in 1938 (divorced, 1952); son: Jan; married Marguerite Williams in 1954; children: Maria, Tina, and Martin. **Career:** Assistant, under Clarence Kennedy, Smith College, Florence, 1931-33; Publicity Photographer, Lloyd Triestino, Trieste, 1934-36; Contract Photographer, *Life* magazine, New York, 1937-41; Photographer, Office of War Information, Washington, D.C., 1942-45; Contract Photographer, under Alexey Brodovitch, *Harper's Bazaar,* New York, 1945-50; Staff Photographer, City Service Oil Company, New York 1951-58; established home and studio, St. Croix, Virgin Islands, 1958; Photographer, European Travel Commission, New York, 1959-62; freelance photographer, in St. Croix, since 1962. Artist-in-Residence, Trinity University, San Antonio, Texas, 1978. Member, Gesellschaft Deutsche Lichtbildner (GDL), 1954-59. Founder Member and Trustee, American Society of Magazine Photographers. **Recipient:** Photo prizes, *Photography,* New York, 1948, 1950, 1951, 1952, 1954, 1955, 1957; Award of Excellence, Art Directors' Club of Philadelphia, 1954; Picture Contest Prize, *Popular Photography,* New York, 1960. **Member:** Virgin Islands Academy of Arts and Letters, 1972. **Agent:** Witkin Gallery, 415 West Broadway, New York, New York 10012, U.S.A. **Died:** (in St. Juan, Puerto Rico) 31 January 1993.

Individual Exhibitions:

1936   *Japan,* Mitsubishi Department Store, Tokyo

1937	*Japan and China,* Rockefeller Plaza Lobby, New York
1943	*Mexico,* private showing in New York
1950	*Hawaii,* Museum of Natural History, New York
1953	New York Camera Club
1954	*Caribbean,* Smithsonian Institution, Washington, D.C. (toured the United States)
1956	*Industrial/Oil Photos,* International Museum of Photography, George Eastman House, Rochester, New York
1957	*Caribbean Movies,* International Museum of Photography, George Eastman House, Rochester, New York
1958	*Caribbean,* Government House, Christiansted, St. Croix, Virgin Islands
1960	*American Virgin Islands in Color,* Government House, Christiansted, St. Croix, Virgin Islands
1962	Staatliche Landesbildstelle, Hamburg
1967	Exhibition Hall, Rollei Werke, Braunschweig, West Germany
1970	Institute of Culture, University of Puerto Rico, San Juan (retrospective)
1971	*American Virgin Islands in Color,* Exhibition Hall, Rollei Werke, Braunschweig, West Germany
1974	New York Cultural Center (retrospective)
1975	Galleria de las Americas, San Juan, Puerto Rico (retrospective)
1976	Galerie am Schloss, Wolfenbuttel, West Germany (retrospective)
1977	Art Museum, Allentown, Pennsylvania (retrospective)
1978	Trinity University, San Antonio, Texas (retrospective)
	Michener Gallery, University of Texas at Austin (retrospective)
1979	*Color Photographs,* Trinity University, San Antonio, Texas
1980	*Fritz Henle: A 50 Year Retrospective,* Witkin Gallery, New York
1981	Galerie Foto-Arts, Basle, Switzerland
1982	*Casals,* Osterreichisches Landerbank, Vienna
1983	Fotomuseum im Stadtmuseum, Munich
1984	Overseas Press Club, New York
	Amerika-Haus, Heidelberg, West Germany
1985	Kunsthaus, Zurich
1986	First Pennsylvania Bank, St. Thomas, Virgin Islands
	America: A Theme in Variations 1936-86, Amerika-Haus, Heidelberg, West Germany (toured Germany)
1989	*Paris 1938,* Museum für Kunst und Kulturgeschichte, Dortmund
1994	Museum für Kunst und Kulturgeschichte, Dortmund (retrospective)

Selected Group Exhibitions:

1968	*2nd World Exhibition of Photography: Woman,* Pressehaus Stern, Hamburg (and world tour)
1978	*Color and Casals,* University of Texas at Austin
	APA International Exhibition of Photography, Tokyo
1980	*Body Electric: Color,* Squibb Institute, Princeton, New Jersey
1981	*Germany: The New Vision,* Fraenkel Gallery, San Francisco
1983	*The Henle Family,* Reichhold Center of the Arts, St. Thomas, Virgin Islands
1984	*Sammlung Gruber,* Museum Ludwig, Cologne
1985	*Das Aktfoto,* Fotomuseum im Stadtmuseum, Munich (toured Germany)

Collections:

Museum of Modern Art, New York; International Center of Photography, New York; International Museum of Photography, George Eastman House, Rochester, New York; Lehigh University, Allentown, Pennsylvania; Gernsheim Collection, University of Texas at Austin; Center for Creative Photography, University of Arizona, Tucson; Foto-Historama Agfa-Gevaert, Leverkusen, West Germany; Landesbildstelle, Hamburg; Museum Ludwig, Cologne; Fotomuseum im Münchner Stadtmuseum, Munich.

Night in the Museum of Modern Art, New York, **1952.** Photograph by Fritz Henle.

Publications:

By HENLE: Books—*This Is Japan,* with text by Takayasu Senzoku, Munich 1937; *China,* with text by Kwok Ying Fung, New York 1943; *Mexico,* Chicago 1945; *Paris,* with text by Elliot Paul, New York 1947; *Hawaii,* with text by Norman Wright, New York 1948; *The Virgin Islands,* with text by Vivienne Winterry, New York 1949; *Fritz Henle's Rollei,* with text by Vivienne Winterry, New York 1950; *Fritz Henle's Figure Studies,* with an introduction

by Jacquelyn Judge, New York 1954, London 1957; *Great Photographs 2: Fritz Henle,* edited by Norman Hall and Basil Burton, London 1954; *Fritz Henle's Guide to Rollei Photography,* with George B. Wright, New York 1956; *The Caribbean: A Journey with Pictures,* with P.E. Knapp, New York and London 1957; *Photography for Everyone,* with H.M. Kinzer, New York 1959; *Holiday in Europe,* with text by Anne Fremantle, and an introduction by Patrick Dennis, New York and London 1963; *A New Guide to Rollei Photography,* with H.M. Kinzer, New York and London 1965; *The American Virgin Islands,* colorprint portfolio, 1971; *Casals,* with text by Pablo and

Marta Casals, New York 1975; *The Rolleiflex SL66 and SLX Way,* with text by L. Andrew Mannheim, London 1975; *Fritz Henle,* with a foreword by Allan Porter, New York 1975; *The American Virgin Islands,* New York 1986; *Paris vor 50 Jahren,* Heidelberg 1989; *Fritz Henle 1909-1993,* Heidelberg und Dortmund 1993.

On HENLE: Books—*Akt International/International Nudes,* with introduction by Otto Steinert, Munich and London 1954; *Photography Today,* edited by Norman Hall, London 1957; *Beauty: Variations on the Theme Woman by Masters of the Camera—Past and Present,* edited by L. Fritz Gruber, London and New York 1965; *Fotografie 1919-1979, Made in Germany: Die GDL-Fotografen* edited by Fritz Kempe, Bernd Lohse and others, Frankfurt 1979; *Sammlung Gruber: Photographie des 20. Jahrhunderts,* exhibition catalogue with foreword by Siegfried Gohr, Cologne 1984; *A Concise History of Photography* by Helmut Gernsheim, New York 1986. **Articles**—"Fritz Henle" in *Popular Photography* (New York), March 1964; "Focus on Fritz Henle" in *Popular Photography* (New York), November 1964; "Fritz Henle" by Beaumont Newhall in *Infinity* (New York), March 1968; "Fritz Henle: Forty Years on Top" by Julia Scully in *Modern Photography* (New York), March 1970; "Fritz Henle" in *Westermann Monatshefte* (Braunschweig, West Germany), February 1972; "Fritz Henle" in *Modern Photography* (New York), March 1972; article by Allan Porter in *Camera* (Lucerne), June 1969; "Fritz Henle" in *Foto Magazin* (Munich), March 1980; "Fritz Henle" in *Humboldt* (Berne), March 1980; "Art: Fritz Henle, Witkin Gallery" by Grace Glueck in the *New York Times,* 2 May 1980; "Who, What, Where" by Grace Naismith in *Overseas Press Club Bulletin* (New York), 15 May 1980.

*

One fact which I never emphasized in articles about myself is that I am actually "self-taught." My studies at the Photographic School in Munich merely added to the knowledge which I had already acquired, and, realizing this, my marvellously intuitive and spontaneous teacher, Hanna Seewald, made it possible for me to enter the second year of the curriculum immediately. Her decision was based on a portfolio of my work which I had shown to her and the school's director, for this made it clear to them that I was more than well acquainted with darkroom techniques and that I had spent a considerable amount of time patiently trying to solve problems to which I had wanted to find my own solutions.

It was never enough for me to simply capture an impression on film. As early as the late 1920s I had been impressed by "craftsmanship," and it was this that had led me to set up a small darkroom in the basement of our house in Heidelberg. I cannot count the numbers of hours I spent there, sometimes late into the night, sometimes on the point of desperation when I seemed unable to print a particularly difficult picture which was important to me!

Much of this early work was lost during the war years, but fortunately I took the pictures which were closest to me in America.

I cannot emphasize too strongly the importance of making the darkroom a vital and integral part of one's domain as a photographer. I have done my own darkroom work throughout my career—even when I was working for *Life,* where we had all the facilities imaginable at our disposal for the production of first-class negatives and prints. Later, during the 1950s, when my interest became focused on the Caribbean, I was lucky enough to make the acquaintance of Pat and Julio Motal: to work with them in the darkroom was a marvellous experience, for they were true artists and their experience and virtuosity led to a relationship in which I felt I could entrust my films and printing to them when I was far away on assignments. This relationship became even more important when I decided to leave New York and settle on St. Croix in the American Virgin Islands, for there is a scarcity of water in these islands which makes it impossible to run a successful darkroom.

Not all my work is in black and white, however, and with the advent of Kodak's Ektachrome films I finally found a medium equal to Kodachrome. (It was impossible to use the latter successfully with my Rolleiflex—a fact which at times caused me some distress.)

During the early 1950s, when I first became acquainted with the Caribbean, I also made my first movies there, and two movies of Trinidadian dancers—Geoffrey Holder and his group—have become classics and are now in the collection of George Eastman House and in the Gernsheim Collection at the University of Texas in Austin.

As a photographer who was fascinated from the very beginning by the large square format of the Rolleiflex, I found it impossible to break away from this camera. I am most enthusiastic about the groundglass and the immediacy of composition which it provides, and I trained myself straight away to fill the frame so completely with the image as I had visualized it that cropping was in most cases not only unnecessary but would have actually spoiled the concept of the picture.

I first became acquainted with the Rolleiflex at the Photographic School in Munich in 1930. Across the street from the school was the store, run by Mr. Letzgus, which provided the school with all the necessary materials. Although I did not have the money to buy the camera, my mind was nevertheless made up, and the more I worked with the school's large studio-type cameras, the less convinced I was that they could provide the means for me to express myself in the future. I remember confiding in a fellow student about my admiration for the Rolleiflex, and her somewhat amused and incredulous reaction hurt my feelings since she was very pretty and we were fond of each other; from then on I decided to keep my other love to myself! In order to become the owner of my first Rolleiflex, I worked long nights in the darkroom doing cheap prints for a drugstore. This was rather an ordeal, since I had to make do with only a few hours' sleep as well as having to prepare for school the next day. But my determination lent me the necessary stamina, and a few months later I was able to surprise my classmates with pictures taken with this "tiny" camera.

Since that time I have stuck to the Rolleiflex. When I came to America in 1936 I realized that very few photographers had broken away from the larger formats, so in order to compete I never showed a sheet of contact prints—that would have been impossible. My editors would look at only 8 x 10 inch pictures, and I was able to produce beautiful enlargements in this size from my Rollei negatives.

The "secret" came out when the famous Swiss photographer and graphic artist Herbert Matter kindly offered me the use of his darkroom in New York and took a picture of me for the photographers' column in *Life* magazine to accompany my story "Texas High School," which appeared on the cover and twelve pages of the magazine. This was in 1937, a time in which such large coverage was unprecedented, and the question of my "small" camera was never brought up again. It would in any case have ceased to be a problem, since many of the European photographers who emigrated to the United States at that time brought with them not only an entirely new and vigorous way of seeing, but also their equipment, which was new for America. At this time, in 1938, I was working with Alfred Eisenstaedt on a revolutionary idea for the world of fashion. We took our models out of the studio into the lovely countryside of New England; Eisenstaedt worked with his Leica and I with my Rollei, and we achieved some beautifully candid results. The editors of *Life* assured us that we had helped to usher in a new era in fashion—"outdoor fashions"—and it appears that they were right.

Like the rest of us "newcomers," I could probably have stayed with *Life* if I had wanted to. But not everyone fits into the same pattern of development, and during my year in Florence in 1932 and long trips to India and the Far East between 1933 and 1936, I tasted a creative freedom which—despite the loneliness and difficulties of these years in which I was entirely dependent on my own ingenuity—I was unable to find again. This became especially clear when I asked *Life* to send me to Paris to photograph the city, and particularly its inhabitants, in a time in which the impending catastrophe of World War II was latent in the atmosphere. My wish was granted, and I remember these weeks as a tense and vitally interesting period. I was fascinated by the people, and they readily accepted me although my French is not fluent. A photographer is like an actor on the stage: the more self-possessed he is, the more successfully he is able to hide his tension and become part of the show—the show which is life itself. To capture this show in a visual form is, for me, the true meaning of photography. Participation of this kind brings both joy and agony, and the necessary self-imposed discipline can sometimes become a torture. The element of the unknown is always present; one can never be sure . . . and this results in a great and—at times—almost unbearable intensity. It is this intensity alone which can lead to the creation of valuable and lasting impressions. I experienced this intensity in Paris, as I had on occasions during my trips to India, China, and Japan, and it became increasingly difficult for me to fit into a preconceived framework. I remember the make-shift darkroom which I set up in an attic in Montmartre, the excitement with which I developed my films, and the endless hours which followed—I only had one small tank in which to develop dozens of rolls. I felt sure that I had captured the people of

Paris, and all that was necessary was for a skilled writer to collaborate in the creation of a fine story for *Life* magazine.

When I returned to New York, however, my collection was returned, complete with the films—an utter failure. I was in despair. How could I ever find happiness expressing myself?

Many years passed, and a most horrible war went into its final stages. Paris was liberated. A call reached me from the *New York Times:* "Have you ever been to Paris?" Back in 1938, in my disillusionment, I had locked up my Paris negatives in a small safe. Now, a few minutes after receiving the call, I set to work enlarging negative after negative—there must have been about 150 prints by the end, and late that afternoon I presented them to the editor of the *New York Times,* Madame Lazareff, herself a French refugee. Few words were exchanged; she was extremely emotional, and so was I. Next Sunday the paper's magazine section published my pictures of the people of Paris on the cover and four inside pages—images which still spoke the same vivid language that they had spoken five years previously. In fact, they now seemed even more alive, because now I had a reason for my story even more eloquent than before.

At this time I worked closely with Alexei Brodovitch—a man whom I greatly admired, and the combination of his fine vision and my creativity resulted in some of the finest pages in *Harper's Bazaar*. This great artist accepted my approach without question, and I well remember how proud I felt when I visited his art department and saw large photostats of my pictures, some of which have since become well known. My photographs of the "Desert Plant, Nievis—Mexican Indian Beauty" and the almost giddy spiral of the "Lights of New York" all covered full pages in *Harper's Bazaar*; but our greatest accomplishment was the book *Paris* for which Brodovitch did the layout. The picture which struck him most was "Madame Niska," and this, too, was published on a full page in the magazine. I was also represented on the fashion pages, and here again I broke away from the usual style by photographing "fashion in motion."

The years I spent with *Life* taught me a lot; the war years spent taking photographs for the government and my years as a fashion photographer were full of exciting experiences. Over and over again, it became clear that I did my best work when left to find my own solutions. I disliked routine work, and what interested me was finding the beauty in seemingly ordinary subjects.

The place where I decided to make my home, the American Virgin Islands, had never really been fully understood. Its magnificence had been largely overlooked, and one of my more recent achievements is the creation of a collection of pictures of these islands which had previously only been known through pretty picture postcards. In order to gain the freedom to devote myself to this project, I applied for a grant from the Council of the Arts in 1969, and I was most gratified when I received support which by far exceeded my expectations. I immersed myself completely in photographing the islands, and the result was published as a portfolio about 13 inches square, with 24 color pictures mounted individually. These pictures were printed in heliogravure in Switzerland in a rather unusual technique—all the photographs were reproduced from original dye transfer prints, a method which enabled the craftsmen at the Bucher publishing house in Lucerne to have complete control of the rendition of all the colors.

In 1970, *Modern Photography* honored me with a ten-page article entitled "Forty Years at the Top." I was slightly embarrassed by this title, since I am a quiet man by nature and I never force myself into the limelight. I was extremely gratified by the article, however, for I must admit that there have been times when I felt that my work has not received the recognition it deserves. The article was beautifully written by Julia Scully, and the title is really intended to attract the amateur. But how can one be really "on the top?" If we forget about the financial implications, it would appear to me that "top" means the success of a creative artist to express himself through the quality and beauty of his work. "Top" is where the never-ending urge for fulfilment is being realized. And, indeed, it is only when I can truthfully say that I have approached a certain pinnacle with some of my photographs that I can be happy as an artist.

As recently as May 1972, I was able to prove this to myself once again. Not far from my home, on the large neighboring island of Puerto Rico, lived the great musician Pablo Casals. The Institute of Culture of the Government of Puerto Rico invited me to exhibit some of my work in the museum in Old San Juan, a magnificent convent which provided a marvellous background for the show. This was just before the *Casals Festival,* and I expressed my desire to photograph the maestro. The result of the first sitting impressed the great artist

and humanitarian so much that he exclaimed, "Beyond photography!" He then went to his cello and repeated the music which he had played while I had photographed him, and, when he had finished, he took the photograph, wrote a few bars of the music—a Bach saraband—and dedicated it to me. This to me *was* the "top," and at the same time I realized how very rare such moments are in the life of a photographer.

To be "on top" is to stand on a hill in 1936 and see the sacred mountain of Fujiyama in the far distance; no pollution hid its beauty then, and it seemed to be floating in the air, like an image on a delicate Japanese silk screen. "On top" is a lonesome plant in the desert—symbol of the eternal struggle for survival. "On top" are the people of Paris—the old man in his almost tragic pose in the deserted street, the "Lady and the God" in a harmony of pose with an element of humor, and the angry "Madame Niska" trying desperately to convince a passer-by of her talents.

These and other pictures are like crystals which have grown over a period of time and now come together to form a composition. They are part of a process of continued development. I consider myself fortunate. "Forty Years on the Top" does not in fact mean much in a lifetime dedicated to photography; more important is the knowledge that, with each step, I can create new possibilities for myself, all of them influenced by a purity of vision and a passionate desire for beauty. Words alone have never satisfied me—it is all too easy to lose oneself in debates on the value of photography. For me, it is the image which counts.

The preceding thoughts, though I wrote them a few years ago, are as fresh in my mind as they would be today. Photography is making great strides. It is a newborn art. 150 years mean little in the history of mankind. The trends which we experience today have existed practically from the moment that photography became reality. Only relatively few photographers will ever reach the top. To many the medium is a constant struggle—the forced desire to express themselves in ever new ways. And how many ways are there really? It seems there is no limit, and that the only true expression is the way we conceive life in its endless variety and beauty.

—Fritz Henle

*   *   *

"The photographer is like an actor on the stage: the more self-possessed he is, the more successfully he is able to hide his tension and become part of the show—the show which is life itself. To capture this show in a visual form is, for me, the true meaning of photography." In this neat statement Fritz Henle summed up the essence of his work. He has been an observer with the camera for five decades, travelling round the world showing the face of cities, the beauty of scenery, and the life of the people. In addition he became known for the first fashion photographs taken out of doors, and for a series of brilliant beach nude studies. Though Henle worked for long periods for *Fortune, Life, Harper's Bazaar* and *Holiday,* he prefers being his own boss, which excludes the necessity of having to adapt one's own ideas to those of an editor.

His first book appeared soon after his student days in Munich. His last books include a portfolio of colour shots of the Virgin Islands where he made his home since 1958, as well as a book to accompany his retrospective. In between there have been the fine reportages of Japan and Paris, the moving series on Pablo Casals shortly before his death, and much else. Throughout his life in photography Henle remained faithful to the same camera-make, which has earned him the nickname "Mr. Rolleiflex." Indeed, his vision has adapted itself so well to the square format that he hardly ever has to crop his pictures.

Surprisingly, Henle's work of the 1930s and 1940s does not look "dated." Quite the contrary, it looks very advanced for the time, for Henle had a liking for unorthodox views and angle shots right from the beginning of his career in 1930. One of his pictures of that year is called "Rain": a corner of a wet road is illuminated by a street lamp; a tree is silhouetted against the faint light; the whole scene is photographed from above. Very concise. Nothing superfluous. Typical Henle. Arriving in New York from Germany six years later, he created one of his first New World pictures: a car radiator grille from below against the backdrop of the towering RCA building. Back in Paris he spotted a woman resting her feet underneath the huge sculpture of a rivergod apparently doing the same. The harmony of pose combined with the humorous element make an unforgettable picture.

Like most of the classic photographers Henle stresses the "Art of Seeing." He finds beauty in everyday subjects, and the world full of beauty. He is of a happy, positive nature and shuns all discord, in life as in work. Having viewed the world through his lens for 50 years, he has found it a novel experience in the last few years to see the public viewing the world through his images, which are "the expression of my love of life in all its variety."

—Helmut Gernsheim

HENRI, Florence.

Nationality: Swiss. **Born:** New York City, 28 June 1893. **Education:** Studied piano, under Egon Petri and Ferruccio Busoni, Berlin, 1911-14; studied painting, Academy of Fine Arts, Berlin, under Schwitters, 1914, Hans Hofmann School of Arts, Munich 1915-19, at the Académie André L'Hote, Paris, 1922-23, and under Fernand Léger and Amedee Ozenfant, at the Académie Moderne, Paris, 1924-25; studied painting and photography, under Josef Albers and László Moholy-Nagy, at the Bauhaus, Dessau, Germany, 1927. **Family:** Married a Swiss national, Charles Coster, in the 1930s; subsequently divorced. **Career:** Freelance portrait, fashion and advertising photographer, Paris, 1929-63: maintained a studio in Paris, and also taught photography there, 1928-47; associated with the Cercle et Carré group of artists, Paris, in the 1930s. Also a painter: exhibitions—Galerie Nebelung, Dusseldorf, 1952; Studio für Neue Kunst, Wuppertal, 1953; Duisburger Bucherstube, Duisburg, 1953; Hanover Gallery, London, 1969; and Galerie Lowepelz, Zurich, 1979. Lived in Compiegne, France, concentrating on painting, 1963 until her death in 1982. **Died:** (in Compiegne, France) in July 1982.

Individual Exhibitions:

1930	Studio 28, Paris
1931	Galerie Laxer Normand, Paris
1933	*Photoausstellung Florence Henri,* Museum Folkwang, Essen (travelled to the Galerie La Pleiade, Paris, 1934)
1974	Galleria Martini & Ronchetti, Genoa
1975	Martini and Ronchetti Gallery, New York
	Galerie M, Bochum, West Germany (with Bernard Descamps)
	Galleria Martano, Turin
1976	Galleria Milano, Milan
	Galleria Pan, Rome
	Aspekte der Photographie der 20er Jahre, Westfälischer Kunstverein, Munster, West Germany
	Staatliche Kunsthalle, Baden-Baden, West Germany
	M.L. D'Arc Gallery, New York
1977	Galleria Martini & Ronchetti, Genoa
1978	University of Parma, Italy
	Musée d'Art Moderne de La Ville, Paris
	Galleria Narciso, Turin
1979	Galleria G7, Bologna
	Aspetti di un Percorso, Banco di Chivari, Genoa
	Villa Romana, Florence
	The Photographers' Gallery, London
1981	*Florence Henri. 70 Photographies 1928-1938,* Musée d'Art et d'Histoire, Geneva
1982	*Florence Henri's Vintage Photographic Works,* Prakapas Gallery, New York
1987	San Francisco Museum of Modern Art

Selected Group Exhibitions:

1925	*L'Art d'Aujourd'hui,* Syndicat des Anti-quaires, Paris
1929	*Photographie der Gegenwart,* Museum Folkwang, Essen
1932	*Modern European Photography,* Julien Levy Gallery, New York
1937	*Foto '37,* Stedelijk Museum, Amsterdam
1970	*Photo Eye of the 20s,* Museum of Modern Art, New York (toured the United States)
1975	*Women of Photography,* San Francisco Museum of Modern Art (toured the United States, 1975-77)
1980	*Avant-Garde Photography in Germany 1919-39,* San Francisco Museum of Modern Art (toured the United States, 1981-82)
1981	*Germany: The New Vision,* Fraenkel Gallery, San Francisco
1982	*Lichtbildnisse: Das Porträt in der Fotografie,* Rheinisches Landesmuseum, Bonn
	Léger et l'Esprit Moderne, Musée d'Art Moderne de la Ville de Paris
1983	*Bauhausfotografie,* Institut fur Auslandbeziehung, Stuttgart (and world tour)

Collections:

Bibliothéque Nationale, Paris; Centre Georges Pompidou, Paris; Museum Folkwang, Essen; University of Parma; Museum of Modern Art, New York; San Francisco Museum of Modern Art; University of New Mexico Art Museum, Albuquerque.

Publications:

On HENRI: Books—*Foto-Auge/Oeil et photo/Photo-Eye: 76 Fotos der Zeit,* edited by Franz Roh and Jan Tschichold, Stuttgart 1929, London 1974; *Germany: The New Photography 1927-33,* edited by David Mellor, London 1978; *Bauhaus Fotografie,* edited by Roswitha Fricke, Dusseldorf 1982; exhibition catalogues—*Florence Henri* by Ester de Miro, Genoa 1974; *Florence Henri: Una Rieflessione sulla Fotografia* by Maurizio Fagiolo, Turin 1975; *Florence Henri: Aspekte der Photographie der 20er Jahre* by Herbert Molderings, Munster, West Germany 1976; *Florence Henri* by Suzanne Pagé and Herbert Molderings, Paris 1978; *Florence Henri: Aspetti di un Percorso* by G. Marcenaro, G. Martini, and A. Ronchetti, Genoa 1979; *Florence Henri—Artist Photographer of the Avant-Garde,* by Diana C. du Pont, organised by the San Francisco Museum of Modern Art, 1990. **Articles**—"Florence Henri" by László Moholy-Nagy in *I 10* (Amsterdam), 1928; "Florence Henri: A Grand Dame of Photography" by Romeo E. Martinez, in *Camera* (Lucerne), September 1967; "Florence Henri" in *Creative Camera* (London), July 1972; "Le Fotografie alla Seconda di Florence Henri" by Claudio Marra in *G7 Studio* (Bologna), January 1979.

* * *

Born in New York in 1893 of a French father and a German mother, Florence Henri, on the death of her mother, left for Silesia where she settled in with her mother's family; there, she learned to play the piano. At the age of 9 she moved to Paris, at 11 to Vienna, at 13 to England (the Isle of Wight). When she was 16 her father died and she settled in Rome. There she was to meet the most brilliant artistic avant-garde of her time: the futurists and in particular Marinetti. Her life was to be a mirror image of her youth: a series of changes and encounters. Her friends, her contacts, were Arp, Moholy-Nagy, Maiakowsky, Lissitsky, Léger, Larionov, Delaunay, Mondrian, Gropius. There were no photographers (or very few) among her artistic liaisons. Her interest changed from music to painting. A determining factor in her future life, however, was a period she spent at the Bauhaus in 1927 where her teacher was Moholy-Nagy. It was probably he who caused her to choose photography as her preferred means of expression.

Almost immediately that she determined what her career was to be, Florence Henri devoted herself to the most exacting research. While pictorialists were trying to ape the painting of 50 years before, applying purely and simply recipes invented by others for another medium, Henri, taking into account the most vital developments in the plastic arts of her time (painting, cinema), invented, along with a few others, a new language for photography at a time when photography was beginning to enjoy a rebirth. Moholy-Nagy dreamed of a camera employing the dark chamber but eliminating the representation of perspective, a camera fitted with lenses and mirrors able to catch an all-round view of the subject, creating "light frescoes," optical compositions that could not be achieved with canvas, brush and paint. Florence Henri followed this direction of research when in her portraits, self-portraits and still-lifes, she used mirrors to multiply the image and its reflections, to distort space and alter planes, awakening our astonished perception with mysterious but simple images, surprisingly rigorous in their subtle luminosity—or when she photographed glass surfaces, transparent and at the same time reflective, recording ready-made superimposed images, in the manner of photos produced 40 years later by Friedlander.

Florence Henri, who spent her last years in a small village in the Oise, had generally been forgotten. But over the past few years—thanks particularly to the Musée d'Art Moderne (ARC) Paris, to Suzanne Pagé and Catherine Thiek—her remarkable and exciting work is gradually being rediscovered. Contact with it evokes in the observer, in its very ambiguity, a feeling of joy and excitement provided today by very few other artists.

—Michel Nuridsany

HERRAEZ GOMEZ, Fernando.

Nationality: Spanish. **Born:** San Fernando, near Cadiz, 26 September 1948. **Education:** Attended a school in San Fernando, 1958-65; self-taught in photography. **Military Service:** Served in Spanish Army, 1967-68. **Career:** Independent photographer, Madrid, since 1972. **Agent:** Canon Gallery, Reestraat 19, Amsterdam, Netherlands. **Address:** Calle San Cristobal no. 10-5, San Fernando, Cadiz, Spain.

Individual Exhibitions:

1978	*Village Festivity in Spain,* Canon Gallery, Amsterdam (travelled to Galerie Trockenpresse, West Berlin)
	Caja de Ahorros, Pamplona, Spain
1979	Galerie Contrejour, Paris
1980	Photographic Center, Athens
1981	Galerie AAA, Brussels
	Galerie Delpire, Paris

Selected Group Exhibitions:

1978	*Ritos y Minorias,* Photogaleria, Madrid
1980	*Madrid: Photojournalism,* The Poetry Centre, London
1985	*Fotografie im Spanien,* Museum Folkwang, Essen, West Germany

Collections:

Museo de Arte Moderno, Cuenca, Spain; Stedelijk Museum, Amsterdam.

Publications:

By HERRAEZ: Book—*España, Años y Leguas,* with Ramón Zabalza, Madrid 1980. **Articles**—"Bloed, Pijn en Pret" in *Panorama* (Haarlem), 3 August 1979; "Het Rijke Roomse Iberie" in *Avenue* (Amsterdam), January 1980.

On HERRAEZ: Book—*Fotografie im Spanien,* exhibition catalogue, by Ute Eskildsen and Joan Fontcuberta, Essen, West Germany 1985. **Articles**—"Photographie Actual en Espagne" by Belen Agosti in *Contrejour* (Paris), March/April 1976; "Fernando Herraez" by Ignacio Barceló in *Arte Fotografico* (Madrid), December 1976; "Portfolio of the Month: Fernando Herraez" by Lorenzo Merlo in *Reflexions* (Amsterdam), January 1978; "Fernando Herraez" by Ramón Zabalza in *Zoom* (Madrid), December 1978; "L'Oeil Iberique" by Jacques Marchois in *Photo-Reporter* (Paris), March 1979; "Bede Vaarten en Processies" by Wim Broekman in *Foto* (Amersfoort, Netherlands), May 1979; "Spanish Photography in the 80s" by Joan Fontcuberta in *European Photography* (Göttingen), April 1980.

*

For several years, I have been working on a single theme—that of fiestas in Spain and Portugal. At present I am working on new projects but still with my own subjective perspective, using the subject merely as a pretext for making photographs.

As far as the type of work I am developing is concerned, there is no official financial support in Spain.

Concerning the world of photography, my preferences include the work of Arbus, Robert Frank, Weegee, Bellocq, but very few others.

—Fernando Herraez Gomez

*   *   *

Among young Spanish photographers committed to creative photography, Fernando Herraez is important for his extremely descriptive style. Basically, his photography concentrates on the man in the street, avoiding bitter social commentary or any other kind of moralistic analysis.

Herraez was born in Andalusia and is a devoted observer of human behavior within communities hardened by the difficulties of agricultural life. Also because of his background, he does not look for extreme attitudes or for obvious expressiveness in his subjects. He is not a spectator (as one without a deep knowledge of his subject would be), ready and over-eager to achieve an easy photographic impact. His works have a deliberate slowness. They describe one kind of common life from the point of view of his own beliefs and his own symbols. The aspects of his subjects that most interest him are those that are least controlled and most casual—but they are full of realism and naturalness, derived from a profound knowledge of tradition.

From this perspective, his depictions of Spanish fiestas are compelling: with great skill, his camera captures images of the street, groups or individuals; there is great sensitivity to the customs involved, but he does not rely on obvious effects. He is interested in ceremonies, temporal rites, particularly those originally inspired by religious fervor that have both penetrated the popular consciousness and eventually lost their liturgical origins and developed a more complex symbolism.

Herraez's images are not so much concerned with a depiction of the celebration itself as with that of the conflict between the daily ambience of a place and its atmosphere during fiesta, when everyday life experiences a temporary transformation. Aesthetic qualities, psychology and existential aspects are mixed in his images. No matter what the subject, however, his camera does not register it rigidly, according to some program; he allows, always, the co-existence of different aspects, the varied facets of human attitudes.

Herraez almost never allows people to pose. He waits for the simple gesture, deep and revealing but not too anecdotic. In the seriousness, distractions, concentration and meetings of his subjects, he finds his images, keys to the manners of a people. His photographs do not depict ebullience; they go directly to the telling of a moment that has to do with communal realities, that manifests all the weight of popular culture—a boy playing with a cross, an Easter procession, the running for *toros,* holy scenes, masked people. . . . Seen by Fernando Herraez they reveal much more than just their external forms.

—M. Teresa Blanch

HERS, François.

Nationality: Belgian. **Born:** Brussels, 20 March 1943; moved to Paris in 1968. **Education:** Attended secondary schools in Belgium, Saint Michel in Brussels and Cardinal Mercier in Braine l'Alleud; self-taught in photography. **Career:** Freelance photographer, working with *Le Monde, Critique, Libération, Corriere della Serra,* etc., Paris, since 1968. Founder Member, with Hervé Gloaguen, Guy Le Querrec, Martine Franck, Claude Raimond-Dityvon, and others, Viva photographers group, Paris, 1972-76; Artistic and Technical Director, Mission Photographique de la DATAR (Délégation a l'Aménagement du Territoire et a l'Action Régionale), Paris, since 1983. **Recipient:** Foundation Nationale de la Photographie Fellowship, Lyons, 1976; Ministére de la

Culture Belge Grant, 1978. **Address:** 5 rue Santos Dumont, 75015 Paris, France.

Individual Exhibitions:

1981	*Intérieurs: Photographies de François Hers et Sophie Ristelhueber,* Centre Georges Pompidou, Paris
1982	Kunstgewerbemuseum, Zurich
1983	*Recit,* The Photographers' Gallery, London
	Musée de Toulon, France
1984	Palazzo delle Esposizioni, Rome
	Galleria Arvis, Palermo, Sicily
	Le dernier reportage, Galerie Samia Saouma, Paris

Selected Group Exhibitions:

1973	*Viva: Familles en France,* Galeria Il Diaframma, Milan (travelled to the French Consulate, New York; The Photographers' Gallery, London; International Cultureel Centrum, Antwerp; and Optica Gallery, Montreal, 1973-76)
1974	*Viva Photographers,* Centaur Gallery, Montreal
1975	*Viva,* French Cultural Center, New York
1976	*Viva Fotografien,* Galerie Wilde, Cologne
1977	*10 Ans de Photojournalisme en France,* Musée Galliera, Paris
	A Certain Image of French Photography, Fondation Nationale de la Photographie (Lyons) travelling exhibition (toured the United States)
1980	*Political Photographs,* Project Studio One, New York
1982	*Photographie Contemporaine en France,* ARC/Musée d'Art Moderne, Paris
1985	*Paysages Photographies,* Palais de Tokyo, Paris (toured France)
1986	*Initiatief,* Abbaye Saint Pierre, Ghent, Belgium

Collections:

Bibliothèque Nationale, Paris; Fondation Nationale de la Photographie, Lyons; Musée de Toulon, France; Fonds Régional d'Art Contemporain, Pasde-Calis, France; Fonds National d'Art Contemporain, Paris.

Publications:

By HERS: Books—*Intérieurs: Photographies de François Hers et Sophie Ristelhueber,* with an introduction by Jean-François Chevrier, Paris 1981; *François Hers: Le Récit,* with text by Jean-François Chevrier, Paris 1981, Brussels and London 1983. **Articles**—"Reportage sur la Police" in *Zoom* (Paris), no. 32, 1975; "Les Reporters pendant la Révolution Portugaise" in *Photo* (Paris), no. 99, 1975.

On HERS: Books—*French Photography from its Origins to the Present* by Claude Nori, Paris 1978, London 1979; *Jeune Photographie,* exhibition catalogue, with introduction by Bernard Chardere, Paris 1980; *Paysages Photographies: La Mission Photographique de la DATAR—travaux en cours 1984/1985,* with texts by Bernard Latarjet, Jean-François Chevrier and others, Paris 1985. **Article**—"Viva Looks at Family Life" in *Amateur Photographer* (London), 7 March 1973; radio broadcast—"François Hers: Photographe," French Radio, November 1980.

*

What is the function of photography? I find the answer to this question, which determines all my work, in certain images. I find it, too in the performances I produce when the opportunity arises or where I find it necessary.

1967: "Take photos or take them from your family albums and tell the story of your life from birth to death." With the selection that resulted I carried out a commission to decorate a large wall in a factory with images.

1969: In a multinational advertising agency on the occasion of a preview, I took a photograph of each employee, enlarged it to the format of an advertising poster and exhibited it in the precise position where each employee worked.

1970: At a workshop in one of the Beaux-Arts schools, on the theme, What is photography? I placed my cameras on a table and asked the students in turn and when they felt like it to be photographer and photographed.

1971: At a center for mentally and physically handicapped children I took photos and projected them without comment. The children recognized themselves as in reality, but the medical personnel didn't recognize the children with whom they lived all the time.

1972: Co-Founder of the Viva group. I suggested that each member report on the theme, "Family Life." Each of us lived for some weeks with a family in France. We produced an exhibition of these reportages that circulated throughout Europe and North America but was rejected in France.

1976: For a commission on the "40th Anniversary of Holidays with Pay" I photographed the French on holiday and composed an ethnographic record under the headings, *Initiation—Memory—Totems.*

1977: Intervention in a retrospective exhibition on photojournalism. I produced a mural panel of 2 x 5 metres made up of six photos which show that all press photography is a fiction—a fiction which I create which does not need captions.

1976/79: I produced a photographic and autobiographical fiction in the form of a book and an exhibition. I returned to my country, Belgium, and searched there for the secular and contemporary myths of my culture.

1980: An exposure of myself as a reporter. I studied the relationship of the photographer and his subject. The subject is naked; my left hand enters the frame and comes into contact with him; my right hand takes the photograph.

1981: *François Hers: Récit*—a book. A summing up and two complex ensembles—images, texts, lay-outs.

—François Hers

*   *   *

François Hers is careful to present his photographs in groups which are relevant to him as "reportage." The term signifies a manner of reflecting on photography; it is also a method of reflecting *by* photography—the contradictions of which he does not try to avoid. His work involves a balance between reasoning and spontaneity, which is not so apparent in each individual photo (as it would be, say, with Cartier-Bresson, who is a rather distant influence) as in the group or movement created by the whole. His improvisation is guided by an initial decision: it defines the aim of the reportage, its final state, and the necessary technical resources, but it also involves the right of freedom along the way.

In his view every photographic investigation is an action: if it is necessary, it is worth carrying through. He defines for himself its preliminary significance. In certain instances this approach could be related to conceptual research and extend far beyond the photographic context. But Hers acknowledges that the "meaning" of the action undertaken is basically unforeseeable.

Hers is not much attracted to that unique and irreplaceable miracle-photography practiced by a large school, more or less successfully, in France. He does not look for that balance between availability and mastery of chance, but he does admit that anyone who works with the instantaneous commits himself to a long and mainly unconscious adventure without reliable points of reference.

Hers is not searching for the photographic "happening." He likes to say that he does not know how to see, that he perceives atmosphere rather than visual organization. He readily goes very close to his subject until he can touch it. These characteristics suggest a comparison with William Klein.

His reportage, in fact, involves two contradictory and yet complementary tendencies: the need for decision, for preliminary and considered choice, and the inability of any image to satisfy a search which is in principle indefinite, because it is, of course, autobiographical. It is not surprising that the greatest number of pictures in his book *François Hers: Récit* are of Belgium where he was born and lived for a long time.

—Jean-François Chevrier

HEYMAN, Abigail.

Nationality: American. **Born:** Danbury, Connecticut, in August 1942. **Education:** Studied at Sarah Lawrence College, Bronxville, New York, B.A. 1964; studied photography under Ken Heyman (no relation) and Charles Harbutt, 1967. **Career:** Freelance photographer, working for *Life, Time,* the *New York Times, Ms.,* etc., New York, since 1967. Co-founder and Director of Picture Project Inc, 1989 to date. Visiting Instructor, International Center of Photography, New York. **Address:** 40 West 12th Street, New York, New York 10011, U.S.A.

Individual Exhibitions:

1975	Friends of Photography, Carmel, California (with Paul Caponigro)
1979	Arizona State University, Tempe
1982	O.K. Harris Gallery, New York
1985	Fine Arts Center, University of Rhode Island, Kingston

Selected Group Exhibitions:

1985	*Espejo: Reflections of One Mexican-American,* Oakland Museum
1987	*Un si grand age,* Palais de Tokyo, Paris
	Photographs from 1987 Books, International Center of Photography, New York
1988	*A Kiss Is Just a Kiss,* Velick Gallery, San Francisco
1992	*Our Town,* Burden Gallery of Aperture Foundation, New York
1993	*Aperture's 40th Anniversary,* Burden Gallery, New York

Publications:

By HEYMAN: Book—*Growing Up Female: A Personal Photo-Journal,* New York 1974; *Butcher, Baker, Cabinet-Maker: Photographs of Women at Work,* New York 1978; *Dreams and Schemes: Love and Marriage in Modern Times,* Aperture 1987; co-editor of *Flesh and Blood: Photographers' Images of Their Own Families,* Picture Project 1992.

On HEYMAN: Book—*Women of Photography: An Historical Survey,* edited by Margery Mann and Ann Noggle, San Francisco 1975. **Articles**—"Abigail Heyman and Imogen Cunningham" by A.D. Coleman in the *New York Times,* 30 June 1974, reprinted in Coleman's *Light Readings: A Photography Critic's Writings 1968-1978,* New York 1979; "Abigail Heyman" in *In/Sights: Self-Portraits by Women,* edited by Joyce Tenneson Cohen, London 1979.

*　　*　　*

Abigail Heyman is known primarily for the feminist-inspired works found in her book, *Growing Up Female: A Personal Photo-Journal,* which is an attempt to document, to capture, a sense of the struggle all women experience growing up in a male-dominated society. As she says in her introduction, "This book is about women, and their lives as women, from one feminist's point of view. It is about what women are doing and what they are feeling, and

Untitled, **from the series** ***Dreams and Schemes,*** **1986.** Photograph ©Abigail Heyman.

how they are relating to their mates, their children, their friends, their interests, and themselves.''

The photographs show girls and women engaged in activities that promote the kinds of stereotyped roles which often lead to isolation, frustration, and alienation. Scenes such as girls playing with dolls; children playing hospital in which the boys are doctors and the girls are nurses; pensive young women tending children while the husband eats by himself; or another woman sitting alone at the laundromat—all present a strong and consciously biased point of view. Because the images come from autobiographical experience and deep personal feeling, they leave little room for debate. Much of their effect comes from the intensity of feeling from which they were created.

When Heyman photographed for ''Espejo,'' a project documenting the Mexican-American culture in California, she naturally focused on the female experience. Weddings and other rituals provided scenes in which to study clothing, attitudes, and expressions of these women who exist in a milieu dominated by an overtly macho sensibility. But because these girls and women come from a different cultural background than she does, Heyman's photographs are somewhat reserved; they are less judgmental than her other works. Nevertheless, her basic sympathy for women's identity struggle in a male-oriented culture still shows through. Her ardent concern for this issue is matched only by her strong desire not to separate her art from her life. She obviously believes that photography should reflect the realities of our lives.

—Ted Hedgpeth

HILL, Paul.

Nationality: British. **Born:** Ludlow, Shropshire, 15 December 1941. **Education:** Ludlow Grammar School, 1952-55; Oswestry Boys' High School, Shropshire, 1955-58; self-taught in photography. **Family:** Married Angela Starkey in 1964; children: Samantha and Dominic. **Career:** Reporter, *Border Counties Advertiser* newspaper, Oswestry, 1959-61; Outdoor Pursuits Instructor, Plas Gwynant, North Wales, 1962; Reporter and Columnist, *Express and Star* group, Wolverhampton, 1962-65; freelance photographer, working for *The Observer, Telegraph Magazine, Financial Times, Radio Times, New Society, The Guardian,* etc., London, 1965-74. Since 1976, Founder-Director, The Photographers' Place workshop and study centre, Bradbourne, Derbyshire. Part-time Lecturer, 1971-74, Senior Lecturer, 1974-76, and Principal Lecturer in Creative Photography, 1976-78, Trent Polytechnic, Nottingham; Visiting Lecturer, Derby Lonsdale College of Higher Education, 1980-81; Visiting Lecturer, Sheffield Polytechnic, 1978-81. Chairman, Photography Committee, West Midlands Arts Association, 1974-75; Secretary, Society for Photographic Education, 1974-75; Member of the Photography Committee, 1977-80, and Chairman of the Support to Photographers Committee, 1978, Arts Council of Great Britain; External Examiner, City of London Polytechnic, London, and West Surrey College of Art and Design, Farnham, 1985-88; External Examiner, University of Humberside, Hull 1989-94; De Montfort University, Leicester 1991-94; Gwent College of Higher Education, 1993-96. External Adviser, Glasgow School of Art, from 1983, and Derbyshire College of Higher Education, from 1985; Vice-Chairman of the Visual Arts Panel, East Midlands Arts Association, 1982-84. Director of East Midlands Arts, Loughborough 1991-96. Elected Fellow of the Royal Photographic Society 1990. Chairman of the RPS Contemporary Group 1989-95 and the Contemporary Distinctions Panel 1992-98. Chairman of the Arts 2000 Derby steering group, *The Year of Photography and the Electronic Image,* 1993-94. Moderator with Business and Technology Education Council since 1992. Awarded major grant by Hasselblad Foundation, Sweden 1993. Adviser Derby Festival of Photography, beginning in 1990. **Recipient:** Midland Press Photographer of the Year Award, 1967. Member of the Order of the British Empire, 1994. **Address:** The Photographers' Place, Bradbourne, Ashbourne, Derbyshire DE6 1PB, England.

Individual Exhibitions:

1971	Wolverhampton Art Gallery
1972	The Photographers' Gallery, London
1973	Birmingham Repertory Theatre
1975	*Remnants and Prenotations,* Arnolfini Gallery, Bristol
	The Warwick Gallery, England (with Thomas Joshua Cooper)
	3 Photographers, Galleria Il Diaframma, Milan (with Thomas Joshua Cooper and John Blakemore)
1976	*Tom Cooper and Paul Hill,* Friends of Photography, Carmel, California (travelled to the University of Oregon, Eugene)
1977	*3 Photographers: Cooper, Hill, Moore,* Focus Gallery, San Francisco (with Thomas Joshua Cooper and Raymond Moore)
	La Photo Galerie, Madrid
	Photographers' Gallery, Melbourne
	Fotogaleriet, Oslo
1978	Robert Self Gallery, London
	Arnolfini Gallery, Bristol
	Canon Photo Gallery, Amsterdam
1979	*Towards the Inevitable,* ffotogallery, Cardiff
	Ian Birksted Gallery, Hampstead, London
	On the Edge of All Things, Spectro Arts Workshop, Newcastle upon Tyne
	Salzburg College, Austria
	Photogallery, St. Leonards-on-Sea, Sussex
1980	Graves Art Gallery, Sheffield
	Sudley Art Gallery, Liverpool
1981	*On Land,* Camden Arts Centre, London
	Contrasts Gallery, London
	Leeds Playhouse Gallery
	Kimberlin Exhibition Hall, Leicester
	Coimbra University, Portugal
1982	Galleri Camera Obscura, Stockholm
	Sir John Cass School of Art, London
	Humberside College, Hull,
	Lonsdale College of Higher Education, Derby
1984	*Land Marks,* Glasgow School of Art, Scotland
	Dundee College of Art, Scotland
	Stirling University, Scotland
	St. Andrews University, Scotland
	Axiom Centre for the Arts, Cheltenham, Gloucestershire
1985	South Hill Park Arts Centre, Bracknell, Berkshire
	Minories Art Gallery, Colchester, Essex
	Newlyn Orion Gallery, Cornwall
	Plymouth Art Centre, Devon
	Midland Group Gallery, Nottingham
	Buxton Museum and Art Gallery, Derbyshire
1986	Gallery of Photography, Dublin
1987	The Metro, Derby
	Northampton College of Further Education
	Chester Fringe Festival
1990	Untitled Gallery, Sheffield
	Buxton Museum and Art Gallery
	Street Level Gallery, Glasgow
	Stills Gallery, Edinburgh
	Metro Gallery, Derby
1991	Gallery of Photography, Dublin
	City Art Gallery, Limerick
	Festival of Photography, Derby
	Royal Photographic Society, Bath
1992	The Photographers' Gallery, London
1994	Pendle Art Gallery, Nelson
1995	Derby Museum and Art Gallery

Selected Group Exhibitions:

1966	*World Press Photo,* The Hague
1973	*Serpentine Photography '73,* Serpentine Gallery, London
1975	*Young British Photographers,* Museum of Modern Art, Oxford (toured Europe and the United States)
1977	*Photography into Art,* Kassel, West Germany (toured Europe and the United States)
1979	*Contemporary European Photography,* at *Venezia '79,* Italy

Tree Shadows and Wall, **Hall Dale, Stanshope, 1989.** Photograph ©Paul Hill.

1980	*Old and Modern Masters of Photography,* Victoria and Albert Museum, London
1981	*Photography as Medium,* British Council, London (and world tour)
1982	*Ten Contemporary British Photographers,* Massachusetts Institute of Technology, Cambridge (toured the United States)
1983	*Faces and Places,* Museum of Fine Arts, Montreal.
1984	*Creation—Modern Art and Nature,* Scottish National Gallery, Edinburgh
	Make 'em Laugh, Open Eye Gallery, Liverpool
1985	*Human Interest,* Cornerhouse Art Centre, Manchester
	The Window, Fox Talbot Museum, Lacock
	Axiom Review, Axiom Centre for the Arts, Cheltenham
	Salzburg College 10th Anniversary, Galerie Fotohof, Salzburg
1988	*Realities Revisited,* Centre Saidye Bronfman, Montreal (toured Canada)
1989	*Through the Looking Glass—British Photography 1945-89,* Barbican Art Gallery, London
	Personal Viewpoints, Rufford Country Park, Nottinghamshire
1993	*Picture Freedom* (S. African voter education), Photographers Gallery, London
	View from Above, GAFF, Rotenburg, Germany
1994	*Family Affairs,* Montage Gallery, Derby

Collections:

British Council, London; Victoria and Albert Museum, London; Arts Council of Great Britain, London; Department of the Environment, London; Graves Art Gallery, Sheffield; West Midlands Arts Association, Sheffield; East Midlands Arts Association, Loughborough; Gwent College of Higher Educa-

tion Library, Newport; Bibliothèque Nationale, Paris; Moderna Museet, Stockholm; Visual Studies Workshop, Rochester, New York; Museum of Fine Arts, Houston; British Film Institute; Suffolk County Museum; Arthur Andersen & Co; Derbyshire Museum Service; Australian National Gallery, Canberra; Japanese Photography Foundation, Tokyo.

Publications:

By HILL: Books—*Young Contemporaries,* Introduction in *Creative Camera Yearbook,* London 1977; *Photographic Truth, Metaphor and Individual Expression* in *3 Perspectives on Photography,* exhibition catalogue, London 1979; *Dialogue with Photography,* with Thomas Cooper, London and New York 1979, Barcelona 1980, Tokyo 1986, Manchester 1992; *Contact Theory,* (ed. Ralph Gibson), New York 1980; *Approaching Photography,* with foreword by Aaron Scharf, London 1982; *Land Marks,* exhibition catalogue, Cheltenham, Gloucestershire 1984; *Second Nature,* edited by Richard Mabey, Sue Clifford and Angela King, London 1984; *White Peak Dark Peak,* Manchester 1990. **Articles**—"Cause for Concern" in *Photography* (London), October 1969; "Covering the Candidates" in *Photography* (London), November 1970; "Is Photography a Non-Art?" in *Artefact* (Loughborough), no. 1, 1972; "Photojournalism—The British Obsession" in *Photographic Journal* (London), November 1973; "Can British Photography Emerge from the Dark Ages?," with Thomas Cooper, in *Creative Camera* (London), September 1974; "Apropos Great Britain" and "Apropos Arles" in *Camera* (Lucerne), August and November 1976; "Photo-initiatives in Europe: The Photographers' Place" in *European Photography* (Göttingen), July/September 1980; "Hill's Hills" in *SLR Camera* (London), September 1983; "Personal View" in *Creative Photography* (Peterborough), May 1985; "Ansel By Himself" in *British Journal of Photography* (London), 17 January 1986; "Why Is Independent Photography so Starved?" *Creative Camera* (London),

July 1986; "What Is Independent Photography?" *Exposure,* (Dublin), December 1990; "Jo Spence—A Personal Tribute," *Contemporary Photography* (RPS Bath), Autumn 1992; "Should Photographers Watch Their Language?" *Contemporary Photography* (RPS Bath), Summer 1993 and *Exposure* (Dublin) May 1993 and *Review* (Newsletter of the Friends of Photography, San Francisco), Sept/Oct 1993; "Watch Your Language!" *The Photographic Journal* (RPS Bath) October 1993. **Film**—script and commentary, with Thomas Cooper, for *Arena: Paul Strand,* BBC Television, 1976.

On HILL: Books—*Serpentine Photography '73,* exhibition catalogue, by Peter Turner, London 1973; *Young British Photographers,* exhibition catalogue, by Chris Steele-Perkins and Mark Edwards, Oxford 1975; *Photography into Art,* exhibition catalogue, edited by Floris Neusüss, Kassel, West Germany 1977; *Geschichte der Photographie im 20. Jahrhundert/History of Photography in the 20th Century* by Petr Tausk, Cologne 1977, London 1980; *Exploring Photography* by Bryn Campbell, London 1978; *Photography as Medium,* exhibition catalogue, by Teresa Gleadowe, London 1981; *About 70 Photographs,* edited by Chris Steele-Perkins and William Messer, London 1981; *The Art of Photography* by Time-Life editors, New York 1982; *Lichtbildnisse: Das Porträt in der Fotografie,* edited by Klaus Honnef, Cologne 1982; *New Photography in Europe,* edited by Andreas Müller-Pohle, Cologne 1982; *Photographers Photographed* by Bill Jay, Salt Lake City, Utah 1983; *Human Interest,* exhibition catalogue, by Norbert Lynton, Manchester 1985; *The Arts of Britain* (ed. Edwin Mullins) London 1983; *World History of Photography* by Naomi Rosenblum, New York 1984 and 1989; *History of Photography* by Peter Turner, London 1987; *Tradition and the Unpredictable* (ed Chasenhoff, Traub, Tucker), Houston 1994. **Articles**—"Camera Flashes of Pure Insight" by Anthony Everitt in the *Birmingham Post,* June 1971; "Paul Hill" by Robert Ray in *The Guardian* (London), June 1971; "On View" by Ainslie Ellis in *British Journal of Photography* (London), 23 May 1975; "Paul Hill and Thomas Cooper" in *Artweek* (Oakland, California), 17 July 1976; "Shows We've Seen" in *Popular Photography* (New York), November 1976; "Three British Photographers" in *Artweek* (Oakland, California), 22 January 1977; "Singular Realities" in *The Guardian* (London), March 1977; "Paul Hill and the New British Photography" by Els Sincebaugh in *Camera 35* (New York), November 1977; "Paul Hill: Dynamic in British Photography" by Inge Bondi in *Printletter* (Zurich), January 1978; "Art Review" by Marina Vaizey in the *Sunday Times* (London), 5 February 1978; "Art: Welds and Weaves" by John McEwan in *The Spectator* (London), 11 February 1978; "Photography" by Caroline Tisdall in *The Guardian* (London), 29 January 1979; "Britain's New Wave" in *Modern Photography* (New York), February 1979; "Photomaster Class" in *The Observer Magazine* (London), 8 April 1979; "Viewed: Paul Hill" in the *British Journal of Photography* (London), 13 July 1979; "Photography: Social and Sensual" by Sarah Kent in *Fotografie als Kunst,* Cologne 1979; "Contemporary European Photography" by Sue Davies in *Photography: Venezia '79,* Milan and New York 1979; "A Breath of Fresh Air" by Marina Vaizey in *The Sunday Times* (London), 1 February 1981; "Paul Hill at Camden" by Ian Jeffrey in *Creative Camera* (London), August 1981; "Paul Hill—On Land" by Rupert Martin in *European Photography* (Göttingen), no.8, 1981; "Whither Documentary?" by Linda Benedict-Jones in *Positive* (Cambridge, Massachusetts), 1982 "A Conversation with Paul Hill" by Robert Holmes in *Darkroom* (San Francisco), November 1985; "Spying on Nature" by Jane Richards in *The Independent* (London) 19 March 1990; "Understanding the Landscape's Secret Language" by Eamonn McCabe in *The Guardian,* London, 3 March 1990; "White Peak Dark Peak" by Bill Bishop *The British Journal of Photography,* 24 May 1990; "Paul Hill" by Ray McKenzie, *Portfolio,* Edinburgh, Summer 1990; "Small Adventures" by Roger Taylor in *Creative Camera,* London Aug/Sept 1990; "Photographic Reviews" by Murdo Macdonald in *The Scotsman,* Edinburgh, 17 August 1990; "Marks of the Peakland Landscape" by Edward Bowman *The Photographic Journal,* Bath, October 1990; "The Sound of One Eye Watching" by Eamonn McCabe in *The Guardian,* 1 December 1990; "White Peak Dark Peak" by Tage Poulsen, *Katalog,* Odense, Denmark, December 1990; "Photography" by Dave Lee *Arts Review* 8 February 1991; "Quality Control" by William Bishop, *The British Journal of Photography,* London, 12 March 1992; "From Photograph to Image," by David Brittain and Jim Harold, *Creative Camera,* London April/May 1993. **Films**—*Exploring Photography,* BBC Television film, by Bryn Campbell,

1978; *Contrasts: Double Exposure,* Central Television film, by Jim Berrow, 1982; *First Night,* Central Television, 1990; *Off the Wall,* BBC Television, 1993.

*

Photography has provided me with a vehicle for exploring and observing both the external and the internal. No other medium can do these things as well as photography can. The symbiotic relationship between form and content in photography gives it great power. But the monumental importance of its unique qualities is rarely considered. This only reflects the myopia of most people when considering something so ubiquitous as photography. This ignorance also reflects badly on the status of visual education, in both practice and theory. Considering the welter of photographic imagery bombarding us each day, this neglect is inexcusable.

Photography is more than Art—and it is more than a vehicle for information. The subject matter in my photographs is crucial, but I hope the images transcend the purely representational. For me, the photographic print *is* the "event," not an objective record of what was in front of the camera at the time of exposure. First-hand experience of the actual world is a *different* "event," which I find too complicated, or too transitory, to record. The camera anchors me to an idea or a place, and this helps me filter out the surplus and superficial elements in order that I might get somewhere near the *essence.*

—Paul Hill

*   *   *

Paul Hill's life in photography has been shaped by his conviction that the photographic record is more than a simple inventory of appearances. The discovery of what, for him, is the nature of that further dimension, and the need to communicate with others about it, led Paul Hill away from commercial photographic documentation towards an area most readily described as a fine art orientated practice, located within the context of photographic education.

Happy coincidences of chance and directed effort have brought about Paul Hill's progress through major institutions, such as Trent Polytechnic and the Arts Council, to a situation in which, running his own small photographic workshops, he has largely reconciled the different aspects of his ambitions.

Certain parallels may be inferred in the evolution of Paul Hill's photographs. Those made during the first phases of his commitment to photography considered as art were presented at the Arnolfini Gallery, during 1975, under the generic title *Prenotations.* Their tenor is urban and technological. The angularities, burn outs and fragmentations bring an atmosphere of the synthetic and the mass-produced even to those images dealing with the natural and the craft-made. Dictates of framing and the effects of abnormal brightness ranges are imposed as a major component of a perceiver's experience of the photographs, and contribute to the sense of stressfulness evoked. Indeed, the title itself refers to the idea that the moments shown contain disquieting, enigmatic prefigurations of impending events.

Although subsequent work remained visually tense, as a result of his concern with the dynamics and ambiguities available through the employment of unconventional framing techniques, certain shifts in emphasis, especially the increasingly domestic subject matter, led to a great reduction in the anxiety to be seen in Paul Hill's images.

Since living in the Derbyshire countryside Paul Hill has made what he considers to be an inevitable further move into photographs dealing with the landscape in terms of man's marks upon it, while continuing to attend to the properties of the photographic medium as a mark-making process. The keynote has tended to be one of contemplation and balance, but the intrusion of modern developments, reservoir construction for instance, returns a degree of anxiety and tension to the work. Distributed across the photographs and accompanying texts, it has resulted in what Paul Hill has remarked is "as much a display of passionate compromise as it is a celebration of where I live."

—Philip Stokes

HILLIARD, John.

Nationality: British. **Born:** Lancaster, 29 March 1945. **Education:** Studied at Lancaster College of Art, 1962-64; St. Martin's School of Art, London, 1964-67, Dip. A.D. 1967. **Career:** Artist and photographer since 1967. Part-time Instructor, Somerset College of Art, Taunton, 1968-71. Part-time Lecturer, Brighton Polytechnic, 1969-76, and since 1979; Rijksakademie van Beeldende Kunsten, Amsterdam, 1994; Chelsea College of Art, 1994. **Recipient:** Visual Arts Fellowship, Northern Arts Association, 1976-78; David Octavius Hill Medal, Gesellschaft Deutscher Lichtbildner, Cologne, 1986. **Agent:** Lisson Gallery, 67 Lisson Street, London NW1; Galerie Durand-Dessert, 28 rue de Lappe, 75011 Paris, France. **Address:** The Vicarage, 49 Chatham Street, London SE17 1PA, England.

Individual Exhibitions:

1969	Camden Arts, Centre, London
1970	Lisson Gallery, London
1971	Lisson Gallery, London
1973	Lisson Gallery, London
1974	Museum of Modern Art, Oxford
	Galleria Toselli, Milan
1975	Lisson Gallery, London
	Galleria Banco, Brescia, Italy
1976	Galerie Hetzler + Keller, Stuttgart
	Galerie Durand-Dessert, Paris
	Robert Self Gallery, Newcastle upon Tyne
1977	Badischer Kunstverein, Karlsruhe
	Galerie Durand-Dessert, Paris
	Paul Maenz Gallery, Cologne
1978	Galerie Akumulatory 2, Poznan, Poland
	Galleria Banco, Brescia, Italy
	Studio Paola Betti, Milan
	John Gibson Gallery, New York
	Lisson Gallery, London
	Laing Art Gallery, Newcastle upon Tyne
1979	Ikon Gallery, Birmingham
	Galerie Foksal, Warsaw
	Galerie Durand-Dessert, Paris
1980	Galerie Max Hetzler, Stuttgart
	Lisson Gallery, London
1981	Orchard Gallery, Londonderry, Northern Ireland
	Galerie Durand-Dessert, Paris
1982	Amano Gallery, Osaka, Japan
	Ryo Gallery, Kyoto, Japan
1983	Galerie Durand-Dessert, Paris
	Kunstverein, Cologne
1984	Kunstverein, Bremen, West Germany
	Kunstverein, Frankfurt
	Kettle's Yard Gallery, Cambridge, England
	Institute of Contemporary Arts, London
	Galerie Media, Neuchatel, Switzerland
	Musée d'Art Moderne de la Ville, Paris (with Dennis Oppenheim)
1985	Galerie Grita Insam, Vienna
1990	Kunstverein, Stuttgart
1992	Galerie Durand-Dessert, Paris
	Art Affairs, Amsterdam
1993	Musée des Beaux-Arts, La Chaix-de Fonds, France
	Galerie Gutsch, Berlin
1994	Galerie de L'Ancienne Poste, Calais, France

Selected Group Exhibitions:

1971	*New English Enquiry,* at the *Bienal de São Paulo*
1972	*The New Art,* Hayward Gallery, London
1976	*The Artist and the Photograph,* Israel Museum, Jerusalem
1977	*Malerei und Photographie im Dialog,* Kunsthaus, Zurich
1979	*Photographie als Kunst 1879-1979,* Tiroler Landesmuseum Ferdinandeum, Innsbruck, Austria (travelled to Neue Galerie am Wolfgang Gurlitt Museum, Linz, Austria; Neue Galerie am Landesmuseum Joanneum, Graz, Austria; and Museum des 20. Jahrhunderts, Vienna)
1980	*Artist and Camera,* Mappin Art Gallery, Sheffield, Yorkshire (travelled to Stoke City Art Gallery; Durham Light Infantry Museum; Cartwright Hall, Bradford)
1981	*Extended Photography,* at the *5th Biennale,* Vienna
1983	*Kunst mit Photographie,* Nationalgalerie, West Berlin
1984	*Construire les Paysages de la Photographie,* Caves Saint-Croix, Metz, France
1985	*Das Aktfoto,* Fotomuseum im Stadtmuseum, Munich (toured Germany)
	New Art, Anthony Reynolds Gallery, London
	Thought Objects, Cash-Newhouse Gallery, New York
	Hand Signals, Ikon Gallery, Birmingham
	Forty Years of Modern Art, Tate Gallery, London
1986	*Kunst-Raum/Raum-Kunst,* Schloss Buchberg, Austria
	Prospect 86, Schirn Kunsthalle, Frankfurt
1987	*Blow-Up,* Württ, Kunstverein, Stuttgart
	Heavenly Embrace, Baskerville & Watson Gallery, New York
	The Other Body, Photographic Resource Center, Boston University
1988	*Photography on the Edge,* Haggerty Museum of Art, Milwaukee
	Starlit Waters, Tate Gallery, Liverpool
	Das gläserne U-Boot, Tabakfabrik, Krems/Stein
	Furkart '88, Furka Pass, Schweiz
	Fotovision, Sprengel Museum, Hannover
	Britannica: Trente Ans De Sculpture, Musée des Beaux-Arts, Le Havre
	That Which Appears Is Good, That Which Is Good Appears, Galerie Tanja Grunert, Köln
	Galleri Contur, Stockholm (with Lum, Kruger, Prince, Wall)
1989	*Beyond Photography,* Krygier/Landau Contemporary Art, Los Angeles
	Foto Biennale, Rijksmuseum, Enschede
	Dart Gallery, Chicago
	Facing the Camera, Galerie Grita Insam, Wien
	Prospect-Photographie, Kunstverein, Frankfurt
	Through the Looking Glass, Barbican Art Gallery, London
	Fotokopie—Fotografie und Imitation, Gewerbemuseum, Basel
	Das Foto als autonomes Bilde, Kunsthalle Bielefeld, Kunstakademie München
	Photo-Kunst, Staatsgalerie, Stuttgart
1990	*Der Collectie Alsnoch,* Provinciaal Museum, Hasselt
1991	*Histoire d'Oeil,* Musée d'Art Contemporain, Lyon
	Nouvel Espace, Galerie Durand-Dessert, Paris
	New Spaces Of Photography, Muzeum Architektury, Wroclaw
1992	*Le Printemps de La Photo,* Chantrerie, Cahors
	Whitechapel Open, Whitechapel Art Gallery, London
	Paysage en Exergue, Espace Art Brenne, Le Blanc
	Sprung In Die Zeit, Berlinische Galerie, Berlin
	International Photo-Triennale, Stadt Museum, Esslingen
1993	*Out Of Sight, Out Of Mind,* Lisson Gallery, London
	Moving Into View, South Bank Centre, London
1994	*Conceptual Photographs 2,* John Gibson Gallery, New York (with Adams, Beckley, Cumming and Le Gac)

Collections:

Tate Gallery, London; Victoria and Albert Museum, London; Leeds City Art Gallery; Centre Georges Pompidou, Paris; Kunsthalle, Hamburg; Kunsthaus, Zurich; Museum of Fine Arts, Lodz, Poland; Art Gallery of South Australia, Adelaide; Museum Moderner Kunst, Vienna; Metropolitan Museum, Tokyo.

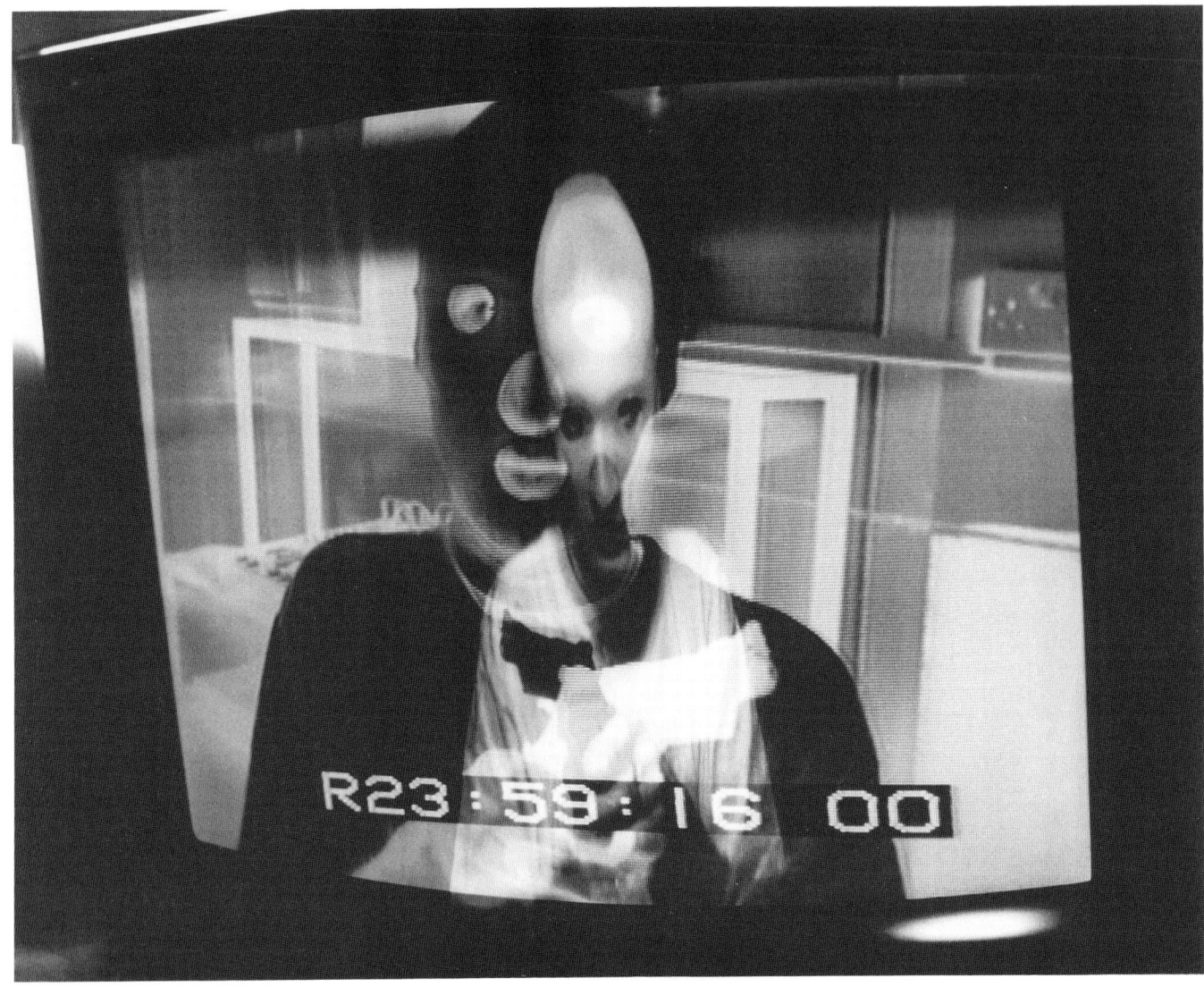

Closed Circuit, **1991.** Photograph by John Hilliard.

Publications:

By HILLIARD: Books—*Elemental Conditioning,* Oxford 1974; *Black Depths, White Expanse,* London 1976; *From the Northern Counties,* London 1978; *Borderland,* exhibition catalogue, Londonderry 1981; *John Hilliard: This. Here. Now.,* exhibition catalogue, Cambridge 1984; *Satellite,* exhibition catalogue, London 1987; *Backwards, Forwards and Sideways,* exhibition catalogue, London 1990. **Articles**—"Unpopulated Rural Black and White Exteriors, Populated Urban Colored Interiors" in *Aspects* (London), Winter 1977; "John Hilliard," interview, with Ian Kirkwood, in *Art Log* (London), Summer 1978; "John Hilliard," interview, with Colin Painter, in *Aspects* (London), Autumn 1978; "Drawings (in anticipation) of Photographs" in *Aspects* (London), no. 16, 1981; "Inverse Correspondences" in *Furor* (Geneva), no. 10, 1983.

On HILLIARD: Books—*The New Art,* exhibition catalogue, by Anne Seymour, London 1972; *Arte Inglese Oggi,* exhibition catalogue, by Luca Venturi and others, Milan 1976; *Analytical Photography* by Manfred Schmalreide, Karlsruhe 1977; *Fotografie als Kunst/Kunst als Fotographie* by Floris Neusüss, Cologne 1979; *Kunst als Photographie* by Peter Weiermair, Innsbruck 1979; *The Artist as Photographer* by Marina Vaizey, London 1982; *John Hilliard,* exhibition catalogue, with texts by Jean Fisher and Wulf

Herzogenrath, Cologne 1983; *Construire les Paysages de la Photographie,* exhibition catalogue, by Jean-Françoise Chevrier, Jean-Marc Poinsot and Michele Chomette, Metz, France 1984; *John Hilliard: Allegories of Law,* exhibition catalogue, with text by Michael Newman, London 1984; exhibition catalogue, Kettle's Yard Gallery, Cambridge 1984; exhibition catalogue, Institute of Contemporary Art, London 1984; exhibition catalogue, Provinciaal Museum, Hasselt 1986; exhibition catalogue, Renaissance Society, University of Chicago 1989; *Vanitas,* exhibition catalogue, Stuttgart 1990; *Scene,* exhibition catalogue, La Chaux-de-Fonds 1993. **Articles**—"3 Pieces by John Hilliard" in *Studio International* (London), April 1972; "Artist as Filmmaker" by Annable Nicolson in *Art and Artists* (London), December 1972; "From Sculpture to Photography: John Hilliard and the Issue of Self-Awareness in Medium Use" by Richard Cork in *Studio International* (London), July/August 1975; "John Hilliard—scenes gelées par des temps differents" by Regis Durand in *Art Press* (Paris), March 1984; "Old Building, New Art" by Brian Haton in *Apollo* (London), May 1990; "John Hilliard: Vanitas" by Johannes Meinhardt in *Kunstforum International* (Cologne), no. 109, 1990; "Le Printemps de La Photo à Cahors" by Régis Durand in *Art Press* (Paris), no 170, June 1992; review by Brian Hatton in *Art Monthly* (London), no. 159, September 1992; review by Frank-Alexander Hettig in *Forum International* (Antwerp), no 15, 1992; "Les Vampires Sortent La Nuit," interview with Patrick Bougelet, Denis-Laurent Bouyer and Richard Klein in *Sans Titre,* No.

25 (Lille), 1994; "Hilliard: Derrière Le Miroir" by Mo Gourmelon in *Beaux-Arts,* No. 21 (Paris), 1994.

*

During the last two or three years, the work that I have produced has sought to be more compressed. In a physical sense, this has entailed a reduction from the diptych to a single panel, and a consequent diminution in overall size. In a structural sense, this singularity has required that the dialectic previously established between juxtaposed modules (through a strategy of comparing and contrasting) must now be operative within one picture area. To this end, three distinct spaces are articulated—an illusory "beyond" the spectator's own space in front of the picture; and the territory of the picture-plane itself. A triad of comparisons is then established between these zones.

Initially, this was achieved by choosing emphatically recessive backgrounds to draw the eye "into" the picture; by optically thrusting picture elements "outwards"; and by masking off areas during printing so that finally the surface of the support itself is revealed to form a third image "across" the other two.

In a second body of work, these spatial divisions have been accommodated through the use of a triple-exposure—addressing a subject from a fixed position, but making separate exposures, one on top of the other, to register in turn the foreground, midground and background. Using a very shallow depth of field, the camera lens, like a probing eye, alights successively at specific points within an otherwise unfocused vista. Most frequently, the camera's view is towards a pane of glass, whose simultaneous capability to function as visible surface, transparent medium and reflective mirror, allows the separated yet overlaid introduction of elements "through," "at" and "in front of" the picture-plane (the third level being available as a reflection).

These methodologies are not ends in themselves, however. They seek to provide an organised dialectical space—an arena into which "innocent" picture elements are politely invited, only to be drawn unwittingly into a loaded conversation, which the spectator, like an eavesdropping detective, reading between the lines, must strive to unravel.

In many of these works the "conversationalists" are indeed men and women, but in the most recent they have been banished, replaced instead by their various sources of illumination (whether electrical bulbs or candles; a television screen or a bonfire). Through these emanations of radiated or reflected light, any narrative suggestion is no longer shouted out loud, but communicated rather as a whisper; any human presence is registered not as an actual sighting, but merely as a trace. The sense of "story," then, is less upfront, less pronounced, signalled only through those same devices that are the luminous providers of the photograph itself. Visible cause and discernible effect are intended to conjoin in a more reflective bond of process and image. If, however, there is any imbalance here, it is the image that is slave to a master strategy—a strict procedure whose structured bidding calls the narrative shots.

—John Hilliard

*   *   *

An approach to photography which takes no account of the traditions built up around the medium by photographers has enabled John Hilliard to build up his own set of premises as he explores its nature.

Prior to 1970, when this systematic exploration began, Hilliard used photography in various contexts to document and to realize the qualities of his sculpture. Although the nature of the photographic medium is a determinant vital to all Hilliard's images produced during that time, its existence as only part of a system whose roots are elsewhere inevitably and effectively masks the specifically photographic issues.

The piece *Sixty Seconds of Light,* 1970, demonstrates the effect upon photographic film of a series of twelve exposures, in increments of five seconds, showing a darkroom timer which indicates the time of each exposure upon its dial. This was the first of a group of pieces related in the sense that all dealt systematically with the photographic process, as revealed in records of progressive change in technical parameters.

The works from 1974, known collectively as *Elemental Conditioning,* differ in that Hilliard elects to hold the photo-chemical conditions constant, and to direct the viewer's attention to the interactions of cropping with titling and their control of the meaning of an image/text unity.

Later, in *From the Northern Counties,* both threads have been brought together by pairing, sometimes joining, prints which each take account only of highlight or of shadow details in the same scene; and, by allowing the same title for both to interact with the different results, to suggest ambiguities of meaning between the two aspects of the image.

This practice of pairing has continued, but Hilliard's meanings, and the potential for significations by viewers have increased in complexity, and acquired filmic resemblances. Indeed, even in the single photographs, where the only interactions are between the image and its title, viewers are prompted at least as strongly to seek out narrative structure for a presumed fiction as to reflect upon Hilliard's investigation of the photographic medium; throwing up a mirror image of his stated priority of concern for the structures of visual language as ground out of which the fictions may grow.

From a traditional photographer's viewpoint, the first impression of the early work is that it is no more than darkroom exercises, a publication of knowledge usually evidenced by graphs and step wedges and assumed in every use of the photographic process. Those pieces where photochemical conditions approximate to a norm can be seen as in a sense not photographic at all, since the medium merely subserves independently existing concepts. The eventual amalgamation of these two aspects might then look like an imposition of non-photographic influences upon sterile didacticism: a coupling inauspicious for its offspring.

Yet it is also the case that from the first, deliberately naive-seeming investigations demonstrate the nature of photographic process more significantly than is likely to be perceived when their counterparts take place incidentally to some other objective. Moreover, the synthesis offered by Hilliard's practice, between the photographic medium and ideas often considered as remote and distinct from it, is such as to prompt valuable thought about the moral dimensions of our visual language. The question "what does this mean?" evolves naturally into "what ought one to think?" and then "what ought one to do?," signifying an aesthetic experience of some elegance and austerity for perceivers able to disembarrass themselves of certain preconceptions, and follow John Hilliard in his journey along the media interfaces.

—Philip Stokes

HIRO.

Nationality: American. **Born:** Yasuhiro Wakabayashi in Shanghai, China, 3 November 1930; moved to Tokyo, 1946, New York, 1954; became United States citizen, 1990. **Education:** Japan Public School, Tsingtao, China, 1937-38; Peking High School, 1942-46; Daiichi High School, Tokyo, 1946-49; studied under Alexey Brodovitch at the New School for Social Research, New York, 1956-58. **Family:** Married Elizabeth K. Clark in 1959; sons: Gregory and H. Clark. **Career:** Assistant to Rouben Samberg, New York, 1954-55; Assistant to Richard Avedon, New York, 1956-57, and Associate, Avedon Studio, 1958-71; Personal Assistant to Alexey Brodovitch, New York, 1958-60. Established Hiro Studio, New York, 1958; freelance magazine and fashion photographer, working mainly for *Harper's Bazaar* and *Opera News,* New York, since 1958 (Staff Photographer, *Harper's Bazaar,* 1966-74; contract photographer, Condé Nast Publications, since 1981). **Recipient:** Gold Medal, Art Directors Club of New York, 1968; Photographer of the Year Award, American Society of Magazine Photographers, 1969; Newhouse Citation, Syracuse University, Syracuse, New York, 1972; Society of Publication Designers Award, 1979; Certificate of Excellence, American Institute of Graphic Arts, 1980 and 1981; Award of Excellence fpr *HIRO,* American Photographer: International Editorial Design Competition, 1982; Photographer Award, Photographic Society of Japan, 1989; The Art Directors Club 70th Annual Exhibition Merit Award for *Farewell My Lovely,* 1991. **Agent:** Norma Stevens, 1075 Park Avenue, New York, New York 10028. Address (studio): 50 Central Park West, New York, New York 10023, U.S.A.

Selected Group Exhibitions:

1959   *Photography in the Fine Arts,* Metropolitan Museum of Art, New York

Donna Mitchell, Craters of the Moon, Idaho, **1968.** Photograph by Hiro.

1968   *One Hundred Years of Harper's Bazaar*, Hallmark Gallery, New York
1972   *Alexey Brodovitch and His Influence*, Philadelphia College of Art
1974   *Color* (American Institute of Graphic Arts), Whitney Museum, New York
1975   *Fashion Photography: 6 Decades*. Emily Lowe Gallery, Hofstra University, Hempstead, New York (toured the United States)
1977   *Fashion Photography*, International Museum of Photography, George Eastman House, Rochester, New York (travelled to the Brooklyn Museum, New York; San Francisco Museum of Modern Art; Cincinnati Art Institute, Ohio; and Museum of Fine Arts, St. Petersburg, Florida)
1982   *Color as Form*, International Museum of Photography at George Eastman House, Rochester, New York
1985   *Shots of Style*, Victoria and Albert Museum, London (toured Britain)
1988   *The Art of Persuasion: A History of Advertising Photography*, International Center for Photography, Midtown, New York
1990   *15th Of My 50th With Tiffany*, Fashion Institute of Technology, New York
        Photographie: de la réclame á la publicité, Centre Georges Pompidou, Paris
        The Indomitable Spirit, International Center of Photography, Midtown, New York
        Modefotografie—Von 1990 Bis Huete, Kuntsforum, Vienna
1991   *54 Masters of Photography*, Japan Toppan Collection (travelled through U.S.A.)
        Appearances, Victoria and Albert Museum, London
1992   *Industrial Elegance*, Pacific Design Center, Los Angeles; Denver; Chicago
        100 Years of Vogue, New York Public Library, New York
        Balenciaga, National Gallery of Victoria, Melbourne, Australia
1994   *Fashion Photography, Avedon, Hiro, Penn*, Art Basel 25 '94 Galerie Zur Stockeregg, Zurich

Collections:

International Museum of Photography, George Eastman House, Rochester, New York; American Telephone and Telegraph Headquarters, New York.

Publications:

By HIRO: Books—*Hiro*, designed by Marvin Israel, New York 1983; *Fighting Birds/Fighting Fish*, New York 1990. **Articles**—''Photo Interviews Hiro'' in *Photo World* (New York), May 1964; ''Hiro,'' interview, with Pucci Meyer, in *Zoom* (Paris), July/August 1972.

On HIRO: Books—*The Magic Image* by Cecil Beaton and Gail Buckland, London and Boston 1975; *The History of Fashion Photography* by Nancy Hall-Duncan, New York 1979; *Color as Form: A History of Color Photography*, exhibition catalogue, with introduction by Robert A. Sobieszek, Rochester, New York 1982; *Shots of Style: Great Fashion Photographs Chosen by David Bailey*, with text by Martin Harrison, London 1985; *Masterpieces of Photography from George Eastman House*, edited by Robert A. Sobieszek, New York 1985; *History of Photography* by Peter Turner, London 1987; *The Art of Persuasion: A History of Advertising Photography*, by Robert A Sobieszek, New York 1988; *Yves St Laurent*, exhibition catalogue, Munich 1988; *54 Master Photographers of 1960-1979*, Tokyo 1989; *Balenciaga*, exhibition catalogue by Marie-Andree Jouve and Jaqueline Demornex, New York 1989; *Hanae Mori 1960-1989*, exhibition catalogue by Yasuko Suita, 1989; *The Idealizing Vision*, New York 1991; *Appearances, Fashion Photographs Since 1945*, by Martin Harrison, London 1991. **Articles**—''Hiro'' by Richard Avedon in *Camera* (Lucerne), August 1965; ''Hiro'' by M. Caen and R. Pledge in *Zoom* (Paris), no. 13, 1972; ''Is This Man America's Greatest Photographer?'' by Owen Edwards in *American Photographer* (New York), January 1982; ''Another Kind of Hiro'' by Lois Slavin in *Photo District News*, volume vi, issue vii, July 1986; ''Eternity'' by Hiroshi Hamaya in *Tosho*, (Tokyo) no 7, 1988; ''The Hiro Enigma'' by Martin Gardlin in *Photo District*

News, Vol. X, Issue IX, July 1990; ''The Zen of Things'' by Owen Edwards in *American Photographer*, November/December 1990; ''The Uncensored History'' by Robert Draper in *Rolling Stone Magazine*, (New York) 1990; in *Graphis, The International Magazine of Design and Communication*, (New York), Mar/Apr 1992; ''The Best Location in America'' in *American Photo*, May/June 1992; ''Ansicht'' in *Das Magazin*, 24 July 1993; ''A Great American Photographer Named Hiro'' in *American Photo*, July/August 1994; ''Hiro Portfolio'' in *Santa Fe Photographic, A Journal of Santa Fe Workshops*, 1994.

*   *   *

Hiro's photographic work combines elegant simplicity and immediate impact. It combines the features of great advertising—clarity and appeal—into masterpieces of fashion and product photography. His ability to transform ordinary objects into items of intense desirability depends in large part on his brilliant use of sumptuous color, pure design and a presentation that affords his product larger-than-lifesize monumentality.

In his use of color Hiro is both a master craftsman and darkroom perfectionist. He is capable of brilliant technical effects with strobe and neon light—which is so easily gaudy or tawdry in the hands of a lesser master—as well as eye-catching combinations of highly-saturated color. This use of color is the stuff of which advertising dreams are made, both more brilliant and more beautiful than reality.

The advertising impact of Hiro's work also lies in his presentation of objects—from a simple scarf to Tiffany jewels—as monumental icons having uncanny presence, scale and importance of their own. One example is the photograph of pyramid-sized Cartier watches set in a luminous lunar landscape of vivid green and shocking blue. Each image incorporates one such eye-catching feature: such ads as the diamond-and-ruby pendant hung on the leg of a Black Angus steer or the diamond necklace circling a silver-scaled fish are unforgettable.

Hiro sees his role of fashion photographer as that of a reporter. ''The beauty of photographs alone,'' he insists, ''doesn't mean anything.'' He aims for contemporary meaning, and his work often incorporates space-age or socially-oriented imagery. To illustrate a lipstick, for instance, he took a close-up of a woman popping a pill, that ubiquitous contemporary commodity, between her lips.

It may come as a surprise to many that Hiro's work includes much serious work beyond fashion and advertising. For many years he has been doing portraiture, still-life, touching informal shots of children, and even landscape. This more personal side of his work, deeply-felt images which nonetheless show the same scrupulous attention to pure design, are part of the monograph that Hiro published in 1983.

—Nancy Hall-Duncan

HOBAN, Tana.

Nationality: American. **Born:** Philadelphia, Pennsylvania; emigrated to France, 1983. **Education:** Graduated from School of Design for Women (now Moore College of Art), Philadelphia, 1938; mainly self-taught in photography. **Family:** Married Edward E. Gallob in 1939 (divorced, 1982); daughter: Miela; married John G. Morris in 1983. **Career:** Began freelance career, first as a graphic artist, then as editorial and advertising photographer, 1940; opened photographic studio in Philadelphia with husband, 1946. Instructor in Photography, Annenberg School of Communications, University of Pennsylvania; devised and conducted experimental therapy with mental patients, using photography and literature as aids to communication, Philadelphia General Hospital, 1966-68. Began creating photographic books for children, 1970. Taught photography, New York University, 1974-76; lectured and gave workshops to school children, teachers and librarians in states of Alaska, Arkansas, Connecticut, Minnesota, Mississippi, Nebraska, New York, Ohio, Pennsylvania, Texas, Virginia and Wisconsin, and in Canada and Europe, 1974-90. **Recipient:** John Frederick Lewis Fellowship, 1938; Gold Medal Award, Chicago Art Directors, 1958; Gold Medal Award, New York Art

Miela, **1956.** Photograph ©Tana Hoban.

Directors, 1962 and 1963; Gold Medal Award, Philadelphia Art Directors, 1962 and 1964; Cine Golden Eagle Award for film *Catsup,* Washington, D.C., 1967; Honorable Mention, New York Academy of Science Award, for *Circles, Triangles and Squares,* 1975; Citation, Brooklyn Art Books for Children, and Certificate of Excellence, American Institute of Graphic Arts, for *Is It Red? Is It Yellow? Is It Blue?,* 1979; Outstanding Science Books for Children, for *More Than One,* 1981; Certificate of Excellence, American Institute of Graphic Arts, for *A, B, See,* 1982; Drexel University Citation, 1983; Award for Non-Fiction, Washington Children's Book Guild, 1983; *Boston Globe* Horn Book Award, and A.L.A Notable List, for *1, 2, 3,* 1985;

George G. Stone Recognition of Merit Award, 1986; Honorable Mention, New York Academy of Science Award, for *Is It Larger? Is It Smaller?,* 1986; *New York Times* Best Illustrated Book Award, for *Look, Look, Look,* 1988; Parents' Choice Foundation Award, for *Of Colors and Things,* 1990; *Boston Globe* Horn Book Award, Parents' Choice Foundation Award, and A.L.A. Notable List, for *Shadows and Reflections,* 1990; Outstanding Science Trade Books for Children, for *Exactly the Opposite,* 1990; Oppenheim Toy Portfolio's Gold Seal Selection, for *26 Letters & 99 Cents,* 1991; Parenting's Reading Magic Award, for *All About Where,* 1991; Pennbook/Philadelphia Children's Literacy Award, 1992; Honorary Doctorate of Fine Arts, Moore

College of Art, Philadelphia, 1992. **Address:** 56 rue des Tournelles, 75003 Paris, France.

Individual Exhibitions:

1948	New York Camera Club
1950	Art Alliance, Philadelphia
1980	Neikrug Gallery, New York
1982	Photographics Unlimited, New York
1985	Galerie Agathe Gaillard, Paris
1989	Espace Van Gogh, Arles, France
1990	Please Touch Museum, Philadelphia
1994	Galerie de l'Arcade, Paris

Selected Group Exhibitions:

1949	Museum of Modern Art, New York (with Margaret Bourke-White, Esther Bubley, Dorothea Lange and Helen Levitt)
1955	*The Family of Man,* Museum of Modern Art, New York
1966	*What Is Man?,* Museum of the Philadelphia Civic Center
1984	*Les Enfants,* Galerie Agathe Gaillard, Paris
1985	Elaine Benson Gallery, Bridgehampton, New York
1992	Musée Carnavalet, Paris

Collections:

Kerlan Collection, University of Minnesota, Minneapolis; De Grummond Collection, University of Southern Mississippi, Hattiesburg; Museum of Modern Art, New York; Musée Carnavalet, Paris; Bibliothèque Nationale, Paris; Mediathèque d'Arles, France; French Ministry of Culture, Paris.

Publications:

By HOBAN: **Books**—*How To Photograph Your Child,* out of print, New York 1955; *Photographing Youth,* out of print, with text by Edna Bennett, New York 1961; *Shapes and Things,* New York 1970; *Look Again!,* New York 1971; *Count and See,* New York 1972; *Push/Pull, Empty/Full,* New York 1972; *Over, Under and Through,* New York 1973; *Where Is It?,* New York 1974; *Circles, Triangles and Squares,* New York 1974; *Dig/Drill, Dump/Fill,* New York 1975; *Big Ones, Little Ones,* New York 1976; *Is It Red? Is It Yellow? Is It Blue?,* New York 1978; *One Little Kitten,* New York 1979; *Take Another Look,* New York 1981; *More Than One,* New York 1981; *A, B, See,* New York 1982; *Round and Round and Round,* New York 1983; *I Read Signs,* New York 1983; *I Read Symbols,* New York 1983; *I Walk and Read,* New York 1984; *Is It Rough? Is It Smooth? Is It Shiny?,* New York 1984; *1, 2, 3,* New York 1985; *What Is It?,* New York and Tokyo 1985; *Is It Larger? Is It Smaller?,* New York 1985; *A Children's Zoo,* New York 1985; *Shapes, Shapes, Shapes,* New York 1986; *Panda, Panda,* New York 1986; *Red, Blue, Yellow Shoe,* New York 1986; *26 Letters & 99 Cents,* New York 1987; *Dots, Spots, Speckles and Stripes,* New York 1987; *Look, Look, Look,* New York 1988; *Of Colors and Things,* New York 1989; *Shadows and Reflections,* New York 1990; *Exactly the Opposite,* New York 1990; *Red, Blue, Yellow Show* (Japanese edition), Tokyo 1990; *Des Couleurs et des Choses,* Paris 1990; *Of Colors and Things* (Danish edition), Copenhagen 1990; *All About Where,* New York 1991; *Ombres et Reflets,* Paris 1991; *Look Up, Look Down,* New York 1992; *The Wonder of Hands,* revised edition, with text by Edith Baer, New York 1992; *Où précisément,* Paris 1992; *Spirals, Curves, Fanshapes & Lines,* New York 1992; *The Moon Was the Best,* with text by Charlotte Zolotow, New York 1993; *Black On White,* New York 1993; *White On Black,* New York 1993; *La Lune de Paris,* Paris 1993; *Who Are They?,* New York 1994; *What Is That?,* New York 1994; *Little Elephant,* with text by daughter, Miela Ford, New York 1994. **Films**—*Catsup,* 1967; *Where Is It?,* 1980; *One Little Kitten,* 1980; *Panda, Panda,* 1987; *Dancing Zoo Zebra,* 1987; *Colors Everywhere,* New York 1995; *Animal, Vegetable or Mineral?,* New York 1995; *Just Look,* New York 1996.

On HOBAN: **Book**—*Something About the Author: Autobiography Series, Volume 12,* Detroit 1991.

*

My pictures are about seeing, about looking, about observing. I make photographs so that I will continue to notice, to look, to observe—thinking perhaps that in revealing things for others, I will also capture them for myself.

I want to remain sensitive to the things around me, including the things of daily life. If one takes these things for granted, they are soon lost. I hope *never* to lose the sense of discovery, of surprise, of wonder.

Photography gives me a chance to capture these discoveries for myself, and to share them with the world.

—Tana Hoban

*   *   *

Tana Hoban is arguably one of the most successful photographers of childhood. Childhood, not just children, in that she has created an impressive and copious body of work for, as well as about, children. Having started as an artist, she opened a photographic studio with her first husband (Edward E. Gallob) in Philadelphia as early as 1946. While women photographers have always had a powerful tradition in portraiture (one has only to consider the Victorian Julia Margaret Cameron's "great heads" of famous men or reflect that, at the turn of the century, more women were employed in English photographic studios than in any profession outside of domestic service), there was a longstanding tendency to ascribe the poorly-named "soft option" of child photography to them. A surprise, then, to find Tana Hoban's first public showing was in company with such stalwarts of the new "socially aware" photography of the Farm Security Administration as Dorothea Lange, Margaret Bourke-White, Esther Bubley and Helen Levitt (New York Museum of Modern Art, 1949).

Her style was indubitably suited to Edward Steichen's creation of the worldwide travelling exhibition, catalogued as the *Family of Man* (1955). This new humanism, following on the horrors revealed by the Second World War and rooted in the aspirations of a United Nations, was set on course to teach humans the unprecedented consequences of two-isms that, it was hoped, would prove to be outdated; nationalism and racism. Now, the attempt looks naive but its premise, that humanism has to be learnt and is not—in some optimistically Rousseau-esque sense, innate—holds truer than ever. From it derived numerous shows in the tradition of *What is Man?* (Philadelphia Civic Centre Museum, 1966) and even *Les Enfants* (Agathe Gaillard, 1984), stressing our common humanity.

Increasingly, in conjunction with her work documenting childhood, youth and the family Tana Hoban was creating a visual discourse for children. She started making films in the 1960s that have continued on until the present day, often based on animals. These signalled a shift also in her voracious output of books—at least a couple of dozen to date, sometimes several a year, many translated into multiple languages—from "how to" photography books to those for under-5s based on colours, shapes, symbols and animals. Now she has started collaborating with her (grown-up) daughter who provides the text for such small delights as *Little Elephant,* shot entirely in an afternoon in a zoo, with a baby elephant endowed with every recognisable human failing and endearment. The text is a novelty, following on many wordless books.

Alongside this considerable area of specialisation, Tana Hoban maintains an entirely different form of personal work. Since the 1980s, when she abandoned her other parallel career teaching photography to school and university students, Tana Hoban moved to a magnificent photographic studio in the old Marais quarter of Paris. This is the area in which she prefers to wander, taking subtle colour images of what she sees in the streets and parks, focusing on seasonal changes and perennial sights. Some even seek to reduce the colour content to a degree where colour film is employed to reveal the range of shades of grey—as in a sequence of wintry leaves or, more curiously, of the rolled rags of the clochards that adorn Parisian gutters. And yet she continues to travel Europe and the United States, ostensibly to teach but also to photograph.

Yet, even as Tana Hoban herself—diminutive, spry, often wearing pointy shoes and with bright spiky hair—appears as a character out of a fairy story, so her pictures sustain a primary connection with childhood and imagination.

(Though it's interesting to learn that French publishers hesitated over her books that they deemed "disturbed the fantasies of childhood" with their realism.) And if you follow her (about-to-be-published) autobiography, it definitely reads like a fairy story: fair cop for a child of Eastern European parents, raised in the States, who makes the return journey to Europe—and whose most reproduced poster is of Alice in Wonderland, aka her daughter Miela.

—Amanda Hopkinson

HOCHOVÁ, Dagmar.

Nationality: Czechoslovakian. **Born:** Prague, 10 March 1926. **Education:** Studied photography, under Jaromìr Funke and Josef Ehm, State Graphic School, Prague, 1942-46; film photography at the Film Faculty of the Academy of Performing Arts (FAMU), Prague, 1947-53. **Family:** Married Zdeněk Reinhardt in 1962. **Career:** Since 1953, freelance photographer, working principally for the Albatros publishing house, Prague, and different journals. In 1953 became a candidate and in 1963 a full member of the Union of Czechoslovak Visual Artists. Since 1989, Member of the Union of Free Photography and Prague House of Photography. Sat as an M.P. in the Czech National Council, 1990-1992. **Address:** Resslova 1, 120 00 Prague 2, Czech Republic.

Individual Exhibitions:

1960	Theatre Rokoko, Prague
1962	Gallery Fronta, Prague
1963	Photographic Cabinet of Jaromir Funke, House of the Lords of Kunstat, Brno, Czechoslovakia
1975	Sonja Henie Kunstsenter, Oslo
1977	Podlipanské Muzeum, Český Brod, Czechoslovakia
1979	Institute for Education of Employees in the Building Industry, Prague
1981	Gallery Foma, Prague
	Gallery Foma, Ostrava, Czechoslovakia
1988	Macromolecular Institute of the Czechoslovak Academy of Science, Prague
1989	Municipal Gallery, House by the Stone Bell, Prague
	Gallery Czechoslovak Writer, Prague
1991	Gallery "U bileho jednorozce," Klatovy, Czech Republic
1992	Czech National Council, Prague
	Theatre of Music, Olomouc, Czech Republic
	Small Gallery of the Saving Bank, Kladno, Czech Republic
1993	Gallery Genesis, Prague
	House of Art, Brno, Czech Republic
	Batschuns, Austria
1994	Czech Center, Vienna

Selected Group Exhibitions:

1952	*Creative Photography,* Union of Czechoslovak Fine Artists, Prague (and 1960, 1970, 1977 and 1984)
1966	*Czechoslovak Photography,* Union of Czechoslovak Fine Artists, Budapest
1968	*Biennale,* Milan, Italy
1970	*100 Pieces of Graphic Art and 100 Photographs from Czechoslovakia,* University Museum of Science and Art, Mexico City
1971	*Československ Photografy 1969-70,* Moravian Gallery, Brno, Czechoslovakia

1973	*Lyrism of Czech Photography,* SICOF, Milan, Italy
1985	*27 Contemporary Czechoslovak Photographers,* The Photographers' Gallery, London (travelled to Bristol)
1987	*Actual Photography 2: Movement,* Moravian Gallery, Brno, Czech Republic (travelled to Cheb, Bechyne and Zdar nad Sazavou)
1988	*Between Elbe and Wolga,* Lenbachhaus, Munich
1989	*Czechoslovak Photography 1945-1989,* Gallery Valdstejnska jizdarna, Prague
	Roads of Czechoslovak Photography, Municipal Gallery, Prague
	150 Photographs, Moravian Gallery, Brno, Czech Republic
	Czechoslovak November 1989, Gallery Foma, Prague (travelled to Ceske Budejovice; Hradec Kralove; Graz; Strassbourg; Nuremberg)
1992	*What's New: Prague,* The Art Insitute of Chicago, Chicago, Illinois
1994	*Czech Photography 1989-1994,* Gallery Manes, Prague

Collections:

Museum of Decorative Arts, Prague; Moravian Gallery, Brno, Czech Republic; Museum Folkwang, Essen, Germany.

Publications:

By HOCHOVÁ: Books—*Hrajte si s námi* (Play With Us), Prague 1960; *Nejen cerné uniformy* (Not Only Black Uniforms), with text by M. Ivanov, Prague 1963; *Všìm jsem byl rád* (I Liked To Be), with text by J. Neruda, Prague 1965; *Terezìn* (The Town of Terezìn), Prague 1965; *Recitujeme 1* (We Recite 1), Prague 1977; *Recitujeme 2* (We Recite 2), Prague 1981; *Dagmar Hochová: Photographs,* with text by Bohuslav Blažek, Prague 1984; *Deset, dvacet, tricet, uz jdu (Ten, Twenty, Thirty—I am Coming),* Prague 1994.

On HOCHOVÁ: Books—*Licht und Schatten/Light and Shadow,* edited by Milos Hrbas, Prague 1959; *Les Arts et la Vie,* Paris 1960; *Frauen der Welt fotografieren,* Leipzig 1964; *Fotoalmanach International,* edited by Knapp Verlag, Dusseldorf 1966, 1970; *Československá Fotografie 1968/1970,* exhibition catalogue, by Antonìn Dufek, Brno, Czechoslovakia 1971; *Photographing Children* by Time-Life editors, New York 1983; *27 Contemporary Czechoslovakian Photographers,* exhibition catalogue, with texts by Jirì Hlušička, Sue Davies and Antonìn Dufek, London 1985; *Encyclopédie internationale des photographes,* by Michele and Michel Auer, Hermance/Genéve 1985; *Cernobila fotografie (Black and White Photography)* by Antonin Dufek, Prague 1987; *Cesty ceskoslovenske fotografie (Roads of Czechoslovak Photography)* by Daniela Mrazkova and Vladimir Remes, Prague 1989; *Dagmar Hochova,* exhibition catalogue by Marie Judlova, Prague 1989. **Articles**—"Barna og hjulet" by K. Evensen in *Dagbladet* (Oslo), 4 April 1975; "Z tvurcì dìlny Dagmar Hochové" by A. Fárová in *Ceskoslovenska Fotografie* (Prague), July 1975; "Dagmar Hochová" by A. Faárováá in *Ceskoslovenska Fotografie* (Prague), November 1977; "Dagmar Hochová" by B. Blažek in *Fotografie 78,* (Prague) 1978; "Dětstvì ve fotografiìch Dagmar Hochové" by D. Mrázková in *Ceskoslovenska Fotografie* (Prague), June 1979; "Rok Dagmar Hochové" by K. Dvorák in *Fotografie 83,* (Prague) 1983; "Fotografka" by D. Mrázková in *Výtvarná kultura* (Prague), May 1986.

*

My whole life I endeavoured to make my photographs correspond with my mental background. I think it is necessary for photography to penetrate every aspect of life. I want to make close contact with all people—children, adults, and the old. I want to base my creative work on the inner self—the emotional as well as the rational. Formal qualities are only important insofar as they enable one to look easily at the photograph without hindrance; form itself is not the main focus of my creative efforts, since I really want to tell people about others outside themselves.

Most of my work is not done on assignment, but when a whole cycle of photos is completed, I then find a client or organization who wants to use it.

—Dagmar Hochová

* * *

She is sometimes called a "photographer of children," perhaps because in children she finds what we all seek and to what we subconsciously long to return but never can: the glorious freedom and total lack of inhibition, the intoxicating feeling of unlimited joy and happiness, the magnificent conviction that any dream, no matter how fantastic or wild, can come true. However, childhood is for the photographer but a beginning, the starting point of the greatest of all adventures, human existence. It is this adventure which remains in the foreground of her interest and it is human life that she studies and observes in its complexity. Holding her camera ready, she enters our ordinary and festive days, freezing the instants which reveal both the ugly and beautiful. She collects these instants, classifies them and assembles them into pictorial messages which tell us who we are and capture the character of our times. The titles of her series are revealing: *Children, Couples, The Power of Age, Uniforms, Holidays and Festivals.*

Naturally, the subjects themselves are not the essential feature of her work, for there are virtually hundreds of photographers whose images capture children, couples, old people, rituals, uniforms, festivals or customs and there are hundreds of those who arrange their pictures chronologically, covering man's life from birth to death. The real value of Dagmar Hochová's work lies in something else: "I just know beforehand what I'm after and if I don't find it, I just don't make the picture," she says. An ardent advocate of photography's spontaneity and authenticity she knows very well when the two qualities contribute to her interpretation of life's drama. Her unusual ability is that she knows precisely how to express this drama using effective brevity, undertone and admirable tension, stemming often from an association of contradictory emotions with which her pictures are charged. She is never descriptive, analytic or epic but rather authenticates man's existential feeling.

She was one of the first students to enroll in the photography department of Prague's Film Academy. It was at a time when Italian Neorealism was still to inspire a chain reaction of various national European waves but was already making its mark as a powerful means of a vital rejuvenation of art due to its social open-mindedness, rawness and internal multivocality of image construction. Dagmar Hochová absorbed these qualities of the style and they have been always apparent from her pictures. Her images are intentionally constructed to have several determinants of meaning simultaneously. She felt similar affinity to the powerful stimuli of the humanist-oriented candid photography of the period. In fact, she has always worked in its spirit and came to be regarded as one of its chief representatives in Czechoslovakia. Her personal programme was adopted by the young Czech post-war generation of photographers who, affected by the great social changes which took place after World War II, started their professional career in the mid '50s.

It was only natural for Dagmar Hochová that from the very beginnings of her career as a photographer she was closely associated with the press. Where else but in the press could she express her discreet comment on the times and the people? There were even times when the press refused to print her pictures, deeming them to be too overt. In time Dagmar Hochová also started producing book illustrations and her photography became a unique and integral part of exhibitions of children's books and toys. Her photographs were also used for films.

A woman of remarkable personality, she seems to be driven by an invisible internal force, in a permanent state of excitement, constantly on the move, always eager to photograph. Whenever she hears that there is something in the making which she feels she should not lack in her never-ending testimonial of the times and the people, she does not hesitate and will even go to the other end of the country never giving a thought to what would immediately spring to the mind of most photographers, i.e. whether she would find publicity for her pictures. She feels it is enough to make the picture. "It is my duty to the times," she says.

—Daniela Mrázková

HOCKNEY, David.

Nationality: British. **Born:** Bradford, Yorkshire, 9 July 1937. **Education:** Studied at Bradford College of Art, 1953-57, and the Royal College of Art, London, 1959-62; mainly self-taught in photography, from 1962. **Career:** Independent painter, graphic artist and photographer, from 1962, and stage designer, from 1966; first composite Polaroid and photographic collages, 1981; worked in London, from 1962, in Paris, 1973-75 and 1979-80, and in Los Angeles, 1964, 1973, and since 1977. Instructor, Maidstone College of Art, Kent, 1962; University of Iowa, Ames, 1963-64; University of Colorado, Boulder, 1965; University of California, Los Angeles, 1966-67. **Recipient:** Guinness Award, London, 1961; Painting Prize, *John Moores Exhibition,* Liverpool, 1961 and 1967; Gold Medal, Royal College of Art, London, 1962; Graphics Prize, *Biennale de Paris,* 1963; First Prize, *8th International Drawings and Engravings Biennale,* Lugano, Switzerland, 1964; Print Prize, *7th International Graphics Exibition,* Liubliana, Yugoslavia, 1965; Graphics Prize, *First International Print Biennale,* Krakow, Poland, 1966; Gold Medal, *6th Norwegian International Print Biennale,* Oslo, 1982; Award of Excellence, Federal Republic of Germany, 1983; Skowhegan Graphics Award, Maine, 1983; Kodak Photography Book Award, Stuttgart, 1984; First Prize, International Center of Photography, New York, 1985. LL.D.: University of Bradford, Yorkshire, 1983; D.F.A.: San Francisco Art Institute, 1985; D.F.A.: Otis Parsons Institute, Los Angeles, 1985. **Agent:** Cavan Butler, The Pantechnicon, 2 Heathfield Terrace, London W4, England. **Address:** 7506 Santa Monica Boulevard, Los Angeles, California 90046, U.S.A.

Individual Exhibitions:

1963	*Paintings with People in,* Kasmin Gallery, London
	The Rake's Progress and Other Etchings, The Print Centre/ Editions Alecto, London
	City Art Gallery, Bradford, Yorkshire
1964	Alan Gallery, New York
	The Rake's Progress, Museum of Modern Art, New York
1965	*Pictures with Frames and Still Lifes,* Kasmin Gallery, London
1966	Stedelijk Museum, Amsterdam
	Drawings for Ubu Roi and Cavafy Etchings, Kasmin Gallery, London
	Palais des Beaux-Arts, Brussels
	Studio Marconi, Milan
	Galleria dell'Ariete, Milan
1967	Landau-Alan Gallery, New York
1968	Kasmin Gallery, London
	Galerie Mikro, West Berlin
	Museum of Modern Art, New York
1969	*Paintings and Prints,* Whitworth Art Gallery, Manchester, England
	Andre Emmerich Gallery, New York
	Recent Etchings, Kasmin Gallery, London
1970	Lane Gallery, Bradford, Yorkshire
	Paintings, Prints, Drawings 1960-70, Whitechapel Art Gallery, London (travelled to Hannover, Rotterdam and Belgrade)
	Kasmin Gallery, London
	Andre Emmerich Gallery, New York
	Galerie Springer, West Berlin
	Kestner-Gesellschaft, Hannover, West Germany
1971	*Zeichnungen, Grafik, Gemalde,* Kunsthalle, Bielefeld, West Germany
1972	Victoria & Albert Museum, London
	Kasmin Gallery, London
	Andre Emmerich Gallery, New York
1973	Holburne Museum, Bath, Avon
	Andre Emmerich Downtown Gallery, New York
	Knoedler Gallery, New York
1974	Kinsman Morrison Gallery, London
	Garage Art, London
	Musée des Arts Décoratifs, Paris

My Mother, Bolton Abbey, Yorkshire, **November 1982.** Photograph ©David Hockney.

Dayton's Gallery 12, Minneapolis, Minnesota
Michael Walls Gallery, New York
Knoedler Contemporary Prints, New York
La Medusa Graphica, Rome
1975 Dorothy Rosenthal Gallery, Chicago
Galerie Claude Bernard Paris
European Gallery, San Francisco
City Art Gallery, Bristol, Gloucestershire
City Art Gallery, Manchester, England
Nishimura Gallery, Tokyo
1976 Nicholas Wilder Gallery, Los Angeles
Sonnabend Gallery, New York
Laing Art Gallery, Newcastle-upon-Tyne
Robert Self Gallery, London
Jordan Gallery, London
Festival Gallery, Bath, Avon
National Gallery of Victoria, Melbourne (toured Australia)
Henie-Onstad Kunstsenter, Oslo (travelled to the
  Kunstmuseum, Goteborg, Sweden)
Waddington Galleries, London
Galeria Juana Mordo, Madrid
1977 Andre Emmerich Gallery, New York
Dorothy Rosenthal Gallery, Chicago
Paintings and Drawings 1961-75, Galerie Neuendorf,
  Hamburg, West Germany
City Art Gallery, Wolverhampton, Staffordshire
1978 Gallery at 24, Miami, Florida
Drawings and Prints, Waddington Galleries, Toronto (trav-
  elled to the Albertina, Vienna; Tiroler Landesmuseum
  Ferdinandeum, Innsbruck; Galerie Bloch, Innsbruck;
  Kulturhaus, Graz; Kunstlerhaus, Salzburg; L. A. Louver
  Gallery, Venice, California)
Travels with Pen, Pencil and Ink, Yale Center for British Art,
  New Haven, Connecticut (travelled to Minneapolis Institute
  of Arts, Minnesota; Cranbrook Academy of Art, Bloomfield
  Hills, Michigan; Nelson Gallery and Atkins Museum, Kansas
  City, Missouri; Hirshhorn Museum, Washington, D.C.; Art
  Gallery of Ontario, Toronto; Toledo Museum of Art, Ohio;
  Fine Arts Museum, San Francisco; Denver Art Museum,
  Colorado; Grey Art Gallery, New York University)
Sudley Art Gallery, Liverpool, Merseyside
1979 Museum of Modern Art, New York
M. H. de Young Memorial Museum, San Francisco
Frances Aronson Gallery, Atlanta, Georgia
Bradford Art Gallery, Yorkshire
Gimpel & Hanover/Andre Emmerich Galleries, Zurich
Britten-Pears School, Aldeburgh, Suffolk
Warehouse Gallery, London
Knoedler Gallery, London
1980 Graves Art Gallery, Sheffield, Yorkshire
Ashmolean Museum, Oxford, England
Laguna Beach Museum of Art, California
Andre Emmerich Gallery, New York
Getler/Pall Gallery, New York
Petersburg Press, New York
Albert White Gallery, Toronto
Knoedler/Kasmin Gallery, London
Tate Gallery, London
Arun Art Centre, Arundel, Sussex
Art and Furniture, Manchester, England
Tyler Graphics, Bedford, New York
1981 Andre Emmerich Gallery, New York
Castelli Graphics, New York
Riverside Studios, London
Galerie Claude Bernard, Paris
Knoedler/Kasmin Gallery, London
Gallery at 24, Miami, Florida
Gallery at 24, Palm Beach, Florida
Galerie Meyer-Ellinger, Frankfurt, West Germany
Ashmolean Museum, Oxford, England

1982 Andre Emmerich Gallery, New York
Christie's Contemporary Art, New York
L. A. Louver Gallery, Venice, California
Photographies 1962-82, Centre Georges Pompidou, Paris
Knoedler/Kasmin Gallery, London
Rex Irwin Gallery, Sydney, New South Wales
Susan Gersh Gallery, Los Angeles
New York Public Library, New York
1983 Andre Emmerich Gallery, New York
Knoedler/Emmerich Gallery, Zurich
Richard Gray Gallery, Chicago
L. A. Louver Gallery, Venice, California
Knoedler/Kasmin Gallery, London
Nishimura Gallery, Tokyo
Bjorn Bengtsson Gallery, Stockholm
Hockney Paints the Stage, Walker Art Center, Minneapolis
  (travelled to Museo Tamayo, Mexico City; Art Gallery of
  Ontario, Toronto; Museum of Contemporary Art, Chicago;
  Fort Worth Art Museum, Texas; San Francisco Museum of
  Modern Art)
Thomas Babeor Gallery, La Jolla, California
William Beadleston Fine Art, New York
Fotografien 1962-82, Kunsthalle, Basle
Hockney's Photographs, Hayward Gallery, London (toured
  Britain)
1984 Milwaukee Art Museum, Wisconsin
Prints, Art and Sport Gallery, Brussels
Prints and Drawings, Bjorn Wetterling Gallery, Stockholm
Selected Prints, Knoedler Gallery, Zurich
New Paintings and Drawings, Andre Emmerich Gallery,
  New York
Photographic Collages, Fraenkel Gallery, San Francisco
Photographic Collages, Greenberg Gallery, St. Louis, Missouri
New Drawings, Richard Gray Gallery, Chicago
Prints and Photographic Collages, Galerie Esperanze, Mont-
  real, Quebec
Photographic Collages, Carpenter/Hochman Gallery, Dal-
  las, Texas
Works on Paper, Patricia Heesy Gallery, New York (with
  Jim Dine)
1985 *Hockney Paints the Stage,* Hayward Gallery, London
Prints and Photocollages, Greg Kucera Gallery, Seattle,
  Washington
Photocollages, Andre Emmerich Gallery, New York
Lithos, Paintings and Collages, Knoedler Gallery, London
Paintings from the 1960s, Andre Emmerich Gallery, New York
Photocollages, State University of New York, New Paltz
New Lithographs and Paintings, Andre Emmerich Gallery,
  New York
New Lithographs, Nishimura Gallery, Tokyo
New Lithographs, Richard Gray Gallery, Chicago
New Lithographs, L. A. Louver Gallery, Venice, California
New Lithos, Photocollages, Drawings and Paintings, Galerie
  Claude Bernard, Paris
Photocollages, State University of New York, Albany
Photocollages, College of Santa Fe, New Mexico
Photocollages, Elaine Horwitch Galleries, Scottsdale, Arizona
  (with Roland Reiss)
1986 *Theatre Sets, Models, Drawings and Etchings,* Contemporary
  Art Center, Honolulu, Hawaii
Photocollages, Paintings, Drawings, Honolulu Academy of
  Art, Hawaii
Photocollages, Cibachromes, Polaroids and Prints, Pasadena
  Art Center, California
Tyler Prints, Harvard University, Cambridge, Massachusetts
Tyler Prints, Tate Gallery, London
Photocollages and Theatre Drawings, Gallery One, Toronto
Photographs by David Hockney, Boca Raton Museum of Arts,
  Florida (travelled to Davenport Art Gallery, Iowa; Spencer
  Museum of Art, Lawrence, Kansas; Elvehjem Museum of

Art, Madison, Wisconsin; Santa Barbara Museum of Art, California; Toledo Museum of Art, Ohio; Ringling Museum of Art, Sarasota, Florida; Akron Art Museum, Ohio; Snite Museum of Art, Notre Dame, Illinois; Philbrook Art Center, Tulsa, Oklahoma)

Paintings and Photographic Collages, University of California, Berkeley

New Lithos and Mexican Hotel Painting, Andre Emmerich Gallery, Zurich

Self-Portraits, Blum Helman Gallery, New York (with Ellsworth Kelly and Francesco Clemente)

1987   Los Angeles County Museum of Art (travelled to the Metropolitan Museum of Art, New York; Tate Gallery, London, 1988)

Selected Group Exhibitions:

1960   *London Group,* RBA Galleries, London
1969   *Pop Art Redefined,* Hayward Gallery, London
1971   *Snap,* National Portrait Gallery, London
1977   *Kunstlerphotographien im XX. Jahrhundert,* Kestner-Gesellschaft, Hannover, West Germany
1979   *Photographie als Kunst 1879-1979,* Tiroler Landesmuseum Ferdinandeum, Innsbruck, Austria (travelled to Neue Galerie am Wolfgang Gurlitt Museum, Linz; Neue Galerie am Landesmuseum Joanneum, Graz; Museum des 20. Jahrhunderts, Vienna)
1981   *Instant Fotografie,* Stedelijk Museum, Amsterdam
1982   *Lichtbildnisse: Das Porträt in der Fotografie,* Rheinisches Landesmuseum, Bonn
1983   *Painter as Photographer,* Camden Arts Centre, London (travelled to Windsor Castle, Berkshire; National Museum of Photography, Bradford, Yorkshire)
1986   *Photomosaics: The Landscape Reconstructed,* Boston University, Massachusetts
1987   *Photography and Art 1946-86,* Los Angeles County Museum of Art

Collections:

Art Institute of Chicago; Arts Council of Great Britain, London; Centre Georges Pompidou, Paris; Los Angeles County Museum of Art; Museum of Modern Art, New York; National Gallery of Victoria, Melbourne; New York Public Library; Stedelijk Museum, Amsterdam; Tate Gallery, London; Victoria & Albert Museum, London.

Publications:

By HOCKNEY: Books—*72 Drawings by David Hockney,* New York and London 1971; *David Hockney by David Hockney,* edited by Nikos Stangos, London 1976; *Twenty Photographic Pictures,* portfolio, edited by Sonnabend Gallery, New York and Paris 1976; *Paper Pools,* edited by Nikos Stangos, New York 1980; *David Hockney: Photographs,* New York, London and Paris 1982; *Cameraworks,* with text by Lawrence Weschler, New York and London 1984; *David Hockney on Photography,* New York 1984, Bradford, Yorkshire 1985; *Martha's Vineyard and Other Places,* London 1985. **Articles**—"An Interview with David Hockney," with Peter Fuller, in *Art Monthly* (London), December 1978/January 1979; "A Conversation with David Hockney," with Mario Amaya, in *Architectural Digest* (Los Angeles), September 1980; "Paper Pools" in *Eastern Airlines Review* (New York), September 1980; "The Art World: True to Life," interview, with Lawrence Weschler, in the *New Yorker,* 9 July 1984; "Vogue par David Hockney" in *Vogue* (Paris), December 1985.

On HOCKNEY: Books—*David Hockney: Paintings, Prints and Drawings 1960-1970,* exhibition catalogue, with text by Mark Glazebrook, London 1970; *David Hockney: Zeichnungen, Grafik, Gemalde,* exhibition catalogue, with text by Gunther Gercken, Bielefeld, West Germany 1971; *David Hockney,* with an introduction by Henry Geldzahler, London 1976; *David Hockney:*

Prints and Drawings, exhibition catalogue, with an introduction by Gene Baro, Washington, D.C. 1978; *David Hockney: Travels with Pen, Pencil and Ink,* with an introduction by Edmund Pillsbury, New York 1978; *David Hockney: Drawings and Prints,* exhibition catalogue, by Peter Weiermair, Vienna 1978; *Pictures by David Hockney* by Nikos Stangos, London 1979; *David Hockney* by Marco Livingston, New York and London 1981; *David Hockney: Paintings and Drawings for 'Parade',* exhibition catalogue, with text by Mark Glazebrook, London 1981; *Hockney Paints the Stage* by Martin Friedman and others, Minneapolis and New York 1983, London 1985; *Hockney's Photographs,* exhibition catalogue, with an introduction by Mark Haworth-Booth, London 1983; *David Hockney: Fotografien 1962-1982,* exhibition catalogue, with text by Alain Sayag, Basle and Paris 1983; *David Hockney: Paintings of the Early 1960s,* exhibition catalogue, with an introduction by Nicholas Wilder, New York 1985. **Films**—*David Hockney's Diaries* by Michael and Christian Blackwood, 1971; *A Bigger Splash* by Jack Hazan, 1974; *Hockney at Work,* BBC television film, by Peter Adam, 1980; *South Bank Show: David Hockney,* London Weekend Television Film, by Don Featherstone, 1983.

* * *

David Hockney and photography might almost be twins. Both are seen everywhere, both gather up and re-present everything that passes before them, and in the public eye both have a bright, jolly surface which seems to mean just what it shows you. Equally, each has followers whispering of hidden depths, endlessly disputing; trading skeletons and crocks of gold.

So perhaps *The Second Marriage,* with its photographic references, was a tiny bit incestuous, and Hockney was simply being moral in his later, slight withdrawal from the medium to a point where, much as had Ruskin, he saw it as informative and interesting, but not quite to be relied upon.

However, the restriction to a business-like commerce between painter and medium did not last, for Hockney's growing awareness of the space-time dialectic within the photograph rekindled his passions. The flow of Polaroids began, rapidly extending Hockney's investigations to embrace the opposition of framed and unframed. In other words, joiners had been born and new perspectives synthesised. But of course, this wasn't so. Photographic journeymen had after all been stolidly joining for longer than anyone could tell, and panoramic photographers, over the decades, had quietly made their long, strange pictures. What happened now was that the baby, easily old enough to be drawing its pension, was plucked by Hockney from the waters and for the first time received sufficient nourishment for it to grow and fill an art gallery.

David Hockney's strengthening brew was compounded of a formidable historical knowledge of art and its techniques, with a particular sensitivity to contemporary visual currents and his remarkable talent for publicity, that the jealous might describe as flagrant opportunism. All of a sudden it really sounded vital and interesting that you could take lots of photographs of people at different moments, and build the pictures into a single, coherent image structure (though Rejlander could have claimed the same). The Cubist notions of simultaneity and fractured perspective were all at once there in the photograph, and exciting (yet what hadn't Muybridge done before?). The very expensiveness of the Polaroids: "How much are they? Nearly 50p a throw? Goodness me, work it out, what did it all *cost* him!" was enough to sanctify the joiners for some. For others, the sheer naughtiness of getting ordinary photoprocessors' prints stuck down and framed on museum walls was a thrill in its own right.

Anyone who comes to the work now, seeing the Polaroids next door to the photocollages, has the further fascination of comparing the effects of the two methods. The square format of Polaroid SX-70 images, combined with their hard physical qualities, makes them somewhat inflexible collage material, and one can hardly imagine Hockney being in the least tempted to do other than lay them out according to the grid indicated by their white borders. That does not preclude the building in of alternatives, an extra face as a phrase in brackets to indicate either an alternative present, or a proposition towards narrative. So it is that in *Don and Christopher in Los Angeles, 6th March 1982* the steadfast, single regard of Christopher Isherwood for the camera, from the visual centre of the image, is countered from away towards the edge of things by the flickering profile, half profile and bits of the head of Don Bachardy, who is himself animated, or being animatedly regarded by Hockney. This animation must be distinguished from a purely optical activation induced by the grid of white borders, which besides disturbing through extreme contrast between its white and the colour seems, in restraining the free passage of the eye, causing it a certain jerkiness, to impose a Cubist disjunction on one's scanning of the whole.

Hockney himself speaks of similarities between the possibilities for modification offered by photographic joining and those of drawing, and when we turn to the later photocollages, this property becomes even more evident, for there is nothing interposed between viewer and constructed perspective, and no inducement to build up to a conventional frame.

Raymond Foye appears to have stood still to look at Brooklyn in November 1982, but Hockney moved around, then integrated the results of two viewpoints, two distances from his subject, into a great rambling, branching thing which scoots across the back of Raymond Foye's shoulders, takes a bite at the window pane, holds on Brooklyn and ends up with a distinct, well integrated full length left profile.

When the progress of Hockney's game of prints embraces subjects such as the unfolding of a Scrabble game, with the play of hands interplaying with progressions of faces, disunified times reconstructed within almost unified space into a painterly abstraction, the optical and imaginative activations add up to a sparkling equivalent of the gold lame jacket he wore to collect his diploma. On the other hand, the joiner showing Mrs. Hockney at Bolton Abbey, with its quiet seriousness and merest flicker of wit, demonstrates the range of Hockney's perceptions. Whoever it was remarked that David Hockney is the Cole Porter of photography may have been near to the truth, indeed.

—Philip Stokes

HOEPFFNER, Marta.

Nationality: German. **Born:** Pirmasens, Pfalz, 4 January 1912. **Education:** Attended the Lyzeum in Pirmasens, until 1927; studied drawing, Kunstgewerbeschule, Offenbach am Main, 1929; painting, graphics and photography, under Willi Baumeister, Kunstschule, Frankfurt am Main, 1929-33. **Career:** Freelance advertising photographer, with own studio, working for *Das Illustrierte Blatt, Das Schweizer Heim, Frankfurter Zeitung,* and McCann advertising agency, Frankfurt, 1934-44; freelance photographer, working for Perutz, Agfa, Adox, Boehringer, etc., in Hofheim in Taunus, 1945-71, and in Kressbronn, Lake Constance, 1971-75, and Alicante, Spain, 1972-75. Since 1975, independent photographer, concentrating on experimental colour works in polarized light, in Kressbronn and Alicante. Founder-Director, Hoepffner School of Photography, in Hofheim, 1950-71, and in Kressbronn, 1971-75. Member, Bundesverband Bildender Künstler, 1956; Gesellschaft Deutscher Litchtbildner, 1967; Bund Freischaffender Fotodesigner, 1970. **Agents:** Galerie Alvensleben, Arcistrasse 58, 8000 Munich 40, Germany; Benteler Galleries, 2409 Rice Boulevard, Houston, Texas 77005, U.S.A. **Address:** Eichendorffweg 56, 7993 Kressbronn, Bodensee, Germany.

Individual Exhibitions:

1949   *Lebendiges Photo,* Kunstverein, Frankfurt
1950   *Fotografik,* Circolo Fotografico Milanese, Milan
1965   *Fotogramme,* Galerie Dorothea Loehr, Frankfurt
1966   *Fotogramme, Lichtobjekte,* Studio Kaluzza, Bad Homburg, West Germany
       Farbfotogramme, Variochromatische Lichtobjekte, Galerie R. Springer, West Berlin
1968   *Farbfotogramme, Lichtobjekte,* Galerie dam Dom, Frankfurt
1969   *Farbfotogramme, Lichtobjekte,* Galerie Senatore, Stuttgart
       Farbfotogramme, Kunstkreis Fulda, West Germany
       Farbfotogramme, Lichtobjekte, Foyer of the Hessische Rundfunk building, Frankfurt
1970   *Lichtobjekte, Farbfotogramme,* Basler Haus, Bad Homburg, West Germany
       Lichtobjekte, Farbfotogramme, Galerie R, Esslingen, West Germany

       Farbfotogramme, Lichtobjekte, Kabinett Dr. Grisebach, Heidelberg, West Germany
1972   *Farbfotogramme, Lichtobjekte,* Galerie Krinzinger, Bregenz, Austria
1973   *Licht und Kinetik,* Kunstverein, Konstanz, West Germany (with Schoffers and Waibel)
1977   *Farbfoto Experimente 1936-76,* Centrum fur Kunst, Vaduz, Liechtenstein
       Farbfoto Experimente, Lichtobjekte, Galerie Holbein, Lindau, West Germany
1978   *Vom Lichtbild zur Lichtkinetik,* Galerie Seebacher, Bludenz, Austria
1979   *Frühe Fotoexperimente und Farbfotogramme,* Osthaus Museum, Hagen, West Germany
       Fotoexperimente, Farbfotogramme, Galerie Altmann-Apeiros, Paris
1980   *Frühe Fotoexperimente, Lichtobjekte,* Kunstkreis Tuttlingen, West Germany
1981   *Frühe Fotoexperimente 1929-46,* Bauhaus Museum, West Berlin
1982   *Das fotografische und lichtkinetische Werk,* Stadtische Galerie, Ravensburg, West Germany
       Lichtobjekte und Fotoexperimente, Galerie Alvensleben, Munich
1983   *Photographs,* Benteler Galleries, Houston, Texas
1984   *Fotografien, Lichtobjekte,* Pfalzgalerie, Kaiserslautern, West Germany
1986   Bodensee-Museum, Friedrichshafen, West Germany (retrospective)
1987   *Konstruktive Farbfotografik,* Galerie in der Lande, Kressbronn, West Germany
1992   *Marta Hoepffner zum 80. Geburtstag, Frühe Portraits und Selbstportraits,* Galerie in der Lände Kressbronn
       Marta Hoepffner, das fotografische und llichtkinetische Werk, Städtische Galerie Konstanz, Wessenberghaus
       Marta Hoepfner zum 80. Geburtstag, fotografische und Lichtkinetische Werke, Galerie Döbele Stuttgart; ART, Cologne

Selected Group Exhibitions:

1950   *Gesellschaft Deutscher Lichtbildner,* Cologne (and annually, until 1966)
1951   *Subjektive Fotografie,* Kunstschule, Saarbrucken, West Germany
1978   *Das Experimentelle Photo in Deutschland,* Galleria del Levante, Munich
1979   *Deutsche Fotografie nach 1945,* Kunstverein, Kassel, West Germany (travelled to Rome and Naples)
1980   *Avant-Garde Photography in Germany 1919-39,* San Francisco Museum of Modern Art (travelled to Akron Art Institute, Ohio; Walker Art Center, Minneapolis; Baltimore Museum of Art, Maryland; Chicago Center for Contemporary Photography, Columbia College; International Center of Photography, New York; Portland Art Museum, Oregon)
1982   *Photo Art 1,* Kunstverein, Cologne
1983   *Lensless Photography,* Science Museum, Philadelphia, Pennsylvania
       Fotogramme—die lichtreichen Schatten, Fotomuseum im Stadtmuseum, Munich
1985   *Das Selbstporträt,* Musée Cantonal des Beaux-Arts, Lausanne, Switzerland
1986   *Foto Fest: The Month of Photography,* Houston, Texas
1987   *Deutsche Lichtbildner,* Museum Ludwig, Köln
1988   *Struktur und Geste,* Suermondt-Ludwig-Museum, Aachen
       Vom Landschaftsbild zur Spurensicherung, Museum Ludwig, Köln
1989   *150 Jahre Fotografie,* Kunstahalle Bielefeld und Bayerische Akademie der schönen Künste, München
       Bild und Lichtbild, Städtische Galerie ''Die Fähre'' Saulgau

Räumliche Stukturen, **1979.** Photograph by Marta Hoepffner.

Subjektive Fotografie 1948-63, Institut für
       Auslandsbeziehungen, Stuttgart
1990   *Das Fotogramm,* Kunsthaus, Zurich
1991   *Das Fotomuseum im Münchner Stadtmuesum,* München
1994   *the camera i,* Photographic self-portraits from the Audrey and
       Sydney Irmas Collection, Los Angeles County Museum
       of Art

Collections:

Muesum für Kunst undGewerbe Hamburg; Sammlung Lütze Stuttgart/
Sindelfingen; Fondazione di Gernheim, Lugano; Regierungspräsidium Stuttgart;

Pfalzgalerie Kaiserslautern; Städtische Sammlung Hofheim/Ts; Kultusministerium
Rheinland-Pfalz; LandrartsamtRavensburg; Kunstsammlung ''Lände''
Kressbronn; Bodensee-Museum Friedrichshafen; Archiv Baumeister Stuttgart;
Städtische Sammlung Konstanz.

Publications:

By HOEPFFNER: Books—*Wogende Wellen, Ragende Gipfel,* Frankfurt
1946; *Ausdruck und Gestaltung,* with introduction by Willi Baumeister,
Stuttgart 1947; *Ten Photograms,* portfolio, with introduction by A. Seide,
Frankfurt 1965; *Frühe Photoexperimente,* with introduction by J. H. Muller,

Hagen, West Germany 1979; *Das fotografische und lichtkinetische Werk*, with introduction by J. A. Schmoll-Eisenwerth, Ravensburg, West Germany 1982; *Marta Hoepffner*, with introduction by G. Fiedler-Bender, Kaiserslautern, West Germany 1984. **Articles**—"Die künstlerischen Moglichkeiten der Fotografie" in *Foto-Spiegel* (Traunstein, West Germany), March 1949; "Solarization—A Process for the Purist" in *American Photography* (Minneapolis), February 1951; "Gestaltungslehre in Fotounterricht" in *Foto-Prisma* (Dusseldorf), June 1954; "Bildkomposition in der Fotografie" in *Foto-Prisma* (Dusseldorf), August 1955; "Solarization" in *Der grosse Brockhaus*, Wiesbaden, West Germany 1956; "Durchsichtige Korper" in *Zauber des Lichts*, Recklinghausen, West Germany 1967; "Meine variochromatischen Lichtobjekte" in *Kunst und Kunststoff*, Wiesbaden, West Germany 1968; "Abstrakte Fotogramme" in *Fotogramme—die lichtreichen Schatten*, edited by Floris M. Neususs, Kassel, West Germany 1983; "Wie lange halten Farbfotos" in *Photopresse* (Hanne-Munden, West Germany), February 1983.

On HOEPFFNER: Books—*Ende der Kunst im Zeitalter...* by O. Bihalji-Merin, Stuttgart 1969; *Depuis 1945, l'Art de Notre Temps* by O. Bihalji-Merin, Brussels 1970; *Die kinetische Kunst* by Frank Popper, Cologne 1975; *Das Experimentelle Photo in Deutschland 1918-1940* by Emilio Bertonati, Munich 1978; *Kunstlerinnen...*, edited by Jorg Krichbaum, Cologne 1979; *The Imaginary Photo Museum* by Helmut Gernsheim, Renate and L. Fritz Gruber, and others, Cologne 1981, London 1982; *Avant-Garde Photography in Germany 1919-1939* by Van Deren Coke, New York 1982; *Deutsche Kunstlerinnen...*, edited by Ulrika Evers, Hamburg 1983; *Kunst der Moderne in der Landschaft Bodensee—Oberschwaben*, by Eva Moser, Friedrichshafen 1984; *A Concise History of Photography* by Helmut Gernsheim, New York 1985; *Frau und Technik*, by Sabina Lessmann, Bonn 1985/86; *Photosammlung*, by Reinhold Misselbeck, Köln 1986; *Leonardo 2000, Kunst im Zeitalter des Computers*, by Herbert W Franke, Frankfurt 1987; *Staging the Self, Self-Portrait Photographie 1840s-1980s* by James Lingwood, Los Angeles 1986/87; *Das Fotogramm in der Kunst des 20. Jahrhunderts*, by Floris M Neusüss und Renate Heyne, Köln 1990; *Frauen kunst Wissenschaft*, by Katarina Sykora, Heidelberg 1992; *the camera i*, by Deborah Irmas and Robert A Sobieszek, Los Angeles 1994. **Articles**—"Foto-Grafik von Marta Hoepffner" by E. Wickenburg in *Frankfurter Zeitung* (Frankfurt), 1940; "Neues Sehen in der Fotografie" by Claus Helbing in *Grafik* (Stuttgart), no. 2, 1949; "Photography as an Art" by Hans M. Wingler in the *Christian Science Monitor* (Boston), 18 June 1949; "Marta Hoepffner, A Light-Artist" by K. Kitano in *Japan Photography* (Tokyo), December 1953; "Marta Hoepffner" by G. Pfeiffer in *Magazin Kunst* (Mainz), January 1968; "Ein Nachtrag zu Marta Hoepffner" by Heidi Knetsch in *Fotogeschichte* (Frankfurt), no. 8, 1983.

*

As a result of the prohibition of modern art under the National Socialist Party in Germany I abandoned painting and concentrated on photography in 1933. I made my first creative photographic experiments: photopaintings, multiple exposures, black and white photograms, solarizations, still-life compositions and portraits. In 1948 I worked on my first interference photograms, employing polarized light. In 1949, I finally succeeded in having about 100 works shown in the Kunstverein Frankfurt am Main and the Circolo Fotografico, Milan.

My aim was to render visual form to realities which cannot be expressed through the medium of painting. Quite early I studied Newton's colour theory and the natural laws governing the behaviour of rays and waves in order to employ and further develop the use of technological advances in my pursuit of artistic achievement.

After the interference photos (e.g., using double layers of woven silk), I created abstract photograms using illuminated material, liquid layers and plastic foils in polarized light. These were shown as a portfolio and as wall pictures in art galleries in 1965. Soon I was also very interested in capturing the fascinating spectral range in print on colourpaper (1958). Since 1966, I have produced strictly geometric constructivist compositions only.

1965 also saw the creation of my "varicoloured light objects" which enable the viewer to experience the darkroom process and its effect of making the invisible visible. In these objects employing polarized light, the colours change according to the gradual shifting of the filter, until they reach their complementary partner. I believe that I have achieved my original aim by showing that light is the source of all colours.

Areas of research: Further experiments in the field of polarized light to lead to new perspectives and new areas of activity.

With my work and my art, I try not to express personal emotion, nor symbols. I want to demonstrate the presence of light and of colour manifestations . . . What I do is a form of poetry, technical and material . . .

—Marta Hoepffner

*   *   *

For fifty years a seeker of new visual forms in photography Marta Hoepffner received many impulses from modern art making the field between painting and photography her domain. This is not surprising considering that she studied for five years painting, graphic art and photography under the avant-garde artist Willi Baumeister who has been called by Michel Seuphor "the least German and, possibly, the most European of the German painters." This transmitter of Bauhaus ideas was dismissed in 1933 from the Frankfurt Art School by the Nazis. Hoepffner thereupon opened an advertising studio in Frankfurt where for the next ten years she specialised in graphic and photographic designs or a combination of both. Much of it was lost when she was bombed out in 1944. For her own pleasure she produced surrealist photomontages, abstract photograms, solarisations and mixed media collages, classified by the Nazis as "decadent." They were publicly exhibited for the first time in 1949 and include "African Art" (1935—masks photo-montaged on a painted background), geometric photograms in "Homage to Kandinsky" and another "to de Falla" (both 1937), a "Composition with an Archipenko sculpture," 1943, etc. This work is, no doubt, the germination of seeds instilled in her receptive mind by her former professor who had been absorbed by constructivist ideas and negro art among other influences. Hoepffner's use of these art impulses for novel photographic compositions is quite original. With Edward and Brett Weston she is also in the forefront of discovering photographic abstract forms in Nature, such as in the bark of a plane tree (1938), in sand dunes, in watered silk and in wood.

From 1949-1974 Marta Hoepffner conducted a distinguished private photo-school, first at Hofheim near Frankfurt, later at Kressbronn on the Lake of Constance, where she instilled new generations of photographers with the need for experimentation, always trying to extend the scope of the medium to the realm of art. Experimenting with colour-film in the mid-fifties led to the production of very original colour-solarisations such as "Glasses with Rose," 1956, and colour-photograms taken in polarised light, 1958. The latter have the appearance of collages with coloured paper, yet are in fact pure, and not so simple, photography without a camera. Thin, colourless and transparent foils of plastic material are laid on photographic colour-paper and taken in polarised light showing spectrum colours not visible to the eye in ordinary light. Whereas in 1958 they were still informal compositions made with torn pieces of foil or cut into shapes, seven years later she conceived the idea of mounting strips of foil on a glass-disc and letting it slowly rotate in polarised light by a motor in a box. This enables the viewer to experience the effects of making the invisible visible. Under the polarised light and movement the colourless foils gradually shift from the primary colours to the complementary colours and vice versa and unfold designs as if by magic. These "vari-coloured light images," as Marta Hoepffner calls them, produce an aesthetic pleasure not altogether dissimilar to the effects obtainable with moveable chromogram slides in the magic lantern—except in those the colours are painted on various glass discs rotating against each other and at different speeds. Reproducing these vari-coloured light images on colour-film results in extraordinary geometric, constructivist designs which have a life of their own, are independent of subject matter and freed from the demands of reality.

—Helmut Gernsheim

HOFER, Volkhard.

Nationality: German. **Born:** Königsberg, Germany (then East Prussia), 15 March 1941. **Education:** Attended schools and university in West Germany; obtained diploma in graphic design, Gesamthochschule Kassel, 1976; self-

From the series *Natural Buildings,* **1991.** Photograph ©Volkhard Hofer.

taught in photography. **Family:** Married Barbara Schätz-Hofer in 1981. **Career:** Began working in agencies. Teacher of Communication, Fachhochschule Hildesheim Holzminden, since 1974, and Professor of Photography at the same school, since 1980. **Recipient:** International Kodak Calendar Award, 1983 and 1990; Member of the Deutsche Gesellschaft der Photografie, 1989. **Address:** Kleine Neustadt 8, 31185 Klein Himstedt, Germany.

Individual Exhibitions:

1970	*Bildungstrieb der Stoffe,* Kunsthalle Nürnberg
1978	*Volagramme,* Stadtsparkasse, Hildesheim
1980	*Der Baum,* Stadtsparkasse, Hildesheim
1981	*Stars and Planets,* Stadtsparkasse, Hildesheim
1982	*Urlandschaften,* Fotogalerie Jausthof, Lehrte
1988	Galerie im Keller, Hannover

Selected Group Exhibitions:

1980	*Polarisierte Symmetrien,* Galerie Zebrastreifen, Würzburg

1983	*Traumberuf Fotograf oder Feuer und Flamme für die Fotografie,* Berlin
1984	*Vor-Bilder,* Roemer-Pelizaeus-Museum, Hildesheim
1989	Galerie Linhof, Munich

Collections:

Gernsheim Collection, Switzerland; Bibliotheque Nationale de France, Paris.

Publications:

By HOFER: Books—*Hannover,* 1984; *Braunschweig,* 1985; *Lebenselement Wasser,* 1992; *Orgeln in Niedersachsen,* 1994.

On HOFER: Book—*Traumberuf Fotograf oder Feuer und Flamme für die Fotografie,* 1981. **Articles**—''Island'' in *COLOR FOTO,* September 1983; ''Bedrohte Naturidylle'' in *Foto-Revue,* September 1983; ''Edle Tropfen'' in *Photo Technik International,* January 1988; ''Canyon des Lichtes'' in *Color*

Foto, June 1990; "Antelope Canyon" in *Photo Technik International,* March 1992; "Das geheimnisvolle Tal" in *Photografie,* April 1994.

*

Beside the experimental photography with its searching for new expressions and the interpretation of commercial information with all its photographic attributes, it was always nature with its inexhaustible fantasy that attracted me and took a great part of my photographic work.

People look at the pictures around them to imagine the idea of life. For me the fascination of photography consists of the fact that the camera gives me a very individual sight of the things I want to see.

The European consumption of pictures is up to six hours a day and the messages and pictures seem to get more and more trivial. In addition to that, pictures and visual media give only second-hand or third-hand information. Only those people who make their own pictures can break through this circulation.

Good photography is often recognized when those who take the pictures give their whole engagement and interest to their motifs—and not only to the equipment. Like a sensitive explorer, I always try to reach this target in the different parts of photography.

—Volkhard Hofer

* * *

Born in Königsberg, East Prussia, in 1941 Hofer spent his school time and university years in West Germany finishing his studies at the Kunsthochschule at Kassel as graphic and photo designer. From 1974 onward he was teacher of communication at the Fachhochschule at Hildesheim being appointed Professor of Photography at the same institution in 1980.

Hofer usually spends the long summer holidays travelling to enrich his work as a creative photographer. In the late '80s he achieved considerable renown with his fascinating colour documentation of the Mono Lake in Southern California, close to the Yosemite National Park. This salt lake in the Sierra Nevada mountains is gradually drying up, revealing bizarre sculptural forms of salt and a fragile architecture of volcanic rock formed by water and wind over thousands of years. It is a strange surrealist world of great aesthetic attraction. Unfortunately, these wonderful monuments of a bygone age now are in danger of being destroyed by unthinking teenagers.

From five visits to the Canyon of Light in Northern Arizona 1988-92 Hofer brought back a majestic series of pictures of the cave-like interior revealing an architect's dream world; sharply chiselled walls and stone cascades carved by rushing water during thousands of years. The light falling in 80-100m above it makes the narrow cavity vibrate with colour ranging from bright yellow to almost black with the whole colour tone range in between. The colour makes a world of difference between Hofer's photographs and those of Bruce Barenbaum taken in monochrome in similar canyon caves. It adds a new dimension.

In 1991/92 Hofer travelled in Iceland producing over one hundred colour photographs on the theme "Water." The result was a superb folio volume of 97 colour photographs divided into five sequences; Falling, Standing, Running Water; the Sea and Ice. Conception, visualisation and design of the book were by the photographer whose hopeful expectation is to be able to devote himself one day entirely to photography without needing the subsidy from teaching.

—Helmut Gernsheim

HONEY, Nancy (Ellen).

Nationality: American. **Born:** Providence, Rhode Island, 6 May 1948; grew up San Francisco, California; moved to England and became British resident, 1972. **Education:** Studied fine art (painting), University of Oregon, 1965-66, and San Francisco Art Institute, 1967-68; studied visual communication, Bath Academy of Art, Corsham, Wiltshire, B.A. (Hons) 1983; post-graduate

Honorary Fellowship in Photography 1984-85, Bath Academy of Art. **Family:** Married James Edward Honey in 1969; children: Jesse James and Daisy Ellen. **Career:** Part-time Lecturer in Photography at many colleges, universities and institutions, including University of the West of England, Bristol, 1989-93; Gwent College of Higher Education, Newport, 1992-93; University of Westminster, and West Surrey College of Art & Design, Farnham, since 1993; University of Brighton, since 1994. Co-opted onto Executive Council, Royal Photographic Society, 1991-92; South West Arts Publishing Advisory Committee Member, 1992-93; *Ten-8* Magazine Editorial Advisor, 1992-94; Arts 2000 Committee Member, 1993; UK Judge for *Kodak European Panorama of Young Photographers,* Paris, 1993; Selection Committee Member for Portfolio Room, Photographers' Gallery, London, 1994. Member IKON Photographers, London, 1994. **Recipient:** South West Arts Project Award, 1988; Arts Council Publishing Award, 1990; Fellowship in Photography, National Museum of Photography, Film & Television, Bradford, and Bradford & Ilkley Community College, 1991-92; Public Art Commission, CityArts, Southampton, 1992. **Agent:** IKON PHOTOGRAPHERS, 3-4 Kirby Street, London EC1 8TS, England. **Address:** 6 Mall Studios, Tasker Road, London NW3 2YS, England.

Individual Exhibitions:

1986	F-Stop Gallery, Bath
1988	Watershed Media Centre, Bristol
	Brewhouse Art Centre, Taunton
	Oldham Art Gallery, Greater Manchester
1990	*Woman To Woman,* Royal Photographic Society, Bath (and tour)
1992	*Entering the Masquerade,* National Museum of Photography, Film & Television, Bradford (and tour)
1993	*Photographie—Nancy Honey,* Maison Pour Tous, Calais, France
	Art on the Buses, Southampton
1994	*Old Enough to Know Better,* Cambridge Dark Room, Cambridge

Selected Group Exhibitions:

1986	*Young Contemporaries,* Institute of Contemporary Arts, London (and tour)
	Royal Photographic Society, Bath
1987	*Regarding Photography,* Ffotogallery, Cardiff (and tour)
	Women Artists Diary Exhibition, London (and tour)
1988	Royal Photographic Society, Bath
	Self Portraiture Exhibition, Women Artists Slide Library, London (and tour)
1991	*A Daughter's View,* Watershed Media Centre, Bristol (and tour)
1993	*Desert Island Pics,* The Photographers' Gallery, London
1994	*Our Bodies Ourselves,* Nottingham Castle Museum

Collections:

The Michael G. Wilson Collection; Union Square Gallery Collection, New York City; Royal Photographic Society, Bath; Polaroid Collection; National Museum of Photography, Film & Television, Bradford; Bradford & Ilkley Community College; Collection de Musée des Beaux Arts, Calais, France.

Publications:

By HONEY: Books—*Woman to Woman,* UK 1990; *Entering the Masquerade,* UK 1992. **CD-ROM**—*Old Enough to Know Better,* 1994.

On HONEY: Articles—"Regarding Photography" in *BJP,* 1988; *Everywoman,* 1988; *The Guardian Women's Page,* October 1990; *PIC Magazine,* 1990; *Women's Art Magazine,* 1991; *Royal Photographic Society Journal,* 1991;

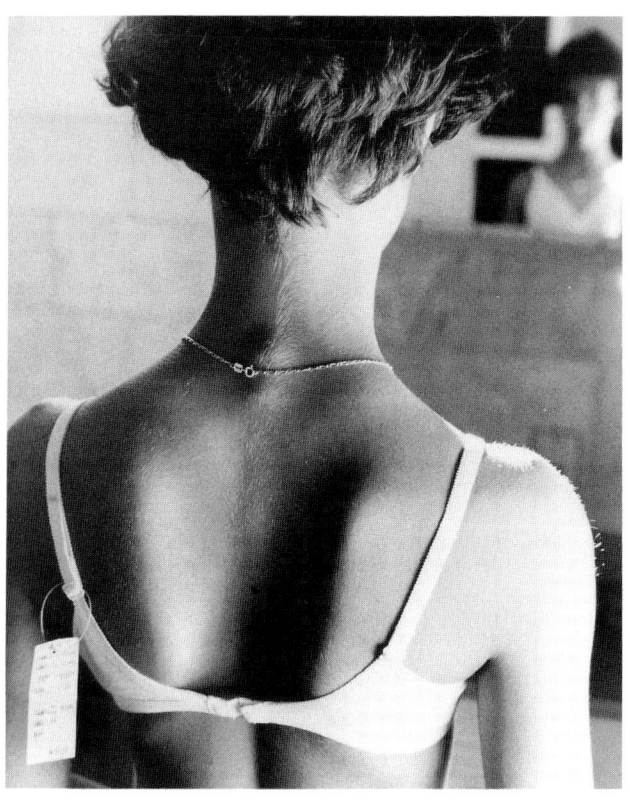

The Apple of my Eye, **1991.** Photograph ©Nancy Honey.

Creative Camera, 1992; *Portfolio Magazine,* 1992; *The Independent,* 1994; *Women's Art Magazine,* No 59, 1994; *Signals Festival* catalogue, 1994.

*

My work stems from an autobiographical root, questioning my identity and then extending to larger questions concerning women and society seen from a very personal and shifting perspective. It has recently become more documentary in nature and is categorised as portraiture by interested observers. I find my work difficult to categorise. I work almost exclusively in colour.

—Nancy Honey

*   *   *

Nancy Honey's imagery is essentially autobiographical. Her photography stems from her own experiences, as a woman and mother. Her early work particularly focussed upon her domestic circumstances, including three linked sequences portraying her family, aspects of her house, and of the immediate urban environment. These pictures are memorable for the use of light, especially in the portraits of her husband and children.

Over the years projects have become more ambitious, requiring more complex research and pre-visualisation. But the themes continue to reflect her subjective approach to questions of gender and identity. Thus, in *Woman to Woman,* a series of triptychs, she reflects "woman," her everyday social experience, and the ways in which the female form and femininity are culturally represented. Images from art, popular culture, pornography, advertising are juxtaposed with more documentary-style shots of "woman," for example, as a child in uniform on her way to school, or elderly out for a walk. Research for this project was diverse including a visit to an amateur photography modelling session where she photographed men photographing the women. (Men came over to explain to her that she was shooting from the wrong place.)

Similarly, *Apple of My Eye,* in which she explores representations of the female breast, stems from personal experience; her daughter as a young teenager, combined with concerns relating to her own health. Here, images of breast-feeding, or the process of mastectomy, are juxtaposed with idealised renderings of the breast in, for example, fine art or on the cover of a magazine. Likewise her major project *Entering the Masquerade,* which was undertaken during the year of her fellowship at the National Museum of Photography (Bradford, Yorkshire), reflected questions about adolescence provoked by considering her daughter and her schoolmates. The project did not stop there; she developed it to include girls from diverse areas of the country.

Aside from the early family portrait sequence, Nancy Honey's work is always in colour. Colour, as a symbolic system, contributes centrally to the rhetoric of her imagery. She prints her own work, and is precise in her visual standards and demands upon herself. She shoots close up, excluding as much as possible other than the most salient visual information. Projects are conceived as series. As such, it is the interplay of imagery that centrally characterises both the aesthetic and the political impact of her work.

Nancy Honey is energetic and hard-working, always simultaneously pursuing a range of projects and objectives, professional and domestic. She is actively committed to fostering work by women artists, and continuously supports initiatives such as the Women Artist's Slide Library in London. But she has a determined impatience with "political correctness" and seeks to challenge unspoken boundaries through her own work and through promoting the work of others.

Having worked with her for a number of years, co-teaching photography courses to undergraduate students of Graphic Design, I am, above all else, aware of the vitality and commitment and, what might be termed "American-style" energy which she brings to all aspects of her work. She never seems afraid to say what she thinks, and to share her personal enthusiasms. As a teacher, by contrast with the more neutral style of many British tutors, she offers a direct, and welcome, challenge to her students (who always rise to the occasion).

—Liz Wells

HÖPKER, Thomas.

Nationality: German. **Born:** Munich, 10 June 1936. **Education:** Attended schools in Munich, Stuttgart, and Hamburg, 1942-56; studied history of art and archaeology at the universities of Göttingen and Munich, 1956-59; self-taught in photography. **Family:** Married the writer-reporter Eva Windmöller in 1968; son: Fabrian. **Career:** Photographer since 1959: Contract Photographer at *Münchner Illustrierte,* 1959-61, *Kristall,* Hamburg, 1961-64, and *Stern,* Hamburg, from 1964; Correspondent for *Stern* in East Berlin, 1974-76, and in New York, 1976-78; Executive Editor of U.S. edition of *Geo,* New York, 1978-81; freelance photographer, New York, since 1981. Art Director, for *Stern* magazine, Hamburg, since 1986. Member, Gesellschaft Deutscher Lichtbildner (GDL), 1956-73. Member, Deutsche Gesellschaft für Photographie (DGPh), and Bund Freischaffender Foto-Designer (BFF). **Recipient:** *Photokina* Award, 1955, 1957; Kulturpreis der DGPh, 1966; Bundesverdienstkreuz, 1975. **Agents:** Anne Hamann, Triftstrasse 10, Munich 22, Germany; and Woodfin Camp, 415 Madison Avenue, New York, New York 10017, U.S.A. **Address:** 250 East 63rd Street, New York, New York 10021, U.S.A.

Individual Exhibitions:

1956   Landesbildstelle, Hamburg
1975   Overbeck Gesellschaft, Lübeck
1977   Stadtmuseum, Munich
1978   Rizzoli Gallery, New York
1979   PPS Gallery, Tokyo
1980   W. Camp Gallery, Washington
1986   *Der Stern-Fotograf: Thomas Höpker,* Fotoforum, Frankfurt
             (retrospective; travelled to Munich, Emden and Hannover)

Selected Group Exhibitions:

1966   *1st World Exhibition of Photography*, Pressehaus Stern,
        Hamburg (and world tour)
1968   *2nd World Exhibition of Photography*, Pressehaus Stern,
        Hamburg (and world tour)
1973   *3rd World Exhibition of Photography*, Pressehaus Stern,
        Hamburg (and world tour)
1975   *Gesellschaft Deutscher Lichtbildner*, Haus Industrieform,
        Essen, West Germany
1976   *Photokina '76*, Cologne
1979   *Fran Jonasson till Armstrong-Jones*, Moderna Museet,
        Stockholm
        Deutsche Fotografie nach 1945, Kasseler Kunstverein, Kassel,
        West Germany
1980   *The Imaginary Photo Museum*, Kunsthalle, Cologne

Collections:

Münchner Stadtmuseum; Bibliothèque Nationale, Paris.

Publications:

By HÖPKER: Books—*Yatum Papa*, Stuttgart 1963; *Horst Janssen*, Hamburg 1967; *Berliner Wande*, with text by G. Kunert, Munich 1976; *Leben in der DDR*, with text by Eva Windmöller, Hamburg 1977; *Expeditionen in Künstliche Gärten*, with Heinz Mack, Hamburg 1977; *Vienna*, London 1978; *Die New York Story*, Hamburg 1983; *Amerika*, Hamburg 1986; *Ansichten*, Heidelberg 1986. **Documentary films for TV**—*Washington: The New Rome?*, 1973; *Canada*, 1974; *Arabati*, 1973; *Rain in Arabati*, 1975.

On HÖPKER: Books—*2nd World Exhibition of Photography*, exhibition catalogue, edited by Karl Pawek, Hamburg 1968; *Geschichte der Fotografie im 20. Jahrhundert/Photography in the 20th Century* by Petr Tausk, Cologne 1977, London 1980; *Fotografie 1919-1979, Made in Germany: Die GDL-Fotografen*, edited by Fritz Kempe, Bernd Lohse and others, Frankfurt 1979; *Deutsche Fotografie nach 1945/German Photography after 1945* by Floris Neusüss, Wolfgang Kemp and Petra Benteler, Kassel 1979; *World Photography*, edited by Bryn Campbell, London 1981; *The Imaginary Photo Museum* by Helmut Gernsheim, Renate and L. Fritz Gruber and others, Cologne 1981, London 1982; *I Grandi Fotografi: Thomas Höpker*, with text by Bryn Campbell, Milan 1983, London 1984. **Articles**—"E Domani si Riparte: Thomas Höpker Obiettivo Tutto" in *Fotografia Italiana* (Milan), April 1973; article in *Camera 35* (New York), April 1981.

*

I have always considered myself a photo-reporter, a journalist who communicates ideas, observations and opinions through photographs. My pictures are primarily meant to be shown on the pages of a magazine or a newspaper—to be viewed and discarded. So I have always felt ill at ease whenever my photographs have appeared on the walls of a museum or gallery, become part of a collection or are discussed or treated like artwork.

Though I have worked mostly in color and the aesthetics of a photograph are very important to me—I know that composition and color can easily become overpowering, decorative elements in an otherwise mindless picture. There are too many good-looking but meaningless photographs around. Any photographer, but especially the photojournalist, should clearly know what he wants to communicate before he lifts his camera. Good photographers have strong opinions and convictions. I don't believe in the cold-eyed "objective" reporter. A balanced view can be as bland to the mind as a balanced composition can be boring to the eye.

—Thomas Höpker

*   *   *

Thomas Höpker's sensitive intelligence, spontaneity and instinct for the right moment have made him into one of the most successful photojournalists

of our time. He was lucky enough to acquire the technical fundamentals as it were by "playing" and step-by-step experimentation at the very early age of 14, without having to burden himself with too much theory. As well, he was greatly interested in art, and that interest is apparent in his early photographs in which he looks for formal aesthetic solutions and pays less attention to content. He found a solution in a severely formed picture construction, which schooled his vision in such a way that the method actually had the effect of emphasising content—to the benefit of his later work as a photojournalist. In his later work, as in his early pictures, Höpker limited himself to the essential and achieved an impressive picture density that became his trademark.

After 6 semesters studying art history, and encouraged by his increasing success as a photographer, Höpker decided to make photography his profession. He became a photojournalist for *Münchner Illustrierte* and *Kristall*, then, after 1964, commissioned by *Stern*, he photographed all over the world his great and now internationally recognized reportages.

Höpker has favored coverage of the constant change in human existence, of anonymous grief in distant lands, famine in India or the leper problem in Ethiopia. He has sought constantly to give expression to his deep sympathy for the grief and suffering of others, and to bring this distress to the attention of readers of the great illustrated magazines of the western world—and to do so as realistically as possible (without repulsing readers), so that support for the distressed might be more quickly and extensively set in motion. Yet, as far as possible, he avoided sensational reports; he also reserved the right to say no to certain commissions.

And Höpker became well-known not only for this kind of reportage but also for his social situation-reports on the monotony of life in a welfare state or on the frightening lack of fantasy among people in countries where no life-threatening poverty prevailed, where there were no droughts or epidemics. Those who have seen his photo-report on the training of American Marines feel through these pictures the senselessness of war more than through any equally gripping coverage of the actual events of war. The brutality of the training has so marked the young recruits that their faces show the dread.

Höpker is also known for his perceptive portraits—for example, of the designer Horst Janssen. Before he created his portraits, Höpker met with Janssen frequently so that the two men could get to know one another more closely. Then, when the time came, Janssen felt that the actual photographing was a joint venture, a new means of expression for himself, in that he and Höpker could stimulate each other with new ideas. And when he was to portray Cassius Clay, Höpker very patiently waited until he was able to persuade this capricious and uncomfortable partner to co-operate, so giving him the pictures that he wanted.

In 1968 Höpker expressed his own opinion of the work of the photojournalist: "I often ask myself what the future of photo-journalism will be. The merry-go-round of sensations turns ever more quickly. Love, birth, death, all human situations have already been photographed in a masterly manner. There are already signs of fatigue. Every taboo in photography is already breached, every shock has been given. Perhaps we shall soon learn once more to appreciate peace and simplicity." And Höpker has always looked for peace and simplicity in his own missions, because those qualities must also be present within the general "loudness," because the merry-go-round must occasionally be slowed down a little.

Höpker's photos show us not only what has happened, that which the technical apparatus of the camera was able to capture, but also the invisible, that which lies under the surface and gives life to a photo. And if a photo provides more than the quickly grasped pictorial information, therein lies the skill of the photographer.

—Jürgen Wilde

HOPKINS, (Godfrey) Thurston.

Nationality: British. **Born:** London, 16 April 1913. **Education:** Attended Salesian College, Burwash, Sussex, 1927-28; Montpellier College, Brighton, 1929-30; studied magazine illustration at the Brighton College of Art, 1931-33. **Military Service:** Served as a photographer with the Royal Air Force, in Italy and the Middle East, 1940-45. **Family:** Married the photographer Grace

The Oldest Inhabitant, Liverpool Slums, **1955.** Photograph by Thurston Hopkins.

Fyfe Robertson in 1956; children: Joanna and Robert. **Career:** Press Photographer, Photopress Agency, London, 1936-37; freelance photojournalist, London, 1946-50; photojournalist, *Picture Post,* London, 1950-57; freelance advertising photographer, with studio in Chiswick, London, 1959-68; now retired. Columnist (''The Professional Scene''), *Photography,* London, 1969-70. Lecturer in Editorial Photographic Studies, Guildford School of Photography, now West Surrey College of Art, 1969-77. **Agent:** The Photographers' Gallery, 8 Great Newport Street, London WC2, England. **Address:** Wilmington Cottage, Wilmington Road, Seaford, East Sussex, England.

Individual Exhibitions:

1974   British Council, London (toured Europe)
1975   *3 From Picture Post,* The Photographers' Gallery, London
               (with Kurt Hutton and Bert Hardy; toured the U.K.,
               1976-77)
1993   *After Dark: Night Photographs from Around the World,* Zelda
               Cheatle Gallery, London

Selected Group Exhibitions:

1955   *Picture Post Photography,* Kodak Gallery, Kingsway, London
               British Press Photographs of the Year, London (and 1957)
1962   *1st International Colour Photography Exhibition,* London
1972   *Personal Views 1850-1970,* British Council, London (toured
               Europe)
1980   *British Art 1940-1980,* The Hayward Gallery, London
1982   *Lichtbildnisse: Das Porträt in der Fotografie,* Rheinisches
               Landesmuseum, Bonn
1983   *Die fotografische Sammlung,* Museum Folkwang, Essen, West
               Germany
               British Photography 1955-65, The Photographers' Gallery,
               London
               Faces and Places: The Montreal Museum of Fine Arts, Canada
1987   *Realities Revisited,* Centre Saidye Bronfman, Montreal
1994   *All Human Life: Great Photographs from the Hulton Deutsch
               Collection,* Barbican Art Gallery, London

Collections:

Victoria and Albert Museum, London; British Council, London; Museum Folkwang, Essen; Arts Council of Great Britain, London; Museum of Fine Arts, Montreal; The Hulton Deutsch Collection, London; The Helmut Gernsheim Collection, Switzerland; The Metropolitan Museum of Art, New York.

Publications:

By HOPKINS: Book—*Thurston Hopkins,* with an introduction by Robert Muller, London 1977. **Article**—review of Tom Hopkinson's *Picture Post* in *British Journal of Photography* (London) 18 December 1970.

On HOPKINS: Books—*Photography Today,* edited by Norman Hall, London 1957; *Geschichte der Photographie im 20. Jahrhundert/History of Photography in the 20th Century* by Petr Tausk, Cologne 1977, London 1980; *Lichtbildnisse: Das Porträt in der Fotografie,* edited by Klaus Honnef, Cologne 1982; *British Photography 1955-1965: The Master Craftsmen in Print,* exhibition catalogue, by Sue Davies, Michael Rand, Mark Boxer and others, London 1983; *Museum Folkwang: die fotografische Sammlung,* exhibition catalogue, with introduction by Ute Eskildsen, Essen, West Germany 1983. **Articles**—''Thurston Hopkins'' by Bill Jay in *Album* (London), April 1970; ''Thurston Hopkins: Man of the Streets'' by G.H. in *Amateur Photographer* (London), 18 May 1977; ''Master of the Leica,'' *Leica Fotografie International,* May 1989; ''Makers of Photographic History,'' *National Museum of Photography,* Bradford 1989; ''After Dark: 80th Birthday Tribute,'' *Leica Fotografie International,* March 1993.

*

I became a photographer by chance, without any training to speak of. Knowing nothing of the technical side of the profession, I allowed myself to be sent on assignments in competition with seasoned Fleet Street cameramen. In my innocence, I would sometimes ask them what exposure to use, since my primitive press camera had no set shutter speeds, and exposure meters were unknown. Only occasionally did they deliberately mislead me!

I never intended to remain in photography. I had trained as a graphic illustrator, and I would probably have gone back to using the pencil and brush but for the war. Service overseas infected me with a desire to travel while at the same time it came to my notice that a particular type of photography—photojournalism—could give me this opportunity. What I really enjoyed about photojournalism was gaining admission to places, and meeting people, otherwise difficult to see. I also enjoyed overcoming difficulties placed in my way, and I've always believed that taking photographs under rough conditions produces a quality—a non-technical quality—often lacking in work produced when everything is going with you. In those days you often heard British photojournalists grumbling at the limited miniature equipment they had to make do with for some time after the war: no super-wide-angle lenses, no through-lens-metering, no zoom lenses then. I myself looked enviously at the masses of glittering equipment *Life* photographers carried around with them.

Undoubtedly, there have been gains from the vastly improved equipment available since that time, but I remain unconvinced that, on the whole, it has enabled photographers to produce more impressive work—at least in the field of photojournalism. Cartier-Bresson could have done his entire life's work on an early Leica, and there would have been no falling off of his quality, his superb quality. Is it too much to suggest that the photographer who has so many exciting items of equipment to choose from has just that little less time to spare for human reaction? The marvellous photographs of Dr. Erich Salomon are human in a way that few photographs are today; I love the *absence* of technical perfection in these moving images. Ruskin suggested that Turner would have produced great art by dipping a blunt stick in mud. Young photographers should ponder this remark; there's a great deal of truth in it.

I no longer use the camera as a means of communication, and I've had my fill of foreign travel. I'm lucky enough to have come full circle: I'm back with the pencil and brush, and no deadlines to meet.

—Thurston Hopkins

*   *   *

Thurston Hopkins is a British photojournalist who spent some of his best years with *Picture Post,* whose service he entered after acquiring a great deal of experience in the Photographic Unit of the Royal Air Force during the war and as a freelancer in London during the late 1940s. His works are rich in a variety of subjects, produced in response to the needs of various editors—yet, despite the great variety, his work does reveal something like a personal style. His usual subject, man, is customarily caught in his typical social environment—for instance, the old woman in the Liverpool slums, the Rev. Reindorp amongst his parishioners, the party-goers in Highgate. Moreover, the pictorial elements of that environment are not ''passive'': they eloquently complement the human subject with pertinent information about the quality of the milieu itself.

His interest in the character and destiny of man led Hopkins to search for significant situations both in his own country and abroad. Like most modern photojournalists, Hopkins has been a great traveller, and always his travels have yielded photographs that convey his particular kind of impression, no matter how different the subject. As usual, his ability to make the one represent the many is obvious, the ability (and not an inconsequential one) to select the right representative from an unknown people in order to vividly characterize all the inhabitants of a certain area. Hopkins has also shown a predilection for musicians and singers, depicting them in situations during performance that express something of their artistic and mental background.

Although the motivation of Hopkins' photography is probably a desire to convey information about human life and human problems in a comprehensible way, he has also created successful images that depict the unique atmosphere of place. Obviously, the two efforts are connected, for Hopkins undoubtedly feels that the spaces in which people live are as important as the people themselves in any integral communication of humanist values.

—Petr Tausk

HOREIS, William (Richard, Sr.).

Nationality: American. **Born:** New York City, 11 October 1945. **Education:** Attended New Utrecht High School, New York, 1962-66; studied graphic arts at New York City Community College, 1968-69; mainly self-taught in photography. **Family:** Married Marjorie Ann Crouch in 1969; son: William Richard (Beejai); married Pamela Grieco in 1985. **Career:** Independent photographer, Toronto, since 1974. Guest Lecturer, York University, Toronto, 1975; Ontario College of Art, Toronto, 1975, 1979; Center for Creative Studies, Detroit, 1976; Camera Canada College, University of Ottawa, 1977. **Recipient:** Ontario Arts Council Grant, 1975, 1977; Canada Council Grant, 1976. **Agent:** Jane Corkin Gallery, 179 John Street, Toronto, Ontario M5T 1X4, Canada. **Address:** 86 Beresford Avenue, Toronto, Ontario M6S 3B1, Canada.

Individual Exhibitions:

1979   Jane Corkin Gallery, Toronto
        National Film Board of Canada, Ottawa (with Suzanne Bloom and Stephen Livick)

Selected Group Exhibitions:

1975   *Exposure,* Art Gallery of Ontario, Toronto (toured Canada)
1976   *21,* National Film Board of Canada, Ottawa
1977   *Arte Fiera '77,* Bologna, Italy
1979   *Opening Exhibition,* Jane Corkin Gallery, Toronto
1980   *Contemporary Photographers,* Jane Corkin Gallery, Toronto
1982   *Le Troisième Salon,* Jane Corkin Gallery, Toronto
1984   *Summer Salon,* Jane Corkin Gallery, Toronto
1985   *Christmas Show,* Jane Corkin Gallery, Toronto
1986   *Twelve Canadians: Contemporary Photography,* Watson Gallery, Houston, Texas

Collections:

Ontario Arts Council, Toronto; National Film Board of Canada, Ottawa; Seagrams Collection, Montreal; Bibliothèque Nationale, Paris; Royal Photographic Society of Great Britain, Bath, Avon.

Publications:

By HOREIS: Article—"Carbon-Carbro: A History and the Method" in *Camera Canada* (Toronto), December 1976.

On HOREIS: Books—*Exposure,* exhibition catalogue, by Glenda Milrod and others, Toronto 1975; *Twelve Canadians,* edited by Jane Corkin, Toronto 1980. **Articles**—"Photography as an Art Form and as an Investment" in *Toronto Life,* September 1975; "The Frozen-Image Renaissance" by Adele Freedman in *Toronto Life,* May 1977.

*

I've been asked for a statement. Writing not being my medium (puts me in an uncomfortable position) I'll leave you with words written by others:

Adele Freedman—"Some photographers go shooting every day, some every week. William Horeis shoots once a year and spends the rest of his time printing. 'I literally spend all my time in a 6 x 12 room in the dark,' he chuckles, but his good humor and geniality prove that the cloistered life hasn't harmed him.

"Horeis makes beautiful images. He thinks there's enough misery in the world without adding more. 'Everything I do is conceptual,' he says. 'When someone buys an image, he's buying something of me.' He does single images only, no series, no stories. He sees, records, passes on.

"Horeis photographs as he finds. Opening the door of a hotel room in Portugal, he sees three oranges bound to a table by cobwebs and a chair at an inviting angle: he takes it. The arrangement is so spontaneous, it looks posed."

Carol Marino—"When photography was first invented, there were many who thought that at last technology could be harnessed in the service of art. Art has proven to be troublesome, and only a small percentage of those who try, succeed. William Horeis is one who succeeds."

—William Horeis

*   *   *

William Horeis creates intimate, precious photographic images of extraordinary beauty using a process that few other photographers would have the patience or inclination to attempt. Horeis works almost exclusively in the demanding technique of the carbon print. By way of a very condensed explanation: carbro prints are made by transferring the photographic image from a conventional silver-bromide print to a carbon pigment sheet, and then placing this carbon image in permanent contact with a paper support. This description does not, however, begin to explain the complexity of the process, the multitude of determining factors involved, and the skill and patience required of the artist who chooses to work with it. Horeis' involvement with and mastery of carbro printing is total. From negative image to finished print, which he mounts on hand-made paper, he controls each detailed aspect of the production of the work. To complete just one of these prints can often require a period of time exceeding one month. During this intense period of involvement with the image, the artist builds, alters and refines the image to its completed state, the print we eventually see on the gallery wall.

When we view Horeis' work, we are immediately aware of the visual signature of the carbro process. Yet at the same time we realize that these images do not rely solely on this intricate and fascinating technology in order to succeed. This art is more transcendent of, than bound to, its process. With an unerring eye for the optimal in composition, Horeis creates photographs that are exquisite explorations of tone. His images can, and often do, re-define black, white and grey as we know them. The dark areas of his prints contain a wealth of visual information, and his mid-tones suggest an opalescent luminosity. Horeis has used this masterful knowledge of light to produce photographs of elegance and serenity, images which convey a strong sense of their own spirituality. This spirituality is further heightened by the carbro process itself—the image seems to float up off the paper towards us in a subtle extension of the traditional dimensionality of the photographic image.

Perhaps no better illustration of the integrity of Horeis' art can be given than the following. In 1980, Horeis travelled to France and lived in and around Paris for about a month, producing during that time 25 new images. Upon his return to Canada, Horeis faced two important realities: firstly, the cost of materials that he required for the carbro prints had been steadily escalating to the point where it had almost become prohibitive; secondly, were he to make only one print of each of his new images, it would take three years to finish the printing. He selected to produce the series as traditional silver prints, although he intends to reprint later in carbro. In these new works we see again the scrupulous attention to detail, the exacting detail and poetic elegance that characterized the earlier work. Little, or nothing, has changed. In a medium that is generally and too often overly occupied with concerns of technique, the photographs of William Horeis are a quiet and extraordinary fusion of art and process.

—Bradford G. Gorman

HORST, Horst P(aul).

Nationality: American. **Born:** Weissenfels, Germany, 14 August 1906; immigrated to the United States, 1935; naturalized, 1942. **Education:** Attend-

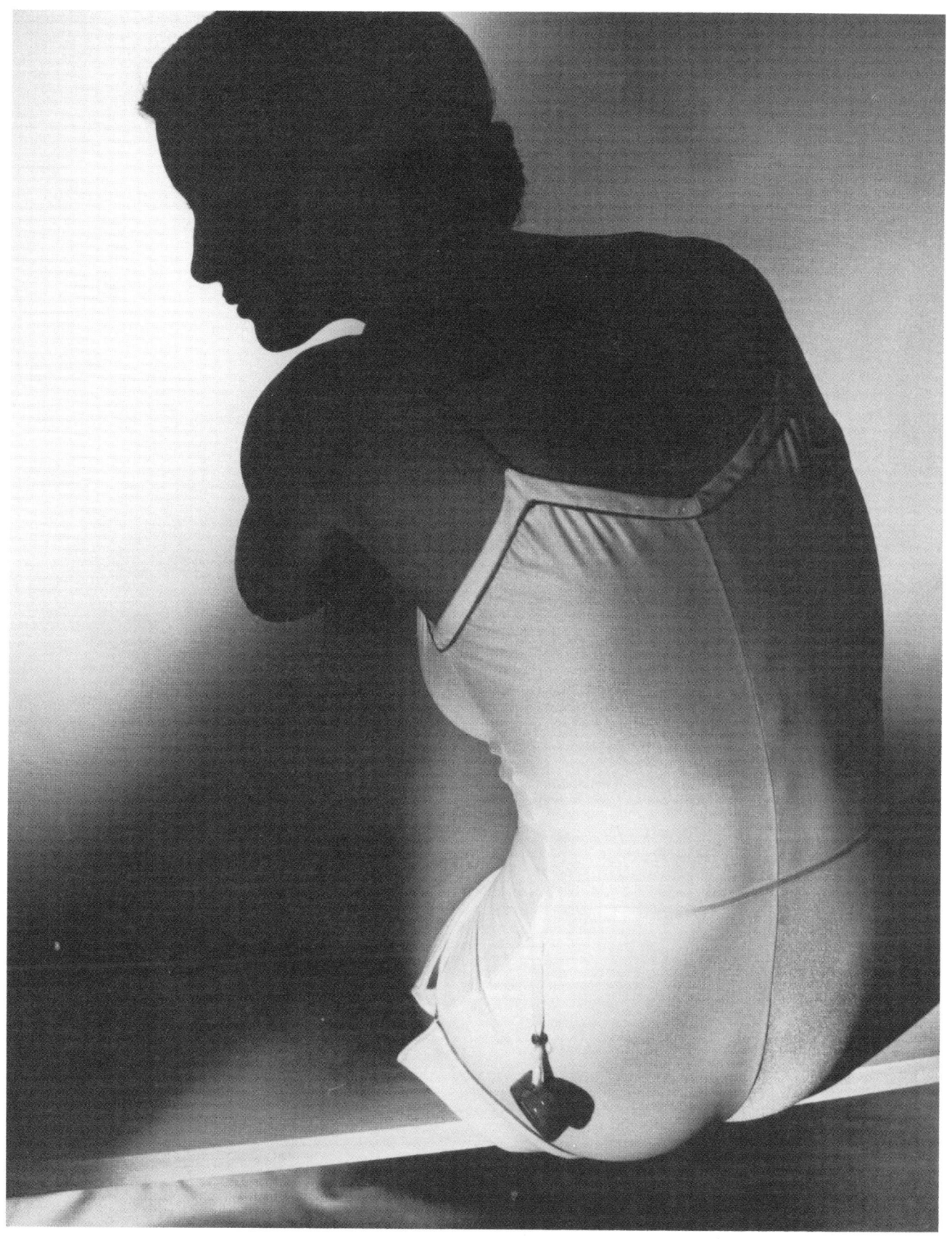

Courreges Bathing Suit, **1979.** Photograph by Horst.

ed the Oberrealschule, Weissenfels, 1912-20; studied architecture at the Kunstgewerbeschule, Hamburg, 1926-28; student-apprentice, studio of the architect Le Corbusier, Paris, 1930. **Military Service:** Served in the United States Army, 1942-45: Technical Sergeant. **Career:** Photographer, with George Hoyningen-Huene, in the *Vogue* magazine studios, Condé Nast Publications, Paris, 1932-35, and in the Condé Nast Studios, New York (*Vogue*), since 1935; maintained Horst Studio, East 55th Street, New York, 1952-70. **Agent:** Staley-Wise Gallery, 560 Broadway, New York, New York 10012, U.S.A.

Individual Exhibitions:

1932	Galerie La Plume d'Or, Paris
1938	Germain Seligman Gallery, New York
1958	Sagittarius Gallery, New York
	Country Art Gallery, Westbury, New York
1974	Sonnabend Gallery, New York
1976	Sonnabend Gallery, New York
1977	Sonnabend Gallery, New York
1978	Galerie Sonnabend, Paris
1980	Sonnabend Gallery, New York
1981	Galerie Contretype, Brussels
1982	Staley Wise Gallery, New York
1984	International Center of Photography, New York (retrospective; travelled to Montreal, Venice, Florence, and London, 1985-86)
	Staley Wise Gallery, New York

Selected Group Exhibitions:

1975	*Fashion 1900-1939,* Victoria and Albert Museum, London
1977	*Fashion Photography,* International Museum of Photography, George Eastman House, Rochester, New York (travelled to the Brooklyn Museum, New York; San Francisco Museum of Modern Art; Cincinnati Art Museum, Ohio; and the Museum of Fine Arts, St. Petersburg, Florida)
1979	*Fleeting Gestures: Dance Photography,* International Center of Photography, New York (travelled to The Photographer's Gallery, London; and *Venezia '79*)
	The Fashionable World, Stephen White Gallery, Los Angeles
1980	*La Mode,* Galerie Zabriskie, Paris
	Allure, International Center of Photography, New York
1982	*Lichtbildnisse: Das Porträt in der Fotografie,* Rheinisches Landesmuseum, Bonn
	Color as Form, International Museum of Photography at George Eastman House, Rochester, New York
1985	*Das Aktfoto,* Fotomuseum im Stadtmuseum, Munich (travelled to Frankfurt, Vienna and Dortmund)

Collections:

Metropolitan Museum of Art, New York; Museum Ludwig, Cologne.

Publications:

By HORST: Books—*Photographs of a Decade,* New York 1945; *Orientals,* editor, New York 1945; *Patterns from Nature,* New York 1946; *Vogue's Book of Houses, Gardens, People,* with text by V. Lawford, New York and London 1963; *Salute to the Thirties,* with George Hoyningen-Huene, New York and London 1971; *Return Engagement: Faces to Remember, Then and Now,* with text by James Watters, New York 1984.

On HORST: Books—*U.S. Camera Annual 1936,* edited by Tom J. Maloney, London and New York 1936; *Fame: Famous Portraits of Famous People by Famous Photographers,* edited by L. Fritz Gruber, London and New York 1960; *Beauty: Variations on the Theme Woman by Masters of the Camera— Past and Present,* edited by L. Fritz Gruber, London and New York 1965; *The Magic Image* by Cecil Beaton and Gail Buckland, London and Boston 1975; *Documenta 6/ Band 2,* exhibition catalogue, edited by Klaus Honnef and

Evelyn Weiss, Kassel, West Germany 1977; *Photographie als Kunst 1879-1979/Kunst als Photographie 1949-1979,* exhibition catalogue, 2 volumes, by Peter Weiermair, Innsbruck, Austria 1979; *The History of Fashion Photography* by Nancy Hall-Duncan, New York 1979; *Visions and Images: American Photographers on Photography,* edited by Barbaralee Diamonstein, New York 1981; *Lichtbildnisse: Das Porträt in der Fotografie,* edited by Klaus Honnef, Cologne 1982; *The Library of World Photography: Portraits,* with introduction by Colin Ford, Tokyo 1982, 1983, London 1983; *Master Photographers: The World's Great Photographers on Their Art and Technique,* edited by Pat Booth, London 1983; *Horst,* exhibition catalogue, by William A. Ewing and Nancy Hall-Duncan, New York 1984; *Horst: His Work and World* by Valentine Lawford, New York 1984. **Articles—**"H.P. Horst" in *The Studio,* by Time-Life editors, New York 1972; "Horst" by P. Beard and R. Kent in *Inter/View* (New York), April 1974; "New York: H.P. Horst, Sonnabend Gallery" in *Artforum* (New York), May 1974; "Horst in Fashion" by Barbara Rose in *Vogue* (New York), May 1976; "Women in Fashion: Horst" in *Photo World* (New York), April/May 1977; "For Horst, Artifice Was Everything" by Gene Thornton in the *New York Times,* 30 September 1984.

*

I like taking photographs, because I like life. And I like photographing people best of all, because most of all I love humanity.

—Horst P. Horst

*   *   *

When Horst P. Horst began to photograph for *Vogue* in 1932, fashion photography was still largely in thrall to the style introduced by Steichen in the 1920s and subsequently refined by Hoyningen-Huene. Horst, who had originally come to Paris to study architecture with Le Corbusier, turned instead to photography after making the acquaintance of Hoyningen-Huene, and his own earliest work echoes Hoyningen-Huene's cool classicism. Models were photographed with meticulous precision under artificial lights; studio sets were austere; backgrounds were plain or severely geometric.

Within a few years, however, Horst developed a more frankly ornamental style that was unmistakably his own. His combination of extravagant visual fantasy and vibrant sensuality sets his fashion photographs quite apart from those of *Vogue's* two other principal photographers of the 1930s, Steichen and Cecil Beaton. Gradually introducing more imaginatively furnished sets and drapery, Horst arranged his tableaux with an eye for elegant undulating lines and sophisticated lighting effects. Amid rich surroundings, his model's face might be thrown unexpectedly into silhouette, giving rise to a mood of calculated mystery and anticipation.

In addition to his fashion photographs, Horst produced during the 1930s a series of highly regarded portraits of the leading personalities of the day, including Dietrich, Dali, Cocteau, and the Duke and Duchess of Windsor. Often done outside the studio, these portraits lack the formal perfection of Horst's fashion work, but effectively transmit the air of sometimes desperate gaiety that marked the period between the wars. Although he remains active, and has published highly successful interior studies and patterned abstractions from natural forms, Horst continues to be irrevocably linked with the sensibility of the 1930s.

—Christopher Phillips

HORVAT, Frank.

Nationality: Italian. **Born:** Abbazia, Italy (now Opatija, Croatia), 28 April 1928. **Education:** Attended secondary school in Lugano, Switzerland, 1939-45; studied drawing at the Accademia di Brera, Milan, 1948-49; self-taught in photography, from 1944. **Family:** Married Maria Terese Lorenzetti in 1956; sons: Michel, Lorenzo and Marco; married Marie Louise Pierson in 1966; son: David; married Alexandra De Leal in 1979; daughter: Sara-Fiammetta.

***Rome,* 1962.** Photograph by Frank Horvat.

Career: Worked as a graphic artist in various advertising agencies, Milan, 1949-50. Freelance photographer, working for *Epoca, Paris-Match, Picture Post, Life, Jardin des Modes, Elle, Vogue, Harper's Bazaar, Glamour, Esquire, Réalités, Revue, Twen,* etc., in Milan, Paris, London and New York, since 1951: settled in Paris, working for the American news agency Black Star, 1956; Associate Photographer, Magnum Photos co-operative agency, Paris, 1959-62; established Frank Horvat Studio, Boulogne-Billancourt, 1968. **Recipient:** Saint Christopher Award, Paris, 1980. **Address:** Frank Horvat Studio, 5 rue de l'Ancienne Mairie, 92100 Boulogne-Billancourt, France.

Individual Exhibitions:

1977	*Trees,* Musée des Arts Décoratifs, Nantes, France (travelled to the International Center of Photography, New York, 1978, The Photographers' Gallery, London, 1979 and Artcurial, Paris, 1980)
1980	Photographers' Gallery, London (retrospective)
1981	Galerie Mamya, Paris (retrospective)
	Galleria Novecento, Palermo, Sicily
	Zeit-Foto Salon, Tokyo
1982	National Museum, Malta
1983	*Arbres,* Centre Georges Pompidou, Paris
	Maison de la Culture, Angouleme, France
	Galerie La Chambre Claire, Paris
	Vraies Semblances, Espace Canon, Paris
1984	Centre Culturel, Toulon, France
	Sander Gallery, New York
1985	Centre d'Art Contemporain, Montbeliard, France
	Arbres, Kunstmuseum, Berlin-Neukölln, West Germany
1986	*Vraies Semblances,* Galleria Novecento, Palermo, Italy
1988	*Fashion Photographs,* French Cultural Center, Prague and Bell Commons, Tokyo
1989	*Fashion Photographs,* Prinz Gallery, Kyoto; Paris Audiovisuel, Paris; Fashion Photography Festival, Trouville, France
	Album de Famille, Comptoir de la Photographie, Paris
1990	*Vraies Semblances,* Fotofest, Houston; French Institute, New York
1991	*Digital Images,* FNAC, Paris
	Fashion Photography, travelling exhibition by FNAC
	Black and White Work, Folio Gallery, Calgary, Canada
	Retrospective at Galerie du Chateau d'Eau, Toulouse, France
1992	*Digital Images,* Picto Gallery, Paris
	Fashion Photography and *Digital Images,* Fotofolies, Rodez, France
1993	*Le Bestiaire d'Horvat,* Centre National de la Photographie, Paris

Selected Group Exhibitions:

1955	*The Family of Man,* Museum of Modern Art, New York (and world tour)
1964	*World Exhibition of Photography: What Is Man?,* Pressehaus Stern, Hamburg (and world tour)
1968	*2nd World Exhibition of Photography: Woman,* Pressehaus Stern, Hamburg (and world tour)
1973	*3rd World Exhibition of Photography: On The Way To Paradise,* Pressehaus Stern, Hamburg (and world tour)
1980	*The Imaginary Photo Museum,* Kunsthalle, Cologne
1982	*Paris-Paris,* Centre Georges Pompidou, Paris
1984	*Sammlung Gruber,* Museum Ludwig, Cologne
1985	*Shots of Style,* Victoria and Albert Museum, London (toured Britain)
	Das Aktfoto, Fotomuseum im Stadmuseum, Munich (toured Germany)
1991	*Appearances,* Victoria and Albert Museum, London
1992	*Photographie et Sculpture,* Centre National de la Photographie, Paris
1993	*Vanites,* Centre National de la Photographie, Paris
1994	*The Select Collection,* Musée de l'Elysée, Lausanne, Switzerland

Collections:

Bibliothèque Nationale, Paris; Musée des Arts Décoratifs, Nantes, France; Fonds National d'Art Contemporain, Paris; Victoria and Albert Museum, London; Centre Pompidou, Paris; Maison Européene de la Photographie, Paris; Museum of Modern Art, New York; Eastman House, Rochester, New York; Ludwig Museum, Koeln, Germany; Kunstbibliothek, Berlin; Select Collection, Lausanne, Switzerland.

Publications:

By HORVAT: Books—*Television,* Lausanne 1962; *Strip-Tease,* Lausanne 1962; *The Tree,* with text by John Fowles, London 1978; *Goethe in Sicilia,* Palermo, Sicily 1982; *Cote Mode,* Paris 1989; *Les Sculptures de Degas,* Paris 1991; *Le Chat Botte,* Paris 1992; *Arbres,* Paris 1994; *Le Bestiaire d'Horvat,* Paris 1994. **Articles**—"Tete a tete avec Frank Horvat," 3 interviews, in *Photo-Magazine* (Paris), September, October and November 1985.

On HORVAT: Books—*Fame: Famous Portraits of Famous People by Famous Photographers,* edited by L. Fritz Gruber, London and New York 1960; *The History of the Nude in Photography* by Peter Lacey, London 1964, 1969; *The Imaginary Photo Museum* by Helmut Gernsheim, Renate and L. Fritz Gruber and others, Cologne 1981, London 1982; *The Library of World Photography: Landscape,* with texts by David Plowden and Ian Jeffrey, Tokyo and London 1984; *Sammlung Gruber: Photographie des 20. Jahrhunderts,* exhibition catalogue, with foreword by Siegfried Gohr, Cologne 1984; *Shots of Style: Great Fashion Photographs Chosen by David Bailey,* with text by Martin Harrison, London 1985; *Appearances: Fashion Photography since 1945,* by Martin Harrison, London and New York 1991. **Articles**—"Les Photographes Aiment-ils les Mannequins" in *Elle* (Paris), 8 April 1974; "Frank Horvat" in *Zoom* (Paris), November 1977; "Les Bonheurs de Horvat" in *Photo* (Paris), February 1981.

*

I must admit that—in the beginning—photography seemed to me the easiest way to express something. This was when I was twenty years old, and just mature enough to realize that my poems were not very good and my drawings even worse.

Rather than sitting in front of a blank page, I would pick up my camera and go searching. There was always something on a contact sheet that seemed worth printing and looked as if I had had something to say. When necessary, I would go to the extreme heresy of enlarging some minute part of a negative (the printer down the street hated the moment when he saw me arriving with detailed instructions about how to do so).

In time, I started to understand the fundamental difficulty of photography—as a counterpart to its fundamental easiness. One can visualize this difficulty by comparing the millions of miles of film that have been made and processed to the few thousand photographs worth being preserved for posterity.

But even now, thirty years later, I feel that I have only begun to understand: had I really understood the difficulty, my film would remain as blank as the paper in front of which I was sitting as a young man.

Actually this happens from time to time: I then say to myself that photography is the art of not pressing the button, of refusing an infinite number of possibilities, expressions, angles, lighting effects, which do not coincide exactly with my accumulated expectation.

For this is the photographer's work, as I see it: to look at things for hours, days, or weeks, to walk and look until something is created in the mind which is not an image or even the negative of an image, but an emptiness, *the need* for an image (for an image like an archetype or an idea in the Platonic sense). And only after this preparation has been completed, lift the camera to the eye and let the millions of possible visual combinations run through the viewfinder, just as a computer lets the endless series of possible figures run through its mechanism, until it clicks and stops at the figure that it was programmed to find.

(This metaphor is only partly correct: a computer can do nothing but accept passively the series of figures that are fed into it, while the photographer can be active in creating the visual combination that fits his "programme" either by explicitly directing what is in front of his lens, or by one of many more subtle, less explicit ways of causing things to happen.)

In fact, photography appears to me now, just as it did thirty years ago, as a job at once too easy and too difficult. It is too easy to have the whole wealth of the visible world laid out in front of oneself, and to be able to own it by merely pressing a button. Too difficult to have to find, within the messy infinity of all possible visual combinations, the one and only instant and angle in which every detail shall have found its order and its place, to coincide with the archetype in the mind.

The word "order" is certainly one of my key words. I feel deeply threatened by the idea of entropy, by the lack of order in general, and by the messiness of the contemporary world in particular. The one thing that I would like to leave behind me is just a tiny bit of order at least within the fragment of the world that I can frame and stop in my viewfinder.

To "stop" would be my second key word—stop *time*, of course. This was most certainly my first and deepest motivation when, at the age of sixteen, I sold my collection of postage stamps in order to buy a second-hand Retinamat camera. There is nothing original about this illusion of stopping time. It makes the stockholders of Eastman Kodak earn the millions of dollars they are earning. It also gives some very high ups and some very low downs, just like a narcotic. One of the downs is the feeling that I get in front of my drawers full of contact sheets and transparencies that I have the courage neither to file nor throw away. Not only because I hate the feeling of dust on my fingers, but also because it is unbearable to have to face a time that is no more.

The third keyword is one that I hesitate to name: "grace"—in an almost theological sense. If I had to estimate how many times I have pushed that button (at an average of a thousand 36-exposure films per year), I would end up with a seven digit figure. I know that through the efforts of my eyes and my legs, through my gimmicks and my stubbornness, I have been able many times to make the composition in the viewfinder coincide with the archetype in the mind. But of some photographs—not many of them, somewhere between ten and fifteen—I know that I did not make them: they have been given to me. They are probably the ones that are worth being preserved.

—Frank Horvat

*   *   *

In common with many reportage photographers who emerged in the 1950s, Frank Horvat was faced, early in his career, with the decline of the established outlets for this kind of work. The demise of magazines such as *Life* and *Picture Post* (for both of which Horvat worked) was accelerated by the emergence of television as the dominant medium for the reporting of news and current events. In these circumstances, his professional survival as a freelance depended on his ability to adapt. His associations with the American Black Star agency from 1956 and with Magnum from 1959 until 1962, though both relatively brief, indicate his willingness to diversify and to operate on the broadest possible front. And although it was first as a photo-journalist and then as a fashion photographer that Horvat eventually became famous, the many other facets of his restless vision continue to attest to the extremely wide range of his interests.

Horvat first visited Paris, where he met Robert Capa and Henri Cartier-Bresson, in 1951, and settled there five years later. In 1957 he made a series with a 35mm camera and long focal-length lenses which was published in *Camera.* Jacques Moutin, art director of the magazine *Jardin des Modes,* saw these photographs and invited Horvat to apply the same techniques to fashion photography. This fortuitous introduction to the world of fashion steered his career in a new direction. Cartier-Bresson advised him against attempting to mix reportage techniques with the illustration of fashions, but Horvat, who had neither a studio nor a deep devotion to the depiction of the latest styles, had to fall back on a way of relating to his new subject matter which came naturally to him. Paradoxically, what grew out of his lack of experience enabled him to become a pioneer in the genre. He was the first to consistently use a 35mm camera in a way that eliminated much of the artificiality associated with fashion photography, but of even greater significance were the qualities of naturalness, affection and wit which characterized his work. Above all, was the respect he maintained for the women in front of his camera as individuals. This was manifested on a level in his horror of the excessive make-up applied to models, his removal of which was a radical step at the time and an important contributory factor in the freshness of his photographs. His ability was soon acknowledged, and his ideas became widely influential through their dissemi-

nation in magazines such as *Harper's Bazaar* in the U.S. and *Vogue* and *Queen* in Britain.

Horvat's disinclination to repeat himself fitted in well with fashion photography's voracious appetite for the new, but eventually disenchantment set in, and he began to concentrate increasingly on projects of greater personal significance. An abiding preoccupation has been his love of trees, which he began to photograph in 1976 and on which subject he has published two remarkable books, *Trees* in 1978 and *Arbres* in 1994. Two books of colour photographs due to be published at the time of writing further confirm the breadth of his interests—one is devoted to the urban landscape of New York, the other to stunning photographs of exotic animals which combine the latest developments in computer-generated imagery.

—Martin Harrison

HOSKING, Eric (John).

Nationality: British. **Born:** London, 2 October 1909. **Education:** Attended the Stationers' Company School, Hornsey, London, 1919-25; self-taught in photography. **Family:** Married Dorothy Sleigh in 1939; children: Margaret, Robin, and David. **Career:** Worked as an apprentice, Stewart and Arden motor-car dealers, London, 1925-26; Clerk/Salesman, George Johnston Ltd., motor parts dealers, London, 1926-29. Freelance bird and wildlife photographer, working for *The Times, Daily Mirror, Weekly Illustrated, Picture Post, Country Life, News Chronicle,* etc., London, since 1929. Photographic Editor, *New Naturalist,* London, 1942-86; Nature Editor, *Daily Mail* School-Aid Publications, London, 1945-47; Photographic Editor, *British Birds* magazine, London, 1960-76. Director of Photography, Coto Donana Expedition, Spain, 1956, 1957; Leader, Cazoria Valley Expedition, Spain, 1959; Director of Photography, British Ornithologists Expedition, Bulgaria, 1960, and Hungary, 1961; Mountfort Expedition, Jordan, 1963; British Expedition in Jordan, 1965, and Pakistan, 1966; World Wildlife Fund Expedition, Pakistan, 1967; Member: Lindblad Expedition, Galapagos Islands, 1970; Kenya and Rhodesia, 1972; Tanzania and Kenya, 1974, 1977; Seychelles, 1978; India, Nepal, Falklands and Antarctic, 1979; New Zealand, Australia and California, 1982; Canadian Arctic and Greenland, 1983; Alaska, 1984; Sri Lanka and Israel, 1985; Madagascar, Coromos, Aldabra and the Seychelles, 1986. Vice-President, Royal Society for the Protection of Birds, 1947-86; Member of the Council, 1950-56, and Member of the Fellowship and Associateship Admissions Committee, 1951-56, 1960-65, 1970-86, Royal Photographic Society; Chairman, Photographic Advisory Committee, Nature Conservancy, London, 1953-73; President, Zoological Photographic Club, London, 1959; President, Nature Photographic Society, London, 1980; Vice-President, British Ornithologists' Union, 1969-72. **Recipient:** Wildlife Photography Medal, *Country Life* magazine, London, 1950; Cherry Kearton Award, Royal Geographical Society, 1968; Kodak Award, 1969; Gold Medal, Royal Society for the Protection of Birds, 1974; Silver Medal, Zoological Society, London, 1975. Fellow, British Institute of Professional Photographers, London; Honorary Vice-President, London Natural History Society, 1959; Honorary Vice-President, British Naturalists' Association, 1962; Honorary Fellow, Royal Photographic Society, 1967. O.B.E. (Officer, Order of the British Empire), 1977. Memorial: The Eric Hosking Charitable Trust, Pages Green House, Wetheringsett, Stowmarket, Suffolk, IP14 5QA, UK, awards bursaries to writers, photographers, painters and illustrators of birds and other natural history subjects. Applications with return mail prepaid only. **Agent:** Frank Lane Picture Agency, Pages Green House, Wetheringsett, Stowmarket, Suffolk, IP14 5QA, England. **Died:** (in London) 22 February 1991.

Individual Exhibitions:

1932   Royal Photographic Society, London
1957   Kodak Gallery, Kingsway, London (and world tour)
1967   Royal Photographic Society, London
1979   Kodak Gallery, High Holborn, London
        Olympus Gallery, London
        Brotherton Gallery, London

Nightjar Hovering, **1949.** Photograph ©Eric Hosking.

1980   Fox Talbot Museum, Lacock, Wiltshire
          An Eye for a Bird, Olympus Gallery, London
1982   *Antarctic Wildlife,* Olympus Gallery, London
1993   The Wildlife Art Gallery, Lavenham
1994   The Gallery, Pensthorpe Waterfowl Trust

Selected Group Exhibitions:

1950   *Country Life International Wildlife Photography Exhibition,*
          London
1981   *Points of View,* Kodak Gallery, London
1986   *Impression of Israel,* Selfridges Department Store, London

Publications:

By HOSKING: Books—*Friends of the Zoo,* with Cyril Newberry, London 1932; *Intimate Sketches from Bird Life,* London 1940; *The Art of Bird Photography,* with C.W. Newberry, London 1944; *Birds of the Day,* London 1944; *Birds of the Night,* London 1945; *More Birds of the Day,* London 1946; *The Swallow,* London 1946; *Masterpieces of Bird Photography,* with H. Lowes, London 1947; *Birds in Action,* with C.W. Newberry, London 1949; *Birds Fighting,* London 1955; *Bird Photography as a Hobby,* London 1961; *Nesting Birds, Eggs and Fledglings,* London 1967; *An Eye for a Bird* (autobiography), with F.W. Lane, London 1970, 1973; *Wildlife Photography,* with John Gooders, London 1973, 1976; *Minsmere,* with Herbert Axell, London 1977; *Birds of Britain,* with Herbert Axell, London 1978; *A Passion for Birds,* with Kevin MacDonnell, London 1979; *Antarctic Wildlife,* with text by Bryan Sage, London 1981; *Eric Hosking's Owls,* with Jim Flegg, foreword by Ian Prestt, London, 1982, 1985; *Eric Hosking's Waders,* with W. G. Hale, foreword by Peter Scott, London 1983; *Eric Hosking's Seabirds,* with text by Ronald M. Lockley, London and Claremont, South Africa 1983; *Just a Lark!,* with David Hosking, text by Jim Flegg, London 1984; *Eric Hosking's Wildfowl,* with Janet Kear, London 1985; *Encyclopedia of Bible Animals,* with David Hosking and Peter France, London 1986; *Which Bird?,* with David Hosking and Jim Flegg, London 1986; *Birds of Prey of the World,* with Jim Flegg and David Hosking, London 1987; *Poles Apart,* with Jim Flegg and David Hosking, London 1990; *Field Guide to the Birds of Britain and Europe,* with Jim Flegg and David Hosking, London 1990; *Field Guide to the Trees of Britain and Europe,* with Jim Flegg and David Hosking, London 1992; *Eric Hosking's Classic Birds,* text by Jim Flegg and David Hosking, London 1993.

On HOSKING: Books—*The Magic Image: The Genius of Photography from 1839 to the Present* by Cecil Beaton and Gail Buckland, London and Boston 1975; *How Famous Photographers Work* by Jack Schofield and others, London 1983. **Articles**—"Eric Hosking" in *Olympus Camera Club News* (London), February 1986; obituary by Val Williams in *The Independent,* February 1991; obituary by Heather Angel in *The Times,* February 1991; Tribute to Eric Hosking by Heather Angel in *The Photographic Journal,* May 1991.

*   *   *

Eric Hosking has been called the world's greatest bird photographer—with good reason. Fine photographers have not overtaken him.

During the 50 years that he was a professional wildlife photographer, Hosking was totally dedicated to nature photography and, apart from his family, had no other interest. At the outset of his career he gained inspiration from Richard Kearton—his boyhood hero—who established a reputation for photographing birds in the early years of the 20th century. Whenever Kearton was scheduled to lecture in North London, Hosking met him at the station and carried his slides for him. Dedication and enthusiasm are vital ingredients, but of themselves they are insufficient to attain the pinnacle of fame; however, these qualities may have produced the mysterious X factor which singles Hosking out from other photographers. He built on the traditions of bird watching initiated by Gilbert White more than two centuries ago, and developed the remarkable ability of knowing bird behavior so intimately that he anticipated the action he wished to photograph in the split second necessary to fire the camera shutter. In addition to knowledge, he had a great love for all living things: "A true bird photographer is primarily interested in the welfare

of the birds and will go to great trouble to disturb them as little as possible. The birds must come first."

Hosking had a natural and unerring "eye for a picture," an inborn aesthetic appreciation of good design, and a remarkable facility for capturing the right moment. The animals, birds or butterflies in his photographs are featured to perfection in appropriate surroundings and many are decorative as well. His photographs give great pleasure, not only because they communicate so well but also because they are aesthetically admirable.

Until 1947 Hosking used a quarter plate Sanderson camera on a tripod, and in 1935 he was the first photographer in Britain to use Sashalite flash bulbs for natural history subjects. He claimed that this technique (advanced for the period) resulted in the production of one his most famous photographs, a barn owl carrying a large rat to its nest. He took the cap off the lens in darkness, waited for the sound of the bird returning to the nest, and then fired the flash bulb.

The biggest problem he faced was the photography of birds in flight. In 1946-47 Dr. Philip Henry of the British Cotton Research Establishment in Manchester built him electronic flash equipment weighing more than 100 weight with another 40 pounds weight of battery. One 5/1,000 of a second gave excellent exposures, but human reactions are not sufficiently quick to fire the shutter at that precise fraction of a second. Henry therefore devised an ancillary system whereby the birds photographed themselves when they passed through the light beam of a photo-electric cell. Hosking's most famous photograph, "Barn Owl in Flight in Heraldic Pose," was produced (in 1948) while he was experimenting with this equipment.

Although modern electronic technology associated with skilled camera operation is essential to the achievement of high standards in nature photography, even more important is the initial visualization of the subject, the determination of viewpoint, and the final decision on selection from the several exposures made of the same subject. Hosking had that kind of vital "know-how." Although birds were his favourite subject, his most outstanding photographs are of owls, and he travelled all over the world photographing animals, insects, fish, wild flowers, trees and the range of animals in captivity. 250,000 black-and-white photographs and 100,000 colour transparencies are recorded, indexed and filed in his archives, which include documentation of 2,000 species of birds. At an age when most people take life more easily, it was still an adventure for Eric Hosking: "It is hard to say what future electronic developments are in store, but the photography of birds in flight becomes more and more exciting as time goes by."

—Margaret Harker

HOSOE, Eikoh.

Nationality: Japanese. **Born:** Toshihiro Hosoe in Yonezawa, Yamagata Prefecture, 18 March 1933. Studied at the Tokyo College of Photography (Tokyo Shashin Daigaku), 1952-54. **Family:** Married Misako Imai in 1962; children: Kenji, Kanako, and Kumiko. **Career:** Freelance photographer, Tokyo, since 1954. Professor of Photography, Tokyo Institute of Polytechnics, since 1975. **Recipient:** Photographer of the Year Award, Japan Photo Critics Association, 1963; Art Award, Ministry of Education, 1970; Honorary Citizen Award, Tucson, Arizona, 1977; Medaille de Vermeil, City of Paris, 1982; Medal of the City of Arles, France, 1983; Photographer of the Year Award, Photographic Society of Japan, 1993. **Agent:** Howard Greenberg Gallery, 120 Wooster Street, New York, New York 10012, U.S.A. **Address:** 2-1-10 Kugayama, Suginami-ku, Tokyo, Japan 168.

Individual Exhibitions:

1956   *An American Girl in Tokyo,* Konishiroku Gallery,
          Ginza, Tokyo
1960   *Man and Woman,* Konishiroku Gallery, Ginza, Tokyo
1969   *Kamaitachi,* Nikon Salon, Ginza, Tokyo
          Man and Woman, Smithsonian Institution, Washington, D.C.
1973   *Eikoh Hosoe,* Light Gallery, New York (partial retrospective)
1975   *Simon: A Private Landscape,* Light Gallery, New York

Witnesses of the End of the 20th Century, **1992.** Photograph ©Eikoh Hosoe.

1977   *Gaudi,* Nikon Salon, Ginza, Tokyo (travelled to the Nikon
        Salon, Shinjuku, Tokyo, and the Nikon Salon, Osaka)
1979   *Eikoh Hosoe: Retrospective,* Photographers' Gallery,
        Melbourne
        *Ralph Eugene Meatyard: Photographs/Eikoe Hosoe:
        Kamaitachi,* Silver Image Gallery, Ohio State University,
        Columbus
1980   *Ordeal by Roses and Kamaitachi,* FNAC Forum, Paris
1981   *Eikoh Hosoe: Retrospective with Recent Works,* Galerij Paule
        Pia, Antwerp
1982   *The Human Figure 1960-1980,* International Museum of
        Photography, George Eastman House, Rochester, New York
        (travelled to the Musée d'Art Moderne, Paris; Rochester
        Institute of Technology, New York)
1983   Light Gallery, New York
        Ordeal by Roses, National Gallery of Canada, Ottawa
1984   *The Cosmos of Gaudi,* Ginza Printemps Gallery, Tokyo
        Zen and Transcendence, Padiglione d'Arte
        Contemporanea, Milan
1985   *Color Works,* Shunju Gallery, Tokyo
        Burden Gallery, New York
        Madison Art Center, Wisconsin
        Vision Gallery, San Francisco (with Johnny Alterman)
1988   *The World of Eikoh Hosoe,* Ikeda Museum of 20th Century
        Art, Ito, Japan; Niigata City Museum of Art, Niigata, Japan
1989   National Museum of Art, Osaka, Japan
1990   *Eikoh Hosoe: META,* Houston Foto Fest, Texas; Center for
        Creative Photography, Tucson, Arizona
1991   International Center of Photography, Midtown, Manhattan,
        New York
1993   *Before Awakening: Toward the End of the Century,* I.C.A.C.
        Weston Gallery, Tokyo
1994   *Eikoh Hosoe: META,* Museum of Arts, University of
        Washington

Selected Group Exhibitions:

1967   *Photography in the 20th Century,* National Gallery of Canada,
        Ottawa (toured Canada and the United States, 1967-73)
1974   *New Japanese Photography,* Museum of Modern Art,
        New York
1976   *Japanese Contemporary Photography,* Städtisches Museum,
        Graz, Austria
1979   *Japanese Photography Today and Its Origin,* Galleria d'Arte
        Moderna, Bologna (travelled to the Palazzo Reale, Milan;
        Palais des Beaux-Arts, Brussels; the Institution of
        Contemporary Arts, London; Museum für Kunst und
        Gewerbe, Hamburg; Gemeente Museum, Arnhem; and
        Pulchri Studio, The Hague)
1980   *The Imaginary Photo Museum,* Kunsthalle, Cologne
1981   *Astrazione e Realtà,* Galleria Flaviana, Locarno, Switzerland
1982   *International Photography 1920-80,* Australian National
        Gallery, Canberra
1983   *New Perspectives on the Nude,* Ffotogallery, Cardiff, Wales
1984   *Sammlung Gruber,* Museum Ludwig, Cologne
1985   *Black Sun,* Museum of Modern Art, Oxford, England (travelled
        to the Serpentine Gallery, London; Philadelphia Museum of
        Art, 1986)
1991   *Beyond Japan,* Barbican Art Gallery, London

Collections:

Shadai Gallery, Tokyo; Nihin University, Tokyo; Museum of Modern Art,
New York; International Museum of Photography, George Eastman House,
Rochester, New York; Smithsonian Institution, Washington, D.C.; National

Gallery of Canada, Ottawa; Victoria and Albert Museum, London; Bibliothèque
Nationale, Paris; National Gallery of Australia, Canberra; Musée d'Art
Moderne, Paris; Tokyo Institute of Polytechnics, Tokyo; Tokyo Metropolitan
Museum of Photography, Tokyo; Kawasaki City Museum, Kawasaki.

Publications:

By HOSOE: Books—*Man and Woman,* with an introduction by Van der
Elsken, Tokyo 1961; *Killed by Roses,* with a preface by Yukio Mishima,
Tokyo 1963, reissued in different form as *Ordeal by Roses,* Tokyo 1971; *Why,
Mother, Why? The Tragedy and Triumph of a Little Girl—in Poetry and
Pictures,* with Miyuki Furuta, Tokyo 1965; *Takachan and I,* with Betty Lifton,
New York 1967; *A Dog's Guide to Tokyo,* with Betty Lifton, New York 1969;
Kamaitachi, with a preface by Shuzo Takiguchi, Tokyo 1969; *Return to
Hiroshima,* with Betty Lifton, New York 1970; *Embrace,* with a preface by
Yukio Mishima, Tokyo 1971; *The Cosmos of Gaudi,* Tokyo 1984; *Barakei, or
Ordeal by Roses,* Aperture, New York 1985; *A Place Called Hiroshima,* with
B. J. Lifton, Tokyo 1985; *The Human Body,* New York 1986. **Article**—
interview in *Photography Between Covers* by Thomas Dugan, Rochester,
New York 1979.

On HOSOE: Books—*Gendai Shashin No Kenkyu/A Study of Contemporary
Photography* by Nobuya Yoshimura, Tokyo 1967; *Photography in the Twentieth Century* by Nathan Lyons, New York 1967; *New Japanese Photography,*
exhibition catalogue, by John Szarkowski and Shoji Yamagishi, New York
1974; *Neue Fotografie aus Japan,* exhibition catalogue, by Otto Breicha, Graz
and Vienna 1977; *De Japanse Fotografie van 1848 tot heden,* exhibition
catalogue, by Attilio Colombo and Isabella Doniselli, Amsterdam 1980; *Nude
Photographs of Japan,* with text by Shiroyasu Suzuki, Tokyo 1981; *Eikoh
Hosoe,* exhibition catalogue, by Claude Nori, Paris 1982; *Sammlung Gruber:
Photographie des 20. Jahrhunderts,* exhibition catalogue, with foreword by
Siegfried Gohr, Cologne 1984; *A Day in the Life of Japan—June 7, 1985,*
edited by Rick Smolan and David Cohen, New York and London 1985;
Masterpieces of Photography from George Eastman House, edited by Robert
A. Sobieszek, New York 1985. **Articles**—"Yukio Mishima/Eikoh Hosoe"
by Mark Holborn in *Artforum* (New York), March 1984; "Black Sun: The
Eyes of Four," special issue of *Aperture* (Millerton, New York), no. 102, 1986.

*

Photography is the way of my life, in which I always seek after anything
that is new to me.

Whenever I am about to take photographs, I devise a hypothesis—in other
words, prejudice or preconception, or perhaps it is a mixture of both. It has to
do with curiosity. I do not care whether the style of my photography is old or
new. What I do care about is that it provides me with a certain kind of
stimulation. If I start with a particular curiosity and decide it is unfair, then I'll
go on to discover something fresh—this often happens. The greater the
metamorphosis, the greater the excitement. If, however, my prejudice is
confirmed, then I realize that it is no longer prejudice but hypothesis. If it is a
true hypothesis, then I must offer the proof in my photography. Because I am a
photographer.

Regarding my works: let me briefly describe some of my experiences.

Man and Woman (1961) began with curiosity, my questioning of *Genesis*
II, 23:

> Now this, at last—
> bone from my bones,
> flesh from my flesh!—
> this shall be called woman,
> for from man was this taken.

Embrace (1971) is an extension of *Man and Woman* in a more developed
form. My question still remains, though. . . .

Ordeal by Roses (1963) was started as an effort at destruction of iconoclasm, that of the great Yukio Mishima; it also involved great respect for my subject. Destruction should be followed by reconstruction, and the project actually grew into a subjective documentary of Mishima based on my own imagination and vision of truth.

Kamaitachi (1969) was started as a record of my memories of World War II when I was evacuated to the countryside at the age of 11. The camera cannot express what you cannot see before your own eyes, yet that is precisely what a photographer often wishes to record with his camera. What does he do then? In my case, I had the co-operation of my friend, a great dancer named Tatsumi Hijikata. This series is also a subjective documentary of Hijikata in the countryside to which I had been evacuated. My intention was to photograph the total background, including the landscapes. Hijikata was a great catalyst. By throwing a stone into a pond you can see a beautiful ripple. I wanted to photograph the ripple, large or small, complete or a portion of it—as well as the dancer himself.

Surprised by the apparition of the dancer, the local farmers were at first apprehensive, but soon they began to laugh and they went on laughing. In their laughter I heard again the same laughter I had heard as a boy in that country. The night was dark and cold. The trees were like monsters in the darkness, and the far mountains were like a gigantic snake lying on the ground. There were many local folktales. Children enjoyed them, but they were often frightened. "Kamaitachi" was one of them: it frightened everyone.

"Gaudi," which has haunted me and on which I am now working, was started in curiosity, by questioning, and prejudice mixed with ignorance, love mixed with hate. I first saw Gaudi's architecture in Barcelona in 1964. I was completely overwhelmed. I could hardly take photographs; I simply stood and observed. When I returned to Barcelona in 1977, thirteen years had passed; I had prepared myself spiritually, I had studied. All of my complex thoughts and emotions regarding Gaudi suddenly became a question, whether what Gaudi had been searching for and had partially realized might have been Zen. Maybe another kind of Zen, produced on the opposite side of the world. That is my simply inspired intuition. During the past four years I have visited Barcelona six times, and my intuition has become firm: Yes, Gaudi must be Zen. This is now hypothesis. It may be just a prejudice. Who knows! But if it is a true hypothesis, then I must give proof of it in my photography. God help me.

—Eikoh Hosoe

*   *   *

Visual perception is kaleidoscopic in nature; that is, it is made of smaller bits of information, and whether they be cultural, personal, innate, or archetypal, they are in a constant state of flux. For Japanese photographer Eikoh Hosoe, born in 1933, his world and its traditions and dreams ran headlong into the Western world of the 20th century, and his photographic interpretations reflect the many facets of this confrontation.

Harmony or "wa," with its aesthetic ideal of a restrained and melancholic beauty, is a very central theme of Japanese life, and was indelibly upset by these changes. The focus now was on more demonic and atavistic aspects of the world, which intensified a naturally subjective and random approach to artistic expression.

The Japanese approach toward photography is also based in the Eastern sensibility of intuitive feeling as opposed to formalized reality. The photographer, Hosoe, through evocation and the power of suggestion, uses the image created as an indication of his personal experiences and intent, and the viewer must be the final interpreter of the picture.

Another important facet of artistic Japanese tradition is the influence of Zen in all aspects of life. It teaches that a seeker can find the eternal, the transcendence, in the simplest finite detail. Reaching Japan in the 12th century, Zen Buddhism stresses the "cultivation of the little," a mode that combines nature and intuition, expressed in terms that are refined, intimate, and disciplined. Devotees seek the ultimate insight, "satori," that Buddha received in Nirvana. This knowledge of non-ordinary reality, or abrupt enlightenment through a sudden grasp of reality, occurred for Eikoh Hosoe on a certain day in 1960. This experience inspired his body of work entitled "Man

and Woman," which has been described by Nobuya Yoshimura as "a work made in a spirit completely opposite to that of pornography." In other words, this "shows a group of naked men and women with every trace of pornography fastidiously removed." Hosoe's contemporary interpretation of eroticism developed from Japanese artistic genre and photographic milieu.

The wood block print—borrowed from the Dutch and known in Japan as "Ukiyo-e," or pictures of the floating world—developed in the 17th and 18th centuries for the emerging lower classes. The "Ukiyo-e" prints by Harunobu, Utamaro, Hokusai, and Hiroshige, with their dynamic composition and their graphically erotic and sometimes pornographic subjects and themes, attained world-wide recognition. Their influence on Western artists, among them painter James Abbott McNeill Whistler, in turn affected the Pictorialists, Coburn, Steichen, and White, whose similar styles are characterized by soft focus, deep shadows, and strong linear compositions.

Photographically, it was not until the 1920s that serious art photography of the nude began in Japan, and the results left some critics viewing the pictures as romanticized and sentimental.

Against the diverse, evolving tapestry of Japanese artistic development, Hosoe chose to continue his photographic exploration of the nude, known as "Embrace," almost immediately after completion of "Man and Woman" in 1961. However, it was not shown until 10 years later because a photographic exhibition of Bill Brandt's "Perspective of Nude" showing in Japan at that time, greatly resembled those in "Embrace," so according to Hosoe, "I stopped working on it for a time."

"Embrace," with its strict adherence to form and graphic detail, depicts Hosoe's confrontation with the Japanese approach to the nude figure and the new attitudes toward sexuality in Japan, and yet maintains a certain classical formality. Much as Weston with his exquisite studies of line and form in his nude photographs saw the need for tension between opposites as necessary, so, too, has Hosoe in the ultra whiteness of woman and the rich, deep blackness of man. In Hosoe's prints the whiteness of the female form as a lyrical reflection of traditional Japanese woman and the blackness of man as in the black things and dark places of primordial fears of mysterious memory are seen as images of classical Japan.

For the Japanese artist, whether it be the painter following the tradition of "emakimono," the long, narrow, horizontal scroll which when unrolled portrays a procession or progressive scenes whose conscious placement reflects the visual narrative, or Hosoe as a contemporary photographer whose many bodies of work are singular images seen in the context of a common theme—these works are meant to be seen as a series or in book form, as is much of post-World War II Japanese photography. This expression—the flow—and the relationship of photographic images in a conscious effort to form a continuity of thought and vision is a particular aspect of Japanese photography today.

Using this form, Hosoe continued to explore allegorical symbols with the publication of *Kamaitachi* in 1969, known also in the world of superstition and legend as "The Weasel's Sickle." Hosoe collaborated in this work with the renowned dancer, Tatsumi Hijikata. Hosoe felt this was not theatrical photography, "but is that rare case where the camera obscura itself becomes the theater." The Kamaitachi, which according to popular legend may be a "lacerated wound caused by a state of vacuum which is produced partially in the air, owing to a small whirlwind," is a drama of madness triggered by jealousy. Recalling the myths and superstitions of his youth, Hosoe recreates episodically this traditional Japanese fable. The villagers are participants as eyewitnesses to a strange dancer—is he an earthly creature or phantasmagorical? Perhaps they see in him the lost image of the magician priest, forgotten in the remote past.

Between "Man and Woman" and "Embrace," Hosoe completed another large body of work, "Ordeal by Roses," for which he used novelist Yukio Mishima as a model. Hosoe once again explored the strengths, fears, and weaknesses of man while luring him to that other reality. As Mishima states, "The world to which I was abducted under the spell of his lens was abnormal, warped, sarcastic, grotesque, savage, and promiscuous . . . yet there was a clear undercurrent of lyricism murmuring gently through its unseen conduits."

Against the recurring themes of pessimism and melancholia, the intuitive and necessarily personal experiencing of reality, Hosoe's view of fantastical and mysterious images emerges in his cinematic approach to photography. His photographs have attained "Shibui," that point where beauty reaches great subtlety and achieves a restrained elegance. Through his visual acuity toward design and his personal expression in the tonality of his prints, Hosoe seeks the universality of form in his photographs and communicates his personal involvement effectively.

—Monica R. Cipnic

HSIEH CHUEN-TE.

Nationality: Taiwanese. **Born:** Taichung, Taiwan, 10 January 1949. **Education:** Self-taught in photography. **Career:** Ironwork apprentice, advertising agent, telephone operator and post office doorman, 1965-67. Began to explore in painting, photography and 16 mm filming, 1968. Photographer, *Fortuen Esquire Monthly,* 1974; Photographer, Cloud Gate Dance Assembly, The Orchid Theatre, New Aspects Art Centre, The Silk-Sound Chinese Opera, The Kingdom of Field Music, The Ancient Boo-Ta Dance Theatre, The Contemporary Legend Theatre, Beijing Central Ballet, American National Orchestra, and New York Philharmonic Orchestra, 1975-92; Founder, *Image* monthly, 1976; Project Director, *Land & People of My Own,* 1977-79; Director of Photography Department, *Taiwan TV Guide,* 1978; Fashion Photographer, working for *China Times Weekly, Di Monthly, Marie Claire, Elle,* and for designers and department stores, 1979-93; Contributing Photographer, *China Times Weekly,* 1979-82, and Director of Photography Department, 1983; Project Co-ordinator, *Culture Innovation Review* and *Taipei Art Season Review,* 1983; Art Director/Director of Photography, Autumn Rain Printing Co., 1984; Founder, Hsieh Chuen-Te Studio, 1984, and Arena Visual Co. Ltd., 1988; Project Director, Taipei Religious Arts Festival, 1992; Director/Producer of 16 mm documentaries and Director/Co-producer of television series and commercial films, 1992-93. **Address:** B1 No. 35, Lane 105, Liao-Ning Street, Taipei, Taiwan.

Individual Exhibitions:

1969	Taipei Fine Arts Gallery
1975	*Meditating Classic,* Taipei American Culture Center (and tour)
1979	*Land and People of My Own,* Taipei Spring Art Gallery (and tour)
1981	*Window and Mirror,* Taipei Print Maker Art Gallery (and tour)
1986	*Faces of Time,* Taipei Spring Art Gallery (and tour)
1988	*Promise Land,* Taipei Hsiuan Shih Art Gallery

Untitled. Photograph by Hsieh Chuen-te.

Selected Group Exhibitions:

1970   *The Modern Nine Exhibition,* Taipei Fine Arts Gallery
1973   *Visual Group Ten: This Is Life,* Taipei Chinese Art Gallery
1976   *Visual Group Ten: 76,* Taipei American Culture Center
1981   *Artists of Our Time Exhibition,* Taipei Print Maker Art Gallery
1985   *Coast Line Exhibition,* Taipei City Fine Arts Museum
1994   *Contemporary Photography from China, Hong Kong and
          Taiwan,* Hong Kong Arts Centre

Collections:

Taipei Fine Arts Museum.

Publications:

By HSIEH CHUEN-TE: Films—*The Chill of the Lakeside This Year,* art director, 1982; *Crossing Ocean in Summer Time,* 1991; *Festival on Religion,* director, documentary film, Taiwan 1992; *Tong Dynasty,* director, television series, Hong Kong 1993; *Chiou Chung's Point of View on Law,* producer and art director, television film, Hong Kong 1994; *A Letter to Taimahah,* director, Taiwan 1994; *Coming Home,* director, Taiwan 1994.

On HSIEH CHUEN-TE: Books—*Hsieh Chuen-Te's Image World: Window and Mirror,* 1981; *Hsieh Chuen-Te's Image World: Writer's Journey,* 1983; *Hsieh Chuen-Te's Works: Faces of Time,* 1986; *Hsieh Chuen-Te's Works: Promise Land,* 1988.

*   *   *

Born into a peasant family in Taichung City in 1949, Hsieh Chuen-Te dreamed as a teenager of becoming a writer, a painter and a film director. Although becoming an artist was a profession unheard of at the time, Hsieh's passion for the arts succeeded in convincing his family, and their later support became the roots of his artistic achievements. The publication of *Homeland* in 1988 is the milestone where the artist pays his tribute to his land and people. Whether in the picture of an aboriginal mother in Lanyu, an empty cradle by the sea of Peng Hu, the railroads of Hua Lien, irrigation in Kinmen or ancestral worship in Pin Tung, *Homeland* reflects Hsieh's social and environmental concerns as part of the process of growing up.

It is perhaps ironic to learn that Hsieh's interest in portraiture was originally therapeutic. He first intended to use photography as a tool to help him communicate with the outside world because he was too "shy" to confront his subjects—a characteristic almost untraceable even in his earlier works *My Land and My People, Writer's Journey* and that eventually vanished in the portraiture series *Faces of Our Time.* In recent years, Hsieh took a further step towards transforming this space between himself and his subjects into instant theatre. This highly dramatized and manipulative photographic process helped Hsieh to interpret his subjects' personalities through his own. Here one can see a constant antithesis between romanticism and realism through the traces of childhood memories, culture and ideals re-enacted by the subjects of his photographs.

It is also no exaggeration to say that the journey of Hsieh Chuen-Te's photography is ever-changing. Over the years his work has gone in many different directions, and this disharmony has not bothered him in the least. From landscape to studio portraits, nature to fashion, social documentary to TV commercials, conceptual nudes to MTV . . . to Hsieh there is no distinction between art and commerce, the distinction only resides in good and bad quality. In fact Hsieh's dedication once he had embarked on a project convinced the public so well that it opened up many new and challenging markets for his photography, among them a MTV for a political campaign and

an anti-drug campaign. But his success has in no way made him self-satisfied. Hsieh's concern for his culture, the social and political as well as the natural environment impels him to explore more means of expression in the practice of photography. As Hsieh keeps himself abreast of the latest technology in computer and electronic imaging, one expects to see a whole new synergy in the collaboration and transaction between Hsieh Chuen-Te and his subjects.

—Becky Cho

HU WUGONG.

Nationality: Chinese. **Born:** Xian, Shannxi province, July 1949. **Education:** Graduated from the affiliated high school of Xian Academy for Arts in 1969; graduated from a tertiary institution, major in painting in the 1970s. **Military Service:** Joined the army and became a photographer. **Family:** Married Sang Guo Qing in 1975; son: Hu Sang. **Career:** Reporter, Shannxi News Photo Agency since 1994; Editor-in-Chief *News Knowledge,* Shannxi Daily, 1994; committee member, China's News Photo Assocation; Chief Secretary, Shannxi News Photo Assocation. **Recipient:** First prize in "China's News Photo Competition"; Special prize in "All China News Photo." **Address:** Shannxi Daily Residence, No. 1 Wan Cheng South Road, East section, Xian Province, Shannxi, Peoples' Republic of China.

Selected Group Exhibitions:

1986   *Joint Exhibition by 17 Photographers,* Beijing
1988   *Chinese Photography in 40 Years*
1994   *Contemporary Photography of China, Taiwan and Hong Kong,*
          Hong Kong

Publications:

By HU WUGONG: Books—*The Eyes of a Photographer,* 1985; *Introduction to Photographic Aesthetic,* 1986; *Chinese Photography in 40 Years,* 1988; *Hu Wugong Photo Album,* 1990. **Articles**—*China Travel Magazine; The Earth Magazine; Chinese Geographic Monthly; China Times Weekly.*

On HU WUGONG: Book—*Contemporary Photographers of China, Hong Kong and Taiwan,* 1993. **Articles**—"Contemporary Youth" in *China Photo News,* 1985; "Chinese Elite," 1993; interviews: by Hong Kong Television Broadcast Ltd, 1993 and 1994.

*

I started working on my own photography for more than ten years and I adore documentary photography. Like water to humans, one can always appreciate its precious and scarce nature no matter how much the supply. It is also basic and yet we cannot live without it. Photography to me resembles this particular nature of water, which regardless of its basic simplicity, contains all sorts of nutrients.

—Wugong Hu

*   *   *

Born in Xian, Shannxi, China in 1949, Hu Wugong joined the army soon after his graduation from high school in 1969 and served as a photographer. He then studied painting in a tertiary educational institution in China from 1970 and worked as a reported for the Shannxi News Photo Agency in 1975. He is presently the Chief Editor of the *News Knowledge* monthly published by the

Untitled. Photograph ©Hu Wugong.

Shannxi Daily. Before he published his monograph *Hu Wugong Photographs* in 1990, Hu was already engaged in essay writing and published *The Eye of a Photographer* in 1985; organized a nationwide exhibition, *Chinese Photography in 40 Years*; and took part in the editorial work of the same catalogue in 1987.

Hu is one of the faithful followers of the Social Documentary School in China, in certain aspects similar to those of the British Documentary school of thought who believe in expressing social concerns through the medium of photography. Hu, through his imagery, seems to entice the viewer to believe what he believes in: a kind of livelihood of the Shannxi peasants. Hu's work, with his acute perception and split-second precision, pounds your heart.

He always describes himself as a dull person, persistent and stern even. Perhaps this is what it takes for a person who stands on this "Loess Plateau" of China with persistence and sternness to do what he thinks must be done!

—Joseph Fung

HUBMANN, Hanns.

Nationality: German. **Born:** Freden/Leine, near Hannover, 21 June 1910. **Education:** Attended schools in Darmstadt until 1928; studied paper engi-

neering at the Technische Hochschule, Darmstadt, 1928-31; photography, at the Staatslehranstalt für Lichtbildwesen, Munich, 1931. **Family:** Married Elisabeth Lisl in 1934; children: Hans Peter, Ursula, and Andreas. **Career:** Worked as a part-time freelance photojournalist, mainly for the *Münchner Illustrierte* and advertising agencies, Munich, 1931-35; Staff Photographer, *Berliner Illustrierte,* 1935-45: war reporter for *Signal* magazine in Berlin and at the front, 1940-45; Chief Photographer, *Stars and Stripes,* United States Army newspaper, Altdorf, Germany, 1945-48. Staff Photographer, 1948-63, and since 1963 Chief Photographer, *Quick* magazine, Munich (also freelanced for *Life,* etc., 1948-78). **Recipient:** Obelisk Award, *Photokina 69,* Cologne, 1969. **Address:** Angersdorf 2, 8311 Kröning 1, Germany.

Individual Exhibitions:

1980	Stadtmuseum, Munich
1983	Fotomuseum im Stadtmuseum, Munich

Selected Group Exhibitions:

1950	*Photokina,* Cologne
1968	*Quick Foto-Expo,* Munich (toured West Germany 1968-71)
1979	*Deutsche Fotografie nach 1945,* Kasseler Kunstverein, Kassel, West Germany

Publications:

By HUBMANN: Books—*Moskau,* Munich 1958; *Moskau, Metropole des Ostens,* Hamburg 1959; *New York, Metropole des Westens,* Hamburg 1959; *Die letzten Cowboys,* Reutlingen, West Germany 1961; *Fotoreporter sehen die Welt,* Munich 1968; *Gesehen und Geschossen,* with an introduction by Franz Hugo Mosslang, Munich 1969; *Kinder—Kinder,* with text by Ruth Gassmann, Rosenheim, West Germany 1970; *Bergfoto heute,* Munich 1971; *Garten der Traüme,* Munich 1973; *Die Stachlige Muse,* Munich 1974; *Und Kein Bisschen Weise,* illustrations, text by Curt Jürgens, Munich 1976; *Augenzeuge 1933-1945,* Munich 1980; *Die Hitler-Zeit 1933-1945,* Munich 1982; *Die Adenauer-Zeit 1949-1967,* Munich 1983.

On HUBMANN: Books—*Photography of the World '60,* edited by Hiromu Hara, Ihei Kimura and others, Tokyo and New York 1960; *Geschichte der Fotografie im 20. Jahrhundert/Photography in the 20th Century* by Petr Tausk, Cologne 1977, London 1980; *Deutsche Fotografie nach 1945/German Photography after 1945* by Floris Neusüss, Wolfgang Kemp and Petra Benteler, Kassel, West Germany 1979; *Bilder vom Krieg* by Rainer Fabian and Hans Christian Adam, Hamburg 1983, as *Images of War: 130 Years of War Photography,* London 1985.

*   *   *

Actually, Hanns Hubmann should have become an engineer in paper technology. But in 1930, inspired by the colorful goings-on at an international "Student Olympics" organized by his university, he photographed the event. The pictures were immediately published, he was paid well for his work, and the student, just ready for his first exams, was advised to devote what a picture editor correctly diagnosed as his natural gift to the (at that time) exciting new profession of press photographer. He went to work as a part-time freelance photojournalist. The most important illustrated journal of the day, the *Berliner Illustrierte* of the Ullstein publishing house, soon noticed and hired him, and his great moment came in 1936 when the Olympic Games took place in Berlin. Today, more than half a century after he began, Hubmann is still at it, still active. Hardly anyone—except, of course, Alfred Eisenstaedt—is as much living proof as Hubmann that press photography keeps one young. But one must be born to it. Whoever has experienced Hubmann in action or whoever has had the opportunity to rummage through his well-stocked picture collection and to listen to his running commentary, will have no doubt about that.

Hubmann is an example of that phenomenon of a man predestined to be completely devoted to his work and to a certain extent sacrificing his whole self to it. In action he is all eye, striving for his goal—here amiably persuasive, there energetically surmounting barriers. Then, in the actual process of taking photographs, there is a complete change of gear: from the eye via the professional subconscious to the shutter finger. With one aim only, in the service of the press: to catch the interesting perspective, the right moment, in such a way that the editorial staff will say, These are just the pictures we need for our story.

Hubmann has always worked in this way, as an illustrator for journals—before Hitler he worked for a Munich photo-agency; after the 1936 Olympics he worked for *Berliner Illustrierte*; during the war for its offshoot *Signal*; after the war for the American *Stars and Stripes*; and when it again became possible to produce German illustrated journals, he played a leading role in 1948 in the founding and creation of *Quick*: he still works for this journal today.

The statesmen, potentates, prominent artists, actors and sportsmen whom he has captured in his pictures are legion—as are also the scenes from working life, from war-time, from the distressing years after the war. They are always striking, appropriate for the requirements of his medium, and often one step ahead of the competition. The skill is in his preparation, in concentrated amiability, in the art of persuasion, but above all in his sure instinct for pictorial form. Hubmann's photos—for which, in fact, he himself has claimed neither a particular "style" nor any conscious desire for form—are as diverse, as colorful and as multifarious as life itself. They are never boring.

—Bernd Lohse

HUCEK, Miroslav.

Nationality: Czechoslovakian. **Born:** Malacky, 18 November 1934. **Education:** Studied mechanical engineering, SPSS School, Prague, 1953-56, and motion-picture photography, FAMU Film and Television Academy, Prague, 1957-58. **Family:** Married Arita Haiduková in 1962; daughter: Barbara. **Career:** Assistant cameraman, Czech Television and Film Production, Prague, 1958-62; Technical Editor, 1962-64, photojournalist, 1964-67, and Head of the Photographic Department, 1967-75, *Mladý Svět* weekly magazine, Prague: worked in Czechoslovakia, Hungary, Greece, Bulgaria, U.S.S.R., Cuba, India, Japan, Scandinavia and Western Europe. Since 1975, freelance photojournalist and advertising photographer, working for *Magazin Mladé Fronty, Slovenka, Sluníčko, Tvorba, The Democrat Journalist, Prace,* Kratky Film, Čedok, Czech Television, etc., in Prague: established his own studio for advertising photography in Prague-Zbraslav, 1983. **Recipient:** Annual Photo Book Award, Prague, 1980. **Addresses:** (studio) U národní galerie 483/25, Prague 5-Zbraslav; (home) Řimská 35, 120 00 Prague 2, Czech Republic.

Individual Exhibitions:

1964	*Tramping and Big-Beat,* Kino Praha, Prague
1966	Wooden Colonnade, Mariánské Lázně, Czechoslovakia
	Municipal House of Culture, Klášterec nad Ohře, Czechoslovakia
1971	*Paris-Youth-Marches des Pices,* D-Club, Prague
1974	*Youth of the World,* House of Culture, Úst-ìnad-Labem, Czechoslovakia
1975	*Spare Time,* House of Culture, Ústì-nad-Labem, Czechoslovakia
1976	*Dance,* House of Culture, Ústì-nad-Labem, Czechoslovakia
1978	*Young People,* House of Culture, Ústì-nad-Labem, Czechoslovakia
1979	*Leisure,* House of Culture, Ústì-nad-Labem, Czechoslovakia
1982	*Villages of Various Countries,* Municipal Museum, Semily, Czechoslovakia
	Fishermen and Harbours, Gallery In-Above, České Budějovice, Czechoslovakia
	Gallery Mladá Fronta, Prague (retrospective)
1983	Fine Art Gallery, Cheb, Czechoslovakia
	House of Culture, Aš, Czechoslovakia
1984	*As We Were?* Gallery Semafor, Prague
	House of Culture, Blansko, Czechoslovakia
1985	*At Home in Zbraslav,* Chamber of Culture, Prague-Zbraslav, Czechoslovakia
	Gallery Fotochema, Prague
	Youth and Spare Time, House of Culture, Ústì-nad-Labem, Czechoslovakia
	Recreation and Travel, Spa Colonnade, Karlovy Vary, Czechoslovakia
1988	Theatre Semafor, Prague
	Gallery Old Town Hall, Brno, Czechoslovakia
	Fotofest, Zdar nad Sazavou, Czechoslovakia
1989	House of Culture, Orlova, Czechoslovakia
	Spa Colonnade, Karlovy Vary, Czechoslovakia
	Spa Darkov, Karvina, Czechoslovakia
1994	Small Gallery of the Saving Bank, Kladno, Czech Republic

Selected Group Exhibitions:

1958	*National Photo Exhibition,* Gallery ÚLUV, Prague
1960	*We Want to See Life in All,* Cinema Lucerna, Prague
1967	*Youth,* Czech Cultural Centre, Budapest
	Czech Photojournalists' Club Exhibition, Prague (and annually, since 1967)
1969	*Union of Czech Creative Artists Exhibition,* Prague (and 1977, 1980, 1984, 1985)
1973	*Current Reportage,* Municipal Gallery, Bratislava, Czechoslovakia

1977   *Child,* Prague (and world tour)
1985   *Czechoslovakia 1985,* Czech Cultural Centre, Warsaw (travelled to Havana, Berlin, Sofia, and Moscow)
        Fathers and Children, Marianske Lazne, Czechoslovakia
1989   *Czechoslovak Photography 1945-1989,* Gallery Valdstejnska jizdarna, Prague
        Roads of Czechoslovak Photography, Municpal Gallery—House by the Stone Bell, Prague
        Czechoslovak Press Photography, Brussels Pavilion, Prague
        Salon of Applied Art, Industrial Palace, Prague
1990   *Slovak Photography of the 1960s,* House of Art, Bratislava
1994   *District Cheb,* Municipal Museum, Cheb, Czech Republic
        Czechoslovak Photography 1989-1994, Gallery Mánes, Prague

Collections:

Museum of Decorative Arts, Prague; Collection of the Union of Czech Photographers, Prague; Moravian Gallery, Brno, Czech Republic; Municipal Museum, Cheb, Czech Republic; Gallery 4, Cheb, Czech Republic; Slovak National Gallery, Bratislava; Bibliothéque Nationale, Paris.

Publications:

By HUCEK: Books—*Má vlast je Krásná,* 1962; *Miádì,* Prague 1965; *Jazz-Festival,* Prague 1965; *Vlatava,* Prague 1966; *Jazz-Practice,* Prague 1967; *Anatomy for Artists,* Prague 1972; *Castle Červená Lhota,* Prague 1979; *Jakou barvu má mládì,* Prague 1980; *Věčné návraty,* Prague 1982; *Město,* Prague 1984; *Čtyři o čtyřech,* Prague 1984; *Jakou barvu má láska,* Prague 1985; *Zbraslav,* Prague 1985; *Svedectvi prazskych zdi,* Prague 1990; *Velka ceska kucharka,* with Barbara Huckova, Prague 1992; *Prazsky hrad—klenotnice* (Prague Castle-Treasury), with Barbara Huckova, Prague 1992; *Zahrady Prazskeho hradu (Gardens of Prague Castle)* with Barbara Huckova, Prague 1993; *St Vitus Cathedral,* Prague 1994; *Detailed Guide of Prague Castle,* with Barbara Huckova, Prague 1994. **Photostories**—"Montmartre," with text by J. Pacovský, in *Mladý Svět* (Prague), no. 17, 1969; "Sport—Athens," with text by Z. Šálek, in *Mladý Svět* (Prague), no. 43, 1969; "USSR Galleries" in *Mladý Svět* (Prague), no. 50, 1969; "India—Bombay," with text by P. Bártìk, in *Mladý Svět* (Prague), no. 20, 1970; "Japan—Expo 70," with text by K. Šmìd, in *Mladý Svět* (Prague), no. 30, 1970; "Egypt," with text by P. Bártìk, in *Mladý Svět* (Prague), no. 16, 1971; "Olympiada Mnichov," with text by Z. Šálek, in *Mladý Svět* (Prague), no. 41, 1972; "Ballet School, Leningrad," with text by J. Janoušek, in *Mladý Svět* (Prague), no. 16, 1974; "Pictures and People," with text by J. Pacovský, in *Magazin Mladé Fronty* (Prague), no. 1, 1974; "Ahoy River," with text by P. Hora, in *Magazin Mladé Fronty* (Prague), no. 1, 1976; "First Dance Lesson," with text by M. Tikalová, in *Magazin Mladé Fronty* (Prague), no. 3, 1980.

On HUCEK: Books—*Učebnice novinářské fotografie* by Petr Tausk, Prague 1984; *The Evolution of Czechoslovak Photography from 1918 to Today* by Petr Tausk, Prague 1986; *Encyclopédie internationale des photographes* by M & M Auer, Hermance/Genéve 1985; *Miroslav Hucek* by Vladimir Remes, Prague 1987; *Black and White Photography* by Antonin Dufek, Prague 1987; *A Short History of Press Photography* by Petr Tausk, Prague 1988; *Roads of Czechoslovak Photography,* by Daniel Mrazkova and Vladimir Remes, Prague 1989; *Who Is Who—Czech Republic,* Prague 1994. **Articles**—"Miroslav Hucek" by J. Boček in *Československa Fotografie* (Prague), No. 5, 1964; "Miroslav Hucek" by Jiñ Macků in *Fotografie* (Prague), no. 4, 1973; "Miroslav Hucek" by Daniela Mrázková in *Maxla Litva* (Riga, Latvia), April 1974; "Miroslav Hucek" by Daniela Mrázková in *Žhurnalist USSR* (Moscow), March 1975; "Miroslav Hucek" by Daniela Mrázková in *Fotografie* (Prague), no. 1, 1976; "Miroslav Hucek" by L. Šolc in *Fotografie* (Prague), no. 4, 1983; "Miroslav Hucek" by Daniela Mrázková in *Československa Novinar* (Prague), August 1985; "Miroslav Hucek" by Ladislav Solc in *MY* (Prague), no. 19, 1991.

*   *   *

I have always been fascinated by changes in life, and have tried to photograph the eloquence of events to which I have been an eye-witness. People depicted in the images from the photographer's camera do not know what he will catch. For this reason I prefer to photograph joyful situations where people are happy and my pictures cannot hurt them. It is therefore quite logical that my favourite themes in photo-stories and reportage deal with leisure, festivals, music and dance, as well as work—themes which inspire pleasure in people.

—Miroslav Hucek

*   *   *

Among mid-generation Czechoslovak photojournalists, Miroslav Hucek is known for his prodigious picture-stories. Some of his series became so extensive that they were transformed into complete books. His production of more than ten picture-volumes testifies to a strength of personal style and ability to exploit photography's eloquence as a visual language.

Originally, Hucek studied as a movie-cameraman at the Prague Film and Television Faculty, but soon found himself more attracted to still photography. It was not possible at that time to study photography at the school, so Hucek worked as an assistant cameraman in the Prague Department of Film Production while learning to photograph independently. Very soon he was contributing as a freelancer to the weekly *Mladý Svět* (Young World), and in 1962 became the magazine's technical editor. This preliminary experience taught him the basic requirements of magazine photography, and two years later he started to work as one of *Mladý Svět's* two full-time staff photographers. Being a young people's magazine employing only young journalists and photographers, the journal has played a key role in the development of Czech press photography since the early 1960s. Here, Hucek was able to work creatively on dynamic photo-stories completed very quickly with live-news pictures and background feature shots. His photographs of artists at work in their studios and all kinds of typical environments and characters became immensely popular for their warm humanity. Always focussing on the positive side of life, Hucek's best work deals with people at leisure or play.

In accordance with *Mladý Svět's* staff policy, Hucek handed over to the new generation in 1975, and embarked on a freelance career once more. Whilst he contributed non-stop to a number of weeklies and monthlies, he now found time to work more frequently in colour and to concentrate on the preparation of his picture-books. His greatest success came in 1980 when his book *What is the Colour of Youth* won him the Award of the Year. Freelancing also opened the way to advertising assignments—a field in which Hucek made good use of his photojournalistic experience. For a chain of Prague restaurants and cafes, he prepared a booklet of snapshots taken reportage-style in several of their establishments, and created a fresh approach to promotional publishing.

Hucek's life is totally permeated by his photography, his whole family being involved. His wife Arita is his full-time collaborator, while his daughter Barbara studies at the Film and TV Faculty in Prague. All three have a common love of photography, the camera being a constant presence in their family life. This amalgamation of work-assignment and leisure time is clearly evidenced by the number of Hucek's exhibitions in which the major theme is autobiographical.

—Petr Tausk

HUJAR, Peter.

Nationality: American. **Born:** Trenton, New Jersey, 11 October 1934. **Education:** Attended New York City schools; High School of Industrial Art, New York, graduated 1952; Trappist novitiate, in Kentucky, for 2 years. **Career:** Worked as a blackjack dealer, Havana, 1955-56; co-owner of a mink ranch in Argentina, 1957-58; worked as an assistant to various commercial photographers, New York, 1958-62; lived and worked in Italy, 1962-65; worked as an assistant photographer, New York, 1965-67; freelance photographer, with own studio, New York, since 1967 (did commercial/fashion work for advertising agencies and magazines, notably *Harper's Bazaar,* until 1971). **Recipient:** Fulbright Grant, 1962; Creative Artists Public Service Grant, 1976; National Endowment for the Arts Grant, 1977, 1980. **Address:** Peter

Will, Char-pei, **1985.** Photograph by Peter Hujar. Courtesy James Danziger Gallery, New York.

Hujar Estate, c/o James Danziger Gallery, 130 Prince Street, New York, New York 10012, U.S.A. **Died:** (in New York) 26 November 1987.

Individual Exhibitions:

1974   *Peter Hujar,* Floating Foundation of Photography, New York
1975   *Portfolio,* Foto Gallery, New York
1977   *New York Portraits,* Marcuse Pfeifer Gallery, New York
         Catskill Center for Photography, Woodstock, New York
1978   *The Male Nude,* Marcuse Pfeifer Gallery, New York

1979   *Recent Photographs,* Marcuse Pfeifer Gallery, New York
         Public Library, Port Washington, New York
1980   *Peter Hujar,* La Remise du Parc, Paris
1981   *Portraits and Landscapes,* Robert Samuel Gallery, New York
1982   *Peter Hujar: Fotos 1974-1981,* Galerie Jurka, Amsterdam (and
         tour, 1982-83)
         Galerie Nagel, Berlin
         Kunstverein, Frankfurt, Germany
         Faces Photographed: Contemporary Camera Images, Grey Art
         Gallery & Study Center, New York University

1985	*Nude Stripped Bare,* Hayden Gallery, List Visual Arts Center, MIT, Cambridge, Massachusetts
1986	*Recent Photographs,* Gracie Mansion Gallery, New York
1987	*Sexual Difference: Both Sides of the Camera,* CEPA Gallery, Buffalo, New York (travelled to Wallach Art Gallery, Columbia University, New York, 1988)
1988	*The Photographs of Peter Hujar,* State University College of New York at Buffalo, New York
1990	*Peter Hujar,* Grey Art Gallery, New York University (travelled to the Fine Arts Gallery, University of British Columbia, Vancouver, Canada)
	Peter Hujar's New York, James Danziger Gallery, New York
1992	*Peter Hujar: Portraits of Animals, 1978-1984,* James Danziger Gallery, New York
1994	Stedelijk Museum, Amsterdam (retrospective)
	Fotomuseum, Winterthur, Switzerland (retrospective)

Selected Group Exhibitions:

1975	*Coming of Age in America,* Midtown YMHA, New York (toured the United States)
1976	*Celebration of Life Below 14th Street,* Floating Foundation of Photography, New York
1977	*New York: The City and People,* Yale School of Art, New Haven, Connecticut
	Contemporary Photographs, Baltimore Museum of Art
1978	*The Male Nude,* Marcuse Pfeifer Gallery, New York
1979	*The Male Image,* Robert Samuel Gallery, New York
1980	*The Figure and Man-made Environments,* Allbright College, Reading, Pennsylvania
1981	*New American Nudes,* Massachusetts Institute of Technology, Cambridge
1982	*3 New Yorker Fotografen: Peter Hujar/Larry Clark/Robert Mapplethorpe,* Kunsthalle, Basel
1986	*The Animal in Photography 1843-1985,* The Photographers' Gallery, London
1988	*Les Splendeurs et Misères du Corps,* at *Mois de la Photo,* Paris
1989	*Witnesses: Against Our Vanishing,* Artist's Space, New York
	Self and Shadow, Aperture Foundation, Burden Gallery, New York
	150 Jahre Basler Kunstverein, 1839-1989, Basle, Switzerland

Collections:

Fordham University, Bronx, New York; Princeton University Museum, New Jersey: New Orleans Museum of Art; San Francisco Museum of Modern Art.

Publications:

By HUJAR: Books—*Portraits in Life and Death,* with an introduction by Susan Sontag, New York 1976, London 1977; *The Grotesque in Photography,* with others, edited by A.D. Coleman, New York 1977.

On HUJAR: Books—*The Photograph Collector's Guide* by Lee D. Witkin and Barbara London, Boston and London 1979; *New American Nudes* by Arno Rafael Minkkinen, New York 1981; *3 New Yorker Fotografen,* exhibition catalogue, with texts by Dieter Hall, Jean-Christophe Ammann and Sam Wagstaff, Basel 1982; *Peter Hujar,* exhibition catalogue, New York 1990; *Peter Hujar: A Retrospective,* with text by Max Kozloff, Hripsimé Visser and Urs Stahel, Zurich, Berlin and New York 1994. **Articles**—"Pictures from the Underground" by Henry Post in *Viva* (New York), April 1976; "Peter Hujar" by Henry Post in *Art in America* (New York), November/December 1976; "Death Leads the Dance with Life" by Owen Edwards in the *Village Voice* (New York), 13 December 1976; "Disfarmer's Naivete and Hujar's Sophistication" by Gene Thornton in the *New York Times,* 16 January 1977; "Peter Hujar and the Nature of Identity" by Richard Whelan in *Christopher Street* (New York), May 1979; "Peter Hujar at Marcuse Pfeifer" by Rene Ricard in *Art in America* (New York), December 1979; "Hujar's Progress" by Ben

Lifson in the *Village Voice* (New York), 10 December 1979; "An Intense Silence" by Hervé Guibert in *Le Monde* (Paris), 3 August 1980.

*

I think of my photographs as pieces of paper that have a life of their own. The whole story has to be on that paper. It is amazing that photographs can have such power.

—Peter Hujar

*   *   *

Like a print taking shape in its tray of developer, the profile of Peter Hujar's place in modern photography is emerging from obscurity and coming clearer. The shape of his art has never been more plain than it is in the book *Peter Hujar, A Retrospective.* Here at last Hujar's achievement can be seen whole. Here critics and curators Max Kozloff, Hripsimé Visser and Urs Stahel have assessed his unique place in the history of photography with fresh accuracy and depth. Peter Hujar is one of the great unknowns in modern art. His hour has come at last and here is the place to begin.

Like Peter's own face, the face of Hujar's art is both handsome and hurt. Kozloff and Visser speak of the "tension" that pulls across the surface of these pictures and gives them their power. The tension one feels in these pictures is a magnificent aesthetic expression of what people invariable felt about the man. Nobody who spent more than an hour with Peter is likely to forget that Hujar edge, cutting into the very air around him everywhere and always. I myself felt it from the first moment I met him, back in Susan Sontag's living room, circa 1965, until the day he died, twenty-two years later. It was only after he died that I could acknowledge how in all my years of friendship with this sad, smart, angry, lonely man, I remained always a little tense myself, always taut, at attention, on edge.

In the pictures, that edge becomes a splendid source of insight and power, felt in every image along with Peter's theatricality and what I call his "classicism." Classicism? This is an era of posturing postmodernism that Peter used to call, with his testy disdain, "looks like art." Hujar is a classical practitioner. He knew the history of his art, and in his unique way saw through it. He was tied to authenticity; he was committed to all the classic values of looking—to insight, beauty, lucidity, grace. And yet what a tense classicism it is! The place Peter found for his own vision was also a solitary one, and that reminds me of Peter's loneliness and all that went with it: Peter's poverty, Peter's conviction—and how right he was!—that he would be appreciated only after death. This is classicism all right, but it is a classicism without complacency; classicism without comfort. This is a classicism that has stared into hell. And that is what gives his pictures their wonderful integrity, intelligence and power.

—Stephen Koch

HURN, David.

Nationality: British. **Born:** Redhill, Surrey, 21 July 1934. **Education:** Attended Hardy's School, Dorset, 1948-52; Royal Military Academy, Sandhurst, 1952-54; self-taught in photography, from 1955. **Family:** Married Alita Naughton in 1964 (divorced, 1971); daughter: Sian. **Career:** Photographer since 1955; Assistant Photographer to Michael Peto and George Varjas at Reflex Agency, London, 1955-57; freelance photographer/photojournalist, working for *Look, Life, Sunday Times Magazine,* etc., in London, 1957-70, and in Wales, since 1971; Member, Magnum Photos cooperative agency, New York and Paris, since 1967. Head of the School of Documentary Photography and Film, Gwent College of Higher Education, Newport, 1973-90. Distinguished Visiting Artist and Adjunct Professor, Arizona State University, Tempe, 1979-80. Editorial Adviser, with Bill Jay, *Album* photographic magazine, London, 1971. Member of the Photography Committee, 1972-77, and of the Arts Panel, 1975-77, Arts Council of Great Britain. Member, Photography Committee, Council for National Academic Awards, London,

Large Bronze Face by Igor Mitoraj, Yorkshire Sculpture Park, **1993.** Photograph ©David Hurn.

1978-87. **Recipient:** Welsh Arts Council Award, 1971; Kodak Photographic Bursary, 1975; U.K./U.S.A. Bicentennial Fellow, 1979-80; Imperial War Museum Arts Award, 1987-88; Bradford Fellowship, 1993-94. **Agents:** Magnum Photos, 72 Spring Street, 12th Floor, New York, New York 10012, U.S.A.; 5 Passage Piver, Paris 75011, France; Moreland Buildings, 2nd Floor, 23-25 Old Street, London EC1V 9HL, England; Vingt-Cinq Building 5F-3-7 Kanda Ogawa-Cho, Chiyoda-Ku, Tokyo 101, Japan.

Individual Exhibitions:

1971	Serpentine Gallery, London
1973	Bibliothéque Nationale, Paris
	Neikrug Gallery, New York
1974	*Wales in Black and White,* National Museum of Wales, Cardiff
	The Photographers' Gallery, London
1976	*Rencontres Internationales de Photographie,* Arles, France
	Centre d'Animation Culturelle, Douai, France
	Ecole Municipale des Arts Decoratifs, Strasbourg
1977	FNAC Etoile Gallery, Paris
	Arnolfini Gallery, Bristol
	Ecole des Beaux-Arts, Angers, France
	Musée du Chateau d'Eau, Toulouse
	Rheinisches Landesmuseum, Bonn
	Rathaus, Augsburg, Germany
	Stadtbucherei, Stuttgart
1978	Städtisches Museum, Bochum, West Germany
	Northlight Gallery, Arizona State University, Tempe
	Culturele Raad, Leeuwarden, Netherlands

	Openbare Bibliotheek, Arnhem, Netherlands
	Canon Photo Gallery, Amsterdam
	Cultureel Centrum, Winterswijk, Netherlands
	University of Idaho, Moscow
	Galeria Spectrum, Barcelona
	Galeria Spectrum, Zaragoza, Spain
1979	San Carlos Opera House, Lisbon
	University of New Mexico, Albuquerque
	Texas Christian University, Fort Worth
	University of Idaho, Moscow
	Midland Group Gallery, Nottingham, England
1980	Fifth Avenue Gallery, Scottsdale, Arizona
	Sterling College of Art, Kansas
1981	Les Recontres d'Olympus, Paris
1982	Contrasts Gallery, London
	Olympus Gallery, London
	Malmo Museum, Sweden
	Palais des Congres, Lorient, France
1983	Olympus Gallery, Tokyo
	Palais des Beaux-Arts, Charleroi, Belgium
1984	Olympus Gallery, Hamburg
	Ffotogallery, Cardiff, Wales
1985	The Photographers' Gallery, London
	National Museum of Photography, Bradford, Yorkshire
1986	Cambridge Darkroom, Cambridge, England
	Axiom Gallery, Cheltenham, Gloucestershire
	Stills Gallery, Edinburgh
1994	*The Last Train,* Newport Museum, Wales

Carving and Controversy—Sculpture Exposed, National Museum of Photography, Bradford

Selected Group Exhibitions:

1971	*Personal Views 1850-1970,* British Council Gallery, London (toured Europe)
1978	*18 Photographes Européens: Images des Hommes,* Belgian Ministry of Culture touring exhibition, (toured Europe)
1980	*Visitors to Arizona 1846-1980,* Phoenix Art Museum, Arizona
1983	*British Photography 1955-65,* The Photographers' Gallery, London
	Images of Sport, Ffotogallery, Cardiff
	Autographs, Cambridge Darkroom, Cambridge
1985	*Quelques Anglais,* Centre Nationale de la Photographie, Paris
	The Miners World, Midland Group, Nottingham (touring)
	Take One: British Film Stills, Photographers Gallery, London (touring)
1989	*Through the Looking Glass: Photographic Art in Britain 1945-1989,* Barbican, London
	In Our Time: The World as Seen by Magnum Photographers, ICP New York, Paris, London
1991	*Distinguished Visiting Artists* (with Wegman), Northlight Gallery, Arizona State University
1994	*Revelations. Male and Female Nudes,* John Jones Gallery, London
	A Positive View, The Saatchi Gallery, London

Collections:

Arts Council of Great Britain, London; Welsh Arts Council, Cardiff; Contemporary Arts Society for Wales, Cardiff; Bibliothèque Nationale, Paris; International Center of Photography, New York; International Museum of Photography, George Eastman House, Rochester, New York; Center for Creative Photography, University of Arizona, Tucson; San Francisco Museum of Modern Art; California Museum of Photography, University of California at Riverside; Museum of Modern Art, New York.

Publications:

By HURN: Books—*Wales in Black and White,* exhibition catalogue, Cardiff 1974; *David Hurn: Photographs 1956-1976,* with an introduction by Tom Hopkinson, London 1979; *Arizona Trip,* with interview by Bill Jay, London 1982. **Articles**—"A Revolution in Photo Teaching?" in *Amateur Photographer* (London), 13 June 1973; "David Hurn," interview, with Martine Voyeux, in *Zoom* (Paris), May/June 1977; "The Picture Story" in *Camerawork* (London), no. 9, 1979.

On HURN: Books—*Photography: Venice '79,* edited by Daniela Palazzoli, Vittorio Sgarbi and Italo Zannier, Milan and New York 1979; *British Photography 1955-1965: The Master Craftsmen in Print,* exhibition catalogue, by Sue Davies, Michael Rand, Mark Boxer and others, London 1983. **Articles**—"David Hurn: Springtime in Paris" in *Photography* (London), April 1958; "David Hurn, Magnum" in *Creative Camera Owner* (London), September 1967; "Photographs by David Hurn, Magnum" in *Creative Camera* (London), April 1971; "Portfolio: David Hurn" in *British Journal of Photography* (London) 28 May 1971; "David Hurn" in *Photo* (Paris), September 1971; "Photogallery" in *Designer* (London), October 1971; "David Hurn" in *British Journal of Photography Annual 1972,* edited by Geoffrey Crawley and Mark Butler, London 1971; "Personal Views 1850-1970" in *Creative Camera* (London), May 1972; "David Hurn" in *Zoom* (Paris), November/December 1972; "Wales in Black and White" by Ainslie Ellis in *British Journal of Photography* (London), 29 November 1974; "What Is Wales?" in *Amateur Photographer* (London), 11 December 1974; "David Hurn: Photographs in Wales" in *Creative Camera* (London), December 1974; "David Hurn ou le Scrupule" in *Photo* (Paris), January 1981; "David Hurn" in *British Journal of Photography* (London), 3 June 1983; "Photos by David Hurn" in *Creative Camera* (London), February 1986.

*

In previous ages the word "art" was used to cover all forms of human skill. The Greeks believed that these skills were given by the Gods to man for the purpose of improving the conditions of his life. In a real sense, photography has fulfilled the Greek ideal of art; it should not only "improve" the world but also "improve" the photographer. It is the goal of man to be actually what he is potentially. Each should be stretching his interest to the limit.

There are many genres in photography—none more inherently important than another. The most important single characteristic of all fine photographers must be a marrying of intellectual and visual integrity, for photography has a peculiar moral problem. Do we have the right to shoot a picture of another human being without their permission? Of one thing I am sure. We do not have the right to abuse others in our pictures, whatever our motives.

Morality must be more important than commerce. Morality must be more important than aesthetics. In the end, the expression of all a photographer's work is really the expression of his life.

—David Hurn

*   *   *

David Hurn is keen to dismiss what he suspects are the largely derogatory associations of the term "photojournalism." The only definition that appeals is that supplied by Henri Cartier-Bresson—"I am a photojournalist insofar as photography is my journal." It is a form of diary-keeping that David Hurn also subscribes to, treating as photojournalism only his early coverage of the 1956 Hungarian Uprising and the following four or five years working on newspapers "learning my craft."

As Director of Documentary Photography at Newport, Gwent, through the 1970s, Hurn maintained his commitment to the importance of learning. For Hurn is someone who learns as he teaches, preparing minutely and continually recovering and discovering photographing influences. It's hard to achieve a comprehensive list of those photographic predecessors he regards as formative: the mention of, say, Koudelka leads into a lengthy explanation of his seminal significance. Even today any journey Hurn makes overseas is preceded by quantities of research into who has worked there before him. Thus a Distinguished Visiting Artist Fellowship to Arizona State University from 1979-80 involved him in examining the work of early North American photographers such as Jackson and O'Sullivan, and in literally comparing the desert he was documenting with their record of a hundred years earlier.

Lest this sound either literal or imitative, Hurn is swift to re-view photography as an art form dealing in the Big Issues (one can hear the capital letters as he says them). His rhetorical *What is art?* brings forth a resistance to and resentment of fine artists who employ photographic processes only as an adjunct in their overall conception. On the other hand, Hurn is fascinated by artistic interfaces and has recently (1993-94) compiled a major exhibition of sculptured images for the National Museum of Photography. As to his follow up, *What is Culture?,* he is working towards 1998 (declared by the various Arts Councils of the UK as the Year of Photography and the Digital Image) on a project that involves working with the National Museum of Wales to display a hundred archival prints alongside his own sets of archetypal portraits (in the tradition of the great early twentieth century German portraitist, August Sander) and local images, taken over the last twenty-five years.

For David Hurn was Welsh-born and, despite long years away (based in England and frequently travelling), remains deeply rooted in a land whose culture has been forcibly altered out of recognition in the space of a single generation. Since the first industrial revolution: "When you thought of Wales you thought of coal mines and steel works. Not any more. All that's replaced them is heritage tourism and a certain number of high-tech office operations." The effect that has had through culture to identity—particularly in the self-image of machismo—is only part of the record.

There's a sense in which David Hurn has reached his ideal way of working. He recognises, more easily in retrospect, the mythology and self-deception involved in remaining a photographer while teaching photography. "I probably kept up with it more than most and, to be honest, that 'most' amounted to becoming a weekend photographer." Also, how out of sympathy he finds himself with current magazine working practices: "It took me a while to realise that an assignment that I regarded as necessitating at least a month or two's input, the picture editor was considering offering me *a day or two* to complete." To achieve large-scale retrospectives on the aesthetic themes that have been absorbing him for years, accompanied by major publications, is to achieve the major priorities. If that can be followed up by decent magazine coverage, then all possible interests are covered.

In a curious way this preoccupation with eternal questions gives David Hurn his feeling of "going back to the future." He talks of the nineteenth century invention of photography as "as important as Darwinism. It came out of an explosion in the age of science: that's its strength and its weakness, what makes it unique." Now that photography can be reduced to the artistic margins or inserted simply in the form of digitally manipulated images, Hurn is all for recovering something of its initial importance, recording memories in the making. Much of his early work, the 1960s "social documentaries" on strip clubs or gay bars taken when such places were hardly seen and even more rarely heard about, ensures that hindsight cannot erase specific places and times. The latter work, in travelling the longer distance, takes a wider geographical and historical sweep in which the individual image is of paramount significance but in which the accomplished whole is definitively more than the sum of its parts.

—Amanda Hopkinson

HUTCHINGS, Roger Lionel.

Nationality: British. **Born:** Winchester, England, on 16 October 1952. **Education:** Attended the University of Portsmouth 1973-76 and studied documentary photography at Newport College of Art 1980-82. **Career:** Worked as a freelance photojournalist since 1982 for *The Observer, The Sunday Times, The Independent, Stern, Der Spiegel.* **Recipient:** Nikon Photoessay of the Year 1990; Nikon News Photographer 1992; World Press People in the News award 1994; Amnesty International Award for Photojournalism 1994; Prague Award 1994. **Agent:** Network Photographers, 3/4 Kirby Street, London EC1N 8TS, England.

Selected Group Exhibitions:

1994   *Drawing the Lines—Joint Exhibition about Bosnia,* Zelda
        Cheatle Gallery (and touring)

Collections:

National Museum of Film, TV and Photography, Bradford.

Publications:

On HUTCHINGS: Article—"To Bosnia and Back" by Neil Burgess in the *British Journal of Photography,* 19 August 1993.

*   *   *

Roger Hutchings graduated as a mature student from the Newport School of Art in Wales in 1982, having studied documentary photography with the Magnum photographer David Hurn. It is in this field that he has continued to make his mark, primarily working as a freelance with the Network agency in London, frequently producing reportage features for the London Sunday newspaper, *The Observer.*

From the early 1980s he has covered such major stories as the civil wars in Sudan and Sri Lanka; the ill-starred Haitian elections in 1987 and those in Pakistan a year later; the collapse of communism in eastern Europe at the end of the decade, and of the Mengistu regime in Ethiopia. Meanwhile he

continued with social documentary reports within the United Kingdom, alternating with long, often heart-rending, trips to cover such stories as the aftermath—and return—of the Pol Pot regime in Cambodia; an essay on the Gurkhas, the mercenary British army in India and a feature on India in Turmoil; and two years spent intermittently working on the Bosnian situation from 1992-4. Of this he said: "This war has been very different. What you've seen here is news organisations equipped with armoured cars, walkie-talkies and body armour. This is a war where journalists and photographers have been targets too. You have to remember that we're dealing with people who understand the power of the media. Serbian soldiers in Belgrade can be watching CNN doing a live report from Sarajevo, and then that same CNN team can be going through a checkpoint and those same soldiers will say: 'We don't like the way you're reporting the war, you're biased' and shoot them." (Interview with Neil Burgess, BJP, 13 April 1994.)

In 1994 Hutchings won first prize for the *People in the News* category of the World Press Photo Awards for work shot on five visits in the previous 12 months. Some of the work was shown in a group show, with Judah Passow and Anthony Suau, at London's Zelda Cheatle Gallery, called *Drawing the Lines.* All proceeds from picture sales went to *War Child,* a new charity founded "in response to the atrocities being committed in the Balkans". For those who question the humanitarianism of reporters in the tradition of humanist photography might reckon that here not only were the photographers not profiting from the civil war but that their lives are also on the line in *Drawing the Lines.* According to Hutchings: "Bosnian snipers might be only 50-100 meters away from you, and using a high velocity rifle with a telescopic sight, they can decide whether to shoot you through the left or the right eye . . . . or just remind you that you're a target by firing just behind you." (Ibid)

According to Zelda Cheatle herself: "Importantly, the pictures show much humanity and warmth in embattled and war-torn zones. There is compassion in the manner in which Hutchings approaches his subjects which translates on to the printed page and the gallery wall. Hutchings' photographs are a perfect example of sensitivity and intelligence and the immediacy of a talented and experienced eye." As we go to press, Hutchings is pursuing another frequently ignored war, that of the Kurds for their own self-determination. Knowing that mere chance dictates when and where we happen to be born on this planet, he is also identifying with their situation, even "trying to convince them that you're taking the same chances that they are."

—Amanda Hopkinson

HUTH, Walde (Waldberta Huth-Schmölz).

Nationality: German. **Born:** Stuttgart, 29 January 1923. **Education:** Studied architectural photography under Professor Walter Hege at the Staatsschule für Kunst und Handwerk, Weimar, 1940-43. **Family:** Married the photographer Karl Hugo Schmölz in 1956 (died, 1986). **Career:** Worked as a colour photographer at AGFA, Wolfen, 1943-45; photographer at the Maschinenfabrik Esslingen, 1945-46; independent photographer, since 1947; opened own studio for fashion photography and commercial photography, 1953; worked for *Haute Couture* magazine in Paris and Florence, 1954-56; studio for commercial photography with Karl Hugo Schmölz, 1958-86. **Recipient:** Honorary Member, Deutsche Fotografische Akademie, Leinfelden, 1993. **Address:** Am Südpark 45, 50968 Köln, Germany.

Individual Exhibitions:

1959   *Mode, Mensch, Dinge,* Landesbildstelle, Hamburg
1970   *Farbfotografische Kompositionen,* Hamburg
1975   *Aus Praxis und Liebhaberei,* DGPH-Galerie, Cologne
        (retrospective with Karl Hugo Schmölz)
1980   *100 ungeschriebene Briefe,* Galerie am Markt, Köln-Porz (and
        tour, 1989)
1981   Galleria Il Diaframma, Milan
        Galerie Zur Stockeregg, Zurich
1984   *Optische Delikatessen,* Heidelberger Kunstverein

Vitez, Bosnia, **April 1993.** Photograph ©Roger Hutchings.

1985	*100 ungeschriebene Briefe—100 festgehaltene Schritte—100 unwirkliche Wirklichkeiten,* Wessenberg-Galerie, Konstanz
1988	*Licht ist alles,* Cologne (and tour, 1989-91)
1993	*Gestalt geworden,* Schwörhaus, Galerie der Stadt, Esslingen
1994	*Augen Weide,* Städtische Galerie Peschkenhaus, Moers

Selected Group Exhibitions:

1970	*Fotografinnen,* Museum Folkwang, Essen
	Landschaften, Kunsthalle, Cologne
1975	*Photographie 1929-1975,* Kunstverein, Stuttgart
1981	*Farbe im Photo,* Kunsthalle, Cologne
1983	*Glamour & Fashion,* Sammlung Gruber, Museum Ludwig, Cologne
1984	*Neuerwerbungen,* Museum Ludwig, Cologne
	Farbphotographie, Galerie Zur Stockeregg, Zurich
	Photographie des 20. Jahrhunderts, Museum Ludwig, Cologne
1985	*Windows,* Fox Talbot Museum, Lacock, Wiltshire, England
1987	*Deutsche Lichtbildner,* Museum Ludwig, Cologne

Collections:

Museum Ludwig, Cologne; Museum Folkwang, Essen; Staatliche Landesbildstelle, Hamburg; Bibliothèque Nationale, Paris; Musée Nicéphore Niépce, Chalon-sur-Saône; Fox Talbot Museum, Lacock, Wiltshire; Galleria Il Diaframma, Milan; Staatsgalerie, Stuttgart; Lehmbruck-Museum, Duisburg; Galerie der Stadt, Esslingen.

Publications:

By HUTH: Book—*Walde Huth—100 ungeschriebene Briefe, fotografische Modulationen,* Cologne 1991.

On HUTH: Books—*Ein Wundergewebe durchwandert die Welt,* Stuttgart 1953; *Fotografinnen,* exhibition catalogue, Essen 1970; *Sammlung Gruber, Photographie des 20. Jahrhunderts, Bestandskatalog Museum Ludwig,* Cologne 1984; *Sammlung Photographie, Bestandskatalog Museum Ludwig,* Cologne 1986; *A Concise History of Photography,* 3rd edition, by Helmut Gernsheim, New York 1986. Articles—in *U.S. Camera,* Vol. 20, No. 4, April 1957; ''Ohne Erotik ist bei mir nichts denkbar—Die Fotografin Walde Huth'' by Friedhelm Röttger in *Eßlinger Zeitung,* 20 March 1993; ''Walde Huth—Laudatio'' by Helmut Gernsheim in *Bulletin der Deutschen Fotografischen Akademie* (Leinfelden), No. 10, 1994.

*

The eye—my camera. To be in constant visual dialogue with the world around me, to speak the language of the wind, feel the touch of music, hear the warmth of passion, and to transform these phenomena into momentary captives of time on my film—this is my work. Only through the knowledge of my years, the wealth of my subconscious treasure chest, am I able to react to the instant, metamorphose the everyday sublime into kinetic compositions of true and void, clarity and texture. It is almost always a split-second decision as to whether the key elements which evoke life in their form, meet my demands for quality. The science of photography merely offers me the medium in which

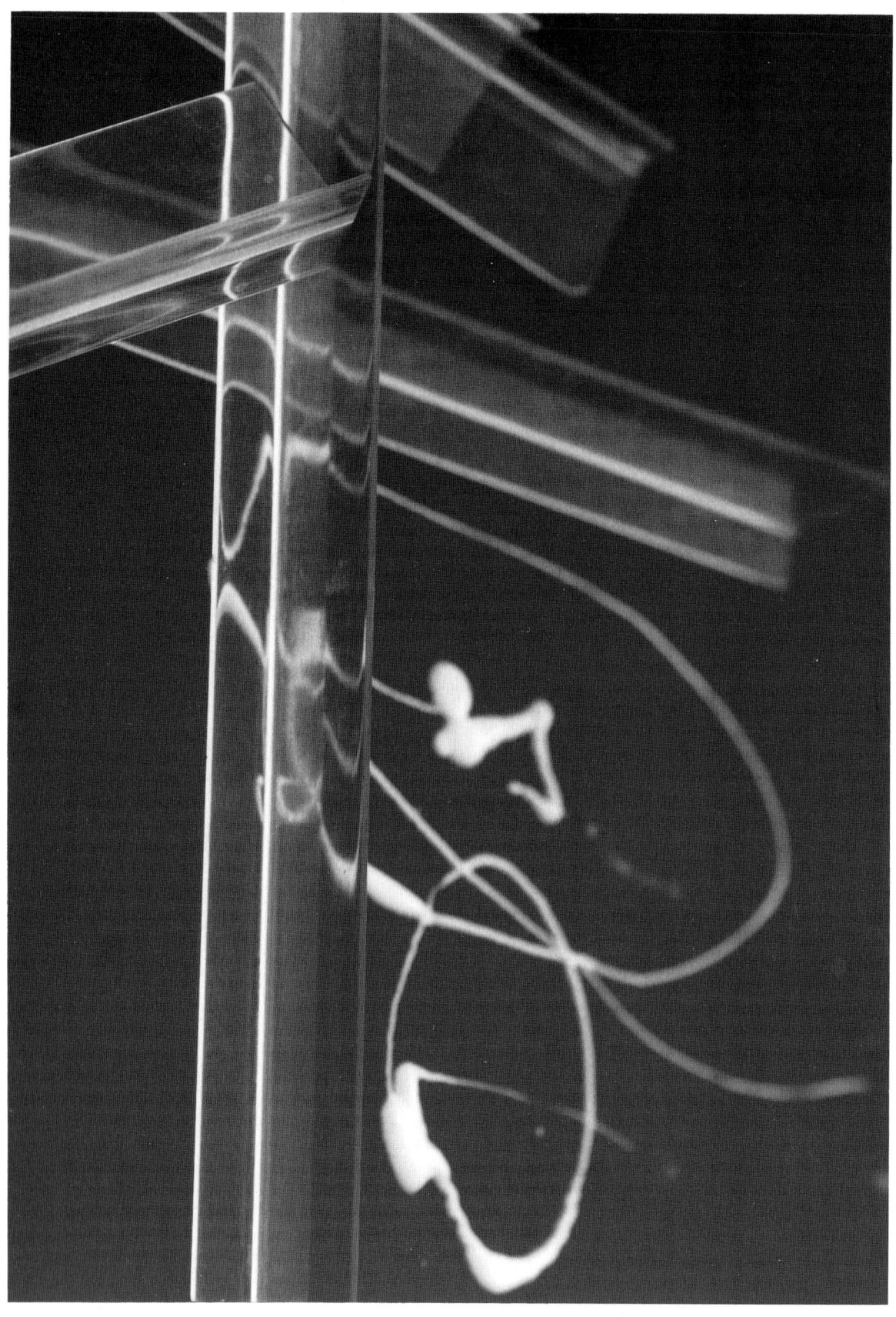

From Me to You, **1992.** Photograph by Walde Huth.

I can translate perspective effects and the interaction of materials in an art which I call my own. The film in my camera is something like my sounding-board.

—Walde Huth

* * *

The Second World War denied Walde Huth her first wish to become a sculptor. So she studied photography with Professor Walter Hege at Weimar from 1940-43, realizing the great possibilities of giving expression to her urge to create by working in that field.

After finishing her studies at the State School for Applied Art Hege asked her to become his assistant. This would probably have turned her into a famous architectural or wildlife photographer like her teacher. Yet this was not considered war work, whereas the colour film department of AGFA filmworks at Wolfen was. In 1945 she managed to flee into the Allied Zone to join her parents at Stuttgart. With portraits and commercial work she kept herself going, no easy work in a country that was half in ruins. By 1953 Walde had a large studio in Stuttgart with eight assistants and drew attention to herself by novel fashion pictures taken in the open air.

Thereupon the well known French fashion magazine *Haute Couture* offered her an exclusive contract necessitating her working partly in Paris and partly in Florence. Walde Huth's open-air fashion pictures were a novum for all fashion houses. Also her style of bringing fashion and architecture into an expressive relationship to each other led her photographs to be published worldwide. She was offered a contract with *Vogue* in 1956, yet instead chose to marry and start life in Cologne with the well known architectural and advertising photographer Karl Hugo Schmölz. Walde's main activity lay now in commercial photography for the textile industry. It usually required costly build-ups in the studio and more work behind the scenes than up front. Her husband had a separate studio mainly faking pictures of furniture. In the sixties they both employed up to twenty people.

After the death of Karl Hugo in October 1986 Walde Huth sold the studios and made herself independent to do what she had always dreamed of doing—creating pictures for her own pleasure. This urge had already manifested itself a few years earlier in their holiday house in the Ligurian Alps, when one day she observed the constantly changing play of light and shadows of the window shutters on the billowing curtains. Instead of answering her correspondence her observation with the camera gave birth to the now well known series of photographs entitled *Hundred unwritten letters*. Soon afterwards there followed another cycle of photos of a decaying, boarded-up wall in a former greenhouse. In the strong headlights of her car passing at night the reality was transposed for a moment into a surreal world becoming a stage for ghostly images. Thousands would pass by without observing anything unusual. Walde Huth stopped the car to fix the haunting vision on film. Known as the *Hundred observed steps*, the images range from a metamorphosis of reality to complete abstraction.

Another time Walde would spot an old sheet of copper, corroded and bent, lying in the street. As she approached she noticed the fascinating reflections of her clothes on the bent metal, looking like a cubist painting. It made a great picture, not looking like a photograph at all. She is a poetess with a camera, exploring new paths in photography. The fascination of her colour images rests chiefly in the great aesthetic pleasure evoked by the artist's eye and partly in their enigmatic expression. They are strong, arresting images, created impromptu by an impulsive artist.

In honour of her 70th birthday in 1993 the Deutsche Fotografische Akademie at Leinfelden made Walde Huth an Honorary Member. In my *Laudatio* I made a comparison to Albert Renger-Patzsch, the pioneer of modern photography in Germany. From 1922 onward he astonished the world with breathtaking images of everyday things. Our way of looking at nature had changed. Sixty years later Walde Huth discovered in ordinary objects new forms by looking at them or lighting them differently. With imagination she breathed life into them and made her vision visible to all. Her mutation of nature enriched our mental image and sharpened our power of observation. Renger-Patzsch's exact, objective representation depended on Light and Realism—apart from his eye. Walde's subjective mutation of an object or scene is achieved by Light and Imagination. Her maxim "Light is everything" does not do her justice.

—Helmut Gernsheim

HYDE, Scott (Frederick).

Nationality: American. **Born:** Montevideo, Minnesota in 1926. **Education:** Studied at the Art Center School, Los Angeles; Art Students League, New York; Columbia University, New York; and Pratt Graphics Center, New York. **Career:** Photographer for Condé Nast Publications, New York, 1947-49. Freelance photographer, New York, since 1950. **Recipient:** Guggenheim Fellowship in Photography, 1965, 1972; New York State Council of the Arts Grant, 1972, 1975. **Address:** 7411 Dreyfuss Drive, Amarillo, Texas, 79121, U.S.A.

Individual Exhibitions:

1964	Gallery Archives of Heliography, New York (with William Clift)
1969	The Darkroom, New York City
1970	Focus Gallery, San Francisco
1971	Witkin Gallery, New York City
1979	Witkin Gallery, New York City
1982	University of New Mexico Art Gallery, Albuquerque, New Mexico
1983	Focus Gallery, San Francisco
1985	Tom Zimmermann Fine Arts, New Hope, Pennsylvania
1986	Ville de Saigon, New York City
1987	P.A.C.A. Gallery, New York City
1988	Center for Photography, Woodstock, New York
	West Texas A & M University, Canyon, Texas
1989	Bound and Unbound, New York City
1993	Center for Contemporary Art, Abilene, Texas

Selected Group Exhibitions:

1967	*Photography in the 20th Century,* National Gallery of Canada, Ottawa (toured Canada and the United States, 1967-73)
1970	*Into the 70s: Photographic Images by 16 Artists/Photographers,* Akron Art Institute, Ohio
1971	*Photo/Graphics,* International Museum of Photography, George Eastman House, Rochester, New York
	Photography Invitational, Arkansas Arts Center, Little Rock
1973	*Photography into Art,* Scottish Arts Council Gallery, Edinburgh
1974	*Synthetic Color,* Southern Illinois Univesity, Carbondale
1977	*On the Offset Press,* Everson Museum, Syracuse, New York
1978	*Mirrors and Windows: American Photography since 1960,* Museum of Modern Art, New York City (toured the United States, 1978-80)
1981	*Master Photographers,* Focus Gallery, San Francisco
1982	*The Alternative Image,* Kohler Art Center, Sheboygan, Wisconsin
1984	*Off the Press,* State University of New York, New Paltz
1985	*City Light,* International Center for Photography-Midtown, New York City
1988	*Through a Plastic Lens,* Northlight Gallery, University of Arizona, Tucson
1991	*Hungers 1990s: Not by Bread Alone,* Square House Museum, Panhandle, Texas (travelled, 1991-93)
1992	*Library,* Granary Books, New York City
1993	*Coffee, Tea and Thee,* Oklahoma City Art Museum, Oklahoma

***Inez and the Feast of Venus,* 1994.** Photograph by Scott Hyde.

Collections:

Museum of Modern Art, New York; Metropolitan Museum of Art, New York; International Museum of Photography, George Eastman House, Rochester, New York; Everson Museum of Art, Syracuse, New York; Smithsonian Institution, Washington, D.C.; High Museum of Art, Atlanta; Pasadena Art Museum, California; National Gallery of Canada, Ottawa; Bibliothèque Nationale, Paris; Musée Français de la Photographie, Bièvres, France; San Francisco Museum of Modern Art, California; The Nelson-Atkins Museum of Art, Kansas City, Missouri; Harry Ranson Center at the University of Texas, Austin; Israel Museum, Tel Aviv, Israel; Cooper Hewitt Museum, New York City; Museum of the City of New York, New York Public Library, New York City; University of California Art Galleries, Los Angeles.

Publications:

By HYDE: Books—*CAPS Book,* New York 1975; *Dust Map,* Jersey City, New Jersey 1979; *The Real Great Society Album,* Jersey City, New Jersey 1979; *CRUMS,* Amarillo, Texas 1992; *Dissolving,* Amarillo, Texas 1993.

On HYDE: Books—*Photography in the 20th Century* by Nathan Lyons, New York 1967; *Into the 70s: Photographic Images by 16 Artists/Photographers,* exhibition catalogue, by Robert Doty and Tom Muir Wilson, Akron, Ohio 1970; *Photo/Graphics,* exhibition catalogue, with text by Van Deren Coke, Rochester, New York 1971; *Photography into Art,* exhibition catalogue, by Pat Gilmour, Edinburgh 1973; *Modern Photography Annual,* New York 1974; *Scott Hyde: Photography between Covers,* by Thomas Dugan, Rochester 1979; *Options for Color Separation: An Artists Handbook,* edited by Philip Zimmermann, Rochester 1980; *A World History of Photography,* by Naomi Rosenblum, New York 1984. **Articles**—"The Color Alchemy of Scott Hyde," in *Popular Photography* magazine, February 1965; "Pictures by Scott Hyde" by Syl Labrot in *Aperture* (Millerton, New York), Summer 1970; article by Henry Korn in *Print Review,* No 2, 1973; *Skew,* Journal of the University of Arizona Graduate Photography Program, Tucson 1981; *Exposure,* Photo-offset issue, Journal of the Society for Photographic Education, No 21:3, 1983.

*

Although I regard myself as a photographer, my medium of first choice is offset lithography. I do not use lithography as a reproductive medium, but rather design the pictures with this medium in mind. Most of my pictures are in color, but I seldom use color films. Instead I photograph in black & white and then print several images together in different colors. Images may be disparate (a montage), or may be a single subject photographed several times with some differences between the images such as: different color filters, subject movements, camera movements, changing light conditions, etc. My original camera negatives are used to make a set of enlarged negatives on litho films for imprinting onto the zinc plates used in offset lithography. When I am invited to have a picture published, as for instance in this book, I submit a set of litho negatives and specify the color each is to be printed. I regard a picture printed in this way as a kind of "original" print, since no "reproductive" steps are involved. If I am satisfied with the way the picture looks, I do not permit that picture to be published again.

There are several advantages to this method of work: the first is that, although the picture may be "mass-produced," it is more directly my picture than a reproduction would be. Secondly, these prints, consisting of only varnish ink on paper are structurally much simpler than conventional photographic color print materials, so they have potentially better archival stability. This advantage naturally depends on the quality of ink and paper used. A third advantage is the low price per print, due to the high speed and efficiency of the presses. And finally, the mass-production of an original art work creates an interesting situation because these prints lose practically all value as Art Objects. The art establishment (including the photographic-art establishment) is predicated on the exhibit and exchange of "unique art objects." Even the limited, numbered-edition print (the invention of 19th century art dealers) is, by definition, limited. What validity, as Art, can a picture retain if it exists in thousands of unsigned copies, yet is not a reproduction? This question interests me.

In recent years I have been experimenting with Xerographic copiers. Within a few years the image, quality and versatility of these new devices will have increased, until they have most of the advantages listed above for offset lithography, plus the additional advantage of allowing smaller editions than is practical with offset printing.

—Scott Hyde

*   *   *

The capacity inherent in photography to generate inexpensive multiples has been a central concern for Scott Hyde. This long-term commitment to photography as a means for the production of economically accessible imagery has led Hyde to the rejection of what he's called "the autograph club"—that approach to photography and its dissemination which emphasizes the unique or limited-edition print, rendered certifiably precious by the authenticated touch of its maker's hand.

As an alternative, Hyde since the 1960s has pioneered in the exploration of offset lithography as a primary vehicle for the photographer, accepting it not simply as a device for reproducing already-existing images but as an end in itself, a key component in the creative act. He has approached offset as a printmaking technique, and has pursued the creation of a body of visual imagery which investigates the distinctive characteristics of the offset process.

Synthetic color, variations on themes, montages created directly on the press and a simple but effective form of stereographic imagery are some of the technical and structural issues which Hyde has successfully addressed. He has consistently stressed the importance of process over product, and has built the elements of experiment and surprise into his working method, through tactics such as submitting image components to printers in forms which require the press operators to become collaborators in the image-making act.

Underlying these strategies has been a dedication to the democratization of the photographic image as object, through the production of multiples in the largest possible quantities. Some of Hyde's images—those which have achieved their final form on the pages of large-circulation magazines and newspapers—have been published in "editions" of 100,000 and more.

Hyde's vision itself is by turns lyric and satiric. His lyricism manifests itself most consistently in his contemplations of the natural landscape, which examine such phenomena as clouds, the rippling of water and the dappling of sunlight on leaves in an attentive, almost pastoral mode. He turns a more bemused eye on the urban landscape, often juxtaposing it to image elements which render the urban scene absurd, as in his montage, "The Judgement of Paris with the Astor Place Luncheonette." Another aspect of his work is directed towards a structural analysis of photographic encoding and offset printing, exemplified by such pieces as the book *Dust Map* and the single-sheet piece "Dust, Scratches, and Newton's Rings meets Hickeys, Streaks, and Misregistrations," a collaboration with printer/poet Larry Zirlin.

Through his persistent inquiry into the possibilities of the offset process, Hyde has directly or indirectly influenced many younger photographers and artists who have come to see the photographic print as an intermediary step en route to an offset print or book, and who have come to understand that the dissemination of one's work is as crucial a matter as its production.

—A.D. Coleman

ICHIMURA, Tetsuya.

Nationality: Japanese. **Born:** Nagasaki, 10 June 1930. **Education:** Studied literature at Nihon University, Tokyo; self-taught in photography. **Family:** Married Ayako Hamaguchi in 1974; daughters: Miku and Mirei. **Career:** Freelance photographer, Tokyo, since 1959. **Recipient:** Special Prize, *International City Photo Exhibition,* Tokyo, 1959. **Address:** 825 Horiuchi, Hamayamachi, Miura-gun, Kanagawa, Japan.

Individual Exhibitions:

1963	*Love and Lost,* Fuji Foto Salon, Tokyo
1972	*The Woman and The Man,* Ginza Matsuya Department Store, Tokyo (with Tatsuki and Kano)
1973	*Messenger, and City of Port Nagasaki,* Canon Salon, Tokyo
	Actress Michiko Saga, Shibuya Seibu Department Store, Tokyo
1976	*The Nude,* Canon Salon, Tokyo
1981	*An Afterimage of Britain,* Olympus Gallery, Tokyo

Selected Group Exhibitions:

1973	*Critics' Choice,* Neikrug Galleries, New York
1974	*New Japanese Photography,* Museum of Modern Art, New York
1977	*Neue Fotografie aus Japan,* Kulturhaus, Graz, Austria (travelled to the Museum des 20. Jahrhunderts, Vienna)
1979	*Japanese Photography 1848 to Today,* Galleria d'Arte Moderna, Bologna, Italy (travelled to the Palazzo Reale, Milan; Palais des Beaux-Arts, Brussels; Institute of Contemporary Arts, London; Museum fur Kunst und Gewerbe, Hamburg; Gemeente Museum, Arnhem; Pulchri Studio, The Hague, 1979-80)
1982	*An Afterimage of Britain,* Olympus Gallery
1989	*Nagasaki,* Yurakucho Marion
	Shinko, Canon Salon, Ginza

Collections:

Museum of Modern Art, New York; Tokyo Municipal Museum of Photography.

Publications:

By ICHIMURA: Books—*Dialogue of Eros,* with Hosoe and Okura, Tokyo 1969; *Salome,* Tokyo 1970; *Come Up,* Tokyo 1971; *The Last Remaining Mystery: The Maya Inca Civilization,* Tokyo 1975; *Thought in Photography,* Tokyo 1978; *Impressions of Japan,* with text by Tsutomu Minakami, Tokyo 1978; *Shinko,* Tokyo 1988. **Article**—"Document of spirit and senses" in *Chuo Koron,* Tokyo 1990.

On ICHIMURA: Books—*New Japanese Photography,* exhibition catalogue, by John Szarkowski and Shoji Yamagishi, New York 1974; *Neue Fotografie aus Japan,* exhibition catalogue, by Otto Breicha, Ben Watanabe and John Szarkowski, Graz and Vienna 1977; *De Japanse Fotografie van 1848 tot heden,* exhibition catalogue, by Attilio Colombo and Isabella Doniselli, Amsterdam 1980. **Articles**—"Tetsuya Ichimura: Nagasaki" in *Camera Mainichi* (Tokyo), August 1973; "New Japanese Photography" in *Camera Mainichi* (Tokyo), June 1974.

*

Photography keeps records; it records objects and events. But there are two ways it may do so.

There is the mechanical photograph, the photograph achieved by mechanical means. One can say of such pictures that they have achieved exact records through mechanics, without human feelings.

But the man who wishes to take a photograph that will truly convey war or the events of history or love—he wishes, too, to convey his thought, his soul, as well as simply create a mechanical reproduction. Such photographs are taken by men who are truly living contemporary life.

However, some people would say that the photograph is the origin and the product of the mass media, that it is just another product and process in the vast quantity of print. What, then, in this age, is the "human" photograph?

When I think about my own themes, I know that I am especially concerned with pollution, nuclear weapons, war, the big gulf between the rich and the poor, racial discrimination and religious war. But, whatever the theme, I would like to think that the photograph is a document of the human soul, the product of human eyes, which are, in turn, the agents of God.

It is my belief that the photographer must be one of his own subjects, one of the human beings in the world before the camera; otherwise, no real photograph happens, even if it seems accurately to record objects and events.

—Tetsuya Ichimura

*   *   *

After completing one year of studies in Nihon University's preparatory course, Tetsuya Ichimura began taking photographs as he worked through as many as ten odd-jobs. In 1959 he won a special prize at the *International City Photo Exhibition.* He turned professional after that success.

Ichimura looks at Japanese sexuality in an idealistic manner. While his photographs are sensuous and erotic, they also focus on the peculiar juxtaposition between life and death.

—Norihiko Matsumoto

IGNATOVICH, (Vjesvolovich) Boris.

Nationality: Russian. **Born:** Slutzk, Ukraine, in 1899. **Education:** Attended schools in Slutzk, 1909-14; mainly self-taught in photography, but studied photographic history and theory and was influenced by the artist Lebedev. **Military Service:** Served as war reporter, on 30th Army newspaper *Boyevove Znamya (Fighting Battalion),* 1941-43. **Family:** Married the photographer Yelizaveta Ignatovich. **Career:** Worked as a journalist, for *Severo-Donezki Kommunist* and *Krasnaya Svezda,* in Charkov, Ukraine, 1918-20; Editor, *Krasnaya Bachkiriya* magazine, Charkov, 1920-21, and *Gornyak (Mineworker)* magazine, Moscow, 1921-22; editor of several humorous magazines, Leningrad, 1922-25; Photojournalist and Picture-Editor, for *Ogonyok (Little Fire), Prozhektor (Reflector), Krasnaya Niva (Red Bank), Bednota (Poverty)* magazines, Moscow, 1926-30; worked as a motion picture cameraman, Moscow, 1930-32; Photo-reporter, working for *SSSR na Stroike (USSR under Construction), Heute, Wetchernaya Moskva* and *Aufbau Moskva (The Development of Moscow)* magazines, 1933-41; freelance photojournalist, working with the Soyuzfoto agency, and concentrating on colour photography, Moscow, from 1945. Delegate, with playwright Majakowski, First Rosta Conference, 1920; Organizer, with Alexander Rodchenko, 1926-28, and Leader, 1928-29, *Oktyabr* creative art group, Moscow; also, Head of Association of Photo-reporters, Press House, Moscow; Leader of "Brigade Ignatovich" photo group, at Soyuzfoto agency, Moscow; and Member, Association of Artists of Grekowstudios, Moscow. **Died:** (in Moscow) *in June 1976.*

Individual Exhibitions:

1947   Prague
1948   *Landscapes of My Homeland,* Moscow
1969   Ignatovich Residence, Moscow (70th birthday retrospective)
1972   Photo Art Society of the Lithuanian SSR, Vilnius
1980   Institute of Art History, Moscow
1986   Majacovsky Museum, Moscow
1994   Alex Lachmann Gallery, Cologne

Selected Group Exhibitions:

1929   *Film und Foto,* Deutscher Werkbund, Stuttgart
1979   *Film und Foto der 20er Jahre,* Württembergische Kunstverein, Stuttgart (travelled to Museum Folkwang, Essen; Werkbundarchiv, Berlin; Kunsthaus, Zurich; Kunstverein, Hamburg; and Museum des 20. Jahrhunderts, Vienna)
         Paris-Moscou 1900-1930, Centre Georges Pompidou, Paris
1984   *Paris-Moscow,* Paris
         Moscow-Paris, Museum of Fine Arts, Moscow
1989   *150 Years of Photography,* Central Exhibition Hall, Moscow
1991   *Soviet Photography of the 20s and 30s,* Alex Lachmann Gallery, Cologne
1992   *The Great Utopia: The Russuan and Soviet Avante-Garde, 1915-1932,* Frankfurt; Amsterdam; New York; Moscow; St Petersburg
1992   *The Utopian Dream: Photography in Soviet Russia, 1918-1930,* Laurence Miller Gallery, New York

Collections:

K. Ignatovich, Moscow; Soyuzfoto, Moscow; Alex Lachmann Gallery Collection, Cologne; Shickler/Lafaille Collection, Los Angeles

Publications:

By IGNATOVICH: Books—*The State Collection of Weapons in the Kremlin,* Moscow 1969; *Boris Ignatovich,* exhibition catalogue, Vilnius 1979.

On IGNATOVICH: Books—*Boris Ignatovich* by Leonid Volkov-Lannit, Moscow 1973; *Fotografie der 30er Jahre: Eine Anthologie,* edited by Hans-Jürgen Syberberg, Munich 1977; *Geschichte der Fotografie im 20. Jahrhundert/ Photography in the 20th Century* by Petr Tausk, Cologne 1977, London 1980; *Film und Foto der 20er Jahre,* exhibition catalogue, by Ute Eskildsen and Jan Christopher Horak, Stuttgart 1979; *Internationale Ausstellung des Deutschen Werkbundes "Film und Foto" 1929,* facsimile reprint, edited by Karl Steinorth, Stuttgart 1979; *Sowjetische Fotografen 1917-40* by S. Morosov, A. Vartanov, G. Tschulakov, O. Suslova and L. Uchtomskaya, Leipzig and West Berlin 1980; *Pioneers of Soviet Photography* by Grigory Shudakov, Olga Suslova and Lilya Ukhtomskaya, London and Paris 1983; *A World History of Photography* by Naomi Rosenblum, New York 1984; *Tvorcheskaya Fotografia/ Creative Photography* by Sergei Morosov, Moscow 1985; *Sowjetische Fotografen 1941-1945* by S. Morosov, A. Vartanov, O. Suslova and others, Leipzig 1985; *20 Soviet Photographers, 1917-1940* by Grigory Chudakov, Amsterdam 1990; *Anthology of Soviet Photography,* Vol. 1 1986, Vol. 2 1987. **Articles**—"Boris V. Ignatovich 1910-1976" in *Photography Year 1977,* by Time-Life editors, New York 1977; "Photographie Creative" by Romeo

Martinez and A.N. Lavrentiev in *Paris-Moscou 1900-1930,* exhibition catalogue, Paris 1979; "Camera Eye" by Allan Porter, and "The International Werkbund Exhibition 'Film und Foto' Stuttgart 1929" by Karl Steinorth in *Camera* (Lucerne), October 1979; "Soviet Photography Between the World Wars 1917-1941" by Daniela Mrázková and Vladimìr Remeš in *Camera* (Lucerne), June 1981.

* * *

Boris Ignatovich started his career in 1918, at the age of 19, as a journalist. He began to photograph in 1923 when he was given a simple Kodak folding camera. The results of his first attempts were surprisingly good, and in 1926 he changed from journalist to photojournalist and went on to work for various illustrated journals. For two years, from 1930 until 1932, he worked in motion pictures as a cameraman. After he returned to photojournalism, he created magnificent images in Donbass about the beauty of human labor. From 1937 until the outbreak of the war he chiefly portrayed life in Moscow. Like most of his colleagues, he spent the first half of the 1940s photographing the front line battles against the German invaders. And in peacetime he again enlarged his interest, this time moving on to color photography, in which he very soon produced significant results.

Ignatovich belonged to the first generation of Soviet photographers who highly esteemed the significance of images showing important situations in human life. He showed an infallible sense for the right choice of moment, the moment at which the photographed event possessed the most narrative intensity. Very early on in his career he recognized the importance of photographs that depicted the various motifs of human life when nothing extraordinary was happening. Simultaneously, he discovered that such work requires solutions of the utmost photographic sensitivity and imagination.

This depiction of everyday life was the significant and very difficult task that inspired Ignatovich, throughout his career, to new photographic methods and means. Earlier than Cartier-Bresson, indeed in the 1920s, Ignatovich was already applying the principle of the "decisive moment." Ignatovich not only tried to mediate epic information, but also he tried to express poetically the atmosphere, the environment, in which an event took place. He seems always to have felt keenly and accurately when it was advisable to come as near as possible to the action in order to distinctly depict the expression of individual persons, or when it was best to move to the wider environment, the depiction of the "outer space" of an event, when that would provide the means, the pictorial elements, necessary to establish the emotional effect that he wanted to convey. Perhaps, in this respect, he had well learned the lessons of his experience in motion pictures.

—Petr Tausk

INFANTE, Francisco (Arana).

Nationality: Russian. **Born:** Moscow in 1943. **Education:** Attended secondary art school, Moscow, 1957-61. **Family:** Married Goriunova Nonna Petrovna; sons Paquito Infante (born 1971) and Platon Infante (born 1978). **Career:** Freelance kinetic artist and photographer, Moscow, since 1962. Member, Dvizenie kinetic art group, Moscow, 1962-68; founder-member, ARGO (Author Working Group), Moscow, since 1970. Has worked on 13 major projects since 1962, including *Galactic* sculpture (1967), *Melomedia* environment (1970), *Participation* kinetic structure (1972), *Luminosity* sculpture (1973), and *Synthetic Image* environment (1974). **Address:** 10/2, Brodnikov per., ap.11, 109180 Moscow, Russia.

Artefacts, **from the series** *Applications,* **1993.** Photograph by Francisco Infante-Arana.

Individual Exhibitions:

1989	*Les Artefacts: Francisco Infante,* Wilhelm-Hack-Museum, Ludwigshafen
1989	*Francisco Infante from Moscow,* Gallery International Images Ltd., Sewickley, Pennsylvania
1991	*Francisco Infante: Dessins, Objets, Artefacts,* Galerie Scheoller, Düsseldorf
1991	*Artefacts,* Gallery Fernando Duran, Madrid
1992	*Artefacts: Francisco Infante,* Galerie Tretiakov, Moscow
1993	*Prodolgénia,* Centre d'Art contemporain, La Base, Levallois

	Francisco Infante: Artefacts 92, Galerie Emilio Navarro, Madrid
1994	*Installation,* Tzarytzino Museum of Applied Arts and Contemporary Art, Moscow
	Francisco Infante, Hillside Gallery and Art Front Gallery, Tokyo
	Artefacts, Chateau de Napoule, France

Selected Group Exhibitions:

1965	*Dvizenye,* House of Architects, Leningrad

1966 *ART—LIGHT—ART,* Eidnhoven, Holland
   Kinetica, Cologne, Germany
1969 *La nueva escuela de Moscu,* Florence, Italy
1973 *Kinetism—What Does It Mean?* House of Artists, Moscow
1977 *Contemporary Russian Art,* Palace of Congress, Paris
   Unofficial Russian Art from the Soviet Union, Institute of
    Contemporary Arts, London
   New Art from the USSR, Washington, D.C. and Ithaca,
    New York
   Biennale, Venice, Italy
1989 *What is Photography?* Prague
1990 *The Logic of Paradox,* Palace of Youth, Moscow
   In der USSR en Erbuiten—28 kunstenaars, 1970-1990,
    Stedelijk Museum, Amsterdam
   Soviet Contemporary Art, Socho, New York
1991 *Back to Square One,* Berman-E.N. Gallery, New York
   Soviet Contemporary Art: From Thaw to Perestroika, Setagaya
    Art Museum, Japan
   Contemporary Russian Artists, Santiago Compostela, Spain
   El Apartamento, el sueno del collecionista, Gallery Fernando
    Duran, Madrid
1992 *The First International Sacharov's Festival of Art,* State
    Museum of Fine Arts, Niznyi Novogorod
   *Herbarium: The Photographic Experience in Contemporary
    Russian Art,* Fotogallery Wien and Kunsthalle Exnergasse,
    Vienna
1993 *Adresse Provisoire,* Post Museum, Paris
1994 *Europa, Europa,* Kunst und Austellunghalle, Bonn, Germany
   Utopia, Schusev Museum of Architecture, Moscow

Collections:

Cremona Foundation, Maryland; Galerie Gmurzynska, Cologne; Collection Russe à Montgéron, France; Collection Kostakis, Athens; Collection Lenz, Schönberg, Austria; Institute of Russian Culture, Los Angeles; McRori Corporation; Gerald Janecek, University of Kentucky.

Publications:

By INFANTE: Books—*Projets de réconstruction du ciel étoilé,* ed. Masline Boutikov, France 1993. **Articles**—"Artificially Created Spaces: The Projects and Realizations of the ARGO Group" in *Journal of Decorative Propaganda Arts* (Miami), 1987 No 5; "An Architecture of Artificial Systems in Cosmic Space" in *The Structurist* (Saskatoon), 1975-76 No 15-16; "Nature and Art. The Natural and the Artificial" in *The Structurist* (Saskatoon), 1983-84 No 23-24; "Introduction to the 'ARTEFACT': A Game Based on the Correspondence Between the Artificial and the Natural" in *Soviet Union* (Tempe) 1980 Vol 7.

On INFANTE: Books—*Progressive Russische Kunst: der Aufbruch bis 1930 + Lev Nusberg und die Moskauer Gruppe Bewegung,* with texts by S. Bojko and M. Ragon, Cologne 1973; *Gruppe Bewegung 'Dvizenie', Moskau 1962-1972,* with text by P. Wember, Krefeld, West Germany 1973; *An Introduction to Russian Art and Architecture,* edited by Robert Auty and Dimitri Obolensky, Cambridge 1980; *Another Russia: Through the Eyes of the New Soviet Photographers* by Daniela Mrazkova and Vladimir Remes, London 1986; *Francisco Infante from Moscow* (catalogue), Sewickley, Pennsylvania, 1989; *Artefacts* (catalogue), Madrid, 1991; *Francisco Infante* (catalogue), Tokyo, 1994. **Articles**—"From the USSR: Francisco Arana Infante" in *Flash Art* (Milan), July/August 1977; "Künstler in Moskau" by E Peschler in *Stemmle* (Zurich) 1988; "Moscow: Francisco Infante. Tretiakou" by John Bowlt in *Art News,* April 1993.

* * *

His experimenting work stems from the heritage of the Soviet avant-garde of the 1920s, from Tatlin's Tower of the Third International, Klucis' monumental billboards, Rodchenko's mobile constructions or El Lissitzky's spatial projects, works infused with the spirit of revolution and a vision of a new life. And thus when Infante's photography first appeared abroad in the Italian magazine *Flash Art,* it immediately captured interest with its manifestation of the idea that action and space are virtually unlimited, unrestricted and infinite.

"I've been involved in mobile art since 1962," says Infante. "I take kinetics as equivalent to a living organism. This is why I have produced various projects, models of moving and lighted spatial constructions, kinetic landscape systems, kinetic theatre, futurist 'architecture' of self-contained man-made space structures. At the same time I made spontaneous performances in which the means of expression or media used were mostly natural materials like snow, grass, fire, soil . . . "

Infante's projects always count on a creative participation of the spectator and his aesthetic experience is *a priori* calculated to be an integral part of the project, construction or action in the making. Photography is then not only a record of the author's activity but often the main goal of Infante's projects which aim at engaging the spectator in the performance and making him participate in the art-making.

Infante's unconventional expression often provokes the uninformed public to attacks. He has been accused of folly, formalism and lack of content. A typical example was his project involving images in nature. Hanging boards of reflective material in various geometric shapes among trees, he produced images of the forest. An unexpected external interference then resulted in a shift from the original intended stylization, leading to an unplanned happening of sorts which has found its permanent record in photography.

Infante's "Images in Nature" as he calls his artificial compositions of carefully arranged mirrors using reflection effects are culminated by photographic record. His monstrous giant lighted and moving mobiles simulating take-offs of space machines symbolizing a post-technological civilization are merely documented photographically. Both, however, are an expression of man's age-old aspiration to conquer the infinite universe. It is an emotional reaction to the culture of the space age, but these fantastic constructions and actions also reverberate with the romantic sentiments of the avant-garde, her one-time need to show visions of a distant future characterized by a complete reconstruction of society according to the revolutionary ideals. And thus Infante, like his predececesors, capitalizes in his work on the conflict of existing reality and its illusive representation.

In 1962 Infante graduated from a secondary art school in Moscow but did not venture into a career of professional artist. He was not interested in conventional means of expression and media but rather in nontraditional spatial constructions obliterating the division line between painting and sculpture and in action in nature. This interest understandably led him also to photography. In 1970 Infante became the central figure of a group of similarly oriented young artists and technicians, named ARGO. Since then the group has prepared 13 projects, 9 of which were actually produced. Since 1976 Infante has also been interested in a kinetic form of Land-Art. "I'm fascinated by the whimsical metamorphism of the relation between man-made objects and living nature," he says. His photographic record of these relations constitutes his private book called *Presence,* a living testimony offering insights into contemporary life.

—Vladimìr Remeš

IONESCO, Irèna.

Nationality: French. **Born:** Paris, 3 September 1935. **Education:** Educated in Constanza, Rumania. **Career:** Painter, since 1951, and photographer, since 1966, in Paris. **Address:** 16 Boulevard Soult, 76012 Paris, France.

Individual Exhibitions:

1970 Jalmar Gallery, Amsterdam
1973 The Photographers' Gallery, London
1974 Le Doigt dans l'Oeil Galerie, Bordeaux
   Galleria Spectrum, Barcelona
   Galerie Nikon, Paris
1980 Canon Photo Gallery, Geneva (with Serge Borner)
1987 Galerie Skopek, Nuremberg, West Germany

Selected Group Exhibitions:

1984   *Sammlung Gruber*, Museum Ludwig, Cologne

Collections:

Museum Ludwig, Cologne.

Publications:

By IONESCO: Books—*Liliacées Langoureuses aux Parfums d'Arbie*, Paris 1974; *Femmes san Tain*, Paris 1975; *Litanies pour une Amante Funebre*, Milan 1976; *Nocturnes*, New York 1976; *Ecstasy*, Chicago 1977; *Temple aux Miroirs*, with Alain Robbe-Grillet, Paris 1977. **Article**—interview, with Mike Treasure, in the *British Journal of Photography* (London), 30 November 1973.

On IONESCO: Books—*Photography Year 1977*, by the Time-Life editors, New York 1977; *Women on Women*, with an introduction by Katharine Holabird, London 1978; *Irèna Ionesco*, with texts by Bernard Letu and André Laude, Paris 1979; *Collection Images Obliques*, vol. 6: *Irèna Ionesco: Cent Onze Photographies Erotiques*, with a preface by Pierre Bourgeade, Lyons 1980; *Sammlung Gruber: Photographie des 20, Jahrhunderts*, exhibition catalogue, with foreword by Siegfried Gohr, Cologne 1984. **Articles**—"Un Monde Mysterieux: Irèna Ionesco" in *Le Nouveau Photocinema* (Paris), April 1973; "Irèna Ionesco: Portraits d'Eva" in *Le Nouveau Photocinema* (Paris), March 1974; "Le Serail d'Irèna Ionesco" by André Pieyre de Mandiargues in *L'Oeil* (Paris), September 1974; "Irèna Ionesco: Style 80" in *Photo* (Paris), December 1979.

*   *   *

Irèna Ionesco directs, and through her photographs presents, *tableaux* from that theatre of femininity in which the acts are, for the most part, played out partly hidden behind the facade of everyday existence. The settings, with their profuse and heterogeneous objects, are in the line of descent running via Flaubert's *Salammbô* and Gustave Moreau's paintings; are from the garden where Joris Huysmans nurtured the etiolated prolixities of *À Rebours*. Yet the women and the heat are Baudelairean entirely.

An uncanny appositeness in Irèna Ionesco's handling of her material offers exact *correspondances* for the heady blend of incense with human and artificial perfumes one apprehends as pervading the heavily enclosed interiors in which she works. The women are, moreover, seen to present themselves as participants in enigmatic acts of ritual, of fetishism, of fantasy or of catatonia. Never, though, does one become even tentatively certain as to what were the larger situations from which the single images have been extracted. One's thoughts are left to migrate into the general Symbolist, Decadent irony of corruption and death as co-extensive with the most perfect, exotic florescence.

Again, the viewer implied as an essential presence outside all Irèna Ionesco's images is, one senses, destined to share the identity of the perceiver of the photograph; and so never participate, but remain invisible, condemned to the febrile passivity suffered by Baudelaire in the presence of his Black Venus.

Irèna Ionesco's choices of subject matter, medium and the mode of combining them, make her images entirely suitable for the visual aspect of a joint excursion with Alain Robbe-Grillet into the *nouveau roman*. Probably, it was only the publication of *Temple aux Miroirs* which fully justified a view of the Ionesco photographs as more than a specialised revival of the Decadent aesthetic. The atemporalities, the initial attractiveness of a *chosiste* reading, and the eventual understanding of the book's images in terms of a visual *écriture*, all lead, as Heath said of Robbe-Grillet's texts, to a response to the activity of the work, rather than to the work as means of arrival at the notion of a story, or other like product.

That such features of interpretation are affirmed by the structuring of the photographs into the *Temple* fiction is not a denial that any of them could have been engendered as a response to earlier encounters with the images: it is a fleshing out of what otherwise would have remained hypotheses cautious in the shadows of conventional readings of this body of work; which, it turns out,

is far from being restricted to the mere expression of nostalgia for a previous Fall.

—Philip Stokes

ISHIMOTO, Yasuhiro.

Nationality: Japanese. **Born:** San Francisco, California, to Japanese parents, 14 June 1921; grew up in Kochi City, Japan; returned to the United States, 1939; emigrated to Japan, 1961: naturalized, 1969. **Education:** Educated in Kochi City (attended agriculture school there) until 1939; studied agriculture at the University of California, 1940-42, and architecture at Northwestern University, Chicago, 1946-48 (interned in a relocation camp, Armach, Colorado, 1942-44); studied photography, under Harry Callahan and Aaron Siskind, Institute of Design, Illinois Institute of Technology, Chicago, 1948-52, B.S. 1952. **Family:** Married Shige Ishimoto in 1956. **Career:** Freelance photographer, Tokyo, 1953-58, Chicago, 1958-61, and Tokyo, since 1961. Lecturer, Tokyo Institute of Photography, 1973. **Recipient:** Young Photographers Contest Prize, *Life* magazine, 1950; Moholy-Nagy Prize, Chicago, 1951, 1952; Society of Japanese Photography Critics Prize, 1958; Mainichi Art Prize, Tokyo, 1970; Minister of Education's Prize, Japan, 1978; Annual Award, Photographic Society of Japan, 1978; Japanese Purple Ribbon Medal, Tokyo, 1983. **Agent:** Photo Gallery International, Tokyo. **Address:** c/o Photo Gallery International, 2-5-18 Toranomon, Minato-ku, Tokyo 105, Japan.

Individual Exhibitions:

1953   Museum of Modern Art, New York
1954   Takemiya Gallery, Tokyo
1960   Art Institute of Chicago
1961   Museum of Modern Art, New York
1962   *Chicago, Chicago*, Shirokiya Gallery, Tokyo
1977   *Den Shingonin Ryokai Mandala*, Seibu Museum of Art, Tokyo
1983   *Yamanotesen 29*, Photo Gallery International, Tokyo
1984   *Katsura: Space and Form*, Seibu Museum of Art,
        Funabashi, Japan
1986   *City, People, Form*, Photo Gallery International, Tokyo
        Chicago, Chicago 1942-1982, Kintetu Department
        Store, Osaka
1988   *HANA*, Photo Gallery International, Tokyo
1989   *KATSURA*, Photo Gallery International, Tokyo
1990   *The Photography of Yasuhiro Ishimoto: 1948-1989*, The Seibu
        Museum of Art
1992   *Fallen Leaves and Crashed Cans*, Photo Gallery International, Tokyo
1994   *Yasuhiro Ishimoto: Katsura and Recent Works*, Recontres
        Internationales de la Photographie, Arles, France

Selected Group Exhibitions:

1967   *Photography in the 20th Century*, National Gallery of Canada,
        Ottawa (toured Canada and the United States, 1967-73)
1974   *New Japanese Photography*, Museum of Modern Art,
        New York
1977   *The Photographer and the City*, Museum of Contemporary Art,
        Chicago
1979   *Japanese Photography Today and Its Origin*, Galleria d'Arte
        Moderna, Bologna (travelled to the Palazzo Reale, Milan;
        Palais dex Beaux-Arts, Brussels; and the Institute of
        Contemporary Arts, London)
1980   *The New Vision*, Cultural Center, Chicago
        Photographers at the Institute of Design, Gilbert Gallery,
        Chicago
1984   *The Art of Photography from the Art Institute of Chicago*,
        National Museum of Art, Osaka, Japan
1988   *Eight Japanese Photographers*, Photo Gallery International

Common Sunflower, **1987.** Photograph ©Yasuhiro Ishimoto.

1991   *Innovation in Japanese Photography in the 1960s,* Tokyo
        Metropolitan Museum of Photography
        Photography 1955-1965, Yamaguchi Prefectural Museum
        *SITE WORK: Architecture in Photography since early
        Modernism,* Photographers' Gallery, London

Collections:

National Museum of Modern Art, Tokyo; Museum of Modern Art, New York;
Art Institute of Chicago; Nihon University.

Publications:

By ISHIMOTO: Books—*Aru Hi, Aru Tokoro* (Someday, Somewhere), with
an introduction by Tsutomu Watanabe, Tokyo 1958; *Katsura,* with texts by
Walter Gropius and Kenzo Tange, New Haven, Connecticut 1960; *Chicago,
Chicago,* with text by Shuzo Takiguchi, Tokyo 1969; *The City,* Tokyo 1971;
Tokyo, Tokyo 1971; *The Document of Human Revolution,* with Haruo
Tomiyama, Tokyo 1973; *The World of Kenmochi,* Tokyo 1976; *Den Shingonin
Ryokai Mandala,* Tokyo 1977; *Journey to the Kunisaki,* Tokyo 1978; *Kura,*
Tokyo 1980; *Islam: Space and Design,* Tokyo 1980; *Dry-Landscape Gar-
dens,* Tokyo 1980; *Master Carver Hiragushi Denchu,* Tokyo 1980; *The
Illusion of Yamataikoku,* Tokyo 1980; *The World of Churyo Sato,* Tokyo 1981;

Juichimen Kannon in Shiga, Tokyo 1982; *Chicago, Chicago: 2,* Tokyo 1983;
HANA, Kyuryudo 1988 and San Francisco 1989.

On ISHIMOTO: Books—*Photography of the World,* edited by Heibonsha
Publishers, Tokyo 1956; *Photography of the World '60,* edited by Hiromu
Hara, Ihei Kimura and others, Tokyo and New York 1960; *Photography in the
20th Century* by Nathan Lyons, New York 1967; *New Japanese Photography,*
exhibition catalogue, by John Szarkowski and Shoji Yamagishi, New York
1974; *The Photographer and the City,* exhibition catalogue, by Gail Buckland,
Chicago 1977; *Japanese Photography Today and Its Origin* by Attilio
Colombo and Isabella Doniselli, Bologna 1979; *Nude Photographs of Japan,*
with text by Shiroyasu Suzuki, Tokyo 1981; *The Art of Photography Past and
Present from the Collection of the Art Institute of Chicago,* exhibition
catalogue, with text by David Travis, Osaka, Japan 1984; *Flora Photographica,*
London 1991; *Innovation in Japanese Photography in the 1960s,* exhibition
catalogue, Tokyo 1991; *Photography 1955-1965,* exhibition catalogue,
Yamaguchi 1991. **Article**—"New Japanese Photography, The Museum of
Modern Art" in *Camera Mainichi* (Tokyo), June 1974.

*

One day during the middle of winter, I was waiting for the traffic signal to
change so I could cross the street in front of a department store in downtown
Tokyo. I happened to glance up. Two dry leaves were being buffeted by the
wind at the top of an otherwise defoliated tree standing near the side of the

road. It was a brave little scene. The signal changed to green, and as I started to walk across, I suddenly started to wonder: how has so slender a stem been able to tether that big, broad leaf to its branch all the way through from spring until autumn?

I asked my wife, who walked alongside me, "Don't you wonder why?" My adversary, who is familiar with my childlike habit of endless questioning when I am wondering about something, quickly made her escape, saying, "Well, I wonder why, too. Shall we ask a botanist?"

Being a bit lazy, I never asked any botanist. To tell the truth, I rather enjoyed keeping this feeling of "wondering" in my mind. Soon after, my wondering spread from leaves to flowers. There are flowers that gradually wither while still on the stem, and there are flowers whose petals fall away. Some flowers have petals that are lushly massed together, and some have petals that are simply and delightfully singular. The creation of such forms is, of course, nothing less than God's own art.

Truth to tell, I am totally ignorant about plants. I am fairly familiar with flower names like plum, cherry, camellia, narcissus and tulip. However, when talk turns to tree peony or Chinese peony, I begin to wonder which is which. When it comes to identifying trees and grasses, I immediately give up. Nevertheless, I boldly began to feel that I wanted to photograph flowers while retaining my naive and wondering feeling.

Right about that time, Mr Ishida of the Kyuryudo publishing house, who happened to notice one photo of mine that was on display at a small private exhibition—an enlarged photo of a leaf that my sense of "why?" led me to shoot—kindly whispered to me: "What would you think about doing a book?" Needless to say, these photos are not botanical studies. Neither are they the result of seeking beauty by going into the field or wandering through the mountains.

While living in the great city of Tokyo, I took pictures of flowers that from time to time caught my eye, using an "instant" studio converted from our living room. Sometimes the flowers were ones we had purchased; sometimes my wife went to procure them from people we didn't even know, bringing them a box of sweets in exchange. Even Ms Sai, a small slender woman from the publisher's office, lugged two bunches of flowers over to me. And friends helped me by bringing flowers, too. I chose the ones whose shapes were least damaged—and this was unexpectedly difficult. Sometimes I carefully allowed a flower to wither. Often our living room was a big mess, with the thriving and the withering all jumbled about.

When I formally arranged these flowers, I could have been laughed at by people saying, "Aren't they just all flowers?" But I was seriously attempting to encounter the creation of the form of the flower through my lens.

You will notice that these images are totally devoid of color. I intentionally avoided colors. The first reason was, of course, that I hoped to take photographs that scrupulously adhered to the flower's form; but looking back, I can also see that I was resisting the usual mundane inundation of color, which seemed to me like nothing less than insanity.

Anyway, I think it is best if people who see the photos tint the flowers with whatever colors come to their minds. Probably that is when my photographs are truly brought to perfection.

—Yasuhiro Ishimoto

* * *

Yasuhiro Ishimoto was born in San Francisco in 1921, to Japanese parents who had immigrated to the United States. He went to Japan with his parents in 1924, and spent his childhood in Kochi City until he graduated from agricultural school. He returned to America in 1939, this time on his own. The next year he entered the Agricultural School at the University of California, but his studies were interrupted by World War II and he spent two years in a detention camp in Colorado. In 1946, after the end of the war, he entered the School of Architecture at Northwestern University, Chicago. Two years later he transferred to the Institute of Design, where he studied photography under the direction of Harry Callahan from whom he learned the creative basics of the medium. While there, he was a prize winner in a contest for young photographers sponsored by *Life* magazine. In 1951 and 1952 he received the Moholy-Nagy Prize. In 1953 he returned to Japan, where he photographed the Katsura Palace. He remained in Japan until 1958, then returned to Chicago with his new wife. During his stay in Japan his work had been exhibited and he had published a book, *Aru Hi, Aru Tokoro* (Someday, Somewhere), in 1958. That

same year he had received the annual prize of the Society of Japanese Photography Critics. In 1960 his book *Katsura* was published by Yale University Press, and it gave him a new impetus to explore Japan. In 1961 he returned to Japan again; in the following year he mounted an exhibition *Chicago, Chicago*. In 1969 he obtained Japanese nationality.

Given his personal background, it is understandable that Ishimoto's photography should be based on a strong plastic sensibility and excellent technique, both of which he learned at the Institute of Design. These skills lend his photographs a very cool, sharp appearance, detached from any kind of romantic involvement. He is able to tackle any subject (man or object) with an almost piercing visual intelligence. Nevertheless, there is a deep-seated humanity about his photographs which ensures for his cool images a contact with reality. Sometimes that humanity even reaches the level of the poetic.

At first, when he came to Japan, Ishimoto had intended photographing traditional Japanese architecture, but as a result of photographing the Katsura Palace he developed an interest in the larger questions of the nature of Japanese-ness and Japanese culture. In 1977 he presented an exhibition, later published in book form, which he called *Den Shingonin Ryokai Mandala* (the Ryokai Mandala, a Treasure from the Shingonin): it has been Ishimoto's most celebrated work. It comprises close-up shots showing every detail of the Ryokai Mandala, which has been stored in the Shingonin, at Toji Temple, Kyoto, for a thousand years. Ishimoto does not simply replicate the mandala but makes us appreciate his creative agility. This will be the future course he will follow, I am sure.

Yasuhiro Ishimoto has been a unique photographer of Japan, and, after Ken Domon, he must be the most important photographer of his generation.

—Takao Kajiwara

ISHIUCHI, Miyako

Nationality: Japanese. **Born:** Gumma in 1947. **Education:** Studied at Tama Art University; self-taught in photography. **Recipient:** Awarded the Ihei Kimura Prize by *The Ashai Daily News* in 1979. **Address:** 1-7-19-607, Midorigaoka Meguro-ku, Tokyo.

Individual Exhibitions:

1977	*Yokosuka Story,* Nikon Salon Ginza, Tokyo
1978	*Apartment,* Nikon Salon Ginza, Tokyo
1980	*Endless Night,* Nikon Salon Ginza
1981	*From Yokosuka,* Cabaret 2nd New, Yokosuka
1982	*Tokyo Dental College,* Nikon Salon Ginza
1984	*Tokyo Bay Cities,* Nikon Salon Ginza
1985	*Tokyo Bay Cities,* Nikon Salon, Osaka
1986	*Tokyo Bay Cities in Yokosuka,* Saikaya Salon, Yokosuka
1988	*From Yokosuka Third Position,* Room 801, Tokyo
1991	*Interior,* Past Rays Yokohama Photo Gallery, Yokohama
1992	*Interior 2,* Gallery Te, Tokyo
1993	*Interior 3,* Gallery Te, Tokyo
1994	*1906 To The Skin,* Gallery Te, Tokyo
	1906 To The Skin, Dickson Foundation Gallery, Charlotte, North Carolina
	1.9.4.7., Laurence Miller Gallery, New York

Selected Group Exhibitions:

1979	*Japan: A Self-Portrait,* International Center of Photography, New York (travelled to Venice)
1984	*Dumont's—Die Japanische Photographie,* Museum Für kunst und Gerwerbe, Hamburg
1985	*Paris/New York/Tokyo,* Tsukuba Photography Museum, Tsukuba

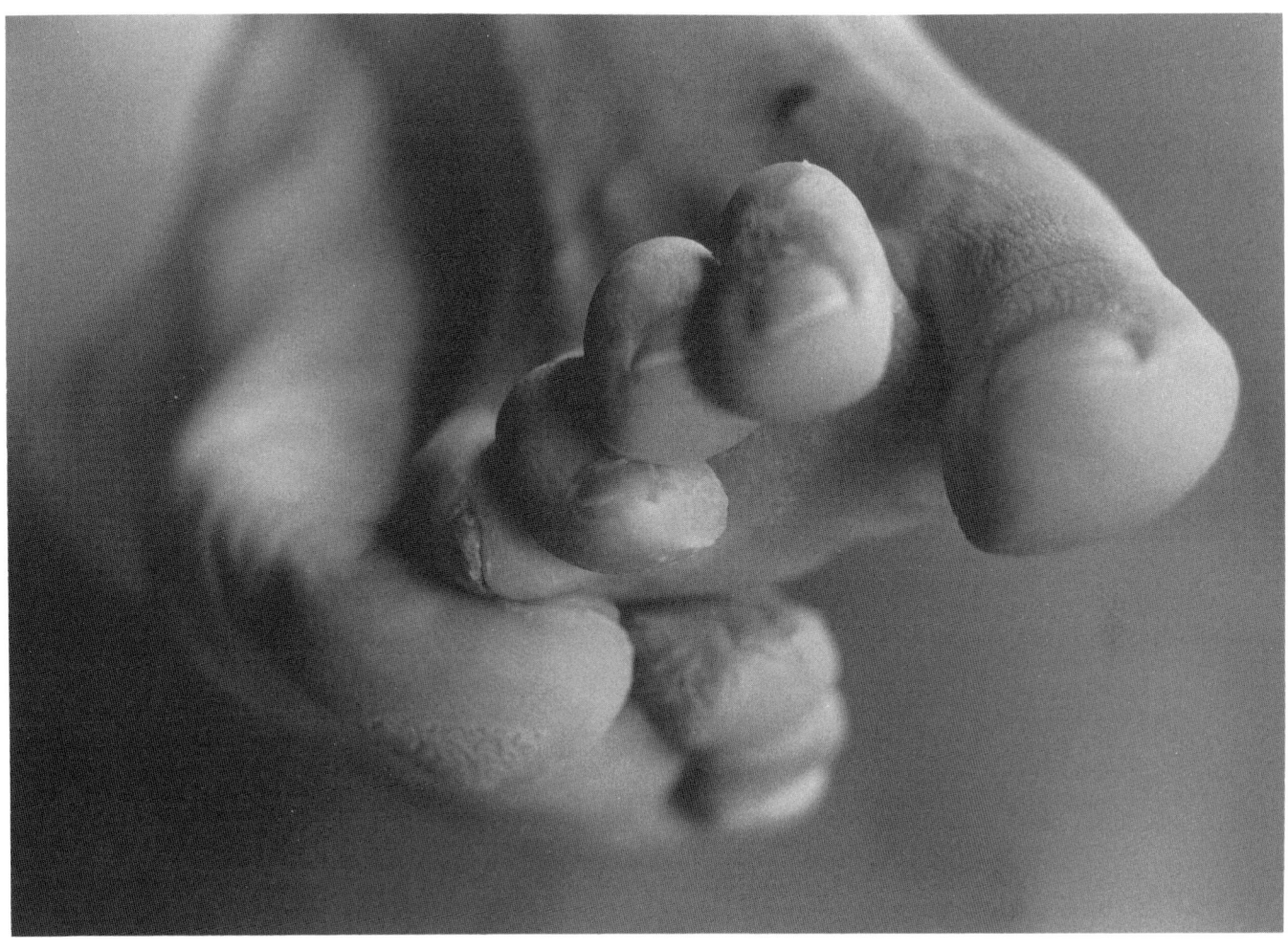

1.9.4.7. **No. 9, 1990.** Photograph by Miyako Ishiuchi.

1986   *World of Super-Image,* Yurakucho Seibu Art Forum, Tokyo
1987   *Japanese Women Photographers,* Lehigh University Art
            Gallery
1989   *Contemporary Japanese Photography,* Center for Creative
            Photography, University of Arizona
1990   *Woman's Perspective in Germany and Japan,* Kawasaki City
            Museum
1991   *Self-Portraits of Contemporary Women,* Tokyo Metropolitan
            Museum of Photography
            Japanese Contemporary Photography, The Photographers'
            Gallery, London
1992   *Symposion über Fotographie 13,* Forum Stadtpark, Graz
1993   *Changing I dense cities,* Shedhalle, Zürich
            Zeitgenössische Japanische Photographie, Kunsthaus, Zürich
1994   *When the Body Becomes Art,* Itabashi Art Museum, Tokyo
            Japanese Art After 1945, The Guggenheim Museum,
            New York
            Inside Out: Contemporary Japanese Photography, The Light
            Factory Photographic Arts Center, Charlotte, North Carolina

Collections:

Center for Creative Photography, University of Arizona; Tokyo Metropolitan Museum of Photography, Tokyo; The Museum of Art, Yokohama; The National Museum of Modern Art, Tokyo; Kunsthaus, Zürich; The Museum of Modern Art, New York.

Publications:

By ISHIUCHI: Books—*Apartment,* Shasin Tsushinsha 1978; *Yokosuka Story,* Shasin Tsushinska 1979; *Endless Night,* Asahi Sonorama 1981; *Tokyo Dental College,* Issei Shuppan 1981; *1.9.4.7.,* Inter Press Corporation 1990; *Monochrome,* Chikuma Shobo 1993; *1906 To The Skin,* Kawade Shobo Sinsha Publishers 1994.

*

Photographs are, after all, what an individual's eye has caught. So any photo has a very private meaning of its own. There may be no point in my stressing this fact, but somehow I feel I must say it: my photographs are my personal history. They reflect my very self-centred and self-absorbed vision and are biased by my subjectivity.

For the 12 months in the production of a book, I go through what few photographs I have taken over and over again. One rarely gets such a chance. Usually one simply keeps on taking them, and they keep piling up and are quickly pushed in to the past and oblivion. I put a stop to this process and place in front of me all of my photographs, from the very first picture I have published to the one I am working on at that time. The resulting book consists of my personal impressions of those photographs and fragments of memories I have put down about them.

There are as many styles of photograph as there are photographers. There is no defining what a photograph is or should be. Only those who take them can decide what their idea of each photograph is. It is all that personal.

In the midst of the deluge of photographs that are being produced, consumed and thrown away every day, I feel I must keep on asking myself the meaning of taking this extreme care and making the best possible effort and being accountable for every single photograph I produce and show to the public.

Photography is a very personal vocation but it involves a lot of people. In that sense, all photographs are social. They bring to light the very brief encounter with all those people who are not me, landscape and society. The sense of distance I feel with them, my own perspective, and sensitivity are the original source of inspiration of my photographs.

—Miyako Ishiuchi

ITO, Yoshihiko.

Nationality: Japanese. **Born:** Yamagata Prefecture, 1951. **Education:** Graduated from Tokyo Collect of Photography, 1977. **Address:** c/o Photo Gallery International, 2-5-18 Toranomon, Minato-ku, Tokyo 105, Japan.

Individual Exhibitions:

1979   *Process Eye,* Gallery OWL, Tokyo
1980   *Eyes,* Gallery OWL, Tokyo
        Eyes 2, Gallery OWL, Tokyo
1981   *Photographic,* Gallery OWL, Tokyo
        Test—Circumference of Consciousness, Gallery OWL, Tokyo
        Eyes 3, Gallery OWL, Tokyo
1987   *Imagery 72—Kumo,* Gallery Yo, Tokyo
1989   *VVV Filmorogie,* FROG, Tokyo
1990   *New Delicate—Shikaku,* Route Gallery, Tokyo
1992   *Contact Print Series,* Gallery Hosomi, Tokyo
        Contact Print Stories, Laurence Miller Gallery, New York
1994   *Contact Prints: To Observe and Continue to Observe,* Photo
        Gallery International, Tokyo

Group Exhibitions:

1979   *Kyodo-Ten (The Collection),* Kanagawa Prefectural Gallery,
        Yokohama
1982   *The Potential of Scenery,* Kanagawa Prefectural Gallery,
        Yokohama
1986   *Photographs Showing Tokyo—Open Graph,* Gallery
        Tamaya, Tokyo
        Off-Mode Off-Code, G Art Gallery, Tokyo
1987   *Exhibition of Shashin,* Yurakucho Asahi Gallery, Tokyo
1987-88 *Photographic Aspects of Japanese Art Tokyo,* Tochigi
        Prefectural Museum of Fine Arts
1989   *Tama Vivant '89,* Seed Hall, Shibuya Seibu, Tokyo
        Playing Shadow, Yokohama City Okurayama Memorial
        Gallery
1990   *Polyphony of Photography,* Talk Gallery, Sapporo
        Assemblage Photography—New Delicate, FROG, Tokyo
        Japanese Contemporary Photography: Twelve Viewpoints,
        Tokyo Metropolitan Museum of Photography, Tokyo
1991   *Speaking through Photography II,* Photography Center, Tokyo
        National Museum of Fine Arts and Music, Tokyo
        Photo Session, Sizuoka Prefectural Gallery, Sizuoka Prefectural
        Museum, Sizuoka
1994   *When the Body Becomes Art,* Itabashi Art Museum, Tokyo
        Contemporary Human Images, Hokkaido Musem of Modern
        Art, Hokkaido
        Cross and Square Grids, The Musem of Modern Art, Saitama

Collections:

The National Museum of Modern Art, Tokyo; The Museum of Fine Arts, Houston, Texas; Center for Creative Photography, The University of Arizona, Tucson; The Art Museum, Princeton University, Princeton, New Jersey.

Publications:

On ITO: Books—*Japanese Contemporary Photography: Twelve Viewpoints,* exhibition catalogue (Tokyo), 1990; *When the Body Becomes Art,* exhibition catalogue (Tokyo) 1994.

*

Having all the family there at mealtimes is great fun. We discuss many topics and sometimes it can go on for quite a time. If the talk turns to past events or to now, the present, problems arise for each person and the pleasant atmosphere disintegrates. If, however, the talk turns to things yet to come, the near future, it suddenly brightens up and the conversation bounds along because problems do not easily arise for individuals talking about the future. One subject that children enjoy is "What would you most like now?" Children really love this "most" idea, and as their faces light up they vie to be the first to answer. They produce names of concrete objects and begin chatting along the lines "If all goes well . . ." The conversation finally moves on to life in the future, but no voice of reproach is heard. Eventually, this conversation too drifts gradually away from reality, and they begin to speak about space, finally jumping to the topic of a time machine. I like times like this. Then comes the turn of myself and my wife to say what we would like most. We answer almost in unison, "Time!" Their answers show concrete things or objects, but ours is something both like and unlike an object, and their response therefore lacks a little enthusiasm.

It is certain that the world contains some things which can be seen and some which cannot—probably determined by what and how one's personal antenna picks up. Whether one understands the manner of things or not depends on this. Also, I believe the signals do not just emanate from outside, but some are transmitted by oneself. It is however exceptionally difficult to perceive these clearly. If definite reception of these signals were possible I am sure that our doubts regarding various questions would abate.

Time is certainly one of those things which we cannot see. It is not true that the instant that one does something it becomes visible . . . rather, it draws away from us in the way of some invisible distance. Yet there are also some that draw closer. Discussing things with such properties can lead to a very satisfying time; past, present and future react with each other instantaneously and simultaneously inside everyone's head to become words which are then uttered. If this incomprehensible entity became visible as an object, I am sure children would fight to be the first to get it. I laugh when I consider such a prospect.

My wife says that a natural life of "working outside when fine, reading inside when wet" is good. I agree with such a lifestyle. However, when I feel I want to understand the manner of things, or when I tell the children that what I want is time, thoughts of such a life vanish completely. My thoughts turn outwards and I continue to observe together with my friends rain, wind, clouds and light.

—Yoshihiko Ito

ITURBIDE, Graciela.

Nationality: Mexican. **Born:** Mexico City, 16 May 1942. **Education:** Sagrado Corazon School, San Luis Potosi, Mexico, 1958-61; Centro de Estudios Cinematograficos (CUEC), Mexico City, 1969-72; private photographic studies, as assistant to Manuel Alvarez Bravo, Mexico City, 1970-72. **Career:** Freelance photographer, working for Instituto Nacional Indigenista, Secretaria de Comunicaciones, and various magazines, Mexico City, since 1970; also filmmaker, Mexico City, since 1969. Founder-Member, Foro de Arte

Contemporáneo, Mexico City; Member, Consejo Mexicano de Fotografia, Mexico City. **Address:** Ortega 20, Coyoacan, Mexico 21, D.F., Mexico.

Individual Exhibitions:

1975	*Three Women Photographers,* Galería José Clemente Orozco, Mexico City
1976	*Three Mexican Photographers,* Midtown Gallery, New York (with Collete Urbajtel and Paulina Lavista)
1979	Casa de Cultura, Juchitán, Oaxaca, Mexico
1980	Casa del Lago, Mexico City

Selected Group Exhibitions:

1976	*10 Photographers,* Salón de la Plástica Mexicana, Mexico City
1978	*Primera Muestra de Fotografia Latinoaméricana,* Museo de Arte Moderna, Mexico City
	Contemporary Photography in Mexico: 9 Photographers, Northlight Gallery, Arizona State University, Tempe (travelled to University of Arizona, Tucson)
1979	*Opera Inconclusa,* Foro de Arte Contemporáneo, Mexico City
1980	*7 Portafolios Mexicanos,* Centre Culturel Mexicain, Paris (travelled to Picasso Museum, Antibes, France)
	Primera Bienal de Fotografia, Auditorio Nacional, Mexico City
1981	*Segunda Muestra de Fotografia Latinoaméricana,* Palacio de Bellas Artos, Mexico City
	Fotografie Lateinamerika, Kunsthaus, Zurich
1982	*La Photographie Contemporaine en Amerique Latine,* Centre Georges Pompidou, Paris
1985	*SIF 85: Semana Internacional de la Fotografia,* Palacio del Infantado, Guadalajara, Spain

Collections:

Consejo Mexicano de Fotografia, Mexico City; Casa de la Cultura, Juchitán, Oaxaca, Mexico; Bibliothèque Nationale, Paris.

Publications:

By ITURBIDE: Book—*Los que Viven en la Arena,* with text by Luis Barjau, Mexico City 1981. **Films**—*The Life of Jose Luis Cuevas,* 1969; *Elecciones,* 1970; *Crates,* with Alfredo Joskowicz, 1971.

On ITURBIDE: Books—*Avándaro,* with text by Luis Carrión, Mexico City 1971; *Contemporary Photography in Mexico: 9 Photographers,* exhibition catalogue, by Terence Pitts and Rene Verdugo, Tucson 1978; *Hecho en Latinoamérica,* edited by Pedro Meyer, Mexico City 1978; *Desnudo Fotográfico,* with text by Mariano Flores Castro, Mexico City 1980; *7 Portafolios Mexicanos,* exhibition catalogue, with text by Raquel Tibol, Mexico City 1980; *Hecho en Latino América 2,* exhibition catalogue, with texts by Pedro Meyer, Lazaro Blanco and others, Mexico City 1981; *La Photographie Contemporaine en Amerique Latine,* exhibition catalogue, by Alain Sayag, Paris 1982. **Articles**—"La Fotografía de Graciela Iturbide" by Alfredo Joskowicz in *Artes Visuales* (Mexico City), Winter 1975; "Graciela Iturbide" in *Photocinema* (Paris), 1977; "Presencias" in *Arquitecto* (Mexico City), no. 10, 1978; "Fotografías de Graciela Iturbide" in *Rehilete* (Mexico City), February 1980; "Graciela Iturbide: La Sembradora de Imagenes" in *La Semana de Belles Artes* (Mexico City), 19 March 1980; "Graciela Iturbide: Artista Fotografa" in *La Letra y la Imagen* (Mexico City), 20 April 1980; "Mexico: New Images of an Ancient Land" in *Camera 35* (New York), February 1981.

*

Photography is a way of life. I write, I draw with light my daily experiences; I retain in images casual external encounters and internal finalities.

I seek to trap life in the reality that surrounds me, without forgetting that therein lie my dreams, my symbols, my imagination.

In human beings I search to discover my own nostalgia.

—Graciela Iturbide

* * *

Photographing people is a very difficult task; it is even more so if the people happen to be Mexican Indians. Socio-economic contrasts are extremely sharp in Mexico, and there is a great deal of mistrust among social classes. The Indians have been mercilessly exploited for the past five centuries. Their culture, their religion, their economic system, their family structure, and their relation to nature and to their fellow men have been continuously subject to the cruellest forms of aggression ever since the Spanish Conquest. Some have tried to assimilate in a hopeless struggle to become white men; others chose to retreat, to shut themselves within their ancient traditions, full of resentment towards the white man and mistrusting any attempt at communication. Besides, there is a belief—not as preposterous as it may seem—that the camera steals the photographed person's soul. Every day the tourist attacks the inhabitants of Indian villages with his brandished camera. He grabs disrespectfully whatever he can as false proof of his presence in these places, as something exotic to show to friends. For the Indian, the white man is someone who steals his land, his traditions, and his soul. It is the accomplishment of Graciela Iturbide that, with all of these obstacles, she has been able to come close to these people.

Iturbide has such tact and respect that her subjects show themselves before her in all their natural poise and dignity. There is, in her work, no search for the picturesque, but only an innocent and somewhat romantic attempt to find human integrity and that vital link with the environment that Indian people still keep. It is this link and this integrity that appeal to Iturbide, for they are traits that have been almost lost by the inhabitants of such chaotic places as Mexico City and the other gigantic capitals of the Western world.

"Nuestra Senora de las Iguanas" is one example. She is an Indian from Juchitan, Oaxaca, a region of scarce economic resources but of great artistic and mythological wealth, the land of the Mixteco-Zapoteca cultures. Accomplishing this photograph required many days. Iturbide had to bridge the gap between herself and this woman so as to reach a kind of communion, subtle and sincere. She even helped her to sell tomatoes and iguanas in the market place until the woman agreed to face the camera without hiding. The similarity between this photograph and some of the work of Francisco Toledo, a painter from Juchitan, is not coincidental. The mysterious unity between man and animal, the poetry and the throbbing myths involved in this bonding, are part of everyday life in Juchitan.

In the few years that Graciela Iturbide has been working in photography she has consistently achieved what many other photographers acquire only in their mature work—a genuine respect for the person facing the camera, a profound sense of his or her existence. This is particularly true when her subject is a woman; indeed, it could be said that Iturbide is particularly a photographer of Woman.

She approaches her subject delicately, and allows herself to be touched to the same extent that she attempts to touch with her camera. She doesn't grab images; she earns them. What Graciela Iturbide obtains—the permission to touch a human being—she returns to whomever stops to contemplate her work. She caresses with her camera, both her subject and the beholder of her work.

—Katya Mandoki

IZIS.

Nationality: French. Born Israel Bidermanas in Mariampole, Lithuania, 17 January 1911; emigrated to France, 1930: naturalized 1946. **Education:** Attended schools in Lithuania, 1921-26; apprentice in a photographic studio. **Career:** Freelance photographer, establishing own portrait studio, Paris, 1930-39; worked as a photo-retoucher, and active in the French Resistance, adopting the name "Izis," Limoges, France, 1940-44; freelance photographer, Paris, 1945-49; Staff Photographer, *Paris-Match* magazine, 1949-69;

Carousel in the Tuileries, Paris. Photograph by Izis. Courtesy of the Art Institute of Chicago.

freelance magazine photographer, Paris, 1970-80. **Died:** (in Paris) *16 May 1980.*

Individual Exhibitions:

1944	*Ceux de Grammont,* Musée du Limoges, France
	Limoges en Novembre, Musée du Limoges, France
1955	Art Institute of Chicago
1957	Limelight Gallery, New York
1966	*Cirques d'Izis,* Musée du Limoges, France
1972	Museum of Modern Art, Tel Aviv
1975	Galerie Agathe Gaillard, Paris
1977	Galerie Nagel, West Berlin
	Fête à Paris, Carlton Gallery, New York
1978	Musée Réattu, Arles, France
1979	*Izis,* FNAC, Paris; Lyon; Mulhouse; Grenoble
1980	*Izis,* Galerie Paule Pia, Anvers
1984	*40eme anniversaire de la Libération: Les Maquisards,* Pavillon du Verdurier, Limoges
1987	*Izis rétrospective,* Caisse Nationale des Monuments Historiques et des Sites, Paris
1989	*L'emotion partagée,* Musée de la Photographie, Charleroi
1990	*Izis,* Musée Nicéphore Niépce, Chalon-sur-Saône
1993	*Izis photographie Chagall. La création d'un Monde,* Joods Historisch Museum, Amsterdam

Selected Group Exhibitions:

1951	*5 French Photographers: Brassaï/Cartier-Bresson/Doisneau/ Izis/Ronis,* Museum of Modern Art, New York
1954	*Great Photographs,* Limelight Gallery, New York
1955	*The Family of Man,* Museum of Modern Art, New York (and world tour)
1957	*Salon National de la Photographie,* Bibliothèque Nationale, Paris (and 1959)
1972	*Boubat/Brassaï/Cartier-Bresson/Doisneau/ Ronis/Iris,* French Embassy, Moscow
1976	*Other Eyes,* Arts Council of Great Britain travelling exhibition (toured the U.K.)
1986	*Crosscurrents II,* San Francisco Museum of Modern Art

Collections:

Bibliothèque Nationale, Paris; Musée Réattu, Arles, France; Musée du Limoges, France; Museum of Modern Art, New York; Art Institute of Chicago.

Publications:

By IZIS: Books—*Paris des Reves,* with text by Jacques Prévert, with foreword by Jean Cocteau, Paris 1950, as *Paris Enchanted,* London 1952; *Grand Bal du Printemps,* with text by Jacques Prévert, Paris 1951; *Charmes de Londres,* with text by Jacques Prévert, Paris 1952, as *Gala Day: London,* London 1952; *Paradis Terrestie,* with text by Colette, Paris 1953; *People of the Queen,* London 1954; *Israel,* with a foreword by André Malraux, Paris 1956; *Le Cirque d'Izis,* with text by Jacques Prévert, Paris 1965; *Paris des Poètes,* with text by Jacques Prévert, Paris 1967; *Le Monde de Chagall,* with text by Roy McMullen, Paris 1969.

On IZIS: Books—*Photography Today,* edited by Norman Hall, London 1957; *Moderni Francouzska Fotografie/Modern French Photography* by J.A.

Keim, Prague 1966; *Other Eyes,* exhibition catalogue, by Peter Turner, London 1976; *Geschichte der Fotografie im 20. Jahrhundert/Photography in the 20th Century* by Petr Tausk, Cologne 1977, London 1980; *Izis de Paris et d'ailleurs,* text by Pierre Borhan, Paris 1988; *Izis photographies,* Paris 1988; *Izis: Les Amoureux du Temps Retrouvé,* Japan 1989; *Izis: Les Enfants du Temps Perdu,* Japan 1989; *Izis photographies 1944-1980,* exhibition catalogue with text by Marie de Thézy, Paris 1993; *Izis Photographs Chagall: A World in the Making,* exhibition catalogue, Amsterdam 1993. **Articles**—"Izis: Paris in the 50s" in *Creative Camera* (London), November 1976; "Izis" in *Camera* (Lucerne), January 1979; "Izis: Un Hommage" by Roger Therond in *Photo* (Paris), June 1980.

* * *

It's certain that in the green pastures that now make up his universe Izis is still a photographer, and his poetic inspiration flowers better there than here below.

He entered photography at the age of 13 by modest means: he worked in the sort of studio where ordinary people have the great moments of their lives fixed on paper. But he took from this kind of apprenticeship an essential rule: truth first. He never forgot it, even though he went on to great success. At the age of 20 he had established his own rather more chic studio in Paris; he was, remarkably, self-employed and successful in a strange city; during the German Occupation, which all but cost him his life, he immortalized in pictures his comrades in the Resistance; he created a number of books; and for 20 years he collaborated on a great magazine, *Paris-Match*—yet he never once departed from those ethics based on honesty. (Well, actually, he did fib once: in a conversation with an editor, Izis assured him that he knew all about color photography, the consequence of which was that he was forced to buy his first color film and his first light meter, and succumb to modernism and artifice!)

In any "who's who" of photography, Izis the remarkable, the loner, should always be perceived as "different." Eternally faithful to his old Rolleiflex (against the generalized style of 24 x 36), always stingy in his shots (against the modern, machinegun approach), he took few pictures; he knew how to wait ("like a fisherman waiting for a nibble," he said) until the exact, significant scene presented itself to him. As for his instinctive technique—without flash and without the famous light meter—it was so sure that he never miscalculated. The results inevitably reveal meaning, construction, balance, and the thought and emotion of the artist. Stillness, tenderness and beauty are evident in those series in which he made himself a specialist: painters, poets, writers, carnival and circus people, illustrious characters, the people of Paris—and above all and always Paris itself, the city that dazzled the immigrant from a difficult past. And there is not a picture of his that does not tell of the gratitude of the heart, the brotherhood and bond between photographer and model, an ardent need to share the joy—or sorrow—of the subject.

Is Izis, then, a pure humanist poet of photography? Yes and no. Yes, because his works have a rare precision and luminescent composition; they are carriers of a dreamlike, diffuse dimension, of a "supplementary soul," sometimes of an unreality which is the heart itself of "poetic realism." His "Cracheur de Feu," for example, is a phantasmagorical flower of which all the fascination, appropriately, comes from the scientific exactitude of presentation. And no, too, because Izis also flays the world: he is deferential with the greats of the world, but he lingers on the forgotten, the castaways of life, the damned (like the writers Céline and Léautaud). At some point one asks oneself: could Izis secretly have been, rather than a poet, a militant philosopher?

—Roger Therond

JACHNA, Joseph D(avid).

Nationality: American. **Born:** Chicago, Illinois, 12 September 1935. **Education:** Chicago Vocational High School, 1949-53; studied art education and photography, under Harry Callahan and Aaron Siskind, at the Institute of Design, Illinois Institute of Technology, Chicago, 1953-54, 1955-61, B.S. Art Ed. 1958, M.S. Photography 1961. **Family:** Married Virginia Kemper in 1962; children: Timothy, Heidi and Jody. **Career:** Worked part-time as a photo assistant, Derwin Studio Darkroom, Chicago, 1953-54; photo-technician, Eastman Kodak Laboratories, Chicago, 1954; photographer's assistant, DeSort commercial photo-illustration studio, Chicago, 1956-58. Freelance photographer, Chicago, since 1961. Instructor in Photography, Institute of Design, 1961-69, and Professor of Art, Photography at University of Illinois at Chicago Circle, since 1969. **Recipient:** Ferguson Foundation Grant, Friends of Photography, Carmel, California, 1973; National Endowment for the Arts Grant, 1976; Illinois Arts Council Grant, 1979; Guggenheim Fellowship for Photography, 1980. **Agent:** Edwynn Houk Gallery, 200 West Superior Street, Chicago, Illinois 60610, U.S.A. **Address:** 5707 West 89th Place, Oak Lawn, Illinois 60453, U.S.A.

Individual Exhibitions:

1961	Art Institute of Chicago
1963	St. Mary's College, Notre Dame, Indiana
1965	University of Illinois, Chicago
1970	Lightfall Gallery, Evanston Art Center, Illinois
	University of Wisconsin, Milwaukee
1974	Center for Photographic Studies, Louisville, Kentucky
	Friends of Photography, Carmel, California
	Tyler School of Art/Moore College of Art, Philadelphia
	Nikon Photo Salon (2 galleries), Tokyo
1975	University of Notre Dame, Indiana
	Afterimage Gallery, Dallas
1977	*Iceland/Wisconsin/Upper Michigan,* University of Illinois at Chicago Circle
1979	Visual Studies Workshop Gallery, Rochester, New York
1980	*Light Touching Silver: Photographs by Joseph D. Jachna,* Chicago Center for Contemporary Photography
1981	Focus Gallery, San Francisco (with George Krause)
	Perihelion Gallery, Milwaukee (with Marija Petrauskas)
1983	Nexus Gallery, Atlanta, Georgia (with Emmett Gowin)
	Photogenesis Gallery, Albuquerque, New Mexico
1984	Andover Gallery, Massachusetts
1985	Northern Kentucky University, Highland Heights
	University of Arkansas, Fayetteville
	Southern Illinois University, Carbondale
	Black, White and Gray, Chicago State University, Illinois
1986	University of Minnesota, Duluth
1988	*Josephson, Jachna and Siegel: Chicago Experimentalists,* San Francisco Museum of Modern Art, San Francisco
1993	*Time Pieces,* Gallery 954, Chicago, Illinois
1994	*Poetic Visions,* Illinois Art Gallery, Chicago; Lockport Gallery, Lockport, Illinois; Illinois State Museum, Springfield

Selected Group Exhibitions:

1963	*Contemporary Photographers,* Art Institute of Chicago

1966	*American Photography: The 60s,* University of Nebraska, Lincoln
1968	*Light 7,* Massachusetts Institute of Technology, Cambridge
1975	*For You, Aaron,* Renaissance Society Gallery, University of Chicago
1977	*Photographers and the City,* Museum of Contemporary Art, Chicago
1978	*Spaces,* Museum of Art, Rhode Island School of Design, Providence
1981	*Second Sight,* Carpenter Center for the Visual Arts, Harvard University, Cambridge, Massachusetts
1983	*Harry Callahan and His Students,* Georgia State University, Atlanta
1985	*Light: From Illumination to Pure Radiance,* San Francisco Museum of Modern Art
1986	*Iceland Sextet,* The National Museum of Modern Art, Kyoto, Japan
	Views and Visions: Recent American Landscape Photography, International Center for Photography, New York
1987	*Photography and Art—Interactions Since 1946,* Los Angeles County Museum of Art
1991	*Echoes: A Chicago Tribute,* Catherine Edelman Gallery, Chicago
1992	*Patterns of Influence,* Center for Creative Photography, Tucson, Arizona

Collections:

Museum of Modern Art, New York; International Museum of Photography, George Eastman House, Rochester, New York; Massachusetts Institute of Technology, Cambridge; Art Institute of Chicago; Museum of Contemporary Art, Chicago; Center for Photographic Studies, Louisville, Kentucky; University of Kansas Art Museum, Lawrence; Center for Creative Photography, University of Arizona, Tucson; Friends of Photography, Carmel, California; San Francisco Museum of Modern Art.

Publications:

On JACHNA: Books—*Photography in the 20th Century* by Nathan Lyons, New York 1967; *Be-Ing Without Clothes,* exhibition catalogue, by Minor White, Millerton, New York 1970; *Untitled 14,* Friends of Photography exhibition catalogue, Carmel, California 1973; *Language of Light,* exhibition catalogue, by James Enyeart, Lawrence, Kansas 1974; *Photography Year 1974,* by the Time-Life editors, New York 1974; *The Target Collection of American Photography,* exhibition catalogue, by Anne Tucker, Houston 1977; *Light Touching Silver: Photographs by Joseph D. Jachna,* exhibition catalogue, with an introduction by Steven Klindt, Chicago 1980; *Landscape as Photograph* by Estelle Jussim and Elizabeth Lindquist-Cook, New York 1985; *Photography and Art—Interactions Since 1946,* exhibition catalogue, by Andy Grundberg and Kathleen M. Gauss, Los Angeles 1987; *Decade by Decade: 20th Century Photography from the Collection of the Center for Creative Photography,* Tucson 1989; *Poetic Visions: Photographs by Joseph D Jachna,* exhibition catalogue, Chicago 1993. **Articles**—"New Talent U.S.A.: Photography" in *Art in America* (New York), no. 1, 1962; "Joseph Jachna" by Charles Desmarais in *Artweek* (Oakland, California), 4 May 1974; "Joseph Jachna," special issue of *Asahi Camera* (Tokyo), April 1975; "Joseph Jachna: Door County Landscapes" by John B. Turner in *Photo-Forum* (Auckland, New Zealand), June/July 1975; "The New Vision: Forty

Years of Photography at the Institute of Design" in *Aperture* (Millerton, New York) no. 7, 1981; "The Armed Vision Disarmed" by Abigail Solomon Godeau in *Afterimage* (Rochester, New York), January 1983.

*

An important aspect of my working attitude is a primary concern with "basics"—tones, focus, light, etc.—and those elements of a picture which are visual, visible, describable and controllable. Certain other aspects, perhaps the really important ones, which deal with its meaning or "spirit" will always enter the picture when the controllable elements are properly attended to, and so it has become, more or less, a credo to pay attention to certain details, to work carefully and intelligently on them, so that the desired result can occur.

The making of a photograph is an act of intelligence and an act of discovery: knowledge is brought to the process so that knowledge can be gained, and none of this knowledge needs a verbal counterpart. A photograph often has a counterpart in life, in music, a poem or a song, but these are never substitutes. The photograph is its own full explanation, and the joy it is to look at it.

—Joseph D. Jachna

*   *   *

Joseph D. Jachna is primarily a photographer of nature. Educated at the Institute of Design under Aaron Siskind and Harry Callahan, he reflects in his early work the Bauhaus simplicity of that institution and combines something of the attention to abstract form of Siskind with the precision and delicacy of Callahan.

Jachna works primarily in black and white, pushing the formal and expressive qualities of tonality to their limits. Black versus white takes on an almost symbolic significance. Many images employ a recurring line, usually a curve, suggestive of the yin-yang symbol, a line which divides yet at the same time admits and accepts the underlying duality, or complementary quality of nature.

His iconography is established through a progression of simple, archetypal juxtapositions: white snow vs. black hill, egg vs. weathered wood, mirror vs. landscape, hand versus cloud, fist versus nude. The earliest landscapes are what we might term non-manipulative, "window" images which are at the same time carefully organized, simplified, condensed, suggesting metaphors. The progression of his work can be seen as that from objective to self-reflexive, from more or less passive photographer to an open acknowledgement of the forming quality of vision.

Self-reflexivity literally breaks through the picture plane in a dramatic series made in 1969 in Door County, Wisconsin. In this series the extended hand of the photographer literally juts into the picture frame and becomes part of the landscape. The series evolves into a progression of hands holding shards, pieces of mirrors, surfaces which reflect, instead of the expected visage of the photographer, the face of nature. Nature is held up for examination, yet at the same time nature and self are merged. The hand holding the mirror is abstracted, reduced to simple, dark, almost phallic shapes, which dance about the reflected image of nature. Through an implied yet restrained eroticism, the metaphor of man's "merging" with nature is consummated in a wonderfully understated, yet visually exhilarating, fashion. This series is spectacular in its sense of energy and in the realization and acceptance of the creative will of the photographer.

Through a grant from the National Endowment for the Arts in 1976, Jachna travelled to Iceland, and continued, in large format land- and sky-scapes, the merging of his own "mark" with the expanse of nature. The tangibility of the grain structure of these images now meshes the protrusion of the photographer, his arm or hand, into an elemental cohesiveness with the Icelandic panorama.

More recently, a series of "snow angels," imprints of the bodies of children upon freshly fallen snow, serves to underscore Jachna's metaphor: nature, and the imprint of the human form, literally, upon that nature. Jachna sees the human impingement upon nature as strong, insistent, giving form, but a form that is also transitory, as it is in itself inextricably meshed with the "stuff" of nature: the clouds will pass, the snow will melt, taking with it the

imprint of human activity. Permanence is gained only through the event of the image-making itself.

—Carole Harmel

JACOBI, Lotte (Johanna).

Nationality: American. **Born:** Thorn, West Prussia, Germany, 17 August 1896; emigrated to the United States, 1935; naturalized, 1940. **Education:** Attended the Königliche Louisenschule, Posen, 1902-12; studied art history and literature, Academy of Posen, 1912-16; Bavarian State Academy of Photography, Munich, and, art history, University of Munich, 1925-27; graphics, art history, French and literature, University of New Hampshire, Durham, 1961-62; etching and engraving, with S.W. Hayter, Atelier 17, Paris, 1962-63. **Family:** Married Fritz Honig in 1916 (divorced, 1924); son: John Frank; married the publisher Erich Reiss in 1940 (died, 1951). **Career:** Director, Jacobi Studio of Photography (family business), Berlin, 1927-35; freelance photographer, with a studio there, New York, 1935-55; also maintained a gallery in New York, 1952-55. Proprietor, Jacobi Studio and Gallery, Deering, 1963-70. A Founder, Department of Photography, Currier Gallery of Art, Manchester, New Hampshire, 1970 (Honorary Curator of Photography, 1972-78). **Recipient:** Silver Medal, Royal Photography Salon, Tokyo, 1931; First Prize, British War Relief Photography Competition, *Life* magazine, New York, 1941; First Prize, New Hampshire Art Association, 1970; New Hampshire Governor's Award for the Arts, 1980; Erich Salomon Prize, West Berlin, 1983. D.F.A.: University of New Hampshire, Durham, 1974; University of Maryland, Baltimore, 1983; Rivier College, Nashua, New Hampshire, 1984; D.H.L.: New England College, Henniker, New Hampshire, 1978; New Hampshire College, Manchester, 1982; LL.D.: Colby-Sawyer College, New London, New Hampshire, 1982. **Died:** (in Concord, New Hampshire) 6 May 1990.

Individual Exhibitions:

1937	Jacobi Studio, 24 West 59th Street, New York
1941	Jacobi Studio, 154 West 54th Street, New York
	Direction Gallery, New York
1948	Norlyst Gallery, New York
1952	Ohio University College, Athens
1953	University College of Education, New Paltz, New York
1955	Jacobi Gallery, 46 West 52nd Street, New York
1957	Sharon Arts Center, Peterboro, New Hampshire
1959	Currier Gallery of Art, Manchester, New Hampshire (retrospective; travelled to Brandeis University, Waltham, Massachusetts, and the University of New Hampshire, Durham, 1960, and the University of Ohio, Athens, 1961)
1962	Colby Junior College, New London, New Hampshire
1964	303 Gallery, New York (retrospective)
	Institute of Arts and Sciences, Manchester, New Hampshire
	Templehof Art Gallery, Temple, New Hampshire
1965	Middlebury College Library, Vermont
	New England College, Henniker, New Hampshire
	University of Chicago
1966	Mr. and Mrs. Roger McCollester House, Irvington-on-Hudson, New York
	Two Photographers, Gropper Galleries, Cambridge, Massachusetts (with Marie Cosindas)
1967	Community Church Art Gallery, New York
1968	New England College, Henniker, New Hampshire
1969	Concord Public Library, New Hampshire
1972	N.H. Belknap College, Center Harbor, New Hampshire
	Staatliche Landesbildstelle, Hamburg
1973	Folkwang Museum, Essen (travelled to the Städtisches Museum, Munich, 1974)
1974	University of New Hampshire, Durham
	Light Gallery, New York

Sharon Arts Center, Peterboro, New Hampshire
Washington Gallery of Photography, Washington, D.C.
1975   University of New Hampshire, Durham
New England College, Henniker, New Hampshire
1976   Photo-Graphics Workshop, New Canaan, Connecticut
Arts and Sciences Center, Nashua, New Hampshire
William Benton Museum of Art, Storrs, Connecticut
1977   Danforth Museum, Framingham, Massachusetts
Kimmell-Cohn Gallery, New York
Allan Frumkin Gallery, Chicago
Manchester Institute of Arts and Sciences, New Hampshire
1978   University of Maryland, Baltimore
New Hampshire Art Association, Manchester
1979   Studio 139, Portsmouth, New Hampshire
1980   Theater on the Sea, Portsmouth, New Hampshire
1981   *Lotte Jacobi: Begegnungen,* Münchner Stadtmuseum, Munich
Gutenberg Museum, Mainz, West Germany
Westbrook College, Portland, Maine
Catskill Center for Photography, Woodstock, New York
1982   Lamont Gallery, Exeter, New Hampshire
The Plus Company, Nashua, New Hampshire
1983   Dryden Galleries, Providence, Rhode Island
Galerie Taube, West Berlin
Associated Artists Gallery, Philadelphia
1984   Currier Gallery of Art, Manchester, New Hampshire
Ledel Gallery, New York
Carl Solway Gallery, Cincinnati, Ohio

Selected Group Exhibitions:

1930   *Das Lichtbild,* Munich
1937   *Dance Photographs,* Brooklyn Museum, New York
1948   *In and Out of Focus,* Museum of Modern Art, New York
1955   *Subjektive Fotografie 2,* State School of Arts, Saarbrucken (and
      Subjektive Fotografie 3, 1958)
1960   *The Sense of Abstraction,* Museum of Modern Art, New York
1975   *Women of Photography,* San Francisco Museum of Art (toured
      the United States)
1979   *Recollections: 10 Women of Photography,* International Center
      of Photography, New York (toured the United States)
1980   *Avant-Garde Photography in Germany 1919-39,* San
      Francisco Museum of Modern Art (toured the United States)
1983   *Fotogramme—die lichtreichen Schatten,* Fotomuseum im
      Stadtmuseum, Munich (toured Germany)
1987   *Photography and Art 1946-86,* Los Angeles County
      Museum of Art

Collections:

University of New Hampshire, Durham; Museum of Modern Art, New York;
Metropolitan Museum of Art, New York; Massachusetts Institute of Technology, Cambridge; Wellesley College Museum, Massachusetts; Addison
Gallery of American Art, Phillips Academy, Andover, Massachusetts; Currier
Gallery of Art, Manchester, New Hampshire; Smithsonian Institution, Washington, D.C.; Folkwang Museum, Essen; Staatliche Landesbildstelle, Hamburg.

Publications:

By JACOBI: Book—*Berlin, New York: Schriftsteller in den 30er Jahren,*
with foreword by Ludwig Greve, Marbach and Stuttgart 1982. **Portfolios**—
Portraits Before 1940, 1978; *Portraits of Albert Einstein 1927-1938,* 1978;
Dance and Theater, 1979; *Photogenics 1946-1955,* 1981; also, illustrations
for numerous books and brochures in Germany and the United States,
since 1938.

On JACOBI: Books—*Designing with Light on Paper and Film* by Robert
W. Cooke, Worcester, Massachusetts 1969; *Photography Without a Camera*
by Patra Holter, New York and London 1972; *Lotte Jacobi: Menschen von
Gestern und Heute—Fotografische Porträts, Skizzen und Dokumentationen,*

exhibition catalogue, Essen 1973; *Lotte Jacobi* by James A. Fasanelli,
Danbury, New Hampshire 1979; *Recollections: 10 Women of Photography,*
edited by Margaretta K. Mitchell, New York 1979; *Avant-Garde Photography in Germany 1919-1939,* exhibition catalogue, by Van Deren Coke, Ute
Eskildsen and Bernd Lohse, San Francisco 1980; *Counterparts: Form and
Emotion in Photographs* by Weston J. Naef, New York 1982; *Fotogramme—
die lichtreichen Schatten,* exhibition catalogue, by Floris M. Neususs, Kassel,
West Germany 1983; *Figure della danza/Visions of the Dance 1859-1982,*
exhibition catalogue, by C. Traub, R. Silverman and G. Ackerman, Reggio
Emilia, Italy 1983.

*

Too much is written about ''Photography!''

I think it speaks for itself. If it doesn't, there is something wrong with ''it''
or with the photographer.

Too many are interested in the ''technique'' of photography. You should
study all you can about technique—but, when you are taking or making
pictures, the technique should be in your fingertips, your body; your mind and
concern should be with your object, your ''victim,'' whether it is a person, an
animal, a landscape, a town or city, or a ''non-objective'' subject.

—Lotte Jacobi

*   *   *

Lotte Jacobi was a fourth-generation photographer in a family of photographers—almost predestined to her profession. (It was around 1840 that her
great-grandfather purchased equipment and a license to practice from
Daguerre himself.) As a child she hoped to be an actress and was thus drawn as
a photographer to make theater portraits; she also worked for magazines and
newspapers. She made portraits full-time for the Jacobi Studio in Berlin until
she left Germany for the United States in 1935. Her early work is in itself a
unique composite portrait of German culture after the First World War.

The photographer's American work is no less important as witness to a
culture. In a career which spans almost 70 years, Lotte Jacobi has made
likenesses of many famous people, and, like it or not, a portraitist is known in
part by the fame of her sitters: Lil Dagover, Sonja Heinie, Peter Lorre, Lotte
Lenya, Kurt Weill, Käthe Kollwitz, Theodore Dreiser, Max Liebermann,
Laszlo Moholy-Nagy, Marc Chagall, Pablo Casals, Yehudi Menuhin, Max
Reinhardt, Kostantin Stanislawski, Edward Steichen, Eleanor Roosevelt,
Alfred Stieglitz, Thomas Mann, Erich Mendelsohn, Marianne Moore, Paul
Tillich, J.D. Salinger, Paul Strand, Mary Wigman, Robert Frost and Albert
Einstein.

Once in New York, she opened a portrait studio with her sister. She was
greatly aided in establishing herself by Albert Einstein who, when approached
by them, told *Life* magazine to use a portrait which Jacobi would take. For
another assignment she was the first woman admitted on the floor of the Stock
Exchange during trading hours.

Lotte Jacobi claimed no special approach to the technique of portraiture
beyond the capacity of the photographer to develop intuition and keep her own
personality out of the portrait as much as possible. Her work was natural,
personal, often casual and conversational. These qualities are hallmarks of the
Jacobi style; like the actress who knows how to disappear into the role she
plays, the photographer becomes a medium for her subject. The subject is
helped to forget the camera. In her own words, ''I only photograph what I see;
my style is the style of the people I photograph. In my portraits I refuse to
photograph *myself,* as do so many other photographers.''

Lotte Jacobi spoke in a disarmingly simple manner of her approach to the
act of photographic portraiture, but the compassion, integrity and unpretentiousness of her artistic intentions was rock-solid. She had an intuitive sense of
design which shows itself most clearly in her early work from Germany; the
American portraits become increasingly informal. But all her work shows an
independent and honest observation of life, one which does not indulge in
generalities but rather embraces individuality. Thus a gesture or an expression
of the sitter was used by Lotte Jacobi to reveal a particular personality, not to
create a preconceived type.

The life-work of Lotte Jacobi also includes a series of light inventions
called ''photogenics,'' distinct from photograms because they are made not
only without a camera but also without any recognizable objects. She

described the technique as drawing on photo-sensitized paper by moving the light source, glass or cellophane to allow subtle nuances in the play of light. It is in this work that the intuition of the artist was most visible as she created a work of art from such minimal materials.

In her life as in her work Lotte kept things simple and straightforward. She left New York in 1955 and lived on a wooded road in New Hampshire where she continued to photograph and frequently met with new generations of student photographers. She encouraged them to see for themselves.

—Margaretta K. Mitchell

JÄGER, Gottfried.

Nationality: German. **Born:** Burg bei Magdeburg, 13 May 1937; son of the photographer Ernst Jäger. **Education:** Apprenticed in handicraft photography, Bielefeld, 1954-57; studied at the Staatliche Höhere Fachschule für Photographie, Cologne, 1958-60, Dip.Ing., M.Photog. 1960; postgraduate mentor: Herbert W. Franke. **Family:** Married Ursel Gawlick in 1957; children: Gabriele and Markus. **Career:** Worked as an assistant industrial and advertising photographer, Siegried Baumann Studio, Bielefeld, 1957-58. Since 1960, freelance photographer and designer, working for AEG, Herder-Verlag, Dr. Oetker, Klimsch und Co., Carl Froh Rohrenwerk, etc., Borgholzhausen, near Bielefeld; established his own studio, Werkstatt für Fotografie und Grafik, Borgholzhausen, 1962; also writer on professional photography training and aesthetics, since 1964. Instructor in Photographic Technology, Werkkunstschule, Bielefeld, 1960-71; Professor of Photography, Department of Design, Fachhochschule, Bielefeld, since 1971. Executive Committee Member, Deutsche Gesellschaft für Photographie (DGPh), 1975-83; Chairman, 1983-86, and President of the Photographic Academy, 1986, Gesellschaft Deutscher Lichtbildner (GDL). **Recipient:** Obelisk Award, *Photokina 66,* Cologne, 1966. **Agent:** Galerie und Edition Jesse, Neustadter Strasse 12, 4800 Bielefeld 1, Germany.

Individual Exhibitions:

1964 *Fotografien, Lichtgrafik,* Kunstsalon Otto Fischer, Bielefeld, West Germany
   Fotografien, Lichtgrafik, Galerie Clasing, Münster, West Germany
1965 *Lichtgrafik,* Disco-Galerie, Basel, Switzerland
1967 *Fotogramme, Fotografien,* Galerie Clarissa, Hannover, West Germany
1971 *Generative Fotografie,* Goethe-Institut, Cairo, Egypt (with H. Gravenhorst)
1975 *Apparative Grafik,* Galerie Jesse, Bielefeld, West Germany
   Apparative Grafik, Galerie Le Disque Rouge, Brussels
1976 *Apparative Grafik,* Lippische Gesellschaft fur Kunst, Detmold, West Germany
1979 *Generative Fotografie,* Werkstatt fur Photographie, West Berlin (with K. M. Holzhauser)
1982 *Lichtbilder—Generative Arbeiten,* Fotomuseum im Stadtmuseum, Munich
1983 *Lichtbilder—Generative Arbeiten,* Galerie Jesse, Bielefeld, West Germany
1986 *Generatywne Fotodzielo,* Galeria Foto Medium Art, Wroclaw, Poland

Selected Group Exhibitions:

1966 *Between Science and Art,* at *Photokina 66,* Cologne
1968 *Generative Fotografie,* Kunsthaus, Bielefeld, West Germany
   Experiments in Art and Technology, Brooklyn Museum, New York
1972 *Wege zur Computerkunst,* Goethe-Institut, Karlsruhe, West Germany (and world tour 1972-74)

1975 *Generatieve Fotografie,* Internationaal Cultureel Centrum, Antwerp, Belgium
1979 *Deutsche Fotografie nach 1945,* Kunstverein, Kassel, West Germany (travelled to Rome and Naples)
1981 *Third International Triennale of Photography,* Musée d'Art et d'Histoire, Fribourg, Switzerland
1983 *Fotogramme—Die lichtreichen Schatten,* Fotomuseum in Stadtmuseum, Munich
   Lensless Photography, Franklin Institute Science Museum, Philadelphia (travelled to the IBM Gallery, New York, 1984)
1986 *Positionen experimenteller Fotografie,* Kunsthalle, Bielefeld, West Germany

Collections:

Fotomuseum im Münchner Stadtmuseum, Munich; Museum Ludwig, Cologne; Museum für Kunst und Gewerbe, Hamburg; Sammlung Etzold, Städtisches Museum, Mönchengladbach, Germany; Kunsthalle, Bielefeld, Germany; Fotomuseum, Burghausen, Germany; Sammlung Galerie Clarissa, Kestner-Museum, Hannover, Germany; Sammlung Fotografis Länderbank, Vienna; Musée d'Art et d'Histoire, Fribourg, Switzerland; International Museum of Photography at George Eastman House, Rochester, New York.

Publications:

By JÄGER: Books—*Apparative Kunst—Vom Kaleidoskop zum Computer,* with H. W. Franke, Cologne 1973; *Generative Fotografie—Theoretische Grundlegung, Kompendium und Beispiele,* with K. M. Holzhauser, Ravensburg, West Germany 1975; *Wetterlage—Bilder aus Ostwestfalen-Lippe,* with J. Bostrom and K. M. Holzhauser, Bielefeld, West Germany 1981; *Carl Struwe—Das fotografische Werk 1924-1962,* Dusseldorf and Bielefeld, West Germany 1982. **Articles**—"Formen der Natur—Verdichtete Formen" in *Camera* (Lucerne), no. 7, 1964; "Verwandlungen" in *Foto Prisma* (Dusseldorf), no. 8, 1965; "Grenzbereiche—Signale eines neuen Programms" in *Foto Prisma* (Dusseldorf), no. 10, 1965; "Programmierte Gestaltung—Serielle Fotografie" in *Foto Magazin* (Munich), no. 1, 1970; "Generative Photography" in *Leica Fotografie* (Frankfurt), no. 4, 1976; "Fotoasthetik" in *DuMont Foto 2,* Cologne 1980; "Exakte Fotografie" in *Format* (Karlsruhe), no. 85, 1980; "Konstruktive Entwicklungen in der Fotografie" in *Camera Austria* (Graz), no. 10, 1982; "Generative Photography" in *Leonardo* (Oxford), no. 4, 1986.

On JÄGER: Books—*Phanomen Kunst—Die naturwissenschaftlichen Grundlagen der Asthetik* by Herbert W. Franke, Munich 1967; *Die Geschichte der Fotografie im 20. Jahrhundert/Photography in the 20th Century* by Petr Tausk, Cologne 1977, London 1980; *Kybernetische Asthetik—Phanomen Kunst* by Herbert W. Franke, Munich and Basel 1979; *Photography as Art—Art as Photography* by Floris M. Neususs, Cologne 1979; *Farbe in Foto—Die Geschichte der Farbphotographie von 1861 bis 1981* by Rolf Sachsse and others, Cologne 1981; *Medien und visuelle Kommunikation,* edited by F. Niggemeier, Hannover 1982; *Theorie der Fotografie III* by W. Kemp, Munich 1983; *Die Kunst der Photographie* by W. Koschatzky, Salzburg and Vienna 1984; *Fotonetz 47,* edited by A. Horlitz and R. Matz, Essen, West Germany 1985. **Articles**—"Generativna Fotografija" by H. W. Franke in *Spot* (Zagreb), no. 2, 1973; "Generative Fotografie—Wege in visuelles Neuland" by H. W. Franke in *Camera* (Lucerne), no. 2, 1975; "Gottfried Jäger—Generative Sachfotografien" by R. Sachsse in *Professional Camera* (Munich), no. 11/12. 1979; "Gottfried Jäger—Schichtungen, Mulrany" by D. Meili in *Photart* (Schaffhausen), no. 1, 1980; "Gottfried Jäger—Multiple Objekte, Kakteen" by D. Meili in *Photographie* (Schaffhausen), no. 11, 1980; "Gottfried Jäger—Schichtungen, Sundern-Hachen" by D. Meili in *Photart* (Schaffhausen), no. 2, 1981; "Gottfried Jäger—Lichtbilder 1980-1982" D. Meili in *Photographie* (Schaffhausen), no. 11, 1983; "Photography's Alter Ego" by C. Hagen in *Camera Arts* (New York), no. 5, 1983; "Gottfried Jäger—Fotoarbeiten 1983, 1984" by J. Brenner and others in *Delfin* (Rheda-Wiedenbruck), no. 5, 1985.

*

From the very beginning photography has never been concerned with realizing an idea; on the contrary, it has always aimed at presenting a specific reality. This also applies to my work in generative photography. To be more precise, I do not produce pictures which have already taken shape in my mind; I allow pictures to emerge which give a sophisticated and visible form to things that are latent and, as yet, undefined in "nature." The aim is to locate a hidden "treasure." The generative process therefore consists in inciting and unleashing forces that can unfold and develop in their own way. The generative process is in itself a process that develops and realizes itself. It is self-realization of the picture: pure photography.

"Generative Photography" gives expression to the aesthetics of transition. It is not the expression of something final or absolute or total. It does not pursue a specific goal; it only believes in the next step. It places its hopes in the next, new generation which has learned to throw overboard the old ideals and replace them with new ones. It is always producing and reproducing in constant alternation. There is no clearly defined beginning or end. All we have is an "inbetween-ness," a state of suspense the creative potential of which needs to be developed.

During the first few years of my artistic career in the early 1960s, I started off by working "experimentally," that is, according to the method called "trial and error." Structural improvement was achieved by sensual impression, according to the classical rules of abstract composition. Light graphic work was the result. It dealt with a specific object, changing it step by step according to a series of compositional principles. In the late 1960s, influenced by the current theory of "exact aesthetics," especially the "generative aesthetic" by M. Bense, I began organizing and systematizing my pictorial structures more stringently. Terms like "program" and "apparatus-based composition" became increasingly important and I found the title "generative photography" for this kind of work in 1968. This development started with the "pin-hole structures," based on the dot as a formal, basic element. I later included the element of chance in my programs. The formal repertoire was extended by lines and geometrical shapes. I am currently working with surfaces that are projected into a given space, and I do this by letting the photographic paper react freely, thus enabling it to give expression to its inner tension.

This kind of composition consists of a system of variable surface elements that are not fixed. They can, for a while, take on a specific shape, for example, for the duration of an exhibition. They can be used again; they can develop, grow, disintegrate and libitum. They are only briefly in a state of repose. Its task, its purpose is to have a *generative* effect, to provoke incessant generations of new forms in a constant process of renewal and regeneration. No standstill, nothing final is envisaged, but rather something that is perpetual, continuous and in a constant state of development: the aesthetics of transition.

—Gottfried Jäger

*   *   *

Many of mankind's driving forces are manifested simultaneously in science, technology and the arts. The theoretical breakthroughs achieved in the last quarter century in microelectronics, nuclear engineering and biotechnology, for instance, might thus also be expected to have their parallels in the realms of art.

In contemporary creative photography, one of the most important innovators of technical applications is the German photographer and teacher Gottfried Jäger. Although much of his work seems revolutionary, he began by making a thorough study of early photographic evolution, since he felt that in history might be found the way for the future. Jäger was especially fascinated by two old principles: the multiple lens system invented by Disderi around 1854 and the pinhole camera. He combined both ideas by constructing a multiple pinhole camera with his own design of interchangeable pinhole plates. With this camera he photographed a system of light spots arranged in a symmetrical pattern, resulting in a composition of separate but overlapping images. By means of changing the pinhole pattern, a whole new series of light-spot images could be created.

The first series of experiments were conducted in black-and-white, but Jäger soon modified his system to make colour pictures based on spots of coloured light and differing filters with varying exposures. He also experimented with the shape and size of the pinholes as well as choice of materials for daylight or tungsten illumination.

Jäger's results encouraged him to develop a new theory valid not only for his own researches but for other non-conventional image-making processes.

An essential feature of the theory was that with the appropriate technical means a large number of wide variations could be effected by making only small alterations to the programme—a programme in which the artist was not only the inventor of the hardware but the originator of the software too. Jäger denominated all these new systems as "Generators," and hence for the whole field of experimentation coined the expression "Generative Photography." His role as a teacher led in the 1970s to the collaborative production of two major books on the subject.

The definition and aims of "Generative Photography" opened up a number of new experiments in other fields of multi-media activity, not because tools from various disciplines were employed, but because Jäger and his collaborators had shown how to amalgamate technical know-how with artistic sensibility.

—Petr Tausk

JAMES, Geoffrey.

Nationality: British. **Born:** St. Asaph, Clwyd, Wales, 9 January 1942; resident in Canada, since 1966. **Education:** Wellington College, Crowthorne, Berkshire, 1955-60; studied modern history, Wadham College, Oxford, England, 1960-64, B.A. 1962, M.A. 1964; self-taught in photography, from 1965. **Family:** Married Ellen Sulkis in 1966 (divorced, 1981); Jessica Bradley in 1981; sons: David and Charles. **Career:** Contributing Editor, *Time* magazine, Montreal, 1967-75; Head of the Visual Arts Section, Canada Council, Ottawa, 1975-82; independent photographer, Ottawa, since 1982. Visiting Professor of Visual Arts, University of Ottawa, 1982-84; Artist-in-Residence, Centre International de Recherche, de Création et d'Animation, Villeneuve-les-Avignon, France, 1985. **Recipient:** Graham Foundation Fellowship in Fine Arts, Chicago, 1984; Canada Council "A" Grant, 1987; Guggenheim Fellowship, 1989; Course A du Ministere des Affaires Culturelles, Quebec, 1990. **Agents:** Galerie René Blouin, 372 Sainte Catherine Street West, Montreal, Quebec H3B 1A2, Canada; Laurence Miller Gallery, 138 Spring Street, New York, New York 10012, U.S.A. **Address:** 4579 Avenue Coloniale, Montreal, Quebec H2T 1W1, Canada.

Individual Exhibitions:

1971	Sir George Williams University, Montreal
1975	Yajima/Galerie, Montreal
1978	Yajima/Galerie, Montreal
1981	Photograph Gallery, New York
1983	Yarlow-Salzman Gallery, Toronto
	Panoramic Photographs, Nova Scotia College of Art and Design, Halifax
1984	*Entrances and Exits,* Queen's University, Kingston, Ontario
1985	*I Giardini Italiani,* Palazzo Braschi, Rome
	I Giardini Italiani, Centre Internationale de Recherche, Villeneuve-les-Avignon, France
	Italian Gardens, University of Kent, Canterbury
	Genius Loci, Graham Foundation, Chicago (retrospective)
1986	*Landscape with Ruins,* RIBA Heinz Gallery, London
	Coburg Gallery, Vancouver, British Columbia (with Glenn Lewis)
	Genius Loci, organised by the Canadian Museum of Contemporary Photography (travelled to various centers in Canada and USA)
1987	Galerie Rene Blouin, Montreal
1988	*Italian Journeys* (two person show with Adolf Benca), Twining Gallery, New York
1989	Equinox Gallery, Vancouver
1990	Galerie Rene Blouin, Montreal
	Equinox Gallery, Vancouver
	Verticale, Quebec City
1991	Twining Gallery, New York
1992	Laurence Miller Gallery, New York

The Aqueduct Claudio, 1989. Photograph ©Geoffrey James. Courtesy Laurence Miller Gallery, New York.

Selected Group Exhibitions:

1977   *13 Canadian Photographers,* Madison Art Center, Wisconsin
1980   *Group Exhibition: Photographers,* Sander Gallery, Washington, D.C.
1983   *Panoramic Photographs,* Equivalents Gallery, Seattle, Washington
1985   *Contemporary Canadian Photography,* National Gallery of Canada, Ottawa
1987   *Classical Concerns,* Twining Gallery, New York
        Elementa Naturae, Musée d'art contemporain, Montreal
        Diverse Secrecies, Presentation House, Vancouver
        Toronto: Le Nouveau, Nouveau Monde, (touring exhibition), Maison de L'Architecture, Paris; Bagatti Valsecchi, Milan; Casa de Architectura, Barcelona
1988   Jan Turner Gallery, Los Angeles
1989   Twining Gallery, New York (with Lee Friedlander, Eugene Atget, Josef Sudek et al)
        Contemporary Canadian Photography, Budapest, Hungary
        Anamnese, Dazibao, Montreal (with Pierre Bogaerts, Annette Messager, The Starn Twins)
1990   *Works for the Garden,* Blum Helman Gallery, Los Angeles
        The Shaping of Nature, Oakville Galleries, Oakville
1991   Galerie Rene Blouin, Montreal
        Corriger Les Lieux, Dazibao, Montreal
        Archipels de Desir, Musée du Quebec
        20th Century Photography, Equinox Gallery, Vancouver
1992   Turner-Krull Gallery, Los Angeles
        North American Photographic Practice after Modernism, Charles H Scott Gallery, Emily Carr College of Art, Vancouver
        Documenta IX, Kassel
        Fotografia Vista da Gae Aulenti, Molle Antonelliana, Turin

Collections:

Musée d'Art Contemporain, Montreal; Public Archives of Canada, Ottawa; Canada Council Art Bank, Ottawa; Edmonton Art Gallery, Alberta; Winnipeg Art Gallery, Manitoba; Canadian Centre for Architecture, Montreal; Bibliothèque Nationale, Paris; Palazzo Braschi, Rome; Art Gallery of Ontario; Canadian Museum of Contemporary Photography; Graphotek, Stuttgart; Museum of Modern Art, New York; National Gallery of Canada; Vancouver Art Gallery.

Publications:

By JAMES: Books—*An Inquiry into the Aesthetics of Photography,* editor, Toronto 1974; *Transparent Things: The Artist's Use of Photography,* Ottawa 1977; *The Legacy of Atget,* coauthor, Edmonton, Alberta 1977; *Visions: Essays on Contemporary Canadian Art,* coeditor, Vancouver 1977; *Entrances and Exits,* Kingston, Ontario 1984; *I Giardini Italiani,* with introduction by I. Pizzetti, Rome 1985; *Genius Loci,* with introduction by Martha Langford, Ottawa 1986; *Morbid Symptoms,* with text by M. Mosser, Princeton, New Jersey 1986; *Landscape with Ruins,* exhibition catalogue, London 1986; *Diverse Secrecies,* exhibition catalogue, Vancouver 1987; *Toronto: Le Nouveau, Nouveau Monde,* exhibition catalogue, 1987; *Anamnese,* exhibition catalogue, Montreal 1989; *La campagna Romana,* Montreal 1991; *13 Essays on Photography,* co-edited and with introduction by Geoffrey James, Ottawa 1991; *The Italian Garden,* New York 1991. **Articles**—introduction to *Tom Gibson: Signature One,* Ottawa 1975; introduction to *A Certain Identity: 50 Portraits by Sam Tata,* Ottawa 1983.

On JAMES: Articles—"Geoffrey James" by Ian Wallace in *Vanguard* (Vancouver), September 1983; "Paradise Lost" by Douglas Chambers in *Canadian Art* (Toronto), Summer 1985; "Geoffrey James" by Pier Luigi Tazzi in *Artforum* (New York), November 1985; "Exposing the Twilight of the Liberal Dreams" review by John Bentley Mays in *Globe & Mail* (Toronto) 16 May 1987; Book review of "Morbid Symptoms & Genius Loci" by Peggy Gale in *Canadian Art,* Summer issue 1987; "Geoffrey James: de l'esprit des lieux" by Monique Mosser in *Beaux Arts* (Paris) May 1988; "Critics Choice" by Gene Thornton in *New York Times* (New York), 10 January 1988; Review of "Equinox" exhibition by Petra Rigby Watson in *C Magazine* (Toronto), Winter 1991 issue; Review of "The Italian Garden" by Ingrid Sischy in *The New Yorker* (New York), 15 July 1991; Review of "Corriger Les Lieux" by Guy Bellevance in *Parachute,* Fall issue 1991; Review of "Twining" exhibition by Gretchen Faust in *Artsmagazine* (New York), February 1992.

*

I am interested in ideal spaces—gardens and certain architectural ensembles—that bespeak Utopian longings. I try to make images that do justice to their subject while being worthy as photographs. The photography that touches me the most is that tradition of utilitarian and un-selfconscious work that began with people like Baldus, continued with Atget and ended ... where? At Alfred Stieglitz or Victor Burgin?

For quite a few years now I have been exploring the garden culture of Italy and France and England. Most of my pictures are taken with a panoramic camera with a curved film plane and 1-to-3 proportion, a format that accommodates the ductile forms of the Baroque and allows for multiple viewpoints. (More recently I have also been working with a more conventional view camera.) I have a sense that the kind of places I have been photographing are being leached of their magic and meaning, in part by the mass tourism industry, in part by our museum culture, which turns everything into Disney World. I increasingly favour publication over exhibition, hoping by this means to share some of my private passions with a broader public than the one that inhabits art spaces.

—Geoffrey James

*   *   *

Suppose that one were to grow up in the orderly, domesticated landscapes of Europe and then eventually make one's home in a place like Ottawa where the dreary tangles of the boreal forest are never far from the city limits. And suppose that after a ten year apprenticeship on a Leica acknowledging Kertesz and Cartier-Bresson, one were to take up a large camera and take on the landscape. What and how would one photograph? In the case of Geoffrey James this path has lead away from the idiot bush and into the great gardens of Europe. If the boreal forest evidences a kind of primordial chaos, the garden signals the civilizing hand of man, the aesthetic impulse, and the drive for order and control. For the picture-maker the garden is a readymade landscape, a small part of the surface of the earth that has been organized into a calculated series of views that mediate between the natural world and culture. For this reason photographers and painters have long loved gardens, even going so far in the case of Monet at Giverny, as to create a garden in order to paint it.

However, where Monet found colour and joy, James has witnessed a series of monochromatic landscapes in decay. The gardens of the Age of Reason are now studies in neglect where aging and solitary custodians helplessly preside over the inexorable return of the bush. If these once private Edens of merchant princes and royalty survive, they do so as public parks and commercial spectacles with railings around the plantings and a turnstile at the gate. Viewing James' photographs one suspects that a part of him sympathizes with Yeats' remark that the politics of democracy is the dirty orange peel on the newspaper editor's stair. Eden, as we all know, was created for the enjoyment of only one couple.

A first viewing of James' garden panoramas inevitably evokes the spirit of Atget. Both photographers share an affection for the same subject matter, the wide angle view, and the pleasures of perspective. Both pointed their antiquated equipment—a wooden viewcamera for Atget, an old Kodak panorama camera for James—toward the vestiges of another time. Writing about Atget, James has asserted that the old man's photographs ultimately extended the working vocabulary of the medium. Building on Atget's legacy, James has taken the subjects of individual Atget photographs—a closeup of an urn, the statue in the middle ground, an horizon line of tree tops—and combined them in single photographs. The former's sense of space, particularly the deep recessions of the Paris street views, have been compounded into double, even triple vanishing points by the rotation of James' panoramic lens. Space is no longer quite as Euclidean.

While James' photographs reflect an affectionate study of the cataloguer of Old Paris, they also recognize the spatial discoveries of the American photographer Lee Friedlander. Taking his own cues from Atget, Friedlander has found it more interesting to peer through the branches of Atget's tree studies than to examine the presence and form of the tree iself. Beginning with this perforated foreground screen, he sets up, through shrewd self-positioning, a series of similar constructs behind it like the scrims and flats of the theatre. As James' inventory of gardens grows, his photographs increasingly employ this kind of spatial complexity. The near and further distant are deliberately confused: whole segments of foreground space are flattened out thus deepening the spatial recessions visible through breaks in the frontal plane. The garden becomes a theatre of illusion.

If James has absorbed much from Atget and perhaps even more from Friedlander's appropriations from the same material, he has unquestionably made all this uniquely his own. What may, if viewed casually, seem to be merely nostalgic views of the picturesque, become cumulatively a series of meditations on space, form, and culture history. They are both celebrations of and lamentations for that most English medium of expression, gardening, as well as a commitment to a currently unfashionable notion of beauty. The

content may be of the past but the sensibility organizing and interpreting it belongs to the present. James' eye is one educated by modern painting and sculpture as well as the quick juxtapositions and disjunctions of contemporary cinema. The honest old purist of Paris would be flummoxed by photographs that comprehend so much at once and play such roulette with description. Some years ago in an essay on Atget, James declared that the failed actor's photographs were "unadorned, authoritative, and ultimately mysterious. . . ." He could just as well have been describing his own.

—Michael Mitchell

JANSEN, Arno.

Nationality: German. **Born:** Aachen, 13 February 1938. **Education:** Studied graphic design at Folkwangschule, Essen, 1957-59, and photography, under Otto Steinert, at the Folkwangschule, 1959-63. **Family:** Married Danièle Chausson in 1974; daughter: Elodie. **Career:** Photographer and commercial artist for the City of Braunschweig, 1964-65. Freelance photographer, Cologne, since 1965. Instructor, School of Fine Arts, Braunschweig, 1964-65. Since 1965, Head of Photographic Studies, Kölner Werkschulen, now the Department of Art at the Fachhochschule, Cologne: Professor since 1973. Member, Deutsche Gesellschaft für Photographie (DGPh), 1971. **Address:** Ubierring 40, D-5000 Cologne 1, Germany.

Individual Exhibitions:

1962	British Council Gallery, Dusseldorf
1967	Galerie Brebaum, Dusseldorf
1970	*Realistik und Phantastik,* Staatliche Landesbildstelle, Hamburg
1971	Studio Dumont, Cologne
1972	Studio 41, Duisburg, West Germany
1979	Art Studio, Cologne
	Work Gallery, Zurich
1980	Werkstattgalerie, Bad Godesberg, West Germany
1981	Galerie Renner, Munich
	Goethe Institut, Toulouse, France
	Galerie Hamma, Dusseldorf
1983	Gallery Wide, Tokyo
1984	Galerie Image, Madrid
	Galerie Imago, Cologne
	Galerie Pro Photo, Nuremberg, West Germany
1985	Photo-Galerie 52, Luxembourg
1986	Lindemanns Galerie, Stuttgart

Selected Group Exhibitions:

1979	*Fotografie 1919-1979,* Stadtmuseum, Munich
1980	*Vorstellungen und Wirklichkeit: 7 Aspekte subjektiver Fotografie,* Städtisches Museum, Leverkusen, West Germany (travelled to the Künstlerhaus, Vienna, Fundació Joan Miró, Barcelona, 1980; and Palais des Beaux-Arts, Brussels, 1981)
1981	*New German Photography,* The Photographers' Gallery, London (toured the U.K., 1981-82)
1982	*Aspectes de la photographie allemande de 1920 à nos jours,* Centre Culturel Pierre Bayle, Besançon, France
1983	*Fotografie in Deutschland Heute,* Akademie voor Schone Kunsten, Ghent, Belgium (travelled to Hasselt, Antwerp and Charleroi, Belgium)
1984	*Contemporary German Photographers,* Santa Fe Center for Photography, New Mexico
1985	*Zeitgenössische deutsche Fotografen,* Museum für Photographie, Braunschweig, West Germany
1986	*Foto Biennale,* Enschede, Netherlands

Collections:

Staatliche Landesbildstelle, Hamburg; Bibliothèque Nationale, Paris; Polaroid Collection, Amsterdam; Stadtmuseum-Fotomuseum, Munich; Museum Ludwig, Cologne; San Francisco Museum of Modern Art; Center for Creative Photography, University of Arizona, Tucson.

Publications:

By JANSEN: Books—*Arno Jansen: Braunschweig*, Braunschweig 1965; *Arno Jansen: Rüsselsheim—Bilder einer Stadt*, Rüsselsheim, West Germany 1969. **Articles**—"Meine Fotografien sind meine Reflexionen," interview with Jörg Krichbaum, in *Fotografie* (Göttingen), no. 6, 1978; "Arno Jansen" in *Dumont Foto 1*, Cologne 1978; "Photos by Arno Jansen" in *Ambit* (London), no. 77, 1979; "Arno Jansen: Portfolio" in *Fotografie* (Göttingen), no. 9, 1979; "Arno Jansen" in *Zoom* (Munich), November 1979.

On JANSEN: Books—*Vorstellungen und Wirklichkeit: 7 Aspekte subjektiver Fotografie*, exhibition catalogue, by Dieter Wellershof, Cologne 1980; *Farbe im Photo: Die Geschichte der Farbphotographie von 1861 bis 1981* by Fritz Binder, Gert Koshofer, Rolf Sachsse and others, Cologne 1981; *Arno Jansen: Fotobilder 1975-1984*, exhibition catalogue, with texts by Jorg Krichbaum and Lothar Romain, Cologne 1984. **Articles**—"Arno Jansen" by L. Fritz Gruber in *Fotografie* (Göttingen), no. 9, 1979; "Vergessene Stilleben" by Jörg Krichbaum in *Zoom* (Munich), November 1979; "Chiffren einer rätselhaften identität" by Rüdiger Müller in *Kölner Skizzen* (Cologne), no. 2, 1983.

*

The photographs that I've taken in the past few years are concerned with still life. This classical theme in art—which is often understood merely as a kind of formal expression and valued for its charm—gains significance for me to the extent that it offers other possibilities beyond the compositional; a sensual play with forms, materials, surfaces and shades of colour; the making of artistic worlds of fantasy comprehensible.

Objects excite my fantasies. I am interested in the interrelationships between subject and object, in the question of inner and outer identity, and in time: a desire to follow up the past by means of its relics. What were the circumstances? Who were the people connected with them at the time. These finds are also fetishes, icons, and souvenirs for me: devoid of their original function, they have become magical objects, independent entities. As the result of new combinations they encounter each other on another level, become very eloquent, conveying complexes of thought and metaphorically reflecting inner fears, aggression, sexuality, death and decay.

The medium of photography is in my view especially suited to stressing the existence of things, to interpreting them in a way different from the painted picture or any other art object, but it can also give to those things a certain documentary presence and permanence.

—Arno Jansen

* * *

Arno Jansen's still-lifes—his principal theme in recent years—represent a particular speciality in contemporary photography in so far as he deals not with compositions of "found" subject matter, which have a tendency to become stylized, but with an exact, almost documentary, reproduction of artistically arranged objects or groups of objects. These photos do not suggest affinities with particular photographic tendencies so much as they remind the viewer of the impressively contained world of the still-life painting of Giorgio Morandi.

To a certain extent, this similarity has to do with Jansen's choice of subject matter: the spare arrangement of color-and rust-speckled tin cans, for example, carefully disposed according to their relative proportions, immediately calls to mind the bottle compositions of the Italian painter. And, at the same time, it is also the restrained manner, the occasional detachment *vis à vis* the subject matter, or, in the color photographs, the atmospheric components of the picture, which in general bring these works close to painted still-life. Yet—and this is a vital point—these features are produced with distinctly

photographic methods. Although the respective objects or groups of objects are not altered by their deliberate arrangement, in the photograph they nevertheless gain a dimension, which clearly goes beyond the purely factual, even if this is occasionally only by suggestion. Ingenious lighting unexpectedly relieves them, in the play of light and shade, of their commonplace banality and brings to such objects suggestions of strangeness and mystery, raises them to the level of the icon—or at least allows them to function as relics of no obvious significance.

Notwithstanding this tendency to "private mythologies," these photographs have documentary aspects, because, for once, the prevailing central perspective corresponds precisely to the presentational character of the arrangement of objects. Central perspective—to quote an observation of Dieter Wellershof—doesn't touch the objects, "it does not cut or distort them," but simply sets things in front of us. That is to say, in a certain sense, it distances the viewer. In this way Jansen achieves stylistic composure in calculated contrast to the thematic over-enhancement of his mainly deliberately simple composition of objects.

This description may suggest a question: if these artistic arrangements are already in themselves complete, autonomous works, why must they also be photographed? The answer is simple: because the direct presentation would leave the things as they stand in their directness, whereas through photography they will at least be brought into the realm of duality.

"Light, for example"—to cite Dieter Wellershof again—"emotionalizes the objects, defines them or lets them fade away, so that in this way photography proves itself an artistic medium, thanks to which objects can be seen better and differently." In other words, the things themselves are not directly Arno Jansen's subject matter; his subject is the associative meanings released by the photograph. Only when photographed do the objects appear—for the photographer as well as for the viewer—as evocative evidence of subjective experience and reality.

—Rolf Wedewer

JASANSKÝ, Pavel.

Nationality: Czechoslovakian. **Born:** Prague, 30 September 1938. **Education:** Studied at Charles University, Prague, 1963; self-taught in photography. **Family:** Married to Jana Salzmann; children: Lukáš and Jakub. **Career:** Freelance photographer and graphic designer, since 1964. Established advertising agency "JAGO," 1991. Teacher at FAMU, Prague, since 1992. Member of "SIGNUM." **Address:** Jasná II, 39, 14700 Prague 4, Braník, Czech Republic.

Individual Exhibitions:

1960	*Fotografie dětí/Photography of the Children*, Divadlo J. Wolkera, Prague
1981	*Paristory*, Galerie Fotochema, Prague
	Dům umění města, Brno, Czechoslovakia
1982	Středoslovenská galerie, Banská Bystrica, Czechoslovakia
	Fotografie z Řecka/Photography from Greece, Galerie F, Banská Bystrica, Czechoslovakia
	Most/Bridge, Divadlo Rubín, Prague
1983	*Masopust*, Malá galerie čs. spisovatele, Prague
1985	*Fotografie*, Galerie Fotochema, Prague
	Nová krajina, noví obyvatelé/New Landscape, New Inhabitants, Correggio, Italy
1987	*Těla/Bodies*, Galerie Fotochema, Prague (travelled to Galerie 4, Cheb, Czechoslovakia, and to Vienna, 1990-93)
1988	Galerie AFC, Paris
1989	Galerie Fotochema, Prague

Selected Group Exhibitions:

1969	*Fotosalon*, Tokyo, Japan
1971	*Bohuslav Reynek*, Staroměstská radnice, Prague

Untitled. Photograph by Pavel Jasanský.

Collections:

Bibliothèque Nationale, Paris; Musée Nicéphore Niépce, Chalon-sur-Saône, France; Moravská galerie, Brno, Czechoslovakia; ICP, New York; Museum Ludwig, Cologne; The Art Institute of Chicago; Howard Goldberg Gallery, New York; The National Gallery, Prague; Beth Hatefutsoth Museum of the Jewish Diaspora, Tel Aviv, Israel; Museet Fotokunst Brandts Klaederfabrik, Odense, Denmark.

Publications:

By JASANSKÝ: Book—*Město (The Town),* Prague 1984.

On JASANSKÝ: Articles—"Commercial Photography Exposed" in *JCA* (Tokyo), 1983; "International Photography Exposed" in *JCA* (Tokyo), 1985; "Photographic Sensuality" in *JCA* (Tokyo), 1987.

*

I use photography when I think it is the best method to express my ideas. Otherwise, I use overpainted photography, graphic methods or sculpture.

—Pavel Jasanský

*   *   *

Pavel Jasanský's photographic work is exceptionally rich and diverse. The documentary part, originating from the 1960s, comprises hundreds of individual photographs and many more compact series. These include *Children* (1962-1965); *Paristory* (1967-1969 and 1977); *Greece* (1982); *Maternity Hospital* (1982-1983); *Senior Citizens' Home* (1983) and others which as a whole form a many faceted portrayal of human life. These photographs, exhibited in Prague in 1985, contrasted with the optimistic picture of joyous life favoured by the ruling communist clan. The book *Město (The Town)* in which Pavel Jasanský played an important role, had been suppressed three years earlier because of its allegedly exaggerated pessimism and was finally published in a considerably censored form.

Pavel Jasanský's photographs are often really raw and harsh due not only to the rough-grained character and limited tonal range of the enlargements, but also to the themes chosen from extreme life situations, portrayed, however, with feeling and understanding. Like Josef Koudelka and Viktor Kolar,

Jasanský was one of the first photographers to bring Czech documentary photography of the 1960s a strongly subjective nature and an entirely individual interpretation of the reality portrayed. He made ingenious use of allusions with multiple meanings based on pictorial symbols and the metaphorical confrontations of different motifs.

The documentary part of his work also includes "New Landscape, New Inhabitants" of the latter half of the 1980s. Here eloquent static details of the most varied environments reveal a great deal about life in Czechoslovakia at that time. A series of work covers the "Velvet Revolution" in Prague in 1989. Later Pavel Jasanský, along with his colleagues from the Sigma agency, documented the devastated Jewish cemeteries in Bohemia, Moravia and Silesia.

In addition to documentary photography, Pavel Jasanský produces artistically orientated photographs, montages and sculptures. The best known photographs is the *Bodies* cycle, which developed gradually from 1985 up to the 1990s. The large pictures of naked figures, couples and whole groups, originally made in cooperation with the painter Jiri Sozanský, were created as separate, individual works as well as in the form of complete, structured sequences. Later Jasanský, like Arnulf Reiner and other artists, began to supplement these symbolic photographs of naked bodies with dynamic black over-painting. Highly expressive intermediary works resulted, with symbolically expressed motifs of yearning, individual identity or violence. His endeavour to find new expression in combining various artistic media also led Jasanský to create video-programmes with similar motifs of throngs of naked figures, and to individual installations combining photography with sculptures and projections.

—Vladimir Birgus

JODAS, Miroslav.

Nationality: Czechoslovakian. **Born:** Prague, 30 November 1932. **Education:** Attended a basic school in Prague, 1938-47; Professional School of Goldsmith's Art, Prague, 1947-50; self-taught in photography. **Family:** Married Marcela Kratka in 1953; children: Marek and Lucie. **Career:** Worked in a hospital in Prague, 1950-54; Goldsmith, for Soluna, Prague, since 1954. Independent photographer, Prague, since 1967. **Recipient:** Silver Medal, *International Photo Exhibition,* Neuchatel, Switzerland, 1959; Gold Medal, 1964, and Bronze Medal, 1966, *Foto-Session,* Prerov, Czechoslovakia. **Address:** Na Ladách 6, Dejvice, Prague 6, Czechoslovakia.

Individual Exhibitions:

1959   *Animals in the Zoo,* Gallery in St. Mary Street, Pilsen, Czechoslovakia
1960   *Photographs by Miroslav Jodas,* Club in Nekázanka Street, Prague
       Animals in the Zoo, Osvětová Beseda Club, Ceská Lìpa, Czechoslovakia
1964   *Photographs by Miroslav Jodas,* Club in Nekázanka Street, Prague
1970   *Photographs 1965-70,* Town Gallery, Ostrov nad Ohri, Czechoslovakia (travelled to the Gallery Dum pánu z Kunštátu, Brno, Czechoslovakia, 1971)
1972   *Jazz in Photography,* Theatre Reduta, Prague
1982   *Roads,* CKD Club Gallery, Prague
1985   *In Praise of Jazz,* Small Gallery of Czechoslovak Writers, Prague
       In Praise of Jazz, at the *Jazz Festival,* Prerov, and Blansko, Czechoslovakia
1986   *In Praise of Jazz,* Rostejn Castle, Czechoslovakia
       In Praise of Jazz, Fotochema Gallery, Hradec Kralove, Czechoslovakia
1987   *In Praise of Jazz,* Thermal, Karlaag Vray OKD, Tilina
1988   TV Studio "J," Prague
       Classic Music in Photograph, Prague

1990   *In Praise of Jazz II,* Prague
1993   *In Praise of Jazz III,* Brno Theater of Mr Polinka

Selected Group Exhibitions:

1959   *International Photo Exhibition,* Neuchatel, Switzerland
1964   *Foto-Session,* Přerov, Czechoslovakia
       Foto-Nova, Photography Club, Bologna (and 1965)
1966   *Foto-Session,* Přerov, Czechoslovakia
       Foto-Nova, Photography Club, Beirut
1967   *7 + 7,* Spála Gallery, Prague
1968   *SČVU Exhibition,* Municipal Building, Prague
1975   *CSSR 1975,* Ministry of Culture, Prague (toured Europe)
1977   *Contemporary Creative Photography,* Fragner's Gallery, Prague
1984   *Czech Creative Photography,* Gallery of Czechoslovak Writers, Prague

Collections:

Moravian Gallery, Brno, Czechoslovakia; Ministry of Foreign Affairs, Prague; Museum Tasdorpen ne Thirkach Umeleckrprumyslareha Murea n Praze.

Publications:

By JODAS: Books—*Udeřila naše hodina (Our Time Has Come),* with poems by various authors, Prague 1964; *Den, který nebyl (The Day That Wasn't),* novel by J. Kadlec, Prague 1965; *Jazz Inspiration,* with poems by various authors, Prague 1969; *Music and People,* with text by A. Hostomská, Prague 1969.

On JODAS: Books—*Licht und Schatten/Light and Shadow,* edited by Milos Hrbas, Prague 1959; *Soucasna Ceskoslovenska Fotografie,* exhibition catalogue, by Antonin Dufek, Brno, Czechoslovakia 1969; *Miroslav Jodas: Fotografie 1965-70,* exhibition catalogue, by Anna Fárová, Ostrov nad Ohri, Czechoslovakia 1970; *Lexikon of Photographers, Czech Republik.*

*   *   *

Miroslav Jodas has created an oeuvre in which there can be found various genres of photography, a great richness of subject matter, and even slightly different photographic approaches, evidence of his search for the appropriate way to depict the chosen subject. Yet, despite the many-sided character of his work, it is possible to feel that all of these images were taken by the same photographer.

From the beginning of his career until the present, Jodas has always shown a predilection for the portrait. He likes to depict the human face both in tranquility and in dynamic movement. Painters, writers, photographers and other artists have posed for him in their studios. He prefers to photograph each person in the "space" in which he logically belongs; he composes the figure with regard to the interesting motifs of his or her environment. Conversely, in his shots of jazz musicians he includes very little of their environment, preferring to concentrate attention on their faces in the dynamic and ecstatic atmosphere of performance. Yet, whatever his method, his solutions are highly individualistic, since Jodas tries always to express his own relationship toward his subject.

In order to delineate the responses of his subjects, Jodas sometimes prepares cycles of portraits of the same person, in which he endeavors to point out some relativity of expression. By moving successively with his camera toward a stationary model, he forms a sequence of responses.

Another kind of subject beloved by Miroslav Jodas is the still-life, a mode he almost approximates in his series of portraits of artists in their studios. Later, he was attracted to similar, chance arrangements in the real world. Among his "found" still-lifes have been faded flowers on tombstones in old cemeteries or an empty cyclists' arena, in which the surprising forms resemble slightly surrealistic pictures.

Jodas has also photographed landscapes of a part of the Czech countryside not very often visited by tourists: he has always been attracted to the beauty of the modest environments of everyday life. In this respect, his work is typical of

Czech photography, in which the poetical interpretation of the real world has a long tradition.

In the early 1980s, Jodas began working in colour, concentrating particularly on ephemeral aspects of the landscape as affected by changes in light, season and weather conditions—most notably in his series on Prague bridges and the newly-constructed express highways. A development of his experiences in photographing jazz performers recently continued in his work on assignment, collaborating with the designer Rathousky on booklets, programmes and posters for the National Theatre in Prague.

—Petr Tausk

JODICE, Mimmo.

Nationality: Italian. **Born:** Sanita, Naples, 29 March 1934. **Education:** Attended the Catholic Sisters elementary and secondary schools, and the Istituto Flavio Gioia, Naples, 1940-50; self-taught in photography, from 1950. **Family:** Married Angela Salomone in 1962; children: Barbara, Francesco and Sebastian. **Career:** Worked in bookshops and publishing houses, in Naples, 1950-67. Since 1967, freelance, professional photographer, working for the magazines *Epoca, Europeo, Panorama, Stern, Merian, Lotus International, Casabella, Abitare, Domus, Gran Bazaar,* and the publishers Rizzoli, Mondadori, Electa, Hachette, etc., in Naples. Established his own studio in the Via Chaia, Naples, 1967. Instructor in photography, Accademia di Belle Arti, Naples, since 1970. **Agents:** Galleria Il Diaframma, via degli Imbriani 15, 20100 Milan, Italy; Galleria Lucio Amelio, Piazza dei Martiri 58,80121 Naples, Italy. **Address:** Via Villanova 16, 80123 Naples, Italy.

Individual Exhibitions:

1967	Libreria La Mandragola, Naples
1968	Teatro del Palazzo Ducale, Urbino, Italy
1969	Libreria DePerro, Naples
1970	Galleria Il Diaframma, Milan
1972	Boston City Hall, Massachusetts
1973	Associazione Fotografica Napoletana, Naples
	Mimmo Jodice: Il ventre del colera, at *SICOF,* Milan
1974	Galleria Pictogramma, Rome
	Galleria Il Diaframma, Milan
1975	Modern Art Agency, Naples
1976	Galleria l'Incontro, Naples
1978	Studio Trisorio, Naples
1980	Studio Fossati, Alessandria, Italy
1981	Museo di Villa Pignatelli, Naples
	Galleria Rondanini, Rome
	Spazio Immagine, Bari, Italy
1982	Biblioteca Marciana, Venice
	Institut Culturel Italien, Paris
	Fonds Nationale d'Art Contemporain, Paris
1983	Institut Culturel Italien, Paris
1985	Villa Borghese, Rome
1986	Museo di Villa Pignatelli, Naples
	National Federal Hall, New York
	Centre Européen Recherche Nucléaire, Geneva, Switzerland

Selected Group Exhibitions:

1970	*Incontro Nazionale di Fotografia,* Teatro dell'Arte, Milan
1971	*Italfotografie,* Interkamera, Prague
1977	*Fotografi e fotografia,* Galleria Lastaria, Rome
1978	*Twentieth Century Photographs,* University of New Mexico, Albuquerque
1979	*Venezia 79: La Fotografia,* at the *Biennale,* Venice
1981	*Expression of the Human Condition,* San Francisco Museum of Modern Art
1982	*21 Photographes Contemporaines en Europe,* Arles, France (travelled to Yokohama City Gallery, Japan)
1983	*La Sperimentazione Fotografica in Italia,* Galleria d'Arte Moderna, Bologna, Italy
1985	*The European Iceberg,* Art Gallery of Ontario, Toronto
1986	*Fotografi a Napoli,* Calcografia Nazionale, Rome

Collections:

Calcografia Nazionale, Rome; Centro Studi e Archivio della Comunicazione, Parma, Italy; Fonds Nationale d'Art Contemporain, Paris; Bibliothèque Nationale, Paris; University of New Mexico Art Museum, Albuquerque; Yale University Art Gallery, New Haven, Connecticut; Detroit Institute of Arts, Michigan; San Francisco Museum of Modern Art.

Publications:

By JODICE: Books—*Napoli, una vicenda,* with text by Giulio De Luca, Naples 1974; *Chi e devoto—feste popolari in Campania,* with text by Carlo Levi, Naples 1975; *Mezzogiorno: questione aperta,* Bari, Italy 1976; *Vedute di Napoli,* with text by Giuseppe Bonini, Milan 1980; *Teatralita quotidiana a Napoli,* with introduction by Luigi Carluccio, Naples 1982; *Naples: une archaeologie future,* with text by Jean-Claude Lemagny, Paris 1982; *Gibellina,* with text by Arturo Carlo Quintavalle, Milan 1982; *Demoni e santi,* with text by R. De Simone, Naples 1983; *Capri,* with text by Cesare De Seta, Rome 1983; *Salemi,* with text by Pierluigi Nicolin, Milan 1984; *Napoli,* with text by Cesare De Seta, Milan 1985; *La Campania,* Milan 1985; *Un secolo di furore,* with text by N. Spinosa, Rome 1985; *Qui come altrove,* with text by G. Raviele, Rome 1985.

On JODICE: Books—*48 fotografie di Mimmo Jodice,* exhibition catalogue, by Antonio Napolitano, Naples 1967; *Mimmo Jodice: fotografie dal Giappone,* exhibition catalogue, with text by Luciano Caruso, Rome 1974; *70 Anni di Fotografia in Italia* by Italo Zannier, Modena, Italy 1978; *Napoli '81: Sette fotografi per una nuova immagine,* exhibition catalogue, by Cesare De Seta, Milan 1981: *I Grandi Fotografi: Mimmo Jodice,* with text by Filiberto Menna and others, Milan 1983; *The European Iceberg,* edited by Germano Celant, Milan 1985; *Mimmo Jodice Tempo Interiore* by Roberta Vattorta, Milan 1994. **Articles**—"Dove va l'avanguardia" by Italo Zannier in *Popular Photography Italiana* (Milan), April 1971; "Dedicato alla Madonna dell'Arco" by Mario Pomilio in *Progresso Fotografico* (Milan), March 1973; "Mimmo Jodice: impressioni di Bangkok" by F. Consigli in *Nuova Fotografia* (Milan), December 1973; "Mimmo Jodice" by Giuseppe Turroni in *Fotografia Italiana* (Milan), September 1974; "La Napoli di Mimmo Jodice," special issue of *Progresso Fotografico* (Milan), January 1978; "I piu bravi, 1979" by Marina Miraglia in *Bolaffi Arte* (Turin), July 1979; "Venezia 79: La Fotografia" by George Tatge in *Artform* (New York), November 1979; "Mimmo Jodice" by Giuseppe Bonini in *Progresso Fotografico* (Milan), March 1980; "Zeitgenossische Fotografie in Italien" by Italo Zannier in *Zoom* (Munich), August 1980; "Mimmo Jodice" in *Camera International* (Paris), no. 6, 1986.

*   *   *

Naples, an image-city par excellence, like Venice or Rome, has been linked with the flowering of photography since the days of its first invention, when scientific interest and popular curiosity in the city provoked certain events which were to become landmarks in the history of Italian photography—like the "Relazione intorno al dagnerrotipo" by Macedonia Melloni at the Academy of Science on November 12th 1893 or the public demonstration of the daguerrotype by Gaetano Fazzani in the presence of journalists and city authorities on November 28th of the same year.

From that time onwards the city, with its bay and the still active Vesuvius, became one of the most frequently photographed subjects, not only by travellers from Northern Europe on the "Grand Tour" which would later lead them to Malta, Athens and Cairo, but also by a small band of serious photographers. People like Giorgio Sommer, Conrad, Chauffourier and Bernoud, also from the North, came to practice their new and magical art, quickly excelling with captivating scenes of that luminous and highly photogenic place. Very much in the tradition of picturesque photos they also shot artful little typical scenes—little scenes of local life which, with no sociological pretensions whatsoever, attempted to reveal the vices and virtues of the lively, creative and flamboyant Neapolitan people, victims not only of a crushing poverty but also of their own everyday theatre. This theatre is a living reality in Naples but is rarely taken too seriously and is usually enacted with a great deal of sarcasm and irony.

Mimmo Jodice returns to the myth of this theatricality which is so prominent in the stereotyped image of Naples—the result of visual pillaging by neorealist reportage often in search of grim scenes from the more infamous ghettos, as were the writers and filmmakers who set out to create a rather superficial folklore of suffering. By contrast Mimo Jodice has tried to capture in photographs the hidden moral tension at the heart of the city.

He reveals it without falling into the trap of a speculative populism but rather adopts more scientific criteria of an anthropological type. Here images are used instead of words and have not only a didactic or illustrative function but also a conceptual one. The photographs strive to express their subjects' philosophy of life through the cathartic, emblematic and revelatory signs which can be captured in images.

"The photography," wrote Luigi Carluccio in relation to Jodice, "has delved into the city in all its aspects: architecture and show, solitude and togetherness, opulence and poverty, wealthy areas and slums, work and inactivity...." Jodice's is a catalogue not only of more or less stereotyped images of the city but also of states of mind, expressed in gestures and signs which the photos have captured with ruthless immediacy and absolute descriptive clarity. They reveal a whole way of life in its documentary indices, a stratified and complex 'story' which Jodice's civilized eye has extracted from the city's public face—everything from local folklore to the falsely humanitarian gutter press.

Mimmo Jodice was able to accomplish this task (and not only in *his* city, Naples, but also in a variety of other places where he has recently worked on assignments) only after a long and painstaking meditation on photography as a language. He initially worked with the cutting and abstract elaboration of images, almost totally destroying the hypothetical objectivity of photographs—something he considered too facile and automatic. From the early montages, cuttings and experimental collages which revealed his talent as a research photographer in the 1960s, Jodice rapidly, almost naturally, moved into the cultural space, opened up by the new American and European avantegarde absorbing the influence of Frank, Friedland and Klein through a complex and comprehensive cultural web—rereading Strand and the realism of Evans and including some of the irony of a Brassai or a Doisneau.

The emphases of post-modernism influenced him profoundly, suggesting new formal and thematic avenues. Jodice has produced photographic images of remarkable clarity, rediscovering the city in other symbols which had at first been excluded (those of classicism which had become kitsch and vice versa; fragments of urban archeology and natural landscape) and which are now, with great figurative rigour, placed firmly in the foreground. In this way these symbols take on the suggestive value of present-day totems, avoiding melancholy, leaving little room for irony, but dense with tragic and magical allusion.

—Italo Zannier

JOHNSON, Tore.

Nationality: Swedish. **Born:** Saint-Leu la Forêt, near Paris, 8 January 1928. **Education:** Viggbyholmsskolan, Viggbyholm, Sweden, 1943-48; apprentice/assistant to Karl W. Gullers, Studio Gullers, Stockholm, 1948. **Family:** Married Marianne Axelsson in 1961 (divorced, 1966); son: Olof. **Career:** Freelance photographer, working for various Swedish and foreign magazines and book publishers, Paris, 1948-51, New York, 1952-53, and Stockholm, 1954 until his death, 1980. Founder Member, Tio Fotografer group, Stockholm, 1958-80. **Recipient:** Swedish-American Society grant, 1952. **Died:** (in Stockholm) 14 May 1980.

Individual Exhibitions:

1989   Todd Weinstein Gallery, New York

	Mois de la Photo, Montreal, Quebec
1990	Lilla Edet, Sweden

Selected Group Exhibitions:

1949	*Unga fotografer,* Rotohallen, Stockholm
1951	*Jeunes Photographes Suedoises,* Galerie Kodak, Paris
	Subjektive Fotografie, Saarbrucken, West Germany
1958	*Fotokonst 1958,* Lunds Konsthall, Lund, Sweden
1959	*Tio Fotografer: Hundra bilder,* Svensk Form, Konstfackskolan, Stockholm
1962	*Svenskarna sedda av 11 fotografer,* Moderna Museet, Stockholm
1964	*World Exhibition of Photography: What Is Man?,* Pressehaus Stern, Hamburg (and world tour)
1971	*Contemporary Photographers from Sweden,* Library of Congress, Washington, D.C.
1977	*Tio Fotografer,* at *Rencontres Internationales de Photographie,* Arles, France (travelled to La Photogalerie, Paris)
1984	*Subjektive Fotografie: Images of the 50s,* San Francisco Museum of Modern Art (travelled to the University of Houston, Texas; Museum Folkwang, Essen; Vasterbottens Museum, Umea; Kulturhuset, Stockholm; Saarland Museum, Saarbrucken; Palais des Beaux-Arts, Brussels)

Collections:

Norsk Fotohistorisk Forening, Oslo; Finska Fotografiska Museet, Helsinki; Bibliothèque Nationale, Paris; Library of Congress, Washington, D.C.

Publications:

By JOHNSON: Books—*Paris hemliga tecken,* with text by Göran Schildt, Stockholm 1952; *Okänt Paris,* with text by Ivar Lo-Johansson, Stockholm 1954; *Skulptur,* Stockholm 1958; *Färdmän Från isarna,* with text by Jan Sundfeldt, Stockholm 1964; *LKAB i bild,* with text by Sven Brunnsjö, Stockholm 1965; *Hallarna i Paris,* with text by Sven Aurén, Stockholm 1967; *Den sociala fotobildboken,* with text by Ivar Lo-Johansson, Stockholm 1977.

On JOHNSON: Books—*Tore Johnson—Still Moments in the River of Life,* with text by Rune Hassner, Stockholm 1987; *Svenskarna sedda av 11 fotografer,* exhibition catalogue, by K.G. Pontus Hultén and Stig Claeson, Stockholm 1962; *Visitor's Views: Swedish Travellers in the U.S. from the 17th to the 20th Century* by Karl Sjunnesson, Trelleborg, Sweden 1976; *Tio Foto Bildbyra,* Stockholm 1983; *Subjektive Fotografie: Images of the 50s,* exhibition catalogue, by Ute Eskildsen, Manfred Schmalriede and Dorothy Martinson, Essen, West Germany 1984.

*   *   *

In the years when Europe began to recover from the wounds inflicted by the Second World War, Paris became an important meeting place—and center for ideas—for a new generation of photographers. Tore Johnson was one of the many who went there. During his stay in Paris at the beginning of the 1950s, he matured as a camera artist—and emerged as a photographic portrayer of Paris in the footsteps of Kertész and Brassaï. But he showed a clearly individual stamp from the very start.

Johnson worked as a freelance photographer and was employed by Swedish magazines; for a time, he was a stringer for Magnum; and, in two books, he produced a fastidious selection of pictures. *Paris hemliga tecken* contains acute observations of everyday events and finely catches the atmosphere of the time. Like Kertész, Johnson had a penchant for the odd, the bizarre. He looked at the world around him with warmth and humour. *Okänt Paris* was produced in collaboration with the Swedish writer Ivar Lo-Johansson. It is a social study of the Paris of the poor, the sick, and the defeated. Johnson depicted the dark side of the metropolis with insight and with respect. Of many picture books about Paris, *Okänt Paris* is one of the very few that contains a penetrating visual report on the social conditions among the

Paris, **1951.** Photograph ©Tore Johnson.

poorer section of the community. It can, in parts, be compared to Lewis Hines' earlier work in the United States, which Johnson did not come to know until later.

Other fine series of photographs were gathered during a visit to New York and during many years of wandering through his home town of Stockholm. It was mainly the big city and its people which Johnson depicted—places and people he came to know intimately—a delicate interpretation of his own

impressions and the "secret signs" of city life. But a severe sense of self-criticism caused him to leave the greater part of this rich material unpublished.

Commissions from magazines often led Johnson to a confrontation with a more brutal reality, which he visualized as a true "concerned photographer": the famine in Kasai during the Congo crisis; a massacre of seals in the Gulf of Bothnia; a mineworkers' strike in northern Sweden. Another interesting area of Johnson's work is his colour studies of nature, collected on long journeys into the Arctic. The grandeur and the silence in the barren landscapes and snowy wastes emerge and are emphasized in forceful compositions and in delicately balanced, subtle colours. And, in his last years, Johnson began to explore, with camera and microscope, a world of images invisible to the naked eye—close-up studies of vitamin crystals, which were published in *GEO* in 1980. Without having to respond to demands for scientific or journalistic significance, Johnson presented in these works his artistic discoveries of form and colour.

The strength of Johnson's work lies, however, in his compassionate, poetic studies in black-and-white of his fellow citizens in happiness and in grief.

—Rune Hassner

JONES, Harold (Henry).

Nationality: American. **Born:** Morristown, New Jersey, 29 September 1940. **Education:** Morristown High School, 1955-59; studied painting at the Newark School of Fine and Industrial Art, New Jersey, 1959-63, photography at the Maryland Institute of Art, Baltimore, 1963-65, B.F.A. 1965, and photography and art history at the University of New Mexico, Albuquerque, 1965-68, M.F.A. 1972. **Family:** Married Frances Ellen Murray in 1970; children: Rebecca and Star Ann. **Career:** Advertising Chairman, Gallery 61, Newark, 1962-63; Wedding Photographer, Udel Studios, Baltimore, 1964; Official School Photographer, Maryland Art Institute, 1964; Portrait Photographer, Jordan Studios, Baltimore, 1965-66; Gallery and Technical Adviser, Quivira Bookshop and Gallery, Corrales, New Mexico, 1966-67; Assistant, University of New Mexico Art Museum, 1966-68; Assistant Curator, 1969, and Associate Curator, 1970-71, George Eastman House, Rochester, New York; Director, Light Gallery, New York, 1971-75. Instructor in Painting and Drawing, Barelas Community Center, Albuquerque, 1966-67; Visiting Lecturer in Photography, University of Rochester, 1970-71, and Cooper Union, New York, 1971-72; Adjunct Associate Professor of Art History, Queens College, New York, 1974-75. Director of the Center for Creative Photography, 1975-77, and since 1977 Director of the Photography Program, University of Arizona, Tucson. **Recipient:** Eastman House Fellowship, 1967; Smithsonian Institution Travel Grant, 1976; Gold Award, University and College Designers Association, 1977; National Endowment for the Arts Grant and Photographers Fellowship, 1977; University of Arizona Centennial Committee Grant, 1982; Publication Grant, University of Arizona Foundation, 1984. **Agents:** B.C. Space, 235 Forest Avenue, Laguna Beach, California 92651; and Dinnerware Artists Cooperative, 272 East Congress, Tucson, Arizona 85701. **Address:** Department of Art, University of Arizona, Tucson, Arizona 85721, U.S.A.

Individual Exhibitions:

1969	University of California at Davis
1970	Photographic Workshop, Rochester, New York
	Barnes Gallery, Loomis Institute, Windsor, Connecticut
1972	Madison Arts Center, Wisconsin
1973	University of Massachusetts at Boston
1974	Soho Photo Gallery, New York
1976	Spectrum Gallery, Tucson, Arizona
	Light Gallery, New York
1977	Kresge Art Center, Michigan State University, East Lansing
	Hang-Up Gallery, Tucson, Arizona
1978	*Lightning,* Neal Slavin Studio, New York
	Bayard Gallery, Orange Coast College, Costa Mesa, California
	Harris 125 Gallery, University of Southern California, Los Angeles
1979	Northlight Gallery, Arizona State University, Tempe
	Slocumb Gallery, East Tennessee State University, Johnson City
1980	Light Factory Gallery, Charlotte, North Carolina
	Light Gallery, New York

	Gallery Atelier 696, Rochester, New York (with Frances Murray)
1982	Etherton Gallery, Tucson, Arizona
1983	B.C. Space, Laguna Beach, California
	Dinnerware Gallery, Tucson, Arizona (with Greg Benson)
1984	B.C. Space, Laguna Beach, California
	Dinnerware Gallery, Tucson, Arizona
1985	*Invisible Photographs,* Performance Projects Inc., Tucson, Arizona (with Dennis Williams)

Selected Group Exhibitions:

1970	*Photosynthesis,* Oakland College of Arts and Crafts, California
1972	*60s Continuum,* International Museum of Photography, George Eastman House, Rochester, New York
1973	*New Images 1839-1973,* Smithsonian Institution, Washington, D.C.
1974	*New Images in Photography,* Lowe Art Museum, University of Miami
1977	*The Great West: Real/Ideal,* University of Colorado, Boulder (subsequently Smithsonian Institution travelling exhibition; toured the United States)
1979	*Attitudes: Photography in the 1970s,* Santa Barbara Museum of Art, California
1980	*Mondo Arizona,* Joseph Gross Gallery, University of Arizona, Tucson
1981	*Contemporary Hand-Colored Photographs,* de Saisset Art Gallery, University of Santa Clara, California
1983	*Arboretum,* Boulder Center for the Visual Arts, Colorado (travelled to Shwayder Gallery, University of Denver, Colorado; Auraria Higher Education Complex, Colorado)
1984	*The Alternative Image II,* Kohler Arts Center, Sheboygan, Wisconsin

Collections:

Museum of Modern Art, New York; International Museum of Photography, George Eastman House, Rochester, New York; Rhode Island School of Design, Providence; University of Louisville, Kentucky; University of Colorado, Boulder; Santa Fe Museum, New Mexico; Arizona State University, Tempe; Center for Creative Photography, University of Arizona, Tucson; Norton Simon Museum of Art, Pasadena, California; University of California at Los Angeles Art Museum; National Gallery of Canada, Ottawa.

Publications:

By JONES: Articles—"The Influence of Thomas Barrow upon Mother Nature's Inventions" in *Album* (London), May 1970; "The 50s: A Renaissance in Photography" in *The Photographer's Choice,* edited by Kelly Wise, Danbury, New Hampshire 1975; "Harold Jones: Interview" in *New Times* (Tempe, Arizona), Summer 1975; "A Touch of Class" in *Tucson Daily Citizen,* 21 December 1976; "Harold Jones and Mark Cohen" in *Popular Photography* (New York), April 1977; "Harold Jones: Interview" in *Perspectives,* San Francisco 1978; introduction to *Contemporary California Photography,* exhibition catalogue, San Francisco 1978; "Harold Jones: Interview" in *Photobulletin* (Los Angeles), January 1978; "Photography" in *Twenty Arizona Artists,* exhibition catalogue, Phoenix, Arizona 1978; "Five Quotations" in *Northlight* (Tempe, Arizona), November 1978; "Photographs and Professionals," interview, in *Print Collectors Newsletter* (New York), July/August 1983.

On JONES: Books—*Vision and Expression* by Nathan Lyons, New York 1969; *The Photography Catalog,* edited by Norman Snyder, New York 1976; *The Alternative Image II,* exhibition catalogue, with introduction by Anita Douthat, Sheboygan, Wisconsin 1984. **Articles**—"Harold Jones" by Van Deren Coke in *Creative Camera* (London), August 1969; "Harold Jones: Leaving the Light" in the *Village Voice* (New York), 16 June 1975; "Harold Jones: Photographs in Balance" in *Artweek* (Oakland, California), 30 October

1976; "Five More Thinking Photographers" by Chuck Nicholson in *Artweek* (Oakland California), 14 April 1984.

*

It is not as simple as black and white. There is no clear, distinct picture in my mind of what photography is or isn't. It generates elegance in so many dialects of vision that I am constantly awed at its flexibility. From Heinrich Kühn's landscapes to Harold Edgerton's stroboscopic wonders, from Weegee's New York to Helmut Newton's sirens, from 19 million snapshots made every day in the U.S.A. to the postcards bought on Harvard Square, photography speaks as an articulate, many-tongued creature. Yet, I fully acknowledge Oscar Wilde's observation, "Photography has the remarkable power to turn wine into water."

While I have been making photographs since 1963, it has only been during the last five years that I have been able to do so on almost a daily basis. From 1968 to 1975, as director of Light Gallery, my time and energy were dedicated to the ideas and work of other photographers; in late 1975, I had an opportunity to devote more time to finding out where my *own* sensibilities began and into what directions they might extend. In late 1977 I changed occupations to a position that intensified my desire for research into the realm of photography. I consciously avoided taking on a "project." I wanted to see what would happen if I allowed my photographs to evolve from within my own visual and intellectual instincts. I photographed a wide range of subject matter intuitively, allowing the direction to reveal itself naturally. The photographs became the markers. They animated memory and my sense of touch for the presence of things. Slowly I discovered a sense for the harmony of parts, and from the pictures I began to realize that a sonata form of observation was emerging, informed with excited wonder.

I work in four modes; that is, I continually have bodies of work in progress in four areas: black and white silver prints; drawings on photographs; black and white Polaroids; and color slides. I constantly make color slides, which function for me as a way of sketching, note-taking. To discuss all the reasons why color slides interest me would consume more space than is practical here. Put briefly, the formal and emotional characteristics by which color animates image matter is of great interest to me. I consider the slides to be an important part of my work. The black and white prints, drawings, and Polaroids deal much more with formal examinations and questions posed by the "optical unconscious." The concept of optical unconscious is mentioned by Walter Benjamin in his *Short History of Photography:* "It is possible, however roughly, to describe the way somebody walks, but it is impossible to say anything about that fraction of a second when a person *starts to walk.* Photography with its various aids (lenses, enlargements) can reveal this moment. Photography makes aware for the first time the optical unconscious. Structural qualities, cellular tissue, which form the natural business of technology and medicine are all much more closely related to the camera than to atmospheric landscape or the expressive portrait. At the same time, photography uncovers in this material physiognomic aspects of pictorial words which live in the smallest things, perceptible yet covert enough to find shelter in daydreams, but which, once enlarged and capable of formulation, show the difference between technology and magic to be entirely a matter of historical variables."

My work is an unfolding biography. The exposure is made when a number of signals swing into a moment of harmony; become coherent to generate a sense of wonder. The photograph is the object that begins and allows recall; it becomes first the point of entry, then the bridge between emotion and intellect. The photograph is the end, and the photograph is the beginning.

—Harold Jones

* * *

Harold Jones speaks of his work as a conversation with photography. There is evidently a lot to be said about vision and history by both partners in the dialogue.

Jones' style of work reveals an inquisitive, restless mind. He moves easily between straight gelatin silver work and the synthetic images. He will paint on or tear a black-and-white photograph, will arrange objects to be photographed as a still life or make a straight 4 by 5 inch contact print of an urban scene. He explores one idea, such as the effect of hand-coloring a particular object, then breaks the pattern and moves on. This searching spirit is in the best tradition of photographic ideas.

In his work of the 1960s—black and white photographs resplendent with green cows or red wrought-iron benches—we are well aware of his presence. The hand (voice?) of the photographer indicates the surface of the print, its potential and shortcomings with candor and wit. In later work the painted additions take on the tonal range of the gelatin silver photograph and perceptual confusion increases. What is photographic? What is the true field of the image?

His subjects are simple and generally unspectacular: a glass of water, his back yard, a gleaming white chair, light from a window at dusk, but each functions as an investigation into and a comment on the possibilities of the medium. This is not an over-intellectualizing of photography. The photographs are organizations of concrete facts, models of reality, or rather photography's transformation of the obvious. Jones remains neutral in his approach to the subject matter—his conversation is with photography itself not the nature of landscape or green cows. One picture appears to be circles within circles. This design can be translated as a glass with ice, laying on its side on a round table without reducing the graphic power of the image.

Harold Jones thinks a good deal about photography. It is part of his everyday life. He has a lot to say and he is also, apparently, a very good listener.

—Marianne Fulton

JONES, Pirkle.

Nationality: American. **Born:** Shreveport, Louisiana, 2 January 1914. **Education:** Lima High School, Ohio, 1928-31; studied photography, under Ansel Adams and Minor White, at the California School of Fine Arts, now the San Francisco Art Institute, 1946-49. **Military Service:** Served as a Warrant Officer, Signal Corps, 37th Infantry Division, United States Army, in the South Pacific, 1941-46: Bronze Star. **Family:** Married Ruth-Marion Baruch in 1949. **Career:** Worked as a machine operator at Lima Sole and Heel Company, 1933-41. Freelance photographer, San Francisco, since 1949. Assistant to Ansel Adams, San Francisco, 1949-52. Instructor in Photography, California School of Fine Arts, 1953-58, and San Francisco Art Institute, since 1970. **Recipient:** Photographic Excellence Award, National Urban League, New York, 1961; National Endowment for the Arts Photography Fellowship, 1977; Award of Honor, San Francisco Arts Commission, 1983; Citizen of the Day Award, KABL Radio, San Francisco, 1983. **Address:** 663 Lovell Avenue, Mill Valley, California 94941, U.S.A.

Individual Exhibitions:

1947	Public Library, Lima, Ohio
1952	Ansel Adams Gallery, San Francisco
1955	International Museum of Photography, George Eastman House, Rochester, New York (retrospective)
1957	*Building an Oil Refinery,* San Francisco Academy of Sciences
1960	*California Roadside Council Exhibition,* The Capital, Sacramento, California
	Death of a Valley, San Francisco Museum of Art (with Dorothea Lange; travelled to the Oakland Museum, California; Art Institute of Chicago; and the University of California at Davis)
1963	*The Story of a Winery,* Smithsonian Institution, Washington, D.C. (with Ansel Adams; toured the United States)
1964	*Walnut Grove: Portrait of a Town,* San Francisco Museum of Art (with Ruth-Marion Baruch)
1965	American Federation of Arts, Carmel, California (retrospective)
1967	Bay Window Gallery, Mendocino, California
	Photography Center, Carmel, California
1968	*Portfolio Two,* California Redwood Gallery, San Francisco
	Photographic Essay on the Black Panthers, De Young Museum, San Francisco (with Ruth-Marion Baruch;

travelled to the Studio Museum, Harlem, New York; Dartmouth College, Hanover, New Hampshire; and the University of California at Santa Cruz)

1969   Underground Gallery, New York (retrospective)
1970   *Gate Five,* Ikon Gallery, Monterey, California (travelled to the Focus Gallery, San Francisco)
1971   Tintype Gallery, Tiburon, California (retrospective)
1972   *Portfolio Two,* The Studio Gallery, Bolinas, California
1973   The Photography Place, Berwyn, Pennsylvania
         Shado' Gallery, Oregon City, Oregon
1977   *Portraits of Adams, Lange, Sheeler, Weston,* San Francisco Art Institute
         The Sculpture of Annette Rosenshine, San Francisco Art Institute
1984   *Vintage Years,* Vision Gallery, San Francisco

Selected Group Exhibitions:

1954   *Perceptions,* San Francisco Museum of Art
1956   *This Is the American Earth,* California Academy of Sciences, San Francisco (and world tour)
1957   *I Hear America Singing,* Kongresshalle, Berlin (travelled to Tokyo)
1959   *Photographer's Choice,* Indiana University, Bloomington
1960   *Photography at Mid-Century,* International Museum of Photography, George Eastman House, Rochester, New York (toured the United States)
1967   *Photography in the 20th Century,* National Gallery of Canada, Ottawa (toured Canada and the United States, 1967-73)
1973   *Octave of Prayer,* Massachusetts Institute of Technology, Cambridge
1975   *The Land: 20th Century Landscape Photographs Selected by Bill Brandt,* Victoria and Albert Museum, London (travelled to the National Gallery, Edinburgh; Ulster Museum, Belfast; and National Museum of Wales, Cardiff)
1980   *New Landscapes: Part I,* Friends of Photography, Carmel, California
1984   *Photography in California 1945-80,* San Francisco Museum of Modern Art (travelled to the Akron Art Museum, Ohio; Corcoran Gallery, Washington, D.C.; Los Angeles Municipal Art Gallery; Cornell University, Ithaca, New York; High Museum of Art, Atlanta, Georgia; Museum Folkwang, Essen; Centre Georges Pompidou, Paris; Museum of Photographic Arts, San Diego, California)

Collections:

Library of Congress, Washington, D.C.; Art Institute of Chicago; Adams Collection, University of Arizona, Tucson; Amon Carter Museum, Fort Worth, Texas; San Francisco Museum of Modern Art; Oakland Museum, California.

Publications:

By JONES: Books—*Portfolio One,* with text by Charles P. Johnson, San Francisco 1955; *Death of a Valley,* with Dorothea Lange, Millerton, New York 1960; *Portfolio Two,* with an introduction by Ansel Adams, Mill Valley, California 1968; *The Vanguard: A Photographic Essay on the Black Panthers,* with Ruth-Marion Baruch, Boston 1970. **Articles**—"House and Home Photography" in *Encyclopedia of Photography,* New York 1957; "Nature Photography XXII" in *Pacific Discovery* (San Francisco), January/February 1967; "In Tandem: Pirkle Jones and Ruth-Marion Baruch," interview with Phiz Mezey, in *Darkroom Magazine* (San Francisco), December 1977.

On JONES: Books—*Subjektive Fotografie: Images of the 50s,* exhibition catalogue, by Ute Eskildsen, Manfred Schmalriede and Dorothy Martinson, Essen, West Germany 1984; *Photography in California 1945-1980* by Louise Katzman, San Francisco and New York 1984. **Articles**—"Pirkle Jones, Photographer" by Ansel Adams in *U.S. Camera* (New York), October 1952;

"Pirkle Jones Portfolio" by Nancy Newhall in *Aperture* (Rochester, New York), vol. 4, no. 2, 1956; "Short Run Color" by Minor White in *Image* (Rochester, New York), March 1957; "Pirkle Jones" by Robert Holmes in *British Journal of Photography* (London), 17 October 1980; "Poet of Images" by Jack McCarty in the *Examiner and Chronicle Living Magazine* (San Francisco), 13 January 1985.

*

I am interested in the single image as an aesthetic expression and in documentary photography. I demand content in my work, and I am not interested in style for its own sake. Examples of my work as single images appear in many publications and collections. *Portfolio Two* are original prints, with a foreword by Ansel Adams, self published in 1968.

Four large bodies of my work have appeared:

1) In 1956 I collaborated with Dorothea Lange on a project in the Berryessa Valley in California. In this rich farm valley homes were being destroyed, people and livestock moved out, trees cut down and burned—everything had to go to make ready for the water that was to come after a large dam was completed. This price for progress was paid for by those who lived in the valley, so that others might have the benefits of more water. This poignant essay is considered an important contribution to photography. Published in *Aperture* and exhibited at the San Francisco Museum of Art, the Art Institute of Chicago, Oakland Museum, California, and the University of California at Davis, this essay appeared as *Death of a Valley.*

2) In 1968 I worked with Ruth-Marion Baruch on the essay called "A Photographic Essay on the Black Panthers." This controversial political essay is on the Black Panther movement in the San Francisco Bay area. We photographed all the top leaders, gatherings, programs and related images of this movement. The exhibition of over 120 photographs was designed and produced by the two of us, shown at the De Young Museum of Art in San Francisco, December 1969 to January 1970, also at the Studio Museum in Harlem, New York, at the Hopkins Center at Dartmouth College, and at the University of California at Santa Cruz. The book, *The Vanguard: A Photographic Essay on the Black Panthers,* was published by Beacon Press in 1970.

3) "Gate Five" is a study of a large houseboat community which lives on the edge of San Francisco Bay in Sausalito, California. This large collection of photographs is in an unpublished form: 44 pages of text and about 125 finished fine prints in the collection of the photographer. Photographs of this alternative lifestyle were made in 1969 and 1970, with a few in 1971. Only small sections of this essay have been exhibited. Six black-and-white photographs from this essay are in the permanent collection of the San Francisco Museum of Modern Art.

4) "The Salt Marsh Series" and "The Rock Series" are two collections of work from nature produced in 1978-79; two additional series of photographs were produced in 1980, "The Tanbark Oak Series" and "The Madrono Series."

—Pirkle Jones

* * *

Although he had exhibited his photographs in pictorial salons before he entered the U.S. Army in 1941, his studies with Ansel Adams and Minor White at the California School of Fine Arts in the late 1940s were decisive influences on Pirkle Jones and his photography. They taught him the technique for which both were to become famous and of which he soon became a master—the production of the full range of tones of which film and paper are capable if exposed and developed according to what has since then become widely known as the zone system. And Adams and White each contributed something more personal to his education, each a different message and each, apparently, equally appealing to Jones's character and temperament. From the example of Adams, the ardent champion of wilderness and park conservation, Jones learned that artistic photographs could also make political statements; from White's work and teaching, he realized how fine an instrument the camera can be for self-exploration and the rendering of personal emotion. The combination of the two, reflecting the oddity of his combined names (Gertrude Stein would have said *induced* by them) have been constant in subsequent years: *Pirkle,* the poet; *Jones,* the social witness.

It is hard to understand, except as a fault in general perception, why his large body of work has not yet received the major recognition that is due it. Perhaps it is his lack of exaggeration. He sees things in their appropriate scale and sense: mountains are not molehills, nor are people isolated zombies. He uses his camera sympathetically, and sympathy is not "exciting" enough for today's jaded taste. His photographs record what a generous temperament as well as a trained eye feels and sees. The style of each photograph is derived from the immediate subject as he experiences it; nothing is stylishly imposed.

His most personally explored subjects have been aspects of the California landscape—wooded and pastured lands, sandy and rocky beaches, plant patterns, and portraits of fellow photographers—Charles Sheeler, Ansel Adams, Edward Weston, Dorothea Lange. His investigations of American, particularly Californian, society have included *Death of a Valley* (with Dorothea Lange), "Walnut Grove: Portrait of a Town" (with his wife, the poet and photographer Ruth-Marion Baruch), and *The Vanguard: A Photographic Essay on the Black Panthers* (also with Ruth-Marion Baruch). Each of these essays includes portraits, architectural details and long views that locate the story. They are combined in a thoughtfully edited sequence to present a powerful interpretation of its subjects. Each is a statement against what the authors considered a social injustice.

Pirkle Jones's most recent project is making photographs on Mount Tamalpais, near his home in Marin County, north of San Francisco. The photographs that he has made so far of the land and growth there, taken at close range, are consistent with his earlier introspective landscapes, and speak as well of his long mastery of photographic form.

—Anita V. Mozley

JONES GRIFFITHS, Philip.

Nationality: British. **Born:** Rhuddlan, Wales, in 1936. **Education:** Educated in local schools; studied pharmacy; self-taught in photography. **Career:** Worked as a freelance press photographer and cameraman for Granada Television, Manchester. Full-time freelance press and reportage photographer, working *The Observer Magazine, Town, Queen, Look, Life, McCall's, The Sunday Times Magazine,* the *New York Times,* etc., in London, Rhodesia, Zambia, Zanzibar, Vietnam, etc., since 1961. Member, Magnum Photos cooperative agency, Paris and New York. Lecturer in Photography, Royal College of Art, London. **Address:** c/o Ed Barber, Half Moon Photography Workshop, 119 Roman Road, London E2, England.

Selected Group Exhibitions:

1967	*Photography in the 20th Century,* National Gallery of Canada, Ottawa (toured Canada and the United States, 1967-73)
1973	*3rd World Exhibition of Photography: On the Way to Paradise,* Pressehaus Stern, Hamburg (and world tour)
1981	*A Day in the Life of Australia,* Sydney, New South Wales (toured Australia)
1983	*British Photography 1955-65,* The Photographers' Gallery, London

Publications:

By JONES GRIFFITHS: Book—*Vietnam Inc.,* New York 1971. Article—"Philip Jones Griffiths," interview, with Andrew de Lory, in the *British Journal of Photography Annual,* London 1975.

On JONES GRIFFITHS: Books—*Photography Today,* edited by Norman Hall, London 1957; *Photography in the 20th Century* by Nathan Lyons, New York 1967; *America in Crisis: Photographs for Magnum,* edited by Charles Harbutt and Lee Jones, with an essay by Mitchel Levitas, New York 1969; *War,* edited by A.R. Leventhal, New York 1973; *The Magic Image* by Cecil Beaton and Gail Buckland, London and Boston 1975; *Geschichte der Fotografie im 20. Jahrhundert/Photography in the 20th Century* by Petr Tausk, Cologne 1977, London 1980; *The Camera at War* by Jorge Lewinski, London and New

York 1978; *A Day in the Life of Australia—March 6, 1981,* with introduction by Thomas Kenneally, Potts Point, New South Wales 1981; *British Photography 1955-1965: The Master Craftsmen in Print,* exhibition catalogue, by Sue Davies, Michael Rand, Mark Boxer and others, London 1983; *Bilder vom Krieg* by Rainer Fabian and Hans Christian Adam, Hamburg 1983, as *Images of War: 130 Years of War Photography,* London 1985. **Articles**—"Philip Jones Griffiths" in *Modern Photography Annual,* New York 1972; "Vietnam Inc.: Philip Jones Griffiths" by S. MacPherson in the *British Journal of Photography* (London), 17 March 1972; "Philip Jones Griffiths: Vietnam Inc." in *Zoom* (Paris), June/July 1974.

*   *   *

Philip Jones Griffiths was born in a small village in Wales in the same year as *Picture Post. Picture Post* and *Illustrated* were his window on the world while he was growing up, and brought him to dream of being a photographer. He studied pharmacy ("counting pills," he calls it) and thought about becoming a freelance photographer, and *Picture Post* and *Illustrated* closed down. Thus he lost his most suitable potential market before he'd even started. Nevertheless, Jones Griffiths did eventually stop counting pills and start freelancing, going full time in 1961. He worked for most of the prestigious picture magazines and travelled the world shooting stories. Eventually he wound up in Vietnam, where he spent about three years from July 1966 to June 1968 plus 1970.

Early on he realized he was not going to sell many of his Vietnam pictures, as the American press was still "gung ho" about the war. However, he had a lucky break when he photographed Jackie Kennedy for a week in Cambodia and the rival Black Star films were sent to Manila by mistake. That left the field clear for him and he made money. He used it to help finance his Vietnam photography, with the idea of eventually publishing it as a book.

Vietnam was a wonderful war for photographers in terms of the cooperation they got in taking their shots. However the media still controlled what was published, and for them it had two main overlapping phases. First there was the war as morally uplifting, supreme spectacle, with the soldiers as the representatives of freedom showing such positive qualities as courage and valour. (David Douglas Duncan had established this genre with his book on Korea, *This Is War.*) As horror was piled on horror and the public became numbed to the violence, this shaded into a second phase where more and more sensational pictures were published, essentially glorifying horror and mindless violence—until revulsion finally set in. (Duncan's Vietnam book was *War Without Heroes.*)

In both these phases, the war was seen from the point of view of the American soldier, and that was not how Philip Jones Griffiths saw it at all. He put the war in the context of how it must look to an ordinary Vietnamese peasant, in the light of the country's history and culture. It must have very quickly become clear to him that the American involvement was doomed to failure, and he methodically photographed the processes by which that failure was to become more and more evident. The resulting pictures—with an essential text—were published as a book, *Vietnam Inc.,* in 1971.

Vietnam Inc. is certainly the most powerful book about the Vietnam war, and probably the best book about any war anywhere. On its publication it must have come as a bombshell to any American readers who were still pro-war, and certainly it provided the anti-war movement of the time with some of its most rational, sensitive and intelligible arguments against continuing the fighting. The book probably saved lives, and would probably have saved more if it had been more widely disseminated. It is the one book that neither glorifies the fighting, nor concentrates on the savagery and horror of the results. It is the one book that shows the utter vulnerability of the Vietnamese in the face of the superior American firepower, yet shows how the underlying resilience of their culture would win out against anything less than total genocide. It was, it is, a great work of humanity, and with every year that passes the essential rightness of Jones Griffiths' judgement becomes more and more clear.

In his excellent book *The Camera at War,* Jorge Lewinski describes it thus: it gives "a balanced viewpoint . . . a comprehensive, profound image of the totality of war, the way it affects soldier and civilian alike, the way the two become intertwined and together create the environment of a country at war. *Vietnam Inc.* is in the nature of a diary, but also a dissection of war into its various segments. Layer after layer, the facets of the war, the groups of people connected or affected by it, are uncovered and magnified under Griffiths' lens. The country, the village, its inhabitants; the American war machine, its origins, operation, constituent parts, its human elements of soldiers and administrators—the interactions and relationships between the cultures of east and west, corruption, graft, drug-taking, prostitution; the degeneration of the soldiers; the misery of the people; the devastation; the slaughter. Jones Griffiths' book has been skilfully assembled—its effect is cumulative; the visual narrative becomes sadder and grimmer as the story progresses. It begins with almost gay pictures of a beautiful, serene Vietnamese village and ends with shattering images of a shattered people, maimed or thrust into insanity by degradation and the constant fear of death. . . . The book is a great documentary on war in its distressing totality.''

Within this structure there is a great variety of pictures of many and various subjects, and they all work to the final end, the impact of the book. To pick out one or two for mention is rather like picking phrases out of a poem—ultimately meaningless. However, there are some pictures embedded in *Vietnam Inc.* that, on their own, are among the most emotionally powerful and memorable war pictures ever published in that they neither glamourize war nor do they work simply by shocking, in the sense of being gruesome to look at. It is the psychological impact, the emotional content, that is significant.

One picture shows a soldier sitting in an ornate chair, with his feet up on a window with his gun pointing out into the street. Clearly he is prepared to shoot anything that moves. Underneath his chair is a child's naked, broken doll. Another picture of a dark interior shows two soldiers about to rape a Vietnamese girl. One of the men has his mouth open as though about to bite, and the girl has twisted her head away. Like many of Jones Griffiths' pictures it is full of vital detail, like the sunglasses left on the bed and the wedding ring on the soldier's hand. A third picture shows a figure holding a terrible hand up to a face that is completely covered in bandages. A label tied to the wrist carries the words ''VNC FEMALE.''

Philip Jones Griffiths has taken many fine war pictures in countries as different as Vietnam, Israel and Northern Ireland. All have deserved a better showing in the national press than they have received. Hopefully, however, he will not produce another book like *Vietnam Inc.*, because no ''end'' can ultimately justify means that deserve this kind of treatment from a great photographer.

—Jack Schofield

JONSSON, (Olof) Sune.

Nationality: Swedish. **Born:** Nyåker, Västerbotten, 20 December 1930. **Education:** Studied English, literature and ethnology at the University of Stockholm, and the University of Uppsala, B.A. 1961; mainly self-taught in photography. **Family:** Married Stina Mobrink in 1959. **Career:** Photographer since the early 1950s. Editor, Swedish Broadcasting company, Umeå, 1962-65; freelance editor/photographer, working on photodocumentary projects, for the LT Publishing Company, Stockholm, 1966-70. Ethnologist, Västerbottens Museum, Umeå, since 1968. **Recipient:** Författarstipendium, 1965; Svenska Turistföreningens Silverplakett, 1970; Samfundet de Nios Stora Pris, 1972; Kungliga Vetenskapsakademien Award, 1973; Tidskriften Fotos Stora Fotografpriset, 1980; Kungl. Gustav Adolfs Adademien Award, 1981; The Hasselblad International Photography Prize, 1993. **Address:** Kungsgatan 37, 903 25, Umeå, Sweden.

Individual Exhibitions:

1960   *In på livet,* Bankpassagen Gallery, Hötorgscity, Stockholm
        (travelled to the Nutida Konst Gallery, Uppsala, and the
        Kopparhatten Gallery, Umeå, 1961)
1962   *Den stora Flyttningen,* Västerbottens Museum, Umeå (travelled
        to the Norrbottens Museum, Luleå, Sweden, Stadsmuseet,
        Sundsvall, Sweden and the Värmlands Museum, Karlstad,
        Sweden)
1965   *Kongo,* Västerbottens Museum, Umeå (travelled to the
        Dalarnas Museum, Falun, Sweden)
1968   *Prag Augusti 1968,* Västerbottens Museum, Umeå (toured
        Sweden)

1975   *Landskap och Redskap,* Västerbottens Museum, Umeå
1980   *Dagar vid havet,* Västerbottens Museum, Umeå (travelled to
        Gallery 1 x 1, Helsingborg)
1987   *Hemmavid 1986-87,* Fotografiska Museet, Stockholm
        (retrospective)
1993   *Sune Jonsson* The Hasselblad Center, Gothenburg
        (retrospective)

Selected Group Exhibitions:

1962   *Svenskarna sedda av 11 fotografer,* Moderna Museet,
        Stockholm
1978   *Tusen och en bild,* Moderna Museet, Stockholm
1979   *Svenskt landskap,* Moderna Museet, Stockholm
1982   *Fotograferna och det Svenska landskapet,* Fotografiska Museet,
        Stockholm
1985   *Samlingarna ca 200 fotografer,* Fotografiska Museet,
        Stockholm
1986   *Bilden berättar,* Fotografiska Museet, Stockholm

Collections:

Västerbottens Museum, Umeå; Moderna Museet, Stockholm; The Hasselblad Center, Gothenburg.

Publications:

By JONSSON: Books (photographs and text, unless noted)—*Byn med det blå huset,* Stockholm 1959, 1972; *Timotejvägen,* Stockholm 1961; *Hundhålet,* short stories, Stockholm 1962; *Bilder av Nådens barn,* Stockholm 1963; *Utmark,* with verse by Sigvard Karlsson, Stockholm 1963; *Bilder från den stora flyttningen,* Stockholm 1964; *Bilder av Kongo,* Stockholm 1965; *Torpet Åsen på Brännsjöskogen,* with drawings by Kurt Sundberg (text by Jonsson), Solna, Sweden 1965; *Sammankomst i elden,* Stockholm 1966; *Bilder från bondens år,* Stockholm 1967; *Bornholm og Bornholmere,* with text by Henning Ipsen, Copenhagen 1967, as *Bilder från Bornholm,* Stockholm 1968; *Prag, Augusti 1968,* Stockholm 1968; *Saltlake och blodvälling* by Lisa Johansson (edited by Jonsson), Stockholm 1968; *Brobyggarna,* novel, Stockholm 1969; *Minnesbok över den svenske bonden,* Stockholm 1971; *Stationskarl Albin E. Anderssons minnen,* novel, 1974; *Karl Lärkas Dalarna,* editor (also wrote introduction), Stockholm 1974; *Jordabok,* Stockholm 1976; *Örtabok,* Stockholm 1979; *Dagar vid havet,* Stockholm and Helsingborg 1981; *Om sommaren om hösten bittida sent,* verse by Bo Johansson, Stockholm 1981; *Blombok,* Stockholm 1983; *Hemmavid,* with introduction by Sverker Sörlin, Stockholm 986; *Tidenviskar: En Småbrukarfamilj 1960-1990,* Stockholm 1992; *Jordqubbar med mjölk,* Stockholm 1994. **Articles**—''Populärt eller dokumentärt'' in *Populär Fotografi* (Helsingborg), no. 10, 1968; ''Om fotografen Olof Perssons Storhet'' in *Konstrevy* (Stockholm), no. 44, 1968; ''Tankar om den dokumentära metoden'' in *Populär Fotografi* (Helsingborg), no. 2, 1970; ''Nio funderingar kring 125-delen'' in *1000 och en bild,* Stockholm 1979.

On JONSSON: Books—*Fotografisk Årsbok* by Kurt Bergengren, Stockholm 1960; *Bländande bilder* by Leif Wigh, Stockholm 1981; *Fotograferna och det svenska landskapet* by Leif Wigh, Stockholm 1982. **Articles**—''Sune Jonsson'' by Pär Rittsel in *Foto* (Stockholm), no. 1, 1981; ''Dokumentärfoto grafens arbete'' by Sverker Sörlin in *Vertex* (Umeå), no. 5, 1981; ''Ivar Lo är min chefsideolog'' by Sverker Sörlin in *FIB/Kulturfront* (Stockholm), no. 18, 1981; ''Den arbetande tiden'' by Sverkel Sörlin in *Film and TV* (Stockholm), no. 3, 1982.

*

As an ethnologist it is my wish to mediate to contemporary and future readers of my books and pictures the people of my own province, Västerbotten in northern Sweden, their environment, way of living, their economic, religious and social conditions and above all to depict the life of such minorities that have got into a scrape, are being slowly ruined and in the end disappearing from the social scene because of new economic structures and

A Crofter's Family, Mötingselberg, Lapland, **July 1994.** Photograph ©Sune Jonsson.

values. With my photographs, short stories and novels I want to make better situated groups in society understand and value those who are not so well off, established and vigorous. The ultimate purpose (I am a museum official) is of course to give future generations (even if imperfect and rhapsodical) an account of some of the ways of living and working in my own time.

—Sune Jonsson

*   *   *

In 1959 Sune Jonsson made his debut with a book about a small village in northern Sweden, which became something of a milestone in Swedish photographic literature. Its format was unpretentious, but it was full of pictures the like of which were at that time rare in Sweden. People with a knowledge of photographic history might well see certain similarities with the pictures of the F.S.A. photographers of the United States in the 1930s and with August Sander's pictures of Germany between the wars. Furthermore, the sensitive stories in the book were of a quality not normally found in photographic books, and the captions were in themselves small poems—limpid in formulation and concise in style.

Sune Jonsson thus established his individuality right from the start, by mastering pictorial as well as written language. The pictures were made with tenderness and showed the simple, quiet life of sparsely populated northern Sweden. As well, the concentration on a limited area and on a few people set this book apart from the very different "tourist picture" books, that were popular at the time. Here the spectator came close to ordinary Swedes, and behind the everyday exterior he found strong personalities whose changing fortunes were brought to life by the text. In these life-stories there is always a central truth, on which the author spins his tale, freely and subjectively. At times the biographies are developed into whole stories. An interesting combination of fact and fiction.

Sune Jonsson's photographic method was soon imitated widely by Swedish amateur photographers. Pictures of immobile, sitting people became numerous in competitions and exhibitions. But in his subsequent books Sune Jonsson showed that he also had the observant press photographer's ability to capture sudden events. The static style of the first book had been determined by its subject: that many old people, for various reasons, are forced into a life of inactivity.

In the early 1950s Sune Jonsson had made pictures of the type which dominated the photo-club movement of the day: car tracks in snow and graphic forms. But his interest in documentary pictures was awakened by the now famous 1955 exhibition *The Family of Man.* In a manifesto he talks of a pictorial language that should be comprehensible to hairdressers and car mechanics. He talks ironically about the photo-clubs' competition photos, their discussions about technique and theories of composition.

After his first book he produced another twelve, in addition to his work as a field technician at the Västerbotten Museum in Umeå, which includes film as well as photography. About the former he has said in an interview: "Film is vastly more documentary. While the still photograph represents a moment caught accidentally and subjectively, film can reproduce a precisely defined passage of time."

Sune Jonsson has also published two colour books of flora, a book with photographs of coastal landscapes, illustrations to a book of poetry and a new novel. He is a versatile person who is able to unite poetical nuances with objectivity.

—Rune Jonsson

JOSEPHSON, Kenneth.

Nationality: American. **Born:** Detroit, Michigan, 1 July 1932. **Education:** Eastern High School, Detroit, 1948-50; Rochester Institute of Technology, Rochester, New York, 1951-53, 1955-57, B.F.A. 1957; Institute of Design, Illinois Institute of Technology, Chicago, under Harry Callahan and Aaron Siskind, 1958-60, M.S. 1960. **Military Service:** Served in the United States Army, 1953-55. **Family:** Married Carol Compeau in 1954 (died, 1958); Sherrill Petro in 1960 (divorced, 1972); and Sally Garen in 1973 (divorced, 1978); children: Matthew, Bradley, and Anissa. **Career:** Photographer, Chrysler Corporation, Detroit, 1957-58. Freelance photographer, Chicago, since 1958. Professor, School of the Art Institute of Chicago, since 1961. Exchange Teacher, Konstfackskolan, Stockholm, 1966-67; Associate Professor, University of Hawaii, Honolulu, 1967-68; Visiting Professor, Institute of Design, Illinois Institute of Technology, 1969, Rhode Island School of Design, Providence, 1973, University of Minnesota, Minneapolis, 1974, and Tyler School of Art, Temple University, Philadelphia, 1975. **Recipient:** Guggenheim Fellowship, 1972; National Endowment for the Arts Grant, 1975, 1979. **Agents:** The Workshop Gallery, Visual Studies Workshop, 31 Prince Street, Rochester, New York 14607; and Young Hoffman Gallery, 215 West Superior Street, Chicago, Illinois 60610, U.S.A. **Address:** 2648 West 21st Place, Chicago, Illinois 60608, U.S.A.

Individual Exhibitions:

1966	Konstfackskolan, Stockholm
1971	Visual Studies Workshop, Rochester, New York
	Art Institute of Chicago
1973	State University of New York at Buffalo
	University of Rochester, New York
	Nova Scotia College of Design, Halifax
1974	291 Gallery, Milan
	University of Iowa, Iowa City
	College of Marin, Kentfield, California
1976	Cameraworks Gallery, Los Angeles
	Galerie die Brücke, Vienna
1977	Purdue University, Lafayette, Indiana
	Barat College, Lake Forest, Illinois
1978	Ulrich Museum of Art, Wichita, Kansas
	Neuberger Museum, Purchase, New York
	University of Southern Illinois, Carbondale
	Fotoforum der Gesamthochschule, Kassel, West Germany
	Gallery Sansmon, Moncton, New Brunswick
1979	P.P.S. Gallery, Hamburg
	The Photographers' Gallery, London
	Open Eye Gallery, Liverpool
1981	Young Hoffman Gallery, Chicago (with sculptor Bruce Nauman)
1982	Northwestern University Gallery, Evanston, Illinois (retrospective)
	Photo Gallery, Orange Coast College, Costa Mesa, California
1983	Museum of Contemporary Art, Chicago
	Northern Illinois University, DeKalb

Selected Group Exhibitions:

1964	*The Photographer's Eye,* Museum of Modern Art, New York
1967	*Photography in the 20th Century,* National Gallery of Canada, Ottawa (toured Canada and the United States, 1967-73)
1977	*The Photographer and the City,* Museum of Contemporary Art, Chicago
1978	*Mirrors and Windows: American Photography since 1960,* Museum of Modern Art, New York (toured the United States, 1978-80)
1979	*American Photography,* Art Institute of Chicago
1980	*A New Vision,* Light Gallery, New York
1983	*Subjective Vision,* High Museum of Art, Atlanta, Georgia

1984	*Exposed and Developed,* National Museum of American Art, Washington, D.C. (toured the United States)
1985	*American Images 1945-80,* Barbican Art Gallery, London (toured Britain)
1987	*Photography and Art 1946-86,* Los Angeles County Museum of Art

Collections:

Museum of Modern Art, New York; Joseph E. Seagram and Sons, New York; International Museum of Photography, George Eastman House, Rochester, New York; Museum of Fine Arts, Boston; Rhode Island School of Design, Providence; Art Institute of Chicago; Museum of Fine Arts, Houston; University of New Mexico, Albuquerque; Center for Creative Photography, University of Arizona, Tucson; University of California at Los Angeles; Bibliothéque Nationale, Paris.

Publications:

By JOSEPHSON: Books—*The Bread Book,* Chicago 1973; *Portfolio: Kenneth Josephson,* with an introduction by Alex Sweetman, Louisville, Kentucky 1975; *Underware,* portfolio, with others, Chicago 1976; *Kenneth Josephson,* postcard portfolio, New York 1980.

On JOSEPHSON: Books—*Photography Yearbook,* Stockholm 1968; *Looking at Photographs* by John Szarkowski, New York 1973; *The Photographer's Choice,* edited by Kelly Wise, Danbury, New Hampshire 1975; *The Photographer and the City,* exhibition catalog, by Gail Buckland, Chicago 1977; *Spaces,* exhibition catalogue, by Diana L. Johnson, Providence, Rhode Island 1978; *Chicago: The City and Its Artists 1945-1978* by Diane Kirkpatrick, Ann Arbor, Michigan 1978; *Mirrors and Windows,* exhibition catalogue, by John Szarkowski, New York 1978; *Kenneth Josephson: The Illusion of the Picture,* exhibition catalogue, by Floris Neusüss, Kassel, West Germany 1978; *Nude: Theory,* edited by Jain Kelly, New York 1979; *World Photography,* edited by Bryn Campbell, London 1981; *The Imaginary Photo Museum* by Helmut Gernsheim, Renate and L. Fritz Gruber, Cologne 1981, London 1982; *Exposed and Developed: Photography Sponsored by the National Endowment for the Arts,* exhibition catalogue, with text by Merry Amanda Foresta, Washington, D.C. 1984; *American Images: Photography 1945-1980,* edited by Peter Turner and John Benton-Harris, London 1985; *Photography and Art 1946-1986,* exhibition catalogue, by Andy Grundberg and Kathleen M. Gauss, Los Angeles 1987. **Articles**—"New American Imagery" in *Camera* (Lucerne), May 1974; "Reading the Bread Book" by Alex Sweetman in *Afterimage* (Rochester, New York), March 1974; "Photos Within Photographs" by Max Kozloff in *Artforum* (Oakland, California) 14 February 1976.

*

The heart of my method is this: a clue from one photograph leads to an idea for another. At times the subject matter suggests a method of working and vice versa. Sometimes I seek out some specific subject matter with a planned picture in mind, but as I become involved with the subject a very different picture may result.

While attempting to resolve an idea, I can never predict which source will supply the clue necessary for its completion. This clue might be furnished by the form and movement of the subject, a type or quality of light observed, an unrelated image viewed somewhere, some music, or a few words read or heard. The best procedure for me to follow is to involve myself completely with a number of problems, then move from one to another, and return to each for the purpose of re-evaluation. Time lapse is the most important factor in this procedure.

Many of my photographs are about the medium of photography, about how photography works. I have a group of images called the "History of Photography Series," which I began about 1970, and to which I've been adding ever since. In the "History Series" I sometimes make a picture in the style of another photographer. Sometimes the subject matter, by itself, carries the idea of someone's work. Then, too, many of the photographs have to do with photographic processes or historical movements; these are images that make a kind of off-handed reference to the evolution of the medium.

I would like to point out that I approach some of my work from a somewhat humorous point of view. I think that's been lacking in the history of photography. It's all too serious. Ultimately, my aim is to make a visual statement rather than a verbal statement about our medium because I think it is an important thing to do.

—Kenneth Josephson

*   *   *

The idea of making photographs about photography is a vital one that has taken numerous forms in the last two decades. The work of Kenneth Josephson examines the act of picture-making and the inherent paradox of photographic representation with humor and wit. From the fact that photographs are illusionistic representations of the exterior world, Josephson extracts comments upon the nature of that illusion and upon the relationship of the object to the object photographed. The automatic tendency of photographs to flatten space and the dissolution of scale when objects are juxtaposed are the basis of Josephson's most successful and widely reproduced images. Josephson describes the range of his pictures when he says, "My work is about the following: expressions of visual ideas made possible by the photographic medium; the special reality of photographs; humor and surrealism; chance and accident; manipulative photography; snapshots."

The pictures in which he uses already existing photographs address the issue of different levels of reality that can be represented at one time, on the same plane. Sometimes Josephson approaches the problem with utter simplicity as in his photograph of a brick wall with a picture of bricks taped to its center. There is no spatial illusion here; in the paucity of elements, one is drawn to the accuracy of scale reproduction between the bricks and the photograph of bricks and to the breakdown in the illusion, where a corner of the photo peels up off the wall, calling attention to its two-dimensional existence. However simple the concept, its illustrations are rich with variations in perspective, scale, illusionistic effect. A hand holds out a postcard view of a castle in Drottningholm, Sweden, comparing it to the actual castle, and despite radical shifts in scale, we have no trouble reading the image for what is going on. Josephson examines what we take for granted—the peculiarity of photographic language, and his point is not that photos lie but that the syntax of the language breaks down, flies apart, and yet still communicates. As Marshall McLuhan noted, photographs and pictures are the means whereby we know the world; one can hardly imagine what it would mean to be a visual illiterate. Thus, a picture of a ship sitting on the horizon of a "real" ocean signals no communication gap whatsoever.

Josephson diagrams this language further in his images that employ the vocabulary of snapshots. A shadow of a man appears to be holding a baby who is really lying on the ground. Taking the classic "mistakes" of amateur photographers, Josephson gives new artistic purpose to misjudged cropping, unsuspected shadows, and centrally placed compositions.

Many of the photographs employ two distinct modes of language, which may confound the meaning of the statement but, remarkably enough, do not confuse the viewer of the photograph. Josephson often uses the device of a hand intruding into the frame from the lower left—a pointing gesture, communication on its most rudimentary level, and yet this hand often holds a measuring tool, signalling the precise, sophisticated language of mathematics. However ludicrous we know the idea to be of measuring the Tetons with a twelve-inch ruler, Josephson makes some sense of it by reducing the comparison between the mountain range and a map of the mountain range to the two-dimensional space of a photograph. Any tourist who has ever photographed a companion holding up the tower of Pisa knows the gag, but Josephson has removed the gag to the realm of art photography and imbued an old joke with new meaning in terms of the medium and how we read it.

On many occasions photographers have expanded our appreciation of the world by looking more closely at something we usually ignore; Josephson continues in that tradition, not necessarily by examining the banal detail, but by taking apart the convention whereby we read and understand the visual documents of the physical world.

—Dana Asbury

JOYCE, Paul.

Nationality: British. **Born:** Winchester, Hampshire, 27 December 1940. **Education:** Dulwich College, London, 1950-59 and London School of Film Technique. **Family:** Two sons and a daughter. **Career:** Managing Director of Lucida Productions, filmmaker, writer and photographer. **Agent:** Witkin Gallery, 415 West Broadway, New York, New York 10012, U.S.A. **Address:** c/o Lucida Productions, 53 Greek Street, London W1V 5LR, England.

Individual Exhibitions:

1977	*Welsh Landscape,* Photographic Gallery, University of Southampton
1978	*Elders,* National Portrait Gallery, London
	Landscape, Galleria Il Diaframma, Milan
1980	*From Edge to Edge,* Photographic Gallery, Cardiff
1988	*New Photographic Work* (a joint show with David Hockney), Hamiltons Gallery, London

Selected Group Exhibitions:

1974	*New Photography,* Midland Group Gallery, Nottingham
1977	*Summer Show 4,* Serpentine Gallery, London
1978	*Singular Realities,* Side Gallery, Newcastle upon Tyne
	Faces and Facades, Institute of Contemporary Arts, London
1979	*9 Contemporary Photographers,* Witkin Gallery, New York
	The Native Land, Mostyn Gallery, Llandudno, Wales
1980	*British Art 1940-1980,* Hayward Gallery, London
	Contemporary British Photographers, Adelaide Festival of the Arts, Australia
1981	*Photographer as Printmaker,* Ferens Art Gallery, Hull, Yorkshire (travelled to the Museum and Art Gallery, Leicester; Cooper Gallery, Barnsley; Castle Museum, Nottingham; Photographers' Gallery, London)
1984	*La Photographie Créative,* Pavillon des Arts, Paris

Collections:

National Portrait Gallery, London; Victoria and Albert Museum, London; Tate Gallery, London; Department of the Environment, London; Welsh Arts Council, Cardiff; Bibliothèque Nationale, Paris.

Publications:

By JOYCE: Book—*From Edge to Edge,* Photographs of the Welsh Landscape, published by the Arts Council in association with the Welsh Arts Council, 1983; *Hockney on Photography,* Jonathan Cape, 1988. **Articles**—in *British Journal of Photography* (London), 19 November 1976; "Wider Still" in *Amateur Photographer* (London), 23 February 1977; "The Photographic Scene in London" in *Contemporary Review* (London), May 1978; "Questioning Landscape: On the Nature of Landscape Photography in General and the Work of Paul Joyce in Particular," interview, with Ainslie Ellis, in *British Journal of Photography* (London), 25 April 1980.

On JOYCE: Books—*Summer Show 4,* exhibition catalogue, by Aaron Scharf, London 1977; *Singular Realities,* exhibition catalogue, by Gerry Badger, Newcastle upon Tyne 1978; *Perspectives on Landscape,* edited by Bill Gaskins, London 1978; *9 Contemporary Photographers,* exhibition catalogue, New York 1979; *Photography Year Book 1979,* London 1979; *The Arts Council Collection,* catalogue, by Isobel Johnstone, London 1980; *Photographer as Printmaker,* exhibition catalogue, with texts by Gerry Badger, Peter C. Bunnell and Ansel Adams, London 1981; *La Photographie Créative* by Jean-Claude Lemagny, Paris 1984. **Articles**—in *Fotografia Italiana* (Milan), June 1977; "Elders" by Walter Nurnberg in *British Journal of Photography* (London), 20 January 1978.

*

Abandoned Building and Drainage Ditch, Eglwysfach, **1977.** Photograph ©Paul Joyce.

There is a primal human response to light, verging on the organic. Eyes, limbs, emotions move towards it. We bathe in it. Small wonder that artists struggle to capture its special qualities. For the photographer, who uses light as a constant tool in trade, the frustrations and rewards can be equally intense. Certain fine prints transmit light so brightly that it is painful to gaze at the source. Perhaps this is the reason so many photographers, who hate darkrooms, spend so much time in them. We practice alchemy with a cold light, and with fine silver as the ultimate goal.

—Paul Joyce

* * *

Paul Joyce began his working life in the Bank of England, became a film director, a theatre director, a writer of television plays, and a still photographer. Recently he directed four episodes of "Dr. Who" for the BBC. When it comes to photography, Paul Joyce told Ainslie Ellis in the *British Journal of Photography* (25 April 1980) that he was more interested in writers like Graham Greene and Thomas Hardy and Father G. M. Hopkins than in photographers. (He will speak only of Paul Nash and Bill Brandt.) He is divorced, has a venerable Morris Minor, has a conservative demeanour, and lives in the Borough of Chelsea in London.

Someone recently sent me a list of what he considered the purposes of reportorial prose: to entertain, amuse, assess, shed light, inform, pay homage and encourage thought. Most members of the Literary Merchants Sodality seem to "sink to the occasion" and write (with difficulty) about themselves only, offering little response to what they are supposedly considering. If you write about Harry Callahan's photography, then write as clear as a bell and light as a syllabub. His work *is light*—in all its engaging senses.

From this desk in the library at Corn Close, I regularly look out across the valley of the River Dee to a cluster of Scotch pines in a field of grass. The light in Dentdale, Cumbria is unusually dim and the pines are inconspicuous and unremarkable. But, let the late sun shine its rays up the dale—particularly in a month like October—and the trees become transfigured, with the forms of the foliage and the trunks and those of the elongated shadows endlessly fascinating to the eye. The air is as cool and palpable as amber. Everything is seen "in a new light." Which is what Paul Joyce's photographs are about—a turn-on, as they say.

Paul Joyce has photographed the landscape in Wales extensively, and also in Lancashire, and, recently, in Cumbria. He writes about light in his statement above. He says another useful thing: "I seldom think about photography, except when I'm doing it, and not much then, come to that. Life goes on around the camera, and you can't capture it all, not even with a panoramic."

An obviously active and attentive man. The mountains and the remote valleys should consider themselves lucky. To give Paul Joyce a last quote: "Have you ever noticed how we are much more concerned with people who ignore us, than those who listen to us with different degrees of intensity? I am obsessed with nature, for it never fails to offer me sublime indifference."

—Jonathan Williams

JUAN I-Jong.

Nationality: Taiwanese. **Born:** Tou-Cheng, I-Lan County, Taiwan, 20 July 1950. **Education:** Graduated from Tou-Cheng High School in 1968; self-taught in photography. **Family:** Married Yao-Yao Yuan in 1977; son: Sea. **Career:** Worked for *ECHO* magazine and started to photograph, 1972-74; worked for *Family* magazine as photo editor, 1975-81; worked as executive producer, scriptwriter, director, background music editor, film editor, producing weekly television documentaries, 1981-87. Established Juan's Darkroom Workshop, 1987. Teacher of photography in Fine Art Department of National College of Arts, 1988. Established *Photographers Publications,* 1990; established *Photographers International Magazine* (English and Chinese bilingual), 1992; established *Image Monthly* photo magazine, 1994. **Agent:** Photographers International Magazine, P.O. Box 39-1265, Taipei, Taiwan, R.O.C. **Address:** P.O. Box 39-1265, Taipei, Taiwan, R.O.C.

Individual Exhibitions:

1985   *Pei Pu,* Hsiung Shih Gallery, Taipei, Taiwan
         Pa Chih Men, Hsiung Shih Gallery, Taipei, Taiwan
1987   *Man and Land,* Hsiung Shih Gallery, Taipei, Taiwan (travelled to Hong Kong Arts Centre, 1988; Musée Français de la Photographie, Bièvres, France, 1990)
1988   *Taipei Rumour,* Hsiung Shih Gallery, Taipei, Taiwan
1990   *Szu Chi,* Hsiung Shih Gallery, Taipei, Taiwan

Taipei Rumor series, 1977. Photograph ©Juan I-Jong.

1993   Musée Nicéphore Niépce, Chalon-sur-Saône, France
        (retrospective)
1994   Galerie du Château d'Eau, Toulouse, France (retrospective)
        Provincial Museum of Taiwan, Taichung, Taiwan
        (retrospective)

Selected Group Exhibition:

1994   *Contemporary Photography from Mainland China, Hong Kong*
        and Taiwan, Hong Kong Arts Centre

Collections:

Musée d'Art Moderne de la Ville de Paris; Musée Français de la Photographie, Bièvres, France; Victoria and Albert Museum, London; Musée Nicéphore Niépce, Chalon-sur-Saône, France; Galerie du Château d'Eau, Toulouse, France; Taipei Museum of Arts; Taiwan Museum of Arts, Taichung.

Publications:

By JUAN: Books—*Twenty Eye-Witnesses of Humanity: An Introduction of Great Photographers,* Taipei 1985; *Pei Pu, Juan I-Jong Photographs,* exhibition catalogue, Taipei 1985; *Pa Chih Men, Juan I-Jong Photographs,* exhibition catalogue, Taipei 1985; *Man and Land, Juan I-Jong Photographs,* exhibition catalogue, Taipei 1987; *The Modern Photographers: An Introduction of 17 World Photographers,* Taipei 1987; *Taipei Rumour, Juan I-Jong Photographs,* exhibition catalogue, Taipei 1988; *Szu Chi, Juan I-Jong Photographs,* exhibition catalogue, Taipei 1990.

On JUAN: Articles—"Juan I-Jong's Eyes" by Paul Shackman in *Free China Review* (Taipei), 1984; "Taiwan's Cartier-Bresson" by Mark Holston in the *Washington Times,* July 1994.

*

To me, photography is photography; there is no need to categorize it. What I care about is whether my works surpass mere documentation and localism. I believe that the camera is an extension of the eye, a means through which a decisive moment can be captured. Other than serving as a testimony of his surroundings, photography is also a way of living for the photographer. Photography must go beyond simple reportage to affirm what it records. Every step of the process, beginning with the choice of subject, aperture, angle, etc., is an act of affirmation that each of us must take, consciously seeking an ideal, as in life, that asserts and affirms the value and meaning of what we shoot. My works are considered—and I agree—a testimony of the island of Taiwan, its change from an agricultural society to an industrial one. In *Man and Land,* I tried to extol the noble qualities man once had; in *Taipei Rumour,* I tried very hard to foreshadow the punishment that mankind will bring down on itself.

—Juan I-Jong

*   *   *

Juan I-Jong is a pure humanist who adheres stubbornly to documentary photography. He also possesses one of the rarest qualities among photographers—the ability to critically organise and edit his own works. Through the years Juan has concentrated on documenting the social phenomenon of Taiwan with great passion and insight. His discipline in always challenging his own limits resulted in numerous book publications and exhibitions since 1985. In recent years, Juan has also helped the promotion of photography in Taiwan by establishing Photographers Publications, a company that exclusively publishes photographic magazines.

But Juan's mission of social documentary started in the 1970s after he first landed himself a job with a magazine in Taipei at the time when the city was just going through the most critical period of urbanisation. This chaotic transformation from agricultural to industrial lifestyle stimulated Juan's urge to escape. For a country boy who resented every bit of his rural childhood experiences, Juan I-Jong considered the history of his photography a self-criticism of his growth. The photo essay *Man and Land* is an observation of the rural lifestyle Juan had rejected as a youth. These images taken during 1974-86 celebrate the joy of the artist as he rediscovered the love and affection of the land and the people with whom he grew up. The humanistic values of the farming community that shaped his early life contrast greatly with the alienation of Taipei city. Through his images we can learn about old Taiwanese beliefs and the lived experience of hardship, family values and, most importantly, attitudes to life which, in Juan's words "learned from the earth."

Man and Land may seem like a happy ending, but it did not stop Juan I-Jong from searching for the next creative statement. While the rural quality of life continued to inspire his creativity, Juan was also taken sadly by the "sickness" of Taipei city. In his collection *Taipei Rumor,* the ugliness of its chaotic infrastructure, traffic congestion, phoney architecture, industrial waste and pollution creeps out behind the glittering advertising billboards and neon signs with uncompromising realism. In a city where "money becomes the passport" as Juan described it, conspicuous consumption became the major characteristic of human values. The "rumor" behind this confusion of true and false values is cynically displayed by the large amount of psychological and social contradictions captured by Juan's camera. Despite his eagerness to criticise the failure of the city and its people, Juan I-Jong also found time to escape to the rural side of the country and photographed *Pei Pu* and *Pa Chih Men* between 1980-1985. But perhaps the most in-depth study among his works on rural Taiwan is the photo essay *Sze Chi*—an aboriginal tribe named Atayal located near I Lan—taken between 1981 and 1990. The honest portrayal of the life and destiny of these local people offer a contemplative pause in this new period of Taiwan's history.

—Becky Cho

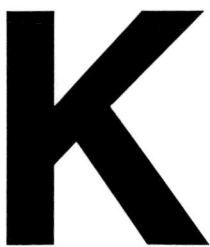

KALISHER, Simpson.

Nationality: American. **Born:** New York City, 27 July 1926. **Education:** Attended Christopher Columbus High School, Bronx, New York, 1939-43; Indiana University, Bloomington, 1943-44, 1946-48, B.A. in history 1948; self-taught in photography. **Military Service:** Served as an infantryman in the United States Army, in Germany, 1944-46; Corporal. **Family:** Married Ilse Kahn in 1954 (divorced, 1968); son: Jesse; married Colby Harris in 1968 (divorced 1989); children: Amy, David and Allon. **Career:** Freelance photographer, New York, since 1948. Secretary, American Society of Magazine Photographers, New York, 1962-63. **Recipient:** Book Award, and Design and Print Award, American Institute of Graphic Arts, 1961. **Agent:** Witkin Gallery, 415 West Broadway, New York, New York 10012; and Keith de Lellis, Fine Art Photography, 141 East 88 Street, New York. **Address:** 5 North Street, P.O. Box 202, Roxbury, Connecticut 06783, U.S.A.

Individual Exhibitions:

1961	Image Gallery, New York
1962	International Museum of Photography, George Eastman House, Rochester, New York
1963	Art Institute of Chicago
1980	Voltaire Gallery, New Milford, Connecticut
1984	*Railroad Men,* Akron Museum of Art

Selected Group Exhibitions:

1951	*Young Photographers,* Museum of Modern Art, New York
1958	*Photography at Mid-Century,* International Museum of Photography, George Eastman House, Rochester, New York (toured the United States)
1964	*Four Directions in Photography,* Albright-Knox Art Gallery, Buffalo, New York
1967	*History of the Picture Story,* Museum of Modern Art, New York
1968	*Harlem on My Mind,* Metropolitan Museum of Art, New York
	12 Photographers of the Social Landscape, Poses Institute, Waltham, Massachusetts
1975	*Photography in America,* Whitney Museum, New York
1978	*Discovering America,* Art Institute of Chicago
	Photography as Social Literature, Farmingham Valley Arts Center, Avon, Connecticut
	Mirrors and Windows: American Photography since 1960, Museum of Modern Art, New York (toured the United States, 1978-80)
1981	*American Children,* Museum of Modern Art, New York
	Summer Stock, Witkin Gallery, New York
1990	*Connecticut Craftsmen,* Pump House Gallery, Hartford, Connecticut
1994	*Poses and Gestures,* Museum of Modern Art, New York

Collections:

Museum of Modern Art, New York; International Museum of Photography, George Eastman House, Rochester, New York; Art Institute of Chicago; Milwaukee Museum of Art.

Publications:

By KALISHER: Books—*Railroad Men: Photographs and Collected Stories,* with an introduction by Jonathan Williams, New York 1961; *Propaganda and Other Photographs,* with an introduction by Russel Baker, and afterword by Allen Schoener, Danbury, New Hampshire 1977; illustrations for *Clinical Sociology* by Glassner and Freedman, New York and London 1979.

On KALISHER: Books—*12 Photographers of the American Social Landscape* by Thomas H. Garver, New York 1967; *Photography in America,* edited by Robert Doty, with an introduction by Minor White, New York and London 1974. **Article**—"Book Review: Railroad Men" by Hugh Edwards in *Infinity* (New York), March 1962.

*   *   *

Simpson Kalisher works out of his studio in Roxbury, Connecticut and makes a living from commercial jobs. To paraphrase Dr. Samuel Johnson: "Any man who takes photographs for reasons other than money is a fool." The only problem is that Kalisher's job-work has tended to obscure the fact that he is a fine ironist and political satirist with a camera, and that he is quite as much of an "art" photographer as, say, Robert Frank. Another problem that follows on from this, now that I think of it, is that it is hard to see many of his prints. He is not on view in many of the galleries where such excellent work might be expected.

Back in the early 1960s I wrote a note for his first book, *Railroad Men,* a sequence of photographs and prose vignettes, an extremely honest and discrete series of observations of an old-fashioned brotherhood of American working men. I liked the way Kalisher saw these (mostly) elderly men as practising a vocation, and that vocation carried with it the idea of service to the body politic. "The conductor and the Pullman porters have that inevitability of presence that the canon and acolytes of a cathedral have. They wear their vestments as a blazon of belief in what they are doing. It is completely tacit."

Kalisher's second book, *Propaganda* (my copy is unfortunately on a mountain in North Carolina while I sit here writing a few words in the Cumbrian Dales) is another matter: social comment, if you like. Plenty of wit and plenty of vitriol. A dark look at our parlous republic. Dark, but not sour. There is an admirable quiet and solemnity in the way Simpson Kalisher sees things. What makes me again think of Robert Frank is the fact that Kalisher is never some tub-thumping Marxist hack. He is never short on "pictorial values," though this is getting to be a sin in some critical quarters, particularly amongst those criticasters who can't hit the floor with their hat as regards literary values.

Mature photographers, unlike aging violinists, do not lose their tone. We need more books from Simpson Kalisher and more attention for a distinguished body of work. Can we afford to ignore photographers this good? We ignore pianists as stylish as Herbie Nichols. Yet, some of us fans vaguely remember "Piano Legs" Hickman, who committed no fewer than 91 errors while playing third base in 118 games for the New York Giants during the season of 1903. A funny country we live in.

—Jonathan Williams

***Untitled*, 1992.** Photograph by Simpson Kalisher.

KALLÁY, Karol.

Nationality: Czechoslovakian. **Born:** Cadca, Czechoslovakia, 26 April 1926. **Education:** Attended the High School of Technology, Bratislava, 1945-49, Dip.Ing. 1949; thereafter studied law for 3 years; self-taught in photography, but influenced by the work of Henri Cartier-Bresson, William Klein, Robert Frank and Bill Brandt. **Family:** Married Zdenka Soukupová in 1950; sons: Karol and Martin. **Career:** Freelance photographer, in Bratislava, since 1950: established studio, 1967; fashion photographer for *Moda*, Bratislava, since 1956, *Saison*, Berlin, 1960-72, *Jardin des Modes*, Paris, 1965-66, and *Sibylle*, Berlin, 1965-76. Member of Bilderberg agency, Hamburg; collaborator at *Geo* magazine, Hamburg. **Recipient:** *Popular Photography* Prize, New York, 1957; Most Beautiful Book on Czechoslovakia Prize, Ministry of Culture, Prague, 1972, 1973; Book Prize, *Internationale Buchausstellung*, Unesco, Leipzig, 1977, 1984. Fellow, Fédération Internationale de l'Art Photographique, 1970. **Agent:** Slovart. **Address:** Fándlyho 12, 80100 Bratislava, Slovakia.

Individual Exhibitions:

1956	Municipal Gallery, Bratislava
1960	Funke Gallery, Brno, Czechoslovakia
1961	Union of Artists Gallery, Bratislava
1965	Municipal Gallery, East Berlin
1967	Municipal Gallery, East Berlin
1968	Czechoslovak Cultural Centre, Baghdad
	Czechoslovak Cultural Centre, Cairo
1969	Czechoslovak Cultural Centre, Sofia
	Czechoslovak Cultural Centre, Budapest
1970	Czechoslovak Cultural Centre, Warsaw
	Czechoslovak Cultural Centre, Bucharest
	Czechoslovak Pavilion, at Expo '70, Osaka, Japan
1973	Municipal Gallery, Prague
	Municipal Gallery, Bratislava
	Lenin Library, Moscow
1974	Municipal Gallery, Bratislava
	Czechoslovak Cultural Centre, Sofia
	Czechoslovak Cultural Centre, Warsaw
1979	Galerie Stadt Berlin, East Berlin
1985	Galerie Grauwert, Hamburg
1986	Centre International de l'Art Modern, Paris
	Municipal Gallery, Bratislava
1989	*Armenia*, House of Czechoslovak-Soviet Friendship, Bratislava
1990	*Armenia*, Bratislava
1991	*Everyday in Albania*, Werkbund-Archiv, Berlin

Selected Group Exhibitions:

1960	*Contemporary Czechoslovak Photography*, travelling exhibition (toured the world, 1960-70)
1969	*Soucasna Ceskoslovenska Fotografie*, Moravian Gallery, Brno, Czechoslovakia
1973	*Ceskoslovenska Fotografie 1971/72*, Moravian Gallery, Brno, Czechoslovakia
	Lyric Sources in Czechoslovak Photography, SICOF, Milan, Italy
1979	*Tschechoslowakische Fotografie 1918-78*, Fotoforum, Kassel, West Germany
1988	*Slovak Photography of the 1980s*, Slovak Radio, Bratislava (travelled to Brno)
1989	*Roads of Czechoslovak Photography*, Municipal Gallery—House by the Stone Bell, Prague
	Czechoslovak Photography 1945-1989, Gallery Valdstejnska jizdarna, Prague
	Meeting 01, Gallery of the Union of Slovak Fine Artists, Bratislava
1990	*Slovak Photography of the 1960s*, House of Art, Bratislava
1991	*The Wild West*, exhibition of Bilderberg agency, Hamburg (travelled extensively throughout Europe)

	Slovak Photography, Industrial Palace, Prague
1992	*Unknown Slovakia*, exhibition of Bilderberg agency, Month of Photogrpahy 92, Slovak National Musuem, Bratislava (travelled throughout Europe)
1993	*Czech and Slovak Photography from Between the Wars to the Present*, Fitchburg Art Museum, Fitchburg, Massachusetts (travelled to Boston and Middlebury)

Collections:

Municipal Gallery, Brno, Czechoslovakia; Slovak National Gallery, Bratislava; Moravian Gallery, Brno.

Publications:

By KALLÁY: Books—*Slovak Rivers*, Martin, Czechoslovakia 1954; *Slovak National Theatre*, Bratislava 1961; *Italy Today*, London 1963; *Slovakia*, Prague 1963; *A Day of Wonders*, Bratislava 1963; *New York*, East Berlin 1967; *Mexico City*, East Berlin 1968; *Moscow*, Bratislava 1972; *Song of Slovakia*, Bratislava 1973; *The Slovak National Uprising 1944*, Bratislava 1974; *Venice*, East Berlin 1976; *Kolumbus in der Tatra*, Leipzig 1979; *Taschkent, Buchara, Samarkand*, East Berlin 1979; *Slovakia*, East Berlin 1980; *Just Stone and Wood*, Bratislava 1980; *Tokyo*, East Berlin 1982; *Los Angeles*, Leipzig 1983; *Peking*, Leipzig 1986; *Albanien*, with Erich Andres and Wolfgang Krolow, Berlin 1991; *Der Wilde Osten*, with Bilderberg agency, Schaffhausen, Switzerland 1991 (English edition under the title *Disorientations—Eastern Europe in Transition*, London 1992); *Die Hohe Tatra und Zipser Umland*, Würzburg, Germany 1992; *Slowakei*, Würzburg, Germany 1992; *Memories of the Slovak National Uprising*, Banska Bystrica, Slovakia 1994; *Die Unbekannte Slowakei (Unknown Slovakia)*, Bratislava 1994. **Article**—"It is a Long Way to Nachodka" in *Geo* (New York), April 1979 and in *Geo* (Paris), July 1980.

On KALLÁY: Books—*Licht und Schatten/Light and Shadow*, edited by Milos Hrbas, Prague 1959; *Karol Kalláy* by Lubor Kara, Prague 1963; *Die Geschichte der Fotografie im 20. Jahrhundert/Photography in the 20th Century* by Petr Tausk, Cologne 1977, London 1980; *Slovak Foto*, with text by Jaroslav Ciljak, Martin, Czechoslovakia 1980; *Karol Kalláy* by Ludovìt Hlaváč, Martin, Czechoslovakia 1983; *Encyclopédie internationale des photographes* by Michéle and Michel Auer, Hermance/Genéve 1985; *History of Photography* by Ludovit Hlavac, Martin, Slovakia 1987; *History of Slovak Photography* by Ludovit Hlavac, Martin, Slovakia 1989; *Roads of Czechoslovak Photography* by Daniel Mrazkova and Vladimir Remes, Prague 1989; *Slovak Photography of the 1960s*, exhibition catalogue by Vaclav Macek 1990; *Czech and Slovak Photography from Between the Wars to the Present*, exhibition catalogue by Vaclav Macek, Antonin Dufek and Vladimir Bigus, Boston 1994. **Articles**—"Karol Kalláy" by Petr Tausk in *Fotografie* (Prague), no. 3, 1981; "Karol Kállay: Los Angeles" by Vladimir Birgus in *Revue Fotografie* (Prague), no. 1, 1986; "Gulliver's fotoaparatem" by Vladimir Remes and "Kallayovo Theatrum vitae" by Anna Gregorova in *Ceskoslovenska fotografie* (Prague), no. 1, 1987.

*

Through my photographs I have always tried to express what I really saw and felt. I saw people in their happiness and misery, in their wealth and poverty.

I always took up an attitude, according to my heart, reason, feelings and morals.

—Karol Kalláy

*   *   *

Only a relatively small number of well-known photographers can be said to be all-rounders in their choice of themes, genres and images. Karol Kalláy is one of these rather exceptional personalities. In his native country Kalláy was known mainly as a top fashion photographer, but he feels offended if anyone attempts to characterize him by so restrictive a label. Besides his fashion work, Kalláy has always been strongly attracted by spontaneous photography, and his greatest joy has been in preparing picture volumes about life in various countries.

When reacting creatively to vivid situations, his approach is based on coming as near as possible to events: he often uses a camera equipped with a wide angle lens. Of no less importance is his sense for the typical in the actions of people in different parts of the world: he is gifted with an ability to record his discoveries in images of great immediacy. It could be said that he belongs to that group of photographers who are specialists in capturing actions that are indicative yet, in fact, reveal nothing extraordinary happening.

Kalláy seems to grasp very well the most important aspect of each different genre of photography. He is as adept at portraying the interesting situation in his "live" images as he is in creating the best formal arrangements in his landscapes.

Kalláy is accustomed to photographing both indoors and outdoors. He maintains a very well equipped studio in which he makes portraits and fashion photographs. From time to time, too, he likes to experiment by using various attachments to his lenses—sometimes bought, sometimes constructed by himself. He wants to search through all the possibilities that photography offers. He is as active in black and white as in colour, and he obviously respects the inherent nature of each medium. He is, in short, an enthusiast. And, like most all-rounders, Kalláy often uses experiences gained in one genre in other genres, in appropriately modified form. Thus, he enriches his work with a surprising freshness.

From the late 1970s, Kalláy has been preoccupied with taking photos for the geographical magazine *Geo* and for a number of illustrated books—an activity he feels gives the best expression to his vision of the world and enables him to react to new environments. More and more, he has focussed on the excitement generated in immediate response to place, time and situation which he communicates to the viewer through his use of both single shot and image sequences.

—Petr Tausk

KALVELIS, Jonas.

Nationality: Lithuanian. **Born:** Kupiskio district, 11 March 1925. **Education:** Studied land organization at the Agricultural Training College, Kaunas, Lithuania, 1953-58; mainly self-taught in photography. **Family:** Married Brone Davolyte in 1958 (divorced, 1971); daughter: Rasa. **Career:** Worked as a technician for the Institute of Forestry of the Lithuanian SSR, Kaunas, 1948-54. Since 1954, Head of the Photo Laboratory, Institute of Planning of Water Resources, Kaunas. **Recipient:** Artist Award, 1976, and Silver Medal, 1977, Federation Internationale de l'Art Photographique (FIAP); Grand Prize, *Amber Land* exhibition, Siauliai, Lithuania, 1977; FNSPF Diploma, *Auteurop '78* exhibition, Paris, 1978; Ministry of Foreign Affairs Medal, *Phot-Univers* exhibition, Bievres, France, 1978; Ifo-Scanbaltic Medal, Rostock, East Germany, 1982. **Address:** c/o (agent) Photographic Art Society of Lithuanian SSR, Universiteto 4, Vilnius 232600, Lithuania. **Died:** (in Kaunas) *27 June 1987.*

Individual Exhibitions:

1974	Photo Salon, Plovdiv, Bulgaria
1975	Photography Salon, Vilnius, Lithuania (travelled to Riga, Leningrad and Moscow)
1979	Palace of Culture, Gorzow, Poland
	Photo Museum, Siauliai, Lithuania
1980	Art Research Institute, Moscow
1985	Photo Gallery, Vilnius, Lithuania

Selected Group Exhibitions:

1973	*Europaische Fotografen,* Rathaus, Charlottenburg, West Berlin
1974	*Trenutak Covjeka,* Fotoklub Maglaj, Yugoslavia
1975	*Fotoforum,* Palace of Culture, Ruzomberok, Czechoslovakia
1976	*IFO-Scanbaltic,* Exhibition Gallery, Rostock, East Germany

1977	*Salon Mondiale de Photographie,* Virton, Belgium
1978	*Auteurop,* Cheminot-Montparnasse, Paris
	Phot-Univers, Musée Français de la Photographie, Bievres, France
1980	*Lithuanian Photography,* The Photographers' Gallery, London
1983	*Fotografie aus Litauen,* Dusseldorf, West Germany
1986	*Salon d'Auteur,* Dijon, France

Collections:

Photography Museum, Siauliai, Lithuania; Musée Français de la Photographie, Bievres, France; Bibliothèque Nationale, Paris; International Center of Photography, New York; Photo Art Society of Lithuanian SSR, Vilnius.

Publications:

By KALVELIS: Book—*Jonas Kalvelis,* with an introduction by Algirdas Gaizutis, Kaunas, Lithuania 1975.

On KALVELIS: Book—*Lietuvos Fotografija,* with an introduction by Romualdas Pacesa, Vilnius, Lithuania 1978. **Article**—"Moment of New Truth" by Viktor Diomin in *Sovietskoye Photo* (Moscow), December 1978.

*

Nature is by itself the author of its own art. The task is to be able to notice it and convey it to others.

—Jonas Kalvelis

*   *   *

Some photographers work continuously and for years on the same subject, developing it and varying it—as musicians who have mastered their instruments may work and re-work their interpretations of particular compositions. In photography such orientation may create not only mastery but also an ability to convey, within the favorite subject, the photographer's inner nature and devotion.

Nature, the environment without people, has been Jonas Kalvelis's main subject. As photos of nature predominate in his work, it is not unfair to call him a "nature photographer." Forests, trees, snowy valleys and sand drifts—they are the environments in which Kalvelis feels at home—as part of the whole, as someone who comes very close to his trees and flowers to study them in detail. Characteristically, he focusses on one part of the whole, and the result is always the opposite of the accidental: the photos are well-composed, purposeful, perfect in their black-and-white tonality. Kalvelis's purity of feeling toward nature expresses itself in the outward appearance of the photos, in a graphic style that stresses his sincerity and at the same time suggests the specific form from within the general. What might be called Kalvelis's intimate relations with nature are so beautiful and so precisely conveyed that they can be enjoyed by those who view his work as well.

If his favorite subject is the forest, then his second love must surely be the sand dunes of the wildlife preserve on the western coast of Lithuania. His great masterpiece of recent years (which has put him in the avant-garde of Lithuanian photographers) is the series *Sand Drifts in Neringa.* In his photos of the dunes we have Kalvelis's characteristic stance—not the cold, emotionless observer but the conveyor of secrets and realities not revealed in the work of his predecessors. These secrets—the essence of the dunes—are not profound; they are available to anyone who pauses for longer than the casual passer-by, who looks for textures, who observes from above or below—the observer, in short, who takes the time to look.

Kalvelis is not just a recorder of the beauty of the simple forms of nature; because of his absolute devotion to his subject, he preserves beauty at the same time that he conveys the joy of discovery.

—Peeter Tooming

KANE, Art.

Nationality: American. **Born:** Arthur Kanofsky in the Bronx, New York City, 9 April 1925. **Education:** Attended New York public schools; studied photography at the Cooper Union, New York, 1940-41, 1946-50. **Military Service:** Served in the United States Army, in Europe, 1942-45. **Family:** Twice married and divorced: sons: Jonathan and Anthony. Layout Designer, *Esquire* magazine, New York, 1950-52; Art Director, *Seventeen* magazine, New York, 1952-56; Art Director, Irving Serwer Advertising Agency, New York, 1956-59; freelance advertising, magazine and television photographer, working for *Look, Life, McCall's, Vogue, Queen,* etc., in New York, 1959-73; Corporate Design Director, *Penthouse* and *Viva* magazines, New York, 1973-74; resumed freelance career, 1975. **Agent:** Staley-Wise Gallery, 560 Broadway, New York, New York 10012, U.S.A.

Individual Exhibitions:

1994   *Art Kane: A Life in Photography,* Staley-Wise Gallery, New York

Selected Group Exhibitions:

1981   *Dog Show No. 1,* Nikon Fotogalerie, Zurich
         Farbe im Photo, Josef-Haubrich-Kunsthalle, Cologne
1985   *Das Aktfoto,* Fotomuseum im Stadtmuseum, Munich (toured West Germany)

Publications:

By KANE: Books—*The Persuasive Image: Art Kane,* with text by John Poppy, Los Angeles and London 1975; *The Great Cities: Rio de Janeiro,* with text by Douglas Botting, New York 1978; *Rare Images: A View J & B,* with text by Clive Sinclair, Zurich 1981. **Articles**—"Too Many Photographers—Too Many Photographs" in *Infinity* (New York), June 1963; "Art Kane," interview, in *Zoom* (Madrid), no. 14, 1978; "Art Kane; I Love Marcella," interview, with Jeanne Brody, in *Camera 35* (New York), May 1978.

On KANE: Books—*Über das Schöpferische in der Photographie* by L. Fritz Gruber, Cologne 1966; *Photographic Communication,* edited by R. Smith Schuneman, London and Toronto 1972; *Geschichte der Fotografie im 20. Jahrhundert/Photography in the 20th Century* by Petr Tausk, Cologne 1977, London 1980; *The Vogue Book of Fashion Photography* by Polly Devlin, with an introduction by Alexander Liberman, London 1979; *The History of Fashion Photography* by Nancy Hall-Duncan, New York 1979, as *Histoire de la Photographie de Mode,* Paris 1979; *Farbe im Photo: die Geschichte der Farbphotographie von 1861 bis 1981* by Fritz Binder, Gert Koshofer, Rolf Sachsse and others, Cologne 1981. **Article**—"Art Kane" by Jacob Deschin in *Popular Photography* (New York), September 1965.

*   *   *

Possibly Art Kane was not the first "Pop" photographer, but only the most famous and the most important. He was Pop in admitting straight away that he was not trying to record the *real* world (if such a thing should exist) in his photographs. He was Pop in simplifying his graphic approach to reproduce bold, simple, direct images, often using bright colours. He was Pop in his willingness to try new lenses (extreme wide-angles and telephotos), to make montages, double-exposures, slide sandwiches . . . "anything goes." He was also Pop in the literal sense, in that he quickly became associated with the musicians of the Swinging 60s, photographing many of them and even illustrating their songs. He photographed Bob Dylan, The Who, Jefferson Airplane (*Life* cover, June 28, 1968) and many more. He illustrated Beatles songs ("A Day in the Life," "Strawberry Fields," "Eleanor Rigby") and Dylan songs ("Blowing in the Wind," "With God on Our Side," "Lay Lady Lay") and many others.

This was a flowering of his first involvement with professional photography. His first assignment was for *Esquire* in 1957: photographing the great jazz-men. He did it brilliantly and it won him the first of many awards. One of the jazz-men was Louis Armstrong. Kane flew him, and an old rocking chair, into the desert and photographed him against the setting sun—a shot inspired by the song "Old Rockin' Chair." Of course it was set up, and of course it was corny, but there was one over-riding factor: *it worked.*

Kane applied himself to advertising and editorial work in similar ways after that, for major clients and the great picture magazines such as *Life, Look, Twen, Vogue* and *McCall's.* Like any commercial artist, he illustrated things. He drew roughs, he manipulated colours, he did what needed doing to make it new. What he did was important because he thought big thoughts and executed them in ways that would reach a big audience. On rare occasions he might tackle reportage work. He once did a feature on truck drivers for *Esquire.* Earlier he had entitled one of his talks "Color Is a Liar!" Not surprisingly he insisted on shooting the feature in black and white.

With benefit of hindsight, one sees that one of his most successful projects was photographing "The Waters of Venice" for *Look.* His approaches ran from the sublime—using a slide sandwich to turn St. Mark's Square into a closed world—to the ridiculous—clogging up a canal with 200 dead pigeons. The "lead" picture of Venice drowning is unforgettable.

In the early 1970s he returned to his original profession—art director—joining *Penthouse* and *Viva* magazines. It turned out to be not the right job for him. Better forgotten now are the exotic "public hairstyles" (worn by Penthouse Pets) which Kane photographed in closeup, and also the "copulation sequence" in a kitchen, which has unfortunately been preserved in the pretentious *Masterpieces of Erotic Photography* collection. However, when he returned to photography it was with renewed vigour. He opened a new studio in 1975 and equipped it with flash—previously he had been known as an available light photographer. Later, working with a new model called Marcella he produced a particularly imaginative portfolio of new work, much of it taken outside at night with hand-held flash.

In spite of all this, it remains difficult to form a just opinion of Art Kane's work: so many of the ideas he pioneered were picked up immediately by other photographers, who promptly worked them to death. Only one of his pictures seems to have been permanently added to the national consciousness, and that is "Star Spangled Banner." It shows the Stars and Stripes dominating the frame, with a thin strip of sky and a group of young people at the top of the frame. The shot was taken for *Look* in 1962 to illustrate the preamble to the American Constitution ("We the people . . . "). The shot has been much mauled by imitators, but it survives.

Nor does Kane seem to have produced any worthwhile personal work during his commercial career. It seems strange that a man who is internationally recognized as an important photographer, and who has had a major influence on commercial photography for over 25 years, should not have produced a definitive work to preserve his memory.

—Jack Schofield

KARSH, Yousuf.

Nationality: Canadian. **Born:** Mardin, Armenia, Turkey, 23 December 1908; emigrated to Canada, 1924: naturalized, 1946. **Education:** Attended public school, Sherbrooke, Montreal, 1925; studied photography under the portrait photographer John H. Garo, Boston, 1928-31. **Family:** Married Solange Gauthier in 1939 (died, 1961); married Estrellita Maria Nachbar in 1962. **Career:** Worked as an assistant in his uncle's portrait photography studio, Sherbrooke, Montreal, 1926-28. Established the Karsh Studio, Ottawa, specializing in portrait photography, since 1932; industrial photographer for Atlas Steel Ltd., Wellington, Ontario, 1950-51, and for Ford of Canada Ltd., 1951. Visiting Professor of Photography, Ohio University, Athens, 1967-69; Visiting Professor of Fine Arts, Emerson College, Boston, 1972-73, 1973-74. Photographic Adviser, *Expo '70,* Osaka, Japan. Trustee, Photographic Arts and Sciences Foundation, since 1970. **Recipient:** Canada Council Medal, 1965; Canadian Centennial Medal, 1967; Master of Photographic Arts Award, Professional Photographers Association of Canada, 1970; U.S. Presidential Citation, 1971; First Gold Medal, National Association of Photographic Art, 1974; President's Cabinet Annual Award, University of Detroit, 1979; Achievement in Life Award, *Encyclopaedia Britannica,* 1980. LL.D.: Queen's University, Kingston, Ontario, 1960; Carleton University, Ottawa, 1960; D.H.L.: Dartmouth College, Hanover, New Hampshire, 1961; Ohio University, Athens, 1966; Mount Allison University, Sackville, New Brunswick, 1968; Emerson College, Boston, 1969; D.C.L.: Bishop's University, Lennoxville, Quebec, 1969; D.F.A.: University of Massachusetts, Amherst, 1979; University of Hartford, Connecticut, 1980; Tufts University, Medford, Massachusetts, 1981. Honorary Fellow, Royal Photographic Society, London, 1970; Member, Royal Canadian Academy of Arts, 1975. O.C. (Officer, Order of Canada), 1968. **Address:** Chateau Laurier Hotel, Suite 660, Ottawa, Ontario KIN 8S7, Canada.

Individual Exhibitions:

1959   National Gallery of Canada, Ottawa
1967   *Men Who Make Our World,* at the Canadian Pavilion, *Expo
         '67,* Montreal(toured Canada, the United States and Europe,
         1967-81; entire exhibition acquired by the Museum of
         Modern Art, Tokyo; National Gallery of Australia, Canberra;
         and the Province of Alberta)
1973   Santa Barbara Museum of Art, California (with Margaret
         Bourke-White)
1980   Zeit-Foto Salon, Tokyo
1983   International Center of Photography, New York (retrospective)
1984   Photographic Museum, Helsinki
         Flint Institute of Arts, Michigan (retrospective)
         Imprimatur Gallery, Minneapolis
         Scottish National Portrait Gallery, Edinburgh

Selected Group Exhibitions:

1967   *Photography in the 20th Century,* National Gallery of Canada,
         Ottawa (toured Canada and the United States, 1967-73)
1977   *Fotografische Künstlerbildnisse,* Museum Ludwig, Cologne
1978   *The Quality of Presence,* Lunn Gallery, Washington, D.C.
1979   *Life: The First Decade 1936-45,* Grey Art Gallery, New York
         University
         *Photographie als Kunst 1879-1979/Kunst als Photographie
         1949-1979,* Tiroler Landesmuseum, Innsbruck, Austria
         (travelled to the Neue Galerie am Wolfgang Gurlitt Museum,
         Linz, Austria; Neue Galerie am Landesmuseum Joanneum,
         Graz, Austria; and the Museum des 20. Jahrhunderts,
         Vienna)
1980   *The Imaginary Photo Museum,* Kunsthalle, Cologne
1982   *Lichtbildnisse: Das Porträt in der Fotografie,* Rheinisches
         Landesmuseum, Bonn
1984   *Sammlung Gruber,* Museum Ludwig, Cologne

Collections:

Government of Alberta; National Gallery of Canada, Ottawa; Museum of Modern Art, New York; Metropolitan Museum of Art, New York; International Museum of Photography, George Eastman House, Rochester, New York; Art Institute of Chicago; St. Louis Art Museum; National Portrait Gallery, London; Museum of Modern Art, Tokyo; Museum Ludwig, Cologne.

Publications:

By KARSH: Books—*Faces of Destiny,* New York and London 1946; *This Is the Mass,* with text by Henri Daniel-Rops and Fulton J. Sheen, New York and Kingswood, Surrey 1958, and with text by Henri Daniel-Rops and Paul-Emile Cardinal Leger, Paris 1959; *Portraits of Greatness,* London, Toronto and New York 1959; *This Is Rome,* with text by Fulton J. Sheen and H.V. Morton, New York 1959, Kingswood, Surrey 1960; *This Is the Holy Land,* with text by Fulton J. Sheen and H.V. Morton, New York 1960, Kingswood, Surrey 1961; *In Search of Greatness: Reflections of Yousuf Karsh* (autobiography), Toronto and New York 1962, London 1963; *These Are the Sacraments,* with text by Fulton J. Sheen, New York 1962; *The Warren Court,* with text by John P. Frank, New York 1965; *Karsh Portfolio,* Toronto and New York 1967; *Faces of Our Time,* Toronto 1971; *Karsh Portraits,* Toronto and Boston 1976;

Karsh Canadians, Toronto 1978; *Karsh: A Fifty-Year Retrospective,* exhibition catalogue, Boston, New York and London 1983. **Article**—interview in *Interviews with Master Photographers* by James Danziger and Barnaby Conrad III, New York and London 1977.

On KARSH: Books—*Fame: Famous Portraits of Famous People by Famous Photographers,* edited by L. Fritz Gruber, London and New York 1960; *Photographs of Yousuf Karsh: Men Who Make Our World,* exhibition catalogue, Montreal 1967; *Photography in the 20th Century* by Nathan Lyons, New York 1967; *Fotografische Künstlerbildnisse,* exhibition catalogue, by Dieter Ronte, Evelyn Weiss and Jeane von Oppenheim, Cologne 1977; *Faces: A Narrative History of the Portrait in Photography* by Ben Maddow, Boston 1977; *Life: The First Decade 1936-1945* by Robert Littman, Ralph Graves and Doris C. O'Neill, New York 1979, London 1980; *Photographie als Kunst 1879-1979/Kunst als Photographie 1949-1979,* exhibition catalogue, 2 volumes, by Peter Weiermair, Innsbruck 1979; *Lichtbildnisse: Das Porträt in der Fotografie,* edited by Klaus Honnef, Cologne 1982; *Master Photographers: The World's Great Photographers on Their Art and Technique,* edited by Pat Booth, London 1983; *The Library of World Photography: Portraits,* with introduction by Colin Ford, Tokyo and London 1983; *Contemporary Canadian Photography* by Martha Langford, Edmonton, Alberta 1984. **Articles**—"A Collection of Photographs" in *Aperture* (Millerton, New York), Fall 1969; "Karsh of Ottawa" in *Image* (Rochester, New York), no. 1, 1973; "Karsh of Ottawa" by G. Hughes in *Amateur Photographer* (London), 4 December 1974; "The Many Faces of Yousuf Karsh" by Adrian Waller in the *Reader's Digest* (New York), December 1976; "Yousuf Karsh, Photographer: The Legend Who Captures Legends" by Hank Whittemore in *Parade* (New York), 3 December 1978.

*

    One of the questions I am asked more frequently is why my best known portraits tend to be those of famous persons, rather than of ordinary people whose faces might provide interesting studies for their own sake. It is true that the photographs that have given me the greatest satisfaction are, with a few notable exceptions, those of people of consequence, although by no means of consequence in the same field or for the same reason. They have included scientists, labour leaders, captains of industry, physicians, film stars, directors, composers, statesmen, clergymen, military leaders, princes and presidents. I have also been interested in the "common man," and have made countless photographs of people of all kinds. But I have not as a rule felt the same challenge when photographing people who have made no special contribution, good or bad, to the world. In fact, my reactions to these people are probably quite similar to the reactions of viewers and readers. I seriously doubt if the interpretation of an unknown face is likely to have interest equal to that of a known personality, either to a photographer or to those who view his work. The best proof of this is that my portraits of famous people are better known than any of my other photographs.

    My quest in making a photograph is for a quality that I know exists in the personality before me, for what I sometimes call the "inward power"; and I am more anxious to capture that, or at least to interpret it to my own satisfaction, than I am to create the facsimile of an interesting figure with no depth of soul. Candid portraiture often has unposed, human interest, but I am seeking more than a study of physical features for their own sake—sometimes this could even be accomplished by using professional models. I am hoping to capture abstract virtues or traits of personality, and I concentrate all my efforts to accomplish this when taking a photograph. Before I begin, I will have studied my subject to the best of my ability, and within broad limits know what I am hoping to find, and what I hope to be able to interpret successfully. The qualities that have attracted me to the subject are those that will satisfy me if I can portray them in the photograph, and that will most probably satisfy viewers of the picture as well. My personal interest in ordinary people is unlimited, but I am fascinated by the challenge of portraying true greatness adequately with my camera.

    Steichen was seeking something quite different when he brought together that unforgettable exhibition *The Family of Man.* This was not a collection of portraits, but was a highly successful record of interpretations of human emotions, and human interests.

    I believe that it is the artist's job to accomplish at least two things—to stir the emotions of the viewer and to lay bare the soul of his subject. When my own emotions have been stirred, I hope I can succeed in stirring those of others. But it is the mind and soul of the personality before my camera that interests me most, and the greater the mind and soul, the greater my interest.

I think it was Bernard Shaw who first observed that even a genius is 98% ordinary. It is the task of the photographer to bring out the remaining 2%. When one sees that residuum of greatness before one's camera, one must recognize it in a flash. There is a brief moment when all there is in a man's mind and soul and spirit may be reflected through his eyes, his hands, his attitude. This is the moment to record. This is the elusive "moment of truth."

—Yousuf Karsh

* * *

In 1918 the massacres in his home town of Mardin, in the Armenian part of Turkey, forced young Yousuf Karsh to flee his native land. He went to Canada to live with his uncle, a studio portrait photographer who introduced his nephew to the rudiments of the profession. A three-year apprenticeship to John H. Garo of Boston, a portrait photographer and fellow Armenian who Karsh remembers as a "stimulating and inspiring teacher," completed his photographic education. In 1931 Karsh returned to Canada, and after briefly debating whether to study surgery, opened the portrait studio in Ottawa that would earn him the world-wide reputation: "Karsh of Ottawa."

Yousuf Karsh has devoted his photographic career to making portraits of famous and powerful leaders of his time. When he first set up his studio, Ottawa was a small but fast-growing city, and Karsh saw to it that his business grew at the same rate. Political connections made a crucial difference. His skill as a portrait photographer was acclaimed by the Governor-General's son, which led to introductions to (and commissions from) members of the government and visiting dignitaries. The Prime Minister, a friend and patron, arranged for Karsh perhaps the most important sitting of his career—with Sir Winston Churchill. This portrait, the result of a two minute session, shows a tough Churchill, leaning forward slightly, with a hard determined look in his eye and a clenched jaw. The picture became symbolic of the British people's indomitable fighting spirit, and it brought Karsh great fame.

Karsh's career of documenting fame and power through portraits of world leaders was launched. The Canadian Government asked him to go to England to do a series of portraits of British wartime leaders. On assignment from *Life* Karsh photographed American war leaders. In 1946, at the close of World War II, Karsh published his first book, *Faces of Destiny*, a collection of portraits of the men who had taken the Allies to victory.

After the war ended, Karsh's interests expanded beyond military and political leaders. He has photographed "people of consequence" who have made a major contribution to the world. His subjects are leaders in all fields: science, industry, the arts, politics, education, sports, religion. Sometimes he travels half-way around the world for a half-hour sitting.

As a portraitist, Karsh's style is formal. He uses light to model the faces before his camera in a sculptural way, rendering the human presence monumental. Karsh in a consummate craftsman. His compositions are tight and exact. The backgrounds used are simple and often solid black. No props or decorations detract from the direct approach to the subject. Karsh's portraits are visual idealizations of the public image and legend of the individuals who confront his camera.

—Sarah Putnam

KAWADA, Kikuji.

Nationality: Japanese. **Born:** Ibaragi Prefecture, 1 January 1933. **Education:** Rikkyo High School, Tokyo, 1948-51; studied economics at Rikkyo University, Tokyo, 1951-55, A.B.D. 1955; self-taught in photography. **Family:** Married Nakako Ohnuki in 1957; son: Norio. **Career:** Freelance photographer since 1959, working for *Shinchosha Art Magazine,* and some speciality camera magazines and press, etc., Tokyo. **Address:** 3-8 Ichigaya-sadoharachyo, Shinjukuku, Tokyo 162, Japan.

Individual Exhibitions:

1959	*The Sea,* Fuji Photo Salon, Ginza, Tokyo
1961	*The Map,* Fuji Photo Salon, Ginza, Tokyo
1968	*Sacré Atavism,* Nikon Salon, Ginza, Tokyo
1976	Shadai Gallery, Shinjuku, Tokyo
1984	*Nude and Ludwig der zwei Collection,* Photo Gallery International, Tokyo
1986	*Los Caprichos,* Photo Gallery International, Toranomon, Tokyo

Selected Group Exhibitions:

1957	*10 Photographers' Eyes,* Konishiroku Gallery, Ginza, Tokyo
1962	*"Non" Exhibition,* Matsuya Department Store, Ginza, Tokyo
1963	*Contemporary Japanese Photographs,* National Museum of Modern Art, Tokyo
1974	*New Japanese Photography,* Museum of Modern Art, New York
1977	*Neue Fotografie aus Japan,* Kulturhaus der Stadt, Graz, Austria, (travelled to Museum des 20. Jahrhunderts, Vienna)
1979	*Japan: A Self-Portrait,* International Center of Photography, New York
1982	*38 Japanese Photographers,* Zeit-Foto Salon, Tokyo
1985	*Paris, New York, Tokyo,* Tsukuba Photo Museum '85 Tsukuba, Ibaragi Prefecture
1986	*L'Art Japonais du XXème Siecle,* Centre Georges Pompidou, Paris
	World of Super Image, Shibuya, Seibu, Seed Hall, Tokyo
1988	*8 Japanese Photographers,* Photo Gallery International, Tranomon, Tokyo
1989	*Photographie Japonaise,* Provincial Museum, Netherlands
1990	*Eye of déjà-vu,* Heineken Village, Shibuya, Tokyo
1991	*Beyond Japan: Photo Theatre,* Barbican Art Gallery, London
	Photographs in Japan 1955-1966, Museum of Modern Art, Yamaguchi Pref.

Collections:

Museum of Modern Art, New York; Princeton University, New Jersey; Kawasaki City Museum, Kanagawa Prefecture, Japan; Nippon University, Tokyo; Shadai Gallery, Tokyo; Georges Pompidou Centre, Paris; Tokyo Metropolitan Museum of Photography; Yamaguchi Pref; Tama Art University Museum, Tokyo.

Publications:

By KAWADA: Books—*The Map,* Tokyo 1965; *Sacré Atavism,* Tokyo 1971; *Cosmos of the Dream King, Ludwig II,* Tokyo 1979; *The Nude,* portfolio, Tokyo 1984.

On KAWADA: Books—*Essays on Contemporary Photography* by Nobuya Yoshimura, Tokyo 1970; *New Japanese Photography,* exhibition catalogue, by John Szarkowski and Shoji Yamagishi, New York 1974; *Neue Fotografie aus Japan,* exhibition catalogue, by Otto Breicha, Graz and Vienna 1977; *Nude Photographs of Japan,* with text by Shiroyasu Suzuki, Tokyo 1981; *38 Japanese Photographers,* exhibition catalogue, edited by Zeit-Foto Salon, Tokyo 1982. **Articles**—"Kikuji Kawada" by Tatsuo Fukushima in *Camera Age* (Tokyo), October 1966; "Kikuji Kawada" by Arthur Goldsmith in *Popular Photography* (New York), June 1975; "Zu Kikuji Kawada Foto-Serie 'Los Caprichos' " by Otto Breicha in *Protokolle* (Vienna), no. 1, 1977.

*

A Floating Fish, from the series *Los Caprichos,* Tokyo 1975. Photograph ©Kikuji Kawada.

I seek for the analogical power and the enlargement of consciousness in photography.

—Kikuji Kawada

KEETMAN, Peter.

Nationality: German. **Born:** Wuppertal-Elberfeld, 27 April 1916. **Education:** Attended the Gymnasium, Wuppertal-Elberfeld, 1926-29, the Hindenburg-Realgymnasium, Wuppertal, 1929-32, Landschulheim, Schondorf am Ammersee, 1932-34, and the Deutsches Kolleg, Bad Godesberg, 1934-35; studied photography, under Hans Schreiner, Bayerische Staatslehranstalt für Photographie, Munich, 1935-37, 1947-48, M. Photog. 1948; also studied in the master-class of Adolf Lazi, Stuttgart, 1948. **Military Service:** Served in the German Army, 1940-45. **Family:** Married Esa Girshausen in 1950; daughter: Regine. **Career:** Photographic assistant in the studio of Gertrud Hesse, Duisburg, 1937-39; industrial photographer, for C. H. Schmeck Company, Aachen, 1939-40. Freelance commercial and industrial photographer, working for Bahlsen, Inka, Gervais, Hipp, etc., in Munich, 1952-79, and in Thiersee, Austria, since 1980: in partnership with the graphic designer Nikolai Borg, since 1964. Founder-member, fotoform group, Stuttgart, 1949. **Recipient:** Silver Medal, 1950, Diploma, 1951, 1956, 1958 and 1980,

Photokina, Cologne; Distinguished Achievement Award, *Weltausstellung der Photographie,* Lucerne, 1952; David-Octavius-Hill Medal, 1981. Honorary Member: Deutsche Fotografische Akademie DFA, 1957; Bund Freier Foto-Designer, 1969. Member: Stuttgarter Photographische Gesellschaft, 1948; Deutsche Gesellschaft fur Photographie, 1951. Bayerische Akademie der Schönen Künste, 1994. **Agent:** Prof. F C Gundlach, Parkallee 33, D-20144, Hamburg, Germany. **Address:** Wurzerweg 1, 83250 Marquartstein, Germany.

Individual Exhibitions:

1961	Staatliche Landesbildstelle, Hamburg
1980	Galerie Photo-Art, Basle, Switzerland
1981	Photomuseum im Stadtmuseum, Munich
1982	PPS-Galerie F. C. Gundlach, Hamburg
	CCD-Galerie, Dusseldorf
	Benteler Galleries, Houston, Texas (with Fee Schlapper)
1983	University of California, Riverside (with Toni Schneiders)
1986	*Eigene Ausstellung* (VW-Photos), Galerie voor industriele Vormgeving, Amsterdam
1987	*Eigene Ausstellung,* Lichtbild Galerie, Ingolstadt
1988	*Eigene Ausstellung,* Galerie Zur Stockeregg, Zurich; Galerie Fotohof, Salzburg
1989	*Fotografien von Peter Keetman,* Fotografie Forum, Frankfurt
	Peter Keetman, form-verlust, form-findung, PPS Galerie Gundlach, Hamburg
	Foto-Forum Böttcherstrasse, Bremen (with Harry Callahan)
1990	Spectrum Photogalerie, Sprengel-Museum, Hannover
1991	Stadtmuseum München. Deutscher Kulturpreis 1991 der DGPh

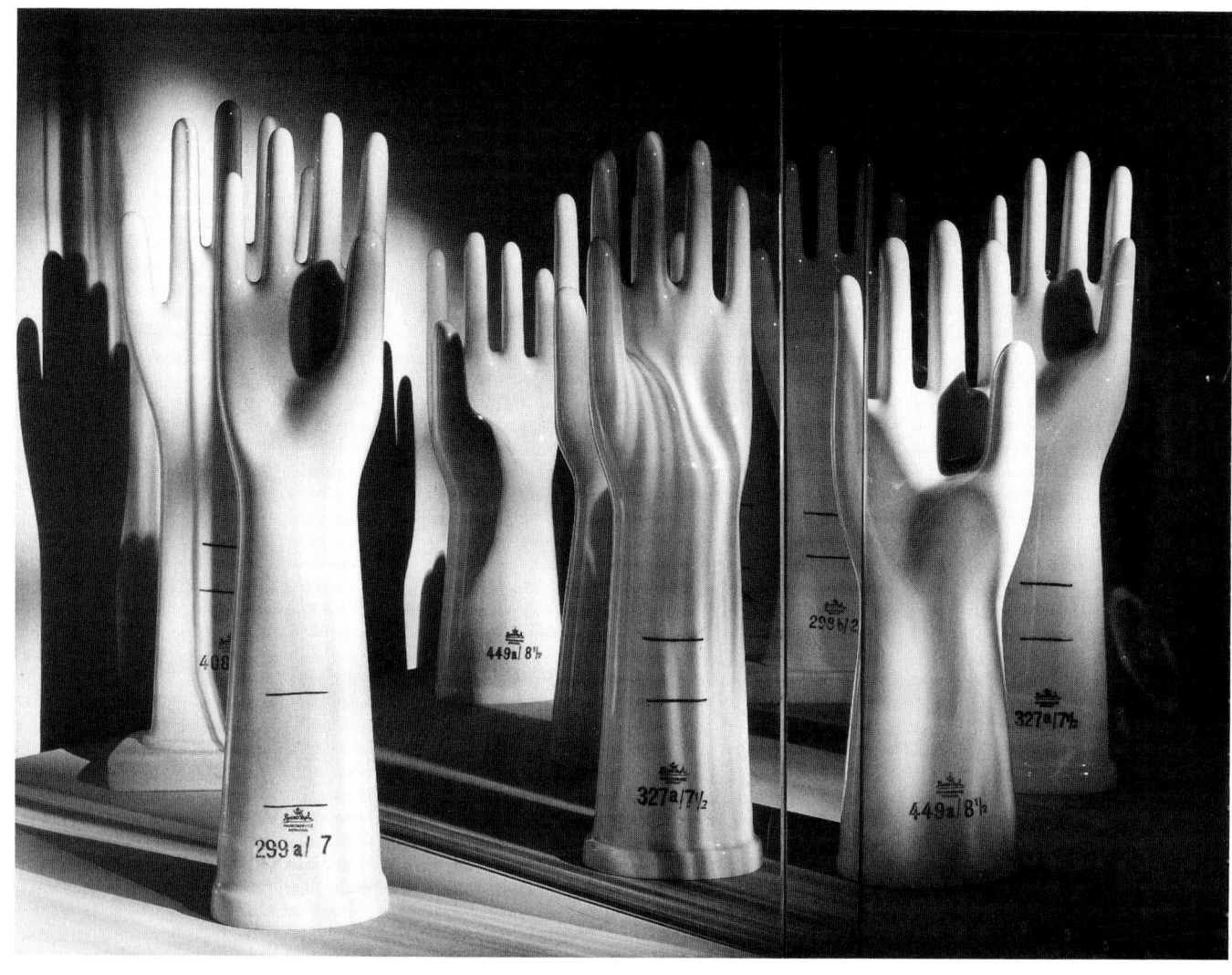

Porcelain Hands, **1958.** Photograph ©Peter Keetman

1994   Von-der-Heydt Museum, Wuppertal

Selected Group Exhibitions:

1948   *Die Photographie,* Landesgewerbemuseum, Stuttgart
1950   *fotoform,* at *Photokina,* Cologne (and 1951, 1953)
1952   *Weltausstellung der Photographie,* Lucerne, Switzerland
1956   *Photography in the Fine Arts III,* Metropolitan Museum of Art, New York
1967   *World Exhibition of Photography,* at *Expo 67,* Montreal
1979   *Deutsche Fotografie nach 1945,* Kunstverein, Kassel, West Germany (toured West Germany)
1980   *fotoform-Ausstellung,* Galerie Rudolf Kicken, Cologne
1983   *Die fotografische Sammlung,* Museum Folkwang, Essen, West Germany
1984   *Subjektive Fotografie: Images of the 50s,* San Francisco Museum of Modern Art (travelled to the Museum Folkwang, Essen; Vasterbottens Museum, Umea; Kulturhuset, Stockholm; Saarland Museum, Saarbrucken; Palais des Beaux-Arts, Brussels)
1988   *Swimmers,* Aperture Gallery, New York
        Fotovision. Projekt Fotografie nach 150 Jahren, Sprengel-Museum, Hannover

1989   Kunstraum im Messepalast, Wien
        Museum für Gestaltung, Zürich

Collections:

Fotomuseum im Münchener Stadtmuseum, Munich; Museum Folkwang, Essen, Germany; Sammlung F.C. Gundlach, Hamburg; Museum für Kunst und Gewerbe, Hamburg; CCD-Galerie, Düsseldorf; IBM-Sammlung, Germany; Sammlung des Volkswagen-Werkes; Museum Ludwig, Cologne; Benteler Galleries, Houston, Texas; Art Institute of Chicago; Busch-Reisinger Museum; Harvard University Art Museum, Cambridge, MA; Metropolitan Museum of Art, New York; San Francisco Museum of Modern Art; Canadian Centre for Architecture.

Publications:

By KEETMAN: Books—*München, Lebenkreise einer Stadt,* with text by Erhard Gopel, Lindau, West Germany 1955; *Bayerisches Seenland,* with text by Dorothee Kiesselbach, Lindau, West Germany 1957; *Berchtesgaden, Reichenhall, Salzburg,* with text by Pert Peternell, Lindau, West Germany 1959; *Spiele mit dem Orff-Schulwerk,* with text by Suse Böhm, Stuttgart 1975; *Eine Woche im Volkswagenwerk,* West Berlin 1985; *fotoform,* Berlin 1988;

Volkswagen: A Week in the Factory, San Francisco 1992. **Article**—"Peter Keetman über Peter Keetman" in *Foto-Prisma* (Dusseldorf), December 1962.

On KEETMAN: Books—*Subjektive Fotografie* by Otto Steinert, Bonn 1952; *Photography of the World,* edited by Heibonsha Publishers, Tokyo 1957; *The Picture History of Photography* by Peter Pollack, New York 1958; *A Concise History of Photography* by Helmut Gernsheim, London 1962; *Apparative Kunst* by Herbert W. Franke and Gottfried Jager, Cologne 1973; *Die Geschichte der Fotografie im 20. Jahrhundert/Photography in the 20th Century* by Petr Tausk, Cologne 1977, London 1980; *Deutsche Fotografie nach 1945/German Photography after 1945* by Petra Benteler, Kassel, West Germany 1979; *Subjektive Fotografie: Images of the 50s,* exhibition catalogue, by Ute Eskildsen, Manfred Schmalriede and Dorothy Martinson, Essen, West Germany 1984; *Portfolio,* edited by CCD-Galerie, Dusseldorf 1985. **Articles**—"Nachwuchs" in *Foto-Spiegel* (Munich), December 1948; "Sichtbar gemachte Schwingungen" in *Graphik* (Stuttgart), December 1950; "Experimentelle Photographien" in *Gebrauchsgraphik* (Munich), December 1950; "Lichtbildkunst auf neuen Wegen" in *Die Kunst* (Munich), January 1951; "Die Grenzen erweitern" in *Foto-Prisma* (Dusseldorf), August 1951; "The Key: Imagination" by Jacquelyn Judge in *Modern Photography* (New York), September 1953; "Peter Keetman" by Werner Suhr in *Gebrauchsgraphik* (Munich), April 1958; "Peter Keetman" in *Modern Photography* (New York), October 1961; "Skizze zu Peter Keetman" by Rolf Sachsse in *Fotografie* (Gottingen), September 1979; "Ein Leben mit der Fotografie" in *Leica Fotografie* (Frankfurt), March 1981; "Erkenntnisse durch das Auge" in *Foto-Scene* (Mainaschaff), March 1981; "Peter Keetman" in *Profifoto* (Dusseldorf), January/February 1983.

*

I have never found it easy to write about myself, about my work and the aims of my photography. I have never been a theoretician. The impulse to represent things through the medium of photography goes beyond what I see and what I feel. My aim being to reduce, to abstract, I have perhaps a closer affinity for black-and-white than for colour photography.

I have always been attracted, for example, by the idea of representing what the eye cannot grasp as a whole. In 1948 I began a series of studies on light-pendulum photography. An electric torch—fastened to the end of a string swinging backwards and forwards—opens up a wonderland of linear structures in no way conceivable without the medium of photography. It makes visible laws, which though they were always there, could only be perceived via photography.

Since the concept of "ambition" is an alien one to me, I have always used my camera—in so far as my non-professional work is concerned—for the sheer joy of doing so. It was curiosity which led me repeatedly to study the dynamics of movement, to observe the laws of light and to arrange the available technical means in such a way that, through the process of simplification, a concentrated statement might—wherever possible—be reached.

Is there anything fundamentally new to be photographed? Is there anything that other—and much better—photographers have not already long ago seen, felt, revealed and structured? What is it that impels us to point our camera again and again at a new object which moves our spirit and urges us to press our finger down on the shutter-button? For me it is, among other things, the experience of the present moment: the experience of something that has never existed before for a particular individual, something that cannot be predicted and cannot be retrieved. Photography can capture this personal experience of a single and unrepeatable moment.

The picture of the porcelain hands might serve as an example of this. I was photographing in a museum, but these hands hadn't made any great impression on me. Then, suddenly, a sunbeam falling through the window bathed the previously "dead" hands in a magical and enchanting light that brought them to life. After just a few minutes this fleeting impression had disappeared, and the scene had once more become lifeless and insignificant. Sheer luck had determined that I was there to click the shutter at precisely the right moment.

—Peter Keetman

*   *   *

There are artists whose designs are so strong that you feel completely bowled over on being confronted with their work for the first time. That's exactly what happened to me on coming across the work of Peter Keetman and Helmar Lerski at the *World Exhibition of Photography* in Lucerne, Switzerland, in 1952.

Keetman was one of six photographers who had founded the "fotoform" group in Germany three years earlier. In each of his pictures the clarity of form was the outstanding element, apart from simplicity of design and strong black and white contrasts in presentation. Having lived with wishy-washy British exhibitions for fifteen years, Keetman's vision and expression were a revelation not to be forgotten. His pictures were also the first abstract designs in photography expressed with the full force of Neue Sachlichkeit. Between 1950-1953 Keetman created a series of oscillation photographs—beautiful designs of geometrical shapes drawn by a pencil-light in the darkroom on an open camera lying in a rotating grammophone, or alternatively swinging over a fixed camera.

Living at one of the large Bavarian lakes it is not surprising that nature should inspire some of Keetman's finest pictures such as "Ice flows during a snowfall," "Reeds on the edge of the lake" or "Fish upon stones." The reeds look like indian ink pen strokes drawn on the paper; the crispy fish, partly disintegrated, forms a surrealist contrast to the rocks on which it is lying, the whole scene bathed in a luminous sidelight which makes you aware of every bone and of every rock-grain. Who would have thought that stinging nettles could provide an interesting picture? Have a look at a group photographed from above by Keetman. The formation of a pattern, their furry leaves catching the glistening light, and the transformation is complete. "Oildrops" is perhaps Keetman's most famous pattern design. Hundreds of drops of all sizes reflect the crossbars of a window. Like semicircular steel-buttons they are an agglomeration of shiny, fascinating shapes. Fascinating also is his wide-angle shot of a stack of steel-pipes, the cylinders, big and small, pointing at you like a multibarrelled cannon. The screw pattern produced by a bouncing table-tennis ball is just another facet of Keetman's gift for turning very ordinary things and observations into captivating images few people can read immediately.

Whereas most of the photographs mentioned so far have been produced for Keetman's own pleasure, the landscapes and cityscapes he takes for book publications, and the occasional industrial work provide his living. This bread-and-butter work is also strong in form and rich in vision and superb craftsmanship. Out of hundreds of photographs taken by him in 1953 of the Volkswagen production, recently published in book form, there are many fine images one would hardly associate with the documentation of a factory. If we consider that Keetman labours under the handicap of severe war wounds, the strength and luminosity of his work is a particularly notable feature.

—Helmut Gernsheim

KEMPADOO, Roshini.

Nationality: British. **Born:** in Crawley, Sussex, on 13 March 1959. **Education:** Graduated with a B.A. in visual communications from the West Midlands College of Higher Education, 1984, and an M.A. in photographic studies from Derbyshire College of Higher Education, 1989; intern at the National Museum of African Art, Smithsonian Institution, Washington, D.C., and the Archive Department of the Schomberg Centre for the Research in Black Culture, Photography and Print Department, New York. **Family:** Married Paul Wilcox 19 April 1986. **Career:** Worked as a picture researcher in London, 1979-80; a photographic assistant, Loughborough, 1980-81; a community photographer for Coventry Resource and Information Service, 1984-86; photographer for Format Partners Photo Library, London, 1984 to the present; co-ordinator and manager for *Ten.8* international photographic magazine, 1986-89; photography officer to West Midlands Arts Board, Birmingham, 1991-94. **Address:** 26 West Avenue, Leicester, LE2 1TR, England.

Colonized, **1993.** Photograph by Roshini Kempadoo.

Individual Exhibitions:

1984	*My Daughter's Mind,* Ikon Gallery (and Ikon Gallery touring service)
1991	*Culture and Identity,* Perspektief, Rotterdam
1992	*ECU: European Currency Unfolds,* Greenwich Art Gallery, London
1994	*A Bit of the Other,* Angel Row Gallery, Nottingham

Selected Group Exhibitions:

1989	*Fabled Territories,* Leeds City Art Gallery
1990	*Black Markets,* Cornerhouse Media Centre, Manchester
1991	*Interrogating Identity,* Grey Arts Center, New York
1992	*Who Do You Take Me For?,* Institute of Modern Art, Brisbane
	Shifting Borders, Laing Art Gallery, Newcastle upon Tyne
1993	*Recontres au Noir,* Arles Photography Festival, France
1994	*Metamorphoses: Photography in an Electronic Age,* Aperture touring show, FIT, New York

Collections:

National Museum of Photography, Film and Television, Bradford; Walsall Museum and Art Gallery; Middlesex University.

Publications:

On KEMPADOO: Books—*Women Photographers* by Val Williams, Virago 1986; *Identity,* edited Johnathan Rutherford, Lawrence and Wishart, London 1990. **Articles**—*Ten.8* (Birmingham), Issue 35, 1989; *Artforum,* (New York), November 1990; *Perspektief Magazine* (The Netherlands), November 1992; *Photography Journal/Asahi Camera* (Tokyo), 1993; *Aperture* (New York), Summer 1994. **Television**—*Shifting Borders,* BBC1, August 1992.

*

As a photographic practitioner or cultural producer, I produce images concerned with individuals and communities of colour living in Europe. I produce work looking at the issue of representation and visibility. My work takes two forms. The first is through the social documentary image using colour and black and white. The second is producing photo-constructions using a computer. I work to commission or originate exhibition pieces for publication, exhibition and collection.

—Roshini Kempadoo

*   *   *

Roshini Kempadoo's contribution to photography in Britain is diverse. First, as a member of FORMAT Photography Agency she concentrates on stories concerning the position and social circumstances of minority groups in Britain and other parts of Europe. Current work includes a project on young Asian women working as prostitutes in Amsterdam. Second, as an artist she has been among the first to incorporate electronic imaging methods within her photographic practice. Third, through her work in arts administration she is actively involved in and committed to supporting others working in photography and electronic imaging. In relation to this, she regularly appears as a visiting lecturer, discussing her own work, or the work of other black British photographers.

Issues of representation, and identity, in the post-colonial context, are central to her work. Her imagery always reflects, and reflects upon, questions of ethnicity and gender. Thus, for instance, she questions the use of black women in advertising to connote the exotic, and ways in which such stereotyping contributes to masking the realities of the exploitation of Third World labour, historically and now. She is concerned to expose discourses whereby the characterisation of black people as "other," both in terms of First World/Third World relations and also in terms of ethnic groupings within Europe, contributes to sustaining ideological dimensions of white superiority. Thematically her work is direct, and politically uncompromising. This is what makes it so memorable.

Her imagery not only reflects clarity of political purpose but also implicitly demonstrates her understanding of the nature of photographic codes and conventions. In her montages, each element is carefully placed within the overall frame, with attention to scale, proportion and ways in which the image conforms to, or refuses, standard conventions, for example, the placing of the horizon. Written text may be incorporated within the image, or as captions or quotes used to anchor meaning. The use of electronic means of synthesising her images allows for productive visual experiment.

—Liz Wells

KEMPE, Fritz (Fried Maximilian).

Nationality: German. **Born:** Greifswald, Germany, 22 October 1909. **Education:** Attended Greifswald Gymnasium, 1915-25; studied photography under his father Max Kempe, Greifswald, 1925-27; Dip. Photog. with distinction, Halle an der Salle, Berlin, 1938. **Military Service:** Served in the German Army, 1939-45 (British prisoner-of-war, Feldwebel, 1945). **Family:** Married Erika Wiegand in 1946; children: Stephan and Elisabeth. **Career:** Proprietor, Photo-Kempe photography shop, Greifswald, 1929-38; Director, Studios für Werbeund Industrie-Photographie, Berlin, 1938-39; press chief of a welfare organization in Humburg, 1945-49, and Editor, *Hamburg Allgemeine Zeitung,* 1946-48; Director, Staatliche Landesbildstelle, Hamburg, 1949-74. Founder, 1952, and Honorary Director since 1977, History of Photography Collection, Museum für Kunst und Gewerbe, Hamburg. **Recipient:** Culture Prize, Deutsche Gesellschaft für Photographie (DGPh), 1964; David Octavius Hill Medal, Gesellschaft Deutscher Lichtbildner (GDL), 1974; Grand Silver Prize, City of Hamburg, 1974; Kodak Photography Book Prize 1976, 1977; Erich-Stenger Prize for photographic history, Deutsche Gesellschaft für Photographie (DGPh), 1979; Senator Biermann-Ratjen Medal, Hamburg, 1981; Kodak Photography Book Prize, 1983; Golden Pin Award, Centralverband des Deutschen Photographenhandwerks, 1984. Member, Freien Akademie der Künste, Hamburg. Honorary Member, DGPh, GDL, Verband Deutscher Amateurfotografen-Vereine, Österreichische Gesellschaft für Photographie, Bundesgremium für Schulphotographie, Hamburger Gesellschaft für Filmkunde, Bund Freischaffender Foto-Designer (BFF), Justus Brinckmann-Gesellschaft, Hamburg, Club Daguerre, Photographic Historical Society of New York, and Fédération Internationale de l'Art Photographique (FIAP). Honorary Professor, City of Hamburg, 1982. **Agent:** PPS-Galerie F.C. Gundlach, Feldstrasse/Hochhaus 1,2000 Hamburg 4. **Died:** (in Hamburg) *1988.*

Individual Exhibitions:

1959	*Hamburger: Hundert Porträts 1949-59,* Museum für Hamburgische Geschichte, Hamburg
1964	*Hamburger: Photographische Porträts,* Museum für Hamburgische Geschichte, Hamburg (travelled to the Deutsche Gesellschaft für Photographie, Cologne, 1965)
1970	*Hamburger und ihre Gäste,* B.A.T. Haus, Hamburg
1972	*Hamburger,* Valokuvamuseon Studio, Helsinki
1973	*Fotografierte Künstler,* Städtisches Museum, Flensburg, West Germany (with Bernd Jansen)
1974	*5 Jahrzehnte Photographie,* Museum für Kunst und Gewerbe, Hamburg
1975	*Portraits,* Galerie Spectrum, Hannover

1976	*Künstlerporträts,* Freie Akademie der Künste, Hamburg
1978	*Fotografierte Fotografen,* Leitz-Galerie, Wetzlar, West Germany
1980	*Die Zeit in den Gesichtern,* PPS-Galerie, Hamburg
1983	*Die Zeit in den Gesichtern,* CCD-Galerie, Dusseldorf
	Hamburger und ihre Gäste, Dresdner Bank, Hamburg
1984	*Sechs Jahrzehnte Photographie 1924-84,* PPS Galerie, Hamburg
1986	*Neue Porträtphotographein,* Freie Akademie der Kunste, Hamburg

Selected Group Exhibitions:

1965	*Gesellschaft Deutscher Lichtbildner,* Institute für Neue Technische Form, Darmstadt (travelled to the Haus am Lützoplatz, West Germany, 1966)
1969	*Foto Selection: 50 Jahre GDL,* Museum für Kunst und Gewerbe, Hamburg
1975	*Gesellschaft Deutscher Lichtbildner,* Haus Industrieform, Essen
1978	*Later 20th Century Photography,* University of New Mexico, Albuquerque
	Tusen och En Bild, Moderna Museet, Stockholm
1979	*Deutsche Photographie nach 1945,* Kasseler Kunstverein, Kassel, West Germany (toured West Germany)
	Fotografie 1919-1979, Made in Germany, Die GDL Fotografen, Fotomuseum, Munich
1982	*Lichtbildnisse: Das Porträt in der Fotografie,* Rheinisches Landesmuseum, Bonn
1983	*Die fotografische Sammlung,* Museum Folkwang, Essen, West Germany

Collections:

Museum für Kunst und Gewerbe, Hamburg; Folkwang Museum, Essen; Det Kongelike Bibliotek, Copenhagen; Fotografiska Museet, Moderna Museet, Stockholm; International Museum of Photography, George Eastman House, Rochester, New York; University of New Mexico, Albuquerque; San Francisco Museum of Modern Art.

Publications:

By KEMPE: Books—*Der Film in der Jugend—und Erwachsenenbildung,* Seebruck, West Germany 1952; *Von Meisterfotos lernen,* Dusseldorf 1958; *Film: Technik, Gestaltung, Wirkung,* Braunschweig, West Germany 1958; *Die Welt der Photographie,* with others, Dusseldorf 1962; *Hamburger,* with text by Bernhard Meyer-Marwitz, Hamburg 1963; *Die anonymen Miterzieher unserer jugend,* Munich 1963; *Fetisch des Jahrhunderts,* Dusseldorf 1964; *Gesellschaft Deutscher Lichtbildner, Eine Dokumentation,* with Heinrich Freytag, Essen 1969; *Das Bild und die Wirklichkeit,* Munich 1974; *One Hundred Years of Photographic History: Essays in Honor of Beaumont Newhall,* with others, edited by Van Deren Coke, Albuquerque, New Mexico 1975; *Vor der Camera: Zur Geschichte der Photographie in Hamburg,* Hamburg 1976; *Photographie: Zwischen Daguerreotypie und Kunstphotographie,* Hamburg 1977; *Daguerreotypie in Deutschland: Vom Charme der frühen Fotografie,* Seebruck and Munich 1979; *Albert Renger-Patzsch: 100 Photographien 1928,* Cologne 1979; *Dokumente der Photographie 1: Nikola Perscheid/Arthur Benda/Madame d'Ora,* Hamburg 1980; *La Photographie Artistique en Allemagne vers 1900, Stuttgart 1980; Dokumente der Photographie 2: Daguerreotypien,* with Bodo von Dewitz, Hamburg 1983.

On KEMPE: Books—*Fritz Kempe: 5 Jahrzehnte Photographie,* exhibition catalogue, by Heinz Spielmann and others, Hamburg 1974 (includes bibliography); *Lichtbildnisse: Das Porträt in der Fotografie,* edited by Klaus Honnef,

Cologne 1982. **Articles**—"Fritz Kempe als Porträtist" by Herman Speer in *Foto-Prisma* (Dusseldorf), October 1963; "Fritz Kempe wird 60" by Liselotte Strelow in *Foto-Prisma* (Dusseldorf), October 1969; "Fritz Kempe: Der Dokumentarische Porträtist" by Günther Lensch in *Fachkontakt* (Dusseldorf), March 1974; "Fotos sollen Menschen nicht demaskieren" by Inge Mösch in *Hamburger Abendblatt,* March 1976; "Laudatio zur Verleihung des Erich Stenger-Preis" by Rolf H. Krauss in *DGPh Intern* (Cologne), February 1979; "Fritz Kempe zum Siebzigsten" by Bernd Lohse in *Photo-Antiquaria* (Frankfurt), March 1979; "Fritz Kempe: Porträtist mit Kamera und Feder" by Hugo Schöttle in *Leica-Fotografie* (Frankfurt), August 1979; "Fotograf, Fotopublizist, Anreger un Förderer" by Karl Steinorth in *81 Format* (Karlsruhe), September 1979; "Fritz Kempe: Der Chronist, der 70 wird" by Bernd Lohse in *Foto-Magazin* (Munich), October 1979; "Seine Fotos hängen in den Galerien der Welt" by Liselotte Strelow in *Die Welt* (Hamburg), October 1979; "Fritz Kempe wird 75" by Karl Steinorth in *Leica-Fotografie* (Frankfurt), no. 7, 1984; "Zu Fritz Kempes Fünfundsiebzigsten Preceptor Photographies" by Bernd Lohse in *Photo Technik International* (Munich), October/December 1984.

*

I was born in the university town of Greifswald, Pomerania, the son of the photographer Max Kempe. Inflation from 1919 to 1923 ate into my father's means and made it necessary for him to take me away from gymnasium to become his apprentice. I was not very happy either as an apprentice or as the owner of a photographic shop (1929-38). The pleasure I had in a studio for industrial and advertising photography (October 1938-November 1939) was upset by the war. After my release from English captivity in October 1945, I found no work as a photo-reporter in Hamburg—even though my Leica was my only possession to have survived the war. So I became the public relations chief of a welfare organization and the editor of a Hamburg newspaper. I wrote about social topics, composed glosses, essays and short stories. Writing became my own quite personal method of expression; I thought no more about photography.

In 1949 I took over direction of the Staatliche Landesbildstelle in Hamburg, where I remained for 25 years. The photographic centres in Germany have the task of providing schools with audiovisual teaching aids, which, in part, they also produce. I extended the technical and pedagogic activity of the Hamburg Landesbildstelle to include an overall pedagogy of the medium of photography. In 1950 I introduced the lecture series "What One Should Know about Film," which was later extended to the three photographic media, photography, film, and television. In 1952 I started to hold exhibitions showing the work of the great masters as well as unknown young photographers and the work of the photo-clubs. The photo gallery of the Staatliche Landesbildstelle is the oldest in Europe. In all, I have organized more than 300 photographic exhibitions in Hamburg.

In 1952 I founded the Hamburg *History of Photography Collection,* which in 1974 comprised more than 30,000 photographs, cameras and books including many incunabula and the whole of *Camera-Work*. Since 1977, in an honorary capacity, I have administered the collection, which is now in the Museum für Kunst und Gewerbe.

In 1949 I also began to take photographs again: I portrayed politicians, businessmen, scholars and artists of importance to the city of Hamburg. In addition, I supported the Hamburg Art and Culture Prizes and local photographers. The collection *Hamburger und ihre Gäste* includes about 1,300 portraits. As I no longer have a studio at my disposal, I work with the Leicaflex and with available light, which has made a considerable difference in the style of my photographs. As I portray in this way people whom I have already photographed in a studio ten, twenty or thirty-years ago, exciting companion pictures arise. My exhibition in 1980 at F.C. Gundlach's PPS-Galerie in Hamburg showed how *Die Zeit in den Gesichtern* leaves its mark. This kind of photography of people fascinates me and has become a passion. Thanks to the support of my friend F.C. Gundlach, I am able to pursue it further.

Everything that I have photographed, investigated, collected or written comes from my historic interest in photography: the biographies that I wrote about friends who are now dead, the many biographic/iconographic reports, the essays about young photographers whom I was able to promote through my exhibitions and publications. Among my late friends I count Albert Renger-Patzsch and Otto Steinert as the closest; I miss them very much. In the meantime some of the younger photographers have become better known, if not yet famous. I look at the sensitive photography of the most recent times with sympathy and with a curiosity to know where it will yet lead us.

—Fritz Kempe

*   *   *

Fritz Kempe learned his craft in Greifswald, that small Pomeranian town well known from the paintings of Caspar David Friedrichs. In the 1930s the town was still steeped in the past, just as the great romantic painter had portrayed it, and Kempe's specialized photography shop was at that time very progressive. Cameras, film and all articles required by the amateur photographer were for sale; clients' films were developed and printed. Kempe's own remaining photographs from those days consist chiefly of bromide emulsion prints which continue the tradition of "fine art photography." Kempe still shows particular affection for that period in photographic history; he has preserved, collected, publicized and interpreted it with an impressive passion since the early 1960s. His own works have, without doubt, paved the way for the growing appreciation of the period, but they, in contrast to him, remained almost unknown until his Hamburg retrospective in 1974.

Because of the political situation, Kempe left the Greifswald shop in 1938 to open his own studio for industrial and advertising photography in Berlin. Apart from the ordinary commissions, he created aesthetically balanced pictures of Berlin and smaller towns in the region. Photographs of the then famous film actress Margot Hielscher were the beginning of his portraits, which after 1950, were to bring Kempe a growing reputation.

As for most young men of his generation, the war was for Kempe a drastic caesura. In the years after 1945 he worked as a journalist. Here he, as it were, rose from the ranks in a second craft, that of writing. Apart from photography, writing is now his most important activity. The sheer number of his publications is impressive: more than 500 books, articles and catalogues have appeared since 1946, including certain monographs that are now standard works in the history of photography. His books *Vor der Camera* and *Photographie: Zwischen Daguerreotypie und Kunstphotographie* were honored with Kodak Prizes in 1976 and 1977, and *Daguerreotypie in Deutschland* received the 1979 Erich Stenger Prize of the Deutsche Gesellschaft für Photographie. Without Kempe's contribution, significant chapters on the German photography of the 19th and early 20th centuries would hardly be known.

And without his introduction many a now well-known photographer of the younger generation would not have found such quick and effective access to the public. From the early 1950s, as Director of the Staatliche Landesbildstelle, Kempe produced exhibitions on an almost monthly basis, the majority of them introducing young photographers. He also organized the larger annual exhibitions at the Museum für Kunst und Gewerbe, many of which travelled to other cities.

In 1952 Kempe took over from the Museum für Kunst und Gewerbe its stock of daguerreotypes and other photographic materials from the time around 1900 and built it up into a comprehensive collection: with around 45,000 pictures and several hundred pieces of photographic equipment, it has become the most important collection of fine art photography in the German Federal Republic. In 1977 it was returned to the Museum für Kunst und Gewerbe, where Fritz Kempe continues as Honorary Director, to maintain and promote it.

Although doing so was certainly not included in his responsibilities as Director of the Landesbildstelle, Kempe has continuously taken photographs of local politicians, celebrities and officials, and, in so doing, has created a first-class documentation of his time and place. There is hardly a personality in the arts, politics and public life who has worked in or had links with Hamburg since 1950 who is not now represented in Kempe's archives, some of them repeatedly over long periods of time. Kempe has never manipulated portraits. His pictures, which are never modified by work in the darkroom, are distinguished by their honesty and spontaneity, by their simplicity, and by his precise observation of appearance, gesture and behavior. His subjects have included Max Ernst and Hans Richter, Oskar Kokoschka and Josef von Sternberg, Albert Renger-Patzsch and Max Bill. Kempe has created, with a suggestive, evocative realism, a portrait of a people of an entire region over a period of more than three decades.

—Heinz Spielmann

KENNARD, Peter.

Nationality: British. **Born:** London on 17 February 1949. **Education:** Studied at The Byam Shaw School of Art, 1965-67; the Slade, 1967-70 and the Royal College of Art, 1976-79. **Career:** Worked as artist in residence at Sussex University, 1971; lecturer in fine art and photography at West Surrey College of Art and Design, 1989-94; senior tutor in photography at the Royal College of Art, 1994; part-time lecturer at North East London Polytechnic, Polytechnic of Central London, Byam Shaw School of Art and Winchester School of Art. **Address:** 13 Lidfield Road, London N16 9NA, England.

Individual Exhibitions:

1968	St Catherine's College, Oxford
1970	Zeez Arts, London
	ICA London
1971	Gardner Arts Centre, Sussex University, Brighton
1973	Photographers Gallery, University of Southampton
1978	*A Document of Chile,* Half Moon Gallery, London
1980	*No Nuclear Weapons,* Camerawork Gallery, London
1981	*Images for Disarmament,* ICA London (travelled to the Arnolfini, Bristol)
1982-83	*Despatches from an Unofficial War Artist,* County Hall, London (travelled to the Museum of Modern Art, Oxford; Gardner Arts Centre, University of Sussex; Reading University; Southampton City Art Gallery; Harlow Town Hall; Southwark Town Hall, London)
1984	*Data 1984,* Barbican Centre, London (travelled to the Wilhelm-Lehmbruck Museum, Duisburg, Germany; Artspace, Aberdeen)
1985	*Images Against War, 1965-1985,* Barbican Centre, London
1987	*In a Right State,* Aspex Gallery, Portsmouth (travelled to Camerawork, London; Bluecoat Gallery, Liverpool)
1989	*Photomontages for Peace,* United Nations, Palais des Nations, Geneva
1990	*Images for the End of the Century,* Gimpel Fils Gallery, London
1992	*Brake up—Eastern Europe,* Laing Gallery, Newcastle
	Stop Paintings and Photomontages 1973-1991, Kent Gallery, New York
	OUR 999, Gimpel Fils Gallery, London
	Welcome to Britain, Towner Art Gallery, Eastbourne
1994	*Welcome to Britain,* Royal Festival Hall, London
	Out of Order, Zone Gallery, Newcastle

Selected Group Exhibitions:

1973	*Photography into Art,* Arts Coucil (touring)
1978	*Art into Society,* Whitechapel Art Gallery, London
1981	*Photographer as Printmaker,* Arts Council (touring)
1983	*Place,* Gimpel Fils, London
1984	*Art of the Comic Strip,* Gimpel Fils, London
1986	*Art Meets Science,* Smiths Gallery, Covent Garden, London
1985-88	*Whitechapel Open,* Whitechapel Gallery, London
1989	*Through the Looking Glass, Photographic Art in Britain 1945-89,* Barbican, London
	Invention D'un Art, Pompidou Centre, Paris
1991	*Shocks to the System,* Festival Hall, London (touring)
	Photomontage Now, Manchester City Art Gallery
1992	*The Cutting Edge,* Barbican, London
1993	International Artists Centre, Poznan, Poland
1994	*Where is Home?,* Kent Gallery, New York

Collections:

Magdalen College, Oxford; St Catherine's College, Oxford; University College, London; Victoria and Albert Museum, London; Imperial War Museum, London; Arts Council of Great Britain; Saatchi Collection, London; National Museum of Photography and Film, Bradford; Science Museum, London.

Publications:

By KENNARD: Books—*No Nuclear Weapons* (with Ric Sissons), London 1981; *Jobs for a Change* (text by GLC Economic Policy Group), London 1983; *Keep London out of the Killing Ground,* London 1983; *Target London,* London 1985; *About Turn* (with Bill Evans), London 1986; *Images for the End of the Century,* London 1990; book covers for Penguin, Pluto Press; Paladin, Verso, Routledge; photomontages for *The Guardian, The Listener, Time* magazine, *New Statesman and Society, The Washington Post, New Scientist, NME, Radio Times, The Sunday Times* (London), *The Observer.* **Television**—Unstable Elements, Channel 4, 1984; "State of Emergency—South Africa," *Bandung File,* Channel 4, 1986; "The People's Flag," Platform Films for Channel 4, 1987; *Heartfield: The Father of Photomontage,* Granada TV, 31 March 1991; photomontages for Labour Party Broadcasts, 1982 and 1983.

On KENNARD: Film—*Photomontage Today,* Arts Council of Great Britain, 1983.

*

The point of my work is to use easily recognisable iconic images, but to render them unacceptable. To break down the image of the all-powerful missile, in order to represent the power of the millions of people who are actually trying to break them. After breaking them, to show new possibilities emerging in the cracks and splintered fragments of the old reality.

I studied as a painter, but after the events of 1968, I began to look for a form of expression that could bring art and politics together to a wider audience. I found paintings increasingly problematic: the sensuality of the medium tended to take over the subject of the painting. The viewer intentionally related the painting back to the problems of art history, whatever the subject. I found however that photography wasn't as burdened with similar art historical associations. People are still forced to link the images back to the actual world (the traces of reality recorded by the camera) rather than to purely formal concerns.

My photomontages are also easily reproducible and this has enabled me to show work in a number of different contexts, from my local launderette to the United Nations in Geneva. They have also been used as an image resource by anti-nuclear, environmental and human rights campaigns. They have appeared in newspapers, on TV and films, posters, tee-shirts, postcards, badges etc. Local campaigning groups have produced their own versions of the images in sculptural form, on banners and murals. For me, getting the work out into the world and used is as important as its production. The photomontages are not only reports on events and possibilities but become part of those events themselves when they are used by the people campaigning for change.

By breaking down elements in photographs, cutting them up and reconstituting them, a critical narrative on opposing futures can be presented visually. The resultant images are not documentary mirrors (although some of my photomontages only exist as a result of the bravery of documentary photographers who go out into the world while I sit in a room trying to make sense of the images they bring back), but visual maps of human choice. My photomontages are constructed to show that events are not natural and inexorable as they often appear to be in photographs, but the result of set of choices and decisions. They aim to subject photographic images to human criticism.

—Peter Kennard

*　　*　　*

Ever since photography began over 150 years ago, debate has raged over whether it constitutes an art, a science or a "technique." Neatly sidestepping the argument between the former two, Peter Kennard adapts the latter by covering his wooden sculptures with photographic images which are printed on to sheet paper, then coated with dust, grime and oil paint and stuck onto rough wooden pallets and placards. This technique not only explains Peter Kennard's resistance to description as a photographer, whatever the traditional

Gulf II, **1991.** Photograph by Peter Kennard.

connotations, but also links his work firmly to the relevant elements of its immediate environment.

At the Royal Festival Hall in London that meant, in his words, "bringing the outside in." Kennard took account of those sleeping rough under the nearby railway arches by making their presence felt within the concert halls covering their subterranean existence. The pallets, on which many of the homeless sleep, bear the ghost of their bodily imprint as surely as the sheets from which most of us rose up this morning bear ours, only in one instance the imprint is photographic and in the other merely physical. Instead of transferring swiftly, obviously, from Waterloo or Charing Cross Station across a bridge and into the soothing warmth of a haven of culture, culture is itself forced into "a relationship with poverty and the actuality of human degradation."

Peter Kennard is not, however, much interested in the idea of exercising the consciences of either the indifferent or the benevolent. The underside of Britain, a country where both poverty and wealth differentials are absolutely increasing, is not to remain hidden placidly on the underside of the South Bank—or even corralled in the Royal Festival Hall Galleries. When Kennard showed similar works at Eastbourne's Towner Art Gallery, he invited a group of young people from a hostel for the homeless and worked with them to create their own exhibition area where their reactions to homelessness were articulated through magazine and newsprint collages of their own. A similar project occurred when the exhibition toured to the Zone Gallery in north-east England, when the disaffected on a run-down Newcastle housing estate were invited in to colour-photocopy and collage their own images of daily life and its preoccupations.

Not since the eighteenth century and Britain's major sea-faring wars with France have we seen such a resurgence of mercantilist values as part of a wider political programme. Peter Kennard's work emphatically stands opposed to the barren morality that today reduces social values to simple equations of profit and loss and refuses to engage with the human losses that unbridled profiteering entails. In doing so, he stands alongside some of the great questioning voices among twentieth century artists in Europe. John Heartfield, Josef Beuys, Anselm Keifer and Jo Spence used mixed media to express their refusal to separate art and life, life from society, society from politics. The theorists are there too, whether in a writer/photographer such as Victor Burgin or in collaborations between writers and photographers such as John Berger and Jean Mohr.

In *Welcome to Britain* Peter Kennard collaborated with a writer for the first time. Words have always been important in an associative dimension to his collages, whether as a vehicle to illustrate politicians being forced to eat their words; to parrot and parody advertising jargon; or in a felicitous coincidence such as allowing a Last Supper of elderly inmates of an old people's home to take place around a loaf of radiantly Sunblest bread. Kennard's visions, already deliberately distorted or distressed to resemble faded paintings, were viewed in conjunction with the words of the poet Peter Reading who linked Britain with the continent of Europe in his revelation of the threat and actuality of deprivation.

By regarding art itself as essentially uncompromising Peter Kennard is unequivocally taking sides. And by aligning himself with the dispossessed, who knows but that he may find himself on the side of the angels?

—Amanda Hopkinson

KEPES, Gyorgy.

Nationality: American. **Born:** Selyp, Hungary, 4 October 1906; emigrated to the United States, 1937; naturalized, 1956. **Education:** Studied art, under Istvan Csok, at the Academy of Arts, Budapest, 1924-28, M.A. 1928; self-taught in photography. **Family:** Married Juliet Appleby in 1937; children: Juliet and Imre Peter. **Career:** Independent painter and filmmaker, associating with Munka Art Group, Budapest, 1929-30; worked as an exhibition, stage and graphic designer, Berlin, 1930-32, 1934-36; Designer, studio of László Moholy-Nagy, London, 1936-37. Independent painter, photographer, and teacher, in the United States, since 1937: designer, for Travelers Insurance Company of Los Angeles, Container Corporation of America, Abbot Laboratories, *Fortune* magazine, etc., 1938-50. Head, Light and Color Department,

New Bauhaus School, later the Institute of Design, Chicago, 1938-43; Professor of Design, North Texas State College, Denton, and Brooklyn College, New York, 1943-45; Professor of Visual Design, 1946-66, Founder-Director of the Center for Advanced Visual Studies, 1967-70, and Institute Professor, 1970-74, Massachusetts Institute of Technology, Cambridge. Visiting Instructor, Art Directors Club, Chicago, 1939; Visiting Professor, Harvard University, Cambridge, Massachusetts, 1965; Visiting Lecturer, University of California at Los Angeles, 1969; Visiting Artist, University of Hawaii, Honolulu, 1970; Painter-in-Residence, American Academy, Rome, 1974; Bicentennial Professor, University of Utah, Salt Lake City, 1975; Andrew Mellon Professor, Rice University, Houston, 1976; Artist-in-Residence, Dartmouth College, Hanover, New Hampshire, 1977; Distinguished Visiting Louis D. Beaumont Professor, Washington University, St. Louis, 1978; Kern Institute Professor in Communications, Rochester Institute of Technology, New York, 1981. **Recipient:** Typographical Arts Award, American Institute of Graphic Art, 1947; Guggenheim Fellowship, 1960; Silver Medal, Architectural League of New York, 1961; Fine Arts Award, American Institute of Architects, 1968; Distinguished Teaching Award, College Art Association of America, 1982. Fellow, Rhode Island School of Design, Providence, 1981. Fellow, American Academy of Arts and Sciences; Member, National Institute of Arts and Letters; Academician, National Academy of Design; Member, Hall of Fame, Art Directors Club of New York. **Agents:** Saidenberg Gallery, New York; and Alpha Gallery, Boston. **Address:** 90 Larchwood Drive, Cambridge, Massachusetts 02138, U.S.A.

Individual Exhibitions:

1939	Katherine Kuh Gallery, Chicago
	Grand Rapids Art Museum, Michigan (with Jean Helion and László Moholy-Nagy)
1944	Art Institute of Chicago
1951	Currier Gallery of Art, Manchester, New Hampshire
	Margaret Brown Gallery, Boston
1952	San Diego Fine Arts Gallery, California
	San Francisco Museum of Art
	University of California, Berkeley
1953	DeCordova Museum, Lincoln, Massachusetts
	Margaret Brown Gallery, Boston
1954	Cranbrook Academy of Art, Bloomfield Hills, Michigan
	Municipal Arts Center, Long Beach, California
	San Francisco Museum of Art
1955	Margaret Brown Gallery, Boston
	Stedelijk Museum, Amsterdam
1956	Fitchburg Art Museum, Massachusetts
1957	Everson Museum of Art, Syracuse, New York
	Museum of Fine Arts, Dallas
1958	Centro Culturale Olivetti, Ivrea, Italy
	Galleria di Via Montenapoleone, Milan
	Galleria Il Numero, Florence
	Galleria dell'Obelisco, Rome
1959	Baltimore Museum of Art
	Hayden Gallery, Massachusetts Institute of Technology, Cambridge
	Howard Wise Gallery, Cleveland
	Museum of Fine Arts, Dallas
	Museum of Fine Arts, Houston
	Swetzoff Gallery, Boston
1960	Saidenberg Gallery, New York
	Swetzoff Gallery, Boston
1962	Swetzoff Gallery, Boston
1963	Saidenberg Gallery, New York
	Swetzoff Gallery, Boston
1965	Swetzoff Gallery, Boston
1966	Marion Koogler McNay Institute, San Antonio, Texas
	Phoenix Art Museum, Arizona
	Saidenberg Gallery, New York
	Swetzoff Gallery, Boston
1967	Phillips Exeter Academy, New Hampshire
	Southern Methodist University, Dallas
1968	Alpha Gallery, Boston

	Galerie Moos, Montreal
	Saidenberg Gallery, New York
1970	Saidenberg Gallery, New York
1972	Alpha Gallery, Boston
	Galerie Moos, Montreal
	Saidenberg Gallery, New York
1973	Museum of Science, Boston
1974	Alpha Gallery, Boston
1975	Galleria dell'Obelisco, Rome
1976	Kunstlerhaus, Vienna
	Mucsarnok, Budapest
1977	Alpha Gallery, Boston
	Baushaus-Archiv Museum für Gestaltung, West Berlin
	Dartmouth College, Hanover, New Hampshire
	Prakapas Gallery, New York
	Robinson Gallery, Houston
	Vision Gallery, Boston
	Stephen Wirtz Gallery, San Francisco
1978	Steinberg Gallery, Washington University, St. Louis
	Hayden Gallery, Massachusetts Institute of Technology, Cambridge
	Henry Gallery, University of Washington, Seattle
1984	*Lightgraphics,* International Center of Photography, New York

Selected Group Exhibitions:

1929	*Artist New Society,* K.U.T., Budapest
1944	*Abstract and Surrealist Art in the U.S.A.,* Cincinnati Art Museum, Ohio (toured the United States)
1946	*Design with Light,* Philadelphia Art Alliance
1959	*The Sense of Abstraction,* Museum of Modern Art, New York
1965	*Photography in America 1850-1965,* Yale University, New Haven, Connecticut
1978	*Das Experimentelle Photo in Deutschland 1918-40,* Galleria del Levante, Munich
1979	*Photographic Surrealism,* New Gallery of Contemporary Art, Cleveland (travelled to Dayton Art Institute, Ohio, and Brooklyn Museum, New York, 1980)
1980	*Avant-Garde Photography in Germany 1919-39,* San Francisco Museum of Modern Art (toured the United States 1981-82)
1983	*Fotogramme—die lichtreichen Schatten,* Fotomuseum im Stadtmuseum, Munich
1985	*Extending the Perimeters of 20th Century Photography,* San Francisco Museum of Modern Art

Collections:

Museum of Modern Art, New York; Whitney Museum, New York; Rhode Island School of Design, Providence; Museum of Fine Arts, Boston; Fogg Art Museum, Harvard University, Cambridge, Massachusetts; Massachusetts Institute of Technology, Cambridge; Art Institute of Chicago; San Francisco Museum of Modern Art; Bauhaus Archiv, Berlin; National Museum of Fine Arts, Budapest.

Publications:

By KEPES: Books—*Tul a Valon,* with Gyorgy Dan, Budapest 1925; *Language of Vision,* Chicago 1944; *Graphic Forms: The Art as Related to the Book,* Cambridge, Massachusetts 1949; *The New Landscape in Art and Science,* Chicago 1956; *The Education of Vision,* editor, New York 1965; *Structure in Art and Science,* editor, New York 1965; *The Nature and Art of Motion,* editor, New York 1965; *Light as a Creative Medium,* with Bernard I. Cohen, Cambridge, Massachusetts 1965; *Module, Symmetry, Proportion, Rhythm,* editor, New York 1966; *Sign, Image, Symbol,* editor, New York 1966; *The Man-Made Object,* editor, New York 1966; *The Center for Advanced Visual Studies,* Cambridge, Massachusetts 1967; *Arts of Environment,* editor, New York 1972; *El Arte y la Technologia,* Bogota 1973; *Gyorgy Kepes Kialliasa,* with an introduction by Eva Korner, Budapest 1976; *Portfolio of Photographs by Gyorgy Kepes,* with an introduction by Philip Hofer, Boston

1977; *Gyorgy Kepes Irasai,* edited by Ferenc Bodri, Budapest 1978; *Gyorgy Kepes: The MIT Years 1945-1977,* with text by Judith Wechsler and Jan Van der Marck, Cambridge, Massachusetts 1978; *Gyorgy Kepes: Lightgraphics,* with text by Anne Hoy, New York 1984. **Articles**—"On Photography" in *Arts and Architecture* (Los Angeles), August 1946; "Form and Motion" in *Arts and Architecure* (Los Angeles), July/August 1948; "New Landscape in Art and Science" in *Art in America* (New York), October 1955; "Creating with Light" in *Art in America* (New York), vol. 80, no. 4, 1960; "Light and Form" in *Arts and Architecture* (Los Angeles), May 1960; "Light as a Creative Medium" in *Arts and Architecture* (Los Angeles), October 1966; "Light and Design" in *Design Quarterly* (Minneapolis), no. 68, 1967; "László Moholy-Nagy: The Bauhaus Tradition" in *Print* (New York), January 1969.

On KEPES: Books—*The Picture History of Photography* by Peter Pollack, New York 1958, 1969; *Das Experimentelle Photo in Deutschland 1918-1940* by Emilio Bertonati, Munich 1978; *Photographic Surrealism,* exhibition catalogue, by Nancy Hall-Duncan, Cleveland 1979; *Avant-Garde Photography in Germany 1919-1939,* exhibition catalogue, by Van Deren Coke, Ute Eskildsen and Bernd Lohse, San Francisco 1980; *Fotogramme: die lichtreichen Schatten,* exhibition catalogue, by Floris M. Neususs, Kassel, West Germany 1983.

*   *   *

In what is generally considered an unusual combination of talents for a visual artist, Gyorgy Kepes talks about his aims for his art as succinctly as his art reveals those ideals. Just as unusually, and just as successfully, Kepes melds his social and personal goals into a giant exploration of the universe. Painter, photographer and architectural redesigner, Kepes turns these—generally conceived—separated, even fragmented parts of human experience into a dynamic thrust that combines art and science and creates a giant explosion of forms. Kepes hopes these forms will awaken, and perhaps help direct, the development of mankind's positive sensibilities. The common denominator for his work, aims and ideas is the presence, and vigor, of light. He is drawn to—one might say consumed by—the way light gives form to the formless.

As a redesigner of spaces, Kepes takes a space such as Boston's harbor and plans to turn that entire space into a Gateway—into a redefined unit of light, his plan reverberating with structuralist/cubist overtones. As a painter, he takes a canvas and registers different degrees of form through tonalities that light alone creates. But it is through his photographs—and their necessary and basic use of light—that he shapes his freest designs with the world. Breaking loose from the given spaces he receives as an architectural redesigner and the predictable spaces he works with as a painter, he freshly conceives of a new world of forms through the camera. In one photograph, an eye rests upon an eye. In another, a moving object is depicted—moving—only to be dispersed through the air in another part of the photograph. The camera allows him to develop layers of experience as he creates and shapes those experiences into forms that would otherwise remain formless in a fragmented world. It also allows him to combine his lyrical and structuralist freedoms into new forms. For, ultimately, it is a world without form—threatening to dissolve into personal, social and creative chaos—that worries and spurs him.

Kepes' photographs are rooted in understandings that come from Moholy-Nagy (he was, in a manner of speaking, a Moholy-Nagy student) and Herbert Bayer, an anti-Fascist German photographer of the 1920s and 30s. Starting with light-expressive collages that expose some of the intensity of a Fascist ideology, on the one hand, and the fears wrought by a socially and economically depressed world on the other, Kepes places objects in these early photographs in a timeless space. Many of these spaces are triangular and trapezoidal, reminiscent of the structuralist forms that infected the consciousness of the 1920s. Becoming more influenced by the world that light creates—rather than illuminates—Kepes experiments with photograms, his photograms depicting the form that objects take when seen as light-filled forms alone. Although these photographs are filled with movement—as visually attractive entities are—for the most part they are not concerned with movement. They are not about movement. They are primarily concerned with, and about, shapes and spaces.

By the 1940s and right through the 1970s, Kepes' photographs develop an interest in the movement that people, but mainly objects, create. Sometimes he depicts that movement as a relatively static phenomenon which has degenerated into pattern alone. At other times, he more excitedly depicts that movement with soaring possibilities. At still other times he catches the flair of that movement by subtly controlling the light and revealing the quiet cultures contained within that movement. It's as if Kepes has become aware of time as an element in his art, as if time has joined his considerations of space and helped shape these objects. It's as if these objects take on a form because of their own history, and their own development as forms. Their own composition—sometimes extravagant—and developed over the ages—now enters their existence. Unswerving in his belief about the way light gives shape to forms, Kepes uses light to give these forms a dimension. As forms alone, they stand over time. More sophisticated than his earlier forms, they echo some of the 1970s formalist concerns. But much more basically, they reflect Kepes' sensibilities. Refined, lyrical and fulsome, they tell the world that chaos has been kept at bay, that it is possible to create a world of dynamic forms that lift the expression of science and art onto new planes.

—Judith Mara Gutman

KEPPLER, Victor.

Nationality: American. **Born:** New York City, 30 September 1904. **Education:** Attended Stuyvesant High School, New York, 1918-22; self-taught in photography. **Wartime Service:** Worked for the United States Treasury during World War II. **Family:** Married Josephine Windmann in 1924; children: Herbert and Victoria. **Career:** Worked as a movie extra, designer, photo-printer, and part-time photographer, New York, 1916-20; photographer, Fingerprint Bureau, New York, 1926-28; freelance advertising and magazine photographer, working for U.S. Steel, Dupont, Westinghouse, Alcoa, General Electric, Corning Glass, Kodak, etc., and for *Saturday Evening Post, American Magazine, Woman's Home Companion, Ladies Home Journal, New York Woman, Hollywood Woman, Better Homes and Gardens, Cosmopolitan,* etc., New York, 1928-61; Founder, Director and President, Famous Photographers School, Westport, Connecticut, 1961-72; now retired. President and Director, The Photographic Administrators, New York, 1972-78; Creative Director, New Security Concept, Fairfield, Connecticut, 1976-78. Consultant, Hartford Insurance Group, Connecticut, since 1964; Creative Consultant, C.B. Dolge Company, Westport, since 1973. Member, Europhot professional photographers group, Brussels, since 1971. Trustee, Photography Hall of Fame. **Recipient:** Harvard Award, 1944; Gold Medal, Art Directors Club, New York, 1958, Cleveland, 1958, Chicago, 1959, Philadelphia, 1959, Boston, 1960; Photographers Hall of Fame Award, Santa Barbara, California, 1970; Distinguished Medal for Achievement, City College of New York, 1980. **Address:** 11 Ferry Lane West, Westport, Connecticut 06880, U.S.A.

Selected Group Exhibitions:

1982   *Color as Form,* International Museum of Photography at
        George Eastman House, Rochester, New York

Collections:

Newhouse Communications Center, Syracuse University, New York; International Museum of Photography, George Eastman House, Rochester, New York; Philadelphia Museum of Art; Nimitz Library, United States Naval Academy, Annapolis, Maryland; Smithsonian Institution, Washington, D.C.

Publications:

By KEPPLER: Books—*The Eighth Art: A Life of Color Photography,* with a foreword by Bruce Barton, New York 1938; *Commercial Photography,* New York 1940; *Your Future in Photography,* New York 1970; *Victor Keppler: Man + Camera: A Photographic Autobiography,* with a foreword by Beaumont Newhall, New York 1970.

On KEPPLER: Books—*U.S. Camera Annual 1936,* edited by Tom J. Maloney, New York and London 1936; *Color as Form: A History of Color*

Photography, exhibition catalogue, with introduction by Robert A. Sobieszek, Rochester, New York 1982. **Articles**—"Victor Keppler: Legend in Our Times" in *Infinity* (New York), August 1971; "Pioneers of Commercial Color: Bruehl, Keppler, Muray, Outerbridge, Steichen" by Diana Edkins in *Modern Photography* (New York), September 1978.

*   *   *

In the 1920s, as advances in printing technology made possible the greatly-improved reproduction of photographs on the printed page, large commercial studios sprang up to meet the photographic needs of advertisers. Victor Keppler, by reason of his striking images, ceaseless energy, and flamboyant personality, became one of New York's best-known advertising photographers. For more than four decades he was an active force on New York's commercial photographic scene.

What makes for a successful advertising photograph? Is it one that wins awards, or one that aims to sell the product? Keppler could boast triumphs on both counts: he won more than his share of recognition from the New York Art Directors Club, yet maintained a reputation for extraordinary attention to the needs of his clients. Keppler knew precisely the value of working on demand for demanding clients, and charged them accordingly; often he taped a couple of aspirin to the bottom of his bill.

From the beginning Keppler proved adept at incorporating into advertising images the trends of the other visual arts. In the 1920s, he combined razor-sharp realism with cubist-derived geometric patterning in cigarette advertisements. In the 1930s, he mastered the elaborate studio lighting techniques popularized by Hollywood, while at the same time bringing the look of documentary photography to his series for the American Tobacco Company. In the 1950s, Keppler learned from photo-journalism how realistic settings, spontaneous action, and natural lighting might be used to great advantage.

From the early 1930s Keppler established a reputation as one of the leading color photographers in advertising. Working primarily in the difficult carbro color process, he produced a great many vivid, eye-stopping photographic illustrations for advertisements and magazine covers. In his book *The Eighth Art,* Keppler demonstrates the understanding of the technical side of color photography that accounted for his success with it.

Keppler's autobiography, *Man + Camera,* is one of the most complete examinations of the career of an advertising photographer. It throws revealing light on the relations between the business and cultural environments and photographic technology, and is marked throughout by Keppler's own high spirits.

—Christopher Phillips

KERN, Pascal.

Nationality: French. **Born:** Paris on 13 June 1952. **Education:** Studied engraving and sculpture at Ecole des Beaux Arts, Paris; gained a doctorate in aesthetics and the history of fine art from the Sorbonne; self-taught as a photographer. **Agent:** Galerie Zabriske, 37 Rue Quincampoix, 75004 Paris; and 724 5th Avenue, New York, New York 10019, U.S.A. **Address:** 167 Boulevard Serurier, Paris 75019, France.

Individual Exhibitions:

1979   *Usine à Bastos,* Paris
1980   *Usine à Bastos,* Musée National d'Art Moderne, Centre George
        Pompidou, Paris
1982   *Cinéma l'Epatant* and *Trois Insallations,* Usine Pali-kao, Paris
1983   *Fictions Colorées,* Axe-sud Art Actuel, Toulouse (travelled to
        Galerie Zabriskie, Paris; FRAC Champagne-Ardennes,
        Chaumont; Thomas Barry Fine Art Gallery, Minneapolis;
        Palais des Congrès et de la Culture, Le Mans; Maison de la
        Culture, Amiens)
1985   *Colored Fiction,* Galerie Anna Leonowens, Halifax, Canada

Sculpture (tryptich), **1992.** Photograph by Pascal Kern.

1986   *Icônes,* Galerie Zabriskie, Paris (travelled to Galerie Zabriskie, New York)
1988   *Icônes et Fiction Colorées,* Galerie de l'Ecole des Beaux-Arts, Rouen (travelled to Institut Français, Cologne)
        Sculpture, Galerie Zabriske, Paris (travelled to Galerie Zabriske, New York; Ecole Municipale d'Arts Plasiques, Châtellerault)
1989   *Icônes et Sculptures,* Centre d'Arts Plastiques, Villefranche-sur-Saone (travelled to Musée d'Art Moderne, Calais)
1990   *Fiction Colorées—Icône—Sculpture et Architecture,* Musée d'Art Moderne, Strasbourg
1991   *Culture et Nature,* Galerie Zabriske, Paris (travelled to Centre National de la Photographie, Palaise de Tokyo, Paris; International Center of Photography, New York)
1992   *Sculpture, Culture, Nature,* Le Parvis, Tarbes et Parvis 3, Pau (travelled to C.A.P. de Royan, Voûte du Port

Selected Group Exhibitions:

1976   *Assemblages,* Palais de Tokyo, Paris
1981   *Sans titre, ou les figures du vide,* Rennes
1982   *XIIe Biennale de Paris*
1983   *Image Fabriquées,* Musée National d'Art Moderne (travelling)
1984   *L'Hôtel Revisté,* Fondation Jourdan, Paris
1985   *Sans Titre,* Houston (travelled to New York, San Francisco and Canada)
1986   *A Visible Order,* Lieberman and Saul Gallery, New York
1987   *The Spiral of Artificiality,* Hallwalls, Buffalo
1988   *Art or Nature,* Barbican, London
1989   *Ateliers et Pratiques d'Artistes,* Musée d'Art Moderne, Strasbourg
1990   *Photographie Français en Liberté,* Fondation Gulbenkian, Lisbon (travelled to I.C.P., New York)
1991   *The Second East-West Photoconference,* Museum of Architecture, Wroclaw, Poland
1992   *Primavera,* Museum of Modern Art, Barcelona.

Publications:

On KERN: Articles—"La sculpture plane de P.K." by Loïs Malle in *Art Press,* No.85 1984; "Des photos en sculpture" by Daniel Soutif in *Libération,* April 1985; "Three French Artists" by Michael Brenson in *The New York Times,* July 1985; "La forme du nouveau" by Elio Grazioli in *Flash Art,* No. 132, 1987; "P.K." by Ginger Danto in *ART News,* No. 88/2, 1989; "N.M., C.B., P.K." by Otto Hahn in *L'Express,* No. 1974, 1989; "N.M., C.B., P.K." by Anne Dagbert in *Art Press,* No. 137, 1989; "P.K." by Catherine Goffaux in *Photographie Magazine,* No. 22, 1990; "P.K." in *The Village Voice,* June 1990.

*   *   *

From the beginning Pascal Kern has worked within a space that has to do with transference: a transfer of signs and information through his edition of texts in his very earliest works (*The Factory at Bastos*); transfers of objects recovered from a specific place in order to accumulate, install and photograph their installation (in his *Colourful Fictions*); but, from the series of *Ikons* onwards, above all to rigorously define and implement a formulary way of working entailing research into industrial objects and materials which the artist photographs in the studio, exactly life-sized, 1/11, head on, without artifice or intervention. These large Cibachrome runs, generally presented through the assembly of a number of elements, have a rare impact in their presence. At the same time there is something enigmatic about them, something that refuses to be reduced to the simple image of what is being represented. Thus it is frequently impossible to say exactly what the subject being represented is, for it's evident that the photographer here uses photography in a manner considerably more complex than in its familiar form as a simple analogous recording process. The importance of overall design, in which the material echoes the fabric of the objects depicted in the images, and whose function clearly goes beyond the decorative, likewise invites us to participate in a prolonged and interrogative contemplation of these works.

If Pascal Kern defines himself as a "sculptor" it's because the real material of his work, his particular domain, raises the issue of volume in every one of its aspects; the relationship between volume and surface, flat and hollowed, depth and evenness. These objects and materials will give birth to numerous series of work tackling various aspects of the representation of volume.

For example, in the series called *Sculpture,* he was to often employ wooden constructions, the "core boxes" used in factories to manufacture the moulds into which liquid metals can be poured. These are remarkable objects in themselves, as they serve as the repositories of history, a history of techniques in the process of vanishing, but above a history of the intricate manipulations to which they give rise, and which function as a veritable lexicon of sculptural operations: positive/negative inversions, passages through the different stages and materials leading to the final casting, the tension between volume and surface and so forth. Pascal Kern also has recourse to industrial objects manufactured in series with moulds or engravings (like buckets, tiles, bathroom fittings, car wings, etc.), in the service of which he attempts to resolve the questions linked to our perception of scale, along with the problem of reproducibility, sculpture and photography having in common, among other attributes, the possibility of reproduction, of multiple runs, something which enters into conflict with the concept of an original, itself the foundation of assessing the value of a traditional work of art.

In his series *Nature and Culture,* Pascal Kern plays, often humorously, with a schoolboy opposition between the two terms, from whence he translates their logic into the language of his personal reflections. Here one can clearly see how far his work remains from the poetics of "found objects" (which doesn't of course, of itself, preclude the objects used from having a remarkable plastic presence of their own). Here it is that certain objects become "moulds" in their turn, with the help of which he models plaster copies, which he then arranges and photographs. Here there are natural objects (cucurbitaceous fruits that he often grows himself) from which he again makes moulds. In these hollowed shapes, he lays down pigments of colour to be absorbed into the material, leaving traces of the colour to create an arresting illusion. Within that triptych the "natural" object is at the centre, enclosed by the two halves of the mould which appears to have "drunk" not only the colour but also the depth, the antithesis of concave and convex, of hollowed and flat. As to the colour, it is by now impossible to ascertain what is of the plant and what deposited by the artist, what, finally, results from the transformation of the fabric of the mould. We are here at the heart of every sort of paradox which the photographic image alone, with the admixture of extreme precision and indifferent distance it permits, is capable of restituting in all its complexity.

—Régis Durand

KERTÉSZ, André.

Nationality: American. **Born:** Andor Kertész in Budapest, Hungary, 2 July 1894; emigrated to France, 1925, and to the United States, 1936; naturalized, 1944. **Education:** Studied at the Academy of Commerce, Budapest, 1910-12; self-taught in photography. **Military Service:** Served in the Austro-Hungarian Army in Poland, Albania, and Rumania, 1914-15. **Family:** Married Elisabeth Sali in 1933. **Career:** Photographer from 1912. Worked as an accounts clerk, Budapest Stock Exchange, 1912-14, 1918-25; freelance photographer, working for *Frankfurt Illustrierte, Berliner Illustrierte, Uhu, Strasburger Illustrierte, Le Nazionale de Fiorenza, Vu, Sourire, The Times* (London), etc., Paris, 1925-35; Contract Photographer, Keystone Studios, New York, 1936-37; freelance magazine photographer, for *Harper's Bazaar, Vogue, Town and Country, American Magazine, Collier's, Coronet, Look,* etc., New York, 1937-49; Contract Photographer, Condé Nast Publications, mainly for *House and Garden* magazine, New York, 1949-62; freelance photographer, New York, 1962 until his death in 1985. **Recipient:** Photography Competition Prize, *Borsszem Janko* magazine, Budapest, 1916; Silver Medal, *Exposition Coloniale,* Paris, 1930; Gold Medal, *4th Mostra Biennale Internazionale della Fotografia,* Venice, 1963; Guggenheim Fellowship, 1974; Mayor's Award, New York, 1977; University of Salford Award, England, 1980. Member of Honor, American Society of Magazine Photogra-

Pont Neuf, Paris, **1931.** Photograph by André Kertész. Courtesy of the Art Institute of Chicago.

phers, 1965. Commander, Order of Arts and Letters, France, 1977. Officer, Légion d'Honneur, France, 1983. **Died:** (in New York) 27 September 1985.

Individual Exhibitions:

1927	Galerie Le Sacre du Printemps, Paris
1946	Art Institute of Chicago
1962	Long Island University, New York
1963	Bibliothèque Nationale, Paris
	Modern Age Studio, New York
1964	Museum of Modern Art, New York
1971	Moderna Museet, Stockholm
	Magyar Nemzeti Galeria, Budapest
1972	Valokuvamuseum, Helsinki
1973	Hallmark Gallery, New York
	Light Gallery, New York
1976	Wesleyan University, Middletown, Connecticut
	French Cultural Institute, New York
1977	Centre Beaubourg, Paris
1978	*Sympathetic Explorations: Kertész/Harbutt,* Plains Art Museum, Moorhead, Minnesota
1979	Serpentine Gallery, London
	Kiva Gallery, Boston
1980	Salford University, England
	Galerie Agathe Gaillard, Paris (with Gilles Ehrmann)
1981	*Vintage Prints,* Galerie Wilde, Cologne
	Susan Spiritus Gallery, Newport Beach, California
	Zeit-Foto Salon, Tokyo

1982	*Still Lifes,* Edwynn Houk Gallery, Chicago
1983	*On Reading,* New York Public Library
	Rarely Seen Images, Neikrug Photographica, New York
	Color, Susan Harder Gallery, New York
	Form and Feeling, Portland Art Museum, Oregon
	Benteler Galleries, Houston, Texas
	Light Factory, Charlotte, North Carolina (retrospective)
1984	University of Miami, Coral Gables
	Early Paris, Edwynn Houk Gallery, Chicago
	Witkin Gallery, New York
	Akron Art Museum, Ohio (retrospective)
1985	*Gardens,* Susan Harder Gallery, New York
	Of Paris and New York, Art Institute of Chicago (retrospective; travelled to the Metropolitan Museum of Art, New York)

Selected Group Exhibitions:

1928	*Premier Salon Indépendant de la Photographie,* Salon de l'Escalier, Paris
1929	*Film und Foto,* Deutscher Werkbund, Stuttgart
1932	*Modern European Photography,* Julien Levy Gallery, New York
1934	*Photographies,* Salon Leleu, Paris
1937	*Photography 1848-1937,* Museum of Modern Art, New York
1967	*The Concerned Photographer,* Riverside Museum, New York (and world tour)
1979	*La Photographie Francaise 1925-1940,* Galerie Zabriskie, Paris (and Zabriskie Gallery, New York)

1982   *Counterparts: Form and Emotion in Photographs,* Metropolitan
        Museum of Art, New York (travelled to the Contemporary
        Arts Center, Cincinnati; Dallas Museum of Fine Arts, Texas;
        San Francisco Museum of Modern Art; Corcoran Gallery,
        Washington, D.C.)
1985   *L'Amour Fou: Photography and Surrealism,* Corcoran Gallery,
        Washington, D.C. (travelled to San Franciscco Museum of
        Modern Art; Centre Georges Pompidou, Paris; Hayward
        Gallery, London)
1986   *The Animal in Photography 1843-1985,* The Photographers'
        Gallery, London

Collections:

Museum of Modern Art, New York; International Museum of Photography,
George Eastman House, Rochester, New York; Smithsonian Institution,
Washington, D.C.; Carpenter Center, Harvard University, Cambridge, Massa-
chusetts; Detroit Institute of Arts; Art Institute of Chicago; New Orleans
Museum of Art; University of Nebraska, Lincoln; Center for Creative Photog-
raphy, University of Arizona, Tucson; Musée d'Art Moderne, Paris.

Publications:

By KERTÉSZ: Books—*Enfants,* with text by Jaboune, Paris 1933; *Paris Vu
par André Kertész,* with text by Pierre MacOrlan, Paris 1934; *Nos Amis des
Bêtes,* with text by Jaboune, Paris 1936; *Les Cathedrales du Vin,* with text by
Pierre Hamp, Paris 1937; *Day of Paris,* with text by George Davis, Paris 1945;
André Kertész, Photographer, with text by John Szarkowski, New York 1964;
On Reading, New York 1971; *Foto,* Budapest 1972; *André Kertész: Sixty
Years of Photography,* with poems by Paul Dermée, New York and London
1972; *J'Aime Paris: Photographs since the 1920s,* New York 1974; *Washing-
ton Square,* with an introduction by Brendan Gill, New York 1975; *Of New
York,* New York 1976; *Distortions,* with an introduction by Hilton Kramer,
New York 1976; *André Kertész,* edited by Aperture, Millerton, New York
1976; *André Kertész: Landscapes* and *Americana* and *Birds* and *Portraits,* all
edited by Nicolas Ducrot, New York 1979; *From My Window,* Boston 1981;
Kertész on Kertész: A Self Portrait, New York and London 1985. Articles—
interview in *Dialogue with Photography* by Paul Hill and Thomas Cooper,
London 1979; interview in *Voyons Voir: 8 Photographes,* edited by Pierre
Borhan, Paris 1980.

On KERTÉSZ: Books—*André Kertész: Photographies,* exhibition cata-
logue, Paris 1963; *André Kertész* by Anna Farova, New York 1964; *André
Kertész,* exhibition catalogue, by Colin Ford, London 1979; *Visions and
Images: American Photographers on Photography,* edited by Barbaralee
Diamonstein, New York 1981; *Master Photographers: The World's Great
Photographers on their Art and Technique,* edited by Pat Booth, London 1983;
André Kertész: Of Paris and New York, with texts by Sandra S. Phillips, David
Travis and Weston J. Naef, Chicago, New York and London 1985. Articles—
"Photo Kertész" by Montpar in *Chantecler* (Paris), 19 March 1927; "La
Photographie, est-elle un art?" by Jean Gallotti in *L'Art Vivant* (Paris), 1
March 1929; "Kertész et son miroir" by Bertrand Guegan in *Arts et Metiers
Graphiques* (Paris), no. 37, 1933; "André Kertész: Day of Paris" by Bruce
Downes in *Popular Photography* (New York), no. 6, 1945; "André Kertész"
by William Hoseman in *Infinity* (New York), no. 4, 1959; "My Friend André
Kertész" by Brassaï in *Camera* (Lucerne), no. 4, 1963; "André Kertész,
Photographer" by Margaret R. Weiss in *Saturday Review* (New York), 20
December 1964; "André Kertész: A Meeting of Friends" by Bill Jay in
Creative Camera (London), August 1969; "A Triumph for the Innocent Eye:
The Work of André Kertész" by Ainslie Ellis in *British Journal of Photogra-
phy* (London), 20 October 1972; "André Kertész at 80" by D.S. Gelatt in
Popular Photography (New York), November 1974; "The Master of the
Moment" by Carole Kismaric in the *Sunday Times Magazine* (London), 13
January 1980; "I Looked, I Saw, I Did" by Douglas Davis in *Newsweek* (New
York), 6 December 1982; "Kertész: The Great Democrat of Modern Photog-
raphy" by Gene Thornton in the *New York Times,* 22 July 1984; "Kertész
Exhibition Celebrates a Vital Visual Force" by Alan G. Artner in the *Chicago
Tribune,* 5 May 1985; "The Bittersweet Exile of André Kertész" by Kathryn

Livingston in *American Photographer* (New York), February 1986. Film—*A
Window on the Square,* BBC Television, directed by Michael Macintyre, 1980.

*

I started photography instinctively. I never tried to imitate or copy any
painting or graphic work; photography itself was the medium by which I
strove to express my impressions and feelings. As with every art, in photography the most important thing is that we feel fully what we are doing.

—André Kertész (1982)

*   *   *

André Kertész was one of the first photographers to work spontaneously
with a small, hand-held camera, catching things as they happened; and he was
always one of the best. But he was never limited; he worked just as well with a
tripod-mounted camera in a studio.

No one seems to think of Kertész as a photographer with a special gift for
design; yet, in an understated way, he excelled at design. Because of that skill,
he is one of the very few first-rank black-and-white photographers whose
pictures do not depend on excellent printing. That's fortunate, because for
many years his darkroom work was done by others and seldom to the standard
that his photographs deserve. Even in technically undistinguished prints, his
pictures keep their strength and much of their subtlety. When printed well, of
course, they get even better. And that is because he photographed consistently
with rigorous, extreme formal clarity. The design does not call attention to
itself. His sense of form seems innate: it is not the kind that can be learned in an
art school. And it is never all there is to the picture. He used it quietly as a
means to an end, and so efficiently that it goes unnoticed. In this he is far
different from those photographers whose pictures shout "design!" and have
little else to show us. They are clever poster-makers; he was a thoughtful and
intuitive artist. They strain for effect; he achieved it without letting the
effort show.

Something seldom noted: another demonstration of Kertész's design
sense. In the 1930s he did the excellent layout for Robert Capa's first book,
Death in the Making, about the Spanish civil war. Capa was then a young
protegé of Kertész. Unfortunately, this book was printed very poorly. It would
be worth republishing with Kertész's layout intact, and this time with good
halftone reproduction.

His work was economical, without waste motion. As one of the first
photojournalists, Kertész would go out to cover a news event and he'd bring
back 8 or 12 exposures, not 59 rolls. And those few frames told the story.
Intelligent and discriminating seeing is more useful than a motor-driven
camera.

Kertész had humor and irony, and needed them. After a brilliant start in
Europe, first as a boy in Hungary and as a young officer in the Austro-
Hungarian Army during World War I (excellent photographs survive from
those times), then after the war in Paris, where he earned prompt recognition,
he came to the United States before World War II. His contract with Condé
Nast seemed to offer full scope for his talent and initiative, but it didn't work
out that way. Through the 1940s and '50s the work he did for them was mostly
the conventional photography of well-decorated houses that is standard in
magazines that specialize in gracious living rather than real life. It was a trap.
He did this work beautifully and became identified with it. (At the time I had
seen nothing else from him and thought of him as one of those highly skilled
hacks who earn a comfortable living by doing what is expected.) Luckily for
us, Kertész never forgot who he was and never stopped doing his own work,
which no one saw, often taking personal pictures on the way to and from the
pretty-house assignments.

In the early 1960s he came out from behind that curtain. Some personal
pictures were published in *Infinity,* the magazine of the American Society of
Magazine Photographers, and some were exhibited at the Museum of Modern
Art in New York. They were revelations.

This emergence must have gratified Kertész: people began to see that he
was a unique and remarkable artist. It did not solve his problems, since the
commercial demand for subtle perception does not exist. But from then on
there have increasingly been outlets for his real work—exhibitions and books.

Kertész had good reason to be bitter, and he kept some bitterness to the
end. He was skeptical, but never descended to cynicism.

His special gift was to see and record the absurd and touching sights of ordinary life with poignance and clarity, on the wing as they fly past, so that the rest of us can see and appreciate them too. His photographs have grace, wit and compassion. They are warm, not cold. The bizarre interested him and he photographed it, but not as a freak show. He smiles; he doesn't sneer. His work reminds us that while people are certainly odd they are not all fools or all evil. They aren't all intelligent or pleasant, either, but something good is there for those who can see it. Kertész shows it to us.

—David Vestal

KESSEL, Dmitri.

Nationality: American. **Born:** Kiev, 20 August 1902; emigrated to the United States, 1923: naturalized, 1929. **Education:** Attended the Nemirov Gymnasium and at the Paltava Military Academy, Poltava, Russia, graduated 1918; studied at the Industrial Chemistry Institute, Moscow, 1921-22; studied at the New York City College, and photography at the Rabinovitch School of Photography, New York, 1934. **Military Service:** Served in the Ukrainian Army, 1918, and as an officer in the Red Army, during the Russian/Polish War, 1919-21. **Family:** Married Shirley Farmer in 1964. **Career:** Worked at various odd jobs, for a fur exporter, and as a correspondent for Russian newspapers, New York, 1923-34; freelance industrial, advertising and reportage photographer, working for *Fortune, Life, Colliers, Saturday Evening Post*, etc., New York, 1934-42; war correspondent, on contract to *Life*, 1942-44; staff photographer, *Life*, 1944-67; contract photographer, Time-Life publications, 1967-72; freelance photographer, working for *Smithsonian Magazine*, Time-Life Books, *Life*, etc., since 1972. **Recipient:** Order of Excellence, Spanish Morocco, 1949; Gold Medal, City of Ravenna, Italy, 1959; Knighthood, Italian Government, 1965; Order of Tadj, Iran, 1966. **Address:** 46 Avenue Gabriel, 75008 Paris, France.

Selected Group Exhibitions:

1951	*Memorable Life Photographs,* Museum of Modern Art, New York
1955	*The Family of Man,* Museum of Modern Art, New York (and world tour)
1979	*Life: The First Decade 1936-45,* Grey Art Gallery, New York University
1982	*Floods of Light,* The Photographers' Gallery, London
1985	*Life: The Second Decade,* Grey Art Gallery, New York University (travelled to Bonn, Paris and Rome, 1985-86)

Collections:

Metropolitan Museum of Art, New York; Time-Life Library, New York.

Publications:

By KESSEL: Books—*The Splendors of Christendom,* Lausanne, Switzerland 1964; *On Assignment: Dmitri Kessel, Life Photographer,* New York 1985.

On KESSEL: Books—*U.S. Camera 1936,* annual, edited by Tom J. Maloney, New York and London 1936; *Memorable Life Photographs,* with text by Edward Steichen, New York 1951; *Words and Pictures: An Introduction to Photojournalism* by Wilson Hicks, New York 1952; *How Life Gets the Story: Behind the Scenes in Photo-Journalism,* edited by Stanley Rayfield 1955; *Life Photographers: Their Careers and Favorite Pictures,* edited by Stanley Rayfield, New York 1957; *Travel Photography,* by the Time-Life editors, New York 1973; *The Magic Image* by Cecil Beaton and Gail Buckland, London and Boston 1975; *Life: The First Decade 1936-1945* by Robert Littman, Ralph Graves and Doris C. O'Neill, New York 1979, London

1980; *Floods of Light: Flash Photography 1851-1981,* exhibition catalogue, by Rupert Martin, London 1982.

*   *   *

Even as a boy, Dmitri Kessel took pictures with a Brownie camera. After he left his father's beet plantation in the Podolia district of the Ukraine at the age of 10, to go to school, he graduated from military academy in 1918 with a commission in the Ukrainian Army. He promptly got himself into trouble for taking amateur photos of the massacre of a Polish Army unit, in which 200 men were killed by Ukrainian peasants. He recalls that an army officer smashed his camera with its heavy glass plates over his head. In the turmoil of the Polish-Russian war of 1920-21, Kessel was twice imprisoned; he finally made his way to the U.S.A., arriving in New York in 1923.

After a series of odd jobs, including working for a fur exporter and manufacturer and as a correspondent for Russian language periodicals, he became interested in the combination of journalism and photography. He took a course in photography from the renowned Rabinovitch, from whom he principally learned self-criticism. Gradually, after photographing the New York streets, buses, overhead railways and unfamiliar people, Kessel specialized in industrial photography on assignments from advertising agencies and American corporations. His first assignment for Time-Life's *Fortune* magazine came in 1935, and he joined *Life's* staff of photographers in 1944.

It is for his work as a news cameraman on these magazines that he is best known. His outstanding pictures of violence—the Congo, the British sweep into Greece, the Greek Civil War, the German retreat of 1945—are the work of a tried-and-tough newsman. At one time during the Greek civil war, Kessel stood directly in the firing line to take pictures, although he knew they stood little chance of getting published. When asked why he had done such a "crazy" thing, he said: "Somebody had to take them." After World War II, Kessel worked mainly out of *Life's* Paris bureau until 1956, covering the Middle East oil crisis, the Haganah Army in Palestine, Franco's post-war Spain, and stories from China, Ceylon, Japan, India, Siam, South and Central America.

But, apart from his hard-hitting news pictures, Kessel has an intense response to beauty: his record of the soaring majesty of many great churches and cathedrals—often taking several long exposure shots to achieve—are world famous. The extraordinary fidelity of his colour studies of the Vatican, the Sistine Chapel, St. Mark's in Venice, the mosaics of Ravenna, the sculpture of Bernini and Michelangelo have a monumental quality that is technically beyond comparison.

—Colin Naylor

KIFFL, Erika.

Nationality: Austrian. **Born:** Karlsbad, Czechoslovakia, 19 December 1939. **Education:** Studied graphics, under Joseph Fassbender, Fachhochschule, Krefeld, West Germany, 1957-59, and graphic design and photography, under Walter Breker, Kunstakademie, Dusseldorf, 1959-61. **Career:** Art Director, *Elegante Welt* fashion magazine, Dusseldorf, 1961-65; Art Buyer, TEAM Publicity Agency, Dusseldorf, 1965-68; freelance representative for foreign photographers in Dusseldorf, 1968-75. Freelance photographer, Dusseldorf, since 1979. **Recipient:** Barkenhoff Stiftung grant, Worpswede, 1982; Kunstfonds grant, Bonn, 1983.

Individual Exhibitions:

1978	Staatsgalerie, Stuttgart
1979	Studio F, Ulm, West Germany
	Kunstmuseum, Dusseldorf
1980	Galerie Heike Curtze, Dusseldorf
	Städtische Galerie, Wolfsburg, West Germany
	Kunsthalle, Kiel, West Germany
	Neue Galerie, Linz, Austria
1981	Sammlung Fotografis, Vienna

Kunstmuseum, Hannover
Galerie Spectrum, Hannover
Kunstverein, Frankfurt
1982 Stadtmuseum, Munich
Stadtmuseum, Dusseldorf
Rheinisches Landesmuseum, Bonn
Galerie Jutta Rössner, Stuttgart
1984 Landessammlung Rupertinum, Salzburg, Austria
Shadai Gallery, Tokyo
Kulturhaus, Graz, Austria
1985 Mala Galeria, Warsaw
Goethe Institute, Tel-Aviv, Israel
1986 ZPAF Gallery, Krakow, Poland
Budapest Gallery, Hungary

Selected Group Exhibitions:

1981 *New German Photography,* The Photographers' Gallery,
London
1985 *Rheingold,* Galleria d'Arte Moderna, Turin, Italy
Process und Konstruktion, Fotomuseum im Stadtmuseum,
Munich

Collections:

Kunstmuseum, Dusseldorf; Stadtgeschichtliches Museum, Dusseldorf; Neue
Sammlung, Munich; Staatsgalerie, Stuttgart; Kunsthalle, Hamburg; Institute
für Moderne Kunst, Nuremberg; Sammlung Fotografis, Vienna; Landessammlung
Rupertinum, Salzburg, Austria; Bibliothèque Nationale, Paris; Institute of
Polytechnics, Tokyo.

Publications:

By KIFFL: Books—*Künstler in ihrem Atelier,* with a foreword by Jörg
Krichbaum, Munich 1979; *Neue Wege in der Fotografie: Foto-Symposion
Schloss Mickeln,* Munich 1980; *Raum-Sequenzen,* with text by Helmut
Heissenbüttel, Munich 1980; *Ist Fotografie Kunst? Gehort Fotografie in's
Museum?,* editor, Munich 1982.

On KIFFL: Books—*Erika Kiffl: Kontakte,* exhibition catalogue, by Anda
Rottenberg, Warsaw 1985; *Erika Kiffl: Das Reich der Zeichen,* exhibition
catalogue, by László Beke, Budapest 1986. **Articles**—"Künstler und Räume"
by Ingrid Bacher in *Professional Camera* (Munich), February 1979; "Erika
Kiffl" by Jörg Krichbaum in *Zoom* (Munich), March 1980; "Räume" by
Christiane Zillinger in *Architekture und Wohnen* (Hamburg), September 1980;
"New Germany Photography" by Rupert Martin in *European Photography*
(Göttingen), December 1980; "Erika Kiffl" by Ekkehard Mai in *Das Kunstwerk*
(Baden-Baden), June 1984.

*

My experience of the world comes from looking, and I try, by giving form
to reality, to come to terms with my own reality and to clarify my point of view.

My photographs are a reaction to my surroundings and an action in the
process I call life by which I capture and create my own reality.

My photographs are a message to people who know how to look, who can,
by looking at my pictures, find themselves in touch with me.

In this way I take part in events.

I take photographs in studios because they are, for me, mysterious places
where something is happening which has a lot to do with my own longing to
express myself.

Artists' studios and what happens in them have always exerted an
extraordinary fascination which either paralyzes or inspires me.

I have discovered my own pictures by travelling as a spectator through
artists' studios.

—Erika Kiffl

* * *

The starting point for Erika Kiffl's photographs is not other photographs,
nor the supposedly continuous contemplation of reality however modified, but
the development of painting in the last two decades. So it follows that her
vision is not to be judged according to traditional photographic criteria—as,
for example, "realistic," "romantic," "poetic," "objective," etc. From her
direct exposure to the artistic work at the Kunstakademie in Dusseldorf over
the past 20 years (Graubner, Girke, Richter, Geiger, Beuys, Haese, Heerich,
Klapheck, Uecker, among others), she has gained a feeling for new artistic
ways of seeing and also found her theme—rooms.

In her series *Künstler in ihrem Atelier* (Artists in Their Studios), Kiffl has
tried to discover and to portray creatively and photographically the ways in
which the room—the studio—influences the work of individual artists. Her
technique, however, is not painterly; she does not "paint" with the camera.
She has made a particular camera lens system her own (quadrangular/square
view-finder), and includes within this field of vision the most important
components of the room and its natural light forms. Apart from the angles and
corners which directly characterize the form (the "cube" of the room), light is
the most important element in her pictures. Like a mute stage manager, light
gives to the objects their significance and their roles, intermingling brilliance
and darkness, the known and the unknown, the present and the past. Within
this field of tension the artist is only occasionally present, and the objects
themselves contribute to the impression of silent communication: empty
chairs, working tools left lying around and specially laid apart, and, above all,
materials. All of these objects and materials emit an intensity appropriate to
our conception of the place in which an artist would set out to create an
atmosphere conducive to his work.

After this series, it was only consistent that Erika Kiffl should completely
renounce people and concentrate on rooms themselves. Her latest series,
Raum-Sequenzen, continues the working methods of *Künstler in ihrem
Atelier,* but here she turns her attention from the materials of the artist (the
particular studio as a source of inspiration) to other questions relating to space.
Some of these photos could have come from the Robbe-Grillet novel/film
Last Year in Marienbad.

—Ulrich Bischoff

KILLIP, Chris(topher).

Nationality: British. **Born:** Douglas, Isle of Man, 11 July 1946. **Education:**
Attended Douglas High School, 1957-62; self-taught in photography.
Career: Worked as a photographic assistant to various photographers, London, 1963-69. Freelance photographer, London, since 1970. Photography
Fellow, Northern Arts, Newcastle upon Tyne, 1975-76; Director, Side Gallery
of Photography, Newcastle upon Tyne, 1977-78; Photographer-in-Residence, University College, Cardiff, 1979-80; Visiting Lecturer, Department
of Visual and Environmental Studies, Harvard University, Cambridge, Massachusetts; Professor, Harvard University, 1994. **Recipient:** Photography
Grant, Arts Council of Great Britain, 1973, 1974, 1977; Henri Cartier-Bresson
Award, Paris 1989. **Address:** Visual and Environmental Studies, Harvard
University, 24 Quincy Street, Cambridge, Massachusetts 02138, U.S.A.

Individual Exhibitions:

1977 *Photos of North East England,* Side Gallery, Newcastle
upon Tyne
1980 *Isle of Man,* Side Gallery, Newcastle upon Tyne (toured the
U.K., 1980-83)
1984 *Seacoal,* Side Gallery, Newcastle upon Tyne
1985 Serpentine Gallery, London
1986 *Another Country,* National Museum of Photography, Bradford,
Yorkshire
Art Institute of Chicago
1987 *Another Country,* Auckland City Art Gallery, Auckland, New
Zealand
1988 *In Flagrante,* Victoria and Albert Museum, London; Landes
Museum, Munster; Atrium Museum, Aachen.

Untitled, **from the book** *In Flagrante,* **1988.** Photograph by Chris Killip.

1989   *In Flagrante,* Museum für Künst und Külturgeschede, Dörtmund; Alter Rathaussaal, Münich; Centrum für Industrie-Kültur, Nüremberg; Landesbildstelle, Stüttgart; Musem Het Princessehof, Leeuwarden.
    Chris Killip, Fotografiska Museet i Moderna Museet, Stockholm

1990   *Working at Pirelli,* Victoria and Albert Museum, London

1991   *Chris Killip Retrospective,* Palais de Tokyo, Paris

Selected Group Exhibitions:

1977   *Concerning Photography,* The Photographers' Gallery, London (travelled to Spectro Workshop, Newcastle upon Tyne)

1980   *Old and Modern Masters of Photography,* Victoria and Albert Museum, London (toured the U.K.)

1982   *Lichtbildnisse: Das Porträt in der Fotografie,* Rheinisches Landesmuseum, Bonn

1985   *Quelques Anglais,* Centre National de la Photographie, Paris

1986   *British Photography,* at the *Foto Fest,* Houston, Texas

1987   *Towards a Bigger Picture,* Victoria and Albert Museum, London
    Photoworks from Great Britain, Forum Stadtpark, Graz, Austria
    Three British Photographers, Consejo Mexicano de Fotografia, Mexico City

1988   *On the Edge of the City,* (with the painter Ken Currie), Manchester City Art Gallery, England
    Britische Sicht! Fotografie aus England, Museum für Gestaltung, Zürich
    Matter of Facts: Photographie Art Contemporain en Grande Bretagne, Musée des Beaux Arts, Nantes and Musée d'Art Moderne, Saint-Etiennes
    Towards a Bigger Picture, Tate Gallery, Liverpool

1989   *The Art of Photography 1839-1989,* Museum of Fine Art, Houston; Australian National Gallery, Canberra; Royal Academy of Arts, London.
    Through the Looking Glass: Photographic Art in Britain 1945-1989, Barbican Art Gallery, London
    Photography: 150 Years, The Australian National Gallery, Canberra
    Photography Until Now, The Museum of Modern Art, New York

1990   *British Photography from the Thatcher Years,* The Museum of Modern Art, New York
    Arbete Pågår, Hasselblad Center, Götenborg

1991   *Shocks to the System,* Royal Festival Hall, London; Northern Centre for Contemporary Art, Sunderland; Ikon Gallery, Birmingham.
    Arbetets Värld, Arbetets Musem, Norrköping, Sweden

1992   *More than One Photography: Works Since 1980 From the Collection,* The Museum of Modern Art, New York

1993   *Encontros de Fotografia,* Coimbra, Portugal

Collections:

Victoria and Albert Museum, London; Bibliothèque Nationale, Paris; Arts Council of Great Britain, London; Museum of Modern Art, New York; Metropolitan Museum of Art, New York; International Museum of Photography at George Eastman House, Rochester, New York; Center for Creative Photography, University of Arizona, Tucson; Harry Ransom Center, University of Texas, Austin; San Francisco Museum of Fine Art; Stedelijk Museum, Amsterdam; I.V.A.M., Valencia, Spain; Museum Folkwang, Essen, Germany; National Gallery of Australia, Canberra; Auckland City Art Gallery, New Zealand.

Publications:

By KILLIP: Book—*Isle of Man: A Book about the Manx,* with an introduction by John Berger, London 1980. **Articles**—"Lewis Hine" in *Side Gallery Bulletin* (Newcastle upon Tyne), 1977; "Sir Roy Strong, Director of the V&A,

Interviewed" in *Creative Camera,* October 1981; "Personal Choice: A Celebration of Twentieth Century Photographs Selected and Introduced by Photographers, Painters and Writers." Victoria and Albert Museum 1983; "Photography Now," review of the exhibition in *Camera Austria,* No. 9, 1989; "Marketá Luskacová: Photographs of Spitalfieds," London 1991.

On KILLIP: Books—*British Image 2,* edited by the Arts Council, London 1976; *Concerning Photography,* exhibition catalogue, edited by Jonathan Bayer, London 1977; *Creative Camera Yearbook,* edited by Colin Osman and Peter Turner, London 1975; *Exploring Photography* by Bryn Campbell, London 1978; *About 70 Photographs,* edited by Chris Steele-Perkins and Bill Messer, London 1981; *Photography: A Concise History* by Ian Jeffrey, London 1981; *Lichtbildnisse: Das Porträt in der Fotografie,* edited by Klaus Honnef, Cologne 1982; *Photography Annual 1986,* New York 1986; *Photography Until Now,* ed. John Szarkowski, New York 1989; *British Photography from the Thatcher Years,* ed. Susan Kismaric, New York 1990. **Articles**—"Chris Killip" in *Creative Camera* (London), May 1977; "Chris Killip" by Shoji Yamagishi in *Camera Mainichi* (Tokyo), July 1978; "Har Finns Mina Rötter" by Peter Turner in *Aktuell Fotografi* (Helsingborg, Sweden), November 1980; "Chris Killip" by Mark Haworth-Booth in *Camera Austria* (Graz), no. 11/12, 1983; "Chris Killip: Scenes from Another Country" by Mark Haworth-Booth in *Aperture* (Millerton, New York), no. 193, 1986; "Chris Killip" interviewed by David Lee in *Creative Camera,* May 1988; "Killip" text by John Morrison in *Photography,* May 1988; "Ihr da Unten" text by John Berger and Sylvia Grant, translated by Martin Hielscher in *Zeit Magazine,* October 1989; "Head to Head: Chris Killip and Bert Hardy" interviewed by Terry Hope in *Amateur Photographer,* June 1990; "Levande Män!" in *Prat Magazine,* Sweden 1990; "Part of the Family: Talking with Chris Killip" text by Christopher Lyon in *MOMA Members Quarterly,* Winter 1991.

*   *   *

Chris Killip is self taught in photography. Not simply in the taking of pictures with a 4 x 5 camera, but also in the way in which photography was served and seen in Britain during the 1970s and 80s. To understand this he was willing to give time, both as a director of the Side Gallery and on various Arts Council committees, to fully understand the status of photography in this country and work for its improvement.

As a social documentary photographer the use of large format is not the easiest of tools. What it does give him is time to balance an immediate impression of a scene and to compose to the full limits of the frame. In an interview with Bryn Campbell he once spoke of the difficulties of showing the impact of a messy situation with clarity so that the viewer is drawn into the picture and is encouraged to study all its detail. Born on the Isle of Man, Killip started with an essay on the TT races and he then progressed to a series of portraits of the islanders where his knowledge of them and their way of life added considerable warmth to a format which encourages a rather formal approach.

He spent a few years in London as a freelance but his real interest has been in the north of England and his best work has been done there. The north suffered first in the growing recession and in this long on-going project Chris has shown its impact on the people and the places in a way which many southerners would prefer to be able to ignore. With the publication of *In Flagrante* in 1988 and in several exhibitions this work received wide acclaim and in 1989 he won the coveted Cartier-Bresson Award. Such long and historically valuable work requires funding and although he had received some earlier bursaries he has also undertaken selected commercial work. In 1991 he became a Visiting Lecturer in the Department of Visual and Environmental Studies at Harvard and has recently been made a Professor there. He continues to photograph during vacations in England and his work is included in the *Documentary Dilemmas* exhibition currently touring in Europe.

Chris Killip does not talk easily about his photography. I imagine he is either a ruthless editor of his work, or takes considerable time in selecting the viewpoint. He prints in a very straightforward manner, not enhancing black or whites but using the whole range of tones to give a full and convincing impression of what he has seen. The results are magnificent photographs that repay close study; nothing is there by accident and everything has its value within the composition.

—Sue Davies

KIRSTEL, Richard.

Nationality: American. **Education:** Studied photography, under Ralph Hattersley and Minor White, Rochester Institute of Technology, Rochester, New York, and, under Aaron Siskind and Harry Callahan, Institute of Design, Illinois Institute of Technology, Chicago. Freelance photographer. Instructor, Maryland Institute College of Art, Baltimore. **Address:** 212 East Biddle Street, Baltimore, Maryland 21202, U.S.A.

Individual Exhibitions:

1969   Exposure Gallery, New York

Selected Group Exhibitions:

1970   *Be-Ing Without Clothers,* Hayden Gallery, Massachusetts
            Institute of Technology, Cambridge

Publications:

By KIRSTEL: Book—*Pas de Deux,* with an introduction by Nat Hentoff, New York 1970.

On KIRSTEL: Articles—''Richard Kirstel: *Pas de Deux*'' by A.D. Coleman in the *Village Voice* (New York), reprinted in Coleman's *Light Readings: A Photography Critic's Writings 1968-1978,* New York 1979; ''Richard Kirstel: Is This the Scopes Trial of Photography?'' by A.D. Coleman in the *New York Times,* 8 November 1970; ''Poetic Justice I'' by A.D. Coleman in the *Village Voice* (New York), 4 March 1971; ''Poetic Justice II'' by A.D. Coleman in the *Village Voice* (New York), 11 March 1971.

*   *   *

Theater, myth and the psychosocial disturbances of our epoch are the linked concerns which run throughout the work of Richard Kirstel. Using such archetypal motifs as darkness, violence and water, his imagery dissects the psychoids of contemporary Western culture.

Because the issues he addresses invariably concern the human condition, the central presences in his images are almost always human—or, if not, such facsimiles thereof as African tribal sculpture (one of his earliest subjects) or dolls, which he has explored for over a decade, using the doll not as a nostalgia-evoking signifier but as a human simulacrum or totem. Agreeing with William Butler Yeats that the only subjects fit for the contemplation of the mature mind are sex and death, Kirstel has considered those themes at length: sexuality in the two sequences which comprise his book *Pas de Deux,* and death in a number of works, most notably the sequences ''Water Babies'' and ''Florida Condo.''

Additionally, his work has explored such corollary concerns as madness and the grotesque. The result is a major body of imagery which has been highly controversial—subject to much debate and even (in the case of *Pas de Deux*) to legal prosecution.

Kirstel employs the silver print exclusively as his vehicle. His studies under Minor White and Ralph Hattersley at the Rochester Institute of Technology, and with Aaron Siskind and Harry Callahan at the Institute of Design, grounded him in the classic tradition of photographic printmaking. Since then he has become a virtuoso printmaker who chooses to work in silver primarily because it makes possible the crafting of an extraordinarily subtle and highly personalized space, which is essential to his imagery.

Perhaps due to this meditative relationship to the printmaker's craft, Kirstel's photographic attitude is a contemplative one. He works with deliberate slowness, allowing little accident into his pictures. Opposed in principle to the so-called ''snapshot aesthetic,'' he believes that ''the camera is not just a net to be used to harvest images like a school of fish, but rather is a probe to explore the space of [my] existence.''

Serial form is also essential to the approach to photography which Kirstel has defined as ''extended realism.'' His stance is that of the epic poet or dramatist. Thus virtually all his imagery is conceptualized and resolved in sequences or suites, a conscious rejection of ''the notion that the individual photograph is a complete statement.'' This commitment has led him to an investigation of the poetics of photography as well as the connections between this visual medium and sculpture, theater, and language itself.

A theorist and teacher as well as an image-maker, Kirstel has lectured and written essays on these and other subjects for a number of publications. A current work-in-progress is a book-length study, *Speculations On Imagery,* directed (like most of his writing) toward defining and analysing the linguistic infra-structure of photography as a communicative process—an attempt to build a comprehensive hermeneutic understanding of the medium.

The combination of his writing, his teaching and his imagery has earned Kirstel a reputation as a ''photographer's photographer.''

—A.D. Coleman

KLEIN, Aart.

Nationality: Dutch. **Born:** Amsterdam, 2 August 1909. **Education:** Attended 8th B.H.S. High School, Amsterdam, 1922-25; self-taught in photography. **Military Service:** Served in the Dutch Army Infantry, 1939-40; Sergeant; and as a Dutch war correspondent (rank of Captain), 1945. **Family:** Married Johanna Magdalena Lindenberg in 1936; sons: Marcel and Edwin. **Career:** Photojournalist and documentary photographer, working for the Polygoon Agency, Amsterdam, 1940, Schimmelpenningh, The Hague, 1940-41, Stadhuisfotograaf, Haarlem, 1941-42, Brusse Bureau, Amsterdam, 1942, and as a freelance photographer for *Algemeen Handelsblad, De Geillustreerede Pers,* etc., Amsterdam, since 1946. **Recipient:** Capi-Lux Alblas Prize, 1981. **Agent:** Lowinsky Gallery, 578 Broadway, New York. **Address:** Amsteldijk 7, 1074 HP Amsterdam, The Netherlands.

Individual Exhibitions:

1964   *Bilder ohne Worte,* Staatliche Landesbildstelle, Hamburg
1965   De Drommedaris, Enkhuizen, Netherlands
1966   Jongerencafé Schuttershof, Heerlen, Netherlands
            Akademie voor Beeldende Kunsten, Arnhem, Netherlands
1968   *Images Sans Mots,* Galerie Montalembert, Paris (travelled to
            the Centre Culturel Communal, Chatillon, France)
1972   Bibliothèque Nationale, Paris
1973   Polytechnical Museum, Moscow
            Stedelijk Museum, Amsterdam
1974   Galerie Fiolet, Amsterdam
            Staatliche Landesbildstelle, Hamburg
1977   *Brandt/Gibson/Klein,* Vrije Universiteit, Amsterdam (with
            Bill Brandt and Ralph Gibson)
1978   Galerij Paule Pia, Antwerp
1981   Stedelijk Museum, Amsterdam
1983   Kasteel Groeneveld, Baarn, Netherlands
1986   *Aart Klein (Foto '86),* Boekhandel Der Verbeelding, Amster-
            dam; De Beyerd, Breda
1992   *Aart Klein in Kleur,* Galeria Dedato, Amsterdam
            Aart Klein 2½ x 4½, Fotogalerie, Amsterdam
1993   Galerie ICPNA-Miraflore, Lima, Peru
            Duch Embassy, Djakarta, Indonesia

Selected Group Exhibitions:

1948   *Foto '48,* Stedelijk Museum, Amsterdam
1952   *Weltausstellung der Fotografie,* Kunsthaus, Lucerne
1954   *Subjektive Fotografie 2,* Staatliche Schule für Kunst und
            Handwerk, Saarbrucken
1961   *Dag Amsterdam,* Stedelijk Museum, Amsterdam
1968   *The Door,* Museum of Contemporary Crafts, New York
1975   *The Land: 20th Century Landscape Photographs Selected by
            Bill Brandt,* Victoria and Albert Museum, London (travelled
            to the National Gallery, Edinburgh; Ulster Museum, Belfast;
            and National Museum of Wales, Cardiff, 1976)

American War Cemetery, Margraten, Netherlands, **1960.** Photograph by Aart Klein.

1978   *Fotografie in Nederland 1940-75,* Stedelijk Museum, Amsterdam
1980   *De ondergedoken camera,* Paleis op de Dam, Amsterdam
1984   *Subjektive Fotografie: Images of the 50s,* San Francisco Museum of Modern Art (travelled to the University of

Houston, Texas; Museum Folkwang, Essen; Vasterbottens Museum, Umea; Kulturhuset, Stockholm; Saarland Museum, Saarbrucken; Palais des Beaux-Arts, Brussels)
1986   *Nederlands Architectuurfotografie 1930-60,* Westersingel 8, Rotterdam

1988   *Roots and Turns. 20th Century Photography in The Nether-
        lands,* Sarah Campbell Blaffer Gallery, Houston
        *Er is geen landschap dat de tijd heeft om te dromen,
        Vormen van Nederlandse landschapsfotografie,*
        Gouvernement, Maastricht

Collections:

Stedelijk Museum, Amsterdam; Prentenkabinett, Rijksuniversiteit, Leiden;
Museum für Kunst und Gewerbe, Hamburg; Bibliothèque Nationale, Paris;
Victoria and Albert Museum, London; Maria Austria Instituut, Amsterdam;
Rijksdienst Beeldende Kunst, Den Haag; Museum of Fine Arts, Houston.

Publications:

By KLEIN: Books—*Zoo leeft Duitschland: Op de puinhpen van het Derde
Rijk,* with Sem Presser, Amsterdam 1945; *Amsterdam/Rotterdam: Two Cities
Rhapsody,* Baarn, Netherlands 1959; *Delta: Poort van Europa,* Amersfoort,
Netherlands 1962; *Nederlands wordt groter,* Amsterdam 1963; *In de tijd
gezet,* Amsterdam 1966; *Delta: Stromen Land in Beweging,* Amersfoort,
Netherlands 1967; *Een eeuw in beweging,* Hengelo, Netherlands 1968; *Philips
professioneel profiel,* with Hans Samson, Amsterdam 1970; *Semper mare
navigandum,* Amsterdam 1970; *Gasunie Engineering: A Profile,* Amsterdam
1977; *Havens van Rotterdam,* Amsterdam 1978; *Aart Klein, fotograaf,* with
text by Pauline Terreehorst, Utrecht 1986; *De Amstel is er gelukkig nog. Een
fotografisch document doodr Aart Klein,* Amsterdam 1991; *Art Klein in Kleur,*
exhibition catalogue, Amsterdam 1992; *Amstel,* Amsterdam 1993.

On KLEIN: Books—*Photography Yearbook,* edited by Norman Hall,
London 1963; *Aart Klein,* exhibition catalogue, by Will Bertheux, Amsterdam
1973; *The Land: 20th Century Landscape Photographs Selected by Bill
Brandt,* exhibition catalogue, edited by Mark Haworth-Booth, London 1975;
Fotografie in Nederland 1940-1975, exhibition catalogue, by Els Barents,
The Hague 1978; *Fotografie in Nederland 1920-1940,* exhibition catalogue,
by Flip Bool and Kees Broos, The Hague 1979; *Subjektive Fotografie: Images
of the 50s,* exhibition catalogue, by Ute Eskildsen, Manfred Schmalriede and
Dorothy Martinson, Essen, West Germany 1984; *Roots & Turns. 20th Century
photography in The Netherlands,* exhibition catalogue, by Ingeborg Th.
Leijerzapf e.o., Houston 1988; *Kleur in Zwart-wit/Kleurcahier,* Amsterdam
1992. **Articles**—"Gesprek met Aart Klein" by Jaco Groot and Paul Mertz in
Streven (Amsterdam), December 1965; "Portfolio: Aart Klein" by Colin
Osman in *Creative Camera* (London), May 1970; "Uber Aart Klein aus
Holland" by Fritz Kempe in *Moderne Fototechnik,* August 1970; "Aart
Klein: Designs with White Light and Black Paper" by Willem Coumans in
Foto (Doetinchem, Netherlands), December 1970; "Aart Klein" by Tineke de
Ruiter and Ingeborg Th. Leijerzapf; "Geschiedenis van de Nederlandse
fotografie in monografieën en thema-artikelen" in *Alphen aan den Rijn,*
Amsterdam 1988; "Wachten op die ene fotot. Een afwijkende standpunt van
fotograaf Aart Klein" by Rik Planting in *Elsevier,* 2 November 1991.

                                        *

I have always asked myself: is a zebra a black horse with white stripes, or a
white horse with black stripes? The question remains.

In photography we speak of black and white photography, or black-on-
white photography. I think it is white on black. Without light for our eye, all is
black; a negative that did not catch light gives a black print. Each photo is the
result of placing or catching light on a plane that is originally black. It depends
on the quantity of light which impression the photo will make. A great quantity
of white on the black brings the picture to the graphic print. But the photo is a
matter of white-on-black.

The men on the moon made a wonderful picture of the world globe in a
black heaven. It is all sharp and colourful. But there was war on earth, and
hunger, and dinners, and demonstrations against the war; there were people
dying, children were born, there was love-making, there was fighting in the
streets. And on this wonderful picture you see nothing of that at all.

It is, therefore, that I say, it is the photographer who must cut pieces out of
reality, or make pieces from his fantasies. In one picture you can't show all that
is going on. Neither is it necessary.

                                                            —Aart Klein

                            *   *   *

It was after 1950 that Aart Klein's photography first acquired its own
unique characteristics. Prior to that time he had occupied himself with ordinary
journalistic and theatre photography. But, from 1950, it became more and
more apparent to him that his most important concern was not so much the
actual subject as the way in which it was printed. He acquired his personal way
of developing, contrasting black/white, sometimes even excluding any grey
tones. His photographs achieved a graphic character.

Klein always refers to white/black photography, rather than black/white,
because, he says, "the light, the white, is put on the black paper." By printing
in this way, he has been able to emphasize that which is important and to allow
unimportant details to disappear. He analyzes the accompanying photograph
as follows: "There is a lawn with a million blades of grass, but you cannot see
any of them because, for me, the light on the crosses was more important for
my photograph."

It is the case, however, that though Klein maintains that his subject is not
important, he is, in fact, attracted to objects that already have a strong black/
white contrast and a certain line structure—for instance, a building in
scaffolding, bridges, viaducts, and also the wrinkled horizontal/vertical
accent. He calls his photographs "images without words."

They do not need any text; they are self-explanatory, because he focuses
always on the essential. Because of his almost playful interest in form and line,
and because of the character of his photographs, his work is often referred to as
"architectural" photography of photographic "construction."

Klein has produced some rather large books in which he has been able to
work out his ideas and principles in detail: the best-known is *Delta: Stromen
Land in Beweging (Delta: Land of Streams in Movement).*

Yet, finally, his photographs lack any social message. Klein uses photography as a means of expressing himself artistically, and his goal is to produce
photographs of graphic quality.

                                        A. de Jonge-Vermeulen

KLEIN, William.

Nationality: American. **Born:** New York City in 1928. **Education:** Studied
social sciences at City College of New York, and art at the Sorbonne, Paris,
1948; studied painting, with the artist Fernand Léger, Paris, 1948-50; self-
taught in photography. **Military Service:** Served in the United States Army,
working as a cartoonist etc. for the *Stars and Stripes* army newspaper,
Germany and France, 1945-48. **Career:** Independent painter, Paris, 1950-54;
Contract Fashion Photographer, under Alexander Liberman, then Art Director, *Vogue* magazine, Paris, and also freelanced for *Domus,* etc., Paris, 1955-
65; abandoned still photography to concentrate on filmmaking, Paris, from
1965. **Recipient:** Prix Nadar, Paris, 1957; Top Photographer Award, *Photokina,*
Cologne, 1963; Grand Prix, *Festival Internationale de Tours,* 1965; Prix Jean
Vigo, Paris, 1967; Grand Prix National de la Photographie, France 1986;
Kulturpreis, Germany 1987; Guggenheim Fellowship, 1989. **Address:** 5 rue
des Medicis, Paris 6, France.

Individual Exhibitions:

1961   Fuji Gallery, Tokyo
1967   Stedelijk Museum, Amsterdam
1978   The Photographers' Gallery, London (toured the U.K.)
        Galerie Fiolet, Amsterdam
        Apeldoorn Museum, Netherlands (toured the Netherlands)
1979   Fondation Nationale de la Photographie, Lyons (toured France)
        Canon Photo Gallery, Geneva

1980	Museum of Modern Art, New York
1981	Centre Beaubourg, Paris
	Galerie Zabriskie, Paris
	Centre Culturel Americain, Paris
	Light Gallery, New York
	Cinematheque, Paris (films)
	Ikona Gallery, Venice
	Light Gallery, Los Angeles
	The Photographers' Gallery, London (audio-visuals)
1983	Centre Beaubourg, Paris
	Retrospective, Georges Pompidou Centre, Paris
1986	Musée d'Art Moderne, Paris
1987	Tokyo
	Osaka
1988	Walker Art Center, Minneapolis (toured U.S., Mexico and Cuba)
1995	*William Klein New York 1954-1955,* Howard Greenberg Gallery, New York

Selected Group Exhibitions:

1964	*World Exhibition of Photography: What Is Man?,* Pressehaus Stern, Hamburg (and world tour)
1967	*Photography in the 20th Century,* National Gallery of Canada, Ottawa (toured Canada and the United States, 1967-73)
1968	*2nd World Exhibition of Photography,* Pressehaus Stern, Hamburg (and world tour)
1977	*Fashion Photography,* International Museum of Photography, George Eastman House, Rochester, New York (travelled to the Brooklyn Museum, New York; San Francisco Museum of Modern Art; Cincinnati Art Institute, Ohio; and the Museum of Fine Arts, St. Petersburg, Florida)
1978	*10 Photographers from Atget to Klein,* Massachusetts Institute of Technology, Cambridge
1979	*Photographie als Kunst 1879-1979/Kunst als Photographie 1949-1979,* Tiroler Landesmuseum Ferdinandeum, Innsbruck, Austria (travelled to the Neue Galerie am Wolfgang Gurlitt Museum, Linz, Austria; Neue Galerie am Landesmuseum Joanneum, Graz, Austria; and the Museum des 20. Jahrhunderts, Vienna)
1980	*Photography of the 50s,* International Center of Photography, New York (travelled to the Center for Creative Photography, University of Arizona, Tucson; Minneapolis Institute of Arts; California State University at Long Beach; and the Delaware Art Museum, Wilmington)
1982	*Floods of Light,* The Photographers' Gallery, London
1985	*American Images 1945-80,* Barbican Art Gallery, London (toured Britain)
1987	*Photography and Art 1946-86,* Los Angeles County Museum of Art
1989	*On the Art of Fixing a Shadow: One Hundred and Fifty Years of Photography,* National Gallery of Art, Washington, D.C.; Art Institute of Chicago, Chicago; Los Angeles County Museum of Art
1990	*A Particular Collection: Photography from the Museum Collection,* Bayly Art Museum of the University of Virginia, Charlottesvile

Collections:

Museum of Modern Art, New York; Metropolitan Museum of Art, New York; Stedelijk Museum, Amsterdam; Bibliothèque Nationale, Paris; National Museum of Modern Art, Tokyo; Museum Ludwig, Cologne; Museum Folkwang, Essen, Germany.

Publications:

By KLEIN: Books—*New York,* Paris and London 1956; *Rome,* London 1960; *Moscow,* New York 1964; *Tokyo,* New York 1964; *William Klein,* portfolio, with text by Alain Jouffroy, Paris 1978; *William Klein: Photo-graphs,* with text by John Heilpern, Millerton, New York, London and Paris 1981; *William Klein: Photographies,* with text by Carole Naggar, Paris 1983; *Photo-poche,* with text by Christian Caujolle, Paris 1985; *William Klein Monograph,* Tokyo 1987; *The Films of William Klein,* text by Bruce Jenkins and Jonathan Rensbaum, Minneapolis 1988; *Close Up,* London, Paris and New York 1989; *Torino 90,* text by Guy Mandery, Milan 1990; *William Klein,* Tokyo 1991; *William Klein,* Stockholm 1992; *In and Out of Fashion,* London 1994. **Films**—*Broadway by Light,* 1959; *Cassius the Great,* 1965; *Qui etes-vous Polly Magoo?,* 1967; *Loin du Vietnam,* with Alain Resnais, Jean-Luc Godard, Chris Marker and others, 1967; *Mr. Freedom,* 1968; *Pan-African Cultural Festival,* 1970; *Eldridge Cleaver, Black Panther,* 1969; *Le Grand Cafe,* television series, 1972; *Muhammad Ali the Greatest,* 1974; *The Model Couple,* 1976; *Hollywood, California,* 1977; *Maydays,* 1978; *Music City U.S.A.,* 1979; *The Little Richard Story,* 1980; *The French,* 1981; *Cibtacts,* 1983; *Slow Motion,* 1984; *Mode in France,* 1986; *Ciné Défense,* 1989; *ID,* 1989; *The Great Arch,* 1989; *Evidence,* 1989; *Babilee 91,* 1991; *In and Out of Fashion,* 1993.

On KLEIN: Books—*Beauty: Variations on the Theme Woman by Masters of the Camera—Past and Present,* edited by L. Fritz Gruber, London and New York 1965; *Photography in the 20th Century* by Nathan Lyons, New York 1967; *2nd World Exhibition of Photography,* exhibition catalogue, edited by Karl Pawek, Hamburg 1968; *The Magic Image* by Cecil Beaton and Gail Buckland, London and Boston 1975; *Concerning Photography,* exhibition catalogue, by Jonathan Bayer and others, London 1977; *Geschichte der Fotografie im 20. Jahrhundert/Photography in the 20th Century* by Petr Tausk, Cologne 1977, London 1980; *Photographie als Kunst 1879-1979/ Kunst als Photographie 1949-1979,* exhibition catalogue, 2 vols., by Peter Weiermair, Innsbruck, Austria 1979; *The History of Fashion Photography* by Nancy Hall-Duncan, New York 1979; *The Vogue Book of Fashion Photography* by Polly Devlin, with an introduction by Alexander Liberman, New York and London 1979; *Old and Modern Masters of Photography,* exhibition catalogue, by Mark Haworth-Booth, London 1980; *Voyons Voir: 8 Photographes,* edited by Pierre Borhan, Paris 1980; *Photography of the 50s: An American Perspective* by Helen Gee, Tucson, Arizona 1980; *William Klein: Photographer, Filmmaker* by Katherine Tweedie, Rochester, New York 1982; *American Images: Photography 1945-1980,* edited by Peter Turner and John Benton-Harris, London 1985; *Photography and Art 1946-1986,* exhibition catalogue, by Andy Grundberg and Kathleen M. Gauss, Los Angeles 1987; *A History of Photography* by Jean-Claude Lemagny and André Rouillé, Cambridge 1987; *American Photography and the American Dream,* by James Guimond, Chapel Hill and London 1991. **Articles**—"William Klein" in *Camera* (Lucerne), March 1969; "William Klein" by Alain Jouffroy in *Zoom* (Paris), July/August 1973; "William Klein" in *Creative Camera* (London), July 1974; "William Klein" in *Photo* (Paris), March 1979; "William Klein: Apocalypse" by Allan Porter, in special monograph issue of *Camera* (Lucerne), May 1981; "Another Star Is Born" by Jan Zita Grover in *Afterimage* (Rochester, New York), January 1982; "Film: Raging Bull" by Katherine Dieckmann in *Art in America,* December 1990; "Close and Wide" in *Popular Photography,* March 1991.

*   *   *

William Klein's most recent publication, *In and Out of Fashion* (1994), clearly refers to his two major bouts with the world of fashion photography. The first occured while he was working for *Vogue* in the 1950s, and the second backstage, while he worked on the film *Made in France* in 1986. *In and Out of Fashion* is also reminiscent of Klein's ambiguous position in the world of still photography. Although his influence on other photographers has been constant since the first publication of his book *New York is Good for You William Klein Trance—Witness—Revels* in 1956, there was a period of over ten years when he and photography turned their backs on each other and he concentrated entirely on film making.

Klein's early career as a painter had started in Paris where he used his GI grant to study at the Sorbonne and spent a short time in the studio of Fernand Léger. Léger's opinion was that Klein ought to emerge from the studio and work with architects as he himself had done. It was as Klein began using a camera to record murals that he became fascinated with the possibilities of photography and wanted to make more experiments. At about this time Alexander Liberman, the art director at *Vogue* was taking on young painters and photographers in an effort to enliven the magazine, then suffering by comparison with its great rival *Harpers Bazaar*. Liberman offered William Klein a job in the art department, which he accepted partly in order to see New York again, but also because he was increasingly losing sympathy with the world of fine art. At first nervous of the work, Klein used the opportunity it afforded both to learn new photographic techniques and to spend his spare time looking at his native city, which he explored with a very basic Leica. The resulting pictures were hated in New York—a city which Klein saw, even in the fifties, as the dangerous slum it has become—and his first book has never been published in America.

He found that although unable to take the fashion world seriously, the surrounding glamour and theatricality both amused and interested him. He had many pictures published in *Vogue*. These were not necessarily the ones he would have chosen, but they certainly changed the look of the magazine and made way for much of the street fashion photography which came to the fore in the sixties. The money he earned enabled him to make his four big city books, *New York*, being followed by *Rome*, *Moscow* and *Tokyo*. The pictures seem aggressive, full of information, close-ups, very grainy; but the seeming chaos is always held in graphic control. It is interesting that Chris Marker, who, already a film-maker, was the first publisher of the New York book, has said that if he edits a single frame from one of Klein's films what he sees is a Klein photograph. "We are faced by the mystery of an eye that instinctively cuts reality into slices of Klein."

Klein made his first film *Broadway by Light* in 1958 and went on to make documentaries for French television, but the final break with *Vogue* came partly due to his lack of sympathy with Diana Vreeland but largely because he was part of the team working on *Far from Vietnam* which was considered too un-American to be associated with *Vogue*, and which marked his increasing interest in politics. The next ten years were spent making film, both features and documentaries but in 1978 he was asked to prepare a retrospective exhibition of his photographs to be shown in London and which later toured in the Netherlands. This led him to re-examine his contact sheet, a process he describes as being like reading a diary, evoking not only the people but the sights and smells that surrounded the taking of the pictures. He had a big exhibition in New York in 1980 and from then on has received continuous photographic assignments for both magazines and books, and has re-entered the world of still photography with enormous energy and renewed interest. Exhibitions and sales of his photographs have grown throughout the world. He has, of course, continued to make films and also has more than 250 TV commercials to his credit which, like his early fashion photography, have been both innovative and helped pay for his personal film and still photography projects.

William Klein has always insisted on controlling the layout of his books and has brought his clear ideas on graphics to all his work. He has not been concerned with following fashion or making the images appear precious by surrounding them with white space. He knows what is right for his own photographs and understands that part of our fascination with them is our perception that life goes on outside and around them. Therefore, the best way to show them is to encourage our imagination to consider what lies just outside the frame.

William Klein is now recognised as a major force in twentieth century photography. It would not be surprising if in another ten years the same will be said of his work as a film-maker.

—Sue Davies

KNORR, Karen Helen.

Nationality: American. **Born:** Frankfurt am Main on 5 January 1954. **Education:** Graduated with a B.A. (Honors) in Film and Photographic Arts from the University of Westminster, 1980; M.A. in Photographic Studies from University of Derby, 1990. **Family:** Married Barry Shaw on 5 May 1990; children: Roland. **Career:** Delivered a master class at Derbyshire College of Higher Education, 1985; freelance photographer until 1986; lecturer in contemporary photographic practices at London College of Printing from 1986-93; visiting Professor at the Academy of Photography at the Konstfack,

Stockholm, October 1993-94; visiting lecturer at Gothenberg University, Sweden, March 1994; visiting lecturer at the University of Lund, Sweden, April 1994; course leader of MA in photographic studies at the University of Derby, 1994. Awarded the Thames TV Bursary, 1979; Arts Council Bursary, 1980; GLAA Award, 1980 and 1985; National Endowment for the Arts, 1986; London Arts Board Grant, 1993. **Agent:** Maureen Paley Interim Art, 21 Beck Road, London E8 4RE, England. **Address:** 6 Springdale Road, London N16 9NX, England.

Individual Exhibitions:

1983 *Gentlemen,* Samia Saouma Gallery, Paris
1984-85 *Country Life,* Samia Saouma Gallery, Paris (travelled to The Photographers' Gallery, London)
1986 *Connoisseurs: Looking at Great Works of Art,* Riverside Studios, London
1987 *Gentlemen,* Salon du Livre, Geneva
 Karen Knorr: Connoisseurs, Samia Saouma Gallery, Paris
 Compostures, Musée d'Art Moderne de la Ville de Paris
1989 *Vues de L'Esprit,* Galerie Art et Essai, Rennes (travelled to Galerie Du Cloître, Rennes; Galeria le Lieu, Lorient)
1991 *Marks of Distinction,* Portfolio Gallery, Edinburgh
 Gentlemen, Country Life, Connoisseurs and *Capital,* Antoine Candau Gallery, Paris
 Capital, Salama-Caro Gallery, London
1992 *Les Délices de Voltaire,* Ferney-Voltaire, France
1993 *Karen Knorr,* Moderna Museet, Stockholm
 The Virtues and The Delights, Interim Art, London

Selected Group Exhibitions:

1991 *Les Couleurs de L'Argent,* Musée de la Poste, Paris
 Connoisseurs, Kunst Rai, Amsterdam
 Shocks to the System, South Bank Centre, London (travelled to Sunderland, Birmingham, Eastbourne, Exeter and Plymouth)
1992 *Invented Worlds,* Internationale Foto-Triennale, Esslingen, Germany
 Capital, European Festival, North Terminal, Gatwick Airport
 The Cutting Edge, Barbican Centre, London
 The Fortune Teller, Rochdale Art Gallery, Lancashire
1993 *Inside/Out,* Museo Pecci, Prato, Italy
1994 *Die Orte, Der Kunst,* Sprengel Museum, Hannover

Collections:

The Arts Council of Great Britain, London; The Victoria and Albert Museum, London; Musée d'Art de la Ville de Paris; National Museum of Modern Art, Kyoto; Cabinet des Estampes, Geneva; Winnipeg Art Gallery, Canada; The Cartier Foundation; FRAC Aquitaine, France; FRAC Bretagne, France; FRAC Lorraine, France; FRAC Normandie, France; The British Council, London; Folkwang Museum, Essen; Warburg Bank; Texaco Corporation.

Publications:

By KNORR: Book—*Marks of Distinction,* London 1991. **Articles**—*Camerawork* (London), Numbers 26 and 29, 1978 and 1984; *Creative Camera,* Numbers 199, 226 and 256; *European Photography,* Numbers 9, 21, 1921, 1985; *Camera Austria,* Numbers 25 and 27, 1987 and 1988; "Karen Knorr Interview" by David Brittain in *Creative Camera,* Number 309, April 1991; Jessica Evans in *Portfolio Magazine,* Summer 1991; "Pictures from Post-Industrial Britain" in *Creative Camera,* June 1992.

On KNORR: Articles—*Artscribe,* Numbers 27, 28, 34, 43, 47; "Beyond the Purloined Image" by John Roberts in *Aspects,* Winter 1983/84; "Magnificent Obsession" by M. Gagnon in *C Magazine,* Fall 1985; "Les Code Perdu du Temps Perdu dans la Photographie de Karen Knorr" by Elisabeth Lebovici in *Art Press,* October 1986; "Second Generation Post-Photography" in *Flash Art,* April 1988; "Vues de l'Esprit" in *Art Press,* March 1991; *Photomagazine* (Paris), May 1991; "Sarah Kent on Karen Knorr" in *Time Out,* 12-19 June

A Vindication of the Rights of Woman, **1994 (original in colour).** Photograph by Karen Knorr.

1991; *Liberation* (Paris), May 1991; "Patrick Roegiers on Karen Knorr" in *Le Monde,* July 1991; "The Order of Things" by John Taylor in *After Image,* September 1991; "L'Art et L'Argent" by Jean-Joseph Goux in *Art Press,* 1992. **Television**—"Britain Your Britain: The Virtues and the Delights," *News SouthEast,* 1993. **Video**—"Vues de L'Esprit," Rennes, Beaux Arts, France 1989.

*   *   *

Born to North American parents of Norwegian, German and Polish extraction, Karen Knorr received her further education in Switzerland and France. This long period of study took in all the fine arts without seriously touching on photography. In 1976, after failing to obtain a place at the Ecole des Beaux Arts in Paris, she decided, instead, to study photography in London. It was there that she graduated with a B.A. in Film and Photographic Arts from the University of Westminster and later finished her education at the University of Derby in 1990. Karen Knorr has been a visiting professor this year at the Konstfack, Stockholm and will be taking up a new position as Course Leader of Postgraduate Photographic Studies at the University of Derby.

Karen Knorr was warned against the mounting commercial pressures of the Thatcherite eighties, that with her giant, glossy colour images she would be working for Benson and Hedges in ten years time. She is proud not to be doing so, though swift to add "not that I got asked." Instead she delights in subverting the smart world of coffee table imagery with its own tools, fascinated by the British capacity for taking umbrage. A body of work in 1980 entitled *Belgravia,* of black and white portraits of residents captioned with their own statements, was jettisoned by Vogue; her Cork Street gallery became dismayed when the show she called *Capital,* 1991, contained visual references not only to the City of London but to Karl Marx. Karen Knorr has learned that you cannot sell a series like *Country Life* with its military memoirs and hunting trophies to *Country Life* magazine itself.

And yet . . . along with a fierce pictorial commitment to applying society's norms to itself, there is an unmistakeably genuine naivety in Karen Knorr's unoffended response to their offended one. Rather, she is intrigued by the apparent lack of that much-vaunted English virtue, a sense of irony: her parents were, after all, living in Belgravia when the photo-series was made, her mother and grandmother both feature. Her work in the past has referred to the photographic style found in the magazines *Country Life* and *Interiors* but also the work of such conceptual artists as Mary Kelly and Victor Burgin. The work of Walker Evans, a seminal photographer of the Depression in the Deep South, and the contemporary Puerto Rican photographer, Joe Delano, have also had a significant effect on her work.

Karen Knorr brings her polyglot background to bear in linking the two sides of the Channel for a view of *Britannia.* Taking the eighteenth century French Enlightenment as her theme, Karen Knorr entwines the sayings of the French *philosophes* with their English contemporaries and followers, presenting a cosmopolitan heritage with a strong feminist twist. She takes the radical writings of the Jean Marie de Condorcet and Emilie du Châtelet, counterposes them with those of Tom Paine and Mary Wollstonecraft and allows her imagination to dress the subjects in period costume, to set them in period settings such as Voltaire's garden and English country mansions. The characters are as androgynous as the cast of a Mozart opera—and who more subversive than Beaumarchais, playwright of *The Marriage of Figaro,* with its cross-dressing cast satirising a decadent aristocracy.

It is a theme well suited to Karen Knorr's preferred techniques of social subversion. During the eighteenth century familiar institutions were heavily questioned—and what more familiar than the institution of marriage with legitimacy, then as now, an open question? Rousseau might have celebrated a return to a mythic state of nature, but it was one where women are created for man's delight. Karen Knorr reviews the Age of Enlightenment's blueprint for a universal morality based on the principle of human perfectibility with a quizzical eye: Newton's experiment is turned on its head and apples are transformed into visibly plastic oranges and lemons; Rousseau's Noble Savage becomes Savage Noble, concealed within a folly of his own devising into which flourishing nature threatens to encroach. Karen Knorr's models recline in their period costumes accompanied by such allegorical emblems as a bowl and pitcher (prudence); a cracked wall mirror (moderation and vanity) and a cracked wall (reason undermined). Narcissm is defeated by *The Other's Gaze,* self-surveying in a non-reflecting mirror.

Photography is of its essence about image and representation. History is about elucidating a mythology suited to the politics of the age. When showing us Voltaire's Garden at Ferney, Knorr focuses on the *L'Aiguillon de Vénus* (Venus's dart or clitoris). This becomes a reference to women's pleasure and to Voltaire's friend and lover Émilie du Châtelet, who was herself a member of the English Academy of Science: The Royal Society. Allusion and ambiguity, inversion and subversion, the play on words, the pun in the picture, an Adam's Apple devouring a Famous Face, the Best of all Possible Worlds at the Frontiers of Utopia; this is photography mutually penetrating philosophy. Never has there been such an elegant encounter between the two. Nor such a fruitful one, plastic lemons notwithstanding.

—Amanda Hopkinson

KO, Alfred Chi-Keung.

Nationality: Chinese. **Born:** Hong Kong, 21 December 1953. **Education:** Studied at the Banff School of Fine Arts, Alberta, Canada, obtaining Senior Diploma in Photography, 1978. **Career:** Freelance photographer. Member of Hong Kong Institute of Professional Photographers. **Recipient:** Photographer of the Year, 1992, awarded by Hong Kong Artists' Guild. **Address:** 11/F, 7 Ho Wing Bldg., Whampoa Est., Kowloon, Hong Kong.

Individual Exhibitions:

1978	American Library, sponsored by American Consulate, Hong Kong
1979	Hong Kong Arts Centre
1982	Palace Museum, Beijing
1988	Hong Kong Arts Centre
1990	Canon Image Plaza, Hong Kong
1991	Hong Kong Fringe Club

Collections:

Banff School of Fine Arts, Alberta, Canada.

Publications:

By KO: Books—*Palace Museum of Beijing,* China 1983; *Nouvelle Cuisine Chinoise,* Hong Kong 1989; *The Old Tea and Horse Road,* 1993.

*

As 1997 approaches, the fate of Hong Kong is called into question. After the Beijing violence of 1989, the date of 1997 is looked upon as doomsday, thinking that the Chinese are more concerned with control than with prosperity. While officials in Beijing have promised that the Hong Kong social and economic system will "remain unchanged for 50 years," that assurance is not widely trusted in the colony. Fearing the worst from unification, millions of citizens marched down the street protesting the Tiananmen Square massacre. Hong Kongers cannot forget the 1989 massacre in Beijing. Many are also angry because their fate has been decided without their participation.

Nevertheless, Hong Kong has always been a place of coming and going. Our history before its time of prosperity—under the Japanese heel in the 1940s, when Mao overran the mainland, and as cultural revolution spilled into the colony . . . all seems to suggest that everything that is going to happen has already happened. Brain drain slowly became an obvious phenomenon on the human side of exodus. But undaunted by such speculation, practical Hong Kong gets on with life. The choice is to emigrate or acquiesce, and since the vast majority do not possess the first option, Beijing may find the tide of reality flowing in its favour.

Given Chinese policies and the mood of the Hong Kong populace, the present prospect is that the dynamism of Hong Kong will decline, economic standards will continue slipping, contentiousness will grow as confidence declines, and social troubles will proliferate as a market economy moves under the shadow of a paternalist regime.

We cannot know for certain what 1997 will bring, if only because China itself is so volatile. Yet the only certainty is that Hong Kong is changing and once again—a "new" Hong Kong will edge out the familiar one. And this is a photo project which reflects the experience and feeling of myself (a local born Hong Kong Chinese)—my fears, disappointments and triumphs in an era of transiency.

—Alfred Ko

* * *

The seriousness of Alfred Ko's involvement with the camera and his dependence on it as a vital means of expression has kept photography inseparable from Ko's life. A graduate in fine art photography from Canada, Ko returned to Hong Kong to work as a commercial photographer in 1977. His knowledge of photography as a skill and as an art form has driven Ko's photography into opposite directions. Despite this contradiction which the artist may not be able to resolve at times, Ko succeeds in developing his career and artistic achievement with absolute devotion and dedication. Part of this devotion has also been diversified into the area of education since Ko's return to Hong Kong. His creative and technical expertise have influenced and benefited many young photographers in the last 15 years.

Perhaps the intensity of commercial work keeps Alfred Ko's consciousness of his own creative work continually alert. Since starting in photojournalism he seldom takes even the shortest walk without a camera and he still continues to observe the social environment to which he belongs. Perhaps the most profound observation one can find in Ko's works is the social documentary photography which he has been working on in Hong Kong and China since 1981. Taken to argue the problematic nature of the society and its environment, these black-and-white photographs subtly reflect the artist's concern and frustration within this intricate relationship between the two social systems. The messages they contain are emotional and explosive. Despite his reluctance ever to intrude upon the scene we are conscious of Ko's presence in every image through its critical composition and unimagined ways of seeing. In his exhibition series on Hong Kong in 1988, *History of Our Future,* Ko explored a new expression by using medium format instead of the usual 35mm, to elevate and transform images of reality into images of aesthetic contemplation. These photographs of the Queen's statue, the New China News Agency, abandoned soccer fields, concrete playgrounds and industrial urban landscapes provoked social concerns for a changing and disorienting world.

Child with a Toy Gun in Ansai, Shaanxi Province, China, **winter 1989.** Photograph by Alfred Ko.

These questions reached a much bigger dimension in the following year which marked the beginning of Ko's next social documentary, taking a much closer look at the intense and yet uncertain period before 1997.

Ko's knowledge and insight in photographing his own country has generated requests for his involvement in projects on local issues and themes in recent years. But these works also often involved extensive travelling and considerable consumption of time taken away from his own creative venture. Nevertheless, we would expect to share Ko's photographic visions of his country at critical moments of history in the very near future.

—Becky Cho

KOLÁŘ, Viktor.

Nationality: Czechoslovakian. **Born:** Ostrava, 7 September 1941. **Education:** Studied at the Pedagogical Institute, Ostrava, 1960-64; mainly self-taught in photography, at his father's photo-studio, Ostrava, from 1955. **Family:** Married Martha Roszkopf in 1975; daughters: Marta and Teresie. **Career:** Independent photographer, Ostrava, from 1965. Worked as a chemist, Vitkovice Steel Factory, Ostrava, 1959-60; teacher in a secondary school, Ostrava, 1964-65; librarian, Ostrava, 1966-68; worked as a molybdenite and nickel mine labourer, laboratory technician, photographer for an Italian minority newspaper, etc., in Canada, 1968-73; labourer in the new iron foundry, Ostrava, 1974-75; stagehand, P. Bezruč Theatre, Ostrava, 1975-84. Since 1984, freelance photographer, working for local construction and other state-owned companies, Ostrava. **Address:** Husovo nám. 3, 701 00 Ostrava 1, Czechoslovakia.

Individual Exhibitions:

1964	*Ostrava,* Černa louka, Ostrava, Czechoslovakia
1973	*Viktor Kolar's Czech Eye,* Centaur Gallery, Montreal, Quebec
1976	*Man Amongst Men,* Fotochema Gallery, Ostrava, Czechoslovakia
1978	*Ostrava 1968-78,* Fotochema Gallery, Ostrava, Czechoslovakia
1981	*Ostrava 1968-80,* Jaromir Funke Fotokabinett, Brno, Czechoslovakia
	New World Encounters, Galerie v podloubì, Olomouc, Czechoslovakia
1982	*Ostrava,* Mala výstavnì sìn, Liberec, Czechoslovakia
	New World Encounters, Galeria F, Bystrica, Czechoslovakia
1983	*Ostrava,* Ústav makromolekul. chemie, Prague
	New World Encounters, Fotochema Gallery, Prague
	From Contemporary Czech Photography, Komornì Galerie, Bratislava, Czechoslovakia (with B. Holomicek)
1984	*Ostrava,* Canon Photo Gallery, Amsterdam
1985	*Ostrava,* Photographic Confrontations, Gorzow, Poland
	Ostrava, Gallery of Photography, Kaunas, U.S.S.R.

Selected Group Exhibitions:

1982	*Aktualni Fotografie,* Moravian Gallery, Brno, Czechoslovakia
1983	*Rencontres Internationales de la Photographie,* Arles, France
1984	*Generation 70,* Fotochema Gallery, Prague
	Czech Creative Photography, Gallery D, Prague
1985	*27 Contemporary Czech Photographers,* Photographers' Gallery, London

Collections:

National Film Board of Canada, Ottawa; International Center of Photography, New York; Moravian Gallery, Brno, Czechoslovakia; Silesian Museum, Opava, Czechoslovakia; Navigator Foundation, Boston, Massachusetts.

Publications:

By KOLÁŘ: Books—*Victor Kolář—A Monograph,* with text by Daniela Mrazkova, Ostrava, Czechoslovakia 1986; *Theatre J. Mynona—Reconstruction of the Theatre,* Opava, Czechoslovakia 1986. **Articles**—"Introducing Victor Kolář" in *Camera Canada* (Toronto), no. 11, 1971; and portfolios in *Czechoslovak Photography* (Prague), no. 10, 1967, and no. 12, 1978; *Photography Review* (Prague), no. 3, 1981; *Creative Camera* (London), no. 228, 1983; *Die Fotografie* (Leipzig), no. 8, 1984.

ON KOLÁŘ: Books—*Black and White Variations,* edited by Ludvik Souček, Prague 1963; *Aktualni Fotografie,* exhibition catalogue by Antonin Dufek, Brno, Czechoslovakia 1982; *Contemporary Canadian Photography* by Martha Langford, Edmonton, Alberta 1984; *27 Contemporary Czechoslovakian Photographers,* exhibition catalogue by Jiri Hlusicka, Sue Davies and Antonin Dufek, London 1985. **Articles**—"Ostrava in Photos by Victor Kolář" by Vladimir Birgus in *Czechoslovak Photography* (Prague), no. 12, 1978; "Kolář's Ostrava" by Vladimir Birgus in *Photography Review* (Prague), no. 3, 1981; "Victor Kolář, CSR" by Vladimir Birgus in *Reflexions* (Amsterdam), no. 12, 1984; "How One Photographer Sees His Town" by Vladimir Birgus in *Die Fotografie* (Leipzig), no. 8, 1984.

*

Photography is endowed with the quality of conducting a dialogue with the world, but with itself at the same time. It involves being a document, sometimes also poetry, it preserves a record of relations and feelings. It is a witness to our transience and eternity. I try to record that which disappears forever on the project of coming days. A change in the style of life, the entry of affluence into people's lives. Even the apparently deep disproportion between the desired and the possible. The persistent effort to change the course of things which are unfavourable to man, the desire to taste the fruit of the tree of life as far as possible, to enjoy its vitality. It is an honour for me constantly to try to make this chronicle of 'human fate', the purpose of which is to show the heritage of the human race, which with its typical persistence imbues the lives of our generation—but not only it—without taking account of the uniqueness of the age in which we live. Behold, what a challenge to the photographer to try and try again to record that which is unique and general in the span of a lifetime . . .

—Viktor Kolář

*   *   *

"I feel an urge to record how an old lifestyle changes into a new one. I want to see how affluence affects people's lives, how man copes with new conditions of life, what makes him happy and what does not," he says. Material for speculation about humanity, which is often psychologically, morally, culturally and even physically unprepared to cope with the rapid progress of civilization can be of course found just anywhere, but Viktor Kolář has decided to seek it in Ostrava, the steel and coal heart of Czechoslovakia where all aspects of the "new" life are most prominent. This is where he was born and where he lives and works, in this promised land of industrial development, a socialist Klondike whose mines and steel plants offer unexpected possibilities and top wages. This is the fabled country of hard men's work and human pettiness, flowery orations and cultural mediocrity. Kolář's photography peers behind the backdrop of the visible world; his series of everyday banalities captured seemingly at random constitutes an essay on contemporary man, his strength, sadness, bravado and dejection, but most of all his humanity. It is an essay on man who loudly, proudly but also painfully seeks his place in the world in which he lives.

Kolář's photography is a direct, spontaneous message about the human deal. However, the reality captured by each of his pictures never lacks an inner plan. It is as if the picture constituted a never-ending confrontation of ideal and reality, of things as they are and as they could or should be, a permanent speculation about the alternatives to human happiness, contentment and values. Kolář's vision is characterized by subtle shifts of meaning, overstatement, humour and irony. The lifestyle of contemporary man, or rather the changing life of urban population, so typical for an advanced technology-dominated civilization has been in the focus of Kolář's interest from the very beginnings of his serious attempts in photography. The same interest dominated his work when he studied on a grant in Canada and photographed in supermarkets of large Canadian cities where purchasing has long ceased to be a vehicle for obtaining one's necessities of life and has grown into a new culture, an inevitable social activity symbolizing one's status, self-realization, means of relaxation and the essential lifestyle of consumer society. Similarly in his native Ostrava, so different from far-away Toronto or Ottawa, Kolář's interest is focused on the essential tokens of changing cultural and lifestyle patterns. He photographs old neighbourhoods where people do not live as comfortably as tenants of modern housing projects in satellite cities, but their existence is still not marked by the uniformity of the latter, and traditional neighbourly relations still survive here. Kolář's camera notes how even these older districts are affected by a growing comfort and affluence, bringing about a change in the lifestyle with which many are still unable to cope. Kolář is a shy man and it is quite symptomatic that he does not pursue his kind of people in the privacy of their homes as do many of his peers, but rather seeks them on the stage of the cityscape, in the streets and public places.

Kolář's pictures brim with contrast, provoking undertone and tension of tacit intimation, a tension often produced by his juxtaposing the real and the imaginary, by his incorporation of the absurd, by his creating an eerie feeling. Kolář's images are carefully composed and even the most minute detail is a significant part of the whole. And thus, although all pictures are invariably a part of a larger monothematic series, each image constitutes an independent, self-contained and aesthetically valid message.

Viktor Kolář is a leading representative of that part of the Czechoslovak generation of photographers who since the mid-70s have been seriously undermining the age-old traditional canons of art photography, emphasizing fact rather than poeticism and aestheticism, attempting instead to analyze and characterize social and psychological aspects of existence.

—Daniela Mrázková

KOLLÁR, François.

Nationality: French. **Born:** František Kollár in Senec, near Pressburg, Hungary (now Bratislava, Czechoslovakia), 8 October 1904; emigrated to France, 1924; naturalized, 1947. **Education:** Educated in Pressburg, 1910-19; self-taught in photography, from 1920. **Family:** Married Fernande Papillon in 1930; children: Jean Michel, Maria Francoise and Jean Bernard. **Career:** Worked for the Czech Railways, Nove Zamky, 1920-24; lathe-operator, Renault car factories, Paris, 1924-26; printer, Bernes, Marouteau et Cie art lithographers, Paris, 1927-28; head of the photographic studios, Draeger fine art printers, Paris, 1928-29; assistant to the industrial and architectural photographer Chevojon, then under the photographer André Vigneau, at Lecram Agency, Paris, 1930. Freelance publicity, fashion and portrait photographer, establishing his own studio on the rue de la Tour, Paris, from 1930: worked for Dunhill, Philips, Frigidaire, the agencies Dorland, Erwin Wasey, Walter Thompson, McCann and Company, and the magazines, *Vu, Voila, Town and Country, Die Dame, Neue Linie, L'Art Vivant, Harper's Bazaar, Plaisir de France, Le Figaro Illustré*, etc., from 1931; established new studio on the rue Chardin, Paris, 1934: worked for the fashion houses Schiaparelli, Maggy Rouf, Chanel, Patou, Balenciaga, Balmain, Dior, Fath, etc., 1934-39. Head of photographic displays, Exposition Internationale, Paris, 1937. Proprietor, radio electrics shop, in Poitiers, France (photographic activity interrupted by World War II), 1940-45; established new studio on the rue Notre-Dame-de-Lorette, Paris, 1945-65: concentrated on colour photography,

working as a photographic book illustrator, and for La Documentation Francaise, Christofle, Les Grands Moulins de Paris, Parfums Schiaparelli, etc., 1947-62. Photo shop proprietor, in Creteil, France, 1965-79. **Recipient:** Bronze Medal and Diploma, Centre National de la Recherche Scientifique, Paris, 1938. **Estate:** Jean Michel Kollár, 145 rue Pelleport, 75020 Paris, France. **Died:** (in Creteil, France) 3 July 1979.

Individual Exhibitions:

1932	*La France Travaille,* Galerie d'Art Contemporain, Paris
1934	*30 Photos,* Galerie de la Pleiade, Paris
1948	Galerie Royale, Paris
1965	National Gallery, Bratislava, Czechoslovakia (retrospective; with Jean-Michel Kollár)
1981	Hotel de Ville, Arles, France
1983	Maison des Associations, Creteil, France
	Galerie F, Banska Bystrica, Czechoslovakia
1984	Komorna Galeria, Bratislava, Czechoslovakia
1985	*La France Travaille,* Bibliothèque Forney, Paris
	La France Travaille, Denain, France

Selected Group Exhibitions:

1930	*Internationale Ausstellung,* Munich
1932	*The Modern Spirit in Photography,* Royal Photographic Society, London
1934	*Art Photographique Publicitaire,* Studio Saint Jacques, Paris
1936	*Exposition des Dix,* Chez Leleu, Paris
1948	*Exposition des Photographes Hongrois de France,* Union Democratique des Hongrois de France, Paris
1957	*Salon Nationale de la Photographie,* Bibliothèque Nationale, Paris (and 1959, 1961)
1977	*The History of Fashion Photography,* International Museum of Photography at George Eastman House, Rochester, New York (travelled to Brooklyn Museum of Art, New York; San Francisco Museum of Modern Art; Cincinnati Art Institute, Ohio; Museum of Fine Arts, St. Petersburg, Florida)
1979	*La Photographie de Mode en France,* Galerie Zabriskie, Paris
1982	*Magazines et Photographies 1928-40,* Centre Georges Pompidou, Paris (toured France)
1985	*Extending the Perimeters of 20th Century Photography,* San Francisco Museum of Modern Art

Collections:

Bibliothèque Nationale, Paris; Centre Georges Pompidou, Paris; Bibliothèque Forney, Paris; National Gallery, Bratislava, Czechoslovakia.

Publications:

By KOLLÁR: Books—*L'Histoire du Pain,* children's album, Paris 1931; *La Fête Foraine,* children's album, Paris 1931; *La France Travaille,* 2 vols., Paris 1932-34; *25 Photos de Kollár,* Paris 1934; *Le Port de Marseille,* Marseille 1935; *Dakar et Senegal,* Paris 1951; *L'Afrique Occidentale Française,* Paris 1951; *Abidjan et la Côte d'Ivoire,* Paris 1951; *Encyclopédie Nationale de la Police,* Paris 1955; and numerous brochures and portfolios for Sarlino Linoleum, 1931-56; Cognac Martell, 1931-32; Electricité de France, 1932-37; Usine de Bromat, 1933; BNCI (Banque Nationale de Paris), 1938; Documentation Francaise, 1947-51; Compagnie d'Assurance Phoenix, 1948-62; Les Fourrures Lionel, 1948; Christoflé, 1950-51; Union Aeromaritime de

Transports, 1953; Mines de Potasse d'Alsace, 1954; Etablissements Rougier, 1955; Les Tannins Rey, 1955; Parfums Schiaparelli, 1957; Poliet et Chausson, 1957-61; Syndicat National des Ciments et Chaux, 1958; Alimentation Equilibrée Comentry, 1962; etc.

On KOLLÁR: Books—*L'Art de Voir et la Photographie* by M. Natkin, Paris 1935; *Le Monde des Affaires de 1830 a nos Jours*, Paris 1952; *The History of Fashion Photography* by Nancy Hall-Duncan, New York 1979; *František Kollár* by Lubo Stacho, Prague 1984; *François Kollár: La France Travaille,* exhibition catalogue, by Francoise Denoyelle, Denain, France 1985; *François Kollár: Regard sur les années trente—La France Travaille,* exhibition catalogue, by Raymond Bacholet and Anne-Claude Lelieur, Paris 1985. **Articles**—"François Kollár," special issue of *Le Professionnel Photographe* (Paris), March/June 1931; "Tschecoslovaquie," special issue of *Diversion* (Paris), May 1935; "Deuxieme Exposition d'Art Photographique Publicitaire," special issue of *Le Professionel Photographe* (Paris), no. 57, 1937; "Projekt La France Travaille" by Lubo Stacho in *Vitvarnictvo* (Bratislava, Czechoslovakia), no. 2, 1985; "Fashion Photography" by Lubo Stacho in *Ceskoslovenska Fotografie* (Prague), no. 3, 1985; "François Kollár, 1904-1979" by Lubo Stacho in *Vitvarni Zivot* (Bratislava, Czechoslovakia), no. 3, 1985.

*   *   *

Kollár emerged from the abyss of history as one of the most important photographers of his time and his work became respected almost overnight. Soon after his death, Paris and then New York saw the exhibition *French Photography 1925-1940* in which he ranked among the most prominent authors. Two years later his photography became the talk of the 1981 International Photography Week at Arles, France. In fact he was the only photographer represented there who won universal acclaim. "Most of the show was just short of disaster," wrote *Le Figaro,* "and the only thing that helped avoid it was Kollár's photography." It should be noted that the praise went to photographs from the series titled *Working France* and dating from fifty years back! "Kollár's photographs have clarity, a geometric style and feeling for the message; they have mystery," wrote *Le Monde.*

František Kollár had originally started as an amateur photographer. Interested exclusively in Hoyningen-Huene, Guyllot and Man Ray, he could not find a job in a commercial studio. Paris was for him but a stopover on his way to America. The young railway clerk from Bratislava just wanted to make enough in Paris to buy his steerage. At fourteen he had received his first camera, a 10 x 15 cm Erneman, and after that dreamed only of becoming a professional photographer. He felt the pitiful circumstances of his native Slovakia so restricting that in 1924 he decided to leave, forgetting even to say goodbye to his parents.

Although his destination was America, he settled in Paris. At first he operated a lathe in the Renault car factory, then spent long hours doing uninteresting, tedious commercial photography. But it was photography at least and he gained invaluable professional experience in reproduction work at a well-known studio. He met with famous people and established contacts with exclusive magazines. In 1930 he married a French girl, started a studio of his own and in three years became famous as a French Sander. The *Horizons de France* Publishers commissioned him to do a documentary project entitled *Working France/La France travaille.* The two thousand pictures, selected carefully from some 10,000 exposed negatives, were to give people assurance shaken by the Depression. They reconfirmed a belief in the positive values of work beneficial to the entire society. The pictures were first published in a series of fifteen consecutive issues, then appeared in two book volumes.

The grand promotion project which included an exhibition paved the way for Kollár's cooperation with the French bureau of *Harper's Bazaar.* Financially secure, he could now afford to live in the centre of Paris. His knowledge of Hungarian, acquired in his bilingual background, brought him among a circle of major avant-garde Hungarian expatriate artists and photographers living in Paris. He participated in their shows, was even thought to be

Hungarian, and was one of the Ten Independent Photographers, a presage of the post-war Magnum Photos. For the 1936 World Exposition in Paris he made a monumental decoration project, a huge 2.5 x 120m frieze for the facade of the French pavilion designed by Le Corbusier. From the same time dates also his documentation of the repainting of *Guernica,* by which Picasso protested in the Spanish pavilion against the Fascist terror unleashed in his native country.

The mainstay of Kollár's photography remained in commercial work, especially fashion and advertisement. Long before the war he took interest in the possibilities of colour photography and after the war he perfected his negative-positive process at the school of applied arts at Vevey. In the 50s he was commissioned by the French government to document the transition of former French colonies in Africa. He ended his professional career as owner of a small photographic shop in the outskirts of Paris.

—Vladimìr Remeš

KON, Michiko.

Nationality: Japanese. **Born:** Kamakura, Kanagawa Prefecture, Japan, 1955. **Education:** Graduated from Sokei Art School, 1978; attended Tokyo Photographic College, 1978-80. **Recipient:** Art Scholar Prize, Kanagawa Prefectural Art Exhibition, 1984; New Artists Prize, Higashikawa International Photography Festival, 1987; The Ihei Kimura Photography Award, 1991. **Address:** c/o Photo Gallery International, 2-5-18 Minato-ku, Tokyo 105, Japan.

Individual Exhibitions:

1985	*Still Life,* Nikon Salon, Shinjuku, Tokyo
1987	*EAT,* Kodak Photo Salon, Tokyo and Osaka
1990	*EAT: Recent Works,* Photo Gallery International, Tokyo
1991	*Michiko Kon Photographs,* Exposure Gallery, PARCO, Tokyo
	Michiko Kon, Portfolio Gallery, Edinburgh
	EAT, Minolta Photo Space, Tokyo and Osaka
1992	*Michiko Kon: Still Lives,* MIT List Visual Arts Center, Massachusetts Institute of Technology, Cambridge, USA
	Michiko Kon, Old Town Hall Arts Centre, Hemel Hempstead, England; Tramway, Glasgow; Focal Point Photography Gallery, Southend, England
1993	*Michiko Kon,* Angel Row Gallery, Nottingham
	Michiko Kon: Still Lives, Virginia Museum of Fine Arts
1994	*Still Lives,* Photo Gallery International, Tokyo

Selected Group Exhibitions:

1979	*Art as Photography, Photography as Art,* Shiba Gallery, Yokohama
1982-84	*Aspects of Fifteen Individuals,* Kamakura Community Gallery, Kamakura
1988	*Speaking through Photography,* Photography Center, Tokyo National University of Fine Arts and Music
	Peace by Peace, Ginza Graphic Gallery, Tokyo
	Japanese Women Photographers, Lehigh University Art Gallery, Philadelphia
1989	*New Age Photography,* Store Days, Roppongi WAVE, Tokyo

Hat of Yellow Tail, **1986.** Photograph ©Michiko Kon.

The Hitachi Collection of Contemporary Japanese Photography, Center for Creative Photography, University of Arizona, Tucson
New Age New Art, Isetan Department Store, Tokyo
TORINO PHOTOGRAFIA, Torino, Italy
151st Year of Photography, Heineken Village Gallery, Tokyo

1990 *FOTOFEST/The International Month of Photography,* Houston Convention Center, Houston

The Silent Dialogue: Still Life in the West and Japan, Shizuoka Prefectural Museum of Art, Shizuoka
Beyond the Photographic Frame—11 Recent Works, Contemporary Art Gallery, Art Tower, Mito, Ibaraki
Japanese Contemporary Photography, Pavillon des Arts, Paris
Japanese Contemporary Photography: 12 Viewpoints, Tokyo Metropolitan Museum of Photography, Tokyo
TOKYO, Seibu Art Forum, Yurakucho, Tokyo

1991   *Art is Fun II,* Hara Museum ARC (Hara Museum of
            Contemporary Art), Gumma Prefecture
          Make-Believe: Contemporary Photography from JAPAN, The
            Photographers' Gallery, London
1992   *Representatives: Women Photographers from the Permanent
            Collection,* Center for Creative Photography, The University
            of Arizona, Tucson
1993   *Make Believe,* Viewpoint Photography Gallery, Salford,
            England
          Fabricated Realities, The Museum of Fine Arts, Houston
          When the Body Becomes Art, Itabashi Art Museum

Collections:

Tokyo Metropolitan Museum of Photography, Tokyo; Itabashi Art Museum, Tokyo; International Museum of Photography at George Eastman House, Rochester, New York; Center for Creative Photography, University of Arizona, Tucson; The Art Museum, Princeton University, New Jersey; Museum of Vincent Van Gogh, France; Museum of Fine Arts, Houston, Texas; M.I.T. List Visual Arts Center, Cambridge, Massachusetts.

Publications:

By KON: Book—*EAT,* 1987, revised (Shogakukan) 1991.

On KON: Books—*Beyond the Photographic Frame—11 Recent Works,* exhibition catalogue, (Ibaraki) 1990; *Japanese Contemporary Photography: Twelve Viewpoints,* exhibition catalogue (Tokyo), 1990; *Make Believe: Contemporary Photography from Japan,* exhibition catalogue (London) 1991; *Michiko Kon: Still Lives,* exhibition catalogue (Cambridge USA), 1992. **Articles**—"Dejà-vu No. 2," in *Photo Planet* (Tokyo), 1993; "Explorations: 10 Portfolios" in *Aperture 130,* (New York) 1993.

* * *

Look at Michiko Kon's photographs. As they stand out against their pitch-black background, such strange and beautiful objets d'art take our breath away. The chilled atmosphere which hovers around these pictures feels poignant, tense. If you have not encountered them before, they will provoke an immediate, involuntary smile. But then after inspecting the objects which silently reside in these pictures, you will be surprised to discover what they are made of. You will be both disgusted and enthralled. They are strange and beautiful objets which could survive in no place other than Michiko Kon's world of photography. Lingerie made from pond herrings' skins. Countless safety pins are fastened to the chest and body, and herring heads are arranged on the shoulder straps and the garters at equal intervals. A sneaker whose canvas is a patchwork of cuttlefish and whose shoelace is imitated by squid tentacles. A chrysanthemum planted in a cabbage wearing pantyhose and high heels. Sardine heads in full bloom on a splash of baby's breath.

A brassiere, a sweater, a hat, shoes, melons, cabbages, fish, fish and fish. These commonplace items are bountiful within daily life. Michiko Kon's cunning hand transforms these insignificant articles of food, clothing and shelter into bizarre objets. Michiko Kon bestows life onto freak objets. Their momentary life, perpetuated by photography, glows vividly within the enclosed space of sensitized paper. As a temporary refreshment from the banality of our conventional way of living, her works quench the thirst of our senses.

Michiko Kon's studio is located near the fish market in the Tsukiji section of Tokyo. After working out an idea (she says this process consumes most of her working hours) she visits the fish market early in the morning to pick out the materials. While selecting them, it is said, she appears so obsessed that no one dare interrupt her. Purchase in hand, she returns to her studio and strips each fish of skin with care so as not to mar its head, scales or eyes. She fondly affixes each piece of fish skin to previously prepared objects such as lingerie, violin, various garments, or even a man's body.

Of the five senses, touch and smell are the first to surface. Fish is a fresh food. It gives off an intense, unique smell and taken in your hands, it feels so solid and substantial it appeals to you with its living existence. In addition to the odor, the feel of slimy matter also penetrates, stimulating our tactile sensitivity. The more beautiful her finished print quality, lighting and arrangement is, the stickier the imagery feels to your skin, causing a strong physiologi-

cal reaction, a kind of repulsion. Her works are sprinkled with a venom which, being sharp and prickly like the safety pins attached to her lingerie, disturbs your senses.

Within the lineage of mainstream Japanese photography, her works are certainly unorthodox and belong nowhere else but within contemporary photography. She is a heretic even among the nation's small number of women photographers, who are mostly portraitists, photojournalists or in the advertising business. She is an outsider not only because she received no formal instruction in photography and has no mentors whatsoever, but also because her works lack the unique emotional intimacy of Japanese photography. Whether male or female, artists like her who are concerned with photography as a mere tool or means for communication, have only recently begun to emerge.

Her choice of photography as a medium happened unexpectedly. In art school she studied wood block printing and produced various types of collage, attracted to unexpected juxtapositions. It was not until she attempted to assemble actual objects instead of working with flat images that the camera played a role in her production process. To her the camera is nothing more than a simple, convenient instrument.

Can her works truly be classified under the term "surrealism," a term often used to describe her work? I feel it is hard to defend this label. Her works do share some affinities with surrealism in its widest sense, i.e. an investigation into the unconscious, or a freedom of the imagination. But her works have nothing to do with French Surrealism, a movement which, being fundamentally rebellious in the fashion of the day, aimed at a total social revolution.

And she has no more relation with Japanese Surrealism than with the French movement, which greatly influenced the local practice. This nation's surrealistic photography evolved around amateur photographers' clubs and is known as "new photography" or "avant-garde photography." This Japanese movement's chief concern was with the "automatism" of photography and photographic techniques, including solarization, photograms, collage, etc. Starting from photographic concerns, the movement ended in photographic technicalities. Great significance may be attached to the fact that they claimed photography as a model of expression before it gained independence as such. But it is absurd to include Michiko Kon's works in the line of Japanese Surrealism.

Her works are representative of this age because she plays in an overserious manner. Her depiction of this age shows an existence in which excessive information, stimuli and images inundate and deaden our five senses. Or perhaps she is depicting us, her contemporaries, who have lost our sensitivity to such information, stimuli and images. And Michiko Kon—one of us—laments "I must say that I really don't like it! I want to express myself and keep sensitive by implementing all the bodily senses such as taste, touch, hearing, sight and smell." She continues to resist the surging waves while sensing with her whole body. Her works pierce our numbed senses to make them tingle.

—Michiko Kasahara

KOPOSOV, Gennadi.

Nationality: Russian. **Born:** Leningrad, in July 1938. **Education:** Attended schools in Leningrad, 1945-55, and the Merchant Marine School in Riga, Latvia, 1955-57; self-taught in photography. **Career:** Served in the Soviet Army, 1957-59. **Career:** Photo Lab Assistant, Research Institute, Leningrad, 1959; Photographer for TASS (Soviet press agency), Leningrad, 1960. Since 1960, Special Photo-Correspondent for *Ogonyok* magazine, Moscow. Chairman, Photojournalists Section, U.S.S.R. Union of Journalists, 1975-78. **Recipient:** First Prize, *World Press Photo Exhibition,* Holland, 1964; First Prize, *Interpressphoto Travelling Exhibition,* 1965. **Address:** Ogonyok Magazine, Moscow-Centre, Russia.

Selected Group Exhibitions:

1964   *World Press Photo,* Gemeente Museum, The Hague (toured
            Europe)

1965   *Interpressphoto* travelling exhibition
1971   *The Soviet Union in Photography* travelling exhibition (toured Prague, Moscow, Budapest, Berlin, Warsaw, Paris, etc.)
Koposov's work has also appeared in the annual exhibitions of *Ogonyok* magazine and the Novosti Agency, Moscow.

Collections:

Ogonyok Magazine, Moscow; Novosti Agency, Moscow; Daniela Mrázková Collection, Prague.

Publications:

By KOPOSOV: Books—*V fokuse fotoreporter* (*In Front of the Photoreporter's Camera*), with Lev Sherstennikov, Moscow 1967; *My/We!,* with Lev Sherstennikov, Moscow 1970; *Pod nogami ostrov ledyannyj* (*Glacial Island*) Moscow 1972; *Hallo Siberia!,* with Lev Sherstennikov, Moscow 1972.

On KOPOSOV: Books—*Foto SSSR,* by the Sovetskoye Foto editors, annually since 1970; *Eye Witness; 25 Years through World Press Photos* by Harold Evans, London 1981. **Article**—"Photo-reporters of Ogonyok" by Daniela Mrázková in *Revue Fotografie* (Prague), no. 4, 1972.

* * *

Gennadi Koposov's work was moulded from the outset by the requirements of Soviet picture magazines—in his case the biggest and oldest of the Soviet weeklies, *Ogonyok,* founded in 1923, where Koposov has been employed since the age of 22. His job has provided him with great opportunities for travel throughout the vast territory of the U.S.S.R., including regions hardly accessible to the rest of the population (Siberia, the North and South poles, the Far East), with generous conditions regarding his time, which have enabled him to devote a great deal of time to work on one theme, and finally with a somewhat exclusive professional and social position; at the same time, however, he was restricted in his work, by the general standard of a journal directed at the broadest section of the population and by propaganda tasks, which are the motive power of Soviet journalism, even pictorial journalism. And yet, finally, Koposov is the principal representative of the Soviet photojournalists of the early 1960s who were able to make their own way and take advantage of the liberalization that came about with the end of the tough Stalinist era.

Instead of the schematic picture stories that had become common in the press, this new generation of photojournalists once again introduced into Soviet photography themes from everyday life, a fresh perception, and emotion. They replaced overtly expressive and thematic photography with work that conveyed the artist's unique partialities and his individual vision. Just like its predecessor, the generation of the 1920s and 30s, it opened up to the public the near and far regions of an immense country; it popularized the country's program of industrialization that had been interrupted by the war; and it propagated the message of settlement on and economic usage of virgin lands and untapped mineral resources. Of course, all of this done with the inevitable pathos of Soviet art.

Koposov and his fellow reporters did not so much focus on man himself and his problems, his changing style of living during the period in which the echoes of war still made themselves felt, as concentrate on the conditions under which a citizen, now seen as a civilian, fulfilled his tasks and contributed to the implementation of the important set aims of the whole of society. That is why Koposov puts such emphasis on expressing the whole atmosphere of the depicted environment, of places fascinating because of their rough and yet romantically imagined exclusiveness and scope. That is why he makes use of arrangement, even montage processes, and various graphic devices, such as graining.

His most typical theme is the North, those places where temperatures drop to minus 50-60 degrees centigrade. Here, in the polar night, amidst snowstorms and blizzards, with scattered light, Koposov can make use of his talent for working under difficult lighting conditions, and give way to his fancy for using light effects to separate the essential from the non-essential, mixing light and darkness, with the silhouettes of people and things turning into spectres.

Koposov introduces artistic elements into reportage—artistic means of expression and artistic schemas of composition. He links his photographs into broader thematic units. With his friend, the editor Lev Sherstennikov, with whom he has worked closely for many years, he has been a pioneer in the U.S.S.R. with his thematic books of photographs, some of which they published themselves at the end of the 1960s and early 70s.

The leadership and influence of the leading reporter of *Ogonyok,* Dmitri Baltermans, an outstanding photographer of the preceding generation, also contributed to Koposov's development, and he in turn became a significant figure in the feature photography of the 60s and early 70s. However, Koposov was unable to keep up or acclimatize himself to the subsequent movement, that of the newest generation of Soviet press photographers, with its interest in the sociological documentary.

—Daniela Mrázková

KORNISS, Péter.

Nationality: Hungarian. **Born:** Kolozsvár, Transylvania, 4 August 1937. **Education:** Attended schools in Kolozsvár until 1949, and in Budapest, 1949-55; studied law, at the Eötvös Lóránt University, Budapest, 1955-57; philosophy, at the Marx-Lenin University, Budapest, 1966-69; mainly self-taught in photography, from 1958. **Family:** Married Edit Wéber in 1966; son: György. **Career:** Assistant in a photo-cooperative, Budapest, 1958-61. Since 1961, staff photographer, and since 1980, Head of the Photo Department, *Nök Lapja* magazine, Budapest. Visiting Lecturer, Rutgers University, New Brunswick, New Jersey, University of Nebraska, Lincoln, and University of Utah, Salt Lake City, 1977. Jury Member, World Press Photo Awards, Amsterdam, 1977-79; International Advisory Committee Member, W. Eugene Smith Memorial Fund, 1983. Since 1991 Freelancing. **Recipient:** Balázs Béla Prize, Hungary, 1975; Grand Prix, United Nations Photo Competition, 1976; Artist of Merit Award, Hungary, 1983. **Agent:** Das Fotoarchiv, Rüttenscheider Str. 36, 45128 Essen, Germany. **Address:** Szt. István Park 22, 1137 Budapest, Hungary.

Individual Exhibitions:

1972   Kluuvi Gallery, Helsinki
1974   Mücsarnok Art Gallery, Budapest
1977   Rutgers University, New Brunswick, New Jersey
        University of Nebraska, Lincoln
        University of Utah, Salt Lake City
1978   House of Friendship, Moscow
        t'Hoogt Gallery, Utrecht, Netherlands
1980   Musée Nicephore Niépce, Chalon-sur-Saone, France
        Tihanyi Museum, Hungary
1981   Fachhochschule, Dortmund, West Germany
1982   Salon Fotografije, Belgrade, Yugoslavia
1983   Canon Gallery, Amsterdam
        Centre Culturel, Toulouse, France
1985   Casa de la Cultura, Quito, Ecuador
1988   Palace of Exhibitions, Budapest
1989   Canon Galery, Amsterdam
        Hollandse Hoogte, Amsterdam
        Rutgers University, New Brunswick, New Jersey
1990   Aspekte Galerie, Münich, Germany

Selected Group Exhibitions:

1961   *International Photography,* Ernst Museum, Budapest
1963   *Women in the 20th Century,* Ernst Museum, Budapest
1968   *Dance in Photography,* National Gallery, Budapest
1976   *Exposicio,* Hatvany Lajos Museum, Hatvan, Hungary
1982   *Hungarian Photography 1840-1981,* Mücsarnok Art Gallery, Budapest
1986   *Studio Nadar,* Ernst Museum, Budapest
1987   *Hungarian Photography Today,* National Museum of Photography, Film and TV, England

New Dance-House Scene, **Transylvania, 1992.** Photograph by Péter Korniss.

Collections:

Hungarian Academy of Science, Budapest; Musée Nicephore Niépce, Chalon-sur-Saone, France; Fotómüvészeti Galéria, Budapest; National Museum of Photography, Film and Television, England.

Publications:

By KORNISS: Books—*The Hungarian National Folk Dance Ensemble,* Budapest 1975; *Heaven's Bridegroom—Hungarian Folk Customs,* with text by Sandor Csoori, Budapest 1975; *Passing Times,* Budapest 1979; *The Land of Red Cloud,* Budapest 1982; *Osi karavánutak földjén/On South Yemen,* Budapest 1985; *The Guest Worker,* Budapest 1988; *Folkloristisch Danstheater,* Amsterdam 1991.

On KORNISS: Books—*The Photographic Memory,* Quiller Press, London 1988. **Articles**—in *Fotómüvészet* (Budapest), February 1974; *Camera 35* (New York), December 1976; *Fotografia Italiana* (Milan), January 1977; *Le Photographe* (Paris), April 1977; *Fotografie* (Leipzig), February 1978, and February 1983; *The New Hungarian Quarterly* (Budapest), Autumn 1985; *Photography* (London), February 1988; *Photography* (London), April 1989; *The British Journal of Photography* (London), 23 November 1989.

*

Photographers have many different ideas about photography, but there is always a link between these ideas and their practical activities. In the mid-60s I started to work in tiny Hungarian and Transylvanian villages, because I realized this was the last chance to photograph disappearing traditional peasant life and culture in East Europe. I have spent fifteen years working with these people. Although their houses could be rebuilt in open-air museums, their songs taped, and their costumes and artifacts preserved in museums, the most important thing—the people—could be captured only by the camera. In this way we can catch and preserve the fast-changing world in photographs for the future. I think that documentation is not merely one possibility for photography; it is one of its most important tasks.

—Péter Korniss

*   *   *

One of the most impressive talents of the middle generation of Hungarian photographers, Péter Korniss is a part of a phenomenon that has never been studied in depth, i.e. the spontaneous Hungarian talent for photography. Korniss' pure photography and deep respect for life one immediately feels from it is an apotheosis of the ordinary man, an epic of man's situation. This high regard for life photography is intimately familiar to us from the work of Korniss' famous predecessors who started the worldwide fame of Hungarian photography in the 1920s and '30s, Kertész, Munkácsi, Escher and other authors whose contribution to photojournalism still remains to be recognized.

Korniss' photography bears a distinct imprint of magazine utilitarianism. It is pictorially effective, formally perfect and highly attractive. It cannot deny that Korniss' growth has been closely associated with his professional career in *Nök Lapja,* the best-known of Hungarian women's picture magazines for which Korniss has been working as reporter since 1961. However, what lends his photography a permanent value surpassing the immediate need of magazine photography is the profundity of his universally human themes. Korniss' work first won international acclaim during the mid-70s but his talent was truly recognized in 1979 when Budapest's Corvina Press published his book *Passing Times.*

The perfectly rendered pictorial essay by the forty-two-year-old author, impressive also for its inner structure, records the traditional lifestyle of rural ethnic Hungarians living in neighbouring countries, i.e. Czechoslovakia, Yugoslavia and Rumania. Korniss compares this lifestyle with that of Hungarian peasant communities and comes to the conclusion that even international borders cannot undermine strong ethnic ties. Korniss' photography, however, does not attempt to preserve a folklore heritage, as is the role of museums or festivals of folk music, song and dance, but rather captures a living ethnic culture surviving in rural communities. And it is the manifestation of this survival despite artificial borders of new administrative and political units, in which lies the strength of Korniss' humanist message.

The project took long to crystallize. The first outline of this extensive work was a 1975 edition of Korniss' book *Heaven's Bridegroom* which recorded the traditional customs of Hungarian country folk. Its culmination, on the other hand, was an exhibition held in 1983 in West Germany within the framework of Hungarian Culture Days and titled *Meeting Hungary.* Korniss seems to prefer extensive serial work, as proven by his next project. It is titled *The Guestworker* and also took years to finish. It captures stories of country men who leave to work in the city every week, coming back home only for weekends, the only time when they can be with their families, work in their gardens or have a friendly drink and chat in the local tavern. Gradually, they grow alienated from their cultural background, their lifestyle and ultimately become uprooted, for they belong neither in the village, nor in the city, feeling strangers in both. Korniss' photographic essay on the guestworkers is a deep probe into contemporary Hungarian life and its socio-psychological conditions and has even a fine socio-critical accent. Korniss has thus ventured into sociologically oriented documentary photography in which the message is borne not only by the pictures themselves but also by precise arrangement and sequence which give it a deeper meaning. No wonder that in 1986 Korniss won the second prize at the top-level photojournalist World Press Photo competition in the Daily Life Series category.

Like Martin Munkácsi, Péter Korniss is a native of Koloszvár. When he was seven, his parents left Transylvania and moved to Budapest. Korniss studied law but in 1958 started working in a photographic laboratory, showing a remarkable talent for the medium. In 1967 he returned to a small Transylvanian village called Szek and started recording the life of its Hungarian minority which he knew so intimately. The project resulted in ten thousand pictures which he donated to the Hungarian Academy of Sciences. In the 1970s his photography won him various major awards and Korniss started exhibiting and lecturing as well as photographing abroad. Yet his best work has always been produced by his intimate knowledge of his home country in which he remains deeply rooted.

—Daniela Mrázková

KOUDELKA, Josef.

Nationality: Czechoslovakian. **Born:** Boskovice, Moravia, 10 January 1938; left Czechoslovakia in 1970, and became British resident, 1971, and French resident, 1980. **Education:** Studied aeronautical engineering at the Technical University, Prague, 1956-61, Dip.Ing. 1961. **Career:** Worked as an aeronautical engineer in Prague, 1961-67; also worked part-time as a freelance photographer, contributing to *Divadlo (Theatre)* magazine, Prague, 1961-65, and as Official Photographer to the Theatre za Branou, Prague, 1965-70 (full-time photographer from 1967). Member, Union of Czechoslovak Artists, 1965-70. Freelance photographer with the Magnum photo agency, Paris and New York, working in London, 1971-80, and in Paris, since 1980. **Recipient:** Annual Award for Theatre Photography, Union of Czechoslovak Artists, 1967; Robert Capa Memorial Award, 1970; British Council Photography Grant, 1972, 1973; Photography Bursary, Arts Council of Great Britain, 1976; Prix Nadar, Paris, 1978; United States National Endowment for the Arts Photography Grant, 1980; Photography Grant, Centre National des Arts Plastiques, France, 1986. **Agents:** Magnum; Galerie Delpire, 13 rue de l'Abbaye, Paris 6, France; Helen Wright, The Atelier Group, 135 East 74th Street, New York, New York 10021, U.S.A.; John Hillelson Agency, 145 Fleet Street, London EC4, England. **Address:** c/o Magnum, 20 rue des Grands-Augustins, 75006 Paris, France.

Individual Exhibitions:

1961	Theatre Semafor, Prague
1967	*Gypsies 1961-66,* Theatre za Branou, Prague
1968	*Theatre Photography 1965-68,* Theatre za Branou, Prague
1975	Museum of Modern Art, New York
	Carlton Gallery, New York

1976	Art Institute of Chicago
1977	Kunsthaus, Zurich
	Tel Aviv Museum
	Galerie Delpire, Paris
	Victoria and Albert Museum, London (toured the U.K.)
1978	Stedelijk Museum, Amsterdam
1979	Musée d'Orange, France
1980	Camera Obscura, Stockholm
1981	Galerie le Trépied, Geneva
	Carpenter Center, Harvard University, Cambridge, Massachusetts
1984	Hayward Gallery, London (toured Britain)
1985	National Museum of Photography, Bradford, Yorkshire
1993	*Vintage Photographs*, Pace/MacGill Gallery, New York

Selected Group Exhibitions:

1967	*Photography: Collective Exhibition,* Spala Gallery, Prague
1968	*Europa '68,* Bergamo, Italy
1971	*Photographs of Women,* Museum of Modern Art, New York
1973	*Two Views: 8 Photographers,* The Photographers' Gallery, London (toured the U.K.)
1974	*Celebrations,* Hayden Gallery, Massachusetts Institute of Technology, Cambridge
1977	*Concerning Photography,* The Photographers' Gallery, London (travelled to the Spectro Workshop, Newcastle upon Tyne)
1978	*18 Photographes Européens: Images des Hommes,* Belgian Ministry of Culture touring exhibition, Brussels (toured Europe)
1980	*Old and Modern Masters of Photography,* Victoria and Albert Museum, London (toured the U.K.)
1983	*Subjective Vision,* High Museum of Art, Atlanta, Georgia
1985	*Magnum Concert,* Musée d'Art et d'Histoire, Fribourg, Switzerland

Collections:

Victoria and Albert Museum, London; Arts Council of Great Britain, London; Ministry of Culture, Brussels; Kunsthaus, Zurich; Stedelijk Museum, Amsterdam; Galerie in Forum Stadtpark, Graz, Austria; Museum of Modern Art, New York; Philadelphia Museum of Art.

Publications:

By KOUDELKA: Books—*Diskutujeme o moralce dneska (Discussion of Contemporary Morals),* Prague 1965; *Alfred Jarry's Ubu Roi,* edited by the Prague Institute of Theatre, Prague 1966; *Koudelka: Gypsies,* edited by Robert Delpire, with text by Willy New, Millerton, New York 1975, as *Koudelka—Gitans: La Fin du Voyage,* Paris 1977; *Portrait of a Film: The Making of White Nights,* with Eve Arnold, Anthony Crickmay and Terry O'Neill, New York 1986.

On KOUDELKA: Books—*Looking at Photographs: 100 Pictures from the Collection of the Museum of Modern Art* by John Szarkowski, New York 1973; *Celebrations,* with text by Minor White, Millerton, New York 1974; *The Magic Image* by Cecil Beaton and Gail Buckland, Boston and London 1975; *Popular Photography Annual,* New York 1976; *British Image 2: Photographs by Ian Berry, Chris Killip, Josef Koudelka, Marketa Luskacova, Dennis Wright, Patrick Ward,* edited by the Arts Council, London 1976; *Concerning Photography,* exhibition catalogue, by Jonathan Bayer, Peter Turner, Ian Jeffrey and Ainslie Ellis, London 1977; *Faces,* edited by Ben Maddow, Boston 1979; *Venezia '79: La Fotografia,* edited by Daniela Palazzoli, Vittoria Sgarbi and Italo Zannier, Milan and New York 1979; *World Photography,* edited by Bryn Campbell, London 1981; *I Grandi Fotografi: Josef Koudelka,* with text by Romeo Martinez, Milan 1982; *Photo Poche: Josef Koudelka,* with text by Bernard Cuau, Paris 1984. **Articles**—"Josef Koudelka: Gipsy" in *Camera* (Lucerne), March 1970; "Josef Koudelka" by Allan Porter

and Daniel Sallenari, special monograph issue of *Camera* (Lucerne), August 1979; "Prague 68" in *Aperture* (Millerton, New York), no. 197, 1984.

* * *

It is next to impossible to get Josef Koudelka to talk about his photographs. What he claims to lack in verbal articulation, he substitutes with his highly sophisticated visual images. It is as though the old cliché "one picture is worth a thousand words" comes to life in Koudelka's work. Photography is his life and there he pursues perfection with single-minded determination. His photographs project a precise visual message and a strong narrative content.

"What has interested me in taking photographs is the maximum—the maximum that exists in a situation and the maximum that I myself can produce from it. Sometimes I may achieve this goal immediately, but usually, for one reason or another, I am just not able to make the most of a situation, and so I have to photograph it time after time until I succeed. This repeated effort also helps to reassure me that I have in fact achieved the maximum."

Koudelka's beginnings in theatre photography taught him a certain discipline which he has applied to his work ever since. The freedom he was given to photograph the stage has enabled him to observe each scene from different angles and photograph it again and again until he achieved a satisfactory result.

In 1962 Koudelka started documenting gypsies in Eastern Slovakia with a dedication and intensity which eventually put him on a firm footing as one of the world's best photographers. This massive essay, which he worked on for nine years until he emigrated to the West, wasn't a sociological study trying to change the world of the gypsies, but a sensitive insight into the lives of people on the margins of society, capturing their essence, their appealing lifestyle, their passions, joys and tragedies. The gypsies in Koudelka's photographs are proud people who preserve their forgotten lives in a materialistic world striving after different values.

Koudelka's photographs of the dramatic events during the invasion of Czechoslovakia by the armies of the Warsaw Pact countries won him the Robert Capa Gold Medal in 1969. Not regarding himself as a photojournalist, Koudelka continued working on his gypsy theme, extended to the continent of western Europe after leaving Czechoslovakia in 1970.

For years Koudelka's lifestyle matched that of the people he photographed and shared his life with—that of dedicated nomads. His work became all-important; taking pictures in the summer, and working in the darkroom in the short dark days of the European winter. Critical as ever of his work, he would only show a photograph which he regarded as perfect.

In 1986 Koudelka's style changed. He started using a panoramic camera, which he first picked up in 1958, and moved to landscape and urban photography. His photographs became devoid of people. The landscapes are stark and uninviting, suffering from the heavy legacy of our modern industrialised society—the environmental damage.

In the middle of the 1980s Koudelka worked on a project sponsored by the French Ministry of Culture, producing a series of images on the environmental changes in northern France as a result of industrialisation, the construction of the Channel Tunnel, and major new road building. The project on the city of Beirut, undertaken with five other well-known photographers, shows Beirut devastated by the civil war. The latest completed project, *The Black Triangle* which Koudelka worked on for five years after the Czech Velvet Revolution in November 1989 enabled him to return to his native Czechoslovakia for the first time since his emigration. It remains a shocking witness to the neglect and devastation of the industrial area of northern Bohemia.

—Liba Taylor

KRAUSE, George.

Nationality: American. **Born:** Philadelphia, Pennsylvania, 24 January 1937. **Education:** Bok Vocational High School, Philadelphia, 1950-54; studied drawing, painting, graphics and design, then photography, at Philadelphia College of Art, 1954-57, 1959-60. **Military Service:** Served in the United States Army, 1957-59. **Family:** Married Patsy Johnson in 1959 (divorced, 1979); children: George and Kathryn. **Career:** Graphics Designer and Photog-

Abuse-Me-Doll, **Rome, 1977, from the series** *I Nudi.* **Photograph**
©George Krause. Courtesy The Museum of Fine Arts, Houston.

raphy Assistant with Samuel Maitin, Seymour Mednick and Dan Moerder, Philadelphia, 1960-67; professional advertising photographer, working for Time-Life Books, Houghton Mifflin publishers, *Show Magazine, Harper's Bazaar, McCall's, Sports Illustrated, Horizon,* etc., New York, 1968-75. Part-time Instructor, Fliesher Art Memorial, Philadelphia, and Swarthmore College, Pennsylvania, 1958-59; Instructor in Photography, Fliesher Art Memorial, Philadelphia, 1970-72, and Brooklyn College, New York, 1972-73; Associate Professor and Head of Photography, Bucks County Community College, Pennsylvania, 1973-75. Since 1975, Professor and Head of the Department of Photography, University of Houston. Visiting Associate Professor, Instituto Allende, San Miguel de Allende, Mexico, 1978; Photographer-in-Residence, American Academy, Rome, 1979-80. **Recipient:** Fulbright-Hays Fellowship, 1963; Guggenheim Fellowship, 1967, 1976-77; Alumni Award, Philadelphia College of Art, 1970; National Endowment for the Arts Grant, 1972, 1979-80, 1985; Prix de Rome, 1976-77; Unicolor Grant, 1983; Cultural Arts Council of Houston, 1986; Artist of the Year, Art League of Houston, 1993. **Agent:** Harris Gallery, 1100 Bissonnet, Houston, Texas 77005; More Gallery, 1630 Walnut Street, Philadelphia, Pennsylvania 19103, U.S.A. **Address:** 420 East 25th Street, Houston, Texas 77008, U.S.A.

Individual Exhibitions:

1970	Museo de Bellas Artes, Caracas
1971	Moravian College, Bethlehem, Pennsylvania
	Photographer's Place, Berwyn, Pennsylvania
1972	Pennsylvania State University, University Park
	International Museum of Photography, George Eastman House, Rochester, New York
	Witkin Gallery, New York
1973	Pennsylvania Academy of Fine Arts, Philadelphia
	Briarcliff College, Briarcliff Manor, New York
1974	Photopia, Philadelphia

	Gallery of Photography, Vancouver
	Museo de Bellas Artes, Caracas
1975	Philadelphia Print Club
1976	Photopia Gallery, Philadelphia
	Museo de Bellas Artes, Bogota
	Afterimage, Dallas
	Cronin Gallery, Houston
	Enjay Gallery, Boston
1977	Gallery of Photography, Vancouver
	American Academy, Rome
1978	Witkin Gallery, New York
	Museum of Fine Arts, Houston
1979	Milwaukee Center for Photography
	Rochester Institute of Technology, New York
1980	American Academy, Rome
	Mancini Gallery, Houston
	Hills Gallery, Denver
1981	Focus Gallery, San Francisco
1982	Pennsylvania Academy of Fine Arts, Philadelphia
	Amarillo Art Museum, Texas
	Milwaukee Center for Photography, Wisconsin
	Burton Gallery, Toronto, Ontario
1983	Chrysler Museum, Norfolk, Virginia
1984	McKillip Gallery, Providence, Rhode Island
1985	Harris Gallery, Houston, Texas
	F.32 Foto Galerie, Amsterdam
	Galleria Torino Fotografia, Turin, Italy
1987	The Photographers' Gallery, London
	Allen Street Gallery, Dallas
1988	Maine Photographic Workshops, Rockport, Maine
	Harris Gallery, Houston
1990	The Art Gallery, Bakersfield College, Bakersfield, California
	New England Photographic Workshops, New Milford, Connecticut
	Harris Gallery, Houston
	Galeria Spectrum, Zaragoza, Spain
1991	Watkins Carter Hamilton Architects, Bellaire, Texas
	Art Institute of Philadelphia, Pennsylvania
1992	*George Krause, A Retrospective,* The Museum of Fine Arts, Houston
1993	Philadelphia Art Alliance, Philadelphia, Pennsylvania
1994	Encontros du fotografia, Portugal
	Harris Gallery, Houston
	More Gallery, Philadelphia, Pennsylvania

Selected Group Exhibitions:

1963	*Five Unrelated Photographers,* Museum of Modern Art, New York
1964	*The Photographer's Eye,* Museum of Modern Art, New York
	Six Photographers, International Museum of Photography, George Eastman House, Rochester, New York
1965	*Recent Acquisitions,* Museum of Modern Art, New York
1967	*Photography in the 20th Century,* National Gallery of Canada, Ottawa (toured Canada and the United States, 1967-73)
1971	*Five Young Americans,* Museum of Modern Art, New York (toured South America)
1975	*Photography in America,* Whitney Museum, New York
1977	*Annual Exhibition,* American Academy, Rome
1978	*Mirrors and Windows: American Photography since 1960,* Museum of Modern Art, New York (toured the United States, 1978-80)
1979	*Self as Subject,* Scudder Gallery, Durham, New Hampshire
1980	*Annual Exhibition,* American Academy, Rome
1981	Washington Project for the Arts, Washington, D.C.
	Salaute! Five Houston Artists, Houston Festival '81, The Alley Theatre, Houston
	New Directions—The Nude, Massachusetts Institute of Technology, Cambridge

Collections:

Museum of Modern Art, New York; International Museum of Photography, George Eastman House, Rochester, New York; Addison Gallery of American Art, Andover, Massachusetts; Museum of Fine Arts, Boston; Philadelphia Museum of Art; Library of Congress, Washington, D.C.; Gernsheim Collection, University of Texas at Austin; Museum of Fine Arts, Houston; Museo de Bellas Artes, Caracas; Bibliothèque Nationale, Paris; Museum of Fine Arts, American Academy in Rome; Campbell Museum of Art, San Antonio; Amon Carter Museum, Texas.

Publications:

By KRAUSE: Books—*Saints and Martyrs,* portfolio, with an introduction by Carol Kismaric, Philadelphia 1976; *George Krause 1960-1970,* portfolio, with an introduction by Mark Power, Philadelphia 1980; *George Krause I,* with an introduction by Mark Power, Haverford, Pennsylvania 1972; *George Krause,* with introduction by Anne Tucker. **Articles**—"Intensification" in *Darkroom,* edited by Eleanor Lewis, New York 1977; "Editing" in *Contact,* edited by Ralph Gibson, New York 1980.

On KRAUSE: Books—*Photography in the 20th Century* by Nathan Lyons, New York 1967; *Looking at Photographs* by John Szarkowski, New York 1973; *Photography in America,* edited by Robert Doty, with an introduction by Minor White, 1974; *Mirrors and Windows: American Photography since 1960,* exhibition catalogue, by John Szarkowski, New York 1978; *The Photograph Collector's Guide* by Lee D. Witkin and Barbara London, Boston 1979; *American Children,* edited by Susan Kismaric, New York 1980; *American Nudes,* edited by Arno Minkkinen, New York 1981; *Scopophilia: The Love of Looking,* edited by Gerard Malanga, New York 1986. **Articles**—"Two Young Philadelphians: Don Donaghy and George Krause" by Murray Weiss in *Contemporary Photographer* (Culpeper, Virginia), Fall 1962; "Young Talent" in *Art in America* (New York), June 1963; "Malaguena" in *Camera* (Lucerne), January 1966; "Saints, Martyrs and Everyday Mysteries" by C. Stevens in *Print* (New York), November/December 1970; "Gallery: I Nudi" in *American Photographer* (New York), April 1981.

                                    *

My work is about the real medium of photography as interpreted through the idea of fantasy.

                                                        —George Krause

                            *   *   *

An artist can be said to have reached maturity when the acclaim for recent accomplishments accords with the glories bestowed upon past achievements. Gems will always stand apart no matter when they are first conceived or executed, but it is a measure of quite some success to be able to maintain recent work on par with the past and vice-versa—have past work easily recollected, like a brand-name, in the face of the new. Only after several decades in a photographer's career can the staying power of singular images or completed bodies of work begin to assert convincing authority. While most 20-year veterans continue to be known primarily for recent hurrahs, there are those, like George Krause, whose past work remains every bit as vital and engrossing as the work they are producing today.

A 1980 photograph of a nude woman swishing a white sheet above her head in Krause's studio in Rome recalls his 1964 photograph of an elderly Spanish woman plodding down the street unknowingly stalked by her own shadow. Form and content are equal collaborators in making the pictures then, and now. The white sheet and the black shadow—the one protean and buoyant, the other coiled and menacing—characterize the life and death impulses that have become the cornerstones of Krause's sensibilities. There is the 1963 photograph of a white stallion rolling in a field. Squeezed into the top half of the frame, the kinetic beast has little room to rise. Echoes of gunshot fill the air. There is the 1970 photograph of the face of a black boy holding his breath underneath a rushing fountain. His round, cherubic features are transformed by the water's flow into stone. And there is the 1971 image of collapsed concrete in a plaza in Buenos Aires that measures the length and width of a coffin.

But Krause's tightest handshake with death, his warmest embrace of life, occurs in his serial works. "Qui Riposa" and "Saints and Martyrs," both from the 1960s, affirm Christianity's inveterate fetishism with the ritual of death, while "i Nudi," from the late 70s, celebrates the mysteries of erotic fantasy.

The "Qui Riposa" photographs, many of which were taken in sunny San Francisco cemeteries, crop close to tombs and cross carrying faded photographs of long gone loved ones. The series permeates our senses with chilling warmth, like the first cold days of spring.

"Saints and Martyrs," by contrast, petrifies. Rummaging through the basement vaults of Indo-Hispanic churches in Mexico and South America, Krause photographed the blood-spattered, white-washed, broken-boned statues of Christ and other worshipped heroes and heroines of the church. Some of these man-made saints are caught clawing their way out of finely-quilted caskets, others are seen wrapped in sheets up to their necks and tagged as inventory, while still others are photographed through cellophane, the cry of their grief and anguish suffocated forever. This, without a doubt, is murder in the cathedral.

Krause's most recent series takes a surprising switch to the subject of the nude. The work coincides with Krause's tenure as photography's first Prix de Rome fellowship recipient. With Rome by his side, it's no wonder Krause imbues these "i Nudi" nudes with the lineaments and atmosphere of Renaissance altarpieces. One bony male nude with knees slightly bent is like the thief beside the savior. Others appear to have just come down from the cross. The female "i Nudi" nudes, on the other hand, are triumphant, full of flesh, or then pitch black with only radiating white cotton panties lowered to the knees or glowing necklaces to reveal their presence in the studio. Lead us not into temptation.

Keenly aware of the camera at his command and the darkroom at his disposal, George Krause has emerged time and again with his tiny prints of dazzling intensity, fantasy and passion. What we see in the world but don't notice, what we feel about life and death but haven't been able to visualize, George Krause buries in our memory with his camera.

—Arno Rafael Minkkinen

KRIMS, Les(lie Robert).

Nationality: American. **Born:** New York City, 16 August 1943. **Education:** Studied at Cooper Union, New York, B.F.A. 1964; Pratt Institute, Brooklyn, New York, M.F.A. 1967. **Family:** Married Leslie Korda in 1968 (divorced, 1972). **Career:** Freelance photographer since 1967. Assistant Instructor in Photography and Printmaking, Pratt Institute, Brooklyn, New York, 1966-67; Instructor in Photography, Rochester Institute of Technology, New York, 1967-69. Since 1969, Professor, State University of New York at Buffalo. **Recipient:** Artistic Decorators Inc. Award, 1969; Research Grant, State University of New York, 1970, 1971; New York State Council on the Arts Grant, 1971; National Education Association Fellowship, 1971, 1972; National Endowment for the Arts Fellowship, 1971, 1972, 1976; Creative Artists Public Service Grant, 1973, 1975. **Address:** 187 Linwood Avenue, Buffalo, New York 14209, U.S.A.

Individual Exhibitions:

1966	Pratt Institute, Brooklyn, New York
1969	Focus Gallery, San Francisco
	International Museum of Photography, George Eastman House, Rochester, New York
	Akron Art Institute, Ohio
	Witkin Gallery, New York (with Wynn Bullock)
	Garrick Fine Arts Gallery, Philadelphia
1970	Galleria Il Diaframma, Milan
	Fictions, Galleri Prisma IV, Lund, Sweden
1971	International Museum of Photography, George Eastman House, Rochester, New York
	Moore College, Philadelphia
	University of Colorado, Boulder
	Silver Image Gallery, Ohio State University, Columbus
	Toronto Gallery of Photography
1972	Witkin Gallery, New York
	Album Fotogalerie, Cologne
	Internationaal Cultureel Centrum, Antwerp
1973	Boston University
	Photogalerie Wilde, Cologne
1974	Galerie Delpire, Paris
	Light Impressions Gallery, Rochester, New York
	Galleria Documenta, Turin
	Galleria Photografica Nadar, Pisa
1975	*Fictcryptokrimsographs*, Visual Studies Workshop, Rochester, New York
	Light Gallery, New York
	Shadai Gallery, Tokyo
	Galerie Die Brücke, Vienna
	Yajima/Galerie, Montreal
	Nina Freudenheim Gallery, Buffalo, New York
1976	University of Colorado, Boulder
	Ohio Wesleyan University, Delaware
	Fictcryptokrimsographs and Kodalith Images, Galerie Jollenbeck, Cologne
	Colgate University, Hamilton, New York
	Suzette Schochet Gallery, Newport, Rhode Island
	Musée Galliera, Paris
	One Eye Open, One Eye Closed, Alberta College of Art, Calgary
	Galerie Nagel, Berlin
1977	*Kodalith Images*, Galerie ABF, Hamburg
	Canon Photo Gallery, Geneva
	Arbus/Krims/Michals, Galerie Schellmann und Kluser, Munich (with Diane Arbus and Duane Michals)
1978	*Academic Art 1974-77*, Canon Photo Gallery, Amsterdam
	Galerij Paule Pia, Antwerp
	Church Street Photographic Centre, Melbourne
	Nova Gallery, Vancouver
1979	Paul Cava Gallery, Philadelphia
1980	*Please*, Phototheque of Thessaloniki, Greece
	Idiosyncratic Pictures, Galerie Fiolet, Amsterdam
1981	*Idiosyncratic Pictures*, Ohio State University Gallery of Fine Art, Sullivant Gallery, Columbus, Ohio
	Les Krims, The Looking Glass Gallery, Detroit, Michigan
1982	*Idiosyncratic Pictures*, Viviane Esders Gallery, Paris
1987	*Les Krims*, The Silver Eye Gallery, Pittsburgh, Pennsylvania
1991	*A Sense of Humor*, New Image Gallery, Harrisonburg, Virginia
1993	*Les Krims*, Centre de la Photographie, Geneve, Geneva, Switzerland

Selected Group Exhibitions:

1969	*Vision and Expression*, International Museum of Photography, George Eastman House, Rochester, New York (toured the United States, 1969-71)
1970	*The Photograph as Object*, National Gallery of Canada, Ottawa
1972	*The Expanded Photograph*, Philadelphia Civic Center
1975	*4 Americanische Photographen: Friedlander/Gibson/Krims/Michals*, Stätisches Museum, Leverkusen, West Germany
1977	*Foto-Sequenties*, Stedelijk Museum, Amsterdam
1978	*Fantastic Photography in the U.S.A.*, Canon Photo Gallery, Amsterdam (toured Europe and the United States, 1978-80)
1980	*Photography: Recent Directions*, De Cordova Museum, Lincoln, Massachusetts
1982	*Lichtbildnisse: Das Porträt in der Fotografie*, Rheinisches Landesmuseum, Bonn
	Color as Form, A History of Color Photography, George Eastman House, Rochester, New York
	Staged Photographs, Lijnbaancentrum, Lijnbaan, Rotterdam, Netherlands
1983	*Portraits from the Musuem Collection*, The Museum of Fine Arts, Houston, Texas
1984	*Maximalism*, Tweed Gallery, Plainfield, New Jersey
	Anxious Interiors, Laguna Beach Museum of Art, Laguna Beach, California
	La Chambre, La Centre National de la Photographie, Palais de Tokyo, Paris
1985	*American Images 1945-80*, Barbican Art Gallery, London (toured Britain)
	The Nude in Photography, Munchner Stadtmuseum, Munich
	A Tribute to Lee D. Witkin, The Witkin Gallery, New York, New York
	Cincinnati Collects Photography, Cincinnati Art Museum, Cincinnati, Ohio
1986	*Staging the Self-Portrait, Photography 1840-1985*, National Portrait Gallery, London
	Commitment to Vision, Museum of Art, University of Oregon, Eugene, Oregon
	Photography, A Facet of Modernism, San Francisco Museum of Modern Art, San Francisco
	Photography As Performance: Message through Object and Picture, The Photographers' Gallery, London
1987	*Photography and Art 1946-86*, Los Angeles County Museum of Art
	Arrangements for the Camera: A View of Contemporary Photography, The Baltimore Museum of Art, Baltimore, Maryland
	True Stories and Photofictions, The Ffotogallery, Cardiff
	Photographs from the National Museum of Modern Art, Kyoto, Kyoto, Japan
	Likeness, Expression, and Character: Presence in Photographs, The Museum of Contemporary Photography, Chicago

Facets of the Collection, San Francisco Museum of Modern
    Art, San Francisco
1988   *Trains and Boats and Planes,* The Witkin Gallery, New York
    150 Years of Photography, Union of Czechoslovak Creative
      Arts, Prague
    Fabricated Photographs, Carpenter Center for the Visual Arts,
      Cambridge, Massachusetts
    NOS 80, III Fofobienal-Vigo 1988, Vigo, Spain
1989   *Light and Shadow: 150 Years of Photography,* Printemps,
      Ginza, Tokyo, Japan
    The Cherished Image: Portraits from 150 Years of Photogra-
      phy, National Gallery of Canada, Ottawa, Ontario
    Photographers' Dialogue, Boca Raton Museum of Art, Boca
      Raton, Florida
1990   *Capturing an Image: 150 Years of Photography,* Fogg Art
      Museum, Harvard University, Cambridge, Massachusetts
    Symbol and Surrogate: The Picture Within, University of
      Hawaii Art Gallery, Honolulu, Hawaii
    American Myth, Sioux City Art Center, Sioux City, Iowa
1993   *Gli anni '70 lo sguardo, la foto,* Galleria Civica, Modena, Italy
1994   *Interiors: A Metaphysical Construct,* Montgomery College,
      Rockville, Maryland
    Centre de la Photographie de Genève, 1984-1994, Galleria
      Gottardo, Lugano, Switzerland
    the camera i, Los Angeles County Museum of Art, Los
      Angeles
    Fotodifusion, Torino, Italy

Collections:

Museum of Modern Art, New York; International Museum of Photography,
George Eastman House, Rochester, New York; Museum of Fine Arts, Boston;
Library of Congress, Washington, D.C.; Minneapolis Institute of Arts; Uni-
versity of Kansas, Lawrence; University of New Mexico, Albuquerque;
National Gallery of Canada, Ottawa; Tokyo College of Photography; National
Museum of American Art, Smithsonian Institution, Washington, DC;
Bibliotheque Nationale, Paris; Whatcom Museum of History and Art,
Bellingham, WA; Australian National Gallery, Canberra; San Francisco
Museum of Modern Art, San Francisco; Museum of Fine Art, Houston, TX;
Centre National d'Art et de Culture, Georges Pompidou Musée National d'Art
Moderne, Paris; The Charles Rand Penny Foundation.

Publications:

By KRIMS: Books—*8 Photographs: Leslie Krims,* New York 1970; *The
Little People of America,* Rochester, New York 1972; *The Deerslayers,*
Rochester, New York 1972; *The Incredible Case of the Stack o'Wheat
Murders,* Rochester, New York 1972; *Making Chicken Soup,* Buffalo, New
York 1972; *Fictcryptokrimsographs,* Buffalo, New York 1975; *Les Krims:
Kodalith Images 1968-1975,* 32 postcards, Vienna 1976; *Previews,* multiple
giveaway book with *Afterimage* (Rochester, New York), May/June 1976;
Idiosyncratic Pictures, portfolio of 15 photos, 1980; *Photo,* Paris 1981;
Idiosyncratic Pictures, 16-card postcard set, Buffalo, NY 1982;

On KRIMS: Books—*The Art of Photography* by Time-Life editors, New
York 1971; *Photography in America,* edited by Robert Doty, with an introduc-
tion by Minor White, New York 1974; *Private Realities: Recent American
Photography* by Clifford Ackley, Boston 1974; *The Photography Catalog,*
edited by Norman Snyder, New York 1976; *Mirrors and Windows: American
Photography since 1960* by John Szarkowski, New York 1978; *Lichtbildnisse:
Das Porträt in der Fotografie,* edited by Klaus Honnef, Cologne 1982; *La
Photographie Créative* by Jean-Claude Lemagny, Paris 1984; *A World
History of Photography* by Naomi Rosenblum, New York 1984; *Masterpieces
of Photography from the George Eastman House Collections* by Robert
Sobieszek, New York 1985; *American Images: Photography 1945-1980,*
edited by Peter Turner and John Benton-Harris, London 1985; *Photography,
A Facet of Modernism,* exhibition catalogue, San Francisco 1986; *The Naked
Eye, Great Photographs of the Nude,* selected and introduced by David Bailey,
with text by Martin Harrison, London 1987; *Fabrications, Staged, Altered and
Appropriated Photographs* by Anne Hoy, New York 1987; *Photography and*

Art 1946-1986, exhibition catalogue, by Andy Grundberg and Kathleen M.
Gauss, Los Angeles 1987; *Photographers' Dialogue,* edited by Gail Roberts
and Steven Caruthers, Boca Raton, Florida, 1989; *Gli anni '70 los guardo, la
foto,* Modena, Italy 1993. **Articles**—"Les Krims: 4 Photographs That Drove a
Man to Crime" by A.D. Coleman in the *New York Times,* 11 April 1971;
"Incisions in History/Segments of Eternity" by Hollis Frampton in *Artforum*
(New York), October 1974; "Violated Instants: Lucas Samaras and Les
Krims" by A.D. Coleman in *Camera 35* (New York), July 1976; "Creating
Photographs" by Peggy Sealform in the *New York Times,* 10 October 1976;
"Pieges à Temps'' in *Nouvel Observateur* (Paris), June 1977; *Camera
Magazine* (Lucerne, Switzerland), September 1978; "Currents: American
Photography Today" by Julia Scully in *Modern Photography* (New York),
March 1979; "Singular Developments" by Allen Robertson in *TWA Ambas-
sador* (St. Paul, Minnesota), December 1979; "The Offset Works of Les
Krims: An Interpretive Critique" by Ted Barrett in *Camera Lucida* (Sun
Prairie, WI), 1982; *Photo Japon* (Tokyo), No. 16, 1985; "In the Wicked
World of Les Krims, Details Spell Trouble" by Abigail Foerstner in the
Chicago Tribune, 11 January 1985; "La Photographie dans L'Art du XXEME
Siecle" by Alain Sayag in *Actualite des Arts Plastiques* (Paris) 1989;
"Instante Postmoderne" by Gianni Riotta in *Corriere Della Sera* (Milan),
June 1990; article by A.D. Coleman in *Fotografisk Tidskrift* (Stockholm),
1990; article by Mette Sandbye in *Det Iscenesatte Fotografi* (Copenhagen),
1992; "L'expérience du simulacre" by Alain Juilliard-Jérôme Hentsch in
Images (Geneva), 1993.

*   *   *

Les Krims remains one of the most controversial of contemporary photographers. His humorous but genuinely provocative photographic series simultaneously engage questions about the nature of the photographic medium, the
relations of art and truth, and about contemporary society. His subject matter
has often attracted more attention from critics (often hostile ones) than his
works' commentary upon photography itself. Yet it is in this last area that his
landmark books of the 1970s and his more recent work are most important.
Krims is one of the photographers whose work in what A.D. Coleman has
called the "directional mode" can be seen today as most predictive of the
work of the self-proclaimed post-modern "artists who use photography" like
Cindy Sherman, William Wegman or Laurie Simmons. Rather than a maverick marginal to the history of photography, he is an important early practitioner of the kind of photographic practice that flowered during the 1980s.

Krims is exceptional for his dedication to the use of photography as a
medium of literal construction of image and world; if his moments are
decisive, it is because he has staged and all but over-determined them. His
camera has always been a deliberately authorial instrument, rather than a tool
for catching the world as it presents itself. This photographic stance is
inherently critical and interrogative of photography's persuasive representations and of power: obsession and violence as they are found in late twentieth
century American society. If the majority of twentieth century photographs are
cast as seductive dreams or memories (that is, advertisements or snapshots),
Krims' are something quite different: jokes, nightmares and parodies.

His *Fictcryptokrimsographs* (1975) explored the relation between the
Polaroid camera and male pornographic fantasy. The images are altered
through the manipulation of the photographic emulsions, a tearing, pulling and
compressing quite commensurate with the fantasized or desired (often violent)
operations upon female bodies. Here, Krims is at his most ambiguous, desire
and criticism are uncomfortably close. In *Stack o' Wheat Murders* (1972)
Krims also presented the erotic politics of femininity in the domestic arena, but
with a very different slant. Here, in images which are made to appear to have
been culled from the tabloids, we see evidence of the progress of a serial
murderer whose signature touch is a stack of pancakes left beside the violated
female victims, each of whom has been messily killed in a different room
(bathroom, laundry room, etc.) while engaged in a different aspect of the
housewife's routine.

Perhaps it was *The Deerslayers* (1972) which finally revealed the deepest
preoccupation of Krims' work—not sex, but violence. These portraits, the
least campy or staged, show red-blooded, all-American hunters with the
spoils of their chase lashed to rooftops or grills of their cars, trophies of a
primal ritual of slaughter. While the *Stack o' Wheat* photos manage a good-
humored parody of the phenomenal misogyny and violence of real life and the
corresponding voyeurism of the media, the *Deerslayers* are more disturbing,

because real. Krims has been a controversial figure because many, including feminist critics, object to the violence and sexual directness of his imagery. Others take refuge behind accusations that he violates the dictates of good taste. Like most artists in any medium who have spoken too directly about the genuine climate of violence and erotic complexity in American society, he has run afoul of the curiously unconvincing vestiges of puritanism that are the dialectical product of just those societal and individual forces that his photographs explore.

—Ellen Handy

KŘÍŽ, Vilem.

Nationality: American. **Born:** Prague, Czechoslovakia, 4 October 1921; emigrated to the United States, 1952: naturalized, 1958. **Career:** Studied photography, under Jaromir Funke, Josef Ehm and František Drtikol. State School of Graphical Arts, Prague, 1940-46; also studied at the Ecole Cinématographique et Photographique, Paris, 1947. **Family:** Married Jarmila Veselá in 1945; children: Gabriel and Dominica. **Career:** Worked as a press photographer and reporter, Prague, 1945-46; foreign correspondent for Czech newspapers, Paris, 1946-48; freelance photographer, associating with surrealistic artists, Paris, 1948-52; settled in Berkeley, California, as freelance photographer, 1952-58, then in Montreal, 1958-60; worked in the photographic department of the Metropolitan Museum of Art, New York, 1960-64; returned to Berkeley, 1964. Has taught photography, since 1964, at various California colleges, including Mills College, Oakland; Holy Names College, Oakland; and University of California, Berkeley. Since 1974, Professor of Photography, California College of Arts and Crafts, Oakland. **Recipient:** Award of Honor, San Francisco Arts Commission, 1986. **Address:** 1905 Bonita Avenue, Berkeley, California 94704, U.S.A.

Individual Exhibitions:

1942	Town Hall, Strakonice, Czechoslovakia
1948	Maison Monaco, Cité Universitaire, Paris
1957	International Museum of Photography, George Eastman House, Rochester, New York
1965	ASUC Studio, University of California, Berkeley
1966	James Kennedy Art Gallery, Oakland, California
1967	M.H. de Young Memorial Museum, San Francisco (retrospective)
	Humboldt State College, Arcata, New York
1968	James Kennedy Art Gallery, Oakland, California (retrospective)
1970	Bathhouse Gallery, Milwaukee, Wisconsin
	Man's Faith, Suffering and Hope, Mills College Chapel, Oakland, California
	University of Lancaster, England
1971	San Francisco Museum of Art
	Santa Barbara Museum of Art, California
1973	Focus Gallery, San Francisco
1976	University of Oregon, Eugene
	Darkroom Workshop Gallery, Berkeley, California
1977	Light Work Gallery, Syracuse University, New York (retrospective)
	Stephen Wirtz Art Gallery, San Francisco
	San Jose Museum of Art, California
	Kimmel/Cohn Gallery, New York
1978	California College of Arts and Crafts, Oakland
	Gilbert Gallery, Chicago
1979	Art Academy, Cincinnati, Ohio (retrospective)
	University of Osaka, Japan
	Sun Gallery, Osaka, Japan
	Friends of Photography, Carmel, California (retrospective)
1983	Bibliothèque Nationale, Paris (retrospective)
1984	Camera Obscura Gallery, Denver, Colorado
	Vision Gallery, San Francisco

1986	Gallery Z-M, Thessaloniki, Greece
1990	Jaromir Funke Gallery, House of the Lords of Kunštát, Brno, Czechoslovakia
	Gallery Foma, Prague
1992	Gallery of Central Bohemia, Prague

Selected Group Exhibitions:

1940	*7 in September,* Smetana Museum, Prague
1949	*International Manifestation of Art,* Maison Monaco, Cité Universitaire, Paris
1953	*Post-War European Photography,* Museum of Modern Art, New York (toured the United States, 1953-56)
1963	*Photography in the Fine Arts,* Metropolitan Museum of Art, New York (toured the United States, 1963-68)
1967	*Photography in the 20th Century,* National Gallery of Canada, Ottawa (toured Canada and the United States, 1967-73)
1978	*Fantastic Photography in the U.S.A.,* Canon Gallery, Amsterdam (toured Europe and the United States)
1980	*Hommage à Giorgio de Chirico,* Art Pavilion, Ljubljana, Yugoslavia (toured Europe)
1984	*Czechoslovakian Photography,* San Francisco Museum of Modern Art
1986	*Commitment to Vision,* University of Oregon, Eugene
1989	*What is Photography—150 Years of Photography,* Gallery Mánes, Prague

Collections:

Metropolitan Museum of Art, New York; Museum of Modern Art, New York; International Museum of Photography, George Eastman House, Rochester, New York; Museum of Fine Arts, Boston; Cincinnati Art Museum, Ohio; Museum of Fine Arts, Dallas; Bibliothèque Nationale, Paris; San Francisco Museum of Art; Crocker Art Gallery, Sacramento, California; Museum of Decorative Arts, Prague.

Publications:

By KŘÍŽ: Books—*Everlasting Beauty,* Prague 1939; *In Another Time,* Prague 1940; *They Come Alive Again,* Prague 1942; *Conversation, Une Invitation au Dialogue,* with an introduction by A. Hyatt Mayor, New York 1963; *Kříž: Surrealism and Symbolism,* with an introduction by Alfred Frankenstein, Berkeley, California 1971; *Sirague City,* Berkeley, California 1975; *Séance,* with an introduction by Thomas Albright, Berkeley, California 1979; *Vilem Kříž: Photographs,* edited by David Featherstone, Carmel, California 1979; *10 Surreal-Postcards,* Berkeley, California 1980; *Vilem Kříž, or The Thickness of Time,* exhibition catalogue, with text by Jean-Claude Lemagny, Paris 1983; *Vilem Kříž—Photographs from a Period 1937-1992,* exhibition catalogue with texts by Jan Sekera and Ladislav Šolc, Prague 1992.

On KŘÍŽ: Books—*Vilem Kříž, Surrealist* by David Featherstone, Carmel, California 1979; *The Library of World Photography: Photography as Fine Art,* with introduction by Douglas Davis, Tokyo 1982, 1983, London 1983; *Czechoslovakian Photography,* exhibition catalogue, by Dorothy Martinson, San Francisco 1984; *What is Photography—150 Years of Photography,* exhibition catalogue, Prague 1989. **Articles**—"Vilem Kříž: A Poignant, Gentle Surrealism" in *Creative Camera* (London), January 1970; "Vilem Kříž's Photographs Have Eyes" by Donald Key in the *Milwaukee Journal,* 20 September 1970; "Photographer's Masterful Spirit of Surrealism" by Thomas Albright in the *San Francisco Chronicle,* 15 January 1971; "Vilem Kříž, Gentle Mystic" by Joan Murray in *Artweek* (Oakland, California), 6 February 1971; "An Old Master of Photography" by Thomas Albright in the *San Francisco Chronicle,* 28 March 1977; "Vilez Kříž: Mythic Surrealism with a Shutterless Camera" by Leslie Goldberg in *San Francisco Bay Guardian,* 2 June 1978; "Surreal Life Drama" by Michael Goldberg in *New West* (San Francisco), 4 June 1979; "Vilem Kříž and His World of Dreams" by Helen Benedict in the *Independent and Gazette Sunday Magazine* (Berkeley, California), 28 December 1980; "Dream World of Photographer Vilem Kříž" by Irene Clurman in *Rocky Mountain News* (Denver), 27 April 1984; "Visionary

Photographs of a Classic Surrealist'' by Kate Regan in the *San Francisco Chronicle,* 4 May 1984; ''Vilem Kříž'' by D. Marable in *Photo Metro* (San Francisco) no. 5, 1989; ''Návrat přesně na den'' in *Tvorba* (Prague), no. 31, 1989; ''Na vystavě v Mánesu'' by Barbara Hucková in *Československá fotografie* (Prague), no. 11, 1989; ''Posledni žák Jaromira Funkeho'' by Vladimir Remeš in *Československá fotografie* (Prague), no. 12, 1989.

*

Ideas do not travel in a straight line from their origin but linger and return to the past.

Their center of gravity does not reside at their moment of conception but in the sum of previous experiences which generated them . . .

Even creativity is determined by a certain order and this order embodies the rule that every advance must depart from the past.

—Vilem Kříž

* * *

After almost a century and a half of photographic practice, and a similar period of critical controversy, it is disappointing to note that popular notions of photographic art continue to hinge on the photographer's role as a recorder of the picturesque. It is not, of course, my purpose to deny that there is any such role, nor to detract from the merit of photographers who are primarily keen observers of the world around us. On the other hand, no art criticism is ultimately viable without some hierarchy of values, and in my hierarchy the imaginative and creative artist outranks the alert recorder of things, no matter how sensitive or ingenious. A painter can begin with an empty canvas, and can proceed to fill it with images which need have no direct relationship with the world outside, images which may be pure products of his mind. That ''art is a process of turning mind into matter'' may be a simplistic definition, but it is for many purposes a very useful one. Certainly, it transcends all notions of art as a natural by-product of technical competence. Photographers can and do live up to this definition, but only with great difficulty, which is after all why really great practitioners are few and far between.

Of all conceivable photographic styles, photomontage represents one of the most congenial ways of following the creative, as distinct from the interpretive, path. The montage artist uses photographs which have their origin in the real world around us, and assembles them in a manner that transcends reality and creates new visual sensations. Objects always become symbols in surrealist hands, but since the component photographs of a montage can themselves be manipulated, photomontage can go beyond surrealism also.

Along these lines Vilem Kříž is an accomplished master. A comparison of his work with the creations of Jerry N. Uelsmann is inevitable, but it is not a simple matter, especially not for an admirer of both artists. Indeed, the comparison raises problems which go to the root of photographic aesthetics. Photographs by Kříž are ''in the same medium,'' but they are in no sense imitative, and whereas Uelsmann often appeals to a sense of grandeur, Kříž touches more intimate human emotions. He does so with unerring and imaginative skill which reveals what we universally admire in an artist: deep insight into the nature of things. In my own view, Vilem Kříž is one of the really outstanding photographers of our time. Among his publications are *Conversation* and *Sirague City.* A representative selection of his work can be found in David Featherstone's monograph *Vilem Kříž: Photographs,* published in 1979 by the Friends of Photography of Carmel, California.

—H.K. Henisch

KRZYWOBLOCKI, Aleksander.

Nationality: Polish. **Born:** Lwów, 23 May 1901. **Education:** Studied architecture, Lwów Polytechnic, 1922-28; photography, under the pictorialist photographer Henryk Mikolasch, Lwów Polytechnic, 1927-28. **Family:** Married; son: Wojciech. **Career:** First photomontages, Lwów, 1926. Independent photographer and photomontagist, in Lwów, 1929-45, in Wroclaw,

1945-71, and in Kraków, 1971-79. Co-founder, Artes artists' group, Lwów, 1925-35, and the Zwiazek Zawodowy Artystow Plastykow, Lwów, 1932. Deputy Director of the Program for the Preservation of Architecture and Monuments, Lwów Region, 1930-39, and Director of the Program, Office of Works, Wroclaw, 1954-58. **Recipient:** Golden Cross of Merit, Kraków, 1978. Honorary Member, Union of Polish Art Photographers, 1970. **Died:** (in Kraków) *24 November 1979.*

Individual Exhibitions:

1949   Muzeum Šlaskie, Wroclaw, Poland
       Muzeum Sztuki, Lódź, Poland
1960   Muzeum Šlaskie, Wroclaw, Poland
1970   Galeria Prezentacje, Toruń, Poland
1974   Galeria BWA, Kraków-Nowa Huta, Poland

Selected Group Exhibitions:

1930   *Grupa Artes,* Lwów, Poland (and exhibitions in Kraków and Warsaw, 1931-32)
1969   *Grupa Artes,* Muzeum Šlaskie, Wroclaw, Poland
1977   *Polska fotografia artystyczna do roku 1939,* National Museum, Wroclaw, Poland
1978   *Portret Polski 1840-1939,* Galeria ZPAF, Warsaw
1979   *Fotografia Polska 1839-1979,* International Center of Photography, New York (travelled to the Museum of Contemporary Art, Chicago; Galeria Zacheta, Warsaw; Whitechapel Art Gallery, London; Museum of Fine Arts, Lódź, Poland)
1981   *Photographie Polonaise 1900-81,* Centre Georges Pompidou, Paris
1984   *Wystawa Fotografii Wspolczesnej,* Galeria Zacheta, Warsaw (travelled to the National Museum, Wroclaw, Poland)

Collections:

Museum of Fine Arts, Lódź, Poland; National Museum, Wroclaw, Poland; Wojciech Krzywoblocki Archive, Kraków, Poland.

Publications:

On KRZYWOBLOCKI: Books—*Artes 1929-1935,* exhibition catalogue, Wroclaw, Poland 1969; *Zrzeszenie artystow plastykow 'Artes' 1929-1935* by Piotr Lukaszewicz, Wroclaw, Poland 1975; *Polska fotografia artystyczna do roku 1939,* exhibition catalogue by Adam Sobota, Wroclaw, Poland 1977; *Portret polski 1840-1939,* exhibition catalogue by Ryszard Bobrowski, Warsaw 1978; *Fotografia Polska 1839-1979,* exhibition catalogue by Julius Garztecki, Adam Sobota, Urszula Czartoryska and others, New York 1979; *Photographie d'Avant-Garde en Pologne,* exhibition catalogue by Urszula Czartoryska, Paris 1981; *Wszystko o fotografii* by Ryszard Bobrowski and others, Warsaw 1984; *Fotografia Polska 1945-1985* by Ryszard Bobrowski, Gorzów Wielkopolski, Poland 1985. Articles—''Pictorialism and Avant-Garde-ism of the Period 1918-1939'' by Adam Sobota in *Fotografia* (Warsaw), special issue 1979; ''Polish Photography'' by Owen Edwards in *American Photographer* (New York), November 1979; ''Fotografia Polska'' by Dan Spinella in *New Art Examiner* (Chicago), November 1979; ''Fotografia Polska 1839-1979'' by Ryszard Bobrowski in *Fotografia* (Warsaw), no. 3, 1980; ''140 lat fotografii polskiej'' by Marcin Gizycki in *Projekt* (Warsaw), no. 4, 1980; ''La Pologne saisie par la photographie'' in *Liberation* (Paris), 14 February 1981; ''Une revelation: la photo polonaise'' by Michel Nuridsany in *Le Figaro* (Paris), 18 February 1981.

* * *

Aleksander Krzywoblocki's photography is part of a trend that exists alongside two major styles of Polish interwar photography, pictorialism and documentary photography. In effect, like all other experimental undertakings, photomontage and photocollage were peripheral to the main interests of Polish photographers and were really closer to the hearts of painters and graphic artists than to the photographic community. If the first examples of Polish photomontage are seen as linked with constructivism and the artists of Warsaw or Łódź, then later examples must be associated with the artists of Kraków and Lwów. Aleksander Krzywoblocki was closely linked with "Artes," a group of artists in Lwów.

"Artes" existed in Lwów in the years 1929-1935. Given the training at the Paris Académie Moderne Leger of several of its members, such as Otto Hans, Marek Wlodarski, Malgorzata Sielska, it was strongly influenced, originally, by the work of F. Leger and A. Ozenfant. However, after the second group exhibition in 1930, these artists tired of constructivism and turned towards a new trend in art—to surrealism. One of the group, M. Wlodarski, even established a close contact with André Breton. Breton's theoretical ideas, however, were never completely accepted by the group. Their connection with surrealism was through a general change of attitude, a rejection of intellect in favour of feeling and imagination. They accepted the new morphology of surrealism, setting boldness and freedom in representing reality and the dynamic interplay of forms and images above the mechanically abstract. However, the "Artes" group were separated from this movement by a lack of trust and understanding of the fundamental principles of the surrealist theory of art with its idea of an internal monologue and its method of automatic registration. Ultimately, for the members of this group, surrealism was primarily an excellent catalyst for imaginative expression.

All the issues that concerned the "Artes" group are illustrated in the photography of Aleksander Krzywoblocki. One section of his work is certainly derived from constructivism and is based solely on conventional criteria. However, although Krzywoblocki began corresponding with Moholy-Nagy in 1929, and was impressed by some of his montages, it is difficult to trace direct influences on his work. The effect of his architectural training, his interest in monuments and his concern with shape was probably more important. At that time, artists were particularly involved with the problem of applying photography to space, with the relationship between illusion and actuality, and with man's ability to strike an attitude to the world of natural objects through photography. This work was meant to simplify visual judgement and to enable parallels to be drawn. This is particularly relevant to Krzywoblocki's series of photographs based on reflections in a mirror. In these, the optical multiplicity of images not only begs the question of what is real and what is illusory, but also questions the principles on which planes are structured, their geometry, depth etc.

Other works produced by Krzywoblocki are certainly related to surrealism. "The new art," one artist stressed, "attempts to reveal inherent values, it tries to move people through a harmony or contrast of colours or shapes and with the power that is generated by two colours chosen by the artist or two shapes harmonized by him." Freely chosen shapes and forms, such as a hand and a book, a glass ball and a leg, now clearly organised, appeared in Krzywoblocki's photographs and, through freedom of association, formed decided expressions of a disquieting and suggestive vision. In this photography, peculiar and disparate features came together into a coherent surrealistic whole.

After the war, Krzywoblocki remained faithful to photomontage although, little by little, he moved from objectivity towards pure abstraction. With that, however, his work lost much of its early authenticity and originality, becoming stiffly mannered and hard to grasp and clearly restrictive of artistic freedom and invention.

—Ryszard Bobrowski

KUMLER, Kipton (Cornelius).

Nationality: American. **Born:** Cleveland, Ohio, 20 June 1940. **Education:** Cornell University, Ithaca, New York, 1958-63, B.E.E. 1963, M.E.E. 1967; Harvard University, Cambridge, Massachusetts, 1967-69, M.B.A. 1969; studied photography, under Minor White, Massachusetts Institute of Technology, Cambridge, 1968-69, and with Paul Caponigro, 1970. **Military**

Service: Served in the United States Navy, 1963-67. **Family:** Married Katherine Alice Coe in 1969; children: Aden and Emily. **Career:** Freelance photographer, Boston, since 1970; studio established, Lexington, Massachusetts, 1976. Senior Consultant, Arthur D. Little Company, Cambridge, 1969-79. Since 1979, President, Lexington Consulting Group. Instructor in Basic Photography, Project Inc., Cambridge, 1969-72; Instructor in Advanced Photography, Image Works, Cambridge, 1974, and Maine Photographic Workshops, Rockport, 1977-80; Field Faculty Adviser, Goddard College, Plainfield, Vermont, 1977-78. **Recipient:** National Endowment for the Arts Survey Grant, 1976, 1980; Massachusetts Arts and Humanities Foundation Grant, 1977. **Agent:** Harcus Krakow Gallery, 7 Newbury Street, Boston, Massachusetts 02116. **Address:** 34 Grant Street, Lexington, Massachusetts 02173, U.S.A.

Individual Exhibitions:

1974	Creative Photography Gallery, Massachusetts Institute of Technology, Cambridge
	Carl Siembab Gallery, Boston
1975	Robert Schoelkopf Gallery, New York
1976	Douglas Kenyon Gallery, Chicago
1977	Jewett Arts Center, Wellesley College, Massachusetts (with the painters Janowitz and Mazur)
	Cronin Gallery, Houston
1978	Grapestake Gallery, San Francisco
	New Jersey Museum, Trenton
1979	The Photography Place, Philadelphia
1980	Cronin Gallery, Houston
	Harcus Krakow Gallery, Boston
	Worcester Art Museum, Massachusetts

Collections:

Metropolitan Museum of Art, New York; Museum of Modern Art, New York; International Museum of Photography, George Eastman House, Rochester, New York; Rhode Island School of Design, Providence; Museum of Fine Arts, Boston; Worcester Art Museum, Massachusetts; Addison Gallery, Andover, Massachusetts; Cornell University, Ithaca, New York; Museum of Fine Arts, Houston; Amon Carter Museum, Fort Worth, Texas; Bibliothèque Nationale, Paris; Victoria and Albert Museum, London.

Publications:

By KUMLER: Books—*Kipton Kumler: Photographs,* Boston 1975; *A Portfolio of Plants,* with an introduction by Hilton Kramer, Lexington, Massachusetts 1977; *Plant Leaves,* Boston 1978. **Article**—interview in *Printletter* (Zurich), November 1977.

On KUMLER: Books—*Janowitz/Kumler/Mazur,* exhibition catalogue, Wellesley, Massachusetts 1977; *Art of the State,* Danbury, New Hampshire 1978; *The Platinum Print,* Rochester, New York 1979. **Articles**—"Kipton Kumler" in *Fox* (New York), May 1972; "Workshops" in *Camera* (Lucerne), June 1972; "Kipton Kumler" in *British Journal of Photography* (London), Spring 1973; "Kipton Kumler" in *Popular Photography* (New York), February 1975.

*

In my photographic work I am interested in what has been called natural symbolism, i.e. the use of objects in/from nature to reveal/suggest another quality or level of experience. This experience resides entirely in the print and not in extraneous apologies.

I see photography as a medium in which old distinctions between "selecting" and "creating" are confounded. The ability within large formal photography to create a new context, coupled with its inherent authenticity, is a powerful tool with which the 20th century artist can work. Clouds, landscapes, still-lifes, plants—all the traditional subject matter of photography and the other arts continue to offer the basic material with which to create contemplative visual experience.

—Kipton Kumler

*   *   *

Kipton Kumler is one of the most sensitive and talented of the younger photographers. Although his work has been exhibited throughout the United States and, to a lesser extent, in Europe, Kumler does not promote himself, nor is he pushed by the galleries that represent him. Slowly and steadily he has established himself as a freelance art photographer.

Kumler's favorite subjects are plants, landscapes and architecture. Mainly working with 8 x 10 cameras, he captures not only detailed visual information, but also, through his emotional relationship with his subjects, creates very personal and true images. His plant pictures, for example, allow the viewer to enter the realm of their "souls," feel their vibrations. Such results are achieved by his prolific artistic vision in combination with his special printing technique. Kumler prefers to produce platinum and palladium prints, which give an almost three-dimensional impression of the subjects; the grey tones are much softer than in the usual silver prints, and depth is not lost in the black areas of the images. He has developed his technique through long tests and intensive studies of the best possible supporting papers and other materials. In 1977, he produced one result of this work, a very beautiful portfolio of 10 images of plants in a limited edition of 50 copies. In his introduction, art critic Hilton Kramer states: "His pictures have the delicacy of chamber music, the intimacy too, and the sustained emotion that comes from being so close to the details of articulation. In these pictures, elegance lives on easy terms with austerity."

Kipton Kumler is currently working on two new series, one realized in Persia, the other consisting of still-lifes of garlic, onions and kitchen implements made directly from negatives shot and processed for platinum printing.

His studies under Minor White and Paul Caponigro gave Kumler a solid base for a career as a traditional photographer. His love for the beauty of nature and his artistic skill have allowed him to grow during the past ten years to a modern and mature photographer with a body of work of lasting value.

—Marco Misani

KURATA, Seiji.

Nationality: Japanese. **Born:** Tokyo, 12 July 1945. **Education:** Studied painting at Tokyo University of Fine Arts and Music, 1964-68; studied at the Photographic Workshop School, under Daidoh Moriyama, Tokyo, 1975-76. **Career:** Freelance photographer, Tokyo, since 1976. **Recipient:** Kimura Ihei Award, Asahi Press, Tokyo, 1980; The Annual Awards of the Photographic Society, 1992. **Address:** 46-8 Oyamakanaicho, Itabashi-ku, Tokyo, 173, Japan.

Individual Exhibitions:

1978   Canon Photo Gallery, Amsterdam
1979   *Street Photo Random,* Nikon Salon, Tokyo (travelled to the Nikon Salon, Osaka, 1980)
1983   DoI Photoplaza, Tokyo
1986   *Random Street Photos II,* Nikon Salon, Tokyo
1990   *Greater Asia,* Minolta Photo Place, Tokyo
1993   Gallery Mole, Tokyo

Selected Group Exhibitions:

1978   *Photokina 78,* Cologne
1979   *Japanese Photography Today and Its Origin,* Galleria d'Arte Moderna, Bologna (toured Europe)
1981   *Photo Session '81; Snapshots,* Konishiroku Gallery, Tokyo

1982   *Floods of Light,* The Photographers' Gallery, London (toured Britain, 1983-85)
1989   *The 150th Anniversary of Photography,* Konika Plaza, Tokyo
1990   *Document Toyama '90,* The Museum of Modern Art, Toyama
1991   *Beyond Japan: A Photo Theatre,* Barbican Art Gallery, London

Collections:

Museum für Kunst und Gewerbe, Hamburg; Yokohama Museum of Modern Art.

Publications:

By KURATA: Books—*Flash Up: Street Photo Random, Tokyo 1975-1979,* with an introduction by Akira Hasegawa, Tokyo 1980; *Photo Carbaret,* with an introduction by Akira Hasegawa, Tokyo 1984; *Greater Asia,* Tokyo 1990; *80s Family: Random Street Photos,* Tokyo, 1991.

On KURATA: Books—*Japanese Photography Today and Its Origin,* exhibition catalogue, by Attilio Colombo and Isabella Doniselli, Bologna 1979; *Nude Photography of Japan,* with text by Shiroyasu Suzuki and Akira Hasegawa, Tokyo 1981; *Floods of Light: Flash Photography 1851-1981,* exhibition catalogue, edited by Rupert Martin, London 1982; *Eye on Photography: Japanese Photographs after World War II,* with text by Akira Hasegawa, Tokyo 1985.

*

I want to make visible the human being and his or her living environment.

—Seiji Kurata

*   *   *

Photography involves selecting small areas of space, time and reality. That this is so is particularly obvious in the photographs of Seiji Kurata. Of course, every photograph must have its share of these properties, for they are, after all, the conceptual frame of photography—but in Kurata's work the power of photography to limit, to "focus," is particularly striking.

Another characteristic of photography is its power of documentary realism, its ability to capture the life of man and the interaction of man and society. This power was notably exploited by the American photographer Weegee—and it is exploited in a similar way by Kurata in his depictions of the scandalous night world of Tokyo. Because his strobe is much stronger than Weegee's flash, Kurata has been able to record all the more vividly the human bodies and objects which float in the night world. His images portray a people somewhere between holiness and tribalism, and the "scandalous" content is not exactly sought out; it is rather the inevitable outcome of the kinds of customs and traditions not just Tokyo man but all of us are trapped in.

—Kineo Kuwabara

KUWABARA, Kineo.

Nationality: Japanese. **Born:** Tokyo, 9 December 1913. **Education:** Tokyo Municipal Dai-Ni High School, 1927-31; self-taught in photography. **Family:** Married Mie Inoue in 1940. Photographer since 1934. Chief Editor, *Ars Camera,* Tokyo, 1948-53; *Sankei Camera,* Tokyo, 1954-59; *Camera Geijutsu,* Tokyo, 1960-65; *The Photo Image,* Tokyo, 1969-73; and *Shyashin Hihyo (Photo Review),* Tokyo, 1974-76. Professor, College of Tama Art School, Kawasaki, 1965-70. Since 1972, Professor at the Tokyo College of Photography. President, Japan Photocritics Association, 1954-65. Director, Japan Photographic Association, 1954-65, and since 1979. **Recipient:** Annual Prize, Japan Photographic Association, 1975. **Agent:** Zeit-Foto Salon, 1-4 Nihonbashi-Muromachi, Chuo-ku, Tokyo. **Address:** 2-711, 2-chome 5, Kamiyoga, Setagayaku, Tokyo 158, Japan.

Individual Exhibitions:

1973   *Tokyo 1936,* Nikon Salon, Ginza (also shown at Nikon Salon,
        Shinjuku, Tokyo, 1973; Shimizu Gallery, Tokyo, and
        Ikebukuro Parco, Tokyo, 1974; and Kitasenju Midoriya,
        Tokyo, 1975)
1975   *Manchuria 1940,* Nikon Salon, Ginza, Tokyo
1976   *Tokyo 1936-1975,* Photo Gallery Prism, Tokyo
1977   *Fantastic Tokyo,* Minolta Photo Space, Tokyo
1979   *Paris Quotidien,* Zeit-Foto Salon, Tokyo
        Canal Cities: Venice and Amsterdam, Olympus Gallery, Tokyo
1980   *Tokyo 1936,* Zeit-Foto Salon, Tokyo
1981   Ufficio dell'Arte, Paris

Selected Group Exhibitions:

1942   *Tokyo Photo Artists,* Ginza Mitsukoshi Gallery, Tokyo
1943   *Tokyo Photo Artists,* Ginza Mitsukoshi Gallery, Tokyo
1975   *First Tokyo-Ten Exhibition,* Metropolitan Art Museum, Tokyo
1979   *Japanese Photography 1848 to Today,* Galleria d'Arte
        Moderna, Bologna, Italy (travelled to the Palazzo Reale,
        Milan; Palais des Beaux-Arts, Brussels; Institute of
        Contemporary Arts, London; Museum fur Kunst und
        Gewerbe, Hamburg; Gemeente Museum, Arnhem; Pulchri
        Studio, The Hague, 1979-80)
1982   *38 Japanese Photographers,* Zeit-Foto Salon, Tokyo

Collections:

Tokyo College of Photography.

Publications:

By KUWABARA: Books—*Tokyo 1936,* with texts by Katsuya Nakamura
and Hiroshi Hamaya, Tokyo 1974; *Manchuria 1940,* with text by Katsuya
Nakamura, Tokyo 1974; *Memories of My Photographic Life,* with text by
Katsuya Nakamura, Tokyo 1977; *Fantastic City,* with text by Katsuya
Nakamura, Tokyo 1977; *Tokyo Days,* with text by Tetsuo Shirai, Tokyo 1978.
Articles—"Conscious and Unconscious of Photo Image" in special issue of
Brain (Tokyo), March 1977; "The Exhibition '15 Photographers' " in *Gendai
no me* (Tokyo) October 1977; "Scenery in Which Human Meets Objects" in
Gendai-Shi Techo (Tokyo), August 1978; "Memory of Photography after
World War II" in special issue of *Asahi Camera* (Tokyo), July 1979; "World
Candid Photography" in *The Mainichi* (Tokyo), 10 July 1980.

On KUWABARA: Books—*Nihon Shashin Shi, 1840-1945* by the Japan
Photographers Association, Tokyo 1971, as *A Century of Japanese Photogra-
phy,* with introduction by John W. Dower, New York and London 1980; *De
Japanese Fotografie van 1848 tot Heden,* exhibition catalogue, by Attilio
Colombo and Isabella Doniselli, Amsterdam 1980; *38 Japanese Photogra-
phers,* exhibition catalogue, Tokyo 1982. **Articles**—"Editorial" in *The Asahi*
(Tokyo), May 1974; "Book Review" by Seijun Suzuki In *Nippoin Dokusho
Shinbun* (Tokyo), June 1974; "Book Review" by Takeshi Yasuda in *Asahi
Journal* (Tokyo), June 1974; "Book Review: Approach II" by Mutsuo Sakata
in *Quarterly Design* (Tokyo), Summer 1974; "About Nostalgia" by Tatsuhiko
Shibusawa in *Umi* (Tokyo), August 1974; "Oval Eye" by Yuko Deguchi in
Chino Kokogaku, Tokyo 1975; "Editorial" in *The Mainichi* (Tokyo), January
1975; "Kineo Kuwabara" in *Zoom* (Paris), June 1981.

*

It is obvious from my biography that I am an essayist on photography as
well as a photographer; also, I've written general articles for newspapers and
magazines.

Since 1974, when I had a photo exhibition entitled *Tokyo 1936*—which
was also published in book form—I've often written about Tokyo during the
period of the 1930s.

I've been a lecturer at photography colleges for the past ten years: it gives
me great pleasure to talk with the younger generation.

And I have also been involved in the editorial planning of a series of
photographic books.

So my daily life in Tokyo is very busy: I like to do as much as I can.

But, more than any of this work, I like taking photographs best. It makes
my mind free.

Since 1930, I have used a Leica camera, which has meant that 35mm has
been my main means of expression. The subjects I shoot are scenes from
everyday life—most of them are snapshots of Tokyo. My files of negatives are
full of this kind of work.

For me, taking photographs is a means of representing what life is about,
and, as a consequence, I don't care about any other "aims" of photography.
But, having been an editor for about twenty years after the end of World War
II, I tend to look at photographs by others in an open-minded way; I try to keep
an objective view about the latest trends.

Whatever else it may be, photography means talking about oneself via the
subjects chosen in the viewfinder. Unable to escape from the domain of
photography, my face can be seen in every image, in every one of my pictures:
and that is my main concern and ideal in photographic art. Yet, if anyone
should ask me, "What, where, is your face?"—well, I could not possibly
explain in this brief statement.

—Kineo Kuwabara

*   *   *

As an amateur photographer during the 1930s, Kineo Kuwabara made the
life of common people his main subject. Since then, he has been noted as a
photography critic, and for his work, for 30 years, as editor of some of the most
influential photography magazines in Japan. Forty years after the time of his
early work, in 1973, his exhibition, *Tokyo 1936,* surprised the world of
photography. There, in these works, the lives of the urban dwellers in the
Tokyo of the 1930s were captured live.

The images reflected the individualism of the masses, and they were raw
documentary beyond the scope of any general thematic definition.

—Norihiko Matsumoto

KUZNETSOVA, Lyalya.

Nationality: Tartarian. **Born:** Uralsk, West Kazachstan, U.S.S.R., 4 August
1946. **Education:** Attended the Institute of Aeronautics, Kazan, 1965-72;
self-taught in photography, from 1976. **Family:** Married the aeronautics
engineer Setsov in 1971 (died, 1976); one daughter. **Career:** Worked in the
photo-laboratory of the Museum of Art, Kazan, 1978-79, and at the Photo Art
Society of the Lithuanian SSR, Vilnius, 1979-80. Since 1980, freelance
photographer, Kazan: worked for *Jalkyn* magazine, Kazan, 1980-82; for the
theatre of Kazan, 1982-83; for *Vecernaya Kazan* evening newspaper, Kazan,
1983; and for the House of Fashion of the Tartarian SSR, Kazan, since 1984.
Address: ul. Marxa 4, kv. 1, Kazan 420111.

Selected Group Exhibitions:

1979-80 Exhibitions organized by the Photo Art Society of the
        Lithuanian SSR
1985   *Three Chapters of Soviet Photography,* Gallery 4, Cheb,
        Czechoslovakia
        The Story of Photography, Fotochema Gallery, Prague
1986   *The Story of Photography,* House of Art, Brno, Czechoslovakia

Collections:

Photo Art Society of the Lithuanian SSR, Vilnius; Daniela Mrazkova and
Vladimir Remes Collection, Prague.

Publications:

On KUZNETSOVA: Book—*Another Russia: Through the Eyes of the New Soviet Photographers* by Daniela Mrázková and Vladimir Remes, London 1986. **Articles**—"The Rising Star" by Daniela Mrázková in *Mlada Fronta* (Prague), April 1985; "The Case of Lyalya Kuznetsova" by Daniela Mrázková in *Ceskoslovenska fotografie* (Prague), September 1985.

*   *   *

Lyalya Kuznetsova comes from the Ural mountains in west Kazachstan and is of Tartar blood. She studied at the Institute of Aeronautics, specialized in aeroplane engines, married an aeronautic engineer and for some time worked with him. Then in 1976 she suddenly became a widow. She was very unhappy and looked for something completely new and different to do, to help her forget. And so, quite by chance, she started to take photographs. Everything that had been resounding within her for years, her passionate admiration of the actions of humanity, the ability to perceive the manifold vibrations of the human soul, the search for real human values, suddenly found their image in her photographs. It was a geyser of oscillating feelings, penetrating vision, and talent, which appears only exceptionally and unexpectedly like a miracle. It was as though she had learnt a new language, more expressive and telling than the one she had been using since her cradle.

In 1980, Antanas Sutkus, the president of the Lithuanian Art Photographic Society, saw her work and invited her to Vilnius. For eighteen months she worked there as an employee of the Society and soon gained recognition at exhibitions. She did not understand Lithuanian, but that was not the main reason why she decided to leave the job thanks to which she had actually been discovered. She felt suffocated by the atmosphere of academism and conventionalism, which the Lithuanians, who had been holding a dominant position in Soviet photography since the sixties, had reached. "All those public appearances, the need to exhibit oneself and the desire to show-off: all that is not my problem," Kuznetsova has said. "I do not want to seize possession of reality, but only quietly approach it. I want to make documents of the human soul."

She returned to the Volga steppes. Having photographed for a children's magazine and for a children's theatre in Kazan, she has since 1980 been working as a freelance. But she really only comes alive with subjects of her own choosing. She is attracted mainly by unconventional people—nomads, circus performers—or people in exceptional circumstances—funerals, holidays and festivities. "I am attracted by the free lives of the gypsies," she has said. "For weeks I wander through the steppe with them and live their kind of life. Usually they are expecting me, because news of me flies from one camp to another, but sometimes a camp does not trust me and rejects me. Once a woman gave me a real beating out of jealousy, but I was not angry. I understood her feelings." Kuznetsova's view of the gypsies' life was at first romantic, but the more she came to understand them the more did her vision of the legendary heroes of the steppe in the midst of unbounded nature recede, together with the taint of Russian realist painting, and her photographs started to reflect the hard reality of people without a home, constantly driven by a sense of unrest. The same can be said about her pictures of circus people, the tight-rope walkers, jugglers, wild-animal tamers and magicians; she photographs them not under the spotlight but in the moments before they put on their glittering costumes and the insouciant masks of courageous professionals.

Lyalya Kuznetsova works easily, quickly and a lot. The exceptional creative passion, even insatiability, with which she has amassed new subjects has, during the few years in which she has been seriously taking photographs, shaped an artistic personality which has such an intuitive feel for subjects and the passing moment that we can infer almost everything about the psychic and social situation of the world in which she lives. In this she is a real master. In her picture series on the traditional Orthodox religion, the May Day celebrations, the last things of man, the rallies for the anniversary of the Socialist Revolution or on such simple things as a woman's soul, Kuznetsova's photographs tell stories like those of only the greatest writers.

—Daniela Mrázková

L

LABROT, Syl.

Nationality: American. **Born:** New Orleans, Louisiana, in 1929. **Education:** Studied at Yale University, New Haven, Connecticut, 1948-49; studied creative photography at the University of Colorado, Boulder, 1956-57. **Family:** Married twice. **Career:** Freelance magazine photographer, in Colorado, associated with the Shostal Agency, New York, and working for *Life, Saturday Evening Post, Ladies Home Journal*, etc., 1954-57; concentrated on own photography, Easton, Connecticut, 1957-59, and on painting, then again on photography, Easton, Connecticut, 1960-72, and in New York, 1972, until his death in 1977. Instructor in Graphics and Photography, Visual Studies Workshop, Rochester, New York. **Died:** (in New York City), in July 1977.

Individual Exhibitions:

1958	International Museum of Photography, George Eastman House, Rochester, New York
1960	*Under the Sun,* Poindexter Gallery, New York (with Walter Chappell and Nathan Lyons)
1977	*3 Photographic Visions,* Ohio University, Athens (with De Lappa and Baltz)

Selected Group Exhibitions:

1958	*Abstraction in Photography,* Museum of Modern Art, New York
1960	*The Sense of Abstraction,* Museum of Modern Art, New York
1962	*10 Photographers,* Schuman Gallery, Rochester, New York
1967	*Photography in the 20th Century,* National Gallery of Canada, Ottawa (toured Canada and the United States, 1967-73)
1974	*Photography in America,* Whitney Museum, New York
1982	*Color as Form,* International Museum of Photography at George Eastman House, Rochester, New York
1987	*Photography and Art 1946-86,* Los Angeles County Museum of Art

Collections:

Museum of Modern Art, New York; International Museum of Photography, George Eastman House, Rochester, New York; Visual Studies Workshop, Rochester, New York; Exchange National Bank, Chicago; National Gallery of Canada, Ottawa.

Publications:

By LABROT: Books—*Under the Sun: The Abstract Art of Camera Vision,* with Walter Chappell and Nathan Lyons, New York 1960; *Pleasure Beach,* Rochester, New York 1976. **Articles**—"Work in Progress" in *Afterimage* (Rochester, New York), September 1974; interview in *Photography Between Covers* by Thomas Dugan, Rochester, New York 1979.

On LABROT: Books—*Photography in the 20th Century* by Nathan Lyons, New York 1967; *Photography in America,* edited by Robert Doty, with an introduction by Minor White, New York 1974; *3 Photographic Visions,* exhibition catalogue, by Arnold Gassan, Athens, Ohio 1977; *Color as Form: A History of Color Photography,* exhibition catalogue, with introduction by Robert A. Sobieszek, Rochester, New York 1982. **Articles**—"Syl Labrot 1929-1977" by Arnold Gassan and "Pleasure Beach," book review, in *Exposure* (New York), September 1977; "Syl Labrot 1929-77" in *Photography Year 1978,* by Time-Life editors, New York 1978.

*   *   *

Syl Labrot began making photographs for the most sentimental of reasons when his first child was born. Having attended Yale for a year and then moving to Colorado, Syl never completed his undergraduate degree but dropped out to become a photographer. Born of a wealthy Louisiana family whose wealth was based on creosote, a wood preservative, Syl bowed to his father's insistence that he make his hobbies pay, and quickly Syl became a successful commercial photographer. He was trained in photography mostly by himself, with inevitable assistance from fellow amateurs and professionals—initially in the Boulder Camera Club, and then in intense discussions with working professionals in Colorado. By the end of a year, Syl was self-supporting, and within three years was one of the best selling photographers in the Shostal Agency collection, a commercial distributing center in New York.

By 1957, three years after he began making pictures, the successful production of elegantly conceived fishing and hunting promotional photographs began to bore him, and he became more interested in formal problems of color, flatness, and the qualities of the color print. After a week's tutoring by a Dye Transfer technician in Colorado Springs, Syl began making his own prints. A few months later he advanced to Carbro printing because that process offered a more suitable print. At the end of 1957 he had a portfolio of 10 prints which he presented to the Museum of Modern Art and other galleries, and found immediate acceptance. Few of his prints survive, however, because of two disastrous fires which successively demolished his house after he moved from Colorado to Connecticut. His photographs keynoted the MoMA exhibit *Abstraction in Photography,* mounted by Steichen in 1958, and he published what he felt were the best examples of the early work in *Under the Sun,* a troika of photographic work by Nathan Lyons and Walter Chappell and himself. In the text, Labrot comments: "From the start of my work in photography I saw the camera image as something quite separate from the reality perceived by the eye . . . it presented its own sense of space. . . .My work moved away from this objective reality to try to discover what the print itself was. . . . "

By the time that book was published, Syl had already stopped photographing and begun painting. For several years he produced photographically detailed, large-scale acrylic paintings that explored the same scenes his camera had recorded but allowed him the tactility of the paint. Later in the 1960s he returned to photography and began working toward a new printmaking which dominated his work until his death: the exploration of direct control of the photo-offset printing process. The conclusion of these explorations was *Pleasure Beach,* a book which he wrote, photographed, and produced himself. The color transparencies, separations, halftones, stripping, typesetting, and printing supervision are all by the photographer. The printing press became his new medium.

His concerns were for discovered relationships between color and form and associations implicit in the photograph as they inter-related to the suggestions of the forms in the picture. The book becomes a subtle, complex narrative beginning with a witty, tongue-in-cheek description by Syl of his "invention of color" (as he recapitulated all the color printmaking processes, he came to half-believe he had invented them anew, a poetic sensation all artists must feel at some point) and concluding with a sequence of double-exposed manipulated images of ancient stones, delicate nudes, patterns like a maze, and a prescient cloud of rubble that floats in indeterminate space. The book recapitulates his entire work, beginning with the same color images that excited Steichen and continuing past the painting done in the 1960s and early

1970s—photographic realism to color-field geometric investigations—and concluding with a personal poetry of photographic printmaking. He compared the book to music in a letter written just before his death in the early summer of 1977: "The book is the most spontaneous piece of work I have ever done, and it was very much the result of major changes going on in my life . . . it is very definitely [like Stravinsky's *Le Sacre*] but things have somehow run away with themselves . . . and there is somehow not the control that exists in all the other work. It seems to be rather a case of there being just enough control to keep things from really running amuck."

Labrot was greatly concerned by what he called the "conceptual poverty" of most color photography. He realized in the late 1950s that he was ahead of the market when he left photography and turned to painting, but when he took up the camera again he found that color had become very nearly a fad. "It does hurt to have Eggleston, Shore, etc., get so much exposure. Not that I mind their work, it just doesn't seem like much and if I were just beginning in the field I would wonder where I was going to get the money to pay for having all my 16 x 20 color prints printed. . . .It turns color photography into a matter or being rich, or having a foundation grant pay for your color." The heart of this plaint was, as always, aesthetics. "I am a printmaker, and see photography as a printmaking medium. . . . The look of the object is what speaks to me. K + L [a commercial laboratory in New York City] may turn out an excellent print, but it's the standard machinery of Kodak—not the expressive prints of a photographer; and the color photographer who goes that route signs an aesthetic contract: he must play within bounds of the conventional look of a 'color photograph'."

—Arnold Gassan

LACH-LACHOWICZ, Natalia.
(Professional Name: NATALIA LL)

Nationality: Polish. **Born:** Zywiec, 18 April 1937. **Education:** Attended schools in Zywiec until 1952; studied at the School of Art Techniques, Bielsko-Biala, 1952-56; Academy of Fine Arts, Wroclaw, 1957-63. **Family:** Married to Andrzej Lachowicz. **Career:** Since 1964, independent artist-photographer, Wroclaw: autoportrait and facial geography series, 1964-69; Intimate Photography series, 1970-72; Consumer Art series of photos, films and actions, 1972-75; Artificial Photography series, 1974-82; performance works, *Dreaming, Pyramid* 1978-80; *States of Self-Communion 1980-83*, concentration on the mystics thought "white" and "black" seances, series of drawings and photographs; *Loose Spaces,* 1986-94 attempts at finding the subjective space of art; video series, photos and paintings, from 1980. Curator, International Drawing Triennale, Wroclaw, 1974-94. **Recipient:** Kosciuszko Foundation Scholarship, to New York, 1977; Artiste, Federation Internationale d'Art Photographique, 1968; Verein Kulturkontakte Scholarship, to Wien, 1991; Pro-Helvetia Scholarship, to Zurich, 1994. **Address:** ul. Mlodych Techników 12, m.9, 53-646 Wroclaw, Poland.

Individual Exhibitions:

1969   *Geography of the Face,* Mücsarnok Museum, Budapest
1971   *Intimate Photography,* Permafo Gallery, Wroclaw, Poland
1972   *The Word,* Permafo Gallery, Wroclaw, Poland
1973   *Problems—Consumer Art,* Arkady Gallery, Krakow, Poland
1974   *Intimate Sphere,* Galerie Paramedia, West Berlin
        Universitario Platense, Buenos Aires
1975   Galeria Wspólczesna, Warsaw
        Galeria Studio 45, Turin, Italy
1976   *Post Consumer Art,* Galleria Diagramma, Milan
1977   *Artificial Photography,* Galerie Milch Strasse, Freiburg, West
        Germany
1978   *Consumer Art,* Studio 16e, Turin, Italy
1979   *Dreaming,* Galeria Mala, Warsaw
        Pyramid, Permafo Gallery, Wroclaw, Poland
1980   *States of Concentration,* Gallery ON, Poznań, Poland
1981   *Adoration,* St. Jean Cathedral, Lyon, France
1983   *The Touch of the Devil,* Gallery BWA, Lublin, Poland

1984   *States of Concentration,* Galerie Galerico, Rosenheim, West
        Germany
1985   *The Scorpion Dance,* Desert of Sabiya, Kuwait
1987   *Art and Liberty,* BWA Gallery, Lublin
1988   *Loose Space,* Mala Gallery, Warsaw
1989   *Painting and Photography,* District Museum, Walbrzych
1990   *Panic Space,* Centre for Art Promotion, BWA, Lodz
        Natalia LL: Painting—Photography—Installation, BWA
        Szczecin
1991   *Vision Space,* Stara Gallery BWA, Lublin
        Natalia LL: Raum der Panik, IFA Friedrichstrasse Gallery,
        Berlin
        Performance EUROPA, Bonner Kunstverein, Bonn
1992   *Natalia LL,* International Cultural Centre, Cracow
1993   *Art and Energy,* National Museum in Wroclaw
1994   *Painting and Installation,* Museum Sloskie, Katowice, Poland

Selected Group Exhibitions:

1966   *Ogólnopolska Wystawa Fotografii I,* CBWA Zacheta Gallery,
        Warsaw
1969   *2nd International Photography Salon,* Tokyo
1971   *Fotografowie poszukujacy,* Gallery Wspolczesna, Warsaw
        (travelled to Milan, Parma and Turin, Italy)
1972   *Photokina,* Cologne, West Germany
1973   *Polish Photography,* Kassel, West Germany (travelled to
        Nuremberg and Tokyo)
1975   *Flash Art Speziale Fotografia,* Galleria del Milione, Milan
1976   *Foto Idea,* Galleria d'Arte Moderna, Parma, Italy
1979   *Fotografia Polska 1839-1979,* International Center of
        Photography, New York (travelled to Museum of Contempo-
        rary Art, Chicago; Zacheta Gallery, Warsaw; Museum of
        Fine Arts, Lodz; Whitechapel Art Gallery, London)
1982   *La Photographie Polonaise,* Centre Georges Pompidou, Paris
1986   *Polish Photography,* Museum of Art, Prague
1988   *Polish Perceptions: Ten Contemporary Photographers 1977-
        1988,* Collins Gallery, Glagow
1989   *Austellung Project,* New Space gallery, Fulda
        What is Photography: 150 Years of Photography, Prague
        Transgression: Borderlands of Photography, BWA Gallery,
        Wroclaw
1990   *Schnelle Bilder, Aktuelle Fotokunst im Gesprach,*
        Kunstlerhaus, Wien
1991   *Passengen der Photographie: Aktuelle Photokunst aus Polen,*
        Schloss Workersdorf
        Kunst-Europa, Schloss Augustusburg, Brühl
        New Space of Photography, Museum of Architekture, Wroclaw
        70 Jahre polnischer Photoavangarde, Kulturforum, Reine
        20th Century Art Collection of Art Museum in Lodz, CBWA,
        Zacheta, Warsaw
1992   *Polish Women Artists,* National Museum in Warsaw
        Mittel Europa: Fin de Sieclès, La Grande Halle-la
        Villette, Paris
        Art Museum in Lodz: Collection-Documentation-Actuality,
        Museè d'Art Contemporain, Lyons
1993   *Skjulte Dimensioner Polsk Samtidsfotografi,* Museet for
        Fotokunst, Odense
        Transgression II, National Museum in Wroclaw
1994   *Hautevolee,* Gallery Rähnitzgasse, Dresden
        Europa-Europa, Kunst und Ausstellungshalle der
        Bundesrepublik Deutschland, Bonn
        Ars Erotica, National Museum, Warsaw

Collections:

Museum Sztuki in Lodz; National Museum, Warsaw; National Museum, Wroclaw, Poland; Museum of Fine Art, Lódź, Poland; Museum Okregowe in Walbrzych; National Museum in Gdansk; Museum Ziemi Lubuskiej in Zielona-Gora; National Museum in Poznan; National Museum in Bratyslava, Umelecko-prumyslove Museum, Prague; Kupferstich Kabinett, Dresden.

Panics Sphere, **Schloss Wolkersdorf, 1991.** Photograph by Natalia Lach-Lachowicz.

Publications:

By LACH-LACHOWICZ: Books—*The Sum,* Wroclaw, Poland 1973; *Hipoteza,* Wroclaw 1979; *Points of Support,* Wroclaw 1979; *Sztuka otwarta-parateatr,* Wroclaw, Poland 1980; *States of Concentration,* catalogue Typisch Frau, Nonn 1981; *Body Art and Performance,* catalogue BWA Gallery, Lublin 1985; *Loose Space,* catalogue Na Ostrowie Gallery 1987 Wroclaw; *Art and Liberty,* catalogue Mala Gallery, Warsaw 1988; *Theory of Head,* EXIT no 6, Warsaw 1991. **Articles**—in *Fotografia* (Warsaw), no. 7, 1970; special issue, with Gislind Nabakowski, of *Heute Kunst* (Dusseldorf), 1974; in *Fotografia* (Warsaw), no. 1, 1976; in *Nurt* (Wroclaw, Poland), no. 12, 1976; "Zdania kategoryczne z obszaru sztuki postkonsumpcynej" in *Stany graniczne fotografii,* Katowice, Poland 1977; "Snienie" in *Fotografia* (Warsaw), no. 1, 1979; "Categorical Statements from the Sphere of Post-Consumer Art" in *Polish Art Copyright,* Warsaw 1979.

On LACH-LACHOWICZ: Books—*Aktuelle Kunst in Osteuropa* by Klaus Groh, Cologne 1971; *NS Perfamo* by Antoni Dzieduszycki, Wroclaw, Poland 1972; *Polska awangarda malarska 1945-1970* by Bozena Kowalska, Warsaw 1975; *Europa/America: Different Avantgardes* by Achille Bonito Oliva, Milan 1976; *Fotografie als Kunst—Kunst als Fotografie* by Floris M. Neususs, Cologne 1978; *Photographie d'Avant-Garde en Pologne,* exhibition catalogue by Urszula Czartoryska, Paris 1981; *Poolse Avant-Garde,* Brussels 1985; *Polish Avant-garde 1918-1980* by Alicja Kepinska in *Flash Art No 102,* Mediolan 1981; *Wspolczesny rysunek polski* by W Wierzchowska WAiF,

Warsaw 1982; *Five Years Performances: Art in Lyon 1979-1983,* Lyon 1984; *Photographers Encyclopedia International 1983 to the present* by M Auer, Editions Camera Obscura, Geneva 1985; *Kunst-Europa,* edition Herman Schmidt, Mainz 1991; *Zywioly* by Kinga Kawalerowicz, exhibition catalogue, Warsaw 1993. **Articles**—"Sztukaifotografia" by Andrzej Lachowicz in *Nurt* (Wroclaw, Poland), no. 10, 1976; "Uwagi o ruchu fotomedialnym" by Bozena Stoklosa in *Fotografia* (Warsaw), no. 4, 1978; "Polish Photography in the Years 1939-1979" by Ryszard Bobrowski in *Fotografia* (Warsaw), special edition, 1979; "The Eye of Poland" by Douglas Davis in *Newsweek* (New York), 13 August 1979; "Wystawa-Fotografia-polska 1839-1979" by Ryszard Bobrowski in *Fotografia* (Warsaw), no. 3, 1980; "L'Air du Temps" by Hervé Guibert in *Le Monde* (Paris), 2 February 1981; "Przestrzenie Natalii LL" by Adam Sobota, *Sztuka,* no 5/6, Warsaw 1988; "Natalia LL" by Ryszard Bobrowski, *European Photography* no 38, Göttingen 1989; "150 lat fotografii w kolekcji Muzeum Narodowego we Wroclawiu" by Adam Sobota, *ODRA,* no 6, Wroclaw 1989; "Znaki obecnoé-Sci" by Andrzej Saj, *ODRA,* no 7-8, Wroclaw 1990; "Natalia LL," *Flash Art,* no 3 Mediolan 1992; "Pojedynek rytualny Natalii LL" by Malgorzata Wendrychowska in *Exit,* no 2 Warsaw 1992; "Natalia LL" by Piotr Krakowski, exhibition catalogue ICC, Cracow 1992; "Przestrzen wizyjna" by Bozena Kowalska in *Format,* no 6-7, Wroclaw 1992; "Natalia LL" by Piotr Krakowski in *Obieg* no 53-54, Warsaw 1993; "Natalia LL—Der Transzendentele Blick" by Reinhold Misselbeck in exhibition catalogue, National Museum, Wroclaw 1993; "Cialo-Sztuka" by Adam Sobota, *ODRA* no 1, Wroclaw 1994; "Natalia LL" by Miroslaw Ratajczak in *Art and Business* no 3/4, Warsaw 1994; "Natlaia LL" by Grzegorz Sztabinski in *Exit,* no 4/16, Warsaw 1993; "Polaritäten und

Konvergenzen der Fotografie'' by Urszula Czartoryska in exhibition catalogue *Europa-Europa,* Bonn 1994.

*   *   *

The almost universal appeal of photography in the late 1960s and early 1970s was one of the most interesting phenomena in Polish art. While interest in photography predates this time, as, for example, with the constructivist movement in the interwar years and the postwar work of Zbigniew Dlubak, it was only with the advent of conceptual art that it took on a completely new dimension. Divisions between artistic and non-artistic means of expression, concerted attempts to find fresh forms of artistic communication, the exploration of systems by which visual information could be conveyed and striving to meta-art were all activities in which photography played a part. Natalia Lach-Lachowicz's work is an interesting example of the ways in which photography can be used to advantage in the creative process.

The beginnings of Natalia LL's conceptual work can be traced to the Wroclaw movement, Perfamo, in the early '70s. This movement, founded on the premise that art is an attempt to reflect reality, promoted the idea of ongoing record of reality in the clear hope of bridging the gap between the commonplace and the artistic, as for example, between an object and its image. In the name of ''ongoing recording,'' Natalia LL spent 24 hours, for example, taking hourly photographs of the dial of an alarm clock—presented as a series under the title of *24 godziny Natalii LL*—and undertook other projects such as *Rejestracja Wyjscie-zejscie* in 1971, and *Miejsce oddalone o 1500 km* in 1973. ''Consumer art'' developed from this concept. ''Consumer art,'' Natalia LL wrote, ''presents itself at every moment of reality, every fact, every second is singular and unrepeatable for the individual. That's why I record common and trivial events such as eating, sleeping, copulation, rest, declaration and so forth.'' In actual fact, she portrayed trivial, everyday activities in such a provocative or perverse way (for example, attractive girls suggestively eating bananas or jelly) that erotic undertones were readily apparent. Her work might equally be placed in the realms of advertising where the task is unequivocally to draw attention and impart selected information.

However, although her work, like all conceptual work, was primarily an intellectual undertaking, Natalia LL did not agree totally with the ideas of many artists in this field. ''The mind's control of visual perceptual processes,'' she stressed, ''is a fiction that art should definitely oppose. The perceptual apparatus—the eye and the brain—is an indivisible whole because we can't see unconsciously. The perceptual process is a complete process and, as such, can only be examined holistically. This leads me to assert that, at the present time, art needs to adjust its ideas as the accepted metalinguistic procedure does not embrace reality in all its diversity and richness. The conceptual movement thoroughly cleaned the spectacles; let's now put them on our noses so that, with their help, we can see the world. I promote art that will be achieved through objective means that are better suited to our thought processes—means, however, that will remain subordinate to artistic intuition. For intellectualisation is proper to science where each hypothesis is based on a carefully proven and described previous hypothesis.''

The result of this position, which can be described as informed intuition, was a succession of series of photographs subsumed by the term ''postconsumer art.'' ''Postconsumer art,'' Natalia LL explains, ''is based on the creation of visual and mental rules which, although non-contradictory in themselves, are possibly very 'artificial' and form a model for complicated intellectual and intuitive processes.'' A good example of this work is a series entitled *Sztuczna fotografia.* This contains photographs that appear to have been created on the basis of superimposing images of the artist sitting in an armchair one on top of another. In these photographs, Lach-Lachowicz has not two but three or four legs, one pair curled under her and the other simultaneously stretched out, etc. The end result of these photographs is to portray people and things whose actual existence is, in fact, impossible while, at the same time, the process by which the pictures are obtained is totally possible, objective and real. ''Photography, therefore,'' Lach-Lachowicz stresses, ''is not a record of reality but a 'real' metareality in which such records as these can exist even if their actual existence in the real world is impossible. Nevertheless, they can be seen—the photograph authentically portrays them—and, accordingly, they can be imagined, all of which we must accept as an isomorphic visual and mental proof. So, I create 'artificial photography' which credibly and authentically records an artificial 'reality'; artificial because it does not, and cannot, exist in our normal, testable and reasonable experience of what is real.'' The merit of

this impossible or artificial photography lies in the assumption that art is intentional artifice yet photography itself is here an objective record of intuition and a way of looking in on the irrational world of artistic consciousness.

From these and other activities, it is clear that Natalia LL is one of the most percipient creative artists working in photography in Poland. While the fundamental and integral feature of her work is intellect, she opposes all over-intellectualisation, pretense, imitation and insincerity in art. Her photography, which is simultaneously intellectual and intuitive, conceptual and visual, constitutes an interesting attempt to integrate or synthesize many artistic values.

—Ryszard Bobrowski

LAIZEROVITZ, Daniel.

Nationality: Uruguayan. **Born:** Montevideo, 27 September 1952. **Education:** Attended España/Iava School, Montevideo, 1958-71; studied psychology at the University of Montevideo, 1972-73; studied photography at the Photo Club Uruguayo, Montevideo, 1974-76, Dip. Photg. 1976. **Family:** Married Judith Isaac in 1973 (divorced, 1976). **Career:** Freelance photographer, Uruguay and Switzerland, since 1976. Advertising Photographer, Consorcio Americano de Publicidad agency, Montevideo, 1977-79; News Photographer, *El Telegrafo* newspaper, Paysandu, Uruguay, 1978-79; Photographer for *Imagenes* magazine, Montevideo, 1978-79. Member, Board of Governors, Foto Club Uruguayo, 1976-77. **Recipient:** Best Photography of the Year Award, Uruguay, 1978.

Selected Group Exhibitions:

1976	*Triennale of Photography,* Zadar, Yugoslavia
1978	*Biennale FIAP,* Athens
	Uruguay Institute of Visual Arts Exhibition, Club Brasilero, Montevideo
	Blanco y Negro, Galeria del Notariado, Montevideo
1979	*1st Latin American Colloquim of Photography,* Mexico City
	Hecho en Latinoamerica, at *Venezia 79 Vivencias,* Galeria del Notariado, Montevideo
	Rencontres Internationales de la Photographie, Arles, France

Collections:

Mexican Photographic Society, Mexico City.

Publications:

On LAIZEROVITZ: Book—*Photography: Venezia 79,* Milan and New York 1979. **Articles**—in *Mundo Color* (Montevideo), 27 August 1978; *El Telegrafo* (Paysandu, Uruguay), 7 October 1978, 20 November 1978, and 6 January 1979; *Imagenes* (Montevideo), no. 16, 1979; *Printletter* (Zurich), July/August 1980.

*

I discovered photography at a difficult stage of my life when it became a most important tool for expressing my feelings and thoughts. After this first stage (in which I experimented mainly in the field of symbolic photography), and feeling that I had to make a choice and define myself in my photographs, I made a 90 degree turn as a photographer, trying to capture images of everyday life.

Being a Latin American, I committed myself to interpreting and analyzing—through my photographs—our society and its symptoms of sickness.

Gradually I started to feel immersed in a common current, together with many other photographers, seeking to face the responsibilites of showing mirror images of conflicts and the struggle of people seeking freedom and justice.

—Daniel Laizerovitz

*   *   *

Every day the mass media offer us two kinds of pictures in violent contradiction to each other: crude and disgusting horror pictures (tortures and massacres, natural disasters and man-made accidents) and, as if by way of contrast, images of grace (beauty, youth, health and economic prosperity). We gradually come to believe that real life is comprised of these two extremes: the first external and removed from us, the second close, inviting imitation. But there is another reality, which is ordinary and likely to be overlooked. Plain daily life has neither the visual impact of the social document nor the glamour of the luxury advertisement. Yet it is precisely through the big and little events of our normal visual world that we are able to know and understand man and society better.

Daniel Laizerovitz depicts in his pictures that world of men and things without a history: unknown people met in the street, everyday happenings, shop windows, walls, posters, notices—all things that we recognize and with which we can identify. Photography is an extremely simple medium of communication, equally accessible to everyone, and Laizerovitz uses it like a language to converse with the public. He likes to play with reality, but he shuns the dogmatism of certain photographers who claim to be giving us an all-embracing, exhaustive picture, in which, in fact, the violence of the visual impact cancels out any other kind of communication. Laizerovitz's work tends instead to establish a relationship of active fellowship, and to suggest that every one of us, if only to a small extent, is responsible for some aspects of the society in which we live.

Yet, even if Laizerovitz's subjects are those people and visual events we come across every day, there is always something disturbing about them. They are, after all, people and events that break the rules of the regulated, composed society we feel it ought to be. The poor, the old, the handicapped—we prefer to ignore them, or, better still, to shut them away in the ghettos of social exclusion. Laizerovitz forces us to become aware of this section of humanity. But his eye is deeply sympathetic; he is not looking for the shocking, nor, on the other hand, has he any moralistic intention. Indeed, his pictures almost always have a touch of humor, which radically upsets the objective situation and lightens the emotional reaction. He does not really set out to move us, or preach to us, just to make us think about the condition of the common man.

And the common man—our next-door neighbor, our colleague at work, the man in the street—is, in Laizerovitz's photographs, oppressed by an almost tangible solitude. And when we consider that his pictures never contain any precise connotation of place or time—they might have been taken in any corner of the earth—we realize that the solitude of the single individual portrayed becomes a metaphor for the solitude of man in contemporary society, man by himself.

We communicate with words and gestures that are wholly inadequate for our actual needs. Complete communication is a Utopia. Photography—at least as it is practiced by Daniel Laizerovitz—tends to break down the barrier of incomprehension.

—Giuliana Scimé

LAKE, Suzy.

Nationality: American. **Born:** Suzanne Marx in Detroit, Michigan, 14 June 1947. **Education:** Attended schools in Detroit, studied at Western Michigan University, Kalamazoo, 1965-66; Wayne State University, Detroit, 1966-68; and Concordia University, Montreal, 1976-78, M.F.A. 1978. Influenced by painter Guido Molinari and sculptor Hugh Leroy. **Family:** Married Roger Lake in 1968 (divorced); Alexander Neumann in 1976; daughter: Danika. **Career:** Independent photographer, since 1971, establishing own studio in Montreal, 1971-74, 1976-78, in Toronto, since 1978. Instructor, Montreal Museum School of Art and Design, 1969-74, 1975-76; Loyola Photography Workshop, Montreal, 1975-78; Concordia University, Montreal, 1976-77; University of Guelph, Ontario, 1978-79, 1981; York University, Toronto, 1980-81. Co-founder, Véhicule Art Inc. art gallery, Montreal, 1971. **Recipient:** Concordia Fellowship, Montreal, 1972; Canada Council Grant, 1972, 1974, 1975, 1978, 1981; Quebec Provincial Grant, 1973. **Agent:** Sable Castelli Gallery, 33 Hazelton Avenue, Toronto, Ontario. **Address:** 1436 Queen Street West, Toronto, Ontario M6K 1M2, Canada.

Individual Exhibitions:

1974	*Transformations,* Galerie Gilles Gheerbrant, Montreal
1976	Loyola Photography Workshop, Montreal
1977	*Choreographed Puppets,* Galerie Optica, Montreal
1978	*Impositions,* Art Gallery of Ontario, Toronto
	Sable Castelli Gallery, Toronto
	imPOSITIONS, Vancouver Art Gallery
	The Image Co-op, Northfield, Vermont
1979	*Are You Talking to Me,* Sable Castelli Gallery, Toronto (travelled to Galerie Optica, Montreal; and Mendel Art Gallery, Saskatoon, Saskatchewan)
1980	Mohawk College, Hamilton, Ontario
1981	Whitewater Gallery, North Bay, Ontario
	Locations Rehearsing, Sable Castelli Gallery, Toronto
	Whitby Art Gallery, Ontario
	Moncton University, New Brunswick (with Sorel Cohen)
1982	Art Gallery of Hamilton, Ontario

Selected Group Exhibitions:

1974	*Camerat,* Galerie Optica, Montreal (travelled to Canadian Cultural Centre, Paris)
1976	*Identité/Identifications,* Centre d'Art Plastiques Contemporains, Bordeaux (toured France)
1977	*Transparent Things,* Vancouver Art Gallery (travelled to London Art Gallery, Ontario; Alberta College of Art, Edmonton; Art Gallery of Greater Victoria, British Columbia; and Dalhousie Art Gallery, New Brunswick)
1978	*New Tendencies,* Musée d'Art Contemporain, Montreal
	Performance Festival, Museum of Fine Arts, Montreal
1979	*Fleeting Gestures: Dance Photographs,* International Center of Photography, New York (travelled to The Photographers' Gallery, London, and *Venezia '79*)
	Winnipeg Perspective 1979: Photo/Extended Dimensions, Winnipeg Art Gallery, Manitoba
1980	*Annual Dalhousie Drawing Exhibition,* Dalhousie Art Gallery, Halifax, Nova Scotia
1981	*Viewpoint 29 x 9,* travelling exhibition (toured Ontario)

Collections:

Art Gallery of Ontario, Toronto; London Art Gallery, Ontario; Canada Council Art Bank, Ottawa; National Film Board of Canada, Ottawa; Musée d'Art Contemporain, Montreal; Montreal Museum of Fine Arts; Southern Alberta Art Gallery, Lethbridge; Winnipeg Art Gallery, Manitoba; Vancouver Art Gallery.

Publications:

On LAKE: Books—*Camerart,* exhibition catalogue, by Chantal Pontbriand, Montreal 1974; *The Winnipeg Perspective 1979: Photo/Extended Dimension,* exhibition catalogue, by Roger L. Selby and Karyn Allen, Winnipeg 1979; *Are You Talking to Me?,* exhibition catalogue, with text by Bruce Ferguson,

Saskatoon, Saskatchewan 1980; *Contemporary Canadian Photography* by Martha Langford, Edmonton, Alberta 1984. **Articles**—"Seven Canadian Photographers" by Ann Thomas in *Artscanada* (Toronto), May 1977; "Suzy Lake and Sorel Cohen" by Diana Nemiroff in *Artscanada* (Toronto), May 1977; "Suzy Lake" by Joanne Danzker in *Vanguard* (Vancouver), March 1978; "Canadian Artists with Cameras" by Bill Ewing in *Art News* (New York), April 1978; "Suzy Lake: Impositions" by Diana Nemiroff in *Parachute* (Montreal), Spring 1978.

*

Before using film or tape, I "bumped through" the more traditional media, only to find these media weren't accommodating "what I was trying to get at." From my standpoint with these media, if the rhythm did become animated enough, the gesture became too graphically beautiful or the image too painterly, etc. (and what did that have to do with Pierre Vallieres, moon shots, the Chicago Seven trial, crushed idealism, "Gunsmoke," anyway?) I wanted to break down the distance between the object and audience; to extend the act of looking to include a more direct act of discovering, experiencing, and making.

Although terms like body art, self-referential art, and autobiographical art tend to crop up, I'm not particularly concerned to keep within those definitions. I use my own image as "someone"; yet, it is important to de-particularize the situation of that person, to allow the viewer to identify with the issue from his or her point of view. Also, by using my portrait as the image to be adapted, I infer the constant as "victim."

Since the early 70s, the work has continued to visually deal with ramifications of identity, angst, vulnerability, etc.... We are a multiplicity of personalities, evolved from our own history of influences, events, or situations, both on voluntary and involuntary levels.

The sequencing of "imPOSITIONS" (1977) and "Are You Talking to Me" (1979) uses a different system of ordering than the early work. The varied sizes and juxtaposition of images set an attitude or environment through an irregular rhythm. Tampering with the negative and the prints' scale also serve to create a sense of disorientation. The single image offers the audience situational (metaphoric) information about the image; whereas, the sequence parallels that information with a sense about that activity.

—Suzy Lake

* * *

Suzy Lake has been immersed in an ongoing analysis which concerns personality and identity and the accompanying ramifications. The earlier work involved the transference of identity through role playing, whereas the current series, "Are You Talking to Me? ...," 1979, focuses on the more basic concerns of "being" and the implied anxiety inherent in those things which are difficult to control.

This complex investigation has led to the creation of symbols of auto-expression and vulnerability in which Lake stages a variety of psychodramas, photo-performances. The "Transformation" series, 1974, focuses on the artist in a state of literal change, for example, "Suzy Lake as Gary W. Smith." The viewer is initially startled by this process with its threatening implications. This exploration of the ambiguities of identity becomes even more compelling in "imPOSITIONS," 1977, a series of largescale photo-murals in which the artist is wrapped and bound, her voice piercing the silence and articulating the fine line between freedom and imprisonment. The psychological implications of this condition are emphasized by the use of techniques and processes such as stretching the negative and longer time exposures. The starkness of the black and white, together with the life-sized scale, contribute to the overall angst.

The sheer scale of the work is compelling, drawing the viewer into an anxious confrontation. Lake has exploited the power of the photographic medium and has utilized its inherent characteristics to a most powerful degree.

The relationship of the work to aspects of theatre—dance, mime, puppetry—is evident. Lake's work is never static. "Vertical Pull," 1977, a series of twelve black-and-white photographs, shows the artist falling down a staircase; it is gripping because of its sense of movement and our apprehension of the potential danger in the act. Furthermore, the serial nature of the work implies that the event is a seemingly endless process (it is like seeing a metaphor for your life passing before your eyes in intervals).

In "Are You Talking to Me? ...," 1979, a series of 63 colour and black-and-white photographs, Lake presents an acutely fine balance between anxious, conflicting sensations: fear and revelation; trust and mistrust; sorrow and relief. It is a kind of silent confessional, a combined process of break*down* and break*through*. The implications of self-portraiture are transferred to a universal realm.

The life-size photographs, of varying scale, are installed in a sequential manner which literally wraps the room in images. Some are stretched and all are registered at the mouth, which is hand-tinted. What results is an evironmental reaction with the viewer that is difficult to ignore. The imagery is filmic, in that the viewer is enveloped by everchanging movement. It is no longer Lake's full body struggling to be released from bondage. Ironically, the bondage is more intense when she is free of physically restraining factors. The highly refined drawing element is ambiguous despite the implied realism. The rhythm set up by the continual flow of images creates a conversational storyline of undetermined content.

The anxiety is one of freedom/captivity. The expression and style of the work underlines the multi-dimensional nature of this quest. Nuances of gesture and the subtle, varying facial expressions and stances are arresting. It is this heightened sense of emotional confrontation—simultaneously direct and open-ended—that is the core of Lake's refined approach and investigation. Although her image is departicularized, the camera allows every detail to be visible. The images are a metaphor for a blurred reality. Subtleties disappear as the viewer is confronted with these images, images with persistent haunting power. "Are You Talking to Me? ..." is an invocation demanding participation of the audience in a manner not unlike a theatrical performance. The series functions as an emotionally rich Greek chorus, which achieves a provisional sort of controlled hysteria.

—Karyn Allen Keenan

LAM, Osbert (Sai Cheung).

Nationality: British. **Born:** in Hong Kong on 26 November 1959. **Education:** Attended Hong Kong Polytechnic, 1978-80, but partly self-taught in photography. **Career:** Worked as assistant photographer to Kevin Orpin, 1980; assistant photographer to Leong Ka Tai, 1981-83. Ran Osbert Lam Photography, 1983-92, and Osbert Lam & Associates Ltd with Wendy Ho since 1992. **Address:** 10B Kam Yuk Mansion, 13 Yuk Sau Street, Happy Valley, Hong Kong.

Individual Exhibitions:

1982   *Dreams of Survival,* Club '97, Hong Kong

Selected Group Exhibitions:

1983   *Looking Pictures, Learning Words,* Landmark, Hong Kong
1987-93   *Annual Exhibition of HKIPP,* Art Centre, Hong Kong
1993   Agfa Fellowship Exhibition, Hong Kong
       Club '97, Hong Kong
       Visage Too, Hong Kong

Untitled. Photograph by Osbert Lam.

1994   *Our Planet,* Tai Koo Shing, Hong Kong

Publications:

On LAM: Articles—*Photography Magazine* (Hong Kong), December 1993; *South China Morning Post,* September 1983; *Photo Pictorial,* October 1990; *Hong Kong Standards,* May 1993; *Photo Asia,* November 1993.

*

My work is so different because I get bored easily. I am a dreamer, a romantic. I will try anything and everything to make a good picture.

Working with my camera is a kind of love-making. The camera is instrumental in expressing my emotional reaction to the subject.

—Osbert Lam

*   *   *

Not surprising for an advertising photographer, each and every little detail in Osbert Lam's photographs is there for a reason although it may look as if chance had a fair say. Another typical Lam feature is the lack of uniformity. His staged images range from illuminating colours to subtle hues and from nostalgic sepia to bold black. That is because his photographs tell a story and include all information which he considers relevant to his subject.

His favourite subject is people. Depending on their personality Lam chooses the atmosphere and setting in which he wants to work. In some respects he displays the characteristics of a movie director. His starting point is his subject; his props are the images that form in his head in connection with this subject. He says "When I view my subjects through the lens, I don't simply see a photograph, I see a story." In other words, he organizes a visual script which "inspires the viewer to think three dimensionally."

Therefore a photograph of a dancer can be as different as a single dynamic figure leaping in the air, or it may become a sedate portrait surrounded by memories of a glorious career. Osbert Lam sees himself as the intermediary who translates a person into an experience, a narration. And because his role is one of an interpreter, none of his pictures look identical. In fact his work is typical because of its variety. His comment: "My work is so different because I get bored easily. I'm a dreamer, a romantic. I'll try anything and everything to make a good picture."

Lam equates the photographic mechanics to a kind of love making, "the camera is instrumental in expressing my emotional reactions to the subject."

627

He chose advertising because it appeals to his desire to create pictures instead of taking them. Although he ventures into computer imaging and commercial video clips, he always returns to basic photography to set his creativity in motion. As he puts it, "I simply enjoy the process of photography—it opens my eyes and mind to possibilities which otherwise don't come about."

—Joyce van Fenema-Tulkens

LAMBETH, Michel.

Nationality: Canadian. **Born:** Toronto, 21 April 1923. **Career:** Studied sculpture, drawing and anatomy at Guildford School of Art, Surrey, England, and Sir John Cass School of Art, London, Atelier Ossip Zakine and Ecole du Louvre, Paris, and University of Toronto (General Arts), 1945-49. **Military Service:** Served in the Canadian Army in Europe, 1942-45. **Family:** Married Fran Lambeth in the early 1950s (later separated). **Career:** Freelance writer, filmmaker, photographer, photojournalist and publisher, Toronto, 1948 until his death, 1977. Also worked as a clerk, Toronto City Hall, 1952-59. Co-Founder, Mind and Sight photography gallery, Toronto, 1972. Tutor in Photography and Fellow of Bethune College, York University, Downsview, Ontario, 1971; Teacher, Ryerson Polytechnic Institute, Toronto, 1972. Associate Artist, Toronto Free Theatre, 1973-77. Member, American Society of Magazine Photographers, 1962-66; Member, Canadian Artists' Representation, and Committee to Strengthen Canadian Culture. **Recipient:** First Amateur Class Award, Canadian Film Awards, Montreal, 1954; Film Honorarium, Young Men's Canadian Club, 1954; Toronto Art Directors Club Award, 1961; Canadian Centennial Medal, 1967; Canada Council Senior Grant, 1968; Ontario Arts Council Grant, 1972, 1974. **Agents:** The Isaacs Gallery, 832 Yonge Street, Toronto; and Canadian Centre of Photography, 596 Markham Street, Toronto, Ontario M5G 2L8, Canada. **Died:** (by suicide; in Toronto) 9 April 1977.

Individual Exhibitions:

1948	Galerie du Dragon, Paris
1961	*50 Photographs,* Towne Cinema, Toronto
1965	The Isaacs Gallery, Toronto
	Art Institute of Ontario travelling exhibition (toured Canada, 1965-66)
1969	*Encounter by Michel Lambeth,* National Film Board of Canada, Ottawa
1970	*Simplicity of Man in an Automated Age,* at *Expo '70,* Osaka, Japan
1971	York University, Downview, Ontario
1972	Canadian Department of External Affairs travelling exhibition (toured New York City boroughs and travelled to the Light Impressions Gallery, Rochester, New York)
	Ryerson Polytechnic Institute, Toronto
1974	*Images of Mexico,* Toronto Free Theatre (exhibition changed and enlarged through 1975)
1979	*Michel Lambeth: A Retrospective,* Photo Gallery, Ottawa (works printed by Michael Torosian; toured Canada, 1979-83)
1986	Public Archives of Canada, Ottawa

Selected Group Exhibitions:

1967	*Gallery Artists,* The Isaacs Gallery, Toronto
1970	*Man and His Drugs Pavilion,* at the *Canadian National Exhibition,* Toronto
1972	*Festival d'Avignon,* France
1973	*Critic's Choice,* Neikrug Gallery, New York
1977	*Photo Festival '77,* National Film Board of Canada, Ottawa
1984	*Responding to Photography,* Art Gallery of Ontario, Toronto

1985	*Contemporary Canadian Photography,* National Gallery of Canada, Ottawa

Collections:

Canadian Museum of Contemporary Photography (formerly National Film Board of Canada), Ottawa; National Photography Collection, Public Archives Canada, Ottawa; Ryerson Polytechnic Institute, Toronto.

Publications:

By LAMBETH: Books—*Made in Canada,* Toronto 1967; *Neuscapes,* portfolio, Toronto 1967; *As We Walk,* with poems by Anastasia Erland, Toronto 1968. **Articles**—"Robert Frank—Americans: Photographs" in *Canadian Forum* (Toronto), August 1960; "Lutz Dille: The Bertold Brecht of the Camera" in *Arts/Canada* (Toronto), December 1969; "The Confessions of a Tree Taster" in *Di'alog Quarterly* (Toronto), Fall 1971; "2-Year Odyssey, Photographing Quebec—Pierre Gaudard" in *The Star* (Toronto), 20 November 1971; "Honesty the Hallmark: B.A. King Photographs at Witkin, New York" in *The Star* (Toronto), 24 December 1971; "Tom Gibson at Merton" in *Proof Only* (Toronto), 15 January 1974; "Art History" in *Carot* (Toronto), June 1975; "Exposure" in *C.A.R.O. Bulletin* (Toronto), November 1975.

On LAMBETH: Books—*Image 2: Photography Canada 1967,* edited by Lorraine Monk, Montreal 1967; *Contemporary Canadian Photography* by Martha Langford, Edmonton, Alberta 1984; *Responding to Photography,* exhibition catalogue, by Maia-Mari Sutnik, Toronto 1984; *Michel Lambeth—Photographer,* exhibition catalogue, by Michael Torosian, Ottawa 1986. **Articles**—"Biographical Note" by P. Pocock in *Canadian Art* (Toronto), November/December 1961; "The Momento-of-Truth Photography of Michel Lambeth" by R. Fulford in *Saturday Night* (Toronto), June 1977; "A Tribute to Michel Lambeth" by J. Wieland in *Artmagazine* (Toronto), December/February 1977-78; "A Belated Recognition for a Street Photographer" by R. Fulford in *The Star* (Toronto), 13 January 1979; "Hard-Edged and Artful Encounters" by D. Livingston in *Maclean's* (Toronto), 26 March 1979; "The Fifties Focus: Retrospective Toronto—The Late Michel Lambeth" by Michael Torosian in *Toronto Life,* June 1981; "Michel Lambeth: Portfolio" in *Photocommunique* (Toronto), Spring 1982.

*   *   *

"So with a negative, salts of iron, one makes one's personal history an almost indelible mark in time a pause, as one great poet said, a pause in the clock."

These meditative words were written in 1974 by Michel Lambeth, an artist and a man of extreme moods and complexity. At once overwhelmingly generous and kind, a romantic at heart, a poet, a teacher, an articulate critic, and a conservationist (of landscapes, trees, and early photography), he was a man of great spirit and enthusiasm whose experience of wartime combat caused him to be frequently melancholy. Passionate in his fight for Canadian cultural independence and a strong nationalist, he was a politicized activist in the service of the disadvantaged. Most significantly, he was a brilliant photographer.

The images he left behind on his death in 1977 aimed at the heart of life, the drama of human beings living very ordinary lives—yet full of and reverberating with emotions: loneliness, pain, anxiety, hope, love, celebrations and illuminating silences. In the immediacy of both personal and external environments, these experiences also became Lambeth's. His photographs never overstated, never indulged or imposed, never sentimentalized, but were full of clarity and compelling directness. His subjects reveal reality with the kind of veracity and integrity that belongs to the truly best in art. Unequivocally, his photographs are indelible marks in time.

Lambeth's main body of work is from the period 1955 to 1970. During World War II he served with a regiment as a tank gunner for the allies in Germany. After demobilization he turned to the study of sculpture and drawing, first in England, then in Paris. In 1948 he returned to Canada, and worked for several years as a clerk in Toronto's City Hall. There he discovered a cache of historical photographs, which were later published as *Made in Canada.* His youthful enthusiasm for trees became a life-long interest, partially because of his rediscovery of the camera, the means to render his fascination in "permanent images." Also, he became familiar with the work of Cartier-Bresson, Brassaï, Kertész, Walker Evans, Bill Brandt, and Robert Frank: he admired them, and their work contributed to his decision to take up photography seriously.

Lambeth respected the unencumbered capabilities of his 35mm Leica, and he was particularly responsive to the temporal in photography. But, though often cited as Canada's Cartier-Bresson, Lambeth expressed, through his own personal struggles, a belief and conviction beyond that of the "decisive moment." Although he too chose to roam the streets and public places (railway stations, markets, parades, gardens, museums, shops), and photographed his friends and fellow artists, progressively in his photographs the most fundamental values of human endeavour quietly transcend external moments of time—moments we see as fractions appear seemingly without an end. His words (in 1971) synthesize his vision clearly:

In his confrontation with reality, esoteric as it may sound, the photographer compounds a totality of work which, for me, is an actual graphic representation of what he really IS. Feeling, as expressed in emotional freedom with photography, becomes at once a diary of a monument to the particular unique existence of one man or woman, much as it does in any other medium but especially when an artist uses it. I believe that what our Greek-derived, science-bound word "photography" fails to say is said succinctly in a two-ideogram character by the Japanese: THE REFLECTION OF EXISTENCE.

As an independent photographer, Lambeth had established his reputation by the mid-1960s. His work appeared prominently in *Star Weekly, Saturday Night, Maclean's, Life, Time* and many daily publications. At intervals he exhibited in group and one-man shows in Canada, the United States and Japan. His last major work was at the Toronto Free Theatre, documenting their productions. In 1974-75 he exhibited there a small selection of images taken earlier in Mexico. But, while Lambeth's work was highly visible during the 1960s, it seldom provided him with a living. He often turned to writing criticism or to giving workshops in creative photography. During the 1970s he drifted from photography to becoming a committed spokesman for Canadian Artists' Representation (C.A.R.), a trade association of artists; at the same time, he was also a member of the Committee to Strengthen Canadian Culture. Often enraged and intensely quarrelsome, Lambeth had, by the mid-1970s, allowed his photographic aspirations to be diminished by his personal anguish, chaos, and deep depressions. After a brief stable period, he died in April 1977 at the age of 53. Ironically, during this time of a resurgent photographic boom he never quite achieved the stature deserved by his great talents. His failure to do so had to do with his mercurial nature and his desire to work independently—sometimes with intense productivity, sometimes faltering in disorder, but always searching within his own nature for that "pause" that so many of his photographs captured.

One of Lambeth's most remarkable images was of a hard-working Quebeçois family in St. Nil, Gaspé, in 1964. His singular observations triggered a series of photographs that combined the story of an event with the unfolding of rich human messages in picture form—reflecting homage to Walker Evans. Yet, Lambeth's work transcended a balance of realism and classical discipline to create a taut and precise synthesis of time and place, of the deeply moving process of life. Tragically, for a person who was so moved by the very process of life and living, Lambeth died alone, forgotten by those he had once served with zest and with his extraordinary photographs, but deeply remembered by those few friends and admirers whose lives his vision and compassion had touched.

—Maia-Mari Sutnik

LARSON, William.

Nationality: American. **Born:** North Tonawanda, New York, 14 October 1942. **Education:** Attended Starpoint Central High School, Pendleton, New York, 1956-60; State University of New York at Buffalo, 1960-64, B.S. in art 1964; studied art and history at the University of Siena, 1964; and photography, under Aaron Siskind, Wynn Bullock and Arthur Siegel, at the Institute of Design, Illinois Institute of Technology, Chicago, 1966-68, M.S. 1968.

Family: Married Catherine Jansen in 1973; daughter: Erika. **Career:** Photographer, Feldkamp-Malloy Design Studio, Chicago, 1967-68. Freelance photographer, Philadelphia, since 1968. Professor, Tyler School of Art, Temple University, Philadelphia, 1967-1988. Visiting Professor, University of Arizona, Tucson, 1980-81; Director of Graduate Studies in Photography, Maryland Institute, College of Art, since 1988. **Recipient:** National Endowment for the Arts Fellowship, 1971, 1979, 1986, 1992; Best Colour Photographer Award, *Triennale de la Photographie*, Fribourg, Switzerland, 1978; Guggenheim Fellowship, 1982; Pennsylvania Council on the Arts Grant 1983, 1988. **Agent:** Light Gallery, 724 Fifth Avenue, New York, New York 10019. **Address:** 120 Hopwood Road, Collegeville, Pennsylvania 19426, U.S.A.

Individual Exhibitions:

1970	Maryland Art Institute, Baltimore
1972	State University of New York at Potsdam
1973	Light Gallery, New York
	Chicago Center for Contemporary Photography
1975	Light Gallery, New York
	Philadelphia Print Club (with Emmet Gowin and Steve Williams)
1976	University of Tennessee, Knoxville
	University of South Dakota, Vermillion
1977	Art Institute of Chicago
	Light Gallery, New York
	Southern Illinois University, Carbondale
	University of Oregon, Eugene
1978	Light Gallery, New York
	Camerawork Gallery, San Francisco
	Pittsburgh Film Makers
1979	Bard College, Annandale-on-Hudson, New York
	Light Gallery, New York
1980	Los Angeles Institute of Contemporary Art
1981	*Joe Deal: The Fault Zone/William Larson: Recent Color Work from Arizona,* Light Gallery, New York
1982	*William Larson/László Moholy-Nagy,* Center for Creative Photography, University of Arizona, Tucson
1985	Institute of Contemporary Art, Philadelphia
1994	Maryland Art Place, Baltimore, Maryland

Selected Group Exhibitions:

1973	*Unique Photographs, Sculpture Multiples,* Museum of Modern Art, New York
1974	*Photography Unlimited,* Harvard University, Cambridge, Massachusetts
1976	*3 Centuries of American Art,* Philadelphia Museum of Art
1978	*Artwords/Bookworks,* Los Angeles Institute of Contemporary Art
	Mirrors and Windows: American Photography since 1960, Museum of Modern Art, New York (toured the United States, 1978-80)
1979	*Attitudes: Photography in the 1970s,* Santa Barbara Museum of Art, California
	Electro Works, International Museum of Photography, Rochester, NY
1980	*Polacolor,* Light Gallery, New York
1981	*Biennial Exhibition,* Whitney Museum of Art, New York
1982	*Color as Form,* International Museum of Photography at George Eastman House, Rochester, New York
1983	*Photography in America 1910-83,* Tampa Museum, Florida
1985	*American Images 1945-80,* Barbican Art Gallery, London (toured Britain)
	The Nude in Photography, Munchner Stadtmuseum, Munich, Germany

Theatre du Monde, **1994 (original in colour).** Photograph ©William Larson.

1987	*Art and Photography, Interactions since 1946,* Los Angeles County Museum of Art
1991	*Artists Choose Artists,* Institute of Contemporary Art, Philadelphia
1993	*Image and Text,* Center for Creative Photography, Tucson, AZ
1995	*The Art of the Emblem,* Yale University Art Gallery, New Haven

Collections:

Museum of Modern Art, New York; Rhode Island School of Design, Providence; University of Hartford, Connecticut; Philadelphia Museum of Art; Princeton University, New Jersey; University of Louisville, Kentucky; New Orleans Museum of Art; American Arts Documentation Centre, University of Exeter, Devon, England; National Gallery of Australia, Canberra.

Publications:

By LARSON: Books—*Fireflies,* Philadelphia 1976; *Big Pictures, Little Pictures,* Philadelphia 1980. **Articles**—"The Figure in Motion" in *Camera*

(Lucerne), April 1970; "Photographic Reality" in *Mundus Artium* (Athens, Ohio), Spring 1971; "The Human Figure in Motion" in *Modern Photography* (New York), April 1971; clour portfolio "Tucson Gardens" in *Aperture* (New York), 1984.

On LARSON: Books—*The Great Themes,* edited by Carole Kismaric, New York 1970; *The Art of Photography,* edited by Carole Kismaric, New York 1971; *Light and Lens,* edited by Donald Werner, New York 1973; *Photographer's Choice,* edited by Kelly Wise, Danbury, New Hampshire 1975; *Three Centuries of American Art,* edited by Will Stapp, Philadelphia 1976; *Spaces,* edited by Aaron Siskind, Providence, Rhode Island 1978; *One of a Kind,* edited by Belinda Rathbone, Cambridge, Massachusetts 1979; *William Larson* (Aperture portfolio) by Michael Hoffman and Carole Kismaric, Millerton, New York 1981; *American Images: Photography 1945-1980,* edited by Peter Turner and John Benton-Harris, London 1985; *Photography and Art 1946-1986,* exhibition catalogue, by Andy Grundberg and Kathleen M. Gauss, Los Angeles 1987; *Post Modern Currents,* edited by Margo Lovejoy, Ann Arbor 1989; *Sequence (con) Sequence,* edited by Julia Ballerini, New York 1991; *Photography at the Dock,* edited by A. Solomon Godeau, Minneapolis 1991; *Photographing in the Studio,* edited by Gary Kolb, Brown and Benchmark 1993. **Articles**—"New Frontiers in Color" by Douglas Davis in *Newsweek* (New York), 19 April 1976; "William Larson: Time and Structure" by Skip

Atwater in *Afterimage* (Rochester, New York), December 1976; article by A.D. Coleman in *Art News* (New York), 1986; portfolio in *Photo Review No. 4* (Langhorne, PA), 1988; photograph in *European Photography* (Göttingen, Germany), 1989.

*

My work currently centers on domestic and local landscape situations which are photographed in color. I like the balance achieved between descriptive photographic detail and a subjective color palette which supports my basic instincts for picturemaking.

—William Larson

* * *

A constant feature of William Larson's work is his use of photography to transmit information about the medium itself. This theme is at least equal in importance to Larson's messages about the outside world, and most of his output displays both aspects in varying degrees.

One of Larson's earlier concerns was with making images that extend the possibilities in photographic rendering of space/time relationships beyond any analogy to human perception yet still within the limits of logical photographic process. Whereas certain work with serial images did involve a fictive element, Larson's series *The Figure in Motion* elegantly demonstrates how the familiar human body, and an innovative if basically self-evident process of photographic recording using travelling film, may together produce images at once wholly strange and wholly true to both the subject and the system that made them.

The direction of Larson's enquiry has since shifted somewhat away from considerations of the medium as total system and more towards an examination of sets of properties within it. In *Fireflies,* the effect of using facsimile machines to transmit photographic and other fragments down telephone lines, and reconstitute them into visual form, draws attention to the nature of the basic information that survives—despite the incompleteness of the component images, and despite the severe filtering and high noise levels introduced by translation from visual to electrical modes and back again via crude transducers and narrow bandwidths.

Larson's excursions into Polaroid—notably *Little Pictures* on SX-70 and *Big Pictures* on 20'' x 24'' Polacolor—demonstrate a progression within the main theme. The early *Little Pictures,* however Matissean the tenor of their content, are unequivocally from SX-70 technology, and from that follows colour rendering and the rationale of lighting effects. Graphic artefacts such as colour patches, grey scales, register marks and waxon crayons in the later *Little Pictures,* focus attention even more sharply on how light has been transmuted to dye, at the same time as the formal composition and tactics of illusionism become complex and purely photographic.

In the *Big Pictures,* presented whole, so that they could only be Polacolor 20'' x 24'', the work is not only photographic in content, consisting almost entirely of studio equipment, but also the principal subjects are the effects and enigmas of lighting, focus and colours. Since then, Larson's work has commented less directly on the medium itself; but his recent subjects have been quieter too, without abandoning the principles established through earlier activity.

Examination of Larson's photography invites the supplementary conclusion that the interactions of the most careful syntax, and the most standardized technical controls, leave intriguing areas of indeterminacy and question about the medium—an encouraging and salutory reminder of the complexity of things.

—Philip Stokes

LARTIGUE, Jacques-Henri (Charles Auguste).

Nationality: French. **Born:** Courbevoie, Seine, 13 June 1894. **Education:** Studied privately—painting, under Jean-Paul Laurens, Decheneau and

Baschet, Académie Julian, Paris, 1915-16; self-taught in photography. **Military Service:** Served as a volunteer in the French Army, 1914-18. **Family:** Married Madeleine (Bibi) Messager in 1919; son: Dani; Marcelle Paolucci in 1934; and Florette Orméa in 1945. **Career:** Took first photographs, Courbevoie, 1902; painter, from 1915 (numerous one-man exhibitions of paintings, 1922-78); particularly known as a photographer since the late 1960s. Vice-President, Gens d'Images, Paris, 1954. Donated life's work to the French nation, 1979. **Recipient:** Gold Medal, City of Paris. Chevalier de la Légion d'Honneur, 1975; Commander des Arts et Lettres, Paris, 1981. **Agent:** c/o Mme. Isabelle Jammes, Conservateur, Association des Amis de Jacques-Henri Lartigue, Grand Palais des Champs-Elyées, Avenue Franklin D. Roosevelt, Porte C, 75008 Paris, France. **Died:** (in Nice, France) 13 September 1986.

Individual Exhibitions:

1963	*The Photographs of Jacques-Henri Lartigue,* Museum of Modern Art, New York
1966	*Photokina,* Cologne
1968	The Photographers Gallery, at Architectural Furniture, New York
1969	*Festival d'Avignon*
1971	L'Oeil de Verre, Lille
	The Photographers' Gallery, London (toured the U.K., and travelled to Marseilles, Le Havre, and Hamburg, 1972-73)
1972	Witkin Gallery, New York
	Neikrug Gallery, New York
1973	Salle des Etats, Dijon
	Centre Culturel et Social, Limoges
	Musée Municipal, Brest
	Friends of Photography, Carmel, California
1974	Galerie de Doigt dans l'Oeil, Bordeaux Center for Photographic Art, Chicago
	Bibliothèque Nationale, Montreal
1975	Galerie Optica, Montreal (travelled to the Yarlow Fine Arts Gallery, Toronto; French Institute, New York; Visual Studies Workshop, Rochester, New York; Art Gallery of Ontario, Toronto; Columbia College, Chicago; and the International Center of Photography, New York, 1975)
	Bibliothèque Municipale, Mulhouse, France
	Witkin Gallery, New York
	Lartigue 8 x 80, Musée des Arts Décoratifs, Paris (travelled to *Europalia 75,* Ghent and Antwerp, 1975; Chambery, France, and Musée de Clamency, France, 1976)
	Galerie Delpire, Paris
	Galerie Municipale du Chateau d'Eau, Toulouse
	Festival d'Arles, France
	Van Gogh Museum, Amsterdam
1976	Centre d'Action Culturelle, Macon
	Nouvelle Bibliothèque, Romorantin, France
	Frantel, Rheims
	Maison des Jeunes et de la Culture, St. Etienne de Rouvay, France
	Seibu Art Museum, Tokyo
	Schiedams Museum, Netherlands
	Arnhems Museum, Netherlands
1977	Centre de la Part Dieu, Lyons
1978	Palais de l'Europe, Menton, France
	Centre International de Grasse, France
	Maison Européenne de la Photographie, Chalon-sur-Saône, France
	Tolarno Gallery, St. Kilda, Victoria, Australia
1979	Grenier à Sel, Honfleur, France
1980	*Bonjour Monsieur Lartigue,* Grand Palais, Paris (restrospective; travelled to the Fondation Nationale de la Photographie, Lyons, 1981; and tour of the United States, 1981-85)
	20 Années de Découverte, Grand Palais, Paris (travelled to Rome, Capri, Potenza, Zurich and Lausanne, 1982-86)
	Contemporary Lartigue, Olympus Gallery, London
1982	*Tennis,* Olympus Gallery, London

Sur la Route de Houlgate, avec Mamie, Bibi et Jean le Chauffeur, Automobile Hispano Suiza 32 hp, **1929.** Photograph ©Jacques-Henri Lartigue.

Grand Palais, Paris
1983   Bibliothèque Municipale, Lisieux, France
        Musée Nicephore Niepce, Châlon sur Saône, France
        Femmes, Grand Palais, Paris (travelled to Olympus Gallery,
            London; Olympus Optical Company, Hamburg)
1984   Couvent des Jacobins, Toulouse, France
        Fondation Nationale de la Photographie, Lyon, France
        Pages d'Albums 1919-22, Grand Palais, Paris (travelled to the
            Kunsthaus, Zurich; Musée de l'Elysée, Lausanne)
        Le Passé Composé, at *Rencontres Internationales de la
            Photographie,* Arles, France (travelled to the Grand Palais,
            Paris)
1986   *Le Troisième Oeil,* Grand Palais, Paris
1987   *Le Bonheur du Jour 1902-1936,* Théâtre Valli à Reggio
            Emilia, Italy
1988   *Moi et les autres,* Grand Palais des Champs-Elysées, Paris
1989   *Les envois de Jacques-Henri Lartigue,* Grand Palais des
            Champs-Elysées, Paris
1990   *Rivages,* Grand Palais des Champs-Elysées, Paris (travelled to
            Musée de la Mer, Ile Sainte Marguerite à Cannes; Théâtre de
            la Passerelle, Gap; Hotel Jouffroy d'Abbans/La Manufac-
            ture, Besançon)
1991   *Jacques-Henri Lartigue à l'ecole du jeu,* Grand Palais des
            Champs-Elysées, Paris (travelled to Taragona, Valence,
            Malaga, Logrono, Pamplona, Gijon, Bilbao, Huesca)
1992   *En Route Monsieur Lartigue,* Grand Palais des Champs-
            Elysées, Paris
1994   *Lartigue a Cent Ans,* Commanderie Sainte Luce, Arles

Selected Group Exhibitions:

1955   *Photographies des Gens d'Images,* Galerie d'Orsay, Paris
            (and 1956)
1964   *World Exhibition of Photography: What Is Man?,* Pressehaus
            Stern, Hamburg (and world tour)
1965   *Un Siècle de Photographie,* Musée des Arts Décoratifs, Paris
1975   *The Land: 20th Century Landscape Photographs Selected by
            Bill Brandt,* Victoria and Albert Museum, London (travelled

to the National Gallery, Edinburgh; Ulster Museum, Belfast;
            and National Museum of Wales, Cardiff, 1976)
        Cents Ans de Couleurs, Salon de la Photographie, Paris
1977   *Photographie Créative du XXème Siècle,* Centre Georges
            Pompidou, Paris
1979   *Fleeting Gestures: Dance Photographs,* International Center of
            Photography, New York (travelled to The Photographers'
            Gallery, London, and *Venezia '79*)
1980   *The Imaginary Photo Museum,* Kunsthalle, Cologne
1984   *Passion and Precision: Grand Prix Racing Photos,* Long
            Beach Museum of Art, California (travelled to Detroit
            Institute of Arts, Michigan)
1986   *The Animal in Photography 1843-1985,* The Photographers'
            Gallery, London

Collections:

Association des Amis de Jacques-Henri Lartigue, Grand Palais, Paris (ar-
chives; 200,000 documents); Museum of Modern Art, New York; Internation-
al Museum of Photography, George Eastman House, Rochester, New York;
Allen Memorial Art Museum, Oberlin, Ohio; Detroit Institute of Arts; Art
Institute of Chicago; Minneapolis Institute of Arts; University of Nebraska,
Lincoln; Center for Creative Photography, University of Arizona, Tucson; San
Francisco Museum of Modern Art.

Publications:

By LARTIGUE: Books—*Les Photographies de J.-H. Lartigue: Un Album
Famille de la Belle Epoque,* edited by Jean Fondin, Lausanne 1966, as
Boyhood Photos of J.-H. Lartigue: The Family Album of a Gilded Age, New
York 1966; *Diary of a Century,* edited by Richard Avedon, New York 1970,
London 1971, as *Photo-Tagebuch unseres Jahrhunderts,* Lucerne 1971, as
Instants de Ma Vie, Paris 1973; *Portfolio J.-H. Lartigue,* portfolio of 10
photos, with an introduction by Anaïs Nin, New York 1972; *J.-H. Lartigue et
les Femmes,* Paris 1973, London and New York 1974; *Das Fest des Grossen
Rüpüskul,* with text by Elisabeth Borchers, Frankfurt 1973; *J.-H. Lartigue et
les Autos,* Paris 1974; *Mémoires sans Mémoires* (extracts from his journal),
Paris 1975; *Mon Livre de Photographie,* Paris 1977; *Portfolio J.-H. Lartigue*

1903-1916, portfolio of 10 photos, New York 1978; *Les Femmes aux Cigarettes,* with a preface by Lartigue, New York 1980; *Les Autochromes de J.-H. Lartigue 1912-1927,* Paris 1980, New York 1981; *L'emerville: écrit a mesure 1923-1931,* Paris 1981; *J. H. Lartigue: Photographs 1970-1982,* with foreword by David Bailey, London 1983; *Le Passé Composé: Les 6 x 13 de J. H. Lartigue,* Paris 1984; *Jacques-Henri Lartigue Album,* Berne 1986. **Articles**—"Jacques-Henri Lartigue," interview, in *Dialogue with Photography* by Paul Hill and Thomas Cooper, London 1979; "Jacques-Henri Lartigue," interview in *Voyons Voir: 8 Photographes* by Pierre Borhan, Paris 1980.

On LARTIGUE: **Books**—*The Photographs of Jacques-Henri Lartigue,* exhibition catalogue, with an introduction by John Szarkowski, New York 1963; *Looking at Photographs* by John Szarkowski, New York 1973; *The Land: 20th Century Landscape Photographs Selected by Bill Brandt,* exhibition catalogue, edited by Mark Haworth-Booth, London 1975; *Lartigue 8 x 80,* exhibition catalogue, Paris 1975; *Histoire de la Photographie 2: J.-H. Lartigue,* Paris and New York 1976; *Photographs: Sheldon Memorial Art Gallery Collection, University of Nebraska,* with an introduction by Norman A. Geske, Lincoln, Nebraska 1977; *Drei Klassiken der Fotografie: Lartigue, Kertesz, Steichen,* edited by Rogner Bernhard, 1978; *The Vogue Book of Fashion Photography* by Polly Devlin, with an introduction by Alexander Liberman, New York and London 1979; *Bonjour Monsieur Lartigue,* booklet to accompany exhibition, edited by the Association des Amis de Jacques-Henri Lartigue, Paris 1980; *Les Grandes Photographes: Lartigue,* with text by Henri Chapier, Paris 1981; *Master Photographers: The World's Great Photographers on their Art and Technique,* edited by Pat Booth, London 1983; *Lartigue Photographs 1970-1982,* London 1983; *Les Femmes,* exhibition catalogue, edited by the Olympus Gallery, London 1984; *Masters of Photography: Jacques Henri Lartigue,* with text by Brian Coe, London 1984; *Le Passé Composé* by Michel Frizot, Paris 1984; *L'oeil de l'oiseieur,* by Jacqueline Kellen, Paris 1985; *L'oeil de la mémoire,* Editions Carère-Lafon, Paris 1986; *Vingt Années de découverte à travers l'oeuvre de Jacques-Henri Lartigue,* exhibition catalogue, Berne 1986; *Bonjour Monsieur Lartigue,* exhibition catalogue, Tokyo 1986; *Les années folles,* by Michel Collomb, Paris 1986; *Le troisième oeil de Jacques-Henri Lartigue,* exhibition catalogue, Paris 1988; *Les envois de Jacques-Henri Lartigue et les débuts de l'aviation,* by Pierre Borhan and Martine d'Astier, Paris 1989; *Rivages,* exhibition catalogue, Paris 1990; *Jacques-Henri Lartigue—La traversée du siècle* by Florette Lartigue, Paris 1990; *Jacques-Henri Lartigue—Le Choix du Bonheur,* Paris 1992. **Articles**—"The Photographs of Jacques-Henri Lartigue" by John Szarkowski in *Museum of Modern Art Bulletin* (New York), no. 1, 1963; "Lartigue: The Happy Man" by Lionel Birch in the *Daily Telegraph Magazine* (London), 19 March 1971; "Spin of Delight: The Photography of Jacques-Henri Lartigue" by Ainslie Ellis in *British Journal of Photography* (London), 14 May 1971; "Jacques-Henri Lartigue: The Pursuit of Humour and Life" in *The Times* (London), 19 May 1971; "Jacques-Henri Lartigue: The Photographers' Gallery" by Oswell Blakeston in *Arts Review* (London), 22 May 1971; "Jacques-Henri Lartigue: Later Pictures" in *Creative Camera* (London), June 1971; "Mercurial Quietude: Cartier-Bresson and Lartigue" by Max Kozloff in *Art in America* (New York), January/February 1972; "The Colour Photographs of Jacques-Henri Lartigue" in the *Sunday Times Magazine* (London), 27 August 1972; "Lartigue: Les Femmes et Moi" in *Photo* (Paris), September 1972; "Lartigue ou l'Oeil du Matin" in *Zoom* (Paris), no. 11, 1972; "Jacques-Henri Lartigue" in *Documentary Photography,* by the Time-Life editors, New York 1973; "New York Letter: Jacques-Henri Lartigue" by S. Schwartz in *Art International* (Lagano), January 1973; "Lartigue in London" in *Photographic Journal* (London), August 1973; "Le Lancelot de Robert Bresson par Lartigue" in *Photo* (Paris), September 1973; "Jacques-Henri Lartigue" in *Photo* (Paris), November 1973; "The Eyes of an Optimist" in the *Sunday Times Magazine* (London), 17 February 1974; "Les Photographes, Aiment-ils les Mannequins" in *Elle* (Paris), 8 April 1974; "J.-H. Lartigue et son piege d'oeil" by Michel Tournier in *L'Oeil* (Paris), December 1974; "Through the Eye of a Loving Lens" by Joan Juliet Buck in *The Times* (London), 19 September 1986. **Films**—*Le Magicien* by Claude Fayard, 1966; *La Famille Lartigue* by Robert Hughes, 1970; *Jacques-Henri Lartigue* by Claude Gallot, 1971-72; *Jacques-Henri Lartigue* by Claude Ventura, 1974; *Jacques-Henri Lartigue, Un Photographe* by Fernard Moscovitz, 1980; *Jacques-Henri Lartigue, Peintre et Photographe* by Francois Reichenbach, 1980.

*

If no one can ever catch the "bluebird," Claude Monet caught his feathers.—1963

Spring is here. The struggle has begun. Struggle against the brightened fog, struggle against the plum trees in bloom, against the wind, against the light, against all the elusive beauties.

We do not "fight" against them. We fight to try to become a hyphen between them and the small human result. And this hyphen, we can become it only if God sends us an angel.

I enter at the back of an old country chapel, like a nest of stones poised in silence....And suddenly, there, God permits it! He permits me to speak to Him about this angel that might come to me.—1965

My memory, a sort of file installed in my brain, keeps things, things in the process of happening that immediately become of the past.

There I recover dates, facts, data, but nothing of the mysterious imponderables that enchant me and that I love and that love me, then escape. So I write (and sometimes I am even reduced to taking pictures), as if I were trying to catch a smoke-ring in a butterfly net, and then my human "intellect" persuades me that all is lost, annihilated, nothingness....Then, a little country bell rings, or a blackbird sings, a fragrance passes by—and all is resurrected. Though, not quite; not resurrected to begin again—I don't deserve that. But resurrected in order to show, to say to me (and therefore to allow me to smile): "Look, I am not dead."

I must choose photographs for my book about women. There are hundreds of 6 x 6's to look at, Florette on one side, me on the other. Subtle colors now washed out, rotten, removed. Dead friends. Countries disfigured by "progress." Desperate, perhaps, this bankruptcy, and yet not completely, this "box of preserves." I will keep for many months the fleeting "blue bird" and make it fly in my imagination, and soon, deaf to the reasons of my reason, I will begin again to search, to recapture, to preserve, the "bluebirds."—1973

—Jacques-Henri Lartigue (from his journal)

* * *

The most popular of French photographers, the one that America "discovered" and covered with honors, the one whose work the French Republic now officially collects and disseminates—that is Jacques-Henri Lartigue, who always claimed that he was not a photographer. On his passport, the description of profession read, "Artist-Painter." He said: "For me, photography is, certainly, a passion. But I am only an amateur." A mischievous nuance, a charming whim perhaps, but it does reveal an authentic modesty, and rather than diminish the public's admiration for him and his work, it enhances it.

At the age of seven, at the beginning of this century, Lartigue received a camera as a gift from his father, and from then on, day after day, he would try to "fix" scenes of his domestic life, having been allowed by the conditions of his life sufficient leisure to do so. These conditions were neither common nor rare. But as Richard Avedon has rightly observed, "Hundreds of children from the same social milieu received cameras, but they never became Lartigues." Only the grace of God and—if one may use the word—an authentic genius explain the difference. Yet there were some fortuitous circumstances.

Some drunks drink sad alcohol; some rich people possess dismal money. Not Lartigue's parents. With them, money was, as it were, merry. The first bit of good luck in his favor was that he learned about money not as the stuff of vanity or deadly pomp but of joyous handouts. For his family, avant-garde for their time, everything was greatly loved; they were intoxicated by their Golden Age, with its arts of living, its discoveries and its naivetés: the automobile, the airplane, the phonograph, the cinema, photography (which his father, a financier, had already discovered), sports of every kind, travel, the sea, the snow—and the array of gadgets, like the inflatable suit which (in theory at least) allowed the wearer to drift in a gentle current without getting wet. There were, in short, a profusion of subjects for Lartigue, a child of that time and class, to capture. When the children—Maurice, the eldest; Jacques-Henri, the younger; and their cousins—devised new toys, we, too, can see them: there is the bobsled on bicycle wheels pulled by a donkey to the top of a hill (a photo), which then comes down the slope at breakneck speed (another photo), producing a series of "sensational scenes," not least of which is its demise (still another photo).

A second bit of good luck was that Lartigue had the opportunity, at 20, to direct his own destiny—to do what he wanted to do, with parental approval. After entering the Académie Julian, thanks mainly to the instruction of the painter Jean-Paul Laurens, he perfected his graphic talent, which was, until then, essentially primitive. And a third bit of good luck was that, in teaching himself photography, he avoided the sterility of pictorial academicism. Perhaps that is the reason for the distinction he made: he called himself a painter and not a photographer because he *learned* one and not the other. The distinction is less specious than it may seem, even though the two disciplines are subject to certain common laws. Lartigue was successful as a painter (his paintings, since 1922, have been highly prized), but when he photographed he did not do so according to any of the rules he mastered as a painter; he created photographs, by pure intuition.

Perhaps too, and not facetiously, one could mention another fortunate circumstance: Lartigue was born under the sign of Gemini, which suggests a gift for social relationships, a great precocity, and, especially, an eternal youthfulness which defies, both physically and mentally, the assault of time. That description does fit Lartigue: the precocious, eternal adolescent, who was at first a little Mozart, who, even as an octogenarian, remained as active, as inquisitive, as mischievous, as impish as when he was eight years old. He and his pictures ignore chronology. His "Interieur en Auvergne," the work one would assume of a mature man, dates from when he was 16; his "Fleurs des Champs," a photo that he could have produced at 12, dates from his last years. In his "albums" youth is presented as of all ages; life, happiness and irony burst forth there with universal simplicity and generosity of spirit. That, finally, is Lartigue's style.

And this is what makes his work so remarkable: his pictures are almost never that which one would actually see in a family album (consider Bibi surprised on the toilet in an indiscreet posture), but neither are they what we expect to find in magazines. He is not really a reporter, he is more like a *paparazzo:* beautiful women walking in the Bois de Boulogne, caught off-guard; losing gamblers leaving Auteuil racetrack. He is also (depending on one's perspective) a fashion photographer *honoris causa,* a theatrical photographer, a photojournalist, a portrait photographer; his subjects include the arts, sciences, technology, society. He photographed anything and everything but not from any creative stance or intellectual imperative but as from his own great curiosity. His pictures are the records, the thoughts, of an emotionally alive and active man. They speak freely and make him, as John Szarkowski has noted, "the precursor of all that has been vital and of interest in the milieu of our times."

Life—that is Lartigue's photographic genre. That is his amusement, his delight—and ours too, of course. An anecdote will illustrate his unalterable "amateurishness" and disarming good-naturedness:

One day, a figure of great importance asked Lartigue to do his portrait, and Lartigue agreed (perhaps the only commissioned portrait of his career). At the appointed time, Lartigue arrived in the courtyard of the palatial home of his potential subject—driving his antique, scrap-metal Citroen 2 CV. Before beginning the session, he put himself at his ease by putting on his slippers, as he would do at home. Between pictures he took a break and, as it was lunchtime, his wife (and assistant) had provided picnic provisions in a basket (a technical detail: the sandwiches prepared by the Lartigues were always encircled at both ends by rubber bands, to avoid incidents).

All of these details are indicative of the Lartigue style, which, on this occasion, was being put at the official service of the former president of the Republic, M. Giscard d'Estaing.

It is true, then: neither he nor his photographs ever aged. When we immerse ourselves in his work, in an album, neither do we. That is the miracle we mean when we say Lartigue.

—Roger Therond

LAU, Grace Pei-Yin.

Nationality: British. **Born:** London, 24 August 1939. Lived in China, 1945-49, and Southeast Asia, 1960-70. **Education:** Gained a Diploma in Applied Photography from Harrow Collage of Higher Education in 1976, a BA in Photographic Media Studies in 1982, and an HND/BTEC in Documentary Photography from Gwent College of Higher Education in 1992. **Family:** Divorced. **Career:** Worked as an occasional visiting lecturer at Westminister University and other colleges; Head of the Photographic Section of the Department of Geology, Imperial College of Science, London, 1979-90; a member of the steering committee for SIGNALS Festival of Women Photographers, 1992-1994; part-time tutor at London College of Printing. Founder of Exposures, Association of Women Photographers, London, from 1993. **Address:** 433 Archway Road, London N6 4HT, England.

Individual Exhibitions:

1987   *Photo Exposures,* Submarine Gallery, London
1988   *The Shape of Things to Come,* BICA Gallery, Brighton,
            England
1994   Chelsea Arts Club, London SW1

Selected Group Exhibitions:

1987   *Behold The Man,* The Photographers' Gallery, London
1991   *Sign of the Times,* Camerawork, London
1993   *Contemporary British Artists,* Les Larmes d'Eros, Paris
1994   *Exposures,* Melkweg Multimedia Centre, Amsterdam
            What She Wants, Impressions Gallery, York (toured)
            Revelations, John Jones Gallery, London
            John Kobal Photographic Portrait Award 1994, National
            Portrait Gallery, London

Publications:

By LAU: Articles—Oxford Union *Debate* magazine, Autumn 1986; *SIYU* (Manchester), 1987; *Discovery* (Hong Kong), 1988; *International Male Photography* (Germany), 1989; "Dirty Looks: Woman, Power and Pornography," BFI (London), 1992; "New Formations" in the *Journal of Culture and Politics* (University of Bristol), 1993; *Social Text* (New York), No. 37, 1994.

On LAU: Book—*Female Fetishism* by Lorraine Gamman and Merja Makinen, London 1994. **Articles**—*Time Out* (London), May 1987; *The Guardian,* 17 June 1987; *The Sunday Times Magazine* (London), 10 September 1989; *The Guardian,* 12 October 1989; Val Williams in the *New Statesman,* 20 October 1989. **Television specials**—*Split Screen,* BBC2, 1986; *01 For London,* ITV, 1989; *Late Show,* BBC2, 1990; *Rude Women,* Channel 4, 1992.

*

My work is about visually exploring contemporary and controversial issues, including cultural diversity, women's radical art, gender identities and sub-cultures. I specifically choose to document the groups and communities that are marginalised or active "on the fringe." I consider my work to be effective if it moves the audience to feel excited or disturbed, and above all—curious. Curiosity provokes questions and leads to a dialogue. Subsequently, communication is created between the photographer and his/her audience. And I believe successful photography is about communication.

I would like my work to reach as wide an audience as possible. But intelligent photography in England is generally limited to precious shows in select galleries while most of the general public remains visually unaware and uninvolved. There should be more accessible public spaces to promote exploratory photography and more informative media coverage.

Zoe, **1993.** Photograph ©Grace Lau.

However, she does not take the view expressed by some radical feminists that the erotic image should be expropriated from men. Lau's work, though always didactic, is never ideologically dogmatic. The world of sado-masochism has taught her that gender identity and sexuality is a myriad of complex shifting feelings, in which notions of masculinity and femininity can be defined in numerous ways. Thus in a feminist sense, Grace Lau might be said to be an integrationist, seeking to liberate men as well as women from the exigencies and rigidity of traditional patriarchy. For example, with her colleague Rosie Gunn and Robin Shaw, she has established the women's photographic co-operative, Exposures, to further her aims. Exposures offers both women and men workshops in photographing nudes of the opposite sex—women photographing naked men for the first time, men re-examining old prejudices and attempting to formulate new answers in a positive interaction with the model and with their colleagues.

In her own work and in her general practice, Grace Lau is in the vanguard of feminist photography. By photographing men as objects of sexuality she undercuts the assumptions of patriarchal society. By broadening the scope of erotic imagery, she helps to liberate both sexes from sexual repression and puritanism.

—Gerry Badger

I try not to compromise my work. An artist has to push boundaries—both their own and that of their audience. My work has been described as "subversive." If so, I am pleased.

—Grace Pei-Yin Lau

* * *

The most important factor unifying the work of Grace Lau is not formal, nor stylistic, nor even a matter of genre. Her diverse imagery is unified by her view of contemporary sexuality and the wider concerns which stem from this fundamental base. She is equally happy fabricating tableaux in the studio, or working on location in the documentary mode as long as the resultant images reflect upon and explore the pressing social issues which obsess her. In a broader sense these issues have gripped an increasing number of women photographers since the 1970s, questions of gender representation and the potentiality of the camera to help empower women in their struggle against male domination of visual culture. Lau is one of a number of feminist photographers who have begun to examine the especially charged area of erotic imagery, whereby women seek to reverse the strong cultural convention of the "male gaze" and depict men as objects of erotic contemplation for the female audience.

In a more particular sense, Grace Lau has forged new, perhaps more controversial territory by focusing upon the sexual subcultures of sado-masochism and rubber/leather fetishism. She documents graphically the activities of these aficionados of the bizarre, both in the studio and in the specialist clubs, beginning recently, for example, an extended series on transvestites. In this work, Lau is never coy, nor overtly prurient, but combines documentary matter-of-factness with a gentle empathy that evokes understanding rather than loathing from those unused to these wilder shores of sexual practice.

Politically, Lau takes the view that the pornographic, or more correctly, the explicitly erotic image is not simply exploitative but can be a potentially liberating vehicle, and as such is a fruitful area of investigation for feminism.

LAUGHLIN, Clarence John.

Nationality: American. **Born:** Lake Charles, Louisiana, 14 August 1905; lived on a plantation near New Iberia, Louisiana, 1905-10, then moved with his parents to New Orleans. **Education:** Attended elementary school and high school (for one year) in New Orleans, 1911-18; self-taught in photography. **Military Service:** Served in the United States Army, at the Signal Corps Photographic Unit, Long Island City, New York, 1942-43, and with the United States Office of Strategic Services, Washington, D.C., 1943-46. **Family:** Married 4 times; children: John, David and Andrea. **Career:** Worked as a bank clerk in New Orleans, 1924-35. Photographer from 1945. Civil Service Photographer, for the United States Engineer Corps, on the Mississippi River, and in New Orleans and Vicksburg, Louisiana, 1936-40; Fashion Photographer, *Vogue* studios, New York, 1940-41; worked for the Photography Department, National Archives, Washington, D.C., 1941-42; freelance architectural photographer, New Orleans, 1946-74. Engaged mainly in writing and creating large personal library (more than 32,000 volumes), mostly on all aspects of fantasy and the fantastic, 1974 until his death in 1985. Associate of Research, University of Louisville, Kentucky, 1968-85. **Recipient:** Distinction in the Arts Award, City of New Orleans, 1978; City of Paris Award, 1980. DHL: Tulane University, New Orleans, 1976. Agent (prints): Robert Miller Gallery, 41 East 57th Street, New York, New York 10022. **Died:** (in New Orleans) 2 January 1985.

Selected Individual Exhibitions:

1936	Delgado Museum of Art, New Orleans
1939	Princeton University Art Gallery, New Jersey
1940	Julian Levy Gallery, New York (with Eugène Atget)
1942	New School for Social Research, New York
1946	Walker Art Center, Minneapolis
	The Camera as a Third Eye, Philadelphia Museum of Art (first personally designed circulating show)

1948   San Francisco Museum of Art
        Ghosts Along the Mississippi, Phillips Gallery, Washington,
            D.C. (toured the United States, 1948-56)
        Seattle Art Museum
1949   Northwestern University, Evanston, Illinois
        The Camera as a Third Eye, with Stieglitz' *Equivalents,*
            Phillips Gallery, Washington, D.C.
1950   Massachusetts Institute of Technology, Cambridge
1951   Stanford University Art Gallery, California
1952   Art Institute of Chicago
1953   *Louisiana Plantation Photos,* United States Department of
            State travelling exhibition (toured Germany)
1954   Cleveland Museum of Art
1956   Wadsworth Atheneum, Hartford, Connecticut
1957   Los Angeles County Museum of Art
        The Bronze Age to Brancusi, Detroit Institute of Art (toured
            the United States)
1962   Smithsonian Institution, Washington, D.C.
1965   *Old Milwaukee Rediscovered,* Milwaukee Public Museum,
            Wisconsin (toured the United States)
1967   *Phoenix Re-Arisen,* Carson Pirie Scott Auditorium, Chicago
            (toured the United States)
1973   *The Personal Eye,* Philadelphia Museum of Art (retrospective)
        New Orleans Museum of Art
1976   Museum of Contemporary Art, Chicago
        Chicago Center for Contemporary Photography
        Minneapolis Institute of Arts
1980   *Louisiana Plantations,* Tulane University Library, New Orleans
        United States Cultural Center, Paris (toured France)
1981   Olympus Gallery, London
1982   *Weston and Laughlin in Louisiana,* New Orleans Museum of
            Art (travelled to the Los Angeles Center for Photographic
            Studies)
1986   *Memorial Exhibition,* Historic New Orleans Collection
        Memorial Exhibition, Robert Miller Gallery, New York

Selected Group Exhibitions:

1940   *Abstract Paintings, Sculpture, Photographs,* Julien Levy
            Gallery, New York
1949   *Mississippi Panorama,* City Art Museum, St. Louis
1955   *4 Photographers: Abbott, Atget, Laughlin, Stieglitz,* Yale
            University, New Haven, Connecticut
1959   *Photography at Mid-Century,* International Museum of
            Photography, George Eastman House, Rochester, New York
            (toured the United States)
1961   *Salon Internationale du Portrait Photographique,* Bibliothèque
            Nationale, Paris
1962   *Subjektive Fotografie 2,* Cologne (toured West Germany)
1976   *Photographs from the Julien Levy Collection, Starting with
            Atget,* Art Institute of Chicago
1977   *Concerning Photography,* The Photographers' Gallery, London
            (travelled to the Spectro Workshop, Newcastle upon Tyne)
1985   *American Images 1945-80,* Barbican Art Gallery, London
            (toured Britain)
1987   *Photography and Art 1946-86,* Los Angeles County
            Museum of Art

Collections:

Historic New Orleans Collection, Louisiana (archives); Metropolitan Museum of Art, New York; Museum of Modern Art, New York; International

Museum of Photography, George Eastman House, Rochester, New York; Phillips Gallery, Washington, D.C.; Smithsonian Institution, Washington, D.C.; Stieglitz Center, Philadelphia Museum of Art; New Orleans Museum of Art; Art Institute of Chicago; Gernsheim Collection, University of Texas at Austin; Bibliothèque Nationale, Paris.

Publications:

By LAUGHLIN: Books—*New Orleans and Its Living Past,* with text by David L. Cohn, Boston 1941; *Ghosts Along the Mississippi,* New York 1948; *Photographs of Victorian Chicago,* Washington, D.C. 1968. **Articles—**"Unexplored New Orleans" in *Magazine of Art* (New York), July 1939; "Poems of Desolation" in *New Directions in Prose and Poetry 1941,* New York 1941; "Ghosts Along the Mississippi" in *Harper's Bazaar* (New York), 1 March 1942; "Speaking of Pictures ... New Orleans Has Lovely Old Ironwork" in *Life* (New York), 6 April 1942; "The Architecture of New Orleans" in *Architectural Review* (London), August 1946; "Plantation Architecture in Louisiana" in *Architectural Review* (London), December 1947; "The Cemeteries of New Orleans" in *Architectural Review* (London), February 1948; "Moss Phantom" in *Mademoiselle* (New York), April 1948; "Variety from Standardization" in *Architectural Review* (London), April 1948; "Symbolic Photography: The Camera as a 'Third Eye' " in *Professional Photographer* (Cleveland), September 1951; "Seven Ways to See a Tree" in *Modern Photography* (New York), September 1952; "Backgrounds and Models," in 2 parts, in *Art Photography Magazine* (Chicago), April and May 1956; "Ultra Modern: Out of Date" in *Harper's Bazaar* (New York), March 1956; "Inner Vision in Photography" in *New World Writing 15,* New York 1959; "Why? Because" in *Modern Photography* (New York), August 1961; "Louisiana Fantasy" in *Architectural Review* (London), May 1967; "American Fantastica" in *L'Oeil Magazine* (Paris), February 1967; "The Third World of Photography: Beyond Documentation and Purism" in *Photo Bulletin* (Los Angeles), March 1979; "Men and Buildings: American Victorian Architecture" in *Perspecta* (New Haven, Connecticut), no. 17, 1981.

On LAUGHLIN: Books—*Modern Photography 1937-38,* edited by C.G. Holme, London and New York 1938; *U.S. Camera 1940,* edited by T.J. Maloney, New York 1939; *Famous Photographs,* edited by Willard Morgan, New York 1948; *A Concise History of Photography* by Helmut and Alison Gernsheim, London 1965; *The Photographer's Eye* by John Szarkowski, New York 1966; *Looking at Photographs* by John Szarkowski, New York 1973; *Clarence John Laughlin: The Personal Eye,* with an introduction by Jonathan Williams, Millerton, New York 1973; *The Magic Image* by Cecil Beaton and Gail Buckland, Boston and London 1975; *American Photography: Past into Present,* edited by Anita Ventura Mozley, Seattle 1976; *Photographs from the Julien Levy Collection, Starting with Atget,* exhibition catalogue, by David Travis, Chicago 1976; *Concerning Photography,* exhibition catalogue, by Jonathan Bayer and others, London 1977; *Light Readings: A Photography Critic's Writings 1968-1978* by A.D. Coleman, New York 1979; *Center for Creative Photography No. 10: Clarence John Laughlin* by Henry Holmes Smith and Terence Pitts, Tucson, Arizona 1979; *The Photograph Collector's Guide* by Lee D. Witkin and Barbara London, Boston and London 1979; *The Imaginary Photo Museum* by Helmut Gernsheim, Renate and L. Fritz Gruber and others, Cologne 1981, London 1982; *The Library of World Photography: Portraits,* with introduction by Colin Ford, Tokyo 1982, 1983, London 1983; *Les Mysteres de la Chambre Noire,* edited by Eduard Jaguer, Paris 1984; *American Images: Photography 1945-1980,* edited by Peter Turner and John Benton-Harris, London 1985; *Photography and Art 1946-1986,* exhibition catalogue, by Andy Grundberg and Kathleen M. Gauss, Los Angeles 1987. **Articles—**"Let's Talk Photography" by Bruce Downes in *Photography Magazine* (New York), April 1951; article by Emil Schulthess in *Du* (Zurich), April 1954; article by Fritz Gruber in *Foto Prisma* (Dusseldorf), February 1960; "3 American Phantasts: Bullock, Sommer, and Laughlin" by Jonathan

Williams in *Aperture* (Millerton, New York), no. 3, 1961; "Potentials of Creative Photography" in *Camera* (Lucerne), July 1968; "Les Fleurs du Mal" in *Arts in Society* (Madison, Wisconsin), no. 3, 1963; "A Significant Magic" in *New Orleans Magazine,* November 1971; "Clarence John Laughlin: Phantoms and Metaphors" by Mary Louise Tucker in *Modern Photography* (New York), April 1977; "Clarence J. Laughlin, Photographer, Essayist" in the *New York Times,* 4 January 1985.

*

The creative photographer should be able to put the stamp of *his* way of seeing on whatever material he touches—just as in the case of the creative painter or poet. This means that the object in the photograph must be so treated, or so grasped (not merely in technical terms, but in terms of the presensitizing of an individual imagination, and the subsequent projection of this individual imagination through the so-called "impersonal" lens) that the object *does* become personal—by acquiring meanings *beyond* itself. In fine, the object is then photographed in terms of what this individual human imagination has *projected* into it. It is *only* when the photograph presents the object so that the meanings conveyed *transcend* the meaning of the object as a *thing-in-itself* that photography becomes art.

It should be stressed that I did not start out as a photographer but, instead, as a writer. Whether for good or ill, this fact has inspired and colored many of my concepts. In addition, through photography I have also tried to tie together and further my active interests in painting, in poetry, in psychology, and in architecture. Whatever value my photography has, it is *only* because of these other interests.

One of my basic feelings is that the mind, and the heart alike, of the photographer must be dedicated to the glory, the magic, and the mystery of light. The mystery of time, the magic of light, the enigma of reality—and their interrelationships—are my constant themes and preoccupations. Because of these metaphysical and poetic preoccupations, I frequently attempt to show in my work, in various ways, the unreality of the "real" and the reality of the "unreal." This may result, at times, in some disturbing effects. But art *should* be disturbing; it should make us both think *and* feel; it should infect the subconscious as well as the conscious mind; it should never allow complacency or condone the status quo.

My central position, therefore, is one of *extreme romanticism*—the concept of "reality" as being, innately, mystery and magic; the intuitive awareness of the power of the "unknown"—which human beings are afraid to realize, and which none of their religious and intellectual systems can really take into account. This romanticism revolves upon the feeling that the world is far stranger than we think; that the "reality"; and that the human imagination is the key to this hidden, and more inclusive, "reality." This position is now completely out of fashion.

As a corollary, I attempt, through much of my work, to animate all things—even so-called "inanimate" objects—with the spirit of man. I have come, by degrees, to realize that this extremely animistic projection rises, ultimately, from my profound fear and disquiet over the accelerating mechanization of man's life and the resultant attempts to stamp out individuality in all the spheres of man's activity—this whole process being one of the dominant expressions of our military-industrial society.

The physical object, to me, is merely a stepping-stone to an inner world where the object, with the help of subconscious drives and focused perceptions, becomes transmuted into a symbol whose life is beyond the life of the objects we know and whose meaning is a *truly human* meaning. By dealing with the object in this way the creative photographer sets free the *human contents* of objects, and imparts humanity to the inhuman world around him.

Everything that I see must become *personal;* otherwise, it is dead and mechanical. Our only chance to escape the blight of mechanization, of acting and thinking alike, of the huge machine that society is becoming, is to restore life to all things through the saving and beneficent power of the human

imagination. This is my personal belief, my hope for humanity, and the power that enabled me to continue my work, under difficult conditions, through many years—despite the indifference, and lack of approval of those who have set themselves up, in this country, as the arbiters of "modern" photography.

—Clarence John Laughlin (1982)

*   *   *

Clarence John Laughlin—in action. . . . Let's see, it must be about nine o'clock in the morning in the Crescent City. Out in the Marigny District near the Lake, the venerable and bodacious one, the greatest master ever to live in New Orleans, is polishing off his version of breakfast: some cold red-beans-and-rice, chased with a big glass of Dr. Pepper, laced with 10,000 units of vitamin-C, the crystalline sort. Refreshed and not dismayed by this fare, he will soon move back to the brick, temperature-controlled studio he has had built behind the house to provide decent quarters for his 15,000 to 20,000 books and a small darkroom for his use. The shelves in the library go to the ceiling and are built as a maze. In the very center is a long table. There CJL will spend this morning studying the recent monumental volume on the Ideal Dream Palace of the Postman Cheval. The book probably costs more than it cost the Postman to build the blessed thing, but money is no object when it helps build fires for the phantasmagorical and fathomless Laughlin imagination. After more red beans at lunch or maybe a poorboy sandwich and celery tonic, back in the labyrinth to study Archimboldo and Grandville and today's new arrival: a tome on the architecture of the Place Stanislaus in Nancy.

Clarence John Laughlin was born in Lake Charles, Louisiana in 1905 and later lived on a plantation near New Iberia. He remained to the end as volatile as Tabasco sauce, though a bad leg slowed him down to a walking speed only twice as fast as most of the earth's population. He looked like Frank Lloyd Wright, with just enough of the ventriloquist's dummy in *Dead of Night* to make it spooky. For there certainly was something preternatural about CJL and his ability to unearth mysteries with his camera. I feel confident you could point Clarence down that street of drab, ordinary, public housing in Chartres and his psychic antennae, like a dowser's rod, would quickly point to La Maison de Picassiette, whose mosaic'd wonders are hidden from plain view. He was the genius of Ignored Ghastliness, the Eldritch, the Psychopompous, the Metamorphic, the Mephitic, the Fearsome, and the Downright Astonishing.

I used to make lists of "People To Talk About The Next Time I See Clarence": viz., St. EOM of the Land of Pasaquan, the Rev. Howard Finster, Boosie Jackson, Virgil Finlay, Abe Merritt, Henry Dorsey, Clarence Schmidt, Edgar Tolson, Atget, Robert Barlow, H.P. Lovecraft, Balthus, Jess Colins, Enid Foster, Henry Clews, Hans Bellmer, Lord Berners, Edward James, Redon, Richard Dadd, Sara Losh, Conlon Nancarrow, Beatrix Potter, Ivan Albright, Tolkien, William Burges, Raymond Isidore, Sorabji, William Hope Hodgson, Raymond Moore, Count Orsini, Delius, Squire Waterton, Barbara Jones, Mervyn Peake, Gallé, Trevor Winkfield, John Furnival, Baron Corvo, Glen Baxter, Lou Harrison, Cyril Scott, and Voysey. . . . Is there enough filé powder in the gumbo to suit you?

I insisted for years that Clarence John Laughlin deserved to be named a "National Treasure," for who has done more to record and salvage and cherish an America that has almost been destroyed in just one generation. I think he worked harder, against more stupid obstacles, than any artist I ever met—nearly 50 years on the job. Never enough space, never enough time, never enough money, never enough serious response. The Ford and MacArthur Foundations will, somehow, never hear of him. The Atgets and Laughlins of this world are both noble and nearly invisible.

The late Weeks Hall, that delightful and impossible painter, raconteur, and occupant of one of the most marvellous of plantation houses, "The Shadows-on-the-Teche," wrote these gracious words about CJL: "The direction of this talent has fortunately been succored by its environment. His city wears an air, confirmed and expressed by its Carnival, of fantasy sobered always by thoughts of mortality. His New Orleans is also the Paris of Meryon, the Bermuda of *The Tempest,* and the Brussels of Ensor. His achievement consists in the fact that these prints are *not* photographs of these places and these things, but are photographed symbols of his thoughts about them. . . . ''

—Jonathan Williams

LEBECK, Robert.

Nationality: German. **Born:** Berlin, 21 March 1929. **Education:** Attended high school in Berlin, until 1943, and in Donaueschingen, 1946-48; studied at the University of Zurich, 1948-49, and Columbia University, New York, 1949-51; self-taught in photography. **Military Service;** Served as an assistant in the German Air Force, and as an artilleryman in the German Army, Berlin and Stettin, 1944-45 (prisoner-of-war, 1945). **Family:** Married Heike Rennert in 1963 (divorced, 1977); daughter: Anna; married Elke Droescher in 1978 (divorced, 1991); married Cordula Reiser, 1991; children: Linda (1992) and Oscar (1993). **Career:** Photographer, *Heidelberger Tageblatt* newspaper, 1952-55; Frankfurt Office Editor, *Revue* magazine, Munich, 1955-59; Staff Photographer, *Kristall* magazine, Hamburg, 1960-61, 1964-65, and *Stern* magazine, in Hamburg, 1962-63, New York, 1966-68, and in Hamburg, 1969-77 and since 1979; Editor-in-Chief, *GEO* magazine, Hamburg, 1977-78. Dr. Erich-Saloman-Price, 1991. **Address:** Hexentwiete 36, D-22559, Hamburg, Germany.

Individual Exhibitions:

1962   *Tokio-Moskau-Leopoldville,* Museum für Kunst und Gewerbe, Hamburg (toured West Germany)
1983   *30 Jahre Zeitgeschichte,* Hamburg (retrospective; toured West Germany, 1983-85).
1991   *Fotoreportagen,* Couvent de Minimes, Perpignan; Museum Ludwig, Cologne (toured Germany 1991-95)
       Portraits 1956-1991, Hamburg (toured Germany 1991-95)

Selected Group Exhibitions:

1968   *2nd World Exhibition of Photography,* Pressehaus Stern, Hamburg (and world tour)
1969   *Vision and Expression,* International Museum of Photography, George Eastman House, Rochester, New York (toured the United States, 1969-71)
1972   *Universalisten,* at *Photokina,* Cologne (with Don McCullin, Jack Garofalo and Mario de Biasi)
1979   *Deutsche Fotografie nach 1945,* Kunstverein, Kassel, West Germany (toured West Germany)
1980   *Das Imaginäre Photomuseum,* at *Photokina,* Cologne
1981   *Farbe im Photo,* Josef-Haubrich-Kunsthalle, Cologne
1982   *Lichtbildnisse: Das Porträt in der Fotografie,* Rheinisches Landesmuseum, Bonn
1983   *Bilder aus der Bundesrepublik,* Kunstmuseum, Hannover
1984   *Wir,* Kunstverein, Frankfurt

Collections:

Museum für Kunst and Gewerbe, Hamburg; Museum Folkwang, Essen; Agfa Foto-Historama, Leverkusen, West Germany; Stadtmuseum, Munich; Inter-national Museum of Photography, George Eastman House, Rochester, New York; Museum Ludwig, Cologne.

Publications:

By LEBECK: Books—*Afrika im Jahre Null: Eine Kristall-Reportage,* Hamburg 1961; *Der Abenteurer,* with text by Georg Stefan Troller, Gutersloh, West Germany 1968; *In Memoriam,* with text by Fritz Kempe, Dortmund 1980; *Busen, Strapse, Spitzenhoschen: erotische Postkarten,* editor, Dortmund 1982; *Augenzeuge Robert Lebeck: 30 Jahre Zeitgeschichte,* Munich 1984; *Romy Schneider,* Zurich 1986; *Begegnungen mit Grossen der Zeit,* Zurich 1987; *Fotoreportagen,* Stuttgart 1993.

On LEBECK: Books—*Beauty: Variations on the Theme Woman by Masters of the Camera—Past and Present,* edited by L. Fritz Gruber, London and New York 1965; *World Exhibition of Photography,* exhibition catalogue, edited by Karl Pawek, Hamburg 1968; *Vision and Expression* by Nathan Lyons, New York 1969; *Famous Photographers Annual,* New York 1969; *Fotografie 1919-1979, Made in Germany: Die GDL-Fotografen,* edited by Fritz Kempe, Bernd Lohse and others, Frankfurt 1979; *Deutsche Fotografie nach 1945* by Floris Neusüss, Wolfgang Kemp and Petra Benteler, Kassel, West Germany 1979; *The Imaginary Photo Museum* by Helmut Gernsheim, Renate and L. Fritz Gruber and others, Cologne 1981, London 1982; *Lichtbildnisse: Das Porträt in der Fotografie,* edited by Klaus Honnef, Cologne 1982; *Wir— Fotografen sehen die Bundesrepublik* by J. Bostrom and R. Gruebling, Frankfurt 1984. **Articles**—"Benjamin" by Fritz Kempe in *Foto Prisma* (Dusseldorf), July 1962; "Robert Lebeck" by Fritz Kempe in *Leica Fotografie* (Frankfurt), March 1963; "Star Photographer" by Derek Stevens in *International Yearbook,* London 1967; "Reportage: Robert Lebeck" by Mary Thomas in *U.S. Camera World Annual,* New York 1968; "Robert Lebeck" by Fritz Kempe in *Foto Magazine* (Munich), June 1970; "Robert Lebeck" by Georg Stefan Troller in *Westermann* (Braunschweig, West Germany), May 1977; "Robert Lebeck" by Fritz Kempe in *Foto Magazine* (Munich), January 1980; "Robert Lebeck" by Fritz Kempe in *Photo* (Munich), June 1981; "Reportagefotografie—Ästhetik zwischen Zufall und Geschichte: Fotografien von Robert Lebeck" by Roland Gross in *Kunstforum International* (Cologne), January 1985; "Foto: Robert Lebeck" by Heinrich Jaenecke in *Stern,* 46, 1991; "Zeitzeuge mit der Kamera" by Michael Koetzle in *Foto Szene,* 6, 1991; "Robert Lebeck covers the world. Germany's most famous photojournalist looks back" by Alex Farnsworth in *Photo District News* (New York), August 1992.

*

I am a journalist.

—Robert Lebeck

*   *   *

Among German photographers of the last quarter of a century there is scarcely another whose notions about pictures have been so influenced by the globe itself, a model of which Robert Lebeck received as a gift when he was eight years old. There are few countries that Lebeck does not know and from which, sooner or later, he has not brought back photographs that have become famous. Seen from today's perspective, Lebeck's progress from unknown to sought-after photographer now seems logical, despite all the leaps and changes: the progression seems logical, that is, from a study of ethnology, to activity for the press in the province of Heidelberg and for an illustrated

***Churchill in Bonn,* 1956.** Photograph by Robert Lebeck.

magazine in Frankfurt, to the Hamburg Press Centre. Hamburg is now his fixed station; it is also an ideal place for him to leave from on his travels and a place to which he gladly returns.

Lebeck's curiosity about the world could have caused him to become a successful ethnologist. That he did not he owes to an American government order to report for the Korean War, which he escaped by returning to Europe in 1951. In the early 50s, not averse to hard work in less attractive fields, he gained experience not only as a photoreporter and editor in all its facets but also, when necessary, as a railway engine cleaner and kitchen hand. His character is now marked by an assurance and matter-of-factness in relation to differing metiers, by a tranquillity born of assurance and an assurance born of tranquillity in the quick reaction to an unrepeatable moment. Lebeck's vision combines practicality and the capacity for artistic perception. His fascination with the instant keeps him from excessive clarity; his aesthetic preserves his "snapshots" from obsolescence.

His almost nonchalant candor about the world as it is determines his choice of themes and motifs. Even his most penetrating pictures, his most serious themes, remain free from pathos. Lebeck catches the greatness of a moment in the portrayal of an unpretentious surprising detail. His most famous picture to date (accompanying this entry) is valid as an example of his photography:

during the Congo's celebration of independence an African snatches away the Belgian king's sabre, and the childlike action of the unknown man makes world history visible and concrete.

And, indeed, Lebeck, with his remarkable flair for events, has often been able to catch that moment of which photojournalists dream. But sometimes, because of late editorial decisions or other circumstances, he has arrived (according to reporter's rules) "too late"—yet the pictures he then achieves show that though Lebeck's talent may respond to the actual event, it is not wholly dependent on some crucial instant—for example, there is his photo of Chou en Lai dancing at the end of a party or his photo of onlookers clambering up walls to get a glimpse of the coffin of the dead Pope. He reacts to the right moment; he reacts just as decisively to its "future"—in either case, without ever losing his composure.

Georg Stefan Troller, with whom Lebeck travelled to Alaska and the South Seas in 1966-67, said of his friend that he is not a man for posterity. The comment may be just, particularly if one considers Lebeck's negligent treatment of his own photographs, which he has never arranged methodically. It is not, however, true of his treatment of the photos of others. Since 1967 he has collected photographs, initially picture postcards (his collection now numbers about 20,000), then unpretentious pictures that gave permanence to particular moments, and still later he concentrated on the early days of photography: in this work, he shows a pronounced flair and a feeling for quality. He has exhibited these photos in Hamburg, and plans an exquisitely printed series of monographs on his collection.

The third sphere that Lebeck commands to perfection is that of editor. When in the late 50s he ran the Frankfurt office of the illustrated magazine *Revue,* he took the photographs, developed and printed them, sought out topical themes, wrote texts, and concerned himself with layout. He made use of this training when he took over the chief editorship of the magazine *GEO.*

Another facet of the man is that he is in constant association with modern art, with painters and sculptors as well as photographers. This interest has persisted from his student days in New York, when he was a constant visitor to the Museum of Modern Art, up to the present: his wife Elke Droescher runs a gallery in Hamburg. It may be that contemporary art, in all its facets, is a decisive correction in all of Lebeck's work and activities.

—Heinz Spielmann

LEE, Russell.

Nationality: American. **Born:** Ottawa, Illinois, 21 July 1903. **Education:** Attended the Culver Military Academy, Indiana, 1917-21; studied chemistry at Lehigh University, Bethlehem, Pennsylvania, 1921-25, and painting at the California School of Fine Arts, now the San Francisco Art Institute, 1929-31, and, under John Sloan, Art Students League, New York, 1931-35; self-taught in photography. **Military Service:** Served as reconnaissance photographer, and Head of the Still Picture Section, United States Army Air Transport Command Overseas Technical Unit, 1943-45. **Family:** Married Doris Emrick in 1927 (divorced, 1939); married Jean Smith in 1939. **Career:** Worked for Certainteed Products Company, Marseilles, Illinois, 1925-29; manager of the Certainteed Roofing Company in Kansas City, Missouri, 1929; independent painter, California and New York, 1929-35; Staff Photographer, under Roy E. Stryker, Historical Section of the Resettlement Administration, later the Farm Security Administration, Washington, D.C. and throughout the United States, 1936-42; Photographer, Office of War Information, throughout the U.S., 1941-42; Medical Report Photographer, Coal Mines Administration, Department of the Interior, Washington, D.C., 1946-47; industrial and magazine photographer, 1947-65; independent photographer, 1965 until his death in 1986. Director, 1949-56, and Instructor, 1956-76, University of Missouri Photo Workshop, Columbia; Instructor in Photography, University of Texas at Austin, 1965-73. **Died:** (in Austin, Texas) 28 August 1986.

Individual Exhibitions:

1965   *Russell Lee: Retrospective Exhibition 1934-1964,* University of Texas at Austin (travelled to the Witte Museum, San

Antonio, Texas, 1965, and the Smithsonian Institution, Washington, D.C., 1966)
1978   Witkin Gallery, New York (retrospective)
1979   Brookdale Community College, Lincroft, New Jersey
1980   *Pie Town, New Mexico,* Side Gallery, Newcastle upon Tyne, England
1986   *Vintage Work of the 30s and 40s,* Silver Image Gallery, Seattle, Washington

Selected Group Exhibitions:

1938   *International Photographic Exposition,* Grand Central Palace, New York
1962   *The Bitter Years,* Museum of Modern Art, New York
1967   *Photography in the 20th Century,* National Gallery of Canada, Ottawa (toured Canada and the United States, 1967-73)
1974   *Photography in America,* Whitney Museum, New York
1976   *A Vision Shared: The F.S.A.,* Witkin Gallery, New York
1979   *Images de l'Amérique en Crise: Photos de la F.S.A.,* Centre Georges Pompidou, Paris
         Photographie als Kunst 1879-1979/Kunst als Photographie 1949-1979, Tiroler Landesmuseum Ferdinandeum, Innsbruck, Austria (travelled to the Neue Galerie am Wolfgang Gurlitt Museum, Linz, Austria; Neue Galerie am Landesmuseum Joanneum, Graz, Austria; Museum des 20. Jahrhunderts, Vienna)
1981   *Farbe im Photo,* Josef-Haubrich-Kunsthalle, Cologne
1982   *Floods of Light,* The Photographers' Gallery, London (toured Britain)
1983   *Roy Stryker, USA 1943-50,* International Center of Photography, New York

Collections:

Museum of Fine Arts, Boston; Library of Congress, Washington, D.C.; National Archives, Washington, D.C.; University of Louisville, Kentucky; Museum of Fine Arts, St. Petersburg, Florida; University of Minnesota, Minneapolis; University of Texas at Austin; Center for Creative Photography, University of Arizona, Tucson; Amarillo Art Center, Texas; San Antonio Museum of Art, Texas.

Publications:

By LEE: Books—*A Medical Survey of the Bituminous Coal Industry,* with others, edited by J.T. Boone, Washington, D.C. 1947; *Image of Italy,* with text by William Arrowsmith, Austin, Texas 1960; *Executive Order 9066: The Internment of 110,00 Japanese Americans,* with text by Maisie Conrat and Richard Conrat, San Francisco 1972. **Article**—"An Interview with Russell Lee," with Rob Powell, in the *British Journal of Photography* (London), 10 October 1980.

On LEE: Books—*Russell Lee: Retrospective Exhibition 1934-1964,* exhibition catalogue, Austin, Texas 1965; *Photography in the 20th Century* by Nathan Lyons, New York 1967; *Portrait of a Decade: Roy Stryker and the Development of Documentary Photography in the 30s* by F. Jack Hurley, Baton Rouge, Louisiana 1972, New York 1977; *The Years of Bitterness and Pride: F.S.A. Photographs 1935-1943,* compiled by Jerry Kearns and Leroy Bellamy, edited by Hiag Akmakjian, New York 1975; *A Vision Shared: A Classic Portrait of America and Its People 1935-1943,* edited by Hank O'Neal, New York and London 1976; *Documenta 6/Band 2,* exhibition catalogue, by Klaus Honnef and Evelyn Weiss, Kassel and Cologne 1977; *Russell Lee: Photographer* by F. Jack Hurley, New York 1978; *Amerika Fotografie 1920-1940* by Erika Billeter, Berne 1979; *A Ten Year Salute* by Lee D. Witkin, with a foreword by Carol Brown, Danbury, New Hampshire 1979; *Les Années Ameres de l'Amérique en Crise 1935-1942,* exhibition catalogue, by Jean Dieuzaide, Toulouse 1980; *Floods of Light: Flash Photography 1851-1981,* exhibition catalogue, edited by Rupert Martin, London 1982; *Roy Stryker: USA, 1943-1950* by Steven W. Plattner, Austin, Texas 1983; *Dust Bowl Descent* by Bill Ganzel, Lincoln, Nebraska 1984. **Articles**—

"Pie Town, New Mexico: Photos by Russell Lee" in *U.S. Camera* (New York), October 1941; "Image of Italy" by William Arrowsmith in *Texas Quarterly* (Austin), no. 4, 1961; "Russell Lee" by F. Jack Hurley in *Image* (Rochester, New York), September 1973; "Russell Lee: Pie Town" in *Creative Camera* (London), July/August 1980.

*

I have been primarily concerned with documenting the social scene at a particular time and place. Ideally, the resulting, captioned photographs should be part of a file accessible to all people. Prints from the original negatives should be available for a small fee.

The Farm Security Administration File in the Library of Congress, Washington, D.C. and the Photographic Files of the National Archives, Washington, D.C., are such examples.

—Russell Lee (1982)

* * *

When Russell Lee joined the Historical Section of the Resettlement Administration (later the Farm Security Administration) in 1936 he had been taking photographs for only a year or two. Trained as a chemical engineer, he became interested in painting and, finding himself to be weak in the skills of draughtsmanship, he bought a 35mm. Contax camera which he intended to use as an aid to drawing. But photography moved from being adjunct to painting to the central and most important means of expression for Lee. By the time he left the FSA Lee had not only taken more photographs than any other member of the Section, he had also laid down the foundation of his approach to the task of documentary photography. He had created a notable body of work and established a reputation that was to grow with the years into the recognition that he is a major figure in the development of American documentary photography.

Roy Stryker, the director of the Historical Section of the FSA, created, with a comparatively small amount of financial assistance from the government, an organization which allowed a number of very important photographers to function and develop. Stryker's personal contribution to this exercise cannot be overlooked, and many people have testified to the importance of his influence. However, no one man no matter how dedicated and inspired could have "produced" Walker Evans, Dorothea Lange, Arthur Rothstein, Russell Lee, et al in other circumstances or in another society. The conditions of social, economic and cultural life in the U.S.A. in the 1930s have been written about in great detail, and no account of Lee's work can ignore the nature of that society or the institutional form through which his early, and shaping, work was achieved.

Especially in Germany, Britain and the U.S.A. the 30s were a very fruitful period for the development of new forms of documentary expression. Poverty and injustice were endemic, but they co-existed alongside wealth, power, and a growing confidence and affluence of certain sections of these societies. The task of the FSA photographer was to record the way of life and condition of certain groups within American society. They were expected to travel around the country, especially in those areas most damaged and broken, and return to Washington evidence which would flesh out the statistics and "objective" accounts of social scientists. This they all did; what the best of them did also was to find new visual forms through which poverty, suffering and human dignity in the face of extreme hardship could be represented. In the process they changed the nature of documentary photography, but more importantly they made visible formerly hidden aspects of American life.

In this process Lee played an extremely important part, yet his work is still not as well-known as that of some of his colleagues at the FSA, such as Walker Evans or Dorothea Lange. One reason for this is that Russell Lee never organized his work around the concept of producing a single striking photograph which would act as a crystallization, a visual summation of a scene or a situation. Rather than imposing meaning on reality by means of a single dramatic photograph, Lee teases meaning out of the appearance of things. In his very informative book, *Russell Lee Photographer,* F. Jack Hurley has written: "Once in a great while, a photographer comes along whose work is so objective and precise that it can almost be called transparent. That is, it represents what existed in front of the camera with very little intrusion by the photographer. Russell Lee's work has often had this quality of transparency."

We know what Hurley means here, for Lee's best photographs do display that shock of apparently unmediated authenticity that all great documentary photographs possess. At the same time we must remember that such works are the product of human skill and artifice, that there is no way of peeling off a photograph directly from reality, only ways of creating images from the available elements of the real world.

Lee's great power as a photographer arises out of the way in which he relates to the subjects of his photographs. We never feel that they have been caught unfairly off-guard, or that the camera lens is functioning as an unwelcome intruder on a scene. Instead, Lee involves himself closely with his subjects and presents us with images that unpick the essence of a task, a moment, a relationship, then re-presents them to us transformed and newly integrated in a way that neither appropriates their uniqueness into a solemn statement about the "human condition" nor loses their sense of transcending the particularity of immediate time and place within which they were taken. There is a quality of calm and of apparent simplicity in many of Lee's images which produces in the spectator a special, often emotionally charged, knowledge about the meaning of things.

This ability of Russell Lee's is the product of great technical skill—an ability to relate to people and a very special way of seeing the world. It makes him a magnificent photographer of community, of the lived relationships between people. But this excellence is not to be found only in his early work. After the war Lee worked for Standard Oil as an industrial photographer, and much of this later work is marked by the same qualities—as is the great body of work produced after that time in several countries and many places.

—Derrick Price

LEIPZIG, Arthur.

Nationality: American. **Born:** Brooklyn, New York, 25 October 1918. **Education:** Attended Erasmus Hall High School, Brooklyn; studied photography, under Sid Grossman, 1942, and Paul Strand, 1946, at the Photo League, New York. **Family:** Married Mildred Levin in 1942; children: Joel and Judith. **Career:** Photographer since 1942: Photography Assignment Editor, 1942, and Staff Photographer, 1942-46, *PM* newspaper, Long Island, New York; freelance press photographer and photojournalist, New York, since 1947. Member, Photo League, New York, 1942-49. Professor of Art and Director of Photography, C.W. Post College, Long Island University, Greenvale, New York, 1968-1990. Professor of Art Emeritus since 1991. Member, Editorial Board, *Infinity* magazine, New York, 1960-63. Member, Fine Arts Board, Nassau County Museum, Long Island, New York, 1973-75; Member, Board of Directors, Long Island Baroque Ensemble, 1978-80. **Recipient:** National Urban League Photography Award, 1962; Annual Art Directors Award, New York, 1969; Research Grant, Long Island University, 1979, 1980; Exhibition Grant, Nassau County Office of Cultural Development, 1981; Cablevision Grant, New York, 1981; Scholarly Achievement Award, Long Island University, 1983 and 1989; David Newton Excellence in Teaching Award, 1989. **Address:** 378 Glen Avenue, Sea Cliff, New York 11579, U.S.A.

Individual Exhibitions:

1975	Nassau County Museum of Fine Art, Roslyn, Long Island, New York (retrospective)
1977	Midtown Y Gallery, New York
1980	Port Washington Library, New York
1982	*Photographs of Jewish Life Around the World,* Nassau County Museum of Fine Art, Roslyn, Long Island, New York
1983	Handwerker Gallery, Ithaca College, New York
	Bass Museum of Fine Art, New York
1984	*Falasha Photos,* Black History Museum, New York
1986	Henry Street Settlement House, New York
1989	*Arthur Leipzig, A Retrospective,* Hillwood Museum
1990	*Arthur Leipzig's New York,* Photofind Gallery, New York
	Arthur Leipzig's People, Frumkin/Adams Gallery
1992	*Arthur Leipzig, Color Photography,* Frumkin/Adams Gallery

Arthur Leipzig Photographs, Salena Gallery
1994   *Arthur Leipzig: Photographs,* Port Washington Library,
         New York

Selected Group Exhibitions:

1946   *New Faces,* Museum of Modern Art, New York
1955   *The Family of Man,* Museum of Modern Art, New York (and
         world tour)
1961   *Photography in the Fine Arts,* Metropolitan Museum of Art,
         New York (and *Photography in the Fine Arts,* 1962)
1967   *Man and His World,* at Expo '67, Montreal
1978   *Photographic Crossroads: The Photo League,* National Gallery
         of Canada, Ottawa (travelled to the International Center of
         Photography, New York; Museum of Fine Arts, Houston;
         and Minneapolis Institute of Arts)
1979   *Urban Open Spaces,* Cooper-Hewitt Museum, New York
1983   *Farmers,* Museum of the Diaspora, Tel Aviv
1985   *Americans at Work,* Transco Gallery, Houston, Texas
1986   *Street Photography,* Daniel Wolf Gallery, New York
         The Jews of Ethiopia, Jewish Museum, New York
1987   *Generations,* Smithsonsian, Washington, D.C.
1989   *The Cherished Image: Portraits from 150 Years of Photogra-
         phy,* The National Gallery of Canada
         150th Anniversary of the Invention of Photography, Manes
         Gallery, Prague, Czech Republic
         History of Photography from California Collections, San
         Francisco Museum of Modern Art
1990   *Games,* Musee De La Civilisation, Quebec City
1992   *The Sporting Life,* High Musuem, Atlanta, Georgia
         ASMP 10,000 eyes, International Center of Photography,
         New York
1994   *Stickball,* Museum of the City of New York

Collections:

Museum of Modern Art, New York; Midtown Y Gallery, New York; Brook-
lyn Museum, New York; International Museum of Photography, George
Eastman House, Rochester, New York; Visual Studies Workshop, Rochester,
New York; Museum of Fine Arts, Houston; National Gallery of Canada,
Ottawa; Pablo Casals Museum, San Juan, Puerto Rico; International Center of
Photography, New York; Nassau Museum of Fine Art, Roslyn, Long Island,
New York; The National Portrait Gallery, Washington, D.C.; National Muse-
um of American Art, Washington, D.C.; The Jewish Museum, New York;
Photography Study Center, Art Institute of Chicago; Brooklyn Public Library,
New York; Long Island University; Bibliotheque Nationale, Paris, France;
Museum Folkwang, Essen, Germany; Consolidated Freightways Collection,
San Francisco, CA; Bank of America Art Program, San Francisco, CA;
Queens College, Queens, New York.

Publications:

By LEIPZIG: Articles—"Old Africa's 'People of the Village' " in *Natural
History Magazine* (New York), April and May 1964; "Arthur Leipzig,"
interview, in *Documentary Photography,* New York 1973; "The Enclave of
Ancianos: An Andean Shangri-La" in *Hospital Practice* (New York),
October 1973; "Six Great Teachers Tell How They Work" in *Popular
Photography* (New York), Summer 1974; "Photography and Social Change"
in *Ventures in Research,* edited by Richard R. Griffith, New York 1979;
"They're Called The Strangers," photo-essay, with text by Sidney C.
Schaefer, in *Newsday* (New York), 8 July 1980.

On LEIPZIG: Books—*The Family of Man,* edited by Edward Steichen, New
York 1955; *Photographic Crossroads: The Photo League* by Anne Tucker,
New York 1978; *New York Street Kids,* with texts by Victor Remer and John
von Harz, New York 1978. **Articles**—"Arthur Leipzig, Photographer" by
Malcolm Preston in *Newsday* (New York), 13 February 1980; "Striking a

Delicate Balance" by David L. Shirey in the *New York Times,* 24 February 1980.

*

For me, photography is an exciting way of making order out of a chaotic
world. Using my camera both as a connection to, and a separation from, the
world, I have been able to observe the world and myself. Photography has
helped me learn much about both.

I have been concerned mainly with exploring the human condition and
human relationships. People are always changing. Photographing them is a
challenge. I am not an intellectual photographer; my images are visceral
responses to the world. However, I study my prints very closely. What I have
done on a pre-conscious level—composition, content, etc.—must be
understood on a conscious level. Only through such a process can I grow. My
work is straightforward and direct. I use no gimmicks or trendy styles to shock
and overwhelm the viewer. If I can communicate my sensitivity to others, if I
can make them see and feel, some of the things I see and feel, then I am
satisfied.

—Arthur Leipzig

*   *   *

Styles in music, art and literature which achieve immediate and enormous
fame frequently fall into disrepute with the next generation of writers,
composers and artists. It is natural and necessary for the next generation to
rebel. Whether or not a style—once discredited—receives attention from
subsequent generations is the true test of its value.

Many of the photographs and photographers which appeared in Edward
Steichen's exhibition *The Family of Man* have been in obligatory eclipse and
are now receiving renewed interest and appreciation. The sweetness of those
pictures and the photographers' compassion toward their subject have been
very much out of fashion for two decades. To say that Arthur Leipzig's work
has been in eclipse is not to imply that he hasn't been working—making new
photographs, exhibiting and publishing his work. It's just that his style of
photography has generally been ignored by the major museums and art
photography magazines in the existentialist, art-for-art's sake decades.

Leipzig is a photojournalist and a teacher. He resists labeling his photographic style, but documentary is the label applied most often. It is the most
appropriate label because collecting evidence is an important part of the
photographic process for Leipzig. But he considers it is even more important
to clearly state his feelings about what he documents.

As a beginning photographer in 1942, Leipzig joined the Photo League, a
group of amateur and professional documentary photographers that existed in
New York City between 1936-1951. He was attracted by the League's low
school fees and darkroom fees and enrolled in Sid Grossman's class in
documentary photography. "Two weeks in Sid's Class," Leipzig said in an
interview, "and I knew what I wanted to be. I photograph the way I feel, and
the League helped me to learn to do that."

He was an active member of the League until 1949, serving on various
committees and teaching in the school. In the spring of 1949 he was one of the
League members admitted to an advanced photography class taught by Paul
Strand. Strand's discipline regarding craftsmanship and composition were an
important influence. The other great influence from the Photo League was W.
Eugene Smith, especially Smith's war pictures. "Smith caught me with much
more feeling than any other photographer had up to that time. I loved Cartier-
Bresson's work, but he never got to me in that emotional way as Smith did."

Leipzig left the League because the success of his free lance career
demanded more and more of his time. As a free lance photographer he has
traveled through the Arabic countries, to India, Africa, South America and the
Arctic. Like most serious journalists, when he travels he makes photographs
for his clients and makes other pictures for himself. He also photographs his
family and the people of Long Island where he lives and teaches.

His photographs are emotive, generous, and frequently humorous.

—Anne W. Tucker

LEITER, Saul.

Nationality: American. **Born:** Pittsburgh, Pennsylvania, 3 December 1923. **Education:** Attended schools in Pittsburgh, Vienna, New York and at Cleveland Theological College, which he left in 1946, moving to New York City to become a painter. **Career:** Worked with abstract expressionist painter Richard Pousette-Dart, whose experiments with photography encouraged Leiter to explore its potential. Street photographer since 1947, including extensive body of 35mm colour work. Exhibited paintings at Tanager Gallery and Samuel Kootz Gallery in the 1950s. Photographed widely for magazines from 1957, including *Esquire, Harper's Bazaar, Queen, Vogue, Nova, Elle, Vanity Fair, Show.* **Agent:** Howard Greenberg Gallery, 120 Wooster Street, New York 10012. **Address:** 111 East 10th Street, New York 10003, U.S.A.

Selected Individual Exhibitions:

1944	Ten Thirty Gallery, Cleveland, Ohio
1984	Gallery Lafayette, New York
1993	*Photographs 1945-1970,* Howard Greenberg Gallery, New York

Selected Group Exhibitions:

1945	Outlines Gallery, Pittsburgh
1947	*Abstract and Surrealist Art,* Art Institute of Chicago
1953	*Always the Young Stranger,* Museum of Modern Art, New York
1991	*Appearances,* Victoria and Albert Museum, London
1994	*Outside Fashion,* Howard Greenberg Gallery, New York

Collections:

Art Institute of Chicago; Museum of Modern Art, New York; Victoria and Albert Museum, London.

Publications:

On LEITER: Books—*Appearances: Fashion Photography Since 1945,* exhibition catalogue, Martin Harrison, London and New York 1991; *The New York School: Photographs 1936-1963,* by Jane Livingston, New York 1992. **Articles**—"Saul Leiter: Souvenirs" by Laurence Wieder in *Camera Arts,* Nov/Dec 1981; "Saul Leiter Rediscovered" by Martin Harrison in *The Correspondent Magazine,* 12 November 1989; "Shadows and Fog" by Vince Aletti in *Voice,* 9 February 1992.

*　*　*

Only Saul Leiter's disdain for self-promotion can account for the fact that it was not until the 1990s that his contribution to photography began to receive the recognition it deserved. But although his remarkable body of "street" photographs, begun in 1947, has now been positioned as an important aspect of the "New York School," its affinities with other products of the "school" scarcely extend beyond their common geography. Where students of Alexey Brodovitch aimed for graphic impact for example, Leiter's photographs, notwithstanding their considerable compositional qualities, are more notable for their reticence, intimacy and quiet lyricism—the result of an oblique, humane but apolitical vision. Unique to him is an extensive corpus of street photography in colour, dating largely from the 1940s/50s. It is especially in these photographs that the relationship with his paintings is evident, in their carefully restricted colour range and subtle combinations of hues; often, as he himself explains, "the colour as much as anything else, is the subject of the photograph."

Leiter cites among early inspirations in photography (in addition to his friendships with painter Richard Pousette-Dart and photographer W. Eugene Smith), Kertesz's book *Day of Paris* (1946) and Cartier-Bresson's 1947 exhibition at the Museum of Modern Art, New York. But he was also "impervious to good advice" and was largely self-taught in photography; he succeeded in forging his own language as a photographer, combining an innate feeling for abstraction with an empathetic and non-judgmental psychological awareness.

In 1952 Leiter opened a small studio, which he mostly used for portraits or the occasional advertising commission. His professional career took off in 1957 when he received his first commission from Henry Wolf, art director of *Esquire.* When Wolf replaced Brodovitch at *Harper's Bazaar* in the following year Leiter was soon established as a leading fashion photographer in the U.S. His influence extended to Europe in the 1960s, and was particularly strong in Britain, where he did distinguished work, both fashion and features, for *Queen* and *Nova.*

Leiter abandoned commercial photography in 1982, though he returned to take widely acclaimed portfolios for *Comme des Garcons* (1990) and *Alberto Aspesi* (1991). Instead he has concentrated both on painting and his personal photography, which he continues to pursue on an almost daily basis.

—Martin Harrison

LEMIEUX, Annette.

Nationality: American. **Born:** Norfolk, Virginia, in 1957. **Education:** Graduated from Hartford Art School, Connecticut, in 1980. **Recipient:** Temple Beth El Sisterhood Award, West Hartford, Connecticut, 1980; Anna Ball Pierce Award, Hartford Art School, 1981; National Endowment for the Arts Drawing Grant, 1983; Pollack/Krasner Foundation Grant, 1986; New York Fellowship for Painting, 1987; National Endowment for the Arts Painting Grant, 1987 and 1991; Mies van der Rohe Stipendium, Kaiser Wilhelm Museum, Krefeld, Germany, 1992; Moonhole Artists Residency, Charles Englehard Foundation, 1994; declined the Bunting Fellowship at Radcliffe College, Harvard University, 1994. **Address:** 228 Winchester Street, Brookline, MA 02146.

Individual Exhibitions:

1980	Joseloff Gallery, Hartford Art School, Connecticut
1984	*3 Artists Select 3 Artists,* Artists Space, New York
	Cash/Newhouse, New York
1986	Cash/Newhouse, New York
1987	Josh Baer Gallery, New York
	Cash/Newhouse, New York
	Daniel Weinberg Gallery, Los Angeles
1988	Lisson Gallery, London
	Matrix Gallery, Wadsworth Atheneum, Hartford, Connecticut
	Rhona Hoffman Gallery, Chicago
1989	Josh Baer Gallery, New York
	The John and Mable Ringling Museum, Sarasota, Florida
	Center for the Fine Arts, Miami
	The New Museum, New York
1990	Galerie Monika Sprüth, Cologne
	Rhona Hoffman Gallery, Chicago
	La Maquina Espanola, Seville
	Mario Diacono Gallery, Boston
1991	Josh Baer Gallery, New York
	Galerie Montenay, Paris
1992	Stichting De Appel, Amsterdam
	Castello di Rivoli, Museo d'Arte Contemporanea, Rivoli
1993	*Work in Editions,* Brooke Alexander Editions, New York
	Josh Baer Gallery, New York
1994	*The Matter of History: Selected Work by Annette Lemieux,* Davis Museum and Cultural Center, Wellesley College, MA

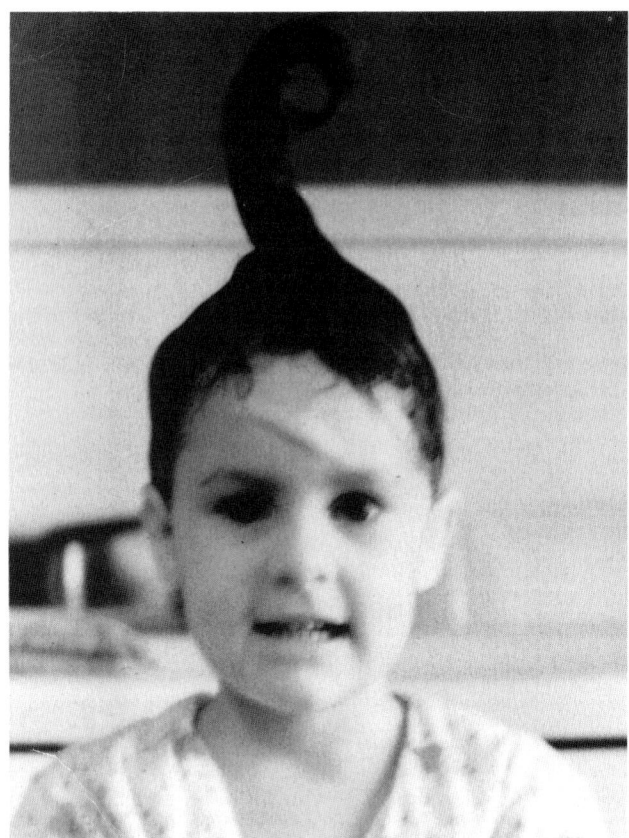 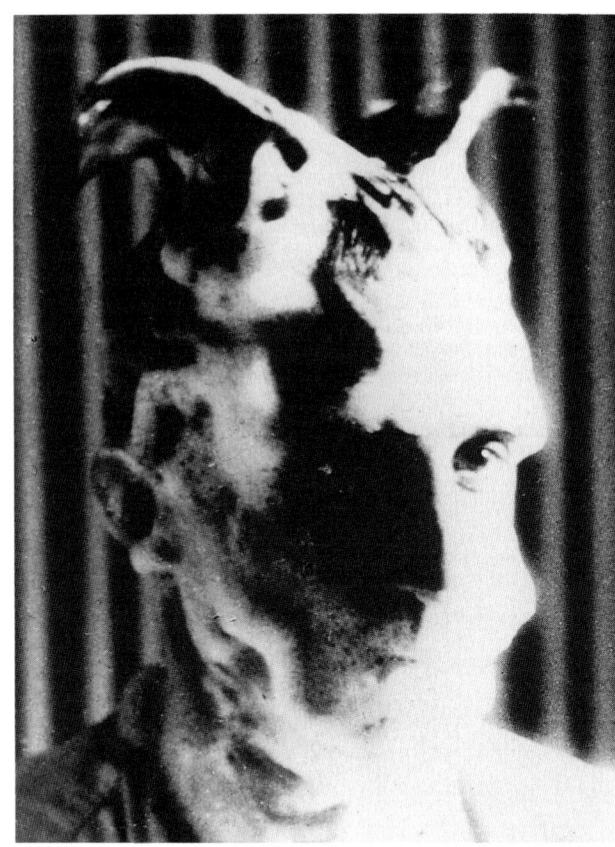

Coincidence, **Dyptich, 1993/94 (left image, original in colour; right image, black and white)** Photographs by Annette Lemieux.

(travelled to Duke University Museum of Art, Durham NC
and Washington University, St Louis, Missouri)
Kaiser Wilhelm Museum, Haus Esters, Krefeld, Germany
Emilio Mazzoli, Galleria d'Arte Contemporania, Modena

Selected Group Exhibitions:

1979   *Hartford Arts Festival,* Hartford, Connecticut
1980   *Beth El Temple Annual Exhibition,* West Hartford, Connecticut
1982   *Contemporary Shields Show,* Gallery des Refuse, New York
1983   *Image Letante,* Alain Bildhaud Gallery, New York
1984   *Symbols Cliche,* A&M Gallery, New York
1985   *Benefit Show,* White Columns, New York
        A Brave New World, A New Generation, Charlottenborg
          Exhibition Hall, Copenhagen (travelled to Lundmuselim,
          Lund, Sweden)
1986   *Currents,* Institute of Contemporary Art, Boston
        Ultrasurd, S.L. Simpson Gallery, Toronto
1987   *1987 Biennial Exhibition,* Whitney Museum of American Art,
          New York
        Extreme Order, Lia Ruma Galerie, Naples
        Coleccion Sonnabend, Centro d'Arte Reina Sofia, Ministerio de
          Cultura, Madrid
1988   *Cultural Geometry,* House of Cyprus, Athens
        Reprises de Vues, Halle Sud/Geneve, Geneva
        Art at the End of the Social, Rooseum, Malmo
        The Binational, The Institute of Contemporary Art, Museum of
          Fine Arts, Boston (travelled to Stadtische Kunsthalle,
          Dusseldorf)
1989   *Prospect '89,* Schirnkunsthalle, Frankfurt

The Silent Baroque, Villa Arenburg, Salzburg
*The Photography of Invention—American Pictures of the
  1980s,* National Museum of American Art, Smithsonian
  Institution, Washington, D.C.
INFAS: 7 Artists, The Space, Hanae Mori Foundation, Tokyo
Image World: Art and Media Culture, Whitney Museum of
  American Art, New York
1990   *All Quiet on the Western Front?,* Galerie Antoine
          Candau, Paris
        A Vint Minuts De Paris, Galeria Joan Prats, Barcelona
        Aperto '90, The Venice Biennale
        Woman Artists of the Day, IMPO, Osaka
        Mind over Matter: Concept and Object, Whitney Museum of
          American Art, New York
        Life-Size: A Sense of the Real in Recent Art, The Israel
          Museum, Jerusalem
1991   *The Sibylline Eye,* Munich Kunsthalle, Germany
        Vertigo II, Galerie Thaddeus Ropac, Salzburg
        Inscapes, Foundation De Appel, Amsterdam
1992   *More Than One Photography,* The Museum of Modern Art,
          New York
        Post Human, Castello di Rivoli, Museo d'Arte Contemporanea,
          Rivoli (travelled to Deste Foundation for Contemporary Art,
          Athens; Deichtorhallen Hamburg; The Israel Museum,
          Jersulem)
1993   *Druksache (Prints & Issues),* Kunst-Werke, Berlin
        Photoplay: Works from the Chase Manhattan Collection,
          Center for the Fine Arts, Miami (travelled to Museo
          Amparo, Puebla, Mexico; Museo de Arte Contemporaneo de
          Monterrey, Monterrey, Mexico; Centro Cultural Consolidado,
          Caracas; Museo de Arte de Sao Paulo, Brazil; Museo

Nacional de Bellas Artes, Buenos Aires; Museo Nacional de Bellas Artes, Santiago)
1994   *Minela Dopitova In Context,* The Institute of Contemporary Art, Boston

Collections:

Castello di Rivoli, Italy; Chase Manhattan Bank, New York; Dannheisser Foundation, New York; DESTE Foundation for Contemporary Art, Athens, Geneva, New York; Fisher Landau Center, New York; Guggenheim Museum, New York; Israel Museum, Jerusalem; Milwaukee Art Museum, WI; Museum of Contemporary Art, Chicago; Oklahoma Art Museum, Oklahoma City; Rooseum, Malmo, Sweden; The Museum of Fine Arts, Boston; The Museum of Modern Art, New York; The Whitney Museum of American Art, New York; Wadsworth Atheneum, Hartford, CT; Washington University Art Gallery, St Louis; Yale University Art Gallery, New Haven; Wesleyan University Art Gallery, Connecticut; Fogg Museum, Harvard University, Cambridge, MA; Olin Arts Center, Bates College, Lewiston, ME.

Publications:

By LEMIEUX: Book—*Memoirs of a Survivor,* ZG Publications 1989. **Article**—"Sonnet" in *Artscribe,* Summer 1987.

On LEMIEUX: Books—*Interpreting Contemporary Art,* IconEditions 1991; *500 Contemporary Artists,* MM Editions, France 1993; *Annette Lemieux,* Kyoto Shoin, ArT Random 1990; *Unexpressionism: Art Beyond the Contemporary* by Germano Celant, Rizzoli Editions 1988; *The History of Art* by H.W. Janson, New York 1991. **Articles**—"Odd Lots" by Walter Robinson in *East Village Eye,* December 1984; "Eluding Definition" by Kate Linker in *Artforum,* December 1984; "57 Between A & D," by Ron Warren in *ARTS Magazine,* April 1985; "Deconstructing" by Beth Biegler in *East Village Eye,* July 1985; "Neutral Trends" by Collins and Milazzo in *East Village Eye,* October 1985; "Talking Back" by Gary Indiana in *The Village Voice,* 11 February 1986; "Formal Wares" by Gary Indiana in *The Village Voice,* 25 March 1986; "Time After Time" by Robert Mohoney in *ARTS Magazine,* March 1986; "Annette Lemieux at Cash/Newhouse" by Gary Indiana in *Art In America,* July 1986; "Space Fictions" by Rosetta Brooks in *Flash Art,* December 1986; *Bomb,* Winter 1987; "Vertical Dreams" by Marie Dyan in *C Magazine,* No. 12, 1987; "Art: Annette Lemieux in Two Mixed Media Shows" by Roberta Smith in *The New York Times,* 17 April 1987; "Art; Annette Lemieux" by Kim Levin in *The Village Voice,* 5 May 1987; "Annette Lemieux" by Monika Spruth in *Eau de Cologne,* November 1987; "Neo/Geo" in *Bijintsu Techno,* December 1987; "Annette Lemieux" by Ronald Jones in *Artscribe,* September/October 1987; "Lemieux Chooses Styles to Fit Concepts" by Alan G. Artner in *The Chicago Tribune,* 27 May 1988; "Blow Ups' Photo Album" by Edith Newhall in *New York Magazine,* 12 December 1988; "Annette Lemieux" by Michael Brenson in *The New York Times,* 31 March 1989; "Annette Lemieux" by Kim Levin in *The Village Voice,* 11 April 1989; "Annette Lemieux at Josh Baer Gallery" by Jack Bankowsky in *Artforum,* Summer 1989; "Annette Lemieux Solo Review" by Joshua Decter in *ARTS Magazine,* Summer 1989; "Annette Lemieux" by Richard Woodward in *Artnews,* September 1989; "Annette Lemieux at Josh Baer" by C. Roger Denson in *Artscribe,* September 1989; "Profile: Annette Lemieux" by Lois Tarlow in *Art New England,* June 1989; "Annette Lemieux" by Kirby Gookin in *Artform,* April 1990; "Found Experience: Annette Lemieux," conversation with Tricia Collins and Richard Milazzo in *Tema Celeste,* April-June 1990; "Annette Lemieux: Monika Spruth" by Jose Lebrero Stals in *Flash Art,* May/June 1990; "Annette Lemieux (Aperto '90 U.S.A.)" by Robert C. Morgan in *New Art International.* 1990; "The Interview: Annette Lemieux" by D.C. Denison in *The Boston Globe,* 26 August 1990; "An Interview with Annette Lemieux by Elizabeith Sussman" in *Noema,* September 1990; "Annette Lemieux" by Christian Leigh in *Contemporanea,* vol.3, no.4, April 1990; "Annette Lemieux, Rhona Hoffman Gallery" by Craig Adcock in *Terma Celeste,* November/December 1990; "Annette Lemieux" by Richard B. Woodward in *ARTnews,* Summer 1991; "Annette Lemieux, Stolen Faces" in *The Print Collector's Newsletter,* September 1991; "Annette Lemieux, Galerie Montenay" by Ami Barak in *Art Press,* December 1991; "Annette Lemieux at De Appel" by Renee Steenbergen in *NRC Handelsblad,* February 1992; "Annette Lemieux/Annette Messager" by Kim Levin in *The Village Voice,* 5

May 1992; "Annette Lemieux/Annette Messager" in *The New Yorker,* 11 May 1992; "Annette Lemieux and Annette Messager" by Holland Cotter in *The New York Times,* 24 April 1992; "Mostra di Annette Lemieux" in *Il Nord* (Italy), 3 December 1992; "Annette Lemieux at Castello di Rivoli" by Trevor Fairbrother in *Terza Pagina* (Bergamo), December 1992; "Annette l'Americana installa a Rivoli i suoi Mega-Collage sulle Guerre d'Oggi" by Francesco di Pasini in *Il Secolo,* 23 January 1993; "Review: Annette Lemieux at Castello di Rivoli" by Guido Curto in *Flash Art* (Milan), February 1993; "Annette Lemieux" by Holland Cotter in *The New York Times,* 2 April 1993; "The Photograph as Art Object" by Andy Grunberg in *Crisis of the Real: Writings on Photography 1974-89,* Aperture Foundation 1990. **Film**—*Mind Over Matter,* Michael Black Wood Productions 1991; videos—*American Art Today: A View from the Whitney 1987 Biennial Exhibition,* Whitney Museum of American Art 1987; *The 7 Artists: INFAS,* Fashion Video Library, Hanae Mori Foundation, The Space, Tokyo; *Art Today,* Vol. II, No. 1, Arts Video, News Service, New York.

*   *   *

Annette Lemieux is seldom considered as a photographer in any of the conventional senses. She works in painting, sculpture and the inter-media genre of conceptual art. Many of her sculptural/photographic pieces are installations more than discrete objects, and her use of photographic imagery is purely in terms of appropriation. Throughout the 1980s Lemieux received a great deal of critical attention for her style-less style, that is to say for a post-modern protean willingness to vary her materials and methods rather than to establish a trademark look for her work.

Lemieux's attention has been approximately equally divided between themes of history and of family. In each case, she harkens back to prior eras of more simply coded power relations. Whatever the subject, the look and finish of each piece is deliberately cool, even cold, in emotional terms. This quality is typical of the appropriation artists of her generation. What is untypical is her refusal of the often too-easy ironies of much post-modern work. But in place of the slick ironies or the strident critiques of her peers and colleagues like Richard Prince or Barbara Kruger, Lemieux's work substitutes no defined quality. Instead, there is an edgy reticence, a kind of blankness at the core of her work.

Some of her works include pieces of furniture, and others incorporate texts. Normally the photographic elements are cropped, captioned or strikingly juxtaposed as part of her aesthetic/critical strategy. For instance, *Mon Amour* of 1987 is a large and striking diptych composed of formally similar images of scattered dead bodies and of 1950s sunbathers at the beach. Here, the shocking pictorial propinquity of two normally segregated categories of history and experience scarcely needs the title to express its message, while in other pieces text is a more dominant element.

Lemieux's work has been widely acclaimed, particularly on the European scene. Truly less a photographer than many others of her cohort who "use photography," it is hard to say whether photographs will continue to be important source materials in her future work. Unlike Sherrie Levine, for instance, Lemieux's appropriations do not take the use and place of photographic images in twentieth century society as a primary subject. She's more interested in content and subject matter, message rather than medium.

—Ellen Handy

LENART, Branko.

Nationality: Austrian. **Born:** Ptuj, Yugoslavia, 15 June 1948; emigrated to Austria, 1954; naturalized, 1961. **Education:** Attended Oeversee Gymnasium, Graz, Austria, 1959-63; studied at the Teachers Training College, Graz, Austria, 1972-77; attended various photography workshops, with Duane Michals, Ralph Gibson, Mary Ellen Mark, Peter Schlessinger, and Lewis Baltz, Arles and Graz, 1976-80. **Military Service:** Served in the Austrian Army, 1967-68. **Family:** Married Friederike Mark in 1979. **Career:** Freelance photographer since 1972. Instructor, Pädagogische Institut, Graz, 1979-80. Instructor, Höhere Technische Bundes Lehranstalt, Graz, since 1979, and

From *Rome or Death*, **1990.** Photograph ©Branko Lenart.

Pädagogische Akademie, Graz, since 1980. Artist-in-Residence, Apeiron Workshops, Millerton, New York, 1980. **Recipient:** Obelisk Award, *Photokina,* Cologne, 1968; French Government Grant, 1973; Photography Grant, Styrian Government, Austria, 1976, 1979; Award for Instant Photography, Polaroid Austria, 1980; Photography Award, Ministry of Education and Art, Austria, 1983; Photography Award, Styrian Government, Austria, 1986; Rupertinum Award, 1988; Grant of the Ministry for Rome, 1990. **Agents:** Fotogalerie Forum Stadtpark, Stadtpark 1, A-8010 Graz. **Address:** Viktor-Kaplan-Gasse 25, A 8045 Graz, Austria.

Individual Exhibitions:

1973   *On the Road,* Ganggalerie im Rathaus, Graz, Austria (travelled to the Galerie im Taxispalais, Innsbruck, 1974)
         Frankreich Subjektiv, Institut Français, Graz, Austria
1975   *Mirrorgraphs,* Galleria Il Diaframma, Milan (travelled to the Fotogalerie Forum, Graz, Austria)
1976   *Selfportraits,* The Photographers' Gallery, London (travelled to the Fotogalerija, Koper, Yugoslavia, and Focus, Ljubljana, Yugoslavia, 1976; and Trockenpresse, West Berlin, and Photowerkstatt, Heddesheim, West Germany, 1977)
         Arles Workshops, Audiovisuelles Zentrum, Graz, Austria
1977   *Presenting Photographers,* Kulturhaus, Graz, Austria
1978   *Ausstellungsbesucher,* Kulturhaus, Graz, Austria
1979   *Seascapes,* Galerij Paule Pia, Antwerp (travelled to the Galerie Lang, Graz, Austria, 1980)

1981   Arhiv TD, Zagreb, Yugoslavia
         Kulturhaus, Graz, Austria
         Fotogalerie Forum Stadtpark, Graz, Austria
1982   Fotografis Landerbank, Vienna
1983   Salzburg College, Austria
         Kulturhaus, Graz, Austria
         Fotogalerie Forum Stadtpark, Graz, Austria
1984   Kulturzentrum bei den Minoriten, Graz, Austria
         Happy Gallery, Belgrade
1985   Fotogalerija, Novo Mesto, Yugoslavia
1988   *Subjektive Topographie,* Libreria Agora, Torino
1989   *Transponderation,* Galerie Faber, Wein
1991   *Wahr Genommen,* Kulturhaus, Graz; Rupertinum, Salzburg
1993   *Res Publica,* Urania, Graz

Selected Group Exhibitions:

1970   *Europäische Fotografen,* Palais Charlottenburg, West Berlin
1974   *Kreative Fotografie Österreich,* Museum des 20. Jahrhunderts, Vienna
1976   *Triennale de la Photographie,* Musée d'Art et Histoire, Fribourg, Switzerland
1977   *Leben mit der Stadt,* Kulturhaus, Graz, Austria
1978   *Hommage á Marcel Duchamp* Moderna Galerija, Ljubljana, Yugoslavia (travelled to the Collegium Artisticum, Sarajevo, Yugoslavia)

1980   *Metaphysical Presence,* Razstavišče Jacopič, Ljubljana, Yugoslavia (travelled to the Paviljon Zuzorič, Belgrade)
1981   *Fotografia Austriaca,* Consejo Mexicano de Fotografia, Mexico City
1983   *New Black-and-White West European Photography,* Northeastern University, Boston (toured the United States)
1985   *La Ciutat Fantasma,* Fundacio Joan Miro, Barcelona, Spain
1986   *Visages, Paysages,* Eiffel Tower, Paris
        Autoscatto, Forum Quattroruote, Torino
1988   *Sloveni Di Confine,* Centro Culturale Pubblico, Ronchi
1989   *Stadtpark Eins,* Kunsthaus, Zug
1990   *Istria e Istriani,* Galleria Fotografica, Fogliano Redipuglia
        Landeskunstpreis für Bildende Kunst 1990, Neue Galerie, Graz
1991   *Im Bilde,* Galeri Hlavnčho, Mesta Prahy, Praha
1992   *Amerika—hin und zurück,* Stadtmuseum, Graz
1993   *Stadtpark eins,* Cullen Center, Houston
1994   *Fotografia austriaca,* Galleria sagittaria, Pordenone

Collections:

Kulturna Skupnost Slovenie, Ljubljana, Yugoslavia; Ministerium für Unterricht und Kunst, Vienna; Sammlung Österreichischer Fotografie, Rupertinum, Salzburg; Bibliothèque Nationale, Paris; Musée Français de la Photographie, Bièvres, France; Photogalerie Jean Dieuzaide, Toulouse; Musée d'Art et d'Histoire, Fribourg, Switzerland; The Photographers' Gallery, London; Sammlung Fotografis Landerbank, Vienna; Archivio fotografico, Trieste, Italy; Fundacio Joan Miró, Barcelona; Musei Comunali, Rimini; Yokohama Museum, Yokohama; Neue Galerie, Linz.

Publications:

By LENART: Books—*Presenting Photographers,* exhibition catalogue, Wien 1977; *Bürgerlicher Realismus,* exhibition catalogue, Wien 1981; *Tito v Reprodukcijah,* exhibition catalogue, Beograd 1984; *Wahr genommen,* monography ed. Otto Müller, Salzburg 1991; *Res Publica,* exhibition catalogue, Graz 1993. **Articles**—''Arles Workshops'' in *Spot* (Zagreb), June 1976; ''Presenting Photographers'' in *Protokolle* (Vienna), August 1977; ''5 Jahre Sammlung Fotografis'' in *European Photography* (Göttingen), October 1980; ''Millerton Project'' in *European Photography* (Göttingen), Spring 1983; ''Project Krkavce'' in *Fotonetz 54* (Essen), December 1985; *Il Territorio,* 16/17, Ronchi 1986; *Sterz,* 38, Graz 1986; *Sloveni di Confine,* Ronchi 1988

On LENART: Books—*Creative Camera Yearbook 1977,* edited by Colin Osman and Peter Turner, London 1976; *Dumont Foto 4: Fotografie in Europa Heute,* Cologne 1982; *La Ciutat Fantasma,* exhibition catalogue, Barcelona 1985. **Articles**—''Non fanno cosi/anche le volpi'' by Giuseppe Turroni in *Fotografia Italiana* (Milan), April 1972; ''Réalité Difformé'' in *Photographie Nouvelle* (Paris), October 1972; ''Styrians'' in *Protokolle* (Vienna), July 1974; ''Branko Lenart'' by Attilio Colombo in *Progresso Fotografico* (Milan), February 1977; ''Ausstellungsbesucher'' in *Protokolle* (Vienna), September 1978; ''Une photographie postmoderne'' by Rudiger Wischenbart in *Art Press* (Paris), no. 1, 1984.

*

I believe that every man has an historical obligation to his culture in general as well as to the specific time and society in which he lives. Hence it follows—in my opinion—that the important function of photography is to document the manifestations of culture.

Formerly, the main interest in my photography was man portrayed in extraordinary situations. Now I am more interested in common situations, in man in his own individual domain, and in the changes that occur through human action in the world around us.

In this regard I see my work as political in a broad sense, as a sociological study with visual means. However, I don't regard my work as being only documentary in the sense that authorship is invisible or interchangeable. I feel that it is not possible (or desirable) to isolate photography totally from the personality of the photographer, his individual experiences and his ideology.

Every classification into categories is problematic and usually confusing. If I were to describe or characterize my photography, I would designate it as ''subjective topography.'' In my view, in photography as well as in reality, the magical and mythological aspect should not be excluded.

—Branko Lenart

*   *   *

Is documentation the essence of the photographic medium? Theoreticians and those versed in the visual arts after Niepce all must have asked themselves this question at one time or another. Recently the question has achieved a new currency, and documentalism appears to have found its place as one of the most solid tendencies of our time. And we must begin to separate the various degrees of documentalism which are being practiced.

Branko Lenart, like many others of his generation, is a late convert to documentalism. The fact that he was previously interested in more experimental creative forms has, without doubt, now left him with a greater subjectivism in the use he makes of the camera. Lenart designates his works as ''subjective topography,'' and with that description he indicates that the establishment of documentalism has hardly supplanted the old polemic between objectivity and subjectivity. It has simply displaced it to another level—a level in which one of the extremes would be represented by those who advocate the total neutrality of the camera—as Bevan Davis says, ''. . . the effort being made to let the camera almost see by itself''—and those who advocate a personal interaction between the theme and creator (a position which Verena von Gagern, for example, has categorized as ''romantic documentalism''). The difference lies in the scope we give to the word ''almost.''

In this panorama, Branko Lenart's contribution comes close to what I would classify as ''existential topographic history.'' I refer to something whose purpose is descriptive of a natural or urban topography, but which supersedes a mere formalism or the mere aesthetic effect of leaving constant the existential environment of the creator. (In this sense, the very statement of the photographer which is included here is sufficiently eloquent.) Therefore we find ourselves looking at interpretations of reality rather than mere reproductions. It is obvious that all photography, including the most apparent reproductions, implies an effort of interpretation, but in the case of Lenart it is so striking as to constitute a transgression of the conventional rules of traditional documentalism: frontal perspective, clarity of composition, distinction between figure and background, etc. To disobey these rules as Lenart does and, for example, to obtain labyrinth-like visual images, with a chaotic density of information, with a compactness of textures, etc., implies dominating the medium rather than allowing it to dominate. It implies, finally, a freedom of expression that radical documentalism represses.

—Joan Fontcuberta

LENNARD, Erica.

Nationality: American. **Born:** New York City, 11 November 1950. **Education:** Attended San Francisco Art Institute, B.F.A. 1971. **Career:** Since 1973, freelance photographer, working for fashion designer Perry Ellis, the magazines *Rolling Stone, Interview, Vogue, Elle, Marie Claire, Mademoiselle, Femme,* etc., in New York and Paris. **Agents:** Sonnabend Gallery, 420 West Broadway, New York, New York 10013; Galerie Agathe Gaillard, 3 rue du Pont Louis-Philippe, 75004 Paris; Jean Gabriel Kauss, 122 East 42nd Street, New York, New York 10017; Catherine Mathis, 20 rue de Renard, 75003 Paris. **Addresses:** 519 West 26th Street, New York, New York 10001, U.S.A.; and 24 rue Charlot, 75003 Paris, France.

Individual Exhibitions:

1974   Galleria Il Diaframma, Milan
1975   Thackrey and Robertson Gallery, San Francisco
1976   Galerie Agathe Gaillard, Paris
        Canon Gallery, Geneva
1977   Galerie Nagel, West Berlin
        Canon Gallery, Amsterdam

Galeria Fotomania, Barcelona, Spain
1979   Thackrey and Robertson Gallery, San Francisco
       Sonnabend Gallery, New York
1980   Galerie Sonnabend, Paris
1982   Galerie Gesellschaft, West Berlin
       Sonnabend Gallery, New York
       Galerie Agethe Gaillard, Paris
1983   Facade Gallery, New York
       Magnuson-Lee Gallery, Boston
1984   Govinda Gallery, Washington, D.C.
1985   Sonnabend Gallery, New York
       Govinda Gallery, Washington, D.C.
       School of the Art Institute of Chicago

Selected Group Exhibitions:

1973   *Women,* Museum of Fine Arts, Boston
1975   *Eight American Women Photographers,* Amerika-Haus,
         Cologne (toured West Germany and Italy, 1976)
1978   *Tusen och en bild,* Moderna Museet, Stockholm
1981   *L'Autoportrait,* Centre Georges Pompidou, Paris
1982   *The Nude in Fashion Photography,* Staley Wise Gallery,
         New York
       Versailles, Grand Palais, Paris
1983   *Photography in America 1910-83,* Tampa Museum, Florida
       La Ville et ses Jardins, Centre Georges Pompidou, Paris
1984   *Roger Vivier Shoes,* Facade Gallery, New York
1985   *FAM Portraits,* Canon Gallery, Paris

Collections:

International Museum of Photography, George Eastman House, Rochester, New York; La Photogalerie, Paris; Bibliothèque Nationale, Paris; Musée Nationale d'Art Moderne/Centre Georges Pompidou, Paris: Stedelijk Museum, Amsterdam; Moderna Museet, Stockholm; Australian National Gallery, Canberra; Albright-Knox Art Gallery, Buffalo, New York.

Publications:

By LENNARD: Books—*Sunday,* with Elizabeth Lennard, New York 1973; *Les Femmes, Les Soeurs,* with introduction by Marguerite Dumas, Paris 1976, as *Women, Sisters,* New York 1978; *Classic Gardens,* New York 1982.

On LENNARD: Books—*Creative Camera Yearbook,* London 1975; *Tusen och En Bild,* exhibition catalogue, by Ake Sidwall, Sune Jonsson and Ulf Hard af Segerstad, Stockholm 1978; *Contact: Theory,* edited by Ralph Gibson, New York 1980; *Fashion: Theory,* New York 1980; *Photography in America 1910-1983,* exhibition catalogue, by Julie M. Saul, Tampa, Florida 1983; *A Day in the Life of London,* London 1984. **Articles**—"Erica et Elizabeth Lennard" in *Le Nouveau Photocinéma* (Paris), January 1974; "The Arms of Venus: Erica Lennard" in *Camera* (Lucerne), September 1975; "Portfolio: Erica Lennard" in the *British Journal of Photography* (London), 3 October 1975; "Erica Lennard" by F. W. McDarrah in the *Village Voice* (New York), 24 December 1979; "Erica Lennard chez Sonnabend" by Herve Guibert in *Le Monde* (Paris), 23 January 1980; "Les photographies d'Erica Lennard" in *Elle* (Paris), 31 January 1980; "Erica Lennard" in *Artforum* (New York), February 1980; "Les paysages sensuels d'Erica Lennard" by Christian Caujolle in *Liberation* (Paris), 3 January 1983; "Gardens of the Mind" by Kelly Wise in the *Boston Globe,* 17 March 1983; "Erica Lennard: Portfolio" by Pierre Borhan, in *Cliches* (Brussels), no. 19, 1985.

*

Over the past few years I have divided my time between doing landscapes from the far-west to archaeological sites including Mexico, Sicily, Morocco and, more recently, India. At the same time I do fashion work for a variety of international magazines, as well as portraits. I suppose this broad spectrum is unusual in this era of photography, but I like the idea of having the work reach an audience outside of the galleries, and the assignments also give me the

freedom to do the kind of work I choose for myself. The photographs always deal with the definition of the idea of beauty, whether it be of a person or of a place.

—Erica Lennard

*   *   *

Precise, calm, and perfectly formed, the photographic world of Erica Lennard clings to moments of visual passion, of striking attitudes. Portraits of women, the body of the beloved, landscapes—everything must be structured by light, by an imperceptible arresting of time, a soft perpetuation of the moment.

Erica Lennard is remarkably professional, typical of those who know how to take advantage of the market for art photography. The exceptional quality of her prints, soft and yet perfectly solid, is the work of a masterful sensibility. Her black-and-white parks, her women in grey, flowing tones—like her fashion photography, everything she does is above all expressive of a certain seductive ambiance: a sensuous world which the photograph protects and which exists only because of the photograph. But isn't this precisely the great strength of photography, to disclose an inner world on rectangles riveted to reality?

—Christian Caujolle

LEONARD, Joanne.

Nationality: American. **Born:** Los Angeles, California, 8 September 1940. **Education:** Attended Hollywood High School, Los Angeles, 1955-58; University of California, Berkeley, 1958-62, B.A. 1962; did post-graduate work at San Francisco State College, 1963-64; studied photography with the anthropological photographer John Collier Jr., San Francisco State College, 1964. **Family:** Divorced; daughter: Julia. **Career:** Freelance photographer since 1964. Instructor in Photography, San Francisco Art Institute, 1973-75, and Mills College, Oakland, California, 1975-78. Since 1978, Professor of Art, University of Michigan, Ann Arbor. **Recipient:** Phelan Award, 1971; National Endowment for the Arts Photo Surveys Grant, 1977; Rackham Faculty Research Grant, 1978, 1982 and 1985, Josephine Nevins Keal Award, 1981, University of Michigan, Ann Arbor; John D. Phelan Foundation Award. **Agent:** Jeremy Stone Gallery, 126 Post Street, San Francisco, California 94108. **Address:** 1319 Pomona Road, Ann Arbor, Michigan 48103, U.S.A.

Individual Exhibitions:

1968   *Our Town,* M.H. de Young Memorial Art Museum, San
         Francisco
       Hopkins Center, Dartmouth College, Hanover, New Hampshire
1969   Seligman Gallery, Seattle, Washington
1971   San Francisco Museum of Art (with Chris Enos and
         Irene Poon)
1973   Wall Street Gallery, Spokane, Washington
1974   Photic Gallery, Maryland Institute of Art, Baltimore (with
         Jacqueline Livingston)
       San Francisco Art Institute
1975   Bristol Polytechnic Art Gallery, England
1977   *Recent Works,* Davis Gallery, Stephens College, Columbia,
         Missouri
1978   *Twins: A Visual Connection,* Lincoln Gallery, Santa Rosa,
         California (with Eleanor Rubin)
1980   *Inside and Beyond,* Laguna Gloria Art Museum, Austin, Texas
1981   *Photo-Trans-Forms by Judith Golden and Joanne Leonard,*
         San Francisco Museum of Modern Art
1985   *Ten Years,* Jeremy Stone Gallery, San Francisco
1987   *Twin Sisters: A Visual Connection,* Sarah Doyle Gallery, San
         Francisco, CA

Book of Names, **1992 (original in colour).** Photograph by Joanne Leonard.

1988   *Photographs and Photo Collage,* Jeremy Stone Gallery, San
        Francisco, CA
1989   *Greenwood/Henke/Leonard: Recent Work,* Detroit Institute of
        Arts, Detroit, MI
1992   *Not Losing Her Memory: Stories in Photographs, Words and
        Collage,* University of Michigan Museum of Art, Ann
        Arbor, MI
1995   *Not Losing Her Memory,* Schlesinger Library, Radcliffe
        College

Selected Group Exhibitions:

1969   *Vision and Expression,* International Museum of Photography,
        George Eastman House, Rochester, New York (toured the
        United States, 1969-71)
1970   *American Photographers,* University of Exeter, Devon, Eng-
        land (toured the U.K.)
1971   *Photo Media,* Museum of Contemporary Crafts, New York
1973   *Women's Image,* Boston University (toured the United States)
1975   *Women of Photography,* San Francisco Museum of Art (toured
        the United States, 1975-77)

1977   *Women See Men,* University of New Mexico, Albuquerque
1979   *Variations on a Theme,* University of New Mexico,
        Albuquerque
1981   *The Nude in Modern Photography,* San Francisco Museum of
        Modern Art (toured the United States)
1983   *Lensless Photography,* Franklin Institute, Philadelphia
1986   *Andy Grundberg, New York Times Critic, Selects,* Detroit
        Focus Gallery, Detroit, MI
1987   *Woman and Memory,* Detroit Artists Market
1988   *Rites of Spring,* The Univesity of Michigan Art Museum
        Children of Our Times, A Photographic Essay: 1900-1988,
        Stephen Wirtz Gallery, San Francisco
        Through the Looking Glass, Bernice Steinbaum Gallery, New
        York City (travelled)
1989   *Urbanology: Social Engagement,* Detroit Focus Gallery,
        Detroit, MI
        Portraits and Self Portraits, Alice Simsar Gallery, Ann
        Arbor, MI
        Post Photo, Hearst Art Gallery, St Mary's College,
        Morago, CA
1990   *Photographers Collect Photography,* Center Galleries, Center
        for Creative Studies, Detroit, MI
        Familial Territory, Hampshire College, Amherst, MA

1992   *Reframing Women's Health,* New Works Gallery, The
          University of Illinois at Chicago
1994   *On Wings of Angels,* sponsored by Aids Interfaith Network of
          Michigan, Bunting Gallery, Royal Oak, MI
1995   *Imagined Children, Desired Images,* Davis Art Museum,
          Wellesley College, Wellesley, MA

Collections:

International Museum of Photography, George Eastman House, Rochester, New York; United States Department of State, Washington, D.C.; Stanford University, California; San Francisco Museum of Modern Art; Crocker Art Museum, Sacramento, California; American Arts Documentation Center, University of Exeter, Devon, England; Oakland Museum, California; Detroit Institute of the Arts, Detroit, MI; The University of Massachusetts Art Museum, Amherst, MA; The Oakland Museum, Oakland, CA; The Monsen Collection of American Photography, Seattle, WA; The Graham Nash Collection, Los Angeles, CA; The Eric Lidow Collection, Los Angeles, CA.

Publications:

By LEONARD: Books—*Joanne Leonard, Photographs and Photo Collage,* San Francisco 1988; *Not Losing Her Memory: Images of Family in Photography, Words and Collage,* New York 1994; *Not Losing Her Memory: Stories in Photographs, Words and Collages,* Baltimore, MD 1995.

On LEONARD: Books—*Vision and Expression,* exhibition catalogue, edited by Nathan Lyons, Rochester, New York 1969; *Women See Men,* edited by Ripp, Kalmus and Wiesenfeld, New York 1977; *In/Sights: Self-Portraits by Women,* edited by Joyce Tenneson Cohen, New York and London 1979; *Inside and Beyond,* exhibition catalogue, with an essay by Lucy Lippard, Austin, Texas 1980; *New American Nudes* by Arno Minkkinen, New York 1981; *Photography in California 1945-1980* by Louise Katzman, New York 1984; *Gardner's Art Through the Ages,* by de la Croix, Tansey and Kirkpatrick, 9th edition, San Diego 1991; *Baby, Baby, Sweet Baby,* by Bruce Velick, San Francisco 1992; *Discourses of Sexuality,* by Domna Stanton, Ann Arbor, MI 1992; *The Politics of Caring,* by Elisabeth Fox-Genovese, Columbia, MO 1992; *The Female Body,* by Laurence Goldstein , Ann Arbor, MI 1992; *Narratives of Change and Continuity: Women Artists Reflect on Their Work,* by Maregery Franklin, Hillsdale, NJ and Hove, UK 1994. **Articles**—"Flash! Here's Looking at You, Kid" by Nancy Stevens in *American Photographer* (New York), January 1979; "Self-Portraits" by Hal Fischer in *Infinity* (New York), Winter 1979; "The Undressed Man" by Vicki Goldberg in *Saturday Review* (New York), 26 May 1979; "The Traditional Side" by Cathy Curtis in *Artweek* (Oakland, California), December 1979; "Photography as Art: Joanne Leonard's Free Photographic Experimentation Redefines the Medium" by Kathryn Bolger in *New American Statesman* (Austin, Texas), 4 February 1980; "Literary Images" by Nancy Rose Kaufman in *Artweek* (Oakland, California), 6 March 1980; "Breaking Barriers" by Julia Rubin in *Ann Arbor News,* 23 March 1986.

*

In my recent work, themes of peace, safety, domestic refuge and adventure are set against suggestions of threat and vulnerability. Real space and invented space are combined, often confounding each other. The resulting ambiguous space and ambiguous reality interests me, and is part of the rationale for combining photography with drawing, photograms and collage. With this composite approach and the resulting ambiguities, I hope to invoke some of the uncertainties and anxieties of everyday life in a nuclear age.

—Joanne Leonard

*   *   *

Joanne Leonard has never been afraid to take on the big ideas, and in *Not Losing her Memory* her themes are loss and memory, mortality and immortality. Its expansive web connects personal and political histories, the Holocaust, genetics, feminism, and photography. The fragile forms that carry all these burdens are the images of three (sometimes four) generations of women:

Leonard's grandmother Ida (also called "Peg") as aristocratically photographed by Edward Weston, Leonard's mother Marjorie—a successful child psychiatrist whose last years were lost in dementia due to Alzheimer's disease—and Leonard herself, her twin sister, artist Eleanor Rubin, and her younger sister, Barbara Handelman, a therapist. Now and then Leonard's daughter Julia appears, but as she herself says in one of the texts, "It was your idea, not mine. I was just there, waiting." Her role in this ongoing story is not yet clear.

The notion of "truth" hovers in the wings of these images, as well as that of "fate" herded along by genetics. Leonard has listed the three "investigations" fundamental to the work in this exhibition: "(1) How text and image function together to construct narrative; (2) How photography, a system of mnemonic cues, functions in the construction of memory and might be employed in the representation of memory loss; (3) How autobiography, very suspect in the realm of research (because of its lack of scientific objectivity) is crucial to photographers and ethnographers as they position themselves critically in their texts/images and in the work they do in the 'field'."

To begin with, the narrative formed by this series is not a linear one; nor is it circular, or even labyrinthine. It is made up of layers, not so much different viewpoints as different possibilities. Drawing parallels between family history and social history, the madness of the Holocaust and the dementia of disease, Leonard repeats texts and images, almost permutationally writing and rewriting, layering and relayering the intertwined stories. The same images of three women appear and reappear in different sizes, contexts and combinations, suggesting new meanings for the words that accompany them. These words are often the screen on which the images are projected, as though anticipating the viewers' verbal responses.

As a child during World War II, Leonard had been told that Hitler was a "monster" and refused to believe a picture she was shown of him because the photograph was obviously that of a *man.* (I too recall childhood nightmares of Hitler chasing me in the dark.) She intertwines her interpretations of personal presence and absence with a critique of social amnesia, the way the stories and contributions of women and minorities are forgotten, the way the Holocaust itself is being denied today in an ominous portent of more lost history. Leonard's father had "suffered devastating losses in the Holocaust" and then years later lost his wife to Alzheimer's—two instances of memory brutally, and physically, disappeared.

Underlying this series and responsible for much of its emotional intensity is the tragic irony of Marjorie Leonard, a woman whose education and erudition made her more visible than most women (and more visible than her wealthy but uneducated mother), only to be pushed back into invisibility by the cloud of unknowing that descended on her. The texts pick up on the multiple ramifications of this situation. "She waited too long to talk about it" reads a recurrent line, cast back into the present in a piece that recalls the Thomas/Hill hearings. It is joined by similar lines: "It's her fantasy," "Forget it," "Completely incredible," "She wanted his attention," "It's an exaggeration," "Her memory is defective." Using the again-layered metaphor of lies, fantasies and delusions, Leonard calls attention to the way women are unheard and unbelieved. (Long before Anita Hill showed everyone how it worked, photographer Lorna Simpson was also making art on this theme of the unheard witness from the perspective of African American woman.)

In some of the collages, photography itself is absent, and the women's now familiar silhouettes are filled in with flowery wallpaper, maps, newspaper, handwriting, colored photographs of faces, flowers, trees. In one, Julia has become a candle in an elaborate candlestick, and Joanne? Elly? and Ida? are "highboys" or bureaus, the drawers suggesting age, experience, perhaps nurture. In another, all three become dalmatian dogs. There is a kind of witchery at work that parallels the instability of female identity across the generations.

Most of the best collages in the series are vignettes on black grounds. A formal strategy for disjunction common since Dada, it holds added meaning in this context. Black suggests depth, infinity, death (and potential life), the abyss. This visual and symbolic darkness *brings out* the photographs and texts as though the lives of these women and the messages they bear were floating to the surface (the present, or memory) of a toy crystal ball. It also emphasizes the cinematic aspect of Leonard's work—the distant echo of a childhood Hollywood.

Leonard has said she uses photographs to suggest "reality" and drawing/collaged elements to suggest fantasy and nightmares. During the years that her father was dying and her mother descending into the prison of Alzheimer's, it was her sister Barbara who took most of the pictures. The situation proved almost too much of a blow to Leonard's insistence if sceptical romanticism. She wrote at the time: "Though photography is my usual expressive form, my camera has always sought the beauty and alight in a moment. I have taken no picture in weeks. Before me are scenes unbearable on first sight—nothing feels as if it could be contained by the camera's frame. The house is filled with an atmosphere of darkness; I am the last person to want to turn on the floodlights or click the shutter now."

In trying to deny the false dichotomy between political and personal reality and fantasy, Leonard touches lightly upon currently pressing issues of class and gender. "In terms of class," she writes, "We have been a downwardly mobile family," ranging from Ida's four or five servants to Marjorie's two or three, to Leonard's single mother/artist status. Yet this is not immediately evident in the photo series, in part because of the displacement of her twin and her daughter into the context of the luxurious Los Angeles house in which Ida lived and where Leonard was partially raised. Leonard's refusal to fix meaning and insistence on avoiding closure permit a certain autonomy to all of her subjects, even as they are seen through the lenses of her love and artistic style. The "empty" backgrounds and texts at "cross purposes" in many of these works could signify an open, or totally unpredictable, ending—one which allows the subjects their own memories even as they are engulfed by the communal circumstances. In the process of documenting memory loss through these works, Leonard has in fact found a longer view, and given her female family a longer life.

—Lucy R. Lippard

LEONARDI, Cesare.

Nationality: Italian. **Born:** Modena, 3 June 1935. **Education:** Liceo Scientifico, Modena; studied architecture, under Quaroni, Ricci, Savioli and Libera, at the University of Florence, 1956-62; self-taught in photography. **Family:** Married Donata Annigoni in 1974; children: Claudia, Elena, Paola, and Guido. Freelance photographer, Modena, since 1950; also practising architect and industrial designer, Modena, since 1961. Professor of Architecture, University of Florence, 1981-82. **Recipient:** First Prize, Public Park Competition, Modena, 1970; Premio Cembureau, Vignola, Italy, 1978; Premio C.O.N.I., Vignola, Italy, 1978. **Address:** Viale E. Po 134, 41100 Modena, Italy.

Individual Exhibitions:

1976	*Cesare Leonardi: Fotografie 1950-1976,* Sale della Rocca, Vignola-Modena, Italy
1977	Magazzini del Sale, Modena, Italy
1978	*Cesare Leonardi: La Città di Modena,* Galleria Civica, Modena, Italy
	Galleria Il Diaframma, Milan
	3 Artistes de L'Ecole de Modène, Galerie Olivetti, Paris
	Segnali, Galleria Civica, Modena, Italy

Selected Group Exhibitions:

1959	*Salon of Photography,* London
1978	*Rencontres Internationales de la Photographie,* Arles, France
1979	*Sequential 77,* New York
1982	*La Città,* Udine, Italy
	Luoghi dell'Immaginario, Galleria d'Arte Contemporanea, Suzzara, Italy

Collections:

Museo della Fotografia, University of Parma, Italy; Bibliothèque Nationale, Paris; Galleria dell'Accademia Collezione Lanfranco Colombo, Bergamo.

Publications:

By LEONARDI: Books—*L'Architettura degli Alberi,* Milan 1982; *Catalogo degli Strumenti Musicali del Museo Civico,* Modena 1983; *Atlanta Fotografico del Duomo di Modena,* Modena 1985; *Il Palazzo Comunale di Modena,* Modena 1985; *La Cultura del Restauro Modena,* Modena 1986.

On LEONARDI: exhibition catalogues—*Cesare Leonardi: Fotografie 1950-1976* by Emilio Mattioli, Modena, Italy 1976; *Cesare Leonardi: La Città di Modena,* with a foreword by Emilio Mattioli, Modena, Italy 1978.

*

I am mainly concerned with the city—signs, objects, streets, houses, etc., as day and night follow each other. I use the camera to the limit of its possibilities and generally in an unorthodox way—with double or triple exposures, as for the *Segnali.*

Another subject is the shadow of buildings on other buildings. I am generally interested in urban "systems."

From 1979 to 1986 my interest moved towards the photographic account of cultural landmarks in an attempt to create a scientific documentation of the subject. In this way were born the photographic studies of the Cathedral at Modena, the Municipal Building of Modena, and of other works now in progress.

—Cesare Leonardi

*   *   *

An architect by training and by profession, Cesare Leonardi uses the camera "like an amateur": photography for Leonardi is not so much an expressive medium as a tool for research into planning, for intellectual enrichment, for investigation of the environment and the architecture of the city. Ever since the time of the photographs he took in the first years of his career (1953-54)—pictures of great buildings mirrored in the shop-windows of Florence—his interest in the details of urban planning and his continual study of the location and the role of green areas have been mixed with a variety of reportages (there is an important one on a district in Turin). But Leonardi is not much interested in recording what already exists; his cities, his green areas, are photographed in series of thousands of pictures that at times become thick wedges of marks, for transformation to project material in due course.

Thus, for example, the 5,000 photographs taken of *Carpinus betulus* (the hornbeam) in spring, summer, autumn and winter at different times of day and night became the base for the design of the Amendola Park at Reggio Emilio, in which Leonardi the architect relies on the research done by Leonardi the photographer in his decision to put a lighthouse 40m (130 ft) high in the park, with searchlights at the top slowly and constantly revolving at night to pierce the dark once every hour, like luminous sundials. Or the city of Modena is photographed in three different seasons at different times of day, when the shadows fall clearly to make distinct patterns that distort the shape of the buildings, almost creating a duplicate of them. Or again, road signs are manipulated by under-exposure and sandwich effect so as to create a new visual code. Taking photographs becomes for Leonardi a way of transforming a park, a city, a system of road signs, of capturing its latent structures, of interpreting it in an unconventional way that contradicts the system of Renaissance perspective.

Urban architecture is subjected to metamorphosis; it fluctuates, creating new forms that produce anomalous results. If it all comes from the research of the architect, there is no doubt that the results can also be of interest to the semiologist or the art critic. Cesare Leonardi's research is basically on the *transcription* of visual features. He uses no additional aids or optical devices, though he does vary the time and manner of the exposures, particularly in his use of unusual angulation. From it all there emerges a sort of challenge that suggests different ways of locating the building, the tree, the road sign in an urban context in which the system of references can be varied—in effect modifying an entire cultural code.

—Attilio Colombo

LEONG, Ka Tai.

Nationality: British (Hong Kong). **Born:** in Hong Kong on 19 November 1949. **Education:** Attended Rice University, Houston, B.A. 1969, M.Eng. 1970; self-taught in photography. **Career:** Worked as an automation engineer in England, 1971-77, and as an assistant in the Flip Morton studio, Paris, 1973-76. **Agent:** Black Star, 116 East 27th Street, New York, NY 10018; Cosmos, 56 Boulevard Latour Maubourg, Paris 75007. **Address:** 32 Wyndham Street, 6/F A Wyndham Mansion, Hong Kong.

Individual Exhibitions:

1976	*Paris Shadows,* Hong Kong Arts Centre
1979	*Everyday Dreams,* Hong Kong Arts Centre
1983	*People of the Yellow River,* The Landmark, Hong Kong
1987	*Tibet,* Da Di Gallery, Taipei, Taiwan
1989	*On China: One to Twenty Four,* Summer Gate Gallery, Taipei (travelled throughout Taiwan)
1994	*A Decade in China,* Empress Place Museum, Singapore

Selected Group Exhibitions:

1987	*Ten Years in a Blink,* China Salon of Modern Photography, Beijing
1988	*Image 88,* Museum of Art, Beijing
1991	*Visits to the Homeland: Photographs of China,* Visual Studies Workshop, Rochester, NY (travelled though America)
1993	*Anatomy of a Sandwich,* Hong Kong Institute of Professional Photographers/Hong Kong Arts Festival

Publications:

By LEONG: Books—*Great Rivers of the World,* National Geographic Society 1984; *Salute of Singapore,* Singapore 1984; *China, The Long March* (with Anthony Lawrence), Australia/China 1985; *Beijing* (with Frank Ching), Singapore 1987; *Macau,* Singapore 1986; *Thailand: Seven Days in the Kingdom,* Singapore 1987; *Tanegashima: Festival of Guns,* Macau 1988; *On China: One to Twenty Four,* Camera 22 Ltd 1988; *Singapore: Island, City, State,* Singapore 1990; *Indonesia, A Voyage Through the Archipelago,* Paris 1990; *A Taste of China* (with Ken Hom), London and New York 1990; *Singapore: the Next Lap,* Singapore 1991; *Here be Dragons: A Portrait of Hong Kong,* New York 1992; *Abode of Peace—Brunei Darussalam,* Singapore 1993. **Articles**—"Ad Durch der Mittel" in *Stern,* May 1989; "China's Youth, waiting for tomorrow" in *National Geographic,* July 1991; "Der entpuppe Luxus" in *GEO,* January 1992; "A Chinese Master" in *The New York Times Magazine,* March 1992; "Vor der Sintflut" in *GEO Special,* February 1994.

*

I try to do the right thing in the right place at the right time.

—Ka Tai Leong

*   *   *

Leong Ka Tai is best known for his pictures of China and its one common denominator—the people—and for the way he documents this vast and varied subject. Always slightly under-exposed, dramatic shadows occupy the larger spaces, whereas the brilliant lights shine like candles in the night, as in Rembrandt's paintings. He controls the art of chiaroscuro to perfection; its use reflects well a dark aspect of life in contemporary China. He says: "Dark is beautiful. Darkness is the mystic side of the Chinese."

Like the majority of Asian photographers, Leong is not a printer and works only with colour film. His use of colour is always subdued, never loud. He even changed his Leica for a Canon EOS "because I'm getting lazy" he claims, but more likely because he knows exactly what he's doing and he wants to do it with the least possible fuss and risks.

A self-taught photographer, Leong made the shift from commercial to documentary photography in 1982. He relies entirely on his intuition, on what he sees, and does not hang around for the light to change to his taste. He blames a good picture for the circumstances: "it just happened that way." When he first travelled into China in the early eighties, he was struck by the profusion of colour and the special northern light: clear yet diffused. He went back, again and again.

Being Chinese there must be a natural bond with the people. He replies: "My parents had always been telling me stories about their ancestral homeland. When I reached there I discovered things to be familiar yet different from what I thought." Everyday life was of an incredible authenticity and directness; it was there for the taking. He says: "My eyes are always drawn by the telling moments of everyday life. The fascinating thing about photography is that people open a bit of their lives to you." His humble and unobtrusive nature must have helped him to get an abundance of extraordinary and intimate shots.

Leong Ka Tai's style is consistent. So much so that he would take a picture identical to an earlier one if he found himself in the same situation. According to Leong a good picture comes about "the moment in which people reveal themselves." And when that moment arrives, Leong is sure to have his camera in position.

—Joyce van Fenema-Tulkens

LEVERANT, Robert.

Nationality: American. **Born:** Boston, Massachusetts, 5 July 1939. **Education:** Attended Brookline High School, Massachusetts, 1953-57; studied philosophy and American literature, Middlebury College, Vermont, 1957-62, B.A. 1962; studied painting with Jack Wolfe, Stoughton, Massachusetts, 1962-63; studied with Zen Master Kirpal Singh Suzuki Roshi, San Francisco, 1963-66; with spiritual master Singh, San Francisco and New Delhi, 1968-74; mainly self-taught in photography. **Family:** Divorced. **Career:** Photographer since 1966. Photo Reporter, *Burlington Free Press,* Vermont, 1963-64; Production Manager, Stover and Associates, Commercial printers, San Francisco, 1964-66; freelance commercial architectural and portrait photographer, San Francisco, 1966-72, 1975-78; Executive Director, 1750 Arch Inc. and Conimicut Foundation, music recording and performance company, Berkeley, California. 1972-75. Production Manager, Addison-Wesley Publishing Company, School Division, Menlo Park, California, since 1978. Founding Board Member, Camerawork Gallery, San Francisco, 1978-80. **Recipient:** Annual Latent Image Award, *Village Voice,* New York, 1969; Mark in Time Award, Glide Foundation, San Francisco, 1971; Best Cover Design Award, American Institute for Graphic Arts, 1973. **Address:** Post Office Box 9444, Berkeley, California 94709, U.S.A.

Individual Exhibitions:

1970	*Color Images,* Images Gallery, San Francisco
1972	*New Works,* Images Gallery, San Francisco
1974	Palmer Gallery, New York

Collections:

Institute of Contemporary Art, Boston; San Francisco Museum of Modern Art.

Publications:

By LEVERANT: Books—*Zen in the Art of Photography,* San Francisco 1969; *On the Transmission of Photography,* San Francisco 1972; *Kirpal Singh: A Visual Biography,* San Francisco 1975; *Photographic Notations,* San Francisco 1980; numerous articles in professional journals.

On LEVERANT: Articles—review by Norman Schreiber in *Modern Photography* (New York), January 1981; "Book Review: Photographic

China, Xinjiang, Kashi, **1991 (original in colour).** Photograph ©Leong Ka Tai.

Notations'' by Mark Melnicove in *Combinations* (New London, Connecticut), March 1981.

*

My work as photographer: 1) commercial (interiors, portraits, locations, print production); 2) occasional teaching; 3) personal or ''art'' (color scapes, portraits, b/w space-time continuums, the book form); 4) writer of articles; 5) service work (founding board member of San Francisco Camerawork Gallery, host/organizer of Photographers for Socio/Political Action, professional services at cost to persons and organizations who cannot afford it).

How did these pursuits come about? I needed to earn a living in a competitive situation; a curious mind. My background? I studied painting and sculpture from ages 8 to 16; thus my eye as to space, tension, surface, texture, depth, illusion, iconography, manner, beauty, etc. had been trained in classical Eastern and Western and contemporary notions long before I entered photography. After some 15 years, my models for photographs still remain some poems, plays, pieces of music, paintings and sculpture, and philosophic tracts.

Some of my considerations when engaged in photography (a contemporary image-gathering, image-making, and image-presentation system) are: the pictorial subject, the ideational subject, the photographic medium, the viewer's headspace. (Degas said he didn't paint what he saw, but what would enable them to see the thing he had.)

Photographically, in my personal work, I'm into allusion, not illusion (my commercial work). To do this, likeness must be shattered: the closer-in to the real (Noumenon), the more the likeness (the Phenomenon, or appearance) needs to be shattered. I do this not through abstraction (and thus violate one of the *sine qua nons* of photography, which is likeness) but by making likeness secondary—the ground rather than figure in the image. The vehicles I'm currently using for this are space and time, modalities natural to the subject, the

medium, the idea, and the viewer's perceptual apparatus. In short: space is my content, and time my form, or vice-versa, depending on the situation.

Thus I produce what could be called inferior and boring, i.e., non-decorative and non-sensation oriented photographs—long sequences, continuums of imperfect moments of life-forms in filled and empty space. The ostensible subject is not viewed in isolation, apart from the whole. The strategy for the image-gathering -making, and - presentation come from the deep and repeated contact with and study of the subject. The strategy arises out of the subject's natural rhythms, not my own or my own sense of them. The photographs are of the co-ordinates of space and time, fixed nodal points which the subject generates. When photographing, I experience the joy of participating in the discovery and sharing of significant relations within reality without the imposition of my subjective ideas, personal whims, concepts, etc. on reality.

In addition, I like the book form. I write, design, illustrate, produce and self-publish texts about once every three years, which are mass-distributed; one has sold some 25,000 copies, another has earned international design and production recognition. Each, in design and concept, involves a different exploration of what now emerges, after 13 years, as a common theme: human scale and the limits of photography. I will soon produce just pictorial books utilizing the sequential nature of the book medium.

—Robert Leverant

*   *   *

Although Robert Leverant has been a professional photographer since 1966, he is more prolific as a writer than as a photographer. His most important book, released in 1969, is *Zen in the Art of Photography,* a statement on photography from a Zen perspective. *Transmission of Photography,* with text and pictures, followed three years later, and his most recent work is *Photographic Notations*—"a thinking book," as he describes it, "one which purposely demands engagement, because I feel the medium keeps us from engagement, trains us not to go below the surfaces, trains us to seek the easy and the obvious. . . . "

Leverant went into photography imagining that he could simultaneously pursue his interest in poetry, but very soon he began to devote himself fulltime to photography. He was also, at the time, studying North Indian music as well as classical Western music, but he came to feel that it would take him years just to get a grasp of these subjects; with photography, he could make a more important contribution. His eye had been trained as a child through painting and later through study with Jack Wolfe.

He started his photographic career in 1967/68 by selling framed color prints. Such photos are now so common that it is hard to conceive what pioneering work he and two of his friends on the West Coast were actually doing then. The public was not ready; the photographic world still thought in black-and-white.

Since then, as a photographer, Robert Leverant has been active in various ways: in commercial work—interiors, locations, and portraits; in personal expression work—from color slides, color prints (largely landscapes, sunscapes, and seascapes) to black-and-white classical and more recently to structural work, space-time continuums for which shutter action is determined by subject; and as a teacher at workshops at centers such as Mendocino, Camerawork Gallery, California College of Arts and Crafts, etc. But, as he wrote to me in a letter, he likes the book form more than gallery walls. He has produced all of his books himself; he will go on to produce others: he now believes that people don't have time to read, that the material of books needs to be presented in more visual terms.

Recently, Robert Leverant took a trip to India, and he continues to challenge the unknown to broaden his spirit and his work.

—Marco Misani

LEVINSTEIN, Leon.

Nationality: American. **Born:** Buckhannon, West Virginia, 1913. **Education:** Studied painting with Stuart Davis and photography with Alexey Brodovitch at the New School for Social Research, New York and studied under Sid Grossman at the Photo League, New York, 1948. **Military Service:** Served with the United States Army in World War II, discharged 1945. **Career:** Worked as catalog lay-out artist. **Recipient:** Guggenheim Fellowship, 1975. **Died:** (in New York) 1988.

Individual Exhibitions:

1956	*Levinstein's New York,* Limelight Gallery, New York
1982	Photographs, New York
1990	Howard Greenberg Gallery, New York
1994	*The Street Walkers* (with Frank Paulin), Howard Greenberg Gallery, New York
1995	*Retrospective,* National Gallery of Canada

Selected Group Exhibitions:

1952	*Photography Then and Now,* Museum of Modern Art, New York
1953	*Always the Young Stranger,* Museum of Modern Art, New York
	Contemporary Photography, National Museum of Modern Art, Tokyo, Japan
1955	*7 Photographers Look at New York,* Photographer's Place, New York
	Family of Man, Museum of Modern Art, New York
1957	*Photographers Look at New York,* Museum of Modern Art, New York

1959	*Photographs from the Museum Collection,* Museum of Modern Art, New York
	Group Show, Limelight Gallery, New York
1960	*Photographs for Collectors,* Museum of Modern Art, New York
1962	*A Bid for Space,* Museum of Modern Art, New York
1964	*The Photographer's Eye,* Museum of Modern Art, New York
1965	*About New York Day and Night,* Gallery of Modern Art, New York
1967	*The Camera as Witness,* Expo'67, Montreal, Canada
1969	*Harlem on my Mind,* Metropolitan Museum of Art, New York
1973	*The Jew in New York,* Midtown Gallery, New York
1977	*Remembering Limelight,* Carlton Gallery, New York
1978	*New Standpoints,* Museum of Modern Art, New York
	Re-opening Show, Floating Foundation
1980	*Photographs of the '50s,* International Center of Photography, New York
1981	*Photography of the Fifties,* Center for Creative Photography, Tucson
1985	*The New York School,* Corcoran Museum of Art, Washington, D.C.
1991	*Sid Grossman and Leon Levinstein,* San Francisco Museum of Modern Art, San Francisco

Collections:

Chicago Art Institute, Chicago, Illinois; Consolidated Freightways, Palo Alto, California; Hallmark Cards, Kansas City, Missouri; Metropolitan Museum of Modern Art, New York, NY; Muesum of Modern Art, New York, NY; San Francisco Museum of Modern Art, San Francisco, CA.

Publications:

On LEVINSTEIN: Book—*The New York School: Photographs 1936-1963,* by Jane Livingston, New York 1992.

*

If I am awarded a Fellowship, I will photograph as wide a spectrum of the American scene as my experience and vision will allow. As always, I will photograph without deception, without embroidery and without intent; allowing whatever comes in my path to incite me to work. I want my photographs to be spontaneous rather than contrived. For that reason, I prefer to work without any one specific idea in mind; I do not want to be the servant of any one project.

I will endeavour to make the energy and the particular quality that I feel in American life, a part of my photography.

This is the way I have photographed in the past; it is the only way I know.

—Leon Levinstein

*   *   *

Leon Levinstein, who died in 1988 after being mugged in the elevator of his South Bronx apartment building, was one of the last survivors of the so-called "New York School" of photography. He was also one of the last great upholders of the Photo League ethic, that typically New York academy and club of the forties and fifties where the philosophy of Middle European humanism was revered and perpetuated. The typical Photo League member tempered a clear eyed view of both life's and nature's inequalities with an empathy for the underdog—those dealt unkindly blows by cruel nature and uncaring society. Thus the brutal candour of Levinstein's snatches of street life tends to be matched by compassion in equal measure.

Like a number of Photo League stalwarts Levinstein could be classified an amateur, but that does not imply lack of commitment. He photographed for love, without concern for style or profit, not caring whether his pictures were to be regarded as photojournalism or fine art or anything else. His freedom from the exigences of the photographic career made him fiercely independent in his views. He was particularly withering in his contempt for the "phonies" of the photographic world, a contempt stemming not from any grievance that he was neglected (he was) but from his own, ineffably high standards.

Levinstein was an archetypal street photographer, spending all his spare time rooting out the foibles of human nature yielded so gratifyingly by the boulevards of New York to the connoisseur of quirky street theatre. Between street excursions, he would patrol that other stamping ground of many Photo Leaguers—Coney Island in its heyday—where on a fine sunny day upwards of a quarter of a million relaxed and largely equable subjects were available to the keen student of human gesture and physiognomy.

Unusually, Leon Levinstein—like his friend and colleague Lisette Model—preferred the more cumbersome Rollei to the more favoured 35mm Leica of most street shooters. This choice of slower and more deliberate instrument lent his images an almost terrifying monumentality. Frequently caught by a closeup lens with the camera cradled innocuously in the crook of his arm, his largely unaware subjects loom out of the frame towards the viewer, emphasising an almost schizoid quality in his work, a quality that matches perfectly the fractured, ferocious feel to New York street life. However, Levinstein's veneer of streetwise toughness and cynicism was only a veneer. Beneath the brittle surface of his images we can glimpse the heart of a true *mensch*.

—Gerry Badger

LEVINTHAL, David Lawrence.

Nationality: American. **Born:** San Francisco, 8 March 1949. **Education:** Studied studio art at Stanford University, 1970; photography at Yale University, 1973; and management science at MIT, 1981. **Recipient:** Awarded Polaroid Corporation Artist Support Grants, 1987-89; a National Endowment for the Arts, Visual Artists Fellowship, 1990-91. **Address:** 251 West 19th Street, #6-C, New York, New York 10011, U.S.A.

Individual Exhibitions:

1977	Southern Light Gallery, Amarillo College, Texas
	California Institute for the Arts, Valencia, California
	Carpenter Center of Visual Arts, Harvard University, Cambridge, Massachusetts
1978	Quivera Gallery, Albuquerque, New Mexico
	International Museum of Photography at George Eastman House, Rochester, New York
1985	Founders Gallery, University of San Diego, California
	Area X Gallery, New York
1986	Blatent Image Gallery, Pittsburgh
	University of Alabama, Birmingham, Alabama
1987	Philadelphia Collage of Art
	303 Gallery, New York
1988	Allied Arts Gallery, Las Vegas
	Clarence Kennedy Gallery, Polaroid Corporation, Cambridge, Massachusetts
	Laurence Miller Gallery, New York
	CEPA Gallery, Buffalo, New York
1989	Jan Kesner Gallery, Los Angeles
	University Art Museum, California State University, Long Beach, California
1990	Laurence Miller Gallery, New York
	Pence Gallery, Santa Monica, California
1991	Forum Bottcherstrasse, Bremen
	Museum fur Gestaltung, Zurich
	Laurence Miller Gallery, New York
	Janet Borden Inc, New York
1993	Pastrays Gallery, Yokohama, Japan
	Laurence Miller Gallery, New York
	Southeastern Center for Contemporary Art, Winston-Salem, North Carolina
	Palm Springs Desert Museum, California
	Gene Autry Western Heritage Museum, Los Angeles
	Galerie H.S. Steinek, Vienna
	Wiener Staatsoper, Vienna

	The Friends of Photography, Ansel Adams Center, San Francisco
1994	The Photographers' Gallery, London
	Gilcrease Museum, Tulsa, Oklahoma
	Center for Creative Photography, Tucson, Arizona
	Modern Art Museum of Fort Worth, Texas

Selected Group Exhibitions:

1983	*In Plato's Cave,* Marlborough Gallery, New York
1985	BC Space, Laguna Beach, California
1986	*Acceptable Entertainment,* Bruno Facchetti Gallery, New York
	Signs of the Real, White Columns, New York
1987	*Photography and Art 1946-86,* Los Angeles County Museum of Art
	Fabrications, International Center of Photography, NY
	Avant-Garde in the Eighties, Los Angeles County Museum of Art
1988	*Selections 4,* Photokina 88, Cologne
	The Constructed Image II, Jones Taylor Gallery, Washington, D.C.
	The Return of the Hero, Burden Gallery, New York
1989	*The New Concept,* Forum Stadpark, Graz, Austria
	Photography of Invention, National Museum of American Art, Washington, D.C.
1990	*Rethinking American Myths,* University of Connecticut
	Odalisque, Jayne Baum Gallery, New York
1991	*Des Vessies et des Lanternes,* La Botanique, Brussels (travelled to Palais de Tokyo, Paris)
	Devil on the Stairs, Institute of Contemporary Art, Philadelphia (travelled to Newport Harbor Museum, California)
1992	*Illusions et Travestissements,* A.B. Gallery, Paris
	Interpreting the American Dream, Galerie Eugen Lendl, Graz, Austria
	Sofort-Bild-Geschichten, Instant-Imaging-Stories, Museum Moderner Kunst, Vienna
	More Than One Photography, Museum of Modern Art, New York
1993	*American Made: The New Still Life,* Isetan Museum of Art, Tokyo
	Dolls in Contemporary Art, Haggerty Museum, Marquette University
	Memories, Facts & Lies, BlumHelman Gallery, New York

Collections:

Museum of Modern Art, New York; Gene Autry Western Heritage Museum, Los Angeles; Whitney Museum of American Art; Art Institute of Chicago; Amon Carter Museum, Forth Worth, Texas; BankAmerica Corporation, San Francisco; Corcoran Gallery of Art, Washington, D.C.; Georgia Museum of Art, Athens; Grand Rapids Art Museum, Grand Rapids, Michigan; Hallmark Collection, Kansas City; Modern Art Museum of Fort Worth, Texas; High Museum of Art, Atlanta, Georgia; International Museum of Photography at George Eastman House, Rochester, New York; Los Angeles County Museum of Art; Museum of Fine Arts, Houston; Museum of Contemporary Photography, Columbia College, Chicago; National Gallery of New Zealand, Wellington; New York Public Library; Norton Gallery, West Palm Beach, Florida; Polaroid Collection, Cambridge, Massachusetts; The Brooklyn Museum, New York; University Art Museum, California State University, Long Beach; Milwaukee Art Museum, Wisconsin; The Minneapolis Institute of Arts; Birmingham Museum of Art, Alabama; Eurostar, Graz, Austria; Continental Insurance, New York; Progressive Art Collection, Mayfield Heights, Ohio; San Jose Museum, California.

Publications:

By LEVINTHAL: Books—*Hitler Moves East: A Graphic Chronicle 1941-43* (with Garry Trudeau), Kansas City 1977; *Modern Romance,* San Diego 1985; *American Beauties,* New York/Los Angeles 1990; *Desire,* San Francisco 1993; *The Wild West,* Washington, D.C. 1993; *Die Nibelungen,* Vienna

Untitled, **from the series** *The Wild West,* **1988.** Photograph by David Levinthal.

1993; *Dark Light,* London 1994. **Article**—"Captain Gallant" in *American Art,* Winter/Spring 1991.

On LEVINTHAL: Books—*Modern Romance: David Levinthal,* Aaron Press 1985; *Fabrications: Staged, Altered and Appropriated Photographs* by Anne H. Hoy, Abbeville Press 1987; *Photography and Art Interactions Since 1946,* by Andy Grundberg and Kathleen McCarthy Gauss, New York 1987; *Avant-Garde in the Eighties* by Howard N. Fox, Los Angeles County Museum of Art 1987; *Exploring Color Photography* by Robert Hirsch, Wille C. Brown Publishers 1988; *Surrogate Selves* by Sultan Terrie, Washington, D.C. 1989; *Centric 35: David Levinthal* by Lucinda Barnes, California State University Long Beach 1989; *Devil on the Stairs* by Robert Storr, Philadelphia 1991; *Des Vessies et des Lanternes* by Francoise Deville and Alain D'Hooghe, Brussels 1991; *The American Dream* by Julien Robson, Graz 1992; *Sofort-Bild-Geschichten/Instant-Imaging-Stories* by Monika Faber, Wien 1992; *The Wild West* by Constance Sullivan, Smithsonian Institution 1993. **Articles**—"Memorable Books" by Joan Murray in *Artweek,* 7 January 1978; "Hitler: A Chronicle of Horror" by Sally Eauclaire in the *Rochester Democrat & Chronicle* 19 February 1978; "Tabletop History" by Michael Costello in *Afterimage,* April 1978; "Photography at the Dock" in *The Art of Memory/The Loss of History,* New York 1985; "Modern Romance" by Michael Starenko in *Afterimage,* January 1986; "Photos Miniature the Old West" by Kelly Wise in *The Boston Globe,* 13 February 1988; "Camera Records Invented Worlds" by Alice Thorson in *The Washington Times,* 21 April 1988; "The Image in Question" in *Center Quarterly,* Summer 1988; "New York City as Subject and Inspiration" in *The New York Observer,* 9 January 1989; "Hitler Moves East" in *European Phography,* Number 47, Volume 12, Issue 3; "Taking Toys Seriously: Mini-Movement or Sideshow" in *The New York Times,* 26 February 1989; "David Levinthal" by Richard B. Woodward in *ARTnews,* March 1989; "David Levinthal" by David Pagel in *Art Issues,* September/October 1989; "Hitler Moves East" in *Camera* (Austria), 1989; "Photographer Levinthal Goes West" by Christopher Knight in the *Los Angeles Herald Examiner,* 14 April 1989; "The Created Event" by Pamela Kessler in *The Washington Post,* 26 March 1988; "Imaged Documents" in *CEPA Quarterly,* Winter/Spring 1988; "Fabrik Der Mythologien" by Peter Illetschko in *Der Standard,* 8 May 1992; "Getting Close to Gotham" by Marvin Heiferman and Carol Kismaric in *ARTnews,* September 1987; "Image and Idea" in *The New York Times Magazine,* 30 August 1987; "Where Blurred Focus Makes Sharp Statements" by Andy Grundberg in *The New York Times,* 20 December 1987; "Absolutely Successful" by Tim Goodman in *Palo Alto Weekly,* 16 August 1989; "Seeking Critical Dialog" by David French in *Artweek,* 28 November 1987; "*Hitler Moves East* Turns Fourteen" by A.D. Coleman, in *Camera & Darkroom,* January 1992; "Enlarging the Photographic Impact" by Lance Carlson in *Artweek,* 29 April 1989; "A Biennial of Our Own" by Rosetta Brooks in *7 Days,* 3 May 1989; "Property, Patriotism and National Defense" by Wendell Berry in *Aperture,* Spring 1988; "Valley of the Dolls" by Vince Aletti in *The Village Voice,* 21 May 1991.

* * *

The experience of viewing David Levinthal's photograph is akin to viewing a series of film stills—isolated frames from a movie, carefully selected for maximum impact, and to induce in the viewer the desire for more information. There is a lot going on but, like coming in on a film half-way through, there is the sneaking feeling that we've missed the vital clue. It's gripping stuff—but tantalisingly so—we have to make do with a transitory moment and come to our own conclusions.

Levinthal started out with a debt to the North American painter, Hopper, in his 1984 series *Modern Romance,* but moved swiftly on, taking with him the cream of Hopper's vision—his sense of colour, light and form—to develop an individual style very much his own. He emerged during the 1980s as one of a group of postmodern photographers who eschewed "perceived reality" instead exploiting photography's potential to construct and reinvent the world with studio set-ups, often using miniature toys. Each of Levinthal's photographic series in the exhibition *Dark and Light 1984-94* has tackled a different theme, but his style remains constant.

Dramatic use of colour and lighting techniques are important defining factors in Levinthal's work, setting the mood and tone of each piece to project his meditations on the dark side of life. Witness the soft orange glow of *The* *Wild West* and *American Beauties,* the harsh blue/greys of *Modern Romance* and the dangerous and sexually alluring connotations of red and black in *Desire* and *Mein Kampf.* Levinthal explores areas and notions that we consider dangerous and oppressive and visits the dark and compulsive side of our collective psyche.

The early series *Untitled (1984)* is really no more than a series of visual notes or sketches—but, as such, it offers valuable clues to the characteristic of Levinthal's later work. Hand-coloured in pale washed out pastels, the images are softly-lit to dissolve rather than describe, to obscure rather than clarify.

With *Modern Romance (1984-86)* Levinthal moved into Edward Hopper territory proper—charting the familiar urban American landscape of lonely bars, diners, hotel rooms and dimly-lit streets. Sad little dramas are viewed through a murky lens—as if through a surveillance camera, recalling the shadowy spaces and ambiguous sexual tensions of film noir. A woman sits on the side of a bed in a dingy motel room, a man is seen through a picture window, at his desk attended by his secretary. There is little optimism here—just a sense of getting through the days and nights—until something or someone snaps.

In his series *The Wild West (1987-89),* Levinthal presents us with a brighter vision, on the surface at least. The images, packages in a nostalgic golden glow, reveal cowboys and indians (miniature toys), in action-packed scenes characteristic of 1950s TV series and John Ford westerns But on closer inspection, this highly romanticised and stylised rendition of western history is revealed to be deeply flawed. All is not well back at the ranch; in one dark, disturbing image, a man hangs from a tree and, most chillingly, a cowboy is seen in silhouette, an ominous shadowy figure, reaching into his holster. Is he really the good guy? Nostalgic golden days are recreated too, in *American Beauties (1989-90).* Here the up-beat nostalgia of locker-room posters is suggested by tiny models of 1950s bathing beauties. But, as with *Wild West,* there is an ominous edge to the daydream: why is the sky black for instance (is it day or night?) and why are the beaches deserted?

In *Desire (1990-91),* Levinthal discards all semblance of surface normality in a more immediately menacing vision altogether. Here, the darker elements of *Modern Romance, American Beauties* and *The Wild West* are brought together in his vision of Sadeian sex. Using Japanese "ready to assemble" sex and bondage dolls, viewed through low light and a blurred lens, it is a frenzied peep show, with only a hint of whips, black leather and shiny red high-heeled shoes. The viewer is forced into the role of voyeur, shown tantalisingly little.

This is a device he uses again in his most recent work, *Mein Kampf (1993-94).* Here he pushes things to the edge, using lurid, glossy colour to present all the horror of the Holocaust as a grotesque piece of theatre. A blatant parade of swastikas, Nazi flags, arms raised in the Nazi salute, figures shoved up against walls, and heaps of bodies, is all the more shocking for the immediacy of colour. (We're accustomed to seeing it in black-and-white—even Steven Spielberg turned to monochrome for *Schindler's List.*) Levinthal's toy soldiers re-enact unspeakable crimes in re-constructions of wartime photographs taken inside concentration camps. Again, Levinthal blurs the images to obscure rather than clarify, but this time the restricted view meets with a marked sense of relief.

—Jane Richards

LEVITT, Helen.

Nationality: American. **Born:** New York City, 31 August 1918. **Education:** Attended New Utrecht High School, New York; studied at the Art Students' League, New York, 1956-57. **Career:** Freelance photographer, New York, since 1939; also, a filmmaker, intermittently, since 1947. **Recipient:** Photography Fellowship, Museum of Modern Art, New York, 1946; Guggenheim Fellowship, 1959, 1960; Ford Foundation Film Grant, 1964; Creative Artists Public Service Fellowship (CAPS), New York, 1974; National Endowment for the Arts, 1976; Friends of Photography "Distinguished Career in Photography," 1987. **Agent:** Fraenkel Gallery, 55 Grant Avenue, San Francisco, California 94108 and Laurence Miller Gallery, 138 Spring Street, New York,

Broken Mirror, **1942.** Photograph ©Helen Levitt. Courtesy Laurence Miller Gallery, New York.

New York 10012. **Address:** 4 East 12th Street, New York, New York 10003, U.S.A.

Individual Exhibitions:

1943	*Helen Levitt: Photographs of Children,* Museum of Modern Art, New York
1949	Photo League, New York (with John Candilario)
1952	Institute of Design, Illinois Institute of Technology, Chicago (with Frederick Sommer)
1954	*3 Photographers,* Caravan Gallery, New York
1963	*3 Photographers in Color,* Museum of Modern Art, New York (with Roman Vishniac and William Garnett)
1974	*Projects: Helen Levitt in Color,* Museum of Modern Art, New York (slide show)
1975	Pratt Institute, Brooklyn, New York
1976	Nexus Gallery, Atlanta, Georgia
1977	Carlton Gallery, New York
1980	Corcoran Gallery, Washington, D.C.
	Sidney Janis Gallery, New York
	Helen Levitt: Color Photographs, Grossmont College, El Cajon, California
1981	*Matrix 66: Helen Levitt,* Matrix Gallery, Wadsworth Atheneum, Hartford, Connecticut
	University of California, Berkeley
1982	Ikona Photo Gallery, Venice, Italy
	Fraenkel Gallery, San Francisco
1983	Museum of Fine Arts, Boston
1984	Robert Klein Gallery, Boston
1985	Fotografiska Museet, Stockholm
1986	Syracuse University, New York
	Eighteen Color Photos, Fraenkel Gallery, San Francisco
1987	International Center of Photography, New York
	Laurence Miller Gallery, New York
1988	The Photographers' Gallery, London
1989	Laurence Miller Gallery, New York
1990	Laurence Miller Gallery, New York
1991	Laurence Miller Gallery, New York
	San Francisco Museum of Modern Art
1992	Metropolitan Museum of Art, New York
	Laurence Miller Gallery, New York

Selected Group Exhibitions:

1949	*6 Women Photographers,* Museum of Modern Art, New York
1955	*The Family of Man,* Museum of Modern Art, New York (and world tour)
1965	*Photography in America 1850-1965,* Yale University, New Haven, Connecticut
1968	*Harlem on My Mind,* Metropolitan Museum of Art, New York
1973	*Landscape/Cityscape,* Metropolitan Museum of Art, New York
1978	*Mirrors and Windows: American Photography since 1960,* Museum of Modern Art, New York (toured the United States, 1978-80)
1981	*The New Color: A Decade of Color Photography,* Everson Art Museum, Syracuse, New York
1982	*Lichtbildnisse: Das Porträt in der Fotografie,* Rheinisches Landesmuseum, Bonn
1985	*American Images 1945-80,* Barbican Art Gallery, London (toured Britain)
1986	*Street Photography, New York 1930-86,* Daniel Wolf Gallery, New York
1988	*No Trumpets-No Swans,* Pratt Institute, New York
	Evocative Presence, Museum of Fine Arts, Houston, Texas
	Convulsive Beauty: The Impact of Surrealism on American Art, Fairfield County, Connetict; Whitney Museum of American Art, New York
	Diamonds are Forever, Smithsonian Museum Travelling Exhibition

1989	*The New Vision: Photography Between the World Wars,* Metropolitan Museum of Art, New York
	The Cherished Image, National Gallery of Canada
	Photography 150 Years, Australian National Gallery
	Fotografiska Museet, Moderna Museet, Stockholm
	On the Art of Fixing a Shadow, National Gallery of Art, Ikona Gallery, Venice
1991	*On the Edge,* New York

Collections:

New York Public Library; Museum of Modern Art, New York; Metropolitan Museum of Art, New York; Corcoran Gallery, Washington, D.C.; Exchange National Bank, Chicago; Springfield Art Museum, Missouri; Museum of Fine Arts, Houston; International Center of Photography, New York; National Museum of American Art, Washington, D.C.; Israel Museum, Jerusalem; Baltimore Museum of Art; Bayly Museum, Charlottesville; Cleveland Museum of Art; Museum of Fine Arts, Boston; San Francisco Museum of Modern Art; Seibu Gallery of Contemporary Art, Tokyo.

Publications:

By LEVITT: Books—*A Way of Seeing: Photographs of New York,* with text by James Agee, New York 1965, 1981; *Helen Levitt: Color Photographs,* exhibition catalogue, El Cajon, California 1980. **Films**—*The Quiet One,* with James Agee and Janice Loeb, 1949; *In the Street,* with James Agee and Janice Loeb, 1952.

On LEVITT: Books—*The History of Photography from 1839 to the Present Day* by Beaumont Newhall, New York 1949; *The Family of Man,* with text by Edward Steichen, New York 1955; *Photography in the Twentieth Century* by Nathan Lyons, New York 1967; *Harlem on My Mind,* edited by Allon Schoener, New York 1968; *Quality: Its Image in the Arts,* edited by Louis Kronenberger, New York 1969; *Looking at Photographs: 100 Pictures from the Collection of the Museum of Modern Art* by John Szarkowski, New York 1973; *The Magic Image* by Cecil Beaton and Gail Buckland, London and Boston 1975; *Faces: A Narrative History of the Portrait in Photography,* edited by Ben Maddow, Boston 1977; *Mirrors and Windows: American Photography since 1960* by John Szarkowski, New York 1978; *Venezia '79: La Fotografia,* edited by Daniela Palazzoli, Vittorio Sgarbi and Italo Zannier, Milan and New York 1979; *The Photograph Collector's Guide* by Lee D. Witkin and Barbara London, Boston and London 1979; *Helen Levitt,* exhibition catalogue, with an introduction by Jane Livingston, Washington, D.C. 1980; *Helen Levitt: Color Photographs,* with an introduction by Roberta Hellman and Marvin Hoshino, El Cajon, California 1980; *American Children: Photographs from the Collection of the Museum of Modern Art,* edited by Susan Kismaric, New York 1980; *Lichtbildnisse: Das Porträt in der Fotografie,* edited by Klaus Honnef, Cologne 1982; *American Images: Photography 1945-1980,* edited by Peter Turner and John Benton-Harris, London 1985; *Photography: A Facet of Modernism* by Van Deren Coke and Diana du Pont, San Francisco and New York 1986. **Articles**—"The Art of Poetic Accident: The Photographs of Cartier-Bresson and Helen Levitt" by James Thrall Soby in *Minicam* (New York), March 1943; "Helen Levitt's Photographs: Children of New York and Mexico" by Edna Bennett in *U.S. Camera* (New York), May 1943; "Sidewalk Primitives" in the *New York Times Magazine,* 22 October 1950; "Photography: New Frontiers in Color" by Douglas Davis and Mary Rourke in *Newsweek* (New York), 19 April 1976; "Levitt Comes in Color Too" by Roberta Hellman and Marvin Hoshino in the *Village Voice* (New York), 24 January 1977; "Fenêtres sur l'Insolite" by Julio Cortazar in *Nouvel Observateur* (Paris), June 1977; "Helen Levitt at Carlton" by Andy Grundberg in *Art in America* (New York), July 1977; "The Photographs of Helen Levitt" by Roberta Hellman and Marvin Hoshino in *Massachusetts Review* (Boston), Winter 1978; "Her Eye Is on the City" by Owen Edwards in the *New York Times Magazine,* 5 April 1980; "Helen Levitt" by Colin Westerbeck in *Art Forum* (New York), May 1980; "A Way of Seeing and the Act of Touching" by Max Kozloff in *Observations,* Carmel, California 1984.

*

I am interested in photographing what I see on the streets. In the 1940s I photographed in black-and-white; for the last 10 years I have been photographing in color and in black-and-white.

—Helen Levitt

*   *   *

Helen Levitt has fashioned an expressive visual reality from the formless flux and movement of street life in New York. At first in black-and-white still photography, subsequently in film and then in color transparency materials, she has used the camera to reveal an unimaginable world of toughness, grace and gaiety, especially among the young. Starting in the late 1930s Levitt has photographed mainly in ethnic and working class neighborhoods because so much of daily life there takes place in the streets. In her effort to seize the most expressive moment, she often has found it necessary to use a prism lens on her Leica so that her own activity would go unnoticed. She is an observer rather than a participant—a passerby who is enchanted with the human panorama and treasures its special moments.

The impetus for Levitt's style was an exhibition during the 30s of the work of Henri Cartier-Bresson at the Julien Levy Gallery. Surrealist images, also shown by Levy, further enlarged her vision of photography's potential for capturing the mysteries of street life. But while the actual moment of exposure is as decisive for Levitt as it is for Bresson, her work is lyrical and poetic rather than ominous and intense. A benign acceptance of the human condition is expressed in images that are informed by wit and humor. Frequently they visually integrate the ordinary and the unexpected, as in a group of children around an empty mirror frame.

At first glance, Levitt's images seem artless, like the most fortunate of snapshots, but hers is a sophisticated sense of organization that does not call attention to itself. Intuitively, she has constructed a seamless unity of form and meaning that is difficult to analyze and impossible to dissect.

In addition to encapsulating poignant moments, Levitt's images serve another purpose. While she would disavow a role as a sociologist or historian, the early photographs, made during the 40s, reveal a texture of communal life that seems light years away from the harsh climate of today. People seem less embattled and the environment less hostile, as children play out their fantasies clothed in handkerchiefs and paper boxes. Toy guns really seem like toys, and the images of street battles have no menace. There is poverty and pain in a number of the photographs, but today's viewer experiences a sense of loss—a feeling of diminished humanity for having allowed the perversion of what was a more humane scenario.

In 1945, encouraged by James Agee and Janice Loeb, Levitt became involved in film. Using simple 16mm equipment that allowed the camera to be used waist high to avoid notice, she and Loeb returned to the same neighborhoods to create In The Street, released in 1952, which projected the same fusion of artless innocence and sophisticated vision that had informed the earlier still photographs. Levitt continued in film, assisting Janice Loeb and Sidney Meyers on The Quiet One and working on several other documentaries.

As the recipient of two Guggenheim grants in 1959 and 60, Levitt began again to work with a still camera using color materials. Her approach continues to be intuitive. While she is still engaged by the entire scene, in which color is only one element, her discriminating eye is now attuned to the harmonies and dissonances of hue as well as to expressive gesture and spatial configuration. As always, the aesthetic structure of Levitt's work is implied rather than brandished as she continues to see buoyant ephemeral moments in an increasingly hostile environment.

—Naomi Rosenblum

LEWCZYŃSKI, Jerzy.

Nationality: Polish. **Born:** Tomaszow Lubelski, 14 March 1924. **Education:** Studied engineering at Silesian Technical University, Gliwice, 1945-51, Dip.Ing. 1951; also studied photography, under Tadeusz Maciejko, Gliwice, 1951-56. **Military Service:** Served as an officer in the Polish Resistance Movement, 1939-45. **Career:** Professional photographer, Gliwice, since 1956. Member, Photographic Association of Gliwice, since 1951, Union of Polish Art Photographers, since 1956, and Fédération Internationale de l'Art Photographique (FIAP), since 1963. Lecturer at The Photographic Academy, Warsaw, 1987-1993; Member of the Artistic Council of ZPAF, Warsaw, 1970-1994. **Recipient:** Award of Merit, Sociedade Fulminense de Fotografia, Rio de Janeiro, 1957; Gold Medal, *Photographers of the New Generation* exhibition, Pescara, Italy, 1960; Voivode Prize, City of Katowice, Poland, 1981; Jan Bulhak Medal, Union of Polish Art Photographers, 1985. **Agent:** Union of Polish Art Photographers, Plac Zamkowy 8, Warsaw. **Address:** Skrytka Post Office, Box 71, 44100 Gliwice, Poland.

Individual Exhibitions:

1958	Krzywe Kolo Gallery, Warsaw
1959	Photographic Association Gallery, Gliwice, Poland
1968	Prezentacje Club, Torun, Poland
1976	*Cimiteria,* Polish Art Photographers Gallery, Cracow, Poland
1979	Wokewódzki Dom Kultury, Legnica, Poland
	Negatives, Foto-Medium-Art Gallery, Wroclaw, Poland
1981	*Wedding Photography,* Municipal Gallery, Gorzow, Poland
	Cimiteria, Photo Gallery, Walbrzych, Poland
1984	*Negatives—Continued,* Mala Gallery, Warsaw
	Cimiteria, Gallery of Katowice, Poland
1987	*FF,* Gallery Lódź
1989	Gallery of the Photographic Society in Gorzow
1990	BWA Gallery in Lublin
	Gallery of the Budapestifotoklub, Budapest

Selected Group Exhibitions:

1960	*Photographers of the New Generation,* Pescara, Italy
1961	*Fotografen aus Polen,* Gesellschaft für Deutsche Photographie, Cologne
1968	*Fotografia Subiektywna,* Biuro Wystaw Artystycznych, Cracow, Poland
1971	*Fotografowie Poszukujacy,* Galeria Wspólczesna, Warsaw
1972	*Schöpferische Fotografie,* at *Photokina,* Cologne
1979	*Fotografia Polska 1839-1979,* International Center of Photography, New York (travelled to the Museum of Contemporary Art, Chicago; Galeria Zacheta, Warsaw; Museum of Fine Arts, Lodz, Poland; and Whitechapel Gallery, London)
1981	*Photographie Polonaise,* Centre Georges Pompidou, Paris
1984	*Wystawa Fotografii Wspolczesnej,* Galeria Zacheta, Warsaw
1986	*Light of Silence/Altitudes,* Museum of Fine Arts, Lodz, Poland
1989	*Nie wieder,* Gallery Stadmuseum, Düsseldorf
	2 x 8, TV Gallery in Berlin
1991	*70 Jahre Polnische Photoavangarde,* Koszalin PL, Bergkamen, Germany
1993	*Antiphotography and Continuation,* National Museum, Wroclaw
1994	*Antiphotography and Continuation,* Warszawa

Collections:

National Museum, Wroclaw, Poland; Museum of Fine Arts, Lodz, Poland. Photographers Society of Gliwice, Poland; Photography Museum, Lausanne; Centrum Regional de la Photographie, Nord-Pas de Calais.

Publications:

By LEWCZYŃSKI: Books—*About the Photo Art of Feliks Lukowski,* 1988; *Zeszyty Gliwickie,* biography of Wilhelm von Blandowski, 1994. articles—''Fotograf Floris Michael Neusüss'' in *Fotografia* (Warsaw), April 1974; ''Zamienilem cale zycie na fotografie'' in *Fotografia* (Warsaw), no. 3, 1980; ''Cialo fotografii'' in *Fotografia polska 1945-1985,* Gorzow Wielkopolski, Poland 1985.

Soldier, **1961.** Photograph ©Jerzy Lewczynski.

On LEWCZYŃSKI: Books—*Penetracje Fotograficzne* by Alfred Ligocki, Cracow 1979; *Photographie d'Avant Garde en Pologne,* exhibition catalogue, by Urszula Czartoyska, Paris 1981; *Wobec fotografii* by Jerzy Busza, Warsaw 1983; *Fotografia polska 1945-1985* by Ryszard Bobrowski and others, Gorzow Wielkopolski, Poland 1985; *Literature,* by Janusz Jaremowicz, Warszawa 1986; *Fotómüvészet* by Abran Laszlo, 1990; *The Atmosphere of the Photographer Jerzy Lewczyński,* by Krzysztof Jurecki, Wroclaw 1991; *Polish Art Studies,* exhibition catalogue with text by Krzysztof Jurecki, Warszawa 1991; *Jerzy Lewczyński,* thesis of Irena Wildner, Warsaw 1994. Articles—"Fotografi della Nuova Generazione" in *Fotografia Italiana* (Rome), no. 9, 1960; "Sztuka Scalania Swiata" by Jerzy Busza in *Kultura* (Warsaw), no. 37, 1977; "Photography: An Interrupted Past" by Ben Lifson in the *Village Voice* (New York), 27 August 1979; "Une revelation: la photographie polonaise" by Michel Nuridsany in *Le Figaro* (Paris), 12 February 1981.

*

I belong to the active originators of the new trend called subjective photography, and produce photos of objects and situations which later serve as a basis for fiction sets. I use old photos and documents to make tales about life and death.

I also make poetic photos. I suggest some new trends such as naive photography, or, recently, the archaeology of the photo based on the sculpture of negatives.

My works are very humanistic and often have a social or sociological background.

—Jerzy Lewczyński

*   *   *

Quite often in the history of art some artist refers to or even to a certain extent copies the art of the past. There are obvious examples of painters who have gone back to the paintings of the old masters and consciously re-created them in a search for new interpretations. The various versions that exist of da Vinci's *Mona Lisa* are a good example. Photography, of course, is a much younger art form, and today is usually a more interesting subject for contemporary photographers than yesterday. Jerzy Lewczyński is an exception, a photographer who doesn't hesitate to take trips into the past. Indeed, his work seems to exist simultaneously in both past and present. Lewczyński is particularly interested in the simple photographs taken by amateurs—often found by chance, often banal, lacking in any special prettiness or ugliness. For him an accidentally uncovered archive, a family album or even a backstreet rubbish heap hold promise of intellectual and artistic adventure.

"On the warm morning of September 6th, 1979," Lewczyński recounts, "I came out of Dom Artysty, the home of the Kosciuszko Studios in New York. In the street I saw an enormous pile of assorted rubbish and immediately noticed the scattered photographs, envelopes and papers amongst it. Trying not to get too excited, I started looking through the photographs and found envelopes full of negatives. The friend who was with me, knowing my interests, encouraged me to take them. He smiled and said that it was quite normal for someone's life and work to be thrown out like this. I put what I could into my bag and made my way to the subway. At home, I glanced through the negatives and, indeed, found a slice of America's private life. I didn't have time to reflect on it but it pleased me to possess such a valuable prize. It was a new step in the development of my 'Discovered Photographs'."

Lewczyński dissects the structure of the photographs that he finds by isolating and enlarging selected fragments, then "re-setting" them with the original; or, he may juxtapose various images similar in form but different in content, thereby giving them a completely new meaning.

In his best known photographic work, "Nysa 1945" (1971), Lewczyński presents a composition that consists of an old photograph showing a typical scene from 1945 in Poland (an overcrowded train standing at a provincial station) with fragments of the same photograph (enlarged portraits of passengers) mounted around the original photograph. In this way, Lewczyński, as he say's himself, hopes to "find out more about the characters represented. It requires an enormous effort but I believe in the mystical power of photography and hope it will lead me to a greater truth."

From his work, it is evident that he wishes to go beyond the confines of a single picture and beyond the range of traditional practice. Over and above this, his desire for ultimate freedom from the influence of pictorialism—strongly felt by Polish photographers, particularly those trained in the 1930s and 1940s—is obvious. This desire to break with tradition and create something new led Lewczyński to ruminate on the advantages of reproductions and to reach for banal negatives and casually encountered photographs.

This kind of presentation reveals two characteristics of photography: realism, with its tendency to oversimplication, and synthesis and the subjective approach, with its tendency to analysis. It also represents a personal reflection on the emotional "potential" inherent in photography. This emotionalism is peculiar to Lewczyński who, despite his experimental and formal interests, differs distinctly from other Polish contemporary photographers, whose work is generally analytical, cool, and self-involved.

—Ryszard Bobrowski

LEWINSKI, Jorge (Jerzy).

Nationality: British. **Born:** Lwow, Poland (now the Ukraine), 25 March 1921. Lived in Britain since 1942; naturalized in 1958. **Education:** Attended Gizycki Gimnasium in Warsaw, matriculating in 1939; graduated from the University of London in 1950; self-taught in photography. **Military Service:** Served with the RAF, taking part in the invasion of Europe. **Family:** Married Emilia Lewinska in 1950; divorced 1974. Married Mayotte Magnus-Lewinski in 1975. Has two children: Ian and Andrew. **Career:** Worked in business 1950-67. Fellow of the Royal Photographic Society 1960. Began photography of artists, 1961. Professional photographer since 1968. Member and exhibitor at the London Salon of Photography since 1970. Part-time teacher at Bath Academy and Harrow School of Photography. Senior lecturer in photography at the London College of Printing 1968-82. Freelance writer-photographer since 1982, mainly concentrating on writing and illustrating articles and books, often in collaboration with his wife Mayotte Magnus. **Agent:** Jennifer Kavanagh, 39 Camden Park Road, London NW1 9AX. **Address:** 78 Trinity Road, London SW17 7RJ.

Individual Exhibitions:

1964	The Royal Photographic Society, London
1965	Reed House, London
1967	San Francisco Museum of Modern Art
1972	National Portrait Gallery, London
1974	Sussex University, Brighton
1977	University of Wales, Cardiff
1979	Photographers' Gallery, London
1980	Camden Art Centre, London
	Gallerie et Fils, Brussels
1987	The Royal Festival Hall, London
1988	The Camera Club, London

Selected Group Exhibitions:

1978	Penwith Galleries (with Mayotte Magnus and Adrian Heath)
1979	Focus Gallery, San Francisco (with Mayotte Magnus)

Collections:

Victoria and Albert Museum, London; National Portrait Gallery, London; Museum of the University of California, Berkeley; Bibliotheque Nationale, Paris.

Publications:

By LEWINSKI: Books—*Byron's Greece* (with Lady Longford), Weidenfeld 1975; *Colour in Focus,* Argus Books 1976; *A Dictionary of Photography,* Arrow Books 1977; *Camera at War—History of War Photography,* W.H. Allen 1978; *Writer's Britain* (with Margaret Drabble), Thames and Hudson

Marcel Duchamp, **1966.** Photograph by Jorge Lewinski.

1979; *James Joyce's Odyssey* (with Frank Delaney), Hodder 1981; *Shell Guide to Photography of Britain,* Hutchinson 1982; *Book of Photographic Portraiture* (with Mayotte Magnus), Ebury Press 1983; *Architecture of Southern Britain* (with Mayotte Magnus and John Julius Norwich), Macmillan 1985; *Wilderness Britain* (with Anthony Burton), André Deutsch 1985; *Architecture of Northern England* (with Mayotte Magnus and J.M. Robinson), Macmillan 1986; *Venice Preserved* (with Mayotte Magnus and Peter Lauritzen), Michael Joseph 1986; *Shell Guide to Archaeology of Britain* (with Jacquetta Hawkes), Michael Joseph 1986; *The Naked and the Nude,* Weidenfeld 1987; *English Heritage* (with Mayotte Magnus and Lord Montagu), Macdonald 1987; *Portrait of the Artist (25 years of British Art),* Carcanet 1987; *By Appointment* (with Mayotte Magnus and Tim Heald), Macdonald 1989; *The Monument Guide to England and Wales* (with Mayotte Magnus and Jo Darke), Queen Ann Press 1991; *The Racing World* (with Julian Wilson), Queen Ann Press 1991. **Articles**—series of some 30 articles for *Amateur Photographer, Good Photography,* and *Photography,* 1964-72; "Modern Portraiture—Philosophy and Practice," *Nikon Manual* 1977.

On LEWINSKI: Book—*Photography in the 20th Century* by Peter Tausk, Focal Press 1980. **Articles**—Peggy Delius in *British Journal of Photography,* December 1964; Ainsley Ellis in *British Journal of Photography,* May 1972; Josef Gross in *Photography Magazine,* June 1991.

*

Portraiture and landscape were always a predominant part of my work. And yet I was never interested in literal description of a face or a place. My landscapes were often closely connected with literature—a specific view or a place seen through the eyes of a writer or a poet who wrote about it. Similary I chose to concentrate on portraits of modern artists, partly because I was myself very much interested in modern art, but mainly, because when photographing a painter or a sculptor in the environment of his studio and surrounded by his or her work, I was hoping to achieve a deeper insight into the imaginative world of my sitter. Consequently, it was not so much outward appearances—their faces—that I concentrated on, but rather the essence of their art—hence their character.

I have often heard a comment that my portraits are very much design orientated. It is true only in a sense that some of my compositions and design were also part of my desire to interpret the personality of the artist and not a "raison d'être" itself.

Since 1961, I have photographed well over 300 artists, many of them several times so that I was able to follow the development of their art over the span of years.

At present, I am again visiting and revisiting studios and exhibitions and photographing old and new artists and working towards a retrospective of portraits of artists of this half of the century.

—Jorge Lewinski

* * *

Long before Jorge Lewinski abandoned his business career in 1967 photography was consuming more and more of his attention—he had been awarded Fellowship of the Royal Photographic Society in 1960.

Lewinski's output has varied widely. In 1961 he began an exhaustive series of portraits of artists, in a curious style which combined a photo-journalistic approach with formal portraiture. The essence of it was based upon reference to the artist-subject's own work. Though it may be too bold to claim his work of this type as pioneering, it is certainly original and, in its way, influential too.

Most of his work has been in book illustration, where his inherently journalistic style is often overlaid with poetic interpretation. In a prodigious output, many books—frequently with Mayotte Magnus—explored landscape and architecture, in which Lewinski's penchant for compositions exploiting dynamic diagonals is clearly displayed.

Writing on composition (*Photography, a dictionary of photographers, terms and techniques,* Arrow, 1977) he hints at his inspirations when quoting Matisse's definition of the discipline—"Composition is the art of arranging,

in a decorative manner, the various elements at the painter's disposal, for the expression of his feeling." In the same work he refers to the Gestalt theoreticians in support of his insistence that order is inherently more attractive than chaos. His view is that in search of simplicity and clarity the photographer must exhaustively explore viewpoints and subject distances.

Lewinski has continued with his photography of artists, and is currently preparing a retrospective of his work in this vein from 1961 to 1994.

—George Hughes

LEWIS, Barry.

Nationality: British. **Born:** London, 23 July 1948. **Education:** Attended the University of Leicester, 1967-71; largely self-taught in photography but "garnished" at the Royal College of Art, London, 1974-76. **Family:** Married Hannah Lewis; daughters: Clare, Anna, Phoebe; son: Jack. **Career:** Worked as a chemistry teacher, 1971-74; freelance journalist since 1976. Founder member of the picture agency Network Photographers, 1980. **Recipient:** Oskar Bernak Award at the World Press Competition 1991 for work on Romania. **Agent:** Network Photographers, 3/4 Kirby Street, London EC4. **Address:** 18 Cromwell Avenue, London N6 5HL, England.

Exhibitions:

1978   *Being disabled,* Photographers' Gallery, Southampton
1979   *Coming and Going,* Museum of London
1981   *Portrait of a City,* Royal Festival Hall, London
1983   *A Week in Moscow,* Photographers' Gallery, London
1989   Museum of Photography, Bradford

Publications:

By LEWIS: Books—*Have Wheels, Will Travel,* Open University 1976; *Working Lives,* 1977; *Into Cuba,* 1985; *Days in the Life of . . .* London, Los Angeles, Ruhr Valley, USA, California, Spain, Italy, Ireland, Hollywood, Vietnam. **Articles**—*British Journal of Photography,* 1978; *Zoom Magazine,* 1979; *The Face,* 1984; *British Journal of Photography,* 1990; also *National Geographic, Sunday Times, Sunday Telegraph, The Observer, Life, Geo, Merian, Business, Forbes, Fortune, Newsweek.*

*

I am a story teller who uses photographs. This is sometimes achieved through use of a single image, where there is a sense of something happening, or about to, outside the frame.

My photographs are more often used as a sequence in books and magazines where my work could be described as traditional photojournalism. The images used in this context are, these days, essentially illustrations, powerful graphic devices to describe and to raise the emotional temperature enough to ensure the viewer reads the text and turns the page to view the advertisements.

Ten years ago, along with eight other photojournalists, I started the agency Network as one way of exercising some control in the use of documentary photography. This has grown, acting as a forum for photographers, picture editors and designers, apart from the more traditional agency role of selling pictures and stories.

In recent years, I find my role as story teller through magazines curtailed, television having taken over the documentary mantle.

Death in the Family—Albania, **1991.** Photograph ©Barry Lewis.

In consequence, my most recent work involves using computers to combine still pictures sequenced with sound and video clips. The resulting stories are put into a CD ROM disk awaiting a new generation of viewers.

—Barry Lewis

* * *

Barry Lewis' reputation is built on his immense energy and a curiosity about everything that crosses his path. These qualities supported by unfailing professionalism combine in a photographer whose repertoire includes gritty reportage, slick corporate colour and some surprising personal projects. Barry is the successful all-rounder, tackling portraiture, news and in-depth reportage with equal panache: a Jack of all trades and master of most. The common characteristic that links his projects is an identifiable energy and dramatic flair that pervades the work, bringing vitality to even the most sombre of subjects.

As a founding member of Network Photographers, Barry is motivated by a never-ending thrill in the still image (with an eclectic appreciation of the work of many photographers) and a solid commitment to the ideals of reportage. Although he is probably best known for the hundreds of perfectly turned magazine features that have appeared in most of the world's leading titles of the last decade, the essence of his portfolio is found in the personal projects—many of which have never been published in the UK. The black and white portrait study of Miami South Beach residents contrasts sharply with the daily life of Albania after the demise of Enver Hoxha; but they are bound by Barry's common interest in the drama of human existence.

Barry holds the delicate balance of sensitivity to his surroundings and steely resolve not to let anything interrupt his progress with wit and humour that is often evident in the pictures. He is rarely without a comment or quip (visual and verbal), and approaches most situations with an unselfconscious stride, (though it might surprise some friends and colleagues to witness the transformation that occurs when he is separated from his camera). With his curiosity always taking him down new paths, we wait to see what Barry will make of the new opportunities offered by today's developing electronic technologies.

—Stephen Mayes

LIBERMAN, Alexander.

Nationality: American. **Born:** Kiev, Russia, in September 1912; lived in Paris, 1924-41; emigrated to the United States, 1941: naturalized, 1946. **Education:** Attended University School, Hastings, Sussex, England, 1921-22; St. Pirans School, Maidenhead, Berkshire, England, 1923-24; Ecole des Roches, Paris, 1924-27; studied philosophy and mathematics, Sorbonne,

Paris, 1927-30; studied painting, under André Lhote, Paris, 1931; studied architecture, under Auguste Perret, at the Ecole Speciale d'Architecture, Paris, 1931-32, and at the Ecole des Beaux-Arts, Paris, 1932-33. **Military Service:** Served in the French Army, 1940. **Family:** Married Tatiana Yacovleff du Plessix in 1942; daughter: Francine. **Career:** Worked as part-time design assistant to Cassandre, Paris, 1931-32; Art Director, then Managing Editor, under Lucien Vogel, *Vu* magazine, Paris, 1933-36; full-time painter since 1936, photographer since 1949, and sculptor since 1958; layout artist, 1941-43, and Art Director, 1943, *Vogue* magazine, New York, then Art Director, 1944-61, and Editorial Director, from 1962, Condé Nast Publications, United States and Europe. Has also had numerous exhibitions of paintings and sculptures. **Recipient:** Gold Medal for Design, *Exposition Internationale,* Paris, 1937. D.F.A.: Rhode Island School of Design, Providence, 1980. **Agent:** André Emmerich Gallery, 41 East 57th Street, New York, New York 10022. **Address:** Condé Nast Publications, 350 Madison Avenue, New York, New York 10017, U.S.A.

Individual Exhibitions:

1959	*The Artist in His Studio,* Museum of Modern Art, New York
1961	Musée des Arts Décoratifs, Paris
1977	Storm King Art Center, Mountainville, New York (retrospective)
1985	*Artists and Studios,* Fort Worth Art Museum, Texas
	Aldrich Museum of Contemporary Art, Ridgefield, Connecticut

Collections:

Museum of Modern Art, New York; Metropolitan Museum of Art, New York; Condé Nast Publications, New York; Yale University, New Haven, Connecticut; Smithsonian Institution, Washington, D.C.; Virginia Museum of Fine Arts, Richmond; Art Institute of Chicago; Bibliothèque Nationale, Paris.

Publications:

By LIBERMAN: Books—*The Art and Technique of Color Photography: A Treasury of Color Photographs by the Staff Photographers of Vogue, House and Garden and Glamour,* editor, with an introduction by A.B. Louchheim, New York 1951; *The Artist in His Studio,* New York 1960; *The World in Vogue,* editor, with B. Holme, K. Tweed and J. Davis, New York 1963; *Greece, Gods and Art,* New York 1968; introduction to *The Vogue Book of Fashion Photography,* edited by Polly Devlin, London 1979. **Film**—*La Femme Francaise dans l'Art,* 1936.

On LIBERMAN: Books—*The History of Fashion Photography* by Nancy Hall-Duncan, New York 1979; *Alexander Liberman: Monograph* by Barbara Rose, New York 1981; *The Library of World Photography: Photography as Fine Art,* with introduction by Douglas Davis, Tokyo 1982, 1983, London 1983; *The Library of World Photography: Portraits,* with introduction by Colin Ford, Tokyo 1982, 1983, London 1983. **Articles**—"Alexander Liberman: Aquatints, Paintings, Photographs and Sculpture" by Frederic Tuten in *Artsmagazine* (New York), June 1977; "Alexander Liberman at Storm King" by Carter Ratcliff in *Art in America* (New York), November/December 1977; "Liberman Staying in Vogue" by Marie Winn in the *New York Times,* 12 May 1979; "Alexander Liberman: photographs of artists" in *Photo Magazine* (New York), July 1982.

*   *   *

Alexander Liberman brings himself as a maker of art to the task of photographing art and artists. His great interest is in recording the excitement of creators and their creations in terms of personality and individuality. Whether it is a ruined masterpiece set in a Greek landscape or a painter's studio in Provence, he means to show us *what it is like.* In the painter's case, he focuses on the most personal of places—the studio. We learn what tools are used, what post cards and reproductions are pinned up for inspiration, what objects collected, what landscape exists nearby. In the case of Greece, we are shown the long known newly: marble against rock, hollyhocks (for color) before columns, grassgrown fragments, sequences of terrain, degrees of ruin.

A picture of the Parthenon at sunset contains a battery of effects worthy of a 19th century Romantic painter. And yet, it is Liberman's intensely modern viewpoint that enables him to risk the banality of famous beauty.

—Ralph Pomeroy

LICHTSTEINER, Rudolf.

Nationality: Swiss. **Born:** Winterthur in 1938. **Education:** Self-taught in photography. **Career:** Freelance photographer, Basel and Zurich, since 1972. Head of the Photography Department, Kunstgewerbeschule, Zurich, 1976-1986. **Recipient:** Swiss Applied Arts Grant (3), 1958-61; Niépce Prize, with M. Garanger, 1966. **Address:** Alte Landstrasse 4, D-79588 Welmlingen, Germany.

Individual Exhibitions:

1973	Galleria Il Diaframma, Milan
1974	Galleria Documenta, Turin
	Canon Photo Gallery, Amsterdam
1975	Wilhelm Lehmbruck Museum, Duisburg, West Germany (retrospective)
1976	Galerij Paule Pia, Antwerp
	Galerie im Forum Stadtpark, Graz, Austria
	Galleria Blu, Milan
1977	Galerie Maurer, Zurich
1980	*Baum-Werke,* Photo-Galerie, Kunsthaus, Zurich
	Canon Photo Gallery, Geneva
1981	*Reisen um mein Zimmer,* Work Gallery, Zurich
1982	The Photography Gallery, Philadelphia
1985	*Tischgeschichten,* Forum Stadtpark, Graz, Austria
	Benteler Galleries, Houston, Texas (with Jerry Uelsmann and Floris Neususs)
1986	*Tischgeschichten,* Galerie Peter Noser, Zurich
1990	*Zeitungsarbeiten, Tischgeschichten,* Galerie Bild, Baden
1991	*Sukessionen, Arbeiten von 1975,* Galerie Anita Neugebauer, Basel
1992	*bildwörtlich—wortbildlich,* Galerie Anita Neugebauer, Basel
	Lebensmittel, Nikon Galerie, Zurich

Selected Group Exhibitions:

1966	*Prix Nicéphore Niepce,* Chalon-sur-Saône, France
1974	*Fotografie in der Schweiz 1840 bis Heute,* Kunsthaus, Zurich
1975	*Photography as Art/Art as Photography,* Maison Européenne de la Photographie, Chalon-sur-Saône, France (and world tour)
1976	*Fantastic Photography in Europe,* at *Rencontres Internationales de la Photographie,* Arles, France, (toured Europe and the United States, 1976-78)
1977	*Photography as Art/Art as Photography II,* Fotoforum, Kassel, West Germany (and world tour)
1978	*Photography as Art/Art as Photography III,* Fotoforum, Kassel, West Germany (and world tour)
1980	*Photographia: La Linea Sottile,* Galleria Flaviana, Locarno, Switzerland
1983	*European Photography,* Gallery of Fine Arts, Ankara, Turkey
1985	*The European Edge,* Museum of Photographic Arts, San Diego, California
1986	*Foco,* Circulo de Bellas Artes, Madrid
1992	Forum für zeitgenössische Fotografie, München
	Helvetia condensed—Fotokunst aus der Schweiz, Hirschberger Kulturage
1993	*Der Traum vom Fliegen,* Frankfurt

Frontiers in and out IX, **1992.** Photograph ©Rudolf Lichtsteiner.

Collections:

Kunsthaus, Zurich; Stedelijk Museum, Amsterdam; National Museum of Modern Art, Tokyo; Center for Creative Photography, University of Arizona, Tucson; Museo de Fotografia, Mexico City.

Publications:

On LICHTSTEINER: Books—*Fotografie in der Schweiz 1840 bis Heute,* exhibition catalogue, by Hugo Loetscher, Walter Binder and Rosellina Burri-Bischof, Zurich 1974; *Fotografie als Kunst* by Floris M. Neusüss, Cologne 1979; *Photographia: La Linea Sottile,* exhibition catalogue, by Rinaldo Bianda and Giuliana Scime, Locarno, Switzerland 1980; *Baum-Werke/ Oevres d'Arbre: Rudolf Lichtsteiner,* exhibition catalogue, with text by Francis Ponge, Zurich and Geneva 1980; *The Imaginary Photo Museum* by Helmut Gernsheim, Renate and L. Fritz Gruber and others, Cologne 1981, London 1982; *Fotografie in Europa heute,* by Andreas Müller-Pohle, Cologne 1982; *Bildgebende Fotografie* by Gottfried Jäger, Cologne 1988; *Swiss Photography from 1840 until Today,* exhibition catalogue, with introduction by Hugo Loetscher, Zurich 1984; *The European Edge,* exhibition catalogue, with text by Arthur Ollman, San Diego, California 1985; *Helvetia (condensed),* exhibition catalogue, with text by Pia Lanzinger, München 1992; *Ueber das Epische in der Kunst,* exhibition catalogue, Hirschberg 1992; *Der Traum vom Fliegen,* exhibition catalogue, with text by Petra Benteler and Michael Wustrack, Frankfurt 1993. **Articles**—"European Edge" by Andreas Müller-Pohle in *European Photography,* (Göttingen) No. 21, 1985; "Neue Schweizer Photografen" by Urs Stahel in *DU, Zeitschrift für Kunst und Kultur* (Zürich), No. 8, 1985; "Rudolph Lichtsteiner Nikon Galerie Zürich Galerie Anita Neugebauer Basel" by Michael Köhler in *Artis, Zeitschrift für neue Kunst* (Bern), November 1992; "Ten Years Later" by Andreas Müller-Pohle in *European Photography* (Göttongen), No. 40 1989.

*

photography has the power
to lend the moment permanence
to capture greatness in a detail
to pinpoint smallness in a close-up
to show repose within movement
to catch time within a lapse
to reveal more than is visible
to light the shadows and wrest shadows from
    the light
to make the night as day
to revert to the witness of the eye
Memento . . . to hold thought in suspense and give
    thought something to hold . . . Death

—Rudolf Lichtsteiner

*   *   *

Rudolf Lichtsteiner stages photographs (most often in series of two to seven photos, sometimes just one) that attract us with their beauty, the clarity of their representation and the enigma of their content. We may simply enjoy looking at them, savouring their mystery, or pause with them to unravel their meaning, which need not coincide with what the author had in mind.

Lichtsteiner originally wanted to become a painter. Much later he began to work with photographs, first as a retoucher, then as an advertising photographer, exploring the manipulated and set-up photograph. Sporadically he did journalistic work. The degree of phantasy in the former and the truncated truth of the latter did not satisfy his need for a more profound reality in his work.

The polarity of emotion and intellect, and that polarity in his own creativity; nature and what man does to it, how he tries to harness it, may misuse it, but cannot conquer it—these are the kinds of considerations that Lichtsteiner endeavors to make visible. He develops his themes by means of a "Script," but his dramatizations do not follow chronological or rational laws. They are arrived at and decoded by associations which may derive from the

common usage of the objects shown, through displacement, as in a dream, or by looking at language in a way akin to that of Freud. The silences or spaces between the photographs accentuate and fertilize the poignancy of his visual messages. Man is not shown. His imprint or intervention—footprints or hands—speak of human existence more eloquently than any specific figure.

As Lichtsteiner's concerns are with making invisible reality physically visible, as in a play on a stage, it follows that he is also interested in setting the stage for his photographs. His catalogue *Baum-Werke* has to be turned around, as he had to turn around words and relationships to arrive at his "Script." Its binding is green, and in the exhibition at the Kunsthaus, plants interacted with his prints in an installation that was, if not unconventional, different, and in harmony with his work.

In the future, Rudolf Lichtsteiner hopes to move more and more, philosophically and physically, into a unified world of words and images related to environment.

For some years, Lichtsteiner has been teaching the Photography Class at the Kunstgewerbeschule in Zurich. He has encouraged individual talent and inclination. Lichtsteiner regards his teaching as an important part of his creative life, an exchange of stimulus, which fertilizes his creative work, though it curtails the time he can give to it.

—Inge Bondi

LIEBLING, Jerome.

Nationality: American. **Born:** New York City, 16 April 1924. **Education:** Attended Lafayette High School, Brooklyn, New York, 1940-42; studied art and photography, under Walter Rosenblum, Ad Reinhardt and Milton Brown, Brooklyn College, New York, 1942, 1946-48; filmmaking, under Lewis Jacobs, Leo Hurwitz and Paul Falkenberg, New School for Social Research, New York, 1948-49; photography, under Paul Strand, Photo League, New York, 1947-49. **Military Service:** Served in the United States Army, in North Africa, Italy, France, England, Ireland, and Germany, 1942-45. **Family:** Married Phyllis Levine in 1949 (divorced, 1969); children: Madeline, Tina, Adam, Daniella, and Rachel. Married Rebecca Nordstrom in June 1990. **Career:** Photographer since 1947, and filmmaker since 1949. Professor of Photography, University of Minnesota, Minneapolis, 1949-69. Since 1970, Professor of Photography, Hampshire College, Amherst, Massachusetts. Visiting Professor, State University of New York at New Paltz, 1957-58, and Yale University, New Haven, Connecticut, 1976-77. Founder Member, Society for Photographic Education, 1961. **Recipient:** Screen Producers Guild Award, 1951; New Talent U.S.A. Award, American Federation of Arts, 1956; First Prize, *San Francisco Film Festival,* 1960; Documentary Award, *Festival dei Popoli,* Florence, 1964; National Endowment for the Arts Grant, 1972, 1979, 1980; Massachusetts Arts and Humanities Award, 1975; Guggenheim Fellowship, 1976-81; Massachusetts Council of the Arts Fellowship, 1984. **Agent:** Howard Greenberg Gallery, 120 Wooster Street, New York City, New York 10012. **Address:** 39 Dana Street, Amherst, Massachusetts 01002, U.S.A.

Individual Exhibitions:

1948	Walker Art Center, Minneapolis
1951	Portland Art Museum, Oregon
1957	International Museum of Photography, George Eastman House, Rochester, New York
1960	Limelight Gallery, New York
1963	*100 Photographs,* Walker Art Center, Minneapolis
1977	Vision Gallery, Boston
1978	Friends of Photography, Carmel, California (retrospective)
	University of California at San Diego
1980	Corcoran Gallery of Art, Washington, D.C.
1982	*Contemporary Color,* Fogg Art Museum, Harvard University, Cambridge, Massachusetts
1983	*Jerome Liebling: Recent Color Photographs,* Hampshire College, Amherst, Massachusetts

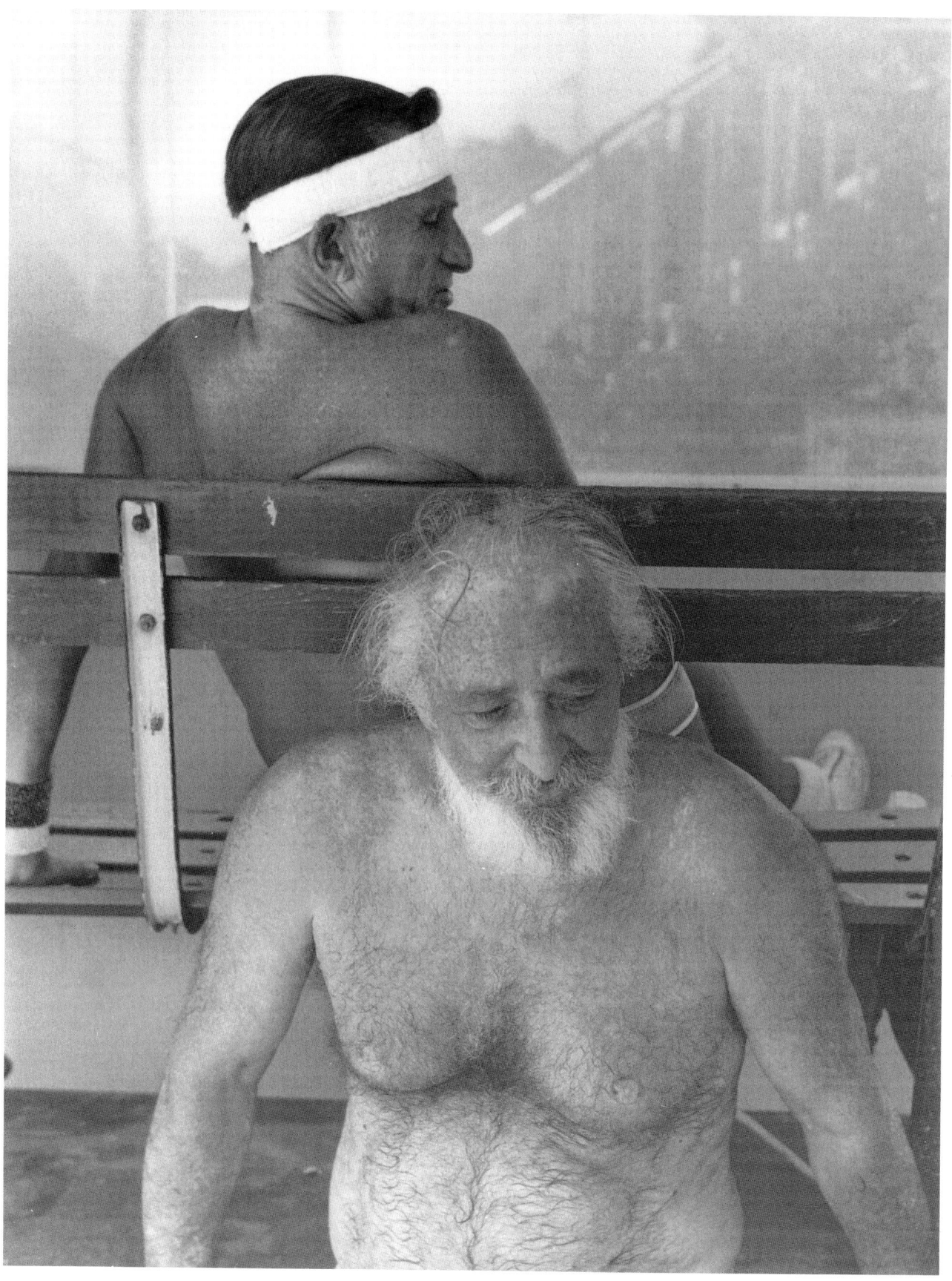

Handball Players, Miami Beach, Florida, **1978.** Photograph by Jerome Liebling.

Portland School of Art, Portland, Maine
1985   Photospace, Department of Art, Northern Illinois Univesity,
        Dekalb, Illinois
1987   The State of Massachusetts Smith College Museum of Art,
        Northampton
1988   Blaffer Gallery of Art, University of Houston
        Photofind Gallery, New York City

Selected Group Exhibitions:

1963   *5 Unrelated Photographers,* Museum of Modern Art,
        New York
1967   *The Camera as Witness,* at *Expo '67,* Montreal
1976   *The Bus Show,* on city buses, New York
1978   *14 New England Photographers,* Museum of Fine Arts, Boston
        Photographic Crossroads: The Photo League, National Gallery
        of Canada, Ottawa (travelled to the International Center of
        Photography, New York; Museum of Fine Arts, Houston;
        and Minneapolis Institute of Fine Arts)
        Photos from the Sam Wagstaff Collection, Corcoran Gallery of
        Art, Washington, D.C. (toured the United States, Canada and
        Europe)
        Mirrors and Windows: American Photography since 1960,
        Museum of Modern Art, New York (toured the United
        States, 1978-80)
1980   *Photo Politic,* Project Studio I (P.S.I.), Queens, New York
1981   *American Children,* Museum of Modern Art, New York
1985   *American Images 1945-80,* Barbican Art Gallery, London
        (toured Britain)

Collections:

Museum of Modern Art, New York; International Museum of Photography,
George Eastman House, Rochester, New York; Museum of Fine Arts, Boston;
Fogg Art Museum, Harvard University, Cambridge, Massachusetts; Yale
University, New Haven, Connecticut; Library of Congress, Washington, D.C.;
Corcoran Gallery of Art, Washington, D.C.; Minneapolis Institute of Art;
Center for Creative Photography, University of Arizona, Tucson.

Publications:

By LIEBLING: Books—*The Face of Minneapolis,* with Don Morrison,
Minneapolis 1966; *Photography: Current Perspectives,* editor, Rochester,
New York 1979. **Articles**—"Jerome Liebling Photographs" *Aperture,* 1989;
"The Evergreens: The Other Dickinson House," text by Masako Takeda and
Gregory Farmer in *Massachusetts Review,* Winter 1993-94; "The People,
Yes!" in *Aperture,* 1994. **Films**—*The Tree Is Dead,* with Allen Downs, 1955;
Pow-Wow, 1961; *The Old Man,* with Allen Downs, 1965.

On LIEBLING: Books—*The Photography Catalog,* edited by Norman
Snyder, New York 1976; *Photographs: Sheldon Memorial Art Gallery
Collection, University of Nebraska,* with an introduction by Norman A. Geske,
Lincoln, Nebraska 1977; *Faces,* edited by Ben Maddow, Boston 1977;
Mirrors and Windows: American Photography since 1960 by John Szarkowski,
New York 1978; *Untitled 15: Jerome Liebling Photographs,* with text by
Estelle Jussim, Carmel, California 1978; *New York Street Kids,* edited by the
New York City Historical Museum, New York 1978; *The Sam Wagstaff
Collection,* edited by Sam Wagstaff, New York 1978; *Jerome Liebling:
Photographs,* exhibition catalogue, with text by Jane Livingston, Washington,
D.C. 1980; *American Images: Photography 1945-1980,* edited by Peter
Turner and John Benton-Harris, London 1985.

*

I would like this series of quotes from three prominent photography critics
to be my statement:

Estelle Jussim, in the monograph *Untitled 15: Jerome Liebling Photographs* (Friends of Photography, 1978): "He has pushed still photography to
its absolute limits as a message system, he has wrenched from paper images,
the utmost which they, as a visual communication medium, can deliver. . . . A
photographer of considerable formal means, with superb ability to make us
feel, whose conscience offers a gripping testament of faith in humanity."

Alan Trachtenberg in his introduction to my portfolio, 1977: "Liebling's
work goes against the grain of contemporary fashion. His pictures are not tense
with ironic subversions. They are not clever statements about photography
itself. They take the world seriously. He is romantic without apology. Human
desire is the unifying motif of his pictures' desire for grace, for transcendence. . . . The unspeakable power of the mundane to move, to impress, to
coerce us into recognitions: this is an authentic power of photography itself."

Jane Livingston, Associate Director of the Corcoran Gallery of Art,
Washington, D.C. in her monograph on my work: "More and more we see that
Liebling's humanity, his heritage and way of life, find literal expression in his
work and communicate to us in the most immediate sense his own experience.
The work is sometimes about guilt and expiation, sometimes about sheer
desire, sometimes empathy. But these 'contents' are not quite in the end the
main point. The color work is really at its best a simple flirtation with esthetic
excitement."

—Jerome Liebling

*   *   *

Jerome Liebling is a photographer of still and motion pictures, an educator
of young photographers, an organizer of photographic colloquia, and a
melancholy humanist. For more than 30 years his imagery has been concerned
with the unenviable and imperative human destinies that most individuals seek
to forget or avoid. His camera lens has sought out the afflicted; he has
photographed individuals in unfathomable occupations and circumstances;
and he has exposed the putrescence of the cadavers that we all become.

A consistent disputant of conventional attitudes, Liebling has refashioned
the affirming humanism of his first teachers—Walter Rosenblum at Brooklyn
College and Paul Strand at the Photo League. His war experiences and the
horror of the Holocaust confirmed his growing awareness of the human
potential for inflicting as well as suffering pain. Since then, his attempt has
been to make these perceptions more than real, through images whose force is
concentrated in rigorously disciplined linear, spatial and tonal relationships.

Liebling's formal visual training in the Bauhaus aesthetic may seem at
odds with his fervent emotional intentions. But just as he redirected the
humanism of his mentors, he has reconceived Bauhaus aesthetic ideas to
encapsulate his own rage and compassion. At times he selects an unusual but
expressive portion of his subject, as in the springing curves of the lower half of
an infant torso to affirm the vitality of new life. The featureless bowed head
and careful hands of a blind man eating becomes a metaphor not only for
sightlessness, but for the photographer's compassionate concern for the
indignities that the afflicted endure. Liebling has made the economy of means
that is at the heart of Bauhaus aesthetic doctrine reverberate with emotional
intensity.

Humor is less apparent in Liebling's work, although one of his earliest
films is a genial spoof of the foolishness of big college football rites. A series
of images of politicians on the hustings, made intermittantly throughout the
1960s and 70s, displays a mordant view that is an unsettling as it is humorous.

In his earliest photographs, made even before his Army service in 1942,
Liebling sought to discomfit his family by presenting them with images of the
urban poor whose existence they had chosen to ignore. He has continued to use
his camera as a prod to complacency, impelling the comfortable viewer to face
the unspeakable. His impolitic images keep presenting reminders of what is
shut away or disregarded until, against our will, we are made to confront both
inhumanity and mortality.

—Naomi Rosenblum

LINDSTRÖM-CAUDWELL, Tuija Lydia Elisabeth.

Nationality: Finish. **Born:** Kotka, Finland, 5 May 1950. Moved to Sweden in 1975. **Education:** Studied photography at the GFU College of Photography in Stockholm in 1979 and at the School of Modern Arts in Stockholm in 1981 and 1984. **Family:** Married to Peter Caudwell in 1975; children: Ilari, Jennifer and Laura. **Career:** Professor of Photography at the Institution of Photography, Gothenberg University, Sweden, working with 16mm black-and-white movie film, incorporating video techniques in her work. **Recipient:** Awarded the Stockholm Museum of Modern Arts Gullers Award in 1982; the Daniel Nyblin Prize in 1988 and the Edstrands Foundation Arts Grant in 1992. Received grants from the Swedish Arts Council in 1983, 1985, 1987-88, 1990 and 1993. **Address:** Aschebergsgatan 25, 411 33 Göteborg, Sweden.

Individual Exhibitions:

1983	Fotograficentrum, Örebro, Sweden
1984	Suomi Gallery, Stockholm
1986	Gallery Mira, Stockholm
	Gallery Billedhuset, Copenhagen
1987	Gallery Hippolyte, Helsinki
	Axiom Centre, Cheltenham, England
	Röda Kvarn, Hälsingborg, Sweden
	Gallery Hybrydys, Warsaw
1988	Rantagalleria, Oulu, Finland
	Galleria Fotokram, Jyväskylä, Finland
	Gallery Hippolyte, Helsinki
1989	Gallery Tornhuset, Luleå, Sweden
	Gallery 2000, Karlstad, Sweden
	Wainö Aaltonen Museum, Turku, Finland
1990	Gallery Fotografica, Copenhagen
	Laterna Magica, Helsinki
	Fotografisk Gallery, Olso
	Gallery Finnfoto, Helsinki
	"Paradigm," Museum of Modern Art, Stockholm
1991	"Finnace," Gallery du Chateau, Nice
1992	Victor Barsokevitz Museum, Kuopio
	Galleri Index, Stockholm
	Fotografisk Gallery, Copenhagen
1992/93	Göteborg Art Museum, Gothenburg
1993	Malmö Museum, Sweden
	Galerie Suzel Berna, Paris
1993/94	Gallery Zebra, Karis, Finland
1994	Gallery Brage, Umeå, Sweden

Selected Group Exhibitions:

1983	International Photo Festival, Malmö, Sweden
1983	*Contemporary Western European B/W Photography,* Amsterdam
1983/84	*Contemporary Swedish Photography,* Cheltenham (travelled to Newcastle, Nottingham and Kendal)
	Ten Swedish Women Photographers, Canon Gallery, Amsterdam (travelled to Belgium, Italy, Nicaragua)
1984	*Camara Obscura,* Stockholm
1985	*Swedish Photography,* Arles
1986	*Images,* New York
	Scandinavian Contemporary Photo Exhibition, Odense, Denmark
1987	*Houston Photo Festival,* Texas
1989	*Photography 150-year Jubilee,* Museum of Photography, Stockholm
1991	*Lika Med,* Museum of Photography
	Gallery Image, Århus, Denmark
	Figuras Feminas, Ecuador (travelled to Mexico)
1992	Speglingar, Oulu, Finland
1992/93	Kvinnliga Fotografer, Arbetets Museum, Norrköping
1993	Pod Ostona Nieba, Warsava, Poland
1993/94	*Combi-Nacion, Imagen Sueca,* Mexico City (travelled to Galleri Enkehuset, Stockholm)
1994	Gallery Stuart Levy, New York

Collections:

Museum of Modern Art, Stockholm; Museum of Photography, Stockholm; Kungligabibliotek, Copenhagen; Wainö Aaltonen Museum, Turku, Finland; Houston Art Museum, Texas; Department of Culture, Paris; Photographic Museum, Helsinki; Galerie Suzel Berna, Paris; Bank of Finland, Helsinki; Malmö Konsthall, Sweden; Gothenberg Art Museum, Sweden; Umeå LänsMuseum, Umeå, Sweden; Lund ArtMuseum, Lund, Sweden.

Publications:

By LINDSTRÖM: Books—*Tiuja Lindström,* ETC Förlag AB Stockholm, 1989; *Sandemar,* Musta Taide/Black Art, Helsinki 1991; *The Girls at Bull's Pond,* Hall & Cederqvist, Stockholm 1993. **Films**—*The Girls at Bull's Pond,* 16mm black-and-white short film, 1992; *The Sleeping Body,* video, 1993.

* * *

Tuija Lindström's photographs are, most of all, encounters—with worlds, others' gazes, faces, bodies, sex. Sometimes comforting, sometimes in despair, her photographs are certificates—and invocations—of presence. As portraits they are not so much about individuals or personalities; they are not "psychological" but rather probes, scrutinies of certain modes of existence. The individual is incomplete, unfinished; let us see what lies in between, what it, she, he, doesn't know of it-, her-, himself.

The human body and the landscape are the two poles in Tuija Lindström's photography. Their borders, their limits are constantly transfigured, transgressed, repositioned: the one always becoming the other. Space in Tuija's photographs is compact, condensed, concentrated; in this way landscapes thicken, become bodies. Time is put aside; it is space, matter, soil, presence. Only two options: the body and the landscape absorb light, become dark dense impenetrable shapes. Or the body and the landscape are illuminated, light passes through, light is emitted by them, they float in light. And sometimes the light turns to water.

Tuija Lindström's world is one of violent beauty. Of a sensualism which could sacrifice anything. Of menace and harmony coexisting. Nakedness is always entirely unmitigated in her photos. Blunt, bold, brutal. Above all, it is the liberating and deadly force of desire and eros which is unleashed in her photography.

—Jan-Erik Lundström

LINK, O. Winston.

Nationality: American. **Born:** Brooklyn, New York, on 16 December 1914. **Education:** Graduated from the Polytechnic Institute of Brooklyn in 1937; self-taught in photography. **Career:** Worked as a public relations photographer, 1937-42; research engineer and photographer for the Airborne Instruments Laboratory, Office of Scientific Research and Development, Columbia University, 1942-45; self-employed industrial and commercial photographer, 1945-87. Major personal project documenting the last of the steam locomotives operating on the Norfolk & Western Railway in Virginia, North Carolina and West Virginia and recording daily life along the railway 1955-60. **Agent:** Thomas H. Garver, P.O. Box 3493, Madison, Wisconsin 53704-0493, U.S.A.

From the series *Preg. Texas,* 1987. Photograph ©Tuija Lindström-Caudwell.

Individual Exhibitions:

1983   *Night Trick,* Photographers' Gallery, London (travelled to
          Bradford, York, Edinburgh, Cambridge, Swansea and
          Lacock)
          Akron Art Museum, Ohio
          International Center for Photography, New York
          Chrysler Museum, Norfolk, Virginia
          Ohio State University
          Museum of Science and Industry, Chicago

Houston Center for Photography, Texas
Museum of Contemporary Photography, Columbia College,
    Chicago
The Madison Art Center, Wisconsin

Collections:

Museum of Modern Art, New York.

Publications:

Mr. and Mrs. Pope Watch the Last Steam-Powered Passenger Train, **1957.** Photograph ©O. Winston Link.

By LINK: Book—*Steam Steel and Stars,* Abrams (New York) 1987; Television—*Trains that Passed in the Night,* Channel 4 (UK) and PBS (USA), 1987.

* * *

While Winston Link was studying civil engineering he also took photographs of various college activities to earn money to help with his studies. This put him in an excellent position to take on the work as Public Relations photographer to the firm of Carl Byoir. During the war his work became more specialised when he had to devise ways to photograph the speed of bullets and solve other scientific as well as photographic problems. One of his most famous pictures after the war was to catch the "after burner" effect of the first jet engines as planes were taking off and he also undertook the documentation of the building of the Verrazano Bridge linking Brooklyn to Staten Island in 1960.

Since childhood Link had a passion for steam trains. He used to spend time watching them in the yards and was fascinated by their size and strength and the fact that they needed feeding, watering and constant attention—in much the same way as horses had done before them. As diesel power began to supercede steam after the war he determined to try and record these monsters while they still existed. His opportunity came, when on a commercial assignment in Waynesboro, West Virginia, he realised the potential in photographing the railway at night. He sent two pictures to the head of the Norfolk and Virginia Railway and asked for permission to make photographs through its territory, and for co-operation in finding the best sites and reaching locations. He promised to include people in all the pictures which would thus record not only the engines but many of those involved in their running and maintenance.

Once this was agreed he spent as much of the following five years as he could, between commercial assignments, working chiefly with one assistant, Thomas Garver, and covering the whole area of the line in Virginia, North Carolina and West Virginia. Except for those areas where the trains only ran in the daytime, all the photographs were taken with a specially designed synchronised series of flash lights at night. These had to be set up well in advance and several days were often needed to take each photograph. As time went by and the railway staff became more involved, they gave him increasing help. He had a key to the phones to connect him with the drivers so that he could, on occasion, ask them to back up for another shot, or make white steam at the appropriate moment. Over 2,000 negatives were made during the five years.

The lasting magic and importance of these pictures lies in the combination of the drama, enhanced by the night and the fact that the trains, while present, are by no means always the main subject of the pictures. These photographs portray a picture of life in one of the more rural areas of America which looked as though it would never change, but has of course done so. Here, we are in Norman Rockwell or Edward Hopper country, with life seemingly stable and, in many ways, unremarkable. The trains connect these people's lives, passing close to their houses down their main streets, past their open air swimming pools and cinemas, ever present and absolutely accepted. The technique and imagination which Link brought to the project, his ability to pre-visualise combined with his passion to get it right, have given us a document which is far more than a series of train pictures, it is a true and loving portrait of a particular time and place in America which would otherwise have passed without record.

—Sue Davies

LIPPER, Susan.

Nationality: American. **Born:** New York on 28 March 1953. Has lived for extended periods in London. **Education:** Attended Skidmore College 1971-75. Took a master class with Lisette Model at the New School in New York in 1979 and an MFA in photography at Yale University 1981-83. **Career:** Worked as assistant to Joyce Baronio and the publisher Pyxidium Press. In 1983, worked on a series of studies of writers and artists in London. Travelled across the US making environmental portraits 1987-89. Began long-term

project in Grapevine Hollow, West Virginia, 1988-93. Taught in a private school in New York 1991-92. **Recipient:** Won a West Virginia Juried Exhibition Award in 1991. **Agent:** Deborah Bell, 137 East 26th Street, New York, New York 10010. **Address:** 178 East 70th Street, New York, New York 10021, U.S.A.

Individual Exhibitions:

1989   Midtown Y Photography Gallery, New York
1990-91   Duane Gallery, Fordham University, New York
1991   Chenango County Arts Council, Norwich, NY (with Andrea Modica)
1994   *Grapevine Hollow,* The Photographers' Gallery, London
                In the Hollows: Susan Lipper and Wendy Ewald, pARTs Gallery, Minneapolis
                Grapevine, Arnolfini Gallery, Bristol

Selected Group Exhibitions:

1981   *American Vision,* Washington Square Galleries, New York University
1982   *16th Annual Central Pennsylvania Arts Festival,* Pennsylvania
1986   *Recent Acquisitions,* National Portrait Gallery, London
1987   *Current Works 87,* Kansas City Art Institute, Missouri
1990   *90 Photographs from the Collection of Tom Strong,* The Taft School, Connecticut
1991-92   *7th Annual West Virginia Juried Exhibition,* Cultural Center, Charleston, West Virginia
1992   *Exhibition of Photography,* Berkshire Museum, Massachusetts
1994   *Who's Looking At The Family?,* Barbican Art Gallery, London

Collections:

Bibliothèque Nationale, Paris; Metropolitan Museum of Art, New York; National Portrait Gallery, London; Sterling Library, Yale University; Museum of Fine Arts, Houston.

Publications:

By LIPPER: Book—*Grapevine,* Cornerhouse Publications (Manchester) 1994. Articles—"The legend of Grapevine Hollow" in the *Telegraph Magazine* (London), 29 January 1994; *Granta* (London), No 47, Spring 1994.

On LIPPER: Books—*Graduate Photography at Yale,* Yale School of Art, New Haven 1983; *Who's Looking At The Family?,* London 1994. Articles—"Bibliotheque Nationale, Paris (collection du XXe avril 84-fevrier 85)" in *Photographies,* No 7, (Paris) May 1985; "If you go down to the woods today" by Tim Hilton in *The Independent on Sunday* (London), 6 February 1994; "The Art of Erotica" by James Hall in *The Guardian* (London), 14 February 1994; "Southern Discomfort" by Gerry Badger in the *British Journal of Photography* (London), 17 February 1994; "Theories of Relativity" by Guy Walters in *The Times Magazine* (London), 21 May 1994; "Mann's Family and other Animals" by Tim Hilton in *The Independent on Sunday* (London), 29 May 1994; "Accentuate the Positive: *Grapevine* by Susan Lipper" by David Brittain in *Creative Camera* (London), No 328, June/July 1994; "Where Women Dare to Tread" by Val Williams in *Women's Art Magazine* (London), No 59, June/July 1994; "Grapevine" by Eddie Marsman in *FOTO,* (Leusden) The Netherlands, Nos 7 and 8, July/August 1994; "A View of Beard's Wild Life: An Appalachian Journal" by A.D. Coleman in *The New York Observer* (New York), 21 November 1994; Susan H. Edwards in the *History of Photography* (London), Vol 9, 1995.

*

My pictures are not an effort to document in any real sense, but rather the collision of my experiences, the tangible world and the nature of photography. I take the viewpoint that reality is fascinating, but that my view of it will be hopelessly subjective and all of this will be articulated by the photographic properties to which pictures are inevitably bound. I photograph to learn both

Grapevine Hollow, **1991**. Photograph ©Susan Lipper.

the appearance of things and also my feelings about them. I prefer images to pose questions and answer in part by returning to the physical world and issues dealt with in the act of photographing.

—Susan Lipper

*   *   *

Chiefly known for her images of a small rural community in West Virginia—Grapevine Hollow—Susan Lipper has been miscast by some as a social documentary photographer. Her photographs are certainly in the ''documentary mode'' as they are undirected in the sense in which that term has come to be understood, and she does not hesitate to show the personal effects and natural *mis en scène* of her subjects. In her portraits she does not concentrate solely upon the face, but utilises the whole body, or even a part of it, together with gesture and interaction with others to make her effect. She is, however, interested not so much in the specifics of geography and social culture as in the nuances of psychological insight. She might be said to be concerned with the more ''universal'' issues of human existence, although to say that should not imply that her images are asocial, rooted merely in formalism or poetics. Her exploration of fundamental issues such as gender relationships within nominally everyday cultural situations gives her work a relevance far beyond those specific contexts.

Lipper refers to her photographs as "works of fiction," stating that any truth within them is her truth. Such a statement is an honest admission that the psychology she explores within her portraits is her own as much as those she pictures. The personal and social issues she investigates are of course relevant to her sitters but the trigger for making her images lies within her own experience and psyche. In every Lipper picture the final tale told is interwoven out of her own and her subject's stories.

In this, and as a woman photographer investigating issues that impinge deeply upon her own gender consciousness, Susan Lipper is no obsessive stalker of "freak" subjects. Her target is the everyday, and she maintains a respectful distance, catching her subjects on the wing rather than in the aggressive stare of a strobe. Nevertheless, Lipper is every bit as sharp as Arbus. Every nuance of gesture and background is explored in the search for evidence of the complex psychological sub-texts underlying daily living. Nothing in a Lipper picture is wasted or meaningless. Like Arbus, she does not attack her subjects, but is entirely sympathetic and non-judgemental at a personal level. Her attack is directed rather to the cloud that envelops them—and us—our culture.

Lipper attacks an excessively male view of things, but in a personal/political sense rather than from a fixed ideological standpoint. When she investigates a community or group of people she is always looking for the relevant parallels with her own existence. Then she can dig deeply and make images that explore her psychological interaction **with** individuals, not simply her superficial impressions **of** human groups. The tensions induced by this often painful process result in Lipper making powerful images with insight and authenticity.

—Gerry Badger

LIST, Herbert.

Nationality: German. **Born:** Hamburg, 7 October 1903. **Education:** Attended Johanneumschule, Hamburg, 1912-20; studied German, briefly, in Heidelberg, 1922; commercial studies, Hamburg, 1923-24; mainly self-taught in photography, but assisted initially by the photographer Andreas Feininger, *q.v.,* from 1930. **Military Service:** Served in the German Army, Norway, 1944-45. **Career:** Worked as clerk-apprentice, Landfried Coffee Company, Heidelberg, 1921-23; assistant buyer, in family coffee import business, Hamburg, 1925-26, travelling in Brazil, Guatemala, San Salvador, Costa Rica and the United States, 1926-28; Company Clerk, then Partner, List and Heineken family company, Hamburg, 1928-36; professional magazine photographer, working for *Vogue, Harper's Bazaar, Verve, Life,* etc., in London, Paris and Athens, 1936-41, and in Munich, working mainly for *Du,* 1945-60; temporary editor, *Heute* magazine, Munich, 1946; gradually abandoned photography to concentrate on collection of Italian 16th to 18th-century drawings, Munich, 1960 until his death, 1975. Member, Gesellschaft Deutscher Lichtbildner (GDL), 1964-73. **Recipient:** David Octavius Hill Prize, Gesellschaft Deutscher Lichtbildner, 1964. Estate: c/o Max Scheler, Bellevue 39A, 22301 Hamburg, Germany. **Died:** (in Munich) 4 April 1975.

Individual Exhibitions:

1937	Galerie du Chasseur d'Images, Paris
1977	Kunsthaus, Zurich
1980	Galerie Lange-Irschl, Munich
	CCD Galerie, Dusseldorf
1981	The Photographers' Gallery, London
	Galleria Il Diaframma/Canon, Milan
	International Center of Photography, New York
	Galerie Lange-Irschl, Munich
	Palazzo Odescalchi, Rome
1985	*Photos 1930-70,* Chicago Public Library, Cultural Center, Chicago

	Pace MacGill Gallery, New York
1988	Charles Cowles Gallery, New York
1992	Fahey Klein Gallery, Los Angeles
	Galerie Zum Stockeregg, Zurich
1994	Glyptothek, Munich
	Musée National du Monument Français, Paris

Selected Group Exhibitions:

1964	*World Exhibition of Photography: What Is Man?,* Pressehaus Stern, Hamburg (and world tour)
1977	*Fotografische Künstlerbildnisse,* Museum Ludwig, Cologne
1978	*Das Experimentelle Photo in Deutschland 1918-40,* Galleria del Levante, Munich
1979	*Photographie als Kunst 1879-1979,* Tiroler Landesmuseum Ferdinandeum, Innsbruck, Austria (travelled to Neue Galerie am Wolfgang Gurlitt Museum, Linz, Austria; Neue Galerie am Landesmuseum Joanneum, Graz, Austria; Museum des 20. Jahrhunderts, Vienna)
	Photographic Surrealism, New Gallery of Contemporary Art, Cleveland (travelled to Dayton Art Institute, Ohio; and Brooklyn Museum, New York)
1980	*Avant-Garde Photography in Germany 1919-1939,* San Francisco Museum of Modern Art (toured the United States)
1981	*Dog Show No. 1,* Nikon Fotogalerie, Zurich
1984	*Subjektive Fotografie: Images of the 50s,* San Francisco Museum of Modern Art (travelled to the University of Houston, Texas; Museum Folkwang, Essen; Vasterbottens Museum, Umea; Kulturhuset, Stockholm; Saarland Museum, Saarbrucken; Palais des Beaux-Arts, Brussels)
1985	*Das Aktfoto,* Fotomuseum im Stadtmuseum, Munich (toured Germany)
1986	*The Animal in Photography 1843-1985,* The Photographers' Gallery, London

Collections:

PPS-Galerie, Hamburg; Museum of Modern Art, New York; Sander Gallery, Washington, D.C.; San Francisco Museum of Modern Art; Museum Ludwig, Cologne.

Publications:

By LIST: Books—*Licht über Hellas,* Munich 1953; *Rome,* with text by Hans Mollier, Munich 1955; *Caribia,* Hamburg 1958; *Dom, Bilder und Eindrücke,* with text by Ingeborg Bachmann, Biberach, West Germany 1960; *Napoli,* with text by Vittorio de Sica, Gutersloh, West Germany 1962; *Bildwerke aus Nigeria/Nigerian Images,* with text by William Fagg, Munich, London, Paris and New York 1963; *Zeitlupe Null,* portfolio, Hamburg 1980; *Fotografia Metafisica,* Munich 1980, New York 1983; *Portraits of the Spirit of Mid Century,* Hamburg 1976; *Junge Maenner,* Los Angeles and London 1988; *Hellas,* Munich, Paris and New York 1993, Italy, Munich and New York 1995.

On LIST: Books—*Akt International/International Nudes,* with introduction by Otto Steinert, Munich and London 1954; *Fame: Famous Portraits of Famous People by Famous Photographers,* edited by L. Fritz Gruber, London and New York 1960; *Photography of the World '60,* edited by Hiromu Hara, Ihei Kimura and others, Tokyo and New York 1960; *The Magic Image* by Cecil Beaton and Gail Buckland, London and Boston 1975; *Herbert List: Fotografien 1930-1970,* with text by Günter Metken, Munich 1976, London 1980, New York 1981; *Fotografie der 30er Jahre,* edited by Hans-Jürgen Syberberg, Munich 1977; *Geschichte der Fotografie im 20. Jahrhundert/ Photography in the 20th Century* by Petr Tausk, Cologne 1977, London 1980; *Herbert List: Portraits,* edited by Max Scheler, with a foreword by Manuel Gasser, Hamburg 1977; *Fotografische Künstlerbildnisse,* exhibition catalogue, by Dieter Rönte, Evelyn Weiss and Jeane von Oppenheim, Cologne 1977; *Italienische Zeichnungen des 16.-18. Jahrhunderts: Eine Ausstellung zum Andenken an Herbert List,* exhibition catalogue, by Herbert Pee and Eckhard Schaar, Munich 1977; *Das Experimentelle Photo in Deutschland*

***Goldfish Glass, Santorini, Greece,* 1937.** Photograph by Herbert List.

1918-1940 by Emilio Bertonati, Munich 1978; *Photographie als Kunst 1879-1979/Kunst als Photographie 1949-1979,* exhibition catalogue, 2 vols., by Peter Weiermair, Innsbruck, Austria 1979; *Fotografie 1919-1979, Made in Germany: Die GDL Fotografen,* edited by Fritz Kempe, Bernd Lohse and others, Frankfurt 1979; *Deutsche Fotografie nach 1945/German Photography after 1945* by Floris Neusüss, Wolfgang Kemp and Petra Benteler, Kassel, West Germany 1979; *Photographic Surrealism,* exhibition catalogue, by Nancy Hall-Duncan, Cleveland, Ohio 1979; *Avant-Grade Photography in Germany 1919-1939,* exhibition catalogue, by Van Deren Coke, Ute Eskildsen and Bernd Lohse, San Francisco 1980; *Herbert List: Fotografia Metafisica,* with text by Günter Metken, edited by Max Scheler, Munich, London and New York 1980; *I Grandi Fotografi: Herbert List,* with text by Max Scheler, Milan 1983; *Subjektive Fotografie: Images of the 50s,* exhibition catalogue by Ute Eskildsen, Manfred Schmalriede and Dorothy Martinson, Essen, West Germany 1984. **Articles**—special issue of *Du* (Zurich), November 1966; "Herbert List," special issue of *Du* (Zurich), July 1973; "Herbert List 1903-1975" in *Photography Year 1976,* by the Time-Life editors, New York 1976; "List's Photographs Acclaimed Once Again" by Inge Bondi in *Print-letter* (Zurich), November/December 1976.

*   *   *

One of his best-known pictures is of a glass of water; in the water there is a fish; the glass is on a balustrade, and behind the balustrade is the glittering sea—"Santorin, 1937." The immeasurable becomes visible in a dreamlike, real, paradoxical cypher. A clearly outlined object becomes the magical subject of our contemplation. Herbert List's best photographs are so simple in their composition and so subtle in their allusions: pictures in which the visible becomes a release for the invisible, for the background of visions. It is not gratuitous that List once wanted to place as a motto in front of a collection of his photographs a quotation from Novalis: "The external is the internal exalted in a mysterious state."

Born in Hamburg in 1903, List was at first active in his father's coffee import business. Interested in a variety of cultural matters, he got to know George Freund Gundolf, Gustav Gründgens, and the young Stephen Spender; he learned the technical basis of photography from Andreas Feininger. A hobby became a profession when the "non-Aryan" List had to leave Germany in 1936. He went to Paris via London, and in a short time was successful; his photos appeared in *Vogue, Verve, Harper's, Life.*

It was the Paris of the surrealists, whose arts of transformation were being taken up even in the refined decor of fashion photography (in the work of Cecil Beaton, for example). The surrealistic inspirations and analogies are recognizable in List's work. "The plastic arts," he wrote (naturally including photography in his definition), "the plastic arts are vision made visible." If Salvador Dali painted "dream photographs" with hyperrealistic sharpness of detail, List, in fact, photographed them, with the declared intention of "catching in pictures the magic of visions."

To describe List's method, Günter Metken coined the term "Fotografia Metafisica," after the paintings of the Pittura Metafisica movement. List himself spoke of the "mysterious marriages that exist between table and chair, glass and bottle." The atmosphere of the metaphysical still-life is common to all his pictures, whether he photographs lodgers at the Casa Verdi listening to music as if in a dream or a trance, or whether he portrays the painter Morandi in his studio. Even if they always had the character of spare-time work, of casual work carried out for pure amusement, portraits were always one of List's principal genres, from the portraits of Parisian artists of the 1940s to those of the cultural elite of East and West Berlin in the 60s.

Licht über Hellas, prepared by List in 1937-38, which first appeared as a volume of photographs in 1953, was not the usual Western retrospective reflection, and reception of the book was belated and uncomprehending. For it was, with its monumental fragments, an hallucinatory Hellas, closer to Piranesi's fantastic ruins than to a worship of classical beauty. And in 1945, in glaring direct light, in snow or sun, List photographed the destroyed city of Munich, the German Athens, the humanist facades of an inhuman regime.

As abruptly as he had begun, List ceased to take photographs. During the last 15 years of his life he dedicated himself only to his collection of Italian drawings of the 16th to 18th centuries—almost as if he himself did not wish to contribute any more to the flood of photographs of our time. Almost unnoticed by the public, List died in 1975—and yet his oeuvre is of equal rank with that of his illustrious contemporaries, Cartier-Bresson, Brassaï and Bill Brandt.

—Peter Sager

LIVICK, Stephen.

Nationality: Canadian. **Born:** Castleford, England, 11 February 1945. **Education:** Attended Rosemount High School, Montreal, 1959-63; Sir George Williams University, Montreal, 1963-67. **Family:** Married Selina Depelteau in 1971 (divorced 1975); married Karen Johns in 1974. **Career:** Worked as photographer, CIP Photo Studio, Montreal, 1965-68; Photo-Place Studio, Montreal, 1968-70; Penthouse Studio, Montreal, 1970-71. TDF Studio, Toronto, 1971-72; color-printer, Benjamin Films, Toronto, 1972-74. Independent photographer, Dorchester, Ontario, since 1974. **Recipient:** Ontario Art Council Photo Award, 1975, 1976, 1978; Canada Council B Award, 1976, 1977, 1979. **Address:** Post Office Box 126, Dorchester, Ontario NOL 1GO, Canada.

Individual Exhibitions:

1972	Centaur Gallery, Montreal
1973	London Art Gallery, Ontario
1975	International Museum of Photography, George Eastman House, Rochester, New York
1976	David Mirvish Gallery, Toronto
	London Regional Art Gallery, Ontario (travelled to local Ontario galleries, 1976-77)
	Photography Gallery, Bowmanville, Ontario
1977	David Mirvish Gallery, Toronto
1978	Baltimore Museum of Art, Maryland
	Lunn Gallery/Graphics International, Washington, D.C.

Gallery Graphics, Ottawa
International Museum of Photography, George Eastman House,
  Rochester, New York (toured the United States and Canada,
  1978-81)
1979   Jane Corkin Gallery, Toronto
        National Film Board of Canada, Ottawa (with Suzanne Bloom
          and William Horris)
1980   Jane Corkin Gallery, Toronto
        Art Gallery of Ontario, Toronto (travelled to local Ontario
          galleries, 1980-81)
1981   Jane Corkin Gallery, Toronto
        McIntosh Gallery, University of Western Ontario, London
1982   George Dalsheimer Gallery, Baltimore, Maryland
1983   MacDonald Steward Art Centre, Guelph, Ontario

Selected Group Exhibitions:

1975   *Permanent Collection Exhibition,* National Art Gallery, Ottawa
1976   *"21,"* National Film Board, Ottawa
1977   *Photographic Landscapes,* International Museum of Photogra-
          phy, George Eastman House, Rochester, New York
1978   *Sweet Immortality,* Edmonton Art Gallery, Alberta
1979   *The Platinum Print,* Rochester Institute of Technology,
          New York
1980   *Invisible Light,* Smithsonian Institution, Washington, D.C.
1981   *Second Sight,* Carpenter Center for the Visual Arts, Cambridge,
          Massachusetts
1983   *Subjective Vision,* High Museum of Art, Atlanta, Georgia
1984   *Seeing People, Seeing Space,* The Photographers' Gallery,
          London
1985   *Contemporary Canadian Photography,* National Gallery of
          Canada, Ottawa

Collections:

National Gallery of Canada, Ottawa; National Film Board of Canada, Ottawa;
Canadian Art Bank, Ottawa; Museum of Modern Art, New York; International
Museum of Photography, George Eastman House, Rochester, New York;
Fogg Art Museum, Cambridge, Massachusetts; Baltimore Museum of Art,
Maryland.

Publications:

On LIVICK: Books—*Photography Year 1978* by Time-Life editors, New
York 1977; *The Platinum Print* by John Hafey and Tom Shillea, Rochester,
New York 1979; *12 Canadians* by Jane Corkin, Toronto 1981; *Persona,* edited
by Karyn Elizabeth Allen, Calgary, Alberta 1982; *Subjective Vision,* exhibi-
tion catalogue, with introduction by A. D. Coleman, Atlanta, Georgia 1983;
Contemporary Canadian Photography by Martha Langford, Edmonton, Alberta
1984. **Articles**—"Stephen Livick" by Allan Porter in *Camera* (Lucerne),
January 1978; "Stephen Livick" by Colin Osman in *Creative Camera*
(London), June 1979; "Photography" by David Livingstone in *MacLean's*
(Toronto), November 1980; "Photography" by David Livingstone in *MacLean's*
(Toronto), September 1981.

*

I stand by a belief that my images reflect any statement I have to make.

—Stephen Livick

*   *   *

Stephen Livick photographs the other half of America—the half Diane
Arbus missed. He finds the same feelings—wonder, dismay, and an overwhelming sorrow—in ordinary people. His close-ups, central images, engage
the viewer, often with the too horribly true, like his mother and baby in
Coshocton, Ohio (1981). Livick's work is a visual history of his insight, like

his image of the girl at a New Wave Rock concert. She looks at the viewer
through oddly shaped glasses, a determined visionary.

Livick photographs with color transparency film, has the transparencies
separated by laser technology then uses watercolour pigments mixed with gum
arabic on Arches paper to get the final result, a full colour gum print.

Recently, he has turned his attention to India, where he has discovered a
joyfulness and a laissez-faire attitude which lends itself to images that are
powerful and yet tinged with a gentle compassion for the culture. The subtle
tones of his new gum prints re-enforce this perception.

Stephen Livick's vision reveals not only his personal passion, but his
sensitivity to the contradictions in what is perceived as true. His work has
impact and monumental scale.

—Joan Murray

LOTTI, Giorgio.

Nationality: Italian. **Born:** Milan, 14 January 1937. **Education:** Studied
Photography at Scuola di Fotografia, Milan. **Military Service:** Served in the
Italian Army for 18 months. **Family:** Married; has 2 children. **Career:**
Freelance photo-reporter, establishing advertising studio, Milan, since 1960;
Photojournalist for *Epoca* magazine, Milan, since 1964. **Recipient:** Montecatini
Prize, 1969; Prora-Canon Prize, 1970; World Understanding Award for
Photojournalism, University of Missouri, Columbia, 1973; Scanno Prize,
1981. **Address:** Via Bordighera 29, Milan, Italy.

Individual Exhibitions in Italy:

1966-67   *Flood in Florence*
1967-77   *Sea*
1968   *Venice Is Dying*
1970   *Pollution in Italy*
1972   *The Poisoned Cathedral*
1973   *China*
1975   *Woman and Sun*
1977   *La Scala Theatre*
1980   *Ballet*
1981   *Earthquake in Irpinia, Italy*

Selected Group Exhibitions:

1968   *2nd World Exhibition of Photography,* Pressehaus Stern,
          Hamburg (and world tour)
1973   *The Concerned Photographer,* at *SICOF,* Milan
1975   *The Land: 20th Century Landscape Photographs Selected by
          Bill Brandt,* Victoria and Albert Museum, London (travelled
          to the National Gallery, Edinburgh; Ulster Museum, Belfast;
          and the National Museum of Wales, Cardiff, 1976)
1977   *10 Italian Photographers/ 10 Japanese Photographers,*
          Modern Art Museum, Tokyo
1979   *Magazzini del Sale,* at *Venezia '79*
        The Italian Eye, Alternative Center for International Art,
          New York
1981   *Omaggio al Fotogiornalismo Italiano: 21 Fotografi,*
          Scanno, Italy

Collections:

Centro Studi, Università di Parma, Italy; Bibliothèque Nationale, Paris;
Victoria and Albert Museum, London.

Publications:

By LOTTI: Books—*Venice Is Dying,* with text by Giorgio Bassani and
Gainfranco Fagiuoli, Milan 1970; *The Poisoned Cathedral,* with text by

Giuseppe Grazzini, Cremona, Italy 1972; *Motocross,* with text by Michele Verrini, Verona 1974; *Ski,* with text by Guido Oddo, Verona 1976; *Basket,* with text by Aldo Giordani, Verona 1976; *Friuli: immagini di una tragedia,* with others, Milan 1976; *La Scala Theatre,* with text by Raoul Radice, Verona 1978; *La Scala Theatre,* pamphlet, Monza, Italy 1978; *The New China,* pamphlet, Como, Italy 1980; *Ballet,* with text by Mario Pasi, Monza, Italy 1981; *Sea Light,* with text by Vittorio G. Rossi, Como, Italy 1981.

On LOTTI: Books—*2nd World Exhibition of Photography,* exhibition catalogue, by Karl Pawek, Hamburg 1968; *Primo Almanacco Fotografico Italiani,* edited by Lanfranco Colombo and Roberta Clerici, Milan 1969; *The Land: 20th Century Landscape Photographs Selected by Bill Brandt,* exhibition catalogue, edited by Mark Haworth-Booth, London 1975; *Photojournalism* by Cliff Edom, Dubuque, Iowa 1976; *Catalogo Nazionale Bolaffi della Fotografia,* Turin 1976; *Geschichte der Fotografie im 20. Jahrhundert/ Photography in the 20th Century* by Petr Tausk, Cologne 1977, London 1980; *70 Anni di Fotografia in Italia* by Italo Zannier, Modena, Italy 1978; *Dument Foto 1,* Cologne 1978; *Exploring Photography,* London 1978; *Venezia: La Fotografia '79,* exhibition catalogue, with text by Carlo Bertelli, Milan 1979; *Dumont Foto 2,* Cologne 1980; *Des Murs dans la Ville,* with text by Gilles de Bure, Paris 1981. **Articles**—"Mare" by Fabio Consiglio in *Nuova Fotografia* (Naples), June 1972; "Il Duomo Avvelenato" by Angelo Schwarz in *Fotografia Italiana* (Milan), December 1972; "Si è Rotto il Vaso Cinese" by Pier Paolo Preti in *Fotografia Italiana* (Milan), May 1973; "Giorgio Lotti World Understanding Award" in *News Photographers,* October 1974; "Giorgio Lotti Culture è Tecnica all Ricerca dei Simboli che Toccano il Sentimento" by M. Capobussi in *Progresso Fotografico* (Milan), December 1975; "Visage de la Photo Italienne: Giorgio Lotti" in *News Reporter,* (Paris), March 1977; "Tre Anni all Scala" by Giampiero Carli Balolla in *Il Fotografo* (Milan), February 1978; "Giorgio Lotti" by Attilio Colombo, special monograph issue of *Progresso Fotografico* (Milan), September 1978; "Una preziosissima Fotografia di Zhou en Lai" by Yuan Huaquin in *Remin Ribao* (Peking, China), March 1979; "Giorgio Lotti" by Carlo Arturo Quintavalle in *Enciclopedia Pratica per Fotografare,* Milan 1979; "Danza è Bello" by Mario Pasi in *Il Diaframma* (Milan), February 1981; "I Nuovi Maestri del Colore" by Daniela Palazzoli in *Bolaffi Arte* (Turin), May 1981.

*

For me photography is an art which allows me to express the joy of living.

—Giorgio Lotti

*   *   *

Giorgio Lotti joined the great illustrated news magazine *Epoca* (of which he is now an outstanding member of the photographic staff) after some concentrated experience in press photography with a number of different agencies. With them he acquired a great professional skill at being "on the spot" and achieving a swift synthesis of events with his camera, often rendering them in pictures of great evocative effect.

There are two basic characteristic in Giorgio Lotti's reportage. First and foremost, his themes: especially with subjects that he has chosen for himself (often working independently of the requirements of his paper), he has a cool capacity for indignation born of a social conscience tempered as it were with a melancholy prudence. In Italy, in particular, he is famous for his work on Venice, dilapidated and abandoned, on Milan Cathedral poisoned by the smog, on the Po delta after the flood. The other feature of Lotti's pictures is his urgent desire to know and to take part, as if his camera were an instrument for sharing other people's experiences rather than simply depicting them. He seldom photographs anyone he has not got to know, and every portrait, every sitting, is preceded by a long dialogue (sometimes face to face, sometimes through scrupulous correspondence) with the subject he is about to face. These characteristics inform his work on the Alaska of Jack London or the China of Chou En-lai, the Scala in Milan, the evidence of corruption that he has pursued all over Italy, his sports reports, and the hundreds of great personages that he has presented to the readers of his magazine.

The extreme respect with which Lotti treats his subjects is all of a piece with the great respect that he accords his public. A most careful craftsman, intolerant of imprecision, he gives us intelligently structured, highly concentrated photographs arranged in a narrative sequence that is concise but of great psychological impact. A master narrator, often by the use of particular details, Lotti displays a notably fresh approach to reportage and to photographic illustration.

In these two fields an essential role is also played by his vivid feeling for color, graphically lively and very carefully controlled in composition and in expressive motives, revealing the spirit not merely of the reporter but also of the artist. And that is something that appears too, not only in some of his journalistic work (his portrait of Chou En-lai, for instance) but in his graphic studies of the sea, the sun, the snow—richly creative and expressive pictures.

—Attilio Colombo

LOUNEMA, Risto.

Nationality: Finnish. **Born:** Pori, 10 April 1939. **Education:** Attended Helsingin Kaksoisyhteislyseo, Helsinki, 1956-59; studied photographic chemistry at the University of Helsinki, 1960-71 (Student Art Prize, 1967; Finnish Cultural Foundation Scholarship, 1969), B.S. 1966, M.S. 1971. **Military Service:** Served in the Finnish Army, 1959-60. **Family:** Married Inari Viljamaa in 1966; children: Tomi and Teppo. **Career:** Took first photographs, 1952; professional freelance photographer, Helsinki, since 1962 (in Lapland, 1971-74). Member, 1962, and Vice-Chairman, 1969-70 and since 1971, and Chairman, 1970-71, Photographic Museum Society of Finland, Helsinki. Member, Finnish Union of Journalists, and International Federation of Journalists, 1971-78. **Recipient:** 3 Silver Medals, 7 Bronze Medals, *World and Its People* photo contest, *World's Fair,* New York, 1964; Photo Artists Personal State Prize, Helsinki, 1967; 2 Silver Medals, Nikon Photo Contest International, Tokyo, 1971; Artist's Award, Lapland District Art Commission, 1972; Journalism Scholarship, Ministry of Education, Helsinki, 1978.

Individual Exhibitions:

1967	*Arctica,* Art Saloon Pinx, Helsinki (travelled to the Library, Rovaniemi, Finland, and the Library, Luleå, Sweden, 1968)
1969	*Reidar Särestöniemi,* Library, Rovaniemi, Finland
1971	*Reindeer,* Murmansk Museum, U.S.S.R.

Selected Group Exhibitions:

1964	*The World and Its People,* at the *World's Fair,* New York
1975	*The Land: 20th Century Landscape Photographs Selected by Bill Brandt,* Victoria and Albert Museum, London (travelled to the National Gallery, Edinburgh; Ulster Museum, Belfast; and National Museum of Wales, Cardiff, 1976)
1985	*Photography Collection of the Union Bank of Finland,* Photography Museum, Helsinki (travelled to Arles, France, 1986)

Collections:

Victoria and Albert Museum, London; Carl Zeiss Collection, Opton, Oberkochen, West Germany; Murmansk Museum, U.S.S.R.; International Museum of Photography, George Eastman House, Rochester, New York; Union Bank of Finland, Helsinki.

Publications:

By LOUNEMA: Books—*Linnanmäki,* Helsinki 1970; *The Ethics of Nature Photography,* lecture paper, Helsinki 1982. **Articles**—"State of Abasement in Our Photobooks" in *Valokuvaaja* (Helsinki), January 1968; "What Is Camera Art and Who Makes It" in *Valokuvaaja* (Helsinki), June 1968; "Critics on Photobooks" in *Uusi-Foto* (Helsinki), March 1978 and February 1979; "Photography as Fine Art" in *Kameralehti* (Helsinki), August 1979; "National Geographic Magazine" in *Kameralehti* (Helsinki), February 1980.

Films—*Linnanmäki,* 1971; *Hirvi,* 1972; *Pakkasen Maa,* 1972; *Koilliskaira,* 1972; *Poroelo,* 1973; *Murmansk,* 1973; *Käsivarsi,* 1973; *Peikko,* 1975; *Maan Arpi,* 1975; *Joutsen,* 1976.

On LOUNEMA: Articles—"Solen" in *Foto* (Stockholm), December 1964; "Risto Lounema" in *Photoalmanach International,* Dusseldorf 1965; "Die Sonne als Bildelement" in *Foto Prisma* (Dusseldorf), July 1965; "Cielo Nordico" in *Foto Magazin Italiana* (Como), July 1965; "Sun" in *Photography Annual,* New York 1966; "Risto Lounema" in *Foto Prisma* (Dusseldorf), November 1966; "Fotografiert, Wenn die Nacht Auffliegt" in *Spiegelreflex Praxis* (Dusseldorf), June 1967; "Kaksi Kuvaa Arctica-Näyttelystä" by Kimmo Eskola in *Valokuvaaja* (Helsinki), June 1967; "Arktista Eksotiikaa" by Hilja Raviniemi in *Kameralehti* (Helsinki), September 1967; "Mit Tele und Weitwinkel auf Renntierfang" in *Spiegelreflex Praxis* (Dusseldorf), February 1968; "Perspective 2000" in *Spiegelreflex Praxis* (Dusseldorf), August 1969; "Moderne Nordlandstudie" in *Spiegelreflex Praxis* (Dusseldorf), December 1969; "Risto Lounema" by Risto Laine in *Kameralehti* (Helsinki), January 1970; "Risto Lounema: Linnanmäki" by P.K. Jaskari in *Kameralehti* (Helsinki), April 1970; "Så här Skall en Fotobok Göras" by Åke Emmer in *Foto* (Stockholm), November 1970; "Na Snimkah-Olenevody" by B. Sokolow in *Polarnaja Pravda* (Murmansk, U.S.S.R.), April 1971; "Gesicht" in *Reflex* (Dusseldorf), October 1972; "Snimki Rasskazyvajut o Prirode i Ljudjah" by A. Telegin in *Arktik Star* (Murmansk, U.S.S.R.), April 1973; "The Era of Magazine Photography's Sorrow and Joy" by Pauli Myllymäki in *Finnish Photographic Yearbook,* Helsinki 1977; "Risto Louneman Kriittinen Puheenvuoro" by Tapani Kovanen in *Kameralehti* (Helsinki), June 1979; "That's Enough, Risto Lounema" by Veikko Rinne in *Kameralehti* (Helsinki), no. 4, 1983; "Behind the pictures" by Seppo Saves in *Finnish Photography* (Helsinki), no. 10, 1983; "Discussion on Nature Photography" by Jorma Luhta in *Finnish Photography* (Helsinki), no. 3, 1984.

*

Local photography critics reckon that Finnish photography is the best in the world. It is a dogma supported by faceless bureaucrats. Here are the facts.

In Finland, creative activity, its form, content and message are regulated by law. The regulations are applied in practice by a government-appointed commission. The commission is made up of commercial technicians and other political officials with even fewer qualifications. These government figures, along with the president, have appointed an academician as supervisor of photographic activity with a number of professors as assistants. At a regional level there are dozens of sinecured art officials. If anyone takes what are deemed improper pictures, he will suffer public reproach and exclusion from official associations. In effect, his work will be ignored.

Finnish photographers are indeed top of the world league in terms of the financial support they receive from state-controlled opinion police. I cannot approve of this system. Co-operation with these art bureaucrats is not the goal of my photographic work, and therefore I do not publish my pictures in Finland. Freedom of creation is more important to the artist than controlled collaboration with state officialdom.

—Risto Lounema

*   *   *

Finland sits high on the forehead of the globe, braced between the Baltic Sea and the Soviet Union. While nearly one-fourth of the country rests above the Arctic Circle, Gulf Stream currents give Finland gentle, civilized summers. Lean and flat, with as much lake surface as birch and pine acreage in some regions, Finland stretches as far as the eye can see.

This land of less than five million people, it is a photographer's paradise. Nights are never dark; twilight merely drifts, unannounced, into dawn. Above the Arctic Circle, it is possible to watch the sun set, then, in the very same minute, watch the sun rise. Land, lakes, and sky create a 24-hour natural light studio.

In winter the laws of darkness prevail. Reciprocity failure becomes a photographer's household word. Luckily, the Finnish language is rich with curses. In northern Lapland, lack of sunlight turns the land into solid, unbroken sheets of ice and snow; a gelid serenity falls upon the landscape several hours

each afternoon as a red dot of sunlight, never high off the horizon, throws its pale fire across the icy blue tundra.

It is not surprising that such schizophrenic visitations of the sun would impassion Finnish photographers, like Risto Lounema, as much as they have aroused and inspired Finland's most beloved poets, painters, sculptors, designers and composers. The awe and affection Finns, in general, feel for their natural environment has always had its greatest impact on the souls of Finnish artists. Indeed, it can be said that some of the very best art of Finland has been an art about nature. Certainly Lounema's determination to arrest the effulgent splendors of Finland's natural forces, as revealed in his grain-textured photographs of the sun and moon—of birds migrating just above the treetops—approaches the very pinnacle of such movitations.

—Arno Rafael Minkkinen

LUSKACOVÁ, Markéta.

Nationality: Czechoslovakian/British. **Born:** Prague, 29 August 1944; emigrated to Britain, 1975. **Education:** Studied social sciences at Charles University, Prague, 1961-67, B.A. 1967; also attended the technical photography course, Academy of Film Arts, Prague, 1967-69. **Family:** Married the writer Franz Wurm in 1971 (separated, 1975); subsequently lived with the photographer Chris Killip; son: Matthew. **Career:** Worked as a freelance photographer for Theatre Behind the Gate, Prague, 1970-71, and for *Zdravi* (Czech Red Cross) magazine, 1972-73; freelance photographer, based mainly in Zurich, 1973-74. Freelance photographer, in London, since 1975. Member, Photography Section, Czech Artists Union, 1969; with Magnum Agency, Paris, 1976-80. **Recipient:** Czech Artists Union Fellowship, 1970-71; Arts Council of Great Britain Award, 1975, 1976; First Prize, Greater London Council Photography Competition, 1985; Kodak Bursary, London, 1985-86. **Address:** 63 Blenheim Crescent, London W11 2EG, England.

Individual Exhibitions:

1972	*Pilgrimages,* Theatre Behind the Gate, Prague
1973	*3 Photographers,* Roudnice, Czechoslovakia
	3 Czechs, Galerie Wilde, Cologne
1974	*3 Photographers,* Bibliothèque Nationale, Paris
1983	*Pilgrims,* Victoria and Albert Museum, London (toured Britain, 1984-86)
1984	*School Sculpture Project,* Museum of Modern Art, Oxford
1985	Malmö Museum, Sweden (travelled to Stockholm and Göteborg)
1989	Bethnal Green Museum of Childhood, London
	Sala Visor, Valencia, Spain
1991	Whitechapel Art Gallery, London
	Dům Ukamenné ho Zuonu, Prague, Czech Republic
	Nottingham Castle, Nottingham, England
1992/93	Touring exhibition by the British Council in Spain to Madrid, Murcia, Salamanca, Las Palmas, Jeréz, Santa Cruz de Tenerife, Palma Majorca.
1994	Stills Gallery, Sydney, Australia
1994	Old Town Hall, Prague

Selected Group Exhibitions:

1969	*Czechoslovakian Photography,* Obecni Dum, Prague
1973	*Ceskoslovenska Fotografie 1971/72,* Moravian Gallery, Brno, Czechoslovakia
1975	*Women of Photography,* San Francisco Museum of Art (toured the United States, 1975-77)

Playground at Francis Holland School, (Citizen 2000) **from the series** *Children in Britain,* **1989. Photograph ©Markéta Luskačová.**

1978	*Beaches in the North East,* Side Gallery, Newcastle upon Tyne (travelled to the University of Cardiff)
1980	*Photographs from the Arts Council Collection,* Hayward Gallery, London
1981	*Leisure Time in North Tyneside,* Side Gallery, Newcastle upon Tyne
1982	*Four Czech Photographers,* Fotografiska Museet, Stockholm (toured Sweden)
1984	*Czechoslovakian Photography,* San Francisco Museum of Modern Art
1986	*Photos from the Side Gallery,* Tampere Museum, Finland

Collections:

Arts Council of Great Britain, London; Victoria and Albert Museum, London; Moravian Art Gallery, Brno, Czechoslovakia; Museum of Decorative Arts, Prague; Philadelphia Museum of Art, Pennsylvania; Stedelijk Museum, Amsterdam; Side Gallery, Newcastle-on-Tyne; Slovakian National Gallery, Bratislava, Czechoslovakia. Bibliothèque Nationale, Paris; San Francisco Museum of Modern Art; Eastman House, Rochester, New York; Museum of Modern Art, New York.

Publications:

By LUSKACOVÁ: Books—*Pilgrims,* exhibition catalogue, with text by Mark Haworth Booth, (V&A Museum) London 1983; *Pilgrims,* with text by John Berger (Arts Council of Great Britain) London 1985; *Photographs from*

Spitalfields, text by David Widgery, Chris Killip, Mark Holborn, London 1991.

On LUSKACOVÁ: Books—*3 Photographers,* exhibition catalogue, by Anna Fárová, Roudnice, Czechoslovakia 1973; *British Image 2,* edited by the Arts Council, London 1976; *Czechoslovakian Photography,* exhibition catalogue, by Dorothy Martinson, San Francisco 1984. **Articles**—"Portfolio: Markéta Luskačová" in *Camera* (Lucerne), August 1969; "Markéta Luskačová" in *Creative Camera* (London), October 1971; article by Daniela Mrázková in *Ceskoslovenska Fotografie* (Prague), March 1973; article in *Creative Camera* (London), November 1973; "Markéta Luskačová" by Allan Porter in *Camera* (Lucerne), July 1974; article in *Du* (Zurich), December 1974; "Markéta Luskacová" in *Creative Camera Yearbook 1976,* London 1975; article in *Camera Mainichi* (Tokyo), December 1976; article in *Photocinéma* (Paris), August 1977; "The Proud Pilgrims of Slovakia" by Mark Haworth-Booth in *Aperture* (Millerton, New York), no. 92, 1983; article in *Creative Camera* by Tom Evans, London, January 1987.

*

I began to take photographs when I needed to illustrate my thesis on traditional religion in Czechoslovakia. After more than 10 years' full-time involvement in photography, I still consider that my work at its best is a way of practising sociology of a rather odd kind.

I am very concerned with the aesthetics of photography, but not for its own sake. My interest is primarily in subject. I like to take my time to get close to the subject. I usually compose my photographs in series of images but work so that each picture, both visually and in human terms, is strong enough to exist on its own.

Since I came to live in Western Europe I have worked as a photo-journalist. I enjoy the experience. I think that *Tagesanzeiger* in Zurich has recognized the nature of my work and used it well.

—Markéta Luskačová

*   *   *

When Markéta Luskačová came to settle in London in 1975 she had already been photographing for nearly ten years. First, in order to illustrate her social science thesis and later to follow up that work on village life and the religious pilgrims of Slovakia. The first series we saw in the west were the Pilgrims which were published in various magazines and later shown by the V & A in London. This series established Markéta as a photographer of great compassion for humanity. Someone who would take time and show people as they were, with their own intrinsic dignity, whatever their social condition might be.

The first years in London were hard ones, and it was not surprising that she gravitated towards the East End markets of Spitalfields and Brick Lane, not simply to photograph but initially because they were cheap places to buy the necessities of life. She got to know many of the people who lived and worked there and has always taken the opportunity of making photographs in the area. This is an ongoing series and many of the pictures were first exhibited together in a big show at The Whitechapel Gallery in 1991. Before that some of the street musicians were put together in a portfolio and shown at The Festival Hall. At about the same time she undertook a series on a House for Battered Women in Chiswick and this marks the beginning of a particular interest in children which has continued to the present day.

Other commissions followed, notably one on the seaside of the northeast of England, where she found many people enjoying what appear to be the rather cold and unfriendly conditions of such places which many of us remember from our childhood holiday excursions. These opportunities to undertake personal work are interspersed with work for particular design groups who appreciate her style of working, and in 1988 she began a continuing series in connection with the television series "Citizen 2000" which is tracing a group of children from Primary School onwards. Through this commission she has been able to reach many other children in different parts of the country. A selection of these photographs were shown in the Bethnal Green Museum of Childhood and, like the Spitalfields photographs, they form a major part of her ongoing work.

Compassion is the common thread through all her photographs, whether they be street traders, musicians or down-and-outs—people who many wish to ignore—she passes no judgement on them, but rather on our society. Where society has seemingly removed the dignity of human beings, Luskačová strives through her photographs to give it back to them. Her pictures of children are joyful and remind us that life promises things that we can make possible only by conscious effort at every level. Her strength lies in her ability to make us feel personally involved in working for a better future for these and all our children.

—Sue Davies

LYON, Danny.

Nationality: American. **Born:** Brooklyn, New York, 16 March 1942. **Education:** Studied history at the University of Chicago, 1959-63, B.A. 1963 (Staff Member and Photographer, Student Non-Violent Coordinating Committee, 1963); self-taught in photography. **Career:** Staff Photographer, Chicago Outlaws motorcyclists' club, 1965-66; independent photographer, Latin America and New Mexico, since 1967; also filmmaker, since 1969. Associate, Magnum Photos co-operative agency, New York, since 1967. **Recipient:** Guggenheim Fellowship in Photography, 1969, in Filmmaking, 1979. **Address:** c/o Bleak Beauty, 191 Chrystie Street, 5A, New York, New York 10002, U.S.A.

Individual Exhibitions:

1966	Art Institute of Chicago
1968	South Street Museum, New York
1969	Art Institute of Chicago
1970	San Francisco Art Institute
	Rice University, Houston
	Fogg Art Museum, Harvard University, Cambridge, Massachusetts
1971	University of Chicago
1972	University of Nebraska, Lincoln
1973	*10 Years of Photographs,* Newport Harbor Art Museum, Newport Beach, California
1980	Simon Lowinsky Gallery, San Francisco
1981	Photograph Gallery, New York
	Equivalents Gallery, Seattle
1982	Philadelphia Museum of Art

Selected Group Exhibitions:

1966	*The Photographer's Eye,* Museum of Modern Art, New York
	Toward a Social Landscape, International Museum of Photography, George Eastman House, Rochester, New York
1967	*12 Photographers of the American Social Landscape,* Brandeis University, Waltham, Massachusetts
	Photography in the 20th Century, National Gallery of Canada, Ottawa (toured Canada and the United States, 1967-73)
1974	*Photography in America,* Whitney Museum, New York
1977	*The Photographer and the City,* Museum of Contemporary Art, Chicago
	Concerning Photography, The Photographers' Gallery, London (travelled to the Spectro Workshop, Newcastle upon Tyne)
1978	*Mirrors and Windows: American Photography since 1960,* Museum of Modern Art, New York (toured the United States, 1978-80)
1983	*Photography in America 1910-83,* Tampa Museum, Florida
1985	*American Images 1945-80,* Barbican Art Gallery, London (toured Britain)

Collections:

Philadelphia Museum of Art; Art Institute of Chicago; University of Nebraska, Lincoln; Museum of Fine Arts, Houston; University of New Mexico, Albuquerque; University of California at Los Angeles; San Francisco Museum of Modern Art.

Publications:

By LYON: Books—*The Movement,* with text by Lorraine Hansberry, New York 1964, as *A Matter of Colour,* London 1964; *The Bikeriders,* New York 1968; *The Destruction of Lower Manhattan,* New York 1969; *Conversations with the Dead,* New York 1971; *The Autobiography of Billy George McCune,* editor, San Francisco 1973; *The Paper Negative,* Bernalillo, New Mexico 1980; *Pictures from the New World,* Millerton, New York 1981. **Films**—*Social Services 127,* 1969; *Llanito,* 1971; *El Mojado,* 1973; *Los Niños Abandonados,* 1975; *Dear Mark,* 1975-80; *Little Boy,* 1977.

On LYON: Books—*The Photographer's Eye* by John Szarkowski, New York 1966; *American Photography: The 60s,* exhibition catalogue, Lincoln, Nebraska 1966; *Toward a Social Landscape: Contemporary Photographers,* exhibition catalogue, by Nathan Lyons, New York 1966; *12 Photographers of the American Social Landscape,* exhibition catalogue, by Thomas H. Garver, Waltham, Massachusetts 1967; *Photography in the 20th Century,* exhibition catalogue, by Nathan Lyons, New York 1967; *America in Crisis: Photographs for Magnum,* edited by Charles Harbutt and Lee Jones, with an essay by Michael Levitas, New York 1969; *Danny Lyon: 10 Years of Photographs,* exhibition catalogue, with text by Thomas H. Garver, Newport Beach, California 1973 (includes bibliography); *Photography in America,* edited by Robert Doty, with an introduction by Minor White, New York and London

1974; *Photographs: Sheldon Memorial Art Gallery Collection, University of Nebraska,* with an introduction by Norman A. Geske, Lincoln, Nebraska 1977; *Concerning Photography,* edited by Jonathan Bayer and others, London 1977; *The Photographer and the City,* exhibition catalogue, by Gail Buckland, Chicago 1977; *Mirrors and Windows: American Photography since 1960* by John Szarkowski, New York 1978; *Light Readings: A Photography Critic's Writings 1968-1978* by A.D. Coleman, New York 1979; *American Images: Photography 1945-1980,* edited by Peter Turner and John Benton-Harris, London 1985. **Articles**—"Danny Lyon" in *Du* (Zurich), October 1965; "Danny Lyon" in *Camera* (Lucerne), February 1977; "The Films of Danny Lyon" by Belinda Rathbone in *Aperture* (Millerton, New York), no. 193, 1986.

*

Photographers traditionally have worked in silence, putting everything into the picture, that small area, measured in inches, that they have staked out. I have never done that, but have usually presented my photographs in books with a text. In the texts I have spoken through other people's voices, sometimes out of respect for what they had to say, and sometimes as a disguise for myself.

—Danny Lyon

*   *   *

Danny Lyon's sympathetic documentary photographs have always been based on direct participation. *The Movement,* his first book, grew out of political involvement rather than artistic or journalistic interest. As a member of the Student Non-Violent Coordinating Committee, he experienced first hand all that he photographed of the early 60s Civil Rights Movement. After that he bought a motorcycle and spent two years riding with a group of bikers to make a sensitive and perceptive book, *The Bikeriders,* which looks past the obvious attraction of bikers as anti-social outlaws to explore the often ritualistic sources of their activity. In these pictures he focuses on their costumes, their expressions and their gestures, and he shows the roles they assume as they gather to laugh and drink together.

In his next well-known project and book, *Conversations with the Dead,* Lyon takes on the difficult task of documenting life in Texas prisons. Always aware of the problematic relationship between photography and social change, Lyon didn't pretend that his study would alter the conditions or that it could even capture the full extent of the inmates' struggles. As he says in the introduction, "The material I have collected doesn't approach for a moment the feeling you get standing for two minutes in the corridor of Ellis." Yet the very completion of the project conveys his commitment to these men living in captivity. His straightforward, sometimes lyrical photographs, which consciously avoid simple condemnation of the ever-present guards or the oppressive regimen, create a vehicle through which the inmates can speak. Lyon's particular strength, then, resides in his willingness to submerge his own personality in order to allow the prisoners a voice.

The autobiographical nature of his later book, *The Paper Negative,* brings to light Lyon's current struggle to produce meaningful images. The text, spoken in the third person using a pseudonym, is a narrative woven loosely around the images which blends realistic occurrence with emblematic event and carries a subtle ambivalence through each of its episodes. His letter to the president of the National Endowment for the Arts (concerning an $8,000 grant he had received) which begins the book, reveals his underlying dilemma: "Finally I can only state that I have failed you in your choice of grantee, for I have not documented life in the Valley of the Rio Grande. I have lived there, but tens of thousands of others have been doing that for years and that alone would hardly qualify them for a grant." Although he is an accepted resident in his community, he is unnaturally separated from its people because of his strange privilege—a privilege he shares with most white Americans.

The photographs of this book are more objective, more detached than his earlier works. They show people and their surroundings as they appear, not as he would like them to appear. The significance of Lyon's message lies in the fact that he doesn't espouse simplistic humanism; he isn't searching for easy answers to social problems, he isn't trying to instill a false sense of solidarity with other peoples. Various pictures of prostitutes and street urchins reflect an acceptance that goes beyond empathy or compassion, and pictures such as the one of two young men working on a car's engine, a father calmly cleaning a gun in front of his wife and child, or others of field workers deny a reading that judges the people or draws any immediate conclusions. The power of these, and all his photographs, comes from the sensitive rendering of particular human situations presented with an unsettling irony that makes you question your own feelings. His images resonate with ambivalence, yet they resonate with life.

—Ted Hedgpeth

LYONS, Joan.

Nationality: American. **Born:** New York City in 1937. **Education:** Attended Alfred University, Alfred, New York, B.F.A. 1957; studied photography at the State University of New York at Buffalo, M.F.A. 1973. **Family:** Married Nathan Lyons *q.v.*; children: Elizabeth, David, Ethan. **Career:** Independent photographer. Instructor since 1971, and Coordinator of the Workshop Press since 1972, Visual Studies Workshop, Rochester, New York. **Recipient:** Creative Artists Public Service Grant, 1975, 1981. **Address:** c/o Visual Studies Workshop, 31 Prince Street, Rochester, New York 14607, U.S.A.

Individual Exhibitions:

1963	Schuman Gallery, Rochester, New York
1965	Schuman Gallery, Rochester, New York
	Alfred University, Alfred, New York (with Nathan Lyons)
1969	Nazareth Arts Center, Rochester, New York
1970	Schuman Gallery, Rochester, New York
1975	Jorganson Gallery, University of Connecticut, Storrs (with Eileen Cowan)
	Moncton Arts Center, New Brunswick, Canada
	Picker Gallery, Colgate University, Hamilton, New York (with Scott Hyde)
1977	University of Colorado, Boulder (with Paul Diamond)
1979	Catskill Center for Photography, Woodstock, New York
1981	Portland School of Art, Oregon
1982	Light Factory, Syracuse, New York

Selected Group Exhibitions:

1963	*Western New York Exhibition,* Albright Knox Gallery, Buffalo, New York
1969	*The Serial Image,* Purdue University, Lafayette, Indiana
1970	*Into the 70s: Photographic Images by 16 Artists/Photographers,* Akron Art Institute, Ohio
1975	*Women of Photography,* San Francisco Museum of Modern Art (toured the United States, 1975-77)
1976	*Photographie: Rochester, New York,* Centre Culturel Américan, Paris
1978	*Mirrors and Windows: American Photography since 1960,* Museum of Modern Art, New York (toured the United States, 1978-80)
1979	*4 Rochester Women Artists,* State University College Gallery, Brockport, New York
1980	*Visual Studies Workshop: The First Decade,* Pratt Manhattan Center, New York
1981	*Photographer as Printmaker,* Ferens Art Gallery, Hull, Yorkshire (travelled to the Museum and Art Gallery, Leicester; Cooper Gallery, Barnsley; Castle Museum, Nottingham; Photographers' Gallery, London)
1982	*Target III: In Sequence,* Houston Museum of Fine Arts, Texas

Collections:

Museum of Modern Art, New York; Seagram Collection, New York; Visual Studies Workshop, Rochester, New York; Memorial Art Gallery, Rochester, New York; International Museum of Photography, George Eastman House,

Rochester, New York; Art Gallery, Princeton, New Jersey; Exchange National Bank, Chicago; Museum of Fine Arts, Houston; Center for Creative Photography, University of Arizona, Tucson; National Gallery of Canada, Ottawa.

Publications:

By LYONS: Books—*Self Impressions,* 1972, *In Hand,* 1973; *Wonder Woman,* with Julie McGrath, 1973; *Busform Shadows,* 1973; *Bride Book Red to Green,* Rochester, New York 1975; *Abby Rogers to Her Grand-Daughter,* with text by Abby Rogers, New York 1977; *Perspectives I to VIII,* 1978; *Full Moon,* 1978; *Sunspots,* 1978; *Spine,* with Philip Zimmerman, New York 1980; *Seed Word Book,* New York 1981. **Article**—interview in *Photography Between Covers* by Tom Dugan, Rochester, New York 1979.

On LYONS: Books—*In the 70s: Photographic Images by 16 Artists/ Photographers,* exhibition catalogue, with text by Tom Muir Wilson, Orrel E. Thompson and Robert M. Doty, Akron, Ohio 1970; *Photographic Process as Medium,* exhibition catalogue, with text by Rosanne T. Livingston, New Brunswick, New Jersey 1975; *The Photographers' Choice,* edited by Kelly Wise, Danbury, New Hampshire 1975; *Geschichte der Fotografie im 20. Jahrhundert/Photography in the 20th Century* by Petr Tausk, Cologne 1977, London 1980; *Mirrors and Windows: American Photography since 1960* by John Szarkowski, New York 1978; *Photographer as Printmaker,* exhibition catalogue, with texts by Gerry Badger, Peter C. Bunnell and Ansel Adams, London 1981; *Target III: In Sequence,* exhibition catalogue, by Anne W. Tucker and Leroy Searle, Houston, Texas 1982; *The Library of World Photography: Portraits,* with introduction by Colin Ford, Tokyo 1982, 1983, London 1983. **Articles**—"New Directions in Photography" in the *Christian Science Monitor* (Boston), 3 January 1977; "Portraits" by Julia Scully in *Modern Photography* (New York), June 1977; in the *Smithsonian Magazine* (Washington, D.C.), October 1980.

*

Work is about process.
The shape it takes is the evidence of process.
The process of forming the work
The process of forming the worker
Are inseparable
I work with what is available, a variety of optical devices.
I work through complexity, to something simple and direct.
This distillation process becomes more evident as time goes on.
I want at those things that are evident;
How I see, not conventions of seeing.
What visual recording is about.
How systems shape data.
It is organic and about growth.

—Joan Lyons

*   *   *

The work of Joan Lyons evades traditional categorization. In her quest for self-expression, she has done copy printing, lithography, xerox drawing, offset printing, and bookmaking. Her images are made using printing and drawing as well as photographic processes. As she said when being interviewed by Tom Dugan in *Photographers Between Covers,* "I can't separate that out in my head and say that one is printmaking and one is photographing—they're all imaging."

Her work of the last decade has concentrated on isolating objects in her immediate environment, preserving and transforming them through process. She has done plant studies, self-portraits, work about fabrics, and a number of books based on women's experience. Prints made with a Haloid-Xerox machine in black and color toners use organic plant forms to create pattern motifs reminiscent of illuminated manuscripts, weaving and architectural decoration. A group of self-portraits, life-size and confrontational, challenge the stereotype of images of women. Because they were pieced together from

multiple transfers they have a slightly awkward, sometimes slightly grotesque presence which suggests that these representations are aspects of the female archetype rather than portraits of an individual.

Lyons is founder and coordinator of the Visual Studies Workshop Press, committed to the development and production of books by artists and photographers. She has printed a number of her own books as well. *Wonder Woman,* a book done in collaboration with poet Julie McGrath, features a housewife at her ironing board who spends her time preparing seduction speeches for male heroes such as Charles Atlas and Sherlock Holmes, but who is later transformed into the comic strip version of Wonder Woman.

Bride Book illustrates the way in which Lyons' subjects and themes grow out of the techniques she employs. Intrigued by the successively lighter copies produced when turning off the ink supply of the printing press, she hit on the idea of simultaneous contrast (developed by the painter Josef Albers) in which two complementary colors of equal value make the image (a found portrait of a 1940s bride) disappear in the center of the page.

One of her more popular works, *Abby Rogers to Her Grand-Daughter,* is based on a letter found by one of her students which described a girl's childhood in a small town in the late 19th century. Since it has to do with the handing down of Abby Rogers' quilt, Lyons illustrated the letter with quilt fragments and other Victoriana. With this book, as with her art in general, she has attempted to move beyond the narrow art audience and appeal to anyone interested in a woman's personal story.

—Ted Hedgpeth

LYONS, Nathan.

Nationality: American. **Born:** Jamaica, New York, 10 January 1930. **Education:** Attended Haaren High School, New York, 1943-47; studied architectural drafting, New York, 1947-48; business administration, Alfred State Technical Institute, New York, 1948-50; philosophy and creative writing, Alfred University, New York, 1950, 1954-57, B.A. 1957; self-taught in photography, from 1946. **Military Service:** Served in photo-intelligence, 1951-53, and as news writer and photographer, 1953-54, United States Air Force. **Family:** Married to Joan Lyons, *q.v.*; children: Elizabeth, David and Ethan. **Career:** Amateur photographer, New York, 1946-50; freelance photographer, New York, 1954-57. With George Eastman House, Rochester, New York, 1957-69; Director of Information, 1957-58; Editor, *Image* magazine, from 1957; Publications Editor, 1958-59; Assistant Director, 1960-63; Director, Office of Extension Activities, 1963-69; Associate Director and Curator of Photography, 1965-69. Founder-Member and Chairman, Society for Photographic Education, 1963-65. Founder-Director, since 1969, and Editor of *Afterimage* magazine, 1972-1977, Photographic Studies Workshop (now Visual Studies Workshop), Rochester, New York. Editor, *Contemporary Photography* series, Horizon Press, and *Modern Photography* series, Prentice-Hall, since 1966; Instructor in private photography workshops, Rochester, New York, since 1959; Visiting Lecturer in Photography, Institute of Design, Illinois Institute of Technology, Chicago, 1963; Rochester Institute of Technology, New York, 1966-67; University of Minnesota, Minneapolis, 1965; Professor 1969-1988, and Director of the Photographic Studies Program, 1969-80, State University of New York, Buffalo; Professor, State University of New York, Brockport, since 1988; Trustee, Center of the Eye, Aspen, Colorado, 1970-73; Trustee, since 1971, and Chairman, 1976-80, Gallery Association of New York State. Trustee, since 1976 and Chair 1976-1993, New York Foundation for the Arts; President, *Montage 93: International Festival of the Image,* 1989-1993; Visiting Scholar, Smithsonian Institution-National Faculty Program, 1994. **Recipient:** New Talent Award, *Art in America,* New York, 1960; National Endowment for the Arts Fellowship, 1974; National Endowment for the Arts Senior Fellowship, 1985; Arts for Greater Rochester Award (for significant contributions to the cultural life of the greater Rochester community), 1986; Lillian Fairchild Award, 1987; New York Foundation for the Arts "Champion of the Arts" Award, 1988; Friends of Photography Peer Award in Creative Photography (for distinguished career in photography), 1989; Award, the Ministry of Culture of the Czech Republic,

From the sequence *Riding First Class on the Titanic,* **1986-87.** Photograph by Nathan Lyons.

1989. **Address:** Visual Studies Workshop, 31 Prince Street, Rochester, New York 14607, U.S.A.

Individual Exhibitions:

1958   *Seven Days a Week,* Glidden Gallery, Alfred University, New York
     Seven Days a Week, International Museum of Photography at George Eastman House, Rochester, New York
1959   Indiana University, Bloomington
     Boston University, Massachusetts
1960   Rochester Institute of Technology, New York
     Under The Sun, Poindexter Gallery, New York (with Syl Labrot and Walter Chappell)
1961   Carl Siembab Gallery, Boston
1962   Arizona State University, Tempe
1963   University of Florida, Gainesville
1964   Institute of General Semantics, New York (with Alice Andrews)
1965   University of Minnesota, Minneapolis
     Alfred University, New York (with Joan Lyons)
1967   Jacksonville Art Museum, Florida
     University of Oregon, Eugene
     Phoenix College, Arizona
     Westbrook Gallery, Minneapolis (with Roger Mertin and Alice Andrews)
1968   University of Iowa, Iowa City
1969   Alfred University, New York

     University of Connecticut, Storrs
     Carl Siembab Gallery, Boston
1971   *Notations in Passing,* University of Colorado, Boulder
1972   Columbia College, Chicago
     National Gallery of Canada, Ottawa (toured Canada)
1973   Addison Gallery of American Art, Andover, Massachusetts
1974   Light Gallery, New York
     Light Impressions Bookstore, Rochester, New York
     Chapman College, Orange, California
1975   Upton Gallery, State University of New York at Buffalo
     Notations in Passing, Carl Siembab Gallery, Boston
     Oakton Community College, Illinois
     Whitney Museum, New York
     University of Colorado, Boulder
1976   Cronin Gallery, Houston, Texas
     University of Colorado, Boulder (with Jack Welpott)
1977   *100 Photos from Notations in Passing,* University of Maryland, Baltimore
     Deja Vu Gallery, Toronto (with Joan Lyons)
1986   *Riding First Class on the Titanic,* Catskill Center for Photography, Woodstock, New York
1987   *Recent Photographs,* Film in the Cities, Minneapolis, Minnesota
     Riding First Class on the Titanic, Light Impressions Spectrum Gallery, Rochester, New York; Albright-Knox Gallery and Center for Exploratory and Perceptual Art (CEPA) Gallery, Buffalo, New York
1988   Photogroup, Miami

1991   *Riding First Class on the Titanic,* Atlanta Photo Gallery,
        Atlanta, Georgia; Studio Internacional de Tecnologicas de
        Imagen, Sao Paulo, Brazil

Selected Group Exhibitions:

1959   *Photography at Mid-Century,* International Museum of
        Photography at George Eastman House, Rochester,
        New York
1961   *The Sense of Abstraction,* Museum of Modern Art, New York
1962   Museum of Modern Art, New York
1963   *Photography in the Fine Arts,* Metropolitan Musem of Art,
        New York
1964   Edward Steichen Photography Center, MOMA, New York
1965   Museum of Modern Art, New York
1966   *American Photography: The Sixties,* University of Nebraska,
        Lincoln
1967   National Gallery of Canada, Ottawa
1968   University of California, Los Angeles
        Museum of Modern Art, New York
        Smithsonian Institution, Washington D.C.
1969   *The Photograph as Object,* National Gallery of Canada, Ottawa
        (toured Canada)
1970   Creative Photography Gallery, MIT, Boston
        Focus Gallery, San Francisco
        Witkin Gallery, New York
        Center of the Eye, Aspen, Colorado
1973   Contemporary Art Festival, Paris
1974   *Photography in America,* Whitney Museum, New York
1976   *Photography: Rochester, NY,* American Cultural Center, Paris
        (toured France)
1977   *The Great West: Real/Ideal,* University of Colorado, Boulder
        (toured the United States)
        Mirrors and Windows, Museum of Modern Art, New York
1982   *Target III: In Sequence,* Houston Museum of Fine Arts, Texas
1985   *American Images,* Barbican Gallery, London (toured Britain)
1986   *City Light,* International Center of Photography, New York
1988   *Mixed Signals: Photographs with Text,* Northlight Gallery
        Arizona State University, Tucson
        Photography and Art: Interactions since 1946, Los Angeles
        County Museum of Art
1989   *The New Documentary,* Washington Project for the Arts,
        Washington, D.C.
1991   *The American City,* Addison Gallery of American Art,
        Andover, Massachusetts
1992   *Patterns of Influence,* Center for Creative Photography Tucson,
        Arizona

Collections:

Museum of Modern Art, New York; International Museum of Photography at
George Eastman House, Rochester, New York; Addison Gallery of American
Art, Andover, Massachusetts; Krannert Art Museum, Urbana, Illinois; Uni-
versity of Minnesota, Minneapolis; Norton Simon Museum, Pasadena, Cali-
fornia; University of California at Los Angeles; National Gallery of Canada,
Ottawa; Bibliothèque Nationale, Paris; Phoenix College, Arizona; Glendale
College, California; Houston Museum of Fine Art; National Museum of
Modern Art, Kyoto, Japan.

Publications:

By LYONS: Books edited—*Under the Sun: The Abstract Art of Camera
Vision,* with Syl Labrot and Walter Chappell, New York 1960, Millerton, New
York 1972; *Photography '63,* exhibition catalogue, Rochester, New York
1963; *Photography '64,* exhibition catalogue, Rochester, New York 1964;
Aaron Siskind, Photographer, exhibition catalogue, with essays by Henry
Homes Smith and Thomas B. Hess, Rochester, New York 1965; *Photogra-
phers on Photography,* New York 1966, 17th ed., 1986; *Contemporary
Photographers: Towards a Social Landscape,* New York 1966; *Photography
in the Twentieth Century,* Rochester, New York 1967; *The Persistence of*

Vision, New York 1967; *Vision and Expression: An International Survey of
Contemporary Photography,* New York 1969; *Notations in Passing,* with
introduction by James Borcoman, Ottawa 1971, Cambridge, Massachusetts
1974; *Verbal Landscapes/Dinosaur Sat Down,* Buffalo, New York 1987.

On LYONS: Books—*Photography at Mid-Century,* exhibition catalogue,
with introduction by Beaumont Newhall, Rochester, New York 1959; *Ameri-
can Photography: The Sixties,* exhibition catalogue, Lincoln, Nebraska 1966;
Photography in America, edited by Robert Doty, with introduction by Minor
White, New York and London 1974; *The Great West: Real/Ideal,* edited by
Sandy Hume and others, Boulder, Colorado 1977; *Die Geschichte der
Photographie im 20. Jahrhundert/Photography in the 20th Century* by Petr
Tausk, Cologne 1977, London 1980; *The Photograph Collector's Guide* by
Lee D. Witkin and Barbara London, Boston and London 1979; *Target III: In
Sequence,* exhibition catalogue, edited by Anne W. Tucker and Leroy Searle,
Houston, Texas 1982. Articles—''New Talent USA: Photography'' in *Art in
America* (New York), no. 1, 1960; ''Photography As Seen from Lyons' Den''
by Margaret Converse in *Upstate Magazine* (Rochester, New York), 15
February 1970; ''Nathan Lyons'' in *Aperture* (Rochester, New York), no. 16,
1971; ''Lyons Show Documents Teacher as Artist'' by John Scarborough in
Houston Chronicle, 3 April 1976; ''Nathan Lyons'' by Angelo Schwarz in
Fotografia Italiana (Milan), June 1977; ''Visual Studies Workshop: Viable
Alternatives in the Pursuit of Interdisciplinary Excellence,'' by Emily Morrison in
Review 20, 1987; ''The Photographer's Photographer: A Portrait of Nathan
Lyons'' by Robert C Morgan in *CEPA Quarterly,* 1987; ''Nathan Lyons on
the Snapshot'' and ''Nathan Lyons Speaks'' by Robert Hirsch in *CEPA
Journal,* Winter 1992 and Spring 1993; ''Eye of the Storm: Montage 93,
Nathan Lyons has the Vision that Made it all Happen'' by Elizabeth Forbes in
the *Rochester Democrat and Chronicle,* 16 July 1993.

*   *   *

Nathan Lyons has multiple careers. He is a photographer, and he is also a
curator, writer, publisher, historian, educator, and archivist. His resume
contains sections on exhibitions he has organized and exhibitions of his own
work as well as articles by him and articles about him and his photographs.
There is an ample precedent in photography for curators to be photographers
too (stronger than in other art media). For instance, John Szarkowski, Director
of the Photography Department at The Museum of Modern Art, received two
Guggenheim Fellowships as a photographer; books and catalogues have been
published on the photographs of Szarkowski, historian Beaumont Newhall,
and curator/directors Van Deren Coke and James Enyeart. But, nonetheless,
there are conflicts and confusions in being both artist and curator. Few choose
to maintain the effort. Lyons, however, insists that he cannot do one without
the other. It is evident that the passions and concerns of photographer Lyons
influence those of critic/curator Lyons and vice versa.

He began to photograph in the late fifties. At Alfred University, he majored
in English literature, wrote poetry and plays, and worked part-time as a
photographer for the university's public relations office. In 1957, he became
Director of Information and Assistant Editor of *Image* magazine at the George
Eastman House in Rochester, New York. In the next three years, he initiated
a highly influential series of small-scale exhibitions of emerging artists and of
one-person and group exhibitions of more established artists. He started a
publications program through which Eastman House catalogues and anthologies were distributed by commercial publishers, and established internships
for photographers and historians to study and work at the Eastman House. A
substantial number of the young photographers whose work Lyons exhibited
are now influential photographers. When he left the Eastman House in 1969 he
was Associate Director and Curator of Photography.

While Lyons worked at the Eastman House, his photographs were featured
with those of Syl Labrot and Walter Chappell in *Under the Sun* (1960). He had
fifteen one-person exhibitions and over a dozen group exhibitions included
his photographs. Throughout the fifties, Lyons used a view camera to
photograph segments of walls and intimate landscapes, expressively juxtaposing texture against tone and light against dark. These images are lyric, somber,
and finely crafted. In response to his work being labeled ''abstract,'' Lyons
wrote, ''Photography is, when used with regard for its inherent directness, a
unique and exacting means of isolating inner realities found in correspondence

with the physical world. This is an important distinction; for the employment of *camera vision* to an area which is commonly labeled 'unidentifiable' or 'abstract' is a misnomer. All photography which reveals existing state of matter is the result of abstraction. . . . It is not the 'thing itself' recorded but a fixed representation of it.''

In 1962, Lyons began an extended body of work which is still in progress. Switching to the 35 mm camera, he plumbs vernacular American culture. Eschewing the cultural keepsakes of another age—covered bridges, split rail fences, colonial homes—he collects embodiments of contemporary values, many of which are too omnipresent and mundane for most of us to notice or find significant. He ''collects'' into his pictures various public displays: lawn decorations, wall posters, advertisements, historical sights, store windows, and billboards. What people display, plus how and where it appears, reveals what they value and often what their community values. Displays are also inherently man-made images, so Lyons' pictures are images about images and about man as an image-maker. Recently, Lyons has pursued his interests in verbal displays, isolating particularly complex, humorous, or painful examples. America has become a cacophany of competing, one-way assertions made to random listeners. Lyons is particularly sensitive to these ''street poems.''

Eventually he expects his post-1962 photographs to form a trilogy of books spanning four decades. The first book of the trilogy, *Notations in Passing,* was published in 1974. The second sequence, *Riding First Class on the Titanic,* nears completion. Both are extended sequences. While each picture has meaning individually, the meanings are cumulative when set in context with other pictures. Each image relies on the previous ones and affects those subsequent.

In 1969, Lyons became founding director of the Visual Studies Workshop, which offers a graduate degree program in photographic studies, and publishes artists books and the magazine, *Afterimage,* as well as books and essays of historical importance. The issues delineated by his photographs and implicit in his photographic style remain central in his other capacities. He has been a major influence on dozens of students who are now curators, critics, gallery dealers, and editors in America and Europe. Working under Lyons, they developed an informed awareness of serial art, vernacular imagery, visual metaphors, visual books and alternative printing processes.

—Anne W. Tucker

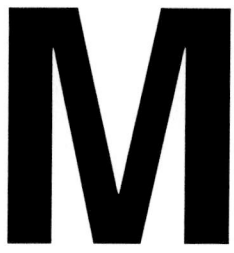

M

MacGREGOR, Greg(ory Allen).

Nationality: American. **Born:** La Crosse, Wisconsin, 13 February 1941. **Education:** Logan High School, La Crosse, 1955-59; studied physics at the University of Wisconsin, Madison, 1959-64; studied photography, under Jack Welpott, Don Worth, Ruth Bernhard, Jerry Uelsmann and Henry Holmes Smith, at San Francisco State University, 1969-70, M.A. 1971. **Career:** Independent photographer since 1966. Research Physicist, Lawrence Laboratory, University of California, Livermore, 1966-70; Assistant Professor of Art, Lone Mountain College, San Francisco, 1970-78. Assistant Professor of Art, University of California at Hayward, since 1980. Vice-President, Camerawork Gallery, San Francisco, 1979-81. Western Region Chairman, 1976-80, and National Conference Chairman, 1981, Society for Photographic Education. **Recipient:** Unicolor Grant, 1982; Purchase Award, *U.S. Biennial,* University of Oklahoma, 1982. **Agents:** O.K. Harris, 383 West Broadway, New York, New York 10012; Equivalents Gallery, 1822 Broadway, Seattle, Washington; and Carson-Sapire Gallery, 1411 Market Street, Denver, Colorado. **Address:** 6481 Colby Street, Oakland, California 94618, U.S.A.

Individual Exhibitions:

1971 Brickwall Gallery, Berkeley, California
  California Silver Rush, Percy West Gallery, California College of Arts and Crafts, Oakland
1972 Memorial Union Art Gallery, University of California at Davis
  Heat Resistant Photographs, Student Union Gallery, University of California, Berkeley
1973 *Silver Eyebright and Epos,* Meramec Community College, St. Louis
  Contemporary Object as Symbol, Silver Image Gallery, Ohio State University, Columbus (travelled to Middle Tennessee State University, Murfreesboro, 1974)
1975 *Deus Ex Machina,* Center for Photographic Studies, University of Louisville, Kentucky
  Friends of Photography Gallery, Carmel, California
1976 *Oddities and the Western Landscape,* Focus Gallery, San Francisco
  The Western Landscape: An Alternative Approach, Mendocino County Museum, California
1977 *Deus Ex Machina,* Canon Photo Gallery, Amsterdam (travelled to the Galerie Image, Liège, and the Photo Redaction Galerie, Paris)
  Remains, Hyppolyte Bayard Memorial Gallery, Orange Coast College, Costa Mesa, California (travelled to the Photo Gallery, New York, 1978)
1979 *Three from California,* Florissant Valley College, St. Louis
  Deus Ex Machina, O.K. Harris Gallery, New York
1980 *Remains,* Lawson-DeCelle Gallery, San Francisco
  Explosions, Tyler School of Art Gallery, Temple University, Philadelphia
1981 *Color,* Pacific Light Gallery, Santa Cruz, California
1982 *Color Photographs,* Foster Goldstrom Fine Arts Gallery, San Francisco
  Color Photos, Colorado Mountain College, Leadville
  Explosions, B.C. Space Gallery, Laguna Beach, California
  Recent Work, Equivalents Gallery, Seattle, Washington
1984 O.K. Harris Gallery, New York

  Technical University, Ruston, Louisiana
  E.J. Bellocq Gallery, New Orleans, Louisiana
1985 *Explosions,* Florida Institute of Technology, Jensen Beach

Selected Group Exhibitions:

1970 *Photomedia U.S.A.,* San Diego State College, California
1972 *Contemporary Photographs,* University of Nebraska, Lincoln
1974 *Photographs from Drug Experience,* Siegfried Gallery, Athens, Ohio
1978 *On the Go,* Fine Arts Museum, San Francisco
1979 *Ten Photographers,* Equivalents Gallery, Seattle
1981 *Contemporary Photoworks,* Albuquerque United Artists, New Mexico
1982 *Contemporary Hand Colored Photographs,* Palos Verdes Art Center, California
1983 *The Eight by Ten Show,* Susan Spiritus Gallery, Newport Beach, California
1984 *Photography in California 1945-80,* San Francisco Museum of Modern Art (travelled to the Akron Art Museum, Ohio; Corcoran Gallery, Washington, D.C.; Los Angeles Municipal Art Gallery; Cornell University, Ithaca, New York; High Museum of Art, Atlanta, Georgia; Museum Folkwang, Essen; Centre Georges Pompidou, Paris; Museum of Photographic Arts, San Diego, California)
1985 *Through the Looking Glass,* Safeco and Pacific Northwest Galleries, Seattle, Washington

Collections:

Museum of Modern Art, New York; International Museum of Photography, George Eastman House, Rochester, New York; Art Institute of Chicago; Middle Tennessee State University, Murfreesboro; Graham Nash Collection, Los Angeles; Pasadena Art Museum, California; Southwestern College, Chula Vista, California; San Francisco Museum of Modern Art; California State University at San Francisco; Oakland Art Museum, California.

Publications:

By MacGREGOR: Books—*Deus Ex Machina,* Berkeley, California 1975; *Darkroom Dynamics,* contributing editor, Marblehead, Massachusetts 1979; *Explosions: A Self-Help Book for the Handyman,* San Francisco 1980.

On MacGREGOR: Books—*Contemporary Hand Colored Photographs,* exhibition catalogue, by Georgianna Lagoria, Santa Clara, California 1980; *California Photography,* exhibition catalogue, by Deborah Johnson, Providence, Rhode Island 1982; *Photography in California 1945-1980* by Louise Katzman, San Francisco 1984. **Articles**—"Heat Resistant Photography" in *Artweek* (Oakland, California), 4 November 1972; "Deus ex Machina" in *Artweek* (Oakland, California), 5 April 1975; "7 Photographers" in *Artweek* (Oakland, California), 19 April 1975; "Photography" in *Artweek* (Oakland, California), 24 January 1976; "Explosions" in *Archetype* (San Francisco), vol. 2, 1979; "San Francisco" in *Artforum* (New York), May 1980; "Proof Sheet" in *Popular Photography* (New York), June 1980; "Playing with Matches" in *Wet Magazine* (Santa Monica, California), December 1980; "A Dialogue on the Work" in *Picture* (Santa Fe Springs, California), no. 17, 1981; "Ambiguous Document" by Ted Hedgpeth in *Artweek* (Oakland,

California), 10 April 1982; "Small Explosions" by Marjorie McCloy in *Darkroom Magazine* (San Francisco), no. 8, 1982.

*

During the past 15 years my involvement with photography has resulted in many apparent changes in the way my actual photographs look. I am referring here to style. I have gone from straight black-and-white to hand-painted toned images, to multiple printing, to straight color type C prints, and now to considering painting onto color photographs. I see these as stylistic changes only, sometimes responding to shifts in what I consider mainstream influences and sometimes just a whim to test out a new technique. This all of course results in a very abrupt change in the way the photograph looks. Beneath all this, however, are some fundamental concerns that I operate within, which serve as my basic subject.

Among them is a commitment to challenge the way we *look* at photographs. To this end I play a lot with the believability of the photo image and challenge it critically, sometimes through recording phoney events. In other cases, such as *Deus Ex Machina,* through the use of believable multiple printing techniques. I challenge the use of the camera as a faithful data-taker, and consequently its ability to tell the truth.

As for specific subject matter: often I deal with some intersection of technology or science and society. I believe art should relate back to life, not art. And since I see a genuine conflict, beauty and confusion between my previous profession as a scientist and my present as an artist, I cannot ignore its influences in my art.

—Greg MacGregor

*   *   *

After working for a number of years as an experimental physicist, Greg MacGregor turned to photography and art in order to explore the world of fantasy and imagination. His images reflect the dual nature of his background, and they exploit the inherent duality of all photographs: they are made believable by a machine-like precision of description which is, in actuality, a total illusion. In his exploration of this paradox, MacGregor's manipulated photographs question the camera's ability to record the world accurately.

His book *Deus Ex Machina* contains a set of black-and-white photographs using multiple printing techniques to create surrealistic scenes pitting man against machine. Real and toy airplanes, helicopters, and automobiles appear in preposterous situations rendered believable by the camera's unblinking eye. *Explosions,* a series of pictures which straightforwardly record absurd events, is a satire on the do-it-yourself craze which swept America. In pseudo-scientific jargon one is instructed in how to herd chickens with fireworks, how to blow up your own office chair, or simply how to create interesting explosions. Showing the influence of performance art as well as earthworks, these pieces mirror our society's cultivation of senseless acts.

Images in a series entitled "Remains" show desolate landscapes littered with strange residue. Hand colored to heighten their fictional quality, they contain a silence in which the debris is charged with an eerie presence. In these prints, the skeleton of an unknown vehicle is made to look like a prehistoric relic, or the black space of a key-shaped hole in a concrete walk becomes an enigmatic symbol of the world's mysteries. Each picture contains a nearly recognizable, but yet unreal scene which seems to be frozen in time like a fossil.

MacGregor's most recent works are large, color photographs of graders, harvesters, dumptrucks, tractors, steamrollers, and other heavy equipment. Inspired by photo-realist painting, these are statically composed, objective pictures treating these American-made vehicles as icons. Using flat areas of primary color and subtly altered perspectives, he makes these objects look like Pop Art toys created for nothing more than pure aesthetic enjoyment. These images, like MacGregor's others, are about our society's love-hate relationship with machines, and they focus on that point where technology intersects normal life.

—Ted Hedgpeth

MACIJAUSKAS, Aleksandras.

Nationality: Lithuanian. **Born:** Kaunas, 16 May 1938. **Education:** Attended the Kaunas Secondary School, 1945-62; studied philosophy at the University of Marxism-Leninism, Kaunas, 1976-77. **Family:** Married Nijole Burdaite in 1959; children: Aukse and Marius. **Career:** Worked in a machine-tool plant, Kaunas, 1956-67. Photographer since 1963. Photo-Correspondent, *Vakarines Naujienos* newspaper, Kaunas, 1967-73. Executive Secretary, Kaunas Branch of the Photographic Art Society of the Lithuanian S.S.R., since 1973. **Recipient:** First Prize, *International Photo Exhibition,* Ruzomberok, Czechoslovakia, 1969; First Prize, *Golden Eye '73* exhibition, Novy Sad, Yugoslavia, 1973; First Prize, *Exhibition of Jokes,* Kapsukas, Lithuania, 1973, 1976, 1979; Grand Prix, *I Salon International,* Orleans, France, 1975; Artist Award, Fédération Internationale de l'Art Photographique (FIAP), 1976; Special Prize, *Triennale of Photography,* Fribourg, Switzerland, 1978; First Prize, *Man and Earth* exhibition, Plateliai, Lithuania, 1980; Gold Medal, XVI Biennale, Poznan, Poland, 1984. **Agent:** National Association of Lithuanian Photographers, Rotuses-1, 3000 Kaunas, Lithuania. **Address:** Taikos pr. 63-56, 3036 Kaunas, Lithuania.

Individual Exhibitions:

1968	Ciurlionis Museum, Kaunas, Lithuania
1969	Union of Journalists, Moscow
1970	House of Print Trades Workers, Riga, Latvia
	Mala Galerija, Bratislava, Czechoslovakia (retrospective)
	Art Museum, Ruzomberok, Czechoslovakia
1971	House of Culture, Siauliai, Lithuania
	People's Ethnographical Museum, Leningrad
1974	Tribina Maldih, Novy Sad, Yugoslavia (retrospective)
	Bibliothèque Nationale, Paris
1975	Hotel de Ville, Arles, France
1976	Galeria Fotografiki, Warsaw (retrospective)
1977	Galeria Fotografiki, Krakow, Poland (retrospective)
	House of Culture, Brno, Czechoslovakia (retrospective)
	Musée Réattu, Arles, France
	Photoclub A.P. 27, Brussels
1979	Museum of Photography, Siauliai, Lithuania
	Galerie et Fils, Brussels
	Art Criticism Institute, Moscow
	House of Culture, Kishinev, Moldavian S.S.R. (retrospective)
	House of Culture, Tiraspol, Moldavian S.S.R.
	Prakapas Gallery, New York
1980	Photography Gallery, Kaunas, Lithuania
	House of Culture, Burgas, Bulgaria
	United Nations Library, New York
	Brandt/Giacomelli/Macijauskas, Galerie et Fils, Brussels
1981	*3 Europeans: Michel Szulc Krzyzanowski, Wilhelm Schürmann, Aleksandras Macijauskas,* San Francisco Museum of Modern Art
	Babylon Cinema, Berlin
	Photo Gallery, Bratislava, Czechoslovakia (travelled to Pribor, Usti nad Laben, Most and Banska Bystrica)
	Valokuva Galleria Finnfoto, Helsinki
	Photo Gallery, Kaunas, Lithuania
	Photo Museum, Siauliai, Lithuania
1986	Galerie Municipale du Château d'Eau, Toulouse, France
	Exhibition House, Vitebsk, USSR
1987	Institute of Russian Language, Moscow
	Culture Centre for Youth, Leningrad
1988	Photo Gallery, Kaunas, Lithuania
	Photo Museum, Siauliai, Lithuania
1991	*My Lithuania,* Portfolio Gallery, London

Series *Memory*, No. 58, 1993. Photograph by Aleksandras Macijauskas.

1992	*This Wild and Small World,* Photo Gallery, Kaunas, Lithuania	1983	*12 Photographes Etrangers,* Maison de la Culture, Namur,

1992   *This Wild and Small World,* Photo Gallery, Kaunas, Lithuania
        This Wild and Small World, Photo Gallery, Vilnius
1993   Gallery ''Les Chiroux,'' Liege, Belgium
        Memory, Photo Gallery, Vilnius
        In the Market, Photo Gallery, Klaipeda, Lithuania
1994   *Memory,* Fujifilm Photo Gallery, Kaunas, Lithuania
        Lithuanian Village Markets, Lithuanian Museum of Art,
            Lemont, Illinois
        In the Veterinary Clinic, Palais des Congres et de la Culture,
            Le Mans, France

Selected Group Exhibitions:

1969   *9 Lithuanian Photographers,* Union of Journalists, Moscow
1973   *Exhibition of Jokes,* Kapsukas, Lithuania (and 1976, 1979)
1975   *Salon International,* Orleans, France
1978   *Triennale of Photography,* Fribourg, Switzerland
        18 Photographes Européens: Images des Hommes, Belgian
            Ministry of Culture travelling exhibition (toured Europe)
1979   *Man and Earth,* House of Culture, Plateliai, Lithuania
1980   *Lithuanian Photography,* The Photographers' Gallery, London
1982   *Fotoforum '82,* Ruzomberok, Czechoslovakia

1983   *12 Photographes Etrangers,* Maison de la Culture, Namur,
            Belgium (toured France)
1984   *La Photographie Crétive,* Pavillon des Arts, Paris
1988   *Another Russia,* Museum of Modern Art, Oxford, England
1989   *Photostroika,* Aperture Gallery, New York
        Experimental and Surrealistic Photography, Ciurlionis Gallery,
            Chicago
1990   *Lithuanian Celebrations,* Ciurlionis Gallery, Chicago
1992   *Six Photographers of Lithuania,* IFA Gallery, Berlin
        Waterscapes, Ciurlionis Gallery, Chicago
1993   *The Memory of Images,* Berlin, Stockholm, Tallinn,
            Vilnius, Kiel
1994   *Exhibition of Photographers of Kaunas,* Tallinn

Collections:

Photography Museum, Siauliai, Lithuania; Bibliothèque Nationale, Paris; Musée Français de la Photographie, Bièvres, France; Musée Réattu, Arles, France; Musée d'Art et d'Historie, Fribourg, Switzerland; University of New Mexico, Albuquerque; San Francisco Museum of Modern Art; Canon Photo Gallery, Amsterdam; National Association of Lithuanian Photographers, Vilnius; International Center of Photography, New York.

Publications:

By MACIJAUSKAS: Books—*My Lithuania*—*Aleksandras Macijauskas,* selected by Daniela Mrazkova and Vladimir Remes, London 1991; *Kaimo Turgus (In The Market),* Vilnius, 1992.

On MACIJAUSKAS: Books—*Aleksandras Macijauskas,* exhibition catalogue, with text by Skirmantas Valiulis, Kaunas, Lithuania 1971; *Aleksandras Macijauskas,* exhibition catalogue, with text by Romuald Losewicz, Warsaw 1976; *Aleksandras Macijauskas,* exhibition catalogue, with text by Daniela Mrazkova, Brno, Czechoslovakia 1977; *Aleksandras Macijauskas,* exhibition catalogue, with text by A. Dabulskis, Kaunas, Lithuania 1977; *Lietuvos Fotografija,* with an introduction by Romualdas Pacesa, Vilnius, Lithuania 1978; *Aleksandras Macijauskas: Veterinary Clinic,* exhibition catalogue, with text by Romualdas Neimantas, Kaunas, Lithuania 1979; *Fotografie: dokument i obraz* by A. Vartanov, Moscow 1983; *La Photographie Créative* by Jean-Claude Lemagny, Paris 1984; *The Story of Photography* by Daniela Mrazkova, Prague 1985, London 1985; *Another Russia* by Daniela Mrazkova and Vladimir Remes, London 1986; *Masters of Photography; A Thematic History,* by Daniela Mrazkova, London, 1987; *Un Regard Sur La Photographie Soviétique Contemporaine,* by Marie-Françoise George, Paris, 1988; *Valokuva CCCP Poto,* Forssan Kirjapaino Oy, Helsinki, 1989; *Aleksandras Macijauskas—Contemporary Masterworks* by Vladimir Birgus, Chicago and London, 1991; *Pflanzenfotografie* by Harald Lange, Leipzig, 1991; *Changing Reality,* by Leah Bendavid-Wal, Starwood Publishing Inc, 1991; *Lithuanian Celebrations,* edited by Algimantas Kezys, Chicago, 1991; *Waterscapes by Lithuanian Photographers,* edited by Algimantas Kezys, Chicago, 1992; *The Horse: Photographic Images 1939 to the Present,* by Gerald Lang and Lee Marks, New York, 1991; "The Memory of Images—Baltic Photo Art Today," Exhibition Catalogue by Barbara Straka and Knut Nievers, Kiel, 1993.
Articles—"Aleksandras Macijauskas and His Dreams" by Daniela Mrazkova in *Fotografie* (Prague), January 1969; "World Photography: Aleksandras Macijauskas" in *Foto Kino Revija* (Belgrade), October 1973; "International Portfolio: Aleksandras Macijauskas in the Market" by Skirmantas Valiulis in *Photography* (London), January 1976; "New Approach, New Solution" by V. Stigneyev in *Sovetskoye Foto* (Moscow), February 1978; "Black-White Markets by Aleksandras Macijauskas" by Barbara Xzczucka in *Fotografia* (Warsaw), February 1978; "A Veterinarian in Close-Up" by Gene Thornton in the *New York Times,* 11 November 1979; "Reality from a Different Angle" by Vladas Braziunas in *Literature and Art* (Vilnius, Lithuania), 15 March 1980; "The Photos of A. Macijauskas" by Vladimir Birgus in *Fotografie* (Prague), no. 1, 1983; "Alexandras Macijauskas" in *Camera International* (Paris), no. 3, 1985; *Freska Zivota* by Daniela Mrazkova in *Ceskoslovenska Fotografie,* Prague, no 5 1988; Laima Skeiviene in *Bulgarsko Foto,* Sofia, no 9, 1988; Many Nations, Many Voices by Daniela Mrazkova in *Aperture,* New York, no 116, 1989; *Le Courrier Professionnel,* Arles, France, no 111, 1990; Animal Farm by Val Williams in *The Independent Magazine,* London, July 27th 1991; Aleksandras The Great by John Green in *Soviet Weekly,* London, July 18th, 1991; Market Forces—Lithuanian Style by John Green, in *Soviet Weekly,* London, September 5th, 1991; My Lithuania by Daniela Mrazkova and Vladimir Remes in *British Journal of Photography,* July 1991; *Life in Photographs* no 3, Moscow; *Foto Megejas,* Kaunas, Lithuania, no 1 1991; My Lithuania by Anna Bartasiena in *Photography/An Argus Specialist Publication,* London, August, 1991; Face of Lithuania by Ria Higgins in *What's on in London,* July-Aug 1991.

*

My purpose is to fix the spirit of a thing instead of the thing itself. I want to generalise human existence instead of just fixing it.

—Aleksandras Macijauskas

* * *

One feels certain that the favorite subject of Aleksandras Macijauskas is man. This was as true at the beginning of his career in the 1960s as it is now,

but his choice of themes has changed and become narrower. In his case, it is reasonable to talk about "themes" and "treatment" because, given his methods and the photographic results, Macijauskas seems variously to be a scientist, an historian, or a sociologist within the field of photography. Long ago he stopped working with single shots, and instead has tried to explore his favorite themes in long series that are created over several years. Perhaps there is nothing new in such a method: every serious and extensive photo series requires solid study of the subject, a "getting into" the spirit of its environment. There are other similar works in world photography. But his various series—such as "Market" or "Veterinary Clinic"—are as striking in their comprehensive essence as in their visual solutions.

Macijauskas shoots only with a wide-angle lens, and he is not afraid of an immediate relationship with his subject. Usually when one tries to shoot "close-up" with a tele-lens, even if the intention is to get to the essentials of the subject, one remains a bystander, an outsider—but Macijauskas, in attempting the same shot, comes very close to his model; there is no effect of distancing. The story is not "observed"; it is very close to him. The result is that his reportage has a unique character and charm. As should happen in any good documentary, the general views and close-ups, the rhythms and moods, change, are orchestrated. And, though the close-up concentration on the model does produce the effect of portraiture, the environment, the background, is always precisely rendered.

Because Macijauskas is never the by-stander, because he is always at the center of the events of his photo, he misses no crucial detail. In "Market" or "Veterinary Clinic" such details are, for example, the "look" of a bird or an animal; a goose in a basket, a sheep or a piglet in a housewife's lap; a kitten or a cow on an operating table. And, always, whatever the immediate interest of the photo, we note the human: as well as the animals in the forefront we can still see clearly, in the background, the active, the enterprising people, the masters of the animals, who may or may not understand them.

Macijauskas is not one of those photographers who shoots "beautiful" scenes; there is always tension and conflict in his works, be it a conflict between people, between man and animal, or between the model and the photographer himself. Unusual shooting angles and the deformations caused by the wide-angle lens also help to raise the tension in his photos.

The work of Aleksandras Macijauskas is a very stimulating example of the dynamism of contemporary photo-reportage.

—Peeter Tooming

MACK, Ulrich (Bernhard Gerhard Antonius).

Nationality: German. **Born:** Glasehausen/Eichsfeld, 19 July 1934. **Education:** Attended primary school in Thorn, West Prussia, 1941-45, and middle school in Freiburg, Neiderelbe, 1946-52; studied graphics, under Alfred Mahlau, and photography, under Eberhard Troeger, Hochschule für bildende Künste, Hamburg, 1956-62. **Family:** Married the painter Katrin Beisert in 1964; children: Julian, Manuel and Mareile. **Career:** Worked as a miner in the Ruhr district, 1952-55, as a fisherman in Spain, 1961-62, and as a lumberjack in Sweden, 1962; freelance photographer, Hamburg, 1962-63; staff Photographer and photojournalist on the magazines *Quick* and *Twen,* Munich, 1963-67, and on *Stern,* Hamburg, 1967-72. Later worked as a freelance advertising photographer and also as a film maker, principally for the Norddeutscher Rundfunk broadcasting corporation. Lecturer in photography, 1975 and Professor of Visual Communications, since 1976 at Fachhochschule, Dortmund. Organizer and moving spirit behind the annual summer academy held at the Abbaye du Gard, Amiens, France, since 1977. Instructor at the Focus Workshops (exchange with students of the Parsons School of Design and the New School for Social Research, New York), Dortmund since 1973. Visiting Professor, College of Communication, Boston University. Founder Member, Verein der Freunde der Photographie, Museum für Kunst und Gewerbe, Hamburg, 1981. **Recipient:** Photo-Story Prize and Artistic Photography Prize, World Press Photo exhibition, The Hague, 1964; Gold Medal, German Art Directors Club, 1970, 1971. **Address:** Chamissoweg 1, D-22587, Hamburg, Germany.

***Der Holm,* 1993.** Photograph by Ulrich Mack.

Individual Exhibitions:

1966   *Bildnisse berühmter Zeitgenossen,* Staatliche Landesbildstelle, Hamburg

1981   *Pellworm,* BAT-Haus, Hamburg (travelled to Schleswig, Moers, Dusseldorf, Kiel, Munich, Husum and Lübeck, West Germany)

1984   *Pellworm-Harkers Island,* Duke University, Beaufort, North Carolina

1985   *Mack on Polaroid,* Hansa-Galerie, Hamburg

1991   *Inselmenschen,* three exhibitions for opening of Inselmuseum, Pellworm

1992   *Old World—New World,* Photokina, Cologne

1993   *Der Holm—ein Familienalbum,* Städtisches Museum, Schleswig

Selected Group Exhibitions:

1964   *World Press Photo '64,* Gemeentemuseum, The Hague

1968   *Weltausstellung der Photographie: Die Frau,* Pressehaus Stern, Hamburg (and world tour)

1969   *Foto-Selection: 50 Jahre GDL,* Museum für Kunst und Gewerbe, Hamburg

1976   *Acht deutsche Photographer,* at *Photokina,* Cologne

1977   *Faces and Facades,* Clarence Kennedy Gallery, Cambridge, Massachusetts

1978   *European Colour Photography,* The Photographers' Gallery, London

1979   *Venezia 79: La Fotografia,* at the *Biennale,* Venice

1981   *Farbe im Photo,* Kunsthalle, Cologne

1982   *Alfred Mahlau und seine Schüler,* Künstlerhaus, Hamburg

1986   *Fifty Years of Colour Photography,* at *Photokina 86,* Cologne

1989   *"Géographies humaines," Pellworm,* Musée de la Photographie, Charleroi, Belgium

1994   *Magic Moments—40 Jahre Leica M*

Collections:

Museum für Kunst und Gewerbe, Hamburg; Altonaer Museum, Hamburg; Museum Ludwig, Cologne; Museum of Modern Art, New York; Fotomuseum im Münchner Stadtmuseum, Munich; Polaroid Collection, Amsterdam; Schleswig-Holsteinisches Landesmuseum, Schleswig, Germany; Photomuseum, München, Munich; Polaroid Collection, Cambridge, Massachusetts; Clarence Kennedy Collection, Cambridge, Massachusetts; Städtisches Museum, Schleswig, and Holm Museum; Inselmuseum, Pellworm.

Publications:

By MACK: Books—*Mack: Pferde,* with text by Peter Sutermeister, Bern and Stuttgart 1966; *Twelve Instant Images,* portfolio, Cambridge, Massachusetts 1974; *Lübecker Kalender: 100 Jahre Thomas Mann,* Frankfurt 1975; *Lübecker Kalender: 500 Jahr Holstentor,* Hamburg 1977; *Lübecker Kalender: Zu Gast in Lübeck,* Hamburg 1978; *Volti,* Paris 1979; *Stille,* portfolio of 6 dye transfers, Braunschweig, West Germany 1979; *Pellworm,* 4 portfolios, Hamburg 1979-81; *Harkers Island,* 4 portfolios, Hamburg 1985; *Pflanzen,* 1987; *Boston University,* portfolios and documentation, 1988; *Photofreunde,* documentation, Hamburg 1988; *Der Holm—ein Familienalbum,,* Kiel, 1993; *Inselmenschen,* Kiel, 1994. **Articles**—"Die Besetzung einer Republik—Das Berliner Philharmonische Orchester" with Werner Burkhardt in *du,* Zurich, January, 1993; "Nachbarn am Meer, durch hundert Horizonte getrennt: Harkers Island und Pellworm" with Uwe Prieser in *Frankfurter Allgemeine Magazin,* 1 October 1993.

On MACK: Books—*2. Weltausstellung der Photographie: Die Frau,* exhibition catalogue, edited by Karl Pawek, Hamburg 1968; *Faces and Facades,* with introduction by Peter C. Bunnell, Cambridge, Massachusetts, 1977; *Mack: Pellworm—eine Insel und ihre Menschen,* exhibition catalogue, with texts by Siegfried Lenz and Christian Rathke, Hamburg 1981; *Sammlung Gruber: Photographie des 20. Jahrhunderts,* exhibition catalogue, with

foreword by Siegfried Gohr, Cologne 1984. **Articles**—"Meister der Leica: Ulrich Mack" in *Leica Fotografie* (Frankfurt), May 1969; "Farbforum der Spitz-fotografen: Ulrich Mack" in *Westermanns Monatshefte* (Braunschweig), July 1969; "Ulrich Mack" by Allan Porter in *Camera* (Lucerne), November 1970; "Document: Ulrich Mack" in *Camera* (Lucerne), May 1973; "Stille" by Michael Neumann in *Westermanns Monatshefte* (Braunschweig), May 1979; "Pellworm—Mack" by Colin Osman and Judy Oldhill in *Creative Camera* (London), November 1979; "Composit: Mack" by Allan Porter in *Camera* (Lucerne), January 1981; "Ulrich Mack" by Don Owens in *Photo Show* (Los Angeles), no. 4, 1981; "Ulrich Mack. Photography: A Love Affair" in *Leica Fotografie,* May, 1994; "Mack—Vom Reporter zum Pädagogen" in *Designers Digest,* no. 50, 1994.

*

Humanity stands the test of time, it is concentrated not only in the exceptional but also in the unpretentious. I'm not important. I'm not an artist and I don't pretend to be one. I am a craftsman, an artisan. It's the work that counts and what it reveals—a passing world changing so rapidly and at the expense of the people who fought the great storms; who stood by each other, nolens volens, who suffered together. As a documentary of its time it is already playing an undeniable role because half the people I photographed are dead.

—Mack

*   *   *

Few photographers who dedicate themselves to contemporary reportage are also able to produce timeless documents of a static world. But one such photographer is Ulrich Mack. Today he devotes his energies to producing series of pictures of peaceful locations, set apart from the hurly-burly of modern life; two decades ago he was acknowledged as one of the best-known German photoreporters, at home in the very heart of world affairs.

Switching from photography of the moment to photography of what is timeless was a conscious step for Mack: as conscious as his experience of the progression from youth to maturity.

The son of a village schoolmaster, he was the sixth in a family of nine children. He trained as a draughtsman in Alfred Mahlau's class at the Hamburg School of Art, subsequently changing over to photography, which he studied under Eberhard Troeger, a colleague of Mahlau's at the Hamburg school. Mack was to turn to photojournalism and work for the magazines *Quick* and *Stern,* but first he retreated for a while into anonymity. For a year he lived as a fisherman in Spain and for a further six months as a logger in Sweden. His reputation was established during the years 1963 to 1971. His series 'Wild Game in Kenya' won him first prize at the World Press Competition in the Hague, and other gold medals and prizes followed. At thirty-four, Mack was elected a member of the German Photographic Society.

After three years, during which he worked in advertising and on television films, Mack was invited by the School of Applied Arts in Dortmund to teach in their visual communications department. Mack became one of the best teachers of photography in the Federal Republic of Germany. The rapid perception of the image, the construction of a picture, the aesthetic craft of photography—few people are able to convey these things to the younger generation as well as Mack does: not only in Dortmund, but also at annual workshops at the Abbaye du Gard near Amiens in France, and with students at the Parsons School of Design in New York.

Two extensive series of pictures sum up Mack's previous work: these are of two islands—Pellworm in the North Sea, and Harkers Island in the Atlantic off the coast of North Carolina. In the apparently incidental and insignificant he discovered the typical beside the individual; the sameness of the everyday and a break with conformity; the inconspicuous beauty that lies a little aside from conventional attractions.

—Heinz Spielmann

Since Heinz Spielmann contributed the note above, Mack has continued his activities as a teacher, still firing the enthusiasm of the younger generation for his craft. Yet at the same time he has brought his skills to bear on book production. *Der Holm—ein Familienalbum,* won the "Best Illustrated Book of the Year 1993" award in Germany. As we go to press, many of the photographs of Pellworm and Harkers Island are about to be re-published in one ingenious volume, enabling them to be compared side by side. Like the work of his Dortmund students, this will certainly stand as a fitting memorial to the "Mack School" of photo-reportage.

MACKU, Michal.

Nationality: Czechoslovakian. **Born:** Brunthal, Czechoslovakia, 17 April 1963. **Education:** Educated at the University of Chemical Technology, Brno, 1981-85, and the Institute of Creative Photography, 1986-89. **Family:** Married Miriam Ondáková, 1986; children: Magdalene and Matthew. **Address:** Velkomoravská 51, 77900 Olomouc, Czech Republic.

Individual Exhibitions:

1990	Kulturní Dům, Bruntál, Czech Republic
	Robert Koch Gallery, San Francisco
	Galerie Centrum, Plzen, Czech Republic
1991	Galerie Pod Podloubím, Olomouc, Czech Republic
	Fotografisk Galleri, Copenhagen
1992	Galerie Bílá Ruze, Prague
	Galerie Caesar, Olomouc
	Umelecká Priemyslovka Palisády, Bratislava, Slovakia
	Galerie Mladych, Brno
1993	Galerie Aura, Olomouc
1994	Prague House of Photography, Prague

Selected Group Exhibitions:

1990	*Tschechoslowakische Fotografie Des Gegenwart,* Cologne (travelled to Erlangen, Metz, Lucenburg, Strasbourg, Odense, Freiburg, Barcelona, Texas, Lawrence)
1991	*Bilder Lust,* Galerie Rhänitzgasse der Landeshauptstadt, Sachsens (travelled to Dresden; Museum Ludwig, Cologne)
	The Male—Contemporary Male Nude Photographs, Portfolio Gallery, London
1992	*What's New: Prague,* The Art Institute of Chicago
1993	*Czech Photography of the 1990s—Fotofeis,* Maclaurin Art Gallery, Ayr, Scotland
1994	*15 Czech & Slovak Photographers: 4 Photos Each,* Photography Gallery, Perth, Australia

Collections:

Museum Ludwig, Cologne; Museum of Modern Arts, Houston; Museet for Fotokunst, Odense, Denmark; The Royal Library of Denmark, Copenhagen; Maison Européen de la Photographie, Paris; Harvard Visual Center, Cambridge, Massachusetts; The Art Institute of Chicago, Illinois.

Publications:

By MACKU: Television—*Process,* Czech TV, 1994.

On MACKU: Book—*Tschechoslovakische Fotografie Der Gegenwart* by Vladimir Birgus and Reinhold Misselbeck, Cologne 1990. **Articles**—"Czech and Slovak Photography Today," Prague 1991; "Disquiet and Anxiety" by Daniela Mrázková in *Fotographie 9,* September 1991; *Bilder Lust* by Ulrich Domröse, Heidelberg 1991; *Encyclopedia of Czech and Slovak Photographers,* Prague 1993; *Graphis Photo,* Zurich 1993. **Television**—*Photography on Moravia: Michal Macku,* Czech TV, 1993.

*

I was interested in details of nature in my earlier work (1980-85). Later I created short cycles using conceptual principles. From 1988 I developed by my creative technique which I have named "gellage" (a mixture of collage and gelatine), laying layers of exposed and fixed photographic gelatine on paper.

I use the nude human body in my pictures, surrounded with abstract patterns and distortions. This allows me to show the human being at more than one level.

—Michal Macků

* * *

Michal Macků distinctively continues the existentially oriented tradition of the mainstream middle generation of Czech fine artists. Yet he is also capable of incorporating the spirituality of contemporary art. His "gellages" use the rare technique of transferring the loosened emulsion from the large-format films to ordinary paper. This technique enables him to give his pictures a final touch of uniqueness and distinctively to stylise the photographed reality.

Michal Macků started his artistic career at the end of the 1970s photographing various static motifs. It was towards the end of his studies at the Institute of Creative Photography that he created fully developed works using this technique of "gellages" which enabled him to rebuild reality in an expressive way—elimination of minor details, distortion of space, multiplication or implanting of main motifs into unusual contexts. Nevertheless, the author does not use this technique "for art's sake" and superficial effects but for artistically effective symbolic utterances on philosophical topics and his own feelings and experiences. Macků, like Jiri Anderle, Jiri Sozansky, Olbram Zoubek and many other members of the mid-generation Czech fine artists does not consider art to be some uncommitted easy game but a kind of creative reaction to serious, sometimes even tragic themes of life's critical situations: loss of identity; polarity of soul and body; the contradictions between eternal ethical rules and a totalitarian power: conflicts of civilisation and nature. From post-modernism he embraced the effort to step over borders of a single art medium but did not accept the claimed distance from the process of creation which the majority of his colleagues displayed through the casualness and lightness of their works.

Among his first "gellages" from the end of the 1980s we can often find an exaggerated freneticism in pictures showing multiple crying heads. At the same time he produced some of his best works—extremely dramatic "gellages" with brutal motifs of torn and naked bodies. They are Macků's answer to the eternal theme of violence, but also contemporary art's growing interest in corporeality. It is not only by accident that he uses with few exceptions his own body because he knows his own body best of all and that helps him to express himself more precisely than working with a model. At the same time he admits that the long term portrayal of his own body is a source of self-identification and self-knowledge.

Another collection of "gellages" is dedicated to the theme of loss of individuality and identity in the crowd. The multiplied archetypal male bodies with expressively raised arms evocative of mysterious and magical signs are gathered in crowds of lonely people occupying an endless empty space, an allegory of futility. They originate in a mightily anxious warning vision of the loss of individual uniqueness at the expense of integration into the crowd. His pictures of solitary, deformed bodies contain an even stronger dramatic accent, symbolising on one hand a violent estrangement and on the other the polarity between carnal and spiritual human elements.

Subsequent photographs, with their motifs of bodies and shadows, are marked by an even stronger interest in the extra-rational spheres of recognition and the duality of form and content of carnality and spirituality. To the receptive observer the shadows represent an ideal state which cannot be achieved by the real physical qualities. At the same time these works show the danger of weakening communication with the spectator, strengthened in the next series by repeated motifs of individuals linked at the arms or elbows. The extremely complicated coded content causes a substantial number of spectators first to notice perfection in technical arrangement, omitting the deeper sense of such features as the overlapping hands resembling bars symbolising the loss of individual freedom. Michal Macků started to make complete multimedia installations, combining photography with three-dimensional objects and music. He began to experiment with film animation as well, when he imaginatively used manipulation of "gellages" in a few shots of his television

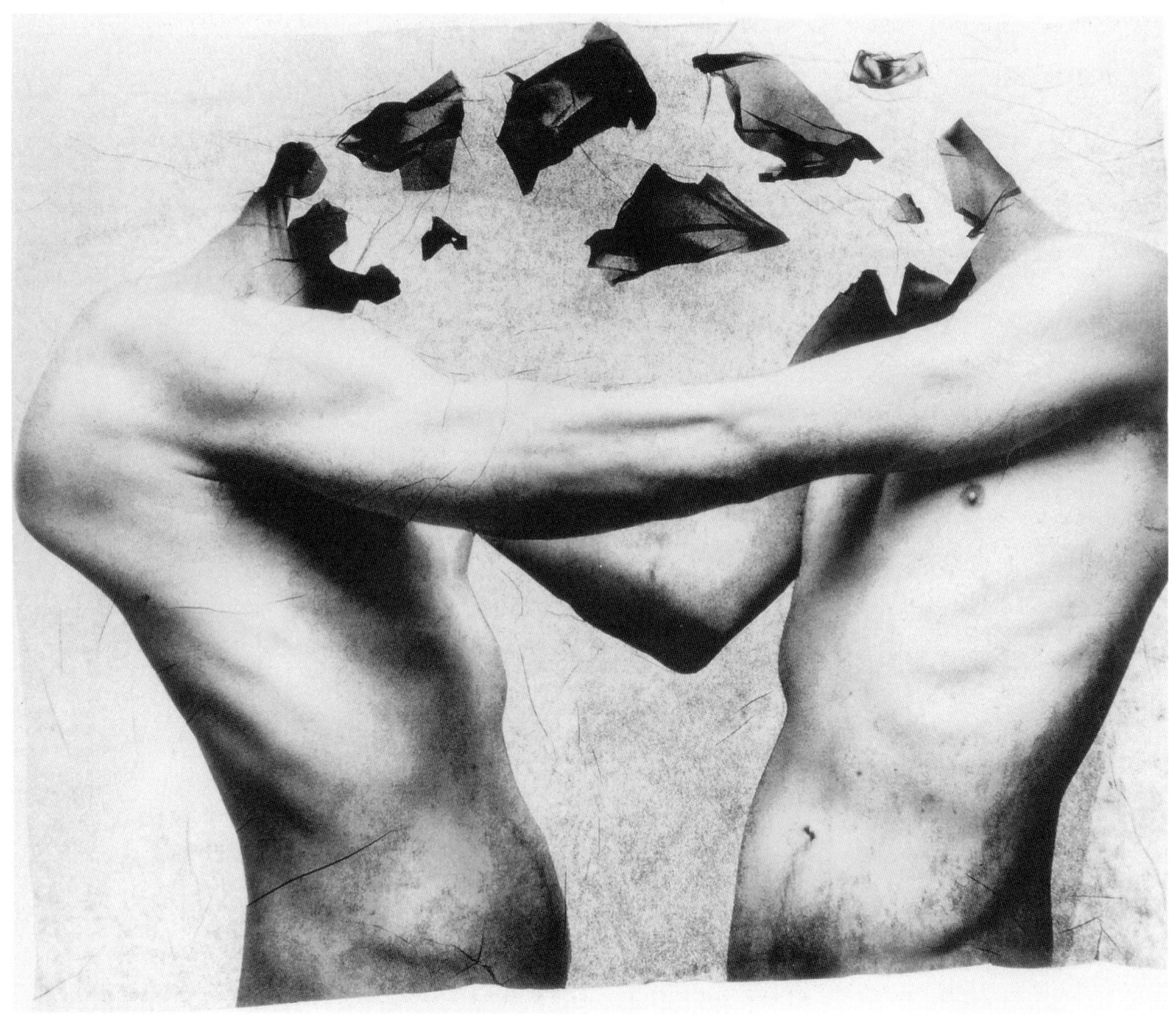

Untitled, **1994.** Photograph by Michal Macků.

profile. Later using this technique, he made a short television film called *The Process,* depicting an allegory of human life in a suggestive symbiosis.

—Vladimír Birgus

MAGGS, Arnaud.

Nationality: Canadian. **Born:** Montreal, Quebec, 5 May 1926. **Education:** Westmount High School, Quebec, 1941-44; studied drawing, Scuola di Belle Arti di Brera, Milan, 1959; Artists Workshop, Toronto, 1974; self-taught in photography. **Military Service:** Served as air gunner in the Royal Canadian Air Force, 1944: Sergeant. **Family:** Married Margaret Frew in 1950 (divorced, 1971); children: Laurence, Toby and Caitlan. **Career:** Worked as freelance graphic designer, Toronto, 1954-63. Freelance photographer and designer, Toronto, since 1966. **Recipient:** Gold Medal, *Canadian Graphica* show,

1966; Canada Council Senior Arts Grant, 1969, 1981, 1985. **Agent:** The Isaacs Gallery, 832 Yonge Street, Toronto, Ontario. **Address:** 24 Noble Street, Toronto, Ontario M6K 2C8, Canada.

Individual Exhibitions:

1971	*Baby Pictures,* Baldwin Street Gallery, Toronto
1972	*Brussels Townsfolk,* Brussels Mainstreet, Ontario
1973	*Movie Directors,* Revue Repertory Theatre, Toronto
1978	*64 Portrait Studies,* David Mirvish Gallery, Toronto
	Nova Scotia College of Art and Design, Halifax
1979	*Ledoyen Series,* YYZ, Toronto
1980	Centre Culturel Canadien, Paris
	Image Co-op Gallery, Montpelier, Vermont
	Three Photographers, Open Space Gallery, Victoria, British Columbia (with Shin Sugino and Jennifer Dickson)
1981	*Downwind,* Mercer Union, Toronto
1982	*48 Views Series,* Jane Corkin Gallery, Toronto
1983	*Turning,* Harbourfront Photo Gallery, Toronto

Joseph Beuys, Optica Galerie, Montreal
1984 *Photographs 1981-83,* Charles H. Scott Gallery, Vancouver,
        British Columbia
      National Exhibition Centre, Castlegar, British Columbia
      Photographs 1975-84, Nickle Arts Museum, Calgary, Alberta
1985 *Dusseldorf Photographs,* The Isaacs Gallery, Toronto
1986 *Photographs 1975-84,* Winnipeg Art Gallery, Manitoba
      Photographs 1975-84, Art Gallery of Hamilton, Ontario

Selected Group Exhibitions:

1977 *Seven Photographers,* National Film Board of Canada, Ottawa
      Five Photographers, York University, Toronto
1978 *Sweet Immortality,* Edmonton Art Gallery, Alberta
      Canadian Connection, Neikrug Gallery, New York
1979 *Photo Extended Dimensions,* Winnipeg Art Gallery, Manitoba
      Opening Exhibition, Jane Corkin Gallery, Toronto
1981 *Realism: Structure and Illusion,* Mac-Donald-Stewart Art
        Centre, Guelph, Ontario
1982 *Persona,* Nickle Arts Museum, Calgary, Alberta
1984 *Seeing People, Seeing Space,* The Photographers' Gallery,
        London
      Responding to Photography, Art Gallery of Ontario, Toronto
1985 *Identités,* Centre national de la Photographie, Paris

Collections:

Edmonton Art Gallery, Alberta; Canada Council Art Bank, Ottawa; National Film Board of Canada, Ottawa; Bibliothèque Nationale, Paris; Department of External Affairs, Ottawa; National Gallery of Canada, Ottawa; Nickle Arts Museum, Calgary, Alberta; Winnipeg Art Gallery, Manitoba.

Publications:

On MAGGS: Books—*Arnaud Maggs,* exhibition catalogue, by David MacWilliam, Paris 1980; *12 Canadians: Contemporary Canadian Photography,* edited by Jane Corkin, Toronto 1981; *Persona,* exhibition catalogue, with text by Karyn Elizabeth Allen, Calgary, Alberta 1982; *Arnaud Maggs: Selected Works 1981-83,* exhibition catalogue, with text by E. Theodore Lindberg, Vancouver 1984; *Arnaud Maggs Photographs 1975-1984,* exhibition catalogue, with text by Karyn Elizabeth Allen, Calgary, Alberta 1984; *Identités: De Disderi au Photomaton,* exhibition catalogue, with texts by Michel Frizot, Serge July and others, Paris, 1985. **Articles**—"64 Portrait Studies at David Mirvish Gallery" by Raphael Bendahan in *Artists Review* (Toronto), May 1978; "Arnaud Maggs at YYZ" by David MacWilliam in *Vanguard* (Vancouver), January 1980; "Calculated Expression" by Martha Fleming in *Afterimage* (Rochester, New York), January 1982; "Issue Talks with Arnaud Maggs" by Barbara Daniel in *Issue* (Vancouver), February 1984; "The Many Faces of Maggs" by John Bentley Mays in the *Globe and Mail* (Toronto), 18 January 1986.

*

When I was forty years old I felt a sudden urge to become a photographer. Up until then I had never been interested in the subject. It wasn't even a hobby of mine. I bought a used Nikon, and in order to earn a living, I started doing fashion pictures for magazines. I had a lot of fun and got quite good at it. I'd been a graphic designer to begin with, so the transition wasn't difficult. I even managed to keep a lot of my same clients. Instead of using my designs and drawings, they started using my photographs. My life seems to run in seven year cycles, and one day I realized that this particular cycle had completed itself and that it was time for a change.

I sold my camera (I had a Hasselblad at this point) and decided to go back to art school. Drawing seemed to be a good place to begin, so I started attending life classes and anatomy classes. It was the type of discipline I needed at this point and it helped me to see, something I'd forgotten how to do. Gradually I became aware of the shapes of people's heads, and this interest led me to start taking pictures of some of the models I'd been drawing.

I think that through drawing and observing the head, I was able to see it in a different way, and I wanted to show what I saw through photography. Edward

Weston did this very successfully with his peppers and cabbages. He taught us to see things with his particular vision. For my part, I began to photograph the head in a very analytical fashion, in an attempt to remove the association with conventional portraiture. My first series, "64 Portrait Studies," showed 32 men and women in four rows of sixteen pictures per row, the first and third row in profile, the second and fourth row in frontal position. After that I began to do pieces where I would take a predetermined number of pictures and show the whole thing, in the order in which it was taken. About a year ago, I exhibited all these works in a big retrospective of over 13,000 images. Somehow it wrapped up that aspect of my work for me, and now I am looking for new ways to make art. Perhaps I'll start drawing again.

—Arnaud Maggs

*   *   *

For Arnaud Maggs, portraits are analytic experiments, variations on a theme. He sometimes predetermines his pieces, using three front and three side portraits against a plain, white background, two people per roll. He often uses the whole shoot unedited, complete with the actual physical evidence of film, as in the twelve rolls with which he photographed André Kertész. (He placed Kertész in a chair that revolved and photographed him in twelve positions according to a clock on the floor.)

Maggs catalogues in a way that recalls August Sander, but his types vary more in their head shapes. He prefers extremes, and is interested by the strangeness of the commonplace. "You'd never guess the front view from the side or vice versa—it's a surprise," he points out.

His "64 Portrait Studies" (1976-78) are the masterpieces of his formal, structured, highly-disciplined work. Almost ugly, the individuals recall news or documentary photographs: they have the same bored, bland look. The repetition of forms is an echo from his long experience in the design field. Arnaud Maggs participates in portraiture's rites—his camera stutters a person who is more real than real.

—Joan Murray

MAGUBANE, Peter.

Nationality: South African. **Born:** Vrededorp, Johannesburg, 18 January 1932. **Education:** the Lutheran School and Western Native High School, Sophiatown, Johannesburg, 1950-55; mainly self-taught in photography. **Family:** Married and divorced twice; children: Fikile, Linda, and Vusi. **Career:** Worked (during school holidays) as a messenger, driver, tea-boy, etc., 1951-54, and as a photographer, under Tom Hopkinson and Jürgen Schadeberg, 1954-63, *Drum* magazine, Johannesburg; freelance press photographer, London and the United States, 1963-65, and in Johannesburg, 1965-66. Began work for *Rand Daily Mail,* Johannesburg, 1967: detained by police and kept in solitary confinement, May 1969-September 1970; placed under Banning Orders and forced to resign from *Rand Daily Mail,* October 1970-October 1975; also detained and kept in solitary confinement for 98 days, 1971; resumed employment with the *Rand Daily Mail,* 1975; again detained, with other Black newsmen, for 123 days during Soweto Riots, 1976. Also, freelance photographer for *Time* magazine, in Johannesburg, since 1978. **Recipient:** First Prize, South African Best Press Picture Contest, 1958; 10 Best British Cameramen Award, 1962; Gold and Bronze Plaque, 1963, and Bronze Plaque, 1964, Professional Photographers Contest, Johannesburg; Enterprising Journalism Award, Stellenbosch Farmers Winery, Johanesburg, 1976; Nicholas Tomalin Award, *The Sunday Times,* London, 1976; Janusz Korezak Literary Award, United States, 1980; Ford Foundation grant, to study cinematography in the United States, 1981; Robert Capa Overseas Press Award, New York, 1986; Erich Salomon Award, West Berlin, 1986. **Agent:** Black Star, 450 Park Avenue South, New York, New York. **Address:** c/o Alfred A. Knopf, 201 East 50th Street, New York, New York 10022, U.S.A.

Individual Exhibitions:

1963   Adler Fielding Gallery, Johannesburg
1964   London School of Printing
1974   Carlton Centre, Johannesburg
1975   Durban Art Centre
1976   Shell House Gallery, Cape Town
1977   Pentax Gallery, Johannesburg
        Pentax Gallery, Tokyo
        United Nations Gallery, New York
1978   International Center of Photography, New York
1980   Interfaith Center, New York
        Bennett College, Greensboro, North Carolina
1981   Cultural Center, Stockholm

Selected Group Exhibitions:

1966   *World Press Photo,* The Hague (and 1967, 1968)
1979   *The Year of the Child,* Carlton Centre, Johannesburg
        World Press Photo, Van Gogh Museum, Amsterdam

Publications:

By MAGUBANE: Books—*The World of Children,* with others, London 1966; *Federation of Black Women in South Africa,* Durban, South Africa 1976; *Black as I Am,* Los Angeles 1978; *Magubane's South Africa,* New York and London 1978; *Soweto,* with Marshal Lee, Cape Town 1978; *Soweto Speaks,* with Jill Johnson, Johannesburg 1979; *The Living Dead: Black South African Children,* New York 1982; *I Grandi Fotografi: Peter Magubane,* Milan 1984; *Soweto Uprisings, 1976,* with foreword by Desmond Tutu, Johannesburg 1986, Grand Rapids, Michigan 1987.

On MAGUBANE: Article—"A Poignant Cry from the Beloved Country" in *Photography Year 1979,* by the Time-Life editors, New York 1979.

*

The kind of work I have been doing since I became a photographer mostly has political implications. Unfortunately in a country like South Africa one is forced to concentrate on more serious subjects than just the ordinary cheesecake, and working in South Africa doesn't give you a very wide scope. I have recently realized that there is quite a lot that I have missed photographically by not having left and worked outside South Africa. Now that I am outside South Africa, I begin to see pictures in a different way. I am exposed to the work of a great number of the world's best cameramen, and in South Africa one does not have that chance. I still hope to improve the little knowledge I have of photography, and once I've done that I will go back to my country and pass it on to the aspiring photographers of all races. My camera does not see color. I also do not see color.

—Peter Magubane

*   *   *

To have become an internationally renowned photographer against all the handicaps of a black South African childhood is a unique achievement. What made it possible for Peter Magubane was, above all, his determined eagerness to learn. Starting as a messenger on the magazine *Drum,* he became tea boy then driver. As driver he would carry Bob Gosani, the cameraman, round on jobs and watch the way he operated. He learned from Bob, from a young German photographer, Jürgen Schadeberg, and from anyone who would teach him anything. After driving all day, he trudged through the streets of Johannesburg at night, shooting pictures with a camera paid for by his father, a vegetable hawker. "I would go back to the office to process, and finally I would sleep there, because there was no transport that would take me back to Sophiatown at that time of night."

Appointed to *Drum's* staff, he was inevitably drawn into photographing black resistance and white oppression, covering African political gatherings, arrests, and the celebrated "treason trials" of the 1950s, during which he was himself arrested three times. But these were to be only the first taste of many painful clashes with authority. At times he would come into the office bruised and bleeding, once so covered in bandages that his editor failed to recognize him.

His courage and endurance became legendary. In all, simply for photographing life as black people experience it in their own country, Magubane has spent 586 days in solitary confinement, plus six further months in jail; he has been beaten up, interrogated for five days without being allowed to sleep, and finally suffered five years of "banning." Among many other hardships, "banning" meant that he could no longer operate as a cameraman because he could never be in the company of more than one person at a time.

Throughout it all he continued to "think photography," even when forbidden to take pictures. In October 1975, when the ban was lifted, he went back to the *Rand Daily Mail* which now employed him: "It was like being back from the dead. But it was uphill, because I had lost my photographer's eye and was not accustomed to mingling with people freely." But, having recovered his eye by constant practice, he now started to take better pictures than he had ever done, and by the time of the great Soweto riots of black schoolchildren which started in June 1976, he had come into his full mastery, above all in the use of space. The amount of sky, the extent of background, room for the fiery action to move into . . . he was allowing it all with the assurance of a great photographer. His pictures from Soweto went round the world. Award after award started to come his way. He was invited to America; editors clamoured for his pictures and publishers for books.

Through it all Peter Magubane has remained completely level-headed, dignified, free from hatred, and still eager to go on learning. He says: "I do not know what will happen next to me. I shall go on working in South Africa, taking the best pictures that I can. I hope they will not all be of violence."

—Tom Hopkinson

MAHR, Mari.

Nationality: Chilean, Hungarian, New Zealander, British. **Born:** Marianne Weiner in Santiago, Chile, 16 March 1941; emigrated to Hungary, 1948; settled in England, 1973. **Education:** Studied at the School of Journalism, Budapest, 1961-64, Dip. Journ. 1964; Polytechnic of Central London, 1972-76, B.A. in photographic arts 1976. **Family:** Married the Hungarian Gyula Mahr in 1959 (divorced, 1972); daughter: Julie; married the New Zealander Graham Percy in 1977. **Career:** Freelance photographer, London, since 1976. **Recipient:** Greater London Arts Association Award, 1980; Fox Talbot Prize, 1989. **Address:** 4 Tibbet's Close, London SW19 6EF, England.

Individual Exhibitions:

1977   The Photographers' Gallery, London
        Canon Photo Gallery, Amsterdam (with Christian Vogt)
1978   Riverside Studios, London
1979   Galerie ABF, Hamburg
        Galerie Art Something, Amsterdam
        Light Factory, Charlotte, North Carolina
1980   Open Eye Gallery, Liverpool
1982   *3 Women,* Moira Kelly Fine Art Gallery, London
1986   *Idle Times,* The Photographers' Gallery, London
1987   The Photography Centre of Athens, Greece.
1988   Artspace, Auckland, New Zealand
        Cupboard Space Gallery, Wellington
        Govett-Brewster Art Gallery, New Plymouth, New Zealand
1989   The Photographers' Gallery, London
        Plymouth Arts Centre, Plymouth, England
        Glynn Vivian Gallery, Swansea, Wales
        Street Level Gallery, Glasgow, Scotland
        Untitled Gallery, Sheffield, England
1990   *Fotofest,* Houston, Texas, USA
        Primavera Fotografica, Barcelona, Spain
        Visor Gallery, Valencia, Spain

Scholarly Virtues, Actual Conversations 1, **1988.** Photograph by Mari Mahr.

Gallery Agora, Turin, Italy
1991   The British Council Gallery, Milan & Rome, Italy
The Photographers' Gallery, London
Les Ateliers Nadar, Marseille, France
1992   Portfolio Gallery, Edinburgh, Scotland
1994   Montage Gallery, Derby, England
Bonni Benrubi Gallery, New York
National Museum of Photography, Film & Television,
    Bradford, England

Selected Group Exhibitions:

1978   *Fantastic Photography in Europe,* at *Rencontres
    Internationales de la Photographie,* Arles, France (toured
    Europe and the United States, 1976-78)
    Hommage à Marcel Duchamp, International Group Junij,
    Ljubljana, Yugoslavia
1979   *European Colour Photography,* The Photographers' Gallery,
    London
1980   *Photography as Art/Art as Photography,* Fotoforum Kassel,
    West Germany (and world tour)
    Photographia: La Linea Sottile, Galleria Flaviana, Locarno,
    Switzerland
    Contemporary Colour Photography/Salford '80, The Photogra-
    phers' Gallery, Salford, England
    Summer Show 2, Serpentine Gallery, London
1983   *Strategies: Recent British Photography,* John Hansard Gallery,
    Southampton, Hampshire (toured Britain)

1984   *Nuovo fotografia inglese,* Milan
1985   *Four British Photographers,* Fay Gold Gallery, Atlanta,
    Georgia
    Landscape/Interior, Coracle Gallery, London
    Revisions, Cambridge Darkroom, England
1986   *Festivals: Domestic Stories,* Camerawork, London
    Rencontres Internationales Photographiques, Arles, France
    New Acquisitions in Photography, V & A Museum, London
    Furniture/Sculpture, Victoria Miro Gallery, London
    First Biennale of Photography, Ein Harod, Israel
1987   *Multiple Originals,* The Photographers' Gallery, London
1988   *Media Show,* Sheffield, England
    Photography on the Edge, Hagarty Museum of Art, Wiscon-
    sin, USA
    My Family: Myself, Untitled Gallery, Sheffield, England
    First Biennale of Photography, Rotterdam, The Netherlands
    Towards a Bigger Picture, V & A Museum, London
1989   *In Celebration of Photography,* Zelda Cheatle Gallery, London
    Through The Looking Glass, Barbican Art Gallery, London
    Anima Mundi: Still Life in Britain, Canadian Museum of
    Contemporary Photography, Ottawa, Ontario, Canada
    Women Focusing, Camerawork, London
    European Women's Imagination, Palazzina Corsini, Rome
    Photo-Sculpture, Watershed Gallery, Bristol, England
1990   National Garden Festival, Gateshead, England
1991   *Constructed Photography,* Padiglioni d'Arte Contemporania,
    Milan, Italy
    De Vierde Wand/Photography as Theatre, Amsterdam

De Composicion, The British Council (touring South America)
Electronic Age, National Museum of Photography, Film &
  Television, Bradford, England
Treading a Fine Line, Zelda Cheatle Gallery, London
1992   *Realta e Surrealta,* Aosta, Italy
Mai de la Photo, Reims, France
Rencontres Internationales Photographiques, Arles, France
Flora Photographica, Serpentine Gallery, London
2 Internationale Foto-Triennale, Esslingen, Germany
1993   *Los Angeles International,* Paul Kopeikin Gallery, Los Angeles
Desert Island Picks, The Photographers' Gallery, London
Moving into View, The South Bank Centre, London
Summer Show, Zelda Cheatle Gallery, London
Phiz 93, The John Kobal Foundation, London
1994   *Who's Looking at the Family?,* Barbican Art Gallery, London
Portrait of my Mother, Institut Français d'Ecosse, Edinburgh

Collections:

Arts Council of Great Britain, London; British Council, London; Bibliotheque Nationale, Paris; Eastern Arts, Norwich, England; V & A Museum, London; FNAC, Lyons, France; National Museum of Photography, Film & Television, Bradford, England; Unilever Collection, London; National Gallery of Australia, Canberra; Contemporary Art Society, London; Warwick University Collection, Coventry, England; Scottish Art Gallery and Museum, Glasgow, Scotland.

Publications:

By Mahr: Books—*A Few Days in Geneva,* London, 1988; *Isolated Incidents,* London, 1989; *Mari Mahr—Photographs; A Collection,* Bradford, 1994.

On MAHR: Exhibition catalogues—*European Colour Photography,* London 1979; *Photographia: La Linea Sottile* by Giuliana Scimé and Rinaldo Bianda, Locarno, Switzerland 1980; *Strategies: Recent Developments in British Photography,* edited by Rupert Martin, London 1983; *Nuova fotografia inglese,* edited by Giovanni Chiaramonte, Milan 1984. **Articles**—in *Creative Camera* (London), February 1980, May 1982, April 1986, 8 & 9 1988, 6/ 1989; *Camera* (Lucerne), August 1980; *European Photography,* 43/1992; *Women's Art Magazine,* 45/1992; *London Magazine,* June/July 1989; *Picabia,* Japan, 12/1990; *Sunday Times,* August, 1993; *Asahi Camera,* Japan, 1/1994.

*   *   *

Photography can be compared to a party game: the players learn the rules, then win or lose depending on their skill. But there will always be some players who want to analyze the rules and try to work out new tactical moves. Experimental photographers are like those players: when they have mastered the basic techniques of the photographic process, they engage in a tireless search for more and new visual solutions. This taste for experiment, this curiosity about the enormous unexplored potential of the photographic medium, is innate in the work of Mari Mahr. Her investigations spring from her need to find perfect forms to represent our interior lives.

Mahr resolves the obvious difficulties of such a goal by trying out different techniques—not chosen capriciously or casually, still less because they are a challenge or an indication of the effectiveness of her manual and inventive skills. She selects a particular photographic process precisely because it is consistent with some visual demand that, formally, can be satified in no other way. The relationship between concept, subject and technique in her work is a very strict one; these three elements in the intellectual and operational execution of her work constitute the essential factors in the creation of the image.

Mari Mahr captures with photography the fugitive pictures that exist in the mind, related perhaps to dreams, the imagination or memory. These pictures can be made "real" in photographs when they can be evoked by some tangible object in our exterior life—sometimes another picture, a drawing in an encyclopaedia, a frame in a film. The picture thus found is the image of the other, interior picture: it has been transformed to make it capable of symbolic representation. To paraphrase Proust, her work is a "search for the lost

picture," which, besides stressing the value of the particular experiment, examines the functioning of visual memory and perception. Her pictures thus function at more than one level, bringing back forgotten acquaintances, sensations and impulses, and often, because of the kind of response they provoke, causing a momentary bewilderment in the beholder. In fact, the persons and objects represented, though they have real outlines and shapes, though they are objects from the "real" world, tend to lose their identity within the memory they suggest, or within recollections that may or may not be true: perhaps the event occurred, perhaps it exists only in our imagination.

The essential concept on which all of Mahr's working experiments are based is a questioning of the mystery and riddle of man's inner life. That question is posed even by the formal expression of the picture, which forces us to flat read it, very much as we interpret dreams or recollections. The picture in fact consists of only a few elements, nearly all on the same plane. The visual field has neither depth nor width. Every detail is in close-up. Nothing is subordinated and nothing is emphasized as we look at the whole, so that the picture seems to swell, to burst out of the spatial limits of which it is composed.

—Giuliana Scimé

MAJORE, Frank.

Nationality: American. **Born:** Richmond Hill, New York, 1948. **Education:** Graduated with B.S. from Philadelphia College of Art in 1969; self-taught in photography. **Recipient:** Photography Fellowship from the New York Foundation for the Arts, 1985; Photography Fellowship from the Aaron Siskind Foundation, 1993; Tiffany Award from the Louis Comfort Tiffany Foundation 1993. **Agent:** Holly Solomon Gallery, 172 Mercer Street, New York, New York 10012, U.S.A. **Address:** 181 Duane Street, New York, New York 10013, U.S.A.

Individual Exhibitions:

1979   C Space, New York
1980   Artists Space, New York
1984   Perspectief, Rotterdam, Netherlands
1986   International Center of Photography, New York
        CEPA, Buffalo, New York
        Nature Morte, New York
        303 Gallery, New York
1987   Holly Solomon Gallery, New York
1989   Holly Solomon Gallery, New York
1990   Josh Baer Gallery, New York
        Rena Bransten Gallery, San Francisco
1991   Holly Solomon Gallery, New York
        Blancpain/Stepczynski Galerie d'Art Contemporain, Geneva,
          Switzerland
        Dreansville, The John and Mable Ringling Museum of Art,
          Sarasota, Florida (travelled to LaForet Museum, Tokyo;
          Fukuoka Atrium, Fukuoka, Japan; The Nagoya Gallery,
          Nagoya, Japan; The Butler Institute of American Art,
          Youngstown, Ohio)
1992   *Early-Late Works,* Holly Solomon Gallery, New York
1994   Thomas Solomon's Garage, Los Angeles

Selected Group Exhibitions:

1977   *Works on Paper,* Katonah Gallery, Katonah, New York
1979   *Personal Visions,* The Bronx Museum of Art, New York
1981   *Fifth International Biennale,* "Erweiterte Fotografie," *Wiener
          Secession,* Vienna
1982   *A Fatal Attraction: Art and the Media,* The Rennaissance
          Society of the University of Chicago, Illinois
1983   *3-D Photographs,* Castelli Graphics, New York (travelled to
          Herman Wunsche Gallery, Bonn, Germany)

Chrysanthemums with Pearls, **1992.** Photograph ©Frank Majore.

1984	*Still Life in Photography,* Rotterdam Arts Foundation, Netherlands
1985	*Between Here and Nowhere,* Riverside Studios, London (travelled to Kettle's Yard, Cambridge; Midland Group Gallery, Nottingham, England; The Orchard Gallery, Londonderry, N. Ireland)
	Biennial Exhibition, Whitney Museum of American Art, New York
1986	*Art and Advertising: Commericial Photographs by Artists,* International Center of Photography, New York
1987	*Avant-Garde in the Eighties,* Los Angeles County Museum of Art, California
1988	*Dwellings,* 56 Bleecker Gallery, New York
1989	*Contemporary Art From New York,* Yokohama Museum of Art, Japan
	Bellevue, Museum Moderner Kunst, Vienna
	The Photography of Invention, National Museum of American Art, Washington, D.C.
1990	*Exchange of Information,* Museum of Modern Art, New York
1991	*Pleasures and Terrors of Domestic Comfort,* Museum of Modern Art, New York (travelled to Baltimore Museum of Art, Maryland; Los Angeles Country Museum of Art, Los Angeles; Contemporary Arts Center, Cincinnati)
1992	*This Sporting Life, 1878-1991,* The High Museum of Art, Atlanta
1993	*Vivid,* Galerie Raab, Berlin
	Commodity Image, International Center of Photography, New York
	American Made/New Still-Life, Isetan Museum of Art, Tokyo (travelled to Hokkaido Obihiro Museum of Art, Hokkaido)
1994	*Desire & Loss,* Carl Solway Gallery, Cincinnati

Collections:

Albright Knox Art Gallery, Buffalo; Allen Memorial Art Museum at Oberlin, Ohio; Baltimore Museum of Art, Maryland; Boston Museum of Fine Arts, Massachusetts; Brooklyn Museum, New York; The Butler Institute of American Art, Youngstown, Ohio; Chase Manhattan Bank, New York; Contemporary Museum of Art, Honolulu; International Center of Photography, New York; International Museum of Photography at George Eastman House, Rochester, New York; Los Angeles County Museum, California; Museum of Fine Arts, Houston; Museum of Modern Art/Palais Lichtenstein, Vienna; Queens Museum, New York; The John and Mable Ringling Museum of Art, Sarasota, Florida; Tamayo Museum, Mexico City; Yokohama Museum of Art, Japan.

Publications:

On MAJORE: Books—*New Directions,* Gallery of World Photography series, Tokyo 1984; *Fabrications: Staged, Altered and Appropriated Photographs,* New York 1987; *Human Space: International Reviewbook of Art and Literature* by Enrico R. Comi, March 1988. Articles—"Shots in the Dark" by Ben Lifson in *The Village Voice,* 19-25 November 1980; "(New) Wave at the Camera" by Andy Grundberg in *Soho News,* 19-25 November 1981; "Couches, Diamonds and Pie" by Ben Lifson in *The Village Voice,* 13-19 May 1981; "Mixing Art and Commerce" by Andy Grundberg in *The New York Times;* "In Today's Photography, Imitation Isn't Always Flattery" by Andy Grundberg in *The New York Times,* 14 November 1982; "On Artificial" by Kate Linker in *Flash Art,* March 1983; "Drifting Off Jamaica" by Douglas Blau in *Arts;* "Tableau America" in *Vogue Bambini,* November/December 1984; "The New Capital at White Columns" by Walter Robinsson in *Art in America,* April 1984; "Hour of the Wolf" by Kim Levin in *The Village Voice,* 17 July 1984; "Frank Majore" by Marietta Haveman in *Perspktief,* November/December 1984; "Sweet Desire, Frank Majore" in *Cafe-Creme Magazine,* Vol. 7, 1986; *The New York Times,* 26 January 23 February, 16 May, 28 September and 28 December 1986; "Review" by Eleanor Heartney in *ART News,* April 1986; "Art and Advertising" by Charles Hagen in *Artforum,* November 1986; "Review" by David Lurie in *Arts,* March 1986; "The Monopoly of Appearances" by Carol Squires in *Flash Art,* February/March 1987; "Guys and Dogs" by Gary Indiana in *The Village Voice,* 22 December

1987; "The Art of Salesmanship" by Vicki Goldberg in *American Photographer,* February 1987; "American Baroque" by Carter Radcliff in *Elle,* December 1988; "The Modern Fetish" by Donald Kuspit in *Artforum,* October 1988; "Frank Majore" by Hiroko Tamako in *Hi Fashion,* March 1988; "Frank Majore at Holly Solomon" by Dan Rubey in *Art News,* March 1988; "Publicita" in *Fotografare,* 1988; "foto" in *Arbeiter Zeitung,* 22 December 1989; "Der Americanische Traum" by Gert Walden in *Falter,* March 1990; "Verfremdungen und Erfindungen" by Maria Von Buchsbaum in *Wiener Zeitung,* 13 December 1989; "Frank Majore: A Photographer Projects Images of Modern Desire" by Carol Squires in *American Photographer,* January 1989; "Gefrorene Bewegung-Sehnsuchte" by Marcus Mittringer in *Die Presse,* 19 December 1989; "Choices (Dwellings)" by Kim Levin in *The Village Voice,* 27 November 1989; "Viewfinder" by Mary Haus in *Interview,* 1989; "Ausstellung 'Bellevue' in Wein" in *Wiener Zeitung,* 8 December 1989; "The Indispensability of Surrealism" by Vivien Raynor in *The New York Times,* 6 May 1990; "Frank Majore at Josh Baer" by Elizabeth Hayt-Atkins in *Art News,* November 1990; "Frank Majore at Josh Baer" by Charles Hagen in *Artforum,* October 1990; "Schnappschuse Aus New York Fotoszene Drei Eigenstandige Amerikaner in Wien" by Gunther Frohmann in *Salzburger Nachrichten,* 13 January 1990; *Cover Magazine,* January 1990; "Choices: Frank Majore" by Vince Aletti in *The Village Voice,* 29 May 1990; "Frank Majore at Holly Solomon Gallery" by Jeff Wright in *Cover Magazine,* April 1991; "Choices: Frank Majore" by Vince Aletti in *The Village Voice,* 16 December 1992; "Frank Majore at Holly Solomon Gallery" by Charles Hagen in *The New York Times,* 1 January 1993; "Frank Solomon at Holly Solomon" by Hovey Brock in *Art News,* February 1993.

*   *   *

From the early 1980s, Frank Majore embraced advertising's suave seductions in his large-scale photographs. Showing no brand name products in his still life, he focused on the icons that Madison Avenue and Hollywood use to whet consumer desire yet leave it ever unsatisfied; the rapturous female, eyes half-closed, mouth half open, who sells everything from soap to cars; the bric-a-brac of elite romance—Martinis and cigarettes in penthouses; the perfect rose, the string of pearls, the flawless antique bust. Like Cindy Sherman, Richard Prince and others of his contemporaries, Majore deconstructed mass media's stereotypes while leaving their allure intact.

For some critics, this group of camera artists seemed to illustrate the thesis of cultural theorist Jean Baudrillard. This teaches that simulation is more compelling than reality in our mediated age, that direct experience has been supplanted by representation in late capitalist society. Photography is no longer an "objectively" descriptive "mirror of nature" but ideologically determined to enforce socio-economic distinctions. Post modern photography shows the puppet strings of mass communication and the artifices of modernism. It is late Pop Art in its absorbtion with representation and its ambiguous attitude. More intrigued by images than objects, it substitutes photographs from *Vogue* and stills from B films for more primitive sources in comic books, billboards and Campbells' soup cans.

Such observations applied to Majore's skillful adoption of advertising's subjects and style. Drawing on his training as a furniture and industrial designer, his work as an art director, he smoothly enhanced his studio setups through lighting and projected images: slides of faces, shot from his TV screen, blue-violet backgrounds of New York skyscrapers, sinuous shadows, speckles of light on crystal and gleams of moonlight through modern windows or venetian blinds. The surfaces of his accessories and of the Cibachromes that seemed to pay homage to them were equally immaculate. Reverently treated, the photograph and its depictions alike were "commodity fetishes" in the period's phrase.

In Majore's work through the 1980s, the sexualization of objects and ojectification of females recalled the media of the 1950s when the Queens-born artist grew up, but also Surrealist with its encounters of disparate objects of desire and its romance with fashion, theatre, and their photography. In his more complex pictures at the end of the 1980s, the level of stylistic quotation was loftier (eggs and biomorphic shapes joined his still lifes, for example), while his control and execution remained as flawless as a product photographer's.

A new simplification and geometric rigor of composition appeared around 1990, as Majore seemed to look beyond his tabletops to his background light projections for ideas. The calligraphic streaks and repeated blobs of colour that signal movement in car ads and time lapse in night cityscapes became a kind of

Abstract Expressionist "camera writing" in his overlaid images. He hovered teasingly close to abstraction.

Around 1992 this New York resident shifted gears again and as advertising revived black-and-white to recall 30s sophistication, he adopted monochrome and a sumptuous tonal range. His subjects were ethereal: clouds, smoke, bubbles, spangled with starbursts of light. Against velvety black grounds, their forms looked baroque. They seemed to send up art photography masterpieces like Stieglitz's Clouds as well as Hollywood visions of heaven. Yet for some viewers they also seemed poignant in their gorgeous immateriality, a reminder that artists were losing growing numbers of friends with AIDS. That Majore's work continues to inspire such multivalent responses testifies to his invention, cultural observation and technical sleight of hand.

—Anne Hoy

MAKAROV, Alexandr.

Nationality: Russian. **Born:** Warsaw, in June 1936. **Education:** Educated in schools in Riga, Latvia; studied play direction at the Moscow Institute of Culture, 1954-58. **Military Service:** Served in the Soviet Army, 1958-60. **Career:** Director for Soviet Television, Moscow, 1960-62. Photo-Correspondent, Novosti Agency, Moscow, since 1962. **Address:** Garibaldy nr. 15, korp. I, Flat 110, 117335 Moscow, Russia.

Individual Exhibitions:

1974   U.S.S.R.: The Country and People, travelling exhibition (toured Budapest, Belgrade, Paris, Prague, Warsaw, Havana, Berlin, Casablanca and Madrid, 1974-77)

Selected Group Exhibitions:

          Annual Novosti Agency Exhibitions, Moscow, since 1962
1976   World Press Photo '76, Amsterdam

Collections:

Novosti Agency Archives, Moscow.

Publications:

On MAKAROV: Books—Photographic Communication, edited by R. Smith Schuneman, London and Toronto 1972; Soviet Photography by Vaclav Jiru, Prague 1974. **Article**—"The New World" in Revue Fotografia (Prague), 1977.

*   *   *

To photograph systematically a special sphere of human activity is essential to most Soviet photojournalists, almost an inevitable adjunct to their main work. And from time to time it happens that what starts as a private hobby with only minimal practical application comes to exert a decisive influence on the photographer's development and growth, creating the foundation for his creative personality. That is the case with Alexandr Makarov and his photographs of the ballet.

The ballet, the traditional expression of culture of the Russian aristocracy, is now in fact as popular with the broad mass of people in the U.S.S.R. as is, say, the circus and its artists. It is the most photographed of artistic activities, and as a result photos of the ballet are often no better than the standard of prefabricated themes, used as journalistic schemas to express high cultural living standards. But thanks to the real masters of photography of stage art—for example, Anatoli Garanin—serious photography of the ballet is on a very high level, and anyone who wishes to excel at it faces fierce competition.

Alexandr Makarov came to take up ballet photography after his professional training. He had shown an active interest as a boy in the theatre; at the same time, he was fond of photography. He cultivated those interests further when studying direction at the Moscow Institute of Culture and while working in television. Two decades of working as an agency photographer developed his abilities as a universal reporter—but at the same time he took the opportunity to follow his interest in a specific field of culture. He has for several years now been taking pictures of some of the outstanding figures in Soviet ballet with such perseverance that it is almost as if he were their personal photographer. Prima Ballerina Nadyezhda Pavlova appears in photographs in his archives when she was still in the 5th form at school, and Makarov has gone from that inspiration to create several large cycles devoted to such contemporary stars as Natalie Bessmertnovova, Yuri Grigorovich, Maris Liepa, etc.

Like Anatoli Garanin, Makarov also focuses his interest primarily on the sources of artistic achievement. He is interested in the environment, the nervous tension and the process of supreme mental and physical concentration. He is fascinated by the peculiar atmosphere of "backstage," that world that is practically inaccessible and unknown to the public. He does not attempt to capture human or artistic individuality; he does not express the unity of the personality and its immediate surroundings; instead, he emphasizes the anonymity, the daily drudgery, fatigue, enthusiasm, and pure joy at success that any other work may bring with it too.

In doing so he makes successful use of the frontal view, and he works with expressive close-ups and contrast grain, but he finds that what offers him most scope is the so-called Garanin "shumy"—two contrast planes of photographs, against a very diffuse background, often creating a closed darker edge framing the picture, against which, with the help of a spotlight with a small stage reflector, the decisive moment of action to which the photographer wishes to draw our attention is accentuated to stand out bright and clear. This method produces the desired effect, evoking the feeling of maximum concentration, revealing the internal mental processes of action which are usually hidden from the audiences's eyes but in reality are only relatively distant. Dynamic photography of this kind, which is slightly reminiscent of looking through a microscope, naturally cultivates all the features of that aesthetic stylization which is usually achieved only afterwards in the laboratory, when deliberate under-exposure is counterbalanced by the drastic effect of developers. The results that Makarov achieves are among the best in Soviet photography.

—Vladimìr Remeš

MALMBERG, Hans.

Nationality: Swedish. **Born:** Stockholm, 20 September 1927. **Education:** Studied photography at Stockholm Vocational School, 1941-43. **Military Service:** Served as photographer, Royal Swedish Navy, 1948. **Family:** Married Margret Gudmundsdottir in 1950 (divorced, 1964); children: Leif, Kristina and Åsa; married Agneta Mälargård in 1970; son: Linus. **Career:** Photographer, with Pressfoto Meyerhöffer, Stockholm, 1943-46; Partner, with Sven Eriksson-Gillsäter, Pressfoto-Bildnytt Agency/Studio, Stockholm, 1947-48; freelance photojournalist, aerial photographer and filmmaker, working for Se, Vi, Stockholms-Tidningen, etc., Stockholm, 1949-77. Founder-Member, Tio Fotografer group, Stockholm, 1958-77. **Recipient:** Kulturpreis, Deutsche Gesellschaft für Photographie (DGPh), 1966. **Estate:** Agneta Malmberg, Allmanna Grand 3B, 115 21 Stockholm, Sweden. **Died:** (in Bergvik, Sweden) 30 August 1977.

Individual Exhibitions:

1975   Hans Malmberg: Bilder 1946-1975, Moderna Museet, Stockholm (travelled to the Sundsvalls Museum, Sundsvall, Sweden, 1976)
1981   Fotograficentrum, Stockholm (retrospective)

Selected Group Exhibitions:

1949   Unga Fotografer, Rotohallen, Stockholm
1951   Jeunes Photographes Suedoises, Galerie Kodak, Paris

1954   *Svartvitt: Svensk fotografi av idag,* Nationalmuseum,
        Stockholm
1958   *Fotokonst 1958,* Lunds Konsthall, Lund, Sweden
1970   *Tenstaborna: Foto/Film/Bild,* Liljevalchs Konsthall,
        Stockholm
1971   *Contemporary Photographs from Sweden,* Library of Congress,
        Washington, D.C.
1976   *Tio Fotografer,* Galerie Aronowitsch, Stockholm
1977   *Tio Fotografer,* Arles, France (travelled to Paris and Bordeaux)
1982   *The Frozen Image,* Walker Art Center, Minneapolis (trav-
        elled to the International Center of Photography, New
        York; University of California at Los Angeles; Por-
        tland Art Museum, Maine, Museum of Contemporary
        Art, Chicago; Tacoma Art Museum, Washington;
        Kjavalsstadir, Reykjavik; Louisiana Museum, Humlebaek;
        Taidehalli, Helsinki; Fotografiska Museet, Stockholm;
        Kunstsenter, Oslo)
1984   *Subjektive Fotografie: Images of the 50s,* San Francisco
        Museum of Modern Art (travelled to the University of
        Houston, Texas; Museum Folkwang, Essen; Vasterbottens
        Museum, Umea; Kulturhuset, Stockholm; Saarland Museum,
        Saarbrucken; Palais des Beaux-Arts, Brussels)

Collections:

Fotografiska Museet, Stockholm; Valokuvamuseon, Helsinki; Norsk Fotohistorisk
Forening, Oslo; Bibliothèque Nationale, Paris; Library of Congress, Washington, D.C.

Publications:

By MALMBERG: Books—*Fädernas kyrka,* with text by Josef Oliv,
Stockholm 1950; *Island,* with text by Helgi P. Briem, Stockholm 1951;
Närmare Dig!, with Bo Setterlind, Stockholm 1951; *Dalälven: Industrifloden,*
with text by Sven Rydberg, Stockholm 1957; *Nils Holgerssons underbara
resa,* with text by Tage and Kathrine Aurell, Stockholm 1962; *I eviga skogen,*
with text by Gunnel Linde, Stockholm 1966; illustrations for *Svensk Färg-TV*
by Bertil Allander, Halmstad, Sweden 1969. **Articles**—"Fotgrafera flyg" in
Foto (Stockholm), September 1949; "Kameraskott i stridslinjen" in *Foto*
(Stockholm), December 1950; "Fotografering förbjuden" in *Foto* (Stockholm), March 1952; "Rapport från Hanoi" in *Vi* (Stockholm), 1968.

On MALMBERG: Books—*Hans Malmberg: Bilder 1946-1975,* exhibition
catalogue, Stockholm 1975; *The Frozen Image: Scandinavian Photography,*
edited by Martin Freeman, Minneapolis and New York, 1982; *Subjektive
Fotografie: Images of the 50s,* exhibition catalogue, by Ute Eskildsen,
Manfred Schmalriede and Dorothy Martinson, Essen, West Germany 1984.
Articles—"Hans Malmbergs bildportfölj" by Tor Alm in *Nordisk Tidskrift
för Fotografi* (Gothenburg), no. 3, 1959; "Helivision och Travelling Matte
hjälpmedel för Nils Holgersson" in *Fotonyheterna* (Stockholm), no. 8, 1962;
"Hans Malmbergs method för trickbild på färgdia skapade unik apparatur" in
Fotonyheterna (Stockholm), no. 9, 1962; "Fotograferade barn" by Ulla
Bergstrand in *Sydsvenska Dagbladet* (Malmo), 12 December 1968; "Hans
Malmberg: En riktig fotograf" by Kurt Bergengren in *Aftonbladet* (Stockholm), 14 June 1975; "Hans Malmberg: Världsfotograf som skildrar förorterna
med ömhet" in *Expressen* (Stockholm), 17 July 1975; "Fotojournalistikens
stora tid före televisionen" by Kurt Bergengren and "Fotografen som fick en
blomma av Onkel Ho" by Lars Westman in *Bildtidning* (Stockholm), no. 3/
4, 1980.

*   *   *

Hans Malmberg belonged to a group of young Swedish photographers
who, after the Second World War, came out in opposition to the ideals of the
older generation of Swedish photographers. The differences between the two
groups were exposed at an exhibition held in 1949: its title, and the motto for
the young photographers, was *Unga Fotografer*—Young Photographers.
Many of these same photographers were later, in 1958, to found the now well-
known Swedish photographers cooperative and picture agency, Tio Fotografer
(Ten Photographers).

What the young photographers principally objected to was the romantic
sentimentality of the older generation. The national romantic style in Sweden
had developed from the neo-classical ideals of the 1930s, influenced by the
German photography published in *Das Deutsche Lichtbild* toward the end of
1930. The young photographers drew their inspiration from the photo-
reportage in such magazines as *Life, Look, Picture Post, Paris Match* and
Réalités, as well as from the *U.S. Camera Annual,* published in 1948. Their
style had developed during the dark years of the war and was intensified during
the years after the war.

Hans Malmberg was the one of the group that was most influenced by the
photographers Henri Cartier-Bresson and W. Eugene Smith. He also shared
Cartier-Bresson's ideal of the "decisive moment."

Malmberg received his education as a photographer at the Stockholm
Stads Yrkesskola (Stockholm Vocational School), and from 1943-46 he was
employed at the Pressfoto Meyerhöffer agency, where he worked out the style
he would later develop to perfection. Together with his friend Sven Gillsäter,
he started Pressfoto-Bildnytt, a photo agency that soon became well-known:
the demand for news photos was great before the TV Age, and editors found
that Malmberg was an outstanding photographer for their needs. He was
thereafter sent round the world with various well-known Swedish reporters.
His photographs from the Korean War attracted a great deal of attention when
they were published in the weekly magazine *Se:* they show the drama of the
front-line with sharp observation and humanity.

During the 1960s Malmberg travelled extensively, around the world, for
various Swedish companies, describing in photos how Swedish products are
used abroad. While doing this work, he was often fascinated by events around
him, and he shot many photos extraneous to his actual missions. His apprehension was of that extraordinary kind that he took his photograph before other
photographers had even got their cameras ready. He always wore his Leica on
his chest and managed to capture vivid and unusual events in the life of the big
cities that he visited. He seemed to "create" photos where no one else could
see anything happening.

Malmberg was a warm and sensible man, but he had an unusual side to his
character. There was a neurotic restlessness that kept him always on the move.
He was always chasing something that few could perceive, and it was only his
closest friends who knew what was driving him. Some people called him a
reporter, others a journalist, or a photo-journalist. Malmberg didn't like titles;
in his opinion, he "collected moments"—an expression he borrowed from the
German author Heinrich Böll in his novel *Ansichten eines Clown.*

In 1975 the Fotografiska Museet in Stockholm showed Malmberg's
pictures in a retrospective exhibition. Documentary photography was then
very important in Sweden, the show was a great success, and Malmberg, with
all his travels and adventures, became an idol for a new generation of Swedish
photographers. Such fame is usually short-lived, but Malmberg's popularity
has been maintained. His photos demonstrate that he was one of Sweden's best
photo-journalists; they are an outstanding record of a whole era, from World
War Two to the death of the great photo magazines.

—Leif Wigh

MAN, Felix H(ans).

Nationality: British. **Born:** Hans Felix Siegismund Baumann in Freiburg im
Breisgau, Germany, 30 November 1893; adopted the professional name Felix
H. Man, 1929; emigrated to England, 1934: naturalized, 1948. **Education:**
Studied fine art and art history at the University of Berlin, 1912-14, University
of Munich, 1914, and the Kunstgewerbeschule, Munich, 1918-21. Served as
an officer in the German Army, 1914-18. **Career:** Took first photos, 1904,
first documentary reportage photos in the trenches on the Western Front, 1915;
professional photographer from 1928. Draughtsman, *Berliner Zeitung am
Mittag* magazine, and freelance photographer for *Tempo* and *Morgenpost,*
Berlin, 1927-28; Production Chief, with Umbo (Otto Umbehr), for Dephot
(Deutsche Photodienst) press agency, Berlin, 1928; Principal Contributor,
Münchner Illustrierte Presse, Munich, 1929-32, and for *Berliner Illustrirte,*
for which he travelled in Finland, Sweden, North Africa, the United States and
Canada, 1932-34; photographer, under Stefan Lorant, *Weekly Illustrated*

magazine, London, 1934; Special Assignments Photographer, under the pseudonym "Lensman," *Daily Mirror* newspaper, London, 1935-36; Chief Contributor, 1938-45, and Colour Specialist, 1948-50, *Picture Post* magazine, London; Special Assignments Photographer, for *Harper's Bazaar,* London, 1942, for Time-Life publications, London, 1951-52, and for the *Sunday Times* newspaper, London, 1957-58. Editor, *Europaeische Graphik* lithography portfolios, Munich, 1961-75. **Recipient:** Culture Prize, Deutsche Gesellschaft für Photographie, 1965; Cross of Merit, First Class, 1968, and Great Cross, 1980, of the Federal Republic of Germany. **Died:** (in London) 30 January 1985.

Individual Exhibitions:

1961	Galerie Loehr, Frankfurt
1965	Deutsche Gesellschaft für Photographie, Cologne
1967	Landesbildstelle, Hamburg
1968	Landesbildstelle, West Berlin
1971	*Felix H. Man: Pionier des Bildjournalismus,* Münchner Stadtmuseum, Munich
1972	Stadtgalerie Schwarzes Kloster, Freiburg im Breisgau, West Germany
1975	Moderna Museet, Stockholm
	Malmö Konsthall, Sweden
1976	Västerbottens Iäns Museum, Umeå, Sweden Biblioteca Germanica, Rome
	Reportage Portraits, National Portrait Gallery, London
	Museum of Decorative Art, Copenhagen
1977	Goethe Institute/National Book League, London
	Source Gallery, Edinburgh
1978	Goethe Institute/Neikrug Gallery, New York
	The Gallery, Toronto
	Goethe Institute, Montreal
	High Museum of Art, Atlanta
	Ulrich Museum, Wichita, Kansas
	Goethe Institute, Buenos Aires
	Museo de Bellas Artes, Cordoba, Spain
	Goethe Institute, Lisbon
	Instituto Aleman, Madrid
	Goethe Institute, Barcelona
	60 Years of Photography, Kunsthaus, Bielefeld, West Germany (travelled to the Kunstverein, Frankfurt, and the Museum Ludwig, Aachen, West Germany)
1979	Kunstverein, Hamburg
	Galleria Il Diaframma, Milan
	Goethe Institute, Naples
	Galleria Giulia, Rome
	Goethe Institute, Bordeaux
	DGPh Kongresshalle, West Berlin
1981	*Canada 50 Years Ago,* Palazzo Braschi, Rome
	60 Years of Photography, Bibliothèque Nationale and Goethe Institute, Paris
	Photos 1929-76, Galerie Photo Art, Basle
1983	*Sixty Years of Photography,* Victoria and Albert Museum, London (travelled to the Staatsbibliothek, West Berlin)
1985	Schwarzes Kloster, Freiburg im Breisgau, West Germany

Selected Group Exhibitions:

1959	*Hundert Jahre Photographie 1839-1939,* Museum Folkwang, Essen (travelled to Cologne, Munich and Frankfurt)
1967	*Photography in the 20th Century,* National Gallery of Canada, Ottawa (toured Canada and the United States, 1967-73)
1968	*Europa '68,* Bergamo, Italy
1977	*Documenta 6,* Kassel, West Germany
1978	*Neue Sachlichkeit and German Realism of the 1920s,* Hayward Gallery, London
	Tusen och En Bild, Moderna Museet, Stockholm
1979	*The 30s: British Art and Design Before the War,* Hayward Gallery, London

1980	*Avant-Garde Photography in Germany 1919-39,* San Francisco Museum of Modern Art (toured the United States)
	The Imaginary Photo Museum, Kunsthalle, Cologne
1983	*Die fotografische Sammlung,* Museum Folkwang, Essen, West Germany

Collections:

National Portrait Gallery, London; Bibliothèque Nationale, Paris; Moderna Museet, Stockholm; Münchner Stadtmuseum, Munich; Museum Folkwang, Essen; Staatliche Landesbildstelle, Hamburg; Foto-Historama Agfa-Gevaert, Leverkusen, West Germany; International Museum of Photography, George Eastman House, Rochester, New York; University of Texas at Austin; San Francisco Museum of Modern Art.

Publications:

By MAN: Books—*150 Years of Artists' Lithographs,* with an introduction by James Laver, London 1953; *Eight European Artists,* with introductions by Graham Greene and Jean Cassou, London 1954; *Lithography in England 1801-10,* New York 1963, Munich 1967; *Europaeische Graphik,* 10 volumes, Munich 1963-75; *Artists' Lithographs: A World History from Senefelder to the Present Day,* London and New York 1970; *The Complete Graphic Works of Graham Sutherland,* catalogue raisonée, Munich 1971; *Homage to Senefelder,* exhibition catalogue, London 1971; *Felix H. Man: Photo Classics IV,* portfolio, edited by Helmut Gernsheim, London 1972; *Felix H. Man: Reportage Portraits,* exhibition catalogue, London 1976; *Felix H. Man: 60 Jahre Photographie,* Bielefeld, West Germany 1978; *Felix H. Man—Bildjournalist der ersten Stunde,* exhibition catalogue, West Berlin 1983; *Man With Camera: photographs from seven decades,* London and New York 1983, as *Felix H. Man: Photographer aus 70 Jahren,* Munich 1983. **Articles**—"Das Europaeische Museum für Photographie" in *Die Welt* (Hamburg), 8 December 1972; "The Beginning of Photo-Journalism" in *Die Welt* (Hamburg), 1 March 1974; "William Henry Fox Talbot, Inventor of the Negative Process" in *Die Welt* (Hamburg), 16 September 1977; "Each Exposure Must Be a Hit" in *Die Welt* (Hamburg), 28 February 1978; "From the Beginning of Photojournalism" in *DGPh Intern* (Cologne), no. 3, 1978; "Reply to Dr. Tim Gidal" in *DGPh Intern* (Cologne), no. 2, 1979; "Der Fotograf im Frack" in *Frankfurter Allgemeine Zeitung,* 12 May 1979.

On MAN: Books—*The Man Behind the Camera* by Helmut Gernsheim, London 1948; *Creative Photography* by Helmut Gernsheim, London and Boston 1962, 1975; *A Concise History of Photography* by Helmut and Alison Gernsheim, London and New York, 1965, 1971; *Photography in the Twentieth Century* by Nathan Lyons, New York 1967; *Felix H. Man: Pionier des Bildjournalismus,* exhibition catalogue, Munich 1971; *Deutschland—Beginn des modernen Photojournalismus* by Tim N. Gidal, Lucerne and Frankfurt 1972; *Photographie et Société* by Gisèle Freund, Paris 1974; *Dictionary of Photography* by Jorge Lewinski, London 1977; *Documenta 6/Band 2,* exhibition catalogue, by Klaus Honnef and Evelyn Weiss, Cologne 1977; *Bilder for Miljoner* by Rune Hassner, Stockholm 1977; *150 Jahre Photographie* by Klaus Honnef, Mainz 1977; *Felix H. Man,* exhibition catalogue, with an introduction by Tom Hopkinson, London 1977; *Geschichte der Photographie im 20. Jahrhundert/History of Photography in the 20th Century* by Petr Tausk, Cologne 1977, London 1980; *Lexicon der Fotografie* by Hugo Schöttle, Cologne 1978; *The Imaginary Photo Museum* by Helmut Gernsheim, Renate and L. Fritz Gruber and others, Cologne 1981, London 1982; *Of This Our Time: A Journalist's Story 1905-50* by Tom Hopkinson, London 1982; *Felix H. Man: Sixty Years of Photography,* exhibition catalogue, with foreword by C.M. Kauffmann, London 1983. **Articles**—"Photographs of Artists" by Tom Hopkinson in *The Spectator* (London), 21 May 1954; "Felix Man: An Appreciation" by Helmut Gernsheim in *Photography* (London), July 1954; "Felix H. Man: Fotograf und Kunstexperte" by Fritz Kempe in *Foto Prisma* (Stuttgart), October 1965; "Felix H. Man, Ein Pionier" by Helmut Gernsheim in *Camera* (Lucerne), April 1967; "Felix H. Man: A 75th Birthday Tribute" by Helmut Gernsheim in *Camera* (Lucerne), November 1968; "The Father of Photojournalism" in the *New York Times,* 14 May 1971; "Photographs by Felix H. Man" by Helmut Gernsheim in *Creative Camera* (London), July 1972; "Felix H. Man Gets Double Exposure" by Vivien Raynor in the *New York Times,* 27 January 1978; "Felix H. Man, Photo-Journaliste" in *La*

Presse (Montreal), 14 October 1978; "Obituary: Felix Man-Pioneer Photojournalist" by Helmut Gernsheim in *The Times* (London), 1 February 1985.

*

No aspect of the history of photography and its principles has been dealt with in such a distorted way as what we call the "new photo-journalism." To go back to the beginning: pictorial journalism was not invented; it came into existence, at the end of the 1920s, as a logical outcome of attempts by editors of illustrated weeklies to join single pictures, mostly travel pictures, into a single unit by adding a lengthy connecting text. But this was not yet photo-journalism, nor can the documentary photographs of such photographers as Lewis Hine or Jacob Riis during the last century be regarded as something other than descriptions of the bare facts of certain conditions or the recording of actual happenings in posed or flashed photographs.

Even in the 1850s draughtsmen were illustrating events through series of pictures for the then proliferating illustrated magazines in Europe and overseas. But these drawings had their origin in most cases in the imagination of their creators, and as such had no real documentary value. As a matter of fact, the idea of describing happenings in pictures in print goes back to the end of the 15th century when the discovery of America by Columbus was illustrated in a sequence of woodcuts.

But the new photo-journalism was built on quite different principles. Though the form of the pictorial essay remained as its basis, as did what was later called "candid camera," which had been practiced long before by Stieglitz, Paul Martin, Benjamin Stone and others in open-air pictures, a number of new facets were added, the result of which was that photography entered an absolutely new phase. New principles hitherto neglected were introduced, and subjects until then thought to be impossible for the camera, particularly in the field of indoor photography, now played the most important part.

Though, as I have said, some attempts to tell a story in pictures had been made before, the actual breakthrough came in 1929 (earlier attempts remained sporadic and did not involve all spheres of life).

The aims of the photo-journalist are similar to those of a writer, but the photo-journalist uses the camera instead of the pen and tells his story with his own means—the lens. While the feature writer of an important newspaper usually specializes in one or another subject, the photo-journalist has to be at home in all fields—in art, literature, science, politics, etc. He has to compose his final essay on the spot, while the writer can do this in comfort at home from notes he has taken; he can even add from his imagination. But the man who works with the camera must have the qualities of a journalist, a reporter and an artist all at the same time. His mastery of the technical side of photography must be complete. His hands must have the skill of an expert, his vision must be a pictorial one, and his knowledge of human nature must be many-sided.

The concept of an appropriate psychological moment at which to take a picture also played an important part in the development of photo-journalism; it was based on Lessing's "fruitful moment," as described by him in *Laocoon*. This concept and its accompanying method were used by the protagonists of pictorial journalism years before the French claimed to have invented this type of picture taking. Great efforts were made to penetrate the surface of things by means of a mechanical gadget in order to give more than a mere optical record; by careful selection, the accidental remained controlled. It has often been said that the camera, a mechanical instrument, can record only what is there. That is true. But not everybody can see what is there, and a creative mind will use the little glass eye with quite a different attitude and outcome, achieving a result not to be compared with optical appearance only.

The great difference was that this new interpretation was not only a selective one to the highest degree—but if the task was to photograph human beings, this task was approached by returning to simplicity, rejecting all artificial means, giving the psychological factor preference. When taking indoor photographs, the photographer had to work only with available light. If additional lamps or flashlight were used, they would disturb the atmosphere and alter the natural forms. At the same time, the photographer tried to remain as unobtrusive as possible. The old method of "smile" and "hold it" were thrown overboard; on the contrary, natural activity was welcomed.

The first photo-journalists had a great sense of responsibility; they did not commit acts of indiscretion. They were invited to important functions as guests, and they mingled with other guests, becoming practically invisible.

There were also technical difficulties which in those early days had to be overcome. Again and again writers on photography say that it was the miniature camera that brought pictorial journalism into existence—a misleading statement. For many months I personally used a Nettle Camera 6:9 cm, fitted with an Ernostar 1:2, 8, with glass plates, for some of the very first indoor essays, changing over to the Ermanox only later and to the Leica in the second half of 1932. But even with the Ermanox, taking photographs indoors by available light was no walkover, as the time of exposure varied between 1/4 and 1 second, and photos could be taken only from a tripod. As the negative material consisted of glass plates only, the number of photographs that could be taken was limited, and every exposure had to be a success. After 1933, when Leitz introduced interchangeable lenses and film became less coarse and of greater sensitivity, the progress of photojournalism was altered for the worse by the new-comers, many of whom never understood the real principles of the movement. Hundreds of photographs were taken, half of which were blown up in order to provide a means of selection of the 10 or 15 best ones. In a book on photo-journalism published by Time-Life, an editor even praised this method of photo-journalism, which is based only on the accidental.

The new photo-journalism broadened their picture of the world for millions of people; the camera penetrated areas which until then had remained obscure for the ordinary spectator. Many of the subjects we discovered 50 years ago were explored later on, again, by television.

With today's highly-developed technical means, it appears easy to photograph what for the first protagonists was new land. However, though one can repeat the outer form, the question still remains: has not the intensity and the strong expressive character of those photographs of 50 years ago been lost? Hasn't the process become more superficial? To observe all the original rules is not sufficient; it is the conception of the man behind the camera and his own recognizable signature that matter.

At the same time as this new development started, portrait photography took an entirely new form. The live portrait came into existence, leaving the posed studio portrait behind. This type of portraiture based on natural facts has today become commonplace, adopted by the majority of newspaper photographers.

The influence of the new photo-journalism on the development of photography has, until now, been grossly under-rated. Critics and historians did not realize that this new vision did not consist only of a new outer form, but that a new pictorial conception was actually the nucleus of such work. To classify this work only as presswork is a devaluation.

—Felix H. Man (1982)

*   *   *

When he died in his 92nd year, Felix H. Man had lived through the dramatic phase of magazine journalism; his active period from the beginning of the First World War covers half the entire history of photography. His contribution to photo-journalism, to colour photography and to art history has been immense; he has also by example and advice helped several generations of younger cameramen to raise the level of their own achievement.

From the late 1920s when he began working in Germany for the *Münchner Illustrierte* and the *Berliner Illustrirte,* Man was always a photographer for the great occasion. He did indeed make many delightful picture series out of simple scenes such as a country shooting party or the life of a village. But the challenge of the unique opportunity, such as his visit to Mussolini at the height of his power—the first by any magazine photographer—brought out his most memorable work. His long-range view of Mussolini at his desk, shot on sudden inspiration from the door when he was expected to come forward and be introduced, has possibly been reproduced more frequently than any other picture of the same period.

Every photojournalist must have acquired the capacity to cut the precise significant action—both in space and time—out of the passing scene, and to do this effectively must have developed a considerable knowledge of people in the public eye, political events, and the current scene in art and sport. But in addition to the essentials, Man had certain qualities apparent to anyone who worked with him.

The first was his intense concentration. Having once established the conditions (of lighting and so on) under which he was operating, he would never look down at his camera. But, leaving all necessary adjustments to his well-trained hands, he would prowl around a theatrical rehearsal or a minister's office, shooting picture after picture without once taking his eyes off the scene in front of him. Second, was his photographic memory, which was extraordinary. No other cameraman, in this writer's experience, could come back from a day's work and hand his films in to the darkroom with the instruction: "On the first film print numbers 8, 12, 14, 19 and 23. On the second, numbers . . ." and so on.

Allied to this was his economy in operation. Trained as an artist and as a layout man, he was constantly visualizing each picture story in page form as he was taking it. As a result he shot very little which was not likely to be used, or at least capable of being used—though he would often shoot the key pictures in both "portrait" and "landscape" shape in order to give the layout editor a choice. Where a less experienced operator would come back with several hundred exposures, Man would be content to have exposed only a couple of films, but all that was needed would be there.

Finally he was, when on the job, extremely patient. By no means the easiest of colleagues in daily life, he showed in pursuit of a picture story the patience and resourcefulness of a practised angler, trying in this and that direction, arguing—even pleading, something quite alien to his everyday nature—to secure some co-operation he required.

To these qualities Man added others which, though not strictly "photographic," made a valuable addition to his general armoury. He had an excellent educational background, which he had extended by wide reading and much travel. He had studied art, practised drawing, painting and etching, and produced authoritative works on the subject of artists' lithographs. All this undoubtedly helped him to get on easy terms with his subjects when he was making his notable series of artists at work—Picasso, Matisse, Chagall, Henry Moore and others. He had an exceptional knowledge and love of music; and his sense of history enabled him to understand the events he was recording day by day, in terms of the past and of the world scene as a whole.

Both in Felix Man's character and his method of approach to any work he undertook, there was a strong element of the scholar and academic. His choice of the arduous life of a photojournalist, when much easier careers were open to him, was due at least partly to his recognition of photography as the most effective medium for expressing and recording the tensions, complexities and dramas of the modern world.

—Tom Hopkinson

MANN, Sally

Nationality: American. **Born:** Lexington, Virginia, 1951. **Education:** Graduated with a B.A. (summa cum laude), from Hollins College in 1974 and an M.A. in writing in 1975; studied photography at Praestegaard Film School, 1971; Aegean School of Fine Arts, 1972; Apeiron, 1973; and the Ansel Adams Yosemite Workshop, 1973. **Career:** Leads workshops and lectures widely. **Recipient:** National Endowment for the Humanities Grant, 1973 and 1976; Ferguson Grant, Friends of Photography, 1974; National Endowment for the Arts Individual Artist Fellowship, 1982; Virginia Museum of Fine Arts Professional Fellowship, 1982; John Simon Guggenheim Memorial Foundation Fellowship, 1987; National Endowment for the Arts, Individual Artists Fellowship, 1988 and 1992; SECCA Artists Fellowship, 1989; Artists in the Visual Arts Fellowship, 1989. Lives and works in Lexington, Virgina. **Agent:** Houk Friedman, 851 Madison Avenue, New York, New York 10021, U.S.A.

Individual Exhibitions:

1988	Southeastern Center of Contemporary Art, Winston-Salem, North Carolina
	Marcuse Pfeifer Gallery, New York
1989	Museum of Photographic Art, San Diego, California
1990	Cleveland Center for Contemporary Art, Cleveland, Ohio
	Edwynn Houk Gallery, Chicago
	The Tartt Gallery, Washington, D.C.
1991	Maryland Art Place, Baltimore
1992	Edwynn Houk Gallery, Chicago

	Immediate Family, Houk Friedman, New York (travelled to the Institute of Contemporary Art, Philadelphia; Contemporary Museum, Honolulu)
1993	Photo Gallery International, Tokyo
	The Center for Creative Photography, Carmel, California
	Still Time, Museum of Contemporary Photography, Chicago (travelled 1994 to Washington and Lee University, Lexington Virginia; Tampa Museum of Art, Florida; Sweet Briar College, Sweet Briar, Virginia.)
1994	Washington and Lee University, Lexington, Virginia
	Hollins College, Virginia
	Immediate Family, Bratislava, Slovakia

Selected Group Exhibitions:

1980	*Not Fade Away: Four Contemporary Virginia Photographers,* Chrysler Museum, Norfolk, Virginia
1981	*New Color,* Southeastern Center for Contemporary Art, Winston-Salem, North Carolina
1982	*The Ferguson Grant Winners Show,* Friends of Photography, Carmel, California
1984	*Alternative Printing Processes: Three Contemporary Photographers,* Chrysler Museum, Norfolk, Virginia
1985	*Big Shots: 20 x 24 Polaroid Photographs,* Visual Arts Gallery, University of Alabama, Birmingham
1987	*Mothers and Daughters,* Aperture Foundation, Inc., New York (travelling exhibition)
1988	*Swimmers,* Aperture Foundation, New York (travelling exhibition)
1989	*The Hand that Rocks the Cradle,* San Francisco Cameraworks, (travelling exhibition)
1990	*Family Photos,* La Grande Halle, la Villette, Paris
1991	*Contemporary Color Photography, Selections from the Collection,* Metropolitan Museum of Art, New York
1992	*The Invention of Childhood,* John Michael Kohler Arts Center, Sheboygan
1993	*Prospect 93,* Frankfurter Kunstverein and the Schirn Kunsthalle, Frankfurt
1994	*Who's Looking at the Family?,* Barbican Art Gallery, London
	The Magic of Play, Los Angeles
1995	*Imagined Children,* Desired Images, Wellesley College, Massachusetts

Collections:

Addison Gallery of American Art, Andover, Maryland; Baltimore Museum of Art, Maryland; Bayley Museum, University of Virginia, Charlottesville; Birmingham Museum of Art, Alabama; Boston Museum of Fine Art, Massachusetts; Chrysler Museum, Norfolk, Virginia; Corcoran Gallery of Art, Washington, D.C.; Dayton Institute of Art, Ohio; Friends of Photography, San Francisco; Hallmark Cards, Inc., Kansas City, Missouri; Harvard University Art Museum, Cambridge, Massachusetts; Hirschhorn Museum and Sculpture Garden; Honolulu Art Institute, Hawaii; Metropolitan Museum of Art, New York; Milwaukee Museum of Art, Wisconsin; Museum of Modern Art, New York; National Museum of American Art, Smithsonian Institution, Washington, D.C.; New Orleans Museum of Art, Louisiana; San Francisco Museum of Art; Tokyo Metropolitan Museum of Art, Japan; Toledo Museum of Art, Ohio; Virginia Museum of Fine Arts, Richmond; Polaroid Corporation, Cambridge, Massachusetts; Whitney Museum of American Art, New York; Harry Winston, Inc., New York.

Publications:

By MANN: Book—*Halloween,* New York, 1993.

Virginia at 6, **1991.** Photograph ©Sally Mann. Courtesy Houk Friedman.

On MANN: Books—*Sally Mann: The Lewis Law Portfolio,* Washington, D.C. 1977; *Second Sight, The Photographs of Sally Mann,* Boston 1982; *Sally Mann: Sweet Silent Thought,* Durham, NC 1987; *At Twelve, Portraits of Young Women,* New York 1988; *Sally Mann: Still Time,* Virginia 1988 (New York 1994); *Women Photographers* by Sullivan, New York, 1990; *Immediate Family,* New York 1992; *A History of Women Photographers,* by Rosenblum, New York, 1994; *Sally Mann: Still Time,* catalogue, New York, 1994. Articles—*Commonwealth Magazine,* October 1975, June 1978; *The Washington Post,* 1984, 1990; *American Photographer,* 1984, 1989, 1990; *Art in America,* 1986, 1987; *Harper's Magazine,* 1987, 1988; *Aperture Magazine,* 1987, 1988, 1989, 1990; *The New York Times,* 1987; *Arts New York,* October 1987; *Flash Art,* December 1987; *Popular Photography,* 1988; *The Village Voice,* 1987, 1988; *Arts Magazine,* December 1988; *LA Times,* March 1989; *Detroit Free Press,* September 1990; *Connoisseur,* November 1990; *The Boston Globe,* December 1990; *The Wall Street Journal,* February 1991; *Photographies Magazine,* May 1991; *Art News,* November 1991; *Art Forum,* November 1991; *The New York Times,* April 1992; *The New Yorker,* June 1992; *The New York Times,* June 1992; *Artforum,* Summer 1992; *The New York Times,* July 1992; *The Village Voice,* July 1992; *Ms. Magazine,* Sept/Oct 1992; *The New York Times Magazine,* September 1992; *The Philadelphia Inquirer,* October 1992; *People Magazine,* October 1992; *Newsweek,* October 1992; *Vogue,* Germany, December 1992; *Elle,* Germany, 1993; *Image Magazine,* Zurich, January 1993; *The New York Times,* February 1993; *Smart Money,* June 1993; *The Chicago Sun Times,* September 1993; *The Chicago Tribune,* September 1993; *The Daily Yomiuri,* November 1993; *New York Review of Books,* February 1994; *History of Photography,* Spring 1994; *Sunday Times Magazine,* London, May 1994; *The Independent on Sunday Review,* May 1994.

*   *   *

Sally Mann has earned wide notice not only for her technical skills but, more recently, for the daring with which she lays out her honest findings about such taboos as puberty and adolescent sexuality. The images of her three children, Emmett, Jessie and Virginia, appear to be typical scenes of family life, or so it seems. There are pictures of barbecues, happy family gatherings, children at play, all shown with uncommon clarity, yet often disturbing, even controversial. At first glance, the black and white photographs look rather realistic. They show the three children in everyday activities, doing what most children enjoy: playing with toys, running around often totally naked, or pretending to be grown up. There are also the usual little disasters and mishaps of childhood, the cuts and bruises, the insect bites. On further inspection the images appear to be contrived, the youngsters posing for the camera—often with a prop—or acting like an adult. These are not recordings of private or precious moments of childhood but that of children growing up fast in front of the camera. No innocence here or playful charm. The look in their eyes confirms they already know that they are sexual creatures. Yet, Mann insists that her utmost responsibility is to protect her children from harm, that they actually enjoy posing for her. Nudity does not bother or embarrass them. They also have the right to veto any photograph taken of them they dislike.

Mann is a documentary photographer of the post-modernist period. Her family portraits began in 1984, when one of the girls, Jessie, came home, her face swollen with gnat bites. That sight gave her mother an overwhelming compulsion to photograph the bitten girl. From then on more pictures followed. Mann uses a large-format camera, her black and white printing technique dates back to the 19th century which is more in common with Victorian photographer Julia Margaret Cameron than with any contemporary artist. Also, she prefers warm tones which give her prints an almost antique look, having spent many years in the darkroom to perfect this skill. She photographs mostly in the summer when the light is at its very best. The remaining months of the year are reserved for a very busy printing period.

Of course there are people who get upset over Mann's family pictures. Does she in fact exploit her children? The answer is "no," because the photographs make it quite clear that the children are no puppets but show the mysteries of childhood and growing up, clearly and beautifully captured by their mother. How they might feel about this intimate portrayal in ten or fifteen years—only time will tell.

—Hildegard Mahoney

MANOS, Constantine (Thomas).

Nationality: American. **Born:** South Carolina in 1934. **Education:** University of South Carolina, B.A. in English. **Career:** Freelance photographer, Boston, since 1964. Member, Magnum Photos co-operative agency, New York, since 1964. **Recipient:** Art Directors Club of New York Award, 1966. Agency: Magnum Photos, 251 Park Avenue South, New York, New York 10010. **Address:** 26 Rutland Square, Boston, Massachusetts 02118, U.S.A.

Individual Exhibitions:

1972	*A Greek Portfolio,* Art Institute of Chicago
	Bibliotheque Nationale, Paris
1985	Pace/MacGill Gallery, New York
1993	*American Slide Show,* South East Museum of Photography, Daytona Beach, Florida

Collections:

Museum of Modern Art, New York; Art Institute of Chicago; Bibliotheque Nationale, Paris.

Publications:

By MANOS: Books—*Portrait of a Symphony,* New York, 1961; *A Greek Portfolio,* New York and London 1972; *Bostonians,* Boston 1975.

On MANOS: Books—*America in Crisis: Photographs for Magnum,* edited by Charles Harbutt and Lee Jones, with an essay by Mitchel Levitas, New York 1969; *The Library of World Photography: Landscape,* with texts by David Plowden and Ian Jeffrey, Tokyo and London 1984. Articles—"Where's Boston" by Bob Schwalberg in *Popular Photography* (New York), November 1976; "Colour Conversion" by Daniel Laskin in *Camera Arts,* May, 1983.

*   *   *

"By his unique nature each human being defies generalities, and no two people are the same. The individual is constantly changing in relation to time, his environment, and other people. Selecting a split second in which to arrest this passage through time is the unique magic of the camera" (from *A Greek Portfolio* by Constantine Manos).

A photojournalist and a commercial photographer, a member of Magnum for 20 years, Constantine Manos is best known for his books, *A Greek Portfolio* and *Bostonians,* and for his work on the multimedia presentation "Where's Boston." These three works display Manos' fine ability to envision the subtleties of the complex lives around him and to render them gracefully on film.

A Greek Portfolio, published in 1972, is a record of Manos' leisurely journey through the Greek countryside. The emphasis of the pictures is on the quiet lives of the people he encountered. Manos, a Greek himself, has infiltrated their lives and used his unobtrusive Leica to record his own experiences with these people. We see them eating, working and worshipping. As he clearly states in his introduction, he does not try to give a vague portrait of this complex culture, but simply tries to make his own journey available to others through these photographs. The book allows us to be very successful tourists. We see the sights and marvel at the manifest differences between our cultures. Most importantly, though, since Manos himself is an insider, we are permitted a glimpse at unguarded and often very personal experiences that we as outsiders would not have experienced.

Manos' book *Bostonians* and the multimedia presentation "Where's Boston" work in a similar fashion. "Where's Boston" is specifically directed at outsiders. Set up in a small theater in a tourist area of downtown Boston, "Where's Boston" is an introduction to the city. Amazingly, even Bostonians (this writer counts himself among that group) have reacted favorably to this p.r. job for the city. Manos, the principal photographer, along with the organizers and writers of the show, have created an astoundingly rich and balanced view of our town. They only half-heartedly repeat the banal praises

July 4 Parade, Boston, **1982.** Photograph ©Constantine Manos.

of ''cultural Boston'' and eagerly delve into a more sophisticated critique of the city. They energetically pursue a view of Boston's ethnic diversity and point out the manifest problems that it has created. They give a good feel for the geography, the climate, the architecture—in short, an overview in 55 minutes of a very complicated subject.

The book *Bostonians* (a spinoff of the ''Where's Boston'' project) clearly demonstrates how Manos was instrumental in producing this excellent show. *Bostonians* is much like *A Greek Portfolio.* Manos deals with the specifics of individual people in non-stereotypical situations. He observes the multifarious textures of the city's people and neighborhoods and presents the reader with a careful balance. He has included everything from a stripper in Boston's famed Combat Zone, to an I.R.A. rally. Manos includes the bluebloods on wealthy Beacon Hill and a baseball game at Fenway Park. The book contains fishermen, firemen, and a bassoon-piano duet.

Bostonians actively records the temporal element of its rapidly changing subject. This is not just any Boston, but Boston in 1974. It is just before the Bicentennial and after the political activism that swept the city. It is a time of particular clothes and hair styles, of particular social problems and cultural attributes. Manos has wisely made this a record of a specific and limited subject, one which works equally well as a tourist guide and as a serious document of our town.

One of the goals of photojournalism so frequently expressed and so infrequently fulfilled is that the photographer should develop an understanding, even a sympathy, for the subject he is documenting. Manos has chosen to photograph the subjects he is already inside. His pictures present that intimate view to those who are not.

—Ken Winokur

MAN RAY.

Nationality: American. **Born:** Emmanuel Rudnitzky, in Philadelphia, Pennsylvania, 27 August 1890. **Education:** Studied art in evening classes at various schools, including the National Academy of Design, New York, 1908-12; studied life-drawing at the Francisco Ferrer Social Center, New York, 1912-13; self-taught in photography, from 1915. **Family:** Married Adon (Donna) Lacroix in 1914 (divorced, 1918); lived with Alice (Kiki) Prin, 1924-30; married Juliet Browner in 1946. **Career:** Independent painter and sculptor, from 1911: worked as part-time designer in an advertising agency, New York, 1913-19; freelance photographer, filmmaker and painter, associating with Surrealist artists, Paris, 1921-40; freelance fashion photographer and painter, Hollywood, California, 1940-50; independent artist, concentrating on own photography and painting, Paris and Cadaques, Spain, 1951 until his death, 1976. Founder-Member, with Marcel Duchamp and Walter Arensberg, Society of Independent Artists, New York, 1915, with Marcel Duchamp and Francis Picabia, New York Dadaist movement, New York, 1917, and with Marcel Duchamp, Katherine Dreier and others, Société Anonyme, New York, 1920. Editor, with Henri S. Reynolds and Adolf Wolff, only issue of *TNT* magazine, New York, 1919, and with Marcel Duchamp, only issue of *New York Dada* magazine, New York, 1921. Instructor in Photography, Art Center School, Los Angeles, 1942-50. **Recipient:** Gold Medal for Photography, *Biennale,* Venice, 1961. **Died:** (in Paris) 18 November 1976.

Individual Exhibitions:

1915   Daniel Gallery, New York (and 1916, 1919)

1921	Librairie 6, Paris
1926	*Rayographs and Objects,* Galerie Surrealiste, Paris
	Photographs and Paintings, Daniel Gallery, New York
1927	Daniel Gallery, New York
1928	Galerie Surrealiste, Paris
1929	*Photographic Compositions by Man Ray,* Arts Club, Chicago
	Galerie Myrbor, Paris
	Rayographs and Paintings, Galerie Quatre Chemins, Paris
	Galerie Van Leer, Paris
1931	Galerie Alexandre III, Cannes
1932	Galerie Chez Dacharry, Paris
	Julien Levy Gallery, New York
	Galerie Vignon, Paris
1934	Lund Humphries and Company, London (and 1935)
	Lund Humphries and Company, London
1935	*Photographs and Rayographs,* Wadsworth Atheneum, Hartford, Connecticut
	Photographs and Drawings, Art Center School, Los Angeles
	Rayographs and Paintings, Galerie Adlan, Barcelona
	Galerie aux Cahiers d'Art, Paris
1936	Curt Valentin Gallery, New York
1937	Galerie Jeanne Bucher, Paris
	Palais des Beaux-Arts, Brussels (with Yves Tanguy and René Magritte)
1939	Galerie de Beaunne, Paris (travelled to the London Gallery)
1941	Frank Perls Galleries, Los Angeles
	M.H. de Young Memorial Museum, San Francisco
1943	Santa Barbara Museum of Art, California
1944	Pasadena Art Institute, California
1945	Los Angeles County Museum of History, Science and Art
	Julien Levy Gallery, New York
1946	Circle Gallery, Los Angeles
1948	Copley Gallery, Hollywood, California
1951	Galerie Berggruen, Paris
1953	Paul Kantor Gallery, Los Angeles
1954	Galerie Furstenberg, Paris
1956	Galerie l'Etoile Scellée, Paris
	Musée de Tours, France (with Max Ernst and Dorothea Tanning)
1959	Galerie Rive Droite, Paris
	Alexander Iolas Gallery, New York
	Mayer Gallery, New York
	Galerie Larcade, Paris
	Institute of Contemporary Arts, London
1960	Esther Robles Gallery, Los Angeles
1962	*Man Ray: L'Oeuvre Photographique,* Bibliothèque Nationale, Paris
	Galerie Rive Droite, Paris
1963	Cordier and Ekstrom, New York
	Musée d'Amiens, France
	Cavendish Gallery, London
	Princeton University, New Jersey
	LGA Austellungsraum, Stuttgart
1964	Galleria Schwarz, Milan
1965	Cordier and Ekstrom, New York
1966	Los Angeles County Museum of Art (retrospective)
1968	Martha Jackson Gallery, New York
	Galerie der Spiegel, Cologne
1969	Hanover Gallery, London
	2 Generations of Photographs: Man Ray and Naomi Savage New Jersey State Museum, Trenton
	Galerie Alphonse Chave, Venice
	Studio Marconi, Milan
	Galleria Il Fauno, Turin
1970	Galerie Richard Foncke, Ghent
	Galleria del Cavallino, Venice
	Galerie XXme Siècle, Paris
	Galleria La Chioccoloa, Padua
	Noah Goldowsky Gallery, New York

	Museum Boymans-van Beuningen, Rotterdam (retrospective; travelled to Musée d'Art Moderne, Paris, and Louisiana Museum, Humlebaek, Denmark)
	Philadelphia Museum of Art
1971	Galleria Milano, Milan
	Salone Annunciata, Milan
	Galleria Il Fauno, Turin
	Galerie Suzanne Visat, Paris
1972	Galleria Gissi, Turin (travelled to Galerie Françoise Tournie, Paris, and Galleria dell'Arte Libreria Pictogramma, Rome)
	Galerie des 4 Mouvements, Paris
	Galleria Il Fauno, Turin
1973	Metropolitan Museum of Art, New York
	Galerie im Lenbachhaus, Munich (with Marcel Duchamp and Francis Picabia)
1974	New York Cultural Center (travelled to Institute of Contemporary Arts, London, and Galleria Il Fauno, Turin)
	Alexander Iolas Gallery, New York
	Galerie Alexandre Iolas, Paris
1975	Mayor Gallery, Athens
	G. Ray Hawkins Gallery, Los Angeles
	Palazzo dell'Esposizione, Rome
	Galleria Il Fauno, Turin, Italy
	Mayor Gallery, London
	Studio Marconi, Milan
1976	*Man Ray: Fotografia,* at the *Biennale,* Venice
1977	Kimmel/Cohn, New York
	Kiva Gallery, Boston
1978	*Vintage Photographs, Solarizations and Rayographs,* Allan Frumkin Gallery, Chicago
	Zeit-Foto Salon, Tokyo
1979	*Man Ray: Inventionen und Interpretationen,* Kunstverein, Frankfurt (travelled to Kunsthalle, Basle)
1980	Prakapas Gallery, New York
	Galeria Eude, Barcelona (toured Spain)
	Man Ray's World, Zeit-Foto Salon, Tokyo
1981	*Man Ray: Photographe,* Centre Pompidou, Paris
	Vintage Photographs, Knoedler Gallery, London
1983	*Mathematical Objects,* Robert Miller Gallery, New York
1985	National Museum of American Art, Washington, D.C.
	Zabriskie Gallery, New York
	77 Fotografien, Museum Villa Stuck, Munich

Selected Group Exhibitions:

1928	*1st Independent Salon of Photography,* Salon de l'Escalier, Paris
1929	*Film und Foto,* Deutscher Werkbund, Stuttgart
1936	*Exposition Internationale de la Photographie Contemporaine,* Musée des Arts Décoratifs, Paris
1959	*Hundert Jahre Photographie 1839-1939,* Museum Folkwang, Essen (travelled to Cologne and Frankfurt)
1964	*The Painter and the Photograph: From Delacroix to Warhol,* University of New Mexico, Albuquerque
1967	*Photography in the 20th Century,* National Gallery of Canada, Ottawa (toured Canada and the United States, 1967-73)
1971	*Photo Eye of the 20s,* University of South Florida, Tampa (travelled to Pasadena, Des Moines, Seattle, Minneapolis and Chicago)
1977	*The History of Fashion Photography,* International Museum of Photography, George Eastman House, Rochester, New York (travelled to Brooklyn Museum, New York; San Francisco Museum of Modern Art; Cincinnati Art Institute, Ohio; and Museum of Fine Arts, St. Petersburg, Florida)
1979	*Photographie als Kunst 1879-1979,* Tiroler Landesmuseum Ferdinandeum, Innsbruck, Austria (travelled to Neue Galerie am Wolfgang Gurlitt Museum, Linz, Austria; Neue Galerie am Landesmuseum Joanneum, Graz; and the Museum des 20. Jahrhunderts, Vienna)

1985   *L'Amour Fou: Photography and Surrealism,* Corcoran Gallery,
        Washington, D.C. (travelled to San Francisco Museum of
        Modern Art; Centre Georges Pompidou, Paris; Hayward
        Gallery, London)

Collections:

Museum of Modern Art, New York; International Museum of Photography,
George Eastman House, Rochester, New York; Yale University, New Haven,
Connecticut, Art Institute of Chicago; New Orleans Museum of Art; University of Kansas, Lawrence; University of New Mexico, Albuquerque; Oakland
Museum, California; Provinciaal Museum voor Kunstambachten, Deurne-Antwerp; Musée d'Art Moderne, Paris.

Publications:

By MAN RAY: Books—*Les Champs Délicieux: Album de Photographies,*
portfolio of rayographs, with a preface by Tristan Tzara, Paris 1922; *Man Ray,*
with text by Georges Ribemont-Dessaignes, Paris 1924; *Man Ray/George
Hoyningen-Huene,* portfolio of fashion photos, Paris 1924-25; *Revolving
Doors, 1916-17,* Paris 1926, Turin 1972; *Kiki Souvenirs,* Paris 1929;
Electricité, portfolio of 10 rayographs, with an introduction by Pierre Bost,
Paris 1931; *Man Ray Photographies, 1920-1934, Paris,* with text and poems
by André Breton, Paul Eluard, Tristan Tzara and others, Paris 1934, reprinted
as *Man Ray: Photographs, 1920-1934,* with an introduction by A.D. Coleman, New York 1975, and as *Man Ray: Photographien, Paris, 1920-1934,*
with text by Andreas Haus, Munich 1980; *Facile,* with poems by Paul Eluard,
Paris 1935; *Les Mains Libres,* with Paul Eluard, Paris 1937; *La Photographie
n'est pas l'Art,* manifesto, with a foreword by André Breton, Paris 1937;
Alphabet for Adults, Beverly Hills, California 1948; *To Be Continued Unnoticed,* Beverly Hills, California 1948; *Man Ray: L'Oeuvre Photographique,*
exhibition catalogue, with text by Jean Adhemar and others, Paris 1962; *Man
Ray: Self-Portrait,* Boston 1963; *Man Ray: 12 Photographs 1921-28,*
portfolio, New York 1963; *Man Ray: Portraits,* with text by L. Fritz Gruber,
Gutersloh, West Germany and Paris 1963; *Man Ray: Tous les Films que J'ai
Réalisé,* Paris 1965; *Les Mannequins,* Paris 1966; *Les Invendables,* portfolio,
Vence, France 1969; *Mr. and Mrs. Woodman,* portfolio, Amsterdam 1970;
Oggetti d'Affezione: Rayographs, with text by C.G. Argan, Turin 1970; *Man
Ray: Les Voies Lactées,* New York 1974; *Man Ray: Femmes 1930-35,*
portfolio of 26 photos, Milan 1981. **Articles**—"Man Ray: Rayograms" in
Surrealisme A.S.D.L.R. (Paris), December 1931; "Sur le Realisme Photographique"
in *Cahiers d'Art* (Paris), no. 10, 1935; "La Photographie qui Console" in
XXme Siècle (Paris), no. 2, 1938; "Is Photography Necessary?" in *Modern
Photography* (New York), November 1957; "Man Ray: The Fiery Elf,"
interview with Morris Gordon, in *Infinity* (New York), October 1962; "Man
Ray on the Future," interview with Ed Hirsch and Ben Zar, in *Popular
Photography* (New York), January 1967; "Man Ray," interview with Paul
Hill and Thomas Cooper in *Camera* (Lucerne), February 1975. **Films**—*The
Return to Reason,* 1923; *Emak Bakia,* 1926; *L'Etoile de Mer,* 1928; *The
Mystery of the Chateau of Dice,* 1929.

On MAN RAY: Books—*Foto-Auge/Oeil et photo/Photo-Eye: 76 Fotos der
Zeit,* edited by Franz Roh and Jan Tschichold, Stuttgart 1929, London 1974;
Un Siècle de Photographie de Niepce à Man Ray, exhibition catalogue, by
Laurent Roosens, Paris 1965; *Man Ray,* with an introduction by Jules
Langsner, Los Angeles 1966; *Man Ray: 60 Years of Liberties* by Louis
Aragon, Jean Arp and others, Milan 1971; *The Painter and the Photograph:
From Delacroix to Warhol* by Van Deren Coke, Albuquerque, New Mexico
1972; *Man Ray* by Janus, Milan 1973; *Photography in America,* edited by
Robert Doty, with an introduction by Minor White, New York 1974; *Man Ray*
by Roland Penrose, London 1975; *The Magic Image* by Cecil Beaton and Gail
Buckland, London and Boston 1975; *American Fashion* by Sara Tomerlin
Lee, New York 1975, London 1976; *Une Histoire du Cinema,* exhibition
catalogue, by Peter Kubelka and others, Paris 1976; *Photomontage* by Dawn
Ades, London 1976; *Man Ray: The Rigour of the Imagination* by Arturo
Schwarz, Milan 1977; *Man Ray: L'Immagine Fotografica/Man Ray: The
Photographic Image* by Janus, Milan 1977, London 1980; *Man Ray: Inventionen
und Interpretationen,* exhibition catalogue, by G. Bussmann and others,
Frankfurt 1979; *Photographen der 20er Jahre* by Karl Steinorth, Munich
1979; *Photographic Surrealism,* exhibition catalogue, by Nancy Hall-Dun-

can, Cleveland, Ohio 1979; *The History of Fashion Photography* by Nancy
Hall-Duncan, New York and Paris 1979; *The Vogue Book of Fashion
Photography* by Polly Devlin, New York and London 1979; *The Photograph
Collector's Guide* by Lee D. Witkin and Barbara London, Boston and London
1979; *Man Ray: Photographe,* exhibition catalogue, with text by Jean-Hubert
Martin, Paris 1981; *The Artist as Photographer* by Marina Vaizey, London
1982; *Atelier Man Ray 1920-1935,* exhibition catalogue, by Alain Sayag,
Paris 1982; *The Great Photographers: Man Ray* by Janus, London 1984;
L'Amour Fou: Photography and Surrealism by Jane Livingston and Rosalind
Krauss, New York 1985.

*   *   *

Although he was familiar with the work of Alfred Stieglitz when he was a
struggling young artist in New York, Man Ray did not take up photography
until he reached Paris in the early 20s; and he did so then, it appears, out of
need rather than desire. Unable to sell his paintings—which were for the most
part crude imitations of the early Cubists—he turned to fashion photography
and, a little later, portraiture. He was extraordinarily successful in both areas,
at least in part because he remembered what he had learned from Stieglitz and
Camera Work. In 1921, Jed Perl explains, his approach caused something of a
sensation: "Man Ray favored natural light, sharp, clear contrast, and informal
poses. All this seemed quite fresh at a time when pictorialism was still the style
favored by commercial photographers in both Europe and the United States. . . .
By the 1920s the soft-focus effects, asymmetrical compositions and anecdotal
subjects that seemed advanced 30 years before no longer had the power to
arrest. Man Ray had known Alfred Stieglitz fairly well back in New York, in
the years when Stieglitz had rejected pictorialism completely, and had been
influenced by the master's dictum: 'No diffused focus. Just the straight goods.'
He was among the first to carry the new, clean-lined photographic work to
Paris and into commercial work." As for the portraits, they are powerful,
uncompromising and anything but flattering in the usual sense. And at least
one of them, a 1932 portrait of Arnold Schönberg, is one of the great
photoportraits of the century.

But it was his new freedom to pursue experimental work which excited
Man Ray. "Photography," he once asserted, "is not art"—a statement which
has to be understood in the context of the period and his close association with
the Dadaists and Surrealists. "Art," as Man Ray uses the term here, means the
bourgeois conception of art, the complacent view that of course the artist
attempts to reproduce "reality" by means of decorum and rational control.
For this conception of art Man Ray, Marcel Duchamp, André Breton, among
many others, had nothing but contempt. It was chance, the irrational and the
deliberate frustration of bourgeois standards which mattered; and it was the
new taste for such things which accounts for the enthusiasm that Man Ray's
Rayographs and Solarizations soon generated. Indeed it was "chance" which
led to the discovery of the Rayographs, as Roland Penrose tells the story:
"[Ray] worked late into the night in his improvised dark-room, developing
the plates he had exposed during the day, and making contact prints on sheets
of paper spread out under the glass negative on a table lit by an electric light
bulb hanging from the ceiling. It was this primitive set-up that made possible a
startling development in photography, when he inadvertently placed a few
objects on a sensitized sheet under the light. To his surprise, an image grew
before his eyes on the paper under the light, 'not quite a simple silhouette of the
objects, as in a straight photograph, but distorted and refracted by the glass
more or less in contact with the paper and standing out against a black
background, the part directly exposed to the light' . . . . 'Taking whatever
objects came to hand,' he tells us, 'my hotel room key, a handkerchief, some
pencils, a brush, a candle, a piece ot twine . . . I made a few more prints,
excitedly, enjoying myself immensely.' . . . On seeing the prints, Tristan Tzara
was at once very excited and claimed that they were 'pure Dada'. Man Ray
tells us, 'Tzara came to my room that night; we made some Rayographs
together, he disposing matches on the paper, breaking up the matchbox itself
for an object, and burning holes with a cigarette in a piece of paper, while I
made cones and triangles and wire spirals, all of which produced astonishing
results.' " The results seem less astonishing today, and the theory behind such
more or less aleatory "creation" naive or even somewhat hypocritical (after
all, someone has to find the found object and label it as such for others). Man
Ray's work has been praised often enough for its spontaneity, as if that were a
good in itself, for its originality (a claim hard to justify, since he may well have
been familiar with Christian Schad's experiments), and for its unexpected wit,

in his paintings and photographs alike (Man Ray refused to distinguish between the two as different "arts"). But viewers who expect to find in these works anything like the inventiveness or wit of Duchamp or Miro and Klee will be badly disappointed. The legacy which Dadaism handed on to photography is a dubious one, as Susan Sontag argues in *On Photography*.

Looking back at his experimental work many years later, Man Ray made some extraordinary statements, now fairly well-known (perhaps for their magniloquence rather than their coherence or descriptive value). In any event, the Rayographs and Solarizations are, in his own words, "oxidized residues, fixed by light and chemical elements, of living organisms. No plastic expression can ever be more than the residue of an experience. The recognition of an image that has tragically survived an experience, recalling the event more or less clearly, like the undisturbed ashes of an object consumed by flames, the recognition of this object so little representative and so fragile, and its simple identification on the part of the observer with a similar personal experience, precludes all psychoanalytical classification or assimilation into an arbitrary decorative system." It is hard to know how far to take rhetoric like this. Man Ray may well have intended these words as a description of his chance, "cameraless" photographs, but they may be even more relevant to his best photoportraits. The notion of the photograph as the residue, the survivor of a mortal experience in time has been developed recently by Roland Barthes with real eloquence. What the authentic photograph tells us—what the photograph of Gertrude Stein or Arnold Schönberg or one's mother as a child tells us—is, finally, *this was and now is gone*.

Man Ray himself would probably be impatient with such theorizing. He was quixotic, playful, and, to quote Jed Perl once again, "cared little for politics, for aesthetics, for the elaborate self-justifications of many of his Surrealist friends. One lived one's life and did what one did. . . . [His work] reflects with pure Dada *esprit* the glee of spontaneous discovery." Yet the nagging question remains: discovery of what? A bit of twine? A shattered matchbox? The freedom Man Ray and his friends revelled in may have been a kind of self-indulgence, a levelling rather than a liberating nihilism.

—Elmer Borklund

MANTE, Harald.

Nationality: German. **Born:** Berlin, 29 March 1936. **Education:** Studied painting and graphic design (on scholarship), under Vincent Weber, Werkkunstschule, Wiesbaden, 1957-61; self-taught in photography, 1960-64. **Family:** Married Eva Witter, sculptress, 1988. **Career:** Freelance photographer, working for *Twen, Stern, Epoca, Bild der Zeit*, etc., since 1965. Instructor in Photography, Werkkunstschule, Wiesbaden, 1967-71, and Fachhochscule, Wuppertal, 1973-77. Since 1974, Professor of Free and Experimental Color-Photography for Photo-Designers, Fachhochschule, Dortmund. Visiting professor at University of Saskatchewan, Saskatoon, Canada, 1978. Member, Deutsche Gesellschaft für Photographie, (DGPh) 1971; Bund Freischaffender Fotodesigner (BFF), 1973; Gesellschaft Deutscher Lichtbilder (GDL), 1974; **Recipient:** Kodak Award for Best Calendar, Graphic Club, Stuttgart, 1980, 1981, 1983, 1990, 1991; Kodak Book Award 1986 and 1994; Bronze Medal, Art Directors Club of Germany, 1981. **Address:** Am Kraftwerk 11, 44227 Dortmund, Germany.

Individual Exhibitions:

1966	*Ireland*, Irish Tourist Board, Frankfurt
1974	*Multiple Objekte*, Galerie "Die Insel," Hamburg
	Multiple Objekte, Galerie im Schauspielhaus, Wuppertal, Germany
1976	*Serien und Sequenzen*, Haus der Kunst, Hamburg
1978	*Serien und Sequenzen*, Galerie Keller-Holk, Wiedenbrück, Germany
	Serien und Sequenzen, PPS-Galerie, Hamburg
	Serien und Sequenzen, Mendel Art Gallery, Saskatoon, Saskatchewan

1979	*Serien und Sequenzen*, Deutsche Gesellschaft für Photographie, Cologne
	Serien und Sequenzen, Galerie 66, Hoensbroeck, Netherlands
1980	*Serien und Sequenzen*, Kunstverein, Bruchsal, Germany
	Serien und Sequenzen, Galerie an der Farbmühle, Wuppertal, Germany
	Toskana, Canada und Sequenzen, Galerie Stadtbildstelle, Würzburg, Germany
1981	*Toskana, Canada und Sequenzen*, Galerie der Deutschen Bank, Berlin
	Toskana, Canada und Sequenzen, Galerie des Rathauses, Aalen, Germany
	Spiegelungen, Canada, Sequenzen, Galerie St. Johann, Saarbrücken, Germany
1985	*Zeitpaare, Sequenzen und Spiegelungen*, Kunstverein, Weingarten, Germany
1987	*Retrospective*, Museum für Kunst und Kulturgeschichte, Dortmund
1992	*Bildräume, Castles in Europe*, (with Eva Witter), Augustiner Museum, Freiburg
	Bildräume, Castles in Europe, (with Eva Witter), Museum für Kust und Kulturgeschichte, Dortmund
1993	*Bildräume*, (with Eva Witter), Goethe Institut, Nancy, France
	Bildräume, (with Eva Witter), Museum für Photographie, Braunschweig, Germany
1994	*Bildräume*, Museum Schloß Arolsen, Arolsen, Germany
	Bildräume, Museum Schloß Rastatt, Rastatt, Germany

Selected Group Exhibitions:

1968	*2nd World Exhibition of Photography*, Pressehaus Stern, Hamburg (and world tour)
1972	*5 Foto-Designer*, Galerie Keresztes, Nuremberg
1975	*Gesellschaft Deutscher Lichtbildner 1975*, Haus Industrieform, Essen, West Germany
1977	*Sequencer und Künstler*, Landesmuseum, Darmstadt
1978	*Form und Farbe im Foto: Harald Mante und Studenten*, Landesbildstelle, Bremen, West Germany (travelled to Höhere Graphische Galerie, Vienna; Landesbildstelle, Stuttgart; and Deutsche Gesellschaft für Photographie, Cologne, 1979-80)
1979	*60 Jahre GDL*, Stadtmuseum, Munich
1980	*30 Member BFF*, Albrecht-Dürer Museum, Nuremberg
1981	*Farbe im Photo*, Joef-Haubrich-Kunsthalle, Cologne
1984	*60 Member BFF*, at *Photokina 84*, Cologne (and world tour)

Collections:

Sammlung Land Baden-Württemberg, Stuttgart; L. Fritz Gruber Collection, Cologne; Saskatoon Art Gallery, Saskatchewan.

Publications:

By MANTE: Books—*Bildaufbau*, Ravensburg, West Germany 1969; *Farb-Design*, Ravensburg, West Germany 1971; *Die Spiegelreflex-Fotografie*, with text by Axel Brück, 1975; *Form und Farbe im Foto*, Munich 1977; *Farbig Sehen und Gestalten*, Schaffhausen, Switzerland 1980; *Toskana-Umbrien*, Munich 1981; *Österreich*, Munich 1982; *Objektive Creativ Nutzen*, photos and text with Josef H. Neumann, Schaffhausen, Switzerland, 1982; *Florenz*, Munich 1983; *Kanada*, Munich 1984; *Irland*, Munich 1986; *Kompositionen* (Monographie), Schaffhausen, 1987; *Filme kreativ nutzen*, photos and text with Josef H Neumann, Schaffhausen, 1988; *Bildräume*, (exhibition catalogue with Eva Witter), Arolsen, 1994. **Articles**—"Bildgestaltung" in *Fotomagazin* (Munich), January-December 1971; "Bewusst Sehen" in *Color-Foto* (Munich), July 1973-June 1975; "Farbig Sehen" in *Photographie* (Schaffhausen, Switzerland), January 1979-December 1980; "Experimental Gestalten" in *Photographie* (Schaffhausen, Switzerland), January-June 1981; "Objektive Creativ Nutzen" in *Photographie* (Schaffhausen, Switzerland), January 1981-December 1982; "Motive Creativ Nutzen" in *Photographie* (Schaffhausen, Switzerland) January 1994.

Bildräume No. 11, **1992.** Photograph by Harald Mante.

On MANTE: Books—*2nd World Exhibition of Photography,* exhibition catalogue, edited by Karl Pawek, Hamburg 1968; *Fotografie 1919-1979, Made in Germany: Die GDL Fotografen,* edited by Fritz Kempe, Bernd Lohse and others, Frankfurt 1979; *Dumontfoto 1,* edited by Hugo Schöttle, Cologne 1978; *Dumontfoto 2,* edited by Hugo Schöttle, Cologne 1979; *Lexikon der Fotografie,* edited by Hugo Schöttle, Cologne 1979; *Amerika-Amerika,* Hamburg 1980; *Farbe im Photo: Die Geschichte der Farbphotographie von 1861 bis 19811* by Fritz Binder, Gert Koshofer, Rolf Sachsse and others, Cologne 1981; *Creative Colour Photography* by Petr Tausk, Martin, Czechoslovakia 1985. **Article**—"Color Harry is 50" in *Photographie* (Munich), no. 3, 1986.

*

In addition to shifts of interest within the medium—e.g., from black/white to color or from the single image to series and sequences—my work has been characterized by its format. During the first phase of my work, I used a Contarex and lenses ranging from 15 to 250mm. Black/white and color photography were equally juxtaposed. I was dedicated largely to the single image, the pursuit of the outstanding photograph (1960-1969). Series came about purely by means of amassing single images—e.g., doors, windows, facades.

Exhibitions and publications on travel themes were supplemented by means of "touristic subjects." My earliest books were illustrated with the best results of this initial phase.

By winning first prize in a photo competition, I was able to buy my first 6 x 6 camera (a Rollei SL 66). The work which followed (1968-74) was a reflection of my fondness for detail in nature, technology and culture. I took photographs of all kinds of structures, colors and forms, involving countless different kinds of subjects. The result, in the space of 6 years, was over 100 series of up to 200 Ektachrome slides. These detailed photographs led eventually to serial (multiple) montages, usually of 8 identical prints mounted around a similar or contrasting center.

A commission from the Minolta Camera Company led me (in 1974) back to the miniature format, and, in turn, to Kodachrome film. With Axel Brück, I was to develop a book for amateurs. This project stimulated in me a renewed search for the single image.

The first series and sequences in color appeared at this time, and this form of expression has since been my favorite in terms of style. The thematic complexities of time/space, light and subject make up the content of the series and sequences—from the smallest, comprised of only 2 photos, to the largest, comprised of 36 or more photos.

Other areas of my work include experimental form and "photography as an art form."

In 1980, I undertook a commission to prepare a photographic picture book on Tuscany/Umbria which was followed by a volume on Austria in 1981, and in 1984 a similarly large book on Canada.

My entire activity can be classified as being within the scope of the formal-aesthetic. My goal is the highest finesse in form and color—the subjects themselves usually take second priority. I tolerate and jest with my colleagues who use the medium of photography differently—e.g., those who are active photojournalists or those who work in the area of new objective photography—and I expect the same tolerance.

I love the medium.

—Harald Mante

*   *   *

Harald Mante's photographic activity is multifaceted—in addition to being a freelance photographer, he also teaches and writes about photography. He began as a self-taught amateur photographer, but was not satisfied with the results and felt that he must express himself differently from the usually prescribed textbook manner. His study of the problems which constitute the basic roots of creativity led him to recognize the underlying nature of photography.

Mante can be viewed as a great master of composition—both in black/white and color. He prefers the latter, no doubt, because he likes to surprise his audience with marvellous arrangements of details found in modest, commonplace subjects. He is able to concentrate his interest on the main aspect of the subject and to omit everything which would detract from the significance of the effect he is trying to achieve. At the same time, he does not manipulate his subjects, but captures them in a situation which enhances his motif.

Mante's creative exploration of the world is closely aligned with his entire intellectual background. He endeavors to react with the world around him, and his choice of subject matter is characteristic of the present state of civilization and the objects of contemporary life. For example, traffic signs or a series of gaily painted cars indicate his effort to interpret, poetically, a particular aspect of modern life. Mante combines similar images into series and sequences, thereby creating a more complex expression.

In his outlook on reality, Mante attempts to respect time, space, light and subject, all of which are aspects of the unique situation which he attempts to depict. While he often concentrates on detail, he does not isolate the subject from its environment—this is particularly evident in sequences where the identity of single images becomes evident by means of comparison.

In the early 1980s Mante made photographs for a number of picture books on various cities and countries. Not only did he depict the most famous buildings and landscape views, but he recalled the entire atmosphere of those places. Characteristic plants, fruits, shop-windows and even details of doorbell pushes feature among his colour images, both in single photos and as sequences displayed across double-page spreads. He photographed at midday, dawn, dusk and at night, sometimes punctuating his vision with live-action reportage images. If Mante's textbooks on photographic composition have proved immensely instructive, then his picture volumes have taught us how to see the world anew.

—Petr Tausk

MANTZ, Werner.

Nationality: German. **Born:** Cologne, 28 April 1901. **Education:** Attended the Oberrealschule, Cologne; studied photography at the Bayerischen Lehr-und Versuchsanstalt, Munich, 1920-21. **Family:** Married Marg. Schmidt in 1939; has 3 children. **Career:** Took first photos, Cologne, 1915; amateur photographer, mainly of the city of Cologne and the Bergisches Land area, Nordrhein-Westphalia, 1915-20; professional portrait photographer, establishing own studio, Cologne, 1921-26; freelance architectural photographer, working for the City of Cologne, and for the architect Wilhelm Riphahn and other architects, Cologne, 1927-38; established second studio, Maastricht, Netherlands, 1932; portrait and child photographer, Maastricht, 1938 until his retirement, 1971. **Agent:** Galerie Rudolf Kicken, Albertusstrasse 1, 5000 Cologne 1, Germany. **Address:** Cramignonstraat 19, NL-6245 Eijsden, Netherlands.

Individual Exhibitions:

1976   Galerie Lichttropfen, Aachen, West Germany
1977   Felicity Samuel Gallery, London
         Galerie Gillespie-De Laage, Paris (with Bernhard and Hilla Becher and P. Weller)
1978   *Fotografien 1926-1938,* Rheinisches Landesmuseum, Bonn

1981   Musée Réattu, Arles, France
1982   *Architekturphotographie in Köln 1926-32,* Museum Ludwig, Cologne
1983   Galleria e Libreria dell'Immagine, Milan (with Heinrich Riebesehl and Reinhart Wolf)

Selected Group Exhibitions:

1931   *Exposition Internationale,* Brussels
1932   *Vereinigung Kölner Fachphotographen,* Kunstgewerbemuseum, Cologne
1975   *Vom Dadamax zum Grungurtel,* Kölner Kunstverein, Cologne
1977   *4 Deutsche Fotografen,* Galerie Spectrum, Hannover
1978   *Neue Sachlichkeit and German Realism of the 20s,* Hayward Gallery, London
1979   *Photographie als Kunst 1879-1979,* Tiroler Landesmuseum Ferdinandeum, Innsbruck, Austria (travelled to the Neue Galerie am Wolfgang Gurlitt Museum, Linz, Austria; Neue Galerie am Landesmuseum Joanneum, Graz, Austria; Museum des 20. Jahrhunderts, Vienna)
1980   *Avant-Garde Photography in Germany 1919-39,* San Francisco Museum of Modern Art (toured the United States, 1980-81)
1981   *Germany: The New Vision,* Fraenkel Gallery, San Francisco
1983   *Photography and Architecture 1839-1939,* Canadian Centre for Architecture, Montreal (travelled to Ottawa, Cologne, Chicago, New York and Paris)
1984   *Sammlung Gruber,* Museum Ludwig, Cologne

Collections:

Museum Folkwang, Essen; Rheinisches Landesmuseum, Bonn; Moderna Museet, Stockholm; Victoria and Albert Museum, London; Gillmann Paper Company, New York; Seagram Company, New York; Sam Wagstaff Collection, New York; Princeton University, New Jersey; New Orleans Museum of Art; University of New Mexico, Albuquerque.

Publications:

By MANTZ: Books—*Portfolio Werner Mantz,* by Galerie Schurmann und Kicken, Aachen, West Germany 1977; *Architekturphotographie in Köln 1926-1932,* exhibition catalogue, Cologne 1982.

On MANTZ: Books—*Vom Dadamax zum Grungurtel: Köln in der Zwanziger Jahre,* exhibition catalogue, Cologne 1975; *Documenta 6/Band 2,* exhibition catalogue, by Klaus Honnef and Evelyn Weiss, Kassel and Cologne 1977; *Geschichte der Fotografie im 20. Jahrhundert/Photography in the 20th Century* by Petr Tausk, Cologne 1977, London 1980; *Neue Sachlichkeit and German Realism of the 20s,* exhibition catalogue, by Wieland Schmied, Ute Eskildsen and others, London 1978; *Werner Mantz: Fotografien 1926-1938,* exhibition catalogue, by Klaus Honnef, Bonn 1978; *Tusen och en Bild,* exhibition catalogue, Åke Sidwall, Sune Jonsson and Ulf Hard af Segerstad, Stockholm 1978; *Photographie als Kunst 1879-1979/Kunst als Photographie 1949-79,* exhibition catalogue, 2 vols., by Peter Weiermair, Innsbruck, Austria 1979; *Avant-Garde Photography in Germany 1919-1939,* exhibition catalogue, by Van Deren Coke, Ute Eskildsen and Bernd Lohse, San Francisco 1980; *Sammlung Gruber: Photographie des 20. Jahrhunderts,* exhibition catalogue, with foreword by Siegfried Gohr, Cologne 1984.

*   *   *

Werner Mantz is a pure professional of the kind that unites the craftsman of art history with the Hollywood film director. The professional photographer arrived in the 1920s when advanced technology brought to an end the epoch of the inventor photographer such as Benjamin, the first epoch in the history of photography.

Mantz began as an amateur. He perfected his knowledge by studying for four terms at the Bayerischen Lehr-und Versuchsanstalt in Munich. His early photographic attempts, while he was still a schoolboy during the First World

War, show that it was to be documentary rather than artistic intentions that would determine his career in photography. And, indeed, Mantz never attempted to obtain the precious artificiality of so-called art photography. His interest was in a contemporary historical statement, not the revelation of aesthetic values in photography. He subordinated art, as it were, to content, until he was able finally to remove any discrepancy between the two components.

Mantz's whole photographic career took place within the framework of the professional photographer. Apart from his first documentations of a Cologne destroyed by bombing raids and damaged by the effect of a flood catastrophe, all his important photographs come from accepted professional practice. He succeeded first as a portraitist, then, thanks to the mediations of a Cologne artist whose sculptures he regularly photographed, he found his photographic destiny as a photographer of architecture. A photographic commission brought him to the notice of the leading Cologne architect Wilhelm Riphahn. Mantz's lucid, sober style corresponded remarkably with Riphahn's ideas about architecture. In the following years he worked exclusively for Riphahn and other important representatives of the new objective manner such as Falck, Kreis, Klotz, Lüttgen, Mendelsohn, Neubert, Bruno Paul, Ruff, Schumacher and Wirminghaus.

His 18 x 24 photographs were expressions of the architectural interpretation of functionalism. Mantz recorded his subjects mainly in morning light. He used the sharply cast shadows to lend to the buildings mass, relief and volume and in so doing created a vivid depiction of structure. He recorded, as photographic motif, from the front or diagonally. With the final "setting" he conveyed the scale of the photographed building complex or interiors, and his way of seeing and photographing demonstrated the functional aspects of the portrayed objects—individual buildings, building complexes, interiors, installations/fittings. The pictorial "idea" does not in any way attempt to make itself independent of these subjects.

Mantz's photographic work not only documents an artistically important building style but also, at the same time, provides a perfect example of functionalist photography in contrast to the "superelevation" of photographic reality in the work of Albert Renger-Patzsch or to the careful diagnosis of a particular time in that of August Sander. Yet, in spite of his functionalism, his interiors in particular convey a magical quality that, above all, is to be attributed to the fact that mathematically calculated scales exist in the relationships between the installed objects and the surrounding space.

For Mantz's precise photographs the concrete, an historic feeling for life, and a vision of reality in which this is reflected, merge steadfastly into one another. They blend together into an indissoluble unity. This seamless accord also guarantees them an importance beyond time.

—Klaus Honnef

MAPPLETHORPE, Robert.

Nationality: American. **Born:** New York City, 4 November 1946. **Education:** Pratt Institute, Brooklyn, New York, 1963-70. **Career:** Underground film-maker, New York, 1965-70; photographer, collagist, assemblagist, New York, 1970-72. Independent photographer, New York, since 1972. **Agent:** Robert Miller Gallery, 41 East 57th Street, New York, New York 10022, U.S.A. **Died:** 9 March 1989.

Individual Exhibitions:

1976	*Polaroids,* Light Gallery, New York
1977	*Portraits,* Holly Solomon Gallery, New York
	Pictures, The Kitchen, SoHo, New York
	Flowers, Holly Solomon Gallery, New York
1978	Corcoran Gallery, Washington, D.C.
	Simon Lowinsky Gallery, San Francisco

	Langdon Street Gallery, San Francisco
	Chrysler Museum, Norfolk, Virginia
	Portraits of Patti Smith, Robert Miller Gallery, New York
	La Remise du Parc, Paris
1979	*Trade-Off,* International Center of Photography, New York (with Lynn Davis)
	Robert Miller Gallery, New York
	Texas Gallery, Houston
	Photos 1970-75, Robert Samuel Gallery, New York
1980	*Blacks and Whites,* Lawson/De Celle Gallery, San Francisco
	Galerie Jurka, Amsterdam
	Vision Gallery, Boston
1981	*Black Males,* Robert Miller Gallery, New York
	Steinernes Haus, Frankfurter Kunstverein, Frankfurt
	PPS Galerie, Hamburg
	Fraenkel Gallery, San Francisco
1982	*3 New Yorker Fotografen: Peter Hujar/Larry Clark/Robert Mapplethorpe,* Kunsthalle, Basel
	Photos aus New York, Kunstverein, Munich
1983	*Photos 1970-83,* Institute of Contemporary Arts, London
	Lady: Lisa Lyon, Olympus Gallery, London
	Centre Georges Pompidou, Paris
	Lisa Lyon, Galerie Rudiger Schottle, Munich
	100 Fotografie, Palazzo Fortuny, Venice
1984	Museum of Modern Art, Oxford
	Erotische Fotografen, Galerie Lietzow, West Berlin
	Next Wave Photography: Mapplethorpe/Simmons/Leatherdale, Jason McCoy Gallery, New York
1985	*Recent Work,* Fraenkel Gallery, San Francisco
1986	*Robert Mapplethorpe: Photographs 1976-1985,* Australian Centre for Contemporary Art, South Yarra, Melbourne, Australia
	Robert Mapplethorpe, Betsy Rosenfield Gallery, Chicago, USA
	Robert Mapplethorpe, Texas Gallery, Houston, Texas
	Palazzo d'Accursion, Bologna
1987	*Robert Mapplethorpe 1986,* Raab Galerie, Berlin
	Robert Mapplethorpe, Obalne Galerije, Piran, Ljubljana, Yugoslavia
	Robert Mapplethorpe, Galerie Pierre-Hubert, Geneva
	Robert Mapplethorpe: Photographs, Claus Runkel Fine Art Ltd, London
1988	*Robert Mapplethorpe,* Stedelijk Museum, Amsterdam (travelled to Pompidou Centre, Paris)
	Mapplethorpe Portraits, National Portrait Gallery, London
	Robert Mapplethorpe, The Perfect Moment, Institute of Contemporary Art, University of Pennsylvania, Philadelphia, (travelled to Chicago, Washington, Hartford, Berkeley, California and Boston)
	Photographien, Mai 36 Galerie, Lucerne, Switzerland
	Hamilton's Gallery, London
	Autoportraits, Au Grand Palais, Paris
1989	*Robert Mapplethorpe,* Baudoin Lebon, Paris
	Robert Mapplethorpe—Een Retrospective, Museum van Hedendaagse Kunst, Ghent, Belgium
1990	*Robert Mapplethorpe,* Martina Hamilton Gallery, New York
1991	*Robert Mapplethorpe,* Galeria Weber, Madrid
	Musée d'Art Contemporain, Lausanne, Switzerland
1992	*Mapplethorpe versus Rodin,* Kunsthalle, Dusseldorf, Germany
	Robert Mapplethorpe, Louisiana Museum of Modern Art, Humlebaek, Denmark (travelled to Palazzo di Rivoli Museo d'Arte Contemporanea, Turin)
	Museo de Monterray, Monterray, Mexico
	Tokyo Metropolitan Teien Museum, Tokyo
1993	Santa Barbara Museum of Art, Santa Barbara, CA
	Robert Mapplethorpe, European Retrospective, Moderna Museet, Stockholm
	Hamilton's Gallery, London
	Museo Pecci Prato, Prato, Italy
1994	Guggenheim Museum, New York
	Xavier Hufkens Gallery, Brussels

715

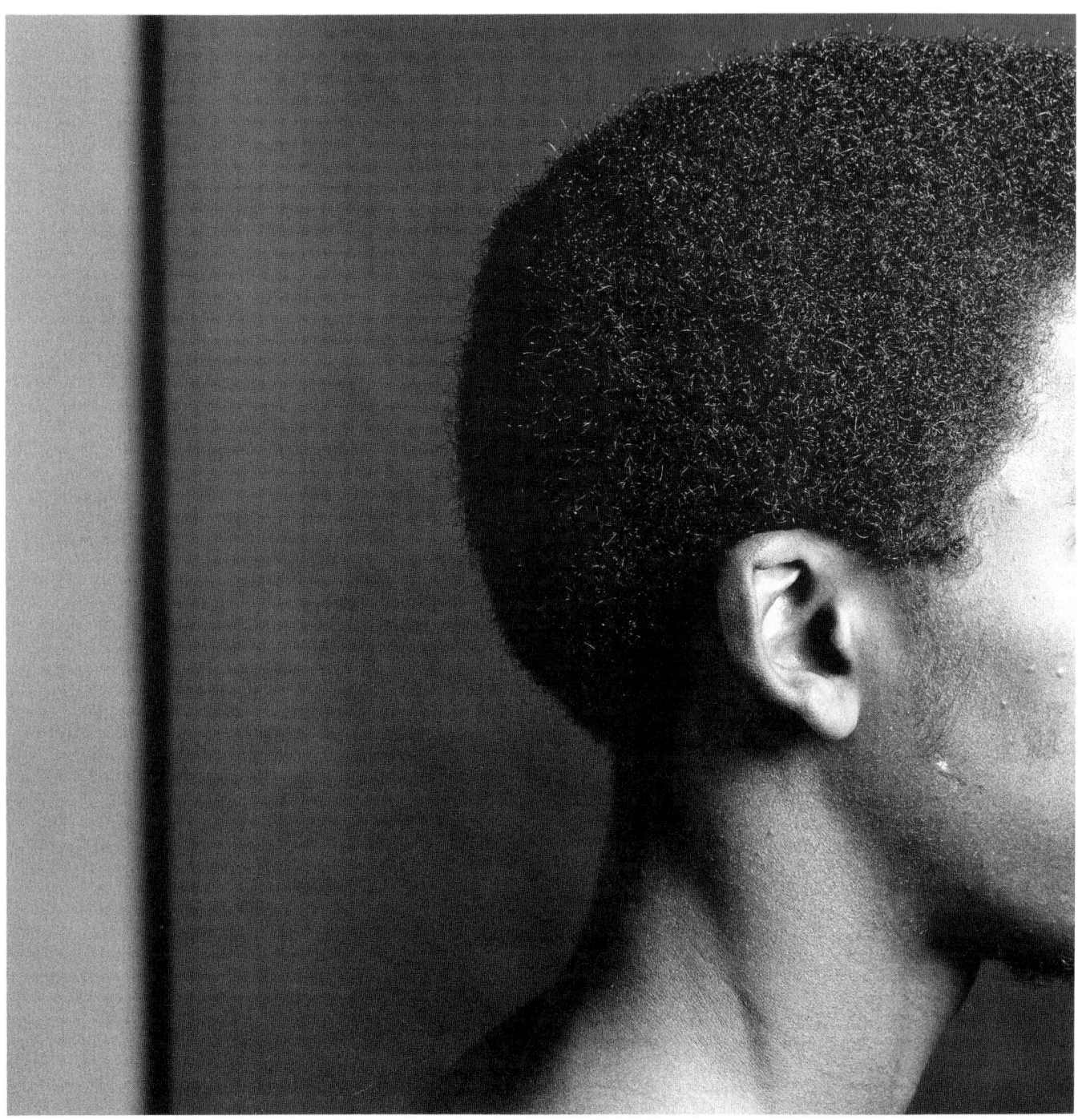

Untitled (profile), **1981.** Photograph by Robert Mapplethorpe. Courtesy Robert Miller Gallery, New York.

Selected Group Exhibitions:

1977   *The Collection of Sam Wagstaff,* Corcoran Gallery, Washing-
        ton, D.C. (travelled to the Grey Gallery, New York
        University)
1978   *Rated X,* Neikrug Gallery, New York
        Mirrors and Windows: American Photography since 1960,
        Museum of Modern Art, New York (toured the United
        States, 1978-80
1979   *Artists by Artists,* Whitney Museum Downtown, New York

Photographie als Kunst 1879-1979, Tiroler Landesmuseum
    Ferdinandeum, Innsbruck, Austria (travelled to the Neue
    Galerie am Wolfgang Gurlitt Museum, Linz, Austria; Neue
    Galerie am Landesmuseum Joanneum, Graz, Austria; and
    Museum des 20. Jahrhunderts, Vienna)
1980   *In Photography: Color as Subject,* School of Visual Arts,
        New York
1982   *Counterparts: Form and Emotion in Photographs,* Metropolitan
        Museum of Art, New York (travelled to the Contemporary
        Arts Center, Cincinnati; Dallas Museum of Fine Arts, Texas;

San Francisco Museum of Modern Art; Corcoran Gallery, Washington, D.C.)
1983   *New Perspectives on the Nude,* Ffotogallery, Cardiff, Wales
1984   *Sammlung Gruber,* Museum Ludwig, Coligne
1985   *Five Years with ''The Face,''* The Photographers' Gallery, London
1986   *Invitation: La Revue Parkett,* Centre National d'Art et de Culture Georges Pompidou, Paris
        Staging the Self, National Portrait Gallery, London and Plymouth Arts Centre, Plymouth, Devon, England
        Art & Advertising, Commercial Photography by Artists, International Center of Photography, New York, NY
1987   *Il Nudo Maschile Nella Fotografia 19th-20th Centurie,* Commune di Ravenna, Ravenna, Italy
        Legacy of Light, International Center of Photography, New York, NY
1988   *Fotofest 88,* Houston, Texas
1989   *Photography Now,* Victoria and Albert Museum, London
        Das Portrait: In Der Zeitgenossischen Photographie, Frankfurter Kunstverein, Frankfurt, Germany; also Kulturzentrum Mainz, Germany
        L'Invention d'un Art, Centre Georges Pompidou, Paris
        Museo De Arte Contemporaneo de Caracas, Caracas, Venezuela
1990   *Vollbild Aids,* Damptzentrale, Bern, Switzerland (travelled to Fondation Deutsch, Lausanne, Switzerland)
        Jan Fabre Theaterarbeiten, Fotografien von Robert Mapplethorpe, Helmut Newton und Carl De Keyzer, Fotografie Forum Frankfurt, Frankfurt, Germany
        Von der Natur in der Kunst, Messelpalast, Vienna
1991   *Fashion Photography Since 1945,* Victoria and Albert Museum, London
        National Gallery of Victoria, Melbourne, Australia
        Erotic Desire, Perspektief, Rotterdam, Netherlands
1992   *Flora Photographica,* travelled to Royal Botanical Garden Edinburgh, Manchester City Art Gallery and Mead Gallery, Coventry, UK
1993   *Almadovar,* Venice Biennal, Venice, Italy
        Supreme Shots-Fashion Photography since 1948, Galleria Photology, Milan, Italy
1994   *Flowers 1850-1994,* Hamilton's Gallery, London

Collections:

Jacksonville Art Museum, Florida; Hayden Gallery, Massachusetts Institute of Technology, Cambridge; Museum Ludwig, Cologne; The Art Institute of Chicago, Illinois; Australian National Gallery, Canberra, Australia; Center for Creative Photography, University of Arizona; Centre Pompidou, Paris; Frankfurter Kunstverein, Frankfurt, Germany; George Eastman House, Rochester, New York; Getty Museum, Malibu, California; Hara Museum of Art, Tokyo; International Center of Photography, New York; Israel Museum, Jerusalem, Israel; Metropolitan Museum of Art, New York; National Archives of Canada, Ottawa, Canada; National Portrait Gallery, London; Stedelijk Museum, Amsterdam, The Netherlands; Tampa Museum of Art; Victoria & Albert Museum, London.

Publications:

By MAPPLETHORPE: Books—*Robert Mapplethorpe Photographs,* with text by Mario Amaya, Norfolk, Virginia 1978; *Robert Mapplethorpe: Fotos/ Photographs,* with an introduction by Rein von der Fuhr, Amsterdam 1979; *Robert Mapplethorpe: Black Males,* with text by Edmund White, Amsterdam 1980; *Lady: Lisa Lyon,* with text by Bruce Chatwin, New York and London 1983; *The Black Book,* with foreword by Ntozake Shange, Munich 1986.

On MAPPLETHORPE: Books—*Documenta 6/Band 2,* exhibition catalogue, by Klaus Honnef and Evelyn Weiss, Kassel, West Germany 1977;

Mirrors and Windows: American Photography since 1960 by John Szarkowski, New York 1978; *Photographie als Kunst 1879-1979/Kunst als Photographie 1949-1979,* exhibition catalogue, 2 volumes, by Peter Weiermair, Innsbruck, Austria 1979; *Contact: Theory,* edited by Ralph Gibson, New York 1980; *Robert Mapplethorpe,* exhibition catalogue, with text by Peter Weiermair, Frankfurt 1981; *3 New Yorker Fotografen,* exhibition catalogue, with texts by Dieter Hall, Jean-Christophe Ammann, and Sam Wagstaff, Basel 1980; *The Library of World Photography: Portraits,* with introduction by Colin Ford, Tokyo 1982, 1983, London 1983; *Counterparts: Form and Emotion in Photographs* by Weston J. Naef, New York 1982; *Private Viewing: Contemporary Erotic Photography,* edited by Terry Jones, with introduction by Jack Schofield, London 1983; *New Perspective on the Nude,* exhibition catalogue, with texts by Susan Butler and Robert Greetham, Cardiff 1983; *Certain People: A Book of Portraits,* Los Angeles 1985; *Some Women,* Boston, Toronto, London 1989; *Robert Mapplethorpe, Early Works* edited by John Cheim, New York 1991; *Mapplethorpe versus Rodin,* text by Germano Celant, Milan 1992; *American Made: The New Still Life,* Tokyo 1993. Articles— ''Hotel Chelsea'' by Gerd Schiff in *Du* (Zurich), May 1971; ''Robert Mapplethorpe,'' special issue of *Creatis* (Paris), 1978; ''The Yin and the Yang of Robert Mapplethorpe'' by Inge Bondi in *Print Letter* (Zurich), January/ February 1978; ''Mapplethorpe: Dick Tracings'' by Sarah Kent and John Gill in *Time Out* (London), 3/9 November 1983; ''Mapplethorpe's Human Geometry'' by Mike Weaver in *Aperture* (Millerton, New York), no. 101, 1985.

*   *   *

In Robert Mapplethorpe's images, the square format dominates, as does stark composition, cold revealing light, precise focus, and a pristine clarity which is reminiscent of the Northern Renaissance painters. He works almost exclusively in black and white.

The idea of ''still life'' is central to Mapplethorpe's work, for whether he is photographing actual still-lifes, or human bodies formally ''arranged'' before his lens, a sense of classical composition prevails. In his still-lifes of flower arrangements, ''posed'' against a plain backdrop, natural colors are reduced to pristine black and white, and emphasis passes to the delineation of form as revealed by the cold light. Everything extraneous is removed—the arrangements exist isolated from their natural origins in a kind of vacuum. There is a definite sense of space, both surrounding the ''arrangement'' and separating the viewer from it. The sensuality evoked addresses itself to the sense of sight, rather than that of touch. We are asked to contemplate, but not participate in, an act of beauty.

The same sense of formal arrangement extends to Mapplethorpe's investigation of the human body, which is his major theme. Generally he poses his models against neutral backdrop paper, often including the edges of the roll to emphasize the sense of ''arrangement,'' of being posed. Bodies are treated as ''objects''—as part of a still-life composition. Often body parts are isolated, such as a pair of hands, a torso, or a pair of feet. The 1981 ''Vincent'' is a minimal, extremely powerful image of masculine, muscled arms folded across a chest. The model poses against a dark background, which merges mysteriously with the shadowed edges of the body. Mapplethorpe often emphasizes the inherent power of the human form through concentration on a glistening musculature, as in his series of black male nudes and the female body builder Lisa Lyon. Many of the later series were shot outdoors, contrasting the landscape of the body with a natural landscape.

Beyond the formal arrangement of limbs, body parts, light and shadow and tonality—Mapplethorpe pursues a disturbing, even shattering investigation of male sexuality and the iconography of power. Concentrating on powerful male bodies, he juxtaposes them with the accoutrements of sado-masochism: chains, leather, binding, etc., building careful still-lifes out of his often shocking material. The formal restraints, the cool scrutiny placed upon this powerful, often disturbing material make these controversial images among his strongest.

Mapplethorpe's portraits exhibit the same sense of arrangement and Vermeer-like clarity of light, even when he moves to locations outside his studio. Especially in his portraits of women, such as the 1971 ''Holly Solomon,'' reclining on a couch, languidly holding a cigarette, a more intimate mood prevails. Attention and sensitivity to fabric and abstract design dominates such images as the 1979 ''Physsis Tweel,'' where the subject faces away from the camera, so that all we see is her long curly hair, polka dot dress, white glove and hat. Mapplethorpe encompasses an extraordinary range, evoking responses which extend from shock and power, to intimacy and tenderness.

—Carole Harmel

MÁRA, Pavel.

Nationality: Czechoslovakian. **Born:** Prague on 20 October 1951. **Education:** Educated at the Secondary School of Graphic Arts in Prague, 1967-71; studied camera and photography at the Film Academy of Performing Arts (FAMU), Prague, 1971-81. **Family:** Married Helena Márová; children: Markéta Mikoláš. **Career:** Worked as an independent art photographer since 1975; worked as an audiovisual director and taught photographic workshops since 1991; started teaching photography at FAMU in 1994. Committee member of the Prague Association of Photographers, 1990-92; member of the Prague House of Photography since 1990. **Address:** Eledrova 7/728, 181 00 Prague 8, Czech Republic.

Individual Exhibitions:

1983	*Mechanical Still Lives,* Cultural Centre, Dobříš, Czech Republic
1985	Dům pánůz Kunštátu, Brno, Czech Republic
1986	Fotochema, Prague
1988	Malá galerie spořitelny, Kladno, Czech Republic
1989	Galerie 4, Cheb, Czech Republic
	Atrium, Prague
1990	Filmgalerie, Regensburg, Germany
1991	Galerie 99, St. Petersburg
1993	*7 Photos,* Galerie R, Prague

Selected Group Exhibitions:

1984	*Czech Artistic Photography,* Čs. spisovatel, Prague
1985	*Photographs of FAMU graduates,* Dům pánů z Kunštátu, Brno, Czech Republic (travelled to the UP Muzeum, Prague; Lithuania)
1986	*Human Body in Czechoslovak Photography,* Muzeum Kroměříž, Czechoslovakia
	Second International Manifestation of Photography, Amsterdam
1989	*Young Czechoslovak Photographers,* Fachschule, Hamburg, Germany
	Czechoslovak Photographers of the Eighties, Nieuwe Kerk, Amsterdam
1990	*Tschechische und Slowakische Fotografie der Gegenwart,* Museum Ludwig, Cologne (travelled to Städtische, Galerie Erlangen, Erlangen, Germany; Musée d'Art et Histoire, Metz; Centre National Audiovisuel, Dudelange; Transit, Strasburg; Brandts Klaedefabrik, Museet for Fotokunst, Odense; Augustinermuseum, Freiburg; Cercle Cultural de la Caixa Penions, Granollers; Stadtmuseum Waldraiburg, Germany; MSC Forsyth Center Galleries, Texas AM University; Spencer Museum of Art, University of Kansas)
	Photographie de L'Est, Palais de Beaulieu, Musée de L'Elysée, Switzerland
	Rencontres internationales de la photographie, Arles, France
	Vision de l'homme, Galerie Municipale du Chateau d'Eau, Toulouse, France
1991	*Ecrans/Icons,* Espace Art Brenne, France
1993	*Fotofest Kolín,* Czech Republic

Collections:

Museum Ludwig, Cologne; Centre of Recontres internationales de la photographie, Arles; Galerie Municipale du Chateau d'Eau, Toulouse; National Gallery, Prague, Czech Republic; UP Muzeum Prague, Czech Republic.

Publications:

On MÁRA: Books—*The Encyclopedia of Czech and Slovak Photographers,* Prague 1993; *Avenues of Czechoslovak Photography,* Prague 1989; *Tschechoslowakische Fotografie,* Heidelberg/Cologne 1990; *Ecrans/Icons,* France 1991; *37 Photographers at Chmelnice* by A. Fárová, Prague 1989; *What is Photography, 150 Years of Photography,* Pragye 1991; *Le jeune photographie tchécoslovaque, Vision de l'homme,* Galerie Municipale du Chateau d'Eau 1990. **Articles**—"Le visage de la Photographie Tcheque" by A. Fárová in *Photographies* magazine, No. 24, 1990; "Tschechoslowakische Fotographie der Gegenwart" in *Profifoto,* No. 4, 1990; "Cent cinquante ans de photographie a Prague" in *Photographies* magazine, No. 19, 1989; "Contemporary Czechoslovak Photography" by V. Birgus in *Fotografiya,* Moscow; "Fotografie an der FAMU Prag" in *Fotografie,* No. 2, 1990; "Mechanical Still Lives" in *Revue fotographie,* No.1 1984; "Pavel Mára 1983-93" by A.Fárová in *Atelier* 24/25 November 1993; "La Tchécoslovaguie á Arles Portraits" in *Camera International,* No. 26, 1990; "Der sker noget i Tjekkoslovakiet" by M. Sandbye in *Katalog,* Denmark, 2 December 1990; "Pavel Mára" by J. Pecák in *Fotographie,* No. 1, 1994; "Czech and Slovak Photography of the 80s" by V. Birgus in *Revue fotografie,* No. 1, 1991. **Film**—*Pavel Mára—More Than Just 7 Photos,* Prague 1994.

*

It is said that the photograph is an existential imprint of reality. Muybridges's photographs are the imprints of real horses. My photographs are the impressions of their hooves.

—Pavel Mára

*   *   *

The photographic work of Pavel Mára is quite varied, both in terms of motifs and styles, as the author has never in his career tried to suppress an urge to experiment, to seek and explore new trends in his art. Following descriptive cycles of pictures from steel works in the latter half of the 1970s, Mára applied himself for a long time to abstract photography, reducing fragments of depicted objects from the world of technical civilization to elementary lines, surfaces, colours and glosses. Thanks to the technical perfection of his large-format enlargements and striking adjustments Mára succeeded in multiplying the artistic impact of those *Mechanical Still Lives,* (the collective name given to several of his cycles from that period).

Mára discovered unexpected artistic values in the monumental spatial details of various metal and plastic objects with sharp contrasts of simple geometric formations with distinct colours. For instance, in the rhythmically recurrent red and white stripes in *Bumpers* from the cycle entitled *Signals* or on the contrary, the soft shades of several colour tones (eg *Yellow Cylinder* or *Blue Cylinder*). In his cycle called *Machines* made between 1976 and 1982 the motifs included red hot metal sheets and ingots. Mára captured intimations of movement and space.

In an overwhelming majority of his pictures from that period (for instance in the cycle *Metal Still Lives*) the photographer was inspired by minimalism in the fine arts. The key motifs of the 1981 cycle *Toys*—cubes from a children's building set—were unlike other collections of pictures from *Mechanical Still Lives* where Mára strove for a stylized representation of reality, arranged by the author with an accent placed on the glosses of geometric surfaces and the resulting counterpoints of light. In his 1984 cycle *Blue Nudes* Mára applied the method of pronounced spatial stylization of details of the female body, reduced to simple lines. A year later, in *Metal Torsos* and *Glass Torsos,* he set out to examine the possibility of processing images by etching on zinc and glass plates and—just like his serigraphic *Torsos*—he accentuated decorative values. Mára made ample use of distinct graphic stylization in the cycle of photo-sculptures entitled *Heads* and made between 1988-1989. The following years his photographic portraits on canvas called *Veils* developed a

Imprints—Veils (Image III), **1990.** Photograph ©Pavel Mara.

metaphor, the biblical theme of the imprint of Christ's face on the cloth, in other black and white photographs on canvas, *Imago* and *Madonnas,* and in large format photographic fragments of the human body called *Corpus.* In recent years Mára has made many impressive series of large format photographs of naked figures in tryptichs portrayed within a short time span, each picture taken with a changed camera angle. In these works he has gone to the greatest lengths in order to examine gnoseological problems and questions of human identity. In addition to this private work, Pavel Mára devotes himself to custom-made photography, ranging from photographs for posters, calendars and catalogues to audiovisual programmes on which he sometimes collaborates with his wife, the photographer Helena Márová.

—Vladimír Birgus

MARCO, Jindřich.

Nationality: Czechoslovakian. **Born:** Prague, 10 May 1921. **Education:** Attended high school, Prague, until 1940; self-taught in photography, from 1940, but influenced by Robert Capa and Alfred Eisenstaedt. **Family:** Married Jindřiška Jirásková in 1962; son: Filip. **Career:** Worked as a reporter, then photographer, for Jan Mikota's news and advertising agency, Prague, 1941-44; photoreporter, Ministry of Information, working for *Svět v obrazech* magazine, Prague Press Agency, Agence France Presse, etcs., in Prague, 1945-48. Imprisoned by Communist Regime 1950-1957 during which time he worked in uranium mines. Since 1948, freelance photographer, working for the agencies Pix and Black Star, and the magazines *Life, Paris-Match, Lilliput, Picture Post, Czechoslovak Life, Regards, Im Herzen Europas,* etc., Prague. **Recipient:** Max Svabinsky Medal, Prague, 1973. **Address:** Soborska 6, 160 00 Prague 6—Dejvice, Czech Republic.

Individual Exhibitions:

1966   *Prague Artists in Photographs,* Union of Czechoslovak Artists, Prague
1967   *A Piece of History and the World,* Gallery Fronta, Prague (retrospective)
1985   *Europe 1945-47,* Gallery Foma, Prague (retrospective)
1991   *Lost Cities,* Chicago Public Library, Chicago

Selected Group Exhibitions:

1958   *All-State Artistic Photography Exhibition,* Gallery ULUV, Prague
1971   *Club de la Photographie,* City Gallery, Limoges, France
1989   *150 Years of Photography, World Exhibition,* Prague
1992   *Czechoslovak Photography from 1915 to 1960s,* Jacques Baruch Gallery, Chicago

Collections:

National Gallery, Prague, Moravian Gallery, Brno, Czechoslovakia; National Gallery, Wroclaw, Poland.

Publications:

By MARCO: Books—*Romantic Prague,* Třebechovice, Czechoslovakia 1948; *England by Word and Picture,* Třebechovice, Czechoslovakia 1948; *Ancient Coins from Olbia and Panticapeum,* Prague and London 1959; *Zoo in Colours,* Prague 1961; *One Round World,* with others, Prague 1963; *Tribal Masks,* Prague and London 1967; *Please Buy My New Song,* Prague 1967; *Comrade Agressor,* Vienna, 1968, (under pseudonym Vaclav Svoboda); *Linz,* Vienna 1970; *Burgenland,* Vienna 1970; *South Bohemia,* Prague 1972; *About Prints,* Prague 1981; *Comrade Agressor,* Prague, 1990; *Israel '48,* Prague, 1990. **Articles**—about 100 illustrated essays in *Svět v obrazech* (Prague), 1945-50, and 60 articles in *Czechoslovak Life* (Prague), 1958-63.

On MARCO: Books—*Postwar Europe* by Vladimir Birgus, Prague 1987. **Articles**—"The World in the Photography of Jindřich Marco" by Vladimir Remeš in *Fotografie* (Prague), November 1973; "Jindřich Marco: Witness of Photography After the War" by Vladimir Birgus in *Ceskoslovenska Fotografie* (Prague), May 1985; "How the Peace Began" by Vladimir Birgus in *Mladý Svět* (Prague), May 1986.

*

The photographer stops time in a fraction of a second and gives us the only faithful and accurate record of that time. Uninteresting events or unphotogenic people don't exist—just good and bad photographers. A good photograph doesn't need a lot of explanation; if a photo needs it, then it's a bad photo.

—Jindřich Marco

*   *   *

Jindřich Marco is one of the most interesting older generation Czech reportage photographers still active. His career began like an illustration of the proverb, "it's an ill wind that blows no good"—for his intended literary studies at Prague's Charles University were forestalled in 1940 by the Nazi occupation, and so Marco had to go and work for a news agency instead. His job there was to write reports mainly about cultural events. One day he was asked to stand in for one of the agency photographers who was unable to make his assignment at a film studio. Marco's pictures turned out to be remarkably good and he was promptly launched on a career as a successful film publicity photographer. The motion picture studio was a brilliant and demanding training ground, and Marco quickly learned how to capture the most telling facial expression or the exact moment to snap open the shutter on an event.

His newly discovered talent was next put to work on a personal subject preparing a record of Prague's beautiful buildings threatened by wartime airraids. Marco was determined to preserve an indelible memory of every part of the city he knew and loved. His homage to Czechoslovakia's capital was eventually published after the war as the book *Romantic Prague.*

In Autumn 1944 Marco was deported to a concentration camp, but in 1945 escaped across the front to the newly-liberated eastern sector of the Czechoslovak Republic. With an old Rolleiflex camera he became a photoreporter with the Czech Ministry of Information, taking photos of every important political event during the last days of World War 2. Back in Prague in 1945, the Ministry commissioned him to work with the weekly *Svět v obrazech* (World in Pictures), for which he produced some of his most penetrating and perceptive visions of everyday life in the war-ravaged areas of Czechoslovakia, Austria, Germany, Hungary and Poland. Apart from his considerable photographic skills and the sharpness of eye, honed during his early days in publicity photography, Marco's immediate postwar work mirrors a sincere human interest rivalling the later work of photojournalists such as David Seymour.

No wonder Marco soon became known beyond the borders of Czechoslovakia. Contracts from major picture agencies such as Black Star and Pix, and commissions from the magazines *Life, Lilliput, Paris-Match* and *Picture Post* came thick and fast. Despite these successes, Marco felt strongly drawn by the desire to bring a coherent summary of his works together in book form. For his systematic picture series on Britain done by working twelve hours a day over a period of seven weeks in 1947, he used both Leica and Rolleiflex cameras. With these, he produced not only a rich panorama of landscape and city images, but combined them with narrative shots of characteristic English behaviour to create an impression of intimate contact with the country and its people.

In the late 1950s, Marco's photojournalism was deeply influenced by employment in the editorial offices of the magazine *Czechoslovak Life.* He was commissioned initially to take pictures of characteristic cultural events, for which he had become well known. In addition, however, Marco started making his own independent series of portraits—a major programmatic study of Czech painters, sculptors, writers and musicians. The series is remarkable for the strong journalistic approach to the portrait genre, Marco's keen eye revealing the inner personality of the artist and his work. Although this series was highly acclaimed when selections of it were first exhibited in 1966, it was his 1967 exhibition of postwar images, closely followed by his book *Please Buy My New Song,* that proved to be his most influential one-man presenta-

An Old Beehive in Moravia, **1989.** Photograph by Jindřich Marco.

tion. The sheer eloquence of those pictures from 1945 and 1946 brought faded memories into sharp focus with a new freshness and clarity.

Today, Marco is still active. Although not as hungrily frenzied as in his youth, he still works on major photo series—his artists portraits numbering some 15,000 exposures taken over a period of twenty-five years—that look set to occupy him for many a year to come.

—Petr Tausk

MARGOLIS, Richard.

Nationality: American. **Born:** Lorain, Ohio, 10 June 1943. **Education:** University of the Americas, Mexico City; studied photo-journalism at Kent State University, Ohio, B.S. 1969; Rochester Institute of Technology, New York, M.F.A. 1978; also attended the Visual Studies Workshop, Rochester. **Family:** Married to Sherry L Phillips. **Career:** Owner/Operator, Photo Graphics commercial and industrial photography studio, Kent, Ohio, 1969-72. Freelance commercial photographer, Rochester, since 1972 (photographic darkroom assistant, International Museum of Photography, George Eastman

House, Rochester, 1975-76). Lecturer in Photography, Nazareth College, Rochester, since 1979; Assistant Professor, Department of Art, State University of New York at Brockport, since 1981. Self employed since 1987. Northeast Region Chairman, Society for Photographic Education, 1982, 1985; Chairman, Photographic Heritage Association/PABIR, Rochester, New York, since 1984. Founding Member: Photo Archives Belong in Rochester, 1984. Member, Phase II Planning Committee, International Museum of Photography, 1986. **Recipient:** Creative Artists Public Service Grant, New York, 1977-78; Photography Grant, New York State Council for the Arts, 1985-86. **Address:** 225 Barrington Street, Rochester, New York 14607, U.S.A.

Individual Exhibitions:

1975	New England School of Photography, Boston
1976	Foto, New York
	Ohio State University, Columbus
	Photographer's Gallery, Saskatoon, Saskatchewan
	Panopticon Gallery, Boston
1977	Gallery Graphics, Ottawa
	Photoworks, Richmond, Virginia
1978	Carpenter Center, Harvard University, Cambridge, Massachusetts

From the series *Bridges—Symbols of Progress,* **High Falls and Portage Viaduct, Letchworth, 1993.** Photograph ©Richard Margolis.

CEPA/Hallwalls, Buffalo, New York
1979 International Museum of Photography, George Eastman House,
Rochester, New York
Antioch College, Yellow Springs, Ohio
Foto, New York
Yuen Lui Gallery, Seattle
1980 Andover Gallery, Massachusetts
Light Factory Gallery, Charlotte, North Carolina
1981 Kathleen Ewing Gallery, Washington, D.C.
Structured Photographs, Foto, New York
English Landscapes, Camden Arts Centre, London
1983 *Middle Landscapes,* Foto, New York
1985 *Bridges—Symbols of Progress,* Monroe Community College,
Rochester, New York
1990 *Bridges—Symbols of Progress,* National Academy of Sciences,
Washington, D.C.
Rochester's Big Trees, Spectrum Gallery, Light Impressions,
Rochester, NY (also at various venues in Canandaigua,
Ogdensburg, Watertown and Rochester, New York)
1991 *Bridges—Symbols of Progress,* The Queen's Museum of Art,
Flushing, New York
Magic Powers, The Powers Building, Rochester, New York
(continuing exhibition)
1992 *Rochester's Public Art,* Dawson Gallery, Rochester, New York
Photographs by Richard Margolis, Walter Street Grill,
Rochester New York (5 year installation)
Bridges—Symbols of Progress, Adirondack Community
College, Glens Falls, New York; Erie Canal Museum,
Syracuse, New York; Tioga County Historical Society,
Owego, New York; Raushenbush Library, Sarah Lawrence
College, Bronxville, New York; Siegel Gallery, Lehigh
University, Bethlehem, Pennsylvania)
1993 *Bridges—Symbols of Progress,* Paul Cava Gallery, Philadel-
phia (travelled to Suffolk Community College, Riverhead,
New York; Hoyt-Potter House, Landmark Society, Roches-
ter, New York)
Rochester's Public Art, Link Gallery, City Hall, Rochester,
New York
1994 *Rochester's Landmarks,* Rochester International Airport (Per-
manent exhibition)
Bridges—Symbols of Progress, Staten Island Institute of Arts
& Sciences, Staten Island, New York; New York City Public
Library, New York
Magic Powers, Hoyt-Potter House, Landmark Society,
Rochester, New York

Selected Group Exhibitions:

1976 *Contemporary Stereo,* Hallwalls, Buffalo, New York
1978 *Some Twenty Odd Visions,* Blue Sky Gallery, Seattle
130 Years of Ohio Photography, Columbus Gallery of
Art, Ohio
1979 *The Residual Landscape,* Addison Gallery, Andover,
Massachusetts
Foto Uno, Casa Aboy, Puerto Rico
1980 *Manipulated Landscape,* State University of New York at
Geneseo
Personal Landscapes, Artworks Gallery, Rochester, New York
1982 *Assembled Photographs,* Catskill Center for Photography,
Woodstock, New York
1983 *Photography Invitational,* Second Street Gallery, Charlottesville, Virginia
1984 *Rochester—A Center of Photography,* International Museum
of Photography at George Eastman House, Rochester,
New York
1986 *Man and the Sea,* 12th International Triennal Exhibition,
People's Museum, Zadar, Yugoslavia
1991 *New York Stories,* Douglas Drake Gallery, New York

1992 *A Picture Perfect Restoration—George Eastman's House and
Gardens,* International Museum of Photography at George
Eastman House, Rochester, New York
1994 *Landscape Show,* Penland School Gallery, Penland School of
Crafts, Penland North Carolina

Collections:

Museum of Modern Art, New York; International Museum of Photography,
George Eastman House, Rochester, New York; St. Lawrence University,
Canton, New York; Yale University Art Gallery, New Haven, Connecticut;
Addison Gallery of American Art, Andover, Massachusetts; Lehigh Universi-
ty, Bethelehem, Pennsylvania; Library of Congress, Washington, D.C.; High
Museum of Art, Atlanta; Victoria and Albert Museum, London; Bibliothèque
Nationale, Paris; The Progressive Corp., Cleveland, Ohio; Visual Studies
Workshop, Rochester, New York; American Red Cross, Rochester, New
York; Exchange National Bank, Chicago; Polaroid Collection, Cambridge,
Massachusetts; Rochester International Airport, Rochester, New York.

Publications:

By MARGOLIS: Books—*Bridges—Symbols of Progress,* catalogue, Flush-
ing, New York, 1991; *Imperial Austria—Treasures of Art, Arms & Armor,*
catalogue, Houston, Texas, 1992. Articles—"Kinds of Photographs" in
Creative Camera (London), April 1978; "Fire at George Eastman House" in
Creative Camera (London), November 1978; "Richard Margolis" in *Ten 8*
(Birmingham, England), Autumn 1979.

On MARGOLIS: Books—*130 Years of Ohio Photography,* exhibition
catalogue, Columbus, Ohio 1979; *Electronic Flash Photography* by Carraher
and Chartier, New York 1980; *Simon's Masterpiece* by James S. La Villa-
Havelin, New York 1983. Articles—"Three on the Edge" by Ben Lifson in
the *Village Voice* (New York), 16 April 1979; "Raveling the Knot" by Owen
Edwards in *Saturday Review* (New York), 28 April 1979; "Connections" in
Exposure (New York), no. 20, 1982; "Seeing Pictures—Photography Teachers Confront the Issue: Can Art and Politics Mix?" by Julia Scully in *Modern
Photography* (New York), June 1985.

*

Thirty years ago I signed up for a journalism course that was already full
and had to settle for photography instead. That was an event that changed my
life. Ten years later I moved to Rochester for graduate school and in the first
month was hired by the curator at Memorial Art Gallery to photograph the
work of Harvey Ellis, a Rochester architect. Rochester's history, architecture
and landmarks have been significant features in my photography ever since.

I had considered architecture as a major when I began college and have
always been interested in it but doubt that I could have survived the discipline,
or the maths, required for that field. Now I find myself photographing it,
arranging buildings and sculpture in my camera to reveal what it is that I find
interesting for others to see.

In the early 1970s I began doing technically complicated landscape
photographs at night that employed multiple light sources, often requiring
exposures of up to an hour. I worked on that project for five years until I
realized I had to move on. Then I photographed *English Landscapes* that could
have been illustrations for the British mysteries that I was reading, followed by
Middle Landscapes, that I described as a blend of natural and artificial
elements based on Thomas Jefferson's notion of the ideal environment.

In 1983 I needed a few prints for a faculty show and could not think of
anything really worthwhile, but the Brooklyn Bridge was celebrating its 100th
birthday with a lot of media attention and I was teaching a course on
"Technology and Society." Bridges seemed like an acceptable academic
subject. Then I got hooked. I discovered that bridges are more interesting than
I had realized. From one angle they are objects, while from another they are
experiences. Mechanical bridges are creative solutions to complicated problems involving transport in two directions that must occupy the same grade.
Among the largest movable things in the world, they are incredible to watch.
They also have a history which is interesting to discover. Since then I have
photographed several hundred historic bridges in seven countries and am

723

continuing to photograph bridges when I travel. I continue doing commercial work, mostly involving historic structures and teaching workshops.

In an open competition I was selected to design a permanent public art project for the new Rochester International Airport. After winning a battle with local conservatives over public funding for art, I have installed ten prints, each 4 x 6 feet, that will introduce visitors to Rochester Landmarks and photography, also one of Rochester's strengths. The Erie Canal, Genesee River, three waterfalls, big trees, a sculpture of Frederick Douglass, and parks designed by Frederick Law Olmstead all contribute to defining the Rochester area for visitors.

My interest in bridges continues and *The Bridge Project* has grown from a little collection of postcards and newspaper clippings to a file cabinet full of treasures. In addition to collecting those stories about bridges I am continuing to photograph them. I recently began working with an 8 x 10 camera in a much slower more deliberate way, making larger and, hopefully, even more beautiful prints.

—Richard Margolis

*   *   *

Richard Margolis is an artist working in the tradition of 19th century Romanticism. His photographs of landscape are transformations of the real world. The light, the formal elements and the treatment of the exposure render a mystical and classical view of a world where all is well and beautiful. Antecedents of Margolis' work are certainly Frederick Evans' evocative images of trees and landscape, while the sylistic impact of his prints comes directly from the work of the Photo-Secessionists, although the techniques differ. Margolis has taken his inspiration from sources considered important historically but not influential in the period of sharp focus Realism, all-consuming Formalism, or manipulation, making Margolis something of a pioneer. He communicates sensation rather than thought.

His work is split into the earlier brown-toned night images and the later daytime images. The nocturnal works are made by long exposure with the focus changed from sharp to soft and the selective addition of flash to the existing ambient light. The night pictures of places have the feeling of a stage set where all of the elements are adjusted to just the right effect. Margolis plays the formal magician to an everyday world.

His later daytime images, mostly of English gardens and landscape, have much the same feeling. In printing these photographs in straight black and white, relying more on unmanipulated exposure, Margolis makes framing most important, although he occasionally uses altered focus and fractured light. He demonstrates a view of landscape which makes the viewer aware of the unseen forces, powers and mythic elements which inhabit those gardens, paths and fields illuminated so strangely.

Richard Margolis is calling forth these spirits in his images with the sensibility of an earlier time, but there's no mistake that his view of either the urban or rural world is populated by contemporary demons. His photographs are beautiful, but the dangers of the present world, urban decay and violence, man seedy and disappearing, lurk in the shadows.

—James L. Sheldon

MARIANI, Anna.

Nationality: Brazilian. **Born:** Rio de Janeiro, 4 July 1935. **Education:** Studied at the Enfoco School of Photography, 1969-70. **Family:** Married Alain Moreau in 1956; married Joaquim Guedes in 1976; single since 1991; children: Daniela, Filipe, André, Gisela and Mariana Moreau. **Recipient:** Aquisition Prize, Museum of Modern Art, Sao Paulo, 1980, and Best Photographer of the Year, awarded by the São Paulo Art Critic Association, 1987. **Agent:** Luiza Strina, rua Padre, João Manuel 974a, 01411 São Paulo, S.P. Brazil. **Address:** rua Bela Cintra 2262/192, 01415-002 São Paulo, S.P. Brazil.

Individual Exhibitions:

1972	Eucatexpo, São Paulo, Brazil
1974	Enfoco, São Paulo, Brazil
1979	Espaçonovo, São Paulo, Brazil
1984	Arco, São Paulo, Brazil
1988	*Des maisons comme des tableaux,* Centre Georges Pompidou, Paris
	Façades, Gallerie FNAC, Paris
1989	*Bahian Talot* Suomen Rakennustaileen Museo, Helsinki
1990	*Facader,* Udstillingsbygningen Charlottenborg, Copenhagen
	Fassaden, Institut für Auslandbeziehungen, Stuttgart, Germany
1992	*Paisagens, Impressoes,* Fundação Roberto Marinho, Rio de Janeiro (travelled to Museu de Arte Contemporanea, São Paulo; Instituto Moreira Salles, Polos de Caldas, Brazil)
	Pinturas e Platibandas, Casa França-Brasil, Rio de Janeiro (travelled to Museu da Cidade, Salvador Bahia, Brazil; Fundação Cultural de Curitiba, Curitiba, Brazil)
1993	*Sob o olhar de Frans Post,* Pinacoteca do Estado, São Paulo, Brazil

Selected Group Exhibitions:

1980	Museu de Arte Moderna, São Paulo, Brazil
1981	Kunsthaus, Zurich, Switzerland
1985	Museu de Arte Moderna, São Paulo, Brazil
1987	*19th São Paulo International Biennale,* Brazil
1988	*Brazil Projects,* The Institute for Art and Urban Resources, PS1, New York
	Staatliche Kunsthalle, Berlin
1989	*Colour in Context,* Serpentine Gallery, London
	U-ABC, Stedelijk Museum, Amsterdam (travelled to Fundãçao C. Gulbenkian, Lisbon)
1991	*A Mata,* Museu de Arte Contemporanea, São Paulo, Brazil
	Homenagem a Frans Post, Museu de Arte Contemporanea, Olinda, Brazil
1994	*Bienal Seculo XX,* São Paulo
	A Hidden View Images of Bahia, Barbican, London
	Coleçáo Pirelli, Museu de Arte de São Paulo, Brazil

Collections:

Pirelli, MASP Collection, São Paulo; Museum of Modern Art, São Paulo; G.B. Silverman Collection, Detroit.

Publications:

By MARIANI: Books—*Pinturas e Platibandas* (with Ariano Suassuna and Lina Bardi), São Paulo 1987; *Façades,* Rio de Janeiro 1988; *Paisagens, Impressoes* (with Antonio Medina and Manuel Andrade), São Paulo 1992.

On MARIANI: Articles—"Anna Mariani" in *El Paseante,* No. 11, 1988; "L'objet pur" by Jan Beaudrillard for Centre Georges Pompidou, Paris 1988; "Anna Mariani" by Caetano Veloso in *El Paseante,* Madrid, December 1988; "Köyhyyden ar rokkaat julkisivut" by Leena Maunula in *Kulttuuri,* 22 February 1989; "Bold Fronts in Brazil" by Bernard Bruce in *The Independent Magazine,* 3 June 1989; "Anna Mariani" by Allister Warman for Serpentine Gallery, London May 1989; "Bunter Protest" by Barbel Kistner in *Kunst Magazine,* May 1990; "Fassaden" by Rainer Zerbst in *Sendung Kultureginal,* 4 May 1990; video—*The Semi-arid Region of Brazil* by Anna Mariani, TV Globo, 1992.

*

In 1971 I initiated a project of documentation of various aspects of the Brazilian north east backlands region (the *Sertão*)—its landscapes, vegetation, villages, human beings and their work. That region has always fascinated me for that was where my Italian forefathers established themselves in 1760.

Camaiura-Xingu, **November 1974.** Photograph by Anna Mariani.

Altogether I took 21 trips in 18 months or 30,000 kilometres. I always took photographs and as time went by these records of my travels became more and more consistent. I had no specific projects initially—the themes being defined as the exhibitions were planned.

From 1976 onwards I concentrated my work on photographing facades of the local houses which are painted with pigmented lime, a very strong tradition of the region. I photographed around 2,000 facades on and around 150 villages. This work became prominent amongst the other themes and 100 photos of facades were exhibited at the 19th Bienal Internacional de São Paulo, where it won the prize of best photographic exhibition of 1987 given by the Associação Paulista de Críticos de Arte.

After the Bienal the exhibition was invited to go to Berlin (1988) and for two years it followed invitations around Europe, including one from the Centre Georges Pompidou in Paris, where the catalogue was rewarded by a text by Jean Baudrillard.

Today this exhibition belongs to the Institut für Auslandsbezilhunger in Stuttgart, which still promotes it in other countries.

Since 1990 I re-initiated the documentation of the Sertão region, concentrating more on its landscapes and vegetation.

—Anna Mariani

*   *   *

Anna Mariani is unusual, particularly among women photographers, in primarily being a landscape artist. Like the great Victorian photographic pioneer, Julia Margaret Cameron, this Brazilian mother of five was given a camera "to amuse herself with" when travelling in Europe. The first pictures she took of Greece were, she claims, so bad that she formulated a personal prohibition to roam outside what she knows in taking images. Snapshots are one thing, but even the places that may inspire you—she agrees with everything said about the skies of Greece or, still more strongly, about the reds of Morocco—but prefers to leave their imprinting to others, preferably Greeks or Moroccans.

What Anna Mariani knows about is her native north eastern region of the Sertão, the wild arid interiors of the remoter fringes of Brazil. Without sweetness or charm but with their own cruel seduction, these backlands have drawn in some of the greatest writers and artists in Brazilian history. Partly inspired by the Sertão itself, partly by the vast sprawling novels of Euclides da Cunha and the dramatic sky and landscapes of the early Dutch painter Frans Post, Anna Mariani has made that wild world her own.

Starting while still a photography student in the 1970s, with a black and white documentation of rural women's work, Anna Mariani began to exhibit her work in São Paulo, where she has lived for the last twenty years. These women were shown working in traditional ways with rudimentary imple- ments, firing pots in open fires, grinding manioc flour with giant stone pestles and mortars or hand binding sisal into brooms and—to the sophisticated eye of a gallery-going urban paulista—must have seemed as remote as the images Mariani also mounted of the indians in their jungle homes.

At the same time, however, Anna Mariani was already starting her documentation of the *caatinga,* the scrubby backwoods of the Bahian hinter- land. Attracted first through the people, the women she'd photographed and their men, the gauchos who still maintain the tradition of dressing from hat to stirrup in leather, she took a closer look at their homes. Just as Frans Post had painted them four centuries earlier, each house (some scarcely more than a hovel) is individuated both by its architecture and its decoration. While the former is worthy of Delft, all crenellated roofs and intricate windows, the latter is vividly showy, clashing colours often arranged in humorous stripes and trompe l'oeil designs. Later, in her book of these *Façades* (1988), Jean Baudrillard would point out the one asymmetrical popular culture ever recorded and declare: "We cannot but salute . . . as the liberating eruption of a pure object, of the most perfect style which isn't a style, of an architecture which isn't an architecture, of a primitivism, a naïvity which likewise isn't one (there's nothing less naïve than this naïvity) of an extreme poverty that refuses to express itself as extreme poverty, but instead as a wealth of lines and appearances and—last but not least—of a photograph which also succeeds in being something considerably more than 'just a photo.'"

If the brilliantly clashing colours of the pseudo-Dutch houses attracted Anna Maraini, so then did those of the natural flora. The following book, *Landscapes and Impressions* (1992) focussed on the miraculous power of the Sertão to appear desertified for months then, within half an hour of a rainfall, to spring back to life in stunning colour. It is these transformations that Anna Mariani has captured, in images of hope and eternal renewal. While her colour work becomes globally known and internationally published, Anna Mariani herself contemplates returning to working in black and white, yet without ever moving outside her beloved Sertão and its peculiarly syncretic worlds of human and natural design.

—Amanda Hopkinson

MARK, Mary Ellen.

Nationality: American. **Born:** Philadelphia, Pennsylvania, 20 March 1940. **Education:** Cheltenham High School, Philadelphia, 1954-58; University of Pennsylvania, Philadelphia, 1958-62, B.A. in Fine Arts, and Annenberg School of Communications, University of Pennsylvania, 1963-64, M.A. in Communications 1964; photographed in Turkey, as a Fulbright Scholar, 1965- 66. **Career:** Freelance photographer. Established studio, New York, 1966; Member, Magnum Photos, New York and Paris, 1976-81. Has also lectured at numerous photographic workshops and in lecture series, throughout the United States, since 1974. **Recipient:** United States Information Agency Grant, 1975; National Endowment for the Arts Photography Fellowship, 1977,

1979; Creative Artists Public Service Grant, New York, 1977; Commission, Bell System Project, 1979; Page One Award, Newspaper Guild of New York, 1980; Feature Picture Story Award, Pictures of the Year Competition, University of Missouri, Columbia, 1981; First Prize, Robert F. Kennedy Journalism Awards, 1981, 1984; Leica Medal of Excellence, 1982; Canon Photo Essayist Award, New York, 1983; Philippe Halsman Photojournalism Award, New York, 1986. **Agent:** Lee Gross Associates, 366 Madison Avenue, New York, New York 10017, U.S.A. **Address:** 143 Prince Street, New York, New York 10012, U.S.A.

Individual Exhibitions:

1975	Photopia Gallery, Philadelphia (with Ralph Gibson)
1976	The Photographers' Gallery, London
	Forum Stadtpark, Graz, Austria
1977	Santa Barbara Museum of Art, California
	Bibliothèque Nationale, Paris
	Port Washington Library, New York
	Creative Photography Library, Massachusetts Institute of Technology, Cambridge (with Burk Uzzle)
1978	Castelli Graphics, New York
	Boise Gallery of Art, Idaho
	Photography Gallery, Yarra, Victoria, Australia
1979	*Ward 81,* Museum of Art, University of Oregon, Eugene
	Ward 81/Bars, Galerie Nagel, Berlin
1981	*Falkland Road,* Castelli Graphics, New York (travelled to the Olympus Gallery, London, 1981; and University of California at Santa Cruz and at Riverside, 1982)
1982	Photography Gallery, Drew University, Madison, New Jersey
1983	Daytona Beach Community College, Florida
	Mother Teresa and Calcutta, Friends of Photography, Carmel, Caliifornia
1985	*Mother Teresa,* Allen Street Gallery, Dallas, Texas
1986	*Mother Teresa,* Northlight Gallery, Tempe, Arizona

Selected Group Exhibitions:

1969	*Vision and Expression,* International Museum of Photography, George Eastman House, Rochester, New York (toured the United States, 1969-71)
1975	*Women Photographers,* Neikrug Gallery, New York
	Women of Photography, San Francisco Museum of Art (travelled to the Sidney Janis Gallery, New York, 1976)
1977	*8 American Female Photographers,* Iran/America Society Cultural Center, Tehran
1979	*American Images: New Work by 20 Contemporary Photographers,* Corcoran Gallery, Washington, D.C. (toured the United States, 1979-81)
	Photographie als Kunst 1879-1979, Tiroler Landesmuseum Ferdinandeum, Innsbruck (travelled to the Neue Galerie am Wolfgang Gurlitt Museum, Linz, Austria; Neue Galerie am Landesmuseum Joanneum, Graz, Austria; and the Museum des 20. Jahrhunderts, Vienna)
1980	*Likely Stories,* Castelli Graphics, New York
1982	*Color as Form,* International Museum of Photography, George Eastman House, Rochester, New York
1983	*International Photographers II,* Eaton/Shoen Gallery, San Francisco
1985	*American Images 1945-80,* Barbican Art Gallery, London (toured Britain)

Collections:

Bibliothèque Nationale, Paris; Australian National Gallery, Canberra.

Publications:

By MARK: Books—*The Photojournalist: Two Women Explore the Modern World and the Emotions of Individuals,* with Annie Leibovitz, New York 1974; *Passport,* New York 1974; *Ward 81,* with text by Karen Folger Jacobs, New York 1979; *Falkland Road,* New York 1981; *Mother Teresa: Her Missions in Calcutta,* Carmel, California 1985; *Streetwise,* Seattle, Washington 1985.

On MARK: Books—*Vision and Expression* by Nathan Lyons, New York 1969; *Great Themes,* by the Time-Life editors, New York 1970; *Geschichte der Fotografie im 20. Jahrhundert/Photography in the 20th Century* by Petr Tausk, Cologne 1977, London 1980; *SX-70 Art,* edited by Ralph Gibson, New York 1979; *American Images: New Work by 20 Contemporary Photographers,* edited by Renato Danese, New York 1979; *Photographie als Kunst 1879-1979/Kunst als Photographie 1949-1979,* exhibition catalogue, 2 volumes, by Peter Weiermair, Innsbruck 1979; *Contact: Theory,* edited by Ralph Gibson, New York 1980; *Lichtbildnisse: Das Porträt in der Fotografie,* edited by Klaus Honnef, Cologne 1982; *Color as Form: A History of Color Photography,* exhibition catalogue, with introduction by Robert A. Sobieszek, Rochester, New York 1982; *American Images: Photography 1945-1980,* edited by Peter Turner and John Benton-Harris, London 1985. **Articles**—"Assignment in Turkey by Mary Ellen Mark" in *U.S. Camera Annual 1968,* edited by Tom Maloney, New York 1967; "The Human Face of Mental Illness" in *Photography Year 1977,* by the Time-Life editors, New York 1977; "Falkland Road: Mary Ellen Mark" in *American Photographer* (New York), April 1981; "Falkland Road" in *Photo* (Paris), October 1981.

*

I've been taking pictures for 23 years. My work has consistently been within the tradition of social documentary photography. Throughout the years I have been striving to find social documentary projects which I both wanted to photograph and felt were important to photography. I have also tried to grow as a photographer and to find original ways of visualizing each new theme.

After graduation, I was awarded a Fulbright Scholarship to spend a year photographing Turkey. This was my first opportunity to work for a long period of time on one theme. It was a year of important development for me; since then I have tried to find the time and means to devote long periods of time to specific projects.

Here is a brief description of a few of the projects that I have worked on in the past:

In the late 1960s I did a series of pictures on the drug problem in England, showing the superficial joys of "shooting up" and the horror of the aftermath. In the early 70s I spent several months in Asia, photographing the pilgrimage of Western youth trying to adapt to a culture completely alien to their own. I also spent time in Northern Ireland photographing both Protestant and Catholic women, to depict the effects of the war on their lives. A number of the pictures from the many different projects that I worked on during my first 10 years of photographing are included in a book I did called *Passport,* published in 1974.

In 1979 I published *Ward 81.* The photographs were taken in 1976 in a maximum security ward for women in the Oregon State Mental Hospital. I was permitted to live in the ward with the women for two months. In my photographs I tried to give some insight into the anxieties and mood changes of these women, as well as show the conditions of their confinement.

In 1977 I spent several months photographing in bars all over the New York and New Jersey area. The pictures were exhibited in Europe and published in *Camera* in September 1977. In 1979 I was asked to participate in the "Commissioned Artist with the Bell System" project. Each of 20 American photographers was asked to produce a portfolio of new work photographed in America. The project I chose was on teenage pregnancy. I photographed a 15-year-old girl and her 14-year-old boyfriend before, during, and after the birth of their baby. The end result was a book of the 20 portfolios called *American Images,* edited by Renato Danese, and also a travelling exhibition.

For the past 18 years I have been travelling to India. I made many trips there and waited several years before I felt I could do difficult documentary statements about this fascinating and complicated culture. During the past eight years I have worked on three large photographic projects in India. In 1978-79 I spent three months with a community of prostitutes in Bombay. This work became the book *Falkland Road.* Later in 1979 I returned to India and worked on two more projects. I spent three months travelling in various parts of the country with snake charmers, street acrobats, monkey trainers, magicians, etc. The street performers of India are in a tradition that has been passed down from father to son over generations. Both the terrible conditions that poverty brings and modern influences are forcing the new generation to abandon their traditional heritage. I chose this subject both because I am fascinated by the art form and also because I felt it was necessary to photograph it while it still exists.

In January 1980 I spent one month photographing Mother Teresa and her Missions of Charity in Calcutta. Since I first travelled to India in 1968, Mother Teresa, the Bengali people that her mission serves, and especially Calcutta itself have represented an aspect of India and its humanity that I desperately wanted to photograph. The photographs I made in January were published in *Life* in July 1980. When I left Calcutta in February 1980 I knew I had to return and make a much longer statement in a book form. I returned in 1981 to complete the project. The photographs were exhibited in 1983 at The Friends of Photography, who published the book *Mother Teresa and Her Missions in Calcutta* in 1985.

In April 1982, I travelled to Seattle to produce a story of runaway children for *Life*. After the published story won a Robert F. Kennedy Award and the Canon Photo Essayist Award, I returned with filmmaker Martin Bell in August 1983 and spent two months filming in Seattle. The film *Streetwise* was completed in September 1984 and was nominated as a documentary for an Academy Award in 1985.

—Mary Ellen Mark

* * *

Mary Ellen Mark is a photojournalist, a photographer who "peels away layers of convention" to report on her subject. It is this ability to find the truth and express it photographically, combined with the compassion of her depiction, that has made her a favorite photographer for magazines such as *Life, Time, Paris-Match, Epoca, Stern, Ms., U.S. Camera, Infinity* and *Leica Magazine.*

Being a photojournalist has meant travelling internationally on assignment for Mark. This aspect of photography has, by her own admission, changed both her personality and her life. "I would die if I felt I had to be confined . . . live in a house and stay in one place. I don't want to feel that I'm missing out on experiencing as much as I can. For me, experiencing is knowing people all over the world and being able to photograph . . . . I think being a transient person . . . manifests itself in every aspect of my life, certainly in my work, in all my relationships . . . . I don't think I was like this ten years ago when I started to photograph" (interview with Eleanor Lewis in *Passport*).

Mark had the "instant recognition" that she wanted to be a photographer while she was studying photojournalism at the University of Pennsylvania's Annenberg School of Communications. A year after graduating, she was photographing in Turkey on a Fulbright Scholarship and two years later *Look* published her first major magazine article, a photographic report on London's St. Clement's Drug Unit and the English approach to treatment of heroin addiction. Since then she has produced numerous articles on a broad range of subjects—from the quality of life in the Women's Army Corps and the militancy of Protestants from the Ulster Defense Alliance to the migration to India of young Americans and Europeans disillusioned with Western culture.

It is the human condition which is the true subject of Mark's photographs. Her focus is on people: people of all ages, professions and nationalities. Her metier is the "journalistic portrait," in which she shows her subjects with honesty and compassion. The difficulty of photographing exotic peoples, she feels, is becoming clichéd, but she overcomes the problem with a very direct method of shooting and by using black-and-white film, which she feels forces her to "get to the essentials."

For Mary Ellen Mark photography is an adventurous experience, a tool of exploration, and a way of relating to the world and its people. Her portraits are formed by journalistic objectivity and are both more factual and more compassionate than those of a photographer like Diane Arbus. This can be seen by comparing Mark's portraits of drug addicts, runaways and transvestites with similar subjects photographed by Arbus. Arbus' work accentuates the deviant and outcast nature of each individual's effort to come to terms with his or her identity; Mark's work is instead relatively non-judgmental, trying to find the truth of each person's existence.

One of Mark's most touching documents is that of the mental patients of Ward 81. An assignment to cover the film *One Flew Over the Cuckoo's Nest,*

shot on location at the Oregon State (Mental) Hospital, led to her interest in the subject. In February 1976 Mark and the writer and social scientist Karen Folger were granted special permission to live for over one month in Ward 81, a women's security ward whose inmates were dangerous either to themselves or others. Seen through photography (published in book form), the cruel existence of these deranged women is both compelling and very real.

It is hoped that Mary Ellen Mark will continue to travel the world with her Leica, producing the type of picture for which she is already well-known. We can only hope, too, that she continues to document our world, thereby telling us something of its scope and meaning through photography.

—Nancy Hall-Duncan

MARON, Knut Wolfgang.

Nationality: German. **Born:** Bonn on 29 December 1954. **Education:** Took an apprenticeship at Fotografschule bei Sachsse, Bonn; studied art at Glasfachschule, Rheinbach; graduated with a diploma in visual communication from Folkwang School in Essen in 1983. **Career:** Founding Member, Trans European Arts Society, 1990. Professor for Experimental Photography at Heiligendamm, 1994. **Recipient:** Grants from Deutsch-Französischen Jugendwerk für Bildende Kunst, Frankreich, 1985; Cite Internationale des Arts, Paris, 1985/86; CIRCA und des Französischen Kultusministeriums, 1989; Bildende Kunst des Kunstmuseums Bonn Stadt, 1989; the Leopold Godowsky Jr. Color Photography Award, 1992. **Agent:** Galerie Bouqueret and Lebon, Paris. **Address:** Hoelderlinstr 21, D-45147 Essen, Germany

Individual Exhibitions:

1981	Museum Folkwang (with Michael Strauss), Essen, Germany
1983	Raum Antrazit, Essen, Germany
	Gesamthochschule, Essen, Germany
1986	Cité Internationale des Arts, Paris
1986	Galerie Jean-Pierre Lambert
1987	Galerie DB-S, Antwerp, Belgium
1990	Galerie Siemandel-Feldmann, Essen, Germany
	Galerie DB-S, Antwerp, Belgium
	C.I.A.L. Strasbourg, France
1991	Stadtmuseum Siegburg, Germany
1992	Galerie Bouqueret and Lebon, Paris
1993	Galerie DB-S, Antwerp, Belgium
	Centre d'Art Contemporain, Quimper, France
1995	École des Beaux Arts, Metz, France
	Kunsthalle, Kühlungsborn, Germany

Selected Group Exhibitions:

1981-82	*Ruhrgebiet,* Stadtmuseum, Düsseldorf (travelled to Städtisches Museum, Mülheim; Museum Folkwang, Essen)
1982	*Junge Deutsche Fotografen,* Graz (travelled to Munich, Germany & Vienna)
	Galerie Kicken, Cologne
1985-86	Junge Europäische Fotografen '85, Frankfurter Kunstverein, Germany
1987	*Les Immagiques,* Musée de Vasarely, Aix en Provence, France
1988	*Le Corps Figuré,* Musée de Roanne, Musée de Saint Etienne, France
	Internationale Triennale der Fotografie, Fribourg, Germany
1989	*Junge Europäische Fotografen '89*
	Museum Ludwig, Cologne
	Forum Böttcherstrasse, Bremen (travelled to the Kunstmuseum, Bonn; Städtisches Museum, Mülheim, Germany)
1990	*Junge Europäische Fotografen '90,* Frankfurter Kunstverein, Germany
	CIRCA, Le Chartreuse, Villeneuve les Avignon, France

Esterel, **1988 (original in colour).** Photograph by Knut Maron.

1991   *Surgence,* Comédie de Reims (travelled to Museé Sainte Croix,
        Poitiers; Museé de Beaux Arts, Rennes; Museé d'Evreux,
        France)
        Zweiter deustcher Photopreis, Stuttgart, Germany
1992   *Surgence,* Zeitgenössische Deutsche Fotografie, Potsdam,
        Germany
        Kunst nach 1945 Fotografie, Kornelimünster/Aachen Manege,
        St Petersburg, Russia
        Rencontre Internationale de la Photo, Arles, France
        Ils collectionnent la Photographie, Bouqueret and Lebon, Paris
1993   International Center of Photography, Boston
        Potsdam-Bonn, Künstlerforum, Bonn (travelled to Staudenhof
        Galerie, Potsdam), Germany
        Werkbund, Frankfurt
1994   *Light Touches,* Calais, France

Collections:

Museum Ludwig, Cologne; Museum Folkwang, Essen; Staatsgalerie, Stuttgart
(Sammlung LGK); Deutsche Leasing Collection, Bad Homburg v.d.H.;
Stadtsparkasse Pforzheim (Foto-Kunst); Kunst nach 1945, NRW,
Kultusministerium; Bundesjustizministerium, Bonn; Bibliothèque Nationale,
Paris; Stadt Museum Sieburg; Stadt Paris, Paris Audiovisuell; Fonds Regional
d'Art Contemporain, Metz, Lorraine; Fonds Regionale d'Art Contemporain,
Rhône-Alpes.

Publications:

By MARON: Book—*Bilder über Landschaften,* Sieburg, Germany

On MARON: Article—Kenneth White in *Creative Camera,* London.

*   *   *

It is common but misleading, to map contemporary German photography
using two "schools" that represent conflicting tendencies in European
photographic Modernism. The Staatliche Kunstakademie, Dusseldorf, under
the Bechers is sometimes discussed as if it were a satellite of Die Neue
Sachlichkeit (Now Objectivity), the pre-war German straight aesthetic.

Meanwhile the Essen Universitäat/Gesamthochschule is considered to be the
flagship of *Subjektive Fotografie*—Otto Steinert's catch-all term to describe
the hotch potch of styles that were marginalised in Europe and the US by
orthodox Modernism. In the 1950s *Subjektive Fotografie* acquired a popularity and moral authority when *Die Neue Sachlichkeit* became tainted through an
association with Nazism. In the late 1970s Knut Maron attended the Universitaat/
Gesamthochschule under the personal tutelage of Steinert, within a few years
of two other important Essen based photographers, Volker Heinze and
Gosbert Adler. His highly subjective style and romantic sensibility seem to
typify Steinert's definition of *Subjektive Fotografie* as a "humanised and
individualised photography."

Maron's training prepared him for a career in applied photography and
immediately after leaving college he started work as a photojournalist. For a
short time this gave him privileged access to cultures and places that were to
shape his ethos and his art. After becoming dissatisfied with the limitations of
reportage, Maron turned from the media to the art world, trading in off-the-
shelf humanism for the ecopolitics of his artistic mentor Joseph Beuys. Since
the late 1980s he has evolved a working method that synthesises the activities
of a photographer, cataloguer and shaman. Each image is an enlarged fragment
of a single Polaroid taken from a personal archive of thousands. Maron
photographs at symbolic places, sacred sites, pagan and Christian settlements,
magnetic rocks, magic circles and pyramids. He is fascinated by androgynes,
wizards, actual or quasi-scientific phenomena. Like Bueys he employs a
symbolic language, suffusing impressionistic representations of symbolic
objects with intense colours that evoke dream-like or drug-induced states. His
post visualisation process relies on chance interventions and intuition, recalling those early surrealist experiments in transcending consciousness. Images
materialise from the darkroom and are pinned up to be considered for days or
weeks before any decisions are made.

Titles identify most of the pictures to be representations of landscapes,
though image quality is deliberately vague making these landscapes appear to
be refracted through a cheap kaledioscope. Maron understands the importance
of context to the realisation of his work and insists on participating in every
stage of a planned catalogue or installation. Prints are usually large scale,
demanding that the viewer accommodate the artist by finding an ideal viewing
distance. Viewers are then invited to reconstitute these sketchy images to their
own requirements.

While Maron's images offer much space for the viewer, a deeply personal,
deeply moral conviction gives the work purpose and direction. Beuys is one of
the most important influences on him (a regular place of pilgrimage is the
Beuys archive in the Hessisches Landesmuseum at Damstadt) though Maron
confesses to be suspicious of the very German phenomenon of the artist's
personality cult. Such processes, whereby one image suggests another or
pictures transform from vague registers of light into meaningful images in the
mind, are analagous to alchemy. Maron also pursues sources of natural or
mystic energy. The transformation of matter into energy is, of course, a motif
in Beuys' work. His work incorporates raw substances that produce energy
(fat, wax, honey, copper) as part of a universe of symbols rendering his work a
metaphor for art as a sustaining medium.

In a recent faxed message Maron explained that he feels that his work
represents an attitude towards the world "based on respect" and concerned
with "loss." The fax included a small image of an elephant that Maron
described as a "projection of loss." Maron belongs to a lineage of German
Romantics which also includes Beuys. He is an extreme romantic and an
optimist who believes in the healing power of art and its potential to reconcile
culture with nature.

—David Brittain

MARTINČEK, Martin.

Nationality: Slovak. **Born:** Liptovský Peter, Slovakia, 30 January 1913.
Education: Studied law at Komenský University, Bratislava, 1932-37, J.D.
1937; self-taught in photography. **Family:** Married the painter Ester Šimerová
in 1946. **Career:** Judge, then State Attorney, Bratislava, 1937-51; Lawyer,
Komunále služby, in Liptovský Mikuláš, 1951-57, and Director of the

Museum of Literature and History, Liptovský Mikuláš, 1957-61. Professional photographer, Liptovský Mikuláš, and Member of the Slovak Union of Artists, Bratislava, since 1961. **Recipient:** First Prize, Tourist Photography Competition, Union of Czech Tourists, 1957; Gold Medal, Musée des Nations, Neuchatel, Switzerland, 1958; Grand Prize, Portrait in Photographic Art Competition, Fenykepesz szovetseg, Budapest, 1959; Silver Medal, *Bienal de Sao Paulo*, 1965; Silver Medal, *International Book Exhibition*, Leipzig, 1965; Artist of Merit Award, from the Czechoslovak Government, 1970; Award of Excellence, Fédération Internationale de l'Art Photographique (FIAP), 1970; Most Beautiful Book of the Year Award, National Literary Art Memorial, Prague, and Slovak Center of Culture, Bratislava, 1970, 1973, 1976, 1979; Memorial Medal, Union of Slovak Artists, 1971; Gold Medal, Association of Czech Photographers, 1983; Gold Medal, Association of Slovak Photographers, 1983; 2 Commemorative Medals, Regional Institute of Liptov, Czechoslovakia, 1983. **Address:** Kukučinova 9, Liptovský Mikuláš, Slovakia.

Individual Exhibitions:

1962	Museum of Literature, Liptovský Mikuláš, Czech Republic
1963	*The Structure of Wood and Water*, Laterna Magica, Prague
	Dum pánu z Kunštátu, Brno, Czechoslovakia
1967	Slovak National Gallery, Bratislava
1968	Municipal Gallery, Prague (in cooperation with the National Gallery, Prague, and the Slovak National Gallery, Bratislava)
	Cultural Center, Budapest (travelled to Sofia, East Berlin, Havana, and Cairo)
1969	*Cycles,* Dum pánu z Kunštátu, Brno, Czechoslovakia (travelled to the Municipal Gallery, Gottwaldov, Czechoslovakia)
	Gallery P.M. Bohúňa, Liptovský Mikuláš, Czechoslovakia
1970	Cultural Center, Baghdad
1973	Interkamera, Prague
1975	Ministry of Foreign Affairs Exhibition, Prague (toured Western Europe and Japan)
1978	*Mountains and Brooks,* Municipal Gallery, Bratislava (travelled to the Municipal Gallery, Prague, 1979)
1981	Czech Pavilion, *Bienal de Sao Paulo*, Brazil
1983	Gallery of Plastic Arts, Banska Bystrica, Czechoslovakia
	Gallery of Plastic Arts, Liptovsky Mikulas, Czechoslovakia
1984	Czech Pavilion, *Biennale*, Venice
1985	Fotogalerie Wien, Vienna (with Magda Robinsonová)
1986	National Gallery, Prague
1988	Municipal Gallery, Pálffy Palace, Bratislava, Czech Republic
1989	House of Art, Bratislava, Czech Republic
	Mikoláš Aleš Gallery of South Bohemia, Hluboká nad Vltavou, Czech Republic
1990	Gallery of Central Slovakia, Banská Bystrica, Czech Republic (with Askold Žáček)
	Gallery of District Kysuce, Oščadnica, Czech Republic (with Askold Žáček)
1991	Novohradská Gallery, Lučenec, Czech Republic (with Askold Žáček)
	Gallery of Artists of Spiš District, Spišská Nová Ves, Czechoslovakia
1993	P M Bohúň Gallery, Liptovský Mikuláš, Slovakia
	M A Bazovský Gallery, Trenčín, Slovakia
	Gallery Studio PKN, Warsaw
	Pusta Gallery, Katowice, Poland
1994	Slovak Embassy, Sofia
	Civic Centre, Annecy, France

Selected Group Exhibitions:

1967	*International Exhibition of Photography*, at *Expo '67*, Montreal
	Photography in the Fine Arts, Metropolitan Museum, New York
1968	*Europa '68*, Bergamo, Italy
1969	*Současna Československa fotografie*, Contemporary Czechoslovak Gallery, Moravian Gallery, Brno, Czechoslovakia
1970	*Czech Graphics and Photography*, Mexico City

1971	*Československa fotografie 1968/70*, Morvian Gallery, Brno, Czechoslovakia
1973	*Lirismo della fotografia cecoslovacca*, at *SICOF 73*, Milan
1975	*Lyrismus in der tschechoslowakischen Fotografie der Gegenwart*, Museum der Stadt, Freiburg im Breisgau, West Germany
1977	*Weltausstellung der Photographie: Kinder dieser Welt,* touring exhibition
1979	*Tschechoslowakische Fotografie 1918-78,* Fotoforum der Gesamthochschule, Kassel, West Germany
1986	*Personalities of Czechoslovak Social Documentary Photography,* Gallery F, Banská Bystrica, Czechoslovakia (travelled to Brno)
1989	*Meeting 01,* Gallery of the Union of Fine Artists, Bratislava, Czech Republic
	Czechoslovak Photography 1945-1989, Gallery Valdštejnská jízdárna, Prague
	Roads of Czechoslovak Photography, Municipal Gallery, Prague
	150 Photographs, Moravian Gallery, Brno, Czech Republic
1990	*Slovak Photography of the 1960s*, House of Art, Bratislava, Czech Republic

Collections:

National Gallery, Prague; Moravian Gallery, Brno, Czech Republic; Slovak National Gallery, Bratislava, Slovakia; Municipal Gallery, Bratislava, Slovakia; Banská Bystrica, Slovakia; J M Bohúň Gallery, Liptovský Mikuláš, Slovakia; M A Bazovský Gallery, Trenčín, Slovakia; Tatranská Gallery, Poprad, Slovakia; Novohradská Gallery, Lučenec, Slovakia; Gallery of the Artists of Spiš District, Spišská Nová Ves, Slovakia.

Publications:

By MARTINČEK: Books—*The Undiscovered World*, Bratislava, 1964, English, French and German editions, Prague, 1964; *Respect is Your Due*, Banská Bystrica, Czechoslovakia, 1967; *People in the Mountains*, text by M Rúfus, Bratislava, 1969; *Lights in Waves*, text by A Plávka, Bratislava, 1969; *Cradle*, with text by M Rúfus, Martin, Czechoslovakia, 1972; *Hill People*, with text by A Matuška, Martin, Czechoslovakia; *Forest*, text by M Rúfus, Martin, Czechoslovakia, 1978; *Praise of Water*, Martin, Czechoslovakia 1981; *Song of Krivăň*, Martin, Czechoslovakia 1988.

On MARTINČEK: Books—*Licht und Schatten/Light and Shadow*, edited by Miloš Hrbas, Prague 1959; *Martin Martinček* by Zora Rampáková, Prague 1976; *Die Geschichte der Photographie im 20. Jahrhundert/Photography in the 20th Century* by Petr Tausk, Cologne 1977, London 1980; *Martinček* by Ludovìt Hlaváč, Martin, Czechoslovakia 1978; *Martin Martinček* by Karel Dvořák, Prague 1979; *Slovak Foto*, with text by Jaroslav Čiljan, Martin, Czechoslovakia 1980; *The Evolution of Czechoslovak Photography from 1918 to Today* by Petr Tausk, Prague 1986; *History of Photography*, by Ľudovít Hlaváč, Martin, Czechoslovakia,1987; *History of Slovak Photography*, by Ľudovít Hlaváč, Martin, Czechoslovakia,1989; *Roads of Czechoslovak Photography*, by Daniela Mrázková and Vladimír Remeš, Prague, 1989; *Slovak Photography of the 1990s*, exhibition catalogue by Václav Macek, Bratislava 1990. **Articles**—"Photographer of His Own Nation" by Vladimìr Remeš in *Fotografie 73* (Prague), no. 1, 1973; "Martin Martinček, Chronist seiner Heimat" by Karel Dvořák in *Fotografie* (Leipzig), no. 9, 1973; "Just Photography" by Ivan Kučma in *Nove Slovo* (Bratislava), 19 June 1975; "A Visit to the Atelier of M. Martinček" by M. Zábojnìková in *Tvorba* (Prague), no. 4, 1975; "Visit to the Atelier M. Martinček" by Ludovìt Hlaváč in *Ceskoslovenska Fotografie* (Prague), no. 12, 1976; "Martin Martinček" by Ludovìt Hlaváč in *Pyramida* (Bratislava), no. 4, 1979; "Tvůrčí podněty Martina Martinćeka" by Jiří Macků in *Československá fotografie*, Prague, No 5, 1983; "Dvě ohlédnutí za výstavou msanželů Martinćekových" by Jiří Pacek and Vladimír Remeš, in *Československá fotografie*, (Prague), No 1. 1987.

*

Liptov—the region in which I live and work—is a lovely place: high mountains with deep romantic brooks and forests. The people in our mountains, especially the older generation, are rich in personality; they possess a significant creative poetic power and an extraordinary vitality.

I have been inspired by talks, discussions, the fates and the activities of the hillside people of Liptov. Their life-style has a special order and a permanent ritual. These people are deeply unified with their mother country. From our mutual understanding came a friendship which taught me the way to show their life in my photo-books *Respect Is Your Due, Hill People,* and *Cradle.*

When the same peoples have remained in a certain region for hundreds and hundreds of years, always respecting everything given and allowed by the country—the relationship gives a special color to that country, and the special face of the country, with its fixed features, remains in the memory of generation after generation. In the symbiosis of landscape and people there appears a reciprocal formation: the land forms the people, and the people create the landscape.

The way of the photographer to photography is rather long. If the photographer feels love toward mankind in his blood, people understand it— particularly the hill people, who are not talkative, but remain withdrawn and suspicious. If someone is kept in their hearts for many years, he has proved himself a friend. I very well understand human pain and problems as a result of my previous profession as a judge, and I have learned to know and appreciate people who can overcome their problems and succeed.

I live in the mountains where, as the poem says, "from the children's spoon up to the altar, everything was made of wood, and death in the saddle was death under a falling tree...." I often think about the written and unwritten traditions of the deep Slovak mountains and their inhabitants. The result was the cycle of photographs *The Undiscovered World* in which I tried to discover the many thousands of faces of wood in which the world's history is written. Wood that has fallen in the mountains, smoothed and piled and chopped, as well as the wood left silent somewhere, undiscovered and beyond our notice.

After *The Undiscovered World* cycle of photos, I worked on a further publication, *Lights in Waves.* I tried to show the unknown face of the river, or just a tiny part of those phenomena appearing in waves/ripples of water for a millisecond before disappearing forever. I was fascinated by the features of chaotic waves.

When I had finished yet another cycle of photos, *Stones Are Alive,* I arrived at a well-known truth, that the landscape and its people are influenced mutually, and that natural structures like wood, stone, water, etc. affect everyday activities—building a house, getting dressed, using tools, making art—everything that involves the use of these materials. The structure of these materials gives the final touch to art. The structure of hillfields resembles the face of piled wood. The same structure is found even in textiles. The rich natural forms that are around us created our famous culture of lace production and inspire the mountain people in their poetic creation of dances and folk songs.

In my latest work I have returned again to the photography of nature, and the result has been the publications *Mountain* and *Praise of Water.* I purposely returned to well-known subjects because I hoped to discover what I still did not know.

To express some truth about my work, I should like to paraphrase the words of T.S. Eliot: "... In photography are many windows which are not magical and through which we do not see a rough and dangerous sea, but in spite of this fact, they are very good windows.... When we talk about our photographers we should not investigate so actively whether they are good or great; we should just consider whether they are authentic, and let the most important judge—time—decide."

—Martin Martinček

* * *

The photographic work of Martin Martinček can be divided into three autonomous parts, differing from each other not only through choice of subjects but also in their approach to reality.

The first is dedicated to the Slovakian landscape and to the old people living in small villages there. In these works Martinček has celebrated in his own way the ancient traditions and spirit of the Liptov district where he was born, a part of Slovakia typical of the whole with its mountains and woods full of nature's beauty. If the driving force of these images is Martinček's sincere love of his native land, it is not surprising that the results tend to a highly emotional interpretation of reality; the very choice of subject, under such circumstances, obviously involves a certain romanticism. For the visualization of his feelings, Martinček has called on all of his photographic skills, yet the images produced are not overwrought but notable for their simplicity and directness.

The second part of this work has to do with his discovery of metaphors on the surfaces of various modest objects. A typical cycle of such images is of textures found on pieces of wood, fantastic forms that resemble human figures and animals. Another series of images suggests the features of a variety of objects found in the patterns formed by the play of light and shadow on the surfaces of mountain brooks. Another is of the surprising configurations on stones which he came across during his long walks in the hills: the integral effect of these images comprises both contour and surface texture. In all of these works, Martinček could be said to have produced his own variation of the surrealist principle of the *objet trouvé*.

The third and most recent set of Martinček's images is based on his current colour work. His first colour photographs of landscapes appeared as a small supplement to the main body of monochrome images in his 1975 book *Hill People.* These few examples were convincing evidence of Martinček's powerful gift for enclosing his vision of the world in fine and hazy hues of a highly cultivated form. His sensitivity to the lives of the hill people was echoed by *Praise of Water,* an all-colour volume on mountain landscapes and streams published in 1981.

In the early 1980s Martinček created three magnificent series in colour. "The Day Coming into Blossom" is composed of brilliant-hued images of flowers—those registered with a breathtaking still-life clarity contrasting against soft, diffuse forms of blossom in movement. The series "Secrets of the Wood," photographed in the vicinity of his home town, follows the destinies of ancient trees as they die and crumble into the earth from whence they grew. Martinček's mastery of camera and colour film gives these photos a truly poetic fascination. Whereas much of his early work signalled an interest in metaphor, his last series, "Praise of Sun," invites no ambiguity or comparative interpretation. The sun, revealed as a total image reflected on still waters, furnishes the earth with light and thermal energy. The viewer is directly confronted by Martinček's vision of wonder and gratitude for nature itself.

—Petr Tausk

MATHYS, Max (Eugen).

Nationality: Swiss. **Born:** Berne, 6 August 1933. **Education:** Attended primary and elementary schools in Alchenstorf/Berne, 1940-49, and public school in Berne, 1950; served apprenticeship as housepainter, 1950-53; studied graphic design, under Armin Hofmann, at the Allgemeine Gewerbeschule, Basle, 1955-60; mainly self-taught in photography. **Military Service:** Served in the Swiss Militia, 1953-83. **Family:** Married Elisabeth Singeisen in 1971; children: Lukas, Johanna, and Samuel. **Career:** Worked as a housepainter, 1950-53; Designer, under Fridolin Muller, Erwin Halpern advertising agency, Zurich, 1960-63. Freelance photographer, Berne, since 1963. Instructor in Photography, Kunstgewerbeschule, Basle, since 1967. **Recipient:** National Stipendium for Photography, Switzerland, 1962, 1966, 1967; Poster of the Year Award, with Armin Hofmann, Switzerland, 1963, 1965, 1967; *Nature '68* Calendar Award, Germany, 1968; Graphic Design Prize, *Deutsche Drucker* and *Graphic Design Germany* magazines, 1967-68. **Address:** Hauptstrasse 17, 4132 Muttenz bei Basel, Switzerland.

Individual Exhibitions:

1967   *Abstract Landscape,* Galerie Leiser Wolpe, Zurich
1969   *Nature's Structure,* Photogallery, New York
1973   *Zeit: Raum,* Josephshaus Kollegium, Schwyz, Switzerland
1975   *2 Landschaften: Emmental und Toscana,* Paulus-Akademie, Zurich
1978   *Stein und Landschaften,* Zumstein Gallery, Berne

1979   *Stein und Landschaften,* Leitz Gallery, Wetzlar, West Germany
1980   *Feldkulturen,* Kulturmühle Gallery, Lützelflüh, Switzerland
1985   *Fotografien,* Galerie Ars Mittenza, Muttenz, Switzerland

Selected Group Exhibitions:

1964   *Leica: Photos from the World,* Leica School of Berlin
1967   *15 Graphic Designers of the Gewerbeschule,* Gewerbemuseum, Basle (toured Boston, Philadelphia, Kansas City, and Chicago)
1970   *Biennale de la Photographie Internationale,* Paris
        Creative Photography, Galerie Impact, Lausanne
1974   *Photography in Switzerland from 1840 to Today,* Kunsthaus, Zurich
1975   *The Land: 20th Century Landscape Photographs Selected by Bill Brandt,* Victoria and Albert Museum, London (toured the United Kingdom)
        Triennale de Photographie, Fribourg
1978   *International Photography Salon,* Tokyo
1982   *18. Kantonale Basellandschaftliche Kunstausstellung,* Muttenz, Switzerland
1984   *Swiss Photography from 1840 until Today,* Pro Helvetia Foundation, Zurich (and world tour)

Collections:

University of Cologne; Kunsthaus, Zurich.

Publications:

By MATHYS: Books—*Nature '68,* calendar, Stuttgart 1967; *Zauber des Flusses,* with text by Max A. Wyss, Lucerne and Frankfurt 1970; *Sky '75,* calendar, Stuttgart 1974; *Four Seasons,* Swissair brochure, Zurich 1975; *Zuruck zur Natur,* with text by Max A. Wyss, Lucerne 1976. **Articles**—"The Stones of a River," with Armin Hofmann, in *Camera* (Lucerne), no. 3, 1967; "Water and Stones" in *Gebrauchsgraphik* (Munich), July 1968; "From Week to Week" in *Du* (Zurich), October 1971.

On MATHYS: Books—*Photography in Switzerland from 1840 to Today,* exhibition catalogue, by Manuel Gasser, Hugo Loetscher, Walter Binder and Rosellina Burri-Bischof, Zurich 1974; *The Land: 20th Century Landscape Photographs Selected by Bill Brandt,* exhibition catalogue, edited by Mark Haworth-Booth, London 1975.

*

My working aims: to show the difference of structures, the colour and composition of places throughout the world, beginning with Switzerland—then Italy—Germany—and so on.
To photograph the moods of the sky at different times and seasons.
To use the camera as an artist does his brush.
To open people's eyes to details they often miss and to reveal Nature's many-sided face—the things that move me.
To reach perfection in my technique—at least the nearest possible to it.

—Max Mathys

*   *   *

Max Mathys came to the fore in the 1960s with a new and individual approach to the concept of landscape photography. He turned towards it with a natural inclination and a rare exclusiveness, becoming, in the two decades of his work, one of the most prominent landscape photographers. Of his own accord he has said: "I make use of my camera as a painter wields his brush." And: "I try to show the difference in structure and colour composition of the most differing places in this world." Indeed we discover in Max Mathys that which, in a painter, we would consider an outstanding quality: the individual touch. These photographs are the result of an artistic perception which has

remained constant for 20 years. Mathys' approach to his pictures stems from a visionary view of landscape which gives an astonishing unity to his work.

Max Mathys is no romantic landscape photographer identifying himself with an all-enveloping experience of nature. He observes composition and colour from a distance and with an unerring eye. He dissolves landscape into structures. It is divided into geometric fields, spreading out like a carpet, flat, without beginning, without end. The eye of the beholder enlarges it, pursues its geometric pattern. One never discovers depth of field, shortenings of perspective. The experience of geometric abstract painting lies behind these photographs.

Colours are used as softly as in many Paul Klee water colours. In his strong attachment to the laws of colour and form there is evidence of the sound artistic education which preceded Mathys' professional life as a photographer. Here is a photographer in search of principles of order in form. Colour is here the starting point of seeing. It is the more substantial element of the composition, without trimmings.

Much is spoken about "form" in photography. Max Mathys shows it. It remains amazing that these landscape compositions do not seem to copy what is actually there—although the camera of course only copies. But Mathys knows how to reveal nature's abstract values. Even in a series of photographs in the Verzasca Valley, in which he follows the river's course, this vision remains preserved in abstract—or should one say absolute—forms. Large is different from small and smaller, from hard and flowing.

And there is something else which is very remarkable in this photographic work: the preoccupation with time. "A Little Landscape Photographed During the Course of a Year" is one of the first substantial works of this unconventional photographer. He photographed the same view for a year. A cycle on the seasons resulted—demonstrated by a single tiny piece of earth. Such work requires patience, perseverance, a feeling for the flow of time. He has also photographed a violent storm. Every two minutes. The storm momentarily alters the landscape. In all the sequences that Max Mathys has produced of a landscape the subject is not only the landscape but also always time.

His work makes one think involuntarily of the cloud studies, the "equivalents," which Alfred Stieglitz produced over the years. Max Mathys is the first photographer after Stieglitz to treat this theme. But with Mathys it belongs to the concept of his photographic vision. He is one of the first photographers to use the sequence as an artistic means. In so doing he placed himself at the beginning of a photographic development which governed the 70s and which, as conceptual photography, started a new chapter in the history of photography.

—Erika Billeter

MATTHEWS, Jennifer.

Nationality: British. **Born:** Plymouth, 1 October 1948. **Education:** Studied at the University of Sussex, 1967-71; largely self-taught in photography, though took City & Guilds examination. **Agent:** Network Photographers, 3/4 Kirby Street, London EC1N 8TS, England. **Address:** 10 St. Philip's Road, London E8 3BP, England.

Individual Exhibitions:

1986   *In the Company of Women,* Impressions Gallery, York (travelled to the Side Gallery, Newcastle; ICA, London; Watershed, Bristol; Plymouth Arts Centre)
1989   *Nambia—Birth of a Nation,* Africa Centre, London
1991   *Brazilian Street Girls,* Guildhall University, London

Selected Group Exhibitions:

1993   *Positive Lives—Responses to HIV,* Photographers' Gallery, London

East London, South Africa, **1992.** Photograph by Jenny Matthews.

Publications:

By MATTHEWS: Books—*Nambia—Birth of a Nation* (with Glenys Kinnock); *Eritrea—Images of War and Peace* (with Glenys Kinnock), London. **Television**—"State of Emergency" for *Bandung File*, Channel 4, 1986; *Moving Stills*, Channel 4, 1989.

*

I am interested in social and political change and the part that photography can play in that. Photographs may not radically effect history but they do play a part in our cultural and social memory and I hope my work will stand as a document of what has happened in certain parts of the world—particularly Africa and Latin America—in the 1980s and 1990s.

—Jennifer Matthews

*　　*　　*

Jenny Matthews is a photographer who wastes nothing of her wealth of previous professional experience. Having read Modern European Studies at Sussex University—"a course so wide you studied film as part of literature"—Jenny Matthews proceeded to art college and 16mm film-making. This, at the turn of the 1970s was the period of the boom in Latin American literature and revolutionary student politics modelled roughly on the lines of the exhortations on the ubiquitous Che Guevera posters. Grafting ideas of Brazilian *cinema novo* onto her own desire for flexibility and "open endings—

and beginnings," Jenny also rapidly "learnt a lot of practical things about handling budgets and working with others."

Again, a certain desire for a practical input turned Jenny away from the "community projects" that were the order of the day at the National Film School, and towards teaching French and Spanish at an innner city secondary modern school. "Those four years of hell taught me that if you can cope with classes of adolescent girls you can take anything." For the twenty years since then Jenny Matthews has been firmly moving away from working in teams (still less in classes) and in the direction of meeting challenges for which her baptism of fire can scarcely have prepared her.

The photographic training she got through City and Guilds evening classes, working out of Paddington Community Darkrooms. That in human relations and organisation, together with familiarity in working in other languages, she obtained from maintaining her work teaching, increasingly also in passing on her newly acquired photographic skills. Still in the 1970s, Jenny became involved in setting up *Camerawork,* one of the first community darkrooms/magazines/gallery spaces, in the East End of London. There it was easy to dissipate energy by focussing on the communal at the expense of personal work, but there was an optimism in collective action at variance with the present bleak economic situation for such ventures.

Project and political work merged through such events as the women's occupation of Greenham Common in protest at the U.S. Cruise missiles based there; in the Peace Movement generally, both in its opposition to nuclear war and the Falklands conflict; and throughout the miners' strikes of the 1980s. "Photography was a way of feeling strongly about things, feeling strongly about the world . . . a way too, of being politically engaged." At the same time anxious "not to be too altruistic, photography is also a very enjoyable way of earning a living."

Also at the start of the 1980s, Jenny Matthews decided to leave teaching and for the first of many times, go to Latin America. In establishing what would soon become a pattern, she obtained commisssions from a cross section of aid agencies, specialist magazines and national newspapers to go to Bolivia. As the news accent shifted towards Central America, so did Jenny Matthews' work, finding expression in features, books and exhibitions particularly related to the daily life in the war zones.

Jennny's commitment to feminism also led to a considerable period of work for the Greater London Council's Women's Committee (until the abolition of the GLC in 1986) and to her involvement in Format Photographers, founded in 1983 and still the only all woman photographic agency in the world. She joined from the start partly from a reluctance to be ghettoised within what she felt was a male dominated macho field of reportage photography "in which you were expected to aggressively track down the World Press Photography prize that would incorporate you into the star system." Paradoxically, of course, any specific field can swiftly become its own ghetto and ten years later, Jenny found it necessay to move on from Format to join Network, one of the major photojournalism agencies in Britain.

In pursuing her quest beyond the ghetto to beyond any form of definitive categorisation, Jenny Matthews has also begun experimenting with her working methods. Known principally for her work across Latin America and Africa, especially that around issues connected with disease (particularly those AIDS-related) and refugees ("women and conflict" being another of her ongoing personal projects), she concludes: "You have to be flexible as world events move on around you. There are only two ways of working; either you commit yourself to a specific issue or region or you take a bit of everything." That "bit of everything" now includes taking her twinned concerns of AIDS-infected children in a Rwandan refugee camp and transforming them from a reportage feature to highly individuated gum biochromate portraits that formed part of a Network travelling exhibition on HIV called *Positive Lives*.

This new way of working is intended to distance herself both from some of the acute pain of immediate involvement in the job of recording, and from the constant pressure that comes with knowing you're only as good as your last job. It goes with the desire not only to follow the interests of the market whether commercially or charitably led, but to create a radically different approach. As she said of her original decision to take up photography; "Through it you can link into a means of expression, whether you're going into a local factory, a new political situation, a country across the world . . . I like the possibility of just getting up and going off and doing it. You're rarely lonely; as long as you're photographing people, there's always someone there with you. When it works it's magic!.''

—Amanda Hopkinson

MATTER, Herbert.

Nationality: Swiss. **Born:** Engelberg, Switzerland, in 1907; emigrated to the United States, 1936. **Education:** Studied painting in Geneva, 1925-27, and painting and drawing at the Academie Moderne, Paris, 1928-29; self-taught in photography. **Family:** Married to Mercedes Matter; son: Alex. **Career:** Photographer since 1929: freelance designer and photographer, working with the poster artist A.M. Cassandre and the architect Le Corbusier, and for Deberny et Peignot design company, Paris, 1929-32; designer of photomontage posters for the Swiss National Tourist Office, Zurich, 1932-36; freelance photographer, working for *Harper's Bazaar, Vogue*, etc., New York, 1936-46; Staff Photographer, Condé Nast Publications, New York, 1946-57. Freelance designer and photographer, New York, 1958 until his death in 1984. Designer, Swiss Pavilion and Corning Glass Pavilion, *World's Fair*, New York, 1939; Design and Advertising Consultant, Knoll International, New York, 1946-66; Design Consultant, New Haven Railroad, 1954-55; Design Adviser, Guggenheim Museum, New York, and Museum of Fine Arts, Houston, 1958-68; Graphics Consultant, New York Studio School, 1964-78. Professor of Photography, Yale University, New Haven, Connecticut, 1958-82. **Died:** (in Southampton, New York) 8 May 1984.

Individual Exhibitions:

1943	Pierre Matisse Gallery, New York (travelled to the Arts Club, Chicago, and the Los Angeles County Museum of Art)
1962	American Institute of Graphic Arts, New York
1978	Yale University, New Haven, Connecticut (retrospective)
	Kunsthaus, Zurich
1979	*Selected Photographs 1929-1979*, Marlborough Gallery, New York

Selected Group Exhibitions:

1932	*Die neue Fotografie in der Schweiz*, Schweizerische Werkbund, St. Gallen, Switzerland (travelled to Berne, Aarau, Lausanne, La Chaux de Fonds, Basle and Zurich, 1932-33)
1969	*Die Fotomontage*, Stadttheater, Ingolstadt, West Germany
1972	*Knoll au Musée*, Musée des Arts Décoratifs, Paris
1979	*Photographie als Kunst 1879-1979*, Tiroler Landesmuseum Ferdinandeum, Innsbruck, Austria (travelled to the Neue Galerie am Wolfgang Gurlitt Museum, Linz, Austria; Neue Galerie am Landesmuseum Joanneum, Graz, Austria; and Museum des 20. Jahrhunderts, Vienna)
1982	*Color as Form*, International Museum of Photography at George Eastman House, Rochester, New York
1984	*Swiss Photography from 1840 until Today*, Pro Helvetia Foundation, Zurich (and world tour)

Collections:

Kunstgewerbemuseum, Zurich; Musée des Arts Décoratifs, Paris; Condé Nast Publications, New York; International Museum of Photography, George Eastman House, Rochester, New York.

Publications:

By MATTER: Book—*13 Photographs: Alberto Giacometti and Sculpture*, portfolio, with Ives-Sillman, New York 1978. **Film**—*The Works of Calder*, 1949.

On MATTER: Books—*Die neue Fotografie in der Schweiz*, exhibition catalogue, by George Schmidt and Peter Meyer, Zurich 1932; *U.S. Camera 1936*, annual, edited by Tom J. Maloney, New York and London 1936; *Herbert Matter: Photographs*, exhibition brochure, with text by James Johnson Sweeney, New York 1943; *Die Fotomontage: Geschichte und Wesen einer Kunstform*, exhibition catalogue, by Richard Hiepe, Ingolstadt, West Germany 1969; *Knoll au Musée*, exhibition catalogue, by Christian Rae, Paris 1972; *Photographie als Kunst 1879-1979/Kunst als Photographie 1949-1979*, exhibition catalogue, 2 vols., by Peter Weiermair, Innsbruck, Austria 1979; *The Vogue Book of Fashion Photography* by Polly Devlin, with an introduction by Alexander Liberman, London 1979; *Neue Sachlichkeit und Surrealismus in der Schweiz 1915-1940*, edited by Rudolf Koella, Berne 1979; *Color as Form: A History of Color Photography*, exhibition catalogue, with introduction by Robert A. Sobieszek, Rochester, New York 1982; *Swiss Photography from 1840 until Today*, exhibition catalogue, with introduction by Hugo Loetscher, Zurich 1984. **Articles**—"Herbert Matter" by V. Borel in *Gebrauchsgraphik* (Berlin), January 1936; "Display Presentations for Architects and Other Designers" in *Architectural Record* (New York), January 1938; "Herbert Matter" in *Arts and Architecture* (Los Angeles), May 1944; "Modern Photography" by Hans Felix Kraus in *TriColor* (New York), June 1945; "Herbert Matter at Work" in *Arts and Architecture* (Los Angeles), March 1953; "Herbert Matter: Designer and Photographer" by E.M. Ettenberg in *American Artist* (New York), March 1956; "Designs that Matter to Matter" in *Print* (New York), March 1962; "Retrospective: Herbert Matter" by Armin Hoffmann in *Graphics* (Zurich), no. 212, 1980; "Herbert Matter" in *The Annual Obituary 1984*, edited by Margot Levy, Chicago and London 1985.

* * *

Herbert Matter was the very opposite of a photographic purist: he considered the photographic process open to experimentation at any point. His approach combined Swiss ingenuity and Swiss precision, revealed in his work's graphic impact, its sophisticated handling of line and form, and the unexpected uses to which he put familiar subject matter. Matter used photography as a bridge between art and industry, and consciously sought out clients who encouraged him to employ the full range of his imaginative capacity.

After training as an academic painter in his native Switzerland, Matter was awakened to the possibilities of modern art in Paris, where he studied under Ozenfant and Le Corbusier in the 1920s. Following the example of Man Ray and Moholy-Nagy, of whose work he was keenly aware, he taught himself photography, and began to employ the camera as an instrument of graphic design. Matter worked for a period in the Paris studio of Charles Peignot, publisher of the periodical *Arts et Metiers Graphiques,* in which some of his earliest photographs appeared. His work first attracted wide attention in the early 1930s, when he designed a series of striking posters combining photography, typography, and applied color in a fresh, light-hearted manner.

When he came to the United States in 1936, Matter at first found his brand of "graphic photography" not much in demand. However, he established himself in New York with the help of Alexey Brodovitch, the innovative art director of *Harper's Bazaar,* who hired him to take fashion photographs. Through the 1960s, Matter's work appeared regularly in the editorial and advertising pages of magazines such as *Vogue, Town and Country,* and *Harper's Bazaar.* His continuing interest in the application of photography to graphic design led him to devise new forms of exhibitions using photographs as the chief element. Matter designed the interior of the Swiss Pavilion at the 1939 New York *World's Fair* using giant photomurals, and later prepared a number of lively installations for Edward Steichen at the Museum of Modern Art.

—Christopher Phillips

MAYES, Elaine.

Nationality: American. **Born:** Berkeley, California, 1 October 1938. **Education:** Stanford University, California, 1955-59, B.A. 1959; San Francisco Art Institute, under Paul Hassel and John Collier, 1959-61; also attended summer photography workshops, under Minor White, 1962, 1963. **Family:** Married Bill Arnold in 1975 (divorced, 1980). **Career:** Photographer since 1960, and filmmaker since 1968. Worked as a freelance commercial photographer, for *Sports Illustrated, Saturday Evening Post, Esquire, Cycle Magazine, Washington Post,* etc., San Francisco, 1960-67; Assistant Professor, University of Minnesota, Minneapolis, 1968-70. Associate Professor of Film and Photography, Hampshire College, Amherst, Massachusetts, 1971-81; Part-Time Instructor, 1970, and Visiting Artist, 1976, 1979, San Francisco Art Institute; Associate Professor, Pratt Institute, Brooklyn, New York, 1979; Instructor, Cooper Union, New York, 1979; Instructor, International Center of Photography, New York, 1979-80; Instructor in film and photography, Bard College, Annandale-on-Hudson, New York, 1982-84; Instructor in photography, Tisch Tschool of the Arts, New York University, since 1984. **Recipient:** Federal Bureau of Public Roads Fellowship, California, 1966; National Endowment for the Arts Photography Fellowship, 1971, 1978; Production Grant, Royal Film Archives of Belgium, 1974; Creative Artists Public Service Grant, New York, 1982; Guggenheim Foundation, Photography Fellowship, 1991-92. **Agent:** Marcuse Pfeifer, 568 Broadway, Suite 102, New York, New York 10012. **Address:** 18 Mercer Street, New York, New York 10013, U.S.A.

Individual Exihibitions:

1969	*We Are the Haight-Ashbury,* Minneapolis Institute of Arts (travelled to Massachusetts Institute of Technology, Cambridge)
1970	*35 Recent Photographs,* San Francisco Art Institute
1972	*Autolandscapes and Rooms on the East Side of the Science Building,* Hampshire College, Amherst, Massachusetts
	Autolandscapes, Williams College, Williamstown, Massachusetts
1973	*Recent Photographs,* Gallery 115, Santa Cruz, California
	20 Photographs, Rhode Island School of Design, Providence
1974	*50 Photographs,* MFA Gallery, Rochester Institute of Technology, Rochester, New York
1975	*Elaine Mayes' Photographs,* Portland School of Art, Maine
	50 Photographs, Bennington College, Vermont
1976	*50 Photographs,* Pratt Institute, Brooklyn, New York
	2 Photographers: Bill Arnold and Elaine Mayes, Lightwork, Syracuse, New York (travelled to the San Francisco Art Institute)
1977	*50 Photographs,* Columbia Gallery of Photography, Missouri
	35 Photographs, Image Space, Cambridge, Massachusetts
1978	*Landscapes,* Marcuse Pfeifer Gallery, New York
1980	*Long Island Photographs,* Hampshire College, Amherst, Massachusetts
1981	*Color Photos,* Maggie Kress Gallery, Taos, New Mexico
1982	*Recent Work,* Sandra Berler Gallery, Chevy Chase, Maryland (and 1984, 1986)
1986	*Flora,* Barbara Giles, Bandon, Oregon
1987	*Things on the Ground,* Art Department Gallery, Northern Illinois University, Dekalb
1989	*Haight Vintage Prints,* Thorne's Third Floor Gallery, Northampton, Massachusetts
1990	Sandra Berler, Chevy Chase, Maryland
	The Atlantis Portfolio, Hampshire College Art Gallery
1992	*Hawaiian Landscapes,* Newton Art Center, Newtonville, Massachusetts; Rhode Island School of Design
1993	*Hawaiian Landscapes,* Interlochen Arts Center, Interlochen, Michigan
1994	*Western Landscapes,* Robert Burge, New York
1995	Sandra Berler, Chevy Chase, Maryland

Selected Group Exhibitions:

1970	*New Acquisitions,* Museum of Modern Art, New York
1971	*Photographs of Women,* Museum of Modern Art, New York
1973	*Landscape/Citycape,* Metropolitan Museum of Art, New York
1974	*8 x 10,* Dallas Museum of Art
1977	*Photography and the Landscape,* International Museum of Photography, George Eastman House, Rochester, New York
1978	*14 New England Photographers,* Museum of Fine Arts, Boston
1980	*The Long Island Project,* Hofstra University, Hempstead, Long Island, New York
1982	*American Photography Today,* University of Colorado, Denver
1984	*Exposed and Developed,* National Museum of American Art, Washington, D.C.
1985	*Photography over the 70s and 80s,* Lightwork, Syracuse, New York
1986	*Fifty Years of Color Photography,* Fotokina, Cologne, Germany
1987	*Photographs of Animals,* Photo Collect, New York
	No Trumpets, No Swans, Pratt Manhattan Gallery, New York
1988	*Garden Imagery in Contemporary Art,* Ft Wayne Museum of Art, Indiana
	City Work, Photographs of New York by Seven Photographers, New York Cultural Center, New York
1990	*American Photography Today,* Basel, Switzerland
1992	*The Country Between Us: Contemporary American Landscape Photographs,* Massachusetts College of Art, Huntington Gallery
1993	*The Cat in Photography,* The Katten Kabinett, Amsterdam
1994	*Town Grown, Town Shown,* Northampton, Massachusetts

Collections:

Museum of Modern Art, New York; Metropolitan Museum of Art, New York; International Museum of Photography, George Eastman House, Rochester, New York; Museum of Fine Arts, Boston; Fogg Art Museum, Harvard

Cane Field, Kekaha, Kauai, **1989 (original in colour).** Photograph ©Elaine Mayes.

University, Cambridge, Massachusetts; Minneapolis Institute of Art; Dallas Museum of Art; San Francisco Art Institute; Philadelphia Museum of Art, Pennsylvania; National Museum of American Art, Washington, D.C; The Dallas Museum of Fine Arts, Dallas, Texas; The Smith College Art Museum, Northampton, Massachusetts; The Class of 1928 Photography Collection, University of Massachusetts; The Denver Museum of Art, Denver, Colorado; The Corcoran Gallery of Art, Washington, D.C.; The Seattle Art Museum, Seattle, Washington; The Reader's Digest Collection, New York; The ITT Collection New York; The Getty Museum of Art, California; The Seagram's Collection, New York; The Santa Barbara Museum of Art, California.

Publications:

By MAYES: Books—*When I Dance,* Lafayette, California 1969; *Love Needs Care,* with text by John Luce and David Smith, Boston 1971; *The City,* with text by Alan Trachtenberg, New York 1971; *San Francisco Viewed,* San Francisco, 1987; *The Cat in Photography,* edited by Sally Eauclaire, 1990; *The Horse, A Photographic History,* edited by Gerald Lang, New York, 1990. **Article**—"Long Tonal Range" in *Darkroom,* edited by Eleanor Lewis, New York 1977. **Films**—*The Clouds,* with Jerome Liebling, 1969; *Fall,* 1972; *Hadley,* 1976; *Living in Hadley,* 1981; *Silver Lake Life, The View from Here,* 1993.

On MAYES: Books—*Darkroom,* edited by Jain Kelly, New York 1977; *Exposed and Developed: Photography Sponsored by the National Endowment for the Arts,* exhibition catalogue, with text by Merry Amanda Foresta, Washington, D.C. 1984. **Articles**—"Elaine Mayes" in *Art in America* (New York), January 1978; "Photography and the Landscape" by Julia Scully in *Modern Photography* (New York), February 1978; "The Wagstaff Collection" in *Horizon* (New York), February 1978; "Aspects of Some Contemporary American Photographers" by Jane Bordon in *Dumont Foto 1: Fotokunst und Fotodesign International,* Cologne 1979; "The Long Island Project" by Andy Grundberg in *Modern Photography* (New York), March 1979; "Color Photography" by Andy Grundberg in *Soho News* (New York), 21 May 1979.

*

I have been working with photographic mediums as art forms for thirty four years. My experience with these mediums leads me to feel they have symbolic, linguistic and historic functions, with creative and aesthetic potentials. Primarily my work has been in straight photography and in "finding" images in the world. Most of my efforts have focused on shooting images spontaneously and using the camera to record aspects of seeing. I also have been interested in a "documentary" approach. Living in mass culture and a world of mediated experiences leads me to believe that basic visual perception (seeing) and direct interaction with the physical world are crucial modes for awareness and human survival as well as for meaningful art endeavours.

—Elaine Mayes.

*   *   *

Although she was a student of painting while she attended the San Francisco Art Institute, Elaine Mayes had had her interest captured by photography by the time she completed her studies in 1961. For the next seven years she worked as a freelance commercial photographer. Her photographs appeared in such national publications as *The Saturday Evening Post, Sports Illustrated,* and *Esquire.* She photographed the Haight Asbury area of San Francisco, documenting the flower children of the late 1960s in a series of sensitive and direct black-and-white portraits. In 1968, when she was offered a position teaching photography at the University of Minnesota, she gave up her commercial work, and moved to Minneapolis. She has been teaching and making personal photographs ever since.

Mayes was appointed to the faculty of Hampshire College in 1971, where she became an associate professor of film and photography. She has made several films, including *The Clouds* (with Jerome Liebling), and *Fall,* an award-winning short film. Her images have been published in many photography magazines. A recipient of numerous grants, Mayes was one of the documentary photographers who worked on *The Long Island Project.*

Mayes considers herself a "straight" photographer. That is to say, she doesn't construct situations or manipulate images—she photographs what is there. In her personal work, this directness of technique both contradicts and contributes to an oblique and abstract quality in the images. At a Mobil station the flying horse sign beams through the mist with an extra-terrestrial glow. The car below it floats out of the dark like some great sea monster. This scenario is ordinary and recognizable, but certainly not familiar. Mayes' subjects are mundane and uneventful landscapes of our daily lives. What brings the images to life is the mystery of light and space conveyed. There is a tension in this mystery, which is in curious juxtaposition to the serenity in the wide range and even gradation of tones.

—Sarah Putnam

MAYNE, Roger.

Nationality: British. **Born:** Cambridge, 5 May 1929. **Education:** Attended the Rugby School, Warwickshire, 1942-47; studied chemistry at Balliol College, Oxford, 1947-51; self-taught in photography. **Family:** Married the playwright Ann Jellicoe in 1962; children: Katkin and Tom. **Career:** Freelance photographer, London, since 1954; moved to Dorset, 1975. Visiting Lecturer, Bath Academy of Art, Corsham, Wiltshire, 1966-69. **Recipient:** Photography Award, South West Arts Association, 1982. **Agent:** Zelda Cheatle Gallery, 8 Cecil Court, London WC2N 4HE, England. **Address:** Colway Manor, Lyme Regis, Dorset DT7 3HD, England.

Individual Exhibitions:

1956	Dryden Gallery, George Eastman House, Rochester, New York; Institute of Contemporary Arts, London
1959	A.I.A. Gallery, London
	Nova Huta, near Kracow, Poland (travelled to Warsaw, 1960)
1960	Royal Court Theatre Foyer, London
1962	*La Strada,* Biblioteca Communale, Milan
1965	Arnolfini Gallery, Bristol
1967	University of Sussex, Brighton
1972	*Daughter and Son,* Half Moon Gallery, London (travelled to the Arnolfini Gallery, Bristol, 1974; Galleria Il Diaframma, Milan, 1977)
1974	*Photographs 1964-73,* The Photographers' Gallery, London
1978	*Landscape Photographs,* Institute of Contemporary Arts, London (travelled to Dorset County Museum, Dorchester, and Plymouth Arts Centre, Devon, 1979; Newlyn Art Gallery, Penzance, Cornwall, 1980; and Parnham House, near Beaminster, Dorset, 1981)
1986	The Photographers' Gallery, London
	Victoria and Albert Museum, London (retrospective)
	Parco Stores, Tokyo
1987-90	*Roger Mayne, Street Photographs,* South Bank Centre (tour to 24 venues including Royal Festival Hall, London 1989)
1989	Prakapas Gallery, New York
1992	Zelda Cheatle Gallery, London

Selected Group Exhibitions:

1955	*Subjective Fotografie 2,* Saarbrucken
1959	*Photography at Mid-Century,* International Museum of Photography, George Eastman House, Rochester, New York
1960	*Fotografi della Nuova Generazione,* Galleria d'Arte Moderna, Milan
1963	*Photography '63,* International Museum of Photography, George Eastman House, Rochester, New York
1967	*Modern Photography,* Victoria and Albert Museum, London (toured England)
1978	*Art for Society,* Whitechapel Art Gallery, London
1979	*Documentary Photography,* Midland Group, Nottingham
1983	*British Photography 1955-65,* The Photographers' Gallery, London
1984	*Subjektive Fotografie: Images of the 50s,* San Francisco Museum of Modern Art (travelled to the University of Houston, Texas; Museum Folkwang, Essen; Vasterbottens Museum, Umea; Kulturhuset, Stockholm; Saarland Museum, Saarbrucken; Palais des Beaux-Arts, Brussels)
1985	*Human Interest,* Cornerhouse Gallery, Manchester, Lancashire
1989	*Through the Looking Glass,* British Photography 1945-89, Barbican Art Gallery, London
1993	*Three Masters Three Decades,* with Henri Cartier-Bresson and Helen Levitt.
	The Sixties—London Art Scene, Barbican Art Gallery, London
	Photographing Children, Scottish National Portrait Gallery, Edinburgh
	Magicians of Light, Photographs from the collection of the National Gallery of Canada, Ottawa
1994	*Street Photography,* Victoria and Albert Museum, London

Collections:

Department of the Environment, London; Victoria and Albert Museum, London; Bibliothèque Nationale, Paris; Museum of Modern Art, New York; International Museum of Photography, George Eastman House, Rochester, New York; Art Institute of Chicago; Los Angeles County Museum of Art; Museum Folkwang, Essen, West Germany; Fox Talbot Museum, Lacock, Wiltshire; Metropolitan Museum of Art, New York; Museum of Fine Art, Huston; New Orleans Museum of Art; Princeton University; National Gallery of Australia, Canberra; National Gallery of Victoria, Melbourne; National Gallery of Canada, Ottawa; National Portrait Gallery, London; Scottish National Portrait Gallery, Edinburgh; University of Parma, Italy.

Publications:

By MAYNE: Books—*Things Being Various,* London 1967; *Shell Guide to Devon,* with text by Ann Jellicoe, London 1975; *Roger Mayne: Landscape Photographs,* exhibition catalogue, Penzance, Cornwall 1980; *Street Photographs of Roger Mayne,* with text by Mark Haworth-Booth, London 1986, reprinted 1993, with revisions, by Zelda Cheatle Press, London. **Articles**—"Pictorialism at a Dead End" in *Amateur Photographer* (London), 24 October 1956; "Photography and Realism" in *Universities and Left Review* (London), Spring 1959; "Great Victorian Photographs" in *Creative Camera* (London), October 1972; "An Unfashionable Opinion" in *Camerawork* (London), no. 6, 1977.

On MAYNE: Books—*Akt International/International Nudes,* with introduction by Otto Steinert, Munich and London 1954; *Subjective Fotografie 2,* exhibition catalogue, Saarbrucken 1955; *Roger Mayne: Photographs 1964-73,* exhibition catalogue, with an introduction by David Piper, London 1974; *The Picture History of Photography* by Peter Pollack, New York 1977; *Geschichte der Photographie im 20. Jahrhundert/History of Photography in the 20th Century* by Petr Tausk, Cologne 1977, London 1980; *British Photography 1955-1965: The Master Craftsmen in Print,* exhibition catalogue, by Sue Davies, Michael Rand, Mark Boxer and others, London 1983; *Subjektive Fotografie: Images of the 50s,* exhibition catalogue, by Ute Eskildsen, Manfred Schmalriede and Dorothy Martinson, Essen, West Germany 1984. **Articles**—"Poetry and Poverty in W10" by Colin MacInnes in *The*

Zoe with Katkin and Ann, **1994.** Photograph by Roger Mayne.

Observer (London), 21 January 1962; "Roger Mayne: Photographs from Spain" in *Creative Camera* (London), March 1972; "Two Men So Different: Roger Mayne and Kurt Hutton" by G. Hughes in *Amateur Photographer* (London), 10 July 1974; "Do You Remember?" in *Amateur Photographer* (London), 11 September 1974; "The British Obsession" by William Messer in *U.S. Camera 77,* New York 1977; "Magical Show: Roger Mayne, ICA" by John Russell Taylor in *The Times* (London), 1 November 1978; "Hey Mister, Take My Picture" by Ian Jack in the *Sunday Times Colour Magazine* (London) 16 February 1986; "Absolute Fifties" by Jane Withers in *Elle* (London), March 1986; "Beginners' Street, W.10" by Colin Ward in *New Society* (London), 21 March 1986; "The Man in the Street" by Ruth Picardie in *The Independent Magazine,* 28 November 1992; "Let Me Take You by the Hand"—Roger Mayne's London Revisited in *The Times Saturday Review,* 28 November 1992

*

My primary interest in photography is as an art—the end product being the print to be exhibited or to be contemplated on a wall. However, I think a confusion has arisen over my personal work because the subject matter was superficially photojournalistic and more recently topographical. Such a confusion can arise because photography is first and foremost a new kind of language, subject to all the uses—mundane or commercial or serious—that any language can be put to. The dividing line between serious photojournalistic and documentary photographs on the one hand and a certain kind of artistic photograph on the other is a narrow and often subtle one. In fact, the only real clue may be that the artistic photograph can sustain endless viewings (but of course to most people a photograph is something looked at once).

In painting today an artistic intent is usually clear (even if nullified by lack of ability, or playing the market). Photography has taken over many of the tasks painting used to do. Thus nobody is going to confuse Lichtenstein with a comic strip; it is recognized that he has used and refined a particular visual language for his own ends.

I see the present state of photography as a rather barren one. Of course a great volume of work is being done, but photography is much too much polarised to two extremes. On the one hand there is the arty, with the traditional "fine print" at one end of the spectrum and the cult of the banal and formless at the other. On the other hand, there is photography where content is all important. This can range from documentary with a very political (left wing) bias, to an attempt to glorify fashion and commercial photography. I find myself in the unfashionable middle road, having come late to the Cartier-Bresson idiom, a consolidator rather than an innovator. It must, however, be remembered that though this idiom is out of fashion in art photographic circles (too straight for the arty; and for the political it is either sneaky to take people unawares, or a liberty to impose a composition on reality—especially if horrendous like war or poverty), the recent Cartier-Bresson exhibitions at Edinburgh and the Hayward received a great response from the public. But then there seems little relation between the tastes of even an informed public and that of the small group that leads artistic fashions.

I think the false state of photography arises from its deep inferiority complex. Photography also shares the isolation of the other arts from society; but I think it has rather chosen to do this—potentially, photography going in the right direction could help to bridge the gap. There is still reason enough for feeling insecure. The battle for photography to be accepted as art is won; but in England certainly, photographs are still not regarded as art objects to be collected or put on walls. The effect of all this is to encourage would be artistic photographers to be arty. They have by various tricks and manipulations to show that they are being creative. I maintain that the photographer must be true to his medium, which is to record reality; and that he shows his creativity by the care with which he selects his imagery and the preciseness with which he organizes it in the picture space. The arty photograph may be visually striking or intruiging at first sight, but will soon pall; good photographs true to the medium often emerge from a context of dullness. For example, I looked at the 400 Atgets in the V & A collection. They are mostly boring architectural records, except to the student of certain kinds of architecture (they were purchased by the museum at the turn of the century purely as record photographs); however, one in ten suddenly takes off, because the subject was right for Atget's marvellous eye. And these photographs can be looked at again and again. In the Cartier-Bresson idiom the less good photographs usually retain the human interest, but are visually a mess. Every so often a photograph occurs where everything falls into its place. In between are the tantalising cases where one wished the virtues of two or three similar images could be combined, for no individual one quite comes off.

There are certain beliefs in photography that I am opposed to. It seems that photography is setting up its own kind of aesthetic, perhaps again out of this sense of inferiority that I have mentioned. There are those in the photographic world (the "specialists" as Hockney calls such people) who accuse the general artistic public of having no real understanding of the medium. I myself would question how much the "specialists" understand art in general. For I feel there is a common ground to all the arts; and that art can be fully appreciated by an interested and experienced public, even if it lacks specific expertise in the medium in question.

The question of size is where I differ most of all from other photographers. For me, finding the correct size of print for the image is of crucial importance. Various things influence the size—e.g., the scale of the subject, the kind of forms in the image, the complexity of the composition. In addition, photographs on a wall require to be larger than when looked at in the hand or in a book. All painters and sculptors are aware of the importance of scale, and will instinctively adapt to whatever scale they happen to be working in. Matisse even went so far as to say that a painter must change the forms somewhat when working up an idea to a larger scale. Thus I find the attitude of the photographic world quite incomprehensible. No doubt I am regarded as a lunatic, but at least I can't be accused of being lazy. I think a lot about the right range of scale for each picture; and do the enlarging myself—up to 4 ft.

A side issue of the standardization of size by most photographers is that most photographic exhibitions are very dull in presentation. The Kertész exhibition, occupying a large space like the Serpentine Gallery—a single line of 10 x 8 prints—is a case in point. Better to look at the pictures in a book. Again, I was very disappointed that Cartier-Bresson's definitive selection of his work should be all at the relatively small size of 13 and a half by 9 inches. Many of the images that had impressed at 36 x 24" in his V & A show 10 years back just got lost.

One side of the photographic aesthetic is the cult of the fine print, and the concept of print quality, but this is a faction within photography similar to those one gets in any art. The fine print implies a small size as part of the feeling of print quality comes from an illusion of seeing more detail than the eye can take in. The danger, however, is that certain things in the picture can easily be missed if the image is insufficiently enlarged (historically, Victorian photographers could make only contact prints and generally speaking used large cameras, which of course gave very fine detail—later a mystique arose that contact prints were superior to enlargements). The large camera approach, with, as often as not, contact prints may suit certain individuals admirably, e.g., Weston, Strand; but I think it is too narrow an idea to become one of the tenets of art photography. It would be rather like saying that an early Flemish portrait leaves no room for the 6 ft. portraits of Velasquez or Goya; or that the handling of paint in Renaissance painting excludes the much rougher handling of impressionism or post-impressionism. Course grain, blurr and out of focus are as much part of the vocabulary of photography as extreme fine detail.

Artistic values will always be controversial. Also I am more certain, the older I get, that shifts of taste are purely a question of fashion, and not necessarily tied up with what the more general artistic public are thinking.

The reasons for taste are complex and often psychological. The broad situation as I see it is that many principles are involved in the creation of art, but that there are divergences of opinion as to what these are—sometimes to the extent that people may hold completely opposite views. Balance, conviction, life are qualities not much in dispute. Skill or craftsmanship I would say

are not always essential—there are times when there is a choice of priorities. Does one have spontaneity at the expense of accuracy or technique? For me, yes. Economy of means is something I value (not to be confused with over-simplification) but which is liable to make a work difficult, for it has to do with expressing the essence of something (not to be confused with a stereotype) rather than surface realism. The two qualities that are really decisive (and as a result give me the feeling that the better my work might become, the less likely it is to be widely appreciated) are austerity and tension. This last idea I find difficult to explain briefly; but for me tension is not only the very life blood of art, but also that which can make art uncomfortable and disturbing.

—Roger Mayne

*   *   *

Roger Mayne's nature has inclined him to respond flexibly to the pressures and opportunites of life. He believes that an artist should tackle anything, and seeks variety rather than obsessive single-mindedness.

A search for "a kind of childhood I didn't have," and being "at the bottom of the pecking order myself" led him early to exercise his passionate engagement with photography, especially in its social documentary aspect. His emphasis was on the life and energy of children and young people, against their decaying urban environments. Roger Mayne believes that he was being carried along by the strength of the subject matter in his street photographs, and that the strength given by his artistic maturity appeared later.

In terms of a major theme: it becomes evident in the photographic record of his children, which began with the birth of daughter Katkin in 1966. Moving from the characteristic documentary stance of an outsider observing less fortunate others, Roger Mayne was now able to produce images whose intensity derived from his intimacy with the subjects, rather than from the drama of adverse circumstances. It is the evocation of the unfolding of ordinary existence which carries over into his recent landscape photography. Even when, as is often the case, it is empty of figures, this work is so definitely and unassumingly about daily human life that to encounter these very specific images is to encounter both the social and universal dimensions of being.

As happens not infrequently to artists whose care is for their work before professional wheeling and dealing, Roger Mayne has found himself with less and less affinity to the photographic scene. Coupled with this has been the realization that there are aspects of the world not readily treated through photography, with its virtually determinate composition and its emphasis on tone and texture before qualities of outline. The characters of drawing and etching, on the other hand, make up this lack; and Roger Mayne is now committed to the pursuit of their possibilities in priority to those offered by the photographic medium. His investigation of landscape continues, and life drawing is a fertile area that nude photography never really was.

—Philip Stokes

McBEAN, Angus.

Nationality: British. **Born:** Newbridge, Monmouthshire, South Wales, 8 June 1904. **Education:** Monmouth Grammar School, 1915-21; self-taught in photography. **Family:** Married Helena Wood in 1923 (separated, 1924). **Career:** Worked as bank clerk, Midland Bank, Newport and Brynmawr, Monmouthshire, 1923-26; shop assistant, Liberty's department store, London, 1926-33; photographic assistant, studio of Hugh Cecil, London, 1934-35. Freelance portrait and theatre photographer, since 1935; established own studio, Victoria, London, 1935-45; in Covent Garden, London, 1945-60; in Islington, London, 1960-66; in Eye, Suffolk, 1966-83; and in Debenham, Suffolk, since 1983. Fellow, Royal Institute of British Photographers. **Died:** (in Ipswich) 9 June 1990.

Individual Exhibitions:

1934   Pirates Den Tea Shop, Hay Hill, London
1964   *Shakespeare's Plays,* Kodak Gallery, London

1971	*Thirty Years of Opera,* The Maltings Opera House, Snape, Suffolk
1976	*A Darker Side of the Moon,* Impressions Gallery, York (retrospective; toured the U.K.; augmented version, National Theatre, London, 1978)
1980	*Photographs 1934-1960,* Rex Irwin Gallery, Sydney
1984	The Photographers' Gallery, London

Selected Group Exhibitions:

1959	*Hundert Jahre Photographie 1839-1939,* Folkwang Museum, Essen (travelled to Cologne and Frankfurt)
1980	*Modern British Photography 1919-1939,* Museum of Modern Art, Oxford (travelled to Leeds Polytechnic; University of East Anglia; University of Sussex; Bolton Museum and Art Gallery; City Museum and Art Gallery, Worcester; Newport Museum and Art Gallery)
1984	*Sammlung Gruber,* Museum Ludwig, Cologne
1989	*Through the Looking Glass,* Barbican Art Gallery, London

Collections:

National Portrait Gallery, London; Victoria and Albert Museum, London; Theatre Museum, London; Royal Photographic Society, London; Kodak Museum, Harrow, London; Australian National Gallery, Canberra; Harvard University, Cambridge, Massachusetts; Museum Ludwig, Cologne.

Publications:

By McBEAN: Books—*Shakespeare Memorial Theatre, 1946-48,* with text by Ivor Brown, London 1949, and following books, every two years, until 1964; *Angus McBean,* with text by Adrian Woodhouse, foreword by Lord Snowdon, London and New York 1984; *Masters of Photography: Angus McBean,* with text by Adrian Woodhouse, London 1985; *Vivien: A Love Affair in Camera,* London 1989. **Articles**—"Results of a Battle" in *British Journal of Photography* (London), 23 February 1940; "Photographing Beauty" in *Picture Post* (London), January 1940; "Restoration Theatre" in *Vogue* (London), August 1980.

On McBEAN: Books—*The Man Behind the Camera,* edited by Helmut Gernsheim, London 1948; *Hundert Jahre Photographie 1839-1939 aus der Sammlung Gernsheim, London,* exhibition catalogue, by Helmut and Alison Gernsheim, Essen 1959; *Fame: Famous Portraits of Famous People by Famous Photographers,* edited by L. Fritz Gruber, London and New York 1960; *Beauty: Variations on the Theme Woman by Masters of the Camera—Past and Present,* edited by L. Fritz Gruber, London and New York 1965; *The Magic Image* by Cecil Beaton and Gail Buckland, London and Boston 1975; *Modern British Photography 1919-1939,* exhibition catalogue, by David Mellor, London 1980; *Angus McBean in Islington,* edited by Mary Cosh, London 1982; *Sammlung Gruber: Photographie des 20. Jahrhunderts,* exhibition catalogue, with foreword by Siegfried Gohr, Cologne 1984; *Through the Looking Glass,* Gerry Badger and John Benton-Harris, London 1989: **Articles**—"Angus McBean" by Helmut Gernsheim in *Photo Monde* (Paris), February 1955; "Angus McBean" by Mark Owen in *British Journal of Photography* (London), December 1964; "Angus McBean" by Val Williams in *Amateur Photographer* (London), June 1976; "Angus McBean" by Stewart Scotney in *Art and Artists* (London), July 1976; "The Works of Angus McBean" by Trevor Gett in *Australian Photography* (Sydney), October 1978; "Angus McBean" by Roger Clark in *British Journal of Photography* (London), 17 August 1979; "Angus McBean" by Jake Wallis in *Creative Camera* (London), February 1980; "The Great Eye" by Sandra McGrath in *The Weekend Australian* (Sydney), 5 July 1980; "Angus McBean" in *Zoom* (Paris), October 1982; "McBean at 80" in *The Times* (London), 8 June 1984.

*

With one Scottish grandfather who provided the name and some genes, I was born and brought up in a colliery village in Monmouthshire and call myself Welsh. After school, I became a bank clerk, but soon—in search of

"Art"—I became a shop assistant in Liberty's in London, where I didn't find art, but learned to handle people—a vital weapon in the armoury of a portrait photographer. Luckily, after seven years I lost this job and, although it was the jobless 1930s, I grew a beard to demonstrate that I was not seeking one. I spent a year at home making masks for both decoration and use on the stage and taking photographs. I had found Art. I held a small exhibition of my work in a small teashop in Hay Hill, London, and there met Hugh Cecil whose temple to photography was next door, and became for a year his assistant, learning a great deal I didn't know before about photography.

After a year, in 1934, I opened my first studio in a basement in Belgrave Road, Victoria, and started photographing theatre shows for no payment, selling the results to the *Sketch* and other magazines—meeting stars like Ivor Novello, Vivien Leigh, Ralph Richardson, and going to the Old Vic every change of play and getting Lawrence Olivier into a corner of the stage and under a light and taking a couple of shots—now the only pictorial record of these historic performances. My publication successes gradually won me the position of official photographer to the Old Vic, Sadlers Wells, Stratford-on-Avon, Glyndebourne, and, finally the great empire of the commercial theatre, H.M. Tennent, under the management of "Binkie" Beaumont.

Now I was probably the no. 1 photographer for 30 golden years of the English theatre. This is most certainly my most important work, a fact recognized by Harvard University Library who bought all my important negatives: 4½ tons of glass, 48,000 exposures which are now cared for and serviced by them. When I gave up stage photography in 1963, I had photographed all of Shakespeare's plays in major productions: *Hamlet,* 14 times, and *Macbeth,* 16 times.

But it is not my stage work which now causes the present interest in my work. It is the series of so-called "surrealist pictures," photographs in the surrealist manner of stage and other personalities, done for the *Sketch* magazine weekly for 3 years before the war, and *The Tatler* for about 2 years after the war. These were perfectly straight photographs of full-sized constructions which included some personality. They were intended seriously only as photography, and although many of them were, I think, pleasing pictures, they were not intended as "fine art." Indeed, I doubt that the camera can aspire to this distinction. They have always caused controversy; when, towards the end of the first series, *Picture Post* asked me to construct and photograph one of these pictures for an article 6 pages long, many people were outraged—*British Journal of Photography* going so far as to call me a "charlatan" and no photographer. Well, they are still calling Dali a charlatan, but no one says he is no draughtsman! As recently as 1980 I had an exhibition in Sydney, Australia, and a critic describing himself as a "purist photographer" dismissed my "surrealist" work as kitsch. This didn't prevent the show being a virtual sell-out, with pictures going to art galleries in Canberra, Sydney and Newcastle.

Of course I know what is meant by a "purist photographer"; for many years I was one, recording what was in front of the camera and developing it to Messrs. Kodak's time-temperature formula. But surely the term is meaningless: a photograph is, by definition, an image produced by light and any such image is a pure photograph, even if a camera is not used at all.

Most of my photography was reasonably straight, but it was with my Christmas cards that I let myself go, using every device known to me—even the adamantly forbidden "mucking about in the dark-room." These went out for 30 years in great numbers, but it was only about 5 years ago when one of them came up at Christies saleroom and sold for £240 that I realized that all those vintage prints in a drawer upstairs were worth a lot of money.

—Angus McBean

* * *

"Theatre is Romance," Angus McBean once declared. Surrealist romance became his trademark in artfully contrived tableaux, sharp-edged reflections of Victorian play acting: in the 1930s his photos created a flavour as heady and strong as the fashionable cocktails of the period. He mixed, and mis-matched, with sardonic elaboration in order to add piquant flavour, a dash of nostalgia, and a knowingness which made spectators collaborators in a world of make-believe. From December 1937, McBean contributed a weekly photo-portrait for the *Sketch,* affectionately quirky.

Born in Wales, McBean worked first as a bank clerk. After coming to London, he worked at Liberty's, and in the 1920s made for himself masks and dolls, marionettes, from real life and the imagination. This sense of how to use props led to the imaginative creation of settings in which to photograph his personalities, settings which underlined interpretations of character. McBean was eventually commissioned by Ivor Novello to make masks for the production of *The Happy Hypocrite* and became a theatrical photographer, supplying the front-of-house photographs that advertised the delights within. These photographs were usually published. However, the majority of McBean's vast audience would absorb his imagery without realizing its authorship: as one commentator put it when discussing McBean, his photographs were "outside almost every theatre in England for 30 years."

Yet McBean carried forward his theatrical traditions to a new world of pop music publicized by the potency of television: in the 1950s and 60s he photographed Tommy Steele, Motown, the Beatles. Stage-struck and camera-mad, McBean has described himself. Rarely can such interests have been so creatively intertwined, and perhaps McBean's interest in the theatre, props, and the creation of illusion led to his ability to use any technique that came to hand, mind and eye for creative, effective photographs. He usually built sets in the studio, and is best known for the use of sand from which fragments of his models might emerge: the face, part of a body. He played about with scale, so that what we would think of as monumental would appear miniature, and vice-versa. He was famous in the profession for his annual Christmas cards, which starting in 1936, were always a photographic joke, playing about with photographic conventions and idioms, with tricky multiple exposures, montages, multiple printings, and of course the use of props, which became his trademark.

He had a fine eye for physical structure and physical appearance; he picked out Audrey Hepburn from a West End chorus line to advertise a beauty product.

Television and a new gritty realism (and a concomitant lack of glamour) in the theatre limited McBean's career: he also felt that the better he got, the duller his images became—a curious paradox. "Anyone can be a photographer," he declared; "it is the subject matter which makes a great photographer." By the end of the 1960s he decided to stop photographing professionally: yet his photographs of the theatre for three decades, his pop record album covers, his surreal portraits of characters and personalities, are all exceedingly well known: his interpretations of his own period have entered the pool of shared visual culture, with imagery he contrived now so accepted as to have become commonplace in advertising campaigns devised in America and Britain by art directors who probably are unaware of the origination of the ideas they use.

—Marina Vaizey

McBRIDE, Will.

Nationality: American. **Born:** St. Louis, Missouri, 10 January 1931. **Education:** Studied illustration under Norman Rockwell at the Academy of Design, New York; also studied at the Art Institute of Chicago, Detroit Society of Arts and Crafts, and Syracuse University, New York; studied German at the Free University, Berlin, 1955-57. **Military Service:** Served as a photographer in the 1st Infantry Division, United States Army, Wurzburg, Germany, 1953-55. **Family:** Married Barbara Wilke in 1959 (separated, 1969); sons: Shawn, Robin, Brian. **Career:** Freelance photographer, working for *Life, Look, Stern, Paris-Match,* and particularly for *Twen,* etc., in Berlin, 1955-61, in Munich, 1961-72; based in Casoli, Italy, working as photojournalist and sculptor, since 1972. **Recipient:** Gold Medal, Art Directors Club of Germany, 1968, 1969, 1972, and of New York, 1970. **Address:** 55060 Casoli di Camaiore, Provincia di Lucca, Italy.

Individual Exhibitions:

1972   Galerie Christoph Durr, Munich
1978   Galleria d'If, Palermo
1980   Commune di Camaiore, Italy
1981   *Will McBride: Autobiographie,* PPS Galerie, Hamburg

1992   *Retrospective,* Kommunikationsfabrik, Frankfurt, Germany
        (travelled to Bonn, Hamburg, Berlin and Munich)

Selected Group Exhibitions:

1957   *5 Young American Artists in Berlin,* Amerika Haus, West
        Berlin
1979   *Deutsche Fotografie nach 1945,* Kasseler Kunstverein, Kassel,
        West Germany (toured West Germany)
1984   *Sammlung Gruber,* Museum Ludwig, Cologne
1985   *Das Aktfoto,* Fotomuseum im Stadtmuseum, Munich (toured
        West Germany)

Collections:

Museum Ludwig, Cologne.

Publications:

By McBRIDE: Books—*Berlin und die Berliner,* with Lynn Millar, West Berlin 1958; *Adenauer: A Portrait,* Munich 1965; *Zeig Mal,* with a foreword by Helmut Kendler, Wuppertal, West Germany 1974; *The Photo-Essay,* with Paul Fusco, text by Tom Moran, New York and London 1974; *Show Me,* with text by H. Fleischauer, New York 1975, London 1976; *The Lord's Prayer,* Wuppertal, West Germany 1978; *Siddhartha,* Kehl am Rhein, West Germany 1982; *Will McBride's Photographic Diary,* 1982. **Article**—"Will McBride: Siddhartha" in *Zoom* (Paris), November/December 1971.

On McBRIDE: Books—*Deutsche Fotografie nach 1945/German Photography after 1945* by Floris Neusüss, Wolfgang Kemp and Petra Benteler, Kassel, West Germany 1979; *Sammlung Gruber: Photographie des 20. Jahrhunderts,* exhibition catalogue, with foreword by Siegfried Gohr, Cologne 1984. **Articles**—"Photographs and Reflections of Will McBride" in *U.S. Camera Annual 1970,* edited by Cranston Jones, New York 1969; "Will McBride" in *Camera* (Lucerne), April 1969; "Das ist der neue Mensch: Eine Vision von Will McBride" in *Twen* (Munich), May 1970; "McBride: Un Certain Regard de Notre Epoque" in *Photo* (Paris), April 1972; "Will McBride: L'Amour aux Cent Visages" in *Photo* (Paris), December 1972; "The Knapsack Classics" in the *Daily Telegraph Magazine* (London), 18 May 1973; "Schottland: Fotos Will McBride" in *Stern* (Hamburg), 20 May 1974.

                              *   *   *

Will McBride was a supernova of a photographer. He was totally unknown in the dark days of the 50s, and he seemed to vanish without trace in the 70s, but in the decade in between he lit up the whole world of contemporary photography, via the pages of *Twen* magazine in Munich and his book *Siddhartha.*

McBride was a painter and sculptor who became a photographer by chance. He discovered David Douglas Duncan's book *The Private World of Pablo Picasso,* and with typically impulsive directness went off to see him. Duncan, not Picasso. Another chance was finding Willy Fleckhaus, who had not yet launched *Twen* but started McBride off with assignments for *Quick.* By such accidents a man who had recently been discharged from the U.S. army and married a German girl, and who had seemed to have few prospects in his adopted country, was set to become one of the most famous figures in the photography of the day.

Twen was the best-designed magazine of all time. It was the most dramatic, the most vivid, the most direct, the freshest, and published photography of a consistent quality and level of imagination that has never been matched. *Twen* did not report on the world, it created it. Fleckhaus filled the large pages with big pictures, relegating the text to neat blocks set off with bold headings and areas of white space: it was revolutionary at the time. The pictures used revolutionary new effects such as supersaturated colours, exaggerated grain, extreme wide-angle distortion and so on. Fleckhaus often reproduced photographs so that the subjects were larger than life—sometimes much larger. A pair of lips in *Twen* could appear over 30cm across! Also, *Twen* had no coyness about showing nudes, and even pubic hair. Fleckhaus showed black men with white women, both nearly naked and touching. It was strong stuff for a respectable magazine in an age when airbrush retouching was still *de rigeur*. The point of all this is that McBride's style was exactly *Twen*'s: they made a combination of the ideal photographer with the ideal magazine. But it must also be observed that *Twen* still looked like *Twen* when it contained no pictures by Will McBride, and McBride still looked like *Twen* even when he did things on his own. (Pete Turner, Art Kane and Hans Feurer were among Fleckhaus's other favorite photographers, and at this time they all had styles that were similar to McBride's. Who knows who influenced who?)

McBride had the ideal mentor and the ideal outlet; all he needed was the ideal subject. Fleckhaus found it for him: Hermann Hesse's *Siddhartha*. McBride strongly identified himself with the hero, and immediately organized a trip to India to shoot the story. As always he sketched out the series of pictures before he shot them—he worked graphically, like an art director. He used all the tricks, shooting many of the pictures with ultra wide (20mm, 24mm) lenses from very close distances. The set was published in *Twen*, and later McBride laid out a brilliant 56-page portfolio in the French magazine *Zoom* including 40 pages from *Siddhartha*.

It was his apotheosis. Shortly after that return from India his wife left him, taking the three children. He gradually lost all his advertising clients. *Twen* went out of business as the bravado and optimism of the 60s gave way to the pessimism of the 70s. McBride simply ran out of money and had to close down his studio. He talked of giving up photography, as he felt he had seen too much, and, anyway, no photograph ever had the passion of his interior world.

Even so, the passion he captured in *Siddhartha* and in his "Dictionary of Sex" project is extraordinary. It is a passion for skin rather than of sex—for acres of skin, full of texture and glowingly warm and human and eminently touchable. McBride photographed skin with a terrifying intensity, and he paid a terrible price for his success. Remember that.

—Jack Schofield

McCORMICK, Ron(ald).

Nationality: British. **Born:** Liverpool, 26 July 1947. **Education:** Studied fine art at Liverpool College of Art, 1964-68, Dip. A.D. 1968; painting, at the Royal College of Art, 1968-71; self-taught in photography. **Family:** Married Linda Bond in 1969; divorced 1985; children: Nancy and Joel. **Career:** Worked in community publishing project, Stepney, London, 1971-72; freelance reportage photographer, London, 1971-79; Director, Half Moon Photography Gallery, London, 1971-73, and Side Gallery of Photography Newcastle upon Tyne, 1976-77. Independent photographer, since 1979. Visiting Tutor, Barking College of Technology, London, 1972-73, North East London Polytechnic, 1972-75, and Sheffield Polytechnic, 1975-78; Artist-in-Residence, Newport College of Art, Wales, 1977-78; Visiting Tutor, Newcastle Polytechnic, Newcastle upon Tyne, 1979. Lecturer in Documentary Photography, Gwent College of Higher Education, Newport, Wales, since 1979. Visiting Fellow, Western Australia Institute of Technology, Perth, 1983-84. Course Leader, BA Hons Photographic Studies since 1990. **Recipient:** Arts Council Award, 1974; Welsh Arts Council Award, 1978; Northern Arts Award, 1979; British Council Travel Award, 1983; Western Australia Arts Council Artist Award, 1983. **Address:** 7 Clifton Place, St. Woolos, Newport, Gwent, NP9 4EX, Wales.

Individual Exhibitions:

1971   *Neighbours: Spitalfields to Whitechapel*, Half Moon Gallery, London
1973   *Oldham: 2 Views*, Oldham Art Gallery and Museum, Lancashire (with Kevin Keegan)
        2 Views: Southend, Beecroft Art Gallery, Southend
        2 Views, The Photographers' Gallery, London
1974   *Festival*, Half Moon Gallery, London
1977   La Photogaleria, Madrid
1979   Oriel/Welsh Arts Council Gallery, Cardiff
        The Photographic Gallery, Southampton

Ceolfrith Arts Centre, Sunderland
1982   *The Wasteland*, John Hansard Gallery, Southampton
1983   Galeire Dusseldorf, Perth, Western Australia
1984   *Australia's West—the man altered landscape*, Western Australia Institute of Technology, Perth
        The Photographers' Gallery, London
1985   *The Valley's Project*, Ffotogallery, Cardiff

Selected Group Exhibitions:

1972   *Summer Show*, Serpentine Galley, London
        This Is Whitechapel, Whitechapel Art Gallery, London
1973   *Inside Whitechapel*, Whitechapel Art Gallery, London
1975   *Young British Photographers*, Museum of Modern Art, Oxford
        Problem in the City, Institute of Contemporary Arts, London
        The Camera and the Craftsman, Waterloo Place Gallery, London
1976   *Rencontres Internationales de la Photographie*, Arles, France
1981   *Evidence of Things Seen*, Newport Museum and Art Gallery, Wales
1982   *Contemporary British Photographers*, Massachusetts Institute of Technology, Cambridge
1983   *Eye of the Beholder—The Prosaic Landscape*, Ffotogallery, Cardiff
1984   *Nuova Fotografia Inglese*, Palazzo Reale, Milan
        National Photographic Exhibition, Albury Arts Centre, Sydney
1987   *Realities Revisited*, Saidye Bronfman Centre, Montreal
1989   *Through the Looking Glass*, Barbican Gallery, London

Collections:

Arts Council of Great Britain, London; Royal Town Planning Institute, London; Crafts Advisory Committee, London; Oldham Art Gallery and Museum, Lancashire; Welsh Arts Council, Cardiff; Bibliothèque Nationale, Paris; National Library of Wales, Aberystwyth; Contemporary Arts Society for Wales; Western Australia Institute of Technology, Perth; Albury City Council, New South Wales, Australia; Ffotogallery, Cardiff.

Publications:

By McCORMICK: Books—*Young British Photographers*, with others, London 1975; *The Camera and the Craftsman*, with others, London 1975; *New British Image*, editor, London 1977; *Newport Survey 4: Industry*, editor, Newport, Wales 1984; *The Wasteland*, exhibition catalogue with introduction by Bill Gaskins, Perth, Australia, 1984; *New Valley Landscapes (the Valley's Project)*, Cardiff, 1985.

On McCORMICK: Books—*Oldham: 2 Views—Photographs by Ron McCormick and Kevin Keegan*, exhibition catalogue, with comment by Arthur Dooley, Oldham, Lancashire 1973; *Ron McCormick*, exhibition brochure, Cardiff 1979; *British Journal of Photography Annual 1980*, London 1979; *DuMont Foto 4, Fotografie in Europa Heute*, Cologne, 1982; *Nuova Fotografia Inglese*, exhibition catalogue, edited by Giovanni Chiaramonte, Milan 1984; *Through the Looking Glass, 40 Years of British Photography*, London, 1989. **Article**—"Southampton—Photography: Ron McCormick" by Hugh Adams in *The Guardian* (London), 10 August 1979; "UN-UK a review of the Wasteland" by John X Berger in *Ten8*, no. 12, 1984.

*   *   *

Ron McCormick has had a variety of roles, sometimes simultaneously, in the world of British photography. Primarily a documentary photographer, although trained as a painter, he has administered photography galleries (Half Moon, London; Side, Newcastle), been a member of Arts Council committees, received awards, and is now a teacher in one of the liveliest photography departments in Britain, that of Gwent, in Newport, Wales.

Several times he received commissions from the Whitechapel Art Gallery, London, to photograph Whitechapel itself, the results effectively exhibited in large exhibitions which contained work by divers hands. McCormick's eye is

New Valley Landscapes. Photograph ©Ron McCormick.

both sensitive and acute, sharply conclusive and imaginative. His eye in particular for the human local colour that makes a locale is discerning, for he manages to be telling and memorable without being sentimental or slick. He can also be reformist: the influential *Problem in the City* exhibition at the Institute of Contemporary Arts, London, laconically demonstrated the self-inflicted horrors of urban planning that have spread in British life.

McCormick is exceptionally effective at composition, in finding what is there, but managing by framing and the exercise of subtle choice, to distill, refine, exaggerate, in such a way that the spectator believes in the truth of what the photographer has found. *Problem in the City,* on which McCormick collaborated with two other photographers, was outstanding because within the documentary tradition, and at a time when vigorous lobbying on the part of disadvantaged groups was a feature of British life, the images managed to tell a scarifying story without being overtly sensational. The photographs were compassionate, dispassionate, "worked" as images without losing or compromising their reportorial quality.

If McCormick's photographs have recently become more private, less documentary-narrative, that is a reflection of the period, which has become more inward. His photographs remain both striking and understated, and the cumulative body of work affecting, substantial, and stimulating. McCormick is gradually evolving from the documentary and reportorial to an attitude which is personal, individual—colour is becoming increasingly important—yet still based on observation. It is more monument, less narrative, with a

natural dignity found in the appearances of things usually passed over and disregarded. McCormick's is an evolving talent.

—Marina Vaizey

McCULLIN, Don(ald).

Nationality: British. **Born:** London, 9 October 1935. **Education:** Tollington Park Secondary Modern School, London, 1945-48; studied painting at Hammersmith School of Arts and Crafts, London, 1948-50 (Trade Arts Scholarship). **Military Service:** Served as a photographic assistant in aerial reconnaissance, Royal Air Force, in Egypt, East Africa and Cyprus, 1953-55. **Family:** Married Christine Dent in 1959; three children. **Career:** Worked as a dining-car attendant, British Railways, London-to-Manchester and London-to-Liverpool trains, 1951-52; colour-mixer, Larkins Cartoon Studios, London, 1952-53, 1956-60; freelance photojournalist, working mainly for *The Observer* newspaper, London, in Berlin, Cyprus, etc., 1961-64; Staff Photographer, *The Sunday Times* newspaper, London, in the Congo, Vietnam, Cambodia, Biafra, India, Pakistan, Northern Ireland, etc., 1964-84. Since

From *East of Aldgate* series, 1984. Photograph ©Don McCullin.

1984, freelance photographer, London. Member, Magnum Photos co-operative agency, Paris and New York. **Recipient:** World Press Photographer Award, 1965; Gold Medal for Photography, Warsaw, 1964; Granada Television Award, 1967 and 1969. **Address:** Redstack, 3 The Square, Braughling, Hertfordshire, England.

Individual Exhibitions:

1980   *Hearts of Darkness,* Victoria and Albert Museum, London
            (travelled to the International Center of Photography, New
            York, 1981)
        The Palestinians, Olympus Gallery, London
1983   *Beirut,* Olympus Gallery, London

Selected Group Exhibitions:

1964   *World Press Photo 64,* Gemeente Museum, The Hague
1972   *4 Internationally Famous Magazine Photographers,* at
            Photokina '72, Cologne
        The Concerned Photographer 2, Israel Museum, Jerusalem
            (toured Europe)
1973   *Third World Exhibition of Photography: On The Way to
            Paradise,* Pressehaus Stern, Hamburg (and world tour)
1979   *Elements,* Olympus Gallery, London
1980   *Old and Modern Masters of Photography,* Victoria and Albert
            Museum, London (toured Britain)
1983   *Il Reportage Fotografico nelle Guerre Contemporanee,* Palazzo
            Fortuny, Venice
1984   *Britain in 1984,* The Photographers' Gallery, London

Collections:

Victoria and Albert Museum, London; Museum of Modern Art, New York; International Center of Photography, New York; International Museum of Photography, George Eastman House, Rochester, New York.

Publications:

By McCULLIN: Books—*The Destruction Business,* London 1971, as *Is Anyone Taking Notice?,* Cambridge, Massachusetts 1973; *The Homecoming,* London 1979; *Don McCullin: Hearts of Darkness,* with an introduction by John Le Carré, London 1980; *The Palestinians,* London 1981; *Beirut: A City in Crisis,* London 1983. **Articles**—"Why Them and Not Me?" in the *Sunday Times Magazine* (London), 12 July 1970; interview, with Bill Jay, in *Zoom* (Paris), January/February 1972. **Film**—*Arena: Home Front,* BBC television film, 1986.

On McCULLIN: Books—*The Face of Life: Photographs Chosen by "The Observer,"* edited by Cliff Hopkinson, London 1959; *Photography of the World '60,* edited by Hiromu Hara, Ihei Kimura and others, Tokyo and New York 1960; *America in Crisis: Photographs for Magnum,* edited by Charles Harbutt and Lee Jones, with an essay by Mitchel Levitas, New York 1969; *The Concerned Photographer 2,* edited by Cornell Capa, New York and London 1972; *The Magic Image* by Cecil Beaton and Gail Buckland, London and Boston 1975; *Geschichte der Fotografie im 20. Jahrhundert/Photography in the 20th Century* by Petr Tausk, Cologne 1977, London 1980; *Old and Modern Masters of Photography,* exhibition catalogue, by Mark Haworth-Booth, London 1980; *Eye Witness: 25 Years Through World Press Photos* by Harold Evans, London 1981; *World Photography,* edited by Bryn Campbell, London 1981; *Donald McCullin* by Mark Hawarth-Booth, London 1983; *Bilder vom Krieg* by Rainer Fabian and Hans Christian Adam, Hamburg 1983, as *Images of War: 130 Years of War Photography,* London 1985. **Articles**—"Don McCullin" in *Album* (London), December 1970; "Photographs by Don McCullin" in *Creative Camera* (London), May 1971; "Two Worlds: The Photographs of Gilles Caron and Don McCullin" by Ainslie Ellis in the *British Journal of Photography* (London), 4 June 1971; "Don McCullin: I Want to Be the Toughest War Photographer in the World" by Robert Y. Pledge in *Zoom* (Paris), January/February 1972; "Donald McCullin: War Photographs" in the *Sunday Times Magazine* (London), 25 June 1972;

"Donald MCullin" in *Zoom* (Paris), no. 10, 1972; "McCullin" in *The Image* (London), no. 12, 1973; "The Concerned Photographer" by Cornell Capa in *Zoom* (Paris), no. 16, 1973; "McCullin: Ici Londres" in *Photo* (Paris), December 1979; "Don McCullin: Taming the Real" by David Moore and "Don McCullin" by Mark Haworth-Booth in *Creative Camera* (London), March/April 1981.

*   *   *

Don McCullin's work emerges from photojournalism, but its importance transcends the journalistic conventions. He has combined cool, effective professionalism with a rare compassion. His photographs were first published in *The Observer* newspaper, and his work developed with the formation of the Sunday colour supplements in London. Throughout the 1960s and early 70s McCullin operated through that most public medium, the magazine, the contrasts of which both exaggerate and insulate the reader from any horror portrayed. *The Sunday Times Magazine,* for which McCullin worked from the mid-1960s, has used his work ambitiously and has given him unprecedented space and emphasis. His great ability has been to find formal, often heroic, single images, the intensity of which question all the surrounding contents of the magazine in which they appear. His work was perfect for challenging the rapidly consumable, ephemeral nature of the medium.

His first published story was of his own street gang, The Guv'nors of Seven Sisters Road, in 1958. They form part of McCullin's raw autobiography. There is a famous picture of the gang posing in a half-demolished house, standing framed by the rafters. From the start McCullin was able to contain the chaos and violence within a structure. His early British pictures are the work of a young man with a bitter conscience looking for a style. He was rapidly absorbing the work of other photographers. The unemployed sifting through coal dust for fuel or wheeling their sacks on bicycles across a northern plain are close to Brandt's work of the 30s. There is his deceptive photograph of the sheep in the early morning from 1961. It appears like a quiet, rural scene, until you realize it is Caledonian market, and they are being herded to their inevitable slaughter at dawn. McCullin's intuition had sensed death, which was to be the significant preoccupation of much of his career.

His work in Cyprus in 1964 won him an international reputation and the World Press Photographer Award. Surrounded by 5,000 Greek irregulars, he charged his pictures in the streets of Liamassol with the adrenalin of the street drama and the appalling grief of the tragedy. The victims were gunned down in their front rooms. He was able to mark his pictures with a domestic intimacy, which touched the most vulnerable areas of our own response. One of the triggers to that response was evident in a quiet, mournful interior, when a boy kneels by the body of his father in silent, suspended grief, close to an iconographic form or a religious passion.

McCullin was in Vietnam during the Tet offensive of 1968. In the midst of the battle, amongst the debris, through a fragmented, dazed two weeks, McCullin found order. Charred uprights frame the athletic gesture of a negro hurling a grenade. A wounded man lies between the silhouette of a bayonet and the line of a drip stand. Details like rings, bracelets and watches glitter amongst the bodies as intimate forms in a zone where everything is smashed. There is his famous picture of the dead Vietcong with ammunition spilled across his open wallet and the photographs of his family. Using all the sentiments of propagandists, McCullin pointed his camera at the other side, at the anonymous adversary. A soldier shot in the legs is carried by his two companions in the form of a Deposition from the Cross. The icon surfaced from the reflexes of battle.

McCullin could contain not only conflict but also history. In the Congo in 1967 in a single photograph of a white mercenary with a gun and a black family with a bowl, he touched a root of colonial conflict. In Biafra, where the history of the Republic was diminished to three years and the children reduced to skeletal forms, he photographed as relentlessly as he has from Beirut to Belfast.

His later work in Britain is an attempt to reestablish himself in the calmer pulses of the English landscape. His *Homecoming* contained photographs of the northern ghetto of Bradford and the East Anglian countryside beneath dark skies. Britain looked like a combat zone.

Don McCullin epitomises the role of witness to the despair of our time.

—Mark Holborn

MEDKOVÁ, Emila.

Nationality: Czechoslovakian. **Born:** Emila Tláskalová, in Ustinad Orlici, Bohemia, 10 November 1928. **Education:** Educated at primary school, Prague, 1934-42; studied photography, under Josef Ehm, State Graphics School, Prague, 1942-43 and 1945-46. **Family:** Married the painter Mikuláš Medek in 1951 (died, 1974); daughter: Eva. **Career:** Independent photographer, associating with the Czech Surrealist Group, Prague, from 1946. Worked for the Barrandov Film Studios, Prague, 1944-45; Institute of Human Work, Prague, 1947-63; Institute of Psychology, Charles University, Prague, 1963-73; Faculty of Philosophy, Charles University, Prague, 1979-81. Estate: Eva Kosáková, Estonská 6, 101 00 Prague 10, Czechoslovakia. **Died:** (in Prague) 19 September 1985.

Individual Exhibitions:

1960	Museum of Hradec Králové, Czechoslovakia
1962	Gallery Krzyve Kolo, Warsaw
1963	House of Art, Kralupy, Czechoslovakia
	Museum of Modern Art, Miami, Florida
	Alšova Jihočeská Galerie, Hluboká, Czechoslovakia
	Vlastivědné Muzeum, Pìsek, Czechoslovakia
	Regional Gallery, Liberec, Czechoslovakia
1964	Fotokabinett Funke, House of Arts, Brno, Czechoslovakia
1965	Aleš Hall, Gallery of Young Artists, Prague
1968	Nova Huta, Krakow, Poland (with Čestmir Krátký and Karel Kuklìk)
1970	Galerie am Klosterstern, Hamburg, West Germany (with Mikuláš Medek)
1973	House of Art, Brno, Czechoslovakia
1978	Minigallery VÚVL, Brno, Czechoslovakia
1979	Fotokabinett Funke, House of Arts, Brno, Czechoslovakia
1980	Gallery of Česká Třebová, Czechoslovakia
1985	Gallery Foma, Prague

Selected Group Exhibitions:

1966	*Surrealism and Photography,* House of Arts, Brno, Czechoslovakia; Museum Folkwang, Essen, Germany
	UDS Thematic Exhibition, Gallery D, Prague
	12 Tschechische Kunstler, Kunstgalerie, Worpswede, West Germany
1967	*Exhibition 7 + 7,* Špala Gallery, Prague
1969	*Present Day,* Moravian Gallery, Brno, Czechoslovakia
1970	*100 Grabados/100 Fotografia CSSR,* Palacio de Bellas Artes, Mexico City
1973	*Presentacje,* Gallery ZPAF, Warsaw
1983	*Die fotografische Sammlung,* Museum Folkwang, Essen, West Germany
1989	*Czechoslovak Photography 1945-1989,* Gallery Valdštejnská jízdárna, Prague
	Roads of Czechoslovak Photography, Municipal Gallery, Prague
1991	*Czech Informel,* Špála Gallery, Prague
1994	*Europa, Europa—Das Jahrhundert der Avantgarde in Mittel- und Osteuropa,* Kunst- und Ausstellungshalle der Bundesrepublik Deutschland, Bonn

Collections:

National Gallery, Prague; Museum of Decorative Arts, Prague; Moravian Gallery, Brno, Czechoslovakia; Museum Folkwang, Essen, Germany; Museum of Modern Art, Miami, Florida; San Francisco Museum of Modern Art; Robert Koch Gallery, San Francisco; The Navigator Foundation Collection, Boston; The Anne & Jacques Baruch Collection Ltd, Chicago; Howard Greenberg Gallery, New York.

Publications:

On MEDKOVÁ: Books—*Emila Medková,* exhibition catalogue, by Jan Kñž, Hluboká, Czechoslovakia 1963; *Fotografie Emila Medková,* exhibition catalogue, by Jan Kñž, Brno, Czechoslovakia 1964; *Emila Medková,* exhibition catalogue, by Jan Kñž, Prague 1965; *Současna Ceskoslovenska fotografie,* exhibition catalogue, by Antonìn Dufek, Brno, Czechoslovakia 1969; *Československá fotografie 1968/1970,* exhibition catalogue, by Antonìn Dufek, Brno, Czechoslovakia 1971; *Československá Fotografie 1971/1972,* exhibition catalogue, by Antonìn Dufek and Ludovit Hlavac, Brno, Czechoslovakia 1973; *Emila Medková,* exhibition catalogue, by Ludvìk Šváb and Albert Marenčin, Brno, Czechoslovakia 1979; *Emila Medková* by Karel Srp, Prague, 1979; *Museum Folkwang: Die fotografische Sammlung,* exhibition catalogue, with introduction by Ute Eskildsen, Essen, West Germany 1983; *Surrealistische Photographie—Zwischen Traum und Wirklichkeit,* by Edouard Jaguer, Cologne, 1984; *Emila Medková,* exhibition catalogue, by Vratislav Effenberger and Alena Nádvornìková, Prague 1985; *Černobílá fotografie,* by Antonín Dufek, Prague, 1987; *Cesty československé fotografie,* by Daniela Mrázková and Vladimír Remeš, Prague, 1989. Articles—"Photography by Emila Medková" by Daniela Mrázková in *Fotografie* (Prague), 1963; "The Face of Czech Photography" by Karel Dvořák in *Československá fotografie* (Prague), 1970; "Les photographies d'Emilia Medková et l'anthropomorphisation de détail" by Alena Nádvorníková in *Surrealisme,* No.1, (Paris), 1977; "Le cycle des interprétations photographiques d'Emila Medková" by Ludvík Šváb in *Le La,* No 12, (Lausanne), 1980; "Hra Emily Medkové" by Jiří Šerých in *Československá fotografie,* No. 4, (Prague), 1985; "Emila Medková" by Ján Šmok in *Fotografie* (Prague), 1985.

* * *

"If photography lacks mystery and its reality lacks a second plane, then it is void," she once stated regarding Surrealist imagery. Emila Medková represents a third wave of interest awakened years ago by André Breton's theory of connecting vessels in which reality and dream flow freely back and forth. Medková entered photography in the late 1940s, right after World War II, a period during which hidden meanings and associations of the real and surreal were a code for longing for freedom, and poetic visions were cryptograms of hatred of the Nazis. Emila Medková joined a goup of artists and poets who rallied round Karel Teige. While the post-war times of great political upheavals and social changes inspired many to new activity, she devoted her efforts to private non-periodical volumes titled *Object,* in which the members of the group confronted her work, thought and insights.

When she married the painter Mikuláš Medek, also one of the members of the group, she became even more firmly convinced of her stance as an artist. Her creative platform was Surrealism; the anxiety-dominated revolt of magical verism which had marked her photography from the very beginning was very much akin to Medek's own Surrealist concepts and even surpassed them. As a photographer, Medková documented all paintings produced by her husband and his friends, and this intimate knowledge of their ambiguous meaning and internal structural order made a deep impression on her and even became decisive in her own creative photography. Its typical feature was enlarged detail and Medková soon discovered its unique function and ability to thoroughly transform reality suddenly perceived at close range, intimately, as if under a magnifying glass. A wall ceases to be just a wall; a door is no more just that, but rather a reality charged with novel meaning. In the drama of introspection, enhanced by poetic vision, reality is the protagonist.

A detail of a wall is still an exact documentary record of masonry with cracked, peeling plaster—but at the same time it acquires also a new appearance which is a product of our activated imagination. The artist thus makes us participate in the making of the ultimate experience, fires our imagination, dynamizes our perception, utilizing the entire system of symbols which we are now able to decode in the primary intention of the author and which we now read with pleasure. One of the characteristic features of Medková's work is cyclic repetition. Using objects that have become obsolete or have ceased to fulfil their original function, as well as phenomena of everyday life, her imagination suddenly lends them diverse appearances, making them unusual and unique, turning them into concrete emotions and notions evoked by unexpected contexts and associations. Medková's series are titled *Heads, Sets, Guard Stones* or *Crevices,* but the common, generic terms represent an urgent appeal, a lasting memento, for they are an expression of anxiety felt by one who lives in the eerie no-man's land between dream and reality.

After her studies at the State Graphic School in Prague, Medková accepted a job as photographer for a research institute. Sixteen years later she took a position with the Psychology Institute of Prague's Charles University. The life-long subject of her creative photography is that cruel phantom which long ago entered her life and never ceased torturing her with its multitude of appearances. In fact, the theme of Inquisitors started appearing in her photography much earlier than it started dominating the work of her painter husband. Hers is a hermetically sealed world of inner, utterly personal experience, an expression voicing her fear of loss of values, death of civilization and culture, as attested by her three illustrations to Vratislav Effenberger's poem *Spectre of the Third War*(1956). The isolation from the external world which did not understand her was aggravated also by personal disasters, including the demise of her husband and greatest soulmate. Medková remained voluntarily in seclusion and did not even feel a need to publish or exhibit. A rare occasion was an exhibition of her selected works which took place during the 10th International Audiovisual Technology Exhibition *Interkamera 85,* which reminded the public of the existence of this major figure in the development of Czech imaginative photography.

—Vladimìr Remeš

MEHTA, Ashvin.

Nationality: Indian. **Born:** Surat, Gujarat, 17 July 1931. **Education:** Studied medical biochemistry, Bombay University, M.Sc. 1955; mainly self-taught in photography, but initially influenced by R.R. Bhardwaj. **Family:** Married Tilottama Dave in 1959. **Career:** Worked as Publicity Manager for Glaxo Laboratories, British Drug Houses and Mac Laboratories, Bombay, 1956-73. Freelance photographer, in Bombay, 1973-81, and in Valsad, since 1981. **Recipient:** Photography Project Grants, Excel Industries, Bombay, 1976 and Kirloskar Oil Engines, 1994. **Agent:** DPA, 13 Vithoba Lane, Vithalwadi, Bombay 400002, India. **Address:** "Tulsi," Tithal-396006, Gujarat, India.

Individual Exhibitions:

1966	*Abstracts and Patterns,* Chemould Art Gallery, Bombay
1968	*The Single Eye: A Second Meaning,* Jehangir Art Gallery, Bombay
1971	*Human Form,* Jehangir Art Gallery, Bombay
1972	*Photo-graphics,* Jehangir Art Gallery, Bombay
1973	*Sea Images One,* Jehangir Art Gallery, Bombay
1975	*Sea Images Two,* Jehangir Art Gallery, Bombay
1977	*Scattered Aeons,* Jehangir Art Gallery, Bombay
1978	*Living with Trees,* Jehangir Art Gallery, Bombay
1980	*Leaves and Grasses,* Chemould Art Gallery, Bombay
1986	*The Other Eye,* Gardner Arts Centre, Brighton, England
1988	*Gifts of Solitude,* Piramal Gallery, Centre for Photography as Art Form, Bombay
1993	*Contemplative Colour,* Piramal Gallery, CPA, Bombay
1994	*Contemplative Colour,* Max Meuller Bhavan, Delhi
1995	*Third Eye,* Piramal Gallery, CPA, Bombay

Selected Group Exhibitions:

1972	*Creative Eye,* the *National Exhibition of Photography,* Rabindra Bhavan, Delhi
1973	*Today's India,* Kodak Gallery, New York
1982	*Festival of India,* The Photographers' Gallery, London
1984	*Indian Photography 1844-1984,* Dermstadt, Germany
1990	*Festival of India,* Russia
1991	*Festival of India,* Germany
1992	*"Another Way of Seeing,"* Netherlands

Collections:

Cabinet des Estampes, Bibliothèque Nationale, Paris; Metropolitan Museum of Art, New York; Centre of Photography as Art Form, Bombay.

Publications:

By MEHTA: Books—*Himalaya: Encounters with Eternity,* London 1985,1991; *Coasts of India,* London 1987; *Gifts of Solitude,* New York 1991; *100 Himalayan Flowers,* New York 1992. **Articles**—"Ashvin Mehta" in *Camera* (Lucerne), January 1967; "Ashvin Mehta: Interview with Saleem Peeradina" in *Youth Times* (Delhi), 11 June 1976; "Apropos India" in *Camera* (Lucerne), May 1978; Interview with the Editor (Marathi) in *Sadhana* (Pune), October 1982.

On MEHTA: Books— *The Other Eye: India, the Land, the Elements,* exhibition catalogue, with text by Keith Robinson, Brighton, Sussex 1986. **Articles**—"Ashvin Mehta—Preserving the eternal on film," Salil Tripathy, *Celebrity,* May, 1985; "Songs of the Crossing" by Geeta Doctor in *Signature,* June 1985; "Ashvin Mehta—Multiplicity & Monism" Keith Robinson introduction to *The Other Eye,* May 1986; "Unravelling Nuances" Kamla Kapur in *Sunday Observer,* March 27, 1988; "Long day's journey into night" by Geeta Doctor in *Signature,* May 1991; "Through a lens, serenely" Sanjiv Saith in *Indian Express,* May 5, 1991; "Manifestations of the infinite" by Chidanada Dasgupta, *Telegraph,* June 14, 1991; Introduction to *Gifts of Solitude,* by Judith Mara Gutman, New York,1991; "Reaching the transcendental through the factual" by Chidanada Dasgupta, *Telegraph,* January, 1992.

*

According to Indian philosophy, the five elements—earth, water, fire, wind and sky (or space)—are the Gods who form the limbs of the Formless. In this sense, my nature-photography is an attempt at His portrayal, and I succeed to the extent that I am able to capture the elements not merely as elements but as His limbs.

One may ignore or strongly disapprove of such an amalgam of photography and vague religious sentiment. But if one pauses to consider the process of creation (in an artist), the final creation can rarely invoke eternity unless one was in touch with it at the time of creation. It matters, therefore, whether one looks upon the elements as just elements or much more. A certain frame of mind can result in "construction," and another, not a frame of mind but a state of communion, results in "creation." All constructions are products of Time, and vanish in Time, in spite of glitter and apparent brilliance. The creations outlive Time and make both the viewer and the creator experience timelessness.

In my photography, I celebrate the Gods, and through them, sing of Him who has neither age nor form. I celebrate, whether I am photographing the ethereal sunshine after a snow-storm in the Himalayas, or a single, tender tree standing resolutely against the shadows of an entire forest. I celebrate, whether I am photographing the mother earth embracing the vast cloudless sky with a few prickly shrubs, or the sea-breakers enticing stolid rocks.

—Ashvin Mehta

*   *   *

Ashvin Mehta's photos are immediately recognizable. Fetchingly alive with unusual combinations of elements, they also become cool, dispassionate abstractions. Even his nudes echo this duality: they lose their identification with human form—for a moment—to become abstract landscapes of the body only to gradually fall into place as representations of human form. Mehta uses a 50mm. lens and comes in close upon his subjects—a pattern in sand is etched by the water's sweep, a massive rock stands on a cliff, a wisp of sea grass bends to the wind in a textured grainy surround. But however commonplace (and beautiful by normal Western standards) these subjects may be, Mehta organizes them into a combination of surprises. A rock, for instance, that stands in the middle distance looms powerfully over a foreground feature, while that foreground feature itself—a tiny tree—upstages that powerful statement to upset our expectations for the role and place of an object in the foreground. The blackened space between a woman's shoulders and her strands of long hair becomes the central organizing feature in a photograph of solids and wisps.

Untitled. Photograph by Ashvin Mehta.

Mehta's photographs thrive on unusual combinations of elements. But more, they gain strength through an unusual organization of these elements. In most Mehta photographs it's difficult to identify a base line. One turns a photo around many times before deciding which is up and which is down. Standard Western notions of how to depict, and where to place, heavy objects are thrown to the winds just as accepted Western understandings of how one normally depicts, and where one normally places, big objects are cast aside. Mehta restructures reality, while viewers look at a cosmic world, a world that goes beyond identifiable worlds of physical reality.

In this sense, Mehta is in the tradition of 19th century Indian photography which overhauled Western traditional understandings of pictorial space—and the camera's use—to create a system of imagery that was related to Indian miniature painting and Indian conceptual systems. In this century, however, and not the last, and giving current form and shape to his ideas, Mehta pays homage to Hindu understandings of godliness. This understanding stresses the Gods, which are seen as five basic elements: wind, water, earth, fire and sky (space), all of which, in turn, are seen as limbs of the Formless. Mehta celebrates the Gods by singing of Him who has neither Form nor age, but who appears (to Mehta) in nature. Producing secular, and sophisticated, representations of the Formless, Mehta creates a photographic portrait of Him.

His success comes from emphasizing space as an entity, and from seeing light, and non-light, as subjects. Many of Mehta's photographs are filled with massive black centers, a rock, for instance, that may be 5 feet away photographed, under natural light, so that is appears as a totally black object midway into the distance, its form played against a whitened sky. Just as characteristically, Mehta turns light itself into an object, many of his photographs growing out of a softened hole of white—as if it were a melded sun—somewhere off-center, molding fragile wisps of grass and textured, grainy sand into a sumptuous and sensuous picture. Still others grow out of a masterfully muted band of white running vertically, horizontally or diagonally through the picture, combining a voluptuous mixture of patterns, textures and objects into a whole. Of humans and nature, abstractions as they are detailed renderings of the world, Mehta's pictures are filled with the generative sources of life.

—Judith Mara Gutman

MEISELAS, Susan.

Nationality: American. **Born:** Baltimore, Maryland, 21 June 1948. **Education:** Educated in public schools, graduated from Colorado Rocky Mountain School, 1966; studied at Sarah Lawrence College, Bronxville, New York, 1966-70, B.A. 1970; Harvard University Graduate School of Education, Cambridge, Massachusetts, 1970-71, M.Ed. 1971; self-taught in photography. **Career:** Worked as assistant film editor to Frederick Wiseman, Cambridge, Massachusetts, 1970-71; photography adviser in New York City public schools, with Community Resources Institute, 1971-73; Artist-in-Residence, for schools throughout South Carolina and Mississippi, 1973-74; consultant, Polaroid Foundation, Cambridge, 1974; photographic adviser in mill town of Lando, South Carolina, 1975; Instructor in Photography, Center for Understanding Media, New School for Social Research, New York, 1975-76. Gahan Fellowship, Harvard University, 1991; Graduate Seminar Instruc-

The Border, **1989.** Photograph by Susan Meiselas.

tor, Cal. Arts 1992; Freelance photographer, working for the *New York Times, Harper's, Time, Life, Geo,* etc., New York, since 1975; Member, Magnum Photos co-operative agency, New York and Paris, since 1976. **Recipient:** Robert Capa Gold Medal, Overseas Press Club, 1978; Leica Award of Excellence, New York, 1982; Photojournalist of the Year Award, American Society of Magazine Photographers, 1982; Photography Grant, National Endowment for the Arts, 1984; Engelhard Award, Boston Institute of Contemporary Art, 1985. D.F.A.: Parsons School of Design, New York, 1986; Lyndhurst Foundation, 1987; MacArthur Fellowship, 1992; Maria Moors Cabot Prize, 1994; Hasselblad Foundation Prize, 1994. **Address:** 256 Mott Street, New York, New York 10012, U.S.A.

Individual Exhibitions:

1974	218 Gallery, Memphis, Tennessee
1975	CEPA Gallery, Buffalo, New York
1976	A.M. Sachs Gallery, New York
	Wellesley College, Massachusetts
1977	Images Gallery, New Orleans
1981	FNAC Gallery, Paris
1982	Camerawork Gallery, London
1983	*New Journalism,* Photography Gallery, La Jolla, California (with Ernesto Bazan)
1984	Museum Folkwang, Essen, Germany
1990	Art Institute of Chicago, Chicago
1994	Hasselblad Center, Gothenberg, Sweden

Selected Group Exhibitions:

1974	*Conference on Visual Anthropology,* Temple University, Philadelphia
	Carnival Strippers, Brockton Art Center, Massachusetts
1975	*International Women's Art Festival,* Fashion Institute of Technology, New York
1976	*Womanview,* University of Iowa, Iowa City
1981	*Color Photography,* Fogg Museum, Harvard University, Cambridge, Massachusetts
	Salvador, Half Moon Gallery, London
1984	*Inside El Salvador,* Museum of Photographic Arts, San Diego, California (travelled to the International Center of Photography, New York)

1985	*Magnum Concert,* Musée d'Art et d'Histoire, Fribourg, Switzerland
1986	*The Indelible Image,* Corcoran Gallery, Washington, D.C.
	On the Line, Walker Art Center, Minneapolis, Minnesota
1989	*The Art of Photography,* Museum of Fine Arts, Houston, Texas
	Los Vecinos, Museum for Photographic Arts, San Diego, California
	In Our Time, International Center of Photography, New York

Collections:

Fogg Museum, Harvard University, Cambridge, Massachusetts; International Museum of Photography at George Eastman House, Rochester, New York; Museum of Photographic Arts, San Diego, California; Museum Folkwang, Essen, Germany; Baltimore Museum of Art, Maryland; The Art Institute of Chicago, Illinois; Birmingham Museum of Art, Alabama; Hasselblad Foundation, Gothenberg, Sweden.

Publications:

By MEISELAS: Books—*Learn to See,* editor, Cambridge, Massachusetts 1975; *Carnival Strippers,* New York 1976; *Nicaragua,* New York 1981; *El Salvador: The work of thirty photographers,* co-editor, New York 1983; *Chile From Within,* editor, New York, 1990. **Articles**—"Appropriation and Documentary Photographs," in *Exposure,* vol.27, no1, 1989; "The Documentary Debate: Aesthetic or Anaesthetic?," in *Camerawork,* Summer, 1992.

On MEISELAS: Book—*A Day in the Life of Australia*—*March 6, 1981,* with introduction by Thomas Kenneally, Potts Point, New South Wales 1981. **Articles**—"Susan Meiselas" by Larry Shames in *American Photographer* (New York), March 1981; "Fragments of History" by Stu Cohen in the *Boston Phoenix,* 30 June 1981; "The Best and the Brightest" by P. Bosworth in *Working Woman* (New York), September 1982; "Susan Meiselas-Photographer" by L Taylor, in *Photography,* Dec. 17 1982; "Susan Meiselas—At War" by G. Emerson in *Esquire* (New York), December 1984."Susan Meiselas: The Frailty of the Frame, Work in Progress" by Fred Ritchin in *Aperture,* 1987; "Susan Meiselas: On Location," *Aperture,* Fall 1993.

*   *   *

Few photojournalists publish two good books by the age of 32—and, it is tempting to add, especially if they are female. Few women win the Robert Capa Prize for the "best photographic reporting or interpretation from abroad requiring exceptional courage and enterprise." Meiselas was only the second woman to have received this award. Clearly she is something of a phenomenon.

The two books are *Carnival Strippers* and *Nicaragua*. It could be argued that the first book covers a "natural" subject for a woman photographer, the strippers being perhaps less apprehensive about being photographed in their off-duty moments than if there was a man behind the camera (I do not argue this view myself.) *Nicaragua*, however, is not open to this kind of attack. Meiselas's colour pictures of the war stand on a par with any war photography in colour by any other photographer, male or female. In neither of these reportages does she flinch from her subject matter, though it is often unpleasant. In other respects, however, the two approaches are quite different—and this is interesting because it illustrates Meiselas's range as a photographer.

Carnival Strippers is a black-and-white reportage on the striptease artistes who travel with fairs round the small New England towns. Meiselas followed them for four summers recording the routines the girls used to attract customers, their performances, and quieter moments such as back-stage card playing. A lot of pictures were taken in low light, and the graininess of the pictures reinforces the seedy atmosphere of bare boards and blankets which surrounds these not-very-beautiful girls with their flabby bodies and crude gyrations. Meiselas does not flatter her subjects, and the results may not be to everyone's taste, but their undeniable qualities were sufficient to propel her into the Magnum picture agency in 1976. She photographed in Chad and Cuba before travelling to Nicaragua. A war had been going on there since 1972, when Sandina raised an army of peasants to fight the U.S. forces, but the west showed little further interest after the Marines were withdrawn. Meiselas went there in 1978 on the strength of an article in the *New York Times*. She was not on assignment (didn't have enough film), but when the revolution erupted she was there. Through Magnum, her pictures were quickly published round the world. She had a head start over the recognized war photographers, and did not let the advantage go.

Unlike *Carnival Strippers,* she photographed Nicaragua largely in colour, producing sharp, bright results. Often she has managed to produce striking compositions, too: a solitary figure balances a tank or a burning car; masked guerillas are counterpointed by watching housewives. Some of the groups are so precisely balanced they could have been posed, but Meiselas manages the same precision in her framing even when capturing an isolated instant (for example, see plates 13, 18, 33 and 39 in *Nicaragua*).

The results ought to look—like so much colour war photography—false, like stills from an expensive movie. They don't, for two reasons. First, Meiselas focuses on atrocities that are beyond even Hollywood's most appalling visualizations. These carry that unarguable stamp of authenticity no art can devise. And second, through her camera, Meiselas generates a sense of fraternity with the rebels. She is clearly on their side, and she is clearly out to enlist the viewer's sympathy for these poor and down-trodden people. It may not square with every photographer's idea of photojournalism, but it certainly produces a powerful result.

Nicaragua is not as comprehensive or as well integrated a condemnation of war as, say, Philip Jones Griffiths' *Vietnam Inc.,* nor is *Carnival Strippers* without its flaws, but many photographers have travelled farther and fared worse. Meiselas has the talent, obviously, and she seems to have the commitment that well could make her, in the future, one of the greatest photojournalists of all.

—Jack Schofield

MENDEL, Gideon

Nationality: South African and German. **Born:** Johannesburg, 31 August 1959. **Education:** Attended the University of Cape Town; self-taught in photography. **Career:** Worked as a school teacher in 1981; a trainee film editor and sound editor at the Independent Film Centre, Johannesburg; freelance photographer, 1983; press photographer for *The Star,* Johannesburg; wire-service photographer Agence France-Presse, 1985-86; freelance photographer with Magnum 1986-91 and with Network since 1992. **Agent:** Network Photographers, 3/4 Kirby Street, London EC1N 8TS, England. **Address:** 87 Oakwood Road, London NW11 6RJ, England.

Individual Exhibitions:

1986   *Broken Landscape,* Market Theatre, Johannesburg
1988   *Living in Yeoville,* Market Theatre, Johannesburg (travelled to
        the Baxter Theatre, Cape Town)
1989   *Beloofde Land (Promised Land),* Market Theatre, Johannesburg
        (travelled thoughout South Africa)

Selected Group Exhibitions:

1984-85   *Cordoned Heart,* ICP, New York (travelled to the
        Photographers' Gallery, London)
1986-87   *The Hidden Camera,* Holland (toured)
1990   *Beyond the Barricades,* United Nations building, New York
        (travelled worldwide)
1992   *World Press Photo,* Amsterdam (toured worldwide)
1993   *Positive Lives: Responses to HIV,* Photographers' Gallery,
        London (toured UK)
1994   *World Press Photo,* Amsterdam (toured worldwide)

Collections:

Johannesburg Art Gallery, South Africa; Gertrude Posel Gallery, University of Witwatersrand.

Publications:

By MENDEL: Books—*Cordoned Heart,* New York, 1984; Beyond the Barricades, New York, 1990; *Positive Lives: Responses to HIV,* London 1993.

*   *   *

Gideon Mendel cut his teeth as a photographer in the political turmoil of South Africa in the last days of apartheid rule. His work at that time, *A Broken Landscape* (1986) and *Beyond the Barricades* (1988), was noted for its passionate involvement with the people he was portraying and for its fearless exposure to physical danger: while other photographers were content to record events from the safety of police lines, Mendel's determination was to capture the experience of the people line of fire.

Before leaving South Africa in 1990, Mendel distanced himself somewhat from actual conflict in preparation of two considerable photographic essays. In *Living in Yeoville* (1988), Mendel explored the routine of daily life in his own suburban environment in Johannesburg, and in *Beloofde Land* (1988-89) he documented the several re-enactments of teh Afrikaner Great Trek and so exposed the pathetic stagemanagement of the symbolic vocabulary of apartheid.

By the time he arrived in England, therefore, Mendel's photography had involved the different strategies of confrontation, anecdote and analysis. Developments within his own life, as well as exposure to new work and of course, the opportunities of new photographic projects have brought considerable maturation to his work in which, to some extent, passionate commitment and engagement are still very much the hallmarks of Mendel's work, but they are tempered, on the one hand, by a need to understand the situation in which he is working, and on the other, by the conviction that private dramas may be as powerful and significant as public spectacles.

The Heart of Soweto, **1993.** Photograph by Gideon Mendel.

The impact on Mendel of his removal to England is perhaps reflected in the series *Immigrants in Israel* (1991) that portrays the first moments of a group of Ethiopian Jews in their adopted home: the photographs record the confusion and bewilderment of the African community as it enters an alien culture. Mendel negotiated his own entry into a new environment by exploring social, rather than political themes and by choosing subjects that themselves are at the margins of English society. His *Teenage Homeless in London* (1991) captures the dejection and despair of the homeless and unemployed victims of Thatcher's England. And his *Positive Lives* project (1993), that was commissioned as part of the Museum of Modern Art, Oxford, travelling exhibition on AIDS, illustrates with extraordinary sensitivity and compassion life in AIDS wards of hospitals in London. In a sense, Mendel's current London project, Claremont Road Ell, for which he is both photographer and designer, is a triumphant assertion of his new identity in its celebration of the right to defend one's home and influence the nature of one's environment.

Mendel's Zimbabwean portfolio on AIDS: *A Challenge for African Health Care* (1993), contrasts powerfully with his London work, in part by drawing attention to the rudimentary nature of some African hospital services, but also by showing how the context of medical treatment can effect the understanding of suffering and, even, of death itself. Other projects in Central Africa—*Zimbabwe, Waiting for Rain* (1993) and *Football Culture in Zambia* (1994)—demonstrate how both work and play may bind communities together and, in different ways, contribute to a sense of national identity. Not suprisingly, perhaps, Mendel's work in South Africa continues to reflect a political interest. He covered the first national elections in 1994 but, characteristically, chose to record this event, not in the limelight, but in the small Karoo community of De Aar that he had previously photographed in a dust storm. His continuing assignments in Johannesburg, Soweto and elsewhere, however,

reveal the political tensions that still permeate every aspect of South African society.

—Michael Godby

MERISIO, Pepi (Giuseppe).

Nationality: Italian. **Born:** Caravaggio, Bergamo, 10 August 1931. **Education:** Attended elementary school in Caravaggio, 1941, Istituto Salesiano Treviglio, Bergamo, 1942-50, and the Università Cattolica, Milan, 1951-55. **Family:** Married Anna Maria Bosio in 1959; children: Luca and Marta. **Career:** Amateur photographer, Bergamo, 1947-60; professional freelance photographer, Bergamo, working for *Du, Camera, Famiglia Cristina, Touring Club Italiano, Paris-Match, Stern, Look, Réalités,* etc., since 1960: Principal Photographic Collaborator, *Epoca* magazine, Milan, 1963-72. **Recipient:** First Prize, Istituto Geografico Militare, Florence, 1957, 1960; First Prize, Centro Turistico Giovanile, Rome, 1957; Special Color Prize, Motta Ferrania, Milan, 1958, 1959; First Prize for Photography, Pondicherry, India, 1958; Carlo Erba Prize, Bambini d'Italia, Milan, 1958, 1961, 1963; First Prize, *Mostra Concorso di Ancona,* 1959; City of Munich Prize, 1959; First Prize,

Il Forno del Pane a Sezze, Lazio, Italy, **1980.** Photograph by Pepi Merisio.

Festival of Color, Como, 1961; First Prize for Photography, Valmalenco, 1962; First Prize for Photography, La Rocca, Assisi, 1963; *Popular Photography* Prize, 1963; First Prize, Racconto e Reportage Fotografico, Fermo, 1963; First Prize, *Mostra Concorso,* Assisi, 1963; First Prize, Premio Nazionale Fotoreporters, Milan, 1964; First Prize, Communicazioni Visive, Genoa, 1965; Premio Rosa Camuna, Milan, 1983. Nominated "EFIAP," 1982; "Maestro della fotografia italiana," 1988. **Address:** Via Noli 4, 24100 Bergamo, Italy.

Individual Exhibitions:

1961	Galleria XX Settembre, Bergamo
1962	Galleria Dalmine, Dalmine, Italy
1965	Circolo Fotografico Veronese, Verona
1966	Galleria La Torre, Lecco, Italy
	Galleria Italsider, Piombino, Italy
	Circolo Fotografico Milanese, Milan
1970	Galleria dell'Immagine, Rome
1976	Circolo Fotografico, Domodossola, Italy
1978	Musée Nicéphore Niepce, Chalon-sur-Saône, France
	Galerie de Ville, Macon, France
	Casino Municipale, San Pellegrino Terme, Italy
1979	Galleria Il Diaframma, Milan

	Galleria La Nuova Fotografia, Treviso, Italy
1980	Helmhaus, Zurich
	Galerie Herder, Freiburg
	Stadtgalerie, Altdorf, Switzerland
1981	Shopping Center Galerie, Emmen, Switzerland
	Shopping Center Galerie, Winterthur, Switzerland
	Galleria Serfontana, Chiasso, Switzerland
	Amicizia dei Popoli Convention, Rimini
	Tenda Circo al Vigentino, Milan
	Il Buco Fotografico, Catania, Italy
	Museo Diocesano, Mantua, Italy
1982	Hasselblad Gallery, Goteborg, Sweden
1983	Galleria L'Agostiniana, Rome
1985	Teatro Sociale, Bergamo, Italy
	Loggia delle Mercanzia, Siena, Italy
	Torre Civica, Castellina in Chianti, Italy
1986	Palazzo Barberini, Rome

Selected Group Exhibitions:

1958	*Expo-Den-X,* Copenhagen
1960	*Italian Photography in Japan,* Tokyo
1961	*Festival of Italian Photography,* Montpellier, France

1965	*Giornalismo e Comunicazione Visiva,* Genoa
1966	*Interpress Photo,* Moscow
1968	*2nd World Exhibition of Photography,* Presshaus Stern, Hamburg (and world tour)
	Europa '68, Bergamo (and *Europa '70*)
1976	*Camera: 10 years,* Lucerne
1979	*Venezia '79*
1980	*SICOF,* Milan

Collections:

Università di Parma; Centro per la Cultura nella Fotografia, Fermo, Italy; Bibliothèque Nationale, Paris; Musée Réattu, Arles, France; Musée Nicéphore Niepce, Chalon-sur-Saône, France; International Museum of Photography, George Eastman House, Rochester, New York.

Publications:

By MERISIO: Books—*Bodini,* Milan 1964; *Lo Sviluppo e la Pace nel Mondo,* Rome 1968; *Terra di Bergamo,* 3 vols., Bergamo 1969; *A Casa sotto il Sole,* Milan 1970; *Architettura del Rinascimento,* Milan 1971; *Prima dell'Ultima Stagione,* Milan 1971; *Lovere Antica. . . . ,* Genoa 1972; *Mi Chiamano Donna,* Milan 1972; *Siena,* Siena 1972; *Il Po,* Milan 1973; *Il Gargano,* Milan 1973; *Immagine di un'altra Lombardia,* Milan 1974; *Italia,* Zurich and Bergamo 1975; *Alla Sera,* Bergamo 1975; *Toscana,* Zurich, Bergamo and Bologna 1976; *Motor,* Milan 1976; *Antiche Città di Lombardia,* Zurich, Bergamo and Bologna 1976; *Puglia,* Zurich, Bergamo and Bologna 1977; *Valle d'Esino,* Bergamo 1977; *Veneto di Terraferma,* Zurich, Bergamo and Bologna 1978; *Marine Marchigiane,* Bergamo 1978; *Vivere nelle Alpi,* Zurich, Bergamo and Bologna 1979; *Sicilia,* Zurich, Bergamo and Bologna 1979; *Montagna Viva,* Milan 1979; *Paolo VI: Le Chiavi Pesanti,* Milan 1979; *Il Cuore della Marca,* Bergamo 1979; *Idea di Bergamo,* Bergamo 1980; *Quei Monti Azzurri,* Bergamo 1980; *I Lieti Colli,* Bergamo 1981; *Liguria,* Bologna 1981; *Il Cantico dell'Umbria,* Bergamo 1981; *Sacri Monti delle Alpi,* Milan 1981; *Palio,* Milan and Siena 1982; *Nostra Lombardia,* Bergamo 1982; *Mestieri di una volta,* Milan 1983; *La terra di Cecco,* Bergamo 1983; *Paesaggio Italiano,* Milan and Zurich 1984; *Piemonte,* Bologna 1984; *Piazze d'Italia,* Milan 1985; *Nel segno di Federico,* Bergamo 1986; *Citta murate,* Milan 1986; *Civiltà rurale,* Rom, 1987; *Civiltà dell'albero,* Rome 1988; *Civiltà artigiana,* Rome 1989; *Civiltà dell'acqua,* Rome 1990; *La Montagna che unisce,* Rome 1991; *L'arte del vendere,* Rome 1992; *Le Orme dell'uomo,* Rome 1993; *Ora et labora,* 1994; *Andrea Fantoni, scultore,* Milan 1994.

On MERISIO: Books—*70 Anni di Fotografia in Italia* by Italo Zannier, Modena 1978; *I Grandi Fotografi: Pepi Merisio,* with texts by Enzo Fabiani and Attilio Colombo, Milan 1982; *Pepi Merisio: 158 Fotografie,* exhibition catalogue, with texts by Roberto Barzanti and Attilio Colombo, Bergamo 1986. **Articles**—"Pepi Merisio," with texts by Attilio Colombo and Alberto Piovani, special issue of *Progresso Fotografico* (Milan), April 1980.

*

What does photography mean to me? So many things—a whole world; let me try to sum it up briefly. I believe that photography is a "discursive" means of expression; it is "writing with the light," one of the most immediate ways of communicating facts and emotions available to man. A means, then, that has merits and limitations derived from its specific qualities. I believe that the first aim of photography is "to seize the *instant,*" as it were, to take possession of the fleeting, changing moment (and this not only in press photography; there is always a moment plucked out from the progress of time in posed photography, in portraits, in landscapes . . .). The delection of the instant is the photographer's first moment of creativity. Every picture, however analytical it may be in the sum of the details of which it consists, is always a synthesis of a "moment" halted and picked out among so many others.

Another specific, fundamental element, I feel, is the search for the best rendering of the *detail* as the element that characterizes the structure and the material of things—"detail" which is not just concentration on the surface material but a study of surfaces, volumes and perspective. It is a deeper understanding of the manifold aspects of reality. That is why I do not care for informal photography, which I feel lacks this basic, concrete link with life and objects.

As a photographer I have long been mainly interested in the Italian country: the people, the work, the land. It is fundamental to me that every picture, every shot, should portray the "environment" and the situations in which the faces, the people and things exist, so as to constitute an accurate arrangement of place and time. So insistent foregrounds are very rare. It is rather a search for cordial participation.

—Pepi Merisio

*   *   *

Pepi Merisio is the singer, the bard, the poet of a small-scale Italy. His world is that of the region of Bergamo, in whose ways he was brought up and which constitutes the recurrent basis of his work as a photographer. He shows the themes of country life, a deeply felt devotion, people confined to the borders of history, a timeless world rooted deep in the millennia. He tells of this world as someone who is part of it, identifying his models—without moralizing or lamenting—in the dignity and humanity of the people he photographs. His many tours of India or Africa, the south of Italy or Turkey, and most of all of his own region, have given us what may be one of the last portraits of country life, living and complete—particularly that life in Italy. His last years of this kind of activity were characterized by a kind of vehement passion, fuelled by his awareness that this world was rapidly crumbling under the blows of our consumer culture. Today, only a few years on, there are many subjects, themes and places that survive only because of his pictures, which portray a way of life that may be lost forever.

Merisio's portrait of Italy (collected in many books of photographs, all marked by his quite unmistakable style) is informed by a method that tends to avoid anything that could be called "news." Even the basic element of the photographic process—its quality of instantaneousness—becomes more an obligatory factor than a freely chosen means of expression. Every picture is, as it were, constructed without reference to time, with a balanced sense of composition. There is little room for dynamic figuration. The photographer's lens evokes archetypes, models, emblems, each of which is a synthesis. What is so surprising is that these effects are obtained by deliberately avoiding emphasis: reduction of light, unusual angles, starkly contrasting tones, compression of planes—all of these devices are foreign to Merisio's style.

The documentary and emotional value of Merisio's photographs does not depend on a particularly brilliant personal style, but appears rather by way of the most normal of expressive instrumentation. He prefers focal depths that do not alter the proportions of shape and volume; he uses a vast range of tonal shades, giving the figuration a compact structure so that each picture approaches the greatest possible objectivity. But every picture forms part of a vast collective panorama, a highly charged view of a unique moment which is slowly fading away. Every picture reveals something of the heart of the rural world. And all Merisio's photographs have an expressive balance that faithfully mirrors the inward form of their creator's own spirit.

—Attilio Colombo

MERTIN, Roger.

Nationality: American. **Born:** Bridgeport, Connecticut, 9 December 1942. **Education:** Studied at the University of Bridgeport, 1960-61; Rochester Institute of Technology, New York, 1961-65, B.F.A. in photography 1965; studied in private workshops, under Nathan Lyons, Rochester, 1963-64, 1965-66, and at the Visual Studies Workshop, Rochester, 1969-72, M.F.A. 1972. **Family:** Married Joan Schultz in 1964 (divorced, 1972). **Career:** Photographer since 1962. Worked as a photographic technician, Eastman Kodak Company, Rochester, 1965-66; Head of the Reproduction Center, 1966-67, and Assistant Curator, 1968-69, George Eastman House, Rochester. Instructor, Rochester Institute of Technology, 1969-74. Instructor, 1973-74, and since 1975 Assistant Professor of Photographic Arts, University of Rochester. **Recipient:** Creative Artists Public Service Fellowship, New York,

1974; Guggenheim Photography Fellowship, 1974; National Endowment for the Arts Photography Fellowship, 1976. **Agents:** Light Gallery, 724 Fifth Avenue, New York 10019; Visual Studies Workshop, 31 Prince Street, Rochester, New York 14607; and Vision Gallery, 216 Newbury Street, Boston, Massachusetts 02116. **Address:** 18 Upton Park, Rochester, New York 14607, U.S.A.

Individual Exhibitions:

1966	International Museum of Photography, George Eastman House, Rochester, New York
1969	University of California at Davis
1970	*Plastic Love Dream,* Do Not Bend Gallery, London
1972	*Photos: August 9-September 12, 1971,* Toronto Gallery of Photography
1973	Light Gallery, New York
1974	Galerie Stampa, Basle
1975	Light Gallery, New York
1976	Afterimage Gallery, Dallas
1978	Center for Contemporary Photography, Chicago
	Visual Studies Workshop, Rochester, New York
1979	Sun Valley Center for Arts and Humanities, Idaho
	Rockwell Kent Gallery, Plattsburgh, New York
	Light Work, Syracuse, New York
1980	Light Gallery, New York
1981	Friends of Photography, Carmel, California (with Larry S. Ferguson and Frank Gohlke)

Selected Group Exhibitions:

1966	*Seeing Photographically,* International Museum of Photography, George Eastman House, Rochester, New York
1967	*Contemporary Photographers IV,* International Museum of Photography, George Eastman House, Rochester, New York
1969	*The Photograph as Object 1843-1969,* National Gallery of Canada, Ottawa (toured Canada)
1974	*Photography Unlimited,* Fogg Art Museum, Harvard University, Cambridge, Massachusetts
1976	*Photographie: Rochester, New York,* Centre Culturel Americain, Paris
1977	*Great West: Real/Ideal,* University of Colorado, Boulder (subsequently Smithsonian Institution travelling exhibition; toured the United States)
1978	*Mirrors and Windows: American Photography since 1960,* Museum of Modern Art, New York (toured the United States, 1978-80)
1980	*The Imaginary Photo Museum,* Kunsthalle, Cologne
1983	*Photography in America 1910-83,* Tampa Museum, Florida
1985	*American Images 1945-80,* Barbican Art Gallery, London (toured Britain)

Collections:

Museum of Modern Art, New York; International Museum of Photography, George Eastman House, Rochester, New York; Visual Studies Workshop, Rochester, New York; Museum of Fine Arts, Boston; Princeton University, New Jersey; Art Institute of Chicago; Minneapolis Institute of Art; Bibliothèque Nationale, Paris; National Gallery of Canada, Ottawa; Australian National Gallery, Canberra.

Publications:

By MERTIN: Book—*Roger Mertin: Records 1976-78,* edited by Charles Desmarais, Chicago 1978.

On MERTIN: Books—*Photography in the Twentieth Century* by Nathan Lyons, New York 1967; *Vision and Expression,* edited by Nathan Lyons, New York 1969; *The Print* by Time-Life editors, New York 1970; *The Great West: Real/Ideal,* exhibition catalogue, edited by Sandy Hume, Ellen Manchester and Gary Metz, Boulder, Colorado 1977; *Mirrors and Windows: American Photography since 1960,* exhibition catalogue, by John Szarkowski, New York 1978; *The Photograph Collector's Guide* by Lee D. Witkin and Barbara London, Boston and London 1979; *One of a Kind: Recent Polaroid Photography,* edited by Belinda Rathbone, Boston 1979; *Nude,* edited by Constance Sullivan, New York 1980; *The Imaginary Photo Museum* by Helmut Gernsheim, Renate and L. Fritz Gruber and others, Cologne 1981, London 1982; *New Color/New York* by Sally Eauclaire, New York 1984; *American Images: Photography 1945-1980,* edited by Peter Turner and John Benton-Harris, London 1985. **Articles**—"Notes upon Rising from a Plastic Love Dream" by Gary Metz in *Album* (London), August 1970; "Hoops: Eight Photographs" by Joe Flaherty in *New Lazarus Review* (Utica, New York) 1979; "Meditations on a Blue Photograph" by Gray Metz in *Untitled* (Carmel, California), no. 23, 1980.

*

It is my conviction that the statement a photographer makes be in the photographs.

—Roger Mertin

*   *   *

All of the works of Roger Mertin bear witness to his respect for the qualities of the unmanipulated photograph. From his early (c. 1967) moderately scaled photographs of shop windows to the more recent (c. 1977) large format images of trees, he has made pictures of great beauty and sensuality. The prints are skillfully made and comparable to the magnificent prints of Minor White and Paul Caponigro. However, comparison with these two photographers is limited to technical excellence. White's and Caponigro's desire for transcendence through abstraction in much of their work is far removed from Mertin's aims, which appear to be concerned with the creation of a variety of cultural catalogues.

When Mertin works with the human figure, elements are introduced that will prevent any contemplation of timelessness or universality. For example, in the series "Plastic Love Dream" (c. 1969) the figures are usually wrapped in plastic sheeting, a contemporary material that obviates any comparison with the romantic figure photography of the turn of the century or even the erotic presence of Edward Weston's photographs of women. In fact, the figure in Mertin's work often appears as incidental to the materials included and the light patterns being created and recorded.

In Mertin's series of pictures of trees and of basketball goals, the meaning again does not reside in the ostensible subject. His images of trees have often been compared to those of Eugène Atget, but they really have very little in common except the subject matter. Atget's trees appear as massive sentinels in the Positivistic French gardens. Conversely, Mertin's trees traverse a range of ambiguities: he observes with a guileless curiosity horticultural forms of bondage; "freakishly" deformed trees; and trees that appear to have no distinguishing characteristics save existence. Herein lies his elegant comprehension of one of photography's fundamental attributes, ambiguity. The pictures are nominally about trees, but they are really an extraordinarily rich documentation of the effluvium that is an everyday component of American culture.

Mertin has obviously looked at a great many photographs and fully understood, for instance, that the central figure in a Lewis Hine portrait is never the "only" thing in the picture. The highly active picture plane that Mertin creates may be interpreted in numerous ways, from Weston's often cited ."..the thing itself" to a virtual palimpsest of our age's methods and mores. But one is never quite certain. The air of ambiguity prevails.

—Thomas F. Barrow

METZKER, Ray K.

Nationality: American. **Born:** Milwaukee, Wisconsin, 10 September 1931. **Education:** Whitefish Bay High School, Wisconsin, 1945-49; studied art at Beloit College, Wisconsin, 1949-53, B.A. 1953; and photography, under Harry Callahan and Aaron Siskind, Institute of Design, Illinois Institute of Technology, Chicago, 1956-59, M.S. 1959. **Military Service:** Served in the United States Army, in Korea, 1954-56. **Career:** Freelance photographer since 1959. Instructor in Photography, 1962-78, and since 1978 Professor, Philadelphia College of Art (Chairman of the Photography/Film Department, 1978-79). Visiting Associate Professor, University of New Mexico, Albuquerque, 1970-72; Adjunct Professor, Rhode Island School of Design, Providence, 1977; Adjunct Visiting Professor, Columbia College, Chicago, 1980-1982; Smith Distinguished Visiting Artist, George Washington University, 1987-1988. **Recipient:** Guggenheim Fellowship, 1966, 1979; National Endowment for the Arts Fellowship, 1974,1988; Bernheim Fellow, 1989. **Agent:** Laurence Miller Gallery, 138 Spring Street, New York, New York 10012. **Address:** 733 South 6th Street, Philadelphia, Pennsylvania 19147, U.S.A.

Individual Exhibitions:

1959	Art Institute of Chicago
1967	Museum of Modern Art, New York
1968	Photographer's Gallery, New York (with Paul Caponigro)
1971	University of New Mexico, Albuquerque
1974	Print Club of Philadelphia
	Dayton College of Art, Ohio
1976	Picture Gallery, Zurich
1978	Marian Locks Gallery, Philadelphia
	International Center of Photography, New York
1979	Center for Contemporary Photography, Chicago
	Light Gallery, New York
	Galerie Delpire, Paris
1980	Pennsylvania Academy of Fine Arts, Philadelphia
	Sand Creatures, Light Gallery, New York
1981	*New Mexico: Pictus Interruptus,* Paul Cava Gallery, Philadelphia
1982	Page and Page Photographic Art, Dallas, Texas
	Film in the Cities, St. Paul, Minnesota (with Tom Arndt)
1983	*City Whispers,* Catskill Center of Photography, Woodstock, New York
	Memphis State University, Tennessee
	City Whispers: Photos 1980-82, Marian Locks Gallery, Philadelphia
	Twenty-Five Years, G.H. Dalsheimer Gallery, Baltimore, Maryland
	Multiple Means/Multiple Ends, Carl Solway Gallery, Cincinnati, Ohio
	Edwynn Houk Gallery, Chicago
1984	*City Whispers,* Laurence Miller Gallery, New York
	Unknown Territory, Houston Museum of Fine Arts, Texas (toured the United States, 1984-86)
1985	Davison Art Center, Wesleyan University, Connecticut
	San Francisco Museum of Modern Art, San Francisco
	Art Institute of Chicago, Illinois
	Philadelphia Museum of Art
	Catskill Center for Photography, New York
	Laurence Miller Gallery, New York City
1986	Allen Street Gallery, Dallas, Texas
	High Museum of Art, Atlanta, Georgia
	International Museum of Photography, Rochester, New York
	National Museum of American Art, Washington, D.C.
1987	Laurence Miller Gallery, New York
	George Dalsheimer Gallery, Baltimore, Maryland
1991	The Art Institute of Chicago
	Cleveland Museum of Art
	Jane Jackson Gallery, Atlanta
1992	Laurence Miller Gallery, New York
	Turner/Krull Gallery, Los Angeles
	Shadai Gallery, Tokyo
1993	Locks Gallery, Philadelphia
	The Art Museum of Princeton University
1994	Halstead Gallery, Birmingham, Michigan
	Laurence Miller Gallery, New York

Selected Group Exhibitions:

1959	*Photography in the Fine Arts I,* Metropolitan Museum of Art, New York
1962	*Photography USA,* DeCordova Museum, Lincoln, Massachusetts
1966	*American Photography: The 1960s,* University of Nebraska, Lincoln
1970	*New Photography U.S.A.,* Museum of Modern Art, New York (and world tour)
1971	*The Figure and the Landscape,* International Museum of Photography, George Eastman House, Rochester, New York
1973	*Landscape/Cityscape,* Metropolitan Museum of Art, New York
1978	*Mirrors and Windows: American Photography since 1960,* Museum of Modern Art, New York (toured the United States, 1978-80)
1982	*Target III: In Sequence,* Houston Museum of Fine Arts, Texas
1985	*American Images 1945-80,* Barbican Art Gallery, London (toured Britain)
1987	*Photography and Art 1946-86,* Los Angeles County Museum of Art
1988	*Art Networks 1950-1970,* Fotofest 1988, Houston
	Photographic Truth, The Bruce Museum, Greenwich, Connecticut
	Swimmers, Burden Gallery, Aperture Foundation, New York
1989	*Invention and Continuity in Contemporary Photography,* Metropolitan Museum of Art, New York
	On the Art of Fixing a Shadow: One Hundred and Fifty Years of Photography, National Gallery of Art, Art Institute of Chicago, and Los Angeles County Museum of Art
1990	*Photography Until Now,* Metropolitan Museum of Modern Art, New York
	City Landscape, Tokyo Museum of Photography
1991	*Motion and Document, Sequence and Time: Eadweard Muybridge and Contemporary American Photography,* ICP, New York, (travelled)
	Poetics of the Real: American Landscape Photography, Columbus Museum of Art
	Departures: Photography 1923-1990, travelling exhibition, organised by Independent Curators
1992	*Special Collections: The Photographic Order from Pop to Now,* ICP Midtown, New York
	Three Decades of Midwestern Photography, Davenport Museum of Art, Davenport, Iowa
1993	*Crossing Territories,* Museum of New Mexico, Santa Fe
	Recent Acquisitions, Museum of Modern Art, New York
	Multiple Images: Photographs Since 1965 from the Collection, Museum of Modern Art, New York

Collections:

Museum of Modern Art, New York; International Museum of Photography, George Eastman House, Rochester, New York; Rhode Island School of Design, Providence; Smithsonian Institution, Washington, D.C.; Art Institute of Chicago; Exchange National Bank, Chicago; Krannert Museum, University of Illinois, Urbana; Sheldon Memorial Art Gallery, University of Nebraska, Lincoln; University of California at Los Angeles Art Galleries; Bibliothèque Nationale, Paris; Addison Gallery of American Art, Andover, MA; Allen Art

Nude, 1966, composite, printed and assembled 1990. Photograph ©Ray K. Metzker. Courtesy Laurence G. Miller Inc., New York.

Museum, Oberlin, Ohio; Australian National Gallery; Beloit College, Beloit, Wisconsin; Fogg Art Museum; IMP/GEH, New York; Los Angeles County Museum of Art; Metropolitan Museum of Art, New York; Museum of Fine Arts, Boston; Philadelphia Museum of Art; Shadai Gallery, Tokyo.

Publications:

By METZKER: Books—*My Camery and I in the Loop,* with text by Hugh Edwards, Chicago 1959; *Portfolio II—Discovery: Inner and Outer Worlds,* Carmel, California 1970; *Sand Creatures,* Millerton, New York 1979; *Unknown Territory,* with text by Anne W. Tucker, Millerton, New York 1984; *Earthly Delights,* 1988. **Article**—"Ray K. Metzker," interview, with Chuck Isaacs, in *Afterimage* (Rochester, New York), November 1978;

On METZKER: Books—*The Persistence of Vision* by Nathan Lyons, New York 1967; *Photography in the 20th Century* by Nathan Lyons, New York 1967; *Bennett, Steichen, Metzker: The Wisconsin Heritage,* with text by Arnold Gore, introduction by Tracy Atkinson, Milwaukee 1970; *Looking at Photographs* by John Szarkowski, New York 1973; *The Photographer's Choice,* edited by Kelly Wise, Danbury, New Hampshire 1975; *Geschichte der Fotografie im 20. Jahrhundert/The History of Photography in the 20th Century* by Petr Tausk, Cologne 1977, London 1980; *Mirrors and Windows: American Photography since 1960,* exhibition catalogue, by John Szarkowski, New York 1978; *Visions and Images: American Photographers on Photography* by Barbaralee Diamonstein, New York 1981; *The Imaginary Photo Museum* by Helmut Gernsheim, Renate and L. Fritz Gruber and others, Cologne 1981, London 1982; *The Gallery of World Photography: Photography as Fine Art, 1983; American Images: Photography 1945-1980,* edited by Peter Turner and John Benton-Harris, London 1985; *Photography and Art 1946-1986,* exhibition catalogue, by Andy Grundberg and Kathleen M. Gauss, Los Angeles 1987. **Articles**—"New Talent U.S.A.: Photography" in *Art in America* (New York), no. 1, 1961; "Ray K. Metzker" in *Aperture* (Millerton, New York), Fall 1967; "Ray Metzker's Consideration of Light" by Christopher Sieberling in *Exposure* (Rochester, New York), September 1977; "Currents: American Photography Today" by Andy Grundberg and Julia Scully in *Modern Photography* (New York), November 1978; "Exhibitions: Ray Metzker" by Owen Edwards in *American Photographer* (New York), November 1978; "Ray K. Metzker at Marion Locks" by Janet Kardon in *Art in America* (New York), November/December 1978; "Ray Metzker" by Peter C. Bunnell in *Print Collector's Newsletter* (New York), January/February 1979; "Ray K. Metzker: Form as Expression" by Andy Brundberg in *Modern Photography* (New York), November 1981; "Photographer Metzker Places Aesthetics Before Subject" by John Dorsey in *The Sun* (Baltimore), 12 September 1983; *Art Forum,* 1985; *Art in America,* May, 1985; *Art News,* September 1987; *New York Times,* 22 May, 1987.

*

"Event" has been a key term for the way a photograph has to work for me. It's been with me a long time. It certainly was important in the Loop, where I would see the street activity, then I would see those relationships developing, and I would feel something fall into place. It wasn't that I came up to something and said, Isn't that a nice arrangement. It was a sense of the tension, of knowing that these things were moving and also that they had come into a position where the tensions were right. After a while, it could happen simply with light. It would have that sense of something coming to place where it wasn't at rest; it wasn't going to be there in a permanent way. For me, a lot of things were just dominant images, like the side of a barn, which is very rich tonally—but there's no event there. I can identify it as being rich material for a photograph, but there's something that's too static about it. In a way, you don't have to wait for anything. I think that's what happens, what continues to happen, but it's become more abstract and more rarefied. I may be only underscoring a photographic interpretation of moment. There's an excitement based on action. In a world where all things seem be changing—either acting on or being acted upon—the camera is best suited to deal with those changes. Photographers are victims of paradox—tracking the impermanent to make it permanent.

There's a kind of duality in me: on the one hand I started out dealing with events, the description of the street, the description of the city, description of situations people find themselves in, people relating to themselves. Let's call it the visible. But there's something else in me that wants to deal with the other side. The results may be read as visual mysteries. I think that's a very strong pull. There's one need, acting out of restraint, that acknowledges the subject, and an attempt to represent it. But other times something else says, Go and leave it behind. I think that maybe the "Pictus Interruptus" series is a sort of mid-point. I'm conscious of that duality, but who knows where it's going?

A lot of my work is about events, but I also think a lot of it is about fragmentation. There's probably a connection between three terms: event, fragmentation, and synthesis. The point of entry for me was the event. But when you go back to so many of the things I've done, even to Chicago, there's always that interest in fragmenting as a way of changing a situation, a means of transforming it. When I finally go into the composite series, I'm willing to synthesize. It's necessary, in the putting-together, to have a sense of structure. Often that is established by identifying and building around an event.

You have to break something down in order to have the parts to synthesize. If something's complete, there's no need to synthesize—it's complete. In journalism, the photograph is *of* an event, whereas in my later work, the photograph *is* the event. The viewer is expected to look into the photography, to see what is there and how it is related—that is, how one part is acting on another.

—Ray K. Metzker

*   *   *

Ray K. Metzker is one of the most inventive and pioneering of contemporary American photographers. Trained by Harry Callahan and Aaron Siskind, influenced by painters and sculptors like Matisse, Frank Stella, and Jean Tinguely and composers such as Stravinsky, Bartok, and Chavez, he displays an original experimental and creative vision. The force of his image selection is as remarkable as his singlemindedness in exploring the photographic medium. Metzker's innovative use of the photographic elements—formal interrelationships, visual patterning, tonal contrasts, print-size, focus, etc.— demonstrate a distinct personal form and style. He challenges habitual and conventional expectations and responses with regard to the image. his "scanning and whooping," as he puts it, is an exciting definitional exploration of the medium. His originality is evidenced in this basic approach—to explore the problems and properties of the medium, to define photography by making images of conviction and resolution. With such determination and imaginativeness, Metzker for more than 20 years has tried and succeeded in manipulating the formal elements to make images that communicate an expressive statement— for photography to stand autonomously as an image yet *be* something simultaneously. By thus inviting viewers to experience a photograph in a radical way, he remains (to quote him) "an intellectual wanderer." But there is a distinct intuitive and visceral force in his imagery which cannot be minimized, clearly illustrated in his series on Chicago and Atlantic City and in the "Pictus" series.

In the 1950s Metzker's photography consisted primarily of single-image prints and a kind of formalism in patterning. But he got tired of the "predictability" and "frozen arrangements" of the single frame. So he moved to "the composite, collected and related moments employing methods of combination, repetition and superimposition." Even in those early photographs one finds his originality and exploratory zeal and determination, for instance in his pictures in the Loop in Chicago. His sense of the spatial geometry, keen patterning, powerful image selection—tracking down the moment to the point of merger of the environment and the people—and the subtlety of interrelationships within a particular image demonstrate Metzker's singleminded approach to the medium as an expressive statement of form and emotive tone. The "Sand Creatures" series is as evocative as it is captivating in its patterning. In his photographs of Chicago, Philadelphia, and Atlantic City the tonal contrasts match in a unique way the juxtapositional patterning of figures and the environment, which instantly directs the viewers to a new way of looking at the images.

Metzker extends this exacting and captivating patterning into his multiple-image photographs depicting the nature of urban living. Starkly lit faces or objects in the midst of stark blackness document particular details as well as, through the method of repetition, juxtaposition, and sequencing, make a metaphoric statement about the city life—its vitality, multiplicity, disconnectedness, and solitude. The abstract designs in his multiple-images, too, express a certain kind of kinetic force and musicality as the entire roll of film unfolds as one single strip with no interruption or as the varied frame-formats present themselves. What also strikes one as extraordinary in these photographs of the 1950s and 60s is the artist's fusion of the intellectual/conceptional attitude and the intuitive power so clearly consummated in his images of the 70s.

Metzker's "Pictus" series records the stunning growth of a visual artist. He has again deliberately and expertly manipulated the medium for newer and more challenging expressive forms and visual experience. In the early 70s Metzker made several photographs in New Mexico; they mark a transition.

The strong contrast and graininess of the print—a distinct tonal richness and luminosity of the middle zones, the manipulation of shadows, and the juxtapositioning of clouds, walls, concrete block buildings, doorways, and plants in his Albuquerque series—reveal an innovative mind, passionate and relentless. The significant aspect of these New Mexico photographs is the way in which Metzker has used the pictorial space and organized the obvious objects in the image not for information or description, for obstruction and interruption are so blatant and deliberate, but to tease us to reflect. These pictures demand a readjustment—a perceptual revolution; each suggests a paradox, as it were, not only in the whimsicality of formats and patterns, but also in the unpredictability and complexity of composition and the dynamics of contrariness.

The 1977 "Pictus Interruptus" series, though compositionally comparatively straightforward, introduces us to a stunning visual experience. In these pictures, taken mostly in Greece and Philadelphia, close objects (hands, papers, etc.) are blurred or flattened out, but the distant objects—clouds, sails, etc.—remain sharp and defined. The close objects are the interrupting elements interposed between the lens and the subject—rooftop nightsky, Greek islandscape, sidewalks, streets, and clouds. The interruptors are kept purposely unidentifiable, "neutral." As such, they simultaneously destroy part of the subject and reconstruct the image. Then there is the device of textual contrast and continuous tonality. In other words, Metzker has now manipulated the properties of the medium in a challengingly paradoxical way. Scales and focus do not mesh; the negative space is used both as void and volume; dematerialization and delineation alternate; and scale and space are in unexpected juxtaposition. Thus he has ventured into one of the most threatening and bewildering areas in any creative endeavour—balancing ambiguity, paradox, and imagination, fusing concept and intuition into an effective expressive mode. And Metzker has triumphed. In intensity and lyricality and through daring imagination, Ray Metzker has radicalized the medium of photography and tantalized viewers to experience his photographs—especially the "Pictus" series—as an act of courage and inventiveness and a state of visual transcendence.

—Deba P. Patnaik

MEYER, Pedro

Nationality: Mexican. **Born:** Madrid, Spain 1935; emigrated to Mexico with his parents in 1937, in 1942 he became a Mexican citizen. **Education:** Self taught photographer. **Career:** Meyer also curates, writes and lectures on photography. Meyer was the founding President of the Mexican Council of Photography—Consejo Méxicano de Fotografiá, Mexico City, 1977.He established and organised the first Colloquium of Latin American Photography, held in Mexico City in 1979, and two further colloquiums held in Mexico City in 1981 and Havana, Cuba in 1984.Since the early 1980s Meyer has increasingly become involved in the world of new technologies and their relationship to photography.In 1990 he produced the first photographic work with narration to be published on a CD ROM—*I photograph to Remember,* the story of the last years of his parents' lives, published by the Voyager Company USA. In 1993, *Truths and Fictions,* a major exhibition of his digital photographic works produced over the last eight years began an international tour. In 1994, an accompanying CD ROM of the same title was published in association with the exhibition. **Recipient:** Purchase Prize, Bienal of Photography Award, Instituto Nacional de Bellas Artes, Mexico City, 1980 and 1983; Premio Internazionale di Cultura Citta di Anghiari, Italy, 1984; Artist in residence Arizona Commission, and first prize by the Organización Internacional del Trabajao, OIT, in Santiago de Chile. John Simon Guggenheim Fellowship Grant, 1987. National Endowments of the Arts award, 1992; US/ Mexico Fund for Culture award to produce *Truths and Fictions* exhibition.

The Border, 1985. Photograph by Pedro Meyer.

Address: Ortega 20, Coyoacan, Mexico DF, Mexico 0400; 1333 Beverly Glen, No. 906, Los Angeles, California 90024, U.S.A.

Individual Exhibitions:

1978   *El Retrato Contemporaneo en Mexico: pintura y fotografía,* Carrillo Gil, INBA-SEP, Mexico DF, Mexico
        Testimonios Sandanistas, Galería de fotografía de la Casa del Lago de la UNAM, Mexico DF, Mexico
        Casa de las Américas, La Habana, Cuba.
1979   *Testimonios Sandanistas—parte II* Nicaragua-Homenaje Plástico, Salón de la Plástica Mexicana, Mexico DF, Mexico
1980   *De Minha Terra: Realidades Lendas e Mitos,* Museu da Imagem e do Som, Sao Paolo, Brazil
1981   *Photographs by Pedro Meyer,* CityScape Foto Gallery, Pasadena, California
        De Minha Terra: Realidades Lendas e Mitos, Centro de Artes, Universidad de Pernambuco, Brazil, Museo de Arte Moderno Salvador, Bahia, Brazil
1982   *Fotografías de Pedro Meyer,* Fachhochschule Bielefeld, Germany, Galeria 666, Paris, France
1983   *Tres Fotógrafos Mexicanos,* Museo Nacional de Bellas Arts de Cuba, La Habana, Cuba
        Fotografía de Pedro Meyer, Nikon Gallery, Zurich, Switzerland, Galeria Spectrum—Cannon, Zaragoza, Spain
        Juchitán: retrato de un pueblo, Casa de Cultura, Ecuatoriana, Quito, Ecuador

1984   *Tres Fotógrafos Mexicanos,* Casa de la Cultura, ''Fernando Gordillo,'' Managua, Nicaragua
1985   *Images of Pedro Meyer,* Palazzo Pretorio, Anghiari, Italy; Centro Ricerca Aperta, Naples, Italy; June's Gallery, Yuma, Arizona
        Juchitán, Casa de la Cultura of Juchitán, Oaxaca, Mexico
1986   *Los Otros y Nosotros,* Museo de Arte Moderno, Bosque de Chapultepec, Mexico DF, Mexico
        Pedro Meyer, Photographe Mexicain, Douchy-les-Mines, Hotel de Ville, Centre Regional de la Photographie Nord-Pas de Calais, France
        Tiempos de America, Sasso di Castalda-Edificio Scolastico, Comune di Sasso di Castalda, (Potenza), Italy
        Planket 86, Centre for Photography, Stockholm
1987   *Photographs by Pedro Meyer,* San Francisco Museum of Modern Art
1988   *Pedro Meyer: Mexican Photography,* Rantagalleria Photo Gallery, Oulu, Finland
1989   *Pedro Meyer: Contemporary Mexican Photography,* Massachusetts College of Art, North Gallery, Boston
        Photographs of Pedro Meyer, Visions Gallery, San Francisco
1993   *Truths and Fictions,* Museum of Photography, Riverside, California
        Museuo de Artes Visuales Alejandro Otero, Caracas, Venezuela
1994   *Truths and Fictions,* Museum of Contemporary Photography, Chicago, IL; Impressions Gallery, York, England; Mexican Museum, San Francisco; Rencontres International de la

Photographie, Arles, France; Centro del Imagen, Mexico City, Mexico

1995 *Truths and Fictions,* Corcoran Gallery of Art, Washington, D.C.; Fotografie Foto Forum, Frankfurt, Germany; Museum of South Texas, Corpus Christi; Houston Center of Photography, Houston, Texas; Foto Massan, Gothenburg, Sweden

Selected Group Exhibitions:

1976 *The Photographers Choice,* Witkin Gallery, New York
1977 *Salón Nacional de Artes Plásticas,* Sección Bienal de Gráfica, Palacio de Bellas Artes, INBA, Mexico DF, Mexico
1978 *Contemporary Mexican Photographers,* Center for Creative Photography, Tucson, Arizona; Meridian House International, Washington D.C.; Nexus Gallery, Atlanta, Georgia
1979 *Hecho en Latinoamérica 1,* Palacio de San Giovani, Turin, Italy; Giardinni de la Biennale, Venice, Italy
1980 *Photographers Contemporaines du Mexique,* Musee Picasso, Chateau D'Antibes, France
1981 *Fotografie Lateinamerika 1860-1980,* Museo Kunsthaus, Zurich, Switzerland
1982 *La Photographie Contemporaine en Amerique Latine,* Musee National D'Art Moderne Centre Georges Pompidou, Paris
1983 *Homenaje a José Clemente Orozco,* Palacio de Bellas Artes, INBA, Mexico DF, Mexico
1984 *La Fiesta de los Muertos,* Musee D'Art Moderne de la Ville de Paris, France
1985 *Fotógrafos Mexicanos en la Revolución,* Asociación Sandanista de Trabajadores de la Cultura, Managua, Nicaragua
L'autoportrait, a l'age de la Photographie, Le Musee Cantonal des Beaux-Arts de Lausanne, Switzerland
1986 *Eight Mexican Photographers,* San Francisco Camerawork Gallery, San Francisco, California
39 Mexican Photographers, Houston Center of Photography, Texas
1987 *Latin American Photography,* Burden Gallery, New York; Society for Photographic Education, San Diego, California; Los Angeles Art Association Gallery, Los Angeles
Encuentro de Grabado '87, Centro Wifredo Lam, Ciudad de la Habana, Cuba
1988 *Imagen de México,* Galeria de Arte del Palacio de Exposiciones, Vienna; Museum of Modern Art, Dallas, Texas
1989 *La Memoria del Tiempo: 150 years of Mexican Photography,* Museum of Modern Art, Mexico DF, Mexico
Ten Years After, The Yuma Symposium, Yuma, Arizona
1990 *What's New: Mexico City,* The Art Institute of Chicago
Between Worlds: Contemporary Mexican Photography, Impressions Gallery, York, England; Camden Arts Centre, London; University of East Anglia, England; International Center of Photography, New York
1991 *Selections from the History of Mexican Photography,* Calvin Morris Gallery, New York
Memoria del Tiempo, Gallery of the Union of Polish Photographers, Varsovia, Poland; Photo Gallery, International Center of Photography, Berlin; Museum of Popular Arts and Traditions, Rome; Sala de Exposiciones del Monumento a los Descubridores Portugueses, Lisbon; Association of Art of Alesund & Rekjavik, Iceland; Bienal de Fotografia, Tenerife, Canary Islands
1992 *Photo Video—Photography in the Age of the Computer,* Impressions Gallery, York, England; Ikon Gallery, Birmingham, England; Photographer's Gallery, London
Breaking Barriers: Revisualising the Urban Landscape, Santa Monica Museum, California
1993 *Montage 1993,* Rochester, New York; Addison Gallery of American Art, Andover, Massachusetts

Collections:

Addison Gallery of American Art, Andover, Massachusetts; Bert Hartkamp Collection, Amsterdam; Bibliotheque National de Paris, Paris; Boston Museum of Fine Arts, Boston; Center for Creative Photography, Tucson, Arizona; Coleccion de Franco Fontana, Milan, Italy; Comuna di Anghari, Palazzo Preorio, Anghiari, Italy; Museum of Modern Art, Mexico DF; Grunwald Graphic Arts Center, University of California at Los Angeles, Los Angeles; International Museum of Photography, George Eastman House, Rochester, New York; International Center of Photography, New York; Museum of Modern Art, New York; Musee Nationale d'Art Moderne, Centre Georges Pompidou, Paris; Riverside Museum of Photography, Riverside, California; San Francisco Museum of Modern Art, California; The Museum of Fine Arts, Houston, Texas; Universidad de Parma, Parma, Italy; Los Angeles County Museum of Art, California; Victoria and Albert Museum, London.

Publications:

By Meyer: Books—*Negromex en Blanco y Negro,* Mexico City, 1977; *Hecho en Latinoamerica,* Mexico City, 1978; *Hecho en Latinoamerica 2,* with Lazaro Blanco and others, Mexico City, 1981; *Pedro Meyer* with introduction by Carlos Monsivais, Mexico City, 1986; *Tiempos de America,* Comune di Sasso di Castalda, (Potenza), Italy, 1985; *Planket 86,* exhibition catalogue, Sweden, 1986; *Espejo de Espinas,* Mexico City, 1986; *Los Cohetes Duraron Todo el Dia,* Mexico, 1988; *Inside the USA- Pedro Meyer, Between Worlds, Contemporary Mexican Photography,* 1990; *I Photograph to Remember,* CD ROM, USA 1990; *Verdades y Ficciones*—catalogue, Venezuela, 1993; *Truths and Fictions,* CD ROM, USA, 1994; *Truths and Fictions,* USA, 1995; *Truth and Fictions,* USA, 1995. **Articles**—"Introduction" to *Memorias del Primer Coloquio Latinamericano de Fotografia,* Mexico City, 1973; "Dignidades" in *Revista Arquitecto,* Mexico City, 1978; "Ernesto Cardenal entre Rifles M-1" in *Uno Mas Uno,* Mexico City, Nov. 1978; Introduction to *XX Aniversario Casa de las Americas,* exhibition catalogue, Mexico City, 1979; article in *Symposium uber Fotografie,* Graz, Austria, 1980; "Letter from Nicaragua" in *American Photographer,* New York, Jan 1980; "Sobre la Fotografia Cubana" in *Semena de Bellas Artes,* Mexico City, July, 1980; "La Fotografia Latinoamericano" in *Fototecnica,* Havana, Jan/March 1984; "Nuevos Espejismos" in *Nexis,* Mexico City, July, 1985; "Inside the USA" *American Art,* Vol 5, No 3, Oxford, England 1991; "La Revolución Digital" in *Luna Cornea,* No 2, 1993; "Los desafíos de la tecnología a la creación fotográfica latinoamericana" in *La Jornada Semenal,* No 267, July 1994.

On Meyer: Books—*The Photographer's Choice,* edited by Kelly Wise, Danbury, New Hampshire, 1971; *Retrospectiva de Pedro Meyer,* exhibition catalogue by Carlos Monsivais, Mexico City, 1980; *Time-Life Photography Year Book 1979,* New York, 1979; *7 Portafolios Mexicanos,* exhibition catalogue, Mexico City, 1980; *La Photographie Contemporaine en Amerique Latine,* exhibition catalogue with text by Alain Sayag, Paris, 1982; *Los Otros y Nostros,* exhibition catalogue by Vicente Lenero, Mexico City, 1986; *Taking New Ideas Back to the Old World—talking to Esther Parada, Hector Mendez Caratini, and Pedro Meyer* by Trisha Ziff; Photo Video—*Photography in the Age of the Computer,* UK, 1991; *Canto a La Realidad—Fotografia,* Erika Billeter, Spain, 1993; *A Shadow Born of Earth, New Photography in Mexico,* Elizabeth Ferrer, USA, 1993. **Articles**—"Foto Imagenes de Pedro Meyer" in *Fotomundo,* Mexico City, March, 1970; "Los Trabajos de Pedro Meyer" by Raquel Tibol in *Gaceta,* UNAM, Mexico City, July 1976; "Le Immagini dell'Anima Messicana" by Edo Prando in *Fotografia Italiana,* Milan, March 1977; "Evocacion Juenos y Metafoeras" by Yolanda Sierra in *El,* Mexico City, March 1977; "Seis Abstracciones Conretas" by Raquel Tibol in *Proceso,* Mexico City, Jan 1978; "Nicaraguan Kuuat" by Marjaana Mykkanen in *Nakopiiri,* Helsinki, Jan 1979; "Obiettivo Mitra de Meyer" in *Il Diario,* Venice, July 1979; "Que Puede Decir La Fortografia de una Revolucion" by Nestor Garcia Canclini in *Casa de las Americas,* Havana, Jan 1980; "Latin American Photography" by Esther Parada in *Afterimage,* Rochester, NY, Nov 1981; "Photography, Art and Politics in Latin America" by Eva Cockcroft in *Art in America,* New York, Oct 1982; "Pedro Meyer Universalfotograf" by Martin Sigrist in *Nikon News,* Zurich, No 4 1984; "Pedro Meyer, Noted Mexico City Photographer" by Patrick McCune in *Yuma Daily Sun,* Yuma, AZ, 15 Feb, 1985; "Rempi d'America: fotografie dei Pedro Meyer" in *L'Illustrazione Italiana,* Milan, May/June 1985; "Latin American Issue"

Aperture Magazine, by Nan Richardson, 1988; ''Truth and Fictions: Photographs by Pedro Meyer'' by Ruben Martinez, *Mother Jones,* Nov/Dec 1993; ''Pedro Meyer'' by Henry Brimmer, *Photo Metro,* USA, Nov 1993; ''Pedro Meyer'' by Sue Weekes, *XYZ Magazine,* UK, Oct 1993; ''Pedro Meyer'' by Rubén Ortiz, *Poliester,* Mexico City, vol 2 no 5, Spring 1993; ''The camera sometimes lies—How Pedro Meyer took his photography into the computer age'' by Derek Bishton, *Telegraph Magazine,* UK 9 April, 1994; ''Rom and Roll'' by Jon Katz, *Rolling Stone,* April 7, 1994; *Reportage,* UK, Issue 4, Spring 1994; ''Interview: Pedro Meyer'' by Jesse Lerner, *Latin American Art,* USA, Vol 5 no 4 1994; ''Wie die Bilder lügen lernen'' by Martin Knapp, *Zeit Magazine,* Germany, September, 1994; ''When in Rom'' by Franllin Odel, *Visions,* Art Quarter, USA, Summer 1994.

*   *   *

In general, when a photographer rejects the more obvious of the variety of possibilities offered to him by the medium and chooses the simplicity and directness of the ''straight shot,'' without subterfuge or special rhetoric, he is someone who believes in his ability to distil with his lens all the expressive nuances of his subject. Pedro Meyer is such a photographer. Without distancing himself from reality, he has created work that is a transparent and vital testimony to his confidence in his own purposes.

Meyer photographs from *within;* he photographs from the ''heart.'' It is an abrasive photography by a modern humanist who sees, who feels, and who thinks, but who, at times, cannot suppress his own impetuousness.

It is also a photography from *without,* from within the body politic yet for the whole community (a particular conflict in Latin America). Throughout its history, documentary photography has not experienced any great aesthetic revolution, apart from technological progress—yet, as far as ideas are concerned, it has involved a virtual unending variety of controversial aesthetic postures. Some critics of ''documentary'' would define the role of the photographer as that of a neutral witness; others would say that he must be a committed spokesman for his time and society. As a Mexican, Meyer is in a peculiar cultural and political situation, and his work always reveals his commitment with an almost belligerent strength.

He manages, however, to transcend that belligerency in his respect for his subject, for the human being on the other side of the camera: his subject is never presented as an instrument of ideological conviction, even if that subject consents to be used for such a purpose. For Meyer is well aware that manifesto-photography is, by its very nature, self-discrediting. (It is worth noting that this feeling of respect, even of affection, between the photographer and his subject is rapidly becoming a sign of distinction shared by very few contemporary photographers.)

Lewis Hine said that everything in need of improvement and deserving of contemplation was worth photographing. That definition has become a cliché. Just the same, taking into account the differences of time, distance, culture and history, it does very well describe the development of Pedro Meyer—a development which would have been hindered by this search for a balance between the demands of his own work and an effort to promulgate the work of other deserving Latin-American colleagues. Meyer has become—or has been made into—the spokesman of Latin-American photography in numerous international circles, but despite this his own work has been advanced rather than held back.

Yet this Latin-American commitment has been interpreted by some critics as a deliberate attempt to 'excavate' a national or South-American style. Photography is certainly a universal language, but this doesn't mean that history, cultural roots and the contemporary political climate do not inspire the work of any creative graphic artist with a set of definitive local traits. In my view, the controversy surrounding this question is resolved in the certainty that Meyer has achieved a personal style, totally international and valid, which not only expresses Mexican tradition but also the whole heritage of documentary photography. The density of detail, the intensity of light, the contrasts and opacity of the dark shades, the wide angles and spontaneous framing are characteristics of a personal expressive rhetoric. The important thing is that when he speaks to us of the vicissitudes of his country and of its exploitation in the hands of its neighbours, and of the problems his fellow Mexicans must face, Meyer achieves true universality.

—Joan Fontcuberta

MEYEROWITZ, Joel.

Nationality: American. **Born:** New York City, 3 June 1938. **Education:** James Monroe High School, New York, 1951-55; studied painting and medical drawing, Ohio State University, Columbus, 1956-59, B.F.A. 1959; self-taught in photography. **Family:** Married Vivian Bower in 1963; children: Sasha and Ariel. **Career:** Worked as advertising art director, New York, 1959-63. Independent photographer, New York, since 1963. Adjunct Professor of Photography, 1971-79, and Mellon Lecturer in Photography, 1977, Cooper Union, New York. Associate Professor of Photography, Princeton University, New Jersey, since 1977. **Recipient:** Guggenheim Fellowship, 1970, 1978; Creative Artists Public Service Grant, New York, 1976; St. Louis Art Commission Grant, 1977; National Endowment for the Arts Grant, 1978; National Endowment for the Humanities Grant, with Colin Westerbeck, Jr., 1978; Photographer of the Year Award, Friends of Photography, Carmel, California, 1981; Ansel Adams Award, American Society of Magazine Photographers, 1986. **Agent:** Witkin Gallery, 41 East 57th Street, New York, New York 10022. **Address:** 817 West End Avenue, New York, New York 10025, U.S.A.

Individual Exhibitions:

1966	International Museum of Photography, George Eastman House, Rochester, New York
1968	*My European Trip,* Museum of Modern Art, New York
1977	*New Color Photographs,* Witkin Gallery, New York
1978	*Cape Light,* Museum of Fine Arts, Boston
1979	University of Arizona, Tucson
	Galerie Zabriskie, Paris
	Akron Art Institute, Ohio
1980	*St. Louis and the Arch,* City Art Museum, St Louis
	San Francisco Museum of Modern Art
	Stedelijk Museum, Amsterdam
	Grapestake Gallery, San Francisco
1981	Greenberg Gallery, St. Louis, Missouri
1982	*New Portraits,* Witkin Gallery, New York
	Yuen Lui Gallery, Seattle
	Provincetown Art Association and Museum, Massachusetts
1983	Grapestake Gallery, San Francisco
1984	Greenberg Gallery, St. Louis, Missouri
	Work from the Same Nature, Witkin Gallery, New York (with Vivian Bower)
1985	Seibu Gallery, Tokyo
	Hong Kong Arts Centre
	Madison Art Center, Wisconsin
	Chapter Arts Centre, Cardiff, Wales (with Stephen Shore)
1986	*A Summer's Day,* Brooklyn Museum, New York
	Time and Light, Daniel Wolf Gallery, New York
	A Summer's Day, Minnesota Museum of Art, Saint Paul
	A Summer's Day, High Museum of Art, Atlanta, Georgia

Selected Group Exhibitions:

1966	*The Photographer's Eye,* Museum of Modern Art, New York
1967	*Photography in the 20th Century,* National Gallery of Canada, Ottawa (toured Canada and the United States, 1967-73)
1970	*10 Americans,* at *Expo '70,* Osaka, Japan
1971	*New Photography U.S.A.,* Museum of Modern Art, New York (toured the United States and Canada)
1977	*Inner Light,* Museum of Fine Arts, Boston
1978	*Mirrors and Windows: American Photography since 1960,* Museum of Modern Art, New York (toured the United States, 1978-80)
1979	*American Images: New Work by 20 Contemporary Photographers,* Corcoran Gallery, Washington, D.C. (travelled to the International Center of Photography, New York; Museum of Fine Arts, Houston; Minneapolis Institute of Arts; and

Indianapolis Institute of Arts, 1980; and American Academy, Rome, 1981)

1981   *American Photographers and the National Parks,* Corcoran Gallery, Washington, D.C. (toured the United States, 1981-83)

1985   *American Images 1945-80,* Barbican Art Gallery, London (toured Britain)

1987   *Photography and Art 1946-86,* Los Angeles County Museum of Art

Collections:

Museum of Modern Art, New York; Joseph Seagram and Sons Inc., New York; International Museum of Photography, George Eastman House, Rochester, New York; Museum of Fine Arts, Boston; Philadelphia Museum of Art; Virginia Museum of Fine Arts, Richmond; Art Institute of Chicago; City Art Museum, St. Louis; Chrysler Museum, Norfolk, Virginia.

Publications:

By MEYEROWITZ: Books—*The Cape,* portfolio of 15 photos, New York 1977; *Cape Light: Color Photographs by Joel Meyerowitz,* with a foreword by Clifford S. Ackley, interview by Bruce K. Macdonald, Boston 1978; *Bay/Sky/ Porch,* portfolio, New York, 1979; *St. Louis and the Arch,* with a foreword by James N. Wood, Boston 1981; *French Portfolio,* 12 photos, San Francisco 1981; *Wild Flowers,* Boston 1983; *A Summer's Day,* New York 1985.

On MEYEROWITZ: Books—*Photography in the 20th Century* by Nathan Lyons, New York 1967; *Vision and Expression,* edited by Nathan Lyons, New York 1969; *New Photography U.S.A.,* exhibition catalogue, by John Szarkowski, Arturo Quintavalle and Massimo Mussini, Parma, Italy 1971; *The City: American Experience,* edited by Alan Trachtenberg and Peter C. Bunnell, New York 1971; *Looking at Photographs: 100 Pictures from the Collection of the Museum of Modern Art* by John Szarkowski, New York 1973; *The Snapshot,* edited by Jonathan Green, Millerton, New York 1974; *Faces: A History of the Portrait* by Ben Maddow, New York 1976; *Mirrors and Windows: American Photography since 1960* by John Szarkowski, New York 1978; *American Images: New Work by 20 Contemporary Photographers,* edited by Renato Danese, New York 1979; *The Photograph Collector's Guide* by Lee D. Witkin and Barbara London, Boston and London 1979; *Joel Meyerowitz,* exhibition catalogue, by Els Barents, Amsterdam 1980; *World Photography* by Bryn Campbell, London 1981; *The New Color* by Sally Eauclaire, New York 1981; *Nude* by Constance Sullivan, New York 1981; *Visions and Images: American Photographers on Photography,* videotape conversations with Barbara Lee Diamonstein, New York 1981; *The Imaginary Photo Museum* by Helmut Gernsheim, Renate and L. Fritz Gruber and others, Cologne 1981, London 1982; *New Color/New York* by Sally Eauclaire, New York 1984; *American Images: Photography 1945-1980,* edited by Peter Turner and John Benton-Harris, London 1985; *Photography and Art 1946-1986,* exhibition catalogue, by Andy Grundberg and Kathleen M. Gauss, Los Angeles 1987. **Articles**—"Joel Meyerowitz: Rainbow" in *Camera Mainichi* (Tokyo), November 1973; "Photography: The Coming of Age of Color" by Max Kozloff in *Artforum* (New York), January 1975; "Joel Meyerowitz" by Max Kozloff in *Aperture* (Rochester, New York), no. 78, 1977; "Joel Meyerowitz" in *Camera* (Lucerne), September 1977; "Two Themes in Stylistic Counterpoint" in *Photography Year 1978,* by the Time-Life editors, New York 1978; "Joel Meyerowitz" in *American Photographer* (New York), August 1978; "Joel Meyerowitz" in *Photo* (Paris), May 1979; "The Masterly Style of Meyerowitz" by Gene Thornton in the *New York Times,* 10 August 1980; "Joel Meyerowitz" by Lisbet Nilson in *American Photographer* (New York), September 1981; "Cape Life" by Gerald Peary in *Camera Arts* (New York), June 1983; "Repeat Performances" by Vicki Goldberg in *American Photographer* (New York, April 1984.

*

I watch; that's my life, a pleasure in watching the way things appear. So I find that I'm scanning all the time; in a way, it's like daydreaming. I enter a new place. I look around. But I look around with a purpose; it's not just aimless. It's a functional curiosity, and I think as I photograph for a longer

period of time I grow more curious about things, because now I've seen how things look when they are transformed by a photograph—they become a new kind of thing. Basically, it's through curiosity and through a kind of perseverance that I see. But that's what photographic intention is: looking to see what will enlarge itself in your life. It's not about looking to make a good photograph. I think there's a real distinction. Because if you search for a good photograph it means you have in mind some notion of what a good photograph should look like, and that's probably a conventional idea. So I try not to think in terms of conventions, but just to be. It's much more an existential approach to photography than a kind of picture-making attitude is.

—Joel Meyerowitz

*   *   *

Joel Meyerowitz began photographing in New York City in the early 1960s, following the tradition of "street" photography in which Cartier-Bresson, Robert Frank—from whom his desire to photograph initially came—and, more recently, Garry Winogrand, Lee Friedlander and Tony Ray-Jones are major figures. He shot initially in black-and-white (slides) using the small 35mm Leica, and, in the Leica tradition of reportage, the focus was generally on behaviour in public surroundings. This style of photograph involves instantaneous decisions which result in images that are unusual, surprising, and often full of the irony and wit which is the essence of life. By using such a camera one is able to be unobtrusive and thereby to capture people and events which do not lose their reality and spontaneity by becoming posed. As Max Kozloff has remarked, "a certain invisibility comes to light, the kind of split-second episode that appears between our normal perceptions and is typically absorbed and erased by them. However mundane, [Meyerowitz's] subject matter exists in this 'Beyond,' an artificial limbo whose unintended grace he pursues with a true mania."

When color film became available, it was generally scoffed at by serious photographers largely because it produced an unrealistic color quality, did not allow the photographer much artistic latitude in the darkroom, and was much too slow for the active photographer. These obstacles were rapidly being overcome—as was some of the prejudice against the use of color film—by the time Meyerowitz began to develop as a photographer. Clifford Ackley has said of Meyerowitz that he is one of those few photographers "who has most successfully made the transition from seeing in terms of black-and-white tonalities to seeing wholly in terms of color." Meyerowitz himself confirms this in his later photographs and says that color is always a part of experience—color film responds to the whole spectrum of visible light: "a color photograph gives you a chance to remember how things look and feel in color. It enables you to have feelings along the full wavelength of the spectrum, to retrieve emotions that were bred in you in infancy.... Color suggests that light itself is a subject.... You don't have to have grand subject matter...."

In shooting his street scenes, Meyerowitz often uses a fast shutter speed (up to 1000/sec.) and a flash. As Max Kozloff points out this "startles out all kinds of information which he himself could not have seen well. It also casts distortions back through spaces that seem freely created.... The film innocently accentuates this hybrid character of light, whether interior or exterior, which the human eye glosses over and averages out. The restoration of such luminous differences—and they can only be realized in color—is an aggressive act. And highly formalized."

In 1976 and 1977, Meyerowitz began to photograph Cape Cod in the area of Provincetown—rather in the tradition of Edward Hopper and Walker Evans—studying the light and landscape. For this he gave up the Leica in favor of a bulky vintage (1938) Deardorff field view camera which allowed him to make negatives which could be printed by contact rather than by enlarging a slide. He also used a slow speed color film (exposures were often 4-10 minutes at f90; and the average daytime exposure was 1/2 second at f90). The results of his sensitive photography and skillful printing produced photographs of a striking clarity and detail which were virtually grainless and recorded the finest nuances of color. There is a much different essence to be found in these photographs in which he has captured the unique juncture of sky, sea and land than in his urban photographs with their distances and irony. Indeed, as Kozloff has said, "the sensibility at work resembles a cross between Henri Cartier-Bresson and Edward Hopper, improbable as that may seem."

—Michael Held

MICHALS, Duane (Stephen).

Nationality: American. **Born:** McKeesport, Pennsylvania in 1932. **Education:** McKeesport Technical High School; studied art at the University of Denver, 1949-53, B.A. 1953; studied at Parsons School of Design, New York, 1956-57; self-taught in photography. **Career:** Assistant Art Director, *Dance Magazine*, New York, 1957; Paste-Up Artist, *Look* magazine, New York, 1957-58; worked in a design studio, New York, 1958. Freelance photographer, working for *Vogue, Esquire, Mademoiselle, Horizon, Scientific American*, etc., New York, since 1958; first sequence photos, New York, 1966. Lecturer, New York School of Visual Arts. **Recipient:** Creative Artists Public Service Award, New York, 1975; National Endowment for the Arts Grant, 1976; Pennsylvania Council of the Arts, 1978; Carnegie Foundation Photography Fellow, Cooper Union, 1979; Medaille de Vermeil de la Ville de Paris, 1982; The Meadows Distinguished Visiting Professor, SMU, Dallas, 1989-90; International Center of Photography Infinity Award for Art, Nissan International Fellow, 1991; Honorary Fellowship, Royal Photographic Society, Bath, 1992; Officier dans l'Ordre des Arts et des Lettres, France, 1993; The Century Award, The Museum of Photographic Arts, San Diego, 1993; Youth Friends Award, School Art League of New York City, 1993; Honorary Doctorate of Fine Arts, The Art Institute of Boston, 1993; Gold Medal for Photography, The National Arts Club, New York, 1994. **Agents:** Sidney Janis Gallery, 6 West 57th Street, New York, New York 10019; and Galerie Wilde, Neiderbergerstrasse 21, 5352 Zülpich-Mülheim, West Germany. **Address:** c/o Sidney Janis Gallery, 110 West 57th Street, New York, New York 10019, U.S.A.

Individual Exhibitions:

1963	Underground Gallery, New York (and 1965, 1968)
1968	Art Institute of Chicago
1970	Museum of Modern Art, New York
1971	International Museum of Photography, George Eastman House, Rochester, New York
1972	Museum of New Mexico, Albuquerque
	San Francisco Art Institute
1973	Galerie Delpire, Paris
	Internationaal Cultureel Centrum, Antwerp
	Kölnischer Kunstverein, Cologne
1974	Frankfurter Kunstverein, Frankfurt
	Galleria 291, Milan
	Galleria Documenta, Turin
	School of Visual Arts, New York
	Light Gallery, New York
1975	Light Gallery, New York
	Broxton Gallery, Los Angeles
1976	Galerie Jacques Bosser, Paris
	Sidney Janis Gallery, New York
	Galerie Die Brücke, Vienna
	Texas Center for Photographic Studies, Dallas
	Contemporary Arts Center, Cincinnati, Ohio
	Ohio State University, Columbus
	Felix Handschin Galerie, Basle
	Douglas Drake Gallery, Kansas City, Missouri
1977	Galerie Breiting, Berlin
	Galerie Paul Maenz, Cologne
	G. Ray Hawkins Gallery, Los Angeles
	Philadelphia College of Art
	Arbus/Krims/Michals, Galerie Schellmann und Kluser, Munich (with Diane Arbus and Les Krims)
	Focus Gallery, San Francisco
1978	Douglas Drake Gallery, Kansas City, Kansas
	The Collection at 24, Miami
	Camera Obscura, Stockholm
	Galerie Fiolet, Amsterdam
	Sidney Janis Gallery, New York
	Galerie Wilde, Cologne
	Akron Art Institute, Ohio

	Duane Michals and Nicholas Africano, Nancy Lurie Gallery, Chicago
1979	La Remise du Parc, Paris
	Canon Photo Gallery, Geneva
	Douglas Drake Gallery, Kansas City, Kansas
	The Collection at 24, Miami
	University of Denver
	Galerie Wilde, Cologne
	Nouvelle Image, The Hague
	Nova Gallery, Vancouver
1980	Carl Solway Gallery, Cincinnati, Ohio
1982	*Photographies 1958-82,* Musée d'Art Moderne de la Ville, Paris
1983	Sidney Janis Gallery, New York
1984	G.H. Dalsheimer Gallery, Baltimore, Maryland (retrospective)
	Photographs 1955-84, Museum of Modern Art, Oxford
	The Journey of the Spirit After Death, Galerie Wilde, Cologne
1985	Sidney Janis Gallery, New York
	Adam Brown, Amsterdam
1986	Studio 8 Gallery, Kalispell, MO
	Dickinson College, Carlisle, PA
	Samia Saouma, Paris
1987	Sidney Janis Gallery, New York
	Southeast Center for Photographic Studies, Daytona Beach Community College, FL
	George Ciscle Gallery, Baltimore, MD
	Art Center College of Design, Pasadena, CA (travelled to Brooks Institute of Photographic Art and Science, Santa Barbara, CA and Meadows Museum and Gallllery, Dallas, Texas in conjunction with the Eastman Kodak Reedy Memorial Lectures)
1988	Fay Gold Gallery, Atlanta, GA
	Allen Street Gallery, Dallas, Texas
	Someone Left a Message for You: Photographs by Duane Michals, Art Institute of Chicago, Chicago
	The Maine Photographic Workshops, Rockport, ME
	Duane Michals: Two Photographers, Blatant Image/Silver Eye, Pittsburgh, PA
	Galerie Fiolet, Amsterdam
	Ugo Ferranti, Rome
	Forum Gallery, Tarragona, Spain
	Duane Michals Photographies, FRAC Aquitaine, Bordeaux, France
	Artoteque de Caen, France
	Oregon Art Institute, Portland
1989	*Duane Michals Photographien 1958-1988,* Museum fur Kunst und Gewerbe, Hamburg (travelled to Museum de Beikerd, Breda, Holland; Chateau d'Eaux, Toulouse, France; Musee de l'Elysee, Lausanne, Switzerland; Museum of Photography, Antwerp, Belgium)
	Photographic Image Gallery, Portland
	Southern Alleghenies Museum of Art, Loretto, Pennsylvania
	Art Kane Photo Workshop, Cape May, New Jersey
	Upside Down, Inside Out and Backwards, Sidney Janis Gallery, New York
	Galerie John A Schweitzer, Montreal, Quebec
	Duane Michals: Portraits, Salt Lake Art Center, Salt Lake City, Utah
	Samia Saouma, Paris
	Spectrum Gallery, Light Impressions, Rochester, New York
1990	Modern Art Center, Calouse Gulbenkian Foundation, Lisbon
	A Gallery for Fine Photography, New Orleans, Louisiana
	Cumberland Gallery, Nashville, Tennessee
	Andrew Smith Gallery, Santa Fe, New Mexico
	Fahey/Klein Gallery, Los Angeles
	Fay Gold Gallery, Atlanta, Georgia
	Vrais Reves, Lyon, France
	Institut de la Communication, Universite Lumiere, Lyon, France

Egypt, The Pyramids by Moonlight, **1978.** Photograph ©Duane Michals.

The Duane Michals Show, Museum of Photographic Arts, San Diego, California (travelled to: Honolulu Academy of Arts, Honolulu, Hawaii; San Francisco Museum of Modern Art, San Francisco; International Museum of Photography, George Eastman House, Rochester, New York; Columbia College, Chicago; Milwaukee Art Museum, Milwaukee, Wisconsin; Boca Raton Museum of Art, Boca Raton, Florida; International Center of Photography, New York; North Dakota Museum of Art, Grand Forks)

1991   Galerie Bodo Niemann, Berlin
Aspen Art Museum, Aspen, Colorado
Poetry and Tales, Sidney Janis Gallery, New York
Robert Koch Gallery, San Francisco
Photograum Fleetinsel, Hamburg, Germany
Busche Galerie, Cologne, Germany

1992   Lynn Goode Gallery, Houston, Texas
Elke Droscher, Fotoram Fleetinsel, Berlin
Espace Photographique de Paris, Paris
Portfolio Gallery, Edinburgh
Paris Stories and Other Follies, Sidney Janis Gallery, New York
Montgomery Glasoe Fine Art, Minneapolis

1993   Ehlers Caudill Gallery, Chicago
Fahey/Klein Gallery, Los Angeles
The Irish Gallery of Photography, Dublin
The Temple Bar Gallery, Dublin
Galerie USVU, Bratislava, Slovakia
Sala Parpallo, Valencia, Spain
University of North Florida, Jacksonville, Florida

1994   Lynn Goode Gallery, Houston, Texas

Selected Group Exhibitions:

1966   *American Photography: The 60s,* University of Nebraska, Lincoln

1967   *Photography in the 20th Century,* National Gallery of Canada, Ottawa (toured Canada and the United States, 1967-73)

1970   *Be-ing Without Clothes,* Hayden Gallery, Massachusetts Institute of Technology, Cambridge

1974   *Photography in America,* Whitney Museum, New York

1975   *4 Amerikanische Photographes: Friedlander/Gibson/Krims/Michals,* Städtisches Museum, Leverkusen, West Germany

1978   *Mirrors and Windows: American Photography since 1960,* Museum of Modern Art, New York (toured the United States, 1978-80)

1981   *Photographer as Printmaker,* Ferens Art Gallery, Hull, Yorkshire (travelled to the Museum and Art Gallery, Leicester; Cooper Gallery, Barnsley; Castle Museum, Nottingham; Photographers' Gallery, London)

1985   *American Images 1945-80,* Barbican Art Gallery, London (toured Britain)

1987   *Photography and Art 1946-86,* Los Angeles County Museum of Art

1988   *First Person Singular: Self Portrait Photography 1840-1986,* The High Museum of Art, Atlanta, Georgia
Black in the Light, Genovese Graphics, Boston
Art of Persuasion, International Center of Photography, New York
Men on Men, Catherine Edelman Gallery, Chicago
Fabrications: Staged, Altered and Appropriated Photographs, Carpenter Center for the Visual Arts, Harvard University, Cambridge, Massachusetts
Language and Photography, California Museum of Art, Luther Burbank Center, Santa Rosa
A Kiss is Just a Kiss, Twining Gallery, New York
Les Photographes en Campagne, Espace J F Guyot, Paris
Splendeurs et Miseres du Corps, Musee d'Art Moderne, Paris
Popular and Preferential Imagery, Boca Raton Museum of Art, Boca Raton, Florida
Influence Show, College of Fine Arts, University of Florida, Gainesville, Florida

Creative Camera, Dayton Art Institute, Dayton, Ohio
50th Anniversary Exhibition, The Contemporary Arts Center,
Cincinnati, Ohio
Identity: Representations of the Self, Whitney Museum of
American Art

1989   *A Garden Walk,* Twining Gallery, New York
Photography and Language, Sheppard Gallery, University of
Nevada-Reno
Fictive Strategies, Squibb Gallery, Princeton, Florida
Flash Point, Art on the Tracks Gallery, Pensacola, Florida
Fantasies, Fables & Fabrications: Photoworks of the 1980s,
Herter Art Gallery, University of Massachusetts-Amherst,
Cliches les Choix des Sens, Centre Culturel de la Communaute
Francais, Wallonie-Bruxelles le Botanique (travelled to
Maison de la Culture d'Amiens; Centre Wallonie Bruxelles;
Piazza Beauborg)
Das Portrait in der Zeitgenossischen Photographie, Frankfurter
Kunstverein, Frankfurt
*Selected Themes: 150 Years of American History by American
Photographers,* Pelham Art Center, Pelham, New York
Six Ideas in Photography, Grand Rapids Art Museum, Grand
Rapids, Michigan
*150Jahre Fotografie das Portrait in der Zeitgenossischen
Photographie,* Galerie Fotohof, Salzburg, Austria
*The Cherished Image: Portraits from 150 Years of Photogra-
phy,* National Gallery of Canada, Ottawa
Object as Subject, Turman Gallery, Indiana State University,
Terre Haute
Fotoritratto—Il Ritratto Nella Fotographia Contemporanea,
Pinacoteca Comunale Logetta Lombardesca, Ravenna, Italy
*Capturing the Image: Collecting 100 Years of Photog-
raphy,* Fogg Museum, Harvard University, Cambridge,
Massachusetts
Acquisitions du FRAC Basie-Normandie, Musee de Coutances,
France
Das Portrait in der Zeitgenossischen, Galerie Krinzinger,
Innsbruck, Austria
Arrangements—Part 1, May 36 Galerie, Lucerne, Switzerland
Vanishing Prescence, Walker Art Center, Minneapolis, Minne-
sota (travelled to The Detroit Institute of Arts, Michigan;
Winnipeg Art Center, Manitoba, Canada; The High Museum
of Art, Atlanta, Georgia; Herbert F. Johnson Museum of Art,
Cornell University, Ithaca, New York; Virginia Museum of
Fine Arts, Richmond)

1990   *New York, New York: The City in Photographs,* Worcester Art
Museum, Massachusetts
The Indomitable Spirit, International Center of Photography,
New York (travelled to Los Angeles Municipal Art Gallery,
Los Angeles; Fraenkel Gallery, San Francisco)
De la Photographie Mis en Scene, Musee de Marseille, Centre
de la Ville Charite, Marseille, France
Word as Image: American Art 1960-1990, Milwaukee Art
Museum, Milwaukee, Wisconsin
Identities: Portraiture in Contemporary Photography, Philadel-
phia Art Alliance, Pennsylvania
Chroniques des Apparences, FRAC de Basse et Haute
Normandie, Abbaye-aux-Dames, Caen, France
Modeles Deposes—1, FRAC du Limousin, Limoges, France
Influences 5/Photography, Birke Art Gallery, Huntington,
West Virginia
Regarding Art: Artworks about Art, John Michael Kohler Arts
Center, Sheboygan, Wisconsin
Personal/Mechanical: Photographs as Support, Graham
Modern Gallery, New York
Stated Upon Eternity, Musee Reattu, Arles, France
Femmes, Galerie Maeght, Paris
Children Should be Seen and Not Heard, Robert Klein Gallery,
Boston
Aids Timeline 1990, Wadsworth Atheneum, Hartford,
Connecticut

1991   *Motion and Document—Sequence and Time: Eadweard
Muybridge and Contemporary American Photography,* Na-
tional Museum of American Art (travelled to Addison Gal-
lery of American Art, Phillips Academy, Andover, Massa-
chusetts; International Center of Photography-Midtown,
New York; Long Beach Museum of Art, California;
Presentation House Gallery, North Vancouver, British
Columbia; Henry Art Gallery, University of Washington,
Seattle)
Extrait d'Une Collection, Centre d'Arte Contemporain de
Basse-Normandie, Herouville, France
Der Fotografierte Schatten, Galerie Rudolf Kicken, Cologne,
Germany

1992   *Voyeurism,* Jayne H Baum Gallery, New York
From Media to Metaphor: Art About Aids, organized by ICI,
New York (travelled to Emerson Gallery, Hamilton College,
Clinton, New York; Center on Contemporary Art, Seattle,
Washington; Sharadin Art Gallery, Kutztown, Pennsylvania;
Musee d'Art Contemporain de Montreal, Quebec; Grey Art
Gallery and Study Center, New York University, New York)
8 Collections of Photographs, Fotografiska Museet, Moderna
Museet, Stockholm
House Without Walls, Buhl Family Foundation, New York
*Something's Out There: Danger in Contemporary Photogra-
phy,* The National Arts Club, New York
*About Face: Photographic Portraits from the International
Center of Photography Permanent Collection, 1900-1991,*
International Center of Photography, New York
Interpretazioni, Eos Arte Contemporanea, Milan, Italy
Fragmente der Erinnerung: Photographie und Reisen, Heidi
Reckermann Photographie, Cologne, Germany
Sprung in die Zeit, Berlinische Galerie, Berlin
Flora Photographica, Vancouver Art Gallery, Vancouver,
British Columbia (travelled to The New York Public Library,
New York City; The Royal Ontario Museum, Toronto,
Ontario; Musee des Beaux Artes de Montreal, Montreal,
Quebec)
Recent Acquisitions, Fonds Regional d'Art Contemporain de
Basse-Normandie

1993   *Expoloring Scale in Contemporary Art,* Laguna Gloria Art
Museum, Austin, Texas
Here's Looking At Me, Art Contemporain, Lyon, France
The Art of Diamonds, Tatistcheff Gallery, New York
The Artist as Subject: Paul Cadmus, Midtown Payson,
New York
Self-Portrait: The Changing Self, New Jersey Center for the
Visual Arts, Summit
The Alternative Eye: Photo Art for the 90s, Southern
Alleghenies Museum of Art, Loretto, Pennsylvania
A La Recherche du Pere, L'Espace Photographique de Paris
Recent Acquisitions, Ecole Maternelle Jacques Prevert,
Argentan, France
Multiple Images: Photographs Since 1965 in the Collection,
Museum of Modern Art, New York

1994   *American Photography: A History in Pictures,* The San
Antonio Museum of Art, Texas
Images Fixed by Light, Jansen-Perez Gallery, San Anton-
io, Texas
*New Acquisitions/New Work/New Directions 2: Photography
from the Collection,* Los Angeles County Museum of Art

Collections:

Museum of Modern Art, New York; International Museum of Photography,
George Eastman House, Rochester, New York; Smithsonian Institution,
Washington, D.C.; Art Institute of Chicago; Museum of New Mexico,
Albuquerque; University of New Mexico, Albuquerque; University of Cali-
fornia at Los Angeles; Norton Simon Museum, Pasadena, California; Akron
Art Institute, Akron, Ohio; Birmingham Museum of Art, Birmingham, Ala-
bama; The Boston Museum of Fine Arts; The High Museum of Art, Atlanta;

Honolulu Academy of Art, Honolulu; The Lowe Art Museum, University of Miami, Miami; Emily Lowe Gallery, Hofstra University, Hempstead, NY; Memphis Brooks Museum of Art, Memphis; Metropolitan Museum of Art, New York; Museum of Fine Arts, Houston; Nelson-Atkins Museum of Art, Kansas City; New Orleans Museum of Art, New Orleans; Ohio State University Collection, Athens, Ohio; Philadelphia Museum of Art, Philadelphia; Princeton University Art Museum, Princeton, New Jersey; Rhode Island School of Design, Providence, RI; San Francisco Museum of Modern Art, San Francisco; University of Delaware, Wilmington, DE; University of Maryland, Baltimore; University of Massachusetts, Boston; Vassar College, Poughkeepsie, New York; Wesleyan University Collection, Middletown, Connecticut; Museum Ludwig, Cologne; Museum Folkwang, Essen, Germany; Australia National Gallery of Art, Auckland, Australia; Bibliotheque Nationale, Paris; L'Espace Nicois d'Art et de Culture, Nice, France; Fonds Regional d'Art Contemporain Basse-Normandie; Fonds Regional d'Art Contemporain Limousin; Fonds Regional d'Art Contemporain, Lorraine; FRAC Nord Pas de Calais, France; Hamburg Museum of Arts and Crafts, Hamburg, Germany; Institute of Polytechnic, College of Photography, Japan; The Israel Museum, Jerusalem, Israel; Kunsthaus Zurich, Zurich, Switzerland; Moderna Museet, Stockholm, Sweden; Musee d'Art Moderne de la Ville de Paris, Paris; Musee d'Art Moderne et Contemporaine, Strasbourg, France; Musee Cantini, Marseille, France; Musee de Nimes, Nimes, France; Museu Calouste Gulbenkian, Lisbon; National Museum of Modern Art, Kyoto, Japan; The National Museum of Canada, Ottawa; National Art Gallery, New Zealand; Republica di San Marino, Italy; Stedelijk Museum, Amsterdam; Vancouver Art Gallery, Vancouver, British Columbia.

Publications:

By MICHALS: Books—*Sequences*, New York and Milan 1970; *The Journey of the Spirit After Death*, New York 1971; *Things Are Queer*, Cologne 1973; *Chance Meeting*, Cologne 1973; *Paradise Regained*, Cologne and Antwerp 1973; *Duane Michals: The Photographic Illusion*, with text by Ronald H. Bailey, Los Angeles 1975; *Take One and See Mount Fujiyama and Other Stories*, under pseudonym Stefan Mihal, New York 1976; *Real Dreams*, Danbury, New Hampshire and Paris 1977; *The Wonders of Egypt*, Paris 1978; *Homage to Cavafy: Ten Poems by Constantine Cavafy/Ten Photographs by Duane Michals*, Danbury, New Hampshire 1978; *Changes*, Paris 1980; *The Book of Sleep and Dreams*, New York 1984; *The Nature of Desire*, Pasadena, 1986; *Portraits*, Pasadena, 1988; *Eros and Thanatos*, Pasadena, 1993; *Upside Down, Inside Out and Backwards*, a Sonny Boy Book, 1993.

On MICHALS: Books—*Toward a Social Landscape: Contemporary Photographers*, edited by Nathan Lyons, New York 1966; *Photography in the 20th Century* by Nathan Lyons, New York 1967; *Photography in America*, edited by Robert Doty, with an introduction by Minor White, New York and London 1974; *The Magic Image* by Cecil Beaton and Gail Buckland, London and Boston 1975; *L'Arte nella Società: Fotografia, Cinema, Videotape* by Daniela Palazzoli and others, Milan 1976; *Kunstlerphotographien im 20. Jahrhundert*, exhibition catalogue, edited by Carl-Albrecht Haenlein, Hannover 1977; *Mirrors and Windows: American Photography since 1960* by John Szarkowski, New York 1978; *Photography Between the Covers* by Thomas Dugan, Rochester, New York 1979; *Light Readings: A Photography Critic's Writings 1968-1979* by A.D. Coleman, New York 1979; *Nude: Theory*, edited by Jain Kelly, New York 1979; *The Vogue Book of Fashion Photography* by Polly Devlin, with an introduction by Alexander Liberman, New York and London 1979; *World Photography*, edited by Bryn Campbell, London 1981; *Visions and Images: American Photographers on Photography* by Barbaralee Diamonstein, New York 1981; *Photographer as Printmaker*, exhibition catalogue, with texts by Gerry Badger, Peter C. Bunnell and Ansel Adams, London 1981; *the Library of World Photography: Photography as Fine Art*, with introduction by Douglas Davis, Tokyo 1982, 1983, London 1983; *Private Viewing: Contemporary Erotic Photography*, edited by Terry Jones, with introdcution by Jack Schofield, London 1983; *Duane Michals Photographs/ Sequences/Texts 1958-1984*, Oxford, 1984; *American Images: Photography 1945-1980*, edited by Peter Turner and John Benton-Harris, London 1985; *Duane Michals*, New York, 1986; *Photography and Art 1946-1986*, exhibition catalogue, by Andy Grundberg and Kathleen M. Gauss, Los Angeles 1987; *Now Becoming Then*, Max Kozloff, Pasadena, 1990; *Duane Michals Photografias 1958-1990*, Valencia, Spain, 1993. **Articles**—''Duane Michals:

People and Places'' by Martin Fox in *Print* (New York), March/April 1966; ''Duane Michals: Sequences'' in *Camera* (Lucerne), July 1969; ''Sequences: Duane Michals'' in *Image* (Rochester, New York), August 1971; ''Duane Michals: How Do You Photograph Chance?'' in *Popular Photography* (New York), December 1971; ''Duane Michals: The Journey of the Spirit After Death'' by A.D. Coleman in the *Village Voice* (New York), 30 March 1972; ''Duane Michals'' by Carter Ratcliff in *Print Collector's Newsletter* (New York), September/October 1975; ''De l'Autre Cote du Miroir, Duane Michals'' by Carole Naggar in *Zoom* (Paris), October 1976; ''Duane Michals Says It Is No Accident That You Are Reading This'' by Shelley Rice in the *Village Voice* (New York), 8 November 1976; ''Real Dreams'' by Vicki Goldberg in *Photograph* (New York), no. 3, 1977; ''Duane Michals: The Sequences and Beyond'' by Julia Scully and Andy Grundberg in *Modern Photography* (New York), March 1979; ''Theater of the Forbidden: Duane Michals and Joel-Peter Witkin'' in *Photo Design*, Jan-Feb, 1988; ''Duane Michals: Fotograafen Schrijver'' by Herman Hoeneveld in *Kunstbeeld*, March 1988; ''Duane Michals'' by Richard B Woodward in *ARTnews*, April, 1989; ''Duane Michals Reale Traume'' by Wolfgang Kemp in *Nikon News* (Zurich), No.3, 1989; ''Duane Michals' Recent Work'' by John H Lawrence in *The New Orleans Art Review*, Jan/Feb 1990; ''Duane Michals: Beyond Appearances'' by Benoit Prieur in *Photo Digest*, Sept/Oct 1990; ''La Galerie Vrais Reve Presente Duane Michals'' by Natalia Luyer in *Vis a Vis*, (Paris), November, 1990; ''Michals Recria a Narrativa Photografica'' by Bernardo Barvalho in *Folha de s. Paulo*, October 19, 1991; ''There's something I must tell you'' in *Tagezeitung*, (Berlin), November 6, 1991; ''Photography & The Sin of Voyeurism'' by Vicki Goldberg in *The New York Times*, March 8, 1992; ''Bringing It All Back Home'' by David Lee in *The Observer*, (London), August 2, 1992; ''Faking It'' by Richard McClure in *Creative Camera*, Aug/ Sept 1992; ''Duane Michals a Paris'' interview by Pierre Borhan, *Photographies*, (Paris) No.44 September 1992; ''Det iscenesatte Fotografi'' by Mette Sandbye, Denmark, 1992; ''Picture Stories of Passion and Feeling'' by David Lee in *The Irish Times*, February 12, 1993; ''Duane Michals' new work is 'serious and also silly''' by Abigail Foerstner in *Chicago Tribune*, March 12, 1993; ''Sequential Photographs'' by Ted Weeks in *Folio Weekly*, (Jacksonville, FL) February 1, 1994 .

*   *   *

Duane Michals can be considered a one-man chart of contemporary photographic fine-art sensibilities. In just over thirty years, his work has moved from street style documentary to carefully staged tableaux, to images combined with text, to photographs which have been painted or drawn upon. If this suggests ecclecticism, a volatile penchant for wild experimentation, such an impression is false, for Michals' oeuvre, whilst rich and complex, is quite distinctive and informed by a very particular sensibility.

Though he has been instrumental in broadening the formal horizons of photography, Michals is not a formalist per se. His primary achievement has been to take the medium forward from the hegemony of the documentary single image to the imaginative multiple image with its greater potential for complex narrative. Even today, Michals will utilise any of the above approaches in his work, for to him formal means are not an end in themselves, but simply a vehicle for expressing what he feels about life.

In his gentle, modest, yet assuredly ambitius way, Michals deals with the big issues—sex, death, spirituality; the nature of human relationships and the inexorable march of time. Thus it is not surprising that his sequences are the most renowned area of his work, both for their innovation, and the fact that in them Michals can investigate several of these concerns at any one time. His single images can, however, also explore complex issues successfully. The sequences are cinematic in quality, continuous in narrative, reading like a series of excerpted still frames from surrealist films. Some are shot outside, but more typically they take place in dark, enclosed interiors that contribute much to their brooding, dreamlike quality.

A key early sequence like *The Spirit Leaving the Body* (1968) is concerned with death and the enduring existence of the immortal soul, themes continued in *Death Comes to the Old Lady* (1969). In these and other series, Michals pursues another obsessive theme, family relationships, especially that between father and son. Another major motif is physical love and desire, including gay themes, as in *Homage to Cavafy* (1979). Whatever the theme, however, the sequences tend to explore psychological matters, frequently featuring apparitions that represent ghosts, spirits or alter egos, and are generally melancholic or elegaic in tone.

Yet though Michals might be serious, he is seldom portentious or solemn and often leavens his darker thoughts with genuine humour—a rare feat in photography. For example, *Take One and See Mount Fujiyama* (1975) features one of Michals' erotic dream sequences, with a comic surreal denouement that plays upon the visual resemblance between the sacred mountain and an erection straining the daydreamer's underpants.

In addition to his sequences and narrative pieces, Michals has not neglected the single image. He is a major photographer of the nude, exploring erotic themes with an early awareness of gender issues from a time when the women's movement began. He is also one of the finest photographic portraitists, managing with great skill to unerringly characterise his subjects while at the same time infusing them with the wistful Michals world view.

In all, Duane Michals has created an important and impressive body of work. Its modest size in the original and generally low-key promotion perhaps has not given him the reputation commensurate with his worth. In future years however, as the originality and depth of his contribution is re-assessed that reputation with surely rise.

—Gerry Badger

MIDORIKAWA, Yoichi.

Nationality: Japanese. **Born:** Okumachi, Okayama Prefecture, Tokyo, 4 March 1915. **Education:** Attended local schools; studied dentistry, Nihon University, Tokyo, 1932-36; self-taught in photography. **Family:** Married Sadako Midorikawa in 1942; children: Mizuko, Koichi and Shoko. **Career:** Dental surgeon, Okayama City, also independent photographer, Okayama, since 1936. Professor, Nippon Photography School, Tokyo. Juror, Nikakai Photographic Competition, annually since 1955; Director, Photographic Society of Japan (PSJ), Tokyo. Member, Nikakai and Japan Professional Photographers Society, Tokyo. **Recipient:** First Prize, 1953, and Prime Minister's Prize, 1973, Nikakai Photographic Competition; First Prize, Camera Geijitsu Photographic Competition, 1960; Society of Photography Critics Prize, 1962; Photographic Society of Japan (PSJ) Award of the Year, 1963. **Address:** 12-23 Ekimotocho, Okayama-shi 700, Japan.

Individual Exhibitions:

1943	*2 Methods of Agriculture,* Chiyoda Gallery, Tokyo
1946	*Okayama Castle,* Temmaya Department Store, Okayama, Japan
1948	*Women,* Fuji Photo Salon, Tokyo
1951	*Kurashiki,* Muramatsu Gallery, Tokyo
1952	*Osaka,* Matsushima Gallery, Tokyo
1959	*Europe,* Takashimaya Department Store, Tokyo (toured Japan)
1964	*The Seto Inland Sea,* Sakura Gallery, Tokyo
1975	*The Landscapes of Japan,* Fuji Photo Salon, Tokyo (toured Japan)
1979	*Setouchi Ryojo,* Minoruta Photo Salon, Tokyo (transferred to Osaka)
1981	*Nihon Hyakkei,* Fuji Foto Salon, Tokyo
1982	*Imperial Palace,* Minoruta Photo Salon, Tokyo (travelled to Osaka and Okayama)
1986	*Four Seasons of Japan,* Pentax Forum, Tokyo

Selected Group Exhibitions:

1957	*6 Photographers,* Fuji Photo Salon, Tokyo (travelled to Osaka)
1970	*Yoichi Midorikawa and Photographers of West Japan,* Pentax Gallery, Tokyo
1975	*The Land: 20th Century Landscape Photographs Selected by Bill Brandt,* Victoria and Albert Museum, London (travelled to the National Gallery, Edinburgh; Ulster Museum, Belfast; and National Museum of Wales, Cardiff, 1976)

Collections:

Victoria and Albert Museum, London; Bibliothèque Nationale, Paris.

Publications:

By MIDORIKAWA: Books—*Woman,* Tokyo 1950; *Kompira,* with an introduction by Yoshinobu Nakamura, Tokyo 1956; *Japon-Japonais,* with text by Charles Henri Favrod, Lausanne 1959; *The Inland Sea,* 10 vols., Tokyo 1962-80; *General Landscapes of Japan,* 9 vols., Tokyo 1967-81; *These Splendored Isles,* Tokyo 1969; *Kyoto,* 2 vols., Tokyo 1970-78; *The Inland Sea,* with an introduction by Donald Ritchie, Tokyo 1971; *The Works of Yoichi Midorikawa,* edited by Toushi Shimizu, Tokyo 1980; *A Hundred Stories of Old Clocks,* 3 vols., Tokyo 1973-76; *Okayama,* 6 vols., Tokyo 1980-81; *Sanshi Suimei* (National Parks of Japan), Tokyo 1983; *The Four Seasons of Japan,* Tokyo 1986.

On MIDORIKAWA: Books—*Photography of the World '60,* edited by Ihei Kimura, Hiromu Hara and others, Tokyo and New York 1960; *The Land: Twentieth Century Landscape Photographs Selected by Bill Brandt,* exhibition catalogue, edited by Mark Haworth-Booth, London 1975.

* * *

Yoichi Midorikawa is one of the most representative of landscape photographers in Japan today. He was born in 1915 at Okumachi, Okayama Prefecture, in the Sanyo District, close to Setonaikai, the inland sea of Japan. The setting in which he grew up was that of a beautiful body of water and its surrounding terrain. When he entered dental school, he began to take photographs; on graduation, he opened a dental clinic in Okayama City, and at the same time his interest in photography grew, and some of his prints were published. His early works featured women as subjects, and these photos have been collected and published. But gradually Midorikawa became more and more interested in landscape, and he set about recording the inland sea he knew so well: the result has been singularly successful.

Perhaps because of his professional role as a dentist, which demands such skills, Midorikawa has always brought to his photography small-scale and subtle techniques, particularly in his early and middle periods. It is rare to find work from this period that isn't both surprising and technically refined. Double exposures are common, as are montages and other methods and techniques. Yet, despite the variety of technical devices, the photographs have a kind of light-hearted vividness and show evidence of his maturing aesthetic.

Shoji Ueda was born and raised in the Sanin District, on the other side of the mountain range dividing Sanin from Midorikawa's birthplace. Ueda's birthplace was a very dark, forbidding landscape that is known as *Ura Nihon* (Back of Japan), and his work generally is solemn, filled with shadows. Obviously, then, for these two wellknown photographers, there is a correlation, almost an entente, between their genius loci and their work. These two contrasting Japanese photographers have substantially opposing characters and styles, yet they understand each other: they have been on good terms since childhood.

In 1959 Midorikawa travelled through Europe for 4 months on a photographic tour. He was struck by the beauty and majesty of the landscapes he encountered, but in the end was forced to conclude that landscapes in Japan were enough for him—they enjoyed the changes of the four seasons; they had a variety of plants, trees, mountains, rivers, etc. When he returned home he began a series of landscapes throughout Japan. It was the time at which color photography came into general use in Japan—and Midorikawa, too, adopted color. And, indeed, his design sense seemed all the more appropriate in color, so much so that he came to be known as "the magician of color."

If one contemplates the work of Midorikawa, then the most appropriate appellation and description of his achievements is as a "designer of landscape." Of late, though, his photographic style has begun to change. Midorikawa has exhibited less decorative, more precise compositions. The photographs have a striking simplicity. It may be that he has come to the conclusion that his final understanding of landscape should be rendered with this kind of directness. In any event, most of Midorikawa's photographs have been published in picture books, numbering to date about 30. He can be said to work basically through the medium of publication, where both the changes and accomplishments of his photography are now available to everyone.

—Takao Kajiwara

MIKHAILOVSKY, Wilhelm.

Nationality: Russian. **Born:** Donetck, 2 October 1942. **Education:** Secondary School 6, 1950-60; Technical College, Konstantinovka, 1960-63. **Family:** Married Vera Makarova in 1967; children: Eduard, Julia, Wilhelm and Jaroslav. **Career:** Worked as a technician at the Latvijas Stikls factory, Riga, 1966-73; Staff Photographer, Project Institute, Riga, 1973-76. Staff Photographer, *Maksla* art magazine, Riga, since 1976. Member, Union of U.S.S.R. Journalists, 1979. Honorary Member of Latvian Photoartists Union 1992. Since 1992 co-founder, co-publisher and artistic editor of weekly newspaper "Baltijskaya Gazeta." **Recipient:** Gold Medal, Photographic Society of America, 1974; Silver Medal, 1975, 1978, 1979, 1980, Gold Medal, 1976, 1978, 1979, 1981, Bronze Medal, 1980, and Artist Excellence Award, 1979, Fédération International de l'Art Photographique (FIAP); Niepce Medal (3), France, 1979; Gold Medal, Fédération Belge des Photographiques, 1977; Gold Medal, Kzakowskie Towarzystwo Fotograficzne, Poland, 1979; Verband Deutscher Amateurfotografen Vereine Prize, West Germany, 1979. **Address:** 12-39 Ilukstes Street, Riga, LV-1082, Latvia.

Individual Exhibitions:

1976	City Historical Museum, Tallin
1977	Poztoky Castle, Prague
	Fotokabinett Jaromir Funke, Brno, Czechoslovakia
1978	House of Friendship, Moscow
1980	Museum of Latvian History, Riga
	Cultural Centre, Colombo, Ceylon
1988	Museum of History, Toheboksary, Russia

Selected Group Exhibitions:

1975	*FIAP Jubilee Exhibition,* Gruppo Fotografico, Turin
	International Salon of Japan, Asahi Shimbun, Tokyo (and annually to 1980)
1978	*Exposition Mondiale d'Art Photographique,* Mairie, Paris (travelled to the Palais des Congrès, Versailles)
	PhotEurop, Kodak Gallery, London
	World Press Photo, Rijksmuseum Vincent Van Gogh, Amsterdam
1979	*Europäische Fotografen,* Rathaus Tempelhof, West Berlin
	Prinfot, Barcelona
1980	*Auteurop '80,* Salle Maine-Montparnasse, Paris
1982	*Fotoforum 82,* Ruzomberok, Czechoslovakia
1985	*Contemporary Latvian Photography,* House of Arts, Bratislava, Czechoslavakia (travelled to Prague)
1989	*150 Years of Photography,* Central Exhibition Hall, Moscow
1990	*L'Année de l'Est,* Lausanne
	Exhibition, Galerievan der Berlage, Amsterdam
1993	*The Third Wave,* House of Journalists, Riga
1993-94	*Baltic Photo Art Today,* Kiel, Rostock, Riga, Talin, Berlin, Vilnius, Stockholm

Collections:

Latvian Society for International Friendship and Culture, Riga; Fotografijos Muziejus, Siauliai, Lithuania; TASS Agency Collection, Moscow; Collection Historique de FIAP, Berne; Musée Français de la Photographie, Biévres, France; Musée d'Élysee, Lausanne.

Publications:

By MIKHAILOVSKY: Books—*Atklasme (Revelation),* Riga 1981; *Wilhelm Mikhailovsky,* Moscow 1981; *Photography,* with texts by Janis Peters and Raimond Pauls, Riga 1982; *Selected Photographs,* Moscow 1988; *Devotion to Riga,* Riga 1992. **Articles**—"The Boundlessness of the Instant" in *Maksla* (Riga), August 1979; "Das Ziel: Einprägsame Aufnahmen" in *Fotografie* (Leipzig), April 1980; "Photography: The Reality of Transformation" in *Maksla* (Riga), June 1980; "Photography My Life" in *Rodnik* (Riga), November 1988; "Photography" in *Sovetskoye Photo* (Moscow), November 1988; "Now a Man From the Crowd Moves Me" in *Maksla* (Riga), November 1988; "Group A Latvia" in *Rodnik* (Riga), October 1990; "How Many Minutes Left Till the X Hour Comes?" in *Maksla* (Riga), July 1992; "Powerlessness and Greatness of Photography" in *Maksla* (Riga), July 1993; "Family Album- The Infinity of the Space" in *Maksla* (Riga), June 1994.

On MIKHAILOVSKY: Books—*Pobaltska sovetska fotografie* by Vaclav Jiru, Prague 1974; *Dumont Foto 1,* edited by Hugo Schöttle, Cologne 1978; *Wilhelm Mikhailovsky,* exhibition catalogue, Riga 1979; *Dumont Foto 2,* edited by Hugo Schöttle, Cologne 1980; *Creative Photography* by Sergei Morozov, Moscow 1985; *Pribeh Fotografie* by Daniela Mrazkova, Prague 1985; *Latvijas Fotomaksla* by Peteris Zeile and others, Riga 1985; *Photographers Encylopaedia International,* Editions Camera Obscura, Switzerland 1985; *Photography in USSR,* Helsinki 1989; *The World of Photography,* Moscow 1990; *Elegie, Le Nudans la Photo d'Art,* Editions, Librarie du Globe, Moscow 1992; *The Memory of Images,* Nieswand Verlag, Germany 1993. **Articles**—"Good Day, Wilhelm Mikhailovsky!" by Ansis Epners in *Literature and Art* (Riga), January 1978; "Wilhelm Mikhailovsky's Secret" by Andris Rozenbergs in *Maksla* (Riga), March 1979; "Wilhelm Mikhailovsky and Contemporary Soviet Photography" by Daniela Mrázková in *Ceskoslovenska Fotografie* (Prague), November 1979; "Mikhailovsky: His Subjects, His Images" by Sergey Vetrow in *Sovetskoye Foto* (Moscow), February 1980; "World Photographers: Wilhelm Mikhailovsky" in *Foto Revij* (Belgrade), September 1980; "A Big Thought Is Coming" by Atis Skalbergs in *Zvaigzne* (Riga), April 1980; "Wilhelm Mikhailovsky" by Josef Mašin in *Fotografie* (Prague), January 1981; "After Montage" by Valentin Mikhalcowich in *Sovetskoye Foto* (Moscow), August 1983; "A Free Improvisation on the Perception of Essence" by Ojars Vacietis in *Maksla* (Riga), January 1984; "Sterile Flowers Witness and Warn" by Janis Peters in *Maksla* (Riga), October 1987; "Wilhelm Mikhailovsky" by Vladimir Birgus in *Review Photography* (Prague), December 1987; "The Dialogue of Drama and Tragedy" by Victor Avotinsh in *Maksla,* 1987, (Riga), "Wilhelm Mikhailovsky: Happy With One Lens" by Seppo Sayes in *Yalokuva* (Helsinki), April 1988; "Give Me Lord Your Understanding" by Janis Baltviks in *Maksla* (Riga), November 1990; "Wilhelm Mikhailovsky: The Song Festival '90, Opus 2" by Mik Sovisko in *Maksla* (Riga), December 1990.

*

I think there is some sense in living your artistic life as a photographer. I can't reject a single work of mine. These works, whether successful or not by my or other people's criteria, were made with the maximum of my potential at the time. Of course if I could go back ten years with my present knowledge of people, I would do many things another way. But now I would not be able to do what I managed to do at that time.

In the process of learning about the world and myself, I pursued several themes: montage and collage photographs; individual portraits (well known figures of culture), and social photography—"Life as a Reality."

In 1986-87, together with film director Gertz Frank, I worked on the documentary "The Supremest Court." I took pictures of and empathised with a prisoner who had been sentenced to be shot for double murder and was awaiting execution. As well as the film, which was shown all over the world, I made a collection of more than 80 pictures about the tragedy of this person and his attempts to atone for his guilt through the suffering of his soul. The death sentence was carried out.

Now I know there is something more frightful than death.

I prepared a book about his life and death—photographs, confession, documents, psychology of the person and psychology of society. The book has not yet been published.

The Supremest Court, **1987.** Photograph ©Wilhelm Mikhailovsky.

All that I've done and that I'm doing now is based on pure free will. Honesty is supreme. Never, ever was I false, insincere or hypocritical with anybody. When people in the portraits I took are beautiful and sublime in their thoughts and feelings then it means that they were really that beautiful and sublime when they were opening themselves for me. If I talked about a person strictly or sublimely then it means that I was talking the only way I could—at the maximum of my potential; on the edge of the possible, morally, ethically, physically and spiritually. To perform at the maximum in any moment of the creative process—as if you are doing your last thing in this life, I understand that. It is necessary to measure self-sufficiency; this work requires less effort, you can take it easier. . . . But nobody knows what will be most interesting and significant eventually in your life's work. Everything will be presented for judgement and nobody will ask you whether you have been saving your energy or burning yourself out. Something will remain of course, but others, not you, will own it. Maybe this is the main point in creating.

If the Lord had given me the chance to choose when to live my life from all the thousands of years, past and future I would have stayed in the present. I have everything in it. People. Events. Life.

—Wilhelm Mikhailovsky

* * *

His work for periodicals has led Wilhelm Mikhailovsky to take up reportage, but his creative personality is brought out fully only in his freelance photographs. Their significance is mainly the result of complex montage processes. By linking unconnected motives and elements, Mikhailovsky provokes meditation on the generally valid, eternal and indisputable truths, those values that do not change with time or geography. He brings them up to date, confronting them according to contemporary life-styles.

In the past his montages were structurally more complicated, not unlike those of his Lithuanian colleague Vitaly Butyrin, attempts at an ideological solution to the mystery of the origin and presentation of life. Later, he passed on to a simpler subject, the contemplations of the natural conflicts between man rooted in tradition and advancing civilization. Towards the end of the 1970s, his work moved into a third phase, a kind of pictorial cosmology, an impressive presentation of the problems of the destiny of man not only as a cosmopolitan terrestrial but also as an inhabitant of the universe. The technique of montage here, too, allows him at will to accentuate the expression of the ecstatic suggestive compositions. These pictorial visions, which are more unambiguous as to their significance and more sober in expression, do not free man from his everyday cares, do not rid him of the humdrum existence of the human race, but they do dramatically present a message that emphasizes how trite all these everyday worries are, how negligible in comparison with the laws and order of the eternal universe.

Mikhailovsky replaces the mystery of our life in nature on earth with a vision of cosmic mystery. Not in order to express a desire for the greater justice of a higher, perfectly-arranged whole, but to celebrate eternal, everlasting life by presenting the question of the dialectical relationship of terrestrial existence in a broader, only recently discovered and explored space. This, of course, is also the creative program of associative photography—to express the sensibility and imagination of contemporary man encountered in many different localities. But Mikhailovsky's lively, inspiring and to a great extent festive expression is unusual in that it does not express the disillusion and scepticism of a member of the consumer society who realizes that, in the end, society turns all the achievements of civilization against man and his naturalness. Mikhailovsky's vision does not involve the usual sense of utter hopelessness; on the contrary, he looks upon this complex set of problems as a challenge, as an inevitable process of changing styles of living, as a means (about which he is optimistic) of seeking after other forms of existence.

Mikhailovsky makes use in his pictorial compositions of the results of his work as a reporter as well as a free-lance photographer. He has a fondness for figures and landscape as well as black-and-white montage. He links his compositions in broad cycles, the captions of which are eloquent in their way and precisely define the boundaries of the artist's intention: Beginning, Sources, Reconstruction Humanus, Sensibility, Renaissance, etc. He has had great success at photographic exhibitions with these works. He has not yet had the opportunity to make other use of them—for example, in book form. His first portfolio about old Riga and its inhabitants is sober; it is based on his reportage. For his second book—which he has been planning for several years—he wants to have more of a free hand. He has called it *Man at Work,* and, in pictorial metaphor and symbol, he intends to deal with the purpose of man's existence. In comparison with the ideologically similar-minded Butyrin, Mikhailovsky's expression is more civil and simple, less pompous and less subject to surrealist transformations.

—Daniela Mrázková

MIKI, Jun.

Nationality: Japanese. **Born:** Kurashiki City, Okayama Prefecture, 14 September 1919. **Education:** Studied economics, Keio University, Tokyo, 1938-43; mainly self-taught in photography, from 1938. **Family:** Married Yasuko in 1950; children: Hiromitsu and Mariko. **Career:** Amateur student photographer, as member of the Photo Friends Society, Tokyo, contributing to the magazines *Shashin Bunka* (Photo Culture) and *Toua Nippo* (Touwa Daily Report); assistant to the photographer Ken Domon, *q.v.,* Tokyo, 1941-42; worked for the Nomura Trading Company, Tokyo, 1943-46; news photographer, Sun News Photos, Tokyo, 1947-48; photographer, International News Photos (INP), Tokyo, 1948-49; Staff Photographer, *Life* magazine (New York), working in Japan, 1949-57. Since 1957, freelance photographer, working for the publishers Time-Life, Iwanami, Chuo-koron-sha, Shinchosha, Kodansha, Bungei-Shuinju-sha, etc., Tokyo. Organizer, with Ihei Kimura and Ken Domon, *Shudan Foto* exhibition, Tokyo, 1950. Director, Nikkor Club, Tokyo, from 1952; Vice-Chairman 1973, and Chairman 1981-88, Japan Professional Photographers Society (JPS), Tokyo; founder and first president Japanese Photographers association 1989. Professor, Nihon University laboratory, Tokyo, since 1977. **Recipient:** Professional Photographer Award, Japan Photo Critics Society, Tokyo, 1952; Kodansha Photographer Award, Tokyo, 1960; Purple Ribbon Award, Tokyo, 1984; 38th Photographic Society of Japan Yearly Award, 1988; The Order of the Sacred Treasure, Gold Rays with Neck Ribbon, 1989; The 40th Meritorious Service Award from Japanese Photographic Society, 1990; Fifth Grade, Senior of Court Rank, 1992; Decoration from Sakata City, Yamagat Prefecture for Meritorious Service, 1993. **Died:** (in Tokyo) 22 February, 1992.

Individual Exhibitions:

1962	*Inca and Brasilia,* Fuji Photo Salon, Ginza, Tokyo
	Mexico—The Expression of a Rising Nation, Takashimaya Department Store, Nihonbashi, Tokyo
1964	*The Story of New York's Fifth Avenue,* Takashimaya Department Store, Nihonbashi, Tokyo
1965	*Samba, Samba, Brasil,* Fuji Photo Salon, Ginza, Tokyo
1973	*Risking the Life,* Nikon Salon, Ginza and Shinjuku, Tokyo
1977	*My New York,* Nikon Salon, Ginza and Shinjuku, Tokyo

1982	*Why I Take Pictures, Part I,* Photo Gallery Wide, Roppongi, Tokyo
	Why I Take Pictures, Part II, Nagase Photo Salon, Ginza, Tokyo
1992	*Liverpool of the Beatles,* Nikon Salon, Ginza and Osaka, Japan
1993	*100 New Sights of Tokyo,* Nikon Salon, Ginza and Osaka, Japan

Selected Group Exhibitions:

1951	*First Shudan Foto Exhibition,* Tokyo
1952	*Gendai Shashin Sakka (Contemporary Photographers) Exhibition '52,* Tokyo
1959	*2nd Biennale,* Venice, Italy
1975	*The History of Japanese Contemporary Photography 1945-70,* Seibu Museum of Art, Tokyo
1979	*Japan: A Self-Portrait,* at the *Biennale,* Venice, Italy
1985	*Japan 1971-84: Man and Society,* Seibu Art Forum, Tokyo
1990	*Image Hong Kong '90,* International Photographers Meeting, Hong Kong

Collections:

Time-Life Library, New York; Museum of Modern Art, New York.

Publications:

By MIKI: Books—*Mexico by Photography—Youth in the Ruins,* Tokyo 1961; *Samba, Samba, Brasil,* Tokyo 1967; *Shashin Sokagakkai* (The New Religious Body by Photography), Tokyo 1968; *Keio Gijuku* (Keio University), Tokyo 1979; *Jun Miki* (Showa Photographers Series), Tokyo 1982; *Kyuchu Saiji-ki,* Tokyo 1984; *Great Britain in Photographs,* Tokyo 1990; *Photographs of Yami Tribesman in Lan Sho Island,* Tokyo 1993.

On MIKI: Books—*Photography of the World,* edited by Heibonsha Publishers, Tokyo 1956; *Photography of the World '60,* edited by Hiromu Hara, Ihei Kimura and others, Tokyo and New York 1960; *Contemporary Photography and Photographers,* with text by Tsutomu Watanabe, Tokyo 1975; *The History of Japanese Contemporary Photography 1945-70,* Tokyo 1977; *Photography: Venice '79,* edited by Daniela Palazzoli, Vittorio Sgarbi and Italo Zannier, Milan and New York 1979; *Showa Photographer Story,* with text by Shozo Kozakai, Tokyo 1983. **Article**—"Jun Miki" in *Asahi Camera* (Tokyo), January 1974.

*   *   *

Born in 1919, Jun Miki was a freelance photographer as well as chairman of both Japan Professional Photographers Society (1986) and Nikkor Club. He started his career as a photographer when he was very young, for he joined the student photographers' circle "Photo Friends" while he was a Keio University student and at the same time became an assistant to Ken Domon, during which he took photos for various magazines. While he worked for Domon, he was greatly influenced by Domon's realist photography. Although photojournalism was little known at the time, he was taught the method of documentary photography by the late photographer Yonosuke Natori who brought it back with him from Germany.

After World War II, Miki immediately restarted his photographic activity, and in 1949, joined the Tokyo branch of Time-Life. The most famous of his photos that appeared in *Life* magazine is the portrait of Prime Minister Shigeru Yoshida shown on the cover of its September 10, 1951, issue. He left Time-Life in 1957, but his days at the magazine can be said his best ones, and he is really the Japanese photographer who did a world-famous job earlier than any others after the war. Furthermore, he made an opportunity for Nikon cameras and Nikkor lenses to become as world-famous as they are now, by introducing the *Life* photographers to the Nikon products which then were not so well-known to the world.

—Takao Kajiwara

Untitled. Photograph ©Jun Miki.

MILI, Gjon.

Nationality: American. **Born:** Kerce, Southern Albania, 28 November 1904; emigrated to the United States, 1923; subsequently naturalized. **Education:** schools in Bucharest until 1920; studied electrical engineering, Massachusetts Institute of Technology, Cambridge, 1923-27, B.S. 1927; mainly self-taught in photography, but worked initially with Harold E. Edgerton. **Career:** Lighting Research Engineer, Westinghouse Electrical and Manufacturing Company, Cambridge, 1928-38; developed biplane tungsten filament lamp and lights for color photography, 1930-35, and worked on experimental and high-speed photography, with Edgerton, at M.I.T., 1938. Freelance photographer, working for *Life* and other magazines, New York, 1939 until his death in 1984; also, a filmmaker, from 1944. Visiting Lecturer, Yale University, New Haven, Connecticut, 1969; Instructor in Photography, Sarah Lawrence College summer project, Lacoste, France, 1972, 1973, 1974; Instructor in Photography, Hunter College, New York, 1973. **Recipient:** American Society of Magazine Photographers Award, 1963. **Died:**(in Stamford, Connecticut) 14 February 1984.

Individual Exhibitions:

1942   *Dancers in Movement,* Museum of Modern Art, New York
1946   Paris Galerie, Paris

1952   *On Picasso,* Museum of Modern Art, New York (with Robert Capa)
1964   Time-Life Building, New York
1970   Lincoln Center for the Performing Arts, New York
        Musée Réattu, Arles, France
1971   Musée des Arts Décoratifs, Paris
1979   Compton Gallery, Massachusetts Institute of Technology, Cambridge
1980   International Center of Photography, New York (retrospective)
1981   Musée Arleton, Arles, France
1994   *Vintage Photographs,* Howard Greenberg Gallery, New York (in collaboration with the *Life* Gallery of Photography)

Selected Group Exhibitions:

1951   *Memorable Life Photographs,* Museum of Modern Art, New York
1975   *Photography Within the Humanities,* Jewett Arts Center, Wellesley College, Massachusetts
1979   *Fleeting Gestures: Dance Photographs,* International Center of Photography, New York (travelled to *Venezia '79,* and The Photographers' Gallery, London)
        Life: The First Decade 1936-45, Grey Art Gallery, New York University
1982   *Color as Form,* International Museum of Photography at George Eastman House, Rochester, New York
        Flooods of Light, The Photographers' Gallery, London (toured Britain)
1986   *Life: The Second Decade,* Grey Art Gallery, New York University

Collections:

Museum of Modern Art, New York; Time-Life Library, New York; Massachusetts Institute of Technology, Cambridge; Bibliothèque Nationale, Paris.

Publications:

By MILI: Books—*Photographs of Picasso by Gjon Mili and Robert Capa,* New York 1950; *The Magic of the Opera,* New York 1960; *Picasso et la Troisieme Dimension/Picasso's Third Dimension,* Paris and New York 1970; *Gjon Mili: Photographs and Recollections,* Boston 1980. **Articles—**in *Life* (New York): "Gjon Mili Photographs Ballet Dancers at High Speed," 19 February 1940; "World Charter," 23 July 1945; "Bad Little Good Girl," 24 December 1951; "World of Sean O'Casey," 25 July 1954; "Queen of Cathedrals," 15 December 1961; "The Relentless Spectre of Brecht," 18 September 1964; "Mr. B. Talks about Ballet," 11 June 1965; "Serenade to 90 Years of Greatness," 11 November 1966; "An American Masterpiece," 3 October 1969; "The Me Nobody Knows," 4 September 1970; "A Mother's Legacy," 26 May 1972; "29 Years Ago in Life," 25 August 1972. **Films—** *Jamming the Blues,* 1944; *Raoul Dufy Paints, New York,* 1950; *Casals, Prades Festival,* 1950; *Jean Babilee, Dancer,* 1951; *Salvador Dali,* 1951; *Stomping for Mili, Brubeck Jazz Quartet,* 1955; *Eisenstaedt Photographs "The Tall Man,"* 1955; *"Tempest": Filmmaking on Location,* 1958; *Henri Cartier-Bresson, Photographer,* 1958; *Homage to Picasso,* 1967.

On MILI: Books—*Gjon Mili,* exhibition catalogue, with an introduction by Jean-Paul Sartre, Paris 1946; *Memorable Life Photographs,* with text by Edward Steichen, New York 1951; *Gjon Mili: Photographies,* exhibition catalogue, Paris 1971; *The Magic Image* by Cecil Beaton and Gail Buckland, London and Boston 1975; *The Photography Catalogue,* edited by Norman Snyder, New York 1976; *Photography Within the Humanities,* edited by Eugenia Parry Janis and Wendy McNeil, Danbury, New Hampshire 1977; *Geschichte der Fotografie im 20. Jahrhundert/Photography in the 20th Century* by Petr Tausk, Cologne 1977, London 1980; *The Vogue Book of Fashion Photography* by Polly Devlin, with an introduction by Alexander Liberman, London 1979; *Life: The First Decade 1936-1945* by Robert Littman, Ralph Graves and Doris C. O'Neill, New York 1979, London 1980; *Flooods of Light: Flash Photography 1851-1981,* exhibition catalogue, edited by Rupert Martin, London 1982; *Color as Form: A History of Color Photography,* exhibition catalogue, with introduction by Robert A. Sobieszek, Rochester, New York 1982; *The Library of World Photography: Photography as Fine Art,* with introduction by Douglas Davis, Tokyo 1982, 1983, London 1983; *Life: The Second Decade,* edited by Doris C. O'Neill, New York 1986. **Articles**—"Gjon Mili: Sauvees du Fe, Quelques Etudes du Patriarche de la Photo" in *Photo* (Paris), July 1971; "Gjon Mili: Photographer King" by Sean Callahan in the *Village Voice* (New York), 26 May 1975; "Photography as Theology" by Sean Callahan in *American Photographer* (New York), November 1980; "Views of Big Cities and Studies of People in Motion" by Gene Thornton in the *New York Times,* 30 November 1980; "Gjon Mili, Life Magazine Photographer, Dies" in the *New York Times,* 16 February 1984; "Gjon Mili" in *the Annual Obituary 1984,* edited by Margot Levy, London and Chicago 1985.

*   *   *

Few photographers are given the privilege (or the talent) to leave a truly distinctive mark on a medium that is available to scores of millions. Photography is based on reality, and its strength lies in its ability to split seconds and to observe dispassionately every detail of the world in front of the lens. Only by his unique, strong vision of the world, or by extending the ability of photography to record what man's limited senses cannot see, can a photographer leave his own stamp on his photography.

The limitations of the medium made it difficult, perhaps impossible, to tell a daguerreotype by Daguerre from one by another early practitioner. The same is true of calotypes by Talbot.

But as materials and equipment loosened their grip on the photographer's vision and imagination, individual workers began to mark their work with a personal style of seeing. Technology became an important factor in releasing individual style as the medium matured. The action studies of Muybridge and Marey, completely removed from the main-stream of their era, come to mind. And the images of the precocious Jacques-Henri Lartigue, combining high-speed photography with a unique way of seeing, are another example of *cachet* apart from contemporary work.

But it remained for Gjon Mili, working in the late 1930s with the then-new stroboscopic electronic flash lamps perfected by Dr. Harold Edgerton of the Massachusetts Institute of Technology, to bring the viewer a new way of looking at the world. Leaving his career as an electrical engineer, Mili experimented for several months with this new light source that could divide a second's worth of action into thousands of individual images, or make a single piercingly sharp image of a bullet in flight. It was a unique marriage of a new technology and a photographer whose vision, understanding and appreciation of it were superbly suited to one another. The imagination of artists working in other media had produced a few memorable pictures that analyzed action by breaking it down into successive pictures. But Mili was the first to provide controlled, clear, scientifically valid yet imaginative and beautiful images that would otherwise have remained hidden from human vision.

Their strength was such that the editors of the two-year-old *Life* magazine began to give him many assignments to picture sports, dance and theater action to be used in its pages. And since these pages reached unprecedentedly large numbers of readers, the new way of seeing soon entered the consciousness of *Life*'s readers across the world.

Mili's association with that magazine continued almost until his death in 1984. And, as a retrospective show at New York City's International Center of Photography bore out, his work was not limited to his strobe-flash specialty.

Over the years Mili photographed famous people—artists, writers, actors, dancers, even historic archcriminals like the infamous Nazi Eichmann. Unlike one by Arnold Newman or Yousuf Karsh, a Mili portrait does not instantly reveal its maker. Many of his people pictures look very much like those by other fellow *Life* staff photographers of the era. But this very fact gives them a variety and appropriateness that are sometimes missing in the work of more stylized photographers. Those of political personalities had often to be done on the spot with little chance to direct or light the subject ideally. But the meticulous craftsmanship, the command of the medium that distinguish a Mili photograph, wipe away the distractions. The technical difficulties are never beyond control.

But perhaps the work that truly shows a masterly combination of both craft and art are Mili's pictures of statuary. His pictures of both ancient Greek and modern statues and bas reliefs truly bring alive the presence and intent of the

sculptor. Mili's means to his end were the same as those of any other photographer—choice of lighting angle to dramatize the sculpture. But the choice! A group of Roman guards on a bas-relief, lit subtly from below, photographed in a close-in composition that concentrates attention on the faces, becomes a menacing, conspiratorial group. Rodin's *The Burghers of Calais,* limned by the light of a setting sun, seem almost to breathe and talk to one another as they consult, faces troubled, within the Hirshhorn Sculpture Garden. Mili's feeling and respect for stone and metal, if not unique, were certainly rare among photographers.

The sustained high level of quality that marks Gjon Mili's output can be credited to his breadth of appreciation for literature and the arts, history, dance and theater. It is a characteristic he shared with a number of his contemporaries, like Cartier-Bresson and Kertész. To this broad cultural base he added a consummate mastery of his medium that made many Mili photographs classics of both innovation and vision.

—Kenneth Poli

MILLER, Lee.

Nationality: American. **Born:** Poughkeepsie, New York, 23 April 1907. **Education:** Studied painting, theatrical design and lighting, Art Students League, New York, 1927-28. **Family:** Married the businessman Aziz Eloui Bey in 1934 (separated, 1939); the painter and art critic Roland Penrose in 1947; son: Antony. **Career:** Worked as a fashion model for Frank Crowninshield and Condé Nast, modeling for the photographers Edward Steichen and Arnold Genthe, New York, 1924-27; photographer, as assistant to Man Ray, Paris, 1929-32; also fashion model, for George Hoyningen-Huene and Horst P. Horst, *Vogue* magazine studios, Paris, 1930-32; established own portrait, fashion, theatre and advertising photography studio, with her brother Eric, working for *Vogue,* Helena Rubinstein, Elizabeth Arden, Camay, Saks of Fifth Avenue, Jay-Thorpe, etc., New York, 1932-33; independent photographer, in Cairo and the Middle East, 1935-37, in England, France, Greece, Bulgaria and Rumania, 1937-40; joins staff of *Vogue* London studios, London, 1940-45: war correspondent, for *Vogue* magazine, in France, Germany, Rumania, Belgium, Austria, Denmark and Luxembourg, 1944-45; freelance journalist and photographer, working for British, French and American editions of *Vogue,* in Chiddingly, Sussex, 1946-54. **Estate:** Lee Miller Archive, Burgh Hill House, Chiddingly, East Sussex BN9 6JF, England. **Died:** (in Chiddingly, Sussex) 21 July 1977.

Individual Exhibitions:

1933	Julien Levy Gallery, New York
1978	Mayor Gallery, London
1984	*Picasso's Gaze,* Photographers' Gallery, London
	Lee Miller in Sussex, Gardner Arts Centre, Brighton, Sussex
1985	*The Lives of Lee Miller,* Staley-Wise Gallery, New York
1986	Photographers' Gallery, London (retrospective)
	Gardner Arts Centre, Brighton, Sussex (retrospective)
1989-90	Corcoran Gallery of Art, Washington (retrospective, toured USA)
1991	Fundacio Joan Miro, Barcelona (retrospective)
1992	Museum Ludwig, Cologne (retrospective, still touring Europe)
	Lee Miller's War, ICA, London (toured UK)

Selected Group Exhibitions:

1931	*Groupe Annuel des Photographes,* Galerie de la Pléiade, Paris
1932	*Modern European Photography,* Julien Levy Gallery, New York
1955	*The Family of Man,* Museum of Modern Art, New York (and world tour)
1976	*Photographs from the Julien Levy Collections,* Art Institute of Chicago (toured the United States)

Portrait of Space, **Siwa, Egypt, 1937.** Photograph ©Lee Miller Archives.

1977   *The History of Fashion Photography,* International Museum of
          Photography at George Eastman House, Rochester, New
          York (travelled to Brooklyn Museum of Art, New York; San
          Francisco Museum of Modern Art, Cincinnati Art Institute,
          Ohio; Museum of Fine Art, St. Petersburg, Florida)
1978   *Dada and Surrealism Reviewed,* Hayward Gallery, London

1982   *Atelier Man Ray 1920-1935,* Centre Georges Pompidou, Paris
1985   *L'Amour Fou: Photography and Surrealism,* Corcoran Gallery
          of Art, Washington, D.C. (travelled to San Francisco
          Museum of Modern Art; Centre Georges Pompidou, Paris;
          Hayward Gallery, London)
        Indelible Image, Corcoran Gallery of Art, Washington, D.C.

1986   *Marseilles,* Musée Cantini, Marseilles, France

Collections:

Lee Miller Archive, Chiddingly, Sussex; Art Institute of Chicago; New Orleans Museum of Art, Louisiana.

Publications:

By MILLER: Books—*Grim Glory: Pictures of Britain Under Fire,* London 1940; *Wrens in Camera,* with introduction by V. Laughton Mathews, London 1945. **Articles**—"Picasso Himself" in *Picasso: Retrospective Exhibition,* catalogue edited by the Tate Gallery, London, 1960; "My Man Ray," interview with Mario Amaya, in *Art in America* (New York), May 1975.

On MILLER: Books—*The Family of Man,* edited by Edward Steichen, with foreword by Carl Sandburg, New York 1955; *Photographs from the Julien Levy Collection, starting with Atget,* exhibition catalogue by David Travis, Chicago 1976; *Fotografen der 30er Jahre: Ein Anthologie,* edited by Hans Jurgen Syberberg, Munich 1977; *Dada and Surrealism Reviewed,* exhibition catalogue by Dawn Ades, London 1978; *Fotografische Kunstlerbildnisse* by Dieter Ronte, Evelyn Weiss and Jeane von Oppenheim, Cologne 1978; *The History of Fashion Photography* by Nancy Hall-Duncan, New York 1979; *Le Numero Barbette: Man Ray, Jean Cocteau,* edited by Jacques Damase, Paris, 1980; *Les Mystères de la Chambre Noire—Le Surrealisme et la Photographie* by Eduard Jaguer, Paris 1982; *Atelier Man Ray 1920-1935: Abbott, Boiffard, Brandt, Miller,* exhibition catalogue with introduction by Alain Sayag, Paris 1982; *The Lives of Lee Miller* by Antony Penrose, London 1985, Tokyo, 1989, and Paris, 1994; *L'Amour Fou: Photography and Surrealism* by Jane Livingston and Rosalind Krauss, New York and London 1985; *Lee Miller Photographer,* by Jane Livingston, California, 1989; *Lee Miller, An Exhibition of Photographs, 1929-1964,* Jane Livingston, California, 1991; *Lee Miller's War,* edited by Antony Penrose, London, 1992; *Lee Miller Photographe et Correspondante de Guerre,* edited by Antony Penrose, Paris, 1994. **Articles**—"The Taking of a Fashion Photograph" by Anne Scott-James in *Picture Post* (London), 26 October 1940; "Obituary: Lee Miller, photographer and model" in the *New York Times,* 24 July 1977; "Obituary: Lee Miller" in *The Times* (London), 25 July 1977.

*   *   *

There is a certain magic to Lee Miller's work, a dark magic. Filled with Surrealist earmarks, it has the swerve and spontaneity of all that makes Surrealism endearing to audiences 50 years after the fact. But filled too, with the darkness of her life, lived with an abandon that never satisfied, it is also touched with constraint and brooding passages.

When she was good, to paraphrase a familiar rhyme, she was very very good. Her fashion, advertising, and theater photographs, a development from her work as a model for Steichen, Horst, and Hoyningen-Huene, are velvety, fresh, and filled with a cool sensuous look. Sophisticated shadows confront, and startle, a lyrical luminescence.

Her World War II photographs, done on assignment for English *Vogue,* are cool, too. But bewilderingly cool in such a period of emotional spleen, they show how she transformed her Surrealist life into this bombardment of "real" surrealism—war. She caught the war's defiant reality by abstracting details associated with total destruction, like the light of bombs, half-standing structures, windows opening nowhere, and amorphous, ominous smoke. With a kind of disbelief, she wove that precarious balance between reality and nonreality into different settings, people, and moments of the war—into, for example, the deadliness of Dachau, the rigor mortis of Nazi-occupied France, the ghostliness of live children almost dead, and into the sight of German opera stars singing into the surround of fallen buildings and failed society. Apparently carefree, she never really was.

But never mind. There was always the famous—Picasso, Max Ernst, Colette—before, during, and after the war. She photographed them all. Before the war, she portrayed them with formal stylistic devices of that time—with dramatic shadows more usually used with the expectation of preserving an individual for posterity. After the war, these people, now even more famous, visited her, with her husband, in their idyllic English rural landscape setting.

And she photographed them again—sometimes continuously. These, however, are the photographs that stretch into posterity. Easy, informal, and done with great skill, they are filled with personal turns of the body, smiles for the familiar, with characteristics that turn a person into the human being the outsider can never see.

She had met these poeple soon after leaving Poughkeepsie, New York, a large town along the Hudson River, to come to Paris in 1925; and worked with as well as learned from them before photographing them. Man Ray, one of this group, and her mentor, also became her closest confidante, the man with whom she mixed love, life, and art. She married Roland Penrose, an art collector and connoiseur in 1947, settled in England, and seemed to be most happy when photographing the friends, like Saul Steinberg, who came to visit. Portraits mainly, and more formally conceived than her family visit photos, they tend, usually quite humorously, to catch the motifs that quite wonderfully embroil an individual in his work.

It was easy for her to mix life and art. She lived that way. So completely, in fact, did she, that she seems the personification of Brett in Hemingway's *The Sun Also Rises.* Hemingway was in Paris when Lee arrived. It is not clear if the two ever met. But Brett's resemblance in that novel to Lee is unnerving—each fleeing madly from demonic spirits, each trying to live with abandon. But where Brett remains a storybook character, Lee's photos tell us of the fun-filled, probing, and unfinished world the Surrealists brought to life.

—Judith Mara Gutman

MINICK, Roger.

Nationality: American. **Born:** Ramona, Oklahoma, 13 July 1944. **Education:** Pacific High School, San Bernardino, California; University of California, Berkeley, 1964-69, B.A. in history 1969. **Family:** Married Joyce Johnson in 1972. **Career:** Worked as a medical orderly, San Bernardino County Hospital, California, 1962-64; Darkroom Assistant, 1965-70, and Director, 1970-75, A.S.U.C. Studio, University of California, Berkeley. Freelance photographer, California, since 1975. Instructor, Academy of Art College, San Francisco, since 1986. **Recipient:** Guggenheim Fellowship in Photography, 1972; National Endowment for the Arts Photo Survey Grant, 1977, 1978. M.F.A.: Universtiy of California, Davis, 1986. **Agents:** Lumina, 251 West 19th Street, #7B, New York, New York, 10011; Thomas V Meyer, 169 Twenty-fifth Ave, San Francisco, California 94121. **Address:** 111 Camino Amigo Court, Danville, California 94526, U.S.A.

Individual Exhibitions:

1971   *Ozark and Delta Images,* Friends of Photography, Carmel,
             California
1975   *Ozark Photographs,* University Art Museum, Berkeley,
             California
             Two Views from the West: Roger Minick and Richard Misrach,
             International Center of Photography, New York
1976   *Rural Photographs,* Creative Photography Gallery, Massachu-
             setts Institute of Technology, Cambridge
1977   *Rural Photographs,* Light Work Gallery, Syracuse, New York
             Roger Minick: Retrospective, Hunter Museum of Art, Chatta-
             nooga, Tennessee
             Roger Minick and Ted Orland, Focus Gallery, San Francisco
1978   *Ozark and Delta Images,* Images Gallery, New Orleans
1980   *Roger Minick: Retrospective,* Douglas Kenyon Gallery,
             Chicago
1981   *Sightseer Series,* Grapestake Gallery, San Francisco
1983   *In The Fields, Undocumented Workers,* Chicago Center for
             Contemporary Photography, Chicago
1991   *Roger Minick Photographs,* Photo Interform, Osaka, Japan

Bryce Canyon National Park, from *Sightseers,* **1979.** Photograph by Roger Minick.

1992   *Recent Photographs and Works on Paper,* Vision Gallery, San
        Francisco

Selected Group Exhibitions:

1968   *Studio '68,* Friends of Photography, Carmel, California
1973   *Places,* San Francisco Art Institute
1976   *L.A. X 6,* Mount St. Mary's College, Los Angeles
1978   *Espejo,* Center for Contemporary Photography, Chicago
1979   *Attitudes: Photography in the 1970s,* Santa Barbara Museum of
        Art, California
1980   *Fotografie im Alltag Amerikas,* Kunstgewerbemuseum, Zurich
        New California Views, Mills College, Oakland, California
1981   *America's National Parks,* Oakland Museum, California
1983   *Landmarks Reviewed,* Pensacola Museum of Art, Florida
1984   *Photography in California 1945-80,* San Francisco Museum of
        Modern Art (travelled to Akron Art Museum, Ohio;

Corcoran Gallery, Washington, D.C.; Los Angeles Municipal
Art Gallery; Cornell University, Ithaca, New York; High
Museum of Art, Atlanta, Georgia; Museum Folkwang,
Essen; Centre Georges Pompidou, Paris; Museum of
Photographic Arts, San Diego, California)
1989   *Picturing California,* Oakland Museum, California

Collections:

Museum of Modern Art, New York; Guggenheim Memorial Foundation, New
York; Fogg Art Museum, Harvard University, Cambridge, Massachusetts;
Museum of Fine Arts, Houston; Center for Creative Photography, University
of Arizona, Tucson; San Francisco Museum of Modern Art; Metropolitan
Museum of Art, New York; Los Angeles County Museum of Art; International
Museum of Photography at George Eastman House, Rochester, New York;
Chicago Center for Contemporary Photography; National Museum of Ameri-
can Art, Smithsonian Institute, Washington DC.

Publications:

By MINICK: Books—*Delta West,* with Dave Bohn, San Francisco 1969; *Hills of Home,* San Francisco 1975; *The Oakland Paramount,* Berkeley, 1981.

On MINICK: Books—*Latent Image* by Joel D. Levinson, San Francisco 1978; *Light Readings: A Photography Critic's Writings 1968-1978* by A.D. Coleman, New York 1979; *New California Views,* exhibition catalogue, by Therese Heyman, Los Angeles 1979; *Photography in California 1945-1980* by Louise Katzman San Francisco 1984; *Picturing California,* by Bill Barich and Therese Heyman. **Articles**—"Roger Minick: Delta West" by A.D. Coleman in the *Village Voice*(New York), 25 June 1970;"Delta West" by Margery Mann in *Popular Photography*(New York),July 1970;"Ozark Exhibition"by Joan Murray in *Artweek* (Oakland, California), 15 February 1975;"Hills of Home"by Michael Kernan in *The Smithsonian*(Washington, D.C.), December 1975; "Exhibit in L.A." by Robert Mautner in *Artweek*(Oakland, California), 13 November 1976; "L.A. Exhibit" by Natalie Canavor in *Popular Photography*(New York), April 1978; "Exhibition at Douglas Kenyon Gallery" by David Elliott in the *Chicago Sun-Times,* 15 June 1980; "Sightseer Exhibition" (exhibition review) by Thomas Albright in *SF Chronicle,* 4 March, 1981; "The Oakland Paramount" (book review) by Allen Temko in *SF Chronicle,* 17 May, 1981; "Picturing California," (exhibition review) by Liz Lufkin in *SF Chronicle,* 16 September, 1989.

*

With my various photographic projects, I have been largely interested in people and how they interact with their environment. Generally, I have concentrated on particular regions that embody unique lifestyles. My approach—as with my project on the Ozarks of Arkansas and the Sacramento Delta—has often been to photograph people amidst surrounding architectural or natural features I feel to be most succinctly representative of a region.

With the mural-portrait series in East Los Angeles, I made portraits that juxtaposed the intensity of the barrio murals with the pride of the Chicano people themselves. In an earlier series from my Southern California work, where I photographed shoppers in shopping malls, I tried to show the tensions resulting from visually bringing together middle-class buyers with the futuristic, hermetically-sealed places of consumerism. Also, in this same project on Southern California, I made a series of photographs of peopleless, urban landscapes, many of which were taken from inside a moving car while driving the freeways. Allowing the interior of the automobile to become an adjunct to the composition, and striving to capture the fleeting configurations caused by the movement, I found this point of view compatible with Southern California's preoccupation with the automobile.

In another project on "undocumented workers," possibly the most photoessay-like of all my work, I have attempted to examine the conditions of agricultural workers in the United States, particularly the Mexican Nationals. By photographing all aspects of their difficult existence, from their meagre camp life to their exhausting work in the fields, I have sought to suggest some of the realities of American agriculture.

In my Sightseer Series (portraits of tourists in the National Parks, 1979-1981) and in a further exploration of shopping malls (1982-1985), I have worked for the first time in color. Since 1985, I have tended to experiment with my work, for example, combining painting and photography into collagelike works on paper. Recently, 1990-1994, I have been working in black and white with double exposed images and negative prints. I feel my newest work has reflected a growing need to make my work more personal.

—Roger Minick

*   *   *

Roger Minick is a thoroughly modern documentary photographer. Since *Hills of Home* and *Delta West,* excellent, traditional photographic studies of people in rural environments, his work has grown increasingly objective, increasingly open. Without turning his back on his earlier work, Minick has changed with the times, updating the tradition of documentary photography.

His work is characterized by fine craftsmanship, extreme sensitivity, and a high degree of integrity. The clarity of detail, the richness of color, and the full tonal range make all his pictures eminently inviting: to view them is to feel part of the real place, to get a sense of the real people they contain. His attention to light quality and compositional nuance emphasize his concern not only for the subjects he has chosen, but also for the viewer he is addressing. Minick does a tremendous amount of work on each of his projects in order to capture and recreate as fully as possible the way in which people interact with their environments. He tries to present them as accurately as possible, and he is always sensitive to their private dreams and desires.

Even though his photographs imply an acceptance of the people, they don't always imply an acceptance of their situations. His images for the "Espejo" project, done in a barrio of East Los Angeles juxtaposing the distinct pride of the Chicano people with vigorous wall murals found in their communities, raise questions about the plight of Chicano peoples in the American culture. And while his study of middle class shoppers in Southern California malls is sympathetic to the people involved in this activity, his photographs reveal the dehumanizing sterility of these environments, and question Americans' odd obsession to consume material goods.

The recent "Sightseer Series" focuses on a common cultural activity (automobile excursions) and documents it in a neutral, almost sociological manner. The photographs show individuals and groups of people standing in front of metal rails and small brick walls on roadside stops which overlook such natural wonders as Monument Valley, Yosemite, and the Grand Canyon. Dressed out of Sears catalogs and gift shops, the people offer an odd contrast to their natural surroundings. An aura of unreality, heightened by the backdrop quality of the vistas, dominates each scene, and as they pose only a little more seriously than they have for hundreds of family snapshots, the people appear oblivious to the incongruity they introduce.

Yet the straightforward, non-ironic tone of these photographs implies an acceptance which transcends social satire. As he enlarges our conception of the landscape to include ourselves and each other, Minick seems to be suggesting that the tourist has become a real, perhaps even natural, part of American scenery. Here, as in his other works, Minick uses photography to present a perceptive examination of societal habits and states of mind.

—Ted Hedgpeth

MINKKINEN, Arno Rafael.

Nationality: American. **Born:** Helsinki, Finland, 4 June 1945; emigrated to the United States, 1951: naturalized, 1967. **Education:** Fort Hamilton High School, Brooklyn, New York, 1959-63; Wagner Collge, Staten Island, New York, 1963-67 (Editor, *Wagner Literary Magazine,* 1965-66), B.A. in English 1967; attended Wagner College Study Program, Bregenz, Austria, 1967; studied photography, under George Tice, at the New School for Social Research, New York, 1970-71, and under John Benson at Apeiron Workshops, Millerton, New York, 1971; studied under Ralph Hattersley at the School of Visual Arts, New York, 1971-72, and, under Harry Callahan and Aaron Siskind, at Rhode Island School of Design, Providence, 1972-74 (Teaching Assistant, 1973-74), M.F.A. in photography 1974. **Family:** Married Sandra Jean Hughes in 1969; son: Daniel. **Career:** Worked as a copywriter in various advertising agencies, New York, 1967-72, 1976-77. Lecturer, Lahden Taideoppilaitos (Art Institute), Lahti, Finland, and Instructor in Photography, Taideteollinen Korkeakoulu (Institute of Industrial Design), Helsinki, 1974-76; Assistant Professor of Photography, Massachusetts Institute of Technology, Cambridge, 1977-81, Since 1981, Assistant Professor, Philadelphia College of Art. Editor-in-Chief, *Views: A Journal of Photography in New England,* Boston, 1980-81. **Agent:** Yuen Lui Gallery, 906 Pine Street, Seattle, Washington 98101. **Address:** 5 Bells Court, Philadelphia, Pennsylvania 19106, U.S.A.

Individual Exhibitions:

1972   Soho Photo Gallery, New York
        Spectrum Gallery, Tucson, Arizona (travelled to Projects Inc.,
            Cambridge, Massachusetts, and Community Darkrooms,
            Syracuse University, New York, 1973)

1973	Woods Gerry Mansion, Rhode Island School of Design, Providence
1974	Valokuvamuseo, Helsinki
1976	Wäinö Aaltosen Museo, Turku, Finland
	Moderna Museet, Stockholm
1977	Red Eye Galley, Rhode Island School of Design, Providence
1979	Yuen Lui Gallery, Seattle
	Canon Photo Gallery, Amsterdam
1980	Crealde School of Art, Winter Park, Florida
1981	Bemidji State University, Minnesota

Selected Group Exhibitions:

1974	*Variety Show II,* Humboldt State University, Arcata, California
	Photography as a Fine Art, University of Florida, Gainesville
1976	*Fantastic Photography in Europe,* at *Rencontres Internationales de la Photographie,* Arles, France (toured Europe and the United States, 1976-79)
1978	*Tusen och En Bild/1001 Pictures,* Moderna Museet, Stockholm
	The Male Nude, Marcuse Pfeifer Gallery, New York
	Photo Exhibition and Print Auction, Neary Gallery, Santa Cruz, California
1979	*The History of the Nude,* Kiva Gallery, Boston
	The Contemporary Photographic Book, Addison Gallery of American Art, Andover, Massachusetts
1980	*Into the 80s: New England Photography,* Keene State College, New Hampshire
	Funny Photographs, Marcuse Pfeifer Gallery, New York

Collections:

Addison Gallery of American Art, Andover, Massachusetts; Rhode Island School of Design, Providence; Center for Creative Photography, University of Arizona, Tucson; Fotografiska Museet, Moderna Museet, Stockholm; Wäinö Aaltosen Museo, Turku, Finland.

Publications:

By MINKKINEN: Books—*Frostbite,* with an introduction by Z. Kwitney, Dobbs Ferry, New York 1978; *New American Nudes: Recent Trends and Attitudes,* editor, Dobbs Ferry, New York 1981. **Articles**—"Young Photographers in America"in *Valokuva*(Helsinki), May 1974; "One by One"in *Valokuva* (Helsinki), November 1976; "The Automobile as Viewfinder"in *Views*(Boston), Fall 1979; "Nixon at Vision" in *Views*(Boston), vol.1, no.2, 1979;"Christopher James"in *Views*(Boston), vol. 1, no.3, 1980; "The Flames of Solos"in *Views*(Boston), Spring 1980; "Merger of the Mediums" in *Views* (Boston), Summer 1980; "The Power of a Single Photograph"in *Views*(Boston), Fall 1980.

On MINKKINEN: Books—*Photography Annual* by the Time-Life editors, New York 1974; *Fantastic Photography in Europe,* exhibition catalogue, by Lorenzo Merlo, Amsterdam 1977; *Self-Portrayal,* edited by Friends of Photography, Carmel, California 1978; *Tusen och en Bild/Thousand and One Pictures,* exhibition catalogue, by Åke Sidwall, Stockholm 1978; *Fantastic Photography,* edited by Lorenzo Merlo and Claude Nori, with an introduction by Attilio Colombo, New York 1979. **Articles**—review by A.D. Coleman in the *Village Voice* (New York), July 1972; "Arno Rafael Minkkinen" in *Foto-Smal-Film* (Copenhagen), April 1974; "Arno Rafael Minkkinen" in *Mellande* (Stockholm), no. 1, 1976; "American Photography" in *Valokuva* (Helsinki), May 1976; "Arno Rafael Minkkinen" in *Popular Photography Annual,* New York 1978; "Arno Rafael Minkkinen" in *Le Nouveau Photocinema* (Paris), June 1978; "The History of the Nude" in the *Boston Phoenix,* 20 March 1979; "Arno Rafael Minkkinen" by James Burns in *Northwest Photography* (Seattle), May 1979; "Arno Rafael Minkkinen" in *Reflections* (Amsterdam), September 1979; "The Photographer as Autobiographer" by Ted Wolner in

Camera 35 (New York), October 1979; "Arno Rafael Minkkinen" by Roberta Valtorta in *Progresso Fotografico* (Milan), June 1980.

*

An artist is much easier to define than art. Paintings, poems, or photographs are works of art in their ability to affect us, strike inward resonances, and eventually remain in our memory. By this definition even a snapshot, carelessly taken yet visually enlightening, can stand on solid ground as a work of art. But is the picture-taker an artist? If he or she can work the same magic over and over again, probably so.

None of my self-portraits are multiple images. But if they appear to have that quality, that's when, to me, they're most successful.

I never see the completed image in the camera, only the background. When the fixer has cleared the negative, that's when I find out how the idea turned out. There is reality. There is imagination. Somewhere in between is my photograph.

Being alone with oneself is central to self-portraiture. There are many who cannot deal with portraits of the self because they cannot deal with being alone.

—Arno Rafael Minkkinen

* * *

For the past decade Arno Rafael Minkkinen has been making self-portraits. His imagery derives from a romantic and surreal imagination and acquires much of its vitality from the winddrenched elements of earth and water in which he the photographer and subject cavort. Born in Helsinki, Finland, holding undergraduate and graduate degrees in English and art, a former copywriter for an advertising agency, Minkkinen embues his work with a personal solitude and fascination with being. Against wide natural expanses he asserts his own form. He makes the viewer shiver with his capers in snow and northland brine.

Drawn from the imagination, contrived with the aid of a tripod, cable release, and an occasional assistant, his photographs are distinctly his own. Almost exclusively, he chooses to appear, whatever part of him, in the nude. His photographs are arresting sometimes because of their sleight-of-hand (feet briskly striding over water; his lower torso hurled like a frozen blanket into the wind) and also because they express feelings that others might leave undisclosed. Photography for Minkkinen is a frank and bracing dialogue with self.

A one-time student of Harry Callahan and Aaron Siskind, Minkkinen creates visual metaphors with his long, sinewy body. Save for a canoe or a paddle or the litter of his own just-shed clothing, he eschews props. His photographs confront the viewer straight-on. Unabashedly open and sexual, they attest to feelings of expansiveness as wide as some of the fjords and deserted lakes which serve as their backdrops. Snow, sea, tide-pools, mist, clouds, waterfall, a frothy beach, an outcropping of rock touching the sea—water in its protean forms is a nourishing element in his work.

His images embrace a spectrum of feelings. The surreal: a leg dangling unaccountably over the bow of a beached boat. The masochistic: a capped swimmer taking a high and downward stroke with a gleaming dagger. The serene and prayerful: a torso levitating before the altar of a softly-lit curtain. The comic: a canoeist surprised that her paddle has dredged up the white derriere of a man. The absurd: a foot thrusting back and out of the snow as though it were a marker for an unlikely burial. The paternal: a baby sitting upright like a ragdoll, lifting his head to a fatherly presence confirmed solely by legs crossed like tent poles and cut off at the knees. The grotesque: a shrunken man squatting on a table, a jacket touching his toes as though he were only half a body. The lyrical: two feet swinging high in a tree against a chalky sky.

Off and on during the 70s, Minkkinen has tried to make other kinds of photographs, removing himself as the subject. Now he has dedicated himself anew to self-portraiture. Both in color and black-and-white, his recent work casts himself again as subject, alone or with a member of his family. These kinds of images, he claims, may engage him for the rest of his life.

—Kelly Wise

MISRACH, Richard (Laurence).

Nationality: American. **Born:** Los Angeles, California, 11 July 1949. **Education:** University High School, Los Angeles, 1964-67; University of California, Berkeley, 1967-71, B.A. in psychology 1971 (Phi Beta Kappa). **Career:** Freelance photographer, California, since 1971. Instructor, A.S.U.C. Studio, University of California, Berkeley, 1971-77; Visiting Lecturer, University of California, Berkeley, 1982, and Santa Barbara, 1984. California Institute for the Arts, Valencia, California, 1990. **Recipient:** National Endowment for the Arts Fellowship, 1973, 1977, 1984, 1992; Western Books Award, 1975; Ferguson Grant, Friends of Photography, 1976; Guggenheim Fellowship in Photography, 1978; American Institute of Graphic Arts Award, 1981; Eureka Fellowship, Fleishaker Foundation, San Francisco, 1991; Distinguished Career in Photography Award, Los Angeles Center for Photographic Studies, 1994. **Agent:** Robert Mann Gallery, 42 East 76th Street, New York, New York 10021, U.S.A. **Address:** 1420 45th Street, Emeryville, California 94609, U.S.A.

Individual Exhibitions:

1975	*Two Views from the West: Roger Minick and Richard Misrach,* International Center of Photography, New York
1976	Madison Art Center, Wisconsin
1977	Oakland Art Museum, California
	ARCO Center for the Visual Arts, Los Angeles
1978	Silver Image Gallery, Seattle
	University of Oregon, Eugene
1979	G. Ray Hawkins Gallery, Los Angeles
	Camera Obscura Gallery, Stockholm
	Cronin Gallery, Houston
	Centre Georges Pompidou, Paris
	Grapestake Gallery, San Francisco
1980	Paul Cava Gallery, Philadelphia
	Silver Image Gallery, Seattle
	Richard Misrach and Debra Bloomfield, The Photographers' Gallery, London
	Young Hoffman Gallery, Chicago
	G. Ray Hawkins Gallery, Los Angeles
1981	*Colour Photographs,* Galerie Claude Givaudan, Geneva, Switzerland (with Jean-Claude Blanc and Jean-Marie Bustamante)
1982	Grapestake Gallery, San Francisco
1983	Los Angeles County Museum of Art
	Grapestake Gallery, San Francisco
1984	*A Decade of Photography,* Friends of Photography, Carmel, California
	Honolulu Academy of Art, Hawaii
	Blue Sky Gallery, Portland, Oregon
	Elizabeth Leach Gallery, Tucson, Arizona
	Etherton Gallery, Tucson, Arizona
1985	Houston Center of Photography, Texas
	Light Gallery, New York
	Film in the Cities, Minneapolis, Minnesota
	Fraenkel Gallery, San Francisco
	Martin Gallery, Washington, D.C.
	University of New Mexico, Albuquerque (with Mark Klett)
1986	*Richard Misrach: Desert Cantos,* Houston Center for Photography, Houston, Texas; The Watson Gallery, Houston, Texas
1987	Fraenkel Gallery, San Francisco
	Oakland Museum, Oakland, California
	Palm Springs Desert Museum, Palm Springs, California
	Philadelphia Museum of Art, Philadelphia, Pennsylvania
1988	Art Institute of Chicago
	Carpenter Center for the Visual Arts, Harvard
	Cleveland Museum of Art
	Gallery Min, Tokyo
	Jan Kesner Fine Arts, Los Angeles
	Las Palmas Museum of Art, Mallorca

	Milwaukee Art Museum
	National Gallery of Art, Wellington, New Zealand *(Desert Cantos,* travelling)
	Santa Barbara Museum of Art
	Santa Monica College, Santa Monica, California
	Seibu Department Store, Tokyo
	Sierra Nevada Museum of Art, Reno, Nevada
1989	University Art Museum, Berkeley, California
	Dominican College, San Rafael, California
	Fotomann Inc., New York
	Fraenkel Gallery, San Francisco
	Toledo Museum of Art, Toledo, Ohio
	University of New Mexico Art Museum, Albuquerque
1990	*Bravo 20: A National Park Proposal,* University of Nevada, Las Vegas, (travelling)
	Fraenkel Gallery, San Francisco
	Jan Kesner Gallery, Los Angeles
	Les Rencontres d'Arles, France
	Parco Gallery, Tokyo, (travelling)
	The Photographers' Gallery, London (travelling)
1991	*Bravo 20: A National Park Proposal,* University of Nevada, Las Vegas, (travelling)
	University of Nevada, Reno
	Friends of Photography, San Francisco
	Fotomann Inc., New York
1992	*Clouds,* Jan Kesner Gallery, Los Angeles
1993	*Clouds,* Robert Mann Gallery, New York
	Fraenkel Gallery, San Francisco

Selected Group Exhibitions:

1977	*Summer Light,* Light Gallery, New York
1978	*Mirrors and Windows: American Photography since 1960,* Museum of Modern Art, New York (toured the United States, 1978-80)
1979	*American Images: New Work by 20 Contemporary Photographers,* Corcoran Gallery, Washington, D.C. (travelled to International Center of Photography, New York; Museum of Fine Arts, Houston; Minneapolis Institute of Arts; Indianapolis Institute of Arts, 1980; and American Academy, Rome, 1981)
	Color: A Spectrum of Recent Photography, Milwaukee Art Center, Wisconsin
1980	*Recent Color Photography,* Sewall Art Gallery, Houston
	Beyond Color, San Francisco Museum of Modern Art
1981	*Photographer as Printmaker,* Ferens Art Gallery, Hull, Yorkshire (travelled to the Museum and Art Gallery, Leicester; Cooper Gallery, Barnsley; Castle Museum, Nottingham; Photographers' Gallery, London)
1982	*International Photography 1920-80,* Australian National Gallery, Canberra
1984	*Photography in California 1945-80,* San Francisco Museum of Modern Art (travelled to Akron Art Museum, Ohio; Corcoran Gallery, Washington, D.C.; Los Angeles Municipal Art Gallery; Cornell University, Ithaca, New York; High Museum of Art, Atlanta Georgia; Museum Folkwang, Essen; Centre Georges Pompidou, Paris; Museum of Photographic Arts, San Diego, California)
1985	*American Images 1945-80,* Barbican Art Gallery, London (toured Britain)
	An Eloquent Light: American Photography from 1945-1980, Barbican Art Gallery, London
	Mark Klett/Richard Misrach, University of New Mexico Art Museum, Albuquerque
	Focus, Santa Barbara, Contemporary Arts Forum, Santa Barbara
1986	*Visions of the West,* (travelling) Etherton Gallery, Tucson, Arizona
1989	Musee d'Art Moderne, (Beaubourg), Paris

Landscape as Thought, Lita Albuquerque and Richard Misrach, California State University at Fullerton
Decade by Decade, Center for Creative Photography, Tucson, Arizona
George Eastman House, Rochester, New York
Fires Sites, Columbia College
Picturing California: A Century of Photographic Genius, Oakland Museum, California
1990 Whitney Museum Annex, New York
Myth of the West, Henry Art Gallery, Washington, D.C.
1991 *Whitney Biennial,* Whitney Museum of Art, New York
1994 *Visions of America: Landscape as Metaphor in the Twentieth Century,* Denver Art Museum, Denver, Colorado (travelling)

Collections:

Museum of Modern Art, New York; Library of Congress, Washington, D.C.; Smithsonian Institution, Washington, D.C.; Kalamazoo Institute for the Arts, Michigan; Museum of Fine Arts, Houston; ARCO Center for the Visual Arts, Los Angeles; San Francisco Museum of Modern Art; Oakland Museum, California; Crocker Art Museum, Sacramento, California; Centre Georges Pompidou, Paris.

Publications:

By MISRACH: Books—*Telegraph 3 a.m.,* Berkeley, California 1974; *A Photographic Book,* San Francisco 1979; *Hawaii,* portfolio, San Francisco 1980; *Richard Misrach: Stonehenge,* portfolio, Emeryville, California 1981; *Graecism,* portfolio, Emeryville, California 1982; *Desert Cantos,* New Mexico, 1987; *Richard Misrach: 1975-1987,* Tokyo, 1988; *Bravo 20: The Bombing of the American West,* 1990; *Violent Legacies: Three Cantos,* New York, 1992. **Articles**—"The Photographer and the Drawing" in *Creative Camera* (London), August 1977; "Richard Misrach," interview, with David Fahey, in *G. Ray Hawkins Newsletter* (Los Angeles), 1979.

On MISRACH: Books—*Mirrors and Windows,* exhibition catalogue, by John Szarkowski, New York 1978; *American Images* by Renato Danese, New York 1979; *World Photography,* edited by Bryn Campbell, London 1981; *The Imaginary Photo Museum* by Helmut Gernsheim, Renate and L. Fritz Gruber and others, Cologne 1981, London 1982; *Photographer as Printmaker,* exhibition catalogue, with texts by Gerry Badger, Peter C. Bunnell and Ansel Adams, London 1981; *International Photography 1920-1980,* edited by Ian North, Canberra 1982; *Photography in California 1945-1980* by Louis Katzman, San Francisco 1984; *American images: Photography 1945-1980,* edited by Peter Turner and John Benton-Harris, London 1985; *History of Photography,* by Peter Turner, 1987; *American Dreams,* by Belinda Rathbone, Spain, 1987; *American Independents,* by Sally Eauclaire, 1987. **Articles**—"Eyes of the West" in *New West* (Los Angeles), November 1978; "Stopping the World: Photograph as Myth" by Irene Borger in *Exposure* (New York), Fall 1979; "Richard Misrach: Words and Images" by Carter Ratcliff in *Print Collector's Newsletter* (New York), January 1980; "Ruins by Night" by Natalie Canavor in *Popular Photography* (New York), May 1980; "Richard Misrach" in *Cliches* (Brussels), no. 8, 1984; "Portfolio—Richard Misrach" by Owen Edwards in *American Photographer* (New York), February 1985; *Darkroom Photography Magazine,* October, 1987; *Connoisseur Magazine,* October 1987; *Harper's Magazine,* July, 1987; *Asahicamera,* May, 1987; "Princesses Against Plutonium," *Life Magazine,* June, 1988; *Los Angeles Times Magazine,* May 22, 1988; *California Magazine,* January, 1988; *Frankfurter Allgemeine Magazin,* March 11, and September, 13 1988; *Conde Nast Traveller Magazine,* April and December 1989; *American Photographer,* April and August, 1989; *Harper's Magazine,* January, 1989; *Frankfurter Allgemeine Magazin,* July, 1989; *American Photo,* March/April and September/October 1990; *Connoisseur Magazine,* November 1990; "Bravo 20: The Park" *Outside Magazine,* October 1990; "The Tainted Desert" *Los Angeles Times Sunday Magazine,* November 4, 1990.

*   *   *

Although he began as a documentary photographer with the book *Telegraph 3 a.m.*—which records the active and unique street life of Berkeley in

the early 1970s—Richard Misrach is known more for his nighttime studies of cactus, stones, and palm trees. This work, important for its experimental and innovative qualities, established Misrach as a major photographic voice of the 70s. His publication, carrying the nontitle *(A Photographic Book),* is an attempt at a purely visual book. It contains not a single word (or number) on its pages that would compete with the visual images; the necessary information of his name, Library of Congress number, publisher, and price is carried on the book's spine. Inside are equally innovative photographs made at night in desolate reaches of the Mojave Desert, using long exposures and a strong flash to capture scenes only a camera could have recorded.

Formally and stylistically bold, these pictures of desert plants flirt with static compositions by placing the main objects in the center of a square format, and by altering the window-like look of most photographs by including the uneven, black border of the negative. Technically they show a successful experimentation with the process of split toning, giving the pictures a combination of warm reddish brown hues and cold, silvery tones; and conceptually they emphasize the act of photographing by changing the time reference within the image. Instead of capturing an instant in the night, they subtly suggest passing time by the shooting stars that appear in the night skies, and by the light of dawn that often begins to erode the darkness of the backgrounds. These photographs transform desert cactus into icons, and they convey a secular sort of mysticism which asks viewers to meditate on the object and the scene in the same way the photographer did as the exposure was being made.

The large, color photographs which followed are less about the act of photographing than about the photograph itself. Although they appear to be similar in conception and intent—straightforward pictures of foliage taken at night using strong flash—they are products of a changing consciousness in photography. These images are about turning the world into pictures. Detached from their subject matter, they examine the process of turning three-dimensional reality into two-dimensional surfaces.

Despite the differences, though, all of Misrach's later works are tied together by his desire to separate photographs from words, ideas, and religious notions. He is an explorer in the realm of the purely photographic image; he wants to strip the image bare until it stands alone, communicating its visual message without the help (or hindrance) of words.

—Ted Hedgpeth

MITCHELL, Michael.

Nationality: Canadian. **Born:** Hamilton, Ontario, 3 November 1943. **Education:** Attended Whitby District High School, Ontario, 1958-63; studied art history, and anthropology, University of Toronto, Ontario 1963-69 (Ontario Graduate Fellowship, 1967-68; University of Toronto Open Fellowship, 1968-69), B.A. 1967, M.A. 1968; anthropological research in Southern Mexico, University of North Carolina, Chapel Hill, 1968-69; photography, Ryerson Polytechnical Institute, Toronto, 1970-72, Advanced Studies Diploma 1972. **Family:** Married Annick Noelle Kassner in 1976; son: Jake. **Career:** Freelance art and magazine photographer, Toronto, since 1972. Instructor, Sheridan College, Toronto, 1974-75; Ontario College of Art, Toronto, 1980-83. Board Member, Harbourfront Art Gallery, Toronto, 1979; President, Toronto Photographers' Co-operative, 1980-81; Editorial Board Member, *Photo Communique* magazine, Toronto, 1980-81; Exhibition Committee Member, Canadian Centre of Photography, Toronto, 1981-83; Director, Fine Art Photography Publications, Toronto, 1983-84. **Recipient:** Ontario Arts Council Grant, 1972, 1982, 1983, 1984, 1985; Art Annual Award, Los Angeles, 1976; Award of Merit, Art Directors Club of Toronto, 1977; Award of Excellence (2), *STA 100 Show,* Chicago, 1978; *Communication Arts* Award of Excellence, Los Angeles, 1981; Certificate of Excellence, American Institute of Graphic Arts, New York, 1981; Award of Merit (twice), Society of Graphic Designers of Canada, Toronto, 1985. **Addresses:** (studio) 641 Queen Street East, Toronto, Ontario M4M 1G4, Canada; (home) 79 Robert Street, Toronto, Ontario M5S 2K4, Canada.

Individual Exhibitions:

1978   *Nightlife,* Art Galley of Ontario, Toronto (travelled to the
           London Regional Art Gallery, Ontario; Kitchener-Waterloo
           Art Gallery, Kitchener, Ontario; Art Gallery of Algoma,
           Sault Sainte Marie, Ontario; and Woodstock Art Gallery,
           Ontario)

1982   *Staying Home,* University of Ottawa, Ontario (travelled to
           the Harbourfront Photography Gallery, Toronto; Southern
           Alberta Art Gallery, Lethbridge; Forest City Gallery,
           London, Ontario)

1985   *Sonora,* York University, Toronto (travelled to the Art Gallery
           of Northumberland, Cobourg, Ontario)
           Nicaragua: After the Triumph, Harbour-front Community
           Gallery, Toronto (travelled to Edmonton Art Gallery,
           Alberta; Vancouver Art Gallery, British Columbia; Nickel
           Arts Museum, Calgary, Alberta; University of Sherbrooke,
           Quebec)
           Structured Paradise, Banff Centre, Alberta (with Douglas
           Curran)

Selected Group Exhibitions:

1973   *Selected Young Artists of Ontario,* Sir Sanford Fleming
           College, Peterborough, Ontario

1975   *Zoosight,* Art Gallery of Ontario, Toronto (toured Canada)
           Exposure, Art Gallery of Ontario, Toronto (toured Canada)

1976   *Focal Point,* Art Gallery of Ontario, Toronto

1978   *Imagées Colorées,* Optica Gallery, Montreal, Quebec
           Tusen och En Bild, Moderna Museet, Stockholm

1980   *Toronto,* Optica Gallery, Montreal, Quebec

1981   *Photojournalism,* National Film Board of Canada Gallery,
           Ottawa

1983   *Production/Reproduction,* A Space Gallery, Toronto

1984   *Contemporary Canadian Photography,* National Gallery of
           Canada, Ottawa (toured Canada)

Collections:

Art Gallery of Ontario, Toronto; Canadian Museum of Contemporary Photography, Ottawa; Whyte Foundation, Banff, Alberta; Moderna Museet, Stockholm.

Publications:

By MITCHELL: Books—*Fighting Back,* portfolio of 20 photos, with text by Graham Fraser, Toronto 1972; *Nightlife,* with an introduction by Allan Porter, Toronto 1978; *Monsters of the Gilded Age: The Photography of Charles Eisenmann,* Toronto 1979; *Singing Songs to the Spirit: The Culture History of the Inuit,* Ottawa 1980. **Articles**—"Legacy" in *Weekend Magazine* (Toronto), November 1977; "At the Grindstone: The Photography of Charles Eisenmann" in *Photo Communique* (Toronto), March 1980; "Round and Round the Telephone Pole: The Photography of Robert Frank" in *Parachute: Art Contemporain* (Montreal), Summer 1980; "The Latinos" in *Today Magazine* (Toronto), October 1980; "The Magic Box" in *Photo Communique* (Toronto), Spring 1981; "Staying Home" in *Photo Communique* (Toronto), Fall 1983; "In the New World: John Gutmann and American Photography" in *John Gutmann,* exhibition catalogue, Toronto 1985.

On MITCHELL: Books—*Exposure,* exhibition catalogue, by Glenda Milrod and others, Toronto 1975; *Tusen och En Bild,* exhibition catalogue, by Ake Sidwall, Sune Jonsson and Ulf Hard af Segerstad, Stockholm 1978; *Contemporary Canadian Photography* by Martha Langford, Edmonton, Alberta 1984; *American Photography One,* annual, New York and London 1985. **Articles**—"Michael Mitchell" by Allan Porter in *Camera* (Lucerne), January 1978; "Nightlife" by Thomas Tritscher in *Artmagazine* (Toronto), March 1978; "Sequencing in Nightlife" by David Harris in *Artists Review* (Toronto), March 1978; "Notebook" by Robert Fulford in *Saturday Night* (Toronto), April 1980; "Production/Reproduction" by Phillip Monk in *Vanguard*

(Vancouver), February 1984; "Nicaragua: After the Triumph" by Geoff Miles in *Vanguard* (Vancouver), May 1985.

*

I came to photography late. When I picked up a camera to learn photography, I thought I had found a congenial if somewhat facile medium. However, I soon discovered that the process of arranging a few tones on a small piece of paper so as to make that paper talk was an extremely difficult undertaking. In a few years I was to compound those difficulties by switching to colour. I now worked in a medium that seemed to have no tradition and no satisfactory models. While my photography has continued to address those things that have always concerned photographers—the extraordinary fact of our presence on this planet and what we do to each other while we are here—it has also been very much a visual enquiry into the making of colour photographs. During the seven years that I have been working exclusively in colour, I have attempted to define colour photography by first making visual jokes in colour, and then through several years of making night photographs by flash that pulled colour out of a black limbo. More recently, I have reversed this strategy by making large format colour photographs of landscapes into which I physically insert a large black cube that is both a man-derived presence in landscape as well as an absence of colour and an absence of the very stuff of photography—light.

Before I turned to photography, I spent a number of years vacillating between working in anthropology and doing painting, sculpture and writing. I was torn between two conflicting directions, the attempt to reach some sort of understanding through the analysis of objective record and the desire to comprehend things by exploring the subjective and the expressionistic. Neither path was completely true nor exclusive of the other, and it seems to me now that photography is the perfect embodiment of this tension. While the individual photograph can be viewed simply as an exquisite two-dimensional record of fact—say appearance of a landscape—it can at the same time resonate with deep associative meanings and provoke new experience. I can't think of a more intractable medium to work in nor one that could be so rich.

—Michael Mitchell

*   *   *

As the preceding biographical information indicates, Michael Mitchell's contribution to Canadian photography includes writing, curating, and teaching as well as his own photography. His photographic work is quite varied and reflects an anthropological perspective and a wide interest in the history and meaning of photography. While this commentary will deal with only four bodies of work from a much larger output, each one has been chosen to reveal an aspect of his overall concerns.

Nightlife (1947-77) consists of twenty-four large (48 x 48 inch) colour portraits and arranged tableaux all taken at night. The images explore the related themes of human isolation and companionship. The working process—working at night, in colour, and with long exposures—necessitated complete control over the situation and the resulting photographs read as poetic, autobiographical constructions. 'Night' becomes a metaphor for the human condition; working at night, a means of isolating figures psychologically and of externalizing memories; and the activity of making portraits, a way of symbolizing the often frail nature of human relationships.

Staying Home (1981-83) is a series of photographs that documents the residue left at the end of the day by Mitchell's two small children. The arrangements of scattered clothing and toys seem chaotic but suggest the kind of order that children create around them: some of the past activities and games can be reconstructed partially while other gatherings remain obscure. In contrast to *Nightlife,* which constructed an order out of the world, *Staying Home* accepts disorder. The photographs are both a poetic evocation of the world of children and (on a more theoretical level) a recognition of the limitations of ever fully recovering knowledge through photography.

In 1984, Mitchell contributed three "Picture Stories" to two circulating exhibitions, *Reading Pictures* and *Production/Reproduction.* Each "story" consisted of a sequence of details lifted from an anonymous early twentieth-century commercial photograph. The details were enlarged and arranged into a linear sequence (accompanied in one case with a text) with the entire photograph reproduced as the final image. Such a process indicates not only the wealth of information normally contained within photographs, but the procedure by which we, as readers, create meaning out of photographs. For example, in *Making Movies,* the details (showing both the scene being filmed and the backstage manipulations) reveal how a movie melodrama is an entirely constructed illusion. Meaning in a film and, by implication in a photograph, lies both within the photograph's frame and in the surrounding cultural context.

Nicaragua: After the Triumph (1984) is a series of forty-eight photographs all made during a one month visit to Nicaragua in February 1984. The photographs survey the country four years after its revolution and show it in the midst of a protracted war along its borders and grappling with such massive problems as literacy, health care, industrialization, and cultural identity. An extensive text accompanies each photograph which situates the subject within the broader social and political forces. In this way, the photographic "moment" is made representative and it partakes of a large history and culture.

While each of these bodies of work arose from a specific occasion, all deal at some level with three larger issues. The first is documentary photography and each body represents a different approach to how photographs (often in conjunction with texts) function in this capacity. The second explores colour as a device for ordering both a photograph and one's experience. The third, which incorporates both of the preceding two issues, concerns the photographers' relationship with his subject matter. While photography deals with our visual and emotional experience of the world on an immediate and often raw level, the photographic apparatus and the entire process successively distances us from that original experience. All of Mitchell's work reveals a strongly analytical ordering of his initial emotional response to his subjects. Such a response is shown in different forms; in his approach to making photographs (as is evident in the opposing approaches found in *Nightlife* and *Staying Home*), in the presentation of photographs (as is seen in the sympathetic text/ image relation of *Nicaragua: After the Triumph*), or in the cultural reading of photographs (as is evident in the constructed "picture stories"). In each of these ways, his work actively deals with the complex processes of making, reading, and understanding photographs.

—David Harris

MIYOSHI, Kozo.

Nationality: Japanese. **Born:** Chiba Prefecture, 1947. **Education:** College of Art, Nihon University, B.F.A. (photography), 1971. **Career:** One year internship at the Center for Creative Photography, University of Arizona; lectured at Seika University of Arts, Kyoto, Japan; California College of Arts and Crafts, Oakland, USA; Society for Photographic Education, National Conference, CA, USA. **Recipient:** New Face 1982, Fine Art Division, *American Photographer,* 1982; Most Promising Photographer Award, The Photographic Society of Japan, 1986; Konica Prize for Photography, Tokyo 1993. **Agent:** Photo Gallery International, 2-5-18 Toranomon, Minato-ku, Tokyo 105, Japan.

Individual Exhibitions:

1979	*Exposure,* Photo Gallery International, Tokyo
1980	*Exposure,* University of California Extention Center, San Francisco
1983	*See Saw,* Photo Gallery International, Tokyo
1985	*Innocents,* Photo Gallery International, Tokyo
1987	*Picture Show,* Photo Gallery International, Tokyo
1989	*Conservatory,* Photo Gallery International, Tokyo
1990	*Roots NE,* Heineken Village Gallery Tokyo
	Roots NE & Conservatory, Bemis Foundation Gallery, Omaha, Nebraska
1991	*Roots NE & Conservatory,* Ffotogallery, Cardiff, Wales
1992	*Kozo Miyoshi: Photographs,* Mark Masuoka Gallery, Las Vegas
	Thailand, Photo Gallery International, Tokyo
1993	*Chapel,* Photo Gallery International, Tokyo

1994	*Far East and Southwest: The Photography of Kozo Miyoshi,* Center for Creative Photography, The University of Arizona, Tucson
	Roots and Cacti, Center for Creative Photography, The University of Arizona, Tucson
	Southwest, Photo Gallery International, Tokyo
	Glass House: Conservatory, Konika Photo Plaza, Tokyo

Selected Group Exhibitions:

1979	*Grain,* Riverside Studios, London & Olympus Gallery, Tokyo
1981	Crown Zellerbach Gallery, San Francisco
1982	*Three Japanese Visions,* Focus Gallery, San Francisco
1984	Light Work, Syracuse, New York
	CEPA, Buffalo, New York
1985	*Paris, New York, Tokyo,* Tsukuba Museum of Photography, Ibaraki, Japan
	Contemporary Photography of Japan, Madrid, Valencia and Barcelona, Spain
1987	*Empathy,* Visual Studies Work Shop, Rochester, New York
	The Federation of Asian Photographic Art: Tokyo Convention, Shadai Gallery, Tokyo
1988	*The Federation of Asian Photographic Art: Invitational Exhibition,* Seoul, Korea
1989	*Night Light: A Survey of Twentieth Century Night Photography,* Nelson Atkins Museum of Art, Kansas City
1990	*Japanese Contemporary Photography,* Pavillon des Arts, Paris
	Japanese Contemporary Photography, Tokyo Metropolitan Museum of Photography, Tokyo
1993	*Contemporary Japanese Photography: In die Felsen bonhren sich Zikadenstimmen,* Kunsthaus, Zurich, Switzerland

Collections:

The National Museum of Modern Art, Tokyo; Tokyo Metropolitan Museum of Photography; Nihon University, Tokyo; International Museum of Photography at George Eastman House, Rochester, New York; Center for Creative Photography, University of Arizona; Hallmark Collection, Kansas City, Missouri: The Museum of Fine Arts, Houston, Texas.

Publications:

By MIYOSHI: Books—*Grain* (editor in Chief), 1977-80; *Far East and Southwest,* exhibition catalogue, Tucson, 1994.

On MIYOSHI: Books—*Japanese Contemporary Photography,* exhibition catalogue, Tokyo, 1990; *Night Light: A Survey of Twentieth Century Night Photography,* exhibition catalogue, Kansas City, 1989; *Contemporary Japanese Photography: In die Felsenbonhren sich Zikadenstimmen,* exhibition catalogue, Zurich, 1993.

*

Picture Show

One morning when the sun is high in the sky, I make a long detour around the town and crossing a ridge which does not look too steep, reach an embankment where one can take in the town in a single view as it lies along the highway linking it to the next town. Here I quench the heat of my body and mind from the solitary games I was enjoying but a moment ago.

I encountered those giant paper lanterns like planets at dusk, when the heat of the day had slightly softened. They emitted a deep and dull light; the array was more than enough to spur on the people of the neighbourhood and local villages. I too pictured myself disappearing into the middle of that ring of light, following the order of my destiny, and sensed an inexpressible tranquillity and terror. Time passed, and the party with it. All that was left was the giant lanterns, a time such that when the sun rose it would be morning and myself already only half alive. A wind bearing the scent of the lanterns and the morning dew was peeping through these harmonious signs at the night dimension of play. It was just as though a stationary universe had suddenly

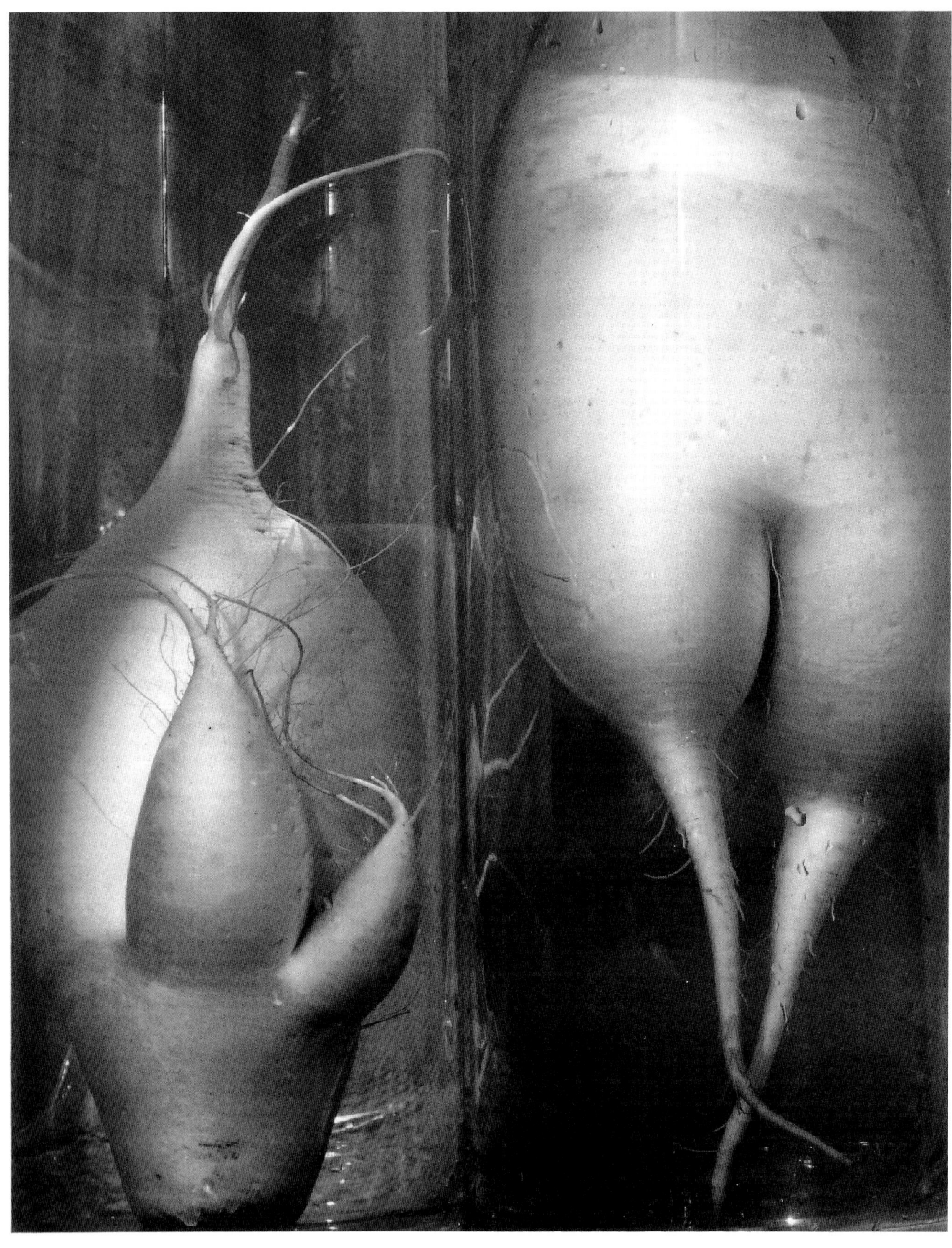

Roots, **1990.** Photograph ©Kozo Miyoshi.

come into action and called up the natural circle of life and rebirth. The things around me were in fear of the rising sun; another nature was breathing. Without doubt it was because my emotions towards them, whether lasting or fleeting, were to be extinguished.

In this season some unusual clouds hang in the sky and envelop the whole town in shade. The borderline between light and shade lies around this embankment. As they watch this town I am looking down on, my pupils are mystified . . . it is impossible to tell whether I am in the midst of light or shade. Yet it seems that some function of the body is already beginning to quest for the town on the other side of the ridge.

Southwest

Two points. On the left, the rocky summit of a mountain, far off and desolate. In the clear blue sky above, devoid of all clouds, a pair of hawks—sometimes visible, sometimes hidden against the light—trace a wide, leisurely path from the middle of the mountain through one part of the afternoon sky.

Pushing through into the semi-desert over two hills, I cower at the source of the vast landscape which spreads out before my feet as though on the threshold of a miniature garden. One step ahead lies a precipice, beyond which the desert stretches out like an expanse of ocean until the distant horizon. What is this sense of distance? It cannot be measured with any ruler based on experience. It is just like bringing a magnet close to a compass, a sense of unease like dizziness or floating. In this world only the twin points formed by the hawks are moving. A primal landscape where nothing stirs, neither in the past nor in the future. Surrounded by this almost perfect creation, what more could one ask for? What can one do with such balanced confrontation? Like those two hawks, beating their wings minutely, I ask for just one instant—to take a photograph.

Chapel

The road just runs on, on across the desert, heading for the village at the foot of the mountains which lie across its path. In this vast terrain, ten miles, twenty miles fall within my field of sight. Yes when I chew over the saying "country roads are near and so far," I can confirm how small my own existence is.

I become embarrassed at this other self, who has already begun to forget the reason for driving and wipe the sweat from my brow. At some point the village comes into view, about 5 miles in front. I prepare myself internally and await the conventional ceremony. In the village I am entering today there are around ten houses. I stop the car in the square. The door of the house furthest away has opened.

"Indian Reservation." I sense expectations and uneasiness lurking within these words along with something which should not be touched upon. These "Native Americans" know natural fears and favours, cultivate great wisdom and continue to exhibit clearly and with pride the co-existence of man and nature. Already many months have passed since I started visiting the villages, dotted around a reservation the size of Japan's Shikoku Island. What is this excitement I feel?

The door was opened by an old man who comes out. Deep wrinkles are chiselled into his forehead. He is probably one of the elders. The old man walks towards me. He is around 300 feet away. I begin to walk too. As always happens 5 or 6 dogs have started to swarm around me. They are in a position such that if I made an even slightly unnatural movement they would attack at once. The distance between the old man and me is down to around 20 feet. He has a slight stoop. His gaze goes through me, full of a self confidence which comes from surviving in the midst of nature's creation. I visit the various villages with the intention of taking photographs, yet I have no licence. I have never yet gone through any paperwork before taking photographs: I have no interest in photographs where one obtains permission first. Encountering something I would like to photograph is a moment which halts time. If it proves impossible, one can give the time back to the flow. In another two or three steps we will be within hand-shaking distance. Now the time has come for me, an Oriental with the same black hair as him, to beg the old man in front of me for such permission to stop the flow of time for 30 minutes, here in this village in the centre of a wilderness. The time to question its importance and its lack of meaning.

—Kozo Miyoshi

*   *   *

One tomato plant at the most bears approximately fifty tomatoes. However, it is cultivated in a zero-gravity space, free from gravitational pull, and given special fertilizers, a tomato plant could bear twenty thousand tomatoes. When I heard this story, I pictured an image of a tomato plant, stretching its stems in all directions, like the legs of an octopus, on which twenty thousand tomatoes grew. It sent a chill down my spine. Life force, hidden in a plant, is hideously excessive. A plant, slowly growing its stems and roots without being noticed, until it covers up the whole space—such a notion tears up our senses with an unexpectedly cruel force.

Kozo Miyoshi's radishes are not like the ones we see at the greengrocers or a supermarket, which are controlled to be of certain shape and size. Seeds, sown in nearby ground, freely spread their roots and when they meet an obstacle like gravel, they change direction, branch out into two or three, and still keep growing. Would you consider that a deformity? No. Clone-like white radishes in plastic bags from supermarkets, should be called a deformity. If there were no dirt or gravel, a radish would grow infinitely in size, with its roots becoming entangled until finally it turns into some monster-like organism beyond the bounds of the aesthetics or morals that we have been building with so much effort. Rather, that is the true and natural state of a plant. When we encounter something incomprehensible, unable to stand its hideousness, what we had been doing was to separate it from its natural environment, cover it up to make it unseen, and put it in a dark place. Therefore, Miyoshi's *Roots NE* is an attempt to put a spotlight on a vital body that had long been emitting a nasty smell, losing its shape and waiting for its death in silence. It is a cruel act. However, this cruelty is far more honest and healthy, compared to the act of leaving the incomprehensible in the dark to "put a lid on the stink." We confront an excess of life in a form we have never seen before. The form is frightening, grotesque and evil looking, but at the same time, is strangely erotic and humorous. Our senses are toned up—like the radishes, photographed by Kozo Miyoshi.

—Kohtaro Iizawa

MODEL, Lisette.

Nationality: American. **Born:** Elise Felic Amelie Seybert in Vienna, Austria, 10 November 1906; emigrated to the United States, 1937, and subsequently naturalized. **Education:** Educated privately in Vienna; studied music with Arnold Schoenberg, Vienna, and for many years associated with his circle, then studied music in Paris; self-taught in photography, from 1937. **Family:** Married the painter Evsa Model in 1936 (died, 1976). **Career:** Photo-laboratory technician, then photographer, under Ralph Steiner, *PM* newspaper, Long Island, New York, 1940-41; freelance photographer, New York, working for *Harper's Bazaar, Look, Ladies Home Journal,* etc., 1941-53; independent photographer, New York, 1953 until her death in 1983. Instructor in Photography, San Francisco Institute of Fine Arts, 1947. Instructor in Photography, New School for Social Research, New York, 1950-82. **Recipient:** Guggenheim Fellowship, 1965. Honorary Member, American Society of Magazine Photographers, 1968; Honored Photographer, *Rencontres Internationales de la Photographie,* Arles, France, 1978. D.F.A.: New School for Social Research, New York, 1981. **Died:** (in New York City) 30 March 1983.

Individual Exhibitions:

1941	Photo League, New York
1943	Art Institute of Chicago
1946	California Palace of the Legion of Honor, San Francisco
1949	Museum of Modern Art, New York (toured the United States)
1975	Focus Gallery, San Francisco
1976	Sander Gallery, Washington, D.C.
1977	Bucks County Community College, Newtown, Pennsylvania
	Galerie Zabriskie, Paris (with Diane Arbus and Rosalind Solomon)
1979	Vision Gallery, Boston
	Port Washington Public Library, New York (with August Sander)

Promenade des Anglais, **1937.** Photograph ©Lisette Model. Courtesy Sander Gallery, Inc.

1980   Galerie Fiolet, Amsterdam
1981   Galerie Viviane Esders, Paris
1984   *Hommage à Lisette Model 1906-83,* Galerie Viviane
        Esders, Paris

Selected Group Exhibitions:

1940   *60 Photographers: A Survey of Camera Aesthetics,* Museum of
        Modern Art, New York
1943   *Action Photography,* Museum of Modern Art, New York
1949   *4 Photographers: Model/Croner/Callahan/Brandt,* Museum
        of Modern Art, New York
1954   *Great Photographs,* Limelight Gallery, New York
1955   *The Family of Man,* Museum of Modern Art, New York (and
        world tour)
1967   *Photography in the 20th Century,* National Gallery of Canada,
        Ottawa (toured Canada and the United States, 1967-73)
1975   *Women of Photography,* San Francisco Museum of Art (toured
        the United States, 1975-77)
1979   *Photographie als Kunst 1879-1979,* Tiroler Landesmuseum
        Ferdinandeum, Innsbruck, Austria (travelled to the Neue
        Galerie am Wolfgang Gurlitt Museum, Linz, Austria; Neue
        Galerie am Landes-museum Joanneum, Graz, Austria; and
        the Museum des 20. Jahrhunderts, Vienna)
1980   *Photography of the 50s,* International Center of Photography,
        New York (travelled to the Center for Contemporary
        Photography, University of Arizona, Tucson; Minneapolis
        Institute of Arts; California State University at Long Beach;
        and the Delaware Art Museum, Wilmington)
1985   *American Images 1945-80,* Barbican Art Gallery, London
        (toured Britain)

Collections:

Museum of Modern Art, New York; International Museum of Photography,
George Eastman House, Rochester, New York; Smithsonian Institution,
Washington, D.C.; New Orleans Museum of Art; Museum Folkwang, Essen,
Germany.

Publications:

By MODEL: Books—*Lisette Model: Portfolio,* 75 photographs, edited by
Lunn Gallery, Washington, D.C. 1976; *12 Photographs,* portfolio, with an
introduction by Berenice Abbott, Washington, D.C. 1977; *Lisette Model: An
Aperture Monograph,* with a preface by Berenice Abbott, designed by Marvin
Israel, New York 1979. **Article**—"Letter to the Editor" in *U.S. Camera*
(New York), October 1944.

On MODEL: Books—*The Family of Man,* edited by Edward Steichen, New
York 1955; *Photography in the 20th Century* by Nathan Lyons, New York
1967; *The Snapshot* by Jonathan Green, New York 1974; *Helen Gee and the
Limelight: A Pioneering Photography Gallery of the 50s,* exhibition catalogue, edited by Jonathan Bayer and others, London 1977; *Tusen och En Bild,*
exhibition catalogue, by Ake Sidwall, Sune Jonsson and Ulf Hard af Segerstad,
Stockholm 1978; *A Book of Photographs from the Collection of Sam Wagstaff,*
designed by Arne Lewis, New York 1978; *Darkroom 2,* edited by Jain Kelly,
New York 1978; *Photographie als Kunst 1879-1979/Kunst als Photographie
1949-1979,* exhibition catalogue, 2 vols., by Peter Weiermair, Innsbruck,
Austria 1979; *Instantanés,* exhibition catalogue, by Michel Nuridsany, Paris
1980; *Photography of the 50s: An American Perspective* by Helen Gee,
Tucson, Arizona 1980; *Lichtbildnisse: Das Porträt in der Fotografie,* edited
by Klaus Honnef, Cologne 1982; *American images: Photography 1945-1980,*
edited by Peter Turner and John Benton-Harris, London 1985. **Articles**—
"Lisette Model, Exploratory Camera: A Rationale for the Miniature Camera"
by Minor White in *Aperture* (Rochester, New York), vol. 1, no. 1, 1952;
"Lisette Model" by Mary Alice McAlpin in *Popular Photography* (New
York), November 1961; "Talking about Lisette" by David Vestal in *Infinity*
(New York), March 1964; "Photographs by Lisette Model" in *Creative
Camera* (London), November 1969; "Lisette Model: Keeping the Legend

Intact" in *Infinity* (New York), January 1973; "Lisette Model" in *Creative
Camera Yearbook,* London 1975; "Lisette with Love" by Louis Stettner in
Camera 35 (New York), June 1975; "The Comparative Art of Lisette Model
and Barbara Morgan" by Benjamin Forgey in the *Washington Star,* 3 October
1976; "Lisette Model: Re-emergence from the Legend" in *Aperture* (Millerton,
New York), September/October 1977; "Lisette Model" by Allan Porter, in
special issue of *Camera* (Lucerne), no. 12, 1977; "Lisette Model, Photographer" (obituary) by Walter H. Waggoner in the *New York Times,* 31 March
1983; "Lisette Model" in *The Annual Obituary 1983,* edited by Elizabeth
Devine, London and Chicago 1984.

*   *   *

Lisette Model made a lasting contribution not only as a photographer, but
also as one of the medium's finest teachers. "It is not important whether one
likes or dislikes a photograph; the important thing is to find out what it's all
about," she said, and the notion underlies a vital aspect of her talent as a
teacher.

She did not talk much about her ways of teaching; she felt about this
subject as she did about interviews: she was willing to tell you everything and
answer all questions, but in the translation from spoken to written word
something is lost—and maybe one should not explain at all.

Diane Arbus was a very close friend and diligent student who started in the
mid-1950s attending classes and then had a steady stream of feedback from
Lisette, constant contact and discussions, understanding and support that
ended only when Arbus died. But Arbus was not at all the only important
student to emerge. Others like Charles Pratt, Larry Fink and Rosalind Solomon
are taking their places in American photography.

—Allan Porter

MOLDER, Jorge.

Nationality: Portuguese. **Born:** Lisbon on 30 October 1947. **Education:**
Graduated with a B.A. in philosophy from University of Lisbon in 1972.
Agent: Galeria Luis Serpa, R. Tenente Raul Cascais, 1B, 1200 Lisbon.
Address: R. Desiderio Beça, 3.1o Dto, 1000 Lisbon.

Individual Exhibitions:

1990   Contretype, Brussels
        Artothèque de Grenoble, Grenoble, France
        The Portuguese Dutchman, Imagolucis, Porto, Portugal
1991   *Trabalhos Anteriores,* Convento de Sao Francisco, Beja,
        Portugal
        The Secret Agent, Galeria Cómicos, Lisbon
1993   *História Trágico-Marítima,* George Pompidou Centre, Paris
        Zerlina, Uma Narrativa, Paço Imperial, Rio de Janeiro
        (travelled to Museu de Arte Moderna de São Pãulo)
1994   *The Sense of Sleight-of-Hand Man,* Jayne H. Baum Gallery,
        New York

Selected Group Exhibitions:

1990   *Ultima Frontera—7 Artistescles Portuguesos,* Centro d'Art
        Santa Mónica, Barcelona, Spain
1991   *Arco,* Galeria Cómicos, Madrid
        The Heart of Science, Centro de Estudos Fotograficos,
        Coimbra, Portugal (travelled to Contretype, Brussels)
        Photography Today, Moderna Galerija, Ljubljana, Slovenia
1992   *Voyeurism,* Jayne H. Baum Gallery, New York
        Arco, Galeria Cómicos, Madrid
        Primavera Fotográfica, Barcelona, Spain
        2.Internationale Foto-Triennale, Esslingen, Germany
        La Première Photo, Galerie du Jour, Paris
        L'échapée Europeene, Pavillon des Arts, Paris

The Hands of Orlac II, **1992.** Photograph by Jorge Molder. Courtesy
Jayne H. Baum Gallery, New York.

	Minimal Relics, University of Amsterdam, Amsterdam
1993	*História Trágico-Marítima,* Galeria Valentim de Carvalho, Lisbon
	Arco, Galeria Cómicos, Madrid
	Minimal Relics, Natural History Museum, Rotterdam, Netherlands
	Image First: Eight Photographers for the '90s, Laura Carpenter Fine Art, Sante Fe, New Mexico
	Gitanes, Arles, France

Collections:

Ajuntamento de Vigo, Spain; Art Institute of Chicago, IL; Artothèque de
Grenoble, France; Bibliotheque Nationale, Paris; Centre of Modern Art—
Calouste Gulbenkian Foundation, Lisbon; Centro Cultural de S. Joao Da
Madeira, Portugal; Everson Museum of Art, Syracuse, New York; Fonds de
l'Etat Belge, Belgium; Fonds National d'Art Contemporain, France; Fundaçao
Luso-Americana para o Desenvolvimento, Lisbon; Musee de l'Elysèe,
Lausanne, Switzerland; Museum of Modern Art, Rio de Janeiro, Brazil;
National Contemporary Art Trust, Paris; Paris Audiovisuel, France.

Publications:

By MOLDER: Books—*Uma Exposiçao* (with Joao Miguel Fernandes Jorge
and Joaquim Manuel Magalhaes), Lisbon 1980; *Seguia o Clamor da Razao
sob as Arvores do Parque* (with Joao Miguel Fernandes Jorge), Lisbon 1982;
six photos for *A Mae de um Rio* by Agustina Bessa Luis, Lisbon, 1982; *Um Dia
Cinzento,* Lisbon 1983; *O Fazer Suave de Preto e Branco* (with Jorge
Martins), Lisbon 1985; *The Secret Agent,* Lisbon 1991; *Joseph Conrad,* Paris
1991; *Zerlina,* Lisbon 1993.

On MOLDER: Book—*Fotografias de Jorge Molder* by Joao Miguel
Fernandes Jorge, Lisbon 1988. **Articles**—"A Ronda da Noite" by António
Pedro Vasconcelos in *Expresso,* November 1980;"Jorge Molder" by Jose
Sousa Machado in *Artforum,* December 1982; "Um Dia Cinzento" by Joao
Miguel Fernandes Jorge in *A Capital,* July 1983; "Um Dia Cinzento" by
Alexandre Pomar in *Diário de Naticias,* June 1983; "Perse: Uma consteleçao
Atlantica" by Jose Sousa Machado in *Jornal de Letras,* May 1984; "Reduzir a

presença à intençao" by Jose Sousa Machado in *O Semanário,* April
1984;"Ethos" by Joao Miguel Fernandes Jorge in *A Capital,* April 1985; "A
Saida do Túnel Expressionista" by António Cerveira Pinto in *Didrio de
Noticias,* February 1985; "Fazer-des/fazer" by Jose Luis Porfirio in
Expresso, November 1985; "O Guerreiro Cinzento" by António Rodrigues in
Jornal de Letras, April 1985; "Contraprovas" by Pedro Miguel Frade in
Expresso, February 1987; "Attente Moderne" by Bernard Genton in *Digraphe,*
No. 43, 1987; "Fotógrafo de Excepçao" by Emídio Rosa de Oliveira,
February 1987; "Le Crépuscule Révélateus" by Charles-Henri Favrod in *Le
Matin,* 1988; "Imagens para uma narrativa" by Pedro Miguel Frade in
Expresso, October 1988; "O texto de Broch Fotografado por Jorge Molder"
by Jose Sousa Machado in *Diário Popular,* October 1988; "Molder e Gaëtan
Expostos e Conjunto" by Emídio Rosa de Oliveira in *O Semanario,* April
1988; "Quelques Morceaux Choisis" by Brigitte Ollier in *Libération,* April
1989; "Les Lumières de la Ville Blanche" by Gabriel Bauret in *Photographics
Magazine,* Paris, 1989; "Um Iogo Suspenso" by Eduardo Paz Barroso in
Jornal de Noticias, Porto, November 1990; "Secretas Ficçoes" by Isabel
Carlos, November 1990; "Oiseaux" by Regis Durand in *Art Press,* 1990;
"Um olhar sobre o olhar" by Jose F. Guimaraes in *O Janeiro,* October 1990;
"The Portugese Dutchman" by Joao Miguel Fernandes Jorge in *O Independente,*
November 1990; "The Portuguese Dutchman" by Teresa Siza in *O Público,*
October 1990; "Olhares Duplos: Molder e Marcas" by Carlos França in *O
Semanario,* November 1991; "Em Beja com Sao Joao Baptista e Jorge
Molder" by Joao Miguel Fernandes Jorge in *O Independente,* May 1991;
"The Secret Agent" by Joao Miguel Fernandes Jorge in *O Independente,*
November 1991; "Relaçoes com o Espaço" by Leonor Nazaré in *Expresso,*
May 1991; "A Deferença de Luz" by Joao Pinharanda in *O Público,* April
1991; "Fragmentos de um Diário" by Joao Pinharanda in *Público,* November
1991; "O Nivel do Acido" by António Cerveira Pinto in *O Independente,*
November 1991; "The Secret Agent" by Teresa Siza in *O Público,* November
1991; "A Marca Molder" by Jose Vegar in *Sábado,* October 1991; "Outras
Ruinas" by Carlos Vidal in *O Independente,* April 1991; "Le Printemps de la
Photographie à Cahors" by Regis Durand in *Art Press,* June 1992; "Jorge
Molder, o Mensageiro" by Regis Durand in *Artes & Leiloes,* No. 15, June
1992; "Jorge Molder" by Regis Durand in *Camera International,* November
1992;"A inocência do detective" by Alexandre Melo in *Artes & Leiloes,* June
1992; "Histoire Photographique de la Photographie" by Henri Van Lier in
Les Cahiers de la Photographie, 1992.

*

My work is concerned with how light is involved in the shaping and
patterns of the world; the impossibility or uselessness of building narratives
through images and, at the same time, the inevitability of trying; and how
photographs are specially suitable to live in a borderline between drama and
irony.

—Jorge Molder

*   *   *

Why pay attention? Why, in particular, pay attention to Jorge Molder's
book of 1991, *The Secret Agent?* Because it promises an interpretation. If
you're astute enough you might read its 46 pictures through to a conclusion.
On the other hand you might fail, because *The Secret Agent* is a complicated
assemblage in four movements involving a variousٍly filled box and a glass
battery or acid bath. The book (published by Difusão Cultural in Lisbon), is
dedicated to—among others—Joseph Conrad, Joseph Cornell and Marcel
Broodthaers. On the dust wrapper it is admitted that Jorge Molder studied
philosophy. In regarding most photography it is possible to understand the
artist's intentions, but here such an understanding is promised and then
disquietingly complicated.

The Secret Agent reveals that you are incapable of a definitive reading, that
you are caught, for example, entertaining the idea that the representation of the
empty box in front of you was the closed box of some moments ago or the half-
filled box overleaf. What exactly is it that you are attending to? Well, if you
were able to put the book aside and think back it might seem that the series has
to do with the insides of containers. However in the act of looking, there is a
constant invitation to look back for verification that the item isolated in the
picture is the self-same item of six frames and twenty seconds ago.

Why should a series of pictures of open and closed boxes, test tubes, coins and a toy labyrinth, all pictured against black backgrounds, be taken as art? Because of its disinterestedness. Photography habitually delivers actionable information and a portable phrase, but in this case there is no conclusion—and in the final frame the evidence is simply pocketed and the show adjourned.

Disinterestedness by itself, though, is not enough. It was certainly less than enough for Cornell and Broodthaers, under whose sign Molder has placed *The Secret Agent*. Broodthaers, via his collections of breakfast eggshells and mussels, negotiated large presentiments touching on life and death. Molder's great idea, by contrast, is The Quest—for clarity and a resolution. At one stage in the proceedings a hand spins a coin, and another is marked by a torn photograph of the dreamer. The Quest is interrupted not only by chance but by an insistent presence in things. Molder's exhibits are centred, dramatically lit and fetishised—evidence got out of hand, become obsessive in a dream or nightmare of epistemology.

The fragments of modernism, narrated by Ezra Pound, James Joyce, Eugène Atget and Robert Frank, for example, related to civilizations in process or never quite forgotten. Molder's fragments, including a white mouse, wrapped sweets, a closed book and a spun coin touch on nothing so magnificent and mainly on a private story which can hardly be surmised. It is a dark series too, and melancholic; but the melencholia stems less from the darkness than from the silence with which everything is imbued. Photography commonly invokes speech, for it represents happenings which can be told, but in *The Secret Agent,* Molder has made a serious effort to bypass speech. When "the detective" appears he muses in isolation on the evidence. What action there is takes place stealthily; flames shimmer in the box and the battery's acid promises to dissolve the artist's few materials. The array of evidence asks for concentration, and concentration precedes speech.

The social, that is to say, is no longer enough. Molder's exhibits belong less perhaps with Cornell and Broodthaers, who enjoyed the social cosmos already articulated, than with Christian Boltanski's stilled relics, where naming is both invited and discoured. Naming, for these later artists, is questionable and even more than enough, for it induces fixity with all its dangers. Molder has monumentalised the moment of concentration, the moment before the descent into words, into the fatal social domain.

Molder's work is both the book with its series, and the individual print in which the all important gravitas of the moment of concentration is emphasised.

—Ian Jeffrey

MONTI, Paolo.

Nationality: Italian. **Born:** Novara in 1908. **Education:** Studied political economics, Università Bocconi, Milan, Dip. 1930; mainly self-taught in photography. **Career:** Worked as a business manager of an industrial company, Venice, 1931-53; amateur photographer, Venice, 1940-53: founder, with Luciano Scattola, Giorgio Bresciani and Gino Bolognini, 1947, and President, 1947-53, La Gondola group of photographers, Venice; professional freelance photographer, working for the magazines *Abitare, Architectural Forum, Bauen und Wohnen, Casabella, Comus, Du, Illustrazione Italiana, Intgeriors, Realites, Stern, Stile e Industria,* and the publishers Alfa, Bompiani, Electa, Fantoni, Comunità, Garzanti, Grafis, Hachette, etc., in Milan, 1953 until his death in 1982. Instructor in photography, Scuola dell'Umanitaria, Milan, 1964-66; Professor of visual Techniques and Aesthetics, Faculty of Letters and Philosophy, University of Bologna, 1970-74. **Recipient:** Award of Excellence, Federation Internationale d'Art Photographique, 1957; Premio Nazionale Zanotti Bianco, Rome, 1980. Istituto Paolo Monti founded in Milan, 1985. Estate: Istituto di Fotografia Paolo Monti, Corso Sempione 28, 20154 Milan, Italy. **Died:** (in Milan) 29 November 1982.

Individual Exhibitions:

1979   *Trent'anni di fotografie 1948-78,* Sala Comunale delle
        Esposizioni, Reggio Emilia, Italy

Selected Group Exhibitions:

1955   *Prima Mostra Internazionale di Fotografia,* Venice
1957   *Fotografie als uitdrukkingsmiddel,* Van Abbemuseum,
        Eindhoven, Netherlands
1958   *Fotografie,* Gemeente Museum, Arnhem, Netherlands
1959   *Photography at Mid-Century,* International Museum of
        Photography at George Eastman House, Rochester,
        New York
1979   *Venezia 79: La Fotografia,* at the *Biennale,* Venice
1980   *Trent'anni di fotografia a Venezia,* Palazzo Fortuny, Venice
        Photographia: la linea sottile, Galleria Flaviana, Locarno,
        Switzerland
1983   *La sperimentazione fotografica in Italia 1930-70,* Galleria
        d'Arte Moderna, Bologna, Italy

Collections:

Fondazione Paolo Monti, Milan.

Publications:

By MONTI: Books—more than 200 volumes illustrated with Monti's photographs, including *Colori e forme nella casa d'oggi,* Como, Italy 1957; *Brunelleschi,* with text by E. Luporini, Milan 1964; *Gli affreschi del Palazzo Rosso di Genove,* with text by G. Mercenaro, Milan 1965; *Storia della letteratura italiana,* 9 vols., with texts by E. Cecchi and N. Sapagno, Milan 1966; *I vetri de Murano,* with text by G. Mariacher, Milan and Rome 1967; *Cattedrali di Puglia,* with text by A. Prandi, Rome 1969; *Venezia Gotica,* with text by E. Arslan, Milan 1970; *Il plazzo Ducale di Venezia,* Turin 1971; *Piazze d'Italia,* with text by C. Brandi, Milan 1979; *Ordine e faghezza,* with text by E. Riccomini, Bologna 1972; *La Tuscia Romana,* with text by J. Raspi Serra, Milan 1972; *Venezia—nascita di una citta,* with text by S. Bettini, Milan 1972; *Venizia e la sua gondola,* with text by G. Chiesa Bellazzi, Milan 1974; *Leon Battista Alberti,* with text by F. Borsi, Milan 1975; *Storia della citta di Bologna,* with text by A. Hessel, Bologna 1975; *Filippo Brunelleschi,* with text by E. Battisiti, Milan 1976, London 1981; *Bologna: storia di un'immagine,* with text by G. Ricci, Bologna 1976; *I centri storici italiani,* with text by M. Fario, Milan 1976; *La Pieta Rondanini di Michelangelo Buonarroti,* Milan 1977; *Vaghezza e furore,* with text by C. Riccomini, Bologna 1977; *Francesco Borromini,* with text by Paolo Portoghesi, Milan 1977; *Chiese e cattedrali,* with text by M. Fagiolo, Milan 1978; *Palazzi di Piacenza dal Barocco al Neoclassico,* with text by A.M. Matteucci, Turin 1979; *Il censimento fotografico dei centri storici: Modena,* Bologna 1979; *L'esperienza sul campo,* Bologna 1981; *Salser: Gli uomini della montagna,* with text by E. Rizzi, Milan 1981; *Antiche case del lago d'Orta,* Milan 1984; *Laboratorio ossolano,* Verbania, Italy 1985; *Fotografia in Venezia,* with M. Alassio, Venice 1985. **Article**—"Otto anni di fotografia Italiana" in *Fotografia Italiana 1955,* Venice 1955.

On MONTI: Books—*Photography Year Book, 1953,* annual, London 1953; *Fotografie Gemeente Museum* by M. Coppen, Arnhem, Netherlands 1958; *Nuova Fotografia Italiana* by Guiseppe Turroni, Milan 1959; *Photography at Mid-Century,* exhibition catalogue, with introduction by Beaumont Newhall, Rochester, New York 1959; *Primo Almanacco Fotografico Italiano,* edited by Lanfranco Colombo and Roberta Clerici, Milan 1969; *Paolo Monti: trent'anni di fotografie 1948-1978,* exhibition catalogue, Modena 1979; *Venezia 79: La Fotografia,* edited by Daniela Palazzoli, Vittorio Sgarbi and Italo Zannier, Milan and New York 1979; *Trent'anni di fotografia a Venezia: il circolo La Gondola 1948-1978,* exhibition catalogue, by Italo Zannier, Venice 1980; *Photographia: la linea sottile,* exhibition catalogue, by Rinaldo Bianda and Guiliana Scime, Locarno, Switzerland 1980; *Paolo Monti e l'eta dei piani regolatori,* Bologna 1983; *La sperimentazione fotografica in Italia 1930-1970,* exhibition catalogue, by Carlo Gentili, Bologna 1983; *Paolo Monti: indice dell'archivio,* Milan 1986; *Paolo Monti: Photographs 1950-1980* compiled by Giovanni Chiaramonte, (Milan), January 1993. **Article**—"La Gondola di Venezia" by Daniel Masclet in *Fotografia* (Milan), November/December 1955.

*

The camera is an instrument of such great technological potential, such wide creative range, that in the hands of a man with just a little imagination it can make extraordinary results possible; this was the starting point for Paolo Monti, who, perhaps because he was aware of the dangers of a frantic, empty "rhetoric of creativity," preferred to confine his photographic activity to the simplest, most documentary possible approach to his subject.

Paolo Monti always photographed sculpture and architecture—that is to say, he photographed *forms*. He worked on dozens of books on Gothic, Renaissance and Baroque architecture, on palaces and cities, on the sculpture of Michelangelo, on the structure of the Venetian gondola, on the basic town-planning of Bologna; for several years he continued to make the first "photographic census" of a city and of a whole region (Emilia—Romagna)—each time mainly concerned to record the shapes and the proportions, not to make a different interpretation of them. And yet "we begin by reproducing, we end by creating"; Paolo Monti has also given us splendid *interpretations* (sometimes technical, but mental and intellectual too) of the buildings and cities that he photographed. But not even the most profound, most essential, most concentrated vision rendered by Paolo Monti's pictures was ever obtained by approaching the subject in a complex way, but only by his correct choice of light, composition, exposure and—above all—printing. The pictures of farmhouses in the province of Bologna, for example, always take in the surrounding countryside, simply to establish links with the environment; a style that some may find excessively objective, but which Paolo Monti used in a masterly way, sometimes employing an emphasis on details (architectonically significant) to produce pictures "which will still be of interest in a hundred years time."

For many years Paolo Monti preferred to work in black and white, the most supple most aristocratic medium that a photographer can ask for. His was a black-and-white technique explored to the fullest, going with the greatest care into every potentiality of the materials and the techniques. Paolo Monti was in fact a highly skillful technician, who tried out in practice every possibility both in exposure and in the dark-room. He did the same in colour photography too, creating some fantastic abstract pictures, using his equipment and materials with complete freedom. Those pictures are ideally seen beside the visual experiments of his first years as a practising photographer, when, as founder of the *Gondola* club in Venice in the late forties he was the teacher of a whole generation of Italian photographers.

—Attilio Colombo

MOON, Sarah.

Nationality: French. **Born:** Marielle Hadengue, in England, 1940. **Education:** Studied drawing in art school; self-taught in photography. **Career:** Worked as a fashion model in Paris during the 1960s. Freelance fashion photographer, working for designer Jean Cacharel, and for *Marie-Claire, Harper's Bazaar, Nova, Vogue, Elle, Votre Beauté, Stern*, etc., Paris, since 1968. **Address:** 19 Avenue du Général Leclerc, Paris 14, France.

Individual Exhibitions:

1975   Galerie Delpire, Paris
1983   *Souvenirs Improbables,* International Center of Photography, New York

Selected Group Exhibitions:

1968   *Modinsolite,* Galerie Delpire, Paris
1972   *Fashion Photography,* The Photographers' Gallery, London
        Photokina '72, Cologne
1974   *Women Photographers,* at *Photokina '74,* Cologne
1977   *Fashion Photography,* International Museum of Photography, George Eastman House, Rochester, New York (travelled to the Brooklyn Museum, New York; San Francisco Museum of Modern Art; Cincinnati Art Institute, Ohio; and the Museum of Fine Arts, St. Petersburg, Florida)

1979   *Elements,* Olympus Gallery, London
1980   *Instantanés,* Centre Georges Pompidou, Paris
1984   *Sammlung Gruber,* Museum Ludwig, Cologne
1986   *The Animal in Photography 1843-1985,* The Photographers' Gallery, London

Collections:

Bibliothèque Nationale, Paris; International Museum of Photography, George Eastman House, Rochester, New York; Fashion Institute of Technology, New York; Museum Ludwig, Cologne.

Publications:

By MOON: Book—*Modinsolite,* Paris 1975.

On MOON: Books—*Geschichte der Fotografie im 20. Jahrhundert/Photography in the 20th Century* by Petr Tausk, Cologne 1977, London 1980; *Women On Women,* with an introduction by Katharine Holabird, New York 1978; *The Vogue Book of Fashion Photography* by Polly Devlin, with an introduction by Alexander Liberman, London 1979; *The History of Fashion Photography* by Nancy Hall-Duncan, New York 1979, as *Histoire de la Photographie de Mode,* Paris 1979; *Instantanés,* exhibition catalogue, by Michel Nuridsany, Paris 1980; *Master Photographers: The Word's Great Photographers on their Art and Technique,* edited by Pat Booth, London 1983; *Sammlung Gruber: Photographie des 20. Jahrhunderts,* exhibition catalogue, with foreword by Siegfried Gohr, Cologne 1984. **Articles**—"Sarah Moon" by Bernard Noel in *Zoom* (Paris), January/February 1972; "A Radical Turn of Fashion" in *Photography Year 1976,* by the Time-Life editors, New York 1976.

*   *   *

The arrival of Sarah Moon in the world of fashion photography happened in a remarkable way in 1968. She participated in the *Modinsolite* exhibition organized by Delpire for Kodak, which presented the avant-garde of fashion photography. She had just arrived on the scene, but she very soon made her impression—a new way to look at women, a new way to treat the photographic image, and a totally subjective vision of space.

To women and to fashion Moon attributed aggressiveness; she objected to the "soft" woman, the woman of nuance, dream and mystery. The photos that she produced then for Woolmark and Cacharel, her first clients, helped to transform the image of femininity and were both the product of, and in harmony with, the feminist movement that rejected the image of woman-as-object.

Sarah Moon's own life does not lack originality. Although she trained in art, circumstances caused her to become a model. It was while seeing fashion photographers at work, watching them set their scenes, adjust their lighting, that she learned the basic principles of the trade. She began to take her own pictures, at first only with friends, but photography soon became more than just an avocation. A professional now for more than fifteen years, Moon always prepares her shots meticulously, very often designing them in detail beforehand. She likes to work with models she knows well with whom she can create a certain intimacy. For her, the quality of relations between people at the moment of the shot is essential to the complicated achievement of her pictures.

The major portion of Sarah Moon's work is commissions for fashion photography or photographs advertising various products for women. In this genre of photography man rarely intrudes his physical presence; instead, he is a mirror, that which makes woman question her own image. As long as the commissions are not too tightly predetermined, with imposed body types or suggestions for how the photos should be accomplished, and as long as there are assurances that the product need not obstruct all other concerns in the photo, then Sarah Moon is willing to take pictures within the constraints of the genre.

A trend in photography is toward a type of work that is more and more interventionist. Moon takes little pleasure in this kind of creation, but she is involved in a personal search. The dream world is very important in her work; her pictures often lead us into a world of little girls who dream of fat cats, a world bewitched. When man appears, then very often the picture moves towards a more disturbing surrealism; a dangerous mystery seems to inhere;

we pass from magic to evil spells. These are photographs in which the bizarre and unusual confront ordinary reality.

Technically, Moon was one of the first photographers to attempt to push the sensitivity of color film to its limit in order to obtain the textured effect which brings a certain softness to her pictures. She also frequently employs cinematic shooting techniques, particularly that of back projection, which permit her to create this exceptional world where reality and the dream, nature and the interior of houses, physical space and memory develop an intimate interweaving—denying Euclidean space and carrying us into her own personal space.

—Ginette Bléry

MOORE, David.

Nationality: Australian. **Born:** Sydney, New South Wales, 6 April 1927. **Education:** Educated at Tudor House School, Moss Vale, New South Wales, 1939-40; Geelong Grammar School, Victoria, 1941-45. **Military Service:** Served as a seaman in the Royal Australian Navy, 1945-46. **Family:** Married Jennifer Flintoff in 1955 (divorced, 1968); children: Karen, Michael, Lisa, and Matthew. **Career:** Assistant, Russell Roberts Photographic Studios, Sydney, 1946-47, and Max Dupain Photo Studio, Sydney, 1947-51. Freelance photographer, in London, 1951-58, and Sydney, since 1958. **Recipient:** Special Prize, *The World and Its People* exhibition, *World's Fair*, New York, 1965; 5 First Prizes, *Pacific Photographic Fair*, Melbourne, 1967; First Prize, Colour Section, Nikon International Photographic Competition, 1971; Commonwealth Award for Service to Professional Photography, Australia, 1979; Denison Award for Architectural Photography, Sydney, 1985. Honorary Fellowship—Australian Institute of Professional Photography, 1989; Australian Artists Creative Fellowship (2 years) 1994. **Agents:** Christine Abrahams Gallery, 27 Gipps Street, Richmond, Victoria 3121, Wildlight, 165 Hastings Parade, Bondi Beach, NSW 2026 and Black Star Inc., 116 East 27 Street, New York, New York 10016, U.S.A. **Address:** 68 Middle Street, McMahon's Point, New South Wales 2060, Australia.

Individual Exhibitions:

1953	*People in Photographs,* Architectural Association, London
1958	*Seven Years a Stranger,* Macquarie Galleries, Sydney (travelled to the Museum of Modern Art, Melbourne)
1976	The Photographers' Gallery, London
	Retrospective 1940-1976, Australian Centre for Photography, Sydney (travelled to the Brummels Gallery, Melbourne, 1976, and the Orange, New South Wales *Festival of the Arts,* 1977; and toured New Zealand, 1978-79)
1977	*Australia,* Australian Embassy, Paris
1980	*Photographs by Design,* Axiom Gallery, Melbourne (travelled to the Macquarie Galleries, Sydney)
1983	*The Landscape of New South Wales,* New South Wales Parliament House, Sydney
	Photographs by Design 2, Australian Centre for Photography, Sydney (travelled to Christine Abrahams Gallery, Melbourne; The Developed Image Gallery, Adelaide)
1985	*Sydney at Mid-Century,* Art Gallery of New South Wales, Sydney (travelled to Christine Abrahams Gallery, Melbourne; the Developed Image Gallery, Adelaide)
	The CRA Pilbara Landscapes, Central Art Gallery, Beijing, China (travelled to the Art Gallery of Shanghai; Cultural and Arts Foundation Centre, Seoul; Metropolitan Teien Art Museum, Tokyo)
1986	*Australian Artists 1960-85,* Christine Abrahams Gallery, Melbourne (travelled to The Print Room Gallery, Sydney)
1988	*Sydney at Mid-Century,* New South Wales House, London
	The Australian Functional Tradition, Christine Abrahams Gallery, Melbourne

1988-89	*David Moore—Fifty Years of Photographs,* retrospective exhibition, Art Gallery of New South Wales, Sydney; Albury Regional Gallery, NSW; Orange Regional Gallery, NSW and Newcastle Region Gallery, NSW
1990	*David Moore—A Survey, 1947-1989,* Christine Abrahams Gallery, Melbourne
	David Moore Photographs, Image Hong Kong 90
1991	*David Moore—Australian Photographer* (The Kodak Collection), Puerto Rico
1992	*David Moore—Australian Photographer* (The Kodak Collection), Shenyang, People's Republic of China
1993	*Sydney Harbour,* State Library of New South Wales, Sydney
1993	*Railway Relics and Romance,* Art Gallery of New South Wales, Sydney
1994	*The Velvet Arena,* Photographers' Gallery, London

Selected Group Exhibitions:

1952	*World Exhibition of Photography,* Kunstmuseum, Lucerne
1955	*The Family of Man,* Museum of Modern Art, New York (and world tour)
1967	*Photography in the Fine Arts,* Metropolitan Museum of Art, New York
1969	*The Perceptive Eye,* National Gallery of Victoria, Melbourne
1973	*Work in Progress,* Brummels Gallery, Melbourne
1975	*Recent Australian Photography,* Department of Foreign Affairs, Canberra (toured South East Asia)
1979	*The Philip Morris Collection,* outdoor exhibition, Sydney
1980	*Ten Australian Photographers,* The Jam Factory, Melbourne
1982	*Heatwave: The Making of a Movie,* Australian Centre for Photography, Sydney
1986	*Australian Landscape Photographed,* Art Gallery of New South Wales, Sydney (travelled to Albury Regional Art Centre, New South Wales; National Gallery of Victoria, Melbourne)
1988	*CSR Photography Project,* Art Gallery of New South Wales, Sydney
1991	*Fine and Mostly Sunny Exhibition,* Art Gallery of New South Wales, Sydney
1992	*Souvenirs of Sydney,* Art Gallery of New South Wales, Sydney
	Recent Acquisitions, Art Gallery of New South Wales, Sydney

Collections:

Art Gallery of New South Wales, Sydney; National Gallery of Victoria, Melbourne; Art Gallery of South Australia, Adelaide; Australian National Gallery, Canberra; Museum of Modern Art, New York; Smithsonian Institution, Washington, D.C.; Bibliothèque Nationale, Paris; Australian Embassy, Paris; CSR Photography Project, Sydney; Australian Parliament House, Canberra; The Polaroid Collection, Cambridge, Massachusetts; The Philip Morris Collection; The National Maritime Museum, Sydney.

Publications:

By MOORE: Books—*Australia and New Zealand,* with Time-Life Editors, New York 1964; *Isles of the South Pacific,* Washington, D.C. 1968; *Life in Australia,* Brisbane 1968; *In the Making,* Melbourne 1969; *Finland Creates,* with Jack Fields, text by Pekka Suhonen, Jyvaskyla, Finland 1976; *Australia: Image of Nation 1850-1950,* with Rodney Hall, Sydney 1983; *The Queen Victoria Building 1898-1986,* Wellington Lane Press, Sydney 1987; *The Australian Functional Tradition,* Five Mile Press, Melbourne 1988; *David Moore—Australian Photographer Vols 1 & 2,* Chapter and Verse, Sydney 1988; *An Australian Place—The Upper Hunter Valley,* Chapter and Verse, Sydney 1991; *Image of New England,* Armidale Development Corporation 1992; *Sydney Harbour,* Chapter and Verse, Sydney 1993. **Article**—in *Max Dupain: An Appreciation,* Sydney 1980.

Migrants Arriving in Sydney, **1966.** Photograph by David Moore.

On MOORE: Books—*Australian Photography—A Contemporary View* edited by Laurence Le Guay, Sydney 1979; *David Moore,* edited by Ian McKenzie, Melbourne 1980; *Silver and Grey: fifty Years of Australian Photography 1900-1950,* edited by Gael Newton, Sydney 1980. **Articles**— "David Moore" in *Camera* (Lucerne), August 1968; "David Moore" by John Williams in *Art and Australia* (Sydney), July/September 1976; "David Moore," in *Photo-Forum* (Auckland), October/November 1977.

＊

Photographers are inevitably influenced by the work of fellow photographers and quite often by other examples of creative expression. Fortunately, my own influences have been many and varied since the late 1940s when I first began to regard photography as a serious occupation.

The study of photographs by Edward Weston and Walker Evans opened doors which led on to Dorothea Lange, Brassaï, Kertész, Brandt, Cartier-Bresson, Newman and Callahan. Additionally, documentary films such as *The River, The Plough That Broke the Plains* and *Louisiana Boy* were strong, early influences.

During the 1960s and 1970s contemporary painters and sculptors imparted a stimulation which tended to alter my perspective to photography. Alexander Calder and Ellsworth Kelly were two such artists.

A family background of architecture, coupled with a close association with designers, has tended to discipline my photography in formal areas. Photojournalism (which I practised for many years) has ceased to hold a position of supremacy in my interest today. Whilst I shall continue to recognize the importance of documentary evidence in photography, I am

personally more interested in what can be done with the photograph from an intellectual point of view.

—David Moore

＊   ＊   ＊

Sydney photographer David Moore was for many years a photojournalist. He was weaned on the images of Edward Weston, Cartier-Bresson, Eugene Smith and many noted World War II photographers, and for a number of post-war years he prowled the precincts of such magazines as *Life, Look* and *Picture Post,* serving a rough apprenticeship, based mainly in London. On his return to Australia in 1958 he continued working as a freelance, on a worldwide basis, for magazine clients and for several agencies.

A great deal of Moore's work is with 35mm, and, like a number of other documentary photographers, he has passed through a number of phases to reach a partial transformation of his personal vision. His present idiom culminated in a recent exhibition of his work, *Photographs by Design.* His new images embrace the abstract and are largely in sharp contradiction to his earlier work.

The son of an architect, Moore very nearly adopted that profession, and his new black-and-white images show variations that embrace a strong architectural theme: he has deliberately cut out and shifted shapes to suit himself in the form of clinical collages, which relate not only to design but also to reality and sometimes deliberately evade the perimeters of the print itself.

These works indicate an acceptance of discipline that distills an essence from the ordinary and an appreciation of pure visual form which indulges in an arbitrary method of manipulating subject matter in tonal and spatial relationships. He embraces form and content as a whole.

Moore feels today that the documentary type photograph "ended up dulling our responses to pictures." He further comments that a "new photographic intellect is emerging" that allows "the viewer to become personally involved instead of becoming a voyeur of life through the open window of the photograph," that the new photographic intellectuals are "concerned with the soft spread of time rather than the selected moment."

Yet, to appraise Moore's work as a whole, it seems necessary, also, to appreciate his earlier stimulating images of people relative to their environment who also communicate with the viewer. Photography is primarily concerned with communication, and although Moore's earlier work may appear more human and emotional, it is perhaps just as valid as his abstract work and may prove more valuable in the future.

—Laurence Le Guay

MOORE, Raymond.

Nationality: British. **Born:** Wallasey, Cheshire, 26 August 1920. **Education:** Studied design at Wallasey School of Art, 1937-40; Royal College of Art, London, 1947-50, A.R.C.A. 1950; studied with Minor White, Massachusetts Institute of Technology, Cambridge, 1970. **Military Service:** Served in the Royal Air Force, 1940-46. **Career:** Freelance photographer since 1955. Instructor in painting and lithography, 1950-55, and lecturer in creative photography, 1956-74, Watford College of Art, Hertfordshire; Senior Lecturer in Creative Photography, Trent Polytechnic, Nottingham, 1975-78. Masterclasses, Derbyshire College of Higher Education; the Photographers Place, Derbyshire; Newcastle College of Art; Glasgow College of Art. **Recipient:** Arts Council Bursary, 1978. **Died:** (Chapel Knowe, Canonbie, Dumfriesshire, Scotland) 6 October 1987.

Individual Exhibitions:

1959	Regent Street Polytechnic, London
1962	Artists International Association Gallery, London
1967	*Modfot 1: Raymond Moore,* R.W.S. Gallery, London (toured the U.K. and Europe)
1968	Welsh Arts Council Gallery, Cardiff (toured the U.K.)
1970	International Museum of Photography, George Eastman House, Rochester, New York
1971	Carl Siembab Gallery, Boston
	Art Institute of Chicago (retrospective)
1973	The Photographers' Gallery, London
1976	Thackrey and Robertson, San Francisco
1977	*3 Photographers: Cooper, Hill, Moore,* Focus Gallery, San Francisco (with Thomas Joshua Cooper and Paul Hill)
1978	The Photographic Gallery, Cardiff
1980	Salzburg College, Austria
1981	Hayward Gallery, London (retrospective)
1982	Royal Photographic Society, Bath, Avon (toured Britain)
1985	Birksted Gallery, London
	Every So Often, Northern Centre for Contemporary Art, Newcastle-upon-Tyne (toured Sweden, Finland and Britain, 1985-86)
1986	*49 Prints,* British Council, Barcelona (toured Spain, France, Canada, Netherlands and West Germany)
1990	*Raymond Moore,* Touring Exhibition organised by Ffotogallery and Oriel, Cardiff

Selected Group Exhibitions:

1975	*The Land: 20th Century Landscape Photographs Selected by Bill Brandt,* Victoria and Albert Museum, London (travelled to the National Gallery, Edinburgh; Ulster Museum, Belfast; and the National Museum of Wales, Cardiff, 1976)
1977	*Photographs: Sheldon Memorial Art Gallery Collection,* University of Nebraska, Lincoln
	Concerning Photography, The Photographers' Gallery, London (travelled to Spectro Workshop, Newcastle-upon-Tyne)
1979	*Three Perspectives on Photography,* Hayward Gallery, London
1980	*Metaphysical Presence,* in *Grupa Junij '80,* Ljubljana, Yugoslavia
	Premfère Triennale Internationale de Photographie, Charleroi, Belgium
1982	*Presences of Nature,* Carlisle Museum and Art Gallery, Cumbria (toured Britain)
1983	*British Photography 1955-65,* The Photographers' Gallery, London
1984	*Creation,* Scottish National Gallery of Modern Art, Edinburgh (toured Scotland)
1986	*The Photographic Art,* Stills Gallery, Edinburgh
1989	*The Art of Photography, 1839-1900,* The Royal Academy of Arts, London
	Towards a Bigger Picture: Contemporary British Photographs from the Victoria and Albert Museum, Tate Gallery, Liverpool
	Through the Looking Glass: Photographic Art in Great Britain 1945-1989, Barbican Art Gallery, London

Collections:

Victoria and Albert Museum, London; Welsh Arts Council, Cardiff; Contemporary Art Society for Wales, Cardiff; University College of Wales, Aberystwyth; Bibliothèque Nationale, Paris; Art Institute of Chicago; Gernsheim Collection, University of Texas at Austin; University of New Mexico, Albuquerque; British Council, London.

Publications:

By MOORE: Books—*Murmurs at Every Turn: the photographs of Raymond Moore,* London 1981; *Every So Often: Photographs by Raymond Moore,* edited by Neil Hanson, Newcastle-upon-Tyne 1983; *Raymond Moore,* essay by Timothy Stevens: catalogue of the travelling exhibition organised by Ffotogallery and Oriel, Cardiff 1990. **Articles**—"Photographs by Raymond Moore" in *Creative Camera* (London), June 1973; interview, with Ian Jeffrey, in *Creative Camera* (London), March/April 1981.

On MOORE: Books—*The Concise History of Photography* by Helmut and Alison Gernsheim, London and New York 1965; *Photographs by Raymond Moore,* exhibition catalogue, Cardiff 1968; *Colour Photography* by Eric de Maré, London 1968; *Art Without Boundaries* by Gerald Woods, London 1972; *The Magic Image* by Cecil Beaton and Gail Buckland, London and Boston 1975; *Concerning Photography,* exhibition catalogue, by Jonathan Bayer, Peter Turner, Ian Jeffrey, and Ainslie Ellis, London 1977; *Photographs: Sheldon Memorial Art Gallery Collection,* exhibition catalogue, by Norman A. Geske, Lincoln, Nebraska 1977; *Geschichte der Photographie im 20. Jahrhundert/History of Photography in the 20th Century* by Petr Tausk, Cologne 1977, London 1980; *Exploring Photography* by Bryn Campbell, London 1978, New York 1979; *Creative Techniques in Landscape Photography* by Gerald Woods and John Williams, London 1980; *Photography: A Concise History* by Ian Jeffrey, London 1981; *Appoaching Photography* by Paul Hill, London and Boston 1982; *British Photography 1955-65: The Master Craftsmen in Print,* exhibition catalogue, by Sue Davies, Michael Rand, Mark Boxer and others, London 1983; *The Library of World Photography: Landscape,* with texts by David Plowden and Ian Jeffrey, Tokyo and London 1984; *British Photography Toward a Bigger Picture,* Aperture Foundation, New York 1988; *Through the Looking Glass, Photographic Art in Britain 1945-1989* exhibition catalogue ed Gerry Badger and John Benton Harris 1989. **Articles**—"The Light and the Vision: The Work of Raymond Moore" by Robert D. McClelland in *British Journal of Photography* (London), 29 August 1969; "Tides of Man and Nature" by Minor White in *Penrose Annual,* London 1971; "Photographs by Raymond Moore" in *Creative Camera* (London), June 1972; "Portfolio: Raymond Moore" in *Camera* (Lucerne), August 1976; "Raymond Moore" in *Creative Camera Yearbook,* London 1977; article by Clive Lancaster in *British Journal of*

Photography (London), 5 June 1981; "Raymond Moore" by Ian Jeffrey in *The London Magazine,* April/May 1985.

*

The single perceptive photograph can suggest the presence of a world that remains almost invisible because of our human limitations defined by time and space. Human fragility and the practical demands of life seldom render us capable of reacting with sufficient awareness to record the image of a happening at maximum intensity. In fact, we spend most of our lives in blinkers, insensitive to the import of what is around us. If we were only capable of transcending our space-time limits to some extent, we could witness happenings undreamt of. At this moment there must be fantastic relationships between the things we call objects, but no-one there to record them. Natural happenings eclipsed and lost in time. All we can do is to cultivate a state of awareness within ourselves, and allow the images to come through unfettered. Amongst the dross, the pertinent ones will serve as hints or signposts to a state of greater visual perception.

Photographs, and particularly groups of photographs, can serve as catalysts to thought and feeling; their limits are measured simply by the persons taking them. Whether the viewer's reaction is exactly the same as the photographer's is immaterial, as long as the photographs are sufficiently provocative to produce some reaction and increased awareness. They occur through the person (both photographer and viewer) just as much as the image is created through the lens. The person is like a very particular lens. Keep the lens clean and uncluttered by preconception. The more preoccupied you are the less freedom you have to act. Only the relaxed mind and body can truly react. Conscious preconception means insensitivity to the ever-present NOW.

—Raymond Moore

*   *   *

Raymond Moore talked about his work sparingly and well. He described his subject as the "no man's land between the real and fantasy—the mystery in the commonplace—the uncommonness of the commonplace" (Welsh Arts Council catalogue, 1968). In an interview with Ian Jeffrey he spoke of being drawn to an "edge of civilization" where obvious valuations do not apply. "If I were dropped into a slum area I don't think I'd want to photograph, I'd have to move out towards the edge. Definite statements have something of preaching about them. I prefer to tease out or to unravel what's going on" (*Creative Camera,* March/April 1981). His photographs are neither documentary nor realist but as a collective whole form a precise and poetic interpretation of chosen aspects of post-war Britain. Moore's Britain is a land of dislocation, spiritual absenteeism, ambiguous signs and economic amnesia. He set himself to discern new patterns and new life in all this. A method of chance collage brought the ordinary evidence of experience into relationship—not by gluing fragments together but by observing symmetries, superimpositions and likenesses.

A critic wrote in response to Moore's major Hayward Gallery exhibition of 1981 that the photographs brought to mind this line from Wallace Stevens: "a little string speaks for a crowd of voices" (Clive Lancaster, *British Journal of Photography* 5 June 1981). The quotation aptly evokes Moore's art of implication, which is strikingly linear and has analogies with music. Speaking of certain passages in Arnold Bax, Moore said that he discovers "other people's work through my own, and generally find more to dwell on and to hold onto within music and poetry than photography." The perfectionism of Moore's use of the tonal scale in his exhibition prints makes them among the most satisfying anywhere in recent times.

The following stylistic pointers may be useful. Moore was trained as a painter in the 1940s and speaks of the style he adopted (he destroyed his paintings later) as deriving from the Euston Road School of the previous decade, which took the surface of urban life as subject. As if in reaction to this, a period of pure abstraction followed in the 1950s. He was impressed by the brave effort to find a new direction for photography of Otto Steinert (*Subjektive Fotografie,* 1952). Other significant points of contact are with aspects of Nash, Kertész, Callahan and Bravo. Moore developed from the experimental geometry of his early photographs (1956) to pictures which are deeply marked by urban life and more intricately ordered in line, plane and tonality. His photographs digested more and more of appearance, notably of the North

West, while assuming more surprising freedom of structure. What Jonathan Williams calls "the pleasing democracy of content" in Moore's photographs involves a place for his achievement in the social as well as art histories of this period.

—Mark Haworth-Booth

MORATH, Inge(borg).

Nationality: American. **Born:** Graz, Austria, 27 May 1923; moved to the United States, 1962: naturalized, 1963. **Education:** Educated in Alsace, Darmstadt and Berlin; studied romance languages at Berlin University, 1941-44, and the University of Bucharest, 1943. **Family:** Married the journalist Lionel Birch in 1951 (divorced, 1954); the playwright Arthur Miller in 1962; daughter: Rebecca. **Career:** Worked as a cleaner, farmhand, etc., on compulsory labor service, East Prussia, and did war service in aircraft factory, Tempelhof Airdrome, Berlin, during World War II; Editorial Translator and Interpreter, United States Information Service Publications, Salzburg, Austria, 1946-49; freelance radio writer for Red-White-Red Radio Network, and Literary Editor, *Der Optimist* magazine, Vienna, 1950; Austrian Editor, *Heute* magazine, Vienna, 1951; photographic apprentice to the photojournalist Simon Guttman, London, 1952. Since 1953, Member of Magnum Photos, Paris and New York, and freelance photographer, working for *Life, Paris-Match, Holiday, Saturday Evening Post,* etc., in Europe and the United States. Researcher and assistant to photographer Henri Cartier-Bresson, on numerous trips throughout Europe and the United States, 1953, 1954. Lecturer, Cooper Union, New York, 1971-72. **Recipient:** Outstanding Accomplishment Award, State of Michigan, 1983; Certificate of Appreciation, Smithsonian Institution, Washington, D.C., 1985. D.F.A.: University of Hartford, Connecticut, 1984. Honorary Member, Austrian Museum of Photography, 1985. Winner Great Austrian State Prize for Photography, 1992. Lives in Roxbury, Connecticut. **Address:** c/o Magnum Photos, 72 Spring Street, New York, New York 10012, U.S.A.

Individual Exhibitions:

1956	Wuehrle Gallery, Vienna
1958	Leitz Gallery, New York
1959	Overseas Press Club, New York
1964	Art Institute of Chicago
1969	Oliver Wolcott Memorial Library, Litchfield, Connecticut
	Russia, Rizzoli Gallery, New York
1971	Andover Art Museum, Massachusetts
1972	University of Miami
1974	Power Center for the Performing Arts, University of Michigan, Ann Arbor
1976	Carlton Gallery, New York
	Neikrug Gallery, New York
1979	*Photographs of China,* Grand Rapids Art Museum, Michigan
1980	*Photographs of China,* Kunsthaus, Zurich
	Photographs of China, Museum des 20. Jahrhunderts, Vienna
1981	*Photographs of China,* Neikrug Gallery, New York
1982	*Fotohof,* Salzburg, Austria (retrospective)
1983	*Photographs of the Theatre,* Alley Theater Festival, Houston, Texas
1984	*Salesman in Beijing,* Hong Kong Theatre Festival, Hong Kong
	Forum Stadtpark, Graz, Austria
1985	Pace/MacGill Gallery, New York
1986	Kunsthaus, Graz, Austria (retrospective; travelled to Salzburg and Vienna, 1987)
	Portraits, Aperture Gallery, New York
1987	*Portraits,* Burden Gallery, Aperture Foundation, NY
1988	*Retrospective,* Moscow Centre of Photojournalists
1989	*Portraits,* Norwich Cathedral, England; American Cultural Center, Brussels

Bella Akhmadulina, Moscow, 1987. Photograph by Inge Morath.

1991	*Portraits,* Kolbe Museum, Berlin; Rupertinum Museum, Salzburg, Austria
1992	*Retrospective,* Neue Galerie, Linz
1993	*Retrospective,* America House, Berlin; Hradcin Gallery, Prague
1994	*Retrospective,* America House, Frankfurt; Hardenberg Gallery, Velbert, Germany; Smith Gallery, Stirling, Scotland; Royal Photographic Society, Bath, England

Selected Group Exhibitions:

1956	*Magnum Photographers,* at *Photokina,* Cologne
1960	*The World as Seen by Magnum,* Takashimaya Department Store, Tokyo (and world tour)
1967	*The Camera as Witness,* at *Expo '67,* Montreal
1981	*Magnum Paris,* Palais du Luxembourg, Paris (travelled to the International Center of Photography, New York, 1982)
1984	*Sammlung Gruber,* Museum Ludwig, Cologne
1985	*Magnum Vintage Prints,* Pace McGill Gallery, New York
1990	*In Our Time,* Travelling Exhibition

Collections:

Metropolitan Museum of Art, New York; International Center of Photography, New York; Rhode Island School of Design, Providence; Fogg Art Museum, Harvard University, Cambridge, Massachusetts; Art Institute of Chicago; Bibliothéque Nationale, Paris; Kunsthaus, Zurich; Ministry of Culture and Education, Vienna; Oesterreichische Fotogalerie Rupertinum, Salzburg, Austria; Santa Monica Museum of Art, California.

Publications:

By MORATH: Books—*Guerre à la Tristesse/Fiesta in Pamplona,* with text by Dominique Aubier, Paris 1954; *Venice Observed,* with text by Mary McCarthy, Lausanne, Paris and New York 1956; *Bring Forth the Children,* with Yul Brynner, New York 1960; *Tunisia,* with Marc Riboud and André Martin, texts by Claude Roy and Paul Sebag, Paris and New York 1961; *From Persia to Iran,* with text by Edouard Sablier, New York 1961, Paris 1967; *Le Masque,* with Saul Steinberg, Paris 1967; *In Russia,* with text by Arthur Miller, Lucerne, New York and London 1969, 1974; *East West Exercises,* with text by Ruth Bluestone, New York 1973; *In the Country,* with text by Arthur Miller, Lucerne, New York and London 1977; *My Sister Life,* with translations of Boris Pasternak poems by Olga Andreyev Carlisle, New York 1977; *Chinese Encounters,* with text by Arthur Miller, New York and Lucerne 1979; *Paris Magnum,* with others, Millerton, New York 1981; *Salesman in Beijing,* with text by Arthur Miller, New York 1983, London 1984; *Saul Steinberg Portfolio,* Salzburg, Austria 1986; *Inge Morath: Portraits,* Millerton, New York 1986; with others, *In Our Time,* 1990; *Russian Journal,* with texts by Yevtushenko, Voznesensky, Olga Andreyev Carlisle Aperture, Sinclair Stenvenson, Christian Brandstaetter, 1991; *Inge Morath: Photographien 1952 to 1992,* Salzburg, 1992; *Inge Morath: Spain in the 50s,* Madrid, 1994. **Articles**—"Anti-Photographer Masks," with Saul Steinberg, in *Creative Camera* (London), February 1969; "Inge Morath in interview" in *Vogue* (Sydney), April 1986.

On MORATH: Books—*Photographie Communication,* edited by R. Smith Schuneman, London and Toronto 1972; *Grosse Photographen unserer Zeit: Inge Morath,* edited by Raoul Martinez, text by Olga Carlisle, Lucerne and Frankfurt 1975; *The Library of World Photography: Portraits,* with introduction by Colin Ford, Tokyo 1982, 1983, London 1983; *Sammlung Gruber: Photographie des 20. Jahrhunderts,* exhibition catalogue, with foreword by Siegfried Gohr, Cologne 1984; *After the War Was Over,* with introduction by Mary Blume, London and New York 1985. **Articles**—"A Collection of Photographs" in *Aperture* (Millerton, New York), Fall 1969; "Inge Morath" in *Camera* (Lucerne), November 1969; "New England Heute: Zehn Aufnahmen von Inge Morath" in *Du* (Zurich), March 1973; "Inge Morath" in *Camera Austria* (Graz), Summer 1986; interview—"Fotographieren ist fuer mich wie atmen" in *Ab 40,* April, May, June, 1994. **Film**—*Copyright by Inge Morath,* made by Sabine Eckhard, Kick Film, shown on German TV and in cinemas.

*

Perhaps I can do my life like a telegram:

Both parents scientists, of old Austrian families, gave me a sense of structure, form, from which to imagine the new. They moved about Europe, so my school was French one year, German next, and I bilingual and patriotically bi-partisan, detached. Longed for China after uncle returned with immense Oriental tales, and grandmother, an early suffragette, occultist, bridge champion further widened doorway to life's infinities. Finished high school in Berlin, followed by Hitler regime's obligatory year of "labor service," cleaning latrines, milking cows, shovelling manure in eastern Prussia. Incredibly idiotic military discipline. Enter Berlin University, studying romance language, plus semester at University of Bucharest, finishing exams under heavy bombing which destroyed home, one younger brother died. Drafted to war service in aircraft factory at Tempelhof Airdrome, finally ended it by joining refugee trek for weeks on foot, reunited with parents in Salzburg, then controlled by U.S. Third Division.

Vienna euphoric then for young people no longer marching in step. Unbounded energy, everything possible, we were like prisoners freed. Job as editorial translator-interpreter U.S. Information Service, radio writing, magazine articles for political-literary *Der Optimist,* finally Austrian editor *Heute* magazine. Text for photographs Erich Lessing, Ernst Trabant brought attention of Robert Capa, who invited Haas and me to join his new photographers' co-operative, Magnum Photos, in Paris. New friends there were David Seymour, George Rodger, Henri Cartier-Bresson, whose assistant and researcher I later became. Still pre-Cold War, we shared common suffering of war and hope of humane consciousness rising, so photography was both tool and its beauty a magical blow against destructiveness, a deep basis for sharp standards and self-discipline. Moving over Europe on stories with Haas, sometimes in box cars on bread and sausage or sumptuously dining in exquisite places when editors came, movie directors, one week Hamburg, the next Italy, now starting to see texts in English, learning to read contact sheets. Reading always—Rilke, Musil, Kafka, Trakl, Mann, Ortega y Gasset when still in Austria, seeing first astounding American play by Saroyan, see Brecht, Hans Weigle's satires, and the education of the coffee house, Ingeborg Bachmann's lyric poems and Arnold Keyserling's Oriental philosophy. Marriage to Lionel Birch, English journalist, spurred reading Shaw, Shakespeare, study of cricket and country pubs and upper class stuttering, but it was a mistake which Houseman, Yeats, Joyce could not mend, and we divorced in a year. The English girls more independent than we were, sexually more related, whimsical, wilful, eccentric. Despite many English friends I missed photographers. At Tate Gallery, British Museum, galleries often looking at paintings to rinse my eyes but I was not a born painter. Finally took out my second-hand Contax, long-owned Christmas present, and found a language. Became apprenticed to Simon Guttmann in London, one of the founders of the *Berliner Illustrierte* considered "Father of Photo-Journalism," quirky and old, had Bob Capa working for him and taught me mercilessly, also how to throw sixpence in gas heater for heating his shaving water, also that a photo comes from inside. Important because I was ashamed to speak German after the War, a millstone of guilt, so a picture was like daring to say "love."

Great event was Robert Capa's inviting me to join Magnum now as a photographer on strength of my pictures and text on French workman priest which was three months in doing. Living in hotels, small digs, did movie coverages, stories, any assignment that came along from roses in the Parc de Bagatelles to Soho and Mayfair. Plus working with Henri Cartier-Bresson as researcher and taking my own pictures. Now I had enough metier to absorb the essence. A hunting, running, flying time; from Bresson and my own education

and spirit came the conviction of composition, the constant alert, truth to the subject, ruthlessness when there was something to photograph. Cartier-Bresson's endless patience till he found the right place from which to photograph a Castilian landscape. Plus reading Aragon now, André Breton and Dad, Gerard de Nerval, Agrippa d'Aubigne, Koestler, Sartre, Gide, de Beauvoir, Camus, Rene Char, Michaud. The Louvre for the eyes, the Orangerie, the provincial museums, the Loire Valley, Normandy, Montherlant, Moliere, Louis Jouvet, the Pitoeffs, the streets of Paris, cabarets, nightclubs, food, wine, bistros. I buy my own apartment in Paris.

And new friends in the Calders, Janet Flanner, editor Robert Delpire, Americans living in Paris, Marie Louise Bousquet, masterful Teriade, editor of *Verve,* struggling with Cartier-Bresson and producing *The Decisive Moment.* His house in St. Jean Cap Ferrat with the tree Matisse painted in his dining room corner to make it look bigger and Chagall's paintings in the salon to match his flowers. For editor Robert Delpire my first book, *Fiesta in Pamplona,* with Dominique Aubier's profound text, and first big story on a woman, Mercedes Formica, Spanish lawyer. Robert Capa announces me as fully fledged.

Fluent now in Spanish, immersion in Spanish culture. Reading Lorca, Gongora, Cervantes, Unamuno, Spinoza. The Prado, the great private collection, the light of Zurbaran, films of Bunuel and others forbidden in Nazi time. All over Spain, on foot, Landrover. Meet Balenciaga and become elegant. *From Persia to Iran,* after *Venice Observed* with Mary McCarthy. Photographing in U.S., South Africa, Middle East, Mexico, South America, another book *Tunisia,* another on refugees with Yul Brynner. Learn much from Gjon Mili in New York, as a person and first great technician I met, musical evenings with Sascha Schneider and great Chinese food, Saul Steinberg, a one-man civilization, meet the New York Magnums, Cornell Capa now in charge after Bob's death, meet Dave Duncan and Bernie Quint from *Life,* that fortress of photojournalism and a room full of photographic equipment like out of a mad dream. Grateful to people at *Holiday* magazine for wonderful assignments. Learn about strobes and posing actors from Mili. Stay no longer anywhere than time needed for photographing, many hellos, adieus, letterwriting, airplane and train reading of American novelists, hear first real jazz in Harlem. My rusty university Rumanian serves well while doing big story of River Danube from source to the Delta embracing North European to Slav to Latin cultures which are combined in my own Austrian family and roots. Back with Cartier-Bresson for a cross U.S. car trip and covering movie *The Misfits* with other Magnums.

Marry Arthur Miller, January 1962, living in Chelsea Hotel at first, continuing work as before until daughter Rebecca is born, then photographing closer to home. A complete record of Kazan's production of Arthur's play *After the Fall,* and begin *Connecticut* as seen by strange European. New friends, the Harrison Salisburys, Robert Osbornes, Olga and Henry Carlisle, Francine and Cleve Grey, Libermans, Styrons and new-old Calders who are neighbors. Growing differently now, more plant-like, in one place. Fascinating to live with the different vision of the writer. Nostalgia for Europe so annually we travel there, twice to Russia. Learn Russian with Olga Carlisle. Book *In Russia* with Arthur's text. We three to Hong Kong, Japan, Thailand, Cambodia just before it blows up. Studying Chinese now, waiting for our visas. Teach two courses at Cooper Union, lecture at Wilson Hicks Conference in Miami. Meanwhile . . . quite fluent in Mandarin (continuous studies at Yale University). Three visits to the People's Republic of China (1978 with Arthur Miller, 1979 with Lois Snow widow of Edgar Snow collaborating on documentation for a book on Edgar Snow, 1983 with Arthur Miller including two months in Beijing working on Chinese production of *Death of a Salesman* and extensive travel). An immense dimension added to my life by this involvement. Also work is Japan with groups of actresses. Spring 1987 I return to both countries with new projects. 1984-85 participation in photographic symposiums, especially Styrian Autumn in Graz and the Smithsonian Institution series on Masters of Portrait Photography. Lectures with slides of China at the International Center of Photography, Columbia University, etc. Am now a photographer for 30 years (hard to believe).

Returned to Russia several times, result was the book *Russian Journal,* 1992. Returned to Spain, working on project "Madrid, End of the Century" with Leonard Freed, Eli Reed, Alex Webb, Miguel Rio Branco. Result book, *Miradas Fin de Siglo,* 1993. Now working on a project about the river Danube from source to delta, repeat of a trip undertaken in the fifties, reporting the changes along this river which is very much part of my background. Continuing to do portraits. Working with young filmmakers, including my daughter,

Rebecca Miller, now directing a movie she wrote herself, "Angela," shooting in New York State.

—Inge Morath

*   *   *

Inge Morath shares with a number of her fellow photographers the gift of "capturing" places and things as well as people. Her images of the Middle East reveal a profound ability to picture things in such a way that we are allowed to see what we haven't actually experienced: ducks perched on a laundry ledge; fabric drying in the sun; an elaborate, people-less room of chandeliers and glass; rug-making and weaving; architectural ruins; "Knights of muscle"; oil-responsible "modernity." She has a brilliant sense of place, of the surprising couched in the commonplace, whether it be Africa or Russia or New England.

Ordinary people at their business of being human or celebrated artists are equally interesting as a result of her insight. A detail of architecture, a cart full of musicians, create for us an instant of participation. In Russia—students, a horse-drawn sleigh, prison guards, a statue against trees, Dostoevsky territory, Onegin's bench, Leningrad seen from a fortress roof, Pasternak's grave strewn with flowers and fruit—all testify to Morath's special talent.

And in her book of "illustrations" for poems by Pasternak she achieves superb "equivalents" to linguistic passion, images of great clarity and enhancement. A blue glass supporting a spray of lilies of the valley. A wedding. The peculiar stare of family photographs. Wild blackberries. A person seated at the piano. All commonplace things brought to rarity.

—Ralph Pomeroy

MORGAN, Barbara.

Nationality: American. **Born:** Barbara Brooks Johnson in Buffalo, Kansas, 8 July 1900. **Education:** Pomona High School, California, 1917-19; studied art at the University of California at Los Angeles, 1919-23; mainly self-taught in photography. **Family:** Married the photographer Willard D. Morgan in 1925 (died, 1967); sons: Douglas and Lloyd. **Career:** Painter and occasional photographer, Los Angeles, 1923-30; also, Art Instructor, San Fernando High School, California, 1923, 1924, and Instructor in Design, Landscape and Woodcut, University of California at Los Angeles, 1925-30, and Writer, Managing Editor, then Editor, *Light and Dark* magazine, U.C.L.A., 1928; moved to New York, 1930, and established studio there, 1931; concentrated on painting, 1925-35 (one-man show of paintings and graphics, Mellon Gallery, Philadelphia, 1934, and Sherman Gallery, New York, 1961); full-time photographer since 1935; established studio in Scarsdale, New York, 1941. Member, Photo League, New York, in the 1930s. Photo Picture Editor, Morgan and Lester, subsequently Morgan and Morgan Inc., publishers, Hastings-on-Hudson, New York, in the 1940s, and Co-Owner, with Willard D. Morgan, Morgan and Morgan Inc., 1950-60. **Recipient:** Trade Book Clinic Award, American Institute of Graphic Arts, 1941; National Endowment for the Arts Grant, 1975. Fellow, Philadelphia Museum of Art, 1970. D.F.A.: Marquette University, Milwaukee, 1978. Awarded Lifetime Achievement Award by American Society of Magazine Photographers, Washington, D.C. 1988. **Died:** (in Tarrytown, New York) 17 August, 1992.

Individual Exhibitions

1938	*Dance Photographs,* Y.M.H.A., Lexington Avenue, New York
1939	*Dance Photographs,* University of Minnesota, Minneapolis
	Duke University, Durham, North Carolina
	Komin Dance Gallery, New York
	A Portfolio of the Dance, Columbia University, New York
	Wheaton College, Norton, Massachusetts
1940	Dock Street Theatre, Charleston, South Carolina
	Greenwich Library, Connecticut
	Photographs of the Dance, Photo League, New York

	Pratt Institute, Brooklyn, New York
	University of Minnesota, Minneapolis
1941	Wesleyan University, Middletown, Connecticut
	Baltimore Museum of Art
1943	*Modern Dance in Photography,* Carleton College, Northfield, Minnesota
	Y.M.H.A., Lexington Avenue, New York
1944	Black Mountain College, Beria, North Carolina
	The Dance, at the *1st Annual Arts Forum,* Women's College, University of North Carolina, Greensboro
1945	Jewish Community Center, Detroit
	Modern American Dance, Museum of Modern Art, New York (travelled to the United Nations Conference, San Francisco, then toured Latin America)
1946	University of Redlands, California
	University of Minnesota, Minneapolis
	University of Wisconsin, Madison
	Dance Photographs, at the *World Youth Festival,* Prague
1952	*Summer's Children,* Bankers Federal Savings and Loan, New York
	Summer's Children, New York Public Library
1955	*Summer's Children,* International Museum of Photography, George Eastman House, Rochester, New York
1956	*Summer's Children,* Kodak Center, Grand Central Terminal, New York
1957	Parents' Magazine Gallery, New York
1959	*Dance Photographs,* at the *12th American Dance Festival,* Connecticut College, New London
1962	Arizona State University, Tempe
1964	International Museum of Photography, George Eastman House, Rochester, New York
	Société Française de Photographie, Paris
1965	Briarcliff Public Library, Briarcliff Manor, New York
	Carnegie Institute of Technology, Pittsburgh
	Paintings and Photographs, Ceejee Galleries, Los Angeles
	Center for Photographic Studies, University of Louisville, Kentucky
1969	Long Island University, Brooklyn Center, New York
	Spectrun 2, Witkin Gallery, New York (with Naomi Savage and Nancy Sirkis)
1970	*Barbara Morgan: Women, Cameras and Images IV,* Smithsonian Institution, Washington, D.C.
	Friends of Photography Gallery, Carmel, California
1971	831 Gallery, Birmingham, Michigan
	Montclair Art Museum, New Jersey
	Phoenix Evening College, Arizona
	Utah State University, Logan
1972	Amon Carter Museum, Fort Worth, Texas
	Focus Gallery, San Francisco
	Museum of Modern Art, New York
	Ohio Silver Gallery, Los Angeles
1973	Pasadena Art Museum, California
1974	Institute of American Indian Art, Santa Fe, New Mexico
1977	Gallery, Hastings-on-Hudson, New York
	Marquette University, Milwaukee, Wisconsin
	University of Nebraska, Lincoln
1979	Ohio University College of Fine Art, Athens, Ohio
	Photomontages, International Museum of Photography, George Eastman House, Rochester, New York
	Baldwin Street Gallery, Toronto
1980	Vision Gallery, Toronto
	Photomontages et Danses, Galerie Zabriskie, Paris
1981	Ikona Photo Gallery, Venice, Italy
	Jeffrey Fuller Gallery, Philadelphia, Pennsylvania
	Kathleen Ewing Gallery, Washington, D.C.
	Zabriskie Gallery, Paris, France
	Jane Corkin Gallery, Toronto, Ontario
	Bruce Museum, Greenwich, Connecticut
	Daniel Wolf Gallery, New York
1982	Arizona State University, Tempe, Arizona

1983   Catskill Center for Photography, Woodstock, New York
        Syracuse University, New York
1984   Queensborough Community College, New York
        Hudson River Museum, Yonkers, New York
1985   University of Oregon, Eugene, Oregon
        Chrysler Museum, Norfolk, Virginia
1986   Philadelphia Museum of Art, Pennsylvania
        Atlanta Ballet Co., Atlanta, Georgia
1988   Marquette University, Milwaukee, Wisconsin
1993   Laurence Miller Gallery, New York

Selected Group Exhibitions:

1938   *International Photographic Exhibition,* Grand Central Palace,
        New York
1944   *A Century of Photography,* Museum of Modern Art, New York
1948   *This Is the Photo League,* Photo League, New York
1954   *This Is the American Earth,* California Academy of Science
        and the Sierra Club, San Francisco (toured the United States)
1955   *The Family of Man,* Museum of Modern Art, New York (and
        world tour)
1960   *Photography in the Fine Arts,* Metropolitan Museum of Art,
        New York
1967   *Photography in the 20th Century,* National Gallery of Canada,
        Ottawa (toured Canada and the United States, 1967-73)
1970   *Be-Ing Without Clothes,* Hayden Gallery, Massachusetts
        Institute of Technology, Cambridge (toured the United
        States)
1979   *Fleeting Gestures: Dance Photographs,* International Center of
        Photography, New York (travelled to the Photographers'
        Gallery, London, and Venezia '79)
1983   *Figure della danza,* Teatro R. Valli, Reggio Emilia, Italy
        Arboratum, University of Colorado, Denver, Colorado
1984   *American Dance Festival,* Duke Art Museum, Durham, North
        Carolina
1985   Aldrich Museum of Contemporary Art, Ridgefield, Connecticut
1986   University of Oregon Museum of Art, Eugene, Oregon
        Port of History Museum, Philadelphia, Pennsylvania
1987   *La Danza Moderna Di Martha Graham,* Teatro Municipale,
        Valli Di Reggio, Emilia, Italy

Collections:

Museum of Modern Art, New York; Metropolitan Museum of Art, New York; International Museum of Photography, George Eastman House, Rochester, New York; Addison Gallery, Andover, Massachusetts; Massachusetts Institute of Technology, Cambridge; Philadelphia Museum of Art; Princeton University, New Jersey; Smithsonian Institution, Washington, D.C.; Library of Congress, Washington, D.C.; Exchange National Bank, Chicago; Amon Carter Museum, Fort Worth, Texas; Bennington College Library, Bennington, Vermont; Detroit Public Library, Detroit, Michigan; Hudson River Museum, Yonkers, New York; Lincoln Center Library and Museum of Performing Arts, New York, NY; Marquette University, Haggerty Museum of Art, Milwaukee, Wisconsin; National Gallery of Canada, Ottawa; National Portrait Gallery, Washington, DC; New Orleans Museum, New Orleans, Louisiana; Phoenix College, Phoenix, Arizona; Rochester Institute of Technology, Rochester, New York; Santa Barbara Museum of Art, Santa Barbara, California; State University of New York, College at Purchase Neuberger Museum, New York; University of California at Los Angeles Library, Los Angeles; University of Colorado, Denver, Colorado; Utah State University Galleries, Logan, Utah; Wesleyan University, Davison Art Center, Middletown, Connecticut.

Publications:

By MORGAN: Books—*Martha Graham: Sixteen Dances in Photographs,* New York 1941, 1980; *Prestini's Art in Wood,* with text by Edgar Kaufmann Jr., Lake Forest, Illinois 1950; *Summer's Children: A Photographic Cycle of Life at Camp,* New York 1951; picture editor and designer of *The World of Albert Schweitzer* by Erica Anderson and Eugene Exman, New York 1955; *Barbara Morgan* (*Aperture* monograph), edited by Minor White, Millerton,

New York 1964; *Barbara Morgan,* with an introduction by Peter C. Bunnell, New York 1972; *Barbara Morgan Dance Portfolio,* 10 photos, New York 1977; *Barbara Morgan: Photomontage,* with an introduction by Marianne Margolis, New York 1980. **Articles**—"Photomontage" in *Miniature Camera Work,* New York 1938; "In Focus: Photography, The Youngest Visual Art" in *Magazine of Art* (New York), November 1942; "Modern Dance" in *Popular Photography* (New York), June 1945; "Photographing the Dance" in *Graphic Graflex Photography* by Willard D. Morgan and Henry M. Lester, New York 1952; "Kinetic Designs in Photography" in *Aperture* (Millerton, New York), no. 4, 1953; "Aspects of Photographic Interpretation" in *General Semantics Bulletin* (Lakeville, Connecticut), nos. 30 and 31, 1963, 1964; "Abstraction in Photography," "Dance Photography" and "Photomontage" in *Encyclopedia of Photography,* New York 1963, 1964; "My Creative Experience with Photomontage" in *Image* (Rochester, New York), nos. 5-6, 1971; interview in the *New York Times,* 19 June 1975.

On MORGAN: Books—*The History of Photography from 1939 to the Present Day* by Beaumont Newhall, New York 1949, 1964; *25 Years of American Dance,* edited by Doris Hering, New York 1954; *Photography in the 20th Century* by Nathan Lyons, New York 1967; *Photography in America,* edited by Robert Doty, with an introduction by Minor White, New York and London 1974; *The Magic Image* by Cecil Beaton and Gail Buckland, London and Boston 1975; *Photographs: Shelton Memorial Art Gallery Collection, University of Nebraska,* with an introduction by Norman A. Geske, Lincoln, Nebraska 1977; *Geschichte der Fotografie im 20. Jahrhundert/Photography in the 20th Century* by Petr Tausk, Cologne 1977, London 1980; *Amerika Fotografie 1920-1940* by Erika Billeter, Berne 1979; *Recollections: 10 Women of Photography,* edited by Margaretta K. Mitchell, New York 1979; *Visions and Images: American Photographers on Photography,* edited by Barbaralee Diamonstein, New York 1981; *Figure della danza/Visions of the Dance 1859-1982,* exhibition catalogue, by C. Traub, R. Silverman and G. Ackerman, Reggio Emilia, Italy 1983. **Articles**—"Barbara Morgan: Painter Turned Photographer" by Etna M. Kelley in *Photography* (New York), September 1938; "Book Review: Summer's Children" by Berenice Abbott in *American Photography* (New York), November 1951; "Great American Photographers: Barbara Morgan" by Fritz Neugass in *Camera* (Lucerne), February 1952; "Barbara Morgan" in *Encyclopedia of Photography,* volume 13, New York 1964; special issue of *Aperture* (Millerton, New York), no. 1, 1964; "Die vielen Geschichten der Barbara Morgan" by Fritz Neugass in *Foto Magazin* (Munich), July 1965; "Barbara Morgan: Permanence Through Perseverance" by Jacob Deschin in *Photography Annual,* New York 1971; "Barbara Morgan: One of America's Great Photographers Reflects a Decade of Dance 1935-1945" by Doris Hering in *Dance Magazine* (New York), July 1971; "Barbara Morgan: Fotografe Tussen Twee Wereldoorlogen" by Jan Coppens in *Foto* (Amsterdam), July 1972; "Barbara Morgan" by Ruth Spencer in *British Journal of Photography* (London), 13 June 1975; "All The Atoms are Dancing" by Deborah Panier in *Washington Calendar Magazine,* 1976; "Barbara Morgan" by Casy Allen in *Camera 35,* May, 1977; "The Essence of Dance" by Diane Loercher in *Christian Science Monitor,* 18 September, 1978; "Taccuino Americano: Barbara Morgan" by Alberto A Salbitani in *Progresso Fotographico,* 1978.

*

Basic to all the themes of my photographs, photomontage, dance, light drawings, people and nature, is my deep interest in expressing life forces of rhythmic vitality. My interest in photomontage comes basically from a philosophical interest in making metaphor comparisons: a fossil or a shell against the forms of the city. Since I was originally a painter and primarily interested in abstraction, the use of visual metaphors in photomontage is one of my primary expressive urges. Photomontage allows me to express the complexity of today's world, its multiplicity and diversity.

The dance photographs were inspired originally by having experienced Southwest Indian rituals during three summers of exploration; their use of dance to unify the people with the life forces, and not merely as entertainment, was a major influence. I saw in Martha Graham's dances a similar interest in the Southwest Indian experiences. This mutual interest between Martha Graham and myself inspired me to do a book of photographs on her dances.

In doing people, I think of them in terms of their relation to today's world, and not merely as individuals. My photographs of people express a concern with human values in our mechanical world. I sometimes find ironic comparisons.

The photographs of children are primarily from a period in my own life when my own children were growing up. Experience of this period inspired my book of photographs, *Summer's Children*.

I see the photographs of nature as metaphors of cosmic dances: the corn leaf, for example, exhibits in rhythmic metre nature's life force.

All of my photographs represent a search for the invisible energies of life. I try to express these inner life forces through the exterior visual forms.

—Barbara Morgan

*   *   *

Five decades of Barbara Morgan's photography demonstrate an unusual versatility, vitality, and richness. With her formal training in painting and design and her later involvement in Asian and Native American thought, her career in photography is one of definite choice, dedication, and an attempt to delineate the magic and mystery of the mind, spirit, and nature. Her photography is an interpretative expression, and in this respect she shows a remarkable independence and originality when compared with other American photographers of the 1930s and '40s.

Inspired by her "whimsical-philosophical" father's idea of "dancing atoms," by her photohistorian husband, Willard Morgan, and by the metaphoric nature of poetry, Morgan's primary concerns in photography have not been formalistic, but symbolic, psychic, and ideational. One may say, she is not a radical experimenter or a towering pioneer. The dynamics of her art work on a different level. Her portraits, light drawings, straight photographs of nature and man-made objects, photomontages, and dance images display an ordering of "material facts raised to imagination," teasing the viewer to thought and reflection. To this chemistry she adds a distinct quality of playfulness, irony, and humor. This gives her imagery—"unforced meditation," to borrow her words—a genuine sense of human concern and value.

Take for instance, the images entitled, "Pure Energy and Neurotic Man," "Hearst over the People," "City Shell," or "Leaf Floating in City." In the first image the abstract light drawing juxtaposed by a grabbing forked hand in the upper right-hand corner of the dark background is a startling patterning of irony, lyricism, and realism. Morgan's social conscience and concern for mankind—a powerful component in almost all of her photomontages—are acutely felt in the "Hearst" image, where the irony is most devastating. "City Shell"—a superb photographic composition with spots of light faintly glimmering in the upper-half dark area of the frame, the lighted shell with four shadowed walking figures on it, and the geometric balance of a half-slanted skyscraper—is a poignant image potent with physical and psychological force. The visual dynamics in "Leaf Floating" are at once lyrical, symbolic, and ironic, a white transparent maple-leaf magnifying, as it were, the skyscraper-jungle of the modern urban habitation. The tiny lighted windows give an eerie feeling of emptiness and blindness rather than of dwelling and looking out.

Though they are not her original invention, Morgan's photomontages carry the emphatic signature of the artist, and certainly constitute, next to the dance images, her most significant contribution to photography. She remarks that they allow her to express "the complexity of today's world;" they grow out of a "philosophical" urge, and are "visual metaphors—metaphoric comparisons." The photomontages are striking for their technical mastery—the keen way the ultimate image has been composed and constructed, the way time and space have been combined and encapsulated. More importantly, they are enduring for their inherent meaning—layers of meanings: social, poilitical, moral, and philosophical—her "vision of the human condition, of human awareness," be it "Spring On Madison Square," "Saeta: Ice on Window," or "Wild-Bee Honeycomb Skyscraper."

When we turn to her images like "Corn Stalks Growing," "Briarlock," "Emerging," or "Martha Graham: Lamentation," we find the same competence and inventiveness fusing elements of whimsy, spiritual metaphors, and human awareness. "Corn Stalks Growing" generates sensations of pure lyricism and whimsy and a kind of "rhythmic vitality" also felt in "Beech

Tree II," "Corn Stalk," and "Corn Leaf Rhythm." "Lamentation" is an absorbing double-image of spiritual and psychic metamorphosis. "City Sound," "Resurrection in The Junkyard," and "Fossil in Formation" convey Morgan's sense of the fantastic and the literal as well as her purposefulness and metaphoric intent. In almost all her photographs, there is authenticity, personal integrity, and simplification of the form so that the subject of her photography does not lose its own vitality and reality in the process of metaphoric suggestion.

Morgan's simplification of form and respect for the subject can be witnessed in her portraits of Sheeler, Le Corbusier, in "Lloyd's Head," "Amaryllis Bud," "Willard's First," and "The Stump" as well as in the pictures in *Summer's Children*. One cannot but perceive her particular vision of life, nature, harmony, and significance. Willard's fist jutting out from the left-hand corner of the picture is a fist at the head of a robust hairy hand; but, it is also a picture of a definite sensation and emotion. Lloyd's dark statuesque head from the back, with the left ear and contour of left cheek showing, goes beyond being just a head propped on a neck. It suggests a process, as do the two amaryllis photographs. In the same way, the photographs of children in a summer-camp are a poetic portrayal of experience and process. What totally undercuts any trace of didacticism in her work is her "whimsicality," her sense of cosmic interrelatedness, and human signification inherent in what she sees, feels, and composes. Her abstract light drawings partake of this vision as fully as do her stunning dance photographs and the photographs in *Summer's Children*, which is not a linear documentation of events, but a subtle evocation of feelings, processes, and experiences.

In the best of her abstract light drawings, such as "Samadhi," "Emanations" and "Cadenza," Morgan's playful imagination creates moments of essentialized feeling and experience. The form, movement, and color—white against black—in these images are indeed, to use her own words, "ecstatic gestures" conveying vitality, harmony, and stillness.

"Except for the point, the still point," writes T.S. Eliot in *Four Quartets*, "there would be no dance, and there is only the dance." Barbara Morgan's dance photographs constitute a visualization of Eliot's thought. The intriguing fact is that in all the different kinds of photographs taken at various points in her career—of a stump, part of a leg, a light drawing, a photomontage composed of discordant and startling elements, or a dance gesture—a sense of awareness and harmony dominates. There is always economy and selectivity—the crystallization of the physical and psychological moment—in these photographs. If her photomontage is prompted by, what she calls, "simultaneous-intake, multiple-awareness, and synthesized-comprehension" inevitable to our Space Age, her dance photographs evoke the feeling and experience our age needs urgently.

Unquestionably, Morgan's dance photographs, started in the 1930s, are extraordinary expressions of those "invisible . . . inner life forces" that all of her photographs endeavour to communicate. They also signify a kind of ritualistic kinetics—dramas of mobility in immobility and immobility in mobility. Isolated gestures and motifs, forms and movements are caught with such vitality and rigour, such austerity and richness, that they inspire a profound realization. She has explained her working method as "previsualization"—emptying mind and allowing the "memorable gestures which inspired the idea to replay," and, thus, attuning oneself to "essentials." This process not only empowers Morgan with a perfect sense of timing, space, light, and an awareness of the most ecstatic and heightened moment of a gesture, but enables her to recreate the moment with a sense of transcendence, for example in "Letter to the World," "Extasis," "Deep Song," "El Penitente," and "Lamentation." The unique feature in these dance-photographs is that the human body and the gesture are so vitally heightened and realized. No part of the body is made into an abstraction or etherealized; on the contrary, it is treated with such eloquence and intensity that hands, feet, necklines, fingers, even veins contribute totally to the climactic experience. Then, there are the folds of the costumes, as in "Imperial Gesture" or "Lamentation" series. Morgan's "Kick," "Swirl," "Chaconne," "El Flagellante," "Torso," "Totem Ancestor," and "War Theme" are but a few of the most powerful and unforgettable examples of "spiritual and esthetic unification." This is the culminating experience—the moment when Barbara Morgan helps us to realize the Yeatsian vision of the dance and dancer becoming one.

—Deba P. Patnaik

MORINAGA, Jun.

Nationality: Japanese. **Born:** Nagasaki City, 11 November 1937. **Education:** Attended a private high school, Ryukoku, Saga-City, 1953-56; studied photography, Nihon University, Tokyo, 1956-60; assistant to W. Eugene Smith, Tokyo, 1961-62. **Family:** Married Yoko Kimura in 1975; daughter: Mayumi. **Career:** Worked as commercial photographer, for Toppan Printing Company, Tokyo, 1963-68; independent photographer, establishing own studio, Shibuya-ku, Tokyo, since 1969. Lecturer, Photography Department, Nihon University, Tokyo, 1970-71. **Recipient:** New Figure Prize, Japan Photo Critics Association, 1970; Japan Photo Association Prize, 1980. **Address:** (studio) 1306-GO, 16-16-5 chome, Sendagaya, Shibuya-ku, Tokyo, Japan.

Individual Exhibitions:

1969   *Moment Is Monument,* Nikon Salon, Tokyo
1971   *Original Prints 1960-71,* Shunju Gallery, Tokyo
1975   *On the Waves,* Nikon Salon, Tokyo
1978   *View of Japanese Cities,* Nikon Salon, Tokyo
1979   *River: Its Shadow of Shadows,* UNAC Salon, Tokyo
1981   *Original Prints,* Akagi Gallery, Fukuoka, Japan
1984   *View of Japanese Cities 2,* Nikon Salon, Tokyo
1988   *On the Waves 2,* Nikon Salon, Tokyo
1991   *Landscape—Water—Sky,* Nikon Salon, Tokyo

Selected Group Exhibitions:

1976   *Original Prints,* Ginza Gallery, Tokyo
1977   *Neue Photographie aus Japan,* Kulturhaus, Graz, Austria
          (travelled to the Museum des 20. Jahrhunderts, Vienna)
1979   *Japan: A Self-Portrait,* International Center of Photography, New York
1982   *38 Japanese Photographers,* Zeit-Foto Salon, Tokyo
1983   *Die Japanische Photographie,* Museum fur kunst unt Gewerbe, Hamburg
1988   PGI Gallery, Tokyo
1991   *Japanese Photography in the 1970s,* Tokyo Metropolitan Museum of Photography

Collections:

Photography Department, Nihon University, Tokyo; Photography Department, Kyushu-Sangyo University, Fukuoka, Japan, Kawasaki City Museum, Kawasaki; Tokyo Metropolitan Museum of Photography, Tokyo.

Publications:

By MORINAGA: Book—*River: Its Shadow of Shadows,* with an introduction by W. Eugene Smith, edited by Kazuhiko Motomura, Tokyo 1980.

On MORINAGA: Books—*Neue Fotografie aus Japan,* exhibition catalogue, by Otto Breicha, Graz and Vienna 1977; *38 Japanese Photographers,* exhibition catalogue, Tokyo 1982.

*   *   *

In 1980 Jun Morinaga published a book, *River: Its Shadow of Shadows,* of photographs selected from a series taken at the beginning of 1960: they show canals and other river-scapes in Tokyo. Although they depict images of river banks and water surfaces, for the most part these pictures are of the waters of pollution, for example, gutters and drains. Morinaga must have had some revolting experiences while taking these photographs, for most of them are in close-up.

Although the book is a photo-portrait of kinds of canals, there is something else present too: as we scan the photographs, we come to see an antiworld of decay and corruption. It is not unlike the cosmos as seen from a satellite. At the same time those strange objects floating in the water call to mind cancer cells, jarring us from time to time.

Having taken those photographs, Morinaga then had the opportunity to act as Eugene Smith's assistant when Smith came to Japan. Morinaga was very impressed with Smith's meticulous print work, and his own prints came to be more carefully composed. His attitude to the original print gave a lead to other Japanese photographers in the 1970s.

Morinaga has been tackling landscape and scenery by means of highly symbolic gestures, some of which have been shown in his one-person exhibitions and in magazine features.

It is reasonable to expect the unexpected from him in the future.

—Kineo Kuwabara

MORIYAMA, Daidoh.

Nationality: Japanese. **Born:** Osaka, 1938. **Education:** Studied design at the Municipal High School of Industrial Arts, Osaka; and studied photography under Takeji Iwayima, Osaka, and Eikoh Hosoe, Tokyo, 1960-63. **Career:** Worked as a graphic designer in Tokyo, 1958-63. Freelance photographer, Tokyo, since 1963. Member, Vivo group of photographers, Tokyo. **Recipient:** Most Promising Photographer Award, Japan Photography Critics Association, 1967. **Address:** 3-6-101 Yotsuya, Shinjuku-ku, Tokyo 160, Japan.

Individual Exhibitions:

1970   *Scandal,* Dick Plaza, Tokyo
1974   *Another Country,* Shimizu Gallery, Tokyo
1975   *Tono Monogatari,* Nikon Salon, Tokyo
1976   *Gosho Gawara,* Nikon Salon, Tokyo
1981   Zeit-Foto Salon, Tokyo
1990   *Moriyama Daido Photo Exhibition,* Zeit Photo Salon, Tokyo
1992   *Moriyama Daido: Works of the 1970s,* Il Tempo, Tokyo
1993   Lawrence Miller Gallery, New York
1994   Ruth Silverman Gallery, San Francisco

Selected Group Exhibitions:

1974   *New Japanese Photography,* Museum of Modern Art, New York
1977   *Neue Fotografie aus Japan,* Kulturhaus, Graz, Austria (travelled to the Museum des 20. Jahrhunderts, Vienna)
1979   *Japan: A Self-Portrait,* International Center of Photography, New York
1982   *38 Japanese Photograpers,* Zeit-Foto Salon, Tokyo
          Twentieth Century Photos from MOMA, Seibu Museum of Art, Tokyo
1985   *Black Sun,* Museum of Modern Art, Oxford (travelled to the Serpentine Gallery, London; Philadelphia Museum of Art, 1986)
1988   *Japanese Contemporary Photographers,* Prague
1989   *Internationale Foto-Triennale,* Esslingen, Germany
          Eleven Photographers 1965-1975, Yamaguchi Prefectural Museum of Art, Japan
          Orientalism, White Museum (World Design Expo '89)
1990   *Fotofest '90,* Houston, Texas, USA
          Foto Biennale Rotterdam '90, Rotterdam, Netherlands
          Tokyo, A City Perspective, Tokyo Metropolitan Museum of Photography, Tokyo
          The Past and Present of Photography, Museum of Modern Art, Tokyo
          Photography and Climatology, Miyagi Museum of Art, Japan
1991   *Beyond Japan,* Barbican Art Gallery, London
          Japanese Photography in the Memories Frozen in Time 1970s, Metropolitan Museum of Photography, Tokyo
1992   *Japanese Pop Art of the 1960s,* Fukui Art Museum, Japan

Untitled. Photograph by Daido Moriyama.

Collections:

National Museum of Modern Art, Tokyo; Museum of Modern Art, New York; International Center of Photography, New York.

Publications:

By MORIYAMA: Books—*Japan Photo Theatre I,* Tokyo 1968; *Goodbye Photography,* Tokyo 1972; *Document,* 6 vols., Tokyo 1972-; *Hunter,* Tokyo 1975; *Tono Monogatari,* Tokyo 1976; *Japan Photo Theatre II,* Tokyo 1978.

On MORIYAMA: Books—*New Japanese Photography,* exhibition catalogue, by John Szarkowski and Shoji Yamagishi, New York 1974; *Neue Fotografie aus Japan,* exhibition catalogue, by Otto Breicha, Ben Watanabe and John Szarkowski, Graz and Vienna 1977; *Japan: A Self-Portrait,* exhibition catalogue, by Shoji Yamagishi, Cornell Capa and Taeko Tomioka, New York 1979; *Nude Photographs of Japan,* with text by Shiroyasu Suzuki, Tokyo 1981; *Twentieth Century Photographs from the Museum of Modern Art,* exhibition catalogue, by John Szarkowski, Tokyo and New York 1982; *Moriyama Daido 1970-1979,* Sohkyu-sha 1989; *Lettre à St Lou,* Kawade Shobo Shin-sha, 1990; *Daido—Hysteric Glamour I,* 1993; *Moriyama Daido—Color,* Sohkyu-sha, 1993; *Daido—Hysteric Glamour II,* 1994. article—"Black Sun: The Eyes of Four," special issue of *Aperture* (Millerton, New York), no. 102, 1986.

* * *

Daidoh Moriyama is the leading exponent of an abrasive new wave of Japanese photography. By challenging accepted photographic conventions, he has moved very close to the chaotic pulse of Tokyo or Osaka, the cities in which he has lived. The form and order of traditional Japanese aesthetics have been discarded by Moriyama, in order to discover a new language of glaring juxtaposition. The strange associations of a dense, multi-layered, hybrid, urban life are his resources. He presents his pictures as disjointed images. They correspond accurately to the fragmented experience of the inhabitants of such a city. It is a dangerous course, for there is no logic, and the city itself contradicts all notions of what an outsider might understand as a "Japanese" quality.

Moriyama worked first as a graphic designer. He studied photography under Takeji Iwamiya in Osaka, then Eikoh Hosoe in Tokyo. Iwamiya is a master of the large format camera, and Hosoe is a meticulous craftsman. Moriyama, however, prints with a grainy, high contrast technique. He photographs from unpredictable angles, often placing his camera very close to his subject. He broke new ground in Japan when he first saw William Klein's "New York," "Moscow" and "Tokyo" series. Klein demonstrated new possibilities beyond previous ideas of form, but Moriyama moved his camera still closer to his subject, dispensing with impressions of scale. He would photograph a cabbage in the market on the same scale as he photographed a volcanic crater.

Tomatsu had opened up a new area of "subjective documentary" and was a great influence in Japan with the Vivo group in the early 1960s. Moriyama's work surfaced at the time when Japanese photography was ripe for a new appraisal outside Japan. In 1974 work from his early series "Japan Photo Theatre I" and "A Hunter" was exhibited together with Tomatsu's Nippon series at the *New Japanese Photography* exhibition at the Museum of Modern Art in New York. The "Nippon Theatre I" series concentrated on travelling actors, including backstage scenes, but produced some frightening associations. Moriyama photographed close to the frenzied mouth of an entertainer on stage, or printed the blurred image of an underground actress together with the sinister glance of a real beggar crawling on his knees. His approach was relentless and direct. In the "Hunter" series he focussed an entire frame on a prowling stray dog, or presented the image of a whore running over the garbage of a Yokosuka alley, a victim of the predatory city where Moriyama himself stalked with his camera.

In a later series "Another Country," his work played tricks of illusion between concrete, immediate reality and a bizarre, alien world, the surface of which his camera scanned without logic. A cow in a field appeared as neither beast nor monument; the roof of a temple was a flattened design next to the flower pattern of kimono cloth. In "Japan Photo Theatre II" all his imagery was derived from Tokyo. It is a dark, grainy, surreal world where the shop window dummy meets the crotch of the passerby, and a giant pig wanders an empty street. The final photograph is of the city lights glaring through a fading sky like a city of an inestimable future.

—Mark Holborn

MORRIS, Wright (Marion).

Nationality: American. **Born:** Central City, Nebraska, 6 January 1910. **Education:** Lakeview High School, Chicago, 1925-28; Crane College, Chicago, 1929-30; Pomona College, Claremont, California, 1930-33; self-taught in photography. **Family:** Married Mary Ellen Finfrock in 1934 (divorced, 1961); Josephine Kantor in 1961. **Career:** Writer and photographer, in California, 1934-38, in Middlebury, Connecticut, 1938-42, in California, 1942-43, in Bryn Mawr, Pennsylvania, 1943-58 and in Mill Valley, California, since 1962. Professor of Creative Writing, California State University, San Francisco, 1962-75; Distinguished Visiting Professor, University of Nebraska, Lincoln, 1975. **Recipient:** Guggenheim Fellowship, 1942, 1947, 1954; National Book Award, 1956; National Institute of Arts and Letters Award, 1960; Rockefeller Foundation Grant, 1967; Marie Sandoz Award, Nebraska Library Association, 1975; American Book Award, 1980; Kirsch Award, *Los Angeles Times,* 1981; Common Wealth Award, 1982; Whiting Award, 1985. Honorary Doctorate, Westminster College, Missouri, 1968; University of Nebraska, Lincoln, 1968; Pomona College, Claremont, California, 1973. Honorary Fellow, Modern Language Association, 1975; Senior Fellow, National Endowment for the Humanities, 1976. Member, National Institute of Arts and Letters, 1970; American Academy of Arts and Sciences, 1972. **Address:** 341 Laurel Way, Mill Valley, California 94941, U.S.A.

Individual Exhibitions:

1940	*The Inhabitants,* New School for Social Research, New York
1975	*Structures and Artifacts: Photographs 1933-54,* Sheldon Memorial Art Gallery, University of Nebraska, Lincoln (retrospective; toured the United States, 1975-80)
1976	Prakapas Gallery, New York
1977	Prakapas Gallery, New York
1979	*Matrix,* University of California at Berkeley
1980	Witkin Gallery, New York
1981	Witkin Gallery, New York
	Northlight Gallery, Tempe, Arizona (with Ralph Steiner)
1983	*Time Pieces,* Corcoran Gallery, Washington, D.C.
	Weston Gallery, Carmel, California (with James Alinder)

Selected Group Exhibitions:

1966	*The Photographer's Eye,* Museum of Modern Art, New York
1974	*Photography in America,* Whitney Museum, New York
1977	*Photographs: Sheldon Memorial Art Gallery Collection,* University of Nebraska, Lincoln

Collections:

Museum of Modern Art, New York; Boston Museum of Art; Sheldon Memorial Art Gallery, University of Nebraska, Lincoln; Houston Museum of Fine Arts; San Francisco Museum of Modern Art.

Publications:

By MORRIS: Books—*My Uncle Dudley* (novel), New York 1942; *The Man Who Was There* (novel), New York 1945; *The Inhabitants* (photo-text), New York 1946, 1972; *The Home Place* (photo-text), New York 1948, Lincoln, Nebraska 1968; *The World in the Attic* (novel), New York 1949; *Man and Boy* (novel), New York 1951, London 1952; *The Works of Love* (novel), New York 1952; *The Deep Sleep* (novel), New York 1953, London 1954; *The Huge*

Season (novel), New York 1954, London 1955; *The Field of Vision* (novel), New York 1956, London 1957; *Love Among the Cannibals* (novel), New York 1957, London 1958; *The Territory Ahead* (essays), New York 1958, London 1964; *Ceremony in Lone Tree* (novel), New York 1960, London 1961; *The Mississippi River Reader,* editor, New York 1962; *What a Way to Go* (novel), New York 1962; *Cause for Wonder* (novel), New York 1963; *One Day* (novel), New York 1965; *In Orbit* (novel), New York 1967; *A Bill of Rites, A Bill of Wrongs, A Bill of Goods* (essays), New York 1968; *God's Country and My People* (photo-text), New York 1968; *Wright Morris: A Reader,* with an introduction by Granville Hicks, New York 1970; *Green Grass, Blue Sky, White House* (short stories), Los Angeles 1970; *Fire Sermon* (novel), New York 1971; *Love Affair: A Venetian Journal* (photo-text), New York 1972; *War Games* (novel), Los Angeles 1972; *A Life* (novel), New York 1973; *Here Is Einbaum* (short stories), Los Angeles 1973; *About Fiction: Reverent Reflections on the Nature of Fiction with Irreverent Observations on Writers, Readers, and Other Abuses,* New York 1975; *The Cat's Meow* (short stories), Los Angeles 1975; *Real Losses, Imaginary Gains* (short stories), New York 1976; *The Fork River Space Project* (novel), New York 1977; *Conversations with Wright Morris: Critical Views and Responses,* edited by Robert E. Knoll, Lincoln, Nebraska 1977; *Earthly Delights, Unearthly Adornments: American Writers as Image Makers,* New York 1978; *Plains Song: For Female Voices* (novel), New York 1980; *Will's Boy,* New York 1981; *Wright Morris: Portfolio of Photographs,* Roslyn Heights, New York 1981; *Picture America,* with James Alinder, Boston 1982; *Photographs and Words,* edited by James Alinder, Carmel, California 1982; *The Writing of My Uncle Dudley,* Berkeley, California 1982; *The Origin of Sadness* (short story), University, Alabama 1984; *Solo: An American Dreamer in Europe 1933-34,* New York 1983, London 1984; *Time Pieces: Photographs and Words,* exhibition catalogue, Washington, D.C. 1983; *A Cloak of Light: Writing My Life,* New York 1985; *Collected Stories 1948-1986,* New York 1986.

On MORRIS: Books—*Wright Morris* by David Madden, New York 1965; *The Photographer's Eye* by John Szarkowski, New York 1966; *Wright Morris* by Leon Howard, Minneapolis 1968; *Quality: Its Image in the Arts,* edited by Louis Kronenberger, New York 1969; *Looking at Photographs* by John Szarkowski, New York 1973; *Photography in America,* edited by Robert Doty, with an introduction by Minor White, New York 1974; *Wright Morris: Structures and Artifacts: Photographs 1933-54,* exhibition catalogue, with texts by Norman A. Geske and Jim Alinder, Lincoln, Nebraska 1975; *Photographs: Sheldon Memorial Art Gallery Collection, University of Nebraska,* exhibition catalogue, with an introduction by Norman A. Geske, Lincoln, Nebraska 1977; *The Novels of Wright Morris: A Critical Interpretation* by G.P. Crump, Lincoln, Nebraska 1978 (includes bibliography); *Light Readings: A Photography Critic's Writings 1968-1978* by A.D. Coleman, New York 1979; *The Photograph Collector's Guide* by Lee D. Witkin and Barbara London, Boston and London 1979; *The Library of World Photography: Landscape,* with texts by David Plowden and Ian Jeffrey, Tokyo and London 1984. **Articles**—"Wright Morris: An Introduction and Photographic Chronology" by Jim Alinder in *Exposure* (New York), February 1976; "Wright Morris: You Can Go Home Again" by James Alinder in *Modern Photography* (New York), March 1978.

*

It is my feeling that the absence of people in my photographs enhances their presence in the structures and artifacts.

The people absent from the photographs are explicitly present in the text in my photo-text books, where verbal images enhance those that are visual.

—Wright Morris

* * *

In sensitive hands, the camera's optically accurate discerning qualities increase our willingness to accept the photograph as evidence and, too, as an object of creation, feeling and emotion.

The photographs of Wright Morris present structures and artifacts of earlier decades photographed in the 1930s, 40s and 50s. The visual organiza-

tion of his photographs is classic: Morris stands face-to-face with these objects. The results are clear, precise and well organized. The photographs inform us of facts and also move us emotionally. It is their intention to be works of art and they are.

Although Morris brought a camera for vacation snaps in 1933, his serious concern with photography began with his purchase of a Rolleiflex in 1935. He then began with a brief foray in the great pictorialist tradition with a series of cloud photographs, but, as the initial magic wore off, Morris shifted his visual concern to the less obviously romantic backyards and alleys of Pomona, California. His roots in Nebraska were also significant in his development, and they serve as well as subject matter for many of his later photographs.

Morris's growth as a photographer paralleled in time his development as a writer. While photography would like to lay first claim to Morris, his larger reputation rests on his pre-eminence as a novelist. Among his eighteen novels, for example, *The Field of Vision* received the National Book Award in 1956 and *Plains Song* won the American Book Award in 1980. His unique contribution to the history of photography lies in the combination of his words with his pictures on an equally powerful level.

In 1938, Morris moved to the East Coast and the auto trip proved a real eye-opener. "I saw the American landscape crowded with ruins I wanted to salvage. The Depression created a world of objects toward which I felt affectionate and possessive. I ran a high fever of enthusiasm and believed myself chosen to record this history before it was gone," he has said. Morris acquired a 31/4 x 41/4 in. view camera, and his photographic documentation of America's structures and artifacts resumed with vigor.

The next year, 1939, a critical creative leap occurred in his work. For some time he had been writing poetically dense prose paragraphs. Suddenly he realized the direct relationship between his writing and his photographs. The meaning of each was enhanced by the other, although the words never directly expained a photograph, nor vice versa. The visual and the written images were joined in the mind's eye. Work on the idea developed into a photo/text project called *The Inhabitants*. Further impetus came from a Guggenheim Fellowship in Photography granted to Morris in 1942 (the first had gone to Edward Weston in 1937). Work on *The Inhabitants* was completed and it was published in 1946.

In 1947, Morris received a second Guggenheim, enabling him to again extend the possibilities of the photo/text. For this work, titled *The Home Place,* Morris used a 4 x 5 in. view camera. The title refers to Morris's Nebraska. Beginning in 1942, Morris had stopped to talk and photograph in and around Chapman, Nebraska. Many of the conversations were with the town barber, Eddie Cahow, who had known Morris's mother and father. Through these Nebraska small-town experiences with lost relatives and old family friends, his roots became concrete and communicable. Previously, he says, "I had known little about my past except what I had conjured up in my fiction." The photographs from these sometimes extended visits are of the fabric of rural American life. *The Home Place* is a small, novel-sized volume rather than a large picture book like *The Inhabitants.* Also, it is designed with a continuous text, rather than having each photograph coupled with a paragraph of text as in *The Inhabitants.*

The Home Place was published in 1948; Morris continued to photograph in the 1950s but with less intensity as the demands of his career as a novelist dominated. Some two decades elapsed before he again combined words and pictures. In part because of the constant demand for *The Inhabitants* and *The Home Place,* which had long been out-of-print, and in part because he felt that time had put different perspectives on his writing, Morris created a new, largely autobiographical text to go with the earlier photographs. This third photo/text is titled *God's Country and My People:* it was published in 1968. While *God's Country* may prove to be the summation of Morris's statement, the previous photo/texts wear well. All three are currently available in reprints.

Each of the photographs makes a particular statement about the objects included within the frame and also a general statement about the ceaseless replacement of objects in our culture. While they have several levels of meaning, Morris's intention was not primarily social comment. In part, these artifacts become secular icons. Though people rarely make personal appearances in Morris photographs, their presence pervades all his work.

The photographs of Wright Morris present with formal elegance, precision and clarity an emotional and intellectual commitment to the commonplace, to the structures and artifacts of a time now disappeared. These pictures are the visible essence of that era, and they may begin to indicate to us what of the present needs to be salvaged.

—James Alinder

MOSES, Stefan.

Nationality: German. **Born:** Liegnitz, Silesia (now Legnica, Poland), 29 August 1928. **Education:** Studied photography, as apprentice to the photographer Grete Bodlee, in Breslau and Erfurt, Germany, 1945-47. **Career:** Theatre photographer, under Lothar Muthel and Hans Robert Bortfeldt, Nationaltheater and Kammerspiele, Weimar, 1947-50; photo-reporter, *Neue Zeitung* newspaper, Munich, 1950-51; freelance photographer, working for *Revue* and *Das Schonste* magazines, Munich, 1951-60; photographer, *Stern* magazine, in Munich, 1960-66. Since 1966, freelance photographer, working for *Stern, Geo, Art,* etc., in Munich. **Recipient:** Kodak Photo Book Prize, 1980. **Address:** Roemerstrasse 21, 8000 Munich 40, Germany.

Individual Exhibitions:

1980   Museum Folkwang, Essen, West Germany
1983   Center for Creative Photography, University of Arizona, Tucson

Selected Group Exhibitions:

1964   *World Exhibition of Photography: What Is Man?,* Pressehaus Stern, Hamburg (and world tour)
1966   *The Photographers's Eye,* Museum of Modern Art, New York
1968   *2nd World Exhibition of Photography: Woman,* Pressehaus Stern, Hamburg (and world tour)
1973   *3rd World Exhibition of Photography,* Pressehaus Stern, Hamburg (and world tour)
1975   *Gesellschaft Deutscher Lichtbildner 1975,* Haus Industrieform, Essen, West Germany
1979   *Deutsche Fotografie nach 1945,* Kunstverein, Kassel, West Germany
1983   *Die fotografische Sammlung,* Museum Folkwang, Essen, West Germany

Collections:

Museum Folkwang, Essen, West Germany; Stedelijk Museum, Amsterdam; Museum of Modern Art, New York; Center for Creative Photography, University of Arizona, Tucson

Publications:

By MOSES: Books—*Manuel,* Hamburg 1967; *Victor Vasarely; Planetary Folklore,* designed by Peter Wilhelm, Munich 1973; *Transsibirische Eisenbahn,* Munich 1979; *Frauen Schreiben,* with text by Jurgen Serke, Marburg, West Germany 1979; *München,* Amsterdam 1979; *Deutsche,* with introduction by Hans Georg Puttnies, Munich 1980; *Die kleine grosse Stadt—Tubingen,* with Joachim Feist, text by Walter and Inge Jens, Stuttgart 1981; *Flic Flac: Andre Heller, Stefan Moses, etcetera,* with text by Andre Heller, Munich 1981.

On MOSES: Books—*The Photographer's Eye* by John Szarkowski, New York 1966; *2. Weltausstellung der Photographie: Die Frau,* exhibition catalogue, edited by Karl Pawek, Hamburg 1968; *Gesellschaft Deutscher Lichtbildner 1975,* exhibition catalogue, by Bernd Lohse, Essen, West Germany 1975; *Bildner for Miljoner* by Rune Hassner, Stockholm 1977; *Deutsche Fotografie nach 1945/German Photography After 1945,* edited Petra Benteler, Floris Neususs and Wolfgang Kemp, Kassel, West Germany 1979; *Fotografie 1919-1979, Made in Germany: Die GDL-Fotografen* by W. Boje, F. Kempe, B. Lohse and others, Frankfurt 2979; *Museum Folkwang: Die fotografische*

Sammlung, exhibition catalogue, with introduction by Ute Eskildsen, Essen, West Germany 1983. **Articles**—"Stefan Moses: The Painter Hundertwasser" in *German Photography Annual,* Munich 1969.

*   *   *

Stefan Moses occupies a special place among the German photographers of the second half of the twentieth century. He is neither a photoreporter—although he has produced a great number of news reports and features—nor is he a so-called art photographer, even though he achieves highly artistic effects with the majority of his pictures. He is known—not without some justification—as a conceptual photographer. But this term too can be misleading, since Moses' photographic method has little in common with a conception of photography in the sense of Conceptual Art, which has left a decisive mark on the development of art since the seventies.

The difficulty of categorizing his work is, among other things, an important indication of Moses' position in the field of German post-war photography. This position can confidently be described as an advanced one, a position that breaks with the slick conventions of photography. Certainly, a number of Stefan Moses' innovations are today the common property of photography, but, far from appearing stale and timeworn, they have retained their freshness and immediacy.

Moses has a certain amount in common with his American colleague Philippe Halsman, a photographer whose significance, like Moses', has not yet been fully recognized. His preferred photographic subjects are people. But his pictures have always been much more than simply naive copies of human beings: Moses has always treated his subjects as actors and agents rather than as the passive victims of photographic practice. Such a procedure presupposes that the photographer has thought out for himself a systematic game-plan before setting his camera in motion. It is in the arrangement of this game-plan that Stefan Moses' decisive creation achievement lies; the rest is determined by technique, of which the photographer naturally has complete command. For one of his most famous series of portraits Moses positioned his models in front of a mirror and put the camera's self-timer in their hands: his own function was that of a quasi-director rather than of a cameraman. In this way he photographed his actors in the course of performance, slipping into the role of a reporter in order to use these same photographs for a different photographic project.

In a series of political portraits, Moses thwarted his models' attempt to appear before the camera in studied statesman-like poses by providing them with dumb-bells, which he had brought along with him, and asking them to do something with them.

His ideas spring from an ironic sense of humour. In the series entitled "Master and Hound," the photos display a startling similarity between the four-legged creatures and their adoring owners. But at the same time the photographer avoids making a joke at the cost of his subjects. In this way an awareness both of the possibilities but also of the limitations of photography runs through the whole of Stefan Moses' photographic work. Moses is an unusually scrupulous photographer, one to whom cynicism and insensitivity are completely foreign.

No photographic representation is able to capture the human personality in all its complexity: each attempt is only an approximation. This insight determines the photographic method of Stefan Moses, and to this extent his photographs are also pictures which reflect the problematic nature of photography as a medium. In short, they are advanced photographic pictures.

—Klaus Honnef

MUDFORD, Grant.

Nationality: Australian. **Born:** Sydney, New South Wales, 21 March 1944. **Education:** Studied architecture at the University of New South Wales, Sydney, 1963-64; self-taught in photography. **Career:** Freelance commercial photographer, in Sydney, 1965-74; also worked as a cinematographer on short films, Sydney; established studio, Los Angeles, 1977. Commercial assignments since 1983 include *House and Garden, Architectural Digest, Interiors,*

The Pike, **from** *Long Beach* **series, 1979-80.** Photograph by Grant Mudford.

Vanity Fair, Architectural Record, Progressive Architecture, Traveller, LA Style, Los Angeles Times, New York Times, Architecture, Los Angeles Magazine and Travel and Leisure. **Recipient:** Visual Arts Board Travel Grant, Australia Council for the Arts, 1974, 1977; Photography Fellowship, National Endowment for the Arts, 1980; Second Prize, Denison Award Exhibition, Sydney, Australia, 1985. **Agents:** Christine Abrahams Gallery, 27 Gipps Street, Richmond, Victoria 3121, Australia; and Rosamund Felsen Gallery, Bergamot Station B4, 2525 Michigan Avenue, Santa Monica, California, 90404, U.S.A. **Address:** 2260 Dundee Place, Los Angeles, California 90027, U.S.A.

Individual Exhibitions:

1972	Bonython Gallery, Sydney
1973	Realities Gallery, Melbourne
	Llewellyn Gallery, Adelaide
1976	Light Gallery, New York
1977	Australian Centre for Photography, Sydney
	Powell Street Gallery, Melbourne
	The Photographers' Gallery, London
	Light Gallery, New York

1979	Hirshhorn Museum and Sculpture Garden, Smithsonian Institution, Washington, D.C.
	Diane Brown Gallery, Washington, D.C.
	Rosamund Felsen Gallery, Los Angeles
	Light Gallery, New York
1983	Rosamund Felsen Gallery, Los Angeles
1984	University of California at Los Angeles
	Project No 46: Grant Mudford, Art Gallery of New South Wales, Sydney
1985	Christine Abrahams Gallery, Melbourne, Victoria
	Roslyn Oxley 9, Sydney, New South Wales
1986	Rosamund Felsen Gallery, Los Angeles
	Macquarie Galleries, Sydney, New South Wales
	Christine Abrahams Gallery, Melbourne, Victoria
	Michael Milburn Gallery, Brisbane, Queensland
1987	Macquarie Galleries, Sydney
	Christine Abrahams Gallery, Melbourne, Australia
1989	Barbara Mann Performing Arts Hall, Edison College, Fort Myers, Florida
	The Urban Monument: The Photographs of Grant Mudford, Southern California Institute of Architecture, Santa Monica

15 Portraits: Photographs, Rosamund Felsen Gallery, Los
 Angeles
1993   Rosamund Felsen Gallery, Los Angeles

Selected Group Exhibitions:

1974   *Aspects of Australian Photography,* Australian Centre for
         Photography, Sydney
1975   *The Land,* Victoria and Albert Museum, London
1976   *New Directions in American Landscape,* Silver Image Gallery,
         Tacoma, Washington
         Photographic Invitational, The Victorian College of the Arts
         Gallery, Melbourne, Australia
1978   *New York, New York,* Light Gallery, New York
1979   *Photographic Directions: Los Angeles 1979,* Security Pacific
         Bank, Los Angeles
         Industrial Sights, Whitney Museum of Art, New York
         Fotographie im Alltag Amerikas, Kunstgewerbemuseum, Zu-
         rich, Switzerland
1981   *Double Take,* International Center of Photography, New York
         1981 Biennial Exhibition, Whitney Museum of American Art,
         New York
1982   *L.A. As Subject Matter,* Los Angeles Center for Photographic
         Studies
         CSR Photography Project—Hunter Valley Coal, The Austra-
         lian Centre for Photography, Sydney, Australia
1983   *A Decade of Australian Photography 1972-82,* Australian
         National Gallery, Canberra
         Available Light, Museum of Contemporary Art, Los Angeles
1984   *La Photographie Créative,* Pavillon des Arts, Paris
         Los Angeles and the Palm Tree: Image of a City, Arco Center
         for Visual Art, Los Angeles
1985   *Images of Australian Buildings,* The Denison Building, Sydney,
         New South Wales
1986   Gallery Min, Tokyo
         The Architecture of Frank Gehry, Walker Art Center,
         Minneapolis (Travelling exhibition)
1988   *New Works on Paper,* Rosamund Felsen Gallery, Los Angeles
1990   *Past & Present—Selected Works by Gallery Artists,* Rosamund
         Felsen Gallery, Los Angeles
1991   *Photographing LA Architecture,* Turner/Krull Gallery, Los
         Angeles
1992   *Louis I Kahn: In the Realm of Architecture,* The Museum of
         Contemporary Art, Los Angeles (travelled to Philadelphia
         Museum of Art; Centre Georges Pompidou, Paris; The
         Museum of Modern Art, New York; The Museum of
         Modern Art, Gunma, Japan; The Museum of Contemporary
         Art, Los Angeles; Kimbell Art Museum, Fort Worth, Texas;
         Wexner Center for the Arts, Columbus, Ohio)
1993   *Not Painting,* The Museum of Contemporary Art, Los Angeles

Collections:

Australian National Gallery, Canberra; Phillip Morris Collection, Melbourne;
National Gallery of Victoria, Melbourne; Victoria and Albert Museum,
London; Museum of Modern Art, New York; International Museum of
Photography, George Eastman House, Rochester, New York; Library of
Congress, Washington, D.C.; Security Pacific Bank, Los Angeles; National
Museum of American Art, Washington, D.C.; Art Gallery of Tasmania,
Hobart; Australian National Gallery, Canberra, Australia; Horsham Art Gal-
lery, Victoria, Australia; Art Gallery of South Australia, Adelaide, Australia;
University of Louisville, Louisville, Kentucky; University of Alabama;
Bibliotheque Nationale, Paris; Art Gallery of New South Wales, Sydney,
Australia; Power Collection, Sydney University, Sydney, Australia; The
Museum of Contemporary Art, Los Angeles.

Publications:

By MUDFORD: Book—*Louis I Kahn: In the Realm of Architecture,* text by
David Brownlee and David G Delong, New York, 1991. **Articles**—''Grant

Mudford'' in *Inter/View* (New York), June 1979; ''Grant Mudford: interview,'' with Mark Hinderacker and Mark Johnson, in *Photofile* (Sydney),
Winter 1983; ''Mudford Proves His Art Can Stand Alone'' by Beatrice Faust
in *The Age,* (Melbourne), February 20, 1985; ''Interview with Max Fulcher''
in *Graphics,* (Sydney), July 1986; ''Interview with Ken Caldwell'' in *LA
Architect,* (Los Angeles), April, 1990.

On MUDFORD: Books—*New Photography Australia: A Selected Survey* by
Graham Howe, Sydney 1974; *The Land,* exhibition catalogue, edited by Mark
Haworth-Booth, London 1975; *Australian Photography,* edited by Laurence
Le Guay, Sydney 1976; *Collecting Photographs: A Guide to the New Art
Boom* by Landt and Lisl Dennis, New York 1977; *Australian Photography: A
Contemporary View,* edited by Laurence Le Guay, Sydney 1979; *Grant
Mudford: Photographs,* exhibition catalogue, by Charles Millard, Washing-
ton, D.C. 1979; *La Photographie Créative* by Jean-Claude Lemagny, Paris
1984; *Visual Instincts: Contemporary Australian Photography,* edited by Max
Pam, Canberra, 1989. **Articles**—''Grant Mudford'' in *Foto File* (New York),
Spring 1973; ''Grant Mudford'' in *The Observer* (London), 30 November
1975; ''Grant Mudford'' in *Creative Camera International Yearbook,* London
1976; ''Grant Mudford'' by Allan Moult in *Australian Camera and Cine*
(Sydney), February 1977; ''Grant Mudford—American Photos'' in *Creative
Camera* (London), April 1977; ''Technology Transformed'' by Nancy Ste-
vens in the *Village Voice* (New York), 23 May 1977; ''Unbeguiled in a
Wasteland Paradise'' in *LAICA Journal* (Los Angeles), October 1978; ''Grant
Mudford'' by Graham Howe and Jacqueline Markham in *Camera* (Lucerne),
April 1979; ''Grant Mudford and Capturing Ascetic Vision'' by Benjamin
Forgey in the *Washington Star,* 8 July 1979; ''Gallery—Grant Mudford'' by
Nancy Stevens in *American Photographer* (New York), September 1979; ''A
Tour of Los Angeles Galleries'' in the *New York Times,* 2 December 1979;
''Single Room, $3.20'' in *Art News* (New York), March 1980; ''Local Boy
Back with his Photographic Painting'' by Arthur McIntyre in *the Age*
(Melbourne), 11 December 1984; ''Picturing Our Elaborate Caves'' by Max
Dupain in *Sydney Morning Herald,* December, 1985.

*		*		*

After studying architecture in the mid-1960s, Grant Mudford became a
commercial photographer in his home town of Sydney, Australia. He soon
turned from advertising to pursue his increasing photographic interest in the
Australian ''outback'' and its rural architecture. It was here that his concerns
for spatial ambiguity and the plasticity of light developed. Mudford's convincingly disciplined photographs fulfill the expectation of compositional elegance, then dematerialize the rational geometry they suggest by challenging
preconceptions about objects represented photographically. These are not
simply sophisticated photographs of buildings, but of the conceptual abstraction advanced by the buildings' existence.

Each large size photograph is a planar arrangement of tone and texture
calmly asserting its perfect geometric alignment, achieved with perspective
correcting lenses and Mudford's point of view. The undetectable landscape
distortion begins the subtle interruption of how to read these pictures.
Mudford's vision describes a knowingly three-dimensional form in confounding, two-dimensional symbols. In ''Los Angeles,'' 1978, the perspective of a
receding wall above an arrow acts less as a dynamic moving through space
than as a flat, calligraphic organizing device like the painted-on arrow itself.
In ''New Orleans,'' 1975, the telephone wires are splayed slashes on a flat
field, losing their functional identity to the atmospheric condition existing
only in Mudford's world of rematerialized matter.

If we cannot be shown what we expect to see, our visual needs must be
satisfied by a unique condition that suspends our ready disbelief. At close
range this is the achievement of Mudford's highly granular surface—going
beyond emulsion on the paper's skin—which at once defines each object and
obliterates it. The success of a Mudford image is the integrity with which these
structures exist in their own rarified envelope of space, defining both the
surface shapes and the spatial atmosphere they become. When looking closely,
we are momentarily unsure if the subject is the film's enlarged granularity or
the mottled articulation of a stucco facade. After all, a photograph is not
''real'' in the sense of a painting's plasticity, not ''real'' in the aspect of
palpable sculpture; a photograph is only the paper on which it is printed.

And yet, any paper that could so masterfully exist between the tactility of
stucco and the expectation of its own enlarged photographic grain participates

in exploring the artist's distinct attitude toward materials and his medium. All things in the photograph exist, at some point, of the same atmospheric matter, constructivist ''tattoos'' where the pigmented forms and flesh are one; and it is Mudford's choice of shapes, meticulously organized and compulsively constructed, that contains this protoplasm in the discrete forms that explain their two-dimensional identity.

In ''Mex,'' 1976, the stucco wall corresponds tonally and texturally to the dirt of the ground, while the distant wall framed by the doorway seems made of sky. All surfaces and spaces seem made of the same protoplasmic ''stuff.'' The tonal quality of this pointillist grain spatially equates areas that are separate and distinct in the ''logical'' world. Negative and positive space frequently invert: sky and wall homogenize tonally, made more compelling by the two-dimensional structural containers that insist it is not so. For Mudford, both the paper and the architectural shapes give up their material identities and functional implications and become substance and surface transformed.

—Jacqueline Markham

MUKHIN, Igor.

Nationality: Russian. **Born:** Moscow, 19 November, 1961. **Education:** Educated in Moscow, until 1982; mainly self taught in photography. **Family:** Married Tanya Lieberman in 1991. **Career:** Worked for the photo agency RAPHO, Paris, 1988; member of the Photographer's Union of Russia since 1993. **Address:** ADC Art & Design Center, Bolshaya Ordinka 14, Moscow, Russia.

Individual Exhibitions:

1987	*One Man Show,* Moscow State University, USSR
1988	*One Man Show,* URALMASH Factory Club, Sverdlovsk, USSR
1989	*One Man Show,* Photo Gallery, Kujbushev, USSR
	One Man Show, Photo Reporters Club, Ukhta, USSR
1990	*One Man Show,* Photo Gallery, Leningrad, USSR
1993	*A Research into the Soviet Monumental Art,* Mary Photo Art Society Exhibition Hall, Yoshkar-Ola, Russia
	What Am I?—The Art of Making a Choice, Shkola Gallery, Union Gallery, Moscow
1994	*Benches: Transformation for the Future,* XL Gallery, Moscow

Selected Group Exhibitions:

1986	*Photo 86,* Malaya Gruzinskaya, Moscow
1987	*Photo 87,* Malaya Gruzinskaya, Moscow
1988	*Contemporary Soviet Photography,* Stockholm
1988-89	*Say Cheese! An Insight into Contemporary Soviet Photography 1968-1988,* Paris, San Diego, Chicago, Moscow
1989	*Russian Show,* Soho Photo Gallery, New York
	150 Years of Photography, Central Exhibition Hall (Manege), Moscow
	Exposition des photographes sovietiques, Theatre de Cherbourg, France
1990	*Looking East,* Image Gallery, Århus, Denmark
	Towards Culture and Recreation, Kashirka Gallery, Moscow
1991	*Changing Reality,* Corcoran Gallery of Art, Washington, USA
	Photo Manifesto, Museum of Contemporary Art, Baltimore, USA
	Photo Manifesto: Photography of Perestroika, Long Island University, Fine Arts Gallery, New York
	Russie—USSR 1914-1991, changements de regards, Paris
	10 x 10—Photo Forum, Zurich, Switzerland and Moscow
	Los Angeles International Art Fair, USA
1992	*Tokyo Art Expo,* Union Gallery, Japan
	Frankfurt International Art Fair, Union Gallery, Germany

	Aktuelle Zeichnung und Fotografie aus Moskau, Gallerie Albecht, Munich
	Litsa. Contemporary Portrait Photography from Russia, Byelorussia and Ukraine, Foundation CIRC, Amsterdam (travelled to other Dutch cities)
	Experiences Photographiques Russes, L'Atrium de Grand Ecran (Mois de la Photo à Paris)
	II International Photo Triennale, Esslingen, Germany
	Premiere Photographie, Galerie du Jour, Paris
1993	*A La Recherche du Pere,* Espace Photographique de Paris, Paris
	Basel Art 24, Basel, Switzerland
	Art MIF, Moscow International Art Fair, Central Exhibition Hall, Moscow
	New Territories of Art, State Museum of Arts, Krasnoyarsk, Russia
	Sixtinian Chapel, Teatro/Art Design Center, Moscow
	ART Hamburg-Eastern Art, Galerie Kicken, Hamburg, Germany
1994	*Art of Contemporary Photography—Russia, Ukraine, Belorus,* Central House of Artists, Moscow
	Who is Who: Celebrities of the New Russia, Central House of Actors, Moscow
	Le Sault dans le Vide, Central House of Artists, Moscow

Collections:

Museum of Contemporary Art, Moscow; Museum of Photographic Collections, Moscow; Victor Barsokevitch Museum, Kuopic, Finland; Pierce Roberts Gallery, San Francisco; J F Bizot, Paris; Michael Pauseback, Cologne; Bernhard Strathman, Hamburg.

Publications:

On MUKHIN: Books—*Seeing Things Differently/ The New Soviet Photography,* Sn-Kirjat Oy, Helsinki, 1988; *Photo Manifesto. Contemporary Photography in the USSR,* New York, 1991; *Changing Reality. Recent Soviet Photography* by Leah Bendavid-Val, Washington DC, 1991; *Mosca la citta del Maestro e diari inediti,* Rome, 1991; *Litsa. Contemporary Portrait Photography from Russia, Belorussia and Ukraine,* Amsterdam, 1992. **Article**—*The Washington Post,* May 1, 1991.

*   *   *

Igor Mukhin stands among the leading Russian photographers. His amateur activities brought him to the Hermitage Association in 1987. This was the first legal institution for contemporary art in the USSR. A first series of portraits of Soviet Artists made Mukhin popular, and was published in magazines throughout the world. His development was influenced by the radical changes in Soviet economic and social life known as perestroika. Mukhin has done several series of portraits of artists and rock and pop musicians as well as scenes of bohemian and demi-monde life, opening this world to the general public.

During the years of perestroika and until recently Mukhin has mainly concentrated his photography on exploring and documenting the cultural signs of the fallen Soviet epoch. Travelling across Russia he took powerful shots of thousands of monuments and architectural landmarks. His studies resulted in several series, *Monuments, Fragments of the Monuments, Kremlin* and *Benches,* which have been successfully exhibited, bringing him positive critical appraisal. His images of recent history have become an invaluable documentary of the vanishing yet nostalgic culture and art works of self-sufficient poetic significance.

Recently, Mukhin has switched from pure photography to actual contemporary art, using his ''monumental'' series as a means of developing various projects and installations. The latest works, organised with support from XL Gallery, undertake serious study of the problems of Soviet cultural heritage, with comparative analysis of the paintings of the Socialist realism style and his own photographic vision of the subject. Thus remarkable photographic chronicles of the former culture assume a new quality, bringing Mukhin to the avant garde of modern Russian photography.

—Elena Selina

MÜLLER-POHLE, Andreas.

Nationality: German. **Born:** Braunschweig, 19 July 1951. **Education:** Herder School, Kassel, 1962-70; studied economics and communications at University of Hannover, 1973-74, and University of Göttingen, 1974-79. **Family:** Married Brigitte Schadwinkel in 1979. **Career:** Independent photographer, Göttingen, since 1974. Founder-Editor of *European Photography,* Göttingen, since 1980. **Address:** Kurt-Schumacher-Weg 18a, D-37075 Göttingen, Germany.

Individual Exhibitions:

1978	Galerie Trockenpresse, Berlin
	Galerie Krebaum, Weinheim, Germany
1979	Art Studio, Cologne
	Work Gallery, Zurich
1981	Galerie Remus, Dusseldorf
	Galerie Renner, Munich
	Galerie Novum, Hannover
	Larry Fink/Andreas Müller-Pohle/Michael Schmidt, Kunstmuseum, Dusseldorf
1982	Galerie Foto Art, Frankfurt
	Benteler Galleries, Houston, Texas
	Galerie Pro Photo, Nuremberg, Germany
1983	Galerie Perspektief, Rotterdam
	Camera Obscura Gallery, Stockholm
	Galerie Studio 666, Paris
1984	Casa do Infante, Porto, Portugal
1985	Fotoforum Bremen, Germany
	Photo-Galerie 52, Luxembourg
	Galerie Jutta Rössner, Stuttgart
1986	Galleria Agorà, Turin, Italy
	Hasselblad Gallery, Göteborg, Sweden
	Galerie Foto Medium Art, Wroclaw, Poland
	Funarte, Rio de Janeiro
	Museu da Imagem e do Som, São Paulo
1987	Espai F, Granollers, Spain
	Marburger Kunstverein, Marburg
	Galeria Fotografii Elementarnej, Ladek Zdrój, Poland
1988	Círculo de Artes Plásticas, Coimbra
	Galerie Jutta Rössner, Stuttgart
1989	Galerie Stará radnice, Brno, Czechoslovakia
1991	Brandenburgische Kunstsammlungen, Cottbus
1992	Fotogalerie Wien, Vienna
1993	Galeria Documenta, São Paulo
	Centre de la Photographie, Geneva

Selected Group Exhibitions:

1978	*Fotografie im Künstlerhaus,* Künstlerhaus, Göttingen, Germany
1980	*Vorstellungen und Wirklichkeit: 7 Aspekte Subjektiver Fotografie,* Städtisches Museum Schloss Morsbroich, Leverkusen, Germany (travelled to the Künstlerhaus, Vienna; Fundació Joan Miró, Barcelona, 1980; and Palais des Beaux-Arts, Brussels, 1981)
1981	*New German Photography,* The Photographers' Gallery, London (travelled to Cardiff, Liverpool, Rochdale, Dublin and Bath)
	Extended Photography, 5th International Biennial, Wiener Secession, Vienna
1982	*European Photography,* Amicizia fra i Popoli, Rimini, Italy

	International Photographers, Eaton/Schoen Gallery, San Francisco
1983	*Photographie in Deutschland heute,* Provinciaal Museum voor Fotografie, Antwerp, Belgium (travelled to Ghent, Hasselt and Charleroi)
1984	*La Photographie Créative,* Pavillon des Arts, Paris
1985	*The European Edge,* Museum of Photographic Arts, San Diego, California
1986	*Fotografie: Abbildung? Einbildung?,* Museum am Ostwall, Dortmund
	Fotografia Elementarna, Galeria Sztuki Współczesnej, Szczecin, Poland
	Foco 86, Circulo de Bellas Artes, Madrid
	Himmelsschreiber, Kunstverein Kassel, Kassel
	Selections 3, Photokina, Cologne
1987	*Le temps d'un mouvement,* Centre National de la Photographie, Paris
	Fotografische Bilder, Deutscher Künstlerbund, Forum Böttcherstrasse, Bremen
1988	*Fotovision—Projekt Fotografie nach 150 Jahren,* Sprengel Museum, Hannover; Kunstraum im Messepalast, Vienna; Museum für Gestaltung, Zurich
1989	*Dokument und Erfindung—Fotografien aus der Bundesrepublik Deutschland 1945 bis heute,* Haus am Lützowplatz, Berlin; Augustinermuseum, Freiburg; Moore College of Art and Design, Philadelphia
	What is Photography? Mánes Gallery, Prague
	Das Foto als autonomes Bild—Experimentelle Gestaltung 1839-1989, Kunsthalle Bielefeld; Bayerische Akademie der Schönen Künste, Munich
	Weitblick—Aspekte einer Kunst mit Fotografie, Universitätsmuseum für Kunst und Kulturgeschichte, Marburg
	Intern—Extern, Galerieforum, Berufsverband Bildender, Künstler, Düsseldorf
1991	*O Coraçao da Ciência,* Centro de Estudos de Fotografia, Coimbra; Espace Photographique Contretype, Brussels
	Européens, Festival Photographique du Trégor, Centre Jean Savidan, Lannion, France
	The Persistence of Memory, Third Israeli Biennale of Photography, Mishkan Le'Omanut, Museum of Art, Ein Harod, Israel
1992	*L'Échappée européenne,* Mois de la Photo, Pavillon des Arts, Paris
	Première Photo, Galerie du Jour Agnès B., Paris
1993	*Deutsche Kunst mit Photographie: Die 90er Jahre,* Deutsches Architekturmuseum, Frankfurt/Main; Rheinisches Landesmuseum, Bonn
	Wiederbegegnung, Marburger Kunstverein
1994	*Photogramme—une pratique contemporaine,* Espace Photographique Contretype, Brussels
	Paysage de l'apparence, Mai de la Photo, Reims

Collections:

Museum für Kunst and Gewerbe, Hamburg; Polaroid Collection, Offenbach; Bibliothèque Nationale, Paris; Musée Cantini, Marseille, France; Sammlung Fotografis Länderbank, Vienna; Rijksuniversiteit te Leiden, Netherlands; Center for Creative Photography, University of Arizona, Tucson; San Francisco Museum of Modern Art; Institut Valencia d'Art Modern, Valencia, Spain; Maison Européenne de la Photographie, Paris; Brandenburgische Kunstsammlungen, Cottbus.

Publications:

By MÜLLER-POHLE: Books-*Dumont Foto 4: Fotografie in Europa heute,* editor, Cologne 1982; *Transformance,* Göttingen 1983; *Was ich nicht sehe, fotografiere ich. Was ich nicht fotografiere, sehe ich. Arbeiten 1976-1991,* Cottbus, 1991; *European Photography Award,* Göttingen 1991; *Andreas Müller-Pohle,* Signa, Vienna, 1992. **Articles—**"Was ist Fotografie?" in

Transformance 7876, **1982.** Photograph by Andreas Müller-Pohle.

Fotografie (Göttingen), no. 5, 1978; "Die Zweite Avantgarde der Fotografie" in *Fotografie* (Göttingen), no. 7, 1978; "Andreas Müller-Pohle: About Visual-Questioning," interview with Marco Misani, in *Printletter* (Zurich), no. 23, 1980; "Serie—Zyklus—Sequenz—Tableau" in *European Photography* (Göttingen), no. 1, 1980; "Uber das Licht: Aspekte einer fotografischen Lichtästhetik" in *Dumont Foto 2*, edited by Hugo Schöttle, Cologne 1980; "Visualismus" in *European Photography* (Göttingen), no. 3, 1980; "Project Photography" in *European Photography* (Göttingen), no. 13, 1983; "Information Strategies" in *European Photography* (Göttingen), no. 21, 1985; "Photography as Staging" in *European Photography*, Göttingen, no 34, 1988; "European Photography" in *ICI Photography Awards 1992*, National Museum of Photography, Film and Television, Bradford, 1992; "The Photographic Dimension" in *European Photography*, no 53, 1993.

On MÜLLER-POHLE: Books—*Vorstellungen und Wirklichkeit: 7 Aspekte Subjektiver Fotografie*, edited by Rolf Wedewer, Cologne 1980; *Die Geschichte der Fotografie im 20. Jahrhundert/History of Photography in the 20th Century* by Petr Tausk, Cologne 1977, London 1980; *Ist Fotografie Kunst? Gehört Fotografie ins Museum?*, edited by Erika Kiffl, Munich 1982; *Fotografia Europea Contemporanea*, edited by Giovanni Chiaramonte, Milan 1983; *La Photographie Créative* by Jean-Claude Lemagny, Paris 1984; *Photographers Encyclopædia International 1839 to the present*, Editions Camera Obscura, 1985; *L'Albufera—Visió Tangencial*, Valencia, 1985; *Selections 3*, Schaffhausen, 1986; *Photographie 1945-1985*, Hamburg 1987; *Bildgebende Fotografie* by Gottfried Jäger, Cologne, 1988; *Fotovision. Projekt Fotografie nach 150 Jahren*, Hannover, 1988; *Dokument und Erfindung—Fotografien aus der Bundesrepublik Deutschland 1945 bis heute*, Jörg Bostrőm, Berlin 1989; *Das Foto als autonomes Bild—Experimentelle Gestaltung 1839-1989*, Gottfried Jäger/ Jutta Hülsewig-Johnen, Stuttgart, 1989; *The Persistence of Memory*, ed. John Stathatos, 1991; *L'Échappée européenne*, Paris, 1992; *Première Photo*, Paris, 1992; *Deutsche Kunst mit Photographie: Die 90er Jahre*, Frankfurt, 1993. **Articles**—"Fotografie—ein gedanklicher Prozess" by Jörg Krichbaum in *Fotografie* (Göttingen), no. 6, 1978; *Photographie*, Schaffhausen no 1, 1979; *Printletter*, Zurich no 23, 1980; *Zoom*, Munich, no.12, 1979; *European Photography*, no 3, 1980; *Printletter*, Zurich no 28, 1980; *European Photography*, no 5, 1981; *Camera*, Lucerne, no 8, 1981; *Photovision*, no 8, Madrid, 1983; *Clichés*, Brussels, no 7, 1984; *Art*, Hamburg, no 7, 1984; *Perspektief*, Rotterdam, no 18/19, 1984; *Photographies*, Paris, no 7, 1985; *European Photography*, no 21, 1985; *Projekt*, Warsaw, no 169, 1986; *Ovo Magazine*, Montreal, nos 59-61, 1986; *European Photography*, no 40, 1989; *Fotografia*, Warsaw, no 51, 1989; *La Recherche Photographique*, Paris, no 11, 1991; *Art Press*, Paris, numero spécial 20 ans, 1992; *Images*, Geneva, no 2, 1993; *Eikon*, Vienna no 7/8, 1993.

*

What I can't see, I photograph. What I don't wish to photograph, I see.

—Andreas Müller-Pohle

*   *   *

Müller-Pohle's photographs are the result of a theoretical reflection. His theory of photography, as expressed in various writings and lectures, needs to be stated, before the pictures themselves are to be considered. There is nothing empirical, naive, about them, and if they seem to be the results of spontaneous motions, this is due to disciplined deliberation. The theory which sustains the photos may be resumed this way:

The camera is an apparatus which was programmed to make pictures. The photographer is expected to act within that program. If he does so, he will be making pictures of the outside world. That world reflects rays which the camera captures on sensitive surfaces, and the photographer who acts within the camera program will "document" the outside world as captured by the camera. But the photographer may refuse to act within the camera program. He may transfer his interest from the outside world toward the camera interior. He may concentrate upon what happens to the rays which come into the camera from the outside world. The pictures which such a photographer will produce will no longer "document" the outside world, but rather the camera program. They will render visible the hidden program, and they will thus whiten the black box. Such pictures are important, because the camera program which

they show is one among the many apparatus programs which are about to structure our perceptions, desires, feelings, our knowledges and our actions. In fact: such a photographer who refuses to go by the camera program is committed to showing the hidden programs of the emerging society of automatic apparatus.

In his book *Transformance* Andreas Müller-Pohle presents the result of such an effort to photograph the inside of the camera, instead of photographing the outside world. His strategy to escape from the camera program is deceptively simple. The camera prescribes a specific sequence of gestures for the photographer to execute: (1) take hold of the camera. (2) look through it toward the outside world. (3) choose one among the visions you have seen. (4) press upon the releaser. Müller-Pohle inverts this sequence thus: (1) take hold of the camera. (2) press upon the releaser. (3) look at the pictures that result. (4) choose one. What happens through this inversion is a true revolution of photographic vision. The outside world disappears from it. The freedom of choice is transferred from the decision to press upon the releaser toward the decision to select one among numerous pictures taken by chance. This freedom is exercised, not within the camera program, but after the camera function, and it acts upon the automatically produced pictures. And the criteria of choice are no longer imposed by the dubious relation between the picture and the outside world, but have become purely formal (esthetic).

If one looks upon the photos presented, one is impressed by their elegance and their "abstractness." The elegance is due to the photographer's criteria of choice: he has selected his photos from among a multitude of automatically produced pictures. Their "abstractness" is due to our difficulty to establish a link between them and the objects of the outside world: since the photos were taken blindly, they do not show the photographer's vision of the outside world, but they show what the moving camera does to the rays it captures. However, this elegance and abstractness of the photos should not divert the observer's attention from the basic message they carry. Which is this: It is possible to escape from the camera program. Left to itself, the camera will photograph blindly, by pure chance, absurdly, without any purpose. And man can then step in, and he can give a meaning to this absurd automatic function, by exercising his freedom of choice. Thus man may use chance as a strategy for freedom.

This is an important message. It goes far beyond the realm of photography, and it concerns a possible attitude in the face of every automatic apparatus. It suggests that freedom, in the immediate future, may not demand from us that we fight apparatus, but that we let it function blindly, and then choose from what the apparatus has produced. Andreas Müller-Pohle's photos say this, in effect: do not photograph as you are supposed to, but let the camera do it. You will then be free to select the pictures you prefer according to criteria which are yours, and not those imposed by the camera program. Andreas Müller-Pohle's photos are proclamations of freedom in the face of automatic apparatus.

—Vilém Flusser

MUÑOZ, Isabel

Nationality: Spanish. **Born:** Barcelona in 1951. **Agent:** Agence Vu, Paris. **Address:** Pajaritos 25, 28007 Madrid.

Individual Exhibitions:

1986	*Toques,* Institut Français, Madrid
1987	*América, América,* Asociación Cultural, Hispano Norteamericana, Madrid
1989	Galeria Spectrum, Zaragoza, Spain
	Primeros Encuentros de la Fotografia, Centro Cultural de Leganés, Madrid
1990	*Tango,* Galeria Jean-Pierre Lambert, Paris (travelled to Université Lumière-Lyon 2, Lyon, France; Fondation Nationale de la Photographie, Lyon, France; Luciegraphie, Strasbourg, France; Bibliothèque-Discothèque Municipal d' Argenteuil, Argenteuil, France; Ex-Convento de la Merced, Tarazona, Spain; Posada del Potro, Córdoba, Spain; Palacio de Revillagigedo, Gijón, Asturias, Spain; Centro Cultural

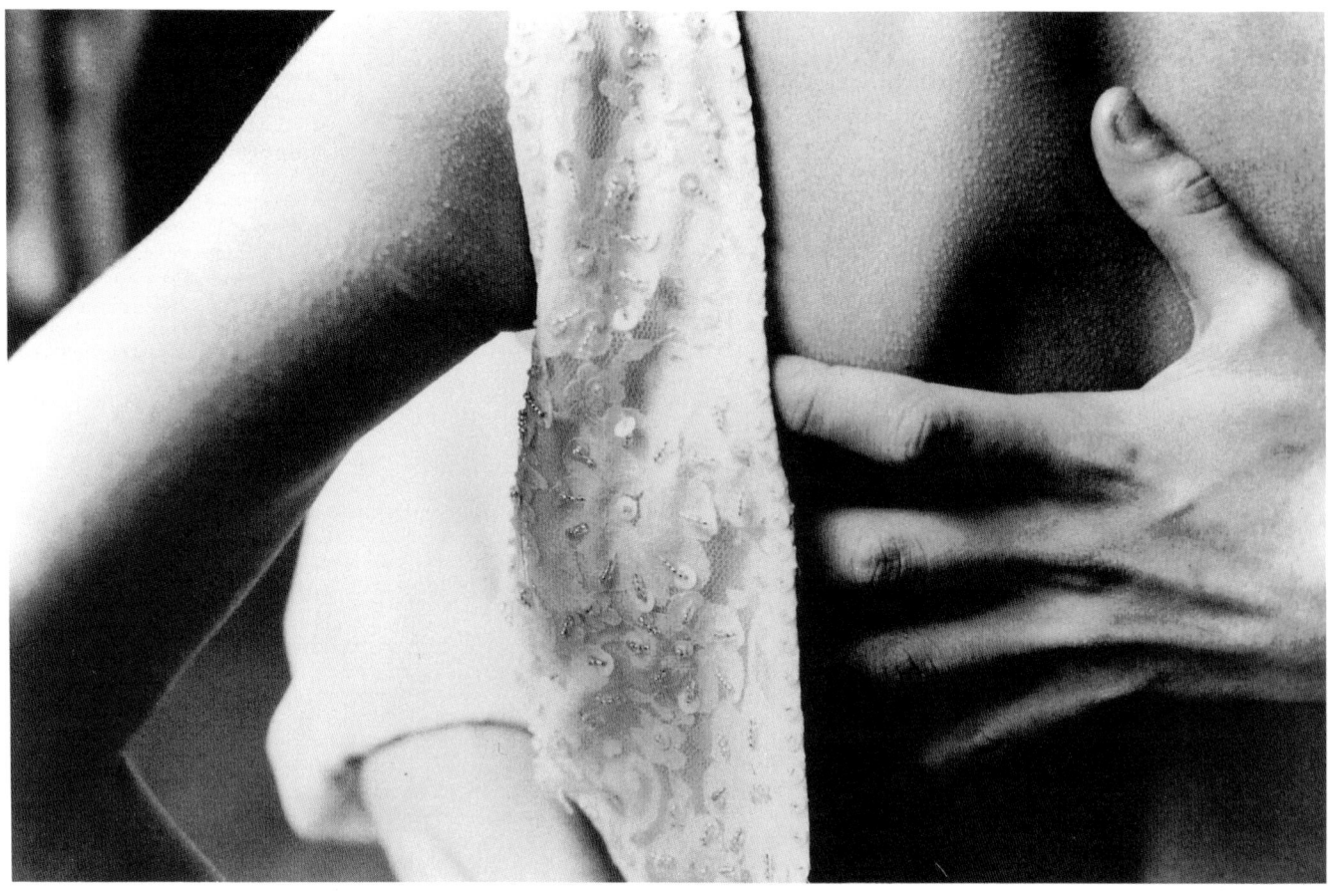

(T6A) Tango, **1993/94.** Photograph by Isabel Muñoz.

Gran Capitán, Ayuntamiento de Granada, Spain; Nouveau Theatre d'Angers, Angers, France; Scene Nationale de Bayonne et du Sud Aquitaine, Bayonne, France; Bunkamura Gallery, Tokyo; Centro Cultural Caleidoscopio, Madrid)

1992 *Flamenco,* Palacio de Revillagigedo, Gijón, Asturias, Spain; The Chrysler Museum, Norfolk, VA, USA; Scene Nationale de Bayonne et du Sud Aquitaine, Bayonne, France; Banque Credit Foncier, Paris; Banque Credit Foncier, Toulouse, France

1993 *Isabel Muñoz,* Ecole des Beaux-Arts, Nîmes, France
Isabel Muñoz, Fotografias, Antiguo Museo, Español de Arte Contemporáneo, Madrid

1994 *Les discours amoureux,* Maison des Jeunes de Saint-Gervais, Geneva, Switzerland
Tango, Centro Cultural Caleidoscopio, Madrid
Flamenco, Banque Credit Foncier, Marseille and Toulouse, France
Tango; Flamenco; Oriental, Julie Saul Gallery, New York

1995 *Tango,* Festival Photosynkria 95, Salonica, Greece

Selected Group Exhibitions:

1989 *Cuando uno y uno son más de dos,* Asociación, Cultural Hispano Norteamericana, Madrid

1991 *Seis propuestas fotográficas,* Galeria Anselmo Alvarez, Madrid

1992 *The Spanish vision: Contemporary art photography, 1970-1990,* The Spanish Institute, New York
Première Photographie, Galerie du Jour, Paris

1993 *Photography is the Medium—Spanish and Dutch Photography,* Enschede, Netherlands

1994 *Trans Europe-Art,* SNCF (travelled to Bordeaux, Grenoble, Lille, Lyon, Marseille, Montpellier, Nantes, Paris, Rennes, Strasbourg, Toulouse, Tours, France)
Autoretratos 93, Galeria Railowsky, Valencia, Spain
Mujeres 10 Fotorafas/50 retratos, TarazonaFoto, Zaragoza, Spain and Fundacion Arte y Tecnologia, Madrid
Entre la Pasion y el Silencio, 25 Rencontres Internationales de la Photographie, Arles, France
Tango, Ayuntamiento de Cordoba, Cordoba, Spain

1995 *10 x 90 = 90,* Galeria Railowsky, Valencia
Entre la Pasion y el Silencio, Palacio de Revillagigedo, Gijon, Spain
Trans Europe—Art, SNCF (Bordeaux, Grenoble, Lille, Lyon, Marseille, Montpellier, Nanters, Paris, Rennes, Strasbourg, Toulouse, Tours), France
Fotografia Española. Un paseo por los 90, Instituo Cervantes, Portugal (United Kingdom, France, Germany, Italy, Greece, Morocco, Tunis, Egypt, Jordan, Lebanon and Syria)

Collections:

Museum of Fine Arts, Houston, USA; Chrysler Museum, Norfolk, Virginia; Bibliothèque Nationale, Paris; Bunkamura Gallery, Tokyo; S.E.I.T.A., Paris; Palace Lumière, Lyon, France; Université Lumière-Lyon 2, Lyon, France; Caja de Ahorros de Asturias, Asturias, Spain.

Publications:

By MUÑOZ: Books—*Parade Nuptiale* (with Gérard Macé), France 1992; *Flamenco* (with Jacques Durand), Paris 1993; *Tango* (with Evelyne Pieiller),

Paris 1994. **Article**—"Madrid es una ciudad muy flamenca, muy taurina" in *El Pais*, 11 November 1993.

On MUÑOZ: Articles—"Isabel Muñoz Revelar a la antigua para crear fotografias en dos dimensiones" by Alfonso Armada in *El Pais*, November 1986; "Imágenes de albúmina, platino y oro" by Manuel Falcés in *El Pais*, 6 November 1987; "Todo lo que necesitas es amor" by Fernando Pacheco in *Panorama*, March 1989; "Parlez-moi de la photographie" by Brigitte Ollier in *Liberation*, 26 October 1990; "El Tango Arrastrado" by Alfonso Armada in *El Pais Semanal*, 4 November 1990; "La Cité des images" by Alain Dister in *Le Nouvel Observateur*, 8 November 1990; "Tango, bis!" in *Liberation*, 11 November 1990; Patrick Rogiers in *Le Monde*, November 1990; "Isabel Muñoz, Galeria Jean Pierre Lambert, Cour intérieur" by Miriam Rosen in *Artforum*, March 1991; "Isabel Muñoz. Una cuestión de tacto" by Jacobo Garcia in *Elle* (Spain), June 1991; "Fotografias de Tango, Flamenco y guerra" by Paché Merayo in *El Comercio*, 28 December 1991; "Isabel Muñoz y Javier Bauluz exponen sus fotografías en Gijón" in *La Nueva España*, 4 January 1992; "Isabel Muñoz, el reto de detener en un instante eterno el movimiento de la danza" by Paché Merayo in *El Comercio*, 7 January 1992; "Flamenco" in *Bunte*, August 1992; "Isabel Muñoz l'exploratice" by Jacques Boudon in *Le Meridional*, July 1993; "Les danses d'Isabel Muñoz" in *Agence France Press*, 12 July 1993; "Les corps sensuels d'Isabel Muñoz" by Michel Guerrin in *Le Monde*, July 1993; "Summer Collections" in *The Village Voice*, August 1993; "Danse" by Faustine de S. Amen in *Vogue*, September 1993; "Flamenco" in *Biba*, October 1993; "Une photo, un livre" in *Le Figaro*, 8 October 1993; "Flamenco Isabel Muñoz—Jacques Durand" by Roger Dumont in *La Republique des Pyrenees*, 10 October 1993; "I. Muñoz et J. Durand Flamenco" by Francis Brochet in *Le Progres*, 17 October 1993; "Portfolio, Isabel Muñoz" in *Diorama*, November 1993; "Isabel Muñoz—Flamenco" by Christian Caujolle in *Foncier Mensuel, Special Mecenat*, November 1993; "Time off" in *The European*, 11 November 1993; "Isabel Muñoz, danzad, danzad" in *ABC*, 12 November 1993; "Isabel Muñoz, fotografías" in *El Punto*, 16 November 1993; "La inteligencia sosegada y quieta de Isabel Muñoz" by Javier López Rejas in *Diario 16*, 18 November 1993; "Photos wrapped in mystery" by Motoko Shimizu in *Ashahi Evening News*, 25 November 1993; "El Flamenco de Isabel Muñoz" by Antonio Molinero in *FV*, December 1993; "Fotos von Tango und Flamencoszenen" by Antje Seifert in *Kontakt*, December 1993; "Isabel Muñoz" by Manul López in *Revista Foto*, December 1993; "Saga Flamenco" in *L'Express*, December 1993; "Flamenco" in *Le Var*, December 1993; "Isabel Muñoz, fotografías. De Tango, Bolero y Oriental" by Fernando Pérez in *Espiral de las Artes*, December 1993; "Isabel Muñoz, Fotófrafía en danza" in *Man*, December 1993; "Actualité" in *Figaro Japon*, December 1993; "Flamenco" in *Nice Matin*, 5 December 1993; "Isabel Muñoz: el baile del cuerpo" in *Epoca*, 6 December 1993; "Isabel Muñoz" in *La Nacion*, 7 December 1993; "Fantasme de Flamenco" by Dominique Frétard in *Le Monde*, 10 December 1993; "Flamenco" in *Le Marseillaise*, 12 December 1993; "Flamenco Pasión" in *Le Courier Picard*, 14 December 1993; "La passion Muñoz" in *Le Quotidien*, 29 December 1993; "Portofolio, Isabel Muñoz" by Manuel López, *Revista Foto*, January 1994; "Isabel Muñoz, Fotografías" by Francisco Vicent Galdón in *Guadalajara 2000*, 10 January 1994; "Isabel Muñoz—Enganchada a la fotografía" in *Man*, February 1994.

*

I work in large format (80 x 120cm) black and white. In order to highlight the powerful sensuality of my subjects, I process all my prints myself, using platinium salts. This old fashioned method of processing enables me to obtain a subtle colouring in brown and bronze tone.

Continuing my work on the body I have produced a major series on tango, flamenco and oriental dance, as well as Islamic architecture, Pharaonic architecture and Gaudí. I have recently finished a new series on bullfighting.

—Isabel Muñoz

*　*　*

Photographers are great swindlers. They cheat with reality, trying to persuade us that what they're revealing is some faithful, reliable trace of reality, that they are the true intermediaries and conduits between the real world and ourselves. They feign interest, for example, in dance, in dances, in certain special dances generally described as folkloric like the flamenco, tango, and belly dancing. They justify their preference by demonstrating how beautiful these dances are, and defend their passion saying how such dances, rooted in popular culture and traditions, have created aesthetic forms, ways of seeing and moving, representative of whole civilisations. Likewise, they capably and correctly inform us (as the above goes to show) that every contemporary choreographer has observed these dances and that they've had a considerable influence over a new generation we are pleased to call 'modern' dance—but that they, the photographers, today desire nothing better than to return to dance's origins.

All this is designed to win us over to the perfection of their images, by persuading us that this is all there is—something which is absolutely not what they would have us believe. What I'd like to do is choose, at random, Isabel Muñoz, a young photographer from Barcelona now living in Madrid. She possesses the wisdom to liberate the tango, the flamenco and oriental dance from the hearsay and exotica that constitute the principal business of so many postcard publishers and all those engaged in running tourism agencies. Using black and white and roaming from Buenos Aires to Cairo, Istanbul to Seville, Isabel Muñoz has observed couples dancing, joining, defying, evoking acts of love—and rejecting the evocation in favour of transforming lovemaking into dancing, into tension. Isabel has singled out something that reflects—in that physical challenge, in those lowering and never-to-be-bestowed kisses, in those ultimately frustrated embraces, in those masculine hands gripping a female thigh, in those secretive swerves out of an eternal coupling, in that skin which rubs another's only to be rebuffed again, in the heightening of desire amid the strictly social character of the occasion. Magnificently, she has known how to frame, to cut those bodies, insert details laden with history and thronged with movement, evocative and suggestive of far more than is ever disclosed. She has shut herself away in her darkroom, struggled with its blackness and there, in the confines of its alchemy, mastered old-fashioned and wearisome techniques which necessitate the production of enormous negatives to copy onto paper, assisted by the oxidation of platinum salts, to realise the images she has succeeded in capturing.

She has taken her passion for texture and fabric to its limit—for the roughness of skin fighting against the weft of the material of a skirt; the sequins sparkling within the sensual folds of a navel that alone seem to feel they have eyes to see. She has known how to endow fixed images with a rhythm and establish a dialogue between the vastness of the spaces and the attention to detail of a hand catching the light of a comb clasped in the black flow of a tortured hairstyle. And she says she wants to show us their dances.

No, Isabel Muñoz doesn't tell us about the dances. She tells us of herself, firstly because she has succeeded in uncovering the most suitable form to convey her emotions when confronted by those bodies, and also because she is generous enough to invite us to share them. Because she *is* inviting us to reach out and touch—with our eyes and hands—the extraordinary tenderness of images that remind us of the moment when we caressed a beloved's skin. Then perhaps with a deeper seriousness, she tells us about photography, telling us that photography is nothing more than a search after images, on the part of someone who, in the most hidden recess of her mind, parades images, other versions of desire, that she would like to realise since at a given moment, those images might have coincided with reality.

Like all true photographers, Isabel Muñoz loves her images but, just like them, lives the moments and individuals she captures, in this case the dancers with who she has worked in order for them to participate in her private world. She loves dance, she loves the dancer, loves photography and since we are truly credulous, since to us photography is a reflection of reality, Isabel Muñoz purports to be telling us about dance, purports to be some kind of mediator between the dance and us.

She has no wish to tell us of anything that doesn't fascinate her personally, anything beyond those bodies, those mysteries that the human body is capable of incorporating, this language of bodies, dialogue of love, the unbounded sensuality experienced by men and women since time began, interminably practised to put the precision of words in their place and to incite us to tumults which only the poets among us know how to achieve.

Isabel is a great photographer simply because she's such a great swindler. Also because she has chosen, for her own personal reasons, to speak of the unspeakable, concealing herself behind the apparent seduction of the images of those bodies she offers us like mirrors, like doubts, like shapes and like wagers.

—Christian Caujolle

MYDANS, Carl.

Nationality: American. **Born:** Boston, Massachusetts, 20 May 1907. **Education:** Medford High School, Massachusetts, 1926; Boston University School of Journalism, 1926-30, B.S. journalism 1930. **Family:** Married Shelley Smith in 1938; children: Seth Anthony and Shelley. **Career:** Worked as a reporter for *American Banker*, New York, 1931-35; photographer with the Farm Security Administration, Washington, D.C., under Roy Stryker, 1935-36; Photographer/Correspondent, *Life* magazine, New York, 1936-72: War Correspondent, Russo-Finnish Winter War, 1939, fall of France, 1940, war in Europe (Casino, Rome, Florence, and France), and war in the Pacific, 1942-45 (prisoner of war in the Philippines and China, 1942-43); Head of the Time-Life Bureau in Tokyo, 1945-48; War Correspondent in Korea, 1950, 1951, and in Vietnam, 1968. Since 1972, Photographer/ Correspondent for *Time* magazine, New York. **Recipient:** Gold Achievement Award, *U.S. Camera*, 1951. D.H.: Boston University, 1960. **Address:** 212 Hemmocks Road, Larchmont, New York 10538, U.S.A.

Individual Exhibitions:

1985   *A Photojournalist's Journey Through War and Peace*, Amon Carter Museum, Fort Worth, Texas (travelled to Boston University; and the International Center of Photography, New York, 1985-86)

Selected Group Exhibitions:

1938   *Farm Security Administration Exhibition*, at the *First International Photographic Exposition*, Grand Central Palace, New York
1951   *Memorable Life Photographs*, Museum of Modern Art, New York
1955   *FSA Anniversary Show*, Brooklyn Museum, New York
1962   *The Bitter Years: FSA Photographs 1935-41*, Museum of Modern Art, New York (toured the United States)
1977   *A Vision Shared: The FSA*, Witkin Gallery, New York
         The FSA: People and Places of America, Santa Barbara Museum of Art, California
1979   *Images de l'Amerique en Crise: Photographies de la FSA*, Centre Georges Pompidou, Paris
         Life: The First Decade, Grey Art Gallery, New York University
1980   *Amerika: Traum and Depression 1920-40*, Kunstverein, Hamburg (toured West Germany)
         Ohio: A Photographic Portrait 1935-41, Akron Art Institute, Ohio

Collections:

Library of Congress, Washington, D.C.; Time-Life Inc., New York

Publications:

By MYDANS: Books—*More Than Meets the Eye*, autobiography, New York 1959; *The Violent Peace*, with Shelley Mydans, New York 1968; *China: A Visual Adventure*, with Michael Demarest, New York 1979; *Carl Mydans: A Photojournalist's Journey Through War and Peace*, with interview by Philip B. Kunhardt, Jr., New York 1985.

On MYDANS: Book—*Memorable Life Photographs*, with text by Edward Steichen, New York 1951; *Words and Pictures: An Introduction to Photojournalism* by Wilson Hicks, New York 1952; *How Life Gets the Story: Behind the Scenes in Photo-Journalism*, edited by Stanley Rayfield, New York 1955; *Das Adenauer Bildbuch/The Adenauer Picture Book*, edited by L. Fritz Gruber, Stuttgart 1956; *Life Photographers: Their Careers and Favorite Pictures*, edited by Stanley Rayfield, New York 1957; *Travel Photography*, by the editors of Time-Life, New York 1973; *The Years of Bitterness and Pride: FSA Photographs 1935-1943*, compiled by Jerry Kearns and Leroy Bellamy, edited by Hiak Akmakjian, New York 1975; *A Vision Shared: A Classic Portrait of America and Its People*, edited by Hank O'Neal, New York and London 1976; *Life: The First Decade 1936-1945* by Robert Littman, Ralph Graves and Doris C. O'Neill, New York 1979, London 1980; *A Ten Year Salute* by Lee D. Witkin, with a foreword by Carol Brown, Danbury, New Hampshire 1979; *Les Années Amères de l'Amerique en Crise 1935-1942*, exhibition catalogue, by Jean Dieuzaide, Toulouse, France 1980; *Bilder vom Krieg* by Rainer Fabian and Hans Christian Adam, Hamburg 1983, as *Images of War: 130 Years of War Photography*, London 1985. **Articles**—"The Story of Carl Mydans" by J.G. Lootens in *U.S. Camera* (New York), December 1939; "Korea: Carl Mydans" in *U.S. Camera Annual 1951*, edited by Tom Maloney, New York 1950; "The History of Carl Mydans" by Ronald H. Bailey in *American Photographer* (New York), August 1985.

*

I am a photo journalist, beginning first with the U.S. Farm Security Administration photo coverage of the United States (1934/35), a government financed project. My photographs on this project, together with those of some dozen other photographers, now reside in the United States Library of Congress, and are viewed as a major historical document of the Depression years.

In 1936 I joined the newly forming *Life* magazine before its first issue appeared. And I remained on its active staff for more than 35 years, until it folded in 1972. Since then I have continued as a photo journalist for *Time* (sister publication) and other publications; and am working on both text and photographic books.

—Carl Mydans

*   *   *

When, in 1935, under the innovative leadership of Roy Stryker, the Farm Security Administration established an "Historical Section," Carl Mydans moved from another branch of the organization in order to work as a photographer on Stryker's team. Trained as a journalist, Mydans bought a Contax 35mm. camera in 1931 and extended his journalism to include the visual recording of events by working as a free-lance photographer. Although his stay with the Historical Section was very brief, he helped to establish its pattern of work and its objectives. Equally, he gained through the experience a way of approaching the task of a photographer that was to influence both the character and the style of his subsequent work.

Mydans made an extended field trip to the southern states of the U.S.A. where his assignment was to document the cotton industry for the Section. He accomplished this task, but few of his exposures were concerned with a cool examination of the techniques of growing and producing cotton. Rather, he recorded with great skill and compassion, and often against the strongly expressed wishes of the white planters, the lives of the poor, the dispossessed and the exploited.

In the fine division of genres into which photographers are often classified, Mydans must be described as a photojournalist rather than a documentary photographer. In 1936 he moved to the newly formed *Life* magazine, which was then known as Project X but was to become a major institution in American life and one of the world's best known and most influential photo magazines. At *Life* Mydans was able to draw on his talents both as a journalist and as a photographer. He was to have a long and distinguished career with the magazine and was a formative influence on its style and aims. He has said of it: "We had an insatiable drive to search out every fact of American life, photograph it and hold it up proudly like a mirror to a pleased and astonished readership. . . . America had an impact on us and each week we made an impact on America.''

—Derrick Price

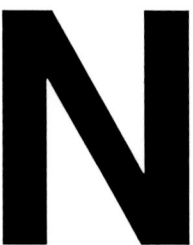

NAGARAJAN, T(ambarahalli) S(ubramania).

Nationality: Indian. **Born:** Hunchadakatte, Karnataka, 13 October 1932. **Education:** Municipal High School, Doddaballapur, 1946-47, Municipal High School, Malavalli, 1947-48, and Maharajah's High School, Mysore, 1948-49; studied English, physics and mathematics at Yuvaraja's College, Mysore, 1949-53, B.Sc. 1953. **Family:** Married Meenakshi Mahalingam Iyer in 1958; daughters: Kalyani and Vasanti. **Career:** Freelance photographer, Mysore, 1953-56; Picture Editor, *Yojana* journal of the Planning Commission, New Delhi, 1956-72; Photographic Officer, Ministry of External Affairs, New Delhi, 1972-75; Director of the Photo Division, Ministry of Information and Broadcasting, New Delhi, 1976-78. Freelance photographer, New Delhi, since 1978; Consultant Photographer, UNICEF and UNFPA in India, since 1978. **Recipient:** Human Interest Photo Award, Press Institute of India, New Delhi, 1968; National Photo Award, All India Fine Arts and Crafts Society, New Delhi, 1976; Unesco Prize, Asian Cultural Centre, Tokyo, 1977. **Agent:** Camera Press Ltd., Russell Court, Coram Street, London WC1, England. **Address:** 6/41 Western Extension, New Delhi 110005, India.

Individual Exhibitions:

1966	*Young Eyes,* All India Fine Arts and Crafts Society, New Delhi
1969	*Around a River, Around a Tower,* All India Fine Arts and Crafts Society, New Delhi
1970	*Banaras-Madurai,* Jehangir Art Gallery, Bombay
1983	*Interiors of Indian Homes,* Art Heritage, New Delhi

Selected Group Exhibitions:

1976	*National Photographic Exhibitions,* All India Fine Arts and Crafts Society, New Delhi
	World Press Photo 76, Amsterdam
1982	*An Eye for India,* National Theatre, London
	The Other India, Museum of Modern Art, Oxford

Publications:

By NAGARAJAN: Books—*The Sikhs Today,* with text by Khushwant Singh, Calcutta 1959; *It Happened in a Village,* New Delhi 1960; *This India,* with text by Sheila Dhar, New Delhi 1973; *Indira Gandhi,* picture editor, text by G.D. Khosla, Faridabad, India 1974; *The Spirit of India,* picture editor, Bombay 1975; *India: Portrait of a People,* picture editor, New Delhi 1976; *Sanjay Gandhi,* editor, text by Maneka Gandhi, Bombay 1980; *Report on the State of Photojournalism in India,* New Delhi 1980; *Exploring Karnataka,* picture editor, photographs by T.S. Satyan, text by H.Y. Sharada Prasad, Bangalore, India 1981. **Articles**—"Transistor in India" in *Illustrated Weekly of India* (Bombay), 10 May 1970; "J. Krishnamurti" in *Illustrated Weekly of India* (Bombay), 31 January 1971; "Ma Anandamaye" in *Illustrated Weekly of India* (Bombay), 30 April 1972; "Taj Watching" in *Pacific Travel News* (San Francisco), November 1974; "In the South of India" in *Pacific* (Tokyo), no. 1, 1976; "Photojournalism in India" in *Illustrated Weekly of India* (Bombay), 28 May 1978; "Doors" in *Pacific* (Tokyo), no. 3, 1980; "Benares: The Eternal City" in *Taj Magazine* (Bombay), March 1980; "Dust Comes to Life" in *Taj Magazine* (Bombay), no. 4, 1982; "The Echoing Interior" in *Swagat* (New Delhi), July 1984; "Design for Living" in *Taj Magazine* (Bombay), no. 4, 1986.

On NAGARAJAN: Articles—"Life Through a Lens" in *Yojana* (New Delhi), February 1969; "Nagarajan" by Chitrangada in *Shankar's Weekly* (New Delhi), 16 February 1969; "Pilgrimage with a Camera" in *The Statesman* (New Delhi), February 1969; "Anti-Glory Nagarajan" in *Enlite* (New Delhi), March 1969; "Assignment India" in *Yojana* (New Delhi), August 1972; "A Ballad Maker in Pictures" in *Sird News Magazine* (New Delhi), October 1972; "T.S. Nagarajan" in *Illustrated Weekly of India* (Bombay), 22 January 1978; "T.S. Nagarajan Analyses the Indian Home" by Keshav Malik in the *Times of India* (New Delhi), 8 February 1983; "Bagarajan's Nostalgia" in *Patrio* (New Delhi), 15 February 1983; "Snaps for Posterity" in *Deccan Herald* (Bangalore), 31 January 1983; "The People's Perspective" by Renu Mittal in *Surya India* (New Delhi), 31 August 1983.

*

I turned to photography by an accidental realization. One day, during my undergraduate days in my home town, Mysore, in the south of India, I was driven by an impish desire to write a piece on the sudden death of "Irawata," the Maharaja's elephant, much loved by the people of Mysore as a dear old friend. A leading Indian weekly published the story ("A Mysore Gentleman Passes Away") with an unsatisfactory photograph of the elephant which I had bought from a local studio. A few weeks later, the editor, an Irishman, sent me a copy of the magazine with my story, along with a cheque and a note urging me to take to the camera "If I had ambitions of making a success of my career as a journalist." I took to photography without a second thought. The years that followed proved in ample measure that the editor was right.

Today, more than 30 years after the death of "Irawata," I have an elephant with a camera on its mount as my professional symbol.

I started as a freelance, but did rather a long stint with the Indian government as its official photographer before I resigned in 1978 to become a freelance once again. It was my privilege as picture editor of *Yojana,* the journal of the Indian Planning Commission, to record for well over a decade the planned economic development of the country. This enabled me to see India as is given to no man, reflecting as my viewfinder did the beauty and the ugliness and the colour and the potential of India; its men and women building their own future, its temples old and new. It was then, while recording this exciting change in the life and landscape of the country, I preferred to be not a photographer of cement and steel and inaugural ceremonies, but a photographer of people.

I believe that a country is people. While photographing people, a photographer neither petrifies them, nor does he make them act. They move, they work, they laugh, they suffer. And he himself becomes part of their movement, their work, their laughter and their pain. He gets involved.

All art, the cynic says, is a form of escapism. The artist creates an image of things as he sees them with his mind and soul, but rarely with his eyes. The photographer, on the other hand, sees life as you and I see it. Most photographers record on bromide that which is obvious, without any effort to discover the poetry and pathos, the joys and sorrows of life. But there are among them, only a few, who use their portable mechanism to capture the beauty and glory of life's rarest moments. Their creations transcend the photographer's routine and become works of art in the truest sense of the term.

My life has been exciting with my camera. I am grateful to have been a photographer. I use Nikons. But my camera does nothing. It neither makes the picture nor prevents me from taking it. It only helps in achieving an idea, an approach, a sort of direction and, perhaps, a philosophy.

—T.S. Nagarajan

*   *   *

T.S. Nagarajan is one of the foremost chroniclers of social change in India. His work encompasses a great variety of themes, places and moods, and is marked by strength and directness. Apart from their high craftsmanship, his pictures have intellectual depth; they make one think. The interaction of tradition and modernity fascinates him. His features on the temple towns of Benares and Madurai are successful essays in capturing the perennial that changes continuously and in subtle ways. His photographs on the induction of technology into rural life and on themes such as family planning and the spread of education have been very widely published. He is more at home in black-and-white, although he has done some notable work in colour.

It is easy for photographers in India to become sentimental and whimsical. Nagarajan avoids both these pitfalls with his self-control and his sturdy sense of context and relevance. He spurns the merely decorative or the contrived. He has an eye, however, for the dramatic, the paradoxical, even the humorous, as long as it is natural. He has not cared to do much "celebrity" photography; he is more interested in society than in Society. To him, photography "is not a poor relation of high art. The photographer should have artistry. But when he pursues aesthetic values too sedulously, the picture he produces will be playing the ape to another art form rather than expressing the true nature of the medium of photography. It is the prerogative of the camera to record the present as a reliable witness."

What has moulded Nagarajan's outlook is his own long experience as a photographer of the Indian Planning Commission's journal, *Yojana*. The position provided him with the opportunity to travel to every part of India and record rural and urban change; even more pertinently, it placed him among sociologists and economists through whom he gained a deep understanding of the development process. Another advantage was that, although he was a government photographer, he was not required to cover the day-to-day events of officialdom. Magazine work and his involvement with exhibitions helped him to develop an editorial eye, which has stood him in good stead in his work as picture editor of photographic essays on Indira Gandhi and Sanjay Gandhi and on *India: Portrait of a People*.

After heading the Photo Division of the Government of India, Nagarajan quit government service to become a freelance photojournalist. He has held exhibitions in New Delhi and Bombay, and his work has appeared in the leading journals of many countries.

—H.Y. Sharada Prasad

NAGATANI, Patrick.

Nationality: American. **Born:** Chicago, Illinois 1945. **Education:** California State University, Los Angeles, B.A., in 1968; and University of California, Los Angeles, M.F.A., 1980. **Career:** Lectures and runs seminars and workshops. **Recipient:** Ford Foundation Travel Grant, 1979; Faculty research grant from Loyola Marymount University, Los Angeles, 1981 and 1983; California Arts Council Artist-in-Residence at the Japanese-American Cultural Center, Los Angeles, 1982-83; National Endowment for the Arts, Visual Artist Fellowship, 1984-85 and 1992-93; commission by the Community Redevelopment Agency of Los Angeles, 1987; Leopold Godowsky Jr. Color Photography Award, 1988; Faculty research grant from the University of New Mexico, 1988 and 1990; California Distinguished Artist Award, National Art Education Associate Convention, 1988; Polaroid Fellowships, 1983-90; Outstanding Faculty Award, College of Fine Arts, University of New Mexico, 1991. **Agent:** Jayne H. Baum Gallery, 588 Broadway, New York New York 10012, U.S.A.

Individual Exhibitions:

1976	Pal Gallery, Evergreen State University, Olympia, Washington
1978	Cityscape Gallery, Pasadena, California
1979	Exploratorium Gallery, California State University, Los Angeles
1980	Orange Coast College, Costa Mesa, California
1981	Susan Spiritus Gallery, Newport Beach, California
1982	Canon Photo Gallery, Amsterdam
1983	*Colorful Cathedrals,* Arco Center for Visual Arts, Los Angeles
1984	*Nagatani and Tracey Polaroid Collaborations 1983-1989,* (with Andree Tracey), Clarence Kennedy Gallery, Boston (travelled)
1985	*Chromo-Therapy Series,* Torch Gallery, Amsterdam
	Jayne H. Baum Gallery, New York (with Andree Tracey)
1986	Fotografie Forum, Frankfurt
1987	Frederick S. Wight Art Gallery, University of California, Los Angeles
	Taped Pieces, Torch Gallery, Amsterdam
	Presentation House Gallery, North Vancouver, British Columbia, Canada
	Museum of Contemporary Photography, Columbia College, Chicago
	Gallery Min, Tokyo
	Jayne H. Baum Gallery, New York
1988	Silver Image Gallery, Seattle
	San Francisco Camerawork, San Francisco
	Koplin Gallery, Los Angeles
1989	Webster University, St. Louis
	Shadai Gallery, Tokyo Institute of Polytechnics, Tokyo
	The Contemporary Museum, Honolulu, Hawaii
	Jayne H. Baum Gallery, New York
1990	Koplin Gallery, Los Angeles
	Art Gallery of Hamilton, Ontario, Canada
1991	*Nuclear Enchantment,* Jayne H. Baum Gallery, New York (travelled to Kyle Roberts Gallery, San Francisco; Andrew Smith Gallery, Santa Fe; Alinder Gallery, Gualala, California; Monterey Peninsula Museum of Art, California; The Albuquerque Museum, New Mexico; University of Tennessee, Knoxville; Photo Mirage Gallery, Denver; Cleveland Center for Contemporary Art, Ohio; South Dakota Museum of Art, Brookings; Koplin Gallery, Los Angeles; Stanford University Museum of Art, California; Royal Photographic Society, Bath; State University of New York, Fredonia)
	Chrysler Museum, Norfolk, Virginia
1992	Orange Coast College, Costa Mesa, California
	Patrick Nagatani: A New Series of Waterless Lithographs, Richard Levy Gallery, Albuquerque, New Mexico
1993	James and Meryl Hearst Center for the Arts, Cedar Falls, Iowa
1994	Jayne H. Baum Gallery, New York

Selected Group Exhibitions:

1976	*Members Exhibition,* Friends of Photography, Carmel, California
1977	*New Photographics,* Central Washington State College, Ellensburg, WA
1978	*Erotica,* SoHo/Cameraworks Gallery, Los Angeles
1979	*Perception—A Field of View,* Los Angeles Center for Photographic Studies, Los Angeles
1980	*Show 5—Five Los Angeles Artists,* Art Rental Gallery, Los Angeles County Museum of Art, Los Angeles
	Sherie Scheer and Patrick Nagatani—Photography from America, Ufficio Dell'Arte/Creatis Galerie, Paris
	Photofusion, Pratt Manhattan Center Gallery, New York
1981	*California Colour,* Photographers Gallery, London
1982	*Studio Work,* Los Angeles County Museum of Art, Los Angeles
	Lately in L.A., Washington Project for the Arts, Washington, D.C.

Fin de Siècle, **Bat Flight Amphitheatre, Carlsbad Caverns, New Mexico, 1989.** Photograph ©Patrick Nagatani. Courtesy Jayne H. Baum Gallery.

1983   *Ten California Photographers,* Sarkis Galleries and Yamasaki
       Gallery, Center for Creative Studies, Detroit
       Hand Colored Photographs, Jayne H. Baum Gallery,
       New York
1984   *What's Happening: Contemporary Art From California,
       Oregon, Washington,* The Alternative Museum, New York
       Selections 2, Polaroid Gallery, Cologne, Germany
       Photography in California: 1945-Present, San Francisco
       Museum of Modern Art (travelled to Akron Art Museum,
       Ohio; The Corcoran Art Gallery, Washington, D.C.; Los
       Angeles Municipal Art Gallery; Herbert F. Johnson Museum
       of Art, Cornell University, Ithaca, New York; The High
       Museum of Art, Atlanta; Museum Folkwang, Essen; Musee
       National d'art Moderne Centre Georges Pompidou, Paris;
       Museum of Photographic Arts, San Diego)
1985   *Off the Street,* Old City Print Shop, Los Angeles
1986   *Selections 3,* Polaroid Gallery, Cologne, Germany (travelled to
       Museum fur Kunst und Gewerbe, Hamburg, Germany;
       Munchener Stadtmuseum, Munich, Germany; The National
       Museum for Photography, Film and Television, Bradford,
       England)
       Contemporary American Photography Part 1, Gallery
       Min, Tokyo

1987   *Greater Than or Equal to 30''x40,''* Jayne H. Baum Gallery,
       New York
       Art Waves, Banner Art Exhibition, Theatre Center, Los
       Angeles
1988   *Two to Tango,* International Center of Photography, New York
       (travelled)
       *Poetic Injury: The Surrealist Legacy in Postmodern Photogra-
       phy,* The Alternative Museum, New York
       L.A. Hot and Cool: The Eighties, M.I.T. List Visual Arts
       Center, Cambridge, Massachusetts
1989   *The Photography of Invention: American Pictures of the 1980s,*
       National Museum of American Art, Smithsonian Institution,
       Washington, D.C. (travelled to the Museum of Contemporary
       Art, Chicago; the Walker Art Center, Minneapolis)
       Selections 4, Polaroid Gallery, Cologne (travelled to Musee de
       l'Elysee, Lausanne, Switzerland; Victoria and Albert Muse-
       um, London; Kunsthalle, Hamburg, Germany; Museo de
       Arte Contemporaneo de Caracas, Venezuela)
1990   *Golden Pool—Asian/Pacific American Perspective,* Los
       Angeles Photography Center, Los Angeles
1991   *Twenty-One Photographers From New Mexico,* Vision
       Gallery, San Francisco
       Cinematic Effects, Lintas Worldwide, New York
1992   *Our Town,* Burden Gallery, New York

New Acquisitions, New Work, New Directions, Los Angeles
County Museum of Art, Los Angeles
California: The Cultural Edge, The Directors Guild of
America, Los Angeles
Americas, Monasterio de Santa Clara, Moguer (Huelva), Spain
1993 *Renewing Our Earth: The Artistic Vision,* Schneider-Bluhm-
Loeb Gallery, Chicago
Taejon International Expo '93, Korea
Breda Fotografica '93, Breda, Netherlands
1994 *Instant Image,* Park Avenue Atrium, New York

Collections:

Albuquerque Museum, New Mexico; Baltimore Art Museum, Maryland;
Bayly Art Museum, University of Virginia; Bibliotheque Nationale, Paris;
Center for Creative Photography, University of Arizona, Tucson; Center for
Graphic Arts, Wright Art Gallery, University of California, Los Angeles;
Graham Nash Collection, Los Angeles; International Museum of Photography, George Eastman House, Rochester, New York; Lehman Brothers, New
York; Los Angeles County Museum of Art; Loyola Marymount College,
California; Metropolitan Museum of Art, New York; Monterey Peninsula
Museum of Art, New York; Museum of Contemporary Photography, Chicago;
Museum of Fine Arts, Houston; Museum of New Mexico, Santa Fe; Museum
of Photographic Arts, San Diego; Newport Harbor Art Museum, California;
Oakland Museum, California; Tampa Museum of Art, Tampa, FL; Tokyo
Institute of Polytechnics; University Art Museum, University of New Mexico,
Albuquerque; University of Virginia Art Museum, Charlottesville.

Publications:

By NATAGANI: Article—*Photographers Forum,* February/March 1980.

On NAGATANI: Articles—"Two Uses of Color" by Dinah Portner in
Artsweek, 18 November 1978; "The Syncretistic Point of View—Photographs by Patrick Nagatani" by A.M. Degtjarewsky in *Color Photo,* March,
1979; "Patrick Nagatani—Kosmopolites" in *Camera Arts* magazine, January/February 1981; "Patrick Nagatani's Symbolism" by Chuck Nicholson in
Artsweek, 10 January 1981; "A Spectrum of Colorists" by Suzanne Muchnic
in the *Los Angeles Times,* February, 1981; "What Happens When You Cross a
Photograph with a Rock?" by A.D. Coleman in *ARTnews,* April 1981; "A
Multicultural Celebration of Photos" by William Willson in the *Los Angeles
Times,* 8 February 1982; "Photos That Are Made, Not Found" by Suzanne
Muchnic in the *Los Angeles Times,* 1 September 1982; "Manipulated Prints"
by Lance Carlson in *Artweek,* 10 September 1983; "On Photography—
Travels Through Time and Space" by Dinah Berland in the *Los Angeles
Times,* 26 June 1983; "Festival" in the *Los Angeles Times,* 15 April 1984;
"Nagatani and Tracey Challenge and Amuse" by Kelly Wise in *The Boston
Globe,* 8 December 1984; "Nuclear Darkroom" in *American Photography,*
September 1985; "Patrick Nagatani: Recent Work and Collaborations with
Andree Tracey" by Robin Hardman in *Views: The Journal of Photography in
New England,* Spring 1985; "Instant Image—Patrick Nagatani and Andree
Tracey" in *Zoom,* August-September 1986; "Patrick Nagatani/Andree
Tracey" by Robert Mahoney in *Arts,* January 1986; "When Tableaux Vivants
Flowered in the Magazines" by Andy Grundberg in *The New York Times,*
March 1986; "Patrick Nagatani and Andree Tracey" in *Marie Claire,* 9
February 1987; "Photography" in *New York Magazine,* 21 September 1987;
"Images from Polaroidland" in *Zoom,* November 1987; "Bilder Von Traum
Und Wahn" by Matthais Matussek in *Stern,* March 1987; "Choices" by
Vince Aletti in *The Village Voice,* 24 November 1987; "L.A., Hot and Cool: A
Rewarding Exhibition" in *The Boston Globe,* 17 January 1988; "Visual
Palette—Patrick Nagatani and Andree Tracey Describe the Atomic Age With
Pop Feeling" in *Asahi Camera Magazine,* April 1988; "Patrick Nagatani and
Andree Tracey at Jayne H. Baum" by Robert Mahoney in *ARTS Magazine,*
January 1988; "Slick Art with a Message" by Elizabeth Grodley in *The
Vancouver Sun,* 24 September 1988; "Photosynthesis" in *L.A. Style,* June
1989; *Harpers Magazine,* November 1989; "Where Photography and Performance Meet" by Kelly Wise in *The Boston Globe,* 25 February 1989;
"Patrick Nagatani and Andree Tracey" by Robert Atkins in *7 Days,* 22
November 1989; "Eve of Destruction" in the *Los Angeles Times,* 16 February
1990; "Polaroid Fusion/Photographs of Patrick Nagatani and Andree Tracey" in

California Magazine, February 1990; "Duck and Cover? 'Radioactive, Inactives
Portraits' by Nagatani and Tracey" by Timothy Murray in *Q: A Journal of Art,*
2 May 1990; "Photographer/Artist: Patrick Nagatani" by Orville Clark Jr in
Southern California Home and Garden, March 1990; "Nuclear Enchantment" by Peter B. Hales in *The New York Times,* 1 December 1991; "The
Ironic Co-Existence of Things Natural, Nuclear" by Zan Dubin in the *Los
Angeles Times,* 2 March 1991; "Patrick Nagatani" by Robert Mahoney in *Arts
Magazine,* March 1992; "Nuclear Enchantment Photographs by Patrick
Nagatani" by Dean Brierly in *Camera and Darkroom,* June 1992; "Letter
from Breda, No. 46" by A.D. Coleman in *Photo Metro,* October 1993; "Breda
Deze Zomer Fotostad" in *Zondag.* 4 July 1993.

* * *

Since the emergence of the "New Topographics" group in the 1970s,
American photographers have been condemning man's abuse of Mother
Nature more often than celebrating her bounty. No more mountain majesties or
dappled glens á la Ansel Adams or Eliot Porter: "new Topographics" artists
like Lewis Baltz and Robert Adams charted the metastasis of tract housing
over western dunes and prairies, and since the 1980s such colour photographers as Richard Misrach, John Pfahl and Barbara Norfleet have decried the
industrial destruction of the American landscape in images of ironic beauty.
All of them are "straight" photographers, unsmiling witnesses to what is felt
as a tragically unnecessary end of an American dream of Eden. It was left to
Patrick Nagatani to stage this story, using studio set ups and collage techniques
with all the artifice of an advertising photographer, and to tell it with mordant
humour as a black comedy of American pop culture. "There are plenty of facts
out there already" he says. "My ideal audience response is first a chuckle and
then a pause."

Nagatani is a Japanese American born in Chicago in 1945 to parents who
had both been interned in US camps for Japanese during World War II. He
brought a sardonic view of the land of the free to Los Angeles, where he earned
his BA and MFA and worked for Hollywood, making miniatures for special
effects filming. This technical skill and his fascination with movie stereotypes
and icons of colliding cultures appeared from the beginning of his career in the
early 1980s.

Working in collaboration with Andrée Tracey from 1983 to 1989, Nagatani
tackled the issues of nuclear proliferation and contamination in tableaux of
elaborate fabrication, combining actors and props in comic-book compositions of shrieking colour, often using the Polaroid 20 by 24 inch camera. In one
of his and Tracey's best-known pictures (1986), Japanese tourists gleefully
photograph an A bomb explosion, an image that captures the brevity of
historical memory and the unthinking, science fiction-fed fascination with
spectacles of Armageddon.

Moving to New Mexico to teach in 1987, Nagatani found himself in the
state where the first atomic bombs were developed and tested, still a dump for
radioactive waste from across the United States. New Mexico is also the
ancestral land of the Pueblo Indians, North America's oldest continuous native
culture.

Riveted and horrified, Nagatani began *The Nuclear Enchantment of New
Mexico,* series in 1989, based on two years of detective-like visits to the
nuclear sites; interviews with military and civilian personnel; and the models
he built of the aircraft and rocketry. The tableaux he composed using these
materials, often in combination with images of Pueblo culture, became a
travelling exhibition of 43 large chromogenic colour prints and a book (1992).
The disturbing contrast of current national values and native American ones,
of two mythologies, especially in their touristic costumes, were among the
themes of the boldly graphic series. It proved that probing social commentary
can come in bright packages, with layers of content made legible for various
attention spans. The artist had used the tools of mass media photography to
reveal mass fictions.

In 1992 Nagatani's attention turned inward with his *Novellas,* an ongoing
autobiographical series influenced by the magical realism of Latin American
authors and focussed on his life as an artist and a Japanese-American. In 1995
he completed a 12 by 25 foot photo mural in various techniques for the Los
Angeles MTA on the theme of transportation. Also that year—the 50th
anniversary of Hiroshima—he completed a two year series on Japanese
American relocation camps. The roughly 140 landscapes documented the state

of these camps today: they were the first unmanipulated colour prints of his career.

—Anne Hoy

NAITOH, Masatoshi.

Nationality: Japanese. **Born:** Tokyo, 18 April 1938. **Education:** Studied chemistry, Waseda University, Tokyo; self-taught in photography. **Family:** Married Kazuko Naitoh in 1969; children: Shizue and Shokichi. **Career:** Worked in the Research Department of Kurashiki Rayon Company, Tokyo. Now, freelance photographer, Tokyo. **Recipient:** Nika Award, 1963; New Photographer Award, Japan Photo Critics Association, 1966; Ken Domon Prize, Tokyo, 1982; Photographic Society of Japan Award of the Year, Tokyo, 1986. **Address:** 2-25-11 Amanuma, Suginami-ku, Tokyo 167, Japan.

Individual Exhibitions:

1966	*Japanese Mummies,* Tokyo
	Homunculus, Tokyo
1970	*Exploding Baba,* Tokyo
1973	*Sanrizuka Heta Buraku,* Tokyo
1980	*Dewa Sanzan,* Shinjuku Minolta Photo Space, Japan
1982	*Dewa Sanzan,* Shinjuku Minolta Photo Space, Japan
1983	*Tales of Tohno,* Nikon Salon, Ginza, Japan
1985	*Tokyo,* Minolta Photo Space, Tokyo

Selected Group Exhibitions:

1971	*10th Modern Japanese Art Exhibition,* Tokyo
1974	*New Japanese Photography,* Museum of Modern Art, New York
1985	*A Day in the Life of Japan,* Tokyo (toured Japan)
	The World of Super Images, Yurakucho Seibu Art Forum, Tokyo
	11 People over 1965-75, Yamaguchi Prefectural Art Museum, Yamaguchi, Japan
	Post War Photography and Tohoku, Miyagi Prefectural Art Museum, Miyagi, Japan
	Japan, Années 60, PICTO, Paris
	International Photo Reporters Festival, Perpignan, France
	Glances at the City—Tokyo, Municipal Museum of Photography, Tokyo
	Beyond Japan, Barbican Centre, London

Collections:

Museum of Modern Art, Tokyo; Museum of Modern Art, New York; Yamaguchi Prefectural Art Museum, Yamaguchi, Japan; Miyagi Prefectural Art Museum, Miyagi, Japan; Kawasaki Civil Museum, Kanawaga, Japan; Yokohama Museum of Art, Kanawaga, Japan; Ken Domon Museum of Photography, Yamagata, Japan; Ideha Cultural Memorial Hall, Yamagata, Japan.

Publications:

By NAITOH: Books—*The Study of Mummy Worship,* Tokyo 1974; *Tales of Tohno,* Tokyo 1978 and 1983; *Baba: Folk Religion of the Tohoku,* with an introduction by Akira Hasegawa, Tokyo 1979; *Dewa Sanzan,* Tokyo 1980; *Tokyo—Look at City Darkness* Tokyo 1985; *The Spiritual Universe of Shugendo,* Tokyo 1991; *Primal Landscape of the Tales of Tohno,* Tokyo 1994.

On NAITOH: Books—*New Japanese Photography,* exhibition catalogue, by John Szarkowski and Shoji Yamagishi, New York 1974; *Nude Photographs of Japan,* with text by Shiroyasu Suzuki, Tokyo 1981; *A Day in the Life*

of Japan—June 7, 1985, edited by Rick Smolan and David Cohen, New York and London 1985.

*   *   *

Masatoshi Naitoh is unique among Japanese photographers. Perhaps it is better, more accurate, to call him a researcher in folklore who uses photography as an instrument, rather than a photographer per se.

Naitoh was born in Tokyo in 1938. While studying applied chemistry in the Faculty of Technology at Waseda University, he enjoyed photography as a hobby and was a member of the University Camera Club. In those days he had already achieved a special kind of expression, which became clearer when he later turned "professional"; he used inventive photographic techniques, contrary to the prevalent realism of the period. When he graduated he entered the Research Department of the Kurashiki Rayon Company. His field of research was in the creation of new life forms, but that was not potentially a very profitable line of enquiry as far as the company was concerned, and after a year he left—though now that the whole field of bio-chemistry is being more widely investigated, Naitoh's work, in retrospect, seems ingenious. Eventually Naitoh went back to things photographic, and his former hobby became his profession.

He began with a series of "S-F Photos," using his expertise as a chemist in the making of surreal fantasies. He quickly lost interest in that series and turned to an examination of the practice of mummification in Japan and elsewhere, an obsession that has lasted to the present time. A collection of his photographs of mummies was shown in 1966: it created a sensation and earned Naitoh the New Photographer Award of the Japan Photo Critics Association. Naitoh's photographs of mummies are very vivid, dynamic, prompting one to imagine that Naitoh has shared the long history of the mummies themselves. Naitoh, who as a chemist first set out to create new bio-chemical life forms, now as a photographer seemed to be aiming to capture the essence of human life forms dormant in the mummies.

These comments may suggest that Naitoh is some kind of monomaniac, but in fact the discovery and investigation of mummies led him to the study of folklore, those kinds of human beliefs without which mummies could not have existed. He concentrated on observances in the Tohoku region as well as the inhabitants of that region. The common idea informing the works he produced is that of recording the fullness of lives of those who have been marginalized in our modern economy, who yet maintain vital links with their own local cultures.

Today, Naitoh is still taking photographs, but he is much more passionately involved with the anthropology of everyday life. Given his history, it is probably reasonable to assume that this study must, in time, find an even newer form of photographic expression within his work.

—Takao Kajiwara

NAKAMURA, Masaya.

Nationality: Japanese. **Born:** Yokohama, 29 March 1926. **Education:** Studied photography at Tokyo Fine Arts High School; studied photochemistry at Chiba University. **Military Service:** Served in the Japanese Army, 1942-46. **Family:** Married Mitsue Sharaishi in 1958; daughter: Mami. **Career:** Professional photographer, working as news cameraman, and portrait and fashion photographer, Tokyo, since 1949; established Masaya Studio, Chinjuku-ku, Tokyo, 1958-64, Minato-ku, Tokyo, since 1966. President, Japan Advertising Photographers' Association, since 1958. Member, Nika-Kai Department of Photography, Tokyo, since 1966. **Recipient:** News Photography Prize, Japan Photo Critics Association, 1957; Art Directors Club of New York 1966. **Address:** Masaya Studio, Kaneko Building, 1-2-9 Nishia-zabu, Minato-ku, Tokyo, Japan.

Individual Exhibitions:

1957	*Young Nudes,* Fuji Photo Salon, Tokyo
1960	*Nudes,* Fuji Photo Salon, Tokyo

***Portrait of the Dead,* from *Tales of Tohno.* Photograph by Masatoshi Naitoh.**

	Nues Japonais, Galerie Oluloy, Paris
1962	*Women,* Fuji Photo Salon, Tokyo
1964	*Nudes,* Fuji Photo Salon, Tokyo
1968	*Girl, Girl, Girl,* Fuji Photo Salon, Tokyo
1969	*Nudes East and West,* Fuji Photo Salon, Tokyo
	Autumn Gale, Nikon Salon, Tokyo
1970	*Nude Photo, Paris and Japanese Women,* Mitsukoshi Department Store, Osaka
1971	*Ema Nude in Africa,* Tokyo Department Store, Tokyo
1972	*Paris Blue,* Gallery Nire, Urawa, Japan
1973	*Flora Flora,* Takashimaya Department Store, Kyoto
	Child Vinci, Getuko Photo Gallery, Tokyo
	Stop and Go, Fuji Photo Salon, Tokyo
1974	*Pandora's Flute,* Ginza Wako, Tokyo
	Miro, Nikon Salon, Tokyo
	Winds of Change, Pentax Gallery, Tokyo
1975	*Woman in Kyto,* Canon Salon, Tokyo
1976	*My Work,* Fuji Photo Salon, Tokyo
1977	*Scenery with Nudes,* Minolta Photo Space, Tokyo
	Bretagne: Sa Lumière et Son Souffle, Contax Gallery, Tokyo
1978	*Spark (Nude),* Canon Salon, Tokyo
1979	*Rainbow Hue,* Canon Salon, Tokyo
	Woman: The Four Seasons, Olympus Gallery, Tokyo
1980	*Slot Machine,* Event Space, Tokyo
1981	*Japanese Spirit ''Iki,''* Fuji Photo Salon, Tokyo
	Kabuki Actor, Tokizio, the Fifth, Minolta Photo Space, Tokyo

Selected Group Exhibitions:

1957	*Eyes of 10,* Konishiroko Gallery, Tokyo
1961	*Group ''Non,''* Matsuya Department Store, Tokyo
1964	*Olympic Art Exhibition,* Matsuya Department Store, Tokyo
1970	*Nudes of the World,* Tokyo
1979	*Japanese Photography Today and Its Origin,* Galleria d'Arte Moderna, Bologna, Italy (toured Europe)

Collections:

San Francisco Museum of Modern Art.

Publications:

By NAKAMURA: Books—*Nues Japonais,* Paris 1960; *Young Nudes,* edited by Koen Shigemori, Tokyo 1961; *Nudes East and West,* with text by Shoji Yamagishi, Tokyo 1969; *Ema Nude in Africa,* with text by Kenichiro Tamada, Tokyo 1971; *My Work,* with text by Shinrio Chono, Tokyo 1976; *Woman's Angle,* with text by Tatsuo Shirai, Tokyo 1977; *Women's Sphere,* with text by Kenichiro Tamada, Tokyo 1978; *Japanese Spirit ''Iki,''* with text by Koen Shigemori, Tokyo 1980; *Kabuki Actor, Tokizio, the Fifth,* with text by Konichiro Tamada, Tokyo 1980. **Articles**—''Multilateral'' in *Asahi Camera* (Tokyo), December 1963; ''Vivace!'' in *Asahi Camera* (Tokyo), April 1969; ''Nude in Okinawa'' in *Asahi Camera* (Tokyo), April 1970; ''Paris, Light and Shadow'' and ''Since Then'' in *Nippon Camera* (Tokyo), February 1971;

"Flora Flora" in *Asahi Camera* (Tokyo), April 1973; "The Blood" in *Asahi Camera* (Tokyo), February 1975; "Twin" in *Nippon Camera* (Tokyo), February 1975; "Autumn in Kyoto" in *Asahi Camera* (Tokyo), September 1976; "Sic Faces" in *Nippon Camera* (Tokyo), January 1977; "As She Is ..." in *Nippon Camera* (Tokyo), June 1977; "Slot Machine" in *Camera Mainichi* (Tokyo), April 1980; "Blown Eve" in *Nippon Camera* (Tokyo), January 1981.

On NAKAMURA: Books—*Japanese Photography Today and Its Origin* by Attilio Colombo and Isabella Doniselli, Bologna, Italy 1979; *Nude Photographs of Japan,* with text by Shiroyasu Suzuki, Tokyo 1981. Article—"A World of Women" in *Popular Photography's Woman 1972,* New York 1972.

* * *

Masaya Nakamura, who was born in 1926 in Yokohama, is a graduate of Tokyo Fine Arts High School, with a major in photography. After working for Yomiuri Newspapers and Eiga Sekaisha, he joined Waseda Studios; he became a freelancer in 1955.

The subject of his work—whether it be commercials, still-lifes, fashion photography or nudes—is always women. His photographs are often symbolic. Such adjectives as "witty," "gentle," "emotional," "passionate" and "sensuous" all appropriately describe his photography.

—Norihiko Matsumoto

NAMUTH, Hans.

Nationality: American. Born: Essen, Germany, 17 March 1915; emigrated to the United States, 1941: naturalized, 1943. Education: Attended the Humboldt Oberrealschule, Essen, 1924-31; studied with Joseph Breitenbach, Paris, 1937-38, and with Breitenbach and Alexey Brodovitch at the New School for Social Research, New York, 1946-47. Military Service: Served in the French Foreign Legion, 1939-40, and in the United States Army Intelligence Service, in Europe, 1943-45: Purple Heart; Croix de Guerre; Medaille du Maroc. Family: Married Carmen P. de Herrera in 1943; children: Tessa and Peter. Career: Freelance photographer, working for *Vu, Life,* etc., Paris and Majorca, 1935-38 (covered Spanish Civil War for *Vu* and other magazines, 1936-37), and for *Life, Look, Time, Newsweek, Harper's Bazaar, Vogue,* etc., New York, since 1946; established studio, New York, 1950; also, freelance filmmaker since 1951. Recipient: Merit Award, Film Council of Greater Boston, 1952; Association of Business Publishers Award, 1955; Art Directors Club of New York Award, 1956, 1959; Public Service Award, United States Department of State, 1958; Art Directors Club of Philadelphia Award, 1959. Agent: Castelli Graphics, 4 East 77th Street, New York, New York 10021, U.S.A. Address: 20 West 22nd Street, New York, New York 10010, U.S.A.

Individual Exhibitions:

1949	*Guatemala: The Land, The People,* Museum of Natural History, New York (travelled to Pan-American Union, Washington, D.C., and the American Federation of Arts, New York, 1950)
1955	*Guatemala: The Land, The People,* American Federation of Arts, New York
1958	*17 American Painters,* at the *World's Fair,* Brussels
1959	*17 American Painters,* Stable Gallery, New York
1967	*Pollock,* Museum of Modern Art, New York
1973	*American Artists,* Castelli Gallery, New York
1974	*American Artists,* Corcoran Gallery, Washington, D.C.
1975	*Early American Tools,* Castelli Gallery, New York (travelled to the Washington Gallery of Photography, Washington, D.C.;

	Water Mill Museum, New York; and Guild Hall, East Hampton, New York, 1975; and the Broxton Gallery, Los Angeles, 1976)
1976	*The Spanish Civil War,* Castelli Graphics, New York
	Living Together, Benson Gallery, Bridgehampton, Long Island, New York
1978	*Small Retrospective,* Himelfarb Gallery, Water Mill, Long Island, New York
1979	*Todos Santos,* Castelli Graphics, New York (travelled to the Parrish Art Museum, Southampton, Long Island, New York)
	Jackson Pollock, Museum of Modern Art, Oxford
	Jackson Pollock: 63 Prints, Musée d'Art Moderne de la Ville, Paris (travelled to the Stedelijk Museum, Amsterdam)
1980	*Pictures from the War in Spain 1936-37,* Galerie Fiolet, Amsterdam
	Pollock Painting, Castelli Graphics, New York (travelled to the Magnuson Lee Gallery, Boston, and the Margo Leavin Gallery, San Francisco, 1981)
1981	*Artists 1950-1981: A Personal View,* Pace Gallery, New York
1982	Leo Castelli Gallery, New York
	Catskill Center for Photography, Woodstock, New York
	Mercer County Community College, Trenton, New Jersey
	Carl Solway Gallery, Cincinnati, Ohio
	Hunter College, New York
	Phoenix II Gallery, Washington, D.C.
1984	Modernism Gallery, San Francisco
1986	Städtische Galerie, Munich

Selected Group Exhibitions:

1975	*The Photographer and the Artist,* Sidney Janis Gallery, New York
1979	*Self-Portraits,* Center for Creative Photography, University of Arizona, Tucson
1982	*Counterparts: Form and Emotion in Photographs,* Metropolitan Museum of Art, New York (travelled to the Contemporary Arts Center, Cincinnati; Dallas Museum of Fine Arts, Texas; San Francisco Museum of Modern Art; Corcoran Gallery, Washington, D.C.)
1983	*Die fotografische Sammlung,* Museum Folkwang, Essen, West Germany
1984	*Portraits of Artists,* San Francisco Museum of Modern Art

Collections:

Metropolitan Museum of Art, New York; Museum of Modern Art, New York; Virginia Museum of Fine Arts, Richmond; Tulane University, New Orleans; Cleveland Art Museum; Center for Creative Photography, University of Arizona, Tucson; Los Angeles County Museum of Art; Fondation de la Photographie, Lyons; Museum Folkwang, Essen.

Publications:

By NAMUTH: Books—*52 Artists,* New York 1973; *American Masters,* with text by Brain O'Doherty, New York 1973; *Early American Tools,* New York 1975; *L'Atelier de Jackson Pollock,* with text by Rosalind Krauss and Francis V. O'Connor, Paris 1978; *Pollock Painting,* New York 1980; *Artists 1950-1981: A Personal View,* New York 1981; *Der Krieg in Spanien 1936,* Munich 1986; films (with Paul Falkenberg)—*Jackson Pollock,* 1951; *Willem de Kooning, the Painter,* 1958; *Homage to the Square,* 1969; *The Brancusi Retrospective at the Guggenheim,* 1970; *Centennial at the Grand Palais,* 1971; *Louis I. Kahn, Architect,* 1972; *Alfred Stieglitz, Photographer,* 1982; *Balthus at the Pompidou,* 1984.

On NAMUTH: Books—*Counterparts: Form and Emotion in Photographs* by Weston J. Naef, New York 1982; *The Library of World Photography:*

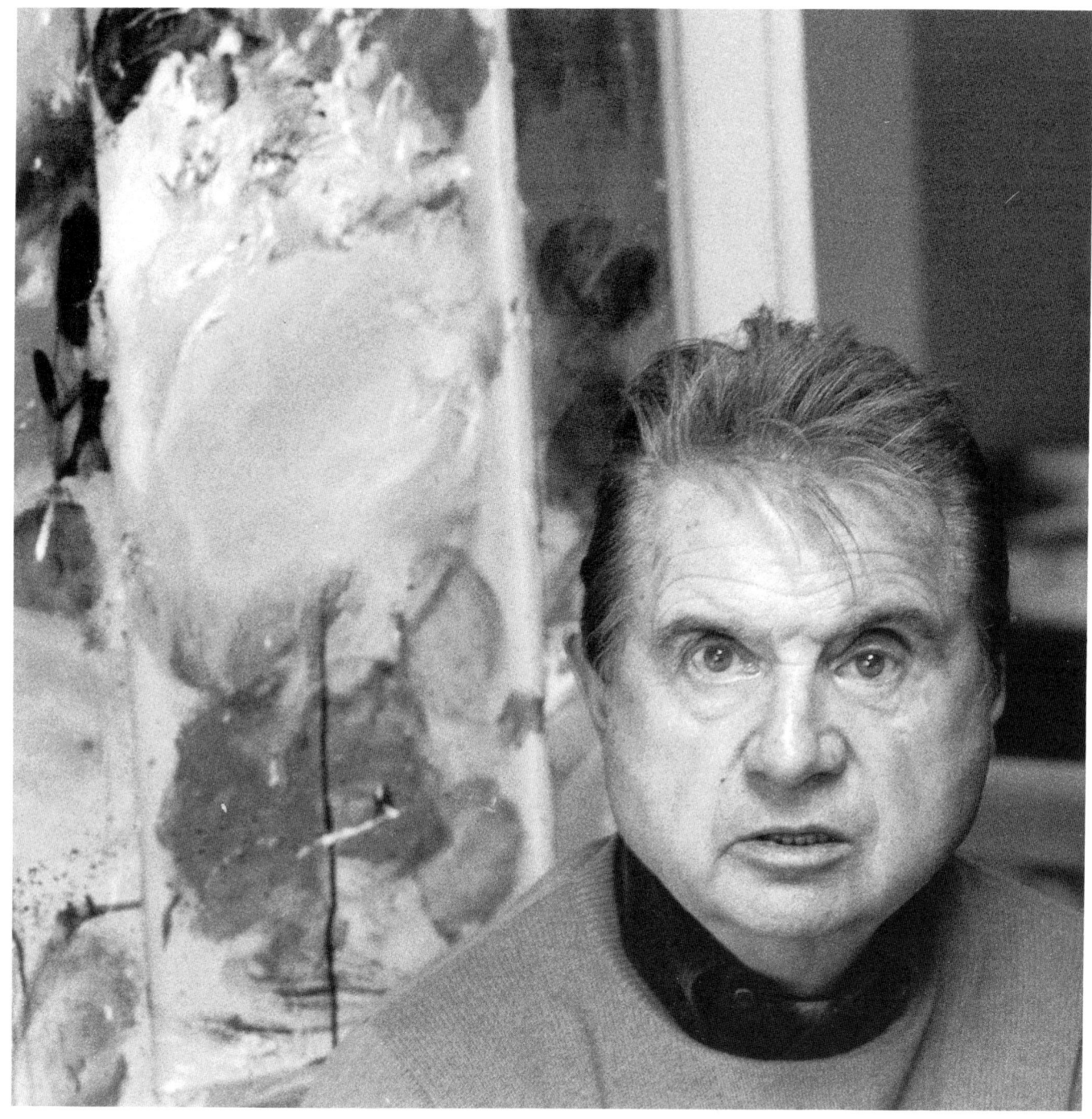

The Painter Francis Bacon, **London, 1984.** Photograph by Hans Namuth.

Photography as Fine Art, with introduction by Douglas Davis, Tokyo 1982, 1983, London 1983; *Museum Folkwang: die fotografische Sammlung,* exhibition catalogue, with introduction by Ute Eskildsen, Essen, West Germany 1983. **Article**—"Hans Namuth" in *Camera* (Lucerne), January 1979.

*

I remember Alexey Brodovitch's words to his class (in 1947 or thereabouts): "You can't be a photographer from 9 to 5. You are a 24-hour photographer or you are not a photographer."

Alexey Brodovitch left his mark on me as he did on everyone whose life he touched.

Today I realize that there are still many fields in art—as in photography—still unexplored. I find new directions and new ideas almost daily.

—Hans Namuth

*   *   *

Hans Namuth's photographs occupy a special position in contemporary photography, balanced between the separate worlds of art and of art photography.

Namuth's earliest published and exhibited images are a series of documentary photographs, made collaboratively with Georg Reisner in Madrid during the Spanish Civil War. In the late 1940s, Namuth began to photograph in Guatemala, documenting areas that he revisits to the present time. But it was in the 1950s, after his studies with Alexey Brodovitch and Joseph Breitenbach, that Namuth began what has become his most widely recognized contribution to photography, the documentation of artists at work. Beginning with his classic study of Jackson Pollock in his studio (1950-51), Namuth continued to document the early Abstract Expressionist painters at work. His style, one of naturalness and freshness, separates his work from other photographers who have covered similar subject matter. Rather than emphasize a formality of composition that would mystify his subjects, Namuth sought a calmer approach—showing artists at work, in their studios, etc. The work succeeds without unnecessary bravado. There is an air of collaboration, not competition, between the artist and the photographer. This pursuit continues to the present date, and has expanded to include photographs of artists of later generations, architects and other art world personages.

In the mid 1970s, Namuth embarked upon another extensive series, titled *Early American Tools*. Using an 8 x 10 camera in an outdoor studio, Namuth has documented the modest tools used to build in the 18th century. Besides merely photographing these objects, Namuth's methods transform the simple objects into sculptural entities, beautiful in form and ambiguous in scale. This body of work, published in 1975, continues as Namuth discovers new pieces to enhance the grouping.

A third example of the serial nature of Namuth's work is a series of portraits made in Todos Santos, a small hill village in Guatemala. In subsequent trips to the area over three decades, Namuth has documented the rituals and local environment. In the late 1970s he began an ambitious project to photograph all the inhabitants of the village. This humane compilation has produced beautiful images and serves as a rich source of anthropological information. All phases of village life are represented by local personages—shamans, farmers, politicians, etc.

Paralleling his interest in portraiture, Namuth has produced a series of films (in association with Paul Falkenberg) on various artists: Jackson Pollock, Josef Albers, Willem de Kooning, Brancusi, Louis Kahn, and Alexander Calder. These films, when considered as an extension of his still photography, secure Namuth an interesting position in the world of the arts, as both artist and artist's witness.

—Marvin Heiferman

NARAHARA, Ikko.

Nationality: Japanese. **Born:** Fukuoka, 3 November 1931. **Education:** Matsue High School, Matsue, 1948-50; Chuo University, Tokyo, B.A. (law). 1954; Waseda University, Tokyo, M.A. (art history), 1959. **Family:** Married Keiko Nakagawa in 1958. **Career:** Freelance photographer, Tokyo, since 1956. Founder Member, with Hosoe, Tomatsu, Kawada, Sato, and Tanno, Vivo Ltd. photographers agency, Tokyo, 1959-61. **Recipient:** Most Promising Photographer Award, 1959, and Photographer of the Year Award, 1967, Japan Photo Critics Association; Mainichi Arts Award, 1967; Arts Award, Ministry of Education, 1968; Award of the Year, Photographic Society of Japan, 1986; Higashikawa Prize, 1987. **Address:** Villa Fresca 702, 2-30-22 Jingumae, Shibuya-ku, Tokyo, Japan.

Individual Exhibitions:

1956	*Man and His Land*, Matsushima Gallery, Tokyo
1958	*Domains*, Fuji Photo Salon, Tokyo (travelled to the Fuji Salon, Osaka)
1959	*Image of Castle*, Marunouchi Gallery, Tokyo
1960	*Blue Yokohama*, Gekko Gallery, Tokyo
	Land of Chaos, Fuji Photo Salon, Tokyo
1965	*España Gran Tarde*, Fuji Photo Salon, Tokyo (and at the Ichi Bankan Gallery and Seibu Gallery, Tokyo, 1970)
1972	*Celebration of Life*, Seibu Gallery, Tokyo
1973	*Ikko*, International Museum of Photography, George Eastman House, Rochester, New York (then at the Neikrug Gallery and Nikon House, New York)
1974	*Ikko's America*, Nikon Salon, Tokyo (travelled to the Nikon Salon, Osaka)
1975	*Ikko*, Light Gallery, New York
1976	*Where Time Has Stopped*, Shadai Gallery, Tokyo
1977	*B'way 1973-74*, Iida Gallery, Tokyo
1979	*Piazza San Marco*, Wako Hall, Tokyo
	Journey to a Land So Near and Yet So Far, Nikon Salon, Iida Gallery, and Unac Salon, Tokyo (travelled to the Nikon Salon, Osaka; and Ban Gallery, Osaka)
1980	*Light in Venezia*, Nikon Salon, Tokyo
	Light and Waves Maruzen Gallery, Tokyo
1981	The Photographers' Gallery, London
1983	*Luminous City: Venezia*, Nikon Salon, Tokyo (travelled to Osaka)
	Aerial Perspective, Seibu Art Gallery, Tokyo
1985	*Humanscape*, Yurakucho Asahi Gallery, Tokyo
	Walker Hill Art Center, Seoul, Korea
1986	*Digital City*, Nikon Salon, Tokyo (travelled to Osaka)
1987	*Human Land*, Photo Gallery International, Tokyo (travelled to Pictur Photo Space, Osaka)
	Stateless Land, Unac Salon, Tokyo
	Stellar Memories, Parco Gallery, Tokyo
	Venezia, Printemps Ginza, Tokyo
1988	*Venezia*, Daimaru Museum, Osaka
1989	*Bergamo*, Unac Salon, Tokyo
1991	*Broadway, Rebirth*, Photo Gallery International, Tokyo
1994	*Blue Yokohama*, Past Rays Photo Gallery, Yokohama, Japan
	Fifteen Thousand Nights, Plaza Gallery, Tokyo

Selected Group Exhibitions:

1957	*The Eyes of 10 Men*, Konishiroku Gallery, Tokyo (and 1958, 1959)
1961	*Non*, Matsuya Gallery, Tokyo
	10 Contemporaries, Museum of Modern Art, Tokyo (and 1966)
1973	*New Japanese Photography*, Museum of Modern Art, New York
1977	*Neue Fotografie aus Japan*, Kulturhaus, Graz, Austria (travelled to the Museum des 20. Jahrhunderts, Vienna)
1978	*Vivo*, Santa Barbara Museum of Art, California
1979	*Japan: A Self-Portrait*, International Center of Photography, New York
1980	*The Imaginery Photo Museum*, Kunsthalle, Cologne
1984	*Six Contemporary Photographers*, Seibu Art Forum, Tokyo
1986	*Houston and the Rodeo*, at the *Foto Fest*, Houston, Texas
	1910-70 Japon des Avant-gardes, Le Center Georges Pompidou, Paris, France
1990	*Tokyo-TOKYO*, Yurakucho-Seibu Art Forum, Tokyo
1991	*54 Master Photographers of 1960-79*, International Center of Photography, New York
	Innovation in Japanese Photography in the 1960s, Tokyo Metropolitan Museum of Photography, Japan
	Photographs in Japan 1955-1965, The Yamaguchi Prefecture Museum of Art, Yamaguchi
	Venice, New Church Museum, Amsterdam, Holland
1993	*Photographers Who Created A New Age 1960s-70s*, Tokyo Metropolitan Museum of Photography, Tokyo
1994	*Reflection of Venice*, The Art Museum Princeton University, New Jersey

Collections:

Nihon University, Tokyo; Tokyo Polytechnic Institute; Kyushu Sangyo University, Fukuoka, Japan; Kyushu Zokei Junior College, Fukuoka; Bibliothèque Nationale, Paris; Museum of Modern Art, New York; International Museum of Photography, George Eastman House, Rochester, New York; Museum of Fine Arts, Boston; Houston Museum of Fine Arts, Texas;

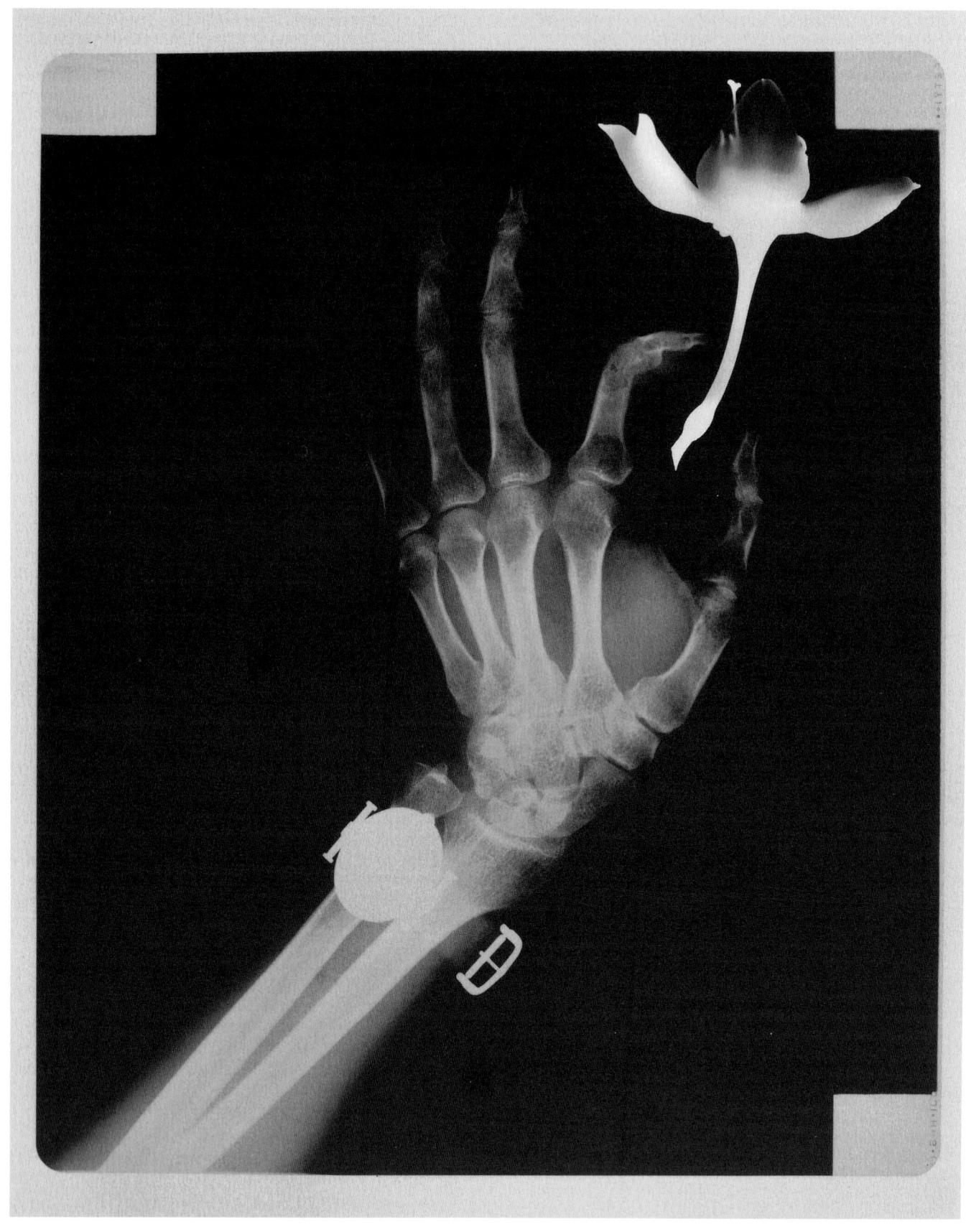

Inner Flower, No 17 Eucharis, **1991 from the book** *Kú-Emptiness,* **1994.** Photograph ©Ikko Narahara.

Museum für Kunst und Gewerbe, Hamburg; The Art Museum, Princeton University, New Jersey; Center for Creative Photography, The University of Arizona; The National Museum of Art, Osaka, Japan; Tokyo Metropolitan Museum of Photography, Tokyo; Yokohama Museum of Art, Japan; Kawasaki City Museum, Japan; The Yamaguchi Prefecture Museum of Art, Japan.

Publications:

By NARAHARA: Books—*Where Time Has Stopped*, Tokyo 1967; *España Gran Tarde*, Tokyo 1969; *The World of Kazuo Yagi*, Tokyo 1969; *Japanesque*, Tokyo 1970; *Man and His Land*, Tokyo 1971; *Celebration of Life*, Tokyo 1972; *Where Time Has Vanished*, Tokyo 1975; *Seven from Ikko*, portfolio, with an introduction by Shuzo Takiguchi, Tokyo 1977; *Domains*, Tokyo 1978; *Journey to a Land So Near and Yet So Far*, Tokyo 1979; *Light and Waves*, with an introduction by J.G. Ballard, Tokyo 1980; *Portici di Luce: Piazza San Marco*, Tokyo 1981; *Trace Space Wonderland*, Tokyo 1983; *Aerial Perspective*, Tokyo 1983; *Aerial Perspective*, portfolio, with poems by Ryuichi Tamura, Tokyo 1983; *Humanscape*, Tokyo 1985; *Venice—Nightscapes*, Tokyo 1985; *Venetian Light*, Tokyo 1987; *Human Land*, Tokyo 1987; *Stellar Memories*, Tokyo 1987; *Broadway*, Tokyo 1991; *Marcel Duchamp Large Glass with Shuzo Takiguchi Cigar Box*, Tokyo 1992; *Kú—Emptiness*, Tokyo 1994; *Japanesque*, Milan, 1994.

On NARAHARA: Books—*Man and His Land* by Masakazu Yamazaki, Tokyo 1971; *Modern Photography Annual*, New York 1972; *New Japanese Photography*, exhibition catalogue, by Shoji Yamagishi, New York 1973; *Creative Camera Yearbook*, London 1978; *Journey to a Land So Near and Yet So Far*, exhibition catalogue, by Koen Shigemori, Tokyo 1979; *Japan: A Self-Portrait*, exhibition catalogue, by Shoji Yamagishi, New York 1979; *De Japanse Fotografie van 1848 tot Heden*, exhibition catalogue, by Attilio Colombo and Isabella Doniselli, Amsterdam 1980; *Nude Photographs of Japan*, with text by Shiroyasu Suzuki, Tokyo 1981; *A Day in the Life of Japan—June 7, 1985*, edited by Rick Smolan and David Cohen, New York and London 1985; *Venezia*, exhibition catalogue by Hiroshi Hamaya, Tokyo 1987; *Innovation in Japanese Photography in the 1960s*, exhibition catalogue by Ryuichi Kaneko, Tokyo 1991; *Photographers Who Created a New Age*, exhibition catalogue by Noriaki Kokubo and Kyoko Jimbo, Tokyo 1993. Articles—by Allan Porter in *Camera* (Lucerne), September 1966; by Julia Scully in *Modern Photography* (New York), March 1968; by Richard Busch in *Popular Photography* (New York), August 1975; by Marline Voyeux in *Zoom* (Paris), June 1978; by Kineo Kuwahara in *Nihon Camera* (Tokyo), July 1987; by Osamu Hiraki in *Asahi Camera* (Tokyo), May 1991; by Ryuichi Kaneko in *Nihon Camera* (Tokyo), November 1991; by Akiko Otake in *Geijutsu Shincho* (Tokyo), August 1993; by Ryuichi Kaneko in *Nihon Camera* (Tokyo), June 1994.

*

Photography is . . .
Photography is window with my mind within, world
     without.
Photography is experience and expression of light.
Photography is visual science fiction.
Photography is fossil of life.
Photography is frozen time and space.
Photography is continuity and discontinuity.
Photography is hidden dimension of cosmos.
Photography is presage of future.
Photography is direct and cryptic.
Photography is intuition.
Photography is dream.
Photography is destiny.
Photography is hands of the Universe.
Photography is KAMIWAZA (the works of God).
Photography reveals myself.

—Ikko Narahara

*   *   *

Ikko's reputation is largely based on his work outside Japan, especially his two major series, *Where Time Has Stopped* and *Where Time Has Vanished*. His travels and exhibitions in America and Europe have gained him wide, international recognition.

After graduating as a student of art history, Ikko Narahara returned to the area of Japan where he had grown up. With no photographic training, he borrowed his father's camera to document two corresponding worlds close to his home, drawing parallels between the village of Kurogami, which had been ruined and isolated by a volcanic eruption, and the artificial island of Hajima, known locally as "Warship Island" because of its strange shape, a coal mine surrounded by a concrete wall 30 feet high. This project was the start of a pattern that was to emerge through much of his later work. Ikko was attracted to the isolated, closed community that encapsulated the forces of a much wider human condition. The correspondence was between the village isolated by nature and the island isolated by the needs of society. He exhibited this work in 1956 in the exhibition *Man and His Land*, which was a surprising success. He continued the theme in 1958 with his document of a women's prison in Wakayama City compared with a Trappist monastery at Hakodate on Hokkaido. The world of silent retreat was compared to one of brutal ostracism. This work was to appear in the book *Man and His Land* and was reprinted in *Domains*.

Ikko's first exhibition did not conform to the predominant style of photorealism, but was unorthodox, subjective and conceptual. The critics viewed it as a challenge to existing photo conventions, and they heralded him as a "new realist." Ken Domon, the master of a classic Japanese realism, was shortly to declare that "the first phase of Realism is over." The critic Tatsuo Fukishima subsequently asked Ikko and Eikoh Hosoe, who had recently held his own first exhibition (the narrative series "An American Girl in Tokyo," 1956), to cover an arts festival. This joint venture lead to the formation of the *Junin-no-me*, The Eyes of Ten.

By the end of the 1950s Japan was undergoing a great social upheaval following in the wake of the Occupation. The new, subjective style of Ikko and Hosoe was most appropriate for recording a country in rapid transition to economic strength and the development of a modern society with all the tensions and contradictions it contained. The critic Fukishima coordinated the work of Ikko, Hosoe and Tomatsu, together with the other members of the *Junin-no-me* group. The group was not an agency, but was formed to participate in collective exhibitions, the first of which was held at the Konishiroku Gallery in Tokyo in May 1957; subsequent exhibitions were held in 1958 and 1959. Ikko went on with Hosoe and Tomatsu to form the Vivo group, a collective agency of six photographers from the core of the *Junin-no-me*. The Vivo group exhibited until January 1962. The formation of these two groups marked the beginning of a modern Japanese photography, which was not imitative of, but quite distinguished from, developments of photography in the West.

Following the breakup of Vivo, Ikko went to Europe for three years. On his return, the results of his travels were published in his first book, *Where Time Has Stopped*. In contrast to the claustrophobic view of his first series, Ikko presented the expansive perspective of man in motion, with all the stimulation of a new, alien culture. He had grown up in a Japan that had been devastated; with the exception of Kyoto, every city had been bombed. In Europe he confronted the fabric of history that had survived the World War: it was a striking contrast to the concrete of his reconstructed native Japan. To hold that perspective, he attempted, as his title suggests, to freeze his image, not as in the minimal time of photographic exposure, but as in a long corridor of history. He photographed the stifled body of the man from Pompeii and framed him in his glass case. He looked for the dark shadows in the lanes of a Renaissance city or the form of arches on a Roman aqueduct. It was an overtly surreal Europe straight out of the conventions of de Chirico, in which classical architecture formed a backdrop to a play of mysterious shadow. These pictures are not inhabited by people but haunted by their shadows as giant, distorted silhouettes on stone walls. Ikko has indicated that the source of this imagery was the silhouette of the disintegrated man whose shadow appears on the wall at the site of the epicentre of the explosion at Hiroshima. "For many decades," he has said, "we will evolve through history in the company of this shadow."

In 1969 he published *España Gran Tarde*, a celebration of Spain and the bullring. Spanish tradition, with its flamboyance and passion, was immensely attractive to anyone from a more austere Japanese background. His Spanish work was closer to subjective or pictorial documentary as exemplified by Eugene Smith's "Spanish Village" series of 1951.

From 1970 to 1974 Ikko lived in New York and travelled widely in America. Unlike his European series, in his American series, *Where Time Has Vanished,* he created the illusion of America as a land with no past but a continual present. Many of the pictures have a flat, expansive sense of space. One is very conscious of his skies, which harbour lightning or neat, white Magritte clouds, which trigger the familiar surrealist connotation. He still found his silhouettes against frosted glass or in the shadow of a child on tarmac. There is the picture of the garbage cans flying down a village street in New Mexico, which was widely published, but more impressive is the shadow of the car driving through the Arizona desert. It is a distorted streak along the American highway, speeding past the surface of things to Ikko's vacant, timeless zone.

The most recent exhibitions of Japanese photography in Europe and New York have included work that Ikko did in 1969 at the Sojiji Temple in Tsurumi, which is a Zen temple of the Soto sect. The series is called ''Silence.'' The exhibition of the series was a result of Ikko's new perspective on his own country on his return from abroad. It forms a logical third part to his other two major series and a reassertion of his Japanese identity, in common with the leading photographers of his generation. In this series he had no need to develop the borrowed imagery of an alien culture, but, true to the spirit of the subject, has found that vacant zone in his observations of the practice of zazen. It is a still world in which even the faces of the statues have been removed to leave a hollowed, black space, and the shaved heads of those who sit in zazen reveal no more than masks.

—Mark Holborn

NAVARRO, Rafael.

Nationality: Spanish. **Born:** Zaragoza, 8 October 1940. **Education:** Self-taught in photography. **Military Service:** Served in the Spanish Army/Air Force, 1960-62. **Family:** Married Rosa Jera in 1965; children: Cesar, Alejandro, Sergio, Eduardo, Isabel and Pablo. **Career:** Worked for ANZA industrial company, Zaragoza, 1962-73. Freelance photographer, Zaragoza, since 1973. Founder Member, with Joan Fontcuberta, Pere Formigera and Manel Escluso, Grupo Alabern photographers, Barcelona, since 1977. President, Sociedad Fotográfica de Zaragoza, 1974; Spanish Representative, Consejo Latinoamerica de Fotografia, 1978; Assessment Council Member, Fundacio Joan Miro, Barcelona, 1985. **Recipient:** Artist Award, Federation Internationale de l'Art Photographique (FIAP), 1976. **Agent:** Mme. Michele Chomette, 240 bis Boulevard Saint-Germain, 75007 Paris, France. **Address:** Marqués de Ahumada 13, 50007 Zaragoza, Spain.

Individual Exhibitions:

1973	Galeria Prisma, Zaragoza, Spain
1974	Galeria Antonio Machado, Madrid
	Galeria Aixelá, Barcelona
1975	Galeria Spectrum, Barcelona
1976	Galeria de C.F.C., Santiago de Chile
	Galeria Spectrum, Ibiza
	Aula de Cultura Guecho, Bilbao, Spain
1977	Galerie de l'Instant, Paris
	Galeria Altre Immagini, Rome
	Galeria Spectrum-Canon, Zaragoza, Spain
1978	Canon Photo Gallery, Geneva
	Galerie 31, Vevey, Switzerland
	Fotomania, Barcelona
	Galeria de Arte de Caja Ahorros Provincial, Tarragona, Spain
1979	Galeria Pepe Rebollo, Zaragoza, Spain
	Galleria II Laboratorio d'If, Palermo, Italy
	Canon Photo Gallery, Amsterdam
	The White Gallery, Tel Aviv
	Sala Bellas Artes, Guadalajara, Mexico
1980	Foto Kit Galeria, Vitoria, Spain
	Galerij Paule Pia, Antwerp

	Photographic Center, Athens
	Night Gallery, London
	Photographic Gallery, Cardiff, Wales
	Galeria Tretze, Valencia, Spain
1981	Sala Zurbaran del Ateneo de Sevilla
	Galeria Costa-3 de Zaragoza
	Instituto Cultural Hispano-Mexicano, Mexico City
	Galerie Suzanne Küpfer, Nidau-Bienne, Switzerland
	Caon Photo Gallery/Le Trepied, Geneva
	Centre Culturel Le Parvis, Tarbes, France
1982	Galleria Il Diaframma-Canon, Milan
	Galeria Spectrum, Gerona, Spain
	Galerie Photo Art, Basle, Switzerland
	Fotogaleria Forum, Tarragona, Spain
	Musée de la Photographie, Charleroi, Belgium
	Instituto de Estudios Riojanos, Logrono, Spain
	Collage Galeria de Arte, Monterrey, Mexico
	Galleria Figura, Biella, Italy
	Studio Fossati, Alessandria, Italy
	Galleria Milano, Milan
	Galeria Album, Sao Paulo, Brazil
	Galleria Agora, Turin, Italy
	Galleria Lotti, Bologna, Italy
	La Chambre Claire, Paris
	Galeria Redor, Madrid
1983	Galleria Fotografiaoltre, Chiasso, Switzerland
	Galerie Alexandre de la Salle, St. Paul de Vence, France
	Berner Photo-Galerie, Berne, Switzerland
	Galerie Le Reverbere, Lyon, France
	Galerie Pro Photo, Nuremberg, Germany
	Instituto Social del Tiempo Libre, Guadalajara, Spain
1984	Galeria Contratalla, Tarragona, Spain
	Kem Damy Gallery, Brescia, Italy
	Fotoforum, Bremen, Germany
	Museum für Photographie, Braunschweig, Germany
1985	Galerie de prêt de Grand Place, Grenoble, France
	Fotogaleria Nueva Imagen, Pamplona, Spain
	Galerie zur Stockeregg, Zurich
	Galeria Petroperu, Lima, Peru
	Spazio Immagine, Bari, Italy
	Maison du Department, Quimper, France
	Centro Nuova Cultura, Lucera Italy
	Centre d'Action Culturelle, Saint-Brieuc, France
	Visor Centre Fotografic, Valencia, Spain
	Centro di Fotoscultura, Castel d'Assaro-Verona, Italy
	Centro d'If, Milan
1986	Galeria Camara Obscura, Logrono, Spain
	Salas del Palacio de Sástago, Zaragoza, Spain
1987	Fotogalleriet, Oslo
	Museo de Bellas Artes, Bilbao, Spain
	Museo Español de Arte Contemporáneo, Madrid
	Perimeter Gallery, Chicago, USA
1988	Le Chateau d'Eau, Toulouse, France
1989	Galerie Faber, Vienna
	Teatro Municipal de San Martin, Buenos Aires, Argentina
	Centre de la Photographie-Gèneve, Maison le Grütli, Geneva, Switzerland
1990	Galeria Spectrum, Zaragoza, Spain
1992	International Week of Photography, Plovdiv, Bulgaria
	Casa dos Crivos, Braga, Portugal
	Escuela Argentina de Fotografia, Buenos Aires, Argentina
1993	Bibliothèque Municipale Part-Dieu, Lyon, France
	Palacio de Exposiciones Kiosco Alfonso, La Coruna, Spain
	Museo Ken Damy, Brescia, Italy
1994	*Fundació Pilar i Joan Miró,* Palma de Mallorca, Spain

Selected Group Exhibitions:

1976	*Seis Fotografos,* Escuela Superior de Bellas Artes, Madrid
1978	*La Fotografia Española,* Centro Juana Mordo, Madrid

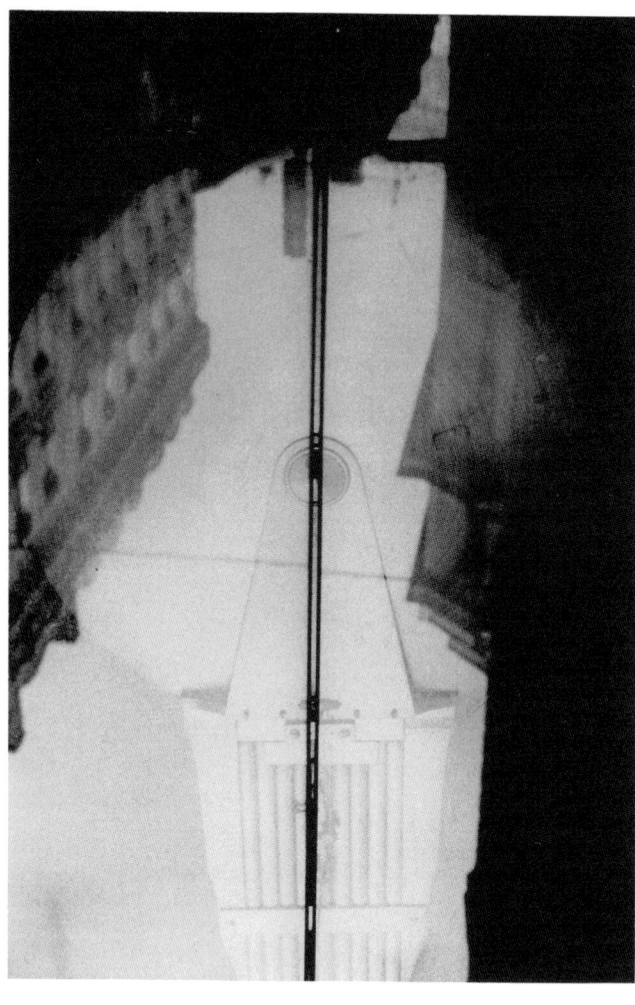

Tempo (n° 1 al n° 10), **1991**. Photograph ©Rafael Navarro.

1979   *New Photographers from Spain,* Spanish National Tourist
        Office, New York
1980   *Hommage à Giorgio de Chirico,* Modern Gallery, Ljubljana,
        Yugoslavia
1981   *Fotografía Subjetiva,* Instituto Aleman, Madrid
1982   *Women in the Magic Mirror,* Padiglione d'Arte
        Contemporanea, Milan
1983   *European Photography,* Northeastern University, Boston
1985   *Construire les Paysages de la Photographie,* Caves Saint-
        Croix, Metz, France
        La Fotografía en el Museo, Español de Arte Contemporaneo,
        Madrid
1986   *Regards Photographiques,* Chapelle de l'Ancien College,
        Montpellier, France
        Contemporary Spanish Photography, University Art Museum,
        Albuquerque, New Mexico
1987   *After Franco,* Marcuse Pfeifer, Gallery, New York
        Facets of the Collection, San Francisco Museum of Modern
        Art, San Francisco
        Le Temps d'un Mouvement, Palais de Tokyo, Paris
        Echos d'Espagne, Espace Lumiere, Bordeaux, France
1988   *Creation Photographique en Espagne 1968-1988,* Musèe
        Cantini, Marseille, France
        *II Biennale International pour la Photographie et Recher-
        che,* Paris
        Cuatro Direcciones, Centro de Arte Reina Sofia, Madrid

1990   *The Spanish Vision 1970-1990,* The Spanish Institute,
        New York
        Visages, Paysages et Autres Rivages, Centre d'Art
        Contemporain, Brussels
        La Photographie dans le Monde, Musèe Nicèphore Nièpce,
        Chalons-sur-Saône, France
1993   *Foto-Biennale Enschede 93,* Enschede, The Netherlands
        Imatges Escollides, (Colección Gabriel Cualladó), IVAM,
        Valencia, Spain
        Recorridos Fotográficos, Colección de fotografias ARCO,
        Fundación Natwest, Madrid
1994   *Entre la pasión y el silencio,* Abbaye de Montmajour, RIP 94,
        Arles, France
        Pictores fictoresques, Galeria Joan Guaita, Palma de
        Mallorca, Spain

Collections:

Bibliothèque Nationale, Paris; Musée Réattu, Arles, France; Musée d'Art
Moderne, Brussels; Museum of Contemporary Art, Skopje, Croatia; Centro
Hidalgo, Mexico City; Musée de la Photographie, Charleroi, Belgium; Galerie
Municipale du Château d'Eau, Toulouse, France; Musée Nicéphore Niepce,
Châlon-sur-Saone, France; Fondos de Arte de las Cortes de Aragon,
Zaragoza, Spain; Università di Parma, Italy; Colección Hartkamp, Amerongen,
The Netherlands; Polaroid Collection, Cambridge, Massachusetts; Museo de
Arte Moderno, México DF, México; Fototeca de la Casa de las Américas, La
Habana, Cuba; Museo de Arte Contemporáneo, Madrid; Yokohama Museum
of Art, Yokohama, Japan; Galleria de Arte Moderna e Contemporanea de
Bergamo, Accademia Carrara, Bergamo, Italy; Museo Nacional Centro de
Arte Reina Sofia, Madrid; Fonds Municipal de Décoration, Geneva, Switzer-
land; Fabio Castelli Collection, Milan, Italy; International Junij Collection,
Ljubljana, Yugoslavia; FRAC Languedoc-Rousillon, Montpellier, France;
Collección Formiguera, Barcelona, Spain; Colección de la Caja de Ahorros de
San Fernando, Seville, Spain; Collección Auer, Geneva, Switzerland; IVAM-
Instituto Valenciano de Arte Moderno, Valencia, Spain; Colección Cualladó,
Madrid; Fototeca de Códoba, Córdoba, Spain; Colección Fontcuberta, Barce-
lona, Spain; Fundación Arco-Ifema, Madrid; Colección Visor, Valencia,
Spain.

Publications:

On NAVARRO: Books—*50 Años de Fotografia en Zaragoza,* Zaragoza,
Spain 1973; *Anuario Fotografico Española 74,* edited by Carlos Perez,
Madrid 1974; *Everfoto 3,* edited by Carlos Perez, Madrid 1975; *Cotecflash 3,*
edited by Francisco Torres, Barcelona 1976; *La Photographie Fantastique* by
Attilio Colombo, Paris 1979; *Hecho en Latino America 2,* with texts by Pedro
Meyer, Lazaro Blanco and others, Mexico City 1981; *Historia de la Fotografia*
by Marie-Loup Sougez, Madrid 1982; *Fotografía Europea Contemporanea,*
edited by Giovanni Chiaramonte, Milan 1983; *Construire les Paysages de la
Photographie,* exhibition catalogue, by Jean-Francois Chevrier, Jean-Marc
Poinsot and Michele Chomette, Metz, France 1984; *Historia de la Fotografia
Española,* Martinez Roca, Barcelona, 1988; *La FotoGalería del Teatro San
Martin,* by Sara Facio, Buenos Aires, Argentina, 1990; *The Spanish Vision:
Contemporary Art Photography 1970-1990,* New York, 1991; *Arco'83,
Arco'84, Arco'86, Arco'88, Arco'91, Arco'92, Arco'93,* Madrid; *Les Con-
serves de Nicéphore-Essai sur la nécessité d'inventer la photographie,*
Chalons-sur-Saône, France, 1992; *Imatges Escollides (Colección Gabriel
Cualladó)* Valencia 1993; *La photographie, histoire d'un art,* by Jean-Pierre
Amar, Aix en Provence, 1993; *Diccionario histórico de conceptos, tendencias
y estilos fotograficos,* by Yañez Polo, Seville, 1994. **Articles**—"Brujas" by
Pablo Perez M. in *Nueva Lente* (Madrid), October 1973; "La Femme
Gelatine" by Claude Nori in Contrejour (Paris), March 1976; "Rafael
Navarro" in *Reflexion* (Amsterdam), May 1979; "Dipticos" by Ignacio
Barceló in *Arte Fotografico* (Madrid), May 1979; "Juxtapositions" in *Petersen's
Photographic Magazine* (Los Angeles), June 1979; "Spanish Photography in
the 80s" by Joan Fontcuberta in *European Photography* (Göttingen), April
1980; "Presencias Metafisicas" by Joan Fontcuberta in *Nueva Lente* (Ma-
drid), October 1980;*Fototécnica,* Cuba, March 1986; *Art,* Hamburg, Germa-

ny, October 1988; *Focus,* Utrecht, The Netherlands, June, 1990; *Lapiz. Cien x 100 Arte Español,* Madrid, No 100 February 1994.

*

"Why are you a photographer?" has been the inevitable question since the very moment I started off; but my answer has undergone several changes through time, and I hope that it will go on changing in the future.

At the beginning I used to think that I had "a special feeling" for photos, and that was why I felt compelled to create pictures.

It didn't take me long to realize that I was actually using my photographs as a means of pouring out something burning inside me which I was not able to recognize, and even less able to tackle.

That made me understand that my flair for photographic expression had been purely casual and had only depended upon the circumstances which made me familiar with photography at the very moment I started needing to express my own self—full of disorder, counterpoints, taboos and inhibitions. Today, I am fully aware that my images have a lot of self-analysis in them, and I can even see among them some lousy self-portraits.

I cannot guess if all this comes true with my audience, but, anyway, I am not really interested in sending specific messages. I simply try to awaken certain emotions in those who observe (or should I say read?) my images— images which I intentionally impregnate with certain sensations. That is how, given a series of scattered clues, the spectator should create his or her own subjective interpretation and build up a personal response to the image.

My tendency towards introversion prevents me from direct communication with the people I happen to meet, and that aspect of my personality is obviously also present in my work—even though I want my photos to act as a counterpoint and not as a continuum of myself.

I openly introduce a lot of personal clues, which are hardly understandable to people who don't know me well; nevertheless, I have luckily had the opportunity to verify that these clues can be discovered by those who, even not knowing me, have a standpoint similar to my own.

I have never tried to stand up as a model of photographic expression, but I should be most glad if I succeeded in achieving sincerity in my work.

—Ravael Navarro

* * *

Within the prolific creativity of Rafael Navarro, it is with "Involución" (1976) and "Agur" (1977) and, most of all, with the series "Dìpticos" (initiated) in 1978) that his photographic expression reaches a true maturity. From this perspective, his earlier works now seem to be exercises to acquire and to discipline his creative potential and, as such, without any special importance for contemporary photography.

In "Involución," however, a message appears along with a more genuine and personal format treatment: the oppression-liberation dialectic of mankind expressed symbolically through the limitations of the negative itself. The confines of the photographic image represent the very same confines of vital space in which the photographic author moves. It is a vital space circumscribed by two principal forces: those dictates, moral and cultural, which form one's subsconscious, and the socio-political reality in which the artist has developed.

A work of art is, of course, a reflection of the artist's personal circumstances. But in the case of Navarro this dependency appears with more clarity than in most artists, suggesting the autobiographical, even the "therapeutic." Photography as an art form becomes equivalent to an arena of freedom wherein lies the possibility of evoking images that the artist can then utilize to escape from his own drama. In this way Navarro is a true representative of the artists and intellectuals of his generation. His attitude and personal contradictions are a sociological product of post-war Spain, that is to say, of the Franco era, characterized by a very difficult restructuring of the economy; culture viewed as subversion; a rigid Catholic morality; authoritarianism and discipline; a respect for tradition; and anachronistic familial values.

The work of Navarro can be compared to that of J.A. Labordeta in popular song and poetry. Although this comparison may seem inappropriate, there can be no doubt that their similarities go beyond that of simply sharing the same geographical and cultural origin—Aragon. In both the idea of rejecting the harsh and oppressive surrounding reality is the same, as is the poetic evasion in which they both take refuge. The "Involución" portfolio certainly contains

the same sentiments as these verses by Labordeta: "So you see/We have gone surging forth/With harsh, uncertain voices/Of despair."

In the "Dìpticos" the poetic space tends to broaden and universalize. Using the same graphic recourse throughout, Navarro arranges two distinct images whose confrontation creates a new meaning which is, according to him, "a subtle sensation, impossible to suggest with only one photograph." In effect, this binary arrangement permits a greater wealth of possibilities and amplifies the thematic and stylistic field enormously. As the Gestalt psychologists have long recognized, in the perception of visual images the whole is greater than the sum of its parts. The system doesn't attempt to develop aesthetic innovations. It simply allows a method of expression from which a whole series of messages emerge through the opposition of two primary concepts: presence vs. absence, materialism vs. spirituality, life vs. death, mobility vs. immobility, tension vs. pacifity, light vs. dark, hot vs. cold, natural vs. artificial, etc. And, naturally, behind this simple mechanism one encounters the complex unfolding of Navarro's inner life: the melancholia, the agony, the solitude, the rage, the placidity, the love, the humor, etc., as though he were taking inventory of his psychic states.

Although Rafael Navarro carefully guards this subjective world of his behind a language of fairly obscure symbolism, there is no doubt that those who have had intensely the same feelings will recognize in "Dìpticos" the keys to these experiences.

—Joan Fontcuberta

NÉMETH, József.

Nationality: Hungarian. **Born:** Budapest, 5 March 1911. **Education:** Studied ceramics and graphics, Technical High School, Budapest, Dip. 1929. **Military Service:** Served as a lieutenant in the Hungarian Army, 1929-30. **Family:** Married Eta Kremsz in 1939; duaghter: Andrea. **Career:** Made first photos, Budapest, 1926. Worked as a graphic designer, Budapest, 1930-34, and as a technical clerk and ceramics designer, Budapest, 1934-38; technical designer and adviser, in the photo laboratories of the Gamma Works, Budapest, 1938-46; freelance photographer, and commercial graphics designer, Budapest, 1946-61; graphic designer, MTI Hungarian News Service, Budapest, 1961 until his retirement in 1971. Editorial Committee Member, *Foto* magazine, Budapest, 1957-73. President, Photo Club of Budapest, 1957-58. **Recipient:** Agfa Grand Prize, 1940; Kodak Silver Wreath, 1942; Photokina Obelisk Award, Cologne, 1966; Béla Balázs Prize, Hungary, 1972; Daguerre and Niepce Memorial Medal, Paris, 1972; Merited Artist of the Hungarian Peoples' Republic, 1978; József Pécsi Prize, Hungary, 1982; Rizzoli Prize, Italy, 1967, 1969 and 1970; Honoured Artist of the Hungarian Republic, 1988; Award of Excellence, Federation Internationale des Artistes Photographes (FIAP). Member, Hungarian Union of Journalists. **Address:** 39 Tóth Lörinc Street, 1126 Budapest, Hungary.

Individual Exhibitions:

1963	Gallery of Art, Warsaw (retrospective; travelled to Krakow and Wroclaw, Poland)
1985	Fotómüvészeti Galéria, Budapest

Selected Group Exhibitions:

1941	*7th International EMAOSZ Photo Exhibition,* Budapest
1956	*International Exhibition,* Luxembourg
1959	*International Exhibition,* Barreiro, Portugal
	2nd Bifota Ausstellung, Berlin
1961	*4th International Artistic Photo Exhibition,* Budapest
1965	*Photoeurop,* Lausanne, Swittzerland
	International Art Salon, Bucharest, Rumania
1966	*125 Years of Hungarian Photography,* Hungarian National Gallery, Budapest
1969	*International Color Photography,* Singapore
1972	*La Ville,* Roubaix, France

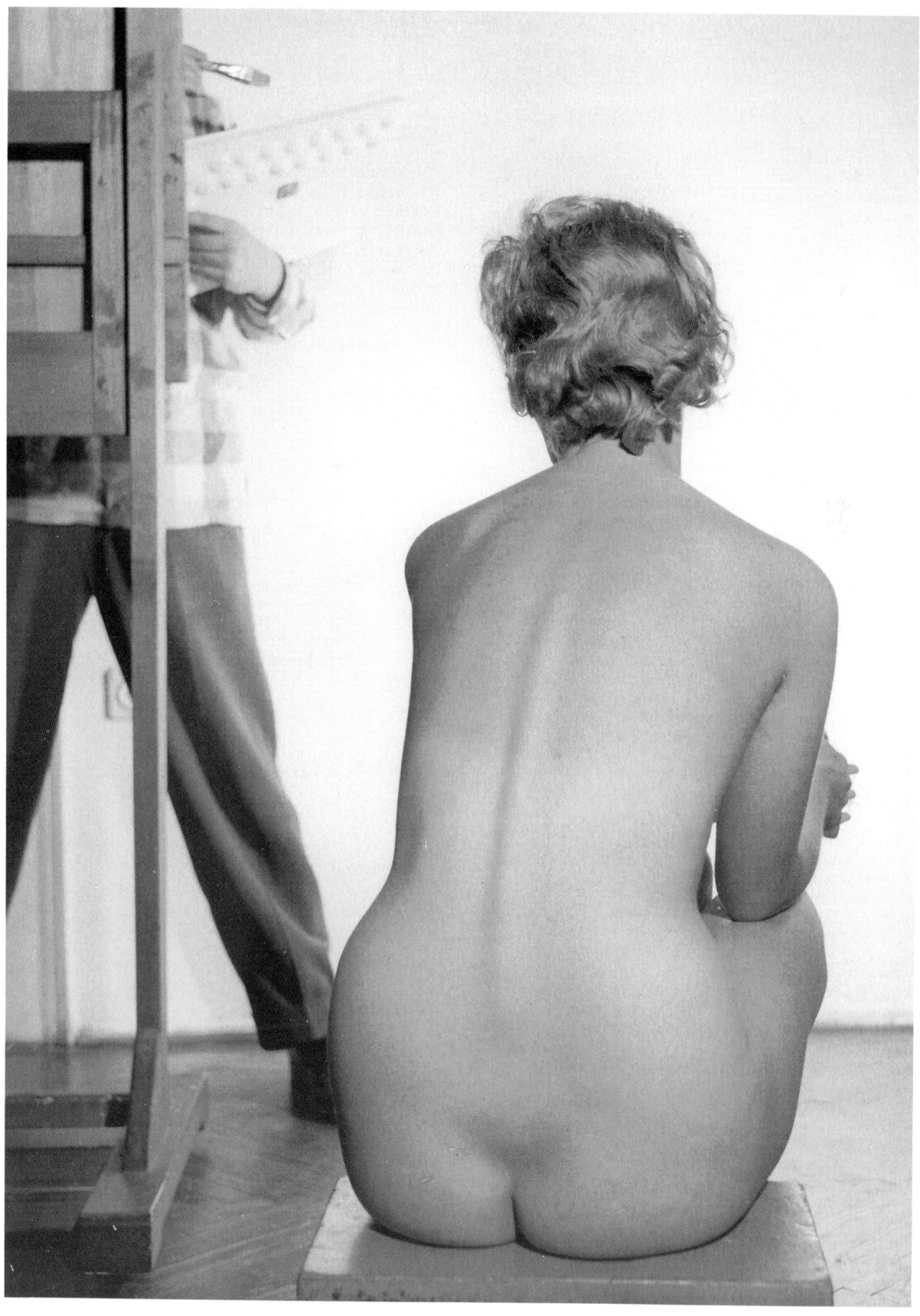

Painter and His Model, **1958.** Photograph by József Németh.

Collections:

Society of Hungarian Artistic Photographers, Budapest; Fotómüvészeti Galéria, Budapest.

Publications:

By NÉMETH: Books—*Wrestling*, with text by László Papp, Budapest 1943; *Leica Pictures*, Budapest 1945; *Pictures and Memories*, Budapest 1947; *Cheap Camera—Good Pictures*, Budapest 1955; *Ceramics of Sarospatak*, with text by János Román, Budapest 1955; *Special Objectives*, Budapest 1958; *China of Hollohaza*, with text by Gyözö Sikota, Budapest 1974; *The Art of Herend*, with text by Gyözö Sikota, Budapest 1976; *Mini Book of Herend*, with text by Gyözö Sikota, Budapest 1977; *China of Zsolna*, with text by Gyözö Sikota, Budapest 1985.

On NÉMETH: Books—*International Photos*, with introduction by Joachim Biebelhausen, Munich 1958; *Photography of the World '60*, edited by Hiromu Hara, Ihei Kimura and others, Tokyo and New York 1960. **Articles**—"József Németh" in *Fotoélet* (Budapest), 1943; "About József Németh" in *Hungarian Review* (Budapest), no. 1, 1962; "Visiting József Németh" by Miklós Csányi in *Fenyképmüvészeti Tájékoztató (Budapest)*, no. 1, 1965; "József Németh" in *Camera Owner* (London), no. 12, 1966; "József Németh" in *Foto Magazin* (Munich), no. 8, 1969; "József Németh: Balázs Béla Prize" by Lajos Végvári in *Fotómüvészet* (Budapest), no. 2, 1971; "Talking with József Németh" by Klára Töry in *Fotómüvészet* (Budapest), no. 4, 1975; "Meeting with József Németh" in *Magyar Hirlap* (Budapest), 1978.

* * *

József Németh belongs to the older generation of contemporary Hungarian photographers. Starting as an amateur in the 1930s, he became a highly skilled specialist in studio techniques, with work on nude studies, advertisement images and promotional brochures, almost exclusively in colour. Although his photographic taste was based on the style of pictures first made in the 1930s, his work reached its high point in the 1940s and 50s. Németh deliberately retained his amateur role in order to have the freedom to work in all the areas of photography that interested him. The books from his first amateur period, *Leica Pictures* and *Pictures and Memories*, show a wide choice of subject— from landscapes to intimate still lifes and portraits.

What differentiates Németh from his mainstream contemporaries is not the choice of subject, however, but his creative temperament. He is not one of those photographers who attempts to capture life's decisive moments. With his training in the fine arts, Németh aspires to no mere entrapment of surface reality; his goal is the formation of a particular ambience. Much of his meticulously controlled work, the result of long consideration and experiment, is therefore of a static character. The creative process in his photographic images does not start and end with the snapping of the camera's shutter. His nudes achieve a sort of universality via a stylization in which the individual and personal features of the body are subdued by the use of careful lighting. The figures present themslves as compositions of pure, decorative line, a cool, clean and non-erotic plasticity. Fond of neoclassical form, Németh harmonizes the shades of silver and grey into homogenous and timeless surfaces.

This timeless quality also touches his advertising and still-life works, the stylization here lending an intimate lyric quality to material beauty. By the precise arrangement of contour, proportion and illumination, and the frequent use of a homogenous white background, Németh transforms the ordinary object into an eternal vision beyond considerations of time or space. The delicate adjustment of soft pastel shades or the introduction of the strong emotional hype of a vivid hue combine with stylized graphic elements in apparently clear and simple compositions so that the final image still retains its original value as a photograph.

Németh's multi-faceted career links him continually with the world of photography. Not only has he exhibited at amateur salons, gaining numerous awards, but has lectured widely and written for specialist magazines. In 1943, he constructed the first reversing prism, used by designer Jeno Dulovits in a number of Duflex mini-cameras, and in the 1950s his book on photographic technique enjoyed widespread popularity.

—Klára Töry

NETTLES, Bea.

Nationality: American. **Born:** Gainesville, Florida, 17 October 1946. **Education:** Attended Yonge High School, Gainesville, 1960-64; University of Florida, Gainesville, B.F.A., 1968; University of Illinois, Champaign-Urbana, M.F.A., 1970. **Family:** Married Lionel Suntop in 1974; children: Rachel and Gavin. **Career:** Freelance photographer, Rochester, New York, 1970-84, and Urbana, Illinois, since 1984. Instructor in Photography, Nazareth College, Rochester, 1970-71, Tyler School of Art, Temple University, Philadelphia, 1972-74, and Visual Studies Workshop, Rochester, 1974-75. Instructor in Photography, Rochester Institute of Technology, 1971-72 and 1976-84; Professor of Photography, University of Illinois, Champaign, since 1984. **Recipient:** Creative Artists Public Service Grant, New York, 1976; National Endowment for the Arts Photography Fellowship, 1979, Illinois Arts Council Fellowship, 1986; Polaroid Corporation Artists Program, 1986; National Endowment for the Arts Fellowship, 1988. **Address:** P.O. Box 725, Urbana, Illinois 61801, U.S.A.

Individual Exhibitions:

1970	*Images and Swamp Dreams*, International Museum of Photography, George Eastman House, Rochester, New York
1971	*Plastic Mythology/Ecology Apology*, Light Impressions, Rochester, New York
1972	*Heart Attacks and Photo Fantasies*, Light Gallery, New York
1973	*Snapshots of the Elements*, Madison Art Center, Wisconsin (travelled to the Spectrum Gallery, Tucson, Arizona, 1974)
1974	*Two Recent Books*, School of the Art Institute of Chicago
1975	*Everyday Oddities*, Center for Photo Studies, Louisville, Kentucky
	Woman's Art Centre of Moncton, New Brunswick, Canada
1976	*Selected Images*, CEPA Gallery, Buffalo, New York
1977	*Moonbeams and Dreams*, Focus Gallery, San Francisco
1978	*Moonbeams and Dreams*, Witkin Gallery, New York
	The Photography Place, Philadelphia
1979	*Flamingo in the Dark*, Orange Coast College, Costa Mesa, California
1980	*Recent Work*, Film in the Cities, Minneapolis
1981	*Recent Work*, Catskill Center for Photography, Woodstock, New York
1982	*Close to Home*, Robert Samuel Gallery, New York
1983	*Gifts*, Moravian College, Bethlehem, Pennsylvania (retrospective)
1984	*Recent Work*, Images Gallery, Cincinnati, Ohio
	Flamingo in the Dark, Texas Women's University, Denton
	Flamingo in the Dark, Western Michigan University, Kalamazoo
	Flamingo in the Dark, Georgia State University, Atlanta
	Flamingo in the Dark, Port Washington Public Library, New York
	Close To Home, Indiana University, Pennsylvania
	Swan Sunset, Daytona Beach Community College, Florida
1985	*Flamingo in the Dark*, Willamette University, Salem, Oregon
	Close to Home, Kalamazoo Institute of Arts, Michigan
	Close to Home, McKissick Museum, Columbia, South Carolina
	Close to Home, Honolulu Academy of Arts, Hawaii
	Flamingo in the Dark, Stevens College, Columbia, Missouri
1986	*Landscapes of Innocence*, University of Dayton, Ohio
	Retrospective, The Museum of Contemporary Photography, Chicago, Illinois
1990	*Life's Lessons: A Mother's Journal*, The Chrysler Museum, Norfolk, Virginia
1991	*Life's Lessons: A Mother's Journal*, State of Illinois Art Center, Chicago, Illinois
1992	*Life's Lessons: A Mother's Journal*, Illinois State Museum, Springfield, Illinois
1993	*Life's Lessons: A Mother's Journal*, Augustana College, Rock Island, Illinois

AppleHouse from *Complexities*, **1992.** Photograph ©Bea Nettles.

Selected Group Exhibitions:

1970	*Photography into Sculpture,* Museum of Modern Art, New York
1971	*Figure in Landscape,* International Museum of Photography, George Eastman House, Rochester, New York
1972	*Photo Media,* Museum of Contemporary Crafts, New York
	60s Continuum, International Museum of Photography, George Eastman House, Rochester, New York
1974	*10 American Photographers,* The Photographers' Gallery, London
1976	*Photographie: Rochester, N.Y.,* Centre Culturel American, Paris
1978	*Fantastic Photography in the U.S.A.,* Canon Photo Gallery, Amsterdam (toured Europe and United States, 1978-80)
1979	*Attitudes: Photography in the 1970s,* Santa Barbara Museum of Art, California
1980	*Photographia: La Linea Sottile,* Galleria Flaviana, Locarno, Switzerland
1981	*Photographer as Printmaker,* Ferens Art Gallery, Hull, Yorkshire (travelled to the Museum and Art Gallery, Leicester; Cooper Gallery, Barnsley; Castle Museum, Nottingham; Photographers' Gallery, London)
	120 Years of Colour, Photokina, Joseph Haubracht Museum, Cologne, Germany
	Photofusions, Pratt Manhattan Center Gallery, NYC
	Altered Image, Center for Creative Photography, Tucson, Arizona
1982	*Photo Collage,* Contemporary Arts Museum, Houston, Texas
	Alternative Image, J M Kohler Arts Center, Sheboygan, Wisconsin (travelled to Toledo Museum, Toledo, Ohio)
	Evocations, Los Angeles Center for Photographic Studies, Los Angeles, California
	Photo Start, The Bronx Museum of the Arts, Bronx, New York
1984	*Alternative Image II,* J. M. Kohler Art Center, Sheboygan, Wisconsin
1987	*Mothers & Daughters,* Burden Gallery, Aperture, New York (travelled three years)
	True Stories & Photofictions, Ffotogallery, Cardiff, Wales
	True Stories & Photofictions, Camerawork, London, England
1988	*Selections 4: from International Polaroid Collection,* Photokina, Cologne, Germany
	Fabrications, Harvard University Carpenter Center, Boston, Massachusetts
	Through a Pinhole Darkly, Fine Arts Museum of Long Island, New York
1989	*The Hand that Rocks the Cradle,* Camerawork, San Francisco, California
	The Hand that Rocks the Cradle, Rose Art Museum, Waltham, Massachusetts
1990	*Flesh and Blood,* The Light Factory, Charlotte, North Carolina
1991	*Self Portraits of Contemporary Women,* Tokyo Metropolitan Museum of Photography
1992	*Photographic Book Art in the USA,* travelled to Center for Creative Photography in Tucson; Houston Center for Photography; and San Francisco Camerawork
1993	*III International Studio of Image Technology,* SESC Pompeia, Sao Paulo, Brazil
1994	*Flesh and Blood,* Friends of Photography, San Francisco

Collections:

Metropolitan Museum of Art, New York; International Museum of Photography, George Eastman House, Rochester, New York; Baltimore Museum of Art; St. Petersburg Museum of Art, Florida; University of Kansas, Lawrence; Museum of Fine Arts, Houston; Center for Creative Photography, University of Arizona, Tucson; Whatcom Museum of History and Art, Bellingham, Washington; Honolulu Academy of the Arts; National Gallery of Canada, Ottawa; Museum of Modern Art, New York; The International Polaroid Collection, Offenbach, Germany.

Publications:

By NETTLES: Books—*Breaking the Rules: A Photo Media Cookbook,* Rochester, New York 1977; *Flamingo in the Dark: Images by Bea Nettles,* Rochester, New York 1979; *Corners; Grace and Bea Nettles,* Urbana, Illinois, 1988; *Life's Lessons; A Mother's Journal,* Urbana, Illinois, 1990; *The Skirted Garden: 20 Years of Images by Bea Nettles,* Urbana, Illinois, 1990; *Knights of Assissi: A Journey through the Tarot,* Urbana, Illinois, 1990; *28 Days: A Deck of Cards,* Urbana, Illinois, 1991; *Complexities: Photographs and Text by Bea Nettles,* Urbana, Illinois, 1992. **Article**—interview in *Photography Between Covers* by Thomas Dugan, Rochester, New York 1979.

On NETTLES: Books—*The Woman's Eye* by Anne Tucker, New York 1973; *In/Sights: Self-Portraits by Women,* edited by Joyce Cohen, Boston and London 1978; *The Photograph Collector's Guide* by Lee D. Witkin and Barbara London, Boston and London 1979; *Gallery of World Photography: New Trends,* edited by Weston J. Naef, Tokyo and New York 1984; *World History of Photography* by Naomi Rosenblum, New York 1984; *The Visionary Pinhole,* edited by Lauren Smith, Layton, Utah 1985, *Fabrications: Staged Altered and Appropriated Photographs,* by Anne Hoy, NYC, 1987; *Mothers and Daughters; That Special Quality,* edited by Diane Lyon, NYC, 1987; *Self Portraits of Contemporary Women,* Tokyo Metropolitan Museum of Photography, 1991; *The History of Photography: An Overview,* by Alma Davenport, 1991.

*

    I first took photography as a senior art major at the University of Florida in 1967. In 1968 I moved to Illinois to begin graduate work in painting. During that two year period I began to incorporate photographic elements in more of my work. It was here that I began to stitch paper photographic prints together and eventually experimented with techniques of making cloth photographs. In the early 1970s I worked extensively in mixed media techniques.

    By the mid-1970s I became fascinated with the possibilities of offset printing, and for almost three years I worked entirely with visual books. In 1975 I returned to work in bichromate printing and created two bodies of work. The first 60 images appear in my visual autobiography, *Flamingo in the Dark: Images by Bea Nettles.* The next group, *Close to Home,* was made using a pinhole camera and documented the years between 1979-83 when I remained near home with my two young children.

    Upon moving to become the Chair of the Photography Program at the University of Illinois in 1984, I began a body of photo-etchings entitled *Landscapes of Innocence.* These etchings addressed events, objects and questions raised by my young children. Since that date several bodies of work dealing with issues of parenting and the role of contemporary women have emerged as photographs and in book form: *Life's Lessons: A Mother's Journal* and *Complexities: Photographs and Text* are the most recent examples. *Complexities* is a book that untangles and examines the complex ties that bind many mothers. In photographs and short stories are blended experiences of childhood, education, pregnancy, childbirth, housework and professional life. Here I demonstrate how intrusions, improvization and balancing have become the basis for my art, an art that is tightly woven with my life.

—Bea Nettles

*   *   *

    Bea Nettles is an innovator. She employs a vast array of processes and techniques to create her autobiographical, fantastic imagery. While studying painting and printmaking she began to include photographic imagery into her canvases and printing plates; soon after that she moved on to explore hand coloring, photo linen, and other photographic mixed media possibilities, until she had done plastic quilts, mirror topped tables, and a whole range of sculpture and collage. Since then she has utilized many of these techniques in a variety of projects. She has self-published (and sometimes actually printed) a number of books—ranging from handmade, limited edition works, including children's books and books of her mother's poetry, to a fairly standard hardbound photographic book—and she has completed a set of original playing cards (Old Maid), and a contemporary interpretation of the Tarot Deck. Finally she has gathered the knowledge from all her experimentation to publish *Breaking the Rules: A Photo Media Cookbook,* which proved to be a popular guide to all sorts of photographic concoctions.

Nettles believes in *making,* rather than *taking* her photographs. She can go for months without using her camera because she often assembles her works from a stock of already existing imagery. Her work finds its source as much in her imagination as in the real world. Her fondness for antiques, fabrics, quilts, and other visual things like illustrated books and rare photographs provides her opportunity to discover intriguing images she might not have found while looking through the lens of a camera. She also values the mental image offered by writers, and the subconscious images that make their appearances in dreams. Like the Surrealists with whom she identifies, Nettles relies on intuition to form and shape her works.

The most common subjects and themes in her prints are the home, familiar landscapes, friends, motherhood, typical events, and a sense of self. Using archetypal symbols—like water, moon, bird, face, tree—in unique combinations, she creates dream-like fantasies in which past and present fuse to invoke a sense of myth. Autobiographical events are transformed into shared experiences, and personal memories become parts of a common consciousness in the public dreams of Bea Nettles.

—Ted Hedgpeth

NEUSÜSS, Floris M(ichael).

Nationality: German. **Born:** Lennep, Germany, 3 March 1937. **Education:** Röntgen-Gymnasium, Lennep, 1948-56; studied at Werkkunstschule, Wuppertal, Germany, 1956-58; Bayerische Staatslehranstalt für Fotografie, Munich, 1958-60; under Heinz Hajek-Halke, Hochschule für Bildende Künste, Berlin. **Career:** Independent artist, exhibition organizer and photographer, Berlin, Vienna and Munich, since 1960. Instructor, then Professor, in Experimental Photography, Hochschule für Bildende Künste (now part of the University of Kassel), 1971—1984; Founder-Director, Fotoforum, Hochschule für Bildende Künste, Kassel, since 1972. **Agents:** Sander Gallery, 19 East, 76th Street, New York, New York, New York 10021, U.S.A.; Gallery Elke Dröscher, Kunstraum Fleetinsel, Admiralitätsstrasse 71, 20459 Hamburg, Germany; Galerie Petra Benteler, Dr Scheid Strasse 3a, 83700 Rottach-Egern, Germany; Galerie Zabristkie, 37 rue Quincampoix, 75004, Paris, France; **Address:** Menzelstrasse 15, 34131 Kassel, Germany.

Individual Exhibitions:

1963	Galerie in der Hiltonkolonnade, West Berlin
	Galerie Brebaum, Dusseldorf
	Photokina '63, Cologne
1964	Staatliche Landesbildstelle, Hamburg
	Galerie Nächst St. Stephan, Vienna
1965	Galerie des Jeunes, Paris
1966	Staatliche Werkkunstschule, Kassel, West Germany
	Galerie im Europa Center, West Berlin
1967	Galerie Nächst St. Stephan, Vienna
1968	Galerie Porta, Wuppertal, West Germany
	Galerie Clarissa, Hannover
1972	Studio Kausch, Kassel, West Germany
1973	Galleria Il Diaframma, Milan
1974	Galerie Nagel, West Berlin
	Galeria Fotografiki ZPAF, Warsaw
1976	Galerie Photo Art, Basel
	The Photographers' Gallery London
1977	Galerie Spectrum, Hannover
	Retrospective 1957-1977, Kasseler Kunstverein, West Germany
1978	*Terre-Eau-Feu-Air,* Canon Galerie, Geneva
	Galerija Suvremene Umjetnosti, Zagreb, Yugoslavia
1980	*Die Fotografie war bereits Erfunden,* Anelie Brusten Galerie, Wuppertal, West Germany
1986	Galerie Texbraun, Paris

1992	Galerie Elke Dröscher, Hamburg
	Heidelberger Kunstverein, Heidelberg
	Beteler-Morgan-Galleries, Houston, Texas
1993	ULO-family, Bildo Gallery, Berlin

Selected Group Exhibitions:

1967	*Biennale de Paris,* Musée d'Art Moderne, Paris
1969	*Vision and Expression,* International Museum of Photography, George Eastman House, Rochester, New York (toured the United States, 1969-71)
1970	*Der Bildungstrieb der Stoffe,* Kunsthalle, Nuremberg, West Germany
1974	*Künstleraktionen in Schaufenstern,* Württembergische Kunstverein, Stuttgart
1976	*Fantastic Photography in Europe,* at Rencontres Internationales de la Photographie, Arles, France (toured Europe and the United States, 1976-79)
1977	*Über Fotografie,* Westfälischer Kunstverein, Munster, West Germany
1979	*Deutsche Fotografie nach 1945,* Kassel, West Germany (toured West Germany)
1981	*Erweiterte Fotografie,* Wiener Sezession, Vienna
1984	*La Photographie Créative,* Pavillon des Arts, Paris
1986	*Crosscurrents II,* San Francisco Museum of Modern Art
1987	*Deutscher Künstlerbund, 35 Jahresausstellung,* Bremen
	Fotografishce Bilder, Mannheimer Kunstverein, Mannheim
	Schrecken und Hoffnung, Hamburger Kunsthalle, Münchner Stadtmuseum, Staatliche Gemäldegalerie, Moscow, Hermitage Museum, St. Petersburg
	Fotogramme 1918 bis heute, Wanderausstellung, Goethe-Institut, Munich
1988	*Photogramme,* Spectrum Photogalerie, Museum Sprengel, Hannover
	Fotovision, Museum Sprengel, Hannover
1989	*Photographie als Kunst—Kunst als Photographie,* Berlinische Galerie, Berlin
	Abstraction in Photography, Zabriskie Gallery, New York
	Toi, photographie, qui es-tu?, Galerie Municipale du Chateau d'Eau, Toulouse, France
1990	*Anwesenheit bei Abwesenheit, Fotogramme und die Kunst des 20 Jahrhunderts,* Kunsthaus, Zurich, Switzerland
	Kultur, Technik und Kommerz, Die photokina-Bilderschauen 1950-1980, Historisches Archiv der Stadt, Köln
1991	*Zwölf Jahre Annelie-Brusten-Galerie,* Kunsthalle, Wuppertal
1992	*Sprung in die Zeit,* Berlinsche Galerie, Martin-Gropius-Bau, Berlin
1994	*Deutsche Kunst mit Photographie,* Rheinisches Landesmuseum, Bonn
	Experimental Vision, Denver Art Museum, Denver, Colorado
	Experimental Vision, Gallery 954, Chicago

Collections:

Museum Folkwang, Essen; Sprengel Museum, Hannover; Museum Ludwig, Cologne; Museum für Kunst und Gewerbe, Hamburg; Münchner Stadtmuseum, Munich; Bibliothèque Nationale, Paris; International Museum of Photography, George Eastman House, Rochester, New York; Visual Studies Workshop, Rochester, New York; Gernsheim Collection, University of Texas at Austin; University of New Mexico, Albuquerque; Museum of Modern Art, New York; Los Angeles County Museum, Los Angeles; Denver Art Museum, Colorado.

Publications:

By NEUSÜSS: Books—*Photography as Art/Art as Photography,* exhibition catalogue, with Peter Böttcher, Kassel, West Germany 1975; *Fotografie an der Gesamtschule Kassel,* Kassel, West Germany 1976; *Figuren und Massstäbe 1961-1976,* exhibition catalogue, London 1976; *Kunstforum, Sonderband: Die Fotografie,* Mainz 1976; *Photography as Art/Art as Photography II,*

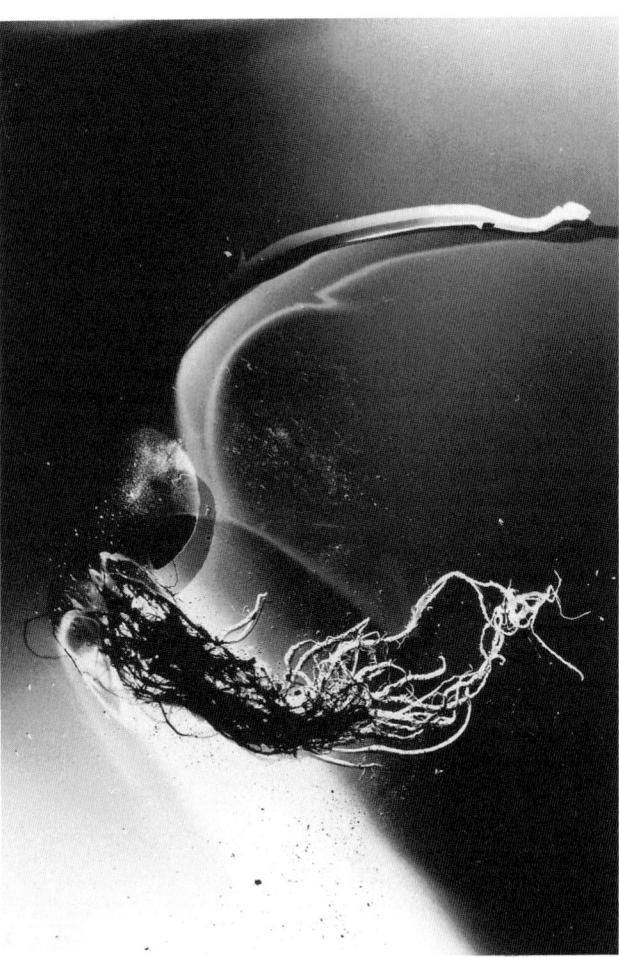

***Flower*, 1993.** Photograph by Floris M. Neusüss.

exhibition catalogue, Kassel, West Germany 1977; *Fotografien 1957-1977,* Kassel, West Germany 1977; *Berufsbild Foto-Design,* with Volker Rattemeyer, Bielefeld, West Germany 1977; *Flugtraum und Körperauflösung,* Kassel, West Germany 1977; *Deutsche Fotografie nach 1945,* editor, with Petra Benteler, Kassel, West Germany 1979; *Fotografie als Kunst/Kunst als Fotografie: Das Medium Fotografie in der bildenden Kunst Europas ab 1968,* editor, cologne 1979; *Fotografie in Kassel 1840 bis Heute—Kassel in Fotografien,* editor with W. Kemp, Munich 1981; *Medium Fotografie,* exhibition catalogue series, editor, Kassel, West Germany 1978-; *Fotogramme—die lichtreichen Schatten,* exhibition catalogue, Kassel, West Germany 1983; with Ecke Bonk, *Sechs Bilder und sechsunddreißig Worte,* Wahlershausen, 1988; *Das Fotogramm in der Kunst des 20 Jahrhunderts,* Köln, 1990; with Michael Glasmeier, *Zweiundsiebzig Gramm,* Zurich, 1994. **Articles**—"Interview: Floris M. Neusüss," with Philippe Dampenon, in *Le Nouveau Grand Angle* (Paris), May 1978; "Interview mit Floris M. Neusüss und Bildbeitrag zu 'Körperauflösungen' " in *Baseler Magazine* (Basle), August 1978; "It's Not a Question of Photography" in *European Photography* (Göttingen), October/November 1980; "From Beyond Vision" in *Experimental Vision,* 1994.

On NEUSÜSS: Books—*Das Deutsche Lichtbild,* annual, by O. Steinert and W. Strache, Stuttgart 1960; *Photography Without a Camera* by P. Holter, New York 1972; *Romain: Die Fotografie* by Klaus Honnef, Frankfurt 1976; *Die Geschichte der Fotografie im 20. Jahrhundert/Photography in the 20th Century* by Petr Tausk, Cologne 1977, London 1980; *Über Fotografie* by H. Molderings, Munster 1977; *Dumont Foto 1,* edited by Hugo Schottle, Cologne 1978; *La Photographie Fantastique* by Lorenzo Merlo and Claude Nori, Paris 1979; *Fotografie 1919-1979; Made in Germany: Die GDL-Fotografen,*

edited by F. Kempe, B. Lohse, H. Fuchs, W. Boje and others, Frankfurt 1979; *Photographia: La Linea Sottile,* exhibition catalogue, by Rinaldo Bianda and Giuliana Scimé, Locarno, Switzerland 1980; *Lichtbildnisse: Das Porträt in der Fotografie,* edited by Klaus Honnef, Cologne 1982; *La Photographie Créative* by Jean-Claude Lemagny, Paris 1984; *Histoire de la Photographie,* by Jean-Claude Lemagny and André Rouillé, Paris, 1986; *Literatur und Photographie,* Erwin Koppen, Stuttgart, 1987; *Kunst heute in der Bundesrepublik Deutschland,* Klaus Honnef et al, Bonn 1988; *Belichtete Welt,* Bernd Buch, Munich, 1989. **Articles**—"Lichtgrafik von Floris M. Neusüss" by Franz Roh in *Gebrauchsgrafik* (Munich), September 1964; "Floris M. Neusüss und seine Skurrilien" by Fritz Kempe in *Foto Rundschau*(Dusseldorf), March 1965; "Floris M. Neusüss" by Kazumi Masaru in *Graphic* (Tokyo), October 1967; "Floris M. Neusüss: Photograms" by Julia Scully in *Modern Photography* (New York), May 1970; "Sequence" in *Camera* (Lucerne), February 1971; "Photo Scale: Floris Michael Neusüss" in *Camera* (Lucerne), February 1975; "Floris M. Neusüss et la Fotoforum" by Gisèle Freunde in *Zoom*(Paris),August/September 1977; "Floris M. Neusüss" by Willem Coumans in *Foto Nederlandse* (Amsterdam), March 1978; articles in *European Photography,* (Göttingen) 1980, 1983, 1985, 1989; "Between Past and Future: New German Photography" by Wilfried Wiegand et al in *Aperture,* (New York), Spring 1991. **Television films**—*Floris M. Neusüss: Experimentelle Fotografie,* directed by Ingeborg Euler, 1968; *Rencontres Internationales de Photographie: Interview with Floris M. Neusüss,* 1977; *Aspekte der Fotografie: Floris M. Neusüss, Schöpfer Neuer Bildweten* by Fritz Gruber, 1978; *An der Wiege der Fotografie: Floris M. Neusüss und Seine Studenten in Chalon-sur-Saône* by Hartmut Schwenk, 1978; *Kunstlerportrait Floris M. Neusüss* by Bettina von Cube, 1979.

*

Photographs are the most important part of my work. The principle of a photogram is that an object is laid on sensitive paper in the dark, is exposed to light, and then developed. This photographic method without a camera portrays the subject—or, as in my work: people—in original size, or rather lifesize, as shadows. The photogram is a process which brings the subject of the picture into direct contact with the photographic basis of the picture—in all other photographic processes the lens comes between the picture-subject and the sensitive material.

From the beginning photography was a decisive factor in my artistic career. I gave up the study of painting in Wuppertal to be instructed in photography, and after that continued my studies at the Hochschule für Bildende Künste, Berlin, in Hajek-Halke's photography class. In the course of my studies I came to know the work of Moholy-Nagy and Man Ray and was particularly fascinated by their photograms. Both added objects to their collages, abstract and constructivist (Moholy) or surreal (Man Ray)—very rarely, a "human reference," a hand or a head, was portrayed, and then not as a reference to reality but rather as an intensification of the surreal and enigmatic aspect.

In three ways my work has gone beyond that of the pioneers of the photogram: first, in my choice of subject, for the portrayal of the whole human body opens up a realistic dimension with a decisive influence on the image; second, in the combination of photography and painting, for the development of the exposed photographic paper in the photographic developer—a process which one cannot carry out afterwards with photographs developed according to the rules—becomes, in some of my works, an act of deliberate control, as in painting: I take the development process "in hand," in that I dip brush, sponge or rag in the developer and bring forth the picture by wiping the paper. In this way I produce a controlled, painterly plane which brings out the photographically registered form and at the same time dissolves it by superimposing the wiped structure on the figure. While Moholy and Man Ray had to decide on the unalterable appearance of their pictures at the moment of exposure, I do not make up my mind even during the development process and in some works do not bring anything to a conclusion in that I do not fix the pictures. ("Wiped photograms originated in 1963-64 during and after a visit to Vienna and contact with the St. Stephan Gallery Group"—Hollega, Mikl, Prachensky, Rainer.)

The third aspect is the production of color: nonfixing means that the undeveloped areas of the pictures are constantly changing color through the years. Moholy's desire for color in the photogram remained unfilled, and he believed that "the greatest hope for the future will be to master the colored photogram.'' He was thinking, certainly, about the production of photograms on a color photography basis. My colored photograms originated, however, from the behavior of color on black-and-white photographic paper developed under specific conditions.

—Floris M. Neusüss

NEWHALL, Beaumont.

Nationality: American. **Born:** Lynn, Massachusetts, 22 June 1908. **Education:** Studied fine arts, Harvard University, Cambridge, Massachusetts, 1926-31, 1933-34, A.B. cum laude 1930, M.A. 1931; Institut d'Art et d'Archaeologie, University of Paris, 1933; Courtauld Institute of Art, London, 1934. **Military Service:** Served as a photo-intelligence officer, United States Army Air Force, in Egypt, North Africa and Italy, 1942-45: Major. **Family:** Married Nancy Wynne Parker in 1936 (died, 1974); married Christy Weston in 1975. **Career:** Independent photographer, from 1926. Assistant, Department of Decorative Arts, Metropolitan Museum of Art, New York, 1933-34; Librarian, 1935-42, Curator of Photography, 1940-45, and Member of the Photography Committee since 1964, Museum of Modern Art, New York; Curator, 1948-58, Director, 1958-71, Director Emeritus, 1971, and Honorary Trustee since 1980, International Museum of Photography at George Eastman House, Rochester, New York; Contributing Editor, *Art in America* magazine, New York, 1957-65; Foot Editor, *Brighton-Pittsford Post,* New York, 1956-65; Associate Curator of the Photography Collection, Exchange National Bank, Chicago, 1968-71. Lecturer, Philadelphia Museum of Art, 1932-33; Instructor, Black Mountain College, North Carolina, 1946-48; Lecturer, University of Rochester, New York, 1954-56; Lecturer, Rochester Institute of Technology, New York, 1956-58; Lecturer in American Film, Salzburg Seminars, Austria, 1958-59; Professor of Art, State University of New York, Buffalo, 1968-71; Professor of Art, 1971-84, and Professor Emeritus since 1985, University of New Mexico, Albuquerque. **Recipient:** Kulturpreis, Deutsche Gesellschaft für Photographie, 1970; Progress Medal, Royal Photographic Society of Great Britain, 1975; Claude M. Fuess Award, Phillips Academy, Andover, Massachusetts, 1979; New Mexico Governor's Award, 1983; Five-Year Fellowship, John D. and Catherine T. MacArthur Foundation, 1984-89. D.F.A.: Harvard University, 1978; State University of New York, 1986. Honorary Fellow: Royal Photographic Society; Photographic Historical Society of New York; Fellow: American Academy of Arts and Sciences; Photographic Society of America; John Simon Guggenheim Foundation; Honorary Master of Photography, Professional Photographers of America; Corresponding Member, Deutsche Gesellschaft für Photographie. **Agent:** Scheinbaum and Russek Gallery, 615 Don Felix Street, Santa Fe, New Mexico 87501, U.S.A. **Address:** Route 7, Box 126-C, Santa Fe, New Mexico 87505-9004, U.S.A.

Individual Exhibitions:

1978	Kay Bonfoey Gallery, Tucson, Arizona
	Galerie Die Brücke, Vienna
	The Frame Company, Santa Fe, New Mexico
1979	G. Ray Hawkins Gallery, Los Angeles
1980	Addison Gallery of American Art, Andover, Massachusetts
	Mattress Factory Gallery, Pittsburgh
	Catskill Center for Photography, Woodstock, New York
1981	Santa Fe Center for Photography, New Mexico
	University of New Mexico, Albuquerque
1982	Portfolio Gallery, Oklahoma City, Oklahoma
	Focus Gallery, San Francisco
	International Center of Photography, New York
	Camera Obscura Gallery, Denver, Colorado
1983	ArtLoft, Honolulu, Hawaii
1984	El Paso Museum, Texas
	Santa Fe Museum of Fine Art, New Mexico
	Polk Community College, Des Moines, Iowa

	International Museum of Photography at George Eastman House, Rochester, New York
	Quincy Art Center, Illinois
	Scheinbaum and Russek Gallery, Santa Fe, New Mexico
1985	Kaiser Art Center Gallery, Oakland, California
	Andrew Smith Gallery, Albuquerque, New Mexico

Selected Group Exhibitions:

1980	*Collector's Exhibition,* Witkin Gallery, New York
	Photography's Response to Constructivism, San Francisco Museum of Modern Art
1981	*Onze Photographes de Santa Fe,* at *Rencontres Internationales de Photographie,* Arles, France (travelled in France, Iceland, Spain, Russia, Turkey and Israel, 1981-84)
1983	*Ten Photographers in New Mexico,* Houston Center for Photography, Texas
1984	*Sammlung Gruber,* Museum Ludwig, Cologne

Collections:

Center for Creative Photography, University of Arizona, Tucson; Victoria and Albert Museum, London; Sammlung Fotografis Länderbank, Vienna; Museum of Modern Art, New York; International Center of Photography, New York; Houston Museum of Fine Arts, Texas; Fogg Art Museum, Harvard University, Cambridge, Massachusetts; Australian National Gallery, Canberra; Santa Fe Museum of Fine Arts, New Mexico; Minneapolis Institute of Arts, Minnesota.

Publications:

By NEWHALL: Books—*Houses of the 1840s, Plain and Ornamental,* portfolio, Tarrytown, New York 1937; *Photography 1839-1937,* New York 1937, as *Photography: A Short Critical History,* New York 1938, as *The History of Photography,* New York 1964, 1972, 1982; *The Photographs of Henri Cartier-Bresson,* with Lincoln Kirstein, New York 1947, as *Photographs by Henri Cartier-Bresson,* New York 1963; *On Photography: A Source Book of Photo History in Facsimile,* Watkins Glen, New York 1956, abridged ed. as *The Art and Science of Photography,* New York 1956; *Masters of Photography,* with Nancy Newhall, New York 1958, 1981; *The Daguerreotype in America,* New York 1961, 1976; *Frederick H. Evans,* Rochester, New York 1964, 1975; *T.H. O'Sullivan, Photographer,* with Nancy Newhall, Rochester, New York 1966; *Latent Image: The Discovery of Photography,* Garden City, New York 1967, 1983; *Airborne Camera: The World from the Air and Outer Space,* New York 1968, London 1969; *William Henry Jackson,* with Diana Edkins, Dobbs Ferry, New York 1974; *Photography: Essays and Images,* New York 1980; *Photography and the Book,* Boston 1980; *Schloss Leopoldskron,* portfolio, Washington, D.C. 1980; *In Plain Sight,* Layton, Utah 1983; *Edward Weston Omnibus,* with Amy Conger, Layton, Utah 1983; *Supreme Instants: The Photographs of Edward Weston,* Boston 1986.

On NEWHALL: Books—*The Picture History of Photography* by Peter Pollack, New York 1958; *Faces: A Narrative History of the Portrait in Photography* by Ben Maddow, Boston 1977; *Sammlung Gruber: Photographie des 20. Jahrhunderts,* exhibition catalogue, with foreword by Siegfried Gohr, Cologne 1984. **Articles**—''People Behind Photography'' by Andrew D. Wolfe in *British Journal of Photography Annual 1967,* London 1967; ''Camera Interview: Beaumont Newhall'' by Paul Hill and Thomas Cooper in *Camera* (Lucerne), May and June 1976; ''The Private Side of Beaumont Newhall'' by Marjorie McCloy in *Darkroom* (San Francisco), July/August 1981; ''A Conversation with Beaumont Newhall'' by Susan Weiley in *Art News*(New York), October 1984.

*

To me it is a constant source of wonder that the world becomes transformed through the finder of my camera. I am forced to concentrate on the forms bounded by the rectangle of the frame. I discover, if I am successful, a structure I could hardly have recognized without my camera. And yet the

***Portrait of Bill Brandt,* London, 1952.** Photograph by Beaumont Newhall.

discovery of that form in no way alters the factual substance of the photographic report. Rather it seems to me to strengthen the image.

I use a 35mm single lens reflex camera exclusively. With it I can see at once from eye level the exact image that will be recorded. I prefer a lens of 50mm focal length, for it approximates that of the eye. I seldom use a tripod because setting it up distracts me from following the subject with the camera. Developing the film and printing I leave to my most competent colleague, David Scheinbaum.

—Beaumont Newhall

*   *   *

From its very first edition in 1937, Beaumont Newhall's *The History of Photography* was a major breakthrough. His original approach to interpreting creative photography's evolution illuminated a profound background to this branch of art. The strength of his argument inspired many to take up the camera and add to this history, so that Newhall acquired through his pioneering work a lot of silent pupils whom he never met.

It always seemed likely that a man with such a comprehension of the nature of creative photography might well be a good photographer himself. Confirmation had to wait until 1978 when Newhall's first one-man show opened at the Kay Bonfoey Gallery in Tucson and shortly after at the Die Brücke Gallery in Vienna. Today his photographic work has become well-known. Although it covers a broad field of themes, Newhall's photography always respects the pure nature of the medium itself. In his boyhood he used the camera like any amateur, and prior to his interest in photographic history, merely registered objects and visual events on film without any creative ambition. This early photographic activity, up to the age of eighteen, may be seen as the important germination period for Newhall's fine sense of image-content and aptness.

His fondness for photographing skyscrapers led Newhall in the late 1920s to discover abstract patterns formed by the intersection of shadows and long straight walls. Much later, in the early 1980s, he photographed these great buildings both by night and day as living sculptures of the big cities. He also made photos of the structure of giant cranes as creatively as he captured the image of sculptures in the gardens of the Rodin Museum.

Newhall's notable interest in still-life subjects is evidenced in pictures of found arrangements in all situations—from shipboard tackle to kitchen implements at Edward Weston's house. Images of graveyard detritus, rooftop details and fragments on Paris billboards reveal his fascination for the *objet trouvé.*

Another major chapter in Newhall's photography is portraiture—particularly pictures of other photographers. Now photographers themselves frequently make poor models, but their customary awkwardness in this situation was overcome by Newhall's close personal friendship and the confidence he inspired, so that he was able to achieve a good number of easy and natural images. Being well acquainted with the work and personalities, Newhall could transform these subtle qualities into the language of the photograph. Thus his portraits of Ansel Adams, Bill Brandt, Henri Cartier-Bresson, Edward Weston, Paul Strand and others represent the quintessential images of great photographers interpreted by a great photohistorian.

—Petr Tausk

NEWMAN, Arnold (Abner).

Nationality: American. **Born:** New York City, 3 March 1918. **Education:** Attended public schools, Atlantic City, New Jersey and Miami Beach, Florida, 1925-36; studied art at the University of Miami, 1936-38. **Family:** Married Augusta Rubenstein in 1949; sons: Eric and David. **Career:** Assistant portrait photographer to Leon Perskie, Philadelphia, and in same chain of studios, Baltimore and Allentown, Pennsylvania, 1938-39; Manager, Tooley-Myron Photo Studio, West Palm Beach, Florida, 1939-41; Director, Newman Portrait Studio, Miami Beach, 1942-45. Owner and President, Arnold Newman Studios Inc., New York, since 1946. Adviser on Photography, Israel Museum, Jerusalem, since 1965. Visiting Professor of Photography, Cooper Union, New York, since 1975. **Recipient:** *Photokina* Award, Cologne, 1951; First Annual Photojournalism Conference Award, University of Miami, 1957; Philadelphia Museum College of Art Citation, 1961; Newhouse Citation, Syracuse University, New York, 1961; University of Miami Citation, 1963; Gold Medal, *Biennale Internazionale della Fotografia,* Venice, 1963; Life Achievement Award, American Society of Magazine Photographers, 1975; Andy Award, Advertising Club of New York, 1983; Honor Medal for Distinguished Service to Journalism, University of Missouri, 1985. D.F.A.: University of Miami, 1981; D.H.L.: Art Center College of Design, Pasadena, 1985. Honorary Fellow, Israel Museum, Jerusalem, 1986; The Lotus Club Medal of Merit Award, New York, 1989; The Ministry of Culture of the Czech Socialist Republic's Honorary Commemorative Medal in celebration of the 150th anniversary of Photography, 1989; Award for "Achievment and Contribution to Photography" from Photographic Society of Japan, 1989; Honorary Degree, Doctor of Fine Arts, Parsons School of Design/the New School, New York, 1990; Named Director's Visitor, Institute of Advanced Study, Princeton, N.J., 1991; Received World Image Award and Scholarship named for him, the New School of Social Research/Parsons School of Design, New York, 1993. **Agent:** Mr. Ronald Kurtz, Commerce Graphics Ltd Inc, 160 East Union Avenue, East Rutherford, New Jersey 17073, U.S.A. **Address:** Arnold Newman Studios Inc., 39 West 67th Street, New York, New York 10023, U.S.A.

Individual Exhibitions:

1941	A.D. Gallery, New York (with Ben Rose)
	Artists Through the Camera, Brooklyn Museum, New York
1945	*Artists Look Like This,* Philadelphia Museum of Art (toured the United States)
1951	The Camera Club, New York
	Photographs 1938-1950, Milwaukee Art Institute
1953	*Color and Black and White,* Ed Weiner Gallery, Provincetown, Massachusetts
	Arnold Newman: Retrospective, Art Institute of Chicago
1955	*Collective Work,* Portland Art Museum, Oregon
1956	Santa Barbara Museum of Art, California
	Photographs 1940-1954, Ohio University, Athens
	Miami Beach Art Center
1958	*Portraits,* Cincinnati Art Museum, Ohio
1961	*Portraits,* Phoenix Art Museum, Arizona
1963	*Portraits,* at the *Biennale Internazionale della Fotografia,* Venice
1972	Light Gallery, New York
	Photographs from Three Decades, International Museum of Photography, George Eastman House, Rochester, New York (toured the United States, from 1972; travelled to Japan, 1980)
1974	Light Gallery, New York
1975	The Photographers' Gallery, London
1976	Galerie Fiolet, Amsterdam
1977	Delaware Art Museum, Wilmington
	Light Gallery, New York
1978	Silver Image Gallery, Seattle
	Fotografiska Museet, Stockholm
	Portraits, Israel Museum, Jerusalem
	Portraits, Tel Aviv Museum of Art

1979	*The Great British,* National Portrait Gallery, London (travelled to the Light Gallery, New York)
1980	Galerie Créatis, Paris
	Artists, Light Gallery, New York
1981	Snite Museum of Art, University of Notre Dame, Indiana
	Atlanta Gallery of Photography
	P.G.I. Gallery, Tokyo
1982	Yuen Lui Gallery, Seattle, Washington
	Hills Gallery, Denver, Colorado
	Clarence Street Lighthouse, Melbourne, Victoria
1983	Images Gallery, Cincinnati, Ohio
	Other Photographs, Daniel Wolf Gallery, New York
1984	Galerie Octant, Paris
	Allen Street Gallery, Dallas, Texas
1985	University of Miami, Coral Gables
1986	Michael Carey Gallery, Austin, Texas
	Museum of Photographic Arts, San Diego, California (retrospective; toured the United States, 1986-89)
	Pori Art Museum, Pori, Finland
	Photographic Museum of Finland, Helsinki, Finland
1986-92	*Arnold Newman: Five Decades,* Museum of Photographic Arts, San Diego, California (travelled to the Art Institute of Chicago; the Minneapolis Museum of Art, Minneapolis; the Massachusetts Institute of Technology Museum, Cambridge, Mass; the Norton Gallery and School of Art, West Palm Beach, Florida; the New York Historical Society, New York City; the Modern Art Museum of Fort Worth, Texas; the Cincinnati Art Museum, Ohio; the Holland Foto Foundation, Amsterdam; the Joan Miro Foundation Museum, Barcelona; Frankfurter Kunstverein, Germany; Musee de l'Elysee, Lausanne, Switzerland; Museum of Modern Art, Oxford, England; and Tokyo)
1988	*Collages and Recent Photographs,* the Sidney Janis Gallery, New York
1989	*Arnold Newman: Portraits, Collage and Abstractions,* Old Town Hall, Prague; the National Gallery, Bratislava; the House of Arts, Brno, Czechoslovakia
1990	*Arnold Newman: Portraits, Collage and Abstractions,* Museum of History, Buda Castle, Budapest, Hungary
1990-94	*Arnold Newman's Americans,* National Portrait Gallery, Washington, D.C. (travelled to Detroit Institute of the Arts, Michigan; the LBJ Library and Museum, Austin, Texas; the Columbus Museum of Art, Georgia; Greenville County Museum of Art, Greenville, South Carolina; Worcester Art Museum, Massachusetts)

Selected Group Exhibitions:

1943	*Masters of Photography,* Museum of Modern Art, New York
1948	*In and Out of Focus,* Museum of Modern Art, New York
1957	*Faces in American Art,* Metropolitan Museum of Art, New York
1959	*Photography at Mid-Century,* International Museum of Photography, George Eastman House, Rochester, New York
1964	*The Photographer's Eye,* Museum of Modern Art, New York
1968	*Photography in the 20th Century,* National Gallery of Canada, Ottawa (toured Canada and the United States, 1967-73)
1972	*Portrait of the Artist,* Metropolitan Museum of Art, New York
1980	*Photography of the 50s,* International Center of Photography, New York (travelled to the Center for Creative Photography, Tucson, Arizona; Minneapolis Institute of Arts; California State University at Long Beach; Delaware Art Museum, Wilmington)
1982	*Lichtbildnisse: Das Porträt in der Fotografie,* Rheinisches Landesmuseum, Bonn
1985	*American Images 1945-80,* Barbican Art Gallery, London (toured Britain)
1988	*Picturing Greatness,* Museum of Modern Art, New York
	The Instant Likeness: Polaroid Portraits, the National Portrait Gallery, Washington, D.C.

Portrait of Sir Cecil Beaton, 1978. Photograph ©Arnold Newman.

Makers of Photographic History, the National Museum of Photography, Film and Television, Bradford, England
Master Photography in the Fine Arts, 1957-1959, International Center of Photography, Prague
5x5 Exhibition, El Musee de Arte Contemporaneo de Caracas, Venezuela

1991   *Artist's Choice—Chuck Close/Head On—The Modern Portrait,* Museum of Modern Art, New York
Art of the Forties, Museum of Modern Art, New York
Exhibition of Contemporary Photographs, 1960-1979, from the Toppan Collection, Tokyo at the International Center of Photography, New York

1994   *Gesture and Pose,* Museum of Modern Art, New York

Collections:

Metropolitan Museum of Art, New York; Museum of Modern Art, New York; International Museum of Photography, George Eastman House, Rochester, New York; Philadelphia Museum of Art; Smithsonian Institution, Washington, D.C.; Art Institute of Chicago; National Portrait Gallery, London; Moderna Museet, Stockholm; Israel Museum, Jerusalem; Victoria and Albert Museum, London; National Portrait Gallery, Washington, DC; National Gallery of Canada, Ottawa; Center for Creative Photography, Tucson, Ariz; Australia National Gallery, Canberra; Nihon University Collection of Art, Tokyo; The Norton Gallery and School of Art, West Palm Beach, Florida; The Sofia Imber Musee de Arte Contemporareo, Caracas,; The Lowe Art Museum, University of Miami, Coral Gables, Florida; Yokahama Museum of Art, Japan; The Worcester Art Museum, Worcester, Mass; The Tel Aviv Museum of Art, Tel Aviv.

Publications:

By NEWMAN: Books—*Happytown Tales,* with Lawrence Tremblay, Coral Gables, Florida 1944; *Bravo Stravinsky,* with text by Robert Craft, Cleveland 1967; *One Mind's Eye: The Portraits and Other Photographs by Arnold Newman,* with an introduction by Robert Sobieszek, and a foreword by Beaumont Newhall, Boston and London 1974; *Faces U.S.A.,* with a foreword by Thomas Thompson, New York 1978; *The Great British,* with text by George Perry, London and Boston 1979; *Artists: Portraits from Four Decades,* with a foreword by Henry Geldzahler, Boston and London 1980; *I Grandi Fotografi: Arnold Newman,* with introduction by Robert A. Sobieszek, Milan and Englewood, New Jersey 1983; *Arnold Newman—Five Decades,* with introduction by Arthur Ollman, San Diego, California 1986; *Arnold Newman in Florida,* USA 1987; *Arnold Newman's Americans,* USA, 1992. **Articles**—"Portrait of an Artist" in *Minicam Photography* (Cincinnati, Ohio), November 1945; "Arnold Newman on Portraiture" in *Popular Photography* (New York), May 1957; "Arnold Newman's Europe" in *Popular Photography* (New York), March 1964; interview in *Interviews with Master Photographers* by James Danziger and Barnaby Conrad III, London 1977; "Peer Group" in *Camera Arts* (New York), January/February 1981; "Masters: Arnold Newman" *US Eye,* premier issue, 1985;

On NEWMAN: Books—*The History of Photography* by Beaumont Newhall, New York 1949, 1954; *Famous Portraits,* edited by L. Fritz Gruber, New York 1960; *The Encyclopaedia of Photography,* edited by H.M. Kinzer, New York 1964; *The Picture History of Photography* by Peter Pollack, revised edition, New York 1969; *Looking at Photographs* by John Szarkowski, New York 1973; *The Magic Image* by Cecil Beaton and Gail Buckland, London and Boston 1975; *Faces: A Narrative History of the Portrait* by Ben Maddow, Boston 1977; *Current Biography,* volume 41, number 10, edited by Charles Moritz, New York 1980; *Photography of the Fifties: An American Perspective* by Helen Gee, Tucson, Arizona 1980; *World Photography,* edited by Bryn Campbell, London 1981; *Lichtbildnisse: Das Porträt in der Fotografie,* edited by Klaus Honnef, Cologne 1982; *The Library of World Photography: Portraits,* with introduction by Colin Ford, Tokyo 1982, 1983, London 1983; *Master Photographers: The World's Great Photographers on their Art and Technique,* edited by Pat Booth, London and New York 1983; *American Images: Photography 1945-1980,* edited by Peter Turner and John Benton-Harris, London 1985. **Articles**—"Arnold Newman" by Fritz Neugass in *Camera* (Lucerne), June 1953; "On Assignment with Arnold Newman" by

Arthur Goldsmith in *Popular Photography* (New York), May 1957; "American Artists" by Nan Rosenthal in *Art in America* (New York), June 1965; "Les Teles Couroness d'Arnold Newman" by Evelyne Jesenof in *Photo* (Paris), June 1973; "A Lesson in Portraiture from a Master" by Arthur Goldsmith in *Popular Photography* (New York), November 1973; "Arnold Newman" by Trevor Gett in *Australian Photography* (Melbourne), October 1980; "Arnold Newman" by Giovanni Calvenzi in *Il Fotografo* (Milan), November 1982; "Arnold Newman der Fotokunstler aus Amerika" by Jordan Mejais in *Frankfurter Allgemeine Zeitung* (Frankfurt), 20 December 1985; "A Conversation with Arnold Newman" *Photo Design,* N.Y. 1986; "Newman's People," *Art News,* New York, 1987; *Newman at Work, American Photographer,* New York, 1988; "Das Auge de Epoche, Der Amerikanische Photographer, Arnold Newman," *Zeit Magazine,* Germany, 1988; "Proudly Presents Arnold Newman," *Fotografisk Tidskrift,* Stockholm, 1988; "One Man's Faultless Camera Eye," *Town and Country,* New York, 1988; "Arnold Newman in Amsterdam—De Grootmeester van het Portret," *Vakblad Voor Visuele Communicate/Porfessionele Fotografie,* Amsterdam, 1989; "Mas que retratos," *Spanish Vogue,* in conjunction with Newman's exhibition in Barcelona, 1990. **Films**—*The Image Makers: The Environment of Arnold Newman,* Nebraska Educational Television Network film, 1977; *The Photographer's Eye: Arnold Newman,* Crosscountry Cable TV film, 1982; *Histoire de la Photographie VI: Arnold Newman,* Production MHF French TV film, 1983; Interview and portrait sitting televised, *The Portrait,* produced by KOCE-TV, USA, 1983; Essay and photographs of Shaker Village in *American Photography,* 1985; Arnold Newman Finally Gets Some Respect, *Photo District News,* New York, 1988; Arnold Newman, *Photographer's Forum,* Santa Barbara, California, 1989; Laureates '89 Arnold Newman, *Northwest Portfolio,* 1989; Arnold Newman, *Photographer's Forum,* Santa Barbara, California, 1989; Subject of *Eastman Kodak Company's "Techniques of the Masters"* television program broadcast in the United States and Europe.

NEWTON, Helmut.

Nationality: Australian. **Born:** Berlin, Germany, 31 October 1920; emigrated to Australia; later settled in Paris and Monaco. **Education:** Heinrich von Treitschke Realgymnasium, Berlin, 1928-32; American School, Berlin, 1933-35. **Military Service:** Served in Australian Army, 1940-45: Private. **Family:** Married the photographer and actress June F. Browne (pseudonyms: June Brunell, Alice Springs) in 1948. **Career:** Apprentice to fashion and theatre photographer Yva (Else Simon), Berlin, 1936-40; freelance photographer, Melbourne, in the mid-1940s; freelance photographer, working for *Jardin des Modes, Elle, Queen, Playboy, Nova, Marie-Claire, Stern Magazine* etc., since 1958, particularly for French and American editions of *Vogue, Vanity Fair and Condé Nast Traveler.* **Recipient:** Best Photography Award, Art Directors Club, Tokyo, 1976; American Institute of Graphic Arts Award, 1977, 1980; Gold Medal, Art Directors Club, Germany, 1978, 1979; Appointed Chevalier des Arts et des Lettres, 1989; Photographers Award for outstanding achievements and Contributions to Photgraphy during the 1960s and 1970s from the Photographic Society of Japan, 1989; Grand Prix de la Ville de Paris, 1989; Grand Prix National for Photography, 1990; World Image Award for Best Portrait Photography, New York, 1991; Das Grosse Verdienstkreuz des Verdienstordens der Bundsrepublik Deutschland, 1992; Chevalier des Arts, Lettres et Sciences, Monaco, 1992 . **Agents:** Hamiltons Photographers Ltd, 35 Fentiman Road, London, SW8 1LD, England; Mr. David Manfredi, TDR, via Bullona 7, 20154 Milan, Italy.

Individual Exhibitions:

1975   Nikon Galerie, Paris
Canon Photo Gallery, Amsterdam

1976   The Photographers' Gallery, London (with Hideki Fujii)
Nicholas Wilder Gallery, Los Angeles

1978   Marlborough Gallery, New York

1979   Centre Culturel Americain, Paris
Canon Photo Gallery, Geneva

Silver Image Gallery, Seattle, Washington
1981   Galerie Daniel Templon, Paris
1982   Galerie Tanit Kunigk und Mollier, Munich
1983   Asher/Faure Gallery, Los Angeles
        31 Nudes/Personalities, Olympus Gallery, London (with Alice
            Springs)
1984   *Retrospective,* Musée d'Art Moderne de la Ville, Paris
        Musée des Beaux-Arts, Nice, France
        I grandi nudi/la moda, Palazzo Fortuny, Venice
        Private Property, G Ray Hawkins Gallery, Los Angeles
1985   *New Work,* G Ray Hawkins Gallery, Los Angeles
        Retrospective, Museo della Automobile, Turin
        Galerie Artis, Monte Carlo
1986   *Retrospective,* Palais de l'Europe, Menton, France
        Retrospective, Foto Foundation, Amsterdam
1987   *Retrospective,* Rheinisches Landesmuseum, Bonn, Germany
        Nus inedits, Galerie Daniel Templon, Paris
        Retrospective, Musee de Groningue, Groningue
1988   *Retrospective,* Museum des 20. Jahrhunderts, Vienna
        Retrospective, Forum Bottcherstrasse, Bremen
        New Nudes, Galerie Reckermann, Cologne
        Retrospective, Berlinische Galerie/Martin-Gropius-Bau,
            Berlin
        New Nudes, Hamilton Gallery, London
        Nouvelles Images, Espace Photographique de Paris
            Audiovisuel, Paris
        Portraits Retrospective, National Portrait Gallery, London
1989   *Fashion Photographs & Portraits,* Metropolitan Teien Art
            Museum, Tokyo
        Fashion Photographs & Portraits, Seibu Art Museum,
            Funabashi, Japan
        Helmut Newton, Neuvas Imagenes, Fundacion Caja de
            Pensiones, Madrid
        Helmut Newton in Moscow, Puschkin Museum & Perwaia
            Galereia, Moscow
        Fashion Photographs & Portraits, Prefectural Museum of Art,
            Fukuoka, Japan
        New Images, Galleria d'Arte Moderna, Bologna, Italy
1990   *New Images,* Carlsberg Glyptotek Gallery, Copenhagen
        Kunstforum Gallery, Vienna
        Hochschule fur Graphik und Buchkunst, Leipzig, Germany
        Fashion Photography & Portraits, The Museum of Modern
            Art, Shiga, Japan
1991   Biennale de Lyon
        Museum of Modern Art, Bratislava, Slovakia
        Naked & Dressed, Hamilton Gallery, London
1992   *Naked & Dressed in Hollywood,* Pascal de Sarthe Gallery, Los
            Angeles
        Helmut Newton, Goro International Exhibition, Tokyo
        Archives de Nuit, sponsored by Credit Foncier de France, Place
            Vendome, Paris
1993   *Helmut Newton,* Carla Sozzani Gallery, Milan, Italy
        Centre Culturel Francaise de Rome (Fashion photographs—
            Acquisitions of Paris Audiovisuel), Rome
        Archives de Nuit, Villa Medici (c/o Credit Foncier de France)
        Helmut Newton aus dem photografischen Werk, Deichtorhallen,
            Hamburg, Germany
1994   Josef-Albers-Museum, Bottrop, Germany
        Fotomusuem Winterthur, Wintherthur; Castello di Rivoli,
            Turin, Italy

Selected Group Exhibitions:

1975   *Fashion Photography: 6 Decades,* Emily Lowe Gallery,
            Hofstra University, Hempstead, New York (toured the
            United States)
1977   *Fashion Photography,* International Museum of Photography,
            George Eastman House, Rochester, New York (travelled to
            the Brooklyn Museum, New York; San Francisco Museum

of Modern Art; Cincinnati Art Institute, Ohio; and Museum
of Fine Arts, St. Petersburg, Florida)
1979   *Fleeting Gestures: Dance Photographs,* International Center of
            Photography, New York (travelled to The Photographers'
            Gallery, London, and *Venezia '79*)
        La Mode, Galerie Zabriskie, Paris
        Photographie als Kunst 1879-1979, Tiroler Landesmuseum,
            Innsbruck, Austria (travelled to Neue Galerie am Wolf-
            gang Gurlitt Museum, Linz, Austria; Neue Galerie am
            Landesmuseum Joanneum, Graz, Austria; and Museum des
            20. Jahrhunderts, Vienna)
1980   *Instantanés,* Centre Georges Pompidou, Paris
1982   *Color as Form,* International Museum of Photography at
            George Eastman House, Rochester, New York
1984   *Sammlung Gruber,* Museum Ludwig, Cologne
1985   *Shots of Style,* Victoria and Albert Museum, London (toured
            Britain)
1986   *The Animal in Photography 1843-1985,* The Photographers'
            Gallery, London
        La femme sur la plage, Palais de l'Europe, Menton, France
1988   *Splendeurs et miseres du corps,* Musee de la Mode, Paris
        Splendeurs et miseres du corps, Musee d'Art Moderne, Paris
        Splendeurs et miseres du corps, Fribourg (Triennale)
        The Art of Photography, Royal Academy of Arts, London
1989   *The Art of Photography,* Museum of Fine Arts, Houston, Texas
        Ministry of Culture of the USSR, Moscow
        Kunstforum Galerie, Vienna
1991   *Appearances,* Victoria & Albert Museum, London
1993   *Regard d'artistes sur la Femme,* Hotel de la Monnaie, Paris
        Vanities, Centre Nationale de la Photographie, Hotel Salomon
            de Rothschild a Paris

Collections:

Condé Nast Publications Inc., Paris and New York; Bibliothèque Nationale,
Paris; Fashion Institute of Technology, New York; Museum of Modern Art,
New York; International Museum of Photography, George Eastman House,
Rochester, New York; Museum Ludwig, Cologne; American Friends of the
Israel Museum, Jerusalem; Baltimore Museum of Art, Maryland; Berlinische
Galerie, Martin Gropius-Bau, Berlin; Brandeis University, Waltham, Massa-
chusetts; Bucknell University, Lewisburg, Pennsylvania; Chamber Opera
Theatre, New York; College of the Holy Cross, Worcester, Massachusetts;
College of William and Mary, Williamsburg, Virginia; Corcoran Gallery of
Art, Washington, D.C.; Fonds Regional d'Art Contemporain, Bordeaux,
France; University of Michigan, Dearborn, Michigan; Michigan State Univer-
sity, East Lansing, Michigan; Musee d'Art Moderne, Saint-Etienne, France;
Musee d'Art Moderne de la Ville de Paris, Paris; Musee des Beaux-Arts, Jules
Cheret, Nice, France; Musee Departemental des Vosques, Epinal, France;
Ohio Wesleyan University, Delaware, Ohio; Rhenisches Landesmuseum,
Bonn, Germany; San Francisco Museum of Modern Art, California; State
University of New York at Albany, New York; University of Pennsylvania,
Philadelphia; University of Wisconsin, Milwaukee; Victoria and Albert
Museum, London; Paris Audiovisuel—Ville de Paris; National Portrait
Gallery, London; House for German History, Berlin.

Publications:

By NEWTON: Books—*White Women/Femmes Secretes,* with an introduc-
tion by Philippe Garner, New York, London, Munich and Paris 1976;
Sleepless Night/Nuits Blanches, New York, London, Munich and Paris 1978;
Helmut Newton: Special Collection: 24 Photo Lithos, New York, London,
Munich and Paris 1979; *47 Nudes,* with introduction by Karl Lagerfeld,
London 1982; *World Without Men,* Paris 1984; *Big Nudes,* text by Karl
Lagerfeld, New York, 1984-86; *Helmut Newton-Portraits,* Preface by Carol
Squires, New York, Paris, Munich, London, 1986; *Helmut Newton's Illustrat-
ed No 1—Sex and Power,* New York, 1987; *Helmut Newton's Illustrated No
2—Pictures from an Exhibition,* Munich, 1987; *Helmut Newton-Portraits,*
Preface by Klaus Honnef, Munich, 1987; *Helmut Newton—Private Property,*
text by Marshall Blonsky, Munich, 1989; *Das Glas im Kopf wird vom Glas,*
Text by Jan Fabre, Uitgevers, Belgium, 1990; *Helmut Newton's Illustrated No*

3—I Was There, Munich, 1991; *Helmut Newton, Pola-Woman,* Munich, 1992; *Immorale,* Japan, 1993. **Articles**—"Helmut Newton: I Think the 'Ideal' Nude Is Erotic" in *Nude: Theory,* edited by Jain Kelly, New York 1979; "Helmut Newton," interview, with Yves Aubry, in *Zoom* (London), November/December 1979; "Helmut Newton Talks to Maud Molyneux," interview, in *Viz* (London), no. 12, 1980; "Helmut Newton," *Photo-Poche,* 1986.

On NEWTON: Books—*Design and Art Direction '68,* London 1968; *Design and Art Direction '69,* London 1969; *The Magic Image* by Cecil Beaton and Gail Buckland, London and Boston 1975; *Photography Year 1976,* by the Time-Life editors, New York 1976; *La Photographie Française des Origines à nos Jours* by Claude Nori, Paris and London 1978; *Geschichte der Fotografie im 20. Jahrhundert/Photography in the 20th Century* by Petr Tausk, Cologne 1977, London 1980; *The Vogue Book of Fashion Photography* by Polly Devlin, with an introduction by Alexander Liberman, New York and London 1979; *The History of Fashion Photography* by Nancy Hall-Duncan, New York and Paris 1979; *Photographie als Kunst 1879-1979/Kunst als Photographie 1949-1979,* exhibition catalogue, 2 vols., by Peter Weiermair, Innsbruck 1979; *SX-70 Art,* edited by Ralph Gibson, New York 1979; *Instantanés,* exhibition catalogue, by Michael Nuridsany, Paris 1980; *Art at Auction 1979-80: Sotheby Parke Bernet,* London 1980; *Contemporary Decorative Arts from 1940 to the Present* by Philippe Garner, London and New York 1980; *Color as Form: A History of Color Photography,* exhibition catalogue, with introduction by Robert A. Sobieszek, Rochester, New York 1982; *Master Photographers: The World's Great Photographers on their Art and Technique,* edited by Pat Booth, London 1983; *Sammlung Gruber: Photographie des 20. Jahrhunderts,* exhibition catalogue, with foreword by Siegfried Gohr, Cologne 1984; *Shots of Style: Great Fashion Photographs Chosen by David Bailey,* with text by Martin Harrison, London 1985. **Articles**—"C'est la Nouvelle Loi de Newton" in *Photo* (Paris), October 1971; "Vogue Paris" by Claude Nori in *Progresso Fotografico* (Milan), December 1973; "Insight: Helmut Newton" in *Camera* (Lucerne), March 1974; "Helmut Newton" in *The Image* (London), vol. 2, no. 5, 1974; "Helmut Newton: Erotica/Fashion Photos" in *Oui* (Paris), August 1974; "My October Child: Helmut Newton" in *Camera* (Lucerne), September 1974; "A Return to Roundness in All the Right Places" by Michael Roberts in *The Sunday Times* (London), 3 January 1976; "Meet the Wife" by Christopher War in the *Daily Mirror* (London), 7 January 1976; "They Bare It All for the Sake of Fashion" by Patricia Morgan in *The Sun* (London), 24 January 1976; "Helmut Newton and Hideki Fujii" by William Packer in the *Financial Times* (London), 29 January 1976; "Helmut Newton: Women Observed" in *Penthouse Photo World* (New York), February/March 1977; "Helmut Newton: Women as Erotica" in *Penthouse Photo World* (New York), April/May 1977; "I Professionati: Helmut Newton" in *Fotografia Italiana* (Milan), September 1977; "Cheres Confrères" in *Photo* (Paris), March 1979; "Brutality Chic" by Rosetta Brooks in *ZG* (London), no. 2, 1980; "La Fine Fleur d'Helmut Newton" in *Photo* (Paris), October 1980. **Films**—*Helmut Newton,* Thames-TV documentary, by Michael White, 1978; *Frames from the Edge,* television documentary by Adrian Maben, 1988; *The Originals,* television documentary, 1992.

* * *

Helmut Newton is first and foremost a fashion photographer, following the tradition created by Adolphe de Meyer and developed by Hoyningen-Huene, Steichen, Munkacsi, Blumenfeld, Horst, Penn and Avedon. His photographs are perfectly suited to the purposes for which they were made—indeed, Newton surpasses the work of his predecessors in this respect and undermines their achievements by introducing an element of social criticism which is subliminal, perhaps unconscious and in any event nearly hidden by the alluring world he depicts: a luxurious, indolent world of *fin-de-siècle* hotels, strange landscapes surrounding French and Italian castles, and the cold, veneered splendors of fashionable New York and Paris apartment buildings. The atmosphere in which his beautiful, intense mannequins move tends to conceal the critical undercurrent, so that his work differs only slightly from that of other great fashion photographers, with the possible exception of Deborah Turbeville.

The critical undertone of his work is apparent in the formal grip he has on the subjects he portrays, his models and the fashionable (and sometimes shady) worlds they inhabit. But the totally artifical atmosphere of traditional fashion photography is missing in Newton's work, and we can begin to sense a latent imaginative realm of fantasies, dreams and nightmares. His photographs are not merely tasteful, thoroughly developed compositions, but reflections of a view of reality full of muted desires, buried memories, aggressive sexual obsessions and forbidden yearnings which appeal directly to the expectations of a decadent culture. These photographs disclose the hidden as well as the overt cruelties of male sexual fantasies and the desire to oppress and subjugate one's partner. They heighten our sense of modern man as a creature caught in the torments of regulated behavior, forced to appear respectable yet at the same time the victim of the desolation and ennui of modern life.

The point of view which governs Newton's camera is that of the voyeur, reducing women to sexual machines always ready to perform. His photographs consciously acknowledge this voyeurism—in fact it is one of his central themes. But the point of view of the photographer himself is ambiguous. He presents his subjects with equalled refinement, suggestive and at the same time supercool, at times almost ritualized. It is difficult to resist these images, with their high degree of affect-potential, but at the same time they radiate something extremely disturbing, as if De Sade's fantasies were suddenly to appear in a fashion magazine. For the viewer the most unsettling part of the experience is that he accepts the manner of representation without blinking an eye—unless, of course, he is already critical of the reality being depicted.

—Klaus Honnef

NICHOLS, Michael. (Nick)

Nationality: American. **Born:** Muscle Shoals, Alabama, 4 September 1952. **Education:** University of North Alabama, B.A. (fine arts, painting and photography), 1976. **Military Service:** Served in the U.S. Army. **Family:** Married Reba Peck in 1977; children: Ian and Thomas. **Career:** Press photographer for the *Florence Times,* 1976-77. Went freelance in 1978, represented by Black Star, working exclusively for *Géo* magazine. In 1983, moved to Magnum agency, worked for *Géo, Rolling Stone,* and *Life.* Since 1990, worked closely with *National Geographic.* **Agent:** Magnum Photos Inc., 72 Spring Street, New York. **Address:** 525 Grove Avenue, Charlottesville, Virginia 22902, U.S.A.

Individual Exhibitions:

1989   *Gorilla, Struggle for Survival in the Virungas,* The California Academy of Sciences, San Francisco (travelled to the Cleveland Museum of Natural History; Atlanta Zoo, Georgia; the Cincinnati Museum of Natural History; New York State Museum, Albany)

Selected Group Exhibitions:

1989-90   *In Our Time, the World Seen by Magnum Photographers,* International Center for Photography, New York (travelled around the United States; Palais de Tokyo, Paris)

Publications:

By NICHOLS: Books—*Gorilla,* New York 1989; *Great Apes, Between Two Worlds,* Washington, D.C., 1993. **Articles**—"Lure of the Abyss" in *Géo,* June 1979; "Venezuela's Lost World" in *Geo,* March 1980; "Riding the Torrent" and "Flying into the Eye of the Hurricane" in *Géo,* August 1980; "Goodbye to El Dorado" in *Géo,* December 1981; "A Tabloid of Savage Innocence" in *Géo,* May 1982; "Faithhealing in the Philippines" in *Géo,* November 1982; "Genetics vs Environment" in *Géo,* May 1981; "The Rope" *Géo,* February 1983; "A Race Against Time" in *Géo,* June 1986; "Expedition in the Tree Tops" in *Géo,* December 1986; "Trance in Bali" in *Geo,* February 1989; "The Last Great Ape" in *American Photographer,* November 1988; "The Skyline that Ate San Francisco" in *California Maga-*

Lechuguilla Cave. Photograph ©Michael Nichols/Magnum.

zine, May 1983; "Hot Spas" in *California Magazine,* July 1983; "The Curse of the Little Round Cans" in *Discover,* September 1985; "Booker Noe" in *Esquire,* September 1987; "Stress, Success, and Samoa" in *Hippocrates,* May/June 1987, "The Great Lighthouse Giveaway" in *Life,* August 1987; "China Strains for Olympic Glory" in *New York Times Magazine,* April 1988; "Once Upon a Time in Rwanda" in *Parenting Magazine,* November 1978; "A Labyrinth called Lechuguilla" in *Smithsonian Magazine,* November 1988; "China Update" in *Travel & Leisure,* February 1984; "Riding the Rapids of the Grand Canyon" in *Travel & Leisure,* April 1986; "Bali High" in *Travel & Leisure,* July 1987; "Death Valley Daze" in *Rolling Stone,* 26 September 1985; "Rolling Thunder" in *Rolling Stone,* 16 July 1987; "Wayward Vets" in *Rolling Stone,* 10 May 1988; "The Scorched Earth" in *Rolling Stone,* 23 February 1989; "Rafting with the BBC" in *Outside,* September 1984; "Sierra Style" in *Outside,* October 1984; "The Naturals" in *Outside* May 1985; "The Old Man and His River" in *Outside,* May 1986; "Seeing the Light" in *Outside,* August 1987; "Gorilla Monsoon" in *Outside,* December 1988; "The Splendors of Lechuguilla Cave" with Tim Cahill in *National Geographic,* March 1991; "Apes and Humans, A Curious Kinship" with Eugene Linden in *National Geographic,* March 1992; "Mountains Lions" with Maurice G. Hornocker in *National Geographic,* July 1992; "New Zoos, Taking Down the Bars" with Cliff Tarpy in *National Geographic,* July 1993. **Film**—*The Ndoki, the Making of a Magazine Story,* National Geographic Explorer, 21 August 1994.

On NICHOLS: Book—*In Our Time, The World Seen by Magnum Photographers* by William Manchester, 1989. **Articles**—"New Faces" in *American*

Photographer; "Wearing the Mask of Photographer" in *America,* Spring 1985; "The Adventures of Nick Danger" by Tim Cahill in *Image Mazagine,* 3 November 1985; "Nick Nichols and the Danger Zone" in *American Photographer,* April 1987; "Flash Points" in *Outdoor Photographer,* April 1987; "Going Ape" in *Outdoor Photographer,* July 1987; "Seeing the Light" in *Outside Magazine,* August 1987; "Up Close with Gorillas" by Debbie Crouse in *International Wildlife,* November/December 1988; "Planet of the Apes" by Christopher Hunt in *Travel & Leisure,* October 1988; "Eyewitnesses" by Michael McRae in *Outside,* October 1992; "Photography's Great Adventures" in *American Photographer,* July/August 1993. **Film**—*Visions,* National Geographic, March 1994.

*   *   *

Nick Nichols is pleased to be a one-note photographer. Ever since making a career change to photography, he has concentrated on working primarily for the *National Geographic.* For them he has produced features, a book and a film on the gorillas and other animals of Central Africa that form the core of his work to date. Living, for weeks or months on end, in the midst of the swampiest jungle inhabited only by a few of Africa's vanishing peoples he proudly claims his work—and the scars and diseases that resulted—as the *studd* that nobody else wanted, or would be crazy enough to go after. Through photography, he was also able to fulfil his love of adventure, of challenging and often harsh living conditions, with social and ecological concerns.

His first contact with photography came when he was drafted into the U.S. military during the last stages of the Vietnam war. He succeeded in getting assigned to the photography unit, and returned home to study the subject at the University of North Alabama. There a former *Life* photographer, Charles Moore, introduced him to the Black Star agency and through them to the French based magazine *Géo* who signed him to cover the Inuit of Canada, the Indus in the Himalayas, the giant Komodo lizards of Indonesia. The French magazine *Photo* bylined him as "the Indiana Jones of photography." In 1983 he joined the Magnum agency as a nominee and five years later became a full member.

Also in 1988 came his first book, *Gorilla, Struggle for Survival in the Virungas.* In 1992 there followed three World Press Photo awards for photographic features on *Lechugilla Cave* and *Apes and Humans: A Curious Kinship.* Then, in 1993 came *The Great Apes: Between Two Worlds* documenting this time, not the mountian gorillas of his earlier work, but the intimate and delicate eco-balance between human and animal primates (for *National Geographic*).

In August 1994 his film *Ndoki*—the local name for the insalubrious Congolese "last Eden" hitherto shunned by all but a few indigenous humans—was shown on U.S. television. Thus his original fusion of photojournalistic assignments with natural history studies has moved into a new medium.

—Amanda Hopkinson

NILSSON, Pål-Nils.

Nationality: Swedish. **Born:** Rome, 7 July 1929. **Education:** Educated in Stockholm; self-taught in photography. **Family:** Divorced; children: Mats-Nils and Paula. **Career:** Freelance photographer, working for Svenska Riksbyggen, *Svenska Turistföreningens Årsbok,* Stockholm, since 1955; also filmmaker, mainly for Swedish television, Stockholm. Member, Tio Fotografer group, Stockholm, since 1958. **Agent:** Tiofoto, Box 3252, 10365 Stockholm, Sweden. **Address:** Lövängsvägen 27, 183 30 Täby, Sweden.

Individual Exhibitions:

1956   Värmlands museum, Karlstad, Sweden
1957   *Life in Sweden Today,* Addo. X Gallery, New York
1959   *New York,* Artek Gallery, Stockholm
1963   Museum Fodor, Amsterdam (with Albert Renger-Patzsch and
           Gabriel Cuallado)

1970	*Samit,* Swedish Institute, Stockholm (travelled to Belgrade, Paris, New York, Helsinki, etc., 1970-75)
1980	*Color Prints,* Lilla Galleriet, Viken, Sweden

Selected Group Exhibitions:

1954	*5 Photographers,* Moderna Musset, Stockholm
1955	*The Family of Man,* Museum of Modern Art, New York (and world tour)
1958	*Fotokonst '58,* Lunds Konsthall, Sweden
1960	*Tio Fotografer på Svensk Form,* Moderna Museet, Stockholm
1962	*Svenskarna sedda av 11 Fotografer,* Moderna Musset, Stockholm
1971	*Contemporary Photographs from Sweden: An Exhibition of the Work of the Tio Photographers,* Library of Congress, Washington, D.C.
1975	*The Land: 20th Century Landscape Photographs Selected by Bill Brandt,* Victoria and Albert Museum (travelled to the National Gallery, Edinburgh; Ulster Museum, Belfast; and National Museum of Wales, Cardiff, 1976)
1982	*The Frozen Image,* Walker Art Center, Minneapolis (travelled to the International Center of Photography, New York University of California, Los Angeles; Portland Art Museum, Maine; Museum of Contemporary Art, Chicago; Tacoma Art Museum, Washington; Kjavalsstadir, Reykjavik; Louisiana Museum, Humlebaek; Taidehalli, Helsinki; Fotografiska Museet, Stockholm; Kunstsenter, Oslo)
1984	*Subjektive Fotografie: Images of the 50s,* San Francisco Museum of Modern Art (travelled to the University of Houston, Texas; Museum Folkwang, Essen; Vasterbottens Museum, Umea; Kulturhuset, Stockholm; Saarland Museum, Saarbrucken; Palais des Beaux Arts, Brussels)
1986	*Jazz pa fotografiska,* Fotografiska Museet, Stockholm

Collections:

Fotografiska Museet, Moderna Museet, Stockholm; Valokuvamuseon, Helsinki; Norsk Fotohistorisk Forening, Oslo; Bibliothèque Nationale, Paris; Victoria and Albert Museum, London; Museum of Modern Art, New York; Library of Congress, Washington, D.C; Museum Folkwang, Essen, Germany.

Publications:

By NILSSON: Books—photographer, illustrator and designer of *Svenska Turistföreningens Årsbok* annual, Stockholm, since 1956; *Landskap,* Stockholm 1956; *Natur,* with text by Bo Rosen, Stockholm 1956; *Duov'dagat ja Bangot,* with text by Israel Ruong, Stockholm 1967; *Hantverkets 60-tal,* Stockholm 1968; *Jojk,* Stockholm 1969; *Dakkan,* Stockholm 1971; *En bok om Barbro Nilsson,* Stockholm 1977. Films—30 documentary films for Swedish Radio-TV.

On NILSSON: Books—*Photography Today,* edited by Norman Hall, London 1957; *Svenskarna sedda av 11 fotografer,* exhibition catalogue, by K.G. Pontus Hulten and Stig Claeson, Stockholm 1962; *Photography Annual 1971,* New York 1970; *Contemporary Photographs from Sweden: An Exhibition of the Work of the Tio Photographers,* exhibition catalogue, Washington, D.C. 1971; *The Land: 20th Century Landscape Photographs Selected by Bill Brandt,* exhibition catalogue, edited by Mark Haworth-Booth, London 1975; *Geschichte der Fotografie im 20. Jahrhundert/Photography in the 20th Century* by Petr Tausk, Cologne 1977, London 1980; *The Frozen Image: Scandinavian Photography,* edited by Martin Freeman, Minneapolis and New York 1982; *Subjektive Fotografie: Images of the 50s,* exhibition catalogue, by Ute Eskildsen, Manfred Schmalriede and Dorothy Martinson, Essen, West Germany 1984.

* * *

For more than 25 years Pål-Nils Nilsson has, on behalf of the Swedish Tourist Association (STF), made voyages of discovery around Sweden with his camera. Each year he has made an intensive study of one specific area or landscape, and for many years his pictures have dominated the STF's illustrated publications.

Nilsson has depicted Swedish cultural history and Swedish nature with insight and objectivity, and thereby splendidly followed the tradition laid down by his prominent predecessors, for example C.G. Rosenberg and Gösta Lundquist. But under Nilsson's leadership, the STF's traditional nature-romanticism and highly nuanced, lyrical pictures—their mainstay in the 1930s and 40s—have given way to a taut idiomatic expression and a journalistic realism. For example, Nilsson has portrayed the changed cultural landscape and the disturbance to the environment that follows in the wake of industrialization.

The 1960s were a productive decade for Nilsson. In addition to his work for the Tourist Association he published picture stories and reportage portraits in magazines such as *Vi* and *Vecko-Journalen,* and he also made a name for himself as an able fashion and advertising photographer. In all of these genres, he combined sober form with a straight journalistic approach and technical perfection.

Like many other Swedish photographers, Nilsson began to work with film in the mid-1960s. In the next decade or so he made more than 30 documentary films for Swedish Television. His personal engagement in social questions became more and more prominent during this period, and the effectiveness of his films can be judged by their impact. For example, his film series about stateless gypsies, who had been forced to leave Sweden for a difficult existence in a Parisian suburban slum, provoked such response that they were granted permission to return.

For a long time Nilsson has also been concerned with the Lapp population's difficulties as a minority in the Swedish welfare state. In films, books, exhibitions and photo stories he has revealed the social injustices, the economic conditions, of their daily lives, at the same time that he has revealed the uniqueness of their traditional crafts. A film which exposed the state's land policy in the Samelat reindeer domains led (among other results) to an official complaint against the activities of Swedish provincial governments.

In other films Nilsson has dealt with the living conditions of the Swedish coastal population, of middle-eastern immigrants, and Finnish gypsies. In this work he has collaborated with the Swedish television journalist Brita Reuterswärd.

In films and picture stories Nilsson has used the image as a weapon in social debate, to inform and to educate. The medium has had to be subordinate to the message. He has treated different subjects with insight and understanding. If one looks at both intent and result, Nilsson must undoubtedly be placed among Europe's outstanding post-war documentary filmmakers and photographers.

—Rune Hassner

NIXON, Nicholas.

Nationality: American. **Born:** Detroit, Michigan, in 1947. **Education:** University of Michigan, Ann Arbor, B.A. (American literature), 1969; University of New Mexico, Albuquerque, M.F.A. (art), 1974. **Family:** Married Bebe Brown in 1971. **Career:** VISTA Volunteer, St. Louis, 1969-70; architectural photographer, Detroit, 1970-71; high school photography teacher, Minneapolis, 1971-73. Independent photographer, Cambridge, Massachusetts, since 1974. Associate Professor, Massachusetts College of Art, Boston, since 1975. **Recipient:** National Endowment for the Arts Photography Fellowship, 1976, 1979; Guggenheim Photography Fellowship, 1977. **Agents:** Light Gallery, 724 Fifth Avenue, New York, New York 10019; Fraenkel Gallery, 55 Grant Avenue, San Francisco, California 94106; and Galerie Rudolf Kicken, Albertusstrasse 1, 5000 Cologne, 1, Germany. **Address:** c/o Massachusetts College of Art, Boston, Massachusetts 02215, U.S.A.

Individual Exhibitions:

1976	Museum of Modern Art, New York
1977	Worcester Art Museum, Massachusetts (with Stephen Shore) Vision Gallery, Boston

1978   Light Gallery, New York
        Color Photographs, Cronin Gallery, Houston (with William
            Eggleston)
        Massachusetts Institute of Technology, Cambridge (with Linda
            Connor)
1979   Light Gallery, New York
        Vision Gallery, Boston
1980   Light Gallery, New York
        Fraenkel Gallery, San Francisco
1981   Light Gallery, New York
        Vision Gallery, Boston
1982   Fraenkel Gallery, San Francisco
        Light Gallery, New York

Selected Group Exhibitions:

1975   *New Topographics: Photographs of a Man-Altered Landscape,*
            International Museum of Photography, George Eastman
            House, Rochester, New York (travelled to the Otis Art
            Institute, Los Angeles, and Princeton University Art
            Museum, New Jersey)
1977   *10 Photographes Américains Contemporains,* Galerie
            Zabriskie, Paris
1978   *Mirrors and Windows: American Photography since 1960,*
            Museum of Modern Art, New York (toured the United
            States, 1978-80)
1979   *Fleeting Gestures: Dance Photographs,* International Center of
            Photography, New York (travelled to *Venezia '79,* and to
            The Photographers' Gallery, London)
        *American Images: New Work by 20 Contemporary Photogra-
            phers,* Corcoran Gallery, Washington, D.C. (travelled to the
            International Center of Photography, New York; Museum of
            Fine Arts, Houston; Minneapolis Institute of Arts; Indianapo-
            lis Institute of Arts, 1980; and American Academy,
            Rome, 1981)
1980   *American Children,* Museum of Modern Art, New York
1982   *International Photography 1920-80,* Australian National
            Gallery, Canberra
1983   *New Work by Eight Photographers,* Daniel Wolf Gallery,
            New York
1985   *American Images 1945-80,* Barbican Art Gallery, London
            (toured Britain)
1987   *Photographs from the Last Decade,* San Francisco Museum of
            Modern Art

Collections:

Museum of Modern Art, New York; Metropolitan Museum of Art, New York;
Joseph Seagram and Sons Inc. Collection, New York; International Museum
of Photography, George Eastman House, Rochester, New York; Museum of
Fine Arts, Boston; Fogg Art Museum, Harvard University, Cambridge,
Massachusetts; Worcester Art Museum, Massachusetts; Art Institute of Chica-
go; Minneapolis Institute of Arts; Museum of Fine Arts, Houston.

Publications:

On NIXON: Books—*New Topographics: Photographs of a Man-Altered
Landscape,* exhibition catalogue, with text by William Jenkins, Rochester,
New York 1975; *Contemporary American Photographic Works,* exhibition
catalogue, by Lewis Baltz, Houston 1977; *Mirrors and Windows: American
Photography since 1960* by John Szarkowski, New York 1978; *American
Images: New Work by 20 Contemporary Photographers,* edited by Renato
Danese, New York 1979; *American Children,* edited by Susan Kismaric, New
York 1980; *International Photography 1920-1980,* edited by Ian North,
Canberra 1982; *American images: Photography 1945-1980,* edited by Peter
Turner and John Benton-Harris, London 1985. **Articles**—"Topographical
Error" by Charles Desmarais in *Afterimage* (Rochester, New York), Novem-
ber 1975; "Route 66 Revisited: The New Landscape Photography" by Carter
Ratcliff in *Art in America* (New York), January 1976; "New York: Nicholas
Nixon, Museum of Modern Art" by Leo Rubinfien in *Artforum* (New York),

December 1976; "A Fascination with Man-Made Settings" in *Photography
Year 1977,* by the Time-Life editors, New York 1977; "Nixon at Vision" by
Arno Minkkinen in *Views* (Boston), no. 2, 1979; "Currents: American
Photography Today: Nicholas Nixon" by Andy Grundberg and Julia Scully in
Modern Photography (New York), May 1979; review by Kelly Wise in
Artforum (New York), April/May 1981.

*   *   *

The facts of Nicholas Nixon's early biography have formed his developing
aesthetic in complex ways. The fact that his earliest photographs were 35mm.
snapshots "in the tradition of Cartier-Bresson," for instance, merely seems to
be an ironic contradiction of the large format which is Nixon's hallmark. The
ease and mobility with which Nixon uses large-format photography, while
retaining the scrupulous detail possible with the 8 x 10 inch camera, has
challenged its potential and opened the format to the possibility of accident
and chance. Nixon has created a unique amalgam by reconciling the spontaneity of Cartier-Bresson with the measure of Walker Evans, another early
favorite.

Seemingly insignificant facts of Nixon's career also hold meaning. Nixon
worked briefly as an architectural photographer, which undoubtedly contributed not only to the choice of cityscape in his 1974-76 views of Boston but also
to his architectonic use of space and precision of detail. The fact that he
volunteered for VISTA signalled the concern and empathy for people which
would surface in his portraiture. Nixon's work is, above all, intensely
American in both its subject and its ruthless honesty of approach. This too has
roots in his past, for he discovered photography while studying American
literature and was initially attracted to the vigorous and forthright images of
Walker Evans, which told the Whitmanesque saga of the American land and its
people.

Honesty is the key to Nixon's work: taken to its extreme, it becomes
almost a disinterested neutrality and anonymity of style which is particularly
unsettling in photographs of people. Concurrent with his cityscapes, Nixon
began a series of family snapshots which combine the artlessness of family
snapshots with a highly developed technical sophistication. Nixon's first
portrait subject was his wife Bebe; gradually he included other relatives in
increasingly complex combinations. The portraits of Bebe and her three
sisters—three of which were included in the Museum of Modern Art's
Mirrors and Windows exhibition of 1978 and are thus among his bestknown
works—are unsettling, even cutting. We are not used to portraits treated so
frankly or women looking so proud and fierce and beautiful. Like all good
photography, this portraiture shakes one to the core.

It is difficult not to say that Nixon's work has matured, for it has and
continues to become increasingly complex and integrated. He has changed his
pictorial structure in the last few years by moving closer to his subject, which
decreases depth recession and allows the subjects to dominate the space. On a
purely formal level, there is a new complexity in the way Nixon uses the
spaces between his subjects, their overlap, and the forms they create on the
picture surface.

These pictures *do* work on an emotional level as well, though not one
usually associated with portraiture. They are infused with an intense calm,
created in part by the fact that the subjects never make eye contact with either
the viewer or each other. Nixon has created an entirely new emotional premise
for portraiture, thereby expanding the very idea of what constitutes this mode
of picture-taking. That these elements have begun to coalesce in Nixon's work
is undeniable; where it will lead, and what form it will take in his increasingly
assured and important production, is uncertain.

—Nancy Hall-Duncan

NOORDHOEK, Wim (Willem).

Nationality: Dutch. **Born:** The Hague, 16 September 1916. **Education:**
Studied art, under Kees Andrea, Christiaan de Moor and Harry Verburgt, Vrije

Akademie, The Hague, 1933-36; studied photography under Meinhard Woldringh. **Family:** Married to Annet van Battum; children: Machteld and Aafje. **Career:** Independent painter and graphic artist, from 1939; freelance photographer, working for Dumont Schauberg Verlag, Leitz, Agfa, Knapp Verlag, etc., from 1950: lived in Mook-Middelaar, 1941-44, in Haps, 1944-45, in Cuyk, 1945-54, in St. Agathe, France, and Erbeek, 1954-60, in Nederhemet, 1961-86, and in Heusden since 1986. Founder, with Enno Brokke, Ap Sok and Jan Gregoor, Cuyk-Group of artists, Cuyk, 1945. Professor of graphics, design and photography, Academie voor Kunst en Vormgeving, Den Bosch, 1950-74; Guest Professor, Rijksuniversiteit, Leiden, and Volkshochschule, Cologne. **Recipient:** Photokina Prize, Cologne; Photobook of the Year Award, 1971, 1974; Province of Brabant Prize, Nivelles, Belgium; Capi-Lux Alblasprijs 1981. Honorary Citizen, City of Stommelen, West Germany. Member, Nederlandse Fotografen Kunstkring; Nederlands Leica Kring; De Grafische Groep, Amsterdam.

Individual Exhibitions:

1957   Gallery of Fine Arts, Someren, Netherlands
1961   Galerie Waag, Nijmegen, Netherlands (with Pan Walther)
1962   Atelier De Greef, Den Bosch, Netherlands
1963   Bas van Pelt, The Hague
1964   Bas van Pelt, Amsterdam
1966   Volkhochschule, Cologne, West Germany
1967   Prentenkabinet, Rijksuniversiteit, Leiden, Netherlands
        Stedelijk Museum De Lakenhal, Leiden, Netherlands
1968   *Poezie en Werkelijkheid,* Technische Hoge-school, Eindhoven, Netherlands
1972   Stadhuis, Zaltbommel, Netherlands
1976   Faculty of Medicine, Erasmus University, Rotterdam
1981   Capi-Lux Building, Amsterdam
1983   Catharinakapel, Harderwijk, Netherlands
        Zie de Mens en De Stilte, De Pronkkamer, Uden, Netherlands
1985   Het centrum voor kunstzinnige vorming Zouavenlaan 77, Den Bosch, Netherlands
1990   *Wim Noordhoek, een overzicht,* Canon Image Centre, Amsterdam

Selected Group Exhibitions:

1961   *Focussalon,* Haarlem, Netherlands
1963   *Nederlandse Fotografen Kunstkring,* Galerie Waag, Nijmegen, Netherlands
        Musement, Utrecht, Netherlands
1964   *Vijf Gelderse Fotografen,* Gemeentemuseum, Arnhem, Netherlands
1966   *Hedendaagse Fotografie,* Meppel, Netherlands
        Fotografie Elementar, at *Photokina 66,* Cologne, West Germany
1976   *De Cuykse Groep na 30 Jaar,* Galerie Kom in de Kring, Bleiswijk, Netherlands
1978   *Fotografie in Nederland 1940-75,* Stedelijk Museum, Amsterdam
1986   *Nederlandse fotografen op reis, een keuze,* Kritzraedthuis, Sittard, Netherlands
1988   *Visies op landschap,* De Gruitpoort-Galerij, Doetinchem
1990   *10 Jaar Capi-Lux Alblas Prijs,* Posthoornkerk, Amsterdam
1994   *Joegoslavië bestaat niet meer, historische foto's van vier Nederlandse fotografen,* Artoteek, Den Haag

Collections:

Prentenkabinet, Rijksuniversiteit, Leiden, Netherlands; Gemeentemuseum, The Hague; Museum Boymans-van Beuningen, Rotterdam; Stedelijk Museum, Amsterdam; Rijksmuseum, Amsterdam; Bibliotheque Nationale, Paris; Royal Museum, Brussels; Landesmuseum, Munster, West Germany; Stichting Nederlands Fotoarchief, Rotterdam.

Publications:

By NOORDHOEK: Books—*Boek van het nieuwe denken,* with others, Amsterdam 1967; *Die Kindernahmaschine,* Cologne 1971; *Beromunster,* Amsterdam 1972; *Grundlehre der Farbfotografie,* Dusseldorf 1978; *Natte cel: verhalen,* Amsterdam 1979.

On NOORDHOEK: Books—*Rekenschap, Aankoop Kunst Rijk 1946-1954,* Amsterdam 1954; *De wereld van het zwart en wit,* Amsterdam 1959; *Vijf Gelderse Fotografen,* exhibition catalogue, Arnhem 1965; *Wim Noordhoek: fototentoonstelling,* exhibition catalogue, with text by J. van Haaren, Eindhoven 1968; *De Cuykse Groep na dertig jaar* by K. Roodenburg, Bleiswijk, Netherlands 1976; *Geschichte der Fotografie im 20. Jahrhundert/Photography in the 20th Century* by Petr Tausk, Cologne 1977, London 1980; *Fotografie in Nederland 1940/1975,* exhibition catalogue, edited by Els Barents, The Hague 1978. **Articles**—"Materie: 4 Meister der asthetischen Fotografie" in *Foto und Film Prisma* (Kulmbach, West Germany), October 1970; "Wim Noordhoek: Winterlandschaft" in *Color Foto Journal* (Munich), December 1974; "Wim Noordhoek retrospectieve expositie" by Wim Broekman in *Foto 45,* jul/aug 1990; "Wim Noordhoek" by Marga Altena in *Geschiedenis van de Nederlandse fotografie in monografieën* en thema-artikelen by Ingeborg Th Leijerzapf (editor) Vol a/d 1992.

*   *   *

The Dutchman Wim Noordhoek originally studied painting, and embarked on a successful career in this field as a fine artist. At the age of thirty-four, he was appointed fine arts teacher at the Royal Academy of Arts in Den Bosch, and at that time began using his art-trained eyes for serious photography. Noordhoek's considerable experience as a visual artist allowed him to make acute comparisions between the disciplines of painting and photography and the specific qualities relative to each. He clearly recognized the primary importance of the artist's attitude, and so began his photographic activity with a relatively simple twin-lens reflex camera. This immediate grasp of photography's basic nature and the spatial qualities inherent in it led Noordhoek to produce pure photos of a very high quality. Recognizing his particular insights into the subject, the Academy soon appointed Noordhoek to teach photography as well as other graphic arts. He engaged his students in unusual pedagogic methods to explain his ideas about the individual's own unique approach to the medium, the application of concepts from widely differing disciplines, and, not least, the evaluation of the photograph as a medium of artistic expression. One of his teaching methods is well illustrated by his 1971 book about a child's sewing-machine, in which he uses the entire volume to show different ways of depicting the one object.

Noorkhoek's own photographic contribution was mainly in the area of colour photography. Since he earned his living as a teacher, he was relatively free to make independent photos for his own interest, only accepting commercial assignments for calendars and book-illustrations particularly suited to his style. He had no preference or prejudice toward any genre or subject, for his photographic choice depended entirely on the emotional excitement generated by his perception of the world around him. The strongest common factor running through the variety of still-lifes, landscapes, urban scenes and action pictures is Noodhoek's frequent use of a sober and limited colour range. The restriction of the palette focusses appreciation on his broad scale of finely modulated shades and tonal values, which enable him, for instance, to produce remarkable images from apparently trivial landscapes. Selecting precisely the right moment and situation for an exposure, he is able to capture the unrepeatable shot both in still-life subject and in transitory events such as children playing in the streets.

A strong regard for his art training and a sensitive awareness permeate his pictures—whose power is not merely perceived by pedagogical speculation. The driving force in Noordhoek's photography is the need to communicate directly and spontaneously his excitement about the world, an emotion supported by his entire visual culture.

—Petr Tausk

NOSKOWIAK, Soyna.

Nationality: American. **Born:** Leipzig, Germany, 25 November 1900; emigrated to the United States, 1915: naturalized, 1922. **Education:** Educated in Chile and California; studied photography with Edward Weston, San Francisco, 1929-34. **Career:** Worked as a receptionist in the Johan Hagemeyer Photo Studio, Los Angeles, 1929; Darkroom Assistant to Edward Weston, San Francisco, 1929-34; Founder Member, with Willard Van Dyke, Imogen Cunningham, and Edward Weston, Group f.64, San Francisco, 1932; independent photographer, with own portrait and architectural photography studio, and working for *Sunset Magazine,* various architects and interior designers, San Francisco, 1935 until her death, 1975. **Died:** (in Greenbrae, California), 28 April 1975.

Individual Exhibitions:

1935	*Portraits by Sonya Noskowiak and Sibyl Arikeeff,* Denny-Watrous Gallery, Carmel, California
1952	Raymond and Raymond, San Francisco
1963	*Photographs of Forms and Places by Sonya Noskowiak,* Stanford Research Institute, California
1978	Center for Creative Photography, University of Arizona, Tucson (retrospective)
1979	*WPA Photographs by Sonya Noskowiak,* San Francisco Museum of Modern Art

Selected Group Exhibitions:

1932	*Group f.64,* M.H. de Young Memorial Museum, San Francisco
1933	*Group f.64,* Ansel Adams Gallery, San Francisco
1939	*Annual Exhibition,* Society of Women Artists, San Francisco (and 1940)
1941	*First Annual Salon: Photography West of the Rockies,* San Francisco Museum of Art
1943	*Photographs from the Federal Art Project,* San Francisco Museum of Art
1977	*Photographs: Sheldon Memorial Art Gallery Collection,* University of Nebraska, Lincoln
1978	*Group f.64,* University of Missouri, St. Louis

Collections:

University of Minnesota, Minneapolis; University of Nebraska, Lincoln; Center for Creative Photography, University of Arizona, Tucson; University of California, Berkeley; San Francisco Museum of Modern Art; San Francisco Public Library.

Publications:

On NOSKOWIAK: Books—*Faces: A Narrative History of the Portrait in Photography* by Ben Maddow, Boston 1977; *Photographs: Sheldon Memorial Art Gallery Collection, University of Nebraska,* with an introduction by Norman A. Geske, Lincoln, Nebraska 1977; *Group f.64,* exhibition catalogue, with texts by Jean S. Tucker and Willard Van Dyke, St. Louis 1978; *Center for Creative Photography No. 9: Sonya Noskowiak,* with texts by Marnie Gillett and William Johnson, Tucson, Arizona 1979.

* * *

A charter member of the influential West Coast group of photographers, Group f.64, the German-American Sonya Noskowiak was an active participant in the struggle to define and practice a progressive, ''straight'' photography in an era still dominated by the conservative outlook of the pictorial esthetic.

Beginning her career as darkroom assistant and student to Edward Weston in 1929, Noskowiak learned Weston's painstaking technical procedures and shared his determination to achieve previsualized prints that could stand uncropped and unenlarged. In the course of her career, Noskowiak developed her vision and her craftsmanship to the point that the master said of her prints: ''Any of these I would sign as my own.''

In the first ''Group f.64'' show at the M.H. de Young Memorial Museum in 1932, Noskowiak exhibited photographs of natural objects—rocks, leaves and sand. The young photographers who formed the group intended its name to signify their preference for small lens apertures that would achieve sharply detailed images. Diverse in subject and style as the group proved to be, each member nevertheless subscribed to Weston's dictum, recorded in his *Daybook,* that ''the camera must be used for recording life, for rendering the very substance and quintessence of the thing itself. . . . ''

Turning from natural subjects as her career progressed, Noskowiak developed the industrial landscape as her particular forte in the early 1930s. In these photographs the surface textures of massive girders, pipes and struts are rendered in tones that range from deep blacks to startlingly pure whites. Although sensitive and sensuous, such full-toned printing of mundane and inexpressive subject matter makes Noskowiak's work occasionally seem something of a tour de force.

As the decade continued, however, Noskowiak turned from this estheticized industrialism, which drew as much on constructivist and German avant-garde photography as it did on Weston's work, toward a somewhat less formalist consideration of architectural subjects. Her later photographs present identifiable architectural details or whole buildings—rather than the anonymous steel of the earlier work—in settings that give a more human sense of the urban social life of the time.

Noskowiak established her own studio in San Francisco in 1935; her commercial work included fashion, portraiture, and architectural views. As a portraitist, she photographed such artists and performers as Jean Charlot, John Steinbeck, and Martha Graham, and throughout her career she continued her landscape and architectural studies in the San Francisco Bay area.

—Maren Stange

NOTHHELFER, Gabriele and Helmut.

Nationality: German. **Born:** Gabriele Nothhelfer born Gabriele Zimmermann in Berlin, 5 March 1945; Helmut Nothhelfer born in Bonn, 3 June 1945. **Education:** Both studied photography at the Folkwangschule, Essen, 1969-70. **Family:** Married in 1973. **Career:** Have worked jointly as freelance photographers, in Berlin and Bonn, since 1973. Held joint Mastership in Photography, Publicity Institute, Free University of Berlin, 1978. **Agents:** Ann and Jürgen Wilde, Niederberger Strasse, 23, Mülheim, 53909 Zülpich, Germany; Galerie Photo Art Basel, St. Alban-Vorstadt 10, 4010 Basle 10, Switzerland; Galerie Agathe Gaillard, 3 rue du Pont Louis-Philippe, 75004 Paris, France; and Sander Gallery, 51 Greene Street, New York, New York 10013, U.S.A.; Galerie Bodo Niemann, Knesebeckstrasse 30, D-10623 Berlin, Germany. **Address:** Weimarer Strasse 32, 10625 Berlin, Germany.

Individual Exhibitions:

1976	Galerie Wilde, Cologne
1977	Galerie Nagel, Berlin
	Galerie Agathe Gaillard, Paris
1978	Sander Gallery, Washington, D.C.
1979	Galerie t'Venster, Rotterdam
	Galerie Breiting, Berlin
	Galerie Wilde, Cologne
1980	Folkwang Museum, Essen
1983	Galerie nei liicht, Luxembourg
	Galerie Wilde, Cologne
	Galerie 2000, Berlin
1985	Galerie Agathe Gaillard, Paris
1986	Galerie Photo Art, Basle, Switzerland
1987	Museum für Photographie Braunschweig, Salzgitter Bad (Katalog)
1992	Galerie Bodo Niemann, Berlin

***Whit Monday on the Winterfeldtplatz,* Berlin, 1988.** Photograph ©Gabriele and Helmut Nothhelfer.

1993   Galerie Agathe Gaillard, Paris
        Rheinisches Landesmuseum, Bonn

Selected Group Exhibitions:

1976   *Porträts und Situationen,* Haus am Waldsee, Berlin (travelled
        to Schloß Morsbroich, Leverkusen and Württenbergischet
        Kunstverein, Stuttgart)
        Berlin Now, Denise René Gallery Downtown, New York
1977   *Documenta 6,* Kassel, West Germany
1978   *Berlin: A Critical View,* Institute of Contemporary Arts,
        London
1979   *Photographie als Kunst 1879-1979,* Tiroler Landesmuseum,
        Innsbruck, Austria (travelled to the Neue Galerie am
        Wolfgang Gurlitt Museum, Linz, Austria; Neue Galerie am
        Landesmuseum Joanneum, Graz, Austria; and Museum des
        20. Jahrhunderts, Vienna)
1981   *New German Photography,* The Photographers' Gallery,
        London
1982   *Lichtbildnisse: Das Porträt in der Fotografie,* Rheinisches
        Landesmuseum, Bonn
1983   *Die fotografische Sammlung,* Museum Folkwang, Essen, West
        Germany
1984   *Kunstlandschaft Bundesrepublik,* Hohenloher Kunstverein,
        Langenburg, West Germany
1986   *Karl-Hofer-Symposion,* Hochschule der Künste Berlin

1989   *Fotografie des 20. Jahrhunderts,* Sammlung Museum, Ludwig
        in der Hochschule für Grafik und Buchkunst, Leipzig
        Photographie als Photographie, Berlinische Galerie, Berlin
1994   *Die 70er Jahre—Meisterwerke der Fotografie,* Musée de
        Elysée, Lausanne
        *Gesture and Pose: Twentieth Century Photographs from the
        Collection,* The Museum of Modern Art, New York

Collections:

Folkwang Museum, Essen; Bibliothèque Nationale, Paris; Stedelijk Museum, Amsterdam; Museum of Modern Art, New York; Berlinische Galerie, Berlin; Museum Ludwig, Cologne; Fonds National d'Art Contemporain, Paris; Metropolitan Museum of Art, New York; Centre National de l'audiovisuel, Dudelange Luxemburg; Fondation Select, Lausanne; Museum of Modern Art, San Francisco; Rheinisches Landesmuseum, Bonn; Sammlung Ann und Jürgen Wilde im Sprengel Museum, Hannover.

Publications:

By the NOTHHELFERS: Books—*Wirklichkeits-vermittlung am Beispiel der Farm Security Administration,* Berlin 1978; *Bildinterpretationen zu Fotografien von Weegee,* Berlin 1978; *Friedrich Seidenstücker,* Berlin 1980.

On the NOTHHELFERS: Books—*Geschichte der Photographie im 20. Jahrhundert/Photography in the 20th Century* by Petr Tausk, Cologne 1977,

London 1980; *Photographie als Kunst 1879-1979/Kunst als Photographie 1949-1979,* exhibition catalogue, 2 volumes, by Peter Weiermair, Innsbruck 1979; *Gabriele und Helmut Nothhelfer,* exhibition catalogue (Folkwang Museum exhibition), by Michael Zimmermann, Berlin 1980; *Zwischenräume: Gabriele und Helmut Nothhelfer,* edited by Ann and Jürgen Wilde, Cologne 1983; *Fotografia Europea Contemporanea,* edited by Giovanni Chiaramonte, Milan 1983; *Gabriele und Helmut Nothhelfer: Photographien 1974-1985,* exhibition catalogue, edited by Anita Neugebauer, Basle 1986; *Lange Augenblicke,* edited by Klaus Honnef, Bonn, 1993. **Articles**—''100 Jahre Photographie'' in *Kunstforum* (Mainz), no. 18, 1976; ''Gabriele and Helmut Nothhelfer'' in *Creative Camera* (London), no. 2, 1977; ''People on Sunday'' by Arnd Schirmer in *Der Tagesspiegel* (Berlin), 28 April 1977; ''The Joyless'' by Hervé Guibert in *Le Monde* (Paris), 20 October 1977; ''Pictures of a Crumbling Society'' by Michel Nuridsany in *Le Figaro* (Paris), 24 October 1977; ''People in Germany Today'' by Thomas Hesterberg in *Kölner Stadtanzeiger* (Cologne), 27 June 1979; ''Wie deutsch sehen die Deutschen aus?'' by Freddy Langer in *Frankfurter Allgemeine Zeitung* (Frankfurt), 9 March 1983; ''Les passants des Nothhelfer'' by François Granon in *Télérama* (Paris), 20 March 1985; ''Gabriele et Helmut Nothhelfer'' by Jean-Christian Fleury in *Photographies Magazine,* (Paris), June 1993; ''Der Durchschnittsmensch in seiner Freizeitnische'' by Roland Gross in *Frankfurter Allgemeine Zeitung,* 10 September 1993; ''Von deutschem Befinden'' by K. von Harbou in *Süddeutsche Zeitung,* 16 September 1993; ''Lange Augenblicke'' by Bettina Thienhaus in *Frankfurter Rundschau,* Edition Braus, 5 February 1994.

*

Our photographs were taken on the occasions of festive events. People are shown detached from their workday life, and they are not captured in snapshot-manner, not caught in the midst of an action, but observed at a moment of pause, of standstill, even of meditation. Often their expressions somewhat contrast with the surrounding festive atmosphere, almost showing melancholy. Maybe the meagreness of everyday life, the insufficient conditions of working and living, show through at these festivities and in that way become apparent.

It is difficult to divide the human being into work and leisure time beings. Signs of unsatisfying work and life situations are evident even on so-called special occasions. Isolation and the unfulfilled longing to please, the vain attempt to preserve a semblance of dignity, and petrified family structures are expressed in features, gestures and dress. Our mutual view of society provides the basis for our teamwork and is evident in the common character of the individual photographs. We photograph together, decide which negatives to print, and determine which croppings have to be made.

—Gabriele and Helmut Nothhelfer

*   *   *

If one designates ''people in everyday life'' as the theme of Gabriele and Helmut Nothhelfer's photographic work, then one must also qualify that statement by saying that their work is not concerned with a representation of everyday work life. Rather, what is meant, is that they depict people in commonplace situations, such as in a garden cafe, during an intermission at the theatre, at an industrial exhibition, or at a national festival. In the Nothhelfers' own words: ''Our pictures show people, not in the midst of carrying out an action, but usually in a moment of pause, of inactivity, or of reflection. Often, the expressions of these figures contrast with the festive atmosphere which surrounds them. A certain melancholia results from this.''

This moment of detachment or of isolation is therefore emphasized, so that the different situations are perceived as being indifferent to one another. Thus, photographs are created which have the effect of being objective and obtrusive; often, at first glance, they even appear to be casual because there is no ''composition'' in the sense of a calculated viewpoint, of an ''interesting'' detail, or of a perspective rich in effect. The photos are, in a word, straightforward and unpretentious. Yet, the choice of subject—which becomes evident on closer examination—is just as precisely as consistently chosen. Everything which is unessential is left aside, and when details appear in the photos—for example, a photo gadget bag or an empty cola can from which a straw protrudes—they are there, not by chance, but are important in a dramaturgical way which becomes immediately evident.

The silent language of the objects corresponds to the facial expressions of the individuals and their mien. Their gaze is often empty, their eyes without focus or interest. This, in combination with the details, produces an atmospherically intense effect which stands in productive opposition to the apparent reality of the representation. The result of this is the above mentioned melancholia, the tone of which almost reduces these images to metaphors of general situations. Patterns of behavior and the conditions of the waiting, the state of loss and emptiness, and the state of being isolated in confusion become, then, thematically realized in a penetrating and meaningful manner.

—Rolf Wedewer

NOWAK, Waclaw.

Nationality: Polish. **Born:** Kraków, 30 December 1924. **Education:** Studied architecture, Kraków Polytechnic, 1948-54; mainly self-taught in photography, from 1956. **Family:** Married Szarota Mol in 1974. **Career:** Worked as an architect, Kraków, 1955-60; independent photographer, Kraków, from 1960. Co-founder, with Zbigniew Lagocki and Wojciech Plewinski, Domino photographers' group, Kraków, 1957. Lecturer in photographic theory, history and technology, Department of Industrial Design, Academy of Fine Arts, Kraków, 1964-70. **Recipient:** 7 photo awards, Dekopan Competition, Berlin, 1956; Bronze Medal, International Photography Exhibition, Adelaide, 1957; Art Award, Ministry of Culture, Warsaw, 1961, 1967; Artiste, 1968, and Title of Excellence, 1976, Fédération Internationale d'Art Photographique (FIAP); Diploma Award, Third Salon of Art Portraits, Gdańsk, Poland, 1970. Member, Union of Polish Art Photographers (ZPAF), 1957. **Died:** (in Kraków) 10 August 1976.

Individual Exhibitions:

1959	*Wystawa Domino,* Kraków, Poland
1961	*Twarze Ludzi,* Galeria Krzywe Kolo, Warsaw
1966	Galeria Krzysztofory, Kraków, Poland
1968	*Tri Polšti Fotografove,* Galeria u Rečickich, Prague
	Galeria ZPAP, Zakopane, Poland
1969	*Prezentacje—Wacław Nowak,* Galeria ZPAF, Toruń, Poland
1970	*Wystawa Grupy Trzech,* Kraków Polytechnic, Poland
	Jeden Fotograf, Galeria Profil, Bratislava, Czechoslovakia
1973	*Projektion,* Galleriet for Creativ Fotografi, Copenhagen
1977	Galeria ZPAF, Kraków, Poland
1987	*Wacław Nowak—fotografie wybrane 1956-1976,* Galeria ZPAF, Krakow
1988	*Wacław Nowak,* Galeria ZPAF, Krakow

Selected Group Exhibitions:

1956	*Grosse Fotoweltbewerb,* VEB Fotochem-Werke, East Berlin
1957	*VII Ogolnopolska Wystawa Fotografii,* Galeria ZPAF, Kraków, Poland
1958	*Austellung der Polnishen Kunstfotografie,* Nuremberg
	Internationale Fotowettbewerb BIFOTA, East Berlin
1959	*Salon Internationale d'Art Photographique,* Kecskemet, Hungary
	VIII Ogolnopolska Wystawa Fotografii, ZPAF, Warsaw
1962	*Nemzetkozi Fotoszalon,* Pecs, Hungary
	Okregowa Wystawa Fotografii, ZPAF, Krakow
1963	*Wystawa Fotografii Uzytkowej,* ZPAF-BWA, Krakow
	Ludzie zza kulis -wystawa fotografii teatralnej, ZPAF, Krakow
1964	*Polnische Fotografie,* East Berlin
1966	*Interpress Photo-Competition,* Moscow
1967	*Foto-Forum, Miedzynarodowy Salon,* Ruzomberok, CS
1968	*Fotografia Subiektywna,* Kraków, Poland (travelled to Warsaw)
	Premfoto—XI Mezinarodni Vystava Fotografie, Prague

1969   *Vision and Expression,* International Museum of Photography
        at George Eastman House, Rochester, New York (toured the
        United States, 1969-71)
        Polnische Fotokunst, Wimpassiger Festtage, Austria
        Subjektiv Fotografi, Stockholm
1970   *Portret—ogolnopolska wystawa fotografii artystycznej,* ZPAF,
        Warsaw
        Mostra della Fotografia Polacca, Torino, Italy
1971   *Searching Photographs,* Galeria Wspolczesna, Warsaw
1972   *Schöpferische Fotografen aus Polen,* Photokina, Cologne
        XII Biennale FIAF, The Hague
1973   *Schöpferische Fotografen aus Polen,* Kunsthalle, Nuremberg,
        West Germany
1985   *Torino Fotografia,* Turin, Italy
        Polska Wspolczesna Fotografia Artystyczna, Galeria Zacheta,
        Warsaw
1989   *What is Photography?* Galerie Manes, Prague

Collections:

Museum Sztuki, Lodz, Poland; International Museum of Photography at
George Eastman House, Rochester, New York; Polaroid Collection, Amsterdam; National Museum, Wrocław.

Publications:

By NOWAK: Articles—"On My Photography" in *Foto-Magazin* (Munich), no. 9, 1969; "Architektura widziana inaczej" in *Architektura* (Warsaw), no. 11, 1970.

On NOWAK: Books—*Prämierte Fotos* by Helmut Grunwald, Halle, East
Germany 1958; *Almanach fotografiki polskiej,* annual, Warsaw 1959, 1960,
1962, 1964, 1967, 1969; *Portret artystyczny fotografii amatorskiej* by Jan
Sunderland, Warsaw 1962; *Internationale Aktfotografie* by Christian Kupfer,
Lipsk, Poland 1966; *Foto-Almanach International* by Karl Knapp, Dusseldorf
1967; *Fotografisk Arsbok,* annual, edited by T. Argangen, Stockholm 1967,
1969; *Vision and Expression: An International Survey of Contemporary
Photography,* edited by Nathan Lyons, New York and Rochester 1969; *Life
Library of Photography: The Great Themes,* New York 1970; *Menschen vor
der Kamera Heute,* Munich 1971; *Views on Nudes* by Bill Jay, London 1971;
Sygnal mijajacej terazniejszosci, exhibition catalogue by Zbigniew Zegan,
Krakow, Poland 1977; *Wszystko o fotografii* by Ryszard Bobrowski and
others, Warsaw 1984; *Fotografia Polska 1945-1985* by Jerzy Busza and
others, Gorzów Wielkopolski, Poland 1985; *Geschichte der Fotografie im 20
Jahrhundert,* by Peter Tausk, Cologne, 1977, 1980; *Waclaw Nowak,* exhibi-
tion catalogue, text by Zbigniew Zegan, Krakow, 1988; *What is Photography?*
exhibition catalogue, Prague, 1989; *Wobec odbiorcow fotografii,* by Jerzy
Busza, Warsaw, 1990; *150 Years of Polish Photography,* Warsaw, 1991.
Articles— *Projekt,* Warsaw, no 1/1969; *Poland,* Warsaw, no 1/1969;
Camera Lehti, Helsinki, no 3/1969; *Photo-Italiana,* Rome, no 7/8/1971;
Schweitzerische Photorundschau, Geneva, no 17/1972; "Architektura widziana
inaczej" in *Architektura,* Warsaw, no 11/1970; "Polish Photography Called
'Explorations'" by Urszula Czartoryska in *Spot* (Zagreb, Yugoslavia), no 4,
1975; "Polish Photography in the Years 1939-1979" by Ryszard Bobrowski
in *Fotografia* (Warsaw), special issue, 1979;"Lekcja fotografii Waclawa
Nowaka" by Zbigniew Zegan in *Fotografia,* Warsaw, no 2/1988.

                              *   *   *

Waclaw Nowak was a photographer of many and varied interests. He
occupied himself with portraits, documentaries and reporting, and with
landscapes. Experimental photography fascinated him. Despite the fact that he
abandoned his original profession—architecture—for photography, he did
not approach the latter with undue gravity. "I take all my affairs," he said,
"half seriously, half jokingly. Photography included. I take photographs for
personal pleasure and that's why I feel friendliness and affection for them."

Evaluating Nowak's achievements with the perspective of time, it has to
be said that he expressed himself best through his experimental work. Nowak
treated his photographic experiments as a process of self-instruction that was
not confined to this particular medium alone but was part of a larger and never-

ending education of mankind. The procedures he used were chosen arbitrarily
and depended on factors such as interest, available time and material and
technical possibilities. In taking photographs, Nowak was always more of a
picturemaker than a picture-taker, preferring to create situations rather than to
wait for them to occur. Single photographs rarely satisfied him. He worked
with series of them, trying to exhaust all the possibilities inherent in the issue
under examination. However, experimentation was never an end in itself.
Nowak saw it, above all, as a means of enriching and perfecting photography,
believing that no amount of theorising could replace actual contact with the
materials of the art.

Nowak's best-known experiments are shown in two series of photographs, one produced with the help of "fish-eye" type objectivity, and the
other on the basis of "sandwiching" pictures together. Aware that, in one
sense, everything possible had already been attempted in photography, Nowak
believed that "it's good to address yourself to a problem or question that has
already been solved or answered. The new solution is bound to be different
and, perhaps, better." For this reason, his "fish-eye" work depended less on
the mechanics of using this type of optical technique to create this form of
photograph than on the penetrating analysis of features and characteristic
images that could be obtained in this way. Similarly, the "sandwich of
negatives" technique raised the possibility of creating, in his view, "photographs within photographs, passing through many stages and becoming, to my
mind, something original."

Nowak knew the difficulties in finding a personal style, in doing something different and original. Despite this, he did not rely on cheap effects that
would shock or cause a sensation. Rather, he attempted to reach the heart of the
phenomenon he was examining and to express it in a visual manner specific to
photography.

                                                          —Ryszard Bobrowski

NYKVIST, Ralph.

Nationality: Swedish. **Born:** Landskrona, 16 December 1944. **Education:**
Educated in Landskrona, until 1960; self-taught in photography. **Military
Service:** Served in the Swedish Army, 1963. **Family:** Daughter: Lisa. **Career:**
Worked as postman, for Swedish Post Office, Landskrona, 1960; Reproduc-
tion Photographer, Kliche and Reklam Company, Landskrona, 1960-68; Press
Photographer, with Eko-Foto agency, Landskrona, 1968-72, and with Studio
Hilding, Landskrona, 1972-80. Freelance photographer, Helsingborg, since
1980. Also freelance writer, contributing regularly to *Aktuell Fotografi,*
Helsingborg, since 1978. Member, MIRA photographers agency, Stockholm,
since 1980. **Recipient:** *Populär Fotografi* Award, Helsingborg, 1971; Press
Photographers Club Award, Stockholm, 1972; Gullers' Grant, Swedish Muse-
um of Photography, 1973; Photography Award, City of Landskrona, 1973;
Photography Grant, Swedish Arts Council 1973, 1976; Swedish Authors
Foundation Grants, 1978, 1979, 1980-85; *Foto* magazine Award, 1981;
Grant, City of Helsingborg Art Prize, 1991; Grant, Swedish Art Council, 1992;
Grant, The Swedish Authors Foundation, 1994-95. **Address:** Karl X
Gustafsgatan 34, S-254 39 Helsingborg, Sweden.

Individual Exhibitions:

1970   *Report from Viarp,* City Theatre, Malmo, Sweden
1971   *In Sweden,* Landskrona Museum, Sweden
1972   *Paris, Easter 1972,* Gallery Athéneum, Lund, Sweden
1974   *Portrait of Painters,* Landskrona Bank Office, Sweden
        In Sweden, Fotografiska Museet, Moderna Museet, Stockholm
1976   *Moscow,* Kursverksamheten, Lund, Sweden
1977   Vehicule Art, Montreal, Quebec
1978   *Ralph Nykvist/Anders Petersen,* Fotogalleriet, Oslo
1981   Fotograficentrum, Örebro, Sweden
        Gallery 1 + 1, Helsingborg, Sweden
        Canon Photo Gallery, Amsterdam
1982   *Ralph Nykvist,* at the *International Photofestival,* Malmo,
        Sweden

Untitled, **1987.** Photograph ©Ralph Nykvist.

Landskrona Museum, Sweden
1984 Nora Museum, Sweden
1985 *The Carnival in Venice,* Fotogalleriet, Lund, Sweden (with Anders Petersen)
The Carnival in Venice, at the Torino Fotografia 85, Turin, Italy (with Anders Petersen)
Fotograficentrum, Stockholm
1987 *1986,* MIRA Gallery, Stockholm
1988 *From Skåne,* Museum of Norrbotten, Luleå, Sweden (with Gerry Johansson & Dawid)
1991 *The Carnival in Venice,* Fotografiska Museet, Museum of Modern Art, Stockholm (with Anders Petersen)
1992 *From Skåne,* Malmö Museum, Malmö, Sweden (with Gerry Johansson and Dawid)
The Carnival in Venice, Landskrona Museum, Landskrona, Sweden (with Anders Petersen)
Recent Photographs, Gallery Föda Kvarn, Helsingborg, Sweden
1993 *The Carnival in Venice,* City Theater, Helsinborg, Sweden (with Anders Petersen)

Selected Group Exhibitions:

1975 *Samlingarna och kop 1971-75,* Fotografiska Museet, Stockholm
1977 *The Swedish Exhibition,* at *Rencontres Internationales de la Photographie,* Arles, France

1981 *Contemporary European Photography,* Museum of Modern Art, Tokyo (toured Japan)
1982 *The Frozen Image,* Walker Art Center, Minneapolis (travelled to the International Center of Photography, New York; University of California at Los Angeles; Portland Art Museum, Maine; Museum of Contemporary Art, Chicago; Tacoma Art Museum, Washington; Kjavalsstadir, Reykjavik; Louisiana Museum, Humlebaek; Taidehalli, Helsinki; Fotografiska Museet, Stockholm; Kunstsenter, Oslo)
1985 *c/o Paris,* Fotograficentrum, Örebro, Sweden
1987 *Nordic Artistic Photography,* The Museum of Photographic Arts, Odense, Denmark
1993 The Hasselblad Centre, Gothenburg, Sweden
1994 *The Photographers Album,* Kuva 94, Åbo, Finland

Collections:

Moderna Museet, Stockholm; Landskrona Museum, Sweden; Fotogalleriet, Oslo; Canon Photo Gallery, Amsterdam; Museum of Modern Art, Tokyo, The Hasselblad Centre, Gothenburg.

Publications:

By NYKVIST: Books—*I Sverige (In Sweden),* Helsingborg, Sweden 1977; *The Carnival in Venice* (with Anders Petersen) Sweden 1991; *Kalejdoskop/ etc* Sweden 1991. **Article—**"Carnival in Copenhagen" in *Fotograficentrums Bildtidning* (Stockholm), no. 3, 1984.

On NYKVIST: Book—*The Frozen Image: Scandinavian Photography,* edited by Martin Freeman, Minneapolis and New York 1982. Articles— "The Street" by Allan Porter in *Camera* (Lucerne), March 1969; "Bilder från Gatan" by Jan Olsheden in *Populär Fotografi* (Helsingborg, Sweden), June 1969; "Ralph Nykvists Svenska Bilder" by Jan Olsheden in *Aktuell Fotografi* (Helsingborg, Sweden), July/August 1973; "Gullersstipendiat" by Rune Hassner in *FMV-Bulletinen* (Stockholm), February 1974; "Så tar Ralph Nykvist Sina Porträtt" by Rune Jonsson in *Aktuell Fotografi* (Helsingborg, Sweden), October 1975; "Visst tar Jag Färgbilder" by Jan Olsheden in *Aktuell Fotografi* (Helsingborg, Sweden), April 1979; "Stora Fotografipriset" by Peder Edstrom in *Foto* (Stockholm), January 1981; "Ralph Nykvist" in *Fotograficentrums Bildtidning* (Stockholm), no. 1, 1985; "Ralph Nykvist pa Fotograficentrum" by Peter Alton in *Dagens Nyheter* (Stockholm), 31 January 1985.

*

It's not easy to write a statement about my own photography, but let me quote from my introduction to my book *I Sverige (In Sweden):* "For me, photography is a way of telling about my own environment and myself, i.e. how I experience the people and places I come in contact with."

—Ralph Nykvist

*   *   *

Ralph Nykvist has mastered not only photography but also the written word. By means of the latter he has presented a large number of young photographers (often French) to readers of Swedish photographic magazines. He has also written fierce contributions to current debates, taking both his contemporaries and younger people to task. One of his arguments has been that in the 1970s Swedish documentary photography had run into a blind alley. Its aims, which often were the portrayal of negative aspects of the welfare state, certainly have his sympathy, but he finds the pictorial language inadequate: mere reproduction, marked by melancholy realism, work in which imagination and humor seem to have been banned.

Nykvist's own photography is comparatively "Un-Swedish." His pictures are often reminiscent of Cartier-Bresson, Robert Frank and Garry Winogrand. Nykvist is the quick-thinking street photographer waiting for the right moment, the moment when his subject, thanks to the right choice of light and angle, becomes suitable for photography. Form and content must combine to make the moderately interested observer susceptible to the picture's message. Nykvist also attempts the synthesis of an event, so as to illustrate it in a minimum number of pictures. He has said in an interview: "The number of pictures can never be a replacement for sensitivity, which is necessary to reach another human being. To communicate feeling by means of pictures, one must respect and exploit the medium."

Nykvist has spent his working life in his native southern Sweden. He began his career as a reproduction photographer and came into daily contact with press photos. In 1968 he began to work as a press photographer himself at an agency that supplied pictures to a number of local newspapers. Here he saw—as have many of his colleagues—how ambitiously composed portraits of local politicians and athletes were cut down to the scale of passport photos by sloppy editors. The fact that the carefully chosen background functioned in both form and content was simply not realized by those responsible for the photo's reproduction. As long as mouth, nose and eyes were there, it passed. Nykvist feels that there has been some improvement during the 1970s. This may be due to the fact that photographers have had more say than used to be the case. And national newspapers have become more picture-conscious: this has clearly also made some impression on the editors of local papers.

In 1976 Nykvist published a book of black-and-white photographs called *I Sverige (In Sweden),* reflecting his travels and walks with the camera from 1964 to 1976. He succeeded in capturing, among other things, the bleakness of small industrial communities and the suburbs of large cities. But it was no depiction of Hell. He looked at his fellow human beings with a touch of humor and with tenderness.

With the help of various grants, among them a five-year working grant from the Swedish Authors Fund, Nykvist has now been able to take leave of professional photography and to concentrate on his own projects.

—Rune Jonsson

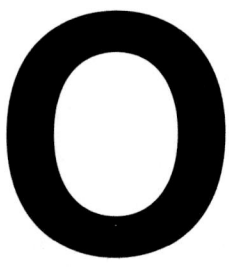

O

ODDNER, Georg.

Nationality: Swedish. **Born:** Stockholm, 17 October 1923. **Education:** Wasa Real School, Stockholm, 1933-39; studied at the Art and Design School, Stockholm, 1940; student-assistant to the photographer Richard Avedon, New York, 1950. **Military Service:** Served in the Royal Svea Life Guards, Swedish Army, 1944-45. **Family:** Married Ewy Malmstrom in 1955; children: Christina, Lisa, Karin, and Frans. **Career:** Worked as a jazz musician, Stockholm and throughout Scandinavia, 1946-49. Freelance photographer, Malmo and Stockholm, since 1951: established studio, Malmo, 1952; Member, Tio Fotografer group, Stockholm, since 1958. Feature film photographer, Copenhagen, 1963-65. Documentary film producer since 1965, and scriptwriter and director since 1971, Swedish Television, Stockholm and Malmo. **Recipient:** Å & Å Publishing House Illustration Prize, Stockholm 1955; Photography Prize, *Biennale,* Venice, 1957; Illustration Prize, *Weekly Vi,* Stockholm, 1957; *Svenska Dagbladets* Prize, Stockholm, 1958; Graphic Art Prize, Royal Library of Stockholm, 1961; Malmo Culture Prize, 1971; Swedish State Artists Scholarship, 1972; Swedish Author-Foundation Scholarship, 1982, 1983; The Culture Prize, *Sydsvenska Dagbladet,* Malmö, 1985; Swedish Author Foundation Special Prize, 1986; The Platinum Egg Award, The Advertising Association of Sweden, 1987; The Author Foundation Scholarship, 1988; Claes Lewenhaupt Scholarship for young photographers, 1993; Swedish State Artists Scholarship 1994-5. **Address:** Jörgen Ankersgatan 20, S-21145 Malmö, Sweden.

Individual Exhibitions:

1957	*Photographic Journey,* Malmo Art Museum (travelled to the Centre Gallery, Copenhagen, 1957, Norrkoping Museum, Sweden, Kalmar Museum, Sweden, and Göteborg Art Museum, Sweden, 1959, and Jonkoping Museum, Sweden, 1960)
1969	*The Eternal Soldier,* Trelleborg Museum, Sweden (travelled to the Fotografiska Museets Vanner, Stockholm, 1970)
1975	*Photographs,* Konstframjandet, Malmo
1982	Gallery Camera Obscura, Stockholm
1983	Gallery Fotograficentrum, Örebro, Sweden
1985	*Photographic Images 1955-85,* Louisiana Museum, Humlebaek, Denmark (travelled to Nordens Hus, Reykjavik; Nordens Hus, Thoshavn, Faroes; Finnish Museum of Photography, Helsinki; and 7 other museums in Sweden, 1986-87)
1986	*30 Jahre Fotografie,* Fachhochschule, Heilbronn, West Germany
	"*Photography from the 50s,*" Foto 86, Amsterdam
1987	*Present,* Kunst Museum, Trondheim, Norway
1988-93	*Present,* at 5 other Museums and Art Galleries in Sweden
1991	*Reality and Vision,* Nordisk Ministerråd Gallery, Copenhagen
1994	*Ingmar Bergman's Theatre Epoch 1952-59,* Malmö Arthall, Malmö

Selected Group Exhibitions:

1951	*Young Photographers of Sweden,* Galerie Kodak, Paris
1954	*Black and White,* National Museum, Stockholm
1958	*Photographic Art Tio,* Konsthall, Lund, Sweden
1964	*World Exhibition of Photography: What Is Man?,* Pressehaus Stern, Hamburg (and world tour)
1967	*International Photography Exhibition,* at *Expo '67,* Montreal
1971	*Tio: Contemporary Swedish Photographs,* Library of Congress, Washington, D.C.
1975	*Samlingarna gavor och kop 1971-75,* Fotografiska Museet, Stockholm
1977	*Swedish Contemporary Art,* Palacio de Bellas Artes, Mexico City
1985	*Ten Swedish Photographers,* Musée Réattu, Arles, France
1986	*Jazz på fotografiska,* Fotografiska Museet, Stockholm

Collections:

Fotografiska Museet, Moderna Museet, Stockholm; Malmo Museum; Oslo Photographic Collection; Helsinki Photographic Collection; Bibliothèque Nationale, Paris; Library of Congress, Washington, D.C.; Lousiana Museum, Copenhagen.

Publications:

By ODDNER: Books—*Good Morning, South America,* with text by P. Persson, Stockholm 1956; *Till Spanien/To Spain,* with text by Klaus Rifbjerg, Copenhagen 1971; *Spanskt Motiv,* with text by Klaus Rifbjerg, Stockholm 1979; *Ah, giv mej en beda,* with text by Max Lundgren, Stockholm 1981; *Kaptenens Verser,* with poems by Pablo Neruda, Stockholm 1983; *Narvarande,* Stockholm 1984; *African Art,* Malmo 1985; *Poesie Suedoise Contemporaine,* anthology, edited by Jacques Outin, Paris 1985; *Japanese Cuttings,* with Klaus Rifbjerg, Copenhagen, 1987; *Queen in Denmark,* with Ninka, Copenhagen, 1989; *Falured and Crocodile,* Höganäs, 1993; *Sankt Petersburg,* with Jan Mark, Helsingborg, 1993. **Articles**—"While the World Becomes Cooler" in *Femina* (Helsingborg, Sweden), April 1975; "Windows" in *Femina* (Helsingborg, Sweden), May 1975; "It's Fun to Play War" in *Expressen* (Stockholm), 15 May 1975; "Malmo New Art Hall" in *Svensk Fotografisk Tidskrift* (Stockholm), September 1975; "Dreamers on a Visit" in *Blixeniana* (Copenhagen), 1981; "Spots of Life" in *Artes* (Stockholm), 1981; "Hon visar oss världen" in *Sydsvenska Dagbladet* (Malmö), 28 July 1985; "Urfadern kameran och apparaturernas terror" in *Sydsvenska Dagbladet,* Malmö, 19/10 1988; "Då öppnas en dörr," *Kulturens Värld,* Stockholm, December, 1987; "Bilder som hörs," *Fotografisk Tidskrift,* no.4, 1988.

On ODDNER: Books—*Creative Photography* by Helmut Gernsheim, London and Boston 1962, 1975; *A Concise History of Photography* by Helmut and Alison Gernsheim, London and New York 1965, 1971; *Tio Foto Bildbyra,* Stockholm 1983. **Articles**—"A Master Shows His Work" by Karl Sandels in *Svensk Fotografisk Tidskrift* (Stockholm), April 1957; "Georg Oddner" by Romeo Martinez in *Camera* (Lucerne), July 1957; "Georg Oddner" by Helmut Gernsheim in *Photography* (London), July 1958; "Faces and Places" by Klaus Rifbjerg in *Vindrosen* (Copenhagen), May 1962; "Georg Oddner" in *Infinity* (New York), September 1968; "Georg Oddner" by Rune Jonsson in *Popular Fotografi* (Helsingborg, Sweden), June 1970; "Till Spanien" by Jan Olsheden in *Aktuell Fotografi* (Helsingborg, Sweden), May 1972; "Master in Picture" by Ture Burglund in *Arbetet* (Malmo, Sweden), May 1980; "Georg Oddners svenska Karen Blixen Film" by Hans Andersen, *Blixeniana,* Copenhagen 1981; "The subjective objectivity" by Klaus Rifbjerg in *Camera Obscura* (Stockholm), no. 2, 1982; "En Masterfotograf" by I. Lekus, and "Det galler att fanga motivet bakom motivet" by J. Werup in *Sydsvenska Dagbladet* (Malmo), 20 October 1985; "Georg Oddner" by Gabriel Bauret in

The Carrier, Peru, **1955.** Photograph ©Georg Oddner.

Camera International (Paris), no. 5, 1985; ''Det medvetna och tillfallige'' by Peter Michael Hornung in *Berlinske Tidene* (Copenhagen), 23 December 1985; ''En berejst sortseer'' by Pierre Lübecher, *Politiken,* Copenhagen, 31 December 1985; ''Magnadar Ljosmyndir'' by Bragi Asgeirsson, *Morgunbladid,* Reykjavik, 16 and 19 March, 1986; ''George Oddner och det visuelle valet'' by Thorild Anbderberg in *Svenska Dagbladet* (Stockholm), 29 January 1986; ''Oddner'' by Ingamaj Beck, *Aftonbladet,* Stockholm, 2 December 1987; ''Fotografiens outhärdliga lätthet'' by Ola Billgren, *Sydsvenska Dagbladet,* Malmö, 3 July 1987; ''Fra Bebop till bilder'' by Bente Haarstad, *Adresseavisen,* Trondheim, 30 January 1988; ''Den fotografiska bilden ... om Oddners dokumentära bilder'' by Helene Schmitz, (treatise), Konstvetenskapliga Institutionen, Stockholms Universitet, 1988; ''Georg Oddner'' by Anders Mildner, *Beckerell,* No.3, 1993; ''Georg Oddner'' by Hasse Persson, *Aktuell Fotografi,* No. 11, 1993.

*

Some thoughts about photography:

The interesting thing about photographing—to depict exteriority—is in trying to catch that which doesn't meet the eye.

A photograph becomes an image when, at every glance, it yields something new. So, the picture cannot be wholly caught by our thoughts, because it is continuously transformed.

The unique power of the picture is that it arrests time and lives in spite of its unalterable form.

But that is also its weakness: the picture is quickly sensed—as is reality—but it demands time to be read. The more time, the more words it suggests, since the feelings react more directly than the intellect.

More simply, one can say that the main difference between words and pictures is that words depict thoughts and indicate exteriority, whereas pictures depict the exteriority and indicate thoughts.

—Georg Oddner

*   *   *

Photographers are commonly divided into two categories—those who make pictures in their heads and those who find their pictures—i.e., those who direct and those who observe and record. Portrait and fashion photographers belong to the former category; documentary and reportage photographers to the latter. ''Cross-overs'' are usually a disaster: most people have probably seen how mediocre the result can be when a studio photographer is made to go out and report a sports event or when the photojournalist attempts fashion photography. But occasionally a photographer excels in both categories: he can construct a picture in a studio and he is also a fast-reacting photographer of the instant. Georg Oddner is such a photographer. Not surprisingly, he has expressed his admiration of, for example, the fashion, film and documentary photographer William Klein.

In the 1950s Swedes who took an interest in such matters knew Oddner as an enviable fashion photographer, who supplied the weeklies with excellent pictures of beautiful girls, often in bathing suits. It probably came as a surprise to many people, therefore, when in his first one-man show, in Malmo in 1957, he exhibited reportage, portraits, and nature studies. Many of these photos were highly realistic, others were dreamingly poetic, and all were a far cry from the paradisical world of the glamorous advertisement. But the effective ability to perceive form and light featured in both Oddner's commercial pictures and in his more personal exhibition material.

Many of the pictures he exhibited in 1957 had been taken on journeys he took to produce advertising pictures for airlines. Alongside the commercial photography he had also continually worked at his more private pictures, closer to everyday life. He said, in 1959: ''I believe in the truth of the photograph. I cannot forget that it always has something to do with reality. But it must, at the same time, be a kind of adaptation of reality, which is ambiguous and meaningful on many levels. A motif which is unambiguous and tritely obvious does not interest me.''

During the 1960s Oddner was hired by several newpapers to produce extensive reportage from Japan, the U.S.S.R., Vietnam, among other places. It turned out that he possessed a highly professional ability as a photojournalist. But like many of his colleagues, he increasingly moved to motion pictures—first as a film photographer, later as a director and scriptwriter. Then, in the early 1970s rather unexpectedly, he produced a book of pictures from Spain—black-and-white pictures with the unmistakable Oddner character—grainy and a little unsharp, but intimate and alive. A combination of playfulness and tautness.

In this book he maintains that, in the twilight of his life, he hopes to devote himself to landscape photography, with tripod and large format camera. A slow and meditative occupation. If one remembers that in the 1940s Oddner was one of Sweden's best jazz drummers—then the contrasts in his various expressive needs emerge even more vividly.

In the autumn of 1984 Oddner published a retrospective photo book, *Narvarande* (Presence), including examples of his photojournalism, portrait and nature studies. Many of the press photographs were taken in the Soviet Union which Oddner had visited for a Swedish magazine as long ago as 1955. These photographs reflect in a human manner the life of the ordinary Soviet citizen. Oddner quotes the philosopher Kant: ''We see the world not as it is, but as we are.''

—Rune Jonsson

OLSON, (Gustaf) Lennart (Eugen).

Nationality: Swedish. **Born:** Göteborg, 21 December 1925; son of the photographer Gustaf Olson. **Education:** Attended secondary school in Borås, until 1941; mainly self-taught in photography, from 1931, but studied printmaking techniques at the Royal Swedish Academy, Stockholm, 1983. **Military Service:** Served in the Swedish Air Force, 1945-46. **Family:** Married Margit Gronblad in 1948 (divorced, 1971); children: Olle, Ingela and Camilla; married Eva von Hanno in 1983; son: Christian. **Career:** Photographer, Donalds Fotografiska studio, Borås, 1942-44, Harry Anderssons Foto, Sodertalje, 1944-48, Henrieds Foto, Stockholm, 1948-52, and Forberg Film AB, Stockholm, 1952-55. Since 1955, freelance architectural, industrial and magazine photographer, working for the architects Paul Hedqvist, Sven Markelius, Klas Anshelm, Anders Tengbom, Peter Celsing, Per-Olof Olsson and Erik Thelaus, the firms Nordiska Kompaniet, Kasthall AB, Nordiska Uppslags-bocker AB, Sveriges Television, and the magazines *Vi, Arkitektur, Form, Industria, Konstrevy,* etc., in Stockholm. Founder-member, with Hans Malmberg, Hans Hammarskiold, Rune Hassner and others, Tio Fotografer group, Stockholm, 1958. Freelance producer/director, as Lennart Olson Film Produktion, for Swedish Television, 1960-80. **Recipient:** Photography Prize, *Svenska Dagbladet* newspaper, Stockholm, 1954; Culture Prize, City of Stockholm, 1954; Gold Medal, *Biennale,* Venice, 1957; Swedish State Grant, 1968, 1969, 1982, 1984, and five-year grant, 1986. **Agent:** Tiofoto AB, Box 3252, 103 65 Stockholm, Sweden. **Address:** Steninge 374, 310 42 Haverdal, Sweden.

Individual Exhibitions:

1980	Galleri Camera Obscura, Stockholm
1982	Stephen White Gallery, Los Angeles
	Galleri Kattsvansen, Sodertalje, Sweden
	Photogravures, Galleri Camera Obscura, Stockholm
1985	Ostergotlands Lansmuseum, Linkoping, Sweden (retrospective)
1986	Lunds Konthall, Lund, Sweden (retrospective)
	Billedhuset, Copenhagen
	Galleri Ullevi, Göteborg, Sweden
1988	Fotograficentrum, Örebro, Sweden
1989	Fotografiska Museet i Moderna Museet, Stockholm, Sweden
1991	Maneten, Göteborg, Sweden
	Båstads Bibliotek, Båstad, Sweden
1992	Kulturverket, Halmstad, Sweden
1993	Hasselblad Center, Göteborg, Sweden
1994	Liljevalchs Konsthall, Stockholm, Sweden

Tjörnbridge IV, **Sweden, 1966.** Photograph ©Lennart Olson/TIO.

Selected Group Exhibitions:

1953	*European Postwar Photography,* Museum of Modern Art, New York
1954	*Subjektive Fotografie II,* Saarland Museum, Saarbrucken, West Germany
1958	*Fotokonst—Tio Fotografer,* Lunds Konsthall, Lund, Sweden
1960	*The Sense of Abstraction,* Museum of Modern Art, New York
1962	*Svenskarna sedda av 11 fotografer,* Moderna Museet, Stockholm
1968	*The Photographer and the City,* Smithsonian Institution, Washington, D.C.
1970	*Tio Fotografer,* Bibliothèque Nationale, Paris
1982	*The Frozen Image,* Walker Art Center, Minneapolis (travelled to the International Center of Photography, New York; University of California at Los Angeles; Portland Art Museum, Maine; Museum of Contemporary Art, Chicago; Tacoma Art Museum, Washington; Kjavalsstadir, Reykjavik; Louisiana Museum, Humlebaek; Taidehalli, Helsinki; Fotografiska Museet, Stockholm; Henie-Onstad Kunstsenter, Oslo)
1984	*Six Swedish Photographers,* Los Angeles Center for Photographic Studies
	Subjektive Fotografie: Images of the 50s, San Francisco Museum of Modern Art (travelled to the University of Houston, Texas; Museum Folkwang, Essen; Vasterbottens Museum, Umea; Kulturhuset, Stockholm; Saarland Museum, Saarbrucken; Palais des Beaux-Arts, Brussels)
1985	*Contemporary European Photography,* Benteler Galleries, Houston, Texas
1988	*Tio Fotografer,* Sandra Berler Gallery, Maryland
1994	*Tres Generaciones de Fotógrafos suecos,* Santiago de Chile, Montevideo, Rio de Janerio, Caracas, Mexico City, Lima and Beijing (China)

Collections:

Fotografiska Museet, Stockholm; Göteborgs Kunstmuseum, Sweden; Centre Georges Pompidou, Paris; Bibliothèque Nationale, Paris; Museum Folkwang, Essen, Germany; Museum of Modern Art, New York; International Museum of Photography at George Eastman House, Rochester, New York; Library of Congress, Washington, D.C.; Boston Museum of Fine Arts, Massachusetts; Art Institute of Chicago; The National Museum of Modern Art, Kyoto, Japan; The Gernsheim Collection, Texas; Skissernas Museum, Lund, Sweden; Upplands Konstmuseum, Uppsala, Sweden; Östergötlands Länsmuseum, Linköping, Sweden; Det Kgl Bibliotek, Copenhagen, Denmark.

Publications:

By OLSON: Book—*Litet Stockholmsalbum,* Stockholm 1961; *Lennart Olson: Fotografier,* introduction by Kristian Romare, 1989. **Articles**—"Abstrakt Bildkonst" in *Svensk Fotografisk Tidskrift* (Stockholm), July 1953; "En Bild ar en Bild" in *Svensk Fotografisk Tidskrift* (Stockholm), June 1954. **Films**—over 50 Swedish television (STV) presentations, including: *Manland,* 1960; *Flamenco,* 1962; *Basker,* 1963; *Gangaram,* 1964; *Familjen,* 1965; *Hello Bobby,* 1967; *Student i Lund,* 1968; *Bagru,* 1971; *Bakat Framat,* 1972; *Tva om Karlek,* 1974; *Samba,* 1977; *Beethoven och Snogerod,* 1979; *Folkbildaren,* 1980.

On OLSON: Books—*Photography of the World,* edited by Heibonsha Publishers, Tokyo 1957; *The Picture History of Photography* by Peter Pollack, New York 1958; *Photography in the Twentieth Century* by Nathan Lyons, New York 1967; *Die Geschichte der Photographie im 20. Jahrhundert/ Photography in the 20th Century* by Peter Tausk, Cologne 1977, London 1980; *The Frozen Image: Scandinavian Photography,* edited by Martin Freeman, Minneapolis and New York 1982; *Tio Fotografer Bildbyra,* Stockholm 1983; *Subjektive Fotografie: Images of the 50s,* exhibition catalogue, by Ute Eskildsen, Manfred Schmalriede and Dorothy Martinson, Essen, West Germany 1984. **Articles**—"Samtidens Bildsprak" by Ulf Hard af Segerstad in *Svenska Dagbladet* (Stockholm), no. 8, 1955; "Lennart Olson" by Ulf

Hard af Segerstad in *Foto* (Stockholm), no. 8, 1955; "Lennart Olson" by Kurt Bergengren in *Fotografisk Arsbok 1961,* Stockholm 1961; "Lennart Olson" by Norman Hall in *Photography Yearbook 1961,* London 1961; "The Bridges of Lennart Olson" by K. Romare in *Camera* (Lucerne), no. 5, 1961; "Wandbilder Bildwande" by Hans Konig in *Camera* (Lucerne), no. 2, 1963; "Lennart Olson" by Rune Jonsson in *Aktuell Fotografi* (Halsingborg), no. 7/ 8, 1979; "Tjornbron var en drom" by Klas Ostergren in *Expressen* (Stockholm), 13 March 1980; "Lennart Olson" by Rune Jonsson in *FMV-Bulletin* (Stockholm), May 1980; "Lennart Olson" by Par Rittsel in *Foto* (Stockholm), October 1980; *Stockholms Tidningen,* by Adam Nycop, 4 August 1982; *Fotografisk Tidskrift* no 2-1993 by Jan Norming, Stockholm; *Damernas,* by Per Ahlmark, no 36, 1983; *Dagens Nyheter,* På Stan by Rolf Broberg, Stockholm, 15 December 1984; Olson at Fotografiska Muséet by Peder Alton in *Bildtidningen,* no 1 1990.

*

When I established myself as a freelance photographer in 1955, I turned more and more to reportage, architectural, industrial and advertising photography. Reportage interested me the most, although from an economic point of view it was the least profitable. Unfortunately, the financial constraints on my reportage assignments hardly ever provided the opportunities for the lengthy and in-depth photo-stories about which I dreamed. This then was the strongest reason for transferring to television documentaries in the 1960s.

As a freelance camera man for Sveriges Television I could choose and carry through my film projects with full control; and this was on a budget which to a great extent allowed me all the time that was necessary. During a good twenty years filming for television I have produced, directed, photographed and edited around fifty films (documentaries, musicals, TV-theatre and drama-documentaries).

My own creative work, which I tried to keep alive alongside my commissioned work, was strongly influenced during the 1950s by non-figurative art. In modern bridges I found a photographic expression for the world of forms which fascinated me. The bridge motif is still important for me today, but the bridge pictures of more recent years carry with them an expression which differs from the earlier ones.

At the end of the 1970s I was shown some photo-lithographs which a friend had made. I was completely captivated by the quality of these pictures. After a short while I taught myself how to master the technique and became so enthusiastic that I eventually left television camera work and returned to still photography. I am there today.

The technique of photo-lithography (and photogravure) allows me to revise and work out the picture with great freedom, to create the expression I aim for. Besides, it is a craft which demands a lot of time, which forces me to work in true conflict with my subject, a struggle which is in itself inspiring and helps to develop creativity. It is during the long work process that I convince myself that the picture holds its own; if the picture has that "mystique" and multiplicity of meaning which allows it to live further.

—Lennart Olson

*   *   *

Even for young Swedish photographers and future photographers, the end of the second World War was a revolutionary experience. After a period of isolation during which romantic landscape photography and descriptive Swedish realism dominated, there opened up an unknown, adventurous and international world for these hitherto vaguely opposed styles. Circumstances were such that Paris became the base for further voyages of discovery. This happened during the golden age of reportage photography and the great illustrated magazines, and in imitation of the masters the young Swedes attempted to describe what they had experienced in "The Decisive Moment." With one exception: Lennart Olson. Urged by a strong, but as yet unarticulated curiosity in cultural events, and not solely of the visual arts, Lennart Olson by chance made contact with a group of artists, writers and art historians in Paris who were particularly interested in the current trend of nonfigurative art. There were for their part interested in the gifted young photographer, and it was not long before Lennart Olson became what he jokingly describes as an "art photographer." He was to do much reportage on the various facets of art life for newspapers and periodicals and was regularly commissioned to photograph art and architecture in Europe for a Swedish publisher. Through this he acquired an extraordinary familiarity with what has happening in the international art world during the 1950s.

One should note that this happened during a so-called formalist period in which the picture's structure and composition was of central interest. Lennart Olson drew from these lessons, and became the first Swedish photographer to transplant the impression of abstract-concrete painting to photographs. It should also be added that he was and remained one of the most prominent, and rapidly enough won an international position within his genre.

In 1952 Olson took his first pictures of a concrete bridge, whose tense play of lines lent itself with great effect to an interpretation in black-and-white photography as a direct parallel to non-figurative painting. In the same year, Edward Steichen came to Stockholm to select photographs for the exhibition *Family of Man.* This experienced judge of images immediately discovered the uniqueness of Olson's pictures and selected four, not for the current exhibition, but for the collection of ''European Post War Photography'' in the Museum of Modern Art in New York. An enlargment, measuring three metres, of one of Olson's photographs of a bridge, later hung for many years in the museum's permanent collection. Still contested in Sweden, the photographer gained encouragement through this, which led him to become even more absorbed by the expressive quality of lines and surfaces. One can even venture to say that within the body of his work he was one of the few who fundamentally felt that, as a pictorial medium, photography offered as much freedom of form as other media. Accordingly, Olson was to continue on this elementary course with his characteristically reflective methods. He developed this genre further until 1964, when he abandoned it for films.

Within Swedish photography it was to a certain extent characteristic that quite a number of the young Swedish reportage photographers from the postwar era were tempted by the development of television and transferred to film. It might appear surprising that Lennart Olson also followed this trend, but he explains that the earlier systematic borderlines between certain types of pictures finally forced him to give up his speciality in order to throw himself into something quite different and new. Within his awreness and perseverance, Lennart Olson has a sensitive personality with a generous interest in humanity, and it is therefore not surprising that during the period from 1964-1981 he made around 50 documentaries throughout the world for STV, among others, reports on developing countries, which have become famous for their insight and genuine local colour. It lies outside the limits of this article to judge Lennart Olson's films in comparison with his still photography, but there is no doubt that even the films are in many cases of very high quality and not only from the pictorial aspect.

When Olson was invited to do a couple of solo exhibitions in Stockholm in 1977, he faced a decision. He took a step backwards to the still image even if in a new form. After the twenty-five years which had passed between the 1950s and 1980s, photographic tolerance had softened. Craft processes, so despised after the war, were revived and knowledge of nineteenth century methods was widely spread. Lennart Olson became interested in and absorbed in the gum bichromate print. At the beginning of the 1950s when Lennart Olson had sought to transfer the line and surface of non-figurative painting to photography, he had accomplished this, in the spirit of his age, by hard black-and-white prints in which arch and bridge lines were drawn with knife-edge linear grace. With the gum-process he acquired a new, flexible and, in a certain sense, more effective tool with which to realise his visual ambitions. At the same time as he extended and developed his earlier visual language, he refined and—if the expression is permitted—deepened it. His new bridge photographs float in a graphic atmosphere, and his repertoire has expanded to also include organic forms. In the spirit of the grand old master, the young radical from the postwar period is permitted now and then to realise his ambitions, to chisel his photography with such infinite care.

—Ulf Hard af Segerstad

OORTHUYS, Cas(parus Bernardus).

Nationality: Dutch. **Born:** Leiden, 1 November 1908. **Education:** Studied architecture at the School voor Bouwkunde, Versierende en Kunstambachten, Amsterdam, 1926-27; also studied architecture in Haarlem and at the Akademie voor Beeldende Kunsten, The Hague; learned photographic technique from the fimmaker Joris Ivens, Amsterdam, in the early 1930s. **Career:** Worked as an assistant in the photo studio of Cock de Graaff, Amsterdam, 1933; established studio with Jo Voskuil, Amsterdam, 1934; advertising photographer, under occasional pseudonym OV 20, Amsterdam, 1934-35; photo-reporter, working for *Het Vrije Volk, Wij,* etc. Amsterdam, 1935-41; freelance war-reporter, also active in documenting conditions in Holland and in producing false identity papers for the Dutch Underground, 1941-45; documentary and industrial photographer, working with Contact Photobooks, Nederlandse Spoorwegen, Hoogovens, Ten Cate, Puttershoek, Deirgeneeskunde, etc., Amsterdam, 1945 until his death, 1975. **Died:** (in Amsterdam) 22 July 1975.

Individual Exhibitions:

1969	*Mensen,* Stedelijk Museum, Amsterdam (toured the Netherlands)
1970	Hoogovens, Ijmuiden, Netherlands
1971	Stedelijk Museum, Amsterdam
	't Meyhuis, Helmond, Netherlands
	Mensen en Nederland, Gallery of Art, Moscow (travelled to Leningrad, Kiev and Minsk)
1974	Galerie Fiolet, Amsterdam
1975	ABN-Galerij, Amsterdam
1980	Gemeente Museum, Arnhem, Netherlands
1982	*The Illegal Camera,* Prakapas Gallery, New York
	Mensen en hun omgeving, De Stichting Wonen, Amsterdam
1984	Galerie Ton Peek, Utrecht, Netherlands
	De Verbeekding, Amsterdam
1988	*Cas Oorthuys Foto's/Fotomontages,* Galerie Duo Duo, Rotterdam
1990	Howard Greenberg Photofind Gallery, New York
1990-91	*Textielportretten van Cas Oorthuys,* Nederlands Textiel Museum, Tilburg
1991-92	*Cas Oorthuys (1908-1975). Vintage Prints,* Amsterdam's Historisch Museum, Amsterdam
1992	*Cas Oorthuys—Guaranteed Real Dutch Congo,* Koninklijk Museum voor Midden-Afrika, Tervuren

Selected Group Exhibitions:

1937	*Foto '37,* Stedelijk Museum, Amsterdam
1945	*Ondergedonken Camera,* Atelier Meijboom, Amsterdam
1953	*European Photography,* Museum of Modern Art, New York
1955	*The Family of Man,* Museum of Modern Art, New York (and world tour)
1961	*Dag Amsterdam,* Stedelijk Museum, Amsterdam
1970	*Kontrasten,* Haags Gemeentemuseum, The Hague
1975	*700 Jaar Amsterdam,* Van Gogh Museum, Amsterdam
1978	*Fotografie in Nederland 1940-75,* Stedelijk Museum, Amsterdam
1980	*Verzet en Vervolging 1933-19nu,* Koninklijk Paleis, Amsterdam
1986	*Nederlandse Architectuurfotografie,* Westersingel 8, Rotterdam
	Het Fotoboek. 4 Nederlandse fotografen in Parijs (Foto '86), Nieuwe Kerk, Amsterdam
1988	*Roots & Turns. Twentieth Century Photography in the Netherlands,* Sarah Campbell Blaffer Gallery, Houston
	De ondergedoken Camera, Verzetsmuseum, Amsterdam
1989	*Ijzersterk mensenwerk,* Gemeentemuseum, Helmond
1989-90	*Foto in omslag. Het Nederlandse documentaire fotoboek na 1945,* De Zonnehof, Amersfoort
1990	*Fotografie Biënnale Rotterdam,* Galerie Duo Duo, Rotterdam
1991	*Confrontaties. Nederlandse fotografen en hun betrokkenheid bij (inter)nationale conflicten,* Grote Kerk, The Hague

1992   *The Illegal Camera*, Houston, Texas
        *Fotografie, geschiedenis, beeldvorming. Nederland en de
        Tweede Wereldoorlog*, Mozes en Aäronkerk, Amsterdam
1992-93 *Rotterdam 1950-1960. Vijf fotografen -vijf boeken*,
        Kunsthal, Rotterdam
1993   *Kinderen van de wereld gezien door Nederlandse fotografen*,
        Grote Kerk, The Hague

Collections:

Archief Oorthus, Amstel en Prinsengracht, Amsterdam; Stedelijk Museum, Amsterdam; Prentenkabinett, Rijksuniversiteit, Leiden; Haags Gemeentemuseum, The Hague; Amsterdams Historisch Museum, Amsterdam; Gemeentearchief, Amsterdam; Rijksinstituut voor Oorlogsdocumentaire (RIOD), Amsterdam; Museum Folkwang, Essen; Stichting Nederlands Foto- & Grafisch Centrum (Spaarnestad Fotoarchief), Haarlem; Museum of Fine Art, Houston; Victoria & Albert Museum, London; New Orleans Museum of Fine Art; Stichting Nederlands Fotoarchief, Rotterdam.

Publications:

By OORTHUYS: Books—*Agriculture in the Netherlands,* with text by D.J. Maltha, Amsterdam 1948; *Amsterdam: Its Beauty and Character,* with Emmy Andriesse, Amsterdam 1949; *De Vlaamse Steden,* with Emmy Andriesse, text by Lode Baekelmans and others, Amsterdam and Antwerp 1950; *Het Water,* with text by E. Zandstra, Amsterdam and Antwerp 1950; *De Steden,* with text by J.T.P. Bijhouwer and others, Amsterdam and Antwerp 1950; *Het Vlaamse Landschap,* with text by Bert Decorte and others, Amsterdam and Antwerp 1951; *This Is Paris from Dawn till Night,* with text by Jan Brusse, Amsterdam and Oxford 1952; *This Is London from Dawn till Night,* with text by Neville Brayburne, Amsterdam and Oxford 1953; *This Is Holland,* with text by C.J. Kelk, Amsterdam and Oxford 1953, 1964; *This Is Amsterdam from Dawn till Night,* with text by H.G. Hoekstra, Amsterdam and Oxford 1954; *This Is Florence,* with text by B. Premsela, Amsterdam and Oxford 1954; *The French Riviera from Marseilles to Menton,* with text by Jan Brusse, Amsterdam and Oxford 1955; *This Is Belgium,* with text by Karel J.B. Jonckheere, Amsterdam and Oxford 1955; *This Is Rome,* with text by R. Patris, Amsterdam and Oxford 1956, 1965; *This Is the Heart of Spain,* with text by Bert Schierbeek, Amsterdam and Oxford 1956; *This Is Austria,* with text by E. Zandstra, Amsterdam and Oxford 1956; *This Is Brussels and the World Exhibition,* with text by Delepinne, Amsterdam and Oxford 1958; *This Is Yugoslavia,* with text by A. den Doolaard, Amsterdam and Oxford 1958; *This Is Greece,* with text by A. den Doolaard, Amsterdam and Oxford 1958, 1960; *This Is Venice,* with text by A. den Doolaard, Amsterdam and Oxford 1958; *This Is the Italian Riviera,* with text by M. Ferro, Amsterdam and Oxford 1958; *Rotterdam: Dynamicsche Stad,* Amsterdam 1959; *This Is Switzerland,* with text by E. Straub, Amsterdam and Oxford 1960; *This Is Brittany,* with text by Pierre Cressard, Amsterdam and Oxford 1961; *This Is Alsace,* with text by Paul Ahnne, Amsterdam and Oxford 1962; *This Is Oxford and Cambridge,* with text by Roger Penrose, Oxford 1962; *This Is Provence,* with text by Maurice Pezet, Amsterdam and Oxford 1962; *Term in Oxford,* with an introduction by Ian Bullock, Oxford 1963; *This Is Naples, Capri, Pompeii, Paestum,* with text by Wim Alings, Amsterdam and Oxford 1964; *This Is Majorca, The Balearic Islands, Minorca, Ibiza, Formentera,* with text by Jean A. Schaelkamp, Amsterdam and Oxford 1964; *Taal en Teken,* with text by Bert Schierbeek, Amsterdam 1965; *Nederland tussen verleden en toekomst,* with text by Albert Alberts, Amsterdam and Antwerp 1966; *This Is Como and the Italian Lakes,* with text by Wim Alings, Amsterdam and Oxford 1966; *Arnhem,* with an introduction by K. Schaap, Amsterdam 1968; *Mensen/People,* with text by Wim Alings and others, Amsterdam 1969; *1944-45 Het Laaste Jaar,* Amsterdam 1970; *Klederdrachten,* with Constance Nieuwhoff, Amsterdam 1976; *Rotterdam, dynamische stad 1950-1990,* Rotterdam 1990; *Guaranteed Real Dutch Congo,* Rotterdam, 1992; *Mensen aan de stroom. Reisimpressies van Cas Oorthuys in Belgisch Congo 1959,* Tervuren, 1992; *Cas Oorthuys. Werken in de bouw 1946-66,* Rotterdam, 1992; *Hotel New York,* Rotterdam,

1993. **Article**—"Cas Oorthuys: Interview" in *Wereldkroniek* (Amsterdam), 27 December 1969.

On OORTHUYS: Books—*Holland and the Canadians* by Norman Phillips and J. Nikerk, Amsterdam 1946; *Amsterdam tijdens de hongerwinter* by Max Nord, Amsterdam 1947; *2nd World Exhibition of Photography,* exhibition catalogue, by Karl Pawek, Hamburg 1968; *Kontrasten,* exhibition catalogue, The Hague 1970; *Fotografie in Nederland 1940-1975,* exhibition catalogue, edited by Els Barents, The Hague and Amsterdam 1978; *Fotografie in Nederland 1920-1940,* exhibition catalogue, by Flip Bool and Kees Broos, The Hague 1979; *Cas Oorthuys fotograaf 1908-1975* by S. Hekking, Amsterdam 1982; *De Arbeidersfotografen: Camera in Crisis in de Jaren '30* by Flip Bool and Jeroen de Vries, Amsterdam 1982; *The Library of World Photography: Photography as Fine Art,* with introduction by Douglas Davis, Tokyo 1982, 1983, London 1983; *Roots & Turns. Twentieth Century Photography in the Netherlands,* by Ingeborg Th. Leijerzapf eo, Houston, 1988; *Foto in omslag. Het Nederlandse documentaire fotoboek na 1945,* by Mattie Boom, Amsterdam, 1989; *De Nieuwe Fotografie in Nederland,* by Kees Broos and Flip Bool, Amsterdam, 1989; Exhibition catalogue, *Cas Oorthuys, Howard Greenberg,* Photofind Gallery, New York, 1990; *Een Beeld van Cas Oorthuys,* by Willem Diepraam, Amsterdam, 1991. **Articles**—"Cas Oorthuys" in *Groene Amsterdam* (Amsterdam), 30 July 1975; "Cas Oorthuys" by Flip Bool in *Ingeborg Th. Leijerzapf,* (red) *Geschiedenis van de Nederlandse fotografie in monografieën en thema-artikelen,* Alphen aan den Rijn, Amsterdam afl. 22, 1993.

*   *   *

One could describe Cas Oorthuys as a concerned photographer. It was his involvement with social causes that was responsible for his becoming a photographer in the first place. He was an out-of-work architect in the crisis period of the early 1930s, and he became involved with the Communist Party and the Association of Labor Photographers: in this environment he received his first lessons in photography from the filmmaker Joris Ivens. His first pictures were published in the left-wing magazine *Afwerfront;* they show a handcuffed negro, the children of an out-of-work seaman, and they demonstrate that his work was already that of reportage—down-to-earth, taken on the spot, without intentional "artistry."

In the work that followed, people were to remain his main theme. He felt that he wanted to photograph people throughout the world as they really were, not sensationally but sincerely portrayed in all situations. And, indeed, his subjects are always shown naturally, unposed, without artifice. His photos are like a momentary flash of vision, and they emphasize movement and action. Their strength is in his ability to choose the right moment at which to shoot: he captures life at a certain moment which is almost symbolic: the "capturing" seems to have been possible only at that moment, only rapidly, before it vanished. And the emotion of a single person, even if that emotion is a general one, becomes in his picture universal. Oorthuys' photo of a woman looking at nothing, blankly, while filling her mouth with a crust of bread conveys "starving" as well as his photograph of a wall on which in white paint the word "hunger" is written—a cyclist passes by, in the instant, apparently looking for food. These are only two examples of the impressive series of war pictures which Oorthuys produced in 1944 while he was a member of the "Underground Cameramen" in Amsterdam, often hiding his camera under his coat or in a bag, secretly taking his pictures. Apart from their photographic value, these photos provide an irreplaceable historical documentary of the time; they were collected by Oorthuys in his book *1944-45 Het Laaste Jaar.*

In his more commercial work—the commissions, the seemingly endless series of books produced after the war—we discover the same kind of intensity. There is, for example, his book *Mensen/People,* published on the occasion of his one-man exhibition at the Stedelijk Museum in 1969. The book is divided into 15 sections, for such subjects as death, birth, youth, hands, observation, discussions, laughter, etc. He himself wrote about the book: "It is a compilation of my work over the last 20 years, a kind of confession if you like, which I have gathered together from my previously unpublished photographs. They are all in black and white, because they were, and are, the colors of my generation."

What he neglected to say, but which we can see for ourselves in his archives in Amsterdam, is that in 40 years of work, Oorthuys revealed all aspects of human life.

—A. de Jonge-Vermeulen

ORKIN, Ruth.

Nationality: American. **Born:** Boston, Massachusetts, 3 September 1921. **Education:** Beverly Hills and Eagle Rock High Schools, Los Angeles, 1935-39; Los Angeles City College, 1940; self-taught in photography. **Military Service:** Served as a Private in the Women's Army Auxiliary Corps, 1943. **Family:** Married the photographer Morris Engel, in 1952; children: Andy and Mary. **Career:** Worked as a messenger at MGM Film Studios, Los Angeles, 1943-44. Freelance photographer, 1945-85; also, filmmaker, with Morris Engel, 1952-55. Freelance photojournalist, in New York, working for *Life, Esquire, Cosmopolitan, Ms., This Week, Collier's, Ladies' Home Journal,* etc. 1947-54. Instructor, School of Visual Arts, New York, 1976-78, and International Center of Photography, New York, 1979. **Recipient:** Silver Lion of San Marco, *Venice Film Festival,* 1953; Ten Best Women Photographers Award, New York, 1959; Manhattan Cultural Award for Photography, 1980; Certificate of Merit, Municipal Art Society, New York, 1984; Memorial Award, American Society of Magazine Photographers, New York, 1985. **Gallery:** Witkin Gallery, 415 West Broadway, New York, New York 10012. **Estate:** Mary Engel, Ruth Orkin Photography, 65 Central Park West, New York, New York 10023, U.S.A. **Died:** (in New York City) January 1985.

Individual Exhibitions:

1974	Nikon House, New York (retrospective)
1977	Witkin Gallery, New York (retrospective)
	Enjay Gallery, Boston
1978	Milwaukee Center of Photography
	Kiva Gallery, Boston
	New York-New York, G. Ray Hawkins Gallery, Los Angeles (with Berenice Abbott and Lou Stoumen)
1979	*Window Photographs,* International Center of Photography, New York
	University of Akron, Ohio
	Rizzoli Gallery, New York (retrospective)
	Afterimage Gallery, Dallas (retrospective)
	Ruth Orkin: Exhibition of 100 Photographs, Rizzoli Gallery, Chicago (retrospective)
1980	Atlanta Gallery of Photography
1981	*A Photo Journal,* Witkin Gallery, New York
	A Photo Journal, International Center of Photography, New York
1985	*Memorial Exhibition,* Witkin Gallery, New York

Selected Group Exhibitions:

1950	*Young Photographers,* Museum of Modern Art, New York
1955	*The Family of Man,* Museum of Modern Art, New York (and world tour)
1964	*The World and Its People,* at the *World's Fair,* New York
1965	*Photography in the Fine Arts,* Metropolitan Museum of Art, New York

1978	*Photographic Crossroads: The Photo League,* National Gallery of Canada, Ottawa (travelled to the International Center of Photography, New York; Museum of Fine Arts, Houston; and Minneapolis Institute of Arts)
1981	*Manhattan Observed,* New York Historical Society
	Art of the Olmsted Landscape, Metropolitan Museum of Art, New York
1985	*American Images 1945-80,* Barbican Art Gallery, London (toured Britain)
	City Light, International Center of Photography, Midtown, New York
1986	*Women Photographers Now,* A.I.R. Gallery, New York

Collections:

Metropolitan Museum of Art, New York; Museum of Modern Art, New York; International Center of Photography, New York; St. Louis Art Museum, Missouri.

Publications:

By ORKIN: Books—*Legacy of Love,* illustrations of poems by Ginsberg, New York 1971; *A World Through My Window: Photographs by Ruth Orkin,* New York 1978; *A Photo Journal: Ruth Orkin,* New York 1981; *More Pictures from My Window,* New York 1983; *Musicians,* with text by Leonard Bernstein, New York 1987. **Articles**—"My Mother the Painter" in the *New York* magazine in the *New York Herald Tribune,* 29 December 1963; interview in *Photographers on Photography* by Jerry La Plante, New York 1979. **Films**—*The Little Fugitive,* with Morris Engel and Ray Ashley, 1953; *Lovers and Lollipops,* with Morris Engel, 1955.

On ORKIN: Book—*The Family of Man* (includes Orkin sequence), edited by Edward Steichen, New York 1955; *The Photograph Collector's Guide* by Lee D. Witkin and Barbara London, Boston and London 1979. **Articles**—"The Incredible Ruth Orkin" by Peter Martin in *Photography Workshop* (New York), Winter 1953; "Ruth Orkin's New York" in *Horizon* (New York), March 1959; "Frontier Woman" by Sarah Webb Barrell in *Camera 35* (New York), May 1975; "Ruth Orkin: Gravure Portfolio" by Nancy Stevens in *Popular Photography* (New York), June 1977; "We Are Not a Muse" by Burt Prelutsky in the *Los Angeles Times,* 28 August 1977; "Invisible Women" by Cecile Starr in *Sight and Sound* (London), Autumn 1980; "Over 40 in the Arts" in *Harper's Bazaar* (New York), September 1982; "The Window is her World" by Jill Neimark in *American Way* (New York), July 1984.

*

Taking pictures is my way of asking people to "look at this—look at that." If my photographs make the viewer feel what I did when I first took them—"isn't this funny/terrible/moving/beautiful?"—then I've accomplished my purpose.

—Ruth Orkin (1982)

* * *

Ruth Orkin was an original and awarded (an Oscar nomination in the 1950s for *The Little Fugitive*) film maker and a distinguished, successful photojournalist. *Life* and *Look,* et al, in their heydays sent her far away, hither and yon, to bring back a bounty of powerful pictures. But probably her finest, most deeply personal work was accomplished in her role as New York City voyeur. Her documentation over a long period of years of what she saw from her Westside window overlooking Central Park resulted in an extraordinary series of images.

This loving spying caught seasons and weather, parades and games, concerts and cars, joggers and cyclists, kites and fireworks. Like some apartment-house deity she observed unobserved, from high up (but not too high), the personal and public activities below her. Included in her sometimes sharp, sometimes impressionistic record are the times of day, times of night, sunrise, sunset, all vividly recognized and composed, and with maximum usage of the drama of nature within towers: the city and park as a tireless, changing stage set.

—Ralph Pomeroy

ORLOPP, Detlef.

Nationality: German. **Born:** Elbing, West Prussia, 14 February 1937. **Education:** Studied photography, Staatliche Fachschule, Cologne, 1955-56; under Otto Steinert, Staatliche Werkkunstschule, Saarbrucken, 1957-59. **Career:** Independent landscape and portrait photographer, in Krefeld and Cologne, since 1959. Instructor in photography, 1959-74, and Professor since 1974, Department of Design, Fachhochschule Niederrhein, Krefeld. Member, Gesellschaft Deutscher Lichtbildner; Deutsche Gesellschaft für Photographie, 1961. **Agent:** Galerie Karsten Greve, Wallrafplatz 3, 5000 Cologne 1, Germany. **Address:** Outrewarche, 87, B 4950 Robertville, Belgium.

Individual Exhibitions:

1957	Galerie Nohl, Siegen, West Germany
1960	Galerie Nohl, Siegen, West Germany
1962	Werkkunstschule, Krefeld, West Germany
1963	Galerie De Ploeg, Bergeyk, Netherlands
1964	Städtische Galerie, Haus Seel, Siegen, West Germany
	Galerie Kuppers, Cologne
1965	Junge Galerie, Kassel, West Germany
	Galerie Jac Eyck, Heerlen, Netherlands
1966	Staatsbad-Galerie, Salzuflen, West Germany
1967	Technische Hochschule, Stuttgart
1968	Galerie Nohl, Siegen, West Germany
	Staatliche Landesbildstelle, Hamburg
1969	Stadtischer Kunstpavillon, Soest, West Germany
	Kunst- und Bucherscheune, Bochum, West Germany
1970	Kultur-Club, Liubliana, Yugoslavia
1971	Galerie S-Press, Hattingen, West Germany
1973	Galerie Mollenhof und Greve, Cologne
	Bibliothèque Nationale, Paris
1974	Kaiser Wilhelm Museum, Krefeld, West Germany
1975	Apenrade Kulturhaus, Denmark
1976	Kunstmuseum, Lahti, Finland
	Galerie Karsten Greve, Cologne
1977	Studio Galleri Engstrom, Stockholm
1983	Benteler Galleries, Houston, Texas
1984	Galerie Lüpke, Frankfurt
1985	Galerie St. Johann, Saarbrücken, West Germany
1990	Galerie Karsten Greve, Cologne
	Galerie Karsten Greve, Paris

Selected Group Exhibitions:

1957	*Exposition Internationale de Photographies,* Palais des Beaux-Arts, Brussels (travelled to The Hague)

1958	*Fotografie als uitdrukkingsmiddel,* Gemeente Museum, Arnhem, Netherlands
1965	*GDL-Ausstellung,* Institut für Neue Technische Form, Darmstadt, West Germany (and GDL exhibitions in Berlin, 1966, Mannheim, 1967, and Hamburg, 1969)
1975	*Fotografie 1929-75,* Wurttembergischer Kunstverein, Stuttgart
1976	*Photography as Art/Art as Photography,* Fotoforum, Kassel, West Germany
1977	*Künstlerische Fotografie,* Saarland Museum, Saarbrucken, West Germany
1979	*Deutsche Fotografie nach 1945,* Kunstverein Kassel, West Germany
1981	*Brosch/Fontana/Kounellis/Manzoni/Orlopp/Twombly,* Galerie Karsten Greve, Cologne
1984	*La Photographie Créative,* Pavillon des Arts, Paris
1985	*Westdeutscher Kunstlerbund,* Karl Ernst Osthaus Museum, Hagen, West Germany
1987	*Photographie 1945-85,* Museum für Kunst und Gewerbe, Hamburg
1988	*/89Fotovision—Projekt Fotografie nach 150 Jahren,* Sprengel Museum, Hannover
	Fotovision—Projekt Fotografie nach 150 Jahren, Kunstraum im Messepalast, Wien
	Fotovision—Projekt Fotografie nach 150 Jahren, Museum für Gestaltung, Zurich
1989	*Westdeutscher Künstlerbund,* Karl Ernst Osthaus Museum, Hagen

Collections:

Fotomuseum im Münchner Stadtmuseum, Munich; Staatliche Landesbildstelle, Hamburg; Museum Folkwang, Essen, Germany; Fotoforum der Gesamthochschule, Kassel, Germany; Kaiser Wilhelm Museum, Krefeld, Germany; Bibliothèque Nationale, Paris; Kunstmuseum, Lahti, Finland; Galerie Karsten Greve, Cologne; Galerie St. Johann, Saarbrucken, Germany; Benteler Galleries, Houston, Texas.

Publications:

By ORLOPP: Books—*Detlef Orlopp: Fotografien,* exhibition catalogue, with text by Helmut Heissenbuttel, Seigen, West Germany 1968; *Detlef Orlopp—Photographien 1961-1974,* exhibition catalogue, with text by Gisela Fiedler, Krefeld, West Germany 1974; *Detlef Orlopp—Photographien,* exhibition catalogue, with text by John Anthony Thwaites, Flensburg, West Germany 1975; *Orlopp,* exhibition catalogue, with text by Helmut Heissenbuttel, Cologne 1976; *Detlef Orlopp Photographie,* text by Peter Weiermeier and Ulrike Lehmann, Cologne, Germany, 1990.

On ORLOPP: Books—*Photography as Art/Art as Photography* by Floris M. Neususs, Kassel, West Germany 1975; *Fotografie 1919-1979, Made in Germany: Die GDL-Fotografend* by W. Boje, F. Kempe, B. Lohse and others, Frankfurt 1979; *Deutsche Fotografie nach 1945/German Photography After 1945* by Petra Benteler, Kassel, West Germany 1979; *Museum Folkwang: Die fotografische Sammlung,* exhibition catalogue, with introduction by Ute Eskildsen, Essen, West Germany 1983; *La Photographie Créative* by Jean-Claude Lemagny, Paris 1984; *Photographie 1945-85,* Museum für Kunst und Gewerbe, Hamburg, 1987; *Bildjebende Fotografie,* Gottfried Jäger, Cologne, 1988; *Fotovision—Projekt Fotografie nach 150 Jahren,* Hanover, 1988; *Westdeutscher Künstlerbund,* Hagen, 1989. **Articles**—"The New Image" by John Anthony Thwaites in *Artsmagazine* (New York), May/June 1964; "Detlef Orlopp und die Fotografie" by Helmut Heissenbuttel in *Foto-Prisma* (Dusseldorf), October 1965; "Detlef Orlopp—Wasserflache" in *Zweitschrift* (Hannover), no. 2, 1976; "Aspekte eines Mediums" in *Kunstforum International* (Mainz), no. 18, 1976; "Seestucke" by Rolf Sachsse in *Professional*

Untitled. Photograph by Detlef Orlopp.

Camera (Munich), no. 5, 1980; "Detlef Orlopp—photographische Bilder" by Viktoria Losche in *Literature in Krefeld,* no. 3, 1985; *Noise, Maeght Éditeur,* Paris no.15/16, 1991; "Werk und Zeit Perspektiven 2," *Landschaftsbilder,* 1994.

*   *   *

Schools of photography are no longer a rarity nowadays. But one in particular stands out from the rest—Otto Steinert's school, which not only marked out a whole era of photography, under the name "Subjective Photography," but also became a school in the traditional sense, engaged in developing individual talent within a programme of compulsory instruction. Detlef Orlopp already occupied a special place among Steinert's pupils when the latter was active in Saarbrücken. In 1959, at the age of twenty-two, Orlopp began working as a photographer in his own right. As well as having his own workshop, he taught at the School of Design in Krefeld, first as an assistant lecturer, and, from 1974, as a professor.

Two themes primarily interested Orlopp from the early sixties: portraiture and landscape. He treated both with absolute directness. His "subjectivity" was bounded by the precision of his perceptions, given their final polish in the darkroom. There is nothing undefined or remotely painterly about these photos, in which every feature is sharply delineated. The faces looking out from the portraits steadfastly hold the spectator's gaze; the landscapes derive their character not from any picturesque quality or coincidental charm, but from their own particular and necessary structure.

Orlopp's first love was for mountains and rock formations; later he became fascinated by water in all its transformations and living dynamism—a theme which he captured particularly well in his pictures of northern Europe. Regardless of whether he chooses a distant perspective or a small detail, the content of these pictures always expresses unequivocally that nature is inseparable from the history of evolution and that we can experience the latter daily if we know how to look properly, without being distracted by the merely coincidental.

—Heinz Spielmann

ORTIZ-ECHAGÜE, José.

Nationality: Spanish. **Born:** Guadalajara, 21 August 1886. **Education:** Educated in Logrono, Rioja, until 1894; studied at Academy of Military Engineering, Guadalajara, 1903-09; self-taught in photography. **Military Service:** Served in Aerial Regiment (balloon service), Spanish Army, in Spain, North Africa and Morocco, 1909-12; Pilot-Officer, Spanish Air Force, 1913-14; Commander, Air Maintenance Corps, Cuatros Vientos, Spain, 1915-17. **Career:** Independent photographer, in Spain, 1900-80; also worked as an engineer for the City Planning Department, Buenos Aires, Argentina, 1912, Metal Industry Factories, France, 1914, and the Escoriaza Company, Zaragoza, Spain, 1916; Founder-Director, Electro-Mechanical Company, La Plata, Madrid, 1917-23; Founder-Director, then Chairman, Construcciones Aeronauticas S.A. (CASA), in Getafe and Cadiz, later in Seville and Madrid, 1923-70; Chairman and Manager, Sociedad Española de Automoviles de Turismo (SEAT), Barcelona, 1950-70. **Recipient:** First Prize, National Competition of Circulo de Bellas Artes, 1915; First Prize, Frederick and Nelson Competition, Washington, D.C., 1924; Silver Medal, *California Pacific International Exposition*, 1935; L. Misonne International Prize, Charleroi, Belgium, 1948; First Prize, *South African Salon of Photography*, Johannesburg, 1958; Medalla de Oro del Trabajo, Madrid, 1958; Gold Medal, Direccion General de Bellas Artes, Madrid, 1962; Gold Medal, Real Sociedad Fotografica de Madrid, 1975. Honorary Fellow, Royal Photographic Society, London, Photographic Society of America, and Hispanic Society of America; Honorary Life Member, Johannesburg Photographic Society; Honorary Member, New Pictorialist Society, U.S.A. **Died:** (in Madrid) 7 September 1980.

Individual Exhibitions:

1928	Piedmontese Photography Group Gallery, Turin
1929	Wasmuth's Verlag, Berlin
1935	Royal Photographic Society, London
1948	Artists' Circle, Turin
1949	Photographic Circle, Milan
1951	Northwest Photographic Salon, Chicago
1952	Smithsonian Institution, Washington, D.C.
1953	Club Fotografico, Mexico City
1955	Johannesburg Photographic, Society, South Africa (toured South Africa)
1958	Royal Photographic Society, London (toured the U.K.)
1959	Photographic Society of America Convention, Louisville, Kentucky
1960	Metropolitan Museum of Art, New York
	Biblioteca Communale, Milan
1961	Centro Cultural FIAT, Turin
1962	Biblioteca Nacional, Madrid
1969	Fine Arts Gallery, South Dunedin, New Zealand
1974	Palacio de la Virreina, Barcelona
1978	Galleria Civica di Cultura, Modena, Italy

1980	Biblioteca Nacional, Madrid (retrospective)

Selected Group Exhibitions:

1935	*California Pacific International Exposition*, San Francisco
1948	*Wisconsin Centennial International Salon*, Milwaukee
1958	*South African Salon of Photography*, Johannesburg
1965	*Un Siècle de Photographie*, Musée des Arts Décoratifs, Paris
1966	*Interpress Exhibition*, Moscow
1977	*RPS Annual Exhibition*, Kodak Gallery, London (travelled to Grundy Art Gallery, Blackpool; Cathedral Nave, Coventry; Howarth Art Gallery, Accrington, 1977-78)
1982	*SIF 82: Semana Internacional de la Fotografia*, Palacio del Infantado, Guadalajara, Spain
1984	*Idas and Chaos: Trends in Spanish Photography 1920-45*, Biblioteca Nacional, Madrid (travelled to the Fundacion Joan Miro, Barcelona; Museo de Bellas Artes, Bilbao; Sala de Exposiciones del Ayuntamiento, Valencia; International Center of Photography, New York; Museum Folkwang, Essen)

Collections:

Biblioteca Nacional, Madrid; SEAT, Barcelona; Royal Photographic Society, London; Smithsonian Institution, Washington, D.C.

Publications:

By ORTIZ-ECHAGÜE: Books—*Spanische Köpfe*, Berlin 1929, as *España, Tipos y Trajes*, Madrid 1933; *España Mistica*, Madrid 1934; *España, Pueblos y Paisajes*, Madrid 1938; *Castillos y Alcazares*, Madrid.

On ORTIZ-ECHAGÜE: Books—*Histoire de la Photographie* by Raymond Lecuyer, Paris 1945; *Jose Ortiz-Echagüe: Photographs*, with text by Gerardo Vielba, Madrid 1978, London 1979; *Semana Internacional de la Fotografia: Guadalajara 82*, exhibition catalogue, by Marie Genevieve and others, Guadalajara, Spain 1982; *Idas and Chaos: Trends in Spanish Photography 1920-1945*, exhibition catalogue, with texts by Joan Fontcuberta, Marta Gili and others, Madrid 1985. **Articles**—"José Ortiz-Echagüe: Fotógrafo de España" by Gerardo Vielba in *Anuario de la Fotografía Española*, León, Spain 1973; "Ortiz-Echagüe" in *Camera* (Lucerne), December 1980; "Spanish Artists Take Their Place on the World Scene" by Gene Thornton in the *New York Times*, 4 February 1986; "Photography in Spain Between the World Wars" by Harvey Fondiller in *Popular Photography* (New York), May 1986.

*   *   *

To refer to José Ortiz-Echagüe is to refer to the internationally best-known Spanish photographer of all time. As a man, he was spiritually aligned with the so-called "Generation of '98" (in 1898 Spain lost its last colonies overseas, and this critical historic moment utterly plunged a group of Castillian intellectuals into the most profound patriotic pessimism). In photography, Ortiz-Echagüe represents what Ignacio de Zuloaga represents in painting: an idealized vision of the Iberian people and their landscape, folklore, religion, etc. The actual country and its people are so sublimated to this vision that the photographer loses all connection with documented reality and in effect creates a fiction—or, perhaps better put, though paradoxically: he creates a remembrance of Spain's mythic past, in which traditions never evolve and everything breathes nobility and solemnity. Yet, despite the evidence of his photographs, Ortiz-Echagüe considered himself a documentalist.

Given the nature of those photographs, it is not difficult to understand the great esteem in which they were held by the Franco regime. For my part, if I had to choose his masterwork from among his very extensive production, I should select "Siroco en el Sahara"(1964), just precisely because, in this picture, his distance from his theme permits him to treat it with more spontaneity than is characteristic of his more celebrated pictures—many of which seem staged—and that spontaneity translated itself, thanks to his uncommon talent, into a very impressive image, clearly detached from the subjects with which he is usually associated.

Although, in fact, in his native country, Ortiz-Echagüe is now the target of polemics that have more to do with ideological than aesthetic questions (if one may separate the two), even his detractors must, I think, recognize the merit of his perseverance in the service of his vision, his great gifts for graphic creation for images, and the mastery with which he used the *fresson* method, which he himself modified and called *al carbón*.

Despite the fact that he insisted that he was not a "pictorialist," it is possible and apt to place Ortiz-Echagüe with the second surge of European pictorialism and with the generation that comprised Pla Janini, Claudi Carbonell, Marqués de Sta. Marìa del Villar, Conde de la Ventosa, etc.—that is, with those photographers who did not attempt to form an avant-garde or to be innovators, but who tried to shape and convey their environment as *they* honestly saw and felt it. It was a generation still interested in romantic values and in classic canons. Gerardo Vielba, who is his best biographer and critic, has said of him: "Ortiz-Echagüe had a fine sensibility, in general baroque, but modified at times by classicism, accented at others with a clear romanticism: what makes his representation so encompassing is the passionate way in which he dominates and, if need be, forces the theme, disclosing it as from within a fantastic aura." There can be no better description of the man or of his photographic style.

—Joan Fontcuberta

ORTIZ MONASTERIO, Pablo.

Nationality: Mexican. **Born:** Mexico City, 2 June 1952. **Education:** Instituto Patria, Mexico City, 1958-70; studied economics at the Universidad Nacional Autonoma, Mexico City, 1970-73; and photography at Ealing Technical College, London, 1974-75, and London College of Printing, 1975-76. **Career:** Photographer, Rhigetti Audio-Visual Company, Mexico City, 1972-74. Photographer and Designer, Troje Taller, Mexico City, since 1978; Chief Editor, Archivio Etnografico Audiovisual, Mexico City, since 1979. Instructor in Photography, Universidad Autonoma Metropolitana, Mexico City, since 1977. **Recipient:** Prize, *Primer Bienal de Fotografia*, Mexico City, 1980. **Address:** Magnolia 38, San Angel Inn, Mexico 20, D.F., Mexico.

Individual Exhibitions:

1976	Creative Camera Gallery, London
	La Photogalerie, Paris
1977	Carlton Gallery, New York
1978	*3 Jovenes Fotografios*, Galeria Juan Martin, Mexico City (with Gabriel Figueroa Flores and Julieta Gimenez Cacho)
1979	*50 Fotografias*, Teatro del Estado, Veracruz, Mexico
1980	Photographers Gallery, Santa Fe, New Mexico

Selected Group Exhibitions:

1975	*Four Letter World*, Weavers Hall Museum, Norwich, England
1978	*Primera Muestra Latinoamerica de Fotografia*, Museo de Arte Moderno, Mexico City
	Triennale de Photographie, Musée d'Art et d'Histoire, Fribourg, Switzerland
1979	*Primera Bienal de Rito y Magia*, Museo de Arte, São Paulo
	Amnesty International, Museo Carrillo Gil, Mexico City
1980	*Primera Bienal de Fotografia*, Galeria del Auditorio, Instituto Nacional de Bellas Artes, Mexico City
	7 Portafolios Mexicanos, Centre Culturel du Mexique, Paris (travelled to the Picasso Museum, Antibes, France)
1981	*Salon de Invitados*, at the *Coloquio Latinoamericano de Fotografia*, Museo Palacio de Bellas Artes, Mexico City
	Hecho en Latino America 2, Palacio de Bellas Artes, Mexico City
1982	*La Photographie Contemporaine en Amerique Latine*, Centre Georges Pompidou, Paris

Collections:

Instituto Nacional de Bellas Artes, Mexico City; Consejo Mexicano de Fotografia, Mexico City; Casa de las Americas, Havana; Bibliothèque Nationale, Paris.

Publications:

By ORTIZ MONASTERIO: Books—*El Mundo Interior*, Mexico City 1979; *El Desnudo Fotografico*, Mexico City 1980; *La Casa en la Tierra*, editor, Mexico City 1980; *Los Pueblos del Viento*, with text by Jose Manuel Pintado, Mexico City 1981; *Los Que Viven en la Arena*, editor, with Graciela Iturbide, Mexico City 1981; *Testigos y Complices*, Mexico City 1984. **Articles**—"Pablo Monasterio" in *British Journal of Photography* (London), July 1975; "Pablo Monasterio: Portfolio" in *British Journal of Photography* (London), July 1976; "El Mimo" in *Revista de Bellas Artes* (Mexico City), July 1976; "Pablo Monasterio" in *Creative Camera* (London), November 1976; "Pablo Ortiz Monasterio" in *British Journal of Photography Annual*, London 1977; "Pablo Ortiz Monasterio" in *Anuario Fotozoom*, Mexico City 1977; "El Cardenal" in *Foto Zoom* (Mexico City), July 1980; "Pablo Ortiz Monasterio" in *Picture Paper* (Santa Fe, New Mexico), no. 5, 1979; "Pablo Ortiz Monasterio" in *Picture Paper* (Santa Fe, New Mexico), no. 9, 1980; "Pablo Ortiz Monasterio" in *Picture Paper* (Santa Fe, New Mexico), no. 10, 1980.

On ORTIZ MONASTERIO: Books—*Bienal de Fotografia*, exhibition catalogue, by the Instituto Nacional de Bellas Artes, Mexico City 1980; *7 Portafolios Mexicanos*, edited by Universidad Nacional Autonoma de Mexico, Mexico City 1980; *Hecho en Latino America 2*, exhibition catalogue, with texts by Pedro Meyer, Lazaro Blanco and others, Mexico City 1981; *La Photographie Contemporaine en Amerique Latine*, exhibition catalogue, by Alain Sayag, Paris 1982. **Articles**—"Pablo Monasterio" in *Nueva Lente* (Madrid), September 1976; "Predomino de lo Formal" by Chely Zarate in *Semana de Bellas Artes* (Mexico City), March 1980; "Mexican Photography" in *Camera 35* (New York), February 1981.

*

I am interested in photography as a form of expression, more precisely as a language with specific characteristics.

Over the years I have been learning and studying the elements one works with in a visual language. These include the technical crafts of photography, such as printing, exposure, etc., as well as the formal elements like composition, light, etc., and of course the meanings that the images convey.

All these elements are techniques that you can learn through observation, investigation and practice.

What remains as the more important question is what to say with the photographic language. The development of technical skills is only important as a tool.

My personal preoccupation is to use this tool (photography) to talk about aspects of our political reality, using different elements to convey meaning with depth, strength and beauty.

—Pablo Ortiz Monasterio

*   *   *

The artistic path of Pablo Ortiz Monasterio has been characterized by his search for self-expression and by his rigorous self-criticism. From 1968 until now, he has passed through a variety of different stages in his development.

He began with the intention of justifying the subject as he photographed art and artists. Then he began to hunt for the photogenic in everyday reality and to investigate the effect of bursting the grain of the film during developing. At times he playfully introduced color with a brush in order to emphasize a detail in the print. At some later stage he encountered Gibson's work and learned to liberate the shutter of his camera, using it as an instrument to tell a story. He tried to create a narrative sequence about a Greek village through several of its most typical characters. When in Portugal, he narrated the various activities of the inhabitants. In these works there was one recurrent element: his subjects were always placed with their backs to a wall (perhaps an unconscious symbol of captivity). Later, he appears to have been seduced by a surrealistic urge. He produced mysterious images of a certain intentional ambiguity in which dimensions, textures, proportions, and positions in space and time are deceptive. These trends in his work—the narrative and the mysterious—became one in the next stage of his work, a series of images about the life of a surgeon of the 16th century, Gaspar Talliacotti.

From then on, Ortiz Monasterio has worked simultaneously in two modes. One involves the development of elements as worked by Hausmann and Heartfield: building, through a single image, a specific political meaning for multiple reproduction. These compact images have a keen semantical accent, and they are distributed outside the usual realm of artistic photography.

The other mode are testimonies (through a sequence of 30 to 50 photographs each) of indigenous Mexican cultures, the Huaves and the Tarahumaras, on the verge of extinction. In these works Ortiz Monasterio has been a follower of Joseph Koudelka in his particular way of constructing photographic discourse around specific subject matter, particularly the way of life and behavior of little-known social groups.

His main resource in these works (apart from his sensibility and obvious technical mastery) is a humble attitude, the result of his inability to directly communicate with these people. This difficulty forces him to recognize that he can capture only a few glimpses of the Indians' historic and cultural complexity. He works, as it were, as through the keyhole of a huge rusty door stuck between the western and indigenous cultures. His attitude is completely genuine, and his outlook is one of wonder, admiration and respect. He does not convey the "superiority" of the "civilized" white man who looks down on peoples of lesser economic development, nor does he give way to the temptation of the picturesque.

The mystery that he sought in his early photographs now comes naturally. It is the mystery that Pablo Ortiz Monasterio conveys in his lyrical and eloquent testimony to a dying culture. His is an aesthetic, political and human commitment.

—Katya Mandoki

OSSWALD, Inge.

Nationality: German. **Born:** Stuttgart on 29 April 1938. **Education:** Studied at the School of Arts and Craft, Saarbrücken, 1957-58; studied graphics at the Folkwangschule für Gestaltung, Essen, 1960-69. **Career:** Assistant at the School of Arts and Craft, Saarbrücken, 1958-59; assistant teacher at Folkwangschule für Gestaltung, Essen, until 1969. Ran her own graphics and photography studio, 1962-85. Worked as a teacher of photography at the University of Wuppertal and Fachhochschule Dortmund and has been Professor of photography at the University of Essen since 1979. Involved in research into the possibilities of the electronic media, 1987. Member of the Gesellschaft Deutscher Lichtbildner (now the Deutsche Fotografische Akademie) and the Deutsche Gesellschaft für Photographie since 1972. Vice-president of the Deutsche Fotografische Akademie, 1989-92; held other positions with Künstlerischer Beirat. **Address:** Bilker Str. 22, D-40213 Düsseldorf, Germany.

Individual Exhibitions:

1991   *Lichtbilder,* Photo Gallery Lajos Keresztes, Nünberg (travelled to Weinsberg), Germany

Selected Group Exhibitions:

1962   *Otto Steinert and Schüler,* Göppinger Gallery, Frankfurt/Main (travelled to Deutsche Gesellschaft für Photographie, Cologne; Museum Folkwang, Essen), Germany
1975   *Gesellschaft Deutscher Lichtbildner,* Haus Industrieform, Essen, Germany
1979   *Fotographie 1919-1979, Made in Germany,* The GDL Photographers
1990   *Personas Exquestas,* Humboldt Institute, Caracas, Venezuela
1991   *Otto Steinert und Schüler. Photography and education from 1948 to 1978,* Museum Folkwang, Essen, Germany
         Mai de la Photo, Reims
1992   *2. Internationale Foto-Triennale Esslingen,* Esslingen, Germany

Collections:

Photo Museum of the town of Burghausen, Germany; Museum Folkwang, Essen (Collection Otto Steinert), Germany; Schleswig-Holsteinisches Landesmuseum, (Collection Fritz Kempe), Schloss Gottorf, Schleswig, Germany; Photo Museum in the Munich Stadtmuseum, Munich; Collection Walter Boje, Solingen, Germany; Collection Helmut Gernsheim, Castagnola, Switzerland; Collection Lajos Keresztes, Nürnberg, Germany; Museum fur Kunst und Gewerbe, Hamburg, Germany; IBM Kunstmuseum.

Publications:

By OSSWALD: Article—*Bildwelt-Weltbild,* 1987.

On OSSWALD: Books—*Otto Steinert und Schüler,* Essen 1965; *Gesellschaft Deutscher Lichtbildner,* Essen 1975; *Mai de la Photo,* Rheims 1991; *2.Internationale Foto-Triennale Esslingen,* Esslingen 1992; *Metamorphoto,* edited by Claudia Gabriele Philipp, Marburg, 1993. **Articles**—"Fotografie

***06/5*, 1988/9 (original in colour).** Photograph by Inge Osswald.

1919-1979, Made in Germany'' in *Die GDL Fotographie* 1979; *Contemporanea,* 1989; ''Otto Steinert und Schüler'' in *Fotografie und Ausbildung 1948 bis 1978,* Essen 1991.

*

The starting point of my own work was that I doubted that facts are more important or more urgent than emotional expressions. In my work as a freelance photographer and graphic designer, I had to identify with the goals and wishes of my clients. I had to use photography and graphics for documentation, idealisation or visualisation of a given context.

In developing my own picture language, I was free to express my own feelings and imagination, and slowly moved away from having to have tangible objects and surfaces in front of the camera. I started to construct my own situations, aiming at a reduction that would allow me to use only light itself in its most immaterial form.

Technically speaking, I add layers of light (and colour), sometimes up to 12 in one negative. This method allows me to add the last layer (a reflection of water) a month later.

Sometimes I build shapes to cover different parts of the light-situation or use models to create room-like impressions. Usually I use a large pin-hole camera, which seems most suitable for the concept of simplicity.

I am not interested in depicting objects. The object is the picture itself. It carries an accumulation of moods and impressions, gathered over a certain period of time. To achieve this, my working process is more like meditation than "picture taking." For the viewer, my pictures are an invitation to go into his/her own inner world of imagination.

—Inge Osswald

*   *   *

Photography is the study of colour, what else? Goethe's image of light differed from Newton's concept of light, but both were full of colour. Image creation with light practised with precision and determination, brings out from the world of appearances the "colourful reflection" like the glimmer of a prism. Shape dissolves into colours: the contours exposed to light, pale streams of fine blue or atomised yellow, become blurred. Colour takes on a contour—light, refracted and simultaneously *hardened* dissolves it: it solidifies into glaring red. Colour is transformed into rays of light.

This process is as elementary as it is abstract, and Inge Osswald, who is fully committed to this "Academy of the Abstract," proves that beyond her sense of form and colour she understands light. Aware that this could appear arrogant, we would nevertheless claim that she is close to discovering the very essence of creating images with light. We want to further claim that in her pictures she encapsulates her capacity to experience her very personal feelings, her ego: the flow of energy between the "inner world" and the colours and shapes which surround the self, between the inner being and the outside world.

Inge Osswald's photographs are influenced by both personal perception and by an awareness of theory, which focuses and advances the medium of photography. Which of these is more influential, the muse or the strict academy teaching? Is it the Freie Waldorfschule she attended as a young woman in Stuttgart or the education for the Diploma in Photography, a diploma stringently supervised by the Photographers' Guild? Or is it discipline, methodical calculation or searching intuition?

Inge Osswald's creative endeavour combines many aspects: didactic talent, and sudden inspiration, the demands of the arts and crafts schools (initially in Saarbrucken and then the Folkwangschule fur Gestaltung, Essen)—and equally work as a freelance graphic designer, producing photographs for advertising and public relations. She is an academic, moved by dreams of creating, a theoretician with the desire for practical design, an individual who acts spontaneously based on broad theoretical knowledge. Anyone who has experienced the way in which she judges and analyses photography in the German Photographic Society (she has been a member of the management committee for many years, and as Vice President of the FA GDL since 1989), values her intuition and her expertise.

So, what effect do her pictures have? Are they a form of subjective photography? Or do they seem to be completely objective? She has been asked whether her creations can still be considered photography. Alternatively, one might assume that this is where photography *truly begins and truly finds itself.* What is happening here—abstraction or sensuality turned into image? Reference to the subjective nature of her work at this point seems reasonable, because this reference brings us to the concept—the guiding maxim—of her great teacher, Otto Steiner, with whom she worked as assistant and senior assistant. Inge Osswald accompanied the strict, abrupt disciple of "subjective photography" during decisive years—from the arts and crafts school at Saarbrucken and Steinert's University Institute there, to the Folkwangschule, Essen. There she learned how one can, with clear, strict adherence to form (as taught by the Bauhaus Movement) overcome the sentimental postwar kitsch, outgrowth of a Nazi photography longing for a continuing existence.

Inge Osswald experiences this design process synaesthetically. "My images" she says, "are not only pictorial, they also often have sound!" Sound can have colour and colour can have sound—and light becomes shape and shape becomes colour, again and again with each new exposure. That is why, as Inge Osswald describes it, the process of taking photographs (used here in the dual sense of taking photographs and taking in/receiving) is a perpetual process, an "inner story" never fully completed. That is why new particles of experience are continually propelled into her photographs, which develop

virtually layer by layer in overlapping exposures (in the language of traditional art: from the first assignment, the grounding to the varnish). These principles are moods which reflect "sound" as well as tactile sensations, including a sense of smell.

In this respect, Inge Osswald has liberated herself from Steinert's rigid theory and has learned to develop her own photographic statement, "a photograph only becomes a photograph when it expresses an idea," Osswald adds, "and the idea is nothing if emotions do not give it life." For photography only becomes photography when in can move us synaesthetically—like light itself.

(from *Metamorphoto,* Jonas Verlag, Marburg, 1993)

—Ruprecht Skasa-Weiß

OSTROVSKY, (Itzhak) Tzachi.

Nationality: Israeli. **Born:** Tel Aviv, 7 July 1945. **Education:** Shalva High School, Tel Aviv, graduated 1963. **Military Service:** Served as a Photographer/Correspondent in the Israeli Army, 1963-66. **Career:** Staff Photographer, United Press International, in Israel, 1966; Senior Photographer, *Ha'aretz* weekly magazine, Tel Aviv, 1966-70. Freelance photographer since 1970: established Studio 500C, Tel Aviv, 1968, and worked with Studio Marco Glaviano, Milan, 1970. **Address:** 14 Ussishkin Street, Tel Aviv, Israel.

Selected Group Exhibitions:

1966   *Capa/Chim Memorial Fund Competition,* Journalists House, Tel Aviv
1967   *The Six-Day War,* Tel Aviv Museum
1969   *Israel: The Reality,* Jewish Museum, New York
1973   *World Press Photo,* Amsterdam (and 1976, 1977)
1974   *One World for All,* at *Photokina '74,* Cologne (travelled to Unesco, Paris, 1975)
1976   *Jerusalem: Types and Sights,* Jerusalem Museum
        J.A. Kamminer Memorial Fund Exhibition, Journalists House, Tel Aviv
1978   *Work and Leisure,* at *Photokina '78,* Cologne
1980   *Israel '80,* Municipal Library, Tel Aviv

Collections:

Tel Aviv Museum; Jerusalem Museum; World Press Photo Foundation, Amsterdam; Bibliothèque Nationale, Paris.

Publications:

By OSTROVSKY: Books—*Israel: The Reality,* with others, edited by Cornell Capa, New York 1969; *Endless War,* with others, Haifa 1970; *Israeli Seaman,* with others, edited by J. Bar Joseph, Haifa 1971; *Sinai Desert,* with others, edited by A. Alon, Haifa 1972; *Bat Chen,* with others, edited by T. Cohen, Haifa 1972; *Israel: Years of Crisis, Years of Hope,* with others, edited by R. Prister, New York 1973; *Israel: 25th Year,* with others, edited by David Pedhetzur, Tel Aviv 1973; *Jerusalem,* with others, edited by E. Kore'n and R. Hecht, Haifa 1974; *Things I Wanted to Tell You,* with poems by Amos Ettinger, Tel Aviv 1981; *Shay Doesn't Hear,* with text by Murit Israeli, Tel Aviv 1981.

*   *   *

"Here," said the slim, intense man almost hidden behind an aureole of curly hair, curly beard, as he pulled five or six photographs from the pile we had just looked through—"if you want to know who I am, look at these. I don't know how to separate Tzachi Ostrovsky the individual from Tzachi Ostrovsky the photographer."

I asked about the particular photograph we were looking at. "It represents my deep love of the desert, of solitude and open space. I'm always looking for simplicity, in my life and in my work. The Sinai is the most beautiful piece of earth I've ever had the chance to see. It's glorious and sacred. The power of nature is incredibly strong there, and I'm fascinated at how human beings adjust.

"I took this picture at a beach south of Nueba. It's inhabited by hippies and wild dogs. The freaks usually don't let photographers in because most of them are only looking for sensationalism, sex, nudity. So I buried my cameras in the sand and just lived with them for two weeks. Then I dug out the cameras, shot for three days and left.

"To me, this picture is relaxation, harmony, quiet. The four animals are so similar, lying in the sand at the end of a hot afternoon when the overpowering sun has finally set. They're trying not to move, to reduce the dehydration. Man, dogs, they're all just lying there, feeling the heat coming from Mother Earth. In the desert you can learn true humility.

"Look, this may sound naive or silly, but I believe the human being is good, even if he is inevitably corrupted by society. I am always seeking for the good and trying to express it, though sometimes it's necessary to show the opposite in order to do that. What I want is to present something that is maybe worth other people's striving for."

—Bonnie Boxer

OWENS, Bill.

Nationality: American. **Born:** San Jose, California, 25 September 1938. **Education:** San Juan High School, Citrus Heights, California, 1953-57; Chico State College, California, 1957-63, B.A. 1963. **Family:** Married Janet Louise Betonte in 1963 (divorced); sons: Andrew and Erik. **Career:** Served in the Peace Corps, 1964-66. Photographer for the *Livermore Independent,* California, 1968-78. Freelance photographer and publisher, Livermore, 1978-83; retired from photography to run his own brewpub in Hayward, California, 1983. **Recipient:** National Endowment for the Arts Grant, 1974, 1977, 1978, 1979; Guggenheim Fellowship in Photography, 1976. **Address:** Buffalo Bill's Brewery, 1082 "B" Street, Hayward, California 94541, U.S.A.

Individual Exhibitions:

1973	Oakland Art Museum, California
1974	Focus Gallery, San Francisco
1977	John Berggruen Gallery, San Francisco
	Drew University, Madison, New Jersey
1978	La Photo Galeria, Madrid
1979	Hippolyte Gallery, Helsinki

Selected Group Exhibitions:

1978   *Mirrors and Windows: American Photography since 1960,* Museum of Modern Art, New York (toured the United States, 1978-80)
          Tusen och En Bild/1001 Pictures, Moderna Museet, Stockholm
1980   *The Imaginary Photo Museum,* Kunsthalle, Cologne
1984   *Photography in California 1945-80,* San Francisco Museum of Modern Art (travelled to the Akron Art Museum, Ohio; Corcoran Gallery, Washington, D.C.; Los Angeles Municipal Art Gallery, Cornell University, Ithaca, New York; High Museum of Art, Atlanta, Georgia; Museum Folkwang, Essen; Centre Georges Pompidou, Paris; Museum of Photographic Arts, San Diego, California)
          La Photographie Créative, Pavillon des Arts, Paris
1985   *American Images 1945-80,* Barbican Art Gallery, London (toured Britain)

Collections:

Museum of Modern Art, New York; Oakland Art Museum, California; Bibliothèque Nationale, Paris; Museum Ludwig, Cologne.

Publications:

By OWENS: Books—*Suburbia,* San Francisco 1973; *Our Kind of People: American Groups and Rituals,* San Francisco 1975; *Working: I Do It for the Money,* New York 1977; *Documentary Photography: A Personal View,* Danbury, New Hampshire 1978; *Publish Your Photo Book,* Livermore, California 1979.

On OWENS: Books—*Mirrors and Windows: American Photography since 1960* by John Szarkowski, New York 1978; *Tusen och En Bild,* exhibition catalogue, by Ake Sidwell, Sune Jonsson and Ulf Hard af Segerstad, Stockholm 1978; *World Photography,* edited by Bryn Campbell, London 1983; *The Imaginary Photo Museum* by Helmut Gernsheim, Renate and L. Fritz Gruber and others, Cologne 1981, London 1982; *La Photographie Créative* by Jean-Claude Lemagny, Paris 1984; *Photography in California 1945-80* by Louise Katzman, San Francisco 1984; *Sammlung Gruber: Photographie des 20. Jahrhunderts,* exhibition catalogue, with foreword by Siegfried Gohr, Cologne 1984; *American Images: Photography 1945-1980,* edited by Peter Turner and John Benton-Harris, London 1985. **Article**—"Bill Owens" in *Camera* (Lucerne), March 1974.

*

The heart of photography is the documentary image, as it is a record of people, places and events. The challenge to the documentary photographer is the highest, as the photograph must be technically perfect and show how people live. The documentary photograph contains the symbols of our society and tells us about ourselves. This type of photography, if properly done, will stand the test of time.

—Bill Owens

* * *

Bill Owens is a lively, California former news photographer who widened his career, turning to self-publishing and helping others to do the same. His trademarks are a fast flow of words and ideas, a fine eye for the folkways of middle-class Americans, and the drive and enthusiasm of a revivalist preacher. His first book, *Suburbia,* sold more than 20,000 copies in 1973, something of a phenomenon at the time, and established Owens as a sort of Weegee of the middle class. *Suburbia* and its descendants, *Our Kind of People* and *Working: I Do It for the Money,* proved to be a kind of photographic litmus paper, testing the acidity of the viewer's attitude toward middle-class America. Some loved the books, some hated them for what each saw in the same groups of photographs of middle-class life.

Bill Owens's newpaper assignments led him into the lodge halls, senior citizens' meetings, business-group lunches, political meetings, school activities, church organizations and tract homes of Californians, in search of news pictures. His sensibility as a photographer led him to shoot his own pictures of these people—his peers—after he had finished his assignments for the newspaper. The people in Owen's photographs take themselves quite seriously for the most part, despite some of their activities in the pictures. And, for the most part, Owens is content not to quarrel with them, visually at least. His images are sharp, clean, well-lit; his subjects are engaged in everything from backyard barbecues to posing in beauty contests.

But, as a working photojournalist, Bill Owens has learned the value of words as corollaries to images. So, he shrewdly includes words, usually those of one or more of the subjects in his pictures, along with the images he presents. In this way, he stays neutral, non-judgemental of his subjects (except in choosing the words he quotes, of course). This neutrality forces the viewer to his own conclusions about what he is seeing and learning about the people in an Owens picture. Whether he loves them or scorns them depends, then, on the viewer's own background, ideas and ideals. In effect, Owens is merely reporting and not editorializing, he claims.

Here's an example of the Owens technique from *Our Kind of People* (subtitle: *American Groups and Rituals*). The photograph shows a line of U.S. beauty contest entrants in clinging, one-piece bathing suits on stage, backs to their audience and the viewer. The photograph is a straight record shot, non-committal. The accompanying text, presumably the words of one of the contestants, says, "A lot of people say we're chunks of meat, like cattle, but we're not. We're all individuals with dreams and aspirations like everybody else. Being a beauty contestant has taught me about myself, other people, poise and public speaking. If I had to do it over again, I would."

Is the photographer sympathetic or unsympathetic to his subject? Whichever you think, can you be sure from what you've seen and read? Or is the decision up to you? Owens's wit and insight have caused him to realize that the most effective editorializing forces the viewer to make his own decisions about the subject.

—Kenneth Poli

PABEL, Hilmar.

Nationality: German. **Born:** Rawitsch, Schlesien, 17 September 1910. **Education:** Studied photography at the Agfa-Fotoschule, Berlin, Dip.Photog. 1929; also studied German culture, philosophy, and journalism, under Emil Dovifat, University of Berlin, 1930-35. **Military Service:** Served in the German Army during World War II (prisoner of war, 1945). **Career:** Freelance photographer, then war correspondent for *Neuen Illustrierten Zeitung,* Berlin, 1935-40; photographer, documenting war-displaced children, for the Bavarian Red Cross and Rowohlt-Verlag publishers, Berlin and throughout Europe, 1945-47; Contract Photographer, *Quick* magazine, Munich, working in Indonesia, Japan, China, Formosa, Africa, Russia and the United States, 1948-60; Staff Photographer, *Stern* magazine, Hamburg, 1961-70. Freelance photographer, West Berlin, since 1970. Honorary Member, Photographic Academy, (Gesellschaft Deutsche Lichtbildne), and BFF, Stuttgart. Founder and sponsor of Hilmar Pabel School in Mueng Thong, Northeast Thailand. Lectures on photojournalism at Chulalongkorn University, Bangkok. **Recipient:** Culture Prize, Deutsche Gesellschaft für Photographie, 1961; World Press Photo Prize, The Hague, 1968; Die Goldene Blende Prize, *Bild der Zeit* magazine, 1972; Photojournalism Prize, Federal Republic of Germany, 1976; Bundesverdienstkreuz am Bande und 1 Klasse (Cross of Merit, Federal Republic of Germany). **Address:** Ratzing Haus 6, 83253 Rimsting/Chiemsee, Germany.

Individual Exhibitions:

1958   *Ich Fotografiere Menschen,* Staatlichen Landesbildstelle, Hamburg (toured West Germany)
1978   Stadtmuseum, Munich
1979   Galerie Nagel, West Berlin
1980   Museum Folkwang, Essen
        Karstadt, Hamburg
1983   Foto-Museum, Burghausen, Germany
1985   *Augenblicke,* Bildarchiv Preussischer Kulturbesitz, Berlin
1986   *Auf Marco Polos Spuren,* Herzogkasten Ingolstadt (toured West Germany for four years)
1992   *Yemen -Arabia Felix,* Sanaa

Selected Group Exhibitions:

1964   *World Exhibition of Photography: What Is Man?,* Pressehaus Stern, Hamburg (and world tour)
1968   *2nd World Exhibition of Photography,* Pressehaus Stern, Hamburg (and world tour)
1975   *Gesellschaft Deutscher Lichtbildner 1975,* Haus Industrieform, Essen, West Germany
1977   *Documenta 6,* Museum Fridericianum, Kassel, West Germany
1979   *Photographie als Kunst 1879-1979,* Tiroler Landesmuseum Ferdinandeum, Innsbruck, Austria (travelled to the Neue Galerie am Wolfgang Gurlitt Museum, Linz, Austria; Neue Galeria am Landesmuseum Joanneum, Graz, Austria; and Museum des 20. Jahrhunderts, Vienna)
1979   *Deutsche Fotografie nach 1945,* Kasseler Kunstverein, Kassel, West Germany
1983   *Die fotografische Sammlung,* Museum Folkwang, Essen, West Germany

1984   *Subjektive Fotografie: Images of the 50s,* San Francisco Museum of Modern Art (travelled to the University of Houston, Texas; Museum Folkwang, Essen; Vasterbottens Museum, Umea; Kulturhuset, Stockholm; Saarland Museum, Saarbrucken; Palais des Beaux Arts, Brussels
        Sammlung Gruber, Museum Ludwig, Cologne

Collections:

Museum Folkwang, Essen; Gesellschaft Deutsche Lichbildner, Cologne; Pressehaus Stern, Hamburg; Fotomuseum im Münchner Stadtmuseum, Munich; Museum Ludwig, Cologne; Bildarchiv Preussischer Kulturbesitz, Berlin; Foto-Museum der Stadt, Burghausen.

Publications:

By PABEL: Books—*Jahre unsereslebens,* Hamburg 1954; *Antlitz des Ostens,* Hamburg 1960; *Der Neben Dir,* Munich 1961; *Bilder der Menschlichkeit,* Munich/Lucerne, 1983; *Auf Marco Polos Spuren,* Munich, 1986; *Abenteuer Kanada,* Munich, 1987.

On PABEL: Books—*Ich Fotografiere Menschen,* exhibition catalogue, Hamburg 1958; *2nd World Exhibition of Photography,* exhibition catalogue, edited by Karl Pawek, Hamburg 1968; *Documenta 6/Band 2,* exhibition catalogue, by Klaus Honnef and Evelyn Weiss, Kassel and Cologne 1977; *Geschichte der Fotografie im 20. Jahrhundert/Photography in the 20th Century* by Petr Tausk, Cologne 1977, London 1980; *Photographie als Kunst 1879-1979/Kunst als Photographie 1949-1979,* exhibition catalogue, 2 vols., by Peter Weiermair, Innsbruck, Austria 1979; *Deutsche Fotografie nach 1945* by Floris Neusüss, Wolfgang Kemp and Petra Benteler, Kassel, West Germany 1979; *Fotografie 1919-1979, Made in Germany: Die GDL-Fotografen,* edited by Fritz Kempe, Bernd Lohse and others, Frankfurt 1979; *Eye Witness: 25 Years Through World Press Photos* by Harold Evans, London 1981; *Sammlung Gruber: Photographie des 20. Jahrhunderts,* exhibition catalogue, with foreword by Siegfried Gohr, Cologne 1984; *Subjektive Fotografie: Images of the 50s,* exhibition catalogue, by Ute Eskildsen, Manfred Schmalriede and Dorothy Martinson, Essen, West Germany 1984.

*   *   *

"I came to photojournalism because I am passionately interested in life and in people all around the globe. I would like to participate in their destiny and contribute to an understanding among them. I would like to help to prevent misfortune by reporting on the tragedy of war and the catastrophes that afflict innocent people." With this simple, short and very honorable statement, photo-reporter Hilmar Pabel describes the philosophy of his life's work with the camera. He has always been a reporter, and there has always been a war to which he has been assigned by some board of editors but on which he has also wished to report. Yet, nothing lies further from his thoughts than to make war heroic; on the contrary, he follows particular destinies, showing individual suffering in the midst of mass murder.

Though some of his best-known picture essays were done on the subject of war, Pabel has always been an all-round photojournalist. He was already at work for illustrated magazines before World War II. His first story appeared in the *Berliner Illustrirte Zeitung* in 1935—strangely with a photograph not taken by himself, but by chimpanzee Tiene of the Berlin Zoo, whom Pabel had given his camera. Tiene managed successfully to take a [slightly blurred] shot of human spectators behind zoo bars. . . . He was an experienced photographer

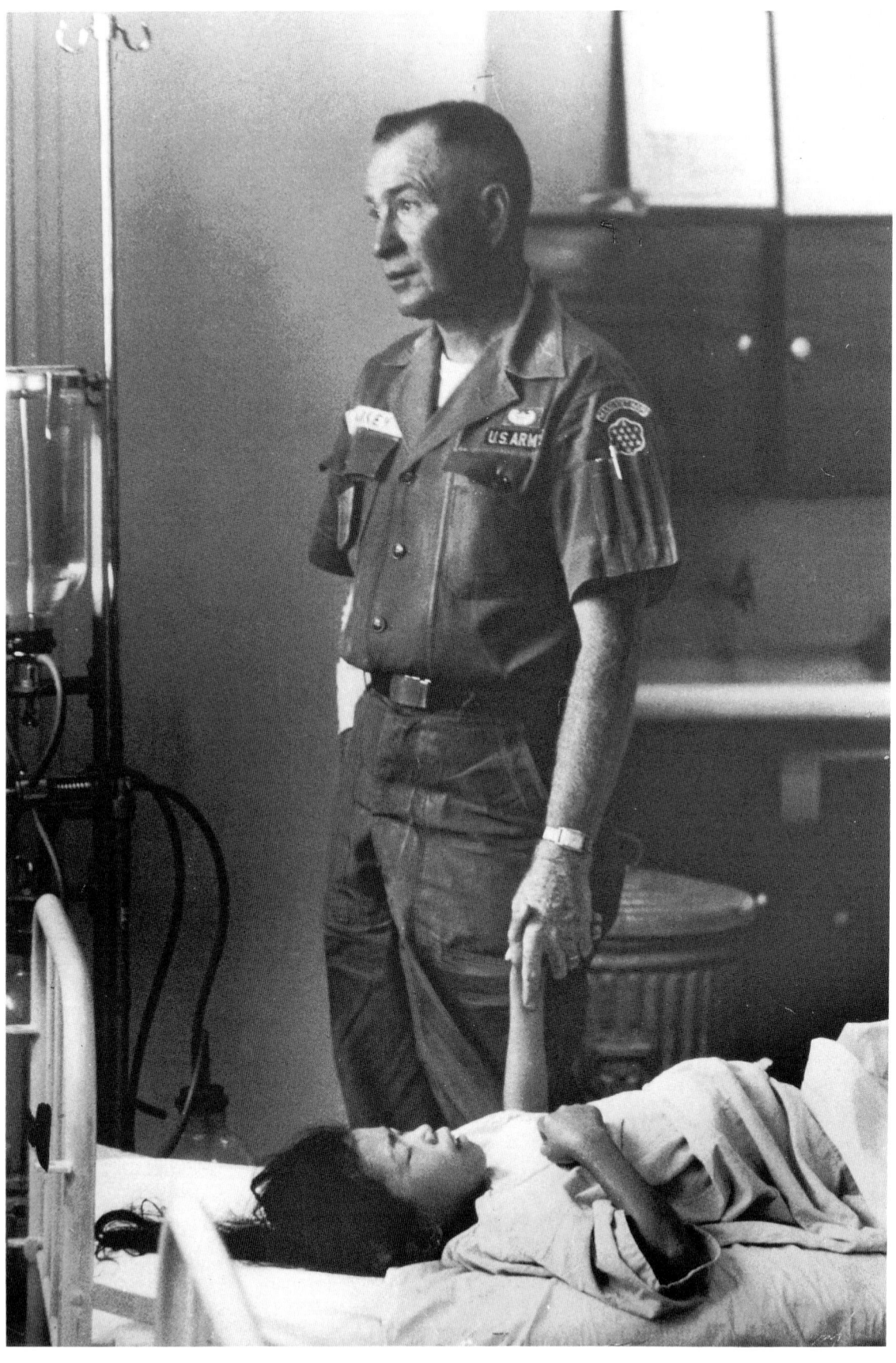

Colonel Markey with the Dying Child Little Orchid, **Mekong Delta, Vietnam, 1964.** Photograph ©Hilmar Pabel.

already when he was assigned as a war correspondent to take pictures for official magazines such as *Signal.* In 1945 he was taken prisoner of war, and right afterwards Pabel undertook an unusual commission that was not very tempting from the standpoint of artistic photography but humanly most rewarding: in the confusion of postwar Germany, he portrayed 2,000 children in orphanages in the effort to find possibly surviving relatives. After that assignment, he moved on to further journalistic work for the illustrated press, first for *Quick* (Munich), then for *Stern* (Hamburg), travelled throughout the world, produced a book of Far East photos, and finally reported on the Vietnam War. It was there in 1968 that Pabel photographed his famous "Die Kleine Orchidee" (The Little Orchid)—the death of a war wounded Vietnamese child whom an American doctor was not able to rescue. In the same year he covered the Russian invasion of Czechoslovakia, and for these photographs Pabel received First Prize in the World Press Photo Competition.

Pabel works unobtrusively, sympathetically, never seeking out the sensational. He has the eye, and the reactions, of the classical reporter. He works for himself and for his fellow creatures and not, in the end, for any picture press. When in 1980 he set out on a second journey to the border camps of Cambodian refugees in Thailand, he had previously collected through contributions a large sum of money for private relief measures.

In spite of the large number of his publications at home and abroad, and in spite of numerous prizes and honors, Hilmar Pabel has not yet been given the international recognition that he deserves—but that may well be due to his personal modesty, not to the quality of his photography.

The Far East, China, Japan, Thailand, the Philippines, India—these countries have become Pabel's favourite places to photograph in recent years, sometimes with an assignment for *Geo* or another magazine. Full of energy at the age of 76 when he returned from some months of colour photography in China, his historically and aesthetically significant negatives were recently acquired by the Bildarchiv Preussischer Kulturbesitz in Berlin.

—Hans Christian Adam

PALFI, Marion (Hermine Serita).

Nationality: American. **Born:** Born, of Hungarian parents, in Berlin, Germany, 21 October 1907; emigrated to the United States, 1940: naturalized, 1944. **Education:** Educated in Berlin until 1932; also trained as a dancer, in Berlin, 1930-34; self-taught in photography. **Family:** Married Martin Magner in 1954. **Career:** Worked as a model and film actress, Berlin, 1932-34; photographic apprentice in a commercial portrait studio, Berlin, 1934-35; freelance industrial and magazine photographer, Berlin, and in Turkey, Lebanon, Syria and Iraq, 1935-36; freelance portrait photographer, establishing own studio, Amsterdam 1936-40; worked as a photo-finisher, Pavelle Laboratories, Los Angeles, 1940-44; freelance professional social documentary photographer, Los Angeles, working for *Ebony* magazine, New York Children's Committee, New York Advisory Committee for the Aged, etc., 1945-78. Instructor in Photographic Social Research, Inner City Institute, Los Angeles, 1971-78. **Recipient:** Council Against Intolerance in America Award, 1945; Ministry of Education Award, Haiti, 1945; Rosenwald Fellowship, 1946; Children's Bureau Award, Federal Security Administration, Washington, D.C., 1950; Government of the Netherlands Award, 1953; New York Mayor's Advisory Committee for the Aged Award, 1956; Taconia Foundation Award, 1963; Guggenheim Fellowship, 1967; National Endowment for the Arts Photography Fellowship, 1974. **Died:** (in Los Angeles), 4 November 1978.

Individual Exhibitions:

1945   *Great American Artists,* Norlyst Gallery, New York
        Museum of Port-au-Prince, Haiti
1949   *Children in America,* New York Public Library (toured the United States, 1949-52)
1953   *Photography: Its Artistic and Social Value,* Curacao, Dutch West Indies (travelled to Aruba)
1961   New School for Social Research, New York

1966   California Art Institute, Los Angeles
1968   *I Too Am America,* Inner City Cultural Center, Los Angeles
1970   El Camino College, Torrance, California
1973   *Invisible in America,* Witkin Gallery, New York
        Invisible in America, University of Kansas, Lawrence (travelled to the Pasadena Art Museum, California, and Friends of Photography, Carmel, California, 1974)
1974   *The Language of Light,* University of Kansas, Lawrence
        Public Landscapes, Museum of Modern Art, New York
1978   Women's Building, Los Angeles

Selected Group Exhibitions:

1974   *Femmes Photographes,* Bibliothèque Nationale du Quebec, Montreal
1975   *Women of Photography,* San Francisco Museum of Art (toured the United States, 1975-77)
        There Is No Female Camera, Neikrug Gallery, New York
        6th Anniversary Show, Witkin Gallery, New York
1976   *Women Look at Women,* Library of Congress, Washington, D.C. (toured the United States)
        Photographic Definitions, Los Angeles Institute of Contemporary Art
1979   *Fotografie in Nederland 1920-40,* Haags Gemeentemuseum, The Hague
        10th Anniversary Show, Witkin Gallery, New York
        Photographic Directions: Los Angeles 1979, Security Pacific Bank Plaza, Los Angeles

Collections:

Palfi Archive, Center for Creative Photography, University of Arizona, Tucson; University of Kansas, Lawrence; Museum of Modern Art, New York; New York Public Library; University of Colorado, Boulder; San Francisco Museum of Modern Art; Museum of Port-au-Prince, Haiti.

Publications:

By PALFI: Books—*Suffer Little Children,* New York 1952; *Invisible in America,* with text by James Enyeart, and a foreword by Lee D. Witkin, Lawrence, Kansas 1973; *Marion Palfi: Language of Light,* Lawrence, Kansas 1974; *Silver See,* portfolio of 21 photos, with others, with an introduction by Victor Landweber, Los Angeles 1977. **Article**—"You Have Never Been Old" in *Transactions* (New York), March 1959.

On PALFI: Books—*Women of Photography: An Historical Survey,* edited by Margery Mann and Ann Noggle, San Francisco 1975; *Art: Anonymous Was a Woman!,* Valencia, California 1975; *Photographic Definitions,* exhibition catalogue, Los Angeles 1976; *Faces: A Narrative History of the Portrait in Photography* by Ben Maddow, Boston 1977; *A Ten Year Salute* by Lee D. Witkin, with a foreword by Carol Brown, Danbury, New Hampshire 1979; *Fotografie in Nederland 1920-40,* exhibition catalogue, by Kees Broos and Flip Bool, The Hague 1979; *The Photograph Collector's Guide* by Lee D. Witkin and Barbara London, Boston and London 1979; *Photographic Directions: Los Angeles 1979,* exhibition catalogue, with introduction by Robert Glenn Ketchum, Los Angeles 1979. **Articles**—in *Minicam Photography* (New York), July/August 1949; "Marion Palfi: Image of Social Change" by Jaki Beshears in *Artweek* (Oakland, California), 13 April 1974.

* * *

Marion Palfi practiced a form of advocacy photojournalism in which her own words and images, combined with textual material from other sources, were merged organically into extended statements on social, economic and political issues. She rejected the label of "documentarian," terming herself a "social research photographer"; her purpose was to provide that information and understanding necessary as the basis for change.

Unlike many of her contemporaries who worked in the documentary mode, Palfi never abandoned responsibility for the relationship between her imagery and its essential accompanying text, maintaining a commitment to exercising editorial control over the context of presentation of her work. In this she most resembled W. Eugene Smith, who also insisted on editorial autonomy of the photojournalist as one who bears witness, in the words of Oliver Wendell Holmes, to "the actions and passions of [her] time."

As a result of her refusal to relinquish control over her work, few of Palfi's extended essays have been published to date. Most of her "social researches" she funded herself; support also came from foundations, social work agencies, and other such organizations—the Rosenwald Foundation, the Council Against Intolerance in America, the Children's Bureau of the Federal Security Administration, the New York Children's Committee, the New York Mayor's Advisory Committee for the Aged and the Guggenheim Foundation among them. Through their sponsorship her works were presented in the forms of reports and exhibitions, serving very practical functions despite their lack of acceptance in the world of commercial publishing. According to James Enyeart, who assembled the major retrospective and monograph on her work, *Invisible in America,* her essays were "twice used by Congress for the enactment of laws that have affected the poor and those subjected to discrimination."

Known to and ardently supported by such diverse figures as Eleanor Roosevelt, Langston Hughes, Edward Steichen and John Collier, Sr., Palfi addressed many of the major issues of her era. Racial discrimination was the subject of *There Is No More Time* and *That May Affect Their Hearts and Minds;* the dispossession of the American Indian was the theme of *My Children, First I Liked the Whites, I Gave Them Fruit...,* which concerns the Hopi, Navajo and Papago tribes; *You Have Never Been Old* examines the plight of the aged in the United States; and *Suffer Little Children*—the only one of her essays to achieve publication in full during her lifetime—is a painful scrutiny of the children of poverty in America.

Despite its general exclusion from the gallery-museum circuit until late in her life, and notwithstanding its commercially "unpublishable" status, Palfi's work was unquestionably successful on its own terms. Coherent, purposeful and pointed, it provided effective ammunition in the ongoing struggle against social injustice on many fronts; its maker was able to direct its usage and to witness its consequence in her time.

—A. D. Coleman

PANJIAR, Prashant.

Nationality: Indian. **Born:** Calcutta, India, 30 March 1957. **Education:** St. Michael's High School, Patna; Fergusson College, Poona, 1973-77; studied political science at Poona University, 1977-81. **Family:** Married Ragini Shankar Deshpande in 1982; son, Rohan. **Career:** Carried out sociological research and photographed peasant communities in the Bihar region 1977-78, then worked as a commercial photographer in Poona 1979-81. Research and photography for book on banditry in central India 1981-83. Freelance photojournalist based in Delhi, 1983-84; photojournalist with the *Patriot* newspaper group in Delhi, 1984-86. Since 1986 has worked as a photojournalist with the fortnightly *India Today,* in Delhi. **Addresses:** C 58 South Extension II, New Delhi 110049, India; *India Today,* F14/15 Connaught Place, New Delhi 110001, India.

Individual Exhibitions:

1984   *Kampuchea Lives Again,* All India Fine Arts and Crafts
        Society, New Delhi, India and Gorky Sadan, Calcutta, India

Selected Group Exhibitions:

1987   *The Endless Wheel—Photography in India,* Schulwarte, Bern,
        Switzerland (travelled to Museum of Trade, Zürich and
        Musée d l'Elysée, Lausanne, Switzerland; Rautenstrauch,
        Cologne, and Ferrari House, Munich, Germany)
1989   *Artists Alert,* Rabindra Bhawan, New Delhi, India
1990   *Second All India Exhibition of Photography,* Chandigarh, India

1991   *Rajiv Gandhi,* All India Fine Arts and Crafts Society, New
        Delhi, India

Publications:

BY PANJIAR: Books—*The Survivors—Kampuchea 1984,* India 1984; *Malkhan—The Story of a Bandit King,* India, 1985; Photographs in: *Das Endlose Rad—Photographie in Indien* by Tim Besserer and Dieter Koeve, Zürich, 1987; *India's Bandit Queen* by Mala Sen, UK, 1991; *Rajiv* by Sonia Gandhi, India, 1992.

ON PANJIAR: Article—Interview by Tim Besserer in *Das Endlose Rad,* Zürich, 1987.

*

The experiences of ordinary people and their struggles have always formed the core of my photographic concerns. For many years I have been working as a full-time photojournalist, doing a mix of news stories and features, both national and international. Over the years my work has evolved in such a way that I find I am concentrating on (and getting more personal satisfaction from) social documentary photography.

Through my photographic work I endeavour to focus on the complexities of the human situation and to convey the emotions and feelings of ordinary people.

—Prashant Panjiar

PAOLINI, Améris M(anzini).

Nationality: Brazilian. **Born:** Améris Manzini in São Paulo, 22 December 1945. **Education:** Ginasio Cristo Rei, São Paulo, 1955-60; did secretarial studies at Mackenzie Institute, São Paulo, 1960-63; studied Italian at the Italian-Brazilian Institute, São Paulo, 1964-67; studied photography, under Uli Bruhn, Institute of Arts and Decoration (IADE), São Paulo, 1970, and under Claudio Kubrusly, Cristiano Mascaro and Maureen Bissiliat, at the Enfoco School of Photography, São Paulo, 1970-72; studied English, University of New York, 1971; advanced photographic technique, Camera Nikon School, São Paulo, 1972-73; Technical Photography Course, Lasar Segal Museum, São Paulo, 1974. **Family:** Married Ivo Paolini in 1968; children: Roberta, Fabio and Sandra. **Career:** Worked as secretary, Swift of Brazil, S.A., São Paulo, 1965; Pfizer Corporation, São Paulo-Guarulhos, 1966-67; Texaco Brazil, S.A., São Paulo, 1967-68; Du Pont of Brazil, São Paulo, 1968. Freelance photographer, São Paulo, working for *Fotoptica, Iris* and *Photocamera* magazines, since 1976, and *Psicologia Agual,* since 1979. Lectured in photography, Zoom School, São Paulo, 1979-80. Member, Association of Graphic and Photographic Artists (AGRAF), São Paulo; Union of Photographers of São Paulo. **Agent:** Galeria Augusto Augusta, Rua Augusta 2161, São Paulo, Brazil.

Individual Exhibitions:

1975   *Slaughterhouses of Campos do Jordão,* Museu de Arte de
        São Paulo
1979   *Landscapes and Abstracts,* Galeria Fotografia, São Paulo-
        Campinas
1980   *Brick Makers,* Faculdade de Artes e Comunicões, São Paulo

Selected Group Exhibitions:

1975   *Ação Valeparaiba '75,* travelling exhibition, (toured Paraiba
        Valley)
        Greater São Paulo, Museu de Arte de São Paulo
1976   *Bienal Nacional '76,* São Paulo
1978   *Hecho en Latinoamerica,* Museo de Arte Moderna, Mexico
        City (travelled to *Venezia '79*)

Earthquake—Bihar, India, **August 1988.** Photograph ©Prashant Panjiar.

International Exhibition of Photography of Santo André, ABC, São Paulo

Pró. Mulher, Fundação Getúlio Vargas, São Paulo

1979　*Post Card Editions,* Galeria Augosto Augusta, São Paulo

Freetime, Fundação Nacional de Arte (FUNARTE), Rio de Janeiro

1980　*1. Triend de Fotografia,* Museu de Arte Moderna de São Paulo

1981　*Astrazione e Realtà,* Galleria Flaviana, Locarno, Switzerland

Collections:

Museu de Arte de São Paulo; Museu de Arte de Porto Alegre, Rio Grande do Sul, Brazil.

Publications:

By PAOLINI: Books—*Hecho en Latinoamerica,* editor, Mexico City 1978; *Memoria e Sociedade,* with others, edited by T.A. Querioz, São Paulo 1979. **Article**—"Depoimento" in *Iris* (São Paulo), April 1976.

On PAOLINI: Books—*Grande São Paulo/Greater São Paulo,* exhibition catalogue, by Roberto Freire and Claudia Andujar, São Paulo 1976; *Trienal de Fotografia,* exhibition catalogue, by Moracy de Oliveira, São Paulo 1980. **Articles**—"Améris Paolini" by Micheline Lagnado in *Fotoptica* (São Paulo), no. 74, 1976; "Améris Paolini" by Paulo R. Leandro in *Fotoptica* (São Paulo), no 75, 1976; "Depoimentos de 7 Fotografos" by Antonio H. Marques in *Iris* (São Paulo), April 1976; "Destruction at Campos de Jordão" by José Nogueira in *Iris* (São Paulo), November/December 1977; "Elderly

People" by José Nogueira in *Iris* (São Paulo), March 1979; "Fotografico da Scoprire" by Giuliana Scimé in *Progresso Fotografico* (Milan), July/August 1979; "Cartão Postal Entre Nessa" by Alberto Neute in *Akropol* (São Paulo), January/February 1980; "Fotografia" by Mauro R. Barros in *Visão* (São Paulo), 23 June 1980; "Realidade para o Espectador Construir" by Stefania Bril in *Oestado de São Paulo,* 13 July 1980.

*

To me, a photograph is essentially a "moment" without past or future. I consider my photographic work as a collection of "moments." There are some examples in which I attempt to display my professional concern with human activities and the presence of human beings (craftsmen at work, for instance)—"portraits" which are always trying to capture the most but never pretending to capture everything. Indeed, as complex as reality is, to capture everything in a single photographic image is impossible. An image is partial and subjective. The photographer is part of the photo; he interferes with reality. I attach most importance to sequences of photographs which reveal more interesting visual elements than a single photograph could suggest on its own.

—Améris M. Paolini

*　　*　　*

In an immense country of violent contrasts of attraction and repulsion, reality is reflected, multiplied and distorted as in a game with mirrors, and the true cannot be distinguished from the false, the imaginary, the exotic, the magical. Brazil is such a country. The Grand Hotel at Bahia, with its impressive size and luxury, is, in the eyes of the tourist, superimposed over cardboard huts, cancelling them out: the bright-colored postcard is ready made. Then there is the Rio Carnival, a powerful soporific for natives and foreigners alike. In such surroundings, there seem to be two traditional ways for the photographer to proceed—either to take on the gaudy surface of a world that is indeed full of visual excitement or enter fully into an alternative world of social, economic and political problems. The choice would seem to be between beautiful photography that is devoid of message and the somewhat bleak testimony of exposure. It is the accomplishment of Améris Paolini to have combined these two opposing attitudes, and to have done so with great originality within an unmistakable visual language all her own.

Aware of and sensitive to the real life around her, Paolini uses photography as an instrument of information, as a link between outer and inner life. The external facts—the actual conditions around her—stimulate a kind of social enquiry that she resolves by a subtle symbolism. The symbol is the expression of the emotional impact, of the personal reaction in the face of reality; and because it is a symbol, it is charged with universal meanings.

In fact, in all the thematic series that Paolini has completed so far— "Slaughterhouses of Campos do Jordão," "Old People's Shelters," "Brick Makers," etc.—the chosen subject becomes a symbol of her disquiet, the grief she feels about a human condition the wretchedness of which is almost beyond endurance. Even in those series in which there are no human figures— "Abstract Views of the Center of Sao Paulo"—there is always a disturbing element (the crooked hook, for instance) that breaks the broad serenity of the picture.

Quite uninfluenced by press photography, Paolini does not simply take pictures of people, events and objects as they appear to the eye of the beholder, but uses them to put over a profound message. Starting from the premise that reality is ambivalent and so impossible to record in a photo, she gets round the obstacle by drawing our attention to the concrete world—the subject represented—and playing with it so skilfully as to communicate her own vision, her own interpretation of the hidden reality.

Her pictures, then, can be read on two different levels: the first, the one we recognize immediately, has to do with our awareness of the objective world; the second is the message to be obtained from the visual representation. In this way photography, having once penetrated the surface of the concrete world and having resisted the temptation to be led astray to other goals, becomes a means of communicating ideas and sentiments.

The sepia coloring that Paolini prefers to the more classical black-and-white smooths the tonal contrasts and gives her pictures a magic touch of unreality. This too, this sepia color, itself becomes a symbolic key, perhaps the first key, to the interpretation of the message.

—Giuliana Scimé

PAPAGEORGE, Tod.

Nationality: American. **Born:** Portsmouth, New Hampshire, 1 August 1940. **Education:** Portsmouth High School, 1954-58; University of New Hampshire, Durham, 1958-62, B.A. in English literature 1962. **Family:** Married Pauline Whitcomb in 1962 (divorced, 1972). **Career:** Photographer since 1962; lived and worked in San Francisco and Boston, 1962-64; travelled and photographed in Spain and France, 1965; worked as a photographer's assistant, New York, 1966-68. Freelance photographer, New York, since 1968. Visiting Instructor in Photography, Parsons School of Design, New York, 1969-72; Visiting Instructor in Photography, Pratt Institute of Art and Cooper Union School of Art, New York, 1971-74; Adjunct Lecturer in Photography, Queens College, New York, 1972-74; Lecturer on Photography, Massachusetts Insitute of Technology, Cambridge, 1974-75; Lecturer on Visual Studies, Harvard University, Cambridge, Massachusetts, 1975-76. Walker Evans Visiting Professor of Photography, 1978-79, and since 1979 Professor of Photography, Yale University, New Haven, Connecticut. **Recipient:** Guggenheim Fellowship for Photography, 1970, 1977; Fellowship-Grant in Photography, National Endowment for the Arts, 1973, 1976. **Agent:** Daniel

Wolf Gallery, 30 West 57th Street, New York, New York 10019, U.S.A. **Address:** 6 Varick Street, New York, New York 10013, U.S.A.

Individual Exhibitions:

1973	Light Gallery, New York
1976	University of Colorado, Boulder
1977	Cronin Gallery, Houston
	Marin College, Kentfield, California
1978	Art Institute of Chicago
1979	Light Gallery, New York
1980	Stills Photography Group, Edinburgh
	Galerie Zabriskie, Paris
1981	Galerie Lange-Irschl, Munich
	Daniel Wolf Gallery, New York
	Sheldon Memorial Art Gallery, University of Nebraska, Lincoln
	Akron Art Museum, Ohio
1985	Daniel Wolf Gallery, New York

Selected Group Exhibitions:

1969	*Vision and Expression,* International Museum of Photography at George Eastman House, Rochester, New York (toured the United States)
1975	*14 American Photographers,* Baltimore Museum of Art
1976	*100 Master Photographs from the Collection of the Museum of Modern Art,* Museum of Modern Art, New York
1977	*10 Photographes Americains Contemporains,* Galerie Zabriskie, Paris
1978	*Mirrors and Windows: American Photography since 1960,* Museum of Modern Art, New York (toured the United States, 1978-80)
1979	*American Photography in the 70s,* Art Institute of Chicago
1980	*American Images,* Corcoran Gallery of Art, Washington, D.C.
1981	*Robert Frank Forward,* Fraenkel Gallery, San Francisco
1982	*Floods of Light,* The Photographers' Gallery, London (toured Britain)
1985	*American Images 1945-80,* Barbican Art Gallery, London (toured Britain)

Collections:

Museum of Modern Art, New York; Seagrams Collection, New York; Museum of Fine Arts, Boston; Yale University Art Gallery, New Haven, Connecticut; Princeton University, Princeton, New Jersey; Akron Art Museum, Ohio; Exchange National Bank, Chicago; Art Institute of Chicago; Museum of Fine Arts, Houston; Bibliothèque Nationale, Paris.

Publications:

By PAPAGEORGE: Books—*Public Relations: The Photographs of Garry Winogrand,* editor and wrote introduction, New York 1977; *Walter Evans and Robert Frank: An Essay on Influence,* New Haven, Connecticut 1981. **Articles**—"On Snapshots" in *Aperture* (Millerton, New York), vol. 19, no. 1, 1974; "Winogrand's Theater of Quick Takes" in the *New York Times Sunday Magazine,* 15 October 1977; "Aesthetics or Truth" in *Photo Communique* (Toronto), vol. 1, no. 6, 1980; "From Walker Evans to Robert Frank" in *Artforum* (New York), April 1981.

On PAPAGEORGE: Books—*The Snaphot,* edited by Jonathan Green, Millerton, New York 1975; *14 American Photographers,* exhibition catalogue, edited by Renato Danese, Baltimore 1975; *Courthouse,* edited by Richard Pare, New York 1978; *American Images: New Work by 20 American Photographers,* edited by Renato Danese, New York 1979; *Floods of Light: Flash Photography 1851-1981,* exhibition catalogue, edited by Rupert Martin, London 1982; *American Images: Photography 1945-1980,* edited by Peter Turner and John Benton-Harris, London 1985. **Articles**—"Photographic Tapestry" by David Elliott in the *Chicago Daily News,* 9 February

1978; "Love-Hate Relations" by Leo Rubinfien in *Artforum* (New York), Summer 1978; "Tod Papageorge" by Rosalind Krauss in *Zabriskie Gallery Newsletter* (Paris), Spring/Summer 1980; "Papageorge's Natural Pauses" by Ben Lifson in the *Village Voice* (New York), 13 May 1981; in *Aperture* (Millerton, New York), no. 85, 1981.

*

As long as photographs are confused with their subjects, we are going to run in circles when we discuss them. This is not to suggest that photographers do not use the camera's mimetic gifts to seduce us: that is where photography—and the photographer's fascination with the medium—begins. Neither could I say that there are not serious photographers, perhaps most of them, who believe that their pictures are true and faithful recordings of the world—or at least believe it at home, away from the frustrating problems of making pictures that seem clear and intentional. Nor will it do to ignore the fact that, unlike other pictures, photographs describe things that once actually stood or moved in front of a machine, and therefore ate memories as well as pictures. None of this, however, denies that photographs *are* pictures, peculiar half-fictions that rise from moments and trace only the surface of things.

This, of course, is a simple point: that the truth photographs contain is at best an adjusted truth, a mediated truth, a collaboration between the photographer, his subject and, finally, photography itself. To extend this, I would suggest that this collaboration is something like the one a poet works with as he attempts to define his experience with language. In fact, I think about photography as a kind of language, one that claims and yet transforms what it describes in much the way that the words of a language both name and recreate their subjects. As W.H. Auden put it: "It is both the glory and the shame of poetry that its medium is not its private language, that a poet cannot invent his words"—something that can as truthfully be said about the photographer and his relation to the importunate need of his medium to embrace our common world.

—Tod Papageorge

* * *

The rather grand dimensions of Tod Papageorge's success in the 1970s are implicit in critics' praise for him: "gorgeous," "pristine," "perfection . . . cold and glittering" critics call his clear, sunny images. Nothing if not self-consciously photographic, and a master teacher and critic of his medium, Papageorge goes beyond formalist experimentation and takes the risk of engagement with the natural and social worlds, with families, beauty, love, and lust as he finds them in his leafy parks, motel pools, beaches and celebrations.

Papageorge's American quotidian associates him with the camera work descended from (in Papageorge's words) Walker Evans' "magisterial and emblematically just" images of America in the 1930s and Robert Frank's claim not only to this lineage but also to a special understanding of it: in his careful, image-by-image comparison of iconography in *Walker Evans and Robert Frank: An Essay on Influence,* Papageorge serves photography in a special way, a way that perhaps only a photographer can, by articulating for the medium the kind of tradition that a practitioner feels it deserves. Frank was not, Papageorge asserts, a "Rimbaud of photography, an anarchic poet who . . . suddenly appeared, flared and then was lost to sight." Rather, his work had precedence in his "knowledge and love" of Evans' work—just as, Papageorge's argument of course implies, the new work of Winogrand, Friedlander, Papageorge and their students can and must be enhanced by appreciation of their own precedents.

Despite his appreciation, however, Papageorge's projects seem to stop short of the ambitions he attributes to his mentors. There is in Papageorge's work nothing recalling the fierce silence that concentrates in the very buildings of Evans' empty southern towns, nor do we recognize allusion to Frank's angry, opaque blur. Perhaps lacking as yet faith in his powers to express strong feelings, Papageorge deals for now in the minor emotions.

Yet, if Papageorge eschews the great, general, inevitably ambiguous and not entirely expressible themes that seem to describe or symbolize a whole country, a whole culture, it is his special gift to present what critic Ben Lifson calls the dream of "nature stilled." Papageorge's truthful photographs remind us by their photographic consciousness and the pleasures they offer that no matter how like nature they seem, such photographs are lovely fictions, never to fulfill the promise of quotidian beauty that they ironically extend.

—Maren Stange

PARKER, Olivia.

Nationality: American. **Born:** Olivia Hood in Boston, Massachusetts, 10 June 1941. **Education:** Winsor School, Boston, 1951-59; studied art history at Wellesley College, Massachusetts, 1959-63, B.A. 1963; mainly self-taught in photography. **Family:** Married John O. Parker in 1964; children; John and Helen. **Career:** Freelance photographer, Massachusetts, since 1971. Artist-in-Residence, Aegean School of Fine Arts, Paros, Greece 1985. Trustee, Friends of Photography, Carmel, California, 1981-1992, Concord Academy, Massachusetts, 1984-1988, MacDowell Colony since 1988 and Art Institute of Boston since 1992. **Recipient:** Artists Foundation Fellowship, 1978; Grant from New Works Commission, The Photographic Resource Center, Boston, MA, 1981. **Agent:** Wooster Gardens-Brent Sikkema, 252 Lafayette Street, New York, New York 10012, U.S.A. **Address:** 229 Summer Street, Manchester, Massachusetts 01944, U.S.A.

Individual Exhibitions:

1973	Harvard Business School, Cambridge, Massachusetts
1976	Vision Gallery, Boston
	Nesto Gallery, Milton, Massachusetts
1977	Vision Gallery, Boston
	F22 Gallery, Santa Fe, New Mexico
1978	Light Work, Syracuse, New York
	Archetype, New Haven, Connecticut
1979	Yuen Lui Gallery, Seattle
	Focus Gallery, San Francisco
	Friends of Photography, Carmel, California
	University of Vermont, Burlington
	The Photography Place, Philadelphia
	Portland Museum Art School, Oregon
	Vision Gallery, Boston
1980	Portland School of Art, Maine
	Marcuse Pfeifer Gallery, New York
	Rhode Island School of Design, Providence
	Bennington College, Vermont
	Halsted Gallery, Birmingham, Michigan
	Boston Atheneum
	Work Gallery, Zurich
	Wesleyan University, Middletown, Connecticut
1981	International Museum of Photography, George Eastman House, Rochester, New York
	Friends of Photography, Carmel, California
	Orange Coast College, Costa Mesa, California
	Clarence Kennedy Gallery, Cambridge, Massachusetts (with William Wegman and Willard Van Dyke)
	Visions Gallery, London
	Camera Obscura, Stockholm
1982	Susan Spiritus Gallery, Newport Beach, California
	Baker Gallery, Kansas City, Kansas
	University of Oregon, Eugene
	Silver Image Gallery, Seattle, Washington
	Light Factory, Charlotte, North Carolina
	Brent Sikkema Inc./Thomas Segal, Boston
	Catskill Center for Photography, Woodstock, New York
	Weston Gallery, Carmel, California
	Art Institute of Chicago
	Edwynn Houk Gallery, Chicago
1983	Marcuse Pfeifer Gallery, New York
	Photo Gallery International, Tokyo
	Halsted Gallery, Birmingham, Michigan

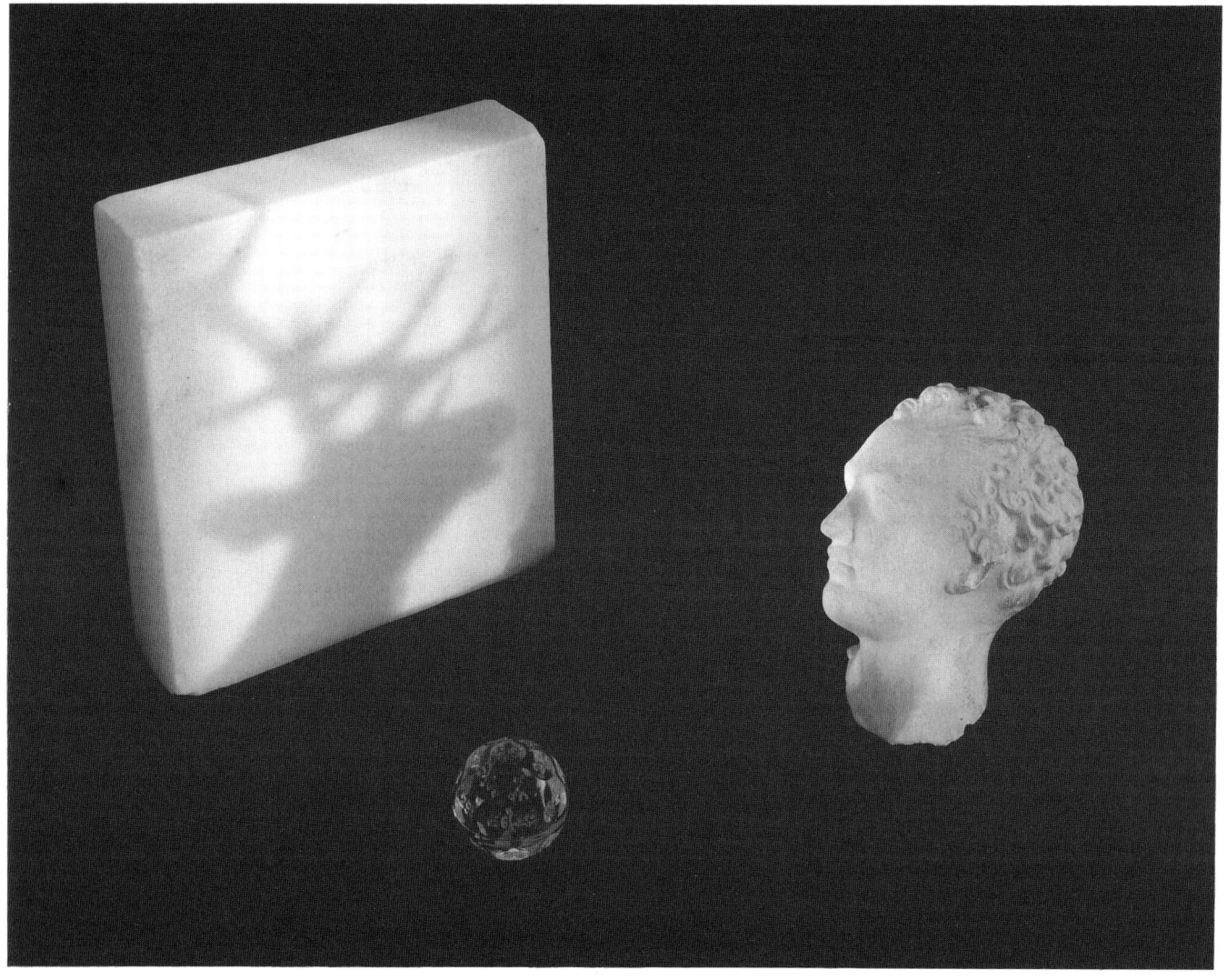

Heads, 1993. Photograph ©Olivia Parker.

Nihon University, Tokyo
Vision Gallery, Boston
Images Gallery, Cincinnati, Ohio
Images Gallery, Boulder, Colorado
New York State University, Plattsburg
Books and Company, New York
G. H. Dalsheimer Gallery, Baltimore, Maryland
1984   Silver Bullet Gallery, Providence, Rhode Island
Smith College, Northampton, Massachusetts
Lowe Art Gallery, Syracuse, New York
Allen Street Gallery, Dallas, Texas
Baker Gallery, Kansas City, Kansas
Photo Gallery International, Tokyo
1985   Fotografie Forum, Frankfurt
Durham Photographic Arts Society, North Carolina
Jones Troyer Gallery, Washington, D.C. (with John Divola and
    Reed Estabrook)
Delta College Galleria, University Center, Michigan
Houston Center for Photography, Texas
1986   Vision Gallery, Boston, Massachusetts
Fotofest, Amsterdam
College of The Redwoods, Eureka, California
Robert Koch Gallery, San Francisco

1987   Photo Gallery International, Tokyo
University of Dayton, Ohio
Ginny Williams Gallery, Denver, Colorado
Picture Photo Space, Osaka, Japan
Texas Woman's University, Denton
Nueva Imagen Gallery, Pamplona, Spain
Circulo Bellas Artes, Madrid
McKissick Museum, University of South Carolina, Columbia
Montserrat College of Art, Beverly, Massachusetts
Vision Gallery, Boston
1988   Hood Museum of Art, Dartmouth College, Hanover, New
    Hampshire
Tweed Museum of Art, Duluth, Minnesota
Lieberman & Saul, New York
1989   Catherine Edelman Gallery, Chicago
University Art Gallery, SUNY, Albany, New York
Huntsville Museum of Art, Alabama
Scheinbaum and Russek, Santa Fe, New Mexico
1990   The Photographers' Gallery, London
Middle Tennessee State University, Murfreesboro
Tower Fine Arts Gallery, SUNY Brockton, New York
1991   Parco Gallery, Tokyo

Brent Sikkema Fine Art, New York
Green Hall, Sagamihara City, Japan
1992   ICAC/Weston Gallery, Tokyo
1993   Light Impressions, Rochester, New York
Fitchburg Art Museum, Massachusetts
Vision Gallery, San Francisco
Robert Klein Gallery, Boston

Selected Group Exhibitions:

1978   *14 New England Photographers,* Museum of Fine Arts, Boston
One of a Kind: Polaroid Color, Corcoran Gallery, Washington, D.C. (toured the United States)
1979   *20 x 24 Light,* Light Gallery, New York
1980   *Nouvelle Nature Morte,* Galerie Viviane Esders, Paris
Farbwerke, Kunsthaus, Zurich
1981   *Photographer as Printmaker,* Ferens Art Gallery, Hull, Yorkshire (travelled to the Museum and Art Gallery, Leicester; Cooper Gallery, Barnsley; Castle Museum, Nottingham; Photographers' Gallery, London)
1982   *Color as Form,* International Museum of Photography at George Eastman House, Rochester, New York
1983   *Student Choice,* Yale University, New Haven, Connecticut
1985   *American Images 1945-80,* Barbican Art Gallery, London (toured Britain)
Boston Now: Photography, Institute of Contemporary Art Boston
1986   *In Spite of Everything, Yes,* Hood Museum of Art, Hanover, New Hampshire
The Poetics of Space, Museum of Fine Arts, Museum of New Mexico, Santa Fe
1987   International Center of Photography, New York
1988   Jones Troyer Gallery, Washington D.C.
The Arts Club of Chicago
1989   Fogg Art Museum, Harvard University
Natuurhistorisch Museum, Leiden, Netherlands
Object as Subject, Turman Gallery, Indiana State University
1990   The Artists' Foundation, Boston
1991   Fitchburg Art Museum, Massachusetts
The Art Institute of Chicago
1992   Anderson Ranch, Snowmass, Colorado
Museum of Fine Arts, Boston
1993   *Close-Up/Still Life,* Museum of Fine Arts, Boston

Collections:

Museum of Modern Art, New York; Metropolitan Museum of Art, New York; Museum of Fine Arts, Boston; Addison Gallery of American Art, Andover, Massachusetts; Smith College, Northampton, Massachusetts; Polaroid Corporation, Cambridge, Massachusetts; Wellesley College, Massachusetts; Art Institute of Chicago; Phoenix College, Arizona; Portland Art Museum, Oregon; Detroit Institute of Arts; Indiana University Art Museum; Vassar College; International Museum of Photography at George Eastman House; Whitehead Institute; Fogg Museum, Harvard University; De Cordova Museum' National Museum of Australia, Canberra; The Victoria and Albert Museum, London; Preus Fotomuseum, Norway; The Israel Museum; The St Louis Art Museum; Bibliotheqe National, Paris; San Francisco Museum of Modern Art; University of Iowa Art Museum; Art Museum, Rhode Island School of Design; Nihon University, Tokyo, Japan; Hood Museum of Art, Dartmouth College; Santa Barbara Museum of Art; Museum of Fine Art, St. Petersburg, Florida; Rose Art Museum, Brandeis University, Waltham, Mas-

sachusetts; University of Oklahoma Art Museum, Norman, Oklahoma; High Museum, Atlanta, Georgia; Bowdoin College Art Museum; Princeton University Art Museum; Milwaukee Museum of Art; California Museum of Photography, Riverside; Tokyo Fuji Art Museum, Tokyo; Museum of Fine Arts, Houston, Texas; Yale University Art Museum.

Publications:

By PARKER: Books—*Signs of Life,* Boston 1978; *Under the Looking Glass,* Boston and London 1983; *Weighing The Planets,* New York, 1987. **Articles**—"Split-Toning" in *Darkroom Dynamics,* edited by Jim Stone, New York and London 1979; "Olivia Parker: Interview," with Eelco Wolf, in *Photo Show* (Los Angeles), September 1980; "New England Landscapes" in *Printletter* (Zurich), January/February 1981.

On PARKER: Books—*One of a Kind: Polaroid Color,* edited by Belinda Rathbone, Boston 1979; *The Print* by Time-Life editors, New York 1981; *Photographer as Printmaker,* exhibition catalogue, with texts by Gerry Badger, Peter C. Bunnell and Ansel Adams, London 1983; *Color as Form: A History of Color Photography,* exhibition catalogue, with introduction by Robert A. Sobieszek, Rochester, New York 1982; *Object and Image* by George M. Craven, New York 1982; *The Library of World Photography: Photography as Fine Art,* with introduction by Douglas Davis, Tokyo 1982, 1983, London 1983; *World History of Photography* by Naomi Rosenblum, New York 1984; *American Images: Photography 1945-1980,* edited by Peter Turner and John Benton-Harris, London 1985; *8 Visions,* edited by Gyoh Suzuki, Tokyo, 1988; *The Modernist Still Life-Photographed,* by Jean S Tucker, St. Louis, 1989; *Flora Photographica,* by William Ewing, London, 1991. **Articles**—"Olivia Parker" by Jacqueline Brody in *Print Collector's Newsletter* (New York), November/December 1977; "The Clear Yankee Eye" by Owen Edwards in *Saturday Review* (New York), March 1979; "Signs of (Still) Life" by Vicki Goldberg in *American Photographer* (New York), May 1979; "Olivia Parker" by Owen Edwards in *American Photographer* (New York), February 1980; "Photography" by Hilton Kramer in the *New York Times,* 29 February 1980; "Shaping Color to Sensibility" by David Featherstone in *Modern Photography* (New York), March 1980; "Today's American Works" in *Photo Japan* (Tokyo), February 1985; article by Susan Weiley in *Art News,* October, 1985; article by Henry Horenstein in *Popular Photography,* December, 1986; article by Evelyn Roth in *American Photographer,* January, 1987; article by Charles Giuliano in *Center Quarterly,* Volume II, no. 3, 1990; review by Nancy Stapen in *Art News,* December, 1993.

*

I will not attempt to explain the meaning of my photographs in verbal terms, because my process is visual, but I can suggest what is on my mind.

I am interested in the way people think about the unknown. For most of human history people have looked to the spirit world to explain what was going on. Animals floated in the night sky and each object had its own "Anima Motrix," its own moving spirit. By the seventeenth century clockwork explanations begin to invade the spirit world, opening doors to modern physics. New ideas form, the old are shattered, and sometimes old ideas pop up again among the new like graffiti on a wall. All is uncertainty and change, but optimists and bingo players are on the lookout for moments of perfect knowledge and perfect cards.

In thinking about the way we understand both contemporary objects and old objects as well as the way people have understood objects at different points in time, I wonder at the vast changes in the human world in an instant of geologic time. In the past, people primarily had to make sense out of the natural world. Increasingly there is a man-made landscape too, some of it beneficial and some of it unforeseen and chaotic. We are learning the rules of the forest, but we know little about the rules of the city dump. Reading objects, archaeologists search for meaning in bones, earth and stone. Today, some anthropologists try to figure us out by checking our garbage. What if each cereal box, grapefruit rind and hubcap were perceived to have its own moving spirit?

Objects rich in human implications are the ones that interest me. I work intuitively, but only part of the time. There is a fluctuation between visual intuition and an editorial process that presses me to throw out what is not working and to go beyond the content level of individaul objects. The objects become a language for me. My intention is not to document objects but to see them in a new context, where they take on a presence dependent on the world within each photograph. Often I use old objects, for as the Polish artist Magdalena Abakanowicz said, ''I am much more interested in an old piece of burlap than a new one, for the beauty of an object is to me, in the quantity of information I can get from it, the stories it has to tell.'' If I use new or organic materials they become interesting only in context; a bone and a machine part must transform each other.

I do not choose objects for sentimental reasons. With the exception of a few rocks, none of them are from childhood collections, and none came from the family attic. I claim no control over other people's attics, their contents and associations. Although I do not use actual objects from my childhood, I am interested in remembered stories and games. No matter how bizarre, a story or photograph can work if its own world rings true. A child's game can be a rehearsal for adult activities, a way of understanding or misunderstanding them, as in playing house and playing war. Games can explore and lead off the map. In the game of telephone, a word starts then ends up as another the same way an image starts and changes in multiple generations on a copier. In the world of play, magic and alchemy are still possible. The rabbit disappears; shadows slide off a page. Light burns white. Light burns black. At the edge of imagination there is a black sun.

Light and silver transform all that is photographed, and yet we expect a photograph to be closer than a painting or a drawing to what we think is real. My constructions do not exist as permanent pieces; they vanish after I make the photograph. Shadows move as the sun moves; flowers decay; forms alter as the light shifts; objects rendered transparent when they are removed during an exposure become solid again. Objects and texts placed on a photocopier yield images of reduced information that I often use as part of my pictures. Also, the toned silver prints are different from what my eye sees in front of the camera because of the character of the print medium I have chosen. The photograph is a tranformation of what I see, caught on an edge in a delicate balance.

—Olivia Parker

*   *   *

Photography, as all of the myriad things we experience during our lives, must be seen in the context of all that has occurred before and all that is yet to come. Olivia Parker is captivated by time and its ceaseless cyclic journeys between life and death and regeneration.

Parker has incorporated in her still-life photographs some of the best artistic traditions. Like the 17th-century Dutch and Flemish painters, whose soft reflective lighting and static arrangements of time-pieces, bottles, and commonplace objects of the day gave still-life painting prestige, Parker has adapted similar aesthetic technique in a number of her 8 by 10 and 20 by 24 Polaroid photographs. Parker's photographs, comprised of objects that are antique, perhaps old photographs against peeling backgrounds, are then combined with the riotous color of flowers picked at that moment or fruit ripest before rotting. In addition, her choice of daylight and tungsten lights allows Parker to conjure up a world remote from our own experiences, the very essence of which nostalgia is born.

Just as 19th-century photographer Charles Aubry looked to 18th-century painter Jean Baptiste Chardin for inspiration on the transitoriness of life in the pictured world versus the real world, so has Olivia Parker benefited from both these artists. Chardin, a Frenchman and possibly one of the finest 18th-century painters, is renowned for his unsurpassed ability to evoke textures in paintings of vegetables, fruits, and game. His use of muted tone, delicate touch, and compositional skill can be seen as an influence in Parker's early work that appeared in the monograph *Signs of Life*. Taken with a view camera, the photographs of subjects ranging from ballet slippers to feathers and parts of radiators to collage combinations that result in whimsically dancing pea-pods on a part of a line drawing of a classical column, combine that personal sensitivity and placement. The crowning touch, however, comes from her contact printing on silver-chloride paper, leaving the opaque richness of the negative carrier as her framework, and then selenium toning the photograph for anywhere from four to twelve minutes. This process, which she calls ''split-toning,'' produces the most sensual tonalities in the beige-gray-platinum gradations of the light areas and a rich brown-gray in the dark areas. Her choice of subject matter in these photographs seems at once to be intensely personal poetry, images evocative of interior dreams and reverently preserved delicate objects.

Charles Aubry, himself successful for his arrangement of elements in such a way as to make details stand out by placing them in direct contrast to one another, can be seen as another predecessor and influence of Parker's in the still-life aesthetic tradition. Her choice of objects in each of her photographs can be seen by the observer at first as disparate, often contradictory and sometimes ironic juxtapositions. And yet, one or more elements can jolt the memory of the past, whether it be historical or personal, and the viewer is enamored with the richness of the metaphor presented.

The surrealism in a number of her photographs and the compartmentalized construction remind one of Joseph Cornell's boxes. Similar in the sense that his work was about a France he never visited, so too are Parker's images which include old, torn, and discarded photographs about a history that now exists only in nostalgic form. And just as the surrealist painters in Paris made the aesthetic pilgrimages to the flea markets of that city seeking beauty in ugliness and the cast-off pieces and discarded items of those times looking for collages in three dimensions, so has Parker sought to include in her photographs objects from attics and junk shops, gardens and greenhouses.

Parker's choice of the instant 8 by 10 or 20 by 24 Polaroid process for image-making fosters her visionary private concerns and forces a certain hermeticism. The givens of the system: virtual grainlessness, rich color, shallow depth of field, the scale factor, and the control of the studio setting are all beneficial and imperative for Parker's photographs.

Parker's chance associations in her photographs create ordered structures just as our minds suggest or more strongly demand. And just as Emily Dickinson, the New England poet, wrote of the themes of nature, love, death, and immortality, perhaps Olivia Parker's own New England roots and her training as a painter allow her to juxtapose the abstract with the concrete and the eternal with the impermanent.

—Monica Cipnic

PARKINSON, Norman.

Nationality: British. **Born:** Ronald William Parkinson Smith in Roehampton, London, 21 April 1913. **Education:** Westminister School, London, 1927-31; apprentice to the court photographers Speaight and Sons Ltd., Bond Street, London, 1931-33. **Family:** Married the actress and model Wenda Rogerson in 1945; son: Simon. **Career:** Opened own studio with Norman Kibblewhite,

Iman with Lucas Samaras Sculpture at Palm Beach, **1983.** Photograph ©Norman Parkinson Limited.

Dover Street, London, 1934; worked for the British edition of *Harper's Bazaar* and for *The Bystander,* 1935-40; did series of photographic essays for the British Armed Services recruitment drive, 1937-39, and reconnaissance photography over France for the Royal Air Force, 1940-45; a portrait and fashion photographer for *Vogue,* 1945-60; first advertising work, 1952; Associate Contributing Editor of *Queen,* 1960-64; moved to Tobago, 1963; currently, freelance photographer for *Vogue, Life, Elle, Town and Country,* etc. Also farmed in Gloucestershire, Worcestershire and Oxfordshire, 1937-60, and in Tobago, since 1964. **Recipient:** Lifetime Achievement Award, American Society of Magazine Photographers, 1983; Gold Award, 1984,

Silver Award, 1985, Design and Art Directors Association, London; Hasselblad Gold Award, Göteborg, Sweden, 1985. D.F.A.: University of Miami, Florida, 1986. Honorary Fellow, Royal Photographic Society, 1968; Fellow, International Institute of Photography, 1975. C.B.E. (Commander, Order of the British Empire), 1981. **Died:** 14 February 1990.

Individual Exhibitions:

1935   Parkinson Studio, Dover Street, London
1960   Jaeger Showrooms, London

1978   The Photographers' Gallery, London
1981   *50 Years of Fashion and Portraits,* National Portrait Gallery,
            London (retrospective)
1983   Sotheby's, New York
            International Center of Photography, New York (retrospective)
1985   *Notable Diamonds,* Art Institute of Chicago (travelled to
            Atlanta, Palm Beach, Detroit, Los Angeles, Dallas, Denver,
            New York, San Francisco and Houston, 1985-86)

Selected Group Exhibitions:

1937   *Exposition Internationale,* Paris
1957   *Biennale di Fotografia,* Venice
1972   *The Mask of Beauty,* National Portrait Gallery, London
1975   *Fashion 1900-1939,* Victoria and Albert Museum, London
            (toured the U.K.)
1977   *Happy and Glorious: 6 Reigns of Royal Photography,* National
            Portrait Gallery, London
1980   *The Queen Mother: A Celebration,* National Portrait Gallery,
            London
            Modern British Photography 1919-39, Museum of Modern
            Art, Oxford (toured the U.K.)
1983   *British Photography 1955-65,* The Photographers' Gallery,
            London
1984   *Sammlung Gruber,* Museum Ludwig, Cologne
1985   *Shots of Style,* Victoria and Albert Museum, London (toured
            Britain)

Collections:

National Portrait Gallery, London; Victoria and Albert Museum, London;
Museum Ludwig, Cologne; Sotheby's, London and New York; Hamilton
Gallery, London; National Museum of Photography, Bradford, Yorkshire.

Publications:

By PARKINSON: Books—*Sisters under the Skin,* with texts by several
authors, London 1978; *Fifty Years of Style and Fashion,* New York 1983, as
Lifework, London 1984; *Would Your Let Your Daughter . . . ?,* New York and
London 1985. **Articles**—"Vogue's Eye View of a Forthcoming Marriage:
Photographs by Norman Parkinson," interview with Polly Devlin, in *Vogue*
(London), November 1973; interview with Roger Clark, in *British Journal of
Photography Annual,* London 1982.

On PARKINSON: Books—*The Art and Technique of Color Photography: A
Treasury of Color Photographs by the Staff Photographers of Vogue, House
and Garden, and Glamour* by Alexander Liberman, with an introduction by
A.B. Louchheim, New York 1951; *Beauty: Variations on the Theme Woman
by Masters of the Camera—Past and Present,* edited by L. Fritz Gruber,
London and New York 1965; *Fashion 1900-1939,* exhibition catalogue, by
Valerie Lloyd and others, London 1975; *The Magic Image* by Cecil Beaton
and Gail Buckland, London and Boston 1975; *The History of Fashion
Photography* by Nancy Hall-Duncan, New York and Paris 1979; *Modern
British Photography 1919-39,* exhibition catalogue, by David Mellor, London
1980; *50 Years of Portraits and Fashion: Photographs by Norman Parkinson,*
exhibition catalogue, London 1981; *British Photography 1955-1965: The
Master Craftsmen in Print,* exhibition catalogue, by Sue Davies, Michael
Rand, Mark Boxer and others, London 1983; *Sammlung Gruber: Photographie
des 20. Jahrhunderts,* exhibition catalogue, with foreword by Siegfried Gohr,
Cologne 1984; *Shots of Style: Great Fashion Photographs Chosen by David
Bailey,* with text by Martin Harrison, London 1985; *Parkinson: Photographs
1935-1990,* by Martin Harrison, London, 1994.

*

I suppose I have had some success—people seem to enjoy my snaps and I
enjoy taking them.

I know very little about the *technique* of photography—all that is for the
expensive amateurs—but I require the camera to be my servant. I master it; it
does not intimidate me.

I have always been aware that the camera is almost as dangerous as a gun.
You can do almost as much damage with it. You can make people happy with
your camera or downright miserable. If you have the responsibility of using
your lens to record people for history, do it well. Everybody can look a little
handsome, a touch beautiful—record them that way. Don't mount them and
destroy them and make them look hideous for the sole purpose of inflating
your own photographic ego. No, don't do that.

Hide inside your photographs; enjoy them—make them enjoyable—make
your snaps full of happiness and sunshine and joy and desirability—it is not
easy but try.

—Norman Parkinson

*   *   *

Norman Parkinson, an "incurable romantic," is unequivocal in his belief
that photography is not art. He advises: "make your [portrait] snaps full of
happiness and sunshine and joy and desirability." While this may suggest a
limited understanding of the possibilities of his "craft," his talent is anything
but limited; for several decades Parkinson has been one of Britain's foremost
portrait and fashion photographers.

Not surprisingly, elegant models, the famous and the glamorous, are the
regular subjects of Parkinson's lens. Nevertheless, some of his work in the
1930s, most notably his poignant study of Welsh mining families during the
Depression, and his photographs for *The Bystander,* demonstrate a keen eye
for reportage.

The pre-war trend to outdoor settings for fashion photography had not
resulted, at least in Britain, in a "natural" look. If anything, the static models
posed at chic society haunts accentuated artificiality. Parkinson wanted
something livelier, and following the footsteps of his innovative European
counterparts, he tried to capture action and spontaneity. By the end of the
1930s he had become a master at suggesting movement in a still photograph.
His fashion work of this time marks a turning point in the genre.

Parkinson's fashion photographs of his wife Wenda Rogerson typify his
early post-war work. The model, smiling and demure, poised in unpretentious
settings, became a new image, one with which British followers of fashion
could readily identify. The new elegance seemed credible and accessible, a
breath of fresh air after the remote, often elitist images of pre-war *haute
couture.* The 1951 picture of his wife in cashmere twinset and pearls seated
next to a cowman in a village pub seems for a moment gimmicky; but the
juxtaposition works: Parkinson's odd couple catch your eye, then hold you
with their sober, unifying gaze. The surreal quality of much of his fashion
work of this period gradually gave way to a more vivacious, energetic style.
The fun and the frolic are attention-getters; the star, almost always, is the
clothes.

Norman Parkinson achieves some striking effects in his photographs of the
famous. Early in his career as a fashionable London photographer he turned
out the usual flattering studio plates that the debutantes of the day required.
But when circumstances permitted, he experimented with unusual compositions created by dramatic lighting arrangements.

One of Parkinson's most memorable works is his 1951 portrait of
Algernon Blackwood, the ghost story writer. Blackwood, seated on a balcony
high above Hyde Park, London, eerily props up his wrinkled head with his
outstretched hands. His hooded, gelatinous eyes stare skyward from dark
sockets; below the modern, mundane world—the gray traffic—slips by.

The 1952 close-up of Montgomery Clift is particularly telling: the
handsome forehead is puckered and careworn; the eyes pensive, puzzled; and
there's something indulgent about the mouth. Mercifully, Parkinson does not
heed his own advice. The Clift picture, like many others, is hardly full of
"happiness and sunshine," although Parkinson's portraits are always elegant
and attractive, and never over-earnest. He does not try to capture especially
"meaningful" expression; he is more interested in the composition, the shape
of the head and the hands, and the texture of skin and material.

As early as the 30s, Parkinson demonstrated a major talent for color
photography and he is still renowned in the field. Using very few colors—
some of his pictures are virtually monochromatic—he achieves some stunning, often highly romantic effects.

Parkinson's vitality, his self-deprecating humor, his delight in beauty but not in prettiness, and above all, his originality, are communicated through his work. Parkinson calls himself a craftsman; many would call him a consummate artist.

—Roland Turner

PARKS, Gordon (Alexander Buchanan).

Nationality: American. **Born:** Fort Scott, Kansas, 30 November 1912. **Education:** Attended public schools in St. Paul, Minnesota, 1918-28; self-taught in photography. **Wartime Service:** Served as a photographer with the Office of War Information, 1943-45. **Family:** Married Sally Alvis in 1933 (divorced, 1961); Elizabeth Campbell in 1962 (divorced, 1973); Genevieve Young in 1973; children: Gordon, Toni, David and Leslie. **Career:** Worked as a busboy, piano-player, lumberback, dining-car waiter and professional basketball player, St. Paul, 1928-37; freelance fashion photographer, Minneapolis, 1937-42; Staff Photographer, under Roy E. Stryker, Farm Security Administration, Washington, D.C. and throughout the United States, 1942-43; photographer and documentary filmmaker, under Stryker, Standard Oil Company of New Jersey, thoughout the United States and in Saudi Arabia, 1945-48; Staff Photographer, *Life* magazine, New York, 1948-61; independent photographer, film writer and director, working for *Show, Vogue, Venture,* and the film companies Warner Brothers/Seven Arts, Metro-Goldwin-Mayer and Paramount Pictures, 1962-71; Editorial Director, *Essence* magazine, New York, 1970-73. **Recipient:** Julius Rosenwald Fellowship in Photography, 1942; National Council for Christians and Jews Award, 1964; School of Journalism Prize, Syracuse University, New York, 1963; Philadelphia Museum of Art Award, 1964; Art Directors Club of New York Award, 1964, 1968; Frederic W. Brehm Award, 1962; Carr Van Anda Journalism Award, Ohio University, 1970; Springarn Award, National Association for the Advancement of Colored People, 1972. D.F.A.: Maryland Institute of Fine Arts, Baltimore, 1968; D.H.: Boston University, 1969; D.Litt.: University of Connecticut, Storrs, 1969; Kansas State University, Manhattan, 1970; H.H.D.: St. Olaf College, Northfield, Minnesota, 1973. **Address:** 860 United Nations Plaza, New York, New York 10017, U.S.A.

Individual Exhibitions:

1953	Art Institute of Chicago
1960	Limelight Gallery, New York
1966	Time-Life Gallery, New York
1979	*Eye Music,* Alex Rosenberg Gallery, New York
1981	Alex Rosenberg Gallery, New York
1984	Baltimore Museum of Art, Maryland
1985	Laguna Gloria Art Museum, Austin, Texas
	Chrysler Museu, Norfolk, Virginia

Selected Group Exhibitions:

1951	*Memorable Life Photographs,* Museum of Modern Art, New York
1964	*World Exhibition of Photography: What Is Man?,* Pressehaus Stern, Hamburg (and world tour)
1967	*Photography in the 20th Century,* National Gallery of Canada, Ottawa (toured Canada and the United States, 1967-73)
1973	*The Concerned Photographer 2,* Israel Museum, Jerusalem (toured Europe)
1977	*Documenta 6,* Museum Friedericianum, Kassel, West Germany
1979	*Images de L'Amerique en Crise,* Centre Georges Pompidou, Paris
1980	*The Imaginary Photo Museum,* Kunsthalle, Cologne
1983	*Roy Stryker: USA 1943-50,* International Center of Photography, New York
1984	*Sammlung Gruber,* Museum Ludwig, Cologne

1985	*American Images 1945-80,* Barbican Art Gallery, London (toured Britain)

Collections:

Museum of Modern Art, New York; International Center of Photography, New York; International Museum of Photography, George Eastman House, Rochester, New York; Library of Congress, Washington, D.C.; Art Institute of Chicago; Museum Ludwig, Cologne; Wichita State University, Kansas.

Publications:

By PARKS: Books—*Flash Photography,* New York 1947; *Camera Portraits,* New York 1948; *The Learning Tree,* novel, New York 1963, London 1964; *A Choice of Weapons,* New York 1966; *A Poet and His Camera,* New York and London 1968; *Whispers of Intimate Things,* New York 1971; *Born Black,* New York 1971; *In Love,* New York 1971; *Moments Without Proper Names,* London 1975; *Flavio,* New York 1978; *To Smile in Autumn: A Memoir,* New York and London 1979; *Shannon,* novel, Boston 1981. **Music**—*Piano Concerto,* 1953; *3 Piano Sonatas,* 1956, 1958, 1960; *Tree Symphony,* 1967. **Films**—*Flavio,* 1962; *The Learning Tree,* 1969; *Shaft,* 1972; *Shaft's Big Score,* 1972; *The Super Cops,* 1974; *Leadbelly,* 1976.

On PARKS: Books—*Memorable Life Photographs,* with text by Edward Steichen, New York 1951; *Life Photographers: Their Careers and Favorite Pictures,* edited by Stanley Rayfield, New York 1957; *Photography in the 20th Century* by Nathan Lyons, New York 1967; *Gordon Parks* by Midge Turk, New York 1971; *Gordon Parks: Black Photographer and Film Maker* by Terry Harnan, Champaign, Illinois 1972; *Social Documentary Photography in the U.S.A.* by Robert J. Doherty, New York 1974; *The Magic Image* by Cecil Beaton and Gail Buckland, London and Boston 1975; *Documenta 6/ Band 2,* exhibition catalogue, by Klauf Honnef and Evelyn Weiss, Kassel and Cologne 1977; *Geschichte der Fotografie im 20. Jahrhundert/Photography in the 20th Century* by Petr Tausk, Cologne 1977, London 1980; *Industry and the Photographic Image: 153 Great Prints from 1850 to the Present,* edited by F. Jack Hurley, New York 1980; *Roy Stryker: USA 1943-1950* by Steven W. Plattner, Austin, Texas 1983; *American Images: Photography 1945-1980,* edited by Peter Turner and John Benton-Harris, London 1985. **Articles**—"The Concerned Photographer" by Cornell Capa in *Zoom* (Paris), no. 16, 1973; "Le Dossier de la Misere" in *Photo* (Paris), February 1980.

*   *   *

A writer and musician, Gordon Parks became interested in photography at an early age, when he was 15. As he points out, his passion for photography slowly became an absorbing one. Seven years after he won the first Julius Rosenwald Fellowship Award in photography in 1942, he was appointed a staff photographer for *Life* magazine. During his years with *Life* (1948-1961), Parks produced remarkable photo-essays on a wide range of events and topics: Harlem street gangs, Winston Churchill, Paris fashions, the civil-rights movement, and South America. His photo-journalism generates power and concern by the very directness and honesty of his art. His work with the Farm Security Administration and the Standard Oil Company of New Jersey also demonstrates his passion for the medium and the dedication with which he uses the camera. A picture of Place de la Concorde seething with automobiles shows the same clarity and force one finds in the picture of a Brazilian slum-child or the Harlem street gangs or the stern face of an old French woman.

For decades Parks' work has been essentially documentary. But his flair for catching the most dramatic and vivid events and faces, and a deep involvement in what he is doing, make these newspictures something significant and unforgettable. His Malcolm X photographs, portraits of Muhammad Ali and Ethel Shariff, and the Fontenelle group of images all bear testimony to Parks' talent as a special kind of photo-journalist. Although the "narrativeness" of his photography has power and directness, it seems to lack the kind of quality one finds in Cartier-Bresson, Brassaï, Dorothea Lange, or Russell Lee. At times he appears to be somewhat distant. However, there is a touch of the poetic in his art, especially the color-photography, particularly in his books combining poetry and photography, *A Whisper of Intimate Things* and *The Poet and His Camera.* He undoubtedly is a competent photographer in color, but the black-and-white photos convey Parks' strength more distinctly. One has the definite impression that he is stronger and better in recording human expressions and gestures as well as events and scenes than in conveying nature. The sort of power his photography reflects is that of a man of urbanity and concern rather than that of the "committed" photographer. Even though he is an Afro American, he is not polemical when he records the people and events of his own background. The Duke Ellington photographs display strong emotion because of his relationship with and admiration for the musician.

Despite his early rejection by many important periodicals in America because of the color of his skin, Gordon Parks has continued to devote his time and energy to photography with unusual commitment. His competence in other expressive forms—music, writing, film—has in no way interfered with his talents as a photographer. The poet, musician, and writer are well fused in the photographer, and he remains an inspiration to both white and black aspirants in photography.

—Deba P. Patnaik

PARR, Martin.

Nationality: British. **Born:** Epsom, Surrey, 23 May 1952. **Education:** Studied photography at Manchester Polytechnic, 1970-73. **Career:** Photojournalist, Manchester Council for Community Relations, 1973-74. Freelance photographer, for magazines, dance and theatre companies, since 1974; established Albert Street Workshop, with Jenny Beavan, Ray Elliott, and Kate Mellor, Hebden Bridge, West Yorkshire, 1974; moved to Ireland, 1980. Part-time Instructor in Photography, Oldham College of Art, 1974-75, and Manchester Polytechnic, 1978. Visiting Lecturer at National College of Art and Design, Dublin and Chelsea School of Art, 1975-82. Visiting Lecturer at School of Documentary Photography, Newport, 1982-84. Visiting Lecturer at West Surrey College of Art and Design, Farnham, 1982. Nominee for Magnum Agency, 1988-92. Visiting Professor of Photography, University of Industrial Arts, Helsinki, 1990-92. Associate Member of Magnum Agency, 1992. Member of Magnum, 1994. **Recipient:** Arts Council of Great Britain Photography Grant, 1975, 1976, 1979; Yorkshire Arts Association Photography Grant, 1978. **Agents:** Magnum Photos, Paris, London, Tokyo and New York. **Dealer:** Janet Borden Ltd., 560 Broadway, New York, New York 10012, U.S.A. **Address:** 7 The Polygon, Clifton, Bristol, BS8 4PW, England.

Individual Exhibitions:

1972	*Butlins by the Sea,* Impressions Gallery, York (with Daniel Meadows; toured the U.K.)
1974	*Home Sweet Home,* Impressions Gallery, York (toured the U.K.)
1975	*The Chimney Pot Show,* Northwest Arts Gallery, Manchester (toured the U.K.)
1976	*Beauty Spots,* Impressions Gallery, York (toured the U.K.)
	3 North West Photographers, Whitworth Art Gallery, Manchester (with Daniel Meadows and Dave Chadwick; toured the U.K.)
1977	The Photographers' Gallery, London
1978	Fotomania, Barcelona
	This Is Your Life, Hebden Bridge Information Centre, Yorkshire
1979	*The Brighouse Commission,* Smith Art Gallery, Brighouse, Yorkshire
	Photogallery, St. Leonard's-on-Sea, Sussex
1980	Canon Photo Gallery, Amsterdam
1981	Gallery of Photography, Dublin
	Abandoned Morris Minors of the West of Ireland, at the Galway Arts Festival, Ireland
	The Non-Conformists, Half Moon Gallery, London (toured the U.K.)
1983	Impressions Gallery, York
1984	*Calderdale Photographs,* Piece Hall Art Gallery, Halifax, Yorkshire

	A Fair Day, Orchard Gallery, Londonderry, Northern Ireland (toured Britain)
1986	Serpentine Gallery, London
	The Photographers' Gallery, London
1987	*Spending Time,* National Centre of Photography, Paris (and subsequent tour)
1988	Kodak Gallery, Tokyo and Osaka
1989	Spectrum Gallery, Hanover, Germany
	The Cost of Living, Royal Photographic Society, Bath (and subsequent tour including Finland, Portugal, Spain, Ireland)
1991	Janet Borden, New York
1992	*Signs of the Times,* Janet Borden, New York and Arles Festival, France
1993	*Bored Couples,* Gallery du Jour, Paris
	Home and Abroad, Watershed Gallery, Bristol (and tour)

Selected Group Exhibitions:

1974	*10 from Co-optic,* Jordan Gallery, London
1978	*YAA Award Winners Show,* Impressions Gallery, York
	Personal Views 1860-1977, British Council, London (toured Europe)
	Art for Society, Whitechapel Art Gallery, London
1979	*3 Perspectives on Photography,* Hayward Gallery, London
1980	*4 Photographers,* at Salford '80, England
1982	*Floods of Light,* The Photographers' Gallery, London (toured Britain)
1983	*Strategies,* John Hansard Gallery, Southampton, Hampshire (toured Britain)
1984	*Nuova Fotografia Inglese,* Milan, Italy
1986	*British Character,* The Photographers' Gallery, London
1987	*Attitudes to Ireland,* Orchard Gallery, Derry, N. Ireland
	Mysterious Coincidences, Photographers' Gallery, London
1988	*A British View,* Museum fur Gestaltung, Zurich
1989	*Through the Looking Glass,* British Photography 1945-89, Barbican Centre, London
1990	*The Past and Present of Photography,* MOMA, Tokyo
1991	*British Photography from the Thatcher Years,* MOMA, New York
1992	*Imagina,* World Fair, Seville
1993	*Photographs from the Real World,* Lillehammer Art Museum, Norway
1994	*From A to B,* 25 Welcome Break Service Stations around UK

Collections:

Arts Council of Great Britain, London; Union Bank of Finland, Helsinki; Museum for Fotokunst, Odense, Denmark; Victoria and Albert Museum, London; George Eastman House, Rochester; Bibliotheque Nationale, Paris; Museum of Modern Art, New York; Philadelphia Museum of Art; Museum of Modern Art, Tokyo; Calderdale Council, Halifax; Getty Museum, Malibu; Walker Art Gallery, Liverpool; Kodak, France; Museum Folkwang, Essen; Seagrams Collection, New York; Museum of Modern Art, Tempere, Finland; British Council, London; Irish Arts Council; Australian National Gallery; Museum of Fine Arts, Houston.

Publications:

By PARR: Books—*Bad Weather,* with text by Michael Fish and Peter Turner, London 1982; *A Fair Day: Photographs from the West of Ireland,* with text by Fintan O'Toole, London and Londonderry, Northern Ireland 1984; *Calderdale Photographs,* exhibition catalogue, Calderdale, Cumbria 1984; *Prescot Now and Then,* catalogue, Merseyside County Council, 1984; *The Last Resort,* Promenade Press 1986; *The Actual Boot, The Photographic Postcard 1900-1920,* (with Jack Stasiack) Jolly Editorial, 1986; *One Day Trip,* catalogue, Editions de la Différence, Centre Regional de la Photographie, Nord Pas de Calais, France, 1989; *The Cost of Living,* Cornerhouse Publications, 1989; *Signs of the Times,* Cornerhouse Publications, 1992; *Bored Couples,* catalogue Gallery du Jour, Paris, 1993; *Home and Abroad,* Jonathon Cape, 1993; *From A to B,* BBC Publications, London, 1994; *Small World,* Dewi Lewis Publishing,

From *The Cost of Living,* **1986-89, Lacock, Wiltshire, (original in colour).** Photograph ©Martin Parr.

1995. **Articles**—"Photographs by Martin Parr" in *Creative Camera* (London), June 1974; "Martin Parr" in *Creative Camera Collection 5,* London 1978; "Martin Parr: Portfolio" in *Popular Photography Annual 1980,* New York, 1979.

On PARR: Books—*3 Perspectives on Photography,* exhibition catalogue, London 1979; *Floods of Light: Flash Photography 1851-1981,* exhibition catalogue, by Rupert Martin, London 1982; *Nuova Fotografia Inglese,* edited by Giovanni Chiaramonte, Milan 1984. **Articles**—"The Slanted Mirror: The Photos of Martin Parr" by Stewart Scotney in *Art and Artists* (London), September 1974; "On View" by Ainslie Ellis in *British Journal of Photography* (London), 6 September 1974; "The Face in the Picture" by Paul Barker in *New Society* (London), 5 January 1978; "Martin Parr" in *Creative Camera* (London), May/June 1980; "End of the Pier" by Robert Morris in *British Journal of Photography,* 15 August, 1986; "The Lost Resort" by David Lee in *Arts Review,* August, 1986; "Comfort and Joy" by Bob Chesshyre and Richard Ehrlich in *Sunday Times Magazine,* 19 November, 1989; "Eloge de la vie quotidienne" by Michel Guerrin in *Le Monde,* 13 March, 1993; interview with M Parr "I'm buggered without my prejudice" by David Brittain in *Creative Camera,* June, 1993; "Up to Parr" by Michael Hallett in *British Journal of Photography, ,* 5 August, 1993; "God Heats at the Supermarket"

by Boyd Tonkin in *New Statesman & Society,* 6 August, 1993; "Ordinary People" by Val Williams in *Independent on Sunday,* 4 December, 1993; "Martin Parr" by David Lee in *Arts Review,* March 1994.

*

The best way to describe my work is subjective documentary.

—Martin Parr

*   *   *

Martin Parr can be considered generally as the leading light of the "New Colour Documentary" School of eighties British and European photography. As such he has been a major influence upon young photographers, both as protaganist and teacher. His style has been imitated extensively, but in the original is marked by an aggressive, typically British coolness and a gleeful propensity for eccentricity and the foibles of human existence. These qualities are presented for our inspection in a manner that seems somewhat insistent and unyielding compared to the methods of the traditional documentary photographer—courtesy not only of Parr's vision but the hyaline lucidity of medium format colour film and the frequent aid of flash lighting.

Gone is the grainy romanticism of available light monochrome, but Parr's work is not ''about'' colour in the manner of some colour formalists. Colour for Parr is simply a ''given,'' an essential element for greater realism and a useful adjunct to hold a dreaded nostalgia at bay.

Gone too is the favourite subject of the ''concerned'' photographer of yesteryear—poverty. Although unemployment and the existence of a poor underclass is as prevalent as ever, some of the sting seems to have been drawn from the class war, as we know it. Photographers like Parr have tended to view all classes, even cultures, as a single homogenised, international, intra-cultural class of consumer. Thus Parr's favoured hunting grounds have shifted from the rainswept, mean streets and shabby back-to-backs of yore to the air-conditioned, micro-climatised supermarkets, out of town shopping malls and ''heritage'' theme parks. The traditional distinctions between classes are largely replaced by a more subtle differentiation, in which class is reduced to a matter of consumer choice—a question of style.

Of course, style is eminently suited to photographic investigation, for style deals with surface appearance, surface appearance with far reaching social implications. Yet Parr and his followers are criticised for celebrating the tawdry and the tacky as much as condemning it, and making superficial pictures in an ephemeral rather than a profound sense. There is something in such a criticism, namely that in concentrating upon the phenomenology of human interaction he captures the effect rather than the cause—but this could be said of many, if not most photographers. Parr is also censured for the direct, even confrontational nature of his approach, and thereby treating his subjects' foibles with sarcasm. While he is a cool, objective photographer, dissecting life with a sharp scalpel, a careful study of his whole oeuvre reveals that he has tended overall to maintain a scrupulous even-handedness towards his material. His humour can be good-humoured as well as ironic.

Over two decades, Martin Parr has compiled a fascinating, wide-ranging portrait of our times, an immense body of work which will stand as one of the leading photographic monuments to this century's end. If he has tended to focus upon the trivial, we must point the finger to the preponderance of the trivial in our society. If we dislike the mirror he has held up to our aggressive, materialist culture, that is perhaps our fault, not his.

—Gerry Badger

PAWELEC, Wladyslaw.

Nationality: Polish. **Born:** Minsk Mazowiecke, 14 October 1923. **Education:** Studied medicine, Marie Curie Sklodowska University, Lublin, 1945-46; mainly self-taught in photography, from 1954. **Family:** Married Irena Pokorska in 1943; daughters: Ilona and Dorota. **Career:** Worked as senior assistant, Polfa-Jelenia Gora, Warsaw, 1947-53; Director of the scientific photography laboratory, Institute of Serums and Vaccines, Warsaw, 1954-64; worked in the editorial section, *Swiatowid* tourism journal, Warsaw, 1966-76. Since 1977, freelance professional photographer, Warsaw. Worked with the Orion Press Agency, Tokyo, 1977, and with the Bernard Letu Gallery, Geneva, 1982. **Recipient:** State Prize for New Medicine, Warsaw, 1952. Member, Union of Polish Art Photographers, 1966. **Address:** Mostowa 22/1, 00-260 Warsaw, Poland.

Individual Exhibitions:

1974	*Monika* Galeria ZPAF, Warsaw
1979	*Natalia,* Galeria ZPAF, Warsaw
	Mala Galeria ZPAF, Torun, Poland
1981	Galeria BWA, Lublin, Poland
1984	Canon Photo Gallery, Amsterdam
	Die romantische Erotik van W. Pawelec, Galerij Paule Pia, Antwerp, Belgium
1985	*Kartki z albumu,* Galeria ZPAF, Kraków, Poland
	Galerie Fotografii Hybrydy, Warsaw
1993	*Erolife '93,* Utrecht, The Netherlands

Selected Group Exhibitions:

1966	*World Press Photo,* The Hague
	Inter-Press Photo, Moscow
1967	*Woman in View,* Amsterdam
1978	*APA International Photography Exhibition,* Tokyo
1985	*Das Aktfoto,* Fotomuseum im Stadtmuseum, Munich
	Wspolczesna fotografia polska, Galeria Zacheta, Warsaw
	East European Nude Photography, at the *Biennale di Fotografia,* Turin, Italy
1992	*Nudes in the Town Hall Prison,* Tallinn, Estonia

Collections:

Lorenzo Merlo Collection, Amsterdam; Franco Fontana Collection, Modena, Italy; Horst Bruggeman Collection, Ludwigshafen, Germany; Verkerke van de Wetering Collection, Amsterdam.

Publications:

By PAWELEC: Books—*Privat,* 5 vols., Nuremberg, West Germany 1984; *The Friends of Zofia,* with text by Jeff Dunas, Los Angeles 1985; *Pawelec,* Tokyo, Japan, 1991.

On PAWELEC: Books—*Wladyslaw Pawelec,* exhibition catalogue, by Romuald Klosiewicz, Warsaw 1974; *Wladyslaw Pawelec,* exhibition catalogue, by Jerzy Busza, Warsaw 1979; *Monika—Natalia,* exhibition catalogue, by Jerzy Busza, Lublin, Poland 1981; *Wszystko o fotografii,* Warsaw 1984; *Fotografia polska 1945-1985,* Gorzow Wielkopolski, Poland 1985; *Photographers Encyclopedia International* by Michel Auer, Hermance, Switzerland 1985; *Wladyslaw Pawelec,* exhibition catalogue, by Ryszard Bobrowski, Warsaw 1985. **Articles**—''Z galerii ZPAF—Wladyslaw Pawelec'' by Romuald Klosiewicz in *Fotografia* (Warsaw), no. 10, 1974; ''Golizna za 160'' by Jerzy Slawomir Lec in *Przeglad Tygodniowy* (Warsaw), no. 3, 1983; ''Le premier calendrier erotique ouvertmenet en Pologne'' by Regis Ganai in *Lausanne—Cities* (Lausanne, Switzerland), 27 October 1983; ''Suites Erotiques Polonaises—La Collections Privée de Wladyslaw Pawelec'' in *Photo* (Paris), April 1984; ''Works in Progress—Pawelec'' by Jeff Dunas in *Collectors Editions Review* (Santa Monica, California), vol. 2, no. 1, 1986; Wladyslaw Pawelec in *The Journal of Erotica,* vol 7, 1994.

* * *

The history of eroticism in Polish photography is long but difficult to recount. Stretching back into the mid-19th century and developing anonymously or semi-legally at first, it did not come into its own until the time of pictorialism when, as with painting, it became seen not as a passion or an obsession but as art. Even then, although it was a subject of occasional interest to several photographers, it never really found its place. Evidence of this was the fact that it was used less confidently and less frequently in photomontage or photocollage than in conventional photography. The situation continued, to some extent, after the war when, despite the fact that nudity was used more freely by avant-gardists than traditionalists, eroticism was still an uncertain subject. Only in the 1960s and 1970s was it consistently and consciously explored through photography. Wladyslaw Pawelec was definitely one of the earliest and most interesting pioneers of this work.

Eroticism was not the first subject that had interested Pawelec. He began with journalistic photography in the tourist magazine *Swiatowid.* In time, *Swiatowid* and other publications gave their cover pages to Pawelec's photographs of women. ''Women,'' he admits, ''have always played an important role in my life. When I was young, my friends were always girls. I was always aware of their sensuality and their beauty.'' In time, this fascination was to transform itself into a great and constantly unfolding passion.

From a photographic point of view, Pawelec was a child of his time representing a generation that had grown up and trained under the influence of pictorialism and journalism. Pawelec's first important exhibition, entitled *Monika,* reflected this influence, portraying a beautiful girl against a background of flowing grass or a romantic mill; idealised—if not simulated—situations. A different kind of idealisation was characteristic of his later works. In the *Natalia* exhibition, for example, a rough country hut took the place of

Untitled, **1985.** Photograph by Wladyslaw Pawelec.

the old mill. Initially, this photography was well received by critics and the general public but, in time it exhausted all possibilities of progress and came to a standstill. Aware of this, Pawelec abandoned the evocative and melancholy and moved in two directions simultaneously—towards the purely visual and towards sharply defined, even aggressive, eroticism.

The women he photographed were no longer captive models artificially set in strange or irrelevant surroundings. On the contrary, they retained their individuality and were clearly "at home" in surroundings that emphasised their reality rather than negating it. Depending on how it is interpreted, this photography marked a sudden and brutal overthrowing of taboos that made it scandalous and contemptible, manifested dynamic vitality or sheer eroticism, or else was a symptom of a decadent era—an era that might be beautiful but was also shallow, exciting but also fallen, an era without mystery but also without value. It showed itself in the same way as fin-de-siècle theatre in which the actresses were Pawelec's nameless models but the real characters of the drama were the members of the audience.

However, the limits of artistic exploration were also reached in this area of Pawelec's work, marked as it is by two books published in the West. The further development of sheer eroticism can only lead to perversity or downright pornography. Mere visual stimulation, however, is not the road best suited to the sensitive nature of a photographer. Within this framework, in his most recent work, Pawelec neither tries to idealise women nor to lay bare their secrets but, rather, to reach the psyche—the fears, dreams and desires that are characteristic of woman's existence but difficult to understand for a man. "The thing that fascinates me most in photography," Pawelec stresses, "is the possibility of carrying the very private and subtly encoded worlds of experience of my models over onto the photographic plate. That's a hard task but also a very bewitching one."

—Ryszard Bobrowski

PEÑA GONZÁLEZ, René.

Nationality: Cuban. **Born:** Havana, Cuba, 1957. **Education:** Studied English at Instituto Superior de Lenguas Extranjeras, Havana. **Agent:** Zone Gallery, 83 Westgate Road, Newcastle upon Tyne, NE1 1SG, England. **Address:** Calle N 111 20, 3ra y E Altahabana, Ciudad Habana, Cuba.

Individual Exhibitions:

1991	Fototeca de Cuba, Havana
1993	Associación Hermanos Saíz, Havana

Selected Group Exhibitions:

1987	Taller Nacional de la Nueva Imagen, Havana
1991	Salón 13 de Marzo, Havana
1992	*Cronicas de la Ciudad,* Fototeca de Cuba, Havana
	Fotografía Cubana, Berlin
	América & Americhe, Italy
1994	*The New Generation,* Houston Fotofest, Texas
	Inconsolable Memories: Contemporary Photography from Cuba, Zone Gallery, Newcastle upon Tyne, England

Publications:

By **PEÑA GONZÁLEZ: Articles**—*Revolución y Cultura,* Cuba 1992; *Revue Noire,* France, No 6 1992; *Creative Camera,* UK, No CC329, 1994.

*　　*　　*

Cuban photography is most closely identified with the "epic revolutionary" documentary styles of the 60s and 70s, perhaps best symbolised by Korda's much reproduced portrait of Ché Guevara. The iconic simplicity of this image belies an acute awareness of the significance of the photograph as a mass communication tool. Photography was consciously employed in the mobilisation of Cuban society and in the creation of a new revolutionary identity. From a broader perspective the Cuban revolutionary experience and the influence of Cuban photographers has extended far beyond the confines of this Caribbean island.

Thirty years on a new world order and the continued U.S. blockade of Cuba has radically altered the cultural and economic climate for Cuban artists. Younger generation of photographers find the deceptive literality of documentary realism insufficient to express the complexities of a society scarred by conflict and dogged with the economic and political problems universally referred to as "our reality." Identity remains a fundamental issue but manifests via more fluid, ambiguous and personal symbolism than concrete heroicism of earlier photographers. Cuban writer and critic, Juan Antonio Molina sees these younger artists using "parody and the hypertextuality of contemporary reality leading to the critical decodification of the discourses of power or the sublimation of cultural codes which until now have been marginalised."

It is the expression of identity in the everyday which is the key to Peña's work. It reveals the complex processes of cultural syncretism that have shaped contemporary Cuba: colonisation by the Spanish and the British, the slave trade from West Africa, the pervasive influence of North America and the struggles for independence. In this context his series of images function as visual maps. Peña locates himself both historically and ideologically within Cuban society via the inter-relationship of symbols and references within his images.

Peña's photographs have been described as baroque in their careful assemblage of people, objects, and borrowed imagery. Critical dialogue in both the single frame and across the series is instigated by the wealth of domestic iconography deployed by the artist. The ubiquitous "coke" can or a pair of sunglasses connotes western imperialism. A bust of a 19th century hero of the struggle for independence or a print of Fidel Castro identifies Cuban political consciousness. More fundamentally, elements from santoria, a devotional image or an unbroken egg, reflect a specifically black experience and suggest an underlying spritual dimension in life. Within this lexicon Peña's family and friends people the images as archetypal characters in a narrative whose significance can only be understood via the decodification of their domestic possessions, from ration cards to a bare electric light.

Peña's more recent works articulate this iconic narrative still further. Forming an ambitious series of self-portraits, they relate personal experience, such as an abortive attempt to travel abroad, to impositions inherent in colonial history and more generalised observations. Borrowing Peter Greenway's film title for the series "The Cook, the Thief, his Wife and her Lover," each image confronts a perceived relationship of exploitation past and present. The seductive conflict between warm and cool tones within the images reflects a fundamental conflict between Afro-Cuban and western cultural frameworks and identities.

Despite the differing cultural environments and modes of representation Peña nevertheless identifies a continuity of development in Cuban photography, which arises from the location of the artist in relation to a wider society. Challenging western perceptions of an isolated individual disconnected from social life Peña argues that "Cuban artists can touch reality because reality touches them. Cuban photographers are more interested in what is happening, what has happened and what will happen in our country than 'what will happen to me'. We are not analysing the artist's position, his person as an artist. When I analyse myself it is myself into a social context without distance between me and our reality." For Peña this provides him with a voice that resonates beyond the immediate boundaries of culture and nation.

—David Sinden

PENN, Irving.

Nationality: American. **Born:** Plainfield, New Jersey, 16 June 1917. **Education:** Studied design, under Alexey Brodovitch, Philadelphia Museum School of Industrial Art, 1934-38. **Military Service:** Served as an ambulance driver and documentary photographer in the American Field Service, with the British

Untitled. Photograph by René Peña González.

Army in Italy and India, 1944-45. **Family:** Married the fashion model Lisa Fonssagrives in 1950; son: Tom. **Career:** Worked as a graphic artist in New York, 1938-41; spent a year painting in Mexico, 1942; designer and photographer for *Vogue* magazine, New York, 1943-44. Photographer, working with Alexander Liberman, for Condé Nast Publications, New York, publishers of *Vogue*, etc., since 1946; also, freelance advertising photographer, New York, since 1952. **Agent:** Pace/MacGill Gallery, 32 East 57th Street, New York, New York 10022, U.S.A.

Individual Exhibitions:

1961   *Photographs by Irving Penn,* Museum of Modern Art of New York travelling exhibition (toured the United States)
1963   Smithsonian Institution, Washington, D.C.
1975   *I Platini di Irving Penn: 25 Anni di Fotografia,* Galleria Civica d'Arte Moderna, Turin
        Recent Works, Museum of Modern Art, New York
1977   *Street Material,* Metropolitan Museum of Art, New York
        Photographs in Platinum Metals—Images 1947-1975, Marlborough Gallery, New York
1980   *Earthly Bodies,* Marlborough Gallery, New York
1981   *60 Photos,* Marlborough Fine Art, London
1983   *Recent Still Life,* Marlborough Gallery, New York
1984   Vision Gallery, Boston
        Museum of Modern Art, New York (retrospective; toured the United States and Europe 1984-87)
1988   *Irving Penn: Cranium Architecture,* Pace/MacGill Gallery, New York

1990   *Irving Penn: Other Ways of Being,* Pace/MacGill Gallery, New York
        Vintage Prints from the Earthly Bodies series 1949-50, Pace/MacGill Gallery, New York
1991   *48 Portraits from 1948,* Pace/MacGill Gallery, New York
1994   *Irving Penn: New York,* Pace/MacGill Gallery, New York

Selected Group Exhibitions:

1955   *The Family of Man,* Museum of Modern Art, New York (and world tour)
1967   *Photography in the 20th Century,* National Gallery of Canada, Ottawa (toured Canada and the United States, 1967-73)
1975   *Photography Within the Humanities,* Jewett Arts Center, Wellesley College, Massachusetts
1976   *Masters of the Camera,* American Federation of the Arts travelling exhibition
1977   *Fashion Photography,* International Museum of Photography, George Eastman House, Rochester, New York (travelled to the Brooklyn Museum, New York; San Francisco Museum of Modern Art; Cincinnati Art Institute, Ohio; and Museum of Fine Arts, St. Petersburg, Florida)
1978   *Tusen och En Bild/1001 Pictures,* Moderna Museet, Stockholm
1979   *Photographie als Kunst 1879-1979,* Tiroler Landesmuseum, Innsbruck, Austria (travelled to the Neue Galerie am Wolfgang Gurlitt Museum, Linz, Austria; Neue Galerie am

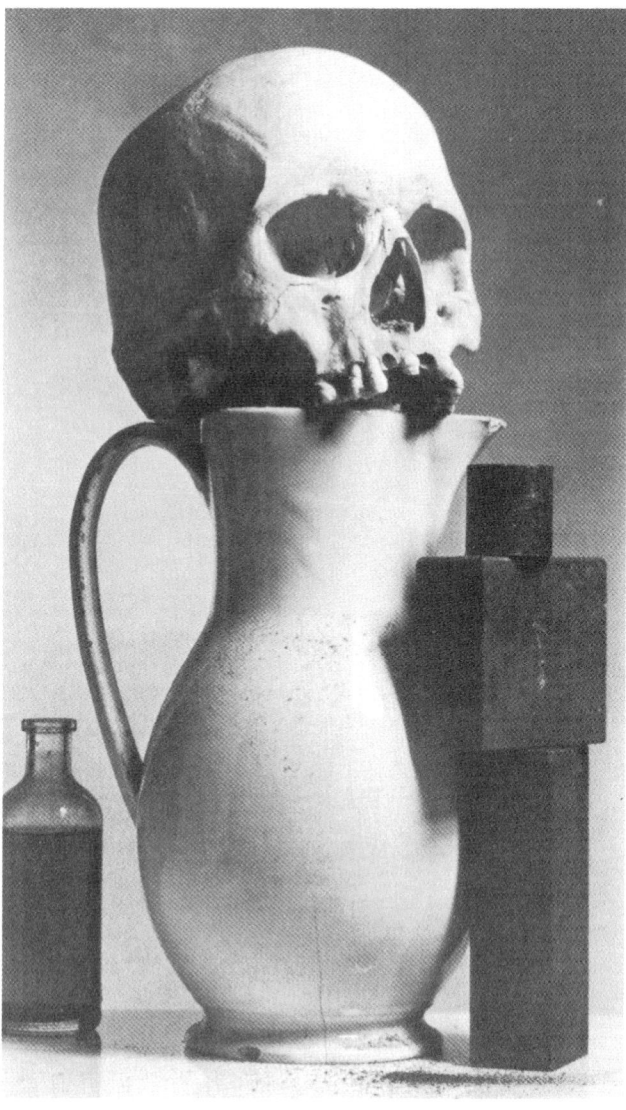

Ospedale, **1980.** Photograph by Irving Penn.

Landesmuseum Joanneum, Graz, Austria; and Museum des 20, Jahrhunderts, Vienna)

1981   *Photographer as Printmaker,* Ferens Art Gallery, Hull, Yorkshire (travelled to the Museum and Art Gallery, Leicester; Cooper Gallery, Barnsley; Castle Museum, Nottingham; Photographers' Gallery, London)

1983   *Selected Images: Abbot/Brandt/Brassaï/Penn,* Marlborough Gallery, New York

1985   *Shots of Style,* Victoria and Albert Museum, London (toured Britain)

1990   Pace/MacGill Gallery, New York

1992   Pace/MacGill Gallery, New York

Collections:

Metropolitan Museum of Art, New York; Museum of Modern Art, New York; International Museum of Photography, George Eastman House, Rochester, New York; Smithsonian Institution, Washington, D.C., Art Institute of Chicago; Galleria Civica d'Arte Moderna, Turin, Italy; Moderna Museet, Stockholm; Stedelijk Museum, Amsterdam; Museum Ludwig, Cologne, Germany; Folkwang Museum, Essen, Germany; Victoria and Albert Museum, London.

Publications:

By PENN: Books—*Moments Preserved: 8 Essays in Photographs and Words,* with an introduction by Alexander Liberman, New York 1960; *Worlds in a Small Room,* New York 1974; *Inventive Paris Clothes 1909-1939: A Photographic Essay by Irving Penn,* with text by Diana Vreeland, New York 1977; *Flowers,* New York 1980; *Irving Penn,* with text by John Szarkowski, New York and Boston 1984; *Penn: A Photographic Essay,* with text by Robert Llewellyn, New York 1986. **Articles**—articles in *Look* magazine, "Provence," 1961; "Provincial Foods of France," 1962; "Portugal," 1963; "Sweden," 1964; "Paris," 1965; "London," 1966; "San Francisco," 1967; in *Show* magazine "Somerset Maugham" (France); "Sophia Loren" (Italy); "Robert Graves" (Majorca); "Henry Moore" (England) all 1962; in *Vogue,* "Japan" and "Scotland," 1963; "Crete," 1964; "Gypsies of Extremadura," 1965; "Dahomey," 1967; "Nepal," 1967; "Cameroon," 1969; "New Guinea," 1970; "Morocco," 1971.

On PENN: Books—*Words and Pictures: An Introduction to Photojournalism* by Wilson Hicks, New York 1952; *Fame: Famous Portraits of Famous People by Famous Photographers,* edited by L. Fritz Gruber, London and New York 1960; *Beauty: Variations on the Theme Woman by Masters of the Camera—Past and Present,* edited by L. Fritz Gruber, London and New York 1965; *The Photographer's Eye* by John Szarkowski, New York 1966; *The Studio* by the Time-Life editors, New York 1972; *Looking at Photographs* by John Szarkowski, New York 1973; *The Magic Image* by Cecil Beaton and Gail Buckland, London and Boston 1975; *Irving Penn: Recent Works,* exhibition catalogue, with an introduction by John Szarkowski, New York 1975; *Irving Penn: Street Material,* exhibition catalogue, with an introduction by Henry Geldzahler, New York 1977; *The History of Fashion Photography* by Nancy Hall-Duncan, New York 1979; *Irving Penn: Earthly Bodies,* exhibition catalogue, with an introduction by Rosalind E. Krauss, New York 1980; *Color* by the Time-Life editors, revised edition, New York 1981; *Irving Penn: Recent Still Life,* exhibition catalogue, with introduction by Colin Eisler, New York 1982; *The Library of World Photography: Portraits,* with introduction by Colin Ford, Tokyo 1982, 1983, London 1983; *American Images: Photography 1945-1980,* edited by Peter Turner and John Benton-Harris, London 1985; *Shots of Style: Great Fashion Photos Chosen by David Bailey,* with text by Martin Harrison, London 1985. **Articles**—special issue of *Camera* (Lucerne), edited by R.E. Martinez, November 1960; "Great Photographers of the World: Irving Penn" by Tom Hopkinson in the *Telegraph Magazine* (London), 17 April 1970; "Certainties and Possibilities" by Janet Malcolm in *The New Yorker,* 4 August 1975; "Irving Penn: New Platinum Photographs" by Thomas B. Hess in *Vogue* (New York), August 1975; "Visual Recycling: Irving Penn's 'Street Material' " by A.D. Coleman in the *Village Voice* (New York), 30 May 1977, reprinted in Coleman's *Light Readings: A Photography Critic's Writings 1968-78,* New York 1979; "Perspectives of Penn" by Owen Edwards in the *New York Times Magazine,* 4 September 1977; "Penn's Earthly Goddesses" by Douglas Davis in *Newsweek* (New York), 22 September 1980; "The Nude According to Penn" by Owen Edwards in *American Photographer* (New York), September 1980; "Irving Penn's People Reign Above the Humdrum World" by Gene Thornton in the *New York Times,* 16 September 1984.

*   *   *

The common denominator of Irving Penn's photographic work is formal intelligence. Penn has no rival in terms of formal complexity, the rich beauty of constructed shape, elegance of silhouette, and abstract interplay of line and volume. The appearance of simplicity Penn achieves through straight-forward poses and natural lighting is a simplicity underpinned by a complex of visual decisions rarely equalled in the medium of photography.

One aspect of Penn's genius for form is the sureness with which he uses the means available to black-and-white photography—pure blacks, stark white, and the subtleties of gray. His oppositions of blacks and whites are sumptuous; grays are used for their subtle colorations. This interest in achieving a full range of blacks and grays explains Penn's choice of rare and difficult techniques that can achieve these ends. These include the platinum process and the complex bleaching technique by which he produces his female nudes. The platinum process, widely used around the turn of the century, is a painstaking process which requires great skill. Because of the nature of the expensive platinum salts that permeate the paper, the platinum process can easily disintegrate into fuzzyness, but well handled, as in Penn's work, it can yield a soft modulation as well as density and luminosity. "A beautiful print," Penn has insisted, "is a thing in itself, not just a halfway house on the way to the page."

Penn is always true to his subject, whether he is shooting fashion or flowers, a famous face or a cigarette butt. An object seen by Penn is unlike any other, presented in a very serene, restful moment. It is his attempt to find truth in a universalized time, the moment he terms "beatitude." Penn sees exactingly and abstractly: he senses the curve and intersection of each line, the weight and implication of each form. The more one looks, the more one realizes that Penn's subjects are not simply seen.

Penn's portraiture combines the simplicity and directness of the 19th century portrait with a modern formal sophistication. In many cases his considerations are those of the portrait photographer of a century ago, favoring a simple studio set-up with natural light from a northern exposure. He has even constructed a portable studio in the tradition of 19th century itinerant photographers in order that he may produce authentic portraits in rural areas of the Cameroons, Peru, and other locales where no studio facilities are available.

The portraits that Penn produces in these places have a straightforward honesty, sharing an anthropological quality as well as a visual resemblance to the work of the German photographer, August Sander. In addition to the single and double portraits that so resemble Sander, Penn excels at the large group portrait: he achieves an ease which transcends the complexity of posing and technical problems inherent in this type of sitting.

The fact that Penn is one of this century's leading fashion photographers has been important to his development and style. Working with designers such as the legendary Alexey Brodovitch of *Harper's Bazaar* and Alexander Liberman, the long-time art director and current creative director of *Vogue*, has undoubtedly influenced Penn's sense of visual design. Working within the commercial requirements of fashion may have contributed to the clarity of Penn's style as well as its inbred elegance, tasteful and controlled.

As Rosalind Krauss has pointed out in *Earthly Bodies,* in an appreciation of Penn's female nudes, there are aspects of Penn's production that "has for him the quality of a covert operation, a kind of privately launched and personally experienced kamikaze attack on his own public identity as a photographer of fashion." Among these more personal and private productions are the female nudes, which are experiments in the formal possibilities and monumental densities possible in nude photography, and the platinum prints of cigarette butts, which question the meaning of subject matter *vis-a-vis* style. What Krauss overlooks, however, is that these partake rather than reject the values of monumentality, formal innovation and quiet truth that Penn has contributed to fashion. Public or private, Penn's work remains dedicated to questions of style and formal discovery as well as realism and depiction. As such, his work is one of the most important productions of our time.

—Nancy Hall-Duncan

PERESS, Gilles.

Nationality: French. **Born:** Neuilly-sur-Seine, 29 December 1946. **Education:** Attended the Institut d'Etudes Politiques, Paris, 1966-68, and 1968-71. University of Vincennes, 1968-70. **Career:** Freelance photographer, Paris and New York, since 1971; Associate, 1972-74, and Member since 1974, Magnum Photos co-operative agency, Paris and New York. Artist-in-Residence, Apeiron Workshop, Millerton, New York, 1977; Vice-President, Magnum Photos Inc., New York, 1984-85; President, 1986-87, 1989-90. **Recipient:** Art Directors Club of New York Award, 1977; National Endowment for the Arts grant, 1978; Overseas Press Club Award, 1981; Page One Award, The Newspaper Guild, 1981; American Institute of Graphic Arts Award, 1981; Best Photo Book Award, City of Paris/Kodak Pathé Foundation, 1981; Prix de la Critique Couleur, 1981; Imogen Cunningham Award,

1983; Photography Grant, Fondation Nationale de la Photographie, France, 1983; W. Eugene Smith Award, 1984; Gahan Fellowship at Harvard University, 1986; Ernst Haas Award, 1989; Art Director's Club Award, 1989; Art Matters Grant, 1990; National Endowment for the Arts Fellowship, 1992; Guggenheim, 1992/93; La Fondation de France Fellowship, 1993. **Addresses:** Magnum Photos, 5 Passage Piver, Paris, 75011, France; 72 Spring Street, 12th Floor, New York, New York 10012, U.S.A.

Individual Exhibitions:

1994   *La Primavera,* Fundacio La Caixa, Barcelona; PS1, New York
            Farewell to Bosnia, Corcoran Museum of Art, Washington,
                D.C.; Fotomuseum Winterthur, Winterthur, Switzerland

Selected Group Exhibitions:

1976   *Other Eyes,* Arts Council of Great Britain travelling exhibition
                (toured the U.K.)
            A Certain Image of French Photography, Fondation Nationale
                de la Photographie, Paris
1980   *The Body Politic,* Institute for Art and Urban Resources,
                New York
1983   *Photographie France Aujourd'hui,* Musée d'Art Moderne de la
                Ville, Paris
1985   *Magnum: Concert,* Musée d'Art et d'Histoire, Fribourg,
                Switzerland
            The Indelible Image, Corcoran Gallery, Washington D.C.
                (toured the United States)
1986   *On the Line: The New Color Photojournalism,* Walker Art
                Center, Minneapolis
            The Catskill Center for Photography, Woodstock
            Carpenter Center for the Visual Arts, Harvard University,
                Cambridge, Massachusetts
            Musée de la Villette, Paris
1987   The Museum of Contemporary Photography, Chicago
1988   Hippolyte Gallery, Helsinki
            Ranta Gallery, Oulu, Finland
            Burden Gallery, New York
1989   Alternative Museum, New York
            International Center for Photography, New York
            International Museum of Photography/Eastman House, Roch-
                ester, New York
            University of South Florida, Tampa
            Canon Image Center, Amsterdam
            Fotograficentrum, Stockholm
            Side Gallery, Newcastle-upon-Tyne, England
            Museum of Photographic Arts, San Diego
            Arbetets Museum, Norrkoping, Sweden
1990   Art Institute of Chicago, Illinois
            Alternative Museum, New York
            International Center for Photography, New York
            Winnipeg Art Gallery, Canada
1992   David Winton Bell Gallery, Brown Univeristy, Providence,
                Rhode Island
1993   Lillehammer Art Museum, Norway

Collections:

Bibliothèque Nationale, Paris; Arts Council of Great Britain, London; Museum of Modern Art, New York; International Museum of Photography at George Eastman House, Rochester, New York; Philadelphia Museum of Art, Pennsylvania; Minneapolis Art Institute, Minnesota; Centre Nationale de la Photographie, Paris; Musée d'Art Moderne, Paris; Galerie Municipale du Château d'Eau, Toulouse, France; The Art Institute of Chicago; Fogg Museum, Cambridge, Massachusetts; Fondation Leitz, Rueil-Malmaison, France; The Metropolitan Museum of Art, New York; The Museum of the Moving Image, New York; The Museum of Fine Arts, Houston, Texas; Victoria and Albert Museum, London.

Publications:

By PERESS: Books—*Telex: Iran—In the Name of Revolution,* with text by Gholam Hassan Saedi, Millerton, New York and Paris 1984; *An Eye for an Eye: Northern Ireland,* with text by Nan Richardson, Millerton, New York, and London 1986; *Farewell to Bosnia,* Berlin, 1994; *Power in the Blood,* text by Nan Richardson, London/Berlin, in press. **Video/film**—*A Peruvian Equation,* part of the series "The Magnum Eye" made for television Tokyo, 1992; *Street Musicians* filmed in New York for Magnum & Co., for Benetton, 1992.

On PERESS: Books—*This is Magnum,* Tokyo 1979; *Magnum: Paris,* with introduction by Irwin Shaw, foreword by Inge Morath, Paris, London, Milan and Millerton, New York 1984. **Articles**—"Paying Guests: Photos, Gilles Peress" by P. Pringle in the *Sunday Times Magazine* (London), 26 May 1974; "Fern der Heimat: Turkische Fremdarbeiter in Deutschland—aufnahmen von Gilles Peress" in *Du* (Zurich), August 1974; "Still Life with Destruction: Photos by Gilles Peress" by L. Garner in the *Sunday Times Magazine* (London), 8 December 1974; "Beirut: The Photographer's Story" by Fred Ritchin in *Camera Arts* (New York), January 1983; "Un Français en Perse" by Christian Caujolle in *Libération* (Paris), 25 May 1984; "The New Truth, Via Telex" by Vicki Goldberg in *American Photographer* (New York), November 1984; "Gilles Peress" by Christian Caujolle in *Libération* (Paris), 1 November 1984.

*

I started shooting in France in 1970, when there were neither grants nor a photography school. First I worked as an assistant in a fashion studio, a job which consisted of setting the cameras and painting the floor, and then as a wedding photographer. I shot my first story about a coal mine strike in 1960: the men occupied the pit, with food lowered down to them, for months before they capitulated. Ten years later the unemployment was so high that the young men of that town spent their days blind drunk on Pernod.

I started working with Magnum in 1971 and became a member in 1974. I covered the deaths and burials of famous statesmen: DeGaulle, Franco, Coco Chanel. I arrived in Portugal three hours after the revolution, trailed behind Popes like an acolyte, went to S and M conventions, mercenary conventions, and Republican conventions. I saw my pictures cropped and people airbrushed away by art directors.

Meanwhile, I have tried to use the magazine world as a vehicle to approach the world and myself in a more sustained way. In 1973 I spent several months documenting immigrant workers in Europe, a story that was published as a portfolio in *Du,* the London *Sunday Times* and other periodicals. In 1970, 1971, 1972, 1973, 1974 and 1979, I found ways to convince editors to send me to Northern Ireland: the material that I gathered has appeared as a portfolio in the *Sunday Times,* the *New York Magazine* and *Photo,* and published as a book.

When I came to America in 1975, I started shooting projects related to the "outsider" element in American society: unemployment in Detroit in 1975 for the London *Sunday Times,* 42nd Street in 1976 for PBS and in 1980 for a Ford Foundation project. I began to shoot, for myself, the way that people drop out of society: the dumping of mental patients on the street, the welfare hotels on the Bowery.

In 1976, while covering the elections for PBS, I became fascinated by the political process and the road to the election. I cornered Carter, watched Wallace, checked Jackson and chewed gum with Ford. I followed many of them, attended conventions and witnessed a million handshakes.

In 1977, I was given an artist-in-residence fellowship at Apeiron, which enabled me to print the work I had done in the U.S. since 1975. In 1977-78 I supported myself with *GEO* stories in Central and South America. That paid for my first darkroom and enabled me to spend six months in the winter of 1978-79 re-editing my work of the last eight years and trying to make sense of a career that seemed like a chaotic compromise between necessity and intention.

In 1979, I applied for and received a $3,000 grant from the NEA. Watching in frustration the television coverage of the hostage crisis, I realized that for the first time in my life I was free, entirely free, to shoot whatever, whichever way I wanted. A day later, I went to Iran, not knowing what I could do, knowing only that I wanted to be there, to see it with my own eyes, without responsibility or commitment (either political, visual or conceptual) to anyone. Although

for many years I tried to escape the preconceived vision of the world that magazine work imposes on you, for the first time I recognized that I didn't have to, as we say in journalism, cover myself. I went to Iran for five weeks, travelled about the country (I did not have to wait in front of the embassy), returned to New York, edited, printed and attempted to make sense of what I had experienced. I published the Iran material as a 74-picture, 10-page layout in *Afterimage.* The *New York Times* decided to run it as well, as a visual portfolio without text, and published it in book form as *Telex: Iran.*

As soon as I came out of the darkroom, I began to shoot the 1980 elections. Apart from the conventions, I have not had either the time or the money to print the bulk of this work. Though I have not yet found a way to make sense of it, this process—at once both absurd and one of the most deadly serious things I have witnessed—continues to intrigue me.

Now more than ever it is essential for me to try to shoot the intersection between the internal and external world, to understand that the closest point to objectivity is the acceptance of subjectivity, to walk the thin line between dreams and events.

—Gilles Peress

*   *   *

As a young photojournalist and member of Magnum, Gilles Peress would seem at first glance to represent the continuity of the tradition of concerned photography, a tradition firmly established in the 1930s and exemplified by Magnum's founders—Robert Capa, David Seymour, and Henri Cartier-Bresson. Certainly the subject of Peress' major photoreportages (for example, Bloody Sunday and its aftermath in Northern Ireland, "New Slaves of Europe: Turkish Workers in Germany," Iran after the Revolution) are precisely those subjects that an "engaged" photographer would be expected to document. A further list of his subjects would include various strikes, demonstrations, political coverage in Europe and the U.S., and a continuing attention to the lives of the poor, the oppressed, the human casualties of the industrialized West. But close examination of the photographs themselves reveals a dissonance between the nominal subject matter, including its implicit political/ social concerns, and increasing abstraction and formalization of the images.

Careful scrutiny of the photographs comprising the reportages on Iran or Northern Ireland, divorced from either accompanying text or captions, elicits little hard information or any political sense of the issues or events they are purportedly documenting. To a certain extent this is a problem implicit in the nature of photographic documentation *per se:* news and documentary photographs are never meant to stand alone; substance, context, and explanation must always be supplied by text. That having been said, one may also assert that there are varying degrees of communicativeness a photograph may possess. While certain events—a rocket launch, an image of combat, a volcano eruption—may require minimal text in order to be instantly legible as pictorial witnesses, most events in the world can never be made comprehensible through images alone. A situation such as obtains in Northern Ireland makes no sense without the knowledge of its history and a political framework that is not presentable in picture form. Peress in Belfast or Londonderry can only show effects, not causes. But within that *a priori* limitation, Peress' particular excellence is his ability to evoke atmosphere—the random violence, the rage, and progressive brutalization of occupied and occupier alike.

The evolution of Peress' photography becomes clear when one compares the Northern Ireland reportage with the one of post-revolutionary Iran. The direction is towards a cryptic, more personal signature style. Excepting certain images of the armed populace, the executed SAVAK officers, and some harrowing photos of their armless and otherwise maimed victims, these photographs can in no way be described as a purely reportorial documentation. In formal terms, they display greater innovation, and are characterized by a nightmare anomic vision, but can only with some difficulty be placed within the category of traditional photojournalism.

This evolution in Peress' work from the relatively straightforward photographs of ten years ago to the more subjective and personal production of the past few years is paradigmatic. For many young photojournalists, it is Cartier-Bresson rather than Robert Capa who is the model, because in Bresson's work subject matter has always been presented in terms of identifiable style. As photographic prestige attaches more and more to art photography—self-referential, personal, and highly formalist—serious photojournalists are caught in a critical bind. If they define their work as the bearing of pictorial witness, they may render themselves invisible; but if they impose a signature style, the events they record may become invisible, the photograph's style and subjectivity having replaced the subject. In certain cases, one can have it both ways: Peress' photographs of French peasants at harvest time are classically composed pastoral celebrations of a vanishing life and culture. The congruence of subject matter and style of depiction is satisfying and appropriate. Judging from his more recent work, it seems reasonable to conclude that the future evolution and direction of Peress' work will be determined by his ability to balance the imperatives of style with those of documentation.

—Abigail Solomon-Godeau

PERKIS, Philip.

Nationality: American. **Born:** Boston, Massachusetts, 12 November 1935. **Education:** Studied at the San Francisco Art Institute, B.F.A. 1962. **Military Service:** Served in the United States Air Force, 1954-58. **Family:** Married Roselaine Perkis in 1960. **Career:** Photographer since 1962. Teacher at Phillips Academy, Andover, Massachusetts, 1964-65; New York Institute of Technology, 1967-68; San Francisco Art Institute, Summers 1968, 1969, 1970; City College of New York, 1971; and New York University Film School, 1971-72. Assistant Professor since 1969, and Chairman of the Photography Department since 1975, Pratt Institute, Brooklyn, New York. **Recipient:** New York State Council on the Arts grants, 1971, 1976; National Endowment for the Arts grant, 1978. **Address:** 171 Steuben Street, Brooklyn, New York 11205, U.S.A.

Individual Exhibitions:

1971	San Francisco Art Institute
1972	Addison Gallery of American Art, Andover, Massachusetts
1976	Nexus Gallery, Atlanta
1977	Portland Art Institute, Maine
1981	*Photografia Actual en Neuva York,* Guadalajara, Mexico

Selected Group Exhibitions:

1967	*12 Photographers of the American Social Landscape,* Brandeis University, Waltham, Massachusetts
1970	*Be-Ing Without Clothes,* Hayden Gallery, Massachusetts Institute of Technology, Cambridge
1973	*Landscape/Cityscape,* Metropolitan Museum, New York
1978	*Photo Landscapes,* International Museum of Photography, George Eastman House, Rochester, New York
1980	*Photography: Recent Directions,* DeCordova Museum, Lincoln, Massachusetts

Collections:

Metropolitan Museum of Art, New York; Sam Wagstaff Collection, New York; International Museum of Photography, George Eastman House, Rochester, New York; Addison Gallery of American Art, Andover, Massachusetts.

Publications:

By PERKIS: Books—*Faces,* with others, New York 1977; *The Warwick Mountain Series,* Atlanta 1979.

*   *   *

All photographs use light in the formation of their images. For many, light is the technical requirement necessary only to document the objects, place or people. Philip Perkis' photographs are about that special quality of light as it is reflected at that one instant of his shutter click. It glows in his images of trees and shadows, discovers people in their backyards and fills with movement and

energy the streets of Tel Aviv. His matt surface images evoke a response similar to opening and looking at daguerreotypes. One discovers a person or an event in an extraordinary intimacy; the light radiates from the plate. His images are illuminated silver worlds which transmit a sensibility tuned to those rare times when the thing photographed and the light which discovers it for the film are in unusual harmony.

Perkis is very much a formalist and has highly developed strategies of controlled picture structure and subdued, modulated mid-tone prints. His subject interests are landscape and street photography which cross influence giving a snapshot feeling to carefully planned images of trees, rocks and rural areas and an archetonic quality of structure and space to people moving and interacting in the street. In his photographs there is always a sense of all the elements having been taken into consideration, examined, solved but not put forth as the most important aspect of his vision. Perkis is interested in giving the viewer a common pebble which one holds, almost discards, then discovers to possess an intricate structure and a surface which seems to emit light. Perkis is unusual among contemporary photographers because he shows us what he sees before he shows us what he thinks.

—James L. Sheldon

PETERSEN, Anders.

Nationality: Swedish. **Born:** Stockholm, in 1944. **Education:** Studied at Christer Stromholm's Photography School, Stockholm, 1966-68; Swedish Filmschool (Dramatiska Institutet), Stockholm, 1973-74. **Career:** Independent photographer, Stockholm. Member, SAFTRA photographers' group. Instructor, Christer Stromholm's Photography School, 1969-71. **Recipient:** Kodak Fotobuchpreis, 1979; Awards from Fotografiska Museets Vänner; Anna Riwkin-Brick Stipendiefond; Författarfonden; Stockholms stad; Konstnärsnämnden. **Address:** Gotgatan 29, 11621 Stockholm, Sweden.

Individual Exhibitions:

1969	*Biennal de Paris,* Musée d'Art Moderne, Paris
1970	*Reeperbahn,* Galleri Karlsson, Stockholm (travelled to the Kunstforeningen, Oslo, 1971)
1973	*Hamburg,* Half Moon Gallery, London
1976	*Circus,* House of Culture, Stockholm
1977	*Cafe Lehmitz,* Musée Réattu, Arles, France
1978	*Bistro d'Hambourg,* FNAC Gallery, Paris
1979	*Anders Petersen Photographiet,* Badischer Kunstverein, Karlsruhe
	Neighbours, City Museum, Stockholm
1980	*Cafe Lehmitz,* Hippolyte Gallery, Helsinki
	Ralph Nykvist/Anders Petersen, Fotogalleriet, Oslo
1982	*Internationella Fotofestivalen,* Mälmö
1983	Fotograficentrum, Linköping
1984	Fotograficentrum, Stockholm
	Fotograficentrum, Örebro
1985	Galleri GAUSS, Stockholm
	Mälmö Museum, Mälmö
	Torino Fotografia, Turin, Italy
1987	Galleri ROM, Oslo
1991	Nordiska Museet, Stockholm
	Fotografiska Museet, Stockholm (with Ralph Nykvist)
	Galleri Tornhuset, Luleå
1992	Arbetets Museum, Norrköping
	Fotograficentrum, Örebro
	Landskrona Museum, Landskrona
	Helsingborgs Stadsteater, Helsingborg
1993	*Rågång till kärleken,* Riksutställingar
1994	Sundsvalls Museum, Sundsvall

Sweden, **1993.** Photograph ©Anders Petersen.

Selected Group Exhibitions:

1967 *Young Photographers,* Moderna Museet, Stockholm
1969 *City in Return,* City Museum, Stockholm
1977 *SAFTRA,* at *Rencontres Internationales de la Photographie,*
   Arles, France
1983 *Den fotografiska bilden,* Universitetshuset, Lund
   Contemporary Swedish Photography, Nottingham, Newcastle,
    Kendal, Cheltenham, England
1985 *Med sikte på verkligheten,* Kulturhuset, Stockholm
   Ten Swedish Photographers, Arles, France
1985 *Jubileumsutställning (SFF),* Fotografiska Museet, Stockholm
1986 *Gruppbilder,* Stockholm Mobile, Stockholm
1988 Houston Fotofest, Houston, Texas
1989 Maison de la Culture Plateau-Mont-Royal, Montreal, Canada
1989 *Contemporary Photographers,* Prague
1991 *LIKA MED,* Moderna Museet, Stockholm
1993 *De refuserede,* Liljevalchs, Stockholm
1994 *Tres Generaciones de Fotografos Suecos,* Museo Nacional
    Bellas Artes, Santiago
   Galleri Fotohuset, Göteborg
   Museo Nacional de Artes Visuales, Montevideo
   Galleri Engman, Umeå
   Galleri Kilen, Luleå
   Smedsby Konstakt, Emtervik
   Fotografens Album, Åbo

Chinese Revolutionary Museum, Peking

Collections:

Fotografiska Museet, Moderna Museet, Stockholm; Bibliothèque Nationale, Paris; Landskrona Museum, Landskrona; Museum of Fine Arts, Houston, Texas; Museum Folkwang, Essen.

Publications:

By PETERSEN: Books—*Grona Lund,* with text by Jan Stolpe, Helsingborg, Sweden 1973; *A Day at the Circus,* with Stefan Lindberg and Mona Larsson, Lund, Sweden 1976; *Cafe Lehmitz,* with text by Roger Anderson, Munich 1978, and Stockholm 1982, as *Bistro d'Hambourg,* Paris 1979; *Fängelse/ Prison,* with text by Leif Persson, Stockholm 1984; *Seychellerna,* text by Folke Isaksson, Stockhom, 1987; *Rågång till kärleken,* text by Göran Odsbratt, Stockholm, 1991; *Karnevalen i Venedig,* with Ralph Nykvist, Stockholm, 1991.

On PETERSEN: Article—''Anders Petersen'' by Peder Alton in *Fotograficentrums Bildtidning* (Stockholm), May 1980.

*

When I'm out taking pictures and meeting people, it is always more important for me to establish a direct dialogue than to be a photographer.

—Anders Petersen

*   *   *

Anders Petersen has often been described as a portrayer of "the damned." He has, for example, taken his motifs from a Hamburg bar (mostly frequented by elderly prostitutes and homosexuals), from a prison, and from a shopping centre where gangs of youths gather to seek warmth and fellowship. And even when he has depicted more usual and more accessible subjects, such as an amusement park or a circus, he is not primarily attracted by the excitement and the festive atmosphere. Generally he keeps to the periphery: he points his camera towards the visitors to the amusement park, who are vacantly seeking a refuge from the drabness and loneliness of everyday life; in the circus he is as interested in the work behind the scenes and life in the caravans as in the circus itself.

Photographers have often been attracted by these subjects, but most have approached the motifs as prying outsiders. They have peeped in stealthily with a tele-objective and have all the time been prepared for a quick retreat. Obtaining a picture of a whore or a drunk bar-guest has become an end in itself. For Petersen the importance lies in the contact with his subject. He has to identify himself with the people he portrays, has to gain their confidence, has to like them. He has to achieve an emotional contact—he says that he "photographs with his belly."

Petersen has often talked of the photographer's responsibility and of the importance of believing in one's work; of explaining properly the purpose of the photo to those whom it affects; of showing them the pictures later and discussing the results, being able to argue for one's pictorial description; but, at the same time, being receptive to the arguments of the subjects. And obviously the photographer must take his share of the responsibility for how the pictures are distributed, in what context they are published, how the captions are written.

Not surprisingly, Petersen often mentions Bruce Davidson as an example. His depiction of gangs of youths in Brooklyn and his documentation of life on East 100th Street show what a receptive photographer can achieve, when he has gained the confidence of people within their surroundings.

"You must have a directness and self-confidence in your way of being with other people in order to make reality visible. With a little luck it then becomes possible to clarify something for others though your pictures" Petersen has said in an interview. He has evolved this working methodology since he documented life in the "Lehmitz" bar in Hamburg in the late 1960s. It took him two years to carry out this project, but it must also be pointed out that many of the people he portrayed there he had known seven years previously. For in the early 60s he had lived in Hamburg (without a camera) to improve his languages.

Anders Petersen has not used the camera as a shield between himself and reality. Photography becomes an integral part of the relationship. His pictures do not function as closed windows, through which we steal a glimpse. They are open, as are the people we meet in his pictorial world.

—Rune Jonsson

PFAHL, John.

Nationality: American. **Born:** New York City, 17 February 1939. **Education:** Butler High School, Butler, New Jersey, 1953-57; Syracuse University, New York, 1957-61, B.F.A. in graphic design 1961, M.A. in communications 1968. **Military Service:** Served in the United States Army, Fort Belvoir, Virginia, 1961-63. **Family:** Married Bonnie Gordon in 1965. **Career:** Adjunct Professor, University of Buffalo, Buffalo, New York, since 1990.

Recipient: Creative Artists Public Service Grant, 1975, 1979; National Endowment for the Arts Photography Fellowship, 1977, 1990; Honororary Doctorate of Fine Arts, Niagara University, Niagara Falls, New York, 1990. **Agent:** Janet Borden Inc., 560 Broadway, New York, New York 10012, U.S.A. **Address:** 797 Potomac Avenue, Buffalo, New York 14209, U.S.A.

Individual Exhibitions:

1970	University of New Hampshire, Durham
1973	East Tennessee State University, Johnson City
1976	Deja Vue Gallery, Toronto
	Visual Studies Workshop, Rochester, New York
1978	*Altered Landscapes,* Robert Freidus Gallery, New York
1979	Princeton University, New Jersey
	Thomas Segal Gallery, Boston
	Canon Photo Gallery, Geneva
	Robert Freidus Gallery, New York
	Danforth Museum, Framingham, Massachusetts
	University of Massachusetts, Amherst
	Divola/Henkle/Parker/Pfahl, Visual Studies Workshop, Rochester, New York (toured the United States)
1980	Jeb Gallery, Providence, Rhode Island
	Bell Gallery, Brown University, Providence, Rhode Island
	Kathleen Ewing Gallery, Washington, D.C.
	Visual Studies Workshop, Rochester, New York
	Picture Windows, Robert Freidus Gallery, New York
1984	*Power Places,* Los Angeles County Museum of Art
	La Jolla Museum of Contemporary Art, California
	Center for Contemporary Arts, Santa Fe, New Mexico
1986	Anderson Gallery, Virginia Commonwealth University, Richmond
	Troyer Fitzpatrick Lassman Gallery, Washington, D.C.
	Nina Freudenheim Gallery, Buffalo, New York
	Castellani Art Museum, Niagara University, Niagara Falls, New York
1988	Fotografie Forum, Frankfurt, Germany
	Visual Studies Workshop Gallery, Rochester, New York
1990	*A Distanced Land: The Photographs of John Pfahl,* The Photographer's Gallery, Palo Alto, California (also travelled to Albright-Knox Gallery, Buffalo, New York, Chicago Art Institute, Illinois, 1991; Friends of Photography, San Francisco, 1992; High Museum, Atlanta, Georgia, 1992; Los Angeles County Art Museum, California, 1993)
1992	Janet Borden Gallery, New York
1993	Linda Cathcart Gallery, Santa Monica, California
1994	International Museum of Photography, George Eastman House, Rochester, New York

Selected Group Exhibitions:

1979	*Color: A Spectrum of Recent Photography,* Milwaukee Art Center
	The American Still Life 1879-1979, Addison Gallery, Andover, Massachusetts
1980	*Polacolor,* Philadelphia Academy of Art
	Aspects of the 70s, De Cordova Museum, Lincoln, Massachusetts
1981	*Photographer as Printmaker,* Ferens Art Gallery, Hull, Yorkshire (travelled to the Museum and Art Gallery, Leicester; Cooper Gallery, Barnsley; Castle Museum, Nottingham; Photographers' Gallery, London)
1982	*Color as Form,* International Museum of Photography at George Eastman House, Rochester, New York
1983	*Photography in America 1910-83,* Tampa Museum, Florida
1984	*La Photographie Créative,* Pavillon des Arts, Paris

Blue Right-Angle, **Buffalo, New York, 1975 (original in colour).** Photograph by John Pfahl.

Construire les Paysages de la Photographie, Caves Saint-Croix, Metz, France

1985   *American Images 1945-80,* Barbican Art Gallery, London
          (toured Britain)
          Images of Excellence, Internaional Museum of Photography,
          George Eastman House, Rochester, New York
          New Color/New Work, Museum of Contemporary Photography,
          Chicago

1986   *Photography: A Facet of Modernism,* San Francisco Museum
          of Modern Art

1987   *Von Landschaftsbild zur Spurensicherung,* Museum Ludwig,
          Cologne
          Photography and Art: Interactions Since 1945, Los Angeles
          County Museum of Art

1989   *On the Art of Fixing a Shadow: One Hundred and Fifty Years
          of Photography,* National Gallery of Art, Washington, D.C.

1990   *The New American Pastoral: Landscape Photography in the
          Age of Questioning,* International Museum of Photography,
          George Eastman House

1991   *Another Side of Progress,* The Light Factory, Charlotte, North
          Carolina

1993   *Commodity Image,* International Center of Photography
          Midtown, New York

Renewing our Earth: The Artistic Vision, United States
Pavilion Taejon International Expo, South Korea
International Effects, The Art Institute of Chicago

1994   *Pictures in the Land,* National Wildlife Art Museum, Jackson,
          Wyoming

Collections:

International Museum of Photography, George Eastman House, Rochester,
New York; Albright-Knox Art Gallery, Buffalo, New York; Smith College,
Northampton, Massachusetts; Princeton University, New Jersey; Minneapolis
Institute of Art; Denver Art Museum; Contemporary Art Museum, Houston;
University of New Mexico, Albuquerque; San Francisco Museum of Modern
Art; Australian National Gallery, Canberra.

Publications:

By PFAHL: Books—*Altered Landscapes,* Carmel, California 1981; *Picture
Windows,* Boston, 1987; *Arcadia Revisited: Niagara River and Falls from
Lake Erie to Lake Ontario,* Alburquerque, 1988; *A Distanced Land: The
Photographs of John Pfahl,* Alburquerque, 1990; *Tainted Photographers and
the Compromised Environment,* Niagara Falls, New York 1991. **Articles**—

"Interview with John Pfahl," with Stuart Rome, in *Northlight* (Tempe, Arizona), April 1981; "Power and Smoke: Two Statements" in *Aperture #120: Beyond Wilderness* (New York), 1990; "Missile/Glyphs" in *Buzzworm: The Environmental Journal* (Boulder), March/April 1991.

On PFAHL: Books—*International Photography 1920-1980*, edited by Ian North, Canberra 1982; *New Color/New York* by Sally Eauclaire, New York 1984; *La Photographie Créative* by Jean-Claude Lemagny, Paris 1984; *The Library of World Photography: Landscape*, with texts by David Plowden and Ian Jeffrey, Tokyo and London 1984; *Landscape as Photograph*, by Estelle Jussim and Elisabeth Lindquist-Cock, New Haven, 1984; *American Images: Photography 1945-1980*, edited by Peter Turner and John Benton-Harris, London 1985; *Masterpieces of Photography from George Eastman House*, edited by Robert A. Sobieszek, New York 1985; *New American Photography*, by Kathleen Gauss, Los Angeles, 1985; *Decade by Decade: Twentieth Century American Photography*, edited by James Enyeart, Tucson, AZ, 1989; *New Landscape* by Kohtaro Iizawa and Natsuki Ikezawa, Tokyo. Articles—"Photography" by Ben Lifson in the *Village Voice* (New York), March 1978; "John Pfahl's Picturesque Paradoxes" by Anthony Bannon in *Afterimage* (Rochester, New York), February 1979; "John Pfahl: Bagles and Rocks" in *Photography Year 1979* by the Time-Life editors, New York 1979; "Binary Fission" by Robert Morgan in *Afterimage*, April 1987; "Unnatural Wonders" by Wayne Draznin in *Art in America*, March 1992.

*

Casual viewers of my "altered landscape" photographs are often misled into believing that there are dotted lines, arrows or other marks drawn on the prints. Closer observation reveals that the markings are actually type, string or foil introduced into the scene in front of the camera *before* the moment of exposure. The illusion created is somewhat related to the anamorphic impulses in painting and drawing that made their first appearances in the early Renaissance.

In this case, however, the illusions are a purely photographic phenomenon and can only be realized by a camera situated at one crucial point in space. A 4 x 5 inch view camera on a tripod was used at selected locations. Simple drawings were traced on the ground-glass and duplicated by placing artificial elements into the scene itself. This procedure involved hours of painstaking trial-and-error adjustments, occasionally with the aid of assistants, and periodically monitored by Polaroid exposures. The "decisive moment" generally turned out to be from two to eight hours long. After the exposures were made, all traces of the activity were removed and the landscape returned to its original inchoate state.

Large format color photography was chosen as the medium because of its great verisimilitude. Perceptual clues denoting depth and distance can be presented with great clarity. Color also permits the introduction of an unabashedly sensuous quality which serves to flesh out the bare conceptual basis for the work.

Locations for the photographs were chosen for their "picturesque" qualities, their formal structure, and their referential possibilities. The added elements suggest numerous markmaking devices associated with photographs, maps, plans, and diagrams. On different occasions, they may pointedly repeat a strong formal element in the landscape, they may fill in information or utilize information suggested by the scene, or they may be only arbitrarily related to the scene but refer instead to the process of making a photograph.

—John Pfahl

*   *   *

John Pfahl is best known for his series of *Altered Landscapes* (c. 1974-77) in which he plays whimsical and often astonishing tricks with our perception. Pfahl, however, has used a number of other approaches to picture-making, including making photographs into sculpture and using materials such as sugar and latex to print photographs; in 1978 Pfahl was the first artist invited to use the Polaroid Corporation's 20 x 24 camera. Although Pfahl goes to great lengths to achieve technically perfect prints, he is constrained in no other way by "photographic purity." His open attitude has allowed him throughout his career to escape the conventions of photographic rendering but, in so doing, to comment upon them.

In *Altered Landscapes,* Pfahl uses a number of methods to enhance his lush views/scenes; with string, yarn, foil, tape, rods, and a variety of other props including bagels, lace, oranges, and a pie pan, Pfahl echoes the forms in the landscape, or uses them as the basis for other forms, or simply applies his own, often arbitrary, system of marks. In the present-day abundance of contemporary photographs that have been drawn on or marked, it is often difficult to remember that Pfahl's designs are part of the picture, rather than applied to the surface. His scenes take hours to set up, require complex figuring to achieve the perfect perspective and illusion he is after, and, unlike other photographs, his compositions "exist" from only one, very precise viewpoint.

Pfahl's imposed designs serve as a system of ordering information that both parallels and contrasts the pictorial system of camera-made imagery. Using the tricks of perspective, Pfahl underscores the nature of photographic illusion and sets up a dialectic between real and abstract, between three-dimensional space and the flat plane of the photograph, and also between photographic clichés and the constant search for novelty, as in his desert scene "Moonrise over Pie Pan." And just as the camera is both personal and mechanistic, Pfahl's unabashed romanticism is belied by the scientific precision of his diagrams.

Pfahl notes that his work represents an exaggeration of the concern, automatic in photography, with how space translates from three dimensions to two. Furthermore, he remarks that most contemporary photographers are concerned primarily with the photographic process itself rather than, simply, with subject matter. Yet, while the world is overphotographed, photographers are finding increasing sustenance in what Pfahl describes as specific detail. Recent advances in color technology, including the 20 x 24 Polaroid camera, have renewed photographers' interest in the idea of inventory, and the idea of setting up solely for the purpose of inventory, as Van Deren Coke's exhibit *Fabricated to Be Photographed* (1979) pointed out. "One of the most beautiful applications of photography," says Pfahl, "is the combination of specific detail with a sense of abstraction." The wit and lushness, the sheer visual appeal of his photographs aside, Pfahl offers in, say, the comparison of a wave breaking on the shore with a strip of lace, a fresh perception, both literally and figuratively, of some of photograph's most favorite, and overworked, motifs. A more recent series of photographs, "Picture Windows," continues to explore the nature of perception using views of backyards, parking lots, mountains, and the variety of scenes for which picture windows were invented. Pfahl reveals that after years of laborious set-ups, the picture windows provide him an exhilarating freedom to accept what is there. The bright rectangles of windows seem to float in the dark interiors, like pictures within a picture, offering an endless series of connections between the camera, the frame, and the world.

Pfahl's greatest contribution lies in his unique ability to combine the conceptual with the pictorial and, perhaps, to pay homage to 19th century ways of viewing the world using modern ideas about perception and the ambiguous line between reality and abstraction.

—Dana Asbury

PIERRE ET GILLES.

Nationality: French. Born: Pierre, born La Roche-sur-Yon, France; Gilles, born Le Havre, France. Education: Pierre, studied in Geneva; Gilles, at the age of 15 entered the Academy of Art in Le Havre and graduated with distinction. Career: Pierre, after military service in France went to Paris in 1973 and started working as a photographer for music and fashion magazines; Gilles, in 1973 moved to Paris and produced collages and paintings as well as illustrations for magazines and advertisements. Pierre and Gilles met in 1976 and in 1977 decided to collaborate. Their first joint work appeared in the magazine Façade. In 1978 the fashion designer Thierry Mugler commissioned work from them as did magazines including *Marie Claire* and *Playboy*. They also designed album covers for Amanda Lear and others. They travelled to India and established a studio in the Bastille quarter of Paris. In 1890/81 they visited Sri Lanka and the Maldive Islands where they did their first open-air work. In 1986, their first video *Naufrage en hiver* was produced. In 1991 they moved to the Paris suburb of Pré Saint-Gervais. From 1991 to 1993 their work

Asian Venus, **1991 (original in colour).** Photograph by Pierre et Gilles. Courtesy Galerie Samia Saouma, Paris.

was shown in numerous exhibitions in Europe, Japan and the Americas.
Address: Galerie Samia Saouma, 16, rue des Coutures St-Gervais, 75003 Paris, France.

Individual Exhibitions:

1983	Galerie Texbraun, Paris
1985	Ginza Gallery, Tokyo
	Galeries Saluces, Avignon, France
1986	Galerie des Arnes, Nîmes, France
	Galerie Samia Saouma, Paris
1988	Galerie Samia Saouma, Paris
1990	Hirschl & Adler, New York
1992	Raab Galerie, Berlin
	Diaghilev Centre of Modern Art, St Petersburg, Russia
	Raab Gallery, London
1993	Galerie Samia Saouma, Paris
	Galerie du Salon, Direction Régionale d'Arts et Culture des Pays de la Loire, Nantes, France
	Galleria Il Ponte, Rome

1994	Le Case d'Arte, Milan, Italy
1995	Roslyn Oxley, Sydney, Australia
	Shiseido, Tokyo
	Retrospective, Maison Europeenne de la Photographie, Paris

Selected Group Exhibitions:

1982	Galerie Viviane Esders, Paris
1984	Galeria Texbraun, Paris
	ARC Musée d'Art Moderne de la Ville de Paris, Centre Georges Pompidou, Paris
1985	Galerie Samia Saouma, Paris
1986	Museum of Contemporary Art, Montreal, Quebec
	Palais des Beaux Arts, Charleroi, Belgium
	Annina Nosei Gallery, New York
1988	Universita Gabriele d'Annunzio, Pescara, Italy
1989	*Das Portrait,* Kunstverein, Hamburg, Germany
	Salzburg Festival, Austria
	Pinacoteca Communale, Ravenna, Italy
	Nos Années 80, Cartier Foundation, Paris

1990	Gulbenkian Foundation, Lisbon, Portugal
1991	*La Photographie française en liberté*, Institute of Contemporary Photography, New York, Museum of Modern Art, Mexico City, Museum of Contemporary Art, New Orleans, Amsterdam Museum, Rotterdam Museum
	Lyon Biennale, Musée Saint Pierre, Lyon, France
	Consorts, Pence Gallery, Santa Monica, California
1992	*Private/Public*, Museum of Modern Art, Oxford, England, also London and Edinburgh.
	Illusions et Travestissements (Images and Travesties), A/B Galeries, Paris
	Images Mtisses, Institute of the Arab World, Paris
	Markhalle Moderne Kunst, Stuttgart, Germany
1993	FAE Museum of Comtemporary Art, Lausanne, Switzerland
	Prospect 93, Frankfurt, Germany
	Galerie Gabrielle Maubrie, Paris
	Histoire de Voir, Château de Villeneuve, Vence, France
	Public/Private, French Institute of Scotland, Edinburgh
	Les Images du Plaisir, FRAC Pays de la Loire, Laval, France
	Discourse of Images, Kunsthistorisches Museum, Vienna
	Austrian Triennale of Photography, Neue Galerie am Landesmuseum Joanneum, Austria
	Personal Jesus, Dooley Le Capellaine, New York
1994	*Cocido y Crudo*, Reina Sophia Museum, Madrid
	The Art of French Portraiture in the 19th and 20th Centuries, Japan (travelled)
	Rencontres Photographiques, Arles, France
	Don't Leave Me This Way: Art in the Age of Aids, National Gallery, Canberra

Collections:

Centre Georges Pompidou, Paris; Fonds National d'Art Contemporain, Paris; City of Paris Art Gallery; Fondation Cartier, Paris; Museum of Contemporary Art, Montreal; FRAC Aquitaine, France.

Publications:

ON PIERRE ET GILLES: Books—*L'Odysée Imaginaire*, Paris, 1988; *Pierre et Gilles*, Paris, 1992. **Articles**— *Art Forum*, March 1983; *Flash Art*, Summer 1986; *Artpress* Nr 108, November 1986; *Actuel*, November 1988; *Le Monde*, 14.12.1988; *Elle (UK)*, January 1991; *Artpress* no. 180, May 1993.

PILLITZ, Christopher J.I.

Nationality: Argentinian and British. **Born:** Buenos Aires, 1 December, 1958. **Education:** Attended St Paul's School, Cordoba, Argentina; studied Hotel Catering & Institutional Management at Dorset Institute of Higher Education; self-taught in photography. **Career:** Since 1983 has worked as a photojournalist/photographer travelling extensively around the world doing stories with a strong social/documentarian emphasis for many of the world's leading magazines such as *The Sunday Times, Geo, New York Times, Telegraph, Stern* and others. Member and part owner of Network Photographers. **Agent:** Network Photographers, 3-4 Kirby Street, London E1, England. **Address:** 39 Church View Road, Twickenham, Middlesex, TW2 5BT, England.

Selected Group Exhibitions:

1989	*Eastern Europe*, Zelda Cheatle Gallery, London; National Museum of Photography, Bradford, England
	The Response to HIV, National Museum of Photography, Bradford, England; Museum of Modern Art, Oxford; Photographer's Gallery, London.

*

I try and be true to the subject.

—Christopher Pillitz

* * *

After training in hotel management, Christopher Pillitz launched unexpectedly and dramatically into photojournalism. Within a few years of deciding on this new life, by the age of 24, he had become a regular feature contributor to the *Sunday Times Magazine* at a time when the *Sunday Times* was leading the field of dynamic photojournalism. Riding the wave of popularity for reportage photography Christopher became one of Britain's busiest feature photographers visiting more than fifty countries in ten years.

This rapid professional development was due in equal parts to a sophisticated visual awareness, intelligent analysis of the themes to be interpreted and a searing intensity of concentration on the matter in hand. Christopher describes himself as a perfectionist and this is evident at every stage of his work: in preparing for a trip, in editing and captioning completed work, in the sales pitch to ensure the best usage of the work and of course in the photography itself. Nobody was surprised that he should use his last drop of energy while in a Belize hospital bed (near death with severe appendicitis) to phone his editor arguing for an hour about the front page use of a picture: it was all part of the job. Watching Christopher work proves the value of sheer hard graft in producing apparently effortless narrative.

Christopher's editorial work has been characterised by dynamic graphic form and astute use of colour. The pictures have a fluid composition which allows the subject matter to project clearly through the confines of the frame.

Christopher is motivated both by the formal aesthetics of the photographic image and by an intense need to communicate about the subject matter. As a perfectionist he is very aware of the limitations of editorial conventions which frequently restrict the content of a story to narrow and simplistic narratives and he has often speculated about the possibility of expanding his repertoire to include film.

In 1990 he began his most ambitious project to date with the first steps in a documentary work that has since become known as *Brazil Incarnate*. Using photography to explore the intangible miasmas of human sexuality and desire with Rio as the raw material for his black-and-white palette, Christopher began to challenge the restrictions of documentary convention. Entirely self-funded and doggedly independent, the work grew over five years to become a wild evocation of abstract experiences: desire and desperation, satisfaction and frustration, beauty and pain. The success of the work has been its liberating effect on Christopher's photography which is now open to all the freedoms of a medium adapted to express the uncertainties, ambiguities and contradictions of human experience.

—Stephen Mayes

PINKAVA, Ivan.

Nationality: Czechoslovakian. **Born:** Náchod, Czech Republic, 1 February 1961. **Education:** Attended the School for Graphics in Prague 1982-86, then studied Photographic Art at the Prague Film Academy. **Career:** In 1989 helped to set up the Foundation of Prague House of Photography. In 1990 lectured at the Rencontres Photographiques festival at Arles, France. In 1991-92, lectured in the Department of Photographic Art at the Prague Film Academy. **Agent:** NOX Contemporary Photography, Na Vypichu 6, 16900 Praha 6, Czech Republic. **Address:** U Svobodárny 10, Praha 9, 190 00, Czech Republic.

Individual Exhibitions:

1990	Fotogalerie in der Brotfabrik, Berlin
1992	*Dynasty*, House of Photography, Prague
1992	Hippolyte Gallery, Helsinki, Finland

Seville, **1988.** Photograph by Christopher Pillitz.

Selected Group Exhibitions:

1988   *Vize,* Moravská Galerie, Brno, Czech Republic
1990   *Choice,* Fotofest, Houston, USA
       Contemporary Czech Photography, Museum Ludwig, Cologne,
         Germany
       Vision of Man, Galerie Municipale du Château d'Eau,
         Toulouse, France
1991   European Photography Award 1991, Berlin
1993   *Presences,* The Photographers' Gallery, London

Collections:

Uměleckoprůmyslové Muzeum, Prague; Moravská Galerie, Brno, Czech Rep;
Bibliothèque Nationale, Paris; Musée de l'Elysée, Lausanne, Switzerland;
Gernsheim Collection, Austin, Texas, USA; Victoria and Albert Museum,
London; Maison Européenne de la Photographie, Paris.

Publications:

By PINKAVA: Book—Ivan Pinkava, *Dynasty* text by Josef Kroutvor,
Prague 1994.

On PINKAVA: Articles—"Ivan Pinkava" by Petr Balajka, *Edice RF* No 1,
Prague 1991; "Ivan Pinkava" by Christian Cajolle, *Clichés* No 64, Brussels
1990; "Noire Melancholie" by Pierre Stiwer and Paul di Felice, *Café-Crème*
Nr 14, Luxembourg 1990; "Ivan Pinkava - Portraits" by Denis Brudna,
Photonews No 2, Hamburg 1994; "Ivan Pinkava/Portfolios", *European
Photography* No 49, Göttingen 1992; "Dynastia" by Aino Martikainen,
Valokuva No 7, Helsinki 1992.

*   *   *

Along with Michal Macků, Robert Portel, and members of the Brotherhood group, Ivan Pinkava ranks among Czech photographers who reject the
playfulness, levity and lack of conflict in the Czechoslovak staged photography of the 1980s, represented primarily by Tono Stano, Miro Švolík, Vasil
Stanko or Rudo Prekop. The fresh ideas of this new generation of post-
modernist photographers were rapidly exhausted, and what had originally
been shocking gradually became commonplace.

Ivan Pinkava and several other contemporary photographers approach
their work with less spontaneity and levity and with a more profoundly
intellectual discipline. They often seek inspiration from decadent turn-of-the-
century symbolism, but they are also interested in mannerism and other more
spiritual trends in art and humanistic thought. Pinkava devotes his attention
almost exclusively to portraits, just occasionally with well-known personalities as their subjects. These are, for example, Allen Ginsberg, Irina Ionesco,
and Anna Fárová, yet even these are to a large extent not only portraits of those

The Head of a Young Man, **1993.** Photograph by Ivan Pinkava.

individuals, but also reflective symbolic self-portraits of the photographer himself.

This approach is even more evident in Pinkava's earlier portraits of anonymous models with closed eyes, from the years 1985-1987 when Pinkava was still a student of the Film & Photography School (FAMU) in Prague. The individual portraits are dedicated to various philosophical, literary, and artistic personalities who were important to him—Dostoyevsky, Nietzsche, Artaud, Wilde, and others. In some cases the portraits outwardly resemble these figures—the ''Photograph for Vladimir Mayakovsky'', for instance, really looks like the Russian avant-garde poet—but usually the parallels are less obvious. These photographs with expressive under-lighting already manifest secrecy as one of the basic attributes of Pinkava's work. In this case it is accented by the constantly repeated motif of closed eyes, suggestive of inner contemplation, meditation, and aloofness from the surrounding world.

The concept of the portrait as symbolic reflection culminates in Pinkava's last cycle, entitled ''Dynasty.'' The photogapher's interest in the spiritual climate of the late 19th and early 20th centuries is even more evident here. Many of the people portrayed are dressed in clothes from this period, while the composition and use of a chiaroscuro background correspond to techniques of that period based on portrait paintings. However, the photographs are supremely contemporary and, owing to their historical references, their astonishing arrangement, and the models' exalted expressions, they rank among the typical manifestations of post-modernist staged photography. This dichotomy of style and the merging of rationality and fantasy emphasize the strong feeling of disquiet evoked in these photographs. This feeling is also enhanced by the models themselves, mostly young men and aging women in whom the typical features of both sexes are combined, but on a far more symbolic plane than in *Modern Lovers* by Bettina Rheims, for example. In Pinkava's photographs they often look like archetypes and mythical figures emerging somewhere from the depths of the subconscious. At the same time, though, they also symbolize the various visions and vibrations in the hypersensitive spirit of the photographer who, through their mediation, clearly betrays more about himself than words could.

As David Chandler observed in the catalogue to *Presences*, ''Pinkava's subjects continually frustrate our efforts to place them—culturally, historically or otherwise. They bear the traces of a timeless conflict, scarred, heavy-lidded, emotionally frayed. They are hardened yet also vulnerable and tender. They appear to us as refugees who have gained temporary sanctuary in Pinkava's imagination, deprived victims or outsiders burned by excess.''

—Vladimír Birgus

PINKHASSOV, Gueorgui.

Nationality: French and Russian. **Born:** Moscow, USSR, 12 August 1952. **Education:** After completing his schooling in 1969 began to take an interest in photography; in 1969 enrolled at the Institute of Cinema (VGIK) in Moscow in the section for cameramen, where he studied until 1971. **Family:** Married Angela Pinkhassov in 1992; children: Daniel. **Career:** From 1973 to 1978 worked as an assistant cameraman at the Mosfilm studios in Moscow. In 1978 joined the Moscow Union of Graphic Arts and gained the status of independent artist. Completed a number of features for the *Soviet Artist* publishing house and other publishers. In the same year was employed by the director Andrei Tarkovski as set photographer on his film *Stalker*. In 1985 he moved to Paris and took French nationality in 1986. In 1988 joined the Magnum agency and in the same year obtained a scholarship from the French Ministry of Culture for his work on minorities in the USSR. He became an associate member of Magnum in 1991. **Recipient:** In 1993 his photojournalism received an Award of Excellence from the Society of Newspaper Design, and his work on Chinese avant-garde artists won the World Press Photo first prize in the Art category. **Agent:** Magnum Photos, 5 Passage Piver, 75011, Paris, France. **Address:** 27, rue de la Villette, 75019 Paris, France.

Individual Exhibitions:

1979   House of Writers, Moscow

          Tallinn, Estonia
1987   Cité Internationale des Arts, Paris
1988   Centre de la Photographie, Geneva, Switzerland
          Exhibition on Central Asia, Galerie Picto, Paris

Selected Group Exhibitions:

1979   Union of Graphic Arts, Moscow
1982   House of Painters, Moscow
1984   *Life through the Lens*, Winter Exhibition, Moscow
1985   *Nine Moscow Photographers*, Malaja Gruzinskaja St, Moscow
1986   Galerie Agathe Gaillard, Paris
1987   Cité Internationale des Arts, Paris
1990   *The Nominees of MAGNUM* (Photos of Armenia), FNAC, Paris
          East with MAGNUM, travelling exhibition starting at the Rencontres Photographiques, Arles, France
1994   Auction of MAGNUM photos at Christies, London

Collections:

Bibliotheque Nationale de Paris, France; Fondation Internationale D'Art Contemporain, Paris; Fondation Shell.

Publications:

By PINKHASSOV: Books—*A l'Est de Magnum,* Paris, 1991; *Indonesia, Malaysia, Brunei, Vietnam,* Paris, 1991; *Livre de Commande sur La Défense de Paris,* Paris, 1992; *Incertain Pays* Paris, 1993; *Sevilla,* Spain 1994. **Photography in magazines**—*Photorevue* (Czechoslovakia) 1978; *Sovietskojé Photo 10* (USSR) 1981; *Technical Aesthetics* (USSR) 1982; *Valukova* (Finland) Sept. 1985; *Creative Camera* (UK) November 1986; *Zoom Nr 143* (France) 1987; *Images 14, L'Hebdo 4, Scènes 16, Emois 9* (Switzerland) 1988; *Actuel 132, 134* (France) 1990; *Actuel 2* (France) 1991; *New York Times Magazine* 1992, 1993, 1994; *Daily Telegraph* (UK) 1994. **Film**—*Russian Prisons*, Little Magic Productions Inc, 1992.

PLEWIŃSKI, Wojciech.

Nationality: Polish. **Born:** Warsaw, 31 August 1928. **Education:** Studied sculpture, Academy of Fine Arts, Kraków, 1949-50; architecture, Kraków Polytechnic, 1951-55, Dip.Arch. 1955; self-taught in photography, from 1955. **Family:** Married Joan Wolska in 1953 (divorced, 1983); Anna Bychawska in 1985; children: Maciej, Anna and Maja. **Career:** Architect, Fine Arts Monuments Maintenance Enterprise, Kraków, 1953-56; photographer, Institute of Zootechnics, Kraków, 1955-59; photoreporter, *Prezkroj* weekly magazine, Kraków, from 1957; also freelance theatre photographer, in Kraków, Warsaw, Katowice, Wroclaw, etc., since 1959. **Recipient:** First Prize, Fotografia prasowa, Warsaw, 1968; First Prize, Artystyczna fotografia rzezby, Warsaw, 1967; Silver Medal, Exhibition of Theatre Photography, Novi Sad, Yugoslavia, 1968; Award of Distinction for Photography, Monte Carlo, Monaco, 1969; Title of Excellence, Fédération Internationale d'Art Photographique (FIAP), 1970; Photography Prize, Madrid, 1971; Gold Medal, Exhibition of Photography, Novi Sad, Yugoslavia, 1971; Press Prize, Pope John Paul in Poland, Kraków, 1979. Member, Union of Polish Art Photographers, 1955; Artiste, Fédération Internationale d'Art Photographique, 1963. **Address:** ul.E. Kwiatkowskiego 10, 30-147 Kraków, Poland.

Individual Exhibitions:

1958   Gallery ZPAP, Kraków, Poland
1961   Gallery Krzywe Kolo, Warsaw
1962   Gallery, MPik, Lodz, Poland
          Gallery Krzysztofory, Kraków, Poland

Armenia—Relief Engine, **1989.** Photograph ©Gueorgui Pinkhassov.

1967   Gallery of Art, Prague
        Gallery Prezentacje, Torun, Poland
        Gallery MPik, Rzeszow, Poland
        Gallery MPik, Lublin, Poland
1971   Art Gallery, Copenhagen
        Gallery PTF, Poznan, Poland
1993   *Photographed in Stary Theatre,* Stary Theatre, Kraków, Poland
        Historical Museum of Kraków, Poland

Selected Group Exhibitions:

1957   *Bienal,* Sao Paulo, Brazil
        Fifth International Exhibition, Royal Gallery of Photography,
            Adelaide, Australia
        International Exhibition, Hong Kong
1958   *Fifth Biennale of Photography,* Antwerp, Belgium
1960   *Sixth FIAP Biennale,* Rijeka, Yugoslavia
1968   *Subjective Photography,* Gallery Wspolczesna, Warsaw
        Triennale of Theatre Photography, Novi Sad, Yugoslavia
1969   *International Exhibition,* Monte Carlo, Monaco
1971   *Researching Photographers,* Warsaw
        Destiny of the Old People, Madrid
1989   *Przemoc, Sex, Nostalgia,* Warsaw, Poland

Collections:

Museum of Fine Arts, Lodz, Poland; National Museum, Wroclaw, Poland;
Historical Museum of Kraków, Poland.

Publications:

By PLEWIŃSKI: Reportages—"Winecja pod woda" in *Przekrój* (Kraków,
Poland), 1957; "Le millionaire de l'Etat Polonaise" in *Paris-Match* (Paris),
1966; "Operacja Zagiel" in *Przekrój* (Kraków, Poland), 1974; "Jan Pawel II
w Polsce" in *Przekrój* (Kraków, Poland), 1979.

On PLEWIŃSKI: Books—*Das Polnische Lichtbild,* with introduction by
Zbigniew Pekoslawski, Halle, East Germany 1961; *Life Library of Photogra-
phy: The Great Themes,* Alexandria, Virginia 1970; *Views on Nudes* by Bill
Jay, London 1971; *Photography in the Twentieth Century* by Petr Tausk,
Cologne 1977, London 1980; *Zeittafel zu Gesichte der Fotografie* by Gerhard
Ihrke, Leipzing 1982; *Wszystko o fotografii* by Ryszard Bobroski and others,
Warsaw 1984. **Articles**—"The Plevinski Pictures" in *Creative Camera*
(London), March 1970; "Polish Photography Called 'Explorations' " by
Urszula Czartoryska in *Spot* (Zagreb), no.4, 1974; "Polish Photography in the
Years 1939-1979" by Ryszard Bobrowski in *Fotografia* (Warsaw), special
issue 1979; "Il nudo nella fotografia del Est Europo" by Franceso Poli in
Torino Fotografia, Turin 1985; TV interview from series *In the Artist's
Workshop,* TVP, Kraków, 1991; TV film *"I am a Photographer of Stills",* by
Dorota Chamczyk, 1993.

*

I consider photography as a document of passing time, places, items,
people, and their appearence, material status, spirits, moods and attitudes.
However, I understand that the way I present it also presents myself. This
means that the photograph presents simultaneously my emotional approach

From the series *Penetrations,* **1966-68.** Photograph by Wojciech Plewiński.

and the object being photographed. For me it is the only way to express myself, my times and the places where I live. For some years now, I have been preparing the series "Self-Portraits", presenting people according to their own wishes. The photographs in this series will present themselves only as a statement of the situation chosen by the subject. It will be a kind of sociological study, presenting people of different social levels and generations in their own daily lives.

—Wojciech Plewiński

* * *

1968 marked an important artistic event in Kraków that is referred to in the history of Polish photography as an exhibition of subjective photography. The idea of subjective photography was, of course, not a new one. Many 20th century photographers accepted that a photograph is something more than a visual record, that what makes photography an art is the exploration and portrayal of man's inner life and its use as a means of artistic expression. The photography of Alfred Stieglitz and Minor White is of this kind and, in Europe, this tradition is associated with the work of Otto Steinert and his Fotoforum of the 1950s which is closely tied to the art of Man Ray, Moholy-Nagy and others.

In Poland in the early 1960s, the work of Wojciech Plewiński and of other photographers indicated the desire for a redefinition of the place of photography among the fine arts and for new ways of thinking about photography

generally. This trend has sometimes been rather loosely termed creative photography. The essence of this photography, which has been contrasted with traditional landscape of documentary work, lay in the principle of interference or deformation on the part of the creator (optically or technically) that resulted in a transformed and unrepeatable photograph to which the same standing attached as to a painted picture. Only then, in the view of its creators, was photography a work of art, unlike the majority of traditional photographs.

This trend was summed up in the above-mentioned exhibition of subjective photography through which certain artists, including Plewiński, renewed their attempts to resolve conventional problems by simultaneous portrayal of symbolic, poetic, and emotional meanings. Unlike the cold, intellectual and formal German subjective photography of Steinert's group, however, Plewiński's photography was closer to the modernist fascination with women and eroticism, symbolism and even mysticism. The statement and drama of the photographs was combined with mystery and enigma and the power of women or eroticism to arouse was sometimes inhibited by fear or indifference.

It should be stressed that Plewiński's interest in this subject was neither novel nor unusual for him. Women had always played an important and significant part in his photographs and both his magazine cover photographs of beautiful girls and his stage photographs bear witness to this. Through this photography, which is as elegant as it is erotic, Plewiński seems to attest that, despite overvaluation and trends, woman unfailingly remains an attractive agent in art, both for the artist as a man and for the artist as photographer.

—Ryszard Bobrowski

PLOSSU, Bernard.

Nationality: French. **Born:** Dalat, South Vietnam, 26 February 1945. **Education:** Educated in Paris; self-taught in photography. **Family:** Married to Kathy Yount (divorced, 1985); son: Shane. **Career:** Photographer, Paris, Mexico, and Santa Fe, New Mexico, until 1985. Lived and worked in Andalusia 1989-92 with Françoise Nunez and their children, Joaquim and Manuela. **Recipient:** Grand Prix National de la Photographie, 1988; Grant, "Villa Medicis-hors-les-murs." **Address:** BP 22, 13701 La Ciotat Cedex, France.

Individual Exhibitions:

1973	Centre Culturel Americain, Paris
	Galerie Multitude, Paris
	Creative Camera Gallery, London
1974	Galeria Spectrum, Barcelona
	Galeria Il Diaframma, Milan
	Friends of Photography, Carmel, California
1975	University of Essen
1976	Galerie Nicephore, Bollwiller, France
	La Photogalerie, Paris
	El Fotocentro, Madrid
	3 Jeunes Photographes: Bruno, Kalvar, Plossu, the Centre Georges Pompidou, Paris (toured France, Spain, Czechoslovakia and Poland)
1977	La Remise du Parc, Paris
	Galerie Aspects, Brussels
	Galerie 31, Vevey, Switzerland
1978	Le Chateau d'Eau, Toulouse
1979	Galerie Contrejour, Paris
	Phot'Oeil Galerie II, Paris
	Maggie Kress Gallery, Taos, New Mexico
	Hill's Gallery, Santa Fe, New Mexico
	Fifth Avenue Gallery, Scottsdale, Arizona
	French Cultural Center, New York
1980	Work Gallery, Zurich
	Stephen White Gallery, Los Angeles
	FIAC Fair, Paris
	Galerie Perspective, Paris
	Church Street Gallery, Melbourne
	Galerie Arpa, Bordeaux
	Santa Fe Gallery, New Mexico
	Galeria Fotomania, Barcelona
1981	Eaton/Shoen Gallery, San Francisco
	Musée Nicéphore Niepce, Chalon-sur-Saône, France (with Djan Seylan)
	Portfolio Gallery, Oklahoma City, Oklahoma
	Photographic Gallery, Cardiff, Wales (retrospective)
	Massachusetts, Institute of Technology, Cambridge (with Gail Skoff)
	Afterimage Gallery, Dallas, Texas (with Max Pam)
1982	Eaton/Shoen Gallery, San Francisco
	Etherton Gallery, Tucson, Arizona
	San Jose State University, California
	Honshour Gallery, Albuquerque, New Mexico
	Susan Spiritus Gallery, Newport Beach, California
	Port Washington Public Library, New York
1984	Oklahoma Museum of Art, Oklahoma City
	Governors Gallery, Santa Fe, New Mexico
	Nagase Photo Salon, Tokyo
	Palm Springs Desert Museum, California
	Bernard Plossu, at the *4th Meeting of Photography*, Coimbra, Portugal
1985	Eaton/Shoen Gallery, San Francisco
	Yuen Lui Gallery, Seattle, Washington
	Benteler Galleries, Houston, Texas
	Eaton/Shoen Gallery, San Francisco
1986	Galerie Credit Agricole, Pujols, France
1988	*Retrospective*, Musée National d'Art Moderne/Centre Pompidou, Paris
1994	Touring Show organised by Association Française d'Action Artistique

Selected Group Exhibitions:

1972	*Photokina '72*, Cologne
1975	*4 Photographes*, Bibliothèque Nationale, Paris (with Bruno, Descamps, and Kuligowski)
1977	*Sequences*, Stedelijk Museum, Amsterdam
1980	*French Photographers*, University of Oklahoma, Norman
1981	*Ten French Photographers*, Santa Barbara Museum of Art, California (travelled to the Lincoln Art Gallery, Santa Rosa; Southwestern College, San Diego)
1982	*Color as Form*, International Museum of Photography at George Eastman House, Rochester, New York
1983	*Europäische Fotografie*, Museum zu Allerheiligen, Schaffhausen, Switzerland
1984	*La Photographie Créative*, Pavillon des Arts, Paris
1985	*Fresson Photographs*, French Cultural Center, New York (travelled to the Contemporary Arts Center, New Orleans; University of Tennessee, Martin; D.D. Patty Museum, Columbus, Missouri; North Carolina State University, Raleigh; Cleveland Contemporary Arts Center, Ohio; Centre Beaubourg, Paris, etc., 1985-87)

Collections:

Bibliothèque Nationale, Paris; Centre Beaubourg, Paris; Musée Cantini, Marseilles; Musée Réattu, Arles, France; Musées Royaux des Beaux-Arts, Brussels; Stedelijk Museum, Amsterdam; International Museum of Photography at George Eastman House, Rochester, New York; Center for Creative Photography, University of Arizona, Tucson; Australian National Gallery, Canberra.

Publications:

By PLOSSU: Books—*Surbanalism*, with text by S. Leone, Paris 1972; *Go West*, with text by Marc Sapotra, Paris 1976; *Creatis No. 2: Bernard Plossu*, with text by J.C. de Feugas, Paris 1977; *Mexique 65-66*, portfolio, Paris 1978; *Le Voyage Mexicain*, with text by Denis Roche, Paris 1979; *Nueva Lente Monograph: Bernard Plossu*, edited by C. Serrano and P.P. Minquez, Madrid 1979; *Egypte*, with text by Carole Naggar, Paris 1979; *Bernard Plossu: 1966-1981*, *Atelier Michel Fresson*, portfolio, with introduction by John Upton, San Francisco 1982; *Voiles d'Afrique*, portfolio, Paris 1984; *Southwest Monuments*, calendar, Albuquerque, New Mexico 1984; *Naples d'un couple*, with Françoise Nunez, Naples, 1988; *Dopo l'Estate*, Naples, 1989; *Théssalonique 1990*, with Françoise Nunez & Pierre Devin, Athens, 1990; *Antwerpen 93*, Belgium, 1993; *L'Oeil de Frère Jean*, with Michel Butor, France, 1993.

On PLOSSU: Books—*Photokina*, exhibition catalogue, Cologne 1972; *Bernard Plossu*, exhibition catalogue, Paris, 1976; *Histoire de la Photographie Française* by Claude Nori, Paris 1978; *Venezia '79: La Fotografia*, edited by Daniela Palazzoli, Vittorio Sgarbi and Italo Zannier, Venice and New York 1979; *Contemporary European Photography* by Claude Nori and Lorenzo Merlo, Tokyo 1981; *Bernard Plossu: Selected Color Photographs 1965-1982*, exhibition catalogue, San Francisco 1982; *Fotografie* by Derek Bennett, Schaffhausen, Switzerland 1983; *La Photographie Créative* by Jean-Claude Lemagny, Paris 1984; *Les Paysages Intermédiaires*, by Alain Sayag & Denis Roche, France, 1988; *Bernard Plossu 1963-1993*, catalogue by Gilles Mora & Maria Filomena Molder, France 1994. **Articles**—*Photo* (Paris), October 1972; *Creative Camera* (London), April 1973; "Realisme: Bernard Plossu" in *Le Nouveau Photocinema* (Paris), September 1973; by Allan Porter in *Camera* (Lucerne), July 1974; by Joan Murray in *Artweek* (Oakland, California), August 1974; in *Progresso Fotografico* (Milan), January 1977; in *Creative Camera* (London), February 1979; by B. Clark in *Rocky Mountain Review* (Denver), October 1979; in *American Photographer* (New York), April 1980; M. Johnson in *Artweek* (Oakland, California), June 1980; "Bernard Plossu" by Matthew Foley in *Artspace* (Albuquerque), April 1981; "Egypt by Bernard Plossu" by Colin Osman in *Creative Camera* (London), January 1982; "Five Views of Paris" by Cathy Curtis in *Artweek* (Oakland, California), 19 May 1984.

*

Photography is all the un-important moments that are in fact so important. Photography does not capture time but evokes it: non-decisive moments.

—Bernard Plossu

*   *   *

Like certain rhythms and refrains of the Beatles, the photographs of Bernard Plossu are the reflecting mirrors of that curious and mobile generation that went to look for its version of truth in the four corners of the globe, mixing different cultures along the way. The wandering so dear to a Kerouac, the fascination with the Orient, the call of the road—all involve a rupture with the ambient milieu, with habitual space, in exchange for a new world, one which, for the photographer, incites and provokes new pictures.

The photograph has always been linked to travel, for photography wants to speak, above all, about displacement, about "going there," so that others can imagine and devise things that they have not seen. Bernard Plossu travels, as it were, between Paul Strand and Edouard Boubat, but he is different from them in that he is more interested to prove by experience the emotions of displacement than merely to record them. True, the influences may be Robert Frank, or the Beat Generation, or the Hippy phenomena, but such comparisons are useful only to a point. For Plossu demands the importance of the "I"; that which happens in his pictures is, above all, a moment of his own life, a personal vibration, a state of his soul, an autobiographical sign. The act of photography is a totally personal experience; it is, each time, the Great Awakening similar to such spiritual experiences as "satori" or "nirvana" but it is, above all, the unique chance to be fully in life, in *his* life. That which Plossu shows us, that which he distills and attempts to transcribe, is the breath of life in the moment of epiphany, the sublime instant: deserts, rain, long roads, tender looks, the transparency of the sun, bustling streets, winking eyes, works of art, a happy tree, a sudden silence, a gust of wind, the smile of a woman early in the morning. . . .

The autobiographical character of Plossu's photographs marks a salutary rupture with the French tradition of photojournalism and the aristocratic stance of Cartier-Bresson in which an abyss separates the photographer from the photograph. In his 1979 book, *Le Voyage Mexicain*, it is a matter, above all, of connivance, of complicity, of an intimacy between a young man who hardly knows how to use the Rétina Kodak that was lent to him and the people he encounters on his way to the great "hallucinatory" experience of Mexico. "We are in the picture instead of looking at it." The characters that parade through the pages of the book tell us their own history; but, even more, they tell us of one that they cherish with the photographer—like the superb young girl with brown skin and a dress lightly turned up: she exudes love. As Kerouac said in his preface to Frank's *Americans:* "We would love to have her phone number."

This sensation of freedom, this emotional relationship, is the result of Plossu's great technical refinement—as if his camera had actually extended the body, making itself a crystallizer of the senses: "I use only the 50mm lens because its normal vision allows me to be self-effacing, and, in so doing, to avoid exercises in style, so that the subject speaks more strongly, by itself, for itself."

After the publication in 1972 of his first book, *Surbanalism*, which was misunderstood at the time, and after numerous trips to Asia and Africa, and after publication of his later two books, *Egypte* and *Le Voyage Mexicain*,

Plossu temporarily settled in Santa Fe, New Mexico. This mythical place for photography (Beaumont Newhall, Paul Caponigro, Eliot Porter, Walter Chappell and others live there), this dry city in the middle of the desert, seemed, for a while, to suit his Mediterranean hedonism. Sensuality inheres in the burning rocks, in the caress of the wind, in the pulsations of the earth, in the soft cushiony folds of a Cadillac.

—Claude Nori

PLOWDEN, David.

Nationality: American. **Born:** Boston, Massachusetts, 9 October 1932. **Education:** Educated at the Collegiate School, New York, 1940-45, Choate School, Wallingford, Connecticut, 1945-46, Trinity School, New York, 1947-48, and Putney School, Vermont, 1948-51; studied economics, Yale University, New Haven, Connecticut, 1951-55, B.A. 1955; studied photography, under Minor White and Nathan Lyons, Rochester, New York, 1959, 1960. **Family:** Married Pleasance Coggeshall in 1962 (divorced, 1976); married Sandra Schoellkopf in 1977; children: John, Daniel, Philip. **Career:** Assistant Train Master, Great Northern Railway, Wilmar, Minnesota, 1955-56; Travel Clerk, American Express Company, New York, 1957; Travel Agent, Nametra Inc., New York, 1958-59. Photographer since 1959: Photographic Assistant, O. Winston Link Studio, New York, 1959, George Meluso Studio, New York, 1960-62; freelance photographer, on assignments from various institutions and for *Architectural Forum, American Heritage, Fortune, Horizon, Life, Newsweek,* etc., in New York, 1962-78, and in Chicago, since 1978. Associate Professor, College of Architecture, Planning and Design, Institute of Design, Illinois Institute of Technology, Chicago, since 1978. **Recipient:** Guggenheim Fellowship, 1968; Benjamin Baroness Award, 1971; Wilson Hicks Award, University of Miami, 1977; Horn Book Award, 1979; Award of Excellence, American Institute of Graphic Arts, 1979. **Agents:** Curtis Brown Ltd., 575 Madison Avenue, New York, New York 10022; Gilbert Gallery, 218 East Ontario Street, Chicago, Illinois 60611. **Address:** 797 Walden Road, Winnetka, Illinois 60093, U.S.A.

Individual Exhibitions:

1962	New York Public Library, Hudson Park Branch
	Steam Engines, Suffolk Museum, Stonybrook, Long Island, New York
1965	*The Route of Lincoln's Funeral Train,* Columbia University, New York
1971	*The Hand of Man on America,* Smithsonian Institution, Washington, D.C. (toured the United States)
1972	*The Great Plains,* Neikrug Gallery, New York
1976	*American Vernacular,* International Center of Photography, New York
	Railroad Men, Smithsonian Institution, Washington, D.C.
	Bridges, Smithsonian Institution, Washington, D.C.
	Bryant Library, Roslyn, Long Island, New York
1977	Port Washington Library, New York
1979	Cincinnati Art Academy
	Witkin Gallery, New York (retrospective)
	Evanston Art Center, Illinois
	Santa Fe Gallery of Photography, New Mexico
1980	The Gilbert Gallery, Chicago
1981	*Steel,* Smithsonian Institution, Washington, D.C.
	The Gilbert Gallery, Chicago

1985   *Industrial Landscape of Chicago,* Chicago Historical Society
        Change and Transformation in America, University of
        Maryland, Catonsville

Selected Group Exhibitions:

1967   *Photography in the Fine Arts,* Metropolitan Museum of Art,
        New York
1976   *The Face of Industry,* Kodak Gallery, New York
        The River, Walker Art Center, Minneapolis
1977   *The Great West: Real/Ideal,* University of Colorado, Boulder
        (subsequently Smithsonian Institution travelling exhibition)
1978   *By the Side of the Road,* Currier Gallery of Art, Manchester,
        New Hampshire
1979   *Industrial Sights,* Whitney Museum, New York
1980   *Photographers of the Institute of Design,* The Gilbert Gallery,
        Chicago

Collections:

Library of Congress, Washington, D.C.; Smithsonian Institution, Washington, D.C.; Art Institute of Chicago; Center for Creative Photography, University of Arizona, Tucson; Museum of Contemporary Photography, Columbia College, Chicago.

Publications:

By PLOWDEN: Books—*Farewell to Steam,* Brattleboro, Vermont 1966; *Lincoln and His America,* New York 1970; *Nantucket,* with text by Patricia Coffin, New York 1970; *The Hand of Man on America,* Washington, D.C. 1971; *Floor of the Sky: The Great Plains,* New York 1972; *Cape May to Montauk,* with text by Nelson P. Falorp, New York 1973; *Bridges: The Spans of North America,* New York 1974; *Commonplace,* New York 1974; *Desert and Plain: The Mountains and the River,* with text by Berton Roneché, New York 1975; *Tugboat,* New York 1976; *The Iron Road,* with text by Richard Snow, New York 1978; *Wayne County: The Aesthetic Heritage of a Rural Area,* with text by Stephen Jacobs, New York 1979; *Steel,* New York 1981; *David Plowden: Photographs,* New York 1982; *Heartland: The Middle West,* New York 1983; *The Library of World Photography: Landscape,* with Ian Jeffrey, Tokyo and London 1984. **Articles**—"Farewell to the Ferry" in *American Heritage* (New York), April 1964; "A Whistle Goodbye" in *American Heritage* (New York), December 1966; "A Workshop for Bridge-Builders" in *Fortune* (New York), August 1967; "Tugboats" in *Fortune* (New York), April 1968; "The Hand of Man on America" in *The Smithsonian* (Washington, D.C.), January 1971; "The Island That Is" in *Audubon* (New York), March 1971; "A Sweep of Bridges" in *American Heritage* (New York), December 1973; "American Vernacular" in *American Heritage* (New York), August 1974; "The End of Innocence" in *Journal of Current Social Issues* (New York), Fall 1976.

On PLOWDEN: Books—*Industry and the Photographic Image: 153 Great Prints from 1850 to the Present,* edited by F. Jack Hurley, New York 1983; *The Library of World Photography: Photography as Fine Art,* with introduction by Douglas Davis, Tokyo 1982, 1983, London 1983. **Articles**—"The Hand of Man in America" by Rene Bruns in *Popular Photography* (New York), June 1971; "Passing Fancies" by Kenneth Poli in *Popular Photography* (New York), June 1973; "View of America" in *Time* (New York), 19 November 1973; "David Plowden" in *Photography Annual,* New York 1976; "David Plowden" by Richard F. Snow in *Modern Photography* (New York), January 1977; "Main Street U.S.A." by Owen Edwards in *American Photographer* (New York), July 1980.

*   *   *

In approaching the work of David Plowden one is struck, most of all, by a sense of balance. There is balance between words and pictures as well as a formal sense of balance within the photographs themselves. Plowden's work has appeared in many magazines, but he is best known for his work with books and it is in the books that his sense of balance best appears. In the book format his words and pictures can work toward a unified whole.

David Plowden's books are always about something other than photography itself. As Plowden puts it, "Photography has never interested me as much as the things I photographed." Make no mistake, Plowden is a very fine photographer, but his camera has generally been used in the service of a specific idea or a personal interest. His basic motivation is documentary.

In his first book, *Farewell to Steam,* Plowden was clearly reaching out to delineate an era (the era of steam locomotion on the railways) that was quickly slipping away. In *The Hand of Man on America* he was protesting the idiotic waste and pollution which has accompanied what we still insist on calling "progress." His major book, *Bridges: The Spans of North America* reflects Plowden's fascination with bridges as one of man's major technical works and also his sensitivity to the idea of the bridge as symbol of man's striving. That book not only contains some of Plowden's finest large-format black-and-white photographs but also a detailed historical analysis of trends in American bridgebuilding which has earned it a respected place in technical libraries all over the country. Other books by Plowden are celebrations of certain aspects of American life which he finds particularly attractive. *Floor of the Sky,* for example, celebrates the Great Plains, while his 1974 book, *Commonplace,* celebrates the life and architecture of small town America.

David Plowden was born in Boston in 1932 and spent his growth years "knocking about the East Coast." He graduated from Yale with every intention of entering a career in business. Already drawn to trains, he took a job with the Great Northern Railway because, "I wanted to be a railroad mogul." By the mid 1950s, however, it was clear that neither the American railway system nor David Plowden was likely to make a great success in the near future. Plowden was drawn more and more to photography and writing.

In 1959 and 1960 he studied with Minor White in Rochester, New York. It was a good experience and important for his visual development, but Plowden found the atmosphere of "art for art's sake" that White engendered somewhat limiting. "I was always the maverick there," he recalls. By the early 1960s he was in New York doing assignments for *Fortune* and working closely with Walker Evans who was then on the staff of that magazine. In this far more congenial atmosphere, Plowden found his stride. *Farewell to Steam* appeared in 1966 and his work has appeared at regular intervals ever since.

Since 1978 he has taught in Chicago at the Institute of Design where he finds the combination of teaching and publishing books particularly satisfying.

—F. Jack Hurley

POIROT, Luis.

Nationality: Chilean. **Born:** Santiago, Chile, 13 December 1940. **Education:** Attended the Alliance Française de Santiago 1946-54; Military College 1955-57; obtained a Bachelor of Letters degree in 1958; from 1959 to 1961 studied at the School of Theatre of the University of Chile; studied in Paris in 1963-64 and worked as a director with French Television; self-taught in photography. **Family:** Married the actress Carla Cristi in 1965; son: Andrés. **Career:** Professional photographer since 1965. From 1969 to 1973 he taught photography in the Catholic University of Chile, where he returned as Visiting Professor in 1989. He was exiled from Chile in October 1973 until September 1985. He lived and worked in Paris 1973-75 and Barcelona 1975-85. From 1983 to 1985 he was a staff photographer for the Spanish newspaper *El Pais* and also contributed photographs and articles on travel, theatre and other

Portrait of Agustín Centeclas, Spanish Photographer, **1982.** Photograph ©Luis Poirot.

topics to magazines in France, Spain and Chile. In 1992-94 he presented a series on creative photography on Chilean television. Throughout his career he has continued to work in the theater, staging more than 20 plays. Was also director of photography on two films, one French and one Spanish. **Address:** Bellavista 0182, Santiago de Chile, Chile.

Individual Exhibitions:

1974	*Imágines del Chile Popular,* Venice Biennale, Italy
1978	Galería Spectrum-Canon, Barcelona, Spain
1979	Galería Spectrum-Canon, Ibiza, Spain
1982	*Portraits of Exile,* Primavera Fotográfica Catalana, Barcelona, Spain
1983	*Rajasthan (India),* Galería Mito, Barcelona, Spain
	Pablo Neruda, Capilla de la Santa Cruz, Barcelona
1984	*Portraits from Within,* Primavera Fotográfica Catalana, Barcelona, Spain
1985	*Postcard from Chile,* Casa Larga, Chile
1986	*Portraits of Photographers,* School of Modern Music, Santiago, Chile
1989	*Landscapes in Black and White,* Instituto Chileno-Norteamericano, Santiago

1991	*Neruda, Absence and Presence,* Centro Cultural de la Villa, Buenos Aires, Argentina
1992	*Neruda, Portrait d'Absence,* Maison de l'Amérique Latine, Paris
	A Chilean in France, Instituto Chileno-Francés, Santiago
1993	*Images of Actors,* Instituto Chileno-Norteamericano, Santiago
	The Ganges, Casa Larga, Santiago
	Ephemera Vulgata, Casa Larga, Santiago
1994	*Portraits in Absence,* Venice, Italy

Selected Group Exhibitions:

1971	*Chile Now,* international travelling exhibition
1982	*Contemporary Photography in Catalonia,* travelling exhibition in Catalonia, Spain
1983	*Contemporary Photography in Spain,* Círculo de Bellas Artes, Madrid
1983-85	Foto-Press in Spain (Madrid, Barcelona)
1984	*Jornadas Fotográficas,* Palacio Generalitat, Valencia, Spain
	Self-portraits, Tartesos, Barcelona, Spain

1987	*Chile Vive,* Círculo de Bellas Artes, Madrid
1990	*Por Qué No* (Why Not), Casa Larga, Chile
1991	*Chile from Within,* travelling exhibition in the USA

Collections:

Museo de Arte Moderno de Madrid; Bibliothèque Nationale, Paris; Museo de Bellas Artes, Santiago de Chile; Various private collections in Chile, Spain and the USA.

Publications:

By POIROT: Books—*Neruda, Retratar la Ausencia,* Santiago 1985; *Neruda, Absence and Presence,* New York 1990; *Logbook of the Iceberg to Seville,* Santiago-Seville, 1992; *Allende, se Abren las Alamedas,* Santiago 1991; *Marta Colvin,* Santiago 1993; *Isla de Pascua,* Santiago 1994; *Chile from Within,* New York 1990; *El Pabellón de Chile en Sevilla,* Santiago 1993. **Article**—"Fotografía en Chile," in *Revista Diseño,* Chile, 1992. **Broadcasts**—Weekly TV series, "Creaciones," introducing photography to the layman. Channel 13, Santiago, Chile, 1992 and 1993.

On POIROT: Books—*Fotografía actual en España,* Madrid 1983; Fotografía Chilena Contemporánea, Chile 1985; *Fotografía Contemporanea en Cataluña,* Barcelona 1982; *Foto-Press 1982/83/85,* Spain; *Primavera Fotográfica en Cataluña 1982-84,* Spain; *Chile Vive,* Madrid 1987. **Articles**—"Luis Poirot" by G. Bardawil, *Photocinema,* (Paris), Feb. 1976; "Lucho Poirot" by J. Mejía, *Flashfoto* (Barcelona), July 1979; "Retratar la Ausencia" by J. Cruz, *El Pais Dominical,* (Madrid), 11 Sept 1983; "Retratas de Luis Poirot" by H. Garfias, *Revista Diseño,* (Santiago), Nov. 1991; "Transfers de Poirot" by J. Mellado, *Revista Diseño,* (Santiago), June 1993; "Postales de Poirot" by E. Lihn, (Santiago), *Apsi,*1985.

*

My photogaphy has to see through memory, in a country which is rapidly forgetting everything in its past, and is left without roots. It is not an exercise in nostalgia; on the contrary, I am seeking lucidity and am trying to understand the nature of the Latin-Americans and Chileans, with our cultural melting-pot of recent immigration.

I take portrait photographs in black and white, which are the colours of photography, in an interplay with the subject, which does not necessarily reveal anything about them, and may even in fact conceal things.

The empty spaces of houses and buildings have a strong attraction for me, because of the traces left in them by their inhabitants, the combination of absence and presence and the play of light on angles and corners.

I explain nothing; I suggest and ask questions.

—Luis Poirot

*   *   *

"Chile is a country without memory." So says one of Chile's foremost photographers—whose medium, by definition, is all about putting things on the record, lest they be forgotten. All the more relevant, too, in this instance in which Poirot was victimized and forced into exile by General Pinochet whose sanitised image abroad was unilaterallly projected by the press of his seventeen year long military dictatorship, and whose continuing presence as head of the armed forces still affords a cover for their repressive record of human rights abuses.

It is against this trend and in favour of the collective memory that is our legacy, our lesson, and our history that Poirot has always worked. Interestingly, his early studies were in the University of Chile's Drama Department, and he has always alternated his photography (including providing the stills for theatrical productions) with directing plays. For thirty years he has also been married to the stage and television actress, Carla Cristi. His preoccupation with truth and memory, then, is also about the multi-layered nature of that truth, of the possible rifts between emotion and drama, disguise and deception, reality and representation. Speaking of a series he took of the Catalan Carnival where men dress as women and identities are masked, he quotes Valle Inclán, "We only bear our true features at our moment of death, the moment when we cannot see ourselves." This concept of a moment of truth at the moment of death haunts Poirot, "In life, our features are concealed between the mask and the face."

Starting in 1964, Poirot soon recognised that street photography was not for him. This in no way diminished his respect for the importance of a documentary tradition, particularly in times of political and social upheaval, but simply led to him favouring a different approach. His cultural connection with writers, for example, led to a close collaboration with the great poet and anti-fascist Pablo Neruda. Following their early encounters at Neruda's home on the island of Isla Negra in 1969, Poirot returned there in 1982 after his own years of European exile were over.

Since Neruda was now dead, Poirot decided on creating a *Portrait of Absence,* inspired by Neruda's own assertion that "there's no such thing as forgetting . . . no oblivion." The book's portraits, then, are of those who knew and appreciated Neruda—writers of the international stature of the Spanish poet Rafael Alberti, the Argentine Julio Cortazar and the Uruguayan Eduardo Galeano—and extraordinarily, of his house on the coast, crammed with *objets trouvés;* even steam engines and mermaids, embossed stirrups and pickled fish, ships' figureheads and fairground horses. Neruda's widow, Matilde, further prevailed on Poirot to document their home in the coastal town on Valparaiso, sacked by Pinochet's armies in retaliation for the intellectual backing given to the Popular Unity government they toppled in 1973. More than any statement made on the streets, this is Poirot's testament to those who kept the faith—with freedom and democracy, against repression and censorship—and a haunting black-and-white record of mute persistence.

After nine years based in Paris and Madrid, Poirot has spent the last decade back home, paradoxically coming full circle. Having been expelled from his teaching at Santiago's Catholic University in 1973, he has now regained his titular position. At the same time he protects his role as a "solitary character." Poitot's interest in human history already stretched back to encompass the early cultural heritage of places as far flung as the Ganges and Easter Island (a book that has sold in tens of thousands and three languages). Increasingly he has moved still further back in time, documenting the transportation of 80 tons of iceberg from its home in Antartica to the Chilean tent at the World Fair in Seville (1992). Like his previous work with rivers and islands, this is another demonstration of Poirot's preoccupation with water, and with history longer than memory, what he calls "the miracle of ordinary magic."

—Amanda Hopkinson

PORTER, Eliot (Furness).

Nationality: American. **Born:** Winnetka, Illinois, 6 December 1901. **Education:** New Trier High School, Kenilworth, Illinois, 1916-18; Morristown School, New Jersey, 1918-20; Harvard University, School of Engineering,

Cambridge, Massachusetts, 1920-24, B.S. 1924; Harvard Medical School, 1924-29, M.D. 1929; self-taught in photography. **Family:** Married Marian Brown in 1927 (divorced, 1934); children: Eliot and Charles; married Aline Kilham in 1936; children: Jonathan, Stephen and Patrick. **Career:** Instructor in Biochemistry and Bacteriology, Harvard University and Radcliffe College, Cambridge, 1929-39. Took first photos, Great Spruce Head Island, Maine, 1913; began serious work as a photographer, 1930; took first bird photographs, 1937; and has concentrated on photography as a career since 1939: freelance photographer, Cambridge, 1939-42; war work on radar development, Radiation Laboratory, Massachusetts Institute of Technology, Cambridge, 1942-44; freelance landscape and wildlife photographer, Winnetka, 1944-46, and in Santa Fe, New Mexico, since 1946. Member, Board of Directors, Sierra Club, San Francisco, 1962-68. **Recipient:** Guggenheim Fellowship, 1941, 1946; Silver Plaque: Wildlife Photography Award, *Country Life International Exhibition,* London, 1950; Conservation Award, United States Department of the Interior, 1967; Maine Commission on Arts and Humanities Award, 1968; Distinguished Son of Maine Award, 1969; Newhouse Citation, Syracuse University, New York, 1973; Governor's Award, New Mexico Arts Commission, 1976; Gold Medal, Academy of Natural Sciences, Philadelphia, 1978. D.F.A.: Colby College, Waterville, Maine, 1969; LL.D.: University of Albuquerque, New Mexico, 1974; D.Sc.: Dickinson College, Pennsylvania, 1979. Associate Fellow, Morse College, Yale University, New Haven, Connecticut, 1967. Fellow, American Academy of Arts and Sciences, 1971. **Agent:** Scheinbaum and Russek, 615 Don Felix Street, Santa Fe, New Mexico. **Address:** Route 4, Box 33, Santa Fe, New Mexico 87501, U.S.A. **Died:** (in Santa Fe, New Mexico) 2 November 1990.

Individual Exhibitions:

1936	Delphic Studios, New York
1939	An American Place, New York
	Georgia Lingafelt Bookshop, Chicago
1940	Museum of Art, Santa Fe, New Mexico
1942	Katherine Kuh Gallery, Chicago
	Bronx Zoological Society, New York
1943	*Birds in Color,* Museum of Modern Art, New York
	Academy of Natural Sciences, Chicago
1952	Museum of Modern Art, New York
1953	Art Institute of Chicago
1955	Limelight Gallery, New York
1957	*Madonnas and Marketplaces,* Limelight Gallery, New York (with Ellen Auerbach)
1958	Fine Arts Museum of New Mexico, Santa Fe (with Laura Gilpin)
1959	Nelson Gallery, Kansas City, Missouri
1960	*Seasons,* International Museum of Photography, George Eastman House, Rochester, New York (retrospective)
	San Francisco Museum of Modern Art
	Baltimore Museum of Art
	Museum of Science, Boston
	Smithsonian Institution, Washington, D.C.
1962	De Cordova Museum, Lincoln, Massachusetts
	Fine Arts Museum of New Mexico, Santa Fe (with Laura Gilpin and Todd Webb)
1963	Art Institute of Chicago
1970	Museum of Fine Arts, St. Petersburg, Florida
1971	Princeton University, New Jersey
1973	Amon Carter Museum, Fort Worth, Texas
	University of New Mexico, Albuquerque (retrospective)
1974	Roswell Museum and Art Center, New Mexico
	Witte Memorial Museum, San Antonio, Texas
1975	Pensacola Center, Florida

1977	*Eliot Porter/Laura Gilpin/William Clift,* Horwitch Gallery, Santa Fe, New Mexico
	Smithsonian Institution, Washington, D.C. (with Daniel Lang)
1979	*Intimate Landscapes,* Metropolitan Museum of Art, New York
1981	*Ansel Adams/Eliot Porter/William Clift,* Cronin Gallery, Houston

Selected Group Exhibitions:

1940	*International Salon of Photography,* American Museum of Natural History, New York
1941	*Image of Freedom,* Museum of Modern Art, New York
1950	*Country Life International Exhibition,* London
1966	*American Photography: The 60s,* University of Nebraska, Lincoln
1967	*Photography U.S.A.,* De Cordova Museum, Lincoln, Massachusetts
1976	*Aspects of American Photography,* University of Missouri, St. Louis
1977	*The Great West: Real/Ideal,* University of Colorado, Boulder (subsequently Smithsonian Institution travelling exhibition; toured the United States)
	Photographs: Sheldon Memorial Art Gallery Collection, University of Nebraska, Lincoln
1978	*Mirrors and Windows: American Photography since 1960,* Museum of Modern Art, New York (toured the United States, 1978-80)
1980	*The Imaginary Photo Museum,* Kunsthalle, Cologne
1983	*Photography in America 1910-83,* Tampa Museum, Florida

Collections:

Museum of Modern Art, New York; Metropolitan Museum of Art, New York; International Museum of Photography, George Eastman House, Rochester, New York; Library of Congress, Washington, D.C.; Art Institute of Chicago; University of Nebraska, Lincoln; University of New Mexico, Albuquerque; Santa Fe Museum of Art, New Mexico; Center for Creative Photography, University of Arizona, Tucson.

Publications:

By PORTER: Books—*American Birds,* with text by Amedon and Murphy, New York 1953; *In Wildness Is the Preservation of the World,* with text by Henry David Thoreau, and an introduction by Joseph Wood Krutch, San Francisco 1962; *The Place No One Knew: Glen Canyon on the Colorado,* edited by David Bower, San Francisco 1963; *Portfolio One: The Seasons,* San Francisco 1964; *Summer Island: Penobscot Country,* edited by David Brower, San Francisco 1966; *Forever Wild: The Adirondacks,* with text by William Chapman White, New York 1966; *Baja California: The Geography of Hope,* with text by Joseph Wood Krutch, San Francisco 1967; *Galapagos: The Flow of Wildness,* 2 volumes, with text by Kenneth Brower and Porter, San Francisco 1968; *Down the Colorado: Diary of the First Trip Through the Grand Canyon, 1869,* with text by John Wesley Powell, New York 1969; *Appalachian Wilderness: The Great Smoky Mountains,* with text by Edward Abbey and Harry M. Caudill, New York 1970; *The Tree Where Man Was Born: An African Experience,* with text by Peter Matthiessen, New York 1972; *Birds of North America: A Personal Selection,* New York 1972; *Iceland: Portfolio II,* New York 1972; *Portraits from Nature,* portfolio, with an introduction by Beaumont Newhall, New York 1973; *Moments of Discovery: Adventures with American Birds,* with text by Michael Harwood, New York

1977; *Antarctica,* New York and London 1978; *Seal Song,* with text by Brian Davies, New York and London 1979; *The Greek World,* with text by Peter Levi, New York 1980; *American Places,* with text by Wallace and Page Stegner, Boston and London 1981; *All Under Heaven: The Chinese World,* with text by Jonathan Porter, Boston 1983, London 1984; *Eliot Porter's Southwest,* Boston 1985; *Maine,* Boston 1986. **Article**—"Eliot Porter," interview, in *Dialogue with Photography,* edited by Paul Hill and Thomas Cooper, London 1979.

On PORTER: Books—*Photography in America,* edited by Robert Doty, with an introduction by Minor White, New York 1974; *The Magic Image: The Genius of Photography from 1839 to the Present Day* by Cecil Beaton and Gail Buckland, Boston and London 1975; *The Great West: Real/Ideal,* edited by Sandy Hume, Gary Metz and others, Boulder, Colorado 1977; *Photographs: Sheldon Memorial Art Gallery Collecton, University of Nebraska,* exhibition catalogue, with an introduction by Norman A. Geske, Lincoln, Nebraska 1977; *Mirrors and Windows: American Photography since 1960* by John Szarkowski, New York 1978; *The Collection of Alfred Stieglitz* by Weston J. Naef, New York 1978; *The Photograph Collector's Guide* by Lee D. Witkin and Barbara London, Boston 1979; *Eliot Porter: Intimate Landscapes,* exhibition catalogue, with text by Weston Naef, New York 1979; *Farbe im Photo: Die Geschichte der Farbphotographie von 1861 bis 1981* by Fritz Binder, Gert Koshofer, Rolf Sachsse and others, Cologne 1981; *The Imaginary Photo Museum* by Helmut Gernsheim, Renate and L. Fritz Gruber and others, Cologne 1981, London 1982; *International Photography 1920-1980,* edited by Ian North, Canberra 1982; *The Library of World Photography: Landscape,* with texts by David Plowden and Ian Jeffrey, Tokyo and London 1984; *Masterpieces of Photography from George Eastman House,* edited by Robert A. Sobieszek, New York 1985. **Articles**—"A Collection of Photographs" in *Aperture* (Millerton, New York), Fall 1969; "Eliot Porter" in *Modern Photography Annual,* New York 1972; "Eliot Porter Retrospective" by R. Mautner in *Artweek* (Oakland, California), 25 May 1974; "Living Masters of Photography: Beaton, Karsh, Porter, Duncan" in *Camera* (Lucerne), June 1974.

*

When color film became available in the 1940s, it was not highly regarded by those photographers who practiced photography as an art. They disparaged color photography as too literal a medium for personal interpretation, which only black-and-white photography permitted. In color photography one was simply copying nature, whereas in black-and-white the hues of the subject could be rendered in almost any desired tone of gray, thus allowing a wide range of interpretation.

As my color photography shifted from the portrayal of birds for proper identification to other nature subjects, I began to realize that their appeal depended very largely on the subtleties of color lost when the subject was rendered in black-and-white; and when I began to make color prints it became apparent that almost infinite possibilities, contrary to the assertions of the disparagers of color, were available for interpretation and individual expression. Why, I wondered, was the remarkable attribute of color vision, not shared by all vertebrates, treated with such disdain by photographers, alone in all the fields of art? Perhaps it is because they feel least secure in their chosen medium and are, by raising restrictive barriers, immuring themselves against invidious comparisons.

Color photography has today become much more generally accepted as a legitimate art, but it has not yet entirely freed itself from an inferiority complex as the self-conscious and self-justifying workshops in color photography indicate. Color perception, color appreciation, color theory, color dynamics, color as medium, color in the natural scene, are taught as though color in photography were a different phenomenon from color in painting.

To say that because a photograph is in color it is less creative than one in black-and-white is to manifest a poverty of perception no less egregious than

to condemn photography as a whole because it is the product of an optical instrument. I suspect that if color photography had been invented before black-and-white, the situation would be reversed.

—Eliot Porter

*   *   *

At a time in American history when the very government agencies charged with the well-being of the country's mountains and forests seem almost inimical to them, the photographs of Eliot Porter seem increasingly valuable. Not just for their worth to investor/collectors, but for their timeless and enduring affection for the landscape and myriad organisms and creatures that inhabit it.

In a society increasingly technical, impersonal and divorced from the realities of working one-to-one with nature to survive each day, Eliot Porter works to keep alive, to share and to kindle in others his own respect and love for the natural world. He knows that man and his surroundings are interdependent, that if man subjugates and steals indiscriminately from nature, he will die along with his victim. From this knowledge and from a love of the positive beauties of the natural world comes the strength of Eliot Porter's photography.

Porter's strength as a photographer of birds and the landscape derives at least in part from his wholeness as a photographer. His physician's skills (he was a doctor before becoming a full-time photographer at age 37) of patience and thoroughness have been put to good work in waiting out the precise moment in the actions of a bird, the exact nuance of light or bloom or foliage in the making of a landscape photograph.

He taught himself mastery of dye-transfer color printing—currently one of the most stable methods of making color images—and for many years made his own prints by this demanding process. Although best known for his work in color, Porter also works powerfully in black-and-white. His book *Summer Island,* a loving biography of a Maine island where he summered as a child, is chiefly photographed in black-and-white, the color exploding like a delicate display of fireworks late in the book, adding its own unique statement to what has gone before.

To his love for and mastery of his medium, both color and black-and-white, Porter adds his livelong love of and familiarity with nature and wild things. This blend of craft, concern and love has produced a life-work that assures Porter a high place among the outstanding nature photographers of the century.

A Porter photograph of a landscape (or detail of one) is, first of all, a contemplation. Typically, it is quiet. But it is the quiet of one who has shrugged off his backpack at trailside to rest a moment. The resulting quiet is not an exhausted but a studious one. The observer, we feel as we ourselves study the image, had looked hard at all within his field of view. He has seen the subtle shadings of different greens in trees and moss and grasses. He has noticed every ripple and reflection nuance on the surface of the quiet pool of water, the position of each leaf that floats on its surface.

And from this raw material he has extracted something that is at once universal and yet highly personal. By the use of his tool the view camera (in most, although not all cases), its lens and shutter, he has controlled his medium to express the mood of flowing water, the saturation of color reflected from leaves, the tone of the sky and other subtleties. He has adroitly edited nature to make it speak even more eloquently. The camera is more perceptive of detail even than the eye. Through the photographer's response to the scene and his capturing of it by the way he uses his medium, the viewer is almost literally given more than meets the eye.

For the most part, what is lacking in a Porter nature photograph is the obviously spectacular. Rather, what sustains and informs is a sense of revelation—the unveiling of what would otherwise perhaps go unseen, or at least unrealized.

In the photography of nature, subject matter that is the very essence of reality, Eliot Porter is able to exercise a vision and an artistry that make his photographs the mark at which his contemporaries must continually aim.

—Kenneth Poli

POST WOLCOTT, Marion.

Nationality: American. **Born:** Marion Post in Montclair, New Jersey, 7 June 1910. **Education:** Attended the Edgewood School, Greenwich, Connecticut, 1925-27; New School for Social Research, New York, 1928-29; New York University, 1929-30; University of Vienna, 1930-32, B.A. 1932; also studied at informal photo workshops, under Ralph Steiner, New York, 1935, 1936. **Family:** Married Leon O. Wolcott in 1941; children: John and Gail (stepchildren), Linda, and Michael. **Career:** Freelance photographer, working for *Life, Fortune,* etc., New York, 1936-37; Staff Photographer, *Philadelphia Evening Bulletin,* 1937-38; Principal Photographer, Farm Security Administration (FSA), under Roy E. Stryker, Washington, D.C. and through the U.S.A., 1938-42; photographic work reduced in favour of parenthood and teaching in Iran, Pakistan, Egypt and New Mexico, 1942-68. Freelance photographer, San Francisco, from 1968. **Recipient:** Dorothea Lange Award, Oakland Museum of Art, California, 1986; Sprague Award, National Press Photographers' Association, 1990; Lifetime Achievement Award, California Museum of Photography, Riverside, Ca., 1990; Lifetime Achievement Award, Society of Photographic Educators, 1991. Estate: Linda Wolcott-Moore, Fine Art, 165 Marguerite Ave, Mill Valley, CA, U.S.A. **Died:** (in California) November 24, 1990.

Individual Exhibitions:

1976	*FSA and Contemporary Color Work,* Hartnell Gallery, Salinas, California
	FSA Work of Russell Lee, Marion Post Wolcott and Walker Evans, Copenhagen
1977	*Contemporary Color, Isla Vista,* Santa Barbara Museum of Art, California
1978	*FSA Photographs,* Berkeley Museum of Art, California
	FSA and New Color Work, Everson Museum of Art, Syracuse, New York (retrospective)
1979	*Contemporary Color and Black and White Photographs,* Focus Gallery, San Francisco
	FSA and Contemporary Photographs, Witkin Gallery, New York
	FSA and Contemporary Color Work, Equivalents Gallery, Seattle
	FSA and Contemporary Photos, Amarillo Art Center, Texas (with Russell Lee)
1980	*American Photography and Social Conscience,* Axiom Gallery, Richmond, Victoria, Australia (with Lewis Hine and Weegee)
	Images of America: Photography from the FSA, Sonoma State University Art Gallery, California
1982	*FSA and Contemporary Color,* San Jose University, California
1984	*FSA Photography,* Fresno Art Museum, California
	FSA Work, Witkin Gallery, New York
	FSA Work, Friends of Photography, Carmel, California
	Three Documentary Photographers, Amon Carter Museum, Fort Worth, Texas (with Robert Frank and Morris Engel)
	FSA and Contemporary Color, Photographer's Gallery, Palo Alto, California
1985	Center for Creative Photography, University of Arizona, Tucson
	FSA Photos, Equivalents Gallery, Seattle, Washington
	Pierce Street Gallery, Birmingham, Michigan (with Jack Delano)

	Vision Gallery, San Francisco (with Don Worth)
1986	*Before and After: The FSA,* Dayton Beach Community College, Florida (with Arthur Rothstein and Jack Delano)
	University of Syracuse, New York (retrospective)
1987	Seattle Art Museum, Seattle, Washington
1988	Santa Barbara Museum of Art, Santa Barbara, California
1990	The Halstead Gallery West, San Francisco, California
	Chicago Art Institute, Chicago, Illinois
	International Center for Photography, New York
1991	Ginny Williams Gallery, Denver, Colorado
	A Gallery for Fine Photography, New Orleans
1992	G Gibson Gallery, Seattle, Washington
	Paul Kopeikin Gallery, Los Angeles
1993	PhotoGroup Gallery, Coral Gables, Florida
	Spectrum Gallery, Light Impressions Corp., Rochester, New York
1994	Lightworks Gallery, Sacramento, California
1995	Santa Barbara Museum of Art, Santa Barbara, California

Selected Group Exhibitions:

1955	*FSA Anniversary Show,* Brooklyn Museum, New York
1962	*The Bitter Years, FSA Photographs 1935-41,* Museum of Modern Art, New York
1968	*Just Before the War,* Newport Harbor Art Museum, California
1977	*A Vision Shared: The FSA,* Witkin Gallery, New York
	Women Look at Women, Library of Congress, Washington, D.C. (toured the United States)
	The FSA: People and Places of America, Santa Barbara Museum of Art, California
1979	*Images de l'Amerique en Crise: Photos de la FSA,* Centre Georges Pompidou, Paris
1981	*Farbe im Photo,* Josef-Haubrich-Kunsthalle, Cologne
1982	*Floods of Light,* The Photographers' Gallery, London (toured Britain)
1984	*Faces Photographed,* San Francisco Museum of Modern Art
1985	Vision Gallery, San Francisco
1988	*Eye on the South,* A Gallery for Fine Photography, New Orleans, LA
1992	*Wine and Food,* Alinder Gallery, Gualala, California
1993	*Women in Photography,* Scheinbaum and Russek, Santa Fe, New Mexico
	More than Meets the Eye, Santa Barbara Museum of Art, Santa Barbara, California
1994	*An American Vision,* Howard Greenberg Gallery, New York
	Billboards/Photographs, Stephen Cohen Gallery, Los Angeles

Collections:

Metropolitan Museum of Art, New York; Museum of Modern Art, New York; International Center of Photography, New York; International Museum of Photography, George Eastman House, Rochester, New York; Library of Congress, Washington, D.C.; Smithsonian Institution, Washington, D.C.; Art Institute of Chicago; San Francisco Museum of Modern Art; National Gallery of Canada, Ottawa; National Gallery of Victoria, Melbourne; Los Angeles County Museum of Art; J Paul Getty Museum, Malibu, California; Center for Creative Photography, Tucson, Arizona; Brooklyn Museum, Brooklyn, New York; The Oakland Museum, Oakland, California; Santa Barbara Museum of Art, Santa Barbara, California; Bibliotheque National de Paris; The Museum of Fine Arts, Houston; Ackland Museum of Art, University of North Carolina at Chapel Hill; Birmingham Museum, Birmingham, Alabama; Seattle Museum of Art, Seattle, Washington; Sarasota Museum, Sarasota, Florida.

Publications:

By POST WOLCOTT: Books—*Washington,* with text by Edwin Rosskam, New York 1939; *Hometown,* with text by Sherwood Anderson, New York 1940; *Vermont: The Green Mountain State,* Burlington, Vermont 1941; *12 Million Black Voices: A Folk History of the Negro in the United States,* with text by Richard Wright and Edwin Rosskam, New York 1941; *Fair Is Our*

Young Cotton Pickers Waiting to be Paid, **Mileston, Mississippi, 1939.** Photograph by Marion Post Wolcott.

Land, edited by Samuel Chamberlain, New York 1942; *Marion Post Wolcott: FSA Photographs,* with introduction by Sally Stain, Carmel, California 1983.

On **POST WOLCOTT: Books**—*The Bitter Years 1935-41* by Edward Steichen, New York 1962; *The History of Photography* by Beaumont Newhall, New York 1964; *Just Before the War: Urban America as Seen by the*

Photographers of the FSA, edited by Thomas H. Garver, New York 1968; *Portrait of a Decade: Roy Stryker and the Development of Documentary Photography in the Thirties* by F. Jack Hurley, Baton Rouge, Louisiana 1972, New York 1977; *In This Proud Land* by Roy E. Stryker and Nancy Wood, Greenwich, Connecticut 1973; *The Years of Bitterness and Pride: FSA Photographs 1935-43,* compiled by Jerry Kearns and Leroy Bellamy, text by Hiak Akmajian, New York 1975; *A Vision Shared: A Classic Portrait of America and Its People 1935-43,* edited by Hank O'Neal, New York and London 1976; *Amerika Fotografie 1920-1940* by Erika Billeter, Berne 1979; *The Photograph Collector's Guide* by Lee D. Witkin and Barbara London, Boston and London 1979; *Floods of Light: Flash Photography 1851-1981,* exhibition catalogue, by Rupert Martin, London 1982; *Marion Post Wolcott: FSA Photographs,* ed. David Featherstone, Carmel, 1983; *Let Us Now Praise Famous Women,* Andrea Fisher, New York, 1988; *Marion Post Wolcott: A Photographic Journey,* Jack F Hurley, Albuquerque, New Mexico, 1989; *Looking For The Light, The Hidden Art and Life of Marion Post Wolcott,* Paul Hendrickson, New York, 1991. **Articles**—"Photographs of the Depression Era" by Robert Doherty in *Camera* (Lucerne), October 1962; "Marion Post Wolcott: FSA Photographs" by James Elliot and Marta Westover in *University Art Museum Bulletin* (Berkeley, California), April 1978; "Marion Post Wolcott's Spectrum of the Depression" by Hal Fischer in *Artweek* (Oakland, California), 27 May 1978; "From the FSA to Today" by Martha Chahroudi in *Afterimage* (Rochester, New York), November 1978; "Not a Vintage Show— Post Wolcott" by Ben Lifson in the *Village Voice* (New York), July 1979; "Marion Post Wolcott" by Joan Murray in *American Photographer* (New York), March 1980; "Photojournalism as Art" by Tony Perry in *The Age* (Melbourne), August 1980; "People Won Out Over Landscapes" by Gene Thornton in the *New York Times,* 24 June 1984; "Wolcott Captured Social Ironies" by Robert Cawthorn in the *Arizona Star* (Tucson), 24 November 1985; "Marion Post Wolcott Portfolio" in *Photo Metro* (San Francisco), February 1986.

*

As an FSA documentary photographer I was committed to change the attitudes of people by familiarizing them with the plight of the underprivileged, especially in rural America. I wanted to show the extent of the gap between the wealthy and the poor; and, despite their marginal and destitute existence, to depict their dignity and courage. To create a general awakening and concern for their appalling conditions, I tried to contrast them with the wealthy and with the complacent tourists in Florida and with the fertility and abundant resources and beauty of our land. These, with the photographs of the positive side of the FSA remedial programs of our government, helped in placing exhibits and winning support for further appropriations from Congress. By informing the American public, the FSA photographs shocked and aroused public opinion to back New Deal policies and projects. They played a part in the social revolution of the 30s. Also, as an ongoing project, whenever possible, I documented, from an historical and sociological viewpoint, small town and rural life in America, especially winter in New England.

Since my final months with the FSA, when I and several others did a little color photography, I've had a long-standing interest in color.

In the early 1970s, following the Vietnam War and the students' burning of the Bank of America and other protests in Isla Vista, California, there was a period of intense re-evaluation—especially by youth—of predominant sociopolitical values. I tried to capture the essence of this new spirit and of changing life-styles, as well as their impact on cultural patterns and mores. I photographed, mostly in color, evidence expressed in their folk art, wall paintings and graffiti, banners, political signs, street fairs, ecology movements and recycling programs and efforts, free medical clinics and health care, etc.

This led to other photography of the California scene, and of some tourists in Hawaii—essentially still documentary in feeling and intent.

I welcome the "new frontier," the new wider vision, the experimentation in contemporary photography, so long as it has integrity and is artistically honest.

During the past few years I have photographed very little because of ill health, involvement in researching and printing of FSA and other old negatives, giving slide lectures, and participating in symposiums and conferences when possible. I am aware of the increasing interest in the FSA documentary project. Many of these photographs, until recently buried in the Library of Congress files, are finding their way into print and exhibitions, etc., including some of mine.

In general, I am pleased with the renewed interest, activity and participation in documentary photography, especially that which deals with environmental and social-political issues, both locally and globally.

—Marion Post Wolcott

*   *   *

Although in the mid-70s she began taking and exhibiting photographs again, Marion Post Wolcott's place in the medium's history rests securely upon the few years she spent in Roy Stryker's Farm Security Administration photography unit. When that project ended, Mrs. Wolcott chose to devote more time to raising her family. Yet, in a mere half-decade, first at the Philadelphia *Evening Bulletin* and after 1938 with the FSA, Marion Post Wolcott created a remarkable and diverse body of work, including some of the most powerful images in the vast FSA collection.

"The fact that I was a late-comer to the FSA photo documentary group," she wrote some years ago, "influenced much the selection of material, the areas, and the assignments given me by Roy (Stryker). . . . I picked up loose ends, filled in holes in areas closer to home base—an example being a series of pictures of mine on New England winter and very early spring, or of a remote back country area in Kentucky: going to school; burying their dead; delivering mail; bringing groceries up the creek bed, barefoot or on horseback; how people spent their leisure, their recreation and games."

As with many catalogs, the detail obscures the accomplishments. In the course of picking up "loose ends," Mrs. Wolcott created beautiful landscapes, particularly in New England and along northern Virginia's Shenandoah Valley. She retraced some of the coal mining regions photographed very early in the project by Ben Shahn, thus providing valuable comparative material. Perhaps most important, she provided an exceedingly rare glimpse of America's upper-middle and wealthy classes at play during the late Depression years.

The FSA file is, apart from Mrs. Wolcott's photographs, silent about those at the upper end of the income scale. She was very much aware of the lacuna: "There was virtually nothing in the files on . . . the elite, on the east or west coasts, or elsewhere. I thought these (pictures) could provide dramatic contrast, help tell our story."

Having been sent, in 1939, to document the life of migrant farm workers in Florida's Lake Okeechobee region, she also spent time in Miami and other areas, photographing wealthy hotel guests, visitors to the Hialeah Racetrack and others in that group for whom the Great Depression was merely an inconvenience. The Miami pictures are among Mrs. Wolcott's best. A particular favorite of mine is a Miami Beach photograph of a tropical-suited, panama-hatted gentleman exiting one of those Rococo Revival facades through a multistoried arch. Another preserves the blasé expression of a wealthy Miami Beach couple showing off their private bar.

I do not mean to imply that these photographs were intended as satire. They scrupulously document what exists; the existence satirizes itself. The photographs were, therefore, a perfectly reasonable addition to the FSA files; it is simply unfortunate that they stand there so much apart. Unfortunate, too, as an indication of what photography lost during Marion Post Wolcott's long sabbatical from the profession. The opportunity to see her later work is thus an event eagerly anticipated.

—Stu Cohen

Marion Post Wolcott took pictures continually, both at home and overseas, many in colour. The legacy of her work in Iran, Egypt, India and Pakistan is, for the most part, still unseen. Her family is editing slides and negatives with a view to presenting a show of post FSA work at the Santa Barbara Museum of Art in late 1995.

—Linda Wolcott-Moore

POWER, Mark.

Nationality: British. **Born:** Harpenden, England, 24 June 1959. **Education:** Obtained First Class, B.A. (Honors) in Graphic Design/Illustration, at Brighton Polytechnic in 1981; self-taught photographer. **Career:** Freelance photographer and Senior Lecturer in Editorial Photography, University of Brighton, Sussex. Joined Network Photographers in 1988. Also founder member of several photographic co-operatives in the Brighton area. **Recipient:** Christian Aid Photography Awards—Best Photograph of Children, 1984; Beefeater Gin Awards winner, 1986; Photographers Gallery bursary, 1986; Ilford Photography Awards Editorial/Features winner, 1990. **Agent:** Network Photographers, 3-4 Kirby Street, London, EC1N 8TS. **Address:** 14 Roundhill Road, Brighton, East Sussex, BN2 3RF, England.

Individual Exhibitions:

1986   *The Childrens Society Photographs,* Brighton Polytechnic
        Gallery, Brighton, England; Watermans Arts Centre, London;
        Open Eye, Liverpool, England; Side Gallery, Newcastle,
        England
1988   *Westminster Childrens Hospital,* The Photographers Gallery,
        London
        But Come and Join the Dance, Photogallery, Hastings, England
1990   *Beyond the Facade,* (with Jim Cooke), Brighton Polytechnic
        Gallery, Brighton, England

Selected Group Exhibitions:

1985   *Human Interest—50 Years of British Art about the Figure,*
        Cornerhouse, Manchester (toured)
        Image and Exploration, The Photographers Gallery, London
        (toured)
1987   *Regarding Photography,* Ffotogallery, Cardiff (toured)
        From Billboards to Postcards, Oldham Art Gallery (toured)
        The State of the Nation, Coventry City Art Gallery (toured)
1989   *Sun Life Photography Awards,* National Museum of Photogra-
        phy, Film and Television, Bradford, England
1990   *The Year of Revolutions—Network Photographers in Eastern
        Europe,* National Museum of Photography, Film and
        Television, Bradford
1992   *Image 90s,* National Theatre, London
1993   *Positive Lives—The Response to HIV,* Photographers Gallery,
        London

Collections:

The Arts Council of Great Britain

Publications:

By POWER: Books—*Westminster Childrens Hospital,* London, 1988; *Positive Lives—Responses to HIV* (one chapter), London 1993.

On POWER: Books—*British Journal of Photography Annuals,* 1985,86, 87, 91, 93, 94. **Articles**—''Power & Poverty'' in *35mm Photography,* UK, June 1985; Interview in *Photography,* UK, March 1988; ''Kirkby—The New Jerusalem'' in *Sunday Times Magazine,* UK, October, 1992; ''The Shipping Forecast'' in *Reportage,* UK, No 5 1994; ''The Shipping Forecast'' in *Telegraph Magazine,* UK, March 1994.

*   *   *

Mark Power's secret is his passionate and steely determination that belies his gentle demeanour and self-effacing manner. Driven by strong beliefs in social justice and an emotional compassion for the people he encounters, Mark has worked in the toughest conditions to produce the gentlest reportages about life at the edges of British society.

Usually working in black and white, his early projects in the mid 1980s were characteristically grainy 35mm photojournalism: heavy and moody representations of homelessness, deprivation and life in poverty. His pictures were used by charities and were widely exhibited, but it was not until the late 1980s that his work found its way into the mainstream media with regular clients including the *Sunday Magazine* and the *Sunday Telegraph.* This brought a welcome income and deserved exposure and the discipline of such work sharpened Mark's abilities as a responsive assignment photographer. However the frustrations of working exclusively to other people's briefs jolted him into a new creative phase.

Mark took off for four months in Spain through the summer of 1992 and suddenly a lyrical core was revealed in his work. The diary of his travels included people and events in a folio rich in wit and visual poetry. As though unchained Mark leapt into a new creative mode and his recent work has been predominantly medium format. Every component of the frame is considered with the ''action'' being only one element of composition, with the form and tone combining in a manner best described as ''construed documentary.''

This style appears to be reaching maturity with the *Shipping Forecast* project. By photographing a fluid mixture of landscape and reportage in every European coastal area he has done more than merely create a visual map of the familiar names (South Utsira, Dogger, Fisher, German Bight etc). The project has developed as a comparative study of European cultures with an emergent introspective quality that marks the work as a very personal interpretation. Together with his moving AIDs related study *Grief and Loss,* Mark's current work is at the forefront of contemporary British documentary photography that is pushing forward into the twenty-first century.

Mark Power is currently dividing his time between teaching photography at Brighton University and making pictures.

—Stephen Mayes

POŽERSKIS, Romualdas.

Nationality: Lithuanian. **Born:** Vilnius on 7 July 1951. **Education:** Studied electrical engineering at Kaunas Polytechnic Institute, 1969-75. **Family:** Married Virginija Grikšaite-Požerskiene, 14 September 1979; children: Povilas and Monika. **Career:** Joined the Photographic Art Society of Lithuania in 1974. Worked as a freelance magazine photographer since 1980. Lectured in the history and aesthetics of photography at Kaunas Vytautas Magnum University since 1993. **Recipient:** Lithuanian National Award, 1991. **Address:** A.Mapu 8-2, Kaunas, 3000 Lithuania.

Individual Exhibitions:

1975   *Youth,* Polytechnical Institute, Kaunas
1976   Photo Gallery, Poznan
1977   International Photo Camp, Gorzow, Poland
        Victories and Defeats, Photo Museum, Siauliai, Lithuania
        (travelled to the Folklore Gallery, Kedainiai)
1979   House of Photography, Plovdiv, Bulgaria
        Photo Gallery, Bialystok, Poland
1981   Mala Galeria, Bratislava, Czechoslovakia
        Art Research Institute, Moscow
1983   House of Culture, Debrecen, Hungary
        Kik in de Kiok Museum, Tallinn, Estonia
        Lithuanian Old Towns, Art Expositions House, Vilnius
1984   Photography Gallery, Kaunas
1985   Photography Gallery, Fotohof, Salzburg
        Bayern Photography Institute, Munich, Germany
1988   Fotogalerie am Helsinforser Platz, Berlin
        Lithuanian Pilgrimages, Ciurlionia Art Gallery, Chicago
        (travelled to The Photo Centre gallery, Moscow)
1990   Broerenkerk te Zwolle gallery, Amsterdam
        Memory Gardens, Salon Photography, Vilnius

Malin, **1993, from** *The Shipping Forecast.* Photograph ©Mark Power.

Selected Group Exhibitions:

1977   Seven Juniors, Photography Salon, Vilnius
1979   Lithuanian Photography, Cannon Photo Gallery, Amsterdam
1986   Young European Photographers, Frankfurt Art Society,
            Frankfurt
1988   La Comptoir de la Photographie Gallery, Paris
1989   World Press Photo, Amsterdam
1990   *World in Focus,* Red Cross Society, Geneva
1991   *Rencontres internationales de la photographie,* Arles, France
1992   *The Nude in Town Holl,* Tallinn, Estonia

            Lithuanian Photography, Finland Photography Museum,
                Helsinki (travelled to Galerie Friedrichstrasse, Berlin)
            Kiss, Galerie du Jour, Paris
1993   *Baltic Photo Art Today,* Stadtgalerie in Sophienhof, Kiel,
                Germany

Collections:

Lithuanian Art Photographers Union, Vilnius; Photo Museum, Siauliai,
Lithuania; Finland Photography Museum, Helsinki; Bibliotheque Nationale,
Paris; Musee Reattu, Arles.

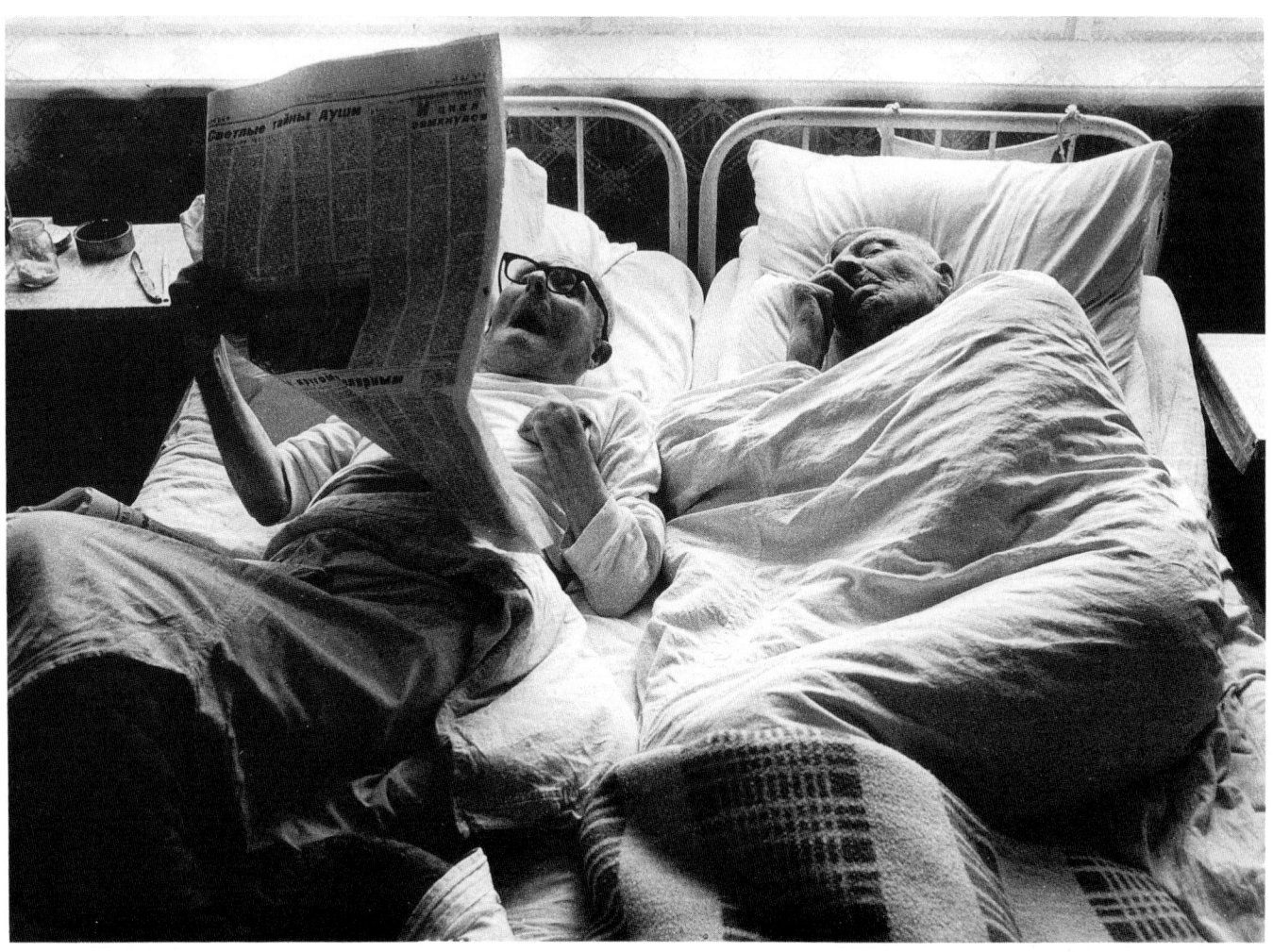

From the series *Last Home - 23,* **1984.** Photograph by Romualdas Požerskis.

Publications:

By POŽERSKIS: Books—*Lithuanian Pilgrimages,* Chicago 1990. **Articles**—*Sovietskoje Foto,* Moscow,No 1, 1978; *Fotografia,* Warsaw; *Bild,* Stockholm, No 2, 1982; *Valokuva,* Helsinki, No 2, 1988.

On POŽERSKIS: Books—*Fotojahrbuch international,* Leipzig 1976, 1979 and 1982; *Lietuvos Fotografija,* Vilnius 1978, 1981, 1986 and 1987; *Photography Year Book,* Surrey, England 1977, 1978, 1981, 1984, 1985, 1987-88, 1989 and 1993; *The Children of This World* by Karl Pawek, Hamburg 1977; *DuMont Foto 4* by Andreas Müller-Pohle, Cologne 1982; *Fotografen aus der USSR,* Baden-Baden 1983; *Photographers Encyclopedia International,* Hermance, Switzerland 1984; *Tvoceskaja Fotografija* by Sergei Morozov, Moscow 1985; *Another Russia* by Daniela Mrazkova and Vladimir Remes, London 1986; *Tsvetenie Zemli* by Viktor Diomin, Moscow 1987; *Il nudo fotografico nell Europa dell Est* by Lorenco Merlo, Bologna 1987; *An insight into contemporary Soviet photography* by Marie-Francoise George, Paris 1988; *FOTO,* Hanover 1989; *Photography in USSR,* Helsinki 1989; *Changing reality* by Benavid-Val, Washington 1991; *The Female Nude in Art Photography* by Irina Bogdanova, Moscow 1992; *Graphis Photo 92,* Zurich 1992; *The Memory of Images,* Kiel 1993. **Articles**—''Students Gallery'' in *Nemunas* magazine, No. 4, 1974; *Bolgarsko Foto,* No. 8,9, 1979; ''Romualdas Pozerskis'' by Halina Murza-Stankiewicz in *Foto;* ''Romualdas Pozerskis'' by Algirdas Gaizutis in *Fotografie,* No. 7, 1981; ''Country Celebrations'' by Vladimir Birgus in *Ceskoslovenska Fotografie,* No. 2, 1982; *Asahi Camera,* No. 12, 1984; *Art and Design,* No.2, 1986; *Color Foto,* No. 2, 1987; *Photographer*

(Paris), November 1988; Geoff Dyer in *Images of the Soviet Union,* No. 8, 1989; Daniela Mrazkova in *Many Nations, Many Voices,* No. 116, 1989; ''Fotograf Romualdas Pozerskis in Nederland'' by Algirdas Gaizutis in *Nederland-USSR Magazine,* No. 5, 1990; ''The Untold Holocaust'' by Victor Gaetan in *Washington and World Arts,* No. 4, 1990; *Red Cross and Red Crescent,* May-August 1990; *Stern,* No. 5, 1991; ''Blick Zuruch nach Vorn'' by Barbara Straka in *Merian,* No. 9, 1992; ''Russland Akte'' by Irina Bogdanova in *New Mag,* No. 1, 1992; ''Two Masters'' by Valerij Stignejev in *Fotografija,* Moscow.

*   *   *

In the 1970s Romualdas Požerskis was, along with his friend Virgilius Šonta, the most outstanding representative of young Lithuanian photography. He followed in the footsteps of a generation of older pioneers of modern documentary photography in Lithuania—Aleksandras Macijauskas, Antanas Lutkus, Vitas Tuckus, Aligimantas Kuncjius and others—who oriented their work to photograph the daily life of ordinary people in the Lithuanian countryside. Romualdas Požerskis also continued in the endeavour to achieve an untouched up portrayal of reality differing in its authenticity from the artificially euphoric portraits of the best workers and happy youth which prevailed in Soviet photography at that time.

Romualdas Požerskis began to photograph in 1963, but it was not until the period of his study of electrical engineering at the Kaunus Polytechnic that together with Šonta he began to approach his photographic work more seriously. Since the 1970s a series of Požerskis's photographs were loosely

911

linked to the work of his then greatest model Macijauskas. In the photographic series *Victories and Defeats,* he was concerned more with depicting the inner world of humanity at moments of hope, victory or defeat than with dramatic moments of sports contests. Similarly, his cycle *In the Hospital* was not merely a document from inside a hospital, but a philospophical deliberation on the fundamental values of human life on our ability to overcome the caprices of fate, pain and the fear of death. In the series *Old Towns of Lithuania* the photographer concentrated on the life of the population of the historic centres of Vilnius, Kaunus and other cities. In a confrontation of several motifs he regularly accented different comical and grotesque elements of otherwise commonplace situations.

The indisputable summit of Požerskis's work is his large series of photographs portraying religious life in Lithuania. Here he depicted widely distinctive wakes and religious festivities, not only in expressing the ancient traditions of his small nation but also his religious feeling, a manifestation of his protest against the official aetheism of the Soviet communist regime which prevailed in Lithuania from the time of the Soviet occupation in 1940 until independence at the end of the Gorbachov era.

His photographs discover the great in the inconspicuous and the dramatic in the ordinary. Behind outer gestures and mimicry he reveals the inner world of ordinary people, their joys, hopes, faith, uncertainty, pain. His subjects are supremely authentic, at the same time full of lyricism and fine poetry. They readily portray fleeting scenes and simultaneously show something permanent and unchanging. They are precisely located by the chosen environment, the type of people, even their clothing; at the same time they say a great deal about common things outside a concrete time and space. They are simple and pathetic. A number of comic elements appear, but Požerskis never lets them manifest themselves in noisy farce or tough satire, but subdues them with a kind and somewhat wistful humour. The closeness between the character of the photographs and the photographer's outlook on life is evident.

In these photographs, mostly presented under the name *Country Holidays* and also published in book form in the USA under the title *Lithuanian Pilgrimages,* Romualdas Požerskis succeeds in combining the ethnographical value of a document about religion in Lithuania in the 1970s and 1980s with a general humanistic overview of the elementary values of human life. A contributory factor lies also in the formal aspect of these photographs, often combining several spatial plans to form a single whole by means of the use of wide-angle lenses. The contrast principle based on the portrayal of several simultaneous happenings and a multiplication of motifs is also reflected in photographs, in which various visual metaphors and symbols appear. In spite of this, however, these photographs can be easily read and interpreted.

Although Romualdas Požerskis's photographic work also includes nude studies, portraits and reportage shots of Kaunus basketball matches or political events taking place in Lithuania during the struggles for independence, humanistic documentary photographs remain dominant. In the 1980s and now in the 1990s—these have been enriched with photographs of children's hospitals, the sad fate of old people dependent on the help of their near ones, or of mourners in cemeteries. They also bear witness to the fact that Romualdas Požerskis ranks among the most outstanding representatives of contemporary Lithuanian photography.

—Vladimír Birgus

PRAZUCH, Wieslaw.

Nationality: Polish. **Born:** 1925. **Education:** Studied at the Academy of Political Sciences, Warsaw. **Career:** Photojournalist for *Swiat* weekly, Warsaw, 1951-69; President, Union of Polish Art Photographers, 1973-76. Since 1976, Chief Editor, *Fotografia* quarterly, Warsaw. **Recipient:** Cross of Merit, 1975; Knight's Cross of the Polish Resurgence, 1980; received several awards from the Ministry of Culture and Arts. **Died:** (in Warsaw) 24 August 1992.

Individual Exhibitions:

1963   *Bliski Wschòd,* Galeria Kordegarda, Warsaw
1964   *Z reportazu,* Klub Ksiazki i Prasy, Torun, Poland

1965   *Z reportazu,* Klub Ksiazki i Prasy, Olsztyn, Poland
1967   *Reportaz,* Galeria Iskra, Torun, Poland
1972   *Faces,* Galeria BWA, Sopot, Poland
1988   *Portraits,* Stara Galeria ZPAF, Warsaw and Klub 13 Muz, Szczecin, Poland

Selected Group Exhibitions:

1975   *The Land: 20th Century Landscape Photographs Selected by Bill Brandt,* Victoria and Albert Museum, London (travelled to the National Gallery, Edinburgh; Ulster Museum, Belfast; and National Museum of Wales, Cardiff, 1976)
1979   *Fotografia Polska 1839-1979,* International Center of Photography, New York (travelled to the Museum of Contemporary Art, Chicago; Zacheta Gallery, Warsaw; Museum of Fine Arts, Lodz, Poland; and the Whitechapel Gallery, London, 1979-80)
          Sztuka reportazu, National Museum in Wroclaw
1980   *I Ogolnopolski Przeglad Fotografii Socjologicznej,* Bielsko Biala, Poland
1981   *Photographie Polonaise 1900-1981,* Centre Georges Pompidou, Paris
1985   *Polska Wspolczesna Fotografia Artystyczna,* Galeria Zacheta, Warsaw
1987   *Fotografia Prasowa lat minionych,* Galeria BWA Gorzow Wlkp., Poland
          Fotografia w tygodniku "Swiat," Galeria BWA Gorzow Wlkp., Poland

Publications:

By PRAZUCH: Article—"Dzial fotografii tygodnika Swiat" in *Fotografia prasowa jako sztuka faktu,* XVII Konfrontacje Fotograficzne, Gorzow Wlkp., 1987.

On PRAZUCH: Books—*Das Polnische Lichtbild,* with introduction by Zbigniew Pekoslawski, Halle, East Germany 1961; *Fotografia i sztuka,* by Alfred Ligocki, Warsaw, 1962; *Sztuka reportazu,* exhibition catalogue, Wroclaw, 1979; *Fotografia Warsawska* by Waclaw Zdzarski, Warsaw, 1974; *The Land: 20th Century Landscape Photographs Selected by Bill Brandt,* exhibition catalogue, by Mark Haworth-Booth, London 1975: *Zawod: fotoreporterzy,* by Jan Kosidowski, Warsaw, 1984; *Fotografia Polska 1945-1985* by Ryszard Bobrowski, Jerzy Busza, Pawel Pierscinski and others, Gorzow Wielkopolski, Poland 1985; *Encyclopedie Internationale des Photographes de 1839 a nos jours,* Geneva, 1985; *Polska wspolczesna fotografia artystyczna,* exhibition catalogue, text by Adam Sobota, Warsaw, 1985; *Czy istnieje fotografia socjologiczna?* by Alfred Ligocki, Krakow, 1987; *Fotografia prasowa jako sztuka faktu,* publication of the seminar: XVII Konfrontacje Fotograficzne, Gorzow Wlkp., 1987; *Wobec odbiorcow fotografii,* by Jerzy Busza, Warsaw, 1990; *150 lat polskiej fotografii,* Warsaw, 1991. **Articles**—"Notatki" by Jerzy Andrzejewski in *Polityka,* Warsaw 17 September, 1960; "Il Salon Zlocistego Jantara" by Marian Szulc in *Dziennik Baltycki,* Gdanzk, no 116/1964;"Wieslaw Prazuch" by Juliusz Garztecki in *Fotografia* (Warsaw), no. 4, 1968; "Portrety—obiektyw w oku" by Grzegorz Nawrocki in *Kontrasty,* Bialystok, no 4/1977; "Chyba po prostu rewolucja" by Witold Pawlowski in *ITD,* Warsaw, no 42/1981; "Wieslaw Prazuch" by Jan Kosidowski in *Fotografia,* Warsaw, no 1/1986; "Wieslaw Prazuch" by Jan Mierzanowski in *Slowo Powszechne,* Warsaw, no 140/1987; "Dzis liczy sie slowo . . . " by Zuzanna Csato in *Express Wieczorny,* Warsaw, no 19/1988; "Wizerunki Wieslawa Prazucha" by Jan Jackowski in the catalogue of the exhibition in Stara Galeria ZPAF, Warsaw, 1988; "Wizerunki" by Krystyna Lyczywek in the exhibition catalogue in Klub 13 Muz, Szczecin, 1988; "Szukam prawdy . . . " by Ryszard Nowicki in *Kobieta i Zycie,* Warsaw, no 6/1988; "Przy okazji wystawy Wieslawa Prazucha" by Joanna Kubica in *Perspektywy,* Warsaw, no 12/1988; "Wizerunki Wieslawa Prazucha" by Andrzej A Mroczek in *Kierunki,* Warsaw, no 10/1988; "Twarze" by Zbigniew Pietrasik in *Polityka,* Warsaw, no 6/1988; "Fotograf Swiata" by c.c. in *Kariera,* Warsaw, no 3/1990; "Prazuch" in *Kobieta i Zycie,* Warsaw, no 33/1993;

"Tygodnik Swiat" by Urszula Czartoryska in *6 x 9—fotografia,* Warsaw, no 7/1993.

* * *

The first years after the Second World War brought to Poland a gradual return to normal, accompanied by great social changes and the gradual reconstruction of the country. Of all the various artistic media, this process found its fullest expression in camera-reportage. In 1951 the first issue of a new illustrated weekly periodical entitled *Swiat (World)* was published. It very quickly developed its own characteristic style in the presentation of human interest features. The style—not so much sensational as reflective, often lyrical—showed a true picture of the people, their everyday life, their worries and their hopes. One of the *Swiat* photographers was Wieslaw Prazuch.

Prazuch worked for *Swiat* throughout its existence, and his photographs excellently represent the characteristic style of the periodical. However, this kind of photo-reportage was initiated in Poland not by Prazuch but by his editorial colleague, Wieslaw Slawny. The photographs of Slawny created a definitive new style in Polish photography, and the essence of this style is easily apparent if one compares Slawny's photographs with those of Polish photographers of the preceding, interwar generation, which were commercial, smooth, elegant, picturing an affluent society (balls, hunts, social events) and essentially addressed only to that society. Nothing—or almost nothing—of that theme found its way into Slawny's photographs, for the simple reason that the country was in ruins, the people were poor, and the socio-political situation was now radically different. Slawny returned to Poland from Paris where he had witnessed the birth of Magnum and had learned first-hand from such illustrated weekly periodicals as *Paris-Match* and *Life* and from the photography of Henri Cartier-Bresson. The new ideas—and the new photographic equipment that Slawny brought with him—caught the imagination of his younger co-workers at *Swiat,* including Prazuch.

A vital role was played in this new Polish photography by the reality of the country's situation. The post-war years in Poland were a period of mass migration of the population, rapid industrialization, and reconstruction. Photographic themes were literally everywhere at hand—on the streets of Warsaw, on large building sites, at political meetings, even deep within the country in the changes in provincial life. But this new photography was not merely a straight-forward record, an ordinary communication of events or activities, but photography with an explicit ethical stance, rich in emotional and often poetic content. It realized the ideas of Edward Steichen, that the "mission of photography is to help a man in understanding other men and also in understanding himself."

The photographic output of the *Swiat* photojournalists created a great and unique document of an epoch, a record of the post-war history of Poland, her people, traditions and culture.

—Ryszard Bobrowski

PRINCE Doug(las Donald).

Nationality: American. **Born:** Des Moines, Iowa, 2 January 1943. **Education:** Attended Johnston Consolidated High School, Johnston Station, Iowa, 1948-61; studied fine arts, 1961-65, and photography, under John Schulze and Ralph Koppel, 1966-68, University of Iowa, Iowa City, B.A. 1965, M.A. 1968. **Family:** Married Rebecca S. New in 1977; children: Brice, Brian (from former marriage) and Case. **Career:** Assistant Art Instructor, University of Iowa, Iowa City 1966-68; Assistant Professor of Art, University of Florida, Gainesville, 1968-76; Assistant Professor of Photography, Rhode Island School of Design, Providence, 1976-79; Adjunct Professor of Photography, Department of Fine Arts, University of New Hampshire in 1994. Freelance photographer since 1979. Lived and worked in Italy, 1980-81. **Recipient:** Prix de la Ville d'Avignon, France, 1972; National Endowment for the Arts Photography Fellowship, 1977, 1979; Light Work Grant, 1986; Artist's Fellowship, New York Foundation for the Arts, 1990. **Agent:** Witkin Gallery, 415 West Broadway, New York, New York 10012. **Address:** 173 Cypress Street, Providence, Rhode Island 02906, U.S.A.

Individual Exhibitions:

1967 Des Moines Art Center, Iowa
1971 Residence, Santa Fe, New Mexico
1973 Light Gallery, New York
1974 University of Tennessee, Knoxville
1975 Light Gallery, New York
   State University of New York at Geneseo
   Print Maker Gallery, Lincoln, Nebraska
   Deja Vu Gallery, Toronto
1976 Woods-Gerry Gallery, Providence, Rhode Island
1980 Witkin Gallery, New York
   Addison Gallery, Andover, Massachusetts
1983 Carl Solway Gallery, Cincinnati, Ohio
   Witkin Gallery, New York
1987 Witkin Gallery, New York
1994 *Twenty Years 1973-1993,* Witkin Gallery, New York

Selected Group Exhibitions:

1965 *Seeing Photographically,* International Museum of Photography, George Eastman House, Rochester, New York
1968 *Young Photographers,* University of New Mexico, Albuquerque
1970 *Photography into Sculpture,* Museum of Modern Art, New York
1973 *Contemporary Photographers,* Princeton Art Museum, New Jersey
   Light and Lens, Hudson River Museum, Yonkers, New York
1974 *10 American Photographers,* The Photographers' Gallery, London
1975 *Artists' Biennial '75,* New Orleans Museum of Art
1978 *Mirrors and Windows: American Photography since 1960,* Museum of Modern Art, New York (toured the United States, 1978-80)
1980 *1st International Photo Exhibition at Salford '80,* England
1981 *Photographer as Printmaker,* Ferens Art Gallery, Hull, Yorkshire (travelled to the Museum and Art Gallery, Leicester; Cooper Gallery, Barnsley; Castle Museum, Nottingham; Photographers' Gallery, London)
1989 Witkin Gallery, New York

Collections:

Museum of Modern Art, New York; International Museum of Photography, George Eastman House, Rochester, New York; Rhode Island School of Design, Providence; Addison Gallery, Andover, Massachusetts; Worcester Art Museum, Massachusetts; Princeton Art Museum, New Jersey; Philadelphia Museum of Art; Exchange National Bank, Chicago; Museum of Fine Arts, St. Petersburg, Florida; University of New Mexico, Albuquerque.

Publications:

By PRINCE: Book—*Photo Sculpture: Doug Prince,* New York 1979. **Article**—"Portfolio: Doug Prince" in *Popular Photography Annual,* New York 1980.

On PRINCE: Books—*Darkroom II,* edited by Jain Kelly, New York 1978; *Mirrors and Windows: American Photography since 1960* by John Szarkowski, New York 1978; *A Ten Year Salute* by Lee D. Witkin, New York 1979; *The Photograph Collector's Guide* by Lee D. Witkin and Barbara London, Boston 1979; *Photographer as Printmaker,* exhibition catalogue, with texts by Gerry Badger, Peter C. Bunnell and Ansel Adams, London 1981. **Articles**—"Photography and Prints" by Peter C. Bunnell in *Art in America* (New York), September/October 1969; "Message into Medium" by Carol Stevens in *Print* (New York), May/June 1970; "Photography into Sculpture" by Peter C. Bunnell in *Artscanada* (Toronto), June 1970; "A Young Illusionist" by Gene Thornton in the *New York Times,* 14 September 1975; "From Fine Art to Plain Junk" by Gene Thornton in the *New York Times,* 14 November 1971; "Lights

On and Chin Up'' by A.D. Coleman in the *Village Voice* (New York), 18 November 1971; ''Photography into Sculpture'' in *Artweek* (Oakland, California), 18 December 1971; ''Doug Prince, Light Gallery'' by William Dyckes in *Artsmagazine* (New York), March 1973; ''Shows We've Seen'' by Harvey V. Fondiller in *Popular Photography* (New York), May 1980.

*

Photography is part of a continuous tradition of image-making in the arts. My work in photography has evolved to share concerns with three areas in this tradition: painting, printmaking and sculpture. In particular, I am attracted to the additive image-making characteristic in these disciplines, which allows the synthesis of elements at a conceptual as well as a process level. For me, this synthesis takes place in a manner closely related to dreams, where events and objects are re-ordered to offer new meanings and appreciations. It is this discovery of successful relationships which is my primary objective in both my black-and-white prints and photo sculptures.

—Doug Prince

* * *

Doug Prince belongs to a generation that has sought to expand the boundaries of the photographic medium through both conceptual and iconographic means. Inspired by 19th century ambrotypes, Victorian Easter eggs with peepholes, and miniature dioramas (all of which are small, hand-held objects which invite viewer participation). Prince began experimenting with 3-dimensional imagery while still in graduate school. He developed the idea of using photographic images on transparencies, placing one behind the other, and containing the images within the closed environment of a small plexiglas box. His further explorations into illusionistic fantasy continued at the University of Florida where he served as Assistant Professor of Photography. Additional influences can be traced to symbolist and surrealist painters, and to the photographer Jerry N. Uelsmann, a colleague at the University of Florida. A major group show, *Photography into Sculpture,* curated by Peter Bunnell, was mounted at the Museum of Modern Art in New York in 1970, and Prince's work in that show shared with others an exploitation of the technology of plastics and a concern with the photograph as a tactile object. His work was included in numerous other group shows in the early 70s focusing on transparent images, ''Small Environments'' or ''Extraordinary Realities.''

Prince's concern has been with examining the graphic qualities inherent in the materials as a means of translating light and space relationships into topographic images. He builds up new tonal relationships not possible with images printed on paper and viewed with refracted light. He has consistently explored the qualities of graphic arts film with its properties of high contrast and potential for solarization of the image.

A number of diverse elements coalesce in Prince's work to make it dynamic and vital. The inherent veracity of the photographic image lends authenticity to the subject represented, and an intriguing tension results from the play between illusion and reality. The fusion and juxtaposition of diverse and unrelated images brings about a new illusionistic reality, creating Prince's own personal symbology. The fabrication of a photographic fantasy—in his words, ''through the synthesis of unconnected images into new spatial and psychological relationships''—has been an on-going concern with him in both his photographic prints and in his boxes. His search for new personal symbols is both intuitive and empirical, and has become the crux of his image-making. Prince associates this ''restructuring of reality'' with dream imagery where ''elements converge in new relationships to offer fresh insights and create personal symbols which further our understanding of ourselves and our environment.'' He works with restructuring the elements of light, time and space and explores the natural order of things (birth, death, evolution and entropy). The content of his boxes ''range from realistic environments, composed of objects in logical spaces, to the more problematic and surreal juxtaposition of elements akin to surrealistic imagery.'' His primary thematic concerns are the ''sensory exploration of the environment by his two sons, the containment and vulnerability of domestic animals in the landscape, and evidence of humanity on the natural environment.'' Prince's union of structural and stylistic concerns, firmly entrenched in a photographic vision, make his work an important contribution to the language of photography.

His body portraits began on a serious level in 1993 and involve a photo resist technique. He first oils a body part, like an arm, then he impresses it onto photo paper. When the paper is dipped into photographic chemicals, the oil creates an area that resists development.

—Jean Caslin

PRINCE, Richard.

Nationality: American. **Born:** Panama Canal Zone in 1949. **Agent:** Barbara Gladstone Gallery, 99 Greene Street, New York, New York 10012, U.S.A.

Individual Exhibitions:

1980	CEPA Gallery, Buffalo, New York
	Artists Space, New York
1981	Richard Kuhlenschmidt Gallery, Los Angeles
	Metro Pictures, New York
1982	Metro Pictures, New York
1983	Baskerville & Watson, New York
	Richard Kuhlenschmidt Gallery, Los Angeles
	Institute of Contemporary Art, London
	Le Nouveau Musée, Lyon, France
1984	Baskerville & Watson, New York
	Feature Gallery, Chicago
	Riverside Studios, London
1985	Richard Kuhlenschmidt Gallery, Los Angeles
	International with Monument, New York
1986	Feature Gallery, Chicago
	International with Monument, New York
1987	Daniel Weinberg Gallery, Los Angeles
	Galeria Isabella Kacprzak, Stuttgart, Germany
1988	Galerie Rafael Jablonka, Cologne, Germany
	Galerie Ghislaine Hussenot, Paris
	Tell Me Everything, One Times Square, New York
	Le Casa d'Arte, Milan, Italy
	Barbara Gladstone Gallery, New York
	Centre National d'Art Contemporain de Grenoble, France
1989	Daniel Weinberg Gallery, Los Angeles
	Barn Gallery, Ogunquit, Maine
	Spiritual America, IVAM Centre del Carme, Valencia, Spain
1990	Arthur Roger Gallery, New Orleans, Louisiana
	Galerij Micheline Szwajcer, Antwerp, Belgium
	Galerie Rafael Jablonka and Galerie Gisela Capitain, Cologne, Germany
1991	Stuart Regen Gallery, Los Angeles
	Galerie Ghislaine Hussenot, Paris
	Galleri Nordanstad-Skarstedt, Stockholm
	Barbara Gladstone Gallery, New York
1992	*Works on Paper,* Le Case d'Arte, Milan, Italy
	Beaver College Art Gallery, Glenside, Pennsylvania
	Whitney Museum of American Art, New York
1993	Galerie Micheline Szwajcer, Antwerp, Belgium
	Girlfriends, Jablonka Galerie, Cologne, Germany
	First House, Stuart Regen Projects, Los Angeles
	Kunstverein and Kunsthalle, Dusseldorf, Germany
	San Francisco Museum of Modern Art, San Francisco
	Museum Boymans-van Beuningen, Rotterdam, Netherlands

1994   Kestner Gesellschaft, Hanover, Germany

Selected Group Exhibitions:

1979   Castelli Graphics, New York
1980   ARC/Musee d'Art Moderne de la Ville de Paris
1981   *Body Language,* Hayden Gallery, MIT, Cambridge, MA, USA
          Erweiterte Fotografie, Fifth Wiener Internationale Biennale, Wiener Secession, Vienna
1982   *Image Scavengers,* Institute of Contemporary Art, Philadelphia, USA
1983   *Science Fiction,* John Weber Gallery, New York
          Biennale of São Paulo, São Paulo, Brazil
          Language, Drama, Source and Vision, The New Museum of Contemporary Art, New York
1984   *The Magazine Stand,* Washington Project for the Arts, Washington, D.C.
          New York: Ailleurs et Autrement, ARC/Musee d'Art Moderne de la Ville de Paris, Paris
1985   *1985 Biennial Exhibition,* Whitney Museum of American Art, New York
1986   *Wien Fluss,* Wiener Festwochen, Weiner Secession, Vienna
          As Found, Institute of Contemporary Art, Boston
          The Sixth Biennial of Sydney, Sydney, Australia
1987   *The Viewer as Voyeur,* Whitney Museum of American Art at Phillip Morris, New York
          Photography and Art: Interactions since 1946, Los Angeles County Museum of Art, Los Angeles
          Fotografien, Galerie Nachst St. Stephan, Vienna
1988   *Aperto '88,* Venice Bienniale, Venice, Italy
          Kunsthalle, Zurich, Switzerland
          Reprises de Vues, Halle Sud, Geneva
          The Object of the Exhibition, Centre National des Arts Plastiques, Paris
          Modes of Address: Language in Art Since 1960, Whitney Museum of American Art, New York
          Gangs of Surrogate Entertainers, Gallerie F.C. Gundlach, Hamburg, Germany
          Galleri Contur, Stockholm
1989   *Arrangements 1,* Mai 36 Galerie, Lucerne, Switzerland
          Horn of Plenty: Sixteen Artists from New York City, Stedelijk Museum, Amsterdam
          Scripta Manent—Verba Volant, Monika Spruth Galerie, Cologne, Germany
          Photography Now, Victoria and Albert Museum, London
          New Acquisitions, New Work, New Directions, International Museum of Photography at George Eastman House, Rochester, New York
          Contemporary Art from New York, Yokohama Museum of Art, Japan
1990   *Disconnections,* Galleri Nordanstad-Skarstedt, Stockholm
          Art et Publicite 1890-1990, Centre Georges Pompidou, Paris
          The Charade of Mastery, Whitney Museum of American Art, New York
          Images in Transition: Photographic Representation in the Eighties, National Museum of Modern Art, Kyoto, Japan
          Life Size: A Sense of the Real in Recent Art, The Israel Museum, Jerusalem
1991   *Rope,* Fernando Alcolea Gallery, Barcelona, Spain
          La Revanche de L'Image, Galerie Pierre Huber, Geneva
          Centraal Museum, Utrecht, Netherlands
          Metropolis, Walter Gropius Bau, Berlin
          Fonds Regional d'Art Contemporain des Pays de la Loire, Clisson, France

          American Art of the 80s, Palazzo delle Albere, Trento, Italy
1992   Rena Bransten Gallery, San Francisco
          Special Collections—The Photographic Order from Pop to Now, International Center of Photography, New York
          Galerij Micheline Szwajcer, Antwerp, Belgium
          Theoretically Yours, Ciesa di San Lorenzo, Aosta, Italy
          Ars Pro Domo, Museum Ludwig, Cologne, Germany
          Documenta IX, Kassel, Germany
1993   Jügen Becker, Hamburg, Germany
          Galerie Johnen & Schottle, Cologne, Germany
          Commodity Image, International Center of Photography, New York
          The Language of Art, Kunsthalle, Vienna
1994   *Tuning Up,* Kunstmuseum, Wolfsburg, Germany

Publications:

By PRINCE: Books—*The Camera Believes Everything,* Stuttgart 1988. **Articles**—*File Magazine,* No. 28. 1987; *Flash Art,* October 1988; "Tell Me Everything: Richard Prince Interviewed by Stuart Morgan" in *Artscribe International,* January-February 1989; *Metropolis,* April 1991.

On PRINCE: Books—"Richard Prince—Rephotographer" by Andy Grundberg in *The Crisis of the Real,* New York 1990. **Articles**—"Thomas Ruff, Richard Prince, Robert Mapplethorpe, Jeff Wall" by Jude Schwendenwein in *Artscribe International,* November-December 1988; "Allan McCollum/Richard Prince: Kunsthalle Zurich" by Christoph Schenker in *Noema,* September-October 1988; "Richard Prince" by Daniela Salvioni in *Flash Art,* October 1988; "Richard Prince: Jokes Epitomize the Social Unconscious" by Daniela Salvioni in *Flash Art International,* Summer 1988; "Richard Prince—Times Square" by Patricia C. Phillips in *Artforum,* April 1988; "Grenoble sur tous les tons" by Michel Nuridsany in *Le Figaro,* 11 October 1988; "Richard Prince: Barbara Gladstone Gallery" by John Miller in *Artscribe International,* September-October 1988; "Americana: Richard Prince" by Maria Luisa Frisa in *Dolce Vita Magazine* (Milan), December 1988; "Richard Prince" by Giulio Ciavoliello in *Flash Art,* October-November 1988; "Richard Prince" by Daniel Canogar in *Lapiz 56,* Ano. VI, 1988; "Comics As Inspiration: Are We Having Fun Yet?" by Richard B. Woodward in *The New York Times,* 23 April 1989; "Richard Prince" by Roberta Smith in *The New York Times,* 1 December 1989; "Richard Prince" by Jeffery Rian in *Bijutsu Techo,* January 1989; "Richard Prince and Hans-Peter Feldmann" by Gregorio Magnani in *Flash Art,* January-February 1989; "Richard Prince: Jablonka Galerie" by Kay Heymer in *Tema Celeste,* January-March 1989; "Prince's Pictures: Made in the USA" by Sophia Defina in *Elle,* November 1989; "Richard Prince" by Dorothy Spears in *Arts Magazine,* February 1990; "Richard Prince: Barbara Gladstone Gallery, Jay Gorney Modern Art" by David Rimanelli in *Artforum,* February 1990; "Richard Prince—Overtaken by his Muse" by Laura Cottingham in *Flash Art,* May/June 1990; "Richard Prince: Suburban Fiction" by Mariuccia Casadio in *Vogue Italia,* March 1990; "Richard Prince at Jay Gorney Modern Art and Barbara Gladstone" by Tiffany Bell in *ARTnews,* April 1990; "Richard Prince" by Jack Bankowsky in *Contemporanea,* March 1990; "Richard Prince at Barbara Gladstone and Jay Gorney" by Brooks Adams in *Art in America,* May 1990; "Review: Richard Prince—Ghislaine Hussenot" by Olivier Zahm in *Artforum,* April 1991; "Richard Prince at Barbara Gladstone" by Roberta Smith in *The New York Times,* 10 May 1991; "Boyfriends, Girlfriends: Richard Prince's Alternative Bondings" by Stuart Morgan in *Artscribe,* March/April 1991; "Review: Richard Prince—Galerie Gisela Capitain & Jablonka Galerie" by Kay Heymer in *Flash Art,* March/April 1991; "Richard Prince/Barbara Gladstone" by Brian D'Amato in *Flash Art,* Summer 1991; "Richard Prince, Art's Bad Boy, Becomes (Partly) Respectable" by Paul Taylor in *The New York Times,* 17 May 1992; "Richard Prince, Questioning the Definition of Originality" by Roberta Smith in *The New York Times,* 8 May 1992; "Richard Prince's Psychopathic America" by Donald Kuspit in *Artforum,* May 1992; "Richard Prince at the Whitney" by Ken Johnson in *Art in America,* November 1992; "Is Richard Prince a Feminist?" by Carol Squires in *Art in America,* November 1993; "Richard Prince" by Eleanor Heartly in *ARTnews,* November 1993; "De-Construction Worker: Richard Prince's First House Launches Regen Projects" by Philip Hunter Drohojowska in *Los Angeles Times,* 10 April 1993; "Richard Prince—Regen Projects" by Michael Cohen in *Flash*

Art, Summer 1993; "Bad Boy der Kunstszene" by Evelyn Schels in *Elle* (Germany), March 1994.

* * *

Perhaps the most absolute of the "appropriation artists" of the 1980s, Richard Prince is a difficult figure to categorise in terms of the photographic medium. His most important work comments upon or provides a critique of the ubiquity of photo-mechanical reproduction in contemporary mass culture. He is clearly very knowledgeable about the history of fine art photography, as well as alert to the ironies and excesses of advertising and pornographic imagery. Indeed, none of his photographs take as their subjects, anything other than such images. In this his method is so radically different from the images resulting from the photojournalism of Robert Capa, the fine art photography of Alfred Stieglitz or the advertising work of Irving Penn, that relating Prince to the mainstream traditions of the medium is highly problematic.

Prince's work is largely admired rather than liked, perhaps because of the chilling effect of his ironic refusal to judge the images he finds and re-photographs, many of which are banal, repellent or obscene by most people's standards. Unlike some appropriations artists, Prince does not always re-photograph images in their entirety when he claims them. His famous series of *Marlborough men,* appropriated from the ubiquitous cigarette advertisements are blurred, isolated, tightly framed and truncated in his renderings, so that they would scarcely be legible if they were not already so familiar. These iconic images of a commodified romanticised western frontier speak to and from mainstream (mass) culture. However Prince's *Girlfriends* are a very different type of image. Re-photographed from the snaps sent in by readers for publication in biker magazines, these amateur porn images depict the motorcyclists' female companions bare-breasted and on or near motorcycles. The tight pictorial conventions of this deviant subculture fascinate Prince as much as the gender coding and eroticism of the images. Another series returns to advertisements for its source images, but rather than focussing on the mythic claims of a single product's marketing campaign, in this work Prince juxtaposes entirely unrelated product or model shots, and finds startling similarities of pose and arrangement.

In this last body of work, Prince's clever unmasking of the grammar of banality and merchandising is most apparent. The clear critique here outweighs the tendency of his work toward a cynical and affectless postmodernism. He is most impressive when most dogmatic. Prince is an influential writer as well as photographer and his cryptic, allusive, personalized musings on art and culture are widely read by younger artists and photographers today.

—Ellen Handy

PROŠEK, Josef.

Nationality: Czechoslovakian. **Born:** Podol u Mšenèho, Czechoslovakia, 19 October 1923. **Education:** Attended public school in Prague, 1929-39; studied photography at the State Graphic School, Prague, 1945-49. **Family:** Married Irena Wenigová in 1959; daughter: Magdalena. **Career:** Editor, *Květy* magazine, Prague, 1950-55. Freelance photographer, Prague, since 1956. Member, Mánes art group, Prague, 1948-53, and Radar art group, Prague, 1960-70. Member, Union of Czech Fine Artists, 1949. **Died:** (in Prague) 9 December 1992.

Individual Exhibitions:

1962	Václav Špála Gallery, Prague (retrospective)
1963	The House of Art, Brno, Czechoslovakia
1967	*Paris,* Gallery of Czech Writers, Prague
1987	Špála Gallery, Prague
1993	Prague House of Photography, Prague

Selected Group Exhibitions:

1965	*Mánes Art Group,* Mánes Gallery, Prague
1961	*Artists Group "Radar,"* Gallery of Czech Writers, Prague
1964	*Artists Group "Radar,"* Mánes Gallery, Prague
1966	*Czechoslovak Photography,* Museum of Art, Belgrade
1969	*Cycles and Series,* Gallery of the City of Prague
1970	*100 Graphics and 100 Photos,* Museo Universitario, Mexico City
1973	*Lyrismo di Fotografia Cecoslovacci,* at *SICOF,* Milan (travelled to the Fotokabinett Jaromir Funke, Brno, Czechoslovakia, and the Städtische Museum, Freiburg, West Germany)
1977	*Members' Exhibition,* Mánes Gallery, Prague
1979	*Tschechoslowakische Photographie 1918-1978,* Fotoforum, Kassel, West Germany
1984	*Czechoslovak Creative Photography,* Gallery of Czech Writers, Prague
1989	*Czechoslovak Photography 1945-1989,* Gallery Valdštejnská jízdárna, Prague
	Fine Artists in Photography, National Gallery, Prague
1993	*Czech and Slovak Photography from Between the Wars to the Present,* Fitchburg Art Museum, Massachusetts (travelled to Boston and Middlebury)

Collections:

Museum of Decorative Arts, Prague; Bibliothèque Nationale, Paris; Moravian Gallery, Brno; Prague House of Photography, Prague; Robert Koch Gallery, San Francisco.

Publications:

By PROŠEK: Books—illustrations for numerous Czech publications, including *Konrád: Na černé hodince,* Prague 1953; *The Work of M. Braun in Kuks,* Prague 1956; *Soujourn in Prague,* Prague 1958; *J. Wilgus: Sculptor,* Ostrava, Czechoslovakia 1965; *M. Braun: Sculptor,* Prague 1965; *Czechoslovakia,* Prague 1966; *Paříž u Paříži,* Prague 1967; *Akty a akty,* Bratislava 1967; *Kuks,* Prague 1970; *Radar: Anatomy of a Group,* Prague 1971; *South Bohemia,* Prague 1980; *Česke Středohoří,* Prague 1980; *Zapadočeské lazně,* Prague 1982; *Ceskomoravská vysocina,* Prague 1986.

On PROŠEK: Books—*Josef Prošek* by Jan Řezáč, Prague 1962; *Czechoslovak Photography* by Karel Dvořák, Prague 1973; *Geschichte der Photographie im 20. Jahrhundert/History of Photography in the 20th Century* by Petr Tausk, Cologne 1977, London 1980; *Dictionnaire des photographes* by C Naggar, Paris, 1982; *Encyclopédie internationale des photographes* by Michel and Michele Auer, Geneva, 1985; *The Evolution of Czechoslovak Photography from 1918 to the Present* by Petr Tausk, Prague 1986; *Černobílá fotografie,* Antonín Dufek, Prague, 1987; *Cesty československé fotografie* by Daniela Mrázková and Vladimir Remes, Prague, 1989. **Articles**—"Josef Prošek" by Petr Tausk in *Revue Fotografie* (Prague), no. 3, 1980; "Kultura a fotografie" by Jiří Šerých in *Československá fotografie,* Prague, No 6, 1980.

*

I started my creative life in an avant-garde of all kinds of young artists. At that time we were fascinated by surrealism. Although my present stand, the result of successive evolution, is very far from that point of view, I have never forgotten that beginning. For similar reasons, I must confess, photography is for me a young, charming, frivolous girl who is climbing Kilimanjaro.

—Josef Prošek

* * *

The mature work of Josef Prošek obviously developed from his original contacts with the artistic avant-garde of his youth. Surrealism, for example, caused him to esteem the poetic possibilities of the *objet trouvé.* The depiction of the surprising poetry discovered in the real world (without any intervention in arrangement from the photographer) was also consistent with the then current trend of coming "closer" to reality. And his use of lighting confirmed that approach: the play of beams and shadows was suppressed; his preference was for a diffuse light coming from above, which allowed the photographed subjects to be represented by themselves without deflecting the viewer's attention from their essential nature to any extraordinary inventive solutions devised by the photographer.

At the beginning of his career, Prošek also devoted much of his time to photographing sculptures. His sense for their forms and volumes seems to have created a kind of mental perspective that has informed his other pictures. Prošek is very adept at interpreting a simple chair in a park or a single house as if they, too, are statues. And in his later work this approach is amalgamated with the old (if slight) heritage of surrealism. An old car covered by an awning may be perceived as both a surrealist *objet trouvé* and as sculpture.

Prošek's work has always involved an effort to achieve, to come closer to, a sober depiction of reality. The decisive step in his evolution toward a more direct photography of the real world was made during a journey to Italy with a tour company in the late 1960s. Keeping up with the group's excursions did not enable Prošek to compose his pictures from carefully considered viewpoints, and he was forced to take photographs immediately of an interesting view if suitable lighting conditions presented itself. The value of these 'uncomposed' quick-reaction shots was not discovered until Prošek returned home.

His pursuit of straight photography in the natural environment finally led Prošek to colour work in the 1970s. Given the nature of his interest, he does not use colour merely to enrich his vision or for its seductive aesthetic qualities alone. Prošek sees the dimension of colour as an information source to achieve a more precise rendition of reality than is possible in black-and-white photography. He has thus been able to expand his vocabulary with three colour books on the Bohemian central highlands, the Bohemian-Moravian uplands, and the West Bohemian spas.

Because he belongs among those photographers for whom the final print is the highpoint of their activity, Prošek eventually began working with Cibachrome prints. The colour ranges he allows himself are only those which will ultimately enhance a more direct contact with the world he photographs.

—Petr Tausk

PROVAZNÍK, František.

Nationality: Czechoslovakian and British. **Born:** Prague, 7 February 1948. Emigrated to the UK in 1980, naturalised in 1990. **Education:** Took one-year course in photojournalism at FAMU, Academy of Art, Prague. **Family:** Married Julia Rees in 1991. **Career:** Worked as assistant director of light on Czechoslovak Television, 1971-72; editor in the telephoto department of the Central Czechoslovak Press Agency, 1972-73; staff photographer in the Prague sports magazine *Stadion,* 1973-75; freelance photographer, 1975-80; technical advisor to the Photographic Department at Oxford Polytechnic, 1981; freelance photographer since 1981. Named "Master of Sport," 1973. Member of the Club of Olympionics; the Czech Union of Artists; Chelsea Arts Club; Association of Professional Photographers. **Agent:** Andy Hudson, 7 Umbria Street, London SW15 5DP, England. **Address:** 274 Woodstock Road, Oxford OX2 7NW, England.

Selected Group Exhibitions:

1982	*The Third Meaning,* Museum of Modern Art, Oxford, England
	Ten Oxford Artists, Museum de Lakenhal, Leiden, Netherlands
1984	*Six Artists,* Oxford Polytechnic, Oxford, England
	Sequences, Cambridge Darkroom, Cambridge, England (travelled to Watershed Gallery, Bristol)
	The Faces, Playhouse Theatre, Oxford, England
	Group Six, Orleans House Gallery, London
1985	*Photographs,* Templeton College, Oxford, England
	Three Cities, Waaggebouw, Leiden, Netherlands
	Five Artists, Trinity College, Oxford, England
	Assemblage, Untitled Gallery, Sheffield, England
	Aspects of Still Life, Axiom Gallery, Cheltenham, England
1986	*Still Life,* Gardner Centre, Brighton, England (travelled to Ffoto Gallery, Cardiff)

1987	*Flowers,* Anne Berthoud Gallery, Cork Street, London
	Salon of Contemporary British Photographers
1992	*Czech Photographers in Exile,* Mánes, Prague
1993	*Introducing,* Association of Professional Photographers, London

Collections:

Victoria and Albert Museum, London.

Publications:

By PROVAZNÍK: Articles—has written articles for the *Daily Mail; The Guardian Art Line; The Spectator; Creative Camera; Time Out; Amateur Photographer; Art & Artists; Photography; Revue K; Sunday Times; Eids Dagblad; Zeit Magazine; De Leidse Post; Oxford Times; Oxford Mail; Vanity Fair;* and *Vogue.*

*   *   *

Franta Provazník is neither a professional Czech nor does he belong to that considerably larger community of professional exiles—those who live off the experiences of an often violent deracination and waxing nostalgia for their place of origin. No, Provazník is a professional photographer and like thousands of others earns a living from weddings, portraits and book jackets. What—again like thousands of others—he doesn't derive a viable income from are the 'art photos' that have been the subject of his exhibitions at Oxford, Cheltenham, Sheffield, Brighton, Cardiff and London.

Not that Provazník himself likes the artistic distinction between his two fields of work. He is nothing if not unworldly in his approach, genuinely perplexed with what he sees as the English obsession with failure, an extension of our near infinite capacity for self-deprecation and embarrassment. Whoever noted that "Mrs. Thatcher made the definition of failure a 40-year-old man standing at a bus stop" would cut little ice with Provazník. Despite having been here since the early '80s, he is proud to live effectively without overheads: "I don't have a car . . . or children . . . I live above a studio I rent for £15 a week . . . If I stopped smoking I'd be rich by my standards—but then since I do smoke, I clearly don't care that much about being rich."

Success for him lies in "finding that essential combination of serenity and intensity through my work." That he seeks in "the everyday," for which Provazník has a great respect and a considerable ability to rearrange. While the egalitarian attention he gives to all his portraits is admirable (the day we met he was complaining of a prima donna four year old who couldn't leave off sucking her thumb, while praising John le Carré for his modesty and pleasant manner), it is clearly in his "grey pictures" that he most closely expresses himself.

Certainly, at least in winter, Prague must be among the greyest cities in Europe: lowered skies, a vast dark river, bleached buildings in staggered ranks up to the greystone castle. Provazník's acknowledged photographic influences are also predominantly Czech, particularly Sudek and Svoboda, for who he organised "unauthorised" exhibitions before the attentions of the military police precipitated his departure in 1980. ("You become a dissident not through your politics but because the police are so stupid they can't bear to leave you alone.") Determinedly apolitical, Provazník's work is the antithesis of the reportage work we have come to associate with contemporary Czech photography. Yet Czechoslovakia is there, both in the wintery trees outlined against cloud-strewn skies and in the choice of subject matter for his still lifes—Bohemian glass, vegetable peppers, clay pipes.

Reminiscences also of Juan Gris, Georges Braque, Picasso during the creation of the Cubist movement? "Yes of course, it's their 2-D world. The Cubists flattened space and began with different assumptions. As a black-and-white photographer you need shades of grey to build up a thin surface." This "thin surface" of the landscapes and still lifes, often expanded into new dimensions through reflections, couldn't be in greater contrast to the very human and 3-dimensional portraits.

Both, however, share a preoccupation with light and space that Provazník suspects is architectural in origin: "When I was at FAMU [The Prague Film and Photography School], we were taught art history by Rejnik. He'd drag us round the cathedrals and there we learnt about such things as depth and shadow." On a more personal note, Provazník is willing to admit that his

Garlic, **1992 (original in colour).** Photograph by Franta Provaznik.

refugee status is also bound to influence his work. ''For me there's no difference between space and freedom, and for a long time I needed freedom of movement—in my life and in my work—and found it hard to put down roots.'' Intellectually, however, what comes through is a sense of wonder that applies to all his photography. ''We're still surprised that light can create picture, we experience the same sense of wonder as Steiglitz or Fuche.''

Alongside the lessons of history lie those of modernity. Despite a battery of cameras that have included a Voigtlander, a Bronica and several Leicas, Provazník emphasises how contemporary developments have liberated photographers from technical shackles. Paradoxically, this links the camera itself to an earlier art-form. ''It's important to get away from the mechanics of photography and use the camera as a paintbrush.'' So says perhaps the first Cubist of the camera—75 years after the advent of Cubism in painting, it has arrived in photography.

—Amanda Hopkinson

PURCELL, Rosamond Wolff.

Nationality: American. **Born:** Rosamond Wolff in Boston, Massachusetts, 28 June 1942. **Education:** Buckingham High School, Cambridge, Massachu-setts, 1953-60; Boston University, 1960-64, B.A. in French literature 1964; studied photography with Kipton Kumler, Lexington, Massachusetts, 1973, and photo-darkroom technique with John Weiss, Arlington, Massachusetts, 1975. **Family:** Married Dennis William Purcell in 1969; sons: Andrew and John Henry. **Career:** Administrative assistant in a primary school, 1966; Instructor in French, Palfrey Street School, Watertown, Massachusetts, 1967-69. Freelance photographer, Medford, Massachusetts, since 1969. **Agents:** The Photographers' Gallery, 8 Great Newport, Street, London WC2, England; Marcuse Pfeifer Gallery, 568 Broadway Avenue, Suite 102, New York, New York 10012. **Address:** 121 Allston Street, Medford, Massachusetts 02155, U.S.A.

Individual Exhibitions:

1972	Creative Photo Gallery, Massachusetts Institute of Technology, Cambridge
1973	Polaroid Gallery, Cambridge, Massachusetts
1974	Zone 4, Watertown, Massachusetts
1975	University of Iowa, Iowa City
	Enjay Gallery, Boston
1976	Madison Art Center, Wisconsin
	Archetype Gallery, New Haven, Connecticut
1977	Roswell Museum, New Mexico
	Galleria Il Diaframma, Milan
	The Photographers' Gallery, London
	Galerie Fiolet, Amsterdam
	Delaware Art Museum, Wilmington
1978	A Photography Place, Stafford, Pennsylvania
	Santa Fe Gallery of Photography, New Mexico
1979	Wah Lui Gallery, Seattle
	Images Gallery, New Orleans
	Archetype Gallery, New Haven, Connecticut
	After the Fact, Clarence Kennedy Gallery, Cambridge, Massachusetts
1980	Marcuse Pfeifer Gallery, New York
	Boston Atheneum
	The Billiard Room, Cambridge, Massachusetts

Selected Group Exhibitions:

1978	*Fantastic Photography in the U.S.A.,* Canon Photo Gallery, Amsterdam (toured Europe and the United States, 1978-80)
	One of a Kind: Polaroid Color, Corcoran Gallery, Washington, D.C. (toured the United States)
1982	*Counterparts: Form and Emotion in Photographs,* Metropolitan Museum of Art, New York (travelled to the Contemporary Arts Center, Cincinnati, Ohio; Dallas Museum of Fine Art, Texas; San Francisco Museum of Modern Art; Corcoran Gallery, Washington, D.C., 1982-83)

Collections:

Metropolitan Museum of Art, New York; Museum of Fine Arts, Boston; Polaroid Corporation, Cambridge, Massachusetts; Delaware Museum of Art, Wilmington; New Orleans Museum of Art; Madison Art Center, Wisconsin; University of Iowa, Iowa City; Victoria and Albert Museum, London.

Publications:

By PURCELL: Books—*A Matter of Time,* with afterword by Dennis W. Purcell, Boston 1975; *Half-Life,* Boston 1980. **Articles**—''Attracted by

Structures and Transformations'' in *Print Letter* (Zurich), July/August 1978; article in *Darkroom Dynamics,* edited by Jim Stone, Boston 1979.

On PURCELL: Books—*Counterparts: Form and Emotion in Photographs* by Weston J. Naef, New York 1982; *The Library of World Photography: Portraits,* with introduction by Colin Ford, Tokyo 1982, 1983, London 1983. **Articles**—''Rosamond Wolff Purcell'' in *Popular Photography Annual,* edited by Jim Hughes, New York 1977; ''Rosamond Wolff Purcell'' in *Creative Camera Year Book,* edited by Colin Osman and Peter Turner, London 1978; ''Rosamond Wolff Purcell'' in *Popular Photography Annual,* edited by Jim Hughes, New York 1979; ''Purcell's Haunting Visions'' by Owen Edwards in *Saturday Review* (New York), November 1980.

*

One day a friend cut the edges off a Polaroid snapshot of converging boulders to show me that angles of rocks pointing inward was all that mattered; the rest should be thrown away. I had always thought that photography consisted of stepping off a tour bus to record the facade of the castle. I didn't know that recording a scene might require having an idea. I began to use a camera. At the time I was writing short stories. Friends were polite about the writing, but enthusiastic about the photographs. Now, aside from absorption with my family, I practice photography in one way or another almost every waking hour.

I do not keep track of what is being *said* about photographic styles, but I already know too much to work in a naive fashion. Although the technical training I received has proved invaluable to me, I am glad that I never spent much time in formal study of the medium. I would remember what had been said rather than how to see. Finding the thin edge again and again on one's own—that is what is hard to do. This is the only reason I can find for pursuing photography. I will learn what I can of various processes in order to continue.

Some of my photographs are one-of-a-kind Polaroid prints. Others are printed from Polaroid negatives or from 2¼ roll film. When using instant materials, I work from print to print rather than more subliminally with negatives, which cannot be examined as the photographic event proceeds. My eyes and emotions select; the camera and prints tell me how much of an illusion will be possible. Although the images occasionally run ahead of consciously applied intelligence; the process is not mysterious. Each print presents itself as an established fact which I must accept, reject, or modify. The method does not allow for wishful thinking. When I go to the darkroom, I almost always know which proof print sent me, and what I want from it.

Probably because of my fondness for instant materials, I have never practiced a long-winded printing technique. I have not yet experimented with some of the time-honored methods (making one's own paper, emulsion, matching each image to its appropriate materials, large format contact printing, etc.). This has, upon a few occasions, seemed a handicap in more esoteric circles.

Prints meant to convey ideas should have a transparent quality. They should be free of technical flaws so as not to excite criticism, and they should support, rather than create, possible ''meanings'' for an image. Technique more loving than content never fails to impress me. It appeals directly. But the visual part of the photograph is just the beginning for me; its potential for creating various levels of meaning is far more significant.

In school I used flash cards to memorize Latin vocabulary. There were three categories of cards: words in which the English revealed itself in Latin; words which after mechanical perseverance could be memorized; and words which unfailingly came apart in my mind between one language and the other, like a piece of fraying rope—words which not only did not reveal their English equivalent, but which seemed to possess a range of seemingly unconnected meanings.

I have a photo of a woman lying in a shaft of light. A writer, having seen it on exhibit, wrote of ''an unconscious astronaut hurtling through space.'' I offered it for exhibition because I liked the way the model had been forced into a narrow band of light but was not confined by it. The model, herself, said, ''I look dead.'' I do not believe that interpretation has anything to do with my conscious intentions. Perhaps the photo is only the front of the flash card, its appearance standing for clusters of thoughts, which if written, would appear on the back.

At our house, among other treasures, we have a 10-foot long plaster mermaid, a year-old egg yolk which looks like amber glass, and a 60-year old piece of bread from a French prison. I often place fragments of paper or glass in available light in the hope that they will transcend recognizability and change into ''something rich and strange.'' I am endlessly greedy for the sight of transformation of objects from one state to another. But I have rarely successfully recorded such a transformation directly.

My great-aunt wore a fox-headed stole and someone else has a hat made from a whole bird. In the zoological museum there is a hippopotamus with a pink plaster throat, a book eaten by worms. I look forward to seeing frescoes from Pompeii, and to buying fish for dinner just to see what might be in the ice-packed case . . . the mundane, the decadent, and the instructive presentations fascinate me equally. But the actual surfaces (with the possible exception of the wormy book) function only as allusions. Usually the memory of an atmosphere will contribute to the photographs I actually take. I have had a great many visual experiences and made relatively few photographs.

I used to take bus trips to different parts of the United States. I travelled alone, to record conversation and to take Polaroid pictures (never of castles). West of Boston the country opens wide, and the hypnotic motion of the bus always released my thoughts from their usual tracks. I never remembered the route, perhaps because extraordinary sights occur regardless of geography and rarely in the same place twice. I have written many records, but the photographs occurred, for the most part, later, at home, inspired by the memory of being adrift.

I heard that a group of photographers crossed the U.S.A. on their own bus, stopping each time one of them ''saw'' a picture. I have often wondered how many photos came home and how many mirages.

There are as many clichés as there always were. In fact, there are *only* clichés. But photographers are travelling in herds these days, and the likelihood of throwing one's own light on commonly used subjects may seem harder, especially when it appears that the less effective version by the betterknown artist receives all the acclaim. It may seem safer to decide to be strongly influenced by someone else's work. It may seem a good idea to subscribe to a popular way of seeing. I don't think so. I think today's school of thought is tomorrow's dead duck.

Periodically I come to believe in groups of my own photographs. They work together as clearly as trains of thought. At such moments I am tempted to refer to them as a ''body of work,'' and the notion that I may be doing the ''right thing'' by photography produces euphoria that may last for days or even weeks.

But, in the end, it doesn't work. As soon as the dimensions of new work become clear to me, it does not seem important. Individual images recede. Exhibiting photographs has always seemed a rather dreamlike exercise to me—I feel both pride and sense of loss, because, of course, the work already seems vaguely suspect. Hopefully, by the time the photographs are on the wall, I will have managed to move along.

I wrote the above a few years ago, and some of the thoughts may now seem dated. The basic message is still, I suppose, that the equilibrium between knowing what has been (and is being done) and maintaining a private world is the best method I have devised for proceeding with my own work. I am working currently on *minding my own business.*

—Rosamond Wolff Purcell

*   *   *

Imagination is a word too loosely hung around artists' necks. To commend a photographer for his or her imagination is usually to say very little. Yet, "imagination," raw and infectious, is exactly what makes Rosamond Wolff Purcell's photographs stand out.

Purcell's photographs imagine a story more complicated than a single photograph can fully explain. Her 1980 book *Half-Life* contains images that intimate bizarre family relationships, or a conspiracy of stuffed animals. The photographs imagine the worlds beyond the one we can directly touch. They imagine death and they explore life that has preceded our own.

The most interesting quality of Purcell's work is the way it proposes illogical or impossible scenarios without lapsing into the surreal. Her photographs gather elements from life which, in combination, speak directly about that life. The interest is not to create wild juxtapositions or to unravel the unconscious, but instead to allow artifacts to comment on the real world.

Purcell's best photographs are a recent untitled portfolio of color prints that utilize manipulated antique portraits. The composite pictures unveil hidden passions and suggest man's primitive nature. Purcell combines the stark and rigid expressions of 19th century portraits with pictures of stuffed animals, other portraits, or with hazy colors. In "Fuegia" and "The Climber" (from the book *Half-Life*), pictures of monkeys combine with portraits of 19th century ladies. These pictures allude to our animal origins which the ladies with their starched dresses and lace would like to deny. In "The Other Woman" a rigid and puritanical-looking man is montaged with the picture of a beautiful woman whose hair is haloed by butterfly wings. Purcell's title suggests an intriguing scenario of illicit love. The man's stern face is his public denial of wrongdoing.

Purcell's photographs work largely because they demand an active participation from the viewer. These strange stories are not fully explained. Purcell supplies the characters, specifies a setting, and then suggests a vague story. The confronting compositions demand an explanation that is not adequately provided. In this way, Purcell's fertile imagination entices the viewer to finish the story with his or her own imagination.

—Ken Winokur

PYKE, Steve.

Nationality: British. **Born:** 21 October 1957. **Career:** Worked as a motorcycle mechanic at production races, a knitting-machine mechanic, a post-office worker and a musician. Steve Pyke has worked for many major publications worldwide. His work has also been featured on BBC TV. **Recipient:** South Bank Photography Award, 1989; The Photographers' Bursary, 1992. **Address:** The Mission, 55 Holywell Lane, London EC2A 3PQ, England.

Individual Exhibitions:

1984   *Poland,* Diorama, London
1985   *Directors,* Filmhouse, Newcastle (travelled to the Filmhouse, Edinburgh), UK
1989   *Triptychs,* Some Bizarre Gallery, London
1990-94 *Philosophers,* Zelda Cheatle Gallery, London (travelled to the National Museum of Photography, Bradford; Derwent Gallery, Derby; F Stop Gallery, Bath; Museum of Modern Art, Oxford; Portfolio Gallery, Edinburgh; Picture House, Leicester; Gallery of Photography, Dublin; Architects Association, London)
1991   *Uniforms,* Wilson Hale Gallery, London (travelled to the Metro Gallery, London)

1993   *Acts of Memory,* Zelda Cheatle Gallery, London
1994   *Veterans,* Imperial War Museum, London; Historiale de la Grande Guerre, Perone, France; Leeds City Art Gallery

Selected Group Exhibitions:

1982   *Midland Group,* Nottingham, England
1984   *Face Photographers,* Photographers Gallery, London
1985   *Stars of the British Screen,* National Portrait Gallery, London
1986   *20 For Today,* National Portrait Gallery, London
1989   *Through the Lens,* Royal Academy, London
1990   *London,* South Bank Arts Centre, London
1991   *The Experts Eye,* National Museum of Photography, Bradford, England
        Fashion Photography, Loft Forum, Tokyo
1992   *Artists Choice,* Angela Flowers Gallery, London
        Tribes, Visa 92, Perpignan, France
        ICI Awards, National Portrait Gallery, London
        The Color of Fashion, Courtyard Gallery, New York (travelled to the American Design Center, Chicago; Center for Creative Imaging, Maine; The Pacific Design Center, Los Angeles), USA
1993   *Positive Lives,* Photographers' Gallery, London (travelled to National Museum of Photography, Bradford; Museum of Modern Art, Oxford; Cornerhouse, Manchester, England)
1994   *Uniforms,* Photographers' Gallery, London
        John Kobal Award, National Portrait Gallery, London
        Back to Basics, Angela Flowers Gallery, London
        A Positive View, Saatchi Gallery, London
        Photo de Mode, Carousel de Louvre, Paris
        Streetstyle, Victoria and Albert Museum, London

Collections:

National Portrait Gallery, London; National Museum of Photography, Bradford, England; Kobe Fashion Museum, Japan.

Publications:

By PYKE: Books—*Poguetry,* London, 1990; *Philosophers,* Manchester, 1993 and London, 1995; *Acts of Memory,* London, 1995. **Articles**—"Philosophers" in *O Magazine,* September 1991; "Uniforms" in *The Face,* January 1991; "Money" in *Granta,* Winter 1994.

On PYKE: Articles—"Philosophers" by Gibson in *The Correspondent,* 21 October 1990; "Veterans" by Faulks in *The Observer,* 7 November 1993; "Veterans" in *Granta,* Autumn 1993; "Faces of our Time" by Peter Hamilton in the *British Journal of Photography,* 13 July 1991. **Television**—"The Human Face" in *Arena,* 1992; "Philosophers" on *The Late Show,* 1993.

*

For me photography is an investigation into the nature of being.

The contents of a photograph are not facts, nor reality, nor truth. They are a means that we have created to extend our way of seeing in our search for "truth."

For some people a photograph is an affirmation of existence. For others, it questions existence. On a most fundamental level one may question a likeness: "How is that me . . . it does not look like me . . . but it is there in front of me . . . it is a photograph of me."

Robert Altman, Film Director, **1993.** Photograph by Steve Pyke.

I do not want my work to be about like or dislike but about "what do you see?"

—Steve Pyke

*   *   *

Photography was born a Victorian medium and to a surprising extent still bears the marks of its upbringing. Just before the invention of photography (and just before Victoria's reign) a whole family of sciences sprang up devoted to the idea of measuring. The nineteenth century became the era of data collection. Reverend clergymen became enthusiastic amateur geologists or lepidopterists and when it arrived (think of Calvert Jones) photographers. Victorian natural science was driven by the idea that if we can only get enough information about the surface of things we can know their interior. Immediately before photography itself, a whole family of image-making systems prefigured it in the business of accurate measurement. The silhouette, the physionotrace, even the cult of death-masks all predate photography as attempts to make ever more precise maps of the human visage, until eventually (it was assumed) the accuracy would be good enough to provide the information sought beneath the surface. As the century wore on the faith in photography as a means of measuring the human psyche grew: Bertillon, the chief of police during the Paris Commune, invented a system of composite portraits which were intended to throw light on the physical appearance of criminal types. If I make a portrait of a dozen known thieves on the same plate, he reasoned in a classically Victorian manner, I will have evidence of what the family characteristics of *genus* thief looks like. Which in turn would enable him to catch the future ones. Physiognomy sounds a little ridiculous now, it smacks of eugenics. However it was a respectable science throughout the early years of photography and Lavater's catalogue of physical types (fleshy lips imply debauch, narrow faces imply weakness and so on in an astonishing detail) was if not a best seller at least a widely-disseminated and widely-read book. Photography grew up in that climate and presented itself as a measuring system so accurate that no artist or collator interfered with it at all. It was no accident that Fox Talbot chose to call his book *The Pencil of Nature.*

The astonishing thing is that precisely the same atmosphere survives around photography where it has dimmed or vanished elsewhere. We still think that a portrait tells us as much about the inner man as it does about his features. With the exception of the delightful idea that "after thirty, a man is responsible for his own face," we know it to be nonsense: a face as round and open as Mr Pickwick's may mask a vicious or cunning man in spite of our physiognomic prejudices. Yet somehow we come to photographs with that certainty suspended and a Victorian faith in the idea that if the photography be well enough made, the psychological innards will be revealed on the surface.

In those terms, Steve Pyke is a great Victorian photographer. He has done other things, and done them well, but his strength and the great bulk of his work is as a black-and-white portrait photographer. He works in series: Philosophers, whatever they think or publish, should look. . . . Is it Socratic? Or like Einstein? So Pyke makes a collection of them and we are confronted not only by the erosion of our unspoken prejudices, but by a specimen-collection which may reveal new genera that we had not understood. It is as though he sets himself an agenda with each series: to understand what we're supposed to think about these people, and then to see if any of it corresponds to reality. Superficially, the photographs look as though they derive from more recent models: a touch of Avedon in the uncompromising lighting and four-square view, a touch of David Bailey in the moonscape of pores and whiskers seen without blinking at such uncomfortably close range, but Pyke's pictures look older than that. He works in one of photography's central arteries, right in the area that photographers strode into from day one. The photographer himself almost disappears: objective solid truth, that most Victorian of commodities, replaces him, or seems to. The magic is that by his self-effacing absence of stylistic frills, Pyke becomes all the more present in his work—just like a Victorian scientist.

—Francis Hodgson

QUIGLEY, Edward W.

Nationality: American. **Born:** Philadelphia, 3 January 1898. **Education:** Self-taught photographer. **Career:** Became a professional photographer in 1918, went into business for himself in 1930. Joined the Photographic Society of Philadelphia in 1929 and became an Artist Member of the Philadelphia Art Alliance in 1932, becoming chairman of the Art Alliance's Photographic Salon in 1938. Widely exhibited in North America and Europe during the 1930s. **Agent:** Houk Friedman, 851 Madison Avenue, New York, New York 10021, U.S.A. **Died:** (in Haddonfield, New Jersey) 6 April 1977.

Individual Exhibitions:

1991   *Edward Quigley: American Modernist,* Houk Friedman, New York; Houk Gallery, Chicago
1995   *Edward Quigley: American Modernist 1898-1977,* Fay Gold Gallery, Atlanta, Georgia

Selected Group Exhibitions:

1991   *Summer Exhibition,* Houk Friedman, New York
1992   *The Twentieth Century City, New York, 1900-1990,* Houk Friedman, New York
1993   *Urban Visions,* Houk Friedman, New York
1994   *Non-Objective Photography between the Wars,* Houk Friedman, New York
        Planes, Trains and Automobiles: Machine Age America, Micheal Rosenfeld Gallery, New York
        New York Images, Michael Fuchs Gallery, Berlin

Publications:

By QUIGLEY: Books—*Edward Quigley: American Modernist,* New York 1991. **Articles**—"Table Top Tricks" in *Good Photography,* No. 3, 1939; "Your Skin is as Important . . . " in *Photo Technique,* June 1941; "What's Worth Shooting" in *Good Photography,* No. 8, 1942; "My Assignment—Industry" in *Good Photography,* No. 9, 1942; "Salad with Milk" and "Billions of Rods" in *American Photography,* February 1942; "Expressive Close-Ups" in *Good Photography,* No. 10, 1943; "Catching Cats with the Camera" in *The Camera,* May 1943; "Wonderment" and "Bearing" in *American Photography,* June 1943; "My Specialty is Everything" in *The Camera,* October and November 1943; "Architectural Photography" in *The Camera,* January 1944; "Architectural Interiors" in *The Camera,* February 1944; "The Circus is Coming" in *The Camera,* April 1944; "Men at Work" in *Photographic Handbook,* 1949; "How to Interpret Sculpture" in *The Camera Magazine,* November 1950; "Problems in Illustration . . . Bottles of Milk" in *The Camera Magazine,* December 1950; "Problems Illustration—Saws" in *The Camera Magazine,* January 1951; "Photographic Interiors" in *The Camera Magazine,* February 1951.

*   *   *

The rediscovery of Edward Quigley may say as much about the understanding of American modernism and its fortunes in the current art and photography market as about his achievements in the 1930s.

Born and based in Philadelphia, Quigley began to photograph professionally in 1918 and opened a commercial studio of his own in 1930. Until 1953, he took almost 13,000 pictures, the majority for advertising commissions. However he also made portraits, architectural and industrial studies and work he considered fine-art photography and presented in solo exhibitions and entered in numerous photographic salons. He printed all his work himself—exquisitely—on warm toned chloro-bromide paper; he wrote frequently for photography magazines (*My Speciality is Everything* in 1943); and he was an active member of prestigious photographers' and artists' associations. The poles of his career may be his light abstractions of 1931, which were exhibited to high praise at the time and are now considered his finest innovations and his photo-book of 1938 on his cat (a bestseller in England).

The prints in between closely resemble those of Coburn, Moholy-Nagy, Strand, Steiner, Sheeler and Stieglitz of a few years earlier—work termed since then "The New Vision" (after Moholy's 1928 text) and gathered in 1929 with other examples of fine-art and commercial photography in the epochal exhibition in Stuttgart *Film und Foto.* Quigley knew this photography directly or through reproductions and he was aware of key modernist photographers in the 1930s. His light abstractions were chosen by Ansel Adams, Edward Weston and Willard van Dyke for the *First Salon of Pure Photography,* at a San Francisco gallery in 1934; the same year Quigley showed his abstractions at New York's pioneering Delphic Gallery, which exhibited Moholy-Nagy, Weston, Anton Bruehl and other modernists in 1929-34; in 1938 he brought Weston's and Moholy-Nagy's photographs to Philadelphia for their first shows there.

Not surprisingly, Quigley's still lifes and industrial landscapes display "New Vision" hallmarks; plunging perspectives and novel vantage points, platonic geometries composed in emphatic patterns and drastic diagonals, sharp and angled lighting creating graphic shadows and playing off reflective surfaces, sharp focus matched by faultless printing, all machine made perfection. His elegant light abstractions and photograms (or camera-less images) can be placed in the same matrix, where the darkroom experiments of Coburn, Man Ray, Moholy-Nagy and Franics Bruguière were sister explorations of what Moholy trumpeted as photography's intrinsic properties.

Quigley was completely fluent in modernist language and his prints have an unearthly beauty. How original was he? The claim rests most heavily on his abstractions, which appear dependent on Brugière's and others. The difficulties of answering may suggest, ultimately, the irrelevance of the question, except for traditional art history and Quigley's prices.

Originality was a retrograde value when modernism first, a means of propaganda, was born during and in the service of the Russian Revolution. Only modernism's goals, not its forms, altered appreciably as its practitioners moved west. In Europe and later in the United States it was co-opted by advertising, which then as now must balance innovation with recognition and acceptance—the market's three-legged stool. Pleasing the art public and clients alike, Quigley's skilful variation can be compared, for example, with Sheeler's River Rouge plant and Stieglitz's New York from the Shelton. The comparison leads to reductive connoisseurship or to a more expansive contextual study of the weave of fine art and commercial photography, especially in the 1930s and their evolving reception to the present. Which direction seems more fruitful? For Quigley, and his colleagues waiting to be discovered it would seem to be the latter.

—Anne Hoy

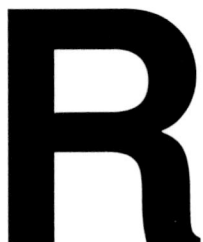

RADOCHONSKA, Lucia (Stanislawa).

Nationality: Belgian/Polish. **Born:** Bolestraszyce, Poland, 9 November 1948; adopted Belgian nationality, 1968. **Education:** Studied photography at the Institut des Beaux Arts Saint Luc, Liège, 1969-72. **Family:** Married photographer Jean-Louis Vanesch, 1974; daughter: Carole. **Address:** 57 rue des Trois Chênes, 4621 Retinne, Belgium.

Individual Exhibitions:

1975	Galeria Colombo, Milan, Italy
1976	Galerie Spectrum, Brussels
1985	Galerie des Chiroux, Liège, Belgium (with Jean-Louis Vanesch)
1986	Galerie J.P. Lambert, Paris
1987	Musée de Charleroi, Belgium
1988	Espace St Cyprien, Toulouse, France
	Maison de la Culture, Amiens, France
1989	Gallerie Pennings, Eindhoven, Holland
1990	Galerie Photo Sephiha, Brussels
1991	*Through Carole's Eyes . . .*, Centre Culturel de Hasselt, Belgium
1992	*Dream in Daylight,* Yokohama, Japan
1993	*Heaven and Earth,* Galerie J.P.Lambert, Paris

Selected Group Exhibitions:

1973	Galerie Wilde, Cologne, Germany (with Susan Baron)
	Salon of Young Belgian Photographers, Palaix des Beaux Arts, Brussels and Antwerp
	Young International Photographers, Bibliothèque Nationale, Paris
1974	Light Impressions Gallery, Rochester, New York
	Musuem of Fine Arts, Boston, Massachusetts
1980	*Camera Belgica,* toured Belgian cities
1983	*Made in Belgium,* Galerie XYZ, Ghent, Belgium
1986	International Festival of Photography, Liège, Belgium
1991	Travelling exhibition in Poland
	La Photographie Belge, CNP, Paris
1993	*Fotopad,* Netherlands
	Belgian Photography, New York

Collections:

Ministry of the French Community of Belgium; Bibliothèque Nationale, Paris; Sterckshof Provincial Museum, Antwerp, Belgium; Galerie Wilde, Cologne, Germany; Museum of Photography, Charleroi, Belgium; Museum of Modern Art, New York; Musée de l'Elysée, Lausanne, Switzerland; Le Château de l'Eau, Toulouse, France; Galerie St Cyprien, Toulouse, France; Museum of Photography, Yokohama, Japan.

Publications:

On RADOCHONSKA: Books—*Creative Camera International Year Book,* 1975; *Le Miroir doté d'une Mémoire,* Antwerp 1983; *International Encyclopaedia of Photographers, 1893 to the Present,* Switzerland 1985; *La Mesure de l'Eau,* Paris, 1994. **Articles**—*Focus,* Nov. 1985; *Fotografia,* Turin 1985; *Clichés* No 26 May 1986; *Photographie,* June 1987; *Un petit pan de mur blanc,* Paris 1984; *Marie-Claire Japan* No 62, Jan 1988; *Clichés* No 60, Nov 1989.

*   *   *

Today there are two types of photographers; Stakhanovites and poets. Lucia Radochonska belongs to the latter category, struggling patiently on behalf of a certain concept of photography, irreducible simply to matter, and where the work obtains its value by virtue of its quality and so of its form, poetic and incorporeal.

Polish by birth, Lucia has succeeded in recreating a universe around herself in which spiritual nourishment is of primary importance. She shares her daily life with the photographer, Jean-Louis Vanesch, measured in an equilibrium composed of music, literature and above all poetry through the writings of, among others, Pierre Reverdy. It is thus on solid foundations such as these that Lucia Rodochonska's photographs are wrought, upon the principles established in their day by Baudelaire, Poe and Eliot.

These principles, adapted and applied to photography, transform the photographer into a wordless poet, open to seeing things in poetic forms.

Lucia would not gainsay T.S. Eliot, for whom "inspiration" is experienced "as the breaking down of strong habitual barriers—which tend to reform very quickly. Some obstruction is momentarily whisked away, the accompanying feeling is less like what we know as positive pleasure, than a sudden relief from an intolerable burden." (T.S. Eliot, *The Use of Poetry and the Use of Criticism*).

This poetic exigence demands total creative freedom of spirit and it comes as no surprise that the intimate relationship Lucia enters into with her photography is most of all apparent in her photographic fairyland, a series developed from 1973 to 1985, in which children are placed centre stage.

With her childhood scenes, Lucia achieves a kind of "photographic fulfilment" in which the body, soul and spirit of photography are found in an almost perfect musical harmony.

Jacques Maritain, reclaiming a directive of St. Paul in the service of art (Thessalonians 1, 5:23), affirms in his *Frontiers of Poetry* that in every work of art one can differentiate *the body* (the language and discourse of the work, the sum of its technical media); *the soul* (the generative idea, the artist's "verbum cordis," born of an expansive heart) and *the spirit,* meaning its poetry. However Maritan also adds there is a fourth element according to which aesthetic appreciation and feelings may surface, one not specifically restricted to beauty but concerned with grace, in that sense in which Plotinus said that grace is superior to beauty. Within that element what counts is the magic of the work.

This magic is omnipresent both in child's play and in the play of light, Lucia's more recent photographic preoccupation. It is the particular quality of surprise, engendering an intense spiritual joy, precisely analogous to Stravinsky's *musical poetics* or Vladimir Jankélévitch's *je ne sais quoi* or *presque rien.*

Because her photographs have that naturally ineffable characteristic we also find in music and because the "simplicity of a look" we associate with music (which recalls Plotinus' *Aeniads*) is her golden rule, Lucia Radochonska belongs to that new catogory of ultra-modern yet *mediaeval* photographers, who will be there to powerfully inaugurate the twenty-first century, about which we say it will—or won't—be a spiritual age.

—Frédéric Ripoll

La Coccinelle, **1985.** Photograph by Lucia Radochonska.

RAGAZZINI, (Vinc) Enzo.

Nationality: Italian. **Born:** Rome, 8 December 1934. **Education:** Attended the Liceo Classico, Rome, 1950-53; studied architecture at the University of Rome, 1953-55; selftaught in photography. **Military Service:** Served in the Italian Army, in the tank battalion, Lecce, Caserta and Verona, 1955-56. **Family:** Married Simonetta Piccone Stella in 1959 (separated, 1963); son: Giuseppe. **Career:** Freelance photographer and photojournalist, Rome, 1958-66, London, 1966-76, and Rome, since 1976. Instructor in Photography, Hornsey College of Art, London, 1969-71. **Recipient:** Documentary Film Prize, Cannes, 1972 (with Enzo Muzii); Photo Book Prize, City of Misano Adriatico, 1981. **Address:** Via Gradisca 13, 00198 Rome, Italy.

Individual Exhibitions:

1965	*Graphics and Photographs,* Libreria Einaudi, Rome
1969	*Spectrum: The Diversity of Photography,* Institute of Contemporary Arts, London
	Museum of Modern Art, Oxford
1971	DM Gallery, London
1975	Galleria Il Diaframma, Milan (retrospective)
1976	Galleria Mara Chiareti, Rome
1981	Galleria Gregoriana, Rome
	Galleria Marconi, Milan
1982	Galleria Il Diaframma, Milan

1988	Cornell Capa Gallery, International Center of Photography, New York

Selected Group Exhibitions:

1963	*Triennale,* Milan
	Biennale, Musée d'Art Moderne, Paris
1967	*Britain Today,* British Pavilion, at *Expo '67,* Montreal
1972	*Biennale,* Venice
1973	*Photography into Art,* Camden Arts Centre, London
1985	*Tsukuba Expo 85,* Tsukuba, Japan
	Vie del ferro, Prato, Italy
1988	Rondanini Gallery

Collections:

Mara Chiaretti Gallery, Rome; The Photographers' Gallery, London; Museum of Modern Art, Oxford; Museum of Modern Art, New York.

Publications:

By RAGAZZINI: Books—*Conversazione in Sicilia,* with text by Elio Vittorini, Milan 1973; *Arno,* with text by Mario Tobino, Milan 1974; *Photographs of Bomarzo,* London 1980; *Tropici: Prima del Motore,* text also by Ragazzini, Milan 1981; *Mediterraneo,* with text by Leonardo Sciascia, Milan 1984; *I giorni e le opera,* text by Attilio Bertolucci, 1988; calendars and diaries—Alenia Group 1991; Italtel 1991, 1992, 1993. **Films**—*La Macchia*

I Giorni e le Opere. Photograph by Enzo Ragazzini.

Rosa, with Enzo Muzii, 1969; *Pensare Brazil,* with Enzo Muzii, 1971; *Impulsi,* with Enzo Muzii, 1972.

On RAGAZZINI: Book—*Photography into Art,* exhibition catalogue, by Colin Osman, Ainslie Ellis and Margaret Harker, London 1973. **Articles**—"He Is a Lone Wolf with a Lens" in the *Daily American* (Rome), June 1965; "Spectrum Photographics: Some of the Work of Enzo Ragazzini Shown at the ICA" in *British Journal of Photography* (London), 25 April 1969; "IBM United Kindgom Ltd.: Anatomy of a Computer" by H. Ochi in *Idea* (Tokyo), September 1970; "Enzo Ragazzini: l'Antifotografo" by Enzo Muzii in *Skema* (Bologna), December 1974; "Dal Peru a Firenze mimeticamente" by Laura Cherubini in *Il Messagero* (Rome), February 1982.

*

Until a few years ago I spent part of my life in photographic research and experiments, and I found no great difference between subjects recorded in the dark-room, with or without lenses, and those taken on film with a camera. In the first case the light, the only active agent (projecting for instance abstract forms onto a sensitive emulsion in movement), left marks and shapes that depended on the speed and intensity with which it fell on the gelatine; in the second case it was still the light, reflected from a face, a landscape, an object, that left other marks and other messages on the film contained in some kind of photographic machine.

I was fascinated by the power of the photographic medium because it could range from the infinitely large to the infinitely small, taking in the scale of human activities; I was convinced, ingenuously perhaps, that this expressive medium was more than just scientifically on account of the ingenious combination of optics and chemistry on which it was based, and for that reason it seemed to me that it ought to be preserved from the evils that afflicted painting.

As time passed my convictions became less "scientific": my love for the abstract has considerably cooled off and the dimension of human activities has now got the upper hand with me.

Nowadays I often find it hard to explain to myself why I like one photo better than another, why certain "artificial" photos are so much more beautiful than some "real" ones. Now I like to photograph human beings and everything on which they have left their mark.

Love for the abstract has been changed into love for perspective, for lights, for composition, for the materials, for focussing and finally for printing. With these means it is possible, barring complications, to control the creative process, which, as Roland Barthes says paradoxically, tends not to explain reality but rather to make it inexplicable, through that very mystery that surrounds everything created when it has life of its own.

—Enzo Ragazzini

*   *   *

Enzo Ragazzini is one of those photographers who are hardly known to the general public, particularly in their native country—in his case Italy—because of their style. Not that that style is ugly; on the contrary, it is too beautiful. To ingratiate oneself into those circles in which photographic criticism is practised, particularly in Italy, it is necessary to find oneself a sponsor, someone who writes for a newspaper or magazine or teaches in some university or institute. Ragazzini is above such little power games. Consequently, he is almost unknown, never mentioned in histories of Italian photography, even the most recent ones which claim to be comprehensively well informed. And among those who talk about recent Italian photography, very few know about him. Luckily for Ragazzini, his ability and his professionalism are well known to many art editors, editors of periodicals and others professionally concerned with photography on a day-to-day basis.

His work—always precise and always of a high standard—ranges from reportage to advertising campaigns. Whether he is photographing a truck for a calendar or doing a feature on the condition of the street-level dwellings of Naples, Ragazzini approaches his subject directly. He deals with each situation in the best way. For, say, the truck for the calendar, he relies on his expert knowledge of photographic technique; for Naples, he relies on his gifts as a human being. He succeeds in coming to some understanding, some comprehension, of even the most difficult subjects. This is, I think, a basic requirement for good work. He is not one of those reporters who "steal" their pictures: he prefers not to take a photograph at all rather than treat his subject improperly.

Ragazzini's reportage recalls the great documentary tradition of the best-known Italian reporters of the postwar period—to photograph an event is to take part in it, to make the viewer take part in it. To produce a clear photograph that everyone can understand, he prefers a documentary exactness to the allusiveness of some modern reportage. His photographic travels are always around the things and persons depicted; they are never excuses for narcissistic withdrawal over purely personal problems.

This love of his for precision through a simple—but not necessarily simplistic—visual communication is also the basis of his success as an advertising photographer. He always exploits the elements of photography to the best effect, for a clarity of information rather than allusion.

—Edo Prando

RAI, Raghu.

Nationality: Indian. **Born:** Jhang, near Lahore, (now in Pakistan) 18 December 1942. **Education:** Studied Civil Engineering at Industrial Training Institute, Punjab University; photography self-taught with initial help from elder brother, S. Paul. **Family:** Married Gurmeet Sangha; children: son, Nitin, daughters, Lagan and Avani. **Career:** Worked as chief photographer for *The Statesman* newspaper, New Delhi, 1966-76; curator/designer of "The Creative Eye" exhibition, New Delhi, 1974; chief photographer for *Sunday Magazine*, Calcutta, 1977-80; joined Magnum with a base in New Delhi, 1977; picture editor for *India Today* fortnightly news magazine, New Delhi, 1981-90; founding member and chairman of "A Forum of Contemporary Photographers," 1992. **Agent:** Magnum Photos, 23-25 Old Street, London, England; or 72 Spring Street, New York, New York; or 5 Passage Piver, Paris, France. **Address:** D-I/One Rabindra Nagar, Near Khan Market, New Delhi, 110003, India.

Individual Exhibitions:

1970	Triveni Art Gallery, Delhi, India
1971	Jehangir Art Gallery, Bombay
	Gallery Delpire, Paris
	St James Church, New York
	Nikon Galleries, Tokyo and Kyoto
1975	*Texture of Our Time,* Delhi
1993	Max Mueller Photo Gallery

Selected Group Exhibitions:

1987	*Forty Years of Magnum Photos,* Paris, London, New York, Tokyo
	Das Endlose Rad, Photographie in India, Musée de l'Elysée, Lausanne, Switzerland; Museum of Trade, Zurich, Switzerland; Ferrari House, Munich, Germany

Collections:

National Gallery of Modern Art, New Delhi, India; Bibliotheque Nationale, Paris, France

Publications:

By RAI: Books—*Delhi: A Portrait,* 1982; *The Sikhs,* 1984; *Indira Gandhi,* 1985; *Taj Mahal,* 1986; *Dreams of India,* 1987; *Calcutta,* 1988; *Tibet in Exile,* 1990; *Khajuraho,* 1991; *Lotus of Bahapur,* 1992; *Raghu Rai's Delhi,* 1993.

RAJZÌK, Jaroslav.

Nationality: Czechoslovakian. **Born:** Hradec Králové, Bohemia, 3 May 1940. **Education:** Studied film and television at the Academy of Arts, Prague, 1959-64, 1974-77, Dip.Film 1964, Dip.Photog. 1977. **Family:** Married the painter Renata Rozsìvalová in 1969; daughter: Denisa. **Career:** Photographer since 1970. Assistant Professor, 1966-80, and since 1980 Associate Professor and 1987-90 Head of the Department of Photography, Film and Television Faculty, Academy of Arts (FAMU), Prague. Presently, Professor of Creative Photography. Associate, 1970, and Member since 1981, Union of Czechoslovak Creative Artists. **Address:** Pod Havránkou 28, 171 00 Prague 7-Troja, Czech Republic.

Individual Exhibitions:

1965	Gallery of Artists, Hradec Králové, Czech Republic
1971	Gallery of Artists, Hradec Králové, Czech Republic (retrospective)
1972	Gallery of Young Artists, Prague
1976	Gallery of Creative Arts, Hodonin, Czech Republic (retrospective)
1977	North-Czech Museum, Liberec, Czech Republic
1983	Gallery V. Kramáře, Prague
1987	Gallery U melounu, Prague
1990	Gallery FOMA, Prague
1992	Museum of Central Bohemia, Roztoky u Prahy, Czech Republic
1994	The Savings Bank Gallery, Kladno, Czech Republic

Selected Group Exhibitions:

1971	*Czechoslovak Photography,* Moravian Gallery, Brno, Czech Republic
1973	*Czechoslovak Photography 1971-72,* Moravian Gallery, Brno, Czech Republic
	Lyrismo di Fotografia Cecoslovacci, at *SICOF,* Milan (travelled to the Fotokabinett Jaromir Funke, Brno, Czech Republic, and the Städtisches Museum, Freiburg, West German)
1977	*Contemporary Art Photography,* Fragner's Gallery, Prague
	Tschechoslowakische Photographie 1918-78, Fotoform, Kassel, West Germany
1980	*Exhibition of Photographs for Sale,* Centrum Gallery, Prague
1982	*Topical Photography,* Moravian Gallery, Brno, Czech Republic
1984	*Czechoslovak Photography,* San Francisco Museum of Modern Art

Untitled (original in colour). Photograph by Raghu Rai.

1985   *27 Contemporary Czechoslovakian Photographers,* The Pho-
        tographers' Gallery, London
1989   *Elementary Photography,* Wroclaw, Poland
        Contemporary Czechoslovak Photography, Amsterdam,
        Holland
        Czechoslovak Photography 1945-1989, Prague
        Roads of Czechoslovak Photography, Prague
1990   *Contemporary Czechoslovak Photography,* Museum Ludwig,
        Köln (repeated)
1992   *Czech Photography,* The Art Institute of Chicago
1993   *Czech Photography of the 1990s,* Maclaurin Art Gallery, Ayr,
        Scotland (repeated)

Collections:

Museum of Art, Prague; Moravian Gallery, Brno, Czech Republic; San
Francisco Museum of Modern Art; North Czech Museum, Liberec, Czech
Republic; Museum Ludwig, Köln; Victoria and Albert Museum, London;
Bibliothèque Nationale, Paris.

Publications:

On RAJŹIK: Books—*Geschichte der Photographie im 20. Jahrhundert/
Photography in the 20th Century* by Petr Tausk, Cologne 1977, London 1980;
Black and White Creative Photography by Petr Tausk, Martin, Czechoslova-
kia 1980; *Dumont Foto 4,* edited by Andreas Muller-Pohle and others,
Cologne 1982; *The Evolution of Czechoslovak Photography from 1918 to the
Present* by Petr Tausk, Prague 1986; *Black and White Photography,* by

Antonín Dufek, Czechoslovakia, 1987; *Roads of Czechoslovak Photography,*
by D Mrázková and V Remeš, Czechoslovakia, 1989; *Czechoslovak Biographical Dictionary,* Prague, 1992; *Encyclopedia of Czech and Slovak
Photographers,* Prague, 1993. Articles—''Jaroslav Rajzìk'' in *European
Photography* (Göttingen), no. 3, 1980; ''Exhibition of Photographs'' by
Vladimír Birgus in *Revue Fotografie* (Prague), no. 3, 1980; Light Compostitions
of Jaroslav Rajzìk by Jan Šmok in *Revue Fotografie* (Prague), no. 4, 1990.

*

The theme of my work is the discovery of thoughts and forms in the reality
of the material world. Nature is full of perfect forms and thoughts: they are
merely hidden in cyphers, needing to be emancipated or freed from the tangled
chaos of the world.

For me, the key to this cypher is composition and light. My principal and
continuing series of works are entitled: *Arches and Labyrinths, Philosophy of
a Landscape, Studies of Light, Light Still Life, Light Apocalyptic Pictures* and
The Diary of Light Pictures.

—Jaroslav Rajzìk

*   *   *

Jaroslav Rajzìk is both a photographer and a teacher of photography, and
his academic background has influenced his own work as a photographer; he
has meditated often on the nature of photography.

Rakzìk was originally trained in secondary school as a chemist, and that
heritage is evident in his work, in his interest in ''explaining'' facts in an exact

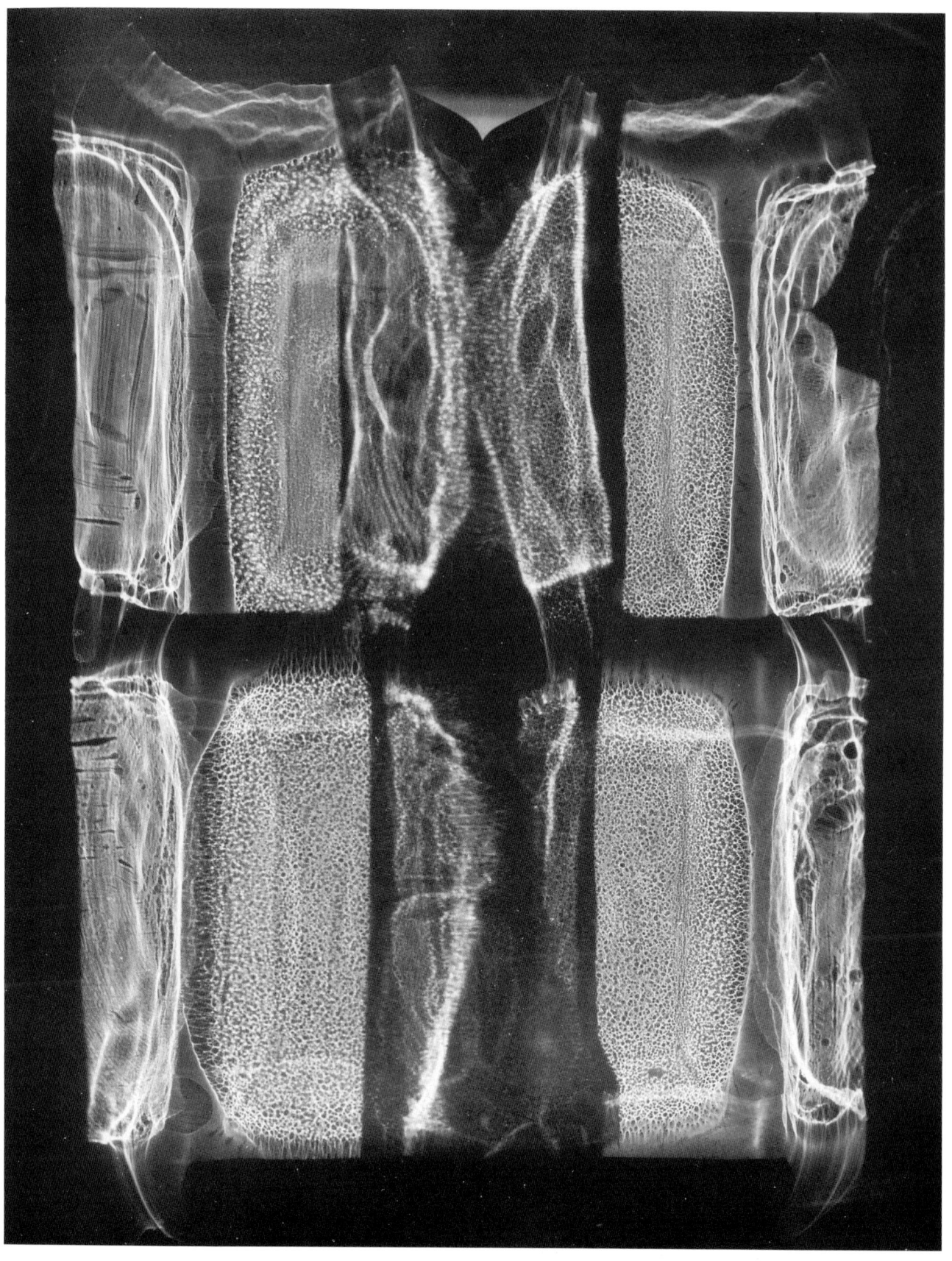

Revelation of the Head, **1992, from cycle** *Diary of Light Pictures,* **1992-93.** Photograph by Jaroslav Rajzík.

way. As a scientist he understands the decisive role of light in the photographic depiction; as a photographer, he respects light for its creative possibilities. Because he esteems the "elements" of his medium, he has regarded research into the various kinds and uses of light as appropriate to his work as a photographer. Rajzìk has carried on and continued the Czechoslovak tradition instigated by Jaromir Funke in the late 1920s of experiments with light and shadow resembling photograms but achieved by pure photography.

Rajzìk began his researches by subjugating the objects that he photographed to the extent that they completely lost their identities: the subject of his creative experiments was, in effect, the path of beams of light within the observed space under conditions that he had carefully prepared in accordance with his own principles of composition. The simple patterns created in this way were very close to the geometrical abstractions successfully achieved by some painters. However, these experiments with composition were not solely the product of intellectual speculation about visually active forms; they involve, too, creative games, as well as a vision of subconscious forces at work in the artist. And, it's probably also true that some admirable results happened by trial and error—changing the paths of light beams, evaluating whether or not the resultant formations were suitable for the image. As a person he tends to be shy, and his work, too, seems modest and in its nobility of forms easily vulnerable. Rajzìk is also keenly interested in small objects as subjects, objects that he photographs from a short distance in order to show vividly those features that to most people usually remain unnoticed.

As a teacher of landscape photography, Rajzìk has concentrated his talents on the genre to produce four different series bonded by an inner logic. *Romantic Landscapes* comprises intimate views of the countryside seen under varying conditions of climate and light, each picture capturing an unrepeatable glimpse of a unique atmosphere. The feeling of intimacy is strengthened by printing the monochrome images in small formats of 5 by 7 inches. The second cycle consists of enlarged colour shots of unemotive landscapes taken in a neutral light—a tactic by which Rajzìk has been able to express a certain modesty characteristic of the everyday panorama. He further experimented by making montage photographs of the land based on an artificial grid drawn onto each image. The symbols and signs appearing in the pictures focus the viewer's awareness on the natural world confronted with a universe constructed by human intellect.

The link between Rajzìk's pedagogic activities and his creative work is most clearly seen in a series of landscapes where two prints have been made from one negative, but exposed for differing periods of time. This series of darkroom mini-sequences connects areas of Rajzìk's concerns about the whole process of photography from the initial idea in front of the camera through to the final print.

—Petr Tausk

RAKAUSKAS, Romualdas.

Nationality: Lithuanian. **Born:** Akmene, 19 August 1941. **Education:** Attended schools in Akmene, 1948-58; studied journalism at Vilnius University, Lithuania, 1958-63. Served in the Soviet Army, 1963-65. Photographer, *Literatura ir menas* weekly magazine, Kaunas, 1962-67; photo-manager, *Nemunas* magazine, Kaunas, Lithuania, since 1967. Member, Lithuanian Society for Art Photography. **Recipient:** Gold Medal, *He and She* exhibition, Vilnius, 1970; Gold Medal, *Man's Moment* exhibition, Maglay, Yugoslavia, 1972; Silver Medal, *Zlatno Oko* exhibition, Novy Sad, Yugoslavia, 1973; Antwerp Prize, Agfa-Gevaert exhibition, Mortsel, Belgium, 1976; Gold Medal, *Ifo-Scanbaltic* exhibition, Rostock, East Germany, 1976, 1984; Grand Prize, *Man and Earth* exhibition, Plateliai, Lithuania, 1986. **Agent:** Photo Art Society of the Lithuanian SSR, Universiteto 4, Vilnius 232600, Lithuania. **Address:** Uršo 26-34, Kaunas 2233-43, Lithuania.

Individual Exhibitions:

1972	Gallery of Fine Arts, Vilnius (travelled to Moscow, Minsk and Riga)
1979	Photo Gallery, Vilnius, Lithuania

	Photo Gallery, Kaunas, Lithuania
	Photo Museum, Šiauliai, Lithuania
1980	Art Museum of Rostock, East Germany (toured East Germany)
1983	Art Research Institute, Moscow
	House of Culture, Sofia, Bulgaria
1984	FAMU Academy of Arts, Prague
1985	House of Arts, Riga, Latvia
	Photo Gallery, Vilnius, Lithuania

Selected Group Exhibitions:

1968	*Four Photographers*, Art Museum, Vilnius, Lithuania
1969	*Nine Lithuanian Photographers*, Journalists' Union, Moscow
1971	*Lithuanian Photography*, USSR People's Ethnographical Museum, Leningrad
1973	*Four Lithuanian Photographers*, The Photographers' Gallery, London
1975	*Lithuanian Photography*, House of Art, Brno, Czechoslovakia
1978	*Contemporary Soviet Photography*, Komorna Galeria, Bratislava, Czechoslovakia
1979	*Lithuanian Photography*, Canon Photo Gallery, Amsterdam
1980	*Lithuanian Photography*, The Photographers' Gallery, London
1981	*Third International Triennale of Photography*, Musée d'Art et d'Histoire, Fribourg, Switzerland
1984	*La Photographie Créative*, Pavillon des Arts, Paris

Collections:

Lithuanian Society for Art Photography, Vilnius; Bibliothèque Nationale, Paris; Daniela Mrázková Collection, Prague; Canon Photo Gallery, Amsterdam; International Center of Photography, New York; R.I.P. Permanent Center, Arles, France; Photo Museum, Siauliai, Lithuania.

Publications:

By RAKAUSKAS: Books—*Everyday Vilnisu*, with Antanas Sutkus, Vilnius 1968; *This Country Is Called Lithuania*, with Antanas Sutkus, Vilnius 1970; *Tenderness*, exhibition catalogue, Vilnius 1972; *Our Kaunas*, Vilnius 1976; *Blossom*, exhibition catalogue, Vilnius 1979; *New Lithuanian Architecture*, Vilnius 1982; *The Light of Hope*, Vilnius 1983.

On RAKAUSKAS: Books—*Lietuvos Fotografija*, Vaga, Lithuania 1967, Vilnius, Lithuania 1969; *Soviet Photo*, by the editors of Sovetskoe Foto, annually, 1970-75; *Pobaltska sovetska fotografie* by Vaclav Jiru, Prague 1974; *La Photographie Créative* by Jean-Claude Lemagny, Paris 1984; *Another Russia* by Daniela Mrázková and Vladimir Remeš, London 1986. **Articles**—"Romualdas Rakauskas" by Daniela Mrázková in *Ceskoslovenská Fotografie* (Prague), no. 11, 1978; "Rakauskas" by Vladimir Birgus in *Fotografie* (Prague), no. 1, 1986.

*   *   *

From about the mid-1960s Romualdas Rakauskas has been one of the leading representatives of Lithuanian photography, which at that time attracted attention for its impressive lyrical qualities and its sincere interest in the well-being of man. With his colleagues at the Lithuanian Society for Art Photography, Rakauskas produced optimistic photographs, attempting to create symbols of feeling of a healthy enjoyment of life. His aim, too, was an artistically modified picture based on reportage. A mother dancing with her children on the wide stretches of a summer meadow; tiny figures of children running across the countryside; a couple of lovers on a path covered with fallen leaves—human beings were shown mostly in motion and dealt with as part of the countryside. These photos are always full of a sparkling purity of emotion and produce an unusually cheerful effect. This effect was partly the result of the way in which Rakauskas dealt with the texture of the countryside and objects, brightly lit by the Lithuanian low spring sun, accentuating even microscopically tiny particles.

Over the past few years, however the lyricism and cheerfulness have been receding in Rakauskas' pictures; the running figures, the ostensible joy, have been disappearing, and he has turned to a more sober but more significantly documentary approach, to the very essence of the people and the countryside, to meditation. This transformation does not come about by chance; it has to do with a change of interest in all of Lithuanian photography from "depiction" to "meditation," from an outward view to philosophical reflection.

Now, too, Rakauskas selects beautiful and pleasing subjects, including some that are, in fact, actually a kind of sweet pseudo-art; he is still known as a romantic who works to evoke a mood. However he brilliantly counterbalances the precisely measured dosage of banality by putting stronger emphasis on the texture of the surface, from which the principal motif stands out, and also by a contrast of romantic and documentary elements. Since 1976, he has been working on a long-term cycle, "Time of the Flower," in which a whitish pointillism of blooms and leaves artistically transforms the picture, giving it a purely photographic structure. Against the background of the white sea of flowers, living subjects are dealt with—an old married couple sitting at a table which has been laid for dining; an orderly line of country children; a boy gently holding a white rabbit in his hand; a family group on a Sunday outing—all in stationary peace in accordance with premeditated arrangement. The confrontation of the romantic motif of flowers and the documentary style employed in the arrangement of subjects evokes excitement and even irritation at the disharmony and unusual approach. The lesson to be drawn from the aesthetic purpose of the photographer is linked with the documentary approach.

The result, however, perfectly expresses the sensibility of contemporary man, his longing for feeling and dream that all the time comes up against reality. It contains the artist's constant reminiscences of his childhood, when life had a clear purpose in the direct merging of man and nature, which in turn suggest criteria essential to living in the world today. The dramatic conflict about truth and the purpose of life in Rakauskas' photographs constitutes a captivating emotion of rediscovering basic values.

Rakauskas is an artist who manages to speak about the basic things in life lightly, joyfully, emotionally and without pathos. The slightly grotesque touches of his latest work introduce a new quality of expression and thought to his photographs.

—Daniela Mrázková

RANKAITIS, Susan.

Nationality: American. **Born:** Cambridge, Massachesetts, 10 September 1949. **Education:** University of Illinois, Champaign-Urbana, B.F.A. (painting), 1971; University of Southern California, Los Angeles, M.F.A. (photography and painting), 1977; studied photography with Bart Parker, Philip Melnick and Robert Flick. **Family:** Married Robert Flick, 5 June 1976. **Career:** Worked as Research Assistant and Art Director at Computer-based Education Research Laboratory (PLATO), University of Illinois, Champaign-Urbana, 1971-75; worked as Graduate Teaching Assistant (Painting, Drawing and Photography) at University of Southern California, Los Angeles, 1976-77; part-time instructor of Art at Chapman College, 1977-81; also as part-time Instructor of Photography at Orange Coast College, 1978-81, and 1982-83; Assistant Professor of Photography at Orange Coast College, 1981-82, becoming Associate Professor of Art at same college in 1983; Chair and Associate Professor, Department of Art, Chapman College, 1984-89 and Research Fellow 1984-87; Fletcher Jones Chair in Art, Scripps College, Claremont, California since 1990; **Recipient:** National Endowment for the Arts Fellowships in Photography 1980 and 1988; Graves Award for Teaching in the Humanities,1985; Djerassi Foundation Residency in Painting (Agnes Bourne Foundation), 1989; USA/France Fellowship at La Napoule Foundation, Cannes, France, 1989. **Agents:** Ruth Bloom Gallery, 2036 Broadway, Santa Monica, California 90404, U.S.A.; and Robert Mann Gallery, 42 East 76th Street, New York, New York 10021, U.S.A. **Address:** 3117 Lansbury, Claremont, California 91711-4146, U.S.A.

Individual Exhibitions:

1983 The Los Angeles County Museum of Art, Los Angeles

    The International Museum of Photography at the George Eastman House, Rochester, New York
1984 Light Gallery, New York
1988 Min Gallery, Tokyo
1989 Myers/Bloom Gallery, Santa Monica, California
1990 Schneider Museum of Art, Ashland, Oregon
    Myers/Bloom Gallery, Santa Monica, California
1991 The Center for Creative Photography, Tucson, Arizona
1992 Ruth Bloom Gallery, Santa Monica, California
1994 Museum of Contemporary Photography, Chicago, Illinois
    Robert Mann Gallery, New York

Selected Group Exhibitions:

1988 *Under Construction: New Photo-montage,* Cranbrook Academy of Art Museum, Bloomfield Hills, Michigan
1989 *Experimental Color in Photography,* San Francisco Museum of Modern Art, San Francisco
1991 *Contemporary Women,* University of New Mexico Art Museum, Albuquerque
1993 *Works from the Permanent Collection,* Princeton University Art Museum, Princeton, New Jersey
1994 *Experimental Vision: The Evolution of the Photogram since 1919,* Denver Art Museum, Colorado

Collections:

California Institute of Technology; Princeton University Art Museum, Princeton, New Jersey; Center for Creative Photography, Tucson, Arizona; Seagrams Bi-Centennial Collection, New York; Los Angeles County Museum of Art; San Francisco Museum of Modern Art; Museum of Modern Art, Lodz, Poland; The International Museum of Photography at the George Eastman House, Rochester, New York; Museum of Israel, Jerusalem; University of New Mexico Art Museum.

Publications:

On RANKAITIS: Books—*New American Photography* by Kathleen Gauss, Los Angeles, 1985; *Photography and Art: Interactions Since 1946* by Andy Grundberg and Kathleen Gauss, New York 1987; *Photography of Invention: American Pictures of the 80s* by Merry Forresta and Joshua Smith, Cambridge, Massachusetts, 1989; *Los Angeles Art and the Photograph 1960-1980,* by Charles Desmarais, Los Angeles, 1992; *Experimental Vision* by Neususs, Barrow and Hagen, 1994. **Articles**—"Susan Rankaitis" Gallery Min exhibition catalog entry with essay by Merle Schipper and preface by Marjorie Perloff, Tokyo, 1988; "Susan Rankaitis" Myers/Bloom Gallery exhibition catalog entry by Susan Kandel, Santa Monica, California, 1990; "Susan Rankaitis' Encounters," Center for Creative Photography exhibition catalog by Terence Pitts, Tucson, 1991; "Photography: Out of the Ghetto" by Pepe Carmel, in *Art News,* April, 1994.

*

My work has always consisted of questions that combined, hybridized and connected my circumstance with the world at large in a visual dialogue. Although trained and positioned as a painter I have always been drawn to the alchemy of photography.

After a studio fire, I found myself bringing fire, water, air and earth into the work, all of them emblematic (symptomatic) of loss, decision-making and retrenchment.

When my studio was underneath the flight path of LAX I used to lie on my roof and photograph the bellies of planes as they went overhead, in part because they were so present and so intrusive but also because they were so beautiful and powerful.

There is a part of me that will always be amazed that something so large as a plane can actually fly. I have an innate fear of flying and am terrified of heights; so thoughts about power and terror and technology have merged and now lead to work which deals with technological issues. I am constantly surprised that something as small as a chromosome can have such startling implications for a human life and how we are in many ways so trapped in our

DNA 6, **1992.** Photograph ©Susan Rankaitis. Courtesy Robert Mann Gallery.

own genetic code. Indeed, I find it almost impossible to be an artist today without caring about the physical and biological sciences.

While working in France at La Napoule Art Foundation in late 1989 I became interested in jargon, possibly as a result of my own convoluted French, but also because of the new technological and scientific words which were constantly brought into everyday language. Many of these words were awkward and funny but most were interesting attempts to hybridize not only language but concepts. I have been trying to do this visually for years and to this day view my own work as a sort of visual jargon.

It was at the time of an illness in 1990 that I first became interested in genetic engineering and the rapidly expanding code of language with regard to DNA discoveries. The biochemical arena is one which continues to draw me into its web. It is both horrific and miraculous and, like everything that I've worked with, both personal and deeply ethical.

My work is about encoding and unravelling information.

—Susan Rankaitis

*   *   *

"It's art but is it photography?" asked an art review in the early 1990s that heralded the art-world acceptance of the term I used as the title of my book *Fabrications: Staged, Altered and Appropriated Photographs.*

This is a question that could be posed about Susan Rankaitis' career of making one-of-a-kind, laboriously worked, sometimes wall-sized and irregularly shaped near-abstractions of photographic images and processes. Their analogies are painterly, distantly to the photo-silkscreens of Robert Rauschenburg with their layered popular icons, to the jagged graphism in Willem de Kooning's Abstract Expressionism of the 1960s and to the vertical build-up of landscape forms in a Chinese Song Dynasty painting. However Rankaitis's works resemble no other photographs on earth.

She studied painting at the University of Illinois, Champaign, and the University of Southern California, Los Angeles where, in 1975 her encounter with the solarized photograms and the theories of Moholy-Nagy and later the cameraless experiments of Man Ray led her to try various photographic techniques. Since then she has used up to a hundred negatives in a single work, applying multiple printing methods along with selective development and processing, adding toner, airbrush, painting, drawing and collage elements, mounting the completed work as geometrically cut shapes or like scrolls and, recently, installing them with objects—a rocket nose cone in 1990—that she finds and paints. Much is lost in reproduction, like the changing reflectivity of her metallic tints and the details in her dark, closely hued harmonies. The sensuous overload is extreme.

Dazzling as her procedures are, however, Rankaitis is more than a technician or formalist. Her work connects with her scientific interests and the sometimes drastic changes in her life. In 1980 a studio fire destroyed all of her current painting and much of her photography. The disaster seemed to free her to start making her hybrids and it also gave them an iconography of the four elements and an aura of threat. Her next studio in the path of flights into Los Angeles County Airport gave her close-up views of jets and so the futuristic theme of flying with its mixed messages of excitement and fear and the aerodynamic forms of planes both entered her work.

Rankaitis's illness in 1990 gave personal meaning to the double helix representing the genetic building blocks of DNA and this spatially rich motif came to represent her sense of all the dynamism in nature. For her it evokes the endless cycles of ecology and molecular and chemical compositions. To such observable patterns she added signs and codes from biology and physics in an attempt to suggest the internal and universal forms of life. Fractals, references to chaos theory, allusions to the perils and promises of genetic engineering and computer jargon lurk in her shadowy layerings and reveal her interest in both the forms and concepts of these recent developments in science and technology. Whether or not one recognises or understands such allusions Rankaitis's works draw the viewer into their sensations of speed and outer space. The very contemporary anxiety they thus create is heightened by the paradox of their seductive beauty.

—Anne Hoy

RAUSCHENBERG, Robert.

Nationality: American. **Born:** Port Arthur, Texas, 22 October 1925. **Education:** Studied at Kansas City Art Institute and School of Design, Missouri, 1946-47; Académie Julian, Paris, 1947; studied art under Josef Albers, and photography under Hazel Larson, Black Mountain College, North Carolina, 1948-49; Art Students' League, New York, 1949-52. **Military Service:** Served as a neuropsychiatry technician, United States Naval Reserve, California Naval Hospital, 1942-45. **Family:** Married Susan Weil in 1950 (divorced, 1952); son: Christopher. **Career:** Independent painter, graphic artist and photographer, since 1950, and stage designer, since 1955: mounted first "Happening," with John Cage and others, Black Mountain, North Carolina, 1952. Technical Director, Merce Cunningham Dance Company, New York, 1955-63; Co-founder, with Billy Kluver, Experiments in Art and Technology (E.A.T.), 1966; President of the Board, Change Inc., New York, 1970; Founder, Untitled Press graphics, studio, Captiva Island, Florida, 1971; President, Trisha Brown Dance Company, New York, 1978. Instructor, Black Mountain College, North Carolina, 1952. **Recipient:** Painting Prize, 1960, and Logan Award, 1976, Art Institute of Chicago; Ohara Prize, National Museum of Modern Art, Tokyo, 1962; First Prize, 1963, and Grand Prize of Honour, 1979, *International Exhibition of Graphic Art,* Ljubliana; First Prize, *Biennale,* Venice, 1964; William A. Clark Gold Medal, *Corcoran Biennale,* Washington, D.C., 1965; Mayor's Award of Honor in Arts and Culture, New York, 1977; Creative Arts Medal, Brandeis University, Waltham, Massachusetts, 1978; Chicago Arts Award, 1978; Special Award, *Biennale of Graphic Arts,* Kraków, 1979; Gold Medal for Graphics, Oslo, 1979; Skowhegan Medal for Painting, Maine, 1982; Grammy Award, New York 1984; Jerusalem Prize for Arts and Letters, Friends of Bezalel Academy, Jerusalem, 1984. D.H.L.: Grinnell College, Iowa, 1967; D.F.A.: University of South Florida, Tampa, 1976; New York University, 1984. Fellow, Rhode Island School of Design, Providence, 1981. Member, American Academy of Arts and Sciences, 1978; Foreign Member, Swedish Royal Academy of Fine Arts, Stockholm, 1980; Officier, Ordre des Arts et Lettres, France, 1981. **Agent:** Pace/MacGill Gallery, 32 East 57th Street, New York, New York 10022, U.S.A.

Individual Exhibitions:

1951	Betty Parsons Gallery, New York
1953	Stable Gallery, New York
	Galleria d'Arte Contemporanea, Florence, Italy
1955	Charles Egan Gallery, New York
1958	Leo Castelli Gallery, New York
1959	Leo Castelli Gallery, New York
	Galleria La Tartaruga, Rome
	Galerie 22, Dusseldorf
1960	Leo Castelli Gallery, New York
1961	Leo Castelli Gallery, New York
	Galerie Daniel Cordier, Paris
	Galleria dell'Ariete, Milan
1962	Dwan Gallery, New York
1963	Leo Castelli Gallery, New York
	Jewish Museum, New York (retrospective)
	Galleria dell'Obelisco, Rome
	Galerie Ileana Sonnabend, Paris
1964	Galerie Ileana Sonnabend, Paris
	Galleria Civica d'Arte Moderna, Turin
	Whitechapel Art Gallery, London (retrospective)
1965	Leo Castelli Gallery, New York
	Amerika Haus, West Berlin
	Contemporary Arts Society, Houston, Texas
	Walker Art Center, Minneapolis
	Moderna Museet, Stockholm
1966	Museum of Modern Art, New York
1967	Douglas Gallery, Vancouver, British Columbia
1968	Leo Castelli Gallery, New York
	Museum of Modern Art, New York
	Stedelijk Museum, Amsterdam
	Peale House, Philadelphia

Jean Tinguely, **Basel, Switzerland, 1984.** Photograph by Robert Rauschenberg. ©Untitled Press, Inc.

Kunstverein, Cologne
Musée d'Art Moderne, Paris
1969   Leo Castelli Gallery, New York
Fort Worth Art Museum, Texas
Douglas Gallery, Vancouver, British Columbia
Newport Harbor Art Museum, Balboa, California
Phoenix Art Museum, Arizona
1970   Seattle Art Museum, Washington
1971   Galerie Ileana Sonnabend, Paris
1972   Leo Castelli Gallery, New York
Galerie Ileana Sonnabend, Paris
Galerie Buren, Stockholm
1973   Galerie Ileana Sonnabend, Paris
Leo Castelli Gallery, New York
Ace Gallery, Venice, California
Southern Illinois University, Carbondale
Israel Museum, Jerusalem
1974   University of South Florida, Tampa
Galerie Buren, Stockholm
Galerie Mikro, West Berlin
Modern Art Agency, Naples, Italy
Museum Museum Haus Lange, Krefeld, West Germany
Castelli-Sonnabend Galleries, New York
Castelli Graphics, New York
Galerie Sonnabend, Geneva
Jared Sable Gallery, Toronto
1975   Castelli Graphics, New York

Visual Arts Gallery, New York
Ace Gallery, Venice, California
Museo d'Arte Moderna Ca'Pesaro, Venice
Art Association, Newport, Rhode Island
1976   Galerie de Gestlo, Hamburg
Galerie H.M., Brussels
Galleria Civica d'Arte Moderna, Ferrara, Italy
Leo Castelli Gallery, New York
Fort Belvidere, Florence, Italy
Ace Gallery, Vancouver, British Columbia
National Collection of Fine Arts, Washington, D.C.
    (retrospective)
Alberta College of Art, Calgary
Galleriet, Lund, Sweden
1977   Galleriet, Lund, Sweden
Galerie Sonnabend, Paris
Museum of Modern Art, New York (retrospective)
Castelli-Sonnabend Galleries, New York and San Francisco
Museum of Modern Art (retrospective)
Albright-Knox Art Gallery, Buffalo, New York
Art Institute of Chicago
Janie C. Lee Gallery, Houston, Texas
Galerie Rudolf Zwirner, Cologne
1978   Galerie Sonnabend, Paris
Mayor Gallery, London
Vancouver Art Gallery, British Columbia
Castelli Graphics, New York

Forth Worth Art Museum, Texas
1979   Sonnabend Gallery, New York (twice)
Akron Art Institute, Ohio
Portland Art Center, Oregon
Kunsthalle, Tübingen, West Germany (retrospective)
Musée de Toulon, France
Multiples-Goodman, New York
Virginia Museum of Fine Arts, Richmond
Gloria Luria Gallery, Bay Harbor Islands, Florida
1980   Conejo Valley Art Museum, Thousand Oaks, California
Edison Community College, Fort Meyers, Florida
Visual Arts Museum, New York
Staatliche Kunsthalle, West Berlin (retrospective)
Leo Castelli Gallery, New York
Galerie Sonnabend, Paris
Staatliche Kunstmuseum, Dusseldorf
Photographers Gallery, Sanibel Island, Florida
Louisiana Museum, Humlebaek, Denmark (retrospective)
Baltimore Museum of Art, Maryland
Children's Hospital, Washington, D.C.
Ace Gallery, Vancouver, British Columbia
Lunds Galleriet, Lund, Sweden
1981   Stadtische Kunstinstitut, Frankfurt (retrospective)
Stadtische Galerie im Lenbachhaus, Munich (retrospective)
Sable-Castelli Gallery, Toronto
Tate Gallery, London (retrospective)
Portfolio of 12 Photographs, Gallery Watari, Tokyo
Rauschenberg in the Rockies, Colorado State University, Fort Collins (travelled to Colorado State University, Denver)
Rauschenberg Photographs, Centre Georges Pompidou, Paris (travelled to the Musée Cantini, Marseille; Musée des Beaux-Arts, St. Etienne; Moderna Museet, Stockholm; Aarhus Kunstmuseum, Denmark)
Arcanum I-XIII, Styria Gallery, New York
Photems, Institute of Contemporary Art, Boston, Massachusetts
Combine Drawings, Mayor Gallery, London
In + Out City Limits: Charleston, Gibbes Art Gallery, Charleston, South Carolina
In + Out City Limits: Boston, Magnuson-Lee Gallery, Boston, Massachusetts
In + Out City Limits: Baltimore, Grimaldis Gallery, Baltimore, Maryland
In + Out City Limits: Los Angeles, Rosamund Felsen Gallery, Los Angeles
1982   *In + Out City Limits: New York*, Sonnabend Gallery, New York
In + Out City Limits: 6 Cities 40, Photographers' Gallery, Sanibel Island, Florida
First Footage of the 1/4 Mile, Edison Community College, Fort Myers, Florida
Prints from Gemini G.E.L., Hara Museum of Contemporary Art, Tokyo
Razorback Bunch I-VIII, Castelli Graphics, New York
Arcanum Series, Lunds Galleriet, Lund, Sweden
Prints, Long Beach Museum of Art, California
Sculpture, Flow Ace Gallery, Paris
Paintings and Works on Paper, van Straaten Gallery, Chicago
Seven Characters, Museum of Modern Art, New York
1983   *Kabal American Zephyr Series*, Sonnabend Gallery, New York (and Castelli Gallery, New York
China Collages, Thomas Babeor Gallery, La Jolla, California
In + Out City Limits: New York, Louisiana Museum, Humlebaek, Denmark (travelled to Tranegaarden, Copenhagen; and Henie-Onstad Kunstsenter, Oslo)
Shigaraki, Prince Hotel, Tokyo
Shigaraki, K.B.S. Kaikan, Kyoto, Japan
Works from the Last Decade, Flow Ace Gallery, Los Angeles
Photographs, Daytona Beach Community College, Florida
Seven Characters/Unique Collages, Jingxian, Anhui Province, China

Second Footage of the 1/4 Mile, Edison Community College, Fort Myers, Florida
Performance 1954-83, Galleria di Franca Mancini, Pesaro, Italy (travelled to Cooper Union, New York; Contemporary Arts Museum, Houston, Texas; Cleveland Center for Contemporary Art, Ohio; North Carolina Museum of Art, Raleigh; Norton Gallery, West Palm Beach, Florida; California State University, Long Beach)
Photos, Douglas Elliot Gallery, San Francisco
Photogravures, Castelli Graphics, New York
Images of China, Dalsheimer Gallery, Baltimore, Maryland
Images from China, Maryland Institute, Baltimore
Drawings, Susanne Hilberry Gallery, Birmingham, Michigan
Important Works, Marianne Friedland Gallery, Toronto
Australian National Gallery, Canberra
1984   *Photogravures*, Harcourts Contemporary Gallery, San Francisco
Galerie Beyeler, Basle, Switzerland (retrospective)
Heland Thorden Witterling Galleries, Stockholm
First 400 Feet of the 1/4 Mile, Miami Center for Fine Arts, Florida
Recent Paintings, Fondation Maeght, St. Paul de Vence, France
Photogravures: China-Mix, Adagio Gallery, Bridgehampton, New York
Sling-Shots Lit, Gemini G.E.L., Los Angeles
Photems: Series I, Allen Street Gallery, Dallas, Texas
Photogravures: America-Mix, Objects Gallery, San Antonio, Texas
Salvage Series, Edison Community College, Fort Myers, Florida
Photogravures: America-Mix, Scheinbaum and Russek Gallery, Santa Fe, New Mexico
New Yorks, Sonnabend Gallery, New York
1985   Fundacion Juan March, Madrid (retrospective; travelled to the Fundacion Joan Miro, Barcelona)
Salvage Series, Ringling Museum of Art, Sarasota, Florida
Rauschenberg Overseas Cultural Interchange (ROCI), Museo Rufino Tamayo, Mexico City (and world tour, 1985-89)
Recent Works, Galerie Daniel Templon, Paris
Works from Four Series, Contemporary Arts Museum, Houston, Texas, (travelled to Marion Koogler McNay Art Museum, San Antonio; Dallas Museum of Art; and Art Museum of South Texas, Corpus Christi)
1986   *Photographs 1949-84*, Contemporary Arts Museum, Houston, Texas
Painter Photographer, Espace Nicois d'Art et de Culture, Nice, France
White and Black Paintings 1949-52, Larry Gagosian Gallery, New York
Newest Continuation of the 1/4 Mile, Edison Community College, Fort Myers, Florida
Drawings 1958-68, Acquavella Galleries, New York
Photos and Photems, School of Visual Arts, New York
Gluts, Castelli Gallery, New York
Rauschenberg Overseas Culture Interchange, Setagaya Art Museum, Tokyo
1987   Pace/MacGill Gallery, New York
Selections from Rauschenberg's 1/4 Mile or 2 Furlong Piece, Metropolitan Museum of Art, New York
Rauschenberg: Paintings on Copper and Stainless Steel— 1985/86, Heland Thorden Wetterling Galleries, Stockholm
Robert Rauschenberg—Recent Work, Kaj Forsblom Gallery, Helsinki
Rauschenberg: Works on Paper, Blum-Helman Gallery, New York
Robert Rauschenberg: New Works, Galerie Denise Rene Hans Meyer, Dusseldorf, Germany
Robert Rauschenberg—Neapolitan Gluts, Galerie Lucio Amelio, Naples, Italy
Robert Rauschenberg—Gluts, Edison Community College, Fort Myers, Florida

Rauschenberg: Tibetan Keys and Locks, Castelli Graphics, New York
Robert Rauschenberg: Summer Gluts, Texas Gallery, Houston
Robert Rauschenberg—Gluts, Waddington Galleries, London
1988   *Robert Rauschenberg: The Glut Series,* Blum-Helman Gallery, New York
Robert Rauschenberg: New Pictures, Pace/MacGill Gallery, New York
Rauschenberg Overseas Culture Interchange, Museo Nacional, Castillo de la Fuerza and Casa de las Americas, Havana, Cuba
Robert Rauschenberg: Currents 1970, Galerie Alfred Kren, Cologne, Germany
Robert Rauschenberg: New Drawings from the Passes Series, Knoedler & Company, New York
Rauschenberg: Gluts, Galerie Isy Brachot, Brussels
Robert Rauschenberg: Beamer Series, BMW Showroom, West Berlin
Rauschenberg: Shiners, Gluts, Urban Bourbons, Knoedler & Company, New York
1989   *Soviet/American Array,* Universal Limited Art Editions Gallery, New York
Rauschenberg Culture Interchange, Central House of Culture, Tretyakov Gallery, Moscow
Robert Rauschenberg, Fabian Carlsson Gallery, London
Rauschenberg: Samarkand Stitches, Castelli Graphics, New York
Rauschenberg Revisited: The Hoarfrost Editions 1974, Ivory Kimpton Gallery, San Francisco
Robert Rauschenberg: New Paintings, Akira Ikeda Gallery, Tokyo
Robert Rauschenberg, The Gemini Works: 1967-1988, Fred Hoffman Gallery, Santa Monica, California and Manny Silverman Gallery, Los Angeles
Robert Rauschenberg, Heland Wetterling Gallery, Stockholm and Gothenberg, Sweden
Robert Rauschenberg Works, Knoedler & Company, New York
A Tribute to Rauschenberg: Works from Dallas Collection, Meadows Museum, Southern Methodist University, Dallas
Robert Rauschenberg, Galerie Jamileh Weber, Zurich, Switzerland
1990   *Rauschenberg Prints,* Lorence/Monk Gallery, New York
Robert Rauschenberg: China Mix, Scott Hanson Gallery, New York
Rauschenberg Overseas Culture Interchange, Neue Berliner Galerie, Alten Museum, Berlin
Rauschenberg: Peintures, Dessin, Editions, Galerie Montaigne, Paris
Rauschenberg: Currents, Castelli Graphics, New York
Rauschenberg Overseas Culture Interchange, National Art Gallery, Kuala Lumpur, Malaysia
Robert Rauschenberg: Works on Paper, Knoedler & Company, New York
Rauschenberg Graphic Works, Pyo Gallery, Seoul, South Korea
Pharmakon '90, Nippon Convention Centre, Makauhari Messe, Japan
1991   Pace/MacGill Gallery, New York

Selected Group Exhibitions:

1957   *Collage in America,* American Federation of Arts, New York (toured the United States)
1961   *American Vanguard,* Guggenheim Museum, New York (toured Europe)
1964   *Black, White and Gray,* Wadsworth Atheneum, Hartford, Connecticut
1968   *Dada, Surrealism and their Heritage,* Museum of Modern Art, New York
1973   *Fotografia Creativa,* Centro La Cappella, Trieste, Italy

1976   *Photographic Process as Medium,* Rutgers University Art Gallery, New Brunswick, New Jersey
1987   *Art about Art,* Whitney Museum, New York
1979   *Photographie als Kunst 1879-1979,* Tiroler Landesmuseum Ferdinandeum, Innsbruck, Austria (travelled to the Neue Galerie am Wolfgang Gurlitt Museum, Linz; Neue Galerie am Landesmuseum Joanneum, Graz; and Museum des 20. Jahrhunderts, Vienna)
1983   *Photography in America 1910-83,* Tampa Museum, Florida
1987   *Photography and Art 1946-86,* Los Angeles County Museum of Art
1990   Pace/MacGill Gallery, New York
1992   Pace/MacGill Gallery, New York

Collections:

Museum of Modern Art, New York; Guggenheim Museum, New York; Whitney Museum, New York; Museum Ludwig, Cologne; Stedelijk Museum, Amsterdam; Los Angeles County Museum of Art; Art Gallery of Ontario, Toronto; National Gallery of Canada, Ottawa; Kunsthaus, Zurich; Kaiser Wilhelm Museum, Krefeld, Germany.

Publications:

By RAUSCHENBERG: Books—*Rauschenberg Photographe,* exhibition catalogue, with interview by Alain Sayag, Paris 1981; *Photos In + Out City Limits: Boston,* Boston 1981; *Photos In + Out City Limits: New York,* New York 1982. **Articles**—''Carnal Clocks'' in *Art Now* (New York), May 1969; ''A Collage Comment by Robert Rauschenberg on his Latest Suite of Prints'' in *Studio International* (London), December 1969; ''Robert Rauschenbert Talks to Maxime de la Falaise McKendry'' in *Interview* (New York), May 1976. **Film**—*Canoe,* 1966.

On RAUSCHENBERG: Books—*Rauschenberg,* exhibition catalogue, with essay by Gillo Dorfles, Milan 1961; *Rauschenberg,* exhibition catalogue, with text by John Cage, Lawrence Alloway and others, Paris 1963; *Robert Rauschenberg: Paintings, Drawings and Combines 1949-1964,* exhibition catalogue, with essays by Henry Geldzahler, John Cage, and Max Kozloff, London 1964; *Robert Rauschenberg: Paintings 1953-64,* exhibition catalogue, with introduction by Dean Swanson, Minneapolis 1965; *Robert Rauschenberg,* exhibition catalogue, by Andrew Forge, Amsterdam 1968; *Robert Rauschenberg* by Andrew Forge, New York 1969; *Robert Rauschenberg in Black and White,* exhibition catalogue, by Thomas H. Garver, Balboa, California 1969; *Rauschenberg: Black Market* by Jurgen Wissman, Stuttgart 1970; *Combattimento per un'immagine: fotografie e pittori,* exhibition catalogue, edited by Daniela Palazzoli and Luigi Carluccio, Turin 1973; *Fotografia Creativa,* exhibition catalogue, by G. Mazzotta and D. Palazzoli, Trieste, Italy 1973; *Rauschenberg at Graphic Studio,* exhibition catalogue, with introduction by Willard McCracken, Tampa, Florida 1974; *Rauschenberg's Pages and Fuses,* exhibition catalogue, with introduction by Joseph E. Young, Los Angeles 1974; *Robert Rauschenberg,* exhibition catalogue, with essays by Guido Perocco, Daniel Abadie and David Bourdon, Venice 1975; *Photographic Process as Medium,* exhibition catalogue, by R.T. Livingston, New Brunswick, New Jersey 1976; *Kunst und Photographie: Kontakt, Einflusse, Wirkungen* by Otto Stelzer, Munich 1978; *Robert Rauschenberg: Zeichnungen, Gouachen, Collagen 1949 -bis 1979* by Gotz Adriani, Munich 1979; *Photographie als Kunst 1879-1979,* exhibition catalogue, by Peter Weiermair, Innsbruck, Austria 1979; *Off the Wall: Robert Rauschenberg and the Art World of Our Time* by Calvin Tomkins, Garden City, New York 1980; *Photography and Art 1946-1986,* exhibition catalogue, by Andy Grundberg and Kathleen Gauss, Los Angeles 1987.

*

My preoccupation in 1949 with photography was supported by a personal conflict between curiosity and shyness; the camera functioned as a social shield. Now I think of the camera as my permission to walk into every shadow or watch while any light changes. Mine is the need to be where it will always never be the same again; a kind of archaeology in time only, forcing one to see whatever the light or the darkness touches, and care. My concern is to move at a speed within which to act.

Photography is the most direct communication in non-violent contacts.

—Robert Rauschenberg

*   *   *

Robert Rauschenberg, one of the pioneers and main representative of pop-art, is today ranked among the most distinguished American painters, designers and graphic artists of the second half of the twentieth century. His works had relatively soon reached resounding success culminating in his being awarded the Grand Prix at the 32nd Biennial in Venice in 1964 (after James Whistler and Mark Tobey, Rauschenberg has thus become only the third American awarded this prestigious prize), several honorary doctor's degrees and membership of the American Academy of Art and Science in 1978. Today, Rauschenberg's paintings and pieces of graphic art are exhibited in many foremost galleries and museums all over the world, while different kinds of history of modern art pay great attention to his work, and a couple of major monographs on Rauschenberg have already appeared. His scenographic work and experiments in the fields of para-theatre and para-ballet have also gained recognition.

However, before the beginning of the 1980s only few knew that Rauschenberg is an outstanding photographer as well. It was not until 1980 that he presented his photographs at smaller exhibitions at Sanibel in Florida and in Boston, and a year later at a great photographic retrospective show at the Georges Pompidou Center in Paris, which was later successfully repeated in several other towns. So it has been proved that Rauschenberg must be ranked with other pop-art representatives, Andy Warhol and David Hockney, who have become successful as photographers, too.

Robert Rauschenberg comes of a family of a German immigrant to the United States and a Native American woman of the Cherokee tribe. He began his art studies at the Kansas City Art Institute relatively early after demobilization and a factory job. He left for Europe after the first year of his studies, attending, among others, the Académie Julien in Paris. The beginning of his creations was greatly influenced by his studies under Josef Albers at the famous Black Mountain College in North Carolina, which, imitating the model of the German Staatliches Bauhaus, had become an important centre of avant-garde art in the United States. It was here that he met music composer and art theoretician John Cage, who roused his interest by demanding abolition of the border-line between art and life. Under his influence, Rauschenberg gradually departed from painting in the style of abstract expressionism and in 1953-55 began to create a collection of "combined paintings" which included picture postcards, newspaper photo cutouts and pieces of cloth. They reflect the inspirational influence of works by Marcel Duchamp and Kurt Schwitters, but in his later works Rauschenberg got rid of this immediate influence by attempting a broad synthesis of many art trends reaching from Dadaism to gestic painting. In his assemblages composed of photographs, newspaper clippings, but also glass bottles or stuffed animals, he tried to realize his idea that "a picture resembles more the real world if it is created of subjects from the real world." These tendencies to paint more realistically were of extraordinary significance after the long years of dominance of abstract art. Absurd configurations of various objects deprived of their usual connections mock at various consumer fetishes and activate the spectators to think over the suggested problems.

Rauschenberg achieved remarkable results, too, in scenography and costume designing (in 1955-63 he cooperated with the Merce Cunningham Dance Company), and also in the fields of variform para-theatrical actions or of creative use of the latest audio-visual means.

He took an interest in photographing even before becoming a painter. According to Rauschenberg's own words, his interest in photography was supported by an inner conflict between curiosity and an inborn shyness, because the camera served him as a kind of social shield. The oldest photographs he included in his Paris retrospective show originated at the turn of the nineteen-forties and -fifties. We can find among them portraits of his closest friends, quiet corners of the flea markets containing seemingly non-photogenic objects, details of interiors, photos from his trips to Italy, bird's-eye-view photographs whose composition follows experiments of the photographic avant-garde of the 1920s and 1930s and also an original set of five shots capturing from various distances fragments of the figure of

Rauschenberg's friend on the Spanish Stairs in Rome, which in certain respects anticipated contemporary photographic sequences. They are mostly sort of scraps from a personal diary, an auto-reflexive expression of his own experiences, subjective views with a strong emotional charge and a sense of discovering surprising creative values in the most simple motifs. The photographs are enlarged from the full size of the negative (6 x 6 cm), because Rauschenberg refuses cutouts and when taking pictures he waits for a suitable moment showing that the field of vision has been best filled. Many works originating in Raschenberg's first photographic period attract by their untraditional composition and courageous segmentation of the depicted realities. Some of the compositions follow the experiments by László Moholy-Nagy and other photographers from the Bauhaus, while, on the contrary, some other "fragments of reality" anticipate, for example, Ralph Gibson. Though in the period context many of these works can be considered outstanding samples of the ever-increasing trend of distinctively subjective photography with a lot of space for picture metaphors and hidden meanings, Rauschenberg has never published them. In the first place, photography offered him the possibility of direct and simultaneously intimate contact with the outer world, but it also often meant for him the starting point in other branches of creation, even though photographs as such appeared in Rauschenberg's paintings and graphics quite rarely.

Rauschenberg's first photographic period ended roughly in 1952. Supposedly the author then felt that he had reached a stage at which he should decide unequivocally either in favour of the fine arts or photography. He had decided for the former. It was not before the turn of the nineteen-seventies and -eighties that he came back to photographing. He continued with his interest in unusual photographic presentation of everyday things by depicting complex and ambiguously interpretable objective and, symbolically, even interpersonal relations.

This did not always originate from a need to create freely but, for example, also from a necessity to acquire a great number of photographs for the scenographic solution to a theatre play. Rauschenberg had brought many photos from his photographic expedition along the U.S. East Coast; many others had been created for photographic exhibitions in various American cities. They are mostly inventive confrontations between several static motifs which, of course, on a second plane of meaning tell something about contemporary America and the world of today, too, often with a considerable ironic tendency.

Not all of Rauschenberg's photographs can stand the most severe evaluation criteria but, considered as a whole, these photographs enrich without doubt the spectrum of contemporary American photography.

—Vladimìr Birgus

RAYMOND, Lilo.

Nationality: American. **Born:** Frankfurt, Germany, 23 June 1922; immigrated to the United States, 1939: subsequently naturalized. **Education:** Studied photography under David Vestal, New York, 1961-63. **Family:** Married Henry A. Schubart in 1943; Herbert D. Raymond in 1954. **Career:** Worked at various odd jobs, as milliner, waitress, tennis coach, etc., as a waitress in Helen Gee's Limelight Gallery, and as an assistant to the photographer Charles Pratt, in New York, 1940-64. Freelance photographer, New York, since 1964. Instructor in Photography, School of Visual Arts, New York, since 1978. Visiting Instructor in Photography, International Center of Photography, New York, 1980. **Agent:** Marcuse Pfeifer Gallery, 568 Broadway Avenue, Suite 102, New York, New York 10012, U.S.A. **Address:** 212 East 14th Street, New York, New York 10003, U.S.A.

Individual Exhibitions:

1971	Floating Foundation of Photography, New York
1976	Schoelkopf Gallery, New York
	Enjay Gallery, Boston
1977	Galerie Zabriskie, Paris
	Marcuse Pfeifer Gallery, New York

Catskill Center of Photography, Woodstock, New York
    (travelled to the Port Washington Library, New York; and
    Wisconsin Art Center, Madison)
1978   831 Gallery, Birmingham, Michigan
    Fredericksburg Gallery of Modern Art, Virginia
    Quidacqua Ltd., Washington, D.C.
    Gilbert Gallery, Chicago
    Christian Vogt/Lilo Raymond, Focus Gallery, San Francisco
    Camera Obscura, Stockholm
1979   Equivalents, Seattle
    University of Texas, Dallas
    Jeb Gallery, Providence, Rhode Island
    Art Ringger/Lilo Raymond, Nikon Gallery, Zurich
    Stephen White Gallery, Los Angeles
    Kamp Gallery, St. Louis
    Focus Gallery, San Francisco
1980   Kamp Gallery, St. Louis
    Drew University, Madison, New Jersey
    Equivalents Gallery, Seattle, Washington
    University of Dallas, Texas
    Jeb Gallery, Providence, Rhode Island
    Nikon Galerie, Zurich
1981   Visions Gallery, London
    Kamp Gallery, St. Louis
1982   Photography West Gallery, Carmel, California
    Galerie Nei Licht, Luxembourg
1983   Marcuse Pfeifer Gallery, New York
    Maine Photographic Workshop, Rockport
    Silver Image Gallery, Seattle, Washington
    Photographer's Gallery, Palo Alto, California
    Photogalerie Der Compagnie, Hamburg
1984   Arkansas Art Center, Little Rock
    Orange Coast College, Costa Mesa, California
1986   Galerie Esperanza, Montreal

Selected Group Exhibitions:

1971   *Festival of Women,* University of Toronto
1972   *Festival d'Avignon,* France
1974   *Women Look at Women,* Floating Foundation of Photography,
    New York
1976   *The Still Life in Photography,* Helios Gallery, New York
1977   *Photographs: Sheldon Memorial Art Gallery Collection,*
    University of Nebraska, Lincoln
1981   *Sixth Anniversary Exhibition,* The Alternative Museum,
    New York
1983   *Twentieth-Century Photography,* Jayne H. Baum Gallery,
    New York

Collections:

Museum of Modern Art, New York; Metropolitan Museum of Art, New York; New Orleans Museum of Art; St. Louis Museum of Art; University of Nebraska, Lincoln; Bibliothèque Nationale, Paris.

Publications:

By RAYMOND: Book—*Lilo Raymond,* portfolio, New York 1976; *A Portfolio of Six,* New York 1981.

On RAYMOND: Books—*The Craft of Photography* by David Vestal, New York 1975; *The Magic Image* by Cecil Beaton and Gail Buckland, London and Boston 1975. Articles—"Lilo Raymond" in *Popular Photography Annual,* New York 1964, 1967, 1968, 1971; "Lilo Raymond" in *U.S. Camera Annual,* New York 1964, 1967, 1970, 1971; "Lilo Raymond: Portfolio" in *35mm Photography* (New York), Winter 1975; review by Hilton Kramer in the *New York Times,* 15 April 1977; "Acrobatics vs. Pastoral Poetry" by Gene Thornton in the *New York Times,* 24 April 1977; "Poems of Order and Intimacy" by Alexandrea Anderson in the *Village Voice* (New York), 9 May

1977; "Lilo Raymond: Gravure Portfolio" by Alicia Wille in *Popular Photography* (New York), July 1977; "Photography: Focusing on the Posed and the Unposed" by Alfred Frankenstein in the *San Francisco Chronicle,* 4 November 1978; "Lilo Raymond: Photographs" by Ted D'Arms in *The Weekly* (Seattle), 21-27 February 1979.

*

My subjects are human in scale, the quieter evidences of people. These are objects people make or put someplace. God makes apples and vegetables, which I love, but I know that I like them because they have something to do with people.

Days with incredible light are like a gift. On a day when the light is right I will photograph God knows what. I prefer inanimate objects, because I can look at what the light is doing, and I am not confused by human beings who move or talk to me.

When you print a photograph you want to get back what you saw. You didn't see it in that glaring light. Film is so contrasty, whereas your eye isn't. That's how my addiction to various forms of backlight and sidelight started. And my photographic experiments led me also to a real awareness of the differences in effects between strong back or sidelight and a milder variety. The latter often occurred when the sun was covered by a light layer of clouds. Then the lighting was still directional, but softer and more subtle rather than harsh.

Later on came an even more intense involvement with light as I started exploring the delight of tone in photographing *things* in my world. The interesting thing about such non-people pictures is that light tends to be an even more important force in the creation of strong images. Take my backlighted shot of a melon on a windowsill. Then consider the importance of that backlight, and how different the effect would have been with even lighting, or with the main light source to one side or somewhere in front.

That melon picture is part of a series on windows, shot from inside and out, that I am still involved with. At this writing, however, the aspect that intrigues me especially is how light from the sun strikes one or more panes of glass to create a dramatic glare.

The longer I work for this kind of delight of tone, the easier I find it is to pre-visualize the effect I want on the print and get it. When I'm kidding around with students, I sometimes say fliply that after a while you begin to see pictures you can print. But, to put this more seriously, there tends eventually to be a closer rapport between your seeing before shooting and the possibilities on the final print. This is because you have learned the limitations of film and paper and have taken them into account ahead of time. And, as a general rule, experienced photographers do this almost automatically.

Good techniques are, of course, essential. Most of the time it pays to use a good lens shade with backlight and sidelight, and to shoot a lot of film of the same subject.

There is so much gross and technical ability necessary initially in the other art forms that are not necessary in photography. I could teach anyone in a few hours how to take a picture, develop it, contact it, and print it—but that is only the beginning. From my experience, photography gets hard after the first five years. Five years are joy, and then it really begins to be hell. When you know more, you begin to demand more of yourself. You take the same picture, and perhaps the ratio of better pictures you take is higher than it was when you started, but what can and must improve is technique.

—Lilo Raymond

*   *   *

Lilo Raymond's photographs convey an insistent stillness. They are exquisitely controlled pictures whose quiet surfaces belie a tension that strains almost to bursting. It is this tension that keeps them from being merely romantic and makes the images transcend their apparent simplicity. Her concern with order, with a simplified and ordered universe, comes from her past and is the motivation in her art. She photographs with intimacy everyday objects usually in an ordinary room illuminated by extraordinary light. "The way I remember incidents or what people have said, is by the setting and the room and the light." Her formalism appeals to painters and in fact she admits to being much more influenced by them than by photographers.

Her still life pictures bring to mind paintings by Cezanne or Braque. The objects she chooses are almost always found the way she photographs them. She relishes the search rather than the manufacture of her images. She is searching for a moment from her childhood when all was well in the world and light streamed in at the window. This was a time before the light exploded and security was torn to pieces by war.

Lilo Raymond is a survivor. She was born in Germany in 1922 to a father who was a Nazi and fought with Rommel and a mother who was Jewish. In 1939 her mother gathered up her two daughters and brought them to America where she supported them by working as a professional tennis player. Raymond did many different things before she found herself in photography. She taught tennis for a time, was an artist's model for Hans Hofmann among others, and was also a waitress in Helen Gee's Limelight Cafe. Finally in her late thirties she turned her full attention to the art in which she is now recognized.

She uses the simplest tools and materials: a 35mm Nikon camera, even though most of her work is still life, and ordinary Polycontrast paper. She gets the most out of her materials, and although her prints vary somewhat according to her mood (''I'm not an automaton''), it is feeling she wants to convey rather than mechanical perfectionism. Light becomes the subject in those images that Hilton Kramer calls her ''white pictures,'' and her subtle printing conveys this appropriately. Because so many of her pictures are painterly, she uses the texture and grain of the prints to advantage.

Since her first major exhibition at The Marcuse Pfeifer Gallery in New York in 1977, Lilo Raymond's photographs have been shown all over the United States and in several European countries. Her work has received critical acclaim everywhere it has been shown.

—John Esten

REAS, Paul.

Nationality: British. **Born:** Bradford, Yorkshire 14 February, 1955. **Education:** Studied at Newport School of Art. **Family:** Married Jane Reas, 1980; son, Tom. **Career:** Since 1988 has been visiting Lecturer at West Surrey College of Art and Design; Trent Polytechnic; Newport College of Art and Design (Documentary Photography); Kent Institute; Royal College of Art; LCP; Stockport College of Art; National Museum of Photography, Bradford. Presently Senior Lecturer in Photography, Editorial Photography Department Brighton University. **Recipient:** Photographers Gallery, London, Bursary, 1987; Vigo Visions, Vigo, Spain, 1990; Arts Council of Great Britain, Publication Award, 1992; ICI Fox Talbot Award Nominee, 1992; The Andy Sproxton Memorial Award, 1993. **Agent:** Network Photographers, 3-4 Kirby Street, London, EC1N 8TS, England. **Address:** 9E Palmeira Avenue, Hove, East Sussex, BN3 3GA, England.

Individual Exhibitions:

1988   Photographers Gallery, London
        Olympus Gallery, Amsterdam
        Fotobienal, Vigo, Spain
1993   Photographers Gallery, London
        Cornerhouse, Manchester, England

Selected Group Exhibitions:

1987   *Young European Photographers,* Frankfurter Kunstverein,
            Frankfurt, Germany
1989   *Fotobienale,* Enschede, Netherlands
        Through the Looking Glass, British Photography 1945-89,
            Barbican Art Gallery, London
        Condemned to Making Sense, Perspektief Gallery, Netherlands
        The Globe, Impressions Gallery, York, England

1990   *Vigo Visions,* Vigo, Spain
1992   *ICI Awards,* The National Museum of Photography, Bradford,
            England
        Arles Rencontre, Arles, France
1993   *Documentary Dilemmas,* British Council (touring exhibition)
        Positive Lives, Photographers Gallery, London (toured)
1994   *Who's Looking at the Family?* Barbican Art Gallery, London
        Positive View, Saatchi Gallery, London
        Foto International, Foto Institute, Rotterdam, Netherlands

Publications:

By REAS: Books—*I Can Help,* Manchester 1988; *Flogging a Dead Horse,* Manchester 1993. **Catalogues**—*Towards a Bigger Picture, British Photography,* New York 1988; *Through the Looking Glass, British Photography 1945-89,* 1989; *Positive Lives,* London 1993; *Documentary Dilemmas,* 1993; *Who's Looking at the Family,* London, 1994; *Dream of England,* Manchester 1994. **Articles**—Creative Camera, no 8 1986; *Ten 8 Magazine,* 1987; *Foto Magazine,* Netherlands 1988; *Aperture,* New York, No 113 1988; *Perspektief,* Netherlands 1988; *Vis a Vis,* France, No 9 1990; *Creative Camera,* London 1994. **Broadcasts**—*The Late Show,* BBC2 TV, 1992; *Kaleidescope,* BBC Radio 4, 1993.

*   *   *

Paul Reas has become one of the ambassadors for the new force of British documentray photography. Working with consistent commitment to political and social ideals Paul has imposed a rigorous creative discipline on his work that balances wit, humour and intellect in the service of serious communication.

While many commentators have been impressed with the style of Paul's photography, his primary committment has always been to the subjects of his work rather than the technique of representation, even while recognising the two are inextricably linked. Paul's photography is a means to an end, not an end in itself. Often choosing his subjects and broad social issues such as the consumer culture, the romantic distortion of history and current sociopolitical obsessions, Paul's talent is to express complex themes through the lives and circumstances of individuals. With an uncanny knack of finding moments in everyday life that reflect the wider mores, Paul constructs sharp commentaries that reveal original thought in original imagery. It is a rare talent indeed that makes critical comment on people's social conditions without making a mockery of the individuals in each frame. There are few cheap laughs in his pictures.

Paul does nothing without careful thought—whether it be choosing a subject, refining the appropriate technique or editing the exposed film. Seemingly casual observations take on greater weight when one appreciates that the frame reveals more than the immediately visible: very litttle is shown by accident, and Paul demands as much of the viewer as he does of himself in understanding the significance of what is seen. However pleased he may be with the formal qualities of an image he will not hesitate to remove it if it could be open to abuse by the viewer. His colleagues were startled when he shelved an expensive project on ''sexploitation'' because he felt that the people in the pictures could become objects of titillation and ridicule. (The pictures remain on file and it is hoped that a constructive use may be found for them in the future.)

Subsequent projects have taken an introspective turn, wrestling with the emotional consequences of social abuse. In 1993 Paul worked with Rupert Haselden, a man with AIDS living in the expectation of an early death; in a collaborative excercise Paul produced a convincing photographic realisation of Rupert's emotional history. In 1994 Paul looked into himself to begin a painful exploration of his relationship with his father and produced an eloquent evocation of a life-time's confusion and conflict. Raw nerves were exposed and taboo subjects broached in a manner that once again touched on common experiences beyond the immediately personal.

Although widely published in the United Kingdom and Europe (with a client list that includes many leading titles and a growing advertising folio) such work does not have a ready editorial context and his significant exposure will probably continue to be in galleries.

—Stephen Mayes

Dickensian Christmas, **from the book** *Flogging a Dead Horse,* **1993 (original in colour). Photograph by Paul Reas.**

REICHMANN, Vilém.

Nationality: Czechoslovakian. **Born:** Brno, 25 April 1908. **Education:** Attended primary and vocational school in Brno; studied architecture, Higher Polytechnic, Brno, 1926-31, Dip.Arch. 1931; self-taught in photography, from 1940. **Military Service:** Served in the German Army, 1942-45: prisoner-of-war, and member of the prison camp anti-fascist committee, Ordzhonikidzeabad, U.S.S.R., 1943-45. **Family:** Married Rudolfina Zukalová in 1933. **Career:** Worked as a teacher at vocational schools in Moravia, 1931-39; employee of the Building Office, Brno, 1939-42; active as anti-fascist cartoonist (under the pseudonym "Jappy") for the left-wing press, Brno, 1939-42; independent painter, exhibiting with the RA artists' group, Brno, 1945-68. Since 1945, freelance photographer, concentrating on macrophotography, and cartoonist, Brno. **Recipient:** City of Brno Prize, 1959; Artist Emeritus Award, Czechoslovakia, 1968; Award of Excellence, Fédération Internationale des Artistes Photographes, 1972. Honorary Associate, Fédération Internationale des Artistes Photographes; Czechoslovakian Union of Photographers. **Died:** (in Brno) 15 June 1991.

Individual Exhibitions:

1959	*Poetry and Life,* House of the Lords of Kunštát, Brno, Czechoslovakia
1960	Little Gallery, Neudeggergasse, Vienna
1964	*Uncommon Day,* Local History Museum, Prostějov, Czechoslovakia
1967	*Uncommon Day,* House of Culture, Ostrava, Czechoslovakia
	Cultural Centre, Frankfurt, West Germany
	Kunstverein, Marburg, West Germany
1968	Little Gallery of Czechoslovak Writers, Prague
	Recent Photographs, House of the Lords of Kunštát, Brno, Czechoslovakia
1969	State Castle, Gottwaldov, Czechoslovakia
1970	*Macrophotographs,* Little Gallery on Česká Street, Brno, Czechoslovakia
	Medallion of Vilém Reichmann, Museum of Hradec Králové, Czechoslovakia
1971	Gallery Profile, Bratislava, Czechoslovakia
1974	*Metamorphoses,* Trade Unions House, Blansko, Czechoslovakia
1975	*Metamorphoses,* State Castle, Uherský Brod, Czechoslovakia
1977	Galerie Schweinebraden, East Berlin

1979	*From Nearby,* Blansko Castle, Czechoslovakia
	Galerie Berlin, East Berlin
1981	*Makroterie,* Minigallery Vúvel, Brno, Czechoslovakia
	Tabularia, Club on Křenová Street, Brno, Czechoslovakia
1982	*Macrophotographs,* Music Theatre, Olomouc, Czechoslovakia
1983	*Message of Trees and Agave,* Galerie OKS, Uherský Brod, Czechoslovakia
	The Gallery, Česká Třebová, Czechoslovakia
	House of the Lords of Kunštát, Brno, Czechoslovakia
1984	*Selected Macrophotographs,* Theatre Foyer, Cěský Těšìn, Czechoslovakia
	Galerie SČF, Česká Lìpa, Czechoslovakia
	Macrophotographs, Galerie Spectrum Plzeň, Czechoslovakia
	Scene, SKN Theatre Foyer, Prague
1985	*Grafogramy,* ÚJEP (university) Gallery, Brno, Czechoslovakia
1986	*Grafogramy* Gallery Upstairs, Cěské Budějovice, Czechoslovakia
	Tabularia, The Gallery, Třebìč, Czechoslovakia
	Hibernalie, The Gallery, Sovinec, Czechoslovakia
1987	*Close-up,* Small Gallery, Liberec, Czechoslovakia
1988	Prague Municipal Gallery, Old Town Hall, Prague
	Fotofest, Žďár nad Sázavou, Czechoslovakia
1989	Museum Bochum, Bochum, Germany
1990	Museum moderner Kunst, Vienna
	San Francisco Museum of Modern Art, San Francisco
	Old Town Hall, Brno, Czechoslovakia
	Jacques Baruch Gallery, Chicago
1992	Galerie Neumann, Düsseldorf, Germany
	Prague House of Photography, Prague

Selected Group Exhibitions:

1947	*Skupina RA,* Brno, Prague and Budapest
	Modern Photography in Czechoslovakia, Zurich (travelled to Vienna)
1966	*AICA: Actual Tendencies in Czechoslovak Photography,* Mánes Gallery, Prague
1967	*Surrealism and Photography,* Museum Folkwang, Essen, West Germany
1970	*Cien Garbados y Cien Fotografias Checoslovaquia,* Mexico City
1973	*Lyrical Tendencies in Czechoslovak Photography,* House of the Lords of Kunštát, Brno, Czechoslovakia (travelled to Prague and Milan)
1982	*Aktualnì Fotografie,* Moravian Gallery, Brno, Czechoslovakia
1983	*Surrealist and Imaginative Painting in Czechoslovakia,* Galerie 1900/2000, Paris
1984	*Czech Photography 1918-1938,* Museum Folkwang, Essen, Germany (travelled to Frankfurt and Vienna)
	Aspects of Czechoslovak Photography, Thackrey and Robertson Gallery, San Francisco
	Facets of Collection: Czechoslovak Photography, San Francisco Museum of Modern Art, San Francisco
1986	*Czech Photography,* Komorná galeia fotografie, Bratislava, Czechoslovakia
	Body in Czechoslovak Photography 1900-1986, Museum Kroměřížska, Kroměříž, Czechoslovakia
1987	*Topical Photography 2—Moment,* Moravian Gallery, Brno, Czechoslovakia
	The Implicit Image, San Francisco Museum of Modern Art, San Francisco
1988	*Town,* The House of Art, Brno, Czechoslovakia
	Group Ra, Prague Municipal Gallery, Dům U kamenného zvonu, Prague
1989	*Contemporary Czechoslovak Photography,* Holland Foto 89, Nieuwe Kerk, Amsterdam
	Roads of Czechoslovak Photography, Prague Municipal Gallery, Dům U kamenného zvonu, Prague
	Czechoslovak Photography 1945-1989, Valdštejnská jízdárna, Prague

	Czech Modernism 1900-1945, The Museum of Fine Arts, Houston; International Center of Photography, New York; Akron Art Museum, Akron
1990	*Czechoslovak Photography Today,* Museum Ludwig, Cologne (travelled to Erlangen, Germany; Metz, France; Luxembourg; Strasbourg, France; Odense, Denmark; Freiburg, Germany; Barcelona, Spain; Waldkreiburg, Germany; Lawrence, Kansas, and Dallas, Texas)
	Progressive Photography in Czechoslovakia, Galerie Robert Doisnea, Vandouvre-les-Nancy, France (travelled to Müllheim, Germany, and Strasbourg, France)
	Das innere der Sicht, Museum moderner Kunst, Vienna
	Czech Avant-Garde, RIP, Arles, France
1992	*Photography from Czechoslovakia from the 1930s and 1940s,* Galerie Carla Stützer, Cologne
1993	*Czech and Slovak Photography from Between the Wars to the Present,* Fitchburg Art Museum, Massachusetts (travelled to Boston and Middlebury)

Collections:

Moravian Gallery, Brno, Czechoslovakia; Aleš Gallery of South Bohemia, Hluboká, Czechoslovakia; Museum Sztuki, Lódz, Poland; Museum Folkwang, Essen, Germany; San Francisco Museum of Modern Art; Museum of Decorative Arts, Prague; Museum of Art, Olomouc, Czechoslovakia; Museum moderner Kunst, Vienna; Paul Getty Museum, Malibu; Victoria and Albert Museum, London; Robert Koch Gallery, San Francisco; Howard Greenberg Gallery, New York; The Navigator Foundation, Boston.

Publications:

By REICHMANN: Books—*Kunštátské aklordy,* with text by Ludvìk Kundera, Brno, Czechoslovakia 1966; *Valaška Suita,* with K.O. Hrubý and J. Tomeček, Brno, Czechoslovakia 1966; *Brno,* with K.O. Hrubý and M. Budik, text by Vladimír Burian, Brno, Czechoslovakia 1968: *Pod Pálavou,* with text by Jaromìr Tomeček. Prague 1970; *Řeka Morava,* with text by Helena Lisická, Prague 1976; *Jižni Morava,* with K.O. Hruby, Prague 1977; *Northy Moravia,* with text by J. Strnadel, Prague 1980; *Raněné město,* portfolio, with text by Antonìn Dufek, Brno, Czechoslovakia 1985; *Vysočina Viléma Reichmanna,* Prague, 1988. **Articles**—''The Author on his Work'' in *Revue Fotografie* (Prague), no. 9, 1959; ''About Artistic Photography of Things'' in *Revue Fotografie* (Prague), no. 2, 1962; ''Vilém Reichmann Speaking'' in *Československá Fotografie* (Prague), no. 5, 1963; ''About Photography: This Time Otherwise,'' interview, in *Československá fotografie* (Prague), no. 7, 1965; ''About Sudek's Work'' in *Československá fotografie* (Prague), no. 1, 1966; ''From Vilém Reichmann's Creative Workshop'' in *Československá fotografie* (Prague), no. 4, 1975; ''Vilém Reichmann-Quasiautomatický text'' in *Revue Fotografie* (Prague) No 1, 1992.

On REICHMANN: Books—*Licht und Schatten/Light and Shadow,* edited by Milos Hrbas, Prague 1959; *Vilém Reichmann: Cykly,* with text by Václav Zykmund, Prague, 1961; *Geschichte der Fotografie im 20. Jahrhundert/ Photography in the 20th Century* by Petr Tausk, Cologne 1977, London 1980; *Aktualnì Fotografie,* exhibition catalogue by Antonin Dufek, Brno, Czechoslovakia 1982; *Museum Folkwang: die Fotografischè Sammlung,* exhibition catalogue with introduction by Ute Eskildsen, Essen, West Germany 1983; *Vilém Reichmann: Portfolio,* with text by Alena Šlachtová, Prague, 1985; *Vilém Reichmann,* by Bronislava Gabrielová, Brno 1988; *Vilém Reichmann* with text by Antonín Dufek, Prague 1988; *Vilém Reichmann* with texts by A Dufek, L Kundera, Z Primus and P Spielmann, Berlin, 1989; *Dictionnaire de surrealisme* by René Passeron, Paris 1979; *Les mysteres de la chambre noire* by Edouard Jaguer, Paris, 1982; *Černobílá fotografie,* by Antonín Dufek, Prague, 1987; *Dejiny fotografie* by Ludovít Hlaváč, Martin 1987; *Cesty československé fotografie* by Daniela Mrázková and Vladimír Remeš, Prague 1989; *Tschechoslowakische Fotografie der Gegenwart,* by Vladimír Birgus, Heidelberg 1990. **Articles**—''Vilém Reichmann'' by Jiñ Jenìcek in *Fotografie* (Leipzig), no. 12, 1958; ''The Poet of Photo Cycles'' by Ludvik Kundera in *Die Galerie* (Vienna), no. 5, 1958; ''Photographic Metaphor'' by Václav Zykmund in *Fine Arts* (Prague), no. 5, 1959; ''Imaginary Interview with Vilém Reichmann'' by Ján Raum in *Science and Life* (Brno, Czechoslovakia), no. 3, 1976; "Photographer and Poet" by Adolf Kroupa in *Fine Arts, Photography, Film* (Bratislava, Czechoslovakia), no. 3, 1980; "Poetry of Everday Life" by Antonìn Dufek in *Revue Fotografie* (Prague), no. 2, 1983; "Zasloužilý umělec Vilém Reichmann jubíluje" by Bronislava Gabrielová in *Československá fotografie* (Prague) no 4, 1983; "Fotografie a folkalky skupiny Ra" by Vladimír Birgus in *Revue Fotografie* (Prague) no 4, 1989.

*   *   *

Surrealism has been an important influence on the development of modern Czechoslovak photography for the period between both World Wars and up to the present day. In a land long steeped in legend and fairy tale, the Surrealist movement found fertile soil. It is notable that Sigmund Freud, scientific precursor of the Surrealists, was born in Pribor (now a town in Czechoslovakia), and that the fantasy painter Guiseppe Arcimboldo worked for several years in the Prague court of Rudolph II. An inherited feeling for the surreal may then logically be found in several forms in the works of several generations of Czechoslovak photographers—even if used unintentionally or subconsiously. Following the contributions in the 1930s of such classic masters as Jaromir Funke, Josef Sudek, Jindrich Styrsky and Frantisek Vobecky, a new generation began to appear in 1945, of which the most accomplished was Vilém Reichmann.

A mid-generation artist born in 1908, his early artistic experience was in architecture and caricature drawings; Reichmann's photographic career began by chance after receiving his first camera in the 1940s as a gift from a Jewish friend departing for a concentration camp. It was as a consequence of the last battles of World War 2 that Reichmann's first important series of photographs came about. In the town of Brno where he lived, he found a lot of haphazard and surreal juxtapositions among the rubble of the war-damaged town. His sensitive art-trained eye was well prepared for such events as the fortuitous *objet trouvé*, and thus his marvellous and powerful photo series entitled *Wounded City* was created.

In common with many surrealist artists, Reichmann was fascinated by country fairs. Amidst the simple booths with their naive posters and props, he felt the overwhelming surge of mysterious and only half-consciously perceived forces at work. His series on fairs was followed by images of unusual cemetery sculptures carved by anonymous stone-masons, and another series on chance juxtapositions occuring in nature. Two tree stumps resemble gossiping girl friends, and rock formations become the skull of some nightmarish beast. Photography reinforced Reichmann's ability to recognize the metaphorical in everyday life, allowing him to communicate his peculiar observations directly to a broad audience.

By the time he had become well-known for his *objet trouvé* photographs, Reichmann had already turned his camera onto the minutiae of the world, discovering in the surface textures of quite small objects an apparently hidden world. He now penetrated this secret universe through the technique of macrophotography. In the holes and crevices among the leaves of an agave plant, for instance, he discovered arrangements which offered remarkable patterns of a quite surreal character when enlarged in the darkroom.

Through the use of relatively straight photography, Reichmann's work is strongly characteristic of the long traditions of Czechoslovakian culture and sensibility—a sensibility based on the interpretation of a subtle poetry of everyday life.

—Petr Tausk

REISEWITZ, Wolfgang.

Nationality: German. **Born:** Thionville (Lothringen, France) 9 September, 1917. **Education:** Apprenticed in commerce, 1936. **Military Service:** Soldier in German Army 1937-45; wounded and taken captive by Russians in 1945. **Family:** Married 1955; daughter: Petra. **Career:** Gained mastership in photography in Munich, 1948, also taking part in first postwar exhibition in Germany. Started working in his father's photographic studio in 1949. Founder member of "fotoform" group. Took over family business, then taught at Staatliche Werkkunstschule, Mainz, 1963. Member DGPh 1971;

Professor of Visual Communications at Fachhochschule des Landes Rheinland-Pfalz; retired 1979. **Recipient:** Second prize, International Photo Exhibition, Rio de Janeiro, 1949; Gold Medal, Belgrade, 1952; Belgian State Prize, 1955; also won many awards in group shows. **Address:** Westring 169, 55120-Mainz, Germany.

Selected Group Exhibitions:

1943-47   Concours Amsterdam; Zaragoza, Spain; Rovaniemi, Finland;]Melbourne, Australia
1948   *Die Fotografie,* Germany
1949   *Photographic Art,* Rio de Janeiro, Brazil
1950   Photokina, Cologne, Germany
1951   Photokina, Cologne, Germany
1952   *I Medunarobna Izlozba Fotografske Umetnosti,* Belgrade, Yugoslavia
1954   Photokina, Cologne, Germany
1955   *Photo 57,* Focus-Salon, Amsterdam
1969   Roubaix, France
1970   Photokina, Cologne, Germany
1980   Photokina, Cologne, Germany

Collections:

Museum Folkwang, Essen, Germany; Victoria and Albert Museum, London; Foto-Historama, Leverkusen, Germany; Museum für Kunst und Gewerbe, Hamburg, Germany; Preussischer Kulturbesitz, Berlin; Bayerische Staatslehranstalt, Munich, Germany.

Publications:

On REISEWITZ: Books—*Encyclopédie International des Photographes 1839-1983,* Paris 1983; *DGPh-Mitgliederverzeichnis,* Germany 1988. **Articles**—*Gebrauchsgraphik,* Germany, No. 9, 1950; *Photorama,* Belgium, No. 11, 1953; *Photorama,* Belgium, No. 23, 1955.

*

I seek through photography to express and give the best definition to my vision while taking care more especially of the rendering of forms, structures and backgrounds . . . of objects.

—Wolfgang Reisewitz

*   *   *

Reisewitz has had a long career but for me he is the photographer of a special moment—the late 1940s. He exemplified the ambitions of "Subjektive Fotografie." The exhibitions and catalogues produced under this title, guided by Dr Otto Steinert, were a brave attempt to revive the Bauhaus spirit in hard times—to insist that non-utilitarian efforts in photography were worthwhile, that imagination could address new subjects with new subjectivities. As a young man, Reisewitz experimented with subtle kinds of montage and negative printing to create a new mix of reality and imagination. Perhaps his early masterpiece is *Glockenzug* or *Hanging the Bells* (1949), which is illustrated here. The subject is acutely symbolic—for the original bells of the 13th-century Evangelical Stifts-kirche in Neustadt (Weinstrasse, Rheinland-Pfalz) were melted down during the Second World War for munitions. Reisewitz photographed the raising of the new bells in 1949. He recalled in 1994, in correspondence with the present writer, that he made two exposures of the raising of the bells. The time was about 5 pm and the exposures were separated by an interval of ten minutes. He placed the two negatives side by side, one of them flipped over, and copied the montage onto transparency film before producing a negative print. His complex image takes some elucidation, because at first sight we appear to be looking at the facade of a church: close analysis reveals that Reisewitz photographed the bell rising at the side of the building. The time interval resulted in different positions for the new bell as it ascended to its home in the church tower. The cast of spectators in the foreground also changed in the ten minute interval. The negative print

Glockenzug, **1949.** Photograph by Wolfgang Reisewitz.

brightens the bells and deepens the mystery of this new space visualised by Wolfgang Reisewitz. *Glockenzug* was shown in many exhibitions around the world during the 1950s.

—Mark Haworth-Booth

REQUILLART, Bruno.

Nationality: French. **Born:** Marcq en Baroeul, 30 December 1947. **Education:** Attended the Pension Saint Joseph, Arras, France, 1955-62; Ecole Superieure de Publicité, Tournai, Belgium, 1962-69. Began photographing in 1968; full-time freelance photographer, Paris, 1969-1979; concentrated on painting, Paris, since 1979. **Recipient:** Prix des Communautées Européenes, *Photokina,* Cologne, 1968; Grand Prix, *Festival d'Arles,* 1976; Fellowship, Fondation Nationale de la Photographie, Lyons, 1980; Fellowship, Ministry of Culture, Paris, 1985. **Agents:** Zabriskie Gallery, 29 West 57th Street, New York, New York 10019, U.S.A.; and 37 rue Quincampoix, 75004 Paris, France. **Address:** 16 rue Bezout, 75014 Paris, France.

Individual Exhibitions:

1970	Auditorium Mail, Brussels
1975	Galleria Il Diaframma, Milan
1976	13 x 15 Gallery, St. Louis
	Photographs by Linda Benedict-Jones and Bruno, Photographic Gallery, University of Southampton
	3 Jeunes Photographes: Bruno, Kalvar, Plossu, Centre Georges Pompidou, Paris (toured France, Spain, Czechoslovakia and Poland)
1977	Galerie Fiolet, Amsterdam
1978	Centre Georges Pompidou, Paris
	Galerie Zabriskie, Paris
1979	Zabriskie Gallery, New York
1982	Massachusetts Institute of Technology, Cambridge (with Deborah Turbeville)
1986	*Photos 1972-79,* Palais de Tokio, Paris

Selected Group Exhibitions:

1968	*Photokina '68,* Cologne
1973	*Séquences et Conséquences,* Musée d'Art Moderne de la Ville, Paris
1975	*4 Photographes,* Bibliothèque Nationale, Paris (with Descamps, Plossu, and Kuligowski)
1976	*Rencontres Internationales de la Photographie,* Arles, France
1977	*French Photographers,* San Francisco Art Institute (also shown at Camerawork Gallery, San Francisco)
1978	*Junge Franzosische Photographen,* University of Kreuzberg, Berlin
1980	*Triennale Internationale de Photographie,* Charleroi, Belgium
1981	*Des Photographies dans le Paysage,* Galerie de France, Paris
1982	*Versailles, palais d'images 1852-1982,* Grand Palais, Paris
1984	*La Photographie Créative,* Pavillon des Arts, Paris

Collections:

Bibliothèque Nationale, Paris; Musée d'Art Moderne, Paris; Centre Georges Pompidou, Paris; Musée Réattu, Arles, France; Musée Cantini, Marseilles; Fondation Nationale de la Photographie, Lyons; Polaroid Collection, Amsterdam; Stedelijk Museum, Amsterdam; Southampton University, Hampshire, England.

Publications:

On REQUILLART: Books—*3 Jeune Photographes,* exhibition catalogue, by Pierre de Fenoel, Paris 1976; *Photographie Actuelle en France,* edited by Carole Naggar, Jean-Claude Lemagny and others, Paris 1976; *Jeune Photographes Francais,* exhibition catalogue, by M. Schmidt, Berlin 1978; *Histoire de la Photographie Francaise* by Claude Nori, Paris 1979; *Triennale Internationale de Photographie,* exhibition catalogue, by Jean-Claude Lemagny, Charleroi, Belgium 1980; *La Photographie Créative,* edited by Jean-Claude Lemagny, Paris 1984; *Siderations: l'atelier photographique francais* by Barnard Lamarche-Vadel, Paris 1985. **Articles**—"Bruno: From February to April" in *Creative Camera* (London), January 1975; "Bruno" in *Nueva Lente* (Barcelona), May 1976; "Bruno: La Photographie n'a pas de Sens" by Arnaud Claass in *Zoom* (Paris), November/December 1976; "Bruno" in *Creative Camera Yearbook 1978,* edited by Colin Osman and Peter Turner, London 1978; "Versailles" by Michel Nuridsany in *Light Vision* (Melbourne), November 1978; "Le photo sans filtre" by Jean-Claude Lemagny in *Révolution* (Paris), October 1984. **Film**—*Droit de Cité: Bruno Requillart,* television film, by Jean Brard, 1976.

*

Since 1979 I have devoted myself entirely to painting, attempting to portray the *human face,* which I have never succeeded in photographing to my satisfaction. This, of all subjects, is the most important.

Photography today seems to me like a series of "notes on day-to-day life," though paradoxically I have *never seen* (in its entirety) what I was photographing. While walking I have been captivated by the grouping of objects (and how they strike the eye), I have been captivated by open spaces, and by sensations. And I have tried to reproduce them while playing on the ambivalence of concreteness and abstraction.

Painting takes the same route, but in reverse! The starting point is abstract (the act of painting, colour, brushstroke) and, proceeding from abstraction to abstraction, I attempt to retain a "limited figuration." (In photography, on the other hand, I started out from concrete reality with the purpose of making it abstract.)

This is the point at which I find myself today: full of uncertainty.

—Bruno Requillart

*   *   *

By his own admission, Bruno Requillart was initially attracted to reportage, then quickly realized that the photos he obtained were inadequate representations of the events he thought he had photographed. He realized, too, that he was not interested in "covering" events, that his real interest was in inventing images. He was one of the first young French photographers to break away from reportage in order to search for a more personal, more immediate reality.

Bruno, as he is familiarly called, is an exacting and concerned photographer. So much so that he was even questioned whether he was right to choose photography as a means of expression. "Whether we like it or not," he says, "photography is always documentary. Yet, when I invent images, I do so by distorting reality." Bruno has not exhibited or published any new images for several years; he has allowed his negatives and contact plates to accumulate, and he has printed nothing.

Since 1968 Bruno has been adept at imposing an original vision in immediately recognizable images that have earned him great respect in international photographic circles. Despite that success, he chose to stand back, to regard his own work objectively. He came to feel that that which produced such strength in his images was a danger to him; he wanted to find a more spontaneous and less reflective method, to rediscover the freer vision of the amateur. The man who has always photographed motionless objects began to take pictures through the windscreen of a moving car. None of this new work has been seen.

Bruno assures us, however, that his new pictures, despite a different approach, will show the same formal characteristics. Preoccupied above all with space and sensations in space, he has gone in a direction diametrically opposed to reportage. He has chosen not the platitudes of graphic composition, but is striving for a unifying atmosphere. He balances values and sensations.

He works with a rather strong grain in order to unify space and suppress detail. Photography for him is still a distortion of reality and a search for balance within this distortion. He looks for movement in immobility, that is, the translation of subjective variations in space.

—Jean-François Chevrier

RESNICK, Marcia (Aylene).

Nationality: American. **Born:** Brooklyn, New York, in 1950. **Education:** Studied at the Cooper Union School of Art, New York, B.F.A. 1972, and California Institute of Arts, Valencia, 1972-73, M.F.A. 1973. **Career:** Freelance photographer, California and New York, since 1973. Instructor in Photography, International Center of Photography, New York, 1977. **Recipient:** National Endownment for the Arts grant, 1975, 1978. **Address:** 530 Canal Street, New York, New York 10013, U.S.A.

Individual Exhibitions:

1977	Lightworks Gallery, New York
1978	Chicago Center for Contemporary Photography (with Larry Williams)

Selected Group Exhibitions:

1977	*Outside the City Limits,* Trope Intermedia Gallery, Spark Hill, New York
	The Extended Frame, Visual Studies Workshop, Rochester, New York
1978	*Punk Art,* Washington Project for the Arts, Washington, D.C.
	Book Art, Art Institute of Chicago
1979	*Kunst als Photographie 1879-1979,* Tiroler Landesmuseum Ferdinandeum, Innsbruck, Austria (travelled to the Neue Galerie am Wolfgang Gurlitt Museum, Linz, Austria; Neue Galerie am Landesmuseum Joanneum, Graz, Austria; Museum des 20. Jahrhunderts, Vienna)
1981	*Photos der 70er Jahre,* Galerie Wilde, Cologne
1982	*Target III: In Sequence,* Museum of Fine Arts, Houston, Texas

Collections:

Museum of Modern Art, New York; International Museum of Photography, George Eastman House, Rochester, New York; Visual Studies Workshop, Rochester, New York; Chicago Center for Contemporary Photography.

Publications:

By RESNICK: Books—*See,* New York 1975; *Tahitian Eve,* New York 1975; *Landscape,* New York 1975; *Landscape-Loftscape,* New York 1977; *Re-Visions,* New York 1977, Toronto 1978. **Article**—"Marcia Resnick: An Interview," with Alex Sweetman, in *Exposure* (New York), Summer 1978.

On RESNICK: Books—*Women on Women,* with an introduction by Katharine Holabird, New York 1978; *Photographie als Kunst 1879-1979/Kunst als Photographie 1949-1979,* exhibition catalogue, 2 vols., by Peter Weiermair, Innsbruck, Austria 1979; *Target III: In Sequence,* exhibition catalogue, by Anne W. Tucker and Leroy Searle, Houston, Texas 1982; *Private Viewing: Contemporary Erotic Photography,* edited by Terry Jones, with introduction by Jack Schofield, London 1983. **Articles**—"Marcia Resnick: Pop-Up People" in *Photography Year 1974,* by the Time-Life editors, New York 1974; "The Layered Eye; Painted Photographs by Marcia Resnick" in *Camera 35* (New York), July 1974.

*   *   *

The general terms used to describe photographers don't work very well with Marcia Resnick. Resnick is a photojournalist and a narrative photographer, she works with sequenced photographs, incorporates text with images, and attempts to document a community. But, Marcia Resnick is better described with terms from outside photography. She is a punk, a bit of a voyeur and, most simply, an artist.

Her work consciously crosses borders. Her serious art photographs are most easily seen in mass circulation newspapers and magazines. Her favorite medium is the artist's book, and her favorite trick (and perhaps the most heretical thing she does) is to be funny.

Resnick sees herself as an iconoclast. Consciously rebelling against the domination of the single image, her first works were three conceptually oriented books: *See, Tahitian Eve,* and *Landscape.* These books used repeating compositions in which only a few elements changed. *See,* for instance, has 35 photographs of people with their backs to the camera, surveying the landscape. The book is a somewhat precious attempt to examine the act of seeing.

Resnick explains that she was frustrated by the limited audience for this type of artist's book, and by the "incestuousness" of the art photography community in general. Her next project, a more elaborate book entitled *Re-Visions,* effectively added an amusing narrative to make the book more accessible.

Re-Visions, an extended self-portrait, is a story of the photographer as an adolescent, anxiously discovering her own sexuality and abandoning her innocent pleasures. Resnick uses a young girl as a model throughout the book, posing her in obviously staged scenes, with appropriate props. Each picture is faced with a single sentence text. A picture of the girl lying on the floor with her dress flying up to cover her face is accompanied by the text: "When her mother first noticed a red stain on her panties and roared, 'You're a woman now,' she promptly fainted." Unlike so many ponderous and formal exercises relating sequences of images, *Re-Visions* is a funny and entirely delightful book. Functioning much like a short novel, the book perceptively explores archetypical adolescent anxieties in a manner that is engrossing and remarkably easy to read.

When she had finished *Re-Visions,* Resnick began working on her current project, *Bad Boys: Punks, Poets, and Politicians.* Resnick describes this project as the "great love work of men" which she undertook because "it was the subject I understood least." *Bad Boys* is a series of informal portraits of "men who look like men, men who look like women, and women who look like men." Many of the "boys" are prominent figures in the New York underground art/music scene: Brian Eno, Diego Cortez, Andy Warhol and others.

Individual photographs from *Bad Boys* have been widely published in magazines and newspapers, a perfect medium for the gossipy tone of the project. Taken as a whole *Bad Boys* is an intelligent look at those outside the system. Resnick, the inconoclast, has found the perfect subject for her talents.

—Ken Winokur

REXROTH, Nancy (Louise).

Nationality: American. **Born:** Washington, D.C., 27 June 1946. **Education:** Wakefield High School, Arlington, Virginia, 1960-64; Marietta College, Ohio, 1964-65; studied English, American University, Washington, D.C., 1965-69, B.F.A. 1969; studied photography, Ohio University, Athens, 1969-71, M.F.A. 1971. **Career:** Freelance photographer, from 1971; also professional massage therapist, since 1985. Instructor, Ohio University, Lancaster, 1975-76; Assistant Professor, Antioch College, Yellow Springs, Ohio, 1977-79. Assistant Professor, Wright State University, Dayton, Ohio, 1979-82. **Address:** 2631 Clearview Avenue, Cincinnati, Ohio 45206, U.S.A.

Individual Exhibitions:

1971	Putnam Street Gallery, Athens, Ohio
1973	Corcoran Gallery of Art, Washington, D.C.
1974	Jefferson Place Gallery, Washington, D.C.

1975	Light Gallery, New York
	Antioch College, Yellow Springs, Ohio
1977	Light Gallery, New York
1978	Silver Image Gallery, Columbus, Ohio
	Grapestake Gallery, San Francisco
1979	Catskill Center for Photography, Woodstock, New York
	Northern Kentucky University, Highland Heights
1980	Light Gallery, New York
1981	Camerawork, San Francisco
1982	Center for Creative Photography, University of Arizona, Tucson

Selected Group Exhibitions:

1973	*New Images: 1939-1973,* Smithsonian Institution, Washington, D.C.
1976	*The Snapshot . . . Then and Now,* Focus Gallery, San Francisco
	Contemporary Photography, Halsted 831 Gallery, Birmingham, Michigan
1979	*Fleeting Gestures: Dance Photographs,* International Center of Photography, New York (travelled to The Photographers' Gallery, London, and to *Venezia '79*)
	Attitudes: Photography in the 1970s, Santa Barbara Museum of Art, California
1980	*The Contemporary Platinotype,* Rochester Institute of Technology, New York
	The Diana Show, Friends of Photography Gallery, Carmel, California
1982	*Color as Form,* International Museum of Photography at George Eastman House, Rochester, New York
1983	*One of a Kind,* Lawrence Miller Gallery, New York
1984	*La Photographie Créative,* Pavillon des Arts, Paris

Collections:

Museum of Modern Art, New York; University of Massachusetts, Amherst; Smithsonian Institution, Washington, D.C.; Library of Congress, Washington, D.C.; Corcoran Gallery of Art, Washington, D.C.; Center for Creative Photography, University of Arizona, Tucson; Santa Barbara Museum of Art, California; Washington State Art Consortium, Seattle; Bibliothèque Nationale, Paris; Houston Museum of Fine Arts, Texas.

Publications:

By REXROTH: Books—*Iowa,* with an introduction by Mark Power, New York 1976; *The Platinotype 1977,* pamphlet, New York 1977.

On REXROTH: Books—*The Snapshot,* edited by Jonathan Green, Rochester, New York 1975; *Photography* by Phil Davis, Dubuque, Iowa 1975; *The Criticism of Photography* by Hugh Davies, Amherst, Massachusetts 1978; *130 Years of Ohio Photography* by Budd Bishop, Columbus, Ohio 1978; *Diana and Nikon* by Janet Malcolm, Boston 1979; *Attitudes: Photography in the 1970s,* exhibition catalogue, by Fred R. Parker, Santa Barbara, California 1979; *The Platinum Print* by John Hafey and Tom Shillea, with an introduction by Marianne Fulton Margolis, Rochester, New York 1979; *The Diana Show,* exhibition catalogue, by David Featherstone, Carmel, California 1980; *Presences: The Figure and Man-Made Environments* by Bruce Sheftel, New York 1980; *Color as Form: A History of Color Photography,* exhibition catalogue, with introduction by Robert A. Sobieszek, Rochester, New York 1982; *La Photographie Créative* by Jean-Claude Lemagny, Paris 1984; *American Photography: A Critical History, 1945 to the Present* by Jonathan Green, New York 1984. **Article**—"The Intimate Visions of Nancy Rexroth and JoAnn Frank" by A.D. Coleman in *Camera 35* (New York), April 1978.

*

My book was called *Iowa*—about dreams, memories . . . the Midwest. . . . Peter Pan said she would never grow up, never grow up. It took six years to make the book, but the photographs came with such ease. A camera that floats. My wishes.

Then it was the "SX-70 Transfer," the process that got harder to do, and there was a lot of illness over five years or so. Isolation. And photography up and gone . . . studied massage for two years, and now earn my living this way. Photography can't be "gone." Hold close again; you were always the *only* one.

—Nancy Rexroth

*　　*　　*

It has been said, often enough and in various ways, that the power of the camera resides in its ability perfectly to delineate visual reality. The "problem" with such statements is that the history of photography has given us too many powerful images which do nothing of the sort. Some photographs make no attempt whatsoever to limn the lines of real objects. Their purpose has little to do with imparting information or describing something. In these photographs, we are not being asked to measure the dimensions of reality, but to enter into a conspiracy, a willing suspension of visual disbelief, and to give up our normal preferences for visual clarity. Various techniques, from very simple to extremely complex, are used to create these images. We often think of them as "mysterious" in some way or another, but only because we have been taught to hold 20/20 vision as superior to any other kind of vision.

The power of art to provoke a conscious recognition of particular feeling or understanding in a viewer resides at least partly in how effectively the artist has used the tools at his disposal. When the tools are simple, basic, or even primitive, the artist's task is all the greater. Obviously, photography requires tools of a very modern nature, and the effectiveness of a photograph cannot wholly be separated from the appropriateness of the techniques used to make it. However, given the particular photograph, the techniques themselves are totally unimportant.

At the beginning of her career, Nancy Rexroth worked with a cheap plastic camera called the "Diana." It was made in Hong Kong, cost a couple of dollars, and is now no longer available. With this camera, Ms. Rexroth made an extensive series of photographs based on two assumptions: a) that a photograph of one specific place could actually be "about" another quite different place, and b) that it was possible consciously to infuse a photograph with a manifest sense of nostalgia. The Diana camera was a tool whose simplicity and primitiveness worked towards destroying most of those elements in a photographic image that we normally think of as "photographic." Its plastic lens vignetted the picture edge, softened focus and contrast, and forced us to imagine in the image about as much detail as was actually given to us. In her book *Iowa*—many of whose images were made in Ohio—Ms. Rexroth wrote that her Diana photographs often appear to her "like something you might faintly see in the background of a photograph." The suggestion in this is that the prominent elements of a family snapshot, when seen many years after its making, have no greater importance for us than the partly hidden, out-of-focus details in the background. Anyone who has looked at old snapshots of his family or himself knows this to be true.

A sense of place is at the core of childhood, which is why a smell, a certain kind of light, the corner of a building—or almost anything—can create a strong feeling of nostalgia in us many years after we have left a place. Ms. Rexroth's "Iowa" photographs evoke those same feelings. Oddly enough, with the super cameras available to us today, we have in a sense forgotten how to see simply, and have consequently become more interested in what a photograph expresses about the medium of photography than in what it expresses about the world. Ms. Rexroth's "simple" photographs tell us a personal "document" need not document anything that is visibly recognizable, and that, occasionally, photography can express visually what the emotions can only hint at.

—Derek Bennett

RIBOUD, Marc.

Nationality: French. **Born:** Lyon, 24 June 1923. **Education:** Attended secondary schools in Lyon; studied engineering at the Ecole Centrale, Lyons, 1945-48, Dip. Ing. 1948; self-taught in photography. **Military Service:** Served with the French Resistance and the Free French Army, 1943-45: Croix de Guerre, 1945. **Family:** Married the artist Barbara Chase (i.e., Barbara Chase-Riboud) in 1961; children: David and Alexis; married the writer Catherine Chaine in 1982; children; Clémence and Théo. Worked as an industrial engineer, in Lyon, 1948-52. **Career:** Freelance photographer and photojournalist, Paris, since 1953. Member, Magnum Photos Inc., Paris and New York, 1953-79: Vice-President, Paris, 1958-75; President, Paris and New York, 1975-76; Chairman of the Board, Paris and New York, 1976-77. **Recipient:** Overseas Press Club Award, New York, 1967, 1970. **Agent:** Galerie Agathe Gaillard, 3 rue du Pont-Louis-Philippe, 75004 Paris, France. **Address:** 3 rue Auguste-Comte, 75006 Paris, France.

Individual Exhibitions:

1963	Art Institute of Chicago
1966	*The Three Banners of China,* Asia House, New York (travelled to the Institute of Contemporary Arts, London, and Galerie Delpire, Paris, 1967)
1974	*Jean-Philippe Charbonnier/Marc Riboud: Reporters-Photographes,* French Institute, Stockholm
1975	International Center of Photography, New York (retrospective; travelled to *Rencontres Internationales de la Photographie,* Arles, France, 1976; The Photographers' Gallery, London, and Galerie Chateau d'Eau, Toulouse, 1977; the Galerie Agathe Gaillard, Paris, 1978)
1981	*China,* The Photographers Gallery, New York (travelled to Galerie Delpire, Paris, The Photographers' Gallery, London, Galerie Le Trepied, Geneva, and FNAC Galerie, Lyons)
1984	*Homage à Marc Riboud,* Centre d'Action Culturelle, Angouleme, France
1985	Musée d'Art Moderne de la Ville, Paris (retrospective) *Photographes photographiés,* Musée Nicéphore Niepce, Châlon-sur-Saone, France

Selected Group Exhibitions:

1957	*Salon National de la Photographie,* Bibliothèque Nationale, Paris (and 1959)
1972	*Behind the Great Wall,* Metropolitan Museum of Art, New York
1973	*The Concerned Photographer II,* Israel Museum, Jerusalem (toured Europe) *Israel 25th Anniversary Exhibition,* Jerusalem
1974	*Celebrations,* Hayden Gallery, Massachusetts Institute of Technology, Cambridge
1977	*Concerning Photography,* The Photographers' Gallery, London (travelled to the Spectro Workshop, Newcastle-upon-Tyne)
1980	*The Imaginary Photo Museum,* Kunsthalle, Cologne
1981	*French Photographers,* Zabriskie Gallery, New York
1983	*Il Reportage Fotografico nelle Guerre Contemporanee,* Palazzo Fortuny, Venice
1984	*Sammlung Gruber,* Museum Ludwig, Cologne

Collections:

Bibliothèque Nationale, Paris; Victoria and Albert Museum, London; Museum of Modern Art, New York; Metropolitan Museum of Art, New York; Art Institute of Chicago; Musée d'Art Moderne de la Ville de Paris; Museum Ludwig, Cologne.

Publications:

By RIBOUD: Books—*Women of Japan,* with text by Christine Arnothy, Amsterdam and London 1959; *Les 3 Bannieres de la Chine/The Three Banners of China,* Paris, London and New York 1966; *The Face of North Vietnam,* New York 1970; *Bangkok,* with text by William Warren, New York, London, Tokyo and Hong Kong 1972; *Instantanés de Voyages Chine,* Paris 1980, as *Visions of China,* New York, 1981.

On RIBOUD: Books—*Photography Today,* edited by Norman Hall, London 1957; *The Concerned Photographer II,* edited by Cornell Capa, New York and London 1972; *Behind the Great Wall of China,* edited by Cornell Capa, with an introduction by Weston J. Naef, New York 1972; *Jean-Philippe Charbonnier/ Marc Riboud: Reporters-Photographes,* exhibition catalogue, Stockholm 1974; *The Magic Image* by Cecil Beaton and Gail Buckland, London and Boston 1975; *Celebrations,* edited by Minor White, Cambridge, Massachusetts and Millerton, New York 1974; *Concerning Photography,* exhibition catalogue, by Jonathan Bayer and others, London 1977; *Geschichte der Fotografie im 20. Jahrhundert/Photography in the 20th Century* by Petr Tausk, Cologne 1977, London 1980; *Voyons Voir: 8 Photographes,* edited by Pierre Borhan, Paris 1980; *The Imaginary Photo Museum* by Helmut Gernsheim, Renate and L. Fritz Gruber and others, Cologne 1981, London 1982; *The Library of World Photography: Landscape,* with texts by David Plowden and Ian Jeffrey, Tokyo and London 1984; *Sammlung Gruber: Photographie des 20. Jahrhunderts,* exhibition catalogue, with foreword by Siegfried Gohr, Cologne 1984; *After the War Was Over,* with introduction by Mary Blume, London 1985. **Articles**—"A Collection of Photographs" in *Aperture* (Rochester, New York), Fall 1969; "Marc Riboud" in *Photography Annual,* New York 1970; "Marc Riboud: Gesichter aus Nord-Vietnam" in *Du* (Zurich), June 1970; "Les Nouveaux Chinois" in *Photo* (Paris), December 1971; "Marc Riboud" in *Modern Photography Annual,* New York 1972; "Power to All Our Friends: Photographs by Marc Riboud, with text by David Caute, in the *Sunday Times Magazine* (London), 10 March 1974; "Marc Riboud: Les Nouveaux Chinois" in *Photo* (Paris), October 1980.

* * *

Marc Riboud makes stunningly beautiful pictures—of land, harbors, cities—that are given an urgency because of the people he sees making these worlds come to life. Riboud saturates a picture. Many of his pictures are filled with five or six areas of activity, the viewer's eye pulled, pushed and drawn in as many directions. In one picture he took of a harbor in China in 1965, the viewer's eye slips over the bend of a man's body as the man hauls a boat to shore from the sea, but does so as if it were caressing, not just seeing, the man. But the scene is more complex. For the viewer's eye suddenly skips over to the woman next to the man. Every part of her body, from an outstretched hand to her foot straining from the haul, writhes as if it were crying out in a bloodless shriek. Meanwhile, the visual organization takes the viewer's eye in a contrary direction, against the lyrical swell and into details—like that tiny outstretched hand—that work against the smooth caresses of a lyrical flow. Riboud gives us visually and emotionally complex pictures, many filled with both smoothly lyrical and explosively furious components. He points to the complex and varying ways that a world takes shape, while his pictures tell us the world comes to life—with all of its beauty, hope and despair—because of the design and shape people give it. His passion for people dominates.

It is possible to analyze Riboud's photographs on formalist principles alone. His use of color in a color photograph is magnificent, both in its expression of contrasting hues and in his expression of the range of tones in any one color. Similarly, his black-and-white photographs, as in a terraced hillside (in China, as many of his best photos are), carry that same infinite expression of tones. His compositions are often filled with soaring shapes and minute sensibilities—as in a picture of a group in a rice paddy; while his use of a sharply isolated figure or an angularly paced object—like a hoe—often darts into a lyrical space to challenge a picture's dominant order only to spur the viewers's eye into new circles, new points of interest, new tonalities and new figures not seen on the first go-around. His control of light and shapes within a given space are of the first order.

But it is the excitement he generates by making those principles work that makes these pictures so powerful—and what those principles reveal that makes his pictures so exciting. Worlds come to life because his pictures are packed with people walking, thinking and doing. They have the lilt of a man walking, the querulousness of a woman lifting her eyebrow, and the passion and fury of young people gathered in a city square. He turns color, form and shape into their servants.

Color, for instance, is conceived as a shape, but a shape that allows the viewer to see the people who have created the picture's momentum. In a photograph of a demonstration in China we see a band of red sweep across the top half of the picture. Irregularly toned—as if it were a banner waving in the wind—it receives, in effect, the jagged edge of the people below who are marching. More than just seeing color as a shape, he sees it mobilized by the people who have mobilized the picture. Sometimes he runs through every tone of blue, green, grey, mauve and brown—in one picture—as in a terraced hillside that lets the hill gracefully unfold behind the foreground figures, making the viewer marvel at such minute gradations of tone. A farmer and his bull—those foreground figures—contain most of those tones, but in the process of registering them more boldly, though solemnly, Riboud heightens the hillside's majesty, the foreground figures themselves heighten the hill's infinite capacities.

It's that capacity to run formal and substantive matter into each other so intricately that one speaks with the voice of the other that mark Riboud's pictures. Add to that his utter and complete control of form and color, and we are given a rare insight into the way people mirror and shape their worlds.

His black-and-white photographs often play on the same control of an expression of an infinite range of tonalities—did we ever know that grey could have so many tones . . . or that it could be so sensual? In a photograph he took in Peking in 1965, looking out of a shop window (the accompanying photo), he organizes the picture plane into six different units, each a complete entity—in tones of grey—at the same time it is joined to the others. Each person in the picture is looking, walking, bending, standing in a distinct fashion, different from the others, while the viewer is treated to a multiplicity of life and forms.

For, finally, Riboud's photographs let us see the many faces, configurations, shades, intensities, hues and desires that are human. Ushering us into magnificently conceived worlds of colors, shapes and movements, Riboud penetrates a static world to let us see the many, minute sensibilities that people develop; and the way that multiplicity—both formal and substantive—develop a power to reveal what we have never before seen.

—Judith Mara Gutman

RICCIARDI, Mirella.

Nationality: Kenyan. **Born:** Mirella Rocco in Kenya in 1933. **Education:** Educated in Kenyan schools; studied photography as an assistant photographer Harry Meerson, Paris, 1953-55. **Family:** Married Lorenzo Ricciardi in 1959; has 2 daughters. **Career:** Freelance photographer, Kenya and London, since 1955. **Address:** 25 Holmead Road, London, SW6, England.

Individual Exhibitions:

1971   Time-Life Building, London
1972   Snack Gallery, Paris
        Nikon Gallery, New York
1973   Tryon Gallery, London
1982   *African Saga,* Olympus Gallery, London

Selected Group Exhibitions:

1972   *Photokina 72,* Cologne

Publications:

By RICCIARDI: Books—*Vanishing Africa,* New York and London 1971, 1974; *The Voyage of the Mir-El-Lah,* with text by Lorenzo Ricciardi, London 1980; *African Saga,* London 1982; *African Rainbow,* with text by Lorenzo Ricciardi, New York, 1989; *Vanishing Amazon,* with text by Mirella Ricciardi and Marcus Colchester, New York, 1991.

On RICCIARDI: Articles—"Women Photographed by Women" in *Photokina 72: Bilder und Texte,* exhibition catalogue, by L. Fritz Gruber, Cologne 1972; "Les Perles Noires de Mirella Ricciardi" in *Photo* (Paris), January 1972; "Mirella Ricciardi: Fashion Photographs" in the *Daily Telegraph Magazine* (London), 23 August 1974; "The wild life of a woman in love with adventure" by Shaun Usher in the *Daily Mail* (London), 26 March 1982.

*

Photography is a democratic art, and most practitioners have fairly ordinary backgrounds. Mirella Ricciardi's is, in contrast, extremely exotic. Her grandfather founded the Panama Canal. Her mother was a pupil of Rodin. She was born and brought up in Kenya, near Lake Naivasha, because this was where her father crashed his plane. She grew up as Miss Rocco, not Ricciardi, and learned her trade in Paris, working as an assistant to the French photographer Harry Meerson, before returning to Africa.

Meanwhile Lorenzo Ricciardi was travelling round the world making films (he'd been an assistant to Fellini and played the part of Christ in the film *Ben Hur*) and was in Kenya to film the flamingoes of Lake Nakuru. In a nightclub he saw a set of prints hung up over the bar: Mirella's pictures. He phoned her, met, wooed and married her, and they had two daughters.

The pictures were of Maasai and Samburu warriors, and they not only impressed Lorenzo, they also impressed a publisher, who coughed up a cheque. Mirella left the children with her parents, bought a Toyota landcruiser, and set off with her sister and Kimuyu (her safari boy) to photograph the "vanishing tribes" of Kenya.

The resulting book, *Vanishing Africa,* was published in 1971 and reprinted in 1972, 1973, 1977 and 1978, as well as being revised in 1974. The pictures were exhibited in London, Paris and New York. Mirella Ricciardi became, on the publication of the book a star almost overnight. She was young, beautiful (she still is), had enjoyed an exotic upbringing, and produced a book full of stylish, graceful and striking photographs. It all combined to make her, in a way, irresistible. However, it hardly equipped her for the often dull and repetitive work of being a commercial photographer in London for such publishers as Condé Nast.

The next major production was her husband's. He fulfilled a dream of sailing a dhow from the Arabian Gulf down the coast of East Africa—like some modern Sinbad. He called the boat Mir-El-Lah (after her, but making it sound Arabic), and she photographed the voyage for the resulting book, with somewhat uneven results.

Recently she has divided her time between London and Los Angeles, photographing colour stories, fashion and beauty for magazines such as *Brides, Beauty* and *Vogue,* photographing Pavarotti for *Life* magazine, and shooting for movies like *Green Ice.* She can throw herself into such jobs with the kind of intensity that only her kind of larger-than-life character can sustain. But do the jobs reciprocate?

None of them can subsitute for the Edenic Kenya of her childhood before the Second World War. That Africa of noble warriors and shy but beautiful young girls full of natural grace was the Africa she embraced—made love to—through her camera, and, like her childhood, it has vanished. However, some unpublished colour photographs of great delicacy, taken through the mists of dawn from a native boat on an isolated South American lake, suggests that a primitive, elemental setting could again provide the natural resonance in response to her artless photography that would raise it once again to the heights reached in *Vanishing Africa.*

—Jack Schofield

*   *   *

Mirella remembers: "Photography became my means of expression and I owe many of the important incidents of my life to it. I was 26 when Lorenzo entered my life." Lorenzo Ricciardi instilled in Mirella the insatiable thirst for travel and to publish the results of their joint ventures. In 1987 they were the first to cross Africa by boat—a 6,000 km voyage from the Indian Ocean to the Atlantic, an undertaking sponsored by the National Geographic Magazine. *African Rainbow,* published in 1989, contains the fascinating story in words and pictures, the latter all monochrome unfortunately. Photographically speaking this is not as great a book as *Vanishing Amazon,* with 150 colour plates which appeared two years later with text by Marcus Colchester, an anthropologist, who replaced Lorenzo Ricciardi on this expedition. Superb, intimate pictures of tribal life, landscape, fauna and plants—the perfect companion volume to Mirella's first publication, *Vanishing Africa,* 1971, of which the *Times Literary Supplement,* wrote: "This volume heralds the arrival of a new photographer of exceptional talent and loving perception."

—Helmut Gernsheim

RICE, Leland.

Nationality: American. **Born:** Los Angeles, California, in 1940. **Education:** Studied at Arizona State University, Tempe, 1960-64, B.S. 1964; Chouinard Art Institute, Los Angeles, 1965; San Francisco State College, 1966-68, M.A. 1968; also attended photography workshops under Oliver Gagliani, Ruth Bernhard, and Paul Caponigro. **Career:** Independent photographer, San Francisco, then Los Angeles, since 1968. Founder Member, with Judy Dater, Jack Welpott and others, Visual Dialogue Foundation, San Francisco, 1968-73. Assistant Professor, California College of Arts and Crafts, Oakland, 1969-72; Lecturer in Art, University of California at Los Angeles, 1972; Co-ordinator and Instructor, U.C.L.A. Extension, 1973-76; Lecturer in Art and Curator of the Photography Gallery, Pomona College, Claremont, California, 1973-79. Professor of Photography, University of Southern California, Los Angeles, since 1980. Trustee, Los Angeles Institute of Contemporary Art; Trustee, Friends of Photography, Carmel, California; Member of the Council, Center for Southern California Studies in the Visual Arts, Los Angeles. **Recipient:** National Endowment for the Arts grant, 1978; Guggenheim Photography Fellowship, 1979. **Address:** P.O. Box 4100, Inglewood, California 90309, U.S.A.

Individual Exhibitions:

1973	Witkin Gallery, New York
1976	Visual Studies Workshop, Rochester, New York
	Tyler School of Art, Philadelphia
	Jack Glenn Gallery, Newport Beach, California
1977	Diane Brown Gallery, Washington, D.C.
	Witkin Gallery, New York
	The Photographic Work of Leland Rice, Hirshhorn Museum, Washington, D.C.
	Orange Coast College, Costa Mesa, California
1978	University of Southern California, Los Angeles
1979	Diane Brown Gallery, Washington, D.C.
	Rosamund Felsen Gallery, Washington, D.C.
	University of Rhode Island, Kingston
1980	Grapestake Gallery, San Francisco
1987	San Francisco Museum of Modern Art

Selected Group Exhibitions:

1966	*Urban Reality,* SPUR, San Francisco
1968	*Young Photographers,* University of New Mexico, Albuquerque
1969	*Vision and Expression,* International Museum of Photography, George Eastman House, Rochester, New York
1970	*California Photographers 1970,* University of California at Davis (travelled to the Oakland Museum, California; Pasadena Art Museum, California)
1976	*Exposing: Photographic Definitions,* Los Angeles Institute of Contemporary Art
1978	*The Photograph as Artifice,* California State University at Fullerton
1980	*Spectrum: New Directions in Color Photography,* University of Hawaii, Honolulu
1981	*Californian Colour,* The Photographers' Gallery, London
1982	*Color as Form,* International Museum of Photography at George Eastman House, Rochester, New York

1984	*Photography in California 1945-80,* San Francisco Museum of Modern Art (travelled to the Akron Art Museum, Ohio; Corcoran Gallery, Washington, D.C.; Los Angeles Municipal Art Gallery; Cornell University, Ithaca, New York; High Museum of Art, Atlanta, Georgia; Museum Folkwang, Essen; Centre Georges Pompidou, Paris; Museum of Photographic Arts, San Diego, California)

Collections:

Museum of Modern Art, New York; Metropolitan Museum of Art, New York; International Museum of Photography, George Eastman House, Rochester, New York; Fogg Art Museum, Harvard University, Cambridge, Massachusetts; Art Institute of Chicago; Center for Creative Photography, University of Arizona, Tucson; Los Angeles Institute of Contemporary Art; San Francisco Museum of Modern Art; National Gallery of Canada, Ottawa; Bibliothèque Nationale, Paris.

Publications:

By RICE: Book—*The Photographs of Moholy-Nagy from the William Larson Collection,* exhibition catalogue, with David W. Steadman, Claremont, California 1975.

On RICE: Books—*Young Photographers,* exhibition catalogue, by Van Deren Coke, Albuquerque, New Mexico 1968; *Vision and Expression* by Nathan Lyons, New York 1969; *California Photographers 1970,* exhibition catalogue, by Fred R. Parker, Davis, California 1970; *Photography in America,* edited by Robert Doty, with an introduction by Minor White, New York 1974; *Photographers' Choice,* edited by Kelly Wise, Danbury, New Hampshire 1975; *The Photographic Work of Leland Rice,* exhibition catalogue, with text by Charles W. Millard, Washington, D.C. 1977; *Mirrors and Windows: American Photography since 1960* by John Szarkowski, New York 1978; *The Photograph Collector's Guide* by Lee D. Witkin and Barbara London, Boston and London 1979; *Spectrum: New Directions in Color Photography,* exhibition catalogue, by Donna Nakao, Honolulu 1980; *Californian Colour,* exhibition catalogue, by Sue Davies, Avery Danziger and James Hugunin, London 1981; *Color as Form: A History of Color Photography,* exhibition catalogue, with introduction by Robert A. Sobieszek, Rochester, New York 1982; *Studio Work: Photographs by Ten Los Angeles Artists,* exhibition portfolio, with text by Kathleen M. Gauss, Los Angeles 1982; *Photography in California 1945-1980* by Louise Katzman, San Francisco 1984. **Articles**—"Kasten and Rice" by M.T. Wortz in *Artweek* (Oakland, California), 23 March 1974; "Enigmatic Portraits of Places" in *Photography Year 1978,* by the Time-Life editors, New York 1978.

*   *   *

In writing of Leland Rice's work, Charles Millard has said that it brings together "what seem to be the most disparate strands of contemporary photography into successful—and increasingly abstract—images." Millard is referring to the unlikely reconciliation of strains of abstraction, surrealism and pictorialism with the large-camera format and zone-system pre-visualization favored by the "straight" photography approach.

Rice's photographs, even when they are most minimal in terms of subject, exhibit a surreal inflection. The evocative quality of the commonplace rather than the manipulated interests Rice and is always created from photographic means—the way space can be used or the camera angled—rather than by oddities of subject matter, as in the work of Diane Arbus. In the early 1970s Rice created distortions through unexpected camera angles and spatial disjunctures by juxtaposing large areas of extreme value contrast.

Rice has also re-translated means derived from orthodox surrealism into ends that are purely photographic. Concurrent with a series of "overripe" and "decadent" portraits taken in extravagantly patterned and object-filled settings, Rice produced a series of "portraits" of unoccupied chairs. The use of furniture to evoke the human presence and animate space, seen commonly in surrealist painting such as that of René Magritte, created a haunting and eerie result. A series which Rice termed "Wall Sites"—interiors "inhabited" by various objects individually or in groups—depended on the same effect. In

1976 the sites gave way to bare interiors or fragments of interiors which often included nearly abstract patches of plaster.

A second concern of Rice's work is the continuing development of his formal means. In reference to this, Millard has written of Rice that ''one is struck by how rapidly he has moved toward broader effects of tone and scale and how painterly his work is, without in any way becoming unphotographic.'' Rice's photography has become increasingly abstract and minimal, stripped progressively of its apparent subject matter but increased dramatically in visual strength. Experimentation with color, which Rice began in 1977, is the most recent development increasing the range of his formalist concerns.

—Nancy Hall-Duncan

RICHON, Olivier.

Nationality: Swiss. **Born:** Lausanne, 12 September 1956; resident in London since 1976. **Education:** Studied film and photographic arts at School of Communication, Polytechnic of Central London, B.A. (honors), 1980, and M.Phil., 1988. **Career:** Worked as Associate Lecturer in photographic studies at Derbyshire College of Higher Education, 1985-91; Senior Lecturer and Course Leader in M.A. photographic studies at University of Derby, England, 1992; Senior Lecturer in the theory and criticism of photography, and Course Leader for M.A. photographic studies at School of Communication, University of Westminster, London, 1993. **Agents:** Samia Saouma, 16 Rue des Coutures, St Gervais, 75003 Paris, France; Jack Shainman, 560 Broadway, New York, New York 10012, U.S.A. **Address:** 18 Rossetti House, London, W1N 5LX, England.

Individual Exhibitions:

1984	Institute of Contemporary Arts, London
1985	Cash/Newhouse, New York
1986	Galerie Samia Saouma, Paris
1987	Galerie Samia Saouma, Paris
1989	Jack Shainman Gallery, New York
	Galerie Samia Saouma, Paris
1990	Jack Shainman Gallery, New York
	Galerie Samia Saouma, Paris
	Lawrence Olivier, Philadelphia
1991	Espace d'Art Contemporain, Lausanne, Switzerland
1992	Galerie des Beaux Arts, Nantes, France
	University Gallery, Essex, England
	Galerie Samia Saouma, Paris
1993	Jack Shainman Gallery, New York
	Galerie de l'Aquarium, Valenciennes, France

Selected Group Exhibitions:

1983	*Beyond the Purloined Image,* Riverside Studios, London
1987	*The Analytical Theatre, New Art from Britain,* Independent Curators Inc., New York
1988	*Presi & Incantamento, La Nuova Fotografia Internazionale,* Padiglione di Arte Contemporanea, Milan, Italy
1989	*Photo Triennale,* Esslingen, Germany
1990	*Images in Transition, Photographic Representation in the '80s,* National Museum of Modern Art, Kyoto and Tokyo, Japan
1993	*Dïskurse der Bilder,* Kunsthistorisches Museum, Vienna

Collections:

Arts Council of Great Britain; Victoria and Albert Museum, London; Cabinet des Estampes, Geneva, Switzerland; Musée de l'Elysée, Lausanne, Switzerland; Brooklyn Museum, New York; Musée d'Art Moderne de la Ville de Paris; Fonds Regionale d'Art Contemporain, Bretagne, France; National Gallery of Modern Art, Kyoto, Japan; Fonds Regionale d'Art Contemporain, Loire, France; Collection da la Ville de Paris; Kunstring, Folkwang, Essen, Germany.

Publications:

By RICHON: Books—*Representation, The Despot, The Harem, in Europe and its Others,* Vol 1., edited by F.Barker, University of Essex, England 1985; *Other Than Itself; Writing Photography,* co-edited with John X. Berger, Cornerhouse Publications 1989. **Articles**—''The Academy'' in *Camera Austria 25* 1988; ''The Imageless Temple'' in *Block 15,* Middlesex Polytechnic (UK), 1989; ''A Devouring Eye'' in *Camera Austria 37,* 1991; ''The Hunt: On the Sophist, Uccello, Animality'' in *Public,* No.6 (Toronto), 1992; ''Orality, Anality, Photography'' in *Fragmente,* No. 41, University of Kassel (Germany), 1993

On RICHON: Books—*Framing Feminism; Beyond the Purloined Image* by Mary Kelly, London 1987; *Visual And Other Pleasures; Magnificent Obsession* by Laura Mulvey, London 1989; *Thinking Art, Beyond Traditional Aesthetics: Mimesis and Abjection* by Michael Newman, edited by P.Osborne, London 1991. **Articles**—''Beyond the Purloined Image'' by Jean Fisher in *Artforum,* December 1983; ''The Analytical Theatre'' by Maureen Bloomfield in *Artforum,* October 1987; ''Imitatio Sapiens'' by Denis Baudier in *Artpress* (France), November 1990; ''A Devouring Eye'' by Olivier Zahm in *Flash Art,* November 1990; ''Et in Arcadia'' by Giorgio Verzotti in *Artforum,* October 1992; ''After D.L.'' by Richard Vine in *Art in America,* May 1994.

*   *   *

We are tolerably well acquainted, by now, with the business of staged photography. By contrast with such things as the documentary, which is supposed to tell the truth, staged photography tells no more than somebody's truth. The business of staging events for the camera goes back at least as far as Hippolyte Bayard's wonderful self-portrait as a drowned man in 1841, even if one excludes the still-earlier composed still lifes of Fox Talbot or Daguerre. Oliver Richon is at first sight a practitioner in this long and distinguished tradition, a photographer who sets things up that we might see them rather than one who goes into the world or the laboratory to report on how they are. Yet we quickly find that Richon's pictures, while quite obviously pregnant with meanings, refuse to yield single cononical readings. We can look and look and never be quite sure that we have understood any final point from these elusive and very complex weavings of culture. We can never confidently distill an image of Richon's into words: they remain images, with all the flashing uncertainty that implies. There is no doubt that Olivier Richon has done this on purpose. Where we are used to unravelling a puzzle and finding something like an answer, in Richon's work the unravelling itself is the pleasure of the picture. His pictures are not there as vessels carrying some idea or pattern of ideas from him to us. Richon says that he regards the ideas behind the making of a photograph as scaffolding, to be removed once the thing itself is built. Which means that however well-disposed, however moved by a particular image, we have no way of recreating with certainty the pattern of thought that gave rise to it. This makes Richon an exceptionally non-communicative photographer. Confronted by his pictures we find ourselves thinking—but we will not be thinking his thoughts.

Richon works in series of photographs, not normally very numerous. Like many photographers, he feels that he has worked in colour since before colour was entirely respectable. He works relatively slowly. It is noticeable that he has recently been using fewer elements in each series, refining them and tautening them. He uses quite astonishing varieties of cultural references in his work, not pompously to deploy his considerable erudition, but rather playfully acknowledging that the full range of previous thought is material for him and for us. Art history is perhaps the lode he mines most easily: his series *Imitatio Sapiens* of 1989 in which a monkey both contemplates and is part of a series of tableaux taken from pre-existing pictures seems to have been started by Chardin's picture of a monkey dressed and equipped as the painter. He will, however, quite happily expect us to dive into deeper waters after him, too. His recent

Imitatio Sapiens, After Joseph Wright of Derby, **1989.** Photograph by Olivier Richon.

series, *After Diogenes Laertius* expects the viewer at the very least to know that certain Greek philosophers are known only by fragments quoted by later authors. That may be too strong: a viewer who did not know would sill find enough of mystery, of wit, of gentle irony in these pictures to enjoy them and set the cogs of his mind in motion in front of them. The sophisticated references are there for anybody who wants to go that way.

Olivier Richon has invented a kind of photography that is wholly modern in its refusal to determine a single ''correct'' interpretation of itself. It might certainly be called post-modern although Richon himself dislikes the term. Inspired as much by philosophical and literary currents of recent years as by anything that has happened in photography, Richon has been primarily interested in looking at representation itself: his tableaux would look odd, maybe even interesting if we saw them in fact, but to make them into images changes them and the way we understand them. It might be called a semantic way of photographing, but it is also more simply a playful, provocative, inventive and ultimately a modest one, where the photographer himself disappears from the recipe, leaving us alone before a rich feast that needs our fullest intellectual participation to be complete.

—Francis Hodgson

RICHTER, Evelyn.

Nationality: German. **Born:** Neukirch bei Bautzen, in 1930. **Education:** Studied photography in the classes of Franz Feidler and Pan Walther, Dresden, 1947-51; Hochschule für Grafik und Buchkunst, Leipzig, 1953-56. **Career:** Freelance photographer, working for Henschel Verlag, Urania Verlag, Fotokinoverlag, *Fotografie* magazine, etc., Leipzig, 1956-80. Since 1980, Head of own photography master class, Hochschule für Grafik und Buchkunst, Leipzig. **Recipient:** Honour Prize for Photography, Kulturbund der DDR, Berlin, 1975; Honour Prize, *Photokina 78,* Cologne, 1978; Fine Arts prize, City of Leipzig, 1984. **Address:** Georgenbadstrasse 31, 01904 Neukirch (L), Germany.

Individual Exhibitions:

1979	Galerie der Kunst, Dresden, East Germany
1983	Fotomuseum im Stadtmuseum, Munich, West Germany
	Galerie P., Leipzig, East Germany
1984	Nationalgalerie, East Berlin

1986   Rencontres de Photographie, Arles, France
1991   Leica Galerie, Solms, Germany
1992   Hochschule für Bildende Künste, Dresden, Germany
        Goethe Institut, Oslo,
        Staatliche Galeire Moritzburg, Halle, Germany
1993   Hochschule für Grafik und Buchkünst, Leipzig, Germany

Selected Group Exhibitions:

1964   *World Exhibition of Photography: What Is Man?* Pressehaus
        Stern, Hamburg, West Germany (and world tour)
1977   *Medium Fotografie,* Staatliche Galerie Moritzburg, Halle, East
        Germany
1978   *Photokina 78,* Cologne, West Germany
1979   *D D R Fotografie,* Galerie Gurzenich, Cologne, West Germany
1985   *Photographes Contemporains en R.D.A.,* Cherbourg, France
        (travelled to Brest and Rheims, France)
1986   *Photographing Women,* Fotogalerie Helsingforserplatz, East
        Berlin
        Fruhe Bilder: Photographie in D D R 1945-65, Leipzig, East
        Germany (travelled to East Berlin)

Collections:

Deutsche Fotothek, Sachsische Landesbibliothek, Dresden, Germany; Fotokino
Verlag, Leipzig, Germany; Hochschule für Grafik und Buchkunst, Leipzig,
Germany; Musée d'Elysee, Lausanne, Switzerland; Sprengel Museum, Hano-
ver, Germany; Fotomuseum Stadthus, Munich, Germany; Berlinische Galerie,
Berlin; Museum für Bild und Kunst, Leipzig, Germany; Staatlich Galerie,
Moritzberg, Germany; Halle Kudferstich Kabinett, Dresden, Germany; Staatlich
Museum, Brunn, Germany; Ludwig Collection, Cologne, Germany.

Publications:

By RICHTER: Books—*David Oistrach—ein Arbeitsportrat,* with text
by Ernst Kraus, East Berlin 1973; *Paul Dessau—aus Geprachen,* East
Berlin 1974; *Entwicklungswunder Mensch—Illustrationen zu einer
Entwicklungspsychologie,* with H.-D. Schmidt, Leipzig 1980; *Niemensland,*
Berlin 1988; *Liepziger Blätter,* Leipzig 1990.

On RICHTER: Books—*Erlebnis, Bild, Personlichkeit—funf Fotografen,
funf Sichten,* edited by B. Beiler and H. Foppel, Leipzig 1973; *Medium
Fotografie,* edited by Andreas Huneke, Gerhard Ihrke, Alfred Neumann and
Ullrich Wallenburg, Leipzig 1979; *Kunst in der DDR,* Eckhard & Rainer
Haarmann, Cologne 1990; *Ostdeutsche Photographie 1945-1989,* Ulrich Hg
von Domröse, Berlin 1992. **Articles**—"Copyright Evelyn Richter" in
Fotografie (Leipzig), no. 4, 1965; "Gruppenbilder von Evelyn Richter" in
Fotografie (Leipzig), no. 3, 1977; "Fotografie als soziale und bilderische
Entscheidung" by Volker Frank in *Bildende Kunst* (East Berlin), no. 4, 1984;
"Die Würde des Bildes, Werke der Fotografin Evelyn Richter in der Dresdner
Kunsthochschule" by Peter Guth in *Frankfurter Allgemeine Zeitung,* 25 May
1992; "Evelyn Richter—Kulturpreisträgerin 1992 der Deutschen Gesellschaft
für Photographie" by Michael Koetzle in *PN-Foto,* Chemnitz, March 1992;
"Es war ein mühsamer Weg" by Michael Koetzle in *Kulturchronik,* Bonn
April 1992; "Evelyn Richter Kulturpreisträgerin" by Jan Tiedge in *Fotodesign
und Technik,* Munich, no. 39 1992.

*   *   *

Evelyn Richter belongs to the first generation of East German photojournalists. Her principal theme is portraiture and her preference is for the
reportage-style portrait, regardless of milieu and background of the photographic subject. Without claiming to be exclusive, this working method, which
enables her to crystallize original situations, is an essential characteristic of

Richter's style. Evelyn Richter's perceptions are highly individual and she has
a great sensitivity towards her environment. This enables her to create pictures
typical of and directly related to the spirit of her time, while still retaining her
marked independence and umistakable individuality.

Taught by Franz Feidler and Pan Walther, Richter owes her photographic
education to humanistic ideals and classical models. The personality of Franz
Fiedler in particular has exerted a significant influence on Richter's development. After his whole collection was destroyed during the Second World War,
Fiedler began working again in Dresden in 1945, and in 1948 Evelyn Richter
began studying under him. Fiedler's belief that it takes much more than merely
technical means to create the stylistic atmosphere of a photograph is evidenced
today by the work of his erstwhile student. While perfectly mastering the
technical aspects of photography, Richter is just as careful to avoid any
contrived technical effects. Her photographs are always simple, even when the
subject matter is highly original.

Her student years in Dresden, her direct experience there of the traditional
art scene and encounter with many famous artists, or artists later to become
famous, were obviously instrumental in determining Richter's strong affinity
with diverse forms of artistic expression. Her portraits of the virtuoso violinist
David Oistrach are among her best achievements in this area. On a par with
these artist-portraits are those compositions depicting encounters between
people and works, particularly, of plastic art. This is a theme which Richter has
treated in numerous variations—from the reaction to contemporary ideological discussions to the abstruse inspiration, executed with superb technical
skill. All Evelyn Richter's photographs of people, be they portraits of
prominent personalities or otherwise, offer the viewer numerous means of
entering into and identifying with the subject of the photograph.

A number of Richter's photographs are considered to be real works of art.
To conclude one way or the other about that is scarcely relevant, however—at
least today. Such a classification adds nothing to the value of photography
itself, nor is it appropriate to the work of Evelyn Richter as some kind of
certificate of excellence. Her best photos record the attitudes, thoughts and
feelings of our time; that's already saying a great deal.

—Uwe Prinz

RIEBESEHL, Heinrich.

Nationality: German. **Born:** Lathen, 9 January 1938. **Education:** Studied
photography under Otto Steinert at the Folkwangschule, Essen, 1963-65,
Dip.Design 1972. **Family:** Married Gisela Remane in 1964; daughter: Catharina.
Career: Worked as an assistant at the Galerie Clarissa, Hannover, 1966;
Reporter, *Hannoversche Presse,* 1967-68. Freelance photographer, Hannover,
since 1968. Dozent, Fachhochschule, Hannover, since 1968; Codirector,
Galerie Spectrum im Sprengel Museum, Hannover, 1971-1992. Member,
Deutsche Gesellschaft für Photographie (DGPh), since 1971. **Recipient:**
Bernhard-Sprengel Prize, Hannover, 1981; Niedersächsisches Künstlerstipendium,
1981. **Address:** Am Kanonenwall 1, Hannover 1, 30169 Germany.

Individual Exhibitions:

1966   *Lokomotiven,* Galerie am Berg, Stuttgart (travelled to Galerie
        Clarissa, Hannover; Staatliche Landesbildstelle, Hamburg;
        and Galerie Form, Zurich, 1967)
1970   *Menschen im Fahrstuhl,* Kunstverein, Hannover (travelled
        to Galleria dell'Immagine, Bergamo, Italy; Staatliche
        Landesbildestelle, Hamburg; and Pressehaus,
        Hannover, 1971)
1975   *Situationen und Objekte,* Galerie im Steintor-Verlag, Burgdorf,
        Germany (travelled to Kunstverein, Unna, Germany, 1976;
        and Werkstatt für Photographie, Berlin, 1977)

Braunschweig, from Railway Landscape, **1981-1993.** Photograph by Heinrich Riebesehl.

1977   *Contemporary Photographs,* Sander Gallery, Washington, D.C.
1979   *Die Norddeutsche Agrarlandschaft,* Sander Gallery, Washington, D.C.
1980   *Agrarlandschaften,* Galerie Kicken, Cologne
       Norddeutsche Agrarlandschaften, Kunsthalle, Bremen
1981   *Norddeutsche Landschaften,* Kunstverein, Celle, West Germany
1982   Sprengel Museum, Hannover
       Wolfgang Gurlitt Museum, Linz, Austria
1983   *Agrarlandschaften,* Städtische Galerie, Nordhorn, West Germany
       Galleria e Libreria dell'Immagine, Milan (with Werner Mantz and Reinhart Wolf)
1984   *Photographien 1963-83,* Museum für Photographie, Braunschweig, West Germany
1985   *Alte Stadt-Moderne Zeiten,* Landesausstellung, Braunschweig, West Germany
       Galerie Phoenix, Würzburg, West Germany
1986   *Photographien 1963-83,* Kunstverein, Wolfenbüttel, West Germany
       Kultural Offices, Poznan, Poland
1987   Hiroshima
1988   Kunstverein Gifhorn
1990   Kunstverein Springe
1992   Sprengel Museum, Hannover

Selected Group Exhibitions:

1969   *10 Photographen in Hannover,* Galerie im Kubus, Hannover
1970   *Sei Fotografi della GDR,* Palazzo dell'Arte, Milan
1973   *Points de Vue sur le Portrait,* Société de Photographie, Paris
1975   *Photographie 1929-1975,* Kunstverein, Stuttgart
1976   *Photographie Hier und Heute,* Kunstverein, Hamburg
1977   *Photographie Créattrice au XX siècle,* Centre Georges Pompidou, Paris
1978   *The Naked Environment,* Salzburg College, Austria
1979   *In Deutschland,* Rheinisches Landesmuseum, Bonn
1981   *New German Photography,* The Photographers' Gallery, London
1986   *Ein Maler—Ein Photograph,* Kunstverein, Vechta, West Germany
1987   *Photographien 1945-1985,* Museum für Kunst und Gewerbe, Hamburg
1988   *Photovision,* Sprengel Museum, Hannover
1991   *Kulturlandschaften,* Museum für Photographie, Braunschweig
       Otto Steinert und Schüler, Museum Folkwang, Essen
       Norddeutsche Kunst, Spitalerhof, Hamburg
1994   *Architektur in der Photographie,* Museum für Kunst und Gewerbe, Hamburg

Nature/Culture, San Francisco Museum of Modern Art,
California
Aspekte deutscher Photographie nach 45, Fotogalerie, Vienna

Collections:

Museum für Kunst und Gewerbe, Hamburg; Museum Folkwang, Essen; Musée d'Art et d'Histoire, Fribourg, Switzerland; Bibliothèque Nationale, Paris; Stedelijk Museum, Amsterdam; Philadelphia Museum of Art; Library of Congress, Washington, D.C.; Boston Museum of Fine Arts; New Orleans Museum of Art; Sprengel Museum, Hannover.

Publications:

By RIEBESEHL: Books—*Photographierte Erinnerung,* Hannover 1975; *Situationen und Objekte,* with text by Jörg Krichbaum, Riesweiler, Germany 1978; *Agrarlandschaften,* with an introduction by Peter Sager, Bremen 1979; *Bilder aus Norddeutschland,* exhibition catalogue, Celle, West Germany 1982.

On RIEBESEHL: Books—*Menschen im Fahrstuhl,* exhibition catalogue, by Manfred de la Motte, Hannover 1970; *Gesellscahft Deutscher Lichtbildner 1975,* exhibition catalogue, by Bernd Lohse, Essen, West Germany 1975; *In Deutschland: Aspekte gegnwartiger Dokumentafotografie,* exhibition catalogue, by Klaus Honnef, Bonn 1979. **Articles**—"Das Leben im Lift" by Ursula Bode in *Hannover Allgemeine,* February 1970; "Menschen im Fahrstuhl" by Rainer Fabian in *Die Welt* (Hamburg), April 1971; "Fotografie Heinrich Riebesehl" by Jiri Machu in *Ceskoslovenska Fotografie* (Prague), March 1973; "Master of the Leica: Heinrich Riebesehl" by Fritz Kempe in *Leica Fotografie* (Frankfurt), April 1973; "Situationen und Objekte" by Winfried Wiegand in *Frankfurter Allgemeine,* July 1979; "Die Unwirtlichkeit der Landschaft" by Manfred Schuchmann in *Frankfurter Rundschau,* December 1979; "Bilder aus einer fremden Welt" by Peter Lebrecht in *Schädelspalter,* December 1990; "Geraffte Zeit-Die Macht des Bildes" by Dieter Lange in *Living,* March 1990; Lichtbildner und akribischer Landvermesser by Jochen Stöckmann in *Hannoversche Allgemeine,* May 1992. **Film**—*Künstlerische Fotografie: Heinrich Riebesehl,* German television film, by Martina Mettner, 1985.

*

I'm interested in photography because I'm interested in the different realities of things and situations, and photography can be a very authentic and spontaneous medium to make a document about my sense of the environment.

—Heinrich Riebesehl

*   *   *

Heinrich Riebesehl is one of the few German photographers who is known internationally from exhibitions and publications. Born in 1938 in Lathen, he has lived in Hannover since 1958. The spareness and sobriety of the north German landscape and its inhabitants may have made an early contribution to his particular vision, and so, perhaps, did Hannover's distinctive artistic tradition: Hannover was one of the centers, with Berlin and Cologne, of the *Neue Sachlichkeit,* the "New Objectivity." But the most decisive influence on Riebesehl's development was his study with Otto Steinert at the Folkwangschule in Essen. What Riebesehl's learned from the master of "Subjective Photography," already a legend in his own lifetime, apart obviously from technical perfection, was above all an emphasis on the artistic quality of photography, individual composition of the picture, and the necessity to make a decision to view an object in one way and no other. Added to this influence and already apparent in his early work—"Lokomotiven" of 1963, for example—was Riebesehl's preference for the series, a system of photographic art beyond the individual picture.

These characteristics are particularly clear in the series "Menschen in Fahrstuhl" of 1969: everyday faces, variations on a commonplace situation, gain an existential quality of expression. No less documentary in method, but more subjective in outcome, is the series "Selbstdarstellungen" of 1972, portraits without the portraitist—people of various professions and ages take photographs of themselves using a lengthened cable release, as unaffected or peculiar as they wish.

Riebesehl published *Situationen und Objekte* in 1978, black-and-white photographs notable for their peculiar atmosphere of suspense and for their paradoxically unspectacular tension. In certain constellations of light and shade—which are as much accidental as calculated—people and things gain a new and disturbing reality. The ambivalence of the situations, the anonymity of the people, and the strangeness of familiar objects, are all increased by heavy cutting, overlapping, and a very fast, almost snap-shot-like, technique. It is photography as fiction of another reality: it casts doubt on what and how we see. Counter movements, mysterious meetings: in *Situationen und Objekte* Riebesehl shows a predilection for people who are cut from the edge of the picture, whose faces are in shade or who turn their backs on us. And at the provisional end of the series, there are pictures totally without people, landscapes with only traces of their inhabitants.

The characteristic perspective of most of the photographs in *Situationen und Objekte* has to do with Riebesehl's attitude, the striking anti-classical concept of the "wrong moment." He says: "The short time before or after the 'right moment' can be just as powerful in its statement. In fact, it is often more powerful; Before and After come from a period of activity, they allow the imagination to consider what could happen or has already happened."

Riebesehl's next book, *Agrarlandschaften,* published in 1979, is based on a series of more than 1,000 photographs of land, farm-houses, fields, machines and feed-silos in North Germany, nature under the aspect of its produce, documented in sober, normal, everyday light. The typology of landscape is apparent, the structure of things. Riebesehl's photographic land survey, with its precision and method, follows in the tradition of August Sander, Albert Renger-Patzsch, and Bernd and Hilla Becher. But here the magical surreal aspect of reality is also visible.

With his particular kind of subjective documentary photography Riebesehl belongs to a group of German photographers—Wilhelm Schürmann, Michael Schmidt, Martin Manz, among others—who have devoted themselves to a new kind of "New Objectivity." Neither photo-journalists nor art photographers, they favor a neutral, diffused light, take eye-level photographs (preferably in black-and-white), mistrust the "beautiful" picture, and set against the Kodachrome of the illustrated magazine a deliberately reserved, spare aesthetic. They renounce sensational motives and spectacular composition; they emphasize the normal, almost the banal. Heinrich Riebesehl is one of the purists of this new aesthetic.

—Peter Sager

RIEFENSTAHL, Leni.

Nationality: German. **Born:** Berra Helene Amalia Riefenstahl in Berlin, 22 August 1902. **Education:** Attended the Realgymnasium, Berlin, 1912-18; studied art at the Kunstakademie, Berlin, 1918-19; classical ballet, under Eduardova, Berlin, and modern dance, under Mary Wigman, Dresden, 1919-23. **Family:** Married Peter Jakob in 1944 (divorced, 1946). **Career:** Worked as a dancer in Germany and throughout Europe, 1923-26; film actress, appearing in *Der Heilige Berg,* 1926, *Der Grosse Sprung,* 1927, *Das Schicksal derer von Hapsburg,* 1929, *Die Weisse Hölle von Piz Palü,* 1929, *Stürme über dem Montblanc,* 1930, *Der Weisse Rausch,* 1931, and *SOS Eisberg,* 1932. Film Producer, Leni Riefenstahl Produktion, Berlin, subsequently Munich, since 1931; has also worked in still photography, Munich, since 1962. **Recipient:** Gold Medal for Film, *Biennale,* Venice, 1932, 1936, 1938; Grand Prix, *Exposition Internationale,* Paris, 1937; Gold Medal, Art Directors Club of Germany, 1975; Order of Distinction, Republic of the Sudan, 1976. **Address:** Leni Riefenstahl—Produktion, Tengstrasse 20, 8000 Munich 40, Germany.

Individual Exhibitions:

1980   *The Nuba,* Seibu Museum, Tokyo

Self-Portrait, **1941.** Photograph by Leni Riefenstahl.

Selected Group Exhibitions:

1973   *3rd World Exhibition of Photography: On the Way to
        Paradise,* Pressehaus Stern, Hamburg (and world tour)
1979   *Biennale of Graphic and Visual Art,* Graz, Austria

Publications:

By RIEFENSTAHL: Books—*Kampf in Schnee und Eis,* Leipzig 1933;
Hinter den Kulissen des Reichsparteitag-films (ghost-written by Ernst
Jaeger), Munich 1935; *Schönheit im Olympischen Kampf,* Berlin 1937; *Die
Nuba,* Munich 1973, as *The Last of the Nuba,* New York 1974; *Die Nuba von
Kau/People of Kau,* Munich and New York 1976; *Korallengarten/Coral
Gardens,* Munich, Paris, London and New York 1978; *Mein Afrika,* Munich
1982, as *Leni Riefenstahl's Africa,* London 1982; *Wonders under Water,*
London 1991; *The Sieve of Time,* London 1992, and as *Leni Riefenstahl: A
Memoir,* New York 1992. **Articles**—''Das Fest der Messer und der Liebe'' in
Stern (Hamburg), 7 October 1975; ''Mein Wildes Leben'' in *Quick* (Munich),
August 1977; ''Leni Riefenstahl: Weltkarriere als Taucherin'' in *Submarine*
(Munich), September 1978; ''Der Trieb, Schön zu Sein'' in *Quick* (Munich), 5
October 1978. **Films**—*Das Blaue Licht,* 1932; *Sieg des Glaubens,* 1933;
Triumph des Willens, 1934; *Tag der Freiheit: unsere Wehrmacht,* 1935;
Olympia, 1938; *Tiefland,* 1954.

On RIEFENSTAHL: Books—*Screen Series: Germany* by Felix Bucher,
New York 1970; *Filmguide to ''Triumph of the Will''* by Richard Barsam,
Bloomington, Indiana 1975; *Leni Riefenstahl, the Fallen Film Goddess* by
Glen Infield, New York 1976; *Leni Riefenstahl* by Charles Ford, Paris 1978;
The Films of Leni Riefenstahl by David Hinton, Metuchen, New Jersey 1978;
Leni Riefenstahl et le 3e Reich by G.B. Infield, Paris 1978; *Leni Riefenstahl* by
Renata Berg-Pan, Boston 1980; *Der Traum vom Sieg: Kampf und Kult in der
Sportfotografie* by Matthias Matussek and Christiane Gehner, Hamburg 1986;
75 Years of Leica Photography 1914-1989, Solms, Germany 1990. **Arti-
cles**—''Leni et le Loup'' by Carl Dreyer in *Cahiers du Cinema* (Paris),
September 1965; ''Comeback for Leni Riefenstahl'' in *Film Comment* (New
York), Winter 1965; ''Leni Riefenstahl'' by H. Weigel in *Filmkritik* (Munich),
August 1972; ''Leni'' by A. Mannheim in *Modern Photography* (New York),
February 1974; ''Zur Riefenstahl Renaissance,'' special issue of *Frauen und
Film* (Berlin), December 1977; ''Directors of the Decade: Leni Riefenstahl''
by John Russell Taylor in *Films and Filming* (London), March 1983; ''The
White Hell of Piz Palu'' by Hans Casparius in *In my View: A Pictorial
Memoir,* Leamington Spa, Hamburg and New York 1986; ''Transposed
Narratives: Leni Riefenstahl's and Robert Mapplethorpe's Forays on the Wild
Side,'' in *Spot,* Houston, Spring 1988; ''Liberated but Illiberal Pioneers'' by
Mark Almond in *The Times,* London, 15 October, 1992; ''The Führer's Movie
Maker'' by John Simon in *The New York Times,* 26 September, 1993;
''Riefenstahl, in a Long Close-Up'' in *New York Times,* October 1993; ''Carry
on Kampfing'' by Gilbert Adair in *The Sunday Times,* London 1993; ''Leni
Riefenstahl, Disingenuous Genius?'' in *Washington Post,* March 1994; ''Just
What Did Leni Riefenstahl's Lens See?'' in *New York Times,* March 1994;
''Triumph of her Will'' in *Washington Post,* May 1994.

*   *   *

Leni Riefenstahl's photographs remind one of movies, as they very well
might. Having spent the better part of her life as a film-maker, it's no accident
that Riefenstahl's pictures pick up some of a film's sensibilities. But they do so
in a curious, and, in some sense, rather sophisticated way. For, instead of
relying on the look of movies—as one might expect a camera to do—they
catch the feel of movies. They allow viewers to think that as they look at the
still picture, they are seeing a movie. Small and large objects, for instance, are
thrown into the same scene without any attention to a ''true'' scale, and,
actually, are rather outlandishly scaled. It's as if Riefenstahl were saying that
the camera is about to change everything you see, that the imbalance in seeing
a small object up front and an overpowering object in the distance is
temporary. The scene is in transition. It's about to change. It suggests a vitality.
Riefenstahl achieves the same effect with her lens, many of her people
unpredictably out of focus in places where we have come to expect them to be
in focus (i.e. in the center of a crowd). Once again, the imbalance is temporary,

as if the scene and people we are looking at are on their way towards being
changed.

When she uses large grain imagery, however, we're stymied. We can't
make an adjustment and, furthermore, feel a discomfort that makes us question
the work's premises. For we have come to understand grainy imagery as a
device for heightening and intensifying physical reality. Grainy imagery does
not do that in Riefenstahl's pictures. The figures, at first, look sculpted and we
stop to take them in and absorb them. But we can't. Although the figures look
like people to begin with, they aren't. Abstracted from humanity, they stand as
forms, as shapes, as constructs that occupy a time and place—as if they were
molded out of clay and made to stand in a particular way. They lack any sense
of internal movement—they don't look as if they can breathe. A scene looks
like a staged representation of reality, much like the ape-like figures in the film
2001—no sense of a pulse ticking away.

This non-human thrust appears throughout her work. In one photograph,
the shapes (resembling people) echo the shapes of rocks and look as inanimate.
In another, silhouetted against the sky, the shapes look mindless. In another,
where people are tattooed, the tattoos take over the faces so completely, the
photograph becomes one over-whelming design, the people from whom that
design originated reduced to raw material for the design.

Only when Riefenstahl broadens her focus to a whole village scene does
one pick up a voluptuous swell of life, as, for instance, in a photograph of a
village where her camera has swept across a land-scape. And only then does
the viewer, once again, pick up the vitality that movies—as a process and
medium—can impart.

—Judith Mara Gutman

RITTS, Herb.

Nationality: American. **Born:** Los Angeles, 1952. **Education:** Attended
Bard College; self-taught in photography. **Career:** Worked for *Rolling Stone,
Vanity Fair, Vogue, Interview, Tatler, Vogue Hommes, French Vogue* and
L'Uomo Vogue, and for advertising campaigns for Giorgio Armani, Calvin
Klein, Gianfranco Ferre, Gap, Levis, Honda, Vittel, Paul Mitchell and Guy
Laroche. Also directed music videos for Madonna, Chris Isaak, Janet Jackson
and Michael Jackson. **Recipient:** The Year's Most Prominent Fashion Pho-
tographer, from the California Fashion Institute, 1989; the Infinity Award for
Applied Photography from the International Center for Photography, 1991.
Agent: Fahey/Klein Gallery, 1-18 North La Brea Avenue, Los Angeles,
California 90036, U.S.A.

Individual Exhibitions:

1988   Staley/Wise Gallery, New York
        Parco Gallery, Tokyo
        Fahey/Klein Gallery, Los Angeles
1990   Staley/Wise Gallery, Los Angeles
        Hamilton's Gallery, London
        Parco Gallery, Tokyo
        PPS Gallery, Hamburg, Germany
        Catherine Edelman Gallery, Chicago
        Jane Corkin Gallery, Toronto, Canada
        Arthur Roger Gallery, New Orleans
        Fahey/Klein Gallery, Los Angeles
1991   PPS Galerie, Hamburg, Germany
        Allene Lapides Gallery, Santa Fe, New Mexico
        Robert Koch Gallery, San Francisco
        Le Printemps de la Photo, Cahors
1992   Kathryn Fleck Gallery, Aspen, Colorado
        Davis/McClain Gallery, Houston, Texas
        Parco Gallery, Tokyo
        Allenes Lapides Gallery, Santa Fe
        Staley/Wise Gallery, New York
        Fahey/Klein Gallery, Los Angeles
1993   G. Gibson Gallery, Seattle

Galleria Photology, Milan, Italy
Catherine Edelman Gallery, Chicago
Arthur Roger Gallery, New Orleans
Robert Koch Gallery, San Francisco
Hamilton's Gallery, London
Fay Gold Gallery, Atlanta, Georgia

Selected Group Exhibitions:

1989-90   *The Christmas Show,* Staley/Wise Gallery, New York
           Censorship, Couturier Gallery, Los Angeles
           Arthur Roger Gallery, New Orleans
1993   *Quatrième Festival International de la Photo de la Mode,*
           Monaco

Publications:

By RITTS: Books—*Pictures,* Twin Palm Publishers 1988; *Men/Women,*
Twin Palm Publishers 1989; *Duo,* Twin Palm Publishers 1991; *Notorious,*
Boston 1992; *Photographs,* Milan 1993; *Africa,* Boston 1994.

*   *   *

Celebrity portraiture is basically a form of advertisement. A celebrity
needs to promote a face and Herb Ritts, the decade's best-known photographer, is the facemaker who makes it visible and easily recognisable in
magazines around the world. He has photographed them all: from statesmen
past and present to the famous and would-be-famous of today. He is one of the
celebrity photographers who has little illusion that photography pictures the
soul. His images are about surfaces which he describes with immense clarity,
for the subjects are symbolic objects, decorative and sexy. The pictures are
strong, rather old-fashioned, very often cheeky and a little provocative. Ritts'
speciality is to obscure the subject's identity: faces are covered almost totally
by hair, hats or objects: some are seen from the back and could as easily have
meanbeen dummies; or he focusses on a specific part of the body, for instance,
the buttocks, making them the obvious area of interest. In the past, photographers who used the caricaturist's ploy to photograph a single feature usually
picked a mouth, eyes or legs.

Ritts, born in 1952 in Los Angeles, California, is self-taught. He was a
furniture sales representative until one summer in the late 1970s when he
bought a camera and began photographing some of his friends. He has not
looked back since. Soon his work appeared in leading fashion magazines
including *Rolling Stone, Vogue, Vanity Fair, Tatler,* and *Interview.* His
pictures have been exhibited in solo and group exhibitions in American,
European and Asian galleries and reproduced in numerous books. He gives
occasional lectures, works for the advertising industry, represents famous
fashion houses and has also directed music videos for Madonna, Chris Isaak,
Janet Jackson and Michael Jackson.

For the elegant portraits he shot for the well-known fashion chain Gap,
Ritts received the Infinity Award for Applied Photography from New York's
International Center for Photography in 1991. In 1989, he became the Year's
Most Prominent Fashion Photographer named by the California Fashion
Institute, Los Angeles.

—Hildegard Mahoney

RIO BRANCO, Miguel.

Nationality: Spanish. **Born:** Las Palmas, Canary Islands, 1946. **Recipient:**
First prize in the First Photography Tiennale, Museu de Arts Moderna, Sao
Paulo, 1980; prize for the best photography, Brazil Film Festival, 1981;
special jury prize and international critics' prize, XI International Film
Festival, Lille, 1982; Kodak Prize for Photography Criticism, Paris, 1982;
special jury prize in the International Festival of Short Films, Salvador, Bhaia,
and best video direction in the Festival of Film and Video, Maranhao; and best

photography for a full-length film at the Brasilia Film Festival. **Address:** Rua
Joquim Naboco 258-302, Copacabana 22080-030, Rio de Janeiro, Brazil.

Individual exhibitions:

1972   Veste Sagrada, Rio de Janeiro
1974   Galerie Grupo B, Rio de Janeiro
1977   Ipanema Gallery, Tel Aviv
1978   Escola de Arts Visuais, Rio de Janeiro (travelled throughout
        Brazil)
1980   Galeria Fotóptica, Sao Paulo (travelled to Fotogaleria Funarte,
        Rio de Janeiro)
1982   Gabinete de Cultura, Bilbao, Spain
1983   *Diálogas con Amaú,* XVIIe Biennale de São Páulo (travelled to
        Rencontres Internationales, Arles)
1985   *Coeur miroir de la chair,* Galerie Magnum, Paris
1987   *Coração espelho da carne,* Fotogalerie Funarte, Rio de Janeiro
1990   *Photo Biennale,* Rotterdam, Netherlands
1991   Chappelle St. Jean de Moustiers, Rencontres
        Internationales, Arles
        IFA Gallery, Bonn, Germany
1992   Stadtische Galerie, Tuttlingen, Germany
        Fotogalerie Friedrichshain, Berlin

Selected Group Exhibitions:

1976   Grande São Paulo, Museu de Arte de São Paulo
1977   Galeria Grafitti, Rio de Janeiro
1979   *Nossa Gente,* Fotogaleria Funarte, Rio de Janeiro
        Foto Bahia, Teatro Castro Alves, Salvador
1980   *Camera Incantate,* Palazzo Reale, Mila, Italy
        First Photographic Triennale, Museu de Arte Moderna, São
        Páulo
1981   *Coleçao Gilberto Châteaubriand,* Museu de Arte Moderna, Rio
        de Janeiro (travelled to São Páulo)
1982   Kodak Centre, Paris
        Contemporary Latin American Photography, Centre Georges
        Pompidou, Paris
1983   *O tempo de olhar,* Museu de Belas Artes, Rio de Janeiro
        (travelled to Sao Paulo)
1984   *First Art Biennale,* Havana, Cuba
1985   *Audio Retrato do Brasileiro,* Museu de Arte Moderna, São
        Páulo
1986   *On the Line, the New Colour Photojournalism,* Walker
        Art Centre, Minneapolis (travelled to Portland, Oakland,
        Spencer, Laguna Museums of Art and the Carnegie Mellon
        Art Gallery)
        50 Jahre moderne Farbfotografie, Fotokina, Cologne, Germany
1987   *Masters of Street Photography III,* Museum of Photographic
        Arts, San Diego
        Latin American Photography, Australian Centre for
        Photography
1989   *Contemporary Art in Uruguay, Argentina, Brazil, Chile,*
        Stedeljik Museum, Amsterdam
1990   *Suadouro,* Galerie 1900-2000, Paris
1992   *Brazilian Colour Photography,* Houston Fotofest
        Fifth Photo-Biennale, Vigo Galeriee Zeno X, Anvers
1994   *A Hidden View,* Concourse Gallery, The Barbican Centre,
        London

Collections:

Museu de Arte de São Páulo; Museu de Arte Moderna de São Páulo; Centre
Georges Pompidou, Paris; Museum of Modern Art, San Francisco; Stedelijk
Museum, Amsterdam; Museum of Photographic Arts, San Diego; Evergon
Collection, Canada; David Rockefeller Collection; Thomas Cohn Collection;
Sammlung Uwe Scheid.

Bahia, **1988.** Photograph ©Miguel Rio Branco/Magnum.

Publications:

By RIO BRANCO: Books—*Dulce Sudro Amargo,* Mexico 1985; *Salvador de Bahia,* Page 1985. **Articles**—"Abandoned Children" in *Geo* (USA), 1980; "Les Olvidados" in *Geo* (France), 1980; "La Cicatrici" in *Il Fotografo,* 1980; "Portfolio," *PhotoMagazine,* 1982; "Beset by a Golden Curse" in *National Geographic,* 1984; "Kapapós en de progrès" in *Geo* (France), 1984; "Rio Branco en Amazonie" in *PhotoMagazine,* 1984; "Ruée vers Carajás" in *Geo* (France), 1986; "Bolivars Traum" in *Stern,* 1990; "Schwarze Glut" in *Stern,* 1990; "Bailando en la Calle" in *El Pais Semanal,* 1990.

On RIO BRANCO: Book—*A Hidden View: Images of Bahia, Brazil,* exhibition catalogue, edited by Amanda Hopkinson, Barkway and London, 1994.

*   *   *

Miguel Rio Branco is both a photographer and an artist or, as he prefers to describe himself, *an author.* Increasingly he refuses to separate out the two worlds not, as more commonly happens, by mixing the media in the artwork itself but by presenting exhibitions where canvases and large scale colour prints alternate on the gallery walls.

In writing "colour," another qualification immediately presents itself. For Rio Branco's use of colour is very specific: he employs a particular palette to suit a particular mood and topic, even a particular texture. Thus, in a recent show commissioned by the Spanish bank Banesto, the images he sought on the city of Barcelona—whether a crucifix in a chapel, a dead bird on a pavement,

even the curl of a stone balustrade—came together with abstract paintings predominantly in shades of grey and oxblood to suggest a still and sinister ambience one could almost reach out and feel.

His native Brazil receives a very different treatment. Whether in his first book *Dulce Sudor Amargo (Bittersweet Sweat)* or his most recent exhibition (for Cuba, 1994) on the boxing gyms of rundown Lapa in downtown Rio de Janeiro, it is the blues and yellows suggestive of sunlight and water (even in ill-lit interiors) that wash the images with a definite light of their own. Immense care and research at every stage of the way, including extreme fastidiousness in the processing and placing of his work, are characteristic of an 'author' whose work hangs—most often and most naturally, it seems—in old monasteries or chapels, converted warehouses or factories, in an interplay that extends the drama of the images.

Of an immensely cosmopolitan background (born into a diplomatic family with varied places of residence); trained in fine art as well as film and photography; erudite regarding the history and cultures within which his work is situated; his work has a depth of content and a poetic realisation that demand serious attention. Now widely exhibited and internationally respected, Miguel Rio Branco defies classification as just a photographer, still less just a Brazilian photographer. Increasingly incorporating his own previous metiers (particularly in film and video) and fantasies (including sound as well as vision in his projects), he is perhaps one of the least typical associates of the prestigious Magnum photojournalist agency. Even though his major contemporary project has to do with the Rio street children who gather around the Candelaria church, it is guaranteed to be something beyond a piece of reportage. In his own words: "The street children are a parable of survival in distress, you can apply it to anywhere you like in Brazil, even as a metaphor of the country as a whole . . . [it's like] what's interesting about the boxing series is that it's not really about boxers. It's like having a map of humanity, all the precariousness and uncertainty of existence."

Parables and preciousness, poetry through photography, these are but a few of the elements composing some of the most interesting artistic diversity we are likely to see in the work of one person.

—Amanda Hopkinson

ROBERTSON, Grace.

Nationality: British. **Born:** Manchester, England, 13 July 1930. **Education:** Kendal High School for Girls, Cumbria and Eothen School, Caterham, Surrey; teacher training at Maria Grey College, Twickenham, West London; self-taught in photography. **Family:** Married photographer Thurston Hopkins 1955; children: Joanna and Robert. **Career:** Started work at the Simon Guttmann "Report" agency, 1949; freelanced, exclusively for *Picture Post,* 1950-57, then for *Life Magazine* and other British picture magazines, principally through the Pictorial Press Agency 1957-60; worked as a teacher 1963-76; continued to work as an independent freelance photographer, 1965-75, and returned to full-time professional photography in 1980s. **Recipient:** Distinguished Photographer Award from *American Women in Photography International,* 1992. **Agents:** Photographers' Gallery, London and Zelda Cheatle Gallery, London, England. **Address:** Wilmington Cottage, Wilmington Road, Seaford, East Sussex, BN25 2EH, England.

Individual Exhibitions:

1989	Zelda Cheatle Gallery, London
	Lansdowne House, Leicester
	Photography Workshop, Edinburgh, Scotland
1990	Dunfermline District Museum, Scotland
	National Museum Of Wales, Cardiff
1991	Clean Break Theatre, London
1992	Cathleen Ewing Gallery, Washington D.C.
1993	Royal National Theatre, London
	Watershed Media Centre, Bristol
	Perth Museum, Perth, Scotland
	Lighthouse Media Centre, Wolverhampton, England
	Battersea Arts Centre, London
	Midland Arts Centre, Birmingham
1994	University of Brighton, Sussex
	The Maltings, Farnham, Surrey
1995	The Towner Art Gallery, Eastbourne, Sussex

Selected Group Exhibitions:

1986	Photographers' Gallery, London
	National Museum of Photography, Film and Television, Bradford, England
1990	Gardener Centre, Sussex University, Brighton, England
1991	Victoria and Albert Museum, London
1993	Royal Scottish National Portrait Gallery, Edinburgh, Scotland
1994	*All Human Life,* The Barbican Centre, London

Collections:

Victoria and Albert Museum, London; National Museum of Film and Photography, Bradford, England; The National Gallery of Australia, Canberra; The Helmut Gernsheim Collection, Switzerland; Side Gallery, Newcastle, England; Hulton Deutsch Collection, London.

Publications:

By ROBERTSON: Books—*Grace Robertson, Photojournalist of the 50s,* 1989; *The Nineties* (London), 1993. **Articles**—Review of Humphrey Spend-

er's work in "Lensman" in *Creative Camera,* 1988; "Women Photographers" in *British Journal of Photography,* 1988; "Women Photographers," in *The Sunday Telegraph,* 1988; Book review of Vicki Goldberg's biography on Margaret Bourke-White in *Creative Camera,* 1989; tribute following the death of Sir Tom Hopkinson in *The Correspondent Magazine,* 1990; catalogue entry for exhibition of Humphrey Spender's work at Bolton Museum and Art Gallery, 1993; Review of Anna Fox's exhibition "The Village" in *Women's Art,* 1994.

On ROBERTSON: Books—*Photography of the Twentieth Century* by Petr Tausk (London), 1977; *Women Photographers. The Other Observers* by Val Williams (London), 1986; *Photographers and Their Images* by Fi McGee (London), 1988; *The Picture Post Album* by Robert Kee (London), 1989; *Makers of Photographic History* from National Museum of Photography, Film and Television in association with The Hulton Deutsch Picture Library, 1989; *Picture Post Women* by Juliet Gardener (London), 1993; *A History of Women Photographers* by Naomi Rosenblum, (New York), 1994. **Articles**—*Image,* September 1988; in *Contact* (UK), 1989; "Master of the Leica" in *Leica Fotografie International,* May 1989; "Caught by Grace" by Tom Hopkinson in *Independent Magazine* (London), October 1989; "Getting the Picture" in *Everywoman,* November 1989; "Picture Story" in *Scotland on Sunday Magazine* (Scotland), January 1990; in *Portfolio Magazine* (Scotland), 1990; "Moving Pictures" by Val Williams in *The Guardian* (London), September 1991; "Acts of Grace" in *What's On* (London), 1993; "Into the Nineties" in *Second Shift,* 1993; "A Nation at Play" in *The Times Magazine* (London), 1993; "About as Old as It Gets" in *The Independent Sunday Review* (London), 1993; "Laughing at the Passage of Time" in *The Birmingham Post* (Birmingham), November 1993. **Video**—*Grace Robertson, Photojournalist* Channel 4 TV documentary, 1986; *The Other Observers* video cassette by The Inner London Education Authority, 1987; interview by Colin Ford for BBC Radio 3 *Master Photographer* Series, 1990.

*

I learned my professionalism out of necessity, disciplined by the expectations of a waiting picture editor and the ever-present deadline. I developed my working method in the belief that as a photojournalist, with strong leanings towards pure documentary, I should not let my personal feelings dictate the picture-making process. I feel that really serious photography, like really serious painting—or really serious any other creative act—is always difficult, and there is good reason to believe that success in photography is, in very large part, the immediate outcome of surmounting every sort of difficulty.

—Grace Robertson

*   *   *

Although Grace Robertson grew up with an intimate knowledge of *Picture Post* because her father worked for the magazine as a journalist, she had not initially imagined becoming involved herself. She became able to recognise the work of individual photographers, particularly that of Kurt Hutton, even though they were not usually credited at the time. When she was sixteen her mother became bed-ridden and Grace left school to run the household. Grace began to see "pictures," people standing in a queue, or getting onto a bus, that she thought would make excellent photographs. Although there was no money to take a course she was given a second-hand Leica and an enlarger and began to teach herself. She sent her first two stories into *Picture Post* under an assumed name and although neither was accepted, both were encouraged. Her father introduced her to Simon Guttman who took her into his agency and sold three stories the first year. Guttman was a very fierce critic of all the young photographers he worked with but, like them, Grace is still grateful and appreciates all she learned at that time.

She began to work regularly as a freelance for *Picture Post,* and other magazines and in 1953 she was asked to join the staff but she refused because she felt it could be construed as nepotism as her father still worked for the paper. Later she also refused to join *Life* because she had just got married and it meant living in the United States for three years. Her work at this time was very varied, including work with a particular women's angle but by no means exclusively so; beginning with stories assigned by the picture editor but increasingly putting up her own ideas and having them accepted. When

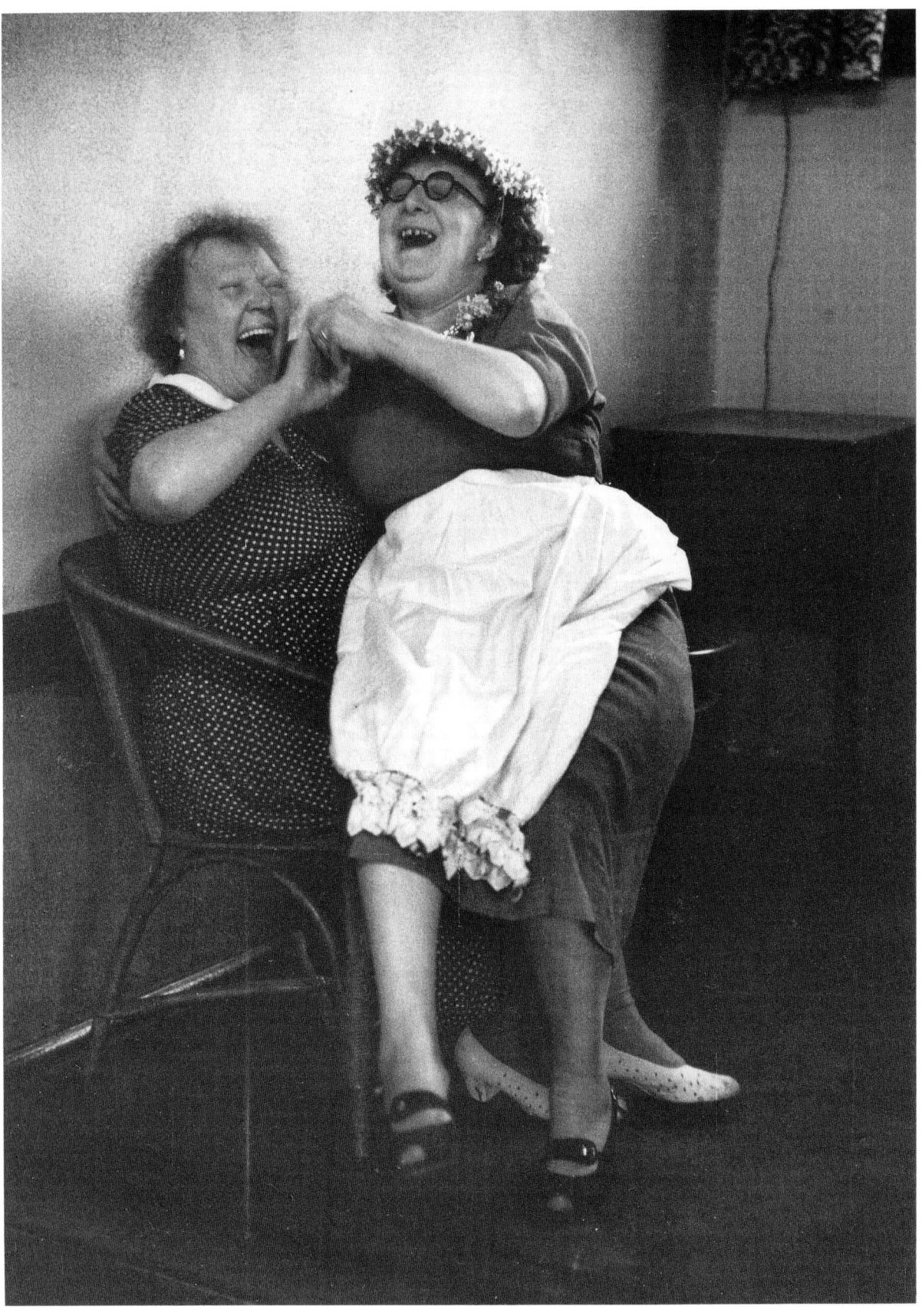

Mothers Day Pub Outing, **1954.** Photograph ©Grace Robertson.

Picture Post closed she continued to freelance for various publications but also acted as driver for her husband, Thurston Hopkins, who had gone into advertising photography. It became impossible to do both so for a time she stopped taking pictures and acted as his girl Friday. Once they had children she decided to re-train as a teacher and gave up serious photography for the following thirteen years.

When interest was revived during the 1970s in the work of *Picture Post* photographers it concentrated at first on the war years. Later this interest expanded to include the younger photographers and Grace Robertson has not only been recognised for her early work but is again taking photographs, accepting commissions and exhibitions and becoming more involved in all aspects of photography, including lecturing, judging and the organisation of photographic events.

Although tough and uncompromising in her photographic standards, Grace Robertson has a natural sympathy and interest in her subjects. This enables her to take pictures of people which are full of information but never exploit or pass judgement on them. Being aware of the possibility of a good picture and able to make good use of it is clearly something she learned early and has never forgotten.

—Sue Davies

RODGER, George.

Nationality: British. **Born:** Hale, Cheshire, 19 March 1908. **Education:** St. Bees College, Cumbria, 1921-25. **Military Service:** Served in the British Merchant Navy, 1927-29. **Family:** Married Cicely Joane Hussey-Freke in 1942 (died, 1949); married Lois Witherspoon in 1953; children: Jennifer, Jonathan, and Peter. **Career:** Worked as a machinist, wool-buyer, steel-rigger, fruit farmer, etc., in United States, 1929-36; worked for the B.B.C., 1936-38; freelance photographer with the Black Star photo agency, London, 1938-39; photographer and war correspondent for *Life* magazine, throughout Europe, North Africa, the Middle East and Burma, 1939-45. Founder Member, with Robert Capa, Henri Cartier-Bresson, and David Seymour ("Chim") of Magnum Photos cooperative agency since 1947. **Recipient:** Arts Council Bursary, 1975, 1977; First Prize, *Peace to the World* exhibition, Moscow, 1985; Fellow of Kent Institute of Art and Design (Hon), 1993; Fellow of Royal Photographic Society, 1993 (Hon); D. Litt (Hon) University of Kent, 1994. **Agent:** Magnum Photos Ltd, 23-25 Old Street, London EC1V 9HL, England. **Address:** Waterside House, Smarden, Kent TN27 8QB, England.

Individual Exhibitions:

1974	The Photographers' Gallery, London (toured the U.K.)
1976	Canterbury Library, Kent (toured Southeast England)
1978	University of South Africa, Cape Town
1979	*Masai Moran,* The Photographers' Gallery, London (toured the U.K.)
	Masai Moran, FNAC Galleries, Paris (toured France)
1981	Contrasts Gallery, London
1982	*Festival Africain,* Galerie de Pret, Grenoble, France
1984	*London Faces the Blitz,* Photo Gallery, St. Leonard's on Sea, Sussex (toured the U.K.)
	Tribal Africa, Magnum Photos Gallery, Paris
	Tribal Africa, Galerie Espace Images, Marseille, France
	The Photographers' Gallery, London
1985	*Tribal Africa,* Ecole Regionale des Beaux-Arts, Dunquerque, France
	Tribal Africa, Galerie FNAC-Montparnasse, Paris (toured France, 1985-86)
1986	*Tribal Africa,* Galeria Fontana d'Or, Gerona, Spain
	Tribal Africa, Galerie Foto, Amsterdam
	Nicosia and Limassol, Cyprus
1987-88	Retrospective at Photographers' Gallery, London and in 1988 on tour in UK at Burnley, Lancs; Folkestone, Kent;

	University of Aberdeen; Oriel Clwyd Wrexham, Wales; Bolton Art Gallery Lancashire; Wakefield Art Gallery, Yorkshire.
1990	Musee d'Elysees, Lausanne; Musee de la Photographie, Charleroi, Belgium; Astley-Cheetham Gallery, Manchester; Stockport Arts Centre, Merseyside.
	Le Blitz at Picto Bastille, Paris
	The Blitz, Zelda Cheatle Gallery, London and at Museum of Film, Photography and TV, Bradford, and at The Navy Museum, Washington DC.
	Africa, Le Port, Reunion
1991	*The Blitz,* Guillaume Gallozzi Gallery, New York
	Retrospective at Portfolio Gallery, Edinburgh
	Africa, at Bretagne 9th Festival Photographe, Lorient, France
1992	*Winston Churchill's Britain at War,* Churchill House, London
1993	Kent Institute of Art and Design, at Maidstone and Rochester, Kent
	Vision Gallery, San Francisco
1994	Lichtbild Gallerie, Bremen
	University of Kent
	Bowhill, Selkirk, Scotland
	The Royal Photographic Society, Bath, England
1995	Barbican Art Gallery, London

Selected Group Exhibitions:

1955	*The Family of Man,* Museum of Modern Art, New York (and world tour)
1960	*The World as Seen by Magnum,* Takashimaya Department Store, Tokyo (and world tour)
1969	*Fotomundi,* Eindhoven, Netherlands
1975	*The Real Thing: An Anthology of British Photographs 1840-1950,* Hayward Gallery, London (toured the U.K.)
1976	*British Photographers,* at *Rencontres Internationales de la Photographie,* Arles, France
1979	*Life: The First Decade 1936-1945,* Grey Art Gallery, New York University
1980	*Magnum Photos,* Galerie Le Cloître, St. Ursanne, Switzerland
1983	*Faces and Places,* Musée des Beaux-Arts, Montreal
1985	*Magnum Concert,* Musée d'Art et d'Histoire, Fribourg, Switzerland
1986	*South Africa,* Galerie FNAC-Montparnasse, Paris (toured France)
1987	*Realities Revisited,* Centre Saidye Bronfman, Montreal
1989	*Through the Looking Glass,* Barbican Art Gallery, London
1990-93	*Magnum Founders,* ICP Gallery, Uptown
	In Our Time, Magnum Exhibition in New York, Paris, London, Tokyo and on tour worldwide
1991	*Year of Tibet,* Portfolio, London, New York, Japan, Los Angeles
1993	*Annees 50, 60, 70,* Musee d'Elysees, Lausanne
1994	Gropper Associates, San Francisco

Collections:

Victoria and Albert Museum, London; Arts Council of Great Britain, London; Rijksmuseum, Amsterdam; University of South Africa, Cape Town; Australian National Museum, Sydney; Bibliothèque Nationale, Paris.

Publications:

By RODGER: Books—*Red Moon Rising,* London 1943; *Desert Journey,* London 1944; *Far on the Ringing Plains,* New York 1944; *Le Village des Noubas,* Paris 1955; *This England,* with others, Washington, D.C. 1966; *The World of the Horse,* with text by Judith Campbell, London 1975; *George Rodger en Afrique,* with text by Carole Naggar, Paris 1984; *The Blitz—The Photography of George Rodger,* Penguin-Viking: July 1990 (reprint 1994). **Articles**—"Television History" in *Photo World* (London), March 1939; "Belsen" in *Time* (New York), 30 April 1945; "Africa's Most Dangerous Shooting" in *Argosy* (New York), August 1953; "Sand in Your Eyes" in

Nuba Girl with Lip Plug, Southern Sudan, **1949.** Photograph by George Rodger.

National Geographic Magazine (Washington, D.C.), May 1958; "Elephants Have Right of Way" in *National Geographic Magazine* (Washington, D.C.), September 1960; "Beginnings of Magnum: Random Thoughts by a Founding Father" in *Creative Camera* (London), March 1969; "A Letter to My Son" in *Album* (London), no. 8, 1970; "Souvenirs en vrac d'un membre fondateur de Magnum" in *Reporter* (Paris), no. 10, 1973; interview in *Dialogue with Photography* by Paul Hill and Thomas Cooper, London and New York 1979.

On RODGER: Books—*The History of Photography* by Helmut and Alison Gernsheim, London and New York 1955, 1969; *Photography Today,* edited by Norman Hall, London 1957; *Personal Views,* exhibition catalogue, London 1972; *The World of Time Inc.,* edited by Robert Elson, New York 1973; *George Rodger* by Inge Bondi, London 1974; *The Real Thing: An Anthology of British Photographs 1840-1950,* exhibition catalogue, by Ian Jeffrey and David Mellor, London 1975; *Life Goes to War,* edited by David Scherman, New York 1977; *The Camera at War* by Jorge Lewinski, London 1978; *British Photography 1955-1965: The Master Craftsmen in Print,* exhibition catalogue, by Sue Davies, Michael Rand, Mark Boxer and others, London 1983; *George Rodger—Magnum Opus,* by Martin Caiger-Smith, UK and Germany 1987; *Humanity and Inhumanity—The Travels of George Rodger,* by Bruce Bernard, Phaidon—London, New York and Paris 1994. **Articles**—"George Rodger, the World's Most Travelled Photographer" in *Creative Camera* (London), February 1968; "L'Afrique Secrete de George Rodger" in *Photo* (Paris), May 1971; "George Rodger" in *Photographic Journal* (London), September 1974; "George Rodger, Photographer for *Life*" in *Orbit* (Eastbourne, Sussex), May 1975; "George Rodger" in *The Guardian* (London), 2 May 1975; "Photography" by Richard Ehrlich in *Art and Artists* (London), March 1979; "George Rodger" by Tom Hopkinson in *You and Your Camera* (London), no. 10, 1979; "Masai Moran" by Carole Naggar in *Le Matin* (Paris), 1 February 1980; "L'Afrique de George Rodger" in *Photo* (Paris), October 1984; "George Rodger: Desert Journey" in *Creative Camera* (London), July/August 1985; "Rodger's Vanishing Africa" in *Readers' Digest,* 1987; "Power, Dignity and Racism?" in *Creative Camera,* 1987; "The Inveterate George Rodger," in *World Magazine,* 1988; two-issue interview in *British Journal of Photography,* 1989; Review of Exhibition in *New York Times,* 1989; "Magnum Opus" in *Expresso,* Lisbon; Review on "Blitz" Exhibition, *Photo,* Paris 1990; "Living Through the Blitz" in *The Telegraph Magazine,* 1990; interview by Amanda Hopkinson, *Photography Magazine,* 1990.

*

From an early age I had an instinctive urge to document all I saw, all that I lived, and, at first, photography—as such or as an art—interested me not at all. It was only a means of expression to supplement my writing. In the beginning my typewriter was as much a part of my recording apparatus as my camera.

This meant that in those early years I had no contact with my contemporaries in the photographic field, nor even knowledge of their work. So I was influenced by no one, and there were no short cuts for me. I was self-taught, the hard way, by trial and error.

Probably this was the embryo stage of a natural "photo-journalist," though I didn't know it and, anyway, the word hadn't been coined yet.

During World War II, as war correspondent for *Life,* I reached my heyday as a photojournalist looking at tragedy, horror, disaster and sometimes glory through the viewfinder—as though my camera were a window on the world, and, instinctively, I founded my own photo philosophy.

Although I wrote detailed captions to my pictures for *Life* and sent lead-in text pieces with each package, I realized at last that the force of what I had to say lay in my pictures. They took on a new measure, and, to maintain their strength, I knew they had to be meticulously factual, honest and true—no staged effects, no Western Desert mockups, no falsity.

And I follow this principle still. It can probably be summed up in one word: "integrity."

I may juggle the composition, as the strength of a picture is in the composition. Or I may play with the light. But I never interfere with the subject. The subject has to fall into place on its own and, if I don't like it, I don't have to print it.

I am saddened sometimes to see among the young photographers of today so much desperate striving for effect, for distortion, for so much gimmickry, and for kudos.

—George Rodger

* * *

The theme of George Rodger's work since the end of World War II has been a noble one—the unity of man with the whole natural world. In many distant places, but above all in Africa, he has made an unforgettable record of the lives, customs and ceremonies of primitive peoples in their own surroundings, following a pattern of existence which has lasted unchanged over the centuries, sometimes indeed over thousands of years. "At school I was a dreamer. I dreamed of faraway places and never really studied. By the time I was 19 I had worked my way as a seaman twice around the world, and established an inability to keep still for long."

Basic to his photographic achievement is Rodger's capacity, not so much for "getting on with" people in remote parts, of whose language he can at best know only a few words, as for allowing himself to be quietly absorbed into their way of life, so that he becomes in spirit the tribesmen or villagers whose manner of life he is recording. Chiefly, he says, "this is a matter of the respect and liking you feel for them, and which somehow they understand and feel towards you in return."

The impulse that launched Rodger off into this special aspect of photography derived from his experiences in World War II. During those five years he crossed the Sahara from the Cameroons and on into Syria; made his way to Burma for the Japanese invasion; covered the North African campaign and the landings in Sicily and Italy; on to the D-Day assault, followed by the drive across France and Germany—to the ultimate horror of being present when the Belsen concentration camp was opened up. *Life* magazine, for which he was then working, made an 8-page story on George Rodger's travels as a war photographer, and so fearful were many of the scenes he photographed that he resolved to have nothing more to do with the coverage of war and violence.

As one of the four "founding fathers" of the Magnum agency in 1947, he chose Africa as his quarter of the globe, with magical effect on his work, as Inge Bondi, who was his colleague at Magnum has described: "To inaccessible valleys, across roadless deserts and bushland, Rodger moved cautiously, observing and absorbing the customs and courtesies of tribal men. Accepting and adopting the local expressions of friendship and hospitality, however strange, opened up to him the wonders of varying village customs, which he has recorded with an accuracy and simplicity unrivalled in photography."

The word "simplicity" is all-important. Many photographers, as is well known, make efforts to establish a personal style which can be recognized as a hallmark on their pictures. But the only style that George Rodger cares about is truth—to catch, with simplicity and naturalness, that aspect of reality which is presented to him through the viewfinder. His pictures are always boldly composed; often, since he operates so much in bright sunshine, strongly lit; and, because his theme is people at home in their own environment, taken from a sufficient distance to allow their setting to appear, so drawing the viewer in to become part of the whole scene.

Operating so much on his own, far away from offices and colleagues, George Rodger took to being his own writer, first in the form of notes for captions, plus a careful diary of events and facts which a journalist later could write up. But after a while he took to writing, and sometimes cabling, his own stories. In addition, despite all the stress and hazard of the war period, he managed to write two books, the first on his experiences in the desert, the second on Burma and the Japanese invasion. Besides being his own writer, he is also his own darkroom worker, and has often spent the whole night printing up his pictures.

Only a few years ago—at the age of 70, though looking 20 years younger—Rodger went back to East Africa, to Kenya, where he used his unique powers of making contact and gaining acceptance to photograph a secret circumcision ceremony among the Masai warrior tribe. The fifty or so pictures made early one morning in the course of a few hours created an unforgettable impression when exhibited in London and elsewhere. Speaking of them, he said: "That was the first story I've felt really happy about since I was living among the Nubas in the Upper Nile thirty years ago. . . . I was much more at home with them than in any city in the world.''

—Tom Hopkinson

ROITER, Fulvio.

Nationality: Italian. **Born:** Meolo, Venice, 1 November 1926. **Education:** Studied chemistry at the Istituto Pacinotti, Venice, 1946-49; self-taught in photography. **Family:** Married Louise Seuntjens in 1938; daughters: Evelyn and Jessica. **Career:** Member, La Gondola group of photographers, Venice, since 1949. Freelance photographer, in Venice, working for *Rivista Pirelli, Du, Réalités, Camera, Schöner Wohnen,* etc., since 1953. **Recipient:** Prix Nadar, Paris, 1956; Best Photobook Prize, Arles, France, 1979. **Address:** Lungomare Marconi 28, Venezia-Lido, Italy.

Individual Exhibitions:

1970	Fondazione Querini Stamalia, Venice
1973	Musée des Beaux-Arts, Brussels
	Musée des Beaux-Arts, Antwerp, Belgium
1979	Galerie L'Oeil, Paris
	Trent'anni di un Fotografo, Galleria Ravagnan, Palazzo delle Prigioni, Venice

Selected Group Exhibitions:

1955	*Subjektive Fotografie,* Saarbrucken, West Germany
1964	*World Exhibition of Photography: What Is Man?,* Pressehaus Stern, Hamburg (and world tour)
1980	*Trent'anni di Fotografia a Venezia 1948-78,* Palazzo Fortuny, Venice
1983	*Die fotografische Sammlung,* Museum Folkwang, Essen, West Germany
1984	*Subjektive Fotografie: Images of the 50s,* San Francisco Museum of Modern Art (travelled to the University of Houston, Texas; Museum Folkwang, Essen; Vasterbottens Museum, Umea; Kulturhuset, Stockholm; Saarland Museum, Saarbrucken; Palais des Beaux-Arts, Brussels)

Publications:

By ROITER: Books—*Venise à Fleur d'Eau,* Lausanne 1954; *Ombrie, Terre de St. François,* Lausanne 1955; *Andalousie,* with texts by Garcia Lorca, Machado, Jimenez and Unamuno, Lausanne 1957; *Bruges,* with poems by Maurice Careme, Brussels 1960; *Naquane,* Lausanne 1966; *Liban: Lumière des Siècles,* with text by Max-Pol Fouchet, Lausanne 1967; *Mexico,* Zurich 1968; *Brasil,* Zurich 1970; *Turquie,* Zurich 1971; *Algarve,* Lausanne 1971; *Espagne,* Zurich 1972; *Tunisie,* Zurich 1973; *Venice,* Zurich 1973; *Essere Venezia,* Udine 1977; *Laguna,* Udine 1978; *Mexico,* Zurich 1979; *Fulvio Roiter,* Milan 1980; *Verona,* Udine 1980; *Carnevale a Venezia,* Padua 1981; *Firenze e Toscana,* Udine 1981.

On ROITER: Books—*The Picture History of Photography* by Peter Pollack, New York 1958; *Nuova Fotografia Italiana* by Guiseppe Turroni, Milan 1959; *70 Anni di Fotografia in Italia* by Italo Zannier, Moderna, Italy 1978; *Trent'anni di Fotografia a Venezia: Il Circolo La Gondola 1948-1978* by Italo Zannier, Venice 1980; *Museum Folkwang: die fotografische Sammlung,* exhibition catalogue, with introduction by Ute Eskildsen, Essen, West Germany 1983; *Subjektive Fotografie: Images of the 50s,* exhibition catalogue, by Ute Eskildsen, Manfred Schmalriede and Dorothy Martinson, Essen, West Germany 1984.

*

Since 1954 my photographic activity has essentially revolved round the production of books of photographs. It has always fascinated me to describe a country or a city by means of pictures. I did not move on to this as my main activity after a long apprenticeship as a newsman (as happens to many photographers), but suddenly, when as long ago as 1953 I decided to go off to Sicily on a bicycle.

It is a hard discipline, because each book is a form of harsh training. The publishers want all they can get with a minimum of outlay, on the grounds of cost, so I am forced to undertake a continual simplifying exercise.

And then the quality of the reproduction: many of these books (for example *Ombre et Terre de St. François*—which won the Prix Nadar in 1956—and *Algarve, Liban, Brasil, Turquie*) were printed in ''heliogravure'' in the great printing works of Heliogravure S.A. in Lausanne and are incomparable examples of quality both in black-and-white and in colour. *Andalousie,* for example, contains some colour pages in heliogravure that look as if they had been printed yesterday—yet they date from 1957!

But the most curious phenomen of the past few years has been the success of the book *Essere Venezia,* an all-colour volume that has sold, in only three years, 150,000 copies in four versions, Italian, French, German and English.

—Fulvio Roiter

*   *   *

It is hard not to recognize one of Fulvio Roiter's photographs at first sight; the presence—excessive, as some think—of his hand ''adjustment'' of the subject (in accordance with classical rules for the expression of forms and lines) is unmistakable. Roiter is without doubt one of the greatest international masters of illustrative photography. Apart from some work (as it were in anticipation) for magazines around the world, all of his vast reportage has been published in books. His pictures are destined to stand the test of time; they hardly ever include any trace of the ephemeral, but depict worlds that are almost timeless, ''as they must have been before they were contaminated by the presence of man.''

Folon has written of him that ''for Roiter the 20th century does not exist''; it does not exist as events in the past or in the present, nor as a series of problems. Roiter is not interested in the news of the day, still less in recording great deeds. What Roiter depicts is sensations, emotions, impressions, in every country in the world from his native Venice or the Umbria of St. Francis to Brazil, Africa, Turkey, Spain. . . . The great merit of his photography lies in the value given to things that commonly go unobserved because we look at them in such a trivial way. Roiter tackles this by seeking to show the environment in which a people has developed, probing into basic features, almost into their archetypal structure. For this purpose he rarely needs human figures in his pictures; when they do appear they are often reduced to mere figures in the composition, hardly recognizable as individuals and virtually never as problems.

The great strength of Fulvio Roiter's language, its remarkable impressiveness, comes from the photographer's continual intervention in the composition, the arrangement, to obtain strict geometrical clarity and to emphasize the right features in the composition—problems that Roiter long worked on in black and white, a very complex discipline, to enable him finally to express himself in colour. Roiter's is a photography of colours, sumptuous, luxuriant and of great evocative power, which appeals to viewers all over the world for its spectacular quality, the dreams it creates, the atmosphere, the wide visions of timeless worlds. An optimistic photography too, if we wish, inseparable from the personality of the photographer, who loves people and is for ever in search of motifs of hope among them.

—Attilio Colombo

RONIS, Willy.

Nationality: French. **Born:** Paris, 14 August 1910. **Education:** Attended the Lycée Rollin, now the Lycée Decour, Paris, 1919-27; Lycée Louis le Grand, Paris, 1928. **Military Service:** Served as a meteorologist in the French Air

Force, at Châteaurous, 1931, and at Châteaudun and Bergerac, 1939-40. **Family:** Married the painter Marie-Anne Lansiaux in 1946. **Career:** Freelance photographer, Paris, since 1936. Instructor, Lycée Louis Lumière, Paris, 1968, Lycée Estienne, Paris, 1968-70, Ecole des Beaux-Arts, Avignon, 1971-76, Faculty of Letters of the University of Aix en Provence, 1972-76, and at the University of Provence St. Charles, Marseilles, 1978-81. **Recipient:** Kodak National Prize, 1947; Gold Medal, *Biennale,* Venice, 1957; National Grand Prize of Arts and Letters for Photography, 1979. Honorary President, Association Nationale des Reporters Photographes Illustrateurs (ANRPI), 1975; Honoured Photographer, *Rencontres Internationales de la Photographie,* Arles, France, 1980; Prix Nadar, Paris, 1981. Commandeur, Ordre des Arts et des Lettres, Paris, 1985. Chevalier de la Légion d'Honneur 1986; Membership of the Royal Photographic Society of Great Britain, 1993. **Agent:** Agence Rapho, 8 rue d'Alger, 75001 Paris, France. **Address:** 46 rue de Lagny, 75020 Paris, France.

Individual Exhibitions:

1936   *Neige dans les Vosges,* Gare de l'Est, Paris
1937   *Paris la Nuit,* Gare de l'Est, Paris
1967   *La Republique Democratique Allemande,* toured France
        Mon Paris, toured the world
        La Provence des Montagnes, toured the world
        L'Alsace, toured the world
1979   *Sur Paris,* Centre Socio-Culturel, Lannion, France
1980   *Willy Ronis: Photographies 1945-1979,* at *Rencontres Internationales de la Photographie,* Arles, France
        Photographic Center of Athens
        Sur le Fil du Hasard, FNAC Gallery, Montparnasse, Paris
1981   Fotogalerie Pennings, Eindhoven, Netherlands
        Le Château d'Eau, Toulouse
        Musèe d'Orange, France
        French Cultural Center, New York
1982   Galerie FNAC, Metz, France (travelled to Raismes, Dreux and Le Mans, France)
        Musée des Beaux Arts, Charleroi, Belgium
1983   Espace Cardin, Paris (travelled to Avignon, Cholet, Bordeaux, Rouen and Arras, France)
1985   Palais de Tokio, Paris (retrospective; travelled to the Fondation Nationale de la Photographie, Lyon, France)
1986   Afterimage Gallery, Dallas, Texas
        Witkin Gallery, New York
1986-90 Exhibitions in France, New York and Moscow
1990   10 exhibitions in France, London. and Lausanne, Switzerland
1992   Centres culturel à Vitré, Aubagne, and Brest, France
1993   St. Benoît-Poitiers, Nancy, Toulouse-Blagnac, Lorient, Aubenas, France and Barcelona, Spain
1994   Hôtel de Sully, Paris (organised by the Ministry of Culture)

Selected Group Exhibitions:

1935   *La Photo qui Accuse,* Maison de la Culture, Paris
1938   *Photos de Neige,* Grand Atelier, Paris
1947   *Groupe des XV,* Paris (and annually until 1961)
1951   *4 French Photographers: Brassaï/Doisneau/Izis/Ronis,* Museum of Modern Art, New York
1955   *The Family of Man,* Museum of Modern Art, New York (and world tour)
1965   *6 Photographes de Paris,* Musée des Arts Décoratifs, Paris
        Photographie Française, French Embassy, Moscow
1978   *Photographies de la Region Provence-Alpes Maritimes,* Ecole d'Art, Luminy, Marseilles (toured France)
1981   *French Photography 1945-80,* Zabriskie Gallery, New York
1983   *Photos de Famille,* Centre d'Art Plastique Contemporain, Bordeaux, France (toured France)

Collections:

Bibliothèque Nationale, Paris; Musée Réattu, Arles, France; Musée de Toulon; Musée d'Orange, France; Museum of Modern Art, New York; Ministry of Culture, Paris; Metropolitan Museum of Art, New York; University of Arizona, Tucson.

Publications:

By RONIS: Books—*Photo-Reportage et Chasse aux Images,* Paris 1951, as *Il Manuale del Perfetto Fotoreporter,* Rome 1953; *Belleville-Ménilmontant,* with text by Pierre MacOrlan, Paris 1954, 1984; *Sur le Fil du Hasard,* Paris 1980; *Willy Ronis,* ed. Fabbri, Milan, 1983; *Mon Paris,* with preface by H. Raczymow, Paris 1985; *12 Photos,* portfolio, with preface by Bertrand Eveno, Paris 1985; *12 photos,* portfolio, edited by Bérard Pinhas, Paris 1986; *Willy Ronis,* ed Photopoche, Paris, 1991; *Willy Ronis 1934-1987,* Japan, 1991; *Toutes Belles,* with text by Régine Deforges, Paris, 1992; *Les Enfants de Germinal,* with a text by Cavanna and photographs by Ronis, Jean Philippe Charbonnier and Robert Doisneau, Paris, 1993; *Quand je serai grand,* Paris, 1993; *Lungo il fume delle domeniche,* Milan, 1994. **Articles**—"Le Reporter et ses Batailles" in *Photo-Cinéa* (Paris), March 1948; "L'Eclair Enchaine" in *Photo-Service* (Antwerp), January/February 1950; "Reverie d'un Chasseur d'Images" in *Photo-Cinéma* (Paris), August 1951; "Ne Tirez Pas sur le Photographe" in *Photorama* (Antwerp), May/June 1952; "Vieilles Pierres . . ." in *Photo-Cinema* (Paris), September 1952; "Comment J'ai Fait Cette Photo" in *Photo Cinéma* (Paris), November 1952; "Vision Naturelle et Vision Photographique" in *Camera* (Lucerne), December/January 1954/55; "A Batons Rompus" in *Camera* (Lucerne), September 1955; "Le Photographe devant la Réalité" in *Photorama* (Antwerp), July 1955; "A Propos de Photo Industrielle" in *Photorama* (Antwerp), January 1958; "Une Vieille Maison" in *Photorama* (Antwerp), October 1958; "Oeil, Objectif, Vision Globale" in *Photographie Nouvelle* (Paris), November 1967; "Willy Ronis," interview, with Jean-Claude Gautrand, in *Le Photographe* (Paris), November 1975; "Histoire d'une photo celebre" in *Photo* (Paris), July 1985; "Willy Ronis," interview, with Herve Guibert, in *Le Monde* (Paris), 4 July 1985.

On RONIS: Books—*U.S. Camera Album,* edited by Tom Mahoney, New York 1953; *Moderni Francousta Fotografie* by J.A. Klein, Prague 1966; *La Photographie Française* by Claude Nori, Paris 1978, as *French Photography,* London 1979; *Voyons Voir: huit photographes,* edited by Pierre Borhan, Paris 1980; *10 photographes pour le patrimoine,* exhibition catalogue, edited by Jean-Claude Gautrand, Paris 1980; *Les Grands Photographes: Willy Ronis,* with text by Bertrand Eveno, Paris 1983. **Articles**—"Our Guest of Honour: Willy Ronis" in *Photography* (London), March 1952; "Willy Ronis" in *Modern Photography* (New York), April 1952; "Willy Ronis" in *Photography* (London), November 1955; "De Parijse Fotograaf Willy Ronis over" in *Foto* (Amersfoort, Netherlands), February 1962; "Il Reportage Umanistico" in *Progresso Fotografico* (Milan), July/August 1977; "Willy Ronis" in *Il Fotografo* (Milan), November 1979; "Willy Ronis" in *Photo-Journal* (Paris), February 1980; "L'Année Willy Ronis" in *Le Photographe* (Paris), February 1980; "Willy Ronis" in *Photo* (Paris), November 1980; "Willy Ronis" in *Photo Cinéma* (Paris), January 1981. **Film**—*Willy Ronis ou les cadeaux du hazard,* Patrice Noia,1986.

*

One of the best introductions to an understanding of my work (it is easy to read and comprehend) is contained in my book *Photo-Reportage et Chase aux Images.* Edward Steichen produced a long extract when he presented my portfolio in *U.S. Camera* in 1953. I have not changed my ideas since those distant days. I worked until 1954 with a 6 by 6 Rolleiflex, then moved, for 99 percent of my work, to small format, and I now maintain, without reservation, that I have always taken very nearly the same photographs with the same look.

As well, an interview with Jean-Claude Gautrand in *Le Photographe* of November 1975 and the article in *Photo-Journal* of February 1980 complete the picture better than I know how to do.

I will not hazard a judgment on contemporary photography. It is multiform and a great deal of it is incomprehensible or of very little interest to me.

My book, *Sur le Fil du Hasard*—published by Contrejour in 1980—begins with a long text which will, I hope, completely clarify my ideas.

Here is that preface, *Level with the Daisies*: When I go out with my camera I do not go in search of the Holy Grail. I do not feel invested with any message for anyone, nor do I perceive any transcendental vibration. I put in order and combine information, which my head and heart, in their fashion, immediately modify. To do this, I have no need to lift my eyes to the heavens for some sign, nor do I feel the emergence of any kind of spiritual approach; my eyes are occupied by scanning my surroundings as well as by the image captured by the viewfinder. This is already a great deal of effort; my attention cannot go further.

My photographs are not a vengeance on death, and I do not suffer from any existential anguish. I don't even know where I am going, except to be in front of—more or less by chance—things or people who please, interest, disturb or offend me. It is afterwards that I try to reflect, when I have my images in front of me. The limits of my intelligence are such that I do not dwell on this work; others, if they want to, will do that better than I can.

At the point I have reached I have acquired no certainty and no anxiety about having none. Nature has given me, purely by chance, a kind of sensitivity that has given me a fair amount of torment but also immense joy. Thank you! I have ploughed my furrow with my instinct, my ordinary decency, singing my song under my breath. I have often had a lot of pleasure and that compensates for the rest that happily is easily forgotten.

Have I found myself. I am not conscious of ever having lost myself, but I know no more about that than did the little boy in the sailor suit, who in 1913 wheeled his hoop in Condorcet Street (Paris 9), who has retained all his artlessness and hopes to preserve it to the end of the run.

—Willy Ronis

*   *   *

The photographs of Willy Ronis cannot be separated from Willy Ronis the man. Ronis is bursting with life, avid for knowledge, a man with a sharp eye, a modest man. His photographs are full, completely, of humanity. Not one of his pictures is without one or more people—men, women, children.

Ronis's real subject is human relationships, relationships experienced in real life as well as those he devises within the rectangular shape of his pictures, relationships between people as well as between people and the field in which they picnic, the walls of the town in which they live, the machines of the factory in which they work.

Ronis's world is not one of contorted faces or violence; it is a harmonious world. This isn't a weakness in his work; it involves a choice. This man wants to have faith in man. The harmony within the pictures is the photographic equivalent of tenderness.

In 1951 Edward Steichen presented an exhibition, *4 French Photographers,* at the Museum of Modern Art in New York. The photographers were Brassaï, Doisneau, Izis and Ronis. A real family. Certainly they are not the only photographers who can be claimed to represent France; just the same, they are the most intensely French, the most completely Parisien, of photographers. And, they remain to this day among the most representative of French photography of the 1950s.

Indeed, for Ronis, the essential, the significant, is never far away; it is where people are—at a dance, at a fair, in a café. "Adventure is not measured by kilometers," he has said. "The strongest feelings of the exotic are not to be found in the bistros of Soho or Prague or Rostock, but in those of Paris among the belote players of the Café-Guingette in the rue des Cascades."

There is music in his photographs—not always accordions, sometimes a little jazz, a strain of violins. There is something that, like music, and better than words, conveys a particular idea, speaks to us of the human soul.

For Stravinsky, music was "the creation of a harmony between man and time." Are Willy Ronis's photographs also a creation of harmony between man and his spatial environment? In fact, he himself says that "to transform chaos into harmony is the constant quest of the seeker of images." A faith that he immediately qualifies by stressing that "the beautiful picture is a geometry modulated by the heart."

—Guy Mandery

ROSENBLUM, Walter.

Nationality: American. **Born:** New York City, 1 October 1919. **Education:** Attended Seward Park High School, New York, 1932-36; City College of New York, 1936-38; studied photography, under Paul Strand and Lewis Hine, at the Photo League, New York, 1937-40. **Military Service:** Served as a photographer in the United States Army Signal Corps, in Europe, 1943-45; most decorated photographer in the Army; Silver Star; Bronze Star; Purple Heart; Presidential Unit Citation; 5 Battle Stars. **Family:** Married Naomi Baker in 1949; daughters: Nina and Lisa. **Career:** Photographer since 1937. Member of the Photo League, New York, 1938-52: Editor of *Photo Notes,* 1939-41; Chairman of the Exhibition Committee, 1941-42; Executive Secretary, 1945-46; Vice-President, 1946-47; and President, 1947-52. Worked as an assistant to the photographer Eliot Elisofon, New York, 1939-40; freelance photographer, working for *Survey Graphic, Mademoiselle,* Federation for the Support of Jewish Philanthropies, etc., New York, 1941-42; Staff Photographer, United States Department of Agriculture, Washington, D.C., 1940-41, and Agricultural Adjustment Administration, throughout the United States, 1942-43; Staff Photographer, Unitarian Service Committee, France and Texas, 1946-47. Joined the photography faculty, Brooklyn College, New York, 1947: Professor of Photography since 1971. Member of the faculty, Yale Summer School of Music and Art, Norfolk, Connecticut, 1952-77; Professor of Photography, Cooper Union, New York, 1956-65. Founder Member, Society for Photographic Education, 1962. Co-Curator, with Naomi Rosenblum, *Lewis Hine Retrospective,* Brooklyn Museum, 1977. Board Member, The Photographers' Forum, New York, 1979, and the Asian American Research Institute, New York, 1980. **Recipient:** National Endowment for the Arts Fellowship, 1977; New York State Council for the Arts Fellowship, 1978; Institute for Art and Urban Resources Fellowship, 1978; Guggenheim Fellowship, 1979; PSC-CUNY Award, New York, 1982 and 1985. **Address:** 21-36 33rd Road, Long Island City, New York 11106, U.S.A.

Individual Exhibitions:

1944	American Red Cross, London
1949	Brooklyn Museum, New York
1950	University of Minnesota, Minneapolis
1955	International Museum of Photography, George Eastman House, Rochester, New York
	2 Photographers: Alfred Eisenstaedt and Walter Rosenblum, Philadelphia College of Art
1957	Whitman Hall, Brooklyn College, New York (retrospective)
	Cooper Union Museum, New York (retrospective)
	3 Photographers: Harry Callahan, Walter Rosenblum, Minor White, White Museum of Art, Cornell University, Ithaca, New York
1964	*Photographs of Haiti,* International Museum of Photography, George Eastman House, Rochester, New York (travelled to the Germantown Arts Association, Philadelphia)
1969	Carr House Gallery, Rhode Island School of Design, Providence (retrospective)
1973	*Haitian Photographs,* Centrum Gallery, Hampshire College, Amherst, Massachusetts
1975	*Walter Rosenblum: Retrospective Exhibition,* Fogg Art Museum, Harvard University, Cambridge, Massachusetts
1976	Milwaukee Center for Photography (retrospective)
	Photopia Gallery, Philadelphia (retrospective)
1978	Witkin Gallery, New York (retrospective)
1979	*People of the South Bronx,* Lincoln Hospital, New York (travelled to the Parsons School of Design, New York, 1980)
1981	University of Maryland, Baltimore (retrospective)
	People of the South Bronx, University of Southern Maine, Portland
	South Africa/South Bronx, State University of New York at Old Westbury (with Peter Magubane)
	People of the South Bronx, Board of Higher Education, New York
1982	*People of the South Bronx,* Uptown Hull House, Chicago

Street Shower, Muclaly Park, **South Bronx, New York, 1981.** Photograph by Walter Rosenblum.

Milwaukee Institute of Art and Design, Wisconsin
Indiana University, Bloomington
1984 *People of the South Bronx,* Lehman College, New York
 People of the South Bronx, Brooklyn College, New York
1986 *Pitt Street 1938-39,* Hebrew College, Boston
 Pitt Street 1938-39, Baruch College, New York
1987 Staatsmuseum, East Berlin (retrospective)
 National Museum, Havana (retrospective)

Selected Group Exhibitions:

1943 *New Photographers I,* Museum of Modern Art, New York
1959 *Photographs by Professors,* Limelight Gallery, New York
1962 *5 Photographers,* A Photographer's Place, Philadelphia
1965 *10 American Photographers,* University of Wisconsin at
 Milwaukee
1966 *21 Photographers,* New Hope Historical Society, Pennsylvania
1967 *Photography in the 20th Century,* National Gallery of Canada,
 Ottawa (toured Canada and the United States, 1967-73)
1968 *13 Photographers,* Pratt Institute, Brooklyn, New York
1972 *Masters of Photography,* Vogel Galleries, Layton School of
 Art, Milwaukee

1979 *International Year of the Child,* Westenhook Galleries,
 Westfield, Massachusetts
1983 *Founding Members,* Society for Photographic Education,
 Philadelphia

Collections:

Museum of Modern Art, New York; Brooklyn Museum, New York; Queens Museum, New York; International Museum of Photography, George Eastman House, Rochester, New York; Yale University, New Haven, Connecticut; Detroit Institute of Art; National Gallery of Canada, Ottawa; Bibliothèque Nationale, Paris; Metropolitan Museum of Art, New York; Carnegie Institute Museum of Art, Pittsburgh.

Publications:

By ROSENBLUM: Books—*Paul Strand: A Retrospective Monograph,* with others, Millerton, New York 1971; *America and Lewis Hine,* with Naomi Rosenblum and Alan Trachtenberg, Millerton, New York 1977; *Photographs by Earl Dotter,* portfolio introduction, New York 1979. **Articles**—"The Quiet One" in *Photo Notes* (New York), Fall 1941; "Image of Freedom" in *Camera Craft* (San Francisco), February 1942; "What Is Modern Photography?'' in *American Photography* (New York), March 1951; ''Five Weeks with a Camera'' in *American Photography* (New York), January 1953; ''Teaching Photography'' in *Aperture* (Millerton, New York), no. 3, 1956; ''Photographic Style'' in *Contemporary Photographer* (New York), July 1963; ''Educating the Young Photographer'' in *Infinity* (New York), April 1970; ''Edouard Boubat'' in *35mm Photography* (New York), July 1975; ''Robert Doisneau'' in *35mm Photography* (New York), January 1977.

On ROSENBLUM: Books—*Walter Rosenblum,* exhibition catalogue, by Paul Strand, Brooklyn, New York 1949; *Walter Rosenblum: Retrospective Exhibition,* exhibition catalogue, by Milton Brown, Cambridge, Massachusetts 1975; *Faces: A Narrative History of the Portrait in Photography* by Ben Maddow, Boston 1977; *Walter Rosenblum: People of the South Bronx,* exhibition catalogue, by Martica Sawin, New York 1980. Articles—''Walter Rosenblum'' by Jerome Liebling in *American Photography* (New York), May 1951; ''Photography in the Classic Tradition'' by Minor White in *Image* (Rochester, New York), December 1955; ''The Art of Teaching'' by Van Deren Coke in *College Art Journal* (New York), July 1960; ''Famous Teachers'' by Barbara Ullman in *Camera 35* (New York), July 1965; ''Photography on the Mind'' by Jack Somers in *New York Magazine,* 28 May 1973; ''Between Teacher and Student'' by Jacob Deschin in *35mm Photography* (New York), Summer 1974; ''Documentary Style'' by Stephen Perloff in *Philadelphia Review,* January 1976; ''Rare Dancer'' by Louis Stettner in *Camera 35* (New York), January 1976.

*

I have always felt that the photographer should remain mute about his own work, since he has chosen the photograph as his means of communication. But I have been invited to make a statement for this book—so I offer the following.

When successful, my photographs convey to others my most profound feelings about the world, in images that are without cant or hypocrisy. There is no conscious imitation of others or attempt to adhere to passing styles. My goal is to be sensitive to the reality I perceive and to be responsible to those people and places I choose to photograph. To celebrate, through my work, the potential, the richness and the mystery of life.

—Walter Rosenblum

* * *

Walter Rosenblum is most widely known for his relationship with the Photo League, but his career has included, besides his work at the League, a multiplicity of impressive accomplishments in photography. There is his extensive and important work as a photographer, his career as a teacher, his friendship with Paul Strand, and his work as archivist of the Lewis Hine Collection and as spirited critic, writer, and organizer for the continuing tradition of documentary photography.

Walter Rosenblum was born in New York City in 1919 on the Lower East Side. His family had come to the United States as immigrants via Ellis Island and could have been photographed by Lewis Hine. He grew up as a child of the streets, his life filled with immigrant poverty and idealism, searching for the American Dream of the ''better world.'' In the late 1930s Rosenblum enrolled in photography classes at the Photo League, a loose organization that provided a center for photographic activity related to the documentary tradition of Lewis Hine and the F.S.A. As a precocious teenager, Rosenblum met many photographers, including Lewis Hine, and began to produce photographs as part of the Photo League's series of documentary projects. His work was quickly recognized for its penetrating insight and formal control, and he was soon successfully free-lancing, eventually assisting Eliot Elisofon, the *Life* photographer. Rosenblum was a combat photographer during World War II, and upon his discharge from the U.S. Army in 1945 he returned to New York City and again became active in the Photo League. This flourishing period for the League (1946-50) would see it become an important influence in establishing patterns of classes, projects, lectures, exhibitions, and publications that have become the commonplace activity of all present-day academic and museum photographic programs.

Art and photography training in academic institutions in the late 1940s had not as yet begun in the United States. There was a photography program in California with Minor White, Chicago with Moholy-Nagy, Clarence White in

Ohio, and Walter Rosenblum at Brooklyn College in New York. He started teaching at Brooklyn College in 1946 when he was 27 years old, succeeding Berenice Abbott, and he has been teaching there until the present. His work as a teacher both at Brooklyn College and at the Yale Summer School in Norfolk, Connecticut, has had significant influence on many students who in turn have become photographers, critics and teachers of reputation.

With the black-listing of the Photo League and its eventual demise in the early 1950s, the need to preserve the Lewis Hine Collection became a major problem. Hine had given most of his collection to the League, and for years volunteers had been slowly cataloging the material and printing a series of small portfolios. Various institutions were offered the collection but were not interested in receiving the work. With much difficulty, Walter and Naomi Rosenblum housed the collection and cared for it until George Eastman House, where it now resides, finally accepted the bulk of the collection. In the late 1970s the Rosenblums undertook a major exhibition of the work of Hine that was exhibited widely in the United States and finally in Canada. In conjunction with the exhibit, Alan Trachtenberg and the Rosenblums produced the definitive book on Hine, published by Aperture.

As a young man in his twenties, Rosenblum met Paul Strand, then in his fifties. Their close relationship was continuous until Strand's death in 1975 and strongly influenced Rosenblum's idea concerning style and direction in the use of documentary photography. Rosenblum's photography is an act of engagement and participation with the subjects of his work. From his early years, working on Photo League projects, the idea of the multi-faceted extended interaction of photographer and place has been the direction of his work. He strongly feels that photography demands social commitment and social responsibility.

Rosenblum continues to photograph actively and in 1979 was the recipient of a Guggenheim Fellowship which permitted him to work for a year on the very important ''People of the South Bronx'' project. These photographs exemplify all of his working principles of extended personal involvement in issues of deep social concern. They reveal an aesthetic control that derives from the force and tension of the subject, and provides clarity, insight and compassion.

—Jerome Liebling

ROSS, Judith Joy.

Nationality: American. Born: Hazleton, Pennsylvania, 1946. Education: Moore College of Art, Philadelphia, B.A. (art education), 1968; Institute of Design, Illinois Institute of Technology, Chicago, M.A. (photography), 1970. Recipient: John Simon Guggenheim Memorial Foundation Fellowship, 1986 (taken 1987-88); Charles Pratt Memorial Award, 1992. Agent: James Danziger Gallery, 130 Prince Street, New York, New York 10012, U.S.A.

Individual Exhibitions:

1987	*Portraits of the United States Congress 1986-87,* Pennsylvania Academy of the Fine Arts, Philadelphia
1991	*Judith Joy Ross: A Survey,* James Danziger Gallery, New York
1993	*New Work,* retrospective, San Francisco Museum of Modern Art, San Francisco

Selected Group Exhibitions:

1985	*New Photography,* Museum of Modern Art, New York
	The Sensuous Image, Paul Cava Gallery, Philadelphia
	Swimmers, Pace/MacGill Gallery, New York
	Eurana Park, Weatherly, Pa., Allentown Art Museum, Pennsylvania
1987	*Recent Acquisitions,* Museum of Modern Art, New York
	Twelve Photographers Look at Us, Philadelphia Museum of Art
1988	*Rethinking American Myths,* Laurence Miller Gallery, New York

Jackie Cieniawa, A. D. Thomas Elementary School, Hasleton, PA, First Grade, **1992.** Photograph ©Judith Joy Ross.

Real Faces, Whitney Museum of American Art at Phillip
Morris, New York

1990 *Photography until Now,* Museum of Modern Art, New York
*The Indomitable Spirit, Photographers and Friends Unit-
ed Against AIDS,* International Center of Photography,
Midtown, New York
Eurana Park, Weatherly, Pa., Laurence Miller Gallery,
New York

1992 *Representatives: Women Photographers from the Perma-
nent Collection,* Center for Creative Photography, Tucson,
Arizona
More than One Photography, Museum of Modern Art,
New York
The Charles Pratt Memorial Award Exhibition, Center for
Creative Photography, Tucson, Arizona
*Intentions and Techniques, Photographs from the Lehigh
University Collection,* Lehigh University, Bethlehem,
Pennsylvania

1993 *Observing Traditions, Contemporary Photographs 1975-93,*
National Gallery of Canada, Ottawa, Ontario
The Body in Nature, James Danziger Gallery, New York
Pennsylvania Photographers, Allentown Art Museum,
Pennsylvania
Photographs from the Real World, Lillehammer Art Museum,
Norway

Collections:

Allentown Museum of Art, Pennsylvania; Birmingham Museum of Fine Arts,
Alabama; Lehigh University Collection, Bethlehem, Pennsylvania; Metro-
politan Museum of Art, New York; Museum of Fine Arts, Houston, Texas;
Museum of Modern Art, New York; National Gallery of Canada, Ottawa,
Ontario; Paul F.Walter Collection, New York; San Francisco Museum of
Modern Art, California; Carlton Willers Collection; Wellesley Art Museum,
Wellesley, Massachusetts.

Publications:

By ROSS: Book—*Judith Joy Ross: A Survey,* exhibition catalog with text by
Vicki Goldberg, James Danziger Gallery (New York).

On ROSS: Books—*Women Photographers* by Constance Sullivan, 1990;
The Indomitable Spirit, exhibition catalog by Marvin Heiferman, Harry N.
Abrams (New York), 1990; *Photography until Now* by John Szarkowski (New
York), 1990; *Photographs from the Collection of Carlton Willers* by Joann
Conklin (Iowa, USA), 1993; *Magicians of Light* by James Borcoman (Otta-
wa), 1993. **Articles**—''Eurana Park, Judith Ross'' by Stephen Perloff in
Philadelphia Photo Review, Spring 1985; ''The Ghosts of War'' by Andy
Grundberg in *The New York Times,* 23 August 1985; ''An Opinionated Survey
of the Week's Events'' by Guy Trebay of *New Photography* in *Village Voice,*
21-27 August 1995; ''The Modern Focuses on Contemporary Photography''
by Andy Grundberg in *The New York Times,* 15 September 1985; Reproduction of 4-part print from ''Portraits at the Vietnam Veterans' Memorial
Washington D.C. 1983-84,'' in *Afterimage,* October 1985; ''Twelve Photographers Look at Us,'' by Eric Levin in *People Magazine,* 18 May 1987; ''We
the People, In Philadelphia, A Well-Constituted National Portrait'' by
Kathryn Livingston in *American Photographer,* July 1987; ''Faces of Power''
by Edward Sozanski in *The Philadelphia Inquirer,* 23 July 1987; ''Snap
Judgements'' by Sandy Sorlien in *The Philadelphia Daily News,* 10 April
1987; ''Twelve Photographers Look at Us,'' exhibition catalog with text by
Martha Chahroudi (Philadelphia), Spring 1987; ''Born in the USA'' by Brian
Paterson in *Afterimage,* October 1987; ''Real Faces'' by Max Kosloff in
exhibition catalog for Whitney Museum of American Art at Phillip Morris,
Spring 1988; Detail from ''Untitled'' portrait in ''Eurana Park, Weatherly
Pa.'' series in *New York Times,* 1 May 1988; ''Portraits Return in a New
Perspective'' by Andy Grundberg in *New York Times,* 26 June 1988; ''Choices''
in *Village Voice,* 16 August 1988; ''Self and Shadow'' in *Aperture* No.114,
1989; Reviews of book ''Photography Until Now,'' by Phillip Gefter in *Photo
Metro,* 1990, by Alan Artner in *The Chicago Tribune,* 25 February 1990, and
by Ed Sozanski in *The Philadelphia Inquirer,* 23 February 1990; ''The Ties

that Bind Judith Joy Ross Redefine Family'' interview by Vince Aletti in *The
Village Voice*; Review by Ingrid Sischy in *The New Yorker,* 28 January 1991.

*

I make portraits because from them, I gain something I need to know.

These portraits are made most often as series and have largely involved
children, either at leisure or in public school rooms, but other series have been
as diverse as *Portraits at the Vietnam Veterans Memorial, Washington, D.C.
1983-84,* or *Portaits of the US Congress 1986-87.*

For me, there are two qualities which, if I am fortunate enough to see
together, allow for the making of a good portrait. These two qualities appear in
life and in some images simultaneously, but in words I can only describe them
as though they existed separately.

One, is the imperfections and frailties which people hope I am overlooking
and which they perhaps think they are better off without. The other is the
ability people have to hold up under the particular momentary or defining
circumstances they bear.

When I am able to see this miraculous combination, the subject and I have
made a portrait, and I have had another chance to reinstate this recognition in
my heart.

—Judith Joy Ross

*   *   *

Judith Joy Ross is one of the finest of the traditionalists among her
generation of photographers. Her restrained, subtle portraits, made with a
large camera and with the conscious collaboration of her subjects, are
unexcelled in their directness and vulnerability. Her pictures look far more like
what one occasionally sees in the mirror than they do like most photographs on
a driving licence, high school graduation or family reunion. Ross's photographs are transcripts of the dialogue that for most people occurs between self
and soul, not face and camera. Her photographs have most often depicted
children, particularly at play in Eurana Park, Weatherly, Pennsylvania—a
perfect instance of small town American life as lived by children during the
long days of summer. These photographs are resonant with youthful uncertainty, but they differ from most touching pictures of children by linking this
quality, apparently indissolubly with strength and dignity. Ross has also
photographed adults with equal poignancy—perhaps an even greater
accomplishment.

Her series *Portraits at the Vietnam Veterans Memorial, Washington DC*
(1983-84) is passionately indirect; it represents the faces of a wide cross
section of American visitors to Maya Lin's famous monument in Washington.
Seen in almost cinematic close-up as they read the columns of names etched
on the memorial, these people are individuals, not representatives, participants
in private moments, not public mourners, yet Ross's photographs movingly
take on the weight of history and a nation's reckoning with its past. A
documentary project of even wider aspiration was Ross's 1986-87 *Portraits of
the US Congress,* a series as sad and funny as it is often moving. The pathetic
ordinariness she found in the corridors of power and the odd juxtapositions of
the few overly famous faces with the virtual anonymity of most of the
legislators make for fascinating viewing. Ross wastes no time pondering the
possible distinctions between documentary and fine art photography and her
group of tense but delicate portraits of U.S. military personnel on the eve of the
war in the Persian Gulf are exceptional works in both categories.

—Ellen Handy

RÖSSLER, Jaroslav.

Nationality: Czechoslovakian. **Born:** Smilov, 25 May 1902. **Education:**
Attended elementary school, Havlíckuv Brod, 1909-17; student-apprentice in
the studio of the photographer František Drtikol, Prague, 1917-21. **Family:**
Married Gertruda Fischerova in 1926 (died, 1976); daughter: Silvia Vìtová.
Career: Photographer in Studio Drtikol, Prague, 1921-26, and Studio Manuel

Freres, Paris, 1926-27; Photographer, *Pestrý týden* weekly review, Prague, 1927-28; Photographer, Studio Lorelle, Paris, 1928-32, Studio Piaz, Paris, 1932-34, and Studio Lucien Lorelle, Paris, 1934-35; maintained own studio, Prague, 1935-51; Photographer, Studio Fotografia, Prague, 1951-64. **Died:** (in Prague) 5 January 1990.

Individual Exhibitions:

1968	Malá Galerie, Prague
1975	Fotokabinett Jaromír Funke, Brno, Czechoslovakia
1985	The Photographers' Gallery, London (with Jaromìr Funke)
1991	Prague House of Photography, Prague

Selected Group Exhibitions:

1923	*Foto-Salon,* rue de Clichy, Paris
1926	*Devětsil Group,* Rudolfinum, Prague
1966	*Surrealism and Photography,* Fotokabinett Jaromìr Funke, Brno, Czechoslovakia
1974	*Personalities of Czech Photography,* Municipal Gallery, Roudnice, Czechoslovakia (travelled to the Museum of Decorative Arts, Prague)
1979	*Tschechoslowakische Photographie 1918-1978,* Fotoforum Kassel, West Germany
1980	*The Imaginary Photo Museum,* Kunsthalle, Cologne
1981	*Germany: The New Vision,* Fraenkel Gallery, San Francisco
1982	*Lichtbildnisse: Das Porträt in der Fotografie,* Rheinisches Landesmuseum, Bonn
1983	*Photographes Tchèques 1920-50,* Centre George Pompidou, Paris
1984	*Tschechische Fotografie 1918-48,* Museum Folkwang, Essen, West Germany (travelled to Frankfurt, Germany; Vienna, Austria and Lódž, Poland)
1985	*Ursprung und Gegenwart tschechoslowakischer Fotografie,* Fotografie Forum, Frankfurt am Main, Germany
1988	*Line, Colour, Form,* Prague Municipal Gallery, Prague
1989	*What Is Photography—150 Years of Photography,* Gallery Mánes, Prague
	Czech Modernism 1900-1945, The Museum of Fine Arts, Houston (travelled to New York and Akron)
1990	*Progressive Photography in Czechoslovakia,* Galerie Robert Doisneau, Vandouvre-les-Nancy, France (travelled to Müllheim and Strasbourg)
	Czech Avant-Garde, RIP, Archbishop's Palace, Arles, France
1993	*The Art of the Avant-Garde in Czechoslovakia 1918-1938,* IVAM Centre Julio Gonzales, Valencia, Spain (travelled to Spain)

Collections:

Museum of Decorative Arts, Prague; Moravian Gallery, Brno, Czechoslovakia; Polaroid Collection, Amsterdam; Bibliothèque Nationale, Paris; Museum of Fine Arts, Houston; Museum of Modern Art, New York; Art Institute, Chicago; San Francisco Museum of Modern Art, San Francisco; Getty Museum, Malibu, California; The Navigator Foundation, Boston; Robert Koch Gallery, San Francisco; Howard Greenberg Gallery, New York; Houk & Friedman Gallery, New York; Musée nationale d'art moderne, Paris; Prague House of Photography, Prague; Galerie Rudolf Kicken, Cologne, Germany; Galerie Neumann, Düsseldorf, Germany; Museum Folkwang, Essen, Germany.

Publications:

By RÖSSLER: Book—*Jaroslav Rössler: 10 Photographien,* portfolio, edited by the Galerie Rudolf Kicken, Cologne 1982.

On RÖSSLER: Books—*Stavba a báseň/Construction and Poem* by Karel Teige, Prague 1927; *Tschechoslowakische Fotografie 1918-1978* by Karel Teige, Prague 1947; *Die Geschichte der Fotografie im 20. Jahrhundert/ Photography in the 20th Century* by Petr Tausk, Cologne 1977, London 1980;

Photographie als Kunst 1879-1979/Kunst als Photographie 1949-1979, exhibition catalogue in 2 volumes, by Peter Weiermair, Innsbruck 1979; *The Imaginary Photo Museum* by Helmut Gernsheim, Renate and L. Fritz Gruber and others, Cologne 1981, London 1982; *Lichtbildnisse: Das Porträt in der Fotografie,* edited by Klaus Honnef, Cologne 1982; *Photographes Tchèques 1920-1950,* exhibition catalogue, by Zdeněk Kirschner and Antonìn Dufek, Paris 1983; *Tschechische Fotografie 1918-1948,* exhibition catalogue, edited by Ute Eskildsen and Antonín Dufek, Essen, West Germany 1984; *Czechoslovakian Photography: Jaromìr Funke, Jaroslav Rössler,* exhibition catalogue, by Jiñ Hlušička, Sue Davies and Antonìn Dufek, London 1985; *The Evolution of Czechoslovak Photography from 1918 to the Present* by Petr Tausk, Prague 1986; *Příběh fotografie,* by Daniela Mrázková, Prague, 1985; *Černobílá fotografie,* by Antonín Dufek, Prague, 1987; *Cesty československé fotografie* by Daniela Mrázková and Vladimír Remeš, Prague, 1989; *Czech Modernism 1900-1945,* exhibition catalogue, Houston, 1989; *The Art of the Avant-Garde in Czechoslovakia 1918-1938,* exhibition catalogue, Valencia, 1993. **Articles**—"Jaroslav Rössler" by Karel Dvořák in *Revue Fotografie* (Prague), no. 1, 1961; "Jaroslav Rössler" by Anna Fárová in *Revue Fotografie* (Prague), no. 2, 1971; "Jaroslav Rössler" by Antonìn Dufek in *Ceskoslovenská Fotografie* (Prague), November 1978; "Jaroslav Rössler" by Petr Tausk in *Revue Fotografie* (Prague), no. 2, 1979; "Three Decades: The Czech Avante Garde" by Jan Christopher Horak in *Afterimage* (Rochester, New York), Summer 1984; "Jaroslav Rössler" by Martin Stein in *Revue Fotografie,*(Prague), No 3 1987; "Nedoceněný Jaroslav Rössler" by Vladimir Birgus in *Československá fotografie,*(Prague), No 5, 1991.

* * *

Jaroslav Rössler started his career as an apprentice in the Prague studio of František Drtikol during the First World War. Although he admired his master, he very soon began looking for his own way. Instead of building artificial scenes into which the model was framed, Rössler used the effects of light and shadow when creating portraits, making them images of self-expression. The most important part of his work, however, was done outside the studio. He tried to discover interesting forms in the immediate vicinity. Very often he concentrated on details in order to create a balance in composition, for which he always had an intuitive sense.

In the mid-1920s Rössler went to Paris. Although his reason for going there was to enlarge his photographic experience by working in some of the city's well-known studios, he also enjoyed Paris itself very much: he found the atmosphere exciting, and it provided the inspiration for many photographs. The driving force of his enthusiasm seems to have been a sensitivity of vision that found stimulation quite universally in the reality of Paris, and his photos of that time are of a great variety of subjects. For instance, besides the views of the details of construction of the Eiffel Tower and the roofs of Paris, there are also photos of the audience at a racetrack, conveyed with Rössler's marvellous facility for depicting the fleeting situation.

Rössler's work of that time even attempted to enrich the conception of certain images by blurring the contours of moving objects—for instance, a car moving down a boulevard. He also experimented with depicting light beams coming through a simple lens, in order to discover, during the creative games, different forms and shapes. At this time Rössler was a very keen experimenter. He had already learned from Drtikol all the old positive techniques, and himself continued his research into methods of combining photomontage with the bromoil overprint process. He prepared particular areas of an image in bromoil, and then connected them into the final picture by overprinting in a simple hand-press.

In 1935 Rössler returned home to Prague and set up his own small studio for portrait photography. The problems connected with the business were such that he did not resume his own work until the beginning of the 1950s. This gap of some 15 years is a real one; it has tended to isolate his "first creative period" in Paris from his subsequent work: the photos of the late 1920s and early 1930s now seem a "closed" work with characteristic signs. And, indeed, since 1951 Rössler has created images quite different from those of the earlier period. He seems to have lost interest in depicting the real world through direct contact, and has preferred instead to experiment with the technical tools and resources of photography.

Rössler started this "new" period by using a prism placed before the frontal lens, enabling him to repeat his subject in a mirror-reverse position. Some of the results he achieved came close to images of fantasy, whilst others reflected his sense of abstract design. In each case, the generating force for the image was the subconscious impulse. This approach is evident in the series of surreal pen-and-ink drawings which Rössler made in the late 1940s and early 1950s.

He also returned to his earlier photomontage experiments, this time using normal photographic techniques, exposing only selected parts of each frame in the darkroom. Sometimes he employed solarisation effects to enhance certain images. All this experience prepared Rössler for his next phase of colour abstract work. Although several types of colour film were available, Rössler preferred experimenting with a montage of three toned extracts based on modified black-and-white photos. The final image was made by overlapping the partial images and mounting the three transparent films on white paperboard.

Dut to his excessive shyness, Rössler's innovative contributions of the inter-war period remained unknown even in his native country until the *Surrealism and Photography* exhibition in 1966. In the late 1970s, however, the Galerie Rudolf Kicken of Cologne began introducing Rössler's work to an audience outside Czechoslovakia. Encouraged by all this new success, Rössler emerged from retirement to work again on some of his old negatives. The use of modern pigment prints for pictures originally produced on bromsilver papers revealed the near-forgotten positive processes in a new light.

—Petr Tausk

ROTHSTEIN, Arthur.

Nationality: American. **Born:** New York City, 17 July 1915. **Education:** Stuyvesant High School, New York, 1929-32; studied under Roy Stryker, at Columbia University, New York, 1932-35, B.A. 1935. **Military Service:** Served as a photo officer, in the United States Army Signal Corps, in India, Burma and China, 1943-46. **Family:** Married Grace Goodman in 1947; children: Robert, Ann, Eve, and Daniel. **Career:** Photographer, under Roy Stryker, Farm Security Administration, Washington, D.C. and throughout the United States, 1935-40; Photographer, *Look* magazine, New York, 1940-41; Picture Editor, Office of War Information (OWI), New York, 1941-43; Director of Photography, *Look* magazine, New York, 1946-71; Editor, *Infinity* magazine, New York, 1971-72; Director of Photography, then Associate Editor, *Parade* magazine, New York, 1972-85. Visual Aids Consultant, United States Environmental Protection Agency, and American Iron and Steel Institute, Washington, D.C., 1971-72. Instructor, Graduate School of Journalism, Columbia University, New York, 1961-70; Spencer Professor, Newhouse School of Communication, Syracuse University, New York. Founder-Member, American Society of Magazine Photographers, 1941 (Vice-President, 1947); President, Photographic Administrators, New York, 1961-63. **Recipient:** First Prize for Color Photography, 1955, and Sprague Award, 1967, National Press Photographers Association; Newhouse Citation, Syracuse University, New York, 1963; Award of Distinction, New York Art Directors Club, 1963; Distinguished Service Award, United States Department of Defense, 1965; Photographic Scientists and Engineers Citation, 1966; International Award, Photographic Society of America, 1968; Lifetime Arts Achievement, New York Council of the Arts, 1985; Progress Medal, Photographic Society of America, 1985. Fellow, Royal Photographic Society, London, 1968; Fellow, Photographic Historical Society of New York, 1979. **Estate:** c/o Grace Rothstein, 122 Sutton Manor, New Rochelle, New York 10805, U.S.A. **Died:** (in New Rochelle) 11 November 1985.

Individual Exhibitions:

1956	International Museum of Photography, George Eastman House, Rochester, New York
1960	Biblioteca Communale, Milan
1963	Smithsonian Institution, Washington, D.C.
1964	*World's Fair,* New York
1966	*Photokina,* Cologne
1967	Kodak Exhibition Center, New York
1972	Michigan State University, East Lansing

1973	University of Massachusetts, Boston
1974	United States Information Service, Washington, D.C. (and world tour)
1975	Washington Photo Gallery, Washington, D.C.
1976	*My Land, My People,* International Museum of Photography, George Eastman House, Rochester, New York
1977	Brigham Young University, Salt Lake City, Utah
1978	Prakapas Gallery, New York
1979	Western Heritage Museum, Omaha, Nebraska
	Empire State Plaza, Albany, New York
	Fine Arts Museum of the South, Mobile, Alabama
1980	Rizzoli Gallery, New York
	Rizzoli Gallery, Chicago
	Tulsa University, Oklahoma
	Sun-Times Gallery, Chicago
	Art Institute, Fort Lauderdale, Florida
	Goddard Art Center, Daytona Beach, Florida
1981	*International Photographic Exposition,* Seattle
	Douglas Elliott Gallery, San Francisco
	Catskill Center for Photography, Woodstock, New York
1983	Salt Lake Art Center, Utah
1986	*Before and After: The FSA,* Daytona Beach Community College, Florida (with Jack Delano and Marion Post Wolcott)

Selected Group Exhibitions:

1938	*1st International Photographic Exposition,* Grand Central Palace, New York
1949	*Exact Instant,* Museum of Modern Art, New York
1959	*Hundert Jahre Photographie 1839-1939,* Museum Folkwang, Essen (travelled to Cologne and Frankfurt)
1962	*The Bitter Years: FSA Photographs 1935-41,* Museum of Modern Art, New York (toured the United States)
1971	*The Artist as Adversary,* Museum of Modern Art, New York
1973	*The Compassionate Camera: Dustbowl Pictures,* Victoria and Albert Museum, London (toured the U.K.)
1977	*New Deal Art,* Delaware Art Museum, Wilmington
1978	*Photographic Crossroads: The Photo League,* National Gallery of Canada, Ottawa (travelled to the International Center of Photography, New York; Museum of Fine Arts, Houston; and Minneapolis Institute of Arts)
1982	*Lichtbildnisse: Das Porträt in der Fotografie,* Rheinisches Landesmuseum, Bonn
1985	*American Images 1945-80,* Barbican Art Gallery, London (toured Britain)

Collections:

Rothstein Collection, Library of Congress, Washington, D.C.; Smithsonian Institution, Washington, D.C.; Museum of Modern Art, New York; International Museum of Photography, George Eastman House, Rochester, New York; Royal Photographic Society, London; University of Kansas, Lawrence.

Publications:

By ROTHSTEIN: Books—*Photojournalism,* New York 1956, 1965, 1974, 1979; *Creative Color Photography,* New York 1963; *Look at Us,* with text by William Saroyan, New York 1967, 1970; *Color Photography Now,* New York 1970; *The Depression Years,* New York and London 1978; *Words and Pictures,* New York 1979; *The American West in the Thirties,* New York and London 1981; *Arthur Rothstein's America in Photographs 1930-1980,* New York 1984; *Documentary Photography,* Stoneham, Massachusetts, 1986. **Articles**—"Photojournalism and Ecology" in *Infinity* (New York), August 1970; "Arthur Rothstein: An Interview," with Bill Ganzel, in *Exposure* (New York), Fall 1978.

On ROTHSTEIN: Books—*Hundert Jahre Photographie 1839-1939,* exhibition catalogue, by Helmut and Alison Gernsheim, Essen 1959; *Great*

News Photos and the Stories behind Them by John Faber, New York 1960, 1978; *The Bitter Years* by Edward Steichen and Grace Mayer, New York 1962; *Portrait of a Decade* by Jack Hurley, Baton Rouge, Louisiana 1969; *In This Proud Land* by Roy Stryker and Nancy Wood, New York 1973; *Social Documentary Photography in the U.S.A.* by Robert Doherty, New York 1974; *The Magic Image* by Cecil Beaton and Gail Buckland, London and Boston 1975; *A Vision Shared: A Classic Portrait of America and Its People 1935-1943,* edited by Hank O'Neal, New York and London 1976; *Documenta 6,* exhibition catalogue, by Klaus Honnef and Evelyn Weiss, Kassel, West Germany 1977; *Faces: A Narrative History of the Portrait in Photography* by Ben Maddow, Boston 1977; *Documentary Portrait of Mississippi: The Thirties,* edited by Patti Carr Black, Jackson, Mississippi 1982; *Dustbowl Descent* by Bill Ganzel, Lincoln, Nebraska 1984; *American Images: Photography 1945-1980,* edited by Peter Turner, London 1985. **Article**—in the *Journal of the Smithsonian Institution* (Washington, D.C.), no. 1, 1977.

*

As a photojournalist for more than forty years, I have had the opportunity to photograph the people and places of this varied and vibrant world.

I have used the visual image to present facts, to register ideas and emotions, for the camera captures the decisive moment and records events with greater accuracy than does the human eye.

My photography is based on the concept of knowing the subject and telling the story as graphically as I can. I use design and composition to enhance the effect and make the message clear. I prefer to portray people with dignity and sympathy and to capture expressions with the greatest meaning. Sometimes I will select a revealing detail or fragment of the whole scene in order to make a more effective statement. My photographs are primarily designed to serve a useful purpose in communication, yet many of them have been considered works of art.

Because powerful images are fixed in the mind more readily than words, the photographer needs no interpreter. A photograph means the same thing all over the world and no translator is required. Photography is truly a universal language, transcending all boundaries of race, politics and nationality.

The photographer who uses this universal language has a great social responsibility. Accepting this challenge, I have probed the problems of our times and used my camera to communicate ideas, facts and emotions.

That is why I am pleased to have my photographs published in *Parade.* Their unique editorial blend of words and pictures permits me to inform, enlighten, persuade and convince a large audience.

For those who see my photographs, I hope that these images will be a remembrance of the past, a record of accomplishment, and an affirmation of faith in humanity.

—Arthur Rothstein (1982)

*   *   *

Arthur Rothstein was at the very center of photojournalism for nearly 50 years. He started running in the 1930s and was still running until his death in 1985. There is virtually nothing in the world of photography—no stylistic mode, technique or aspect of the craft of photography—that Rothstein had not attempted and mastered. In terms of early 20th century philosophical thought, Rothstein can be classified as a John Dewey "experimentalist." Rothstein greeted the world with all the awe and enthusiasm of a young child entering Times Square for the first time.

Rothstein began his photographic career while still a student at Columbia University assisting his teacher, Roy Stryker, in preparing teaching tools. Stryker believed photographs could add more reality to his economics classes. When Stryker left Columbia to form the Historical Section of the Resettlement Administration (later the Farm Security Administration: RA/FSA), Arthur Rothstein was one of the first photographers he hired to document the work of this agency in meeting the problems of drought, a declining farm market, depression and the mechanization of farming. Anyone who remembers the 1930s depression also remembers the dustbowl. *The* symbol of the dustbowl is Rothstein's photograph (accompanying this entry) of two children and a man caught in a dust storm in Cimarron, Oklahoma in 1936. It is a powerful and gripping, unforgettable image of this dismal period in American history.

An actual count of Rothstein's work at RA/FSA has never been made, but it is certain that he was one of the most prolific photographers of the group. He was sensitive yet aggressive, and while he was sympathetic to and understanding of the plight of his subjects, he maintained the essential detachment that allowed him to remain objective in his work. A study of Rothstein's work will quickly show that he learned many lessons from others in the field and utilized what he learned to perfect his craft. In his work, one occasionally encounters a Walker Evans by Arthur Rothstein, but there is usually a new wrinkle in the Rothstein: an element of whimsy or humor appears in the Evans-like picture. Sometimes Rothstein's zeal for the perfect picture caused panic. Rothstein photographed a parched skull on the mudflats of South Dakota in the spring of the 1936 national election year. Rothstein was not pleased with the position of the skull, so he moved it to get better shadows. A Dakota newspaper editor found the same skull in two different pictures and called foul. This issue reverberated in the American press throughout the summer and fall, being silenced only by the reelection of Roosevelt.

Rothstein left RA/FSA in spring 1940 to work for *Look* magazine. Two years later he returned briefly to government service with the New York office of the Office of War Information prior to entering military service during World War II as a photographer in the China-Burma-India theatre. Upon discharge from the service, Rothstein worked for the United Nations photographing in China. Rothstein rejoined the staff at *Look* and remained with the magazine until its demise. For most of his career at *Look* Rothstein was director of photography. Under his direction, some very outstanding photography, covering a much broader range and scope than *Life,* was undertaken. *Life* was much more narrowly photo-journalistic in its coverage. *Look* covered everything from fashion to furniture and architecture to cooking trends, and the level of the photo essays brought the reader a wider variety of picture experiences. Many of these were brilliant examples of the use of the camera, reflecting Rothstein's skill in assigning photographers.

In his search for new and novel, Rothstein spent much effort in reviving, perfecting and publishing the mass use of the 19th century parallax stereogram, a three-dimensional picture which appeared in the pages of *Look.* It was a bright, but short lived, experiment.

Rothstein was a teacher too. And, in his desire to share his experience with others, he published widely and for many years at Florida and later at the University of Maryland, where he organized highly successful symposia in photojournalism. These symposia brought the student together with the stars of the field in a vital and fruitful forum.

As a photo-journalist, one senses Rothstein's awe, enthusiasm, sometimes wit and, always, his high level of craftsmanship.

—Robert J. Doherty

RUBEN, Ernestine Winston.

Nationality: American. **Born:** Detroit, 19 July 1931. **Education:** Graduated with B.A. from the University of Michigan, Ann Arbor, in 1953, and an M.A. from Wayne State University, Detroit, in 1956; studied photography at Princeton University, Mercer County Community College and, briefly, with Nathan Lyons, Lee Friedlander, Frederick Sommer and Andreas Muller-Pohle. **Family:** Married Herbert S. Ruben in 1958; children: Phillips, Caroline, Lisa and Erica. **Career:** Worked as an art teacher at the Detroit Institute of Art and public and private schools in New York and New Jersey; conducts workshops and lectures. **Address:** 644 Pretty Brook Road, Princeton, New Jersey 08540, U.S.A.

Individual Exhibitions:

1982	FNAC Galleries, France (travelled to Paris-Montparnasse, Nice, Toulouse, Marseille, Colmar)
1983	Rubiner Gallery, Detroit
	Photographer's Gallery, Paule Pia, Antwerp, Belgium
	Profoto Gallery, Nuremburg
1984	*Primavera Fotografica,* Tartessos Gallery, Barcelona, Spain
	Le Reverbere, Lyon, France

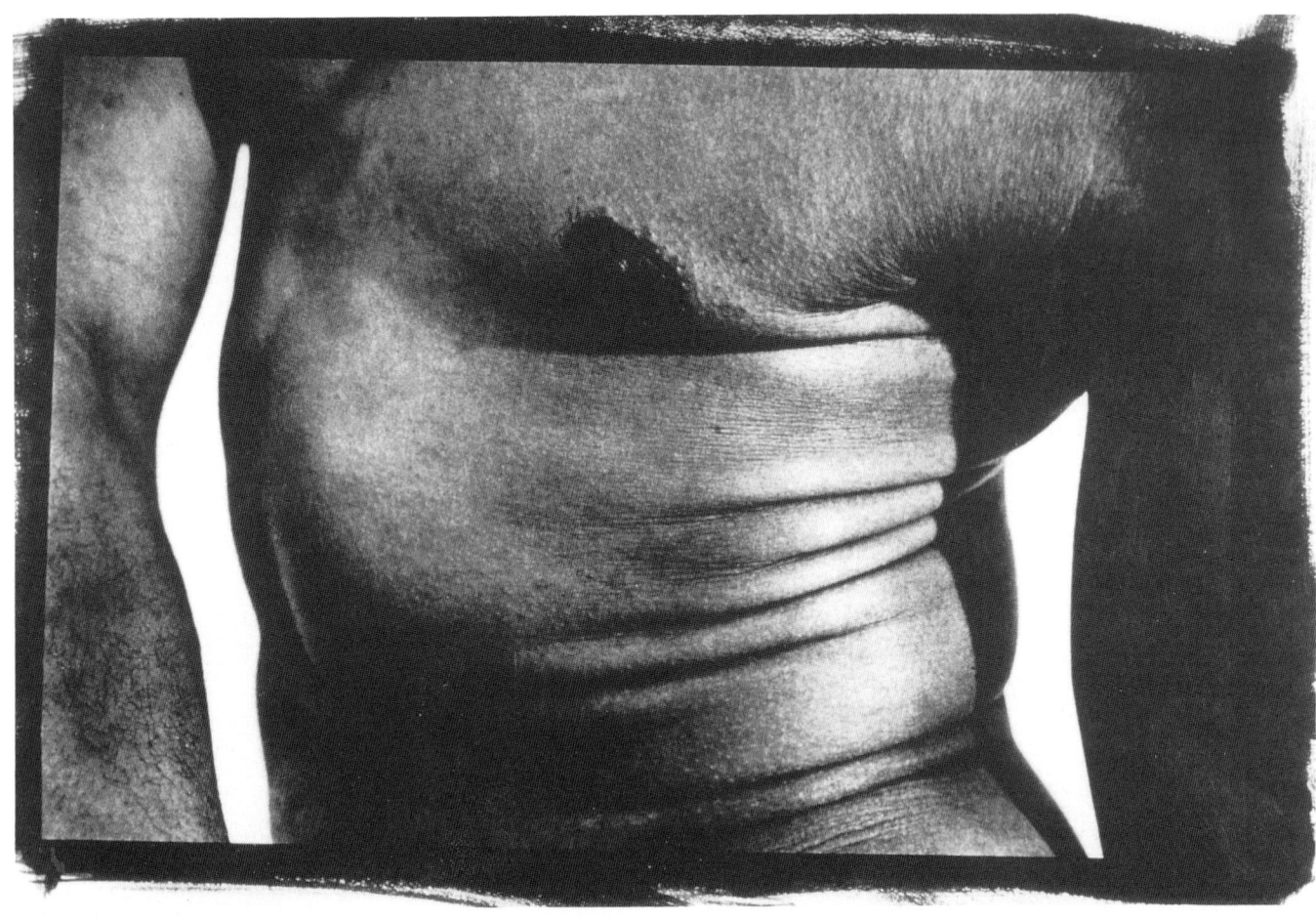

Big Chest, **1993.** Photograph by Ernestine Ruben.

Etre Humain, Bateau Lavoir, France
1985   Photographic Centre of Athens, Athens
        The American Cultural Center, Brussels
        Corps Humain, Musée Fabre, Montpelier, France
        Contemporary Women's Exhibit, Volvic, France
1986   Salzburg College, Salzburg, Austria
        Ken Damy Gallery, Brescia
        Al Ferro di Cavallo, Rome
        Ken Damy Gallery, Milan, Italy
        IV Mois de la Photo, Lisieux, France
1987   Le Chambre Claire, Paris
1988   Wilfrid Israel Museum, Haifa, Israel
        Museum, Aurillac, France
        Marcuse Pfeifer Gallery, New York
        Centre de la Culture, Amiens, France
        Galerie Charles Sablon, Paris
1989   Canon Image Centre, Amsterdam
        Forum Gallery, Tarragona, Spain
1990   ICP Midtown, New York
        Johnson and Johnson, New Brunswick, NJ
        Espace Photo de la Ville de Paris, Paris
        Chateau D'Eau, Toulouse, France
        Sephia Gallery, Brussels
1991   *Form and Feelings* (toured twelve German cities)
        Gallery of Union of Czech Photography, Prague
1992   Gallery 6X7, Mainz, Germany (travelled to *ArtEXPO,*
            Frankfurt)
1993   The Walters Gallery, Rutgers University

1994   Gallery MR, Angouleme, France

Selected Group Exhibitions:

1980   Monmouth Gallery, Monmouth College, New Jersey
1982   Soho Gallery, New York
1983   Municipal Museum, Bologna, Italy
        Galerie Marion Valentine, Paris
        Nimbus Gallery, Dallas
1984   *Amsterdam Photo Festival*
        Les Plus Belle Images du Mois de la Photo, Galleries
            Lafayette, Paris
        Rubiner Gallery, Detroit
1985   Espace Austerlitz, Paris
1986   *Perros, Ses Rochers,* Perros-Guirec, France
1987   *The Male Nude in the 19th and 20th Centuries,* Pinacoteca
            Comunale, Ravenna Italy
        Image du Corps, Chateau d'Eaux, Toulouse
1988   *Creation en France, Le Corps, La Galère,* Musée des Beaux
            Arts, Toulon
        Ombres de Chair, Bibliothèque Nationale, Paris
        Splendeur Misère du Corps, Musée d'Art Moderne, Paris
        Graz City Hall, Austria
1989   Nikon Live Gallery, Zurich
        Salle de Musee Botanique, Brussels
1992   Noyes Museum, New Jersey
        En Avion, Palais Tokyo, Paris
1993-94 Noyes Museum, New Jersey

Collections:

Brandenburgische Kunstsammlungen, Museum für Zeitgenössische Kunst, Cottbus, Germany; Maison Europeenne de la Photographie, Paris; The Museum of Fine Arts, Houston; Museum of Modern Art, Paris; Stedlijk Museum, Amsterdam; Detroit Institute of Arts; Bibliothèque Nationale, Paris; Bibliothèque Historique de la Ville de Paris; Artothèque, Toulouse; Israel Museum, Jerusalem; Johnson and Johnson, and Merrill Lynch Corporate Collections.

Publications:

By RUBEN: Books—*Ernestine Ruben Photographs,* Kassel 1982; *Camera Obscura,* 1986; *Entre Deux* (with Pierre Borhan), Paris 1987; *Ernestine Ruben: Form and Feelings,* Schaffhausen 1989; *Ernestine Ruben: A Retrospective Exhibition of Photography,* New Brunswick 1993. Articles—*Progresso Fotographie* (Milan), July/August 1986; *Photographie* (Switzerland), 1988 and November 1986; *Brutus* (Japan), Spring 1988; *NewMag* (Munich), May 1992.

On RUBEN: Articles—Vladimír Birgus in *Interview* (Czechoslovakia), April 1994; *Der Spiegel,* 1991; *Tvorba,* October 1991; "A Corps perdu. Les abstractions sculpturales d'Ernestine Ruben" by Patrick Roegiers in *Le Monde,* 26 June 1990; "Deux Architectes du Corps (Ruben and Minkinnen) by Patrick Roegiers in *Le Monde,* November 1988; *Images* (Geneva), June 1986; *Samourai* (Paris), June 1985; *Liberation,* October 1984; *Art Press,* November 1984; *European Photography,* June 1983; *Zoom,* Summer 1983. Television—*Assiette Anglaise,* Antenne Deux, Paris, November 1988.

*

When I plunged into photography, I brought with me my interest in sculpture, dance, architecture and the history of art. I logically chose the human as my subject matter so that I could apply all the experience I had accumulated. Whether dealing strictly with the body, or working with the landscape, portrait, dance, still life or architecture, it is my primary objective to render the image three dimensional, moving in space and able to come alive and breathe. I have carried this work far exploring many different media, formats and techniques (photography merged with glass blowing, dance performance, paper making, sculpture etc). The motivating force behind my photography remains consistent. I persist in the endeavour to bring an experience (through its image) to life by rendering it human, dynamic and sentient. Often I investigate only the remaining environment of the human, to see what effect the human has had. I often seek out the phantoms of yesterday still dwelling among us, and evoke the auras and atmospheres of the human and natural world. Often I work with mere suggestions or fragments in order to give birth to a full blown up idea or to a new object. I am fascinated by how inanimate objects can become animate. Through the many diverse realities, I ponder the seen and the unseen and I continually seek questions about existence. I always wish to challenge the viewer to participate with me in the various wonders of our visual experiences.

—Ernestine Ruben

*   *   *

Photography is only one of the branches of art—among sculpture, glass design, painting, drawing, architecture, dance and music—to which Ernestine Ruben devotes active attention or in which she is intensely interested. She was born into a family closely connected with art. Her grandfather was the outstanding Detroit architect Albert Kahn, who designed a number of buildings for the Ford Motor Company. Her mother, the ceramist Lydia Winston Malbin, was a leading American collector of modern art. Ernestine grew up surrounded by works by Picasso, Kandinsky, Mondrian, Balla, Leger, Miro, Arp, Gabo, Brancusi and other renowned artists. It is not surprising that she herself took up an artistic career. She concerned herself with sculpture, painting and drawing and taught the history of art at a number of state and private schools. Later however she inclined away from artistic work and the educational sphere for many years and devoted her attention to bringing up her children.

She returned to art as late as her forty-seventh year, when she began to photograph intensively. She attended the photography courses of Emmet Gowin, Frederick Sommer and Peter Bunnell at Princeton University, worked at Nathan Lyons' workshop and later also ran various workshops herself. She rapidly gained numerous successes in her own work and held a number of successful solo exhibitions at leading museums and galleries. Apart from this, she has also published several monographs.

The best-known of her older works are her characterful nudes, which create a surprisingly chaste and fine effect in the flood of ever harsher erotic and pornographic photographs. In these works Ernestine Ruben concentrates on symbolic meanings and the artistic value of details of the human body, in which she frequently emphasizes their parallels with nature. However unlike, for example, Bill Brandt, she does not orient her photographs to confrontations of nudes with static objects, created by nature or human beings, and she also does not use spatial distortions. She is more interested in visual metaphors. She believes that nature has its own soul and therefore seeks symbolic analogies between the forms of the human body and the shapes of trees, stones or plants. These parallels are clearer in her composition photographs, created by means of double exposures on one negative, but we can also come across them in unusually composed fragments of male and female bodies.

In these Ernestine Ruben reduces the photographed motifs to elementary lines, often accepted by suggestive contrasts and lights and shades. She is not concerned here merely with aesthetic values and consequently she does not idealize her models, but also portrays them with minor skin defects. This contributes to the way we perceive her male and female models as real people of flesh and bones. By means of untraditional cut-outs and unusual views of the human body she tries to relativize conventional perception and invite the viewer to his own interpretation of the theme of one's attitude towards one's own body and of the relations between a man and a woman or between humanity and nature. The artist herself compares a photograph to a bridge along which viewers move between imaginary poles and real worlds; emotions and intellect; details and the whole; as well as logical and illogical antitheses.

Ernestine Ruben does not content herself with the classical form of a gelatine silver print on paper. On the contrary, she constantly experiments with non-traditional photographic techniques and combines photography with the other artistic media. Quite often she tones and colours her photographs by hand. She uses photographic emulsions applied to ceramics or canvas. She has created original objects with mechanically rotating round photographs of details of the human body, taken with a fish-eye lens. She has projected her photographs at various dance performances, thus creating suggestive confrontations of real and halted movement.

Ernestine Ruben has also turned her interest to novel ways of installing and presenting her photographs. These include her exceptionally well thought out, original and emotionally strong installations of images of the Old Jewish Cemetery in Prague at an exhibition held at the Walters Gallery at Rutgers University in 1993, created in co-operation with the architect Meira Kowalsky.

Ernestine Ruben returned to motifs of human bodies in the 1990s, when she again began to take a close interest in the possibility of combining sculpture and photography and the use of palladium prints on various hand-produced papers with a conspicuous structure. At the Rutgers Center for Innovative Printmaking she co-operated with the papermaker Gail Deery in creating suggestive photographic reliefs with an ingeniously composed mosaic of detailed shots of the human body. These indisputably rank among the best of the works she has produced hitherto.

In her strikingly stylized cycle of photographs with a motif of ancient ruins, in which she combines the world of photography, papermaking, printmaking, sculpture and painting, she continues to pursue her investigation of original possibilites of the use of palladium prints on handmade papers.

—Vladimír Birgus

RUBENSTEIN, Meridel.

Nationality: American. Born: Detroit, Michigan, 26 March 1948. Education: Mumford High School, Detroit; Cambridge School, Weston, Massachu-

Edith's House, **1993.** Photograph ©Meridel Rubenstein.

setts, 1961-65; Sarah Lawrence College, Bronxville, New York, 1965-70, B.A. 1970; studied photography, under Minor White, Massachusetts Institute of Technology, Cambridge, 1972-73, and under Beaumont Newhall and Van Deren Coke, University of New Mexico, Albuquerque, 1973-77, M.A. 1974, M.F.A. 1977. **Career:** Worked as a holographer, PTR Optics Company, Waltham, Massachusetts, 1972-73. Professional photographer since 1973. Lecturer in Photography, University of New Mexico, 1976, 1977-78, 85 and College of Santa Fe, New Mexico, 1976-80; Visiting Lecturer, University of Colorado, Boulder, 1980-83; Associate Professor and Head of the Photography Program, San Francisco State University, 1985-1990; Professor of Art, Institute of American Indian Arts, Sante Fe, New Mexico, beginning in 1990. **Recipient:** Matching grants received from the NEA, New Mexico Bicentennial Commission, New Mexico Arts Commission, UNM Research Fellowships and Loan Committee for exhibition of *La Gente de la Luz,* New Mexico Museum of Fine Arts, catalogue and travelling exhibition, 1975-77; Ferguson Grant, Friends of Photography, Carmel, California, 1977; John Simon

Guggenheim Fellowship, 1981-82; NEA Photographic Survey Grant, 1982; NEA Photographer's Fellowship—Emerging Artist, 1983; Art Matters Inc., New York City, 1987; NEA Inter-Arts Grant (with Steina and Woody Vasulka and Ellen Zweig), 1988-89; New Forms Regional Initiative Grant, Diverse Works, Houston, Texas, 1990; Western States Regional Media Arts Fellowship, Portland Art Museum/Northwest Film Center/AFI, Portland, Oregon, 1991; NEA Photographer's Fellowship, 1992. **Agents:** Horwitch Lewallen Gallery, 129 East Palace, Santa Fe, New Mexico 87505, U.S.A.; Troyer Fitzpatrick Lassman Gallery, 1710 Connecticut Avenue N.W., Washington D.C. 20009, U.S.A. **Address:** Route 2, P.O. Box 305A, Santa Fe, New Mexico 87505, U.S.A.

Individual Exhibitions:

1975   *Meridel Rubenstein/Baldwin Lee,* Creative Photo Laboratory, Massachusetts Institute of Technology, Cambridge
1977   *La Gente de la Luz,* Museum of Fine Arts, Santa Fe, New Mexico (toured the western United States)
1978   *A Personal Landscape,* Hill's Gallery, Santa Fe, New Mexico
1979   *La Gente de la Luz,* Museum für Kunst und Gewerbe, Hamburg
      51 Portraits of Craftspeople, Museum of Albuquerque, New Mexico
      From a Personal Landscape, Brattleboro Museum and Art Center, Vermont
1980   *The Lowriders,* Museum of Fine Arts, Santa Fe, New Mexico
1981   *Meridel Rubenstein/Joan Myers,* Galerie Arpa, Bordeaux (travelled to Galerie Montesquieu, Agens, France)
      Orange Coast Community College Gallery, Costa Mesa, California
      Neikrug Gallery, New York
      Yuen Lui Gallery, Seattle
      Galerie Ufficio dell'Arte/Créatis, Paris
      Port Washington Library, New York
      Eclipse Gallery, Boulder, Colorado
      Colorado Mountain College, Breckenridge, Colorado
      The Lowriders, Artists Space, New York
1982   Consejo Mexicano de Fotografia, Mexico City
      Louisville School of Art, Kentucky
      Susan Spiritus Gallery, Newport Beach, California
      Heydt-Bair Gallery, Santa Fe, New Mexico
      A/UN Ranch, Museum of Fine Arts, Santa Fe, New Mexico
      New World College, Montezuma, New Mexico
      Colorado Mountain College, Leadville
1983   Center for Creative Photography, University of Arizona, Tucson
      University of Colorado, Boulder
1984   Sebastian-Moore Gallery, Denver, Colorado
      Philadelphia College of Art, Pennsylvania
1985   California Museum of Photography, Riverside
      Film in the Cities, St. Paul, Minnesota
1986   Jack Meier Gallery, Houston, Texas
      University of Rhode Island, Kingston
1987   Santa Fe Center for Contemporary Art, New Mexico
1988   *Two Person,* Jones Troyer Fitzpatrick Gallery, Washington, D.C.
      Fuller-Gross Gallery, San Francisco, California
1990   *Labyrinths,* with Barbara De Genevive, University of Texas, Arlington
      Amarillo Art Center, Amarillo, Texas
      LewAllen Butler Gallery, Santa Fe, New Mexico
1992   *Selections from Critical Mass,* Rena Bransten Gallery, San Francisco, California
      They Spoke to the Angels, Lewallen Gallery, Santa Fe, New Mexico
1993   *Critical Mass,* New Mexico Museum of Fine Arts, Santa Fe, New Mexico
      Tickling the Dragon's Tail, LewAllen Gallery, Santa Fe, New Mexico

1994   *Critical Mass,* MIT's List Center for the Visual Arts, Boston; Southeast Museum of Photography, Daytona Beach, Florida; University Art Museum, Laramie, Wyoming; Scottsdale Center for the Arts, Arizona

Selected Group Exhibitions:

1974   *Photography Unlimited,* Fogg Art Museum, Harvard University, Cambridge, Massachusetts
1977   *The Great West: Real/Ideal,* University of Colorado, Boulder (subsequently Smithsonian Institution travelling exhibition; toured the United States)
1979   *History of Photography in New Mexico,* University of New Mexico, Albuquerque
      Attitudes: Photography in the 1970s, Santa Barbara Museum of Art, California
1980   *The Portrait Extended,* Museum of Contemporary Art, Chicago
1981   *10 Photographes de Santa Fe, Nouveau Mexique,* Centre Culturel Americain, Paris (travelled to *Rencontres Internationales de la Photographie,* Arles, France)
1983   *Arranged Image Photography,* Boise Gallery of Art, Idaho
1985   *The Essential Landscape,* New Mexico Museum of Fine Arts, Santa Fe
1986   *Visions of the West,* Etherton Gallery, Tucson, Arizona
1987   *Myth/Ritual,* San Francisco Camerawork, San Francisco
      Cultural Assimilation and Isolation, The Boston Photographic Resource Center, Boston, Massachusetts (travelled)
1989   *Witness,* Fuller Gross Gallery, San Francisco, California
      Nature and Culture: Conflict and Reconciliation in Recent Photography, The Friends of Photography, Ansel Adams Center, San Francisco, California
      Fantasies, Fables and Fabrications: Photoworks from the 1980s, University of Massachusetts (travelled)
      Photography in the Eighties, National Museum of Modern Art, Smithsonian, Washington D.C.
1990   *Shelters and Structures,* Rena Bransten Galleries, San Francisco
      Robichon Gallery, Denver, Colorado
1991   Bentley Tomlinson Gallery, Scottsdale, Arizona
      Selections from the Permanent Collection: The Big Picture, San Francisco Museum of Modern Art, San Francisco
      Critical Reactions, Rena Bransten Gallery, San Francisco
      Identity Crisis: Portraits in the Eighties, Center for Creative Photography, University of Arizona, Tucson
      Nuclear Matters, San Francisco Camerawork, San Francisco
1992   *Too Hot to Handle,* Copeland Rutherford, Santa Fe, New Mexico
      Jones Troyer Fitzpatrick Gallery, Washington D.C.
      The Country Between Us: Contemporary American Landscape Photographs, Massachusetts College of Art, Cambridge
      Between Home and Heaven, National Museum of American Art, Smithsonian Institution, Washington, D.C.
1994   Jonson Gallery, Albuquerque, New Mexico
1995   *Long and Belonging,* SITE, Sante Fe, New Mexico

Collections:

Denver Museum of Art; University of Colorado, Boulder; Minneapolis Institute of Arts; Museum of New Mexico, Santa Fe; University of New Mexico, Albuquerque; Museum für Kunst und Gewerbe, Hamburg; Bibliothèque Nationale, Paris; Center for Creative Photography, University of Arizona, Tucson; San Francisco Museum of Modern Art; California Museum of Photography, University of California at Riverside; American Telephone and Telegraph; Houston Museum of Fine Arts, Texas; Santa Barbara Museum of Art; Museum of Albuquerque; National Museum of American Art, Washington, D.C.; New Mexico Museum of Fine Arts, Santa Fe; Rocky Mountain Energy Co., Denver, Colorado; Valley National Bank of Arizona, Phoenix; Vesti Corporation, Boston, Massachusetts; The Wheelwright Museum, Santa Fe, New Mexico.

Publications:

By RUBENSTEIN: Thesis—*The Circles and the Symmetry: The Mutual Influences of Georgia O'Keeffe and Alfred Stieglitz,* thesis, University of New Mexico, Albuquerque 1977. Books—*One Space: Three Visions,* edited by Dextra Frankel, Albuquerque, New Mexico 1979; *The Lowriders,* portfolio, Santa Fe, New Mexico 1980; "Georgia O'Keefe as a Role Model" in *From the Faraway Nearby: Georgia O'Keefe as Icon,* ed Christopher Merrill and Ellen Bradbury, 1992; *Critical Mass,* exhibition brochure, 1993. Articles—"Holography as Art," "Ellen Landweber" and "Eileen Cowin" in *Light and Substance,* exhibition catalogue, Albuquerque, New Mexico 1973; "Photography in New Mexico" in *Afterimage* (Rochester, New York), January 1977; "The Great West: Real/Ideal" in *Afterimage* (Rochester, New York), January 1978; statement in *Friends of Photography Newsletter* (Carmel, California), April 1978; "Alternative Images" in *Afterimage* (Rochester, New York), September 1979; "The Feminine Portrait: Photographs by Gilpin, Noggle and Rubenstein, by Steve Yates in *El Palacio,* Santa Fe summer/fall 1986. Video/audio projects—*The Lowriders,* 1981; *Unravelling Sound,* 1982; *A Spirited Place: The Arts of New Mexico,* New Mexico Museum of Fine Arts, 1991; *The Desert is No Lady,* BBC, London, 1993; *The Big Shell,* Santa Fe, 1993; *Critical Mass,* New Mexico Museum of Fine Arts, 1993.

On RUBENSTEIN: Books—*La Gente de la Luz,* exhibition catalogue, with texts by Beaumont Newhall, Van Deren Coke and John Nichols, Santa Fe, New Mexico 1977; *The New Mexico Portfolio,* Santa Fe, New Mexico 1977; *The Great West: Real/Ideal,* exhibition catalogue, by Gary Metz, Ellen Manchester, and Sandy Hume, Boulder, Colorado 1977; *Five Photographers,* exhibition catalogue, by Katherine Chafee, Denver 1977; *Attitudes: Photography in the 70s,* exhibition catalogue, by Fred Parker, Santa Barbara, California 1979; *Photography in New Mexico* by Van Deren Coke, Albuquerque, New Mexico 1979; *The Portrait Extended,* exhibition catalogue, by Charles Desmarais, Chicago 1980; *Photography for Collectors: The West* by James Alinder and others, Carmel, California 1980; *American Photography: A Critical History* by Jonathan Green, New York 1984; *Landscape as Photograph,* edited by Estelle Jussim, New Haven, Connecticut, 1985; *Reclaiming Paradise: American Women Photograph the Land,* ed Gretchen Gardner, Duluth, 1987; *Artists Response to Architecture,* ed James Edwards, Texas, 1987; *The Photography of Invention—American Pictures of the 1980s,* eds Joshua P Smith and Merry A Foresta, Cambridge MA and London, 1989; *Fantasies, Fables and Fabrications: Photo-Works from the 1980s,* exhibition catalogue, Amherst, MA, 1989; *Artists of the 20th Century: The Museum of Fine Arts Collection,* New Mexico, 1992; *Mapping American Culture,* ed Wayne Franklin and Michael Steiner, Iowa City, 1992. Articles—"Meridel Rubenstein: Portfolio" in *Untitled* (Carmel, California), Spring 1978; "Report from Santa Fe" by Marcy Dickman in *American Photographer* (New York), November 1979; "Report from New Mexico" by Joan Simon in *Art in America* (New York), June 1980; "Photography in the West" in *Rocky Mountain Magazine* (Denver), July 1980; "Places in the Sun" in *Rocky Mountain Magazine* (Denver), September 1980; "The Lowriders" in *Native Arts* (Santa Fe, New Mexico), October 1980; "The Lowriders" in *Santa Fe Reporter* (New Mexico), October 1980; "Meridel Rubenstein: The Lowriders" in *Artspace* (Albuquerque, New Mexico), Spring 1981; "New Mexico Now" in *Creative Camera* (London), September 1985; "Myth/Ritual" in *San Francisco Camerawork Quarterly,* Fall 1987; interview by John Bloom in *Photo Metro,* September 1988; "Images of Power and Grace" by Rebecca Solnit in *Artweek,* 1 October 1988; in *Art News,* December 1988; "Uncommon Perceptions" by Rebecca Solnit in *Sierra Magazine,* July/August 1989; "A Portrait is not a Likeness" in *The Archive,* 1991; "Myth/Ritual" in *San Francisco Camerawork Quarterly,* Fall 1987; "Trauma or Style—Critical Reactions at Rena Bransten Galley" in *Artweek,* 25 April 1991; "Meridel Rubenstein: Critical Mass" by Rebecca Solnit in *Artspace,* July/August 1992; "Meridel Rubenstein's Insights into Atoms, Scientific Method" by Diane Armitage in *Pasatiempo: The New Mexican,* 13-19 November 1992; "Unsettling the West" by Rebecca Solnit in *Creative Camera,* Dec/Jan 1993; interview in *Photography at Bay,* New Mexico 1993; "Scrambling the Codes: Art in the Atomic Age" by Rebecca Solnit in *El Palacio,* vol. 99, nos. 1 & 2; "Philosophical Fallout" by Lucy R Lippard in *Z Magazine,* April 1994.

*

For 20 years I've resisted traditional categories in making my artworks. In my work, history, culture and myth intertwine with nature's threatened landscape. Contrary materials: elegant palladium prints, raw steel and video imagery exist within works side by side. My working situation has evolved from that of the lone palladium printer to the opening of my studio to collaborators who have introduced me to extended video imagery and sound.

From the beginning I've worked in an additive sense trying to increase the levels of information that one can absorb visually from an image or a larger work. I've looked at my subjects as having a past, present and future; as having a physical presence affected by time and by the elements; as having a social and cultural level, as well as an internal or private side where hidden rituals can occur. The physical environment nurtures and informs us. I'm still struggling to understand how we are connected to this place that we call home.

Initially I was concerned with breaking photographic boundaries. Perhaps my most pivotal body of work concerned the Lowriders (1980). For this initially documentary project, color environmental portraits were made of this Hispanic subculture who paint and decorate their cars inside and out using contrary materials (hi-tech surfaces with metallic candy apple colours, lush velvets and painted imagery) to make rich allusions to ancient religious and sexual rituals. To deal properly with this material I found that the photographs alone were inadequate. I conceived of an installation on Santa Fe's main plaza (1980) where the actual cars and makers flanked the photographs to provide different levels of reality and information. This event was the largest single opening in Santa Fe because it touched so many different communities. When the photographs travelled to New York (Artist's Space 1981), I installed a video and parts and paraphenalia from the cars, to make up for their absence. The lessons I gleaned from the Lowriders, about their use of contrary materials, the function of myth within everyday life, and the involvement of communities in portrait projects, have been with me to this day. The Lowrider Show was my first interactive, intermedia project. I did receive a Guggenheim Fellowship in 1982 for this work. Since then palladium and steel, combined with audio and moving imagery, have been some of the materials and techniques I've worked with to create my own multivalent resonances.

My most recent work (1988-93) is truly an intemedia project. In the collaborative installation *Critical Mass,* photography, video and language come together to examine the forces of history and domesticity that went into the making of the first atomic bomb at Los Alamos. We use the story of a woman at whose home the Native American world and that of the Nuclear Physicist intersected during this historic time.

I began this project in 1988 upon receiving an NEA Interarts grant with Ellen Zweig, a performance and installation artist from New York. We knew from our team teaching of Image/Text classes at San Francisco State University that we wanted to make work combining photography, sound, video and text. We asked pioneer video artists Steina and Woody Vasulka to help us put our ideas into moving imagery. What followed for the next five years was a very deep and richly rewarding collaboration among the four of us. We were able to match our NEA grant with many additional grants. I personally received a Western States Media Arts Fellowship to make one of the videos in our installation and a New Forms Regional Initiative Grant from NEA/Rockefeller to begin the large portrait piece "The Meeting." These two grants, along with the NEA Interarts grant, validated me as an Intermedia artist. I also received, in 1992, a NEA Photographer's Fellowship which helped me to complete the photographic pieces in time for the opening of our exhibition on November 6, 1993.

Like the Lowrider Project, *Critical Mass* involved intense interaction with diverse communities. Since one of its central themes is the intersecting of the Native American world with that of the Nuclear Scientist, both groups were consistently consulted and included in events surrounding the exhibition. "The Meeting" is a piece about this interaction and includes photographs of portraits and objects from both these worlds and includes a video "hearth."

In *Critical Mass,* our individual participation extended beyond our original skills. I have created and edited some of the videos, written some of the texts, and conceptualized the video installations. Ellen has contributed to the thinking behind the photoworks. I was in fact the Artistic Director for all of the video, so if there's a visual image, I selected it. But our collaboration goes beyond these archaic assigning of tasks. In truth two of us for several years aided, encouraged, and researched together a mutual project, while two others helped technically. As our project has benefited from this multiple attention, so have we all as artists. I in fact have produced more as a result of the attention I received from my partners. At the time of the opening of *Critical Mass,* I opened a second exhibition of my own related works, *Tickling the Dragon's Tail,* at my gallery in Santa Fe. This included two installation pieces, one with an audio work. While the larger installation will travel for several years opening its tour at MIT's List Center, October 1994, these other works will be exhibited in my galleries in Washington D.C. and Santa Fe.

Presently I'm working on a new installation to open July, 1995 at SITE, Santa Fe, an international art exhibition featuring the work of 30 artists, curated by Bruce Ferguson.

—Meridel Rubenstein

*   *   *

The diverse cultural heritages and magnificent expansive landscape of New Mexico are ongoing photographic concerns for Meridel Rubenstein. Few places in America can offer such an exotic and exciting visual array of people: Hispanic, Indian, and Anglo. And to compliment them, the ever-changing dramatic landscape of the South West. It's a magical, enchanted and often difficult land, one in which Ms. Rubenstein, an easterner, seems eminently at home.

She can be defined as a portrait photographer, but her portraits encompass more than just a likeness of her subject. They are environmental portraits in the largest sense, utilizing the person's own home, the land on which he or she lives, personal possessions, and sometimes handwriting. These are complex images. They are layered and textured by the various printing combinations that she employs. Unsatisfied with simply photographing a person in a particular place, she combines a portrait of her subject in one situation with part of a negative taken in another. Sometimes other objects are placed directly on the printing paper—a bit of lace, ribbon, or dried corn, for example. This combining of elements results in a multi-dimensional portrait.

The most recent works of Meridel Rubenstein may seem startling if one is familiar with her earlier work. They are straight-forward, large format color portraits of Lowriders in New Mexico posed with their cars. These pictures have a documentary quality but go beyond the ordinary document. The rich color of the New Mexico landscape coupled with the bright and garish colors of the Lowrider cars does give a vivid description of this small but highly visible group of Mexican Americans.

The project culminated in an exhibition in the downtown plaza in central Santa Fe. Portraits of the Lowriders were displayed along with the Lowriders and their cars. This type of presentation transformed what could have been a gallery showing into an event. Viewers were free to examine the photographs, wander about the cars, and talk to the Lowriders.

—Judy Dater

RUBINSTEIN, Eva.

Nationality: American. **Born:** Born, of Polish parents, in Buenos Aires, Argentina, 18 August 1933; lived in Paris, 1933-39; immigrated to the United States, 1940: naturalized, 1946. **Education:** Westlake School for Girls, graduated 1950; attended Scripps College, Claremont, California, 1950-51; studied acting at the University of California at Los Angeles, 1952-53; also attended photo workshops, under Lisette Model, Jim Hughes, Ken Heyman and Diane Arbus, New York, 1968-71. **Family:** Married the Rev. William S. Coffin, Jr., in 1956 (divorced, 1968); children: Amy; Alexander (died 1983); David. **Career:** Performed as a dancer and actress, in New York and Europe, 1953-56 (in *Diary of Anne Frank,* New York, 1955-56). Freelance editorial, documentary and portrait photographer, New York, since 1968. Instructor in Photography, School of Visual Arts, New York, Spring 1972, and Manhattanville College, New York, 1974; Guest Teacher, 1977-81, and Member of the Faculty since 1980, New School for Social Research, New York. **Agents:** Lee

Gross Associates, 366 Madison Avenue, New York, New York 10017, U.S.A.; Neikrug Photographica, 224 East 68th Street, New York, New York 10021, U.S.A. **Address:** 145 West 27th Street, New York, New York 10001, U.S.A.

Individual Exhibitions:

1970	Focus Gallery, San Francisco
1971	Ogilvy-Mather Agency, New York
1972	Underground Gallery, New York
1973	Dayton Art Institute, Ohio
	Archetype Gallery, New Haven, Connecticut
1974	Neikrug Galleries, New York
1975	Canon Photo Gallery, Amsterdam
	Festival of Arles, France
	Garrett Theological Seminary, Evanston, Illinois
	La Photogalerie, Paris
	Friends of Photography, Carmel, California
1976	Madison Art Center, Wisconsin
	Galerie 5.6, Ghent
	The Portfolio Gallery, Boston
	Gallery of Photography, Washington, D.C.
	The Infinite Eye, Milwaukee
	Willette Gallery, Fort Lauderdale, Florida
1977	Drew University, Madison, New Jersey
	Galerie Trockenpresse, West Berlin
	Frumkin Gallery, Chicago
1978	University of Vermont, Burlington
	Imagination, Seattle, Washington
	Port Washington Public Library, New York
1979	Galleria Sinisca, Rome
	Atlanta Gallery of Photography, Georgia
	Neikrug Galleries, New York
	Woodman Gallery, Morristown, New Jersey
1980	Soho Gallery, New York
	John Young Museum of Science and Astronomy, Orlando, Florida
	Film in the Cities, St. Paul, Minnesota
1981	Neikrug Galleries, New York
	Signet Fine Arts, St. Louis, Missouri
1982	*Light Years 1967-82,* Neikrug Photographica, New York
	Hermitage Foundation Museum, Norfolk, Virginia
	Zenith Gallery, Pittsburgh
	Christopher Scheiter Gallery, Kalamazoo, Michigan
	Camera Obscura, Denver, Colorado
1983	The Photographers' Gallery, London
	Galerie Forum Labo, Arles, France
	Catch Gallery, Utrecht, Netherlands
	Galerie Nicéphore, Lyon, France
1984	Image Galeria, Madrid
	Muzeum Sztuki, Lodz, Poland
	Arpa Gallery, Bordeaux, France
	Union of Artist Photographers Gallery, Kraków, Poland (travelled to Warsaw and Katowice)
	Image Gallery, Cincinnati, Ohio
1985	Galleria Il Diaframma/Canon, Milan
	Neikrug Photographica, New York
	Galerie Demi-Teinte, Paris
	Galerie Municipale du Château d'Eau, Toulouse, France
	Lodz Photographic Socity, Poland
1986	ZPAF Gallery, Kraków, Poland
	Gdansk Photographic Society, Poland
	Galeria Foto/Medium/Art, Wroclaw, Poland
	Vision Gallery, San Franciso
	Espace Canon, Paris
1987	*SICOF 912th Salone Internatzionale,* Milan, Italy
	''The Nave of St Christopher's'' Gallery, Lodz, Poland
	L'Image Fixe, Lyon, France
	1988L'Artothéque, Galerie de Prêt, Grenoble, France
1989	*Elegies—1984-1988,* Neikrug Photographica, New York City

Table, Arles, **1986.** Photograph ©Eva Rubinstein.

Heuser Art Center Gallery, Bradley University, Peoria, Illinois
3-os Encontros da Imagem, Braga, Portugal
Bibliothéque Nationale, Galerie Colbert, Paris
Galerie Picto-Bastille, Paris
1990   Portfolio Gallery, (with Lilo Raymond), London
     Vaison-la-Romaine, France
1993   *Mai: Photographies,* Galerie Artem, Quimper, France
1994   FNAC-Étoile, Paris (travelling in Europe until 1997)
     Centro Culturale Pier-Paolo Pasolini, Agrigento, Sicily

Selected Group Exhibitions:

1972   *Images of Concern,* Delgado Museum, New Orleans
1974   *Photography U.S.A.,* U.S.I.A., Washington, D.C. (toured the
     United States and Europe, 1974-77)
     Femmes Photographes, OVO Photo, Monreal
1975   *Breadth of Vision,* Fashion Institute of Technology, New York
1977   *Creative Photography of the 20th Century,* Centre Georges
     Pompidou, Paris
     Women Photograph Men, International Center of Photography,
     New York
1978   *Tusen och En Bild/1001 Pictures,* Moderna Museet,
     Stockholm
1980   *The Imaginary Photo Museum,* Kunsthalle, Cologne
1983   *New Perspectives on the Nude,* Ffotogallery, Cardiff, Wales
1984   *La Photographie Créative,* Pavillon des Arts, Paris
1985   Quay Arts Centre, Isle of Wight, England
     Canon Gallery, Amsterdam

Diaframma/Canon Gallery, Milan, Italy
Swimming Pools, Arles, France
Atelier 29, Mont de Marsan, France
Faculty Show, Ecole Nationale de la Photographie, Arles,
     France
1986   Cultural Center of Asist Belgium
     Women Photographers NOW, travelling exhibition, United
     States
     2nd International Invitational Salon, Lodz House of Culture,
     Lodz, Poland
1987   *L'Imagerie de Michel Tournier,* Musée d'Art Moderne de la
     Ville de Paris
     *The Male Nude in Photography of the XIXth and XXth
     Centuries,* Pinacoteca Communale, Ravenna, Italy
1988   *Intimate Places,* Pierce St. Gallery, Birmingham, Michigan
     The Arts in Honor of van Gogh, Espace van Gogh, Arles,
     France
     Behold the Man, Stills Gallery, Edinburgh; Photographers'
     Gallery, London; Plymouth Arts Centre, Plymouth; Aberdeen
     Art Gallery, Aberdeen; Orchard Gallery, Londonderry,
     Northern Ireland
     Stairways and Empty Chairs, Ledel Gallery, New York City;
     Silvermine Gallery, Stamford, Connecticut
     Images of the 20th Century, St. Louis, Missouri
     A Kiss is Just a Kiss, Twining Gallery, New York City
1989   *L'Homme dans sa Fenêtre,* Chateau d'Eau, Toulouse, France
     Popular and Preferred Images, Boca Raton Museum, Boca
     Raton, Florida
     Galerie PICTO Bastille, Paris
     Les Correspondants, Galerie Arena, Arles, France

1990   Settimana della Fotografia, Terrasini, Palermo, Italy
1993   *Festival de l'Image, (Natures Mortes)*, Le Mans, France,

Collections:

Metropolitan Museum of Art, New York; International Center of Photography, New York; Library of Congress, Washington, D.C.; Bibliothèque Nationale, Paris; Musée Réattu, Arles, France; Museum Het Sterckshof, Deurne-Antwerp; Israel Museum, Jerusalem; Hermitage Foundation Museum, Norfolk, Virginia; Museum Ludwig, Cologne; Fotografiska Museet, Stockholm; Kalamazoo Institute of Arts, Michigan; Muzeum Sztuki (Museum of Modern Art) Lodz, Poland; Museum of the History of the City of Lodz, Poland; University of Parma, Italy; Library of the University of Lodz, Poland; Musée d'Art Moderne de la Ville de Paris; L'Artotheque, Bibliotheque Grand'Place, Grenoble, France; Fondation van Gogh, Arles, France; The Imaginary Museum, Fritz Gruber Collection, Köln, Germany.

Publications:

By RUBINSTEIN: Books—*Eva Rubinstein,* with a preface by Sean Kernan, New York 1974; *Eva Rubinstein: Portfolio 1,* 12 photos, with an introduction by John Vachon, New York 1975; *Eva Rubinstein Portfolio,* slides/cassettes, Garfield, New Jersey 1976; *Explore and Express,* slides/cassettes, Minneapolis 1980; *Eva Rubinstein: Portfolio 2,* with an introduction by André Kertész, New York 1981; *I Grandi Fotografi: Eva Rubinstein,* Milan 1983; *Portfolio,* Paris 1990. **Article**—"Notes from Two Irelands" in *Camera 35* (New York), November 1972.

On RUBINSTEIN: Books—*Leica Manual,* edited by Douglas O. Morgan, New York 1973; *Women Photograph Men,* edited by Danielle B. Hayes, introduction by Molly Haskell, New York 1977; *10 Photographers,* with text by Michael Edelson, New York 1978; *Tusen och En Bild,* exhibition catalogue, by Ake Sidwall, Sune Jonsson and Ulf Hard af Segerstad, Stockholm 1978; *Venezia '79: La Fotografia,* edited by Daniela Palazzoli, Vittorio Sgarbi and Italo Zannier, Milan and New York 1979; *Photographers on Photography,* edited by Jerry C. LaPlante, New York 1979; *The Photograph Collector's Guide* by Lee D. Witkin and Barbara London, Boston and London 1979; *The Male Nude in Photography,* edited by Lawrence Barns, Waitsfield, Vermont 1980; *The Imaginary Photo Museum* by Helmut Gernsheim, Renate and L. Fritz Gruber and others, Cologne 1981, London 1982; *La Photographie Créative* by Jean-Claude Lemagny, Paris 1984. **Articles**—"How Do You Photograph Chance" in *Camera 35* (New York), October 1971; "Meaningful Portraiture" by Ralph Hattersley in *Popular Photography* (New York), December 1971; "Eva Rubinstein" in *Camera*(Lucerne), January 1973; "Eva Rubinstein" by Jim Hughes in *Popular Photography* (New York), September 1975; "Eva Rubinstein" by Attilio Colombo in *Progresso Fotografico* (Milan), April 1977; "What Price Fame" by Alice Williams in *35mm Photography* (New York), Winter 1978. **Films**—*Cudzoziemka (The Foreigner),* by Michal Maryniarczyk, Lodz, Poland 1986; *Chwilowe Spotkania (Brief Encounters),* by Jacek Marczewski, Lodz Film School, Poland 1987.

*

I have always felt the need to leave footprints . . . perhaps because those of my family have been so blurred or simply swept away during the recent past. I am a keeper and a gatherer . . . my room, house, apartment has always looked like the home of the Queen of the Pack-Rats. Obsessed by the ephemeral quality of everything in my life (I even wrote really terrible poetry about it at 14 . . . stuff about looking back where I'd walked along the beach and seeing that the tide had washed away my footprints!), I've always lived rather too intensely in the moment, but longed for something like roots, permanence . . . perhaps making photographs is for me a way of satisfying my need both for an "outward and visible sign," something solid which will not "melt, thaw, and resolve itself into a dew," and a way to hold on to the momentary, the fleeting, the emotionally charged or serene . . . and the need to have something to share with others, without benefit of translator, choreographer, script, or director.

Photography became for me a way of hanging on to the moments of my life when I was moved by anything from a wonderful or startling face or person, to the quality of light in an empty place, a conflict between people or forms of a

nude body. The camera is for me both a means of reaching people, and, when I need it, a sort of refuge.

I am glad and grateful when someone likes, understands, is amused or moved by a photograph I have made, because each time I feel a little root go down into some sort of common ground, which makes me feel more as though I were a card-carrying member of the human race and less like a figment of my own imagination.

—Eva Rubinstein

*   *   *

When Eva Rubinstein came to photography in 1967, she entered and carved a spot in a tradition that was largely dying out. The failing picture magazines left a void in the market for talented photojournalists, and serious photographers had to find other outlets for their expression. Eva Rubinstein managed to continue in the shrinking, ever more competitive field of the humanist documentarian while supporting her travels with magazine assignments.

Her monograph (1974) presented a selection of her personal photographs at the time when her work was not only gaining her assignments but also artistic recognition in the gallery world. The book opens with her portraits of children whose friendly and concentrated cooperation she has elicited with unusual skill. Suffused with the overcast light of northern Europe, these portraits are unmistakably localized yet timeless in their removal from mundane detail. Two small Spanish girls, well-behaved and carefully posed in their straw hats and pleated dresses, belong to the 19th century daguerreotype studio as much as to their town of Marbella in 1973. The grace and sensitivity Rubinstein brings to her subjects enables her to transcend the time-locked specificity of most photographs (especially journalistic illustration) and achieve that rare condition where the literal becomes universal. Rubinstein's photographs of adults similarly remain undated in terms of time or place; yet, the open, forthright faces and the few carefully chosen details satisfy our curiosity as to who they are and how they live. Rubinstein's eye is compassionate and never intrusive; it is simple human dignity which she spots and records with apparent ease.

Her photographs of interiors capture the same warmth of human presence even while the compositions are stark and austere. The light functions in these pictures as the principal character, a palpable presence as tangible as the familiar faces of her portraits. Many of these pictures are nearly empty, yet loaded with significance; they are, as one reviewer noted, repositories of archetypal memory. Light and fabric, light and wallpaper, light and peeling paint, or, even more simply, light on the empty spaces of waiting rooms and stages—these are images which recall the sounds and bustle of activity in the same way poetry can. Rubinstein uses visual elements as precisely and economically as a poet uses the well-chosen word; the response she triggers is lyrical and this side of sentimental.

Eva Rubinstein belongs to a tradition uncommon for contemporary photographers; her work is classicist. She seeks and arranges an orderly world; the studied formality of her compositions places her as a direct descendant of photography's grandest tradition, from Paul Strand to Henri Cartier-Bresson, In a world glutted with photographs, Eva Rubinstein's are enduring by virtue of her humanism and compassion and the trueness of her ability to translate that quality onto film.

—Dana Asbury

RUSCHA, Edward (Joseph).

Nationality: American. **Born:** Omaha, Nebraska, 16 December 1937. **Education:** Classen High School, Oklahoma City, 1954-56; Chouinard Art Institute, Los Angeles, under Richard Rubin, 1956-60. **Military Service:** Served in the United States Navy, Los Angeles, 1956-64. **Family:** Married Danica Knego in 1967; son: Edward Joseph V. **Career:** Independent painter, photographer and book creator, since 1960. Lecturer in Painting, University of California at Los Angeles, 1969-70. **Recipient:** National Council on the Arts Award, 1967, 1978; Guggenheim Foundation Fellowship, 1971; Skowhegan Medal in

Graphics, Maine, 1974. **Agent:** Leo Castelli Gallery, 420 West Broadway, New York, New York 10012. U.S.A. **Address:** 35 South Venice Boulevard, Venice, California 90291, U.S.A.

Individual Exhibitions:

1970	Galerie Heiner Friedrich, Munich (books)
	Nigel Greenwood Gallery, London (books)
1973	*Projection,* Galerie Ursula Wevers, Cologne (books)
1974	Francoise Lambert Gallery, Milan (film *Premium* and books)
1975	University of Arizona, Tempe (books)
	Leo Castelli Gallery (Rizzoli Screening Room), New York (film *Miracle*)
	Fox Venice Theatre, Venice, California (films *Premium* and *Miracle*)
	Arts Council of Great Britain, London (prints and books; toured Britain)
1976	Stedelijk Museum, Amsterdam
1977	University of Calgary Art Gallery, Alberta (prints and books)
	David Hockney: Photographic Pictures; Edward Ruscha: Photographic Books, Nova Gallery, Vancouver, British Columbia
1978	Galerie Rudiger Schottle, Munich (books)
1982	*The Works of Edward Ruscha,* San Francisco Museum of Modern Art (toured the United States, 1982-83)
1985	James Corcoran Gallery, Los Angeles
	Tanja Grunert, Cologne, Germany
1986	Fuller Goldeen Gallery, San Francisco
1987	Robert Miller Gallery, New York
	Contemporary Art Museum, Houston
1988	Karsten Schubert Gallery, London
	Museum of Contemporary Art, Chicago
	Institute of Contemporary Art, Nagoya, Japan
	Lannan Museum, Lake Worth, Florida
1989	Musee National d'Art Moderne, Paris
	Castelli Gallery, New York
1990	Galerie Ghislaine Hussenot, Paris
	Thomas Segal Gallery and Rhone Hoffman Gallery, Chicago
	Centre Cultural de la Fundacio Caixa de Pensions, Barcelona
	Museum of Contemporary Art, Los Angeles
1991	Modernism, San Francisco
	Castelli Graphics, New York
1992	Galerie Thaddaeus Ropac, Salzburg, Austria
1993	Gagosian Gallery, New York
	Amarillo Art Center, Amarillo, Texas
	Gund Hall, Harvard University, Cambridge, Massachusetts
1994	Laura Carpenter Fine Art, Santa Fe, New Mexico

Selected Group Exhibitions:

1969	*Series Photographs,* School of Visual Arts, New York
1970	*Artists and Photographs,* Multiples, New York
1975	*60's and 70's: Trends of 6 California Artists,* Ruth S. Schaffner Gallery, Los Angeles
1976	*The Artist and the Photograph,* Israel Museum, Jerusalem
1977	*Some Color Photographs,* Castelli Graphics, New York
	The Extended Frame, Visual Studies Workshop, Rochester, New York
1978	*Mirrors and Windows: American Photography since 1960,* The Museum of Modern Art, New York (toured the United States, 1978-80)
1980	*Aspects of the 70s: Recent Directions in Photography,* De Cordova Museum, Lincoln, Massachusetts
1982	*International Photography 1920-80,* Australian National Gallery, Canberra
1987	*Photography and Art 1946-86,* Los Angeles County Museum of Art

Collections:

Whitney Museum of American Art, New York; Hirshhorn Museum and Sculpture Garden, Washington, D.C.; Art Institute of Chicago; Minneapolis Institute of Arts; Art Museum of South Texas, Corpus Christi; The Fort Worth Art Museum, Texas; Los Angeles County Art Museum; Norton Simon Museum of Art, Pasadena, California; Stedelijk Museum, Amsterdam; Auckland City Art Gallery, New Zealand; Museum of Modern Art, New York; Musee Nationale d'Art Moderne, Paris; Denver Art Museum; Museum of Contemporary Art, Los Angeles

Publications:

By RUSCHA: Books—*26 Gasoline Stations,* 1962; *Various Small Fires,* 1964; *Some Los Angeles Apartments,* 1965; *The Sunset Strip,* 1966; *34 Parking Lots,* 1967; *Royal Road Test,* 1967; *Business Cards,* with Billy Al Bengston, 1967; *Nine Swimming Pools,* 1967; *Crackers,* 1968; *Real Estate Opportunities,* 1969; *A Few Palm Trees,* 1970; *Records,* 1971; *Colored People,* 1971; *Hard Light,* with Lawrence Weiner, 1972—all published in Hollywood, California. **Articles**—"They Shoot Corners, Don't They?" in *Esquire* (New York), January 1977; "Ed Ruscha on V-Various S-Subjects" in *Stuff Magazine* (Los Angeles), no. 24, 1980. **Films**—*Premium,* 1974; *Miracle,* 1975.

On RUSCHA: Books—*Photography as Art* by Volker Kahmen, Tübingen, West Germany 1973, London 1974; *Mirrors and Windows: American Photography since 1960,* exhibition catalogue, by John Szarkowski, New York 1978; *Photography als Kunst 1879-1979/Kunst als Photographie 1949-1979,* exhibition catalogue, 2 vols., by Peter Weiermair, Innsbruck, Austria 1979; *Guacamole Airlines,* edited by Hugh Levin, New York 1980; *International Photography 1920-1980,* edited by Ian North, Canberra 1982; *Scopophilia: The Love of Looking,* edited by Gerard Malanga, New York 1985; *Photography and Art 1946-86,* exhibition catalogue, by Andy Grundberg and Kathleen M. Gauss, Los Angeles 1987. **Articles**—"The Magic of Raw Life: New Photography" by Douglas Davis in *Newsweek* (New York), 3 April 1972; "Photography: 'My Books End Up in the Trash' " by A.D. Coleman in *New York Times,* 27 August 1972; "Photography: 'I'm Not Really a Photographer'" by A.D. Coleman in *New York Times,* 10 September 1972, reprinted in *Light Readings: A Photography Critic's Writings 1968-1978* by A.I. Coleman, New York 1979.

*

My work in photography has been mostly limited to a series of books and two 16 mm films. First of all, with any medium I choose using a camera, it is no miracle for me to actually do the shutter snapping. Photography for me is not an end in itself, but a means to an end. My books are books first and not pages of paper housing a collection of photographs. The films are films first and not exercises in cinematography—they are stories told in such a way as to make the camera as non-existent as possible.

I do not make photographic prints and for this reason may be disqualified as being a photographer. The camera has to be the workhorse of another medium, not an end in itself.

—Edward Ruscha

*   *   *

Well-known as a pop/conceptual artist through his paintings and prints, Ed Ruscha has also strongly affected the world of photography with his ingenious series of books. Mimicking the way in which Americans use their cameras, these collections of snapshot-like pictures question the medium's artistic potential and raise broader issues about our society's strange affair with photography.

Ruscha's books are so simple they become profound. Similar to Andy Warhol's Brillo Boxes, his *26 Gasoline Stations* shocked viewers with its conscious lack of artistic content and its refusal to make any judgments about its subject matter. The book is no more than the title implies: it contains 26 straightforward pictures of gasoline stations. That brand of Pop irony can be found in many of his other books as well. *Nine Swimming Pools, 34 Parking Lots,* and *A Few Palm Trees* are purposely so uninspiring that they raise the question of why someone went to the trouble to publish them. Copying the look of a real estate brochure, *Real Estate Opportunities* shows a series of unappealing vacant lots in the L.A. area in order to make a viewer consider the activity of business from a fresh perspective. *Some Los Angeles Apartments* works similarly. It presents examples of the worst L.A. architecture in a way that neither romanticizes nor condemns, thus allowing the viewer to reach his or her own conclusions.

In terms of its effect on photography, the most significant book has been *Sunset Strip,* which contains a picture of each building joined together in accordian fashion so it can be folded out and displayed as a continuous strip 27 feet long. This piece pokes fun at the documentary impulse of the snapshot takers as well as the art photographers, because the desire to capture every important person, place, event, or feeling on film creates just such a surrogate reality. By actually completing such a silly project, Ruscha proves that the result of these desires is inevitably an illusion of the real experience.

Since Ruscha does not consider himself a photographer, he holds no commitment to the history or the traditions of the medium, and he openly questions its use as a purely artistic endeavor. When questioned by Howardena Pindell in the *Print Collectors Newsletter,* he said, "I have special reservations about the limits of the photograph, and I couldn't cross it into any other medium. . . . The photographs are very simple things. They really don't mean that much to me. It's the making of the entire book that's important—the collecting of all those things. . . . I would never frame one of my photographs and put it in an art exhibit. The book is the look, not the photograph."

The irony of this stance, of course, is that as he denies photography's artistic potential, he uses it to make his own artistic statements. So again, he leaves the photographers and viewers on their own to ponder what it all might mean.

—Ted Hedgpeth

RUSSO, Marialba.

Nationality: Italian. **Born:** Giugliano, Naples, 14 August 1947. **Education:** Studied at the Accademia di Belle Arti, Naples, 1968-72. **Career:** Freelance photographer, Naples, since 1968. Professor of Photography and Ethnography, University of Salerno, 1972-73. Professor, Liceo Artistico, Naples, since 1973; Professor of Photography, Department of Visual Communication Sciences, Universita Popolare, Naples, since 1975. **Address:** via Santa Agata dei Goti 32, 00184 Rome, Italy.

Individual Exhibitions:

1972	*La Festa Popolare,* University of Bologna
1973	*Madonna dell'Arco,* Museo Nazionale delle Artì e Tradizioni, Rome
1981	*130 figure di spalle,* Museo Diego Pignatelli Cortes, Naples
	Sala delle Colonne, San Marco, Venice
1982	Teatro San Carlo, Naples
1983	Galleria Spazio Immagine, Bari, Italy
	Galleria San Fedele, Milan
1984	Galleria Lotti, Bologna
	Palazzo Massari, Ferrara, Italy
	Centre Culturel d'art moderne, Troyes
1985	Centre Culturel Municipal, Cherbourg
	Collège de la Rochette, Chaumont

1986	Theatre Mediterranée, Toulon
1989	Galleria d'Arte Moderna G Morandi, Bologna
1992	*On the Face of Europe,* Derby Photography Festival, London
	Mai de la Photo, Ville de Reims
1993	Fonds Régional d'Art Contemporain, a cura di Laurence Imbernon
	Fondazione Mudima, Milan
1994	*Roma Fasti Moderni. Il Disordine del Tempo,* Palazzo delle Esposizioni, Rome

Selected Group Exhibitions:

1970	*Incontri di Sorrento,* Sorrento, Italy
1971	*Fotografia e Informazione Visiva,* Atelier 70, Naples
1972	*Naples and Its Region,* Italian Tourist Office, Boston
1977	*Carnevale,* at *SICOF '77,* Milan
1979	*Fotografia come Bene Culturale,* Commune di Modena, Italy (travelled to Venice and Florence)
1980	*L'Abete e il Faggio,* Museo Nazionale Arte Moderna, Rome
1981	*La danza,* Museo in Trastevere, Rome
1984	*Mediterranean Photography,* Centre Cultural de la Caixa, Barcelona, Spain
1985	*Trace de Memoire,* Fond Regional d'Art Contemporain de Champagne Ardenne, France
1986	*50 anos de color,* Circulo de Bellas Artes, Madrid
	Trouver Trieste, Tour Eiffel, Paris
	Cartoline da Napoli, Ministero per i Beni Culturali e Ambientali, Rome
	Tra sogno e bisogno, Palazzo Isimbardi, Milan
1987	*Soucasna Cernobila Zapadoevropska fotografie,* Ledna
1989	*Torino Fotografia 89,* Turin
	L'insistenza dello sguardo, Palazzo Fortuny, Venice
	150 Years of Photography, Ministerstvo kultury CSR, Prague
	Latvian Photo Art Society, Riga
	Nature—Everybody's Home, Fotofest, Houston, Texas
1990	National Association of Lithuanian Photographers, Vilnius
	L'orizzonte della quotidianità, Galleria d'Arte Moderna, Bologna
1991	*The Circle of Life,* California Academy of Sciences, San Francisco
1993	*Il divenire della fotografia, 1839-1990 a cura di Italo Zannier,* Mestre, Venice
	Tutte le strade portano a Roma, Palazzo delle Esposizioni, Rome
1994	*Segni di Luce—La Fotografia Italiana Contemporanea,* Biblioteca Classense, Ravenna

Collections:

Museo Nazionale delle Arti e Tradizioni Popolari, Rome; Museo Nazionale d'Arte Moderna, Rome; Centro Studi e Archivo della Comunicazione, University of Parma; Archivio dell'Istituto Geografico De Agostini, Milan; Fonds Regional d'Art Contemporain de Champagne Ardenne, France; Bibliothèque Nationale, Paris.

Publications:

By RUSSO: Books—*Immagini della Madonna dell' Arco,* with an introduction by A. Rossi and R. De Simone, Rome 1974; *Al Ristorante il 29 Settembre 1974,* Naples 1976; *Carnevale si Chiamava Vincenzo,* with an introduction by A. Rossi and R. De Simone, Rome 1977; *Giornale Spray,* with an introduction by Daniela Palazzoli, Naples 1977; *Gli Eretici dell' Assunta,* with an introduction by J. Recupero, Rome 1978; *In fondo al Sud,* with text by Arturo Fratta, Turin 1981; *Carnevali in Campania,* with text by Filiberto Menna, Naples

Italy, 1981. Photograph by Marialba Russo.

1982; *La strada occulta,* with text by Jacques Defert and V. Delouya, Milan 1984; *Il paese delle meraviglie,* edited by Francesco Indovina and Gaddo Morpurgo, Milan 1984; *Il presepe napoletano nella collezione del Banco di Napoli,* Naples 1987; *Isole d'estate* by Norman Douglas, Naples 1988; *Marialba Russo—fotografie 1980-87,* text by A Moravia, Milan 1989; *Capua Antica,* text by Werner Johannowsky, Ed. Guida, 1989; *Sardegna,* text by Valeria Gigante Lanzara, Ed. Guida 1989; *Benetton,* with Franco Batacchi, 1991; *Roma, Fasti Modern il Disordine del Tempo,* Milan 1993. **Articles**— "Dove Rinasce il Folk" in *Radiocorriere TV* (Turin), 9 October 1975; "Il Mondo delle Favole" in *Fotografia Italiana* (Milan), September 1976; "I Nuovi Graffiti" in *Paese Sera* (Naples), September 1977; "Carnevale" in *Paese Sera* (Rome), December 1977; "Libri di B. Alario" in *Nuova Fotografia* (Naples), January 1979; "Carnevale come Evasione" in *Vogue Italia* (Milan), February 1980; "Di Giovedi Rinasce . . . " in *Europeo* (Rome), February 1980; "Vedi Napoli e le sue Mostre" in *L'Uomo Vogue* (Milan), May 1980.

On RUSSO: Books—*Violence and Aggression,* by the Time-Life editors, New York 1976; *Catalogo Bolaffi della Fotografia n.2,* Turin 1977; *L'Opera dei Pupi,* Palermo 1977; *SICOF '77,* exhibition catalogue, by Lanfranco Colombo, Milan 1977; *Gli Eredi della Terra,* exhibition catalogue, Milan 1979; *SICOF '79,* exhibition catalogue, by Lanfranco Colombo, Milan 1979; *Venezia '79: La Fotografia,* edited by Daniela Palazzoli, Vittorio Sgarbi and Italo Zannier, Milan and New York 1979; *Enciclopedia per Fotografare,* Milan 1980; *Arte e Critica 80,* Rome 1980; *11 Italian Women Photographers,* exhibition catalogue, edited by Lanfranco Colombo, Cologne 1984; *La giovane fotografia europea,* exhibition catalogue, with text by Gerardo Pedicini, Naples 1985; *Visages Paysages hier et aujourd'hui,* with text by Italo Zannier, Milan 1986; *Storia della fotografia italiana,* text by Italo

Zannier, Bari, 1986; *Tra sogno e bisogno,* preface by A C Quintavalle, Milan, 1986; *Ritorno a Bach,* Venice, 1986; *Storia della fotografia,* by Jean Claude Lemagny and André Rouillé, Milan, 1988; *L'insistenza dello sguardo, fotografie italiane 1839-1989,* Alinari, 1989; *150 let fotografie,* Ministerstvo Kultury, Prague, 1989; *Encontros da imagen,* Braga, 1990; *Mitterauer. I giovani in Europa dal Medioevo a oggi,* Ed, Laterza, 1991; *The Circle of Life,* Ed. by David Cohen, New York, 1992; *Il divenire della fotografia,* Venice, 1993; *Tutte le strade portano a Roma,* Ed. Carte Segrete, 1993; *Aperture. Immagini Italiane,* Ed. Charta, 1993; *Segni di Luce. Fotografia Italiana Contemporanea,* Ed. Longo, Ravenna, 1994. **Articles**—"Riscoperta del Carnevale" by R. Lejdi in *Europeo* (Milan), March 1976; "Tre Modi di Intendere la Fotografia" by Edo Prando in *Fotografia Italiana* (Milan), May 1976; "Tra Pittura e Fotografia" by Lea Vergine in *Fotografia Italiana* (Milan), October 1977; "I Nuovi Fotografi" by Daniela Palazzoli in *Europeo* (Rome), June 1979; "L'Arte Impura" by M. Luisa Agnese in *Panorama* (Milan), June 1979; "Marialba Russo" by Attilio Colombo in *Progresso Fotografico* (Milan), October 1979; "El nuevo color" in *Photovision* (Madrid), no. 14, 1986.

*

I scarcely transcribe the shadows, more or less clear, of the different experiences of the eye.

They do not want only to be the evidence of my experiences; these images would like to remain at the same level of liveliness, of ambiguity, as the figures and events that provoked them.

This desire does not come from love of the phenomena, but from fear that institutions of the eye could always capture in the secure net of their rules those rituals and those cultures that they do not yet grasp.

Meanwhile, the camera has captured them, enlightening the scene in which some rituals unfold in dim light their figures of origin, of diversity and of survival.

I will then stop my eye on the image of the rules so that like a negative on a positive it will make more uncertain the signs of the positive.

—Marialba Russo

* * *

Marialba Russo was born, and lives, in the south of Italy. Her field of vision is wholly comprised within the borders (historical and psychological, perhaps, rather than geographical) of southern Italy, where she has been investigating religious festivals and archaic rites, and peasant customs and way of life, for more than a decade. She is specially interested in an anthropological situation that escapes any hasty recording, that goes beyond the mere recording of phenomena to become a synthesis of a people's complex spirit.

What interests Russo is not simply folklore, but the psychology of the depths, the motivations, that lie behind the archaic carnivals of the Campania, the religious ceremonies in the sanctuaries in the little villages of the Apennines—in short, the spirit of a civilization. For this purpose her photography must be more than pure documentation; she herself often uses the term "registration" to describe her work. In addition to collaboration with university institutions, "registration" involves the need to read, when considering a particular event, all the layers of cultural background that have kept it alive.

Russo's expressive instrumentation is individual and extremely effective. Her style of photography avoids the forms of classical documentary (expressive cutting, correct angulation, modulation of tones, clarity of detail and so on), choosing rather the methods of sequence and especially movement, with the pictures taken from an angle that allows her to "enter" into the actual event. Her pictures seem to be shots in a film taken with the camera shoulder-high; but it is quite wrong to think that she regrets being unable to use the ciné-camera. What seems at first to be a limitation in still photography, the difficulty of reproducing movement, becomes the real virtue, the significance of her photographs. What takes place before her lens is not crystallized, simply because a ritual is unfolding whose profound comprehension sometimes escapes the photographer; it is a succession of vital moments in which the action evokes a mystery, the vitality adds up to ambiguity.

In rejecting formal perfection in her photographs, Marialba Russo defines the limitation of her research and at the same time declares her refusal to capture within the safe nets of photographic records, with their visual rules, those rituals and cultures that still escape understanding and rationalization. Russo's photographs, nearly always in series, upset people who are accustomed to rational certainties. They are, after all, transfigurations born of the encounter between their author's powerful sensibility and the very roots of her culture, endlessly probed but never adequately clarified.

—Attilio Colombo

RYDET, Zofia.

Nationality: Polish. **Born:** Stanislawów, 5 May 1911. **Education:** Attended primary school in Warsaw, 1918-21, and a public school in Stanislawów, 1921-24; studied economics, Lwów University, 1930-34; self-taught in photography, from 1937. **Career:** Independent sociological and artistic photographer, since 1957. Lecturer in Photography, Department of Architecture, Silesian Polytechnical University, Gliwice, 1961-78. **Recipient:** 10 First Prizes and 7 Gold medals, XII Exposition, Kraków, Poland, 1960; Silver Medal, Concours Photocinema, Paris, 1960; Bronze Medal, XIII Salon International d'Art, Bordeaux, Fance, 1962; Bronze Medal, Australian Museum of Modern Art, 1962; Gold Medal, IV FIAP Biennale, Gdańsk, Poland, 1968; Gold Cross of Merit, Poland, 1976; Ministry of Culture Prize, Poland, 1981; Union of Polish Art Photographers (ZPAF) Prize, 1985; W. Kucki Prize, Gorzów, Poland, 1985; Bishop's Grand Prize, Poznań, 1985. Order of Polonia Restituta, Ministry of Culture, Warsaw, 1985. Member, Photographic Society of Poland, 1954; Artiste, 1960, and Title of Excellence, 1976, Federation Internationale d'Art Photographique (FIAP); Member, Union of Polish Art Photographers (ZPAF), 1961. **Address:** Wybrzeze Wojska Polskiego 5, Gliwice 44-100, Poland.

Individual Exhibitions:

1961	*The Little Man,* Club G.T.F., Gliwice, Poland
	The Little Man, Galeria Krzywe Kolo, Warsaw
1962	*The Little Man,* BWA, Katowice, Poland
	The Little Man, Silesian Museum, Bytom, Poland
	The Little Man, BWA, Sosnowiec, Poland
1963	*The Little Man,* BWA, Chorzów, Poland
1964	*Time of Passing,* BWA Zacheta Gallery, Warsaw
1965	*Time of Passing,* BWA, Katowice, Poland
1967	*Time of Passing,* Club G.T.F., Gliwice, Poland
	The Little Man, Asociata Artista Fotografia, Bucharest, Rumania
1968	*Time of Passing,* Galeria Prezentacje, Toruń, Poland
1975	*The World of Feelings and Imagination,* Club G.T.F., Gliwice, Poland
	The World of Feelings and Imagination, Galeria K.T.F., Katowice, Poland
	The World of Feelings and Imagination, Galeria Z.P.A.F., Kraków, Poland
	The World of Feelings and Imagination, BWA, Poznán, Poland
	The World of Feelings and Imagination, BWA, Tychy, Poland
	The World of Feelings and Imagination, Galeria Z.P.A.F., Szczecin, Poland
1978	*The Little Man,* Gallery of Contemporary Art, Leszno, Poland
1979	*Sociological Record A.D. 1978,* Galeria KMPIK, Warsaw
1980	*Infinity—A Long Way,* Galerie G.N., Poznán, Poland
1981	*Infinity—A Long Way,* Galeria Od Nowa, Gdańsk, Poland
1982	*Standing Women,* Galeria BWA, Gorzów, Poland
1983	*The World of Feelings,* Dom Kultury, Swidnica, Poland
1984	*Sociological Record AD 1978-84,* Pedagogical Institute, Rzeszów, Poland
	Presence—Call Against War, BWA, Gorzów, Poland
1985	*Sociological Record,* Gallery of the Academy of Art, Katowice, Poland
1986	*Home,* Gallery in the Nave of St. Christopher's, Łòdź, Poland
	Infinity/World of Feelings/Presence, Galeria BWA, Lublin, Poland
1990	*Zapis socjologiczny 1978-1990,* Galeria FF, Łòdź, Poland
1991	*Swiat uczuè i wyobraźni,* Galeria ZPAF, Katowice, Poland
1993	*Nieskończonośè dalekich dróg/Zwykły człowiek,* Portrety Museum, Gliwice, Poland

Selected Group Exhibitions:

1960	*Fotografia della Nuovo Generazione,* Galleria d'Arte Moderna, Milan
1961	*Salon International du Portrait Photographie,* Bibliothèque Nationale, Paris
1968	*Fotografia subiektwyna,* Galeria BWA, Kraków
1969	*Fotografowie Poszukajacy,* Galeria BWA, Kraków, Poland
1971	*II Wystawa Fotografia Poszukujacy,* Galeria Wspolczesna, Warsaw
1972	*Schöpferische Fotografen aus Polen,* Photokina, Cologne

Image from *A Sociological Record, A.D. 1978-84.* Photograph by Zofia Rydet.

1973	*Modern Polish Photography,* Kunsthalle, Nuremberg, West Germany (travelled to Kassel, West Germany)
	Modern Polish Photography, Patio Foundation, Geneva
	Modern Polish Photography, Kosciuszo Foundation, New York
	Modern Polish Photography, Chalon sur Sâone, France
	Modern Polish Photography, Tokyo
1975	*Modern Polish Photography,* Jose Clement Gallery, Orozco, Mexico
1977	*Contemporary Polish Photography,* Gallery of Contemporary Art, Zagreb
	Contemporary Polish Photography, Il Diaframma, Milan and Rome
1978	*78 APA International Exhibition of Photography,* Tokyo
1979	*Fotografia Polska 1839-1979,* International Center of Photography, New York (travelled to the Museum of Contemporary Art, Chicago; Zacheta Gallery, Warsaw; Museum of Fine Arts, Łódź, Poland; Whitechapel Art Gallery, London)
	Sztuka reportazu, National Museum, Wrocław
1980	*I Ogòlnopolski Przeglad Fotografii Socjologicznej,* BWA Bielsko, Biała, Poland
1981	*La Photographie Polonaise 1900-81,* Centre Georges Pompidou, Paris

1983	*17th Biennal,* Sao Paulo, Brazil
	The Cross in the Universum of Art, Church of God's Charity, Warsaw
1985	*Polska Wspòłczesna Fotografia Artystyczna,* Galeria Zacheta, Warsaw
	Polish Avantgarde, Guy Schranen, Antwerp, Belgium
1986	*The Second International Portfolio of Artists' Photography,* Liget Galeria, Budapest
1987	*Out of Eastern Europe—Private Photography,* List Visual Art Centre; Rosa Esmon Gallery, New York; Artspace, San Francisco
	Modern Photography and Beyond, National Museum of Modern Art, Kyoto, Japan
1988	*L'immagine delle Donne,* Siena, Italy
	Photographie Polonaise, Denain, Douchy, France
	Zwischen Elbe und Volga, Lenbachaus, Munich, Germany
	Out of Eastern Europe, The Baxter Gallery, Portland
	Out of Eastern Europe, Randolph Street Gallery, Chicago
	Polish Perceptions, Glasgow
	Polska fotografia intermedialna, BWA, Poznań
1989	*Zwischen Elbe und Volga,* Kunstamt Schoneberg, Haus am Kleistpark, Berlin
1990	*Fotoberichte aus Polen,* Gasteig Galerie, Munich

1991 *Mai de la Photo,* Reims, France
1994 *Konstelacje—Wystawa fotografii polskiej 1993-1994,* Galeria FF, Lòdz

Collections:

Bibliothèque Nationale, Paris; Museum Sztuki, Lódź, Poland; Muzeum Narodowe, Wrocław, Poland; Pushkin State Museum of Fine Art, Moscow; Slovenske Narodne Muzeum, Bratislava, Slovakia; Muzeum Etnograficzne, Kraków, Poland; Federation of Photographic Associations, Gorzów Wlkp; Eva Pape Collection, New York; International Center of Photography, New York; Museum of Modern Art, New York; The National Museum of Modern Art, Kyoto, Japan; National Museum of Photography, Film and TV, Bradford, England; Circoscrizione 2, Comune di Siena, Italy; Gliwice Museum, Poland.

Publications:

By RYDET: Books—*Maly czlowiek/The Little Man,* Warsaw 1964; *Swiat wyobrzani/The World of Imagination,* Warsaw 1980; *Obecnosc/Presence,* Kalwaria Zebrzydowska, Poland 1986; *Masters of Polish Photography: Zofia Rydet,* Geneva 1986; *Zofia Rydet o swojej twrczości/ Zofia Rydet on her Creative Work,* Gliwice, 1993.

On RYDET: Books—*Frauen der Weltfotografie* by Rita Mass, Leipzig 1964; *Czas przemijania,* exhibition catalogue, text by Alfred Ligocki, Katowice, 1965; *500 zagadek fotografii/500 Photo Puzzle* by H. Latós, Warsaw 1974; *Zofia Rydet—mitologia dalekich podròzy,* by Jerzy Busza, Gdansk, 1980; *Fotograficzne penetracje* by A. Ligocki, Kraków, Poland 1983; *Wobec fotografii/In the Face of Photography* by J. Busza, Warsaw 1983; *Wszystko o fotografii/All About Photography* by R. Bobrowski and others, Warsaw 1984; *Fotografia polska 1945-1983* by R. Bobrowski, J. Busza and others, Gorzów Wielkopolski, Poland 1985; *Encyclopedie Internationale des Photographes de 1839 à nos jours,* by Michel Auer, Geneva, 1985; *Nieskończoność dalekich dròg/Swiat uczuć i wyobrazni,* exhibition catalogue, Lublin 1986; *Czy istnieje fotografia socjologiczna?* by Alfred Ligocki, Kraków, 1987; *Formy i ludzie: almanach fotografiki śląskiej* by Alfred Ligocki, Katowice, 1988; *Zwischen Elbe und Volga—Sechzehn Fotografen aus Osteuropa und der DDR,* exhibition catalogue, Munich, 1988; *Wobec odbiorców fotografii,* by Jerzy Busza, Warsaw, 1990; *Zapis socjologiczny 1978-1990,* exhibition catalogue, text by Urszula Czartoryska, Lòdz. 1990; *Mai de la Photo,* exhibition catalogue, text by Jacqueline Salmon, Reims, 1991; *150 lat fotografii polskiej,* Warsaw, 1991; *Nieskończoność dalekich dròg/Zwykły człowiek/Portrety,* exhibition catalogue, Gliwice, 1993. **Articles**—"maly czlowiek—Zofia Rydet" by U. Czartoryska in *Fotografia* (Warsaw), no. 7, 1961; "Photographs from Poland" in *PhotoGuide Magazine* (London), no. 5, 1962; "Szacunek dla dziela" by J. Garztecki in *Perspektywy* (Warsaw), no. 2, 1977; "Zofia Rydet" by L. Sosnowski in *Magazyn Kulturalny* (Kraków, Poland), no. 2, 1977; "Zofia Rydet Talks with the Editor" in *Projekt* (Warsaw), no. 2, 1979; "Ten swiat" by Juliusz Garztecki in *Perspektywy,* Warsaw, no 45/1980; "Zofia Rydet" by I.A. Guillon in *Art Press* (Paris), no. 6, 1983; "Portret we wnetrzu" by T. Szyma in *Tygodnik Powszechny* (Kraków, Poland), no. 17/18, 1984; "Niezwykłá Obecnośc" by Henry Kuś in *Kierunki,* Warsaw, no 11/1986; Nowy album fotografii Zofii Rydet, by Henryk Kuś in *Kierunki,* Warsaw, no 15/1989.

*

The origin of my interest in photography stemmed, most probably, from my interest in art. As a child, I preferred drawing and painting to playing with other children or skating. Regretfully, for reasons independent of myself, my actual studies had nothing to do with art which, however, did not cease to be the most important of my dreams. Then came the war, so tragic to all of us. When it was over, it was too late for me to make a fresh start. I bought a camera in 1957 and soon realized that it offered me a chance to return to my dreams. Rudolf Anrheim says that photography, connected with the nature of the landscape and man's surroundings, with the world of animals and inanimate objects, of people, their triumphs, sufferings and joys, has the privilege of presenting man to himself, of deepening and fixing sensations and informa- tion. It is a superb instrument. I do not think my works may be defined as documentary. A photographic report is a record of an event, and this is not my

purpose. My main interest is in man, his psyche, his thoughts and feelings. Even if I witness an event, a celebration, or an accident, I take photographs of people's reactions, of how an event impresses itself on their minds. This is the material from which I build a new, perhaps exclusively my own, reality. I kept searching for a novel means of expression, and that is why I went in for photomontage, as it creates a unique chance of transforming one's own hidden thoughts, feelings and experiences into a new image, apparently unreal, but in fact composed of real elements. Montage photographs are surrealistic in their atmosphere, and though in painting surrealism is a classical style, it has quite different prospects in photography. The photographic equipment causes reality to enter a picture that is composed of authentic elements, and thus it penetrates the sphere of our dreams and nightmares.

Boundlessness of Different Roads made in 1980 is a metaphorical story about life and the roads we must walk which are always different and, although there are guiding signs around us, they are meaningless illegible and wrapped up. Only the crosses we meet so often are real and only one direction of movement, towards death, is certain. The composition as a whole is crowned with a gate opening up wider and wider towards the vast waste of the ocean. The concluding pictures are a mystification of life after life—picture of a road, blurred, solarized, taken in motion with a bright point in the horizon where Christ appears.

In 1978 I took up my *Sociological Record.* Andre Bazin once wrote "to artificially fix the appearance of a human being means to deliver him from the river of passing away onto the boat of life." This very "Record" of mine was meant to be such an embalmment of time, was, or rather is, to fix what is already changing and what, although still being the actual reality, keeps fading away and may be hard to imagine. It has to faithfully show man in his everyday environment but which also shows his psyche and sometimes tells us more about him than he himself does. Home is a place where we return, where we find our own selves. No matter whether it is a palace or a shanty, a villa, a mud hut, or a skyscraper, home is always man's shelter from unrest and worries gnawing at him. Home reflects the personality of its owner and it also reflects the society, civilisation and culture which shaped him. Home con- forms to the wish of its creator, the man who lives in it. Home is so intensely permeated with the personality of its master that eventually the home and its master are one. No two similar people or two similar homes exist. Each has exclusively characteristic features. Man instinctively and subconsciously adjusts his home to himself. Point of everyday return, sanctuary of relaxation after torment and joy of each consecutive stage of this journey—*The Hub of the Universe.*

My initial assumption was: things, the interior itself, are more important and the man is merely an element determining such an interior; he is to be static as if being one of those things himself. Thus he is to sit opposite the camera and look directly into the lens. The pictures should always be taken from the same point of view. After all it was intended to be the simplest possible, objective and authentic recording of stagnant reality taken coolly and at a distance. Meanwhile, in the course of working on it I realised that it started growing in quite different colours; that this ordinary document was turning in my eyes into some great truth of human fate and that I was not able to maintain that cool distant attitude any more. Quite the opposite, it engaged me more than anything I had done before and it gradually became a sort of new love and passion providing me with new prospects and strength.

Man, who was supposed to be a mere element, proved to be the most important feature. Furthermore, that direct look into the lens results in a very strong model-camera-photographer link. Looking straight into the lens, the model realized the "importance of the moment," this sort of immortalization, this retaining of his personality which is characteristic of himself only, raising him to the rank of some symbol, although he himself was not great at all. The photographer seemed to be a powerful magician with an ability to stop time and reveal, even if only for an instant, the hydra of death. The camera was the essential instrument—a magic box retaining the picture.

So it became almost an addiction. Walking day after day round villages and towns, entering houses and meeting a great variety of people I kept forgetting the burden of the heavy camera I was carrying, my aching back and how hard it was to keep walking around all day.

I took over 30,000 pictures in 20 voivodships, mainly in the country which changes rapidly year by year; old thatched cottages and tiny wooden houses, so typical of various regions, their interiors with rows of holy pictures, keep vanishing. These trips of mine (without a car) and meeting such a variety of people are still equally fascinating. With my camera I take from them what I find precious, extraordinary and characteristically pretty and I deeply hope thus to transmit to others what I experience myself.

—Zofia Rydet

* * *

The work of Zofia Rydet is of great interest to Polish contemporary photography. Her photography is extremely varied and spans many different areas—from photographic report, through surrealist photomontage, to avant-garde. Rydet has a place in all these areas but, at the same time, goes beyond them because of her individuality and exceptionality. The common denominator, and at the same time, the distinctive feature, of Rydet's photographs is her obvious interest in man, his world, psyche and truth.

Rydet's most important achievement is, without doubt, the series of photographs she began in 1978 and called ''Zapis socjologiczny.'' This collection portrays people and their homes, most commonly, in distant areas of Poland. ''Zapis socjologiczny,'' Rydet says, ''was to be a way of embalming time, it was meant—or rather, is meant—to hold or secure things that change and, despite their present reality, fade from existence so that, in a short time, perhaps, they will be hard to imagine. It is supposed to be an accurate portrayal of man in his everday surroundings among the things that he creates for himself—things that, on the one hand, become decorative artifacts of his immediate environment and that, on the other hand, reveal his psyche, sometimes saying more about him than he would want.''

On the basis of this idea, Rydet assumed that the things that man surrounds himself with and amongst which he lives are more important than he himself is. Because of this, man had to remain static and immobile; to sit directly in front of the camera, like an object, and always be photographed, from more or less the same perspective and in the same light. ''Meanwhile,'' Rydet admits, ''all of this took on a completely different aspect as I worked: in my eyes, this new document began to appear as a new truth of man's fate. Man, who was supposed to be a mere feature, became the most important motif and the direct gaze of the model began to form a strong link between us. The photographer was like a sorcerer with the ability to stop time and point to the spectre of death and oblivion. The photographic camera was the chief instrument in this process.''

Rydet's photography, lying on the border between documentation and contrived photography, shows man and his world with sympathy and understanding. These photographs, grouped around subjects such as children, women, families, etc., form a beautiful story about man, the hardship of his daily life, his beliefs and dreams his truth. The combinations of photographs presented always reveal what actually exists in various areas of the country (Podhale, for example) but, at the same time, show a world that is already fading into the past, inevitably pushed to the periphery of life by the evolution of civilisation and technology. This photography shows the world with a cold clarity of vision that bears witness to its decline and its seeming unreality and, simultaneously, to its charm and undeniable beauty.

—Ryszard Bobrowski

S

SÁGL, Jan.

Nationality: Czechoslovakian. **Born:** Humpolec, 25 March 1942. **Education:** Attended secondary school in Humpolec, until 1959; mainly self-taught in photography, from 1952. **Family:** Married Zorka Jirousová in 1964; daughter: Alena. **Career:** Worked as a storekeeper in a car factory, Humpolec, 1969-61; lighting technician, 1961-62, and assistant cameraman, 1962-63, TV Prague television studios, Prague; stagehand, National Theatre, Prague, 1963-64. Since 1964, freelance advertising promotional, editorial and postcard photographer, working for *Creative Work, Creative Art* magazines, etc., Prague. Since 1989, represented by the Anzenberger Agency in Vienna. Publishes in magazines *Geo, Merian, Globo* and others. **Recipient:** Best Book of the Year Award, Ministry of Culture, Czechoslovakia, 1985 and 1987. **Address:** Chodská 31, 120 00 Prague 2, Czech Republic.

Individual Exhibitions:

1969   V. Špála Gallery, Prague
1979   Institute of Macromolecular Chemistry, Prague
          Galerie ve věži, Mělnìk, Czechoslovakia
1981   CVJM Schroeder-Saal, Hamburg, West Germany
1985   House of Culture (ÚKDŽ), Prague
1987   *The Coloured World,* Marienbad (with J. Saudek and M. Švolìk)
          Museum of Czech Literature, Prague (with Otakar Jiránek)
          Junior Club Na chmelnici, Prague (with Jaroslav Kořán)
          Karel Čapek Bookshop, Prague
1990   Galerie Coupole, Neu Isenburg, Germany (with Zorka Ságlová)
1992   Prague House of Photography, Prague
          House of Arts, Brno

Selected Group Exhibitions:

1965   *Seven Photographers,* Manés Club, Prague
1970   *Young Artists' Exhibitions,* Mánes Club, Prague
1973   *8e. Biennale des Jeunes,* Paris
1979   *Media Practice,* AI Gallery, Tokyo
1982   *Topical Photography,* Moravian Gallery, Brno, Czechoslovakia
1983   *Rencontres Internationales de la Photographie,* Arles, France
1984   *Czech Creative Photography,* Galerie D, Prague
          Aspects of Czech Photography, Thackrey and Robertson Gallery, San Francisco
1985   *27 Contemporary Czechoslovakian Photographers,* Photographers' Gallery, London
          Contemporary Czech Photography, DoI Photoplaza, Tokyo
1986   *Modern Colour Photography 1936 to 1986 (Photokina),* Köln
          Selections 3 (Polaroid), Köln
          The Body in Czechoslovakian Photography 1900-1986, Kroměříž
1989   *The Ways of Czechoslovakian Photography,* House at the Stone Bell, Prague
          Czechoslovakian Photography 1945-1989, National Gallery, Prague
          Czechoslovakian November 1989, Fotochema, Prague, and seven other European towns in 1990

1990   *Contemporary Czechoslovakian Photography,* Museum Ludwig, Köln, and 12 other towns in Europe and USA in the years 1990-94
1992   *What's New: Prague,* The Art Institute of Chicago

Collections:

Bibliothèque Nationale, Paris; Moravian Gallery, Brno; Polaroid Collection, Frankfurt am Main; German Photographic Society; Museum of Applied Arts, Prague; Victoria and Albert Museum, London; Museum of Fine Arts, Houston.

Publications:

By SÁGL: Books—*South Bohemian Landscape,* with introduction by Pavel Vrba, Prague 1985; *North-West Bohemia,* with text by Eva Juzová, Prague 1985; *Paris,* with text by Jan Řezáč and Jaroslav Kořán, Prague 1986; *Paris,* with Otakar Jiránek, Slovart Publishers, 1989.

On SÁGL: Books—*Aktuálnì Fotografie,* exhibition catalogue by Antonìn Dufek, Brno 1982; *27 Contemporary Czechoslovakian Photographers,* exhibition catalogue by Jiřn Hlusička, Sue Davies and Antonìn Dufek, London 1985. **Articles**—"Colour Creation of Jan Ságl" by Martin Hruška in *Ceskoslovenska Fotografie* (Prague), no. 11, 1985; "Simple Effects of Jan Ságl" by Antonìn Dufek, in *Revue Fotografie* (Prague), no. 2, 1986; "Images d'Est en Ouest" in *Photos* (Paris), May 1986; "You will not steal" by Jan Lacina in *Reflex,* no 6, 1992; text in exhibition catalogue, Prague House of Photography by Jana and Jiří Ševčìk, 1992; exhibition catalogue by Jana Vránová, House of Arts, Brno 1992; Jan Ságl-from the Cycle Polachrome in *Fotografie,* no 7, 1993; Jan Ságl by Martin Hruška in *Revue Fotografie,* no 2, 1993.

*

I got my first camera in 1952, and have been photographing ever since. I left secondary school in Humpolec in 1959, and have lived in Prague since 1961. I have been a professional photographer since 1964, working regularly for the art magazines *Creative Work, Creative Art,* etc. Since 1970 I have worked in colour, making picture postcards, calendars, advertisements and tourist guides to earn a living. At the same time, I make my own independent photos. During 1967-76 I made black-and-white photographs of the music groups "The Primitives," "The Plastic People of the Universe" and "DG 307." In 1969 I went to photograph in the Soviet Union, and this work was published in catalogues and magazines in Cologne and Nuremberg. A cycle of black-and-white contact prints entitled "House Search" was made in 1974. I made several trips to Slovakia between 1974 and 1977, photographing in black-and-white the disappearing landscape and traditional lifestyles. In Poland, I photographed the Baltic sea coast (1978, 1979, 1980) and the pilgrimage at Czestochowa (1978), the Island of Rugen, DDR (1982, 1983), and throughout Tunisia (1985) and France (1986). Since 1979 I have worked exclusively in 24.35mm colour transparencies and Cibachrome paper prints. I worked on three cycles of photographs: landscapes photographed by extreme illumination; light and reflections; photography and creative art. In the 1990s I have prepared six books for publication: "Landscape," "Beaubourg," "Paris," "Bretagne," "Provence" and "Tunisia." However, the publishers who ordered them have—due to the changes in the Czech Republic—gone

Nice, **1991.** Photograph by Jan Ságl.

bankrupt. That is the reason why at the moment I have returned to advertising photography and magazine work.

—Jan Ságl

* * *

Jan Ságl maintains that he is unable to express himself by words and his proverbial taciturnity would seem to corroborate this statement. However, what he once wrote in an exhibition catalogue proves him wrong, since it fully and aptly characterizes his stance as a creative artist and the character of his work: "I think that the place of photography depending on illusive imagery—as in case of visual poetry—lies somewhere between art and literature. That photography which deprives itself of the literary aspect tries in vain to achieve what has been long achieved by art. What I'm interested in is a dialogue, not imitation."

Ságl's photography is thoroughly modern, for his pictures are as much real as unreal and their inner truth lies in the ever-changing correlation of reality and the soul, sensory perception and imagination, the conscious and the subconscious. And although Ságl strictly adheres to the documentary method, his images nevertheless constitute a flux of personal reflection, moods, speculation and meditation. Yet they are determined by time and place and reveal the conflict of man and his world, his desires and frustrations, anxieties and joys. It is not by chance that Ságl, wanting to state his message as precisely as possible, arranges his pictures in sequences in which the images acquire other possible meanings.

Since the late 1970s his imagery has been based on colour. In fact he adopted colour in his creative work only by necessity since he felt that the

canon of life photography restricted him too much. In time he turned the necessity into a virtue, for colour succumbed to his vision and began playing a major role in the symbolics of his message. And thus colour in the multitude of its metamorphoses and light with its tendency to transcend things lend Ságl's imagery a unique mystique of the incessant blending of the real and the imaginary and rank Ságl among the very top in contemporary colour photography. It is as if colour set the essential tone of the feeling, for it shines, permeating everything, lending meaning and order to things, supplying the time base. The same goes for his reflections, his images within images drawn by light and shadow. Ságl's colour and light constitute a challenge, a mystery, a promise, a question mark. They are living things and play a significant semantic role in his imagery.

Ságl first started with landscapes. Landscape is always available to offer comfort to a torn soul seeking refuge. His landscapes, however, were of the never-never land of dream, a stage for a dialogue between man and the elements, exciting and romantic. As if his landscapes opened the gate to the very essence of the land, and nature became rejuvenated by human spiritual values. And yet it is as if these landscapes were aware of the real time and place, spinning their message of the world of contemporary man. They range from primordial landscapes governed only by the elements to symbols of the human quest for the universe, from the mythical setting of burning of evil wintry symbols in the twilight of the May Day eve to a spectre of a space research centre produced by the megalomania of a technocratic civilization. It was here in colour landscapes that Jan Ságl has found the key to his new mode of expression and regained his balance and inner security.

And thus he started returning to places which he had left behind, to the city and among people, a world which irritates, provokes and wounds him and revives his sadness and irony. All this gave birth to his so far most emotionally charged images. 1984, nothing but the year is the ideologic keystone of one of his series. Its subject is an authenticated feeling of an actual human being living in actual time and space. Although Ságl's photography starts with preconceived messages, the real objects discovered during the making of a picture are always presented in their purest and most direct form.

Jan Ságl has learned about life the hard way. A native of Humpolec, Bohemia, he is a son of an insurance company clerk turned tractor driver who was blinded when his vehicle toppled in an accident. As Ságl says, lack of information made him study civil engineering at the Czech Technical University in Prague. After a year he dropped out, because technology was but a word to him. Thus he entered life, so to speak. He started trundling bales of wool in a warehouse, operated a drilling machine in a gearbox factory and cut sheet metal. Then came his National Service. When he was discharged from the army, he worked as a TV studio gaffer, theatre stagehand and from time to time, when he received a commission, he also photographed for an art magazine, doing art photography and reportages from show openings. He became fascinated with reportage, because he saw it as a chance to comment on life and the times.

It took him ten years to find out that times had changed and his type of reportage had meanwhile ceased to be able to express what he felt. And thus he sought refuge in the landscape, in those familiar places which he used to photograph commercially for a picture card manufacturer. He now started photographing landscapes in his own way. Such was the way of Jan Ságl to colour photography, his speculations about contemporary man and his relation to the world he has helped shape, but also speculation about photography's relation to modern art, for this is also one of Ságl's prime subjects. The roots of his imagery lie somewhere in the past, in boyhood when he first discovered Surrealism in objects and structures captured by his Flexareta camera, a time when he was not even aware that there was a thing called Surrealism or that there was an Emila Medková.

—Daniela Mrázková

SALGADO, Sabastiao Ribeiro.

Nationality: Brazilian. **Born:** in Aimorés, Brazil, 8 February 1944. **Education:** Studied economics at Sao Paulo University; Ecole Nationale de Statistique et de l'Administration Economique, Paris; and Paris University. **Family:** Married; two children. **Career:** Worked as an economist for the Ministry of Finance, São Paulo, 1968-69, and at the International Coffee Organisation, London, 1971-73; freelance photographer, 1973-75; photographer for the Gamma Agency, 1975-79, and Magnum, 1979. **Recipient:** Eugene Smith Award for Humanitarian Photography from the French Ministry of Culture, 1982; the City of Paris/Kodak Award for *Other Americas,* in 1984; the World Press Photo Award, Holland, and the Oskar Barnack Prize, West Germany, 1985; the Ibero-American Photography Award, Spain, 1986; Photojournalist of the Year Award from the International Center of Photography, New York, 1986; prize for the Best Photography Book of the Year for *Sahel,* 1986; Best Exhibition award for *Other Americas* at the Paris Audio Visual, 1986; American Society of Magazine Photography's Photographer of the Year, 1987; Maine Photography Workshop Photographer of the Year, 1987; New York Overseas Press Club's Olivier Rebbot Award, 1987; West Germany's Jounalistenpreis Entwicklungspolitik, 1987; France's Ministry of Foreign Affairs' Villa Médicis Award, 1987; West Germany's Erich Salomon Prize, 1988; King of Spain Award, 1988; Photojournalist of the Year Award, International Center of Photography, New York, 1988; New York Art Directors Club's Gold Award, 1988; Erna and Victor Hasselblad Award for life achievement, 1989; Czechoslovakia's Art of Merit Josef Sudek Medal, 1989; Maine Photographic Workshop Award for the Best Photography Book for *An Uncertain Grace,* 1990; International Festival of Photojournalism Gold Visa Award, 1990; Delaware's Common Wealth Award for Mass Communication, 1991; Le Grand Prix de la Ville de Paris, 1991; New York Art Directors Club's Gold Award, 1991; Honorary member of the American Academy of Arts and Science, Massachusetts, 1992; Germany's Oskar Barnack Prize, 1992; Germany's Art Directors Club Award, 1992; Arles International Festival's prize for Best Photography Book of the Year for *Workers,* 1993; Paris Match Gold Award, 1993. **Agent:** Amazonas images, 5 Cité Popincourt, 75011 Paris, France.

Individual Exhibitions:

1986   *Sahel L'Homme en Détresse,* Palais de Tokyo, Paris (travelled to Festival International d'Arles, France; Musée de l'Elysée, Lausanne; Museu de Arte de Sao Paulo, Brazil; National Gallery of Art, Beijing)

    Other Americas, Museo de Arte Contemporaneo de Madrid (travelled to Maison de l'Amérique Latine, Paris; Musée de l'Elysée, Lausanne; Tornio Arts Museum, Oulou, Finland; Museum Mishkan Le'Omanut, Israel; Museum Voor Land in Volkenkunde, Rotterdam; Fundaçao Nacional da Arte, Rio de Janeiro; Palace of Youth, Shanghai)

1989   *Retrospective,* Hasselblad Centre, Götenborg (travelled to Bienal de Cuba, Havana; Künsthalle, Dusseldorf; Photographers' Gallery, London; Stills Gallery, Edinburgh; Royal Albert Memorial Museum, Exeter; Fotogallery, Cardiff; Glasgow Arts Centre; National Museum of Modern Art, Tokyo)

1990   *An Uncertain Grace,* Modern Art Museum of San Francisco (travelled to Wight Art Gallery, University of California, Los Angeles; International Center of Photography, New York; Corcoran Gallery, Washington, D.C.; Carpenter Center, Harvard)

1993   *Workers,* Philadelphia Museum of Art (travelled to Palais de Tokyo, Paris; Centro Cultural de Bélem, Lisbon; Biblioteca Nacional, Madrid; National Gallery Slovakia, Bratislava)

Publications:

By SALGADO: Books—*Sahel: L'Homme en Détresse,* Paris 1986; *Other Americas,* Pantheon Books 1986; *Sahel, El Fin del Camino,* Madrid 1988; *Les Cheminots,* France 1989; *An Uncertain Grace,* Aperture 1990; *The Best Photos/As Melhores Fotos,* Brazil 1992; *Photopoche,* France 1993; *Workers,* Aperture 1993.

*   *   *

Sebastião Salgado is one of the foremost and widely known of contemporary working photojournalists in the world. His style of work takes an epic theme, such as Workers: a Paean to the people labouring in traditional manufacturing industries at the close of a century, an industrial epoch. Pursued with single-minded dedication to unfold multiple visual testimonies, each epic is cast in the best reportage tradition to have emerged between the Wars. He uses his medium to tell the story of people's lives, lives he perceives with respect however harsh their circumstances.

His own life began fifty years ago in the provincial town of Aimores, Minas Gerais, where his parents still have a modest cattle farm. He trained as an economist with a particular interest in transnational companies and exchange commodities and emerged as a political radical, exiled when the military seized power in the late sixties. Salgado became a Parisian by adoption who still feels he has never lost his particular vision of relationships between the First and Third Worlds.

"The world is changing everywhere, entering a new post-industrial revolution. The traditional working-class was so formative for me and my generation that this book and exhibition are a homage to them as well as a portrait of the work they do—a mechanical way of working that is rapidly being superseded. I try constantly to provoke a debate, a discussion, concerning the working-class and especially those workers on the South side."

This South-informed attitude to his subjects has raised discussions of another kind. In the West, Salgado is coming under increasing critical attack for refusing to view his subjects as objects of charity. Mention distress and he responds by addressing the dignity of his subjects; talk of all they lack and he considers their nobility, their concern, their grace. But isn't this precisely what his critics complain of, the icons he makes of people whose lives are at best pitiable, often desperate?

"Sometimes we from the Southern hemisphere wonder why you in the North think you have the monopoly of beauty, of dignity, of riches. Ethiopia is

Construction of the Rajasthan Canal, India, **1990.** Photograph ©Sebastião Salgado.

a country in crisis, where the people are suffering so acutely, yet Ethiopians are probably among the most beautiful, most noble people in the world. There is really no point in going there to deny this reality." His particular vision is informed by a belief in a fundamental law.

"I believe this: that the poor people of the world are not those who lack basic material goods. At any given moment in their history, the presently rich nations have been poor and vice versa. Now it is the West that is suffering economic recession and the countries that formerly governed huge empires experience poverty."

"There is no monopoly either of wealth or of beauty in the world. I believe we must not destroy recognition of human dignity and beauty." Besides having spent two years creating a book whose title was *Sahel, Man in Distress,* he reminds us that "it's nonsense to say that I don't see—or show—distress in the world."

Nor is he prepared to view those undergoing material deprivation one-dimensionally, only as victims. "After all, we all see ourselves as the agents of our own lives, not simply as the 'victims' of external agencies." Perhaps the onus is on the viewer to avoid "that very dangerous imperialism of ideas that permits you to travel the world to judge others and confirm to yourself how right and rich and important you are."

The eternally triangular relationship between photographer, subject and viewer is one that Salgado has subverted in other ways. Not since the heyday of photojournalism 50 years ago has there been a photographer who has so single-mindedly—and single-handedly—insisted on presenting his work not as individual portraits but as a series that tells a story.

Salgado doesn't care how he gets his message across, only that the process of communication and consciousness-raising occurs. "Most of the informa-tion we now get is through television and is mutilated. Photography offers the opportunity to spend much more time on a topic. It's a relatively cheaper medium, and can allow a photographer really to live in another place, show another reality, get closer to the truth."

In a world where we've grown accustomed to being told there's no one truth, but only our variable versions, Salgado has a number of categorical affirmations to make: that man is less the producer than the product of his labour and that the desire to work, pride in one's work, are part of being human. For this image-maker accused of creating biblical icons is an atheist humanist with a profound faith in the universality of human experience. "I believe" is one of the most common prefixes to his sentences, which often close on a note of unpredicted hopefulness.

Finally on a note that summarises the far-reaching scope of his enterprise and optimism, there is the conclusion: "I believe there are really few barriers of race, language or culture. How old are most of them anyway? We have barely 6,000 years of recorded history, in which many different cultures mix together to form what we now call 'Japanese' or 'British' .... I have a hope that within 200 years at most we'll be one race, speaking one language, rid of all our layers of oppression." Images worthy of a man of vision.

—Amanda Hopkinson

SAMARAS, Lucas.

Nationality: American. **Born:** Kastoria, Macedonia, Greece, 14 September 1936; emigrated to the United States, 1948: naturalized, 1955. **Education:**

Memorial High School, West New York, New Jersey, 1951-55; studied, under Allan Kaprow, at Rutgers University, New Brunswick, New Jersey, 1955-59, B.A. 1959; Columbia University, New York (Woodrow Wilson Fellow), 1959-62. **Career:** Artist and photographer, New York, since 1964: first "autopolaroid" photographs, 1970; first "photo-transformations," 1973. Visiting Instructor in Sculpture, Yale University, New Haven, Connecticut, 1969; Instructor, Brooklyn College, New York, 1971-72. **Agent:** Pace/ MacGill Gallery, 32 East 57th Street, 9th floor, New York, New York 10022, U.S.A.

Individual Exhibitions:

1955	Rutgers University, New Brunswick, New Jersey (and 1958)
1959	Reuben Gallery, New York
1961	*Dinners, Liquid Aluminum, Pastels and Plasters,* Green Gallery, New York
1962	*Pastels,* Sun Gallery, Provincetown, Massachusetts
1964	*Boxes, Constructions,* Dwan Gallery, Los Angeles
	Bedroom, Boxes, Plastics, Green Gallery, New York
1966	*Samaras: Mirror Room: Selected Works 1960-66,* Pace Gallery, New York
1968	*Transformations, Mirror Stairs, Paintings and Drawings,* Pace Gallery, New York
1969	*Book,* Museum of Modern Art, New York
	Mirror Room 3, Boxes and Drawings, Galerie der Spiegel, Cologne
1970	*Chair Transformations,* Pace Gallery, New York
	Mirror Room 3, Kunstverein, Hannover
1971	*Stiff Boxes and Autopolaroids,* Pace Gallery, New York
	Acrylics, Pastels, Inks, Phyllis Kind Gallery, Chicago
	Lucas Samaras' Boxes, Museum of Contemporary Art, Chicago
1972	*Chicken Wire Boxes,* Pace Gallery, New York
	Whitney Museum, New York (retrospective)
1974	*Photo-Transformations,* Pace Gallery, New York
1975	*Pastels,* Museum of Modern Art, New York
	Makler Gallery, Philadelphia
	Samaras and Some Others, Pace Gallery, New York
	Photo-Transformations, California State University at Long Beach
1976	University of North Dakota Art Gallery, Grand Forks
	Wright State University Art Gallery, Dayton, Ohio
	Institute of Contemporary Art, Boston
	Seattle Art Museum
	A.C.A. Gallery, Alberta College of Art, Calgary
	Phantasmata, Pace Gallery, New York
	Margo Leavin Gallery, Los Angeles
1977	*Photo-Transformations,* Galerie Zabriskie, Paris
	Photo-Transformations, Walker Art Center, Minneapolis
1978	*Reconstructions,* Pace Gallery, New York
	Mayor Gallery, London
	Reconstructions and Photo-Transformations, Akron Art Institute, Ohio
1979	Richard Gray Gallery, Chicago
1980	*Reconstructions,* Pace Gallery, New York
	Reconstructions, Photo-Transformations and Word Drawings, Pace Gallery, Columbus, Ohio
	Polaroid Photographs, Pace Gallery, New York
1982	*Pastels,* Lowe Art Museum, University of Miami (travelled in USA)
1983	*Polaroid Photographs 1969-83,* Centre Georges Pompidou, Paris (travelled to International Center of Photography, New York; Frankfurter Kunstverein, Frankfurt, Germany; Musee d'Art et d'Histoire, Fribourg, Switzerland; Center of Creative Photography, University of Arizona, Tucson; Phoenix Art Museum, Phoenix, AZ; Krannert Art Museum, Champaign, IL; Lowe Art Museum, University of Miami, Coral Gables, FL; Serpentine Gallery, London; Kennedy Gallery, Cambridge, MA; Photographic Research Center, Boston)
1985	Madison Art Center, Wisconsin
1986	*Polaroid Photographs,* Serpentine Gallery, London
	Mayor Gallery, London
	Lucas Samaras: Recent Panoramas, Pace/MacGill Gallery, New York
1988	Pace/MacGill Gallery, New York
	Lucas Samaras: Objects and Subjects 1969-86, Denver Art Museum (travelled to National Museum, Washington and to Atlanta, Miami, Richmond, Boston)
1991	Pace/MacGill Gallery, New York

Selected Group Exhibitions:

1961	*The Art of Assemblage,* Museum of Modern Art, New York
1968	*The Obsessive Image,* Institute of Contemporary Arts, London
1974	*Photography in America,* Whitney Museum, New York
1977	*Documenta 6,* Kassel, West Germany
1978	*Mirrors and Windows: American Photography since 1960,* Museum of Modern Art, New York (toured the United States, 1978-80)
1979	*One of a Kind: Polaroid Color,* Corcoran Gallery, Washington, D.C. (toured the United States)
1980	*La Photo Polaroid,* Musée d'Art Moderne, Paris
1982	*Color as Form,* International Museum of Photography at George Eastman House, Rochester, New York
1985	*American Images 1945-80,* Barbican Art Gallery, London (toured Britain)
1986	*Photography as Performance,* the Photographers' Gallery, London
1990	Pace/MacGill Gallery, New York
1992	Pace/MacGill Gallery, New York

Collections:

Metropolitan Museum of Art, New York; Museum of Modern Art, New York; Whitney Museum of American Art, New York; Guggenheim Museum, New York; Albright-Knox Art Gallery, Buffalo, New York; Larry Aldrich Museum, Ridgefield, Connecticut; Wadsworth Atheneum, Hartford, Connecticut; Art Institute of Chicago; Walker Art Center, Minneapolis; Los Angeles County Museum of Art; National Gallery of Art, Washington, D.C.

Publications:

By SAMARAS: Books—*Samaras Album, Autobiography, Autointerview, Autopolaroids,* New York 1971; *Lucas Samaras: Photo-Transformations,* with text by Arnold B. Glimcher, New York 1975; *Lucas Samaras,* with text by Kim Levin, New York 1975; *Lucas Samaras: Photos, Polaroid Photographs 1969-1983,* exhibition catalogue, New York 1984. **Articles**—"An Exploratory Dissection of Seeing" in *Artforum* (New York), December 1967; "Greece 1967; A Reconstituted Diary" in *Artforum* (New York), October 1968; "Autopolaroids and Autointerview" in *Art in America* (New York), November/December 1970; "The Art of Portraiture, in the Words of Four New York Artists" in the *New York Times,* 31 October 1976; "Conversation with a Work of Art," interview, with Peter Plagens, in *Aperture* (Millerton, New York), no. 96, 1984. **Film**—*Self,* 1969.

On SAMARAS: Books—*Samaras: Selected Works 1960-66,* exhibition catalogue, with text by Lawrence Alloway, New York 1966; *Chair Transformations,* exhibition catalogue, New York 1970; *Samaras: Selected Works 1960-1969,* exhibition catalogue, with text by Joan Siegfried and Lawrence Alloway, Chicago 1971; *Lucas Samaras' Boxes,* exhibition catalogue, with text by Joan Siegfried, Chicago 1971; *American Art in the 20th Century* by Sam Hunter, New York 1973; *Photography in America,* edited by Robert Doty, with an introduction by Minor White, New York and London 1974; *Mirrors and Windows: American Photography since 1960* by John Szarkowski, New York 1978; *Farbe im Photo: die Geschichte der Farbphotographie von 1861 bis 1981* by Fritz Binder, Gert Koshofer, Rolf Sachase and others, Cologne 1981; *Color as Form: A History of Color Photography,* exhibition catalogue, with introduction by Robert A. Sobieszek, Rochester, New York 1982; *The Library of World Photography: Portraits,* with introduction by Colin Ford, Tokyo 1982, 1983, London 1983. **Articles**—"Samaras'

Autopolaroids'' by Bruce Kurtz in *Artsmagazine* (New York), December 1971; ''Violated Instants: Lucas Samaras and Les Krims'' by A.D. Coleman in *Camera 35* (New York), July 1976; ''Lucas Samaras'' by Shoji Yamagishi in *Camera Mainichi* (Tokyo), July 1977; ''Lucas Samaras: The Self as Icon and Cultural Development'' by Barbara Rose in *Artsmagazine* (New York), March 1978; ''Modernism Turned Inside Out: Lucas Samaras' Reconstructions'' by Carter Ratcliff in *Artsmagazine* (New York), November 1979; ''Singular Developments: Polaroid's Paean to Color'' by Allen Robertson in *TWA Ambassador* (St. Paul, Minnesota), December 1979.

* * *

The art of protean Lucas Samaras is singularly an extended metaphor—of his own self. Voraciously, passionately, and obsessively, he has explored various media to fabricate art-objects which constantly push the limits and possibilities of the particular art-form to stunning realizations. He is both original and fascinating, particularly with regard to the medium of photography.

Samaras' involvement with photography can be traced to the early use of self-portraits taken by others and used in his ''Boxes.'' In Spring 1969 he made the film *Self*—his own self-image, alternating, duplicating, transforming. ''I am,'' he says, ''my own investigation territory;'' the statement unquestionably applies to Samaras' entire artistic and creative endeavour. Most blatantly he has performed—''basically I'm a performer''—in this regard in his photography from ''Autopolaroids,'' begun in December 1969, and continuing through ''Photo-Transformations,'' started in 1973. Repeating themselves, photographic images continually acquire different transformations and symbolisms through new materials and contexts. An enormous lens-reflected face held in his own hand in a photograph of 1968 reappears in ''Photo-Transformations'' as a distorted snarling figure holding a sharp-focussed image in a shaving mirror. This again appears in 1974 in another form and context—under a conical lens on a chiffon cloth between a fork and spoon. The yarn ''Box 36'' with a photo-lined lid and acrylic fingers emerging from a jewelled quicksand field anticipates the image of his mouth transformed into an incinerator consuming the fingers from the edges of his lips.

As one examines Samaras' photography several features emerge: the kind of camera used (Polaroid), the technique employed, the materials and contexts, the main subject (his own self), and the particular use of the medium. He first used Polaroid 360; since 1973 he has used SX-70. It could be suggested that he deliberately exploits the amateurish associations and the temporal immediacy of the Polaroid to tease us to look at the medium from a more philosophical and untraditional viewpoint. Unlike a roll of film with its flat, transparent continuous surface, each shot of Polaroid produces a box of a separate and distinct image. At the same time, his ''Autopolaroids'' and ''Photo-Transformations,'' consisting of series of self-images, each constitute a single iconic enigma. In other words, what he tried to do with his earlier ''assemblage'' techniques to fuse the difference between the idea/concept and the mode/result of expression has come to fruition in a medium that offers the promise of such a possibility. The double and multiple images are created by manipulating (tricking) the electric eye of the camera for approximately 20 seconds to manage the number of exposures. Electronic strobe is used with red mylar, green mylar, and broken coloured glasses, effecting a surrealistic cartoon-world imagery—a kind of painting with coloured lights. By uplighting his pictures he reverses the expected order of highlights and shadows; frequently his images are photographed from below, magnifying the image. All this is not a matter of technical innovation; rather, it is a way of revolutionizing and transforming the system of communication for complex patterns of attitude, thought, and response. The ''Autopolaroids'' and ''Photo-Transformations'' become objects and the system—the process in its entirety; photographic medium is appropriated as an authentic, personalized way of seeing and communicating the reality/realities. The camera as well as the images serve as mirrors—mirrors which Samaras uses often in his sculptural art.

The decor of his images is the very environment, which is only an extension of himself, be it pieces of furniture, silverware, or broken glass. The central and primary subject is Samaras himself—his body: legs, hands, fingers, genitals, buttocks, etc; Samaras spitting out silverware; Samaras kissing, embracing himself; Samaras making love to himself; Samaras as embryo, as a female, as a transvestite, a hermaphrodite, etc. etc. The monstrous exaggerations and distortions—faces becoming phalluses, faces with two mouths and four eyes, and his body turned into weird abstract shapes—expose him so totally and obsessively that the impact on the viewer is one of occultic

reflection. Comic and grotesque, erotic and pornographic, realistic and surrealistic, these images at once evoke contrary and contradicting emotions and thinking. They embody a process of ''transformation''—simultaneously divine and diabolic—a theatre of the absurd and the real, which constantly threatens and challenges our normal conceptual and perceptual categories. Samaras creates a tableau which in exposing him exposes the viewer. The mirror in revealing him reflects us in the caves of our mind and soul. Thus, Samaras' photography transforms itself to an artifice, a ritual, a process of *catharsis,* a mirror, and a theatre of silence with primordial sounds and intimations.

—Deba P. Patnaik

SANDELS, Karl.

Nationality: Swedish. **Born:** Stockholm, 5 November 1906; son of the photographer Knut Hjalmar Sandels. **Education:** Södra Latin High School, Stockholm. **Family:** Married Astrid Stilling in 1930; children: Curt, Björn and Rolf. **Career:** Freelance news photographer, Stockholm, 1923-26; Photographer, *Stockholms Dagblad* newspaper (merged with *Stockholmstidningen,* from 1932), 1926-33; Founder and Director, Sandels Illustrationsbyrå picture agency, Stockholm, 1934-48; ceased active work as a photographer, 1942; served as Secretary and Executive Director, Svenska Fotografernas Förbund (Swedish Photographers Association), Stockholm, Editor of *Svensk Fotografisk Tidskrift* magazine, Stockholm, and Course Leader and Craft Instructor, Swedish Government Institute for Handicrafts, Stockholm, all 1942-60; Founder and Chief Editor, *Fotonyheterna* journal for professional photographers, Stockholm, 1961-80 (now edited by Björn Sandels). Founder Member, Press Photographers Club, Stockholm, 1930 and Bildleverantörernas Förening (Picture Suppliers Association), Stockholm, 1932; Member, Swedish Photographers Association, 1934. **Recipient:** Florman Medal, Stockholm, 1945; Royal Gold Medal, Swedish Government Institute for Handicrafts, 1960; Prisma Award, National Association of Swedish Photography, 1974. **Died:** (in Stockholm) 26 January 1986.

Individual Exhibitions:

1977   *Fotografer: Curt Götlin, Anna Riwkin, Karl Sandels,* Moderna Museet, Stockholm

Selected Group Exhibitions:

1934   *Internationell Fotografiutställning,* Liljevalchs Konsthall, Stockholm
        Annual Press Photographers Club Exhibition, Ekströms Konstsalong, Stockholm
1939   *Det Nya Ögat: Fotografien 100 År,* Liljevalchs Konsthall, Stockholm
        Den Store Nordiske Fotografiudstilling: Fotografien i 100 År, Charlottenborg, Copenhagen
1942   *Ögonblicket Räddat åt Framtiden,* Esseltehallen, Stockholm
1955   *The Family of Man,* Museum of Modern Art, New York (and world tour)
1981   *Sekunder, Centimetrar, Passningar och Mal,* Fotografiska Museet, Stockholm
1982   *The Frozen Image: Scandinavian Photography,* Walker Art Center, Minneapolis (travelled to the International Center of Photography, New York; University of California at Los Angeles; Portland Art Museum, Maine; Museum of Contemporary Art, Chicago; Tecoma Art Museum, Washington; Kjavalsstadir, Reykjavik; Louisiana Museum, Humlebaek; Taidehalli, Helsinki; Fotografiska Museet, Stockholm; Kunstsenter, Oslo)

Collections:

Moderna Museet, Stockholm.

Publications:

By SANDELS: Books—illustrations for *Löpande band* by Waldemar Hammenhög, Stockholm 1939; *Fotografens värld: en vägledning i fotografyrket,* Stockholm 1958; *Sjuttiofem år i fotografins tjänst,* Stockholm 1959; *Edvard Welinder: en minneskrift,* editor, Stockholm 1959. **Articles**—"Bildreportage" in *Foto* (Stockholm), no. 4, 1939; numerous articles and editorials in *Svensk Fotografisk Tidskrift* (Stockholm), 1942-60; "Det fotografiska bildreportaget genom tiderna" in *Fotografisk Årsbok,* Stockholm 1950; "Sweden" in *Focal Encyclopaedia of Photography,* London 1956, 1970; numerous articles and editorials in *Fotonyheterna* (Stockholm), 1961-80; "Att samla fotografisk litteratur" in *Fotografisk Årsbok,* Stockholm 1963; "För 40 år sedan" in *Fotografica '67,* Stockholm 1967; "Att göra fototidningar: Fotonyheterna—tidningen för proffsfoto" in *Fotografisk Årsbok,* Stockholm 1968.

On SANDELS: Books—*Fotografer: Curt Götlin, Anna Riwkin, Karl Sandels,* exhibition catalogue, by Åke Sidwall, Pär Frank, Leif Wigh, Carl-Adam Nycop and Ulla Bergman, Stockholm 1977; *Sekunder, Centimetrar, Passningar och Mal,* exhibition catalogue, by Ake Sidwall, Bengt Ahlbom and Jan Lindroth, Stockholm 1981; *The Frozen Image: Scandinavian Photography,* edited by Martin Freeman, Minneapolis and New York 1982. **Article**—"Karl Sandels 50 år" by Edvard Welinder in *Svensk Fotografisk Tidskrift* (Stockholm), no. 10, 1956.

*

When Sandels Illustrationsbyrå eventually got going in 1934, we took lots of sports pictures. We were known for making good prints, and it was said that on Sunday evenings newspaper editors would wait until our pictures arrived. The whole secret of the thing was our negatives. We used a very fine Illford paper. We knew precisely what could be achieved with it. It was a matter of developing the negative to suit that paper. That was the whole secret. During my Association time, I saw so many bad negatives in portrait photographers' studios that it scared me to death. They were over-exposed. So, the photographers were forced to seek out a suitable paper. Well, that was all wrong, of course. They already had the paper. It was the negative they should have been working on.

I left the profession of photographer simply because it was clear to me that I could accomplish a bit more in the field of photography by first becoming Secretary and then Executive Director of the Association. It was a larger task. Whether it was the correct decision is debatable, I suppose. But I definitely believe it was correct—and, well, I guess I was tired of taking pictures, too. I'd been at it for so long, and who says that just because a person happens to be a photographer, he's got to keep doing the same thing all his life?

I started working for the Association in 1942. At first, it was mainly a half-time job (I still had my firm). Quite early on, I became interested in photographers' purely professional concerns: their being able to receive reasonable payments for their work. In the Association paper I wrote a column for many years—"Just Among Us Photographers." And for a couple of years, I also wrote about various colleagues. The work became more and more a full-time thing, and so it was pretty natural that I relinquished my firm in 1948.

I started the journal *Fotonyheterna* in 1961, and it's been a tremendous success. It's entirely professional-oriented and available only by subscription, and our subscription list includes the entire industry. My book, *Fotografens värld,* I wrote as a kind of guide, a general treatment of the profession of photographer. It was the first book of its kind.

—Karl Sandels (1982)

* * *

Karl Sandels's grandfather, uncle and father were all photographers. His grandfather taught himself the profession in the 1870s, and by the beginning of this century the family ran one of Stockholm's most popular portrait studios. It would therefore seem inevitable that Karl Sandels would also become a photographer. But he found portrait photography in a studio of only moderate interest and chose to become a clerk, who in his spare time took unpretentious snapshots with a simple amateur camera. It was due to sports that he became a professional photographer at all. He was interested in all kinds of sports, was himself an active sportsman, and he often had his camera with him and photographed his friends. In 1924 he managed to sell a picture of a victorious relay team to a morning paper in Stockholm. The fee of 6 kr. was then a large sum to a 17-year-old, and he decided to augment his clerk's income with fees for pictures.

There were at that time about ten daily papers in Stockholm, but only four employed permanent photographers. So the field was open for freelance photographers, and Karl Sandels specialized in sports and feature photos. By 1926 he had become so well known in the newspaper world that he was offered permanent employment at *Stockholms Dagblad.*

Sandels became one of the pioneers of photography in natural light. His great idol was a photographer at the English newspaper *Graphic* and naturally also Erich Salomon, who, with his Ermanox camera, attended political conferences in Europe. By buying *Das Deutsche Lichtbild* each year, as well as regularly reading the *British Journal of Photography, Berliner Illustrirte* and the *Daily Mirror,* Sandels kept himself well informed about international photography and the developments in press photography.

Like other successful press photographers, Sandels had the ability to sense the climax of an event before it occurred. In the decisive moment he had his finger on the release, and many of his sports pictures from the 1930s stand up well in comparison to the work of today's photographers. And it must not be forgotten, that he worked with a large and clumsy camera, and was only able to produce one exposure per event.

Karl Sandels thought, quite early on, that photographers lacked a fighting spirit in professional matters, and he was therefore among the founder members of the Press Photographers Club in 1930. Between 1942 and 1960 he was also Secretary and Executive Director of the Swedish Photographers Association, which before his time had been dominated by portrait photographers and had looked down on press and advertising photographers.

His many administrative concerns resulted in a less active career as a photographer. In 1934 he had started a picture agency, Sandels Illustrationsbyrå, but in 1948 he sold it in order to give his time completely to the Association. At the same time he worked as a highly respected teacher and lecturer all over Sweden.

In 1961 he started his own photographic magazine, *Fotonyheterna,* which is primarily for professional photographers and photographic retailers. Since the end of the 1970s his son Björn has been its Editor-in-Chief. Karl Sandels, the sports photo specialist, the press photo pioneer and the trades association man, spent the greater part of his last years at libraries compiling a bibliography of photographic literature published in Sweden. He always had a great interest in the printed page and considered that books and magazines were excellent media for illustrative communication.

—Rune Jonsson

SAUDEK, Jan.

Nationality: Czechoslovakian. **Born:** in Prague, 13 May 1935. **Education:** Attended Gymnasium School, Prague; studied at the School for Industrial Photography, Prague, 1950-52. **Military Service:** Served as a Corporal in the Czech Army: Exemplary Soldier's Medal. **Family:** Married Marie Saudek in 1958 (divorced, 1972); children: Samuel, David, Marie, Karolina, and Tom. **Career:** Worked at various jobs on farms and in factories, Czechoslovakia, 1952-80. Freelance photographer, Prague, since the early 1950s. **Recipient:** Chevalier des Arts et Lettres, France, 1990. **Agent:** Art Unlimited, P.O. Box 1760, NL-1000 BT, Amsterdam, Holland.

Individual Exhibitions:

1963	Divadlo Na Zábradlì, Prague
1969	University of Indiana, Bloomington
1971	Fotochema, Prague
	House of Lords of Kunstat, Brno, Czechoslovakia

1972	Gallery of Fine Art, Olomouc, Czechoslovakia
1973	Shado' Gallery, Portland, Oregon (and 1974, 1975)
1975	Studentské Koleje, Brno, Czechoslovakia
1976	Art Institute of Chicago
1977	National Gallery of Victoria, Melbourne
	Rencontres Internationales de la Photographie, Arles, France
	Australian Centre for Photography, Sydney
	La Photogalerie, Paris
	Church Street Photo Centre, Melbourne
1978	Photo Art Gallery, Basle
	Photogallery, Wroclaw, Poland
	Kresge Art Center, Michigan State University, East Lansing
	Galleria Il Diaframma, Milan
	Galerie im Riek, Essen
1979	*The World of Jan Saudek,* Jacques Baruch Gallery, Chicago
	Galerie Fiolet, Amsterdam
	Galerij Paule Pia, Antwerp
	Pratt Manhattan Center Gallery, New York
1980	*New Colour Work,* Church Street Photo Centre, Melbourne
	Camden Arts Centre, London
	FNAC, Paris
	Equivalents Gallery, Seattle
1981	Marcuse Pfeifer Gallery, New York
	Jacques Baruch Gallery, Chicago
1982	Galerie Cs. Spisovatele, Czechoslovakia
	Evanston Art Center, Illinois
	Galerie Het Pepertje, Diepenbeek, Belgium
1983	University of Iowa, Iowa City
	Idaho State University, Pocatello
	Equivalents Gallery, Seattle
1984	Galerie Lange, Siegburg, West Germany
	Watari Gallery, Tokyo
	Centre Georges Pompidou, Paris
	Jacques Baruch Gallery, Chicago
1985	Nei Liicht Galerie, Dudelange, Luxembourg
	Jacques Baruch Gallery, Chicago
	Galerie La Reverbere, Lyon, France
	Alvar Aalto Museum, Jyvaskyla, Finland
	Finnish Photography Museum, Helsinki
1986	Caves Sainte-Croix, Metz, France
	Fotografie Forum, Frankfurt
	Torch Gallery, Amsterdam
	Gallery of Fine Photography, New Orleans, Louisiana
1987	Musee d'Art Moderne de la Ville de Paris, Paris
	Fotografie Forum Büttcherstrasse, Bremen, Germany
	Robert Koch Gallery, San Francisco
1988	Fundacio La Caixa, Primavera Fotografica, Barcelona, Spain
	The Second Israeli Photography Biennale, Ein Harod, Israel
	Galerie Urbi et Orbi, Paris
1989	*Fotografie Forum Frankfurt,* Frankfurt, Germany
	Robert Koch Gallery, San Francisco
	Yokohama Gallery, Yokohama, Japan
	Foto 89, Galerie Steltman, Amsterdam
	Galerie Nikki Diana Marquart, Paris
	Jan Kesner Gallery, Los Angeles
1990	Robert Koch Gallery, San Francisco
	Rencontres Internationales de la Photographie, Arles, France
	Yokohama Gallery, Yokohama, Japan
1991	Portfolio Gallery, London
	Galerie Steltman, Amsterdam
	Galerie Fronta, Prague
1992	Galerie La Reverbere, Lyon, France
	Galerie Municipale du Chateau d'Eau, Toulouse, France
	Galerie Thierry Salvador, Paris
1993	Municipal Gallery at Palffy Palace, Bratislava
	Fine Art Gallery of East Slovakia, Kosice, Slovakia
	Vision Gallery, San Francisco
	Halle, Germany
1994	Galerie in Focus, Cologne, Germany

Galerie Aura, Olomouc, Czech Republic
Gdansk, Poland
Prinz Gallery, Kyoto, Japan
Parco Gallery, Tokyo

Selected Group Exhibitions:

1971	*Ceskoslovenska Fotografie 1968/70,* Moravian Gallery, Brno, Czechoslovakia
1977	*X-Rated,* Neikrug Gallery, New York
	Women, Jacques Baruch Gallery, Chicago
1978	*Faces of My Land,* Jacques Baruch Gallery, Chicago
	Collector's Choice, Cincinnati Art Museum, Ohio
	Photographic Collecting, Past and Present, in the United States, Canada, and Europe, International Museum of Photography, George Eastman House, Rochester, New York
1980	*Fine Art Photography,* Assocation of International Photography Art Dealers, New York
1982	*Lichtbildnisse: Das Porträt in der Fotografie,* Rheinisches Landesmuseum, Bonn
1984	*Czechoslovakian Photography,* San Francisco Museum of Modern Art
1985	*Ursprung und Gegenwart Tschechoslowakischer Fotografie,* Fotografie Forum, Frankfurt, Germany
	In Time, Galeria na okraji, Bratislava, (travelled to Cheb, Czechoslovakia and Prague)
	The Nude in Photography from Eastern Europe, Accademia Albertina, Torino Fotografia 85, Turin, Italy (travelled to Amsterdam, 1987)
1986	*Theatre of Life,* Centre National de la Photographie, Palais Tokyo, Paris
	Body in Czechoslovakian Photography, Muzeum Kromerizska, Kromeriz, Czechoslovakia
1989	*Czechoslovak Photography 1945-1989,* Valdstejnska Jizdarna, Prague
	Roads of Czechoslovak Photography, Municipal Gallery, House by the Stone Bell, Prague
	150 Photographs, Moravian Gallery, Brno, Czechoslovakia
1990	*Czechoslovak Photography Today,* Museum Ludwig, Cologne, Germany (travelled to Erlangen, Metz, Luxembourg, Strasbourg, Odense, Freiburg, Barcelona, Waldkreiburg, Texas University Museum, Lawrence)
1991	*Bilder Lust,* Altes Museum, Berlin (travelled to Dresden and Cologne)
1992	*What's New: Prague,* The Art Institute of Chicago, Illinois
1993	*Czech Photography of the 1990s,* Maclaurin Art Gallery, Ayr, Scotland (travelled to London, Lisbon, Porto, Coimbra, Salamanca and Alcata de Hanares)
	Erotic Photography? Robert Koch Gallery, San Francisco
1994	*Names of Prague House of Photography,* Prague House of Photography, Prague
1995	*Masters of Czech Photography,* Karolinum, Prague

Collections:

Bibliothèque Nationale, Paris; Musée Nicéphore Niepce, Chalon-sur-Saône, France; National Gallery of Victoria, Melbourne; International Museum of Photography, George Eastman House, Rochester, New York; Museum of Fine Arts, Boston; Library of Congress, Washington, D.C.; Cincinnati Art Museum, Ohio; Kresge Art Center, Michigan State University, East Lansing; Art Institute of Chicago; Museum of Decorative Arts, Prague; Prague House of Photography, Prague; Moravian Gallery, Brno, Czech Republic; Stedelijk Museum, Amsterdam; Art Unlimited, Amsterdam; Museum Ludwig, Cologne, Germany;Fotografie Forum, Frankfurt, Germany; Musee Nationale d'Art Moderne—Centre Georges Pompidou, Paris; Musee d'Art Moderne de la Ville de Paris, Paris; The David and Alfred Smart Gallery of the University of Chicago, Illinois.

Publications:

By SAUDEK: Book— *The World of Jan Saudek*, exhibition catalogue, with an introduction by David Travis, Chicago 1979; *Il teatro de la vita*, edited by Giuliana Scime, Milan 1982; *Die Welt des Jan Saudek/The World of Jan Saudek*, with foreword by Anna Farova, Geneva and Millerton, New York 1983.

On SAUDEK: Books— *The Imaginary Photo Museum* by Helmut Gernsheim, Renate and L. Fritz Gruber and others, Cologne 1981, London 1982; *Lichtbildnisse: Das Porträt in der Fotografie*, edited by Klaus Honnef, Cologne 1982; *Sammlung Gruber: Photographie des 20. Jahrhunderts*, exhibition catalogue, with foreword by Siegfried Gohr, Cologne 1984; *Czechoslovakian Photography*, exhibition catalogue, by Dorothy Martinson, San Francisco 1984; *The Nude in Photography from Eastern Europe*, Bologna 1988; *Cesty ceskoslovenske fotografie (Roads of Czechoslovak Photography)*, by Daniela Mrazkova and Vladimir Remes, Prague 1989; *What is Photography?—150 Years of Photography*, Prague 1989; *Tschechoslowakische Fotografie der Gegenwart (Czechoslovak Photography Today)* by Vladimir Birgus, Heidelberg 1990; *Bilder Lust*, Heidelberg, 1991; *Month of Photography 1993*, exhibition catalogue, Bratislava 1993. **Articles**—"Photo's Suggestions Tantalize" by Don Morrison in the *Minneapolis Star*, 27 February 1976; article by Alan Artner in the *Chicago Tribune*, 9 May 1976; "Allegories of Jan Saudek" by Edward M. Uzemack in *Midwest Art* (Milwaukee), Summer 1976; "Photokina '76" by Pavel Vacha in *Revue Fotografie* (Prague), no. 1, 1977; "Akt & Erotik" by Anna Farova in *Fotografie* (Göttingen), no. 4, 1977; "Jan Saudek" by Gisele Freund in *Zoom* (Paris), October 1977; "Jan Saudek: I'm Led by Instinct" by Derek Bennett in *Printletter* (Zurich), March/April 1978; "Saudek's Eye Snaps World of Truth" by Alan Artner in the *Chicago Tribune*, 23 February 1979; "Pictures to Evoke Emotional Response" by Harold Haydon in the *Chicago Sun-Times*, 20 April 1979; "De Praga a Chicago" in *Bolaffiarte* (Turin), June 1979; "Jan Saudek" by David Fahey in *Picture Magazine* (Los Angeles), June/July 1979; "Portfolio Jan Saudek: Le Grand Photographe Tcheque" by Pierre Borhan in *Photo-Cinéma* (Paris), January 1980; "The Trend Is a Backward Look" by Gene Thornton in the *New York Times*, 24 August 1980; "The World of Jan Saudek" by Colin Osman in *Creative Camera* (London), December 1983; "Posen für den Poeten mit der Kamera" by Astrid Gerling in *Stern* (Hamburg), 15 December 1983; "Fotos von Keuschheit und Schamlosigkeit" by Alwin-Georg Maibach in *Konder Stadt-Anzeiger* (Cologne), 8 February 1984; "Jan Saudek" in *Valokuva* (Helsinki), No 9, 1985; "Jan Saudek" in *Focus*, (Amsterdam), No 1, 1986; "Jaky je Jan Saudek?" by Milan Skala in *Revue Fotografie* (Prague), No 4 1990; "Porusene Ticho" by Marianna Cerna in *Ceskoslovenska fotografie*, (Prague), No 7, 1990; "Zena je dukazem existence bozi—O zenach s Janem Saudkem" by Michaela Remesova in *Reflex* (Prague), No 18 1990; "Jan Saudek—La Vie, l'amour, le mort & outres broutilles" in *Vis a Vis* (Paris) No 10, 1991; "The Lust and the Vision" by Susanna Jech in *Prognosis* (Prague), 10 July, 1992.

*

I think that *The Family of Man* hasn't been surpassed so far. I admired it as a collection of photographs and it completely changed my life. I decided then that I was going to do a book like that myself, which was crazy. Later I realised that I would never be able to do a book like that, not even a fraction of the book, but I would still very much like to be able to. Steichen chose from thousands of photographs. I spent the whole day in the factory and I didn't have much time left to do photography. *The Family of Man* did show me the way. Even today when I finger through the book, not often, just from time to time, I am just as touched as I was as a younger man.

—Jan Saudek

* * *

Jan Saudek is undoubtedly the most provocative figure in the history of Czechoslovak photography. On the one hand he is surrounded by admiration almost to the point of worship, on the other by dislike to the point of damnation. He and his work excite a strange mixture of tenderness and violence, lyricism and irony, romanticism and an ostentatious eroticism that comes close to obscenity. And perhaps the most exciting thing about him is the fact that he attained world fame by taking phtographs for his own pleasure in whatever time was left after his everyday job as a worker.

Jan Saudek's life could be seen as a pilgrimage of pain, starting with a childhood tragically branded with Hitler's hallmark of non-Aryan birth, a time of humiliation when he and his twin brother Karel found themselves in a special children's concentration camp somewhere on the Polish border. This experience permanently determined Saudek's insatiable longing for certainty and warm relationships between people.

In the 1960s Saudek's photography was greatly inspired by Edward Steichen's "Family of Man" exhibition. His works from that time are full of humanity—a child pressed to his mother's breast, an infant resting on his father's muscular chest, lovers embracing on the ground. They show the poetry of childhood and youth and glorify parenthood. Saudek, whose own childhood was ruthlessly stolen, is pursued by an abiding vision of a promised land, where people have room to live out their dreams and sadnesses, a land that is free from indifference, cruelty, fear. That is why he leaves nothing to chance in his photographs, which are without exception posed. They form a theatre, an artificially built world. Jan Saudek loves contrasts. It is mainly on these that he rests the poetry of his pictures. A little girl in the pose of a woman, a provocative young wanton with a doll under her arm, the over-blown body of a mature woman with the shy gesture of a girl. Children behave like adults and the signs of childhood are visible in the adults. On top of all that are the costumes and the scenery, the puppets, bouquets of flowers, straw hats, corsets, wreaths, masks, ballet shoes . . . essential props that serve to simplify and liberate.

He loves nakedness; for him it is a promise of freedom. "Nakedness makes a woman a woman and a man a man, no matter whether today or a hundred years ago. I undress a woman to make her eternal." Saudek knows the female psyche perfectly and masters it easily. Women willingly allow themselves to be undressed, turn themselves into profligates or even clowns. They enjoy helping him to build his world—a world of delicious sins, fiery emotions, secret wishes. They like to accept the roles he offers them, for they feel that in them, regardless of their appearance, social position or age, they will taste the highest value of all—the magic of their own womanhood.

Saudek's romanticism is undergoing changes with advancing time. His demonstrative glorification of family ties, like his tenderness in relation to women, takes on a more and more distinctive new flavour—aggressiveness. A man appears on the stage of his theatre of life. He is no longer just a protector, a supporter, a source of inspiration in the exploration of womanhood, but a strength, an element to be admired. Saudek's gentle irony, with which he observes human passions and relationships, grows more obvious, his eroticism more ostentatious, his liking for the eloquence of contrasts outgrows individual pictures into multiple series. The transformations of girls' developing bodies; the confrontations between girls' figures and those of their mothers; another series in which a charming woman is transformed into a monkey; or one in which the photographer in the uniform of a soldier of the Austro-Hungarian army, is successively caught, stripped, executed and buried . . . Saudek's photographs are urgently penetrated by the phenomenon of time and anxiety at its passage, the fear of death. Time becomes the main protagonist of his photographic series, and he takes inspiration from, and also echoes North American comics. Kitsch? Cheap taste? Banality? Saudek is a masterly juggler, balancing on the knife-edge between art and kitsch, between what is aesthetic and what is not.

The influence of "The Family of Man" on Saudek is a fateful one. His naive, youthful desire to photograph this grandiose theme himself achieves that fulfilment. For what else are his works, in total, than the story of the family of man? What else is his "theatre of life," portraying the changing reproduction—the Woman, the Man, the Child?

Jan Saudek is a great producer of his "theatre of life," into which he constantly projects himself. These are his own dreams, passions, anxieties and sadnesses that he photographs. Jan Saudek cannot really be sure even today whether he has formulated his life according to the dreams he has phtoographed, or whether his photography is a reflection of, or indeed the way of life that he lives, so intertwined are his life and his work. Whichever way it is, his work as a whole so far is an exciting human drama. A drama that, despite an endless multitude of images, in essence constantly repeats itself. It is a picture of our picture. Comedy and tragedy. In this summary of truth lies the provocative form of Saudek's photography.

—Daniela Mrázkova

SAVELEV, (Boris Savelieu)

Nationality: Russian. **Born:** Chernowitz, Ukraine, 30 December 1947. **Family:** Married Elena Bazikovich, 1980; children: Vadim and Rodiou. **Career:** Started taking pictures as an amateur in 1964; president of the Novator photographic club in Moscow, 1978-80; professional freelance photographer since 1983. **Agent:** Oliver Cescotti, Davidgasse, 79/3 A-1100 Vienna, Austria. **Address:** Prospect Mira M6-B Apt 52, 129626, Moscow, Russia.

Individual Exhibitions:

1981   Museum of Photography, Shaulay, Lithuania
1992-93 Tretakov Gallery, State Museum, Moscow
1994   Art Gallery, State Museum, Kaliningrad-Königsberg, Russia

Selected Group Exhibitions:

1986   Museum of Modern Arts, Oxford
1987   *City Lights,* Goldsmith's Gallery, London
1988   *Say Cheese,* Comptuare de la Photographie, Paris
1989   Museum of Photography, San Diego
        Photostroika, Burden Gallery, New York (travelled to Carnegie
           Mellon Art Gallery; Huntsville Museum, Worcester Art
           Museum, Crocker Art Museum; Bass Museum of Arts)
1990   *What's Photography,* Maneze, Prague
1991   Roy Boyd Gallery, Chicago
        Corcoran Museum, Washington, D.C.
1992   Museum of Fine Arts, Santa Fe, New Mexico
        Rosa Esman Gallery, New York
1993   *Über die grossen Städte,* Berlin
1994   *Art of Contemporary Photography,* Exhibition Centre, Moscow

Collections:

Museum of Fine Arts, Santa Fe, New Mexico; Tretakov Gallery, State Museum, Moscow; South-West Bank Collection, London; Museum of Photograhic Collections, Moscow.

Publications:

By SAVELEV: Books—*Secret City,* introduction by Ian Jeffrey, London 1988.

On SAVELEV: Books—*Another Russia* by Daniela Mrazkova, London 1986; *Changing Reality,* Washington, D.C. 1991. Articles—"Photographing as a Life Necessity" by Daniela Mrazkova in *Ceskoslovenska Fotografie,* Portfolio 11, 1986; "City Camera" by Ian Jeffery in *Creative Camera,* Portfolio 5, 1987; "Soviet Fine Arts" by Thomas Johnson in *Actuel,* Portfolio 10, 1987; "Photocartochky" in *Aperture,* Fall 1989; "It's a Small World" by Charles Hagen in *Art News,* May 1990; "Capturing Soviet Sensations on Film" by Cathy Young in *The World and I,* Washington, D.C. 1990.

*   *   *

Western observers of Moscow stand apart and represent the place as breath taking and marvellous; Boris Savelev, by contrast, discovers a self-denying idiom, part of the place itself and of its fabrication, immanent and impersonal. He makes available something like a general pictorial language, although it is far from being a language which might be read through for meaning or message.

Savelev's attention is held by constructions, by gauges, grids and templates through and across which the weather hesitates and flickers. No one in the history of the medium has been as engrossed by bus windows, for example, or by tiles, railings and brickwork. Primarily he makes pictures, and his art declares how pictures might be made to survive the dangers of a fall into mere observation and commentary. Picture-making involves framing which Savelev declares in many window images; or, if there is no window frame to hand, he refers to the next best thing, to a grid or frame which might function as a window in miniature; and, as the frame is a container, its job might be done by any other kind of container, such as a flagon or basket. Nor does looking merely take place via a frame but through atmosphere which might be neither transparent nor innocent; and the artist, with these inevitable conditions of perception in mind, refers as frequently to mirrors, glass, haze and darkness. In his more complicated vein a view through a vehicle window, itself a moving frame, might be interrupted by a rear-view mirror holding a miniature of elsewhere, all set alongside a windscreen wiper, itself a sign of a provisional transparency. Some of the photographs are hard to make out, with dark bands of shadowed interior separating bright inset window landscapes; or fragments of a figure might project from a dark field into light. Perception is not to be taken for granted, but comes about by virtue of that understanding which would attach a body to that foot isolated in the glare. In addition to inscrutable shadow, perception is hindered by walls and screens; again, less for the sake of any declaration of an absolute blackout than for an underlining of perception as a process of reading or understanding of the signs. The pictures can be read through as though they are texts, or gauged as diagrams, with inferences to be drawn from whatever social emblems or significant fragments they might contain.

His pictures are formats, rectangles enclosing frames and sub-frames with examples of transparent and opaque surfaces, and such signs as advertising and traffic direction leave on city streets. Obviously Savelev delights in rhetoric, in the potential for meaning, for instance, of a scrap of torn paper by a gap in a fence. But there is nothing arcane about his arrangements, no suggestion of a very recherché turn of mind; mainly he works as if to demonstrate how various signifying devices might function in a picture. Why should he be so disinterested? It would be a travesty simply to read his photographs as technical demonstrations of pictorial semiotics, for they obviously carry far more weight than that. What the semiotic dimension does is to confer stability, and to cast the pictures into the public domain as examples of a photographic language repeating itself. The pictures propose a job of work and hold no threat or promise of mystifying depths, and then in their discreet way begin to speak of God knows what.

Savelev deploys his language—and then something happens, a moment of transition. In one powerful detail from a Moscow street a road-roller makes a dynamic diagonal into the shadows, as the sun catches a pale upright seat and an orange segment of rusted iron, bright like a harvest moon or the evening sun. Colour on that heavy metal image is interrupted by colour, as steady reading might be interrupted by a shout, raw noise. In these designed, discursive pictures it is colour which penetrates his capacity of apprehension with a pathos and a sense of the Infinite. Colour makes wild accents incommensurable with the prosaic discursiveness of designer's monochrome and with those judicious formats which Savelev deploys as his points of departure. The formats are commonly held, from a shared syntax of art, but colour is original, fierce, bright and unconstructed.

Savelev is, or would be, a modernist; or at least he is closer to the idea than his contemporaries in Paris, London and New York. The possibility of an elision between mankind (or culture) and nature remains one of his premises. New Yorkers, photographed in the 1980s, are more than likely to be shown afloat among signifiers, among extravagant promises frayed at the edges, whereas Savelev's personnel still live in a milieu which might just have been designed for them. In optimistic high modernism of the 1920s, for example, design comes endorsed by nature, or by an abstract or distillation of nature expressed in terms of ratios. The social stage was to have been apt, arranged in accordance with an immanent right reason; and then that belief was ousted in its turn by one in which we feature as a tabula rasa, infinitely open to suggestion. Savelev registers a memory of modernism in images where there are sympathies between figure and ground, although he is far from insistent. Leger's modernists, back in the old days, might have been put together in the factory which assembled the furniture; Savelev's are more tentative, and only rhyme in part with their places. He has second thoughts. In one of the most striking of his pictures a woman operative in a head scarf smiles from the cab

Gorki Park, Moscow, **1984.** Photograph ©Boris Savelev.

of some sort of heavy plant; she might have stepped out of the great days of the *USSR in Construction,* except that the cab is beautifully, aetherially tinted, as much a dressing table as a work-site. He encompasses as much of art and culture as any photographer in the 1980s, although he works across a far wider range than most. It is the modernist residuum which give his art another term, and an added scope and tension; perhaps it was only in the Soviet Union that the modernist idea could still play a determining part.

(From *Secret City,* Thames and Hudson, 1988)

—Ian Jeffrey

SAVAGE, Naomi.

Nationality: American. **Born:** Naomi Siegler in Princeton, New Jersey, 25 June 1927. **Education:** Studied photography, under Berenice Abbott, New School for Social Research, New York, 1943; studied at Bennington College, Vermont, 1944-47; student-apprentice to her uncle, the photographer Man Ray, Los Angeles, 1948-49. **Family:** Married architect/sculptor David C. Savage in 1950; children: Michael and Lourie. **Career:** Freelance photographer, working for *Vogue, Bucks County Traveler,* Ted Gothelf Advertising Association, Elizabeth Arden, Tom Tru Corp., Denby-Versfeld Associates, Demarais Studio, etc., since 1950. **Recipient:** Cassandra Foundation Award, 1970; National Endowment for the Arts Photography Fellowship, 1971; Silver Award, Art Directors Club of New York, 1976. **Agent:** Witkin Gallery, 415 West Broadway, New York, New York 10016. **Address:** 41 Drakes Corner Road, Princeton, New Jersey 08540, U.S.A.

Individual Exhibitions:

1968	*Three Women Photographers,* Moore College of Art, Philadelphia, (with Marie Cosindas and Barbara Crane)
1969	*Spectrum 2,* Witkin Gallery, New York (with Barbara Morgan and Nancy Sirkis)
	2 Generations of Photographs: Man Ray and Naomi Savage, New Jersey State Museum, Trenton
1974	Ulster County Community College, New York
	School of the Art Institute of Chicago
1975	Center for Photographic Studies, University of Louisville, Kentucky
1976	*Photographic Works,* Princeton Gallery of Fine Arts, New Jersey
	Camera Works Gallery, Los Angeles
1977	Madison Art Center, Wisconsin
	Artemesia Gallery, Chicago
	Witkin Gallery, New York (with Evelyn Hofer)
1983	Noyes Museum, Oceanville, New Jersey

Selected Group Exhibitions:

1953	*Always the Young Stranger,* Museum of Modern Art, New York
1959	*Photography at Mid-Century,* International Museum of Photography, George Eastman House, Rochester, New York (toured the United States)
1962	*Photography U.S.A.,* De Cordova Museum, Lincoln, Massachusetts
1966	*Photographs for Collectors,* Museum of Modern Art, New York
1972	*New Photography U.S.A.,* Museum of Modern Art, New York
1975	*Women of Photography,* San Francisco Museum of Art (toured the United States, 1975-77)
1977	*Subjective Photography,* Kimmel/Cohn Gallery, New York
1978	*Mirrors and Windows: American Photography since 1960,* Museum of Modern Art, New York (toured the United States, 1978-80)

1981	*Photographer as Printmaker,* Ferens Art Gallery, Hull, Yorkshire (travelled to the Museum and Art Gallery, Leicester; Cooper Gallery, Barnsley; Castle Museum, Nottingham; Photographers' Gallery, London)
1985	*Design 85,* Delaware River Mill Society, Stockton, New Jersey

Collections:

Museum of Modern Art, New York; Ulster County Community College, New York; Princeton University, New Jersey; Youth Tennis Foundation, Princeton, New Jersey; New Jersey State Museum, Trenton; Fogg Art Museum, Harvard University, Cambridge, Massachusetts; University of Illinois, Urbana; Madison Art Center, Wisconsin; University of Kansas, Lawrence; University of Texas at Austin; Museum of Fine Arts, Houston.

Publications:

By SAVAGE: Book—*Man Ray from 8 Sides,* portfolios, Princeton, New Jersey 1976. **Article**—"Images of Man Ray" in *Print Collector's Newsletter* (New York), November/December 1974.

On SAVAGE: Books—*Two Generations of Photographs: Man Ray and Naomi Savage,* exhibition catalogue, by Peggy Lewis, Trenton, New Jersey 1969; *New Photography U.S.A.,* exhibition catalogue, by John Szarkowski, New York 1972; *Looking at Photographs* by John Szarkowski, New York 1973; *Women See Women,* New York 1976; *The Photography Catalog,* edited by Norman Snyder, New York 1976; *Innovative Printmaking* by T.R. Newman, New York 1977; *Mirrors and Windows: American Photography since 1960,* exhibition catalogue, by John Szarkowski, New York 1978; *Photographer as Printmaker,* exhibition catalogue, with texts by Gerry Badger, Peter C. Bunnell and Ansel Adams, London 1981; *A World History of Photography* by Naomi Rosenblum, New York 1984. **Articles**—"Naomi Savage" in *Album* (London), October 1970; "Variations" in *Print* (New York), January/February 1971.

*

Although advised long ago by a wise man to "learn to be articulate" I am still uneasy when asked to make a statement about my work. On the theory that a thousand words are worth one picture, is a writer ever asked to draw, paint, or photograph his meaning?

With this objection voiced, I can explain one form of communication in another only by "freely" translating my visual beliefs. The foundation of these is the desire to preserve the life around me in a way that distills the familiar in the unexpected, and vice versa. By juxtaposing improbably subjects or exposing them out of context, and by exercising intuition based on knowledge as well as allowing for an ample measure of chance, I have combined old and new techniques, and explored many directions in an effort to extend the range of photographic experience and interpretation with humor, beauty, and novel variation.

—Naomi Savage

* * *

On first encounter with the work in photography for which Naomi Savage is known internationally, the new viewer's reaction is very likely to be, "It's *different* from anything I've seen before!" Indeed, such reaction may continue even after having seen more of her work. It is different because it *begins* with a photograph and ends with a print from an etched metal plate; many things happen between the beginning and ending.

Naomi Savage's interest in art commenced with classes in high school. This interest was encouraged when in 1943, at 16 years of age, she studied photography with Berenice Abbott at the New School for Social Research in New York City. Her background was enriched with studies at Bennington College (Vermont) in art, photography and music during 1944-1947. The year following, she worked in Hollywood with Man Ray, her uncle, during which time she was encouraged and influenced by the spirit and methods of this innovative artist. Artistic development for Savage continued in a variety of ways. Beginning in 1948, over a period of 10 years she made 35 photographic portraits of composers for music publications. This work demanded particular attention to composition, lighting of the subject and exposing the negative at the proper instant to express personality. As a free lance photographer she executed assignments for companies marketing pharmaceuticals, greeting cards, beauty products and record albums, all of which required resourcefulness and creative discipline.

Subsequent to her marriage to David Savage, an architect and sculptor, she lived in Paris for many years of work and study. In her photography, Naomi Savage concentrated on the environment with particular attention to trees and statues. However, she continued studio work, and being abroad did not prevent her from exhibiting in the United States or her work from appearing in publications there.

Subjects for Savage's photographs include portraits, human figures, landscapes, sculpture, toys and kitchen utensils. She is not dependent upon new or recent work to start a project, often finding subjects and inspiration in her photographs on hand. Subject matter is important to every artist, and for Savage it is the starting point from which adventures with technique begin.

The techniques and methods of working devised by Savage created a new art form. The techniques, both old (etching) and new (photography), utilize the modern photo-etching process. Basically, her method is: from photograph to photo-etching on a metal plate to a pulled print of it; but there are variations—often many of them. For example, one project passed through sixteen stages, including rephotographing, new etchings and tonings. Each stage is studied and considered to be visually interesting. The etched plates may be coated with acrylic paint or silver-plated, oxidized (for patina) and clear-lacquered (to prevent further oxidization). Before printing, the etched plates may be inked, as is traditional, or they may not be inked. In the latter case, an impression from the plate is made into the paper, using more pressure and padding, producing a bas-relief or inkless intaglio print. The etched plates, with their reversed images plated or painted, are exhibited with their prints and the photographs used in a project to make a complete statement about the subject.

Two Generations of Photographers was the title of an exhibition of the works of Naomi Savage and Man Ray at the New Jersey State Museum, Trenton, in 1969. In this exhibition Savage's range of interest in media and techniques may be noted: photo-collage, negative/positive combination, photo-engraving, intaglio print, rayograph (photogram), solarization, color toner, negatives on silver and gold foil, multi-layered negatives and double exposure.

Seldom does an artist have the opportunity to do significant work in monumental dimensions. For Naomi Savage this opportunity was realized when she was commissioned, in 1971, to create the mural for the Lyndon Baines Johnson Library at the University of Texas in Austin. The subjects were of Mr. Johnson's political life and portraits of him and the four immediately preceding presidents of the United States. Mr. Johnson selected the news photographs which Savage used for enlargement and creative treatment with various techniques. The medium is five deeply etched panels of magnesium, each measuring 8 by 10 feet; the mural is 8 by 50 feet.

Savage's work continues to be included in a ranging schedule of exhibitions with varying themes which relate to her interests. Some examples are: *New Directions, Photography: A Personal View, Repeated Exposure, The Alternative Image, Elements of Abstraction,* and *Design 1985.* Likewise, her work frequently serves to illustrate aspects of creativity in photography magazines and reference books in the United States and abroad.

—Robert W. Cooke

SCHAD, Christian.

Nationality: German. **Born:** Miesbach, Upper Bavaria, 21 August 1894. **Education:** Educated in Munich, Germany, until 1913; studied painting, under Heinrich von Zügel, Akademie der Bildenden Künste, Munich, 1913-14. **Military Service:** Served briefly in German Army, Munich, 1915. **Family:** Married Marcella Arcangeli in 1923 (separated, 1927); son: Nikolaus; married Bettina Mittelstädt in 1947. **Career:** Independent painter, working for Walter Serner's *Sirius* magazine, Zurich, 1915-16, and with other Dadaist artists and writers: Hans Arp, Hugo Ball, Emmy Hennings, Tristan Tzara, etc.,

in Geneva, 1916-20; experimentation with photographic processes, first "Schadograph" photograms, Geneva, 1918; independent painter, associating with Jules Evola, Enrico Prampolini and the Casa d'Arte Bragaglia avant-garde artists' group, in Rome, 1920, travelling with Walter Serner throughout Italy; in Naples and Rome, 1920-25; in Vienna, 1925-27; in Berlin, establishing own studio, 1927-43 (destroyed, 1943): worked at various professions including picture-restorer, theatre critic, teacher, etc., and as manager of a brewery office, 1935-42; lived and worked in or near Aschaffenburg, Germany, from 1943: concentrated on painting, from 1951, and on new "Schadographs," from 1960. **Recipient:** Cross of Merit First Class, Republic of West Germany, 1979; Honorary Professor Award, Bürgermeister of West Berlin, 1980. **Agent:** Kunstkabinett G.A. Richter, Königstrasse 33, Haus Englisch, 7000 Stuttgart 1. **Died:** 25 February 1982.

Individual Exhibitions:

1964	*Präsentation zum 70. Geburtstag,* Galerie Dorothea Loehr and Hessischer Rundfunk, Frankfurt
1969	*Bilder und Graphik nach 1945,* Neue Münchner Galerie, Munich
1970	*Schad/Dada,* Galleria Schwarz, Milan
1971	Städisches Museum, Trier, West Germany (retrospective)
	Galerie Loehr, Frankfurt (with Boris Keint)
1972	Palazzo Reale, Milan (retrospective)
1973	Galleria Stivani, Bologna
	Galleria Fant Cagni, Brescia, Italy
	Schadographien, Galleria del Levante, Munich
1974	Galerie G.A. Richter, Stuttgart
1975	*Schadographien 1918-1975,* Von der Heydt-Museum, Wupptertal, West Germany
1976	*Christian Schad,* Kunstkabinett G.A. Richter display, *Art 7,* Basle
	Christian Schad, Kunstkabinett G.A. Richter display, at the *Internationaler Kunstmarkt,* Dusseldorf
	Galerie Hilger, Vienna
	Galerie Piro, Frankfurt
1977	*Schadographien,* Kunstkabinett G.A. Richter display, at *Art 8,* Basle
	Kunstkabinett G.A. Richter, Stuttgart (2 exhibitions)
	Galerie Karin Brass, Aschaffenburg, West Germany
1978	*Das Graphische Werk und Schadographien,* Museum des 20. Jahrhunderts, Vienna (travelled to Kulturhaus der Stadt Graz, Austria)
	40 Schadographien von Christian Schad, Stadtmuseum Linz/Donau, Austria
	Goethe Institut, Munich (and world tour)
1979	Museum Stadt Miesbach, West Germany
	Vom Expressionismus bis zum Magischen Realismus, Kunstkabinett G.A. Richter, Stuttgart
1980	*Schadographien,* Galerie Beck, Augsburg, West Germany
	Staatliche Kunsthalle, West Berlin (retrospective)
1981	*Etchings, Woodcuts, Schadographs,* Leinster Fine Art, London
1984	Galleria Civica d'Arte Moderna, Palermo, Sicily

Selected Group Exhibitions:

1936	*Fantastic Art, Dada and Surrealism,* Museum of Modern Art, New York
1951	*Abstraction in Photography,* Museum of Modern Art, New York
1958	*Dada: Dokumente einer Bewegung,* Kunstverein, Düsseldorf
1968	*Dada, Surrealism and Their Heritage,* Museum of Modern Art, New York (toured the United States)
1970	*Photo Eye of the 20s,* Museum of Modern Art, New York (toured the United States)
1977	*Malerei und Photographie im Dialog,* Kunsthaus, Zurich
1980	*The Imaginary Photo Museum,* Kunsthalle, Cologne
1981	*Photographer as Printmaker,* Ferens Art Gallery, Hull, Yorkshire (travelled to the Museum and Art Gallery,

Leicester; Cooper Gallery, Barnsley; Castle Museum, Nottingham; Photographers' Gallery, London)

1983   *Fotogramme—die lichtreichen Schatten,* Fotomuseum im Stadtmuseum, Munich
1984   *Sammlung Gruber,* Museum Ludwig, Cologne

Collections:

Württembergische Staatsgalerie, Stuttgart; Museum Ludwig, Cologne; Kunsthalle, Basle; Kunsthaus, Zurich; Museum of Modern Art, New York; Gernsheim Collection, University of Texas at Austin.

Publications:

By SCHAD: Books—*Christian Schad: 10 Woodcut Prints,* portfolio, Zurich 1915; *Christian Schad: Hommage à Dada 1916-1976,* portfolio of 10 schadographs, Stuttgart 1976; *Christian Schad: Gaspard de la nuit oder Die Hochzeit der Romantik mit dem Geist Dadas,* portfolio of 20 schadographs, Stuttgart 1978; *Gauguins und Seidenstrümpfe,* Stuttgart 1981. **Articles**—"Köpfe" in *Sirius* (Zurich), December 1915; "Graphik" in *Sirius* (Zurich), January 1916; "Mein Legensweg" in *Christian Schad,* exhibition catalogue, Vienna 1927; "Grünewald-Kopie in der Stiftskirche zu Aschaffenburg" in *Maltechnik* (Munich), vol. 2, 1961; "Zürich/Genf: Dada" in *Imprimatur III,* Frankfurt 1962; "Appunti Autobiografici" in *Schad/Dada,* exhibition catalogue, edited by Arturo Schwartz, Milan 1970; "Relative Realitäten: Erinnerungen um Walter Serner" in *Die Tigerin* by Walter Serner, Munich 1971; "Dada, Surrealisme et Autre Chose" in *Gradiva* (Brussels), May 1971; "Arte 80 intervista Christian Schad" in *Arte 80* (Rome), Autumn 1973.

On SCHAD: Books—*Der Maler Christian Schad* by Max Osborn, Berlin 1927; *Fantastic Art, Dada and Surrealism* by Alfred H. Barr Jr., New York 1936, 1937; *Photography: A Short Critical History* by Beaumont Newhall, New York 1938; *Histoire de la Photographie* by Raymond Lecuyer, Paris 1945; *The History of Photography* by Beaumont Newhall, New York 1949, 1964; *Dada: Monographie einer Bewegung* by Willy Verkauf, Teufen, Switzerland 1957, New York and London 1973; *Creative Photography* by Helmut Gernsheim, London 1962; *The Painter and the Photograph* by Van Deren Coke, Albuquerque, New Mexico 1964, 1972; *Dada à Paris* by Michel Sanouillet, Paris 1965; *A Concise History of Photography* by Helmut and Alison Gernsheim, London 1965; *Le Futurisme et le Dadaisme* by José Pierre, Lausanne 1966; *Kunst und Photographie* by Otto Stelzer, Munich 1966; *Art and Photography* by Aaron Scharf, London 1968; *Die Collage* by Herta Wescher, Cologne 1968; *Designing with Light on Paper and Film* by Robert W. Cooke, Worcester, Massachusetts 1969; *Pioneers of Modern Typography* by Herbert Spencer, New York 1969; *The Picture History of Photography* by Peter Pollack, New York 1970; *Christian Schad,* exhibition catalogue, by Giovanni Testori, Milan 1970; *Photography without a Camera* by Patra Holter, New York 1972; *Schadographien,* exhibition catalogue, by Daniela Palazzoli, Munich 1973; *Photographie als Künstlerisches Experiment* by Willy Rotzler, Lucerne and Frankfurt 1974; *Schadographien 1918-75,* exhibition catalogue, with text by Kah Jagals, Wuppertal, West Germany 1975; *Photomontage* by Dawn Ades, London 1976; *Dictionnaire du Dadaisme 1916-1922* by Georges Hugnet, Paris 1976; *Almanacco Dada,* edited by Arturo Schwarz, Milan 1976; *Geschichte der Fotografie im 20. Jahrhundert/ Photography in the 20th Century* by Petr Tausk, Cologne 1977, London 1980; *Malerei und Photographie im Dialog,* exhibition catalogue, by Erika Billeter, Berne 1977; *Das Experimentelle Photo in Deutschland 1918-1940* by Emilio Bertonati, Munich 1978; *Dada und Surrealism Reviewed,* exhibition catalogue, by Dawn Ades, London 1978; *40 Schadographien von Christian Schad,* exhibition catalogue, with text by Arnulf Rohsmann, Linz, Austria 1978; *Photographie als Kunst 1879-1979/Kunst als Photographie 1949-1979,* exhibition catalogue, 2 vols., by Peter Weiermair, Innsbruck, Austria 1979; *Christian Schad: Gaspard de la Nuit,* exhibition catalogue, with text by Kurt Leonhard, Stuttgart 1979; *Avant-Garde Photography in Germany 1919-1939,* exhibition catalogue, by Van Deren Coke, Ute Eskildsen and Bernd Lohse, San Francisco 1980; *Das imaginäre Photo-Museum,* by Renate und L. Fritz Gruber, Cologne 1981; *Monographie Christian Schad,* edited by G.A. Richter, Stuttgart 1981; *The Artist as Photographer* by Marina Vaizey, London 1982; *Fotogramme—die lichtreichen Schatten,* exhibition catalogue, by Floris M. Neususs, Kassel, West Germany 1983; *Sammlung Gruber:*

Photographie des 20. Jahrhunderts, exhibition catalogue, with foreword by Siegfried Gohr, Cologne 1984. **Articles**—"Salon Wolfsberg: Christian Schad" by Hans Trog in *Neue Zürcher Zeitung,* 10 October 1915; "Christian Schad" by R.R. Milrad in *Prager Tagblatt,* 22 December 1915; "Developpement de l'Art Dadaiste" by Alexandre Partens in *Le Mondain* (Geneva), 14 February 1920; "Christian Schad" by Max Roden in *Volkszeitung* (Vienna), 25 January 1927; "Christian Schad im Frankfurter Kunstverein" by Godo Remszhardt in *Frankfurter Rundschau,* 20 July 1956; "Christian Schad" by Gottfried Sello in *Die Zeit* (Hamburg), 6 November 1964; "Christian Schad" and "Neue Sachlichkeit" by Blida Heynoldvon Graefe in *Weltkunst* (Munich), 15 December 1972; "Les Grands Maitres de l'Art Photographique: Christian Schad" by Jean-Claude Gautrand in *Point de Vue* (Paris), 1 March 1974; "Renaissance of the Schadograph" by Inge Bondi in *Printletter* (Zurich), March/April 1976; "Medium Foto" by Günther Wirth in *Das Kunstwerk* (Stuttgart), July 1976; "Metamorphosis of the Schadograph" by Inge Bondi in *Printletter* (Zurich), May 1979; "Christian Schad" by Irmelin Lebeer in *Cahiers du Musée National d'Art Moderne* (Paris), July 1979; "Revelations of the Weimar Era" by Hilton Kramer in the *New York Times,* 5 October 1980; "The Twenties' Bleak New World" by Robert Hughes in *Time* (New York), 10 November 1980.

                                        *

Schadographie occupies a special place in my complete work, next to painting and the graphic arts. As far as I am concerned, it lies very close to graphic art, although it is classed with the art of photography—a medium which I have never used as an artistic means of expression. A photogram is created—if one disregards the use of the light sensitive surface of the photographic paper as the image carrier—in a multi-layered technique which has a far greater similarity to the creation of a graphic print. It approximates the process of aquatint drypoint rather than the very different processes involved in the creation of a photograph.

My first photograms, made in 1918 during my Dada period in Geneva, were something entirely new. My friend Walter Serner was the first to recognize this, and Tristan Tzara gave it the name "Schadographie."

As I began anew to make Schadographs in 1960, the daylight paper which I had used in 1918 was no longer available. It had allowed me to view the slow process of development, and I could intervene by directing or altering the process. Since then I have been forced to work in the darkroom with artificial light, "blind" so to speak, relying entirely on my imagination and conception of what effect I want to achieve. But, I am also open-minded as concerns the chance occurrences which this procedure allows. There can always result from these—controlled—chance occurrences new and unforeseen possibilities for further experimentation.

The first of the Schadographs made since 1960 were still closely related to my attempts from 1918 on, but the mere play with surface and form no longer satisfied me completely. As I came across the work of the French poet Aloysius Bertrand—who died in Paris in 1841 at the age of 34—I became fascinated with the spiritual kinship between his prose-poems in *Gaspard de la Nuit* and the new dimension of my Schadographs: in the one as in the other, a fantastic world is created in which the present seems timeless, as if one were fetched by means of a sudden light for an instant and sharply yanked from the darkness of night during which the past and future remain forever hidden.

The absolute sense of the present in Bertrand's prose-poems—without past or future—occupied me again and again in the 15 years which followed and most of the Schadographs which have originated within this time span carry either directly or indirectly the mark of *Gaspard de la Nuit.*

—Christian Schad (1981)

                        *   *   *

Christian Schad was an artist molded in the environment of the historic avant-garde, and, from the 1920s on, one of the most representative painters of the New Objectivity and German Realism. His contribution to photography took shape within the realm of the Dadaist movement, with the invention of a kind of picture which the Dada theorist and poet Tristan Tzara christened "Schadograph" after its creator's name.

Schad has told us that, upon finding himself in Geneva in 1918, he began to be fascinated by materials and objects that he came across in the streets, in shop windows, even in dustbins. With the aim of discovering new aspects and relationships in these, the typical products and sub-products found in every town, he began to put them together and arrange them over a photosensitive glass or paper surface and then to expose these kinds of collages to the light, sometimes with appropriate filters. That was how he obtained his Schadographs, or photograms, without the use of a camera. The technique (which goes back to the very beginning of photography—Talbot's ''talbotypes'' were, of course, obtained by placing objects directly on photosensitive paper) was developed both by Schad and by other artists of the modern movement like Man Ray with his ''Rayographs'' and Moholy-Nagy with his ''Photograms.'' The first Schadographs—one of which, ''Arp and Val Serner in the Royal Crocodarium in London,'' was published in the seventh and last number of the review *Dada,* issued in Paris in 1920—deliberately avoided any association with geometric forms and all identification with recognizable figures and objects; the outlines were shifted and cut about, recalling Arp's work with the blot technique in the same period. Only later, when he resumed this technique in the 60s, was Schad to depict materials like pieces of string and paper, bits of writing, miscellaneous objects, netting and lace, making more open use of their physical and semantic characteristics—the transparency of the nets and lace, the recognizability of fragments of writing and pictures, the outlines and shapes of identifiable objects.

Schadographs, like the other manifestations of Dada, must be judged in the same spiritual sphere and philosophy which gave rise to them. Launched in 1916/17 by a group of intellectuals and artists who had taken refuge in Switzerland to escape from the war, Dadaism went further than the production of new works of art aimed at confounding the bourgeois fashion of conceiving art as a separate form of existence. According to Dadaist criticism, the bourgeois mentality conceived art as an ideal work in which the beauty and the values, made impossible in everyday life by the very social system that the bourgeoisie followed and defended, could actually be sought. In unmasking the hypocrisy and idealism implicit in traditional art, some artists developed new techniques and new creative strategies. Notable among these was the collage, a new way of looking at objects by placing the objects themselves directly on the pictures instead of painting them; another was the use of photography as a technique of creative manipulation, which, in turn, changed the collage into the transcription of light.

—Daniela Palazzoli

SCHADEBERG, Jurgen.

Nationality: German. **Born:** Berlin, 18 March 1931. **Education:** Studied at the School of Optics and Phototechnics, Berlin, 1946-47; volunteer-apprentice, German Press Agency, Hamburg, 1948-50. **Family:** Married Claudia Horvath in 1984; children: Charlie, and from Schadeberg's previous marriages, Wolfgang, Martine, Frankie, Bonnie and Leon. **Career:** Photographer and Picture Editor, *Drum* magazine, Johannesburg, 1951-59; freelance photographer, working for the Johannesburg *Sunday Times,* London *Sunday Times, Observer, Telegraph, New Society, Marketing, Architectural Journal, Campaign,* the Hamburg *Die Zeit,* etc., in Johannesburg, 1960-64, in London, 1964-68, in Spain, 1969-72, in London, 1973-83, in Cannes, France, 1984-85, and in Randburg, South Africa, since 1985. Editor, *Camera Owner* magazine, London 1964-65. Part-time tutor, Central School of Art and Design, London, 1973-80; tutor, Newport Art College, Wales, 1983. **Address:** 21 Kangnussie Road, Randburg, Transvaal, South Africa.

Individual Exhibitions:

1969   The Gallery, Allo Castello, Spain (retrospective)
1970   *Kalahari Bushmen,* La Palette Bleu, Paris
1971   *Kalahari Bushmen,* Woodstock Gallery, London
1979   *Faces,* Air Gallery, London
1980   Central School of Art and Design, London (retrospective)
1981   The Photographers' Gallery, London (retrospective; toured Britain)

Selected Group Exhibitions:

1962   Faces and Places, Adler Fielding Gallery, Johannesburg
        Faces and Places, Associated Galleries, Cape Town
1976   *Inside Whitechapel,* Whitechapel Art Gallery, London
        The Quality of Life, National Theatre, London
1979   *Lives,* Hayward Gallery, London

Collections:

Bibliothèque Nationale, Paris.

Publications:

By SCHADEBERG: Books—*Jurgen Schadeberg,* exhibition catalogue, with introduction by Tom Hopkinson, London 1981; *The Kalahari Bushmen Dance,* with text by George Hulme, London 1982.

On SCHADEBERG: Articles—''Photographs by Jurgen Schadeberg'' in *Creative Camera* (London) November 1972; ''Portfolio: Jurgen Schadeberg'' in *British Journal of Photography* (London), 15 December 1972; ''Never Mind the Quality'' by Tom Picton in *Camerawork* (London), November 1976.

*   *   *

''I was born in 1931 and grew up in Berlin during the war. Stunned, I emerged from the ruins of the wrecked city and decided to become a photographer. I studied at the School for Optic and Phototechnic in Berlin and worked as an apprentice for the German Press Agency in Hamburg.''

Schadeberg's life has been one of frequent, often sudden, changes of direction, but all centering round that original decision ''to become a photographer.'' At the age of 19, he decided to go to South Africa where he joined the staff of the recently-founded *Drum* magazine. *Drum* was something new in the life of that tormented country—a magazine staffed mainly by blacks and produced for a black readership. For the few whites involved this was a strange experience for it meant living on the narrow borderline between black and white, distrusted in the main by both sides, in Johannesburg, centre and focus of twentieth century colour antagonism. The *Drum* office was one of very few buildings in the city in which the restrictions ordered by apartheid—separated entrances and lifts, separate lavatories, even separate teacups washed up separately—were disregarded. Everyone pitched in together.

It was on *Drum* that Schadeberg discovered a new capacity, that of teacher. Peter Magubane, later to become a cameraman of world reputation, had qualified by slow degrees from messenger to tea-boy, tea-boy to driver, driver to darkroom helper, finally attaining his goal of photographer with a camera paid for by his father out of money saved by hawking vegetables.

''Our picture editor,'' he records, ''was a young German, Jurgen Schadeberg, who was very good at taking pictures and very strict to those like me who were learning. He used to let me make thirty, forty prints at a time. If one was not properly made, I would have to repeat the lot. Often I would sleep in the office because there was no transport for me to get home. I did not mind because all the time I was learning from him.''

During his years with *Drum* Schadeberg took many of his own finest photographs, including those mysterious and evocative pictures of the Bushman dance in the Kalahari desert. This was in 1959 when he joined an expedition organised by the University of the Witwatersrand. Professor Tobias, leader of that expedition, wrote of his pictures; ''They portray, as has never been portrayed before, some aspects of life among the little hunters, the 'harmless people' of the desert. This is where art and science lose their bounds and meet: for these pictures are priceless scientific documents no less than photographic works of highest artistry.''

In 1964 Jurgen came to London, where for twelve months he edited the magazine *Camera Owner,* later to become *Creative Camera.* Then, after a spell in photojournalism working mainly for the Sunday supplements, he went for four years to Spain, where he applied himself to experimenting with colour, both as painter and photographer.

Africa, however, was still calling and in the early 1970s he made two long journeys, one to take photographs for Christian Aid, and the second, an epic hitch-hike from Senegal and Mali, down the West Coast and across Zaire and Kenya to Tanzania. ''My aim was to show the life of Africa apart from its two stereotypes—the primitive life of villages and tribesman, and the violence which so many cameramen set out to look for. I wanted to show the Africa of the market place, the towns, the life of the dusty roads with their bus-stops and river-crossings.''

Back in London once more, he took a post at the Central School of Art and Design, at which he did not so much 'teach photography' as cooperate with groups of students in various forms of workshop experiment. Two of these produced memorably successful exhibitions. First *Inside Whitechapel* in 1973, in which students work together with a group of talented professionals, and *The Quality of Life* in 1976. Planned to coincide with the opeining of the new London National Theatre complex—in which it was displayed to dramatic effect—the exhibition had involved two years work with students from various parts of the world, living together in a disused warehouse near London Bridge which served them as home, workshop, studios and darkroom.

Schadeberg spent the early 1980s mainly in freelancing for British, American and German magazines. But today he is back again in South Africa, trying to identify and file something like a hundred thousand negatives taken by *Drum* photographers up and down the African continent during three decades.

The result, it is hoped, will be a whole series of books.

—Tom Hopkinson

SCHELER, Max.

Nationality: German. **Born:** Cologne, 28 December 1928; son of the philosopher Max Scheler. **Education:** Attended primary and secondary school in Cologne, until 1948; studied art history and literature, University of Munich, 1949-51; Sorbonne, Paris, 1951; mainly self-taught in photography, with the assistance of photographer Herbert List, from 1949. **Career:** Freelance photographer, for *Neue Zeitung* and *Heute* magazines, Munich, working with Herbert List in Italy, Spain, Greece and Yugoslavia, 1950-52; reportage photographer, with Magnum Photos co-operative agency, Paris, working for *Epoca, Look, Paris-Match, Picture Post,* etc., in Munich, Paris, Rome, the United States, Middle East and Far East, 1953-58; photographer, for *Münchner Illustrierte,* Munich, 1958-59; Staff Photographer, working in the United States, Central America, Japan, China, North Africa and Eastern Europe, 1959-75, and a photo-editor, 1975-76, *Stern* magazine, Hamburg; Managing Editor, *Geo* magazine, Hamburg, 1976-80. From 1980-1992 Chief Editor, *Merian* magazine, and editor of the photographic books of Hoffmann und Campe Verlag, Hamburg. Member, Gesellschaft Deutscher Lichtbildner (GDL), 1965; Deutsche Gesellschaft für Photographie (DGPh), 1966. Owns the Estate of Herbert List 1903-1975, produces books and exhibitions of Herbert List. **Address:** Bellevue 39A, 22301 Hamburg, Germany.

Selected Group Exhibitions:

1964	*World Exhibition of Photography: What Is Man?,* Pressehaus Stern, Hamburg (and world tour)
1969	*Ost-West Reportagen,* Museum für Kunst und Gewerbe, Hamburg
1979	*Deutsche Fotografie nach 1945,* Kunstverein, Kassel, Germany *Fotografie 1919-1970,* Fotomuseum im Stadtmuseum, Munich
1983	*Fotografische Sammlung,* Museum Folkwang, Essen, Germany

Collections:

Museum für Kunst und Gewerbe, Hamburg; Fotomuseum im Münchner Stadtmuseum, Munich; Museum Ludwig, Cologne; Museum Folkwang, Essen, Germany.

Publications:

By SCHELER: Book—*Liverpool Days,* London 1994; books edited—*Herbert List: Photographien 1930-1970,* Munich 1976; *Herbert List: Portraits,* Hamburg 1976; *Herbert List: Fotografia Metafisica,* Munich, London

and New York 1983; *Portfolio Herbert List: Zeitlupe Null,* Hamburg 1980; *I Grandi Fotografi: Herbert List,* Milan 1983; *Junge Maenner, Herbert List,* London 1988; *Hellas, Herbert List,* 1993; *Liverpool Days,* London 1993; *Italy, Herbert List* 1995.

On SCHELER: Books—*Fotografie 1919-1979, Made in Germany: Die GDL-Fotografen,* with texts by W. Boje, F. Kempe, B. Lohse and others, Frankfurt 1979; *Deutsche Fotografie nach 1945/German Photography After 1945,* exhibition catalogue, edited by Petra Benteler, Floris M. Neususs and others, Kassel, West Germany 1979; *Museum Folkwang: Die fotografische Sammlung* exhibition catalogue, with introduction by Ute Eskildsen, Essen, West Germany 1983. **Articles**—"Max Scheler" in *U.S. Camera Annual,* New York 1957; "Max Scheler" by Wolf Strache in *Das Deutsche Lichtbild* (Stuttgart), no. 56, 1976.

*

While as a photographer I was mainly interested in social issues, covering such events as political crises, upheaval, revolution, as well as statesmen in their encounters, travels and campaigns, and later focussed on general social conditions all over the world, I have lately been more interested in cultural aspects and the aesthetic side of good reportage—which I produce and publish in *Merian* magazine. While as a young man I thought I could help to improve the world, I am happy now to be able to show what beauty is left in it.

—Max Scheler

* * *

Born in Cologne on 28 December 1928, the son of a philosopher, Max Scheler first took a course in German studies and art history at the University of Munich. At this time, around 1950, he was already studying photography intensively under the guidance of Herbert List, who influenced Scheler's conception of the photographic medium by his visual precision and his way of combining reality and unreality. He continued his studies in Paris where he got to know Robert Capa and became a junior member of the Magnum photographic group, and finally decided on a photographic career. He had already had some success in Munich with publications of his work in the *Neuen Zeitung*; the photo-reportages from Europe, the Middle East, and East Asia, followed by reports made during his eight-month stay in the United States, were to make his name famous. Pictures by Scheler appeared before 1958 in *Look, Paris-Match, Epoca* and *Picture Post,* while the German public got to know his work through the magazine *Stern.* Political crisis and international reports—particularly from the United States, Central America, Japan and China, as well as North Africa—formed the subject matter of these photographs, which combine the immediacy of their message with an effect of aesthetic distancing. This ability to create distance between the subject and the viewer made Scheler a precise photo-reporter who confronts the present moment but never loses himself in it. Scheler's marked objectivity allowed him to find a new focal point for his work from the mid-sixties: he worked as deputy art director of the well-known magazines *Stern* (alongside Rolf Gillhausen), and later *Geo* and *Merian.* His years of travel experience and well-developed visual judgement strongly influenced the character of these publications. Scheler is also responsible for overseeing the illustrated books published by the Hamburg firm Hoffman & Campe, among them a book on Herbert List, whose work Scheler has succeeded in publicizing through a number of exhibitions.

—Heinz Spielmann

SCHMIDT, Michael.

Nationality: German. **Born:** Berlin, 6 October 1945. **Education:** Attended the Hauptschule, Berlin, 1951-60; self-taught in photography: passed external examination as graduate photo-designer at Fachhochschule, Dortmund,

Illusion and Reality at the Height of the Cultural Revolution, **1965.** Photograph by Max Scheler.

1980. **Family:** Married Angelika Miersch in 1968 (divorced, 1974); daughter: Olivia; married Karin Kopto in 1982. **Career:** Freelance photographer, Berlin, since 1965. Instructor in Photography, Volkhochschule, Berlin-Kreuzberg, since 1969 (Promoter and Leader, Werkstatt für Fotografie, Volkhochschule Kreuzberg, 1976-77). Instructor, Pädagogische Hochschule, Berlin, 1976-78, and Universität FB 4, Essen, 1979-80. Member, Deutsche Gesellschaft für Photographie (DGPh), and Gesellschaft Deutsche Lichtbildner (GDL). **Agent:** Galerie Rudolf Springer, Fasanenstrasse 13, 1000 Berlin 12, Germany. **Address:** Wartenburgstrasse 16a, 1000 Berlin 61, Germany.

Individual Exhibitions:

1973   *Michael Schmidt: Berlin-Kreuzberg,* Berlin Museum, West Berlin

1975   *Michael Schmidt: Photographien,* Galerie Springer, West Berlin
1977   *Michael Schmidt: Stilleben und Lifefotografie,* Landesbildstelle, Hamburg
1978   *Michael Schmidt: Berlin-Wedding,* Kunstamt Wedding, West Berlin
1979   *Michael Schmidt: Fotografien 1965-67,* Galerie Springer, West Berlin
1981   *Larry Fink/Andreas Müller-Pohle/Michael Schmidt,* Kunstmuseum, Dusseldorf
        Museum Fodlkwang, Essen, West Germany
1982   Forum Stadtpark, Graz, Austria
1983   Forum Stadtpark, Graz, Austria
        Poll Studio, West Berlin

1984   Dryphoto Prato, Italy
1985   Museo di Rimini, Italy

Selected Group Exhibitions:

1978   *Aspekte Deutscher Landschaftsfotografie,* Stadtmuseum
          München, Munich
1979   *In Deutschland,* Rheinisches Landesmuseum, Bonn
          Photographie 1839-1979, Galerie Rudolf Kicken, Cologne
1980   *Michael Schmidt und Schüler,* Werkstatt für Fotografie der
          VHS Kreuzberg, West Berlin
          Absage an das Einzelbild, Museum Folkwang, Essen
1982   *Photographie en Allemagne 1920-82,* Musée de Besançon,
          France
1983   *Photographie in Deutschland Heute,* Brussels
1984   *Photography from Berlin,* Castelli Graphics, New York
          (travelled to Washington, D.C. and Los Angeles)
1985   *Das fotografische Selbstporträt,* Kunstverein, Stuttgart
1986   *Reste des Authentischen,* Museum Folkwang, Essen, West
          Germany

Collections:

Berlinische Galerie, Berlin; Stadtmuseum München, Munich; Musée d'Art et d'Histoire, Fribourg, Switzerland; Bibliothèque Nationale, Paris; Museum Folkwang, Essen, Germany; Museum für Kunst und Gewerbe, Hamburg.

Publications:

By SCHMIDT: Books—*Berlin-Kreuzberg,* West Berlin 1973; *Michael Schmidt Photographien,* West Berlin 1975; *Berlin: Stadtlandschaft und Menschen,* with text by Heinz Ohff, West Berlin 1978; *Berlin-Wedding,* with text by Heinz Ohff, West Berlin 1978; *Michael Schmidt: Stadtslandschaften,* Essen, West Germany 1981; *Benachteiligt,* with text by Ernst Klee, West Berlin 1982; *Michael Schmidt: Berlin-Kreuzberg Stadtbilder,* West Berlin 1983. **Articles**—"Gedanken zu meiner Arbeitweise" and "Aufgabe und Ziele der Werkstatt für Photographie der Volkshochschule Kreuzberg" in *Camera* (Lucerne), March 1979; article in *Thomas Leuner: Notizen aus einer Stadt,* exhibition catalogue, West Berlin 1980.

On SCHMIDT: Exhibition Catalogues—*In Deutschland,* with text by Klaus Honnef, Bonn 1979; *Michael Schmidt und Schüler,* West Berlin 1980; *Museum Folkwang: die fotografische Sammlung,* with introduction by Ute Eskildsen, Essen, West Germany 1983.

*   *   *

Michael Schmidt is an unusual phenomenon among German photographers of the 1970s. After studying painting, he became a city official, but the constraints connected with that kind of work were contrary to his lively nature. In 1965 he began to take photographs with a miniature camera; by 1969, self-taught, he had become a lecturer in photography at the Volkhochschule in Berlin-Kreuzberg; in 1970 he organized a photography seminar which by 1976-77 had developed into a photography workshop. The enthusiastic teacher (he freed himself from his municipal job in 1973) attracted many students, amateurs of all ages who wanted to learn how to take photographs. Schmidt taught them with the aim that they should, in their pictures, record reality as precisely as possible and so come to an understanding of it; at the same time, he hoped that with and through photography his students would discover something to which they could respond. A very human attitude.

His books of photographs provide a guide to his own development. *Berlin-Kreuzberg* presents, side by side with photographs of streets and houses, many photographs of people. It is a forceful and thrilling small format photography concentrating more on subject than on faultless reproduction. The social tendency is obvious, and a certain ruggedness of style is evidence of the photographer's temperament.

Substantial variations are discernible in *Berlin: Stadtlandschaft und Menschen.* The pictures of the Berlin city landscape are separated from those of people, and the pictures of people have lost their anecdotal quality. The

"shots" show people going for a walk or standing around, and what appears accidental has a strong touch of reality; as well, the observer has a lot to look at in the pictures. This is also true of the city landscapes. Instead of "interesting" or picturesque detail, there are now views where many details are to be seen, which the eye is asked to discover. Neither focus nor lighting is accentuated.

These photos suggest a style that comes to maturity in *Berlin-Wedding.* Trees and concrete, wire netting and wooden huts, decay and modernity are all equally valid. In these photos the sun never shines: they are taken in refracted daylight in soft tones of grey with full focus by means of a 9 x 12 cm camera. Even though he could be said to be taking "notes," Schmidt sets a high value on technical precision. Here, too, people are found in a separate section. Schmidt documents, in a deliberate confrontation of people and camera, how people appear in their offices or workshops or at home. His people offer themselves in icy seriousness. They appear sterile, and their rooms, in general, are no less sterile. It is a terrifying analysis of modern uniformity.

One can only speculate on Michael Schmidt's future development, but it is certain that the social and critical aspects of his work will continue to take precedence over aesthetics.

—Fritz Kempe

SCHRÖTER, Wolfgang G(ünther).

Nationality: German. **Born:** Wolfen, 7 May 1928. **Education:** Attended the Oberschule, Bitterfeld, until 1947; studied photography, under Johannes Widmann, Hochschule für Grafik und Buchkunst, Leipzig, 1949-53, Dip. Photog. 1953. **Family:** Married Rita Grosse in 1954; son: Erasmus. **Career:** Worked in the film checking department of Agfa-Filmfabrik, Wolfen, 1945-48. Since 1953, freelance magazine, book, industrial and commercial photographer, working for *DDR im Aufbau, Freie Welt, Jenauer Rundschau,* Leuna-Werke, Orwo/Agfa-Filmfabrik, Carl-Zeiss-Jena, Insel-Verlag, Union-Verlag, Verlag Edition, Urania-Verlag, Fotokinoverlag, etc., in China, India, Mongolia, Denmark, West Germany: established studio at Wolfgang-Hewinze-Strasse 19, Markkleeberg, in 1976. Instructor in Applied Color Photography, Hochschule für Grafik und Buchkunst, Leipzig, since 1973. Founder-member, Action Fotografie group, Leipzig, 1950-60. Vice-President since 1977, and President of the Working Group of Photographic History since 1980, Gesellschaft für Fotografie der DDR, Berlin; Photojournalism Committee Member, Verband der Journalisten (VDJ), Berlin, 1953. **Recipient:** Title of Honour, Fédération Internationale d'Art Photographique, 1965; Gold Honour Award for Photography, 1966, Johannes R. Becher Silver Medal, 1966, and Honor Prize for Photography, 1977, Kulturbund der DDR. **Address:** Fritz-Reuter-Strasse 5, 7113 Markkleeberg, Germany.

Individual Exhibitions:

1972   *Farbige Industriefotos,* Klub der Intelligenz, Leipzig, East
          Germany

Selected Group Exhibitions:

1957   *Action Fotografie,* Galerie Capitol, Leipzig, East Germany
          Weltfestspiele, Manege Gallery, Moscow
1963   *Erste Pressefotoschau der DDR,* Ausstellungszentrum,
          Friedrichstrasse, East Berlin
1966   *Interpressfoto,* Manege Gallery, Moscow
1973   *DDR-Farbreport,* Ausstellungszentrum, Friedrichstrasse, East
          Berlin (and Fernsehturm, Berlin, 1974; University of
          Hamburg, 1977)
1977   *Medium Fotografie,* Staatliche Galerie Moritzburg, Halle, East
          Germany
1981   *Fotografie in der DDR,* Galerie Gürzenich, Cologne, West
          Germany
1985   *Frühe Bilder,* Informationszentrum, Sachsenplatz, Leipzig, East
          Germany (and Fotogalerie Lichtenberg, East Berlin, 1986)

Collections:

Technisches Museum, Dresden, Germany; Fotohistorische Sammlung, Fotokinoverlag, Leipzig, Germany.

Publications:

By SCHRÖTER: Books—*Das grosse Colorpraktikum*, Leipzig 1966; *Louis Held-Hofphotograph im Weimar, Reporter der Jahrundertwende*, with others, Leipzig 1985; *Herman Walter: Fotografien von Leipzig 1853-1909*, edited, with Rose-Marie Frenzel, Leipzig 1987. Articles—"Farbe—ein Gestaltungsmittel der realistischen Fotografie" in *Fotojahrbuch International 1966*, Leipzig 1966; "Das Ästhetische im Bild der Wissenschaft" in *Fotografie* (Leipzig), September 1970; "Strobochromatografie" in *Fotografie* Leipzig), November 1971; "Farbfotografie ohne Magie und Verfremdung" in *Fotojahrbuch International 1974*, Leipzig 1974; "Das Report—Prinzip" in *Fotografie* (Leipzig), January 1974; "DDR-Farbreport 74—ein Erfahrungsbericht" in *Fotografie* (Leipzig), September 1974; "Metamorphosen am Densitron" in *Fotografie* (Leipzig), February 1975; "Medium in der Prüfung" in *Fotografie* (Leipzig), December 1976; "August Sander—Karl Blossfeldt" in *Beiträge: Symposium zu geschichtlichen und theoretischen Aspekten des Mediums Fotografie der 20er Jahre*, Leipzig and Dessau 1980, East Berlin 1981; "Louis Held" in *Fotografie* (Leipzig), January 1985.

On SCHRÖTER: Books—*Medium Fotografie*, edited by Andreas Hünecke, Gerhard Ihrke, Alfred Neumann and Ullrich Wallenburg, Leipzig 1979; *Frühe Bilder: eine Ausstellung zur Geschichte der Fotografie in der DDR*, catalogue, Leipzig 1985. Articles—"Auftrag Farbfotografie" in *Fotografie* (Leipzig), September 1967; "Ehrenpreis fur Fotografie" in *Mitteilungsblatt* (East Berlin), no. 11, 1977.

*

Completely distinct from the traditional pictorial arts of painting and graphics, photography occupies a place of its own alongside literature and fine art. Photography is probably closer as a medium to literature than to painting. The physical-mechanical genesis of a photograph is the source of its authenticity, an authenticity that belongs to no other medium.

The subject matter is far more important in photography than in any of the other arts. My role as structurer of the creative work is subordinate to the role of the object, and is determined by it. Herein lies creativity that is true to its medium.

The photographic image is taken (physically) out of reality—but thereby removed from the process of reality. It is therefore, as has so often been misunderstood, neither a conservation nor a substitution of reality, but simply an image: nothing more, nothing less.

That demands a different set of principles for the ordering of the picture's surface than those which are conventionally associated with the painted image. My first task in objective-documentary photography is to bring out the distinctness of the image, to lift the subject out of the banality of time and place.

In applied photography I submit willingly to the alluring and fantastic possibilities offered by colour techniques and now also by electronics.

In my work in the field of advertising, where authenticity is not a prime concern, I use all the possibilities of distancing and montage until I find new principles of illustration, such as colour photofinish, strobochromatography, or densitogrammetry.

—Wolfgang G. Schröter

*   *   *

Wolfgang Schröter was born in Wolfen, a German town with a big factory producing photographic film. His birthplace was apparently to influence his destiny, for, having completed his secondary school education, he went to work for approximately a year in the colour-film checking department of the local factory. With this experience, he began to study photography at university level in Leipzig—at the same school in which Johann Wolfgang von Goethe had once learned to draw. Receiving his diploma in 1953, Schröter embarked on the career of a freelance photographer, initially contributing to the journals

DDR im Aufbau and *Freie Welt*. Although at first he concentrated on taking high quality black-and-white pictures, he became more and more interested in colour photography. Both his educational qualifications and his contacts back in Wolfen enabled him to work with the positive-negative technique based on Orwocolor materials. With them, he endeavoured to achieve absolutely perfect results, even sometimes using cameras of large 18 x 24 centimeter formats.

Schröter's high level of technical skill combined with an ability to make creative interpretations of the essential nature of those subjects selected soon brought him the chance to collaborate with publishing houses specializing in picture-books on art. He also made excellent photographs of the ballet and other dance subjects, some taken directly on stage during rehearsal or at the actual performance. Alongside these, more complex pictures were then made using a system of flashes with a large format camera. With this system, Schröter's images of the African ballet visiting Leipzig achieved a particular fame.

Eager to travel, Schröter made photographic trips to the U.S.S.R. in 1956 and to China in 1959. Later, he added series of images on Bulgaria, India and Poland.

He has always been fascinated by the carefully controlled colour shot, so inventively arranged for his dance scenes, and eventually he turned to applied scientific and technical photography. It was not the mere satisfaction of finding ingenious solutions to complicated problems which attracted Schröter, but the discovery of quite surprising dimensions of beauty to be found in the current era of technological revolution. Assignments to develop new methods of applied photography have opened up for Schröter good contacts among scientific institutes, factories and laboratories. He has been able to use colour photography to make eloquent visual statements about the high-tech environment as well as its psychological impact on society.

—Petr Tausk

SCHULTHESS, Emil.

Nationality: Swiss. **Born:** Zurich, 29 October 1913. **Education:** Attended public primary school, Zurich, 1919-25; and public secondary school, Zurich 1925-28; student/apprentice in graphics, under Alex Walter Diggelmann, Zurich, 1928-32; studied photography, under Hans Finsler, *q.v.*, Kunstgewerbeschule, Zurich, 1932; art, Académie de la Grande Chaumière, Paris, 1932. **Military Service:** Served in the Swiss Army, 1940-66. **Family:** Married Bruna Castellini in 1937; children: Alfred and Elisabeth. **Career:** Worked as freelance graphic artist, Zurich, 1932-36; Graphic Designer, Conzett and Huber publishers, Zurich, 1937-41, and Art Director, Picture Editor and Photographer, *Du* magazine (Conzett and Huber), Zurich, 1941-57. Freelance photographer, art director and writer, working mainly for Artemis publishers, Zurich, since 1957. **Recipient:** US *Camera*-Achievement Award, 1951, 1967; Annual Award, American Society of Magazine Photographers, 1958; Prix Nadar, France, 1960; Culture Prize, Deutsche Gesellschaft für Photographie (DGPh), 1964; Goldene Blende Award, *Bild der Zeit*, Stuttgart, 1972; Golden Letter, Best World Books Competition, Leipzig 1983; Josef Sudek Medal, Prague 1989. **Address:** Langacher 5, 8127 Forch/Zurich, Switzerland.

Individual Exhibitions:

1958	*Africa*, American Museum of Natural History, New York
1961	*Antarctica: The White Continent*, Jelmoli Department Store, Zurich (toured Europe, the United States, Latin America and India)
1963	*Africa-Antarctica-The Amazon*, IBM Gallery, New York
1965	*Africa-Antarctica-The Amazon*, Smithsonian Institution, Washington, D.C.
	Afrika-Amerika-Antarktis, Amerika-Haus, Hamburg
1966	*China*, Galerie Form, Zurich
	China: Mensch und Natur im Reich der Mitte, Galerie 58, Rapperswil, Switzerland

1972   *Unspoiled Nature,* U.S. Kodak travelling exhibition (toured
        Europe, South America, and the Far East, 1972-74)
        Unberührte Natur, Swiss Kodak travelling exhibition (toured
        Switzerland and France, 1972-75)

Selected Group Exhibitions:

1961   *Photography in the Fine Arts,* Metropolitan Museum of Art,
        New York
1964   *World Exhibition of Photography: What Is Man?,* Pressehaus
        Stern, Hamburg (and world tour)
1974   *Photographie in der Schweiz von 1840 bis heute,* Kunsthaus,
        Zurich (toured Europe and the United States)
1980   *The Imaginary Photo Museum,* Kunsthalle, Cologne
1981   *Stiftung für die Photographie,* Kunsthaus, Zurich
1984   *Swiss Photography from 1840 until Today,* Pro Helvetia
        Foundation, Zurich (and world tour)

Collections:

Kunsthaus, Zurich; Metropolitan Museum of Art, New York; Smithsonian
Institution, Washington, D.C.

Publications:

By SCHULTHESS: Books—*U.S.A.,* with texts by Emil Birrer, Doris Flach,
Golo Mann, Fred M. Packard, Schulthess and others, Zurich 1955; *Africa I:
From Mediterranean Sea to the Equator,* with texts by Otto Lehmann, Fritz
Morgenthaler, and Schulthess, Zurich 1958; *Africa II: From the Equator to the
Cape of Good Hope,* with texts by Otto Lehmann, Heini Hediger, Schulthess
and others, Zurich 1959; *Africa,* with text by Emil Egli, London and New York
1959, revised edition, Zurich, Munich, London and New York 1969; *Antarctica,* with texts by Raymond Priestley, George J. Dufek, Henry Dater and
Schulthess, Zurich, Munich, London and New York 1960; *The Amazon,* with
text by Emil Egli and Schulthess, Zurich, Munich, London and New York
1962; *China,* with texts by Hans Keller, Emil Egli, Edgar Snow, Harry Hamm
and Schulthess, Zurich, Munich, London and New York 1966; *Soviet Union,*
with text by Klaus Mehnert and Schulthess, Zurich and Munich 1971, with text
by Harrison Salisbury, London and New York 1971; *Midnight Sun,* Berne
1973; *Matterhorn,* Berne 1974; *Zurich,* Berne 1975; *Lucerne,* Berne 1978;
Manhattan-New York, Zurich 1978; *Swiss Panorama,* Zurich 1982; *Landschaft
der Urzeit,* 1988.

On SCHULTHESS: Books—*The Imaginary Photo Museum* by Helmut
Gernsheim, Renate and L. Fritz Gruber and others, Cologne 1981, London
1982; *The Library of World Photography: Photography as Fine Art,* with
introduction by Douglas Davis, Tokyo 1982, 1983, London 1983; *Swiss
Photography from 1840 until Today,* exhibition catalogue, with introduction
by Hugo Loetscher, Zurich 1984. **Articles**—"Emil Schulthess" by Philippe
Halsman in *Infinity* (New York), June 1958; "Africa" in *Camera 35* (New
York), February 1959; "Amazon by Emil Schulthess" by Arthur Goldsmith
in *Infinity* (New York), May 1963; "Emil Schulthess und Seine Fotos" by L.
Fritz Gruber in *Foto-Magazin* (Munich), March 1965; "Lynkeus mit der
Kamera" by Helmuth de Hass in *Die Welt* (Hamburg), March 1965; "Chroni-
cler of Continents" in *Modern Photography* (New York), April 1969; "Das
Pedantische Objektiv" by Volkmar E. Strauss in *Bild der Zeit* (Hamburg),
November 1971; "Des Affiches pour Rever" by L. Antonietti in *Typographische
Monatsblätter* (St. Gallen, Switzerland), November 1972; "Emil Schulthess"
in *Photography as a Tool,* by Time-Life editors, Amsterdam 1972.

*   *   *

As one of six children of a gardener for the city of Zurich, before affluence
came to Switzerland, Emil Schulthess learned early how to make the best of
things. In those days it was not taken for granted that a child would be given the
opportunity to learn a trade. Schulthess considers himself lucky to have been
allowed to take up an apprenticeship as a graphic designer.

He had been working for 12 years with Conzett and Huber as layout man
and production supervisor for Arnold Kübler, then editor-in-chief of *Du,*

when it was decided to dedicate an issue to the sun. Fired up by discussions
with the editorial staff, Schulthess sketched in an 8-page layout the sine curve
of the midnight sun. With an astronomer friend he checked out calculations for
the 24 positions of the sun during 24 hours. The house technician built him a
moving contraption to block out the sun's centre, so that its light would not
eclipse the color in his photographs. He did not know what the landscape
would look like in North-Norway, but set off for the Polar Circle to find on an
island a spot where an extended water horizon would allow him to show the
sun's full sine curve, with its low point just above it. Rarely does the sun
remain uncovered by clouds for 24 hours, but this time it smiled throughout.
Back in Zurich, Schulthess cropped his 24 photographs and fitted them
together into a new historic layout that won awards and is constantly being
republished in schoolbooks and atlases.

This panoramic view of the sun was the beginning of Schulthess' photographic life. In the 30 odd years since, he has published books on his travels
across the United States and America, Antarctica, the Amazon, China and
Russia. His photographs, almost always in color, are sensitive to man, beast,
city and landscape. The primitive stimulates his visual nerve, as does danger
and the grandeur of those manifestations of nature that man cannot conquer.
Schulthess believes in following with dogged determination his own path and
in finding along it solutions for photographing in a new vision what is close to
his heart. Always, after he has conceived a plan, he prepares its execution
down to the last detail. He designs his own books and supervises their printing.
Since 1957, when he began to freelance, he has financed on his own all his
complex projects. Schulthess is a man who along the road of life knows how to
make friends, to whom he remains loyal, friends with whom he cooperates and
who add expertise to his soundly executed work.

One of his unique contributions is his photography of the sun and its paths.
During a 10-month trip he photographed a circular eclipse in Africa and
tracked the vertical ascent of the sun at the Equinox on the Equator.
Ingeniously he solved his predilection for showing the sun's progress in one
image. For the eclipse he stripped together five diagonally cropped photographs, with the desert horizon providing a unified base. For the path of the sun
at the Equator, he used a self-built fish-eye-lens camera, which shows the
whole firmament, and exposed the position of the sun every 20 minutes for 12
hours—from East to the West—on the same sheet of film.

Schulthess had now followed the sun from the polar circle to the Equator.
The International Geophysical Year of 1958 presented an opportunity for the
fulfillment of a long-held dream: to continue his researches in Antarctica. He
was able to join the U.S. Navy's Research Mission "Operation Deep Freeze
IV." In the below-freezing cold, with his broken English, Schulthess was
nevertheless in his element. Not only was he able to track in one horizontal
color picture the midnight sun over the Ross Sea, but also he added to his
researches a series of fish-eye studies showing the sun's path during 18 hours
as a perfect circle over the Pole.

Antarctica is an apex of what Emil Schulthess wants to achieve in his
work. As opportunities to photograph in that uninhabited land are virtually
nonexistent, his work provides unique information of an unexplored, important part of the world, a part where the mysterious laws of nature assert
themselves with beauty and virulence. In acknowledgement of his work there,
the U.S. Board of Geographic Names has called the geographical point
84°47'S Latitude, 115°00'W Longitude "Schulthess-Buttress."

After twenty years of photographing powerful and primitive nations, 57-
year-old Emil Schulthess found himself working at home on a mountain tip.
Swissair had asked him to provide a souvenir for the Osaka *World's Fair.* He
conceived the idea of a panoramic view from the highest point in Switzerland,
the "Top of Switzerland." Although the 360° view taken at 4,634m. from
the tiny peak, big enough only to hold the tripod of his camera with its 3
rotating Japanese lenses, became a best seller, thereafter Emil Schulthess
forsook mountain tops and took to the air, always working in panoramic views,
which have been published as posters. The challenges of overcoming helicopter vibration, so that levelling remains perfect, proved staggering. Years
passed in designing and perfecting specially built camera equipment. Visualizing and finding points in the air that can be composed into vistas both exciting
to look at and informative, requires incredible imagination, precision and skill.
Working it all out in advance with a map, Schulthess now knows exactly from
what angle to approach, say, the Matterhorn, to show it at its most beautiful,
while making sure that none of the other most important mountains will be
hidden in his circular composition. Schulthess is now preparing a book of
this work.

From 1949 on, Emil Schulthess has been on a fertile voyage of photographic imagery and popular scientific knowledge, as orderly and mysterious as the path of the sun. It has involved a progression from a 360 degree view in 24 negatives, taken from one place on the earth, to 360 degree views in one negative taken from the air. His purpose has been to provide new visual information, serving the mind as well as the eye.

—Inge Bondi

SCIANNA, Ferdinando.

Nationality: Italian. **Born:** Bagheria, near Palermo, Sicily, 4 July, 1943. **Education:** Classical School, Bagheria, until 1962; studied literature and philosophy, University of Palermo, 1962-65; mainly self-taught in photography, from 1962. **Family:** Married Carmela Bologna in 1966; daughters: Francesca and Fernanda; married Paola Bergna in 1983; daughter, Eleonora. **Career:** Freelance photographer, in Palermo and Milan, 1963-67; journalist and photographer, 1967-74, and Paris Correspondent, 1974-83, *L'Europeo* magazine, Milan. Since 1983, freelance photographer, as member of Magnum Photos agency, Paris and Milan: established studio on via Castelfidardo, Milan, in 1983. **Recipient:** Prix Nadar, Paris, 1966. **Agent:** Magnum Photos, 5 Passage Piver, 75011 Paris, France. **Address:** 6 via Giannone, 20154 Milano, Italy.

Individual Exhibitions:

1962	*Feste in Sicilia,* Circolo di Cultura, Bagheria, Sicily
1963	*Feste in Sicilia,* Biblioteca Comunale, Milan
1973	*Glorioso Alberto,* at *SICOF,* Milan
1975	*Gitans,* at *SICOF,* Milan
1977	*Les Siciliens,* Institut Culturel Français, Naples, Italy
	I Siciliani, Institut Culturel Italien, Paris
1979	*Sicilia e dintorni,* Galleria Il Diaframma, Milan (retrospective)
1980	*Sicilia e dintorni,* Galleria Arte al Borgo, Palermo, Sicily
	Ten European Photographers for Half a Century, Salford University, UK
1981	*Sicilia e dintorni,* Galleria d'Arte Moderna, Bagheria, Sicily
	Sicilia e dintorni, Landesbildstelle Württemberg, Stuttgart
1989	*Kami,* Musée de l'Elysée, Lausanne, Switzerland
1992	*Le Forme del Caos,* Château d'Eau, Toulouse, France
	Le Forme del Caos, Villa Medicis, Rome

Selected Group Exhibitions:

1973	*3rd World Exhibition of Photography,* Pressehaus Stern, Hamburg (and world tour)
1978	*La Photographie Italienne,* at *Rencontres Internationales de Photographie,* Arles, France
	The Italian Eye, Alternative Center for International Arts, New York
1979	*Fotografia Italiana,* at the *Biennale,* Venice
1980	*Ten European Photographers,* Salford University, Lancashire
	Political Photographs, P.S. 1, New York
1982	*Antropologia Visual,* Museu da Imagen, São Paulo, Brazil
	Italian Photography, Beijing Museum, China

Collections:

Bibliothèque Nationale, Paris; Fonds National de la Photographie, Paris; Galleria d'Arte Moderna e Contemporanea, Bagheria, Sicily; Salford University, Lancashire.

Publications:

By SCIANNA: Books—*Feste religiose in Sicilia,* with text by Leonardo Sciascia, Bari, Italy 1965; *Il Glorioso Alberto,* with text by Leonardo Sciascia, Milan 1971; *Palermo Liberty,* with text by Leonardo Sciascia, Caltanissetta, Sicily 1971; *La villa dei mostri,* with introduction by Leonardo Sciascia, Turin 1977; *Les Siciliens,* with text by Dominique Fernandez and Leonardo Sciascia, Paris 1977; *I Grandi Fotografi: Ferdinando Scianna,* with introduction by Leonardo Sciascia, Milan 1983; *Il grande libro della Sicilia,* Milan 1985; *Kami,* Milan, 1988; *Le Forme del Caos,* Udine, 1989; *Marpessa,* Milan, Paris, 1993.

On SCIANNA: Books—*Primo Almanacco Fotografico Italiano,* with introduction by Pier Paolo Preti, Milan 1970; *Venezia 79; La Fotografia,* edited by Daniela Palazzoli, Vittorio Sgarbi and Italo Zannier, Milan and New York 1979. **Articles**—"Occhio nuovo" in *Popular Photography Italiano* (Milan), January 1963; "Scianna—Portfolio" in *Popular Photography Annual,* New York 1966; "Scianna" in *Foto Film* (Milan), February 1967; "Les Siciliens" in *Nouvel Observateur* (Paris), 11 July 1977; "Italian Photographers" in the *New York Times,* 9 April 1979; "Scianna" in *Corriere della Sera* (Milan), 11 April 1979; "Ferdinando Scianna," special issue of *Progresso Fotografico* (Milan), February/March 1980; "Scianna" in *Corriere della Sera* (Milan), 1 April 1983.

*

I think a lot about photography and I have written a lot about it too. But I try not to think about it while I do it. I agree with Robert Doisneau when he says that a photographer should be "stupid" while he is taking photographs. Stupid in the sense of "innocent," because he has known how to digest all that he has seen and thought before and after having taken his photograph.

That photography should be the mirror of reality is a metaphor that seems false to me: I think rather that it is reality which is the mirror of the photographer. This relation with reality is of course, ambiguous. Photography, an instrument of expression and communication, is ambiguous, like all instruments of expression and communication. The world is absurd, the world is ambiguous, we are absurd and ambiguous in this world. There is no other way to account for our relation to the world than to try to give form to this absurdity, each one with his own intrument. This does not mean, naturally, that form is an end in itself, or that the instrument is. The grape is used to make wine, the instruments of communication and expression to express and communicate.

Every man, therefore also the photographer, searches for his style, and style, obviously, is in form. But what can style in photography be beyond the choice of what is the photograph? I used to believe that photography could change the world or at least improve it. Now I know that photography is too poor a thing to expect of it great powers of resistance, opposition or even explanation of the world. It is, however, my impression that the furious efforts dictators put into censoring photographs is ample testimony of their crimes.

A poor thing, certainly, photography, but for me a great part, but not all, of life. Now I believe that it has become for me the instrument, perhaps even more ambitious, of understanding, of understanding myself, in the hope that perhaps someone else will recognize something of the very little that I have been able to grasp of life in this age old attempt, absurd and foolish in which, as Borges says, we pursue "a third tiger which is not in the verse."

—Ferdinando Scianna

* * *

Ferdinando Scianna's renown as a photographer came with the publication of a book—*Religious Festivals in Sicily* (1965)—which caused a certain stir because of the remarkable ease of its visual narrative; a narrative punctuated by sequences of images which broke, in their vitality and daring, with a number of rules of traditional illustrative both those referred to under the heading of "craftsmanship" and those of committed realism, the latter known for its static, emblematic quality in the style of Strand, the most loved and imitated photographer in Italy ever since the publication of his photoessay *A Village,* by Einaudi.

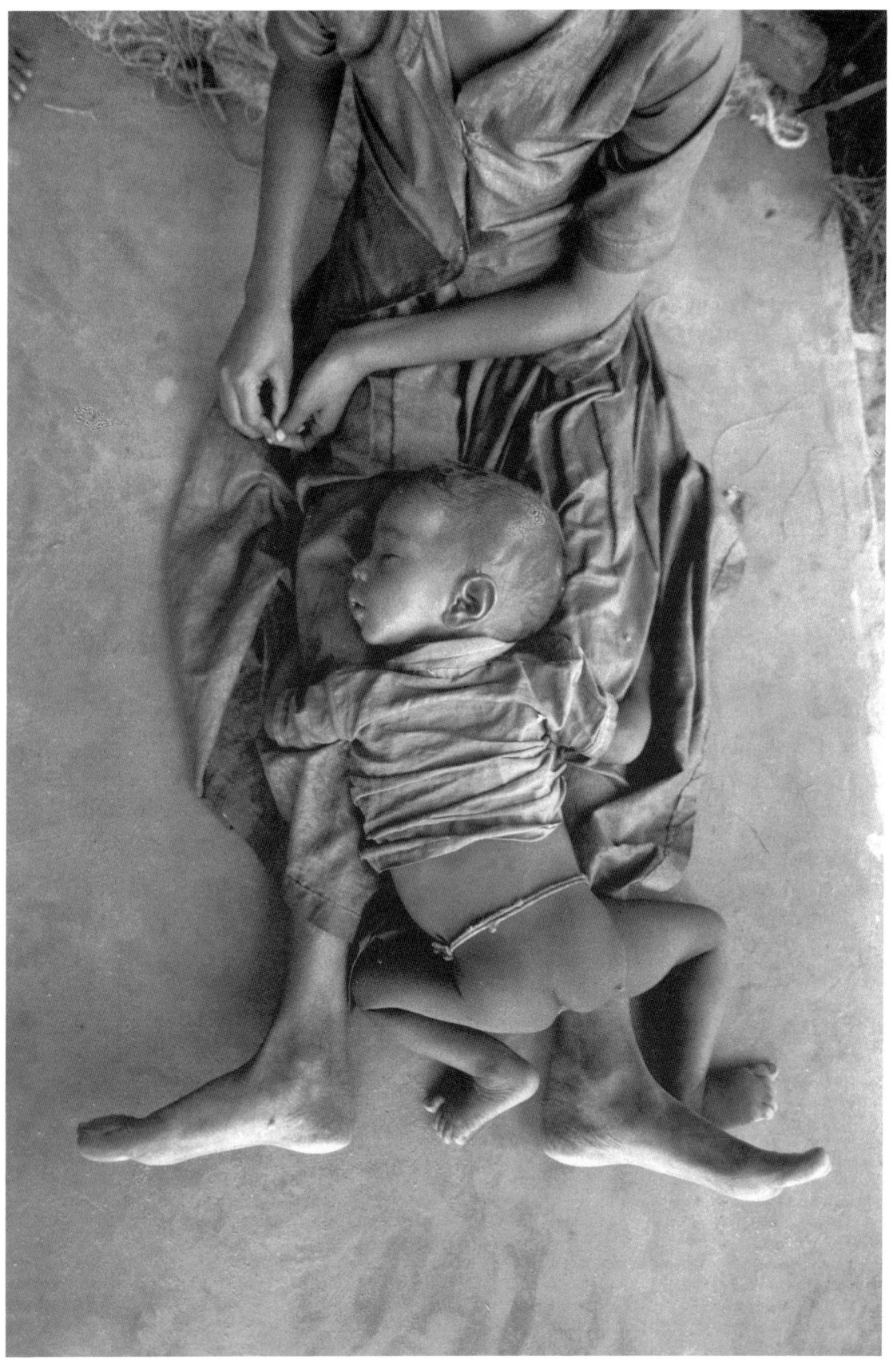

Madras, India, **1989.** Photograph ©Ferdinando Scianna.

Avoiding the debates in photography between formalists and neorealists which had preoccupied young Italian photographers since the war (on one side there was Giuseppe Cavalli with his aristocratic group "La Bussola" [1947] and on the other Pietro Donzelli and his friends in the "Unione Fotografica" [1951] known for their commitment to the left and their great enthusiasm for sociology), Scianna affiliated himself with the style of international photojournalism and, above all, with the style of Cartier Bresson, who was barely recognized in Italy, where the pretensions of artistic photography were still widespread. He insisted on the distinction between creative images (which were so often amateurishly pictorial) and documentary images—the stock in trade of the photojournalist. This latter style of photography had been condemned, above all, by Cavalli and those sharing his ideological stance (Veronesi, Leiss, Finazzi and Vender) who, following the obscurities of the aesthetic proposed by the philosopher Benedetto Croce, tended to refute anything that had too much to do with information.

Scianna, who at the time was studying literature in Palermo, saw a clear way ahead for photography, which was already becoming a powerful mass medium in Italy through the press—the most powerful because so widely distributed, up until the absolute establishment of television throughout the country in the late 1960s.

By showing the development of a particular event (the religious festivals of the South, with their pagan undertones, were the first stories produced by the young intellectual Sicilian photographer) in a sequence of photos remarkable for their spontaneity and immediacy, Scianna successfully moved beyond the limitations of traditional technique. He accepted only the expressive image and, notwithstanding the use of movement, distorted focus or excessive contrast and granulation, used this as the most important means to expressing the significance of the event.

Humanist intellectual as well as craftsman, Scianna has followed his path in photography with a sureness remarkable amongst Italian photographers, combining word and image as a journalist on some of the biggest weeklies (amongst them L'Europeo) and contributing some important reporting as a special correspondent overseas.

It was the photographic book, however, after that wonderful work on the religious festivals with its text by the talented Leonardo Sciascia, which provided Scianna with the ideal space in which to construct an organic assemblage of photographs which fleshed out striking stories and combined to form part of his long visual romance with the land and people of Sicily. Like Enzo Sellerio, one of his teachers and also a photographer for Life in the 1960s, Scianna avoided the facile picturesque approaches to local folklore or pretty Mediterannean landscapes which for almost a century had marked photographic attitudes to the area from Von Gloeden to Fulvio Roiter. Scianna strove in his images to represent people in their daily life—never as the sublime or romantic beings that photography had so often tried to make them. For this reason he has always rejected, as the worst of all evils, the hedonism of the pretty image and has opted instead for a photography where creativity (beauty, one could say) was expressed through the rigorous choice of theme, space and gesture determined by the cultural and political ideology of the author—while at the same time still searching for the archaic cosmos still discernible in his antique and mythic Sicily.

—Italo Zannier

SECCHIAROLI, Tazio.

Nationality: Italian. **Born:** Rome, 26 November 1925. **Education:** Studied, to the 3rd grade, at Commerciale School, Rome, 1941; self-taught in photography, from 1941, but a pupil of Adolfo Porry Pastorel at the V.E.D.O. agency, Rome, 1951. **Family:** Married Rosanna Tolomei in 1962 (divorced, 1977); children: David and Lucille. **Career:** Worked in the radiology department of the University of Rome's Orthopedic Clinic, 1947-51. Photojournalist, for evening newpapers in Rome, from 1952; founder-director, with Sergio Spinelli, Roma Press Photos agency, Rome, 1955-62; freelance photographer, from 1962. Photographer/Reporter of filmmaking, Rome, particularly of the films of Federico Fellini, since 1959. **Address:** Via dei Platani 129, 00172 Rome, Italy.

Individual Exhibitions:

1980	Palazzo delle Stelline, Milan
1982	Anni '60 e dintorni, Pordenone, Italy
1984	A come Ava..., Libreria Agora, Turin, Italy
1985	Qualche foto, Galleria Al ferro di Cavallo, Rome
	60 immagini, Spazio foto San Fedele, Milan
1986	Tra cronaca e cinema, Agrigento, Italy Overstudio, Turin, Italy
	10 foto, Galleria Adria, Rome

Selected Group Exhibitions:

1968	2nd World Exhibition of Photography: Woman, Pressehaus Stern, Hamburg (and world tour)
1970	Venezia 79: La Fotografia, Venice
1981	L'informazione negata: il fotogiornalismo, Pinacoteca Provinciale, Bari, Italy
1982	Fellini, FNAC-Montparnasse, Paris
1983	Incontri sulla fotografia: da Via Veneto a Cinecitta, Istituto Scienze dello Spettacolo, University of Rome
1984	Reflex: la fotografia a Roma, Rome
1985	Expo 85: Image Continue, Tsukuba, Japan
1986	1956-86: trent'anni di fotografia e automobili, Libreria Agora, Turin, Italy

Collections:

Musée d'Art Moderne, Paris; Art Institute of Chicago; Fototeca 3M, Milan; Centro Studi delle Communicazioni, University of Parma, Italy.

Publications:

By SECCHIAROLI: Book—I Grandi Fotografi: Tazio Secchiaroli, with text by Attilio Colombo, Milan 1983.

On SECCHIAROLI: Books—70 Anni di Fotografia in Italia by Italo Zannier, Modena, Italy 1978; L'informazionew negata: il fotogiornalismo in Italia 1945/1980, edited by Uliano Lucas and Maurizio Bizziccari, Bari, Italy 1981; Vita, Dolce Vita by A. Nemiz, Rome 1983; Enciclopedia pratica per fotografare by Arturo Carlo Quintavalle, Milan 1984. **Articles**—"Paparazzi on the Prowl" in Time (New York), 14 April 1961; "Tazio Secchiaroli" in Progresso Fotografico (Milan), November 1977; "Contemporary Italian Photography" by Italo Zannier in Venezia '79, Milan and New York 1979.

*   *   *

It doesn't often happen that a photographer becomes so famous that his name appears in all the newspapers. It happened to Tazio Secchiaroli. His name actually became the symbol of a whole generation of photographers—not his real name, of course, but his nom de guerre: who hasn't heard of Paparazzo? Paparazzo, alias Tazio Secchiaroli, the assault photographer, the human photographic machine-gun, the bounty killer of Rome's Via Veneto in the 1950s, immortalized by Federico Fellini in his film La Dolce Vita. Events in Rome in those days—when Rome was the international capital of the cinema, of the nobility, of the jetset—had in Tazio Secchiaroli their own quite uninhibited chronicler, and Fellini's film was based on the milieu that Secchiaroli had documented: film stars of both sexes bringing actions against each other, illicit love affairs, colossal orgies, Arabian Nights feasts in papal Rome.

Tazio Secchiaroli's basic achievement is to have created, quite deliberately, a style of news photography that in turn became the basis of a worldwide school: he made "assault photography" an essential chapter in photographic history. The scoop is now obtained not only from long ambushes, pursuits and disguises but also from situations actually "provoked" by photographers who have thus become personalities in their own right. Their pictures, filling the columns of the yellow press and scandal weeklies all over the world, have the distinctive mark of the flash, used to make a subject stand out in the style of the best of Weegee.

But it would be wrong to think of Tazio Secchiaroli as being important only in those days when he was Paparazzo as deified by Fellini. Secchiaroli's great capacity for synthesis, his nose for news, his expressive devices, gradually refined over the years—they have enabled him to continue his work on a new scale, no less characteristic and still typically Roman. Still working in the film world, Secchiaroli has shown us since 1960 the same personalities as before, with the same artful style and the same debunking irony. But celebrities who once chased him in the Via Veneto now shake hands with him at cocktail parties or invite him to record their work on the film set. His notable capacity for figuration and his highly trained eye, which can sum up a whole story in a single picture, have enabled Secchiaroli to move on from press photography to a more profound and truthful study of the film personalities (Fellini, Sophia Loren, Marcello Mastroianni and many other actors and producers) whose activities he has long reported so acutely.

—Attilio Colombo

SEMAK, Michael.

Nationality: Canadian. **Born:** Welland, Ontario, 9 January 1934. **Education:** Bloor, Oakwood and Parkdale high schools, Toronto, 1948-53; studied architectural technology, Ryerson Institute of Technology, now Ryerson Polytechnical Institute, Toronto, 1954-58, Dip.Arch. 1958; mainly self-taught in photography, from 1959. **Family:** Married Annette Antoniuk in 1960; children: James and Arlene. **Career:** Freelance photographer, working for *Transaction, Reader's Digest, Time, National Geographic, Cosmopolitan,* Foster Advertising Agency, Alcan, Polaroid Corporation, etc., Toronto, since 1963. Part-time Lecturer, 1971-72, Sessional Lecturer, 1972-73, Lecturer, 1973-74, Assistant Professor, 1974-75, and since 1976 Associate Professor, Department of Visual Arts, York University, Toronto. Chairman of Interarts, Canada-USSR Association, 1974-76; Member of Nominations Committee and Executive Council, Royal Canadian Academy of Art, 1974-78. **Recipient:** Canada Council grants, 1967, 1969, 1971, 1973, 1974, 1979, 1982; Gold Medal, 1969, and grants, 1971, 1975, National Film Board of Canada; Award of Excellence, American Communication Arts, 1969; *Pravda* Award of Excellence, Moscow, 1970, 1971; International Fund for Concerned Photography Award, 1971, 1972; Ontario Countil for the Arts grant, 1972; Award of Excellence, Fédération Internationale d'Art Photographique (FIAP), 1972; York University grants, Toronto, 1973, 1974, 1975, 1977, 1978, 1979, 1981, 1982, 1986; USSR-Canada Society grant, to Moscow, 1975, and to the Ukraine, 1981. Member, Royal Canadian Academy. **Address:** 1976 Spruce Hill Road, Pickering, Ontario L1V 1S4, Canada.

Individual Exhibitions:

1963	Gladstone Public Library, Toronto
1965	Toronto City Hall
1969	*Image 4: Ghana,* National Film Board of Canada, Ottawa (toured Canada, 1969-79, Ghana, 1970, and the U.S.S.R., 1980-81)
1971	Image Gallery, New York
1972	Image Gallery, New York
	York University Art Gallery, Toronto
	Ryerson Polytechnical Institute, Toronto
1973	Galleria Il Diaframma, Milan
	Gallery Oseredok, Winnipeg, Manitoba
1975	The Shado Gallery, Oregon City, Oregon
1976	Galleria Il Diaframma, Milan
	3 Photographers, Deja Vu Gallery, Toronto (with Barbara Astman and Jerry Uelsmann)
	The Dark Room Gallery, Chicago
1977	Enjay Gallery, Boston
1978	University of Calgary Art Gallery, Alberta
1979	Secession Gallery of Photography, Victoria, British Columbia
1980	Resolution Gallery of Photography, Toronto
	Ukrain Society, Kiev, U.S.S.R.

1981	Ukrainian Society for Friendship, Kiev, U.S.S.R.
1982	Conestoga College of Applied Arts and Technology, Kitchener, Ontario
	Edmonton Public Library, Alberta
1983	Confederation College of Applied Arts and Technology, Thunder Bay, Ontario
1984	John M. Cuelenaere Public Library, Prince Albert, Saskatchewan
	Photo Union Gallery, Hamilton, Ontario
	Centre Eye Gallery, Calgary, Alberta
	Production de la Huitième, Noranda, Quebec
	Vanier College, Montreal

Selected Group Exhibitions:

1965	*Canadian National Exhibition,* Toronto
1966	*World Press Photos,* Moscow
1967	*Bytown International,* Ottawa
	People Tree, at Expo '67, Montreal
1969	*Vision and Expression,* International Museum of Photography, George Eastman House, Rochester, New York (toured the United States, 1969-71)
1970	*ASMP 25th Anniversary Show,* New York Cultural Center
1974	*6th Bifota Exhibition,* East Berlin
1976	*Calgary Stampede Exhibition,* Flare Square, Calgary, Alberta
1980	*Words and Images,* National Film Board of Canada, Ottawa
1985	*Contemporary Canadian Photography,* National Gallery of Canada, Ottawa

Collections:

National Film Board of Canada, Ottawa; National Gallery of Canada, Ottawa; Public Archives of Canada, Ottawa; Department of External Affairs, Ottawa; York University, Toronto; Museum of Modern Art, New York; International Museum of Photography, George Eastman House, Rochester, New York; Bibliothèque Nationale, Paris; Musée Nicéphore Niépce, Chalon-sur-Saône, France; Ukraina Society, Kiev.

Publications:

By SEMAK: Books—Image 4, with text by Lorraine Monk, Ottawa 1969; *Michael Semak: Monograph,* Toronto 1974; *Michael Semak: Photographs 1960-87,* Ottawa 1987. Articles—"Statement" in *Impressions* (Toronto), Fall 1974; "Exposure Exhibition" in *Afterimage* (Rochester), July/August 1976; "Semak/USSR" in *Camera* (Lucerne), July 1978.

On SEMAK: Books—*Vision and Expression: An International Survey of Contemporary Photography* by Nathan Lyons, New York 1969; *Contemporary Canadian Photography* by Martha Langford, Edmonton, Alberta 1984. Articles—"Masters of the Leica: Michael Semak" by Heinrich Stöckler in *Leica Fotografie* (Frankfurt), February 1969; "Brooklyn/Semak" by Allan Porter in *Camera* (Lucerne), November 1970; "A Photographer Involved with Life's Human Drama" by Michael Edelson in *Popular Photography* (New York), November 1970; "Each Photo Should Tell a Story" by Don Long in *Canadian Photo Annual 1975/76,* Toronto 1975; "Street Scenes of Russia" by Ed Spiteri in *Photo Life* (Toronto), February 1978.

*

I wish to advocate socio-economic change in our society, using photography as part of my arsenal for that political end. Since photography alone cannot fully explain man and his society, why not change the uniform or role of photographic images, using them in another way? The intention is to increase our awareness of our relationships with others, victims and the victimizers. Coupling words, words directed at us from the mass media, with my images can provide more effective shells for the task ahead.

The system looks upon all of us as just one deep pocket, always ready to buy the dreams and goods it tirelessly dangles and spews out at us day in and day out. Mediocrity seems to be the norm—seeping into every keyhole of our mind. Words are hurled at us from everywhere—what do they really mean? When we unwrap the words we often end up with corpses called empty words. I see many contradictions around us, social realities which I believe rob us of our self-esteem and individuality. Must we continually accept and succumb to the never-ending hot baths for the mind society offers us? I wish my photography and words to disturb the complacent and the sleeper. I offer you cold showers for the mind.

—Michael Semak

*   *   *

If in the Canadian context of more than twenty years ago, the choice of photography as a career can be seen as an ordinary (or even practical) decision, then Michael Semak's professional beginnings can be deemed conventional. He worked on assignment for *National Geographic,* the National Film Board of Canada and Time-Life Books, travelling a great deal, training his camera on things primitive and non-North American as craved by a North American public. On completion of an eight week stint in Ghana, which yielded an exhibition and a book, Semak stated: "When I see, feel and photograph, I am interested in and want to stress the common denominator of people, the similarities of people rather than the petty differences." *Ghana* had poetically described a proud and dignified people of preoccupations so basic to survival, simplicity and ease that Semak's common denominator seemed to be a state of grace. His subsequent journeys through asylums, slaughterhouses and the streets gave evidence of a new conclusion: that we are guided not by gentleness but by a paucity of human contact and compassion. Semak began to see it in all of us and to place it accusingly before the viewer in metaphoric images. Documents of faith gave way to despair.

Semak's compositional tools are not uncommon in photography: the nude, the gesturing hand, the stone. As well, these groupings have been made before: the nude and the smooth stone; the element of self-portrait which is the hand inserted in the landscape—the photographer's presence intruding on his subject. As structured in his photographs, they are both traditional and revolutionary and they introduce the troubling paradox of Semak's work.

The image is often contained by a black line that both vaunts it as untampered with (as an event that actually took place—Semak in the room with the model and the stone) and stresses its photographic (therefore fictional) nature. There is a human presence here, two in fact, but the image while stemming from this human pairing does not suggest a portrait or divulge an introductory or concluding narrative. They are here gathered to be photographed.

The nude, whose outstretched arms are not welcoming but are pinned back in Christian archetype, is a woman in a man's pose. She stands on a rumpled bed. The stone is smooth, round and beautiful, yet it threatens the nude like an unexploded grenade. The bed becomes a battle-ground. The hand brutally thrust into the image and into the head of the figure conceals the identity of the woman. It is a man's hand, the photographer's left hand. This might be an act of chivalry or the theft of individuality.

If we look through the eyes of the awakening Adam, rising to God's touch through Michelangelo's conception, we look down the barrel of a left arm whose downturned hand closely resembles Semak's. Cradled in God's arms, the unspoiled, still unambitious Eve is about to be delivered to her partner in the Garden. In Semak's renewal of this image, the apple of Knowledge is revealed for its sterility. The woman stands condemned and crucified. She is beautiful, faceless and tainted with original sin.

Whose conventions are these that Michael Semak both adopts and challenges? This work and Semak's more recent work wherein he captions his own classic imagery with consumer slogans, sexist labels, political and religious propaganda, are so entrenched in irony that the viewer may be left confused and disaffected. The same measure of faith that we once brought to his utopian exotica must now be applied against this reprehensible typecasting.

Semak uses models and slogans that we have come to find distasteful and turns them against liberal complacency. His work is difficult. Most of us would prefer to turn our backs on such usage and find a new vocabulary for our angers and our perceptions of inequity.

—Martha Langford

SERRANO, Andres.

Nationality: American. **Born:** New York City, 15 August 1950. **Education:** Attended Brooklyn Museum Art School, 1967-69; self-taught in photography. **Family:** Married Julie Ault, 24 December 1980. **Recipient:** Grant from the National Studio Program at P.S.1 in 1985; National Endowment for the Arts in 1986; New York Foundation for the Arts in 1987; Awards in the Visual Arts in 1988; Cintas Foundation and Louis Comfort Tiffany Foundation in 1989; New York State Council on the Arts, 1990. **Agent:** Paula Cooper Gallery, 155 Wooster Street, New York, New York 10012, U.S.A.

Individual Exhibitions:

1985	Leonard Perlson Gallery, New York
1986	*The Unknown Christ,* Museum of Contemporary Hispanic Art, New York
1988	Greenberg/Wilson Gallery, New York
	Stux Gallery, New York
1989	Stux Gallery, New York
1990	The Seibu Museum of Art, Tokyo
	Gallery Hibbel, Tokyo
	BlumHelman Gallery, Santa Monica, California
	Fay Gold Gallery, Atlanta, Georgia
	Gallery Cellar, Nagoya, Japan
	Stux Gallery, New York
1991	Saatchi Gallery, London
	Gallery Via 8, Tokyo
	Nomads, Denver Museum, Colorado
	KKK Portraits, University of Colorado at Boulder
	Thomas Segal Gallery, Boston
	Galleri Susanne Ottesen, Copenhagen
	Galleri Riis, Oslo
	Seibu, Tokyo and Kyoto
	Galerie Yvon Lambert, Paris
1992	Zone Gallery, Newcastle-upon-Tyne, England
	Institute of Contemporary Art, Amsterdam
	The Morgue, Yvon Lambert Gallery, Paris (travelled to La Tete d'Obsidienne, Fort Napoleon, La Seyne-sur-Mer; Palais du Tau, Rheims; Grand Hornu, Mons, France; Paula Cooper Gallery, New York)
1993	*Selected Works: 1986-1992,* Feigen Gallery, Chicago
1994	Grand-Hornu, Hornu, Belgium
	Centre for Contemporary Art, Ujazdowski Castle, Warsaw, Poland (travelled to Moderna Galerija Ljubliana, Slovenia; Magazin 4, Bregenz, Austria)
	The Church Series, Paula Cooper Gallery, New York
	Alfonzo Artiaco, Naples, Italy
	Institute for Contemporary Art, University of Pennsylvania, Philadelphia (travelled to The New Museum of Contemporary Art, New York; Center for the Fine Arts, Miami; Contemporary Art Museum, Houston; Museum of Contemporary Art, Chicago)
	The Morgue, Museum of Contemporary Art, Montreal, Quebec
	Budapest, Paula Cooper Gallery, New York
	Budapest, Galerie Yvon Lambert, Paris
	The Morgue, Galleri Charlotte Lund, Stockholm

Selected Group Exhibitions:

1984	*Indigestion,* P.P.O.W., New York
1985	*Americana,* Whitney Museum of American Art, New York
1986	*Past, Present, Future,* The New Museum of Contemporary Art, New York

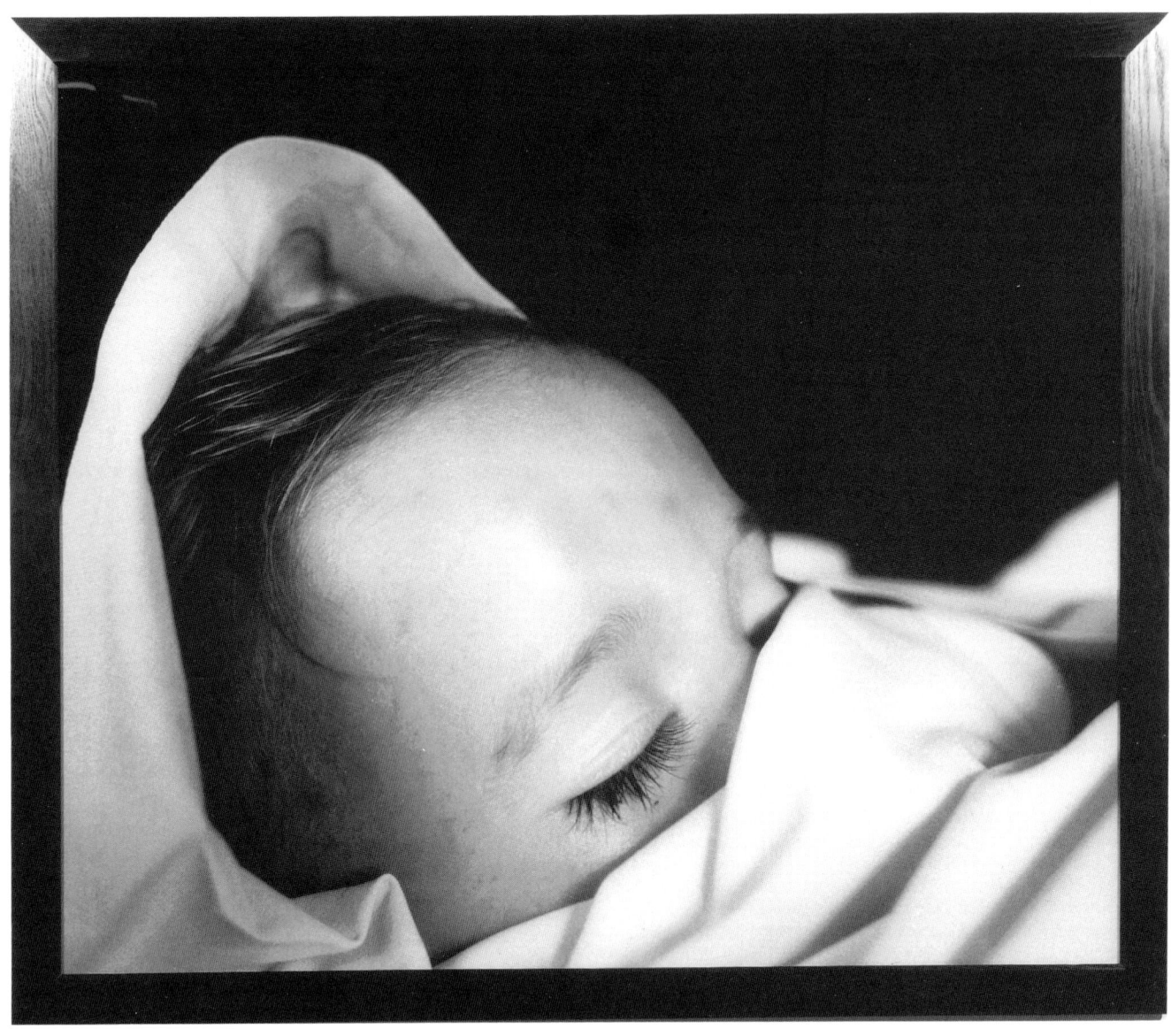

The Morgue (Fatal Meningitis II), **1992, by Andres Serrano.** Photograph by Geoffrey Clements.

1987	*Scared to Breathe,* Perspektief, Rotterdam, Netherlands
1988	*FOCO,* Circulo de Bellas Artes, Madrid
	Female (Re)Production, White Columns, New York
1989	*The Photography of Invention,* National Museum of Art, Smithsonian Institution, Washington, D.C.
	The Indominatable Spirit, International Center of Photography, Midtown, New York
1990	*U.S.A. Annees, 90,* Galerie Antoine Candau, l'Espace-Dieu, Paris
	Figuring the Body, Museum of Fine Arts, Boston
1991	*Sguardo Di Medusa,* Castillo di Rivoli, Turin, Italy
	Erotica Desire, Con Rumore, Rotterdam, Netherlands
1992	The Saatchi Collection, London
	Dirt and Domesticity: Constructions of the Feminine, Whitney Museum of American Art, New York
1993	*Aperto 93,* Venice Biennale
	The Naming of the Colors, White Columns, New York
1994	*GIFT,* The InterArt Center, New York
	Printemps de la Photo a Charos, Cahors Festival, France

Don't Leave Me This Way: Art in the Age of Aids, National Gallery of Australia, Canberra
Black Male, Whitney Museum of American Art, New York
The Little House on the Prairie, Marc Jancou Gallery, London
Face Off: The Portrait in Recent Art, Institute of Contemporary Art, University of Pennsylvania (travelled)
Pour les Chapelles de Vence, Espace des Arts de Chalon-sur-Saône, France; Musée d'art contemporain de Bordeaux, Bordeaux, France
Many Dogs Run Wild. . . . Adlercreutz-Björkholmen, Stockholm

Collections:

University of Alabama; Institute of Contemporary Art, Amsterdam; Baltimore Museum of Art, Maryland; Capc Musee d'Art Contemporain, Bordeaux, France; Institute of Contemporary Art, Boston; Art Institute of Chicago; FRAC, Cluny, France; Israel Museum, Jerusalem; Cintas Foundation, Miami;

Centro Cultural Arte Contemporaneo, Mexico; New Museum of Contemporary Art, New York; Allen Art Museum, Oberlin, Ohio.

Publications:

On SERRANO: Book—*Actes Sud, Andres Serrano Le Sommeil de la Surface,* texts by Daniel Arasse, Jean-Louis Schefer, Jean-Michel Rey, Philippe Blon and Stephen Bann, 1994. **Articles**—"Andres Serrano" by Vince Aletti in *The Village Voice,* 22 March 1988; "Serrano—Ain't Seen Nothing Yet" by Liz Lufkin in *San Francisco Chronicle,* 21 September 1989; "Taboo Artist: Serrano Speaks" by Derek Guthrie in *New Art Examiner,* September 1989; "Serrano's New Photos Achieve Blasphemy by Gossip" by D.D. Coleman in *The New York Observer,* 18 December 1989; "Andres Serrano" by Dennis Cooper *ArtForum,* March 1989; "Andres Serrano" by Tobey Crockett in *Splash,* April 1989; "Andres Serrano: Provocation and Spirituality" by Michael Brenson in *The New York Times,* 29 December 1989; "Serrano Answers Congressional Critics" by Allen Parachini in *The Los Angeles Times,* 13 August 1989; "Reviews/Andres Serrano" by Frances De Vuono in *Art News,* April 1990; "Andres Serrano" by Josh Decter in *Flash Art,* March/June 1990; "Andres Serrano" by Gretchen Faust in *Arts,* March 1991; "Andres Serrano Eye on the Klan" by Dianne Zuckerman in *Daily Camera,* 18 January 1991; "Andres Serrano" by Megumi Sasaki in *Esquire,* June 1991; "Andres Serrano" by Ben Lifson in *ArtForum,* April 1993; "Andres Serrano: The Morgue" by Mark Durden and Jim Harold in *Creative Camera,* February-March 1992; "L'Amerique, Ses Senateurs et Ses Tabous" by Andrew Decker in *Beaux Arts,* February 1993; "Andres Serrano: In Conversation with Simon Watney" in *Talking Art I, ICA Documents 12,* London 1993; Essays by Melissa E Feldman and Benjamin H D Buchloh in *Face-Off: The Portrait in Recent Art,* University of Pennsylvania, 1994.

*   *   *

Andres Serrano is best known for the astonishingly virulent right-wing maelstrom that raged around him in the late 1980s. A coalition of American ideologies, including leading figures from the Church and from the far-right in politics, took exception to his *Piss Christ* (1987) and in particular to the idea that government (through the National Endowment for the Arts) should finance work of Serrano's type. He was not alone. Martin Scorsese's film *The Last Temptation of Christ* ran into the same trouble as famously did, Robert Mapplethorpe, Sally Mann and Jock Sturges. Certain types of expression (notably pornography in its various forms, but also blasphemy and lack of patriotism) were deemed un-American by such experts in the arts as Senator Jesse Helms. It was in many ways an infantile debate, and the election of Bill Clinton and resultant muting (however temporary) of the extreme right did a great deal to tone it down. It is not fanciful to think that the late 1980s routing of Communism led those whose political strength lies in fear to seek an enemy within. Artists provided the perfect target and Serrano happened to be one of them.

The censorship panic was deeply unpleasant, with its moral majority language and its overt style of the witch-hunt, but in the end it did mostly good to the artists involved. The National Arts become a little more timid, but government spending on the arts in the United States is so small a proportion of the whole that it hardly mattered. It simply made it harder to make fair judgement on the art concerned.

Andres Serrano is a Catholic of mixed descent whose art has long sprung from the ritual and iconographies of the Church in which he was brought up. He has said and it is a perfectly honourable position for an artist to adopt, that "I've always believed there was no such thing as the sacred without the profane—and in some cases it's hard to tell the difference." He has chosen to operate in the gap between the two. His use of bodily fluids could be explained by the simple desire to shock that his detractors assume (and there is no doubt that in his less successful pieces it is hard to explain satisfactorily), but at best he uses those fluids as pigments heavily laden with meaning. Blood, sperm and milk are psychologically laden substances which conjure a wealth of responses in the viewer, of which only one may shock or distaste. The fuss of the late 1980s made it necessary to take sides about Serrano's imagery before the full analysis had been made.

Serrano is a highly technically competent photographer whose pictures have the kind of seductive surface perfection that we expect from advertising. He has made quite a few images which pretend to a depth of sophistication that

they simply do not have—his *Morgue* series from 1992 remains a catalogue of the effects of death upon the frame rather than any kind of meditation upon them—but he has also made images whose assured power and (in this postmodern day most unfashionably) whose beauty class them well outside the ordinary. Further, it is clear that Serrano's concerns are utterly appropriate to the time and the society in which he lives. To make a series of pictures called *Ejaculate in Trajectory* in the era of AIDS might have been the nastiest kind of band wagon jumping, but has been made to work brilliantly. It seems so obviously right to be concerned about the things that Serrano is concerned about that it would have been pleasant to judge the pictures without having to nail one's colours to the mast.

At the root of Serrano's work are powerful opposing pairs: faith and iconoclasm, certainty and doubt. He has invented a spartan, pared down way of photographing these things which is properly his own. He has managed to make art about the strange shape of religion in the United States now, spirituality and commercialism welded. He has made some wonderful series and some very much less so. He has neither horns and forked tail nor wings and a white robe, which is exactly how it should be; and who can blame him if from time to time he makes a piece which gets him a little more notoriety? He may not have been an innocent, but the notoriety was thrown at him all the same.

—Francis Hodgson

SHERMAN, Cindy.

Nationality: American. **Born:** Glen Ridge, New Jersey, 19 January 1954. **Education:** Graduated with a B.A. from New York State University College at Buffalo. **Family:** Married to Michel Auder. **Agent:** Metro Pictures, 150 Greene Street, New York, New York 10012, U.S.A.

Individual Exhibitions:

1979	Hallwalls, Buffalo
1980	Contemporary Arts Museum, Houston
	Metro Pictures, New York
	The Kitchen, New York
1981	Metro Pictures, New York
	Saman Gallery, Genoa, Italy
	Young/Hoffman Gallery, Chicago
1982	Galerie Chantal Crousel, Paris
	Larry Gagosian Gallery, Los Angeles
	Metro Pictures, New York
	Texas Gallery, Houston
	The Stedelijk Museum, Amsterdam (travelled to Gewad, Ghent, Belgium; Watershed Gallery, Bristol, England; John Hansard Gallery, University of Southampton, England; Palais Stutterheim, Erlangen, Germany; Haus am Waldsee, Berlin; Centre d'Art Contemporain, Geneva; Sonja Henie-Niels Onstadt Foundation, Copenhagen; Louisiana Museum, Humlebaek, Denmark)
1983	Fine Arts Center Gallery, State University of New York at Stony Brook (travelled to Zilka Gallery, Wesleyan University)
	Galerie Schellmann & Kluser, Munich, Germany
	Metro Pictures, New York
	Musee d'Art et d'Industrie de Saint Etienne, France
	Rhona Hoffman Gallery, Chicago
	The St. Louis Art Museum
1984	Akron Art Museum (travelled to the Institute of Contemporary Art, Philadelphia; Museum of Art, Carnegie Institute,

Untitled, **1989 (original in colour).** Photograph by Cindy Sherman.

Pittsburgh; Des Moines Art Center; Baltimore Museum
of Art)
Monika Spruth Galerie, Cologne, Germany
Laforet Museum of Tokyo, Tokyo
Seibu Gallery of Contemporary Art, Tokyo
1985   Metro Pictures, New York
Westfalischer Kunstverein, Munster, Germany
1986   Galerie Crousel-Hussenot, Paris
Portland Art Museum, Oregon
The New Aldrich Museum, Ridgefield, Connecticut
Wadsworth Atheneum, Hartford
1987   Hoffman-Borman Gallery, Los Angeles
Metro Pictures, New York
Provinciaal Museum, Hasselt, Belgium
Whitney Museum of American Art, New York (travelled to the
Institute of Contemporary Art, Boston; Dallas Museum
of Art)
1988   Galeria Comicos, Lisbon
Monika Spruth Galerie, Cologne, Germany
La Maquina Espanola, Madrid
Galeria Lia Ruma, Naples, Italy
1989   Galerie Crousel-Robelin, Paris
Galerie Der Wiener Secession, Vienna
Galerie Pierre Hubert, Geneva, Switzerland
Metro Pictures, New York
National Art Gallery, Wellington (travelled to the Waikato
Museum of Art and History, New Zealand)
1990   Monika Spruth Galerie, Cologne, Germany
Kunst-Station, St. Peter, Cologne, Germany
Linda Cathcart Gallery, Santa Monica
Metro Pictures, New York
Padiglione d'arte contemporanas, Milan, Italy
University Art Museum, Berkeley
1991   Basel Kunsthalle, Switzerland (travelled to Staatsgalerie
moderner Kunst, Munich, Germany; Whitechapel Gallery,
London)
1992   Monika Spruth Galerie, Cologne, Germany
Galerie Six Friedrich, Munich, Germany
Linda Cathcart Gallery, Santa Monica
Metro Pictures, New York
Museo de Monterrey, Mexico
1993   Galerie Ascan Crone, Hamburg, Germany
Galerie Ghislaine Hussenot, Paris
Galleri Susanne Ottesen, Copenhagen
Tel Aviv Museum of Art, Tel Aviv, Israel
Texas Gallery, Houston
Wall Gallery, Fukuoka, Japan
Centre Pompidou, Paris
1994   *Cindy Sherman Untitled 1987-1991,* Galerie Borgmann
Capitain, Cologne, Germany

Selected Group Exhibitions:

1976   *Hallwalls,* Artists Space, New York
1977   Albright-Knox Gallery, Buffalo
1978   *Four Artists,* Artists' Space, New York
1979   *Re-figuration,* Max Protetch Gallery, New York
1980   *Ils se Disent Peintres, Ils se Disent Photographes,* Musee d'Art
Moderne, Paris
1981   *Autoportraits,* Centre Pompidou, Paris
1982   *Urban Kisses,* Institute of Contemporary Art, London
1983   *Biennial Exhibition,* Whitney Museum of American Art,
New York
1984   *Color Photographs: Recent Acquisitions,* Museum of Modern
Art, New York
1985   *Anniottanta,* Galleria Comunale d'Arte Moderna,
Bologna, Italy

1986   *Staging the Self: Self-Portrait Photography 1840s-1980s,*
National Portrait Gallery, London (travelled to Plymouth
Arts Centre; John Hansard Gallery, Southampton; Ikon
Gallery, Birmingham)
1987   *Avant-Garde in the Eighties,* Los Angeles County Museum of Art
1988   *Presi Per Incantamento,* Padiglione d'Arte Contemporanea di
Milano, Milan, Italy
1989   *The Photography of Invention: American Pictures of the 1980s,*
National Museum of American Art, Smithsonian Institution,
Washington, D.C.
1990   *Energies,* The Stedelijk Museum, Amsterdam
1991   *Self-Portraits of Women in the Eighties,* Tokyo Metropolitan
Museum of Photography, Tokyo
1992   *Pleasures and Terrors of Domestic Comfort,* Museum of
Modern Art, New York
1993   *Commodity Image,* International Center for Photography, New
York (travelled to ICA, Boston)
1994   Galerie Samia Saouma, Paris

Collections:

Art Gallery of New South Wales, Australia; Art Gallery of Ontario, Canada;
Burchfield Art Center; Carnegie Museum of Art, Pittsburgh; Centre Georges
Pompidou, Paris; Centro de Arte Reina Sofia, Madrid; Moderna Museet,
Stockholm; Mount Holyoke College Art Museum, South Hadley, Massachu-
setts; Musee d'art Contemporain, Montreal, Canada; Museum Boymans-van
Beuningen, Rotterdam, Netherlands; Museum Folkwang, Essen, Germany;
Museum of Art, Carnegie Institute, Pittsburgh; The Corcoran Gallery of Art,
Washington, D.C.

Publications:

By SHERMAN: Articles—*Bomb,* spring/summer 1985; *Flash Art,* October/
November 1985; *Art Press,* January 1992.

On SHERMAN: Articles—"Cindy Sherman" by Valentine Tatransky in
Arts Magazine, June 1980; "Cindy Sherman, Metro Pictures" by Richard
Flood in *Artforum,* March 1981; "Cindy Sherman, Metro Pictures" by Lynn
Zelavansky in *Flash Art,* March/April; "Cindy Sherman: A Playful and
Political Post Modernist" by Andy Grundberg in *The New York Times,* 22
November 1981; "Cindy Sherman Untitled Film Stills" in *Paris Review,*
November 1982; "Cindy Sherman" by Grace Glueck in *The New York Times,*
22 October 1982; "One Woman Show: Cindy Sherman Puts Her Best Face
Forward" by Rosemary Robotham in *Life Magazine,* June 1984; "Moi Cindy
Sherman" by Anne DeMargerie and Alain Lopez in *Liberation,* 12 August
1984; "Quel est le vrai visage de Cindy Sherman" by Herve Guibert in *Le
Monde*; "Cindy Sherman" by Freddy Langer in *Frankfurter Allgemeine
Magazin,* September 1984; "Cindy Sherman" in *Camera Austria,* 15/16;
"Cindy Sherman" in *Apres Magazine,* Japan, January 1985; "Today's
American Works: Cindy Sherman" in *Photo Japan,* February 1985; "Cindy
Sherman's Dark Fantasies Evoke a Primitive Past" by Andy Grundberg in *The
New York Times,* 20 October 1985; "Cindy Sherman at Metro Pictures" by
Deborah Drier in *Art in America,* January 1986; "Cindy Sherman" in
Kunstforum, June-August 1986; "Cindy Sherman's Tales of Terror" by
Larry Frascella in *Aperture,* Summer 1986; "Cindy Sherman" by Kim Levin
in *The Village Voice,* 19 May 1987; "Sherman's March" by Gerald Marzorati
in *Vanity Fair,* August 1987; "Photographer Cindy Sherman Shoots Her Best
Model—Herself" by Michael Small in *People,* November 1987; "Cindy
Sherman: Uno Es Siempre Otro" by L. Brea in *Sur Express,* Madrid,
December/January; "About Face: Cindy Sherman's self-transforms" by
Lisa Liebman in *Mirabella,* October 1989; "Art: Cindy Sherman's Latest
Series" by Kay Larsen in *New York Magazine,* 29 January 1990; "Cindy
Sherman" by Laura Cottingham in *Contemporanea,* May 1990; "Cindy

Sherman: A Painted Lady" by Christopher Knight in *The Los Angeles Times,* 8 June 1990; "Cindy Sherman at Metro Pictures" by Charles Hagen in *The New York Times,* 24 April 1992; "Sherman's Inferno" by Elizabeth Hess in *The Village Voice,* 5 May 1992; "Cindy Sherman: Burning the House Down" by Jan Avgikos in *Artforum,* January 1993; "The New Cindy Sherman Collection" by Jim Lewis in *Harper's Bazaar,* May 1993; "Cindy Sherman at Ghislaine Hussenot" by Francoise-Claire Prudhon in *Flash Art,* November/ December 1993; "Cindy Sherman and the Female Grotesque" by Emily B. Greenberg in *Art Criticism,* Vol. 9, No. 2, 1994.

*   *   *

Cindy Sherman is the representative new photographer of the 1980s. Although she has frequently and publicly disclaimed the title "photographer," preferring the rubric of "artist who uses photography." Her remarkably sustained and inventive work has made an indelible impression upon the photographic medium. Sherman's brilliance at translating the critical preoccupations of her time into purely pictorial currency has made her a success among collectors, critics, curators and the general public. Her talent is for making the ubiquitous "issues" and "theory" of the early 1980s art world into compelling and subjective works of art. Unlike Sherrie Levine, the other major figure of American photographic postmodernism, Sherman comments very little on her own work, which itself communicates more in subjective than in analytical, critical terms.

Sherman's photographic work has been an astounding string of photo-theatrical impersonations. Occasionally wrongly described as self-portraiture, Sherman's work has nothing at all to do with self (Sherman's self, that is) but everything to do with role-playing. At first, as in her landmark *Untitled Film Stills* of the late 1970s, Sherman costumed and photographed herself in the guises of feminine roles assigned or invented by society, as represented in B-movies. Her early 1980s colour work continued to inventory characters and plot lines socially constructed for women, and in 1983-84 she began to explore and erase the boundaries between fashion photography, contemporary femininity and fine art photography, by photographing herself in high fashion clothing, in a series of images commissioned by a fashion designer for advertising purposes, but also exhibited by Sherman as her work. Later work then took a dramatic and darker turn into more purely psychological versions of identity and emotion. These powerful photographs seemed less to describe characters, roles and careers than to investigate the inner states of the characters already created.

In 1985 Sherman varied her themes by portraying idiosyncratic and gender-bending images derived from fairy tales. In 1988 she began her series *History Portraits* in which—with even more extraordinary make up and costuming than before—she portrayed herself literally as a series of art historical images, rather than as fictional individuals. This series included images that combined various portraits by Ingres, and others that reached farther back into the history of old master painting. In 1986, an apocalyptic violence swept through the closed world of Sherman's portrayals, and her photographs became complex tableaux rather than merely portraits. Garbage became prominent in the foreground of her images and disgusting foods as well as pools of vomit suggesting a violent purgative body rather than the decorative, seductive ones of her earlier works. The figures in these photographs, still played by Sherman, fell victim to unexplained disasters (including what seem to be explosions) and tumbled into more fearful and disturbing postures than in any previous images.

Throughout Sherman's career to date critics have applauded her work, but also often asked "what next?" The photographs of 1986-88 seemed an almost impossible act to follow, and indeed they marked a turning point in Sherman's career, after which she discontinued the use of her own presence in the photographs. Earlier works had frequently included prostheses of various types, but in 1992, suddenly her photographs were inhabited only by plastic dolls of the sort sold as sexual toys.

She then moved from sex toys to mail order teaching aids, often of internal organs, used in medical schools. The photographic field was no longer a space that she or any real individual could inhabit and her next series of photographs employed medical and plastic models of body parts exclusively. Some of the photographs, in tight close up, focussed only upon strange still life arrangements of plastic sex organs, often painted and adapted so as to suggest painful and diseased conditions. These images reached far beyond the conventions of pornography to a terrifying and intense investigation of the conditions of bodily repulsion, desire and fear as found within the individual, no longer as represented on the wider screen of mass cultural imagery. In little more than fifteen years, Sherman's work has changed from being clever and critical to become intense and almost possessed in its expressionism. She has neither repeated herself nor failed to produce work which vindicated her renown and it is impossible to predict what will come next.

—Ellen Handy

SHINOYAMA, Kishin.

Nationality: Japanese. **Born:** Tokyo, 3 December 1930. **Education:** Studied photography at Nihon University, Tokyo, 1961-63. **Family:** Married Akemi Shinoyama in 1979; child: Naonori. **Career:** Photographer, Light Publicity Company, Tokyo, 1961-68. Freelance photographer, Tokyo, since 1968. **Recipient:** New Photographer Prize, Japan Photo Critics Association, 1966; Photographer of the Year Award, Japan Photographic Society, 1970; New Talent Award, Japan Art Academy and Ministry of Education, Tokyo, 1973; Annual Prize, Kodansha Publishing Company, Tokyo, 1973. **Address:** 6-3-6 Roppongi, Minatoku, Tokyo 106, Japan.

Individual Exhibitions:

1968	*The Birth,* Ginza Salon, Tokyo
1970	*Nudes,* Ginza Matsuzakaya Department Store, Tokyo
1972	*Kabuki Theater: Tamasaburo,* Daimaru Department Store, Tokyo
1973	*Iramours 106,* Daimaru Department Store, Tokyo
1976	*House,* Odakyu Department Store, Tokyo (travelled to the Biennale, Venice, and the Galerie Municipale du Chateau d'Eau, Toulouse, France)
	Arabia, Mitsukoshi Department Store, Tokyo
1977	*The Universe of Tamasaburo,* Seibu Department Store, Tokyo
	Momoe Yamaguchi, Ao Gallery, Tokyo (with Hajime Sawatari)
1979	*Dai Geki-Sha,* Seibu Department Store, Tokyo
1980	*Momoe Yamaguchi, The Actress,* Seibu Department Store, Tokyo
1981	*Silk Road: China,* Seibu Department Store, Tokyo
	Minolta Photo Space, Tokyo

Selected Group Exhibitions:

1970	*Photokina,* Cologne
1975	*Rencontres Internationales de la Photographie,* Arles, France
1977	*Neue Fotografie aus Japan,* Kulturhaus, Graz, Austria (travelled to the Museum des 20. Jahrhunderts, Vienna)
1979	*Japanese Photography Today and Its Origin,* Galleria d'Arte Moderna, Bologna (travelled to the Palazzo Reale, Milan; Palais des Beaux-Arts, Brussels; and Institute of Contemporary Arts, London; Museum für Kunst und Gewerbe, Hamburg; Gemeente Museum, Arnhem; Pulchri Studio, The Hague, 1979-80)
	Japan: A Self-Portrait, International Center of Photography, New York
1980	*The Imaginary Photo Museum,* Kunsthalle, Cologne
1982	*38 Japanese Photographers,* Zeit-Foto Salon, Tokyo
1983	*Die fotografische Sammlung,* Museum Folkwang, Essen, West Germany
1984	*Sammlung Gruber,* Museum Ludwig, Cologne

Collections:

Museum of Modern Art, New York; Museum Ludwig, Cologne; Museum Folkwang, Essen, Germany.

Publications:

By SHINOYAMA: Books—*Kishin Shinoyama and 28 Girls,* Tokyo 1968; *Nudes,* Tokyo 1970; *The World of Kishin Shinoyama,* Tokyo 1970; *Olele Olala (Carnival of Brazil),* Tokyo 1971; *Kabuki Oyama (Male Actress) Tamasaburo,* Tokyo 1972; *Hi, Marie,* Tokyo 1972; *Iramours 106,* Tokyo 1973; *A Fine Day,* Tokyo 1975; *Meaning of the House,* Tokyo 1975; *Paris,* Tokyo 1977; *Tamasaburo,* Tokyo 1978; *135 Girl Friends,* Tokyo 1979; *Venice,* Tokyo 1980; *Momoe Yamaguchi,* Tokyo 1980; *Silk Road,* Tokyo 1981.

On SHINOYAMA: Books—*4 Meister der Erotischen Fotografie* by Alain Robbe-Grillet and Yukio Mishima and others, Munich 1970; *Neue Fotografie aus Japan,* exhibition catalogue, by Otto Breicha, Ben Watanabe and John Szarkowski, Graz and Vienna 1977; *Japan: A Self-Portrait,* exhibition catalogue, by Shoji Yamagishi, Cornell Capa and Taeko Tomioka, New York 1979; *Japanese Photography Today and Its Origin* by Attilio Colombo and Isabella Doniselli, Bologna 1979; *The Imaginary Photo Museum* by Helmut Gernsheim, Renate and L. Fritz Gruber and others, Cologne 1981, London 1982; *Nude Photographs of Japan,* with text by Shiroyasu Suzuki, Tokyo 1981; *Sammlung Gruber: Photographie des 20. Jahrhunderts,* exhibition catalogue, with foreword by Siegfried Gohr, Cologne 1984. **Articles**—"Kishin Shinoyama" in *Camera* (Lucerne), April 1969; "Madchen: 3 Meister der Erotischen Fotografie" in *Film und Foto Prisma* (Munich), September 1970; "Kishin Shinoyama: Women as Design" in *Modern Photography Annual,* New York 1971; "4 Masters of Erotic Photography" by G.S. Whittet in *Art and Artists* (London), August 1971; "Shinoyama" in *Photo* (Paris), January 1972; "Kishin Shinoyama" in *Asahi Camera* (Tokyo), May 1972; "Une Couple et l'Enchanteur Shinoyama" in *Photo* (Paris), May 1972; "Kishin Shinoyama: Maria's Seven Days in Molokai" in *Asahi Camera* (Tokyo), October 1972; "A Dazzling Slide Show" in *Photography Year 1976,* by the Time-Life editors, New York 1976.

*

Naturally, a photographer cannot see the world after his death or before his birth. Therefore, I want to gaze at the period in which I live, and to record it.

—Kishin Shinoyama

*   *   *

The popular success of Kishin Shinoyama in Japan goes beyond recognition as a photographer of diverse talent to that of celebrity. Shinoyama is both the exponent and product of a photographic market that has exploded on the wave of the flamboyant commercialism of Japanese economic prosperity. He is a household name; his face frequents the television commercial or the illuminated billboard. His reputation has been sustained by a prolific output of work as well as by his enormous variety of style and subject.

He came from a background in advertising. His first work was published in *Camera Mainichi* in 1966, including the series "Dancer." In the same year he was awarded the New Photographer Prize by the Photo Critics Association for the "Sisters of Vajra." His first exhibition, *The Birth,* was held in the Nikon Salon in 1968. By 1970 his reputation as a photographer of nudes was established with an exhibition in the Ginza and the publication of his first two books by Mainichi. His early work also included a series on tattoos, executed in the style of Ukiyo-e prints. As opposed to the commercial style of much of his nude work, such as the "Twin" series, the tattoo studies are evidence of a curious exploration of the strange survival of an Edo aesthetic. The photographs are intimate and uncontrived portraits of a Tokyo subculture.

In September 1970 Shinoyama photographed Yukio Mishima only two months before the writer's suicide. The series was to be called "Death of a Man" and was intended for publication in a magazine called *Blood and Roses.* Shinoyama did not release the series, though several of the pictures later appeared in the *Sunday Times Magazine* in London. The series constituted a

morbid theatre under the direction of the writer. Shinoyama unknowingly staged a dress-rehearsal for the writer's death, including the famous portrait of Mishima enacting the martyrdom of Saint Sebastian after Guido Reni. Two years later Shinoyama exhibited and published another theatrical series of studies of the Kabuki actor Tamasaburo.

Shinoyama has travelled widely, publishing work from the Middle East, Brazil, Paris and Australia, where he worked for Qantas. His most outstanding achievement is the large and ambitious series on the Japanese house, exhibited in Tokyo and at the Venice *Biennale* in 1976. Here he used large format colour to produce studies of the Japanese domestic environment in total contrast to normal architectural photography. While exploring the spaces of Japanese interiors, he has included all the details of daily life and juxtaposed traditional arrangements with the mundane utensils of modern Japan. He has not photographed houses as models of design, but as revealing statements of their inhabitants.

Kishin Shinoyama's output is both enormous and unpredictable.

—Mark Holborn

SHIRAKAWA, Yoshikazu.

Nationality: Japanese. **Born:** Kawanoe City, Ehime Prefecture, 28 January 1935. **Education:** Kawanoe High School, 1950-53; studied photography at Nihon University College of Art, Tokyo, 1955-57. **Family:** Married Kazuko Miyamoto in 1964; daughter: Eri. **Career:** Literature and Arts Program Producer, Nippon Broadcasting System, Tokyo, 1957-58; Chief Cameraman, Fuji Telecasting Company, Tokyo, 1958-60. Freelance photographer, Tokyo, since 1960. Lecturer, Nihon Photography School, Tokyo, 1960, and Japan Photographic Academy, Tokyo, 1967; Chief Instructor and Chairman of the Board of Directors, Kanto Photo Technique Academy, Tokyo, 1974. **Recipient:** Japanese Ministry of Health and Welfare Award, 6 times, 1956-61; Special Prize, National Park Photo Contest, Tokyo, 1960; First Prize, *Nika Exhibition,* Tokyo, 1968; Annual Award, Japan Professional Photographers Society, 1970; Art Prize, Mainichi Newspapers, Tokyo, 1972; Ministry of Education Award, 22nd Fine Art Grand Prix, 1972; Photographer of the Year Award, American Society of Magazine Photographers, 1981. **Agent:** The Image Bank, Orion Service and Trading Co. Inc., 55-1 Kanda-Jimbocho, Chiyoda-ku, Tokyo 101, Japan. **Address:** 2-12-15 Takanawa, Minato-tu, Tokyo 108, Japan.

Individual Exhibitions:

1957	*Landscapes,* Konishiroku Gallery, Tokyo
1969	*Mountains,* Tokyu Department Store, Tokyo
1970	Nikon Salon, Tokyo (commemorating Japan Professional Photographers Society Annual Award)
1971	*The Seat of the Gods,* Odakyu Department Store, Tokyo (toured Japan)
1975	*Eternal America,* Odakyu Department Store, Tokyo (toured Japan and the United States)
1979	*The Land of the Bible,* Odakyu Department Store, Tokyo (toured Japan)
1981	*The World of Yoshikazu Shirakawa,* Nikon House, New York (toured Japan)

Selected Group Exhibitions:

1968	*Nika Exhibition,* Tokyo
1975	*The Land: 20th Century Landscape Photographs Selected by Bill Brandt,* Victoria and Albert Museum, London (travelled to the National Gallery, Edinburgh; Ulster Museum, Belfast; and National Museum of Wales, Cardiff, 1976)
1979	*Japanese Photography Today and Its Origin,* Galleria d'Arte Moderna, Bologna, Italy (travelled to the Palazzo Reale, Milan; Palais des Beaux-Arts, Brussels; and the Institute of Contemporary Arts, London; Museum für Kunst und

Gewerbe, Hamburg; Gemeente Museum, Arnhem; Pulchri
Studio, The Hague, 1979-80)
1980   *The Imaginary Photo Museum,* Kunsthalle, Cologne

Collections:

Victoria and Albert Museum, London; Museo de Arte Moderno, Mexico City.

Publications:

By SHIRAKAWA: Technical books—*Cameras and How to Use Them,*
Tokyo 1956; *Exposure and Its Determination,* Tokyo 1957. **Books of photographs**—White Mountains, Tokyo 1960; *The Alps,* with text by Jeen Kruuse
and Max A. Wyss, Tokyo 1969, Lucerne, Frankfurt and London 1973;
Mountains, Tokyo 1971; *The Himalayas,* with text by Arnold Toynbee and
others, Tokyo 1971, New York 1973; *The Seat of the Gods,* Tokyo 1971;
Mountain Photography, Tokyo 1973; *Eternal America,* with text by Fred M.
Paccard, Tokyo 1975, New York 1976; *The Land of the New Testament,* with
text by Asajiro Satowaki, Tokyo 1979; *The Life of Jesus Christ,* Tokyo 1980;
The Land of the Old Testament, with text by Virgil Gheorghui, Tokyo 1980.

On SHIRAKAWA: Books—*The Land: 20th Century Landscape Photo-
graphs Selected by Bill Brandt,* exhibition catalogue, edited by Mark Haworth-
Booth, London 1975; *Japanese Photography Today and Its Origin,* exhibition
catalogue, by Attilio Colombo and Isabella Doniselli, Bologna, Italy 1979;
The Imaginary Photo Museum by Helmut Gernsheim, Renate and L. Fritz
Gruber and others, Cologne 1981, London 1982. **Articles**—"Yoshikazu
Shirakawa: Himalayas" in *Camera* (Lucerne), July 1972; "Alps" in *The
Observer Magazine* (London), 18 November 1973; "Himalayas" by Edward
Hoagland in the *New York Times,* 2 December 1973; "The Majesty of 'House
of Snow' " by Edmund Fuller in the *Wall Street Journal* (New York), 5
December 1973; "The Himalayas" in the *Washington Post,* 9 December
1973; "From Snow Peaks" in *Time* (New York), 17 December 1973;
"Himalayas" in *Newsweek* (New York), 17 December 1973; "Yoshikazu
Shirakawa" in *Camera Mainichi* (Tokyo), February 1974; "Shirakawa Reaches
the Peak" by R. Bradbury in the *Los Angeles Times,* 8 December 1974.

*

Twenty-two years ago, in 1959, I took a leave of absence from the
television station where I was working to make my first trip around the world.
During the trip I stopped in Switzerland and saw the Matterhorn. It changed
my life. On the surface of the lake, like a mirror, there was a red symmetrical
reflection of the mountain at sunrise, and the sky was a beautiful golden color.
It was like an image of the Buddhist world of "higan." After I returned to
Japan, I immediately left the TV station and returned to the Alps. Since then, I
have photographed the Alps on and off for more than 12 years.

I was in a different world when I saw the sunrise over the Monch and
Wetterhorn; the sunset over the Mont Blanc mountains and the scenery
surrounding them were so beautiful that I felt faint, I was so moved. Each day I
became more deeply moved. What impressed me was the beauty and the
greatness of the earth on which we live. I dreamed of showing that emotion to
all the people in the world through my photography. It was the start of the
series "Rediscovery of the Earth."

Then, in 1967, I began to photograph the Himalayas from Bhutan in the
East to Afghanistan in the West. I spent four years travelling almost 3,000
kilometers along these gigantic mountains across seven countries. There are
14 mountain peaks of 8,000m (24,000 feet), more than 300 peaks of 7,000m
(21,000 feet), and there were so many 6,000m mountains (18,000 feet) that it
was impossible to count the exact number of them. A huge chain of mountains,
completely separated from the world of men. During my travels, sometimes I
became sick from the high altitude and lost consciousness. Other times, I was
locked in the snow. For a week I was without food and almost died of hunger.
But I made up my mind to escape from death. I walked and walked for two
days and nights in the deep, threatening snow. It was not a few times that I
thought I was going to die. I experienced the knowledge that one's life is very

small within the vastness of the universe. It was in the Himalayas that I
realized I believed in God.

I started shooting in America in 1971. I wanted to photograph the world of
God there. I wanted to photograph God's world in places where people lived,
not separated from the world of man. I thought of doing that because I
wondered what our ancestors saw when they first started living on this planet
Earth. I believe that they did not see the desert of Death Valley, the Grand
Canyon or Mt. McKinley only as material; I believe that they saw Nature and
the universe behind Nature; I believe they saw the existence of the great spirit
and they respected it. When they felt reverence for that spirit, then they were
not apes but men. And it made them develop spiritually. That realization of the
great spirit in the universe was the one and only absolute reason for mankind to
have become what we are now. Therefore, I excluded from my pictures of the
American landscape all men and man-made objects such as roads, dams,
homes, etc., in order to pursue the nature that our ancestors (apes) had when
they started living here 1,800,000 years ago. It was my effort to find some way
to recover the essence of our humanity.

Some may say that people of our age have already lost these pure feelings
towards Nature and the universe. However, as far as we are human beings, it
exists in the depths of our hearts. If not, and if men are mere physical beings,
then words like "dignity" and "rights" have no meaning. And, when I came
to feel that way, there was only one straight way to go further—the Bible.

In 1977 I started working toward visualizing the words of God. I spent
three years visiting 251 holy places in 14 countries to put into images the
important sayings of the Old and New Testament, including my own favorite
chapter and verse. In the Old Testament, Genesis starts with the following: "In
the Beginning, God created heaven and earth. And the earth was without form
and void, and darkness was upon the face of the deep. And the spirit of God
moved upon the face of the waters." My book also starts with a picture that
says the same words. However, I had days of anxiety because the actual Holy
Land is a wilderness of scattered pebbles. It was far from photogenic, yet I had
to take pictures that expressed images at the time of the Bible; otherwise, my
photography would have lost its meaning. (Photographing the Alps and the
Himalayas was less difficult in this respect, as I tried to photograph them just
as they are.)

In the case of Jerusalem, for example, pictures of a beautiful Jerusalem
would not be enough; they would also have to depict a Jerusalem of blood and
war, because after the death of Christ, that city was invaded and destroyed by
enemies more than 10 times. Another example: in order to recapture the
natural calamities that occurred on the death of Christ, as recorded in the Bible,
I climbed to the top of Mount Olive about 50 times to photograph lightning
striking the land.

Have there been other times when people talked about the necessity of
recovering human nature as we do today? Do we talk about it more now
because we have lost the holy spirit? Destruction of spiritual values is surely
one of today's greatest problems. If my photography has helped make people
think of these spiritual values and has caused even one person to reflect on God
as a result of seeing my pictures of the world of the Bible, then my efforts were
not meaningless. "To recover human nature by rediscovering the earth"—
that is my ideology, and that is the foundation of my photography. The
important thing for mankind now is not progress in science but the recovery of
humanity—the renaissance of the human spirit. It is my task to think about
what human beings are, what it means to live, and to share those thoughts with
others.

—Yoshikazu Shirakawa

*   *   *

Yoshikazu Shirakawa injects an intense personality into his portrayal of
the severe and stern side of nature. He bases his work on two themes: the
rediscovery of the earth and the rejuvenation of humanism.

Shirakawa's works precisely record nature's grandeur and its torturous
side in a noble yet mystical approach. He attempts to capture the most minute
details, beyond the usual range of human vision.

—Norihiko Matsumoto

SHISHKIN, Arkadii (Vasilyevich).

Nationality: Russian. **Born:** Kukarka, Vyatka, now Kirov, 6 February 1899. **Education:** Attended primary school in Kukarka, 1906-10; studied with the portrait photographer Nikolai Richter, Kazan, 1910-11. **Military Service:** Served as a volunteer with the Red Army, 1918-22, as a war correspondent and ordinary soldier, 1941-43, and as a photographer for the political department of the 174th Riflemen's Division of the Red Army, 1943-45. **Career:** Worked as an apprentice photo-printer, Petrograd, 1912-13; photo-printer, Petrograd, 1913-16; independent photographer, establishing own photo studio, Ekaterinburg, now Sverdlovsk, 1917-18; freelance magazine photographer, working for the local press, Vyatka, 1923-25; Photo-Reporter, *Krestianskaia Gazeta (Peasant Newspaper),* Moscow, 1925-39; Picture Editor, *Krestianka (Peasant Woman)* magazine, Moscow, from 1945. **Recipient:** Second Prize, *Color Photography* exhibition, Moscow, 1954; First Prize, *The 7th Five Year Plan in Action* exhibition, Moscow, 1960; First Prize, *International Competition for a Socialist Photo-Art* exhibition, East Berlin, 1964; Silver Medal, *50 Years of the Great October* exhibition, Moscow, 1967. **Address:** c/o Novosti Press Agency, 2 Pushkin Place, Moscow, Russia.

Individual Exhibitions:

1963	*Arkadii Shishkin 1923-1963,* Moscow (retrospective)
1964	*40 Creative Years,* Minsk
1967	*50 Years of the Soviet Countryside,* Kirov
1969	*Jubilee Exhibition: 70th Birthday,* Moscow
	A Photo-Chronicle of the Soviet Countryside, Tambov
1971	*Photo-Work by S.A. Lobovikov and A. Shishkin,* Moscow

Selected Group Exhibitions:

1935	*Works by Moscow Photo-Masters,* Moscow
1937	*All-Union Exhibition of Photo-Art,* Moscow
1954	*Color Photography,* Moscow
1956	*Works by Moscow Photo-Reporters,* Moscow
1958	*Soviet Photography after 40 Years,* Manezhnaya Gallery, Moscow
1960	*The 7th Five Year Plan in Action,* Moscow
	International Photo-Exhibition, Toronto (toured Europe and travelled to Hong Kong)
1964	*International Competition for a Socialist Photo-Art,* East Berlin
1967	*50 Years of the Great October,* Moscow
1977	*Interpressphoto,* Moscow
1989	*150 Years of Photography,* Central Exhibition Hall, Moscow
1992	*The Utopian Dream: Photography in Soviet Russia, 1918-1939,* Laurence Miller Gallery, New York

Collections:

Novosti Press Agency, Moscow; Shickler/Lafaille Collection, Los Angeles; Museum of Photography, (The Russian Union of Art Photographers), Moscow.

Publications:

By SHISHKIN: Book—*Izbrannye fotografii,* Moscow 1979.

On SHISHKIN: Books—*Arkadii Shishkin* by Anatolii Fomin, Moscow 1979; *Sowjetische Fotografen 1917-1940,* edited by S. Morosov, A. Vartanov, G. Chulakov, O. Suslova and L. Uchtomskaya, Leipzig and Berlin 1980; *Die Sowjetunion Zwischen den Kriegen 1917-1941,* edited by Daniela Mrázková and Vladimìr Remeš, Oldenburg, West Germany 1981; *Pioneers of Soviet Photography* by Grigory Shudakov, Olga Suslova and Lilya Ukhtomskaya, London and Paris 1983; *Anthology of Soviet Photography, Vol. I,* Moscow 1986.

*   *   *

Arkadii Shishkin is one of the Soviet Union's outstanding documentary photographers of agricultural life, and his career encompasses the entire history of the Soviet countryside. Of particular interest are Shishkin's records of the various stages of Soviet farming—the introduction of American and then Soviet tractors in the 1920s and 1930s, the decision "to join or not to join" the state and collective farms as the collectivization program began in 1929, the role of the new Soviet woman on the farm, the development of huge state farms such as "Giant," and the exploits of the various shock-workers who, allegedly, have made records in production and yield. Born in a small village, Shishkin—like his fellow countrymen, the painters Ivan Shishkin (no relation) and Apollinarii and Viktor Vasnetsov—knew the countryside from his earliest childhood, and his photographs betray a deep, psychological understanding of the peasant, the village, the land, the animals.

Although Shishkin did not experiment with the formal devices of the camera, except for a few diagonal compositions and ground level perspectives in the 1920s (e.g., "Collective Sowing in the Crimea," 1933 and "The 'Rusko' Commune," 1931), his photographs are exciting, vivid and appealing. Shishkin was interested in documenting Soviet life. Indeed, the public for whom he created his photographs—the peasants—especially in the 1920s and 1930s—demanded images that were simple, readable and "relevant," and Shishkin did not disappoint them. That is why Shishkin scored an immediate and lasting success as a press photographer for the popular *Krestianskaia gazeta* [Peasant Newspaper], which he joined in 1925, and for other journals such as *Krestiana* [Peasant Woman]. His individual photographs such as "The First Woman Tractor Drivers" and his photographic series such as "Collective Farm Workers—Heroes of the Soviet Union" are clear demonstrations of his commitment.

Shishkin enlisted as a common soldier in 1941, and he stayed at the front until the end of the War. In 1943 he was appointed photographer for the Political Section of the Staff of the 174th Riflemen's Division. But, unfortunately, Shishkin's war photographs were practically all destroyed during action and only a handful survive (e.g., "Victory Has Come!" 1945).

—John E. Bowlt

SHORE, Stephen (Eric).

Nationality: American. **Born:** New York City, 8 October 1947. **Education:** Mainly self-taught in photography, but studied under Minor White, Hotchkiss Workshop, 1970. **Family:** Married Ginger Cramer in 1980, son Nicholas. **Career:** Photographer since 1953. Since 1982, Chairman, Photography Department, Bard College. **Recipient:** National Endowment for the Arts Grant, 1974, 1979; Guggenheim Fellowship, 1975; Special Fellowship, American Academy, Rome, 1980; MacDowell Colony Fellowship, 1993. **Agent:** Pace/MacGill Gallery, 32 East 57th Street, New York, New York 10022, U.S.A.; **Address:** 32 Montgomery Street, P.O. Box 295, Tivoli, New York 12583, U.S.A.

Individual Exhibitions:

1971	Metropolitan Museum of Art, New York
1972	Light Gallery, New York
	Thomas Gibson Fine Arts, London
1973	Light Gallery, New York
1975	Light Gallery, New York
	Phoenix Gallery, San Francisco
	Galerie Schürmann und Kicken, Aachen, West Germany
1976	Museum of Modern Art, New York
	Aaron Siskind/Harry Callahan/Stephen Shore, Silver Image Gallery, Tacoma, Washington
	National Collection of Fine Arts, Washington, D.C.
1977	Delahunty Gallery, Dallas
	Worcester Art Museum, Massachusetts (with Nicholas Nixon)
	Galerie Schürmann und Kicken, Aachen, West Germany
	Kunsthalle, Dusseldorf
	Light Gallery, New York

Luzzara, Italy, **1993.** Photograph by Stephen Shore.

1978   Galerie Gundlach, Hamburg
        Light Gallery, New York
        University of Akron, Ohio
        Galerie Gillespie-De Laage, Paris
        Photogalerie Lange-Irschl, Munich
        Robert Miller Gallery, New York
        Vision Gallery, Boston
1979   La Photogaleria, Madrid
        Ewing Gallery, Washington, D.C.
        Susan Spiritus Gallery, Newport Beach, California
1980   Light Gallery, New York
        Light Gallery, Los Angeles
        Werkstatt für Photographie, West Berlin
        Catskill Center for Photography, Woodstock, New York
        Eloquent Light Gallery, Rochester, Michigan
1982   *Photographs 1974-1981,* Fraenkel Gallery, San Francisco
1984   Art Institute of Chicago
1985   Center for Creative Photography, Tucson
1989   Pace/MacGill, New York
1992   J Paul Getty Museum, Malibu
1995   Westfälischer Kunstverein, Münster, Germany
        Sprengel Museum, Hannover, Germany
        America House, Berlin
        Pace/MacGill Gallery, New York

Selected Group Exhibitions:

1973   *Landscape/Cityscape,* Metropolitan Museum of Art, New York
1975   *New Topographics,* International Museum of Photography,
        George Eastman House, Rochester, New York (travelled to
        the Otis Art Institute, Los Angeles, and the Princeton
        University Art Museum, New Jersey, 1976)
1976   *100 Master Photographs from MOMA,* Baltimore Museum of
        Art (toured the United States)
1977   *Court House: A Photographic Document,* Art Institute of
        Chicago (toured the United States, 1978-79)
1978   *Mirrors and Windows: American Photography since 1960,*
        Museum of Modern Art, New York (toured the United
        States, 1978-80)
1979   *American Photography in the 70s,* Art Institute of Chicago
1980   *Color Works,* Kunsthaus, Zurich
1982   *Counterparts: Form and Emotion in Photographs,* Metropolitan
        Museum of Art, New York (travelled to the Contemporary
        Arts Center, Cincinnati, Ohio; Dallas Museum of Fine Art,
        Texas; San Francisco Museum of Modern Art; Corcoran
        Gallery, Washington, D.C.)
1985   *American Images 1945-80,* Barbican Art Gallery, London
        (toured Britain)
1987   *Photography and Art 1946-86,* Los Angeles County
        Museum of Art
1989   *On the Art of Fixing a Shadow,* National Gallery, Washington
        D.C., and Art Institute of Chicago
1991   *The Pleasures and Terrors of Domestic Comfort,* Museum of
        Modern Art, New York

Collections:

Metropolitan Museum of Art, New York; Museum of Modern Art, New York;
International Museum of Photography, George Eastman House, Rochester,
New York; Museum of Fine Arts, Boston; Library of Congress, Washington,
D.C.; Art Institute of Chicago; Center for Creative Photography, University of
Arizona, Tucson; Stedelijk Museum, Amsterdam; Neue Sammlung, Munich;
Australian National Gallery, Canberra; Whitney Museum, New York.

Publications:

By SHORE: Books—*Andy Warhol,* Boston and Stockholm 1968; *The City,*
New York 1971; *12 Photographs,* portfolio, New York 1976; *The Gardens at
Giverny: A View of Monet's World,* with introduction by John Rewald, New
York and Oxford 1983; *Uncommon Places,* Millerton, New York 1982;

Stephen Shore: Luzzara, Arcadia Edizioni, 1993; *Stephen Shore, Photographs
1973-1993* with essays by Enyeart, Liesbrock & Wesk, Munich 1995; *The
Velvet Years,* London 1995. Articles—"Stephen Shore" in *Camera* (Lucerne),
January 1976; article in *Quest/77* (New York), May 1977.

On SHORE: Books—*Photography Year 1977* by the Time-Life editors,
New York 1977; *Mirrors and Windows: American Photography since 1960,*
exhibition catalogue, by John Szarkowski, New York 1978; *Court House: A
Photographic Document,* edited by Richard Pare, New York 1978; *American
Images* by Renato Danese, New York 1979; *The Imaginary Photo Museum* by
Helmut Gernsheim, Renate and L. Fritz Gruber and others, Cologne 1981,
London 1982; *Counterparts: Form and Emotion in Photographs* by Weston J.
Naef, New York 1982; *New Color/New York* by Sally Eauclaire, New York
1984; *American Images: Photography 1945-1980,* edited by Peter Turner and
John Benton-Harris, London 1985; *Photography and Art 1946-1986,*
exhibition catalogue, by Andy Grundberg and Kathleen M. Gauss, Los
Angeles 1987. Articles—"Photography: The Coming of Age of Color" by
Max Kozloff in *Artforum* (New York), January 1975; "Route 66 Revisited"
by Carter Ratcliff in *Art in America* (New York), January 1976; "New
Frontiers in Color" by Douglas Davis in *Newsweek* (New York), 19 April
1976; "Color Photography" by Carol Squires in *Artforum* (New York),
November 1978; "The Framing of Stephen Shore" by Tony Hiss in *American
Photographer* (New York), February 1979.

*   *   *

Stephen Shore's photographs are often described in terms of what they do
not contain. In his travels through small-town America, he presents a cross-
sectional view of the country that is mutely straight-forward. As much an
anthropologist as an artist, Shore seems to eschew the quirks of individual
identity that, in the past, have attracted the photographer's attention. In his
empty, nearly desolate scenes, we find no trace of an obvious esthetic,
sociological, or psychological theme. What attitude we can detect is one of
ambivalence. Shore has been criticized for the banality of his subject matter
and his detachment from and seeming boredom with it, but such a criticism
does not account for the refinement and beauty of the prints themselves.

Szarkowski noted in his introduction to *William Eggleston's Guide* that
"today's most radical and suggestive color photography derives much of its
vigor from commonplace models." In Shore's photographs, the reverse may
be true; that the commonplace derives its vigor from the clear, elegant color
Shore achieves. In any case, the color sets Shore apart from his contemporaries
loosely grouped together by the show and catalogue *New Topographics,* which
included, among others, Joe Deal, Lewis Baltz, Henry Wessel and Robert
Adams. Similarities in the group have been noted in the tension between the
photographers' sophisticated picture-making skills and the urban wasteland to
which they apply them. Shore's approach differs, however, in his careful
avoidance of any trace of social commentary.

This difference between the quality of vision and the banality of subject
matter has inspired a comparison between Shore's photographs and Photo-
Realist painting, but there is, it seems to me, a crucial difference between the
Photo-Realists' uninflected painting of shiny, reflective, often dazzling
modern urban surfaces, such as chrome, steel and glass, and Shore's tasteful
treatment of the mundane. Furthermore, whereas both use the vocabulary of
the American vernacular, the Photo-Realists' use derives from Pop art and
from reproduced, commercial imagery—that is, photographs. Shore's use of
vernacular imagery owes a debt to Walker Evans.

Like Evans, Shore searches for the flattest possible statement; his reticence
results in an austere casualness and a deadpan beauty. Like Evans, he
photographs the structures and artifacts of middle class America in a clear,
direct light, but his interest is evidently not in the implied humanism of the
scenes, but simply in how they look. Garry Winogrand's famous dictum—"I
photograph in order to see what something will look like on film"—is more
plausible when applied to Shore's photographs. His use of color and the 8 x 10
camera does seem to bring to the most inert scene a measure of dignity and an
artistic authority. Shore's presence behind the camera is both powerful and
entirely unobtrusive.

—Dana Asbury

SIEFF, Jeanloup.

Nationality: French. **Born:** Paris, 30 November 1933. **Education:** Attended the Lycée Chaptal, Paris, 1945-52; Lycée Decours, Paris, 1953; studied photography at the Vaugirard Photographic School, Paris, 1953, and at the Photography School, Vevey, Switzerland, 1954. **Military Service:** Served in the Colonial Artillery of the French Army, in Paris, 1958. **Family:** Married Barbara Williams in 1979; daughter: Sonia. **Career:** Professional photographer, Paris, since 1954. Fashion Photographer, *Elle* magazine, Paris, 1955-58; photographer with Magnum Photos co-operative photo agency, Paris, 1959-60; freelance photographer, working with *Harper's Bazaar, Esquire, Vogue,* etc., Paris and New York, since 1961; established permanent studio in the rue Ampere, Paris, 1967. **Recipient:** Prix Niépce, 1959; Silver Medal, Art Directors Club, London, 1967; Gold Medal, Museum Espiritu Santo, Brazil, 1968; Gold Medal, *Zadar Exhibition,* Yugoslavia, 1969; Gold Medal, Museum of Modern Art, Skopje, Yugoslavia, 1971; Silver Medal, *Advertising Film Festival,* Cannes, 1975. **Agents:** Galerie Agathe Gaillard, 3 rue Pont Louis-Philippe, 75004 Paris, France; Galerie Fiolet, Herrengracht 86, Amsterdam, Netherlands; and The Photographers' Gallery, 8 Great Newport Street, London WC2, England. **Address:** 87 rue Ampere, 75017 Paris, France.

Individual Exhibitions:

1967	Kodak Gallery, London
1969	Galerie La Demeure, Paris (retrospective)
1970	Maison de la Culture, Amiens (toured France)
1971	Underground Gallery, New York (retrospective)
	Modern Art Academy, Ghent (retrospective)
1972	*Sad Landscapes and Lazy Nudes,* Nikon Gallery, Paris
1973	Philosophers' Gallery, Geneva (retrospective)
	Nikon Gallery, Tokyo (retrospective)
1974	Centre Culturel, Toulouse
	Spectrum Gallery, Barcelona
1975	Canon Photo Gallery, Amsterdam
	Silver Image Gallery, Tacoma, Washington
	20 Years, Oh Nicéphore!, FNAC Galerie, Paris
1976	Pentax Gallery, Tokyo (retrospective)
	Aspects Galerie, Brussels (retrospective)
	Galerie Jean Dieuzaide, Toulouse (retrospective)
	Portraits of 43 Ladies, Galerie Agathe Gaillard, Paris
	Foster White Gallery, Seattle (retrospective)
1977	Galerie Paula Pia, Antwerp (retrospective)
1978	*Death Valley,* Galerie La Hune, Paris (travelled to the Portfolio Gallery, Lausanne; Galerie Voir, Toulouse; and Sunprint Gallery, Madison, Wisconsin)
1979	Galerie Fiolet, Amsterdam
1981	*Jean-Pierre Sudre/Jeanloup Sieff,* Musée d'Orange, France
	Galerie Suzanne Kupfer, Nidau-Bienne, Switzerland
1982	Galerie Municipale du Château d'Eau, Toulouse, France

Selected Group Exhibitions:

1964	*World Exhibition of Photography: What Is Man?,* Pressehaus Stern, Hamburg (and world tour)
1966	*Fashion Photography,* at *Photokina,* Cologne
1971	*Salon National de la Photographie,* Paris
1973	*Confrontation 1973,* University of Dijon, France
1975	*Photo Festival,* Harze, Belgium
1977	*Fashion Photography,* International Museum of Photography, Rochester, New York (travelled to Brooklyn Museum, New York; San Francisco Museum of Modern Art, California; Cincinnati Art Institute, Ohio; Museum of Fine Arts, St. Petersburg, Florida)
1979	*French Fashion Photography,* Galerie Zabriskie, Paris
1980	*French Photographers,* University of Oklahoma, Norman
1984	*Sammlung Gruber,* Museum Ludwig, Cologne
1985	*Das Aktfoto,* Fotomuseum im Stadtmuseum, Munich (toured West Germany)

Collections:

Bibliothèque Nationale, Paris; Musée Réattu, Arles, France; Musée de Toulon; Museum Ludwig, Cologne.

Publications:

By SIEFF: Books—*La Danse,* Lausanne 1961; *Jeanloup Sieff,* portfolio, Ghent 1971; *La Photo,* with Chenz, Paris 1976; *Erotic Photography,* London 1977; *Death Valley,* Paris 1978; *Best Nudes,* Tokyo 1980. **Article**—"A Bâtons Rompus" in *Zoom* (Paris), December 1979.

On SIEFF: Books—*Photographic Communication,* edited by R. Smith Schunemann, London and Toronto 1972; *The Magic Image* by Cecil Beaton and Gail Buckland, London and Boston 1975; *The History of Fashion Photography* by Nancy Hall-Duncan, New York 1979; *Clefs et Serrures* by Michel Tournier, Paris 1979; *The Imaginary Photo Museum* by Helmut Gernsheim, Renate and L. Fritz Gruber and others, Cologne 1981, London 1982; *Jeanloup Sieff,* exhibition catalogue, edited by Jean Dieuzaide, Toulouse, France 1982; *How Famous Photographers Work* by Jack Schofield and others, London 1983; *Private Viewing: Contemporary Erotic Photography,* edited by Terry Jones, London 1983; *Sammlung Gruber: Photographie des 20. Jahrhunderts,* exhibition catalogue, with foreword by Siegfried Gohr, Cologne 1984. **Articles**—"Young Photographers" by Romeo Martinez in *Camera* (Lucerne), June 1958; "Jeanloup Sieff: Death Valley Days" in *American Photographer* (New York), September 1979; "Jeanloup Sieff: Fashion" by Gabriel Bauret in *Zoom* (Paris), 1980.

*

Today I am 46 and my daughter is two months old. This is probably not a world-shaking occasion, but these little events fill the passing days and, like photographs, serve as reminders. They are like so many small whitestones helping us, according to our mood, rediscover feelings and forgotten faces.

I have been taking photographs for more than 30 years, but I have the curious feeling that I have only just finished an introductory apprenticeship which allows me now, at last, to get on with more serious matters—as if the past, and its thousands of images, have been only a sort of prelude.

For years I have been thinking about a "summing-up" book, one that will perhaps free me from the past. I have gone over and over its title—*Portraits of Seated Ladies, of Sad Landscapes and Indolently Weary Nudes, with Certain Selected Moments and Accompanied by Texts Having No Connection with the Images,* and as this will displease a lot of people I shall certainly keep it as it is. I have even signed a contract with an editor, but months and years have gone by and it is still not finished, hardly begun; perhaps I shall never do it. So when I was offered these pages in *Zoom* I said to myself that it would be a good opportunity to dive in and try, with a selection of a dozen or so images, to produce a kind of sketch of what the book might be.

But to choose 15 photographs out of 200 is a difficult and dangerous task. Why choose one image rather than another? Because of its plastic quality? Because of the memory that it evokes? Because one was happy on the day one made it, or in love with the person it portrays? I really don't know.

So the choice, like all choices, was laborious. All photography is a moment, of oneself and of others, of things and of the world; it is, at one and the same time, the eternalizing of an emotion and its erosion, a perfume that fades or, on the contrary, is strengthened by passing time.

Everyone imbues an image with his own substance—yet, one can share nothing, or very little, of one's deepest feelings. If one thinks otherwise, that is only a misunderstanding, like love, which sometimes lasts a long time and is called happiness. So why show one's work, publish, write books? Perhaps for the same reason that one, sometimes, spontaneously talks to a stranger: it is sometimes thanks to someone else that one comes to an understanding of oneself.

Taking photographs is a strange occupation: daring to want to stop time, to capture for oneself moments in life and things past, an absurd revenge on death to try to preserve, so that they outlive us, a loved face or a pleasant landscape.

The other evening there was a program on television dedicated to Gérard Philipe. His daughter, who had not known him, tried to discover him through his films, old photographs, and the memories of those who had worked with him. All the old actors and wrinkled directors were consoling her for a sadness she did not feel by telling her how marvellous it was that her father had died young, a man who had personified youth itself. As if it were not possible to be and to have been, and as if death were the greatest gift to overprovocative youth. A touching if necessary naiveté to think of life as fixed forever by a photographic representation. One perceives only the appearance; there remains only a beautiful butterfly pinned forever in its case—but where is its flight and the summer scents that enveloped it?

A photograph is only a clue. As Marcel Duchamp said, the spectator is the co-author of every work through the experience he brings with him from his own life. My photographs hardly belong to me any more; they live their own lives, good or bad they have grown up, so perhaps if I put them in this book I shall free myself of them altogether! My daughter Sonia will also leave me when she grows up, but I hope that we shall stay friends.

Robert Doisneau came a little while ago to give me his new book. Two splendid gifts, his book and his visit. He didn't know that it was my birthday, but he must have suspected something. No sooner had he arrived than he was already gone, shy, smiling, not wanting to disturb. I spent two hours reading and keeping company with him through his book. Thanks to him I am in a good mood; thanks to him I again want to do something. It is impossible to talk about Robert Doisneau: words are clumsy compared to his light-heartedness; jokes are boorish faced with his humour; and, as for his talent, it is so conspicuous that I dare hardly write the word and I can already see his eyes creasing with laughter!

Trois Secondes d'éternité is the title of his book, and whoever doesn't possess it will no longer deserve to be greeted!

—Jeanloup Sieff (from *Zoom*, December 1979)

* * *

Jeanloup Sieff is two persons at once: he conceals (quite well) the flame of an inner life rich in emotion and sensuous response behind a screen of measured coldness or surrealist humor. His pictures are like himself: they seem to confess only with regret the feelings from which they were born: a nude model appears from behind, transfixed or simulating an escape; the savage magnitude of Death Valley is demythologized by a foreground where we see a stupid bit of technology, the dashboard of the car of the travelling photographer; the poetry of an almost pictorial composition is denied by a falsely fortuitous presence—a cat passing by, for example; or, the potential lyricism of a shot is undercut by the strict documentary style of the print. Moreover, the man abounds in ambiguities. He is a lover of photography who in his youth slept with his camera, who now (unsuccessfully) discredits himself and his work by announcing that it is merely "the means to make a living," he is a pretend-prude who says he refuses others the right to share or understand the fervor of his heart as he creates this or that picture. Yet Sieff is in fact a truly gifted photographer, gifted in portraiture, fashion, nudes, advertisements, landscapes, even the cinema. The charm—of the man, of his work—is in the ambiguities. He seems fragile; in fact, he is strong. He seems sociable, yet is fiercely independent.

Once, while taking his "entrance exam" at Magnum, he had to present his works to a man he revered, Henri Cartier-Bresson. Cartier-Bresson conspicuously examined the photos upside-down, conveying thereby that their content was of little importance to him: he wanted to see if the lines of force withstood such a test. Sieff was on the verge of rage. This reaction pleased the master, who had, of course, with this method, simultaneously evaluated both the work and the character of the candidate. It should be added, incidentally, that, even upside-down, Sieff's photographs did "withstand."

Today, they withstand even better, for Sieff is an excellent technician, and over the last 30 years he has explored and mastered all the techniques of shooting: large format, medium format, 35mm format, black-and-white, color, long and particularly short focus distances (a mode he has used, without abusing it, since 1959). The formal quality is a hallmark of all of his work.

But why does that work so deeply move us? Because of the absence of that very armor that Sieff would like to construct to protect himself. Because of that which he allows to escape from himself into his work—inspiration, memories, impressions, loves, intimate mysteries. He must be aware of this "presence," for he once said: "Primitive people hid from the camera, to avoid the theft of their souls. But they are mistaken; it is, rather, the soul of the photographer that is captured by the photograph." It is from just that perception that we

understand our own response: to like the photographs of Jeanloup Sieff is to like him.

—Roger Therond

SIEGEL, Arthur (Sidney).

Nationality: American. **Born:** Detroit, Michigan, 2 August 1913. **Education:** Educated in Detroit public schools; studied sociology, University of Michigan, Ann Arbor, 1931-33, and, Wayne State University, Detroit, 1934-35; studied photography, under László Moholy-Nagy, *q.v.*, New Bauhaus School, now Institute of Design, Illinois Institute of Technology, Chicago, 1937-38. **Military Service:** Served as photographer, under Roy E. Stryker, Office of War Information, Washington, D.C., 1942-43, and in the United States Air Corps Aerial Photography Department and Office of Assistant Chief, Air Staff Intelligence, Chanute Field, Rantoul, Illinois, 1944-46. **Family:** Married Barbara Upshaw in 1946 (divorced, 1954); married Irene Yarovich in 1954; children: Julie, Adam and Ezra. **Career:** First photographs, Detroit, 1927; first experimental abstract photographs, Chicago, 1937. Freelance magazine and industrial photographer, working for *New York Times, Wide World, Time, Life, Fortune, Sports Illustrated,* and for Farm Security Administration, and Associated Press Photo Bureau, based in Detroit, 1935-42, Chicago, 1946-68; gradually abandoned professional photography to concentrate on teaching, from 1968. Instructor, Department of Visual Education, Wayne State University, Detroit, 1934-37; Organizer and Head of Photography Department, 1946-49, Professor of Photography, 1949-54, 1965-78, and Chairman of the Department, 1971-78, Institute of Design, Chicago. **Recipient:** American Institute of Architects Award, 1979. **Agent:** Adam Siegel, 1200 West Webster, Chicago, Illinois 60614. **Died:** (in Chicago) 1 February 1978.

Individual Exhibitions:

1949	Wayne State University, Detroit
1954	Art Institute of Chicago
1955	International Museum of Photography, George Eastman House, Rochester, New York
1957	*Abstract Photography,* American Federation of Arts, New York (with Harry Callahan and Aaron Siskind; toured the United States)
1967	*Light and Color Photography,* Art Institute of Chicago
	2 Illinois Photographers, Hyde Park Art Center, Chicago (with Aaron Siskind)
1975	*Aaron Siskind and Arthur Siegel,* Oakton Community College, Morton Grove, Illinois
1981	*Arthur Siegel: A Life in Photography 1913-1978,* Chicago Historical Society
1982	*Vintage Photographs and Photograms 1937-73,* Edwynn Houk Gallery, Chicago (retrospective)

Selected Group Exhibitions:

1950	*Six States of Photography,* Milwaukee Art Institute, Wisconsin
1967	*Photography in the 20th Century,* National Gallery of Canada, Ottawa (toured Canada and the United States, 1967-73)
1974	*Photography in America,* Whitney Museum, New York
1975	*Color Photography: Inventors and Innovators 1850-1975,* Yale University Art Gallery, New Haven, Connecticut
1977	*The Photographer and the City,* Museum of Contemporary Art, Chicago
1980	*The New Vision,* Public Library Cultural Center, Chicago
1982	*Counterparts: Form and Emotion in Photographs,* Metropolitan Museum of Art, New York (travelled to the Contemporary Arts Center, Cincinnati, Ohio; Dallas Museum of Fine Art, Texas; San Francisco Museum of Modern Art; Corcoran Gallery, Washington, D.C.)

1983   *Fotogramme—die lichtreichen Schatten,* Fotomuseum im
        Stadtmuseum, Munich
1985   *The New Spirit in American Photography,* University of
        Illinois, Urbana
1987   *Photography and Art 1946-86,* Los Angeles County
        Museum of Art

Collections:

Museum of Modern Art, New York; Metropolitan Museum of Art, New York; International Museum of Photography, George Eastman House, Rochester, New York; Museum of Fine Arts, Boston; Library of Congress, Washington, D.C.; Art Institute of Chicago; Exchange National Bank, Chicago; University of Chicago; Pasadena Art Museum, California; Chicago Historical Society.

Publications:

By SIEGEL: Book—*Chicago's Famous Buildings,* editor and photographer, Chicago 1965, 1979. **Articles—**"Creative Color Photography" in *Modern Photography* (New York), vol. 16, nos. 1/2/3, 1952; in *Life* (New York), 11 November 1957; "Photography Is" in *Aperture* (Rochester, New York), vol. 9, no. 2, 1961; "Anonymous Art and Choice: The Photographer's World" in *Aperture* (Rochester, New York), vol. 11, no. 2, 1964; "Fifty Years of Documentary" in *Photographers on Photography,* edited by Nathan Lyons, New York 1966.

On SEIGEL: Books—*Photography in the Twentieth Century* by Nathan Lyons, New York 1967; *Photography in America,* edited by Robert Doty, with an introduction by Minor White, New York and London 1974; *The Photography Catalog,* edited by Norman Snyder, New York 1976; *The Photographer and the City,* exhibition catalogue, by Gail Buckland, Chicago 1977; *Arthur Siegel: Retrospective,* exhibition catalogue, with text by John Grimes, Chicago 1982; *Fotogramme—die lichtreichen Schatten,* exhibition catalogue, by Floris M. Neususs, Kassel, West Germany 1983; *Photography and Art 1946-1986,* exhibition catalogue, by Andy Grundberg and Kathleen M. Gauss, Los Angeles 1987. **Articles—**"Experiment in Color" in *American Annual of Photography,* New York 1952; "A Collection of Photographs" in *Aperture* (Rochester, New York), Fall 1969; "Arthur Siegel" in *Camera* (Lucerne), February 1978; "Arthur Siegel: A Short Critical Biography" by John Grimes in *Exposure* (New York), Summer 1979; "Arthur Siegel: A Life in Photography, 1913-1978" by Larry A. Viskochil in *Chicago History,* Summer 1981.

*   *   *

Arthur Siegel's half-century involvement in photography took him into almost every branch of the profession. While he began his career as a photojournalist and commercial photographer, it was as a teacher and experimenter with creative uses of 35mm color and the photogram that brought him the most recognition. The complex images that he produced throughout his career were influenced heavily by his relationship with László Moholy-Nagy and with the New Bauhaus and Institute of Design schools that Moholy had founded in Chicago. Siegel had come from Detroit in 1937 to be one of Moholy's first students of photography. The year he spent at the New Bauhaus proved to be one of the pivotal experiences in his life.

Returning to Detroit the next year, Siegel applied what he had learned when he resumed his commercial work specializing in documentary photography. His "The Right of Assembly," which he made in 1941 while documenting a meeting of auto workers during a Chrysler strike, was certainly his most published image. During the early 1940s Siegel worked briefly for Roy Stryker as a freelance toward the end of the FSA survey and for the Office of War Information documenting industry's contributions to the war effort. This work, and later work that he did independently for a number of industrial clients, shows the influences of his contacts with Moholy and his own development based upon his experimental studies and his knowledge of the history of the medium.

After the war, in which he had served as a photographer at an Air Corps base in Rantoul, Illinois, Siegel returned to Chicago to teach at the Institute of Design. The photography program that he developed over the years, along with Harry Callahan and, later, Aaron Siskind, the two other famous teachers in the ID photographic trinity, still has a far reaching effect on photographic education nationwide.

Siegel spent much of the 1950s and 1960s away from teaching earning a living as a freelance for *Time, Life, Fortune* and other publications and doing advertising and annual report photography. His versatility, and his belief that his commercial work was as important as his personal work, made him a highly sought-after and successful professional. He also gained much public recognition for his architectural photography for, and his editorship of, *Chicago's Famous Buildings,* published by the University of Chicago in 1965. Most of the negatives and prints from Siegel's long career as a commercial photographer are now located at the Chicago Historical Society.

Siegel was a pioneer in the creative use of 35mm color in both his commercial and personal work. One color series of dye transfer prints made in the early 1950s called "In Search of Myself" was important both for its autobiographical implications and for its innovative use of strong colors and motion in complex organization. These elements were Siegel's subject matter as much as the neon signs, window displays, reflections, automobiles, and pedestrian traffic on Chicago's State Street. These images, like his earlier photograms and combination prints and his later "lucidagrams" and SX 70 prints, all include the same design elements he used throughout his career. These include the inevitable circles, layers, modified patterns of light and shadow and other inventions, adaptions, and adoptions that formed his own brand of Moholy's "new vision."

Siegel returned to full time teaching in 1967 and became head of the ID photography program again in 1971. Until the end of his life in 1978 he devoted his energies to teaching, inspiring a generation of photographers and future teachers to carry the ID's methods and messages around the world. In the end he rightly considered this contribution to be his greatest achievement.

—Larry A. Viskochil

SINGH, Dayanita.

Nationality: Indian. **Born:** New Delhi, 18 March 1961. **Education:** Studied Visual Communication at the National Institute of Design, Ahmedabad, 1980-86; studied Photojournalism and Documentary Photography at International Center of Photography, New York, 1987-88. **Career:** Worked as an independent photojournalist since 1988; worked as assistant to Mary Ellen Mark on six month Indian Circus project, 1991; member of invited group of photographers commissioned to document the changing family situation in North East England, 1993; also took part in group photographers' tour of Punjab for Contemporary Photographers Forum book project, 1994; **Recipient:** Alliance Française Award, 1993. **Agent:** J B Pictures, 313 East 74th Street, New York, New York 10021, U.S.A. **Address:** 15 Guru G S Marg, New Delhi 110005, India.

Selected Group Exhibitions:

1994   *The Changing Family Situation in North East England,* Cheb,
        Czech Republic (travelled to Essen, Germany and Brittany,
        France)

Publications:

By SINGH: Books—*Zakir Hussain,* India, 1986. **Film—**coproducer, *Indian Circus* for *National Geographic,* 1992.

Family of Magicians, **New Delhi, 1993.** Photograph ©Dayanita Singh.

On SINGH: Articles—in *Time, Newsweek* (USA), *The Independent, The Times, The Daily Telegraph* (UK), *Aera* (Japan), *Liberation* (France) and *Altag, Du Magazine* (Switzerland).

*

Since I started photography professionally, I have always chosen to work on projects that led me into a close relationship with people, whether it was with the prostitutes on my AIDS work, the Sikh families whose men were killed in the 1984 riots, the eunuchs who are social outcasts, bonded children in the carpet industry, street children on drugs, people in Old Age Homes, street performers or master weavers trying to survive in this mechanical age. Often these projects led to my living with various families, in all sorts of homes, and a deep sharing occurred; secrets were told, fears expressed, joys celebrated. Access was unlimited and conversations personal—way beyond the project in hand.

In this vast social landscape that I tried to document, I found I felt closest to, and invariably gravitated toward, what happened in the family, in a home. I shared the domestic experience, observed the material culture and the patterns of behaviour amongst the members of the family, and wondered about the changes within my own family, as did the others for themselves.

In 1993 I had the opportunity to share my work on families with photographers and editors in Europe and America. It was only then I realized the other aspects of my work. I was presenting an image of India rarely seen in the Western media. In fact, I was often asked if these were pictures of Indians in London or New York. India is, for many westerners, poverty, disasters and the exotic—yet here I was showing a totally different image of a middle class

and upper class, well over 200 million people. This only furthered the urgency of my working on this project, as did my returning to India, finding changes happening from week to week.

—Dayanita Singh

SINGH, Raghubir.

Nationality: Indian. **Born:** Jaipur, 22 October 1942. **Education:** St. Xavier School, Jaipur; studied arts at the Hindu College, New Delhi; self-taught in photography. **Family:** Married Anne de Henning in 1972 (divorced 1990.) **Career:** Worked as a photojournalist in India until 1971. Independent photographer, New Delhi, Hong Kong, Paris and London since 1972. **Agent:** Holly Solomon Editions, 24 West 57th Street, New York, New York 10019, U.S.A. **Address:** 11 rue de Siam, 75016 Paris, France; and 3 Connaught Square, London, W2 2HG, England

Individual Exhibitions:

1981   *India,* Holly Solomon Editions, New York (retrospective)
1982   *Images de l'Inde,* Galerie Nouvel Observateur/Delpire, Paris
            (retrospective)
1983   Camerawork Gallery, San Francisco (with Sacha Haber)
1984   Arnolfini Gallery, Bristol, Avon

Fogg Art Museum, Boston, Massachusetts
Rhode Island School of Design
University of California Museum, Berkeley
1985   Pace MacGill, New York
1989   Arthur M Sackler Gallery of the Smithsonian Institution,
        Washington, D.C.
1991   Center for Creative Photography, Tucson, Arizona
1992   Rice University, Houston, Texas
        Dallas Museum of Art, USA
1994   Aperture Gallery, New York

Selected Group Exhibitions:

1973   *3rd World Exhibition of Photography: On the Way to
        Paradise,* Presshaus Stern, Hamburg (and world tour)
1981   *Lichtbildnisse,* Rheinisches Landesmuseum, Bonn, West
        Germany
1984   *Britain in 1984,* The Photographers' Gallery, London
1989   *The Art of Fixing A Shadow,* Art Institute of Chicago

Collections:

Metropolitan Museum of Art, New York; Museum of Modern Art, New York;
San Francisco Museum of Modern Art; Arthur M Sackler Gallery, Smithsoni-
an Institution, Washington, D.C.; Williams College Museum of Art, Williamstown,
Massachusetts.

Publications:

By SINGH: Books—*Ganga: Sacred River of India,* Hong Kong 1974;
Calcutta, Hong Kong 1975; *Rajasthan: India's Enchanted Land,* with an
introduction by Satyajit Ray, London and New York 1981; *Kumbh Mela,* Paris
1981; *Kashmir: Garden of the Himalayas,* London 1983; *Bananas,* London,
Paris, New York 1986; *Kerala,* London, Paris, New York 1987; *Calcutta, The
Home and the Street,* London, Paris, New York 1988; *Ganges,* London, New
York, Tokyo, Munich and Milan 1992; *Bombay,* New York and Bom-
bay 1994.

On SINGH: Articles—"Raghubir Singh: The Reality of Color" by William
Gedney in *Modern Photography* (New York), October 1976; "A Certain
Sweep: The India of Raghubir Singh" by Max Kozloff (with accompanying
interview), *Asian Art,* Washington D.C. 1989; "Passage To India" by Mark
Harris in *Camera and Darkroom,* July 1993.

*

My interest has always been to photograph in the documentary style where
the viewfinder is a window to two worlds: the internal as well as the external
world.

—Raghubir Singh

*   *   *

Raghubir Singh's *Ganga* is easily the most famous book by an Indian
photographer. No river in the world, not even the Nile, has been the object of
such veneration as the Ganges (to call it by its Anglicised name), and Singh,
after six years of photographing, has brought out the deep emotions the river
evokes, as well as its beauty and grandeur as it makes its way from the high
Himalayas to the Bay of Bengal. "The river of India," Nehru called it,
"whose story is the story of India's civilisation and culture." *Ganga* is one of
the most perceptive pictorial statements on Indian life, beliefs and customs.
Besides seeing this panorama through the camera lens, Singh has felt it as with
a pilgrim's heart. The result is a sacrament and a celebration.

Some of Singh's photographs in *Ganga* (as elsewhere) can be faulted for
being conventional, for it is hard to avoid stereotypes about India. But he
manages to invest almost all of his pictures with unusual detail and an element
of contemplation which, combined with picturesqueness and vividness of
colour, give them distinction and staying power. Among the more memorable

pictures in *Ganga* are those showing sadhus above a waterfall at Gangotri,
village women huddled in the rain on a bank of the river, a herd of elephants
being given a wash, and pilgrim boats where the river meets the sea.

Singh maintains the same mood in *Kumbh Mela,* an exploration of the
mammoth fair which is held once in 12 years at the confluence of Ganga and
Jamuna. Very different in texture is *Calcutta,* in which he deals with urban
realities at their most acute. Many adjectives—all uncomplimentary—have
been used to describe the city of Calcutta, but Singh shows its grace as well as
its garbage. The faces in the endless crowds reveal not only intensity, anger
and despair but also acceptance and hope. *Calcutta* is a tribute to life battling
against squalor and death, to the interplay between song and harshness.

In *Rajasthan* Singh has given himself over to nostalgia. Documenting the
region of his birth, he relives his childhood dreams and memories. The pictures
are declarations of his love for palaces and peacocks, for humble village homes
with mud walls and decorated doorways, and for the very dust that hangs in the
summer air. One of the finest pictures in the book is a scene around a village
well, with camels and oxen and women in garments of postbox red. The
composition is reminiscent of mediaeval miniatures. In his introduction to the
book, Satyajit Ray has rightly extolled Singh for the searching curiosity and
craftsmanship which his photographs reveal.

Kashmir is the landscapists' delight and the photographer's snare. All
tourist places are becoming less idyllic. Raghubir Singh's *Kashmir* is more full
of autumnal serenity than the surprises of spring and summer. He has shown
apple blossoms, but the red chillies drying in the sun are more after his heart,
for he has chosen the latter for the cover. Two photographs are particularly
haunting—one of an interior in a saffron-seller's home, which has a Vermeer-
like interaction of light, and another which shows a bedridden papier-mache
craftsman with his grandson.

Singh worked in earlier years for newspapers in India, but he now lives in
Paris. His work is published in many leading pictorial journals, whose editors
demand pictures that conform to their own preconceptions. But Singh superimposes his own vision, achieving an unusual amalgam of objectivity and
attachment. Above all, he is a master of colour and subtlety, most at home in
mellowness.

—H.Y. Sharada Prasad

SINSABAUGH, Art(hur Reeder).

Nationality: American. **Born:** Irvington, New Jersey, 31 October 1924.
Education: Studied photography under László Moholy-Nagy, Harry Callahan
and Aaron Siskind, at the Institute of Design, Illinois Institute of Technology,
Chicago, 1945-49, 1964-67, B.A. 1949, M.A. 1967. **Military Service:**
Served as a sergeant-photographer in the United States Army Air Force, in the
Far East, 1943-45. **Family:** Married twice; daughters: Katherine and Eliza-
beth. **Career:** Independent photographer, Chicago, then Urbana, Illinois,
1945-83. Instructor in Photography, Institute of Design, Chicago, 1951-59.
Associate Professor, then Professor of Art, University of Illinois, Urbana,
from 1959 (Head of the Photography/Cinematography Department; also,
Associate Member, University of Illinois Center for Advanced Studies, 1972-
73). Founder Member, Society for Photographic Education. **Recipient:** New
Talent Award, *Art in America,* New York, 1962; Society of Typographic Arts
Award, 1964, 1965, 1966; Art Directors Club of Indiana Award, 1964; Art
Directors Club of Los Angeles Award, 1964; Illinois Arts Council Award,
1966; Graham Foundation Award, 1966; Guggenheim Fellowship, 1969;
National Endowment for the Arts Photography Fellowship, 1976. **Agent:**
Daniel Wolf Inc., 30 West 57th Street, New York, New York 10019, U.S.A.
Died: (in Chicago, Illinois) 27 September 1983.

Individual Exhibitions:

1959   St. Mary's College, Notre Dame, Indiana
1963   Art Institute of Chicago
1965   Gallery 500D, Chicago (with Harold Walter)
1970   Underground Gallery, New York
        Carl Siembab Gallery, Boston

1973	Williams College Museum of Art, Williamstown, Massachusetts
1978	Museum of Modern Art, New York
1980	Daniel Wolf Gallery, New York
1984	*The Last Work,* Daniel Wolf Gallery, New York

Selected Group Exhibitions:

1983	*The Photographer and the American Landscape,* Museum of Modern Art, New York
1966	*American Photography: The 60s,* University of Nebraska, Lincoln
1967	*Photography in the 20th Century,* National Gallery of Canada, Ottawa (toured Canada and the United States, 1967-73)
1968	*Photography U.S.A.,* De Cordova Museum, Lincoln, Massachusetts
1971	*New Photography U.S.A.,* Museum of Modern Art, New York (toured the United States and Canada)
1977	*Concerning Photography,* The Photographers' Gallery, London (travelled to the Spectro Workshop, Newcastle upon Tyne)
1978	*Mirrors and Windows: American Photography since 1960,* Museum of Modern Art, New York (toured the United States, 1978-80)
1982	*Color as Form,* International Museum of Photography at George Eastman House, Rochester, New York
1985	*American Images 1945-80,* Barbican Art Gallery, London, (toured Britain)
1987	*Photography and Art 1946-86,* Los Angeles County Museum of Art

Collections:

Art Sinsabaugh Archive, University of Indiana, Bloomington; Museum of Modern Art, New York; International Museum of Photography, George Eastman House, Rochester, New York: Rhode Island School of Design, Providence; Williams College, Williamstown, Massachusetts; Smithsonian Institution, Washington, D.C.; Art Institute of Chicago; Exchange National Bank, Chicago; University of Nebraska, Lincoln; University of California at Los Angeles.

Publications:

By SINSABAUGH: Book—*6 Mid-American Chants/11 Midwest Landscapes,* with Sherwood Anderson, Highlands, North Carolina 1964. **Articles**—"Midwest Landscapes: Low, Wide and Handsome" in *International Harvester World* (Chicago), no. 10, 1963; "Chicago: City of Endless Horizons" in the *Sunday American Magazine* (Chicago), 3 July 1966; "Prairie Landscapes: Rural and Urban" in *Design and Environment* (New York), Fall 1970.

On SINSABAUGH: Books—*The Photographer and the American Landscape,* exhibition catalogue, by John Szarkowski, New York 1963; *American Photography: The 60s,* exhibition catalogue, Lincoln, Nebraska 1966; *Photography in the 20th Century* by Nathan Lyons, New York 1967; *New Photography U.S.A.,* exhibition catalogue, by John Szarkowski, New York 1971; *Concerning Photography,* exhibition catalogue, edited by Jonathan Bayer and others, London 1977; *The Photographer and the City,* exhibition catalogue, by Gail Buckland, Chicago 1977; *Photographs: Sheldon Memorial Art Gallery Collection, University of Nebraska,* with an introduction by Norman A. Geske, Lincoln, Nebraska 1977; *70s Wide-View,* exhibition catalogue, by Elaine A. King, Evanston, Illinois 1978; *A Book of Photographs from the Collection of Sam Wagstaff,* designed by Arne Lewis, New York 1978; *Nude Photographs 1850-1980,* edited by Constance Sullivan, New York 1980; *The Library of World Photography: Landscape,* with texts by David Plowden and Ian Jeffrey, Tokyo and London 1984; *American Images: Photography 1945-1980,* edited by Peter Turner and John Benton-Harris, London 1985; *Photography and Art 1946-1986,* exhibition catalogue, by Andy Grundberg and Kathleen M. Gauss, Los Angeles 1987. **Articles**—"A Collection of Photographs" in *Aperture* (Rochester, New York), Fall 1969;

"Art Sinsabaugh" in *Camera* (Lucerne), June 1972; "Found Horizon" by Greg Daugherty in *Professional Photographer* (Chicago), November 1978; "Art Sinsabaugh's Landscapes" by Gene Thornton in *Camera* (Lucerne), April 1979.

*   *   *

Arthur Reeder Sinsabaugh was a garrulous, hairtrigger Dutchman who loved nothing better than sitting in a cafe, having coffee and talking to absolutely anyone and everyone in sight. Oddly, when it came to providing information about his life and his important career in photography, he clammed up in the manner of Uncle Remus's Tar-Baby. (One is reminded of another sociable man, Erik Satie. After his death, they looked under the bed and found a twenty-year collection of mail he had received. It was all unopened.)

First, then, I quote from a note by Hugh Edwards, former Curator of Photography at the Art Institute of Chicago, provided for *Six Mid-American Chants,* by Sherwood Anderson, a Jargon Society publication of 1964 which contained 11 midwest photographs by Art Sinsabaugh: "Although, from now on, Art Sinsabaugh may be identified with the Midwestern environment, he did not come to Illinois until the 1940s. He was born in Irvington, New Jersey in 1924, and like so many photographers began taking pictures with the famous Brownie. During high school he worked first in a photography studio and later as a Junior Photographer for the War Department, commuting to New York City to attend a photography trade school. In 1943 he was drafted and served for three years in the Army Air Force in the United States and Asia. After his return he came to Chicago to the Institute of Design and was a graduate in 1949. He taught there from 1951 until 1959 when he went to the University of Illinois in Urbana as Professor of Art and where he is now organizing a photography program. His work has been published in England and America and exhibited by the Museum of Modern Art and the American Federation of Arts. In 1963 a one-man show was held at the Art Institute of Chicago and had much success." To up date that account very briefly, Sinsabaugh remained at the University of Illinois but resigned as head of the department. His health was indifferent for some years and his energies for new work sadly curtailed. A Sinsabaugh Archive has been established at Indiana University, Bloomington. Besides Hugh Edwards, his closest colleagues over the years included Arthur Siegel, Harry Callahan, Aaron Siskind, Henry Holmes Smith, and John Szarkowski.

One summer at Champaign-Urbana, Art Sinsabaugh found the "banquet" camera with which he made his primary reputation. It enabled him to photograph the Illinois and Indiana landscape with sheet film 12 x 20 inches in size. As Hugh Edwards says: "One wonders how our horizontal landscape could ever have been represented before, except in these low, wide rectangles suggesting an infinity on either side of our vision as well as one before us in depth." Some have joked that the Sinsabaugh format is like viewing the world through a Venetian blind. But, he had other cameras and used them all in masterly style. His clusters of farm buildings and telephone poles on the dark soil of Champaign County are as refined as the intelligence that Basho brought to bear in his haiku visions. Basho would have loved lugging a banquet camera along the narrow back roads of 17th century Japan.

—Jonathan Williams

SISKIND, Aaron.

Nationality: American. **Born:** New York City, 4 December 1903. **Education:** DeWitt Clinton High School, New York; City College of New York, B.S.S. in literature 1926; self-taught in photography. **Family:** Married Sidonie Glaller in 1929. Instructor in English, various public schools, New York, 1926-49. Took first photos, Bermuda, 1930; professional freelance photographer since 1932. Member of the Film and Photo League, New York, 1932-35, 1936-41. Part-time Instructor in Photography, Trenton College, New Jersey, 1950; Instructor in Photography, with Harry Callahan, Black Mountain College, Beria, North Carolina, 1951; Professor of Photography, 1951-71, and Head of the Department of Photography, Institute of Design,

1961-71, Illinois Institute of Technology, Chicago. Adjunct Professor, Rhode Island School of Design, Providence, 1971; Visiting Lecturer, Harvard University, Cambridge, Massachusetts, 1973. Co-Editor, *Choice* poetry and photography magazine, Chicago, 1961-70. Founder Member, Society for Photographic Education, 1963; Trustee, Gallery of Contemporary Art, Chicago, 1964. **Recipient:** Guggenheim Fellowship, 1966; Distinguished Career in Photography Award, Friends of Photography, Carmel, California, 1981; Photography Award, St. Botolph Club Foundation, Boston, 1982; Governor's Arts Award, Rhode Island State Council of the Arts, 1983. Honorary doctorates: Columbia College, Chicago, 1971; Northwestern University, Chicago, 1980; Bard College, Annandale-on-Hudson, New York, 1981; Rhode Island School of Design, Providence, 1981. **Agent:** Light Gallery, 724 Fifth Avenue, New York, New York 10019. **Died:** (in Rhode Island) 8 February 1991.

Individual Exhibitions:

1941	*Tabernacle City,* Photo League, New York (travelled to Dukes County Historical Society, Edgartown, Massachusetts)
1947	*30 Recent Photographs,* Egan Gallery, New York
	California Palace of the Legion of Honor, San Francisco
1948	Santa Barbara Museum of Art, California
	Old Houses of Bucks County, Delaware Gallery, New Hope, Pennsylvania
	Black Mountain College, Beria, North Carolina
	Egan Gallery, New York
	Queens College Library, Flushing, New York
1949	Egan Gallery, New York
	Institute of Design, Illinois Institute of Technology, Chicago
1951	*New Photographs,* Egan Gallery, New York
1952	*Photographs,* Seven Stairs Gallery, Chicago
	Portland Museum of Art, Oregon
1954	*Recent Photographs by Aaron Siskind,* Egan Gallery, New York
	Menemsha Gallery, Martha's Vineyard, Massachusetts
	International Museum of Photography, George Eastman House, Rochester, New York
1955	Northwestern University, Evanston, Illinois
	Denver Art Museum
	Santa Barbara Museum of Art, California
	Art Institute of Chicago
1956	Cincinnati Art Museum, Ohio
	Photographs by Aaron Siskind, Evanston Township High School, Illinois
1957	*Harry Callahan/Aaron Siskind: Photographes Americains,* Centre Culturel Americain, Paris (travelled to Algiers and London)
1958	Alfred University, New York
	San Francisco State College
1959	*Photographs,* Martha Jackson Gallery, New York
	Carl Siembab Gallery, Boston
	Holland-Goldowsky Gallery, Chicago
1960	*Aaron Siskind/Harry Callahan,* The Cliff Dwellers, Chicago
1961	*3 Photographers,* Kalamazoo Institute of Arts, Michigan (with Wynn Bullock and David Vestal)
1962	John Gibson Gallery, Chicago
	Hanamura's, Detroit (with Toshiko Takaezu)
1963	International Museum of Photography, George Eastman House, Rochester, New York
1964	*Photographs 1954-1961,* Art Institute of Chicago
	Michigan State University, East Lansing
1965	*Photographs,* Pomona College Gallery, Claremont, California
	Aaron Siskind, Photographer, International Museum of Photography, George Eastman House, Rochester, New York (toured the United States and Canada)
	Twenty-Five Photographs, Reed College Photography Association, Portland, Oregon
	Siskind Recently, Museum of Modern Art, New York
1966	Kendall College, Evanston, Illinois
1967	*2 Illinois Photographers,* Hyde Park Art Center, Chicago (with Arthur Siegel)

1968	*Recent Photographs,* Carl Siembab Gallery, Boston
	Friends of Photography, Carmel, California
	Aaron Siskind, Photographer, Paul Arts Center, University of New Hampshire, Durham
1969	*An Exhibition of Photographs,* University of Louisville, Kentucky
1970	*Photography by Aaron Siskind,* Portland University, Oregon
	The Work of Aaron Siskind, Huntington College, Indiana
1971	*Photographs,* Milwaukee Art Center, Wisconsin
	Phoenix Evening College, Arizona
1972	*Aaron Siskind, Photographer,* Art Museum of the Rhode Island School of Design, Providence
1973	*Photographs 1935-1970,* Fogg Art Museum, Harvard University, Cambridge, Massachusetts
	Homage to Franz Kline: Photographs by Aaron Siskind, Bell Gallery, Brown University, Providence, Rhode Island
	Friends of Photography, Carmel, California
	3 Photographers, University of Colorado, Boulder (with Wynn Bullock and Edmund Teske)
1974	*Photographs by Aaron Siskind,* Washington Gallery of Photography, Washington, D.C.
	Light Gallery, New York
1975	*Aaron Siskind and Arthur Siegel,* Oakton Community College, Morton Grove, Illinois
	Art Institute of Chicago
	Photographs of Aaron Siskind in Homage to Franz Kline, Smart Gallery, University of Chicago
1976	*Aaron Siskind/Harry Callahan/Stephen Shore,* Silver Image Gallery, Tacoma, Washington
	Cronin Gallery, Houston
	Vision Gallery, Boston
1978	*Photographs by Aaron Siskind,* Worcester Art Museum, Massachusetts
	Recent Work, Bard College, Annandale-on-Hudson, New York
	Photographs 1976-77, Light Gallery, New York
1979	*Aaron Siskind: Retrospective Exhibition,* Chrysler Museum, Norfolk, Virginia
	Secuencia Fotogaleria, Lima, Peru
	Photographs 1932-1978, Museum of Modern Art, Oxford
1981	*Aaron Siskind: Harlem Project,* Chicago Center for Contemporary Photography
	The Photography Place, Philadelphia
	New Work: Mexico, Peru, Hawaii, Light Gallery, New York
1982	*Photographs from the 1930s,* Rice University, Houston, Texas
	Aaron Siskind: Fifty Years, Center for Creative Photography, Tucson, Arizona (toured the United States)
1983	*Recent Photographs,* Vision Gallery, Boston
	Urban Landscapes, Susan Harder Gallery, New York
	Light Gallery, New York
	Jeb Gallery, Providence, Rhode Island (with Charles Traub)
1984	Museum of Fine Arts, St. Petersburg, Florida
	Homage to Franz Kline, National Museum of American Art, Washington, D.C.
	The Early Years, G.H. Dalsheimer Gallery, Baltimore, Maryland
1985	Brent Sikkema/Vision Gallery, Boston
	Anne Weber Gallery, Georgetown, Maine
1986	*Recent Photographs,* Los Angeles County Museum of Art
1992	*Divers,* Pace/MacGill Gallery, New York

Selected Group Exhibitions:

1940	*Harlem Document,* New School for Social Research, New York
1941	*Image of Freedom,* Museum of Modern Art, New York
1951	*Abstraction in Photography,* Museum of Modern Art, New York
1957	*Abstract Photography,* American Federation of Arts, New York (toured the United States)

1959   *Photography at Mid-Century,* International Museum of
         Photography, George Eastman House, Rochester, New York
         (toured the United States)
1962   *Photography U.S.A.,* De Cordova Museum, Lincoln,
         Massachusetts
1973   *The Photographer as Poet,* Arts Club, Chicago
1978   *Amerikanische Landschaftsphotographie,* Neue Sammlung,
         Munich
1984   *Exposed and Developed,* National Museum of American Art,
         Washington, D.C. (toured the United States)
1985   *American Images 1945-80,* Barbican Art Gallery, London
         (toured Britain)

Collections:

Center for Creative Photography, University of Arizona, Tucson (Siskind Archive); Museum of Modern Art, New York; International Center of Photography, George Eastman House, Rochester, New York; Carpenter Center and Fogg Art Museum, Harvard University, Cambridge, Massachusetts; Art Institute of Chicago; Minneapolis Institute of Art; Museum of Fine Arts, Houston; National Gallery of Canada, Ottawa; Bibliothèque Nationale, Paris.

Publications:

By SISKIND: Books—*Aaron Siskind: Photographs,* with an introduction by Harold Rosenberg, New York 1959; *Spring of the Thief,* poems by John Logan, New York 1963; *Terrors and Pleasures of Levitation,* portfolio, New York 1972; *Bucks County: Photographs of Early Architecture,* with text by William Morgan, New York 1974; *Places: Aaron Siskind Photographs,* with an introduction by Thomas B. Hess, New York 1976; *75th Anniversary Portfolio,* New York 1979; *Volcano,* portfolio, New York 1980; *Harlem Document: Photographs 1932-1940,* with foreword by Gordon Parks, New York 1981; *Aaron Siskind: Limited Edition,* portfolio, New York 1981; *Olive Trees,* portfolio, New York 1981; *Rome Hieroglyphs,* portfolio, New York 1981; *Seaweed,* portfolio, New York 1981; *Tabernacle City 1935-1939,* portfolio, New York 1981; *Viterbo Broom, Italy 1967,* portfolio, New York 1981. **Articles**—"The Drama of Objects" in *Minicam Photography* (New York), June 1945; "When I Make a Photograph" in *American Photography* (New York), March 1951; "Local Color: Book Review" in *ASMP News* (New York), April/May 1951; "Book Review: The Decisive Moment" in *Saturday Review* (New York), 20 December 1952; "This Is My Best" in *Art Photography* (New York), June 1954; "The Essential Photographic Act" in *Art News* (New York), December 1955; "Learning Photography at the Institute of Design," with Harry Callahan, in *Aperture* (Millerton, New York), no. 4, 1956; "Credo 1950" and "Notes on the Photographic Art" in *Spectrum* (Providence, Rhode Island), May 1956; "Where I Find My Pictures" in *Modern Photography* (New York), February 1958; "Education at the Institute of Design," with Harry Callahan, in *Infinity* (New York), February 1960; "A Conversation Between Diana Johnson and Aaron Siskind" in *Spaces,* exhibition catalogue, Providence, Rhode Island, 1978; "An Interview with Aaron Siskind," with Alan Teller, in *Journal of American Photography* (New York), January 1984; "Credo 1950" in *Arts Quarterly* (New Orleans), April/June 1985.

On SISKIND: Books—*Tabernacle City,* exhibition leaflet, by Henry Beetle Hough and Alex R. Stavenitz, New York 1941; *Aaron Siskind,* exhibition catalogue, by Hilda Loveman Wilson, New York 1948; *New Photographs,* exhibition catalogue, with an essay by Elaine de Kooning, New York 1951; *Aaron Siskind, Photographer,* exhibition catalogue, edited and introduced by Nathan Lyons, with essays by Henry Holmes Smith and Thomas B. Hess, Rochester, New York 1965; *Photographers on Photography,* edited by Nathan Lyons, New York 1966; *The Photographer's Eye* by John Szarkowski, New York 1966; *Photography in America,* edited by Robert Doty, with an introduction by Minor White, New York and London 1974; *Photographs by Aaron Siskind in Homage to Franz Kline,* exhibition catalogue, with text by Carl Chiarenza, Chicago 1975; *Aaron Siskind and His Critics 1946-66* by Carl Chiarenza, entire issue of *Center for Creative Photography* (Tucson, Arizona), no. 7/8, September 1978; *Aaron Siskind: Retrospective Exhibition,* exhibition catalogue, with text by Eric Zafran, Norfolk, Virginia 1979; *Aaron*

Siskind: Photographs 1932-1978, exhibition catalogue, with text by Peter Turner and others, Oxford 1979; *Visions and Images: American Photographers on Photography,* edited by Barbaralee Diamonstein, New York 1981; *Aaron Siskind: Pleasures and Terrors* by Carl Chiarenza, Boston 1982; *Photographers Photographed* by Bill Jay, Salt Lake City, Utah 1983; *American Photography: A Critical History 1945 to the Present* by Jonathan Green, New York 1984; *Exposed and Developed: Photography Sponsored by the National Endowment for the Arts,* exhibition catalogue, by Merry Amanda Foresta, Washington, D.C. 1984; *Aaron Siskind and Linda Connor,* exhibition leaflet, by Gay Block, Houston, Texas 1985. **Film**—*Aaron Siskind* by Theodore R. Haimes 1981.

*

When I make a photograph I want it to be an altogether new object, complete and self-contained, whose basic condition is order—unlike the world of events and actions whose permanent condition is change and disorder.

The business of making a photograph may be said in simple terms to consist of three elements: the objective world (whose permanent condition is change and disorder), the sheet of paper on which the picture will be realized, and the experience which brings them together. First, and emphatically, I accept the flat plane of the picture surface as the primary frame of reference of the picture. The experience itself may be described as one of total absorption in the object. But the object serves only a personal need and the requirements of the picture. Thus, rocks are sculptured forms; a section of common decorative iron-work, springing rhythmic shapes; fragments of paper sticking to a wall, a conversation piece. And these forms, totems, masks, figures, shapes, images must finally take their place in the tonal field of the picture and strictly conform to their space environment. The object has entered the picture, in a sense; it has been photographed directly. But it is often unrecognizable; for it has been removed from its usual context, disassociated from its customary neighbors and forced into new relationships.

What is the subject matter of this apparently very personal world? It has been suggested that these shapes and images are underworld characters, the inhabitants of that vast common realm of memories that have gone down below the level of conscious control. It may be they are. The degree of emotional involvement and the amount of free association with the material being photographed would point in that direction. However, I must stress that my own interest is immediate and in the picture. What I am conscious of and what I feel is the picture I am making, the relation of that picture to others I have made and, more generally, its relation to others I have experienced.

—Aaron Siskind

*   *   *

It is more than likely that, when the history of 20th century photography is written, Aaron Siskind will emerge as one of its most significant figures. Of particular note will be the judgement that Siskind forced photographers to confront the physical reality of their product—the photographic print within the boundaries, and on the surface, of a flat sheet of paper. "Siskind," wrote critic Henry Holmes Smith some years ago, "addressed himself to the central problems traditional photography still left unresolved," and provided "the missing answers for which photographers, many of them without realizing it, had been waiting."

Not that the photographer would claim so exalted a position for himself. "I'm thinking I'm a little out of fashion right now," Siskind told me, all evidence to the contrary, in 1977, "maybe my pictures are pictures for old men; something to contemplate."

That characteristic self-effacement does not, however, extend to an underestimation of purpose. "I've tried to get photographers (through both personal example and years of teaching) to accept the space that they're given to work with as a kind of realism. You're given a flat piece of paper; that's what you work with. Accept it, deal with it, and *be conscious* of it, instead of always having illusionary space or just not even thinking about it—just letting the damn image kind of bounce on it."

That realization was the result of Siskind's personal odyssey through photography. The gift of a $12 camera at age 28, his subsequent membership and leading role in the Film and Photo League of Depression-era New York, were but the first steps. Founder and active participant of the League's documentary unit, Siskind worked in a traditional documentary style during these years, and the resulting photographs contain both charm and power. Little of this work has been published; at least one volume is now planned for publication.

During summers on Martha's Vineyard off the Massachusetts coast, however, the elements of Siskind's mature vision were coalescing. Photographing a documentary about the Island's religious community, *Tabernacle City,* he found himself drawn to the formal architectural properties rather than traditional documentary subjects. This emphasis continued in his Bucks County, Pennsylvania photographs. The complete break with the past would come a few years later. Again, Martha's Vineyard would provide both setting and stimulus.

Returning to the island frequently during the early 1940s, Siskind began working with natural objects, composing on a flat plane with geometric organization. By eliminating the deep focus that other photographers cherished, he found the objects in his images taking on added significance. The "breakthrough" for Siskind occurred on a day in 1944, not on the island, but in the coastal community of Gloucester, Massachusetts.

Photographing an old glove against wood, Siskind "realized that I had to take that picture looking straight down . . . wiping out all perspective." He did so, with memorable results ("The Glove," 1944). "Then I realized just how powerful an object it was," he continued, at more than three decade's remove from the event, "I made an object which confronts you, not an object that you're just looking at—it's parallel to you." The object (and this remains true of Siskind's most recent photographs as well) had become both more and less important, both super-real and abstract, simultaneously. The photograph had become the object.

With this personal style of gesture and nuance, this new form of visual calligraphy, Siskind went on to create a remarkable body of work which orders the conflicts and tensions inherent in the subject matter. The imposed order, however, is always a fragile one, all too ready to break down at the edges.

If such characteristics are reminiscent of abstract expressionism, it should not be surprising. For many years, the world of painting showed far more understanding of and receptivity to Siskind's work than did his fellow photographers (indeed, the strict documentarians of the League greeted *Tabernacle City* with cries of "sellout!"). Siskind's photographs were, after all, *about* photography, in the same sense that Jackson Pollock's paintings were about his medium. Aaron Siskind's first major exhibit, in 1947, was at New York's Egan Gallery, a home for the most contemporary painting. His first book, with an introduction by respected art critic Harold Rosenberg, was published only because Franz Kline and other friends from the world of painting provided financial support for the project.

Photographers may have lagged behind, but they caught up in time. As Henry Holmes Smith suggested, other photographers finally perceived in Siskind's work, new possibilities, new answers for unavoidable (if persistently unasked) questions. Through all of this, Siskind continued doing what it gave him pleasure to do: making photographs and teaching young photographers.

Cryptic though some of his images may be at first glance (see, for example, the bits and pieces of wall graffiti from which many Siskind pictures are composed), their internal logic is overwhelming. It is necessary only to suspend the belief that there exists a world on the other side of the photographic image. Siskind's photographs are not windows looking out upon another reality; rather, each is a singular object, flat, irrevocably bounded by its borders—a self-contained reality.

"You know," Aaron Siskind mused in 1977, "for the first time in my life, I'm really free. I'm 73 now and I've made it. It should have happened when I was 71 and could really appreciate it."

—Stu Cohen

SJÖSTEDT, Ulf (Georg).

Nationality: Swedish. **Born:** Karlstad, 7 April 1935. **Education:** Attended schools in Kristinehamn and Borlange, Sweden, 1948-57; studied graphics and photography at the School of Arts and Handicrafts (Konstindustriskolan),

Göteborg, 1959-62; also studied at the Institute of Higher Marketing Education, Göteborg, 1971-73, Dip. 1973. **Military Service:** Served in the Swedish Army Infantry, in Falun and Stockholm, 1957-59: Captain, 1969. **Family:** Married Brita Karäng in 1970 (divorced, 1985); daughter: Katarina. **Career:** Photographer since 1950. Studio Manager, Tre Tryckare publishing company, Göteborg, 1962-64; Editor, *Nordisk Tidskrift för Fotografi* magazine, Göteborg, 1964-66. Editor-in-Chief, *Hasselblad Magazine,* Göteborg, 1967-75. Advertising Manager,1969-1982. Regional Sales Manager 1983-1991, Victor Hasselblad AB photo equipment company, Göteborg. Since 1992 freelance photographer and writer, from 1994 editor of Hasselblad *FORUM.* Photography Correspondent, *Göteborgs Tidningen,* 1971-79. Secretary, National Association of Swedish Photography, 1964-65; Chairman, Photographic Society of Göteborg, 1967-70. **Recipient:** Municipal Culture Award, Göteborg, 1967; Welinder Award, Swedish Photographers Association, 1967; Swedish Authors Fund Award, 1972, 1976, 1979, 1982, 1985, 1989, 1993. **Address:** Valnötsgatan 6, S-426 74 V. Frölunda, Sweden.

Individual Exhibitions:

1966	*Swedish Artisans,* Historical Museum, Göteborg, Sweden
1975	*Pictures,* Pentax Gallery, London
1976	*Photographs 1961-1975,* Fotografiska Museet, Stockholm (travelled to the Varmlands Museum, Karlstad, Sweden, and the Museet-Kulturhuset, Borås, Sweden)
	Portfolios, Galleri Nordenskiold, Göteborg
1978	*Pictures,* Pentax Gallery, Amsterdam
1981	Galerie Reflex, Brussels
1982	Instituto Fotografico, Buenos Aires
1988	Innsbrucker Photoschau, Austria
1990	Uppsala Konsthall, Sweden
	Lycksele Konstförening, Sweden
1991	Galleri Mazarin, Söderhamn, Sweden
	Art Photo Galleri, Gstaad, Switzerland
1993	Galleri Fotohuset, Göteborg, Sweden
	Galleri Rosengången, Lerum, Sweden

Selected Group Exhibitions:

1958	*How We Live,* at *Photokina,* Cologne
1961	*Two Generations,* Art Museum, Göteborg (toured Sweden)
1967	*Silver-Textil-Keramik-Foto,* Konsthall, Skovde, Sweden
	Young Photographers, Moderna Museet, Stockholm
1968	*Young Form—Once Again,* Rhösska Museum, Göteborg
1976	*Fantastic Photography in Europe,* Fondacion Joan Miro, Barcelona (toured Europe)
1977	*From Today Painting Is Dead,* Maneten, Göteborg
	The Children of This World, Unicef/*Stern* travelling exhibition
1978	*A Thousand and One Pictures,* Moderna Museet, Stockholm
1979	*The History of Photography,* Art Museum, Göteborg
1982	*Fotograferna och det Svenska landskappet,* Fotografiska Museet, Stockholm
1992	*Naturfotografi i Sverige,* Hasselblad Center, Göteborg

Collections:

Fotografiska Museet, Moderna Museet, Stockholm; Varmlands Museum, Karlstad, Sweden; Borås Museum, Sweden; Pentax Gallery, London; Pentax Gallery, Amsterdam; Instituto Fotografico, Buenos Aires.

Publications:

By SJÖSTEDT: Books—*Min Bilderbok,* Göteborg 1961; *Modern Reklam,* with text by Lars Foxe, Göteborg 1967; *En Bok om Några Vanner,* Göteborg 1971; *Katarina: Stina och Sommaren,* Göteborg 1976; *Sjön Suger,* with text by Bengt Petersen, Göteborg 1976; *Mina Mest Subjektiva Bilder,* Alingsas, Sweden 1979; *Den Fotografiska Bilden,* Halmstad, Sweden 1979; *Barn på Bild,* Halmstad, Sweden 1981; *Foto på Resaw,* Halmstad, Sweden 1981; *Nya Bilder,* Alingsås, Sweden 1981; *Vid Stranden,* by Erland Svenungson, Göteborg 1981; *Fotokomposition,* Halmstad, Sweden 1984; *Färgfotografi,* Halmstad

Portrait of My Very Good Friends, the Painters Ake R. Nilsson and Roj Friberg, **Veddige, Sweden, 1994.** Photograph ©Ulf Sjöstedt.

1990; *Poetisk Bilderbok*, Göteborg 1994; *Fotografiskt Bildtänkande*, Halmstad 1994. **Articles**—"2 Generations" in *Nordisk Tidskrift för Fotografi* (Göteborg), no. 7/8, 1961; "The Problems of the Countryside Photographer" in *Foto* (Stockholm), no. 5, 1963; "My Best Pictures" in *Foto* (Stockholm), no. 12, 1965; "Schwedische Fotografie" in *Leica Fotografie* (Frankfurt), no. 6, 1967; article in *Amateur Photographer* (London), January 1976; "Foto di Gruppo" in *Nuova Fotografia* (Naples), January 1978; "Motion" in *Petersen's Photographic Magazine* (Los Angeles), May 1978; "Ma ... cos'e una buona fotografia" in *Nuova Fotografia* (Naples), July 1978; "Wellenspiele" in *Photo Revue* (Munich), no. 12, 1978; also numerous other articles in *Nordisk Tidskrift för Fotografi* (Göteborg), 1964-66, *Hasselblad Magazine* (Göteborg), 1965-80, *Fotonyheterna* (Stockholm), 1966-74, and *Photolife* (Toronto), 1978-79; "Le regard en noir et blanc d'Ulf Sjöstedt paysagiste suedois" in *Vautier* (Brussels), August/September 1982; "Los grandes maestros" in *Fotomundo* (Buenos Aires), December 1982; "Melancholischer Nordern" in *Photo Technik International* (Munich), no. 4, 1985; *Hasselblad Forum*, (Göteborg) 1985-1993; The photographic history *FOTO*, (Stockholm) nos. 3,4,5,6,7,8, 1991; *Aktuell Fotografi*, (Helsingborg), nos. 5,6,7,8, 1993.

On SJÖSTEDT: Books—*Fotograferna och det Svenska landskappet*, exhibition catalogue, by Leif Wigh, Stockholm 1982. **Articles**—"Ulf Sjöstedt, Realist" by Bengt Gustafson in *Foto* (Stockholm), no. 8, 1962; "Der Weitwinkel" by Evald Karlsten in *Camera* (Lucerne), February 1968; "Vidvinkel, det dramat. obj." by Helge Jacobsen in *Foto og Smallfilm* (Copenhagen), no. 4, 1969; "The Egg Comes First" by Jane Dreyfuss in *Modern Photography* (New York), January 1970; "Ulf Sjöstedt: Egg Pictures" in *Creative Camera* (London), no. 5, 1971; "Ulf Sjöstedt" by Jean Target in *Phototribune* (Antwerp), no. 6, 1971; "Matador der Kamera" by Joachim Giebelhause in *Color Foto* (Munich), no. 7, 1972; "Ulf Sjöstedt, Tecnica del Sandwich" in *Nuova Fotografia* (Naples), no. 4, 1973; "Ulf Sjöstedt" by Knut Försund in *Fotografi* (Råholt, Norway), December 1975; "Ulf Sjöstedt" in *Flash* (Barcelona), January 1976; "Ulf Sjöstedt" by Evald Karlsten in *Svensk Fotografisk Tidskrift* (Stockholm), no. 1, 1976; "Ulf Sjöstedt Frammenti ... " by Manlio Cammarata in *Nuova Fotografia* (Naples), February 1976; "Forum Junger Fotografen" by Evald Karlsten in *Foto Magazin,* (Munich), no. 6, 1976; "Han vandrar not strommen" by Lars Fahlén in *Foto* (Stockholm), August 1976; "Fotografen en hun werk" in *Foto* (Amersfoort, Holland), March 1977; "Portfolio, Ulf Sjöstedt" by Jean-Pierre Vorlet in *Schweizerische Photorundschau* (Visp, Switzerland), March 1978; "Ulf Sjöstedt" in *Le Nouveau Grand Angle* (Paris), May 1978; "Ulf Sjöstedt" by Per Lindström in *Aktuell Fotografi* (Helsingborg, Sweden), April 1979; "Im Frühtau mit der Kamera" in *Photo Revue* (Munich), May 1981; "A Photographic Purpose" in *Photo Life* (Toronto), December 1981; "Ulf Sjöstedt: het geromantiseerde naakt" in *Foto* (Hilversum, Netherlands), no. 9, 1982; "Form und Spannung" in *Photo Revue* (Munich), February 1983; "Fotografiet som illustration" in *Fotonyheterna* (Stockholm), May 1984; "Windows and Walls" in *Petersens' Photographic* (Los Angeles), May 1985.

*

Photography is a young medium—only about 150 years old—and therefore just in the beginning of its development. No doubt the main purpose of this medium has hitherto been and probably is still to give a realistic description of the world in which we are living—to tell people of today and tomorrow about justice and injustice ...

Most of my pictures are documentary, but, as photography can be used in many different ways, I am more interested in creative photography, in what Professor Otto Steinert called "subjective photography." Painters, draughtsmen and graphic artists can use their media in order to capture a man's mood or his experience, and so can the photographer. It is true that photography has not yet produced a Leonardo, a Rembrandt or a Picasso, but be sure there will be one, someday.

Like the brush, the camera is just a tool, and the quality of all the equipment—camera, film, developer, enlarger, etc. must be of a sort that gives you the exact result of the vision you had at the moment of shooting. Technique and composition are interesting only as means to reach the goal: the contents of the picture; but, on the other hand, should you fail to master skills and technique, that failure will inevitably show up.

International photography is in rapid progress, but whether it is going straight ahead or sideways is not possible to say. I am afraid that in many countries—for instance, Sweden—it is moving sideways.

The great number of photo-galleries that have opened during the last ten years all over the world will, I hope, increase the quality of creative—or, if you will, subjective—photography in every country.

It is sad and almost ridiculous that photography must be hung in fine art galleries within glass and gold frames in order to be taken seriously as a medium for expressing feelings and moods. The picture-book is the best means of presenting photographic pictures—if the printing is of a high quality. You can, in peace and quiet at home, in the most comfortable armchair, take part in and study pictures produced through a medium which is suited more than any other for printing. For me, text and picture are one. The support that the two media can give each other is, I think, often needed. It is very seldom that a picture can manage alone. That generalization also applies to "subjective" pictures. Yet, there are pictures that can stand alone. I don't mean that the text should be "directions"; rather, it should be a guide for the imagination. To read pictures is not easy. Too many of us are picture-illiterates.

One photographer has said that you do not take more than 200-250 good pictures during a lifetime. I believe him. I am not sure that I will reach that number myself. I have not taken more than 50 good pictures. Hardly that.

There is no doubt that I am influenced by the international style of taking pictures. Each month I go through more than a hundred of the world's photo magazines, and I keep in touch with many of the world's leading photographers and photo writers. But I am also influenced by my Swedish friends working with painting, drawing and graphic art, and by their way of making pictures.

In my opinion photography is not more remarkable than painting. Everyone can take photographic pictures as well as draw funny drawings—each one according to their own conditions. Every pictorial medium has its own distinctive character. As I've said, photography is a young medium with enormous possibilities for development. Now is the time for those of us with a camera in hand to take advantage of those possibilities.

—Ulf Sjöstedt

*   *   *

Ulf Sjöstedt has sometimes been called "Sweden's best-known amateur photographer." It is an honorable title, and no doubt there's some truth in it. In spite of a very prolific photographic activity, Sjöstedt has succeeded in preserving the amateur's curiosity and delight in experiment. This is reflected in his picture-world. Nor has he ever been a professional photographer in the accepted sense of the term. He has never derived the main part of his income from selling pictures or from undertaking photographic commissions.

On the other hand, Sjöstedt has been involved with photos for the whole of his working life. After his studies at the School of Arts and Handicrafts in Göteborg, he was engaged as the head of a drawing office for a publishing company; between 1964 and 1966 he was the editor of the Göteborg photoclub's journal; and since 1967 he has been employed by Hasselblad in Göteborg: he was the editor of their journal from 1967 to 1974. In his daily work he has thus had a great deal of opportunity to come into contact with pictures and to reach people interested in pictures. Partly through his articles, partly through his own pictures. In addition, he has written and illustrated several books, and he is also a very popular lecturer in the photo-clubs. Photography has, in effect, become a full-time occupation for Sjöstedt. But he still modestly calls himself an amateur.

Thanks to that amateur status, Sjöstedt's picture-world has remained a private one. Much of what he does can be classified as family and holiday photos. But the technical and artistic quality of his work is certainly higher than what one normally associates with those kinds of pictures.

Names that he normally mentions with great respect are those of the Russian constructivists Rodchenko and Kandinsky. Sjöstedt attempts to adapt their composition theories of diagonals and points to a world of "subjects," and the results emerge sometimes as Scandinavian-romantic, sometimes as surrealistic.

Although many of his best-known pictures were taken in the 1970s, they are reminiscent of the 50s. The conscious idiomatic expression combined with a deep seriousness in many of his pictures reflect the epoch of "Subjective

Photography''—and Otto Steinert is, not surprisingly, another pictorial theoretician to whom Sjöstedt refers.

In recent years he has worked on two large projects—birches and the sea. He sees the birchtree as a symbol of Sweden. In the 1930s and 40s it was almost a symbol of Swedish amateur photography as well, but at that time it was more the natural/lyrical and romantic aspects of the tree that were stressed in exhibition photos. Sjöstedt hopes in his series to combine romanticism and mysticism with a taut and decorative idiomatic expression.

The sea is limitless, and, as a resident of the West Coast, he comes into daily contact with it. It is a challenge to extract something new from that which is so well known. Sjöstedt likes such challenges.

—Rune Jonsson

SKOFF, Gail.

Nationality: American. **Born:** Los Angeles, California, 27 September 1949. **Education:** Hamilton High School, Los Angeles, 1964-67; University of California, Berkeley, 1967-69; Boston Museum School, 1969-71; San Francisco Art Institute, 1971-72, B.F.A. 1972, M.F.A. 1979; also studied at University of California Extension, San Francisco, 1972-73. **Career:** Freelance photographer, Berkeley, since 1973. Instructor in Photography, University of California Extension, Berkeley, since 1976; Instructor since 1976, and Darkroom Supervisor and Photo Curator, 1977-85, A.S.U.C. Studio, University of California, Berkeley. Lecturer, College of Visual Design, Department of Architecture, University of California, Berkeley, Summer 1980. **Recipient:** National Endowment for the Arts Photography Fellowship, 1976. **Agent:** Jones Troyer Gallery, 1614 20th Street N.W., Washington, D.C. 20009, U.S.A.

Individual Exhibitions:

1973   University of California Extension, San Francisco
1974   *Introductions '74,* Phoenix Gallery, San Francisco
1977   Centre Culturel Americain, Paris
        Images of Bali, Simon Lowinsky Gallery, San Francisco
1979   Washington State University, Pullman
1980   Simon Lowinsky Gallery, San Francisco
1981   Simon Lowinsky Gallery, Los Angeles
1982   Equivalents Gallery, Seattle
1983   Delahunty Gallery, Dallas, Texas
        Ledel Gallery, New York
1984   Jones Troyer Gallery, Washington, D.C.

Selected Group Exhibitions:

1975   *Hand-Colored Photographs,* Ohio Silver Gallery, Los Angeles
        Exchange DFW/SFO, Fort Worth Museum of Art, Texas
           (travelled to the San Francisco Museum of Modern Art)
1976   *The Photographers' Choice* (toured the United States,
           1976-79)
1977   *Radical Photography and Bay Area Innovators,* Sacred Heart
           Schools Gallery, Menlo Park, California
1978   *Threads of Tradition,* University of California Art Museum and
           Lowie Museum, Berkeley
1979   *Attitudes: Photography in the 1970s,* Santa Barbara Museum of
           Art, California
1980   *SECA Photography Invitational,* San Francisco Museum of
           Modern Art
1981   *Four California Views,* Oakland Art Museum, California
        American Photographers and the National Parks, Oakland
           Museum, California (toured the United States, 1981-83)
1983   *In Color: Ten California Photographers,* Oakland Museum,
           California
1984   *Exposed and Developed,* National Museum of American Art,
           Washington, D.C. (toured the United States)

1985   *The Colored Image,* Friends of Photography, Carmel,
        California

Collections:

Smith College Art Gallery, Northampton, Massachusetts; Center for Creative Photography, University of Arizona, Tucson; Oakland Art Museum, California; Bibliothèque Nationale, Paris; National Museum of American Art, Washington, D.C.

Publications:

On SKOFF: Books—*Celebrations* by Minor White, New York 1974; *The Photographer's Choice,* edited by Kelly Wise, Danbury, New Hampshire 1976; *Alternative Photographic Processes* by Kent Wade, New York 1978; *The New Landscape,* edited by Friends of Photography, Carmel, California 1981; *The Print* by Time-Life editors, New York 1981; *Photographer as Printmaker,* exhibition catalogue, with texts by Gerry Badger, Peter C, Bunnell and Ansel Adams, London 1981; *Landscape as Photograph* by Estelle Jussim and Elizabeth Lindquist-Cock, New Haven, Connecticut 1985. **Articles**—"The Young Romantics" by Douglas Davis in *Newsweek* (New York), March 1979; "Northern California Photography" by Hal Fischer in *Picture Magazine* (Los Angeles), no. 11, 1979; "Reviews" by Hal Fischer in *Artforum* (New York), May 1980; "Contemporary Hand Colored Photography" in *Picture Magazine* (Los Angeles), no. 17, 1981.

*

My interest in the magical transformation of reality through hand coloring photographs has remained consistent over time although my subject matter has changed considerably. I try to create photographs where time and space are suspended, and a new world emerges separate from my everyday life.

My involvement with these ideas began in earlier hand-colored work, where I photographed costumed models in environments that had an illusion of timelessness. Subsequently, I photographed people in foreign places and exotic cultures, where contemporary life as I know it was nonexistent. Every clue to date was removed from the photographs.

My recent work with the landscape seems to transcend the specificity of time and human presence even more dramatically. I am fascinated with photographing uninhabited spaces: oceans, deserts, prairies and unique natural land formations. Sometimes, when clouds appear in the sky, or in the light of dawn or dusk, the landscape takes on an unworldly glow. To reproduce the visual reality of these places at such moments is not enough. I use the processes of toning and hand-coloring to transform the black-and-white image by selectively emphasizing certain of its elements. When everything comes together in the finished piece, the feeling of being in these places is recreated.

—Gail Skoff

*   *   *

Gail Skoff's consuming passion is the land. Not any land, but the great, sprawling, uncultivated earth of western America. Her safaries into this environment have become a personal odyssey, "the great adventure." Few women in the history of photography have dealt with the landscape as a major concern. Skoff is one of a growing number of women venturing back to this rediscovered frontier. Wanderlust is nothing new to her. She has traveled widely, and some of her best early work was done in France and Bali. But there is a freshness and mature assurance in the more recent American landscapes, an insight and understanding of the nature of the territory.

Gail's automobile excursions resemble the stage-coach journey that Mark Twain writes about in *Innocents Abroad.* He describes the vastness of the western American landscape in the early 1900s which today remains much the same. "The first 700 miles a level continent, its grassy carpet greener and softer and smoother than any sea and figured with designs fitted to its magnitude—the shadow of the clouds.... Then 1300 miles of desert solitudes; of limitless panoramas of bewildering perspective; of mimic cities, of pinnacled cathedrals, of massive fortresses, counterfeited in the eternal rocks and splendid with the crimson and gold of the setting sun; of dizzy altitudes among fog-wreathed peaks and never-melting snows, where thunders and lightnings and tempests warred magnificently at our feet and the storm clouds above swung their shredded banners in our very faces!''

Skoff's images embody this landscape. The way in which she hand colors, heightens and enriches the dramatic effects of light, space, and earth surface. Her hand coloring techniques were used in her earlier work, but have been refined and polished in her more recent work. She uses combinations of paints and dyes, rubbing, blending, masking, drawing and painting on the original black-and-white image. This produces sometimes subtle, sometimes striking, always exquisite results.

—Judy Dater

SKOGLUND, Sandy.

Nationality: American. **Born:** Quincy, Massachusetts. **Education:** Smith College, Northampton, Massachusetts, B.A. 1968, University of Iowa, Iowa City, M.F.A. 1972. **Career:** Worked as teacher at Hartford Art School, University of Hartford, Connecticut, 1973-76; Visiting Professor at Hartford Art School since 1976, and at Newark College of Arts and Sciences, Rutgers, The State University of New Jersey, since 1992. **Recipient:** National Endowment for the Arts grant, 1980; New York Foundation for the Arts grant, 1988. **Agent:** Janet Borden, Inc., 560 Broadway, New York, New York 10012, U.S.A.

Individual Exhibitions:

1981   *Revenge of the Goldfish,* Castelli Graphics, New York; Fort Worth Art Museum, Fort Worth, Texas; Greenberg Gallery, St Louis, Missouri
        Radioactive Cats, Addison Gallery of American Art, Andover, Massachusetts
1982   *Revenge of the Goldfish* and *Radioactive Cats,* Minneapolis Institute of Art, Minneapolis, Minnesota
        Revenge of the Goldfish, Wadsworth Atheneum, Hartford, Connecticut
1983   Galerie Watari, Tokyo
        Maybe Babies, Leo Castelli, New York; Greenberg Gallery, St Louis, Missouri
1987   *True Fiction,* Castelli Uptown Gallery, New York
        Neo Auto, Sharpe Gallery, New York
        Real Art Ways, Hartford, Connecticut
        Fay Gold Gallery, Atlanta, Georgia
1988   *Installation with still life sculptures,* Lorence-Monk Gallery, New York
        A Breeze at Work, Damon Brandt Gallery, New York
1989   Stephen Wirtz Gallery, San Francisco
        Galerie Urbi et Orbi, Paris
1990   *The Green House,* Temple Gallery, Tyler School of Art, Philadelphia, Pennsylvania; Janet Borden, Inc., New York; G H Dalsheimer Gallery, Baltimore, Maryland
        Radioactive Cats, and retrospective of photographs, Parco Gallery, Tokyo
        Fox Games, The Denver Art Museum, Colorado
        True Fiction & Fox Games, International Museum of Photography, George Eastman House, Rochester, New York
1991   *The Green House,* The Tampa Museum of Art, Tampa, Florida; Memphis Brooks Museum, Memphis, Tennessee; The Morgan Gallery, Kansas City, Missouri; Fay Gold Gallery, Atlanta, Georgia
        Gathering Paradise, (two person show with Jack Coplans), Hartford Art School, Harry Jack Gray Center, West Hartford, Connecticut; P.P.O.W. Gallery, New York; Carl Solway Gallery, Cincinnati, Ohio
        Radioactive Cats and retrospective of photographs, Staatsgalerie, Erlangen, Germany, (then travelled to Bremen and Zurich)

Ehlers Caudhill Gallery, Chicago, Illinois
1992   *The Green House,* Aspen Art Museum, Aspen, Colorado; The Museum, Coral Gables, Florida
        Radioactive Cats and retrospective of photographs, travelling to Frankfurt, Barcelona, Paris and Aurillac

Collections:

Addison Gallery of American Art, Andover, Massachusetts; Akron Art Museum, Akron, Ohio; American Petroleum Partners, Dallas, Texas; Art Museum, University of Massachusetts, Amherst, Massachusetts; Baltimore Museum of Art, Baltimore, Maryland; Boise Gallery of Art, Permanent Collection, Boise, Idaho; The Brooklyn Museum, Brooklyn, New York; Center for Creative Photography, University of Arizona, Tucson, Arizona; Centre Pompidou, Paris, France; Tampa Museum of Art, Tampa, Florida; Wadsworth Atheneum, Hartford, Connecticut; Wake Forest University, Winston-Salem, North Carolina; Walker Art Center, Minneapolis, Minnesota.

* * *

Since 1980 Sandy Skoglund has been giving viewers a fun-house *frisson* with her lifesize, candy-coloured, painstakingly crafted tableaux and the large scale Cibachromes she makes of them. Animals are her favorite characters and run amok in everyday interiors: in *Radioactive Cats* (1980) dozens of neon-green felines swarm over an elderly couple's all-gray kitchen; in *Fox Games* (1989) twenty-two red fur-bearers invade an all-gray restaurant; in *The Green House* (1990) thirty-three dogs in purple or green reign in a bourgeois living room covered with artificial grass. The sets and props are real and mundane, and the creatures are modelled to an uncanny verisimilitude, while their manic multiplication and saturated two-colour palette turn them into a satirical pop nightmare. In the airless boxes of middle-class American culture the animals personify anarchic energy as they rebel against their domestication. Disneyland (where Skoglund worked for a summer as a teenager) welcomes Swift and Surrealism in this artist's exuberant imagination.

From 1969-72 Skoglund studied painting, printmaking and film at the University of Iowa and she took up Conceptualism when she came to New York in 1972. Like many of her generation, she eventually found it "too thin" and resumed drawing as she discovered the vitality of illustration and other non-art forms designed for communication. Commercial photography, with its hyped hues and deceptively faux-casual still lifes of food, inspired her first camera work in 1978, the photographs of frozen peas and carrots she carefully arranged on patterned plates. "Pop Art Meets Op Art at the Food Fair" read Vince Aletti's review, catching her broad humour about American tastes, both culinary and aesthetic and her ability to mock both by combining their genres.

Skoglund began constructing tableaux in 1980 and she continues to install them with the limited edition photographs she takes of them, thus dramatizing their differences. "I don't think this whole fabrication business is about the cynicism of how we've lost touch with reality," she says "but how the world of ideas and the world of appearances come together." Each tableau can take six months or more to produce as Skoglund models her animals, then casts them in polyester resin, locates just the right props, then arranges, paints and, after adding human actors, lights and shoots the totality. The results, she observes, combine sculpture, photography, set design and film. Each Cibachrome is "a film in one frame."

In the 1985-86 series she called *True Fiction,* Skoglund investigated photo-collage as another means of "making the familiar unfamiliar," the Surrealist strategy of *depaysement.* Here she stages friends in domestic scenes, photographed them in black and white, printed the negatives in various colours, then cut out silhouettes and collaged new scenes together to rephotograph. This method let her colour her ingredients in the darkroom and gain drastic jumps of scale without loss of detail, but it lacked the horror-movie literalism of her tableaux photographs. What she retained from the series was its focus on suburban folkways and fetishes, like Waring blenders and junk food.

In her 1994 installation called *The Wedding* again preserved in an edition of Cibachromes, Skoglund covered the gallery floor with orange marmalade and the walls with strawberry preserves. Set amid a pattern of grey ceramic roses, her bridal mannequins and cake were uniformly red. In the photograph the live bride tried to walk across the floor to her groom but got stuck in the

The Green House, **1990.** Photograph by Sandy Skoglund. Courtesy Janet Borden, Inc.

jam. Is middle-class marriage in a jam or are romantic rituals disgustingly synthetic-sweet? Whatever Skoglund meant, she again satisfied a popular appetite for satire of American customs and for decorative excess.

—Anne Hoy

SLAVIN, Neal.

Nationality: American. **Born:** Brooklyn, New York, 19 August 1941. **Education:** the Music and Art High School, New York, 1955-59; studied painting, graphic design and photography, Cooper Union, New York, 1959-63, B.F.A. 1963; Renaissance painting and sculpture, Lincoln College, Oxford University, England, 1961. **Military Service:** Served in the United States Army Reserve, 1963-64. **Career:** Freelance photographer and graphic artist, working for *New York Times, Sunday Times* (London), *Stern, Fortune, Esquire, Newsweek,* etc., since 1963; established studio, New York, 1975. Instructor in Photography, Manhattanville College, Purchase, New York, 1970-74; Queen's College, New York, 1972; Cooper Union, New York, 1972-74; and School of Visual Arts, New York, 1973. **Recipient:** Fulbright

Photography Fellowship, 1968; National Endowment for the Arts Grant, 1972, 1976; Creative Artists Public Service Award, 1977. **Agent:** Barbara Von Schreiber, 315 Central Park West, New York, New York 10025, U.S.A. **Address:** 62 Greene Street, New York, New York 10012, U.S.A.

Individual Exhibitions:

1967	The Underground Gallery, New York
1968	National Museum of Ancient Art, Lisbon
1970	Museu Machado de Castro, Coimbra, Portugal
1971	The Underground Gallery, New York
	Royal Ontario Museum, Toronto
1972	Focus Gallery, San Francisco
	831 Gallery, Birmingham, Michigan
1976	Silver Image Gallery, Tacoma, Washington
	University of Maryland, Baltimore
	Oakland Museum, California
	Matrix, Wadsworth Atheneum, Hartford, Connecticut
	Center for Creative Photography, University of Arizona, Tucson
	Light Gallery, New York (2 exhibitions)
1978	Galerie Spectrum, Hannover

	Galerie Gothaer, Cologne
1979	Shadai Gallery, Tokyo
	Milwaukee Arts Center, Wisconsin
1980	Akron Art Institute, Ohio
1986	International Center of Photography, New York
	National Museum of Photography, Bradford, Yorkshire

Selected Group Exhibitions:

1971	*The Concerned Photographer,* Riverside Museum, New York
1975	*National Photography Invitational,* Virginia Commonwealth University, Richmond
1976	*Rooms,* Museum of Modern Art, New York
1978	*Tusen och en bild,* Moderna Museet, Stockholm
1979	*Photographie als Kunst 1879-1979,* Tiroler Landesmuseum Ferdinandeum, Innsbruck, Austria (travelled to Neue Galerie am Wolfgang Gurlitt Museum, Linz; Neue Galerie am Landesmuseum Joanneum, Graz; Museum des 20. Jahrhunderts, Vienna)
1980	*Aspects of the 70s,* DeCordova Museum, Lincoln, Massachusetts
1981	*Aspects of American Photography,* Galerie Spectrum, Hannover
1982	*Counterparts: Form and Emotion in Photographs,* Metropolitan Museum of Art, New York (travelled to the Contemporary Arts Center, Cincinnati, Ohio; Dallas Museum of Fine Art, Texas; San Francisco Museum of Modern Art; Corcoran Gallery, Washington, D.C.)
1984	*Sammlung Gruber,* Museum Ludwig, Cologne
1986	*The History of Color Photography,* at *Photokina 86*

Collections:

Metropolitan Museum of Art, New York; Museum of Modern Art, New York; New York Public Library; International Museum of Photography, George Eastman House, Rochester, New York; University of Maryland, Baltimore; Akron Art Institute, Ohio; Exchange National Bank, Chicago; Center for Creative Photography, University of Arizona, Tucson; University of California at Los Angeles; Moderna Museet, Stockholm.

Publications:

By SLAVIN: Books—*Portugal,* with an afterword by Mary McCarthy, New York 1971; *When Two or More Are Gathered Together,* New York 1976; *Johnny's Egg,* with text by Earlene Long, illustrations by Charles Mikolaycak, Reading, Massachusetts 1980; *Britons,* with introduction by Auberon Waugh, London and New York 1986.

On SLAVIN: Books—Photographs: Sheldon Memorial Art Gallery Collection, *University of Nebraska,* with an introduction by Norman A. Geske, Lincoln 1977; *Geschichte der Fotografie im 20. Jahrhundert/Photography in the 20th Century* by Petr Tausk, Cologne 1977, London 1980; *Documenta 6, Band 2,* exhibition catalogue, by Klaus Honnef and Evelyn Weiss, Kassel, 1977; *Tusen och en bild,* exhibition catalogue, by Ake Sidwall, Sune Jonsson and Ulf Hard af Segerstad, Stockholm 1978; *Dumont Foto 1,* edited by Hugo Schöttle, Cologne 1978; *Darkroom 2,* edited by Jain Kelly, New York 1978; *Faces* by Ben Maddow, Boston 1979; *Photographie als Kunst 1879-1979/ Kunst als Photographie 1949-79,* exhibition catalogue, 2 vols., by Peter Weiermair, Innsbruck 1979; *The Photograph Collector's Guide* by Lee D. Witkin and Barbara London, Boston and London 1979; *Farbe im Photo: Die Geschichte der Farbphotographie von 1861 bis 1981* by Fritz Binder, Gert Koshofer, Rolf Sachsse and others, Cologne 1981; *Lichtbildnisse: Das Porträt in der Fotografie,* edited by Klaus Honnef, Cologne 1982; *Sammlung Gruber: Photographie des 20. Jahrhunderts,* exhibition catalogue, with foreword by Siegfried Gohr, Cologne 1984; *A Day in the Life of Japan—June 7, 1985,* edited by Rick Smolan and David Cohen, New York and London 1985. **Articles**—"New American Imagery: Neal Slavin" in *Camera* (Lucerne), May 1974; "The Coming to Age of Color" by Max Kozloff in *Artforum* (New York), January 1975; "America '76," special issue of *Du* (Zurich), January 1976; "When Two or More Are Gathered Together" by Sheila Turner Seed in

Popular Photography (New York), February 1976; "New Frontiers in Color" by Douglas Davis in *Newsweek* (New York), 19 April 1976; "Looking at Groups, Defining America" by Joan Murray in *Artweek* (Oakland, California), 9 October 1976; "All Things Small and British" by Erla Zwingle in *American Photographer* (New York), July 1986.

*

There are the emotions and there is the intellect—somewhere in the middle there is my photography.

—Neal Slavin

*   *   *

Neal Slavin is one of the most versatile and intelligent commercial photographers in America. Known as an imaginative problem-solver, he works with equal ease on location or in his Manhattan studio, producing images which appear regularly on book jackets and magazine covers, in essay form in such diverse publications as *New York* and *Geo,* and elsewhere.

Alongside his commercial work, Slavin periodically undertakes self-assigned projects of a professional nature, which generally resolve themselves in book form. To date, these extended works have shared a common sociological thrust, but have made radically divergent demands on Slavin's capabilities as an image-maker.

The first of these essays, *Portugal,* is a somber meditation on a repressed culture in the grip of a political dictatorship. For this study, Slavin chose to utilize the 35mm camera and black-and-white film; this enabled him to work in an unobtrusive, fluid, intuitive and responsive manner under virtually any lighting conditions. The resulting sequence of images, a revealing and highly personal interpretation of his subject, showed Slavin to be adept at the small-camera documentary mode as defined by Cartier-Bresson and redefined by Robert Frank. Carefully structured for all their informality, and printed with an awareness of the emotional resonance of darkness, this set of pointed glimpses of Portuguese life cumulatively made a clear statement about the effect of political oppression on those who live under it.

Slavin's next project was conceived on a much larger scale, and involved a considerably different set of craft imperatives. Published as *When Two or More Are Gathered Together,* it is a lengthy suite of posed formal color portraits of American social and professional groups.

Slavin's particular concern in this work was to find and make evident those means by which the members of a group define themselves, in sociologist Erving Goffman's term, as "a *with*"—that is, the ways in which they signal their shared identity. Because clothing and such appurtenances of decor as banners are among those signals, Slavin chose to work in color, which enabled him to render full information on the groups' self-presentation to the camera. The ritualistic aspect of that conscious transaction between photographer and subjects virtually mandated the use of large-format cameras and (in most cases) controlled lighting. The ensuing large negatives provided greater detail—and thus more information—about the groups' dress, body language, hierarchical positioning and other matters.

Thus Slavin's adroit handling of a dramatically different photographic approach—different in its relation to subject matter and different in its materials and techniques—gave evidence of a remarkable adaptability, indicative of the photographer's capacity to conceptualize his projects carefully and bring to them a level of craft which permits the use of whatever tools, materials and techniques are appropriate to the work at hand. Slavin's is a clear case of the benefits which the rigorous demands of professional work bestow on the creative photographer.

—A.D. Coleman

SMITH, Henry Holmes.

Nationality: American. **Born:** Bloomington, Illinois, 23 October 1909. **Education:** Attended primary and secondary schools in Bloomington; studied at the State Normal College, Bloomington, 1927-29, 1930-31; School of the Art Institute of Chicago, 1929-30; Ohio State University, Columbus, 1932-33, B.S. 1933. **Military Service:** Served in the United States Army, in Hawaii, the Gilbert Islands and Iwo Jima, 1942-45. **Family:** Married Wanda Lee Phares in 1947; sons: Christopher and Theodore. **Career:** Independent photographer, Chicago, 1934-46, Bloomington, Indiana, 1946-77, and Lake Tahoe, Navada, 1977-81, and in San Rafael, California, 1981 until his death in 1986; worked on color synthesis photography from 1947. Instructor of Photography, with Gyorgy Kepes and László Moholy-Nagy, New Bauhaus School, Chicago, 1937-38; Instructor of Photography, 1947-65, and Professor, 1965-77, Indiana University, Bloomington. Visiting Professor, Maryland Institute College of Art, Baltimore, 1967. Associate Editor, *Minicam Photography,* Cincinnati, Ohio, 1940-42, and *College Art Journal,* Bloomington, 1955-64. Founder Member, 1963, Vice-Chairman, 1963-67, and Member of the Board of Directors, Society for Photographic Education. Trustee, Friends of Photography, Carmel, California, 1975-83. **Recipient:** Herman Frederick Lieber Distinguished Teaching Award, Indiana University, 1968. D.F.A.: Maryland Institute College of Art, 1968; Indiana University, 1982; Philadelphia College of Art, 1983. **Estate:**c/o Ted R. Smith, 5 Sequoia Road, Fairfax, California 94930, U.S.A. **Died:** (in Marin County, California) 24 March 1986.

Individual Exhibitions:

1946	Illinois Wesleyan University, Bloomington
1947	Indiana University, Bloomington
1956	University of North Dakota, Grand Forks
1958	State University of New York at New Paltz
1959	Indiana Art Directors Association, Indianapolis
1960	Akron Art Institute, Ohio
	Merchants Bank Building, Indianapolis
1962	Institute of Design, Illinois Institute of Technology, Chicago
1964	San Francisco State University
1971	Skidmore College, Saratoga Springs, New York
	Polaroid Corporation, Cambridge, Massachusetts
	University of California, Berkeley
1972	Phos/Graphos Gallery, San Francisco
	Center for Photographic Studies, Louisville, Kentucky
	New Orleans Museum of Art, Louisiana
1973	*Henry Holmes Smith's Art: 50 Years in Retrospect,* Indiana University, Bloomington
1974	Friends of Photography, Carmel, California
	J.B. Speed Museum, Louisville, Kentucky (with Ralph Eugene Meatyard)
	Indiana National Bank, Indianapolis
1975	Addison Gallery, Andover, Massachusetts
	Fort Wayne Art Institute, Indiana
1978	University of Oregon, Eugene
1982	Indiana University, Bloomington
1983	Philadelphia College of Art, Pennsylvania
1984	Silver Image Gallery, Seattle, Washington
	Robert Klein Gallery, Boston
1985	Focus Gallery, San Francisco
	Works 1974-84, California State University, Fresno
1992	*Photographs 1931-1986: A Retrospective,* Howard Greenberg Gallery, New York

Selected Group Exhibitions:

1951	*Abstract Photography,* Museum of Modern Art, New York
1959	*Photographer's Choice,* Indiana University, Bloomington
1960	*Sense of Abstraction,* Museum of Modern Art, New York
1967	*Photography in the 20th Century,* National Gallery of Canada, Ottawa (toured Canada and United States, 1967-73)
1975	*Contemporary American Photographs,* University of California, Los Angeles
1976	*Photographer's Choice,* Witkin Gallery, New York
1980	*Photography of the 50s,* Center for Creative Photography, University of Arizona, Tucson
1985	*American Images 1945-80,* Barbican Art Gallery, London (toured Britain)

1987	*Photography and Art 1946-86,* Los Angeles County Museum of Art
	50 Jahre New Bauhaus, Bauhaus-Archiv, Berlin
	Extending the Boundaries of Photography, University of Arizona, Center for Creative Photography, Tucson
	Modern Photography and Beyond, The National Museum of Modern Art, Kyoto, Japan
1988	*Photographic Legacy: The Influence of Henry Holmes Smith at Indiana University,* Indiana University Fine Arts Museum, Bloomington
1989	*Decade by Decade: Twentieth Century American Photography,* Center for Creative Photography, Tucson, Arizona
1990	*Personal Engagements: Abstract Photography of the Sixties,* The University of Rochester and the International Museum of Photography at George Eastman House, Rochester, New York
1991	*Patterns of Influence,* Center for Creative Photography, The University of Arizona, Tucson

Collections:

Indiana University, Bloomington (Henry Holmes Smith Archive—photographs); Museum of Modern Art, New York; International Museum of Photography, George Eastman House, Rochester, New York; Library of Congress, Washington, D.C.; New Orleans Museum of Art; Museum of Fine Arts, St. Petersburg, Florida; Center for Creative Photography, University of Arizona, Tucson (Henry Holmes Smith Archive—papers); University Art Museum, University of New Mexico, Albuquerque; Oakland Art Museum, California; San Francisco Museum of Modern Art; Museum of the Art Institute of Chicago, Illinois; Museum of Fine Arts, Houston, Texas; Cincinnati Art Museum, Ohio; Kalamazoo Art Institute, Michigan; Crocker Art Museum, Sacramento, California; Metropolitan Museum of Art, New York; Sheldon Memorial Art Gallery, University of Nebraska, Lincoln; Princeton University Museum, Princeton, New Jersey; Bibliotheque Nationale, Paris; Victoria and Albert Museum, London; Bauhaus Archive, Berlin; National Gallery of Canada, Ottawa; The National Museum of Modern Art, Kyoto, Japan.

Publications:

By SMITH: Books—*Henry Holmes Smith: Selected Critical Writings,* edited by Terence R. Pitts, Tucson, Arizona 1977; *Henry Holmes Smith: Collected Writings 1935-1985,* edited by James L. Enyeart and Nancy Solomon, Tucson, Arizona 1986. **Articles**—"Photographs and Public" in *Aperture* (Rochester, New York), 1953; "Frederick Sommer: Collages and Found Objects" in *Aperture* (Rochester, New York), 1956; "The First Indiana University Workshop" in *Aperture* (Rochester, New York), vol. 5, no. 1, 1957; "The Education of Picture-Minded Photographers" in *Aperture* (Rochester, New York), 1957; "Two for the Photojournalist" in *Aperture* (Rochester, New York), vol. 8, no. 4, 1960; "Museum Taste and the Taste of Our Time" in *Aperture* (Rochester, New York), 1962; "The Photographs of Van Deren Coke" in *Photography* (London), 1963; "The Photography of Jerry N. Uelsmann" in *Contemporary Photographer* (Culpepper, Virginia), vol. 5, no. 1, 1964; "New Figures in a Classic Tradition" in *Aaron Siskind, Photographer,* edited by Nathan Lyons, New York 1965; "Photography in Our Time" in *Photographers on Photography,* edited by Nathan Lyons, New York 1966; "An Access of American Sensibility: The Photographs of Clarence John Laughlin" in *Exposure* (Chicago), November 1973; "Critical Difficulties: Some Problems with Passing Judgement and Taking Issues" in *Afterimage* (Rochester, New York), Summer 1978; "Henry Holmes Smith," interview, in *Dialogue with Photography,* edited by Paul Hill and Thomas Cooper, London 1979.

On SMITH: Books—*The New Vision* by László Moholy-Nagy, New York 1938; *Photographer's Choice,* exhibition catalogue, Bloomington, Indiana 1959; *Invitational Teaching Conference at the George Eastman House,* Rochester, New York 1962; *Photography in the 20th Century* by Nathan Lyons, New York 1967; *Henry Holmes Smith's Art: 50 Years in Retrospect,* exhibition catalogue, Bloomington, Indiana 1973; *Photographs: Sheldon Memorial Art Gallery Collection, University of Nebraska,* with an introduction by Norman A. Geske, Lincoln, Nebraska 1977; *The Photograph Collector's Guide* by Lee D. Witkin and Barbara London, Boston and London 1979; *The New Vision: Forty Years of Photography at the Institute of Design* by Charles Traub, New York 1982; *Henry Holmes Smith: Non-Camera Photographer,* exhibition catalogue, Bloomington, Indiana 1982; *Henry Holmes Smith: Man of Light* by Howard Bossen, Ann Arbor, Michigan and Epping, Essex 1982; *Henry Holmes Smith Papers,* Tucson, Arizona 1983; *American Images: Photography 1945-1986,* exhibition catalogue, by Andy Grundberg and Kathleen M. Gauss, Los Angeles 1987; *Decade by Decade: Twentieth Century American Photography,* Boston, 1988; *Das Fotogramm in der Kunst des 20 Jahrhunderts* by Floris M Neususs, Cologne, Germany, 1990. **Articles**—"Photography: Henry Holmes Smith" by Joan Murray in *Artweek* (Oakland, California), 23 September 1972; "Henry Holmes Smith: Speaking with a Genuine Voice" by Betty Hahn in *Image* (Rochester, New York), December 1973; "Teacher's Legacy: My Teacher, Myself" by Mark Johnstone in *Artweek* (Oakland, California), 3 November 1979; "Cliché-Verre: Investigating the Interstices" by Ed Hill in *Afterimage* (Rochester, New York), Summer 1981; "Photographic Legacy: The Influence of Henry Holmes Smith at Indiana University" by Sharon L Calhoon in *Arts Indiana,* September, 1988.

*   *   *

Henry Holmes Smith, innovative photographer, writer and renowned teacher—whose students include Jerry Uelsmann, Robert Fichter, Betty Hahn and Jack Welpott—began taking simple photographs with a box camera in 1923. During his early years of development he was influenced by the photographs of Edward Weston (particularly the "Pepper"), Francis Bruguière and Edward Steichen. When Moholy-Nagy's *The New Vision* appeared, it was a key book for him, as he says in an interview with Paul Hill and Thomas Cooper: "There was nothing like it. The book had proposals for life, and it had proposals for ways of artistic behavior. It introduced me to certain possibilities, and I promptly went to work; on my own I tried to practice some of these things—doing them ineptly, but doing them."

Thus, by the time he met Moholy-Nagy in 1937 in Chicago, he was already experimenting with his ideas and was involved with experimental color. Moholy-Nagy had written in the catalogue for his first photographic exhibition that "the concretization of light phenomena is peculiar to the photographic process and to no other technical invention. The photogram is a realization of spatial tension in black-white-gray. Through the elimination of pigment and texture it has a dematerialized effect. It is a writing with light, self-expressive through the contrasting relationship of the deepest black and lightest white with a transitional modulation of the finest grays. Although it is without representational content the photogram is capable of evoking an immediate optical experience, based on our psycho-biological visual organization." As Betty Hahn has pointed out, in quoting the above, "Smith understood and shared Moholy's insight into this method of image making. Moreover, he was able to connect his own understanding of photograms to color when he made color separation negatives and dye transfer prints." Moholy-Nagy, impressed by Smith's ideas and his work in color experimentation, invited him to teach at the New Bauhaus in Chicago. Unfortunately, the institute did not survive long, and it was not until after World War II that Smith could return to his experimentation.

In 1946, he bought an enlarger and began to experiment with ideas he had proposed to Moholy-Nagy ten years earlier—ideas which were designed to release color photography from the burden of the camera. In 1947, on his way to Indiana University, where he was to teach until 1977, Smith planned a course of study on the light principles of refraction and reflection. This led to a body of work—refraction prints—which Betty Hahn has called his "particular gift and extraordinary contribution to the visual archive of photography." Smith describes the process by which he makes these prints in the interview with Hill and Cooper: " . . . the basic way that you do it is to have a fairly clean piece of glass; then you pour a not-too-heavy gesture of syrup on the glass, and then you either print it, or throw some water on it and print it. Some distance from the glass there will be a light source which gives a very clean kind of light that casts crisp shadows. The glass may be three or four inches or more from the paper, and the light is in such a position that the shadows and the refracting elements from the syrup and water will print on the paper. Then you turn the light on and give it an exposure that is appropriate in length, and you develop it just like a piece of normal photographic paper. Now you've got your key element in the process, and from that point on, you can do anything you

want with it. You can leave it alone, you can copy it on a negative, you can make a positive from it, you can print it on a matrix film with different degrees of density, and you can dye them, then transfer them in any combination you care to in multiple printing." He stated once that "in my work I would like to praise heroes and enable some persons to remember the firm link between past and future that acts of the imagination provide us," and, indeed, such mythological figures as the Phoenix or Castor and Pollux are to be found among his images.

Speaking of his images in general, Mark Johnstone has the following to say: "His images have consistently involved elements that deal directly with the interplay of light and relational aspects of color. . . . The images suggest the space and flow of light, and function as both reproductive and poetic devices. Like parables, their careful construction can reveal many meanings. They offer an appreciation of light and color with a rare contemplative beauty, should we as spectators choose to become participants, and not just look at them but *see* them."

—Michael Held

SMITH, Keith.

Nationality: American. **Born:** Tipton, Indiana, 20 May 1938. **Education:** Mansfield Senior High School, Mansfield, Ohio; School of the Art Institute of Chicago, 1963-67, B.A.E. 1967; studied photography at the Illinois Institute of Technology, Chicago, 1968, M.S. Photog. 1968. **Career:** Instructor, University of California at Los Angeles, 1970; Assistant Professor, School of the Art Institute of Chicago, 1971-74; Coordinator of Printmaking, Visual Studies Workshop, Rochester, New York, 1975-83. Various visiting artist and summer workshops, 1978-92; **Recipient:** Guggenheim Fellowship, 1972, 1980; National Endowment for the Arts Award, 1978; New York State Artists Grant, 1985; New York State LIFT grant in literature. **Address:** 22 Cayuga Street, Rochester, New York 14620, U.S.A.

Individual Exhibitions:

1968	Art Institute of Chicago
1970	International Museum of Photography, George Eastman House, Rochester, New York
	Visual Studies Workshop, Rochester, New York
1971	Light Gallery, New York
1973	Galleria Civica d'Arte Moderna, Turin
1974	University of Illinois, Urbana
	Light Gallery, New York
	Sonia Sheridan and Keith Smith, Museum of Modern Art, New York
1975	*Irene Siegel and Keith Smith,* Barat College, Lake Forest, Illinois
1976	Visual Studies Workshop, Rochester, New York
	Lichtropfen, Aachen, West Germany
	Light Gallery, New York
1977	Vision Gallery, Boston
1978	Stuart Wilber Inc., Chicago
	Chicago Center for Contemporary Photography
1979	Stuart Wilber Inc., Chicago
1980	Stuart Wilber Inc., Chicago
1988	*Retrospective of My Books,* Minnesota Center for Book Arts, Minneapolis

Selected Group Exhibitions:

1976	*Photographie: Rochester,* Centre Culturel American, Paris
1978	*Fantastic Photography in the U.S.A.,* Canon Photo Gallery, Amsterdam (toured Europe and the United States, 1978-80)
	Mirrors and Windows: American Photography since 1960, Museum of Modern Art, New York (toured the United States, 1978-80)

1979   *Attitudes: Photography of the 1970s,* Santa Barbara Museum of
        Art, California
        American Photography of the 70s, Art Institute of Chicago
1980   *Cliché Verre: 1939 to the Present,* Detroit Institute of Arts
        Hand-Colored Photographs, Philadelphia College of Art
1981   *Photographer as Printmaker,* Ferens Art Gallery, Hull,
        Yorkshire (travelled to the Museum and Art Gallery,
        Leicester; Cooper Gallery, Barnsley; Castle Museum,
        Nottingham; Photographers' Gallery, London)
1986   *Photographs by Artists in Mid-Career,* San Francisco Museum
        of Modern Art
1987   *Photography and Art 1946-1986,* Los Angeles County
        Museum of Art

Collections:

Museum of Modern Art, New York; International Museum of Photography, George Eastman House, Rochester, New York; Fogg Art Museum, Harvard University, Cambridge, Massachusetts; Art Institute of Chicago; Arnold H. Crane Collection, Chicago; Center for Creative Photography; University of Arizona, Tucson; National Gallery of Canada, Ottawa; Galleria Civica d'Arte Moderna, Turin; Museum of Geelong, Victoria, Australia; Tokyo Metropolitan Museum of Photography; Victoria and Albert Museum, London; Istvan Kiraly Museum, Budapest, Hungary; Museum of Fine Arts, Houston; San Francisco Museum of Modern Art; Ryerson Institute, Toronto.

Publications:

By SMITH: Books—When I Was Two, Rochester, New York 1977; *Book 91,* Rochester, New York 1982; *Lexington Nocturne,* with Poem by Jonathan Williams, Rochester, New York 1983; *Patterned Apart, Book 89,* Rochester, New York 1983; *Structure of the Visual Book, Book 95,* Rochester, New York 1984; *Book 102,* Rochester, New York 1984; *Construct, Book 106,* Rochester, New York 1985; *Out of Sight, Book 107,* Rochester, New York 1985; *Back and Forth, Book 108,* Rochester New York 1985; *Bobby Book 100,* Rochester, New York 1985; *White Caps, Book 109,* Rochester, New York 1986; *Overcast, Book 112,* Rochester, New York, 1986; *Swimmers, Book 114,* Rochester, New York 1986; *Snow Job, Book 115,* Rochester, New York 1986; *In Between Lines, Book 126,* 1988; *Text in the Book Format, Book 120,* 1989; *Drawn from Reality, Book 123,* 1989; *Drawing upon My Reality of Photography, Book 129,* 1989; *Non-Adhesive Binding, Book 128,* 1991; *Structure of the Visual Book,* 1992; *Solitary Source, Book 125,* 1992; *With It, Book 134,* 1992; *Facing Dorothy, Book 166,* 1992; *Sewing Variations, Book 169,* 1994. **Article**—interview in *Photography Between Covers* by Thomas Dugan, Rochester, New York 1979.

On SMITH: Books—*Photographer as Printmaker,* exhibition catalogue, with texts by Gerry Badger, Peter C. Bunnell and Ansel Adams, London 1981; *Photography and Art 1946-86,* exhibition catalogue, by Andry Grundberg and Kathleen M. Gauss, Los Angeles 1987.

*

Throughout my life I have spent a great deal of time examining the properties of line, tone, texture, color, space, suggestion of 3-dimensional space on 2-dimensional surfaces, pattern, repetition, symbolism, motif, transitions from picture to picture in diptychs, polytics, in groups, series, sequences, as books. I am concerned about mood, movement, and a sense of time. These involvements have been expressed through photography, drawing, collage, non-silver and photo-related printmaking on paper and various surfaces, but just as importantly in day-to-day activities of sex, cooking, home, controlled, non-drug hallucination and dreams.

This discipline is basic, but just as important as hunches, accidents, intuition and allowing the work to speak freely.

Process is never an end for me, merely the means of expression. I am not in love with photography.

I spend a large portion of my time making pictures, underpinned by exercises and a constant vigil of learning to see clearly and freshly and the courage to throw away old ways of seeing.

I exercise how to concentrate, how to evolve my imagination to help me more vividly image the page with energy, boldness, sincerity and openness.

—Keith Smith

*   *   *

Keith Smith lives in a simple late-Victorian row house in Rochester, New York. The interior woodwork he has decorated as richly and exuberantly as did that sport of an architect, Billy Burges. Window frames and door frames are like clusters of different-colored marble. The Outside World requires him now and then to walk over to the Visual Studies Workshop, where he is a legendary teacher of print-making, unstinting with the students who want to work. And then it is straight back to the house, where he works day and night and twice on Sunday on his images. Lithography, etching, engraving, screen-printing, photography—the mix is incredible and it is constantly being extended. In Chicago at the Art Institute Keith Smith studied with Aatis Lillstrom. He remains collaborator, friend and critic, one of the few people Keith Smith sees. Another is Fritz Klemperer (nephew of Otto), a former student, who photographs in Cleveland. The friends are a tiny set; the house is peopled with thousands of visual companions.

Keith Smith makes the kind of prints that would make Jesse Helms grow four tits if he ever happened to encounter one in the wild. Which is a downhome way of saying that perhaps Keith Smith is not a photographer for all five seasons or for all tastes. He is a very important gay artist and it seems fair enough to dwell on this fact at a time when the Oral Majority is busy trying to consign all us Country Genitalists to the fiery furnace. Accordingly, he runs the risk of not being taken ''seriously'' by a commodity society full of prudes, prunes and drones. Keith Smith is the shyest and quietest of men. Very small and wistful, off a farm in Indiana. His imagination is wholly *cathectic* (look it up, damn it . . .). His working life is devoted to the making of images of erotical boys. I do not think it impious to say that he is as devoted to his singular task as a good Trappist is devoted to his. Mr. Smith celebrates spirit *and* flesh. The images are companionable, in a world that too seldom is.

I grew up with friends who were enthralled arse-over-tit with the obsessions of Petty and Vargas in the old *Esquire.* There wasn't much skin for those whose tastes were otherwise constituted, though now one knows that George Platt Lynes and Paul Cadmus and Tchelitchew were busy delineating a male sensuality for east-coast, ivy-league sophisticates. Today, the artist who calls himself Tom of Finland fills magazines with those grotesquely endowed macho gods who ''turn him on.'' World Without End. . . . The writer Stephen King knows that, like himself, most of us were frightened of Daddy and of going into the Dark Cellar. He gives us a book a year and can't ever hope to spend all the money that piles in. But, few of us have obsessions that pay off. Trappists aren't abundant. They're not making money. Neither is Keith Smith.

Is the audience for this work ''restricted?'' I doubt it. People's sexual fantasies are more various than we know. And society has seen to it—up 'til now—that most quote homosexuals unquote were married, just like whitefolks. Aaron Siskind, for example, admires what Keith Smith makes. With so many sultry Shulamite damsels on his mind, can there be many less likely readers of *Blue Boy* in the nation? I suggest that *anyone* may look at Keith Smith's prints, precisely because they are full of aesthetic delight and the quality of one man's longing. Let Old Jesse get uptight. Jesse ain't read the *Greek Anthology,* where some wise ancient has told us: ''Women for use; boys for pleasure; goats for delight . . . '' Somebody else will give you the ladies and the capricorns. Take what you're offered—and be polite!

—Jonathan Williams

SMITH, W(illiam) Eugene.

Nationality: American. **Born:** Wichita, Kansas, 30 December 1918. **Education:** Catholic parochial school, Wichita, 1924-30; Catholic High School, Wichita, 1930-35; studied photography, University of Notre Dame, Indiana, 1936-37. **Family:** Married Carmen Martinez in 1940 (divorced); children: Juanita, Marissa, Shana, Patrick, and Kevin; married Aileen Mioko in 1970.

Career: First photographs, under advice from news photographer Frank Noel, Wichita, 1933-35; part-time press photographer, contributing to *Wichita Eagle* and *Wichita Beacon* newspapers, Wichita, 1935-36; staff photographer, *Newsweek* magazine, New York, 1937-38; freelance photographer, with Black Star Agency, contributing to *Life, Colliers, American Magazine, Harper's Bazaar* and the *New York Times*, New York, 1938-39; Staff Photographer, *Life* magazine, New York, 1939-41, as war correspondent, 1944-45, and 1947-54; Staff Photographer/War Correspondent, Ziff-Davis Publishing Company, in the Pacific, 1942-44; Member, Magnum Photos co-operative agency, worked on a Pittsburgh photographic survey, and contributed to *Life, Pageant, Sports Illustrated,* etc., New York and Pittsburgh, 1955-58; freelance photographer, worked for Hitachi Company, *Life* magazine, etc., New York and Japan, 1959-77; Special Medical Reportage Editor, *Visual Medicine* magazine, New York, 1966-69. Photography Instructor, New School for Social Research, New York, 1958; private classes in photojournalism, New York, 1960; School of Visual Arts, New York, 1969; University of Arizona, Tucson, 1978. **Recipient:** Guggenheim Fellowship, 1956, 1957, 1968; Honor Award, American Society of Magazine Photographers, 1959; Award Plaque for Photojournalism, and Clifford Edom Founders Award, University of Miami, 1959; National Endowment for the Arts Award, 1971. **Died:** (in Tucson, Arizona) 15 October 1978.

Individual Exhibitions:

1944   Museum of Modern Art, New York
1948   Museum of New Mexico, Santa Fe
1957   *10 Buildings in America's Future,* National Gallery of Art,
        Washington, D.C.
        Limelight Gallery, New York
1960   University of Oregon, Eugene
1969   Rochester Institute of Technology, New York
1970   International Museum of Photography, George Eastman House,
        Rochester, New York (toured the United States and Europe)
1971   *Let Truth Be the Prejudice,* Jewish Museum, New York
        (retrospective)
        Witkin Gallery, New York
1974   City Auditorium, Minamata, Japan
1975   International Center of Photography, New York
        University of Oregon, Eugene
1976   Witkin Gallery, New York
1977   State University, Wichita, Kansas
1978   Center for Creative Photography, University of Arizona,
        Tucson (memorial exhibition)
1979   Hippolyte Gallery, Helsinki
        Kunsthaus, Zurich
        West Virginia University, Morgantown
1980   Douglas Kenyon Gallery, Chicago
        Early Work, Center for Creative Photography, University of
        Arizona, Tucson
1981   Photograph, New York (retrospective)
        Eclipse Photographics, Boulder, Colorado
        Clarence Kennedy Gallery, Cambridge, Massachusetts
1982   Photograph Gallery, New York
1983   International Center of Photography, New York
1985   *Let Truth Be the Prejudice,* Philadelphia Museum of Art,
        Pennsylvania (travelled to the International Center of
        Photography, New York; Museum of Contemporary Art, Los
        Angeles; Amon Carter Museum, Fort Worth, Texas; High
        Museum of Art, Atlanta, Georgia; Minneapolis Institute of
        Arts, Minnesota; Cleveland Museum of Art, Ohio; Glenbow
        Museum, Calgary, Alberta; Indianapolis Museum of Art,
        Indiana; Center for Contemporary Photography, Tucson,
        Arizona, 1986-89)

Selected Group Exhibitions:

1951   *Memorable Life Photographs,* Museum of Modern Art,
        New York
1954   *Great Photographs,* Limelight Gallery, New York

1955   *The Family of Man,* Museum of Modern Art, New York (and
        world tour)
1967   *Photography in the 20th Century,* National Gallery of Canada,
        Ottawa (toured Canada and the United States, 1967-73)
1970   *The Concerned Photographer 2,* Israel Museum, Jerusalem
        (toured Europe)
1974   *Photography in America,* Whitney Museum, New York
1979   *Life: The First Decade 1936-1945,* Grey Art Gallery, New
        York University
1980   *Photography of the 50s,* International Center of Photography,
        New York (travelled to the Center for Creative Photography,
        University of Arizona, Tucson; Minneapolis Institute of Art;
        California State University at Long Beach; and Delaware Art
        Museum, Wilmington)
1982   *Lichtbildnisse: Das Porträt in der Fotografie,* Rheinisches
        Landesmuseum, Bonn
1985   *American Images 1945-80,* Barbican Art Gallery, London
        (toured Britain)

Collections:

W. Eugene Smith Archive, Center for Creative Photography, University of Arizona, Tucson; Life Magazine Picture Collection, New York; Museum of Modern Art, New York; International Center of Photography, New York; International Museum of Photography, George Eastman House, Rochester, New York; Boston Museum of Fine Arts; Carpenter Center, Harvard University, Cambridge, Massachusetts; Dayton Art Institute, Ohio; Art Institute of Chicago; University of Colorado, Boulder.

Publications:

By SMITH: Books—*Eugene Smith Photography,* Minneapolis 1954; *Hitachi Reminder,* Tokyo 1961; *Japan: A Chapter of Image,* with Carole Thomas, text by Smith under pseudonym Walter Trego, Tokyo 1963; *Pittsburgh: The Story of an American City,* edited by Stefan Lorant, New York 1964; *Hospital for Special Surgery,* with Carole Thomas, New York 1966; *W. Eugene Smith: His Photographs and Notes,* with text by Peter C. Bunnell and Lincoln Kirstein, New York 1969; *Minamata: Life—Sacred and Profane,* portfolio of 12 photos, with Aileen M. Smith, text by Michiko Ishimura, Tokyo 1973; *Minamata,* with Aileen M. Smith, New York 1975; *Ten Photographs,* portfolio, Roslyn Heights, New York 1977; *W. Eugene Smith: Early Work,* with text by William S. Johnson, Tucson, Arizona 1980; *W. Eugene Smith: Master of the Photographic Essay,* with text by William S. Johnson, Millerton, New York 1981; *The W. Eugene Smith Papers,* edited by Charles Lamb and Amy Stark, Tucson, Arizona 1983. **Articles**—"Photographic Journalism" in *Photo Notes* (New York), June 1948; "Photography Today" in *Photography Annual 1954,* New York 1953; "The Walk to Paradise Garden" in *Croton-Harmon News* (Croton, New York), 31 March 1955; "W. Eugene Smith Talks about Lighting" in *Popular Photography* (New York), November 1956; "Pittsburgh," with an introduction by H.M. Kinzer, in *Modern Photography Annual 1959,* New York 1958; "One Whom I Admire, Dorothea Lange (1895-1965)" in *Popular Photography* (New York), February 1966; "Minamata, Japan: Life, Sacred and Profane," with Aileen M. Smith, in *Camera 35* (New York), April 1974.

On SMITH: Books—*Memorable Life Photographs,* with text by Edward Steichen, New York 1951; *Words and Pictures: An Introduction to Photojournalism* by Wilson Hicks, New York 1952; *How Life Gets the Story: Behind the Scenes in Photo-Journalism,* edited by Stanley Rayfield, New York 1955; *Photography Today,* edited by Norman Hall, London 1957; *Fame: Famous Portraits of Famous People by Famous Photographers,* edited by L. Fritz Gruber, London and New York 1960; *Photography in the 20th Century* by Nathan Lyons, New York 1967; *The Concerned Photographer 2,* edited by Cornell Capa, New York and London 1972; *Photography in America,* edited by Robert Doty, with an introduction by Minor White, New York 1974; *Masters of the Camera* by Gene Thornton, New York 1976; *Photographs: Sheldon Memorial Art Gallery Collection, University of Nebraska,* with an introduction by Norman A. Geske, Lincoln 1977; *Darkroom,* edited by Eleanor Lewis, New York 1977; *Photography within the Humanities,* edited by Eugenia Parry Janis and Wendy MacNeil, Danbury, New Hampshire 1977; *Geschichte der Fotografie im 20.*

Jahrhundert/Photography in the 20th Century by Petr Tausk, Cologne 1977, London 1980; *Light Readings: A Photography Critics Writings 1968-1978* by A.D. Coleman, New York 1979; *Dialogue with Photography,* edited by Paul Hill and Thomas Cooper, London 1979; *Venezia '79: La Fotografia,* edited by Daniela Palazzoli, Vittorio Sgarbi and Italo Zannier, Milan and New York 1979; *Life: The First Decade 1936-1945* by Robert Littman, Ralph Graves and Doris C. O'Neill, New York 1979, London 1980; *Photographie als Kunst 1879-1979/Kunst als Photographie 1949-1979,* exhibition catalogue, 2 vols., by Peter Weiermair, Innsbruck, Austria 1979; *Old and Modern Masters of Photography,* exhibition catalogue, by Mark Haworth-Booth, London 1980; *Photography of the 50s: An American Perspective* by Helen Gee, Tucson, Arizona 1980; *Bilder vom Krieg* by Rainer Fabian and Hans Christian Adam, Hamburg 1983, as *Images of War: 130 Years of War Photography,* London 1985; *Let Truth Be the Prejudice—W. Eugene Smith: His Life and Photographs* by Ben Maddow, New York 1985. **Articles**—"Wonderful Smith" by Tom Maloney and others in *U.S. Camera* (New York), August 1945; "Gene Smith Meeting" by Jo Chaslin and others in *Photo Notes* (New York), November 1947; "W. Eugene Smith's Spain" by Jacquelyn Judge in *Modern Photography* (New York), December 1951; "W. Eugene Smith" by Fritz Neugass in *Camera* (Lucerne), June/July 1952; "W. Eugene Smith Teaches Photographic Responsibility" by Bill Pierce in *Popular Photography* (New York), November 1961; "Gene Smith in Japan" in *Popular Photography* (New York), November 1962; "W. Eugene Smith" by H.M. Kinzer in *Popular Photography* (New York), February 1965; "A Great Unknown Photographer—W. Eugene Smith" by David Vestal in *Popular Photography* (New York), December 1966; "Why Does W. Eugene Smith Write on Walls?" by John Durniak in *Photography Annual 1971,* New York 1970; "W. Eugene Smith: Let Truth Be the Prejudice" by R. Porter in *Infinity* (New York), May 1971; "Notes on Walker Evans and W. Eugene Smith" by Van Deren Coke in *Art International* (Lugano, Switzerland), June 1971; "W. Eugene Smith: Minamata" in *Asahi Camera* (Tokyo), May 1973; "Eugene Smith: Les Morts Vivants de Minamata" in *Photo* (Paris), November 1973; "Rebel with a Camera" by Jim Hughes in *Quest/77* (New York), March/April 1977; "The Passion of St. Eugene" by Ben Maddow in *American Photographer* (New York), December 1985.

* * *

"Humanity," the late Eugene Smith liked to tell his students, "is worth more than a picture of humanity that serves no purpose other than exploitation." A fit epitaph, those words, for a premier master of photojournalism, an area of the medium in which exploitation of one's subjects is a line all too easily transgressed.

Yet, during much of his productive life, Smith clung passionately to his chosen side of that line; it was a basic belief underlying his work (both the successes and the arguable failures). Basic, too, and problematic from time to time, was an equally passionate belief in the integrity of his photographs, of the individual statements in which form, tone, and humanity coalesced with such grace and power.

Smith's early photographs, those of his apprenticeship years in the late 1930s and early 1940s are mere footnotes, the traces of his evolution into a mature artist (although, characteristically, he included a roomful of these early efforts in his massive 1971 New York Jewish Museum retrospective). That maturity, both photographic and, perhaps, moral, was moulded in the cauldron of World War II. Until suffering near-critical wounds on Okinawa in 1945, Smith produced image after image in what he hoped might be "an indictment of war."

Two years later, barely recovered from those wounds (physical disaster, including a near blinding while photographing *Minamata,* stalked Smith throughout his life, culminating in the fall from which he died), fearing an inability to again hold a camera, Smith created his most famous single image, "The Walk to Paradise Garden." A sentimental, heavily romantic evocation of the journey from paradise lost to paradise regained, it became the most memorable feature of Steichen's *Family of Man* exhibit.

Fears assuaged, from 1947 to 1954, Smith worked with *Life* magazine and, in so doing, changed our perceptions of the photo-essay. If some, such as "Country Doctor," simper rather too much, others (i.e., "Spanish Village" and "Nurse Midwife") are exemplars of how the form might best be used. The 1951 essay, "Spanish Village," is perhaps the most striking example of a photo-essay in which the traditional subordination of pictures to words is essentially reversed. Without *Life*'s captions, Smith's pictures retain their communicative power; without the pictures, the words die.

Smith's relationship with *Life,* tenuous at best, was severed more than once. Two years after the last major photo-essay, Smith took advantage of a Guggenheim Fellowship (the first of three) to further one of his most ambitious endeavours: a massive photographic study of Pittsburgh, one of America's industrial capitals.

The results of those Pittsburgh years have been published only in fits and starts. The big book that Smith envisioned, *Pittsburgh: A Labyrinthian Walk,* never came to fruition. In the bowels of the U.S. Library of Congress, however, may be found three thick binders containing a complete record, in contact sheets, of Smith's Pittsburgh labors. Their publication, if permissible, would be of singular value.

Perhaps his most famous major project, *Minamata,* completed in the early 70s, is a lineal descendent of the wartime photographs. This, too, was an indictment, not of the abstraction of war, but of the harsh reality of individuals and institutions which foul the environment and, in the process of profit maximization, wreak unbelievable human suffering. Its value to the people of Minamata, its importance in stimulating the environmental movement, are among Smith's greatest legacies to the humanity from which he drew his subjects.

There is a photographic legacy, as well. The exacting standards he set for himself and the degree to which those standards were, time and again, met, are both inspiration and challenge to his survivors.

Smith's prints are marked by their subtle tonal changes, brilliant highlights (sometimes achieved with local application of bleaching agents), and full, rich-toned blacks. His attention to lighting is revealed most fully in the death bed scene from the Spanish village series. Relying upon strategically positioned candles to augment the light, Smith created a tone poem about life and death, a poem in which each human face speaks its stanza. From the same series, Smith's portrait of three young members of the *Guardia Civil,* demonstrates his mastery of individual light in even its harshest form.

As printmaker, as well as photographer, Smith was exceptional. There is a richness and lustre to even the greatest enlargements, a smoothness of grain (achieved by printing through silk and other diffusers) and a subtle tonality.

In his own work, and by his example, W. Eugene Smith helped transform photojournalism at midcentury. Though the great picture magazines that nourished the form have gone, an army of street photographers, documentarians and photojournalists remains. Whether consciously or not (although consciously in many cases), they are the heirs to Smith's legacies. Both in aesthetic and moral terms, his standards remain the best guideposts for those who follow.

—Stu Cohen

SNOW, Michael (James Aleck).

Nationality: Canadian. **Born:** Toronto, Ontario, 10 December 1929. **Education:** Upper Canada College, Toronto, 1946-51; Ontario College of Art, Toronto, 1951-55. **Family:** Married the artist and filmmaker Joyce Wieland in 1959. **Career:** Independent artist, musician, filmmaker and photographer, Toronto, since 1955. Professor of Advanced Film, Yale University, New Haven, Connecticut, 1970; Visiting Artist, Nova Scotia College of Art and Design, Halifax, 1970, 1974, and Ontario College of Art, Toronto, 1973, 1974, 1976. Also, a musician: member of the CCMC, Toronto, since 1974. **Recipient:** Purchase Award, *Winnipeg Exhibition,* 1958; Canada Council Arts Grant, 1959, and Senior Arts Grant, 1966, 1973, 1980; Henry Street Settlement Exhibition Award, New York, 1964; First Prize, Knokke-le-Zoute Film Festival, Belgium, 1967; Guggenheim Fellowship, 1972; Best Independent Experimental Film Award, Los Angeles Film Critics Association, 1983. LL.D.: Brock University, St. Catherines, Ontario, 1975. Order of Canada, 1981. **Address:** c/o The Isaacs Gallery, 832 Yonge Street, Toronto, Ontario M4W 2H1, Canada.

Individual Exhibitions:

1956   Hart House, University of Toronto
1957   Isaac Gallery, Toronto (and 1958)
1959   Art Gallery of Ontario, Toronto
1960   Isaacs Gallery, Toronto (and 1962)
1963   Gallery XII, Montreal Museum of Fine Arts
        Hart House, University of Toronto
1964   Isaacs Gallery, Toronto
        Poindexter Gallery, New York
1965   Poindexter Gallery, New York
1966   20/20 Gallery, London, Ontario
        Isaacs Gallery, Toronto
1967   *Retrospective '63-'66,* Vancouver Art Gallery
1968   Poindexter Gallery, New York
1969   Isaacs Gallery, Toronto
1970   *Michael Snow: A Survey,* Art Gallery of Ontario, Toronto
        Canadian Pavilion, *Biennale,* Venice
        Bykert Gallery, New York
1972   Center for Inter-American Relations, New York
        Bykert Gallery, New York
1973   *Camera Works by Michael Snow,* University of Manitoba,
           Winnipeg
1974   *Projected Images,* Walker Art Center, Minneapolis
        Isaacs Gallery, Toronto
1976   Museum of Modern Art, New York
1977   *7 Films et Plus Tard,* Centre Georges Pompidou, Paris (toured
           France, 1977-79)
1978   *Michael Snow,* Centre Georges Pompidou, Paris (travelled to
           the Kunstmuseum, Lucerne; Rheinisches Landesmuseum,
           Bonn; Städtische Galerie im Lenbachhaus, Munich; Musée
           des Beaux-Arts, Montreal; and the Vancouver Art Gallery,
           1978-80)
1979   Isaacs Gallery, Toronto
        Museum Boymans-van Beuningen, Rotterdam (with Richard
           Hefti)
1982   Isaacs Gallery, Toronto
1983   *Snow in England,* Canada House, London
        University of California, Los Angeles
        Walking Woman Works 1961-67, Agnes Etherington Art
           Centre, Kingston, Ontario (travelled to Ithaca, New York;
           Halifax, Nova Scotia; London, Ontario; Victoria, British
           Columbia; and Toronto)
1984   Isaacs Gallery, Toronto
        Still Living, Vu Centre de la Photographie, Quebec City
1986   Isaacs Gallery, Toronto

Selected Group Exhibitions:

1966   *The Satirical in Art,* York University, Toronto
1969   *Anti-Illusion: Procedures and Materials,* Whitney Museum,
           New York
1970   *Festival International du Film,* Cannes
1971   *Prospect '71,* Kunsthalle, Dusseldorf
1973   *Options and Alternatives,* Yale University, New Haven,
           Connecticut
1977   *Another Dimension,* National Gallery of Canada, Ottawa
           (toured Canada, 1977-78)
1979   *Re-Visions,* Whitney Museum, New York
1982   *Photoalchemy,* Robert Freidus Gallery, New York
1984   *Seeing People—Seeing Space,* The Photographers' Gallery,
           London
1985   *Aurora Borealis,* Centre d'Art Contemporain, Montreal

Collections:

National Gallery of Canada, Ottawa; Canada Council Art Bank, Ottawa; Art
Gallery of Ontario, Toronto; Montreal Museum of Fine Arts; Winnipeg Art
Gallery; Museum of Modern Art, New York; Philadelphia Museum of Art;

Milwaukee Art Center, Wisconsin; Albright-Knox Art Gallery, Buffalo, New
York; Musée d'Art Contemporain, Montreal.

Publications:

By SNOW: Books—*Place of Meeting,* with text by Ray Souster, Toronto
1962; *Michael Snow: A Survey,* with text by P. Adams Sitney, Toronto 1970;
Cover to Cover, Halifax, Nova Scotia, Toronto 1980; *High School,* Toronto 1980.
Article—"Passage" in *Artforum* (New York), September 1971. **Films**—*A to
Z,* 1956; *New York Eye and Ear Control (A Walking Woman Work),* 1964;
Short Shave, 1965; *Wavelength,* 1967; *Standard Time,* 1967; *Back and Forth,*
1969; *One Second in Montreal,* 1969; *Dripping Water,* 1969; *Side Seat
Paintings Slides Sound Films,* 1970; *La Region Centrale,* 1970-71; *Table Top
Dolly,* 1972; *Rameau's Nephew by Diderot (Thanks to Dennis Young) by
Wilma Schoen,* 1974; *Presents,* 1980; *So Is This,* 1982; sound recordings—
The Artists Jazz Band, 1974; *CCMC,* 5 vols., 1974-80; *Michael Snow: Music
for Whistling, Piano, Microphone, and Tape Recorder,* 1975; *The Artists Jazz
Band: Live at the Edge,* 1977.

On SNOW: Books—*Expanded Cinema* by Gene Youngblood, New York
1970; *Negative Space* by Manny Farber, New York 1971; *Experimental
Cinema* by David Curtis, London 1971; *Visionary Film* by P. Adams Sitney,
New York 1974; *Une Histoire du Cinéma* by Peter Kubelka and others, Paris
1976; *Documenta 6/Band 2,* exhibition catalogue, by Klaus Honnef and
Evelyn Weiss, Cologne 1977; *Michael Snow,* exhibition catalogue, Lucerne
1979; *Snow Seen* by Regina Cornwell, Toronto 1980; *Walking Woman Works:
Michael Snow 1961-1967,* exhibition catalogue, Kingston, Ontario 1983.
Articles—"Wavelength" by Bob Lamberton in *Film Culture* (New York),
Autumn 1967; "Conversations with Michael Snow" by Jonas Mekas and P.
Adams Sitney in *Film Culture* (New York), Autumn 1967; "Critique: Glass
and Snow" by Richard Foreman in *Art and Artists* (London), February 1970;
"Towards Snow" by Annette Michelson in *Artforum* (New York), June 1971;
"Michael Snow on 'La Region Centrale' " by Charlotte Townsend in *Film
Culture* (New York), Spring 1971; "Michael Snow Framed" by Simon Field
in *Art and Artists* (London), November 1972; "The Other Tradition" by
Barbara Rose in *New York,* 11 December 1972; "Doubled Visions" by Amy
Taubin in *October* (New York), Fall 1977; "Michael Snow: The Decisive
Moment Revised" by Regina Cornwall in *Artscanada* (Toronto), April/May
1980; "The Complete Films of Michael Snow" by Catherine Goldsmith in
The Gallery (Toronto), March 1981; "Michael Snow's World" by Stephen
Dale in *Now* (Toronto), May/June 1982; "Michael Snow: Impresario of
Thought" by Adele Freedman in *Artnews* (New York), January 1983; "Ghost
Lustres: Michael Snow's Holographic Visions" by Rene Blouin in *Canadian
Art* (Toronto), Summer 1986.

*

My work relates more to the tradition of painting and sculpture than it does
to that of printmaking/"fine" photography. Yet I concentrate on the aesthetic/
philosophical potential of processes or effects which are particular to photography. In several works I have created both the subject and its representation.

—Michael Snow

*   *   *

In 1961 Michael Snow began his "Walking Woman" series. This "cut-
out" figure functioned as a device in repeated explorations of framing,
serialization, spatial and illusionary relationships expressed in a variety of
media, forms and environments. Snow's earliest photographic piece, "Four to
Five" (1962), consists of a montage of the "Walking Woman" placed in the
surroundings of various public places. Twelve rectangular photographs are
arranged in a grid formation of three horizontal lines; on the fourth (bottom)
line the two central photographs are placed as verticals, flanked on each side
with a horizontal photograph. In this very simple but remarkable piece, the
photographs mirror real events, transferring particular realities into a photographic process. The situating of process and reorganization within its own
constructed space conditions the work, no longer as a record, but as a response
to the making of a record that reveals its own representation of a new
"reality"—the final photographic object.

Very few of Snow's photographic works are "reproducible." They are frequently structured pieces constituted of, or including, photographic prints, in black/white or colour; 35mm slides; Polaroids; and photo-offset printing in conjunction with other materials and objects. All of the elements are in specific placement in relationship to one another. Of his piece "Tap" (1969), Snow says, "I wanted to make a composition which was dispersed, in which the elements would be come upon in different ways and which would consist of (1) a sound, (2) an image, (3) a text, (4) an object, (5) a line, which would be identified but the parts of which would be of interest in themselves if the connections between them were not seen (but better if seen)." The photographic pieces often occupy space for the eye and the mind to synthesize memory and visual elements which cancel or annual and present themselves again, or repeat to establish a logic in perception of the sum-total.

Snow is best known for his highly acclaimed film work. His photographic pieces share many of the generative elements of investigation seen in the films, and, like his films, reverberate with masterly intellectual control. How the camera functions and the process of photography as an image making instrument; the relationship of the image to light, sequence, series and self-reference; the relativity of sight, sound and memory; the intensity of focusing and the transformation of representation—all are central concerns. In Snow's *Venice Biennial* catalogue (1970), Brydon Smith states that for Snow, "the content of his art follows from the process of its realization. It is realism of process." While this reference is to the piece "Authorization" (1969), the same basic tenets are characteristic of many of Snow's later photographic pieces in colour. Underlying references exist to his earlier period of painting: control of subject and relationship to final form, size, scale, and abstraction. Camera images are frequently used to aid representation and reorganization of surface, at the same time the pieces project recurring gestures of parody, punning and wit.

Snow's continued investigation into the process of perception has recently led to holography. *The Spectral Image,* a work commissioned for *Expo '86,* consists of more than 45 components that convey dimensionality, the sense of depth, width, height, and time through illusion. In this large 929 feet holographic installation, Snow has successfully created a reconstruction of representation through the properties of light, vision and the perceptual process. Individual units and sections of the installation depict thematic connections to transportation, communication and industry; resolved as holographic images they transform the viewer's perception of the objects by variations in arrangement. Illumination systems explore the materiality of light that alter perceptions of space and colour. As the viewer is thrust into a participatory experience, the process of looking and seeing is affirmed and verified by Snow's mastery of a new and complex visual technology.

Snow's overall creativity, evident throughout his paintings, sculpture, film, photography, and in his music, are specific visualizations and concepts constituting highly intelligent investigations that have generated into an authoritatively analytical body of work.

—Maia-Mari Sutnik

SNOWDON, (The Rt Hon the Earl of, GCVO).

Nationality: British. **Born:** Antony Charles Robert Armstrong-Jones in London, 7 March 1930. **Education:** Attended Sandroyd Preparatory School, Surrey, 1938-42; Eton School, Buckinghamshire, 1943-48; studied architecture at Jesus College, Cambridge, 1949-50. **Family:** Married H.R.H. Princess Margaret in 1960 (divorced, 1978); children: David Albert Charles, Viscount Linley, Lady Sarah Frances Elizabeth; married Lucy Lindsay-Hogg in 1978; daughter: Lady Frances. **Career:** Partner, Owen Lloyd Car Hire Ltd., London, 1950; Photographic Assistant to Baron (Nahum), London, 1950-51. Freelance photographer, working for *Sketch, Tatler, Country, Life, Picture Post, Vogue, Queen, Harper's Bazaar, Sunday Times,* etc., London, since 1951: maintained photographic studio, Pimlico Road, London, 1953-60. Artistic Adviser, *Sunday Times* newspaper and publications, London, 1962-1990; Consultative Adviser, Design Council, and Editorial Adviser, *Design* magazine, London, 1962-1987; Consultative Adviser, *The Telegraph Magazine,* since 1990. Designed the Snowdon Aviary, London Zoo, 1965, and Electric Chair

(Chairmobile) for the disabled, 1972. Has also produced television films since 1968. Constable of Caernarvon Castle, 1963. President: Contemporary Art Society for Wales; Civic Trust for Wales; Welsh Theatre Company; and Greater London Arts Association; Hon DUniv of Bradford, 1989; Hon Dr of Law, University of Bath, 1989; Hon DLitt University of Portsmouth, 1993; Patron: National Youth Theatre, London; Metropolitan Union of YMCA's; British Water Ski Federation; Welsh National Rowing Club; Physically Handicapped and Able Bodied; and Circle of Guide Dog Owners. **Recipient:** 2 Emmy Awards, for film, Hollywood, 1968; *Prague Film Festival* Award, 1968; *Barcelona Film Festival* Award, 1968; Diploma, *Venice Film Festival,* 1968; Certificate of Merit, Art Directors Club of New York, 1969; Certificate of Merit, 1970, and Award of Excellence, 1973, Society of Publication Designers; Society of Film and Television Arts Award, 1971; Hugo Award, *Chicago Film Festival,* 1971; Wilson Hicks Certificate of Merit for Photocommunications, 1971; Design and Art Directors Award, London, 1978; Hood Award, Royal Photographic Society, 1979. Fellow, Society of Industrial Artists and Designers, Royal Photographic Society, Royal Society of Arts, and Manchester College of Art and Design; Royal Designer for Industry, 1978. G.C.V.O. (Knight Grand Cross, Royal Victorian Order), 1969. **Address:** 22 Launceston Place, London W8 5RL, England.

Individual Exhibitions:

1958	*Photocall,* London
1972	*Assignments,* at *Photokina '72,* Cologne (travelled to London, 1973; Brussels, 1974; Los Angeles, St. Louis, Kansas City, New York and Tokyo, 1975; Sydney, Melbourne and Copenhagen, 1976; Paris and Amsterdam, 1977)

Selected Group Exhibitions:

1968	*2nd World Exhibition of Photography: Woman,* Pressehaus Stern, Hamburg (and world tour)
1981	*One in Ten,* The Photographers' Gallery, London
	Points of View, Kodak Gallery, London
1982	*Lichtbildnisse: Das Porträt in der Fotografie,* Rheinisches Landesmuseum, Bonn
1983	*British Photography 1955-65,* The Photographers' Gallery, London

Collections:

National Portrait Gallery, London.

Publications:

By SNOWDON: Books—*Malta,* with text by Sacheverell Sitwell, London 1958; *London,* London 1958; *Private View,* with text by John Russell and Bryan Robertson, London 1965; *Assignments,* Cologne and London 1972; *A View of Venice,* London 1972; *The Book of the Goons,* with others, London 1974, 1984; *Inchcape Review,* London 1977; *Pride of the Shires,* with text by John Oaksey, London 1979; *Personal View,* London 1979; *Snowdon Tasmania Essay,* with text by Trevor Wilson, Hobart, Tasmania 1981; *Snowdon Sittings 1979-1983,* with introduction by John Mortimer, London 1983; *My Wales,* in collaboration with Viscount Tonypandy, 1986; *Israel: A First View,* London 1986; *Stills: 1984-1987,* London 1987; *Public Appearances 1987-1991,* London 1991; articles—interview in *Photo* (Paris), December 1972; interview in *Interviews with Master Photographers* by James Danziger and Barnaby Conrad III, New York and London 1977. **Television films**—*Don't Count the Candles,* 1968; *Love of a Kind,* 1969; *Born to Be Small,* 1971; *Happy Being Happy,* 1973; *Mary Kingsley,* 1975; *Burke and Wills,* 1975; *Peter, Tina and Steve,* 1977.

On SNOWDON: Books—*Lord Snowdon* by Helen Cathcart, London 1968; *The Magic Image* by Cecil Beaton and Gail Buckland, London and Boston 1975; *Lichtbildnisse: Das Porträt in der Fotografie,* edited by Klaus Honnef, Cologne 1982; *Snowdon: A Man for Our Times* by David Sinclair, London 1982; *British Photography 1955-1965: The Master Craftsmen in Print,* exhibition catalogue, by Sue Davies, Michael Rand, Mark Boxer and others,

Nursing the Mentally Ill, **1968.** Photograph ©Lord Snowdon.

London 1983. **Articles**—"Lord Snowdon's Workroom" in *Vogue* (London), 15 April 1971; "Great Photographers of the World: Snowdon" in *Réalités* (Paris), September 1971; "Lord Snowdon" in *Photography Yearbook 1972,* edited by John Sanders, London 1971; "Photographs: Snowdon" in *U.S. Camera Annual,* New York 1972; "Snowdon: Assignments" in *Du* (Zurich), September 1972; "Profil de Snowdon" by M. Naumann in *Zeit Magazin* (Hamburg), 20 October 1972; "Snowdon, Photographer" by G. Hughes in *Amateur Photographer* (London), 7 March 1973; "A View of Venice: Photographs by Snowdon" in the *Sunday Times Magazine* (London), 29 April 1973; "Great Portraits: Snowdon" in *Amateur Photographer* (London), 29 August 1973.

*   *   *

Snowdon is an all-round man of the arts, interested in every aspect of design and expert in a number of them. In architecture; in designing for industry; in settings for ballet and the theatre; in the layout of magazines and newspapers; and in the direction and production of television films, he has achieved enough success to have launched a number of careers.

As a still photographer he combines a sharp perceptive eye with great technical ingenuity. Already as a schoolboy he had constructed his own enlarger out of soup cans and astonished his friends with trick photography, including one of matches falling out of a box, made by gluing them together.

Later, requiring an area where his subjects could "walk about and not look lit," in a studio which had no window, he designed a light box. Standing six feet high and holding some sixty 100-watt bulbs, it could be folded to fit into the back of his Morris Minor.

Snowdon's early work was distinguished from that of other talented beginners by irreverence and humour. Fully confident in himself and his own methods, he shattered the conventions of fashion magazines by posing his models in ludicrous or catastrophic situations, slipping on a banana skin or overwhelmed by junked automobiles in a car dump. Sent to cover social events, he concentrated on their ludicrous aspect, disregarding whatever was impressive or imposing.

About his own photography too he has always shown a refreshing lack of vanity. Just the opposite of those photographers who seek to stamp their own "personality" on everything they do, he approaches each new task with an open mind and a readiness to improvise. He will work on the negative, crop his prints to any extent, even attack the surface with a razor blade if that is going to give him the effect he wants.

But at times Snowdon's ingenuity is his enemy. His portraits of celebrities, taken at leisure, too often turn out gimmicky—interpretations of a public personality through setting and contrivance, rather than allowing the subject's true character to appear. His pictures of actors or opera singers on the other hand, taken during stage productions which leave little opportunity for cleverness, are full of tension and vitality.

As a photojournalist he has always been ready to go anywhere and cover any assignment he finds interesting. He likes working to a deadline, which imposes a discipline he appears to want: "If I'm given a completely free hand I either turn the job down or quickly become uninterested." On his foreign assignments in particular, he has worked a good deal in colour. His colour pictures reveal his acute sense for tone and pattern, but appear to owe much to his knowledge of the various schools of painting.

During the last ten years a new and welcome note, a warmth of human feeling, has come into his work. When he started photographing stories for the *Sunday Times* magazine on the old, disabled, or on handicapped children, he showed only one concern—to convey what he saw in the most sympathetic manner. Gimmickry went out; simplicity and directness took over. "I thought if these things were recorded . . . then perhaps people would think more deeply about what it meant and about what might be done." It is this attitude also which has produced his affecting documentary films for television.

Hitherto Snowdon's main concentration has always been on still photography, but it seems far from certain that this will always captivate so versatile a mind and far-ranging an interest.

—Tom Hopkinson

SOMMER, Frederick.

Nationality: American. **Born:** Fritz Sommer in Angri, Italy, 7 September 1905; grew up in Brazil; emigrated to the United States, 1931; naturalized, 1939. **Education:** Educated in German schools, Rio de Janeiro and Sao Paulo, 1911-16; Benedictine Gymnasium, Rio de Janeiro, 1916-21; studied landscape architecture at Cornell University, Ithaca, New York, 1926-27, M. Landscape Arch. 1927; self-taught in photography but influenced by Alfred Stieglitz and Edward Weston. **Family:** Married Frances Watson in 1928. **Career:** Worked as a landscape architect and city planner, with his father Carlos Sommer, Rio de Janeiro, 1927-30; independent painter and occasional photographer, Arizona, 1931-35. Independent photographer, Prescott, Arizona, since 1935. Founder-Instructor, with Lucy Marlow, Studio of Art School, Tucson, 1931-35; Lecturer in Photography, Institute of Design, Illinois Institute of Technology, Chicago, 1957-58, 1963; Coordinator of Fine Arts, Prescott College, 1966-71. **Recipient:** Gold Medal, Pan American Congress of Architects, Rio de Janeiro, 1930; Guggenheim Photography Fellowship, 1974. **Agent:** Pace/MacGill Gallery, New York, New York 10022, U.S.A. **Address:** P.O. Box 262, Prescott, Arizona 86302, U.S.A.

Individual Exhibitions:

1934	Increase Robinson Gallery, Chicago (paintings)
1937	Howard Putzel Gallery, Hollywood, California (paintings)
1946	Santa Barbara Museum of Art, California
1949	Egan Gallery, New York
1957	Institute of Design, Illinois Institute of Technology, Chicago
1959	Wittenborn Gallery, New York
1963	Art Institute of Chicago
1965	Washington Gallery of Modern Art, Washington, D.C. (travelled to the Pasadena Art Museum, California)
1967	Museum of Northern Arizona, Flagstaff
	San Fernando State College, Northridge, California (with Wynn Bullock and Edmund Teske)
1968	Philadelphia College of Art
1972	Light Gallery, New York
1973	Center for Contemporary Photography, Chicago
1977	Light Gallery, New York (with Michael Bishop and Carl Toth)
	Arizona Bank Galleria, Phoenix (with Ansel Adams)
1979	Princeton Art Museum, New Jersey Light Gallery, New York
1980	*Frederick Sommer at 75,* California State University at Long Beach (retrospective; toured the United States, 1980-81, and travelled to London, 1981)
	Venus, Jupiter and Mars: The Photographs of Frederick Sommer, Delaware Art Museum, Newark

1981	Serpentine Gallery, London
1985	High Museum of Art, Atlanta, Georgia
1986	*Frederick Sommer: Photographs and Drawings,* Pace/MacGill Gallery, New York
1992	*Frederick Sommer: Horizonless Landscapes,* Pace/MacGill Gallery, New York
1994	*Recent Collages,* Pace/MacGill Gallery, New York

Selected Group Exhibitions:

1949	*Realism in Photography,* Museum of Modern Art, New York
1950	*Photography at Mid-Century,* International Museum of Photography, George Eastman House, Rochester, New York
1951	*Abstraction in Photography,* Museum of Modern Art, New York
1953	*Contemporary Photography: Japan and America,* National Museum of Modern Art, Tokyo
1965	*Photography in America 1850-1965,* Yale University, New Haven, Connecticut
1967	*Photography in the 20th Century,* National Gallery of Canada, Ottawa (toured Canada and the United States, 1967-74)
1979	*Photographic Surrealism,* New Gallery of Contemporary Art, Cleveland (travelled to the Dayton Art Institute, Ohio, and the Brooklyn Museum, New York)
1980	*Photography of the 50s,* International Center of Photography, New York (travelled to the University of Arizona, Tucson; Minneapolis Institute of Art; California State University at Long Beach; and the Delaware Art Museum, Wilmington)
1985	*American Images 1945-80,* Barbican Art Gallery, London (toured Britain)
1987	*Photography and Art 1946-86,* Los Angeles County Museum of Art
1990	Pace/MacGill Gallery, New York
1992	Pace/MacGill Gallery, New York

Collections:

Museum of Modern Art, New York; International Museum of Photography, George Eastman House, Rochester, New York; Princeton University, New Jersey; Fogg Art Museum, Harvard University, Cambridge, Massachusetts; Art Institute of Chicago; University of Illinois, Urbana; Dayton Art Institute, Ohio; University of New Mexico, Albuquerque; Center for Creative Photography, University of Arizona, Tucson; Norton Simon Museum of Art, Pasadena, California.

Publications:

By SOMMER: Book—*The Poetic Logic of Art and Aesthetics,* with Stephen Aldrich, Prescott, Arizona 1972.

On SOMMER: Books—*Fame: Famous Portraits of Famous People by Famous Photographers,* edited by L. Fritz Gruber, London and New York 1960; *Aperture 10:4: Frederick Sommer,* edited by Minor White, Rochester, New York 1962; *The Painter and the Photograph: From Delacroix to Warhol* by Van Deren Coke, Albuquerque, New Mexico 1964, 1972; *Frederick Sommer,* exhibition catalogue, with text by Gerald Nordland, Washington, D.C. 1965; *Photography in the 20th Century* by Nathan Lyons, New York 1967; *Frederick Sommer: An Exhibition of Photographs,* exhibition catalogue, by Gerald Nordland, Philadelphia 1968; *Light and Lens: Methods of Photography,* edited by Donald L. Werner and Dennis Longwell, New York 1973; *Photography in America,* edited by Robert Doty, with an introduction by Minor White, New York and London 1974; *The Magic Image* by Cecil Beaton and Gail Buckland, London and Boston 1975; *Photographic Process as Medium,* exhibition catalogue, with text by Rosanne T. Livingston, New Brunswick, New Jersey 1975; *Dada and Surrealism Reviewed,* exhibition catalogue, by Dawn Ades, London 1978; *Amerikanische Landschaftsphotographie 1860-1978,* exhibition catalogue, with an introduction by Klaus-Jürgen Sembach, Munich 1978; *Photographic Surrealism,* exhibition catalogue, by Nancy Hall-Duncan, Cleveland 1979; *Photography of the 50s:*

An American Perspective by Helen Gee, Tucson, Arizona 1980; *Frederick Sommer at 75,* edited by Constance W. Glenn and Jane K. Bledsoe, Long Beach, California 1980; *Venus, Jupiter and Mars: The Photographs of Frederick Sommer,* exhibition catalogue, edited by John Weiss, Newark, Delaware 1980; *Frederick Sommer: Photographs, Drawings and Musical Scores,* exhibition catalogue, London 1981; *Visions and Images: American Photographers on Photography,* edited by Barbaralee Diamonstein, New York 1981; *Sommer/Words Sommer/Images,* Center for Creative Photography, 1984; *American Images: Photography 1945-1980,* edited by Peter Burner, London 1985; *Photography and Art 1946-86,* exhibition catalogue, by Andy Grundberg and Kathleen M. Gauss, Los Angeles 1987. **Articles—** "Three Phantasists: Laughlin, Sommer, Bullock" by Jonathan Williams in *Aperture* (Rochester, New York), 9:3, 1961; "Frederick Sommer: 1939-1962 Photographs" by David Heath in *Contemporary Photographer* (Culpeper, Virginia), Summer 1963; "Frederick Sommer" in *Aperture* (Rochester, New York), 16:2, 1971; "Frederick Sommer" by J. Kelly in *Art in America* (New York), January/February 1973; "New York Letter: Frederick Sommer" by S. Schwartz in *Art International* (Lugano), January 1973; "Frederick Sommer" in *Exposure* (New York), February 1977.

* * *

The ostensible subject matter of Frederick Sommer's photographs includes portraits, peeling walls, landscapes, found objects and sculpture. Formally, he favors flat, two dimensional planes, often layered and always punctuated by precise details. His compositions, though often frontal and emblematic, more often than not use a sense of "field," a textured, middle grey background which extends beyond the edge of the frame. Beyond this, his images suggest the dissolution of matter: precise surfaces are shown wearing away to reveal layers beneath. As such, they may be read as metaphors for the process of time, or even, in a more extended sense, as the process of analysis (psychological) or the search for inner truth. Many of the images evoke horror, but usually the physical precision of the surfaces is such that they seem "beautiful" at the same time, and thus hang, dialectically poised, between these two extremes.

The 1948 portrait of the child "Livia" exhibits all these qualities. Although the child is beautiful, her pose, her stare, her juxtaposition against a peeling weathered wall, evoke a state of uneasiness in the viewer. The photograph is framed horizontally. The child is posed emblematically dead center, cut off just below the waist, her hands crossed, almost as if in death. Her white summer pinafore seems almost ceremonial, and accents the whites of her eyes, focused on the viewer in a disconcerting stare. The peeling wall behind her forms a flat two-dimensional surface, but also suggests layering and dissolution. The age of the child contrasts with the old, weathered wall. An interesting counterpart to "Livia" is "Medallion," done in the same year, in which a doll's head is substituted for the child, intensifying the sense of death and decay. The other qualities remain: the wall, middle grey and precisely textured, the flat space, the sense of "field" and past time.

A prototype for the "field" of the flat, peeling, middle grey wall (or other texture) may be found in the "Arizona Landscapes" done in the early 1940s. Shot from above with nothing to suggest scale, these panoramas of rocks, cacti and spare tufts of vegetation become almost abstract. The sense of three-dimensionality is modified onto a single plane; they are precisely textured and middle grey.

Found objects, especially those which are man-made, become part of many of Sommer's images, especially dolls, skeletons, old posters, (glass, pipes, machine parts, particularly those which might suggest body parts). Sommer arranges these artifacts against the ever present grey background. In "Valise d'Adam," a doll becomes, through positioning, a phallus, and a machine part becomes an animal head. What appear to be the arms and legs of a mannikin of small carved sculpture complete the totem-like figure. The amalgam of human, child, toy and animal references becomes a mythological "personage" which is both whimsical and terrifying at the same time. By using "real" objects, and rearranging them Sommer creates an alchemical world which is always changing before our eyes.

The most horrifying of Sommer's images involve real objects—often decayed beyond recognition. He seems fascinated by the process of probing, of peeling away, and uses the camera like a surgeon's scalpel. In many of these images Sommer faces death and the ravages of physical matter with a cool stare. Most viewers will flinch from the extraordinary clarity of this vision. In

"Detail," an amputated, partially dissected leg is examined, in excrutiating detail, classically centered against a black background. In "Coyotes," the dessicated carcasses of four of those animals are arranged against dry, cracked soil. The details are spellbinding: the grace of the skeletal forms, the juxtaposition of slender limbs, the terrible fangs, the clinging tufts of hair. In "Artificial Leg" (1944), the primitive leather and straps of the prosthetic device merge with a shadowed version of the "grey field." The decaying "boot" of the leg begins to merge with this background, flattening out, becoming a plane itself. The terrifying 1939 "Chicken" is a sickening, yet ultimately fascinating image of a glistening, unborn chicken embryo. Sommer spares us nothing: the pale wash of blood adds a delicate tonality to the stark white background.

In a gentler, more romantic mode, Sommer's photographs of old posters, usually containing human figures, repeat the theme of dissolution. In "Venus, Jupiter and Mars" (1949), two men and a woman sit at a tea table in what appears to be an advertising poster for some unidentified product. They form a classic triangle as they gaze longingly into each other's eyes. The poster is ripped, and peels away to reveal the wall beneath. At the same time the peeling process partially obliterates the features of the three figures. The image suggests the transience of human passion and beauty.

This theme takes another form in the out-of-focus images of statues done in the 1960s. In "Capitoline Museum," a classical, draped nude statue appears to dance because of the slight movement of Sommer's camera at the moment of exposure. It is another way of giving the appearance of transparency and evanescence to something that is solid and man-made (a marble statue).

Sommer's images range from the delicate and ephemeral to the terrible and traumatic. He turns his lens unequivocally on death and decay; indeed, his great theme is that of the impermanence of matter, especially artifacts. He leaves us precise records of the dissolution of the physical world, the work of time, and the gradual progress of death.

—Carole Harmel

SONNEMAN, Eve.

Nationality: American. **Born:** Chicago, Illinois, 14 January 1950. **Education:** South Shore High School, Chicago, 1959-63; University of Illinois, Urbana, 1963-67, B.F.A. 1967; University of New Mexico, Albuquerque, 1967-69, M.A. 1969. **Career:** Freelance photographer, with studio in New York City, since 1969. Lecturer, Cooper Union, New York, 1970-71, 1975-78, 1985; Visiting Artist, Rice University, Houston, 1971-72; Lecturer, City University of New York, 1972-75, and School of Visual Arts, New York, 1975-89. **Recipient:** Boskop Foundation Grant, New York, 1969; National Endowment for the Arts Award, 1972, 1978; Institute for Art and Urban Resources Grant, New York, 1977; Polaroid Corporation Grant for work in Polavision, 1978; Polaroid Corporation Grants, 1988, 1989; Fondation Cartier pour l'Art Contemporain, France, 1989. **Agents:** Castelli Graphics, 4 East 77th Street, New York, New York 10021; Rudiger Schottle, Martiusstrasse 7, 8 Munich 40, Germany; Texas Gallery, 2439 Bissonet, Houston, Texas; and Galerie Farideh Cadot, 11 rue du Jura, 75013 Paris, France. **Address:** 684 Avenue of the Americas, New York, New York 10010, U.S.A.

Individual Exhibitions:

1970	*A Survey,* Cooper Union, New York (travelled to the Media Center, Rice University, Houston, 1971)
1972	Art Museum of South Texas, Corpus Christi
1973	Whitney Museum Art Resources Center, New York
1974	*Coney Island Series,* The Texas Gallery, Houston
	College of St. Catherine Museum, St. Paul, Minnesota
1975	*Subway Series,* The Texas Gallery, Houston
1976	Bard College, Annandale-on-Hudson, New York
	Observations: 1/4 Mile in the Sky, Castelli Gallery, New York
1977	*New Work,* Artemisia Gallery, Chicago
	New Work, Galerie Farideh Cadot, Paris
	New Work, The Texas Gallery, Houston
	New Work, Diane Brown Gallery, Washington, D.C.

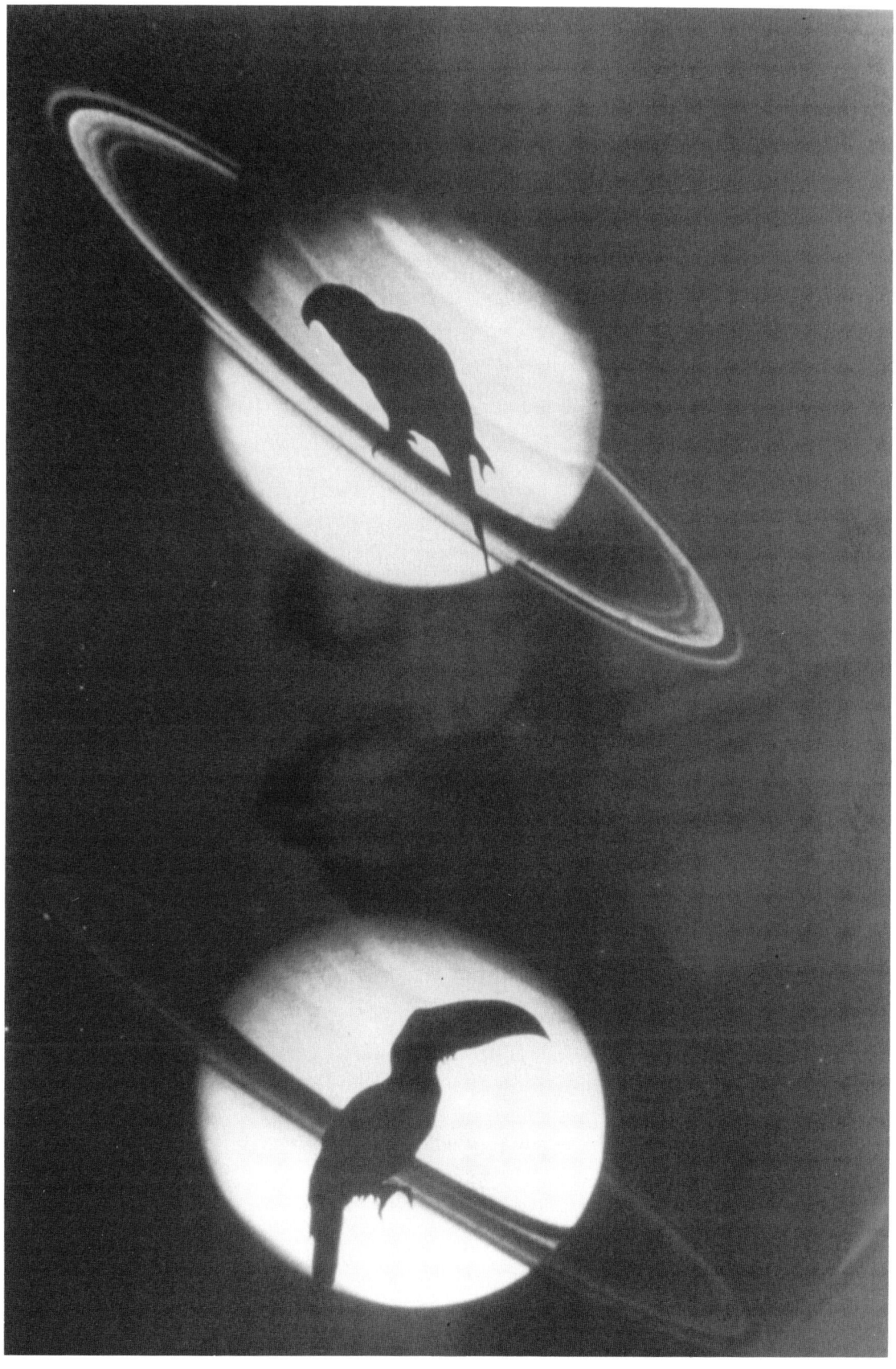

Macaw and Toucan on Saturn, **1990 (original in colour).** Photograph by Eve Sonneman.

A Survey, College of Wooster, Ohio
1978   *New Work,* Castelli Gallery, New York
1979   *Color Work,* Thomas Segal Gallery, Boston
       3 Americans, Moderna Museet, Stockholm (with Lewis Baltz and Mark Cohen; travelled to the Alborg Kunstmuseum, Denmark; Kunstpavillionen, Esbjerg, Denmark; Tranegarden, Gentofte, Copenhagen; and Henie-Onstad Museum, Oslo, 1980)
       Color Work, Rudiger Schottle Gallery, Munich
1980   *Color Work,* La Nouveau Musée, Lyons
       5 Year Color Show, Contemporary Arts Center, New Orleans (travelled to the Contemporary Arts Center, Cincinnati, Ohio)
       Work from 1968-1978, Minneapolis Institute of Arts
       New Work and Polaroids, Galerie Farideh Cadot, Paris
       The Texas Gallery, Houston
       Polaroid Work, Young Hoffman Gallery, Chicago
       New Work, Francoise Lambert Gallery, Milan
       New Work: New York, Castelli Gallery, New York
1981   *Future Memories,* Cirrus Gallery, Los Angeles
       Work from 1968-1978, Tucson Museum of Art, Arizona
       Galerie Peter Noser, Zurich
       Burton Gallery, Toronto
       Locus Solus, Genoa, Italy
1982   Leo Castelli Gallery, New York
       The Texas Gallery, Houston
       Hudson River Museum, New York
       Cirrus Gallery, Los Angeles
1983   Galerie Farideh Cadot, Paris
       The Photographers' Gallery, London
       Musée de Toulon
1984   Centre Georges Pompidou, Paris
       Leo Castelli Gallery, New York
       Schloss Mickeln, Dusseldorf
       Gloria Luria Gallery, Miami, Florida
       Mattingly Baker Gallery, Dallas, Texas
       Santa Barbara Art Museum, California
       The Texas Gallery, Houston
1985   Museum of Modern Art, Costa Rica
       Galerie Peter Noser, Zurich
       Gloria Luria Gallery, Miami, Florida
       Galleria Francoise Lambert, Milan
       Galerie Imago, Cologne
       Gallery for Fine Photography, New Orleans, Louisiana
1986   Castelli Graphics, New York
       Tyler School of Art, Philadelphia
1988   Peter Noser Galerie, Zurich, Switzerland
       Elizabeth Galasso Gallery, Ossining, New York
1989   A Gallery for Fine Photography, New Orleans, Louisiana
       Cirrus Gallery, Los Angeles
       Jones Troyer Fitzpatrick Gallery, Washington, D.C.
       Lieberman & Saul Gallery, New York
1990   Gloria Luria Gallery, Miami
       Zabriskie Gallery, New York
1991   Grand Central Terminal, New York
1992   Charles Cowles Gallery, New York
1993   Jones Troyer Fitzpatrick, Washington, D.C.
       Cirrus Gallery, Los Angeles
1995   The Art Museum of New Mexico, Albuquerque

Selected Group Exhibitions:

1969   *Recent Acquisitions,* Museum of Modern Art, New York
1977   *Bookworks,* Museum of Modern Art, New York
1978   *Mirrors and Windows: American Photography since 1960,* Museum of Modern Art, New York (toured the United States, 1978-80)
1979   *Attitudes: American Photography in the 1970s,* Santa Barbara Museum of Art, California
1980   *One of a Kind,* Corcoran Gallery of Art, Washington, D.C.

1982   *Counterparts: Form and Emotion in Photographs,* Metropolitan Museum of Art, New York (travelled to the Contemporary Arts Center, Cincinnati; Dallas Museum of Fine Art, Texas; San Francisco Museum of Modern Art; Corcoran Gallery, Washington, D.C.)
1983   *Photography in America 1910-83,* Tampa Museum, Florida
1984   *Exposed and Developed,* National Museum of American Art, Washington, D.C. (toured the United States)
1985   *Rare Books of the 20th Century,* Bibliothèque Nationale, Paris
1987   *Photography and Painting 1946-86,* Los Angeles County Museum of Art
1988   *Saletta Conumale de Sposizone,* Francoise Lambert Galleria, Milan, Italy
       Le SAGA 88-FIAC Editions, Grand Palais, Paris
1989   *Artist Books,* Victoria and Albert Museum, London
1991   *The Imaginary Library,* The National Gallery of Canada, Ottawa, Ontario
       The National Museum of Women in the Arts, Washington, D.C.
1992   *Illuminations,* Museum of Modern Art at Pfizer Co, New York
       Contemporary Collection, Centre Georges Pompidou, Paris
1993   *A Private Collection,* Galerie Cadot, Paris
1994   *Flowers,* Museum of Modern Art, New York

Collections:

Museum of Modern Art, New York; Metropolitan Museum of Art, New York; Princeton University, New Jersey; Art Institute of Chicago; Museum of Fine Arts, Houston; de Menil Foundation, Houston; Centre Georges Pompidou, Paris; Bibliothèque Nationale, Paris; Rheinisches Landesmuseum, Bonn; National Gallery of Australia, Canberra; The Museum of Contemporary Art, Los Angeles, California; National Gallery of Australia, Canberra, Australia; Center for Creative Photography, Tucson, Arizona; Dallas Museum of Fine Arts, Dallas, Texas; San Francisco Museum of Modern Art, California; Le Nouveau Musee, Lyon, France; Fondation Cartier for Contemporary Art, France; Toppan Museum, Tokyo.

Publications:

By SONNEMAN: Book—*Real Time,* New York 1976; *Roses are Read,* with text by Klaus Kertess, Paris 1982; *America's Cottage Gardens* with text by Patricia Thorpe, New York 1990; *Where Birds Live,* with introduction by Adam Gopnik, New York 1992.

On SONNEMAN: Books—*Mirrors and Windows: American Photography since 1960,* exhibition catalogue, by John Szarkowski, New York 1978; *One of a Kind: Recent Polaroid Color Photography* by Belinda Rathbone, Boston 1979; *Diana and Her Nikon: Essays on the Aesthetic of Photography* by Janet Malcolm, Boston 1980; *Eve Sonneman: Work from 1968-81,* exhibition catalogue, with text by Bruce Kurtz, New York 1982; *Counterparts: Form and Emotion in Photographs* by Weston J. Naef, New York 1982; *American Photography: A Critical History, 1945 to the Present* by Jonathan Green, New York 1984; *Eve Sonneman,* exhibition catalogue, with text by Jeffrey Deitch, San Jose, Costa Rica 1985; *A World History of Photography* by Naomi Rosenblum, New York 1985; *Photography and Art 1946-86,* exhibition catalogue, by Andy Grundberg and Kathleen M. Gauss, Los Angeles 1987; *Sequence: Con Sequence,* New York 1989; *Eve Sonneman: Work from '68-'78* by David Shapiro, New York 1991; *A History of Women Photographers* by Naomi Rosenblum, New York 1994; *The Power of Style,* New York 1994. **Articles**—"Eve Sonneman at Castelli" by Bruce Kurtz in *Art in America* (New York), January 1977; "Alternatives from New York" in *Flash Art* (Milan), February/April 1977; "A View from Kassel" by David Shapiro in *Artforum* (New York), September 1977; "Eve Sonneman" by Jonathan Crary in *Arts* (New York), November 1978; "Photography: Two Roads" by Janet Malcolm in *The New Yorker,* December 1978; "Eve Sonneman's Progressions in Time" by Tiffany Bell in *Artforum* (New York), October 1979; "Eblouissante Eve Sonneman" in *Le Figaro* (Paris), 23 January 1980; "Eve Sonneman's Explorations" by Andy Grundberg in the *New York Times,* 18 April 1982; "Eve Sonneman and the World in Color" by William Zimmer in *Arts* (New York), September 1984; "Eve Sonneman" by Klaus Honnef in *Kunstforum International,* March/April 1986; *Photographie; International*

Magazine fur Fotografie, no. 6 1989; "Eve Sonneman at Zabriskie" by Carl Little in *Art in America,* New York October 1990; "Art That Lays Bare the Pain of Loss" by Nancy Stepen in *The Boston Globe,* April 1992.

*

My work as an artist includes photography. A photograph is a magical moment crossing time and open to the world.

—Eve Sonneman

* * *

Since 1968 Eve Sonneman has been making photographs in Europe and America. Her work characteristically contains pairs or quartets of images having some formal or thematic relationship to one another. In the earliest of these series, black and white quartets made in and around New York between 1968-1974, Sonneman began to explore subtle shifts in visual perspective and chronology and the effects of such manipulation on the viewer. At the conclusion of this period, the quartets were further complicated by the juxtaposition of pairs of color and black-and-white photographs within the same work. In the "Coney Island" photographs, made at this time, tightly framed variations on beach and street scenes, located within a quadruple image, give these vernacular subjects an analytical weight generally reserved for more heroic material.

Sonneman's investigations of formal mannerism in relation to subject and locale continued through 1976 in "Observations; 1/4 Mile in the Sky" (the title of her one-woman show containing a series of diptychs made at the World Trade Center observation deck during the Bicentennial celebration) as well as in the second group of photographs made in Europe during 1980.

In May 1980 Sonneman showed a group of paired photographs made in Europe and America over a period of two years; they demonstrate that photography need not be either a cold document of reality or a poetic evocation of the world processed through the photographer's manipulative intelligence. Each Sonneman diptych insists on vernacular situations which are simultaneously mysterious. The viewer's participation, apparent in the impulse to reconcile or paraphrase the joining of visually related information, is thus strongly encouraged by the formal strategy of this work. Through this strategy, Sonneman presents documents in which reality is not distilled or manipulated into a single privileged view, but is a progression excerpted from life. Her multiple images underscore the temporal process and activity of vision as it continues to select, revise, and edit what is ultimately taken to be real.

A number of pieces in this exhibition seemed at first to fall within the traditional category of the *nature morte,* but Sonneman's views of elaborately contrived displays (whether of magazines, seed packets, or chemical glassware in a shop window) are more accurately the means by which she denies that it is the photographer who composes. In point of fact, she records the works of those who invent and contrive such arrangements as part of their daily lives. Similarly, her views of the landscape (a gas station over which the rising moon intrudes, the progression of a plane as it dusts crops, or a frieze of chalk drawings in an urban gutter) maintain that reality, as seen and defined in these photographs, is a series of provisional, interchangeable, material situations in which viewers actively consider and synthesize what Sonneman has merely seen first.

Sonneman's work since 1981 has begun to emphasize the effect of scale rather than counterpoint in the impact of her work. In addition to her new diptychs, she has also shown 20 x 24 inch Cibachrome single images.

—David Corey

ŠONTA, Virgilijus.

Nationality: Lithuanian. **Born:** Panenéžys, Lithuania, 16 February 1952. **Education:** Attended the Polytechnical Institute, Kaunas, Lithuania, 1970-76, Dip.Ing. 1976; self-taught in photography, from 1974. **Family:** Married Vaitkevičiuté Vida in 1980; daughter: Miglé. **Career:** Photojournalist, for the TASS Agency and Elta Telegram Agency, U.S.S.R., 1976-77; staff worker, Photo Art Society of Lithuania, Vilnius, 1977-81. Freelance photographer, working for Intourist and other publicity companies, Kaunas, 1981-1984. Returned to work at the Society of Photo Artists in Vilnius, 1985. Acquired U.S. citizenship, 1990. **Recipient:** Bronze Medal, *Man's Moments* exhibition, Maglay, Yugoslavia, 1977; Photo Prize, *Man and Nature* exhibition, Novosibirsk, U.S.S.R., 1978; Medal, *Phot-Univers* exhibition, Bievres, France, 1978; Grand Prize, *Junij* exhibition, Belgrade, 1979; Medal, *Europaische Fotografen* exhibition, West Berlin, 1982. **Agent:** Romualdas Požerskis, A Mapu 8—2, Kaunas, 3000, Lithuania. **Died:** (in Vilnius) July 28, 1992.

Individual Exhibitions:

1977	House of Culture, Šiauliai, Lithuania
1980	Photo Gallery, Poznan, Poland
1981	Art Research Institute, Moscow
1982	Residence of TASS Agency, Moscow
1983	Photography Salon, Vilnius, Lithuania
	Photo Gallery, Kaunas, Lithuania
	Photo Museum, Šiauliai, Lithuania
1984	House of Photography, Plovdiv, Bulgaria
	Scientist House, Vladivostok, Russia

Selected Group Exhibitions:

1979	*Lithuanian Photography,* Canon Photo Gallery, Amsterdam
1980	*Lithuanian Photography,* Photographers' Gallery, London
	Junij-80, Belgrade, Yugoslavia
1983	*Photography in Europe Today,* Gallery of Fine Arts, Ankara, Turkey
1985	*Contemporary Lithuanian Photographers,* at *Rencontres Internationales de la Photographie,* Arles, France
	Lithuanian Photography, at *Torino-85,* Turin, Italy
1988	*An Insight into Contemporary Soviet Photography,* La Comptoir de la Photographie Gallery, Paris
1989	*Foto dialog,* Halle, Germany
1990	Photography Gallery, Portland, Oregon
1991	Altes Museum, Berlin
1993	Stadtgalerie im Sophienhof, Kiel, Germany
	Kunsthalle, Rostok, Germany
	Exhibition Hall, Riga, Latvia
1994	Photography Gallery, Tallinn, Estonia

Collections:

Bibliothèque Nationale, Paris; Photo Museum of Šiauliai, Lithuania; International Center of Photography, New York.

Publications:

On ŠONTA: Books—*Lietuvos fotografija,* with introduction by Romualdas Pacesa, Vilnius, Lithuania 1975, 1978, 1981; *Fotojahrbuch International,* Leipzig 1979, 1982; *Dumont Foto 2,* Cologne 1980; *Photography Year Book,* London 1981; *Fotografie in Europa heute,* Cologne 1982; *Fotografen aus der UdSSR,* Baden-Baden, West Germany 1983; *Dumont Foto 4,* Cologne 1983; *Photographers Encyclopaedia International,* Switzerland 1984; *Lietuvos fotografija annual,* Vilnius 1986, 1987; *Tsvetenie Zemli/A Blossom of the Earth,* by Viktor Diomin, Moscow 1987; *An Insight into Contemporary Soviet Photography,* Paris 1988; *Photography in USSR,* Helsinki 1989; *FOTO, Ein fotografischer Dialog,* Hannover, Germany 1989; *Changing Reality* by Bendavid, Washington 1991; *Bilder Lust, Erotische Photographien,* Berlin 1991; *The Female Nude in Art Photography,* Moscow 1992; *The Memory of Images, Baltic Photo Art Today,* Kiel, Germany 1993. **Articles**—in *Foto* (Warsaw), no. 2, 1980; *Fotografie* (Leipzig), no. 9, 1980; *Fotografie* (Prague), no. 4, 1983; *Photographer,* (Paris), November 1988; *The Independent Magazine,* (London), April, 1989; *Aperture,* no. 116, (New York), 1989; *Photo,* (Paris), July 1989.

*

The language of photography enables me to describe an inner state that is impossible to put into words. From apparently unimportant minor events the camera helps me to feel and diagnose the dramas and conflicts in interhuman relations. Constantly raising the question of human existence, it makes bridges between people and arouses the feeling of not being alone.

—Virgilijus Šonta

*   *   *

Vigilijus Šonta is perhaps the most significant of the younger generation Lithuanian photographers. His recent work departs considerably from the commonplace and often overwhelming lyricism of the Lithuanian School and from its dominant interest in the certainties of harmonious village life. More than any fellow Lithuanian, Šonta reacts individually to the inspirational impulses of contemporary international work, thus enriching Soviet photography with non-traditional themes and styles.

At first, he devoted himself to music and then to amateur film, and it was not until his studies at a polytechnic school in Kaunas that he began to photograph. He was greatly influenced by his schoolfriend photographer Romualdas Pozerskis and by his acquaintance with the already renowned photographer Aleksandras Macijauskas, whom he frequently accompanied on photographic excursions to village markets. Šonta's own village photos, however, were of a quite undistinctive nature owing to a shyness which did not permit him to move in with the telling personal close-up. Instead, he felt more drawn to landscape photography, in which he followed the style of Jonas Kalvelis. In 1974-78 Šonta created a large cycle of romantic pictures entitled *Lithuanian Landscapes,* paying tribute to the beauty of his native land with its far horizons of endless plains, lakes and pine forests. From the lyrical and academically classic style of these photographs, he soon moved to a more stylized form of landscape detail. A decisive break in this development came in 1978 with his scholarship trip to the Far East near Vladivostok and Kamchatka. From this two-month stay on the Soviet Union's Pacific coast, Šonta brought home *Stones* and *Cycles,* two cycles of great importance for his further creative efforts. The first cycle, creatively captured the bizarre shapes of giant boulders and rocks. often juxtaposed against a quiet water surface. Šonta's concern was not only with the aesthetic qualities of elementary line and tone, but also with symbolic meaning and deeper philosophical content. In the cycle *Flights,* a series of images that captured children in the act of diving, people appeared in Šonta's photographs for the first time. With their otherworldly atmosphere, the pictures caught figures in mid-flight so that they often appear suspended in a mysterious void.

In the same year, Šonta developed his sense of metaphor in a collection of compositions depicting various articles washed up on the sandy beaches of the Lithuanian coast—glass bottles, electric light bulbs, plastic containers and the remnants of old wooden crates. Out of these he created strongly stylized "metaphysical landscapes" based on counterpoints of nature, represented by the sea, beach, skies darkened by cumulus clouds, and fragments of man-made objects. Many of these imaginary landscapes, whose emotive charge is accentuated by unusual perspective, tonality and evocative shadows, remind one of paintings by Giorgio de Chirico.

It was in 1980 that Šonta began photographing in a boarding-school for mentally handicapped children in the Lithuanian town of Šiauliai. He spent a long time preparing for this difficult task and took no pictures at all during his first six months there, but made himself familiar with the children and their life stories. Influenced as he was by the Milos Forman film *One Flew Over the Cuckoo's Nest* and the photographs of Diane Arbus, Šonta nevertheless first tried to gain his own personal view of this peculiar microworld. The Soviet critic Anninskij has rightly observed that Diane Arbus had indicated where to look, but Šonta himself knew what to look for. For three years Šonta worked on this cycle entitled *My School, My Home* not only in Šiauliai but in other similar schools, endeavouring to show how the mentally handicapped experience their joys and griefs, and seek understanding and friendship. He photographed the sick children as if they were healthy, without embellishment or pity. The photos reflect a human sympathy and often an admiration for their subjects' unconventionality and freedom. A certain aesthetic distance is established by the use of wide-angle distortion and raw flash illumination—a distancing not found in thematically similar photographs of Mary Ellen Mark's *Ward 81,* for instance.

Šonta had been working on subjectively conceived documentary photographs that relied on visual metaphors whose content cannot be sufficiently transformed into words. The unusually composed images, frequently a little mysterious and always carrying multiple possibilities of interpretation, open wide the door to imagination. A confrontation of several antagonistic motifs in one photograph create a dreamlike atmosphere whose very oddity causes the spectator to suddenly see everyday phenomena anew, to look beneath the conventional for a deeper meaning. The conception, first seen in the pioneer 1950s work of William Klein and Robert Frank, and rarely emerging in Soviet photography, asserted itself ever more distinctly in the work of Virgilius Šonta.

—Vladimìr Birgus

SPENCE, Jo.

Nationality: British. **Born:** South Woodford, Essex, 15 June 1934. **Education:** Graduated with a B.A. in film and photographic arts from the Polytechnic of Central London. **Family:** Married David Roberts, 13 May 1992. **Career:** Worked as a secretary for a commercial photographer, before becoming a printer's assistant 1951-66. Established own portrait studio, Joanne Spence Associates, in Hampstead 1967. Cofounded, with Terry Dennett, Photography Workshop in 1974, which later combined to become Half Moon Photography Workshop and started *Camerawork* magazine. **Estate:** The Jo Spence Memorial Archive, c/o Terry Dennett, 152 Upper Street, London N1 1RA, England. **Died:** 24 June 1992.

Individual Exhibitions:

1973	*Children Photographed* (with the help of Arts Council Grant)
1985	*Review of Work,* Cambridge Darkroom (travelled)
1990	*Silent Health,* Camera Work Gallery, London
1991	*Collaborative works* (toured Australia and the United States)
	Missing Persons/Damaged Lives, Leeds City Art Gallery
1994	*The Cancer Project,* Gallery d'Art Santa Monica, Barcelona
	Jo Spence: Matters of Concern Collaborative Images 1982-1992, Festival Hall, London and Impressions Gallery, York

Selected Group Exhibitions:

1975	*Women Musicians* travelling exhibition
1979	*Beyond the Family Album,* Cockpit Gallery, London
	The Worker Photographer, travelling exhibition
1982	*Family, Fantasy and Photography,* Cockpit Gallery, London (travelled)
	Re-Modelling Photo History, M.I.T. (toured the United States and England)
1983	*Fairy Tales and Photography,* travelling exhibition
1985	*The Picture of Health,* Photography Workshop (travelled)
	The Phototherapy Road Show, Photography Workshop (travelled)
1987	*Staging the Self,* National Portrait Gallery, London
1988	*Sexual Difference,* Miriam and Ira Wallach Art Gallery, Columbia University
1989	*Through the Looking Glass,* Barbican, London
1990	*Libido Uprising,* Photography Workshop, London (travelled)
1991	*Exploring the Unknown Self,* Tokyo Metropolitan Museum of Photography
	Missing Persons/Damaged Lives, Leeds Art Gallery (travelled)
1992	*The Crisis Project: Scene of the Crime* in "Real Stories," Museet for Fotokunset, Denmark
1993	*Class Shame projects* in "Re Negotiations," Norwich Gallery (travelled)
1994	*The Cancer Project in Different Stories,* Rotterdam Photofest, Rotterdam, Netherlands

Return to Nature, 1984. ©The Jo Spence Memorial Archive.

Our Bodies Ourselves, Nottingham Castle (touring 1995)
Matters of Concern, Collaborative Images 1982-92, Royal
　　Festival Art Gallery, London

Publications:

By SPENCE: **Book**—*Putting Myself in the Picture,* London 1986. **Television**—"Putting Ourselves in the Picture—the Work of Jo Spence" in *Arena,* BBC 20 March 1987; *Opening up the Family Album,* Channel Four, August 1988; *Tip of the Iceberg,* 1989; *Video Diary,* BBC 1991.

*　　*　　*

Jo Spence's reputation has grown and consolidated since her early death, not in the academic circles where she knew her innovative "phototherapy" work would receive short shrift; nor in the galleries where fine art photogaphy "proper" is increasingly invading. To them she was always something of an amateur; neither a qualified counsellor nor a gallery based artist, her work was most widely disseminated through books and exhibitions (often informally displayed), lectures and conferences and increasingly through television. For Channel 4 she made a whole series which she ultimately repudiated as a travesty of her original concept; for BBC 1, an Arena programme about the interpenetration of her life and work; and, perhaps most successfully, shortly before she died, a BBC 2 Video Diary renewing her contact with her long separated brother.

For the family, that now most fashionable current of artistic preoccupations, was the basis of all of Jo's late work. Curiously, it did not become an issue through her early, usually collective, projects directly on political themes

related to housing, poverty and community organisation. Nor through her, perhaps, inevitable preoccupation in the 1970s with the feminist movement and "ways of seeing" the female nude through her chosen medium of portraiture. This shift of focus onto the importance of the family progressed with the diagnosis in 1982 of her breast cancer—the disease that killed her mother. Feeling the need to look within herself both for the sources of her cancer and for the resources to deal with it, Spence deliberately abandoned documenting the outside world. In dealing with her illness and mortality, Jo discovered she needed also to deal with the family she had "ingested."

At this point Spence began reviewing the facts she thought she had reflected on so many times before. How she had been born into a downwardly mobile working class home and bought her upward mobility through education and middle class boyfriends who she explained, even when they decided she probably would not make a suitable wife, at least treated her to people and places she would not otherwise have known. How the trauma of separation, through wartime evacuation, even from parents with whom she felt resolutely little in common, had left her with the scars of abandonment, however rigorously she tried to intellectualise the historical context. How the onset of asthma coincided with other pubescent agonies and recurred most aggressively at times of intense psychic stress (for example, after her hounding at the first National Photography conference at Salford in 1987, when her selected theme was hotly disputed).

It was in the last decade of her life, when Jo was directly and daily fighting to stay alive, that she found her theme. This incorporated not only the inevitable feelings about life and death but also those about her origins and her future; her preoccupation with what she could leave to the future was paramount. In developing the rich complexity of phototherapy, devised to give the sitter/subject permission to devise an image, together with the photographer/

1053

therapist a way in which family relationships could be explored in order to throw light on what ultimately constitutes the individual.

The essentially agitprop nature of her work combined with the community politics of the period gave rise to a sporadic proliferation of work across a spectrum of visual, literary and oral media. Never one to be too precise in the cataloguing of her work, Spence would proceed with untidy albums of loose photographs under her arms ready to be shown to anyone who seemed interested or simply to pull out to punctuate her always animated conversation at points when her effervescence could pause. Once she became chronically ill with cancer, however, the work gained a different momentum in which it was a tool used less for politicised consciousness-raising—a term she came to call unconscious-raising.

In a reversal of the personal-is-political maxim, Spence refused to relinquish her self-definition as a working class woman concerned "with just about issue of importance" that might create a better, safer and fairer world. Having learnt to mistrust political parties, she lamented the fact that "there are no cultural groups around the politics of leukaemia or cancer." Yet health was, for her, the microcosm of a larger political view in which she felt she could intercede as a *cultural sniper*. She even pondered on her role as artist, noting how "artists are incredibly badly paid and under validated" even as she commented on the different reception she was accorded as "one of them" rather than as a cultural worker, or even as a photographer. Yet, in seeking to incorporate so much, increasingly straddling a wider field to contribute her views on subjects as diverse as the culture of feminism and cult of fitness, she touched an extraordinary amount of the issues of our time and of the people who sought her out.

—Amanda Hopkinson

SPENDER, Humphrey.

Nationality: British. **Born:** London, 19 April 1910. **Education:** Greshams School, Holt, Norfolk, 1923-27; studied at University of Freiburg im Breisgau, Germany, 1927-28; and at the Architectural Association School, London, 1929-34, AA Dip. 1933; also studied anthropology, under Raymond Firth, London School of Economics, 1938; mainly self-taught in photography, but learned techniques with brother Michael, London, 1920-24. **Military Service:** Trained in Royal Army Service Corps (Tanks), Salisbury Plain, Wiltshire, 1941, then served as War Office Official Photographer and subsequently transferred as Photo-Interpreter, Theatre Intelligence Service, London and Medenham, Buckinghamshire, 1942-46: Captain. **Family:** Married the architect Margaret Low in 1937 (died, 1945); son: David; married Pauline Wynne in 1947; son: Quentin. **Career:** Worked as a portrait and commercial photographer, establishing studio with Bill Edmiston, London, 1934-39; Staff Photographer, as "Lensman," *Daily Mirror* newspaper, London, 1936-38, and *Picture Post* magazine, London, 1938-41 and 1946-49; also photographer on Tom Harrisson's Mass Observation project, London and Blackpool, 1937-39, and for the Ministry of Information, London, 1941; gradually abandoned photography to concentrate on painting and textile design, from 1949 (individual exhibitions at Redfern Gallery, London, 1943, 1945, 1947, 1949, 1951, 1963; Leicester Galleries, London, 1953, 1958; and New Art Centre, London, 1975). Tutor in Textile Design, Royal College of Art, London, 1953-75; Visiting Lecturer, West Surrey College of Art and Design, Farnham, Camberwell School of Art, London, and Hornsey College of Art, London, 1960-75. **Recipient:** Design Award, Council of Industrial Design, London, 1951, 1953, 1955, 1961. Associate, Royal Institute of British Architects (ARIBA), London, 1934-70; Fellow, Society of Industrial Arts and Designers (FSIAD), 1960-75. Honorary Fellow, Royal College of Art, London, 1975. **Address:** The Studio, Ulting, near Maldon, Essex CM9 6QX, England.

Individual Exhibitions:

1977   *Worktown 1937-38,* Gardner Art Centre, University of Sussex, Brighton

1978   *Mass Observation Photographs,* Brewery Arts Centre, Kendal, Cumbria

1979   *Mass Observation,* Impressions Gallery, York

1981   *Photographs of the 30s,* Prakapas Gallery, New York

           Arnolfini Gallery, Bristol (retrospective; travelled to John Hansard Gallery, Southampton; Geffrye Museum, London; Royal College of Art, London; Kettles Yard Gallery, Cambridge; Playhouse Gallery, Harlow; Museum of Modern Art, Oxford)

           Stepney and Whitechapel 1934-36, Museum of London

1984   *People: Portrait Photographs,* Oliver Bradbury and James Birch Fine Art, London

1986   The Photographers' Gallery, London

1987   National Museum of Photography, Bradford, Yorkshire

1988   *Comptoir de la Photographie,* Paris

1992   Trinity Studios, Colchester

           Hayletts Gallery, Colchester

Selected Group Exhibitions:

1975   *The Real Thing: An Anthology of British Photographs 1840-1950,* Hayward Gallery, London (toured the U.K.)

1976   *Young Writers of the 30s,* National Portrait Gallery, London

1979   *The 30s: British Art and Design Before the War,* Hayward Gallery, London

1980   *Portraying People,* Sandford Gallery, London

           Modern British Photography 1919-39, Museum of Modern Art, Oxford (toured the U.K.)

1981   *The British Worker,* Mappin Art Gallery, Sheffield (toured the U.K.)

1982   *Lichtbildnisse: Das Porträt in der Fotografie,* Rheinisches Landesmuseum, Bonn

Collections:

Victoria and Albert Museum, London; National Portrait Gallery, London; Museum of London; Arts Council of Great Britain, London; Mass Observation Archive, University of Sussex, Brighton; Chelmsford Museum, Essex.

Publications:

By SPENDER: Books—*Britain in the '30s,* London 1977; *Worktown People: Photographs from Northern England 1937-38,* with transcriptions of taped interviews, Bristol 1981.

On SPENDER: Books—*Mass Observation* by Tom Harrisson and Charles Madge, London 1937; *Mass Observation: The First Year's Work,* edited by Tom Harrisson, London 1938; *Britain by Mass Observation,* edited by Tom Harrisson, London 1939; *Britain Revisited,* with text by Tom Harrisson, London 1961; *Britain in the 30s,* with text by Tom Harrisson, London 1975; *The Real Thing: An Anthology of British Photographs 1840-1950,* exhibition catalogue, by Ian Jeffrey and David Mellor, London 1975; *Humphrey Spender: Worktown: Photographs of Bolton and Blackpool Taken for Mass Observation 1937-38,* exhibition catalogue, with text by Ian Jeffrey, David Mellor and Derek Smith, Brighton 1977; *Thirties: British Art and Design Before the War,* exhibition catalogue, by Ian Jeffrey, William Feaver, Brian Lacey and others, London 1979; *Modern British Photography 1919-1939,* exhibition catalogue, by David Mellor, London 1980; *Lichtbildnisse: Das Porträt in der Fotografie,* edited by Klaus Honnef, Cologne 1982; *Humphrey Spender: People,* exhibition catalogue, with introduction by Lewis Biggs, London 1984; *A World History of Photography* by Naomi Rosenblum, New York 1985. **Articles**—"Humphrey Spender: MO Photographer," interview, by Tom Picton and Derek Smith in *Camerawork* (London), September 1978; "The Quiet Observer" by Stephen McClarence in *Photographers* (York), August/October 1979; "Humphrey Spender" in *Creative Camera* (London), May/June 1980; "The British Worker: Photographs of Working Life 1839-1939" by Colin Osman in *Creative Camera* (London), May/June 1981; Double

Sudbury Suffolk, Market Day, **1934.** Photograph by Humphrey Spender.

spread interview with Michael Hallett in *British Journal of Photography,*
June 1992.

*

Looking through all my past work as photographer, I come increasingly to
the conclusion that the most valid and proper use of a camera is as a means of
recording aspects of human behaviour; as time passes, social-documentary
photographs gain in interest, whereas the "beautiful" photograph (and I have
taken many such) progressively loses interest, becomes boring.

Endless discussions go on about "Photography as Art," and I find these
rather tedious, just as tedious as the type of photograph which manipulates
photographic techniques to produce highly personal and individual statements
deriving from the elements of contemporary painting, surrealism, abstract
expressionism, etc. Occasionally, such manipulations produce seductively
ravishing results if handled by a truly creative thinker, but too often the
potential of the modern camera's superb technology seems not to have been
exploited.

As disclosed by publications like Camera Workshop's journal *Camerawork,*
there are many highly skilled young documentary photographers around,
superbly exploiting the true potential of their cameras; but there are many
distressing aspects of the contemporary photographic scene: e.g., 50 photographers stand in a regimented row to shoot the same subject (such as our future
queen), each exposing ten frames—what an absurd waste; or, the tourist,
victim of the sharp dealer's sales talk, loaded with a pack of expensive
equipment which he doesn't understand (how many such photographers know
how to use the depth-of-focus scale?); and the escalating inflated prices
imposed by wheeler-dealers in the auction/collector/dealer world.

Finally, I become more and more aware of the power of the photographic
image, and thus more and more aware of the responsibility of the individual
photographer. The poet Wystan Auden is quoted as saying "the camera
always lies: it just ain't art." That is a somewhat sensational exaggeration, but
it is an alarming thought that in the wrong hands (those of Goebbels, for
instance) the camera can be a bomb.

—Humphrey Spender

* * *

Humphrey Spender played an extremely important part in the development of British documentary photography during the 1930s and 1940s. Like a
number of other English writers and artists of the time, he became interested in
the social, political and artistic life of Germany and spent some time in that
country during the 1920s. As a student of architecture in Freiburg he was
exposed to the New Objectivity movement in art and photography and also the
major German photo documentary magazines, notably the *Berliner Illustrierte
Zeitung* and the *Arbeiter-Illustrierte-Zeitung.* One of his brothers, Michael,
worked for the Leitz company which manufactured the Leica camera, so that
Spender was also introduced to an improved technical means through which
documentary photography might be extended. On his return to England
Spender became an exemplar of and apologist for the new German styles of
photography. He was, in addition to working as a press photographer for the
Daily Mirror, to become a significant member of two important institutions of
the time—Mass Observation and the illustrated magazine *Picture Post.*

Founded in 1937, Mass Observation brought together poets, painters,
social scientists and documentary filmmakers who (aided by scores of

volunteers) aimed to observe and record the pattern of ordinary life in Britain. Its purpose was to bridge the gulf between ruler and ruled, to establish a new basis for social democracy based on an educated, informed and participating public. Spender became the official (and unpaid) photographer for Mass Observation, which although it wanted to record the minutiae of daily life, was unable to use many photographs in its published reports, or indeed to employ any other photographer, because of its lack of finance.

Spender worked in the manner of Erich Salomon, using a concealed camera in order to produce photographs in conditions of secrecy. His subjects, however, were not kings, politicians and leaders, but ordinary people usually photographed in public places—in streets, pubs, buses and cafes. Spender was instrumental in helping to establish this mode of documentary photography in Britain. Although captured with a hidden camera, his photographs are rarely badly composed, and it is clear that he used his interest in painting and architecture to good purpose so as not to sacrifice the formal characteristics of his photographs. Unsentimental and undramatic, they have a fine quality of suspended time in which the transposition from the mundane to the extraordinary is made through the representation itself.

When he was sacked from the *Daily Mirror* for refusing to work on an assignment which he found offensive, Spender joined *Picture Post*, the most interesting and successful of British illustrated magazines. From the late 1930s and throughout the years of war he continued to work for the magazine but abandoned photography after the war in order to devote more time to painting and textile design.

—Derrick Price

SPLÌCHAL, Jan.

Nationality: Czechoslovakian. **Born:** Sloupnice, 17 December 1929. **Education:** Studied at the School of Decorative Arts, Jablonec nad Nisou, 1945-49; Academy of Fine Arts, Prague, 1949-50. **Family:** Married Libuše Struplová in 1953 (died, 1986); children: Daniel and Věra. **Career:** Graphic artist for Polygrafia, Prague, and freelance photographer, Prague, since 1950. Associate Member, Union of Czechoslovak Artists, 1964: Member since 1977. **Address:** Ladova Street, 7, CZ-12800 Prague, 2- Nově Město, Czech Republic.

Individual Exhibitions:

1964	Club of the Arts, Cheb, Czechoslovakia
1967	Gallery Dromedaris, Enkhuizen, Netherlands
1968	Bunker Ulmenwall, Bielefeld, West Germany
	Gallery of the Castle, Duchcov, Czechoslovakia
1969	Gallery Dromedaris, Enkhuizen, Netherlands
	University of Purmerend, Netherlands
	Municipal Gallery, Wieringerwerg, Netherlands
1970	Gallery Fronta, Prague
1975	Municipal Gallery, Hodonìn, Czechoslovakia
1979	Zentrum ZIF, Bielefeld, West Germany
1980	Jaromir Funke Studio, Brno, Czechoslovakia
1983	Fotogalerie Lindemann, Stuttgart
1984	Gallery of Rumanian Creative Artists, Bucharest
	Gallery Fotochema, Prague
1986	Galerie Bünde, Dammhaus, West Germany
	Galerie Fotoforum, Frankfurt am Main
1987	Municipal Museum, Hořice, Czech Republic
1988	Czech Cultural Centre, Havana, Cuba
	Boedelschwinggemeinde, Bielefeld, Germany
1989	Goethe Institut, Cordoba, Argentina
1990	Municipal Museum, Freiburg, Germany
1991	Gallera Genesis, Prague, Czech Republic
1992	Fotogalerie Lindemanns, Stuttgart, Germany
	Gallery Genesis, Prague, Czech Republic
1993	Ravensberger Spinerei, Bielefeld, Germany
	European Parliament, Strasbourg, France
	Land Parliament, Düsseldorf, Germany

	Rathauspavillon, Brackwede, Germany
1994	Prague House of Photography, Prague, Czech Republic
	Goethe Institut, Santiago de Chile, Chile

Selected Group Exhibitions:

1958	*Creative Photography,* House of Exhibition Services, Prague
1965	*Fotosalon,* Municipal Gallery, Prague
	Czechoslovak Photography, Palac Kultury i Nauky, Warsaw
1966	*Surrealism and Photography,* Museum Folkwang, Essen
1973	*Proměna Artists Group,* Capek's Gallery, Prague
	Lyrismo di Fotografia Cecoslovacci, at *SICOF,* Milan (travelled to the Fotokabinett Jaromir Funke, Brno, Czechoslovakia, and the Städisches Museum, Freiburg, West Germany)
1977	*Contemporary Photography,* Fragner's Gallery, Prague
1979	*Tschechoslowakische Photographie 1918-1978,* Fotoforum, Kassel, West Germany
1982	*Aktualnì Fotografie,* Moravian Gallery, Brno, Czechoslavakia
1984	*Czechoslovak Creative Photography,* Gallery of Czechoslovak Writers, Prague
1990	*Tschechoslowakische Photografie der Gegenwart,* Köln; Erlangen; Metz; Freiburg; Odense; Barcelona; Luxembourg; Texas; Kansas.
1991	*Festival Photography,* Žd'ár n/s, Czech Republic

Collections:

Moravian Gallery, Brno, Czechoslovakia; Municipal Gallery, Hodonìn, Czechoslovakia; Town Hall, Bielefeld, Germany.

Publications:

By SPLÌCHAL: Books—*The Sculptor František Bìlek,* with an introduction by Marcela Mrázová, Prague 1966; *Jan Splìchal: Photographs,* with an introduction by Petr Tausk, Prague 1971; *Tau und Regen zu sein,* Evang, Berlin; *Praha našich snů,* Vyšehrad, Prague 1980; *Naúpatí hory,* Kalich 1984; *Jan Šplìchal—Photography,* Foto Mida, České Budějovice 1993. **Article**—"On Photomontage," with Karel Dvořák, in *Fotografie '73,* Prague 1973.

On SPLÌCHAL: Books—*Soucasna Ceskoslovenska Fotografie,* exhibition catalogue, by Antonìn Dufek, Brno, Czechoslovakia 1969; *Encyclopedia of Practical Photography* by Petr Tausk and others, Prague 1972; *100 Temi di Fotografia* by Petr Tausk and H. Hofstätter, Milan 1977; *Geschichte der Photographie im 20. Jahrhundert/History of Photography in the 20th Century* by Petr Tausk, Cologne 1977, London 1980; *Aktualnì Fotografie,* exhibition catalogue, by Antonìn Dufek, Brno, Czechoslovakia 1982; *Contemporary Photographers,* by Petr Tausk, Macmillan, 1982; *Photographers' Encyclopedia International 1839 to the present,* Edition Camera Obscura, 1985; *Die Drei Künstler in Prag,* by H H Hofstätter in Münster 1986; *The Evolution of Czechoslovak Photography from 1918 to the Present Day* by Petr Tausk, Prague 1986. **Articles**—"On the Photographs of Jan Splìchal" by Petr Tausk in *Fotografia* (Bratislava), no. 1, 1969; "Photomontages of Jan Splìchal" by Karel Dvořák in *Ceskoslovenska Fotografie* (Prague), no. 9, 1972; "From the Works of Art of Jan Splìchal" in *Ceskoslovenska Fotografie* (Prague), no. 10, 1976; *Fotomontáže Janna Šplíchala* by Jiří Šerých in *Ceskoslovenska Fotografie* no. 8, 1983; *Manipulierte Wirklichkeit* by Rudolf Hillebrandt in *Fotoheft,* no. 5, 1989; *Fotografie jako smysl existence* by Martin Hruška in *Česká a slovenská fotografie dnes,* Orbis 1991; *Jan Šplíchael—fotografie,* diploma work *FAMU,* Prague 1991

*

In my work I prefer the photomontage. Photomontage means for me multiplied expression of a creative character that can depict events and visions that could not be mediated by means of pure photography.

—Jan Splìchal

*   *   *

From the cycle *Landscape of My Home*, 1993. Photograph by Jan Šplíchal.

Jan Splìchal's most significant works, and those which best convey his artistic and philosophical orientation, are his photomontages. In his first attempts at this form he endeavored to connect images of various subjects, the surface structures of which differed considerably. His experiments in the laboratory enabled him to unite elements from various negatives into a new and fully autonomous image during enlarging. Although there was always obviously a certain idea at the beginning of the creative process, Splìchal did his main creative work in the darkroom, playing a game inspired by impulses from the subconscious as to choice of proper picture-elements and their placement in the montage.

After having mastered the "grammar" of the right combination of various images from a few negatives into one resulting enlargement, Splìchal was free to move away from the technical, formal side of the process and devote himself to expressing more complex ideas. A large cycle was inspired by his effort to create portraits of painters and sculptors in confrontation with their works: his goal was to show a unity of artist and art.

Splìchal lives in Prague, and the atmosphere of the city has challenged him for many years; he has searched for elements that could be the symbols of his vision of the city. Toward the end of the 1960s he found one solution in connecting images of various towers without regard to their particular loca-tion. A newer series of montages was of cathedrals. It was close to the previous cycle in its intellectual impetus: Splìchal admired both the architectonic forms and the significance of all these buildings in the shape of the present town.

His philosophic approach to the world is perhaps best conveyed in his cycle of landscapes, in which the organic and inorganic fuse with each other. Petrification projected onto a meadow reveals in a vortex a kind of hope for further development of the live. The problems of the environment, the ecology, have influenced numerous contemporary artists; Splìchal is no exception. He has not expressed his views in images of regions devastated by industry but in images that manifest his sincere trust in the creative forces of nature. In the cycle "Landscapes," he offers a kind of cautious optimism.

His continuing landscape series led in the early 1980s to the two audiovisual presentations *Creation* and *Landscapes*. The use of music to complement the projection of monochrome slides evoked strong emotional impressions of a powerful narrative character.

A topic which recurs in Splìchal's work is his favourite city, Prague. His latest series of pictures do not merely describe Prague's external face but evoke an inner nature touched by the contributions of the artists and writers who have lived there. Conceived as an homage to Franz Kafka, Splìchal's cycle of photomontages are of another Prague which might have been experienced by the great writer (who died some five years before Splìchal was born). Employing skilful photomontage techniques, Splìchal has combined images of old houses with their ancient garchways and staircases in quite different arrangements to those existing today. In some of these dreamlike images, he has even incorporated small ethereal portraits of Kafka himself.

Currently Splìchal pursues his visions of Prague, but not in any particular serial form. Most of his montages have an experimental quality—sometimes using fanlike arrangements of pictorial elements, or fragments of night-time Prague views. It seems that the great variety of montage devices that Splìchal is now exploring are steps into a new area for further cycles of serial works yet to come.

—Petr Tausk

SPURIS, Egons.

Nationality: Latvian. **Born:** Riga, 5 October 1931. **Education:** Studied radio-engineering at the Riga Polytechnical Institute, 1956-62, Dip.Eng. 1962. **Family:** Married Lia Kimene in 1953; son: Egils. **Career:** Worked as a locksmith, laboratory assistant, radio technician and engineer-designer in the VEF electro-technical factory, Riga, 1947-62; Design Leader, Rigas Radioizotopu Aparatu Buves Zinatniski Petnieciskais Institut, Riga, 1960-72; Chief Designer of Projects, 1972-76, and Chief Artist/Photographer, 1976-78, Specialais Maksli-Nieciskas Konstru Esanas un Technologisko Projektu Biro JS, Riga. Lecturer in Radio Engineering, Riga Polytechnical Institute, 1962-64. Member since 1968, Honorary Member since 1977, and Art Director since 1975, People's Photo Studio, Riga; Leader of the Ogre photoclub, 1975-1990; Member of the Latvian Designers Society from 1988. **Recipient:** Gold Medal, *Premio Michelangelo,* Petrasanta, Italy, 1970; Prix de la Ville de Monaco, 1970; Grand Prize, *Dzintarzeme* (Amber Land), Siauliai, Lithuania, 1970, Riga, 1979; Gold Medal, Norwegian Photo Federation, 1971; Gold Medal, Photographic Society of America, 1971; Charles Kingsley Memorial Award, Toronto, 1971; Medal, *12 Top Photographers,* Ghent, 1971; Artist Award (AFIAP), Fédération Internationale de l'Art Photographique, 1975; Grand Prize, *Latvia '75,* Riga, 1975, and *Latvia '77,* Riga, 1977. Honorary Artist, Art-Photo Society of Ceylon (ANPAS); Honorary Member, Natron, Maglay, Yugoslavia. **Died:** (in Riga) May 20, 1990.

Individual Exhibitions:

1973	City Museum, Tallinn, Estonia
1974	People's Photo Studio Exhibition Gallery, Riga, Latvia
	City Museum, Valmiera, Latvia
	City Museum, Cesis, Latvia
	Town Museum, Dikli, Latvia
1975	Museum of Photography, Lithuanian Society of Art Photographers, Vilnius
1976	U.S.S.R. Palace of Culture, Prague
1978	U.S.S.R. Palace of Culture, Helsinki
1979	*Gunar Binde/Egons Spuris/Peeter Tooming,* Dum Panu z Kunstatu, Brno, Czechoslovakia (travelled to the Museum of Olomouc, Czechoslovakia, 1979, and Kiek in de Kök, Tallinn, Estonia, 1980)
1981	Bremen, Germany
	Ogre, Latvia
1983	Kaunas, Lithuania
1985	Bremen, Germany
1986	Tallin, Estonia
1993	Latvian Photography Museum, Riga

Selected Group Exhibitions:

1968	*4th Exhibition of Latvian Photographers,* Kaunas, Lithuania
1969	*Vision and Expression,* International Museum of Photography, George Eastman House, Rochester, New York (toured the United States and Canada, 1969-71)
1971	*12 Top Photographers,* Ghent
1973	City Museum, Liepāja, Latvia
1989	*Photographers Dialogue,* Bielefeld, Germany
	Moscow, Russia
	Three Days of Awakening, Museum of Pharmacy, Riga
1990	*L'Année de l'Est,* Musée d'Elysée, Lausanne, Switzerland
	Galerie Van der Berlage, Amsterdam
1991	*Photographs from Latvia & Other Soviet Republics,* Santa Barbara, California
1992	*Parmijas—Contemporary Art from Riga,* City Exhibition Hall, Münster, Germany
	Baltisk Fotografi, Museum of Photographic Art, Odense, Denmark
1993	*The Memory of Images—Baltic, Photo Art Today,* Kiel & Rostock, Germany & Riga, Latvia
1994	*The Memory of Images—Baltic Photo Art Today,* Gdansk, Poland

Collections:

Museum of Photography, Siauliai, Lithuania; Bibliothèque Nationale, Paris; International Museum of Photography, George Eastman House, Rochester, New York.

Publications:

By SPURIS: Books—*The Woman I Left,* Riga 1971; *Sacred Is Your Land* (Armenian poetry), Riga 1971; *Dance around a Steam Engine,* with text by Mats Traat, Riga 1972; *Empress Ficke,* text by Ivanov, Riga 1972. **Article**—''Photography in Design'' in *Māksla* (Riga), October 1973.

On SPURIS: Books—*Vision and Expression,* edited by Nathan Lyons, New York 1969; *Pobaltska sovetska fotografie* by Vaclav Jiru, Prague 1974; *Dumont Foto 1,* edited by Hugo Schöttle, Cologne 1978; *Dumont Foto 2,* edited by Hugo Schöttle, Cologne 1980; *The History of Latvian Art Photography* by Peteris Zeile, Riga 1981; *Masters of Latvian Art Photography* by Atis Skalbergs, Riga 1981; *Latvijas Fotojaksla* by Peteris Zeile and others, Riga 1985; *Another Russia* by Daniela Mrázková and Vladimir Remes, London 1986; *Creative Photography* by Sergei Morozov, Moscow 1989; *Poetics of Photography* by V.I. Mihalkovic and V.T. Stigneev, Moscow 1989; *The World of Photography* by Varlerij Stigneev and Aleksandr Lipkov, Moscow 1989; *Three Days of Awakening* by Vilnis Auzinš, Riga 1989; *Comrades & Cameras* by Glen R Serbin and Karen Sinsheimer, Santa Barbara 1991; *Stepping Out of Line,* exhibition catalogue, by Boris Mangolds, 1992; *Pārmijas,* exhibition catalogue, Münster 1992; *The Memory of Images* by Barbara Straka, Helena Demakova and Knut Nievers, Kiel 1993. **Articles**—''Concerning the Photos of Egons Spuris'' by J. Janackova in *Revue Fotografie* (Prague), November 1970; ''Searching for an Individual Means of Expression'' by Mihail Leontjev in *Sovetskoye Foto* (Moscow), February 1974; ''Searching for the Essence of Creativity'' by S. Daugovish in *Māksla* (Riga), October 1974; ''Erst Kommt Mir die Idee'' in *Sputnik* (Moscow), May 1976; ''A Poet of Versatile Form'' by Daniela Mrázková in *Revue Fotografie* (Prague), May 1978; ''Searcher after the Simplest Truth'' by P.K. Jaskari in *Kamera Lehti* (Helsinki), June 1978; ''The Tracks of Time'' by Vjaceslav Jegorov in *Sovetskoye Foto* (Moscow), April 1979; ''Egon Spuris 5/10/1931-20/05/1990'' by Uldis Briedis and Andrejs Grants in *Literatūra un Māksla,* Riga, May 1990; ''To Determine Oneself in the World'' by Vilhelms Mihailovskis in *Māksla,* Riga 1990; ''Egon Spuris's Confession of Love'' by Vilnis Auzinš in *Literatūra un Māksla,* 18/06/1993; ''Photographs of Proletarian Districts in Riga'' by Vilnis Auzinš in *Diena* 5/06/1993; ''Proletarian Districts in Photography'' by E. Valtere in *Latvijas Jaunatne,* Riga 8/06/1993.

*

I am interested in photography only as an art. Though I pay attention to technical means and devices, they serve *only* to enrich my photographic vocabulary. To my mind, the task and duty of an artist is not to multiply already extant beauty (nice landscapes, outstanding people, celebrities, beautiful girls, interesting events, etc.). I gain satisfaction by creating an effective picture, creating values from a material which plays a tiny role in our lives, and which has no (apparent) value of its own.

I try to avoid the so-called literary movement in my work—i.e., the outer and visual dynamism. Usually there is no action in my photographs. Compositions are mainly stable, even static. I try to see and reflect the character (not characteristic) of things or environment, the fascinating mood, inner dynamism or stillness.

I have been much engaged in photomontage (especially in 1969-71). I have acquired different special techniques in colour photography, too, and this knowledge serves me in my professional work. Since 1976, I have stopped using these particular technical means when creating works for myself or for exhibitions, as their use seems an easy way to success. That is why I create my works only in black and white, and though the technique is rather simple (I use masking, bleaching, etc., to get the necessary intensity and correspondence of tones), it often takes me several days to create a copy of my work (a good print).

Overcoming these difficulties is not an aim in itself; it is the test of my abilities—who am I?

—Egons Spuris

*   *   *

Egons Spuris started photographing as an amateur, and even today his attitude is basically that of an amateur. To Spuris, photography has never been his means of earning a living but just a hobby, a fulfillment of a life's ambition, a love to which he completely devoted himself. It seems almost as if he were deliberately cultivating such an attitude, for it allows him to photograph only when he wishes to: he does not have to accept commissions, and he does not have to give way to the views of others.

Spuris' work is essentially modern, for with precise urgency it expresses the way of life of contemporary man. It does not reproduce reality as such; it does not aim at conveying illusions but at communicating sentiments about reality. Moreover, the work is based on Latvian national feelings. The span of themes and expressions in his work ranges from an inner experience of the landscape to the intimate style of portraits to still-lifes of urban nooks. The most striking feature of his style is the sharp contrast between black and white and the very high standard in presenting shape. He fondles, kneads and models the shapes of things and phenomena by the angle of the shot, with the help of views from below or above, and he communicates their internal sense mainly with the help of light. This method gives rise to expressive dramatic pictures in which the main motif emerges like a sudden spectre against the dark background, and also to an impressive optical magic that conveys the world of dreams, myths and fairytales. A strong sensibility, a perfect comprehension of the rhythmic arrangement of space, a deep admiration for ordinary things, a creative knowledge and an intellectual background—all these things have contributed towards making Egons Spuris one of the most striking personalities not only of Latvian but also of "Soviet Baltic photography"—the term now applied to the work of Latvian, Lithuanian and Estonian photographers.

The roots of Spuris' work are closely linked with the rugged, melancholy seaside of the Baltic. This accounts also for the gentle nostalgia of his landscapes, in which the vast, almost deserted, stretches of the seacoast are usually photographed with a wide-angle lens. The rough structure of the windswept sand, rocks, coarse tufts of grass, and the dark surface of the sea, with the silhouette of a boat, a boulder or a fish on the foreground: these are Spuris' symbols of the land in which he lives. From this impetus, too, springs his meditative portraits in which the knowledgeable eyes of contemporary man usually gaze straight into the lens.

From about the mid-1970s the poetical quality of Spuris' prints, closely linked with domestic cultural traditions, suddenly became more sober, civil and matter-of-fact. Spuris withdrew from the natural themes of seaside landscapes and portraits to concentrate on problems of urban civilization. He became interested in architectural structures, both modern and historical, and in the urban environment—the geometry of roofs, paved streets, the surfaces of walls. He traces the sharply contrasting relationship between the products of technical progress and traditional life: the modern car or prefabricated house are alien in the environment of the streets and yards of ancient Riga and yet symbolize change in ways of living. Spuris, given his intellectual concerns, is still not merely interested in the bare system of form and structural agglomeration of urban shapes; rather, his interest is in an objective testimony of the

process of civilization. Spuris' vision has suddenly become more cosmopolitan. His photographs are now psychological pictures of the world of modern man.

—Daniela Mrázková

STECHA, Pavel.

Nationality: Czechoslovakian. **Born:** Prague, 20 December 1944. **Education:** Attended secondary school in Prague, 1959-63; studied photography at FAMU (Arts Academy), under Anna Fárová and Ján Smok, Prague, 1967-71. **Military Service:** Served in the Czech Army, 1963-65. **Family:** Married Alice Bubníková in 1969; daughter: Martina; grandaughter: Johana. **Career:** Photographer, Prague, since 1971. Assistant Lecturer, 1975-78, and since 1978 Senior Lecturer FAMU, Prague; Associated Dean since 1990. Left FAMU, 1990, to found Department of Photography at Prague University of Arts, Design and Architecture, 1994. **Recipient:** Youth Photography International Prize, *Photokina*, Cologne, 1968; World Press Photo, Amsterdam, 1992. **Address:** V Horce 189, Cz-25228 Černošice, Czech Republic.

Individual Exhibitions:

1978	*Weekend Houses,* Cinohernì Klub Theatre, Prague
1980	*Traffic,* Cinohernì Klub Theatre, Prague
1982	Hippolyte Gallery, Helsinki
1989	Istanbul, Turkey
1990	Jerusalem Theatre, Israel
1992	Fronta, Prague
1993	Dortmund, Germany
	Berlin, Germany

Selected Group Exhibitions:

1968	*Youth Photography Exhibition,* at *Photokina,* Cologne
1971	*The Rest Home at St. Thomas,* Roudnice Art Gallery, Czechoslovakia (travelled to the Fotokabinett Jaromir Funke, Brno, Czechoslovakia, 1972)
1973	*Fotoforum 73,* Ruzomberok, Czechoslovakia
1979	*Tschechoslowakische Fotografie 1918-78,* Fotoforum der Gesamthochschule, Kassel, West Germany
1981	*9 + 9,* Plasy, Czechoslovakia
1982	*Topical Photography,* Moravian Gallery, Brno, Czechoslovakia
1984	*Czechoslovakian Photography,* San Francisco Museum of Modern Art
1985	*27 Contemporary Czechoslovakian Photographers,* The Photographers' Gallery, London
1989	*37 Photographers*
1990	*Choice,* Houston Fotofest

Collections:

Museum of Decorative Arts, Prague; Moravian Gallery, Brno, Czechoslovakia; San Francisco Museum of Modern Art; ICP New York; National Gallery, Prague.

Publications:

By STECHA: Books—*Prague Housing Signs,* Panorama, Prague; *Heart of Europe,* Artia; *Listopad '89,* Odeon; *Prague Passages and Galleries,* Norma, France; *Prague—Hidden Splendours,* Flammarion, France. **Articles**—"Documentary Photography at FAMU" in *Revue Fotografie* (Prague), January 1978; "Timo Kalaranta and the Finnish Photographic School" in *Fotografie* (Prague), no. 1, 1983; "Photography and Rock" in *Fotografie* (Prague), no. 3, 1983; "Christer Stromholm, Swedish Photographer" in *Fotografie* (Prague), no. 2, 1984; "The Group Antrazit" in *Fotografie* (Prague), no. 4, 1984.

On STECHA: Books—*Aktualnì Fotografie,* exhibition catalogue, by Antonìn Dufek, Brno, Czechoslovakia 1982; *Through Ten Lenses* by Kristian Suda and Rudolf Křeśťan, Prague 1983; *Prague House Signs* by L. Petránová, Prague 1986; *Prague Ghetto* by M. Vilìmková, Prague 1986; *The Evolution of Czechoslovak Photography from 1918 to the Present Day* by Petr Tausk, Prague 1986. Articles—"Photography and Sociology" by J. Andel in *Ceskoslovenska Fotografie* (Prague), July 1974; "Stecha's Tábor" by A. Dufek in *Ceskoslovenska Fotografie* (Prague), June 1975; "Prague: At the Heart of Europe" by Daniela Mrázková in *Ovo Magazine* (Montreal), no. 30/31, 1979; "At the Foyer Theatre Cinohernì Klub" by Anna Fárová in *Camera* (Lucerne), July 1980.

*

I suppose that the most important thing about photography is the possibility of stopping time—Cartier-Bresson's "decisive moment."

I believe in the power and narrative potential of thematic photography, as opposed to the single, all-encompassing picture.

—Pavel Stecha

*   *   *

Among the middle generation of photographers in Czechoslovakia, Pavel Stecha is known for his attempts to solve, or at least creatively explore, complex sociological questions by means of images.

Stecha's main interest has been man living in the town. In collaboration with social scientists, he examined the environment close to old houses destined for demolition in the near future. In an attempt at a complete characterization, his images involve both typical exteriors and views into average flats. As well, he created a gallery of portraits of the inhabitants—useful documentation of the kinds of people living in such an environment. But this is not to suggest that his work is either indiscriminate or inartistic. With great care and comprehension Stecha has applied the principle of *pars pro toto:* he has chosen the precisely right details to depict the whole, and his photos are fresh reminders of the most important conclusions reached in the study. Quite often, too, he has been very skilful in choosing the typical situation, the characteristic event that reveals the style of living within the environment.

At the other extreme, but with the same intention, and with equal success, Stecha has also photographed the environments of new dwellings and their inhabitants. The mere comparison of the two series is illuminating, and new facts emerge from each viewing of these complex cycles.

Because of the greater distance of modern districts from the center of the city, Stecha has also been interested in all kinds of municipal transportation. This interest has provided the occasion for more dynamic images. Again, his interest is sociological, and his touch exact: he carefully selects the key situation, that which informs, say, not only about the density of traffic but also about the groups of people using cars, buses and the subway.

In another series, Stecha follows the urban dweller to his weekend cottage in the country. He confronts town-man in his log cabin. These photos have both documentary strength and creative charm: the approach might be described as a modern variation on the heritage of August Sander.

Stecha well understands the effects of juxtaposed single images within the logic of an enclosed cycle. In his series on owners of weekend cottages, he took pictures of the same people standing in front of their log cabins as he had photographed some ten or fifteen years previously. It was thus possible to document the changes in facial and bodily features was well as in the houses so keenly improved and refurbished by their owners. In a number of cases, Stecha asked the subjects to hold in their hands enlargements of those earlier photographs to accentuate both the pictorial and narrative aspects of the work.

Stecha's studies of life-styles have not just been limited to Prague and its vicinity. Taking his experience in sociological communication to the big industrial centre of Ostrava enabled him to discover the particular ambience of the newly emergent suburbs and modern housing developments, a chapter that serves to reinforce his work in the old districts of the capital city.

—Petr Tausk

STEELE-PERKINS, Chris(topher Horace).

Nationality: British. **Born:** Rangoon, Burma, 28 July 1947. **Education:** Christ's Hospital School, Sussex, 1959-65; studied psychology at the University of Newcastle upon Tyne, 1967-70, B.Sc. 1970. **Career:** Freelance photographer, working for *Fortune, Geo, Newsweek, Observer Magazine, Paris-Match, Stern, Time, Sunday Times,* etc., London, since 1970. Member, Exit group of photographers, London, since 1975; Associate, Viva photo agency, Paris, 1976-78; Nominee 1979-83, and Member since 1983, Magnum photo agency, London, Paris and New York. Lecturer in Photography, Polytechnic of Central London, 1976-77. Member, Photography Committee, Arts Council of Great Britain, 1976-79. **Recipient:** Gulbenkian Foundation Grant, 1975; Oskar Barnak Award—World Press, 1988; Tom Hopkinson Award, Photographers Gallery, London 1988; Robert Capa Gold Medal, ICP New York 1989; Cooperative Award for film "Dying for Publicity," 1994. **Agent:** Magnum Photos, 5 Old Street, London, EC1V 9HL **Address:** 5 St. John's Buildings, Canterbury Crescent, London SW9 7QB, England.

Individual Exhibitions:

1974 *The Face of Bengal,* Camerawork Gallery, London (with Mark Edwards; toured Britain)

1977 *Film Ends,* Photographers Gallery, Southampton, Hampshire (with Mark Edwards; travelled to Spectro Workshop, Newcastle upon Tyne; Photographers' Gallery, London; Centre Culturel du Marais, Paris; International Center of Photography, New York)

   Mixed Photos, Prakapas Gallery, New York

1979 *The Teds,* Camerawork Gallery, London (travelled to Side Gallery, Newcastle upon Tyne; National Theatre, London)

1982 *Survival Programmes,* Side Gallery, Newcastle upon Tyne (with Paul Trevor and Nicholas Battye)

1983 *Beirut,* Camerawork Gallery, London

1985 *Lebanon,* Magnum Gallery, Paris

   Famine in Africa, Barbican Art Gallery, London

1990 *The Pleasure Principle,* Toured U.K. and France

Selected Group Exhibitions:

1974 *The Inquisitive Eye,* Institute of Contemporary Arts, London

1975 *Young British Photographers,* The Photographers' Gallery, London (toured Europe, the United States, and Canada)

1982 *Maritime England,* The Photographers' Gallery, London

   Terre de Guerre, Victoria and Albert Museum, London

1985 *Contemporary British Photography,* Centre National de la Photographie, Paris

   The Indelible Image, Corcoran Gallery, Washington, D.C. (toured the United States)

1986 *South Africa,* FNAC-Montparnasse, Paris

1990 *In Our Time,* Magnum Photos World Tour

1994 *A Terrible Beauty,* Artists Space, New York

Collections:

Victoria and Albert Museum, London; Bibliothèque Nationale, Paris; Arts Council of Great Britain, London; Side Gallery, Newcastle upon Tyne; Photographers' Gallery, London; National Gallery of Victoria, Melbourne; FNAC, Paris.

Publications:

By STEELE-PERKINS: Books—*The Teds,* London 1979; *About 70 Photographs,* editor, London 1981; *Survival Programmes,* with Paul Trevor and Nicholas Battye, Milton Keynes, Buckinghamshire 1982; *Beirut Frontline Story,* with texts by Selim Nasib and Caroline Tisdall, London 1982; *The Pleasure Principle,* London 1989; *St Thomas's Hospital,* London 1992.

Ghana—Bread Distribution. Photograph by Chris Steele-Perkins.

On STEELE-PERKINS: Books—*Young British Photographers,* exhibition catalogue, London 1975; *Die Geschichte der Photographie im 20. Jahrhundert/Photography in the 20th Century* by Petr Tausk, Cologne 1977, London 1980; *The Indelible Image* by Jane Livingston and Frances Fralin, New York 1985; *Creative Camera,* 1987.

*　　*　　*

Chris Steele-Perkins obviously esteems photography for its ability to communicate in easily understood images and, simultaneously, for its ability to provoke emotional responses.

He strives for the expressive image, and his chief interest is what could be called the "live" photograph. He has based a large part of his work on the right evaluation of situations discovered by him in daily life, photos that suggest a non-intervention from the photographer. This kind of approach is apparent not only in his reportage but also in his portraits within environments typical of his subject.

He has a profound knowledge of the narrative qualities of the image, so much so that he has been able to use photography as a means of providing sociological information—for instance, his large cycle *The Teds.* In this series he works in the genre of the journalistic portrait: many of the photos are of Teds' faces. Other photos in the series are "live," depicting typical situations from their lives, their amusements. The series as a whole, which has been published, is modern reportage at its best.

His comprehension of the significance of the eloquent situation might be called the driving force for a great part of his work. Simultaneously, Steele-Perkins seems to be aware that the capturing of important "events" can also

be the result of luck and chance. Probably these points-of-view are what have led him to an interest in what might be called *object trouvé* appropriately modified by the demands of reportage.

A special and very unusual kind of demonstration of the eloquent event discovered by chance is his work in the exhibition *Film Ends.* The ends of film are often automatically exposed by the photographer, and within these chance shots there might be, now and then, some interesting images. Having made this discovery with Mark Edwards, the two of them searched through about 5,000 "film ends" and chose 40 of the best for the exhibition. The creative act, obviously, was not in the careless exposing of film ends, but in discovering what a treasure of chance events of significance might be hidden in such photos. In its own way the cycle was very near in spirit to Conceptual Art.

Although he has shown some regard for the diffusion of ideas from avant-garde art into photography, Steele-Perkins' main interest has always been in reportage and his particular brand of human interest imagery. New contacts at Magnum (as a nominee in 1979, an associate in 1981 and a full member from 1983) enabled him to work in Africa, the Middle East and Central America. His earlier experience as a teacher at the Faculty of Communication of the London Polytechnic helped him translate his ideas on human suffering into readily understandable photographs. This honest approach to a difficult subject saved his work from the sensation-seeking effect so commonplace in current journalism, since his aim was not to excite the imagination but to persuade the viewer that the necessary reaction should be more than mere sympathy. In his images of Beirut and South Africa, Steele-Perkins not only enlarges his considerable repertoire but fulfils a human duty.

—Petr Tausk

STERENBERG, Abram.

Nationality: Russian. **Born:** Zhitomir, Russia, in 1894. **Education:** Attended the Jewish School, Zhitomir 1901-09. **Military Service:** Served in Tsarist Army, 1915-17, in photographic department, Red Army, 1919-22, and as a war photographer, Red Army, 1941-45. **Family:** Married; had no children. **Career:** Apprentice in photo-order studio, Zhitomir, 1911-15; Photographer, studio of Boris Kapustianski, Taschkent, 1917-19, Sojuzfoto picture agency, Moscow, 1926-41, and Novosti Press Agency, Moscow, 1945-78. **Died:** (in Moscow) 6 December 1978.

Selected Group Exhibitions:

1924	*Annual Exhibition,* Russian Photographic Society, Moscow
1928	*Soviet Photography After 10 Years,* Moscow
1933	*Social Photography,* Metro, Prague
1935	*Works by Moscow Photo Masters,* Moscow
1936	*International Exhibition of Photography,* Mánes Gallery, Prague
1938	*International Photo Exhibition,* Royal Photographic Society, London
1958	*Soviet Photography After 40 Years,* Manezhnaya Gallery, Moscow
1980	*Soviet Photography Between The World Wars 1917-1941,* Dumumenì House of Art, Brno, Czechoslovakia
1982	*Early Soviet Photographers,* Museum of Modern Art, Oxford, England (and world tour)
1989	*150 Years of Photography,* Central Exhibition Hall, Moscow
1992	*The Utopian Dream: Photography in Soviet Russia, 1918-1932,* Lawrence Miller Gallery, New York
1992-93	*The Great Utopia, The Russian and Soviet Avante Garde, 1915-1937,* Frankfurt, Amsterdam, New York, Moscow, St. Petersburg

Collections:

Novosti Press Agency, Moscow; Lubomìr Linhart, Prague; Daniela Mrázková/Vladimìr Remeš Collection, Prague; Shickler/Lafaille Collection, Los Angeles; Museum of Photography, (The Russian Union of Art Photographers) Moscow.

Publications:

By STERENBERG: Book—*Goskinoizdat,* Moscow 1939. **Article**—"Terrible Assignment" in *Sovetskoye Foto* (Moscow), January 1934.

On STERENBERG: Books—Soviet Art Photography by Sergej Morozov, Moscow 1958; *Die Sowjetunion zwischen den Kriegen 1917-1941* by Daniela Mrázková and Vladimìr Remeš, Oldenburg 1981; *Pioneers of Soviet Photography* by Grigory Shudakov, Olga Suslova and Lilya Ukhtomskaya, London and Paris 1983; *The Story of Photography* by Daniela Mrázková, Prague 1985, London 1986; *Sowjetische Photographie 1919-1939,* Zurich 1986; *Anthology of Soviet Photography, Vol I,* Moscow 1986. **Article**—"Portraits by Abram Sterenberg" by Lubomŕ Linhart in *Revue Fotografie* (Prague), March 1977.

*   *   *

In contrast to the majority of outstanding figures of Soviet photography engaged in documentary, reportage or artistic experiments in the period between the two world wars, Abram Sterenberg focused throughout his life on three genres: portrait, still life and landscape. It was especially portraiture that made him famous. He devoted himself to it from the beginning—while working on photoagency assignments and during his work in the photo department of the Red Army, which he joined after the Revolution—until his death in the 1970s. The only time when he did not engage in portraiture was during the second half of the 1930s, a time when the portrait as well as still life and landscape photography were declared "useless rubbish." For a time, like his friends of the progressive Oktyabr group—Alexander Rodchenko, Eleazar

Langman, Boris Ignatovich and others—he engaged in reportage photography, believing that it alone could express the greatness of the time. He tried to depict the social, political and economic changes taking place in the country.

Sterenberg produced a number of outstanding portraits of both well-known and unknown personalities. Characteristic of these portraits is the heightened detail of the head or face. He made artistic use of light (usually side-lighting, but sometimes front lighting) and emphasized the structure and texture of the surface, thereby highlighting the character and expressing the individual qualities of the subject; he would emphasize essential factors and eliminate all that was unnecessary or distracted from his subject. He deliberately eliminated light from the background causing the face to stand out dramatically against a black background. While, for example, the photograph of the poet Vladimir Mayakovski (1919) still has a ring of light around the face and the photo of the violinist (1925) makes use of lighting effects which bring out not only the line but the surface of the hand and the instrument, the portrait of the photographer and painter Yuri Yeremin (1935) focuses solely on the demonically lit face of the artist, and the portrait "Mother" (1926) focuses on the shape and expression of the wrinkled face which stands out plastically against the dark background. We find a similar effect in the portraits of Henri Barbusse (1934) and Rabindranáth Thákur (1929) in which only the illuminated faces fill the entire area of the picture.

Sterenberg, however, also makes use of other elements to bring out the characteristic features: the movement of the head in the photograph of the Georgian ballet dancer Maka Macharadze (1969), the traditional collar used with fine irony in the portrait of the British actor, producer and theatre theoretician Edward Gordon Craig (end of the 1930s) and the delicate conventionality of the direct look at the face of the film genius Sergej Eisenstein (1940).

Sterenberg's portraits are as much studies of the mind as of the physiognomy of the subject. Each photograph by the artist was created as a unique work, an original worked out in detail and destined for exhibition rather than reproduction. He therefore recognized only those copies made by the artist himself, where an important role is played by the selection of the paper and chemicals or by cropping. Sterenberg was therefore unique in Soviet photography between the two world wars as well as in the postwar period, when stress was laid on multiplication and on the massive propaganda effect of photography.

—Daniela Mrázková

STERN, Bert.

Nationality: American. **Born:** Brooklyn, New York, 3 October 1929. **Education:** Brooklyn High School, 1942-46; self-taught in photography from 1948. **Military Service:** Served as a movie cameraman/photographer in the United States Army, in Japan, 1951-53. **Family:** Married the dancer Allegra Kent in 1959 (divorced, 1975); children: Trista, Susannah and Bret. **Career:** Worked as a clerk, Wall Street Bank, New York, 1946-47; mailroom clerk, etc., *Look* magazine, New York, 1947-48; assistant to art director Herschel Bramson, *Look* magazine, New York, 1948-51; art director, *Mayfair* magazine, New York, 1951; freelance photographer, initially with Herschel Bramson at L.C. Gumbiner Agency, working for Smirnoff, DuPont, Arpege, IBM, Pepsi-Cola, U.S. Steel, American Cyanamid, Volkswagen, etc., New York, 1953-71, 1973; also magazine photographer, for *Vogue, Esquire, Look, Life, Glamour, Holiday,* etc., New York, 1959-71; Founder-President, Libra Productions television commercial company, New York, 1961-71 (established studios at 80 West 40th Street, 1954-59, East 39th Street, 1959-64, 63rd Street and First Avenue, 1964-71, and 54th Street, 1974). Closed studio, and lived in Mijas, Spain, 1974-75. Since 1976, resumed commercial and magazine photography in New York, working for Polaroid, Pirelli, *Vogue* and *New York* magazines, etc. Faculty Member, Famous Photographers' School, Westport, Connecticut, 1964-71. **Recipient:** Documentary Film Award, Venice Film Festival, 1960; Art Directors Club Awards, New York, 1964-71. **Agent:** Staley Wise Gallery, 560 Broadway, New York, New York 10012, U.S.A.

Individual Exhibitions:

1958	Limelight Gallery, New York
1982	*The Last Sitting,* Xenon Gallery, New York
	Monique Knowlton Gallery, New York
1992	Rudolf Mangisch Gallery, Zurich, Switzerland
1993	*Marilyn,* Staley Wise Gallery, New York

Selected Group Exhibitions:

1971	*Photo-Graphics,* International Museum of Photography, George Eastman House, Rochester, New York
1977	*The History of Fashion Photography,* International Museum of Photography, George Eastman House, Rochester, New York (travelled to the Brooklyn Museum, New York; San Francisco Museum of Modern Art; Cincinnati Art Institute, Ohio; and Museum of Fine Arts, St. Petersburg, Florida)
1984	*Sammlung Gruber,* Museum Ludwig, Cologne
1992	*Mois de la Photographie,* Paris

Collections:

Museum of Modern Art, New York; Fashion Institute of Technology, New York; International Museum of Photography, George Eastman House, Rochester, New York; Museum Ludwig, Cologne.

Publications:

By STERN: Books—*Marilyn Monroe,* portfolio of silkscreen prints, New York 1967; *Marcel Duchamp: Electronic Prints,* portfolio, New York 1968; *The Pill Book,* New York 1979; *The Last Sitting,* with text by Annie Gottlieb, New York and London 1982. **Film**—*Jazz on a Summer's Day,* 1968.

On STERN: Books—Polaroid Portfolio No. 1, edited by John Walbarst, New York 1959; *Fame: Famous Portraits of Famous People by Famous Photographers,* edited by L. Fritz Gruber, London and New York 1960; *Beauty: Variations on the Theme Woman by Masters of the Camera—Past and Present,* edited by L. Fritz Gruber, London and New York 1965; *The Documentary Tradition: From Nanook to Woodstock* by Lewis Jacobs, New York 1971; *Photo/Graphics,* exhibition catalogue, with text by Van Deren Coke, Rochester, New York 1971; *The Vogue Book of Fashion Photography* by Polly Devlin, with an introduction by Alexander Liberman, London 1979; *The History of Fashion Photography* by Nancy Hall-Duncan, New York 1979; *Sammlung Gruber: Photographie des 20. Jahrhunderts,* exhibition catalogue, with foreword by Siegfried Gohr, Cologne 1984. **Articles**—"The Return of Stern" by Laurence Shames in *American Photographer* (New York), August 1981; "Photography: Bert Stern," interview, in *Manhattan* (New York), no. 10, 1985.

*

Advertising was the way I became a professional photographer, but I was taking photographs on my own for five years before. Photography is the closest thing to seeing for me. Even before I got interested in photography I was always moving around and reframing things in front of me. Sometimes things wouldn't look right, so I changed my position or angle to please myself. I'm always changing seats in a restaurant, and I used to change rooms in hotels a lot. I have calmed down a bit, but I find my mood is affected by the environment around me.

My feelings are now tempered by experience. Some things you can only feel once—like falling in love the first time. You may fall in love more than once, but that first time is more profound because it is new. Some photographs can be taken only once.

Now we are living and working in a more hightech world. We don't just take pictures—we make pictures. So the question should be: "What kind of photos do I want to make?" I like to make pictures that *I* like. If a photograph pleases me, it usually pleases others. A good photo should be well-executed graphically, and have an emotional element.

—Bert Stern

*   *   *

It is hardly possible to confine Bert Stern to a specific section of photography. Basically a commercial photographer, Stern belongs to that elite class of photographers for whom the expression of beauty pervades everything they choose to touch. Essentially a dreamer, Stern has that rare gift of making his dreams come true in his photographs and, at the same time, of being a huge commercial success. In achieving this he has been helped by an unusual sense of understanding of both his subject and the purpose of the picture as well as by an unusual ability to translate ideas into images. He has also been helped by a relentless urge to achieve perfection, irrespective of the time factor or possible inconveniences involved.

In 1955 he went to Egypt to photograph a glass of martini in front of the pyramid of Gizeh. It was for one of his numerous Smirnoff ads. The picture became legend, his own legend.

During the twenty-odd years of Stern's fame, from approximately the mid-1950s to the mid-1970s, he was a pioneer in his field. He liberated commercial photography from unwanted clutter and lifelessness. He religiously followed the famous motto: less is more. With tremendous insight, patience and respect for a model's needs, he obtained the desired results, the visions he wanted to convey. He worked with Dian Parkinson for nearly two years before obtaining the symbolic expressions he knew he could extrapolate from her: the image he carried with himself of the American Dream Girl.

Lighting was Stern's main tool. Combined with his own spontaneous reactions, his ingenuity, the choice of camera and film, there was nothing which did not become unforgettable: the photographs of Audrey Hepburn, of Marilyn Monroe, the wonderful series of "Romantic Little Girls," the picture of "What to give to a woman who has everything," the symbolic image of "Lolita" wearing heart-shaped sunglasses. His constant urge to create led to experiments with printing processes, silk-screening, video-taping and photo-collage.

Bert Stern has been true to his beliefs and to his dreams. He has been an innovator and a leader.

—Ruth Spencer

STERNFELD, Joel (Peter).

Nationality: American. **Born:** New York City, 30 June 1944. **Education:** Studied at Dartmouth College, Hanover, New Hampshire, 1961-65, B.A. 1965; self-taught in photography, from 1965. **Career:** Independent landscape, industrial, architectural and portrait photographer, New York, since 1966. Associate Professor of Photography, Stockton State College, Pomona, New Jersey, 1971-84; Instructor in photography, Yale University, New Haven, Connecticut, 1984-85, and Sarah Lawrence College, Bronxville, New York, since 1985. Artist-in-Residence, Dartmouth College, Hanover, New Hampshire, 1985. **Recipient:** Guggenheim Fellowship, New York, 1978, 1982; Photographer's Fellowship, National Endowment for the Arts, Washington, D.C., 1980; Fellowship, New York State Council for the Arts, 1980; Emerging Artist Award, American Council for the Arts, 1983; Grand Prize, Higashiwa Festival of Photography, Japan, 1985; Grand Prix de Rome, Rome. **Address:** c/o Pace/MacGill, 32 East 57th Street, New York, New York 10022, U.S.A.

Individual Exhibitions:

1976	Pennsylvania Academy of Fine Arts, Philadelphia
1981	Daniel Wolf Inc., New York
	The Photography Gallery, La Jolla, California
	San Francisco Museum of Modern Art (with Larry Fink)
1982	Brent Sikkema Gallery, Boston, Massachusetts

Grapestake Gallery, San Francisco
Looking Glass Gallery, Royal Oak, Michigan
California Museum of Photography, University of California at
    Riverside
Blue Sky Gallery, Portland, Oregon
1983   G. Ray Hawkins Gallery, Los Angeles (with Joel Meyerowitz)
1984   Visual Studies Workshop, Rochester, New York
Daniel Wolf Inc., New York
Friends of Photography, Carmel, California
Museum of Modern Art, New York (with Robert Adams and
    Jim Goldberg)
1985   Museum of Contemporary Photography, Columbia College,
    Chicago
Afterimage Gallery, Dallas, Texas
Michael Carey Gallery, Austin, Texas
Halsted Gallery, Birmingham, Michigan
Fotografien 1978-84, CCD-Galerie, Dusseldorf
Dartmouth College, Hanover, New Hampshire
Joel Sternfeld, at the Higashikawa International Festival, Japan
1986   Chrysler Museum, Norfolk, Virginia (with David Allison)
1987   *American Prospects, The Photography of Joel Sternfeld,*
    Museum of Fine Arts, Houston, Texas (travelled in U.S.A.
    and to The National Gallery of Canada, Ottawa, Canada)
1989   *Contemporary Photographs,* Pace/MacGill Gallery, New York
1991   *Campagna Romana: The Roman Countryside,* Pace/MacGill
    Gallery, New York (travelled to Museum of Fine Arts,
    Boston and Art Institute of Chicago, Chicago)
1994   *On This Site,* Pace/MacGill Gallery, New York

Selected Group Exhibitions:

1976   *Photographs of the American Landscape,* Print Club,
    Philadelphia
1977   *The Second Generation of Colour Photographers,* Festival
    d'Arles, France
1978   *Fotografie im alltage Amerikas,* Kunstgewerbemuseum, Zurich
1979   *One of a Kind,* Houston Museum of Fine Arts, Texas (travelled
    to the De Cordova Museum, Lincoln, Massachusetts;
    Minneapolis Institute of Arts, Minnesota; University of
    Arizona, Tucson; Los Angeles Institute of Contemporary
    Art; Corcoran Gallery, Washington, D.C.; Denver Art
    Museum, Colorado; Art Institute of Chicago)
1981   *The New Color,* Everson Museum of Art, Syracuse, New York
1982   *Color as Form,* International Museum of Photography at
    George Eastman House, Rochester, New York
1983   *Subjective Vision,* High Museum of Art, Atlanta, Georgia
    Photography and the Industrial Image, New York University
1984   *Political Photographs,* Museum of Modern Art, New York
1985   *American Images,* Barbican Art Gallery, London (toured
    Britain)
1987   *Photography and Art 1946-86,* Los Angeles County
    Museum of Art
1989   *On the Art of Fixing a Shadow, 150 Years of Photography,*
    The National Gallery of Art, Washington D.C. (travelled to
    The Art Institute of Chicago, Chicago, The Los Angeles
    County Art Museum)
    The Art of Photography, 1839-1989, The Museum of Fine
    Arts, Houston, Texas (travelled to The Royal Academy of
    Art, London and the Australian National Gallery of Art,
    Canberra)
1991   *Pleasures and Terrors,* Museum of Modern Art, New
    York City
1992   *More Than One Photography,* Museum of Modern Art, New
    York City
1993   *About Big Cities,* New Society for Fine Art, Berlin

Collections:

Museum of Modern Art, New York; San Francisco Museum of Modern Art;
Houston Museum of Fine Arts, Texas; Dallas Art Museum, Texas; Akron Art

Institute, Ohio; Seattle Art Museum, Washington; High Museum of Art,
Atlanta, Georgia; Worcester Museum of Art, Massachusetts; Massachusetts
Institute of Technology, Cambridge; California Museum of Photography,
University of California at Riverside; Art Institute of Chicago, Chicago;
Fotomuseum Winterthur, Winterthur, Switzerland.

Publications:

On STERNFELD: Books—*One of a Kind: Recent Polaroid Color Photography,* exhibition catalogue, by Belinda Rathbone and Eugenia Parry Janis,
Boston 1979; *The New Color* by Sally Eauclaire, New York 1981; *Color as
Form: A History of Color Photography,* exhibition catalogue, with introduction by Robert A. Sobieszek, Rochester, New York 1982; *Subjective Vision,*
exhibition catalogue, with text by A.D. Coleman, Atlanta, Georgia 1983; *New
Color/New York* by Sally Eauclaire, New York 1984; *Photography and Art
1946-1986,* exhibition catalogue, by Andy Grundberg and Kathleen Gauss,
Los Angeles 1987. **Articles**—"Joel Sternfeld" in *Camera* (Lucerne), July
1977; "Photographis Interruptus: Mark Cohen, Joel Sternfeld, Larry Fink" by
Allan Porter in *Camera* (Lucerne), November 1977; "Inhabited Terrain:
Photographs by Joel Sternfeld" by Andy Grundbert in *Modern Photography*
(New York), March 1980; "Recent Landscapes by Joel Sternfeld" in *Camera
Arts* (New York), November 1980; "The Incredible Commonplace" by Andy
Grundberg in the *New York Times,* 25 October 1981; "A Call to the Colors"
by Douglas Davis in *Newsweek* (New York), November 1981; "Joel Sternfeld
at Daniel Wolf" by Pepe Karmel in *Art in America* (New York), February
1982; "A Respect for Tradition" by Andy Grundberg in the *New York Times,*
8 February 1983; "Fall Preview" in *New York Magazine,* September 1984.

*   *   *

Joel Sternfeld began to photograph shortly after he graduated from
Dartmouth College in 1965. Self-taught, he began to work solely with color
photographs in 1968, receiving his first one-man exhibition at the Pennsylvania Academy of Fine Arts in Philadelphia in 1976. The exhibition included
photographs from a trip across the Gulf coast states to New Orleans (1974),
from a summer in Nags Head, North Carolina (1975), and of New York City
and its environs (1974-75). Most of them were 35mm photographs of city
life—black men around a juke box, a couple with aqua blue sun glasses in an
aqua blue convertible—but the pictures from Nags Head were about summer
light and spatial fluidity, and only secondarily about people and their interactions at the beach.

In 1976-1977, Sternfeld worked with 35mm and 4 x 5 inch press cameras
and with strobe to photograph on street corners at rush hour. He let people pass
him at close range. The pedestrians don't notice being photographed any more
than they interact with the commuters around them. They are preoccupied; a
few seem anxious. Their gestures express being hurried and a desire to be
anonymous. With the foreground figures illuminated by strobe, and the
background exposed by daylight, three dimensional space becomes so shallow
as to be claustrophobic. Tonal contrasts are harsh; the colors of their clothes
are often garish.

With the assistance of two Guggenheim Fellowships and other grants,
Sternfeld has spent six years crisscrossing America, photographing magnificent vistas, small towns, cities and suburbs with an 8 x 10 inch view camera
and in luxuriant color. These pictures are radically different than his previous
series. The current series shares the softer color tones and concerns for light
and space of his Nag's Head photographs. Now his primary tools are distance,
color, disjunction and humor. He frequently gets up high and distant so that the
picture's foreground starts 40 to 60 feet out from the camera. The distance
allows him to incorporate more information. Because he is so distant, what is
one detail in his photographs is significant enough to be the entirety of
someone else's photograph of the same subject. Thus frequently, Sternfeld's
most significant details are not what the viewer first notices. The beauty of the
land first catches the eye, then the viewer perceives a twist of irony or the signs
of an actual or foreboding disaster. Some of the disasters or threats are man-
made, such as military weapons; others are naturally occurring catastrophes,
such as flash floods, volcanic eruptions and tornadoes. His distance also
allows him to make more complex pictures, rich with incongruous juxtapositions
to humorous effect. Sternfeld's most popular photograph is *Mclean, Virginia*
which shows a fireman shopping for pumpkins while a farmhouse burns on the
hill before him. Flames rising from the roof dwarf other fireman precariously

perched in a mechanical bucket above the fire; with one pumpkin in his arm, this modern day Nero considers other possible purchases.

He has called the series *American Prospects* referring both to America's future and its commanding views. Looking out is both physical and mental, phenomenological and psychological. By identifying the specific location of each landscape, he makes it clear that these are *American* landscapes to be perceived in the cultural and historical context of America. Sternfeld has studied the crops, industries, seasons, geology, and vegetation natural to each region. He's read American literature attentively for detail of regional life. His photographs record abandoned mills and river towns in New England, military bases and retirees in the South, ranchers and dude-ranch riders in the West, abode brick makers and Indians in the Southwest, and colonial homes with dogwood trees in the Southeast. "The photographs which I made," he wrote, "represent the efforts of someone who grew up with a vision of classical regional America and the order it seemed to contain, to find beauty and harmony in an increasingly uniform, technological and disturbing America." It became a matter of reconciling himself to new, increasingly homogenized America and of finding new sources of beauty.

He searches for beauty in unexpected places. Eschewing America's remaining wilderness, Sternfeld concentrates instead where man has altered the land for purposes of domesticity, agriculture, industry or pleasure. He focuses on man as the earth's caretaker and photographs where man and nature interact with varying degrees of concern. He searches for beauty in the ordinary aspects of life. In part because he believes that an ordinary life has sufficient visual content if he has the clarity of vision to extract it. But also because he wants his audiences to pay attention to scenes and details which they habitually neglect to notice on the premise that what you are taught to praise you will not maim or exploit or destroy.

—Anne W. Tucker

STETTNER, Louis.

Nationality: American. **Born:** Brooklyn, New York, 7 November 1922. **Education:** Abraham Lincoln High School, New York, 1938-39; studied engineering at Princeton University, New Jersey, 1940-42; studied at the Institut des Hautes Etudes Cinematographiques, Paris, 1952-56, B.A. in photography and cinematography 1956. **Military Service:** Served in the United States Army, 1942-45. **Family:** Married 4 times; has 3 children. **Career:** Freelance photographer, New York, since 1949, working as contract and freelance photographer for *Time, Fortune, Du, Paris-Match, Réalités, National Geographic* etc., and advertising photographer for various American and European agencies; Photojournalist for *M.D. Magazine,* New York, 1965-70. Adjunct Lecturer in Photography, Brooklyn College, Queensborough College, and Cooper Union, all New York, 1972-73; Professor of Art, C.W. Post Center, Long Island University, New York, 1973-79; Visiting Lecturer, International Center of Photography, New York, and Bennington College, Vermont, 1976. **Recipient:** Creative Photography Fellowship, Yaddo, Saratoga Springs, New York, 1956, 1957; Creative Artists Public Service Grant, New York, 1973; National Endowment for the Arts Photography Fellowship, 1974; First Prize, Pravda International Photography Contest, 1975. **Agent:** Howard Greenberg Gallery, 120 Wooster Street, New York 10012, U.S.A. **Address:** 46 rue Mathieu, 93400 Saint-Ouen, France.

Individual Exhibitions:

1954	Limelight Gallery, New York
1958	E. Leitz Gallery, New York
1959	Moderna Museet, Stockholm
1964	Village Camera Club, New York
1971	International Museum of Photography, George Eastman House, Rochester, New York
1973	Witkin Gallery, New York
1974	Neikrug Gallery, New York

1975	Gallery 1199, New York
1979	Yellowstone Art Center, Billings, Montana
1980	Milwaukee Center for Photography (retrospective; with Brad Temkin)
1981	*40 Photographs,* travelling exhibition (toured France, 1981-83)
	Photograph Gallery, New York
1982	The Photographers' Gallery, London
1983	Berner Photo-Galerie, Berne, Switzerland
	Midtown Y Gallery, New York
1985	Neikrug Gallery, New York
1986	Centre de la Photographie, Geneva
1987	Photofind Gallery, New York
1989	Comptoire de la Photographie, Paris
	Kate Heller Gallery, London
	Berenson Gallery, Berlin
1990	Galerie Agathe Baillard, Paris
	Gallery Zaragoza, Spain
	Vision Gallery, San Francisco
1992	Center of Photography, Geneva
	Howard Greenberg Gallery, New York
	Photography Gallery, Malaga, Spain

Selected Group Exhibitions:

1953	*Subjektive Fotografie,* Saarbrücken
1967	*The Camera as Witness,* at *Expo '67,* Montreal
1983	*Die fotografische Sammlung,* Museum Folkwang, Essen, West Germany
1984	*Subjective Fotografie: Images of the 50s,* San Francisco Museum of Modern Art (travelled to the University of Houston, Texas; Museum, Folkwang, Essen; Vasterbottens Museum, Umea; Kulturhuset, Stockholm; Saarland Museum, Saarbrücken; Palais des Beaux Arts, Brussels)
1985	*City Lights,* International Center of Photography, New York

Collections:

Museum of Modern Art, New York; International Museum of Photography, George Eastman House, Rochester, New York; Hopkins Center, Dartmouth College, Hanover, New Hampshire; Victoria and Albert Museum, London; Bibliothèque Nationale, Paris; Museum Folkwang, Essen, Germany; Metropolitan Museum of Art, New York; Smithsonian Museum, Washington D.C.; Museum of Fine Arts, Boston; Art Institute of Chicago, Illinois; San Francisco Museum of Art, California; Musée Carnavalet, Paris; Musée d'Elysée, Lausanne, Switzerland.

Publications:

By STETTNER: Books—*Paris Street Stories,* with an introduction by Brassaï, Paris 1949; *35mm Photography,* New York 1956; *History of the Nude in American Photography,* New York 1966; *Workers: 24 Photographs,* with an introduction by Jacob Deschin, New York 1974; *Women: Portfolio,* New York 1976; *Weegee the Famous,* editor, New York 1978; *Sur le Tas,* with an introduction by Cavanna, Paris 1979; *Streetwork,* portfolio of 12 photos, New York 1981; *Early Joys,* (Photographs from 1947-72), New York 1987; *Sous Le Ciel de Paris,* introduction by Cavanna, Paris 1994.

On STETTNER: Books—*Museum Folkwang: die fotografische Sammlung,* exhibition catalogue, with introduction by Ute Eskildsen, Essen, West Germany 1983; *Subjektive Fotografie: Images of the 50s,* exhibition catalogue, by Ute Eskildsen, Manfred Schmalriede and Dorothy Martinson, Essen, West Germany 1984. **Articles**—"Un Artiste Americain et son Conception de l'Art" by Paul Montel in *Photo Cinema* (Paris), no. 12, 1948; "Collaboration" by Jacob Deschin in the *New York Times,* 13 October 1964; "Framing the Photos" by James Auer in the *Milwaukee Journal,* 2 March 1980.

*

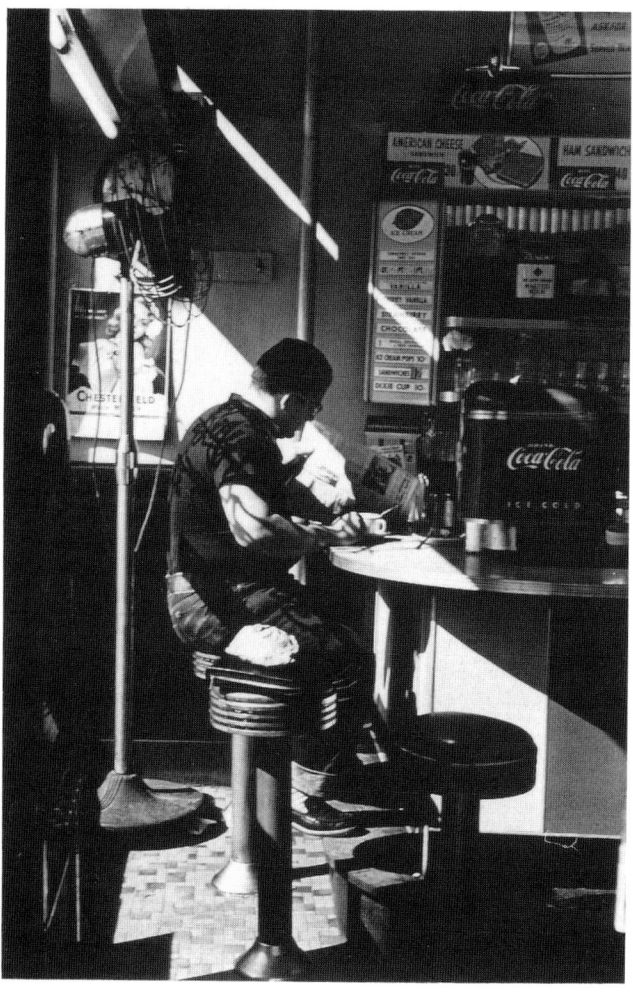

Diner, **New York City, 1954.** Photograph ©Louis Stettner. Courtesy of
Howard Greenberg Gallery, New York.

Photography has always been to me a passionate way of interpreting the
world around me. Human beings (whether they are in the photograph or not)
have always been the central theme of my work.

—Louis Stettner

*   *   *

Louis Stettner's photographs have spoken for more than three decades in a
quiet but firm and confident voice in behalf of the essential goodness of
mankind. In an era of self-expressive, self-involved and, alas, self-indulgent
photography, Stettner's camera chooses to reveal his fellows' rather than his
own preoccupations. And at a time when assaults upon the image with brush,
pigment pointed stick and razor blade are counted "creative," Louis Stettner
has held to straight photography. Rather, he creates by his insight and choice of
moment and lighting.

As a writer and teacher as well as a photographer, Stettner has always
championed humanism as photography's most important goal. Since photography, more than any other medium, excels at presenting outer reality—the
world and its people—as opposed to the photographer's inner reality, he has
chosen to do with it what it does most strongly. But, of course, he is no mere
recorder of the passing scene.

From the first, Stettner's photographs have had a pared-down simplicity in
composition, a strong feeling for light and a directness that communicates
swiftly, like a poster. Affection for mankind flows through a Stettner photo—

sentiment but not sentimentality, however. And his eye is quick to find the
memorable segments of an otherwise unmemorable scene. One such that
comes to mind shows a small girl in the dimness of a large city railroad
terminal. Oblivious to scurrying figures in the background, she is stepping
from one to another of a series of bright circles of light, circles which are out-
of-focus images of the sun framed by pinholes in the ceiling far above. In a
frilly, uncomfortably dressed-up outfit, the little girl is nevertheless acting her
age. She is enjoying striding from spot to spot, stepping only into the circles of
light. Although her back is to us, we know her. We know that she is still
mistress of childhood's ability to make its own world, to extract magic from
the mundane. And we know it because Louis Stettner knows it and also
recognizes how to show us what he knows.

His feeling for people also comes through in two portfolios which he has
published: *Women* and *Workers.* The titles, like the photographs, are direct.
Stettner's women are real women. There is no idealized beauty among them.
They are on picket lines. Age and trouble and poverty have marked some of
them. They are the women we pass on the street on our way to work and in the
checkout lines in the supermarket. And, although life has marked each, each
has a kind of beauty because Stettner has seen it, captured it and pointed it
out to us.

His workers are also seen and photographed with the sympathy for
humankind that pervades Stettner photographs. Frequently he relates the
worker to his work, combining in one image a portrait and a strong, spare,
dramatic composition that presents us at once with an individual and a symbol.

Louis Stettner has an abiding faith in man. It showed in his early work; it
shows in his most recent. He is an unquenchable humanist, preserving the
strengths of his medium—immediacy, detail and the ability to seize the
moment—in an era of photographic self-indulgence and navel contemplation.

—Kenneth Poli

ŠTREIT, Jindřich.

Nationality: Czechoslovakian. **Born:** Vsetín, Czechoslovakia 5 September
1946. **Education:** Studied Art Education at Teacher Training Department of
Palacký University, Olomouc, Czechoslovakia, graduating in 1967; learned
photography from father from 1964 and subsequently from Professor Jan
Bukovan; also studied photography through correspondence courses at Institute of Creative Photography, 1974-77. **Family:** Married Agnes 20 April
1971; daughter: Monika. **Career:** Started work as a primary school teacher in
Rýmařov in 1967 and later became Headmaster of a village school in Sovinec
and Jiříkov. From 1973 directed a gallery in Sovinec specialising in the work
of avant-garde artists; participated as sole photographer in an exhibition of
alternative art scheduled for presentation on tennis courts in Prague, 1982;
arrested by secret police, sentenced to 10 months imprisonment for "Defama-
tion of the Republic and and the Head of State," after examination of whole
photographic archive (published and unpublished); prints, negatives and
camera confiscated as "instruments of crime"; kept under surveillance and
banned from photographic activity or, after release from prison, from teaching; worked as librarian, then as an agricultural foreman on a state farm until
1989; following collapse of Communist regime, worked for district authorities
in Bruntál, and in Sovinec; external lecturer in photography at the Film and TV
Academy (FAMU) of Prague and at the Institute of Creative Photography of
the Theatre of Music, Silesian University in Opava since 1990; during 1991
and 1992 worked by invitation for various periods in France, documenting the
Red Cross Settlement at Reims and life in the town of Saint Quentin and the 13
villages constituting its District. **Address:** Sovinec 6, Autopošta Bruntál,
cz79201, Czech Republic.

Individual Exhibitions:

1967   *Tension,* University Club, Olomouc, Czechoslovakia
1974   *The Man,* Theatre of Music, Olomouc, Czechoslovakia
1975   *Gypsies Without Romanticism,* Gallery V Podloubí, Olomouc,
            Czechoslovakia

From the book *The Village Is a Global World,* **1986.** Photograph by Jindrich Streit.

1978	*The Theatre of Life,* Gallery V Podloubí, Olomouc, Czechoslovakia
1979	*Photographs from Journies,* Factory Club, Uničov, Czechoslovakia
1980	*Photographs,* Bruntál, Czechoslovakia
1981	Theatre, Činoherní klub, Prague
1988	J. Chloupka Gallery, Brno, Czechoslovakia
	The Chamber Gallery of Photography, Bratislava, Czechoslovakia
1989	House of the Lords of Kunštát, Brno, Czechoslovakia
	Gallery Foma, Prague
1990	Side Gallery, Newcastle upon Tyne, England
	Gallery 4, Cheb, Czechoslovakia
	Small Gallery, Liberec, Czechoslovakia
	Galerie Lelieu, Lorient, France
1991	Mai de la Photo, Reims, France
	Theatre of Music, Olomouc, Czechoslovakia
	Povážská Gallery, Žilina, Czechoslovakia
	Gallery of Middle Slovakia, Banská Bystrica, Czechoslovakia
	Art Gallery, Ždár nad Sázavou, Czechoslovakia
	Cultural Centre, Opole, Poland
	Festivales photographiques du Tregnol, France
1992	Prague House of Photography, Prague
	District de Saint-Quentin, France
	Sommevoire, France
1993	Špála Gallery, Prague

Gallery Caesar & Gallery Aura, Olomouc, Czech Republic
House of Art, Opava, Czech Republic
Palisády Gallery, Bratislava, Slovakia
Ann Arbor Studio, Michigan
Saint Remy sur Busy, France

Selected Group Exhibitions:

1982	*Actual Photography,* Moravská Gallery, Brno, Czechoslovakia
1985	*27 Contemporary Czechoslovak Photographers,* The Photographers Gallery, London (travelled to Bristol)
1986	*Personalities of Czechoslovak Social Documentary Photography,* Gallery F Banská, Brno, Czechoslovakia
1989	*Czechoslovak Photography 1945-1989,* Gallery Valdštejnská jízdárna, Prague
	150 Photographs, Moravian Gallery, Brno, Czechoslovakia
	1st International Photo Triennial, Esslingen, Germany
	On the Art of Fixing a Shadow, Smithsonian Institute, Washington, D.C., (travelled to Chicago and Los Angeles)
	Contemporary Czechoslovakian Photography, Foto 89, Nieuwe Kerk, Amsterdam
	Czechoslovakian November 1989, Gallery Foma, Prague (travelled to České Budějovice, Hradec Králové, Graz, Strasbourg and Nuremburg)
1990	*Choice,* Houston Fotofest, Houston, Texas
	A Year of the East, Musée de l'Elysée, Lausanne, Switzerland

Tschechoslovakische Fotografie der Gegenwart, Ludwig Muse-
   um, Cologne, Germany (travelled to Erlangen, Germany;
   Metz, Strasbourg, France; Luxembourg; Odense, Denmark;
   Freiburg, Waldkreiburg, Germany; Barcelona, Granollers,
   Spain; Texas and Kansas)
1991   *Contemporary Czechoslovak Photographers*, Shwayder Gallery,
   Denver University, Colorado
   Contemporary Czechoslovak Photography and Art of Glass,
   Kunsthall, Hamburg, Germany
   Recent Acquisitions, The Museum of Modern Art, New York
1992   *More Than One Photograph*, The Museum of Modern Art,
   New York
   What's New: Prague, The Art Institute of Chicago, Illinois
1993   *Czech Photography of the 1990s*, Fotofeis, Ayr, Scotland
   (travelled to London, Lisbon, Porto and Salamanca)
   *Czech and Slovak Photography from Between the Wars to the
   Present*, Fitchburg Art Museum, Fitchburg, Massachusetts
1994   *Another Continent*, Tokyo Metropolitan Museum of Photography, Tokyo

Collections:

Moravian Gallery, Brno, Czech Republic; Museum of Decorative Art, Prague;
Collection of the Union of Czech Photographers, Prague; Sztuki Museum,
Lodž, Poland; Ludwig Museum, Cologne, Germany; The Museum of Fine
Arts, Houston, Texas; The Art Institute of Chicago, Illinois; The Museum of
Modern Art, New York; District de Saint-Quentin, France; Side Gallery,
Newcastle, U.K.; Stanford University Museum of Art, California; The Har-
vard University Museum of Art, Cambridge, Massachusetts; International
Center of Photography, New York; Victoria and Albert Museum, London; The
National Gallery of Art, Washington, D.C.; Metropolitan Museum of Photog-
raphy, Tokyo; Bibliothèque Nationale, Paris; Musée de l'Elysée, Lausanne,
Switzerland.

Publications:

By ŠTREIT: Books—*14 Regards Sur Le District de Saint-Quentin* Saint-
Quentin, France), 1992; *Saint-Quentin: 14 Views of the Region*, in collabora-
tion with A. Dufek, (Brno), 1993; *The Village is a Global World* with text by
Antonin Dufek, Prague, 1993; *La Quai de Rohan—Nouvelle Ville* with text by
Patrick Bernier, Lorient, France, 1994; *Myšlenky do kapsy*, Olomouc, Czech
Republic, 1994.

On ŠTREIT: Books—*On the Art of Fixing a Shadow* by Sarah Greenhough
and others, Washington, 1989; *Tschechoslowakische Fotografie der Gegenwert*,
by Vladimír Birgus, Heidelberg, 1990. Articles—"Mladá generace: Jindřich
Štreit" by Vladimír Birgus, in *Československá fotografie*, Prague, no. 6, 1978;
"Nekonečná hladania Jindřicha Štreita" by Marta Bezúchová in *Výtvarníctvo-
fotografia-film*, Bratislava, no. 10, 1988; "Fotograf ze Sovince" by Jiři
Šerých in *Československá fotografie*, Prague, no. 12, 1989; "Nechci žít z toho,
co jsem prožil" by Ladislav Solc in *Revue Fotografie*, Prague, no. 4, 1990;
"Jindřich Štreit" by Vladimír Birgus, in *Tvorba*, Prague no. 38/9 1991;
"Nejsem typ hrdiny" by Daniela Mrázková in *Fotografie*, Prague, no. 10
1991; "Dvě knihy Jindřicha Štreita" by Vladimír Birgus, in *Revue Fotografie*,
Prague, no. 4, 1993. Films—3 documentary films about Štreit's work,
produced by Jan Špata for television.

*　*　*

Jindřich Štreit began to photograph seriously during his university studies
in Clomouc in the mid sixties. After his graduation he and his wife left to take
up teaching at the small remote village of Sovinec, where in the course of time
he created a cycle of suggestive portraits of the local inhabitants under the title
Man. In his next collection, called *Gypsies without Romanticism*, 1974/5 he
avoided superficial enchantment with the life of gypsies and endeavoured to
portray more general characteristics typical of all people, which his predecessor, Josef Koudelka had emphasized in his photographs with a gypsy theme.
At the conclusion of his studies at the Institute of Creative Photography in
1977 he created a cycle of photographs from the theatre environment in which
he portrayed actors not only on stage, but also in their dressing rooms where

instead of being dramatic heroes they once again become ordinary people with
everyday problems, above all exceptionally sensitive to their own personal and
artistic successes and failures.

Jindřich Štreit rid himself definitively of a degree of exaggerated aestheticism and artificiality through creating his supremely authentic photographs
portraying country life at Sovinec and its surroundings during the late 1970s.
With an intimate knowledge of the environment and people, facilitated by his
sincere nature and teaching profession, Štreit captured cracked houses, muddy
paths, delapidated yards and the cheerless stereotype of new prefabricated
houses. He also photographed boring meetings and formal celebrations of
various communist festivals and the sincere relationships of people in a
convivial rural community where everyone knows everyone else. He portrayed the cyclical events of a calendar year in human life such as weddings,
funerals or wakes. Other subjects include people at work in the fields or
watching television in their homes and documented how elements of modern
civilisation with its consumer fetishes penetrate to a growing extent into
traditional country life. How traditional folk culture mixes with industrially
produced trash, and how purely formal and wholly dehumanized relations
appear next to natural interhuman ones. How bombastic communist slogans
penetrate even into remote villages, how even there people learn to live lies
and pretences and how not only the surrounding countryside but also the living
values of the villagers are devastated.

During the communist regime no other Czech photographer depicted
village life in Czechoslovakia in the 1980s in such a raw manner. These
photographs are widely remote from the idyllic pictures which appeared in
official newspapers and magazines. Thus it is not surprising that Jindřich Štreit
became dangerous to Gustáv Husák's communist regime. A contributory
factor was also the immeasurable activity he showed in organizing exhibitions,
concerts and theatre performances of nonconformist artists in the tiny village
in which he lived. For this reason Štreit was arrested in the spring of 1982 and
finally given a suspended sentence of ten months for allegedly insulting the
president and slandering the republic. He was thus obliged to give up teaching
and become a packer on the State Farm at Rýžoviště. Even under these
circumstances he did not cease to photograph and organise cultural events.

In spite of their naturalism Jindřich Štreit's photographs are not all
pessimistic. The photographer firmly believes that devastation of the environment and even of the physical aspect of human life need not necessarily mean
devastation of the human spirit. He by no means idealises people in his
photographs. Quite often he depicts them drunk or dirty, but at the same time
tries to find positive values at their core, indicated perhaps by means of a
tender gesture towards a child or animal, sincere laughter or a longing to
escape from deadly reality into the glowing world of the television screen. As a
result his photographs are not simply a penetrating sociological probe into the
life of a village population. They also say a great deal about the threat to the
fundamental values of life and about the ability to prevent its realisation.

At the end of 1989, after the fall of the Communists, Štreit began to teach in
the department of photography at the Faculty of Film and Television in Prague
and at the Institute of Creative Photography of the Silesian University in
Opava. He also undertook to care for the reconstruction of the mediaeval castle
at Sovinec and additionally to continue organizing various cultural events. He
radically widened the sphere of his activity as a photographer—he photographs villages in North Moravia and Silesia, and during long sojourns, he has
also provided penetrating photographs of life in Reims, in the neighbourhood
of the French town of Saint-Quentin, in the countryside in the north of England
and on a farm in Austria. An entirely new experience for him is his
photographic project based on a women's prison. The resulting photographs
are of an earthy and unbeautified nature, but once again they express Jindřich
Štreit's profound love of people.

—Vladimír Birgus

STRELOW, Liselotte.

Nationality: German. Born: Redel bei Polzin, Lower Pomerania, 11 September 1908. Education: the Volksschule, Neustettin, 1915-17, and a private
lyceum, Neustettin, 1917-20; later studied agriculture; studied photography,

Lette-Verein, Berlin, 1930-32. **Career:** Worked in the photo studio of Sys Byk, Berlin, 1932-33; Staff Photographer, Kodak AG, Berlin, 1933-38; freelance portrait and magazine photographer, working for *Frankfurter Allgemeine Zeitung, Rheinisches Post, Die Welt, Der Spiegel, Die Zeit, Theater der Zeit,* etc., and establishing own studio, in Berlin, 1938-43, in Neustettin, 1943-44, in Detmold, 1945-50, in Dusseldorf, 1950-66, in West Berlin, 1966-68, in Munich, 1969-76, and in Hamburg, 1977-81. Staff Theatre Photographer, under Gustaf Grundgens, Schauspielhaus, Dusseldorf, 1947-54; Official Photographer, *Richard Wagner Festival,* Bayreuth, 1952-61; Chief Photographer, City Theatres, Cologne, 1959-62. Member, Gesellschaft Deutsche Lichtbildner, 1959-61 and 1979-81. **Recipient:** Silver Medal, *World Photo Exhibition,* Rochester, New York, 1935; Handwerkskammer Prize, Berlin-Brandenburg, 1938; International Art Photo Diploma, Salzburg, 1950; Plaque, *Photokina,* Cologne, 1951, 1952; City of Hamburg Prize, 1951; Diploma, *Camera* magazine, Lucerne, 1951; Diploma, *World Exhibition of Photography,* Lucerne, 1952; Gold Chain, Centralverbandes des Deutschen Photographen-handwerke, 1952; Gold Medal, *Biennale di Fotografia,* Venice, 1957; Honor Award, *World's Fair,* Brussels, 1958; Adolf-Grimme Prize, with S. Mohrhof, WDR Broadcasting, Cologne, 1966; David Octavius Hill Prize, Gesellschaft Deutsche Lichtbildner, 1969; Culture Prize, with R. Clausen and R. Relang, Deutsche Gesellschaft für Photographie, 1976. **Died:** (in Hamburg) 30 September 1981.

Individual Exhibitions:

1949	Galerie Mutter Ey, Dusseldorf
1952	Galerie de Parnass, Wuppertal
1958	German Pavilion, *World's Fair,* Brussels
1961	Deutsche Gesellschaft für Photographie, Cologne
1962	Kunstverein, Dusseldorf
1973	Münchner Stadtmuseum, Munich
1977	Galerie Kuhling, Hamburg
	Galerie Nagel, West Berlin
	Liselotte Strelow: Porträts 1933-1972, Rheinisches Landesmuseum, Bonn

Selected Group Exhibitions:

1935	*World Photo Exhibition,* International Museum of Photography, George Eastman House, Rochester, New York
1950	*Photo-Kino Ausstellung (Photokina),* Cologne
1951	*Subjektive Fotografie,* Saarbrücken
1957	*Biennale di Fotografia,* Venice
1964	*World Exhibition of Photography: What Is Man?,* Pressehaus Stern, Hamburg (and world tour)
1969	*50 Jahre GDL,* Museum für Kunst und Gewerbe, Hamburg
1970	*Fotografinnen,* Museum Folkwang, Essen
1979	*Deutsche Fotografie nach 1945,* Kasseler Kunstverein, Kassel, West Germany (toured West Germany)
1982	*Lichtbildnisse: Das Porträt in der Fotografie,* Rheinisches Landesmuseum, Bonn
1984	*Sammlung Gruber,* Museum Ludwig, Cologne

Collections:

Strelow Photo Archive, Rheinisches Landesmuseum, Bonn; Museum Folkwang, Essen; International Museum of Photography, George Eastman House, Rochester, New York; Museum Ludwig, Cologne.

Publications:

By STRELOW: Books—*Gustaf Grundgens,* with text by Werner Vielhaber, Bad Honnef, West Germany 1953; *Das Manipulierte Menschenbildnis,* Dusseldorf and Vienna 1961, as *Photogenic Portrait Management,* London 1966. **Articles**—"Das Geschicht einer Landschaft" in *Photo-Graphik* (Berlin), no. 10, 1936; "Lichtbildner unserer Zeit" in *Suddeutscher Zeitung* (Munich), 2 April 1952; "Fotoschau Vorbildlich Aufgebaut" in *Die Welt* (Berlin), 21 June 1952; "Eine Ketzerin an ein Dunkelkammergenie" in *Foto Magazin* (Mu-

nich), March 1953; "Ensusste Kinderbilder" in *Frankfurter Illustrierte,* 4 April 1953; "Hof-Fahig" in *Die Welt* (Berlin), 9 March 1960.

On STRELOW: Books—*Fame: Famous Portraits of Famous People by Famous Photographers,* edited by L. Fritz Gruber, London and New York 1960; *Beauty: Variations on the Theme Woman by Masters of the Camera—Past and Present,* edited by L. Fritz Gruber, London and New York 1965; *Liselotte Strelow: Porträts 1933-1972,* exhibition catalogue, with text by Klaus Honnef, Bonn 1977; *Geschichte der Fotografie im 20. Jahrhundert/ Photography in the 20th Century* by Petr Tausk, Cologne 1977, London 1980; *Fotografie 1919-1979, Made in Germany: Die GDL-Fotografen,* edited by Fritz Kempe, Bernd Lohse and others, Frankfurt 1979; *Deutsche Fotografie nach 1945* by Floris Neusüss, Wolfgang Kemp and Petra Benteler, Kassel, West Germany 1979; *Lichtbildnisse: Das Porträt in der Fotografie,* edited by Klaus Honnef, Cologne 1982; *Sammlung Gruber: Photographie des 20. Jahrhunderts,* exhibition catalogue, with foreword by Siegfried Gohr, Cologne 1984. **Articles**—"Liselotte Strelow" by Hanns Riss in *Camera* (Lucerne), January 1959; "Die Augenblick is ihr Fetisch" by Fritz Kempe in *Die Welt* (Berlin), vol. 5, no. 1, 1966; "Photographic Portraiture" by Jacob Deschin in the *New York Times,* 3 March 1968; "Photographinnen" by Peter Sager in *Die Zeit* (Hamburg), 16 September 1976.

*   *   *

The ascent and decline of the portrait in art are closely connected with the development of bourgeois society. In the individual likeness of his own person the self-confident bourgeois showed his sovereign attitude towards his environment. Photography brought a final flowering of the classical portrait, to a certain extent its apotheosis and perfection. The portrait in the post-bourgeois age of postmodernism signifies something other than it did in the vast stretch of "modern times" from the Renaissance to the mid 20th century. The self-assured, composed personality, perennial subject of the artistic portrait, has given way to the vast faceless masses of industrial civilization: individual behavior and appearance, adapt to prevailing conditions. Only recently does there appear to be a change in direction, yet, admittedly, one cannot yet foresee which course it will take.

Liselotte Strelow is one of the last great practitioners of portrait photography in the classical sense. Yet even her portraits reveal a radical change, even if that change is not apparent at first sight. For with vast psychological powers of intuition, she is ingenious in her understanding of how to work to the individual core of her "model," to release the contemporary individual from his cocoon. Strelow's portraits, unpretentious in formal arrangement, free from any distracting accessories (so that they dispense with an external aid to characterization) and free furthermore from any conspicuous striving after "reality," trace out the personality structure of the people portrayed as well as their physiognomy. Strelow tries to make visible the human psyche, human experience and human fate. She rarely takes the whole human body into the pictures; she restricts herself throughout to the head, though now and then some motif may be reiterated by the hands. In contrast to the older August Sander, Liselotte Strelow defines people not primarily as social types, but as autonomous, independent subjects.

Her photographic portraits still suggest something of the humanism of Renaissance portraits: to paraphrase Walter Benjamin, they make us ask after those who have passed safely and irrevocably from sight, regardless of whether or not they were prominent in politics, trade and industry, or culture. Precisely this factor lends even those images that people take of themselves in photo-booths—which can't properly be called "portraits"—a painful and almost desperate dimension. And this—forgivable?—self-assertion of the human individual from within the levelling clutch of the social workforce, paradigmatically evidence by the omnipresence of those clichés of reality that the technical and electronic photographic media spew forth daily—this is Liselotte Strelow's particular theme, the basis of her artistic vision. Her photographic work lays stress on the active portrait, so that the likeness, which resists the levelling out tendencies of the medium, may gain ascendency—though that goal is frequently met only with the vehement support and deliberate and circumspect direction of the photographer.

—Klaus Honnef

SUDA, Issei.

Nationality: Japanese. **Born:** Kanda, Chiyoda-ku, Tokyo, 24 April 1940. **Education:** Tokyo University, Department of Economics, Tokyo, 1960-61; studied at the Tokyo College of Photography, 1961-62. **Family:** Married Sachiko Nakagawa in 1969. **Career:** Worked as a freelance photographer for various magazines, Tokyo, 1962-67; Photographer, Tenjo Sajiki Play Laboratory, Tokyo, 1967-70. Freelance photographer, contributing to *Asahi Camera, Camera Mainichi, Nippon Camera, Camerart*, etc., Tokyo, since 1971. Tutor, Tokyo College of Photography, Yokohama, since 1979. **Recipient:** New Photographer of the Year Award, Japan Photographic Society, 1976. **Address:** 4-5-9 Tendai, Inage-ku, Chiba-shi, Chiba 263, Japan.

Individual Exhibitions:

1977	*Fushi Kaden,* Nikon Salon, Tokyo
1978	*A Photographic Exhibition of Issei Suda,* CAMP Gallery, Tokyo
	Anonymous Men and Women: Tokyo 1976-78, Nikon Salon, Tokyo
1979	*Issei Suda: Views of Shinano,* Minolta Photo Space, Tokyo
	Original Prints of Issei Suda, Tsukaido Gallery, Fukuoka, Japan
1981	*My Tokyo,* at *SICOF,* Milan
1988	*Taipei White Heat,* Doi Photo Plaza, Tokyo
1989	*Tokyo 1980,* Photo Gallery International, Tokyo
	Block 1988 Hong Kong, Olympus Gallery, Tokyo
	4chome, Ginza, Tokyo 1983-1986, Ginza Nikon Salon, Tokyo
1991	*Yokohama,* Frog, Tokyo
	In the Storehouse, Fuji Photo Salon: Professional Space
	Dog's Noses, Minolta Photo Space, Tokyo
	Kiryu, Hiranaga-cho Bridge Gallery, Tokyo
	Wet Sand in August, Hiranaga-cho Bridge Gallery, Tokyo
	Utsunomiya, Frog, Tokyo
1992	*Hakodate,* Hakodate History Plaza, Hokkaido, Japan
	Tokyo/Osaka, Picture Photo Space, Osaka, Japan
	Hong Kong Scan, Hiranaga-cho Bridge Gallery, Tokyo
1993	*Family Diary,* Hiranaga-cho Bridge Gallery, Tokyo
	Naked City, Doi Photo Plaza, Shibuya, Tokyo
	Taipei, Hiranaga-cho Bridge Gallery, Tokyo
1994	*Trance,* Zeit Photo Salon, Tokyo
	Challenge of Light, Polaroid Gallery, Tokyo

Selected Group Exhibitions:

1977	*Neue Fotografie aus Japan,* Kulturhaus, Graz, Austria (toured Europe, 1977-79)
1978	*Photokina '78,* Cologne
1979	*Japanese Photography Today and Its Origin,* Galleria d'Arte Moderna, Bologna (travelled to the Palazzo Reale, Milan; Palais des Beaux-Arts, Brussels; the Institute of Contemporary Arts, London; Museum für Kunst und Gewerbe, Hamburg; Gemeente Museum, Arnhem; Pulchri Studio, The Hague)
	Five Photographers, Santa Fe Gallery of Photography, New Mexico
	Japan: A Self-Portrait, International Center of Photography, New York (travelled to *Venezia '79*)
1982	*38 Japanese Photographers,* Zeit-Foto Salon, Tokyo
1985	*A Day in the Life of Japan,* Tokyo (toured Japan)
1988	*8 Japanese Photographers,* Photo Gallery International, Tokyo
1989	*Eleven People over 1965-75,* Yamaguchi Prefectural Art Museum, Yamaguchi, Japan
	The Hitachi Collection of Contemporary Japanese Photography, Center for Creative Photography, The University of Arizona, Tucson
	150 Years of Photography, Konika Plaza, Tokyo
	Europaria 89 Japan, Antwerp, Belgium

1990	*Fotografie Biennale,* Rotterdam, Netherlands
	Glances at the City, Tokyo, Tokyo Municipal Museum of Photography, Tokyo
1991	*Japanese Photographs: the 1970s,* Tokyo Municipal Museum of Photography, Tokyo
1992	*What Did Photographers Express? 1960-1980,* Konika Plaza, Tokyo
	Post-war photography and Tohoku 2: Essays on Primal/ Japanese Landscapes, Miyagi Prefectural Art Museum, Miyagi, Japan
1995	*Photographic City TOKYO* (draft title), Tokyo Municipal Museum of Photography, Tokyo

Collections:

Tokyo College of Arts and Crafts; Museum für Kunst und Gewerbe, Hamburg; Yamaguchi Prefectural Art Museum, Yamaguchi; Tokyo Municipal Museum of Photography, Tokyo; Osaka University of Arts, Osaka; Miyagi Prefectural Art Museum, Miyagi; Paris Museum of Photography, Paris.

Publications:

By SUDA: Books—*Fushi Kaden,* edited by Tatsuo Shirai, Tokyo 1978; *My Tokyo,* edited by Yusaku Kamekura, Tokyo 1979; *Dog's Noses,* Tokyo 1991.

On SUDA: Books—Neue Fotografsie aus Japan, exhibition catalogue, by Otto Breicha, Graz and Bienna 1977; *The Era of Photography* by Taeko Tomioka, Tokyo 1979; *Japanese Photography Today and Its Origin* by Attilio Colombo and Isabella Doniselli, Bologna 1979; *A Day in the Life of Japan—June 7, 1985,* edited by Rick Smolan and David Cohen, New York and London 1985. **Articles**—"Fushi Kaden: A Season of Festivals" by Masao Tanaka in *Photo Art* (Tokyo), April 1976; "Issei Suda: Profile" by Masao Tanaka in *Camera Mainichi* (Tokyo), July 1976; "Fushi Kaden" by Taeko Tomioka in *Camera Mainichi* (Tokyo), June 1977; "A Theatre of Images" by Koji Taki in *Asahi Camera* (Tokyo), November 1977; "Trusting a Thought to an Image" by Masao Tanaka in *Camera Mainichi* (Tokyo), March 1979; "New Photo Theory" by Shiroyasu Suzuki in *Asahi Camera* (Tokyo), February 1980.

*

The act of taking a picture is just one of the many manifestations of being alive.

My confrontations with life are like a pendulum—to be touched, not to be touched, to be betrayed, not to be betrayed, the progress of which seems to me to constitute my photography.

My sense of sight usually takes precedence over my sense of touch; it is, at any rate, difficult to know all of one's senses. However, in everyday occurrences, that to which I respond, I often feel a kind of strangeness about me or feel attracted to some object. In trying to take pictures as within the perspective and response to such feelings, I verify myself and try to practice according to a certain model of Japanese action and spirit.

—Issei Suda

*   *   *

After graduation, Issei Suda found work as a stage photographer, supplying background photographs for the productions of poet/playwright Shuji Teryama's theatrical troupe, which was known as "Tenjo-Sajiki." His photographs did not, however, appear in published form until 1971 when they were shown in the contribution section of *Camera Mainichi* called "Album." After that, series of his photographs appeared independently in *Camera Mainichi* under the title *Fushi Kaden.* But it was not until he produced the photographs using mirrors that Suda established his own style. Thereafter, each time that his photographs appeared in *Camera Mainichi*, recognition of

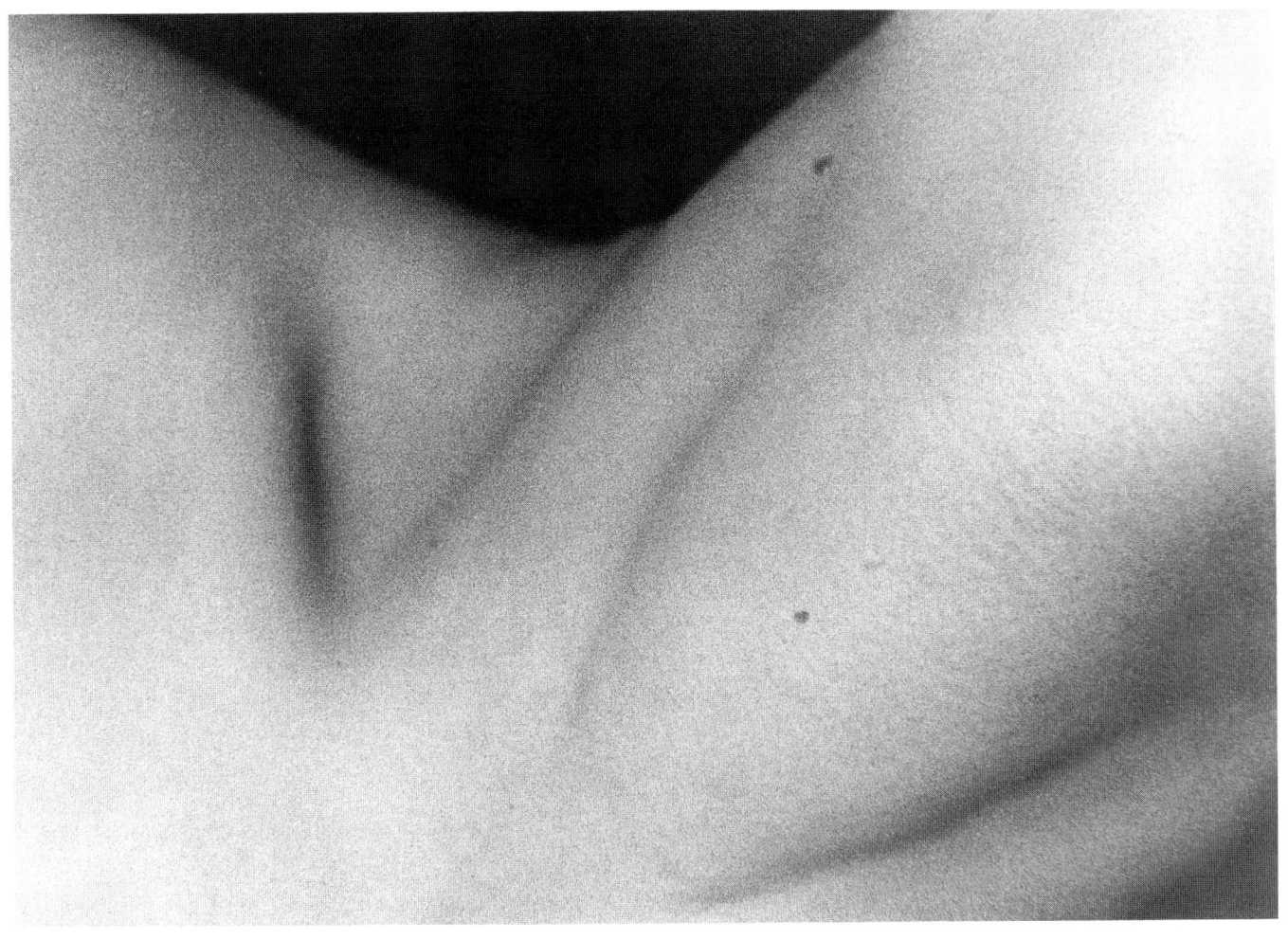

Trance, **1994.** Photograph by Issei Suda.

them grew, and in 1976 he won the "New Photographer of the Year Award" of the Photographic Society of Japan. Now, Suda's works are highly valued in the world of Japanese photography for their artistic merit and uniqueness.

Fushi Kaden has been translated as "Transmission of the Flower of Art." The term was originally the title of a 15th century literary work by Zeami on the classical Japanese theatre of the *Noh.* Zeami, an accomplished actor himself, wrote the work to preserve the teachings of his father, Kanami, the most highly revered actor, composer, instructor and playwright of the time. In addition to his father's teachings, the work also includes Zeami's own interpretations of the Noh, as well as his theories on acting, production, play composition, practice and other techniques. Although it was written mainly as a guide for transmission of the oral teachings of the Kanze school of the Noh, the work has also come to be widely read today as a philosophical classic on artistic technique and human nature. In the original *Fushi Kaden,* Zeami described the ultimate accomplishment which the actor must strive for in Noh as a "flower" which, in effect, refers to the attainment of total beauty in the actor's level of performance.

The main reason why *Fushi Kaden* was borrowed as the title for Suda's best-known work is that Suda himself is an avid reader of Zeami's original *Fushi Kaden.* The Noh and photography are, of course, different modes of expression. Yet, Suda has found much to learn about art in the teachings of Zeami that he feels may also be applied to photography. Suda undoubtedly feels this way because he himself is an exceptionally accomplished photographer in quest of the "flower" that Zeami spoke of in the world of the Noh.

—Akira Hasegawa

SUDEK, Josef.

Nationality: Czechoslovakian. **Born:** Kolín, Bohemia (Czechoslovakia), 17 March 1896. **Education:** Kolín, until 1911; apprentice bookbinder, Prague, 1911-13; studied photography, under Karel Novák, State School of Graphic Arts, Prague, 1922-24. **Military Service:** Served in the Czech Army, in Italy, 1915-20 (wounded and hospitalized, 1917-20). **Career:** Independent photographer, Prague, 1920-76; Official City Photographer, Prague, 1928; worked as commercial advertising and portrait photographer, working with Druzstevni Prace publishing company, Prague, 1928-36; Coeditor and Illustrator, *Panorama* magazine, and later, *Žijeme* magazine, 1928-36. Member, Amateur Photographers Club, Prague, 1920-24; Founder-Member, with Jaromir Funke, and others, Czech Photographic Society, Prague, 1924. **Recipient:** Artists of Merit Award, Czech Government, 1961; Order of Work, Czech Government, 1966. **Died:** (in Prague) 15 September 1976.

Individual Exhibitions:

1933   Krásná Jizba, Prague
1958   Alšova sin Umělecke besedy, Prague
1959   House of Arts, Brno, Czechoslovakia
1961   Slezské Museum, Opava, Czechoslovakia
        Frenštat pod Radhoštěm, Prague
1963   Gallery of Czechoslovak Writers, Prague

1964	Regional Gallery, Olomouc, Czechoslovakia
1966	Severočeské Museum, Liberec, Czechoslovakia
1971	Moravian Gallery, Brno, Czechoslovakia
	Bullaty-Lomeo Studio, New York
1972	Neikrug Gallery, New York
1974	International Museum of Photography, George Eastman House, Rochester, New York
	Light Gallery, New York
	Corcoran Gallery, Washington, D.C.
1976	Moravian Gallery, Brno, Czechoslovakia
	Roudnice, Czechoslovakia (retrospective)
	Museum of Decorative Arts, Prague (retrospective; toured Europe and the United States)
	Neue Galerie, Aachen, West Germany
	The Photographers' Gallery, London
	Impressions Gallery, York, England
1977	International Center of Photography, New York
	Light Gallery, New York
	International Museum of Photography, George Eastman House, Rochester, New York (retrospective)
1978	Moderna Museet, Stockholm
	Allan Frumkin Gallery, Chicago
	National Gallery, Prague
	Finnish Photographic Museum, Helsinki
1979	Museum of Decorative Arts, Prague
1980	Kunstindustrimuseet, Copenhagen
1981	Daytona Beach Community College, Florida
	Prakapas Gallery, New York
	Stephen White Gallery, Los Angeles
	Galerie Municipale de Château d'Eau, Toulouse, France
1982	Jacques Baruch Gallery, Chicago
	Cykly 1, Castle Kozel, Czechoslovakia
	Preus Fotomuseum, Horten, Norway
1983	*Cykly 2,* Castle Kozel, Czechoslovakia
	Sudek-Saudek: Images from Czechoslovakia, University of Iowa, Museum of Art, Iowa City
1984	*Cykly 3,* Castle Kozel, Czechoslovakia
1985	Pushkin Museum, Moscow
	Cykly 4, Castle Kozel, Czechoslovakia
1986	*Cykly 5,* Castle Kozel, Czechoslovakia
	Poet of Prague, Ledel Gallery, New York
1988	San Francisco Museum of Modern Art, San Francisco
	Art Institute, Chicago
	University of Pittsburg Gallery, Pennsylvania
	Cleveland Museum of Art, Ohio
	Jan Kesner Gallery, Los Angeles
	Museum of Decorative Arts, Prague
	Musée National d'Art Moderne, Centre Georges Pompidou, Paris
1989	Mücsarnok Gallery, Budapest
1990	Primavera Fotográfica, Barcelona
	Philadelphia Museum of Art, Pennsylvania
	North Carolina Museum of Art, Raleigh
1991	*Fotofest,* Ždár nad Sázavou, Czechoslovakia
1992	The Toledo Museum of Art, Ohio
	The High Museum of Art, Atlanta, Georgia
1993	*Poetic Images,* Sander Gallery, New York
	Drtikol + Sudek, Dobra Galerie, Prague
1994	*RIP,* Arles, France

Selected Group Exhibitions:

1930	*Modern Czech Photography,* Mansard of Aventinum, Prague
1936	*International Exhibition of Photography,* Palace Mánes, Prague
1939	*One Hundred Years of Photography,* Museum of Decorative Art, Prague
1958	*National Exhibition of Photography,* Prague
1960	*Sudek in the Arts,* Mladá Fronta, Prague (homage by painters and graphic artists)
1967	*Czech Photography Between Two World Wars,* Prague

1975	*Lyrismus in der tschechoslowakischen Fotografie der Genenwart,* Stadtische Museum, Freiburg im Breisgau, West Germany
1979	*Tschechoslowakische Fotografie 1918-78,* Fotoforum der Gesamthochschule, Kassel, West Germany
1983	*Sudek et la Photographie Tchèque,* Centre Georges Pompidou, Paris
1984	*Tschechische Fotografie 1918-48,* Museum Folkwang, Essen, West Germany (travelled to the Kunstverein, Frankfurt; Museum Moderner Kunst, Vienna; Muzeum Sztuki, Lódź, Poland)
	Facet of the Collection: Czechoslovak Photography, San Francisco Museum of Modern Art
1985	*Ursprung und Gegenwart tschechoslowakischer Fotografie,* Fotografie Forum Frankfurt, Germany
1988	*Tschechische Kunst der 20er + 30er Jahre,* Mathildenhöhe, Darmstadt, Germany
1989	*What is Photography—150 Years of Photography,* Mánes, Prague
	Czechoslovak Photography 1945-1989, Valdštejnská jízdarna, Prague
	Czech Modernism, Moravian Gallery, Brno, Czechoslovakia
	150 Photographs, Moravian Gallery, Brno, Czechoslovakia
	Czech Modernism 1900-1945, Museum of Fine Arts, Houston (travelled to New York and Akron)
	The Art of Photography 1839-1989, Museum of Fine Arts, Houston; Australian National Gallery, Canberra; Royal Academy of Arts, London
	On the Art of Fixing a Shadow, National Gallery of Art, Washington; The Art Institute of Chicago; Los Angeles County Museum of Art
1990	*Czech Avantgarde,* Archbishop's Palace, Arles, France
1991	*Czech Avantgarde,* Howard Greenberg Gallery, New York
	Photographie der Moderne in Prag 1900-1925, Neue Galerie, Linz, Austria (travelled to Vienna; Frankfurt and Paris)
1993	*Czech and Slovak Photography Between the Wars to the Present,* Fitchburg Art Museum, (travelled to Boston and Middlebury)

Collections:

Museum of Decorative Arts, Prague; National Gallery, Prague; Museum of Czech Literature, Prague; Dobra Galerie, Prague; Moravian Gallery, Brno, Czech Republic; Silesian Museum, Opava, Czech Republic; Gallery of Fine Art, Hodonín, Czech Republic; The Philadelphia Museum of Art; Museum of Modern Art, New York; The Metropolitan Museum of Art, New York; International Center of Photography, New York; The Art Institute of Chicago; The Collected Image, Chicago; Jacques Baruch Gallery, Chicago; University of New Mexico, Albuquerque; High Museum of Art, Atlanta; Center for Creative Photography, Tucson, Arizona; Museum of Fine Arts, Boston; Victoria and Albert Museum, London; The Royal Photographic Society, Bath, England; Musée National d'Art Moderne, Paris; Museum Folkwang, Essen, Germany; Stedelijk Museum, Amsterdam; Sammlung Fotografis, Bank Austria, Vienna.

Publications:

By SUDEK: Books—*Svaty Vit (Saint Vitus),* portfolio of 15 photos, with an introduction by J. Durich, Prague 1928; *Praha—Československo (Prague—Czechoslovakia),* with text by Cyril Merhout and others, Prague 1929; *Calendar of Družstevni Práce for the Year 1933,* Prague 1932; *Baroque Prague,* with text by Arne Novák, 3rd edition with others, Prague 1938, and 4th edition, Prague 1947; *Pražký Hrad (Prague's Castle),* with text by Rudolf Rouček, Prague 1945, 1947; *Magic in Stone,* with text by Martin S. Briggs, London 1947; *Praha: Josef Sudek,* with text by Vitezslav Nezval, Prague 1948; *Nač Hrad (Our Castle),* with text by A. Wenig and J.R. Vilimek, Prague 1948; *Lapidarium Narodniho Muzea (Lapidarium of the National Museum),* with text by V. Denkstein, Z. Drobná and J. Kybalová, Prague 1958; *The Sculptor Josef Mařatka*, with text by Anna Masaryková, Prague 1958; *Praha panoramatická (Prague Panoramas)*, with poems by Jaroslav Seifert, Prague 1959; *Karlův Most (Charles Bridge)*, with text by Emanuel Poche and Jaroslav Seifert, Prague 1961; *Pražské Ateliery (Prague Studios)*, Prague 1961; *Mostecko-Humboldtka*, set of 11 postcards, Prague 1969; *Wychowanie Muzyczne (A Musical Education)*, with text by Alojz Suchanek, Prague 1970; *Janaček-Hukvaldy*, with an introduction by Jaroslav Šeda, Prague 1971; *Walker of Prague*, with text by Vítězslav Nezval, Prague 1981.

On SUDEK: Books—*Pražske Paláce (Prague Palaces)*, by Alois Kubiček, Prague 1946; *Josef Sudek: Fotografie*, with an introduction by Lubomir Linhart, Prague 1956; *Light and Shadow*, edited by Miloš Hrbas, Prague 1959; *Memory in Black and White* by Jan Řezáč and Josef Prošek, Prague 1961; *Josef Sudek Profily*, set of 12 postcards, with text by Jan Řezac, Prague 1962; *Sudek: 96 Photographs*, with an introduction by Jan Rezac, Prague 1964; *Five Photographers*, exhibition catalogue, Lincoln, Nebraska 1968; *Great Photographers* by Time-Life editors, New York 1971; *Octave of Prayer*, exhibition catalogue, by Minor White, Cambridge, Massachusetts 1972; *The Magic Image* by Cecil Beaton and Gail Buckland, London and Boston 1974; *Sudek*, exhibition catalogue, with text by Anna Fárová, Prague 1976; *Josef Sudek*, exhibition catalogue, with text by Antonìn Dufek, Brno, Czechoslovakia 1976; *Josef Sudek*, exhibition catalogue, with text by Petr Tausk and Werner Lippert, Aachen, West Germany 1976; *Photographs: The Sheldon Memorial Art Gallery Collection, University of Nebraska*, with an introduction by Norman A. Geske, Lincoln, Nebraska 1977; *Concerning Photography*, exhibition catalogue, edited by Jonathan Bayer and others, London 1977; *Documenta 6/Band 2*, exhibition catalogue, edited by Klaus Honnef and Evelyn Weiss, Kassel and Cologne 1977; *Josef Sudek: Portfolio*, 13 photos, with an introduction by Petr Tausk, Prague 1976; *Sudek*, with text by Sonya Bullaty, introduction by Anna Farova, New York 1978; *Josef Sudek: Portfolio*, 18 photographs, with introduction by Petr Tausk, Prague 1980; *Geschichte der Fotografie im 20. Jahrhundert/Photography in the 20th Century* by Petr Tausk, Cologne 1977, London 1980; *The Photograph Collector's Guide* by Lee D. Witkin and Barbara London, Boston and London 1979; *Praha objektivem mistru/Prague Through the Lens of Masters*, with an introduction by Ludvik Baran, Prague 1981; *Josef Sudek*, Leipzig 1982; *Josef Sudek: 10 Fotos*, portfolio, edited by Galerie Rudolf Kicken, Cologne 1982; *Josef Sudek*, with text by Zdeněk Kirschner, Prague 1982, 1986; *Photographes Tchèques 1920-1950*, exhibition catalogue, by Zdeněk Kirschner and Antonìn Dufek, Paris 1983; *I grandi fotografi: Josef Sudek* by Anna Fárová, Milan 1983; *Tschechische Fotografie 1918-1948*, exhibition catalogue, edited by Ute Eskildsen, Essen, West Germany 1984; *Ceska Fotografie 1918-1938*, exhibition catalogue, by Ryszard Stanislawski, Antonìn Dufek and Urszula Czartoryska, Lodz, Poland 1985; *Josef Sudek* by Allan Porter, Zurich 1985; *The Evolution of Czechoslovak Photography from 1918 to the Present Day* by Petr Tausk, Prague 1986; *Josef Sudek* by Anna Fárová, Paris 1990; *Josef Sudek—Poet of Prague* by Anna Fárová, New York 1990; *Josef Sudek* by Zdeněk Kirschner, Tokyo and New York 1993; *Josef Sudek—Poetic Images*, exhibition catalogue, by Matthew Witovsky, New York 1993; *A World History of Photography* by Naomi Rosenblum, New York 1984; *Příběh fotografie* by Daniela Mrázková, Prague 1985; *A History of Photography* by Jean-Claude Lemagny and André Rouillé, Cambridge 1986; *History of Photography* by Peter Turner, London 1987; *Cesty československé fotografie* by Daniela Mráková and Vladimír Remeš, Prague 1989; *Czech Modernism 1900-1945*, exhibition catalogue, Houston 1989; *Photographie der Moderne in Prag 1900-1925* by Monika Faber and Josef Kroutvor, Schaffhausen 1991; *The Art of the Avant-Garde in Czechoslovakia 1918-1938, exhibition catalogue*, Valencia 1993. Articles—"Josef Sudek" by Vaclav Sivko in *Zpravodaj* (Prague), Fall/Winter 1956; "Josef Sudek: 60 Years" by V. Jiru in *Výtvarna Práce* (Prague), no. 5, 1956; "An Artist/Photographer" in *Fotografie* (Prague), no. 4, 1961; "Josef Sudek: 70 Years" in *Československa Fotografie* (Prague), no. 2, 1966; "Sudek" by Allan Porter in *Camera* (Lucerne), no. 3, 1966; "Josef Sudek" in *Camera* (Lucerne), no. 4, 1967; "Gallery: Josef Sudek: Poet of Prague" in *Life* (New York), 29 May 1970; "Josef Sudek" in *Fotografia Italiana* (Milan), July 1974; "Josef Sudek: The Birthplace of Janáček" in *Creative Camera* (London), October 1975; "Josef Sudek: A Monograph" by Allan Porter and Anna Fárová in *Camera* (Lucerne), no. 4, 1976; "Josef Sudek: The Czech Roman-

tic" by Charles Sawyer in *Modern Photography* (New York), September 1976; "Josef Sudek: A Tribute" by Ruth Spencer in *British Journal of Photography* (London), 3 December 1976; "Josef Sudek: Poet of Prague" in *Photography Year 1977* by Time-Life editors, Alexandria, Virginia 1977; "Backyard Romantic" by Ilka Normile in *Afterimage* (Rochester, New York), May/June 1977; "Josef Sudek's Poetic Reveries" by Gene Thornton in *New York Times*, 19 July 1977; "Josef Sudek: Photographs" by Carter Ratcliff in *Print Collector's Newsletter* (New York), September/October 1977; "Sudek: A Monk of Photography" by Vicki Goldberg in *American Photographer* (New York), 3 March 1979; "Josef Sudek" in *Creative Camera* (London), April 1980; "Josef Sudek: His Life and Work" by Petr Tausk in *History of Photography* (London/Philadelphia), January 1982; "Cykly Josefa Sudka" by Zdeněk Kirschner in *Revue Fotografie* (Prague), no. 3, 1986; "Sudek a Funke" by Zdeněk Kirschner in *Revue Fotografie* (Prague), no. 4, 1986; "Poznámky o Josefu Sudkovi" by Antonin Dufek in *Revue Fotografie* (Prague), no. 1, 1994.

*　　*　　*

Even though belated, the recent international recognition of Josef Sudek in western Europe and America has added an artist of consummate quality to the pantheon of photography's pioneer masters. Among them, all born before the turn of the century, he is most like Eugène Atget in the simplicity of his vision and the unity of his life's work. Like Atget he was always and exclusively concerned with the imagery of his immediate experience, the streets and buildings of Prague, the objects in his studio and garden, the landscapes of his native Bohemia. In the prints of Atget, however, the object, be it buildings, streets, trees or human beings, is seen objectively: the artist's response is held delicately within the bounds of an affectionate familiarity. In Sudek the quality of the response is of a different kind. It is warm with the subjective emotion of a true romantic. The subject is imbued with a sense of wonder. In a sense the subject is not the object itself but the light and atmosphere in which it exists. Atget the realist, Sudek the romantic is perhaps too simple a formulation, but there is no doubt of the difference between them. In the miraculous seizure of time which is the essence of their photography, Sudek is the enchanted one.

The numerous prints taken within the darkened interior of his studio, the still lifes of eggs and bread, plates of fruit, glasses of water, are impeccable in form and dense with sensory associations. They remind one of the miraculous still lifes of Chardin. It is, however, in the equally marvelous views through a window clouded with condensation or rain, that Sudek's definitive imagery may be found. These windows are more than windows. They act as filters for the artist's imagination. From within the security of self, through a fluctuating veil of moisture and light, he sees his world in terms of uncertainty, mystery and flux. In a larger sense, Sudek's camera almost always provides a transition from one reality to another. His landscapes have the hushed and waiting atmosphere of dawn or dusk. His deserted garden with its spectral white chairs arranged in the accidental patterns of contemplation or conversation, waits for the entry of an animating presence. It is in these prints that Sudek declares himself most noticeably as poet and magician. The light of burning kerosene lamps penetrates the tangled vegetation of the garden. A man's hat lies on the ground among stones and pebbles placed with a knowing but undeclared purpose. Sudek's most personal device is his use of glass eyes, often inserted into still life arrangements to invest them with a spiritual presence. In one of his best known prints such an eye is lodged in the gnarled trunk of a dead tree thus creating a fantastic creature to engage in a demonic conversation with the artist himself who sits with his back to the viewer, but with his spectacles reversed on the back of his head.

In these instances there is something of the exquisite horror of the surreal, but this same peculiarity of mood may be seen as present in varying degrees in most of Sudek's work. Throughout the range of his work; in the hundreds of views of Prague seen in all seasons and times of day and night; in the veritable archive of trees, forests, groves, storm-struck survivors (again reminding us of Atget); in the almost terrifying views of Prague's Jewish cemetery, known as Mala Strana; even in his few portraits and nudes of magisterial quality, there is an extraordinary sensibility at work, performing magic of a kind that is rare, not merely in photography, but in art.

—Norman A. Geske

SUDRE, Jean-Pierre.

Nationality: French. **Born:** Paris, 27 September 1921. **Education:** Attended the Lycée Montaigne, and the Lycée Saint Louis, Paris, 1931-38; Ecole Nationale de Cinématographie, Paris, 1941-43; Institut des Hautes Etudes Cinématographiques (IDHEC), Nice and Paris, 1943-45. **Family:** Married Claudine Richard in 1947; children: Dominique and Fanny. **Career:** Independent photographer, since 1946. Instructor, Ecole des Arts Appliqués de la Ville de Paris, 1957-58, and Ecole Supérieure Nationale d'Architecture et des Arts Visuels (La Cambre), Brussels, 1965-70; Founder-Director, Photography Department, Ecole Supérieure des Arts Graphiques, Paris, 1968-72; Founder, Photography Department, Galerie La Demeure, Paris, 1968; Founder-Instructor, Stage Expérimental Photographique (research center for experimental photography), with Claudine Sudre, Paris, 1968-73, and in Lacoste, Vaucluse, France, 1974-81; Founder, History of Photography Course, Université Saint Charles, Marseilles, 1976-77, and at Ecole des Beaux-Arts de Luminy, Marseilles, 1977-81. Member, Board of Directors, Société Française de Photographie, 1968-72, and Fondation Nationale de la Photographie and Comité Pédagogique, Paris, 1979. Member, Board of Directors, *Rencontres Internationales de Photographie*, Arles, France, since 1978. **Recipient:** Gold Lion Medal, *Biennale di Venezia*, 1957; Prix de l'Association des Critiques d'Art, Brussels, 1963; Davanne Medal, Société Française de Photographie, 1970. Chevalier de l'ordre des Arts et des Lettres, 1981. **Address:** 5 rue Felibre Gaut, 13100 Aix-en-Provence, France.

Individual Exhibitions:

1952	*Sous-Bois,* Galerie La Demeure, Paris
1955	*Végétal et Natures Mortes,* Musée National, Amiens, France
1956	*Natures Mortes,* Galerie Morian, Courtrai, Belgium
1957	*Végétal et Natures Mortes,* Société Française de Photographie, Paris
1961	*Matériographies,* Galerie Veranneman, Courtrai, Belgium
1962	*Aventure de Matière,* Galerie Montaigne, Paris (with Denis Brihat)
	Matériographies, Palais des Beaux-Arts, Brussels
1963	*Matériographies,* Galerie Huidevettershuis, Bruges, Belgium
1964	*Matériographies,* Galerie La Demeure, Paris
1965	*Grands Panneaux et Tryptiques,* Institut Français, Cologne (toured Germany)
1966	*Grands Panneaux et Tryptiques,* Galerie Les Contards, Lacoste, France
1967	*Denis Brihat/Pierre Cordier/Jean-Pierre Sudre,* Galerie Artek, Helsinki
1968	*Végétal et Minéral,* Centre Culturel, Toulouse, France
1969	*Végétal et Minéral,* Galerie Les Contards, Lacoste, France
	Apocalypse, Galerie La Demeure, Paris
1971	*Murals,* Arras Gallery, New York
1972	*Paysages Matériographiques,* Galerie Les Contards, Lacoste, France
	Paysages Matériographiques, Galerie Die Brücke, Vienna
1975	*Paysages Matériographiques,* Galerie Fiolet, Amsterdam
	Galerie Municipale du Château d'Eau, Toulouse, France (retrospective)
1976	Musée Nicéphore Niepce, Chalon-sur-Saône, France (retrospective)
	Matériographies et Natures Mortes, Atelier Galerie, Aix-en-Provence, France
1978	*Natures Mortes,* Marcuse Pfeifer Gallery, New York
	Musée de Besançon, France (retrospective)
1980	Galerie Les Métiers, Biot, Alpes-Maritimes, France (retrospective)
	Galerie Philippe Médard, Avignon, France (retrospective)
	Work Gallery, Zurich (retrospective)
1981	*Natures Mortes,* French Institute, New York
	Galerie Portefolio, Lausanne, Switzerland (retrospective)
	Jean-Pierre Sudre/Henri Cartier-Bresson, Stephen Wirtz Gallery, San Francisco

	Jean-Pierre Sudre/Jeanloup Sieff, Musée d'Orange, France
	Natures Mortes, Galerie Photogramme, Quebec
	Galerie Reflex, Brussels (retrospective)
	Galerie Le Grand Cachot de Vent, Neuchâtel, Switzerland (retrospective)
	Musée Ancien de Grignan, France (retrospective)
1983	Santa Fe Center for Photography, New Mexico
1984	Galerie Marijke Winnubst, Amsterdam
	Susan Spiritus Gallery, Newport Beach, California (retrospective)
	Centre Culturel de Lannion, France
	Centre Culturel de Papeete, Tahiti
1985	*Temps Materiographes,* Alexandre de la Salle Galerie, Saint Paul de Vence, France
1986	*Travelling,* Société Française de Photographie, Paris
1987	*Natures Mortes,* RIP, Arles, France
1988	Marcuse Pfeiffer Gallery, New York
	Natures Mortes, Barbican Art Gallery, London
1989	Union des Artistes Plastiques, Prague
	Bielefeld Museum, Germany
	Maine Workshop
	Bibliothèque Nationale, Paris
1990	*Retrospective 1948-1990,* Busto Arsizio Museum, Italy
1992	*Imaginaire Planetaire,* Galerie de la Gare, Bonnieux, France
1993	*12 Natures Mortes,* Musée de Tesse, Le Mans, France
1994	*Petite Rétrospective 1948-1992,* Galerie Picto Bastille, Paris
	Fondation Veranneman, Kruishoutem, Belgium

Selected Group Exhibitions:

1957	*Salon National de la Photographie,* Bibliothèque Nationale, Paris
1960	*Salon Comparaisons,* Musée d'Art Moderne, Paris (and to 1966)
1968	*L'Oeil Objectif,* Musée Cantini, Marseilles (with Denis Brihat, Lucien Clergue and Robert Doisneau)
1972	*La Photographie Française,* National Museum, Moscow
1973	*Photography as Art,* Scottish Arts Council Gallery, Edinburgh
1980	*Photographia: La Linea Sottile,* Galleria Flaviana, Locarno, Switzerland
1984	*La Photographie Créative,* Pavillon des Arts, Paris

Collections:

Bibliothèque Nationale, Paris; Musée Nicéphore Niepce, Chalon-sur-Saône, France; Musée Cantini, Marseilles, France; Museum of Modern Art, New York; Gernsheim Collection, University of Texas at Austin; Center for Creative Photography, University of Arizona, Tucson.

Publications:

By SUDRE: Books—*Bruges: Bau Berçeau de la Peinture Flamande,* with text by F. Cali, Paris 1963; *Diamantine,* Paris 1964; *Pralinne,* Paris 1967; *Argentine,* Paris 1968; *Apocalypse,* exhibition catalogue, Paris 1970; *Paysages Matériographiques,* portfolio, Paris 1975; *Nus,* portfolio, Paris 1978; *Natures Mortes No 1, 1948-1953,* portfolio, Paris, 1990; *Natures Mortes, No 2, 1953-1960,* portfolio, Paris, 1994; *Sous-Bois, 1948-1951,* portfolio, Paris, 1995.

On SUDRE: Books—*Dictionnaire Pittoresque de la France,* Paris 1955; *Aventure de Matière,* exhibition catalogue, Paris 1962; *L'Oeil Objectif,* exhibition catalogue, Marseilles 1968; *Histoire de la Photographie* by J. Keim, Paris 1970; *Photography into Art,* exhibition catalogue, by Pat Gilmour, Edinburgh 1973; *Jean-Pierre Sudre,* exhibition catalogue, by Jean Dieuzaide, Toulouse 1975; *The Magic Image* by Cecil Beaton and Gail Buckland, London and Boston 1975; *Jean-Pierre Sudre,* exhibition catalogue, by Paul Jay, Chalon-sur-Saône, France 1976; *Geschichte der Fotografie im 20. Jahrhundert/ Photography in the 20th Century* by Petr Tausk, Cologne 1977, London 1980; *Photographia: La Linea Sottile,* exhibition catalogue, by Rinaldo Bianda and Giuliana Scimé, Locarno, Switzerland 1980; *La Photographie Créative* by

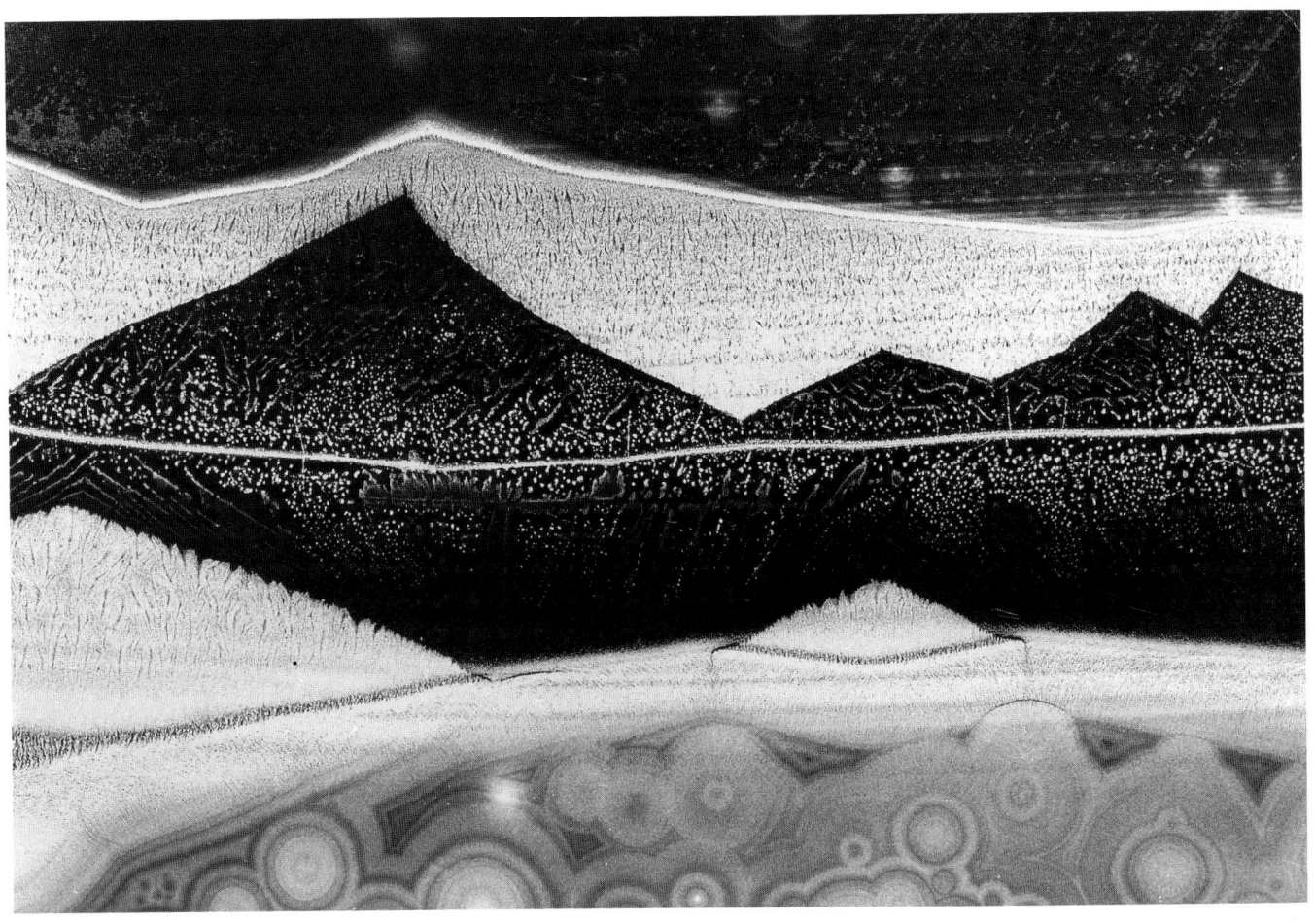

From *Paysages Matériographiques, 1972-75.* Photograph by Jean-Pierre Sudre.

Jean-Claude Lemagny, Paris 1984. **Articles**—"Jean-Pierre Sudre" in *Camera* (Lucerne), August 1956; "Jean-Pierre Sudre" in *Terre d'Images* (Paris), no. 3, 1964; "Jean-Pierre Sudre" by Romeo E. Martinez in *Camera* (Lucerne), November 1966; "Jean-Pierre Sudre" in *Techniques Graphiques* (Paris), July/August 1966; "Jean-Pierre Sudre" by Michel Kempf in *Photo Revue* (Paris), December 1976; "Jean-Pierre Sudre" by Guy Mandery in *Le Photographe* (Paris), no. 4, 1977; "Jean-Pierre Sudre" in *Photo Jeunesse* (Paris), February 1979. **Television film**—*Chambre Noire* by Michel Tournier, 1967.

*

Start with a general view of the forest.
Approach a tree.
Analyze its branches,
count its leaves,
scrutinize its bark,
slip into its trunk
and wander
the enchanted paths of its veins.
Then plunge
into the darkness of its roots
and glide softly while
travelling to the centre of matter;
this, photographically,
is the fantastic journey
that I have taken for fifteen years.
Will I ever discover

the palace of Diamantine, Queen of the night,
whose thousand crystallized towers
scintillate obliquely
when the hidden suns
are gradually dispersed?

—Jean-Pierre Sudre

*   *   *

The photography of Jean-Pierre Sudre is a search. Having begun during the 1950s by questioning ordinary everyday objects and plant life, he has gone on to push his investigations to the limit, to the very substance of photography.

"Without wishing to forget the great charm of the vegetable kingdom, the world of crystallographic silence brings to this age, the era of the atom, a pleasure and an inexhaustible source of inspiration. To prepare a crystallization for the purpose of making pictures that seem vital is to go back to the art of still-life where objects are arranged with precision" (Preface to *Apocalypse,* 1970).

This original attitude to photography requires special means of investigation. The main photographic tool used by Sudre, other than large format plates, is an unequalled photochemical knowledge. Together with his wife Claudine, Sudre works as a researcher in photographic art, producing everything himself, sometimes even down to the light sensitive surfaces. In his laboratory pictures develop in his manipulation of flasks containing rare substances.

Naturally, Sudre's work is not entirely to be perceived as chemistry. The objects and plants of his early work and his more recent nudes frame a long series of "matériographies," which are sometimes suggestive of the countryside and sometimes of anthropomorphic details—but that is not the point. What matters are the prints, the photographic object itself. And Sudre's prints are among the most exquisite that one is privileged to see.

A leading spirit of the French school of pure photography, Sudre has pursued the artistic adventure to its ultimate consequences, even to the point of making it into a kind of ritual practice somewhere between alchemy and the martial arts. In all ways, a noble exercise.

His artistic work cannot be disassociated from his decisive role in France as a teacher at the highest level. He was also, during the 1950s and 1960s, one of a handful of French photographers who fought for the recognition in their country of photography as an art in itself.

Jean-Pierre Sudre is, in other words, one of the most completely original figures in the international gallery of photographers.

—Guy Mandery

SUSCHITZKY, Wolf(gang).

Nationality: British. **Born:** Vienna, Austria, 29 August 1912; emigrated to Britain, 1935: naturalized, 1947. **Education:** Studied photography, Graphische Lehr- und Versuchsanstalt, Vienna, 1930-33. **Family:** Married Puck Voute in 1934 (divorced, 1936); Ilon Donat in 1939 (divorced); married Beatrice Cunningham; children: Peter, Misha and Julia. **Career:** Freelance photographer since 1933: established studio with Puck Voute, Amsterdam, 1934-36; freelance photographer, working for *Illustrated Animal and Zoo Magazine* and *Geographical Magazine*, London, 1936-42; film cameraman, with Paul Rotha, London, 1937, 1942-44, and for Data Film Unit, 1944-53; freelance film and television cameraman, London, since 1953. Associate, Royal Photographic Society, London. **Address:** Flat 11, Douglas House, 6 Maida Avenue, London W2 1TG, England.

Individual Exhibitions:

1940	*Animal Pictures,* Ilford Galleries, London
1982	The Photographers' Gallery, London (retrospective)
1985	Joods Historisch Museum, Amsterdam
1988	Camden Arts Centre, London
1989	Zelda Cheatle Gallery, London
1991	British Academy of Film and TV Arts, London
1992	*Three Generations of Suschitzky* at Zelda Cheatle Gallery, London

Selected Group Exhibitions:

1959	*Hundert Jahre Photographie 1839-1939,* Museum Folkwang, Essen, West Germany (travelled to Cologne and Frankfurt)
1964	*World Exhibition of Photography: What Is Man?,* Pressehaus Stern, Hamburg (and world tour)
1968	*2nd World Exhibition of Photography: Woman,* Pressehaus Stern, Hamburg (and world tour)
1979	*Fotografie in Nederland 1920-1940,* Haags Gemeentemuseum, The Hague
	The 30s: British Art and Design Before the War, Hayward Gallery, London
1984	*Subjektive Fotografie: Images of the 50s,* San Francisco Museum of Modern Art (travelled to the University of Houston, Texas; Museum Folkwang, Essen; Vasterbottens Museum, Umea; Kulturhuset, Stockholm; Saarland Museum, Saarbrücken; Palais des Beaux Arts, Brussels)
1985	*The Miner's World,* Castle Museum, Nottingham
1986	*Art in Exile in Great Britain,* Volkshochschule Kreuzberg, West Berlin (toured West Germany)
	The Animan in Photography 1843-1985, The Photographer's Gallery, London

Collections:

Archives of the City of Amsterdam; Haags Gemeentemuseum, The Hague; Gernsheim Collection, University of Texas, Austin.

Publications:

By SUSCHITZKY: Books—*Photographing Children,* London and Glasgow 1940, 1948; *Photographing Animals,* London and New York 1941; *An Animal Tour,* with text by Cecilia Davies, London and Glasgow 1944; *That Baby,* with text by L. Frank, London and Glasgow 1946; *Open Air ABC in Colour Photography,* London and Glasgow 1947; *Faithfully Ours: Cats and Dogs Photographed by Wolf Suschitzky,* with text by Cecil Smyth, Norwich 1950; *The Flying Poodle,* with text by Roland Collins, London 1951; *Baby Animals,* with others, London and Glasgow 1952; *All About Taking Baby and Your Camera,* London and New York 1952, 1958; *Kingdom of the Beasts,* with text by Julian Huxley, London 1956; *Animal Babies,* London 1957; *Island Zoo,* with text by Gerald M. Durrell, London 1961; *Brendan of Ireland,* with text by Bryan MacMahon, London 1961, 1965. **Article**—in *Photography* (London), June 1954. **Films**—(as cameraman/director of photography) *Power for the Highlands,* 1943; *Children of the City,* 1944; *The Bridge,* 1945; *Adventure in Sardinia,* 1950; *No Resting Place,* 1950; *The Oracle,* 1952; *The Bespoke Overcoat,* 1955; *Small World of Sammy Lee,* 1962; *Lunch Hour,* 1962; *Ulysses,* 1966; *Ring of Bright Water,* 1968; *Entertaining Mr. Sloane,* 1969; *Get Carter,* 1970; *Living Free,* 1971; *Something to Hide,* 1971; *Theatre of Blood,* 1972; *Moments,* 1973. **Documentaries**—*Cradle of Genius,* 1959; *From Stone into Steel,* 1959; *Trinidad and Tobago,* 1964; *The River Must Live,* 1965; *Design for Today,* 1965; *The Tortoise and the Hare,* 1965; *Carbon,* 1967; *Poussin,* 1967; *Claude Lorraine,* 1969; has also worked on numerous television commercial films and on series for British television, including: *Sailor of Fortune,* 1956; *Charlie Chan,* 1957; *Worzel Gummidge,* 1979, 1980, 1981; *Staying On,* 1980; *Owain Glyndwr,* 1982; *Good and Bad at Games,* 1983; *The Young Visiters,* 1984; *The Chain,* 1984; *Claudia's Story,* 1985. *Charing Cross Road in the Thirties,* Verlagnishen 1988

On SUSCHITZKY: Books—*The Man Behind the Camera* by Helmut Gernsheim, London 1948, New York 1979; *Great Photographs 1: Suschitzky,* edited by Norman Hall and Basil Burton, London 1954; *Photography Today,* edited by Norman Hall, London 1957; *Hundert Jahre Photographie 1839-1939 aus der Sammlung Gernsheim, London* by Helmut and Alison Gernsheim, Essen 1959; *Fotografie in Nederland 1920-1940,* exhibition catalogue, by Flip Bool and Kees Broos, The Hague 1979; *Thirties: British Art and Design Before the War,* exhibition catalogue, by Ian Jeffrey, William Feaver, Brian Lacey and others, London 1979; *Subjektive Fotografie: Images of the 50s,* exhibition catalogue, by Ute Eskildsen, Manfred Schmalriede and Dorothy Martinson, Essen, West Germany 1984. **Articles**—"Wolf Suschitzky" in *U.S. Camera Annual,* New York 1962 and 1972.

*

I prefer straightforward, honest photography—the selective eye waiting for the right moment. A photograph should make some statement, and it should be aesthetically pleasing. I'm afraid that I'm old-fashioned enough not to like the modern trend of obscure pictures, taken without knowledge of the photographer's craft.

My main work, in the last thirty years or more, has been cinematography. I grew up in documentary films, and I was cameraman on a good number of features like: *Ulysses* (1966), *Ring of Bright Water* (1968), *Entertaining Mr. Sloane* (1969), *Get Carter* (1970), *Living Free* (1971), and *Something to Hide* (1971).

I have worked on films for television and countless commercials.

While I still take photographs, it is rarely as a professional photographer— more for pleasure and interest.

—Wolf Suschitzky

*   *   *

Wolf Suschitzky came to Britain from Vienna before the war. He had gone first to Holland for a brief spell, but soon settled in England and began work as a film cameraman and it is for this work that he is probably best known today. All the while, however, he has taken stills for himself and on assignment and he was often published in photography magazines in the 1950s and 1960s. His range is wide, from reportage to portraits and there are, in his work, many marvellous photographs of animals and birds.

Early on he made a series of pictures of the Charing Cross Road, which show not only the place, its bookshops, and the cross-section of activities to be found there, but also records the various people and itinerant tradesmen as well as buildings that have now sadly disappeared. The area fascinated him; so did the East End where he also photographed extensively, producing a marvellous series of people both in portraits and groups. Children play in streets that have now been blocked with cars, if not pulled down altogether, and throughout these photos there is a sentiment without sentimentality, a rare quality in pictures of an intrinsically emotive place and time.

His documentary filming has taken him to many parts of the world, and it is interesting to compare pictures taken in Thailand before the war with those taken in the early 1980s; so much has not changed, and Suschitzky's trained eye and sympathetic vision can produce images that do actually evoke a place and make one long to see it for oneself without their ever being ''picaresque'' or creating the impression that it is simply a tourist's view. The work is real, it is interesting, it is evocative without being either despairingly seedy or romaniticised as the geographical magazines can sometimes make of such places. It is this realism that is the most enduring and stimulating thing about these photographs. There is a consistency between the early and later work that is reassuring and though the portraits may now be of more famous people, they are still done with respect but not adulation and with a certain sense of humour. This humour is probably most apparent in some of the animal pictures, also done with respect and without any overt attempt to anthropomorphize creatures out of their own characters.

Early on his film work widened from the purely documentary to include films, television series and commercial work. Since the early eighties his still photographs have been seen in many one-man and group exhibitions both in London and in other parts of Europe. He is widely acknowledged and appreciated in the film world and it is a real bonus for those of us who work with still photographs that he has continued to produce and to show such an enduring interest in this side of his life, for many of his still images remain vividly in the mind long after they have first been seen.

—Sue Davies

SUTKUS, Antanas (Motiejaus).

Nationality: Lithuanian. **Born:** Kluoniskiai, Kaunas, 27 June 1939. **Education:** Studied journalism at Vilnius State University, Lithuania. **Family:** Married Mardjosaite Aukse in 1964 (divorced); children: Simas, Giedre and Indre; married Rima Sutkiene in 1993. **Career:** Worked at the Eserelis Peat-Works, Lithuania, 1956-58. Full-time photographer since 1958: Reporter-Cameraman, *Literatura ir Means (Literature and Art)* weekly magazine, Vilnius, 1960-62; Photo-Reporter, *Tarybine Moteris (Soviet Woman)* magazine, Vilnius, 1962-69; independent photographer, with studio in Vilnius, since 1969. President of the Organizing Committee, 1969-74, Vice-President of the Praesidium, 1974-80, and President of the Praesidium, 1980-1990; Photography Art Society of Lithuania, Vilnius. **Recipient:** Michelangelo Gold Medal, Italy, 1970; First Prize, *Fotoforum,* Ruzomberok, Czechoslovakia, 1970; Grand Prize, *Golden Eye '73* exhibition, Novy Sad, Yugoslavia, 1973; Grand Prize, *Man and His World* exhibition, Katowice, Poland, 1973; Artist Award, 1976, and Gold Medal, 1979, Fédération de l'Art Photographique (FIAP); Macumba Cross, Ndola, Zambia, 1980; Merited Worker in Culture Award, Supreme Soviet of the Lithuanian S.S.R., 1980; Socialist Photography Prize, Bucharest, 1982; Lithuanian State Prize for Art Works, Vilnius, 1985. **Address:** Algirdo 39-412, Vilnius 2006, Lithuania. **Studio:** Kauno 10-18, Vilnius 2006, Lithuania.

Individual Exhibitions:

1969   Bratislava, Czechoslovakia

1970   Novi Sad, Yugoslavia
1974   Photo Gallery, Vilnius, Lithuania
1975   Sofia, Bulgaria (toured Bulgaria)
1978   Rostock, East Germany (toured East Germany)
        Helsinki, Finland (travelled to Pori, Finland)
1979   United Nations Building, New York
        Photographs by Antanas Sutkus and Aleksandras Macijauskas, Prakapas Gallery, New York
        Photo Gallery, Vilnius, Lithuania
1980   Photo Gallery, Kaunas, Lithuania
        House of Photography, Plovdiv, Bulgaria (travelled to Sofia, Varna and Burgas)
        Art Research Institute, Moscow
1981   Finnish Photography Museum, Helsinki (travelled to Joensuu, Finland, and Goteborg, Sweden)
1982   Fotografiska Museet, Stockholm (toured Sweden)
1985   Zango Fotoforum Gallery, Munich
1986   Musée Nicéphore Niepce, Chalon-sur-Saône, France
1991   Travelling Exhibition, United States
1994   Photo Gallery, Kaunas, Lithuania
        Photo Gallery, Vilnius, Lithuania
        In Memory of Kaunus Jewish Ghetto, Synagogue, Kaunus, Lithuania
1993   *Jean-Paul Sartre and Simone de Beauvoir in Lithuania in 1965* (Travelling exhibition)

Selected Group Exhibitions:

1968   *Four Photographers,* Art Museum of Vilnius, Lithuania
1969   *Nine Lithuanian Photographers,* Journalists' Union, Moscow
1973   *Four Lithuanian Photographers,* The Photographers' Gallery, London
1979   *Lithuanian Photography,* Canon Photo Gallery, Amsterdam (travelled to Paris and London)
1973   *Lithuanian Photography,* Dusseldorf, West Germany
1984   *Quinze Ans des Passions,* at *Rencontres Internationales de Photographie,* Arles, France
1985   *Contemporary Lithuanian Photographers,* Musée Reattu, Arles, France
        Lithuanian Photography, Museo Civico, Turin, Italy
1986   *Lithuanian Photography,* Galerie Municipale du Château d'Eau, Toulouse, France
1991   *East-West,* Munich, Germany
1992   Aspekte Litauisher Pfotographie, Berlin
        Memory of Images, Berlin
1993   Rostock, Germany
        Riga, Latvia
1994   Vilnius, Lithuania
        Copenhagen, Denmark

Collections:

Photography Museum, Siauliai, Lithuania; Bibliothèque Nationale, Paris; Musée Français de la Photographie, Bièvres, Paris; Valokuvamueseon, Helsinki; Musée Nicéphore Niépce, Châlon-sur-Saône, France; International Center of Photography, New York; National Art Museum, Vilnius, Lithuania; Art Institute of Minneapolis, Minnesota.

Publications:

By SUTKUS: Books—*Everyday Vilnius,* with text by Romualdas Rakauskas, Vilnius, Lithuania 1968; *Souvenirs of Native Meadows,* Vilnius 1969; *This Country Is Called Lithuania,* with text by Romualdas Rakauskas, Vilnius 1970; *Lazdynai,* Vilnius 1975; *Fragments of Old Vilnius,* Vilnius 1975; *Colors of the Native Land,* Vilnius 1976; *Soviet Lithuania,* with texts by several authors, Vilnius 1976; *Lithuania from a Bird's-Eye View,* Vilnius 1981; *Lithuania,* Vilnius 1981, 1983; *Neringa,* Vilnius 1982, 1994; *Daina Lietuvai,* Vilnius 1984; *Draugyste/Friendship/ Album,* Vilnius, 1988; *Natur Paradies Kurische Nehrung,* Germany, 1988; *Lithuania,* Vilnius, 1991, 1993; *Lietuva,* 1993.

Vilnius 23 August, **1991.** Photograph by Antanas Sutkus.

On SUTKUS: Books—*Pobaltska sovetska fotografie* by Vaclav Kiru, Prague 1974; *The Story of Photography* by Daniela Mrázková, Prague 1985, London 1986; *Another Russia* by Daniela Mrázková and Vladimìr Remeš, London 1986. **Articles**—in *Fotografie* (Leipzig), no. 5, 1977; *Valokuva,* (Helsinki), no. 3, 1979; *Ceskoslovenska fotografie* (Prague), no. 8, 1979; *Sovetskoye Foto* (Moscow), no. 10, 1979, no. 11, 1985.

*

Let's leave technology and professional culture aside. They are an alphabet that is a must to each professional photographer.

Photography must be needed by people. The main direction of my effort in photography is rehabilitation of old topics. I try to find generosity, kindness, love and dreams in people. I look for thoughtfulness and heartiness. My aim, like that of a number of other Soviet photographers, is to take part in painting a big canvas on contemporary spiritual life, and my main purpose is to make an attempt at drawing a psychological portrait of contemporary man. I work mostly on portraits. I contribute regularly to my series *People of Lithuania,* commenced in 1976.

Generations succeed one another, and man's perception of the world also changes. I try to express, by means of photographic language, things and notions that are irrevocably leaving our times. I feel it is my responsibility, because future generations will judge our way of life, our culture and our inner world on the basis of photographs.

The part played by photography in the contemporary world is unusually great. Often it is by means of photography that we try to overcome alienation, to come to better mutual understanding. Although it is the youngest branch of art, photography has a considerable informational significance. That significance is so great that often it's hard to tell the difference between informative and art photography. Sometimes a trend emerges, determined by the historical period, in which there is a transition of informative photography into art photography.

I believe in photography that not only informs about main world events, serves scientific purposes, decorates public buildings and private apartments, advertises goods, etc., but also influences our feelings and thoughts by its beauty, emotive qualities, inner power and broadness of generalization. I am most of all interested in art photography. In general, I think more theoretical work is needed in the subject to prevent any merely good photography from being automatically classified as art. Such cases, by the way, are quite frequent in the various international salons, where enthusiastic jury panels lavishly decorate any picture, whatever its quality, with medals or citations. And, once determined, standards in photography travel quickly from continent to continent. Yet, in my view, this fashion of standards is a hindrance to the development of genuine photographic art, and salon photography often retards the progress of thought and resource in the field.

When a predestination of value exists, and when that value was determined in the first place by fashion, then there will inevitably be a devaluation of significant topics and of photography itself. Sometimes the criteria for assessing photography remind one of those for sports.

Like any other branch of art, photography requires sacrifice, the artist's entire lifetime. Names and personalities—similar to those in painting, literature, music or cinematography—are needed in photography. Their emergence would certainly reinforce the position of photography as art.

Photography must be loyal to its times; it must help to solve contemporary problems. It must be an efficient champion of peace, friendship among nations, and ideas of internationalism and their dissemination. It must struggle for social progress and humanism, for the clean and bright face of the Earth, man's planet. Nevertheless, in my opinion, art photography should not serve only a particular brief moment, or—what's even worse—surrender to expediency. It should never be used to stress violence or sex or be guilty of pure advertising and formal experiment as a means of shocking the world. Art photography ought to be involved with accumulating stable artistic values. Modern photographic artists must be able to differentiate between the essential and the accidental. They must be particularly sensitive to human truth, the truth of life. Finally, photographers must choose the important moments of our restless planet's life, and consider, too, the view of coming generations.

—Antanas Sutkus

* * *

Antanas Sutkus is a photographer whose main subject is man in all his situations and moods. Like a first-rate photojournalist, Sutkus "fixes" everyday life. Recognizing the power of photography for just that kind of "fixing," he primarily applies that particular feature in his work. Only the camera is able to preserve our contemporaries and we ourselves as we really exist—and to capture one moment of our lives is still to generalize. Sutkus doesn't indulge in tricks; deformations caused by the wide-angle lens are not conspicious; his photos of our environment are normal, ordinary and familiar, though, as photography, still very stylish. Because of his profound photographic culture and his mastery of the medium, Sutkus can photograph well in every situation—from the planned sculptural form to the sudden snapshot.

A large series, "People of Lithuania," is a good example of his strenuous efforts over a long period of time to depict the people of his native country for posterity. These photos are often produced in what seems to be the mode of the photojournalist, but in fact Sutkus is adept at asking his model to stand, sit or act, and in a certain place—to behave in a way that is, in his view, most characteristic. As a result of his technique, Sutkus has created many memorable photos of artists, composers, cultural figures, artists, and ordinary country people. Sutkus loves the countryside, as is revealed by close-up photos that range from ploughing the fields to the folds in the faces of old people. Most of all, his mastery is revealed in those photos taken during trips across Lithuania or trips as a tourist where there was no time for long preparation and planning and where he had to react quickly and resolutely. In such a situation only a real professional can remain himself—and with Sutkus, that means capturing something essential in a rapidly changing situation. His series about Bulgaria and her people is a good example of his skill.

During the last ten years Sutkus has been an officer—he is now the President—of the Photography Art Society of Lithuania. He has had to deal continuously with problems connected with the whole of Lithuanian photographic life, and the greatness of the task has left him little time for his own creative work. Nevertheless, exhibitions by the President have taken place in several foreign countries, and he has been involved in producing several photography books. During recent years he has published and has now collected a great series of aero-photos, taken from a helicopter, of the rivers and lakes, forests and fields, villages and towns of Lithuania. These photos reveal that Sutkus, whatever his other responsibilities, continues with what has become his life's work—photographing Lithuania. Because of his accomplishments, Sutkus has been honored with the title of Merited Worker in Culture of the Lithuanian S.S.R.

—Peeter Tooming

SUZUKI, Risaku.

Nationality: Japanese. **Born:** Wakayama Prefecture, Japan, 1963. **Education:** Graduated from Tokyo College of Photography, 1985; graduated from the Research Institute, Tokyo College of Photography, 1987. **Agent:** Photo Gallery International, 2-5-18 Toranomon, Minato-ku, Tokyo 105, Japan.

Individual Exhibitions:

1990   *True Fiction,* Kichijoji PARCO Gallery, Tokyo
1991   *Sun City,* Kanda Hiranagacho-bashi Gallery, Tokyo
1992   *White Sands, True Fiction,* Photo Gallery International, Tokyo
1993   *Double Life,* Photo Gallery International, Tokyo
1994   *Torii and its Surroundings,* Polaroid Gallery, Tokyo

Selected Group Exhibitions:

1985   *15 Contemporary Photographic Expressions 8th,* Annex Hall
        Gallery, Tsukuba University, Japan
1986   *Tokyo College of Photography, Research Institute Exhibition,*
        Olympus Gallery, Tokyo
1987   *Photography 87: Possibility of a New Photography,* Setagaya
        Museum of Art, Tokyo

From the series *White Sands,* **c. 1980.** Photograph ©Risaku Suzuki.

*

I am very fond of traveling America by driving a car. The car's current velocity multiplied by the distance to the next town lets me know that the time has passed. When I cruised a highway stretching straight in a never-ending monotonous scenery, I really felt that I swam a long-distance swim in amnesia.

It was on such an occasion that I first visited White Sands. White Sands gave me a false impression that I was in a sugar jar, and when I found myself standing alone amid the desert under the domed sky, I really felt completely released from irritations. Though I had thought that when I ran out of a place I could find another world, White Sands taught me that the world itself would not change at all and I knew the joy of life under the shelter of the sky. When I click the shutter, a time of one-several hundredths is fixed on the film. It is quite enjoyable to be always able to see the moment in the print which I saw in the past.

The world I can see by my eyes is fully colored. Therefore, when I watch and catch the world I wanted, the colours, the shape and the feeling of atmosphere are among the decisive factors to locate the objects. When I took photos at White Sands, the fact that I am a Japanese and that White Sands is a place in the United States of America did not bother me at all. Neither did the fact that White Sands is the place where the world's first explosion experiment of the Atomic bomb was performed. But now, I wonder how dazzling the flash of explosion was over those white sands of the desert.

—Risaku Suzuki

At Risaku Suzuki's personal photo exhibition under the title of *White Sands* many photos of white sands against blue sky were displayed to make a long, long line in a small gallery. On his photos, I could not find any cloud, any shadow or an uneasiness, and there existed no humidity, no weariness and no stain. You could only see the sky of deep blue, pure white sands and the people moving around in the space configured by the sky and the sands.

It's really a world in itself.

How did Suzuki get this brightness without any harmful intention and the innocence without any prejudice expressed in the photos?

Suzuki's photos do not convey the moisture of scenery photos commonly taken by Japanese photo artists. His pieces are completely removed from any self-satisfied intention of environmentalist enlightenment derived from an excessive admiration of the scenery, from fear of Mighty Nature and from reference to the industrialized society carefully hidden in the scenery photographed. We can only see the usual colours of skies, an extent of sky, fully dried air and white sands, all found in New Mexico, United States of America.

Suzuki successfully gives us a feeling of atmosphere of a non-real world by presenting photos of common scenery of the real world.

—Kasahara Michiko

SVOBODA, Jan.

Nationality: Czechoslovakian. **Born:** Bohuňovice, Moravia, 27 July 1934. **Education:** Apprenticed to a porcelain modelling workshop, Stará Role, 1949-50; studied stage design, under Z. Balas, R. Lander, F.V. Mokrý and J. Solar, School of Applied Art and Industry, Prague, 1950-54; mainly self-taught in photography, from 1956. **Military Service:** Served in the Czech Army, 1954-56. **Family:** Married Anna Horáčková in 1965. **Career:** Worked as a draughtsman, Stavoprojekt building industry plant, Prague, 1956; graphic designer, Sovětska Kniha publishers, Prague, 1957-60, and Obuv shoemaking company, Prague, 1960-71; Staff Photographer, Museum of Decorative Arts, Prague, 1971-83. Since 1983, freelance photographer, as member of the Foundation of Czechoslovak Artists, Prague. Member, Máj artists' group, Prague, 1963. **Died:** (in Prague) 1 January 1990.

Individual Exhibitions:

1968	Galerie na Karlově nám., Prague
	Fotokabinett Funke, House of Arts, Brno, Czechoslovakia
1969	Gallery of Fine Arts, Ostrov nad Ohřì, Czechoslovakia
1970	Regional Gallery, Olomouc, Czechoslovakia
1971	House of Arts, Brno, Czechoslovakia
1975	Dum pánu z Kunštáu, Brno, Czechoslovakia
1978	*Portret rzezbiarza*, Galerie Fotografii, Wroclaw, Poland
1979	Galerie Print, Worpswede, West Germany
1980	*Portret rzezbiarza*, Salon Fotografiki, Łódž, Poland
1982	The Photographers' Gallery, London (travelled to the Museum of Modern Art, Oxford)
1983	*Komparace I*, Gallery of Fine Arts, Roudnice nad Labem, Czechoslovakia (with Josef Sudek)
1986	Malá Galerie, Kladno, Czechoslovakia
	Galeria Foto-Medium-Art, Wroclaw, Poland
1987	Gallery Foma, Prague

Selected Group Exhibitions:

1964	*Máj*, Nova Sìň, Prague
1969	*Cykly a serialy*, Gallery of the Capital City of Prague
1970	*Cykly a serialy*, House of Arts, Brno, Czechoslovakia
	Cien grabados y cien fotografias Checoslovaquia, Museo Universitario, Mexico City
1971	*Ateliéry*, Galerie U Recickych, Prague
1973	*Československá fotografie 1971/72*, Moravian Gallery, Brno, Czechoslovakia
1978	*Strom*, Dum pánu z Kunštátu, Brno, Czechoslovakia
1983	*Okno*, Gallery of Art, Karlovy Vary, Czechoslovakia
1984	*Československá fotografie*, Galerie D, Prague
1986	*Elementary Photography*, Sczecin, Poland
1989	*Contemporary Czechoslovak Photography*, Holland Foto, Nieuwe Kerk, Amsterdam
	Czechoslovak Photography 1945-1989, Valdštejnská jízdárna, Prague
1990	*Czechoslovak Photography Today*, Museum Ludwig, Cologne (travelled to Erlangen, Germany; Metz, France; Luxembourg; Strasbourg, France; Odense, Denmark; Freiburg, Germany; Barcelona, Spain; Waldkreiburg, Germany; Dallas, Texas; Lawrence, Kansas)

Collections:

Museum of Decorative Arts, Prague; Moravian Gallery, Brno, Czechoslovakia; Regional Gallery, Olomouc, Czechoslovakia; Muzeum Sztuki, Łódž, Poland; Museo Universitaria de Ciencias y Arte, Mexico City.

Publications:

By SVOBODA: Book—*Fotografie*, edited by Karel Srp, Prague 1980.

On SVOBODA: Books—*Československá Fotografie 1971/72*, exhibition catalogue, by Antonìn Dufek and Ludovit Hlavac, Brno, Czechoslovakia 1973; *O Janu Svobodovi, o fotografii, o uměnì*, thesis, by Arnošt Nosek, Famu College of Photography, Prague 1981; *Jan Svoboda*, exhibition catalogue, with text by Antonìn Dufek, Prague 1982; *Černobílá fotografie*, by Antonín Dufek, Prague 1987; *Cesty československé fotografie* by Daniela Mrázková and Vladimír Remeš, Prague 1989; *Tschechoslowakische Fotografie der Gegenwart*, by Vladimír Birgus, Heidelberg 1990; *Jan Svoboda*, by Petr Balajka, Prague, 1991. **Articles**—"Maj" by Jiřì Šetlìk in *Vytvarná práce* (Prague), no. 12, 1964; "Ze sbìrek UPM" by Anna Fárová in *Československá fotografie* (Prague), no. 7, 1973; "Ztvurěci Jana Svobody" by Jaroslav Anděl in *Revue Fotografie* (Prague), no. 3, 1975; "Ztvurěci, dílny Jana Svobody" by Jan Křìž in *Československá fotografie* (Prague), no. 11, 1975; "Stul ve fotografiìch Jana Svobody" by Jan Křìž in *Revue Fotografie* (Prague), no. 1, 1978; "Jan Svoboda," interview, by Liba Taylor in *British Journal of Photography* (London), 18 June 1982; "Form and Reality" by John Goto and Craigie Horsfeild in *Creative Camera* (London), December 1983; "Porovnáni" by Zdeněk Kirschner in *Revue Fotografie* (Prague), no. 1, 1984; "Rzeczy, jakimi sa?" by Jerzy Olek in *Projekt* (Warsaw), no. 6, 1985; "Soukromé krajiny Jana Svobody" by Antonìn Nový in *Československá fotografie* (Prague) no 10, 1986; "Svobodův pokus o dialog" by Ladislav Šolc in *Československá fotografie* (Prague) no 11, 1987; "Jan Svoboda" by Petr Balajka in *Revue Fotografie* (Prague) no 3, 1989; "Za Janem Svobodou" by Petr Balajka in *Československá fotografie* (Prague) no 8, 1990.

*

I believe that one day photography will be, among other things, a part of our culture and not something separate, something useless, stupid and empty. The fact is that a world which is running towards alienation doesn't interest me. Because the world of brutality is terrible for me.

What irritates me most is that I am represented as a minimalist. Minimalism which originated in America is something totally different. In Czech we say "less is more" and that's not minimalism. If a person photographs a nail on the wall which before had a picture hung on it—one asks whether the wall is more beautiful with the nail or without the nail, even with the photograph. But that's not a minimalistic photograph. In Czech *less is more*. That has nothing to do either with the History of Art or with fashion. Less is simply more. It's as if somebody wanted to compare a still life by Cezanne with a Baroque still life. So I am a minimalist! I am a terrible modernist! I am a complete idiot. I am either a traditional man or I am nothing at all! That's what I think.

—Jan Svoboda

*   *   *

Jan Svoboda said to me in an interview once that he wasn't a photographer, he was just a man who took photographs. He was right—not only was he self-taught which, in his native Czechoslovakia didn't provide him with good enough credentials to qualify as a professional, but he was also a person who abhorred conventions and his unorthodox photographs put him on the fringe of mainstream Czechoslovak photography.

For Svoboda photography was a way of expressing himself and not a mechanical means of making a living. He saw photography as an art form and he was deeply upset by the lack of respect, appreciation and the general devaluation of the craft of photography through mass accessibility.

Svoboda was born a rebel. As a child he showed considerable artistic talent, especially at drawing, and later worked as a painter of porcelain at the famous Carlsbad porcelain factory. But he was frustrated; the work was not creative enough and he wanted to study painting at an Art College in Prague.

But he never finished his studies because he did not find a teacher whom he could respect.

After working as a graphic designer in the advertising industry, he finally got a job as a professional photographer documenting the art collections in the Museum of Decorative Arts in Prague. Svoboda the photographer was at long last officially recognised and for him it was a dream come true—he could photograph the things he liked as a job. However, his enthusiasm was soon quashed by the realisation that his labour of love was not appreciated, his commitment to create images which would match the objects photographed in their artistic merit was wasted.

"My problem is that when I do something, I put everything into it. I enjoy it and at the same time I create a strange relationship within myself; it's almost a form of destruction. I can get so involved that I am not interested in anything else, I don't know anything else and in the end I don't get anything out of it. Those are the results of a determination which eventually reaches the point of collapse. And what for?"

That shocking experience made him realise that his only real security was his own creativity and the strange world of his own photographs.

Svoboda's earliest photographs date back to his early twenties when he considered becoming a poet and used photography to illustrate his poetry. That was the beginning of his exploration of the meditative aspects of photography which stayed with him for the rest of his life.

Svoboda's photography is a symbiosis of his interest in, and a thorough knowledge of, other art forms, and his friendship with sculptors and painters from the artistic group MAJ of which he was also a member and with whom he first exhibited in 1964.

The influence of Josef Sudek, the great Master of Czech photography, on Jan Svoboda, was enormous. They met in 1957, and it was not just the beauty of Sudek's photogaphs which fascinated Svoboda, but his entire personality as well—his culture, his sensitivity, his big heart. Foreign influences on Svoboda's work were minimal, mainly because of the difficulties in having access to the work of artists and photographers outside the eastern bloc. His work originates from the intimate knowledge of the familiar, the things he lived with. His old love of poetry reflects in his photographs—they are meditative, gentle, quiet. They show an obsessive involvement with the subject of his enquiry—his inner relationship with the outside world, his confrontation with the world of everyday reality, materialism and conventions that emphasise basic values such as simplicity, modesty and humility.

Svoboda's photographic series move from the exploration of the subjective to the more general aspects of photography such as the problem of composition, light and the two-dimensional space of his pictures. He developed photographic techniques to complement his vision—the pictures are soft and grey rather than traditionally black and white. Some of his photographs were enlarged to attain a sense of monumentality. Svoboda destroyed many of his negatives during his lifetime.

Jan Svoboda's work is quite unique in the history of Czechoslovak photography, in his honest testimony of the complexity of twentieth century man dealing with philosophical problems, in its immense contribution to contemporary visual arts. His work can be regarded as one of the major contributions to modern Czechoslovak art history.

—Liba Taylor

ŠVOLÍK, Miro.

Nationality: Czechoslovakian. **Born:** in Zlaté Moravce, Czechoslovakia, 13 April 1960. **Education:** Studied commercial photography at the Secondary School of Applied Arts in Bratislava, 1975-79, and art photography at FAMU film school in Prague, 1981-87. **Family:** Married Alexandra, 19 May 1990; children: Tereza and Oliver. **Career:** Artist in residence in Newcastle-upon-Tyne, 1991; taught photography at Folkhojeskole, Samso, Denmark, in 1992, and at the Prague House of Photography, in 1993. **Agent:** Darek Votruba, Nox Agency, Na Vypichu 6, 169 Praha 6, Czech Republic. **Address:** Chvalova 9, 13000 Praha 3—Zizkov, Czech Republic.

Individual Exhibitions:

1984	FAMU, Praha, Czechoslovakia
1985	Arhiv Toso Dabac, Zagreb
1986	Galerija Fotografija, Split
1988	Mala Fotografska Galerija, Ljubljana
1989	Fotografie Forum, Frankfurt am Main
	Robert Koch Gallery, San Francisco
1990	Dum Kultury, Plzen, Czech Republic
	Liget Galeria, Budapest
1991	Galerie 4, Cheb
	Stuart Levy Gallery, New York
	Zone Gallery, Newcastle-upon-Tyne, UK
1992	Focal Point, Southend-on-Sea, UK
	Untitled Gallery, Sheffield, UK
	Photofusion, London
	Portfolio, Edinburgh, Scotland
	Open Eye, Liverpool, UK
	Galerie Stara Ranice, Brno, Czech Republic
	Fotografisk Gallery, Copenhagen
	Mala Galerie Sporitelny, Kladno, Czech Republic
	Occurrence Gallery, Montreal, Quebec, Canada
1993	Palais Montcalm, Quebec, Canada
1994	Mestske Divadlo, Kolin, Czech Republic

Selected Group Exhibitions:

1985	*27 Contemporary Czechoslovak Photographers,* London
1986	*Fotografie z Prahy,* Bratislava, Czechoslovakia
1988	*Questioning Europe,* Rotterdam, Netherlands
1989	*First Internationale Foto Triennale,* Esslingen, Germany
1991	*Fotobiennale,* Enschede, Netherlands
1993	*Preview (Marzee),* Nijmegen, Netherlands

Collections:

Umélecko, Průmyslové Muzeum, Praha, Czech Republic; Severoceske Muzeum, Liberec; Moravská Galerie, Brno; Slovenska Narodna Galeria, Bratislava, Slovakia; Museum of Modern Art, New York; Artotheque de Saint-Fons, France.

Publications:

On ŠVOLÍK: Book—*Miro Švolík—One Body, One Soul,* Bratislava 1992.

*

I take only portrait photographs. Under each photograph I write a caption to give the photograph some further dimension. I then put them together into small series (approximately six to ten), so that each one, as a link in the series, is enhanced by other expressive possibilities. Furthermore, I am attempting to demonstrate through these series of photographs a new and creative form. Through my photographs, I believe I am able, precisely and frankly, to express my inner mood and feelings.

—Miro Švolík

SWARUP, Manish.

Nationality: Indian. **Born:** Bhopal, Madhya Pradesh, India, 28 April 1968. **Education:** Obtained University Degree in Economics and Commerce, 1989; mainly self-taught in photography, with help from T. Kashinath and S. Rajan. **Family:** Married Aasha Gulrajani on 24 October 1993. **Career:** Started work as a freelance news photographer in 1986, joined *The Sunday Mail* (India) as staff photographer in 1989; moved to *The Pioneer* as staff photographer in 1991, becoming Senior photographer, June 1994. Major assignments include

Neither Fish nor Fowl, **1992.** Photograph ©Miro Švolík.

Dreams in Debris, **May 1993.** Photograph by Manish Swarup.

coverage of the Ayodha riots, 1990, Rajiv Gandhi's funeral, 1991 and a photographic tour of Punjab for a book project for Contemporary Photographers' Forum, 1994. **Address:** DII/310, Vinay Marg, Chanakya Puri, New Delhi, 110021, India.

Selected Group Exhibitions:

1991   *Rajiv Gandhi,* Aifacs Hall, New Delhi
1992   *The Best of Pioneer,* Hotel Maurya Sheraton, New Delhi

Publications:

On SWARUP: Article—Interview with Raghu Rai in *Hindustan Time,* February 1993.

*

Most of my better photographs focus on persons reacting in extreme situations, such as fire, riots, or picking up the frame from day to day life, especially capturing emotions on bromide. My other preference is portraiture, be it of a politician or a model. Children play a very important role in my photography, and I love shooting them.

In several assignments I have also explored the mysteries of contrasts, be it in nature or general news photography.

—Manish Swarup

SYKES, Homer.

Nationality: Canadian. **Born:** Vancouver, 11 January 1949. **Education:** Sidcot School, Somerset, England, 1960-68; studied at the London College of Printing, 1969-71. **Family:** Married Juliet Watson in 1974; children: Theo, Jacob and Tallulah. **Career:** Freelance photographer since 1971, major editorial assignments for *The Sunday Times Magazine,* London; *The Observer Magazine,* London; *Merian Magazine,* Hamburg; *Geo Magazine,* Hamburg; *Globo Magazine,* Munich; *Newsweek Magazine,* New York; *GQ Magazine,* Tokyo. **Recipient:** Deadline Award, Society of Professional Journalists, New York, 1985. **Agents:** Network Photographers Ltd., 3-4 Kirby Street, London EC1, England. **Address:** 19 Kenilworth Avenue, London SW19 7LN, England.

Party, South London, **1983.** Photograph by Homer Sykes.

Individual Exhibitions:

1977   *Traditional British Calendar Customs,* Arnolfini Gallery,
        Bristol (toured the U.K.)
1986   *The English Season,* South Bank Gallery, London

Selected Group Exhibitions:

1970   *Personal Views 1850-1970,* British Council, London (toured
        Europe)
1972   *Young British Photographers,* Museum of Modern Art, Oxford
1976   *Rencontres Internationales de la Photographie,* Arles, France
1978   *Reportage Fotografen,* Museum des 20. Jahrhunderts, Vienna
        (travelled to Forum Stadtpark, Graz, Austria)
1985   *A British Eye on the World,* Museum of Modern Art, Rio de
        Janeiro

Collections:

Arts Council of Great Britain, London; Keflex Collection, London.

Publications:

By SYKES: Books—*Facts about a Pop Group,* with text by Dave Gelly,
London 1976; *Once a Year: Some Traditional Country Customs,* London
1977; *The English Season,* with text by Godfrey Smith, London 1986; *The
Best of British* (a 24-page colour supplement) published by The Menswear
Association of Great Britain, 1988; *The Village Pub,* with Roger Protz,

London 1992; *Mysterious Britain—Fact and Folklore,* London 1993; *The
Great Stones of England,* London 1994; *The Storm is Passing Over,* with Roy
Kerridge, London 1995.

On SYKES: Books—*Creative Camera International Yearbook,* edited by
Colin Osman and Peter Turner, London 1975; *British Image 1,* London 1975;
Special Effects in Photography by Robert Haas, London 1985; *Me and My
Camera* by Joe Partridge, London, 1985. **Articles**—"Homer Sykes" by Peter
Turner in *Creative Camera* (London), December 1971; "Pictures of Ameri-
ca" by David Litchfield in *The Image* (London), no. 3, 1972; "Photographs by
Homer Sykes" by Peter Turner in *Creative Camera* (London), March 1974;
"Homer Sykes: Special Occasions" in *London Magazine,* April 1977; "Une
Fois l'An, Quelques Coutumes Britanniques" in *Zoom* (Paris), December
1977; "Our Violent Society" by George Hughes in *Amateur Photographer*
(London), May 1978; "Homer Sykes: Law and Order" in *London Magazine,*
August 1978; "Fotograficke Svedectvi Homera Sykese" in *Revue Fotografie*
(Prague), no. 2, 1979; "Homer Sykes" in *British Journal of Photography*
(London), 15 March 1985. **Film**—*Me and My Camera,* Yorkshire Television
film, 1985; "Homer Sykes: What Is He Doing Now?," by Kate Salway in
British Journal of Photography, March 1985; "Wasps in the Pimms" by John
Morrison in *Photography,* London, August 1987; "Homer Sykes: Een
Luchthartig Vleugje England" by Ellen Kok in *Focus,* Amsterdam, January,
1988; "Tips from the Top—Homer Sykes," in *Amateur Photographer,*
January, 1994; "The Pro Approach—Homer Sykes" in *Photo Answers
Magazine,* August, 1994.

*

What I enjoy most about photography is learning, understanding and meeting people on their territory, seeing how they live, love and cope with life, and then trying to convert what I have learnt and know into a picture or set of pictures that captures the spirit of this mini adventure. Having said that, in my book *Mysterious Britain—Fact and Folklore* there are no photographs of people. I got enormous pleasure working on this project, watching and waiting for those elusive magic moments when the light was just so, turning what could be considered ordinary into the extraordinary. Finally, to have control of the work, so when it is published it is true to my truth and concept, in a form that I am proud of. This makes all the effort worthwhile, and this is the impetus to move on and forward to perhaps the next adventure.

—Homer Sykes

*   *   *

Homer Sykes' particular interest is centred on Britain, its people and its places. He first came to be widely known with the publication of *Once a Year— Some Traditional Country Customs,* in 1977. Here he explored the various events and happenings that take place regularly each year in different parts of the country. Some of them date from pre-Christian times but many were revived or invented by the Victorians. While he was working on these he felt that many of them would die out, but as time has passed and we become increasingly a tourist-seeking society, it seems more likely that they will increase and communities seek out new "old" customs to revive. His next major book dealt with high society and their traditional customs in *The English Season,* and this also marked a move to colour photography.

Sykes' photographs can be quite complex in construction and contain a great deal of information. He does like to get close to his subjects and though there is humour it is never cruel or mocking. He is not a believer in aggressive use of flash in daylight and works with the people he is photographing rather than as an outsider. In later books he has described particular areas of British life but also in *Mysterious Britain—Fact and Folklore,* those parts of the island that are linked with the past through myths and legends as well as religion. This and *The Great Stones,* do not involve people directly but their absence and contribution to the landscape is clearly felt. In his latest book he explores another aspect of life in Britain through the congregations of four black community churches, two with mainly West Indian congregations and two for the Nigerian-British community.

This thread of exploring British life is a continuing passion and each project necessarily takes a considerable time to complete. While this personal work progresses Homer Sykes undertakes assignments, mainly editorial, for many magazines and for the occasional advertising or corporate client. He is an excellent example of the best of free-lance photographers, having the skill to take on a wide variety of work and an abiding love of photography which enables him to continue to research and produce his valuable record of life in Britain.

—Sue Davies

SZABO, Stephen (Lee).

Nationality: American. **Born:** Berwick, Pennsylvania, 17 July 1940. **Education:** Studied at Pennsylvania State University, University Park, 1958-62; Art Center School of Design, Philadelpia, 1964-66. **Military Service:** Served in the United States Army, 1963: Private. **Career:** Staff Photographer, *Virgin Island Times* newspaper, U.S. Virgin Islands, 1963-64; and *The Washington Post* newspaper, Washington, D.C., 1966-71. Freelance photographer, Washington, D.C., since 1971. Instructor in photography, Corcoran School of Art, Washington, D.C., since 1979. **Recipient:** World Press Photography Award, The Hague, 1968; White House News Photographer Award, Washington, D.C., 1968, 1969, 1970, 1971. Fellowship Grant, National Endowment for the Arts, 1986. **Agent:** Kathleen Ewing Gallery, 1609 Connecticut Avenue, Washington, D.C., 20009, U.S.A. **Address:** 3615 Ordway Street N.W., Washington, D.C. 20016, U.S.A.

Individual Exhibitions:

1973	Phillips Collection, Washington, D.C.
1976	Afterimage Gallery, Dallas
	University of Kansas, Lawrence
1977	Gallery of Photographic Art, North Olmsted, Ohio
	Springfield Art Museum, Missouri
	Fisher Gallery, Nantucket, Massachusetts
	Silver Fantasy Gallery, Camden, Maine
	Hunter Museum of Art, Chattanooga, Tennessee
	International Center of Photography, New York
	Fine Arts Museum of the South, Mobile, Alabama
	Academy of the Arts, Easton, Maryland
	Baltimore Museum of Art
1978	Focus Gallery, San Francisco
	Kathleen Ewing Gallery, Washington, D.C.
1979	Madison Art Center, Wisconsin
1980	*3 Washington Photographers,* Kathleen Ewing Gallery, Washington, D.C.
1981	Atelier Galerie, Aix-en-Provence, France
	Steve Szabo: Urban Landscapes, at *Rencontres Internationales de la Photographie,* Arles, France
	Contrasts Gallery, London (with Mark Power)
1982	The Mariners' Museum, Newport News, Virginia
1986	Kathleen Ewing Gallery, Washington, D.C.
1991	Kathleen Ewing Gallery, Washington, D.C.
1995	Sheldon Memorial Art Gallery, Lincoln, Nebraska

Selected Group Exhibitions:

1972	*Washington Photographers,* University of Maryland, College Park
1979	*The Contemporary Platinotype,* Rochester Institute of Technology, New York
	Auto as Icon, International Museum of Photography, George Eastman House, Rochester, New York
1980	*Non-Silver and Hand-Made Photographs,* Kathleen Ewing Gallery, Washington, D.C.
1981	*Portrait d'Arbes,* Centre Culturel de Boulogne, Paris, France
	Acquisitions 1973-80, International Museum of photography at George Eastman House, Rochester, New York
1982	*Environnement Urbain,* Charleroi, France
	Washington Photography: Images of the Eighties, Corcoran Gallery of Art, Washington, D.C. (travelling)
1983	*Hommage a la Terre Natale,* Hungarian National Museum, Budapest
	L'architecture: Sujet, Objet ou Pretexte?, travelling exhibition, Agen, Bayonne and Bordeaux, France
1985	*The Washington Show,* Corcoran Gallery of Art, Washington, D.C.
	The First Nine Years, Kathleen Ewing Gallery, Washington, D.C.
1986	*A Breath of Light—The Contemporary Platinum Print,* New Jersey State Museum, Trenton (travelling)

Collections:

Museum of Modern Art, New York; International Center of Photography, New York; International Museum of Photography, George Eastman House, Rochester, New York; Library of Congress, Washington, D.C.; Corcoran Gallery of Art, Washington, D.C.; Exchange National Bank, Chicago; Sheldon Memorial Art Gallery, University of Nebraska, Lincoln; Fine Arts Museum of the South, Mobile, Alabama; High Museum, Atlanta, Georgia; Bibliothèque Nationale, Paris; Madison Art Center, Madison, Wisconsin; National Museum of American Art, Washington, D.C.; Sheldon Memorial Art Gallery, Lincoln, Nebraska; Canadian Centre for Architecture, Montreal, Canada; Museum of Fine Art, Houston.

Arthur #13, October 6, 1990, 1:38 p.m., from the series *Icons of the Great Plains*. Photograph by Steve Szabo.

Publications:

By SZABO: Books—*Where We Live: Photographs of Housing in America Today,* Washington, D.C. 1973; *The Eastern Shore,* Danbury, New Hampshire 1976. **Article**—"Steve Szabo: An Interview" by Melissa Shook in *Photograph* (New York), April 1978.

On SZABO: Books—The Platinum Print by John Hafey and Tom Shillea, with an introduction by Marianne Fulton Margolis, Rochester, New York 1979; *Acquisitions 1973-1980, George Eastman House,* exhibition catalogue, by Robert A. Sobieszek, Marianne Fulton and Philip Condax, Rochester, New York 1981. **Articles**—"Taking Pictures" by Tom Zito in *Washington Post* (Washington, D.C.), April 1973; "Dialogue . . . Document the Past" in *Camera* (Lucerne), May 1976; "Photo Giant and Ascendant" by H. Cullinan in *Plain Dealer* (Cleveland), August 1977; "Photography Books" by Andy Grundberg in *Art in America* (New York), November 1977; "The Eastern Shore" in *Photo Revue* (Paris), November 1978; "Three Washington Photographers" in *American Photographer* (New York), November 1980; "Art Portfolio" by C. Wittenberg in the *Washington Revue* (Washington, D.C.), July 1980; "From LA to DC" by Marguerite Welch in *New Art Examiner,* June 1982; "Washington's Strongest" by John Brumfield in *Artweek,* July 2, 1983; "The Four Steve Szabo's," by Paul Richard in *The Washington Post,* 27 September 1990; "Booted Up" by Lee Fleming in *Museum & Arts Washington,* May/June 1991; "The Heart & Sole of the Great Plains" by Michael Welzenbach in *The Washington Post,* May 18, 1991; "Icons of the Great Plains" by Pat Kolmer in *Washington Review,* June/July 1991.

*   *   *

Steve Szabo started his career as a newspaper photographer in the fast moving, electric Washington scene. Considering that background, his current photography is all the more remarkable. Szabo is the master of the romantic landscape. His photographs are quiet, contemplative, classically composed, and very reminiscent of the work of some late 19th century English and American landscape photographers.

The principal subject of Szabo's work is Maryland and especially the world of the watermen along Chesapeake Bay. Szabo does not photograph the people directly nor does he photograph any contemporary 20th century scenes. Instead, he captures old skipjack sailboats lying on the mudbanks and in salt marshes, empty houses hidden in among burgeoning foliage, abandoned cars settling back into the earth, and silent rocking chairs. Szabo's world is arcadian and pastoral.

The absence of people is deliberate. This region was once a land of small salt water farms and crab and oyster fishermen. The small farms were uneconomical, and the oyster beds gave out. The artifacts of this culture are returning to nature. They have the same fascination for Szabo that crumbling abbeys had for 18th and 19th century Englishmen. In Szabo's photos we always expect nymphs and shepherds to gambol from off camera across the scene. The works of man are dead but haunted with rich memories. Nature is alive and filled with a presence encroaching on the mouldering remnants of man's past.

Most of Szabo's current work is printed on platinum paper. Many contemporary photographers have experimented with platinum paper, but few have mastered it. Szabo is perhaps the best of all. The difficulties are formidable: since platinum paper is no longer commercially available, the photographer must make his own. Since the only practical way to use it is by contact printing, the photographer must use a large format camera. Szabo uses 4 x 5 and 8 x 10 view cameras. Since platinum paper requires a very contrasty negative, the photographer must expose and develop with platinum especially in mind.

Even more difficult for most photographers is using platinum paper in a way that justifies its nuisance and expense. Platinum paper has a very low range of brillancy but a very long and subtle range of tones. The blackest black is a deep brown. The whitest white is a pale gold. But within those limits it beautifully delineates the slightest variation in tone.

Szabo makes excellent use of this tonal richness, and the warm golden tone of the paper is especially suitable to his arcadian vision. The pale gold highlights evoke the warm hazy skies of Chesapeake Bay. The soft brown shadows arouse a remembrance of things past.

Steve Szabo is a regional photographer who has made a universal statement that transcends geography to depict a dream of a pastoral golden age common to all men.

—Mike Rowell

SZÉKESSY, Karin.

Nationality: German. **Born:** Essen, 17 April 1939. **Education:** Attended a school in Hertfordshire, England, until 1957; studied, under Hans Schreiner, at the Institut für Photojournalismus, Munich, 1957-59. **Family:** Married the painter Paul Wunderlich in 1972; children: Oliver, Natascha and Laura. **Career:** Photojournalist, *Kristall* magazine, Hamburg, 1963-66; Instructor in Photography, Art Academy, Hamburg, 1967-70. Freelance photographer, Hamburg, since 1970: established studio, 1974. Member, Gesellschaft Deutsche Lichtbildner (GDL), 1970-77, and since 1979. **Recipient:** Special Prize, *Triennale of Photography,* Fribourg, Switzerland, 1977; Kodak Prize, 1976, 1978, 1979, 1984, 1985. **Agents:** PPS Photo Gallery, 1 Feldstrasse, 2000 Hamburg 4; and Redfern Gallery, 20 Cork Street, London W1, England. **Address:** Haynstrasse 2, 20249 Hamburg 20, Germany.

Individual Exhibitions:

1966	Landesbildstelle, Hamburg
1968	Galerie Brusberg, Hannover (with Paul Wunderlich)
1969	Städtische Kunsthalle, Recklinghausen, West Germany (with Paul Wunderlich)
	Städtische Galerie, Oberhausen, West Germany
	Phoenix Gallery, Berkeley, California
	Kunst und Photographie, Stadtmuseum, Munich
1971	Galerie Niedlich, Stuttgart
1972	Canon Photo Gallery, Amsterdam
1973	*Art as Photography,* Städtische Kunsthalle, Recklinghausen, West Germany
1974	Galleri 1 + 1, Helsingborg, Sweden
1975	Galerie Levy, Hamburg
	American Associated Artists, New York
	Redfern Gallery, London
1976	Watari Gallery, Tokyo
	Staempfli Gallery, New York
	Kunsthalle, Kiel, West Germany
1977	Galerie Levy, Hamburg
	Galerie Kunze, West Berlin
	Yamaki Gallery, Osaka, Japan
1979	Huntley Gallery, Canberra, Australia
	Watari Gallery, Tokyo
1980	Goethe Institut, Brussels
	Junge Galerie, Cologne
1981	Galerie Negru, Paris
1982	Benteler Galleries, Houston, Texas
	Redfern Gallery, London
1983	Galerie Photo-Art, Basle, Switzerland
	Galerie Nikon, Zurich
1984	Galerie Schaefer, Giessen, West Germany
1985	Galerie Pro Photo, Nuremberg, West Germany
	Goethe Institut, Copenhagen
	Galleri 1 + 1, Helsingborg, Sweden
1986	Museum of Tondern, Denmark
1987	Photomuseum, Bremen, Germany
1988	Redfern Gallery, London
1989	BAT Hamburg
1990	Ming Gallery, Tokyo

Simone, **1994.** Photograph ©Karin Székessy.

Selected Group Exhibitions:

1964   *The Painter and the Photograph: From Delacroix to Warhol,*
        University of New Mexico, Albuquerque
1966   *8 German Photographers,* Leningrad
1975   *Gesellschaft Deutscher Lichtbildner 1975,* Haus Industrieform,
        Essen, West Germany
1976   *8 German Photographers,* at *Photokina '76,* Cologne
1978   *2a. Triennale della Fotografia,* Musée d'Art et d'Historie,
        Fribourg, Switzerland
1979   *Deutsche Fotografie nach 1945,* Kunstverein, Kassel, West
        Germany (toured West Germany)
        Best Nudes, Witkin Gallery, New York
1984   *Sammlung Gruber,* Museum Ludwig, Cologne
1985   *Das Aktfoto,* Fotomuseum im Stadtmuseum, Munich (toured
        West Germany)
1993   Fotoforum, Frankfurt (took part in three shows)

Collections:

Staedel Museum, Frankfurt; Stadtmuseum, Munich; Kunsthalle, Kiel, Germany; Museum Folkwang, Essen; Bibliothèque Nationale, Paris; Musée des Beaux-Arts, Brussels; University of California at Berkeley; Museum Ludwig, Cologne; Museum für Kunst und Gewerbe, Hamburg; Fotografiska Museet, Stockholm; Schleswig Holstein Landsmuseum; Museum für Kunst und Gewerbe, Hamburg; Museum of Photography, Tokyo; Museum Ludwig, Cologne.

Publications:

By SZÉKESSY: Books—*Les Filles dans l'Atelier,* Paris 1969; *Correspondenzen/ Transpositions,* with Paul Wunderlich, Stuttgart and Zurich 1976, London 1980; *Pariser Zeichen,* introduced by Max Bense and Marie Cardinal, Stuttgart 1977; *Best Nudes,* with Irèna Ionesco, Tokyo 1979; *Madchen im Atelier,* with afterword by Max Bense, Dortmund, West Germany 1985; *Mädchen wie Stilleben,* Schaffhausen, 1990; *Sylt ein Inselleben,* with Wolfgang Klähn, Dortmund,1990.

On SZÉKESSY: Books—*The Painter and the Photograph: From Delacroix to Warhol* by Van Deren Coke, Albuquerque, New Mexico 1964, 1972; *Karin Székessy,* exhibition catalogue, by Fritz Kempe, Hamburg 1975; *Women on Women,* introduced by Katharine Holabird, London 1978; *Deutsche Fotografie nach 1945/German Photography After 1945* by Floris Neusüss, Wolfgang Kemp and Petra Benteler, Kassel, West Germany 1979; *Sammlung Gruber: Photographie des 20. Jahrhunderts,* exhibition catalogue, with foreword by Siegfried Gohr, Cologne 1984. **Article**—"Karin Székessy" in *Zoom* (Paris), June 1981. Calendar, Museum Ludwig Group of Photographers, 1994.

*

I leave it to others to speak or write. My small statement on my life—or, life in general—well, I try to do it with the lenses of my camera.

—Karin Székessy

*   *   *

A blonde from Essen who married Paul Wunderlich (the German artist whose visuals of fantasist contortions once brought him into trouble with the police, a brush with authority that failed to hinder his inclusion in the top ranks of his country's art hierarchy), Karin Székessy has discovered a way of coping with a family, acting as purveyor of inspirations that have sparked off some of her husband's finest works, besides gaining for herself a position amongst the world's foremost investigatory photographers.

Her purposeful and exploratory control of nude photography, either of a solitary figure, a couple, or a throng, has frequently helped the composition of Wunderlich's extraordinary paintings and, on more than one occasion, man and wife have combined, he to prompt her with the strangeness of his

imagination, she to carry out with personal contributions her own considerable craft as photographer.

Double images, focus manoeuvrability, introduction of fantasist and surrealist elements, together with point-of-impact figuration and an understanding she shares with her husband of the shock-sensation of realist/ figurative contortion, all reflect her powers as a camera artist.

The nude brunette, her arms languidly resting on the back of an easy chair, curves her haunches langourously towards camera, one leg extended over the chair's arm while, beside a massive Fernando Botero picture of a woman, a mysterious naked male stands tautly half hidden by the plump upholstery. This is nude photography beguiling for its composition and, because of its story-line, redolent with carnal quietus, magnetic and daunting.

But parallel with this eye-catching experimentation Székessy is also a straight verité-realist, capable of effecting the transition few can attain that transforms a "photo" into a meaningful and enduring "portrait" (creating records, psychologically sound, of such artists as Hans Bellmer, Richard Lindner, her husband Wunderlich of course, Hundertwasser, Jan Voss, Bernhardt Schültze, Jens Lausen and Johannes Grützke—pictures in which the subjects do not so much pose as comfortably fall into a personality attitude). She also has the Cartier-Bresson knack of replacing "reportage" with absolute moments of life—such as her "Woman with a Gold Tooth," "Lolitas 1964," "Alcohol" and "Morning at the Mainline Rail Terminus."

The vital and principal *rôle* that Karin Székessy has come to play in the development of modern photography lies in her rejuvenation of the "Lichtdruck," the Heliograph. In a determined effort to shrug off the familiar routines of photo-production, she made her way to a little workshop in Lübeck (which specialized in printing heliographic postcards) some two years after she had met her husband and he asked her if he could use one of her photographs as a "silent model." At Lübeck in 1967 she was able to do her printing only once— shortly before the workshop closed down—but the little studio taught her the heliograph techniques that have been the hallmark of so much of her work since then.

Of course the nudes (very successfully) invaded the sphere of what this half-forgotten but now-revived photographic system had to offer: one result, a collaboration with her husband, was the book *Correspondenzen* in 1976.

The special value of the heliographs is that in their final states (and they can end up in a series of different colour combinations), they have the finish of a "work of art" rather than that of a photograph. Even to the print connoisseur they possess the character of a mezzotint or a lithograph, or a mixture of both. (Photographer and printer work in close contact right the way through to production of the final state.)

However, it is in a recent venture, a haunting selection of heliographs of Paris for the volume *Pariser Zeichen,* which she calls "natures mortes," that Karin Székessy has one of her greatest triumphs. Direct pictures of a shuttered house in the rue Montbrun, an SNCF metal safe, the red-and-white notice on a red garage door advising constant use and forbidding parking, a grotesque double-snake doorknocker, a *trompe-l'oeil* perspective of marble tiling in different shades of blue—these images are simultaneously touching and magnificent.

—Sheldon Williams

SZILASI, Gabor.

Nationality: Canadian. **Born:** Budapest, Hungary, 3 February 1928; emigrated to Canada, 1957; naturalized, 1964. **Education:** Evangélikus Gimnázium, Budapest, until 1944; studied medicine, University of Budapest, 1945-47; photography, School of Modern Photography, Montreal, 1959-61; Thomas More Institute, Montreal, 1967. **Family:** Married Doreen Lindsay in 1962; daughter: Andrea. **Career:** Worked at various jobs in Budapest, 1949-57; Cartographer, Ministère des Terres et Fôrets, Quebec, 1957-59; Photographer, Office du Film du Québec, Montreal, 1959-71. Instructor in Photography, Collège du Vieux Montréal, 1971-79. Professor of Photography, 1979-84, and Chairman of the Department of Cinema and Photography since 1984, Concordia University, Montreal. **Recipient:** Canada Council Grant, 1970, 1973, 1976-77, 1986; Fellowship, Ministère des Affaires Culturelles du

Québec, Montreal, 1979. **Agent:** Art 45, 1460 Sherbrooke Street West, Montreal, Quebec H3G 1K4. **Address:** 483 Grosvenor Avenue, Montreal, Quebec H3Y 2S5, Canada.

Individual Exhibitions:

1967	Loyola Bonsecours Centre, Montreal
1970	*Charlevoix*, Studio 23, Montreal (travelled to Baldwin Street Gallery, Toronto, and Institute of Design, Illinois Institute of Technology, Chicago, 1971; National Film Board of Canada, Ottawa, 1972; and Gallery of Photography, Vancouver, 1973)
1974	*La Beauce*, McCord Museum, Montreal
1977	*Images du Québec*, National Film Board of Canada, Ottawa
1978	Yajima/Galerie, Montreal
1980	Musée d'Art Contemporain, Montreal
	The Photographers Gallery, Saskatoon, Saskatchewan
	Toronto Photographers Co-op at Harbourfront Gallery
	Images du Québec, Memorial University, St. John's, Newfoundland
1981	*Portraits/Interiors*, Art Gallery of Cobourg, Ontario
	Maritime Photographic Workshops, Fredericton, New Brunswick
1982	*Panoramas de Montréal*, Galerie Art 45, Montreal
1984	*Enseignes Lumineuses*, Galerie Art 45, Montreal
1985	*Charlevoix*, Musée Laure Conan, La Malbaie, Quebec
1986	*Colour Photographs 1978-85*, Toronto Image Works, Ontario

Selected Group Exhibitions:

1967	*Montréal Insolite*, Bibliothèque National du Québec, Montreal
1973	*Le Groupe d'Action Photographique*, Musée d'Art Contemporain, Montreal
1978	*Tusen och En Bild/1001 Pictures*, Moderna Museet, Stockholm
1980	*Aspects de la Photographie Québecoise Contemporaine*, Musée d'Art Contemporain, Montreal
	Environments, National Film Board of Canada, Ottawa
1981	*Points of View: Architectural Photographs*, Musée des Beaux-Arts, Montreal
	Photojournalism, National Film Board of Canada, Ottawa
1982	*Esthétiques actuelles de la photographie au Québec*, at *Rencontres Internationales de la Photographie*, Arles, France
1983	*Photographie actuelle au Québec*, Saydie Bronfman Centre, Montreal
1985	*Portraits*, Articule, Montreal

Collections:

Mount Allison University, Sackville, New Brunswick; McCord Museum, Montreal; Musée d'Art Contemporain, Montreal; Musée des Beaux-Arts de Montreal; The Art Bank, Canada Council, Ottawa; Public Archives of Canada, Ottawa; National Film Board of Canada, Ottawa; National Gallery of Canada, Ottawa; Edmonton Art Gallery, Alberta.

Publications:

By SZILASI: Article—"You Only Have to Look and See . . . " in *Foto-Canada* (Montreal), October/November 1967.

On SZILASI: Books—Keepsake: Selections from the Archives of a Photographic Project, *Alberta 1980*, Calgary, Alberta 1981; *Contemporary Canadian Photography* by Martha Langford, Edmonton, Alberta 1984; *A World History of Photography* by Naomi Rosenblum, New York 1985. **Articles**—"Gabor Szilasi Photographs Charlevoix Country" by Geoffrey James in *Vie des Arts* (Montreal), no. 62, 1971; "Gabor Szilasi" in *Camera* (Lucerne), August 1973; "Gabor Szilasi: Portraits de Beauce" in *Ovo* (Montreal), May 1974; "Responding to Photographs: A Canadian Portfolio" in *Artscanada* (Toronto), December 1974; "Gabor Szilasi: Photographies Récentes" by

Sandra Marchand in *Atelier* (Montreal), December 1979-March 1980; "L'Objectif Humain de Gabor Szilasi" in *Vie des Arts* (Montreal), no. 100, 1980; "Exhibitions: Gabor Szilasi" by Louise Abbott in *Artscanada* (Toronto), December 1980; "The Physiognomy of Building/Photography and Architecture" by Peter Wollheim in *Vanguard* (Vancouver), May 1981; "Petrobucks and Prairie Oysters" by Peter Wollheim in *Vanguard* (Vancouver), Summer 1981.

*

My three main interests in photography are people, interiors and architecture. The latter two are closely related to the first in that they are made by man to serve as space in which to live and work. For me to find the subject interesting to photograph, there has to be some trace of men present.

When I came to Quebec in 1957, I used a 35mm camera exclusively, working in a journalistic tradition. In the late sixties, I started using a 4 by 5 inch view camera and for nearly ten years visited the people of rural Quebec, documenting their lives, the interiors and the architecture.

I was much influenced by Paul Strand's *Tir a' Mhurain*, a book of photographs with text on the outer Hebrides. His carefully composed, clear, simple images impressed me for their honesty and straightforwardness in depicting the land and its people. I regard colour in a photograph as interesting if it surprises me. I find that in most cases the abstraction of black and white conveys aspects of the subject that are far more important than colour. In interiors, however, the colour provides an additional set of information that is absent in black and white. It may indicate individual tastes, cultural traits or social position. Colour composition has no interest for me. When photographing an interior with, for example, a great deal of orange in the lower left, if I were concerned with pictorial matters I would put, let's say, a complementary blue in the upper right. But I am not interested in formal colour composition. I respect the individual taste of someone who has spent a great deal of time arranging his or her room. I simply set up the camera and let the colours speak for themselves.

After having worked in the documentary mode for the last fifteen years or so, my interest in photography is shifting towards the exploration of a more personal world. I am now using the medium as a means of subjective expression.

—Gabor Szilasi

*   *   *

Gabor Szilasi is committed to making people aware of their environment. Relationships are his subject, either through portraits or through photographs of interiors—settings which, for Szilasi, mirror the soul. His vision is simple and straightforward. Curiosity has in his case become art.

"Portraits/Interiors" is Szilasi's major statement on the theme which preoccupies him. Begun in 1977, the series elaborately contrasts and juxtaposes black-and-white Roleiflex portraits of people who interest him with interiors shot in colour using a 4 x 5 view camera. The paired pictures complement each other—the portraits are flat; the interiors have great depth. The portraits require the viewer's concentration but reveal the psychological aspect of the subject. The furnished spaces add an unexpected dimension—not only the surface of the subject's life, but also their individual tastes, cultural traits and social position.

For Szilasi, certain furnished rooms reveal the folk artist in Everyman. Over the last ten years, he has documented life in rural Quebec. In his work in this area, he has used the scale of his sitter in his composition to define the physical space of the room. Even in empty rooms, the human presence is evident. His urban views of Montreal taken in 1981-82 with an 8 x 20 camera reveal the city as a setting for the individual, an outdoor echo of the subject he has always loved. In his most recent work Szilasi concentrates on intimate views of people and places all of which form part of a personal world.

—Joan Murray

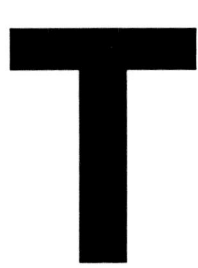

TABARD, Maurice.

Nationality: French. **Born:** Lyons, 12 July 1897. **Education:** Studied-violin, Lyons, 1903-13; studied fabric design in father's silk manufacturing plant, Lyons, until 1918; studied photography, under Emil Brunel, New York Institute of Photography, 1918; studied portraiture, under the painter Carlos Baca-Flor, in New York, 1927, in Paris, 1928. **Career:** Worked as silk fabric designer, Lyons, 1914-18; delivery boy for Shoe Craft Company, New York 1918-20; Assistant Photographer, Bachrach Studio (New York), working in Baltimore, Cincinnati and Washington, D.C., 1922-28; freelance magazine, fashion, advertising and portrait photographer, working for *Jardin des Modes, Vu, Bifur, Art et Decoration, Arts et Metiers Graphiques,* etc., Paris, 1928-38; organized photo studio for advertising, Deberny-Peignot publishers, Paris, 1930-31; darkroom man for Pathó Films, Paris, 1932; still photographer and motion picture photographer for Gaumont Films, Paris, 1936; filmed news-*cum*-propaganda films for the French Government, 1936; freelance photographer in south of France, 1939-45; Staff Photographer, *Harper's Bazaar,* under editor Carmel Snow, travelling to England and Scotland, 1946-48, in America, under Alexey Brodovitch, 1948-50; worked for Paul Linwood Gittings Studio, New York, 1948-49, 1968; freelance photographer, working for *Femina, Elle, Album du Figaro, Silhouette, Marie-Claire, Paris-Match,* etc., 1948-65 (returning to Paris, 1950); Instructor of Photography, Winona School for Professional Photographers, Indiana, 1950; gradually gave up photography and retired, living in Paris, 1965-80, and in Nice, France, 1980-84. **Died:** (in Nice) 23 February 1984.

Individual Exhibitions:

1933	Galerie de la Pléiade, Paris
1948	Professional Photographers Association of America, Chicago
1976	Marlborough Gallery, New York
1977	Sander Gallery, Washington, D.C.
1978	Salon International de la Photographie, Porte Versailles, Paris
1979	Institut Français, Cologne
1981	Sander Gallery, Washington, D.C.
1984	Galerie Marion Meyer, Paris
	Galerie Wilde, Cologne
1985	Sammlung Fotografis Landerbank, Vienna
1990	Musée Municipale, Paris

Selected Group Exhibitions:

1929	*Film und Foto,* Deutscher Werkbund, Stuttgart
1931	*Annual Exhibition of Photographs,* Galerie de la Pléiade, Paris (and annually until 1934)
1932	*Modern European Photography,* Julien Levy Gallery, New York
1936	*Exposition Internationale de la Photographie Contemporaine,* Musée des Arts, Decoratifs, Paris
1957	*Salon National de la Photographie,* Bibliothèque Nationale, Paris
1976	*Photographs from the Julien Levy Collection, Starting with Atget,* Art Institute of Chicago
1979	*Photographic Surrealism,* New Gallery of Contemporary Art, Cleveland (travelled to the Dayton Art Institute, Ohio, and the Brooklyn Museum, New York)
1983	*Fotogramme—die lichtreichen Schatten,* Fotomuseum im Stadtmuseum, Munich
1985	*L'Amour Fou: Photography and Surrealism,* Corcoran Gallery, Washington, D.C. (travelled to San Francisco Museum of Modern Art; Centre Georges Pompidou, Paris; Hayward Gallery, London)
1987	*The Implicit Image,* San Francisco Museum of Modern Art

Collections:

Condé Nast Publications, Paris; Bibliothèque Nationale, Paris; Museum Folkwang, Essen; Fashion Institute of Technolgoy, New York; International Museum of Photography, George Eastman House, Rochester, New York; Art Institute of Chicago; St. Louis Art Institute; New Orleans Museum of Art; San Francisco Museum of Modern Art; J. Paul Getty Museum, Malibu, California; Sammlung Fotografis Landerbank, Vienna.

Publications:

By TABARD: Article—"Notes on Solarization" in *Arts et Metiers Graphiques* (Paris), 1933.

On TABARD: Books—*Foto-Auge/Oeil et photo/Photo-Eye: 76 Fotos der Zeit,* edited by Franz Roh and Jan Tschichold, Stuttgart 1929, London 1974; *Photographs from the Julien Levy Collection, Starting with Atget,* exhibition catalogue, by David Travis, Chicago 1976; *Fotografie der 30er Jahre: Eine Anthologie* by Hans Jürgen Syberberg, Munich 1977; *Paris-Berlin 1900-1933,* exhibition catalogue, by H. Molderings, W. Spies, G. Metken and others, Paris 1978; *Paris-Moscou 1900-1930,* exhibition catalogue, by Romeo Martinez, A.N. Lavrentiev and others, Paris 1979; *Photographen der 20er Jahre* by Karl Steinorth, Munich 1979; *Film und Foto der 20er Jahre,* exhibition catalogue, by Ute Eskildsen and Jan Christopher Horak, Stuttgart 1979; *The History of Fashion Photography* by Nancy Hall-Duncan, New York and Paris 1979; *Photographic Surrealism,* exhibition catalogue, by Nancy Hall-Duncan, Cleveland 1979; *Fotogramme—die lichtreichen Schatten,* exhibition catalogue, by Floris M. Neususs, Kassel, West Germany 1983; *L'Amour Fou: Photography and Surrealism* by Rosalind Krauss and Jane Livingston, Washington, D.C. and New York 1985; *Maurice Tabard 1897-1984,* exhibition catalogue, Vienna 1985; *Maurice Tabard,* Paris 1987. **Articles**—"Maurice Tabard" in *L'Art Vivant* (Paris), January 1930; "Focus Your Brain First: The Story of Maurice Tabard of Paris" by Paul Linwood Gittings in *PSA Journal* (New York), vol. 14, 1948; "Tabard" in *Modern Photography* (New York), January 1950; "Tabard" in *Photo* (Paris), June 1976; "Camera Eye" by Allan Porter and "The International Werkbund Exhibition Film und Foto Stuttgart 1929" by Karl Steinorth in *Camera* (Lucerne), October 1979.

* * *

A warm, friendly man with merry, sparkling eyes opened the iron door to a darkly situated room facing the street in a quiet and elegant residential district of the 16th quarter of Paris. We found ourselves in a makeshift workroom, not particularly comfortable—actually rather damp and repelling—which was, nevertheless, the latest refuge of the photographer Maurice Tabard. He appeared to be pleased that I was repaying his 1974 visit to me, and he was happy to be able to show me a portfolio of photographs spanning his long career in photography.

I had many questions about that highly celebrated "golden age" of the 1920s and 1930s. At that time Tabard had been acquainted with almost all of his colleagues—those who in the meantime have taken their places in the history of photography and whose works have been extensively exhibited and published. (To date, Tabard has had no book published on or about his work. On the one hand he regretted this, but on the other excused it on the basis of his restlessness and the new interests that he was constantly pursuing.) Tabard maintained close contact with very few of his colleagues; most of the time they met one another at exhibition openings at the Galerie de la Pléiade, Galerie de la Plume d'Or or the Galerie d'Art Contemporain, where almost everyone who worked for the important magazines of the era had several pictures. Everything that was exhibited and offered for sale in a gallery was signed by its creator—in Paris it would have been unthinkable to do otherwise. Yet very few photographs were sold: photography had not yet found recognition as an art form. To live in Paris then was expensive, as it is at any time, and one had to earn money somehow. Tabard worked for various advertising studios and magazines. Of particular interst to him were unique lines of automobiles, and he succeeded in producing impressive photographs by using exaggerated perspectives—that is, when he was given complete freedom to do as he wished.

Toward the end of the 1920s Tabard experimented with double exposure: usually he used two negatives which he continued to slide around against one another until the arrangement of the individual parts confirmed his mental image of what the whole picture should be. He produced not only highly interesting portrait and life studies, but also pictures of objects which could be classified as within the realm of Surrealism. Tabard had a fine sense for nuance in his compositions, in the various superimposed layers. The attraction of these works lies particularly in the possibility of multiple meanings and symbolic relationships between persons and situations. Alienation of reality by means of printing various negatives one on top of the other to photomontage or to the photogram was only a small step. Even if some of his photographs produce the effect of montage because of their geometric abstraction, the few preserved photomontages are more expressive and more advanced in their symbolic functioning than similar works of the time. Indeed, Tabard succeeded in expanding the boundaries of the photographic medium through the diversity of his experimentation. He constantly astonished visitors to the numerous exhibitions of the time with his newest work.

Unfortunately, most of his work, including his entire negative archive, was lost during the war, and Tabard has hardly been given the place in the history of photography which he has earned. Until now, one has looked in vain for his name in the well-known works on the history of photography.

—Juřgen Wilde

TAHARA, Keiichi.

Nationality: Japanese. **Born:** Kyoto, Japan, 21 August 1951. **Education:** Attended high school, Osaka, Japan, 1968-70; self-taught in photography, but influenced by his grandfather, the photographer Yoshitaro Miyagawa. **Career:** Lighting designer and photographer, Red Buddha theatrical group, throughout Europe, 1971-72. Freelance photographer, Paris, since 1972. **Recipient:** Young Photographer Prize, Rencontres Internationales de la Photographie, Arles, France, 1977; Kodak Prize, France, 1978. **Agents:** UNAC, 112-1-1-20 Azabudai Minato-ku, Tokyo, Japan; Marcuse Pfeifer Gallery, 568 Broadway, Suite 102, New York, New York 10012, U.S.A. **Address:** 21 avenue Alphand, 94160 St. Mandé, France.

Individual Exhibitions:

1975   *Environment,* Canon Photo Gallery, Amsterdam (travelled to Galleria II Diaframma, Milan, and La Photogalerie, Paris, 1975; and Galleria Nadar, Pisa, Italy, 1976)

1978   *Window,* UNAC, Tokyo (travelled to Iida Gallery Annexe, Tokyo, and Bibliothèque Nationale, Paris, 1978; Galerie Pennings, Eindhoven, Netherlands, 1979; and Marcuse Pfeifer Gallery, New York, 1980)

Selected Group Exhibitions:

1974   *Sur la Ville,* Bibliothèque Nationale, Paris *Festival of Royan,* France

1977   *Tendences Actuelles de la Photographie en France,* Musée d'Art Moderne de la Ville (ARC 2), Paris

        The Naked Environment, Salzburg College, Austria (toured Italy)

1979   *Les 3 Lauréats du Prix Kodak,* Centre Kodak, Paris

        Japanese Photography Today and Its Origin, Galleria d'Arte Moderna, Bologna (travelled to the Palazzo Reale, Milan; Palais des Beaux-Arts, Brussels; Institute of Contemporary Arts, London; Museum für Kunst und Gewerbe, Hamburg; Gemeente Museum, Arnhem; Pulchri Studio, The Hague)

1980   *7 European Photographers,* University of Oklahoma, Norman

        Transparency, Galerie Viviane Esders-Rudzinoff, Paris

1981   *Des Photographies dans le Paysage,* Galerie de France, Paris

1984   *La Photographie Créative,* Pavillon des Arts, Paris

Collections:

Bibliothèque Nationale, Paris; Musée Réattu, Arles, France; Asahi Pentax Gallery, Tokyo; Nikon Salon, Tokyo; University of Oklahoma, Norman.

Publications:

By TAHARA: Book—*Keiichi Tahara 1973-1983,* with text by Bernard Lamarche-Vadel, Tokyo 1984. Articles—"Windows" in *Clef* (Paris), no. 2, 1978; "Keiichi Tahara," with Jean-Claude Lemagny, in *Asahi Camera* (Tokyo), August 1978.

On TAHARA: Books—Tendances Actuelles de la Photographie en France, with text by Michel Nuridsany, Paris 1978; *Transparences: Photographies,* exhibition catalogue, with text by Gilbert Lascault, Paris 1980; *De Japanse Fotografie van 1848 tot Heden,* exhibition catalogue, by Attilio Colombo and Isabella Doniselli, Amsterdam 1980; *La Photographie Créative* by Jean-Claude Lemagny, Paris 1984. Articles—"Keiichi Tahara: Environment" in *Nouveau Photocinema* (Paris), no. 29, 1974; "Keiichi Tahara" by Roberto Salbitani in *Progresso Fotografico* (Milan), no. 82, 1975; "Keiichi Tahara" by Julia Scully in *Modern Photography* (New York), March 1976; "Keiichi Tahara: Environment" in *Creative Camera* (London), no. 152, 1977; "Discoveries: Keiichi Tahara" in *Time-Life Photography Year,* New York 1978; "Keiichi Tahara: Fenêtre" in *Zoom* (Paris), no. 53, 1978; "Keiichi Tahara: Window" by Seigo Matsuoka in *Camera Mainichi* (Tokyo), April and June 1978; "Keiichi Tahara: Environment" in *Yu* (Tokyo), no. 1002, 1978; "Keiichi Tahara: Window" by Naomi Yanagimoto in *Bijutsu Techo* (Tokyo), August 1978; "Keiichi Tahara" in *Pentax Photography* (Paris), March 1979; "Keiichi Tahara: Window" in *L'Album Photographie I,* Paris 1979; "K. Tahara: Windows" by Emès Manuel de Matos in *Alternes* (Paris), no. 1, 1980; "Keiichi Tahara" by Julia Scully in *Modern Photography* (New York), July 1980.

*

When I arrived in Europe, I noticed a great strength in the energy of light which I had never previously experienced. This archetypal image is, in fact, caused by the harsh and cavernous blackish blue sky, pierced by the light which illuminates buildings aligned like walls under this sky as well as by the charm of the very sharp contrast between light and shade. The violence of the light, particularly at sun set, was so keen that I had the illusion that the molecules of light possessed a formidable destructive power attacking all existing forms and colours and reducing the world to black and white.

Perhaps because my astonishment was so great and because I was continually conscious of it at the back of my mind, all landscapes in the light began gradually to transform themselves into a reality that one could call a "scene": buildings outlined in the erosion of light, the chiaroscuro seemed to exude from these walls. . . . The walls and the stone streets were absorbed with the energy of the light as if they obtained life from it—they themselves exhaled light, creating shadows, detaching themselves and developing a great and ponderous existence swarming with life.

How useful were the windows of my apartment to observe this meeting with the light! From dawn to sunset one could watch as much as one wanted to.

By watching continually, I realised a very interesting thing: that which I see is sometimes the air between me and the window, sometimes the powder glued to the windowpane, sometimes the windowframe, sometimes the landscape in the distance, sometimes the air between the window and the landscape, or even sometimes the light itself that dominates all these things. That said, my gaze moves all the time in search of what is called "distance," and the visual field grows or diminishes, even if one is not conscious of it. Momentarily, space and things present are no longer within the framework of the "object" and dissolve into thoughts and sensibilities evoked by the vision. Consequently, places particular to me, one can probably say to my existence, have very often become ambiguous. . . .

For the past seven years, I have performed this daily action of looking through the window at landscapes, and I leave the window of my apartment with photographs in order to confirm the places that I could have.

—Keiichi Tahara

*   *   *

Keiichi Tahara, who is from Kyoto, went to France in 1971 as director of lighting and imagery for the theatre company "Red Buddha" led by Tsutomu Yamashita. He remained in Paris to pursue photography, as in a relatively short time his work has been shown at the Bibliothèque Nationale and Musée d'Art Moderne in Paris as well as in Amsterdam, Pisa and Tokyo.

His series entitled "Mado/Fenêtre/Window," in two parts, has received wide critical acclaim. Tahara photographed images seen through the window of the attic where he has resided during his Paris years. He has captured the beauty of shadows and shades in a manner reminiscent of ink painting.

—Norihiko Matsumoto

TAS, Filip (Josef).

Nationality: Belgian. **Born:** London, England, 11 March 1918. **Education:** Attended primary school in Mortsel, Antwerp, 1924-32; Academy of Fine Arts, Antwerp, 1935-39; studied chemistry at the School of Industry, Antwerp, 1939-46, Dip.Chim. 1946. **Family:** Married Mélanie Barentsen in 1945 (divorced, 1965); children: Joris, Els, Hilde, and Bruno. **Career:** Worked as a chemist for Gevaert Photo Products, Mortsel, 1937-44. Freelance photographer, Antwerp, since 1945. Founder-Member, G 58-Hessenhuis plastic arts group, Antwerp, 1958. Film director for Flemish Television, Antwerp, since 1960. Photography Editor, *De Standaard* newspaper, Brussels, since 1965. Professor of Photography, National Higher Institute for Architecture and Town Planning (NHIBS), Antwerp, since 1968. **Recipient:** Gold Medal for Photography, San Sebastian, Spain, 1948; First Prize for Photography, Province of Antwerp, 1951, and Province of Limburg, Belgium, 1952; Gold Workshop Prize, Belgian Government, 1977; State Award for the Arts, Brussels, 1983; Award for Special Merit, Province of Antwerp, 1983. **Agent:** Galerij Paule Pia, Kammenstraat 57,2000 Antwerp, Belgium. **Address:** Kleine Beerstraat 42,2000 Antwerp, Belgium.

Individual Exhibitions:

1957	Gallery Ulysses, Antwerp
1959	G 58-Hessenhuis, Antwerp
1960	Celbeton, Dendermonde, Belgium
	Discothèque, Antwerp
	Deutscher Bücherbund, Bonn
	Galleria del Disegno, Milan
	Gallery Het Venster, Rotterdam
1961	Hessenhuis, Antwerp

1962	Gallery Het Venster, Rotterdam
1968	Patati, Vlassenbroek, Belgium
1971	Celbeton, Dendermonde, Belgium
1975	*Dreams*, Galerij Paule Pia, Antwerp
1976	*Bad Weather*, Arenberg, Antwerp
	Heroes' Place, at the *Biennale*, Venice
1979	*Statues of Brussels*, Palais des Beaux-Arts, Brussels
1981	*Art in our Environment*, Penzoil Place Tower, Houston, Texas
1983	*Nus á la façon de grand-père*, Galerij Paule Pia, Antwerp
	Middelheim, Gemeentekrediet van België, Antwerp
1984	International Cultureel Centrum, Antwerp (retrospective)
1985	*Strange Countries, Queer Graves*, Cultural Centre, Hasselt, Belgium
	Leuven on 400 ISO, Town Hall, Leuven, Belgium
	Aperture on the Equator, Galerij Paule Pia, Antwerp
	Travel Pictures, Cultural Centre, Knokke, Belgium
1986	*Hurrah, It's an Automobile!*, Cultural Centre, Bierbeek, Belgium
1987	*Mini Retro*, House Bellemans, Edegem, Belgium
	Photo/Slide Salon, (as guest of honour), Beringen, Belgium
	Architecture of Marc Dessauvage, Cultural Centre deSingel, Antwerp, Belgium
1988	*Recent Work*, Gallery Lorenzo, Antwerp, Belgium
1991	*Photograms*, Musée de la photographie, Charleroi, Belgium
	Free Work, Higher Architecture Institution of the State, Antwerp, Belgium
1993	*The Glamour of a City: Fifty Years Photos of Antwerp*, Archives and Museum of Flemish Cultural Life, Antwerp
	Artists from Antwerp, (portraits 1960-1970), Province Hall, Antwerp

Selected Group Exhibitions:

1958	*Group G 58*, Middelheim, Antwerp
1959	*Foto '59*, G 58-Hessenhuis, Antwerp
1960	*7 Artisti del G 58*, Galleria Bruno Danese, Milan
1963	*Zeigt Europäsche Avantgarde*, Galerie d, Frankfurt
1976	*Fünfzehn Photographen aus Flandern*, Künstlerhaus, Vienna (travelled to the Palais des Beaux-Arts, Brussels)
1977	*Photography in Flandern*, Centrum voor Kunst en Kultuur, Ghent
1980	*Photography in Belgium 1940-1980*, Het Sterckshof Museum, Deurne-Antwerp
1983	*Reflections on America*, American Centre, Brussels
1985	*Flemish Photography*, Cultural Centre De Brakke Grond, Amsterdam
1986	*G/58 Artists Retrospective Exhibition*, Hessenhuis, Antwerp
1989	*Images inventées*, Contretype, Brussels
1990	*Images inventées*, Musée d'art moderne de la ville de Paris, Paris
1991	*Image d'une époque*, Palais des beaux-arts, Brussels
1992	*Chelsey*, Belgian Centre of the Comic Strips, Brussels
1993	*Photographie en Belgique depuis 1839*, Musée de la photographie, Charleroi, Belgium

Collections:

Het Sterckshof Museum, Deurne-Antwerp; Museum of Photography, Brussels; Ministry of Culture, Brussels; Museum of Fine Arts, Bruges; Provincial Museum, Limburg, Belgium; Musée de la photographie, Charleroi, Belgium; Museum of Fine Arts, Ostend, Belgium.

Publications:

By TAS: Books—*Antwerp: City on the River*, Tielt, Belgium 1965; *De Keygnaert: A Residence in the Polder*, Tielt, Belgium 1975; *The Catholic University of Louvain-Kortrijk*, Tielt, Belgium 1975; *South America: People and Tribes*, Amsterdam 1977; *Filip Tas: Portfolio*, Antwerp 1980; *Antwerpen provincie: foto's*, with Anton Hardy and Raoul ven den Boom, Tielt, Belgium 1980; *Filip Tas: Portfolio*, Antwerp 1983; *Antwerp Behind the Scenes*, Tielt,

From *Heroes' Place,* **1976.** Photograph ©F. Tas.

Belgium 1986; *Antwerpen,* Mortsel, Belgium, 1986; *Portfolio, Maastricht,* Netherlands, 1988; *Kunstenaars in Antwerpen,* Antwerp, Belgium, 1993; *Architectuur, Leon Stijnen,* Antwerp, Belgium, 1993. **Articles**—"Haiti" in *Avenue* (Amsterdam), November 1972; "Bolivia" in *Libelle-Rosita* (Antwerp), October 1973; "Bolivia" in *Avenue* (Amsterdam), December 1974; "Bolivia" in *Avenue* (Amsterdam), February 1976; "Mexico" in *Avenue* (Amsterdam), January 1977.

On TAS: Books—*The Imaginary Photo Museum* by Helmut Gernsheim, Renate and L. Fritz Gruber, Cologne 1981, London 1982; *Foto- en Film Encyclopedie,* Amsterdam/Brussels, by K van Deuren, 1981; *Encyclopédie internationale des photographes de 1839 jusqu'à nos jours,* Switzerland, 1985; *Grote Winkler Prins Encyclopedie* (9th ed., Vol 22), Amsterdam/Antwerp, by K van Deuren, 1990; *Pour une histoire de la photographie en Belgique,* Charleroi, Belgium 1993; *F J Tas, beeldene kunstenaar. De poëzie van een stad,* by K van Deuren, Antwerp, Belgium 1993; *Filip Tas, fotograaf. Kunstenaars in Antwerpen 1960-1970,* Antwerp, Belgium 1993. **Articles**—"The Photography of Filip Tas" by Eduard Braun in *Flemish Pockets,* Hasselt, Belgium 1964; "Photographs by Tas" by Karel van Deuren in *Fototribune* (Antwerp), no. 2, 1965; "Tas and Statues of Brussels" by Xavier Rombouts in *Foto* (Amersfoort, Netherlands), March 1980; "Portfolio—Tas" by Karel van Deuren in *Foto* (Amersfoort, Netherlands), April 1980; "Filip J. Tas" in *Foto-Magazine* (Brussels), April 1980; "Tas: Un Promeneur Visionnaire" by Guy Vaes in *Spécial* (Brussels), September 1980.

*

A few short contemplations on photography as a means towards the liberation of mankind:

In the evolution of human emancipation photography has a very important role to play. Above all that which separates races and nations it has become a universal language understandable to every human being.

Photography takes a very important part in our era of images and visualization, which have—as everyone knows—a strong unifying influence on mankind. Prejudices, ignorance and fixed ideas are gradually cleared away through information (provided it is not abused, used to achieve contrary goals).

More, important, however, is the liberating effect that photography can have on individuals: particularly those who, through lack of certain skills (in sketching, painting, etc.), feel their creative urges limited or even thwarted in other media—for them, photography permits a form of visual artistic expression. In this way, the so-called "non-artistic" contribute to the cultural development of mankind.

—Filip Tas

*   *   *

Filip Tas is one of the most noteworthy figures of contemporary photography. He has produced an extensive, varied and prestigious body of work over the past 50 years.

Tas sees photography as a discipline that belongs to the plastic arts, a point of view that is certainly discernible from his work. In the 1950s his first exhibition was devoted entirely to geometric/abstract photographic prints that were made directly under the enlarger as monotypes without camera. Since then his purely artistic work has evolved under the influence, on the one hand, of the subjective photography of Otto Steinert (more through Steinert's ideas and concepts than through his actual work) and, on the other hand, the photomontage of the Bauhaus. These influences are especially apparent in those of his works that seen like quick sketches of a personal response.

Tas is a photographer of incomparable technical prowess, which he employs to formulate his wonder at the bizarre world in which we live. His work has the deepest roots in reality, yet it is also a photography of poetic, impressionist reportage, endowed with a touch of the surrealist—as, for example, in his montage series *Heroes' Places.* His work is the reflection of an attitude of constant surprise at what he sees around him, a continual exploration of the instrument of the photograph, with which, in his work, the organic is fused with art.

—Karel van Deuren

TATA, Sam (Bejan).

Nationality: Canadian. **Born:** Born of Indian parents in Shanghai, China, 30 September 1911; emigrated to Canada, 1956; naturalized, 1961. **Education:** Shanghai Public School, 1919-30; studied at Hong Kong University, 1931-32; mainly self-taught in photography, from 1935: influenced by the photographer Henri Cartier-Bresson, from 1948. **Family:** Formerly married to

Marketa Langer, 1952; daughter: Antonia. **Career:** Worked as an assistant, D.C. Tata and Company family cotton business, Shanghai, 1933-46; amateur street photographer, 1936-39, and studio portrait photographer, 1940-46, in Shanghai, and reportage photographer, working with *Trend* and *Flashlight* magazines, Bombay, India, 1946-48; freelance reportage and documentary photographer, in Shanghai, 1949-55, and in Kashmir, India, 1955-56. Since 1956, full-time freelance photojournalist, working with *Maclean's, Chatelaine, Montrealer, Star Weekly, Perspectives, Globe Magazine, Time Canada, Canadian Fiction,* etc., in Montreal. Co-editor, *Foto Canada* magazine, Montreal, 1967-68. **Recipient:** Gold Medal, 1947, Bronze Medal, 1948, *All-India Exhibition,* Bombay; Silver Medal, Bombay Art Society, 1948; Queen's Silver Jubilee Medal, Ottawa, 1977; LL.D.: Concordia University, Montreal, 1982; Life-Member, Royal Photographic Society of Great Britain, 1947; Member, Royal Canadian Academy, 1976. **Address:** 1750 Crevier, Apt. 7, St. Laurent, Quebec H4L 2X5, Canada.

Individual Exhibitions:

1946	Sun Sun Department Store, Shanghai (with Long Chin-San)
1947	Bombay Art Society Salon, Bombay
1949	Alliance Francaise, Shanghai
1957	Royal Ontario Museum, Toronto
	Phoenix Art Center, Arizona
1958	International Museum of Photography at George Eastman House, Rochester, New York
1959	University of Boston, Massachusetts
	Museum of Fine Arts, Montreal, Quebec
1968	Studio 23, Montreal (with Anthony Graham and Jeremy Taylor)
	End of an Era: Shanghai 1949, Sir George Williams University, Montreal (toured Canada)
	National Film Board, Ottawa (with Gunter Karkutt and John Flanders)
1971	Perception Gallery, Montreal
1974	*A Certain identity,* Centaur Gallery, Montreal
1977	*Hasidim,* WS Gallery, Montreal
1978	Centre Culturel Canadien, Paris (with Gabor Szilasi)
1980	Deja Vue Gallery, Toronto
1981	Yajima Galerie, Montreal

Selected Group Exhibitions:

1947	*All-India Exhibition,* Conference Room, Electric House, Bombay (and 1948)
1959	*Photography at Mid-Century,* International Museum of Photography at George Eastman House, Rochester, New York
1967	*Photography Canada 1967,* National Film Board, Ottawa
1968	*Other Places,* National Film Board, Ottawa
1970	*Contemporary Photography in Canada,* National Film Board, Ottawa
1971	*Magic World of Childhood,* National Film Board, Ottawa
1977	*Photo '77,* Conference Centre, Ottawa
1978	*La Fete,* at *Rencontres Internationales de Photographie,* Arles, France

Collections:

National Gallery of Canada, Ottawa; Public Archives, Ottawa; Canadian Museum of Contemporary Photography; Canada Council Art Bank, Ottawa; Musée d'Art Contemporain, Montreal; Edmonton Art Gallery, Alberta; Winnipeg Art Gallery, Manitoba; Concordia University, Montreal; Museum of Modern Art, New York.

Publications:

By TATA: Books—*Montreal,* with text by Frank Lowe, Toronto 1963; *Expo 67: Sculpture Dadanana,* Montreal 1967; *Marcel Braitstein,* with others, text by Jean Simard, Montreal 1970; *A Certain Identity,* with foreword by Geoffrey

James, Ottawa 1983. **Articles**—"Photo-journalism in Canada" in *Foto Canada* (Montreal), September 1967; "Portraiture" in *Foto Canada* (Montreal), October/November 1967; "On Assignment: John Max" in *Foto Canada* (Montreal), August 1968; "On Assignment: Henri Paul" in *Foto Canada,* (Montreal), September 1968; "Colleagues" in *Canadian Fiction* (Toronto), Spring 1986.

On TATA: Articles—"Sam Tata's Rebellion" by Norman Hall in *Photography* (London), October 1956; "One Man Show: Sam Tata" by John Linder in *Photoage* (Montreal), April 1962; "The Work of Sam Tata" by Margaret Teal in *Industrial and Commercial Photographer* (London), October 1970; "Sam Tata: l'artiste vu par l'artiste" by Geoffrey James in *Vie des Arts* (Montreal), Spring 1973; "Sam Tata: la lezione di Bresson" in *Nuova Fotografia* (Naples), July/August 1976; "Sam Tata" by Geoffrey Hancock and Hugh Hood, special issue of *Canadian Fiction* (Toronto), no. 29, 1979; "Sam Tata: Montreal 1956-1967" by Denyse Gerin-Lajoie, special issue of *Ovo Magazine* (Montreal), no. 42, 1981; "Sam Tata: Shanghai in the Throes of 1949" by Lorne Fromer in *Photo Communique* (Toronto), Fall 1982; "I'm Somebody with a Camera" by Sooni Taraporevala in *Express Magazine* (Bombay), February 1984; "Sam Tata, International Photographer" by Havovi Anklesaria in *Debonair Magazine* (Bombay), May 1985.

                                    *

My work follows the tradition of photographers such as André Kertész, Bill Brandt, Eugene Smith, Lord Snowdon, and of Henri Cartier-Bresson whose influence has been the strongest and the most direct, thanks to a close friendship of almost four decades. I suppose in the eyes of today's young photographers in *avant-garde* directions, I would be regarded as a traditionalist, but I can find nothing more fascinating than working in the streets, constantly recording the whys and wherefores of Mr. Everyman. The reality all around us is a constant and challenging theatre for the camera.

Though I have worked in photo-reportage for many years and enjoy the sequence of a photographic essay, I am particularly fascinated by the single image that I may suddenly happen on, something not anticipated but fortuitously there. My greatest pleasure is in this moment of discovery when memory, experience and the accident of time combine to realise a good photograph.

I have also had the good fortune of having been an eye-witness to history before and after the advent of the Peoples Liberation Army in Shanghai in 1949. The resulting essay in depth has been shown throughout Canada since 1970 under the aegis of the National Film Board's Still Division (since 1985 renamed the Canadian Museum of Contemporary Photography).

The environmental portrait, too, is an abiding passion, almost an obsession. My preferred subjects are artists (a term used in its broadest sense), both the creative as well as the interpretive.

I much prefer working in black-and-white: I find colour a difficult medium. Colour tends to vitiate any statement I try to make and even succeeds in endowing the direst poverty with a certain elegance.

With photography's seeming need to categorise, I have been labelled a documentary photographer, a social photographer, a photo-journalist. Best of all, I have been called a humanist which I feel sums it up very well.

—Sam Tata

                              *   *   *

Sam Bejan Tata's photographs record the collective drama of human existence from the banal moments passed by ordinary people on the streets and sidewalks of cities to the excitement of parades and the more historically profound occasions, such as the takeover of Shanghai by the Communists from the Kuomintang in 1949. They also depict the portraits of artists, actors, musicians, dancers, photographers and other members of predominantly Canada's cultural community. These latter images, rather than portraying the individuals in a heroic mould, are gentle visual explorations of individual identities. In passing from a reportage of the collective life of people to the making of specific portraits, Tata communicates his impressions of the world around him with graceful affection and a strong sense of being inseparable from the events and from the lives of the subjects that pass before his lens.

It was at the age of 25, in 1936, that Sam Tata was first introduced to photography. Although he received much of his early exposure to photography and his technical knowledge of the medium from the Shanghai Camera Club members, Tata's first camera, on the advice of local journalist/photographer Alex Buchman, was a Leica. The subjects of his early photographs were the landscape around Nanking and members of his immediate family, but the motivation behind the work at that point remained strictly that of the amateur.

Born in Shanghai in 1911, of Indian parents, Sam was the oldest of five children and, as such, primed from early on to assume a role in the operation of two cotton mills, a family business managed by his father, Bejan Tata. As part of his training for this role, he attended Hong Kong University, where he studied for a degree in Commerce, an undertaking which did not work out either to the satisfaction of Sam's talents or to the benefit of the family business. Although he did not entertain thoughts about becoming a commercial photographer, Tata worked conscientiously at increasing his knowledge of photography and regularly submitted work to newspaper contests and Salons. A turning point for him was a fortuitous meeting with Henri Cartier-Bresson in February of 1948. At the end of 1946 Tata had left Shanghai for a visit to India and found himself some fourteen months later attending an exhibition of Cartier-Breson's work, with the photographer in attendance. The revelation of spontaneity that Cartier-Bresson's photographs communicated to Tata had a lasting effect on how he was to assess his own photographs and develop his own vision. A friendship developed between the two photographers and in 1949 Tata and Cartier-Bresson were to explore the streets of Shanghai together.

Not only had Tata by this time abandoned his struggle with mastering an array of large format cameras and batteries of lights, but had begun to exploit the freshness of vision that had already been evident in some of his photographs taken in 1937, during the Japanese bombing of Chapei bordering the International Settlement of Shanghai. Tata's photographs taken on the streets of Shanghai during the days of the Kuomintang withdrawal from Shanghai and the Communist takeover, provide an extraordinary visual and historic document of that period. As Geoffrey James, writer and photographer, has appropriately noted, these images are "clear, visually unforced and without rhetoric."

Between the final year of the Revolution and 1956, when Tata emigrated with his wife, Marketa Langer (married Shanghai, 1952) and daughter Toni (born, 1953) to Canada, were not without event. In 1952 he moved to Hong Kong and while resisting his father's earlier suggestion that he acquire the photography studio of Oscar Seepol, a Latvian born portrait photographer with a commercial studio in Shanghai and ties with India, it was there that Tata undertook his first commercial photography commission: to produce a catalogue for a jewellery company. In 1955, he travelled to Kashmir with his family and produced a body of black and white photographs of the annual Hindu pilgrimage to Amarnath, which in conjunction with an article by Christopher Rand, was published in *National Geographic*.

In 1956 Tata arrived in Canada, receiving his Canadian citizenship in 1961. After an initial period of adjustment, Tata began to explore his new environment with a journalistic hunger for the facts of daily life: people at lunch counters, street parades, the annual Saint Jean Baptiste Day festivities and life as generally lived on the streets of his new city, Montreal. He also began in the sixties that series of portraits of artists, that was still being added to more than 25 years later. Tata, armed with camera, became a familiar figure in Montreal and a friend to many of the members of the Canadian artistic community, whose portraits he recorded. By now his livelihood was tied to photography and he supplied photographs for a number of magazines, such as *Time, Life, Fortune, National Geographic, Perspectives, MacLeans, Star Weekly, Weekend* and *Chatelain*. In November of 1983 Tata visited India once again, with the specific intent of producing a body of photographs which in his own words would be "in search of his roots." With a Naipaul-like feeling for the curious juxtapositions of cultural facts and a sense of timelessness that seems to characterize the street life of these cities, Tata explored the streets of Bombay, Goa, Ernakulam, Bangalore, Udaipur, Delhi, and returned in March 1984 to Canada with a commendable record of his stay.

—Ann W. Thomas

TAUSK, Petr.

Nationality: Czechoslovakian. **Born:** Prague, 24 January 1927. **Education:** Studied chemical engineering, Technical University, Prague, 1946-50; mainly self-taught in photography, but initially instructed by his father Arnošt Tausk, from 1937. **Family:** Married Dana Šperlová in 1959; daughter: Darina. **Career:** Independent photographer, Prague, since 1956. Senior Technical Scientist, Central Institute for Scientific, Technical and Economic Information, Prague, since 1951. Visiting Lecturer, Department of Creative Photography. Academy of Performing Arts, Prague, since 1967. Advisory Board Member, *History of Photography* magazine, Philadelphia and London, since 1986. Associate Member, Union of Czechoslovak Creative Artists, 1967; Honorary Member, European Society for the History of Photography, 1981, and Union of Slovak Photographers, 1984. **Died:** (in Prague) 3 May, 1988.

Selected Group Exhibitions:

1965   *Czechoslovak Photography,* Split, Yugoslavia
1967   *My Favourite Photograph,* Gallery Fotochema, Prague
1979   *People and Time,* Town Hall, Prague
1984   *Czechoslovakian Photography,* Thackrey and Robertson Gallery, San Francisco

Collections:

Bibliothèque Nationale, Paris; International Center of Photography, New York; International Museum of Photography at George Eastman House, Rochester, New York; Museum of Modern Art, New York; Kunsthaus, Zurich; Preus Fotomuseum, Horten, Norway; Royal Library, Copenhagen; Museum für Kunst und Gewerbe, Hamburg; San Francisco Museum of Modern Art; Collection of the Union of Czech Photographers, Prague.

Publications:

By TAUSK: Books—*Photography with Interchangeable Lenses,* with B. Biskup, Prague 1961; *Fundamentals of Creative Colour Photography,* Martin, Czechoslovakia 1973; *An Introduction to Press Photography,* Prague 1976; *Josef Sudek,* with W. Lippert, Aachen, West Germany 1976; *Photography in the 20th Century,* Cologne 1977, London 1980; *100 Temi di Fotografia,* with H.H. Hofstatter, Milan 1977; *It Is Not Enough To Press The Button,* Prague 1978; *Black-and-White Creative Photography,* Martin, Czechoslovakia 1981; *Textbook of Press Photography,* Prague 1981; *Creative Colour Photography,* Martin, Czechoslovakia 1985; *Josef Ehm—Profily,* Prague, 1979; *Josef Sudek—Profily,* Prague, 1980; *Vilém Heckel—Profily,* Prague, 1981; *Přehled současné fotografie v zahraničí,* Prague, 1985; *Přehled vývoje československé fotografie od roku 1918 až po naše dny,* Prague, 1986; *A Short History of Press Photography,* Prague, 1988. **Articles**—"Fotografia i realnost" in *Foto-kino revija* (Belgrade), no. 9, 1964; "Tschechoslowakische Fotografie" in *Foto Prisma* (Dusseldorf), no. 9, 1966; "Josef Sudek" in *Foto Prisma* (Dusseldorf), no. 4, 1970; "Mutual Influences Between Photography and Painting" in *British Journal of Photography Annual,* London 1973; "Jaromir Funke" in *Camera* (Lucerne), no. 1, 1977; "The Object Trouvé in Photography" in *Creative Camera* (London), no. 2, 1977; "Roots of Modern Photography in Czechoslovakia" in *History of Photography* (Philadelphia/London), no. 3, 1979; "Jaromír Funke" in *European Photography* (Gottingen), no. 4, 1980; "Jan Lauschmann and Czechoslovak Photography" in *History of Photography* (Philadelphia/London), no. 5, 1981; "Josef Sudek—His Life and Work" in *History of Photography* (Philadelphia/London), no. 6, 1982; "Jubileum Petra Tauska" by Martin Hruška in *Československá fotografie,* (Prague) no 1, 1987; "Petr Tausk šedesátiletý" by Ján Šmok in *Revue Fotografie,* (Prague) no 1, 1987; "Zemřel Petr Tausk" by Ladislav Šolc in *Revue Fotografie* (Prague) no 4, 1988; "Vzpomínká na Petra Tauska" by Ján Šmok in *Československá fotografie,* (Prague) no 10, 1988.

On TAUSK: Books—*Dictionnaire des Photographes* by Carole Naggar, Paris 1982; *Encyclopedia of Photographers* by Michel and Michéle Auer, Hermance, Switzerland 1985. **Articles**—"Beichte eines Fotoautors" in *Photo Revue* (Munich), July 1980; "Petr Tausk—Farvefilmen er bedst til

Cornell Capa, **1983.** Photograph by Petr Tausk.

afdaempede motiver'' by Tage Paulsen in *Foto* (Copenhagen), July/August 1982; ''Avtor knig—Peter-Tausk'' by A.Diordienko in *Sovetskoye Foto* (Moscow), October 1985.

*

In my approach to photography, I distinguish two standpoints: that of a photo-historian and that of a photographer. As a photo-historian, my duty to my students is to explain what are the main currents in the evolution of photography up to the present, without necessarily declaring what photographs I prefer personally. As a photographer, I believe it is necessary to have a high regard for the essential properties of the medim, and to employ them accordingly.

Goethe wrote after visiting the Dresden painting collection that, ''the task of the artist is to teach the people to see.'' Latterly, Max J. Friedlander stated that there is an important difference between mere ''perceiving'' and ''seeing.'' I think the photographer is well placed to assist people not only to perceive reality but to see it with all their mental faculties. It is possible in this respect to use both the documentary precision of photography and its ability to register a latent image on a light-sensitive layer in the fraction of a second. Photography is thus able to react to the aesthetic properties of life's many and varied situation. It can also satisfy another classical requirement of art as defined by Hegel: ''It has always been the most important purpose of art to find interesting situations . . . ''

In my own photographic work, I have tried to discover both interesting situations in my immediate vicinity (especially in my youth) and the haphazard formations of still-life arrangements that appeal directly to me. As well as these fortuitous motifs, I occasionally came into contact with well-known photographers and made portraits of them. The first whom I photographed in this way was Otto Steinert in 1966, and since then I have continued this work as an ongoing series.

Initially I photographed only in black-and-white, but now I much prefer working with colour images. It was the work of Joel Meyerowitz that persuaded me of the colour photograph's autonomy as a work of art. After all, the real world in all its aesthetic aspects is coloured, too.

—Petr Tausk

*   *   *

Petr Tausk is known primarily as a historian of photography, a teacher, a publicist, and organizer of several exhibitions. It is less known that he is also a good photographer.

He obtained his first camera from his father when he was only 10, but during this early period took only snapshots of Prague, including a number made after the city's liberation from Nazi occupation in 1945. He took up photography more seriously almost twenty years later. As a chemistry graduate, he was initially interested in the technical possibilities of photography, the qualities of different sensitive materials and methods of developing. He was also fascinated by the possibilities of changing photographic composition through the use of various telescopic lenses. He wrote his first book on the subject in 1961.

In this period his photos consisted mainly of snaps taken from everday life in a classic humanist style as exemplified by the work of photographer and journalist Vaclav Jiru with whom Tausk often associated. During the 1960s, Tausk travelled in the U.S.S.R., Hungary, Italy, France, Britain and Scandinavia where he made photographs reminiscent of the ideas enshrined in Steichen's project *The Family of Man.* Some of these photo essays from Tausk's travels were published in prominent Czech magazines.

The late 1960s saw Tausk devoting more time to studying the history of photography and its current state all over the world. He began publishing an extensive series of articles about photography from different countries in the journal *Československá fotografie.* He also became interested in the connections between painting and photography (he had himself just taken up painting), and began publishing portfolios by prominent Czech and foreign photographers. During Otto Steinert's visit to Prague, Tausk made several portrait photographs of the famed West German photographer and teacher. This was the beginning of a series of portrait studies of famous photographers, including Josef Sudek, Jaroslav Rössler, Josef Prošek, Jan Šplìchal, Cornell Capa, Bill Brandt, Joel Meyerowitz, Sam Haskins and many others. These portraits, expressing the subject's personality and suggesting aspects of their photographic style, were taken with a large format camera.

At the same time, Tausk focussed his talents once more on the theory and practice of photography, combining his experiences of portraiture and a recent move into colour film. As well as writing books on colour photography, he made a number of prototypical instructive colour photos in addition to those of a creative character. His favourite motifs continue to be those found in hidden corners of towns and landscapes. Frequently he turns his camera onto the intriguing view of an apparently ugly object, discovering remarkable interest in either colour harmonies or contrasts. A subtle melancholy permeates his fragmented landscapes in which reality is condensed into an economy of few lines, forms and hues. Alongside these outdoor photographs, Tausk creates still lifes redolent of surreal poetry.

Although not an extensive oeuvre or a heterogenous one, Tausk's photographic work—in its best examples—shows its author to be not only a talented historian but a photographer of rare sensitivity and creative power.

—Vladimìr Birgus

TELBERG, Val.

Nationality: American. **Born:** Vladimir Telberg-von-Teleheim in Moscow, 14 February 1910; family emigrated to China in 1918; emigrated to U.S., 1938. **Education:** Won scholarship to Wittenberg College, Springfield, Ohio, 1928, graduating with BSc in chemistry, 1932; took up painting and attended Art Students League, New York City, 1942; self-taught in photography with assistance from Kathleen Lambing. **Family:** Married Kathleen Lambing in

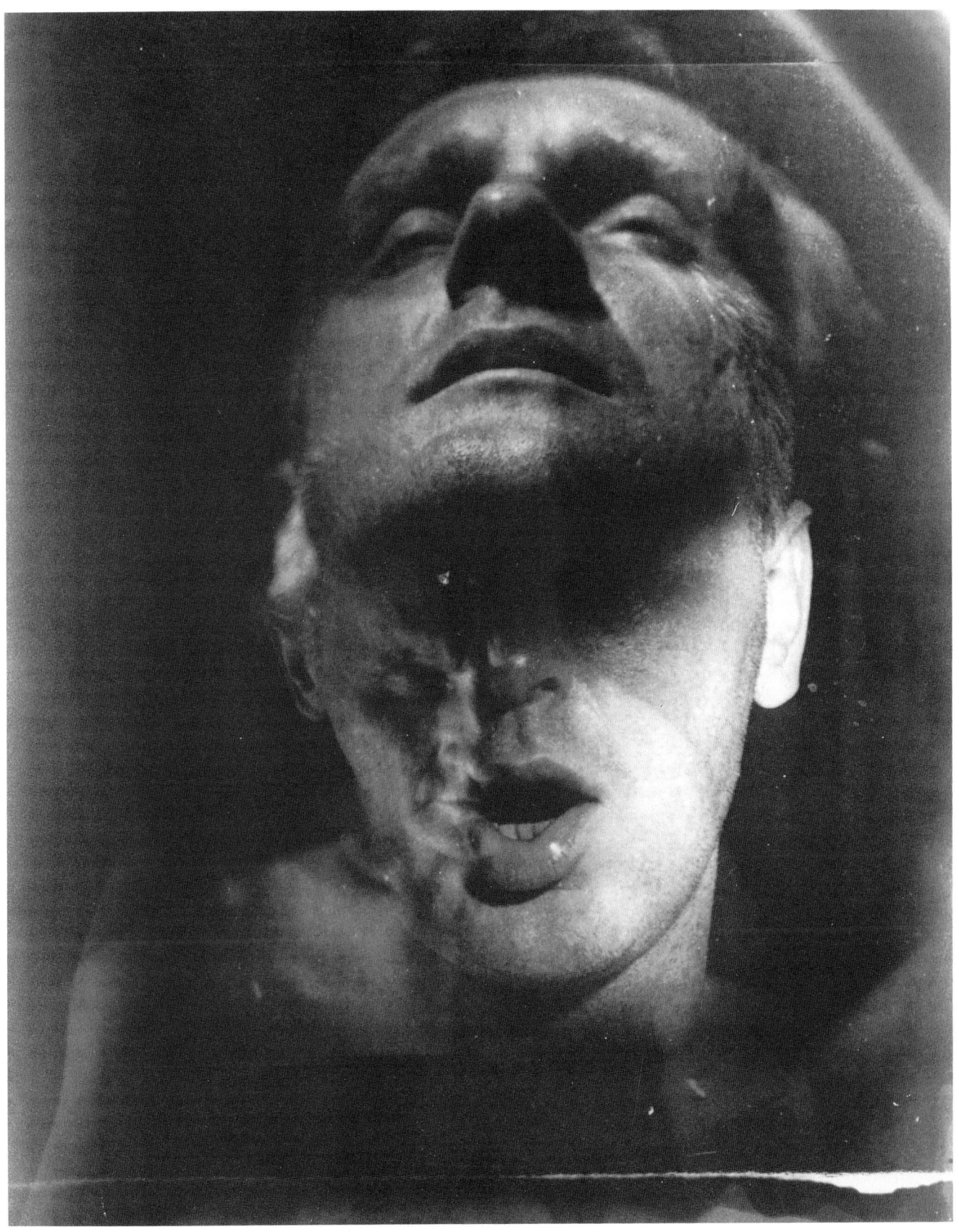

Triple Self-portrait, **c. 1950.** Photograph ©Val Telberg. Copy photograph by D. James Dee. Courtesy of Laurence Miller Gallery, New York.

1944 (later divorced); married Lelia Katayen, dancer and choreographer, in 1955; children: son, Rurick, and daughter, Tamara. **Career:** In China, engaged in various business activities including book publishing, magazine editing, multi-lingual broadcasting and pharmaceutical sales; in U.S., worked in administration at a New Jersey pharmaceuticals company until 1941; worked as night-club photographer in Florida, also ran a photo-fun portrait concession in Lincoln Park, Fall River, Massachusetts, 1944; returned to New York to work full-time as independent photographic artist, 1948, developing novel technique of multi-negative printing, now known as Multiple Imagery, first exhibited at the Brooklyn Museum in New York, 1948. **Recipient:** Huntington Hartford Fellowship (first photographer so honoured), 1952; Yaddo Fellowship, 1953. **Agent:** Laurence Miller Gallery, 138 Spring Street, New York, New York 10012, U.S.A. **Address:** P.O. Box 920, Sag Harbor, New York 11963, U.S.A.

Individual Exhibitions:

1948	Brooklyn Museum, New York
1948	Colorado Springs Fine Arts Center
	Henry Gallery, University of Washington, Seattle
	Tacoma Art League, Washington
	Eastern Washington State Historical Society, Spokane, Washington
1950	San Francisco Museum of Art, California
	Santa Barbara Museum of Art, California
	Fine Arts Gallery of San Diego, California
	Munson-Williams-Proctor Institute, Utica, New York
	Norton Gallery of Art, West Palm Beach, Florida
1951	Smithsonian Institute, Washington, D.C.
	Galérie Huit, Paris
	University Gallery, University of Minnesota
1952	New York Public Library, New York
1953	Instituto Allende, San Miguel, San Miguel de Allende, Mexico
	Central School of Arts and Crafts, London
	Yaddo Gallery, Saratoga Springs, New York
	Talladega College, Talladega, Alabama, Georgia
1954	DeCordova Museum of Art, Lincoln, Massachusetts
	Boston Museum of Art School, Boston, Massachusetts
	Art Gallery, University of Maine, Orono
1955	Hacker Gallery, New York
1960	Art Gallery, University of Maine, Orono
1965	Parrish Art Museum, Southampton, New York
1966	Hudson River Museum, Yonkers, New York
1978	Gillan Gallery, Bridgehampton, New York
1979	Pittsburgh Film Institute, Pennsylvania
1982	Guild Hall, East Hampton, New York
1983	San Francisco Museum of Art, California
1984	Laurence Miller Gallery, New York
1985	Fine Arts Gallery, Long Island University, Southampton, New York
1987	Benton Gallery, Southampton, New York
1991	Laurence Miller Gallery, New York
1993	Art House Odeon, Sag Harbor, New York
1994	Rathbone Gallery, Sage Junior College, Albany, New York
	Fine Arts Gallery, Long Island University, Southampton, New York

Selected Group Exhibitions:

1948	*In and Out of Focus,* Museum of Modern Art, New York
1951	*Abstraction Photography,* Museum of Modern Art, New York
1953	*Japan and America,* National Museum of Modern Art, Tokyo
1960	*A Sense of Abstraction,* Museum of Modern Art, New York
1982	*Form, Field and Feelings,* San Francisco Museum of Modern Art, California
1983	*Nus,* Galérie Adrien Maeght, Paris
1985	*Photography; A Facet of Modernism,* San Francisco Museum of Modern Art, California
	Guild Hall, East Hampton, New York
1988	*Montage,* Hillwood Art Gallery, Brookville, New York

1989	*Out of Bounds,* Guild Hall, East Hampton, New York
1990	*El Surrealismo Entre el Viejo y Nuevo Mundo,* Centro Atlántico de Arte Moderno, Las Palmas, Canary Islands, Spain
1991	*Dreams, Lies and Exaggerations: Photomontage in America,* University of Maryland Art Gallery
1991-93	*Departures,* Cantor Art Gallery, College of the Holy Cross, Worcester, Massachusetts
	Denver Art Museum, Colorado
	Joslyn Art Museum, Omaha, Nebraska
	Pittsburgh Center for the Arts, Pittsburgh, Pennsylvania
	Goldie Palie Gallery, Moore College of Art and Design, Philadelphia, Pennsylvania
	Tel Fair Academy of Arts and Sciences, Savannah, Georgia
1994	*American Surrealist Photography,* Museum of Modern Art, New York
	Self-Portraits, Los Angeles County Museum of Art, California

Collections:

Brooklyn Museum, New York; Guild Hall Museum, East Hampton, New York; The Minneapolis Institute of Arts, Minneapolis; The Museum of Modern Art, New York; Princeton University Art Museum, New Jersey; San Francisco Museum of Modern Art, California; Santa Barbara Museum of Art, California; Smithsonian Institute, Washington, D.C.; University Art Museum, Albuquerque, New Mexico; Metropolitan Museum of Art, New York; Museum of Fine Arts, Houston, Texas; Getty Museum, Malibu, California; New Orleans Museum of Art, Louisiana; Los Angeles County Museum of Art, California.

Publications:

By TELBERG: Articles—"Art and the Subconscious" in *American Artist,* January 1949; *American Photography,* October 1950; "Composite Photography" in *American Artist,* February 1954; "Pittsburgh: Symposium on Overlooked Photography" in *Afterimage,* May 1979.

On TELBERG: Books—*U.S. Camera Annual,* (1949); *Say It With Your Camera: An Approach to Creative Photography* by Jacob Deschin (New York), 1950; *American Annual of Photography,* 1953; *House of Incest* by Anaïs Nin (Chicago), 1958; *Elements of Design* by D.Anderson (New York), 1961; *Photography in the 20th Century* by Nathan Lyons (New York), 1967; *Far-Out Prints of the Avant-Garde* (New York), 1970; *Who's Who in American Art,* (1984); *Photography and Art* by Andy Grundberg and Kathleen McCarthy Gauss (Abbeville), 1987. **Articles**—"Two Kinds of Work" by Jacob Deschin in *The New York Times* (New York), 26 September 1948; "Une Nouvelle Voie en Photographie" in *Photo Ciné Revue,* September 1951; "Une Forme d'Art Photographique" in *Photo-Cinema,* September 1951; *Photo-Guide Magazine* (London), 1952; *Functional Photography* (London), 1951; *Design* (London), September-October 1952; *American Photography,* May 1953; "Val Telberg" in *Arts,* January 1955; "Ein Photograph Schreibt uber Sich" in *Photo Magazine* (Munich), September 1957; *Picture Post* (London), 15 December 1959; "Avant-Gardist with A Loyal Underground" by Edwin Fancher in *Village Voice* (New York), May 1959; *Fortune Magazine,* January 1961; *Field of Vision* (Pittsburgh), Summer 1979; *The New York Times* (New York), 12 August 1979; "16 Feet of Dreamlike Imagery" by Helen Harrison in *The New York Times* (New York), 15 August 1982; "Val Telberg" catalog preface for *San Francisco Museum of Modern Art* by Coke Van Deren, 1983; Review by J.Tarshis in *Art in America,* December 1983; "Unsettling Dreams" by Janis Bultman in *Darkroom Photography,* January 1983; "Nus: Photographies de Ballocq, Telberg, Steinberg," exhibition catalog essay for *Galeries Andrien Maeght* (Paris), 1983; Review by Albright in *The San Francisco Chronicle,* 12 May 1983; Review by K.Stiles in *California Voice,* 20 May 1983; Interview by Darwin Marable in *Photo Metro,* May 1985; "Val Telberg Recent Sequential Photographs" catalog essay by Yolande Trincere for Fine Arts Gallery, Long Island University, Southampton (New York), July 1985; "Photography: A Facet of Modernism" catalog review for San Francisco Museum of Modern Art, 1985; "Photographers Dialog" catalog entry for Boca Raton Museum of Art, 1988; "Montage" catalog entry for Hillwood Art Museum (New York), 1988; "Out of Bounds" catalog entry for Guild Hall Museum (New York), 1989; "El Surrealismo Entre el Viejo y Nuevo Mundo" catalog entry for Centro Atlantico da Arte Moderno (Las Palmas), 1990; "Dreams, Lies and Exaggerations: Photomontage in America" by Cynthia Wayne in exhibition catalog for University of Maryland Art Gallery, 1991; *Anaïs: An International Journal,* 1992; "Val Telberg's Wizardry, 50 Years of Superimposed Images" by Phyllis Braff in *The New York Times,* 26 September 1993; "Arts Facts and Artifacts" by Donald Kennedy in *The Independent* (Sag Harbor), 22 September 1993; "From The Studio" by Rose C.S. Slivka in *The East Hampton Star,* 30 September 1992; "Senses Working Overtime" by Rich Kreiner in *Metroland,* 20 January 1994; "Val Telberg and House of Incest" by Gunther Stuhlmann in *Annaïs: An International Journal,* 1994; "Photomontage exhibit at Sage in Albany a unique visual, intellectual treat" by Joseph Andrew Phillips in *Schenectady Daily Gazette,* 10 January 1994; "Val Telberg-Anaïs: House of Incest Exhibit" by Joan Crandall in *Sage Times,* 21 January 1994; "Telberg montages in spotlight at Sage JCA" by Michael Eck in *Albany Times Union,* 23 January 1994; "A Batch of Dreams" by Doreen Tiernan in exhibition brochure for Sage JCA, January 1994.

*

My pictures should be felt rather than pronounced, and an effort to translate them into words may only bring on frustration.

—Val Telberg

TENNESON, Joyce.

Nationality: American. **Born:** Boston, Massachusetts, 29 May 1945. **Education:** Studied at Regis College, Weston, Massachusetts, 1963-67, B.A. 1967; George Washington University, Washington, D.C. 1967-69, M.A. 1969; Antioch College, Yellow Springs, Ohio, 1976-78, Ph.D. 1978; mainly self-taught in photography, from 1970. **Career:** Independent photographer, Washington, D.C., 1971-83. Since 1983, freelance portrait, fashion and magazine photographer, working for *Vogue Italia, Interview, New York Magazine, In Fashion,* the *Washington Post,* etc., in Washington, D.C. and New York City: established studios on Biltmore Street, Washington, D.C., in 1971, and on West 27th Street, New York, in 1984. Professor of Art, Corcoran School of Art, Washington, D.C., and Northern Virginia Community College, 1971-83. Photo-editor and critic, *Washington Review of Arts,* Washington, D.C., 1975-80. **Recipient:** Ford Foundation Grant, 1979; District of Columbia Commission on the Arts Grant, 1982; International Center for Photography's Infinity Award, 1989; Named Photographer of the Year by the international organization, Woman in Photography, 1990. Member of Society for Photographic Educations; College Art Association of America. **Agents:** Galerie Viviane Esders, 12 rue Saint Merri, 75004 Paris, France; Marie Martin, 18th Street N.W., Washington, D.C. 20009, U.S.A. **Addresses:** 1915 Biltmore Street N.W., Washington, D.C. 20009, U.S.A.; and 114 West 27th Street, New York, New York 10001, U.S.A.

Individual Exhibitions:

1974	Corcoran Gallery of Art, Washington, D.C.
1975	Foundry Gallery, Washington, D.C.
1977	Washington Gallery of Photography, Washington, D.C.
1980	Phillips Collection, Washington, D.C.
1981	Marcuse Pfeifer Gallery, New York
	Centre Culturel Americain, Paris
	Galerie Viviane Esders, Paris
1983	*Joyce Tenneson,* at *SICOF 83,* Milan
1984	*Joyce Tenneson,* at *Rencontres Internationales de Photographie,* Arles, France
1985	Canon Photo Gallery, Amsterdam
	Galerie Municipale du Château d'Eau, Toulouse, France
1986	Martin Gallery, Washington, D.C.
1987	Musée d'Art Moderne, Paris
1988	Marcuse Pfeifer Gallery, New York City
	Boca Raton Museum of Art, Florida
	Agathe Gaillard Gallery, Paris
	International Photography Congress, Rockport, Maine
1989	Ken Damy Photogaliery, Milan
	Fendrick Gallery, Washington, D.C.
	Special Photographer's Gallery, London
	Agathe Gaillard Gallery, Paris
1990	Vision Gallery, San Francisco
	Museo Ken Damy, Bresia, Italy
	Daniel Inoue Gallery, Osaka, Japan
	Torino Photographica Biennale, Torino, Italy
	Seattle University, Seattle, Washington
1991	Frederick Gallery, New York/Washington, D.C.
	Special Photographer's Gallery, London
	Fredericksoborg Museum, Copenhagen, Denmark
	Laguna Beach Gallery of Photography, California
	Daniel Inoue Gallery, Osaka, Japan
	Festival International de la Photographie, Barcelona, Spain
1992	International Center of Photography, New York
1993	G Ray Hawkins Gallery, Los Angeles, California

Selected Group Exhibitions:

1984	*La Photographie Créative,* Pavillon des Arts, Paris

Collections:

Library of Congress, Washington, D.C.; Smithsonian Institution, Washington, D.C.; Corcoran Gallery of Art, Washington, D.C.; Women's Interart Center, New York; Bibliothèque Nationale, Paris; Collection of the City of Paris, Musée Reattu, Arles, France; Rufino Tamayo Museum of Contemporary Art, Mexico City.

Publications:

By TENNESON: Books—*In-Sights: Self-portraits by Women,* editor, with text by Patrician Meyer Spacks, Boston 1978, London 1979; *Transformations,* introduction by Vicki Goldberg, Boston, 1983; *Joyce Tenneson—Black and White Photos,* with introduction by Phillip Jason, Boston 1985; *Au Dela—Joyce Tenneson,* Paris, 1989.

On TENNESON: Book—*La Photographie Creative* by Jean-Claude Lemagny, Paris 1984.

*

When I photograph for myself, what excites me is seeing something in my camera that moves me; something awesomely beautiful or even terrifying which seems to appear without my interference or prodding.

There is usually an intense unspoken intimacy at these times which cannot be explained or talked about afterwards. These "passionate" inspiring moments are what makes me love photography and keep pushing me to go further.

—Joyce Tenneson

*   *   *

The figures in Joyce Tenneson's evocative images perform in a peculiarly light-filled void; like Bernini's Saint Theresa they are both spiritual and sensual. Tenneson is a photographer who currently divides her time between Washington, D.C. and a studio in New York City. Her first book, *In-Sights: Self-portraits by Women,* was published in 1978. This innovative collection pre-dated much of the current interest in photography towards women's images of themselves. During the early 1980s she produced a suite of fragmented, high-key figure studies which were published as a monograph by David Godine in 1984.

Untitled (original in colour). Photograph ©Joyce Tenneson.

These studies, of nude and semi-nude figures swathed in flowing white gowns, invoke Tenneson's experience as a child growing up in her parent's convent. By printing on a silver emulsion coated on water-color paper, and precisely controlling development, Tenneson was able to produce an incredibly nuanced tonal range of grays and white. The figures bathe in an intense, dappled light. Often we see only fragments, a foot or an arm, which stand out in sculptural relief against a ground of white linen. This body of work comprised a kind of metaphorical journey which mixed images of birth, death and rebirth. It left Tenneson feeling both "drained and vulnerable." She has always seen photography as co-extensive with the most fundamental aspects of her own life; the emotional stakes are high.

In her more current work the fragments of limbs and bodies have begun to compose themselves into indentifiable figures, often full portraits. Her subjects now have faces, some gaze implacably out at us, others look inward or away. Always the hands and arms are as expressive as the faces, they grasp, twine, and hold in a curious, rapturous embrace. Although more traditionally "composed" than her earlier work these new portraits benefit from an increasing sensitivity to personality, and to Tenneson's rapport with her subjects. For Tenneson the portrait becomes a "closed field of forces," to use Roland Barthes' term, made up of an interconnected series of "looks." As Barthes comments in *Camera Lucida* on the process of having his portrait taken, "In front of the lens, I am at the same time: the one I think I am, the one I want others to think I am, the one the photographer thinks I am, and the one he makes use of to exhibit his art." While retaining resonances of classical sculpture and a finely modulated sense of light, these newer works are less visually complicated but more psychologically complex.

Tenneson taught at the Corcoran School of Art, in Washington, D.C., for over ten years. She has exhibited both nationally and internationally, and has participated in photographic workshops around the world. With her success as a fine artist and teacher Tenneson has also felt free to pursue more "commercial" work in fashion photography. Yet her sensuous color studies for *Italian Vogue* seem an absolutely natural extension of her own, more private work. She stopped teaching in 1984 and has since supported herself throuth her own photography, commissioned portraits, and fashion assignments.

Tenneson sees her involvement with photography as a kind of performance designed to elicit an "intense, unspoken intimacy" a "passionate moment" in the act of making a photograph, which reveals as much of herself as it does of her subject. Certainly Tenneson's images transmit an eroticism, yet it is an eroticism that borrows from the body as well as the spirit, an intense longing-after that cannot be satisfied.

—Grant Kester

TESKE, Edmund (Rudolph).

Nationality: American. **Born:** Chicago, Illinois, 7 March 1911. **Education:** Attended Chicago public schools, 1916-28; self-taught in photography. **Career:** Photographer since 1928; also worked in the family business, Chicago, 1928-33, and as a designer, actor, make-up artist, and photographer, Theatre Department, Hull House, Chicago, 1933-34; Assistant Photographer, A. George Muller's Photography Inc., commercial photo studios, Chicago, 1934-36; established photo workshop, as an honorary Taliesin Fellow, Frank Lloyd Wright's Taliesin, Spring Green, Wisconsin, 1936-37; Instructor, New Bauhaus Institute of Design, under László Moholy-Nagy, Chicago, 1937-38; assistant, Katharine Kuh Gallery, Chicago, 1937-38; Instructor, Federal Arts Project, Chicago, 1939-40; assistant to the photographer Berenice Abbott, New York, 1940-41; worked for the United States Engineers, at Rock Island Arsenal, Illinois, 1941-43; settled in Los Angeles, 1943; worked in the photographic department, Paramount Pictures, Hollywood, 1944; assistant to Aline Barnsdall, Los Angeles, 1945-46; actor in the film *Lust for Life,* 1956; Instructor, Chouinard Art Institute, Los Angeles, 1962-64; Visiting Professor, under Robert Heinecken, University of California at Los Angeles, 1965-70; Visiting Instructor, Immaculate Heart College, Los Angeles, 1974; Visiting Professor, California State University at Los Angeles, 1979. **Recipient:** Certificate of Recognition, Photographic Society of America, 1969. **Address:** 1652 North Harvard Boulevard, Los Angeles, California 90027, U.S.A.

Individual Exhibitions:

1950	Third Street Gallery, Los Angeles
1954	Cafe Galeria, Laurel Canyon, Los Angeles
1961	Pasadena Art Museum, California
	Santa Barbara Museum of Art, California
1963	San Francisco Museum of Art
	Ceejee Gallery, Los Angeles
1965	Palos Verdes Community Association, California
1968	Camera Work Gallery, Costa Mesa, California
	3 Photographers, San Fernando State College, California (with Wynn Bullock and Frederick Sommer)
1970	Art Institute of Chicago
	Sheldon Memorial Art Gallery, University of Nebraska, Lincoln
1971	International Museum of Photography, George Eastman House, Rochester, New York
	Witkin Gallery, New York
	Mammoth Gallery, Mammoth Lake, California
1972	Ohio Silver Gallery, Los Angeles
1973	*3 Photographers,* University of Colorado, Boulder (with Wynn Bullock and Aaron Siskind)
	University of Southern California, Los Angeles
1974	Focus Gallery, San Francisco
	Light Impressions Gallery, Manhattan Beach, California
	Shado' Gallery, Oregon City, Oregon
	Municipal Art Gallery, Barnsdall Park, Los Angeles
1975	Friends of Photography, Carmel, California
	Revision Gallery, Santa Monica, California
1976	Susan Spiritus Gallery, Newport Beach, California
1977	Visual Studies Workshop, Rochester, New York
1985	Vision Gallery, San Francisco (with Colette Bravo)

Selected Group Exhibitions:

1960	*Sense of Abstraction,* Museum of Modern Art, New York
1962	*Contemporary Photographs,* University of California at Los Angeles
1964	*Purchase Award Photos from Krannert,* University of Illinois, Urbana (toured the United States)
1970	*Continuum,* Downey Museum of Art, Los Angeles
1973	*Light and Substance,* University of New Mexico, Albuquerque
1974	*Through One's Eyes,* Muckenthaler Cultural Center, Fullerton, California
1979	*A Survey of the Nude in Photography,* Witkin Gallery, New York
1981	*Photographer as Printmaker,* Ferens Art Gallery, Hull, Yorkshire (travelled to the Museum and Art Gallery, Leicester; Cooper Gallery, Barnsley; Castle Museum, Nottingham; Photographers' Gallery, London)
1984	*Photography in California 1945-80,* San Francisco Museum of Modern Art (travelled to the Akron Art Museum, Ohio; Corcoran Gallery, Washington, D.C.; Los Angeles Municipal Art Gallery; Cornell University, Ithaca, New York; High Museum of Art, Atlanta, Georgia; Museum Folkwang, Essen; Centre Georges Pompidou, Paris; Museum of Photographic Arts, San Diego, California)
1987	*Photography and Art 1946-86,* Los Angeles Country Museum of Art

Collections:

Museum of Modern Art, New York; International Museum of Photography, George Eastman House, Rochester, New York; Art Institute of Chicago; Krannert Art Museum, University of Illinois, Urbana; New Orleans Museum of Art; University of Nebraska, Lincoln; Center for Creative Photography, University of Arizona, Tucson; University of New Mexico, Albuquerque; San Francisco Museum of Art; Norton Simon Museum of Art, Pasadena, California.

Publications:

By TESKE: Book—*Untitled 22: Images from Within—The Photographs of Edmund Teske,* with an introduction by Aron Goldberg, Carmel, California 1980.

On TESKE: Books—Edmund Teske, exhibition catalogue, with text by Gerald Nordlund, Los Angeles 1974; *Photographs: Sheldon Memorial Art Gallery Collection, University of Nebraska,* with an introduction by Norman A. Geske, Lincoln, Nebraska 1977; *Photographer as Printmaker,* exhibition catalogue, with texts by Gerry Badger, Peter C. Bunnell and Ansel Adams, London 1981; *Counterparts: Form and Emotion in Photographs* by Weston J. Naef, New York 1982; *Photography in California 1945-1980* by Louise Katzman, San Francisco 1984; *Photography and Art 1946-1986,* exhibition catalogue, by Andy Grundberg and Kathleen M. Gauss, Los Angeles 1987. **Articles**—"Neglected Photographer" by Gerald Nordland in the *Los Angeles Mirror,* 21 August 1961; "Teske—Realist of Reverie" by Rosalind G. Wholden in the *Beverly Hills Times* (Los Angeles), 18 January 1963; "Edmund Teske" by Rosalind G. Wholden in *Artforum* (New York), February 1964; "The Work of Edmund Teske" by Aron Goldberg in the *Los Angeles Free Press,* 2 September 1966; "Little Seen, Less Said" by A.D. Coleman in the *Village Voice* (New York), 1 April 1971; "Edmund Teske" by Leland Rice in *Artweek* (Oakland, California), 27 October 1973; "Edmund Teske" by Lois R. Fishman in *Artweek* (Oakland, California), 27 April 1974.

*

Photography!
Summation of the life experience
Exquisite focal point of all being
Aromatic distillation
Inmost
And ultimate
Light.
From out of Darkness
Ascending, once again,
God alone.
Photography?
Realization,
Identity,
My religion of
Organic infoldment.
Spaciously
In the lap of
Mother alone
Full blown as a rose
Organic unfoldment.

—Edmund Teske

*   *   *

Suffused with a lyric mysticism, the photography of Edmund Teske is directed toward a spiritual investigation of the photographer's own psyche.

Dream, memory, sexuality and nature are among the primary components of Teske's introspective vision. Concerned as much with the printmaker's craft as with camera vision, Teske makes virtuosic use of photomontage, solarization and split-toning (or, in his term, "duo-toning") to create one-of-a-kind prints whose unique subtleties render them iconic. Within the context of Teske's work as a whole, they take on the role of religious objects, embodying the emotional and psychological nuances of the photographer's relationships to other people, to himself and his past, and to the natural and spiritual worlds.

These images are then organized into extended sequences and suites which are the photographer's preferred means of presentation. This makes possible the reiteration of central motifs, the presentation of variations on themes, and even the recurrence of specific image components—since, like many photographers who work with photomontage, Teske utilizes a file of negatives from

which his final images are built, and a particular key negative may be printed into numerous different image structures.

Such reiteration gives a cyclical, time-suspended ambience to Teske's oeuvre, and creates a coherence and continuity within it. Thus images from diverse areas and periods of Teske's life co-exist, combine and recombine in an ongoing exploration of personal experience.

The homoerotic has been a central issue in Teske's life and work, and his courageous insistence on manifesting it in his imagery dates back at least to the 1950s. Since at that time this aspect of self and sexuality was considered unacceptable, the professional repercussions of Teske's "coming out" were considerable, and its impact on his career severe. Now that this taboo has been lifted somewhat, Teske can be seen as a pioneer in that regard, to whom such photographers as Duane Michals, Arthur Tress and Robert Mapplethorpe are indebted directly.

Teske's willingness to address the intimate issues of autobiography in a frankly romantic and emotional fashion, and his embrace of photographic techniques (such as solarization) which the medium's dominant historians—Beaumont Newhall among them—have labelled "aberrations," have been inspirational to a younger generation of photographers seeking to claim as their birthright the full scope of the medium's possibilities. Through his role as a teacher, Teske has since the 1960s promulgated an approach to photography which encourages an openness to chance, experimentation, and the resonance of personal history. His advocacy of this position has been as influential as his imagery has been exemplary of its potential.

—A.D. Coleman

THOMAS, Lew(is Christopher).

Nationality: American. **Born:** San Francisco, California, 19 December 1932. **Education:** Studied under Robert Kirk, University of San Francisco, 1958-63, B.A. 1963; self-taught in photography, from 1967. **Family:** Married Natalie Joyce Simon in 1960; daughter: Kesa Louize. **Career:** Worked as a clerk, warehouseman, etc., in San Francisco, 1952-59. Independent photographer, San Francisco, 1967-85, and in Houston, Texas, since 1985. Manager, Legion of Honor Bookshop, San Francisco, 1963-82; Publisher and Editor, NFS Press, San Francisco, 1975-83; Director, Joseph Gross Gallery, University of Arizona, Tucson, 1983-84; Executive Director, Houston Center of Photography, and editor of *Spot* quarterly, Texas, since 1985. Visiting Artist, 1977, and Photography Instructor, 1981, San Francisco Art Institute; Photography Instructor, City College of San Francisco, 1982-83; Lecturer in Photography, San Francisco State University, 1983, and University of Arizona, Tucson, 1983-85; also Visiting Lecturer at several American universities from 1977. Member of the Artists' Committee, San Francisco Art Institute, 1979-83. **Recipient:** Ilo Liston Publications Award, Mills College/Western Association of Art Museums, 1974; Graphic Arts Award, Printing Industries of America, 1974, 1980; Publications Grant, SECA/San Francisco Museum of Modern Art, 1976; National Endowment for the Arts Photography Fellowship, 1975, 1980, 1981, and Exhibitions Grant, 1980, Washington, D.C.; Ellison Book Award, University of Cincinnati, Ohio, 1979. Member, College Art Association of America, 1982; Society for Photographic Education, 1982. **Agents:** Fraenkel Gallery, 55 Grant Avenue, San Francisco, California 94108, U.S.A.; Asher/Faure, 612 N. Almont, Los Angeles, California 90069, U.S.A. **Address:** 1441 West Alabama, Houston, Texas 77007, U.S.A.

Individual Exhibitions:

1973   *Photography of Ennui,* University of Santa Clara, California
1974   *Photographic Corners,* San Francisco Art Institute
1975   *8 x 10,* Lamkin Camerawork Gallery, Fairfax, California
         8 x 10, Mills College, Oakland, California
         Bracketing, Darkroom Workshop, Berkeley, California
1976   *Photographic Works,* William Sawyer Gallery, San Francisco
         Outside/Inside, Coffee Gallery, San Francisco
         Vitruvian Context 1482-1976, San Jose State University, California

1979   *Bibliography(s),* Lawson De Celle Gallery, San Francisco
        Scale, Washington Project for the Arts, Washington, D.C.
1980   *Installation,* Zriny Hayes Gallery, Chicago
        Bookspines, Asher/Faure Gallery, Los Angeles
        Bookspines, Fraenkel Gallery, San Francisco
        Reproductions of Reproductions, Center for Creative Photography, University of Arizona, Tucson
1981   *Installation,* Ohio State University, Columbus
1985   *VCR Film Stills,* Asher Faure Gallery, Los Angeles
1986   *VCR Film Stills,* Modernism Gallery, San Francisco
        University of Texas, Arlington
        Graham Gallery, Houston, Texas
        Artists League of Texas, Abilene

Selected Group Exhibitions:

1976   *Photography and Language,* LaMamelle Gallery, San Francico
1978   *Mirrors and Windows,* Museum of Modern Art, New York
1980   *Absage an das Einzelbild,* Museum Folkwang, Essen, West Germany
1981   *Erweiterte Fotografie,* at the *Biennale Wiener Sezession,* Vienna
1982   *Target III: In Sequence,* Houston Museum of Fine Arts, Texas
1983   *Big Pictures by Contemporary Photographers,* Museum of Modern Art, New York
1984   *Photography in California 1945-80,* San Francisco Museum of Modern Art
1985   *Arizona Photographers,* Arizona State University, Tempe
1986   *Stills: Cinema and Video Transformed,* Seattle Art Museum, Washington
1987   *Cross Currents,* Los Angeles County Museum of Art (toured the United States)

Collections:

Aschenbach Foundation, San Francisco; Museum of Modern Art, New York; Princeton University, New Jersey; University of Santa Clara, California; Washington Project for the Arts, Washington, D.C.; Center for Creative Photography, University of Arizona, Tucson; Houston Museum of Fine Arts, Texas; Chase Manhattan Bank, New York.

Publications:

By THOMAS: Books—*The Thinker,* exhibition catalogue, San Francisco 1974; *8 x 10,* San Francisco 1975; *Photography and Language,* editor, San Francisco 1976; *Eros and Photography,* co-editor, San Francisco 1976; *Photography and Ideology,* editor, Los Angeles 1977; *Gay Semiotics,* editor, San Francisco 1978; *Structuralism and Photography,* San Francisco 1979; *18th Near Castro Street x 24,* editor, San Francisco 1979; *Pages from a Child's Documentary,* co-author, San Francisco 1980; *Still Photography: The Problematic Model,* co-editor, San Francisco 1981; *The Restless Decade: John Gutmann's Photographs of the Thirties,* co-author, New York 1984. **Articles**—"Notes" in *San Francisco Camera* (San Francisco), no. 5, 1972; "Michael Snow: Cover to Cover" in *Art Contemporary* (San Francisco) no. 2/3, 1976; "The One ... The Other (sic)" in *San Francisco Bay Area Photography,* exhibition catalogue, San Francisco 1976; "Photography and Ideology: Theory, Review and Correspondence" in *Art Contemporary* (San Francisco), no. 4, 1977; "Analogical Aesthetics" in *Intermedia Broadside* (Los Angeles), no. 1, 1977; "In the Beginning Was the Word—And Since Then There's Been the Quote" in *U-Turn Supplement* (Los Angeles), no. 1, 1984; "Forgetting Camerawork" in *SF State Photo Group Newsletter* (San Francisco), no. 5, 1985; "What Was/Is NFS Press" in *Exposure* (New York), Spring 1985; "Desire of the Other" in *Spot* (Houston, Texas), no. 6, 1986.

On THOMAS: Books—*Mirrors and Windows: American Photography Since 1960* by John Szarkowski, New York 1978; *An Introduction to Modern Times: Culture and Anarchy* by George Myers, Jr., Westerville, Ohio 1983; *Photography in California 1945-1980* by Louise Katzman, San Francisco 1984. **Articles**—"Taking Pictures" by Martha Charoudi in *Afterimage*

(Rochester, New York), April 1977; "Lew Thomas' Library" by Joan Morgan in *Artweek* (Oakland, California), August 1980; "You Can't Tell a Book by Its Cover" by Robert C. Morgan in *LAICA Journal* (Los Angeles), September 1980; "A Structuralist Trilogy" by James Hugunin in *Catskill Center Quarterly* (Woodstock, New York), Summer 1983; "Metropolis" by James Hugunin in *Afterimage* (Rochester, New York), December 1984; "Art" by Michael Lawrence in *West Hollywood Paper* (Hollywood, California), 12 December 1985; "Reshaping the Familiar" by Mark Johnstone in *Artweek* (Oakland, California), 21 December 1985.

*

Since 1971 my work as a photographer, and later as an editor, curator and teacher, can best be described as a commitment to photography based on ideas or concepts, particularly as they parallel the sign systems of language. This commitment can be followed in the work from its earliest period dealing with the photograph as a systemic object whose relationship to time was as important as any considerations of space, light or the autonomy of single image photography.

As I learned to trust the conceptual aspects of working with photography from a structural point of view, the work evolved into installations and collaborative ventures which culminated in a series of exhibitions and publications produced chiefly through the auspices of the NFS Press, San Francisco, 1976-1983: *Photography and Language, Eros and Photography, Structuralism and Photography,* and *Still Photography: The Problematic Model.* Concomitant with the progress of the work was an increased awareness of how to combine issues related to language, literature, and philosophy with the processes of image making. For me, the power of photography comes from its capacity to unite these issues in personal forms of expression. This is obviously different than simply making pictures of ineffable beauty or ugliness.

Extremely important to whatever success these projects sustained was the creative support of Donna-Lee Phillips, editor of *Eros and Photography,* and the production and design person who worked ceaselessly with me on all the NFS publications. Other significant collaborators were Hal Fisher, author of *Gay Semiotics* and *18th Near Castro Street x 24,* Meyer Hirsch, publisher of the *New Commercialist,* Harley Lond, publisher of *Intermedia,* and the indefatigable James Hugunin, critic, editor and publisher of *Dumb Ox* and *U-Turn.*

In 1976 I had the rare opportunity to become friends with John Gutmann whose work fascinated me because of its implicit reliance on language and because of its unique style of representing the 1930s in America, especially the City of San Francisco where I was born. These photographs of San Francisco affected me deeply since they seem to offer a look into the world of my parents and my childhood, so authentic was the mood and texture of the times conveyed to me by these remarkable images.

John allowed me the use of his photographs in many of our publications, and together we were able finally to create the first comprehensive monograph of his work, *The Restless Decade,* published by Harry N. Abrams, Inc., of New York.

My recent work, completed while teaching at the University of Arizona in 1985, employs video and color still photography which represents for me current issues involving the transition of our society to an electronic environment and the diminishment of analogical experience. All this engages the critique and breakdown of classical codes that have ruled historically through the male dominant agencies of education, law, politics, and the social relations among different economic, racial and sexual classes of people.

—Lew Thomas

*   *   *

In the 1970s most people called what Lew Thomas did "conceptual photography," meaning it relied on a prior concept or idea and was often formally predetermined, unlike the experientially motivated "expression" of modernist pictorial photography. Although this perceived dichotomy was useful in provoking some of the most lively and substantive dialogue in recent photographic history, it was never adequate to an understanding of Thomas's work. In fact, the pre-determined forms were always a way to more directly experience and express photographic meaning and content. To this end,

Thomas performed radically simple operations with his camera, going back to the most basic images and arrangements in order to strip the language down to its constitutive structure and uncover (recover) the *basic elements* of the linguistic system of photography.

Thomas came to photography taking *nothing* for granted. *Everything* was questioned, everything tested. As he's said, his method was derived in large part from observing his young daughter "at play." In much of his early work an attempt was made to simplify images, to limit the variables in acts of measurement, location and limitation. Time, light and shadow, perspective, framing (8 x 10, 16 x 20, 36 frames) and scale—all were isolated and investigated as constituents of meaning.

Structuralism and Photography (NFS Press, 1978) is a text formed of photographs, letters, reviews, theoretical writing and quotes, documenting Thomas's concerns and early practice. It can also be read as a sort of pedagogical sketchbook. Thomas has always been one of the most literate of contemporary artists. His "Bibliography" pieces emphasize *reading,* and involve photography of books, books of photography, writing and editing of books, quotes from books, readings traced, and "reproductions of reproductions." The *photographed word* was one of his initial attractions to John Gutmann's photographs from the Thirties, with their billboards, signs and graffiti all screaming out from the urban landscape, making claims across time: "Sit in Your Car—See and Hear TALKING PICTURES!" The collection of Gutmann's photographs that Thomas edited for Abrams in 1984, *The Restless Decade,* is a triumph of editorial historical reclamation. Thomas's influential work as editor, curator, teacher and writer comes directly out of and extends his work as photographer—all are acts of selection, recognition and attention, revealing constitutive connections among representational and linguistic systems. In the belief that conventional (repressive) structures necessarily carry repressive (conventional) messages, he has interrogated such structures as ideological tools in the politics of representation, and has countered such structures with a "photography that advances itself by theoretical use."

Over the years, Thomas's concern with what Hans Haacke calls "the consciousness industry"—the conglomerate apparatus for influencing public opinion through words and images ("mass media")—has become more focussed, and has resulted in work which is more mimetic of popular techniques, and more broadly "communicative" than the earlier groundwork.

His most recent work reproduces images from the electronic environment in the static form of still photography in order to slow down the ideological barrage for analysis and transformation. His "VCR Film Stills" translate iconic black and white movie stills through a half inch video camera and manipulate them by adding color in the camera. 16 x 20 inch color photographs are made by photographing these altered stills from a TV monitor. This process mimics the currently popular practice of watching Hollywood movies at home by way of a VCR. The "VCR Film Stills" are beautiful objects, seductive enough to enter the image environment competitively. The mimicry is interrupted and transformed by the addition of captions, computer-generated onto the photographed TV screen. These short captions comment on and contradict the language of pictorial rhetoric evident in the original images, and interrogate their methods. A still from "High Noon" pictures lawman Gary Cooper with his hands full, holding "the woman" close in submissive protection with one hand, while preparing to shoot someone with the gun in his other hand. He gazes purposefully in the direction the gun is pointed. She gazes helplessly, adoringly at him. The image is split into upper and lower halves, each half TV-framed. The caption above reads "Whose Gaze," below, "Hose Law." The strong feminist statement is coupled with a trenchant question concerning the politics of pictorial representation. Throughout the series, the racism, sexism and economic class bias of the original messages are laid bare by the addition of conscious captions, which seem to be generated out of the images themselves—more *readings* than writings. The process of TV viewing is slowed down and problematized. The dominant ideology carried by the originals is short-circuited as is the passive gaze of the TV viewer.

Thomas's photographic/text work has always encouraged *reading* as opposed to more passive "viewing." He persistently recognizes photography as a language which can and must be used to reach and *act on* the world.

—David Levi Strauss

THORMANN, Ernst.

Nationality: German. **Born:** Breslau (now Wroclaw, Poland), 29 May 1905. **Education:** Educated in Berlin, until 1919; mainly self-taught in photography, from 1920. **Family:** Married Frieda Schneider in 1945. **Career:** Amateur photographer, Berlin, from 1929: member, 1926-33, and picture technician, 1929-33, Vereinigung der Arbeiter-Fotografen Deutschlands (German Worker-Photographers' Union), Berlin. Worked as an engraver, Firma Brugman, Berlin-Neukolln, 1920-24; unemployed, 1925-30; printing plate retoucher, Druckerei Carl Sabo, Berlin, 1930-43; worked for the German Democratic Republic mass media, in East Berlin, 1949-70. **Died:** (in East Berlin) in 1985.

Individual Exhibitions:

1981   Galerie Otto-Nagel-Haus, East Berlin

Selected Group Exhibitions:

1977   *Medium Fotografie,* Staatliche Galerie Moritzburg, Halle, East
            Germany

Collections:

Deutsche Fotothek, Sachsisches Landesmuseum, Dresden, East Germany; Gesellschaft für Fotografie—Zentralverband, East Berlin; Fotokinoverlag, Leipzig, East Germany.

Publications:

By THORMANN: Book—*Ernst Thormann,* with introduction by Rainer Knapp, Leipzig 1981.

On THORMANN: Books—*Medium Fotografie,* edited by Andreas Huneke, Gerhard Ihrke, Alfred Neumann and Ullrich Wallenburg, Leipzig 1979; *Fotografie im Klassenkampf* by Erich Rinka, Leipzig 1981. **Article**—"Ernst Thormann—Ein Arbeiterfotograf" in *Fotografie* (Leipzig), no. 9, 1978.

*   *   *

Ernst Thormann belongs in the ranks of the most important representatives of German social documentary photography between the two World Wars. An early childhood talent for painting, drawing and modelling led to an apprenticeship in steel-engraving. It was at the age of 16, on completion of his apprenticeship, that a friend drew Thormann's attention to photography in the form of a 9 x 12 cm format camera. Naturally, his earliest efforts revolved around simple depictions of his immediate family, but Thormann soon found his way to the amateur photo group of the Naturfreunde Association—a movement very popular throughout Germany at the time. Here, Thormann came into contact with the remnants of the now fading pictorialist movement, and even admired its painterly qualities in soft bromoil tones and classical rules of composition. Before long, however, he perceived the importance of training his photographic eye, and a realization of photography's sharp documentary powers. The idea of expressing socio-critical messages in photographs did not impress itself on Thormann's mind until he joined the left-wing youth movement. His photographic evolution was further determined by the German economic crisis, in which the young Thormann found himself unemployed.

He now spent his time collaborating as an occasional reporter for the *Arbeiter-Illustrierte-Zeitung (AIZ)* journal. His contacts there, especially with noted writers such as Egon Erwin Kisch, provided a stimulating intellectual climate in which to evolve as a live-action photographer. As soon as the Verein der Arbeiter Fotografen Deutschlands (German Worker Photographers' Union) came into existence, Thormann enlisted his services as one of its most energetic organizers. Being relatively skilled (as a *nearly* professional reporter) he used his experience to teach new members about photographic techniques and the art of getting the effective message into the viewfinder. The role as trainer of younger colleagues helped hone Thormann's already considerable critical acumen, and he became a kind of mediator between the club's newcomers and the editorial staff of *AIZ*.

Thormann's own photographic interests principally turned on the life of the streets. He took powerful shots of roadmenders renewing asphalt surfaces, of poor children on pavements and of traders in the market place. The eloquence of these photos stemmed from his acute understanding of the ordinary person's everyday life. Images from a variety of social milieux made effective counterpoint in his photo essays, although his interest in workers and their families always prevailed. Eager to master every aspect of the medium to the degree that each photograph would effectively render his vision permanent, Thormann explored the shady world of depression nightclubs as well as of the beggars awaiting the appearance of people from cinemas and theatres. When racist propaganda became public policy, Thormann made foreboding images of Nazi thugs persecuting gypsy families—a premonition of future atrocities.

Under the Nazi government, all left-wing organizations, including the Arbeiter-Fotografen, were suppressed in Germany. At this time Thormann went underground as an illegal activist in the anti-nazi movement and managed to avoid discovery. After World War II, his poor health did not permit him the active life of a photoreporter, and he gained employment in the Democratic Republic's mass media. It was thus that Thormann's remarkable photographic oeuvre of the 1920s and 1930s became a closed chapter.

—Vladimìr Birgus

TICE, George A(ndrew).

Nationality: American. **Born:** Newark, New Jersey, 13 October 1938. **Education:** Studied commercial photography at Newark Vocational and Technical High School, 1955. **Military Service:** Served as a photographer's mate in the United States Navy, in Memphis, Tennessee, and on the *U.S.S. Wasp*, 1956-59. **Family:** Married Joanna Blaylock in 1958 (divorced, 1960); Marie Tremmel in 1960 (divorced, 1976); children: Christopher, Loretta, Lisa, Lynn and Jennifer. **Career:** Worked as a home portrait photographer, Americana Portraits Inc., West Orange, New Jersey, 1960-69. Freelance photographer, since 1969. Instructor in Photography, New School for Social Research, New York, since 1970. **Recipient:** Grand Prix, *Festival d'Arles,* 1973; National Endowment for the Arts Photography Fellowship, 1973; Guggenheim Fellowship, 1973; Joint Fellowship in Photography at The National Museum of Photography, Film and Television, Bradford and Ilkley, Community College, 1990-91. **Agent:** Witkin Gallery, 415 West Broadway, New York, New York 10012, U.S.A. **Address:** 323 Gill Lane, No. 9B, Iselin, New Jersey 08830, U.S.A.

Individual Exhibitions:

1965	Underground Gallery, New York
1966	Gallery 216, New York
1970	*The Amish Portfolio,* E. Weyhe Gallery, New York
	831 Gallery, Birmingham, Michigan
	Fields of Peace, Witkin Gallery, New York
1971	*Paterson,* New Jersey Historical Museum, Newark
1972	*Paterson, New Jersey,* Metropolitan Museum of Art, New York
1973	*Seacoast Maine,* Witkin Gallery, New York
	The Photography Place, Berwyn, Pennsylvania
1974	Silver Image Gallery, Tacoma, Washington
	Festival d'Arles, France
1975	Rutgers University, New Brunswick, New Jersey
	Witkin Gallery, New York
1976	New Jersey State Museum, Trenton
	Afterimage Gallery, Dallas
	Susan Spiritus Gallery, Newport Beach, California
	Pedro Meyer and George Tice, Enjay Gallery, Boston
1977	Milwaukee Center for Photography
	Werkstatt für Photographie der VHS Kreuzberg, Berlin

	Artie Van Blarcum, Witkin Gallery, New York
1978	Cronin Gallery, Houston
	Atlanta Gallery of Photography
	Columbia Gallery, Missouri
1979	*Liberty Park,* Museum of Modern Art, New York
	Maitland Art Center, Florida
	North Carolina State University, Raleigh
	Jeb Gallery, Providence, Rhode Island
	The Photography Place, Philadelphia
1980	Robeson Center Gallery, Newark, New Jersey
	Metropolitan Museum, Miami Beach
	Gallery Exposures, Coral Gables, Florida
1981	Hills Gallery, Denver, Colorado
	The Photographs of George Tice 1953-1981, Witkin Gallery, New York
1982	Images Gallery, Cincinnati, Ohio
1983	Governor's State University, Park Forest South, Illinois
	Lone Star Photographic Workshops, Austin, Texas
	Simon Gallery, Montclair, New Jersey
1984	*Lincoln,* Witkin Gallery, New York
1985	Hermitage Foundation Museum, Helsinki
	Barron Arts Center, Woodbridge, New Jersey
	Main Street to Red Square, Drew University, Madison, New Jersey
1986	*Photographs of the Amish,* Susan Spiritus Gallery, Newport Beach, California
1987	*Seacoast Maine,* Bentler-Morgan Galleries, Houston
	Seacoast Maine, 253 Gallery, Norfolk, Virginia
1988	*Seacoast Maine,* Photo Gallery International, Tokyo
	Hometowns, The Chrysler Museum, Norfolk, Virginia
	Hometowns, The Witkin Gallery, New York
1989	*Hometowns,* The Photographer's Gallery of Palo Alto, California
	Photographs, SCP Gallery, Kansas City, Missouri
	Hometowns, Photo Gallery International, Tokyo
	Hometowns, Susan Spiritus Gallery, Costa Mesa, California
	A Retrospective: 1961-1988, Photo Forum, Pittsburgh
1990	*Hometowns,* The Afterimage, Dallas, Texas
	Photographs, A Gallery for Fine Photography, New Orleans
	Hometowns, Oklahoma City Art Museum, Oklahoma
1991	*Stone Walls, Grey Skies,* National Museum of Photography, Film and Television, Bradford, England
1992	*Stone Walls, Grey Skies,* The Photographer's Gallery of Palo Alto, California
	Stone Walls, Grey Skies, The Witkin Gallery, New York
	Stone Walls, Grey Skies, Photo Gallery International, Tokyo
1993	*Photographs,* Fay Gold Gallery, Georgia

Selected Group Exhibitions:

1971	*Obsolete Processes/Contemporary Practitioners,* Art Institute of Chicago
1973	*Landscape/Cityscape,* Metropolitan Museum of Art, New York
1974	*Photography in America,* Whitney Museum, New York
1976	*Aspects of American Photography,* University of Missouri at St. Louis
1977	*Concerning Photography,* The Photographers' Gallery, London (travelled to the Spectro Workshop, Newcastle upon Tyne)
1978	*Mirrors and Windows: American Photography since 1960,* Museum of Modern Art, New York (toured the United States, 1978-80)
1980	*The Imaginary Photo Museum,* Kunsthalle, Cologne
1983	*Arboretum,* University of Denver, Colorado
1984	*The Documentary Photograph,* Southern Illinois University, Carbondale
1985	*Visions and Vistas,* 253 Gallery, Norfolk, Virginia
1990	*Money Matters: A Critical Look at Bank Architecture,* Museum of Fine Art, Houston, Texas
1992	*George Tice and Richard Benson,* Scheinbaum & Russek Ltd, Santa Fe, New Mexico

Buckstones, Scamonden Moor, Yorkshire, from *Stone Walls, Grey Skies: A Vision of Yorkshire,* **1990.** Photograph by George Tice.

Collections:

Metropolitan Museum of Art, New York; Museum of Modern Art, New York; New Jersey State Museum, Trenton; Library of Congress, Washington, D.C.; Art Institute of Chicago; Minneapolis Institute of Arts; University of Kansas, Lawrence; Amon Carter Museum Fort Worth, Texas; Victoria and Albert Museum, London; Bibliothèque Nationale, Paris; Nihon University, Japan; Whitney Museum of American Art, New York; High Museum of Art, Atlanta, Georgia.

Publications:

By TICE: Books—*Fields of Peace: A Pennsylvania German Album,* with text by Millen Brand, New York 1970; *Goodbye, River, Goodbye,* with poems by George Mendoza, New York 1971; *Paterson,* New Brunswick, New Jersey 1972; *Seacoast Maine: People and Places,* with text by Martin Dibner, New York 1973; *George A. Tice: Photographs 1953-73,* with an introduction by Lee Witkin, New Brunswick, New Jersey 1975 (includes bibliography); *Urban Landscapes: A New Jersey Portrait,* New Brunswick, New Jersey 1975; *Artie Van Blarcum: An Extended Portrait,* Danbury, New Hampshire 1977; *Urban Romantic,* Boston 1982; *Lincoln,* New Brunswick, New Jersey 1984; *Hometowns, An American Pilgrimage,* Boston, 1988; *Stone Walls, Grey Skies: A Vision of Yorkshire,* Bradford, England, 1991 (second edition/ expanded 1993). **Articles**—"The Lost Art of Platinum" in *Album* (London), no. 11, 1970; "George Tice," interview, with J. Novak, in *Camera 35* (New York), February 1978; interview in *Photography Between Covers* by Thomas Dugan, Rochester, New York 1979; "Conversation with George Tice," with

W. Abranowicz, in *Photography Forum* (Santa Barbara, California), May/ June 1980.

On TICE: Books—*The Print* by Time-Life editors, New York 1970; *Photography Year 1973* by Time-Life editors, New York 1972; *Photography in America,* edited by Robert Doty, with an introduction by Minor White, New York and London 1974; *Darkroom* by Eleanor Lewis, Rochester, New York 1977; *Concerning Photography,* exhibition catalogue, by Sue Davies and others, London 1977; *Mirrors and Windows: American Photography since 1960,* exhibition catalogue, by John Szarkowski, New York 1978; *The Darkroom Handbook by Curtin, DeMaio and London,* Marblehead, Massachusetts 1979; *The Photograph Collector's Guide* by Lee D. Witkin and Barbara London, Boston 1979; *A Ten Year Salute,* edited by Lee D. Witkin, Danbury, New Hampshire 1979; *The Platinum Print* by J. Hafey and T. Shillea, Rochester, New York 1980; *Landscape: Theory,* edited by Carol Di Grappa, New York 1980; *Signs of Life* by Alfred Appel, New York 1983; *A World History of Photography* by Naomi Rosenblum, New York 1984; *The Library of World Photography: Landscape,* with texts by David Plowden and Ian Jeffrey, Tokyo and London 1984. **Articles**—"Fields of Peace" by P. Killer in *Du* (Zurich), December 1971; "Book Review: Paterson" by S. Schwartz in *Art International* (Lugano), November 1972; "George Tice: Craft and Vision" by Julia Scully in *Modern Photography* (New York), February 1975; "Book Review: Urban Landscapes" by Peggy Sealfon in *Camera 35* (New York), November 1976; "Recent Books—Urban Landscapes" by Gerry Badger in *British Journal of Photography* (London), 25 March 1977; "The Native Eye" by N. Sullivan in *New Jersey Monthly* (Princeton), January 1980; "Magic and the Fine Print" by R. Hilliard in *Darkroom/Photography* (San Francisco), July/August 1980; "Romantic Notions" by Barbara London in *Camera Arts* (New York), June 1983; "George A. Tice" by Harri Hietala in *Valokuva* (Helsinki), May 1984; "Photos of George A. Tice" by M. Leonteiv in *Sovetskoye Photo* (Moscow), March 1985; reviews of "Hometowns" by Andy Grundberg, *The New York Times,* 4 December, 1988; Ralph Novak, *People Magazine,* 9 January, 1989; James Kaufman, *Photographer's Forum,* November, 1988.

*

Photography is whatever you want it to be.

—George A. Tice

* * *

Any consideration of George A. Tice's photographs must include the word "unusual"—with the caution not to use the word too often. His formal education ended abruptly in vocational high school which had fostered his interest in photography, begun at the age of 14 in a local camera club. A short time as darkroom assistant for a commercial photographer was followed by enlistment at 17 years of age in the United States Navy as Photographer's Mate. When Tice returned home to New Jersey, he joined the Vailsburg Camera Club in Newark and became active in competitions and judgings that helped develop his aesthetic attitudes. For several years following, he made his livelihood as a photographer of infants in New Jersey and California. However, during the time Tice was in the Navy he had photographed an explosion aboard the *U.S.S. Wasp*; in 1959 this photograph came to the attention of Edward Steichen, then director of the photography department at the Museum of Modern Art in New York, who acquired a print for the museum's collection. This event marked the first national recognition for Tice's work and the beginning of his relationship with Steichen, for whom he became protégé and printmaker. Tice's determination for personal growth is highlighted in his self-assignment to perform the major experiments and discoveries in the history of photography. His many and diverse experiences, beginning early in life, have served to broaden his vision, provide a continuum for building technical competencies and shape professional opportunities. The late Lee Witkin, a long-time friend of Tice, referred to him as having taught himself everything, gaining a firm place in his art which contains spare romanticism in seeking perfection and beauty.

Tice's essential interest in places is illustrated in his study of Paterson, New Jersey, which was published in a book with the same name. Using an 8 x 10 inch format camera, he recorded parts of this city in his straight-forward manner, providing icons of the urban condition of many cities. Without nostalgia for Paterson's more fortunate historic past, he did not overlook its spectacular falls (the Passaic River), trees and bluffs. Almost as a footnote, he photographed, with a hand-held 35mm camera, local people on downtown streets. This book is another of Tice's self-assignments and illustrates his complete dedication to a project, sensitiveness to a subject and thoroughness of effort; a commercial assignment of this type might have been completed in one week or so. His vision grew as he developed insights about the city as it was revisited and photographed over several years.

A review of Tice's work to date reveals that most subjects have been places, rather than people. However, his "places" emit emotional content that includes feelings of human presence—that someone may have just left or is about to appear. There is also a sense of intrigue suggested by the tonal ranges (often low key) and the placement of light in the negative and/or induced in the darkroom. Color is not essential in Tice's photographs, partly because of the choice of subject matter—but more important is the aura which takes its place. He does not use color materials because of their general impermanence; he believes that black-and-white photography is immortality.

Characteristic of artists and typical of Tice's work is that, with time, it becomes more difficult to generalize about him. This condition results from new interests which produce change and inconsistencies in the choice of subject matter and how it is interpreted. His photographs in *Fields of Peace* are revealing and straight reporting of both the Pennsylvania German people and their farmlands. Another departure from "places" is Tice's photo-essay *Artie Van Blarcum,* which has the subtitle, "An Extended Portrait." And that it is: a selection of photographs about one person by the photographer, who is again on self-assignment, over a long period of time. Here the emphasis is upon one subject: a person. That person was the focus of Tice's attention, and, as with

Paterson, time let him reflect and review what he had done and needed to do in presenting his subject while still in the process of doing it. With Tice's informal photographs of a factory worker, Artie, and written comments, intimacy and identification merge to reveal that "there's a little bit of Artie in all of us."

Tice's book *Lincoln* features places and things which bear the name of the (U.S.) Civil War president Abraham Lincoln. Objects photographed include local bars, parks, motels, statues and, of course, outdoor signs.

His newest project, over three years in the making, has the working title *Hometowns, An American Pilgrimage.* Featured are three small towns which he senses have qualities that contribute to natives upon becoming adults. Selected are Dixon, Illinois, Fairmount, Indiana, and Hannibal, Missouri—boyhood locales of Ronald Reagan, James Dean and Mark Twain, respectively. In personal and diverse ways these men incurred Tice's pictorial interests.

Much of Tice's work has historical themes. He seems to prefer subjects with significant pasts; when selecting subjects, he not only considers their romantic/aesthetic appeal, but also the opportunity to display his masterly technical skills.

George A. Tice's mastery of photographic techniques can be accounted for by his interest and diligence in the study of equipment, materials and processes plus the practice of what he has learned. The unusual range of subjects he selects for painstaking portrayal naturally follows his inclination, in his fifties, not to develop a personal style: an artist can have many visions.

—Robert W. Cooke

TOMASZEWSKI, Tomasz.

Nationality: Polish. **Born:** Warsaw, 6 May 1953. **Education:** Studied physics, Warsaw University, 1973-74; studied optics, Technical University, Warsaw, 1974-78; self-taught in photography from 1975. **Family:** Married the journalist Malgorzata Niezbitowska in 1978; daughter: Maryna. **Career:** Photojournalist, *ITD* weekly paper, Warsaw, 1975-76; staff photographer, *Razem,* 1976-77, and *Perspektywy* weekly magazines, Warsaw, 1977-81; also freelance commercial and theatre photographer, working with the Polish Jazz Association, Pagart Art Agency, Alex Band, Kombi, Ewa Bem, Laboratorium and Stefan Zach pop musicians, and the Poznan Polski Theatre, Gdynia Music Theatre and Warsaw Jewish Theatre, 1978-81. Since 1981, freelance photographer, working with *Solidarity Weekly,* Warsaw, 1981, and *National Geographic* magazine, Washington, D.C., from 1985. Work for Polish underground press 1982-1985. Photography Editor, *Przeglad Katolicki* magazine, Warsaw, 1984-85. Publications in magazines such as *Stern, Paris Match, Welt Woche, La Croix, La Vie, Famiglia Christiana, Die Zeit.* Lecturer on Photography, Film and Television College, Katowice, 1985. Lectures at the Film and Television School, Poland, 1988-90. Lectures at the International Photographic Workshop, Bulgaria, 1991. Lectures at the International Photographic Workshop, Hungary, 1992. Member, ANA Photo Agency, Paris, since 1981; deputy chairman, Union of Polish Art Photographers, (ZPAF), Warsaw, since 1985; member of the jury of World Press Photo, Amsterdam, 1992-93; member of the German Photo Agency-VISUM Archiv 1994. **Recipient:** First Prize, 20th Press Photography Competition, Warsaw, 1977; Solidarity Award, Warsaw, 1985, 1986; honourable mention for the category Magazine-News-Series, in *Washington Journalism Review,* first annual photojournalism competition, 1992. **Address:** 05-510 Konstancin-Jeziorna, ul Batorego #19, Poland.

Individual Exhibitions:

1975	*Pokoje na godziny,* Technical University, Warsaw
1976	*Korytarz,* Klub Akademik, Warsaw
	Sytuacje rodzinne, Klub Mechanik, Warsaw
1985	*The Last Polish Jews—Remnants,* ZPAF Gallery, Warsaw
1986	*The Last Polish Jews—Remnants,* ZPAF Gallery, Krakow, Poland (travelled to Katowice, Poland)
	National Geographic Society, Washington, D.C.
	International Center of Photography, New York

Spring Cleaning after Communist Rule, **Kozlowka, 1991.** Photograph by Tomasz Tomaszewski.

1987   Prince Gallery, Detroit, Michigan
         Robert Kahn Gallery, Houston, Texas
         Beth Tzedec Museum, Toronto, Ontario
         National Press Club, Washington, D.C.
1988   Beth Hatefutsot Museum, Tel Aviv, Israel
         Culture Centre, Jerusalem
1989   Zacheta Gallery, Warsaw
1990   Canon Gallery, Amsterdam

Selected Group Exhibitions:

1976   *Press Photography,* ZPAF Gallery, Warsaw
1978   *Photo-Reports,* Photo-Medium-Art Gallery, Wroclaw, Poland
1979   *Art Photography—Jantar 79,* ZPAF Gallery, Gdansk, Poland
1980   *Polish Photography,* Polish Cultural Institute, Stockholm
         Socially-Engaged Photography, Bydgoszcz Art Gallery,
          Poland
1983   *Holy Father's Second Pilgrimage to Poland,* St. Hyacinthus
          Church, Warsaw
1984   *Photos for the Catholic Review,* God's Grace Church, Zytnia
          Street, Warsaw

1985   *Contemporary Polish Art Photography,* Zacheta Gallery,
          Warsaw
         Photographies Polonaises du XXe Siecle, Forum du Credit
          Mutuel, Digne, France

Collections:

Museum of Art, Lodz, Poland; National Library, Warsaw.

Publications:

By TOMASZEWSKI: Books—*Cofni wskazowe zegara/Put the Clock Back,* with text by A. Rowinski, Warsaw 1980; *Die verbannten Dichter,* with text by J. Serke, Hamburg 1982; *Cyganie Polscy/Polish Gypsies,* with text by J. Ficowski, Warsaw 1985; *The Last Jews of Poland—Remnants,* with text by Malgorzata Niezbitowska, New York 1986; *Die Letzen Juden in Polen,* Zurich, 1987; *Day in the Life of America,* New York, 1987; *Day in the Life of Spain,* New York, 1988; *Day in the Life of Soviet Union,* New York, 1988; *Odyssey, the Art of Photography,* Washington, D.C., 1989; *Power to Heal,* New York, 1990; *Remnants, the Last Jews of Poland,* Warsaw, 1993; *In Search of America,* Warsaw, 1994. **Reportages and photos—***ITD* (Warsaw), 1976; *Razem* (Warsaw), 1977; *Perspektywy* (Warsaw), 1977; and in *Stern*

(Hamburg), *La Vie* (Paris), *Weltwoche* (Zurich), La Croix (Paris), *Famiglia Christiana* (Rome), *Paris-Match* (Paris), 1981-83, and *National Geographic* (Washington, D.C.), 1986.

On TOMASZEWSKI: Articles—"Remnants of Polish Jewry Sit for a Bleak Photo Portrait" by Mathew Vita in *Chicago Tribune,* 6 December 1985; "Ostatni" by Tadeusz Szyma in *Tygodnik Powszechny* (Krakow, Poland), 8 December 1985; "Dlaczego ostatni" by Jan Saber in *Kultura Niezalezna* (Warsaw), December 1985; "Nieostra fotografia" by Jerzy Busza in *Kultura* (Warsaw), January 1986; "Epitafium," interview with Malgorzata Niezbitowska, in *Niewidomy Spoldzielca* (Warsaw), February 1986; "Nagrody Solidarnosci—Tomasz Tomaszewski" in *Kos* (Warsaw), 23 February 1986; "Nie wszystek umre" by Irena Frackowiak in *Nowiny* (Rzeszow, Poland), 7 October 1986.

*   *   *

It has been said that contemporary Poland is a country in which nothing is possible. As soon as this is the case, however, anything and everything can happen. Recent history is the best proof of this. Hence, a cardinal from a communist country has become the head of the Catholic Church yet a communist country legalised a non-communist "Solidarność" only to make it illegal, through unlawful means although in the name of the law, when it grew strong and invincible. Photography is not exempt from these kinds of events, and when in the autumn of 1985, Tomasz Tomaszewski exhibited his work in Warsaw, everyone was in for a big surprise.

Polish Jews, or rather, those few amongst them who live in Poland, are the subject of Tomaszewski's most recent photography. The subject is not an easy one. The relationship between Poles and Jews has a long and difficulty history. It is drenched, particularly in the last hundred years, in bitterness and accusation. At the heart of the conflict lie mutual reproaches: over Polish antisemitism and the hostility of Catholicism to Judasim, on the one hand and, on the other, over the privileged socio-economic standing of the Jews, their indifference and, sometimes, downright hostility, to issues of independence and patriotism that are so important in Poland. There is right on both sides and each can—and does—air justifiable grievances. Emotion, resentment and bias prevail against any kind of coherent, objective appraisal. Stereotyped views about Polish antisemitism and absurd accusations about the role of the Poles in the extermination of Jews in the last war—popularised in the West, particularly—need to be acknowledged as an important factor. Such is the situation.

While, as far as the West is concerned, the major issue appears to be that of Polish anti-semitism—the existence of which it is hard to deny at such times as the late-19th and early-20th centuries and the interwar years—the major issue in Poland is over the identity of the Jewish community and the very fact of its existence. For Poland, historically a religiously and socially tolerant as well as culturally cosmopolitan country and a promised land for Jews from the whole continent (in 1800, 75% of the world's Jewish population lived on Polish soil), is, today, a country that, by comparison, has no Jewish community. The Jewish population forms such an inconspicuous minority that there are no estimates of its size, as many Polish Jews simply do not know which tradition and culture they identify with most, or which feels closer to them. Probably, both are equally close. Tomaszewski's photography deals with these lost, orthodox Jews who are searching for an identity and seeking to preserve a dying tradition.

"What is left," asks Tomaszewski who carried out this study with the help of his wife, "of the great and plentiful Jewish civilisation in this country? The question was a tempting one but trying to answer it also involved coming to terms with painful and complicated issues. First, we had to overcome our own ignorance and our often unconscious prejudices and stereotypes, not only about the Jews, but also about the Poles and about relations between the two. Looking at it from a different angle, we also had to break through the distrust of many Jews living in Poland and to gain acceptance in closed Jewish communities. Neither of us is anti-semitic or pro-Jewish. We're quite ordinary and at least we try. And we were able to convince many of the people we met of this. Had it been otherwise, this photography would not exist. The work took us five years and, in that time, we travelled all over Poland. The result was this—over seven thousand photographs and hundreds of pages of text, all of which can be most simply described as a history of absence."

It must be emphasised that Tomaszewski portrays this history with exceptional honesty and objectivity. In no way is his photography photogra-phy with a message. He does not select facts or bend them to support his views and he neither dramatises nor beautifies. We are shown life itself, literally and metaphorically. He shows us people of various social classes, representatives of diverse traditions and numerous orientations—even the most contradictory. The photographer portrays this whole mosaic of Polish Judaism with sympathy and understanding. We are aware of his astonishment, curiosity and interest. The most interesting thing about this study of today's Polish Jews by a non-Jew, however, is not, as it might seem, the exoticism that attaches to saving this world from extinction—a world which, anyway, is totally unknown to those born after the war—but, rather, the question that invariably accompanies this colourful, if not at times over-colourful, photography—a question about the future. What will happen to this tradition and this culture, once so alive and now so peripheral? Will it survive despite the enormous losses it has suffered, or is it doomed to a slow death? How can a world so out of step with today's be reconciled with contemporary life? In the final analysis, who are these people—irretrievably lost Jews or Poles who are trying to rediscover themselves through Judaism? There are many such questions but their theme is always the same—the defence of one's own identity and the search for one's own place.

The merit of Tomaszewski's photography lies in the fact that he never tries to answer these questions, never falls back, on propaganda and never succumbs to catastrophic visions. Put most simply, he bears witness to the truth. The ingenuousness and perseverence that lies behind these photographs appear to indicate that an understanding of communities that share painful experiences is possible and that, despite everything, more unites than divides them.

—Ryszard Bobrowski

TOMATSU, Shomei.

Nationality: Japanese. **Born:** Nagoya-shi, 15 January 1930. **Education:** Science and Engineering High School, Nagoya, 1942-46; studied economics at Aichi University, 1954; self-taught in photography. **Family:** Married Matsuko Inoue in 1960 (divorced, 1975); son: Izumi; married Yasuko Nakano in 1986. **Career:** Photographer since 1951. Founder, with Eikoh Hosoe and others, Vivo group of photographers, Tokyo, 1959. Director, Japan Professional Photographers Society, since 1959. Professor, Tokyo University of Art and Design, since 1966. **Recipient:** Most Promising Photographer Award, Japan Photo Critics Association, 1958; Photographer of the Year Award, Japan Photo Critics Association, 1961; Photographic Society of Japan Award, 1975; *Mainichi* Art Award, 1976; Art Encouragement Award, Ministry of Education, 1976. **Address:** 6149 Ichimiya-cho, Chosei-gun, Chiba, Japan.

Individual Exhibitions:

1959	*The Japanese,* Fuji Photo Salon, Tokyo
1962	*11:02 Nagasaki,* Fuji Photo Salon, Tokyo
1964	*Kingdom of Mud,* Fuji Photo Salon, Tokyo
1981	*The World of Shomei Tomatsu,* Special Gallery, Yatsusiro, Japan (toured Japan, 1981-84)
1984	*Japan 1952-81,* Fotogalerie im Forum Stadtpark, Graz, Austria
1985	Museum Moderner Kunst, Vienna
1986	Galerie im Körnerpark, West Berlin
	Museum Fotoforum, Bremen, West Germany
1988	*Irohanioedo Chirinuruwo,* Polaroid Gallery, Tokyo and Picture Photo Space, Osaka, Japan
	Japanese Landscapes, Toyonaka Central Public Hall, Japan
1989	*Plastics,* Parco Gallery, Shibuya, Japan (travelled to Parco Parade Gallery, Sapporo and Parco Gallery, Shinsaibashi)
1990	*11.02 Nagasaki, Chewing Gum and Chocolate,* Perspektief No 38, Rotterdam, Netherlands
	Sakura/Sakura/Sakura, Umeda Loft, Osaka, Japan
1991	*Time Becomes Weathered,* Maikata Civic Gallery, Osaka, Japan
1992	*Sakura + Plastics,* Metropolitan Museum of Art, New York
1993	*Pencil of the Sun,* Konika Photo Gallery, Nagoya, Japan

New World Map + Golden Mushroom, Inax Gallery, Tokyo
Sakura/Kyo; Original Nippon, Konika Plaza, Tokyo

Selected Group Exhibitions:

1957	*The Eyes of 10 People,* Konishiroku Photo Gallery, Tokyo
1960	*Modern Photography,* National Museum of Modern Art, Tokyo (and 1963)
1974	*New Japanese Photography,* Museum of Modern Art, New York (toured the United States)
1975	*Modern Photography of Japan,* Seibu Art Museum, Tokyo
1977	*Neue Fotografie aus Japan,* Kulturhaus, Graz, Austria (travelled to the Museum des 20. Jahrhunderts, Vienna)
1978	*Vivo,* Santa Barbara Museum of Art, California
	Reportage Fotografen, Forum Stadtpark, Graz, Austria
1979	*Japan: A Self-Portrait,* International Center of Photography, New York (travelled to *Venezia '79*)
1981	*A Day in the Life of Australia,* Sydney, New South Wales (toured Australia)
1985	*Black Sun,* Museum of Modern Art, Oxford, England (travelled to the Serpentine Gallery, London; Philadelphia Museum of Art, Pennsylvania)
1989	*Photography Until Now: Okinawa,* Museum of Modern Art, New York and Cleveland Museum of Art
	Hitachi Collection of Contemporary Japanese Photography (Pencil of the Sun), University of Arizona, Tucson, Arizona
	Photographie Japonaise, Provinciaal Museum Voor Fotografie, Antwerp and Musee de la Photographie, Charleroi, Belgium
1990	*Glances at the City, Tokyo,* Tokyo Municipal Museum of Photography and 16e Arrondissement Festival Hall, Paris
	Photographs of the 1940s and 1950s, Metropolitan Museum of Art, New York
1991	*Toppan Collection Exhibition,* International Center of Photography, New York
	Photographs 1955-65: Independent Groups of Images, Yamaguchi Prefectural Art Museum, Japan
1992	*More Than One Photography,* Museum of Modern Art, New York
1993	*Photographs from the Real World,* Lillehammer Art Museum, Norway
1994	Bergen Kunstforening, Bergen, Norway
	Museet for Fotokunst, Odense, Denmark
	Avantgarde Art in Postwar Japan, Yokohama Museum of Art, Japan

Collections:

Museum of Modern Art, New York

Publications:

By TOMATSU: Books—*11:02 Nagasaki,* with text by Motoi Tamaki, Tokyo 1966; *Nihon,* with Taroh Yamamoto and Takahiko Okada, Tokyo 1967; *Salaam Aleikoum,* Tokyo 1968; *Okinawa, Okinawa, Okinawa,* Tokyo 1969; *Oh! Shinjuku,* Tokyo 1969; *The Asahi Camera Class of Photography,* with others, Tokyo 1970; *A History of Japanese Photography,* editor, with others, Tokyo 1971; *Après-Guerre,* with text by Akiyuki Nosaka, Tokyo 1971; *Modern Art: The Expanding World of Design,* with others, Tokyo 1972; *I Am a King,* Tokyo 1972; *The Pencil of the Sun: Okinawa and South-East Asia,* Tokyo 1975; *Akemodoro No Hana,* Tokyo 1976; *Kingdom of Mud,* with text by Koh-ichi Tanigawa, Tokyo 1978; *A Brilliant Wind,* with text by Kineo Kuwabara, Kenichi Tanigawa and others, Tokyo 1979; *Collection of Works,* Tokyo, 1989; *Sakura, Photo Family,* Konika, 1994. **Articles**—"Ideas of an Image Explorer" in *Photo Contest* (Tokyo), February 1965; "In Search of Punctual Coordinates 'P'" in *Camera Mainichi* (Tokyo), December 1966; "Can Imagery Be on Its Own?" in *Asahi Camera* (Tokyo), April 1967; "Mother Nature of Japan" in *Camera Mainichi* (Tokyo), July 1967; "A Stake on 'Seeing'" in *Yomiuri* (Tokyo), 24 April 1969; "Kitch" in *Shashin Eizo* (Tokyo), Spring 1972; "A Photographic Ego Identity" in *Camera Mainichi* (Tokyo), Autumn 1973; "An Interview: Kishin Shinoyama Speaks Up" in

Asahi Camera (Tokyo), June 1975; "Primer on Photography" in *Riyubou* (Tokyo), April 1977; "Keep Taking Pictures" in *Chunichi* (Tokyo), 6 April 1979; "Okinawa Diary" in *Nihon Camera* (Tokyo), Summer 1979; "The Photographer as Story Teller" in *Asahi Camera* (Tokyo), March 1980; "Plastics" in *Nihon Kamera,* (Tokyo), April 1989; "Motionless Sakura—Teaching the Photographer about Themselves" in *Yomiuri Shinbun,* (Osaka), May, 1990; "Okinawa, Nagasaki etc." in *La Recherche Photographique,* (Paris), October 1990; "Shomei Tomatsu" in *Cimaise,* (Paris), December 1990.

On TOMATSU: Books—*Imagery and Languages* by Kougin Kondoh, Tokyo 1965; *The Photographer's Quest in a Shutter Chance* by Shinichi Tsdua, Tokyo 1968; *Dual Notions: Photographers at Work* by Hiroshi Osada, Tokyo 1969; *Demolition and Eruption* by Nagisa Ohshima, Tokyo 1970; *A Study of the Best Modern Photographs* by Nobuya Yoshimura, Tokyo 1970; *Act and Art* by Taeko Tomioka, Tokyo 1970; *100 Photographers: Profiles and Photographs* by Daido Moriyama, Tokyo 1973; *Camera Eye* by Kohen Sigemori, Tokyo 1974; *Modern Photographs and Photographers* by Tsutomu Watanabe, Tokyo 1975; *Photographic Age* by Taeko Tomioka, Tokyo 1980; *A Day in the Life of Australia—March 6, 1981,* with introduction by Thomas Kenneally, Potts Point, New South Wales 1981; *A Day in the Life of Japan—June 7, 1985,* edited by Rick Smolan and David Cohen, New York and London 1985. **Articles**—"Shomei Tomatsu" by Koubou Abe in *New Current of Art* (Tokyo), June 1960; "Shomei Tomatsu" by Tatsuo Fukushima in *Notebook of Art* (Tokyo), February 1961; "An Essay on Shomei Tomatsu" by Gohzoh Yoshimasu in *Camera Mainichi* (Tokyo), March 1963; "On Shomei Tomatsu" by Kohgi Taki in *The Camera Age* (Tokyo), July 1966; "New Trends in Documentary" by Toshio Matsumoto and others in *The Camera Age* (Tokyo), October 1966; "Image: Its Prime Point" by Kougi Taki in *Design Critique* (Tokyo), February 1967; "On Shomei Tomatsu" by Shiroyasu Suzuki in *Photographic Images* (Tokyo), February 1969; "I Saw a Land in Its Nakedness Right in Front of My Eyes" by Gohzo Yoshimasu in *Camera Mainichi* (Tokyo), April 1975; "Shomei Tomatsu" by Tatsuo Fukushima and Daido Moriyama, special number of *Photo Art* (Tokyo), 1976; "Tomatsu: Japan 1952-1981" in *Camera Austria* (Graz), March 1984; "Black Sun: The Eyes of Four," special issue of *Aperture* (Millerton, New York), no. 102, 1986; "Clouds of Dreams and Mud" by Toshiharu Ito in *Nihon Kamera,* (Tokyo), June 1989; "Tomatsu's Sakura for Ever" by Nagisa Oshima and others in *Sakura,* (Tokyo), June 1990; "Cherry Blossoms, Plastics, Morality Plays" by Vicki Goldberg in *New York Times,* December 1992; "Shomei Tomatsu—Reality in Ruins" by Toshiharu Ito catalogue for Lillehammer Art Museum, November 1993; "Japanese People's Photographs: History and Present: Around 1960, the Era of Images" by Kotaro Iizawa in *NHK,* (Tokyo), June 1994.

*

Photography is life itself. What I feel influences my photographs; and my taking photographs affects my life. I exist within this reciprocity.

—Shomei Tomatsu

*   *   *

Shomei Tomatsu's photography is a most explicit demonstration of the predominant social forces of post-war Japan. Emerging from photojournalism, Tomatsu developed a form of documentary reportage that aims beyond illustration to personal polemic. He records an environment of abrasive contrasts, where he contains chaos and decay in formal abstractions and where human scar tissue can be photographed with graphic detail. His work developed with the post-war economic recovery and exposed the conflicts obscured by the rapidly expanding economy and by the Occupation. His subjective documentary is an assertion of a national identity; it exposes the conflict of a country caught between a native and an alien culture.

In 1959 Tomatsu formed the Vivo group with Hosoe, Ikko and others, which marked the beginning of a new Japanese photography. In 1961 he worked with the leading Japanese photographer Ken Domon on the Hiroshima-Nagasaki document. His own book, *11:02 Nagasaki,* which was published in 1966, refers to the time of the atomic explosion. He confronted the victims directly and formally, exposing suppurating sores, mutilated flesh and the contours of ravaged human features. His technique went far beyond clinical, medical evidence. In his photograph of the melted beer bottle he transformed glass into contorted flesh—like an image from a slaughterhouse. The following year his great series *Nihon* was published. It was revolutionary in that it dismissed the image of Japan as a source of traditional aesthetic order. He photographed the mud of riverbeds, the melted asphalt of a Tokyo street, and the aftermath of a typhoon in Nagoya, where human debris and objects had been scattered by the violence of the storm. It was a volatile landscape, not the Japan of harmonious order. His portraits from the same series include the mask-like faces of the Tokyo sandwich men, poor shopkeepers, or the psychic medium in a trance. Tomatsu was focussing on the exploited or those displaced to the outer periphery of society. In 1969 a political and cultural crisis exploded on the streets of Tokyo, which Tomatsu recorded in his series *Oh! Shinjuku.* He juxtaposed imagery of riots with the overt sexuality of that area of the city.

Since the late 1960s Tomatsu has concentrated on the conflicts surrounding the American bases in Japan and Okinawa. In Okinawa itself he has found the roots of a society with which he can identify at the same time as he has come to see the mainland of Japan as an increasingly contaminated culture. His sympathies are evident in his recent book *The Pencil of the Sun: Okinawa and South-East Asia.*

Tomatsu has been of seminal importance in the development of Japanese photography, and a great influence on the new generation of photographers, notably Moriyama and Tsuchida.

—Mark Holborn

TOOMING, Peeter.

Nationality: Estonian. **Born:** Rakvere, Estonia, 1 June 1939. **Education:** Attended secondary school in Rakvere, 1953-57; studied journalism at the State University of Tartu, Estonia, 1968-74. **Family:** Married Sirje Ong in 1963; daughter: Lee. **Career:** Photographer since 1961. Lighting Director, 1961-63, Cameraman, 1963-72, and since 1972 Producer and Director of Photography, Tallinnfilm film studios, Tallinn, Estonia. Since 1993, Producer, Estonian Television. Founder and manager of the Photo Gallery "Lee," Tallinn, Estonia 1993. **Recipient:** Best Director of Photography, 1980, Special Prize, 1986, *Film Festival of Tallinn*; First Prize, Rakvere Film Festival, Estonia, 1983; Special Prize, Nature Film Festival, Sundsvall, Sweden, 1993. **Address:** Harju 1-7, 200 001 Tallinn, Estonia.

Individual Exhibitions:

1967	*Selected Photos,* University of Kaunas, Lithuania
1972	*A Summer's Story,* Kiek in de Kök, Tallinn, Estonia
	Selected Photos, Fotograficka Galerie, Dečin, Czechoslovakia
1976	*Selected Photos,* Kiek in de Kök, Tallinn, Estonia (travelled to the Museum of Rakvere, Estonia; Museum of Võru, Estonia; and the House of Culture, Haapsalu, Estonia)
	3 Photographers, Kiek in de Kök, Tallinn, Estonia (with A. Dobrovolsici and P. Kraas)
1977	*Selected Photos,* Focus Gallery, Ljubljana, Yugoslavia (travelled to the Dolenjska Galereja, Novo Mesto, Yugoslavia)
	One Day's Story, Kiek in de Kök, Tallinn, Estonia
1978	*Selected Photos,* KTF Photo Gallery, Cracow, Poland (travelled to the Panther Passage, Linz, Austria)
1979	*Returning Home,* Kiek in de Kök, Tallinn, Estonia
	Selected Photos, Photography Museum, Siauliai, Lithuania (travelled to the Municipal Museum, Riga, Latvia; Municipal Museum, Steyr, Austria; and the Gallery of Modern Art, Warsaw)
	Selected Photos, Photography Gallery, Prjbor, Czechoslovakia
	Gunar Binde/Egons Spuris/Peeter Tooming, Dum Panu z Kunstatu, Brno, Czechoslovakia (travelled to the Museum of Olomouc, Czechoslovakia, 1979, and Kiek in de Kök, Tallinn, Estonia, 1980)

1980	*Every Coming Consists of the Leaving,* Kiek in de Kök, Tallinn, Estonia (travelled to the House of Culture, Kaapsalu, Estonia)
	Selected Photos, Urania-Schaufenstergalerie, Vienna
	Selected Photos, Photo Gallery, Kaunas, Lithuania
1981	*Selected Photos,* Club of Artists, Turin, Italy (travelled to Milan and Florence)
1982	*Fotorondo,* Kiek in de Kök, Tallinn, Estonia
	Fotorondo and Nudes, Museum of Kohtla-Jarva, Estonia (travelled to Viljandi, Estonia)
	New Photos, House of the Cinema, Tallinn, Estonia
1983	*Every Path Ends in the Sea,* Kiek in de Kök, Tallinn, Estonia (travelled to Kohtla-Jarva and Kardla, Estonia)
	House of Culture, Johvi, Estonia (retrospective)
	One Day's Story, Photo Gallery, Vilnius, Lithuania
1984	*Selected Photos,* Dnepropetrovsk, Russia (travelled to Maikop, Krasnodar and Cheljabinsk)
	Nude and Nature, Kiek in de Kök, Tallinn, Estonia
1985	*Selected Photos,* Voru, Estonia (travelled to Haljala, Estonia)
	You—The River, Kiek in de Kök, Tallinn, Estonia
	The Story of the Island, House of the Cinema, Tallinn, Estonia
	New Photos, Tallinn, Estonia (travelled to Khotla-Jarva, Estonia,
1986	*Approaching the Tree,* Kiek in de Kök, Tallinn, Estonia
	The Story of the Island, Museum of Viljandi, Estonia
	Trip from Tartu to Viljandi, Kiek in de Kök, Tallinn, Estonia
	Selected Photos, Perm, Russia
1987	*50 Years Later: Virumaa,* Kiek in de Kök, Tallinn
	Selected Photos, Sotschi, Sevastopol and Kuibyshev, Russia
1988	*Selected Photos,* Rostov, Russia; Riga, Latvia; Prjbor, Czechoslovakia
	34 Photos, Tallinnfilm, Tallinn
1990	*50 Years Later: Virumaa,* Kadrina and Tallinn
	Switzerland and Canada, Haljala, Estonia
1991	*Two Size Hallo,* Tallinn
	Faroe Islands, Haljala, Estonia
1992	*Sun Games,* Kiek in de Kök, Tallinn

Selected Group Exhibitions:

1966	*Stodom: Maal; Graafika; Foto,* Academy of Sciences, Tallinn, Estonia
1973	*Fotoforum 73,* Ruzomberok, Czechoslovakia
1976	*World Press Photos 76,* the Hague
1979	*Fotoimpressionen,* Künstlerhaus, Vienna
1980	*Stodom,* Dom Kultury ROH, Pribor, Czechoslovakia
1982	*Sprechende Bilder,* Kongresshaus, Vienna
1984	*Seven Photographers from Tallinn,* Fotografiska Museet, Stockholm
1985	*25 Topfotografen aus aller Welt,* Stadtische Galerie, Traun, Austria
1986	*Photos from Ten Peters,* Kiek in de Kök, Tallinn, Estonia
1992	*Images from Borderlands,* Saaremaa Fotofestival, Estonia
1993	*Borderlands, Street Level,* Scotland
	The Memory of Images, Stadtgalerie im Sophienhof, Kiel, Germany

Collections:

Municipal Museum, Tallinn, Estonia; Photography Museum, Siauliai, Lithuania; Musée Francais de la Photographie, Bièvres, France; Australian Photography Society; Hengl-Kabinett, Traun, Austria; Bibliothèque Nationale, Paris.

Publications:

By TOOMING: Books—25 Fotot, Tallinn, Estonia 1975; *Rakvere,* Tallinn, Estonia 1976; *Fotolood,* Tallinn, Estonia 1979; *Peatu, meenuta,* Tallinn, Estonia 1980; *Saaremaa,* Tallinn, Estonia 1982; *Foto! Foto? Foto . . . ,* Tallinn, Estonia 1983; *Sina, jogi,* Tallinn, Estonia 1984; *Sketches from the Past of Estonian Photography, 1840-1940,* Tallinn, 1986; *Silvery Way,*

My Homeland, **1976.** Photograph by Peeter Tooming.

Tallinn, 1990; *55 Years Later: Virumaa,* Tallinn, 1993; *Highway Attracts,* Tallinn, 1993; *55 Years Later: Saaremaa,* Tallinn, 1994. **Articles**—numerous in Estonian periodicals, and "Aadu Treufeldt, Estonian Photographer" in *History of Photography* (University Park, Pennsylvania), January 1978; "Ein Fotomuseum in Tallinn" in *Fotografie* (Leipzig), May 1980. **Films**—*Moments,* 1976; *Fotorondo,* 1978; *Troubles in Photography,*1989; *Concerto Grosso,* 1990; also director of over 50 documentary films, since 1969.

On TOOMING: Book—*Pobaltska sovetska fotografie* by Vaclav Jiru, Prague 1974. **Articles**—"The Ideas of Peeter Tooming" by A.G. in *Fotografie* (Prague), no. 4, 1969; "A Baltic Pictorialist" by F.T. Merkler in *New Pictorialist* (Spartanburg), no. 2, 1977; "Wplywologia stosowana" by Juliusz Garztecki in *Perspektywy* (Warsaw), no. 11, 1979; "Estonian Photographer Peeter Tooming: We Must Love Our Roots" by Mary Ann Lynch in *Combinations* (New York), no. 5, 1980.

*

Taking photos is actually opening one's soul to the whole world. With a glance one can say with certainty who the author is—a realist or romanticist, a sensitive person or an indifferent one. We see here very different works; some of them affect us like the work of a news reporter, whereas others seem to be deliberately staged; we become aware of a searching for new decorative elements, or of attempts to penetrate to the inner world of men.

A photographer has the right to make use of the most diverse means for expressing his thoughts and feelings. An artistic photo is not only the recording of a fact but also one of the forms of expression of an artist. A photo

ought not to be dull, but it should enrich our emotional world and help us to understand life. And that is a noble aim to strive for.

—Peeter Tooming

*   *   *

Peeter Tooming's introduction to photography was connected with the creative activity of the 1960s, which in the Soviet Union was particularly marked in the Baltic Republics—Lithuania, Latvia and Estonia. This activity was based on the historic artistic culture of the region and its folk art tradition. It enhanced the revival of creative photography with striking national elements. Peeter Tooming is an outstanding figure in this significant cultural transformation in one of these republics, Estonia.

As cameraman of the film studio Tallinnfilm and an active member of the photographic group known as Stodom, he devoted himself mainly to artistically felt and deliberately composed photography. At the same time Tooming was also working as a journalist and photographer for the daily press. These were the bases of his further development, which logically went from emotional symbolism to a kind of vital authenticity. However, even now he has not entirely renounced poetic arrangements, special lighting, a certain stress (which, incidentally, form part of the arsenal of all of Baltic photography), and a certain aesthetic quality regarding man's relationship with nature which retains all the features of the former natural symbiosis.

These characteristics inform his latest works, particularly the series known as "Returning Home." But though these photographs are no less attractive than his previous work, they are much less "constructed." They are also much less dependent on tradition, a tradition that at one time had to be promoted in photography (as in the other arts) if continuity was to be maintained after the forceful interruption of the country's political development. That is why Tooming, like so many other photographers of the Baltic Republics, experimented so extensively with photographic techniques, investigating the qualities of light on shapes, so important for expressing the specific atmosphere of the Baltic region and, following the example of representatives of the post-revolutionary artistic avantgarde, he also took up collage. Even in the combination of such incongruous elements as the juxtaposition of a coloured surface with newspaper cuttings, it was possible to find a unique expression, a novel idea.

The versatility with which Tooming approached photography and which he has cultivated for decades is still with him. It allows him to make use of the experiences he has gained in a variety of ways. He is one of few photographers in the U.S.S.R. who is aware of and exploits the many uses of photography—in communications, books, exhibitions, and in films. For example, in his composition ''Fotorondo,'' he makes use of the pleasant custom of Baltic artists to stage exhibitions of photos in the open air: he arranged such a display in a village street and, like the Polish ''expansive photographers,'' at the same time he took pictures of the photos and the immediate reaction of onlookers. Also, Tooming does not hesitate to use conceptual methods, the purpose of which he describes as ''training expression.'' He collects and saves unique photographs, and he is preparing a *History of Estonian Photography.* But, above all, he is a passionate lover of photography, through the modern practice of which he opens up a window to his native land.

—Vladimìr Remeš

TOROSIAN, Michael.

Nationality: Canadian. **Born:** Fort Erie, Ontario, 31 October 1952. **Education:** Ridgeway-Crystal Beach High School, Ridgeway, Ontario, 1966-70; studied photography at the Ryerson Polytechnical Institute, Toronto, 1970-73, Diploma in Photography, 1973. **Career:** Independent photographer, Toronto, since 1973. Also, cinematographer, and proprietor of Lumiere Press, Toronto. **Recipient:** Ontario Arts Council Grant, 1973, 1975, 1976, 1981, 1982, 1985, 1986; Canada Council Grant, 1973, 1974, 1979. **Address:** 19 Fermanagh Avenue, Toronto, Ontario M6R 1M4, Canada.

Individual Exhibitions:

1974	*A Manual Alphabet,* National Film Board Gallery, Ottawa
	A Manual Alphabet, Robert McLaughlin Gallery, Oshawa, Ontario
1975	*Nocturne,* Cafe La Barge Gallery, Toronto
	Nocturne, National Film Board Gallery, Ottawa
1976	Photo Arts Gallery, Ryerson Polytechnical Institute, Toronto
	Conestoga College, Kitchener, Ontario
	Photography Gallery, Bowmanville, Ontario
1977	Owen Sound Public Library, Ontario
	Photo Arts Gallery, Ryerson Polytechnical Institute, Toronto
	Kelowna Art Gallery, British Columbia
	Penticton Arts Centre, British Columbia
	Seaway Valley Libraries, Cornwall, Ontario
1978	Vanier College, Montreal
	Greater Victoria Public Library, British Columbia
	Atikoken Centennial Museum, Ontario
1979	Vanier College, Montreal
	National Film Board Gallery, Ottawa
	Conestoga College, Kitchener, Ontario
	Sanctuary, University of Oregon, Eugene
1981	Burton Gallery of Photography, Toronto
1985	York University, Toronto
1986	University of Toronto, Ontario
	Marcuse Pfeifer Gallery, New York

Selected Group Exhibitions:

1975	*Exposure,* Art Gallery of Ontario, Toronto (toured Canada)
1978	*Canadians,* Mount St. Vincent University, Halifax, Nova Scotia (toured Canada, and travelled to London)
1983	*Latitudes and Parallels,* Winnipeg Art Gallery, Manitoba
1984	*Contemporary Canadian Photography,* Edmonton Art Gallery, Alberta
1986	*Maine Photographic Workshops Annual Exhibition,* Puck Building, New York
	A Commitment to Vision, University of Oregon, Eugene

Collections:

Canadian Museum of Contemporary Photography, Ottawa; National Library of Canada, Ottawa; National Photography Collection, Public Archives of Canada, Ottawa; Ontario Arts Council, Toronto, Winnipeg Art Gallery, Manitoba; Ryerson Polytechnic Institute, Toronto.

Publications:

By TOROSIAN: Books—*Michael Torosian: Portfolio 1976,* portfolio of 10 photos, Toronto 1976; *Signature 3: Michael Torosian: Nocturne,* Ottawa 1977; *Lunarglyphics,* Toronto 1981; *The Reflections of Existence: A Selection of Fifteen Photographs by Michel Lambeth,* editor, Toronto 1982; *Michel Lambeth: Photographer,* editor, Ottawa 1986. **Articles**—''Collecting Photographs'' in *Financial Post Magazine* (Toronto), February 1979; ''Newsbreak: The Controversy Continues'' in *Photo Communique* (Toronto), September 1979; ''Memento Mori'' in *Photo Communique* (Toronto), November 1979; ''Thinking of Hippolyte'' in *Photo Communique* (Toronto), May 1980; ''Sanctuary'' in *Descant* (Toronto), no. 24, 1980; ''The Fifties Focus'' in *Toronto Life,* June 1981; ''Aurora'' in *Descant* (Toronto), Summer 1985; ''March Tide, The Op's Last Case'' in *Descant* (Toronto), Winter 1985/86.

On TOROSIAN: Books—*Exposure,* exhibition catalogue, Toronto 1975; *Latitudes and Parallels,* exhibition catalogue, Winnipeg 1983; *Contemporary Canadian Photography* by Martha Langford, Edmonton, Alberta 1984; *Commitment to Vision,* exhibition catalogue, by David Featherstone, Eugene, Oregon 1986. **Articles**—''Michael Torosian'' by Michel Lambeth in *Proof Only* (Toronto), 22 February 1974; ''Two Angles on Photography'' by Vicky Sanderson in *Globe and Mail* (Toronto), 20 October 1981.

* * *

Michael Torosian's first works in photography were largely concerned with the evidence and insight into human nature afforded by detail. ''A Manual Alphabet,'' a work first exhibited in 1974, gathered together photographs of hands. It was described at the time and in a gallery setting dominated by colour landscapes of Canada as ''a real documentation of unposed gesture,'' a statement which stresses informational qualities ascribed by the viewer from the clues of age, the tension in the hand or the dress of the wrist.

It was clear from the next major series that what Torosian was after was something far less concrete, as elusive perhaps as a line of light along a torso and something that separated flesh and shadow by as little as a tone. He followed ''A Manual Alphabet'' with ''Nocturne,'' the title of which, describing ''a dreamy or pensive piece of music,'' set the mood for small, dark, black-and-white Polaroid images of female bodies and faces. Torosian experimented with exposure and development of these images, extending the chemical action for as long as 30 minutes to alter the surface and depth of the shadows. His model, sometimes partially draped or enclosed in a black leotard, was deliberately posed and shaped before textured or neutral backgrounds. Torosian strove for and found a richness in the unplumbed depths of Polaroid, making works pleasing for their sensuality and preciousness.

Back on the street and drawing from the moodiness of ''Nocturne'' and the intuitive characterizations of his first works, Torosian began making expressionist portraits. These were not decisive moments but sections of them, shards of the interaction that had characterized the photography of human contact since the inception of the unseen 35 mm camera. Torosian collected incidents of recessed sensibility. He found a population of sleep-walkers deep in thought or listening to their inner voices. These are people that we do not see but who are always quietly in the background. The photographs of "Sanctuary" are again details. What is shocking, even saddening, is that his subjects are whole human beings, coexisting but mutely, in ordinary lives.

In his theatre/studio, Torosian is using the nude as a starting point for a series of tableaus. His current format and content are without softness and without compromise. They glare and they challenge.

—Martha Langford

TRAGER, Philip.

Nationality: American. **Born:** Bridgeport, Connecticut, 27 February 1935. **Education:** Wesleyan University, Middletown, Connecticut, 1952-56, B.A. 1956; studied law, Columbia University School of Law, 1956-60, J.D. 1960; self-taught in photography. **Family:** Married Ina Shulkin in 1957; children: Julie and Michael. **Career:** Attorney, with Bernard H. Trager, Trager and Trager counsellors-at-law, Fairfield, Connecticut, since 1960. Independent photographer, Fairfield, Connecticut, since 1966. **Recipient:** Book of the Year Award, American Institute of Graphic Arts, 1977; 25 Best Books Award, Association of American University Presses, 1977; Recommended Book of the Year Citation, *New York Times* Annual Review of Books, 1977, 1980; Distinguished Alumnus Award, Wesleyan University, 1981; Lay Person Award, Connecticut Society of Architects, 1981. **Address:** 20 Rolling Ridge Road, Fairfield, Connecticut 06430, U.S.A.

Individual Exhibitions:

1970	Underground Gallery, New York
	Davison Art Center, Wesleyan University, Middletown, Connecticut
1972	831 Gallery, Birmingham, Michigan
	Witkin Gallery, New York
1974	*Philip Trager and Ron Stark,* San Francisco Museum of Art
	Davison Art Center, Wesleyan University, Middletown, Connecticut
1975	Photopia Gallery, Philadelphia
	Washington Gallery of Photography, Washington, D.C.
1977	Baltimore Museum of Art
	Focus Gallery, San Francisco
	University of Connecticut, Storrs
	Witkin Gallery, New York
1978	Photographics Workshop, New Haven, Connecticut
	Friends of Photography, Carmel, California
	Milwaukee Center for the Arts
1979	Camera Work Gallery, New York
	Boston Center for the Arts
1980	Witkin Gallery, New York
	Museum of the City of New York
1981	Photo Gallery International, Tokyo
	Ufficio dell'Arte, Paris
	Centre Internacional de Fotografia, Barcelona
	Davison Art Center, Wesleyan University, Middletown, Connecticut
1982	American Institute of Architects, Washington, D.C.
1984	Milwaukee Center for Photography, Wisconsin
	Orange Coast College, Costa Mesa, California
	Aldrich Museum, Ridgefield, Connecticut
1986	Witkin Gallery, New York
1987	Wesleyan University, Middletown, Connecticut
	Centro Internazionale di Studi di Architettura Andrea Palladio, Vicenza, Italy

Selected Group Exhibitions:

1971	*Members Exhibition,* Friends of Photography, Carmel, California
1972	*Photo-Vision '72,* Boston Center for the Arts
1979	*Attitudes: Photography in the 1970s,* Santa Barbara Museum of Art, California
	Photographers Look at Buildings, Yale University Art Gallery, New Haven, Connecticut
1980	*The Photographer and the Frame,* Wesleyan University, Middletown, Connecticut
1981	*New Acquisitions,* Corcoran Gallery of Art, Washington, D.C.
	Manhattan Observed: 14 Photographers Look at New York 1972-1981, New York Historical Society
1982	*Five Years at the Creative Photography Gallery,* Massachusetts Institute of Technology, Cambridge
1983	*Rancho de Taos: A Photographic History,* Santa Fe Museum of Fine Art, New Mexico
1984	*La Photographie Créative,* Pavillon des Arts, Paris

Collections:

Museum of Modern Art, New York; Metropolitan Museum of Art, New York; Museum of the City of New York; Wesleyan University, Middletown, Connecticut; Yale University Gallery of Art, New Haven, Connecticut; William Benton Museum of Art, University of Connecticut, Storrs; Smith College Museum of Art, Northampton, Massachusetts; Corcoran Gallery of Art, Washington, D.C.; Baltimore Museum of Art, Maryland; Bibliothèque Nationale, Paris.

Publications:

By TRAGER: Books—Echoes of Silence, Danbury, Connecticut 1972; *Photographs of Architecture,* with an introduction by Samuel M. Green, Middletown, Connecticut 1977; *Philip Trager: New York,* with an introduction by Louis Auchincloss, Middletown, Connecticut 1980. **Article**—"Following the Beat of an Inner Drummer," interview, with Pèggy Sealborn, in *Print Letter* (Zurich), May/June 1978.

On TRAGER: Books—*Philip Trager and Ron Stark,* exhibition catalogue, by John Humphrey, San Francisco 1974; *A Ten-Year Salute* by Lee D. Witkin, New York 1979; *The Photograph Collector's Guide* by Lee D. Witkin and Barbara London, Boston and London 1979; *La Photographie Créative* by Jean-Claude Lemagny, Paris 1984. **Articles**—"The Pursuit of Excellence" in *The Art of Photography* by Time-Life editors, New York 1971; "Trager and Stark" by Joan Murray in *Artweek* (Oakland), California, 2 February 1974; "Philip Trager" in *Creative Camera* (London), September 1975; "Ageless Architecture" by David L. Shirey in the *New York Times,* 10 April 1977; "Philip Trager" by Don Owens in *Photoshow* (Los Angeles), no. 2, 1980; "A Gossamer Gotham" by Owen Edwards in *American Photographer* (New York), September 1980; "Our Town" by Richard Shepherd in the *New York Times,* November 1980; "Cityscapes" by Carol Halebian in *Camera 35* (New York), November 1980; "Philip Trager: New York" by Marco Misani in *Print Letter* (Zurich), November/December 1980; "City Shapes" by Louis Auchincloss in *Camera Arts* (New York), November/December 1980; "Philip Trager at Witkin" by Lynn Enton in *Art in America* (New York), February 1981; "Philip Trager: New York" by Hilton Kramer in the *New York Times,* 27 March 1981; "Wesleyan Photographs" in *Creative Camera* (London), October 1982; "Works of State Residents Shine in Three Shows" by Vivian Raynor in the *New York Times,* 21 October 1983.

* * *

Very generally, the photography of architecture falls into three categories: the commercial, most often commissioned by architects or builders; the documentary, a systematic depiction of the architecture of particular places or styles; and the aesthetic, the photography of buildings which, quite simply, appeal to the artistic sensibilities of the particular photographer. The first is characterized by stylistic judgements mortgaged to "standards" well known to any junior assistant photographer at any commercial studio anywhere. The second is characterized by its blind adherence to the assumption that all buildings are inherently interesting (and by its occasionally conclusive capacity to bore). And the last is characterized by its innate belief in the "music" of architecture, in the *idea* of architecture.

Philip Trager has concerned himself with walking a thin line between the latter two categories. In Trager's work, it is at times a very thin line, though his images clearly manifest the differentiation between photographs of architecture and photographs whose visible and nominal subject is a building. Recent documentary photographs of architecture are less interested in the buildings themselves than in how they are representative of something else—culture, social class, style, whatever. Trager's, though, are invariably interesting buildings in themselves, existing within their own framework. His judgements are always aesthetic and architectural, never social.

Even so, there are some anomalies in his two large series to date, the first published as *Photographs of Architecture* in 1977, the second as *Philip Trager: New York* in 1980. In the former, even those buildings which are photographed straight on, from the front, are decidedly three-dimensional. They have substance, "body;" there is no question of their reality as buildings. In the latter, we are confronted with a curious insubstantiality; even though most of the New York photographs are taken from oblique angles, creating perspective, the buildings are façades, strangely delicate. In the Manhattan photographs, Trager has succeeded (magically?) in depicting a nearly Augustinian essence of "city," while simultaneously denying it any "body." It is a depiction of city that is as close to the Gothic as one is likely to come—a city seen as sculptured, hewn from a single huge stone, rather than built. It is a city in Trager's eyes in which one form is irrevocably connected to every other form, as a single chaotic whole hovering in the chancel of an immense cathedral. Trager's Manhattan floats. And its absence of people ("empty" is neither objectively sad nor negative) makes it nearly mythic, a city of the departed gods. It is in this that Trager's photographs document something more truly "architectural" than the mere form or function of a building: the essential nature of architecture as an intellection of the most primitive and sophisticated sort.

—Derek Bennett

TRAKHMAN, Mikhail (Anatol'evich).

Nationality: Russian. **Born:** Moscow in March 1918. **Education:** Attended a grammar school in Moscow until 1933. **Family:** Married Lalya Trakhmanova; son: Igor. **Career:** Cameraman in a documentary film studio, Moscow, 1934-39; Photo-Reporter, Sovinformburo/Soviet Information Bureau, Moscow, 1939-41; War Photo-Correspondent, with the Red Army, for TASS, 1941-42, and for Sovinformburo, 1942-45; activities unknown, 1945-58; Chief Photo-Correspondent, *Literaturnaja Gaseta*, Moscow, 1958-76. Also, creator and editor of books for Planeta, Moscow. **Died:** (in Moscow) 1976.

Selected Group Exhibitions:

1972   *Photographes de l'URSS: Le Pays, Les Hommes,* Galerie
        Nationale du Grand Palais, Paris
1975   *Soviet War Reportage 1941-45,* House of Soviet Science and
        Culture, Prague
1977   *The Russian War,* International Center of Photography,
        New York
1978   *Russian War Photography,* Side Gallery, Newcastle upon Tyne,
        England
1989   *150 Years of Photography,* Central Exhibition Hall, Moscow

Collections:

Novosti Press Agency, Moscow; National Film and Photo Archives, Moscow; Daniela Mrázková/Vladimìr Remeš Collection, Prague.

Publications:

By TRAKHMAN: Books—*Zarevo,* with photographs by Trakhman and others, poems, and text by Andrei Voznyesensky, Moscow 1970; *Osvobozhdenye (Liberation),* editor, with text by Boris Polevoy and Konstantin Simonov,

Moscow 1974; *Das der Mensche ein Mensch Sei,* Berlin 1975; *Srdcem přítete* (on Prague and Moscow), Prague 1975.

On TRAKHMAN: Books—*Fotografovali Válku,* by Daniela Mrázková and Vladimìr Remeš, Prague 1975, published as *The Russian War 1941-45,* with an introduction by Harrison Salisbury, New York 1977, published as *The Russian War 1941-45,* with text by A.J.P. Taylor, London 1978; *Von Moskau nach Berlin,* edited by Daniela Mrázková and Vladimìr Remeš, with an introduction by Heinrich Böll, Oldenburg, West Germany 1979; *Bilder vom Krieg* by Rainer Fabian and Hans Christian Adam, Hamburg 1983, published as *Images of War: 130 Years of War Photography,* London 1985; *The Story of Photography,* by Daniela Mrázková, Prague 1985, London 1986. **Articles**—"Sovětská valecná fotoreportáz 1941-45" by Daniela Mrázková and Vladimìr Remeš in *Revue Fotografie* (Prague), March 1975; "A Cry of Anguish from Wartime Russia" in *Photography Year,* by the Time-Life editors, New York 1976; "Il Soldato Fotografo" in *Fotografia Italiana* (Milan), April 1976; *Anthology of Soviet Photography,* Vol II, Moscow, 1987.

* * *

If he could have remained a war correspondent, Mikhail Trakhman would have become a great star in his field. For, in his war photographs, he knew perfectly how to combine the images of war and its impact on the broad masses of the population with an ideological and symbolic significance. But the young Trakhman had had enough of war: he had had such a dose of it that he virtually refused the opportunity to photograph war after the victory in Europe and in the Far East, where he was one of very few Soviet photo-reporters. As a photographer in uniform, he had had to obey military commands, and his refusal to obey orders considerably complicated his start in post-war life. But even without these personal complications, Trakhman would have found it difficult to find a photographic program in keeping with his former personal, partial, sensitive and pensive vision of the war holocaust that had played havoc with the lives of millions of people, uprooted from their environment and forced to fight for their mere existence.

Before the war Trakhman had worked as a documentary film cameraman. This experience is obvious in his photographs: his approach to reality and his spontaneity imprint his photographs with a special quality; they are often composed like shots in a film. Trakhman photographs in great detail—the whole, or half, at the same time—confronting the action on the first and second plane. Not infrequently he also links several dominant features of the action in mutual significance, the combination of which leads to an almost complete testimony. Such a richly articulated presentation does not so much create an epic as a photo full of internal significance from which it is actually possible to obtain a number of equally valuable prints by cropping.

And each photograph does not seem a complete, smooth action, but the record of an event that will continue: the dynamics and depth in space of his prints indicate what has preceded the recorded action and how it is going to develop further.

The photos of the war events, devoted to the lives of guerrilla fighters, men, women and children behind the enemy lines, were taken when Trakhman, as special correspondent for Sovinformburo, was travelling throughout the Soviet Union, and in most cases they were not meant for publication. And yet they are his masterpieces, though, unlike most other Soviet war photographers, he does not deliberately look for the drama of war in battle but in a quiet social analysis of the everyday events. This work is supremely dramatic and effective, above all in its unique emotional and ideological quality, which is in sharp contrast to Trakhman's post-war work, which is completely "adjusted" to the official canon.

In the 1960s and especially in the 1970s, when circumstances made it possible, Trakhman became the author and editor of a number of photographic books and publications that made full use of photography. Here, in this work, his effort during the war came into its own, though he did search the archives for the work of other photographers. Of his picture books on a war theme, the most significant is *Zarevo,* which he edited with the poet Andrei Voznyesensky. It contains his own as well as other war photos, together with Soviet war and post-war poems. Trakhman was also the coinstigator of several volumes on the war for Planeta, Moscow, in which, however, the photographs play only a minor role, being used purely as illustration, to the detriment of the books.

It's fair to say that in Russia Mikhail Trakhman is one of the pioneers in the creation of books endeavoring to speak in the language of photography. He continued to photograph tirelessly until his death, and his books were published not only in the U.S.S.R. but also in Czechoslovakia, Poland and the G.D.R. However, Trakhman's importance as an artist lies entirely in that short period of his war photographs. Neither before nor after did he succeed in again producing outstanding photographs; mostly, they were average. The war was his legacy, which he used successfully throughout his career.

—Vladimìr Remeš

TRAUB, Charles (Henry).

Nationality: American. **Born:** Louisville, Kentucky, 6 April 1945. **Education:** Louisville High School, 1960-63; University of Illinois, Champaign, 1963-67, B.A. in literature 1967; University of Louisville, 1967-69; studied photography, under Aaron Siskind and Arthur Siegel, at the Institute of Design, Illinois Institute of Technology, Chicago, 1969-71, M.S. 1971. **Military Service:** Served in the United States Army, 1969. **Family:** Married Mary Cadden in 1969; son: Aaron. **Career:** Photographer, Chicago and New York, since 1971. Instructor in Photography, 1971-75, Chairman of the Photography Department, 1975-78, and Founder and Chairman, Center for Contemporary Photography, 1975-78, Columbia College, Chicago; Director of the Light Gallery, New York, 1978-80. Visiting Lecturer, International Center of Photography, New York, since 1978. **Address:** 39 East 10th Street, New York, New York 10003, U.S.A.

Individual Exhibitions:

1971	Center for Photographic Studies, Louisville, Kentucky
1972	Dayton Art Institute, Ohio
	Cincinnati Art Institute, Ohio
1974	New England School of Photography, Boston
1975	*Cajun Photographs,* Louisiana State University, Baton Rouge (travelled to Columbia College Photography Gallery, Chicago)
	Bradley University, Peoria, Illinois
	Art Institute of Chicago
	University of Michigan, Ann Arbor
	University of California, Berkeley
1976	Illinois Wesleyan University, Bloomington
	Tyler School of Art, Philadelphia
	University of Northern Iowa, Cedar Falls
1977	Light Gallery, New York
1978	Metro State College, Denver
	Camera Work, San Francisco
	Speed Art Museum, Louisville, Kentucky
1979	Allan Frumkin Gallery, Chicago
	Catskill Center for Photography, Woodstock, New York
	Center for Contemporary Photography, Chicago
1980	Visual Studies Workshop, Rochester, New York
	Addison Gallery, Phillips Academy, Andover, Massachusetts
1982	*Recognitions: Faces and Places,* Hudson River Museum, Yonkers, New York
1983	Jeb Gallery, Providence, Rhode Island (with Aaron Siskind)

Selected Group Exhibitions:

1972	*Gamma I,* John Hancock Gallery, Chicago
1973	*Children 1874-1973,* Exchange National Bank, Chicago
1975	*Windy City Open,* Exchange National Bank, Chicago
	Naked or Nude, Darkroom Gallery, Chicago
1976	*New Photographics,* University of Washington, Seattle
	12 Contemporary Photographers, Halsted Gallery, Birmingham, Michigan
1977	*Contemporary Photography,* Fogg Art Museum, Harvard University, Cambridge, Massachusetts

The Photographer and the City, Museum of Contemporary Art, Chicago

4 Photographers, Rizzoli Book Store Gallery, Chicago

1979   *Photography in the 1970s,* Santa Barbara Museum of Art, California

Collections:

Museum of Modern Art, New York; International Center of Photography, New York; International Museum of Photography, George Eastman House, Rochester, New York; Visual Studies Workshop, Rochester, New York; Art Institute of Chicago; Center for Contemporary Photography, Chicago; Speed Museum, Louisville, Kentucky.

Publications:

By TRAUB: Book—*Charles Traub: Beach,* New York 1978. **Articles**—"Charles Traub: Cajun Photographs" in *Southern Voices* (Atlanta), June 1974; "Charles Traub: Photographs" in *Creative Camera* (London), December 1978; "Portfolio: Charles H. Traub" in *Modern Photography* (New York), November 1979.

On TRAUB: Books—*Photographing Children* by the Time-Life editors, New York 1971; *The Photographer and the City,* exhibition catalogue, by Gail Buckland, Chicago 1977.

*

As a photographer I am concerned with the welfare and growth of the medium of contemporary photography in all its parts. I attend to the business of photography management and the administration of affairs of teaching with the same vigor and creative energy that I apply to my own photographic endeavors. This is done out of deep-felt obligation to the community of photographers and well being of the state of the art. For many years the best endeavors in the medium's promotion were made by photographers themselves; I would hope to be able to contribute to this tradition. Our history is still not yet properly written, our critical literature is too little and our audience is still yet to be properly informed. To these ends I feel we should all contribute.

As an artist it is my intention to simply express those needs and urges which come to me out of a process of working in the medium—something I have done for approximately 17 years. In photographic work one idea is generated by another, one picture begets another, and so on, until a body of work is achieved. Out of that body a great amount of selection must be done, and from that selection comes a core idea which is then built upon anew. The total experience of work should be a synergistic one, something bigger than the sum of its parts.

So far in my career as a photographer I have done what I feel are five significant bodies of work. I am currently engaged in working with color and the idea of random descriptive portraiture. I attempt to extend the nature and the history of portraiture itself, as I feel that this is a proper challenge for all photographers in their work.

My current works are confrontational, spontaneous portraits, all with the agreement and participation of their subjects. They are about gestures, body language, sensuality and, indeed, the idea of confrontation itself. People are what they seem; their gestures and responses are in accordance with their personalities. If one knows how to look, one can read much from a picture about an individual. I also look for relationships between one person and another. I am curious at the repetition of types or the repetition of particular personal styles.

Photography is the most exciting act I can engage in. I am totally out of myself while I am photographing. There are powers and controls gained through the act of photography which are truly exceptional. To recognize those feelings is a great release and is, of itself, enough reason to pursue making pictures.

—Charles Traub

* * *

The photographs of Charles Traub challenge the underlying concerns of photography's portraiture and documentary traditions. Although there are people in most of them, his photographs do not exude the standard humanist attitude we have come to expect from such pictures. What was partisan sympathy on the part of the traditional photographer has, in Traub, become cool objectivity: he is not so much interested in who the people are as he is in what they look like.

The influence of Traub's study at the Illinois Institute of Technology with Aaron Siskind can be seen in the strong design qualities present in all his images. Odd perspectives and points of view dominate photographs that often flirt with pure formalism before giving in to their subject matter. The black vignette in the beach pictures functions primarily as a graphic device, giving the series a strong sense of continuity, but then it adds meaning as it begins to look more and more like a TV screen in the act of monitoring real life. A fascination with the body's form, shape, and gesture as it translates into two-dimensional pictures creates sometimes unpleasant close-ups of male and female bodies engaged in leisurely activities. Made with a wide angle lens at very close range, Traub's pictures are aggressively voyeuristic, and they reveal the slightly perverse sexuality prevalent in beach scenes.

Traub's color photographs are even more challenging than his black-and-white ones. What he calls "confrontational, spontaneous portraits" are very straightforward pictures of people on public pathways taken at close range in daylight using strong flash. Unlike traditional portraits, which are meant to reveal some inner quality of the subject, these portraits characterize people by their appearance. Their focus on posture, hair style, hand gesture, facial expression, and clothing seems to be an attempt to redefine the message of photographs. The underlying statement in these—and many other images by Traub—is that since the camera reveals nothing, it is best used to record outward appearance.

—Ted Hedgpeth

TRESS, Arthur.

Nationality: American. **Born:** Brooklyn, New York, 24 November 1940. **Education:** Attended Abraham Lincoln School, Coney Island, New York, 1954-58; studied painting and art history, under Heinrich Bluecher, Bard College, Annandale-on-Hudson, New York, 1958-62, B.F.A. 1962; travelled and studied the arts in Japan, Mexico, and Europe, 1962-66. **Career:** Photographer, Stockholm Ethnographical Museum, 1966-68. Freelance photographer, New York, since 1968. Visiting Instructor, New School for Social Research, New York, 1976. **Recipient:** New York State Council on the Arts Grant, 1971, 1976; National Endowment for the Arts Grant, 1972; Reva and David Logan Foundation Grant, 1974. **Address:** 2610 Marlborough Lane, Cambria, California 93428, U.S.A.

Individual Exhibitions:

1968	*Appalachia: People and Places,* Sierra Club Gallery, New York (travelled to the Smithsonian Institution, Washington, D.C., 1969)
1970	*Open Space in the Inner City,* Sierra Club Gallery, New York
1972	*The Dream Collector,* Raffi Photo Gallery, New York (travelled to the Focus Gallery, San Francisco, 1973; Galleria Il Diaframma, Milan, *Rencontres Internationales de la Photographie,* Arles, France, and Canon Gallery, Amsterdam, 1974; and Galerij Paule Pia, Antwerp, 1976)
1973	*Vision Seekers,* SoHo Gallery, New York
1975	*Shadow,* Neikrug Gallery, New York (travelled to La Photogalerie, Paris, Gallery of Photography, Washington, D.C., and Shadow Gallery, Portland, Oregon)
1976	Canon Photo Gallery, Geneva
1977	Galerie Trockenpresse, Berlin
	Foto Gallery, New York
1978	Friends of Photography, Carmel, California
	Galerie Die Brücke, Vienna

1979	Robert Samuel Gallery, New York
	Galerie Agathe Gaillard, Paris
	Canon Photo Gallery, Geneva
1980	G. Ray Hawkins Gallery, Los Angeles
	Arthur Tress: A Twelve Year Survey, Robert Samuel Gallery, New York
1981	Galerie Agathe Gaillard, Paris
1984	*Images of Childhood and Adolescence,* Madison Art Center, Wisconsin
1986	*Talisman,* the Photographers' Gallery, London
1989	Galerie Urbi et Orbi, Paris
	Bronson Rollins, Los Angeles
	Vision Gallery, San Francisco
1990	*Fish Tank Sonata,* Kiren Plaza, Osaka
	Shati Gallery, Tokyo
	LA Galerie, Frankfurt
	Andrea Ross Gallery, Los Angeles
1991	*Fish Tank Sonata,* Twining Gallery, New York
	Fish Tank Sonata, Zelda Cheatle Gallery, London
	Fish Tank Sonata, Portfolio Gallery, Edinburgh
	Talisman, Alvan Alto Museum, Tyvasula, Finland
	Talisman, Photogallery, Stockholm
1992	*Fish Tank Sonata,* Visual Studies Workshop, Rochester
	Dream Collection, Howard Greenburg Gallery, New York
	Fish Tank Sonata, National Museum of Photography, Bradford
	Fish Tank Sonata, Royal Photographic Society, Bath
	Chinese Shadows, Gallery Veralto, Milan
	Fish Tank Sonata, Salla Parpallo, Valencia
1993	*Retrospective,* Fay Gold Gallery, Atlanta
	Retrospective, Steven Cohen Gallery, Los Angeles
	Requiem for a Paperweight, LA Galerie, Frankfurt
	Requiem for a Paperweight, Portfolio Gallery, Edinburgh
	Fish Tank Sonata, Center for Photographic Art, Carmel
	Wurlitzer Trilogy, Galerie Reisel, Rotterdam
1994	*Fish Tank Sonata,* Santa Barbara Contemporary Arts Forum
	Requiem for a Paperweight, University Art Museum, Long Beach, California
1995	*Wurlitzer Trilogy,* Center for Creative Photography, Tucson

Selected Group Exhibitions:

1969	*Vision and Expression,* International Museum of Photography, George Eastman House, Rochester, New York (toured the United States, 1969-71)
1978	*Self-Portrait,* Friends of Photography, Carmel, California
1979	*Attitudes: Photography in the 1970s,* Santa Barbara Museum of Art, California
	Photographic Surrealism, New Gallery of Contemporary Art, Cleveland (travelled to the Brooklyn Museum, New York)
1981	*The Nude,* Massachusetts Institute of Technology, Cambridge
1983	*Subjective Vision,* High Museum of Art, Atlanta, Georgia
1984	*La Photographie Créative,* Pavillon des Arts, Paris
1986	*The Animal in Photography 1843-1985,* The Photographers' Gallery, London
1990	*Decade by Decade,* Center for Creative Photography, Tucson, Arizona
1991	*Self Portraits,* Center for Creative Photography, Tucson
1992	*Selections from the Ruttenberg Collection,* Art Institute of Chicago
1993	*Mexico Through Foreign Eyes,* ICP, New York
	Breaking Barriers, Frankfurt
1994	*Erotic Photography,* Robert Koch Gallery, San Francisco

Collections:

Museum of Modern Art, New York; Metropolitan Museum of Art, New York; International Museum of Photography, George Eastman House, Rochester, New York; Center for Contemporary Photography, Chicago; Bibliothèque Nationale, Paris; Centre Pompidou, Paris; Stedelijk Museum, Amsterdam; Los Angeles County Museum of Art, LA; Museum of Fine Art, Houston.

Boy in Flood Dream, Ocean City, New York, **1971.** Photograph by Arthur Tress.

Publications:

By TRESS: Books—*Songs of the Blue Ridge Mountains,* New York 1968; *Open Space in the Inner City,* New York 1970; *The Dream Collector,* with text by John Minahan, Richmond, Virginia 1972, New York 1973; *Shadow: A Novel in Photographs,* New York 1975; *The Theatre of the Mind,* with an introduction by A.D. Coleman, New York 1976; *Tress: Facing Up,* with an introduction by Yves Narvarre, Geneva and New York 1980; *Reves,* with an introduction by Michele Tournier, Brussels 1980; *Tress II: Nature Morte,* with an introduction by Michele Tournier, Geneva and New York 1981; *Arthur Tress, Talisman,* edited by Marco Livingstone, London 1986; *Machinations,* London, 1988; *The Teapot Opera,* New York 1988; *Les Crepuscules des Masques,* Paris, 1992; *The Homoerotic Photographic,* New York, 1992; *A la Recherche du Père,* Vivian Esteres, 1993; *Mexico Through Foreign Eyes,* New York, 1993.

On TRESS: Books—*Vision and Expression* by Nathan Lyons, New York 1969; *The Best of Life,* New York 1973; *Terrorist Chic* by Michael Selzer, New York 1979; *Clefs et Serrures* by Michel Tournier, Paris 1979; *Subjective Vision,* exhibition catalogue, with introduction by A.D. Coleman, Atlanta, Georgia 1983; *La Photographie Créative* by Jean-Claude Lemagny, Paris 1984. **Articles**—"Arthur Tress" in *Photography Annual,* New York 1970; "Arthur Tress: Open Spaces in the Inner City" in *Creative Camera* (London), December 1970; "Portfolio: Arthur Tress" in *Photography Annual 1972,* New York 1971; "Arthur Tress" in *Modern Photography Annual,* New York 1973; "Arthur Tress" in *Photo* (Paris), December 1973; "Arthur Tress" in *Photographing Children,* by the Time-Life editors, Amsterdam 1973; "Insolite Tress" by Michel Tournier in *L'Oeil* (Paris), October 1974; interview in *Photo Revue* (Paris), July 1975; "Shadow," interview with Sheila Turner, in *Popular Photography* (New York), August 1976; "Further Adventures of Arthur Tress," interview with Marcia Caro, in *35mm Photography (New York),* Summer 1978; *Frankfurter Allgemeine Magazine,* September 21 1990; Fish Tank, *The Observer,* June 1991; Interview in *American Photographer,* 3/91; "Fish Tank" in *Los Angeles Times,* 16 August 1992; "Fish Tank" in the *International Photograph,* no 2 1992; Interview, *Art News,* March 1992; Requiem, *La Fotographia,* no 36, Barcelona; Review, *Art and Antiques,* Summer 1993; Requiem, *Foto Magazine,* May 1993, Munich; Interview, *Photo Review,* Summer 1993.

*

A photographer could be considered a kind of magician—a being possessed of very special powers that enable him to control mysterious forces and energies outside himself. The photographer's intensely heightened sense perception, product of the brutal discipline of constantly seeing at 1/250th of a second, unevenly evolves his visual facilities to an almost superhuman degree. With these highly-developed instincts, he seems to be able to almost anticipate the activities of his subjects and sometimes actually appears to cause their occurrence by some mental will power of his own that projects outward, making reality conform to his mentally-conceived image of it that he records on film. Often his best photographs are taken in a trance-like state, where there is an almost unspoken mystical communication between his subject and himself, and action is directed through non-verbal gesture and psychic transference. As a trained observer, he can foretell the potential movements of his subjects and perhaps even by mental intimidation and expansion actually cause them to happen. The photographer participates in an almost ritual dance with the world, whereupon his own intense response to its rhythms corresponds to his being able to predict its following certain predetermined patterns.

The photographic image itself has great magical possibilities. Like the ceremonial mask, the ritual incantation, the protective amulet, or magical mandala, the photograph has the potency of releasing in the viewer preconditioned reactions that cause him to physically change or be mentally transformed. In fact, because of our intense belief in the factual literalness of the photograph, it can provoke even stronger reactions than other graphic media. A photograph can more often "grab our guts" or arouse our sexual desires than other art forms because of its purported realness, but it can also more subtly stimulate unconscious responses that we are hardly aware of. The grotesque or frightening image may stir forgotten animal instincts of primordial helplessness and fear, reaching back to the basic insecurity of early man and our own personal childhoods. Images of great peace and harmony have the

curative possibility of restoring tranquility and balance to a disturbed soul or agitated body. The photographic image which hints to the essential mystery of growing things and the unknown qualities of life itself can make the viewer aware of higher states of nature to which we are faintly sensitive. The magical photograph is simply one that attempts by its mere assertive presence to go beyond the immediate context of the recorded experience into realms of the undefinable. The photographer as magician is just someone who is more acutely aware of the subliminal "vibrations" of the everyday world which can call forth hidden emotions or states of feeling that are usually tightly wrapped up in our unconscious selves. He is, himself, totally "opened" to the multiplicities of association that are submerged behind the appearances of the objective world. He uses the repressed mythology of dreams and the archetypal designs of geometry to magically conjure up deep and irrational reactions from the viewer.

Perhaps why so much of today's photography doesn't "grab us" or mean anything to our personal lives is that it fails to touch upon the hidden life of the imagination and fantasy which is hungry for stimulation. The documentary photographer supplies us with facts or drowns in humanity, while the pictorialist, avant-garde or conservative, pleases us with mere aesthetically correct compositions—but where are the photographs *we can pray to, that will make us well again, or scare the hell out of us?* Most of mankind's art for the past 5,000 years was created for just those purposes. It seems absurd to stop now.

—Arthur Tress

* * *

An essentially theatrical attitude has been a hall-mark of Arthur Tress' imagery since his public debut as a photographer.

The first themes he addressed were nominally topical ones: pollution, ecology, and the claustrophobia of life in urban sinks. One of Tress' primary concerns has always been the various ways in which the world (the physical world, in this case) impinges upon the individual's sense of freedom and psychic territory. Tress photographed his understandings of the causes and effects of these problems—and their possible solutions—in several fashions. Though sometimes his observations were presented in conventional photographic terms, as often as not he found ways and means (through the use of volunteer actors, props and other devices) to dramatize those conditions and situations which he found to be most significant.

This penchant for photographic *tableaux vivants* became even more pronounced in his next extended work, a suite of photographs depicting the fantasies and dreams of children. Almost without exception, these were carefully staged productions of specific scenarios which had been recounted by children to the photographer. Tress scouted appropriate locations, provided the necessary props and costumes, and photographed the children acting out their own inner visions. The photograph became the proscenium arch; the viewer became the audience.

This series was followed, several years later, by a "novel in photographs" whose protagonist was Tress himself, portrayed through his own shadow in an extended sequence of ingenious and intelligent images, all set up and acted out. *Shadow* is an ambitious experiment in photographic storytelling, reminiscent on several levels of the wordless wood-block-print novels of Lynd Ward and Franz Masereel. Like many of those books, this one is also an account of a picaresque spiritual voyage; in Tress' work the adventurer travels through time and space in a symbolic, allegorical and (one presumes) autobiographical narrative.

His next book, *The Theater of the Mind,* was a collection of tableaux and portraits in which adults as well as children revealed intimate aspects of self and acted out fantasies, both the photographer's and their own. In the past few years, Tress has explored at length in books and exhibitions the homosexual subculture and the realm of homoerotic fantasy.

The evolution of Tress' imagery, then, has been towards an increasingly directorial approach and increasingly personal themes. If *The Dream Collector* is (albeit by proxy) an expression of the photographer's own childhood traumas, and *Shadow* the tale of his coming of age, then the work of the past few years has been about Tress in the here and now, a catalogue of his own ongoing concerns and obsessions.

It is not coincidental that the photographer's background includes the study of film directing and Kabuki theater; the impact of these disciplines on his work is apparent. Similarly it is appropriate that his interests include psychology, ethnography, eastern philosophy, magic and the supernatural; his imagery is consistently attuned to the manifestations of power in personal and cultural mythology, and the harmonies and discords between the two.

—A.D. Coleman

TSUCHIDA, Hiromi.

Nationality: Japanese. **Born:** Fukui Prefecture, 20 December 1939. **Education:** Fukui University, 1959-63, B.S. in dyeing chemistry 1963; studied photography, under Koen Shigemori, at the Tokyo College of Photography, 1965-68. **Career:** Worked as a researcher, 1963-68, and Publicity Manager, 1968-71, Pola Cosmetics Company, Yokohama and Tokyo. Freelance photographer, Yokohama, since 1971. Instructor, Tokyo College of Photography, since 1972; Established Nirvana Ltd, 1989; Appointed Principal of Tokyo College of Photography, 1992. **Recipient:** Newcomer's Prize, Camera Jidai, 1967; Grand Prize, *Taiyo Magazine,* 1971; Nobuo Ina Award, 1978. **Address:** 3-16-23-2D, Nishiazabu Minato-ku, Tokyo, Japan 106.

Individual Exhibitions:

1962	*Ku,* Bon Gallery, Fukui, Japan
1964	*Black Rhapsody,* Shizuoka Industrial Hall, Shizuoka, Japan
1971	*Self-Autism Space,* Nikon Salon, Tokyo (travelled to Nikon Salon, Osaka)
1977	*Gods of the Earth,* Doi Gallery, Fukuoka, Japan (toured Japan; travelled to the Canon Photo Gallery, Amsterdam, 1978)
1978	*Hiroshima: 1945-1978,* Nikon Salon, Tokyo (travelled to Nikon Salon, Osaka)
	The Crowd, Minoruta Gallery, Tokyo
1979	*Hiroshima Monument,* Nikon Salon, Tokyo (travelled to Nikon Salon, Osaka)
	Shoal, Eye-heart Gallery, Tokyo
1980	*Tokyo Dolls,* Minoruta Gallery, Tokyo
1982	*Hiroshima Collections,* Nikon Salons, Tokyo and Osaka
1985	*Counting Grains of Sand,* Nikon Salons, Tokyo and Osaka
	Hiroshima, travelled the world sponsored by UNESCO
1985-90	*Hiroshima,* Visual Studio Work Shop, Rochester, New York (toured the United States)
1989	*Hiroshima,* Gallery DB-S, Antwerp, Belgium
1990	*Party,* Minoruta Photo Salon, Tokyo
1991	*Zokushin,* Paris Bibliotheque Nationale, Paris
1993	*Hiroshima Monument II,* Nikon Salons, Tokyo and Osaka
1994	*Tent,* Nikon Salons, Tokyo and Osaka

Selected Group Exhibitions:

1974	*New Japanese Photography,* Museum of Modern Art, New York (toured the United States)
1977	*Neue Fotografie aus Japan,* Kulturhaus, Graz, Austria (toured Europe, 1977-79)
1979	*Japan: A Self Portrait,* International Center of Photography, New York (travelled to *Venezia '79*)
	Japanese Photography Today and Its Origin, Galleria d'Arte Moderna, Bologna (travelled to the Palazzo Reale, Milan; Palais des Beaux-Arts, Brussels; the Institute of Contemporary Arts, London; Museum für Kunst und Gewerbe, Hamburg; Gemeente Museum, Arnhem; Pulchri Studio, The Hague)
1982	*38 Japanese Photographers,* Zeit-Foto Salon, Tokyo
1983	*Symposionn uber Fotografie V,* Graz, Austria
1986	*Japon des Avant Gardes,* Center Georges Pompidou, Paris
1987	*Empathy: Japanese Contemporary Photography '87,* Visual Studio Work Shop, Rochester, New York

1989	*Photographie Japonaise,* Provineiall Museum voor Fotografie, Antwerp, Belgium
	Photography Now, Victoria and Albert Museum, London
1990	*Oppositions: Fotografie Biennale Rotterdam II,* Rotterdam, Netherlands
	Tokyo, A City Perspective, Tokyo Metropolitan Museum of Photography
1992	*Wasteland; Fotografie Biennale Rotterdam III,* Rotterdam, Netherlands
1993	*Hiroshima,* Canada Museum of Contemporary Photography, Ottawa, Ontario
1994	*Fotofest '94,* Houseton, Rotterdam, Netherlands

Collections:

Tokyo Sogo Institute of Photography, Yokohama; Japan Professional Photography Society, Tokyo; Museum of Modern Art, New York; Visual Studio Workshop, Rochester, New York; George Eastman House, Rochester, New York; National Gallery of Canada, Ottawa, Ontario; Center Georges Pompidou, Paris; Bibliotheque Nationale, Paris; Princeton University, Princeton, New Jersey; Tokyo Metropolitan Museum of Photography, Tokyo; Kawasaki Art Museum, Kawasaki, Japan.

Publications:

By TSUCHIDA: Books—*Zokushin: Gods of the Earth,* with an introduction by Goichi Matsunaga, Yokohama 1976; *Hiroshima: 1945-1978,* edited by Tatsuo Shirai, Tokyo 1979; *Tokyo Dolls,* Tokyo 1981; *Testimonies of Hiroshima,* Tokyo, 1982; *Sanctuaries of Japan-Ise Shrine,* Japan 1982; *Hiroshima,* Japan 1983 & 1985; *Zen,* Japan 1988; *Ise Shrine,* Japan 1988; *The Road to North Japan,* Japan 1989; *Counting Grains of Sand,* Japan 1990; *Party,* Japan 1990.

On TSUCHIDA: Books—*New Japanese Photography,* edited by John Szarkowski and Shoji Yamagishi, New York 1974; *Neue Fotografie aus Japan,* exhibition catalogue, by Otto Breicha, Graz and Vienna 1977; *Japanse Fotografie van 1848 tot Heden,* exhibition catalogue, by Attilio Colombo and Isabella Doniselli, Amsterdam 1980; *38 Japanese Photographers,* exhibition catalogue, Tokyo 1982. **Articles**—"The Visible and the Invisible" by Kohi Taki in *Asahi Camera* (Tokyo), September 1977; "The Other Face" by Koji Taki in *Asahi Camera* (Tokyo), January 1978; "Freedom from the Gods of the Earth" by Kazuo Nishii in *Camera Mainichi* (Tokyo), May 1978; "Encounter with the Children of Hiroshima" by Satoshi Hidaka in *Camera Mainichi* (Tokyo), January 1979; "Crossing of the Consciousness of Self" by Shiroyasu Suzuki in *Asahi Camera* (Tokyo), April 1980; "Le drame et l'aprés drame" by Inuhiko Yomota in *La Recherche Photographique,* 1990; "Hiromi Tsuchida and his World of Eternal Ambiguity" by Jean Claude Lemagny in exhibition catalogue of *Zokushin,* 1991; "A crowd whose name is Japan" by Inuhiko Yomota in exhibition catalogue of *Zokushin,* 1991.

*

Before my interest in photography comes my concern with the mentality of the Japanese people. This is why, for the last fifteen years, I have toured the country (in particular, the rural areas) and documented people as they participate in festivals and ritual ceremonies. I have tried to record the basic elements of Japanese culture as it manifests itself in such extraordinary time-space situations as festivals.

You could say that my photographs constitute a type of visual "Japanology." The reason I have focussed upon folk culture in particular is that it most clearly expressed itself in visual terms. Another motive lies in the fact that I myself am a product of that culture. My work has become a confirmation of my own identity. The results of this effort have been brought together in my book of

Student uniform

Akio Tsukuda (13 at the time) was engaged in fire prevention work about 800 meters from the hypocenter. His father found his school uniform hanging on a branch of a tree on August 8, 1945. His body was not found.

Hiroshima, **1979.** Photograph by Hiromi Tsuchida.

photographs, *Zokushin.* At present, I have changed the setting of my work from the country to a metropolis (Tokyo) and am pursuing the theme of people as they appear in groups, swarms, and shoals.

Since 1975 I have been documenting the subject of "Hiroshima." In photographing the present-day scenery of the city and the remaining "hibakusha" (victims of the A-bomb) as they live today, I have tried to become conscious of the way a tragedy of the past survives and changes in nature with time. The great changes that have occurred in Japanese culture forty years after the year may be enacted on the stage of "Hiroshima." This subject also provides me with a framework in which to contemplate the Japanese mentality as well as to ponder the tragic nature of a nuclear explosion in this present day. My documentation of "Hiroshima" has continued along the following themes: 1) 1975-78—Hibakusha: interviews and photographs; II) 1978-79—Hiroshima landscape: relics of the blast (buildings, trees, etc.) standing within a 3 km. radius of the bomb site; III) 1980—Documents and exhibits inside the Hiroshima Peace Memorial Museum; and IV) At present—Investigating other photographic possibilities.

As for the future, I myself am not sure in which direction my camera will turn; but basically the crux of my photography will continue to be an investigation into Japanese culture and the Japanese people.

—Hiromi Tsuchida

*   *   *

In the early 1970s the young photographer Hiromi Tsuchida travelled throughout the remoter areas of Japan, from Aomori and Hokkaido in the north to southern Kyushu. He was ostensibly recording festivals and pilgrimages. Under the guidance of Shoji Yamagishi, Tsuchida returned from his travels with an extraordinary body of work, which was published in 1976 as *Zokushin: Gods of the Earth.*

"I suppose what I was trying to do was to find myself again as a Japanese," said Tsuchida. This assertion of a Japanese identity was a preoccupation he shared with many of his contemporaries. After the prosperity of the 1960s, a cultural crisis was evident at the start of the new decade. The distinguished novelists Mishima and Kawabata both committed suicide. The photographers Hosoe and Tomatsu, who had surfaced with Vivo in the early 1960s, had overthrown the first phase of post-war realism. They now directed their work into areas that strongly emphasized the exploration of Japanese tradition as well as the cultural conflicts that resulted from western influence. Tsuchida was to emerge with a new generation, including Shinoyama and Moriyama, all of whom were exploring the roots of their native culture.

In *Zokushin* the pre-war notion of the purity of the Yamato race—as Matsunaga puts it in his preface, "that pitiful fabrication of the ruling powers linking the myth of the descent from the Gods with reality"—is dismissed. The Gods of the Earth are the people of Japan, balanced between the profane—the sake and sex—and the spiritual devotion of the pilgrimage. Tsuchida found his subjects either in the outer, wilder regions of Japan or else on the outer periphery of society. The Shinto devotions of the festivals are coupled with the assertion of the communal spirit celebrated through dance and drink, not through the traditional concept of holiness or abstinence. Against such a background the characters in *Zokushin* are often anachronistic. In the mist on Mount Fuji a pilgrim in white robes peers through his dark glasses as if on the edge of the 20th century. Following the backroads of Japan, Tsuchida found the actors, the bar girls, the transvestites, the widow on the beach and the wedding couple on the outskirts of town; they all appear as displaced people. Like Robert Frank's American journey Tsuchida's *Zokushin* moves across an often desolate landscape with an abrasive technique that challenges many previous concepts of photographic order.

Between 1976 and 1978 Tsuchida worked on a portrait project called "Children of Hiroshima." The series was based on a text of interviews with child victims of the atomic explosion, which had been published in 1951. He integrated his portraits taken 30 years after the explosion with the original interviews. The series is a sign of the spirit of recovery. Many of the portraits have an intimate, domestic calm; they are, however, violently juxtaposed with the revelations of the text. The trauma of 1945 remains a deep scar across modern Japan, which Tsuchida has exposed with understatement as he strips back the veneer of Japanese post-war prosperity.

—Mark Holborn

TUGGENER, Jakob.

Nationality: Swiss. **Born:** Zurich, 7 February 1904. **Education:** Sekundärschule, Zurich, 1916-19; studied drawing, Reimann Kunstschule für Gestaltung, Berlin, 1930-31; self-taught in photography. **Military Service:** Served in the Swiss Army, 1931-32. **Family:** Married three times; two sons (one deceased). **Career:** Apprentice draughtsman, 1919-23, then machine draughtsman, 1923-30, Maag Zahnräder AG, Zurich; freelance industrial photographer, working for Maschinenfabrik Oerlikon, Steckborn Kunstseide, Jakon Rieter und Co., Sprecher and Schuh, etc., Zurich, 1932-51 (established own photo studio, Zurich, 1935). Freelance magazine and advertising photographer, Zurich, working for *Du* and other magazines, since 1951. Also, independent documentary and fantasy filmmaker, and painter, Zurich, 1937-70. **Recipient:** Gold Medal, *Biennale di Fotografia,* Venice, 1957; City of Zurich Cultural Achievement Award, 1981. **Address:** Titlistrasse 52, 8032 Zurich, Switzerland.

Individual Exhibitions:

1969	*Ballnächte,* Neue Sammlung, Munich
1974	*Photographien 1930 bis Heute,* Helmhaus, Zurich
1978	*Fotografien 1930 bis Heute,* Museum der Stadt Solothurn, Switzerland
1980	Work Gallery, Zurich
1981	Kunsthaus, Zurich
	Galerie zur Stockeregg, Zurich

Selected Group Exhibitions:

1951	*Collegium of Swiss Photographers,* Helmhaus, Zurich (and annually, to 1954)
1954	*Great Photographs,* Limelight Gallery, New York
1955	*The Family of Man,* Museum of Modern Art, New York (and world tour)
1957	*Biennale di Fotografia,* Venice
1963	*Die Grossen Fotografen unseres Jahrhunderts,* Cologne
1964	*Lausanne Exposition,* Pavilion of Woods and Wine, Lausanne, Switzerland
1981	*Photographs from European Collections,* Kunsthaus, Zurich (toured Europe)
1980	*The Imaginary Photo Museum,* Kunsthalle, Cologne
1983	*Die fotografische Sammlung,* Museum Folkwang, Essen, West Germany
1984	*Subjektive Fotografie: Images of the 50s,* San Francisco Museum of Modern Art (travelled to the University of Houston, Texas; Museum Folkwang, Essen; Vasterbottens Museum, Umea; Kulturhuset, Stockholm; Saarland Museum, Saarbrücken; Palais des Beaux Arts, Brussels)

Collections:

Stiftung für die Photographie, Kunsthaus, Zurich; Museum der Stadt Solothurn, Switzerland; Museum Folkwang, Essen, Germany.

Publications:

By TUGGENER: Books—*Fabrik: Ein Bild Epos der Technik,* Zurich 1943; *Zürcher Oberland,* with text by Emil Egli, Zurich 1956; *Forum Alpinum,* Lausanne, Switzerland, 1965; films (all 16mm, black/white, silent)—*Flugmeeting (Dubendorf),* 1937; *Zürich Stadt und Land,* 1937-40; *Die Maschinenzeit,* 1938-70; *Abbruch der Tonhalle,* 1938; *Rosmarie,* 1942; *Die Schiffmaschine,* 1943; *Wir Fordern,* 1943; *Die Seemühle,* 1944; *Der Weg aus Eden,* 1946; *Dazio Grande,* 1947; *Uerikon-Bauma Bahn,* 1948; *Die Strassenbahnen im Kt. Zug,* 1952; *Hyronimus* 1953; *Illusion,* 1954; *Die Muse,* 1957; *Das Grab des Kelten* (unfinished), 1959; *Palace Hotel, St. Moritz,* 1960; *Dornröschen,* 1961; *Wien, Nur Du Allein,* 1960-62; *Mortimer,* 1962; *Die*

Versuchung des Hl. Antonius, 1963; *Die Hölzfäller,* 1963; *Ciel Naif,* 1967; *Roberto Niederer, der Glasbläser,* 1970.

On TUGGENER: Books—*Schweizer Künstler: Fotografie,* Zurich 1963; *Jakob Tuggener: Fotografien 1930 bis Heute,* exhibition catalogue, by André Kamber and Kurt Ulrich, Solothurn, Switzerland 1978; *Neue Sachlichkeit und Surrealismus in der Schweiz 1915-1940,* edited by Rudolf Koella, Berne 1979; *The Imaginary Photo Museum* by Helmut Gernsheim, Renate and L. Fritz Gruber and others, Cologne 1981, London 1982; *Museum Folkwang: die fotografische Sammlung,* exhibition catalogue, with introduction by Ute Eskildsen, Essen, West Germany 1983; *Subjektive Fotografie: Images of the 50s,* exhibition catalogue, by Ute Eskildsen, Manfred Schmalriede and Dorothy Martinson, Essen, West Germany 1984. **Articles**—by Hans Kasser in *Camera* (Lucerne), October 1949; in *Schweizer Journal* (Zurich), no. 1/2, 1952; in *Du* (Zurich), May 1954; by Arnold Kubler in *Du* (Zurich), January 1957; "Jakob Tuggener" by Norman Hall in *Photography* (London), September 1962; "Palace Hotel" by Manuel Gasser in *Du* (Zurich), February 1968; by Oswald Ruppen in *Schweizerische Photorundschau* (Visp), no. 24, 1974; "Tuggener Stimme aus der Stille" in *Schweizerische Photorundschau* (Visp), December 1978. **Film**—*Zum Beispiel Tuggener* by Dieter Bachmann, 1974.

*   *   *

Only the greatest among photographic storytellers have in their single pictures an easily recognizable handwriting. This is true of Jakob Tuggener, astute and gentle observer of humanity at work and at play. Tuggener is a warm and perceptive person who delights in what he sees, reports on it with empathy and feeling, totally non-judgmental in his attitude toward rich and poor, reacting with fresh imagery to whatever is real. His response is immediate, his personality effacing, resulting in photographs that are intimate and true.

Tuggener's main subject is Switzerland, its nooks and crannies, its private places, where only God has had time to look. In the past 50 years he has woven a unique tapestry. It has been his custom to work for himself for decades on themes that please him and to assemble photographs from these into albums. He considers his oeuvre not single photographs, but the 70 or so bound books, which he has composed of photos in a visual rhythm, mounted and bound. The books contain up to 108 photographs. His main themes are Industry (13 for industry itself, 10 on technology), Ballnights (8), and Farmers (9). Many more are devoted to various parts of Switzerland, his travels and European capital cities.

His imagery is not influenced by any photographer. Perhaps it was stimulated by the many silent films he has made and by his painting, for he is a master at varying range and scene of a chosen subject, and his composition was from the beginning unfailingly right. Between his early and late pictures there is no difference in concept, feeling, composition or quality. Perhaps, he volunteers, the early themes are more monumental.

Social criticism has been ascribed to him, but his intention is purely photogenic: soot and dirt, pomp and glitter he likes because they make pictures. "My domain," he says, "is the soul; my photography, the shortest route to the heart."

Stimulus comes to Tuggener from the past. As others transform reality into a private vision, Tuggener draws on his strong sense of identity with his great Swiss ancestors. To their noble deeds as advisors and captains of French King's bodyguards, to their mercy shown in battle centuries ago, he ascribes the equanimity with which he photographs all.

It was an army encounter that turned the amateur from an unemployed draughtsman into a professional photographer with unheard of freedom, working for the house organ of one of Switzerland's greatest machine builders. Tuggener's specialty developed into self-designed anniversary books for Swiss companies. His oeuvre thus includes a unique coverage of Swiss industry, by now, because of automation, archeology.

At 77 Tuggener is still in love with seeing. When the light is right, his heart overflows into poignant photographs, which endear themselves with the simplicity and rightness of their conception. From the minutiae of every day life, familiar objects and places, he distills poetry.

—Inge Bondi

TUNBJÖRK, Lars

Nationality: Swedish. **Born:** Borås, 15 February 1956. **Career:** Has worked as a freelance photographer since 1977; employed at "Stockholm-Tidningen," 1983-1984. **Agents:** Tiofoto, Box 3252, S-10365 Stockholm, Sweden; Agence Vu, 11 Rue Beranger, 75003 Paris, France. **Address:** Smedsuddsvägen 10, 112 35 Stockholm, Sweden.

Individual Exhibitions:

1989	Fotograficentrum, Gothenburg
1990	Mira Gallery, Stockholm
	Lansmuseet, Kristianstad, Sweden
1991	Fotohurst, Gothenburg
1992	Travelling exhibition in Russia
1993	Hasselblad Center, Gothenburg
	Landskrona Museum, Sweden
1994	Nordiska Museet, Stockholm
	Bildmuseum, Umeå, Sweden
	Gdansk, Poland

Selected Group Exhibitions:

1983	*Picture of the Year,* Kulturhuset, Stockholm
1984	*Picture of the Year,* Lund, Sweden
	Portraits, Fotografiska Museet, Stockholm
	Stocken, Fotograficentrum, Stockholm
1990	*To Poland,* Krakow, Poland
1991	*Machine of Sight,* Leningrad
	Lika Med, Moderna Museet, Stockholm
	Gothenburg Photographic Fair, Gothenburg, Sweden

Collections:

Fotografiska Museet, Stockholm; Hasselblad Centre, Gothenburg.

Publications:

By TUNBJÖRK: Books—*Photography Unbound,* 1987; *Paris—200 Years After* with Herman Lindquist, 1989; *Landet Utom Sig (The Country Beside Itself)* with Thomas Tidholm and Göran Greider, 1993; **Television**—*Liverpool,* Swedish Television 1984.

On TUNBJÖRK: Articles—"Inpå Livet Med Distans" by Hasse Persson in *Aktvell Fotografi & Foto,* No. 12, 1992; "Folkzin i Otakt" by Mikael Van Reis in *Göteborgs-Posten,* 29 August 1993; "Vardagas Landet Med Omhet Olm Sorg" by Karin Berglund in *Dagens Nyheter,* 21 August 1993; "En av de Stora Berättarna" by Mika Larsson in *Fotografisk Tidskrift,* No. 4-5, 1993.

*

I am a storyteller.

I worked for eight years as a press photographer and now work mostly with longer personal projects. I have travelled widely on assignments, but in the past few years have concentrated mostly on Sweden. I think that a photographer does his most important work where he has his roots.

In my latest book, *Landet Utom Sig (The Country Beside Itself),* I have tried to show how Sweden has changed from an egalitarian society to a more commercially oriented one. This crumbling of the "Swedish model" has resulted in a feeling of widespread alienation.

I have travelled around Sweden and photographed shopping centres, camping grounds and the land and city-scapes where people meet. I left the 35mm at home and instead started to work with medium format and colour in order to highlight details—a poster in the background is just as important to the picture as a funny man in the foreground.

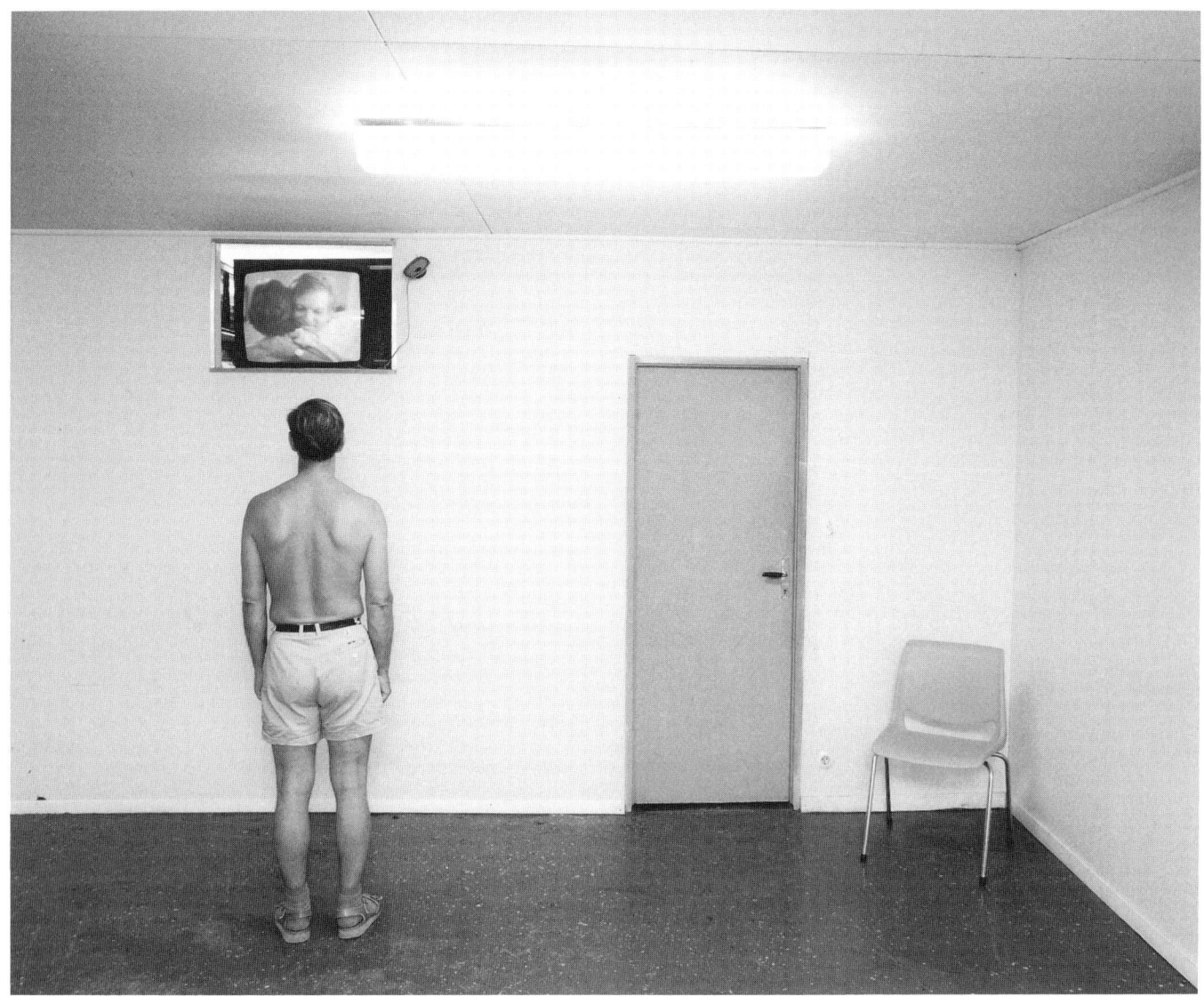

Oland, **1991 (original in colour). Photograph ©Lars Tunbjork.**

I believe that many of my pictures have a typical Swedish atmosphere, a mixture of sadness, humour and self-irony.

—Lars Tunbjörk

*   *   *

An emptiness permeates our cities and smaller towns and moves along the roads. It used not to be there. When it began to emerge, it went undetected for some time, supressed beneath a kind of dizzy tipsiness that spread across the country and was everywhere and which perhaps transformed the very fundamentals of Sweden.

In the mid-1970s, Swedish society turned around completely. It happened during sleep, however, so the inhabitants did not realize when they woke up on the other side. This marked the culmination of the process set in motion way back in the 1930s. The engine behind the previous system change—the welfare state ideal—ebbed and left behind an emptiness of eroded equality which was soon to be filled by a current of commercial euphoria. When the economic boom finally peaked, fifteen years of accumulated alienation came rushing towards us. I, and many with me, stood there, dead sober in the dawn,

surrounded by the punctured Swedish model which had made up our whole society. What happened?

Looking through Lars Tunbjörk's work is an intriguing experience. It completely lacks images from public life, from hospitals or communal sports halls, from waiting rooms at the national social security offices or from the steps of city halls, from the community houses or even police stations, from public memorials or public artworks in a town square during the Saturday morning rush. Not even Systembolaget (the government liquor monopoly), the peculiar state-run institution with its department-store fatigue is represented. Instead, I see the powers that emerged victorious from this period, roughly 1987 to 1992, when these photographs were shot. The perspective is strong. In the end, the images are accusatory. Taken together, the photographs form a kind of giant soap bubble with a glossy surface on which an artificial rainbow floats around and around. They tell of something missing. Sweden abandoned its progress toward something worthier and more humane.

The sadness brought on by Lars Tunbjörk's photographs is not rooted in any failure to establish the welfare state ideals because of fundamentally flawed blue-prints. Rather, it reflects the abrupt end of the movement, or that the effort was denied continuation because the industrial power elite said "No." Step by step we came to a time of reduced collective expectations. We arrived one by one in the free-market paradise, and nowadays even some local elections simulate marketing campaigns. Hence the emptiness; every citizen has a business card.

Everywhere in these images I see people who have been hindered in the progress towards something, and that brings on the distress. They often look out-of-place, and they seem to be aware of it. I want to argue that there is common ground here where political visions of equality and fairness walk hand in hand with the fact that photographers, artists and writers are once again beginning to discover this country and the people who live here. That is why my feeling for Lars Tunbjörk's photographs suddenly turns away from the emptiness I initially felt. They are not merely a bleak reminder of life's isolation, but they also encompass a folksy Sweden, obvious perhaps to a majority but something that nonetheless prompts the cultural middle-class in the inner-city ghettos to back off. Central Stockholm projects the official Sweden-image, and it would be strange if this image was not affected by the journalists and cultural workers who shape it. In August Strindberg's time, a half-hour walk through central Stockhom sufficed to traverse the entire class spectrum. Fewer people live within the city limits now than at the turn of the century but the number of white-collar workers is clearly over-represented.

The segregation is not, however, just a question of city versus suburbia. Statistics show that as much as 46 percent of the most revered cultural elite grew up in one of the major cities, as compared with 14 percent of the population as a whole. How could this world and its elite inhabitants understand the firework of experience that radiates so clearly from several of Lars Tunbjörk's photographs? I, who grew up in this world but ended up outside looking in, must, in the end, describe the experience as carnival-like. Santa Clauses appearing in the midst of a summer heatwave. Hamburgers as bloated as the sausages during a carnival week in Germany in the middle ages. Rebates, special offers and discount shopping malls are not exactly the vocabulary of cultural circles. In the eyes of the cultural middle-class this carnival is at best exotic; at worst, tasteless. But the aversion is nothing other than the erosion of democracy. The public sphere, where our common problems must be dealt with, corrodes when whole lifestyles are forced to the fringes. It runs the risk of turning into a salon for an elitist few, horrified by threatening populism.

When I sat for about a week and leafed through these pictures, Sweden seemed dreamlike and unreal. I saw people in supermarkets, department stores and shopping centres, as if explorers in a jungle of colours and offers, as if in an aggressive paradise. But then the pages turned silently inside me, paving the way for a much larger Sweden—as if all the vacation snapshots of the nation were coming forward for recognition. It really is about the very foundation on which democracy is based. There is life on this planet, in this country.

—Göran Greider

TURBEVILLE, Deborah.

Nationality: American. **Born:** Medford, Massachusetts, 6 July 1937. **Education:** Attended Brimmer and May Preparatory School, Boston, 1949-54; studied photography in seminars with Richard Avedon and Marvin Israel, New York. **Career:** Design Assistant to Claire McCardell, New York, 1956-58; Editorial Assistant, *Ladies' Home Journal*, New York, 1960-62; Fashion Editor, *Harper's Bazaar*, New York, 1962-65; Associate Fashion Editor, *Mademoiselle*, New York, 1967-71. Freelance fashion photographer, working for *Vogue, Marie-Claire, Nova, Harpers, House and Garden, Lei, Viva* etc., Paris and New York, since 1972. **Recipient:** American Book Award, 1981. **Agent:** Staley Wise Gallery, 560 Broadway, New York, New York 10012, U.S.A. **Address:** c/o Janice Goodman, Attorney-at-Law, 36 West 44th Street, New York, New York 10036, U.S.A.

Individual Exhibitions:

1976	Cameraworks, Beverly Hills, California
	Camera Gallery, Sydney
1977	Sonnabend Gallery, New York (retrospective)
	Kölnischer Kunstverein, Cologne
1978	Newport Museum, Rhode Island

	Weston Art Gallery, Massachusetts
	Wallflower, Sonnabend Gallery, New York
1980	*Collages,* Paul Cava Gallery, Philadelphia (travelled to the Stephen Wirtz Gallery, San Francisco)
1981	*John Baldessari/Deborah Turbeville,* Sonnabend Gallery, New York
	Clock Tower Gallery, New York
	La Remise du Parc, Paris
	Pierce Street Gallery, Birmingham, Michigan
1982	Delahunty Gallery, Dallas, Texas
	La Remise du Parc, Paris
	Il Ponte, Rome
1985	Parco Galleries, Tokyo
1986	Centre Georges Pompidou, Paris
1987	Pierce Street Gallery, Birmingham, Michigan
	Staley Wise Gallery, New York
1994	Staley Wise Gallery, New York

Selected Group Exhibitions:

1975	*Fashion Photography: 6 Decades,* Emily Lowe Gallery, Hofstra University, Hempstead, New York (toured the United States)
	Fashion and Fantasy, Rizzoli Gallery, New York
1977	*Fashion Photography,* International Museum of Photography, George Eastman House, Rochester, New York (travelled to the Brooklyn Museum, New York; San Francisco Museum of Modern Art, California; Cincinnati Art Institute, Ohio; Museum of Fine Arts, St. Petersburg, Florida)
1980	*Surrealism in Photography,* Cleveland Art Museum (travelled to the Brooklyn Museum, New York)
1982	*Lichtbildnisse: Das Porträt in der Fotografie,* Rheinisches Landesmuseum, Bonn
1983	*Versailles—19th Century to Present,* La Grande Palais, Paris
1986	*Fashion Retrospective,* Victoria and Albert Museum, London
1988	*Collaboration Between Designers & Photographers,* Musee de Costume, Arles, France
	The Art of Commercial Photography, Musee de la Mode, Paris
1989	*Body Language,* Staley Wise Gallery, New York

Collections:

Paul Walter Collection, New York; Sam Wagstaff Collection, New York; Bruno Bischoffberger, Zurich.

Publications:

By TURBEVILLE: Books—*Maquillage,* New York 1975; *Wallflower,* edited by Marvin Israel and Kate Morgan, New York and London 1978; *Unseen Versailles: Photographs by Deborah Turbeville,* with text by Louis Auchincloss, New York 1981; *Les Amoureuses du Temps Passé,* Paris, 1985; *Photographes Contemporains I,* Paris, 1986.

On TURBEVILLE: Books—*Time-Life Photography Year,* New York 1976; *Women on Women,* edited by Katharine Holabird, London 1978; *The History of Fashion Photography* by Nancy Hall-Duncan, New York 1979; *Lichtbildnisse: Das Porträt in der Fotografie,* edited by Klaus Honnef, Cologne 1982; *Surrealism,* exhibition catalogue, Cleveland, Ohio, 1980. **Articles**—"Deborah Turbeville" in *Zoom* (Paris), June/July 1976; "Deborah Turbeville" by Allan Porter in *Camera* (Lucerne), 1976; "Deborah Turbeville" by Andrea Skinner in the *New York Times,* January 1977; "Deborah Turbeville" by Gene Thornton in the *New York Times,* May 1977; "Deborah Turbeville" in *Zoom* (Paris), March 1978; "Deborah Turbeville: Wallflower" in *The Guardian* (London), May 1979; "Wallflower" by Carter Ratcliff in *Art in America* (New York), June 1979; "Deborah Turbeville: Wallflower" in *Zoom* (Paris), July 1979; "Unseen Versailles" by Christian Caujolle in *Liberation,* Paris, October, 1981; "The Hidden Versailles" by Vicki Goldberg in *New York Times Magazine,* 20 September 1981; "Musees

Paris—Deborah Turbeville" in *Connaissance des Arts,* Paris, July 1986; "The Charm & Grace of Deborah Turbeville" in *Le Monde,* Paris, July 1986.

*

In 1972 I moved away from New York to live in Paris and while packing and sorting I came across a piece of paper on which I had written several years ago. It went like this: "Through a series of vignettes in stills, I wish to use the medium of photography to explain a group of rather eccentric people ... sometimes one or two, sometimes many ... placed in settings that help describe them. These people perform like a repertory company, often reappearing in different roles."

My pictures walk a tightrope. They never know. At 50 I am one of the very few "enfants terribles" still claiming to take fashion photographs. I am not a fashion photographer; I am not a photojournalist; I am not a portraitist.

The photographs are like the women you see in them: a little out of balance with their surroundings, waiting anxiously for the right person to find them, and thinking perhaps they are not of their times. They move forward clutching their past around them, as if the ground of the present may fall away. Their exteriors endless ... airless. The very print quality reflects something in the women that is hesitant, a little faded and scratched. Or that, having emerged into a light too harsh, stand frozen in space—overexposed.

It is interesting to me that the definition of the rather old-fashioned word "wall-flower" is: a pale yellow or brownish-red flower that clings, wild, to the sides of walls—and someone who chooses not to, or is not chosen to, dance: a spectator.

—Deborah Turbeville

* * *

Former fashion editor Deborah Turbeville breaks all the traditional fashion photography rules when she takes her pictures. She neither portrays the aloof statuesque woman featured by high fashion magazines nor the vapid and featureless girl-next-door featured by magazines for the middle class; her models are interesting women—haunted, desperate, and beautiful. You want to know them. Though elusive and lonely, they are real flesh and blood, not two-dimensional objects. Their expressions are brooding and anxious. The deep set eyes do not sparkle and contain no flirtatious come-on or put-down. It is the whole woman who dominates the scene; her clothes are part of her.

The traditional tendency of fashion photography, to reduce women to erotic objects, is missing. Turbeville likes women, and she does not fear them.

A photographer of proven courage, Turbeville produces prints that are grainy and often scratched. Her photographs contrast sharply with the perfect creamy prints of fashion, the kind produced by large cameras and complicated studio lighting. You are aware of the air that surrounds her models. Outdoors, they peer at us through mist and fog; inside, they wander through empty spaces in light filtered by dirty and cracked windows. Her color pictures are full of odd muted tones.

Turbeville chooses her locations with care and originality. Abandoned mansions, greenhouses lying in ruins, deserted public bathhouses, empty corridors, and jumbled warehouses replace the seamless backdrops and the elegantly furnished society manors that we are accustomed to. Her settings seem more appropriate to a mystery play than to the selling of clothes. The mood is one of menace and uncertainty. The sense of theatre prevails—something is about to happen in this soft focus dream world.

Are clothes the meaning of these pictures? Turbeville appears to be more interested in the making of interesting and eye-stopping pictures. It is often difficult to get a clear idea of the details of the garments being worn. Yet, the magazine reader's eye is caught, the women are real and appealing, and the reader can identify with them. Perhaps these haunting pictures do sell clothes.

If Turbeville's view of fashion is about its time, then women live in a world of malaise, of uncertainty, angst, boredom, loneliness, and terror. They are victims. Turbeville's evocative photographs reflect the women in them and are a strong criticism of our culture. Her care in choice of model, location, staging, camera, lens, and printing all contribute to her view of the anxious isolation of even the most beautiful of women placed in a disquieting time.

—Barbara Norfleet

U

UEDA, Shoji.

Nationality: Japanese. **Born:** Sakaiminato, Tottori Prefecture, 27 March 1913. **Education:** Yonago Public High School, Tottori Prefecture, 1924-30; studied, under Toyo Kikuchi, at the Oriental School of Photography, Tokyo, 1930-31. **Family:** Married Norie Shiraishi in 1932; children: Hiroshi, Kazuko, Mitsuru, and Touru. **Career:** Photographer since 1933, with studio in Sakaiminato; Member, Chugoku Photographers' Club, Okayama, 1934-37, Ginryusha Photographers' Club, Tokyo, 1948, and Nika-kai Photographers Club, Tokyo, 1955. Professor of Photography, Kyushyu Sangyo University, Fukuoka Prefecture, 1975-1994. **Recipient:** Photography Prize, Nika Exhibition, Tokyo, 1955; Photographic Society of Japan Award, Tokyo, 1975; Cultural Merit Award, Tokyo, 1978. **Agent:** Zeit-Photo, Yagicho Bld. 5F 1-4, Muromachi, Nihonbashi, Chuo-ku, Tokyo. **Address:** 85-3 Higashi-kurayoshi-machi, Yonagoshi, Tottori-ken 683, Japan.

Individual Exhibitions:

1953	*Shoji Ueda/Youichi Midorikawa*, Muramatsu Gallery, Tokyo
1971	*Children the Year Round*, Asahi Pentax Gallery, Tokyo
1972	*Sketch Album in Europe*, AO Gallery, Tokyo
1975	*Shoji Ueda's World*, Nikon Salon, Tokyo (travelled to the Nikon Salon, Osaka)
1979	*Shoji Ueda*, Asahi Pentax Gallery, Tokyo
	Matsue, Olympus Photo Plaza, Tokyo
1980	*Izumo*, Minolta Photo Space, Tokyo
	Europe, Asahi Pentax Gallery, Tokyo
	Shoji Ueda, Nikon Salon, Tokyo
	Paysage et Hommes, Zeit-Foto Salon, Tokyo
1981	*Marchenland*, Zeit-Foto Salon, Tokyo
1984	*Shoji Ueda's Fifty years*, Pentax Forum, Tokyo
1988	*Vintage*, Zeit Photo Salon, Tokyo
	Shoji Ueda, Seibu Art Gallery, Tokyo
	Shoji Ueda, The Museum of Contemporary Photography, Columbia College, Chicago, Illinois
	Foto Fest '88, Houston, Texas
1989	*With the Light and Wind of Andalucia*, Pentax Forum, Tokyo
1990	*Tales of Scenery and Still Life*, Konika Plaza, Tokyo
	Part I. Vintage Prints Exhibition; Part II. Monochrome Works; Part III. Colour Works, Picture Photo Space, Osaka, Japan
	With the Light and Wind of Andalucia, Takashimaya Hall, Yonago, Japan
1991	*Modernist of the Dunes*, Il Tempo, Tokyo
1992	*Dune Theatre*, JCII Photo Salon, Tokyo
	Still Life, Nihonbashi Mitsukoshi Select Gallery, Japan
1993	*Dye Transfer Prints*, Picture Photo Space, Osaka, Japan
	Tokyo Station Gallery, Tokyo

Selected Group Exhibitions:

1948	*Ginryu-sha Exhibition*, Matsuya Department Store, Tokyo
1949	*Ginryu-sha Exhibition*, Matsuya Department Store, Tokyo
1960	*Japanese Photography*, Museum of Modern Art, New York
1970	*Six Photographers*, Fuji Photo Salon, Tokyo
1979	*Japanese Photography 1848 to Today*, Galleria d'Arte Moderna, Bologna, Italy (travelled to the Palazzo Reale, Milan; Palais des Beaux-Arts, Brussels; Institute of Contemporary Arts, London; Museum für Kunst und Gewerbe, Hamburg; Gemeente Museum, Arnhem; Pulchri Studio, The Hague, 1979-80)
	Japan: A Self-Portrait, International Center of Photography, New York (travelled to *Venezia '79*)
1980	*The Imaginary Photo Museum*, Kunsthalle, Cologne
1982	*38 Japanese Photographers*, Zeit-Foto Salon, Tokyo
1984	*Sammlung Gruber*, Museum Ludwig, Cologne
1990	*Postwar Photographs: Rebirth and Development: Dune Series*, Yamaguchi Prefectural Art Museum, Japan
	The Era of Art Photographs, Yonago City Museum of Art, Tottori Prefecture, Japan
	Japon-Années 60, PICTO Bastille, Paris
1992	*Shoji Ueda and Friends—1935-55*, Yonago City Art Museum, Tottori Prefecture, Japan

Collections:

Museum of Modern Art, New York; Bibliothèque Nationale, Paris; Museum Ludwig, Cologne, Germany; Tokyo Municipal Museum of Photography; Tokyo National Museum of Modern Art; Yokohama Museum of Art; Kawasaki Civil Museum; Yamaguchi Prefectural Art Museum; Yonago City Museum of Art; Shoji Ueda Photographic Art Museum, Kishimoto Town, Japan.

Publications:

By UEDA: Books—*Izumo Myths*, with Masaaki Ueda, Tokyo 1965; *Oki*, with Tatsuya Naramoto, Tokyo 1967; *Children the Year Round*, Tokyo 1971; *The Legend of Izumo*, Tokyo 1974; *Sketch Album in Europe*, Tokyo 1974; *Sand Dunes*, Tokyo 1978; *Izumo Fudoki*, Tokyo 1980; *Brilliant Scenes*, Tokyo 1981; "In the Initial Era of Modern Japanese Photography" in *Shoji Ueda and his Friends 1935-55*, Yomago City, Japan, 1992.

On UEDA: Books—*Akt International/Internationald Nudes*, with introduction by Otto Steinert, Munich and London 1954; *Photography of the World*, edited by Heibonsha Publishers, Tokyo 1956; *Nihon Shashin Shi 1840-1945*, edited by the Japan Photographers Association, Tokyo 1971, as *A Century of Japanese Photography*, with introduction by John W. Dower, New York and London 1980; *Japanese Photography* by Shoji Yamagishi, Tokyo 1979; *Japanse Fotografie van 1848 tot Heden*, exhibition catalogue, by Attilio Colombo and Isabella Doniselli, Amsterdam 1980; *Nude Photographs of Japan*, with text by Shiroyasu Suzuki, Tokyo 1981; *Sammlung Gruber: Photographie des 20. Jahrhunderts*, exhibition catalogue, with foreword by Siegfried Gohr, Cologne 1984; "Shoji Ueda" in *Showa Photographers* by Tetsuro Kato, Tokyo 1990; *Literary Fragments about Shoji Ueda -the route to Theme: My Family* by Noriko Tsutatani, research bulletin of Osaka Kyoiku University Art Course, 1990; *Shoji Ueda and his Friends—1935-55* by Noriko Tsutatani, Yomago City, Japan, 1992; "The golden age of photography clubs: Shoji Ueda" in *A Walk Through Japan's Photographic History* by Kotaro Lizawa, Tokyo 1992. **Articles**—"The World of Shoji Ueda" in *Photo Art Annual*, Tokyo 1974; "Shoji Ueda: Cute Stories" in *Camera Mainichi* (Tokyo), January 1974; "Shoji Ueda" in *Camera International* (Paris), November 1984.

*

Photography has been placed in a lower position and evaluated less in Japan than the other arts—for instance, painting. Although there may be many reasons for this attitude and neglect, the main ones seem to be that there prevailed a wrong way of thinking in the past, when the majority of people had a biased view that recognized photography in graphic journalism but not in other fields, and that Japanese graphic journalism itself did not show any particularly positive attitude in communicating with foreign countries.

Recently, however, these tendencies have been gradually rectified by progressive photographers and journalists. Evidence of this change is that a movement to found a photography museum in Japan has become one of the dominant concerns of the Japan Professional Photographers Society.

It is, indeed, encouraging and delightful that we are moving into a new age, leaving behind the old narrow and regional way of thinking, exchanging communication broadly with photographers and photographic circles throughout the world.

My photographs in graphic journalism are, of course, an important part of my work. But I also regard the original prints made for exhibitions and my other works as important as well.

Needless to say, we must evaluate and respect the masterpieces of the past. But it is also the duty of present-day photographers to direct our work as from the realization that our significance lies in how well we produce photographs appropriate to the new age.

—Shoji Ueda

*   *   *

The most appropriate description of Shoji Ueda must be ''poet of images.'' There is an authentic poesie in his photographs.

Ueda was born in 1913 in Sakaiminato City in Tottori Prefecture. From childhood he took a delight in photography, and he went on to set up his own photographic studio in Sakaiminato. He worked continually on his most personal of prints, which came to be published widely. His prime subjects have been landscapes and people, rendered in the particular local colors of the Sanin District. The unique Ueda-style is an amalgam of a strong compositional sense and a feeling of spaciousness; another factor is an almost childlike simplicity. Ueda himself has said that he was influenced by the paintings of Rousseau, and this influence would seem to be borne out by his series, *Sand Dunes.*

Recently Udea has expanded his range from the limited imagery of Sanin; he has now gone so far as to include western and even Chinese elements. Nevertheless, whatever the subject-matter, the Ueda-style is still there, ready to surprise the observer. On the evidence of these latest works, his vision as a photographer is still both strong and original.

Ueda has matured; he has been a practicing photographer for a long time; and he is now treated as a senior member of the Japanese photographic fraternity—and yet neither his sensitivity nor his freshness has left him. Rather, he seems to be getting younger by the day, possibly because his enthusiasm and curiosity are still those of a young boy. Whatever the reasons, Ueda still shows an interest in anything new—not just new techniques of developing and printing but new clothes, new ideas, new products; at present he is growing an orchard and breeding Afghan hounds.

In his own profession he is currently fascinated by soft focus color prints taken through a customized lens fitted to a single lens reflex Pentax. These most recent photographs were published in 1981.

From the beginning of his career, Ueda has regarded photography as an art, and it is perhaps owing to that attitude that his own work has always set a standard for excellence. Almost by himself, Shoji Ueda pioneered serious photography in Japan, and he is still at the forefront of that photography today.

—Takao Kajiwara

UELSMANN, Jerry N(orman).

Nationality: American. **Born:** Detroit, Michigan, 11 June 1934. **Education:** Cooley High School, Detroit, 1948-52; studied photography, under Ralph Hattersley and Minor White, at Rochester Institute of Technology, Rochester, New York, 1953-57, B.F.A. 1957; audio visual communication, 1957-58, and photography, under Henry Holmes Smith, 1958-60, at Indiana University

Graduate School, Bloomington, M.S. 1958, M.F.A. 1960. **Family:** Married Marilynn Kamischke in 1957 (divorced, 1974); married Diane Farris in 1975; son: Andrew. **Career:** Photographer since 1953. Interim Instructor in Photography, 1960-62, Instructor, 1962-64, Assistant Professor, 1964-66, Associate Professor, 1966-69, Professor, 1969-74, and since 1974 Graduate Research Professor, University of Florida, Gainesville. Visiting Professor, Nihon University College of Art, Tokyo, October 1979. Founder Member, 1962, and Member of the Board of Directors, 1966, Society for Photographic Education. Advisory Trustee, Friends of Photography, Carmel, California, since 1975. **Recipient:** Guggenheim Fellowship, 1967; Faculty Development Grant, 1971, and Teacher/Scholar of the Year Award, 1975, University of Florida; National Endowment for the Arts Fellowship, 1972; City of Arles Medal, France, 1973; Bronze Medal, *International Exhibition of Photography,* Zagreb, 1979. Fellow, Royal Photographic Society, London, 1973. **Agent:** Witkin Gallery, 415 West Broadway, New York, New York 10012. **Address:** 5701 South West 17th Drive, Gainesville, Florida 32608, U.S.A.

Individual Exhibitions:

1960	Indiana University, Bloomington
1961	University of Florida, Gainesville
	San Francisco State College
	Illinois Institute of Technology, Chicago
1962	School of the Art Institute of Chicago
	Indiana University, Bloomington
1963	Kalamazoo Art Institute, Michigan
	Jacksonville Art Museum, Florida
	3 Photographers, International Museum of Photography, George Eastman House, Rochester, New York
	University of Florida, Gainesville
1964	Arizona State University, Tempe
	Heliography Gallery, New York (with Wynn Bullock)
1965	University of South Florida, Tampa
1966	Pratt Institute, Brooklyn, New York
	Lowe Art Gallery, University of Miami
1967	University of New Hampshire, Durham
	Museum of Modern Art, New York (toured the United States)
1968	Ringling Museum of Art, Sarasota, Florida (toured the United States)
	Refocus, University of Iowa, Iowa City
	Long Island University, Brooklyn, New York
	University of Oregon Art Museum, Eugene
	Creative Photography Gallery, Massachusetts Institute of Technology, Cambridge
	Phoenix College, Arizona
	Minneapolis Institute of Arts
	Ayer Gallery, Philadelphia
	Container Corporation of America, Chicago
1969	University of South Florida, Tampa
	Friends of Photography, Carmel, California
	Recent Photographs, Carl Siembab Gallery, Boston
	Camera Work Gallery, Costa Mesa, California
1970	Philadelphia Museum of Art (retrospective; toured the United States)
	International Museum of Photography, George Eastman House, Rochester, New York (toured the United States)
1971	College of Idaho, Caldwell
	Southern Illinois University, Carbondale
	Boise State College, Idaho
1972	Witkin Gallery, New York
	Stetson University, DeLand, Florida
	Barry College, Mt. Barry, Georgia (with Todd Walker and Doug Prince)
	Art Institute of Chicago
	Vanderbilt University, Nashville, Tennessee
1973	Western Carolina University, Cullowhee
	Camera Work Gallery, Portland, Oregon
	University of Northern Iowa, Cedar Falls
	SoHo Photo, New York
1974	The Photographic Place, Berwyn, Ilinois

Untitled, **1985.** Photograph ©Jerry Uelsmann.

Middle Tennessee State University, Murfreesboro
Eastern Washington State College, Cheney
Art Academy of Cincinnati, Ohio
Center Culturel Americain, Paris (toured France)
1975 Rochester Institute of Technology, Rochester, New York
Washington Gallery of Photography, Washington, D.C.
Jack Glenn Gallery, Newport Beach, California
Witkin Gallery, New York
1976 Deja Vue Gallery, Toronto (with Barbara Astman and Michael Semak)
Center for Creative Photography, University of Arizona, Tucson
J. Hunt Gallery, Minneapolis
Texas Center for Photographic Studies, Dallas
University of Texas, Dallas
1977 *Jerry N. Uelsmann Retrospective,* San Francisco Museum of Modern Art
Grapestake Gallery, San Francisco
Susan Spiritus Gallery, Newport Beach, California
Pennsylvania State University, University Park
Recent Work, Witkin Gallery, New York
1978 Worcester Art Museum, Massachusetts
Cronin Gallery, Houston

Museum of Fine Arts, Santa Fe, New Mexico
Galerie Fiolet, Amsterdam (in conjunction with Canon Gallery)
Nova Gallery, Vancouver
Photographers Gallery, South Yarra, Victoria, Australia
1979 The Photography Place, Philadelphia
Atlanta Gallery of Photography
Thomas Center, Gainesville, Florida
Silver Image Gallery, Ohio State University, Columbus
Nihon University Gallery, Tokyo
Deja Vue Gallery, Toronto
Photo Gallery International, Tokyo
1980 *Photographs from 1975-79,* Center for Contemporary Photography, Chicago
Read Centre, Indiana University, Bloomington
Witkin Gallery, New York
Impressions Gallery, York, England
Photography Place, Philadelphia
Louisiana State University, Baton Rouge
Atlanta Gallery of Photography, Georgia
Thomas Center, Gainesville, Florida
Deja Vue Galleries, Toronto
Gallery Exposures, Coral Gables, Florida
Silver Image Gallery, Seattle, Washington

Stephen White Gallery, Los Angeles

1981   Edison Community College, Fort Myers, Florida
        Jeb Gallery, Providence, Rhode Island
        Baker Art Gallery, Kansas City, Missouri
        International Museum of Photography at George Eastman
            House, Rochester, New York
        Gallery of Fine Arts, Daytona Beach, Florida
        Gilbert Gallery, Chicago (with Diane Farris)

1982   Eclipse Gallery, Boulder, Colorado
        Keystone Gallery, Santa Barbara, California
        Lansing Community College, Michigan
        Images Gallery, Cincinnati, Ohio
        Witkin Gallery, New York
        University of Florida, Gainesville

1983   Virginia Miller Galleries, Coral Gables, Florida
        Atlanta Gallery of Photography, Georgia
        Weston Gallery, Carmel, California
        G.H. Dalsheimer Gallery, Baltimore, Maryland
        Columbia College, Chicago
        LeMoyne Center for the Visual Arts, Tallahassee, Florida
        Port Washington Public Library, New York
        Des Moines Art Center, Iowa
        Center for Creative Photography, University of Arizona,
            Tucson
        Douglas Elliott Gallery, San Francisco (with Todd Walker)

1984   Photographer's Gallery, Palo Alto, California
        Eclipse Gallery, Boulder, Colorado
        Silver Image Gallery, Seattle, Washington
        United States Cultural Center, Istanbul
        Emily Edwards Gallery, San Antonio, Texas
        Susan Spiritus Gallery, Newport Beach, California (with
            Thomas F. Barrow)

1985   Daytona Beach Community College, Florida
        Silver Visions Gallery, Boston
        Boston Atheneum, Massachusetts

1986   University of Florida, Gainesville
        Museum of Fine Arts, St. Petersburg, Florida
        Fotografie Forum, Frankfurt (with J. Splìchal and I. Ben-
            Arieh)

1991   *A Selective Retrospective, 1960-1991,* Witkin Gallery,
        New York

Selected Group Exhibitions:

1959   *Photography at Mid-Century,* International Museum of
        Photography, George Eastman House, Rochester, New York
        (toured the United States)

1967   *Photography in the 20th Century,* National Gallery of Canada,
        Ottawa (toured Canada and the United States, 1967-73)

1969   *The Photograph as Object 1843-1969,* National Gallery of
        Canada, Ottawa (toured Canada)

1972   *4 Directions in Modern Photography: Paul Caponigro, John T.
        Hill, Jerry N. Uelsmann, Bruce Davidson,* Yale University
        Art Gallery, New Haven, Connecticut

1974   *Photography in America,* Whitney Museum, New York

1975   *The Land: 20th Century Landscape Photographs Selected by
        Bill Brandt,* Victoria and Albert Museum, London (travelled
        to the National Gallery, Edinburgh; Ulster Museum, Belfast;
        and National Museum of Wales, Cardiff, 1976)

1978   *Mirrors and Windows: American Photography since 1960,*
        Museum of Modern Art, New York (toured the United
        States, 1978-80)

1982   *Counterparts: Form and Emotion in Photographs,* Metropolitan
        Museum of Art, New York (travelled to the Contemporary
        Arts Center, Cincinnati; Dallas Museum of Fine Arts, Texas;
        San Francisco Museum of Modern Art; Corcoran Gallery,
        Washington, D.C.)

1985   *American Images 1945-80,* Barbican Art Gallery, London
        (toured Britain)

1986   *The Animal in Photography 1843-1985,* The Photographers'
        Gallery, London

Collections:

Museum of Modern Art, New York; International Museum of Photography, George Eastman House, Rochester, New York; Philadelphia Museum of Art; Art Institute of Chicago; Center for Creative Photography, University of Arizona, Tucson; San Francisco Museum of Modern Art; National Gallery of Canada, Ottawa; National Museum of American Art, Washington, DC; Boston Museum of Fine Arts; Victoria and Albert Museum, London; Bibliothèque Nationale, Paris; Moderna Museet, Stockholm.

Publications:

By UELSMANN: Books—*8 Photographs: Jerry Uelsmann,* with text by William E. Parker, New York 1970; *Jerry N. Uelsmann,* with an introduction by Peter C. Bunnell, fables by Russell Edson, Millerton, New York 1970, 1973; *Jerry N. Uelsmann,* portfolio, New York 1972; *Jerry Uelsmann: Silver Meditations,* with an introduction by Peter C. Bunnell, Dobbs Ferry, New York 1975; *Jerry N. Uelsmann: Twenty-Five Years, A Retrospective,* with text by James L. Enyeart, Boston 1982; *Uelsmann: Process and Perception,* with text by John Ames, Gainesville, Florida 1985. **Articles**—"Inter-relationship of Image and Technique" in *Invitational Teaching Conference at the George Eastman House,* edited by Nathan Lyons, Rochester, New York 1963; "Post-Visualization" in *Florida Quarterly* (Gainesville), Summer 1967, reprinted in *Creative Camera* (London), June 1969, and included in *The Camera Viewed: Writings on 20th Century Photography,* edited by Peninah R. Petruck, New York 1979; "Wynn Bullock: Tracing the Roots of Man in Nature" in *Modern Photography* (New York), May 1970; statement in *Into the 70s,* exhibition catalogue, Akron, Ohio 1970; article in *Infinity* (New York), September 1970; article in *Color,* by the Time-Life editors, New York 1970; "Some Humanistic Considerations of Photography" in *The Photographic Journal* (London), March 1971; comments in *Modern Photography* (New York), July 1973; "How Jerry Uelsmann Creates His Multiple Images" in *Popular Photography* (New York), January 1977, reprinted as "Multiple Images" in *Darkroom,* edited by Eleanor Lewis, New York 1977; statement in *American Photographer* (New York), November 1979.

On UELSMANN: Books—*The Persistence of Vision* by Nathan Lyons, New York 1967; *Jerry N. Uelsmann,* illustrated checklist, by John Szarkowski, New York 1967; *The Criticism of Photography as Art: The Photographs of Jerry Uelsmann* by John Ward, Gainesville, Florida 1970; *Photography in America,* edited by Robert Doty, with an introduction by Minor White, New York and London 1974; *The Land: 20th Century Landscape Photographs Selected by Bill Brandt,* exhibition catalogue, edited by Mark Haworth Booth, London 1975; *Masters of the Camera* by Gene Thornton, New York 1977; *Geschichte der Fotografie im 20. Jahrhundert/Photography in the 20th Century* by Petr Tausk, Cologne 1977, London 1980; *Mirrors and Windows: American Photography since 1960* by John Szarkowski, New York 1978; *Light Readings: A Photography Critic's Writings 1968-1978* by A.D. Coleman, New York 1979; *The Photograph Collectors's Guide* by Lee D. Witkin and Barbara London, Boston and London 1979; *Jerry N. Uelsmann: Photographs from 1975-79,* exhibition catalogue, with an introduction by Steven Klindt and an essay by Jim Enyeart, Chicago 1980; *Counterparts: Form and Emotion in Photographs* by Weston J. Naef, New York 1982; *The Library of World Photography: Landscape,* with texts by David Plowden and Ian Jeffrey, Tokyo and London 1984; *American Images: Photography 1945-1980,* edited by Peter Turner, London 1985. **Articles**—"Jerry Uelsmann" in *Infinity* (New York), May 1962; "The Photographs of Jerry N. Uelsmann" in *Contemporary Photographer* (Culpeper, Virginia), no. 1, 1964; "Color, Candids, Novelty" by Jacob Deschin in the *New York Times,* 22 November 1964; "Jerry N. Uelsmann: Involved with the Celebration of Life" by H.M. Kinzer in *Popular Photography* (New York), November 1965; "Notes on Uelsmann's Invented World" by William E. Parker in *Infinity* (New York), February 1967; "Uelsmann's Unitary Reality" by William E. Parker in *Aperture* (Rochester, New York), no. 3, 1967; "Sense and Perception" by Margaret Harker in *The Photographic Journal* (London), May 1968; "Jerry N. Uelsmann: New Symbols" in *Modern Photography Annual,* New York 1971; "Jerry Uelsmann" in *Infinity* (New York), May 1972; "An Album of

Cryptic Impressions" in *Photography Year 1976,* by the Time-Life editors, New York 1976; "The Inclusion of Medieval and Victorian Art in Jerry Uelsmann's Photographs: A Reading of Associations" by Susan Dodge Peters in *Image* (Rochester, New York), March 1979; "Tarnished Meditations: Some Thoughts on Jerry Uelsmann's Photographs" by James Hugunin in *Afterimage* (Rochester, New York), May 1979; "Jerry Uelsmann's Recent Work" in *Afterimage* (Rochester, New York), April 1980.

*

I try to begin working with no preconceived ideas. Each click of the shutter suggests an emotional and visual involvement and contains the potential of establishing greater rapport with some quintessential aspect of the subject and my feelings toward it, both conscious and preconscious. My contact sheets become a kind of visual diary of all the things I have seen and experienced with my camera. They contain the seeds from which my images grow. Before entering the darkroom, I ponder these sheets, seeking fresh and innovative juxtapositions that expand the possibilities of the initial subject matter. Ultimately, my hope is to amaze myself. The anticipation of discovering possibilities becomes my greatest joy.

—Jerry N. Uelsmann

*   *   *

Images of astounding variety, mystery and enigma characterize the photographs of Jerry Uelsmann. His ability to produce works of great interest in regularity is the hallmark of his style. In the past, when the energy of viewers and critics alike has lagged in the face of the enormity of his body of work, attempts to pigeonhole or categorize his photographs as Surrealist, Jungian, Neo-romantic, or literary has taken precedence over more detailed analysis of its content.

Uelsmann's photography is singularly none of these, yet encompasses all of them and more. As a body, his photographs defy any categorization which is all inclusive, just as each individual photograph defies exact referential interpretation. What most often appears as surreal in his work is the dominance of absurd or unbelievable juxtaposition of subject matter. However, actual stream of consciousness method is rarely employed. One can perceive through a large cross-section of his photographs several repeated choices of juxtaposed subject matter which contradict the surrealist dictum of automatism. Further, Uelsmann makes the inappropriate appear appropriate and the unbelievable, believable—qualities rarely found in Surrealism.

Because his images are generally mysterious, there is a temptation to find intellectual security in sweeping generalizations like Surrealism. While Uelsmann may be predisposed to contain Surrealist tendencies like free-association, he nevertheless makes aesthetic judgements of what will and will not work together in creating an image. It is this process which places his work in a contemporary realm and accounts for the repetition of certain visual associations in his imagery. The visual associations I refer to are based on recurrent use of subject motif and iconographic devices. Among the motifs he consistently uses are hands, eyes, the nude, objects of antiquity, the mirror, water, rocks. The iconographic devices include floating objects, metamorphosis and positive/negative combinations.

The primary method by which Uelsmann arrives at his imagery, what he calls "in process discovery," is in essence a gestalt position in which creativity is viewed in terms of one's ability to associate dissimilar elements in meaningful ways and in terms of restructuring the entire stimulus field. To disassociate known subject relationships (reality) and associate them in new but perhaps mysterious ways is the modus operandi of "in process discovery." To this point Uelsmann has said: "It seems to me that life abounds with mystery, that it is central to life, that when you are truly alive there are many kinds of questions . . . and it is the challenge of these questions that makes life interesting. It is important that we maintain a continual open dialogue with our materials and process; that we are constantly questioning and in turn being questioned. . . . In terms of my own development I have found the recognition of questions more provocative than the provision of answers. Often, confident that we have the right answers, we fail to ask enough questions, and then our seeming confidence fogs our vision, and the inconceivable remains truly unconceived."

It has never been easy and remains difficult to tell exacting what is going on in Uelsmann's imagery (even for him), except in his overtly humorous and portrait works. These two manifestations of his photographs have generally been straightforward and without allegory, myth or mystery.

Whereas Uelsmann's photographs up to 1975 may have been interpreted from various personal biases relating to psychological theories, it should not be ignored that they were also more simply symbolic. Uelsmann himself often pointed to that symbolism by his use of titles to reinforce the symbol, as in "Massacre of the Innocents" or "Apocalypse." In his work since 1975 the use of titles has become less frequent and less meaningful. Although some aspects of symbolism may remain in even the most recent work, it is no longer pervasive or obvious. As early as 1971 Uelsmann made it clear that his use of symbol existed, but with qualifications. "I think of many of my photographs as being obviously symbolic, but not symbolically obvious." His twisting of words is no less enigmatic than his mixture of humor and symbol. He claims to believe in angels and adores strawberries because they do not hide their seeds.

On rare occasions Uelsmann has expressed his own interpretation or intention in the use of symbolism in his work—as in the "Massacre of the Innocents" of 1971: "Being basically from the Midwest I developed certain prejudices toward the South. I moved there and I found myself in the position of being very upset by certain attitudes of Southerners, particularly relative to racial concerns, and at the same time there was a gentleness among the people, there was a pace that I found very human and very appealing. I think 'Massacre of the Innocents' deals with the South that is very much going through a painful transition. It was also done at the same time that three civil rights workers were killed in Mississippi."

In this image, as in all of Uelsmann's imagery, the use of symbol is not specific and certainly not brutal. He did not document the fact or event in media-style violence. Rather, he attempted to represent in a larger context the pertinent human condition.

If pictorialism dressed up as classicism in the first part of this century in order to make eroticism acceptable, then Uelsmann may be seen as making the symbol pictorial in order to provoke simultaneously the intellect and emotions. In this sense, his photographs would not differ so greatly from Robert Heinecken's earlier sensitized canvas renderings of our socio-sexual environment. For that matter, it would place him squarely in the center of contemporary photography, the concern of which seems to be devoted to beautiful objects whether drawn from banal subjects or hand treated intellectualizations. The primary difference would be that Uelsmann has chosen not to disregard emotion as a part of his aesthetic goal: "By our cameras we are introduced to an endless array of trees, clouds, rocks, objects, people, feelings, experiences, and so on. We wander through this varied landscape as contemporary archeologists, anthropologists, poets and explorers essentially serarching in our own internally directed way. Each click of the shutter becomes an emotional investment, and a part of the world becomes our visual possession."

As an alternative to psychologizing about Uelsmann's imagery, I would like to suggest viewing his recent work in terms of mythology. When Uelsmann states that we are as contemporary archeologists, anthropologists, poets and explorers in a search for internally directed meaning of our environment, there is a correlation to spontaneous myth-making, the creation of symbolic stories to represent the inexpressible verbalizations of our visions and emotions. What is drawn from our psychic sources finds difficulty existing elsewhere, and for Uelsmann, as for the ancient Greeks, myth can represent what cannot really exist. Uelsmann's controlled choices in organizing his subject combinations, and the rhythmic repetition thereof, make me less satisfied with the possibility of aleatory or dream consciousness in his work than the more structured elements of mythology.

Uelsmann is careful in the making of his photographs not to invoke the purely personal vernacular of Surrealism. His final choice of subjects and their combinations reflect instead associative forms in super-realistic terms, which may in turn and in part be archetypal. In fact, mythological subject divisions of Uelsmann's work would often be analogous to or incorporate traditional archetypes: cosmogony, hero, earth woman, mother goddess, flood, death, apocalypse, paradise and morphology. In most cases the archetype would simply serve as a symbol within the visual myth.

The mythology I suggest does not relate to any extant narratives, classical or primitive, but would be individual to each photograph and contemporary to its creation. Uelsmann's mythology could then represent a kind of story-telling about a personal journey between visual discovery and visual creation. Within its sphere emotions would be set free, humor and seriousness would be inseparable, and enigma would be god-head of associative form. To use Uelsmann's words: "If one accepts the fact that you can impose yourself on subject matter, then perhaps you can literally create subject matter."

The scenario for each myth introduced in each of Uelsmann's photographs is contained completely therein. There is no beginning and no end as in verbalized or written myths. Rather, these are visual mythologies which contain elements of unlived, but psychically recognizable, experiences.

Uelsmann's faith in "in-process discovery" and his evolution from simple symbol to myth invokes the spirit of a Latin phrase painted by Giorgio de Chirico on his self-portrait in 1908. *Et quid amabo misi quod aenigma est*—And what am I to love, if not the enigma?

—James Enyeart

UMBO.

Nationality: German. **Born:** Otto Umbehr in Dusseldorf, 18 January 1902; adopted the name "Umbo" in 1924. **Education:** Educated in Saarland, Stuttgart, Duisberg and Dusseldorf, 1908-16; studied art, under Johannes Itten, Walter Gropius, Wassily Kandinsky, Paul Klee, etc., at the Staatliches Bauhaus, Weimar, Germany, 1921-23; self-taught in photography. **Military Service:** Served as a driver in the German Army, 1943-45. **Family:** Married Irmgard Hirz in 1943 (divorced, 1950); daughter: Phyllis. **Career:** Worked as coal-miner, Essen, 1920; as potter with Kuno Jaschinsky, Goslar, Germany, 1920; as actor in Maria Heide's mystery performance group, in several German towns, 1921; in workshops of Muck Lamberty, Naumberg, Germany, 1921; with Friedel Dicker and Franz Singer in Arts and Crafts Workshops for Theater Berthold Viertel, Berlin, 1923-24. Worked as film editor and cameraman with Kurt Bernhardt and Walter Ruttmann; also, film-poster designer, glass- and alabaster-worker, clown, photomontagist, etc., Berlin, 1924-26; freelance photographer, establishing own studio, Berlin, 1926-45; studio photographer and photojournalist, under Simon Guttmann, Dephot (Deutscher Photodienst) co-operative photo agency, Berlin, 1928-33; Staff Photographer, Ullstein Verlag publishers, Berlin, 1938-43; freelance press photographer, working for *Quick, Der Spiegel, Picture Post*, etc., Hannover, 1945-80: House Photographer, Kestner-Gesellschaft, Hanover, 1948-72. Instructor in Photography, Landesversehrtenberufsschule, Bad Pyrmont, West Germany, 1957-74; Werkkunstschule, Hannover, and Werkkunstschule, Hildesheim, West Germany, 1965-74. Member, Gesellschaft Deutsche Lichtbildner (GDL), 1977-80. **Agent:** Rudolf Kicken, Albertusstrasse 47-49, 5000 Cologne 1, Germany. **Died:** (in Hannover), 13 May 1980.

Individual Exhibitions:

1927   Kneipe (pub) "Die Lunte," Berlin
1928   Kabarett "Im Toppkeller," Berlin
1979   *Umbo: Photographien 1925-1933*, Galerie Spectrum in Kunstmuseum, Hannover (retrospective)
        Galerie Rudolf Kicken, Cologne (with Paul Citroen)
1981   Centre Georges Pompidou, Paris (with Herbert Bayer)

Selected Group Exhibitions:

1929   *Film und Foto*, Deutscher Werkbund, Stuttgart
1932   *Modern European Photography*, Julien Levy Gallery, New York
1969   *Zehn Photographen in Hannover*, Galerie im Kubus, Hannover
1978   *Das Experimentelle Photo in Deutschland 1918-1940*, Galleria del Levante, Munich
1979   *Dada-Fotografie und Fotocollage*, Kestner-Gesellschaft, Hannover

Photographic Surrealism, New Gallery of Contemporary Art, Cleveland (travelled to Dayton Art Institute, Ohio; and Brooklyn Musuem, New York)
1980   *Avant-Garde Photography in Germany 1919-1939*, San Francisco Museum of Modern Art (toured the United States, 1981-82)
1981   *Germany: The New Vision*, Fraenkel Gallery, San Francisco
1982   *Lichtbildnisse: Das Porträt in der Fotografie*, Rheinisches Landesmuseum, Bonn
1983   *Bauhausfotografie*, Institut für Auslandsbeziehung, Stuttgart (and world tour)

Collections:

Kunstbibliothek der Staatlichen Museen, Berlin; Ullstein-Archiv, Berlin; Kestner-Gesellschaft, Hannover; Art Institute of Chicago; San Francisco Museum of Modern Art.

Publications:

By UMBO: Article—"Knieschuss Ohne: Nur Drei Haare Fehlten" in *Spiegel-Almanach* (Hannover), 25 October 1950.

On UMBO: Books—*Es Kommt der Neue Fotograf!* by Werner Graeff, Berlin 1929; *Foto-Auge: 76 Fotos der Zeit* by Franz Roh and Jan Tschichold, Stuttgart 1929; *Die Fotomontage: Geschichte und Wesen einer Kunstform*, exhibition catalogue, by Richard Hiepe, Ingolstadt 1969; *10 Photographen in Hannover*, exhibition catalogue, with introduction by Bernhard Haake, Hannover 1969; *Deutschland: Beginn des Modernen Photojournalismus* by Tim N. Gidal, Lucerne 1972; *Fotografie der 30er Jahre: Eine Anthologie*, edited by Hans-Jürgen Syberberg, Munich 1977; *Geschichte der Fotografie im 20. Jahrhundert/Photography in the 20th Century* by Petr Tausk, Cologne 1977, London 1980; *Das Experimentelle Photo in Deutschland 1918-1940* by Emilio Bertonati, Munich and Milan 1978; *Germany: The New Photography 1927-33*, edited by David Mellor, London 1978; *Tusen och En Bild*, exhibition catalogue, by Åke Sidwall, Sune Jonsson and Ulf Hard af Segersted, Stockholm 1978; *Fotografie 1919-1979, Made in Germany: Die GDL-Fotografen*, edited by Fritz Kempe, Bernd Lohse and others, Frankfurt 1979; *Photographie als Kunst 1879-1979/Kunst als Photographie 1949-1979*, exhibition catalogue, 2 vols., by Peter Weiermair, Innsbruck, Austria 1979; *Film und Foto der 20er Jahre*, exhibition catalogue, by Ute Esildsen and Jan Christopher Horak, Stuttgart 1979; *Photographen der 20er Jahre* by Karl Steinorth, Munich 1979; *Photographic Surrealism*, exhibition catalogue, by Nancy Hall-Duncan, Cleveland 1979; *Dada Photomontage*, exhibition catalogue, by Carl-Albrecht Haenlein and others, Hannover 1979; *Umbo: Photographien 1925-1933*, exhibition catalogue, by George Reinhardt, Hannover 1979; *Experimental Photography*, exhibition catalogue, by Dawn Ades, London 1980; *Avant-Garde Photography in Germany 1919-1939*, exhibition catalogue, by Van Deren Coke, Ute Eskildsen and Bernd Lohse, San Francisco 1980; *Bauhaus Fotografie*, edited by Roswitha Fricke, Dusseldorf 1982; *Lichtbildnisse: Das Porträt in der Fotografie*, edited by Klaus Honnef, Cologne 1982; *Bauhausfotografie*, exhibition catalogue, by Wulf Herzogenrath, Stuttgart 1983. **Articles**—"Exhibition in Stuttgart, June 1929, and Its Effects" by Andor Kraszna-Krausz in *Close-up* (London), 29 December 1929; "Bildjournalismus: Die Legendaren Zwanziger Jahre" by Bernd Lohse in *Camera* (Lucerne), April 1967; "Umbo" by Karl Steinorth in *Color Foto* (Munich), November 1975; "Der Dopplelte Umbo: 75. Geburtstag des Fotografen Otto Umbehr" by Dirk Tils in *Hannover'sche Allgemeine Zeitung*, 18 January 1977; "Otto Umbehr—Genannt Umbo" by George Reinhardt in *Professional Camera* (Munich), February 1979; "Umbo: Fotos 1927" in *Zweitschrift* (Hamburg), no. 4/5, 1979; "Umbo (Otto Umbehr): Mit der Kamera Durchs Leben" by George Reinhardt in *Neues Rheinland* (Cologne), vol. 22, no. 8, 1979; "Umbo Ist Tot" by Dagmar Figl in *Foto-Scene* (Mainaschaff, West Germany), June 1980.

*   *   *

Otto Umbehr, or Umbo, was a versatile and innovative photographer, specializing in photoreportage; he belonged to that group of German photoreporters which includes other pioneers of modern photojournalism such as Erich Salomon and Felix Man. Yet he was far more than a documentary photoreporter—his interest in experimentation and his artistic sense create aspects in common with the Surrealists; his interest in collage and photomontage, his experimentation with camera angle and perspective, and his use of the negative print and prints from X-ray film provoke comparisons with such people as Christian Schad and Franz Roh.

In 1925, Umbo met Paul Citroen with whom he became lifelong friends. Citroen built him his first darkroom, and Umbo began to make images using a 13 x 18 cm field camera which his father had used to take family photographs. This led to his becoming a freelance portrait photographer for several years: his photos of the actress Rut Landshoff brought him sufficient recognition and customers from the circle of the Berlin salons that he was able to open up his own studio and photo laboratory in Berlin-Charlottenburg.

His interest in photojournalism did not really begin until 1928 when he met Simon Guttmann who was then Director of Dephot, the German photoreportage cooperative news agency. Umbo worked for Dephot (with such other notable figures as Fritz Goro, Andreas Feininger and Felix Man) until its demise as an indirect result of the Hitler regime in 1933. His versatility as a photographer, combining current avant-garde trends of the artistic and experimental with solid documentary reportage and portraiture, caused him to be a great asset to Guttmann. After the Dephot had ended, Umbo continued as a freelance photographer, doing local reportage, advertising photographs, and overseas assignments which carried him to North Africa and Italy.

Umbo's Berlin studio, complete with negatives and photographs, was destroyed in 1945, and he moved to Hannover, freelancing for various periodicals, and eventually becoming the house photographer for the Kestner-Gesellschaft in Hannover. While he enjoyed the experimental and artistic aspects of photography, Umbo was first and foremost a documentary reportage photographer.

Although he did not study photography at the Bauhaus—no formal course in it was offered there—Umbo's photographic career was certainly influenced by his years spent there. His experimental work in several areas of photography, e.g., political and social photomontage and collage, produced notable results as did his multiple exposures of subjects in different positions (e.g., his "Simultanporträt" of Rut Landshoff, as well as many of his other female portraits). A further unique aspect of many of these photos is that he either used X-ray film (which did not produce halftones) or printed a negative image.

In 1935 Umbo began a series—"Die Wolkenkamera sieht sich auf der Erde um"—using a fisheye camera with an angle of 180 degrees. The camera itself was originally designed for meteorological studies because it was capable of showing the whole sky with cloud formations in one image. By experimenting with picture angle and distorted perspective in this and another series entitled "Die unheimliche Strasse," he was able to produce unusual effects with his photos. There is a surrealistic, abstract, almost "Dali-esque" quality to these and other photos of the same period. In the former series, this is created by unusual camera angle (above or below the line of sight) as well as by the distorted perspective caused by the 180-degree lens; in the latter, it is produced again by distorted perspective, but this time caused by the angle of light in many cases, producing shadows which are greatly elongated. The result is that the subjects appear dwarfed, causing the observer to concentrate on the 2-dimensional shadows rather than on the subjects—the effect of this is to make the subjects (i.e., shadows) appear to blend right into the street.

As Georg Reinhardt points out, Umbo's photos, like Salvador Dali's paintings, combine real elements with fantastic abstractions. His more conventional portraits and photoreportages also contain elements of the artist and experimenter at work. The photos come to life because he attempted to capture the spontaneous as well as the feverish qualities of life which are reflected in his choice of theme and location for photographing: persistent restlessness or excitement and sensation-filled atmosphere (although this is not to say that he doesn't take photographs where the opposite sense of total peace and calm prevails), dance, cabaret, masses coming together for some social ritual, scenes of misfortune, and—certainly not to be forgotten—his fascination for scenes at the circus, particularly the trapeze artists.

—Michael Held

URBAN, João Aristeu.

Nationality: Brazilian. **Born:** Curitiba, 21 April 1943. **Education:** Grupo Escolar Professor Cleto, Curitiba, 1950-54; Colégio Santa Maria, Curitiba, 1954-56; Colégio Estaduel do Parana, 1956-63. **Family:** Married Adelaide Fortes in 1969 (divorced, 1980); children: Dora and Vladimir. **Career:** Worked as a store clerk for the family business Urban Ltd., Curitiba, 1957-59; bank teller in Bamerindus, Curitiba, 1959-67; maintained own studio, Photon Photos Ltd., Curitiba, 1967-69. Since 1969, photographer for Phototecnica, Curitiba. **Recipient:** Prize, *Bienal de Sao Paulo*, 1977; Banco do Brasil Prize, 1978. **Address:** Rua Angelo Zeni, 1048, 80520 Curitiba, Paraná, Brazil.

Individual Exhibitions:

1978	*Boias-Frias, Vista Parcial,* Federation of Rural Workers (FETAEP), Curitiba, Brazil (travelled to Fernando Moreira Gallery, Curitiba; Faculty of Agronomy, University of Parana, Brazil; Pontificia Universidade, Parana, and *Bienal de Sao Paulo,* 1979; and Pontificia Universidade, Sao Paulo, 1980)
1980	*Os Polacos,* Pope John Park II Park, Curitiba, Brazil
1987	*Pinho e Polacos (Pines and Poles),* SESC/Pompéia, São Paulo
1988	*Male Pamiiatki—Polonia W. Brazilli (Small Rememberances—Poland in Brazil),* Warsaw, Krakow and Kochalin, Poland
1990	*Bóias-Frias, Vista Parcial,* Instituto Goethe, Curitiba, Brazil
	Bóias-Frias, Vista Parcial, Palácio da Abolição, Fortaleza, Brazil
1991	*Bóias-Frias, Vista Parcial,* Teatro São Pedro, Porto Alegre, Brazil
1993	*Curitiba, Paisagens Urbanas (Curitiba, Urban Landscapes),* Fundação Cultural de Curitiba, Curitiba, Brazil
	Curitiba, Paisagens Urbanas (Curitaba, Urban Landscapes), Galeria de Fotografia J B Scalco -Solar dos Camâras, Porto Alegre, Brazil
	Sonhos e Fantasias (Dreams and Fantasies), Solar do Rosário, Curitiba, Brazil

Selected Group Exhibitions:

1973	*35th Exhibition,* Paraná Exhibition Hall, Paraná, Brazil
1976	*Photojournalism Exhibition,* Cultural Foundation, Curitiba, Brazil (and 1977, 1978, 1981)
1977	*Biennial de São Paulo*
	Luvas, Mãos, Ferramentas, Biennial of São Paulo, Brazil
1978	*38th Exhibition,* Paraná Exhibition Hall, Paraná, Brazil
	Latin American Exhibition, Museo de Arte Moderno, Mexico City
1979	*Our People,* Fundación Nacional de Bellas Artes, Rio de Janeiro
	Venezia '79
	O Espaco Habitado, Brazilian Institute of Architecture, Brasilia
	Biennial of Ecologic Photography, Porto Alegre, Brazil (and 1981)
	Biennial of São Paulo
1980	*Triennial of Photography,* Museu de Arte Moderno, São Paulo
1981	*SICOF '81,* Milan
	Buscando Raízes, group exhibition with André Zallis, Galeria do Instituto Nacional da Fotografia, Rio de Janeiro
1982	*La Photographie Contemporaine en Amerique Latine,* Centre Georges Pompidou, Paris
1994	*5th Biennial International de Havana—Tu i Tam,* Havana

Collections:

Fundación Nacional de Bellas Artes, Rio de Janeiro; Casa Romario Martins, Curitiba; Culture Foundation of Curitiba, Paraná, Brazil; IBAC—Brazilian Art and Culture Institute, Rio de Janeiro; Art Museum of São Paulo; French

Niño en el barrio chino (Boy in Chinatown), **Havana, 1994.** Photograph by João Urban.

Museum of Photography, Paris; Kunsthaus, Zurich; Collection Joaquim Paiva, Brasilia; Collection Lili Sverner, São Paulo.

Publications:

By URBAN: Books—*Hecho en Latino-America,* with others, edited by Consejo Mexicano de Fotografia, Mexico City 1978; *O Espaco Habitado,* with others, edited by the Institute de Arquitetos do Brasil, Brasilia 1979; *Our People,* with others, Rio de Janeiro 1979; *The Child in Latin America,* with others, edited by Unicef, Santiago, Chile 1980; *Hecho en Latino-America II,* Mexico 1981; Fotosul 83, Brazil, 1983; *Bóias-Frias, Tagelöhner in Süden Brasiliens,* text by Tereza Urban, Switzerland, 1984; *Bóias-Frias—Vista Parcial,* Culture Foundation of Curitiba, 1988; *Tropeiros,* published with support from INCEPA, 1992. **Articles**—series of articles in *Grafia, O Jornal da Foto* (Curitiba, Brazil), 1978-79.

On URBAN: Books—*Venezia '79: La Fotografia,* edited by Daniela Palazzoli, Vittorio Sgarbi and Italo Zannier, Milan and New York 1979; *La Photographie Contemporaine en Amerique Latine,* exhibition catalogue, by Alian Sayag, Paris 1982; *General Art History in Brazil,* São Paulo, 1983; *Enciclopédia Internacionale des Photografes,* Edition Camera Obscura; *Around Brazilian Photography,* Pietro Maria Bardi, São Paulo, 1987; *The Dam and the Settler,* Brazil, 1989; *Canto a la Realidad—Fotografía Latinoamericana (1860-1993),* Erika Billeter, Spain, 1994.

*

My relation to photography is to produce it so that it can be both documentary, in the long term, and informative in the short term. Although I can't always obtain such a result (still less with just one shot), that is the aim which I pursue.

I place myself among the photographers who see photography as a result of a co-production between the photographer and reality—that is, as co-author of the photograph with the subject.

I am looking for a balance, with either a single or several photographs, between an absolute record which would bring about a kind of naturalism and a photography of an excessive discursive kind, which may distort reality. Of course, sometimes the photographs are rather descriptive, and in other cases they clearly avoid description in favour of a personal and often subjective opinion. Generally, I try to avoid extremes of either kind, so that the viewer can have his own opinion, and even discuss the photographer's commentary.

I see exhibitions at galleries and other cultural centres as a necessity for the photographer to keep the public and colleagues well in touch with his work, so that there is an exchange of information, and so that the work may be criticized and thereby developed and improved.

However, I think there are other larger and more particular media that will expose the photographer's work. There is a public in schools, trade unions, factories, in large commercial areas and even on the streets which the photographer must find and to which he must exhibit his work.

—João Aristeu Urban

*   *   *

In recent years the photography of social documentary has been more and more a cold and calculated reportage, with pictures that, though they depict obvious facts, have more in them of demagogy than of human fellowship. João Aristeu Urban is an exception. He has not only recorded facts, events and conditions; he has also been able to represent that mass of feelings—hopes and sorrows—that are the inward nature of man.

The "boias frias"—the itinerant agricultural laborers—who seek work day after day on the enormous estates of Parana number at least 800,000; they constitute a social factor of great importance to the Brazilian economy. Exploited, regarded as no more than hired hands, they each day, contribute to the foundation of the entire country's prosperity. In four successive journeys between 1977 and 1979, Urban investigated the day-to-day existence of the boias frias. And if his original intention was born of a profound desire to "expose," his record, in fact, has been transformed into a portrait of a community. This transformation is the result of Urban's attitude, to use the camera as an instrument—as a language, rather—of communication between men, as a medium for the exchange of sentiments.

The invisible curtain that the cold glass eye of the lens erects between the subject and the photographer has been obliterated. The people in his pictures do not feel or see any such impediment, because Urban, modestly and with warmth, has got close to them and discovered their lives. They do not feel their intimacy to have been violated, and they feel no shame for the state of poverty in which they live: they are neither judged nor patronized. The photographer has established a relationship of understanding. The black box of his camera disappears; the scenes of life in their simple spontaneity are sensitively recorded.

Yet Urban remains faithful to reality; there is no sentimentalized exaggeration or ideological orchestration; he achieves an harmonious synthesis of emotion and truth. It's often said that truth in photography is wholly subjective, but the truth of Urban's pictures avoids excessive subjectivity and succeeds in being an objective record and an expressive portrait.

And, in fact, he does not start from any preconceived idea which he is obliged to follow or demonstrate. His is a sort of "candid camera" operation, in which, however, he still follows the thread of his story. As in every good novel, the characters, the background, the everyday objects, the way of life are all described exactly, incisively, in such a way as to furnish the reader/beholder with the material he needs to understand.

Urban's visual story is a great epic poem of our anti-heroic times: instead of wondrous deeds, he describes the heroism of daily survival.

—Giuliana Scimé

UZZLE, Burk.

Nationality: American. **Born:** Raleigh, North Carolina, 4 August 1938. **Education:** Dunn High School, North Carolina; self-taught in photography. **Family:** Divorced; children: Tad and Andy. **Career:** Staff photographer, *News and Observer* newspaper, Raleigh, 1955-56; Contract Photographer, Black Star news agency, New York, working in Atlanta, Houston and Chicago, 1957-62. Contract Photographer, *Life* magazine, Chicago and New York, 1962-68. Member, Magnum Photos co-operative agency, New York, 1967-83 (President, 1979-80). Independent photographer based in New York 1984-94. **Recipient:** Page One Award, Newspaper Guild of New York, 1970; National Endowment for the Arts Photography Fellowship, 1975; Second Place Award, Photographic Book of The Year (All American), 1985. **Agent:** Leica Gallery Inc, 670 Broadway, 5th Floor, New York, NY 10012, U.S.A.

Individual Exhibitions:

1970	*Typically American,* International Center of Photography, New York
1973	Witkin Gallery, New York
	University of Massachusetts, Boston
1974	Dayton Art Institute, Ohio
	831 Gallery, Birmingham, Michigan
1977	Aperion Workshops, Millerton, New York (toured the United States)
	Center for Contemporary Photography, Chicago
	Hayden Gallery, Massachusetts Institute of Technology (with Mary Ellen Mark)
1979	Witkin Gallery, New York
	Galerie Fiolet, Amsterdam
	Galerie Agathe Gaillard, Paris
	Art Institute of Chicago
1980	*News from Cambodia,* International Center of Photography, New York
1985	*Burk Uzzle,* Open Eye Gallery, Liverpool, Merseyside Ffoto Gallery, Cardiff, Wales
1985	*All American,* Philadelphia Museum of Art, Pennsylvania
1986	253 Gallery, Norfolk, Virginia

1992	*A Progress Report on Civilisation,* The Chrysler Museum, Norfolk, Virginia
1994	*Burk Uzzle: Three Decades of Photography,* Leica Gallery, New York
	Burk Uzzle: Recent Work, The Photography Gallery, Drew University, Madison, New Jersey

Selected Group Exhibitions:

1968	*Photography '68,* International Museum of Photography, George Eastman House, Rochester, New York
1969	*Spectrum One,* Witkin Gallery, New York
1971	*Contemporary Photographers,* Fogg Art Museum, Harvard University, Cambridge, Massachusetts
1974	*100 Years of American Photography,* La Maison de Port Deauville, France
1975	*The Impact of Design,* Nikon House, New York
1976	*Festival d'Automne,* Musée Galliera, Paris
1978	*Contemporary Photographers,* Stedelijk Museum, Amsterdam
1979	*Contemporary Photographers,* Santa Barbara Museum of Art, California
1984	*La Photographie Créative,* Pavillon des Arts, Paris
1985	*Samlingarna ca 200 fotografer,* Fotografiska Museet, Stockholm

Collections:

International Center of Photography, New York; Metropolitan Museum of Art, New York; Museum of Modern Art, New York; International Museum of Photography, George Eastman House, Rochester, New York; Fogg Art Museum, Harvard University, Cambridge, Massachusetts; Smithsonian Institution, Washington, D.C.; Art Institute of Chicago; Santa Barbara Museum of Art, California; Bibliothèque Nationale, Paris; Stedelijk Museum, Amsterdam; Chrysler Museum, Norfolk, Virginia; Philadelphia Museum of Art, Philadelphia, Pennsylvania.

Publications:

By UZZLE: Books—*Burk Uzzle: Landscapes,* with an introduction by Ronald Bailey, New York 1973; *All American,* Millerton, New York 1985. **Article**—''New York'' in *Du* (Zurich), September 1977.

On UZZLE: Books—*America in Crisis: Photographs for Magnum,* edited by Charles Harbutt and Lee Jones, New York 1969; *Photographic Communication,* edited by R. Smith Schunemann, London and Toronto 1972; *Album Photographique 1,* Paris 1979; *The Photograph Collector's Guide* by Lee D. Witkin and Barbara London, Boston and London 1979; *World Photography,* edited by Bryn Campbell, London 1981; *Visions and Images: American Photographers on Photography,* edited by Barbaralee Diamonstein, New York 1981; *La Photographie Créative* by Jean-Claude Lemagny, Paris 1984. **Articles**—''Burk Uzzle'' in *Camera* (Lucerne), October 1970; ''Burk Uzzle'' in *Photo* (Paris), May 1971; ''Burk Uzzle'' in *35mm Photography* (New York), Spring 1973; ''Burk Uzzle'' in *Camera* (Lucerne), November 1973; ''Transposing the Ordinary'' by Julia Scully in *Modern Photography* (New York), March 1974; ''Burk Uzzle: Marines'' in *Reporter Objectif* (Paris), November 1974; ''Burk Uzzle'' in *Zoom* (Paris), April 1976; ''Burk Uzzle'' in *Photo* (Paris), October 1976; ''Burk Uzzle: The Hustle Comes of Age'' by James Baker Hall in *Aperture* (Millerton, New York), no. 77, 1976; ''Burk Uzzle'' in *Photo* (Paris), April 1978; ''Burk Uzzle'' in *Zoom* (Paris), December 1978; ''Burk Uzzle'' by Ronald Bailey in *American Photographer* (New York), March 1980; ''Men in Sequins, Grandmothers with Batons'' by Rosemary Ranck in the *New York Times Book Review,* 7 July 1985; ''Burk Uzzle: All American'' by Claire Peeps in *Friends of Photography Newsletter* (Carmel, California), no. 10, 1985; by Rob Powell in *British Journal of Photography,* 1985.

*

I give to photography as photography gives to me; and one turns into the other, as myself and my medium form the ground from which the harvest comes.

Life has been a rich diet of trial and error and knowledge through experimentation. I know what I can do because that's what's left that feels natural.

Photography is robust, vital, and demands honesty. Too many tools can be divisive, obscuring primary relationships between photographer and subject.

Dogma is the declaration of shallowness, while discipline—if used instead of worshipped—is liberating.

The imperatives of a visual medium have everything to do with the dynamics of graphics and composition and are among a photographer's strongest tools. Others are instinct, intelligence, humor and energy.

The work of a complex photographer using simple equipment compares favorably to the work of a simple photographer using complex equipment. We give our mechanical medium its life by the contribution of our humanity, while responding to the essence of ourselves and the properties of our materials.

America is my home; it's what formed me, and it's those values I take every place I go. Many countries and many people have offered later layers of experience that later become pictures.

My work is a collage of sometimes contradictory, sometimes harmonious, parts in search of meaning, order and beauty.

I love humor, beauty, silliness, and the greatness of meaningful commitment. My life is a swirl of parts that are both accidental/circumstantial and personally controlled. I use them all; I put them together. They are me, they are my pictures. My work is my visible love.

—Burk Uzzle

*   *   *

If Eugène Atget was the gentle poser of surreal questions, Burk Uzzle delivers the Surrealist answer: yes, the photographed world is full of marvels; yes, its beauty is convulsive; and yes, both its humour and its chance are entirely objective!

The photographs are technically immaculate, direct views of ordinary events in the familiar world. Like a good philosopher, Burk Uzzle tends to select trivial examples so that the form of his argument shall not be confused by the importance of the content.

Extraordinarily enough, the elegance and simplicity which dominate a first sight of the photographs, are not the signposts to understanding which might be anticipated. For, as the pictures are studied, the certainties of the finely matched optics and materials lead only to ambiguities of reading. The very objectivity of Burk Uzzle's description of the people and the people inflatables, milling around the outside of a public lavatory, paradoxically obscures the differences between them; and however much it ought to undercut the resemblances, the fact that the inflatables are together, about ten feet above their breathing counterparts does nothing to weaken the association. Truly, his photography is as humorous, chancy and convulsive as it is objective.

Perhaps, though, the concept of humour does not fit snugly enough across the range of images to leave the term unchallenged as a description. For many of Burk Uzzle's ambiguities of space and identity leave one, either at first recognition or as an aftertaste, with that sense of having entered his dream on the point of balance at which things will either continue as a pleasant adventure, or shift through territories of unspecific menace, into the horrors of nightmare.

It is wit that forms the truest quality of these photographs. Sometimes warm, sometimes very chill indeed, and occasionally all things mixed; it is born out of the precise enunciation of uncertainty and incongruity, an apparently nonchalant proof of André Breton's contention that ''it is only at the approach of the fantastic, at a point where human reason loses its control, that the most profound emotion of the individual has the fullest opportunity to express itself.''

For Burk Uzzle to have achieved thus, in straight photography, without contrived whimsy or melodrama, is no mean feat.

—Philip Stokes

VACHON, John.

Nationality: American. **Born:** St. Paul, Minnesota, 19 May 1914. **Education:** St. Thomas College, St. Paul, 1930-34, B.A. 1934; self-taught in photography. **Military Service:** U.S. Army, 1943-45. **Family:** Married Penny Vachon (died); children: Brian, Ann and Gail; married Françoise Fourestier; children: Christine and Michael. **Career:** Assistant messenger, 1936-37, junior file clerk and unofficial photographer, 1937-40, and junior photographer, 1940-42, under Roy E. Stryker, Farm Security Administration (FSA), Washington, D.C.; photographer, under Roy E. Stryker, Office of War Information, Washington, D.C., 1942-43; photographer, under Roy E. Stryker, Standard Oil Company of New Jersey, 1943, and for the *Jersey Standard,* in New Jersey and in Venezuela, 1945-47; staff photographer, *Life,* magazine, New York, 1947-48; *Look* magazine, New York, 1948-71; freelance photographer, New York 1971-75. Visiting Lecturer in Photography, Minneapolis Art Institute, 1975. **Recipient:** Guggenheim Fellowship, 1973. **Died:** (in New York) 20 April 1975.

Individual Exhibitions:

1972   Imageworks, Cambridge, Massachusetts (retrospective)

Selected Group Exhibitions:

1942   *Road to Victory,* Museum of Modern Art, New York
1955   *FSA Anniversary Show,* Brooklyn Museum, New York
1962   *The Bitter Years: FSA Photographs,* Museum of Modern Art, New York (toured the United States)
1967   *Photography in the 20th Century,* National Gallery of Canada, Ottawa (toured Canada and the United States, 1967-73)
1968   *Just Before the War,* Newport Harbor Art Museum, Newport Beach, California (travelled to Library of Congress, Washington, D.C.)
1976   *A Vision Shared: FSA Photographers,* Witkin Gallery, New York
1979   *Images de l'Amérique en Crise,* Centre Georges Pompidou, Paris
1980   *Les Années Ameres de l'Amérique en Crise 1935-1942,* Galerie Municipale du Chateau d'Eau, Toulouse
1982   *Floods of Light,* the Photographers' Gallery, London (toured Britain)
1983   *Roy Stryker: USA, 1943-50,* International Center of Photography, New York

Collections:

New York Public Library; Museum of Modern Art, New York; International Museum of Photography, George Eastman House, Rochester, New York; Library of Congress, Washington, D.C.; Minneapolis Art Institute.

Publications:

By VACHON: Books—*Just Before the War: Urban America from 1935 to 1941 as Seen by the Photographers of the Farm Security Administration,* with Arthur Rothstein and Roy Stryker, with an introduction by Thomas Garver, Boston 1968; *John Vachon Memorial Portfolio,* New York 1977. **Articles**—

"John Vachon: A Realist in Magazine Photography," interview, with Edna Bennett, in *U.S. Camera* (New York), December 1960; "Tribute to a Man, an Era, an Art" in *Harper's Bazaar* (New York), September 1973.

On VACHON: Books—*The Bitter Years,* edited by Edward Steichen, New York 1962; *Fame: Famous Portraits of Famous People by Famous Photographers,* edited by L. Fritz Gruber, London and New York 1965; *Photography in the 20th Century* by Nathan Lyons, New York 1967; *The Years of Bitterness and Pride: FSA Photographs 1935-1943,* complied by Jerry Kearns and Leroy Bellamy, edited by Hiak Akmakjian, New York 1975; *A Vision Shared: A Classic Portrait of America and Its People 1935-1943,* edited by Hank O'Neal, New York and London 1976; *Amerika Fotografie 1920-1940* by Erika Billeter, Berne 1979; *Les Années Ameres de l'Amérique en Crise 1935-1942,* exhibition catalogue, by Jean Dieuzaide, Toulouse 1980; *Industry and the Photographic Image: 153 Great Prints from 1850 to the Present,* edited by F. Jack Hurley, New York 1980; *Floods of Light: Flash Photography 1851-1981,* exhibition catalogue, edited by Rupert Martin, London 1982; *Roy Stryker: USA, 1943-1950* by Steven W. Plattner, Austin, Texas 1983; *Dust Bowl Descent* by Bill Ganzel, Lincoln, Nebraska 1984. **Articles**—"John Vachon; Profile of a Magazine Photographer" by Sean Kernan in *Camera 35* (New York), December 1971; "John Vachon 1914-1975" in *Photography Year 1976* by the Time-Life editors, New York 1976; "John Vachon" by Brian Vachon in *American Photographer* (New York), October 1979; "Le Dossier de la Misère" in *Photo* (Paris), February 1980.

*   *   *

"Strange things happen to me when I look at these pictures again," said John Vachon while considering some of the work that resulted from his participation in the Farm Security Administration's Historical Section.

Vachon was among Roy Stryker's "second generation" of photographers and, quite remarkably, it was his first experience with a camera. He had been hired, in 1936, by the FSA as a messenger, which translated into writing captions on, mounting, and filing the photographs turned in by Evans, Lange, Shahn, Mydans, Lee, and the other photographers hired and nourished by Stryker.

Bored, as Vachon later recounted the story, he began looking at and being captivated by the photographs he had been rather cavalierly handling. "About that time, Roy Stryker decided he would like to mold a photographer in his own image. He put a camera in my hand, breathed upon me, and told me to see what I could do (but only on weekends, of course)."

In the beginning, Vachon spent a great deal of time scouring the world for the real-life analogs to Walker Evans' photographs. In a strange way, he admitted later, the pictures were defining the world and the master's style defining the disciple's. The mold was broken in 1941, however, when Vachon (now officially classified as a photographer) was sent by Stryker to the West (an area never visited by Evans).

It was in the West, midst the loneliness of the Great Plains, dotted with small towns, that Vachon's style developed. He produced stark, beautiful images of the plains; evocative, often gentle pictures in the small towns and cities; and, in the closest that any FSA photographer ever came to pure abstraction, a remarkable series of grain-elevator-and-railroad-car photographs. Among the best known, and most typical, pictures from this period is one of a farmer and his dog riding after cattle across a storm-swept landscape. Its simple, yet powerfully dynamic composition exemplifies the degree to which Vachon had developed his own style.

In later years, Vachon would be a mainstay of *Look* magazine's photo staff (whose director was another FSA alumnus, Arthur Rothstein). However, with one exception, Vachon's best work remained his FSA work. He felt this, too, in the years before his death (several other FSA colleagues have expressed similar feelings about their careers).

The exception, and I saw these pictures only once, in Vachon's apartment, are photographs made in Europe after the Second World War for the United Nations Relief and Rehabilitation Agency (UNRRA). They are gritty documents of anger and humanitarian concern and, as with much of Vachon's *oeuvre,* richly deserve publication.

—Stu Cohen

VALLHONRAT, Javier.

Nationality: Spanish. **Born:** Madrid, 14 June 1953. **Education:** High School in Sagrados Corazones, Madrid and University of Fine Arts, Madrid graduating in 1986. **Family:** Married Cynthia Waldren, 1987; sons, Pablo and Martin. **Career:** Freelance photographer since 1973. Photographer for Italian, British and French Condé Nast since 1984. Takes workshops in Creative Photography. **Address:** San Vicente Ferrer 72, 28015 Madrid, Spain.

Individual Exhibitions:

1983	Aele Gallery, Madrid
1984	Fotonostra, Lérida, Spain
	Forum Gallery, Tarragona, Spain
1985	Il Diaframma Gallery, Milan, Italy
	Círculo de Bellas Artes, Madrid
1986	Buades Gallery, Madrid
	Visor Gallery, Valencia, Spain
	Porin Taidemuseo, Porin, Finland
	Museo Nacional de Bellas Artes Caracas, Venezuela
1987	Les Somnambules Gallery, Toulouse
1988	Van Melle Gallery, Paris
	Fotobienal, Vigo, Spain
1989	Abbaye de Montmajour, Arles, France
	Forum Gallery, Tarragona, Spain
1990	Parco Photographers Gallery, Tokyo
	Juana Mordó Gallery, Madrid
	Museo de Arte Moderno, Huelva, Spain
1991	*Bienal Internacional de Fotografía,* Tenerife, Canary Islands
	Centro de Cultura Sa Nostra, Palma de Mallorca, Majorca
	L.A: Galerie, Frankfurt, Germany
1992	Forum Gallery, Tarragona, Spain
	La Recova, Centro de Arte, Tenerife, Canary Islands
	Hamiltons Gallery, London
1993	*Art Fair,* Hamiltons Gallery, Basel, Switzerland
	Prinz Gallery, Kyoto, Japan
	Monasterio de Veruela, Zaragoza, Spain
	Spectrum Gallery, Zaragoza, Spain
	Juana Mordó Gallery, Madrid
	Espacio Caja de Burgos, Burgos, Spain
	Antigua Escuela de Artes y Oficios, Valencia
1994	Juana Mordó Gallery, Madrid
	Hamiltons Gallery, London

Selected Group Exhibitions:

1985	*FOCO 85,* Círculo de Bellas Artes, Madrid
1986	*Recent Spanish Photography,* University of Alburquerque, New Mexico
	Museo de Arte Moderno, Tarragona, Spain
1987	Marcuse Pfeifer Gallery, New York
	Photographie Mediterranéenne Contemporaine, La Vieille Charite, Marseille, France
1988	*Mois de la Photo,* Musée d'Art Moderne, Paris
1989	*Clichés, Le Choix des Sens,* Le Botanique, Brussels
1990	The Special Photographers Company Gallery, London

	Spanish Eyes, Clarence Kennedy, Gallery, Cambridge, Massachusetts
1991	*On the Shadow Line—Ten Spanish Photographers,* Australia
	Cuatro Direcciones: Fotogracia Contemporánea Española 1970-1990, Museo Nacional Centro de Arte Reina Sofía, Madrid
1992	*Leave the Balcony Open,* Fotografía en el Arte Contemporáneo, Fundación La Caixa, Barcelona, Spain
	Les Europeans, Encuentros Internacionales de Arles, Arles, France
1993	*Enschede Photo Bienal,* Enschede, Netherlands
1994	Fundación Cartier, Cahors, France

Collections:

Maison Européene de la Photo, Paris; Musée Cantini, Marseille, France; Museo Palacio de Sástago, Zaragoza, Spain; Collection Paris Audio-Visuel, Paris; FRAC Rhône-Alpes, Lyon, France; Colección Fondo de Cultura, Vigo, Spain; International Polaroid Collection, Boston, Massachusetts; Centro de Arte Reina Sofía, Madrid; Collection Caja de Burgos, Spain; Collection Banesto, Madrid; Museo de Bellas Artes de Alava, Spain; Fundación Tous-de Pedro, Barcelona, Spain.

Publications:

By VALLHONRAT: Books—*Animal-Vegetal,* Madrid 1986; *The Possessed Space,* Munich 1992; *Autograms,* Munich 1993.

On VALLHONRAT: Book—*Entre Vues* by Frank Horvath, Paris, 1990. **Articles**—*Camera International,* (Paris) No 4 1985; "50 años de color" in *Photovision* (Madrid), No 14 1985; *Perspektief* (Rotterdam) No 26/27 1987; *Photovision* (Madrid) No 16 1987; *Camera International,* (Paris) No 17 1988; *Clichés,* (Brussels) No 52, 1988; *Nude,* Tokyo 1988; *Artics,* (Barcelona) No 2 1989; *European Photography,* (Göttingen) No 42 1990; "Conversation with Salomé Cuesta," in *Lapiz Magazine,* (Madrid) no 101 1994.

*

For several years I have developed different projects which share some common elements: they try to be an exploration of photography as a symbol of our way of perceiving the world, a cultural expression of the illusion of domination over reality, how it conditions our western culture, influencing the way we relate to reality.

In every project I have tried to underline critically the ambivalence of the elements which determine the nature of the photographic media.

Some of the projects explore the hybrid status of photography, in its ambivalence between the world of the icons and the world of the objects.

Precarious Objects follows up and develops some ideas that I started in the previous series *The Possessed Space* 1987-1991, and *Autograms,* 1991. In *The Possessed Space,* I worked with the idea of photography as a three dimensional object. In *Autograms,* time, light, chance, photography as a condensation of an experience as opposed to fragmentation, the implications of what photography means as participation of events, leaving my position as "teller" or spectator, were the elements that gave configuration to the work.

In *Precarious Objects,* I kept underlining and exploring certain elements inherent to the essence of the photographic media: the tension existent between surface and representation of three dimensional space, the "narrative character" culturally attributed to photography, the possible materiality of the physical nature of the "photographic object." In other words, the difficulty of definition of their status as icons and as objects.

The elements and objects photographed, allude to some degree of sensory experience. Their weight, hardness, fluidity, density and their dynamics are opposed to the fragile and tense material nature of these "photographic objects"

—Javier Vallhonrat

* * *

Untitled, from *Precarious Objects,* **1993-94 (original in colour).** Photograph by Javier Vallhonrat.

Javier Vallhonrat is swift to admit a dearth of photographic influences, even to admit a liking for the work of a heterogenous collection of photographers, including the controversial Helmut Newton and Joel-Peter Witkin. Comparisons with these are, although frequent, hardly fair. Unlike them, Vallhonrat was formed and trained as a fine artist, (at the Madrid art school where his fellow national Christina Garcia Rodero was also trained and now teaches). His work has moved through distinct phases and subjects—with titles such as *Animal-Vegetal* and *Homages*—although the human and particularly the female form remains integral. Unlike Man Ray's famous dictum about painting what he could not photograph and vice versa, Vallhonrat is closer to "painting with the camera," and anticipates a day when he may well again take up the paintbrush and "combine form with the abstract."

The voyeuristic exploitation of a Newton or a Witkin, whether or not intended as tongue-in-cheek, simply doesn't enter into his very differently disciplined manner of working. In *The Possessed Space,* the Hamilton's exhibition, there was only one subject: the dancer Dominique Abel with whom Vallhonrat is at pains to point out he works in collaboration. On record as saying he considers even the most 'dispassionate' work of a Nadar or a Sander are a revelatory of them themselves as of their sitters, Vallhonrat is not afraid to demonstrate his own obsessions but links them to a project essentially undertaken in partnership. This strips the result of both objective and voyeuristic elements and allows a rare tenderness of interaction to enter into even the most formalised poses.

Vallhonrat's vocabulary in discussing his work is not that one immediately associates with a photographer whose primary concern is the female nude. Its terminology could take issue with the most intellectual Cartesian, relishing such categories as 'objectual' (not objective), dichotomy and contradiction, precision and extension, inversion and confrontation. 'Objectual', a term that

exists in both French and Spanish, refers not to the objectivity of the photographic eye but to the work as object. This is something which fascinates Vallhonrat: he works in a studio with his brother (who's by now really fed up with all my reworking of the image), enlarging and refining the image now into an elipse, now a circle, to test the boundaries not only of the human form, but its physical extension in space. It emerges pushed up hard against the frame, again precisely selected to set a 'natural' limit in richly chestnut hued wood.

Such a meticulous process puts the type of work undertaken by Vallhonrat at the opposite extreme to that of photojournalism, a medium he also greatly admires. However he acknowledges that "street photography is something I've tried but never succeeded at. Yet the problem remains the same however you take the photographs: what a subject is in reality and what it is in photography". By removing the photographic medium from its associative realism, Vallhonrat turns the process into one less of recording reality than on creating a photograph.

The degree of rift between the two depends on the presence, some would say the intervention, of the individual photographer. Vallhonrat talks enthusiastically about a new assignment he has just completed in Mexico. Working alonside fellow photographer Carlos Somonte, he with his modern Hasselblad, Somonte with an ancient Chinese square format camera, the two photographers spent four days shooting a colour series called *Latino* at the lagoons of Manialtepec. "I still haven't seen the contacts yet, but there's one thing I can guarantee: our images of every same subject will be entirely different. The oceans between us (Somonte is Mexican; Vallhonrat of Catalan origin) mean we come from two different universes."

As to the dichotomy that recurs throughout our conversation, Vallhonrat repeatedly couches it in terms of the space between the observer and observed, objectifier and subject and as the contained space from within which Dominiqe Abel's viewer and image questions the whole issue of possession. Is the dancer/model possessed by the limits of space, or does the whole become the possession of the viewer/interpreter/purchaser? Or does she take possession of the space around her, and of the interest, aesthetic or financial, the viewer/purchaser has in her?

As Vallhonrat himself says "We always refer a photograph to its subject." In some sense, he wishes the work to be seen as an artefact, as a whole—and as an object. At the same time, he sees its fragmentation as natural: "I broke the object not the woman. The body bends in movement and I use its movement to take advantage of the different possibilities of vertical and horizontal space." The dyptich now leans proudly hinged at the dancer's waist between floor and wall. Another that looks shattered into six fragments by the glass is likewise explained "When I divide a single image into a hexagram, it's because that's the way it looks to me in a mirror."

The concept of photography as mirror rather than window is hardly new. Vallhonrat is taking it one stage further with a sequence of colour self portraits "which will, however, leave me quite unrecognizable."

The fascination here is motion rather than space, building on a series of reflective images in which fire and light blaze the trail. In this Vallhonrat believes he is following in the tradition of the earliest 'sun pictures' made over 150 years ago, and accredited as being 'from the perfect pencil of light' or 'with the precise eye'.

Further back still, Vallhonrat sources his work in the Renaissance, which he sees as the cradle of pure science, its perspective most truly that of the camera obscura. The task is to create a two dimensional object with a three-dimensional appearance through a new medium of mathematically refracting light. "It's the precise aspect of such an undertaking that fascinates me. A mathematical system allows you to fragment reality and to witness the confrontation of science and art." Science he sees according to a more nineteenth than fifteenth century stereotype as "cold and detached, objectifying reality." He enjoys the contrast between this and the subject of this exhibition: "I wanted to underline this idea of dichotomy. I chose a subject that attracted me by sensuality and plasticity of the dancer's movements and also the drama she could put into her body."

The Renaissance is renowned for believeing in the goal of reproducing reality in a perfect manner. For Vallhonrat photography is the ideal medium to explore this inside-outside relationship of reality and its reproduction. If we as viewers, have become accustomed to the lack of objectivity in much of what has passed for photographic realism and to the implicit subjectivity of every photographer in their work, then maybe this third dimension is not too much to grapple with either: the synthesis of Renaissance theory, Baroque style and contemplatory practice more than bear seeing and pondering on.

—Amanda Hopkinson

VAN DER ELSKEN, Ed(uard).

Nationality: Dutch. **Born:** Amsterdam, 10 March 1925. **Education:** Attended schools in Amsterdam; mainly self-taught in photography, but took correspondence lessons from the Nederlandse Fotovakschool, The Hague. **Family:** Married several times; has several children. **Career:** Freelance photographer, in Amsterdam, 1947-50, Paris, 1950-55, and in Edam, Netherlands, since 1955; also freelance filmmaker, Edam, since 1959. **Recipient:** Staatsprijs voor de filmkunst, The Hague, 1971; David Roëll Prijs, 1988. **Died:** (in Edam, The Netherlands) 28 December, 1990.

Individual Exhibitions:

1955	Art Institute of Chicago
1956	Steendrukkery de Jong, Hilversum, Netherlands
	Galerie 't Venster, Rotterdam
1959	Stedelijk Museum, Schiedam, Netherlands
	Zonnehof, Amersfoort, Netherlands
	Museum voor Stadt en Lande, Groningen, Netherlands
1960	Galerie De Waag, Nijmegen, Netherlands
1966	Stedelijk Museum, Amsterdam
1968	De Vishal, Haarlem, Netherlands
1977	Stedelijk Museum, Amsterdam
1979	*Amsterdam 1946-70*, Historisch Museum, Amsterdam
1981	*Paris of the Fifties*, Canon Photo Gallery, Amsterdam
1984	Historisch Museum, Amsterdam
	Een liefdesgeschiedenis in Saint Germain des Prés, Stedelijk Museum, Amsterdam
1986	Printemps Department Store, Tokyo
	Une Histoire d'amour à Saint-Germain-des-Pres (Mois de la Photo 1986), Institut Néerlandais, Paris
1987	*Jong Nederland*, Canon Photo Gallery, Amsterdam
	Canon Rotown Gallery, Rotterdam
1988	Canon Image Centre, Amsterdam
1988-89	Canon Image Centre, Amsterdam
	De ontdekking van Japan. Foto's van Ed van der Elsken 1961-1988, Canon Image Centre, Amsterdam
	De andere kant van Japan. Foto's van Ed van der Elsken 1959-1960, Rijksmuseum voor Volkenkunde, Leiden
1989	Museum voor Schone Kunsten, Gent
1991	Stedelijk Museum, Amsterdam
1993	*Ed van der Elsken—Autoportrait*, Citroën-galerie, Amsterdam
1994	*Ed van der Elsken Once Upon a Time*, Fotomuseum, Winterthur
	Ed van der Elsken in kleur. Foto's 1950-1990, Bloom Gallery, Amsterdam

Selected Group Exhibitions:

1954	*Subjektive Fotografie 2*, Saarbrücken
1955	*The Family of Man*, Museum of Modern Art, New York (and world tour)
1967	*Expo '67*, Montreal
1968	*2nd World Exhibition of Photography: Woman*, Pressehaus Stern, Hamburg (and world tour)
1972	*World Press Photo 1971/72*, Amsterdam
1973	*5 Masters of European Photography*, The Photographers' Gallery, London
1977	*Fotos voor de Stad*, Historisch Museum, Amsterdam
1978	*Fotografie in Nederland 1940-75*, Stedelijk Museum, Amsterdam
1979	*Fotografie in Nederland 1920-40*, Gemeentemuseum, The Hague
1980	*Gebonden Kunstenfederatie (fotografen)*, Stedelijk Museum, Amsterdam
1981	*De stad in zwart/wit*, Museum Fodor, Amsterdam
1985	*Amsterdam 1950-1959 20 fotografen*, Gemeentearchief, Amsterdam
1986	*Het Fotoboek. 4 Nederlandse fotografen en Parijs (Foto '86)*, Nieuwe Kerk, Amsterdam
1987	*Naakt voor de camera, 1840-1987*, De Meervaart, Amsterdam
1988	*Roots & Turns. Twentieth Century Photography in The Netherlands*, Sarah Campbell Blaffer Gallery, Houston
1989/90	*Foto in omslag.Het Nederlandse documentaire fotoboek na 1945*, De Zonnehof, Amersfoort
1990	*Col.Lecció. Un recorregut per la fotografia europea*, Palau Robert, Barcelona

Collections:

Stedelijk Museum, Amsterdam; Bibliothèque Nationale, Paris; Museum of Modern Art, New York; Art Institute of Chicago; Print Room, University of Leiden, Netherlands; Capi-Lux Alblas Stichting, Amsterdam; Gemeentearchief, Amsterdam; Rijksmuseum, Amsterdam; Rijksdienst Beeldende Kunst, Den Haag; Stichting Nederlands Foto-& Grafisch Centrum, Haarlem; Museum of Modern Art, Kawasaki, Japan; Stichting Nederlands Fotoarchief, Rotterdam.

Publications:

By van der ELSKEN: Books—*Love on the Left Bank,* Amsterdam, London, New York and Paris 1954; *Een liefdesgeschiedenis in Saint Germain des Prés,* Amsterdam 1956; *Nederlands Danstheater,* Amsterdam 1958; *Jazz,* Amsterdam 1959; *Bagara, Central Africa,* Amsterdam and Paris 1959; *De werkelijkheid van Karel Appel,* Amsterdam 1962; *Sweet Life,* Amsterdam, New York and London 1963; *Musique barbare van karel Appel,* Amsterdam 1963; *Ed van der Elsken,* exhibition catalogue, Amsterdam 1966; *Vrouwen van Amsterdam,* with Mattheus Engel and others, Amsterdam 1970; *Zomar in een sloot ergens bij Edam,* Bussum, Netherlands 1977; *Eye Love You,* Amsterdam 1977; *Life of a Swan Family,* Amsterdam 1977; *Hallo!,* Amsterdam 1978; *Amsterdam: Old Photographs,* Amsterdam 1980; *Avonturen op het land,* Amsterdam 1980; *Amsterdam! Oude foto's 1947-1970,* Amsterdam 1980; *Parijs! Foto's 1950-1954,* Amsterdam 1981; *Amsterdam?,* Amsterdam 1984; *Are You Famous?,* Amsterdam 1985; *Elsken: Paris 1950-1954,* Tokyo 1985; *San-jeruman-de-pure no koi (L'amour à Saint Germain des prés).* Photo exhibition, Tokyo, 1986; *Jong Nederland, adorable rotzakken 1947-1987,* Amsterdam 1987; *Nippon Datta,* Tokyo, 1987; *Jazz 1955-1959.61,* Tokyo, 1988; *De ontdekking van Japan,* Amsterdam, 1988; *Afrika,* Tokyo, 1990; *Jazz,* Amsterdam, 1991; *Once Upon a Time,* Amsterdam, 1991.

On van der ELSKEN: Books—*The Picture History of Photography* by Peter Pollack, New York 1958; *Fotografie in Nederland 1940-1975,* edited by Els Barents, The Hague 1978; *Roots & Turns. Twentieth Century Photography in the Netherlands,* by Ingeborg Th. Leijerzapf e.o., Houston, 1988; *Foto in omslag. Het Nederlandse documentaire fotoboek na 1945,* by Mattie Boom, Amsterdam, 1989. **Articles**—"Ed van der Elsken" by Evelyn de Regt in Ingeborg Th. Leijerzapf (red), *Geschiedenis van de Nederlandse fotografie in monografieën en thema-artikelen,* Alphen aan den Rijn/Amsterdam, afl. 16, 1991.

*

I have been a freelance roving photographer since 1947. I have lived most of my life in Holland except for four years in Paris (1950-55). With Amsterdam as a home base and, later, the small Dutch town of Edam as home, I travel a lot.

In 1959 I started filming as well, mainly for television. In filming, part of my activity is designing and developing new cameras and other equipment which make spontaneous, lightweight reportage—like filming—easier. My pride is that I was working professionally with my own self-blimped 16mm sync camera before the famous Eclair NPR camera came onto the market. For six years now I have worked with "professional super 8, direct sound." And, of course, I work with low budget video. I am also making slides with sync things.

I think it characteristic that I make personal things with low budget techniques, which makes me as independent as possible of the money people.

—Ed van der Elsken

* * *

In the 1950s Ed van der Elsken became known for his pictures of the Paris district of St. Germain. This series of romantic, sensitive photographs impressed Edward Steichen when he was looking for material for the exhibition *Family of Man* in 1955. American critics praised van der Elsken's work for his sharp eye, for the dramatic situations in the lives of the bohemians in the Paris of Sartre and Sagan, and for the strong personal impact of the images. The pictures were taken with extremely sensitive materials, without flash, and van der Elsken's way of developing them augmented the dramatic effect. He had already shown the series at various international exhibitions before he published it in book form in 1954, a self-invented love story expressed in photographs and a short text, *Love on the Left Bank*—and in so doing he invented a new kind of photographic book: fiction in documentary photography.

After *Love on the West Bank* van der Elsken was established as a photographer, and he went on to photograph—only people—all over the world. He sometimes emphasizes the sensational: he has tried to convey the boredom and depression that exists in life in the cities. His intention is to show how other people feel and what they do, and that intention comes over in the photographs. He says that his photographs are a product of days of "wandering around." "In Hong Kong I wandered every day for six weeks through the streets. I did not create or invent anything: I hoped that I would suddenly see something fantastic happen and that I would have my camera with me." Because of this method, his pictures seldom possess well-balanced composition. They also lack a social or political message. He captures everyday emotions. And he knows how to capture the most typical features in every city and country—later, he selects for a book. For most of his career he has worked outside the Netherlands, in Europe and beyond.

His books reflect his life-style and working methods: *Bagara,* a report about the people and their way of life in Equatorial Africa; *Jazz,* in which jazz musicians, with their shining instruments and emotional facial expressions, are dramatically captured in light and dark effects; *Sweet Life,* the result of a 14-month tour around the world. Van der Elsken has always opposed the usual practice in publishing, that for commissions photographers must make concessions. He is rigorous in his own demands. All the photographs in his books are his own choice, and the layout of each book has been worked out in close collaboration with the graphic designer.

In the 1960s van der Elsken also began to film, choosing the same subject-matter as for his photographs. In recent years he has remained in Edam, a small town near Amsterdam, concentrating on photographing and filming the nature surrounding him.

—A. de Jonge-Vermeulen

VAN DER ZEE, James (Augustus Joseph).

Nationality: American. **Born:** Lenox, Massachusetts, 29 June 1886. **Education:** Attended Lenox public schools; self-taught in photography. **Family:** Married Kate Brown in 1906 (divorced, 1914); children: Rachel (died, 1923) and Emile (died, 1911); married Gaynella Greenlee in 1920 (died, 1970); married Donna Mussenden in 1978. **Career:** Worked as busboy, waiter, elevator man, etc., New York, 1906-07; dining-room waiter, etc., Hotel Chamberlain, Old Point Comfort, Virginia, 1907-09; worked as waiter, and musician, with Fletcher Henderson Band and John Wanamaker Orchestra, New York, 1909-15; darkroom assistant and photographer, Gertz's Department Store, Newark, New Jersey, 1915-16; opened own photographic studio (Guarantee Photos, and later, GGG Photo Studio), New York, 1916-68; ceased professional photography, New York, 1969; resumed photography, New York, 1980 until his death in 1983. **Recipient:** American Society of Magazine Photographers Award, 1969; Life Fellowship, Metropolitan Museum of Art, New York, 1970; Pierre Toussaint Award, 1978; President's Living Legacy Award, Washington, D.C., 1978. D.H.L.: Howard University, Washington, D.C., 1983. James Van Der Zee Institute established by Reginald McGhee and Charles Innis, now under care of Metropolitan Museum of Art, New York, 1969. **Estate:** James Van Der Zee Institute, 103 East 125th Street, New York, New York 10035, U.S.A. **Agent:** Howard Greenberg Gallery, 120 Wooster Street, New York 10012, U.S.A. **Died:** (in Washington, D.C.) 15 May 1983.

Individual Exhibitions:

1970   Lenox Library, Massachusetts
1971   Studio Museum, Harlem, New York
1974   Lunn Gallery/Graphics International, Washington, D.C.
1979   *The Legacy of James Van Der Zee: A Portrait of Black Americans,* Alternative Center for International Arts, New York
         Delaware Art Museum, Wilmington
1983   Camera Club of New York, New York City
         Idaho State University, Pocatello
1994   *Retrospective,* National Portrait Gallery, Washington, D.C.
         Vintage Photographs of Harlem, Howard Greenberg Gallery, New York

Selected Group Exhibitions:

1969   *Harlem on My Mind: Cultural Capital of Black Ameria 1900-*
        1968, Metropolitan Museum of Art, New York
1978   *The Quality of Presence,* Lunn Gallery, Washington, D.C.
1979   *The Black Photographer,* San Francisco Museum of Mod-
        ern Art
        Fleeting Gestures: Dance Photographs, International Center of
        Photography, New York (travelled to The Photographers'
        Gallery, London)
1982   *Lichtbildnisse: Das Porträt in der Fotografie,* Rheinisches
        Landesmuseum, Bonn
1985   *Gifts from the Ramer Collection,* San Francisco Museum of
        Modern Art
1987   *Harlem Renaissance,* Studio Museum in Harlem, New York
        (toured the United States, 1987-89)

Collections:

Metropolitan Museum of Art, New York; Baltimore Museum of Art, Mary-
land; Library of Congress, Washington, D.C.; University of Michigan, Ann
Arbor; Cleveland Museum of Art; Minneapolis Institute of Arts; University of
Nebraska, Lincoln; Museum of Fine Arts, Houston; Center for Creative
Photography, University of Arizona, Tucson; University of California at Los
Angeles.

Publications:

By VAN DER ZEE: Books—*The World of James Van Der Zee: A Visual*
Record of Black Americans, with an introduction by Reginald McGhee, New
York 1969; *James Van Der Zee,* edited by Liliane De Cock and Reginald
McGhee, with an introduction by Reginia A. Perry, New York 1973; *James*
Van Der Zee: 18 Photographs, portfolio, with an introduction by Reginia A.
Perry, Washington, D.C. and New York 1974; *The Harlem Book of the Dead,*
with poetry by Owen Dodson and text by Camille Billops, Dobbs Ferry, New
York 1978.

On VAN DER ZEE: Books—*Harlem on My Mind: Cultural Capital of*
Black America 1900-1968, exhibition catalogue, edited by Allon Schoener,
New York 1969; *Photographs: Sheldon Memorial Art Gallery Collection,*
University of Nebraska, with an introduction by Norman A. Geske, Lincoln
1977; *The Legacy of James Van Der Zee: A Portrait of Black Americans,*
exhibition catalogue, with a preface by Gino Rodriguez, foreword by Robert
W. Brown, New York 1977; *The Photograph Collector's Guide* by Lee D.
Witkin and Barbara London, Boston and London 1979; *Lichtbildnisse: Das*
Porträt in der Fotografie, edited by Klaus Honnef, Cologne 1982; *The Library*
of World Photography: Portraits, with introduction by Colin Ford, Tokyo
1982, 1983, London 1983; *Harlem Renaissance: Art of Black America,* with
introduction by Mary Schmidt Campbell, New York 1987; *Van Der Zee:*
Photographer 1886-1983, by Deborah Willis-Braithwaite, New York and
London, 1994. **Articles**—"Harlem's 'Picture-Taking Man'" by Val Wilmer
in *The Observer Magazine* (London), 21 September 1980; "James Van Der
Zee Dies: Photographer of Harlem" in the *New York Times,* 16 May 1983;
"James Van Der Zee, 1886-1983" in *Afterimage* (Rochester, New York),
June 1983. **Film**—"James Van Der Zee" in *Black Journal,* educational TV
series, New York 1972.

*   *   *

"The message of Van Der Zee's photography is a universal one," wrote
Prof. Regina A. Perry some years ago. "To the Black viewer, the revealing
glimpses of people and activities in America's most unique Black community
are bound to instill an element of pride and self-respect. To the non-Black
viewer, Van Der Zee's photographs represent Black Americans in all their
grace and dignity—an impressive point of view which should help dispel
existing misconceptions. Above all, Van Der Zee was a photographer of
people, and his works are both raceless and timeless."

James Van Der Zee lived and photographed in Harlem for decades.
Equally important, however, is that he lived and worked in Harlem during that
community's remarkable decade of cultural flowering, the "Harlem Renais-

sance" from approximately 1919-1929. This was the period of Marcus
Garvey's back-to-Africa movement (for which Van Der Zee served as official
photographer), of Countee Cullen's poetry, of James P. Johnson's piano, and
Duke Ellington's orchestra. It is unclear whether every celebrity of the period
passed before Van Der Zee's lens, or merely "almost" every celebrity.

Harlem's political, religious and cultural figures, therefore, comprise a
large block of Van Der Zee's carefully preserved archive. So, too, do the
groups around which much of everyday life was organized, the fraternal
lodges, and sports and social clubs. As with the community itself, celebrations
are prominent. Van Der Zee photographed weddings, dinners, and (especially
in the years of the great influenza pandemic) many funerals. Perhaps above all,
he photographed individuals, especially women, and families.

Although many of Van Der Zee's photographs were made "on location,"
he was a studio photographer in the truest sense. Much of his vision, indeed
much of his time, was devoted to posing his subjects, to providing the right
backgrounds, to structuring the moment. His portraits are deeply psychological, providing rich insights into sitter and photographer alike.

Among other qualities, Van Der Zee's pictures reveal his romanticism and
unashamed sentimentality. Asked to photograph the funeral of Blanche Powell
(sister of Adam Clayton Powell, Jr.), he deemed the picture incomplete until he
had double-printed the image of Blanche, herself, towering above the choir.
Such combination printing and the deft use of the air brush were hallmarks of
Van Der Zee's technique.

But if such manipulated compositions project a "period piece" aura,
many of Van Der Zee's "straighter" efforts are as contemporary now as when
they were made. Indeed, the straight portrait of Blanche Powell, from which
the overprint was made, is a lovely image of a charming young woman.

However, Van Der Zee's photographs inhabit two realms of importance.
They are a record of the life's work of one of America's first great Black
photographers. At the same time, they are an historical archive, a picture of
Harlem in an era in which that name conjured visions of jazz, art, and
literature, not grinding poverty and occasional rebellion.

—Stu Cohen

VAN DYKE, Willard (Ames).

Nationality: American. **Born:** Denver, Colorado, 5 December 1906. **Education:** Self-taught in photography, but influenced by Edward Weston, Ansel
Adams, and Ralph Steiner. **Family:** Married Mary Gray Barnett in 1938
(divorced, 1950); children: Alison and Peter; married Margaret Barbara
Murray Milikin in 1950; children: Murray and Cornelius. **Career:** Independent social documentary photographer from 1930, and filmmaker from 1935
(in San Francisco, 1930-45; New York, 1945-81, settled in Santa Fe, New
Mexico, 1981-86): Founder Member, with Edward Weston, Ansel Adams,
Sonya Noskowiak and Imogen Cunningham, Group f/64, San Francisco,
1932; photographer for the Public Works Administration Art Project, San
Francisco, 1934, and for *Harper's Bazaar,* New York, 1935; Technical
Director, Film Section, Office of War Information, Washington, D.C., 1940-
45; Producer, Affiliated Film Producers, New York, 1946-58; President, Van
Dyke Productions Inc., New York, 1958-81; Director, Film Department,
Museum of Modern Art, New York, 1965-72. Professor of Film, 1972-77,
and Professor Emeritus 1977-86, State University of New York at Purchase.
Member of the Visiting Committee, Rhode Island School of Design, Provi-
dence, 1969-86, Carpenter Center, Harvard University, Cambridge, Massachusetts, 1980-86, and School of the Museum of Fine Arts, Boston, 1981-86.
President, New York Film Council, 1947, Screen Directors International
Guild, New York, 1960-62, and International Film Seminars, New York,
1965-72. **Recipient:** First Prize, *Camera Craft,* 1927; Silver Cup, George
Eastman House, Rochester, New York, 1978. **Died:** (in Jackson, Tennessee)
23 January 1986.

Individual Exhibitions:

1932   M.H. de Young Memorial Museum, San Francisco
1933   San Diego Museum of Art, California

1969   Hetzel Center, Pennsylvania State University, University Park
1971   Hungarian National Gallery, Budapest
1977   *Photographs 1930-37*, Witkin Gallery, New York
        Wirtz Gallery, San Francisco
        Archetype Gallery, New Haven, Connecticut
        Neuberger Museum, Purchase, New York
1978   International Museum of Photography, George Eastman House,
           Rochester, New York
        Carpenter Center, Harvard University, Cambridge,
           Massachusetts
        Stephen White Gallery, Los Angeles
1980   Milwaukee Center for Photography
        Film in the Cities Gallery, St. Paul, Minnesota
        Clarence Kennedy Gallery, Cambridge, Massachusetts (with
           William Wegman and Olivia Parker)
1981   Douglas Kenyon Gallery, Chicago (with Mark Godfrey)
        Museum of Modern Art, New York (testimonial screening of
           films)
        Whitney Museum, New York (retrospective screening of films)

Selected Group Exhibitions:

1932   *Group f/64*, M.H. de Young Memorial Museum, San
           Francisco
1933   *Group f/64*, Ansel Adams Gallery, San Francisco
1978   *Group f/64*, University of Missouri, St. Louis
1979   *Life: The First Decade 1936-45*, Grey Art Gallery, New York
           University
        One of a Kind, Museum of Fine Arts, Houston (toured the
           United States)
1982   *Images of America*, San Francisco Museum of Modern Art
           (travelled to St. Louis Art Museum, Missouri; Baltimore
           Museum of Art, Maryland; Des Moines Art Center, Iowa;
           Cleveland Museum of Art, Ohio)

Collections:

Museum of Modern Art, New York; Neuberger Museum, Purchase, New York; Polaroid Corporation, Cambridge, Massachusetts; Detroit Institute of Fine Arts; Art Museum of St. Louis; Museum of Fine Arts, Houston; Center for Creative Photography, University of Arizona, Tucson; San Diego Museum of Art, California; Oakland Museum, California; San Francisco Museum of Modern Art.

Publications:

By VAN DYKE: Books—*Group f/64*, with Jean S. Tucker, St. Louis 1978; introduction to *A Point of View* by Ralph Steiner, Middletown, Connecticut 1978. **Films**—*The River*, as cameraman, with Stacey Woodward and Floyd Crosby, directed by Pare Lorentz, 1937; *The City*, with Ralph Steiner, 1939; *Valley Town*, 1940; *The Children Must Learn*, 1940; *Sarah Lawrence*, 1940; *To Hear Your Banjo Play*, 1941; *Tall Tales*, 1941; *The Bridge*, 1942; *Oswego*, 1943; *Steeltown*, 1943; *Pacific Northwest*, 1944; *San Francisco*, (official film on founding of the United Nations), 1945; *Journey into Medicine*, 1946; *The Photographer*, 1947; *This Charming Couple*, 1949; *Mount Vernon*, 1949; *Years of Change*, 1950; *New York University*, 1952; *Working and Playing to Health*, 1953; *There Is a Season*, 1954; *Recollections of Boyhood*, 1954; *Cabos Blancos*, with Angel Rivera, 1954; *Excursion House*, 1954; *Life of the Molds*, 1957; *Skyscraper*, with Shirley Clarke, 1958; *Tiger Hunt in Assam*, 1958; *Mountains of the Moon*, 1958; *Land of White Alice*, 1959; *The Procession*, 1959; *Ireland: The Tear and the Smile*, 1960; *Sweden*, 1960; *So That Men Are Free*, 1962; *Harvest*, 1962; *Depressed Area*, 1963; *Rice*, with Wheaton Galentine, 1964; *Frontiers of News*, 1964; *Pop Buell: Hoosier Farmer in Laos*, 1965; *Taming the Mekong*, 1965; *The Farmer: Feast or Famine*, with Roger Barlow, 1965; *Frontline Camera 1935-1965*, 1965; *Shape of Films to Come*, 1968.

On VAN DYKE: Books—*U.S. Camera 1936*, annual, edited by Tom J. Maloney, New York and London 1936; *The Picture History of Photography*

by Peter Pollack, New York 1958; *The Documentary Tradition: From Nanook to Woodstock* by Lewis Jacobs, New York 1971; *Faces: A Narrative History of the Portrait in Photography* by Ben Maddow, Boston 1977; *One of a Kind: Recent Polaroid Color Photography*, with a preface by Belinda Rathbone, introduction by Eugenia Parry Janis, Boston 1979; *Life: The First Decade 1936-1945* by Robert Littman, Ralph Graves and Doris C. O'Neill, New York 1979, London 1980; *Film on the Left* by William Alexander, Princeton, New Jersey 1981; *Cinema Strikes Back: Radical Filmmaking in the United States 1930-1942* by Russell Campbell, Ann Arbor, Michigan 1982; *Images of America: Precisionist Painting and Modern Photography*, exhibition catalogue, by Karen Tsujimoto, Seattle, Washington 1982. **Articles**—"Focus on Willard Van Dyke" by Art Zuckerman in *Popular Photography* (Boulder, Colorado), April 1965; "Willard Van Dyke" by Helen Morse in *Image* (Rochester, New York), June 1978; "Master Lensman Willard Van Dyke Reflects on a Remarkable Career" by Alan G. Artner in the *Chicago Tribune*, 14 April 1985; "Willard Van Dyke, Ex-Head of Films at Modern Museum" by Douglas C. McGill in the *New York Times*, 24 January 1986. **Film**—*Conversations with Willard Van Dyke* by Amalie Rothschild, 1981.

*

I believe that photography is the most important way of seeing the meaning of society, and its most potent form is documentary photography.

—Willard Van Dyke (1982)

*   *   *

Willard Van Dyke began young and was good from the beginning. He even had the friendship of such colleagues as Edward Weston, Imogen Cunningham and Ansel Adams, all of whom joined him for a time in a loosely formed working group called "f/64" that he founded with them in San Francisco in 1932. Sharp focus and depth of field were the main things they were all after, a kind of "straight" photography devoid of the influence of traditional painting all too prevalent in photography at that time. They were aided in their efforts by the clarity of California light, pollution-free in the 1930s.

Van Dyke was also an active filmmaker, and made numerous films, including such distinguished works as *The Bridge, The Skyscraper,* and one on Weston, *The Photographer*. Van Dyke's still photographs deal with a wide range of subject matter. He photographed sand dunes and dried bones; store fronts; poor people and poor streets; a boxer wrapping his hands—all curve of trouser folds and fingers; a fence post with abstracting arabesques of barbed wire. Ironically, although his esthetic abjured that of painting, Van Dyke's cool compositions of ship funnels link him to such modern painters as the Precisionists Sheeler and Demuth. In contrast, his portraits are full of warmth and knowledge—a thoughtful Ansel Adams musing over a tea cup, a smiling, extrovert William Saroyan. Among his most powerful pictures are those revealing an unblinking look at victims of the Depression—despairing people and abandoned buildings—in which depths of meaning find an equivalent to depth of technique.

—Ralph Pomeroy

VANESCH, Jean (Louis).

Nationality: Belgian. **Born:** Liège, Belgium, 28 May 1950. **Education:** Studied photography at the Institut Supérieur des Beaux Arts St. Luc, Liège. **Family:** Married Lucia Radochonska, 1974; daughter: Carole. **Address:** 57 Rue des 3 Chênes, 4621 Retinne, Belgium.

Individual Exhibitions:

1983   Galerie Sogno di Carta, Liège, Belgium
1986   Galerie le Réverbère, Lyons, France
1987   Galerie J.P. Lambert, Paris

From the *Arbos* series, **1988.** Photograph by Jean-Louis Vanesch.

1988	Maison de la Culture d'Amiens, Amiens, France
	Galerie Pennings, Eindhoven, Holland
	Galerie Le Cirque Divers, Liège, Belgium
1990	Galerie St. Cyprien, Toulouse, France
1990	Galerie J.P. Lambert, Paris
1993	Galerie Artecoppo, Verviers, Belgium
1994	Galerie Contretype, Brussels
	Galerie J.P. Lambert, Paris

Selected Group Exhibitions:

1988	Galerie XYZ, Gand, Belgium
1989	Musée de la Photographie, Charleroi, Belgium
	Forum de l'Image, Toulouse, France
1990	Musée de la Photographie d'Anvers, Belgium
1991	Salon de la Découverte, Paris
1992	Mai de la Photographié, Reims, France
1993	*Histoire de la Photographie Belge Carte Blanche á J.L Godefroid,* Musée de la Photographie, Charleroi, Belgium
1994	*La Matiere, L'Ombre, La Fiction,* Bibliothéque Nationale, Paris

Collections:

Musée de la Photographie, Charleroi, Belgium; Musée de la Photographie de l'Elysée, Lausanne, Switzerland; Le Chateau d'Eau, Toulouse, France; FRAC, Aix en Provence, France; Bibliothèque Nationale, Paris; Arthotèque de Lyon, France.

Publications:

By VANESCH: Book—*Ce Sentiment à la Fois d'Exil et d'Ivresse,* portfolio, with text by J.P.Otte. **Articles**—"Un petit pan de mur blanc," ed. J.P. Lambert with text by Guy Mandery; in *Cliché,* No.62; with text by J.C. Renault, in *Art Press,* special photography edition, 1990; "La Recherche Photographique" in *La Photographie Europeenne*; in *Art Press,* special number *20 Ans, L'Histoire Continue*; with text by G.Karikeze in *Sogno di Carta*; with text by J.M. Sarlet in *Contretype.*

*

Once I used to take pictures of suburbs, then of roads, of the countryside, and of trees too. Quite sharp photos, well composed. Then, as a chance result of a series of photos of graminaceous grasses, I discovered some aberrations, some "vibrations," which I have researched, explored. So I started to explore the different elements which combine to form an image; these aberrations, the blurring, the limits of sharpness, the density. And the deep blackness. This was done fairly methodically in the series *Arbos* (1988-90). A subject deliberately condensed into a series, allowing concentration on each part of the image, to delve always deeper, to enlarge my vocabulary, to progress towards the limit.

At the end of this series, I resumed taking pictures of the places which I had photographed before. But now with a richer palette, and incorporating therein the knowledge of the above series, with the idea also of including these images as "respirations" in the *Arbos* series. Like those moments when one can "blow, breathe, shed the weight of the world." Hence the title *Reposoirs (Resting Places),* for this series which is still evolving. Bringing objects and things closer, trying to capture their presence, their weight. A way of seeking an accord with the world, of finding within it one's place.

—Jean-Louis Vanesch

*   *   *

The work of Jean-Louis Vanesch is among the most representative in the creative photography movement that developed in Belgium in the second half of the 1960s. It also possesses a remarkable coherence.

Jean-Louis Vanesch received his professional training in photography at the Saint-Luc Fine Arts Institute in Liege at the end of the 1960s. He has however still never engaged in industrial or commercial photography.

His images are only shown in the context of exhibitions or portfolios of original prints. It is clear that he attaches considerable importance to their quality.

His work falls into several distinct periods. First of all, until 1977/8 he photographed solitary places, city outskirts, suburban corners, peaceful districts or ports. These are images devoid of documentary intent. Vanesch carefully avoids the picturesque or dramatic and the extremities of life in society. These photographs are of minute size (approximately 10 x 15 cms) but their plastic qualities already evince with a definite concern for light, often the oblique light of morning or the close of an afternoon.

Then, during the first half of the 1980s Vanesch left the urban environment to seek out places in which vegetation, nature itself, has greater importance. Not nature in grandiose or mythic terms; he was concerned, rather, with 'familiar green places' near to his home or in the districts he regularly frequented in Languedoc or Larzac. In the course of this period the borders close in, the veiwpoint also gets closer, a photographic interest in luminous variations is ever more manifest.

Vanesch concerns himself with representing the micro-elements marking the passage of time upon the world: drops of rain upon leaves; a breath of dust on a pane of glass, branches catching at a ray of sunlight in the foreground of a Causses landscape.

Many photographs from this period are accompanied by a brief manuscript text and these fragments of suspended sentences look as if they were lifted from a private journal ("... and at times chaos, like a call from beyond. . . .the other side of silence . . . ") that perhaps remains unwritten.

Around 1985/6 Vanesch passes, progressively, into a different style. His chosen subjects and places remain largely the same, but now the camera moves in very close as he carves little fragments of reality; twigs, sprigs, grasses. From now on it is the texture of the world's surface which interests him more than its space. The size of his prints increases (to around 24 x 30 cms) and today it seems that this fairly short series assured his progression to the next which, something new again, was endowed with a title—Arbos—from the outset.

The period of Arbos began around 1986 and closed in 1990. It consists of images of trees, with a close focus but with a print format that is still growing larger (to around 40 x 50 cms). Massive black tree trunks or fine outlines of branches against a pale grey background are featured. There is no concern with the rendition of the woody substance yet the images are never reduced to the plain graphics of an engraving or ink drawing. They still retain something particular to photography, a certain haziness in depth of field and above all those micro-aberrations originating in optics at the shadowy boundaries of forms and resembling the traces left by vibrations affecting even the most visually heavy and solid matter.

These images juggle on the frontier between the figurative and the abstract, sometimes becoming one and sometimes the other. It comes as no surprise to learn of the photographer's interest in painters such as Pollok, Newman, Rothko, Hartung and Soulages, though it is also necessary to note his interst in musicians such as Thelonius Monk, John Coltrane and Keith Jarret.

Finally, since 1991, Vanesch has returned to the countryside with a series called Reposoirs (Resting Places); a return to familiar places, banale even, where people finally emerge—the photographer's wife and daughter. However, recent images—and these are also large (around 40-50cms) present a considerable deviation from the relatively literal rendition of landscapes before Arbos.

Here the dark effectively invades the image, sometimes to the point of barely permitting a few traces of dark or silvery grey to remain. (It is necessary to remember that in photography every image is created according to Genesis: "In the beginning was darkness. Then came light." Nonetheless, this extreme blackness does not lead to a form of dramatisation; it lacks even the emphasis of being a sign of anguish. Perhaps it is more the case that black here serves as a sign of serenity, the product of a meditation at the end of which the image of reality might resurface. In Arbos the photographer had virtually suppressed all reference to reality.

Thus the image of reality rediscovered has much in common with the mental images which people our dreams, our moments of absence or abandon ("... the moments when one can sigh, breathe deeply, set down the weight of the world," according to Vanesch). From my point of view, as a writer, the series Reposoirs is what Jungian terminology refers to as "the shadow self."

One can perhaps say that Vanesch's complete work (except perhaps for the Arbos series), evokes the concept of "genius loci," of dreaming breadth, propounded and plainly described by Jean-Claude Lemagny (in Les Cahiers de la Photographie 14, le Terretoire) from which I will quote no more than the following excerpt: "What appears empty is nonetheless poetically inhabited. What appears visible is still dreamt. What appears offered to the view of us all in a contingent manner, is still experenced as a secret belonging to each one of us . . . "

—Jean-Michel Sarlet

VERONESI, Luigi (Mario).

Nationality: Italian. **Born:** Milan, 28 May 1908. **Education:** Studied painting under the painter Carmello Violante and the critic Rafaello Giolli, Milan, 1924-29; studied painting and experimental photography with Fernand Léger, Paris, 1932-35, but essentially self-taught in photography, from 1925. **Military Service:** Served in the Italian Resistance, 1940-45. **Family:** Married Ginetta Nicora in 1945; son: Silvio. **Career:** Independent graphic artist, associating with Léger and Georges Vantongerloo, Milan and Paris, from 1928; first abstract photographs, 1930, photographic stage designs, 1934. Member, Campo Grafico artists group, Milan, 1933-36; Abstraction-Création artists group, Milan and Paris, 1934-36; and Gruppo Milione artists group, Milan, 1935-40; Founder Member, with Giuseppe Cavalli, Mario Finazzi, Ferruccio Leiss and Federico Vender, La Bussola group of photographers, Milan, 1947-56; Member, Gruppo MAC artists group, Milan, 1948-57. **Recipient:** First Prize for Color, International Film Festival, Knokke-le-Zoute, Belgium, 1949; Prix St. Gobain, Milan, 1966; Grand Prix, Quadriennale d'Arte di Torino, 1968. **Agent:** Galleria Milano, Via Manin 13, Milan, Italy. **Address:** Via Bellotti 2, 20129 Milan, Italy.

Individual Exhibitions:

1932	Galleria il Milione, Milan
1934	Galleria il Milione, Milan
1939	Galerie Equipe, Paris
	Galleria Schettini, Milan
1956	Oeuvres Recentes, Galerie de l'Institut, Paris
1957	Galleria Apollinaire, Milan
1958	Galleria del Grattacielo, Milan
1960	Silografie e Litografie, Galleria Salto, Milan
1962	Galleria delle Cre, Milan
	Galleria Ciranna, Milan
1963	Galleria Ciranna, Milan
1965	Galleria Lorenzelli, Milan
	Galleria Marciso, Turin
	Galleria del Corco, Padua
1966	Galleria La Polena, Genoa
	Galleria San Petronio, Bologna
1967	Galleria Milano, Milan
	Galleria Pegaso, Milan
1968	Galleria il Grattacielo, Legnano, Italy
	Galleria Vismara, Milan
	Galleria La Colonna, Como

Galleria il Bilico, Rome
Galleria Martano, Turin
Centro Rosmini, Trento, Italy
1970   Musée Municipal, St. Paul de Vence, France
Galleria Peccolo, Livorno
Galleria La Chioccola, Padua
Galleria Ghelfi, Vicenza, Italy
1972   Studio Marconi, Milan
Galleria Milano, Milan
Galleria Martano, Turin
Galleria La Polena, Genoa
Galleria Pourquoi-pas, Genoa
Galleria Eunomia, Milan
Galleria dei Mille, Bergamo, Italy
1974   Galleria Pictogramma, Rome
Städtisches Museum, Leverkusen, West Germany
Museo del Teatro della Scala, Milan
Galleria Milano, Milan
Galerie Friedrich, Munich
Galerie Liatowitsch, Basel
1975   Galleria Milano, Milan
Galleria Martano, Turin
Salone della Pilotta, Parma (retrospective)
Studio Marconi, Milan
1978   Galleria Civica, Palazzo dei Diamanti, Ferrara, Italy
        (retrospective)
1981   Galleria Flaviana, Locarno, Switzerland
Galleria Radice, Lissone, Italy
Galleria Toninelli, Rome

Selected Group Exhibitions:

1934   *Mostra Internazionale di Scenografia,* Circolo Nuova Vi-
        ta, Milan
1947   *Arte Astratta e Concreta,* Palazzo Reale, Milan
1955   *Bienal de Sao Paulo,* Brazil
1964   *44 Protagonisi della Visualita Struttura,* Galleria
        Lorenzelli, Milan
1973   *Medium Fotografie,* Städtische Museum, Leverkusen, West
        Germany
1979   *Photographie als Kunst 1879-1979,* Tiroler Landesmuseum
        Ferdinandeum, Innsbruck, Austria (travelled to the Neue
        Galerie am Wolfgang Gurlitt Museum, Linz, Austria; Neue
        Galerie am Landesmuseum Joanneum, Graz. Austria; Muse-
        um des 20. Jahrhunderts, Vienna)
1980   *Photographia: La Linea Sottile,* Galleria Flaviana, Locarno,
        Switzerland
1981   *Photographie Futuriste Italienne 1911-39,* Musée d'Art
        Moderne de la Ville, Paris
1983   *La Sperimentazione Fotografico in Italia 1930-70,* Galleria
        d'Arte Moderna, Bologna, Italy
1984   *Futurism and Photography,* Long Island University, Greenvale,
        New York (travelled to the University of Miami, Coral
        Gables; University of California, Riverside; University of
        New Mexico, Albuquerque)

Collections:

Museo della Fotografia, Università di Parma; Galleria Civica d'Arte Moderna, Turin; Galleria Civica d'Arte Moderna, Ancona; Gallerià Civica, Palazzo dei Diamanti, Ferrara; Galleria Civica, Avezzano; Calcografia Nazionale, Rome; Musée de Saint Paul de Vence, France.

Publications:

By VERONESI: Books—Quaderno di Geometria, with text by Leonardo Sinisgalli, Milan 1936; *14 Variazione di un Tema Pittorico 1936: 14 Variazioni di un Tema Musicale,* with text by Riccardo Malipiero, Milan 1939; *Del Film Astratto,* Milan 1948; *Voyelles,* with text by Arthur Rimbaud, Milan 1959; *15 Disegni di Veronesi,* with text by Osvaldo Patani, Milan 1961; *Le Stelle sono i*

Fiori della Notte, with text by Osvaldo Patani, Milan 1963; *Veronesi,* with text by Osvaldo Patani, Milan 1965; *Veronesi: La Ragioni Astratta,* edited by Paolo Fossati, Turin 1972; *Luigi Veronesi: legni colorati 1977-78,* with text by Miklos N. Varga, Bologna 1978. **Films**—*Caratteri,* 1939; *Viso e Colore,* 1939-40; *Film No. 4,* 1940; *Film No. 5,* 1940; *Film No. 6,* 1941; *Film No. 9,* 1951; *Film No. 13,* 1980-81.

On VERONESI: Books—*Luigi Veronesi: Oeuvres Recentes,* exhibition catalogue, with text by Alain Dalembert, Paris 1956; *Pittura Italiana del Dopoguerra* by Tristan Sauvage, Milan 1957; *Arte Italiana dal Futurismo ad Oggi* by Guido Ballo, Rome 1958; *Nuova Fotografia Italiana* by Giuseppe Turroni, Milan 1959; *Luigi Veronesi: Silografie e Lithografie,* exhibition catalogue, with text by Giulia Veronesi, Milan 1960; *Disegno Moderno in Italia* by Osvaldo Patani, Milan 1960; *Veronesi,* exhibition catalogue, with text by Osvaldo Patani, Milan 1962; *Strutture di Visione,* exhibition catalogue, Rome 1964; *Nuovi Materiali, Nuove Techniche,* Caorle, Italy 1969; *Aspetti del Primo Astrattismo Italiano 1930-1940,* exhibition catalogue, by Luciano Caramel, Monza, Italy 1969; *L'Immagine Sospesa: Pittura e Scultura Astratti in Italia 1934-1940* by Paolo Fossati, Turin 1971; *The Non-Objective World 1939-1955,* exhibition catalogue, edited by George Rickey, London 1972; *Medium Fotografie,* exhibition catalogue, by Rolf Wedewer and L. Romain, Leverkusen, West Germany 1973; *Luigi Veronesi,* exhibition catalogue, with texts by Guido Ballo, Paolo Fossati and others, Parma 1975; *Photographie als Kunst 1879-1979/Kunst als Photographie 1949-1979,* exhibition catalogue, 2 vols., by Peter Weiermair, Innsbruck, Austria 1979; *Photographia: La Linea Sottile,* exhibition catalogue, by Rinald Bianda and Giuliana Scimé, Locarno, Switzerland 1980; *Luigi Veronesi* by Glauco Viazzi, Rome 1980; *Photographie Futuriste Italienne 1911-39,* exhibition catalogue, by Giovanni Lista, Paris 1981; *The Imaginary Photo Museum* by Helmut Gernsheim, Renate and L. Fritz Gruber and others, Cologne 1981, London 1982; *Luigi Veronesi* by Piero Quaglino, Ravenna, Italy 1983; *Futurism and Photography,* exhibition catalogue, by Yolanda Trincere, Greenvale, New York 1984. **Articles**—"Come la Musica puo Diventare Colore" by S. Danese in *Bolaffiarte* (Turin), March 1972; "Sette Schede di Carico" in *Arte Milano* (Milan), May 1972; "Italia" in *NAC* (Milan), May 1972; "Veronesi e Bonfanti" by F. Vincitorio in *NAC* (Milan), November 1972; "Parma: Luigi Veronesi" by Daniela Palazzoli in *Bolaffiarte* (Turin), Summer 1975.

*

I am a painter; for 50 years I have been painting non-representational pictures and for the same time I have also been seeking to express myself in another medium: photography.

The technique of the "photogram"—the picture obtained without using a camera, only with light on the sensitive material—is the one that interests me most and that answers best to what I am aiming for.

The picture that I obtain is never a likeness; to describe or portray an object, I transform the image of the object into a pure design of light and shade.

The "photogram" really originated the first time a ray of light fell on some object and made a shadow.

In the majority of cases the photogram forms part of that "metaphysical" or "abstract" orientation that has influenced and conditioned so much of all modern art. In the photogram objects rediscover their primordial expression; we can see them beyond their actual shape, in pictures that are not apparent to us and yet are true, and that change instantaneously at the movement of the least glimmer of light.

—Luigi Veronesi

*   *   *

Born in 1908, Luigi Veronesi studied art in Milan while still a boy under the guidance of the painter Violante and the avant-garde critic Rafaello Giolli, who were at that time at the center of many of those intellectuals, architects and painters who were later to set the tone of anti-Fascist Italian art. It was not until 1932, however, after long experience in many artistic genres—painting, photography, film, illustration—that Veronesi mounted an exhibition of his work at the Galleria il Milione in Milan.

He then began to travel. He was particularly attracted by Paris, by the sparkling cultural climate stimulated in those years by the protagonists of the historic avant-garde. The avant-garde immediately became the arena of Veronesi's work, animated as he was by a never-satisfied curiosity about research in all the visual arts—a contrast to that academicism in Italy which was chained to the myth, the mythomania, of the Fascist regime.

The friends he made during his stay in Paris were members of the "Abstraction, Création, Art Non-Figuratif" group of 1934, among whom George Vantongerloo was particularly close to him; at the same time he came in contact with other members of the avant-garde, such as László Moholy-Nagy, Max Bill, and Joseph Albers; while in Italy he consorted with Lucio Fontana, Atanasio Soldati, Rene Radice, Mauro Reggiani and Fausto Melotti, men who, at that period, as Giulio Carlo Argan has written, "launched in a disciplined way, with no sensational polemics, a purely formal, non-figurative research."

Veronesi had begun to interest himself in photography as early as 1925, encouraged by his father, who was himself an amateur photographer; but his studies were immediately directed towards a picture freed from the theories of naturalism, seeking a self-sufficient experimentation with new expressive techniques such as the photogram and investigating the language of photography not as a means of "documentary reproduction" but as a creative instrument. In this, Moholy-Nagy was his most authentic master: his work, as Paolo Fossati has written, "not only became a reference point always to be kept in view but, by setting Veronesi outside every Italian context, made him a very special case in events in Italy."

Photography, painting, cinema, illustration—Veronesi used all these techniques in a search for new figurative solutions, which in this artist tend to be essentials, cleansed of every traditional semantic superstructure. In the Italian cultural climate of those years, when "19th centuryism" and, in photography, "pictorialism" were dominant, Veronesi's actions were inevitably provocative—but they seemed less so because of his association with various rationalist authors, who together with certain other photographers (Scopinich, Lattuada, Comencini) and some book-creators (Steiner, Boggeri, Grignani), were building a new cultural foundation which, in the case of photography, was to be given voice by the magazine *Domus* in its yearbook *Fotografia* of 1943, still an invaluable source of information about historic events in Italian photography.

In 1937, besides producing abstract photograms, Veronesi employed solarization techniques (the Sabbatier effect), which Man Ray had already experimented with in the 1920s but the effects obtained by the Italian photographer were less dramatic than Ray's, often decorative, sometimes making use of advertising layouts, with which he was concerned at the time. Photography also had its part in the many stage sets that Veronesi designed in those years for leading theatres, including La Fenice in Venice and La Scala in Milan. In 1941 his remarkable sets for Malipiero's *Balletto* appeared, which included the projection of an abstract film. For a long time Veronesi concentrated on experimental films, and in 1949 he won the prize for the "best utilization of color" at the *International Film Festival* at Knokke-le-Zoute.

In Luigi Veronesi's research, writes Giuliana Ferrari, "the *experimental* aspect is stressed in an examination of the artistic operation, which he tends to organize as a methodology of vision . . .": Veronesi's creativity, which is both fresh and tireless, is not an end in itself but has as its goal the establishment of a new semantic parameter, of a hitherto unknown lexical element to be added to his stimulating, hypothetical grammar of seeing.

It is a "grammar" that he has constructed not only through the alchemy of the laboratory but also by means of a direct reading of elementary objects such as rocks or the bark of trees, bringing to light hidden forms in them quite foreign to their surroundings, so as to suggest a different reading of reality, always to the limits of abstraction, in a visual space which in Veronesi's pictures appears fantastic.

With macrophotography and microphotography (the latter a technique that he has been using for a long time), Veronesi has tried to retrace the affinities and formal analogies of the "very small" and the microscopic, putting forward a visual "continuum," as it were an idea of the *infinite,* which would be symbolized by the inexhaustibility of forms that the picture can include, different only because of their conventional dimensions, but confirmed by the photographic relief. It is as if Veronesi found his natural "landscape" in the microscope, as if he found himself very much at ease in this dimension, where the optical instrument or polarized light revealed to him an inexhaustible universe of forms, surprisingly similar to those of his photograms, executed directly on sensitized photographic paper in the darkroom.

Luigi Veronesi—who is best known as a painter—has since his early youth sought out in photography and films the languages that are perhaps most congenial to him, but he has had a great struggle to get these "machine-made" pictures appreciated on the same level as painting and drawing in the Italian cultural environment, where these techniques have always been looked at askance, as if their use involved a sort of secondary "minor art." Veronesi's activity has thus been a kind of witness to his faith in the photographic medium. With his friends, he has been involved in a long battle—in promoting photography, collaborating in the organization of photographic exhibitions, and in the publication of books and articles on photography. In 1947, with Giuseppe Cavalli, Mario Finazzi, Ferruccio Leiss and Federico Vender, he founded the Bussola Group, which had a notable influence on post-war Italian photography in the period when the foundations of a culture which had been the victim of Fascism, which now sought to be integrated with art throughout the Western world, making up for lost time, were being rebuilt.

Veronesi, then, has been among the very few artists in Italy in a position to suggest a line of research in the field of photography, with his work influenced by the experiments of the avant-garde outside Italy, of which he has been a member since the start of the 1920s. His contribution has been fundamental to the development of Italian photography, its purging of provincialism, and Veronesi has certainly worked as few others have, as Wladimiro Settimelli writes, to "chuck out photography of Fascist stamp"—which in Italy has long been taken to mean the representational.

—Italo Zannier

VESTAL, David.

Nationality: American. **Born:** Menlo Park, California, 21 March 1924. **Education:** University High School, Urbana, Illinois, 1938-41; studied painting at the Art Institute of Chicago, 1941-44; photography, privately, with Sid Grossman, New York, intermittently 1947-55. **Family:** Married Ann Treer in 1961; daughter: Anne Doherty. **Career:** Photographer since 1947. Assistant to Ralph Steiner, New York, 1955-57; freelance magazine photographer, New York, 1957-63. Private teacher in photography since 1956. Dean, New York Institute of Photography, 1965-66; Instructor in Photography, School of Visual Arts, New York, 1967-72, 1986-1993; Visiting Artist in Photography, Art Institute of Chicago, 1972-73; Visiting Lecturer in Photography, University of New Mexico, Albuquerque, 1974; Instructor in Photography, College of Santa Fe, New Mexico, 1975-77; Instructor, Parsons School of Design, New York, 1984-1994. Instructor in Photography, Pratt Institute, Brooklyn, New York, 1987-present. Freelance writer on photography since 1961. Associate Editor, 1967-69, and Contributing Editor 1975-86, *Popular Photography* magazine, New York; Associate Editor, *Travel and Camera* and *Camera 35* magazines, New York, 1969-71, Associate Editor, *Camera Arts* magazine, New York, 1982-83. Contributing Editor, *Darkroom Techniques* magazine, Niles, Illinois, 1988-present. Writer and publisher, *Grump,* newsletter on photography, 1988-present. **Recipient:** Guggenheim Fellowship in Photography, 1966, 1973. **Agent:** Frances Collin, P.O. Box 33, Wayne, Pennsylvania 19087-0033, U.S.A. **Address:** P.O. Box 309, Bethlehem, Connecticut 06751-0309, U.S.A.

Individual Exhibitions:

1954	Limelight Gallery, New York
1955	A Photographer's Gallery, New York
1958	American Institute of Graphic Art, New York (with Ann Treer)
1959	Smithsonian Institution, Washington, D.C.
	Image Gallery, New York
1961	Limelight Gallery, New York
	3 Photographers, Kalamazoo Institute of Arts, Michigan (with Wynn Bullock and Aaron Siskind)
1963	University of Maine, Orono
1967	Temple University, Philadelphia
1971	Witkin Gallery, New York
	Museum of New Mexico, Santa Fe (with Wayne Lazorik)

Rio de Janeiro, Brazil, **1960.** Photograph by David Vestal.

Focus Gallery, San Francisco (with Ralph Gibson)
1975   East Street Gallery, Grinnell, Iowa
Midtown Y Gallery, New York (with Larry Siegel)
1979   MFA Gallery, Rochester Institute of Technology, Rochester,
New York
1984   A Personal Gallery, Greensboro, North Carolina
1985   Tom Zimmerman Fine Arts, New Hope, Pennsylvania
1987   Salon de la Plástica Mexicana, Mexico City
Galeria del Bosque, Guadalajara, Mexico
New England Photo Workshops, New Milford, Connecticut
1988   Casa de la Cultura Jalisciense, Guadalajara, Mexico
New England Photo Workshops, New Milford, Connecticut
1989   Daytona Beach Community College, Florida
New England Photo Workshops, New Milford, Connecticut
1990   New England Photo Worskhops, New Milford, Connecticut

Selected Group Exhibitions:

1967   *Photography U.S.A. '67,* De Cordova Museum, Lincoln,
Massachusetts
1969   *Vision and Expression,* International Museum of Photography,
George Eastman House, Rochester, New York (toured the
United States, 1969-71)
1978   *Photographic Crossroads: The Photo League,* National Gallery
of Canada, Ottawa (travelled to the International Center of
Photography, New York; Museum of Fine Arts, Houston;
and Minneapolis Institute of Arts)
1979   *The Great West: Real/Ideal,* University of Colorado, Boulder
(subsequently Smithsonian Institution travelling exhibition;
toured the United States)
1985   *The Photo League,* Photofind Gallery, Woodstock, New York
The New York School, Corcoran Gallery, Washington, D.C.

Collections:

Museum of Modern Art, New York; International Museum of Photography,
George Eastman House, Rochester, New York; Art Institute of Chicago; High
Museum of Art, Atlanta; Museum of Fine Art, St. Petersburg, Florida;
Museum of New Mexico, Santa Fe; University of New Mexico Art Museum,
Albuquerque; Houston Museum of Fine Arts, Texas; Metropolitan Museum of
Art, New York; New York Public Library; Rochester Institute of Technology,
Rochester, New York; Center for Creative Photography, University of Arizo-
na, Tucson; University of Louisville, Kentucky; National Gallery of Canada,
Ottawa, Ontario, Canada.

Publications:

By VESTAL: Books—Cape Cod, portfolio of 6 photographs, New York
1960; *U.S. Camera Annual 1971,* editor, New York 1970; *Leica Manual,*
editor, with others, New York 1972; *The Craft of Photography,* New York
1975; *The Art of Black-and-White Enlarging,* New York 1984. **Articles**—
numerous, mainly in *Popular Photography* (New York), *Camera 35* (New
York), *Infinity* (New York), since 1962; and *Darkroom Techniques,* (Niles,
Illinois), since 1987.

*

I try to evoke feeling both by form and by information given in the
pictures. The mode is conventional ''straight'' photography in black and
white.Subjects are whatever I feel like photographing: places and conditions
more often than people and events, but nothing is ruled out.

I try for accuracy, without understatement or melodrama; the result is often
mistaken for understatement. I'm after depth and am indifferent to impact.

I work mostly in single pictures as they present themselves; not projects. I
don't plan work, but improvise it. No rules or systems.

I do not work on assignment: to quote Berenice Abbott's quotation from
Atget, ''People don't know what to photograph.'' I recognize mine when I see
it, not before.

The criteria are feeling and clarity.

—David Vestal

*   *   *

David Vestal is perhaps best known to American photographers as a writer
whose wise and often iconoclastic views have appeared in many photographic
magazines. In fact, however, he is an accomplished and award winning
photographer who also writes and teaches.

After a short period at the Art Institute of Chicago, where he studied
painting, Vestal moved to New York in 1946. There he ''discovered photography,'' becoming an active member of the Photo League and a student of Sid
Grossman. From 1955 to 1957 he worked as assistant to Ralph Steiner while
also starting to develop his own career. His quiet, introspective photographs
have appeared in most of the major magazines in the United States and his
pictures are in the permanent collections of the George Eastman House and the
Museum of Modern Art.

Vestal has held two prestigeous Guggenheim Awards, the first in 1966 and
the second in 1973-74. These have allowed him to travel in the southwestern
United States seeking ''the places that people ignore.''

In the late 1950s Vestal began to teach private seminars in photography to
small groups of serious students. This, and more institutional teaching, has
continued. From 1967 to 1972 he taught at the School of Visual Arts in New
York. In 1972-73 he taught at the Art Institute, ''which was fun, because I had
dropped out of there years ago.''

Vestal began to write free lance articles for *Popular Photography* in 1963,
becoming a member of the staff in 1967. He is now contributing editor of the
magazine. He has also written for *Travel and Camera* and *Camera 35*. His
book, *The Craft of Photography,* is a lucid discussion of straight black-and-
white still photography. He is currently writing a book on fine printing
techniques.

—F. Jack Hurley

VISHNIAC, Roman.

Nationality: American. **Born:** Pavlovsk, Russia, 19 August 1897; emigrated
to the United States, 1940; naturalized, 1946. **Education:** Studied zoology and
medicine at Shanyavsky University, Moscow, 1914-20, Ph.D. 1920; also
studied oriental art at the University of Berlin in the 1920s; self-taught in
photography. **Military Service:** Served in the Tsarist, Kerensky and Soviet
Armies, Russia, 1914-17. **Family:** Married; one son and one daughter.
Career: Lived in Berlin, 1920-30: worked at various odd jobs and as a
medical/scientific researcher, 1920-35; freelance photographer, documenting
Jewish life and problems in Germany and Eastern Europe, 1935-39; moved to
France, 1939: imprisoned as stateless person at Du Richard, Annot, France,
1940. Freelance portrait and medical microphotographer, New York, from
1940. Chevron Professor of Creativity, Pratt Institute, New York; Visiting
Professor of Art, Rhode Island School of Design, Providence. **Recipient:**
Honor Award, American Society of Magazine Photographers, 1956. **Died:** 27
January 1990.

Individual Exhibitions:

1939   Musée du Louvre, Paris
1941   Teachers College, New York
1962   *Through the Looking-Glass,* IBM Gallery, New York
1963   *3 Photographers in Color,* Museum of Modern Art, New York
(with Helen Levitt and William Garnett)
1971   *The Concerns of Roman Vishniac,* Jewish Museum, New York
1973   The Photographers' Gallery, London
1977   *Jewish Ghettos of Eastern Europe 1936-39,* Witkin Gallery,
New York
1979   Photopia Gallery, Philadelphia
1985   Chrysler Museum, Norfolk, Virginia

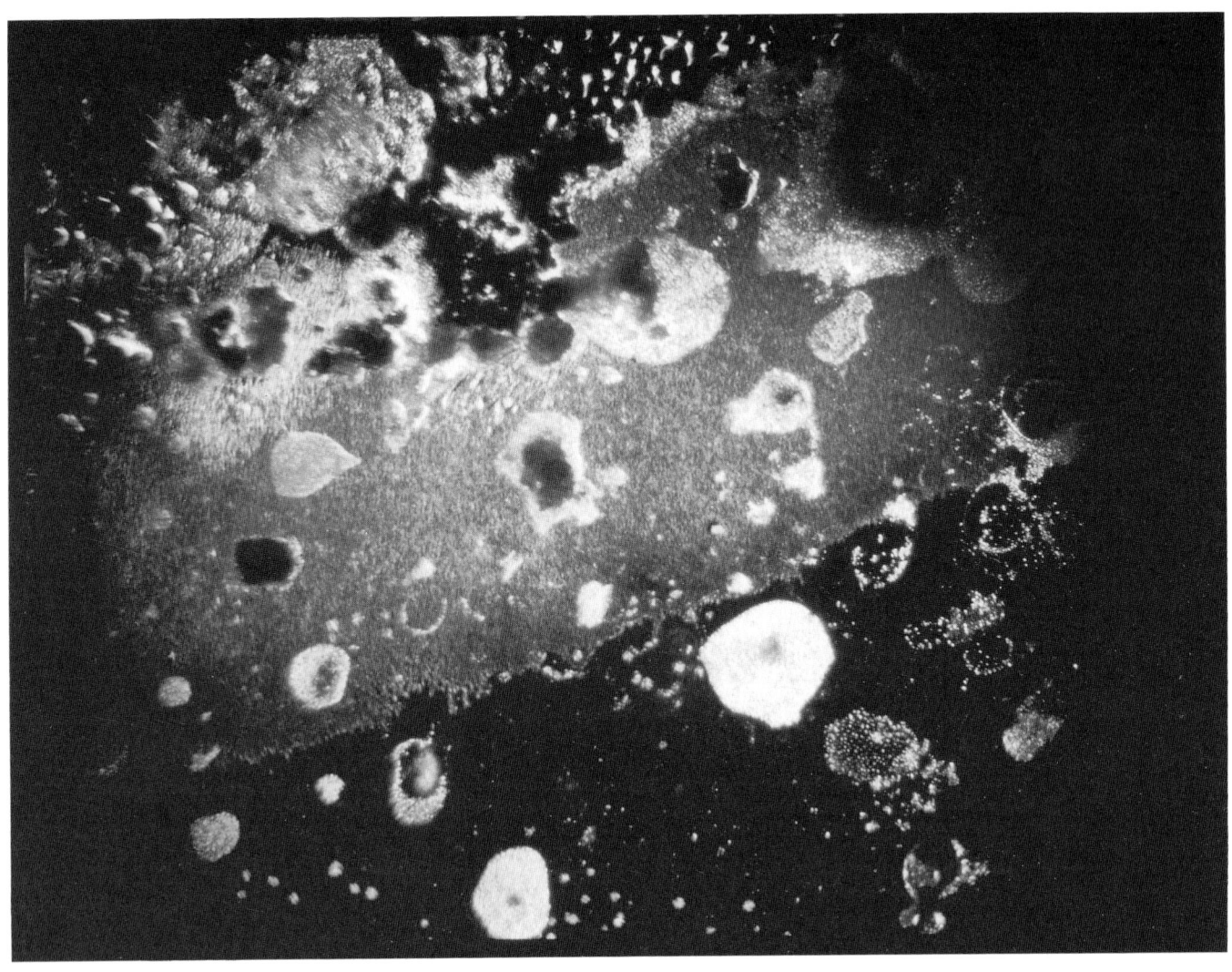

48 Vitamin C/Ascorbic Acid (original in colour). Photograph by Roman Vishniac.

1993   *The Photographs of Roman Vishniac: Man, Nature and Science 1930-1985,* International Center of Photography, New York

Selected Group Exhibitions:

1960   *The Sense of Abstraction,* Museum of Modern Art, New York
1973   *The Concerned Photographer II,* Israel Museum, Jerusalem (toured Europe)
1979   *10th Anniversary Show,* Witkin Gallery, New York
        Life: The First Decade 1936-45, Grey Art Gallery, New York University
1980   *The Imaginary Photo Museum,* Kunsthalle, Cologne
1982   *International Photography 1920-80,* Australian National Gallery, Canberra
        Lichtbildnisse: Das Porträt in der Fotografie, Rheinisches Landesmuseum, Bonn

Collections:

Museum of Modern Art, New York; Jewish Museum, New York; Library of Congress, Washington, D.C.; Smithsonian Institution, Washington, D.C.; Roman Vishniac Archive, International Center of Photography, New York.

Publications:

By VISHNIAC: Books—*Polish Jews: A Pictorial Record,* with text by Abraham Joshua Heschel, New York 1942, 1965, as *Les Juifs de Passe,* Paris 1979; *A Day of Pleasure,* with text by Isaac Bashevis Singer, New York 1969; *Building Blocks of Life,* New York 1971; *Roman Vishniac,* with text by Eugene Kinkead, New York 1974; *Roman Vishniac: The Vanished World of the Shtetl,* portfolio of 12 photos, New York 1978, as *The Life That Disappeared,* New York 1980; *Roman Vishniac: Einstein,* portfolio of 7 photos, New York 1980; *A Vanished World,* with foreword by Elie Wesel, New York and London 1983.

On VISHNIAC: Books—*How Life Gets the Story: Behind the Scenes in Photo-Journalism,* edited by Stanley Rayfield, New York 1955; *Polaroid Portfolio No. 1,* edited by John Walbarst, New York 1959; *The Concerned Photographer II,* edited by Cornell Capa, New York 1972; *The Magic Image* by Cecil Beaton and Gail Buckland, London and Boston 1975; *A Ten Year Salute* by Lee D. Witkin, foreword by Carol Brown, Danbury, New Hampshire 1979; *Life: The First Decade 1936-1945* by Robert Littman, Ralph Graves and Doris C. O'Neill, New York 1979, London 1980; *The Photograph Collector's Guide* by Lee D. Witkin and Barbara London, Boston and London 1979; *The Imaginary Photo Museum* by Helmut Gernsheim, Renate and L. Fritz Gruber and others, Cologne 1981, London 1982; *Lichtbildnisse: Das*

Porträt in der Fotografie, edited by Klaus Honnef, Cologne 1982. **Articles—** "The Concerns of Roman Vishniac" by M. Edelin in *Infinity* (New York), October 1971; "The Magnification of Roman Vishniac" by M. Edelson in *Camera 35* (New York), October 1974; "The Concerned Photographer" by Cornell Capa in *Zoom* (Paris), no. 16, 1973; "Roman Vishniac" by Inge Bondi in *Die Weltwoche* (Zurich), 20 September 1978; "The Photomicrographic World of Roman Vishniac" by Francene Sabin in *Omni* (New York), October 1978; "Roman Vishniac" by Erla Zwingle in *American Photographer* (New York), July 1981.

* * *

Personal experience, culture, family and ethnic traditions, even a particular mother tongue—all of these factors constitute the connecting tissue of the personality of an individual. In the artist in particular these "biographical" characteristics have a deep influence on the individual's chosen mode of expression. And certain choices, apparently casual, can lead to the discovery of working tools, lifelong passions. In photography there seems to be almost an infinity of examples—from Lartigue to Bill Brandt to Aaron Siskind, all of whom became photographers because they found themselves with a camera in their hands by chance, and chance resolved an inward questioning. And so it was with Roman Vishniac, who was given a camera and a microscope when he was only six; he was already intensely curious about nature.

That trivial episode—long ago in 1904—was the first step to a destiny: science and photography have been interwoven throughout the whole of Vishniac's life. He is one of the great humanists of our time, a man in the tradition of the Italian Renaissance, when the figure of the scientist-artist was the key to the thought of the epoch that opened the door to the modern world. Science and art, then, were not in conflict—and neither are they in conflict for Vishniac: a simultaneity of expression of pure reason and abstraction is a reflection of the sublime expression of nature itself. A rare exponent of the new humanism, Vishniac has replaced empirical research with the modern tools of technology and the brush with the camera. Vishniac has a particular love for natural history, from the microscopic world of the life of insects to the world of the life of man. Patience, scrupulous reasoning, strict documentation, organized reasearch—he applies all of these gifts to the magic instrument of photography which he uses for the recording of truth.

Internationally recognized for this work, for his outstanding research and photographic records, Vishniac entered the world of creative photography with a remarkable historical account of the Jewish communities of Eastern Europe, communities that were later completely wiped out by the methodical barbarity of the Nazis. In fact, this step involved no break in Vishniac's photographic methods: his scientific records and his human records spring from the same philosophy of life, a regard for every organism as an essential and irreplaceable part of the harmony of the universe. There is nothing casual about Vishniac. In four years, starting in 1936, he made a series of journeys to the eastern European ghettos, journeys that covered 5,000 miles, to record a world that he knew would disappear: "And I thought maybe years and years after the killing, maybe the Jews will be interested to hear of the life that disappeared, of the life that is no more, and I went from country to country, from town to village. . . . It was a terrible task; I was many times in prison, but I returned again and again because I wanted to save the faces." He thus preserved the memory of what could no longer exist. Urged on by a conscious foresight based on a knowledge and analysis of past history, he responded to an inward necessity in himself which, as an individual belonging to an ethnic group, he transformed into the necessity of an entire community.

What is so extraordinary about Vishniac's account (apart from its enormous historical value) is the way in which he has made visual records as if in a sketchbook, a series of minute observations of customs that enables him to reconstruct the everyday history of a people. Accustomed to move about in the world of nature as if he were invisible, so as to leave its life undisturbed, he now moved unseen among people recording their attitudes, expressions, movements. In order not to interfere with their everyday activities he kept his camera concealed, operating it with his delicate hands by loving instinct. He became an integrated member of the community. His pictures record life as it was and, even though 40 years have passed, have the life and spontaneous freshness of pictures made today. Vishniac's transcends the limitations he imposed on himself: we are no longer looking at a historical record—"The life that disappeared; the vanished world of the Shtetl"—but at memory, which art can make eternal.

Every picture has a quality so tangible that we can feel the piercing cold in our bones and ourselves experience the worry that wrinkles the face of a woman, the disappointment of an unhappy little girl, the thoughtful wisdom of a studious old man, the shy smile of a youth setting out on a life that will never be—the fear, the desperation of not understanding the reason for the cruelty. And over it all, the song of prayer. . . . The testament of Vishniac is the visual counterpart of the tradition of mystically inspired Jewish culture, a historical cycle that ends in tragedy. The tales of Sholem Aleichem, the stories of Isaac Bashevis Singer, the philosophy and teaching of Hassidism collected by Martin Buber: these tell of men and places, of conditions and customs, of beliefs and sentiments—a whole world wiped out that can never be rebuilt. Vishniac grasps this world in its last moments, photographs it, fixes it forever. It is a heritage for everyone in the world who, through his work, may know that which they were never able to see.

Vishniac's words, "Nature, God, or whatever you want to call the creator of the universe comes through the microscope clearly and strongly. Everything made by human hands looks terrible under magnification—crude, rough and unsymmetrical. But in nature every bit of life is lovely"—these words reveal the man to us, Vishniac the scientist and artist, and the profound value of his work.

—Giuliana Scimé

VOGT, Christian.

Nationality: Swiss. **Born:** Basel, 12 April 1946. **Education:** Studied photography at the Schule für Gestaltung, Basel, 1964-67. **Career:** Worked as an assistant to the photographer Will McBride, Munich, 1968. Established own studio, Basel, 1969. **Recipient:** *Photokina* Award, Cologne, 1972; Swiss National Scholarship, 1974, 1975; Grand Prix, *Triennale of Photography,* Fribourg, Switzerland, 1975; Lion's Club Art Award, 1976; Canada Council Grant, 1977; Art Directors Club Award, (Germany), 1978; Photography Grant, Erziehungsdepartement Basel-Stadt, 1984, 1986. Art Directors Club Award (Switzerland), 1987; Silver Award for "Baudokumentation" Calendar, Architectural Information Services, Switzerland, 1987; Art Directors Club Award (Los Angeles), 1988; Art Directors Club Award (New York), 1988; Clio Award, New York, 1988; Golden Egg Award, Sweden, 1988; Kunstpreis der Stadt Basel, 1992; Art Directors' Awards "Aids Campaign," 1993. **Agent:** Sue Allatt, 30C Great Sutton Street, London EC1, England. **Address:** Augustinergasse 3, 4051 Basel, Switzerland.

Individual Exhibitions:

1972	Galerie Hilt, Basel
1973	Galeria Il Diaframma, Milan
1974	Canon Gallery, Amsterdam
	Galleria Il Diaframma, Milan
	Galleria Documenta, Turin
	Galleria Schillerhof, Graz, Austria
1975	The Photographers' Gallery, London
	Galerie Christine, Paris
	Galerie Rivolta, Lausanne
1976	Kunsthaus, Zurich
	Galerie in der Altstadt, Zug, Switzerland
	Galerie im Forum Stadtpark, Graz, Austria
	Photoselection, Dusseldorf
	Hotel de Ville, Lausanne
1977	Galerie Jean Dieuzaide, Toulouse, France
	Canon Galerie, Geneva
	Yajima Galerie, Montreal, Quebec
	Salzburg College, Austria
	Art '77, Basel
	Focus Gallery, Ljubljana, Yugoslavia
1978	Galerie Handschin, Basel
	International Center of Photography, New York
	Focus Gallery, San Francisco

Untitled. Photograph ©Christian Vogt.

	Trudelhaus, Baden, Switzerland
1979	University of North Dakota, Grand Forks
	Galerie Trockenpresse, West Berlin
	Tel Aviv Museum
1980	Galerie Photo Art, Basel
	Jacques Baruch Gallery, Chicago
	Boris Gallery, Boston
	Rencontres Internationales de la Photographie, Arles, France
	Nikon Galerie, Zurich
1981	Galerie Watari, Tokyo
	Preus Fotomuseum, Horten, Norway
	Blixt Gallery, Ann Arbor, Michigan
	Galerij Paule Pia, Antwerp
	Netzhaut Photogalerie, Frankfurt
	Paule Pia Gallery, Antwerp, Belgium (and Brussels)
1982	Galerie Le Reverbre, Lyon, France
	Work Gallery, Zurich
	Galerie Suzanne Kuepfer, Nidau-Bienne, Switzerland
	Portfolio Gallery, San Francisco
1983	CCD Galerie, Dusseldorf, West Germany
	Kunstmuseum, Hannover
	Edwynn Houk Gallery, Chicago
	Berowergut, Kunstverein Riehen, Switzerland
	Vienne La Photographie, Vienne, France
	Kornshutte, Lucerne, Switzerland
	Fotogalerij 't Peppertje, Diepenbeek, Belgium
	Galerie XYZ, Ghent, Belgium
	GGK Galerie, Vienna
	Galerie Gabriel, Vienna
	Galerie Der Ring, Vienna
1984	Netzhaut Galerie, Frankfurt
1985	Galleria Nostra Descrittiva, Rimini, Italy
	Galerie Fotografia Oltre, Chiasso, Switzerland
	Olympus Galerie, Hamburg
	Galerie für Fotografie, Stuttgart
	Galerie Photo Art, Basel, Switzerland
	Galerie Pro Photo, Nuremberg, West Germany
1986	Gewerbemuseum, Basel, Switzerland
	Museum für Gestaltung, Basel
1987	Fotoforum, Lucerne, Switzerland
1988	Musée de l'Elysée, Lausanne, Switzerland
	Neikrug Gallery, New York
	Fotoforum Pasquart, Bienne
1989	Galeria del'Arte Moderna, Bologna, Italy
	Gallery Draajer and Fiolet, Amsterdam
	Swiss Institute, New York

1990	*Innenräume,* Architekturmuseum in Basel
	Les Halles, Paris Audiovisuel, Paris
1991	*Schlachtfelder,* Galerie Littmann
	Espaces interieure, Ecole Polytechnique Féderale de Lausanne, Lausanne
1992	Museo Ken Damy, Brescia, Milan
	Banca di Vicenza, Italy

Selected Group Exhibitions:

1972	*Photokina '72,* Cologne
1975	*Art as Photography/Photography as Art,* Musée Nicéphore Niepce, Chalon-sur-Saône, France
1977	*Festival Internationale d'Art,* Royan, France
1979	*Photographie als Kunst 1879-1979,* Tiroler Landesmuseum Ferdinandeum, Innsbruck, Austria (travelled to the Neue Galerie am Wolfgang Gurlitt Museum, Linz, Austria; Neue Galerie am Landesmuseum Joanneum, Graz, Austria; and Museum des 20. Jahrhunderts, Vienna)
1980	*Photographia: La Linea Sottile,* Galleria Flaviana, Locarno, Switzerland
1981	*Farbe im Photo,* Josef-Haubrich-Kunsthalle, Cologne
1983	*In Grand Perspective: Polaroids,* The Photographers' Gallery, London
1985	*Swiss Photography from 1840 until Today,* Pro Helvetia Foundation, Zurich (and world tour)
	Das Aktfoto, Fotomuseum im Stadtmuseum, Munich (toured West Germany)
1986	*Fifty Years of Colour,* Galeria Foto Vision, Madrid
	L'Art et le Regard, Musée de l'Elysée, Lausanne, Switzerland
	Landschaften, Fotogalerie in der Schwanenberg, Kleve
	10 Jahre, Galerie Photo Art Basel, Basel
1987	*Encontros de Fotografia,* Coimbra, Portugal
	Galerie für Fotografie, Stuttgart, Germany
	Hettinga De Lang Possel DeBoers Galerie, Amsterdam
	Aktfoto, Zurich, Switzerland
1988	*L'Arc Lemanique,* Musée de l'Elysée, Lausanne, Switzerland
	Behold the Man, Stills Gallery, Edinburgh
	La Gloire et Misère du Corps, Musée d'Art et d'Histoire, Fribourg, Germany
	Mois de la Photo, Paris
	FotoPorto, Casa de Serralves, Porto, Portugal
1989	*Arrangements,* Mai 36 Galerie, Lucerne
	Contemporary Swiss Photography, Galerie zur Stockeregg, Zurich
1990	*Wichtige Bilder,* Museum für Gestaltung, Zurich

1991	*The Fourth Wall—Photography as Theatre,* Amsterdam, (travelling)
	Überall ist Jemand, Museum für Gestaltung, Zurich
1992	*Sonderfall,* Schweizerisches Landesmuseum, Zurich
1993	*Bali,* Museum of Anthropology, Basel
	Fototage Frankfurt, Frankfurt
	A la Recherche du Père, Paris Audiovisuel, Paris
1994	*Tabu—Love and Aids,* Galerie Fabian Walter, Basel

Collections:

Stiftung für Photographie, Kunsthaus, Zurich; Hoffmann Stiftung, Gegenwartsmuseum, Basel; Die Neue Sammlung, Munich; Bibliothèque Nationale, Paris; Moderna Museet, Stockholm; Preus Fotomuseum, Horten, Norway; Tel Aviv Museum; Museum Ludwig, Cologne; Musei Comunali di Rimini, Italy; Università di Parma, Italy; Polaroid Collection, Cambridge, Massachusetts, USA; Getty Foundation (Sam Wagstaff Collection), Los Angeles; Hartkamp's Collection, Amsterdam; Ilford Collection, London; Polaroid International Collection, Amsterdam; Fritz Gruber Sammlung, Cologne; Centro Studi e Archivo della Communicazione, University of Parma, Parma; Grupa Junij, Ljubljana, Yugoslavia; Albert Sammlung, Vienna; B Schürch, Fondation, Nestlé, Diener und Diener Architekten, Basel; Sammlung Ludwig, Frankfurt; Museé de l'Elysée, Lausanne.

Publications:

By VOGT: Books—*Christian Vogt: Photographs,* with text by Sue Davies, Fritz Gruber and Allan Porter, Geneva 1980; *Christian Vogt,* portfolio, Chicago 1981; *Photoedition 5: Christian Vogt,* Schaffhausen, Switzerland 1982; *In Camera, 82 Images by 52 Women,* Geneva 1982; *Fotografische Notizen und notierte Zufalle,* Basel 1984; *Katzenschattenhase,* Basel, 1988; *Catshadowhare,* 1989; *Schlachtfelder,* catalogue, Basel, 1991; *Christian Vogt—Light Fingering the Piano Cover,* Zurich, 1991; *Bilder einer Ausstellung,* Basel, 1992; *Århus—Seen Through the Eyes of Christian Vogt and Poul Ib Henricksen,* Denmark, 1992.

On VOGT: Books—*Photokina '72: Bilder und Texte,* edited by L. Fritz Gruber, Cologne 1972; *Women by 10,* Chicago 1973; *Four Masters of Erotic Photography,* London 1972; *SX 70 Art,* edited by Ralph Gibson, New York 1979; *Photographie als Kunst 1879-1979/Kunst als Photographie 1949-1979,* exhibition catalogue, 2 volumes, by Peter Weiermair, Innsbruck 1979; *Dumont Foto II,* edited by Hugo Schottle, Cologne 1980; *Photographia: La Linea Sottile,* exhibition catalogue, by Giuliana Scimé and Rinaldo Bianda, Locarno, Switzerland 1980; *Women in the Magic Mirror* by Giuliana Scime, Milan 1981; *The Imaginary Photo Museum* by Helmut Gernsheim, Renate and L. Fritz Gruber and others, Cologne 1981, Cologne 1982; *Private Viewing: Contemporary Erotic Photography,* edited by Terry Jones, London 1983; *Swiss Photography from 1840 until Today,* exhibition catalogue, with introduction by Huto Loetscher, Zurich 1984; *Der erotische Augenblick* by Hans Freyermuth and Rainer Fabian, Hamburg 1984; *Nude Photography: The Art and Technique of Nine Modern Masters,* edited by Peter Lacey, New York 1985; *Männer Sehen Männer,* Schaffhausen, 1987; *Professionelle Beleuchtungstechnik,* Jost Marchesi, Schaffhausen, 1987; *The Naked and the Nude,* Jorge Lewinski, London, 1987; *Rooms,* B & R Khatir Editori, 1990; *Unerwartete Schweizer,* Zurich, 1993; *Graphis Photo,* New York, Zurich, 1993. **Articles**—"Vogt" in *Camera* (Lucerne), August 1970; "Sequence" and "Sequence, part 2" in *Camera* (Lucerne), February 1971 and October 1972; "Christian Vogt: Zwischen Hirsingue und Werentzhouse" in *Du* (Zurich), April 1971; "Christian Vogt: Dreams and Reality" in *Photography Year,* by the Time-Life editors, New York 1973; "Christian Vogt" in *Camera* (Lucerne), March 1973; "Baselr Zuhause: 19 Aufnahmen von Christian Vogt" in *Du* (Zurich), February 1974; "Christian Vogt" in *British Journal of Photography* (London), 25 October 1974; "Christian Vogt: Wohnungsportraets" in *Werk* (Zurich), December 1974; "Bilder aus dem Jura," special issue of *Du* (Zurich), no. 7, 1981; "Schweizer Fotografen" in *Du* (Zurich), no. 8, 1985; "Basel," special issue of *Du* (Zurich), no. 2, 1986; *Direction Magazine,* London, September, 1987; *Photographie,* No. 2, 1987; *Schweizerische Photo Rundschau,* July, 1987; *Graphis International,* Interview and Portfolio, Nov/Dec, 1988; "Black and White Portfolio," *Schori & Partner Media Agentur und Verlag,* no. 2, 1990; "documenta ix," Special Issue, *Basler Zeitung,*

1992; "Donne con oggetti," *Zoom,* No. 118, 1992; "Kunst in der Schweiz," *Ars Helvetica,* Vol.XII, 1992; "20 Jahre Nikon-News," *Nikon-News,* No. 2, 1994.

*

I think that there is almost nothing that I identify with. I sometimes feel as if something good happens through me, and this I enjoy. I just play and work: I learn to understand only through doing.

—Christian Vogt

*   *   *

Christian Vogt has combined an intellectual and technical approach in his photography to produce "made" rather than "taken" photographs. Working from an early age in the medium of advertising, he has been aware of the value of subliminal ideas concealed beneath a beautiful surface image. Surrealism has always intrigued photographers and on the face of it appears sometimes an easy option and over-exploited by the advertising fraternity. Because Vogt has always been interested in exploring the evocation of associations in his own work and in pushing the possibilities to the limits of photography, making use of the qualities of reality which the medium carries with it, he has been able to continue his own work while utilising some of the simpler ideas for his clients. The "frame" series explored not only the limitations of the rectangular frame, an old problem for both painters and photographers, but by the addition of the nude or scantily dressed figure, also discussed the role of women as caged objects. In the same way the "red" series not only used the great swathes of colour in a dramatic way but also as a series held some of the ritualistic associations of this colour with the female cycle.

Now that his work is selling well, Vogt is able to try to explore more complex ideas. He appears to believe in the collective unconscious and in his search to visualise ideas that are common to us all, the early work is being overtaken by less easily assimilable images. Since his technique is prodigious and the perfectionism of his finished image is important to him, the problem arises that the viewer can be seduced by the surface quality of a print and thus prevented from seeing or absorbing the more complicated message it may contain. To help avoid this, he has created pictures recently that are less obviously beautiful and require more effort on the part of the viewer.

Unlike many other European photographers working in fashion and advertising, Christian Vogt has not completely changed his style or methods when undertaking personal projects. By using all his expertise he has explored ideas which in themselves are the opposite and balancing factors to the positive and cheerful images required by clients. His photographs of museum objects and their settings produced a rather bleak look at those things which our forebears felt to be important to save and collect. He then undertook research and in 1991 produced a book on Swiss battlefields through the ages in which he appears to be searching for any remaining frisson in places where there has been massive and sudden death. He is currently engaged on a series of portraits taken in a portable studio around the world. It will be interesting to see the sort of people he selects for this excercise, and what he will bring to it that is different from previous series done by Penn and Avedon.

—Sue Davies

von GAGERN, Verena.

Nationality: German. **Born:** Verena Merkl in Bonn, 1 December 1946. **Education:** Humanistisches Gymnasium, Cologne, 1956-65; studied architecture at the Technical University, Aachen, 1966-70, and architecture and planning at Pennsylvania State University, University Park, 1970-72, M.A.Arch. 1972. **Family:** Married Michael von Gagern in 1968; children: Franziska and Moritz. **Career:** Freelance photographer, Munich, since 1972. Teaching

Assistant, Pennsylvania State University, 1972-73; Instructor, Salzburg College of Photography, Austria, 1975-79. **Recipient:** Young Photographer's Prize, *Rencontres Internationales de la Photographie,* Arles, France, 1975. **Address:** Genterstrasse 13, 8 Munich 40, Germany.

Individual Exhibitions:

1975	Galleria Il Diaframma, Milan
	Galerij Paule Pia, Antwerp
	Galerie Fiolet, Amsterdam
1976	Salzburg College Gallery, Austria
1977	Galleria Nadar, Pisa, Italy
	Salzburg College Gallery, Austria
1978	*Öffentliche Bilder von Privatem und Private Bilder von Öffentlichem,* Work Gallery, Zurich
1979	*Kamera Fotografie: Raoul Haussmann und Verena von Gagern,* Neue Sammlung, Munich
1980	*Zufälle in Erinnerung,* Photogalerie Lange-Irschl, Munich

Selected Group Exhibitions:

1976	*8 German Photographers,* at *Photokina '76,* Cologne
1978	*4 Femmes Photographes,* Centre Culturel, Bordeaux
	Exhibition de la Collection, Musée Réattu, Arles, France
1979	*Incontri di Fotografia,* Prato, Italy
1980	*Vorstellung und Wirlichkeit: 7 Aspekte Subjektiver Fotografie,* Städtisches Museum, Leverkusen, West Germany
	Neue Wege in der Fotografie, Kunstmuseum, Leverkusen, West Germany
	Triennale de la Photographie, Charleroi, Belgium

Collections:

Neue Sammlung, Munich; Kunstgewerbemuseum, Hamburg; Musée Réattu, Arles, France.

Publications:

By von GAGERN: Articles—"Verena von Gagern: Notes" in *Le Nouveau Photocinéma* (Paris), October 1975; "Notes on My Work" in *Photorevue* (Paris), 1975; "Notes" in *Popular Photography* (New York), Obtober 1976; "Verena von Gagern" in *Camera* (Lucerne), October 1977; "The Camera as a Notebook" in *Photo* (Munich), May 1978; "Against German Photographic Ideologies" in *Fotografie* (Göttingen), October 1978; "To Photograph Is the Decision to Remember," with Ralph Gibson and André Gelpke, in *Fotosymposium Dusseldorf: Reader I,* Munich 1980.

On von GAGERN: Books—*Photokina '76,* exhibition catalogue, with an introduction by Fritz Gruber, Cologne 1976; *Kamera Fotografie: Raoul Haussmann und Verena von Gagern,* exhibition leaflet, Munich 1979; *Vorstellung und Wirlichkeit,* exhibition catalogue, by Dieter Wellershof and Rolf Wedewer, Cologne 1980; *Triennale Internationale de la Photographie,* exhibition catalogue, Charleroi, Belgium 1980.

*

The points of departure for my photographs have been actual private realities at home, in cities, on trains. The printed images, however, show memories of unknown images behind these actual highlighted moments.

The language of photography to me is most interesting in its relationship to time, the doorway between language and reality. In photographs I rediscover a hidden knowledge of the stored traces of past images, both individual and collective, which we call memory. In a single photograph—executed at the peak of presence—I read about a part of reality of which I know only traces, signs and codes within one chosen frame of beautiful memory.

—Verena von Gagern

*   *   *

Stylistically, the photographs of Verena von Gagern are difficult to characterize. They portray "subjective" moments captured autonomously, so that the subject as a dramatic motif is less important than the mysterious articulation of light, shadow, surfaces and space. These are followed by narrative moments in which everything is comparatively clear. The subject is suspended—in most instances between representation and associative freedom—so that it becomes ambiguous and evocative.

Verena von Gagern herself speaks of "romantic documentation" and in this context means photography as the "documentation of suggested images, formed recollections, products of visual perception, which is also a type of experience—an experience in which a single visual phenomenon unites with a particular thought.... Images feed memories and hopes and become the occasion for reflections and their control." A good illustration of this point is one of her best-known photographs, "Untersberg" (1976).

It is evident throughout von Gagern's work that her photographs are caught in a characteristic flux between direct likeness and creative freedom which will support different kinds of interpretation and emphasis. We can see this, for example, in a photograph in which we have the rear view of a girl wearing pig-tails who is looking from the foreground into a room with an interior staircase and a wall lined with books. Two girls are standing in the middle ground, facing the viewer but not looking at him. Obviously one of the girls is looking to the right of the girl in the foreground, but the latter is clearly looking in a different direction. What the first girl is looking at lies completely outside the range of the photograph itself. The occasion for this assemblage of figures is not apparent, nor can it be deduced from the photograph. Because of this, the viewer has a certain space which he is free to fill with his own recollections and associations. Yet no matter how he fills that space, his interpretation will not contradict what is in the photograph itself.

Verena von Gagern realizes this "romantic" dimension of things stylistically, by reflections and displaced perspectives. By means of her art she produces in her photographs a precarious tension between the determinate and the ambiguous which the viewer is unable to resolve. Opposed to the realized artistic fact is always something casual and fortuitous which is nevertheless completely convincing. (Take for example the position of the ravens, in one photograph, in relation to the whiteaproned figure of a waiter, or another photograph in which a dog is sitting on the floor so that patches of sunlight and shadow give us a distorted perspective of its two pairs of legs.) In theme and intention, then, Verena von Gagern achieves a persuasive stylistic synthesis.

—Rolf Wedewer

WAHLBERG, Arne.

Nationality: Swedish. **Born:** Orebro, near Stockholm, Sweden, 4 November 1905. **Education:** Educated in local schools, 1911-20; self-taught in photography. **Family:** Married Margareta Lindeborg in 1938. **Career:** Worked as assistant to commercial photographer Anders Karnell, Gothenburg, 1927-28, and to Herman Sylwander, Atelier Jaeger, Stockholm, 1928-29; freelance portrait, advertising and industrial photographer, establishing own studio, in Stockholm, 1929-59, in Blekinge, Sweden, 1959-73; retired, lived in Asarum, Sweden, since 1973. **Died:** (in Asarum) 27 May, 1987.

Individual Exhibitions:

1985   Fotografiska Museet, Stockholm (retrospective)
           Volvo Works, Olofström, Sweden

Selected Group Exhibitions:

1928   *Andra Internationella Fotografiska Salongen,* Stockholm
1930   *2. Internationale Fotografiutstalling,* Trondheim, Norway
1944   *Moderna Svensk Fotokonst,* Nationalmuseum, Stockholm
1950   *Internationale Tentoonstelling: Vak Fotografie 1950,* Van Abbemuseum, Eindhoven, Netherlands
1952   *5th Annual Masters Exhibition,* Photographers Association of America, Chicago
1967   *Vi i Bild,* Stadsmuseum, Stockholm
1977   *Fotografer: Heilborn, Järlås, Sundgren, Wahlberg,* Moderna Museet, Stockholm
1979   *Svenskt Landskap,* Moderna Museet, Stockholm
1982   *The Frozen Image: Scandinavian Photography,* Walker Art Center, Minneapolis (travelled to the International Center of Photography, New York; University of California, Los Angeles; Portland Art Museum, Maine; Museum of Contemporary Art, Chicago; Tacoma Art Museum, Washington; Kjavalsstadir, Reykjavik; Louisiana Museum, Humlebaek, Denmark; Taidehalli, Helsinki; Fotografiska Museet, Stockholm; Kunstsenter, Oslo)
1985   *Samlingarna ca 200 fotografer,* Fotografiska Museet, Stockholm

Collections:

Nationalmuseum, Stockholm; Moderna Museet, Stockholm.

Publications:

By WAHLBERG: Articles—"Nagot om bildmassighet" in *Nordisk Tidskrift för Fotografi* (Enebyberg, Sweden), no. 3, 1931; "Materialatergivning vid foremalsfotografering" in *Nordisk Tidskrift för Fotografi* (Enebyberg, Sweden), no. 3, 1938; "Den 'Konstnarliga' fotografiska bilden" in *Nordisk Tidskrift för Fotografi* (Enebyberg), no. 3, 1940; "Brollopsfotografering" in *Svensk Fotografisk Tidskrift* (Stockholm), no. 10, 1943; "Forernalet och

Kameran" in *Fotografisk Arsbok,* Stockholm 1950; "Fototryck pa tyg," "Principerna för Formgivning med Ijus," and "Kommersiell fotografering" in *Fotografisk Handbok,* vol. 12, Stockholm 1958.

On WAHLBERG: Book—*The Frozen Image: Scandinavian Photography,* edited by Martin Freeman, Minneapolis and New York 1982. **Exhibition catalogues**—*Fotografer: Emil Heilborn, Sven Järlås, Gunnar Sundgren, Arne Wahlberg* by Ulla Bergman and Ake Sidwall, Stockholm 1977; *Tusen och En bild* by Ake Sidwall, Sune Jonsson and Ulf Hard af Segerstad, Stockholm 1978. **Articles**—"Arne Wahlberg: amatören som blev yrkesfotograf" by K.O. Sjostrom in *Nordisk Tidskrift för Fotografi* (Enebyberg, Sweden), no. 1, 1945; "De gamla som unga: Arne Wahlberg" in *Foto* (Stockholm) no. 6, 1953.

*   *   *

At the beginning of this century the international photographic exhibitions were dominated by pictures produced as bromoil prints, gum prints, carbon prints etc. The 1920s saw an avant-garde emerge in reaction, with its roots in Germany: people were now photographed from below; factories were, more often than not, placed diagonally across the picture; and there was a return to photographic clarity and distinctness. Photographers such as Hans Finsler and Renger-Patzsch made razorsharp pictures of plant fragments and architectural detail—the term "new objectivity" was coined.

Sweden, however, was somewhat isolated culturally, and here "pictorial" photography continued to be dominant for a little longer. The advertising and portrait photographer Arne Wahlberg was one of the first to take up the new ideas from Germany. He had been there on a study tour in 1931 and had made valuable contacts with, among others, the great portrait photographer Hugo Erfurth and the versatile Franz Fiedler. At this time Wahlberg was still making lyrical bromoil pictures, but very soon his trade mark became photographic sharpness and compositional purity. In addition to his German contacts he had also come across the American f/64 group. He was an early subscriber to American photographic magazines, and Edward Weston became another source of inspiration, as did the painter Paul Klee. Wahlberg was always very open to different artistic modes of expression and for this reason he became a highly regarded photographer in the fields of modern architecture, interior design and Swedish craft and design. Few were as adept as he in letting the material and the subject speak for themselves, and soon he became something of a specialist in metal and glass.

His lighting was often exquisitely simple—mostly just a window and some reflecting screens. "It is better to move the subject to the light, than the light to the subject" was one of his basic rules. But when the darkness of the northern winter descended on Stockholm he did, of course, have to resort to artificial light. With the camera stopped down to 32 or 45 he then often worked with flexible lighting. He "painted" with the lamp over the subject, with the shutter left open, in order to avoid hard shadows. And he was also a master of complicated interior photography, for example of mines and large industrial spaces.

During the years many pupils and colleagues worked with him in his studio and later came to establish themselves as prominent advertising and architectural photographers. Arne Wahlberg was an excellent teacher, and he was also much in demand as a lecturer and teacher at courses all over Sweden.

At the end of the 1950s he moved to southern Sweden, to finish his work in milder climes.

—Rune Jonsson

WALKER, Robert.

Nationality: Canadian. **Born:** Montreal, Quebec, 8 June 1945. **Education:** Studied painting, Sir George Williams University, Montreal, 1964-69, B.A. 1969; mainly self-taught in photography from 1975, but studied at workshops of Lee Friedlander in Montreal, 1975, and Gary Winogrand in New York, 1980. **Family:** Married Ania Swietlik in 1985. **Career:** Independent photographer in Montreal, 1975-77, and in New York, since 1977. Curator, *Camerart* exhibition, Galerie Optica, Montreal, 1974, and *Philippe Halsman '79* exhibition, International Center of Photography, New York, 1979. **Recipient:** Canada Council Arts Grant, 1976, 1979, 1980, 1981 and 1991. Bursary from the Ministère de la Culture, Québec, 1990. **Address:** 1477 Rue Viau, Montreal, Quebec HIV 3G8, Canada.

Individual Exhibitions:

1975	Espace 5, Montreal
1977	Galerie Mira Godard, Montreal
	Cross-Cultural Referents, Galerie Optica, Montreal
1978	Vancouver Art Gallery, British Columbia
	Bertha Urdang Gallery, New York
	Galerie Nouvel Observateur/Delpire, Paris
1979	Bertha Urdang Gallery, New York
	Galerie Gilles Gheerbrant, Montreal
	Eye Level Gallery, Halifax, Nova Scotia
	The Gallery, Stratford, Ontario
	Canadian Cultural Centre, Paris
1980	Union of Polish Art Photographers Gallery, Warsaw (travelled to Krakow and Katowice, Poland)
1981	Fotogalerie Pennings, Eindhoven, Netherlands
	Canadian Cultural Centre, Brussels
	Splash Gallery, Ottawa
	Canadian Centre of Photography, Toronto
1983	White Water Gallery, North Bay, Ontario
1984	Gotham Book Mart, New York
1985	International Center of Photography, New York (book launch)
1991	Saidye Bronfman Centre, Montreal
1992	Galerie Brenda Wallace, Montreal

Selected Group Exhibitions:

1975	*Camerart,* Galerie Optica, Montreal
1976	*Transparent Things,* Vancouver Art Gallery, British Columbia
1978	*Encapsulated Landscapes,* National Film Board, Ottawa
1980	*Contemporary Works,* Atlanta Gallery of Photography, Georgia
1982	*Color as Form,* International Museum of Photography at George Eastman House, Rochester, New York
	Esthetiques actuelles de la photographie au Quebec, Arles, France
1983	*Color in the Street,* California Museum of Photography, University of California at Riverside
	Personal Choice, Victoria and Albert Museum, London
1984	*Canada/New York,* 49th Parallel Gallery, New York
1985	*New York: The City and its People,* Beijing Workers Cultural Palace, China
1987	*New American Photographs,* Fogg Art Museum, Harvard University, Cambridge, Massachusetts
1989	*City Lights—Colour Photographs,* Goldsmiths' Gallery, University of London
1993-94	*Flora Photographica,* New York Public Library and the Montreal Museum of Fine Arts

Collections:

Musée d'Art Contemporain, Montreal; Canadian Museum of Photography, Ottawa; Canada Council Art Bank, Ottawa; International Center of Photography, New York; Victoria and Albert Museum, London; Bibliothèque Nationale,

Paris; Chiat/Day/Mojo Advertising, New York, Los Angeles; Ivanhoe Corporation, Montreal.

Publications:

By WALKER: Books—*Camerart,* exhibition catalogue, editor, Montreal 1974; *Halsman '79,* exhibition catalogue, editor, with Cornell Capa, New York 1979; *New York Inside Out,* with introduction by William Burroughts, Toronto 1984.

On WALKER: Books—*L'Art au Quebec depuis 1940* by Guy Robert, Montreal 1973; *Photography: A Concise History* by Ian Jeffrey, London 1981; *Color as Form: A History of Color Photography,* with introduction by Robert A. Sobieszek, Rochester, New York 1982; *Annie on Camera* by Anne H. Hoy, New York 1982; *Canadian Contemporary Photography from the Collection of the NFB,* with introduction by Hugh Maclennan, Edmonton, Alberta 1984; *Flora Photographica,* London, 1993; *The Body: Photoworks of the Human Form,* by William Ewing, London, 1994. **Articles**—"Quebec '75" by David Burnett in *Artscanada* (Toronto), July 1976; "Canada's Artists with Cameras" by William Ewing in *Art News* (New York), April 1978; "Cross-Cultural Referents" by Paul Heyer in *Parachute* (Montreal), Winter 1978; "Robert Walker: Embracing Photography on its own Terms" by Nancy Stevens in *American Photography* (New York), January 1979; "Walker at Bertha Urdang Gallery" by Colin Westerbeck Jr. in *Artforum* (New York), September 1980; "Street Photography—Walker's New York" by Ian Jeffrey in *Creative Camera* (London), February 1985; "Il colore di Walker" by Anna Winand in *Progresso Fotografico* (Milan), June 1985; "Street Smart" by William Burroughs in *Popular Photography* (New York), August 1985; "Robert Walker's Spliced New York" by William Burroughs in *Aperture* (Millerton, New York), Winter 1985.

*

I have always photographed in colour, and this, in retrospect, is probably due to the fact that I felt the black-and-white work of contemporary masters such as Frank, Klein, Friedlander and Winogrand would be too difficult to improve upon. Colour creates a new ball game, where the old rules don't apply. One is gratuitously handed a "clean slate" and can work without the demon of History gawking over your shoulder. Colour also adds another complex dimension to the delicate act of balancing form and content. In the jumbled chaos of New York City where I usually work, I like my pictures to have the crisp, clean colour, the choreography and humour of a Disney cartoon.

—Robert Walker

*   *   *

The advent of photographers interested in a fresh approach to colour in artistic photography was one of the most interesting phenomena of art in the 1970s. In actual fact, attempts to use colour can be found throughout the history of photography (hand-coloured daguerreotypes and visiting cards, and coloured resins, might be mentioned as examples here) but colour was not really treated seriously until after the last war. Even then, with a few exceptions such as Eliot Porter or Ernst Haas, colour photography remained secondary to traditional black-and-white. The reason for this was obvious—it was simply unclear how to avoid merely taking black and white photographs in colour or how to express colour in a purely photographic way. One of the photographers who attempted to resolve these issues was Robert Walker.

Walker's photography, beginning in Montreal and continuing thereafter in Manhattan, was influenced by two trends in contemporary American photography. The first was the so-called street photography that, in America, began with the work of Robert Frank and was perfected by Garry Winogrand. Walker took a great deal from this tradition both in his choice and selection of subjects and in his use of the photographic processes themselves. However one looks at his photographs, one sees a huge picture in which, as if reflected in a shattered mirror, there are various fragments of New York streets, events encountered there and people, captured quickly but thoughtfully. The other influence that meant a great deal to Walker came from photographers concerned with colour—most notably, William Eggleston and Joel Meyerowitz. Skilful use of

Cricoland, Poland, **1994 (original in colour).** Photograph by Robert Walker.

colour fascinated Walker who, at the beginning of his career, was also a painter. At the same time, he was also aware of the new direction in which photography was heading. He carried features from both the above trends into his own photography.

Colour is fundamental and crucial to Walker's photography and everything else is subordinate to it: objects, situations, events and even people. ''People are only incidental to my photography,'' Walker says. ''They mean nothing more to me than do shadows or post-boxes.'' He makes use of features rather than of objects, using them as carriers of colour through which he can achieve the appropriate figural construction and the required tension. Colour, useful in portraying rapidly conceived ideas rather than in recording even the most interesting visual events, is used by the photographer to organise his picture.

However, there are certain dangers inherent in this attitude. The attractiveness of the colour used does not automatically make the picture it is used for equally attractive from a visual or photographic point of view. The treatment of colour solely as a building block for a unidemensional picture draws photography dangerously close to painting (for example, geometric abstracts) and the desire to use colour in order to create a photographic picture around it perhaps erases the differences between coloured photography and black and white.

Walker, it seems, is aware of the dangers that exist here. His photography, therefore, is an incessant battle to steer clear of such extremes while developing the area between them—and in which he continues to work—as far as possible. His best works are numbered amongst those achievements of contemporary photography that epitomise developments in this area and, in so doing, lay the foundations for the further growth of colour photography.

—Ryszard Bobrowski

WALKER, (Harold) Todd.

Nationality: American. **Born:** Salt Lake City, Utah, 25 September 1917. **Education:** Hoover High School, Glendale, California, 1930-34; Glendale Junior College, 1939-40; Art Center School, Los Angeles, under Edward Kaminski, 1939-41. **Military service:** Served as an Air Cadet, then as a Flying Instructor, United States Army Air Corps, 1943-45: 2nd Lieutenant. **Family:** Married Betty Mae McNutt in 1944; children: Kathleen and Melanie. **Career:** Worked in the Scenic Department of RKO Film Studios, Hollywood, 1934-42. Photographer, Tradefilms Inc., Hollywood, 1941-43; freelance advertising, industrial and magazine photographer, in Los Angeles, 1946-51, and Beverly Hills, California, 1951-70. Since 1970, independent photographer, in Gainesville, Florida, 1970-77, and in Tucson, Arizona, since 1977. Instructor in Photography, Art Center College of Design, Los Angeles, 1966-70, and University of California Extension, Los Angeles, 1969-70; Associate Professor of Art, California State University at Northridge, 1970; Associate Professor of Art, Printmaking and Photography, University of Florida, Gainesville, 1970-77. Since 1977, Professor of Art at the University of Arizona, Tucson. **Recipient:** National Foundation for the Arts Grant, 1971; Florida Council on the Arts Fellowship, 1976. **Address:** 2890 North Orlando Avenue, Tucson, Arizona 85712, U.S.A.

Individual Exhibitions:

1963	*Resemblances of Reality,* California Museum of Science and Industry, Los Angeles
1965	*3 Photographers,* at the *World's Fair,* New York
1969	International Museum of Photography, George Eastman House, Rochester, New York (with Oliver Gagliani)
	Camera Work Gallery, Costa Mesa, California
1970	Focus Gallery, San Francisco
	Utah State University, Logan
	Friends of Photography Gallery, Carmel, California
	Phoenix Gallery, Arizona
1971	Bathhouse Gallery, Milwaukee, Wisconsin
	Chicago Center for Contemporary Photography

	University of Nevada Art Gallery, Reno
1972	Rhode Island School of Design, Providence
	3 Photographers, Berry College, Mt. Berry, Georgia (with Jerry Uelsmann and Doug Prince)
	University of Rhode Island, Kingston
	University of Iowa, Iowa City
	Silver Image Gallery, Ohio State University, Columbus
	Light Gallery, New York
1973	Clemson University, South Carolina
	University of Northern Iowa, Cedar Falls
	Visual Studies Workshop, Rochester, New York (toured the United States)
	Uelsmann/Prince/Walker, University of Alabama (with Jerry Uelsmann and Doug Prince)
	3 Photo-Printmakers, Western Illinois University, Macomb
	3 Photographers, Pennsylvania State University, University Park (with Jerry Uelsmann and Doug Prince)
1974	University of Notre Dame Art Gallery, Indiana
1975	University of Oregon, Eugene
	University of Florida, Gainesville (retrospective)
	Camerawork Gallery, Fairfax, California
	Madison Art Center, Wisconsin
	Utah State University, Logan
	Center for Photographic Studies, Dallas
1976	Center for Photographic Studies, University of Louisville, Kentucky
	Light Work Gallery, Syracuse, New York
	Nexus Gallery, Atlanta
	Silver Image Gallery, Tacoma, Washington
1977	Deja Vue Galleries, Toronto
	Visual Studies Workshop, Rochester, New York
	Center for Creative Photography, University of Arizona, Tucson
1978	Northern Kentucky State College, Highland Heights
	Florida Technological University, Orlando
	Daytona Beach Community College, Florida
	Fichter/Walker/Wood, Light Factory, Charlotte, North Carolina (with Robert Fichter and John Wood)
1979	Orange Coast College, Fullerton, California
	One Thing Just Sort of Led to Another, University of Arizona Art Museum, Tucson
	Photographs by Steve Cromwell and Todd Walker, Colorado College, Leadville
1980	Daytona Beach Community College, Florida
1981	Chicago Center for Contemporary Photography
1983	International Museum of Photography at George Eastman House, Rochester, New York
	Douglas Elliott Gallery, San Francisco (with Jerry Uelsmann)

Selected Group Exhibitions:

1963	*Biennale,* Venice
1968	*Contemporary Photographers,* University of California at Los Angeles
1971	*Photo/Graphics,* International Museum of Photography, George Eastman House, Rochester, New York (travelled to the University of New Mexico, Albuerque)
1973	*Light and Lens,* Hudson River Museum, Yonkers, New York
1974	*Photography in America,* Whitney Museum, New York
1976	*Premeditated Fantasy,* University of Colorado, Boulder
1978	*Mirrors and Windows: American Photography since 1960,* Museum of Modern Art, New York (toured the United States, 1978-80)
1981	*Photographer as Printmaker,* Ferens Art Gallery, Hull, Yorkshire (travelled to the Museum and Art Gallery, Leicester; Cooper Gallery, Barnsley; Castle Museum, Nottingham; Photographers' Gallery, London)
1984	*Photography in California 1945-80,* San Francisco Museum of Modern Art (travelled to the Akron Art Museum, Ohio; Corcoran Gallery, Washington, D.C.; Los Angeles Municipal

Art Gallery; Cornell University, Ithaca, New York; High Museum of Art, Atlanta, Georgia; Museum Folkwang, Essen; Centre Georges Pompidou, Paris; Museum of Photographic Art, San Diego, California)

1985   *American Images 1945-80,* Barbican Art Gallery, London (toured Britain)

Collections:

Museum of Modern Art, New York; International Museum of Photography, George Eastman House, Rochester, New York; Fogg Art Museum, Harvard University, Cambridge, Massachusetts; Philadelphia Museum of Art; Museum of Fine Arts, St. Petersburg, Florida; Minneapolis Institute of Arts; Center for Creative Photography, University of Arizona, Tucson; University of California at Los Angeles; Norton Simon Museum of Art, Pasadena, California; Bibliothèque Nationale, Paris.

Publications:

By WALKER: Books—(published by Walker from the Thumbprint Press, Los Angeles) *8 Shakespeare Sonnets/8 Todd Walker Photographs,* 1965; *John Donne,* 1966; *The Story of an Abandoned Shack in the Desert,* 1966; *An Abandoned Shack,* portfolio, 1967; *How Would It Feel to Be Able to Dance Like This,* 1967; *John Donne,* portfolio, 1968; *Melancholy,* 1968; *Portfolio III,* 1974; *27 Photographs,* 1975; *For Nothing Changes,* 1976; *The Edge of the Shadow,* 1977; *A Few Notes,* 1977; *Three Soliloquies,* 1977; *See,* 1978. Articles—"Photo Fun Indoors—with a Pound of Salt" in *U.S. Camera* (New York), June 1949; "Patterns from Your Negatives" in *Popular Photography* (New York), September 1952; "Trends for Photographers," in 2 parts, in *The Rangefinder* (Los Angeles), August and September 1960; "Todd Walker," interview, with Charles Kelly, in *Afterimage* (Rochester, New York), March 1974.

On WALKER: Books—*Photography in America,* edited by Robert Doty, with an introduction by Minor White, New York and London 1974; *The Photographers' Choice,* edited by Kelly Wise, Danbury, New Hampshire 1975; *Mirrors and Windows: American Photography since 1960* by John Szarkowski, New York 1978; *Tusen och En bild,* exhibition catalogue, by Ake Sidwall, Sune Jonsson and Ulf Hard af Segerstad, Stockholm 1978; *One Thing Just Sort of Led to Another,* exhibition catalogue, with texts by William S. Johnson and Susan E. Cohen, Tucson, Arizona 1979; *The Photograph Collector's Guide* by Lee D. Witkin and Barbara London, Boston 1979; *Photography for Collectors: Volume 1, The West,* San Francisco 1979; *Photographer as Printmaker,* exhibition catalogue, with texts by Gerry Badger, Peter C. Bunnell and Ansel Adams, London 1983; *Photography in California 1945-1980* by Louise Katzman, San Francisco 1984; *American Images: Photography 1945-1980,* edited by Peter Turner, London 1985. Articles—"Advertising's Natural Look" in *Infinity* (New York), October 1959; "We Look at Todd Walker" in *PSA Journal* (Chicago), January 1964; "The Restless Eye of Todd Walker" in *U.S. Camera* (New York), April 1964; "Todd Walker" by Leland Rice in *Artweek* (Oakland, California), 3 April 1971; "Todd Walker" in *Camera* (Lucerne), December 1971/January 1972; "Todd Walker" in *Creative Camera* (London), May 1973; "Retrospective: Photographer Walker's Personal Vision" in *Gainesville Sun* (Florida), 6 April 1975; "Beyond the Negative" by Ed Scully in *Modern Photography* (New York), November 1975; "Walker Pictures Life in His Art" in *Gainesville Sun* (Florida), 27 December 1976; "Two from Todd," book review, by Michael Lonier, in *Exposure* (New York), May 1977; "Nudes" in *American Photographer* (New York), December 1978.

*

I am a photographer, firmly grounded in the California tradition of photography. That is where I learned photography and worked for many years. The function of working with a camera is to produce not merely an image, as it is now called, but a picture. A dictionary tells me what I mean by those words—*image:* the optical counterpart of an object produced by a lens; *picture:* the representation of something in visible or symbolic form.

For me, the image from the camera needs to be transformed into a picture. That transformation is an important part of my work. In addition to being

involved with the image while using the camera, I must then concentrate on that image, with my reaction to the illusions that I have about my environment, and form a concrete picture that attempts to describe and delineate my illusion.

When, from among the many incomplete or inadequate pictures that I have done, one seems to support the illusion that I had while using the camera, or now may have, this becomes the particular one from which I evolve my representation of that illusion. *Representation:* to present again.

In the "purist" tradition of photography, this representation of the picture had certain restrictions, and the direct print from the negative was among them. Although I have come from that tradition, I have not gone far. The alteration of my images has to do with light, chemistry, and pigments other than silver. Yet my concern is strongly with the ability of the photographic process to reveal subtle differences in tone, the way that light is reflected and absorbed, and the marvellous extension of vision that results.

I came to photography with the desire to conquer this machine, the camera, and make it my slave. Instead, I have now a respect for it and for other machines as expanders of my awareness. The printing press, the process camera, photomechanical methods are now part of my photography and are teaching me what else is latent in the negative that comes from the camera.

Through all of this I am trying to make pictures, to re-present something in visible and/or symbolic form.

—Todd Walker

*   *   *

From childhood on, Todd Walker has been interested in photography. He has also been fascinated by machines and by the way things work, understanding them after the briefest examination—a talent that has had a great impact on his development as a photographer. He worked for a time as a painter's apprentice at RKO studios in Hollywood where he observed the creative power of light; he then attended the Art Center School in Los Angeles part-time in order to learn commercial photographic skills. Never content, but always patient, Walker went on to master the skills of each type of photography he encountered. He came from the California School of "straight" photography and found a creative outlet in the boom of commercial photography in Southern California in the 1950s, becoming a much admired and sought-after commercial photographer as a result of his knowledge of how to capture reality in an appealing and eye-catching manner. He also studied and experimented with the "Dorothea Lange" or documentary school of photography as well as the editorial school, although his participation in these areas was minimal.

While he was at the Art Center School, Walker took a course from Eddie Kaminski which introduced him to cubism and surrealism. By the early 1950s he had achieved sufficient success to allow himself to return to those things which were of private interest to him. According to Susan Cohen, "Todd's primary drive [is] to match in visual form his personal response to the phenomenal world, to confirm what he calls his 'illusion of reality.'" After a reassessment of his work and goals, Walker gave up the security and prosperity of the commercial world of photography in the late 60s to pursue his own artistic interests, which attests to his strong commitment to his art and to his belief in the "individual."

His break with traditional "straight" photography and his skill and ingenuity in using such techniques as the Sabbatier line, solarization, posterization, the offset lithographic press or the collotype allow him to play with space, line, motion, alterations in color, repetition, use of blur, etc. By way of experimentation and by mastering such various and diverse techniques, Walker has successfully revitalized the clichéd tropes of the nude and the landscape. In his work with the female nude, for example, he does not dwell on the sexually provocative or the voyeuristic aspect, but rather often creates a soft intimacy with the subjects by placing them in "caves" or "artificial structures" (in addition to the natural environment) to explore how "people relate to themselves rather than there being an outside reference to something else." It should be noted, perhaps, that his use of diverse techniques is not to correct a "failed" image, but to enhance a perfectly good image and give it a new significance.

Walker's photographs are constantly becoming more and more complex—perhaps this is because it is not easy to successfully "match in visual form [one's increasingly complex] personal response to the phenomenal world." Regardless, Walker's photography is exciting and invigorating—whether he is photographing machines, still-lifes, people, leaves or nudes—because he is never afraid to continue experimenting and attempting to redefine the boundaries of modern photography. He has been able to move away from the purely objective to surrealism as an alternative approach to the medium, yet without losing an important link with reality. As William Johnson has noted, "Todd has always been attracted to surrealism, or rather to a certain aspect of the surrealist message—that there is more to the world than what is physically there; that there can be a world of cause and consequence not structured by normal expectations; that the world can have a sense of poetry, of elusiveness, of mystery that can never be quite categorized or defined. . . . This sense of the power of mystery is conveyed in his 'salt table' photographs in the late 1940s and again in the best of the solarized prints of the later 1960s. Gradually, however, Todd has been able to strip away the forms of surrealism to achieve the substance of its idea. He no longer has to make images that look surreal; now he has reached the point where he can embody the sense of mystery within the most quotidian images." Ultimately, then, as is often the case, it is not the specific subject matter which is so important, but the overall coherent effect which the artist has achieved.

—Michael Held

WANG, Miao.

Nationality: Chinese. **Born:** Beijing, 29 January 1951. **Education:** Graduated with photography degree at the The Chinese University in 1985. **Family:** Married He Di; son He Zhao. Photojournalist of the Chinese News Agency, Beijing 1979. **Career:** Since 1986, photojournalist and editor of *China Tourism,* magazine, Hong Kong. Now Editor-in-Chief and Vice Director of Hong Kong Tourism Press. **Agent:** Hong Kong Tourism Photo Agency. **Address:** c/o Hong Kong China Tourism Press, 20 Westland Road, 24/F Westland Centre, Quarry Bay, Hong Kong.

Individual Exhibitions:

1986	*Tibet,* Hong Kong
1987	*Journey through Sichuan and Tibet,* California, USA
1988	*The Works of Chinese Photographer: Wang Miao,* Taipei, Taiwan

Selected Group Exhibitions:

1979-81	*Nature, Society and Men,* Beijing, China
1984	*Chinese Photographers Exhibition,* Hong Kong and Macau
1985-88	Group exhibitions by Modern Photography Society, China
1991	*Twenty Photographers from China and Japan Group Exhibition,* Beijing, Shanghai and Zhuhai
1992	*Chinese Photographers Exhibition,* USA
1994	*Contemporary Chinese Photography in China, Taiwan and Hong Kong,* Hong Kong Art Centre

Publications:

On WANG: Books—*The Dunhuang Frescoes, Luoyang Lungmen, Datong,* China, 1979; *The Young Chinese Photographer Series—Wang Miao Photo Collection,* China, 1985; *Poems of Nature,* Hong Kong, 1991; *The Works of Chinese Photographer—Wang Miao,* China, 1991; *Tibet: A Mysterious Land,* Taiwan, 1992; *Tracing Back in History—The Silk Road by Marco Polo,* Hong Kong, 1993. **Articles**—various articles in *Discovery Magazine, Geo, Photo, Popular Photography.*

*

I would like to observe the world with my vision, feel it with my heart, learn to understand it with my knowledge and express the world I know with photography.

My job as a reporter requires me to take photographs of many different subjects, but at the same time my career also allows me the opportunity to photograph the things I enjoy taking. I always feel like a child facing the world. I love nature and mankind. Despite how mysterious it can be sometimes, I still would like to use my heart and soul to feel it, and record this intricate relationship between human and nature.

—Wang Miao

*   *   *

It is probably not an exaggeration to say that Wang Miao has travelled and photographed the places and people of China more than any single photographer previously. Once a reporter, an editor and now director of *China Tourism Magazine;* readers of the world are fascinated by the stunning images of China through Wang Miao's eyes. The feeling of life and warm humanity which she imparted into every picture captured the soul of many who share her visions of China. Nature, people, lifestyles and culture . . . we are drawn to her acknowledgement of the rare beauty of the spaces that hold these elements and embrace them in radiance.

A founding member of two professional organizations of photographers in China—The April Photo Meet and Modern Photo Salon, Wang Miao was among the first group of formally trained photographers since China relaxed its policy in art education in the early 1980s. Perhaps Wang's most profound photographic achievement is her ability to connect the images and photographers of her own country with the rest of the world. Shortly after her photojournalism career started in 1979 Wang Miao was stationed in Hong Kong where she worked as a reporter for *China Tourism Magazine.* The job required extensive travelling within China, but at the same time opened up a new channel through which Wang could communicate and exchange with the outside world. In this first internationally distributed Chinese magazine with a strong emphasis on photography Wang Miao was able to publish her images as well as those from her fellow mainland Chinese photographers. There are, however, many obstacles which Wang encounters as a woman photographer in China. Her mission is to reach the parts of China which are of interest to the readers and that means undiscovered locations. Unfortunately they usually coincide with reporting difficulties, whether it be the wilderness of mother nature or the primitive livelihood of ethnic minorities. Her exhibition series, *Journey through Sichuan and Tibet* in 1987 is a true reflection of how Wang celebrates the intimacy and charm of the human environment. In 1993 she ventured into the heart of Chinese Turkestan and documented *Tracing Back in History—The Silk Road by Marco Polo*—a desert journey which hardly any other photographers would have attempted to accomplish.

In her book *Poetic Sketches of Nature* one can feel the joy in nature that Wang Miao's photographs communicate. Excited by the magnificence of the scenery, Wang is fascinated by the design or botanical nature of the plants but the beauty of such poetic nature is not her only photographic language. Wang's portraits of people succeed in capturing part of a human soul and her gift in establishing a warm human relationship after the briefest encounter with her subjects is visible within each single frame. The nomads of Taklamakan, the children of Xinjiang, a stage artist in Shanbei and a mountain boy in Sichuan are examples of the subjects captured by Wang Miao's natural and honest way of seeing.

—Becky Cho

WAPLINGTON, Nick.

Nationality: British. **Born:** Scunthorpe, England, 25 July 1965. **Education:** Studied foundation studies at Worthing Art College, West Sussex, until 1986; Trent Polytechnic, B.A. (photography), 1989; Royal College of Art, M.A. (with distinction), 1992. **Recipient:** Kodak British and European Awards 1990; EC Eurocreation Bursary (Naples) 1991; ICP New York Young Photographers' Award 1993. **Address:** 69A Hartham Road, Islington, London N7 9JJ, England.

Yellow Earth Plateau. Photograph ©Wang Miao.

Individual Exhibitions:

1990   *Family Pictures,* Pomeroy Purdy Gallery, London
        Living Room, The Photographers' Gallery, London
        Picture House, Leicester
1991   Nikon Live Gallery, Zurich, Switzerland
        Burden Gallery, New York
1992   *Living Room,* Philadelphia Museum of Art, Pennsylvania
        The Isaac Mizrahi Pictures, James Danziger Gallery,
            New York
1992-94 *Living Room,* FNAC, Paris, (travelled to many other galleries
            in France)
1993   *Half Lives,* Royal Photographic Society, Bath, England
        Living Room 2/Documentary, The Museum for Photography,
            Braunscheweig, Germany
        Natural Resources, Mark Boote Gallery, New York
1994   *Living Room,* Wood Street Gallery, Pittsburgh, Pennsylvania
            and Norton Museum, Palm Springs, California

Selected Group Exhibitions:

1989   Colour Work, Photographers' Gallery, London
1990   *Relative Values,* Center for Creative Photography, Houston,
            Texas,
1991   *Enter the Others,* Strasbourg, France
1992   *Nenos,* Vigo Photography Centre, Spain
        Enter the Others-2, Lisbon

        Our Town, Burden Gallery, New York
1993   *Aperture 40th Anniversary Exhibition,* Burden Gallery,
            New York
        About Big Cities, Neue Gesellschaft, Berlin
        Air Alexander, Kunsthalle, Rotterdam, Netherlands
        Montpelier Photography Festival, Montpelier, France
        Krieg, Neue Galerie, Graz, Austria
        Mesiac Fotografie, Bratislava, Slovakia
1994   *Who's Looking at the Family?* Barbican Art Gallery, London
        Present/Future, Jackson Fine Art, Atlanta, Georgia
        Forum Stadtpark, Graz, Austria (With Erich Lazar and Jindrich
            Streit)

Collections:

Philadelphia Museum of Art, Philadelphia, USA; Australian National Gallery,
Sydney.

Publications:

By Waplington: Books—*Living Room,* with essays by Richard Avedon and
John Berger, New York 1991; *Other Edens,* with Marianne Wiggins, New
York 1994. **Exhibition catalogues**—*Uber die Grossen Stadt* Berlin 1993;
Mesiac Fotografie Bratislava 1993; *Die Alexanderplolder* Thoth, Bussum,
Holland 1993; *Kreig* Austria 1993. **Articles**—*British Journal of Photogra-
phy,* (London), June 1989; *Photographies,* (Paris), October 1990; *Das Zurich
Magazin,* December 1990; *British Journal of Photography,* (London), Decem-
ber 1991 and February 1992; *American Photo,* March 1992; *Photo* (US),

Untitled, **from** *Other Edens,* **1990 (original in colour).** Photograph by Nick Waplington.

Spring 1992; *New York Times,* 9 April 1992; *Philadelphia Inquirer,* 1 May 1992; *Creative Camera,* (London), August/September 1992; *Photographers International,* (Taiwan), December 1992; *Art Forum,* (New York), March 1993; *British Journal of Photography,* (London), June and November 1993; **TV/Video**—*England Mine,* directed by Waplington for CA Sept (France), broadcast November 1990; *Living Room,* directed by Waplington, broadcast on Premiere channel, (Germany), December 1994.

*

I began taking pictures in the early 1980s. I undertook an art foundation course in 1985/6 and the following year I attended Trent Polytechnic, Nottingham. While studying for my degree, I began to work with my friends and neighbours on the estate where I lived with my grandfather on the outskirts of the city. The first stage of the work appeared as the book *Living Room* in 1991. The work is an on-going project and its second stage will appear as a book in 1995. It deals with my time spent with my friends, and I will continue to work there indefinitely.

Other Edens was published in November 1994. In this work I try to deal with my own responses to the world which we inhabit. Using cultural, social and political sites as a backdrop, I hope with these pictures to ask questions about the direction we seem to be taking as we move towards the millennium.

At the time of writing I am doing work which looks at cultural and imperial colonialism and its repercussions on my life as a Western white male.

—Nick Waplington

*   *   *

Nick Waplington emerged at the end of the 1980s as a fully formed photographer without having gone through the chrysalis stage as a follower of anybody before him. Still a very young man, it is already clear that his is one of the major talents. He has found notable supporters, not least Richard Avedon, who has publicly expressed his admiration for Waplington's pictures on many occasions. His first book was a triumph; a study of the living-life-to-the-full that could be managed by ordinary people at the sharp end of Margaret Thatcher's Britain. Its apparently chaotic style, of clashing colours in cramped interiors, of violent upheavals of pose and gesture, is less haphazard by far than it appears. Waplington re-invented a kind of documentary in which the truth is not claimed as objective; he was a participant, a player in his own drama. The feet that appear in the corners of the pictures are as likely to be his as the sitters', and the joie-de-vivre certainly is.

The panoramic format has become his chosen tool, the lightweight Fuji 617 that can be hand-held as Josef Koudelka discovered for some years before. In the next book, *Other Edens,* done in panoramic format, Waplington appears in all the pictures, in a hostile world of mysterious monuments and confused cultures and disintegrating ecology. It is a series of stage sets made out of the actual world.

Nick Waplington keeps on expanding and is already an innovative and much sought after film maker, whose first film *Mon Angleterre Jamais Oubliée,* was made for La Sept in France. In his photography, he combines a profound knowledge of his own art-form with an utter refusal to be bracketed within it. There is no more avid buyer of photographic books and no more studious observer of movements in contemporary photography. Yet he never allows his great knowledge to take the heart out of the pictures. Never original for originality's sake, Nick Waplington is yet one of the great original photographers of recent years.

—Francis Hodgson

WARHOL, Andy.

Nationality: American. **Born:** McKeesport, Pennsylvania, 6 August 1928. **Education:** Studied at Carnegie Institute of Technology, Pittsburgh, 1945-49, B.F.A. 1949. **Career:** Worked as illustrator for *Glamour Magazine,* New York, 1949-50, and as a commercial artist, New York, 1950-57. Independent artist, New York, from 1957: concentrated on making paintings derived from strip comics and advertisements, 1960-61; first silk-screen paintings, 1962; first films, mainly with Paul Morrissey, 1963. Editor, *Inter/View* magazine, New York. **Recipient:** Art Directors Club of New York Medal for shoe advertisements, 1957; 6th Film Culture Award, New York, 1964; *Los Angeles Film Festival* Award, 1964. **Agent:** Leo Castelli Gallery, 4 East 77th Street, New York, New York 10021, U.S.A. **Died:** (in New York) 22 February 1987.

Individual Exhibitions:

1952	Hugo Gallery, New York
1956	Bodley Gallery, New York
1957	Bodley Gallery, New York
1958	Bodley Gallery, New York
1959	Bodley Gallery, New York
1962	Ferus Gallery, Los Angeles
	Stable Gallery, New York
1963	Ferus Gallery, New York
1964	Leo Castelli Gallery
	Stable Gallery, New York
	Galerie Sonnabend, Paris
1965	Leo Castelli Gallery, New York
	Galerie Sonnabend, Paris

Galerie Rubbers, Buenos Aires
Galerie M.E. Thelen, Essen
Gian Enzo Sperone Arte Moderna, Milan
Institute of Contemporary Art, Philadelphia
Galerie Buren, Stockholm
Jerrold Morris International Gellery, Toronto
Gian Enzo Sperone Arte Moderna, Turin
1966   Galerie M.E. Thelen, Essen
Gian Enzo Sperone Arte Moderna, Milan
Institute of Contemporary Art, Boston
Contemporary Arts Center, Cincinnati, Ohio
Galerie Hans Neuendorf, Hamburg
Ferus Gallery, Los Angeles
Leo Castelli Gallery, New York
1967   Galerie Rudolf Zwirner, Cologne
Galerie Sonnabend, Paris
1968   Galerie Rudolf Zwirner, Cologne
Stedelijk Museum, Amsterdam
Galerie der Spiegel, Cologne
Rowan Gallery, London
Galerie Heiner Friedrich, Munich
Kunstnernes, Oslo
Moderna Museet, Stockholm
1969   Neue Nationalgalerie der Staatlichen Museen Preussischer
      Kulturbesitz, West Berlin
Irvin Blum Gallery, Los Angeles
Leo Castelli Gallery, New York
1970   Galerie Folker Skulima, West Berlin
Museum of Contemporary Art, Chicago
Stedelijk van Abbemuseum, Eindhoven, Netherlands
Musée d'Art Moderne de la Ville, Paris
Pasadena Museum of Art, California (toured the United States
      and Europe)
1971   Galerie Bruno Bischofberger, Zurich
Gotham Book Mart Gallery, New York
Institute of Contemporary Arts, London
Musée d'Art Moderne, Paris
1972   Castelli Downtown Gallery, New York
Multiples Gallery, New York
1973   Margo Leavin Gallery, Los Angeles
1974   Mayor Gallery, London
Musée Galliera, Paris
1975   Baltimore Museum of Art
1976   Württembergischer Kunstverein, Stuttgart (travelled to
      Kunsthalle, Dusseldorf)
1980   *Andy Warhol: Photos,* Lisson Gallery, London
1981   *Portrait Screenprints 1965-1980,* Gloucestershire College of
      Arts and Technology, Cheltenham, England
1982   Galerie Schellmann und Kluser, Munich
Stadtische Galerie im Lenbachhaus, Munich
1983   Fraenkel Gallery, San Francisco
1984   Scottsdale Center for the Arts, Arizona
Edition Schellmann und Kluser, Munich
Flow Ace Gallery, Los Angeles
Judith Goldberg Gallery, New York
Galerie Kammer, Hamburg
Galerie Schellmann und Kluser, Munich
1986   Galerie Daniel Templon, Paris
Edition Schellmann, Munich
Anthony D'Offay Gallery, London
1987   Galerie Bernd Kluser, Munich
1992   *Polaroids 1971-86,* Pace/MacGill Gallery, New York

Selected Group Exhibitions:

1964   *The Painter and the Photograph: From Delacroix to Warhol,*
      University of New Mexico, Albuquerque
1966   *11 Pop Artists: The New Image,* Galerie M.E. Thelen, Essen
1971   *Photo/Graphics,* International Museum of Photography,
      George Eastman House, Rochester, New York

1975   *Photographic Process as Medium,* Rutgers University, New
      Brunswick, New Jersey
1977   *Paris-New York,* Centre Georges Pompidou, Paris
1978   *Mirrors and Windows: American Photography since 1960,*
      Museum of Modern Art, New York (toured the United
      States, 1978-80)
1980   *La Photo Polaroid,* Musée d'Art Moderne, Paris
      Instantanés, Centre Georges Pompidou, Paris
1982   *Lichtbildnisse: Das Porträt in der Fotografie,* Rheinisches
      Landesmuseum, Bonn
      Painter as Photographer, John Hansard Gallery, Southampton,
      Hampshire (travelled to Wolverhampton Art Gallery; Muse-
      um of Modern Art, Oxford; Royal Albert Memorial
      Museum, Exeter; Camden Arts Centre, London, 1982-83)

Collections:

Museum of Modern Art, New York; Whitney Museum, New York; Corcoran Gallery of Art, Washington, D.C.; Walker Art Center, Minneapolis; County Museum of Art, Los Angeles; Norton Simon Museum of Art, Pasadena, California; Art Gallery of Ontario, Toronto; Tate Gallery, London; Moderna Museet, Stockholm; Museum of Contemporary Art, Chicago.

Publications:

By WARHOL: Books—*Andy Warhol's Index Book,* New York 1967; *A: A Novel,* New York 1968; *Andy Warhol: Transcript of David Bailey's ATV Documentary,* London 1972; *A to B and Back Again,* London and New York 1975; *Ladies and Gentlemen,* Milan 1975; *Andy Warhol: Photographs,* portfolio of 12 photos, New York and Zurich 1980; *Popism: The Warhol '60s,* with Pat Hackett, New York 1980, London 1981; *Andy Warhol: Schweizer Portraits,* with text by George J. Dolezal, Thun, Switzerland 1982; *Andy Warhol's Children's Book,* Zurich 1983; *America,* New York 1985. **Articles**—"My Favorite Superstar: Notes on My Epic, *Chelsea Girls,*" interview, with Gerard Malanga in *Arts* (New York), February 1967; "Andy Warhol Tapes Roman Polanski" in *Inter/View* (New York), November 1973; "Andy Warhol: Interview" in *Photo* (Paris), May 1979; "Warhol: Mon Carnet Mondain" in *Photo* (Paris), March 1980. **Films**—*Kiss,* 1973; *Tarzan and Jane Regained Sort Of,* 1963; *Dance Movie,* also known as *Roller Skate,* 1963; *Haircut,* 1963; *Eat,* 1964; *Blow Job,* 1963/64; *Batman Dracula,* 1964; *Empire,* 1964; *Henry Geldzahler,* 1964; *Soap Opera,* also known as *The Lester Persky,* 1964; *Couch,* 1964; *Shoulder,* 1964; *Mario Banana,* 1964; *Harlot,* 1964; *13 Most Beautiful Women,* 1964/65; *13 Most Beautiful Boys,* 1964/65; *50 Fantastics and 50 Personalities,* 1964/66; *Ivy and John,* 1965; *Suicide,* 1965; *Screen Test 1,* 1965; *Screen Test 2,* 1965; *The Life of Juanita Castro,* 1965; *Drunk,* 1965; *Horse,* 1965; *Poor Little Rich Girl,* 1965; *Vinyl,* 1965; *Bitch,* 1965; *Restaurant,* 1965; *Kitchen,* 1965; *Prison,* 1965; *Face,* 1965; *Afternoon,* 1965; *Beauty 2,* 1965; *Space,* 1965; *Outer and Inner Space,* 1965; *My Hustler,* 1965; *Camp,* 1965; *Paul Swan,* 1965; *Hedy,* also known as *Hedy the Shoplifter* and *The 14 Year Old Girl,* 1965; *The Closet,* 1965; *More Milk, Evette,* also known as *Lana Turner,* 1965; *Lupe,* 1965; *Bufferin,* also known as *Gerard Malanga Reads Poetry,* 1966; *Eating Too Fast,* 1966; *The Velvet Underground,* 1966; *Chelsea Girls,* 1966; *Bike Boy,* 1967; *Nude Restaurant,* 1967; *Lonesome Cowboys,* 1967; *Blue Movie,* 1969; *Schrafft's Commercial,* 1969.

On WARHOL: Books—*The Painter and the Photograph: From Delacroix to Warhol* by Van Deren Coke, Albuquerque, New Mexico. 1964, 1972; *Andy Warhol,* John Coplans, Pasadena, California 1970; *Andy Warhol* by Rainer Crone, London 1970; *The Autobiography and Sex Life of Andy Warhol* by John Wilcock, New York 1971; *Andy Warhol: Films and Paintings* by Peter Gidal, New York 1971; *Photo/Graphics,* exhibition catalogue, with text by Van Deren Coke, Rochester, New York 1971; *Photographic Process as Medium,* exhibition catalogue, with text by Rosanne T. Livingston, New Brunswick, New Jersey 1975; *L'Arte nella Società: Fotografia, Cinema, Videotape* by Daniela Palazzoli and others, Milan 1976; *Mirrors and Windows: American Photography since 1960* by John Szarkowski, New York 1978; *SX-70 Art,* edited by Ralph Gibson, New York 1979; *Voglio essere una macchina: la fotografia di Andy Warhol* by Paolo Barozzi, Milan 1979; *Instantanés,* exhibition catalogue, by Michel Nuridsany, Paris 1980; *Lichtbildnisse: Das*

Porträt in der Fotografie, edited by Klaus Honnef, Cologne 1982; *The Artist as Photographer* by Marina Vaizey, London 1982.

* * *

The photographic image is central to the art of Andy Warhol: without it his imagery, his intent and his result would differ entirely. Much of Warhol's impact as an image-maker depends on his use of the dream figures, horrific events, and the products of the advertising world. Furthermore, he presented these subjects in the way most 20th-century consumers understand—through the advertisement, the media image and the photograph. All photography has the uncanny ability to appear as an unmediated record of objects and events: we take it to be real. Warhol played upon this quality. His art seems not to represent interpreted objects (as paintings and drawings do) but objects merely one step away from reality, seen through the lens. Pop art deals with images that already exist as signs, such as comics or brand goods; Warhol's art deals with the power of images and how we perceive the sign-system of photographic images which is this century's most powerful and ubiquitous formal language.

Both Warhol's imagery and his art form are derived from popular culture. His subjects are well-known: Brillo boxes, Campbell soup cans, Coca-Cola bottles, Marilyn, Liz, Elvis, the Mona Lisa. His mass-media sources are meant to question the elitist, purist attitude toward art: his subjects show Warhol's willingness to treat our whole culture as if it were art. He thus questioned not only the meaning of "taste" but also the value of "art." The banality of his artistic subject, his choice of the garish hues of a cheap color reproduction, and his choice of the cheapest reproductive process, the silkscreen, all speak of Warhol's opposition to the idea of artistic purity.

The silkscreen process—which is the simplest and technically most straightforward as well as the cheapest printing process—offered Warhol results which look not like "art" but like common reproduction. The artist reputedly once said that he "thought somebody should be able to do all his paintings for him." This desire for the "artist" to be minimized is possible with silkscreen: Warhol's artistic imput consisted merely of sending a selected image, which has been ripped from a newspaper or magazine, to commercial silkscreenmakers with his size and color specifications. Ultimately, he was implying that an "artist" is not needed to make anti-art.

However, the mechanical anonymity of Warhol's art is, to some extent, a sham. Even in the most repetitious of Warhol's images—row upon row of Campbell soup cans or bland repeats of Liz Taylor—there are numerous variations made in the print according to the amount of ink and the amount of pressure applied in its making.

Both this technique and Warhol's subject were aimed to hit the "center of a communal nerve": his images are instantly recognizable to everyone. Many are images which under normal circumstances elicit violent emotional response: they are figures who are idolized and lusted after or the horrifying symbols of instant death and violent destruction. His people no less than his objects are icons and totems of contemporary life. They are media presentations—people we know and sometimes feel we know intimately, only through photography.

Warhol's art forces us to rethink the meaning of photographic images and the uses of photography as a form-language in our society. By serializing his images—stacking row upon boring row—he has shown us the emotional and intellectual impact caused by repetition of even the most shocking and startling images. He made us look again at both the content of our world and the content of our art by presenting the "contentless" image. Warhol presented his viewer with only the "thingness" of a thing (*just* a soup can) rather than any implicit or explicit content. He showed how images *can* and have been stripped of content in our daily lives.

—Nancy Hall-Duncan

WASSERMAN, Cary (Robert).

Nationality: American. **Born:** Los Angeles, California, 27 November 1939. **Education:** Los Angeles High School, 1954-57; University of California at

Los Angeles, 1957-63, B.A. in English literature 1961, M.A. 1963; studied literature, 1963-66, art history, education, and contemporary music, 1966-69, and photography, under Henry Holmes Smith, 1967-70, Indiana University, Bloomington. **Career:** Freelance photographer, with studio in Cambridge, Massachusetts, since 1970. Instructor, Indiana University, Indianapolis, 1966-70; Art Institute of Boston, 1971-74; Phillips Academy, Andover, Massachusetts, 1973; Northfield-Mt. Hermon School, Northfield, Massachusetts, 1976; University of Maine, Portland-Gorham, 1976-77; University of Lowell, Massachusetts, 1977-79 and 1982-83; Phillips Academy, 1979; Martha's Vineyard School of Photography, Massachusetts, 1980; New England School of Photography, Boston, 1984-85. Massachussets College of Art, Boston, Artist in Residence, 1989-90; Visiting Assistant Professor, 1990-92; Columnist ("Photoart"), *Boston Globe,* 1970-73. **Recipient:** Polaroid Corporation Grant, 1974; Cambridge Arts Council Open Competition Prize, 1975; Blanche E. Coleman Award, 1982, 1989. Director, Amiga Video Users Group, Boston Computer Society, 1990-94. **Address:** 6 Porter Road, Cambridge, Massachusetts 02140, U.S.A.

Individual Exhibitions:

1970	*Urban Color Photographs,* Arthur D. Little Corporation, Cambridge, Massachusetts
	Mexican Photographs, Polaroid Gallery, Cambridge, Massachusetts
1971	*Recent Photographs,* Art Institute of Boston
1972	*Photographs 1969-71,* Addison Gallery of American Art, Andover, Massachusetts
1974	*Photographs,* Belknap College, Center Harbor, New Hampshire
	Recent Photographs, Mather House, Harvard University, Cambridge, Massachusetts
	Rural Values, Enjay Gallery, Boston
	Charlestown: In Progress, Charlestown YWCA, Massachusetts
	Photographs 1970-74, Portland Museum of Art, Maine
1975	*Changes: Boston Area Architecture,* Harvard School of Design, Cambridge, Massachusetts
1976	*Cambridge Memories,* City Hall, Cambridge, Massachusetts
	Cyanotypes (In Memory of Minor White), Newton Free Library, Massachusetts
1978	*Color Photography,* Williams College, Williamstown, Massachusetts (retrospective)
	Color Photographs 1971-74, Portland School of Art, Maine
1979	*SX-70 Photographs,* Pine Manor College, Chestnut Hill, Massachusetts
	Kwik-Prints, North Cambridge Library, Massachusetts
1980	*SX-70 Photographs,* Next Move Theatre, Boston
1983	*SX-70 Prints,* Project Arts, Cambridge, Massachusetts
1986	Galerie Texbraun, Paris
	The Eiffel Tower and All That Jazz, French Library, Boston
1990	*SX-70 Manipulations,* Brooks Institue, Santa Barbara, California
1993	*Landscapes,* Dana Hall Art Gallery, Wellesley, Massachusetts

Selected Group Exhibitions:

1972	*Points of View,* Institute of Contemporary Art, Boston
	The New England Experience, De Cordova Museum, Lincoln, Massachusetts
1974	*Private Realities,* Museum of Fine Arts, Boston
1975	*Color Photography Now,* Wellesley College Museum of Art, Massachusetts
1976	*The Photographers' Choice,* Witkin Gallery, New York (toured the United States, 1976-79)
	New Blues (Cyanotypes), Arizona State University, Tempe
1977	*Color Photography,* Photoworks, Richmond, Virginia
1978	*Artists' Books,* Boston Visual Arts Union Gallery
1980	*Urban/Suburban Color Photographs,* Addison Gallery of American Art, Andover, Massachusetts
1981	*Photography/New Visions,* Lopoukhine/Nayduch Gallery, Boston

1982	*44 Cambridge Photographers,* Project Arts, Massachusetts
1985	*Hospitable Art,* Gallery 57, Cambridge, Massachusettts
1989	*Boston Visions,* BVAU at Prudential, Boston
1990	*The Endangered Earth,*Boston Visual Artists Union Gallery
	Censorship Show, Boston Visual Artists Union Gallery
1992	*Site #1 Revisited, (Blue Sky/Falling Car),* Mural installation proposal for Reclamation Artists, Boston
1993-94	*Beam Me Up: A Simplified Approach to the Space Time Continuum,* photography/computer/video event for First Night, Boston (31 December)

Collections:

Museum of Fine Arts, Boston; Cambridge City Hospital, Massachusetts; Polaroid Collection, Cambridge, Massachusetts; Smith College Museum of Arts, Northampton, Massachusetts; Wellesley College Museum of Art, Massachusetts; Portland Museum of Art, Maine.

Publications:

By WASSERMAN: Articles—"SX-70 Manipulation" in *Petersen's Photographic Magazine* (Los Angeles), December 1976; "Ben Shahn, Photographer" in *Maine Sunday Telegram* (Portland), November 1977; "Photographs of Architecture" in *New Age Journal* (Boston), April 1978; "Bruguière" in *New Age Journal* (Boston), June 1978; "Edward Weston Nudes" in *Boston Visual Artists Union Newsletter,* no. 10, 1978; "Steichen: Master Prints" in *New Age Journal* (Boston), December 1978; "Minor White: Rites and Passages" in *Parabola* (New York), Winter 1979; "Duane Michals" in *New Age Journal* (Boston), April 1979; "Man Ray" in *New Age Journal* (Boston), May 1979; "Expressive Toning" in *Darkroom Techniques* (Chicago), Winter 1980; "SX-70 Image Manipulation" in *Darkroom Techniques* (Chicago), March/April 1983.

On WASSERMAN: Books—*Points of View,* exhibition catalogue, edited by Susan Channing and John Snyder, Boston 1972; *Private Realities* by Clifford S. Ackley, Boston 1974; *The Photographers' Choice,* edited by Kelly Wise, Danbury, New Hampshire 1975; *New Blues,* exhibition catalogue, edited by Che Du Puich, Tempe, Arizona 1976; *Creative Camera International Yearbook 1977,* edited by Peter Turner, London 1976; *The Color Photographs of Cary Wasserman* by Susan Dodge Peters, Portland, Maine 1978. **Articles**—"Cary Wasserman: Active Experimenter" by Jonathan Goell in the *Boston Globe,* 7 November 1971; "Wasserman's View" by Jonathan Goell in the *Boston Globe,* 18 January 1974; "Rural Values" by Vladimir Gulevich in *Popular Photography* (New York), July 1974; "Private Realities: Recent American Photography" by Vladimir Gulevich in *Popular Photography* (New York), August 1974; "'Color Photography Now' Belongs to the Experimentalists" by David Akiba in the *Boston Globe,* 12 October 1975; "A Decade of Dramatic Progress" by Jessica Bethoney in the *Boston Globe,* 31 July 1980; "Photography/New Visions" by Rosamond Purcell in *Views* (Boston), Winter 1981/82; "SX-70 Surprises" by Robin Winter in *Views* (Boston), Spring 1983; "Wasserman at Large" by Kelly Wise in the *Boston Globe,* 15 January 1983.

*

My concerns involve expressively documenting aspects of time and facets of space that describe a felt reality.

Photography enables me to set my perceptions, memories, feelings, aspirations and ideals into an accessible, communicable form.

I assume that art emerges from the interaction of freedom of expression and aesthetic choice. Photography offers a broad range of materials and traditions, of camera formats, light sensitized materials, and diverse subject matter, each choice having its own implications.

I work with conventional camera optics and formats from 35mm to 12 x 20 contact negatives; perceptually natural curvilinear lenses; conceptual materials such as stereo (3-D cameras and prints); with assemblage sculpture; and with the sequential time delineation of movie film. I am interested in capturing a feeling of life in my work and describing our psychic environment.

Much of my work in the past decade has been involved with the urban experience most often reflected in shop names, storefronts and neon. The Time-Zero SX-70 print material, with its initially malleable emulsion, has been a frequent photographic starting point, allowing, as I begin altering the image to more personally satisfying configurations, certain figures or spirits to emerge that suggest conversations and relationships, interactions that have been a principal theme in my work.

My first serious interest in photography in the early 1960s was related to the possibilities of color, at first in descriptive modes, and later in more allusive, metaphoric ways. It was my great fortune to have been able to study with Henry Holmes Smith, whose innovative work, as well as his personal integrity and committment to a vision, continues to stimulate and inspire.

—Cary Wasserman

*   *   *

Speaking of black-and-white photography during a recent conversation, but in terms equally applicable to his color work, Cary Wasserman said: "There must be an awareness of all the possibilities of experimentation for black-and-white—including transformation to color. Sometimes a black-and-white negative goes beyond the possibilities in silver."

"Experimentation" is the key word in, and the key to, both the work and the photographic lineage of this artist. Wasserman readily admits to the influences of Henry Holmes Smith, Atget and Cartier-Bresson, among other 20th century masters; as well, there is a more antique influence at play (and "play" is a most appropriate characterization). Like Bayard, Fox-Talbot, and countless others, both named and anonymous, Cary Wasserman is chiefly concerned with understanding the technology at his disposal, utilizing it, and pushing it ever further in the service of creating an evolving imagery.

Thus, a given lens-made or chemically-created image may exist in a stream of technical incarnations over time. A carefully crafted "straight" black-and-white photograph of Ranchos de Taos Church (also the subject of one of Paul Strand's most beautiful pictures) will later be toned in yellow or otherwise altered, with each alteration producing a new experience for photographer and viewer alike.

This fascination with photographic experimentation has yielded a rich and diverse body of work since the late 1960s (when Wasserman studied with the abstract-color master Henry Holmes Smith in Indiana). Of particular note, both because of their photographic and pure color qualities, is a series of gum bichromate prints from 1974. Of this antique technology, Wasserman says: "It's such a magical process; the point was to create color which looks natural, even if manipulated."

A more recent endeavor, although one that is coming to an end because of changes in available Polaroid materials, consists of several groups of SX-70 prints, each of which has been manipulated, by pressing with an awl, before the surface hardened. Whether built upon constructed elements (i.e., "Death and the Maiden," 1976) or natural, environmental ones (i.e., "Ciudad de Los Angeles," 1978), these delicate images evoke the colors and imagery of Hundertwasser without abandoning a strong loyalty to the medium from which they spring.

Most recently, Wasserman has been experimenting with stereographic pairs of SX-70 images; it is very much a work in progress but one with interesting possibilities.

I have dwelt upon Wasserman's color work because it is the area of his greatest contribution. However, this thoroughgoing belief in experimentation and the sense of joy and playfulness that mark his work are valuable lessons no matter what the tonal range in which one works.

—Stu Cohen

WATANABE, Yoshio.

Nationality: Japanese. **Born:** Sanjo, Niigata Prefecture, 21 April 1907. **Education:** Studied at the Tokyo School of Photography, 1925-28. **Family:** Married Yoshiko in 1948. **Career:** Worked in the photography department, 1928-30, and editor of *Photo Times* monthly magazine, 1930-34, Oriental Photo Industry Company, Tokyo; established Watanabe Studio in Ginza,

Tokyo, 1935-36, working for government departments, including the International Tourist Bureau (Ministry of Transportation), International Culture Promotion Organization, and the Foreign Ministry Intelligence Bureau; photographer, as member of the International Report Photographers Society (IRP), Tokyo, 1936-40. Since 1940, freelance photographer, Tokyo. Director, Japan Press Photography Society, Tokyo, 1941-45; part-time employee of the International Culture Promotion Organization, Tokyo, 1943. Lecturer, 1950-52, Assistant Professor, 1952-58, and Professor of Art from 1958, Nihon University, Tokyo; Director, Tokyo Institute of Technology, since 1978. Chairman, 1958, and Honorary Chairman since 1981, Japan Professional Photographers Society (JPS), Tokyo; Director, 1959, and Vice-Chairman, 1973, Photographic Society of Japan (PSJ), Tokyo. Director Tokyo Municipal Museum of Photography, 1990; Founder President of Japan Photographic Arts Society 1992. **Recipient:** Photographic Society of Japan Award, Tokyo, 1957; Art Encouragement Award, Ministry of Education, Tokyo, 1958; Photographic Society of Japan Service Award, 1970; Purple Ribbon Medal, Tokyo, 1972; Mainichi Art Award, Tokyo, 1973; Third Order of Merit and Order of the Sacred Treasure, Tokyo, 1978; Sixth Tokyo Municipal Culture Award, 1990; designated Person of Cultural Merit, 1990. **Agent:** Yoshio Watanabe Photography Office, Midhill, 8 Motoshio-cho, Shinjuku-ku, Tokyo 160, Japan. **Address:** Midhill, 8 Motoshio-cho, Shinjuku-ku, Tokyo 160, Japan.

Individual Exhibitions:

1933	*Stage Photographs,* Takarazuka Theatre Basement Hall, Tokyo
1938	*Nanking/Shanghai Press Photos,* Ginza Mitsukoshi Department Store, Tokyo (with Ihei Kimura)
1950	*The Emperor and the Imperial Palace,* Nihonbashi Mitsukoshi Department Store, Tokyo (with Tatsuo Kumagai)
1957	*Travelling in Italy,* Konishiroku Photo Gallery, Tokyo
	Asian Nations, Takashimaya Department Store, Nihonbashi, Tokyo (travelled to Peking, China)
1958	*People in Europe,* Gekko Gallery, Tokyo
	Konishiroku Photo Gallery, Tokyo (with Ihei Kimura)
1965	*Tombstones in Kyoto,* Gekko Gallery, Tokyo
1985	*Grand View of Old Temples,* Wako Hall, Ginza, Tokyo (travelled to Peking, China)
1987	*Ise,* Kodak Photo Salon, Ginza, Tokyo
1989	*Yoshio Watanabe, Photographer,* Niigata Prefectural Art Museum, Japan
1991	*Yoshio Watanabe,* Yokohama Museum of Art, Japan; Tokyo Institute of Polytechnics, Shadai Gallery, Tokyo

Selected Group Exhibitions:

1975	*The History of Japanese Contemporary Photography 1945-70,* Seibu Museum of Art, Tokyo
1985	*Japan 1971-84: Man and Society,* Seibu Art Forum, Tokyo
1988	*Beautiful Japan,* Tokyo Municipal Garden Art Museum, Tokyo
1992	*A Day in Moscow, 1956,* Nikon Salon, Shinjuku, Tokyo

Collections:

Museum of Modern Art, New York; Toppan Collection, Tokyo.

Publications:

By WATANABE: Books—*Bunraku,* with others, Tokyo 1940; *the Imperial Palace,* Tokyo 1949; *A Day in the Life of Moscow,* Tokyo 1957; *Katsura Detached Palace,* Tokyo 1958; *Japanese Temples,* 5 vols., Tokyo 1959-61; *Ise—The Original Form of Japanese Architecture,* Tokyo 1962; *Ise,* Cambridge, Massachusetts 1965; *Togu Imperial Palace,* Tokyo 1968; *The Palace,* Tokyo 1969; *Grand View of Nara's Six Old Temples,* 6 vols., with others, Tokyo 1969-72; *Ise Shrine,* Tokyo 1973; *The Guest House,* Tokyo 1975; *Grand View of Yamato Old Temples,* 3 vols., with others, Tokyo 1977-78; *Ise-*

Ji and Shrine, Tokyo 1979; *The Imperial Palace and Guest House,* Tokyo 1980; *Japanese Pagoda,* Tokyo 1982; *Overview of the Byodoin—Vol 1: Architecture,* (co-author), Tokyo 1988; *Ise Shrine and Izumo Shrine,* (co-author), 1993; *Ise Shrine through Yoshio Watanbe's eyes,* Tokyo, 1994.

On WATANABE: Books—*Photography of the World,* edited by Heibonsha Publishers, Tokyo 1956; *Photography of the World '60,* edited by Hiromu Hara, Ihei Kimura and others, Tokyo and New York 1960; *Contemporary Photography and Photographers,* with text by Tsutomu Watanabe, Tokyo 1975; *The History of Japanese Contemporary Photography 1945-1970,* Tokyo 1977; *Showa Photographers Story,* with text by Shozo Kozakai, Tokyo 1983; *Yoshio Watanabe, Photographer,* exhibition catalogue, 1989; *Yoshio Watanabe Photography Exhibition,* catalogue, Yokohama, 1991.

*   *   *

Born in 1907, Yoshio Watanabe is one of Japan's oldest photographers. When he was young, he took news and stage photos, but from 1945 or so, began to specialize in architectural photography, and is now widely known as Japan's foremost architectural photographer.

His most important work is *Ise Shrine.* Since the shrine is a very holy one where the Emperor's ancestors are enshrined, nobody else but him can photograph the shrine. At Ise Shrine, from olden times, the new sanctuary is built every twenty years, when the event called "Sengu" is held and the object of worship is moved to the new sanctuary. When the event was held in 1953, Watanabe was permitted to shoot it for the first time, and he shot it again in 1973. The architectural style of Ise Shrine is said to be the prototype of Japanese architecture, and is a complete wooden house. Watanabe's camera-eye precisely captured the simple Japanese formative beauty which the plain wood has. In addition, he shot many old temples in Nara, but he consistently captures the constructive beauty of the architecture as it is, and is not so subjective in photographing things. This is where he, by contrast, differs from Ken Domon who has taken the same subject. Therefore, at the first glance, his photos seem an ordinary expression, but he intentionally uses such a technique in order to capture the beauty of the architecture precisely.

The beauty of his photos lies in the composition and the expression in soft, monochrome tone. When shooting, therefore, he pays careful attention to light, and when also making a print, he makes every effort to reproduce all the tones of the negative film on a printing paper.

In commemoration of his own sixty years as a photographer, he held a grand exhibition of photo memoirs entitled "Grand View of Old Temples" in 1985, and as he continues to shoot as an active photographer, he is still in important posts such as chairman of Japan Professional Photographers Society, vice president of Photographic Society of Japan, etc.

—Takao Kajiwara

WEBB, Alex(ander Dwight).

Nationality: American. **Born:** San Francisco, California, 5 May 1952. **Education:** Harvard University, B.A. (history and literature), 1974; learned photography originally from father, then through Apeiron Workshop with Charles Harbutt, 1972; also at Carpenter Center for the Visual Arts at Harvard University, 1972-74. **Family:** Married Susan J. O'Connor on 23 September 1982; child: Max. **Career:** Started work as a freelance professional photojournalist, 1974; joined Magnum Photos as associate member 1976; carried out numerous reportage assignments in southern United States, Caribbean, and Mexico in mid-1970s, and also throughout Africa and Latin America in 1980s; during 1993 carried out a photographic survey of the Amazon River. **Recipient:** Overseas Press Club Award, 1980; Leopold Godowsky Jr. Color Photography Award, 1988. **Agent:** Magnum Photos, 72 Spring Street, New York City, New York 10012, USA. **Address:** 135 Eastern Parkway 5D, Brooklyn, New York 11238, USA.

US-Mexico Border, **1990 (original in colour).** Photograph ©Alex Webb/Magnum.

Individual Exhibitions:

1983   Gallerie Magnum, Paris
1986   California Museum of Photography, Riverside, California
1987   Torino Fotografia, Museo dell'Automobile, Turin, Italy
1989   Sala de Exposiciones del Canal de Isabel II, Madrid
1991   Focale Gallery, Nyons, Switzerland
1992   Studio Marangoni, Florence, Italy
        L'Espace Nationale, Bayonne, France

Selected Group Exhibitions:

1975   *Contemporary Photographers V,* Fogg Art Museum, Cambridge, Massachusetts
1980   *Color Photography,* Fogg Art Museum, Cambridge, Massachusetts
1983   *Color in the Street,* California Museum of Photography, Riverside California
1986   *On the Line: The New Color Photojournalism,* Walker Art Center, Minneapolis, Minnesota, then travelling to Portland Museum of Art, Portland, Maine; Spencer Museum of Art, Lawrence, Kansas; Laguna Gloria Art Museum, Austin, Texas; Carnegie Mellon University Art Gallery, Pittsburgh, Pennsylvania; Toledo Museum of Art, Toledo, Ohio
1987   *Masters of the Street,* Museum of Photographic Arts, San Diego, California
        Museum of Contemporary Photography, Chicago, Illinois

1989   *Haiti: Revolution in Progress,* Museum of Photographic Arts, San Diego, California; also at Sterling Art Center, Texas Southern University, Houston, Texas
        In Our Time: The World as Seen by Magnum Photographers, International Center of Photography, New York; also at Centre Nationale de la Photographie, Palais de Tokyo, Paris
1991   *Biennial Exhibition,* Whitney Museum of American Art, New York
1992   *Mexico Through Foreign Eyes,* Tamayo Museum, Mexico City
1993   *Mexico Through Foreign Eyes,* International Center of Photography, New York

Collections:

Davison Art Center, Wesleyan College, Middleton, Connecticut; Fogg Museum of Art, Cambridge, Massachusetts; Fuji Museum, Japan; International Center of Photography, New York City, New York; Museum of Contemporary Photography, Chicago, Illinois; Museum of Photographic Arts, San Diego, California; Portland Museum of Art, Portland, Maine; University Gallery, University of Massachusetts, Amherst, Massachusetts; Whitney Museum of American Art, New York; Bohen Foundation, New York City, New York; Fundación Cultural Banesto, Madrid, Spain; Southland Corporation, Dallas, Texas.

Publications:

By WEBB: Books—*Hot Light/Half Made Worlds: Photographs from the Tropics* (New York), 1986; *On the Line: The New Color Photojournalism,* exhibition catalogue for Walker Art Center (Minneapolis), 1986; *In Our Time: The World As Seen By Magnum Photographers,* with other contributors (New York), 1989; *Under A Grudging Sun: Photographs from Haiti Liberé* (New York), 1989; *Alex Webb: Fotografias: From the Tropics,* exhibition catalog for Sala de Exposiciones del Canal de Isabel II, (Madrid), 1989; *Biennial Exhibition Catalog* for Whitney Museum of American Art (New York), 1991; *Mexico Through Foreign Eyes,* with other contributors (New York), 1993; *Madrid Visto Por: Miradas Fin de Siglo,* with other contributors (Madrid), 1993. **Articles**—"On the Border: Life Begins on the Other Side" with text by Tom Miller in *Geo,* November 1979; "Palm Trees and Paranoia" with text by Ken Labiche in *Geo,* May 1980; "Uganda's Road to Ruin" with text by Kevin Buckley in *Geo,* September 1980; "Das Schwarze Meer Von Mexiko" in *Geo,* August 1984; "Haiti" in *Stern* (Germany), December 1986; "Tatorte der Exilados" in *Geo,* August 1988; "Freiheit Nein Danke—Puerto Rico" in *Geo,* September 1991; "Barcelona" in *El País* (Spain), 7 June 1992; "Sevilla" in *El País* (Spain), 14 June 1992; "Madrid" in *El País* (Spain), 21 June 1992; "Paraguay: Plotting A New Course" in *National Geographic,* August 1992; "Quand Vanuatu Retourne A La Coutume" in *Geo,* March 1993.

On WEBB: Articles—*Creative Camera* (England), December 1975; "Between Expression and the Document" in *Modern Photography,* March 1979; "Photojournalism: It's Back with a New Face" by Andy Grundberg in *Modern Photography,* June 1980; *Photo Magazine* (France), September 1982; "India: Ritual and The River" in *Aperture,* Winter 1986; *Photo Magazine* (France), April 1988; *Foto* (Spain), July 1989; "Picturing the Killing Fields" by Max Kozloff in *Art in America,* June 1991; "Haiti" in *Aperture,* 1992; *Aperture,* 40th Anniversary Issue, 1992.

*

My work comes out of the tradition of street photography. Though it is sometimes referred to as photojournalism, (and indeed some of my photographs do appear in various journalistic publications, and my photographic projects do at times touch on current events,) its essence lies elsewhere; in a more personal and interpretative vision of the world. I quite simply see myself as exploring the world with my camera, following certain passions and obsessions. In the mid to late 70s these obsessions led to black and white work in Haiti, along the US/Mexico border, and in particular in the American South. However in the late 70s and early 80s, as I began photographing increasingly in the Caribbean, Mexico, and Africa, I started working more in color. There were (and are) certain kinds of emotional essences in these tropical lands that I felt (and still feel) that I could deal with best in color. It is the light, the heat, the color, the vibrancy, the rawness and disjointedness of much of the tropical world that has fascinated and disturbed me. I continue to photographically explore these worlds in color.

—Alex Webb

*　　*　　*

Alex Webb is a photographer cast firmly in the Magnum mould. An inveterate traveller, particularly across the Americas, Africa, India and the Caribbean, he now works mainly in colour though principally still within a reportage tradition. His infatuation with the tropical regions of the world has given rise to his two books to date; *Hot Light/Half-made Worlds* (1986) and *Under a Grudging Sun* (1989).

Both boast a political awareness of "Third World" issues as well as visual sophistication and proven photographic versatility. *Hot Light* pays tribute to fellow Magnum photographer, Eugene Richards, as well as to the subjects of his images, taken across all the tropical regions of the world (India to Ivory Coast, Grenada to Tobago, Costa Rica to the Dominican Republic, with a preponderant affection for Mexico and the borderlands, the theme of some of his early work in the 1970s). Without captions, but with a brief quotation from the Mexican writer Carlos Fuentes ('. . . lulled by the sweet novelty with which the tropics receives its visitors before unsheathing the claws of its petrified desperation. . .') the pictures, though carefully married across page-spreads, are clearly intended to speak for themselves. Strikingly, sometimes stridently, they do so.

The latter book controversially celebrates a brief period of democracy in Haiti's bloody history. From having been the first colony to take the egalitarian message of the French Revolution to heart (in Toussaint l'Ouverture's overthrow of imperialist despotism), Haiti sank into becoming the poorest country of the western hemisphere, a fit topic for Graham Green's cruelly titled *Comedians.* Alex Webb saw it differently, in the brief period before its democratically-elected President Aristide's violent expulsion (1986-89) as 'the sad and vibrant Haiti I had always known, but with a curtain pulled back, the curtain that had inhibited speech . . . (sometimes) referred to as a "moment of nudity" when the skeletal strucure of Haitian society is suddenly revealed'. Because of the greater concentration on a narrower theme, the juxtaposed images of cock fights and funerals for victims of army violence; survival on the rubbish-ridden streets of Cité Soleil and pounding on the windows of a police station; the sultry silence of the graveyard and the street on which a freshly shot body lies ignored, *Under a Grudging Sun* comes across all the more strongly. Again, the familiarity with the lives of his subjects is balanced with the explicit tribute paid to fellow Magnum members for their support.

All this is a far cry from a San Francisco childhood, a Harvard education (majoring in history and literature) and a track record of exhibiting in such prestigious venues at the Museum of Photographic Arts, the Walker Art Centre, the International Centre of Photography and the Whitney Museum of American Art. With a personal reputation that leaves some of his colleagues wondering whether it's an Ivy League manner or simply shyness that keeps Webb quiet and hard-working, Webb's rapid manoeuvres to catch the exact shot—and his flaming red beard—do little to minimise his presence from his subjects. Now working on a lengthy project following the Amazon River from mouth to source, Webb is building on that capacity both to establish a rapport with his subjects and to insist upon getting the colour, the composition and the shock value so characteristic of his work at its best.

—Amanda Hopkinson

WEBB, Todd.

Nationality: American. **Born:** Charles Clayton Webb in Detroit, Michigan, 15 September 1905. **Education:** Newmarket High School, Ontario, 1920-24; University of Toronto, 1924-25; studied photography, under Ansel Adams, photography workshop, Detroit, 1940. **Military service:** Photographers mate first class, U.S. Navy, in the South Pacific, 1942-45. **Family:** Married Lucille Minqueau in 1949. **Career:** Freelance photographer since 1946: worked with Roy Stryker, Standard Oil Company, New York, 1947-49; in Paris and throughout Europe, 1949-54; and for the United Nations, New York, 1955-69. **Recipient:** Guggenheim Fellowship in Photography, 1955, 1956; National Endowment for the Arts Photography Fellowship, 1979. **Address:** 120 North Street, Bath, Maine 04530, U.S.A.

Individual Exhibitions:

1946	*I See a City,* Museum of the City of New York
1947	Delgado Museum, New Orleans
	Louisiana State University, Baton Rouge
1950	*Paris Architecture,* Architectural Center, Wuppertal, Germany (travelled to the Münchner Standtmuseum, Munich)
1951	*Photographs of Paris,* U.S. Embassy, Paris
1954	*80 Photographs by Todd Webb,* International Museum of Photography, George Eastman House, Rochester, New York
1956	*90 Photographs by Todd Webb,* Art Institute of Chicago
1962	Kalamazoo Art Institute, Michigan
	University of Indiana, Bloomington
	Fine Arts Museum of New Mexico, Santa Fe (with Laura Gilpin and Eliot Porter)
1965	*Todd Webb: Photographs,* Amon Carter Museum, Fort Worth, Texas (travelled to Texas A and M College, College Station, Texas, 1966)
1966	*19th Century Texas Homes,* Amon Carter Museum, Fort Worth, Texas (travelled to the Museum of the Southwest, Midland, Texas, 1967)

Selected Group Exhibitions:

Collections:

Center for Creative Photography, University of Arizona, Tucson (Webb archive of photos and letters); International Center of Photography, New York; Westbrook College, Portland, Maine; Museum of Modern Art, New York; New York Public Library; Worcester Museum of Art, Massachusetts; Art Institute of Chicago; Amon Carter Museum, Fort Worth, Texas; New Mexico Museum, Santa Fe; Bibliothèque Nationale, Paris.

Publications:

By WEBB: Books—*Gold Strikes and Ghost Towns,* New York 1961; *The Gold Rush Trail and the Road to Oregon,* New York 1961; *Todd Webb: Photographs,* Fort Worth, Texas 1965, 1979; *19th Century Texas Homes,* Austin, Texas 1966; *19th Century Texas Public Buildings,* Austin, Texas 1974; *Georgia O'Keeffe: The Artist and Her Landscape,* Pasadena, California 1984; *Photographs of New York and Paris 1946-1960,* Kansas City, Missouri 1985.

On WEBB: Books—*The History of Photography* by Beaumont Newhall, New York 1964; *Photography in the 20th Century* by Nathan Lyons, New York 1967; *Harlem on My Mind,* exhibition catalogue, New York 1968; *The Picture History of Photography* by Peter Pollack, New York 1969; *Industry and the Photographic Image: 153 Great Prints from 1850 to the Present,* edited by F. Jack Hurley, New York 1980; *Roy Stryker: USA, 1943-1950* by Steven W. Plattner, Austin, Texas 1983; *Subjektive Fotografie: Images of the 50s,* exhibition catalogue, by Ute Eskildsen, Manfred Schmalriede and Dorothy Martinson, Essen, West Germany 1984. **Article**—"The Photography of Todd Webb" by Betty Bryce in *El Palacio* (Santa Fe, New Mexico), March 1971.

*

In my opinion, photography is:

Photography means many different things to different people and has many aspects and uses. It can be a means of communication, illustration, education, expression, conservation and more. It can be simple, complex, thoughtful, trite, realistic, abstract, humorous or sad.

The craft of photography is not difficult to learn but it is vitally important. It takes a well-exposed and properly-developed negative to make a fine print. Weston Meter instructions carefully read and followed give the same results with roll film as the complicated zone system that has confused and frustrated so many neophytes. I think the tendency now is to put the instructions into words that are vague and sometimes incomprehensible. Technical aspects of photography can be talked to death and often are. Photography is not a bag of tricks. It does help if you have someone capable of showing you what a good print and good negative look like.

A photograph can often be used to illustrate a statement. But a photograph can be a statement without any explanatory treatise. Creative photography does not have anything to do with location, projects or causes as such—yet it can involve any one of them. It is a need to express something within the photographer. A creative photograph is one seen *through* the photographer. The reason for making the photograph is often unexplainable.

My personal photography seems to have more to do with what man does to nature than with nature itself. I do have a sense of history, and I am concerned about the disappearance of relics. I think that over the past forty years I have photographed unconsciously many objects and aspects of living that have already disappeared.

—Todd Webb

* * *

The three predominating elements in the photography of Todd Webb are humanity, sense of time and place, and humor. Todd Webb was drawn into photography in the first place by the lure of far-off people and places. His first inspiration came not from photographers but from globe trotting writers such as Richard Halliburton and Lowell Thomas. He soon discovered that photography could open up a new way of viewing the world and that even his hometown of Detroit could be seen in a new fashion.

From the first Todd Webb did most of his work with large format view cameras. As a result people actually appear in only about 30 percent of his photographs from the late 1930s, the 1940s and early 1950s. When someone criticized Todd's photos for this, his friend Alfred Stieglitz defended him by saying that no one put more "people" into his photographs than Todd Webb. Even in the emptiest of scenes, we have the feeling that someone has just left and will step back into view any second. For example, in a view of a Parisian side alley that Todd Webb did in the mid-1970s, a baby carriage sits prominently in the scene, and we have the impression that a mother will emerge from a door to collect it momentarily.

Todd Webb first came to national attention for his photographs of New York in the 1940s. He photographed the bustling crowds of people, the exuberant marketplaces, and most of all the elevated railway system that shuttled people roof-high through the metropolis. All of this he staged against a backdrop of towering skyscrapers, teeming tenements and soaring bridges. He created a portrait of a dynamic city filled with power and creative energies that was uniquely New York in the late 1940s.

In the early 1950s he photographed in Paris in a very different style. The photos are mellow and quiet and less staccato than the New York prints. He portrayed an aging Paris that was gentle and tolerant to artists, lovers and those seeking a quiet existence. In 1954, he photographed Ibiza in the Balearic isles. For a change he abandoned his 5 x 7 and 8 x 10 view cameras in favor of a little

Leica 35mm. The resulting photographs of stately women in black shawls parading past dazzling white facades bleached by the Mediterranean sun are very striking. It is like intruding upon a mystic ritual that has continued unchanged since the beginning of time.

Todd Webb has photographed in England, Ireland, Spain, Portugal, Southern France, North Africa, Mexico, New Guinea, the Amish country of Pennsylvania, the American Southwest, and many other places. To each he has brought his special artistry, the ability to capture the essence of time and place while at the same time defining a little further what it is to be human.

There are many recurring subjects in Todd Webb's photography: cars, doorways, bridges and most importantly signs. In his work these things always represent themselves. Whereas many modern photographers depict signs or portions of signs as symbols fractured of their original meanings, in Todd Webb's pictures a sign always stands for itself and means exactly what it says. The insight, humor, or pathos comes from the situation itself.

Despite Todd Webb's retiring nature and the limited access the public has had to his work, his reputation as an artist is steadily rising because of his universal appeal and unique vision.

—Mike Rowell

WEBER, Wolfgang.

Nationality: German. **Born:** Leipzig, 17 June 1902. **Education:** Studied ethnology, philosophy and music, University of Munich, 1920-26; also trained as a conductor, Akademie für Tonkunst, Munich, 1922-26; self-taught in photography, from 1919. **Family:** Married Gertrud Bierhals in 1936; daughters: Cosima and Claudia. **Career:** Assistant to Erich von Hornbostel, Phonetic Institute of the University of Berlin: commissioned to record music of the Vadjaggas, Kilimanjaro, Africa, 1924-25; freelance photoreporter, working for the *Berliner Tagblatt, Berliner Illustrierte Zeitung, Munchner Illustrierte Presse,* and the agencies Kultur-Korrespondenz für deutsche Zeitungen, Berlin, the Deutsche Presse Korrespondenz, Hannover, and Presseverlag Dr. Dammert, Berlin, 1925-32; staff photographer, Ullstein Publications, working chiefly for the *Berliner Illustrierte,* Berlin, 1932-45; chief reporter, *Neue Illustrierte,* Cologne, 1946-63; freelance documentary film producer, for WDR Television, Cologne, and SWF Television, Baden-Baden, 1964-81; also photographer for Burda Verlag publishers, Cologne 1964-85. **Died:** (in Cologne) 5 March 1985.

Individual Exhibitions:

1982   *Reisen ohne Ende: Fotos 1935-39,* Historisches Archiv der
          Stadt Koln, Cologne
1984   *Barcelona 1928,* Caixa de Barcelona, Spain

Selected Group Exhibitions:

1950   *Photo-kino Ausstellung,* cologne
1977   *Documenta 6,* Museum Fridericianum, Kassel, West Germany
1983   *Die fotografische Sammlung,* Museum Folkwang, Essen, West
          Germany

Collections:

Stadtbibliothek, Cologne; Museum Folkwang, Essen, West Germany.

Publications:

By WEBER: Books—*Das Gesicht der Stadte: Barcelona,* Berlin 1928; *Hotel Affenbrotbaum,* Berlin 1936; *Abenteuer einer Kamera,* Berlin 1938; *Reisen ohne Ende—Wolfgang Weber sieht die Welt,* Bonn 1952; *Abenteuer meines Lebens,* Munich, Vienna and Basle 1960; *Auf Abwegen um die Welt,* Gutersloh, West Germany 1964; *Hinter den Kulissen des Fernsehens,* Baden-Baden, West Germany 1975, Ravensburg, West Germany 1980.

On WEBER: Books—*Deutschland: Beginn des modernen Photojournalismus* by Tim N. Gidal, Frankfurt and Lucerne 1972, as *Modern Photojournalism: Origin and Evolution 1910-1933,* New York 1973; *The Magic Image: The Genius of Photography from 1839 to the Present Day* by Cecil Beaton and Gail Buckland, London and Boston 1975; *Documenta 6: Band 2,* exhibition catalogue, edited by Klaus Honnef and Evelyn Weiss, Kassel, West Germany 1977; *Die Geschichte der Fotografie im 20. Jahrhundert/Photography in the 20th Century* by Petr Tausk, Cologne 1977, London 1980; *Wolfgang Weber: Reisen ohne Ende—Fotos aus den Jahren 1935 bis 1939,* exhibition catalogue, Stuttgart 1982; *Museum Folkwang: die fotografische Sammlung,* exhibition catalogue, with introduction by Ute Eskildsen, Essen, West Germany 1983; *Wolfgang Weber* by Joan Fontcuberta, Barcelona 1984. **Articles**—"First Man Wolfgang" by Hanns Hubmann in *Foto-Magazin* (Munich), no. 6, 1969; "Wolfgang Weber—Barcelona 1926-27" by Colin Osman in *Creative Camera* (London), February 1975; "Photojournalism: Wolfgang Weber" by Bernd Lohse in *Camera* (Lucerne), October 1976; "Ausstellung: Reisen ohne Ende" in *Color Foto* (Munich), no. 12, 1982; "Ein Blick in eine Welt von Gestern" in *Foto Szene* (Mainaschaffen, Germany), no. 10, 1982; "Im Kleinen Grosses erkennen: Wolfgang Weber—Bildjournalist der ersten Stunde" by Karl Steinorth in *Leica Fotografie* (Wuerzbach, Germany), no. 4, 1984.

*   *   *

Remarkably, Wolfgang Weber is always referred to as one of the founding fathers of the "new photojournalism" that arose in the late 1920s, despite there being very little written on his work, and only shortly before his death were some of his photos exhibited. The main reason for this apparent neglect was probably due to Weber's overriding interest in projects for the future, practically all his energy being spent on planning and preparing for the next assignment. In all those years he never took time to reflect on his past work or put his negatives in any kind of order. Only when a heart attack made further television work impossible just before his eightieth birthday did he consider life's work.

Weber was born in Leipzig in 1902 and brought up in a remarkable household: his father—a well-to-do industrialist—had a passion for ethnology. His mother was a painter having close contacts with many other artists of her time. At the end of World War I, Weber's father sold his business and took the family to Munich where he now worked full-time with the explorer Leo Frobenius and the philosopher Oswald Spengler.

Wolfgang Weber was fascinated by his father's work, but also interested in music—so it was decided that he should study both. This combination, plus a talent for languages, led to his first job: an expedition to record the music of the Vadjaggas living in the region of the Kilimanjaro in East Africa. To get extra money for the trip, Weber accepted an assignment to bring back stereo views—his first professional job as a self-taught photographer. On his return to Berlin, he offered some of the pictures with a text to various newspapers: suddenly, there were twenty published articles in fourteen different periodicals—and an unexpected sum of money.

This experience was the beginning of Weber's career as a photoreporter. At first, he concentrated on articles about visits to foreign countries, but then took assignments for many other subjects.

In 1926/27 Weber was commissioned to do a book about Barcelona, and in 1929 the *Munchner Illustrierte Presse* published fourteen reports (with 70 photos) about his trip to the United States. By 1932, Weber had become a staff photographer for Ullstein Publications, chiefly working with the *Berliner Illustrierte Zeitung*—a job with which he continued until the end of World War II. Even when several of his friends and colleagues had left Germany in 1933, Weber stayed on to continue the work he loved. In his travels and reports from faraway places, his education and international experience gave a cosmopolitan view of the world.

When the new magazine *Neue Illustrierte* was founded in the autumn of 1946, Weber became its chief reporter. Travelling to England (1947), Italy (1948), and a world tour (1949) taking in the United States, India, China and other East Asian states he had visited some ten years earlier, Weber continued his work with the magazine until 1963 when new owners tried to increase circulation by swamping the pages with pin-ups girls.

At this time came the opportunity to work in television. founding his own production company, Weber was able to make documentaries in Cuba, China, Outer Mongolia as well as various Third World countries. His last production was a report on factory work in China, shown on several German channels in 1981.

Any future study of Weber's work will certainly have to deal with his astonishing ability to tell a story in pictures. Apart from its photographic professionalism, the quality of the work draws on Weber's educational background, extensive knowledge and international expertise. His ethnological studies and interests made him especially suited to report on the great changes occurring in many of the new independent states. His many contacts with people later playing a major role in world affairs gave Weber a front seat to record the end of one era and the beginning of the new.

—Karl Steinorth

WEEMS, Carrie Mae.

Nationality: American. **Education:** California Institute of the Arts, Valencia, B.A., 1981; University of California, San Diego, M.F.A., 1984; studied folklore at the University of California, Berkeley, 1984-87. **Career:** University tutor 1983-91. Artist in Residence at the Visual Studies Workshop, Rochester, New York, 1986; Light Work, Syracuse, New York. **Recipient:** Los Angeles Women's Building Poster Award; University of California Fellowship Award, 1981-85, University of California Chancellor's Grant, 1982; California Arts Council Grant, 1983 and Louis Comfort Tiffany Award, 1992. **Agent:** Penny Pilkington-Wendy Olsoff, 532 Broadway, New York, NY 10012.

Individual Exhibitions:

1984   *Family Pictures and Stories,* Multi-Cultural Gallery, San
            Diego, California
1987   Hampshire College Art Gallery, Amherst, Massachusetts
1989   Rhode Island School of Design, Providence
1990   *Calling Out My Name,* CEPA Gallery, Buffalo
            PPOW, New York
1991   Institute of Contemporary Art, Boston
            Trustman Gallery, Simmons College, Boston
            And 22 Million Very Tired and Very Angry People, The New
                Museum of Contemporary Art, New York (travelled to
                Walter/McBean Gallery, San Francisco Art Institute, Matrix
                Gallery, Wadsworth Atheneum, Hartford, CT)
            Family Pictures and Stories, Albright College, Reading,
                Pennsylvania (travelled to Art Complex Museum, Duxbury,
                Massachusetts)
            Carrie Mae Weems: Two Works, University of Southern
                California at Irvine
1992   Greenville County Museum of Art, Greenville, South Carolina
            Sea Islands, PPOW, New York (travelled to Linda Cathcart
                Gallery, Santa Monica; Rhona Hoffman Gallery, Chicago)
            New Langton Arts, San Francisco
            The Fabric Workshop, Philadelphia
1993   *Carrie Mae Weems,* National Museum of Women in the Arts,
                Washington, D.C. (travelled to The Forum, St Louis;
                Museum of Modern Art, San Francisco; Afro-American
                Museum, Los Angeles; Contemporary Arts Center, Cincin-
                nati; Center for Fine Arts, Miami; Walker Art Center,
                Minneapolis; Portland Art Museum, Oregon; Institute of
                Contemporary Art, Philadelphia)
1994   The Hood Museum of Art, Dartmouth College, Hannover, New
                Hampshire
            Dakar Biennial, Senegal

Selected Group Exhibitions:

1980   *Contemporary Black Photographers,* San Francisco State
                University
            Multi-Cultural Focus, Barnsdall Art Gallery, Los Angeles

1983   *Four West Coast Photographers,* Vanderbilt University Art
                Gallery, Nashville
1985   *Analysis and Passion: Photography Engages Social and
                Political Issues,* Eye Gallery, San Francisco
1986   *Past, Present, Future,* The New Museum, New York
1987   *Documenta B,* The Castle, Kassel, Germany
1988   *Prisoners Image, 1800-1988,* Alternative Museum, New York
1989   *Black Photographers Bear Witness: 100 Years of Social
                Protest*
1990   *Black Women Photographers,* Ten-8, London
1991   *Whitney Biennial,* The Whitney Museum of American Art,
                New York
1991-92 *Dirt and Domesticity: Constructions of the Feminine,* Whitney
                Museum of American Art at Equitable Center, New York
1993   *Urban Masculinity,* Longwood Arts Center, Bronx, New York
1994   *Bad Girls, Part 1,* The New Museum of Contemporary Art,
                New York

Publications:

By WEEMS: Books—*Blasted Allegories: An Anthology of Writings by Contemporary Artists,* New York 1988; *Black Photographers 1940-88,* Gardner Press 1988. **Article**—*Atelier* magazine, (Japan), January 1991.

On WEEMS: Articles—*Aperture,* May 1988; ''Carrie Mae Weems: The Right Questions'' by Marguerite VanCook in *Village Beat,* December 1990; ''Carrie Mae Weems'' by Lois Tarlow in *Art New England,* August/September 1991; ''Down-Home Look Belies Power of Carrie Mae Weems' Works'' by Cathy Curtis in *The Los Angeles Times,* 21 October 1991; ''The Isms Brothers, Carrie Mae Weems at SFAI'' by Jeff Kelley in *Artweek,* 7 May 1992; ''Dark Passage'' by Vince Aletti in *The Village Voice,* 22 December 1992; *The New Yorker,* 21 December 1992; ''Lessons in the Stories: The Engaging Voice of Carrie Mae Weems'' by Jo Ann Lewis in *The Washington Press,* 7 January 1993; ''Weems's World'' by Ruby Rich in *Mirabella,* February 1993; ''Carrie Mae Weems: Indictments of racism in black and white'' by David Hamilton in *Art and Antiques,* September 1993.

*   *   *

Californian photographer, Carrie Mae Weems' images engage with black culture. They deal with women, self portrayal or issues related to documentation of grotesque everyday artefacts. Provocative and critical, the visual and verbal narratives range from racial stereotypes to gender politics and are striking but also moving at the same time, and they offer hope and optimism for a better world.

Weems' first retrospective exhibition at the National Museum of Women in the Arts, Washington, in 1993 was simply called *Carrie Mae Weems*. The pictures, dating from 1978 to 1992 are about gender, class and race in America. Not only a photographer but also a fine and gripping story teller with an engaging voice, she does not mince her words. This becomes especially apparent when she speaks directly to the viewer via an audio tape describing her family's migration from a Mississippi sharecropper's plantation to Portland in Oregon, her place of birth. Here, her father worked in a factory sorting cowhides while her sister ''Tough Cookie'' helped to bring her up. Weems does not hide skeletons, in fact she tells of her own teenage pregnancy, her mother's angry reaction to it, and of a drunken gunfight between her father and her brother ''Son-Son.'' This offering of confidential personal detail and honesty to strangers can only establish human connections.

Many of Weems' photographs are posed. *The Kitchen Table Series 1990,* for instance, is an invented love story taking place around a kitchen table. Other stories are based on racist jokes. In fact, the question of colour always plays a vital part in her work. Many of the portraits illustrate variations, real or unreal of black skin. There is *Honey Coloured Boy, Chocolate Coloured Man, Golden Yella Girl* and *Magenta Coloured Girl* not forgetting *Blue Black Boy,* a blue-tinted triptych. Taken with a Polaroid camera, then hand tinted in different colours, the images illustrate the immense beauty of black faces, thus creating an extraordinary haunting presence. Called *Coloured People,* the title becomes a double-entendre.

The pictures of African-American folklore, entitled *Sea Island Series,* with the focus on distinctive black culture and its rich history, are perhaps

Weems' most original work to date. The images are beautiful and lavish. They are enriched by captions written out on plates in ceramic which are placed at random.

—Hildegard Mahony

WEGMAN, William.

Nationality: American. **Born:** Holyoke, Massachusetts, 12 February 1942. **Education:** Massachusetts College of Art, Boston, B.F.A., 1965; University of Illinois, Urbana, M.F.A., 1967. **Family:** Married to Gayle Wegman; son: Man Ray. **Career:** Artist and freelance photographer, California and New York. Instructor, University of Wisconsin at Wausau, 1967, and at Waukesha, 1968-69; Assistant Professor, University of Wisconsin, Madison, 1969-70; Lecturer, 1970-71, and Visiting Artist, 1978, California State University at Long Beach. **Recipient:** Guggenheim Fellowship, 1975 and 1986; National Endowment for the Arts Grant, 1975-77 and 1982; Creative Artists Public Service Grant, 1979. **Agent:** Pace/MacGill Gallery, 32 East 57th Street, New York, NY 10022, USA.

Individual Exhibitions:

1971	Galerie Sonnabend, Paris
	Pomona College, California
1972	Sonnabend Gallery, New York
	Galerie Ernst, Hannover
	Situation, London
	Galerie Konrad Fischer, Dusseldorf
	Courtney Sale Gallery, Dallas
1973	Galerie Sonnabend, Paris
	Texas Gallery, Houston
	Los Angeles County Museum of Art
	Francoise Lambert and Claire Copley Gallery, Los Angeles
1974	Modern Art Agency, Naples
	Galerie D, Brussels
	Galleria Toselli, Milan
	112 Greene Street Gallery, New York
	Texas Gallery, Houston
1975	Mayor Gallery, London
	Galleria Alessandra Castelli, Milan
	Galerie Konrad Fischer, Dusseldorf
1976	The Kitchen, New York
1977	Sonnabend Gallery, New York
	Bruno Soletti Gallery, Milan
1978	Rosamund Felsen Gallery, Los Angeles
	Robert Cumming/William Wegman, California Intitute of Technology, Pasadena
1979	Holly Solomon Gallery, New York
	Arnolfini Gallery, Bristol
	Galerie Konrad Fischer, Dusseldorf
	Otis Art Institute, Los Angeles
	William Wegman: Retrospective, Fine Arts Galleries, University of Wisconsin at Milwaukee
1980	*William Wegman: Selected Works 1970-1979,* University of Colorado Art Galleries, Boulder (travelled to the Aspen Center for Visual Arts, Colorado)
1981	Clarence Kennedy Gallery, Cambridge, Massachusetts (with Willard Van Dyke & Olivia Parker)
1982	Dart Gallery, Chicago
1983	*Wegman's World,* Corcoran Gallery, Washington, D.C.
1984	*William Wegman's Instant Miami,* University of Miami, Coral Gables
1985	*Photographs and Videotapes,* Albright College, Reading, Pennsylvania
1986	*Improved Photographs,* Daniel Wolf Gallery, New York
	Texas Gallery, Houston, Texas

	Beaver College Art Gallery, Glenside, Pennsylvania
	William Wegman: Color Photographs, Cleveland Museum of Art, Ohio
1987	*Works by William Wegman,* Honolulu Academy of Arts, Hawaii
	Massachusetts College of Art, Boston
1988	The Stuart Collection, University of San Diego, La Jolla
	William Wegman: Recent 20 x 24 Polaroid Photographs, Pace/MacGill Gallery, New York
	William Wegman: Polaroids & Videos, San Francisco Museum of Modern Art, San Francisco
1989	Maison de la Culture et de la Communication de Saint Etienne, Saint-Etienne, France
	William Wegman: Peintures, Dessins, Polaroids, Photos Retouchees, Galerie Durand-Dessert, Paris
	William Wegman: Photographies, Baudoin Lebon, Paris
1990	*The History of Travel,* The Taft Museum, Cincinnati
	William Wegman: Painting, Drawings, Photographs, Video-tapes, Kunstmuseum, Lucerne, Switzerland (travelled to Stedelijk Museum, Amsterdam; Frankfurt Kunstverein, Frankfurt, Germany; Centre National d'Art et de Culture Georges Pompidou, Paris; Institute of Contemporary Art, London; Institute of Contemporary Arts, Boston; Contemporary Arts Museum, Houston Texas; JM Ringling Museum, Sarasota; Whitney Museum of American Art, New York.)
	New Polaroids and C-Prints, Mai 36 Galerie, Lucerne, Switzerland
	Galerie Wanda Reiff, Maastrich, Belgium
	Salama-Caro Gallery, London
	Galerie Philippe Kriwin, Brussels
1991	*Outdoor Photographs,* Neuberger Museum State University of New York at Purchase, New York
	Galeria 57, Madrid, Spain
	William Wegman: L'oeuvre photographique 1969-1976, Fonds Regional d'Art Contemporain, Limousin, France
1992	*New Polaroids,* Holly Solomon Gallery, New York
	Early Black and White Photographs, Pace/MacGill Gallery, New York
	New Paintings, Sperone Westwater Gallery, New York
1993	*The Alphabet and Little Red Riding Hood,* Pace/MacGill Gallery, New York

Selected Group Exhibitions:

1969	*Place and Process,* Edmonton Art Gallery, Alberta
1971	*Prospect '71,* Dusseldorf
1973	*Whitney Annual,* Whitney Museum, New York
1977	*Photography as an Art Form,* Ringling Museum of Art, Sarasota, Florida
1978	*23 Photographers,* Walker Art Gallery, Liverpool
1979	*The Altered Photograph,* Project Studio 1, Long Island City, Queens, New York
1980	*Artist and Camera,* Mappin Art Gallery, Sheffield, Yorkshire (travelled to Stoke City Art Gallery; Durham Light Infantry Museum; Cartwright Hall, Bradford, 1980-81)
1983	*Subjective Vision,* High Museum of Art, Atlanta, Georgia
1986	*The Animal in Photography 1843-1985,* The Photographers' Gallery, London
1987	*Photography and Art 1946-86,* Los Angeles County Museum of Art
1988	*Fabrications: Staged, Altered and Appropriated Photographs,* Carpenter Center for the Arts, Harvard University, Cambridge, Massachusetts; Haifa Museum, Israel
1989	*Biennial Exhibition,* Whitney Museum of American Art, New York
	Photography Now, Victoria and Albert Museum, London
	Contemporary Art from New York, Yokohama Museum of Art, Yokohama, Japan
	Sesame Street: The First Generation, Museum of Modern Art, New York

1990   *Painting Beyond the Death of Painting,* USSR Artists Union, Moscow

Photography Until Now, Museum of Modern Art, New York (travelled to The Cleveland Museum of Art)

Les Annees 80 La Photographie, Galerie Langer Fain, Paris, France

Points of Departure: Origins in Video, The Carnegie Museum of Art, Pittsburgh, Pennsylvania

1991   *Videos et Films d'Art,* ELAC Art Contemporain, Lyon, France

La Revanche de L'Image, Galerie Pierre Huber, Geneva, Switzerland

Robert Mapplethorpe, Richard Prince, Cindy Sherman, William Wegman, Blum Helman Gallery, New York

Collections:

Whitney Museum of American Art, New York; Museum of Modern Art, New York; Ed Ruscha Collection, Los Angeles; International Museum of Photography at George Eastman House, Rochester, New York; Albright-Knox Gallery, Buffalo, New York; Allen Memorial Art Museum, Oberlin College, Ohio; Australian National Gallery, Canberra; Brooklyn Museum, New York; Carnegie Institute, Museum of Art, Pittsburg, Pennsylvania; The Contemporary Museum, Honolulu; Honolulu Academy of the Arts; Archer M Huntington Gallery, University of Texas, Austin; Minneapolis Institute of Arts; Museum of Fine Art, Houston; San Francisco Museum of Modern Art; Saint Louis Museum of Modern Art; Stuart Collection, University of California, San Diego; Walker Art Center, Minneapolis.

Publications:

By WEGMAN: Book—*Man's Best Friend,* New York, 1983. **Articles**—"Shocked and Outraged" in *Avalanche* (New York), Winter 1971; *Prints & Liquid Light Photographs,* New York, 1991.

On WEGMAN: Books—*Photography as Art* by Volker Kahmen, Tubingen, West Germany 1973, London 1974; *Subjective Vision,* exhibition catalogue, with introduction by A.D. Coleman, Atlanta, Georgia 1983; *Photography and Art 1946-1986,* exhibition catalogue, by Andy Grundberg and Kathleen M. Gauss, Los Angeles 1987. **Articles**—"Photography" by Ben Lifson in the *Village Voice* (New York), 9 April 1978; "Everything You Wanted to Know about William Wegman but Didn't Dare Ask" by Stuart Morgan in *Arnolfini Review* (Bristol), May/June 1979; "William Wegman" by Ian Walker in *Art Monthly* (London), no. 27, 1979; "William Wegman: Altered Photographs" in *Domus* (Milan), July 1979; "Postmodern TV: Wegman and Smith" by Patricia Mellercamp in *Afterimage* (Rochester, New York), December 1985.

*   *   *

William Wegman belongs deliberately to that large area between strictly defined photography and strictly defined art that has been so consciously fertilized and exploited as a major result of the intentions behind minimal and conceptual art. The whole idea of posing for photographs and arranging effects, so contrary to the concepts of documentary photography, harks back neatly and poignantly to the tenets of "art" photography current in the 19th century. We might almost consider that that desirable goal of having one's cake—and eating it, too—has come near realization.

Wegman began as a painter; his dog, who has featured in many a photographic sequence, was appropriately named Man Ray. Wegman has moved easily among a variety of techniques and media: he has used video extensively as well as photography and drawing. There are hints of the storyboard, surreal autobiographical content, and sardonic use of the artifacts of consumer culture, as well as a subliminal take-off of the culture-vulture aspects of American culture.

Thus his imagery, often hilarious, sardonic and ironical, can be rather emotional too, and intricately baroque. The deliberate set-ups that he creates to photograph can be elaborate put-downs, a visual commentary on Madison Avenue culture laced with West Coast exuberance.

What makes Wegman so unusual is that without being punky or funky, he is funny, amusing, wry. There is surprisingly little humour in "art" or in "photography." Wegman will, say, produce something like "Family Combi-nations," in which eyes, hair, nose, mouth are matched in various combinations—harking back to Victorian face games—which is both telling and hilarious. His work is domestic, sometimes fetchingly silly and absurd: in "Untied On Tied Off" one hairy leg wears an untied boot, the other has tied to it a boot. In an image called "The Morphy Richards Problem" (shades of sociological pomposity) an electric radiator of that make keels over. In "Before Learning to Write with His Own Sweater He Learned to Write with His Hand," we see just that: a sheet of paper, bearing upon it one besweatered arm through which a pen is writing, and one hand, not writing.

It is absurd, arresting, a freshly surreal look at reality, in intimate mode.

—Marina Vaizey

WELPOTT, Jack (Warren).

Nationality: American. **Born:** Kansas City, Kansas, 27 April 1923. **Education:** primary and secondary schools, Bloomington, Indiana; studied photography under Henry Holmes Smith, painting under Leon Golub and Harry Engle, and design under George Rickey, University of Indiana, Bloomington, 1946-59, B.S. 1949, M.S. in Visual Communication 1955, M.F.A. 1959. **Military Service:** Served in the 13th Intelligence Unit, U.S. Air Force, 1943-46; Staff Sergeant, 3 combat stars. **Family:** Married Doris Jean Franklin in 1949 (divorced, 1968); children: Jan Marie and Matthew David; married the photographer Judy Dater, *q.v.,* in 1971 (divorced, 1977). **Career:** Production Supervisor, Audio-Visual Center, Indiana University, Bloomington, 1949-59. Independent photographer since 1959. Assistant Professor of Photography, 1959-60, Associate Professor, 1961-70, and Professor since 1971, San Francisco State University. Lecturer, University of California Extension, San Francisco, 1966-69. Member, Board of Trustees, Friends of Photography, Carmel, California, and Society for Photographic Education, since 1963. **Recipient:** Medal of Arles, France, 1973; National Endowment for the Arts Grant, 1979. **Address:** 281/2 Precita Avenue, San Francisco, California 94110, U.S.A.

Individual Exhibitions:

1961   Kalamazoo Institute of Art, Michigan

1962   University of California at Davis

1963   Florida State Museum, Tallahassee

University of Florida, Gainesville

1966   International Museum of Photography, George Eastman House, Rochester, New York

1969   Phoenix College, Arizona

1970   Friends of Photography, Carmel, California

1972   Art Institute of Chicago

1973   Wall Street Gallery, Spokane, Washington

Ohio Silver Gallery, Los Angeles (with Judy Dater)

Sisters: A Photographic Exhibition, Focus Gallery, San Francisco (with Judy Dater)

Ms.: Portraits of Women, International Museum of Photography, George Eastman House, Rochester, New York (with Judy Dater)

1974   Gallery 113, Santa Cruz, California

Witkin Gallery, New York (with Judy Dater)

1975   Washington Gallery of Photography, Washington, D.C. (with Judy Dater)

Shadai Gallery of Photography, Tokyo (with Judy Dater)

International Center for Photography, New York (with Judy Dater)

Jack Welpott: The Artist as Teacher/The Teacher as Artist: Photographs 1950-1975, San Francisco Museum of Art (retrospective; travelled to Indiana University Art Museum, Bloomington and University of Southern California at Los Angeles, 1977)

University of Colorado, Boulder (with Nathan Lyons)

1976   Musée Réattu, Arles, France (with Judy Dater)

1977	Silver Image Gallery, Seattle
1978	Ohio State University, Columbus
1979	Center for Creative Photography, University of Arizona, Tucson
1980	Colorado Mountain College, Leadville
	Equivalents Gallery, Seattle
1981	Jehu Gallery, San Francisco
	Bard College, Annandale-on-Hudson, New York
	O.W. Gallery, Dallas, Texas
	Jeb Gallery, Providence, Rhode Island
1984	Vision Gallery, San Francisco

Selected Group Exhibitions:

1966	*Contemporary Photography since 1950,* International Museum of Photography, George Eastman House, Rochester, New York (toured the United States)
1967	*Photography in the 20th Century,* National Gallery of Canada, Ottawa (toured Canada and the United States, 1967-73)
	Photography in the Fine Arts, Metropolitan Museum of Art, New York (and 1968)
1969	*Recent Acquisitions,* Pasadena Art Museum, California
1970	*California Photographers 1970,* University of California at Davis (travelled to the Oakland Museum, California; and Pasadena Art Museum, California
1974	*Photography in America,* Whitney Museum, New York
1977	*Photographs: Sheldon Memorial Art Gallery Collection,* University of Nebraska, Lincoln
	The Great West: Real/Ideal, University of Colorado, Boulder (subsequently Smithsonian Institution travelling exhibition; toured the United States)
1979	*Teacher's Legacy: My Teacher, Myself,* Susan Spiritus Gallery, Newport Beach, California (homage to Henry Holmes Smith)
1984	*Photography in California 1945-80,* San Francisco Museum of Modern Art (travelled to the Akron Art Museum, Ohio; Corcoran Gallery, Washington, D.C.; Los Angeles Municipal Art Gallery; Cornell University, Ithaca, New York; High Museum of Art, Atlanta Georgia; Museum Folkwang, Essen; Centre Georges Pompidou, Paris; Museum of Photographic Art, San Diego, California)

Collections:

Museum of Modern Art, New York; Whitney Museum, New York; International Museum of Photography, George Eastman House, Rochester, New York; Art Institute of Chicago; Center for Creative Photography, University of Arizona, Tucson; University of New Mexico, Albuquerque; Norton Simon Art Museum, Pasadena, California; Oakland Art Museum, California; San Francisco Museum of Modern Art; Bibliothèque Nationale, Paris.

Publications:

By WELPOTT: Book—*Women and Other Visions: Photographs by Judy Dater and Jack Welpott,* with an introduction by Henry Holmes Smith, New York 1975. **Articles**—"Genre Photography: Jack Welpott," in *Camera* (Lucerne), May 1975; "Judy Dater and Jack Welpott," interview with Gilles Walinski, in *Zoom* (Paris), November/December 1979.

On WELPOTT: Books—Photography in the 20th Century by Nathan Lyons, New York 1967; *California Photographers 1970,* exhibition catalogue, by Fred R. Parker, Davis, California 1970; *The Print,* by the Time-Life editors, Amsterdam 1972; *Photography in America,* edited by Robert Doty, introduction by Minor White, New York 1974; *The Photographers' Choice,* edited by Kelly Wise, Danbury, New Hampshire 1975; *The Artist as Teacher/The Teacher as Artist: Photographs 1950-1975,* exhibition catalogue, with text by Henry Holmes Smith and Rodney C. Stuart, San Francisco 1975; *Photographs: Sheldon Memorial Art Gallery Collection,* University of Nebraska, with an introduction by Norman A. Geske, Lincoln 1977; *The Great West: Real/Ideal,* edited by Sandy Hume and others, Boulder, Colorado 1977;

Concerning Photography by Jonathan Bayer and others, London 1977; *The Photography Collector's Guide* by Lee D. Witkin and Barbara London, Boston and London 1979; *La Photographie Créative* by Jean-Claude Lemagny, Paris 1984; *Photography in California 1945-1980* by Louise Katzman, San Francisco 1984; *the Library of World Photography: Landscape,* with texts by David Plowden and Ian Jeffrey, Tokyo and London 1984.

*

Part of the fascination that photography holds is its ability to unlock secrets kept even from ourselves. Like dreams, the photograph can uncork a heady bouquet of recognition which can escape into the cognitive world. Sometimes the aroma is sharp, sometimes dry. This "shock of recognition" can be, at times, unsettling. It can also be sublime.

—Jack Welpott

*   *   *

Jack Welpott is a part of the recent, post-World War II, generation of photographers that has been able to "study" photography formally at the University level. He attended Indiana University as a student of Henry Holmes Smith and soon became acquainted with other influential photographers— Aaron Siskind, Minor White, Roy Stryker, Harry Callahan, Jerry Uelsmann, etc. He himself has since become a respected photographer and teacher whose main photographic themes are "the psychological landscape" and the "attempt to define changing reality in terms of human psychology."

For a period of time in the 1970s, Welpott and his former wife, Judy Dater, worked together, often photographing women, sometimes even photographing the same subjects to bring out the subtle differences in interaction between the subject and the male photographer and the subject and the female photographer. As Welpott says in the introduction to *Women and Other Visions,* "Portrait photography is an experience between two human beings, an experience shared with the viewer through the resulting photograph. If the moment was charged with feeling, the image can be personal and revealing." The people whom they photographed were people who "we found fascinating and who, in some manner, expressed something about the 'feminine mystique.' Most were strangers to us. We discovered them in cafes, banks, shops, and on the streets—anywhere we happened to be. We usually spent several hours photographing them in their own environment. In every case, the few hours spent with these people were intense and, at times, progressed to extended friendships."

Mark Johnstone in *The Print* provides a mild criticism of Welpott's work, describing his imagery as "quiet in a nice Midwestern way. As reflections of a moment, rather than staggering revelations of a time, the works exist as meditations. But the meditative 'softness' comes across as content without substance—neither a pictorial quality that might enhance the image nor a classic composition that mirrors more than the subject matter depicted. Instead, a consideration of his photographs implies that his way of working is one that has been passed over not only by the 70s but by the 60s as well. ... Welpott's imagery lacks the verve which might otherwise transform it into an active living vision."

Several years later, Henry Homes Smith, writing in the catalogue for *The Artist as Teacher/The Teacher as Artist* exhibition, took a more favorable view of Welpott's development and work: "He offers us today a child's eye view of the world, seen as through the mind of a kindly, sophisticated, secure adult. Welpott has ripened as have the times as well. The increasing frequency of pictures reminding us of the pleasures of mind and body were long foretold in earlier work. Those of us who know the earlier pictures may feel the chagrin that accompanies belated recognition of overlooked earlier truths. This passage back to joy, rewarding both artist and a sympathetic audience, lies through thorn bush and dark groves during a time of troubles. Our arrival is all the better for it. ... Culturally commonplace, culturally oversaturated visual matter was reached and passed through quite early in his career. These include the security of simple geometric picture structure, the appeal of made-up good looks, the unmeant poses of fashion models and the insecure stance of hometown beauty. Beyond these come the pressure generated by the intense feeling of being alone, the need to achieve one's greatest potential, contemplation of certain dark mysteries that generate fear and awe and probably most important of all the longings that males tend to believe are theirs exclusively.

We can see from [his] pictures the trail of a journey far from finished, toward uneasy insights about how men and women fare together and the place of nature in our . . . environment.''

—Michael Held

WESSEL, Henry, Jr.

Nationality: American. **Born:** Teaneck, New Jersey, 28 July 1942. **Education:** Northern Valley Regional High School, Demarest, New Jersey, 1956-60; studied psychology, Pennsylvania State University, University Park, 1960-66; B.A. 1966; photography, State University of New York at Buffalo/ Visual Studies Workshop, Rochester, New York, 1969-72, M.F.A. 1972. **Career:** Independent photographer, since 1966: proprietor, Images commercial photo studio, at Pennsylvania State University, 1966; cinematographer on U.S. Department of Health, Education and Welfare documentary film *The Retreads*, 1967; director, Photographic Resources commercial documentary photo business, San Francisco, 1978. Instructor, Department of Art, Pennsylvania State University, University Park, 1967-69; Instructor in Photography, San Francisco Art Institute, since 1973; Assistant Professor, 1974, and Lecturer, 1985, San Francisco State University; Visiting Artist, University of California at Davis, and California College of Arts and Crafts, Oakland, 1977. **Recipient:** Guggenheim Fellowship, 1971, 1978; National Endowment for the Arts Grant, 1975, 1977, 1978. **Agent:** Fraenkel Gallery, 49 Geary Street, San Francisco, California 94108-5730. **Address:** Box 475 Point Richmond, California 94807, U.S.A.

Individual Exhibitions:

1973	Museum of Modern Art, New York
1974	Pennsylvania State University, University Park
1976	Grossmont College, El Cajon, California
1977	Visual Studies Workshop, Rochester, New York
1981	Charles Cowles Gallery, New York
	Fraenkel Gallery, San Francisco
1987	Gallery Min, Tokyo
	International Museum of Photography, Osaka, Japan
1988	Museum of Art, Rhode Island School of Design, Providence, USA
1989	Fraenkel Gallery, San Francisco, USA
1992	Fraenkel Gallery, San Francisco, USA

Selected Group Exhibitions:

1969	*Vision and Expression,* International Museum of Photography, George Eastman House, Rochester, New York (toured the United States)
1970	*Contemporary Photographers V,* International Museum of Photography, George Eastman House, Rochester, New York (toured the United States)
1975	*New Topographics: Photographs of a Manaltered Landscape,* International Museum of Photography, George Eastman House, Rochester, New York (toured the United States)
1978	*Mirrors and Windows: American Photography since 1960,* Museum of Modern Art, New York (toured the United States, 1978-80)
1981	*Robert Frank Forward,* Fraenkel Gallery, San Francisco
1982	*Slices of Time: California Landscapes,* Oakland Museum, California (travelled to the Security Pacific Bank Plaza, Los Angeles)
1984	*Photography in California 1945-80,* San Francisco Museum of Modern Art (travelled to the Akron Art Museum, Ohio; Corcoran Gallery, Washington, D.C.; Los Angeles Municipal Art Gallery; Cornell University, Ithaca, New York; High Museum of Art, Atlanta, Georgia; Museum Folkwang,

	Essen; Centre Georges Pompidou, Paris; Museum of Photographic Art, San Diego, California)
1985	*American Images 1945-80,* Barbican Art Gallery, London (toured Britain)
1987	*The Insistent Object: 1845-1986,* Fraenkel Gallery, San Francisco
	Contemporary American Figurative Photography, Center for the Fine Arts, Miami
	Midtown Review, International Center of Photography Midtown, New York
	Photographs from the Last Decade, San Francisco Museum of Modern Art
1988	*Road and Roadside: American Photographs 1930-1986,* San Francisco Museum of Modern Art
1989	*Picturing California: A Century of Photographic Genius,* Oakland Museum, California
1990	*Shelters and Structures,* Rena Bransten Gallery, San Francisco
1991	*The City Life of Flora and Fauna,* Joseph Seagram and Sons Inc., New York
	The American Scene: Contemporary Photographs, Rena Bransten Gallery, San Francisco
	Pleasures and Terrors of Domestic Comfort, Museum of Modern Art, New York
1993	*In Camera,* Museum of Fine Arts, Museum of New Mexico
1994	*One Hundred Years of Street Photography,* Wright State University, Dayton, Ohio

Collections:

Museum of Modern Art, New York; Seagram Collection, New York; International Museum of Photography, George Eastman House, Rochester, New York; Visual Studies Workshop, Rochester, New York; University of Maine, Gorham; Philadelphia Museum of Art; University of Nebraska, Lincoln; Norton Simon Art Museum, Pasadena, California; National Gallery of Canada, Ottawa, Ontario; American Arts Documentation Center, Exeter, England; Art Institute of Chicago; National Gallery of Australia, Canberra; California Museum of Photography, University of California, Riverside; Center for Creative Photography, University of Arizona, Tucson; Crocker Art Museum, Sacramento; Denver Art Museum; Fogg Art Museum, Harvard University, Cambridge, Massachusetts; Metropolitan Museum of Art, New York; Museum of Fine Arts, Boston; Museum of Fine Arts, Houston, Texas; San Francisco Museum of Modern Art; Victoria and Albert Museum, London.

Publications:

On WESSEL: Books—*Vision and Expression* by Nathan Lyons, New York 1969; *New Topographics: Photographs of a Man-altered Landscape,* exhibition catalogue, with text by William Jenkins, Rochester, New York 1975; *Henry Wessel, Jr.,* exhibition catalogue, with an introduction by Ben Lifson, El Cajon, California 1976; *Photographs: Sheldon Memorial Art Gallery Collection, University of Nebraska,* with an introduction by Norman A. Geske, Lincoln, 1977; *Mirrors and Windows: American Photography since 1960* by John Szarkowski, New York 1978; *Nude Photographs 1850-1980,* edited by Constance Sullivan, New York 1980; *Slices of Time: California Landscapes 1860-1880, 1960-1980,* exhibition catalogue, by Therese Thau Heyman and Ted Hedgpeth, Oakland, California 1981; *Photography in California 1945-1980* by Louise Katzman, San Francisco and New York 1984; *American Images: Photography 1945-1980,* edited by Peter Turner, London and New York 1985. **Article**—"New American Imagery: Henry Wessel, Jr.'' in *Camera* (Lucerne), May 1974.

* * *

The imagery of Henry Wessel, Jr. is part of a split in the tradition of documentary photography. Unlike earlier members of this tradition such as Walker Evans or Robert Frank, Wessel is not trying to reveal that which is particularly American, he is not trying to persuade his viewers to recognize the wrongs of our society. His is a more detached point of view, a more dispassionate tone. His images carry a new attitude toward the significance of the photographic message. In this contemporary branch of photography the photographer is no longer expected to concentrate on the beauty, the drama, or the tragedy of life; here the photographer is free to explore unnoticed aspects of modern life.

When photographing, Wessel is attracted to ordinary, almost mundane, subjects he encounters in his daily life. His photographs are full of telephone poles, chain link fences, TV antennas, tract houses, patios, and parking lots. When people are included in his photographs, they are never aware of the photographer's presence; they are immersed in routine activities such as walking, sunbathing or talking on the phone. Although the photographs are titled with the name of a city, state, and the date, they have very little to do with specific places or times. The tree in a picture titled "Tempe, Arizona, 1974" or the house in "Albany, California, 1972" could be found anywhere. In these photographs, then, the subject matter is less important than the way in which it is presented.

The formal arrangement and printing of Wessel's pictures are understated. An overall grayness, created by a preponderance of midtones, gives way to a subtle interplay of rich tones throughout each print where silvery gray poles and surfaces of sand and sidewalk suddenly command attention. Similarly, what appear to be random compositions eventually reveal a highly organized structure. Palm trees, poles, and wires are used to fracture the picture plane as well as to join diverse elements together. Shadows, from both seen and unseen objects, take on a life of their own as they appear in the most unexpected places and shapes. After some exploration, one can see that these photographs are full of surprising visual intricacies.

In the end, the world of Hank Wessel's photographs is far from mundane. Unlike many artists who are disturbed by "normal life," Wessel finds sustenance in it. His pictures remind us that forlorn banality is part of life, and with their quiet sense of acceptance and their unique sense of humor, they allow us to ponder those oddly common moments and places we can so easily forget.

—Ted Hedgpeth

WESTON, Brett (Theodore).

Nationality: American. **Born:** Los Angeles, California, in 1911. **Education:** Educated in California schools; studied photography with his father from 1925. **Careeer:** Established studio with Edward Weston, San Francisco, 1929; later moved to Carmel, California; freelance photographer, working for film studios and aeroplane factories, California, 1941-43, in New York, 1943-45; worked with Edward Weston on Edward's photographic portfolios, Carmel, California, 1948-58. **Recipient:** Guggenheim Fellowship, 1946. **Died:** (in Hawaii) 22 January 1993.

Individual Exhibitions:

1927	Los Angeles Museum (with Edward Weston)
1930	Jake Zeitlin Gallery, Los Angeles
1932	M.H. de Young Memorial Museum, San Francisco
1935	Julien Levy Gallery, New York
1966	Amon Carter Museum of Western Art, Fort Worth, Texas
	Museo de Arte Moderno, Mexico City (with Edward Weston)
1971	Witkin Gallery, New York
	Carl Siembab Gallery, Boston (with Edward Weston)
1975	Thackrey and Robertson, San Francisco
1976	G. Ray Hawkins Gallery, Los Angeles
1977	Cronin Gallery, Houston
	Modesto Junior College, California (with Edward Weston and Paul Strand)
1979	Fifth Avenue Gallery of Photography, Scottsdale, Arizona
1981	Hills Gallery, Denver (retrospective)
1983	*Photographs 1925-30, 1980-82,* San Francisco Museum of Modern Art
	Douglas Elliott Gallery, San Francisco
1985	Vision Gallery, San Francisco (with Henry Bianchini)

Selected Group Exhibitions:

1929	*Film und Foto,* Deutscher Werkbund, Stuttgart
1963	*The Photographer and the American Landscape,* Museum of Modern Art, New York
1967	*Photography in the 20th Century,* National Gallery of Canada, Ottawa (toured Canada and the United States, 1967-73)
1974	*Photography in America,* Whitney Museum, New York
1975	*The Land: 20th Century Landscape Photographs Selected by Bill Brandt,* Victoria and Albert Museum, London (travelled to Edinburgh, Belfast and Glasgow)
1979	*Photography Rediscovered: American Photographs 1900-1930,* Whitney Museum, New York (travelled to Art Institute of Chicago)
1980	*Photography of the 50s,* International Center of Photography, New York (travelled to University of Arizona, Tucson; Minneapolis Institute of Arts, Minnesota; California State University at Long Beach; and Delaware Art Museum, Wilmington)
1983	*American Photographers and the National Parks,* Los Angeles County Museum of Art
1984	*Exposed and Developed,* National Museum of American Art, Washington, D.C.
1985	*American Images 1945-80,* Barbican Art Gallery, London (toured Britan)

Collections:

Museum of Modern Art, New York; International Museum of Photography, George Eastman House, Rochester, New York; Carpenter Center and Fogg Art Museum, Harvard University, Cambridge, Massachusetts; Library of Congress, Washington, D.C.; Art Institute of Chicago; New Orleans Museum of Art; Amon Carter Museum of Western Art, Fort Worth, Texas; University of New Mexico, Albuquerque; Norton Simon Museum of Art, Pasadena, California; Oakland Art Museum, California.

Publications:

By WESTON: Books—*San Francisco,* portfolio of 12 prints, Carmel, California 1938; *White Sands,* portfolio of 10 prints, Carmel, California 1949; *New York,* portfolio of 12 prints, with a foreword by Beaumont Newhall, Carmel, California 1951; *Brett Weston Photographs,* with text by Merle Armitage, New York 1956; *10 Photographs,* portfolio, Carmel, California 1958; *Aperture Monograph: Brett Weston,* New York 1960; *Baja California,* portfolio of 15 prints, Carmel, California 1967; *Japan,* portfolio of 15 prints, Carmel, California 1970; *Europe,* portfolio of 12 prints, Carmel, California 1973; *Brett Weston: Voyage of the Eye,* with text by Beaumont Newhall, New York 1975; *Oregon,* portfolio of 15 prints, Carmel, California 1975; *Portraits of My Father,* portfolio of 10 prints, with an introduction by Ansel Adams, 1976; *20 Photographs,* 1970-1977, portfolio, with a foreword by Rosario Mazzeo, Carmel, California 1977; *Brett Weston: Photographs from Five Decades,* with text by R.H. Cravens, New York and London 1980; *Brett Weston Photographs: 1925-1930 and 1980-1982,* exhibition catalogue, with text by Van Deren Coke, San Francisco 1983.

On WESTON: Books—*Edward Weston—Brett Weston,* exhibition catalogue, Los Angeles 1927; *The Photographer and the American Landscape,* exhibition catalogue, by John Szarkowski, New York 1963; *Fotografías de Edward Weston/Brett Weston,* exhibition catalogue, with an introduction by Carmen Barreda, texts by Eleanor Green and Nancy Newhall, Mexico City 1966; *Photography in the Twentieth Century* by Nathan Lyons, New York 1967; *A Collection of Photographs* by Beaumont and Nancy Newhall, Millerton, New York 1969; *Photography in America,* edited by Robert Doty, with an introduction by Minor White, New York and London 1974; *The Land: 20th Century Landscape Photographs Selected by Bill Brandt,* exhibition catalogue, edited by Mark Haworth-Booth, London 1975; *The Magic Image* by Cecil Beaton and Gail Buckland, London and Boston 1975; *Interviews with*

Master Photographers by James Danziger and Barnaby Conrad III, New York and London 1977; *Photographs: Sheldon Memorial Art Gallery Collection, University of Nebraska,* with an introduction by Norman A. Geske, Lincoln 1977; *Geschichte der Fotografie im 20. Jahrhundert/Photography in the 20th Century* by Peter Tausk, Cologne 1977, London 1980; *Photography Rediscovered: American Photographs 1900-1930* by David Travis, New York 1979; *A Ten Year Salute* by Lee D. Witkin, with a foreword by Carol Brown, Danbury, New Hampshire 1979; *Dialogue with Photography* by Paul Hill and Thomas Cooper, London 1979; *The Photograph Collector's Guide* by Lee D. Witkin and Barbara London, Boston and London 1979; *Landscape: Theory,* edited by Carole di Grappa, New York 1980; *American Photographers and the National Parks,* exhibition catalogue, by Robert Glenn Ketchum, Los Angeles 1983; *Exposed and Developed: Photography Sponsored by the National Endowment for the Arts,* exhibition catalogue, with text by Merry Amanda Foresta, Washington, D.C., 1984; *American Images: Photography 1945-1980,* edited by Peter Turner, London and New York 1985. **Articles**—"Brett Weston: Japan 1970 and Other New Pictures" in *Creative Camera* (London), February 1970; "Brett Weston" in *Camera* (Lucerne), June 1973; "Brett Weston and Edward Weston: An Essay in Photographic Style" by Roger Aikin in *Art Journal* (New York), Summer 1973; "Group f/64" in *Camera* (Lucerne), February 1973; "New York, Established Style" by D. Turner in *Artweek* (Oakland, California), 23 February 1974; "Profile: Brett Weston" by Joan Murray in *American Photographer* (New York), April 1980; "Brett Weston: Looking at the Beginning" by Joan Murray in *Artweek* (Oakland, California), 12 February 1983.

*   *   *

If abstract expressionism has a master in modern photography, Brett Weston would be a logical choice for the title. Unfortunately, the terms that we use to define artistic styles are never precise. Some would even argue that a photograph by its very nature cannot be abstract. And yet, Brett Weston's work has a consistent, dark and penetrating quality that is derived from the fact that like an expressionist, or a Japanese landscape painter, Brett is relatively unconcerned with simply recording the surface phenomena of nature. In fact it's not unusual to find yourself thoroughly perplexed as to the subject matter of one of his photographs, while fully appreciating it nevertheless. In many of Brett Weston's photographs, highlights, shadows, and reflections are simply points of departure, abstracted in order to better express his deep and essentially emotional reactions to nature. Normal shades of gray give way to dramatic contrast; glimmers of light become startling brilliance. Brett Weston's skill as a printer is such that he manages to exploit every nuance of richness and texture that the medium has to offer. His photographs are not simply black and white, they are brooding darkness and polished silver, a beautiful combination of formal elegance and masculine intensity.

Brett Weston has a gift for using his art to transform details of the natural world into personal statements. His father, the great photographer Edward Weston, also photographed nature, but Brett has developed a style that is distinctly his own. While Edward's work embodies the sensuality, the order and the harmony of nature, Brett's photographs seem to penetrate to a more primal source. In some of his work one feels as if all traces of the soft, surface elements of nature have been removed in order to reveal the solid and poetic beauty beneath. His little known sculptures in wood also have this quality. They are stylized, simplified natural forms that, like the work of Constantin Brancusi, transform the complex structures of nature into symbols of unity and grace. And in fact, it is perhaps the persistent search for a stable and elegant truth that motivates Brett Weston's creative life. This motivation is expressed by his remarkably prolific output. He photographs and prints constantly, travelling and enjoying his time and friends with the robust enthusiasm of a man wholly committed to life and art.

The sheer visual impact of Brett Weston's photographs is obvious, but it's also important to note the quality of awe that pervades his work. Brett doesn't attempt to dominate nature with his perceptions, but rather to discover the infinite variety of form and meaning that the natural world reveals to an artist with vision. Aesthetic discovery in nature requires sensitivity, perseverance, and a profound respect for art and its ability to inspire and delight. Brett Weston has these qualities, and it is for this reason that his work is so important.

—Chris Johnson

WESTON, Cole

Nationality: American. **Born:** in Los Angeles, California, 30 January 1919; fourth son of the photographer Edward Weston. **Education:** Graduated from University High School, Los Angeles, 1937; studied theatre arts at the Cornish School, Seattle, 1937-40; studied photography with his father. **Military Service:** Served as a photographer, in the United States Navy, in Norman, Oklahoma, 1943-45. **Family:** Married Dorothy Hermann in 1940 (divorced); married Helen Prosser in 1951 (divorced); children: Ivor, Kim, Cara and Rhys; married Margaret Woodward in 1963; son: Matthew. **Carer:** Worked for Lockheed Aircraft Corporation, 1940-43; photographer with *Life* magazine, Los Angeles, 1945-46; photographic studio assistant to his father Edward Weston, Carmel, California, 1946-58 (executor of his father's estate, including printing from original negatives, from 1958). Independent photographer, concentrating on color landscape photography, Carmel, California, since 1958. Independent Progressive Party candidate for United States Congress, 1948; started Weston Trout Farm, Garrapata Canyon, Monterey County, 1949; Stage Director, Forest Theatre, Carmel, 1951; started Old Mill Stream Trout Farm, at Knott's Berry Farm, Buena Park, California, 1959; Cultural Director, Sunset Center, Carmel, 1966-69. **Agents:** Afterimage Gallery, The Quadrangle no. 250, 2800 Routh Street, Dallas, Texas 75201; Halsted Gallery, 560 North Woodward Avenue, Birmingham, Michigan 48011; and the Weston Gallery, P.O. Box 655, Carmel, California 93921. **Address:** Box 22155, Carmel, California 93922, U.S.A.

Individual Exhibitions:

1971	Focus Gallery, San Francisco (with Edward Weston)
1973	Focus Gallery, San Francisco
1974	Afterimage Gallery, Dallas
1975	Halsted 831 Gallery, Birmigham, Michigan
1976	Witkin Gallery, New York
1977	Halsted 831 Gallery, Birmingham, Michigan
1978	Leiserowitz Gallery, Des Moines, Iowa
1979	Deja Vue Gallery, Toronto
1981	Susan Spiritus Gallery, Newport Beach, California
1985	Focus Gallery, San Francisco
	Equivalents Gallery, Seattle, Washington
1986	Daytona Beach Community College, Florida

Selected Group Exhibitions:

1981	*Photographer as Printmaker,* Ferens Art Gallery, Hull, Yorkshire (travelled to the Museum and Art Gallery, Leicester; Cooper Gallery, Barnsley; Castle Museum, Nottingham; Photographers' Gallery, London)

Collections:

Museum of Modern Art, New York; International Museum of Photography, George Eastman House, Rochester, New York; Fogg Art Museum, Harvard University, Cambridge, Massachusetts; Philadelphia Museum of Art; Los Angeles Museum of Art.

Publications:

By WESTON: Book—*Cole Weston: 18 Photographs,* with a foreword by Ben Maddow and an introduction by Charis Wilson, Salt Lake City, Utah 1981. **Articles**—"Edward Weston: Dedicated to Simplicity" in *Modern Photography* (New York), May 1969; "Printing Dad's Negatives" in *Popular Photography* (New York), October 1978. **Film**—*Escape to Reality,* 1974.

On WESTON: Books—*The Picture History of Photography* by Peter Pollack, New York 1958; *Darkroom 2,* edited by Jain Kelly, New York 1978; *Photographer as Printmaker,* exhibition catalogue, with texts by Gerry Badger, Peter C. Bunnell and Ansel Adams, London 1981; *The Library of*

World Photography: landscape, with texts by David Plowden and Ian Jeffrey, Tokyo and London 1984.

* * *

The work of Cole Weston has long been overshadowed by the more famous photos of his father, Edward Weston, and his older brother, Brett Weston. Many observers feel that this is only a temporary situation, and that Cole Weston's beautiful sensuous color work will find a place of its own in the world's great photography.

Part of Cole Weston's obscurity is due to his quieter nature, which pales beside that of the more flamboyant Edward and Brett. Part is due to a certain self-abnegation. But most comes from the fact that Cole's work is so closely derived from that of his father that it seems to be just a logical continuation of the father's style.

Until World War II Cole worked by his father's side and under his father's close direction. During the conflict Cole served as a Navy photographer, and afterwards went out on his own as a photojournalist. But the ailing and elderly Edward Weston called Cole back to his side. Edward could no longer print his great black-and-white work himself, so he instructed Cole in the precise techniques for printing his negatives. From that time until today, Cole has provided prints from the Edward Weston negatives. He has become so well known for this work that many are surprised to discover that Cole is a photographer in his own right.

Late in his career, Edward Weston began photographing a little in color. Cole was with him, and took to the new materials immediately. Cole Weston, one of the master black-and-white printers of our day, has done the bulk of all his own photography in color.

Cole Weston's color photographs were amazingly beautiful yet restrained right from the beginning. In those early days of color, most photographers were anxious to make their prints "colorful:" they drowned every scene in a sea of blazing oranges, vibrant yellows and searing reds. Cole was the first to realize that color could be subtle, delicate, and gentle. He photographed much of what his father had photographed, including Point Lobos and the Big Sur country, but he captured it in color with soft browns, pale blues, and quiet greens.

The bulk of Cole Weston's color has been done with large format cameras, and is very much in the f/64 school tradition with its love of the perfectly sharp ground glass image. Cole has continued this emphasis with precise and exquisite dye transfer printing.

At a time when many young photographers are turning to large format color photography, Cole Weston is beginning to be seen as the real pioneer of color photography as an art form.

—Mike Rowell

WHITE, Minor (Martin).

Nationality: American. **Born:** Minneapolis, Minnesota, 9 July 1908. **Education:** public schools in Minneapolis, 1913-28; studied botany, University of Minnesota, Minneapolis, 1928-31, 1932-33, B.S. 1933; art history and aesthetics, Columbia University, New York, 1945-46; mainly self-taught in photography, from 1916, influenced by Beaumont and Nancy Newhall, New York 1945-46. **Military Service:** Served as infantryman, United States Army, in the Philippines, 1942-45: Bronze Star. **Career:** Worked as a waiter and barman, University Club, University of Minnesota, 1933-37; hotel night clerk and assistant in photographic studio, Portland, Oregon, 1937-38; instructor in photography, YMCA, Portland, 1938; secretarial assistant, People's Power League, Portland, 1938; photographer, Works Progress Administration (WPA), Portland, 1938-39; Instructor in Photography, then Director, La Grande Art Center, Oregon, 1940-41; Photographer, Museum of Modern Art, New York, 1945; Instructor in Photography, California School of Fine Arts, now San Francisco Art Institute, 1946-52; Founder-Editor with Dorothea Lange, Ansel Adams, Barbara Morgan, Beaumont and Nancy Newhall and others, and Production Manager, *Aperture* magazine, San Francisco and New York 1952-75; Exhibitions Organizer, 1953-57, and Editor, *Image* magazine,

George Eastman House, Rochester, New York, 1953-57; Instructor in Photography and Photojournalism, Rochester Institute of Technology, New York, 1955-64; Editor, *Sensorium* magazine, Cambridge, Massachusetts, 1965 (not published); Visiting Professor, Department of Architecture, Massachusetts Institute of Technology, Cambridge, 1965-76. Member, Oregon Camera Club, Portland, 1938; Photo League, New York, 1947; Founder Member, Society for Photographic Education, 1962. **Recipient:** Guggenheim Fellowship, 1970. **Died:** (in Boston) 24 June 1976.

Individual Exhibitions:

1939   *Portland Iron Front Buildings,* W.P.A. Exhibition, Portland, Oregon (toured the United States)
        Portland Waterfront, W.P.A. Exhibition, Portland, Oregon (toured the United States)

1942   *Grande Ronde Valley Photographs,* Portland Art Museum, Oregon
        Two Portland Houses, Portland Art Museum, Oregon
        First Sequence, YMCA, Portland, Oregon

1948   *Song Without Words,* San Francisco Museum of Art (toured the United States)

1949   The Record Shop, San Francisco

1950   *Intimations of Disaster,* Photo League, New York
        Two Portland Houses, Portland Art Museum, Oregon
        Mendocino, San Francisco Museum of Art

1952   *Fourth Sequence,* Raymond and Raymond Gallery, San Francisco
        Fifth Sequence, Sequence 6, Intimations of Disaster, San Francisco Museum of Art

1954   *Sequence 7, Sequence 8,* International Museum of Photography, George Eastman House, Rochester, New York
        Sequence 7, 8, 9, Limelight Gallery, New York
        Sequence 8, Santa Barbara Museum of Art, California

1955   *These Images,* International Museum of Photography, George Eastman House, Rochester, New York
        The Photographers Gallery, San Francisco
        Sequence 11, Village Camera Club, New York

1957   Limelight Gallery, New York
        3 Photographers: Harry Callahan, Walter Rosenblum, Minor White, White Museum of Art, Cornell University, Ithaca, New York
        Sequence 10/Rural Cathedrals, Sequence 12/Doors, San Francisco Museum of Art (with Dorothy Norman)

1959   Gateway Gallery, San Francisco
        Sequence 13/Return to the Bud, International Museum of Photography, George Eastman House, Rochester, New York
        Sequence 13/Return to the Bud, Henry Ford Museum, Dearborn, Michigan
        Fourth Sequence, Sequence 12/Doors, Song Without Words, Image Study, Boston University
        Sequence 15A, Limelight Gallery, New York (with Paul Caponigro)
        Sequence 13/Return to the Bud, Oregon Centennial Celebration, Portland

1960   *Sequence 13/Return to the Bud,* Art Institute of Chicago
        Sequence 15A, Smithsonian Institution, Washington, D.C.
        University of Buffalo, New York

1961   *Song Without Words,* Carl Siembab Gallery, Boston

1962   *Sequence 15A,* Pennsylvania State University, University Park

1964   *Sequence 17/Out of Love for You I Will Try to Give You Back to Yourself,* Humboldt State College, Arcata, California
        Sequence 17, Ellsworth Museum, St. Lawrence University, Canton, New York
        Underground Gallery, New York

1965   Gallery 216, New York
        Everything Gets in the Way, Reed College, Portland, Oregon
        Sequence 17, Massachusetts Institute of Technology, Cambridge

1966   *Everything Gets in the Way,* Lotte Jacobi Gallery, Hillsboro, Massachusetts

1967   *It's All in the Mind,* Carl Siembab Gallery, Boston
1968   *Sequence 16/Sound of One Hand Clapping,* Ringling Museum,
        Sarasota, Florida
1970   Philadelphia Museum of Art (retrospective)
1973   *The Photograph as Object, Metaphor and Document of
        Concept: Robert Heinecken, Minor White and Robert
        Cumming,* California State University at Long Beach
1975   U.S.I.A. Gallery, Paris (toured Europe)
1980   Visions Gallery, London
1983   *Jupiter Portfolio,* San Antonio Museum of Art, Texas

Selected Group Exhibitions:

1959   *Photography at Mid-Century,* International Museum of
        Photography, George Eastman House, Rochester, New York
        (toured the United States)
1964   *The Photographer's Eye,* Museum of Modern Art, New York
1967   *Photography in the 20th Century,* National Gallery of Canada,
        Ottawa (toured Canada and the United States, 1967-73)
1968   *Light7,* Massachusetts Institute of Technology, Cambridge
1975   *The Land: 20th Century Landscape Photographs Selected by
        Bill Brandt,* Victoria and Albert Museum, London (travelled
        to Edinburgh, Belfast and Cardiff)
1979   *Photographie als Kunst 1879-1979,* Tiroler Landesmuseum
        Ferdinandeum, Innsbruck, Austria (travelled to Neue Gallery
        am Wolfgang Gurlitt Museum, Linz, Austria; Neue Galerie
        am Landesmuseum Joanneum, Graz, Austria; and Museum
        des 20. Jahrhunderts, Vienna)
1980   *Photography of the Fifties,* International Center of Photogra-
        phy, New York (travelled to Center for Contemporary
        Photography, University of Arizona, Tucson; Minneapolis
        Institute of Arts,; California State University at Long Beach;
        and Delaware Art Museum, Wilmington)
1982   *Target III: In Sequence,* Houston Museum of Fine Art, Texas
1984   *Subjektive Fotografie: Images of the 50s,* San Francisco
        Museum of Modern Art (travelled to the University of
        Houston, Texas; Museum Folkwang, Essen; Vasterbottens
        Museum, Umea; Kulturhuset, Stockholm; Saarland Museum,
        Saarbrucken; Palais des Beaux Arts, Brussels)
1987   *Photography and Art 1946-86,* Los Angeles County
        Museum of Art

Collections:

Minor White Archive, Princeton University Art Museum, New Jersey; International Museum of Photography, George Eastman House, Rochester, New
York; Carpenter Center, and Fogg Art Museum, Harvard University, Cambridge, Massachusetts; Library of Congress, Washington, D.C.; Kalamazoo
Institute of Arts, Michigan; Art Institute of Chicago; University of Louisville,
Kentucky; New Orleans Museum of Art; University of New Mexico, Albuquerque; Oakland Art Museum, California.

Publications:

By WHITE: Books—*Sequence 6,* portfolio of 14 photos, San Francisco
1951; *Exposure with the Zone System,* New York 1956, as *Zone System
Manual,* New York 1961, 1965, 1968; *Photographers on Photography,* with
others, edited by Nathan Lyons, New York 1966; *Light7,* editor, New York
and Cambridge, Massachusetts 1968; *Mirrors, Messages, Manifestations,*
New York 1969; *Be-Ing Without Clothes,* exhibition catalogue, New York
and Cambridge, Massachusetts 1970; *Octave of Prayer,* New York and
Cambridge, Massachusetts 1972; *Celebrations,* with Jonathan Green, preface
by Gyorgy Kepes, New York and Cambridge, Massachusetts 1974; *Jupiter
Portfolio,* 12 photos, with text by Peter Rasun Gould, New York 1975; *The
New Zone System Manual,* with Richard Zakia and Peter Lorenz, New York
1976; *Minor White: Rites and Passages,* with an introduction by James Baker
Hall, New York 1978. **Articles—**"When Is Photography Creative?" in
American Photography (New York), January 1943; "Photography Is an Art"
in *Design* (Minneapolis), December 1947; "What Is Photography?" in *Photo
Notes* (New York), Spring 1948; "How to Find Your Own Approach to

Photography" in *American Photography* (New York), July 1951; "Analysis
of Five Prints" in *Universal Photo Almanac,* New York 1951; "The Camera
Mind and Eye" in *Magazine of Art* (New York), January 1952; "How
Creative Is Color Photography?" in *Popular Photography Color Annual,* New
York 1957; "On the Strength of a Mirage" in *Art in America* (New York),
Spring 1958; "The Craftsmanship of Feeling" in *Infinity* (New York),
February 1960; "Call for Critics" in *Infinity* (New York), November 1960;
"Photography: An Undefinition" in *Popular Photography* (New York), April
1962; "Pictorial Photography" in *The Encyclopaedia of Photography,* New
York 1964; "Extended Perception Through Photography" in *Ways of Growth,*
edited by Herbert Otto and John Mann, New York 1968; introduction to
Photography in America, edited by Robert Doty, New York 1974; interview in
Interviews with Master Photographers, edited by James Danziger and Barnaby
Conrad III, London and New York 1977; interview in *Dialogue with Photography,* edited by Paul Hill and Thomas Joshua Cooper, London 1979;
numerous writings in *Image* (New York), 1956-57, and *Aperture,* 1952-75.

On WHITE: Books—*Photography in the 20th Century* by Nathan Lyons,
New York 1967; *Photography in America,* edited by Robert Doty, New York
1974; *The Magic Image* by Cecil Beaton and Gail Buckland, London and
Boston 1975; *The Land: 20th Century Landscape Photographs Selected by
Bill Brandt,* exhibition catalogue, edited by Mark Haworth-Booth, London
1975; *Geschichte der Fotografie im 20. Jahrhundert/Photography in the 20th
Century* by Petr Tausk, Cologne 1977, London 1980; *Photographs: Sheldon
Memorial Art Gallery Collection, University of Nebraska,* with an introduc-
tion by Norman A. Geske, Lincoln 1977; *Amerikanische Landschaftsphotographie
1860-1978,* exhibition catalogue, with an introduction by Klaus-Jürgen
Sembach, Munich 1978; *Photographie als Kuns 1879-1979/Kunst als
Photographie 1949-1979,* exhibition catalogue, 2 vols., by Peter Weiermair,
Innsbruck, Austria 1979; *The Photograph Collector's Guide* by Lee D. Witkin
and Barbara London, Boston and London 1979; *Light Readings: A Photogra-
phy Critic's Writings 1968-1978* by A.D. Coleman, New York 1979;
Photography of the Fifties: An American Perspective by Helen Gee, Tucson,
Arizona 1980; *The Library of World Photography: Photography as Fine Art,*
with introduction by Douglas Davis, Tokyo 1982, 1983, London 1983;
Subjektive Fotografie: Images of the 50s, exhibition catalogue, by Ute
Eskildsen, Manfred Schmalriede and Dorothy Martinson, Essen, West Germa-
ny 1984; *Lives I've Never Lived: A Portrait of Minor White* by Abe Frandlich,
Cleveland, Ohio 1984; *American Images: Photography 1945-1980,* edited by
Peter Turner, London and New York 1985. **Articles—**"Minor White" in
Camera (Lucerne), August 1959; "Minor White" by Allan Porter in *Camera*
(Lucerne), January 1972; "From Minor White: A Choice Collection" by
Gene Thornton in the *New York Times,* 14 October 1973; "Minor White
Gathers Final M.I.T. Show" by Hilton Kramer in the *New York Times,* 1
March 1974; "On the Invention of Photographic Meaning" by Allan Sekula
in *Artforum* (New York), January 1975; "Minor White (1908-1976): Signifi-
cance of Formal Quality in His Photographs" by Janet E. Buerger in *Image*
(Rochester, New York), vol. 19, no. 3, 1976; "Remembering Cunningham
and White" by Hilton Kramer in the *New York Times,* 1 August 1976; "Minor
White 1908-1976" by David Vestal in *Popular Photography* (New York),
October 1976; "Minor White—Mystic and Mentor" in *Photography Year
1977,* by the Time-Life editors, New York 1977; "Minor White" in
Progresso Fotografico (Milan), November 1977; "The Quest for Angelic
Vision: The Photographs of Minor White" by David Bartlett in *Camera
Lucida* (Milwaukee), Winter 1980; "Minor White: A Living Remembrance,"
special issue of *Aperture* (Millerton, New York), no. 95, 1984.

*   *   *

A bright, energetic tactician, one versed in the politics of art and the
museum and publishing worlds, a teacher with provocative classroom strategies, and a photographer of richly metaphoric images, Minor White was fully
conscious of the uniqueness and privacy of his vision and of the roles he
maintained as the passing years thinned his hair to diaphanous, white strings:
arbiter of photographic tastes, lecturer, director of vigorous workshops,
entrepreneur, and editor of quoted and problematical books (*Be-Ing Without
Clothes* and *Octave of Prayer*).

He brought to his students at Massachusetts Institute of Technology,
where he taught from the mid-60s almost up until his death, a vast experience
and knowledge. The standards that he created and upheld for others were

standards that he also observed for himself. As with the format and design of *Mirrors, Messages, Manifestations,* the extensive *Aperture* monograph of his work published in 1969—the spatter of quotes and poetry, the orchestration of rhythms and enlightening juxtapositions—he was an imaginative and fastidious editor.

For White, a photograph was not simply food for senseless consumption. Its offering of nourishment was more delicate and substantive. Its craft, its shapes, and composition, often predicated by the subject, its unarticulated and subliminal facets of being—some of these, at times most of these, could be deciphered, in fact *read,* or determined by the exercise of an engaged and watchful intellect. A photograph could also be seen as a metaphorical mirror, reflecting for the viewer as well as for the photographer and critic, *feelings-states* and resonances that defy facile descriptions.

Through his editorship of *Aperture,* an influential journal of photography begun in 1952, his curatorial judgements, his own experimentation and creativity, his generous and astute critiques of the work of his colleagues and students, White insisted that if a photograph were worth viewing, it required bold and probing viewing. In White's teaching, scrutiny of a photograph was soulful endeavor; joyful and intense, an often solemn activity that could alter and enlarge one's critical perception, one's creative energies and productivity, and occasionally even one's attitude toward life. Such scrutiny required dedication, integrity, patience, a burgeoning sensibility, and a game covenant with the unknown. As his students were shown, a photograph could be appraised in countless ways—first, for its craft, its elements of composition, its format and print qualities, its freshness of conception; then later for its deeper apprehensions and acknowledgements.

In a public sense, White came to think of photographs principally as either objects to be exhibited in galleries and museums or presented in compelling arrangements in magazines and books. In a private and pedagogic sense, there was an alternative use of photography, that being the opportunity of exploring the interiority of oneself or of studying the exploration and achievement of another human being, at least through the visual manifestation of that exploration and achievement.

During the last phase of his life, this alternative use of photography absorbed more and more of his creative energy and thought. It is what he labored with in his myriad workshops by employing at times provocative silences and cryptically abrasive comments. His students suffered his preoccupations and unsparing aspirations; they were urged to disengage themselves from preconceptions, inhibitions, defense mechanisms, and the telltale smudges of ego. Dance, mime, classical music, readings from esoteric masters, the *I Ching*—all were used to promote self-discovery and to provide a new context for perception.

"I have been defining *creative* ever since I came to M.I.T.," he observed late in his life, "as anything which brings us into contact with our Creator, either inwardly or outwardly." The source for White's spirituality and some of his workshop techniques came from a Russian, George Ivanovich Gurdjieff (1870s-1949). Gurdjieff proposed energizing the three centers of being: intellectual, emotional, and instinctual. After fifty, White adopted Gurdjieff's discipline and philosophy, and they provided lasting sustenance for his intense and hungry spirit.

A poet himself, White thought of poetry as one kind of expression, a harvesting of knowledge within oneself—and of photography as another, as symbolized by one of his supreme images, "The Sandblaster," in which a man is pictured at work, excavating, with only his helmet and shoulders visible. White admitted special fondness for this image; it was a remembrance of himself, digging away at life.

White's early work shot in Portland, Oregon and along the California coast is direct and earthbound—images of rock formations at Point Lobos and of sea flung like wet snow and of streets and buildings that glisten like freshly painted brick and steel. Almost all of his work after 1945, though, yearns in one way or another for the spiritual. The best seem to gain a purchase on mystery and spirit without deserting the mundane. In "Two Barns and Shadow," for instance, the shadow of a telephone pole falls obliquely across a field and points up toward two barns, whose visual arrangement seems something more than ordinary. The image possesses immediate visual coherence, as most of White's images do, and then there is the recognition of another mode. The shadow reads as a black cross and the two barns suggest two sides, one darker and one lighter, of spiritual or psychic being. That image like so many created by White—"Ritual Branch," "Birdlime and Surf," "Long Cloud," "Christ-

mas Ornament," and "Rings and Roses"—abides first in the subtle articulation of light and form.

The non-narrative photographic sequence is White's conceiving. In White's hands a sequence often enacted a dialogue between two people or manifested changing moods and complex feeling-states. For thirty odd years he worked with sequences. Some preserved their original shapes over the years, while others were altered again and again—as often by the inclusion of a new image as by an internal adjustment in sequential order. The individual images were not conceived as from a schedule or filmmaker's script, but first as separate children with equal love and pampering. Scattered about his floor or laid out along the tiers of his wall rack, there were profound differences among them in pitch, density, and velocity. These differences became some of the hidden strings of formal arrangement that ordered images in his sequences.

In his mature sequential work, White achieved a context both indecipherable and as tactile as the rock and snow and frosted glass appropriated as canvas. The context was often highly personal—"Sequence 4" and "Sequence 17," for instance—disclosures of sexuality and states of mind whose lives depend upon revelation but not upon precise identification. "Sound of One Hand Clapping," no doubt his finest sequence, originated from meditations on a Zen koan. Composed of ten images, most of which were frost configurations on the windows of his flat in Rochester, New York, the sequence is a visual equivalent of sound. Covertly hinged together, the images pass from an initial closed and ineffable form to an open showering form. Forces as commanding as hands guide the viewer through the sequence. It is as if the individual images are forms in their secret effulgence, awaiting scrutiny and meditation. Circles, hands, eyes, heads, stars, icicles, scallops of frost, snowbursts—these forms rise and subside, take body and resonance in subtle recurrence. The images seem at first simple and inert, but upon closer scrutiny they break into untutored vitality. They gambol, and chatter, igniting the imagination, exploding into objects of new being.

The bedrock of White's work is self. After 1964, he steadfastly embraced the personal and esoteric. All of his interests and inclinations urged him in that direction: his sexuality; poetry; pedagogy; Stieglitz's equivalence concept, which for him became dogma; oriental ritual, diet, and thought; Gurdjieff work; and the developing concept of non-narrative sequence. Like most of his sequences, "Sound of One Hand Clapping" evades literary reduction and interpretation. Through its sound, the liveliness of its forms, the rhythmical and poetic nature of its arrangement, it provokes the viewer in ways that a single image could not. It passes from a static and enigmatic form, one that affronts almost with its amplitude, through various stages of lyrical calm, unrest, joyful disturbance, bold peace, to the lovely and, perhaps for White, redemptive release of the final image. "Frost Wave," in scale both microcosmic and macrocosmic, communicates as eternally alive.

White may best be remembered for the intensity of his commitment to photography and for the boldness of his vision. With his teaching and his own creative photography, he asserted the significance of the human and the personal. A number of his images and sequences are among the treasures of 20th century photography.

—Kelly Wise

WILLOUGHBY, Bob (Robert).

Nationality: American. **Born:** Los Angeles, California, 30 June 1927. **Family:** Married to Dorothy; sons Christopher, Stephen, David; daughter Catherine. **Career:** Attracted in his early years to photographing dancers and the local jazz scene, he built a substantial library of images (1949-54). An offer from a photographic agent, following his first exhibition in Los Angeles, led rapidly to assignments for *Harpers Bazaar* in New York. He also shot social documentary stories and his journalistic style was later incorporated into film

Dustin Hoffman and Ann Bancroft from *The Graduate,* **Paramount Studios, Hollywood, 1967.** Photograph by Bob Willoughby.

production coverage for various magazines. The first special photographer to be hired by a major Hollywood studio (Warner Brothers on *A Star is Born*— 1954), his career in films blossomed and he went on to work for every major Hollywood studio, producing stories for magazines world-wide. During that period (1954-71), he covered over 100 major feature films including *From Here to Eternity; The Man with a Golden Arm; Raintree County; Can Can; My Fair Lady; Marnie; The Great Race; Who's Afraid of Virginia Woolf?; The Graduate; Rosemary's Baby; The Lion in Winter; Goodbye Mr Chips; Catch 22; They Shoot Horses Don't They?; Klute; The Cowboys* etc. Moving his family to the south of Ireland in 1972 he lived and worked there for the next seventeen years. He now lives in the south of France with his wife, where he continues to photograph, producing a series of books, as well as advertising images for clients in Europe, Japan and the USA. **Address:** Villa l'Aravista, 312 Bd Joseph Ricord, 06140 Vence, France.

Individual Exhibitions:

1958	California Museum of Science and Industry, Los Angeles
1978	*The Platinum Years,* Kiva Gallery, Boston
	The Gallery of Photography, Dublin
1978-79	Centre Culturel Americain, Paris (travelling show)
1980	*Beauty and Mystery,* Niekrug Gallery, New York
	The Platinum Years, Canon Gallery, Amsterdam
	The Yuen Gallery, Seattle, Washington
1986	*The Ilford Calendar,* Il Diaframa, Canon Gallery, Milan, Italy
	31st Cork Film Festival, Triskel Arts Centre, Cork, Ireland
1987	*Agrigento Film Festival,* Sicily
1988	The Kerlin Gallery, Dublin
	Ilford Exhibition, Photokina, Cologne, Germany

1990	*Black and White and Blue,* The Photographers Gallery, London
1992	Stephen Cohen Gallery, Los Angeles
1994	*Tribute to Audrey Hepburn,* Kentetsu Art Museum, Osaka, Japan (travelling exhibition)

Selected Group Exhibitions:

1953	*The Family of Man,* Museum of Modern Art, New York
1955	*Always the Young Strangers,* Museum of Modern Art, New York
1959	*Photography at the Mid Century,* George Eastman House, Rochester, New York
1964	*World Exhibition of Photography,* Hamburg
1967	*The Camera as Witness,* Canadian World Fair
	World's Exhibition of Photography, East Berlin
1968	*World Exhibition of Photography,* Hamburg
1971	*World's Exhibition of Photography,* East Berlin
1973	*World Exhibition of Photography,* Hamburg
1977	*World Exhibition of Photography,* Hamburg
1985	*Stars of the British Screen,* National Portrait Gallery, London (travelling exhibition)
1986-87	*Hollywood Legend and Reality,* Smithsonian Museum (SITES travelling exhibition)
1987	Musée de la Photographie de Charleroi, Belgium
	Masters of Starlight, Los Angeles County Museum

Collections:

The National Portrait Gallery, London; The Museum of Modern Art, New York; National Museum of Photography, Film and Television, Bradford,

England; The Bibliothèque Nationale, Paris; Musée de la Photographie, Charleroi, Belgium.

Publications:

By WILLOUGHBY: Books—*The Platinum Years,* 1974; *Voices From Ancient Ireland,* 1981; *Jazz in LA,* Kiel; *Die Reifeprufung,* Kiel, 1990; *Nur Pferden gibt man den Gnadenschufs?,* Kiel 1990; *War Hat Angst vor Virginia Woolf?,* Kiel 1991; *Rosemary's Baby,* Kiel 1992; *The Hollywood Special,* Tokyo 1993; *Audrey Hepburn, A Tribute,* Tokyo 1993.

*

Hollywood and the movie industry in the late 1940s were a Mecca for creative talent from across the world. Born and brought up close to the "tinsel city," I was drawn like a magnet to the heart of the business.

Although my love of the international jazz scene has never left me, I know that my social documentary picture stories were an important element in the development of my career. But it was the the movie industry and its people that gave me the opportunity to mature my photojournalistic style. On movie sets in the 1950s I was known as the special photographer and for some time I was the only freelance permitted work on major productions by the powerful unions controlling employment in the Hollywood movie business.

I was fortunate. My commissions from leading picture magazines had awoken producers and directors to the advantage of publicity generated from an independent source. From the start, producers were impressed that my pictures were being published regularly in many of the magazines that fed off Hollywood's unending stream of entertainment stories.

Over the period in which I worked on major film productions, I had the good fortune to record, on film, the life and times of producers, directors and "stars" alike. Moving amongst them I documented the massive pool of Hollywood greats in a period, the like of which will never be seen again.

—Bob Willoughby

* * *

It is all too easy for arm chair critics to eulogise, or for that matter denigrate the career and creative talent of a professional photographer. Yet it is only since it became fashionable for a precious few to promote themselves as personalities, that most working professionals have been deemed worthy of a critic's second glance.

In the absence of substantial private means, or an indulgent backer in the style of a medieval patron of the arts, photography as a profession is a serious money-earning business. Without a gut instinct for survival, a lively interest in people, a good technical grounding and an eye for the main chance, photographic talent can be strangled at birth.

Feeding on an inner strength born of relatively humble beginnings Bob Willoughby, a major photographic talent, strode across the international movie scene for many years, working with relentless intensity to create images in the photojournalistic genre.

Fired with enthusiasm for the medium he had, it seems, an unerring instinct for identifying areas in the human zoo that offered consistently rewarding opportunities for creative photography. Even as a young assistant to a studio photographer, he recognised the influence of contemporary jazz musicians on the future of popular music and set about documenting them with sympathy and charm. His library of jazz images are still in great demand today.

Los Angeles jazz and the contemporary dance scene made a superb proving ground. His personality and confidence grew apace and narrative photography became an obsession. Casting further afield, he started shooting social documentary stories.

Once allowed to work where angels fear to tread, the movie industry became his backdrop. His ebullient, yet caring personality helped make his name synonymous with the exciting sensitive photographic interpretation of Hollywood's "platinum years."

We first met in 1957, on the set of Otto Preminger's *Saint Joan* at Shepperton Studios. The film, he advised me, was not going to work. The director, who had selected the young girl in the title role from 8,000 applicants, seemed incapable of appreciating the young Jean Seberg's innocent, childlike qualities. Explosive, devious, theatrical Preminger could not appreciate, let

alone work with her directness and simplicity of thought. The result, off stage was, all too often, Austrian rage and American tears. Watching the way in which Bob handled that fragile and subsequently tragic personality, I recognised a man, already a master of his craft.

Like his capacity for caring, his photographic output was prolific, his picture quality superb, and over a period of twenty years there was not a single week without the Willoughby by-line being seen somewhere in the world's media.

No other freelance, to my knowledge, has so consistently created such a stream of art photography from the heart of the entertainment industry. It may seem strange that such a gifted professional should conduct a search for honesty, elegance and actuality in what is effectively an artificial world, but he revelled in the uniqueness of his skills. Firstly, he was (and still is) a natural photojournalist with the ability to identify opportunities, create stories and sell them to publishers when the official stills men's work lay gathering dust. Secondly, he blended with the invisible fabric of the production unit, without becoming part of it. He also avoided the intrusive egoism that can disrupt the creative atmosphere on the studio floor.

Most importantly he remains his own master. Happiest seeking out beauty at its zenith, he has always been truly in his element when shooting stars.

—John Chillingworth

WILMER, Valerie (Val).

Nationality: British. **Born:** Harrogate, Yorkshire, England, 7 December 1941. **Education:** Streatham Hill & Clapham High School, London, 1953-56 and at Putney High School, London, 1956-59; Photography partly self-taught with one year of IBP studies (IBP Prelim [Hons]) at the School of Photography, The Polytechnic, Regent Street, London, 1959-60. **Career:** Worked as a darkroom assistant for other photographers, and as receptionist at *Tropic,* an early Black British monthly magazine, 1960-62; joined National Union of Journalists in 1964 and was active in organising photographers both inside and outside the NUJ. Sat on Committee of London Freelance Branch 1980-1985; from 1974 worked as photographer for *The Times,* and as newsroom reporter for *Time Out,* London, in 1978-9; worked as a member of *Spare Rib* Visual Group, planning design and visual content of the magazine, 1978-80. Member of a ground-breaking group of women photographers, organising two exhibitions at Half Moon Gallery, London, 1974-75; also worked as a member of Exit (with Nick Battye, Chris Steele-Perkins and Paul Trevor) documenting poverty and inner city deprivation in Great Britain, 1974; Co-founder (with Maggie Murray) of Format women's picture agency, 1983. Works equally as writer and photographer. **Address:** 10 Sydner Road, London N16 7UG, England.

Individual Exhibitions:

1973   *Jazz Seen—the Face of Black Music,* Victoria and Albert Museum, London

1984   *Sorrow Songs to Soulful Shout,* (with David Corio), Town Hall, Lewisham, London

1986   *Jazz Photographs,* Perugia Jazz Festival, Perugia, Italy
        Sorrow Songs, Soulful Shout, Augusta Savage Gallery, University of Massachusetts, Amherst

1990   *Val Wilmer: Jazz Photographs,* Poseurs Gallery, Birmingham, England

1991   *Deep Like the Rivers: Portraits of Black Writers,* Sojourner Truth Library, State University of New York, New Paltz, New York

1993   *Jazz: Roots and Branches,* Special Photographers Company, London

1994   *Sun Ra Omniverse,* Swiss Jazz Museum, Arlesheim, Switzerland

Albert King Plays the Blues, **"Jazz Expo" Odeon, Hammersmith, London, 1969.** Photograph ©Val Wilmer.

Selected Group Exhibitions:

1972	*Music Exhibition,* National Museum of Wales, Cardiff
1974	*Women* by Women Photographers, Half Moon Gallery, London
1975	*Men* by Women Photographers, Half Moon Gallery, London
	Young British Photographers, Photographers Gallery, London
1979	*Three Perspectives on Photography,* Hayward Gallery, London
1983	*Jazz et Photographie,* Musée d'Art Moderne, Paris
1984-85	*Staying on: An Historical Survey of Immigrant Communities in London,* Photographers Gallery, London
1985	*Opportunity Knocks,* Greater London Council touring show
1986	*Jazz på Fotografiska,* Fotografiska Museet, Stockholm
	Same Difference, Camerawork, London
1990	*Jazz in Photography,* Pictures Gallery, Willow, New York
1992	*A Moment in Time,* Smith's Gallery/Cafe Casbar, London

Collections:

Victoria and Albert Museum, London; Arts Concil of Great Britain; Musée d'Art Moderne, Paris; Fotografiska Museet, Stockholm; Schomberg Center for Research in Black Culture, New York.

Publications:

By WILMER: Books—*Jazz People,* London 1970; *The Jazz Scene,* with text by Charles Fox, London 1972; *The Face of Black Music,* New York 1976; *As Serious as Your Life: The Story of the New Jazz,* London 1977; *The Illustrated Encyclopaedia of Jazz,* with texts by Stan Britt and Brian Case, London 1978; *Jazz at Ronnie Scott's* with text by Kitty Grime, London 1979; *Deep Blues,* with text by Robert Palmer, London 1981; *Black Talk,* with text by Ben Sidran, Hofheim 1985; *Mama Said There'd be Days Like This,* (illustrated Autobiography), London 1989; *Auf der Suche nach Cecil Taylor,* with texts by Meinrad Buholzer and Abi S.Rosenthal, Hofheim 1990; *Anthony Braxton: Sein Leben, seine Musik, seine Schallplatten,* with text by Peter Niklas Wilson, Waarkirchen 1993; Introduction in Terry Cryer's *One in the Eye,* Castleford, Yorks 1993; *Omniverse Sun Ra,* with text by Hartmut Geerken and Bernhard Hefele, Wartaweil 1994. **Articles**—''The Jazz Scene in Focus'' in *Amateur Photographer* (London), 1962; ''Jazz Seen—The Face of Black Music,'' exhibition catalogue notes for individual show at Victoria and Albert Museum (London), 1973; ''Valerie Wilmer—The Face of Black Music'' in *Creative Camera* (London), July 1973; ''They Make Such Beautiful Shapes!'' in *British Journal of Photography* (London) 1974; ''The Unretouched Woman,'' in *Spare Rib* (London) 1976; ''Smell of Coal Dust,'' in *Time Out* (London) 11-

17 August 1978; "The Russian War 1941—1945," in *Time Out* (London) May 1978; "Mississippi Women," in exhibition catalogue *Three Perspectives on Photography* at Hayward Gallery (London) 1979; "Harlem's Picture-Taking Man," in *The Observer Magazine* (London) 21 September 1980; "Two Working Photographers," (co-written with Maggie Murray) in *City Limits* (London) 24-30 September 1982; "American Pictures," in *City Limits* (London) 25 November 1983; "Van DerZee: Harlem Photographer" in *Ten.8* (Birmingham) Issue No.16 1985; "No Crystal Stair" in *New Statesman,* (London), 22 January 1988; "Real People" in *City Limits* (London) 21 January 1988; "The Sweet Flypaper of Life; Black Photographers 1830-1940: An Illustrated Bio-Bibliography," in *Ten.8* (Birmingham) Issue No.20; "Chuck Stewart's Jazz Files," in *Ten.8* (Birmingham) Issue No.22; "Editorial," "Beuford Smith: In the Humane Tradition" (interview), "Coreen Simpson: Taking Care of Business" (interview), "Evidence: New Light on Afro-American Images," all in *Ten.8* (Birmingham) Issue No.24 (issue edited by Wilmer); "Roy DeCarava: An Uncommon Beauty," in *Ten.8* (Birmingham) Issue No. 27: "Barboza: The Music of Ourselves," in *Ten.8* (Birmingham) Issue No.28; "Through a Lens, Darkly," in *Wire,* (London) April 1989; "Mama Said There'd Be Days Like This," in *Ten.8* (Birmingham) Issue No.36; "Milt Hinton: A Musical Vision," interview in *Ten.8* (Birmingham) Vol 2 No.1; "Photo Gallery; Val Wilmer" in *Juke Blues* (London) Summer 1992; "Early Days of Rage," in *The Independent on Sunday Review* (London) 22 November 1992; "Jazz: Roots and Branches," notes for exhibition at Special Photographers Company (London) 1993.

On WILMER: Articles—"Jazz Seen—the Face of Black Music" Victoria and Albert Museum exhibition catalogue notes by Humphrey Lyttelton, London 1973; Many reviews of exhibition "Jazz Seen—the Face of Black Music," including Ainslie Ellis in *The British Journal of Photography* (London), 7 September 1973; "Part of my concern with Women's Liberation has come out of the Black Liberation Movement" interview by Rosie Parker in *Spare Rib* (London), September 1973; Many reviews of book "The Face of Black Music," including by Philippe Bas-Rabérin in *Jazz Magazine* (Paris), December 1976, by Amy O'Neal in *Living Blues* (Chicago), 1976, by Bill Smith in *Coda* (Toronto), December 1976 and by John Fordham in *Time Out* (London), 6 May 1977; "Art is a Luxury. Music is a functional thing" interview by Brian Case in *New Musical Express* (London), 7 May 1977; "Cerná Amerika Objectivem Valerie Wilmerové" by Vladimir Birgus in *Československa Fotografie* (Prague), 1981; "Clicking to the Beat" interview by John Fordham in *The Guardian* (London), 7 September 1989; book reviews of autobiography including "Resolute in Crimplene" by David Widgery in *New Statesman* (London), 15 September 1989, and "Mama Said There'd Be Days Like This" by Douglas H. Daniels in *Elimu,* Black Studies Department Newsletter of University of California (Santa Barbara), Winter 1990; "Jazz Diary" by Jane Richards in *The Independent* (London), 7 September 1992; "Shots in the Dark" by John Fordham in *The Guardian* (London), 17 June 1993; "Shooting Straight in the Dark" by Liz Jobey in *The Independent on Sunday Review* (London), 13 June 1993; "Shooting the Blues" interview by Clare Farrow in *Parallel Structures (Art & Design Profile No.33)* (London), Winter 1993. **Films**—*Jazz is Our Religion* based on Wilmer's stills, first shown London Film Festival 1972, produced and directed by John Jeremy, *Silverscreen* (London), 1972.

*

As a documentary photographer, my main concern has been with showing the inside rather than the outside of the individual. This view came from listening to Jazz as a teenager, and getting to know the musicians who played it. While still at school, I began a lifelong documentary of the music, initially writing about it in little magazines and using my early snapshots as illustration.

Taking on board the concerns of another community influenced me greatly—personally and socially, as well as in the aesthetic sense. My photographs of musicians, probably the best known aspect of my work, range from those that are purely a record to attempt to explain and describe the musicians' community and concerns. These photographs however form only part of my work. I have been a general news and documentary photographer, working for *The Times,* as well as numerous African and Caribbean publications, work that has taken me into British coal-mining communities and the palaces of West African Emirs. My interest in Black history led to a photographic documentary on Black women in Mississippi, for which I

received two Arts Council grants and has involved me in writing about and photographing Caribbean, African, African-American and African-British artists in fields other than music. These include a series begun in the 1960s when Ida Kar was a major influence, starting with portraits of writers Langston Hughes and Wole Soyinka and the sculptor Ben Enwonwu.

Apart from Kar, the photographers who first influenced me were Margaret Bourke-White and Dorothea Lange, because they were women who proved I could do it, (vitally important in 1960), and Edward Steichen because of *The Family of Man.* I was inspired by Wayne Miller's book *The World is Young* and Sanford Roth's candid shots of James Dean, related to Cartier-Bresson for his *joie-de-vivre* and Snowdon for his sensitivity. Eugene Smith and Roy DeCarava became my models when I began to think more clearly about what I was doing. Finally, respect is due to the British jazz photographers of the 1950s and 60s, Terry Cryer, Ron Cohen, Eric Jelly and Marc Sharratt, who taught me by their example.

—Val Wilmer

*   *   *

Valerie Wilmer began taking pictures with her mother's Brownie and then graduated to a small Agfa. As a teenager she became increasingly interested in music and took every opportunity to take pictures of musicians as well as asking for their autographs. When she left school she wanted to be a journalist but there was not much money at home and it was felt she might make a more successful career as a photographer, so she was sent to the Polytechnic of Central London in 1958. She left after a year because the course was upgraded and she didn't have enough money to stay the full three years. Her first job was in the darkroom at the National Gallery where she had to work with large glass plates and learn to make enormous enlargements. Her love of music, particularly jazz and blues continued and she went to Paris to take more pictures of musicians but also earned her living doing all kinds of work, from industrial photography to weddings. Valerie also took various non-photographic jobs and worked for a while in the office of *Tropic* where she became more aware of the difficulties that West Indians were having as they arrived in Britain and how their problems of representation echoed those of women in many fields.

Valerie's initial interest in written journalism has continued and she really enjoyed working for *Time Out,* in this capacity. When she is asked to do a story with both words and pictures she prefers to make two dates, one for the interviews and one for the pictures as she finds it produces better results—perhaps because people feel more confident with the two specialised approaches but also because it must be irritating to see a good picture just when your hands are full of pen and paper!

During her career Valerie has undertaken a wide variety of work. Some of her photographs of sculptors and their work have been used in catalogues and cards for long periods and she is very open to new ideas and assignments. The fact remains that for many people she is best known as a photographer of musicians and particularly black musicians. She did a lot of this work when not many people were doing it and set a very high standard. It is extremely helpful in such work to know the music and be able to impart confidence and trust in your subject and this Valerie is well equipped to do. This is the part of her work which is most often published and from which images are called for on a regular basis. This combining of two passions, photography and music, has provided an archive of immense and lasting value for which we should be very grateful.

—Sue Davies

WINNINGHAM, Geoff(rey L.).

Nationality: American. **Born:** Jackson, Tennessee, 4 March 1943. **Education:** Studied English at Rice University, Houston, 1961-65; photography, at Illinois Institute of Technology, Chicago, 1965-68, M.S. 1968. **Family:** Married Judy Gordon in 1973; children: Elizabeth, Alyson, Charles, and Michael. **Career:** Freelance photographer, working for *Esquire, Atlantic Monthly, Life, Time, Newsweek, Photo,* etc., Houston, since 1968. Instructor,

New Trier Township High School, Winnetka, Illinois, 1966-68, and University of St. Thomas, Houston, 1968-69. Member of the faculty, Rice University, Houston, since 1969; currently, Professor of Art and Master of Wiess College. **Recipient:** Public Broadcasting Corporation grant, 1971; Guggenheim Fellowship, 1972, 1978; Documentary Prize, *U.S. Film Festival*, 1973; Public Grant, 1974, and Photography Fellowship, 1975, 1977, National Endowment for the Arts; American Society of Art Directors Award, 1975. **Agent:** Harris Gallery, 1100 Bissonnet, Houston, Texas 77004. **Address:** Post Office Box 2011, Houston, Texas 77001, U.S.A.

Individual Exhibitions:

1968	Rice University, Houston
1972	Rhode Island School of Design, Providence
	Institute of Design, Chicago
	Art Institute of Chicago
1973	Pan Opticon Gallery, Boston
1974	Museum of Fine Arts, Houston
1975	Witkin Gallery, New York
	Madison Art Center, Wisconsin
1976	Halsted 831 Gallery, Birmingham, Michigan
	Afterimage Gallery, Dallas
1977	Cronin Gallery, Houston
	Southwestern College Gallery, La Jolla, California
1979	Cronin Gallery, Houston
1980	Wah Lui Gallery, Seattle
	Harris Gallery, Houston
	Allen Street Gallery, Dallas
1981	First Federal Savings and Loan Association, Little Rock, Arkansas (permanent exhibition of 124 photographs of the vernacular architecture of Arkansas)
1983	San Antonio Museum of Art, Texas

Selected Group Exhibitions:

1969	*Vision and Expression*, International Museum of Photography, George Eastman House, Rochester, New York (toured the United States, 1969-71)
1971	*Photography Invitational '71*, Arkansas Arts Center, Little Rock
1975	*On Time*, Museum of Modern Art, New York
1976	*Light Is the Theme*, Kimbell Art Museum, Fort Worth, Texas
	Masters of the Camera, American Federation of Arts travelling exhibition
1977	*Contemporary American Photographic Works*, Museum of Fine Arts, Houston (travelled to the Museum of Contemporary Art, Chicago; La Jolla Museum of Contemporary Art, California; and Newport Harbor Art Museum, Newport Beach, California)
	The Great West: Real/Ideal, University of Colorado, Boulder (subsequently Smithsonian Institution travelling exhibition: toured the United States)
	4 American Photographers, Whitney Museum, New York
1978	*Mirrors and Windows: American Photography since 1960*, Museum of Modern Art, New York (toured the United States, 1978-80)
1981	*Southern Eye, Southern Mind*, Memphis Academy of Art, Tennessee

Collections:

Museum of Modern Art, New York; Seagrams Foundation, New York; International Museum of Photography, George Eastman House, Rochester, New York; Museum of Fine Arts, Boston; Carpenter Center, Harvard University, Cambridge, Massachusetts; Princeton University Art Museum, New Jersey; Museum of Fine Arts, Houston; Rice University, Houston; San Antonio Museum, Texas; Dallas Museum of Fine Arts.

Publications:

By WINNINGHAM: Books—*Friday Night in the Coliseum*, Houston 1977; *Going Texan: The Days of the Houston Livestock Show and Rodeo*, with text by William C. Martin, Houston 1972; *A Texas Dozen: 15 Photographs by Geoff Winningham*, portfolio, with an introduction by Robert Adams, Houston 1976; *Houston Ballet*, with others, Houston 1977, 1978; *Rites of Fall*, with text by Al Reinert, Austin, Texas 1979. **Films**—*Friday Night in the Coliseum*, 1972; *The Pleasures of This Stately Dome*, 1975.

On WINNINGHAM: Books—*Vision and Expression* by Nathan Lyons, New York 1969; *Geoff Winningham: Photographs*, exhibition catalogue, with an interview by E.A. Carmean Jr., Houston 1974; *Contemporary American Photographic Works*, edited by Lewis Baltz, Houston 1977; *The Great West: Real/Ideal*, edited by Sandy Hume and others, Boulder, Colorado 1977; *Faces: A History of the Portrait in Photography*, edited by Ben Maddow, New York 1977; *Mirrors and Windows: American Photography since 1960* by John Szarkowski, New York 1978; *Light Readings: A Photography Critic's Writings 1968-1978* by A.D. Coleman, New York 1979; *The Photograph Collector's Guide* by Lee D. Witkin and Barbara London, Boston and London 1979. **Article**—"Deep in the Heart of Texas" in *Camera* (Lucerne), August 1977.

* * *

Geoff Winningham's photographs set before us the improbable customs, costumes, characters, and architecture of the state of Texas. In Winningham's images, Texas is a mixture of outsized myth and scarcely more credible reality. His Texans are exuberant, unrestrained; they are also poignant and sometimes heart-breaking. Winningham has a fine ironic eye for details of dress and nuances of situation, but his curiosity is too wide-ranging and systematic to settle for a superficial recording of isolated, extravagant gestures. It's his willingness to enter deeply and fully into Texas culture—to suspend his disbelief, and ours—that makes his photographs so valuable.

Winningham is perhaps best known for two books which examine the Texan predilection for hard-hitting sport. *Friday Night at the Coliseum* devotes equal attention to big-time wrestling and its fervent fans. *Rites of Fall* takes a vivid look inside the world of Texas high-school football.

The wrestling arena provides Winningham with the chance to observe the exaggerated tumult of the contest and the wildly uninhibited response of its audience. Although he shows us the broad, often ludicrous strokes with which the action is staged, Winningham still makes us share the exhilaration of the elaborately choreographed—but by no means predictable—antics in the ring. The photographs are set off by long statements from the wrestlers themselves, who become no longer one-dimensional heroes or villains but flesh-and-blood people with whom we begin to feel strong ties.

Winningham's photographs of Texas high-school football and the elaborate social ritual which has grown up around it provide the occasion for pictures crowded with incident and emotion. His use of electronic flash helps transfer the raw, unbridled energy of the young players to the photographs themselves. Caught in stylized postures of victory or defeat, the young men and women in these pictures unexpectedly convince us that their emotion is the genuine article. Winningham's photographs are as high-spirited and full of surprises as the game he portrays.

—Christopher Phillips

WINOGRAND, Garry.

Nationality: American. **Born:** New York City in 1928. **Education:** Studied painting at City College of New York, 1947-48; Columbia University, New York, 1948-51; studied photography, under Alexey Brodovitch, New School for Social Research, New York, 1951. **Military Service:** Served in the United States Air Force, 1945-47. **Family:** Married the dancer Adrienne Lubow in 1952 (divorced); children: Lauri and Ethan; married Eileen Winogrand; daughter: Melissa. **Career:** Freelance photographer (initially a commercial photographer, working with the Pix agency, then Brackman Associates), New York and Los Angeles, from 1952. Teacher from 1969: taught at the School of the Art Institute of Chicago; Instructor of Photography, University of Texas at Austin, 1973. **Recipient:** Guggenheim Fellowship, 1964, 1969, 1978; New York Council on the Arts Award, 1971; National Endowment for the Arts grant, 1975. **Agent:** Pace/MacGill Gallery, 32 East 57th Street, New York 10022, USA. **Died:** (in Tijuana, Mexico) 19 March 1984.

Individual Exhibitions:

1960	Image Gallery, New York
1963	Museum of Modern Art, New York
1967	*New Documents,* Museum of Modern Art, New York (with Diane Arbus and Lee Friedlander; toured the United States, 1967-75)
1969	*The Animals,* Museum of Modern Art, New York
1975	Light Gallery, New York
1976	Light Gallery, New York
	Cronin Gallery, Houston
1977	*Public Relations,* Museum of Modern Art, New York
1979	Orange Coast Gallery, Costa Mesa, California
1983	*Celebrities 1960-80,* Fraenkel Gallery, San Francisco
1984	Light Gallery, New York
	Zabriskie Gallery, New York
1985	Williams College, Williamstown, Massachusetts
1986	*Little Known Photographs,* Fraenkel Gallery, San Francisco
1987	Pace/MacGill Gallery, New York
1992	*Garry Winogrand, One Unrelated Photographer, Vintage Prints 1956-63,* Pace/MacGill Gallery, New York

Selected Group Exhibitions:

1955	*The Family of Man,* Museum of Modern Art, New York (and world tour)
1959	*Photographer's Choice,* Workshop Gallery, New York
1963	*Photography '63,* International Museum of Photography, George Eastman House, Rochester, New York
1966	*Contemporary Photography since 1950,* International Museum of Photography, George Eastman House, Rochester, New York
1967	*Photography in the 20th Century,* National Gallery of Canada, Ottawa (toured Canada and the United States, 1967-73)
1968	*5 Photographers,* Sheldon Memorial Art Gallery, University of Nebraska, Lincoln
1979	*Fleeting Gestures: Dance Photographs,* International Museum of Photography, George Eastman House, Rochester, New York (travelled to The Photographers' Gallery, London)
1982	*Floods of Light,* The Photographers' Gallery, London (toured Britain)
1985	*American Images 1945-80,* Barbican Art Gallery, London (toured Britian)
1987	*Photography and Art 1946-86,* Los Angeles County Museum of Art
1988	*Fragments From the Real World,* Museum of Modern Art, New York (travelled to Chicago, Pittsburgh, Austin, Los Angeles & Tucson)
1990	Hayward Gallery, London

Collections:

Museum of Modern Art, New York; International Museum of Photography, George Eastman House, Rochester, New York; Baltimore Museum of Art; Library of Congress, Washington, D.C.; University of Michigan, Ann Arbor; Museum of Fine Arts, Houston; University of Nebraska, Lincoln; Center for Creative Photography, University of Arizona, Tucson; University of California at Los Angeles; National Gallery of Canada, Ottawa.

Publications:

By WINOGRAND: Books—*The Animals,* with text by John Szarkowski, New York 1969; *A Photographer Looks at Evans,* exhibition catalogue, Austin, Texas 1974; *Women Are Beautiful,* with text by Helen Gary Bishop, New York 1975; *Public Relations,* with texts by Tod Papageorge and John Szarkowski, New York 1977; *Stock Photographs: Fort Worth Fat Stock Show and Rodeo,* with an introduction by Ron Tyler, Austin, Texas 1980; *Photography Speaks: 66 Photographers on Their Art,* New York, 1989. **Articles**—"Monkeys Make the Problem More Difficult: A Collected Interview with Garry Winogrand" in *Image* (Rochester, New York), July 1972; "An Interview with Garry Winogrand," with Charles Hagen, in *Afterimage* (Rochester, New York), December 1977.

On WINOGRAND: Books—*Photography in the 20th Century* by Nathan Lyons, New York 1967; *5 Photographers,* exhibition catalogue, Lincoln, Nebraska 1968; *New Photography USA,* exhibition catalogue, by John Szarkowski, Arturo Quintavalle and Massimo Mussini, Parma, Italy 1971; *Documentary Photography,* by The Time-Life editors, New York 1973; *New Images in Photography: Object and Illusion,* exhibition catalogue, Miami 1974; *The Magic Image* by Cecil Beaton and Gail Buckland, London and Boston 1975; *Peculiar to Photography,* exhibition catalogue, by Van Deren Coke, Albuquerque, New Mexico; *Aspects of American Photography, 1976,* exhibition catalogue, St. Louis 1976; *Concerning Photography,* exhibition catalogue, by Jonathan Bayer, Peter Turner, Ian Jeffrey and Ainslie Ellis, London 1977; *Photographs: Sheldon Memorial Art Gallery Collection, University of Nebraska,* with an introduction by Norman A. Geske, Lincoln, Nebraska 1977; *Mirrors and Windows: American Photography since 1960* by John Szarkowski, New York 1978; *Photographie als Kunst 1879-1979/Kunst als Photographie 1949-1979,* exhibition catalogue, 2 vols., by Peter Weiermair, Innsbruck, Austria 1979; *The Photograph Collector's Guide* by Lee D. Witkin and Barbara London, Boston and London 1979; *Old and Modern Masters of Photography,* exhibition catalogue, with an introduction by Mark Haworth-Booth, London 1980; *Visions and Images: American Photographers on Photography,* edited by Barbaralee Diamonstein, New York 1981; *Floods of Light: Flash Photography 1851-1981,* exhibition catalogue, by Rupert Martin, London 1982; *American Images: Photography 1945-1980,* edited by Peter Turner, London 1985; *Photography and Art 1946-1986,* exhibition catalogue, by Andy Grundberg and Kathleen M. Gauss, Los Angeles 1987; *Fragments from the Real World,* by John Szarkowski, New York, 1988. **Articles**—"Garry Winogrand" by Arthur Goldsmith in *Photography* (New York), October 1954; "Garry Winogrand" by Mary Orovan in *U.S. Camera* (New York), February 1966; "Photographs by Garry Winogrand" in *Creative Camera* (London), August 1969; "The Animal Kingdom: Myth and Reality" in *Print* (New York), March/April 1970; "Winogrand's Women" by Dan Meinwald in *Afterimage* (Rochester, New York), January 1976; "Garry Winogrand Dies at 56—An Innovator in Photography" in the *New York Times,* 22 March 1984; "Life Seized on the Fly" by Andy Grundberg in the *New York Times,* 23 December 1984.

*   *   *

Garry Winogrand was perhaps the epitome of the modern street photographer, the mode many regard as photography at its basic best. One of the finest virtuosos of the 35mm camera after Cartier-Bresson, he was a fast talking, fast shooting New Yorker, who took the lively, unschooled "snapshot aesthetic" and elevated it into a sophisticated game—or art—of fast reflexes, chance, intuition, and insight. In the course of his career he exposed well over two million frames, training his Leica at anything and everything—but chiefly the manners and mores of his fellow Americans, discreetly catching them on the wing in the city streets, stealthily capturing every nuance of their social gatherings.

"I photograph to see what the world looks like in photographs" was his favourite maxim, which suggests he was a formalist. He was a leading light of the so-called "social landscape school" of the nineteen-sixties and seventies, a loose grouping of photographers who aimed their cameras at the social landscape of America but who were more concerned with the language of the photographic medium, nominally documentary realists who were in effect mirroring their own, somewhat malcontent soul rather than the society which surrounded them.

Intent and effect in photography are frequently two different things, for the real world constantly frustrates those with purely formalist or self-referential motives. However subjective, indulgent or historical Winogrand's view, it remains a view of society. Winogrand's world view, after all, was New York Jewish, and what could be more worldly than that?

His pictures, particularly of those gatherings to which one might append a socio-political "spin," reflect all the scepticism and alienation of the common New York *mensch*, particularly one whose views were born out of the dark days of Eisenhower and the Cold War. They are often humorous, usually cruelly humorous, with sharp, pungent punchlines that reflect very much the crackle of street conversation. There is little sentimentality in Winogrand and a lot of casual cynicism, only occasionally leavened by a streak of schmaltz, which he seemed to reserve mainly for animals.

In searching for what he had not seen before, Winogrand extended profoundly our notions of the formal potential of photography, and through the agency of these new forms extracted new meanings from the world. The nature of these meanings—fragmentary, elliptical, intensely personalised—do not make for comfortable viewing. We are disturbed by the hardness of Winogrand's mind even as we cherish his keen eye. We must continually ask whether sour misanthropy wins out over existential despair, finely judged satire over self-indulgent irony.

Garry Winogrand—by his own admission psychologically scarred yet at the same time liberated by such events as the Cuban Missile Crisis and the Kennedy assassination—seems the bleakest of the social landscapists, his lack of belief in the "truth" of photography the most complete. Nevertheless, the vast gallery of characters photographed by Winogrand seems to tell a particular, if jaundiced truth about a particular era in America—an era of brief hope followed by disillusion; of surface glitter delivering empty promises. Winogrand was one of the great photographic existentialists, as adrift as Robert Frank in an America with which he could not quite connect; the wandering Jew lost in the boundlessness of America and the convoluted yet wholly original meanderings of his work.

—Gerry Badger

WISE, Kelly.

Nationality: American. **Born:** New Castle, Indiana, 1 December 1932. **Education:** New Castle High School, 1948-51; Purdue University, West Lafayette, Indiana, 1951-55, B.S. in creative writing 1955; Columbia University, New York, 1957-59, M.A. in contemporary literature 1959. **Military Service:** Served in the United States Navy, in the South Pacific, 1955-57: Lieutenant Junior Grade. **Family:** Married Sybil Zulalian in 1959; children: Jocelyn, Adam and Lydia. **Career:** Photographer since 1968. Instructor of English and Cinematography, Mount Hermon School, Massachusetts, 1960-66. Instructor of English and Chairman of the English Department, Phillips Academy, Andover, Massachusetts, since 1966. **Recipient:** Kenan Grant, Phillips Academy, Andover, Massachusetts, 1985/86; Creative Photography Grant, and Project Director's Grant, Polaroid Corporation, Cambridge, Massachusetts, 1985/86. **Agents:** Vision Gallery, 216 Newbury Street, Boston, Massachusetts 02116. **Address:** 22 School Street, Andover, Massachusetts 01810, U.S.A.

Individual Exhibitions:

1973	Hewitt Gallery, University of New Hampshire, Durham
1974	Southern Illinois University, Carbondale
	Washington Gallery of Photography, Washington, D.C.
	Portland Museum of Art, Maine
1975	Silver Image Gallery, Ohio State University, Columbus
	Addison Gallery, Andover, Massachusetts
1977	Shado Gallery, Eugene, Oregon
	Canon Photo Gallery, Amsterdam
1978	Andover Gallery of Art, Massachusetts
	University of Massachusetts, Amherst
1979	University of Dayton, Ohio

	Portland School of Art, Maine
	Neikrug Gallery, New York
1980	Sheldon Memorial Art Gallery, University of Nebraska, Lincoln
	Yuen Lui Gallery, Seattle
	Middle Tennessee State University, Murfreesboro
1981	Jeb Gallery, Providence, Rhode Island
	Rose Art Museum, Brandeis University, Waltham, Massachusetts
	Blixt Gallery, Ann Arbor, Michigan
1983	Harvard Bookstore Cafe, Cambridge, Massachusetts
1984	Andover Gallery of Art, Massachusetts
1985	Currier Gallery of Art, Manchester, New Hampshire
	Addison Gallery of American Art, Andover, Massachusetts
1986	Yuen Lui Gallery, Seattle, Washington
	Middle Tennessee State University, Murfreesboro
	Connecticut College, New London
	Depauw University, Greencastle, Indiana

Selected Group Exhibitions:

1972	*Points of View,* Institute of Contemporary Art, Boston
	Octave of Prayer, Hayden Gallery, Massachusetts Institute of Technology, Cambridge
1974	*Private Realities,* Museum of Fine Arts, Boston
1977	*Warm Truths and Cool Deceits,* Sidney Janus Gallery, New York (toured the United States)
1984	*Massachusetts Photographers 1984,* Federal Reserve Bank, Boston

Collections:

International Museum of Photography, George Eastman House, Rochester, New York; Yale University, New Haven, Connecticut; Museum of Fine Arts, Boston; Fogg Art Museum, Harvard University, Cambridge, Massachusetts; Addison Gallery of American Art, Andover, Massachusetts; Library of Congress, Washington, D.C.; Museum of Fine Arts, Houston; Bibliothèque Nationale, Paris; Baltimore Art Museum, Maryland; National Portrait Gallery/Smithsonian Institution, Washington, D.C.

Publications:

By WISE: Books—*The Photographers' Choice,* editor, Danbury, New Hampshire 1975; *Still Points,* with a foreword by Duane Michals, Danbury, New Hampshire 1977; *Lotte Jacobi,* editor, Danbury, New Hampshire 1979; *Midwest Photo '80,* exhibition catalogue, Elkhart, Indiana 1980; *Appraisals,* editor, Danbury, New Hampshire 1981; *Portrait: Theory,* editor, New York 1981. **Articles**—"The Addison Gallery and Photography" in *Views* (Boston), Fall 1979; "Frederick Sommer" in *Creative Arts* (New York), no. 2, 1980; "Nude: Theory" in *Print Collector's Newsletter* (New York), March 1980; "A Ten Year Salute" in *Camera* (Lucerne), Summer 1980; "Diana and Nikon" and "Steve Grohe: An Interview" in *Views* (Boston), Summer 1980; "Carl Zahn: An Interview" in *Views* (Boston), Fall 1980; "Manuel Alvarez Bravo and Alen Mac-Weeney" in *Art New England* (Boston), October 1980; "Sand Creatures" in *Views* (Boston), Winter 1980; "1980: A Vintage Year for Photography Books" in *Art New England* (Boston), December 1980; "Nick Nixon" in *Artforum* (New York), April 1981.

On WISE: Books—*Private Realities,* edited by Clifford S. Ackley, New York 1974; *Photography and Fascination* by Max Kozloff, Danburg, New Hampshire 1979. **Articles**—"Points of View" by Michael Bry in *Popular Photography* (New York), February 1972; "Private Realities" by Deac Rossell in the *Boston Sunday Globe,* 31 March 1974; "Eye Is a Camera" by Douglas Davis in *Newsweek* (New York), 29 April 1974; "Private Realities" by Vladimir Gulevich in *Popular Photography* (New York), August 1974; "The Photographers' Choice" by Michael Edelson in *35mm Annual,* New York 1977; "Introductions to New Artists" by Alfred Frankenstein in the *San*

Francisco Chronicle, 14 July 1977; "Kelly Wise" by Nancy Dickinson in *Art New England* (Boston), February 1981.

*

Photography came late to me, at 36. I am thankful, deeply so, that the muse came at all. With harlequin eyes, she lured me into interior spaces, places I had visited, if at all, with only the safety and distance of the intellect.

Perhaps because I love books and am an English teacher, there is a recurrent literary integer in my work. The funny, the absurd, the terrifying, the sensuous, the tender—all merge. My early work was in black and white, private metaphoric imagery of my family and friends. In 1976 I got into color by using the SX-70 camera. Objects and peopleless spaces—in large and small format color—have become a fascination. Lately, I have been making black and white and color portraits of artists, writers of all types, editors, and publishers.

—Kelly Wise

*   *   *

Out of the first century of photographic development, with its contests between classic and romantic, emotion and objectivity, pictorialism and science, has come an international practice which includes them all. Not only is it possible to find distinguised exponents of all the possibilities of photographic vision; it is also frequently possible to find a significant degree of variation within the work of individual artists and, even more interestingly, within the compass of a single print. It is certainly a characterizing mark of this moment in photographic history that a significant number of photographers can and do work with notable fluency in what might well be described as a repertory of styles.

Kelly Wise is one of these multilingual artists. He was first known as a "straight" photographer, catching his subjects in normal contexts but with the second sight enhancements of light and space seen subjectively. Objects seen through a window seem to share the space of other objects in the foreground. A wall and a closed door are invaded and made animate by a floating oval of light emanating from an unseen source. In such imagery, to seem is to be. Cognitive magic has taken place, and the observer has, firmly in his optical grasp, an enlargement of his visual experience, creativity shared with the artist. Subsequently, or perhaps independently, Wise became involved, along with many others among his contemporaries, with the exploration of color, not the color of verisimilitude but color peculiar to the widening range of films and processes. With this involvement his subjects become more exclusive, single objects seen against the simplest of backgrounds, fragments or details of forms, seen without an information context, the abstracted minutiae of experience. Again, however, the transmitted intelligences is that form in and of themselves are rich with implication and act as sensors for an enormous range of experience.

Wise has most recently undertaken that most demanding of photographic problems, the portrait, in a series devoted to living artists and literati. The precedents are formidable: Abbott, Stieglitz, Freund, Avedon and, even more so, the noncelebrity portraits of Sander and Arbus. Again, however, Wise's distinctive point of view established the integrity of his likenesses. Characteristically, they are not "up tight" in their projection of either personality or celebrity. The familiarity of the photographer with his subject is visible in the easy, relaxed naturalism of the image. It is portraiture taken, as it were, from inside the relationship, without pretense and as natural as a look exchanged.

—Norman A. Geske

WITKIN, Joel-Peter.

Nationality: American. **Born:** Brooklyn, New York, 13 September 1939. **Education:** Saint Cecilia's School, Brooklyn, 1945-53; Grover Cleveland High School, Brooklyn, 1953-57; studied sculpture, Cooper Union, New York, 1970-74, B.F.A. 1974; photography, University of New Mexico,

Albuquerque, 1975-76 and 1978-85, M.A. 1976, M.F.A. 1986. **Military Service:** Served as a combat photographer, U.S. Army, in Texas and Europe, 1961-64. **Family:** Married Cynthia Witkin in 1978; son: Kersen-Ahanu. **Career:** Independent photographer, from 1956. Worked as a color photo printer, New York, 1958-61; owner of an artwork photography business, New York, 1964-70. Instructor in photography, University of New Mexico, Albuquerque, 1976-81; visiting lecturer in photography at numerous universities and institutes throughout the United States, since 1981. Contributor to the magazines *Infinity, Aura, Creative Camera, Advocate,* etc., since 1968. **Recipient:** Creative Artists Public Service Grant in photography, New York, 1974; Ford Foundation Photography Grant, 1977; National Endowment for the Arts Photography Grant, 1981, 1986 and 1992; American Institute of Graphic Arts Book Grant, 1986; First Prize, Art/Quest National Photography Competition, 1986; Art Matters Photography Grant, 1986; Chevalier Des Arts et de Lettres, 1990. **Agents:** Pace/MacGill, 32 East 57th Street, New York, New York 10022; Fraenkel Gallery, San Francisco, California 19408, U.S.A.

Individual Exhibitions:

1969	Moore College of Art, Philadelphia
1972	Cooper Union School of Fine Art, New York
1973	Lake Erie College of Art, Cleveland, Ohio
1980	Projects Studio One, New York
1982	Camerawork Gallery, San Francisco
	Galerie Texbraun, Paris
1983	Kansas City Art Institute, Missouri
	Stedelijk Museum, Amsterdam
	Fraenkel Gallery, San Francisco
	Provinciaal Museum voor Actuele Kunst, Hasselt, Belgium
	Fay Gold Gallery, Atlanta, Georgia
	C.E.P.A. Gallery, Buffalo, New York
1984	Paul Cava Gallery, Philadelphia
	Pace/MacGill Gallery, New York
1985	Butler Gallery, Houston, Texas
	Institut Franco-Americain, Paris
	Pace/MacGill Gallery, New York
	Gallery Watari, Tokyo
	Galerie Texbraun, at *FIAC 85,* Grand Palais, Paris
	Aspen Museum, Colorado
	San Francisco Museum of Modern Art (retrospective)
1986	Tartt Gallery, Washington, D.C.
	Museum of Contemporary Photography, Columbia College, Chicago (retrospective)
	Hiram Butler Gallery, Houston, Texas
	Fay Gold Gallery, Atlanta, Georgia
	Brooklyn Museum, New York (retrospective)
	University of New Mexico, Albuquerque (retrospective)
1987	La Jolla Museum of Contemporary Art, California (retrospective)
	Pace/MacGill Gallery, New York
1988	Kunstverein, Frankfurt (retrospective)
1989	Palais D'Tokyo, Paris
	Pace/MacGill Gallery, New York
1991	Pace/MacGill Gallery, New York
	Hamiltons Gallery, London
	Museum of Modern Art, Haifa, Israel
1993	Galerie De La Tour, Basel, Switzerland
	Pace/MacGill Gallery, New York
	Fraenkel Gallery, San Francisco
	Picture Photo Space, Osaka, Japan
1995	*Recent Photographs and Encaustics,* Pace/MacGill Gallery, New York

Selected Group Exhibitions:

1959	*Great Photographs from the Collection,* Museum of Modern Art, New York
1973	*IX International Biennale of Photography,* Lisbon, Portugal
1976	*New Photographics/76,* Central Washington State College, Washington, D.C.

1977 *Photoerotica,* Camerawork Gallery, San Francisco
1980 *Contemporary Photographers of New Mexico,* Art Institute of
   Chicago
1981 *Photographer as Printmaker,* Ferens Art Gallery, Hull,
   Yorkshire (travelled to the Museum and Art Gallery,
   Leicester; Cooper Gallery, Barnsley; Castle Museum,
   Nottingham; Photographers' Gallery, London)
1982 *New New York,* Florida State University, Tallahassee
   Mois de la Photo, Musee d'Art Moderne, Paris,
   Staged Photo Events, Rotterdamse Kunstichting, Netherlands
1983 *Images Fabriquées,* Centre Georges Pompidou, Paris
1985 *American Images,* Barbican Art Gallery, London (toured
   Britain)
1986 *The Biennial of Sydney,* Sydney, Australia
1987 *American Masters,* Whitney Museum, New York
   Crosscurrents, Forty Years of Photographic Art, Los Angeles
   County Museum of Art, Los Angeles
1989 *The Photography of Invention,* National Museum of American
   Art, Washington, DC
1990 Pace/MacGill Gallery, New York
1992 *Objects O Trouves d'Artiste,* Galerie Urbi et Orbi, Paris
   The Crucifixion through the Modern Eye, Hearst Art Gallery,
   Saint Mary's College of California, Morgana
   Pace/MacGill Gallery, New York

Collections:

Museum of Modern Art, New York; International Museum of Photography at George Eastman House, Rochester, New York; University of New Mexico Art Museum, Albuquerque; National Gallery of Art, Washington, D.C.; University of Arizona, Tucson; Walker Art Center, Minneapolis, Minnesota; Bibliothèque Nationale, Paris; Musée d'Art Moderne, Paris; Stedelijk Museum, Amsterdam; Victoria and Albert Museum, London.

Publications:

By WITKIN: Book—*Joel-Peter Witkin,* Pasadena, California 1985. **Article**—"Modern Masters: Joel-Peter Witkin," interview, with David Fahey, in *Interview* (New York), July 1985.

On WITKIN: Books—*Eros and Photography,* edited by Lew Thomas and others, San Francisco 1976; *Photographer as Printmaker,* exhibition catalogue, with texts by Gerry Badger, Peter C. Bunnell and Ansel Adams, London 1981; *Life Library of Photography: The Great Themes* by Time-Life editor, Alexandria, Virginia 1982; *Masterpieces of Photography from the George Eastman House Collections,* edited by Robert A. Sobieszek, Rochester, New York 1985; *Facets of Modernism,* exhibition catalogue, by Van Deren Coke, San Francisco 1986; *Selected Writings* by Max Kozlof, Alburquerque, New Mexico 1986. **Articles**—"The Trend is a Backward Look" by Gene Thornton in the *New York Times,* 3 August 1980; "Beyond Arbus and Bacon: The Photographs of Joel-Peter Witkin" in *Zein* (Rotterdam), no. 45, 1983; "Dancing with Death" by Owen Edwards in *American Photographer* (New York), August 1983; "Witkin by Witkin" in *the Manipulator* (Dusseldorf), no. 1, 1984; "Witkin, l'amour, la souffrance, la mort" in *Clichés* (Brussels), no. 5, 1985; "Joel-Peter Witkin" by Owen Edwards in *American Photographer* (New York), November 1985; "Joel-Peter Witkin's Bizarre Photos" by Jo Ann Lewis in the *Washington Post,* 15 February 1986.

*

My work reflects the insanity of life. The majority of Western Art shows that we don't know how to live. I make this work in the hope that we, or some other form, will see this work as part of the history of a diverse and desperate time.

—Joel-Peter Witkin

* * *

The photographs of Joel-Peter Witkin are marked by two distinct qualities. Firstly, the viewer cannot fail to note the rawness of his subject-matter. Witkin's iconography comprises a wholly original, personalised gallery of chimerical monsters, marginal freaks, assorted sexual deviants. Transvestitism, bestiality, coprophilia, and even necrophilia appear to be not simply suggested but flagrantly enacted within his grotesque and terrible tableaux. Secondly, in apparent and pointed contradiction to his *grand guignol,* one is struck—almost guiltily—by the sheer seductiveness of his prints, which are amongst the most stunning in all contemporary photography. The surface allure is quite calculated. It reinforces the ambivalence Witkin wants us to feel about his imagery, and iconises, fetishises, makes an object of desire of that which speaks about death of desire. Witkin mitigates the initial shock of his demonic subject-matter, filtering it through a series of allusive marks, a virtuoso screen of tissue veils, scratches, drips, and chemical stains—without diminishing the horror in any way. Needless to say, these two qualities in conjunction—beauty and horror—produce a powerful and haunting art.

It is also an ambitious art. The unedifying subject-matter speaks, no less, of Witkin's torment at his own existence, his anguish concerning the whole human condition. Rarely today, we find a major artist dealing in these major questions, not just in metaphysical but in directly religious terms. Witkin exploits the seam of Judeo-Christian and other mythologies, particularly the myth of sin, expiation and redemption as it relates to sexuality and power. Religious experience is linked to sadomasochism. The sadeian orgasm is raised to the level of a sacrament, representing an annihilation of the self, the release from earthly pain towards which we all inexorably head.

Witkin reinterprets some of the great images of Western art and photographic history in terms of his own diabolical, realistic and deeply pessimistic world view. The rubric of his images is fairly consistent. Figures, usually singly or in pairs, are imprisoned in the contained space of the photographic frame—a close relation of Francis Bacon's 'room' or 'cell'—there to be worked upon, violated by the artist's 'twisted, cruel, fiendish imagination'.

Witkin creates a photography that not only shocks, but one which puzzles, teases, provokes and questions. Thus his pictures, rarely for a male artist talking about the darker recesses of his sexuality, refer beyond personal obsession, beyond even a universal, natural state, to engage political, historical issues. So the words of Angela Carter might answer those who accuse Witkin of pornography and sexism in his work: "The moral pornographer would be an artist who uses pornographic material as part of the acceptance of the logic of a world of absolute sexual license for all the genders, and projects a model of the way such a world might work. A moral pornographer might use pornography as a critique of current relations between the sexes. . . . Such a pornographer would not be the enemy of women, perhaps because he might begin to penetrate to the heart of the contempt for women that distorts our culture, even as he entered the realms of true obsenity as he describes it."

And as an unnamed colleague wrote of the work after Witkin's first semester at UNM: "They are not about horror and suffering, but are the profound emotion which arises when a man is conscious of the potential of horror and suffering that is always present in the reality of the human condition. Here we are confronted with the depths that a conscious man can probe in his search to find himself what makes us human beings."

—Gerry Badger

WOJNECKI, Stefan.

Nationality: Polish. **Born:** Poznań, Poland, 6 April 1929. **Education:** Studied Physics at Poznań University graduating with MSc, 1959; self-taught in photography. **Family:** Married Barbara Malinowska, 5 November 1955; son: Ryszard. **Career:** Started work as a physicist in a factory in Wrocław, 1953-56, then as a secondary school teacher, 1956-75; elected Chairman, Poznań Photographic Society, 1969-75, and Vice-Chairman of the Polish Federation of Non-Professional Photographic Associations, 1974-79; became Chairman of the Great Poland District of the Union of Polish Artists/Photographers in Poznań, 1976-78; Chairman of the Art Council of that Union in Warsaw, 1985-87; Vice-Chairman of the Union, 1987-89; President of the Union since 1989; also Dean (since 1989) and Professor (since 1991) of the Faculty of

Painting, Graphics and Sculpture at the Academy of Fine Arts in Poznań. **Recipient:** Ministry of Culture and Art Prize, Poland, 1975, 79, and 83; Gold Cross, Poland, 1986; Josef Sudek Artist of Merit Medal, Czechoslovakia, 1989. **Address:** Sw Marcin 29/34, PL-61-806 Poznań, Poland.

Individual Exhibitions:

1959	Salon PTF, Poznań, Poland
	KMPiK, Szczecin, Poland
1969	*Faces,* Salon PTF, Poznań
	Salon FASF, Warsaw
1972	*Duograms,* Salon PTF, Poznań
1974	*Alternative Art,* Salon PTF, Poznań
1978	*Hyperphotography,* Gallery BWA Arsenał, Poznań
	Foto-Medium Art Gallery, Wrocław, Poland
	KMPiK, Piła, Poland
1980	*Free Photography,* Jaszczury Photographic Gallery, Cracow, Poland
1981	*Photography of Indentity,* BWA Gallery, Gorzów Wlkp, Poland
1983	*Photography of Indentity,* The Little Gallery of Photography, Toruń, Poland
	Photographic Gallery, Konin, Poland
1984	*Photography of Indentity,* BWA Gallery, Piła
	Bielsko-Biała Photographic Gallery, Poland
	ZPAF Gallery, Katowice, Poland
1986	*I Inscribe My Own World Order,* Little Gallery, Warsaw
1987	*I Inscribe My Experience of the World,* FF Gallery, Lòdz, Poland
	BWA Gallery, Lublin, Poland

Selected Group Exhibitions:

1957	*A Step Towards Modernity,* Salon PTF, Poznań
1971	*Searching Photographs,* Contemporary Gallery, Warsaw
1980	*Anniversary Exhibition of the State Academy of Art in Poznań,* National Museum, Poznań
1985	*Contemporary Polish Art Photography,* Zachęta Gallery, Warsaw
	National Museum, Wrocław, Poland
1986	*Polish Photography 1955-84,* Art and Technology Museum, Prague, Czechoslovakia
1988	*Polish Inter-Media Photography of the 80s,* BWA Arsenał Gallery, Poznań
1989	*Eco Art,* Zamek Ujazdowski Centre for Contemporary Art, Warsaw
	150 Years of Photography from the Collection of the National Museum, National Museum, Wrocław
1990	*Eco Art,* BWA Gallery, Poznań
	BWA Gallery, Częstochowa, Poland
	Eko Art—Ecology in Art, Polish Information and Cultural Centre, Leipzig, Germany
	Quick Pictures: Contemporary Photographic Art in Conversation, Art Gallery, Vienna
	2 X 8—Contemporary Photographic Art from Poland and DDR, TV Tower Exhibition Centre, Berlin
	Art Gallery, Rostock, Germany
1991	*70 Years of Polish Avant-Garde Photography,* Stadtsparkasse, Rhein, Germany
	BWA Gallery, Koszalin, Poland
	Photography of Imagination, Old Gallery, and Little Gallery, Warsaw
1992	*XX Ifo-scanbaltic,* Stadthalle, Rostock, Germany
1993	*Hidden Dimensions - Contemporary Polish Photography,* Museum of Photographic Art, Odense, Denmark
1994	*Contemporary Polish Photography,* Voipaalan taidekeskus, Valkeakoski, Finland

Publications:

By WOJNECKI: Articles—"New Shapes of Photo Exhibitions" in *Fotografia* (Warsaw), No 2, 1970; "Duograms" in *Fotografia* (Warsaw), No 10, 1970; "Avant Garde: A Margin of Social Development or A Development Factor?" in *Fotografia* (Warsaw), No 5, 1973; "Alternative Art" exhibition catalogue entry for Salon PTF (Poznań), 1974; "Photography of Identity" exhibition catalogue entry (Toruń), 1984; "A Glance at the Future" in *Fotografia* (Warsaw), No 2, 1984; "A Slow Camera of the Blue Art" exhibition catalogue, Little Gallery (Warsaw), 1986; "I Inscribe My Experience of the World" exhibition catalogue (Lòdz), 1987; "A Double Star of Culture" catalogue text for *Polish Inter-Media Photography of the 80s* exhibition (Poznań), 1988; "Zuruck in die Zukunft—Fotografie in den 80er und 90er Jahren" in *European Photography* (Gottingen), 1989; "An Interview—150 Years of Photography" in *Fotografia* (Warsaw), 1989; "Debut: A Teacher's Choice" interview in *European Photography* (Gottingen), 1991; "European Currents—The 3rd Arts Council National Photography Conference" interview in *UK Innovative Arts and Media* (Nottingham, UK), 1991.

On WOJNECKI: Books—*Third Eye* by Juliusz Garztecki (Kraków), 1979; *Fotograficzne Penetracje* by Alfred Ligocki (Kraków), 1979; *In the Face of Photographers* by Jerzy Busza (Warsaw), 1990; *The State Academy of Art in Poznań 1979-89* (Poznań), 1992; articles—"Towards the End of Art Photography" by Alfred Ligocki in *Fotografia* (Warsaw), 1971; "Alternative Art" by Romuald Kłosiewicz in *Fotografia* (Warsaw), 1976; "Fotografia ekspansywna" by Jerzy Olek in *Opole* (Opole), 1977; "Confrontation of Polish Photography" by Vladimir Birgus in *Ceskoslovenska Fotografie* (Prague), 1979; "Stefan Wojnecki" by Jerzy Busza in *Fotografia* (Warsaw), 1983; "Gorzów '83" by Barbara Kosińska in *Fotografia* (Warsaw), 1983; "Contemporary Polish Photography 1944-1984" by Jerzy Busza in *Foto* (Warsaw), 1984; "Gorzowskie Konfrontacje" by Barbara Kosińska in *Fotografia* (Warsaw), 1984; "New Faces of Photography" by Andrzej A. Mroczek in *Kierunki* (Warsaw), 1987; "Avant-Garde in Photography" by Krzysztof Jurecki in *Projekt* (Warsaw), 1987; "Toward a Photographic Avant-Garde" by Krzysztof Jurecki in *Projekt* (Warsaw), 1987; "Intermedia Photography" by Iwona Rajewska in *Sztuka* (Warsaw) 1988; "Letter from Warsaw" by Ryszard Bobrowski in *European Photography* (Gottingen), 1988; "Rozptylena fotografie" by Vladimir Birgus in *Fotografie Revue* (Prague), 1988; "Polish Photography of the 80s" by Krzysztof Jurecki in *Exit* (Warsaw), 1990; "Mid-European Tradition" in *AZ* (Vienna), 21 August 1990; "Poland Before and Now" by Wojciech Laskowski in *Katalog* (Odense), 1990.

*

I started my artistic work in 1956 with socially engaged photography. Since 1957 I have turned my interests toward alternative spaces. In 1970 I became interested in the reality generated by computers. Since 1980 I have become interested in the space beyond an object. My works created in 1985 and 1986 entitled *I Inscribe My Experience of the World* also touch upon this range of problems.

In the 1970s my main interests ran parallel to analytical art. The exhibition *Faces* in 1969 opened the phase of going beyond a picture. The exhibition *Alternative Art* held in 1974 was a proposition of inner alternative nature of work of art. In 1978, at the exhibition *Hyperphotography*, I presented multi perspective works, synthesized from many negatives.

In 1979 I initiated in my artistic work a self-reflection tendency with a theoretical statement entitled *Impulse-graphic Picture*. I formulated the opinion that photography expresses our inner models of the world. In the same year I started exploring in my work the problem of identity which resulted, two years later, in the exhibition *Photography of Identity*. In the two exhibitions *I Inscribe My Experience of the World* and *I Inscribe my Order of the World* I expressed my own "inner model" of the world.

—Stefan Wojnecki

*   *   *

Stefan Wojnecki—photographer, theoretician of photography, teacher and a leading figure in Polish artistic photography of the last three decades—is an artist whose work eludes critical attempts at classification.

Wojnecki's approach to his art and his way of perceiving the world are closely tied in with his academic background in physics. He himself believes that in the age of computer science and breakthroughs in psychology the sciences provide the best groundwork for an understanding of a world that otherwise remains inaccessible to the liberal and visual arts.

Theoretical reflection has accompanied his work from the very beginning: texts about photography have come to assume the role of autonomous artistic manifestations on a par with exhibitions.

His earliest exhibitions affirmed an interest in the technical side of photography: experimenting with technology in a search for new means of expression and ways of putting it to scientific use. He designed an ultra-fast miniaturised shutter (1965) and a stereoscopic A4 enlarger with a half-tone screen lens, later used in his *Duogrammes* series.

Successive exhibitions and theoretical texts published between 1974 and 1980 addressed the issue of the ambiguity of photography and ways of influencing the viewer's perception. In the following years the artist openly renounced claims regarding the neutrality of photography by demonstrating various methods of acting upon light sensitive emulsion and attempting to confront photographs with objects in order to evoke specific associations, and to place photography within new semantic contexts.

In 1981, doubtless affected by the social climate prevailing in Poland at the time, he turned his interest towards the functioning of photographic media, paying particular attention to the printed image as an expression of external memory, a way of transmitting and recording visual information about personal experience and social developments. This new approach was presented at the ''Photography of Identity'' exhibition where the author brought out the previously unappreciated value of banal, often anonymous photographs that assume a new dimension over time and elicit associations not originally intended, while manifesting in their own way the identity of the author of the exhibition.

In the first half of the 1980s Wojnecki produced a number of important texts tracing the evolution of his philosophical and artistic views (*Post-Opportunist Art—1983; Revision of Art in the Holistic-Transcendental Spirit—1984; Photography as Communiqué—1985*). In these he outlines the condition of photography, seen as linked to the current condition of art in the face of changes underway in civilization that involve a shift towards the interior of humanity, towards an understanding of the multi-faceted nature of the human condition, ''a stressing of the world of meanings, placing greater emphasis on sense than on construction.'' In the text accompanying his *I Inscribe My Ordering of the World* exhibition (1986) Wojnecki wrote that: ''the meaning of art is to convey convincingly the inner experience of a system of values [. . . .] Art therefore is the social consequence of the properties of the mind, while photography is a reflection of our inner model of the world.''

Tracing draw shapes and forms in space with a point of light, and recording them on film so as to produce ''something that did not exist in the reality being photographed'' led the artist to embark upon an elaborate meditation on the nature of photography.

Wojnecki's sensitivity to technological change and new developments in image technology made him aware early on of the potential offered by the electronic generation of images. He was one of the first photographers in Poland to show the possible implications the new technology brought to bear upon the identity and status of photography, and its foreseeable influence on the thinking and imagination of people as users and beneficiaries of the medium. ''The computer-generated image,'' he wrote in 1988, ''destroys the connection photography has with presence here and now; it puts the magical power of photography, construed as a fragment of reality, in danger of disappearing. . . . The hitherto obvious status of photography is undermined, becoming blurred and uncertain.''

The artist gives expression to his views in the course he conducts at the State Higher School of Art in Poznań, where he stresses the essential interrelation of photography and the fine arts, educating skilled painters and engravers familiar with the technical and creative potential of photography. Owing to Wojnecki's efforts are the Inter-faculty Department of Photography at the Poznań School of Art and departments of photography at universities in several European countries.

Any presentation of Stefan Wojnecki's work would be incomplete without a mention of the role he played in postwar Polish photography, both amateur and professional, holding important posts in photographers' associations and later in the governing body of the Union of Polish Artists/Photographers.

—Barbara Kosińka

WOLF, Reinhart.

Nationality: German. **Born:** Berlin, 1 August 1930. **Education:** Attended the Barkhof Gymnasium, Bremen, 1942-50; studied literature, art history and psychology, as an exchange student, Wabash College, Crawfordsville, Indiana, 1950-51; photography, Bayerische Staatslehranstalt für Photographie, Munich, 1955-56, M.Photog. 1956. **Career:** Since 1958, freelance fashion, advertising and magazine photographer, working for Volkswagen, Oetker, Tschibo, Reemstsma, etc., in Hamburg; established Reinhart Wolf commercial photography studio, 1958, and Wolf und Partner GmbH film company, 1969. Lecturer in Photography, Meisterschule für Mode college of fashion design, Hamburg, 1956-57; also visiting lecturer at numerous schools and universities in West Germany, since 1957. Founder-member, from 1964, and President, 1975-76, Art Directors Club of Germany. Member, Gesellschaft Deutscher Lichtbildner (GDL), 1954. **Recipient:** Europhot Master of Photography Award, 1971; Kulturpreis, Deutsche Gesellschaft für Photographie (DGPh), 1982; Prize of Honour, Kulturbund der DDR, East Berlin, 1982; Kodak-Steuben Award, 1984; also several gold and silver medals from the Art Directors Club of Germany and New York. Honorary Member, Bund freischaffender Foto-Designer (BFF), 1983.

Individual Exhibitions:

1972	Galerie Spectrum, Hannover
1977	Galerie Lange-Irschl, Munich
1980	Editions du Moniteur, Paris
	Galerie Levy, Hamburg
1983	Galerie Pro Photo, Nuremberg, West Germany
	Galleria e Libreria dell'Immagine, Milan (with Werner Mantz and Heinrich Riebesehl)
1984	Fotografie Forum, Frankfurt
	PPS-Galerie, Hamburg
1986	Benteler Galleries, Houston, Texas (with Toni Catany and Cay Lang)

Selected Group Exhibitions:

1973	*3rd World Exhibition of Photography: On the Way to Paradise*, Pressehaus Stern, Hamburg (and world tour)
1976	*The Faces of Buildings*, at *Photokina 76*, Cologne
1979	*Fotografie 1919-1979*, Fotomuseum im Stadtmuseum, Munich
1980	*New York*, at *Photokina 80*, Cologne
1984	*Bildraume*, Karl Ernst Östhaus Museum, Hagen, West Germany
	Sammlung Gruber, Museum Ludwig, Cologne
1986	*Foto Fest*, Houston, Texas

Collections:

Museum Ludwig, Cologne; Museum Folkwang, Essen, West Germany.

Publications:

By WOLF: Books—*Gesichter von Gebauden*, with text by Manfred Sack, Bremen and Hamburg 1980; *New York in Photographs*, with texts by Edward Albee and Sabine Lietzmann, Hamburg and New York 1980, Paris 1982; *Castles in Spain*, New York 1983; *Die neue alte Küche*, Hamburg 1983; *Drei-Sterne-Küche für Zuhause*, Munich 1984; *Gekochte Geschenke*, Munich 1985; *Agnes Amberg's Kochbuch*, Munich 1985; *China's Food: A Photo-*

graphic Journey, New York 1985; *Himmelzeichen*, with text by André Heller, Munich 1986.

On WOLF: Books—*Faces and Facades*, with introduction by Peter C. Bunnell, Cambridge, Massachusetts 1977; *Fotografie 1919-1979, Made in Germany: Die GDL-Fotografen*, with text by W. Boje, F. Kempe, B. Lohse and others, Frankfurt 1979; *Deutsche Fotografie nach 1945/German Photography After 1945*, exhibition catalogue, with texts by Floris M. Neususs, Petra Benteler and others, Kassel, West Germany 1979; *Sammlung Gruber: Photographie des 20. Jahrhunderts*, exhibition catalogue, with foreword by Siegfried Gohr, Cologne 1984. **Article**—"Reinhart Wolf" in *Camera* (Lucerne), July 1977.

*   *   *

Reinhart Wolf is one of those photographers who has gone beyond the level of technical and practical expertise to become masters of their craft. His work is exemplary proof that photography is capable of development similar to those which Goethe described for painting: namely, that colour-grinders can often become excellent painters. In Reinhart Wolf's case, an outstanding technician, professionally involved in the tasks of advertising, became a photographic stylist using to the full possibilites of his medium.

Born in Berlin and brought up in north Germany, Wolf studied in the USA. After completing his studies he went to Munich, where he did advertising photography. He worked in a variety of different fields: for the Volkswagen firm, for coffee and cigarette factories, and in the fashion industry. He made use of moving pictures as well as photographs and after 1956 he taught in Hamburg and in a number of other German art academies, though he remained something of a "mystery man" up until the publication of his exciting New York pictures. These colour photographs brought Wolf international fame in 1980 when they were exhibited at the Cologne *Photokina* (a film strip was also made). It was a long time since New York had been seen this way: in this demonic metropolis, this cement wasteland, Wolf had discovered a city of unreal beauty: one—it might almost be said—which demanded its rightful place in the history of art.

Wolf chose a traditionally artistic theme with his pictures of Spanish castles, published in 1983. Once again he was fascinated by the unreality of mightly walls and towers, but this was architecture standing untouched by time, in a landscape devoid of human life. As in the New York pictures, it was light and its colourful enchantment of reality which provided Wolf with his essential theme.

It would have been easy to produce similar pictures of other monumental building structures, such as the step-temples of Mexico or the Egyptian pyramids, but Wolf avoided doing so. Instead—to many people's surprise—he returned to his original job as an advertising photographer, working in particular on photographic illustrations of cookery books. From the unreality of a visionary architectural aesthetic he thus switched to the robust reality of attractive menus.

We might say that anyone who knows how to take photographs can photograph any subject matter they choose. Such a statement would be correct, but in Wolf's case inadequate. Anyone who looks carefully at the chronology of his photographic work will soon see that fantastic pictures always follow ones rooted in reality, and pictures of personal inspiration—such as the 1986 series "Celestial Signs," for which André Heller wrote the text—follow others produced on commission. Wolf seems to welcome the alternation as a stimulus which helps him to escape from the purely routine.

—Heinz Spielmann

WORTH, Don.

Nationality: American. **Born:** in Hayes Center, Nebraska, 2 June 1924. **Education:** Attended Chariton High School, Iowa; University of Arizona, Tucson, 1945-46; studied piano at the Juilliard School of Music, New York, 1946-47, and Manhattan School of Music, 1947-51, B.Mus. 1949, M.Mus. 1951; studied photography with Ansel Adams, San Francisco, 1956-60.

Career: Instructor in Music, Hartnett Studios, New York, 1947-52, and Manhattan School of Music, 1949-51; Engineering Surveyor, Southern Pacific Railroad, Tucson, 1952-56; Instructor in Music, Mills College, Oakland, California, 1955; Assistant to Ansel Adams, San Francisco, 1956-60. Professor of Art, San Francisco State University, since 1960. **Recipient:** Guggenheim Fellowship, 1974; National Endowment for the Arts Photography Fellowship, 1979. **Agents:** Witkin Gallery, 415 West Broadway, New York, New York 10012; Weston Gallery, 6th and Dolores, Carmel, California 93921; and G. Ray Hawkins Gallery, 9002 Melrose Avenue, Los Angeles, California 90069. **Address:** 38 Morning Sun Avenue, Mill Valley, California 94941, U.S.A.

Individual Exhibitions:

1957	International Museum of Photography, George Eastman House, Rochester, New York
	Nexus Gallery, Boston
1958	California Academy of Science, San Francisco
1959	San Francisco Museum of Art
1963	Carl Siembab Gallery, Boston
	Arizona State University, Tempe
1965	Washington State University, Pullman
1966	San Francisco State University
1967	Santa Barbara Museum of Art, California
	M.H. de Young Museum, San Francisco
	Pasadena Museum of Art, California
	University of California at Davis
1968	Lawson Galleries, San Francisco
1969	Phoenix College, Arizona
1970	Hancock College, Santa Maria, California
	Halsted 831 Gallery, Birmingham, Michigan
	Ohio State University, Columbus
1973	Strybing Arboretum, San Francisco
	San Francisco Museum of Art (retrospective)
	Addison Gallery, Andover, Massachusetts (retrospective)
	University of Nebraska, Lincoln (retrospective)
	Evergreen College, Olympia, Washington
1974	Witkin Gallery, New York (retrospective)
	Spectrum Gallery, Tucson, Arizona
1976	Camerawork Gallery, San Francisco
	Mills College Art Gallery, Oakland, California
	Falkirk Gallery, San Rafael, California
1977	Ohio State University, Columbus
	Plants, Friends of Photography, Carmel, California
1978	Focus Gallery, San Francisco
1979	Afterimage Gallery, Dallas
1980	Photography Southwest Gallery, Scottsdale, Arizona
	Blixt Gallery, Ann Arbor, Michigan
	Vision Gallery, Boston
	Photo Graphics Workshop, New Canaan, Connecticut
1981	Northern Arizona University, Flagstaff
	Photo Gallery International, Tokyo
1982	*Landscapes*, Douglas Elliott Gallery, San Francisco
1988	Witkin Gallery, New York

Selected Group Exhibitions:

1959	*Photography at Mid-Century*, International Museum of Photography, George Eastman House, Rochester, New York (toured the United States)
1961	*7 Contemporary Photographers*, International Museum of Photography, George Eastman House, Rochester, New York
1963	*Photography in the Fine Arts*, Metropolitan Museum of Art, New York (and 1967)
1966	*American Photography: The 60s*, Sheldon Memorial Art Gallery, University of Nebraska, Lincoln
1968	*Light7*, Massachusetts Institute of Technology, Cambridge

| 1970 | *Be-Ing Without Clothes*, Massachusetts Institute of Technology, Cambridge (toured the United States) |

1970   *Be-Ing Without Clothes*, Massachusetts Institute of Technology, Cambridge (toured the United States)

1974   *Photography in America*, Whitney Museum, New York

1981   *American Photographers and the National Parks*, Corcoran Gallery, Washington, D.C. (toured the United States, 1981-83)

1982   *Color as Form*, International Museum of Photography at George Eastman House, Rochester, New York

1984   *Photography in California 1945-80*, San Francisco Museum of Modern Art (travelled to the Akron Art Museum, Ohio; Corcoran Gallery, Washington, D.C.; Los Angeles Municipal Art Gallery; Cornell University, Ithaca, New York; High Museum of Art, Atlanta, Georgia; Museum Folkwang, Essen; Centre Georges Pompidou, Paris; Museum of Photographic Art, San Diego, California)

Collections:

Museum of Modern Art, New York; Guggenheim Foundation, New York; International Museum of Photography, George Eastman House, Rochester, New York; Addison Gallery, Phillips Academy, Andover, Massachusetts; Massachusetts Institute of Technology, Cambridge; Art Institute of Chicago; Center for Creative Photography, University of Arizona, Tucson; San Francisco Museum of Modern Art; Bibliothèque Nationale, Paris; National Gallery of Australia, Canberra.

Publications:

On WORTH: Books—*Photography in the 20th Century* by Nathan Lyons, New York 1967; *Light7*, edited by Minor White, Rochester, New York 1968; *California Photographers 1970*, exhibition catalogue, by Fred R. Parker, Davis, California 1970; *Don Worth: Photographs*, exhibition catalogue, San Francisco 1973; *Photography in America*, edited by Robert Doty, with an introduction by Minor White, New York and London 1974; *Don Worth: Plants*, exhibition catalogue, Carmel, California 1977; *A Ten Year Salute* by Lee D. Witkin, foreword by Carol Brown, Danbury, New Hampshire 1979; *Color as Form: A History of Color Photography*, exhibition catalogue, with introduction by Robert A. Sobieszek, Rochester, New York 1982; *Photography in California 1945-1980* by Louise Katzman, San Francisco 1984. **Articles**—"Don Worth" in *Aperture* (Rochester, New York), 9:3, 1961; "Gallery: Don Worth" in *Life* (New York), 7 May 1971.

*

A well-known younger photographer who once was speaking to a prestigious group of people was asked to make a statement regarding the purpose of his work. In reply he said, "I take photographs in order to see what something looks like when I take a photograph of it." His answer must have seemed shocking, in this situation where a "profound" reply was expected.

Photography is used for many obvious reasons, both superficial and "profound." We use the camera to preserve a moment, a place or an event; we use it to convey our feelings and our experiences to other people; it is used to stop the flow of time and thereby make ourselves seem god-like. We also use the camera to explore our psyche and the psyches of others; we many times use it to create an escape route to a never-never land. And some photographers use the camera to express deep affection for the subject (animate or inanimate). This affection may become so intense that we might even think of the camera as a unique instrument used for "making love."

But apart from all these reasons, most of which could provide inexhaustible material for psychological treatises, lies the simply trait of curiosity: what will this subject look like when it is reduced to black, white, shades of gray and also confined to a small, two-dimensional piece of paper?

But, finally, thinking of one more aspect, there are some of us who take photographs that may please the eye on an abstract level. Relating this idea to music, we should remember that a Beethoven piano sonata or a Bach fugue, which greatly intrigues the mind with its complex and mathematical ordering of melodies, harmonies, meters and rhythms, was written basically to appeal to the ear. Perhaps the ideal approach to photography implies involvement, to some degree, with all of these seemingly disparate reasons for using the camera.

—Don Worth

*   *   *

The direct vision and impeccable technique of Don Worth's photographs have led to his being associated with the "West Coast" tradition in photography, yet the variety of his photographic interests has always been much broader than the conservative stance that the west coast label has come to imply. He is motivated to make photographs that please the eye, but he is not restrained by a limiting concept of what might constitute that pleasure.

Initially trained as a musician, Worth spent 16 years studying music, performing and composing. In photography he found an expressive medium that provided a creative experience less transitory than that of music. The photographer's ability to have a lasting record of his creativity had appeal for him. Undoubtedly his association with Ansel Adams, also a musician, for whom he worked as an assistant during the late 1950s, helped him make the transition from one creative field to another.

Worth is perhaps best known for his extensive series of photographs of plants. These range from close-up studies of the structure of an individual plant to images of entire forested hillsides. It is an indication of Worth's broad interest in photography that these plant photographs were made using color as well as black-and-white material. He is deeply involved with plants as both a botanist and a gardener; this intensity and understanding of growing things are fully conveyed in his plant photographs.

Worth's photographs are unified through two formal characteristics. Most apparent is his attraction to soft, overall light. The majority of his exposures have been made on overcast or even fog enshrouded days with no direct sunlight. Rather than reflecting light, the subjects of his photographs appear to be glowing, often a source of light itself. The second unifying aspect of his work is seen in his tendency to compose his subjects as a part of a larger whole. What is beyond the borders of the frame is almost always implied by the arrangement of objects within the image; the photograph is constructed as a part of a larger reality. This is particularly true in the plant photographs, where there is rarely a distinct center of interest. The eye is left free to search and discover the particular attribute of a plant or a group of plants.

The same characteristics are evident in Worth's other images. He has traveled throughout the world and has photographed many kinds of subjects in addition to plants. Over a number of years he has made a group of self-portraits, many of which portray him nude as a partially blurred form moving through an otherwise still environment. He has used other models in similar contexts, and has photographed buildings and other structures as well. In recent years both his plant photographs and his images made in urban areas have assumed an interest in the commonplace or mundane, expressed through a more environmental point of view that maintains the soft light and the feeling for objects beyond the edges of the frame, but places less importance on the specific objects depicted.

The motion found in his self-portraits reappears in a group of color photographs made during the late 1960s. In these, Worth made three successive exposures on color film using three different colored filters. Still objects are portrayed in their natural colors, while moving elements such as streams, clouds or waves take on an almost pointillist coloration.

From very early in his career Worth considered working in color to be a integral part of his photographic activities. Throughout the late 1950s and 1960s, and into the 1970s, he regularly made color prints as well as black-and-white, not viewing the two as separate activities as many photographers today have come to do. This color work was done at a time when color was not accepted as relevant to fine-art photography by most museums, galleries and dealers, or even by other photographers. As color was "discovered" by photographers during the late 1970s, Worth's interest in working in that medium became distilled. In recent years he has returned to photographing solely in black-and-white.

—David Featherstone

WU Jia Lin.

Nationality: Chinese. **Born:** Zhao Tong Gu Cheng, Yunnan province, 22 October, 1942. **Education:** Self-taught in photography from 1969. **Family:** Married Wu Yue Hua in 1964; sons: Zhao Kun and Zhao Ying; daughters: Zhao Hong and Zhao Xia. **Career:** Chief reporter at Yunnan News Photo Service since 1987; Assistant Chief Executive at Yunnan News Photo Service since 1993. **Address:** No 3 Wa Cangzhuang, Dongfeng West Road, Kunming, Yunnan Province, Peoples Republic of China.

Individual Exhibitions:

1989   *Yunnan Journey*, Taiwan

Selected Group Exhibitions:

1988   *Red Earth, Rhythym & Life Style*, Beijing Chinese Art Museum
1994   *Contemporary Photography of China, Taiwan and Hong Kong*,
        Hong Kong Art Centre

Publications:

By WU: Book—*Wu Jia Lin Photo Collection: Yunnan's Mountain People*, 1993.

On WU: Photo essay—*Chinese Photographers*, critique by Zhang Fu Yan entitled *Unveil*, 1989. **Article**—"Mainland Photographers Special" in *Echo Magazine*, 1989.

*

My work can be divided into two stages:

Before the 80s I placed more emphasis on basic technique and tried the many different areas of photography.

After 1980, besides photographing the minority culture in Yunnan for our publication, I have also been doing documentary work in black and white, photographing the mountain people of Yunnan and their life style. This work reflects my natural response and reaction to the environment. I prefer the more spontaneous and yet profound photographic style over self consciousness in creativity.

—Wu Jia Lin

*   *   *

Wu Jia Lin was born in the year 1942, in Yunan Province, China and went to school in the city of Kun-ming; got married and started teaching himself photography in 1969.

Wu joined the Yunan News Photo Agency in the 1970s and became Chief Photographer in 1987. In 1993 Wu was again promoted to Deputy Director responsible for the Photography and Editorial Departments.

Starting in 1981, Wu began exhibiting his work throughout China, Taiwan and Hong Kong and was considered an important figure in the school of social documentary photography which emerged from the late 1970s and soon entered mainstream photography in China. In most of his self-initiated projects of the 1980s Wu dedicated himself entirely to revealing aspects of daily life in his home town, Yunan. Wu prefers to work in monochrome in

order to elicit the depths of his chosen subjects. These relate closely to his own experiences of life and intepret the character of places where nature and man are closely entwined. In certain respects this work pays homage to the series on *The Norfolk Broads* by the early Pictorialist P.H. Emerson. Wu's images consistently display a sense of closeness with both the people and the land beyond simply showing an objective record of a place.

—Joseph Fung

WU YINXIAN.

Nationality: Chinese. **Born:** Su Yang County, Jiangsu Province, 28 September 1900. **Education:** Studied painting, Fine Arts School, Shanghai, 1920-22. **Military Service:** Served as Film Team Leader, 8th Route Army, Yian An, China, 1938-46. **Family:** Married Wang Zifei in 1940; daughter: Wu Zuging. **Career:** Worked as a fine arts teacher, Middle School, Su Yang County, 1923-30; photographer, Red Lantern Studio, Shanghai, 1931-32; photographer for Dian Tong and Ming Xing Film Corporations, Shanghai, 1935-38; Director, The Film Studio, Chang Chun, 1949-54; Deputy Director, China Film College, Beijing, 1955-66; Film Bureau Adviser, Ministry of Culture, Beijing, 1974-81. Vice-President, China Photographers' Association, Beijing, since 1964; President, China Cinematographers' Society, Beijing, since 1985. **Recipient:** Best Film Award, Chinese Ministry of Culture, Beijing, 1965. Honorary President, China Veteran Photographers' Society, from 1985; Member, China Federation of Literary and Art Circles, from 1960. **Address:** Al. Xuang Wai Street, Beijing, People's Republic of China.

Individual Exhibitions:

1935   Shanghai Youth Society, China
1961   Beijing Museum, China
1985   Beijing Museum, China

Selected Group Exhibitions:

1957-86   *China Photo Exhibitions* (nos. 1-14), Beijing Museum, China
1961-84   *China Portrait Exhibitions* (nos., 1-5), Beijing Museum, China
1962   *Huong Mountain Scenery*, Beijing Museum, China
1983   *Beijing Photographers' Society*, Beijing Museum, China
           Veteran Soldiers Exhibition, Beijing Museum, China
1984   *Flowers*, Beijing Museum, China
           China Photoarts, Exhibition Centre, Hong Kong
1985   *China Photoarts*, Intertrade Building, Singapore
           Chinese Photography, International Center of Photography,
           New York

Collections:

Museum of the Chinese Revolution, Beijing; Archives of China, Beijing; Revolutionary Exhibition Hall, Yan An, China; Xin Hua News Agency, Beijing.

Publications:

By WU YINXIAN: Books—*Techniques of Expression in Photography*, 2 vols., Beijing 1963-65; *Light Selection for Photography*, Beijing 1979, rev.

Yunnan, 1992. Photograph by Wu Jia Lin.

ed. 1986; *Portrait Photography*, Beijing 1982; *Composition for Photography*, Beijing 1983, rev. ed. 1984; *Wu Yinxian's Photo Album*, 2 vols., Beijing 1983-85; *Scenery Photography*, Beijing 1985.

On WU YINXIAN: Articles—"Photo Pictorial" in *Photo Pictorial* (Hong Kong), no. 185, 1980; article in *Photo Pictorial* (Hong Kong), no. 196, 1981; "Comment on Wu Yinxian's Photo Album" in *Yomiuri News* (Tokyo), 18 July 1982; "Witness to History" in *Minolta Mirror* (Tokyo), no. 2, 1984; "Wu Yinxian—Meister der chinesische Photographie" in *China das Neue* (Beijing), no. 1, 1983.

*

I produce my works of art according to socialist principles; they are intended to serve the people and socialist construction. Although the technique of expression depends on the particular subject, my expression in general is of a realistic kind. My intention is to concentrate on expressing the daily life of the Chinese people as they strive for modernization. At the same time, I also like to take landscape photos because China has a long history and many areas of scenic interest.

I think we should not copy foreign photography, but should learn from it to develop a national style. Nor should we imitate Chinese painting, but should work within the specific characteristics of photography itself.

Photography is the real record of our times, a witness of history. So we photographers should place emphasis on photography's social effects, and

should play an important role in encouraging our people to strive for development and social construction. Using photography to expose the backwardness in Chinese society is improper, since it is merely a remnant from the past and not a reflection of today.

—Wu Yinxian

*   *   *

Beyond doubt, knowledge of Chinese photography in the West is fragmentary, random and uncertain. This is so both because of the self-isolation imposed by the so-called cultural revolution of the 1960s and 1970s and because of the true individuality of Chinese culture. In Western Europe, knowledge of this is not great and, despite appearances, does not exceed pure information or documentation. In the light of this, all attempts at a better understanding of Chinese photographers and their art should be met with particular attention and interest, One such photographer, who certainly merits attention, is Wu Yinxian.

Wu Yinxian is the doyen of Chinese photography. Involved in both photography and film since the 1930s, he and his art have experienced Chinese culture in all its stages—from prerevolutionary China, through the war and the Long March, to the various periods of the People's Republic. Against this background, Wu Yinxian is better equipped than anyone else to say: "photography is the real record of our times, a witness of history."

He was concerned with many forms of photography during his long career, two of which deserve special mention. The first is documentary photography of a clearly social character and best described by Wu Yinxian himself in his comment that "photographers should place emphasis on photography's social effects, and should play an important role in encouraging our people to strive for development and social construction." In this way, he not only expressed the popular socialist belief in the necessity of involving photography in pertinent affairs but also the opinion that photography has various responsibilities to live up to. Conceived in this way, photography becomes not only a record of evolving changes but also a means by which social awareness is reconstructed, attitudes and customs are shaped and a new man is formed. Even if photography of this kind unavoidably attempts to show the good rather than the bad aspects of man and only displays successes, it nevertheless forms a great historical record of the life and times of a country and draws a wonderful picture of the struggles of a nation and its aspirations to a better future.

It would be unfair, however, to suggest that Wu Yinxian's photography is confined solely to these issues or that more conventional concerns are removed from it. Like other Chinese photographers, Wu Yinxian is not indifferent to customary problems in photography although he certainly conceives them differently from his Western colleagues. For, here, the conventional strikes the artist most of all as beauty and harmony of landscape, the resonance of nature's shapes and colours and the singular moment, or singular point of view, that compels the shutter to be dropped. In this sense, this photography is often—and may be—classed as conventional or straightforward despite the fact that, for the photographer, it primarily represents the question of how to capture and relay the beauty of the Chinese land. This is equally true of Wu Yinxian's distant landscapes and perspectives and of his large close-ups representing fragments of various plants or flowers (for example, his Blooming Cactus Series).

All in all, Wu Yinxian's photography is varied and interesting. In acknowledging it as a symbolic presentation and an introduction to Chinese photography, the hope must be expressed that it heralds closer acquaintance with this art and marks the beginning of its admittance to its rightful and assuredly deserved place among other achievements in this medium.

—Ryszard Bobrowski

YAMPOLSKY, Mariana.

Nationality: Mexican. **Born:** Chicago, Illinois, 6 September 1925; moved to Mexico, 1944: adopted Mexican citizenship, 1958. **Education:** Studied Humanities at University of Chicago obtaining B.A. degree, 1944; studied Art at the Escuela de Pintura y Escultura La Esmeralda, Mexico City, 1945-48, and Graphic Arts at the Escuela de Artes Gráficos, Mexico City, 1948-49; photography self-taught with encouragement and help from Lola Alvarez Bravo. **Family:** Married Arjen van der Sluis in 1967. **Career:** Worked as Engraver and Exhibition Curator at the Taller de Gráfica Popular, 1945-58 and as a secodary school English literature teacher, 1946-56. Coordinator and editor of photography books since 1960; Director of Children's Literature, Secretaría de Educación Pública, Mexico, 1978-80; Curator of various exhibitions including: *Gran Muestra de la Obra del Taller de Gráfica Popular*, 1956, *Memoria del Tiempo*, Museo de Arte Moderno, Mexico City, 1989, *Bailes y Balas, Mexico City, 1921-1931*, and *Archivo General de la Nación*, Mexico City, 1991. **Agent:** Zelda Cheatle Gallery, 8 Cecil Court, London, WC2 N4HE, England. **Address:** San Marcos 65, Tlalpan, 14000 Mexico, D.F., Mexico.

Individual Exhibitions:

1960	*Imagenes del Medio Oriente,* José María Velasco Gallery, Mexico City
1976	Casa del Lago, Mexico City
	Universidad Nacional Autónoma de México, Mexico City
	Museo de la Alhóndiga, Guanajuato, Mexico
1978	*Madurodam,* The Hague, Holland
1979	University of Manchester, England
1983	Galería Cannon, Milano, Italy
1985	Photographers' Gallery, London
1986	Bayly Art Museum, University of Virginia, Charlottesville, USA
	Las Estancias del Olvido, Museo del Chopo, Mexico City
1988	Sunderland Arts Development Agency, Washington Arts Centre, Washington, England
	La Mujer Mazahua, Museo de Arte Moderno, Mexico City, and Centro Cultural, Instituto Mexiquense de Cultura, Toluca, Mexico
	Eternal Mexico: Photographs by Mariana Yampolsky, Queens College, The City University of New York, USA
1989	Galería de Arte Contemporáneo, Mexico City
	Richland College, Dallas, Texas
1990	*Altars and Idols—The Life of the Dead in Mexico,* University of Essex, England
1991	Sin Fronteras Gallery, Austin, Texas
	Club Fotográfico, Mexico City
1992	*Al Filo del Tiempo,* Curare, Mexico City
	Haciendas de Hidalgo, Fototeca del Instituto Nacional de Antropología e Historia, Pachuca, Mexico
1993	*Constructores de Sueños,* Universidad Veracruzana, Xalapa, Mexico
	Mazahua, University of Groningen, Netherlands and Museo Mural Diego Rivera, Mexico City
	Casas Acariciadoras, Museo Nacional de Antropología, Mexico City

	Traditional Mexican Architecture, The Hafnarfjördur International Arts Festival, Iceland
	Mariana Yampolsky, A Retrospective, Zelda Cheatle Gallery, London
	Encuentro de Fotografía Latinoamericana, Caracas, Venezuela
1994	*Mariana Yampolsky,* Rhode Island School of Design, Providence, Rhode Island

Selected Group Exhibitions:

1975	*International Year of Women,* Mexico City
1978	*First Latin American Photography Colloquium,* Mexico City
1980	*Hecho en Latinoamérica,* Palacio de Bellas Artes, Mexico City
1981	*Latin American Photography,* Kunsthaus, Zurich, Switzerland
	Artists of Mexico, Kunstlerhaus Belhanien, Berlin, Germany
1982	*Artists in Mexico,* Galerija Bih, Sarajevo, Yugoslavia
	10 X 10: Contemporary Mexican Photography, travelling exhibition shown in Austin, Texas, San Francisco and Los Angeles, California, and New York
	Exhibition of Mexican Photography, Stockholm, Sweden, and Oslo, Norway
1983	*Photography as Photography,* Museo de Arte Moderno, Mexico City
1984	*Portraits of Distant Lands: Aspects of Contemporary Latin American Photography,* Sydney, Australia
1985	*La Fête des Morts au Mexique,* Musée d'Art Moderne de la Ville de Paris and Musée des Enfants, Paris, France
	Third Latin American Photography Colloquium, Havana, Cuba
1986	*Inside Mexico,* Sicily, Italy
	Retrato de lo Eterno, Museo de Arte Moderno, Bogotá, Colombia
1987	*Ten Mexican Photographers,* travelling exhibition sponsored by the Ministry of Foreign Affairs, Mexico, shown in New Delhi, India, and in China
1988	*Images of Mexico,* Schirn Kunsthalle, Frankfurt, Germany; Messepalast, Vienna, Austria; and Dallas Museum of Art, Dallas, Texas
	Diverse Images of Mexico, Mexican Fine Arts Museum, Chicago, Illinois
	Exhibition for the Quincentennial of the Discovery of America (with Lola Alvarez Bravo and Flor Garduño) Huelva, Spain
	E Ora di Messico, Galería Il Diaframma, Milan, Italy
	Realités Magiques, Hotel de Ville de Nivelles, Brussels, Belgium
1989	*Polo Donna,* Galería Civica d'Arte Moderna, Palazzo del Diamante, Padiglione d'Arte Contemporanea, Palazzo Massari, Ferrara, Italy
	Graciela Iturbide and Mariana Yampolsky, Museum of Anthropology, Ferrara, Italy
1990	*Between Worlds: Contemporary Mexican Photography,* Impressions Gallery, York, England; Camden Arts Centre, London, and International Center for Photography, New York
	What's New: Mexico City, Art Institute of Chicago, Illinois
	Women in Mexico, National Academy of Design, New York; Museo de Monterrey, Monterrey, Mexico; Centro Cultural/Arte Contemporáneo, Mexico City

Caress. Photograph by Mariana Yampolsky.

Other Images, Other Realities—Mexican Photography since 1930, Sewell Art Gallery, Rice University, Houston, Texas

1991   *Festival of Photography,* Arles, France

1992   *Encountering Difference—Four Mexican Photographers,* Woodstock Center for Photography, New York, and Falkirk Cultural Center, San Rafael, California

Photographic Mexico 1920/1992, Europalia, Brussels, Belgium

El Hechizo de Oaxaca, Palacio de Bellas Artes, Mexico City, and Marco Museum, Monterrey, Mexico

1993   *Oaxaca—Magia de México,* Kunsthal Museum, Rotterdam, Holland

On the Elbow, Witkin Gallery, New York

La Escritura de las Fotografías, Haus der Kulturen der Welt, Frankfurt; Frankfurt Book Fair, Frankfurt, Germany; Book Fair, Bogotá, Colombia

La Mujer en México, Musée d'Art Moderne, Liège, Belgium

Collections:

Center for Creative Photography, University of Arizona; Houston Museum of Fine Arts, Houston, Texas; Southwestern Texas State University, San Marcos; Museo de Arte Moderno, Mexico City, Mexico.

Publications:

By YAMPOLSKY: Books—*Lo Efímero y lo Eterno del Arte Popular Mexicano,* in two volumes with Leopoldo Mendez, Mexico 1974; *La Casa en La Tierra,* with text by Elena Poniatowska, Mexico 1981; *La Casa que Canta,* Mexico 1982; *La Raíz y el Camino,* with text by Elena Poniatowska, Mexico 1985; *Tlacotalpan,* with text by Elena Poniatowska, Xalapa, Mexico 1987; *Estancias del Olvido,* with text by Elena Poniatowska, Mexico 1987; *Bailes y Balas,* with text by Elena Poniatowska, Mexico 1991; *Haciendas Poblanas,* Mexico 1992; *Mazahua,* with text by Elena Poniatowska, Mexico 1993; *Traditional Mexican Architecture,* with text by Chlöe Sayer, London 1993.

On YAMPOLSKY: Books—*La Photographie Contemporaine en Amérique Latine,* Paris 1982; *Plotting Women: Gender and Representation in Mexico,* by Jean Franco, New York 1989; *Compañeras de México: Women Photograph Women,* by Amy Conger and Elena Poniatowska, Riverside 1990; *Between Worlds: Contemporary Mexican Photography,* edited by Trisha Ziff, New York 1990; *Fotografía Latinoamericana: Tendencias actuales,* a series of catalogues, La Rábida, University of Seville 1991; *Desires and Disguises: Five Latin American Photographers,* edited by Amanda Hopkinson, London 1992; *Die Schrift Mexikanische Fotografen, 13x10, La escritura fotógrafos mexicanos,* by Raquel Tibol, Frankfurt 1992; *Textured Lives: Women, Art and*

Representation in Modern Mexico, by Claudia Schaefer, Tucson 1992; *Surviving Beyond Fear: Women, Children and Human Rights in Latin America,* edited by Marjorie Agosin, Fredonia (New York) 1993; *Nachdenken Über Mexiko,* by Erika Billeter, Bern 1993. **Articles**—Book Review of *La Casa en la Tierra (Yampolsky)* by Elena Urrutia in *Fem* Vol 5 No 17, 1981; "Six Women Artists of Mexico" by Shifra M. Goldman in *Woman's Art Journal* Vol 3 No 2, 1983; "Marianna Yampolsky-Urbach" by John Stathatos in *Creative Camera* No 245, May 1985; "Río de Luz" by Esther Parada in *Aperture* No 109, Winter 1987; "Mariana Yampolsky: Drinking from the Roots" by David Brittan in *Creative Camera* No 5 1989; "Masters of Modern Mexican Photography" by Elizabeth Ferrer in *Latin American Art* Vol 2 No 4, Fall 1990; "Mariana Yampolsky: El acto fotográfico" by Juan Coronel Rivera in *Artes de México* No 12, 1991; "Encountering Difference" by Elizabeth Ferrer in *Center Quarterly* No 53 (The Center for Photography, Woodstock), 1992; "Images of Identification" by Celeste Connor in *Artweek,* 19 August 1993; TV-"Mariana Yampolsky, Fotógrafa" interview for Channel 11, Mexico 1994.

*

It would seem easy to press the button and hope for the best. However, there are so many factors that make for a memorable image that I feel exalted when a single one truly captures a profound moment. Manipulation, nostalgia, and the exotic do not interest me.

Most of my time is spent travelling around the Mexican countryside. The abandoned haciendas are filled with light and shadows, evoking a way of life cut short by the Mexican revolution. Popular architecture in its great variety shows the creativity of men and women who live close to the earth. Most fascinating of all are the people themselves, as they work and celebrate. As things unfold before my lens, I try not to intrude and, if anyone is uncomfortable before the camera, I desist.

Mexico is a continual surprise, full of energy, the way people move, their brutality. It is sun and light. Things supposedly in bad taste move me. Even the plastic flowers have character.

—Mariana Yampolsky

*   *   *

Everyone should watch Mariana taking her photos, how she gets close, she selects the right shot, she gets excited, she shoots, she looks for the perfect light, she opens a window, she comes and goes, always smiling, yet concerned that the instant will escape. "Oh time, please stop, you're so beautiful." A key leaning against a wooden door in a certain sunlight, the gleaming back of a rocking chair, a farm woman who protests: "I'm going to comb my hair I look ridiculous" (we always look ridiculous when anyone wants to take our photo), all is part of the creative process. After twelve shots, Mariana feels around in her bag for the next roll. Although it doesn't seem that she would even have time to think, but again, emotion fills her face, the face of a woman who participates, who knows how to see, who sees, understands the essential, captures and above all, loves her country, with a profound afflicted love. There is the expectant mother with another child in her arms. How can she possibly have the strength to have another child? Well, she does, and Mariana and the mother, one in front of the other, the artist and her subject both become inextricably linked. Communicating vessels, we look at them mesmerized; the photograph and the mother, the river of light between the two, the umbilical cord that must be broken because Mariana the sojourner keeps walking on the strong legs of a woman who knows where she is going ... Everything is sculptural as it was for the artists Leopoldo Méndez and Pablo O'Higgins, her most evident sources of influence.

It is this way of looking at life that is Mariana Yampolsky's major contribution to the culture of Mexico; it incorporates days and hours, festivals and objects of daily use, the toil and sorrow of great art, just as Diego Rivera knew how to convey them in his murals and Orozco was able to capture rage and indignation for all times. Mariana is less violent, but is equally incisive. The expression of the young boy working on the pulque-producing hacienda reflects centuries of the exhaustion of the exploited child. The same desolation appears on the face of the young, old girl in the grain storeroom. Another recurring theme is the survival of syncretic pre-Hispanic forms, the weight of religion and the imprint of Mexican hands in everyday labours; whether in the home or in ceremonies. Mariana's whites emerge from the shadows, an untouched white, the young girl in her first communion dress, the little indigenous boy holding on to his father, the young woman, who turns her head covered by a cloth to look out at us, as if a Joan of Arc or a novice on the verge of delivering her soul to God.

—Elena Poniatowska

YAVNO, Max.

Nationality: American. **Born:** New York City, 26 April 1911. **Education:** Evander Childs High School, Bronx, New York, until 1927; studied (evenings), City College of New York, 1927-32; studied business administration and political science, Columbia University, New York, 1932-34; studied cinematography, University of California at Los Angeles, 1972-73. **Military Service:** Served in the U.S. Army Air Force, 1942-45. **Family:** Married Alyse Abrams in 1930 (divorced, 1934). **Career:** Worked as a page boy, New York Stock Exchange, 1927-32; social worker, New York City Relief Bureau, 1935; employed by the Works Progress Administration (WPA), New York, 1936-42. Freelance landscape, documentary and commercial photographer, working for *Vogue, Harper's Bazaar, etc.,* in San Francisco, 1945 until his death in 1985; established commercial photography studio, San Francisco, 1954-75. President, Photo League, New York, 1938-39. **Recipient:** Guggenheim Fellowship, New York, 1953; Art Directors Club Award, New York, 1954, 1955. **Died:** (in San Francisco) 4 April 1985.

Individual Exhibitions:

1946	American Contemporary Gallery, Los Angeles
1948	California Palace of the Legion of Honor, San Francisco
1976	G. Ray Hawkins Gallery, Los Angeles
1977	Halsted Gallery, Birmingham, Michigan
1978	G. Ray Hawkins Gallery, Los Angeles
	Gallery for Fine Photography, New Orleans, Louisiana
1979	Gallery for Photographic Arts, North Olmstead, Ohio
	Marcuse Pfeifer Gallery, New York
1980	Equivalents Gallery, Seattle, Washington
	G. Ray Hawkins Gallery, Los Angeles
	Fine Arts Museum, San Francisco
	Simon Lowinsky Gallery, San Francisco

Selected Group Exhibitions:

1939	*Pictorial Photographers of America,* New York
1947	*Seventeen American Photographers,* Los Angeles County Museum of Art
1976	*Exposing: Photographic Definitions,* Los Angeles Institute of Contemporary Art
1977	*Photographic Corssroads: The Photo League,* Museum of Fine Arts, Boston
	Cityscapes, Fine Arts Museum, San Francisco
1979	*New Directions,* Museum of Modern Art, New York
	The Photograph as Artifice, Independent Curators Inc., travelling show, U.S.A.
	Photographic Directions: L.A. 1979, Security Pacific Bank, Los Angeles
1984	*Photography in California 1945-80,* San Francisco Museum of Modern Art (travelled to Akron Art Museum, Ohio; Corcoran Gallery, Washington, D.C.; Los Angeles Municipal Art Gallery; Cornell University, Ithaca, New York; High Museum of Art, Atlanta, Georgia; Museum Folkwang, Essen, Germany; Centre Georges Pompidou, Paris; Museum of Photographic Arts, San Diego, California)

Collections:

San Francisco Museum of Modern Art; Oakland Museum, California; Center for Creative Photography, University of Arizona, Tucson; Indiana University Art Museum, Bloomington; New Orleans Museum of Art, Louisiana; Fogg Art Museum, Harvard University, Cambridge, Massachusetts; University of Michigan Museum of Art, Ann Arbor; Detroit Institute of Arts, Michigan; University of New Mexico Art Museum, Albuqueque; International Museum of Photography at George Eastman House, Rochester, New York.

Publications:

By YAVNO: Books and portfolios—*The San Francisco Book,* with Herb Caen, Boston 1948; *The Los Angeles Book,* with Lee Shippey, Boston 1950; *The Story of Wine in California,* with text by M.F.K. Fisher, Berkeley and Los Angeles 1962; *Natzler Ceramics,* Los Angeles 1968; *Portfolio One: Image as Poem,* with introduction by Ben Maddow, Los Angeles 1977; *Silver See,* portfolio with others, introduction by Victor Landweber, Los Angeles 1977; *The Photography of Max Yavno,* with text by Ben Maddow, Berkeley, California 1981.

On YAVNO: Books—*Exposing: Photographic Definitions,* exhibition catalogue, with introduction by Robert Mautner, Los Angeles 1976; *Faces: A Narrative History of the Portrait in Photography* by Ben Maddow, Boston 1977; *Photographic Directions: Los Angeles 1979,* exhibition catalogue, with introduction by Robert Glenn Ketchum, Los Angeles 1979. **Articles**—"Max Yavno" in *Camera* (Lucerne), April 1966; "Resurrection in Black and White" by J. Beshears in *Artweek* (Oakland, California), 14 February 1976.

*   *   *

Max Yavno's photography spans a period of over 40 years. He began working with the Photo League in New York during the late 1930s. The sense of cultural and social detail he acquired there remained with him, and formed the foundation of his *oeuvre.* The same themes: storefronts, gas stations, and the nuances of crowded street life continued to occupy him throughout his career. Yavno was a choreographer of the urban scene, a choreographer of endless patience who would wait steadfastly for just the right posture or fall of light. He was also a master craftsman of the black and white print.

Yavno moved from New York to San Francisco after World War II, and in 1948 he produced a book of photographs of that city for Houghton-Mifflin. The wider spaces of San Francisco encouraged a more expansive documentary vision. Yavno's view camera carved out huge chunks of the coastal skyline. In 1950 he worked with Lee Shippey on a second book, about Los Angeles. This book included such classic images as the klieglit "Premiere at Carthay Circle," and the huge, Popart "Leg." The exuberant southern California architecture encouraged Yavno's eye for vernacular irony.

In 1952 Yavno sold several prints to Edward Steichen at the Museum of Modern Art. And in '53 he was awarded a Guggenheim fellowship, having been recommended by Steichen and Edward Weston. Despite this much deserved recognition the early 1950s were not an encouraging time to be a "fine-art" photographer. Yavno was forced to turn to commercial photography. He worked for over 20 years, doing mostly advertising and product shots. He brought the same sense of craftsmanship and attention to detail which characterized his landscape work to his commercial still-lifes. His work appeared in *Vogue* and *Harpers,* and in 1954 and '55 he won Gold Medals from the New York Art Directors Club.

Then, in 1975 Yavno experienced an epiphany of sorts during a trip to Death Valley. He came upon a scene which re-awakened his desire to photograph the landscape, as he recalls, "It was almost a mystical thing. I'm a pretty down to earth guy and I was amazed at the feeling that came over me." Yavno again plunged into photography as an art and met with almost immediate success, having a one-man show at the G. Ray Hawkins Gallery in Los Angeles in 1976. From this point on he photographed almost continuously. Although he did much of his work in Los Angeles he also took trips back to New York, and in 1979 he was able to photograph in both Egypt and Israel on an NEA grant.

In the midst of the "photo-boom" Yavno found a far more receptive audience for his work. In December of 1980 the Fine Arts Museum in San Francisco gave him a one-man show and in 1981 the University of California

Press published a lavishly reproduced monography of his work. Yavno died in 1985, leaving a valuable body of photography. His work represents a direct link between the classical Photo League tradition of sociological portrayal and the more private and introspective school of the fine-art urban landscape.

—Grant Kester

YOSHIDA, Tomohiko.

Nationality: Japanese. **Born:** Tokyo, 1960. **Education:** Graduated from Tokyo College of Photography, 1982 and from Research Institute, Tokyo College of Photography, 1985. **Agent:** Photo Gallery International, 2-5-18 Oranomon, Minato-ku, Tokyo 105, Japan.

Individual Exhibitions:

1985	*Night Watching,* Photo Gallery International, Tokyo
1987	*Tomohiko Yoshida Photographs 1980-1987,* Picture Photo Space, Osaka, Japan
1989	*Light Up,* Photo Gallery International, Tokyo
1993	*Isolated Landscape,* Photo Gallery International, Tokyo

Selected Group Exhibitions:

1983	*Contem Polaroid—IV,* Polaroid Gallery, Tokyo
1984	*Contem Polaroid—V,* Polaroid Gallery, Tokyo
1985	*Dye-Transfer Exhibition,* Olympus Gallery, Tokyo
	Concerning Landscape, Olympus Gallery, Tokyo
1987	*Exhibition of Shashin,* Yurakucho Asahi Gallery, Tokyo
1988	*New Primitive Photographers,* Minolta Photo Space, Tokyo
1990	*20 Promising Photographers,* PARCO Gallery, Tokyo
1992	*Slides on the Wall,* ICAC Weston Gallery, Tokyo
1994	*Liquid Crystal Futures: Contemporary Japanese Photography,* The Fruitmarket Gallery, Edinburgh, Scotland

Publications:

On YOSHIDA: Exhibition catalogue—*Liquid Crystal Futures: Contemporary Japanese Photography,* Edinburgh, 1994.

*

The other day I watched an NHK documentary entitled *The Beat Kids: 150,000 songs with messages from young people,* and was moved by one young person who on seeing the factory belt at Komakomai in Hokkaido said "My heart relaxes when I see this scenery." I am surprised at the number of people other than myself who do relax on seeing factories or wasteland or find them beautiful.

Future cities as portrayed in films or novels inevitably feature wastelands or landfill sites. Now blocks of flats cower on top of such reclaimed areas just like giant tombstones. This is how far the human race has come. Now that they no longer have anywhere to go, I wonder where the animals and plants will move their homes.

—Tomohiko Yoshida

*   *   *

Tomohiko Yoshida had a chance to dabble in photography from an early age because his uncle ran a camera store, and he entered photography school intending to "work taking photographs." He began by taking black and white street scenes, which led him to develop a fixed observation point. He shot

Isolated Landscape, **1985.** Photograph ©Tomohiko Yoshida.

pictures of the two neighbouring houses that he could see right outside the window of his flat. One day the house on the left was partially destroyed by a fire and was left in a half-ruined state. Then, in the course of one night, the house on the right was demolished. Yoshida displayed several photographic ditychs recording the changing states of these two houses over the short time period.

Ruptured, abnormal landscapes captured as photographs fascinated Yoshida. When he sought out abnormal landscapes, he turned to night scenes. One reviewer has called his photographs 'picture postcards of the 21st century city', and this image fully encompasses their sense of futuristic anonymity.

Yoshida explores straightforward, composed settings among the unpopulated urban areas of the night-highways, construction sites and parks. Using a minimum of filter effects and long exposure times, otherwise natural colours are mystically intensified and the detailed constructs of the normal city are dramatically transformed into sci-fi landscapes. Yoshida's receptive personality then draws forth their tranquillity and poetry.

''Colour is important—gaudy intense colours as if the viewer was hallucinating.'' Yoshida had an operation when he was a student, and he speaks of his colour experiences under the influence of morphine. The feeling aroused by deforming the world and transforming it into a demonic, dramatic thing are layered with the expectations of the several hour wait to see what is happening in the dark box of the camera.

Yoshida's photographs show the world's awareness of its own form. The urban night first senses its own beauty through Yoshida's quiet perseverance.

—Yuko Hasegawa

Z

ZELMA, Georgij (Anatolyevich).

Nationality: Russian. **Born:** Uzbekistan, Tashkent, July 1906. **Education:** Attended primary and secondary schools, Tashkent, until 1921; studied photography in school photo-club, Moscow, 1921-22; studied camerawork at Proletkino film studio, Moscow, 1922-23; apprentice at Russfoto agency, Moscow, 1923-24. **Military Service:** Served as war correspondent/photographer, with Red Army, and for *Isvestiya* newspaper, Stalingrad, Odessa and at the front, 1941-45. **Family:** Married Zina in 1934; son: Timur. **Career:** Photographer, Russfoto agency, Moscow and Tashkent, 1924-47; with Soyuzfoto agency, freelancing for *SSSR na Stroike, Krasnaya Svezda, Izvestiya,* etc., 1929-36; also worked as filmmaker/cameraman, with Roman Kamen, Soyuzfoto agency, Moscow, 1930-36; staff publicity photographer and photojournalist, *Izvestiya* newspaper, 1936-45; photographer, *Ogonjak,* 1946-62, Novosti Press Agency (APN), Moscow, 1962-84. **Died:** (in Moscow) in 1984.

Individual Exhibitions:

1966	Retrospective Exhibition, Moscow
1973	*Stalingrad,* Moscow
1975	Retrospective Exhibition, Mali (travelled to Nigeria and Nepal)
1983	Photo Art Society of the Lithuanian SSR, Vilnius

Selected Group Exhibitions:

1935	*Works by Moscow Photo Masters,* Moscow
1975	*Soviet War Reportage 1941-1945,* House of Soviet Science and Culture, Prague
1977	*The Russian War 1941-1945,* International Center of Photography, New York
1978	*Soviet War Photography 1941-1945,* Side Gallery, Newcastle upon Tyne, England
1980	*Soviet Photography between the World Wars,* House of Art, Brno, Czechoslovakia
1982	*Early Soviet Photography,* Museum of Modern Art, Oxford, England (and world tour)
1989	*150 Years of Photography,* Central Exhibition Hall, Moscow
1992	*The Great Utopia: The Russian and Soviet Avente Garde, 1915-1993,* Frankfurt, Amsterdam, New York, Moscow, St. Petersburg
	The Utopian Dream, Photography in Soviet Russia 1918-1939, Lawrence Miller Gallery, New York
1994	C Ray Hawkins Gallery, Santa Monica, California

Collections:

Novosti Press Agency, Moscow; Daniela Mrázková and Vladimìr Remeš Collection, Prague.

Publications:

By ZELMA: Books—*Stalingrad: July 1942-February 1943,* with text by Konstantin Simonov, Moscow 1966; *Living Legend,* Moscow 1967.

On ZELMA: Books—*Foto 71: Photographs by Soviet Professionals and Amateurs,* with introduction by M.I. Bugaev, Moscow 1971; *Fotografivalu Valku,* edited by Daniela Mrázková and Vladimìr Remeš, Prague 1975, as *The Russian War,* with an introduction by Harrison Salisbury, New York 1977, with an introduction by A.J.P. Taylor, London 1978, as *Von Moskau nach Berlin,* with an introduction by Heinrich Böll, Oldenburg, West Germany 1979; *Geschichte der Fotografie im 20. Jahrhundert/Photography in the 20th Century* by Petr Tausk, Cologne 1977, London 1980; *Georgij Zelma: Izbrannye Fotografie (Selected Photos),* with text by Boris Vilenkin, Moscow 1978; *Sowjetische Fotografen 1917-1940* by S. Morosov, A. Vartanov, G. Chudakov, O. Suslova and L. Uchtomskaya, Leipzig and West Berlin 1980; *Die Sowjetunion zwischen den Kriegen 1917-1941,* edited by Daniela Mrázková and Vladimìr Remeš, Oldenburg, West Germany 1981; *Pioneers of Soviet Photography* by Grigory Shudakov, Olga Suslova and Lilya Ukhtomskaya, London and Paris 1983; *The Story of Photography* by Daniela Mrazkova, Prague 1985, London 1986; *Sowjetische Fotografie 1919-1939,* Zurich 1986; *Anthology of Soviet Photography, Vol 1,* Moscow, 1986; *Vol II,* Moscow, 1987; *Allies,* Hugh Lauter Levin Associates Inc. New York, 1989; *20 Soviet Photographers, 1917-1940,* Chudakov, Crigory, Amsterdam, 1990. **Articles**—"Soviet War Reportage" by Daniela Mrázková and Vladimìr Remeš in *Revue Fotografie* (Prague), March 1975; "A Cry of Anguish from Wartime Russia" in *Photography Year 1976,* by the Time-Life editors, New York 1976; "Il Soldato Fotografo" in *Fotografia Italiana* (Milan), April 1976; "The Eighth Miracle of the World" by Daniela Mrázková in *Revue Fotografie* (Prague), September 1977; "Classic Images of the Russian Front" in the *Sunday Times* (London), April 1978; "Soviet Photography Between the World Wars 1917-1941" by Daniela Mrázková and Vladimìr Remeš in *Camera* (Lucerne), June 1981.

* * *

Georgij Zelma was one of the pioneers of Soviet documentary photography. Starting in the first half of the 1920s he became involved in depicting the profound changes taking place in his country, particularly in the non-Russian areas of the Soviet state. His basic qualifications as a reporter (which enabled him to become a correspondent for Central Asia for the Russfoto Agency) were: a thorough knowledge of the problems of Soviet Central Asia with its countless nationalities; understanding of the mentality and way of life of its people, many of whom were still living in medieval conditions, with all the social, economic and political implications of that situation; and a knowledge of their language (Zelma himself came from Uzbekistan). The young photographer did not just record the outward transformations taking place in those distant parts of the country in the period between the October Revolution and the beginning of the Second World War; he also penetrated to the depth of meaning of those changes to provide a social analysis. He conveyed, particularly, a general theme of the time, the gradual liberation of women, who for thousands of years had lived in bondage in a traditional inequality with men, for on the fate of that tradition depended the further fate of the revolutionary process in the country. He devoted himself also to other no less important subjects: the fight against illiteracy; the first introduction of technology into the region; the dependence of the progressive development of the country on the construction of an irrigation system that might force the ever-moving sands of the desert to give way at last to vegetation.

Zelma mastered the contrasts inherent in the coming into being of a new way of life—for example, in the accompanying photo, which is of one of the first civil weddings in Uzbekistan: the bride's face and all her charms are still carefully covered by the traditional parandzha veil, yet the couple is being married by an Uzbekistan woman, and there is the picture of Lenin on the wall looking down at the whole scene. Another photograph based on contrast is that of an Uzbekistan sportsman who has taken off the top of his national costume to do exercises on a bar made of roughhewn tree trunks. There is fine irony, too, in the picture of a man looking surprised and almost full of adoration, holding the earphone of a crystal radio-set to his ear; the caption reads, ''Moscow Calling.'' Zelma's pictures of Central Asia are valuable historical documents, photographically valid, which are being appreciated only now: after the topical aspects serving propaganda purposes have receded into the past, they are now being evaluated for what they are, a profoundly erudite social study.

In the 1930s Zelma continued to deal with the problems of Central Asia—in fact, he continued to do so throughout his life—but simultaneously he also devoted himself to depicting the great building projects of the first economic Five-Year Plan. Acquainted with the formal approaches of Soviet experimental photography of those years, and like Rodchenko and his friends who held similar views, Zelma composed his pictures into diagonals, used steep angles when viewing the object from below or above, used expressive large details—but his approach is cooler. This work does not have the extremely strong personal involvement of his photographs of Central Asia. It was not until the Second World War that Zelma again produced photographs based on deep personal experience: he created a unique testimony of the Battle of Stalingrad and life in that besieged city. The documentary photographer proved to be an alert reporter, active and ready to fight, who took risks to be with the soldiers in the front line as to be able to capture the most critical moments of the historic battle.

Georgij Zelma untiringly devoted his long life to the work of the committed social reporter, but it is because of his documentation of Central Asia of the 1920s and 30s and his reportage of the war that he stands out as a remarkable personality in the world of photography.

—Daniela Mrázková

ŽIDLICKÝ, Vladimír.

Nationality: Czechoslovakian. **Born:** in Hodoníně, Czechoslovakia, 26 July 1945. **Education:** Studied at FAMU, Prague, 1970-75. **Address:** Stojanova 3, Brno 602 00, Czech Republic.

Individual Exhibitions:

1987	Art Museum, Århus, Denmark
	Galerie Image, Denmark
	La Maison Internationale, Rennes, France
	Museum of Photographic Art, Odense, Denmark
	Photographic Encounters, Lorient, France
1988	Maison Photographique, Quimper, France
	Východoslovenská Gallery, Košice, Czechoslovakia
	Robert Koch Gallery, San Francisco
	Forum Les Photographiques, Toulouse, France
	Hyppolyte Gallery, Helsinki, Finland
1989	Fronta Gallery, Prague
	Stavoprojektu Gallery, Brno, Czechoslovakia
1990	Saint Cyprien Gallery, Toulouse, France
	Groll Gallery, Naarden, Netherlands
	Le Parvi Gallery, Tarbes, France
	Picaron Editions, Amsterdam
	Galérie Vrais Rêves, Lyon, France
	Espace Gérard Philippe, Jarny, France
	Galérie Le Triangle, Rennes, France
1991	Gallerie Cons Arc Chiasso, Švýcarsco, Czech Republic
	Henri Vincent Library, Talant, France
	Robert Doisneau Gallery, Nancy, France
	Arts Gallery, Amsterdam
1992	Faber Gallery, Vienna
	Groll Gallery, Naarden, Netherland
	Musée de la Photographie, Charleroi, Belgium
	The Cultural Centre, Hennebont, France

Sephiha Gallery, Brussels

Selected Group Exhibitions:

1984	Museum of Modern Art, San Francisco, California
1985	*27 Contemporary Czechoslovakian Photographers,* London and Bristol, England
1987	*The Time of a Movement,* National Centre for Photography, Tokyo Palace, Paris
1988	*Czechoslovakian Photography,* touring to Paris, Toulouse, Rennes, France
1989	*Photo '89,* Amsterdam
	Czechoslovakian Photography, Ludwig Museum, Cologne, Germany
1990	*Czechoslovakian Photography,* Tours, France
1991	*Photography in Fragments II,* Centre Georges Pompidou, Paris
1992	*2nd International Photo-Triennale,* Esslingen, Germany

Collections:

Moravian Gallery, Brno, Czechoslovakia; Museum of Modern Art, San Francisco; Sztuki Museum, Lodž, Poland; JCA, Tokyo, Japan; Bibliotheque Nationale, Paris; Museum of Fine Arts, Houston, Texas; Museum of Photographic Art, Odense, Denmark; Museum of Modern Art, New York; Art Institute, Chicago; Centre Georges Pompidou, Paris; Ludwig Museum, Cologne, Germany; Photography Museum, Charleroi, Belgium; Museum of Photography, Antwerp, Belgium.

*

The actual materials portrayed and those destroyed by the impact of the artist's individual manipulations are placed side by side within the picture. Populated with unspecified human forms; problems with determining the gender. The scenes lack an epic element and create living pictures reverberating with immediacy in a frozen moment. Stress is laid on the strength of the visual perception. The pictures are not geographically identifiable, only the formal structure hints at a European connection. The surfaces of materials and volumes, being particularly suitable visual receptors, have luminous traces running through them, are torn and scratched by sharp points of an individual, and a multitude of peaks of rough materials leave a wide characteristic trace on the surface. Human shapes, like bowling pins symetrically located on an axis, are spinning along their orbits. Minor collisions of individuals along the tangent leave them with reddish spots and hardly visible bruises. Major collisions of pairs and groups; individual stages of a dramatic sequence. Human forms lie separately or wedged together in pairs pointing away from the epicentre, and we meet with them during catharsis or an expectation of another blow. Heaped side by side and also across one another, they constitute a crowd of permanent premières. They do not suffer from hunger, and are not swallowed up by consumers' phobias. Like a pulsing island of living matter that does not claim individual faces, connected by the primeval bonds of increased temperature radiated and overlapping in a finite and resisting compact fabric at a distance of only a few centimetres away from the source. Clusters of human forms are found irregularly but frequently in all infected areas. Visual defects (grooves and scratches, unidentifiable human forms, sinking space and missing matter) are points of transfer, and the artist uses them to point out the appellative aspect of manipulations and at the same time the common fate of all human clusters.

—Vladimír Židlický

ŽVIRGŽDAS, Stasys

Nationality: Lithuanian. **Born:** in Balbieriskis, Lithuania, 13 September 1941. **Education:** Studied history at Vilnius State University and studied photography for the communal services in 1970. Graduated from the department of photography at the Moscow Institute of People's Art and Culture.

The Dramatic Scene-Stage, No 128, **1991.** Photograph by Vladimir Zidlicky.

Member of the Photographic Art Society of Lithuania since 1989. **Address:** Universitete str. 4, Vilnius 2600.

Individual Exhibitions:

1981	Photography Gallery, Kaunas, Lithuania
1982	Palace of Culture, Chisinau, Moldova
	Palace of Culture, Yevpatoriya, Ukraine
1983	Palace of Culture, Tiraspol, Moldova
	Museum of Photography, Siauliai, Lithuania
	Photography Gallery, Marijampole, Lithuania
1984	Sala gil Marraco, Zaragoza, Spain
1985	Palace of Culture, Moscow
	Palace of Culture, Nida, Lithuania
1986	Photography Gallery, Marijampole, Lithuania
1987	House of Officers, Severomorsk, Russia
1988	Academy of Sciences Library, Novosibirsk
	Museum of Art, Ulan Ude, Russia
1989	Museum of Art, Chita, Russia
1990	Artist's Union Exhibition Hall, Homel, Belarus
1991	Photography Gallery, Vilnius
	Gallery "AL," Palanga, Lithuania

	Photography Gallery, Marijampole, Lithuania
	Jurgen Bekker Gallery, Hamburg
1992	Museum of Photography, Siauliai, Lithuania
	Photography Centre, St. Petersburg, Russia
	Museum of Art, Tel Aviv, Israel
1993	Photography Gallery, Panevezys, Lithuania
	Amber Photo Art Gallery, Portland, Oregon

Selected Group Exhibitions:

1978	*Fourth International Exhibition of Photography,* Belarus
1979	*Third International Exhibition of Photography,* Ndola, Zambia
1982	*Mini-Photos '82,* Mahilyow, Belarus
	24th International Salon of Photography, Sydney, Australia
1983	*59th International Salon of Photography,* Zaragoza, Spain
1985	*Foto jokes '85,* Gabrovo, Bulgaria
1986	*Fotoforum '86,* Ruzhomberok, Czechoslovakia
	17th Landscape Photography Biennal, Poznan, Poland
1987	*24th International Salon of Photographic Art,* Luxembourg
	Belomorje '87, Archangel, Russia
1988	*43rd International Salon of Photographic Art,* Buenos Aires
1989	*Sixth International Salon of Photography,* Minsk, Russia

Metamorphoses of Civilization - 2, 1986. Photograph by Stasys Žvirgždas.

Publications:

On ŽVIRGŽDAS: Books—*Photography Year Book,* London 1983; *Photography in the Structure Mass Communication* by V. Borev, Vilnius 1986; *Naturafotographie unterwegs* by W. Fiedler, Leipzig 1980; *Poetics of Photography* by V.I. Mikhalkovich, Moscow 1989; *Elegy,* Moscow 1993. **Articles**—Nemunas, No. 12 1980, No. 2 1992, No. 1 1994; *Kulturos barai,* No. 9 1981, No. 3 1991; *Jaunimo gretos,* No. 10, 12 1986, No. 1, 2, 5, 6, 12 1987; No. 3, 8 1988; No. 8 1991; *Photokino Magazin,* No. 3 1986; No. 4, 12 1989; No. 2 1990; *Sovetskoyo,* No. 5 1988, No. 12 1991; *Belarus,* No. 4 1991; *Noi,* No. 11 1989, No. 5, 11 1990, No. 2 1991; *The Economist of Lithuania,* No. 3 1991; *Terminator,* No. 1 1992, No. 1, 4 1993; *Tik vyrams,* No. 6 1992, No. 3 1993; *Fantastika ir detekyvai,* No. 2 1990, No. 4 1992; *Boletin informative para los*

senores socios, July-August 1984; *Hellininki fotographia,* October, November, December 1987; *Keturi vejai,* No. 1, 3 1990, No. 5, 6 1991; *Fotografija,* No. 1 1990; *Foto and Doka,* No. 10 1988.

*   *   *

The photoartist Stasys Žvirgždas is one of the most distinct figures in the second wave of the Lithuanian photographic school. The term "Lithuanian Photographic School" was first introduced in 1974 in articles by such well known Russian art and literary critics as Lev Aninskij, Anri Vartanev, Vladimir Berev, Vikter Diemin and others. They stress the universality of Lithuanian photography, a richness of genres and considered Lithuanian photography as a bridge for the newest ideas from West to East. The first series of photographies by Stasys Žirgždas—*Courtyards of Vilnius* (1980-82) was an intriguing declaration by a young author. The black and white shadows in the narrow streets of Vilnius resemble the ancestral souls returning to life. They keep wandering, quivering and, finding no place to rest, they disappear elsewhere. Such an impression arises from the careful composition of Žvirždas' photographs. It is as impossible to forget them as it is impossible to forget the past of the old capital with all its grandeur and historical drama.

In 1986 Stasys Žvirgždas created the series *Metamorphoses of Civilisation* where he reflects on the fate of the world and the grimness of civilisation. In masterly montages, coarse human constructions compress the spaces, suck out the air and only a primordal force driving helpless clouds in a gale resists the rational greediness and vanity of human nature. Investigating the problem Stasys Žvirgždas was rigorous and even cruel to the men who were at fault, who were occupiers and who banished him—the young man—for anti-soviet activities to the Mordovian gulag, not only snatching the most beautiful years of his youth but also hardening him. The years spent in exile gave him new insight into the polyhedral and many layered world. That's why in 1987 he arranged a series called *Fairy Tales are not Fairy Tales* in which he is more indulgent to human fallacies and failings. The heroes taken from Lithuanian folk tales and living in surreal environments are a bit sad, a bit funny, but never banal.

One morning having escaped from the laboratory of his interminable work and ideas Stasys was amazed at the sight of the sun and at the pattern of sunlight on the grey face of old mother earth. It was 1987 and the beginning of his series on the fragile landscapes. Looking at the works at art exhibitions you are afraid to touch them, you are forced to hold your breath, because it seems that the clouds may immediately darken the sun and the water of the river Vilnia will blacken and its banks will harden. Stasys knows when to stop the light and with a blow of the sunbrush he paints his vision of a landscape full of leaping hills and fluid fields full of the sad smell of grass. The more kilometres walked at the weekends, the more photographs fill the bag, the playful content of which will soon lie on the pages of the album now being created.

There is a Lithuanian proverb saying "the carter gets the heavier load" equivalent to a donkey travels best loaded. This must be the reason why this energetic artist has been elected president of the National Association of Lithuanian Photographers by his colleagues. These new duties have burdened him at a time of economic crisis in Lithuania, as a result some promising young artists have joined commercial enterprises and a great number of galleries have closed, but Stasys Žvirgždas is an optimist. He knows for sure that night will be followed by dawn and a long and mature day of Lithuanian photography will last.

—Aleksandras Macijauskas

ZWART, Piet.

Nationality: Dutch. **Born:** Zaandijk, 28 May 1885. **Education:** Studied at the Rijksschool voor Kunstnijverheid, Amsterdam, 1902-07; Technische Hogeschool, Delft, 1913-14; mainly self-taught in photography and photomontage, from 1924. **Military Service:** Served in the Dutch Army, at Den Helder, 1908. **Family:** Married Nel Cleyndert; 4 children. **Career:** Furniture and interior designer, from 1911, and graphic and industrial designer, architect and photographer, from 1919; Assistant Architect, office of Jan Wils, Voorburg, 1919-21, and office of H.P. Berlage, The Hague, 1921-27; freelance graphic designer, concentrating on photography, and working for Posts and Telecommunications, Schevingen Radio, Nederlandse Kabelfabriek (NFK), Bruynzeel Company, etc., in Delft, The Hague, and Rotterdam, 1928-39, and from 1945. Instructor in Drawing and Art History, Industrie-en Huishoudschool voor Meisjes, Leeuwarden, 1909-19; Instructor in Design and Ornament, Academie van Beeldende Kunsten en Technische Wetenschappen, Rotterdam, 1919-33. Visiting Instructor, Technische Hochschule, Delft, 1929, and Bauhaus School, Berlin, 1931. Architecture Correspondent, *Het Vaderland* magazine, 1925-28; Organizer, Dutch Section, *Film und Foto* exhibition, Stuttgart, 1929. **Recipient:** Quellinus Prize for Typography, 1959; David Roell Prize, 1964. Honorary Royal Designer for Industry, London, 1966. **Died:** (in Leidschendam, Netherlands) 24 September 1977.

Individual Exhibitions:

1933	Drukkerji Trio, The Hague
1961	*Piet Zwart—typotekt*, Stedelijk Museum, Amsterdam
1968	*Piet Zwart en PTT*, Haags Gemeentemuseum, The Hague
1973	Haags Gemeentemuseum, The Hague (travelled to Dortmund and Zurich, 1974)
1974	Wassenaarse Galerie-Bibliotheek, Wassenaar, Netherlands
1980	*Piet Zwart: Typotekt*, Ex Libris, New York
1985	*Het Boek van PTT*, Gemeentemuseum, The Hague
1989	*Piet Zwart (1885-1977)*, Galerie Bianca, Wassenaar

Selected Group Exhibitions:

1929	*Film und Foto*, Deutscher Werkbund, Stuttgart
1930	*Das Lichtbild*, Munich (travelled to Essen)
1931	*Fotomontage*, Kunstgewerbemuseum, Berlin
	Foreign Photography, New York Cultural Center
1932	*Exposition Internationale de la Photographie*, Palais des Beaux-Arts, Brussels (travelled to Lakenhal, Leiden, and the Kunstzaal van Hasselt, Rotterdam)
1933	*Nieuwe Richtingen in de Fotografie*, I.O.O.F. Building, Amsterdam
1969	*Nederlandse Fotografie—De Eerste 100 Jaar*, Noord-Brabants Museum, 'S Hertogenbosch, Netherlands (travelled to Philips Ontspanningscentrum, Eindhoven; Dordrechts Museum; De Zonnehof, Amersfoort; Gemeentemuseum, Arnhem; De Lakenhal, Leiden; Bonnefantenmuseum, Maastricht, 1969-70)
1977	*Fotografie der 20er und 30er Jahre*, Galerie Breiting, West Berlin
1979	*Fotografie in Nederland 1920-40*, Haags Gemeentemuseum, The Hague
1983	*Fotogramme—die lichtreichen Schatten*, Fotomuseum im Stadtmuseum, Munich (toured West Germany)
1984	*Bauhaus Fotografie*, Galerie Marijke Winnubst, Amsterdam
1988	*Roots & Turns: Twentieth Century Photography in the Netherlands*, Sarah Campbell Blaffer Gallery, Houston

Collections:

Piet Zwart Archive, Prentenkabinet, Leiden University; Haags Gemeentemuseum, The Hague; Stedelijk Museum, Amsterdam; Museum Folkwang, Essen; Kestner-Gesellschaft, Hannover.

Publications:

By ZWART: Books—*Filmreclame*, Rotterdam 1933; *Het boek van PTT*, The Hague 1938, 1985; *Piet Zwart*, with text by F. Muller and P.F. Althaus, Teufen, Switzerland 1966; *Piet Zwart: 12 Photographien*, portfolio, with an introduction by Kees Broos, Cologne 1974. **Photomontages and designs**—De Absolute Film by Ter Braaks, Rotterdam 1931; *De Techniek van de Kunstfilm* by Mannus Franken and Joris Ivens, Rotterdam 1931; *Wij Slaven Van Suriname* by Anton de Kok, Rotterdam 1934; and other books in the series *Monografien over Filmkunst* for W.L. and J. Brusse publishing company, Rotterdam, 1931-34. **Article**—"Gemeinigde Fotografie" in *Foto '48*, exhibition catalogue, Amsterdam 1948.

On ZWART: Books—*Foto-Auge: 76 Fotos der Zeit* by Franz Roh and Jan Tschichold, Stuttgart 1929; *Gefesselter Blick*, exhibition catalogue, by Hugo and Bodo Rasch, Stuttgart 1930; *Fotomontage*, exhibition catalogue, Berlin 1931; *Piet Zwart—typotekt*, exhibition catalogue, designed by Otto Treumann and Wim Crouwel, Amsterdam 1961; *Sleutelwoorden/Keywords: Piet Zwart*, edited by Jurriaan Schrofer and Will Sandberg, The Hague 1965; *Piet Zwart* by Fridolin Muller, New York 1966; *Piet Zwart en PTT*, exhibition catalogue, by Karst Zwart, The Hague 1968; *Nederlandse Fotografie: De Eerste 100 Jaar* by Claude Magelhaes, Utrecht and Antwerp 1969; *Piet Zwart*, exhibition catalogue, with text by Kees Broos, The Hague 1973; *Photomontage* by Dawn Ades, London 1976; *Tendenzen der Zwanziger Jahre*, exhibition catalogue, by D. Honisch, U. Prince, E. Roters and W. Schmied, Berlin 1977; *Fotografie in Nederland 1920-1940*, exhibition catalogue, by Flip Bool and Kees Broos, The Hague 1979; *Photographen der 20er Jahre* by Karl Steinorth, Munich 1979; *Film und Foto der 20er Jahre*, exhibition catalogue, by Ute Eskildsen and Jan Christopher Horak, Stuttgart 1979; *Dada Photomontagen*, exhibition catalogue, by Carl-Albrecht Haenlein and others, Hannover 1979; *Piet Zwart: Typotekt*, exhibition catalogue, with introduction by Arthur A. Cohen, New York 1980; *Retrospective Fotografie: Piet Zwart* by Kees Broos, Dusseldorf 1981; *De Arbeidersfotografen: Camera in Crisis in de Jaren '30* by Flip Bool and Jeroen de Vries, Amsterdam 1982; *Piet Zwart 1885-1977* by Kees Broos, Amsterdam 1982; *Piet Zwart en het gezicht van Bruynzeel's potloden industrie,* by F. Huygen, Rotterdam 1984; *Piet Zwart en Het Boek van PTT. Een commentaar,* by P Hefting, The Hague, 1985; *Fotosammlung. Museum Ludwig,* by Reinhold Misselbech, Keulen, 1986; *Roots & Turns. Twentieth Century Photography in the Netherlands,* by Ingeborg Th. Leijerzapf e.o., Houston 1988. **Articles**—"Piet Zwart" bij Kees Broos in Ingeborg Th. Leijerzapf (red), *Geschiedenis van de Nederlandse fotografie in monografieën en thema-artikelen,* Alphen aan den Rijn/Amsterdam, afl.12, 1989.

* * *

At the beginning of the 1920s Piet Zwart, together with Paul Schuitema, gave a great forward impetus to Dutch photography. In 1923, when "pictorial" art photography still flourished in the Netherlands, Zwart, already an architect and interior and graphic designer by profession, met El Lissitzky who taught him the principles of the photogram and of photo-fixing. A few years later Zwart used a photogram for an advertisement booklet for a cable factory in Delft. In 1928, in a catalogue for the same company, he purposely chose photography as the means of illustration: he had realized that what he really wanted to do was to produce thoughtful, exact, extremely sharp commercial photographs, in line with the "New Objectivity" and in accordance with Moholy-Nagy's views about the integration of image and text. In effect, from 1923, he taught himself photography: all the optical, technical and chemical problems he encountered he solved by consulting German technical literature. Together with Schuitema and G. Kiljan, he tried out all the various photographic possibilities: light-shadow effects, reflections, movements, etc.

In 1929 Zwart, Schuitema and Kiljan took part in the important exhibition, *Film und Foto,* in Stuttgart. Zwart was responsible for the Dutch submissions.

Works by such participants as the American Edward Weston, the German Walter Peterhans and the Russian Rodchenko overwhelmingly impressed Zwart—for their technique, expression, composition: confronted with such artistry, he felt keenly how much the Netherlands was behind, and what little photographic education there was in his own country. The experience stimulated his own work. So did his stay as guest lecturer in photography at the Bauhaus in 1931. In the years that followed he tried inexhaustibly to bring Dutch photography up to an international standard. Describing his work, he said: "We used the camera only as a means of expression and as a visual medium that offers possibilities found in no other artistic technique, possibilities that the eye can not catch in their totality. We tried to establish a characteristic vision of photography."

Zwart created an extensive archive of technical photographs from his commercial commissions and of his own personal work. His own work very often involves reproductions of structures of great clarity of line—tree-bark, cobwebs, ice formed in a ditch, waterdrops on a branch, a misted window. They are dynamic because of a diagonal line, an unusual angle, or unexpected composition.

In the many articles that he wrote Zwart also stressed the importance of photography in social and scientific life.

His work paved the way for a new generation of photographers—Emmy Andriesse, Eva Besnyö, Cas Oorthuys, and Carel Blazer—none of whom did any commercial photography, but all of whom used and built on his principles in their documentation of people.

—A. de Jonge-Vermeulen

NATIONALITY INDEX

AMERICAN

Berenice Abbott
Ansel Adams
Robert Adams
Lucien Aigner
James Alinder
Eve Arnold
Barbara Astman
Ellen Auerbach
Richard Avedon
Oscar Bailey
John Baldessari
Lewis Baltz
Tina Barney
Thomas F. Barrow
Lillian Bassman
Herbert Bayer
David P. Bayles
Peter Beard
Jim Bengston
Derek Bennett
Ferenc Berko
Ruth Bernhard
Ilse Bing
Michael Bishop
Donald Blumberg
Anton Bruehl
Edna Bullock
Wynn Bullock
Jerry Burchard
Bill Burke
Nancy Burson
Debbie Fleming Caffery
Harry Callahan
Jo Ann Callis
Cornell Capa
Paul Caponigro
Walter Chappell
Sarah E. Charlesworth
Larry Clark
William Clift
Mark Cohen
Van Deren Coke
John Collier
Linda Connor
Thomas Joshua Cooper
Carlotta M. Corpron
Marie Cosindas
Eileen Cowin
Barbara Crane
Donigan Cumming
Robert Cumming
Imogen Cunningham
Robert D'Alessandro
Louise Dahl-Wolfe
Judy Dater
Bruce Davidson
Bevan Davies
Joe Deal
Roy Decarava
Liliane Decock

Jack Delano
John Dominis
Ed Douglas
David Douglas Duncan
Allen A. Dutton
Harold E. Edgerton
William Eggleston
Alfred Eisenstaedt
Elliott Erwitt
Barbara Ess
Walker Evans
Andreas Feininger
Robert W. Fichter
Larry Fink
Steve Fitch
Leonard Freed
Jill Freedman
Lee Friedlander
Benno Friedman
Toni Frissell
Oliver Gagliani
William A. Garnett
Charles Gatewood
Ralph Gibson
Bruce Gilden
Laura Gilpin
Burt Glinn
Frank Gohlke
Judith Golden
Fritz Goro
John R. Gossage
Emmet Gowin
Jan Groover
John Gutmann
Betty Hahn
Phillippe Halsman
Charles Harbutt
Erich Hartmann
David Heath
Robert Heinecken
Fritz Henle
Abigail Heyman
Hiro
Tana Hoban
Nancy Honey
William Horeis
Horst P. Horst
Peter Hujar
Scott Hyde
Joseph D. Jachna
Lotte Jacobi
Harold Jones
Pirkle Jones
Kenneth Josephson
Simpson Kalisher
Art Kane
Gyorgy Kepes
Victor Keppler
André Kertész
Dmitri Kessel
Richard Kirstel

Willard Van Dyke
James Van Der Zee
David Vestal
Roman Vishniac
Todd Walker
Andy Warhol
Cary Wasserman
Alex Webb
Todd Webb
Carrie Mae Weems
William Wegman
Jack Welpott
Henry Wessel, Jr.
Brett Weston
Cole Weston
Minor White
Bob Willoughby
Geoff Winningham
Garry Winogrand
Kelly Wise
Joel-Peter Witkin
Don Worth
Max Yavno

ARGENTINIAN
Alicia D'Amico
Sara Facio
Christopher J.I. Pillitz

AUSTRALIAN
Bob Davis
Max Dupain
Rennie Ellis
David Moore
Grant Mudford
Helmut Newton

AUSTRIAN
Ernst Haas
Erika Kiffl
Branko Lenart

BELGIAN
Paul Ausloos
Pierre Boogaerts
Dirk Braeckman
Pierre Cordier
Carl De Keyzer
Antoon Dries
Martine Franck
Harry Gruyaert
François Hers
Lucia Radochonska
Filip Tas
Jean Vanesch

BRAZILIAN
Mario Cravo Neto
Anna Mariani
Améris M. Paolini
Sabastiao Ribeiro Salgado

João Aristeu Urban

BRITISH
Heather Angel
Gerry Badger
David Bailey
Cecil Beaton
Ian Berry
Zarina Bhimji
John Blakemore
Dorothy Bohm
Bill Brandt
Victor Burgin
Bryn Campbell
John Chillingworth
Almond Chu
Calum Colvin
Stephen Dalton
John Davies
Ian Dickson
Mark Edwards
Anna Fox
Hamish Fulton
Helmut Gernsheim
Fay Godwin
Ken Grant
Joy Gregory
Brian Griffin
David Hamilton
Bert Hardy
Sam Haskins
Nick Hedges
Nigel Henderson
Paul Hill
John Hilliard
David Hockney
Thurston Hopkins
Eric Hosking
David Hurn
Roger Lionel Hutchings
Geoffrey James
Philip Jones Griffiths
Paul Joyce
Roshini Kempadoo
Peter Kennard
Chris Killip
Osbert Lam
Grace Pei-Yin Lau
Ka Tai Leong
Jorge Lewinski
Barry Lewis
Felix H. Man
Jennifer Matthews
Roger Mayne
Angus McBean
Ron McCormick
Don McCullin
Raymond Moore
Norman Parkinson
Martin Parr
Mark Power

Denis Brihat
Henri Cartier-Bresson
Jean-Philippe Charbonnier
Arnaud Claass
Lucien Clergue
Raymond Depardon
Bernard Descamps
Jean Dieuzaide
Claude Dityvon
Robert Doisneau
Tom Drahos
Gilles Ehrmann
Bernard Faucon
Alain Fleischer
Gisèle Freund
Jean-Claude Gautrand
Albert Giordan
Hervé Gloaguen
Irèna Ionesco
Izis
Pascal Kern
François Kollár
Jacques-Henri Lartigue
Sarah Moon
Gilles Peress
Pierre et Gilles
Gueorgui Pinkhassov
Bernard Plossu
Bruno Requillart
Marc Riboud
Willy Ronis
Jeanloup Sieff
Jean-Pierre Sudre
Maurice Tabard

GERMAN
Walter Ballhause
Horst H. Baumann
Bernhard and Hilla Becher
Hans Bellmer
Erwin Fieger
Roland Fischer
Arno Fischer
André Gelpke
Heinz Hajek-Halke
Robert Häusser
Eugen Heilig
Jürgen Heinemann
Marta Hoepffner
Volkhard Hofer
Thomas Höpker
Hanns Hubmann
Walde Huth
Gottfried Jäger
Arno Jansen
Peter Keetman
Fritz Kempe
Robert Lebeck
Herbert List
Ulrich Mack
Harald Mante

Werner Mantz
Knut Wolfgang Maron
Stefan Moses
Andreas Müller-Pohle
Floris M. Neusüss
Gabriele and Helmut Nothhelfer
Detlef Orlopp
Inge Osswald
Hilmar Pabel
Wolfgang Reisewitz
Evelyn Richter
Heinrich Riebesehl
Leni Riefenstahl
Christian Schad
Jurgen Schadeberg
Max Scheler
Michael Schmidt
Wolfgang G. Schröter
Liselotte Strelow
Karin Székessy
Ernst Thormann
Umbo
Verena von Gagern
Wolfgang Weber
Reinhart Wolf

GUATEMALAN
Luis Gonzalez Palma

HUNGARIAN
Tamás Féner
Péter Korniss
József Németh

INDIAN
Mitter Bedi
Sujoy Das
Ashim Ghosh
Ashvin Mehta
T. S. Nagarajan
Prashant Panjiar
Raghu Rai
Dayanita Singh
Raghubir Singh
Manish Swarup

IRANIAN
Abbas

ISRAELI
Micha Bar-Am
Werner Braun
Avi Ganor
Tim N. Gidal
Tzachi Ostrovsky

ITALIAN
Vasco Ascolini
Gianni Berengo-Gardin
Romano Cagnoni
Lisetta Carmi

Franco Fontana
Luigi Ghirri
Mario Giacomelli
Paolo Gioli
Franco Grignani
Frank Horvat
Mimmo Jodice
Cesare Leonardi
Giorgio Lotti
Gideon Mendel
Paolo Monti
Enzo Ragazzini
Fulvio Roiter
Marialba Russo
Ferdinando Scianna
Tazio Secchiaroli
Luigi Veronesi

JAPANESE
Shotaro Akiyama
Ken Domon
Hideki Fujii
Masahisa Fukase
Hiroshi Hamaya
Naoya Hatakeyama
Eikoh Hosoe
Tetsuya Ichimura
Yasuhiro Ishimoto
Miyako Ishiuchi
Yoshihiko Ito
Kikuji Kawada
Michiko Kon
Seiji Kurata
Kineo Kuwabara
Yoichi Midorikawa
Jun Miki
Kozo Miyoshi
Jun Morinaga
Daidoh Moriyama
Masatoshi Naitoh
Masaya Nakamura
Ikko Narahara
Kishin Shinoyama
Yoshikazu Shirakawa
Issei Suda
Risaku Suzuki
Keiichi Tahara
Shomei Tomatsu
Hiromi Tsuchida
Shoji Ueda
Yoshio Watanabe
Tomohiko Yoshida

KENYAN
Mirella Ricciardi

LATVIAN
Gunar Binde
Egons Spuris

LITHUANIAN
Jonas Kalvelis
Aleksandras Macijauskas
Romualdas Pozerskis
Romualdas Rakauskas
Virgilijus Šonta
Antanas Sutkus
Stasys Zvirgzdas

MEXICAN
Manuel Alvarez Bravo
Lázaro Blanco
Enrique Bostelmann
Gabriel Figueroa Flores
Flor Garduño
Graciela Iturbide
Pedro Meyer
Pablo Ortiz Monasterio
Mariana Yampolsky

NEW ZEALANDER
Brian Brake

NIGERIAN
Oladele Ajiboye Bamgboye

PANAMANIAN
Sandra Eleta

POLISH
Mieczyslaw Berman
Anna Beata Bohdziewicz
Leszek Brogowski
Adam Bujak
Zbigniew Dlubak
Benedykt Jerzy Dorys
Krzysztof Gieraltowski
Edward Hartwig
Aleksander Krzywoblocki
Natalia Lach-Lachowicz
Jerzy Lewczynski
Waclaw Nowak
Wladyslaw Pawelec
Wojciech Plewinski
Wieslaw Prazuch
Zofia Rydet
Tomasz Tomaszewski
Stefan Wojnecki

PORTUGUESE
Jorge Molder

RUSSIAN
Yuri V. Abramochkin
Max Alpert
Dmitri Baltermans
Vitaly Butyrin
Boris Ignatovich
Francisco Infante
Gennadi Koposov

NOTES ON ADVISERS AND CONTRIBUTORS_____

ADAM, Hans Christian. Essayist. Freelance picture researcher and photo-historian, Göttingen. Vice-chairman of the History Section, Deutsche Gesellschaft für Photographie (DGPh). Author of *Masters of Early Travel Photography,* 1981; *Images of War,* 1983; *Reiseerinnerungen von damals,* 1985. **Essays:** Bennett; Häusser; Pabel; Saudek.

ALINDER, James. Entrant and essayist. See his own entry. **Essays:** Bernhard; Robert Cumming; Morris.

ALLARA, Pamela. Essayist. Assistant professor, Fine Arts Department, Tufts University, Medford, Massachusetts, since 1978 (lecturer, 1973-77). Boston Correspondent, *ARTnews,* New York, since 1977. **Essays:** Dahl-Wolfe; Robinson.

ALLTHORPE-GUYTON, Marjorie. Essayist. Director of visual arts, Arts Council of England, London, since 1993. Critic and curator, formerly editor, *Artscribe;* contributing editor, *Art Forum,* and author of numerous catalogue essays, most recently Helen Chadwick *Effluvia,* Serpentine Gallery, London and tour, 1994. Author of *A Happy Eye,* a history of Norwich School of Art 1839-1989. **Essay:** Baldessari.

ASBURY, Dana. Essayist. Editor, University of New Mexico Press, Albuquerque. Teacher of photography, University of New Mexico, Albuquerque, 1978-80. Contributor to *Artweek, After-image, Artspace, Progresso Fotografico,* etc. **Essays:** Barrow; Burchard; Callis; Fichter; Hahn; Josephson; Pfahl; Rubinstein; Shore.

BADGER, Gerry. Entrant and essayist. See his own entry. **Essays:** Baltz; Gilden; Lau; Levinstein; Lipper; Michals; Parr; Winogrand; Witkin.

BALDWIN, Roger. Essayist. Instructor in photography and photographic history, since 1979, and director of cooperative education, arts, since 1981, University of Bridgeport, Connecticut; instructor of photography, Fairfield University, Connecticut, since 1979. Editor of the exhibition catalogue *First They Wrought: New England's Teaching Photographers,* 1981; and author of *Jack Sal: Mark Making,* 1981, and *Discovering Photographic History,* with Mark Roskill (forthcoming). **Essay:** Gibson.

BALTZ, Lewis. Entrant and essayist. See his own entry. **Essays:** Davies; Gossage.

BARRETT, Nancy. Essayist. Curator of photography at New Orleans Museum of Art. Author of *Ilse Bing: Three Decades of Photography,* 1985. **Essay:** Bing.

BARROW, Thomas F. Entrant and essayist. See his own entry. **Essay:** Mertin.

BASKAKOV, Andrey. Advisor. President of The Russian Union of Art Photographers, Moscow.

BENNETT, Derek. Entrant and essayist. See his own entry. **Essays:** Rexroth; Trager.

BILLETER, Erika. Essayist. Director, Kunsthaus, Lausanne, Switzerland, since 1981. Chief curator, Museum Bellerive, Zurich, 1968-

75; deputy director of the Kunsthaus, Zurich, 1975-80. Author of *Malerei und Photographie im Dialog von 1840 bis Heute,* 1977; *Amerika Fotografie 1920-40,* 1979; *La Femme et le Surrealisme,* 1988; *Hola Alvarez Bravo,* 1992; *Mariana Yampolsky,* 1993; and *Graciela Iturbide's Mexico,* 1994. **Essay:** Mathys.

BIRGUS, Vladimìr. Adviser, entrant and essayist. See his own entry. **Essays:** Jasanský; Macku; Mara; Pinkava; Pozerskis; Rauschenberg; Ruben; Šonta; Streit; Tausk; Thormann.

BISCHOFF, Ulrich. Essayist. Curator of the Kunsthalle, Kiel. **Essay:** Kiffl.

BLANCH, M. Teresa. Essayist. Art critic, *AVUI* newspaper, Barcelona, since 1975. Editor-in-chief, *Batik* magazine, Barcelona, 1976-80; Barcelona correspondent for *Arteguia* magazine, Madrid, 1977-79; director, art section, *Mundo* magazine, Barcelona, 1978. Author of *Human and Pictorial Meaning in the Landscapes of Hernandez Pijuan,* 1979. **Essay:** Herraez Gomez.

BLANCO, Lázaro. Entrant and essayist. See his own entry. **Essay:** Corrales.

BLÉRY, Ginette. Essayist. Freelance photography critic, Paris, since 1977, contributing to *Le Photographe, Photo,* and *Photo-Revue.* Formerly worked in public relations for Kodak. Author of *Photography,* with Jean Prinet, 1978, and *Pictures for Children,* 1978. **Essays:** John Batho; Dieuzaide; Dityvon; Moon.

BOBROWSKI, Ryszard. Adviser and essayist. Art and photography critic, Warsaw. Editor and publisher of *Central European Review* bi-monthly, Warsaw. Formerly director of the Galeria Fotografii Hybrydy at Warsaw University. Formerly, deputy editor-in-chief, *Fotografia* quarterly, Warsaw. Curator of numerous exhibitions, including, recently, *Fotografia Polska 1839-1979,* shown in New York, Chicago, Warsaw, Lodz, and London, 1979-80; and *Photographie Polonaise 1900-1981,* Paris 1981. Co-curator *Mozenierungen: Zeitgenossische Fotografie aus der Bundesrepublik Deutschland,* Warsaw and tour, 1988. Co-author of *Wszystko o fotografii,* 1984; *Fotografia polska 1945-85,* 1985; *Masters of Polish Photography,* 1986; *Contemporary Masterworks,* 1991. **Essays:** Berman; Bourdin; Brogowski; Bujak; Dlubak; Dorys; Gieraltowski; Giordan; Hartwig; Krzywoblocki; Lach-Lachowicz; Lewczynski; Nowak; Pawelec; Plewinski; Prazuch; Rydet; Tomaszewski; Robert Walker; Wu Yinxian.

BONDI, Inge. Essayist. Freelance critic, historian, teacher and curator of photography, and film consultant on films dealing with photography, since 1968. Associated with Magnum Photos Inc., New York, 1950-70 (one of two non-photographer shareholders in the cooperative; secretary-treasurer of the corporation; director for special projects); taught twentieth-century history of photography, Fairleigh Dickinson University, Rutherford, New Jersey, 1971-72. **Essays:** Bosshard; Groebli; Haas; Lichtsteiner; Schulthess; Tuggener.

BOOTH, Robert. Essayist. Freelance abstract photographer, paints with light to produce "vehicles for the imagination," Oxford; photographic essayist; European Master of Photography; formerly head of the Faculty of Art and Design, Croydon College, London. **Essay:** Dalton.

BORKLUND, Elmer. Essayist. Professor of English, Pennsylvania State University, University Park (member of the faculty since 1962). Author of *Contemporary Literary Critics,* 1977, 1982, and editor of *Great Thinkers of the Twentieth Century,* 1983. **Essays:** Freund; Gidal; Man Ray.

BOWLT, John E. Essayist. Professor, Slavic Department, University of Texas at Austin, since 1971; also, Director of the Institute of Modern Russian Culture at Blue Lagoon, Texas. Books include: *Russian Formalism,* editor, with Stephen Benn, 1973; *The Russian Avant-Garde: Theory and Criticism 1902-34,* editor and translator, 1976; *Russian Art 1870-1970,* 1976; *Benedikt Livshits: "The One and a Half-Eyed Archer,"* translator and commentator, 1977; *The Silver Age: Russian Art of the Early Twentieth Century,* 1979; *The Life of Vasilii Kandinsky in Russian Art,* with Rose-Carol Washington, 1980. **Essay:** Shishkin.

BOXER, Bonnie. Essayist. Freelance writer and critic, Tel Aviv. Foreign rights editor, Zmora, Bitan, Modan Publishers Ltd., Tel Aviv, since 1980. Director of sales, production and distribution, *American Showcase,* New York, 1977-78; American editor, *Zoom,* Paris, 1979. **Essays:** Bar-Am; Braun; Ganor; Ostrovsky; Shemtov.

BRITTAIN, David. Specialist in photography and curator, London. Attended Glasgow School of Art, 1972-76. Co-curator of *New Scottish Photography* (Houston Fotofest 1990) and co-author of the catalogue. Assistant editor for *Creative Camera,* 1990-1991. Editor 1991-present. Since 1990 producer and director of numerous BBC-TV documentaries about photographers for the *Late Show,* including profiles of Duane Michals, Lee Friedlander, Garry Winogrand, William Klein, Don McCullin. Producer of *The Decisive Moment,* a 40 minute special for BBC 2, 1993, and *The Decisive Moment,* a 60 minute special, BBC 2, 1994. **Essay:** Maron.

BRY, Doris. Essayist. Writer, consultant and art dealer; Publisher of Atlantis Editions, New York, since 1967. Assisted Georgia O'Keeffe with disposition of Alfred Stieglitz estate, as well as related matters in the arts, 1946-54; freelance writer and editor, 1954-57; assistant to the vice-president, Fund for the Advancement of Education, and administrative assistant, Ford Foundation, New York, 1957-61; writer and researcher, Time Inc., 1961-65; representative for the sale of O'Keeffe paintings, 1965-77; guest curator, Whitney Museum's Georgia O'Keeffe retrospective, New York, 1969-71. Author of the catalogues *Alfred Stieglitz: Photographer,* 1958 and 1965; editor of *Georgia O'Keeffe: Drawings,* 1968, and of *Some Memories of Drawings* by O'Keeffe, 1974; author of the book *Georgia O'Keeffe,* with Lloyd Goodrich, 1970. **Essay:** Clift.

CARROLL, Alison. Essayist. Curator of prints, drawings and photographs, Art Gallery of South Australia, Adelaide. **Essay:** Douglas.

CASLIN, Jean. Essayist. Assistant director, Photographic Resource Center, Boston, since 1979. Lecturer in the history of photography, Clark University, Worcester, Massachusetts, 1980, and University of Massachusetts Harbor Campus, Boston, 1981. Contributor to *Afterimage, Views,* and *Sojourner* magazines. **Essay:** Prince.

CAUJOLLE, Christian. Essayist. Photography critic since 1978, and picture editor since 1981, *Liberation,* Paris. Author of the exhibition catalogues, *Les Petits Enfants de Robert Doisneau,* 1980; *La Jeune Photographie Suisse,* 1981; and author of the books, *Album Photographique No. 1,* with Pierre de Fenoyl, Paris 1980; *Jenny de Vasson: Une Femme Photographe au Debut du Siècle,* 1982; *Jacques-Henri Lartigue,* 1982; *Manuel Alvarez Bravo,* 1982. **Essays:** Claude Batho; Charbonnier; Drahos; Faucon; Hamilton; Lennard; Munoz.

CHEVRIER, Jean-François. Essayist. Freelance photography critic, Paris. **Essays:** Baltauss; Gloaguen; Hers; Requillart.

CHILLINGWORTH, John. Entrant and essayist. See his own entry. **Essay:** Willoughby.

CHO, Becky. Adviser and essayist. Founder, Hong Kong Institute of Professional Photographers (HKIPP), 1987. Editor of HKIPP annual publication *Images,* 1987-1993. Business development manager, Pro-File Photo Library, 1990-1994. Group exhibition, *Our Planet,* 1994. **Essays:** Chang; Fung; Hsieh; Juan; Ko; Wang.

CIPNIC, Monica R. Essayist. Picture editor, *Popular Photography* magazine, *Camera Arts* magazine and *Photography Annual* (on staff of *Popular Photography* since 1973); also, director, Popular Photography Photo Gallery, New York, since 1976. **Essays:** Hosoe; Parker.

COKE, Van Deren. Adviser and entrant. See his own entry.

COHEN, Stu. Essayist. Photography critic, *Boston Phoenix,* since 1973; also, public affairs writer, Office of Health Policy Information, Harvard School of Public Health, Boston, since 1979. Photography editor, *Boston Review of the Arts,* 1971-72; instructor in the history of photography, Art Institute of Boston, 1976-78. **Essays:** Alvarez Bravo; Post Wolcott; Siskind; W. Eugene Smith; Vachon; Van Der Zee; Wasserman.

COLEMAN, A. D. Essayist. Contributing editor, *Camera 35,* New York, since 1976. Vice-president, Photography Media Institute Inc., since 1977; instructor, Department of Undergraduate Film and TV, New York University, since 1978; member, board of directors, Photographic Resource Center, since 1979. Photography critic, *Village Voice,* New York, 1968-73; photography critic, *New York Times,* 1970-74; founding editor, *Views: A New England Journal of Photography,* 1979-80. Author of *The Grotesque in Photography: A Critical Survey,* 1977; *Light Readings: A Photography Critic's Writings 1968-1978,* 1979; *Lee/Model/Parks/Samaras/Turner: Five Interviews Before the Fact,* 1979; and *The Photography A-V Program Directory,* with Patricia Grantz and Douglas Sheer, 1980. **Essays:** Aigner; Hyde; Kirstel; Palfi; Slavin; Teske; Tress.

COLOMBO, Attilio. Essayist. Editor of *Progresso Fotografico,* Milan. **Essays:** Berengo-Gardin; Leonardo; Lotti; Merisio; Monti; Roiter; Russo.

COOKE, Robert W. Essayist. Art professor emeritus, The William Paterson College of New Jersey in Wayne, since 1977 (Professor of art, 1958-77; chairman of the department, 1958-68). Contributor of the monthly feature "Photography" in *School Arts* magazine, 1973-76. Author of *Designing with Light on Paper and Film,* 1969. **Essays:** Savage; Tice.

COREY, David. Essayist. Lecturer in Humanities, Brooklyn College, City University of New York, since 1967. Member of the faculty, Lehigh University, Bethlehem, Pennsylvania, 1966-67. Author of *Fearful Symmetries,* 1979. **Essay:** Sonneman.

DATER, Judy. Entrant and essayist. See her own entry. **Essays:** Ansel Adams; Rubenstein; Skoff.

DAVIES, Laura Lee. Essayist. Music editor of *Time Out* magazine, London. **Essay:** Dickson

DAVIES, Sue. OBE, Hon FRPS. Adviser and essayist. Founding director, The Photographers' Gallery, London, retired 1991. Freelance writer. **Essays:** Abbas; Angel; Badger; David Bailey; Blakemore; Brihat; Cagnoni; Calvin; Campbell; Cooper; John Davies; Davis; Edwards; Freedman; Goldblatt; Griffin; Killip; William Klein; Link; Luskacová; Robertson; Suschitzky; Sykes; Vogt; Wilmer.

de JONGE-VERMEULEN, A. Essayist. Freelance photo-historian and writer, Leiden. **Essays:** Blazer; Den Hollander; Aart Klein; Oorthuys; van der Elsken; Zwart.

DOHERTY, Robert J. Essayist. Chairman of the Department of Design, New York State College of Ceramics at Alfred University; also, publisher, International Archives of Photography, and the Clandestine Press. Formerly director of Salt Lake Art Center and School, and director, Allen R. Hite Art Institute, University of Louisville; founder, University of Louisville Photography Archives, 1962. Director, George Eastman House, Rochester, New York, 1972-79. Picture editor of *Portrait of a Decade* by F. Jack Hurley, 1972; author of *Sozialdokumentarische Photographie in den USA,* 1973, and *The Complete Photographic Work of Jacob A. Riis,* 1981. **Essays:** Rogovin; Rothstein.

DURAND, Regis. Essayist. University lecturer and art critic. Inspector of artistic creation at the Ministry of Culture (the Delegation of Plastic Arts), Paris, France. Author of *La Part de l'Ombre: Essais Pavese,* 1994. Artistic director of *Printemps de Cahors* (the photography and visual arts spring festival) since 1992. **Essays:** Fleischer; Kern.

EELBODE, Erik. Essayist. Course organiser and lecturer, AMARANT, Ghent, Belgium. Photography correspondent for *De Witte Raaf,* Ghent. **Essay:** Braeckman.

ENYEART, James L. Essayist. Director, Center for Creative Photography, University of Arizona, Tucson, and editor of the *CCP Journal,* since 1978. Charter director, Albrecht Gallery of Art, St. Joseph, Missouri, 1967-68; curator of photography, University of Kansas Museum of Art, 1968-76, also lecturer, 1968-69, assistant professor, 1969-75, and associate professor, Department of Art History, University of Kansas; executive director, Friends of Photography, Carmel, California, 1976-77. Author *Francis Bruguière,* 1977; *Michael Smith, Landscapes, 1975-79,* 1981; *Jerry Uelsmann: Twenty-Five Years,* 1982; *Edward Weston's California Landscapes,* 1984; *Judy Dater: Twenty Years,* 1986; and of numerous exhibition catalogues, including *Karsh,* 1970; *Kansas Landscape,* 1971; *Invisible in America,* 1973; *Language of Light,* 1974; *No Mountains in the Way,* 1975. **Essay:** Uelsmann.

ERICSSON, Lars O. Essayist. Swedish correspondent for *Artforum* and an art critic for *Dagensnyheter.* He is currently associate professor of philosophy at the University of Stockholm. **Essay:** Dawid

ESKIND, Andrew. Essayist. Director of interdepartmental services, George Eastman House, Rochester, New York. **Essay:** Crane.

ESTEN, John. Essayist. Freelance design and writer, New York. Art director, *Harper's Bazaar,* 1971-78; art director, *L'Officiel U.S.A.* magazine, 1979. Editor and designer of *Style in Motion: Photographs by Martin Munkacsi,* with Nancy White, 1979; designer of *Long Island Landscape Painting 1820-1920,* by Ronald G. Pisano, 1985; author and designer of *Blue and White China: Origins and Influences,* 1987. **Essay:** Raymond.

EVANS, Tom. Essayist. Painter and photographer, London. Visiting lecturer, London College of Printing, since 1972. Photography correspondent, *Art and Artists,* London, 1979-80. Contributor to *Camerawork* and *Art Monthly.* Author of *Shunga: The Art of Love in Japan,* with Mary Anne Evans, 1975; *Guitars: From the Renaissance to Rock,* 1977. **Essays:** Jumonji; Edward Weston.

FEATHERSTONE, David. Essayist. Executive associate, The Friends of Photography, Carmel, California, since 1977. Curator, historical photography collection, University of Oregon Library, Eugene, 1974-77, and co-director, Image Point Gallery, Eugene, 1975-76. Author of *Vilem K í : Photographs,* 1979; *The Diana Show: Pictures through a Plastic Lens,* 1980; and *Postures: The Studio Photographs of Marsha Burns,* 1982. **Essays:** Garnett; Worth.

FLUSSER, Vilém. Essayist. Independent writer, and visiting professor at universities in Europe, Brazil and the United States. Formerly, professor of communication at the School for Communications and Humanities, São Paulo. Author of *Lingua a Realidade,* 1963; *Historia do Diabo,* 1965; *Da Religiosidade,* 1967; *La Force du Quotidien,* 1972; *Le Monde Codifié,* 1972; *Natural: mente,* 1979; *Pos-Historia,* 1982; *Fuer eine Philosophie der Fotografie,* 1983; *Ins Universum der technischen Bilder,* 1985; *Schrift: hat Schreiben Zukunft?,* 1986; *Vampyrotheutis Infernalis,* 1986. **Essay:** Müller-Pohle.

FONTCUBERTA, Joan. Entrant and essayist. See his own entry. **Essays:** Catany; Centelles; de Nooijer; Descamps; Gelpke; Ghirri; Lenart; Meyer; Navarro; Ortiz-Echagüe.

FREEMAN, Tina. Essayist. Freelance writer and exhibition organizer. Formerly, curator of photography, New Orleans Museum of Art. **Essay:** Oscar Bailey.

FUAD-LUKE, Alistair. Adviser. Photojournalist. Head of operations, Mirror Syndication International, London.

FULTON, Marianne. Essayist. Associate curator, photographic collection, George Eastman House, Rochester, New York, since 1978 (researcher at Eastman House, 1976-78); has curated numerous exhibitions at Eastman House, including *Symbolism in Photography 1890-1920,* 1978; *Steichen: A Centennial Tribute,* 1979; and *Barbara Morgan: Photomontage,* 1979. Editor and author of introduction, *Camera Work: A Pictorial Guide,* 1978; also wrote introductions to *Muray's Celebrity Portraits of the 20's and 30's,* 1978;

The Platinum Print, 1979; *Barbara Morgan: Photomontage,* 1980; *The Wise Silence: Photographs of Paul Caponigro,* 1983; *Lucien Clergue,* 1985. **Essays:** Gowin; Harold Jones.

FUNG, Joseph. Entrant and essayist. See his own entry. **Essays:** Hu; Wu.

GASSAN, Arnold. Essayist. Author of *A Chronology of Photography,* 1972; *Handbook for Contemporary Photography,* 1977; *The Color Print Book,* 1981; *Report: Minor White Workshops,* 1983. **Essays:** Chappell; Heinecken; Labrot.

GERNSHEIM, Helmut. Adviser, entrant and essayist. See his own entry. **Essays:** Bayles; Berko; Fieger; Garduno; Gianella; Heitmann; Henle; Hoepffner; Hofer; Huth; Keetman; Ricciardi.

GESKE, Norman A. Essayist. Director, Sheldon Memorial Art Gallery, University of Nebraska at Lincoln, since 1953 (assistant director, 1950-53, and acting director, 1953-56, University of Nebraska Art Galleries, Lincoln). Director, Hennepin County Historical Society, Minneapolis, 1940-41; curator, Walker Art Center, Minneapolis, 1947-50. **Essays:** Alinder; DeCarava; Gilpin; Sudek; Wise.

GIDLEY, G.M. Essayist. Reader in American studies and director of the Centre for American and Commonwealth Arts and Studies, University of Exeter, Devon. Author of *Catalogue of American Paintings in British Public Collections,* 1974; *With One Sky Above Us: Life on an Indian Reservation at the Turn of the Century,* with photographs by Dr. E.H. Latham, 1979; *Kopet: A Documentary Narrative of Chief Joseph's Last Years,* 1981; *American Photography,* 1983; *Representing Others,* 1992; and *Modern American Culture: An Introduction,* 1993. Editor of *The Vanishing Race: Selections from Edward S. Curtis' "The North American Indian,"* 1976. **Essay:** Collier.

GILI, Marta. Essayist. Curator of photography at the Joan Miró Foundation, Barcelona; also freelance curator of photography exhibitions in Spain and France. **Essay:** Renau.

GODBY, Michael. Essayist. Professor of the history of art at the University of Cape Town. He has lectured and published on Italian Renaissance art, Hogarth and English eighteenth-century art, South African colonial art, contemporary South African art, ethnographic photography and contemporary South African photography. **Essay:** Mendel.

GOLDBERG, Vicki. Essayist. Editor of *Photography in Print: Writings from 1816 to the Present,* 1981. **Essays:** Erwitt; Michals.

GOLDSMITH, Arthur. Essayist. Editorial director, *Popular Photography, Camera Arts,* and *Photography Annual,* New York. Executive editor, *Popular Photography,* 1953-60; picture editor, *This Week,* 1960-62; president and director, Famous Photographers School, 1962-72. Author of *The Eye of Eisenstaedt,* 1969, and *How to Take Better Pictures, The Photography Game, The Nude in Photography,* and *The Camera and Its Images.* **Essays:** Halsman; Newman.

GORMAN, Bradford G. Essayist. Communications specialist, Apple Computer Inc., Toronto, since 1985. Coordinator, "Cana-

dian Images: A National Conference on Photography and Filmmaking in Canada," at Trent University, Peterborough, Ontario, 1977-79; director and curator of contemporary photography, Canadian Centre of Photography, Toronto, 1980-81; assistant to the director, Art Gallery of Hamilton, Ontario, 1981-85. **Essay:** Horeis.

GRCEVIC, Nada. Essayist, freelance art and photography critic and historian, Yugoslavia, since 1960. Member of the advisory board, *History of Photography,* since 1977. Collaborator, Yugoslav Lexicographic Institution, 1964, Arts and Crafts Museum, 1965, and the Zagreb Center for Photography, Film and Television, 1977. Author of *Nineteenth-Century Photography in Croatia,* 1980. **Essays:** Djordjevic; Grcevic.

GREIDER, Göran. Essayist. Poet and journalist, Stockhom. He has published five volumes of poetry and is on the staff of *Dagens Nyheter.* **Essay:** Tunbjörk.

GUTMAN, Judith Mara. Essayist. Guest curator, International Center of Photography, New York, since 1980; also freelance writer, contributing to the *International Herald Tribune, Washington Post, Book World, New York Times Magazine,* and *Vanity Fair.* Co-producer, art director and scriptwriter, Current Affairs Films, Wilton, Connecticut, 1973-78; adviser, Oxford University Press, New York, 1975-76; director of the research project, "The Photograph as a Cultural Artifact: India 1850-1920," 1976-80. Author of *The Colonial Venture,* 1966; *Lewis W. Hine and the American Social Conscience,* 1967; *The Making of American Society,* with Edwin Rozwenc, 1972-73; *Lewis Hine: Two Perspectives,* 1974; *Is America Used Up?,* 1973; *Buying,* 1975; and *Through Indian Eyes,* 1982. **Essays:** Cornell Capa; Kepes; Mehta; Miller; Riboud; Riefenstahl.

HALL-DUNCAN, Nancy. Essayist. Curator of art, Bruce Museum, Greenwich, Connecticut, since 1985. Assistant curator, International Museum of Photography, George Eastman House, Rochester, New York, 1975-76; guest curator, *Photographic Surrealism,* New Gallery of Contemporary Art, Cleveland, and national tour, 1979-80, and *E.O. Hoppé: One Thousand Exposures,* New York University, 1982. Author of *The History of Fashion Photography,* 1979, and of the exhibition catalogue for *Photographic Surrealism,* 1979, *E.O. Hoppé,* 1982, and *American Icons: Selections from the Chase Manhattan Collection,* 1985. **Essays:** Avedon; Edgerton; Groover; Hiro; Mark; Nixon; Penn; Rice; Warhol.

HANDY, Ellen. Essayist. Art historian and critic, New York. Teaches at La Guardia College, City University of New York. Guest curator of Pictorial Effect/Naturalistic Vision: The Photographs and Theories of Henry Peach Robinson and Peter Henry Emerson, Chrysler Museum, Norfolk, Virginia, 1994. **Essays:** Busson; Krims; Lemieux; Prince; Ross; Sherman.

HÅRD af SEGERSTAD, Ulf. Essayist. Art, architecture, design and photography critic of *Svenska Dagbladet* newspaper, Stockholm. Formerly, editor of the design magazine, *Form,* and vice-president of ICSID International Council of Societies of Industrial Design. Author of *Scandinavian Design,* 1961; *Modern Scandinavian Furniture,* 1963; *Modern Finnish Design,* 1968; *Carl Larsson's Home,* 1975. **Essay:** Olson.

HARKER, Margaret. Essayist. Photographic historian. Emeritus professor, University of Westminster and formerly pro-rector,

Polytechnic of Central London. Author of *The Linked Ring: The Secession in Photography 1892-1910,* 1979; *Henry Peach Robinson, Master of Photographic Art 1830-1901,* 1988 and *The Photographers of Malta, 1840-1990,* 1995. **Essay:** Hosking.

HARMEL, Carole. Essayist. Assistant professor of humanities, Harry S. Truman College, Chicago, since 1972. Chicago correspondent, *Afterimage,* Rochester, New York, since 1979. **Essays:** Jachna; Mapplethorpe; Sommer.

HARRIS, David. Essayist. Assistant to the curator of photography, Canadian Centre for Architecture, Montreal, since 1986. Assistant archivist, Art Gallery of Ontario, Toronto, 1975-78; lecturer in the Department of Cinema and Photography, Concordia University, Montreal, since 1983. **Essay:** Mitchell.

HARRISON, Martin. Essayist. Author, designer, lecturer, photographer and exhibition curator. Contributing editor, *Freize* magazine; director of Olympus Photo Gallery, London, 1982-85. Books include *Black and White Memories (David Bailey),* 1983; *Appearances: Fashion Photography Since 1945,* 1991; *Louis Faurer,* 1993; *Norman Parkinson: Photographs 1935-1990,* 1994. Organised two exhibitions, Victoria & Albert Museum, London: *Shots of Style,* 1985 and *Appearances,* 1991. **Essays:** Bassman; Horvat; Leiter.

HASEGAWA, Akira. Essayist. Freelance photographic critic, Tokyo. **Essay:** Suda.

HASEGAWA, Yuko. Essayist. Curator of Setagay Art Museum, Tokyo; curator of exhibition *Beyond the Photgraphic Frame,* Art Tower Mito, 1990; co-curator of *Liquid Crystal Futures: Contemporary Japanese Photography,* The Fruitmarket Gallery, Edinburgh, Scotland, 1994. **Essay:** Yoshida.

HASSNER, Rune. Adviser, entrant and essayist. See his own entry. **Essays:** Johnson; Pål-Nils Nilsson.

HATTERSLEY, Ralph. Essayist. Contributing editor, *Popular Photography* magazine, New York, since 1970. Associate professor, Rochester Institute of Technology, New York, 1948-61. Author of *Discover Your Self Through Photography, Photographic Printing, Photographic Lighting, Beginner's Guide to Photography, Beginner's Guide to Darkroom Techniques, Beginner's Guide to Photographing People, Beginner's Guide to Color Photography, Beginner's Guide to Color Printing,* and *Andreas Feininger.* **Essay:** Feininger.

HAWORTH-BOOTH, Mark. Adviser and essayist. Curator of photographs, prints, drawings and paintings collections, Victoria and Albert Museum, London since 1977. Edited and introduced *The Land: 20th Century Landscape Photographs Selected by Bill Brandt,* 1975; *Personal Choice: A Celebration of 20th Century Photographs,* 1983; *Bill Brandt's Literary Britain,* 1984; *Hockney's Photographs,* 1984; *The Golden Age of British Photography (1839-1900),* 1984; and other volumes. Co-author with Brian Coe of *A Guide to Early Photographic Processes,* 1983. Author of *E. McKnight Kauffer,* 1979; *Photography Now,* 1989; *Camille Silvy's River Scene, France,* 1992. **Essays:** Raymond Moore; Bhimji; Reisewitz.

HEDGPETH, Ted. Essayist. Contributing editor, *Artweek,* Oak-

land, California; contributing writer, *Artbeat,* San Francisco, *Photoshow,* Los Angeles, and *San Francisco Review of Books.* Member of the board of directors, Camerawork Gallery, San Francisco. Co-editor of *Latent Image: A Quarterly of Fine Art Photography,* 1977-79. **Essays:** Coke; Dater; Dutton; Fitch; Golden; Heyman; Lyon; Joan Lyons; MacGregor; Minick; Misrach; Nettles; Ruscha; Traub; Wessel.

HEIFERMAN, Marvin. Essayist. Publisher and dealer, New York. Assistant director, Light Gallery, New York, 1972-74; director of photography, Castelli Gallery, New York, 1975-82. **Essays:** Robert Adams; Namuth.

HELD, Michael. Essayist. Freelance writer and book editor, Chicago. **Essays:** Meyerowitz; Henry Holmes Smith; Umbo; Todd Walker; Welpott.

HENISCH, H.K. Essayist. Professor of the history of photography, Pennsylvania State University, University Park, since 1974, and fellow of the Institute for the Arts and Humanistic Studies, Pennsylvania State University, since 1978 (professor of physics, 1963). Editor of the international research quarterly *History of Photography,* since 1977. Author of *Chipmunk Portrait,* with B.A. Henisch, 1970; and *Crystal Growth in Gels,* 1970. **Essay:** Kríz.

HILL, Elena. Essayist. BFA in film and photography, Concordia University, Montreal, Canada. Recipient of an award by the Canada Arts Council for a photo installation on the sexuality and representation of the elderly female, working with Age Concern, London. **Essay:** Donigan Cumming.

HODGSON, Francis. Essayist. Formerly head of the print room, Photographers' Gallery, London, and founder of Zwemmer Fine Photographs. Occasional lecturer, Royal College of Art, London. Author of a monograph on David Hiscock. **Essays:** de Keyzer; Pyke; Richon; Serrano; Waplington.

HOLBORN, Mark. Essayist. Freelance writer and critic, New York (specialist in Japan). Contributor to the *British Journal of Photography, Camerawork, London Magazine,* and *Aperture.* Author of *The Ocean in the Sand,* 1978. **Essays:** Domon; Fukase; McCullin; Moriyama; Narahara; Shinoyama; Tomatsu; Tsuchida; Tucker.

HONNEF, Klaus. Essayist. Director of exhibitions at the Rheinisches Landesmuseum, Bonn. **Essays:** Becher; Mantz; Moses; Neusüss; Newton; Schürmann; Strelow.

HOPKINSON, Amanda. Consultant editor, adviser and essayist. Curator, translator, critic and writer on photography, London. Author of *Julia Margaret Cameron,* 1986, and the exhibition catalogues *The Forbidden Rainbow,* 1992; *Desires and Disguises,* 1993; and *A Hidden View: Photography from Bahia, Brazil,* 1994. Regular broadcaster for BBC TV and radio. **Essays:** Cravo Neto; Errazuriz; Etchart; Gonzalez Palma; Ken Grant; Gregory; Hoban; Hutchings; Kennard; Knorr; Mariani; Matthews; Nichols; Poirot; Provaznik; Rio Branco; Salgado; Spence; Vallhonrat; Alex Webb.

HOPKINSON, (Sir) Tom. Essayist. President of The Photographer's Gallery, London. Assistant editor, *Weekly Illustrated,* London, 1934-38; assistant editor, 1938-40, and editor, 1940-

50, *Picture Post,* London; also editor of *Lilliput,* London, 1941-46; editor, *Drum* magazine, Johannesburg, 1958-61; director for Africa, International Press Institute, 1962-66; senior fellow in press studies, University of Sussex, 1967-69; visiting professor in journalism, University of Minnesota, Minneapolis, 1968-69; chairman, British National Press Awards, 1968-77; director, Centre for Journalism Studies, University College, Cardiff, 1970-75. Author of novels, collections of short stories and various nonfiction works, and of *Bert Hardy, Photojounalist,* and *Treasures of the Royal Photographic Society,* 1980; editor of *Picture Post 1938-50,* 1970, 1979. Died June 1990. **Essays:** Berry; Hardy; Henderson; Hurn; Magubane; Man; Rodger; Schadeberg; Snowdon.

HOY, Anne H. Essayist. Adjunct lecturer in art history, New York University. Curator, International Center of Photography, New York, 1983-90. Author of *Fabrication: Staged, Altered and Appropriated Photographs,* editor of *The Art Bulletin,* 1970-94, and consulting editor of *Studies in the Decorative Arts* since 1993. **Essays:** Edna Bullock; Burke; Charlesworth; Cowin; Ess; Majore; Nagatani; Quigley; Rankaitis; Skoglund.

HUGHES, George. Essayist. Features editor of *Amateur Photographer,* London, 1967-79, editor of *Camera Weekly,* 1979-89 and editor-in-chief of *Amateur Photographer* and *Video Camera,* 1989-91. Author (text only) of *David Bailey's Book of Photography* and *Begin with Bailey,* 1983. **Essay:** Lewinski.

HURLEY, F. Jack. Essayist. Professor of history, Memphis State University (member of the faculty since 1966). Author of *Portrait of a Decade: Roy Stryker and the Development of Documentary Photography in the Thirties,* 1971; and *Russell Lee, Photographer,* 1978; editor of *Industry and the Photographic Image,* 1980; and *Southern Eye, Southern Mind: A Photographic Inquiry,* 1981. **Essays:** Plowden; Vestal.

IIZAWA, Kohtaro. Essayist. Critic and writer on photography. Author of *Art Photography in Japan, 1900-1930,* 1986; *La Force de la Photographie,* 1989; and *Photography 1983-1992,* 1993. **Essay:** Miyoshi.

JANTJES, Gavin. Essayist. Painter and printmaker. Senior lecturer, Chelsea College of Fine Art, London. **Essay:** Hallett.

JEFFREY, Ian. Essayist. Historian of photography and of art, London. Teaches art history in the Central European University, Prague. During the 1980s he taught in the University of London, Goldsmith's College. Author of *Concise History of Photography,* 1984. Organiser of the exhibition *Bill Brandt* at the Barbican Art Gallery, London, 1994. **Essays:** Bohm; Molder; Savelev.

JOHNSON, Chris. Essayist. Instructor in photography since 1977, and chairman of the department since 1981, California College of Arts and Crafts, Oakland. Assistant instructor, Ansel Adams Yosemite Workshops, 1973-74; curator and adviser to the Imogen Cunningham Trust, 1975-79. **Essays:** Bullock; Brett Weston.

JOHNSON, William. Essayist. Freelance curator, teacher and author. Public Services librarian for the Fine Arts Library, 1967-76, and lecturer in the history of photography, 1970-76, Harvard University, Cambridge, Massachusetts; instructor in the history of photography, Tufts University for the School of the Museum of Fine Arts, Boston, 1975-76; instructor in the history of photography, Visual Studies Workshop, Rochester, New York, 1976-78; curator, W. Eugene Smith Archive, Center for Creative Photography, University of Arizona, Tucson, 1978-81. Author of *W. Eugene Smith: Early Work 1937-51,* 1980; *W. Eugene Smith: A Chronological Bibliography 1934-1980,* 2 volumes, 1980-81; *W. Eugene Smith: Master of the Photographic Essay,* 1981; and of the exhibition catalogue, *The Photographs of Todd Walker,* 1980; editor of *An Index to Articles on Photography 1977* and *1978,* 1978, 1980. **Essay:** Heath.

JONSSON, Rune. Essayist. Teacher at the Konstfackskolan, Stockholm, since 1969; also, lecturer at Uppsala University, Sweden, since 1975, and Göteborg University, since 1983. Freelance writer for various Swedish photography magazines, since 1960. Author of *Vi börjar fotografera,* 1961; *Fotografera i svartvitt,* 1964; *Bilder av nuet,* 1966; *Hans Hammarskiöld,* 1979; *Hammarby,* pictures by Curt Larsson, 1980; and *Fotografi,* with Werner Noll and Jan Olsheden, 1980; editor of *Fotografisk Årsbok,* 1967, 1968, 1969, 1970. **Essays:** Baum; Hammarskiöld; Hassner; Jonsson; Nykvist; Oddner; Petersen; Sandels; Sjöstedt; Wahlberg.

KAJIWARA, Takao. Essayist. Editor-in-chief, *Nippon Camera,* Tokyo, since 1975. Freelance photographer, Tokyo, 1955-75; professor, Tokyo Photo College, 1959-70. Editor of *Brilliant Scenes by Shoji Ueda,* 1981. **Essays:** Akiyama; Fujii; Hamaya; Ishimoto; Midorikawa; Miki; Naitoh; Ueda; Watanabe.

KASAHARA, Michiko. Essayist. Curator of Tokyo Metropoiitan Museum of Photography; curated exhibitions, including *Self-Portraits of Contemporary Women: Exploring the Unknown Self,* 1991 and *Border/Borderless, Japanese Contemporary Photography,* 1993. Co-translator of *Nude and Naked* by Jorge Lewinski. **Essays:** Kon; Suzuki.

KEENAN, Karyn Allen. Essayist. Supervisor of visual arts, XV Olympic Winter Games, Calgary, 1985. Cultural affairs officer, Government of Ontario, Toronto, 1973-74; special projects officer, Art Gallery of Ontario, Toronto, 1974-77; associate curator of contemporary art, Nickel Arts Museum, University of Calgary, 1981-85. Author of *Colour Xerography,* 1976; *The Winnipeg Perspective,* 1979; *The RCA Exhibition,* 1980; *Barbara Astman: Red,* 1982; *Persona,* 1982; *William Townsend in Alberta,* 1982; *Michael Hayden: Trikha,* 1983; *Arnaud Maggs: Photographs 1975-84,* 1984, editor of *Artists with their Work,* 1977. **Essays:** Astman; Lake.

KEMPE, Fritz. Entrant and essayist. See his own entry. **Essay:** Schmidt.

KESTER, Grant. Essayist. Whitney Museum Studies Fellow, New York. Formerly, contributing editor, *Art Papers,* Atlanta, Georgia. **Essays:** Tenneson; Yavno.

KIL, Wolfgang. Essayist. Freelance art and culture publicist, East Berlin. Formerly practising architect, and editor of an art and architecture journal. Author of *Photographes Contemporains en R.D.A.,* 1985; *Heritage and Beginning: The Years After World War II Seen by German Photographers,* 1987. **Essay:** Fischer.

KNIGHT, Hardwicke. Essayist. Freelance photographer and writer, Dunedin, New Zealand. Director of medical photography, Enfield

Group Hospitals, England, 1948-57; and University of Otago Medical School and Dunedin Hospital, New Zealand, 1957-77. President, Otago Anthropological Society, 1960; photographer and surveyor, National Science Foundation Pitcairn Island Expedition, 1963-64; president, New Zealand Institute of Medical Photographers; president, Dunedin Film Society; vice-president, New Zealand Archives and Records Association, 1978-80. Author of *Photography in New Zealand: A Social and Technical Study,* 1971; *Dunedin Then,* 1974; *Matanaka,* with Dr. Coutts, 1975; *History of the Broad Bay School,* 1977; *Princes Street by Gaslight,* 1976; *Otago Peninsula: A Local History,* 1978, 1979; *Cutten,* with Dr. Grief, 1979; *Burton Brothers, Photographers,* 1980; *Brief Biographies of Dunedin Photographers,* 2 volumes, 1979-80; *The Ordeal of William Larnach,* 1981; *Otago Cavalcade,* 8 volumes, 1981-86; *Dunedin Early Photographs,* 1984, 1985. **Essay:** Brake.

KOCH, Stephen. Essayist. Professor, Columbia University, New York. Contributor to *Peter Hujar: A Retrospective,* 1994. **Essay:** Hujar.

KOETZLE, Michael. Essayist. Writer and curator, Munich. Author of *Bertolt Brecht beim Photografen, Doisneau/Renault, Fotografie an der HFG,* and of articles in *Zoom, European Photography* and *Photo Technik International.* **Essay:** Fischer.

KOSINSKA, Barbara. Essayist. Editor and writer for *Fotografia,* Warsaw, 1972-90 and for *6 x 9 - fotografia,* 1991-94. Chief editor, National Gallery of Art, Zacheta, Warsaw, since 1994. **Essays:** Bohdziewicz; Wojnecki.

KUWABARA, Kineo. Entrant and essayist. See his own entry. **Essays:** Kurata; Morinaga.

LANGFORD, Martha. Essayist. Chief curator, Canadian Museum of Contemporary Photography (formerly Still Photography Division of the National Film Board of Canada), Ottawa, since 1981 (exhibition producer, 1977-80; senior producer 1980-81). Editor of the exhibition catalogue, *Separate from the World,* 1979; and author of the catalogues, *Atlantic Parallels,* 1980; *Paradise/Le Paradis,* 1980; *Contemporary Canadian Photography,* 1984. **Essays:** Semak; Torosian.

LE GUAY, Laurence. Essayist. Freelance photographer and writer, Sydney, since 1938. Editor of *Contemporary Photography* (first independent photographic journal in Australia), 1946-49. Author/photographer of *Sydney Harbour,* 1960; *Sailing Free around the World,* 1976; and *Shadows in a Landscape,* 1980; editor of *A Portfolio of Australian Photography,* 1950; *Australian Photography,* 1975; and *Australian Photography: A Contemporary View,* 1980. **Essay:** David Moore.

LEMAGNY, Jean-Claude. Adviser. Curator of Photography, Bibliothèque Nationale, Paris.

LEPPARD, Lucy. Essayist. **Essay:** Leonard.

LEWINSKI, Jorge. Essayist and entrant. See his own entry. **Essay:** Griffin.

LIEBLING, Jerome. Entrant and essayist. See his own entry. **Essay:** Rosenblum.

LOHSE, Bernd. Essayist. Photographic critic and historian, Burghausen, West Germany. Picture editor, Verlag Scherl, Berlin, 1932-34; freelance photographer, 1934-42, 1951-53; editor, *Foto-Spiegel,* 1947-49, and *Photo-Magazin,* 1949-50; book editor, Umschau Verlag, Frankfurt, 1955-65; editor, *Photoblätter,* 1965-75; now retired. Author of *Cameras from Germany,* 1950; *Australien und Südsee heute,* 1953; *Kanada: Land der Zakunft?,* 1954; and *Hugo Erfurth, Photograph der Goldenen 20er Jahre,* 1977; and editor of numerous books, including *Monumente des Abendlandes,* 9 volumes, 1958-65. **Essays:** Baumann; Heinemann; Hubmann; Windstosser.

LUNDSTROM, Jan-Erik. Essayist. **Essay:** Lindström-Caudwell.

MACIJAUSKAS, Aleksandras. Entrant and essayist. See his own entry. **Essay:** Zvirgzdas.

MACK, Michael. Adviser. Photographer, curator and writer. Editor of Zelda Cheatle Press, London. Photography editor of *The Art Book.*

MAHONEY, Hildegard. Essayist. Photographer and photographic librarian. Formerly worked in newspapers and photographic agencies. Librarian, The Photographers' Gallery, London. **Essays:** Mann; Ritts; Weems.

MANDERY, Guy. Essayist. Photographic exhibition organizer in Paris. Writer for the magazine *Le Photographe,* Paris, 1975-80; Paris correspondent for *Il Diaframma,* Milan, 1978-81; editor-in-chief, *Photo Magazine,* Paris, 1981-85. Contributor to numerous French photo magazines. **Essays:** Boucher; Ehrmann; Ronis; Sudre.

MANDOKI, Katya. Essayist. Professor at the Universidad Autonoma Metropolitana, Mexico City, since 1979; art critic for *Uno Mas Uno* daily newspaper, Mexico City, since 1979; also, correspondent in Mexico for *American Photographer.* **Essays:** Bostelmann; Iturbide; Ortiz Monasterio.

MARKHAM, Jacqueline. Essayist. Independent artist, Los Angeles, since 1969; freelance writer for art and photography publications, since 1978; exhibitions designer and photographer, Aesthetech Corporation, Paso Robles, California, since 1980. Author of *Two Views of Manzanar: Ansel Adams and Toyo Miyatake,* 1978; and *The Graham Nash Collection,* 1978; co-author of *Paul Outerbridge: Photographs,* 1980. **Essay:** Mudford.

MATSUMOTO, Norihiko. Essayist. Freelance photographer, critic and editor, Tokyo. Editor of the *History of Japanese Photography 1940-1945* and *1945-56.* **Essays:** Ichimura; Kawada; Kuwabara; Nakamura; Ohara; Sawatari; Shirakawa; Tahara.

MAYES, Stephen. Essayist. Writer, broadcaster and lecturer, London. Served as chair, World Press Photo Jury. Former managing editor, Network Photographers. Group creative director, Tony Stone Images, since January 1995. **Essays:** Lewis; Pillitz; Power; Reas.

McINTYRE, Arthur. Essayist. Artist and freelance writer, Sydney. Lecturer at N.I.D.A., University of New South Wales, since 1979; Sydney art critic for *The Age,* Melbourne, since 1980. Sydney art critic for *The Australian,* 1977-78. Co-author of *The Visual Arts,* 1980. **Essay:** Ellis.

MESSER, William. Essayist. Freelance photographer, exhibition curator and critic, Cincinnati. Formerly, director of The Photographic Gallery, Cardiff. **Essay:** Claass.

MEYER, Pedro. Adviser and entrant. See his own entry.

MINKKINEN, Arno Rafael. Entrant and essayist. See his own entry. **Essays:** Baltermans; Callahan; DeCock; Frank; Gohlke; Krause; Lounema.

MIRALLES, Francesc. Essayist. Freelance photographic critic, Barcelona. **Essay:** Freixa.

MISANI, Marco. Essayist. Freelance writer and photography critic, Switzerland. Editor and Publisher of *Printletter,* Zurich, 1976-80. **Essays:** Kumler; Leverant.

MITCHELL, Margaretta K. Essayist. Freelance photographer, writer, teacher and photo historian. Guest curator of the exhibition *Recollections: 10 Women of Photography,* International Center of Photography, New York and national tour, 1979-82. Author of *Gift of Place,* 1969; *To a Cabin,* with Dorothea Lange, 1973; introduction to *After Ninety* by Imogen Cunningham, 1977; *Recollections: 10 Women of Photography,* 1979; *Dance for Life,* 1985. **Essays:** Abbott; Corpron; Frissell; Jacobi.

MITCHELL, Michael. Entrant and essayist. See his own entry. **Essays:** Curran; James.

MOORE, David. Entrant and essayist. See his own entry. **Essay:** Dupain.

MOZLEY, Anita V. Essayist. Curator of photography, Stanford University Museum of Art, California. **Essays:** Connor; Cunningham; Deal; Pirkle Jones.

MRÁZKOVÁ, Daniela. Essayist. Editor, Czechoslovaktelevision, Prague, since 1979. Assistant editor, 1966-71, and editor-in-chief, 1971-78, *Revue Fotografie,* Prague. Author, with Vladimìr Remeš, of *They Photographed the War: Soviet War Photography 1941-45,* 1975; *The Russian War,* 1977; *The Russian War 1941-45,* 1978; *Von Moskau nach Berlin,* 1979; *Irena Blüh,* 1980; *Die Sowjetunion Zwischen den Kriegen 1917-1941,* 1981; *Tschechoslowakische Fotografen 1900-1939,* 1982; *Josef Sudek,* 1983; *Jaromìr Funke,* 1986; *Another Russia: Through the Eyes of the New Soviet Photographers,* 1986; author of *The Story of Photography,* 1985; *Jan Lauschmann,* 1986; *Viktor Kolá,* 1986. **Essays:** Binde; Grygar; Hochová; Kolár; Koposov; Korniss; Kuznetsova; Mikhailovsky; Rakauskas; Ságl; Spuris; Sterenberg; Teige; Zelma.

MÜLLER-POHLE, Andreas. Entrant and essayist. See his own entry. **Essay:** Fontcuberta.

MURRAY, Joan. Essayist. Director, The Robert McLaughlin Gallery, Oshawa, Ontario, since 1974. Research curator, 1969, curator of Canadian art, 1970-73, and acting chief curator, 1973, Art Gallery of Ontario, Toronto. Art editor, *The Canadian Forum,* 1970-74. Author of *The Art of Tom Thomson,* 1971; *Impressionism in Canada 1895-1935,* 1973; *Dennis Burton Retrospective,* 1977; *Louis de Niverville Retrospective,* 1978; *Gordon Rayner Retrospective,* 1979; *Painters Eleven in Retrospect,* 1979; *Ivan Eyre Exposition,*

1980; *The Beginning of Vision: The Drawings of Lawren S. Harris,* 1982; *Letters Home 1859-1906: The Letters of William Blair Bruce,* 1982; *Kurelek's Vision of Canada,* 1983; *The Last Buffalo: The Story of Frederick Arthur Verner,* 1984; *Daffodils in Winter: The Life and Letters of Pegi Nicol Macleod,* 1984; *The Best of the Group of Seven,* 1984; *The Best of Tom Thomson,* 1986. **Essays:** Bourdeau; Lynne Cohen; Gagnon; Livick; Maggs; Szilasi.

NAEF, Weston J. Adviser. Curator of photography, J. Paul Getty Museum, Malibu, California. Formerly, curator of photography, Metropolitan Museum of Art, New York. Author of *Era of Exploration: The Rise of Landscape Photography in the American West 1869-1885,* with James N. Wood, 1975; and *The Collection of Alfred Stieglitz: 50 Pioneers of Modern Photography,* 1978; *Counterparts: Form and Emotion in Photographs,* 1982.

NAYLOR, Colin. Essayist. Editor of *Contemporary Artists,* 1977, 1989; associate editor of *Contemporary Architects,* 1980, and of *Contemporary Designers,* 1984. Formerly editor, *Art and Artists,* London. Died 1992. **Essays:** Burri; Dekkers; Dibbets; Kessel.

NORFLEET, Barbara. Essayist. Lecturer in visual and environmental studies since 1970, and curator of photography at the Carpenter Center for the Visual Arts since 1972, Harvard University, Cambridge, Massachusetts; also a photographer (individual exhibitions at Carl Siembab Gallery, Boston, 1980; Houston Center for Photography, 1984; Friends of Photography, Carmel, 1984; Massachusetts College of Art, 1985; Oregon Museum of Art, Eugene, 1986). Author of *The Champion Pig,* 1979; *Wedding,* 1979; *Killing Time,* 1982; *All the Right People,* 1986. **Essays:** Cosindas; Eggleston; Turbeville.

NORI, Claude. Essayist. Correspondent in Paris for *Progresso Fotografico,* Milan, since 1971. Founder, Contrejour (journal, publishing house and gallery), Paris, 1974. Organized the exhibitions *Photographie Actuelle en France* and *La Photographie Française des Origines à Nos Jours,* 1978. Author of *Les Masques Humains,* 1970; *Lunettes,* 1973; *Histoire de la Photographie Francaise,* 1975; *Je Vous Aime,* 1978; and *Une Fille Instantanée,* 1981. **Essays:** Boubat; Franck; Gautrand; Plossu.

NURIDSANY, Michel. Essayist. Photography critic, Paris. Author of the exhibition catalogue *Instantanés,* 1980. **Essays:** Boltanski; Brassaï; Henri.

OLLMAN, Arthur. Essayist. Director, Museum of Photographic Arts, San Diego, California. **Essay:** Caffery.

ORIVE, Maria Crìstina. Essayist. Founder and director, with Sara Facio, Editorial La Azotea, Buenos Aires, since 1973; correspondent of the Gamma Press Agency in Argentina, 1974-84; founding member, Latin American Photographic Council, since 1978; founding member, Argentinian Photographic Council, since 1979. Editor-in-chief, art section, *El Imparcial,* Guatemala, 1954-57; Latin-American desk, French Radio-Television, Paris, 1961-69; correspondent in Latin America for SIPA Press, Paris, 1972-74. Author, with Sara Facio, of *Actos de Fe en Guatemala,* with text by Miguel Angel Asturias, 1980. **Essay:** Eleta.

PALAZZOLI, Daniela. Essayist. Professor of theory and method of mass media, Academy of Brera, Milan. Editor in charge of the photographic book section, Electa Editrice, Milan. Curator/organizer of numerous exhibitions, including *The Fight for the Image;* 1973, *Fantastic Photography in Europe,* 1976. Author of *Fotografia, Cinema, Videotape: L'Uso Artistico dei Nuovi Media,* 1977, and *Giuseppe Primoli,* 1979; editor of *Combattimento per un'Immagine: Fotografi e Pittori,* 1973; *Venezia '79: La Fotografia,* with others, 1979; and *La Fotografia Italiana dell'800,* 1979. **Essay:** Schad.

PATNAIK, Deba P. Essayist. Director of the Third World House and professor of English, Oberlin College, Ohio, since 1980. Professor of religious studies, University of North Carolina, 1975-76; special consultant, George Eastman House, Rochester, New York, 1975-79; writer-in-residence, Le Moyne College, Syracuse, New York, 1976-77; professor of English, Briarcliff College, 1979-80. Author of *Geography of Holiness: Thomas Merton's Photography,* 1980, and editor of *Concelebration: A Poetic Tribute to Thomas Merton,* 1980. **Essays:** Bedi; Caponigro; Morgan; Parks; Samaras.

PHILIPS, Christopher. Essayist. Freelance writer. Contributor to *American Photographer* and *Exposure.* Curatorial assistant, department of twentieth-century photography, International Museum of Photography, George Eastman House, Rochester, New York, 1979-80. Author of *Steichen at War: Naval Aviation in the Pacific,* 1981. **Essays:** Bayer; Bruehl; Horst; Keppler; Matter; Winningham.

POLI, Kenneth. Essayist. Consultant editor of *Popular Photography,* New York, since 1984 (senior editor, 1968-70; editor, 1970-84). Freelance magazine photographer, 1949-51; editor, *Leica Photography* magazine (U.S.A.), 1954-65. **Essays:** Mark Cohen; Davidson; Eisenstaedt; Mili; Owens; Porter; Stettner.

POMEROY, Ralph. Essayist. Poet, painter, critic and curator, New York. Associate director of the Forum Gallery, New York, since 1979; contributing editor, *Arts* magazine, New York, since 1980; lecturer on modern painting, New York School of Interior Design, since 1983. Director, Anna Leonowens Gallery, Halifax, Nova Scotia, 1968-69; staff critic, *ARTnews,* New York, 1963-68; contributing editor, *Art and Artists,* London, 1966-71; San Francisco correspondent, *Art and Artists,* 1973. Author of (poetry) *Book of Poems,* 1948, *Stills and Motives,* 1961, *The Canaries as They Are,* 1965, and *In the Financial District,* 1968, and (other) *Stamos,* 1974, *The Ice Cream Connection,* 1975, and *First Things First,* 1977. **Essays:** Beny; Duncan; Liberman; Morath; Orkin; Stock; Van Dyke.

PONIATOWSKA, Elena. Essayist. Writer and journalist, Mexico. In response to political disturbances in Mexico in September 1968, developed a characteristic style, blending eye-witness accounts with historical background in *La Noche de Tialeloloco, Fuerte es el Silencio* and *Nada, Nada.* Author of the biography of Tina Modotti, *Tinissima,* 1992 and the introduction to *Desires and Disguises,* 1992. **Essay:** Yampolsky.

PORTER, Allan. Essayist. Formerly, editor of *Camera,* Lucerne. Editor and publisher of the *Photothema* series of books, Zurich. **Essays:** Model; Steinert.

PRANDO, Edo. Essayist. Journalist in Turin, specializing in photography. Editor of the fortnightly *Fotogiornale.* Freelance photographer, 1969-73; member, editorial staff, Teletorino TV, 1973-75; editor, *Fotografia Italiana,* Milan, 1976-79. Author of *Guida alle*

Grotte d'Italia, 1973; *Fotografia Speleologica e Archeologica,* 1977; *La Famiglia Barolo,* 1978; *Valtellina,* 1978. **Essays:** Almasy; Clergue; Freed; Gagliani; Lennart Nilsson; Ragazzini.

PRASAD, H.Y. Sharada. Essayist. Information adviser to the Prime Minister of India, 1968-78, and since 1980. Contributor on Indian events to the *Britannica Yearbook,* since 1963. News editor, *The Indian Express,* Bombay, 1948-55; chief editor, *Yojana,* 1959-66; deputy information adviser to the prime minister, 1966-68; director, Indian Institute of Mass Communication, 1978-80. Editorial consultant to the *Nehru Exhibition,* 1964-65, the Indian Pavilion at *Expo '67,* Montreal, and the *Gandhi Centenary Exhibition,* 1969. **Essays:** Nagarajan; Singh.

PRICE, Derrick. Essayist. Principal lecturer in media studies, Bristol Polytechnic, England. Member of the Centre for Contemporary Cultural Studies, University of Birmingham. **Essays:** Delano; Lee; Mydans; Spender.

PRINZ, Uwe. Essayist. Freelance photo-historian and writer, Leipzig. **Essays:** Heilig; Richter.

PUTNAM, Sarah. Essayist. Freelance photographer, Boston, since 1978; photo editor for *Sojourner* since 1980. Exhibition editor, *Views: The New England Journal of Photography,* 1980-81. **Essays:** Beaton; Karsh; Mayes.

READ, Shirley. Essayist. Freelance curator, researcher and project facilitator, London. Founder member of Camerawork and a director of Signals: The Festival of Woman Photographers. Co-curated the exhibitions *Jo Spence: Matters of Concern* and *Women on the Streets.* **Essays:** Doisneau; Gupta.

REMEŠ, Vladimìr. Essayist. Chief dramatist, play section, Czechoslovak Radio, Prague, since 1972. Member of the cultural section, Czechoslovak Radio, 1960-68; film critic for various magazines in Czechoslovakia and writer for Czechoslovak films, 1968-72. Writer on photography, and collaborator with Daniela Mrázková on *Revue Fotografie,* Prague, since 1971. Author, with Mrázková, of *They Photographed the War: Soviet War Photography 1941-45,* 1975; *The Russian War,* 1977; *The Russian War 1941-45,* 1978; *Von Moskau nach Berlin,* 1979; *Irena Blüh,* 1980; *Die Sowjetunion Zwischen den Kriegen 1917-1941,* 1981; *Tschechoslowakische Fotografen 1900-1939,* 1982; *Josef Sudek,* 1983; *Jaromìr Funke,* 1986; *Another Russia: Through the Eyes of the New Soviet Photographers,* 1986. **Essays:** Abramochkin; Havránková; Infante; Kollár; Makarov; Medková; Tooming; Trakhman.

RICHARDS, Jane. Essayist. Freelance writer on photography and journalist with *The Guardian,* London. **Essay:** Levinthal.

RIPOLL, Frédéric. Essayist. Coordinator, Galerie du Château d'Eau, Toulouse, France. **Essay:** Radochonska.

ROMER, Grant B. Essayist. Freelance photographer, daguerreotypist, lecturer and writer. Assistant director of exhibitions, 1976-77, intern coordinator, 1978, and conservator, 1979, International Museum of Photography, George Eastman House, Rochester, New York. **Essay:** D'Alessandro.

ROSENBLUM, Naomi. Essayist. Adjunct professor of art history, Parsons School of Design, New York, since 1976, and Tisch School of the Arts, New York University, since 1985. Formerly adjunct associate professor of art history, Brooklyn College. Co-curator of the *Lewis Hine Retrospective,* Brooklyn Museum, 1977, Venice Biennale, 1979, and China, 1980. Author of *America and Lewis Hine,* with Walter Rosenblum and Alan Trachtenberg, 1977; *American Art,* with Milton Brown, Sam Hunter, John Jacobus, and David Sokol, 1979; *A World History of Photography,* 1984. **Essays:** Levitt; Liebling; Strand.

ROWELL, Mike. Essayist. Freelance photojournalist, since 1970; photography critic, *Maine Sunday Telegram,* since 1973. Automotive editor, Chilton Book Company, 1970; editor, *Maine Racing Annual,* 1974-79, and *Super Stock and Drag Illustrated,* 1979-80. Editor of books on auto repair; author of the forthcoming *Auto Racing Photography.* **Essays:** Szabo; Webb; Cole Weston.

SAGER, Peter. Essayist. Journalist: member of staff of the weekly *Die Zeit,* Hamburg, since 1975. Author of *Neue Formen des Realismus,* 1973; *Sud-England,* 1977; *Schottland,* 1980; *Wales,* 1987, *Die Besessenen Begegnungen mit Kunstsammlern twischen Aachen und Tokyo,* 1992. **Essays:** Hajek-Halke; List; Riebesehl.

SARLET, Jean-Michel. Essayist. Writer, photographer, and television film director, Liège, Belgium. Graduate of the School of Fine Art, Saint-Luc, Liège, and of the University of Liège. **Essay:** Vanesch.

SCHARF, Aaron. Adviser and essayist. Professor of the history of art, Open University (U.K.), 1969-82. Member, Arts Council of Great Britain Photography Sub-Committee, 1972-78. Author of *Creative Photography,* 1965; *Art and Photography,* 1968; and *Pioneers of Photography,* 1975. **Essays:** Ascolini; Cordier.

SCHOFIELD, Jack. Essayist. UK editor of *Zoom,* Paris, since 1978; editor of *Omni: The Book of the Future* weekly magazine, London, since 1981. Editor of *Photo Technique* monthly magazine, London, 1973-78, and *You and Your Camera* weekly magazine, London, 1979-80. Consultant editor of *The Darkroom Book,* 1981, and *Nude and Glamour Photography,* 1982. **Essays:** Gatewood; Gerster; Harbutt; Jones-Griffiths; Kane; McBride; Meiselas; Ricciardi.

SCIMÉ, Giuliana. Essayist. Freelance art and photography critic, and historian, Milan. Regular contributor to *European Photography, Corriere della Sera, Progresso Fotografico, Zoom, Corriere del Ticino.* Curator and author of the exhibition catalogues, *The Thin Line,* 1980; *The Line in Movement,* 1980; and *Women in the Magic Mirror,* 1981; *L'imaginaire d'apres nature,* 1983; *Object: Man,* 1984; *Italian Experimental Photography,* 1985; *Il Laboratorio dei fratelli Bragaglia,* 1986; *Immagini famose,* 1989; *John Florea— The Legend - Life 1940-1950,* 1990; *La specchio (in)fidele,* 1991; and *Bauhaus e Razionalismo,* 1993. **Essays:** Blanco; D'Amico; Facio; Figueroa Flores; Laizerovitz; Mahr; Paolini; Fontana; Schawinsky; Urban; Vishniac.

SHELDON, James L. Essayist. Freelance photographer and filmmaker. Curator of photography, Addison Gallery of American Art, Phillips Academy, Andover, Massachusetts, since 1977. Author of the exhibition catalogues, *Beaumont Newhall: Photographer,* 1980; *Aspects of the 70's,* 1980; and *Looking at America,* 1981. **Essays:** Blumberg; Margolis; Perkis.

SELINA, Elena. Essayist. **Essay:** Mukhin.

SINDEN, David. Essayist. Founder of Zone Gallery, Newcastle upon Tyne, UK. Specialist in photography from socialist and post-socialist countries and curator of exhibitions by artists from the Czech and Slovak Republics, Poland and Cuba. **Essay:** Peña González.

SINGH, Radhika. Adviser, New Delhi, India.

SJÖSTEDT, Ulf. Entrant and essayist. See his own entry. **Essay:** Gillsäter.

SKASA-WEISS, Ruprecht. Essayist. Contributor to Metamorphoto. **Essay:** Osswald.

ŠMOK, Jan. Essayist. Photographer, film operator, writer. Professor of the film and television faculty of the Academy of Performing Arts, Prague, and of the Institute of Creative Photography of the Silesian University, Opava. **Essay:** Birgus.

SOLOMON-GODEAU, Abigail. Essayist. Freelance photography critic, Paris and New York, since 1978; contributor to various photographic journals. Formerly a photo editor. **Essays:** Burgin; Clark; Friedman; Peress.

SPENCER, Ruth. Essayist. Photo-historian; picture researcher, Time Inc. Picture Collection, New York. Regular contributor to the *British Journal of Photography,* London. **Essays:** Goro; Stern.

SPIELMANN, Heinz. Essayist. Professor, University of Münster, since 1984. Director of the Schleswig-Holsteinisches Landesmuseum, Schloss Gottorf, since 1986. Formerly, chief curator for modern art, Museum für Kunst und Gewerbe, Hamburg. Author of *Oskar Kokoscha: Das Schriftliche Werk,* 4 volumes, 1972-76; *Spektrum der Kunst,* 1974, 1982; *Epochen, Künstler, Meisterwerke,* 13 volumes, 1975-77. **Essays:** Kempe; Lebeck; Mack; Orlopp; Scheler; Wolf.

STANGE, Maren. Essayist. Assistant professor of communications and American studies, Clark University, Worcester, Massachusetts. Regular contributor to the *New Boston Review, Massachusetts Review,* and *Prospects.* Author of *Symbols of an Ideal Life: Social Documentary Photography in America 1890-1950,* 1987. **Essays:** Beard; Bishop; Dominis; Fink; Glinn; Hartmann; Joel; Noskowiak; Papageorge; Silk.

STEINORTH, Karl. Essayist. Press chief of Kodak AG, Stuttgart. Also freelance writer and photo-historian. Author of *Photographen der Zwanziger Jahre,* 1979. **Essay:** Weber.

STOKES, Philip. Essayist. Photographer and historian. Senior lecturer, department of visual and performing arts, The Nottingham Trent University. England. **Essays:** Godwin; Hedges; Hill; Hilliard; Hockney; Ionesco; Larson; Mayne; Uzzle.

STOTT, William. Essayist. Professor of American studies and English, University of Texas at Austin, since 1971. Foreign service officer, United States Information Agency, 1964-68. Author of *Documentary Expression and 30's America,* 1973; co-author of *On Broadway: Performance Photographs by Fred Fehl,* 1978. **Essay:** Evans.

STRAUSS, David Levi. Essayist. Independent poet and freelance writer on photography and film, San Francisco. Editor and publisher of the literary journal *Acts*. **Essay:** Thomas.

SUTNIK, Maia-Mari. Adviser and essayist. Photographic coordinator, Art Gallery of Ontario, Toronto, since 1973. Audio-visual librarian, 1969-73. Author of the exhibition catalogues *Eisenstein Drawings from Theatre to Film*, 1974, and *E. Haanel Cassidy: Photographs 1933-1945*, 1981. **Essays:** Gutmann; Lambeth; Snow.

TAUSK, Petr. Adviser, entrant and essayist. See his own entry. **Essays:** Alpert; Ballhause; Bauret; Bengston; Chochola; Dias; Ehm; Garcia Joya; Gernsheim; Giacomelli; Haskins; Helmer-Petersen; Hopkins; Hucek; Ignatovich; Jager; Jodas; Kallay; Mante; Marco; Martincek; Newhall; Noordhoek; Prosek; Rajzìk; Reichmann; Rössler; Schröter; Splìchal; Stecha; Steele-Perkins.

TAYLOR, Liba. Essayist. Freelance photographer, writer and critic, London. **Essays:** Koudelka; Svoboda.

THEROND, Roger. Essayist. Photography critic, *Le Monde,* Paris. **Essays:** Cartier-Bresson; Depardon; Izis; Lartigue; Sieff.

THOMAS, Ann W. Essayist. Curator of photography, National Gallery of Canada, Ottawa. **Essay:** Tata.

TOOMING, Peeter. Entrant and essayist. See his own entry. **Essays:** Butyrin; Kalvelis; Macijauskas; Sutkus.

TÖRY, Klára. Essayist. Instructor in photography and photographic history, High School of Fine Arts, and at the School of Journalism, Budapest. Formerly, press photographer for *Nepfront* illustrated newspaper, Budapest. Author of *The Great Creators of Photography,* 1982. **Essays:** Féner; Németh.

TUCKER, Anne W. Essayist. Photographic historian, critic and lecturer. Gus and Lyndall Wortham Curator, Museum of Fine Arts, Houston, since 1976. Research assistant, International Museum of Photography, George Eastman House, Rochester, New York, 1968-70; photography consultant, Creative Artists Public Service Program, New York, 1971-72; director, photography lecture series, Cooper Union Forum, New York, 1972-75. Author of *Rare Books and Photographs: Catalogue 1,* with Lee Witkin, 1973, and *The Target Collection of American Photography,* exhibition catalogue, with William C. Agee, 1977; editor of *The Woman's Eye,* 1973; *The Anthony G. Cronin Memorial Collection,* 1979; *Suzanne Bloom and Ed Hill* (manual), 1980; *Target II: 5 American Photographers,* 1981; *Unknown Territory: Photography by Ray K. Metzker 1957-83,* 1984; *Robert Frank: New York to Nova Scotia,* 1986. **Essays:** Leipzig; Nathan Lyons; Sternfeld.

TULKENS, Joyce. Adviser and essayist. Curator and writer. Since 1991, first art director, and then editor, *Photo Asia,* Singapore. **Essays:** Chen; Chu; Lam; Leong.

TURNER, Roland. Essayist. Senior editor, St. James Press, Chicago. Formerly, director of the reference books department, St. Martin's Press, New York. Author/editor of *The Grants Register, The Annual Obituary,* and *Thinkers of the Twentieth Century,* 1987. **Essay:** Parkinson.

VAIZEY, Marina (Lady Vaizey). Essayist. Art critic, *The Sunday Times,* London, since 1974. Art critic, *The Financial Times,* London, 1970-74. Member of the arts panel, 1973-78, member, 1976-78, and chairman of arts films, 1976-78, Arts Council of Great Britain; trustee, National Museums and Galleries of Merseyside, since 1986. Author of *100 Masterpieces of Art,* 1979; *Andrew Wyeth,* 1980; *The Artist as Photographer,* 1982; *Peter Blake,* 1985. **Essays:** Fulton; McBean; McCormick; Wegman.

VAN DEUREN, Karel. Essayist. Writer, curator and critic. Corresponding editor for Belgium, *Foto,* Hilversum, Netherlands, since 1977; editor of *Vlaanderen* arts review, since 1977; editor of *Photohistorica,* bibliographical review of the European Society for the History of Photography, 1978-93. Editor and press officer for Agfa-Gevaert, Morstel, Belgium, 1954-81, and editor of the Gevaert publication *Photorama,* 1954-58; also, editor of *Photo-Tribune,* Deurne, Belgium, 1959-64; member of the working party on photo and film, Museum of Photography of the Province of Antwerp, 1974-83. Author and photo-editor of thematic and historical photobooks and catalogues such as *Belgian Photography 1940-1980.* **Essays:** Ausloos; Dries; Reusens; Tas.

VESTAL, David. Entrant and essayist. See his own entry. **Essays:** Kertész; Steiner.

VISKOCHIL, Larry A. Essayist. Curator, prints and photographs collection, Chicago Historical Society, since 1977 (head of library reference and reader services, 1967-77). Chairman, Picture Division, Special Libraries Association, 1981-82, 1982-83. **Essay:** Siegel.

VON ZITZEWITZ, Ingeborg. Essayist. Translator and critic, New York. Formerly worked as a journalist and in public relations. **Essay:** Ellen Auerbach.

WARBURTON, Nigel. Essayist. Lecturer in philosophy, the Open University, Milton Keynes, Buckinghamshire, England. Editor of *Bill Brandt: Selected Texts and Bibliography,* 1993. **Essay:** Brandt.

WEDEWER, Rolf. Essayist. Curator, Museum Leverkusen, West Germany. **Essays:** Jansen; Nothhelfer; von Gagern.

WEIERMAIR, Peter. Essayist. Founder and first director, the Institute of Contemporary Art, Innsbruck, 1969-79. Taught at the Vienna Academy of Art, 1979-80. Director of the Frankfurter Kunstverein since 1980. Author of *The Hidden Image,* 1979 and editor of the anthologies *Männer sehen Männer,* 1984; *Frauen sehen Männer,* 1983; *The Image of the Body,* 1993; and *The Liberated Image,* 1995. **Essay:** Bamgboye.

WELLS, Liz. Essayist. Senior lecturer, School of Media, The London College of Printing, UK. Editor of *Camerawork,* (issues 31 and 32). Curator of the exhibition and editor of the book *Viewfindings - Women Photographers: Landscape and Environment,* 1994, and editor of *Photography: A Critical Introduction* (in preparation). **Essays:** Fox; Honey; Kempadoo.

WIGH, Leif. Essayist. Assistant curator, Fotografiska Museet: Swedish Museum of Photography, Stockholm, since 1977. Part-time writer for the magazines *Fotonyheterna* and *Aktuell Fotografi,* since 1976. Freelance photographer, 1963-77; teacher, School of Photography, Stockholm, 1965-69; photographer/information officer, Swedish National Theatre Centre and the Cullberg Ballet, 1972-77. Has collaborated with curator Åke Sidwall on numerous exhibition catalogues at Fotografiska Museet, since 1974; author of *Fotograferna och det svenska landskapet,* 1981. **Essay:** Malmberg.

WILDE, Jürgen. Essayist. Photographic critic, historian and archivist. Director of the Galerie Wilde, Cologne. **Essay:** Tabard.

WILLIAMS, Jonathan. Essayist. Poet, publisher, photographer and writer on photography. Director of a writers' press, The Jargon Society, Highlands, North Carolina, since 1951. Contributing editor of *Aperture,* Millerton, New York. Author of numerous volumes of verse, and of books, *The Appalachian Photographs of Doris Ulmann,* 1971; *Clarence John Laughlin: The Personal Eye,* 1973; *The Family Album of Lucybelle Crater,* 1974; *Hot What? Collages, Texts, Photographs,* 1975; *"I Shall Save One Land Unvisited": 11 Southern Photographers,* 1978; *Portrait Photographers,* 1979; *The Photographs of Lyle Bonge,* 1982; *Letter in a Klein Bottle,* 1994; and *The Neugents,* 1994. **Essays:** Joyce; Kalisher; Laughlin; Sinsabaugh; Keith Smith.

WILLIAMS, Sheldon. Essayist. Cultural adviser to RONA, London. Secretary to the Société Européene de la Culture, 1965-73; editor of *Art Illustrated,* 1968-70. Sometime arts correspondent with *Contemporary Review, Pall Mall Gazette, Apollo, Arts Voices, Questions d'Art, Artis,* etc. Author of *Situation Humaine,* 1967; *Verlon,* 1968; *A Background to Sfumato,* 1969; *Voodoo and the Art of Haiti,* 1971; *Twentieth-Century British Naive and Primitive Artists,* with Eric Lister, 1975; editor of *RONABOOK,* 1978, and *A Quiet Thunder,* 1978. **Essays:** Bellmer; Székessy.

WINOKUR, Ken. Essayist. Freelance writer and photographer, Boston. Managing editor/feature editor of *Views: The Journal of Photography in New England,* Boston, 1979-81; photo critic for *The Real Paper,* 1980-81. **Essays:** Manos; Purcell; Resnick.

WISE, Kelly. Entrant and essayist. See his own entry. **Essays:** Friedlander; Minkkinen; White.

WORDSWORTH, Christopher. Essayist. Writer and critic, Warminster, Wiltshire, UK. Editor of and contributor to numerous magazines, including the *British Journal of Photography* since 1976. **Essay:** Chillingworth.

ZANNIER, Italo. Essayist. Professor of communications since 1971, and professor of the history of photography since 1983, Faculty of Architecture, Venice. Director, *Fotologia* quarterly, Venice. Professional photographer, specializing in architectural photography, 1952-76; taught photography at the Corso Superiore di Disegno Industriale, Venice, 1960-70; professor of photography, University of Bologna, 1974-83. Has published numerous volumes of photographs; also, author of *Breve Storia della Fotografia,* 1962, 1974; *Fotografia dell'Architettura,* 1969; *Conoscere la Fotografia,* 1978; *70 Anni di Fotografia in Italia,* 1978; *Fotografia in Friuli,* 1979; *Ferruccio Leiss, Fotografo a Venezia,* 1979; *I Manuali del Fotografo: Lo Sport,* with M. Cappon, 1980; *Storia e tecnica della fotografia,* 1982; *Cultura fotografica in Italia,* with P. Costantini, 1985; *Manuale del fotografo,* 1985; *Venezia nella fotografia dell'800,* 1986. **Essays:** Carmi; Gioli; Grignani; Jodice, Scianna; Veronesi.